PENGUIN REFERENCE BOOKS

THE PENGUIN GUIDE TO COMPACT DISCS

EDWARD GREENFIELD, until his retirement, in 1993, was for forty years on the staff of the *Guardian*, succeeding Neville Cardus as Music Critic in 1975. He still contributes regularly to the record column which he founded in 1954. At the end of 1960 he joined the reviewing panel of *Gramophone*, specializing in operatic and orchestral issues. He is a regular broadcaster on music and records for the BBC, not just on Radios 3 and 4 but also on the BBC World Service, latterly with his weekly programme, 'The Greenfield Collection'. In 1958 he published a monograph on the operas of Puccini. More recently he has written studies on the recorded work of Joan Sutherland and André Previn. He has been a regular juror on International Record awards and has appeared with such artists as Dame Elisabeth Schwarzkopf, Dame Joan Sutherland and Sir Georg Solti in public interviews. In October 1993 he was given a *Gramophone* Award for Special Achievement and in June 1994 received the OBE for services to music and journalism.

ROBERT LAYTON studied at Oxford with Edmund Rubbra for composition, and with Egon Wellesz for the history of music. He spent two years in Sweden at the universities of Uppsala and Stockholm. He joined the BBC Music Division in 1959 and has been responsible for such programmes as *Interpretations on Record*. He has contributed 'A Quarterly Retrospect' to *Gramophone* for a number of years and he has written books on Berwald and Sibelius and has specialized in Scandinavian music. He has written a monograph on the Dvořák symphonies and concertos for the BBC Music Guides, of which he was General Editor for many years. His translation of the first two volumes of Erik Tawaststjerna's definitive study of Sibelius was awarded the 1984 Finnish State Literary Prize. The third volume was published last year. In 1987 he was awarded the Sibelius Medal and in the following year was made a Knight of the Order of the White Rose of Finland for his services to Finnish music. His short *Grieg: An Illustrated Life* will be published this autumn.

IVAN MARCH is a former professional musician. He studied at Trinity College of Music, London, and at the Royal Manchester College. After service in the Central Band of the RAF, he played the horn professionally for the BBC and travelled with the Carl Rosa and D'Oyly Carte opera companies. Now director of the Long Playing Record Library, the largest commercial lending library for classical music on compact discs in the British Isles, he is a well-known lecturer, journalist and personality in the world of recorded music. As a journalist he contributes to a number of record reviewing magazines, including *Gramophone*, where his regular monthly 'Collector's Corner' deals particularly with important reissues.

The present volume is dedicated with affection and gratitude to

ROGER WELLS

He was our indefatigable Penguin copy editor during the decade from 1988 to 1998, during which time he acted as our most patient and expert mentor. Together we pioneered a new computerized system of formatting, collating and assembling the final copy for the realization of ten consecutive *Penguin Guides*. It was Roger who guided us through the hazards of an unfamiliar word-processing package. And when our efforts – especially in the early days – fell well short of perfection, he was always at the end of a phone line to rescue us (and sometimes our 'lost copy' also) and set us back on course. Most importantly, the Editor became able to draw at will on all the earlier files, so that when recordings were reissued, the original review came instantly to hand for revision as necessary.

Alongside his long experience as a copy editor and as an eagle-eyed proof-reader, Roger is a lover of good music himself, and a collector who, to our delight, was always being tempted to go out and buy our recommendations at first sight. He liked to edit our reviews to a background of classical music, and later, when he also took on *The Penguin Jazz Guide*, he would choose a stimulating alternation of the two genres. We wish him well and remember our long association with warmth and admiration.

The Penguin Guide to Compact Discs
Completely revised and updated

Ivan March, Edward Greenfield and Robert Layton
Edited by Ivan March

PENGUIN BOOKS

PENGUIN BOOKS
Published by the Penguin Group

Penguin Books Ltd, 27 Wrights Lane, London W8 5TZ, England
Penguin Putnam Inc., 375 Hudson Street, New York, New York 10014, USA
Penguin Books Australia Ltd, Ringwood, Victoria, Australia
Penguin Books Canada Ltd, 10 Alcorn Avenue, Toronto, Ontario, Canada M4V 3B2
Penguin Books (NZ) Ltd, Private Bag 102902, NSMC, Auckland, New Zealand

Penguin Books Ltd, Registered Offices: Harmondsworth, Middlesex, England

This edition first published 1999
10 9 8 7 6 5 4 3 2 1

Set in 8/9.5 pt PostScript Monotype Times New Roman
Typeset, from material supplied, by Rowland Phototypesetting Ltd, Bury St Edmunds, Suffolk
Made and printed in Great Britain by Clays Ltd, St Ives plc

Contents

Foreword

This book is about excellence in recorded music, irrespective of cost. Our current survey gathers together the very finest CDs issued over the last sixteen years. They have survived in the catalogue because their excellence is recognized. If an outstanding recorded performance is deleted, it is unusual for it to remain out of the catalogue for very long. The majority of the very best discs are in the premium-price range, and they are usually well worth it.

Remastered reissues

The major companies have found various resourceful ways of re-marketing their outstanding older recordings. Sometimes they are gathered together in boxes (one thinks of DG's 87-disc 'Beethoven Edition', packed in a cardboard suitcase, and the more recent Bach 'Masterworks', less comprehensively spreading to only 26 CDs). But more often they are offered in the now well-established two-discs-for the-cost-of-one format. In effect, each such reissue is still in the premium-price range, and is packaged in a single jewel-case, but doubling the amount of music offered. Indeed the playing time is often very generous indeed, and the collector rightly senses a bargain. But it is a pity that too often the documentation is far from matching the quantity of music in liberality.

This *Duo* format was pioneered by Philips, with Decca and DG soon following with *Doubles*. Then came the *fortes* from EMI, to be more recently rechristened *double ffortes* – a logo first used in the USA. The *Dyads* are from Hyperion, and the least elegantly named *Twofers* come from BMG/RCA. Warner Classics *Ultimas* draw on the Erato, Teldec and Finlandia catalogues, and most recently the *2-for-1* series have arrived from Chandos. The Virgin Classics *Veritas x 2* reissues are even more tempting, drawing on quite recent digital recordings, and with the pair of CDs offered for the cost of a single mid-priced disc.

The reissue of single CDs of outstanding recordings, often of great historical and artistic interest, has brought special mid-priced logos. DG's 'Originals', Decca's 'Classic Sound', and RCA's 'Living Stereo' led the way, followed by the newer Decca 'Legends' series, EMI's ambitiously titled 'Great Recordings of the Century', and Sony's more expensive but nostalgically packaged 'Heritage' series. In most cases the recordings have been carefully reprocessed to give the collector a reproduced sound as near as possible to the original master.

Historical recordings

Specialist historical labels like Biddulph and Testament have licensed even earlier material from the majors, and taken great care to ensure that the original mono quality is not degraded by the CD analogue-to-digital transfers. But standing head and shoulders above all other such enterprises is the 'Dutton Lab.' series. Mike Dutton is the supreme magician of CD remastering: almost everything he processes seems to turn to gold and the results are sometimes little short of miraculous. One thinks especially of his Barbirolli and Beecham transfers. Most remarkable of all is the astonishing Sargent *Messiah* of 1946. It was transferred from countless 78s and, helped by fine solo and choral singing and the warmly resonant acoustics of Huddersfield Town Hall, gives the listener the impression of listening to a continuous 'live' performance (which it was not). More recently Dutton has produced a superb CD, deriving from Decca *ffrr* 78s, of Ida Haendel in 1945, at the very beginning of her recording career, playing the Saint-Saëns *Introduction and Rondo capriccioso* and the Tchaikovsky and Dvořák *Violin concertos*. The Tchaikovsky concerto, in particular, is wonderfully warm and spontaneous. Miss Haendel went on to re-record the work quite admirably later in her career. But there is something very special about this early version, which has the fresh inspiration of youth. The recording is wonderfully warm and natural, with the 78 hiss quite banished.

Composer entries new to the current *Guide*

Our current survey introduces a remarkable number of new composer entries. From the 15th century comes the highly individual Jean Richafort; from the 16th and 17th centuries we meet Sebastien de Brossard and Francisco Guerrero (this year is the quatro-centenary of the latter's death, in 1599). Aurelio Signoretti lived in Reggio, Italy, while Antony Holborne, Thomas Morley, Adrian Willaert and John Wilbye were all home grown.

The 17th and 18th centuries also bring Henricus Albicastro, Benedikt Aufschnaiter, Carlos Baguer, Franz Beck, Jiří Antonin Benda, the remarkable clarinettist/composer Alessandro Besozzi (whom Mozart travelled to Italy to hear), Johann Cannabich, Evaristo Dall'Abaco, Antoine Dauvergne, Domenico Mazzocchi, Benedetto Platti, Johann Abraham Schulz. In the further exploration of this period we must mention a most enterprising new label, distributed by Chandos, called Tactus (which introduced us to both Besozzi and Signoretti). These intriguing CDs only came to hand just as we were going to press, and we hope to include many more in our next edition.

From the 19th century we meet Ignaz Brull, Oscar Byström, Johann Frolich, Asger Hamerik and Alberto Nepomuceno; but it is the 20th century which brings the largest group of all, led by Thomas Adès (a swiftly rising star in the British firmament). Other new names include Theodor Adoro, Sir Thomas Armstrong (a talented British academic), Arno Babadzhanian, William Baines, Hakon Børresen, Edward Confrey, Maurice Delage, Hanns Eisler, John McCabe, Fernando Obradors, Wilhelm Peterson-Berger, Gabriel Rodó, Joly Brago Santos, Humphrey Searle, Khaikhosra Sorabji, Loris Tjeknavorian, Egon Wellesz and Eric Zeisl. Almost every one of these new names brings unfamiliar music which is well worth the attention of the serious collector.

The Great Interpreters from the Past

In recorded terms, the great names of the past are still very much with us. Currently EMI have an ongoing 'Klemperer Legacy' which has just reached the Brahms Symphonies (and which includes one of the greatest performances of the *First* ever put on record). Bruno Walter and Szell still maintain a strong presence in the catalogue, as do Barbirolli, Bernstein, Karl Boehm, Boult (a much greater interpreter than his reputation outside the British Isles would suggest) and Dorati, who gave us the first set of Haydn Symphonies on record. Giulini and Kempe still have a foothold on the catalogue, Jochum's Bruckner interpretations remain very special, and Solti's Wagner has stood the test of time. Stokowski is celebrated for his sensuously rich orchestral textures, but offers much else besides, including a sensational account of Falla's *El amor brujo*, recorded live at a BBC Promenade concert.

In the late 1950s and early 1960s, Ansermet's extraordinary ear for detail gave his records considerable influence, because of their spontaneity of feeling and clear, but warmly atmospheric Decca sound; it is good that they stand up so well today. Both Cluytens and Martinon had something special to contribute in French music, as did Arthur Fiedler in American classical 'Pops'. Ferenc Fricsay conducted some of the very finest DG mono LPs of the early 1950s: his *Háry János suite* (now on a DG Original) remains a demonstration disc *par excellence*. Haitink in Amsterdam, Mravinsky in Leningrad, Munch in Boston, Ormandy in Philadelphia, Paray in Detroit, and that superb Straussian, Fritz Reiner, in Chicago, have all left us a distinguished permanent legacy.

Karajan still remains dominant in the basic German repertoire, Kubelik almost equally so in the field of Czech music. Pierre Monteux was most notable for his extraordinary versatility. Furtwängler, one of the greatest conductors of all, a musician who could give the impression of re-creating the music in front of the listener, too often received indifferent recording, but fortunately not always. Koussevitzky, who was so influential in pioneering and promoting new 20th-century music, suffered from harsh sound, and Toscanini's electrifying RCA records, especially those recorded in the notoriously dry NBC Studio 8H (the conductor's own ill-chosen venue), seem even more intractible. But the RCA transfer engineers are currently managing to achieve a more listenable quality from these old masters, and the Carnegie Hall sessions give a better idea of what live audiences actually heard at a Toscanini concert in the 1930s and 1940s.

The new interpretative style of the digital era

As one looks through the major works which are at the heart of concert hall repertoire and compares new recordings with old, one is aware of a distinct change in the style of the performances. The new generation of interpreters are less willing to superimpose their own personalities on the music-making and are more concerned to present it freshly, in a way that follows the composer's intentions as closely as possible.

This new – more direct – style was pioneered with great success by Neville Marriner with the Academy of St Martin-in-the-Fields in the 1960s and 1970s. In the early days of the group, democratic discussions were held between conductor and orchestra over the finer points of ensemble, phrasing and interpretation. But that was a short-lived experiment, for most orchestral players prefer a strong authoritative direction, with clear – yet not egocentrically wayward – interpretative ideas.

The roll-call of conductors of this new generation is both extensive and distinguished, including Karajan's successor, Abbado, together with Blomstedt, Chailly, Myung-Whun Chung, Colin Davis, Ivan Fischer, Järvi, Gergiev, Vernon Handley, David Lloyd-Jones, Jansons, Mackerras, Menuhin, Minkowski, Previn, Simon Rattle, Sanderling, Sawallisch, Schwarz, Sinopoli, Tennstedt, Georg Tintner, Jan Pascal Tortelier, Wand, Zander, and David Zinman, whose recent Zurich recordings of the Beethoven Symphonies are so arrestingly fresh, and authentic, in using Jonathan Del Mar's newly edited texts.

Perhaps most typical of the new wave is Richard Hickox who has recorded an enormously wide range of repertoire with consistent success and, like Marriner before him, has continually demonstrated that special gift of bringing performances vividly alive in the recording studio, as if communicating to an audience.

Solo instrumentalists

Our experience with solo instrumentalists has not been dissimilar. The great names of the early and middle decades of the century (Adolph Busch, Casals, Cortot, Edwin Fischer, Gieseking, Godowsky, Kreisler, Lhévinne, Lipatti, Rachmaninov, Schnabel and Solomon) remain with us on mono discs, and others like Arrau, Curzon, Kempff, Fournier, Gilels, Heifetz, Horowitz, Michelangeli, Milstein, Piatigorsky, Sviatoslav Richter, Rostropovich, Rubinstein, Schneiderhan, Segovia, Stern and Tureck have lived long enough to span the years through to our own stereo era.

But who would suggest that the newest generation of soloists perform with less-interpretative insights? Some like Argerich, Cziffra, Glenn Gould, Kremer, Perlman and Pollini seem to belong to the older self-aware school of virtuosi. Others are more self-effacing, dedicated first and foremost to the composer's interests, and once again the list is impressively long. One thinks, for instance, of artists of the calibre of Andsnes, Amoyal, Ashkenazy, Bell, Berezovsky, Brendel, Kyung-Wha Chung, Cliburn, Cole, Coombes, Collard, Frith, Gould, Grumiaux, Hamelin, Hewitt, Hough, Kovacevich, Lin, Jando, Janis, Kissin, Kocsis, Little, Lupu, Mutter, Perahia, Queffélec, Pletnev, Rogé, Schiff, Stott, Thibaudet, Tirimo, Vogt, Uchida, Vengerov and Zimerman.

Period-instrument performances

The most significant change in performance styles of our own time is the return to the use of authentic original instruments for early music. Together with conjectural attempts to simulate period playing-techniques (in terms of timbre and phrasing) and – in the case of stringed instruments – very restricted use of vibrato, the immediate effect on the sound of baroque music in particular has been unparalleled.

The new movement was pioneered by artists like Nadia Boulanger (who virtually rediscovered Monteverdi), the influential, but little-known keyboard player Violet Gordon Woodhouse (who made barely a handful of electrical recordings), her contemporary Wanda Landowska, and the Dolmetsch family (who built their own instruments), then followed a little later by scholar/harpsichordist Thurston Dart and by Rafael Puyana.

The first, great modern counter-tenor (and conductor), Alfred Deller, made a profound contribution, especially in the music of Purcell, as did August Wenzinger's Schola Cantorum Basiliensis, and the imaginatively spirited David Munrow who, with his Early Music Consort of London, explored the new colour combinations of baroque (and earlier) wind instruments. It was Julian Bream who re-established the lute as a solo instrument, to be followed by Jordi Savall who was to bring the viola da gamba fully back to life.

The authentic performance revolution gathered pace, stimulated by various instrumental ensembles, notably those associated with Harnoncourt and Leonhardt, plus Franz Brüggen's Concerto and Quadro Amsterdam. Very soon others joined them, led by Christopher Hogwood and his Academy of Ancient Music, Trevor Pinnock and his English Consort, and Anthony Rooley and the Consort of Musicke.

They all have their own ideas about authenticity, and performances of the same music by different artists bring different solutions. Roy Goodman's Hanover Band – later taken over by Anthony Halstead for a comprehensive exploration of the music of J. C. Bach – Koopman's Amsterdam Baroque Orchestra, Parrott's Taverner Consort, Philip Pickett's New London Consort, Rifkin's Bach Ensemble – each has its own distinct character. They were joined by Harry Christophers' Sixteen (which can expand or contract at will), Simon Standage's Collegium Music 90 and (on American Vanguard) Paul Dombrecht's Il Fondamento. The chamber repertoire was well served by groups like Florilegium and Fretwork (with Christopher Wilson on lute).

At first the great problem was the difficulty of playing early instruments (especially vibrato-less violins) in tune, and creating a pleasing timbre – indeed, any kind of timbre at all. The initial lack of experience of valveless hand horns and period trumpets sometimes produced an only sketchy approximation of the more elusive upper harmonics in very florid passages. And apart from suspect intonation and poor technique, too often the strings seemed to fight shy of expressive warmth in slow movements, in favour of inelegant bulges in the melodic line. With some groups the acid edge on the violins and heavily accented rhythms became almost painful. Yet the specialist critical fraternity, captured by the basic character of authenticity, with its undoubted vitality and transparency of texture, were prepared to be amazingly tolerant of such inadequacies, and the public went along too.

Several decades later, things have greatly improved. The early instrumental techniques have been mastered, violins usually play in tune, timbres and phrasing are far smoother and pleasing to the ear, and the horns, woodwind and brass articulate the right notes without too many problems. The results can be very stimulating indeed.

Roger Norrington and his London Classical Players, among others, moved on further to the 19th century, to offer fresh light on the symphonies of Beethoven with 'authentic' sounds and subsequently, the New Queens Hall Orchestra, directed by Roy Goodwin, has come right into our own century, offering a thrilling performance of Holst's *Planets*, using gut strings, wooden flutes, French bassoons and piston horns, and narrow-bore brass instruments, which is what the composer would have expected to hear.

Throughout our survey, a dominating name is that of John Eliot Gardiner, who began his career with modern-instrument ensembles, but opportunely crossed over into period performance in the manner born. Whether in the major choral works of Bach, the symphonies of Beethoven and Schumann, or the operas of Handel and Mozart, he is very successful indeed. His musical presence is very tangible in all he does: if you respond to his positive, vibrant style, then you will probably find many of his recordings will be a first choice, but if you do not, there are always plenty of alternatives.

Early vocal music

It was David Willcocks and the King's College Choir who in the 1960s achieved a breakthrough with a best-selling Argo record of the three-part and four-part Masses of William Byrd. Even so, early vocal music took a little longer to take off. A Hyperion collection of music by the remarkable 12th-century poet/composer, Abbess Hildegard of Bingen marked the turning point. Sung by the Gothic Voices under Christopher Page, it gradually became a bestseller, and Page and his group went on to record an ongoing survey of medieval music stretching to more than a dozen individual CDs.

But the real breakthrough came with an EMI two-disc set of Gregorian Chant, with its affectingly simple melismas, sung by the Monks of the Benedictine Monastery of St Domingo de Silos. It suddenly made a great cross-over success to sell two million copies world-wide, and almost overnight the record companies discovered that they had a new market for vocal music which went much further back in time than their successful instrumental repertoire.

The music of the great Elizabethan composer Thomas Tallis had, like Byrd, been pioneered by the King's College Choir under Willcocks, and his choir had discovered the extraordinarily spectacular and moving 40-part motet, *Spem in alium*, which was later to become a top classical hit. The composer's name was subsequently appropriated by the Tallis Scholars, directed by Peter Phillips, who were to record a number of very successful collections of his and other Elizabethan music, several of which won international awards.

England has a great tradition of cathedral-trained male choristers who then grouped together to take advantage of the new interest in early music. So arrived the Clerkes of Oxenford, under Davis Wulstan, the Cardinall's Musick directed by Andrew Carwood, who have already given us a complete survey of the music of Robert Fayfax and are up to Volume II of a projected complete recording of all the music of Byrd. But it is the Chapelle du Roi under Alistair Dixon who have embarked on a comprehensive coverage of Tallis's music, and they have now reached their third CD.

Guillaume Du Fay, Josquin Des Prés, Guillaume de Machaut, Obrecht, Ockeghem, Palestrina and Victoria are all among the European Medieval and Renaissance composers well performed by the above ensembles, plus the Clerk's Group under Edward Wickham, Hespèrion XX, the Hilliard Ensemble directed by Paul Hillier, the darker-voiced Ensemble Organum under Marcel Pérès, the Medieval Ensemble of London, and (most economically on Naxos), the versatile Oxford Camerata directed by Jeremy Summerly. A fine American female vocal group, the Anonymous Four, have also successfully crossed over with a series of anthologies of medieval chant and polyphony, carols and motets, which have brought a remarkable public response. And suddenly, Emma Kirkby, with her delightfully fresh soprano voice, ideal for baroque repertoire, has become a star.

For Marc-Antoine Charpentier, and other 17th-century French composers, one can turn to Harry Christophers with Les Arts Florissants, Il Seminario Musicale, and René Jacobs and his Concerto Vocale. Jacobs has also given us some fine Monteverdi madrigals, an area covered more comprehensively by Anthony Rooley, and even more idiomatically by the superbly blended Concerto Italiano directed by Rinaldo Alessandrini, while the King's Consort under Robert King are embarking on a complete coverage of Vivaldi's vocal music, and have just reached Volume 5.

The Standard repertoire

By far the greater part of our survey is the continual reassessment of major recordings of the standard orchestral instrumental and vocal repertoire. The range of alternatives is astonishing. Bach, with the 250th anniversary of his death coming up in the Millennium, is particularly well covered. His organ music is now represented by no fewer than seven complete or ongoing surveys (Marie-Claire Alain, Kevin Bowyer, Christopher Herrick, Peter Hurford, Ton Koopman, Simon Preston and Wolfgang Rübsam), and the cantatas by four.

The complete Teldec cantata cycle directed jointly by Leonhardt and Harnoncourt, and the pioneering but unfinished Karl Richter/DG series are now joined by new recordings from Ton Koopman on Erato, Helmuth Rilling on Hässler and, most unexpectedly, a superb ongoing survey from Japan on the BIS label, directed with continuing freshness and convincing authenticity by Masaaki Suzuki, which looks set to trump all the others. Suzuki has also given us outstanding sets of the *Christmas oratorio* and the *St John Passion*, and most notably, an extraordinarily compelling and beautiful performance of Handel's *Messiah*, as fine as any on record.

This year is the centenary of Poulenc's birth, and both Decca and EMI are offering a generous celebration, covering all his major orchestral and vocal music, and much else besides. The British composer, John McCabe, who is just 50, has returned to the catalogue with CDs of his orchestral, vocal and piano music, while Chandos's coverage of Percy Grainger continues apace.

Ongoing cycles

Among the other ongoing series, the Kodály Quartet's complete Haydn cycle has reached its conclusion on Naxos, while the Mosaïques Quartet – with new recordings of Mendelssohn, Mozart and Schubert – are continuing to show that they are now without peer among period-instrument string quartets. Leslie Howard's coverage of the piano music of Liszt is also nearing its culmination, and has reached Volume 55, with some of his most recent discoveries among the most fascinating, while Graham Johnson's Schubert odyssey on Hyperion has reached the song cycles, with Ian Bostridge's superb *Die Schöne Müllerin* and (Volume 30) Mathias Goerne's equally memorable *Winterreise*.

Marco Polo's Josef Strauss series continues to make attractive new discoveries, and is now up to Volume 18. Another illumination comes on the CPO label which is exploring the orchestral music of Wolf-Ferrari, a composer hitherto only known for his tuneful operatic Preludes and Intermezzi, and of course the sparkling *Susanna's secret overture*. His haunting, unashamedly romantic *Violin* and *Cello concertos* are equally melodic and beautiful, the former has quite a bit in common with the Max Bruch *G minor concerto*: both works deserve to find an immediate place in the concert hall.

Elgar's *'Third' Symphony* and the BBC archives

One of the more controversial events of the year was the completion by Anthony Payne of Elgar's '*Third' Symphony*. The story of its gestation is given within our pages by R. L. who, while working at the BBC was involved in the early part of the saga. Whatever the rights and wrongs of the affair, it has given us some more glorious Elgar, undoubtedly inspired, and Payne has put the symphony together with uncanny skill and prescience. The BBC are now burrowing seriously into their archives with the launch of their Legends series, and have already uncovered a treasure trove from artists of the calibre of Barbirolli, Beecham, Britten, Curzon (with the Amadeus Quartet), Horenstein and Stokowski.

It has been a good year for opera, ranging from the delightful *Dame Blanche* of Boieldieu, sparkling under the baton of Mark Minkowski, to a superb new *Fliegende Holländer* (Bernd Weikl with Cheryl Studer) from Sinopoli. Sir Charles Mackerras gives us a definitive account of Dvořák's *Rusalka* on Decca (with Renée Fleming), and on EMI the celebrated tenor/soprano partnership of Roberto Alagna and Angela Gheorghiu brings great charm to Gounod's *Roméo et Juliette* (Plasson) and romantic passion to Puccini's *Il Trittico* (Pappano). There is a fine Handel *Semele* from Nicholas McGegan and Mozart's *Mitridate* marks Christophe Rousset's successful debut on the operatic podium. Intriguing novelties include Hindemith's *Sancta Susannah*, Korngold's *Die Kathryn*, Menotti's *The Consul*, a new Danish set of Nielsen's *Maskarade*, Previn's *A Streetcar named Desire*, Prokofiev's *Betrothal in a monastery* and Salieri's *Falstaff*.

Gergiev's Kirov opera is the source of a fascinating combination of the 1869 and 1872 versions of Mussorgsky's *Boris Godunov*; Verdi is represented by new versions of *Don Carlos* (Haitink), *Ernani*, with Sutherland, Pavarotti and Nucci and the Welsh National Opera under Bonynge, which Decca recorded in the mid 1980s but have only just released, while Pavarotti is also featured as Oronte in Levine's much more recent Met. version of *I Lombardi*.

With the support of the Peter Moores Foundation, Chandos's 'Opera in English' series is expanding further with the taking over from EMI of Dame Janet Baker's *Mary Stuart* (Donizetti) and *Julius Caesar* (Handel). There is also a first-class English language *La Bohème* with Cynthia Hayman as Mimi and Dennis O'Neil an ardent Rudolph. And we should not forget Hyperion's new recording of Sidney Jones's *The Geisha*, a Gilbert and Sullivan look- and sound-alike which nevertheless is tuneful and very entertaining.

Finally there is Philips' ambitious coverage of the 'Great Pianists of the Twentieth Century', masterminded by John Deacon. Not everyone will agree with his roster of artists, and one of the snags is that of the repertoire included, too much is already in the catalogue. But these generously filled, handsomely packaged and well documented 'Duos' are certainly value for money. There are a hundred altogether, with the most celebrated artists given more than one set each. The series is to be completed for the Millennium, and so far we have been able to cover about two-thirds of them; they are listed together at the end of the book.

Ivan March
Editor

A Personal Choice from the 1999 *Guide*

Each of the three contributors has made a personal choice of a dozen recordings which are new to the current edition:

Edward Greenfield

BEETHOVEN *Symphonies Nos. 1-9*. Soloists, Swiss Chamber Choir, Zurich Tonhalle Orchestra, David Zinman. Arte Nova 74321 65410-2 (5).

Leonore. Hillevi Martinpello, Christian Oelze, Kim Begley, Michael Schade, Franz Hawalata, Alistair Miles, Matthew Best, Monteverdi Choir, ORR, John Eliot Gardiner. DG 453 461-2 (2).

BRUCKNER *Symphonies Nos. 0 in D min. (Die Nulte) & 8 in C min.* (1887 version). National Symphony Orchestra of Ireland, Georg Tintner. Naxos 8.554215/6 (2).

DELIUS *Violin sonatas Nos. 1–3 & 4, Op. Posth.* Tasmin Little, Piers Lane. Conifer 75605 51315-2.

DVORAK *Rusalka*. Renée Fleming, Ben Heppner, Franz Hawlata, Dolora Zajick, Hühn Chorus, Czech PO, Mackerras. Decca 460 568-2 (3).

ELGAR *Symphony No. 3* (completed from sketches by Anthony Payne). BBC SO, Sir Andrew Davis. NMC NMCD 053.

Violin sonata, Op. 82; Canto popolare; La Capriceuse, Op. 17; Chanson de matin; Chanson de nuit, Op. 15/1–2; Mot d'amour, Op. 13/1; Offertoire, Op. 11; Salut d'amour, Op. 12; Sospiri, Op. 70; Sursum corda, Op. 11. Lydia Mordkovitch, Julian Milford. Chandos CHAN 9624.

PUCCINI *Il Trittico (Il Tabarro; Suor Angelica; Gianni Schicchi)*. Angele Gheorghiu, Maria Guleghina, Cristina Gallardo-Domas, Bernadette Manca di Nissa, Felicity Palmer, Roberto Alagna, Carlo Guelfi, Neil Shicoff, José van Dam, London Voices, LSO or Philh. Orchestra, Pappano. EMI CDS5 56567-2 (3).

SCHUMANN *Symphonies: in G min.(Zwickau); Nos. 1–3; 4 (Original 1841 and revised 1851 versions); Konzertstück for 4 horns, Op. 86*. Soloists, ORR John Eliot Gardiner DG 457 591-2 (3).

TIPPETT (i) *The Rose Lake*. (ii) *The Vision of St. Augustine*. LSO, (i) Sir Colin Davis. (ii) Composer. Conifer 76505 51304-2

VAUGHAN WILLIAMS *The Pilgrim's Progress* (complete). Gerald Finley, and soloists, ROHCG Ch. & O, Hickox. Chandos Dig. CHAN 9825 (2).

WALTON *Symphony No. 1. Belshazzar's Feast.* Thomas Hampson, CBSO Chorus, CBSO, Sir Simon Rattle EMI CDC5 56592-2.

Robert Layton

BERLIOZ Overtures: *Béatrice et Benédict; Benvenuto Cellini; Le carnaval romain; Le Corsaire; Les francs-juges; Le roi Lear; Waverley*. Dresden Staatskapelle, Sir Colin Davis. RCA 09026 68790-2.

HENZE *Undine* (complete ballet). London Sinfonietta, Oliver Knussen. DG 453 467-2 (2).

HOLMBOE *Epilog, Op. 80; Epitaph (Symphonic metamorphosis), Op. 68; Monolith, Op. 76; Tempo variabile, Op. 108*. Aarhus Symphony Orchestra, Owain Arwell Hughes. BIS CD 852.

LISZT *Faust Symphony*. Hans Peter Blochwitz, Hungarian Radio Chorus, Budapest Festival Orchestra, Iván Fischer. Philips 454 460-2.

Sonata in B minor. Années de Pèlerinage, 2nd Year: Après une lecture de Dante (Dante Sonata). Concert study: Gnomenreigen. Harmonies poétiques et religieuses: Funérailles. Mikhail Pletnev DG 457 629-2.

RACHMANINOV *Symphony No. 1 in D minor*. St Petersburg Philharmonic Orchestra, Mariss Jansons. EMI CDC5 56754-2.

RAVEL *Concerto for piano left-hand; Piano concerto in G. Valses nobles et sentimentales*. Krystian Zimerman, Cleveland Orchestra or LSO, Pierre Boulez. DG 449 213-2.

RUBBRA *Symphony Nos. 3 & 7*. BBC National Orchestra of Wales, Richard Hickox. Chandos CHAN 9634.

William SCHUMAN *Symphonies Nos. 3; 5 (Symphony for strings) & 8*. New York Philharmonic Orchestra, Leonard Bernstein. Sony SMK 63163.

SHOSTAKOVICH *Symphony No. 8 in C min*. Leningrad Philharmonic Orchestra, Mravinsky. BBC Legends BBCL 4002-2.

SIBELIUS *Karelia suite, Op. 11*; *King Christian II* incidental music, Op. 27; *Pelleas and Melisande* incidental music, Op. 46. Lahti, SO, Vänskä. BIS CD 918.

TCHAIKOVSKY *Sleeping Beauty* (ballet; complete). Russian National Orchestra, Mikhail Pletnev. DG 457 634-2 (2).

Ivan March (Editor)

BACH *The Well-tempered Clavier, Books I–II (complete), BWV 846-69*. Hyperion Dig. *Book I* CDA 67301/2; *Book II* CDA 67303/4, Angela Hewitt (piano).

HANDEL *Messiah* (complete). Midori Suzuki, Yoshikazu Mera, John Elwes, David Thomas, Bach Collegium, Japan, Masaaki Suzuki. BIS 891/2 (2).

LULLY Les Comédies ballets: excerpts from: *Les Amants magnifiques; L'Amour médecin; Le bourgeois gentilhombre; George Dandin (Le grand divertissement royal de Versailles); Monsieur de Pourceaugnac (Le divertissement de Chambourd); Pastoral comique; Les Plaisirs de l'île enchantée. Phaëton* (tragédie en musique; complete). Poulenard, Mellon, Crook, Yakar, J. Smith, Gens, and soloists, Sagittarius Vocal Ens., Musiciens du Louvre, Minkowski. Erato/Warner Ultima 3984 26998-2 (2).

MOZART *String quartets Nos. 21 in D, K. 575; 22 in B flat, K. 589; 23 in F, K. 590*. Leipzig Quartet. MDG Double MDG 307 0936-2 (2).

PISTON *Violin concertos Nos. 1–2; Fantasia for violin and orchestra*. James Boswell, Ukraine National Symphony Orchestra, Theodor Kucher. Naxos Dig. 8.559003.

RAMEAU *Pygmalion* (Acte de ballet); (ii) *Nélée et Myrthis* (Acte de ballet). Howard Crook, Sandrine Piau, Agnès Mellon, Michel-Dansac Donatienne, Jérôme Corréas, Françoise Semellaz, Caroline Pelon, Chorus, Les Arts Florissants, Christie. Harmonia Mundi Dig. HMT 7901381

RICHAFORT *Requiem Mass* (with GUERRERO: *Gradual & Tract*). Chapelle du Roi, Alistair Dixon (with: GOMBERT: *Dicite in magni*. INFANTAS: *Domine ostende*. JOSQUIN DESPRES: *Nimphes nappés*. LOBO: *Versa est in luctum; Libera me*). Signum SIGCD 005.

TCHAIKOVSKY *Violin concerto in D, Op.35*. SAINT-SAENS: *Introduction and Rondo capriccioso*. DVORAK: *Violin concerto*. Ida Haendel, National Symphony Orchestra, Basil Cameron or Karl Rankl. Dutton Lab. CDK 1204.

Symphony No. 5 in E min., Op. 64. Vienna Philharmonic Orchestra, Valery Gergiev Philips 462 905-2.

WOLF-FERRARI *Violin concerto, Op. 26; Serenade for strings*. Ulf Hoelscher, Frankfurt Radio SO, Alun Francis CPO CPO 999 271-2

The Editor, having made only ten choices also wishes to include as a joint recommendation two outstanding new series covering Elizabethan vocal music:

The BYRD Complete Edition on ASV Gaudeamus, from Andrew Carwood and Cardinall's Musick, of which Volumes I (CDGAU 170) and II (CDGAU 178) are praised below in the body of the book. Volume III (CD GAU 179) is announced as we go to press.

The TALLIS Complete Edition on Signum, from Alistair Dixon's Chapelle du Roi, has already reached three Volumes (see below, under their composer entry): Volume I: *The Early works* (SIG 001); Volume II: *Music at the Reformation* (SIG 002); and Volume III: *Music for Queen Mary* (SIG 003).

Introduction

As in previous editions, the object of *The Penguin Guide to Compact Discs* is to give the serious collector a comprehensive survey of the finest recordings of permanent music on CD, irrespective of price. As many records are issued almost simultaneously on both sides of the Atlantic and use identical international catalogue numbers, this *Guide* should be found to be equally useful in the UK and the USA as it will in Australia, Canada and New Zealand. The internationalization of repertoire and numbers now applies to almost all CDs issued by the major international companies and also by the smaller ones. Many European labels are imported in their original formats, both into Britain and the USA. Where recordings available in Britain are not issued in America (and vice versa), this will be indicated. Those CDs that are only available in Britain can be easily obtained by overseas collectors via the Web address given on page xxi.

The sheer number of records of artistic merit now available causes considerable problems in any assessment of overall and individual excellence. What is now very clear is that most major works are available in many recordings of comparable distinction, yet usually conveying different insights. While we always try and indicate a 'best buy', the final choice will often be subjective, and may depend on a collector's personal reaction to the style of the performance as described by us, and perhaps an individual allegiance to the artists concerned.

We feel that it is a strength of our basic style to let our own conveyed pleasure and admiration (or otherwise) for the merits of an individual recording come over directly to the reader, even if this produces a certain ambivalence in the matter of such a final choice. Where there is disagreement between us (and this rarely happens), readers will find an indication of our different reactions in the text.

We have considered (and rejected) the use of initials against individual reviews, since this is essentially a team project. The occasions for disagreement generally concern matters of aesthetics – in the manner of recording balance for instance, where a contrived effect may trouble some ears more than others, or in the matter of style, where the difference between robustness and refinement of approach appeals differently to listening sensibilities rather than involving a question of artistic integrity. But over the years our views seem to have grown closer together rather than to have diverged; perhaps we are getting mellower, but we are seldom ready to offer strong disagreement following the enthusiastic reception by one of the team of a controversial recording, providing the results are creatively stimulating. As performance standards have advanced, our perceptions of the advantages and disadvantages of performances of early music on original (as against modern) instruments seem fairly evenly balanced.

EVALUATION

Most major recordings issued today are of a high technical standard and offer performances of a quality at least as high as is experienced in the concert hall. In adopting a star system for the evaluation of records, we have decided to make use of from one to three stars. Brackets around one or more of the stars indicate some reservations about a recording's rating, and readers are advised to refer to the text. Brackets around all the stars usually indicate a basic qualification: for instance, a mono recording of a performance of artistic interest, where some allowances may have to be made for the sound quality even though the recording may have been digitally remastered.

Our evaluation system may be summarized as follows:

- *** An outstanding performance and recording in every way;
- ** A good performance and recording of today's normal high standard;
- * A fair or somewhat routine performance, reasonably well performed or recorded;

Our evaluation is normally applied to the record as a whole, unless there are two main works or groups of works, and by different composers. In this case, each is dealt with separately in its appropriate place.

ROSETTES

To certain special records we have awarded a Rosette: ❁.

Unlike our general evaluations, in which we have tried to be consistent, a Rosette is a quite arbitrary compliment by a member of the reviewing team to a recorded performance which, he finds, shows special illumination, magic, a spiritual quality, or even outstanding production values, that place it in a very special class. Occasionally a Rosette has been awarded for an issue that seems to us to offer extraordinary value for money, but that presupposes that the performance or performances are outstanding too. The choice is essentially a personal one (although often it represents a shared view) and in some cases it is applied to an issue where certain reservations must also be mentioned in the text of the review. The Rosette symbol is placed before the usual evaluation and the record number. It is quite small – we do not mean to imply an 'Academy Award' but a personal token of appreciation for something uniquely valuable. We hope that once the reader has discovered and perhaps acquired a 'rosetted' CD, its special qualities will soon become apparent. There are, of course, more of them now, for our survey has become a distillation of the excellence of CDs issued and reissued over a considerable time span.

DIGITAL RECORDINGS

Nearly all new compact discs are recorded digitally, but an increasingly large number of digitally remastered, reissued analogue recordings are now appearing, and we think it important to include a clear indication of the difference:

Dig. indicates that the master recording was digitally encoded;

Analogue/Dig. (or Dig./analogue) applies to a compilation where recordings come from mixed sources.

LISTINGS AND PRICE RANGES

Our listing of each recording assumes that it is in the premium-price category, unless it indicates otherwise, as follows:

(M) Medium-priced label;
(B) Bargain-priced label;
(BB) Super-bargain label.

See below for differences in price structures in the UK and the USA.

LAYOUT OF TEXT

We have aimed to make our style as simple as possible. So, immediately after the evaluation and before the catalogue number, the record make is given, sometimes in abbreviated form. In the case of a set of two or more CDs, the number of units involved is given in brackets after the catalogue number. Cassette catalogue numbers, if they exist, are denoted by being given in *italic type*.

AMERICAN CATALOGUE NUMBERS

The numbers which follow in square brackets are US catalogue numbers, while the abbreviation [id.] indicates that the given number is used internationally, which is often the case. Even RCA has moved over to completely identical numbers, although a few earlier issues have an alphabetical prefix in the UK which is not used in the USA. Where a record is available in the USA but *not* the UK, *it will appear in square brackets only*, and that applies especially to RCA's budget 'Basic 100' series and EMI's comparable 'Red Line Classics'.

There are certain other small differences to be remembered by American readers. For instance, EMI use extra digits for their British compact discs; thus the British number CDM7 63351-2 becomes CDM 63351 in the USA (the -2 is the European indication that this is a compact disc). Prefixes can alter too. The British EMI forte and double fforte CZS5 68583-2 becomes CDFB 68583 in the USA; and Virgin Classics VBD5 61469-2 becomes CDVB 61469. We have taken care to check catalogue information as far as is possible, but as all the editorial work has been done in England there is always the possibility of error; American readers are therefore invited, when ordering records locally, to take the precaution of giving their dealer the fullest information about the music and recordings they want.

The indications (M), (B) and (BB) immediately before the starring of a disc refer primarily to the British CD, as pricing systems are not always identical on both sides of the Atlantic. But if we are aware of a difference in price for the American issue, that is indicated within the square brackets, e.g.:

(B) *** EMI CD-EMX 2055 [(M) id.].

This means that the disc is on a bargain label in the UK but is at mid-price in the USA.

When CDs are imported by specialist distributors into the USA, this again usually involves a price difference, e.g.:

(B) *** Decca Eclipse Dig. 448 710–2 [(M) id. import].

This means that the disc is on a bargain label in the UK and is a mid-priced import in the USA. (When mid-priced CDs on the smaller labels are imported into the USA, they often move up to the premium-price range.)

Where no American catalogue number is given, this does not necessarily mean that a record is not available in the USA; the transatlantic issue may not have been made at the time of the publication of this *Guide*. Readers are advised to check the current *Schwann* catalogue and to consult their local record store.

ABBREVIATIONS

To save space we have adopted a number of standard abbreviations in listing orchestras and performing groups (a list is provided below), and the titles of works are often shortened, especially where they are listed several times. Artists' forenames are sometimes omitted if they are not absolutely necessary for identification purposes. Also we have not usually listed the contents of operatic highlights and collections.

We have followed common practice in the use of the original language for titles where it seems sensible. In most cases, English is used for orchestral and instrumental music, and the original language for vocal music and opera. There are exceptions, however; for instance, the Johann Strauss discography uses the German language in the interests of consistency.

ORDER OF MUSIC

The order of music under each composer's name broadly follows the following system: orchestral music, including concertos and symphonies; chamber music; solo instrumental music (in some cases with keyboard and organ music separated); vocal and choral music; opera; vocal collections; miscellaneous collections. Within each group our listing follows an alphabetical sequence, and couplings within a single composer's output are *usually* discussed together instead of separately with cross-references. Occasionally (and inevitably because of this alphabetical approach), different recordings of a given work can become separated when a record is listed and discussed under the first work of its alphabetical sequence. The editor feels that alphabetical consistency is essential if the reader is to learn to find his or her way about.

CATALOGUE NUMBERS

Enormous care has gone into the checking of CD catalogue numbers and contents to ensure that all details are correct, but the editor and publishers cannot be held responsible for any mistakes that may have crept in despite all our zealous checking. When ordering CDs, readers are urged to provide their record-dealer with full details of the music and performers, as well as the catalogue number.

DELETIONS

Compact discs regularly succumb to the deletions axe, and many are likely to disappear during the lifetime of this book. Sometimes copies may still be found in specialist shops, and there remains the compensatory fact that most really important and desirable recordings are eventually reissued, often costing less!

EMI's Special UK Import Service, which began in the UK in August 1995, means that the whole EMI international bargain catalogue is available to UK customers. CDs which are available only through this service are indicated with the abbreviation SIS. EMI suggest that such records will no longer cost more than those in the standard UK catalogue, although recent experience suggests that SIS CDs can take a long wat to obtain. This does not affect the American equivalent issue where indicated as available.

Polygram have now followed suit with their own import service, and these CDs are indicated with the abbreviation IMS. Polygram, however, do currently make a small extra charge for those discs which have to be obtained from Germany or Holland.

COVERAGE

As the output of major and minor labels continues to expand, it is obviously impossible for us to mention every CD that is available within the covers of a single book; this is recognized as a practical limitation if we are to update our survey regularly. Indeed, we have now to be very selective in choosing the discs to be included, and some good recordings inevitably fall by the wayside. There is generally a reason for omissions, and usually it is connected with the lack of ready availablity. However, we do welcome suggestions from readers about such omissions if they seem to be of special interest, although we cannot guarantee to include them in a future survey!

ACKNOWLEDGEMENTS

Our thanks are due to our zealous new Penguin copy editor, Helen Williams, who was initially faced with the unenviable task of collating countless earlier reviews from three different sources, before they were pruned and revised by the three authors. Kathleen March once again carefully checked the proofs for errors and reminded us when the text proved ambiguous, clumsily repetitive in its descriptive terminology, or just plain contradictory, occasionally removing reviews that had somehow appeared twice!

Alan Livesey and Roy Randle contributed to the titling – never an easy task, and especially complicated in the many anthologies involving a bouquet of different performers. Alan Livesey also cast an eagle eye over the proofs, in particular looking for mistakes in the musical listings; he also helped with both titling and retrieval of earlier material (connected with reissues) especially in the hectic period immediately before we sent off our final copy. Paul Westcott and Barbara Menard both gave invaluable assistance in helping to check *every* CD against the manufacturer's inventories, to try and ensure that deleted recordings are not included. Our team of Penguin proof-readers have once again proved themselves indispensable.

Grateful thanks also go to all those readers who write to us to point out factual errors and to remind us of important recordings which have escaped our notice.

The American Scene

CDs are much less expensive in the USA than they are in Great Britain and because of this (so we are told), many bargain recordings available in England are not brought into the USA by their manufacturers. This applies especially to the Polygram group, so that Decca Eclipse, DG Classikon and Philips Virtuoso labels have to be imported by the major US record stores and mail order outlets. What this means is that while almost any recording mentioned in these pages will be available in the USA, sometimes it will cost more than the buyer might reasonably expect.

Duos and Doubles, where available, remain at two discs for the cost of one premium-priced CD in both countries, and here US collectors have a price advantage. However, according to *Schwann*, many excellent lower-priced discs are not issued in the USA. Where a recording is of extra special interest American collectors can obtain it readily by mail order from England, through the Web-site address given. However it will inevitably cost more than it would domestically.

The RCA Basic 100 series and EMI's Red Line Classics are specifically selected for the US market. We have tried to include the best of them but have ignored some of the others, where the performances and recordings seem uncompetitive.

From your many letters, and from visiting record stores in the USA, we know that our *Penguin Guide* is read, enjoyed and used as a tool by collectors on both sides of the Atlantic. We also know that some transatlantic readers feel that our reviews are too frequently orientated towards European and British recordings and performances. In concentrating on records which have common parlance in both Europe and the USA, we obviously give preference to the output of international companies, and in assessing both performers and performances we are concerned with only one factor: musical excellence. In a 400-year-old musical culture centred in Europe, it is not surprising that a great number of the finest interpreters should have been Europeans, and many of them have enjoyed recording in London, where there are four first-class symphony orchestras and many smaller groups at their disposal, supported by recording producers and engineers of the highest calibre. The early-music period-instrument revolution is also presently centred in London, which seems to add another bias, which is not of our making.

However, the continuing re-emergence of earlier recordings by major American recording orchestras and artists is slowly redressing the balance. Our performance coverage in the present volume – helped by the huge proportion of reissued older records – certainly reflects the American achievement, past and present and particularly the 1930s to 1960s. Then Koussevitzky was in Boston; Frederick Stock, and after him Fritz Reiner were in Chicago; Mitropoulos, Bruno Walter and Bernstein directed the New York Philharmonic in its heyday; Stokowski and Ormandy were in Philadelphia, and George Szell was creating astonishing standards of orchestral virtuosity in Cleveland. At the same time, Heifetz and Horowitz, Piatigorsky, Rubinstein and Isaac Stern were carrying all before them in the instrumental field. With the current phenomenal improvements in transferring technology, we hope that increasing numbers of the recordings made by these great names from the past will enjoy the attention of the wider public.

Price Differences in the UK and USA

Retail prices are not fixed in either country, and various stores may offer even better deals at times, so our price structure must be taken as a guideline only. Premium-priced CDs cost on average approximately the same number of dollars in the USA as they do pounds in the UK. The Vanguard CD label (except for the 8000 Series, which retails at around $15) is now mid-price in both the USA and UK. Harmonia Mundi's Musique d'Abord label (prefix HMA) is described as budget – which it is in the UK – but the American list-price is $9.98.

Duos and Doubles, Delos Doubles, Double Deccas, double ffortes, Dyads, Finlandia 'Meet the Composer', Chandos 2-for-1 sets, BMG/RCA 'twofers', Warner Classics Ultimas where available (although they cost less west of the Atlantic) are two-for-the-cost-of-one premium-priced disc the world over. CDCFPD, and Carlton Doubles and the new Virgin Classics 2 X 1 Doubles are two-for-the-price-of-one mid-priced-CD.

Other comparable prices in the UK and USA

Here are comparative details of the other price-ranges (note that sets are multiples of the prices quoted):

(M) MID-PRICED SERIES

Includes: Avid; Carlton 30366 series; Chandos (Collect; Enchant); Classic fM (UK only); CPO/EMI Operas (UK only); CRD; Decca/London including Classic Sound and Legends; DG (including Originals); Dutton CDEA (USA only); Dutton CDAX, CDCLP, CDK, CDLX (UK only); EMI (Classics, British music series, and Great Recordings of the Century); Erato/Warner (UK), Erato/WEA (USA); DHM; Harmonia Mundi Musique d'Abord (USA), Suite; Mercury; Oiseau-Lyre; Philips; RCA Gold Seal and Living Stereo; RCA Melodiya; Revelation; Sony; Teldec/Warner (UK), Teldec/WEA (USA); Tring (USA only); Unicorn UKCD; Vanguard; Virgin.

UK: Under £10; more usually £9;

USA: Under $13; usually under $12.

(B) BARGAIN-PRICED SERIES

Includes: Calliope Approche (UK only); Carlton (30367, 30368; more expensive: 30369, 30371); CfP; Debut; Decca Eclipse (UK only); DG Classikon (UK only); Dutton CDEA (UK only); Eminence (UK only); Harmonia Mundi Musique d'Abord (UK only); Solo; HMP; Hyperion Helios; Naxos Opera; Philips Virtuoso (UK only); Sony Essential Classics; Tring (UK only).

UK: £5.50–£7;

USA: Under $7.

(BB) SUPER-BARGAIN SERIES

Includes: Arte Nova; Arts; ASV Quicksilva (UK only); DHM Baroque Esprit; Naxos; Polygram Belart; RCA Navigator (UK only).

UK: £5; some (including Navigator) cost slightly less;

USA: $5–$6.

The Australian Scene

Not long before going to press we were fortunate in obtaining for review some recordings from the Australian branch of Universal Classics (which is responsible for the three key labels, Decca, DG and Philips). Under the artistic direction of its enterprising Australian Marketing and Repertoire Manager, Cyrus Meher-Homji, Australian Decca have been making a series of local issues of Decca Doubles of great interest.

They include what is to be a complete coverage of the mono and stereo recordings of Julius Katchen, many of which are musically and technically outstanding. These we have been able to include as an appendix to the Philips 'Great Pianists of the Twentieth Century' series.

Another current best-selling Australian Decca five-CD set is called 'The Art of Joan Sutherland' (466 474-2), which includes some of her most famous recital discs: '*French romantic arias*', '*Command performance*', and a rare Wagner recital. There is also a valuable five-CD set of organ repertoire called 'The Art of Gillian Weir'. We hope to review this and other unique Australian Universal reissues in our next Yearbook.

Editor's Note

The current range of recorded classical repertoire is overwhelmingly huge! And even though our new double-column format means that we are now able to include – within the same number of pages – far more CDs than ever before, we still only have space to consider the very finest, irrespective of price. This accounts for the very high proportion of *** listings. It also means that there are many admirable CDs covered in our companion *Penguin Guide to Bargain Compact Discs*, which cost very little and for which there there is simply no room in the present survey. So, for the serious collector it is useful to have access to the *Bargain Guide* as well as the present book.

An International Mail-order Source for Recording in the UK

Readers are urged to support a local dealer if he or she is prepared and able to give a proper service, and to remember that obtaining many CDs involves expertise and perseverance. However, in recent years many specialist sources have disappeared and for that reason, if any difficulty is experienced in obtaining the CDs you want, we suggest the following mail-order alternative, which offers competitive discounts in the UK but also operates worldwide, and is under the direction of the Editor of *The Penguin Guide to Bargain Compact Discs*, whose advice on choice of recordings is always readily available to mail-order customers:

Squires Gate Music Centre (PG Dept)
(LPRL Ltd.),
Rear 13 St Andrew's Road South,
St Annes on Sea, Lancashire FY8 1SX
U.K.
Tel.: (+44) (0) 1253 782588
Fax: (+44) (0) 1253 782985
Full Web-site Address:
http://www.lprl.demon.co.uk/index.html
Basic Web-site Address:
www.lprl.demon.co.uk

You can find out more about us on our Web site. We can supply any recording available in Britain and also the Australian CDs of Julius Katchen. This organization patiently extends compact disc orders until they finally come to hand. A full guarantee of safe delivery is made on any order undertaken. Please write or fax for further details, or make a trial credit-card order, by fax, e-mail or telephone.

❁ The Rosette Service

Squires Gate also offers a try-before-you-buy weekly loan service (within the UK only) so that customers can try out rosetted recordings at home, plus a hand-picked group of some 3,000 recommended key-repertoire CDs, for a small charge, without any obligation to purchase. If a CD is subsequently purchased, it will be discounted and the trial charge waived. Full details sent on request. The Rosette service Catalogue can be accessed via the lprl Web site. We are hoping that this service may be extended to overseas customers.

Squires Gate Music Centre also offers a simple three-monthly mailing, listing a hand-picked selection of current new and reissued CDs, chosen by the Editor of the *Penguin Guide*, Ivan March. Regular customers of Squires Gate Music Centre, both domestic and overseas, receive the bulletin as available, and it is sent automatically with their purchases. It will also be displayed on our Web site.

Abbreviations

AAM	Academy of Ancient Music
Ac.	Academy, Academic
Amb. S.	Ambrosian Singers
arr.	arranged, arrangement
ASMF	Academy of St Martin-in-the-Fields
(B)	bargain-price CD
(BB)	super-bargain-price CD
Bar.	Baroque
Bav.	Bavarian
BBC	British Broadcasting Corporation
BPO	Berlin Philharmonic Orchestra
BRT	Belgian Radio & Television (Brussels)
Cal.	Calliope
CBSO	City of Birmingham Symphony Orchestra
CfP	Classics for Pleasure
Ch.	Choir; Chorale; Chorus
CO	Chamber Orchestra
COE	Chamber Orchestra of Europe
Col. Mus. Ant.	Musica Antiqua, Cologne
Coll.	Collegium
Coll. Aur.	Collegium Aureum
Coll. Voc.	Collegium Vocale
Concg. O	Royal Concertgebouw Orchestra of Amsterdam
cond.	conductor, conducted
Cons.	Consort
DG	Deutsche Grammophon
DHM	Deutsche Harmonia Mundi
Dig.	digital recording
E.	England, English
ECCO	European Community Chamber Orchestra
ECO	English Chamber Orchestra
ENO	English National Opera Company
Ens.	Ensemble
ESO	English Symphony Orchestra
Fr.	French
GO	Gewandhaus Orchestra
HM	Harmonia Mundi
Hung.	Hungaroton
[id.]	same record number for US and European versions
IMS	Import Music Service (Polygram – UK only)
L.	London
LA	Los Angeles
LCO	London Chamber Orchestra
LMP	London Mozart Players
LOP	Lamoureux Orchestra of Paris
LPO	London Philharmonic Orchestra
LSO	London Symphony Orchestra
(M)	mid-price CD
[(M)id. import]	mid-price; same catalogue number, only available as an import
Mer.	Meridian
Met.	Metropolitan
min.	minor
MoC	Ministry of Culture
movt	movement
N.	North, Northern
nar.	narrated
Nat.	National
NY	New York
O	Orchestra, Orchestre
OAE	Orchestra of the Age of Enlightenment
O-L	Oiseau-Lyre
Op.	Opera (in performance listings); opus (in music titles)
orch.	orchestrated
ORR	Orchestre Révolutionnaire et Romantique
ORTF	L'Orchestre de la radio et télévision française
Ph.	Philips
Phd.	Philadelphia
Philh.	Philharmonia
PO	Philharmonic Orchestra
Qt	Quartet
R.	Radio
RLPO	Royal Liverpool Philharmonic Orchestra
ROHCG	Royal Opera House, Covent Garden
RPO	Royal Philharmonic Orchestra
RSNO	Royal Scottish National Orchestra
RSO	Radio Symphony Orchestra
RTE	Radio Television Eireann
S.	South
SCO	Scottish Chamber Orchestra
Sinf.	Sinfonietta
SIS	Special Import Service (EMI – UK only)
SNO	Scottish National Orchestra
SO	Symphony Orchestra
Soc.	Society
Sol. Ven.	I Solisti Veneti
SRO	Suisse Romande Orchestra
Sup.	Supraphon

trans.	transcription, transcribed
V.	Vienna
Van.	Vanguard
VCM	Vienna Concentus Musicus
VPO	Vienna Philharmonic Orchestra
VSO	Vienna Symphony Orchestra
W.	West
WNO	Welsh National Opera Company

Abel, Carl Friedrich (1723–87)

6 Symphonies, Op. 7.
**(*) Chandos Dig. CHAN 8648 [id.]. Cantilena, Shepherd.

The six *Symphonies* of Op. 7 speak much the same language as J. C. Bach or early Mozart. The performances are not the last word in elegance, but they are both lively and enjoyable as well as well recorded.

Abrahamsen, Hans (born 1952)

Märchenbilder; Winternacht; (i) *Lied in Fall.*
(N) ** Marco Polo Dacapo Dig. 8.224080 [id.]. (i) Christopher van Kampen; London Sinfonietta, Elgar Howarth (with NIELSEN: *Three Pieces, Op. 59* arr. ABRAHAMSEN).

The Danish composer Hans Abrahamsen belongs to the same generation as Poul Ruders, and like him studied with Per Nørgård. The earliest piece on the disc is *Winternacht* (1976–8), a poetic, dreamy work with subtle and imaginative textures. But most of his music, including the *Lied in Fall*, written for the cellist Christopher van Kampen, while full of fantasy is primarily static in feeling. The disc is completed with an unconvincing transcription of the three late piano pieces of Nielsen. Admirers of the 'new simplicity' of which Abrahamsen is a committed advocate need not hesitate. Good recording.

Abril, Anton Garcia (born 1933)

Concierto Mudéjar.
(N) *** Analekta Fleur de lys Dig. FL 2 3049 [id.]. Rémi Boucher, Amati Ens., Raymond Dessaints – TORROBA: *Sonatina; Interludes.* ***

This highly enjoyable coupling provides an excellent début for the French-Canadian label, Fleur de lys, which, like the artists featured here is based in Québec. The guitarist, Rémi Boucher, studied in Spain as well as Canada and is a complete master of this repertoire. The *Concerto* by the Aragonese composer Anton Abril is attractively idiomatic. After an enticingly ruminative opening, the main theme of the first movement is developed most inventively and the haunting central *Andante* clearly draws on slow movements by predecessors, Castelnuovo-Tedesco and Rodrigo. There are sinuous Moorish influences in the lyrical moments of the dancing zapateado finale which is also highly individual. The performance is superb in all respects, for Dessaints and his Amati Ensemble prove to be first-class accompanists. The recording too is truthful, warm and pleasing. Highly recommended.

Adam, Adolphe (1803–56)

Le Corsaire (ballet): complete.
*** Decca (IMS) Dig. 430 286-2 (2) [id.]. ECO, Richard Bonynge.

Le Corsaire is agreeably colourful and amiably melodic, but has little of the distinction of *Giselle.* Bonynge conducts it with finesse, warmth and drama, and the recording is out of Decca's top drawer.

Giselle (ballet) complete
(B) *** Decca Double Dig. 452 185-2 [id.]. ROHCGO, Richard Bonynge.
Giselle (older European score).
(BB) *** Naxos Dig. 8.550755/6 [id.]. Slovak RSO, Mongrelia.
(M) **(*) Mercury 434 365-2 (2). LSO, Fistoulari – OFFENBACH: *Gaîté Parisienne*; Johann STRAUSS: *Graduation ball.* *

Giselle (1841) is the first of the great classical ballet scores. Andrew Mongrelia's complete recording uses the normal performing edition. The orchestral playing has grace, elegance and plenty of life: the brass are not ashamed of melodrama. The recording is resonantly full and warm in ambience, yet well detailed.

Bonynge's performance on Decca restores Adam's original and is that bit more strongly characterized, while the Decca sound has a slightly sharper and brighter profile. That remains first choice (at Double Decca price), but the Naxos set costs slightly less.

Mercury's complete recording, like Mongrelia's, draws on the score that was in general use before the war. Fistoulari was a great ballet conductor and the LSO play superbly for him: there is drama in plenty, while in the gentle lyrical music his magical touch consistently beguiles the ear. The CD transfer is very successful, and the early stereo sounds remarkably modern, full-bodied and has plenty of bloom. The snag is that the quite logical Offenbach and Johann Strauss fill-ups were among Mercury's least successful Minneapolis recordings.

Le Toréador (opera) complete.
(N) *** Decca Dig. 455 664-2 [id.]. Sumi Jo, Michel Tremont, John Aler, WNO, Richard Bonynge.

Richard Bonynge is the first hero of this enchanting set of *Le Toréador* by Adolphe Adam, giving this delightful cross between opera and operetta just the sparkle and lift needed, with excellent WNO forces vividly recorded. This is a very Parisian piece built on a farcical love plot which results at the end in a convenient if highly immoral *ménage à trois*. Adam here offers the frothiest score, full of zest, crowned by a great coloratura show-piece, the variations on *Ah vous dirai-je maman* ('Twinkle twinkle, little star'). That inspires Sumi Jo to a dazzling performance, with John Aler as the flautist–lover and Michel Tremont as the old toreador–husband equally idiomatic. Spectacular sound with the copious spoken dialogue well coordinated.

Adams, John (born 1947)

(i) *Chamber concerto; Shaker loops* (chamber version). (ii) *Phrygian Gates* (Piano).
(N) *** RCA Dig. 09026 68674-2 [id.]. (i) Ens. Modern, Sian Edwards; (ii) Hermann Kretzschmar.

Even more than the composer's own version, Sian Edward's performance of the *Chamber concerto* establishes its popular credentials. Under her direction the Ensemble Modern creates a dazzling wildness, with the polyphonic tapestries of the outer movements catching both the Stravinskian rhythmic influences in the one, and the composer's vernacular jazzy leverage on the other. In between, the central walkabout – gathering textural complexities as it proceeds – becomes quite haunting. The string septet version of *Shaker loops* is just as compelling as the version for string orchestra, especially when presented with the present combination of intimacy and concentration of atmosphere. *Phrygian Gates*, written in the same year (1978), is certainly a convincing exploitation of the minimalist idiom in an extended (24-minute) piano work, even if some listeners may feel it could have been more concise. Hermann Kretzschmar's bravura performance holds the listener's attention throughout its gradual shifts of mood and elliptical metamorphoses, but Gloria Cheng-Cochran (see below) is more imaginative in her tonal shading. Excellent recording throughout.

Chamber symphony; Grand pianola music.
*** Elektra Nonesuch/Warner Dig. 7559 79219-2 [id.]. L. Sinf., composer.

This Elektra coupling combines the *Grand pianola music*, one of the most immediately accessible and inspired examples of minimalism, with a piece that is initially more intractable, the *Chamber symphony*, written for 15 instruments and inspired by Schoenberg's Opus 9 (the choice of instrumentation is both comparable and different). It is surely given a definitive performance here. In the composer's hands *Grand pianola music* projects with overwhelmingly thrilling impact, and with extensive and illuminating notes from John Adams himself, this is a key issue in the Adams discography.

(i) *Violin concerto;* (ii) *Shaker loops.*
*** Nonesuch/Warner Dig. 7559 79360-2 [id.]. (i) Kremer, LSO, Nagano; (ii) O of St Luke's, composer.

This concerto makes a strong impression, and undoubtedly Gidon Kremer's account of the fiendishly demanding solo part is dazzling. The performance is superb and the dreamlike *Chaconne* which forms the central slow movement offers aural and spiritual balm but, with the soloist closely balanced, not all listeners will find it easy to last out the bravura battering provided by the 15-minute opening movement. *Shaker loops* is hypnotically involving, and the atmospherically recorded performance by the composer tends to trump previous versions.

(i) *El Dorado*; (ii) *Berceuse élégiaque* (arrangement for chamber orchestra of Busoni's *Cradle song of the man at his mother's coffin*). *The black gondola* (orchestration of Liszt's *La lugubre gondola*).
(N) *** Nonesuch/Warner Dig. 7559 79359-2 [id.]. (i) Hallé O, Kent Nagano; (ii) L. Sinf., John Adams.

El Dorado is a diptych of paired orchestral canvases inspired (in 1991) by two giant paintings the composer saw side-by-side at the time of the 500th anniversary of the Spanish 'discovery' of the New World. Adams sums up his intentions in his notes, which are always illuminating: the first part is 'a musical embodiment of aggressive growth, beginning in a pre-dawn forest and culminating thirteen minutes later in a vast crescendo of brutal force'; the second, *Soledades*, is 'a landscape without man, the governing form a grand arch'. This is also about growth but undistorted, with wavelike undulations and a dreamlike character that is curiously life-enhancing and, unlike the first evocation, essentially serene and optimistic in its closing diminuendo. The two arrangements confirm Adams's skill as an imaginative orchestrator. Whereas Busoni's affecting *Berceuse élégiaque* gains a touching added intimacy from its more economical scoring, Liszt's essentially pianistic *La lugubre gondola* is expanded and transformed into a darkly sensuous tone-painting of the gondola, gliding through sluggish Venetian waters carrying a coffin. John Adams is a splendid advocate of his own music and Nagano's Hallé version of the major work is equally committed and compelling.

(i) *Gnarly buttons*. (ii) *John's Book of Alleged Dances*.
(N) *** Nonesuch/Warner Dig. 7559 79465-2 [id.]. (i) Michael Collins, L. Sinf., composer; (ii) Kronos Qt.

The clarinet was the composer's own instrument and his concertante work, *Gnarly Buttons* is autobiographical and fashioned in three sections. The monodic line of *The perilous shore* is 'a trope on a Protestant shape-note hymn'; it twists and turns and then gathers texture as it proceeds on its relatively intimate journey. *Hoe down (Mad cow)* is even more intricately energetic, but ends nostalgically to make way for *Put your loving arms around me*, a touchingly 'simple song, quiet and tender upfront'. The work was written for Michael Collins who gives a haunting performance which the composer describes as ideal. *John's Book of Alleged Dances* (alleged 'because the steps for them have yet to be invented') opens and closes with a catchy rhythmic ostinato – 'vehicular music, following the streetcar tracks out into the fog and ultimately to the beach' and the composer's two-room cottage. The nine dances which come in between are bustling with creative energy, six of them 'accompanied by a giddy rhythm track made of prepared piano sounds'. Even the graceful Pavane, *She's so fine*, eventually gathers impetus, but the *Habanera* is seductive and the slithering scales of *Alligator's escalator* provides further bizarre contrast. The composer's minimalist imagination knows no bounds and the Kronos players respond with much bravura to his kaleidoscopic ideas. The witty documentation from Adams himself is a delight.

Grand pianola music; Short ride in a fast machine (arr. for wind band by Lawrence T. Odom).
**(*) Chandos Dig. CHAN 9393 [id.]. Netherlands Wind Ens., Stephen Moscow (with LANG: *Are you experienced?* etc. (***)).

John Adams's *Short ride in a fast machine* brings great exhilaration and sounds splendid in the clever arrangement for wind ensemble by Lawrence T. Odom. *Grand pianola music* also suits the Netherlands group and is very seductively played, even if detail is less well defined than in the composer's own recording, and Stephen Moscow's account of the last movement also misses some of the sheer physical exhilaration of the climax. The couplings, too, are a highly debatable proposition.

Harmonielehre; The Chairman dances; (i) *2 Fanfares: Tromba Lontana; Short ride in a fast machine.*
*** EMI Dig. CDC5 55051-2 [id. import]. CBSO, Simon Rattle; (i) with Jonathan Holland, Wesley Warren.

Harmonielehre is an extraordinary, large-scale (39-minute) work in three parts. Its minimalist progress is powerfully sustained by Rattle. *The Chairman dances* his foxtrot for a full 13 minutes, if with unabated energy. The *Two Fanfares* mystically and hauntingly pay their respects to Ives as well as Copland while the *Short* (exhilarating) *ride in a fast machine*, is just as described in the title and has an agreeably unstoppable momentum. The performances bring the most persuasive advocacy and the excellent recording is clear, vivid and spacious.

Shaker loops.
✿ (M) *** Virgin/EMI CUV5 61121-2 [id.]. LCO, Warren-Green – GLASS: *Company* etc.; REICH: *8 Lines;* HEATH: *Frontier.* ***
(N) (B) *** Ph. Virtuoso 412 214-2 [id. import]. San Francisco SO, De Waart – REICH: *Variations for winds, strings and keyboards.* ***

The inspired performance by Christopher Warren-Green and his London Concert Orchestra is full of imaginative intensity, and understandably it received the composer's imprimatur. Outstandingly vivid recording.

The alternative San Francisco version is also first rate and very well recorded, and if the coupling is less generous in time, the Philips reissue is in the bargain range.

PIANO MUSIC

China gates; Phrygian gates.
(N) *** Telarc Dig. CD 80513 [id.]. Gloria Cheng-Cochran – RILEY: *Heavenly ladder, Book 7; Walrus in memoriam.* ***

The miniature, *China gates* is a companion piece to the major work here. It has moments of charm somehow reminiscent of Liadov, and some may feel its briefness is an asset. However Gloria Cheng-Cochran makes a very good case for *Phrygian gates*, which is (in the words of the composer) 'a 26-minute tour of half the cycle of keys, modulating by a circle of fifths rather than stepwise'. The performance here is impressive in its control of mood and Miss Cheng-Cochran's veiled timbre in the music's reflective sections is seductively warm – especially so in the sustained chorale-like passage before her crescendo leads into a final burst of virtuosic energy, followed by a long closing tenuto which is very telling. Excellent recording. An important disc for those interested in minimalism.

CHORAL MUSIC

Harmonium.
*** Telarc Dig. CD 80363 [id.]. Atlanta Ch. & SO, Robert Shaw – RACHMANINOV: *The Bells.* ***

Harmonium is a setting of three poems. John Donne's curiously oblique 'Negative love' opens the piece, with the orchestra lapping evocatively round the chorus. The other two poems are by Emily Dickinson. Robert Shaw's performance is very impressive and the Telarc recording is suitably atmospheric and spectacular in its spaciousness and amplitude in the closing *Wild nights*. Coupled with Rachmaninov, this easily displaces the earlier, San

Francisco version under Edo de Waart (ECM 821 465-2) which had no coupling at all.

OPERA

The Death of Klinghoffer (complete).
*** Elektra-Nonesuch/Warner Dig. 7559 79281-2 (2) [id.]. Sylvan, Maddalena, Friedman, Hammons, E. Op. Ch., Op. de Lyon, Nagano.

The Death of Klinghoffer is far closer to a dramatic oratorio than to an opera, with its lack of incident and its sequence of meditative solos and choruses of comment. Kent Nagano conducts Lyon Opéra forces with the original singers who directly inspired the composer. The treatment of the story, based on the age-old conflict between Palestinians and Jews, is conscientiously dispassionate. The closing scene brings the one solo of fully operatic intensity, the bitter concluding lament of Klinghoffer's wife, Marilyn. The mezzo, Sheila Nadler, rises to the challenge superbly, and the baritone Sanford Sylvan is comparably sensitive as Klinghoffer himself, well matched by James Maddalena as the Captain, an Evangelist-like commentator, and by Thomas Hammons and Janice Felty in multiple roles. The recorded sound is excellent, but the booklet reproduces an unrevised version of the libretto.

I was looking at the ceiling and then I saw the sky.
(N) **(*) Elektra-Nonesuch/Warner Dig. 7559 79473-2 [id.]. de Haas, Mazzie, McDonald, McElroy, Muenz, Teek, Yang, composer.

Inspired by the 1994 California earthquake, using for its title a quotation from one of the survivors, this theatre-piece is an intriguing amalgam of opera and musical. It starts with persistent ostinatos in Adams's early minimalist style, then launches into melodic lines echoing pop and jazz. The first and last of the fifteen numbers are ensembles for the whole cast, with separate numbers for each character in between, whether solo or duet. The dramatic point is lessened on the disc, when no linking dialogue is included, but the mixture is undemanding and agreeable, often moving. Even so, it can hardly compare in its impact with Adams's mainstream operas. Conducted by the composer, the performance with a characterful line-up of singers, is persuasively idiomatic, confidently spanning the divide between classical, popular and jazz. Vivid, upfront sound.

Addinsell, Richard (1904–77)

Film and theatre music: *Fire over England: suite. Goodbye Mr Chips: theme* (arr. Alwyn). *Journey to Romance* (radio feature): *Invocation. The Prince and the Showgirl:* selection (arr. Felton Rapley). *Ring round the Moon: Invitation waltz* (orch. Alwyn). (i) *A Tale of Two Cities: Theme* (arr. Gamley). *Tom Brown's Schooldays: Overture* (arr. Alwyn). (ii) *Trespass: Festival* (beguine). *The Isle of apples;* (ii) *Smokey Mountain concerto;* (i) *Tune in G.*
**(*) Marco Polo Dig. 8.223732 [id.]. BBC Concert O, Kenneth Alwyn, with (i) Roderick Elms; (ii) Philip Martin.

Kenneth Alwyn has pieced a good deal of the material together here where original scores are lost, notably in the 'Overture' from the film music for *Tom Brown's Schooldays* and the charming introductory sequence for *Goodbye Mr Chips*. Not all Addinsell's invention is distinguished, but the *Invitation waltz* for Christopher Fry's translation, *Ring round the Moon*, of Jean Anouilh's *L'Invitation au château* is quite haunting, as is the gentle idyll, *The Isle of apples*, and the simple *Tune in G* with its piano embroidery. These pieces, like the *Smokey Mountain concerto*, were independent compositions. Alwyn and the BBC Concert Orchestra are thoroughly at home in this repertoire and they present it all freshly, the recording bright but with rather a brash sonority.

Warsaw concerto.
(B) *** Ph. Virtuoso Dig. 411 123-2 [id.]. Misha Dichter, Philh. O, Marriner (with Concert of concertante music ***).
(M) *** Decca Dig. 430 726-2 [414 348-2]. Ortiz, RPO, Atzmon – GERSHWIN: *Rhapsody* **(*); GOTTSCHALK: *Grand fantasia* ***; LISZT: *Hungarian fantasia* *** (with LITOLFF: Scherzo).

Richard Addinsell's pastiche miniature concerto, written for the film *Dangerous moonlight* in 1942, is perfectly crafted; moreover it has a truly memorable main theme. It is beautifully played here, with Marriner revealing the most engaging orchestral detail. The sound is first rate and the Virtuoso reissue has an attractive new livery.

The alternative from Cristina Ortiz is a warmly romantic account, spacious in conception If the couplings are suitable, this is a rewarding collection, more substantial than Dichter's. The recording is first class.

(i) *Warsaw concerto* (orch. & arr. Roy Douglas). Film music: *Blithe spirit (Waltz theme).* (ii) *The Day will Dawn (Tea-time music). Greengage Summer: suite* (arr. Philip Lane). (ii) *Highly Dangerous: Theme. The Lion has Wings: Cavalry of the Clouds (march). Out of the Clouds: Theme. The Passionate Friends: Lover's moon. Sea Devils (Prologue). Under Capricorn: Theme.* Radio themes: *Britain to America: March of the United Nations.* (ii) *Journey into Romance: Invocation for piano and orchestra.*
(N) (M) *** ASV Dig. CDWHL 2108 [id.]. R. Ballet Sinf., Kenneth Alwyn; with (i) Martin Jones; (ii) Peter Lawson.

Richard Addinsell had the precious gift of melody, and as this delightful collection shows, they came tumbling out unstintingly. He needed others to help with arrangements and scoring, and it is good that Roy Douglas here receives belated recognition for his work in fashioning Addinsell's musical ideas and cleverly scoring them as a Rachmaninov pastiche for the justly famous *Warsaw concerto*. Its utterly memorable second subject was apparently written many years earlier when Addinsell was an Oxford undergraduate, and it was judiciously 'slowed down' to provide the lyrical centre-piece. But there are many other good things here, and Philip Lane's cleverly fashioned suite from the film *The Greengage Summer* brims over with delightful ideas. Douglas Gamley assisted the composer in this instance, and other credits include Leonard Isaac and Ron Goodwin (who scored the *Cavalry of the Clouds* march). Perhaps Addinsell's melodic gift was slight, but when trifles like the *Tea-time music* from *The Day will Dawn* and the delicious *Waltz* from *Blithe Spirit* are played with such affection and polish under the understanding Kenneth Alwyn, their gentle spirit is life-enhancing. The *Warsaw concerto* is treated as a miniature masterpiece and given a performance which is as dramatic as it is heart-warming. Martin Jones is the splendid soloist, and Peter Lawson contributes equally sensitively to the several other concertante numbers. The recording is first class in every way. Not to be missed.

Adès, Thomas (born 1971)

(i; ii) *Asyla, Op. 17;* (i; iii) *. . . but all shall be well, Op. 10;* (iii; iv) *Chamber symphony for 15 players, Op. 2;* (iii; iv; v) *Concerto conciso for piano and chamber orchestra, Op. 18;* (i; iii) *These premises are alarmed, Op. 18.*
(N) *** EMI Dig. CDC5 56818-2 [id.]. (i) CBSO; (ii) cond. Sir Simon Rattle (iii) cond. Composer; (iv) Birmingham Contemporary Music Group; (v) with Composer (piano).

Rattle's superbly compelling account of *Asyla* (plural of 'asylum') is a live recording, made in Symphony Hall Birmingham in August 1998, confirming that this is Adès's major orchestral work so far, one which surely will join the repertoire. It opens with a soaring horn solo over tuned percussion and in the same way another memorable lyrical theme appears in the second movement, soon to be sung by the bass oboe. Perhaps the most striking movement of all is the Scherzo, marked *Ecstasio*, which also begins gently, but soon develops a Stravinskian rhythmic furore and at its climax produces an orchestral *coup* – a thrilling drum and fife march to set the demons dancing. The finale opens sombrely, but finds a positive resolution. The *Chamber symphony*, is extraordinarily intricate in its rhythmic ideas, developing ear-tickling colouristic patterns, reaching a shrill climax in the third movement, but with the finale reflective. The *Concerto conciso* has the solo piano well integrated into the instrumental group, where rhythms are free and jazzy, but brings a calm central chaconne before the closing 'Brawl'. *These Premises are Alarmed* is a brief witty apoplexy, designed as a brilliant orchestral showpiece for the Hallé Orchestra. Balance is restored in . . . *but all shall be well*, the title coming from *Little Gidding*, the last of T. S. Eliot's *Four Quartets*. It opens out of infinity, again against exotic percussion, moves ruminatively up and down a scale, and is hauntingly and intricately varied before a final 'consolation'. Remarkable music, splendidly played, and most vividly and atmospherically recorded.

(i) *Living toys, Op. 9.* (ii) *Arcadiana, Op. 12*; (iii) *The Origin of the harp, Op. 13*; (iv) *Sonata da caccia, Op. 11*; (v) Anthem: *Gefriolsae me, Op. 3b.*
(N) (B) *** EMI Début CDZ5 72271-2 [id.]. (i) L. Sinf., Markus Stenz; (ii) Endellion Qt.; (iii) Marsh, Robson, Richards, Busbridge, Knight, Boyd, Hopkins, Watkins, Tunnell, Benjafield, cond. composer; (iv) Niesemann, Clark, Composer; (v) King's College, Cambridge Ch., Cleobury; Quinney.

This second disc of Thomas Adès's music in EMI's Debut series offers four substantial works from 1993 and 1994, plus a hushed, deeply devotional motet which he wrote in 1990 for King's College Choir. If that is harmonically more conventional than the rest, it is still most original, while conversely, even when Adès's writing is at its most abrasive, its communicative power is never in doubt. *Living toys* is a brilliant and colourful sequence of eight movements inspired by the naively heroic ambitions of a Spanish child. *Arcadiana*, in a sequence of seven short movements, is Adès's first string quartet, regularly exploiting original timbres and textures, and paying direct tribute in turn (without direct quotation) to Mozart's *Die Zauberflöte*, Schubert's *Aus dem Wasser zu singen* and – most movingly – Elgar's *Nimrod*. The *Sonata da caccia* is a trio for baroque oboe, horn and harpsichord, written in devotion to Couperin, which in its neo-classicism rises well clear of pastiche. The *Origin of the harp* is more enigmatic, an evocation of a symbolic Victorian painting for trios of clarinets, violas and cellos, plus percussion. Excellent performances and recording. Whatever he does, Adès cannot help creating original sounds.

Powder her face (opera; complete).
(N)*** EMI Dig. CDC5 56649-2 [CDC 56649] (2). Gomez, Anderson, Morris, Bryson, Almeida Ens., Composer.

For his first opera Thomas Adès, most brilliant of the younger generation of British composers, presents what might be described as a cabaret opera.

He bases it on the life of the notorious Duchess of Argyll, toast of smart London society in the 1930s, seen in a sequence of flashbacks from the scene in 1990 when, in final penury, she is evicted from her penthouse suite at the Dorchester hotel. Flashy and superficial, she yet emerges as a pathetic, often ridiculous, yet finally touching figure, with Adès's music regularly echoing the popular music of the 1930s, grotesquely distorted. Forces are modest, with three of the four singers taking multiple roles. With voices overlapping, words are not always clear, but the progress of the plot is never obscured, and the result is both offbeat and attractive, with Adès's idiom always approachable and his timing adding the necessary point. Under the composer's energetic direction, with the original cast powerfully headed by Jill Gomez as the Duchess, the recording can be warmly recommended, with colourful chamber textures vividly caught.

Adorno, Theodor (1903–69)

String quartet; 2 Pieces for string quartet, Op. 2; 6 Studies for string quartet.

(N) *** CPO Dig. CPO 999 341-2 [id.]. Leipzig Qt – EISLER: *Prelude and fugue on B-A-C-H, Op. 46; String quartet.* ***

Before he embarked on his career as a philosopher, Theodor Wiesengrund Adorno nourished musical ambitions. The *Six Studies*, composed when he was seventeen in 1920 show an awareness of Schoenberg's musical language. There are many imaginative touches both here and in the *String quartet* of the following year. Neither is negligible even if neither possesses a significantly personal voice. In 1925 he became a pupil of Alban Berg who exerted some influence on the *Two Pieces for string quartet, Op. 2*. The music is much less impenetrable than much of his prose to which he devoted his mature life. The performances and recordings qualify for a three-star rating though the music itself is another matter!

Aho, Kalevi (born 1949)

(i) *Violin concerto; Hiljaisuus (Silence); Symphony No. 1.*

*** BIS Dig. CD 396 [id.]. (i) Manfred Gräsbeck; Lahti SO, Vänskä.

Aho's *First Symphony* betokens an impressive musical personality at work. *Silence* is an imaginative piece. It is related to (and was conceived as an introduction to) the post-expressionist and more 'radical' and trendy *Violin concerto*; it is a work of considerable resource and imaginative intensity. Good performances and recording.

Symphonies Nos. 2; 7 (Insect Symphony).

(N) *** BIS Dig. CD 936 [id.]. Lahti SO, Osmo Vänskä.

The Finnish composer, Kalevi Aho has just turned fifty and already has ten symphonies to his credit. The *Second* is a powerfully conceived and cogently argued work in one movement, predominantly fugal in texture indebted to the world of Shostakovich and Bartók. It was composed in 1970 when he was still a pupil of Rautavaara, though Aho made a number of small revisions in 1995. The *Seventh Symphony* derives its material from an opera, *Insect Life* (based on a play by Karel Čapek). Written in 1985–7, and facing little prospect of performance as the new Finnish National Opera House was being built, Aho decided to refashion its ideas in symphonic form. Each of the six movements is programmatic with titles like *Fox-trot* and *Tango of the Butterflies*, *The Dung beetles* and so on. It is more of a symphonic suite than symphony but scored imaginatively and with flair. Impeccable performances and extremely fine recording.

(i) *Bassoon quintet;* (ii) *Quintet for alto saxophone, bassoon, viola, cello and double bass.*

(N) *** BIS Dig. CD 866 [id.]. (i) Sinfonia Lahti Ch. Ens.

This is part of BIS's ambitious ongoing project to record the complete output of Aho. The *Bassoon quintet* comes from 1977, when the composer was still in his twenties and its six movements played without a break run to 37 minutes. It shows great understanding of the instruments though it has its longueurs. The *Quintet for alto saxophone, bassoon, viola, cello and double bass* – an unusual combination but one rich in tonal variety – is the more concentrated of the two and leaves no doubt as to Aho's instrumental resource and imagination in writing for this ensemble. Virtuoso performances and natural, vivid recording.

Alain, Jehan (1911–40)

Complete organ music

Andante; Aria; Ballade; Berceuse sur deux notes qui cornent; Choral cistercien; Choral dorien; Choral phryien; Climat; 3 Danses; 2 Danses à Agni Yavishta; Grave; Monodie; Premier Fantaisie; Deuxième Fantaisie; Intermezzo; Le jardin suspendu; Lamento; Litanies; Petite pièce; Postlude pour l'office des Complies; Premier Prélude; Deuxième Prélude; Prélude et fugue; Suite; Variations sur l'hymne 'Lucis Creator'; Variations sur un thème de Clément Jannequin.

(N) ✽ *** Erato/Warner Ultima 3984 26996-2 (2) [id.]. Marie-Claire Alain (Valtrin-Callinet-Schwenkedel organ of Basilique Saint-Christophe, Belfort, France).

Vol. 1: *Ballade en mode phrygien; Choral cistercien; Choral phrygien; Climat; 2 Danses à Agni Yavishta; Deuxième Fantaisie; Le jardin suspendu; Litanies; Monodie; Petite pièce;*

Préludes profanes 1–2; Suite; Variations sur un thème de Clément Jannequin.
(BB) *** Naxos Dig. 8.553632 [id.]. Eric Lebrun (Cavaillé-Coll organ of the Church of Saint-Antoine des Quinze-Vingts, Paris).

Vol. 2: *Aria; Berceuse sur les deux notes qui Cornent; Choral dorien; 3 Danses; Grave; Intermezzo; Lamento; Postlude pour l'office des Complies; Prélude et fugue; Première Fantaisie; Variations sur l'hymne 'Lucis Creator'.*
(BB) *** Naxos Dig. 8.553633 [id.]. Eric Lebrun (Cavaillé-Coll organ of the Church of Saint-Antoine des Quinze-Vingts, Paris).

Jehan Alain was killed in action in the early days of the Second World War, thus cutting short a career which had already shown enormous promise. His output reveals a distinctive and powerful voice. Eric Lebrun is completely attuned to Alain's sound-world. His Cavaillé-Coll at the Church of Saint-Antoine des Quinze-Vingts in Paris is ideal. Readers who have yet to discover this music should lose no time in making its acquaintance: Alain's writing has virtuosity and harmonic resource to commend it. Try *Le jardin suspendu*, which has a Messiaen-like atmosphere. These performances are thoroughly recommendable and at the price make a splendid bargain.

However, the reissue of Marie-Claire Alain's outstanding 1972 set on an Erato Ultima Double, quite upstages the Naxos discs, fine as they are. The composer was her brother and she plays his music with extraordinary dedication and concentration. In her hands, pieces like *Le jardin suspendu* and the *Postlude pour l'office des Complies* are hauntingly mystic in atmosphere, and the three *Chorals* have a palpable inner radiance. The chosen organ is ideal for her purposes, and she conjures a marvellous range of bright colours from it. The opening of the *Première Fantaisie* brings a riveting burst of luminescence. These performances are unsurpassed and surely unsurpassable.

Prière pour nous autres charnels.
*** Chandos Dig. CHAN 9504 [id.]. Martyn Hill, Neal Davies, BBC PO, Yan Pascal Tortelier – DUTILLEUX: *Violin concerto etc.* ***

Jehan Alain composed this short but beautiful setting of a prayer by Péguy for two soloists and organ. It is a moving piece, modal yet rich in its musical language, and it makes an admirable makeweight to the Dutilleux works.

Albéniz, Isaac (1860–1909)

Iberia (suite; orch. Arbós).
*** Chandos Dig. CHAN 8904 [id.]. Philh. O, Yan Pascal Tortelier – FALLA: *Three-cornered hat.* ***

The Philharmonia's response brings glowing woodwind colours and seductive string phrasing, well projected by the warmly resonant recording.

Iberia (Books I–IV) complete (orch. Arbós and Surinach).
(M) **(*) Telarc Dig. 2CD-80470 [id.]. Cincinnati SO, Jésus López-Cobos.

The four Books of piano pieces (with three in each), which make up Albéniz's *Iberia*, were written between 1906 and 1908 and are regularly heard and recorded in their original format. But this is the recording première of the complete orchestral version. Jésus López-Cobos is thoroughly at home in this repertory, and the Cincinnati orchestra responds to his flexible rubato very persuasively; the Mediterranean atmosphere is agreeably sultry, with some lovely warm Cincinnati string-playing. The rhythms too are often nicely bounced. The 'Fête-Dieu' climax of *El Corpus en Sevilla* is very spectacular indeed, with the bass drum coming through as one expects from this label; and many will like the relative lack of garishness here. But the playing, though warmly committed, could ideally be more gutsy. The Telarc recording is sumptuous but at times one longs for more transparent and subtle textures – and indeed for a little more glitter. The set comes with two discs costing the same as one premium-priced CD, but with an overall timing of only 82 minutes.

Iberia: Triana; Fête-dieu à Seville. Navarra (all orch. Arbós).
(M) *** RCA 09026 62586-2 [id.]. Chicago SO, Reiner – FALLA: *El amor brujo* etc.; GRANADOS: *Goyescas: Intermezzo.* ***

This vintage Reiner collection of Spanish music is especially notable for the remarkably idiomatic account of these Albéniz pieces. The Latin passion of the climax of *Navarra* is matched by the climax of *Fête-dieu à Seville*, in which Reiner captures the boisterous vulgarity of a Spanish religious procession with superb aplomb. Vintage Chicago recording from 1958, still sounding amazingly ripe and vivid.

(i) *Iberia* (suite; orch. Arbós); *Navarra* (completed De Sévérec); (ii; iv) *Rapsodia española* (arr. Halffter); (iii; iv) *Suite española* (orch. Frühbeck de Burgos).
(N) (B) *** Decca Double Analogue/Dig. 433 905-2 (2) [id.]. (i) SRO, Ansermet; (ii) de Larrocha, LPO; (iii) New Philh. O; (iv) Frühbeck de Burgos – TURINA: *Danzas fantásticas; La oración del torero; Rapsodia sinfónica.* (With GRANADOS: *Goyescas: Intermezzo; Danza española No. 5.* SARASATE: *Aires gitanos*: Ricci, LSO, Gamba. ***)

This collection, as part of Decca's '*Música española*' series gathers a great deal of attractive music together, some of it already available separately (see below). It restores to the catalogue Ansermet's early stereo version of the Arbós orchestral suite from *Ibéria*, and the 1960 Geneva recording still sounds remarkably full and vivid. Ansermet's natural spontaneity combines meticulous care with colouring and balance, so that inner detail is sharper than with Reiner, but the latter scores with more polished, more opulent orchestral playing. The Sarasate *Aires gitanos* from Ricci, with Gamba and the LSO, played with genuine panache, date from the same recording period and are no less vivid. The Granados encores are very successful too: Frühbeck de Burgos conducts the *Goyescas Intermezzo* seductively, and Argenta is no less colourful in the most famous of the *Danzas españolas*.

Rapsodia española (arr. Halfter).
(B) *** Decca Eclipse Dig. 448 243-2 [(M) id. import]. Alicia de Larrocha, LPO, Frühbeck de Burgos – RODRIGO: *Concierto de Aranjuez* etc.; TURINA: *Rapsodia sinfónica*. ***

Albéniz's *Rapsodia española*, originally written for solo piano, is heard here in Cristobal Halfter's arrangement for piano and orchestra. Alicia de Larrocha's performance is both evocative and dazzling, and she is given splendid support by Frühbeck de Burgos and brilliant Decca sound.

Suite española (arr. Frühbeck de Burgos).
(M) *** Decca 448 601-2. New Philh. O, Frühbeck de Burgos – FALLA: *El amor brujo* (with GRANADOS: *Goyescas: Intermezzo*. ***)

Albéniz's early *Suite española* offers light music of the best kind, colourful, tuneful, exotically scored and providing orchestra and recording engineers alike with a chance to show their paces, the sound bright and glittering, and fully worthy of reissue in Decca's Classic Sound series.

GUITAR MUSIC

Cantos de España: Cordoba, Op. 232/4. España (6 Hojas de album), Op. 165. Iberia (excerpts): *El Puerto; Evocación; El Abaicín; Triana; Zambra Granadina. Mallorca (Barcarola), Op. 202; Suite espanola: Aragón.*
(N) **(*) Channel Classics Dig. CCS 10397 [id.]. Peter and Zoltán Katona.

The Katona twins are a highly talented duo and they find plenty of colour and atmosphere in this familiar piano repertoire, very effectively transcribed. The recording too is warm and pleasing, although the resonance blunts the upper range just a little. A most attractive recital just the same.

Cantos de España: Córdoba, Op. 232/4; Mallorca (Barcarola), Op. 202; Piezás características: Zambra Granadina; Torre Bermeja, Op. 92/7, 12; Suite española: Granada; Sevilla; Cádiz; Asturias, Op. 47/1, 3–5.
*** Sony Dig. SK 36679 [id.]. John Williams (guitar).

Some of Albéniz's more colourful miniatures are here, and John Williams plays them most evocatively.

Cantos de España: Córdoba, Op. 232/4; Mallorca (Barcarola), Op. 202. Suite española: Cataluña; Granada; Sevilla; Cádiz, Op.47/1–4.
❁ (BB) *** RCA Navigator Dig. 74321 17903-2. Julian Bream (guitar) – GRANADOS: *Collection;* RODRIGO: *3 Piezas españolas*. *** ❁

Julian Bream is in superb form in this splendid recital (apparently his own favourite record), vividly recorded in the pleasingly warm acoustic of Wardour Chapel, near his home in Wiltshire. The playing itself has wonderfully communicative rhythmic feeling, great subtlety of colour, and its spontaneity increases the impression that one is experiencing a 'live' recital. The performance of the haunting *Córdoba*, which ends the group, is unforgettable. The new super-bargain Navigator reissue includes additionally the *Tres piezas españolas* of Rodrigo and is a bargain of bargains.

Suite española, Op. 47 (extended suite, arr. Barrueco).
(M) *** EMI Dig. CDM5 66574-2 [id.]. Manuel Barrueco – TURINA: *Guitar music*. ***

Although written for the piano, the *Suite española* sounds equally effective (if not more so) in transcription for guitar, especially in the hands of a master-guitarist. Barrueco's playing combines warmth with a pleasing intimacy and a natural, relaxed sense of spontaneity. The more famous evocations, *Castilla*, *Granada* and the closing *Sevilla*, are subtle in nuance and colour, while the vibrant *Asturias* brings a haunting, improvisational feeling in its calm middle section. The recording is beautifully judged, not over-projected.

PIANO MUSIC

Azulejos; Cantos de España (Preludio (Asturias); Oriental; Bajo la palmera (Cuba); Córdoba; Seguidillas (Castilla)). Malagueña; Mallorca (Barcarola); La Vega; Zambra Granadina; Zaragoza.
(M) *** EMI CDM7 64523-2 [id.]. Alicia de Larrocha.

Dating from 1959, this recital is a stimulating example of the younger Alicia de Larrocha playing with enormous dash and a glowing palette – the famous *Córdoba* is full of atmospheric poetry, helped by the warm bass resonance of the recording.

Cantos de España; Suite española.
(N) (B) *** Decca Double Analogue/Dig. 433 923-2 (2) [id.]. Alicia de Larrocha –

GRANADOS: *Allegro de concierto; El pelele; 12 Danzas españolas.* ***

This makes a most rewarding bonus for the coupled Granados collection, and Alicia de Larrocha's playing is imbued with many subtle changes of colour and has refreshing vitality.

Iberia (complete); *Alhambra* (suite): *La vega; Azulejos: Prelude; Navarra* (both completed Martin Jones). *6 Hojas de Album, Op. 165: Tango. Suite española, Op 47.*
(N) (BB) *** Nimbus Dig. NI 5595/8 (4) [id.]. Martin Jones – GRANADOS: *Allegro de concierto; Goyescas* etc. ***

Until now the recordings of Alicia de Larrocha have dominated this repertory, but now comes a real challenge from the British pianist, Martin Jones. He penetrates the ethos of these pieces with a natural feeling for their Spanish atmosphere, and he has sufficient and justified confidence in his own special insights to offer these new completions of both *Navarra* and the composer's very last, ruminative piece, *Azulejos*. His pianism is brilliantly coloured, rhythmically charismatic, and often quite magical in its gentle evocation; moreover, these performances, even though they were recorded in the studio, have the continuing spontaneity of live music-making. This is apparent from the very opening of *Iberia*, and Jones's poetic sensibility illuminates and holds convincingly together the longest single piece, *La vega* from the *Alhambra suite* of 1898. The series of descriptive vignettes of the *Suite española* are given a new dimension by the lilting freshness and subtlety of this remarkable playing. The recording is wholly natural, the ambience warm but not too resonant. This would be highly recommended even if it cost far more.

Iberia; Navarra; Suite española.
❁ *** Decca Dig. 417 887-2 [id.]. Alicia de Larrocha.

On her digital Decca version, Alicia de Larrocha brings an altogether beguiling charm and character to these rewarding miniature tone-poems and makes light of their sometimes fiendish technical difficulties. The recording is among the most successful of piano sounds Decca has achieved.

Iberia (complete); *Suite española No.1; Suite española No. 2 (Zaragonza Sevilla).*
(N) (BB) **(*) Naxos Dig. 8.554311/2 [id.]. Gullermo González.

Born in Tenerife, Gullermo González plays this music with genuine idiomatic feeeling. As the opening *Evocación* of *Iberia* shows, his lyrical style brings a freely romantic rubato, and he can produce an exotic brilliance in the bravura pieces. There is no want of sultry Mediterranean atmosphere, and the miniature portraits of Spanish cities which make up the *Suite española* are vividly depicted, with the Andalusian and Castillian dance rhythms falling naturally into place. He is very well recorded and this Naxos set has a distinct appeal, even if the playing does not always find quite the degree of spontaneity which illuminates the alternative versions from Alicia de Larrocha and Martin Jones.

Iberia (complete); *Suite española* (excerpts): *Granada; Cataluña; Sevilla; Cádiz; Aragon; Navarra. Pavana capricho, Op. 12; España (6 Hojas de album): Tango* (only); *Recuerdos de viaje: Rumores de la caleta; Puerta de Tierra.*
(M) *** EMI CMS7 64504-2 (2) [id.]. Alicia de Larrocha.

The EMI set offers de Larrocha's earliest stereo recording of Albéniz's great piano suite, *Iberia*, made for Hispavox in 1962. The younger de Larrocha is far tougher, more daring, more fiery and if anything even more warmly expressive than she was later. The EMI discs include the haunting *Tango*, deliciously done, the most celebrated of all Albéniz's music, making this a more popular collection.

Iberia (complete); *Navarra. 6 Hojas de album, Op. 165: Malagueña; Tango. Pavana-Capricho, Op. 12. Recuerdos de viaje, Op. 71: Puerta de Tierra; Rumores de la caleta (Malagueña).*
(N) (B)*** Decca Double 433 926-2 (2) [id.]. Alicia de Larrocha – FALLA: *Fantasia bética; 4 Piezas españolas.* ***

Iberia (complete); *Navarra.*
(B) *** Decca Double 448 191-2 (2) [id.]. De Larrocha – GRANADOS: *Goyescas.* *** ❁

Alicia de Larrocha's second analogue set of *Iberia* was made in 1972, a decade after her earliest stereo version for Hispavox. As in that version, she plays with full-blooded temperament and fire, and although there are occasional touches of wilful rubato her natural overriding spontaneity carries the day, both here and in *Navarra*. The piano recording is excellent in its realism, and the Double Decca reissue, coupled with Granados's *Goyescas*, makes a formidable bargain, for on both artistic and technical merits *Iberia* loses little ground to her later, digital set which has rather more subtlety.

The other Decca Double offering more of Albéniz's colourful genre pieces, played with comparable understanding (and coupled with Falla) makes an alternative collection, reissued as part of Decca's '*Música española*' series.

Suite española, Op. 47.
(BB) **(*) ASV CDQS 6079. Alma Petchersky – FALLA: *Fantasía bética* (with GRANADOS: *Allegro de concierto*). **(*)

Alma Petchersky plays engagingly and with a natural spontaneity that gives pleasure. The recording is generally faithful, without being in the top bracket. At super-bargain price this is worth considering.

Albéniz, Mateo de (*c.*1755–1831)

Sonata in D.

(N) (B) *** Decca Double 433 920-2 (2) [id.]. Alicia de Larrocha – GRANADOS: *Escenas románticas; Goyescas; 6 Piezas sobre cantos populares españoles.* SOLER: *Sonatas.* ***

Mateo Albéniz was a Basque church musician who is remembered mainly for this brief one-movement *Sonata* with its obvious homage to Domenico Scarlatti. It has great character and is beautifully played and recorded.

Albert, Eugen d' (1864–1932)

Piano concertos Nos. 1 in B min., Op. 2; 2 in E, Op. 12.

*** Hyperion Dig. CDA 66747 [id.]. Piers Lane, BBC Scottish SO, Alun Francis.

The *Piano concerto No. 1 in B minor* (1884), the inspiration of a twenty-year-old, is the more ambitious of the two works, a 45-minute span, written in a style half-way between Liszt and Rachmaninov, a warmly lyrical mix, lacking only the sharp memorability of a masterwork. Piers Lane plays with delicacy and virtuosity and is well supported by the BBC Scottish Symphony Orchestra. Its musical substance may not be immediately memorable, but there is a rather extraordinary fugal outburst towards the end of the work. The *Piano concerto No. 2 in E major* is a one-movement piece, though in four sections, following the style of Liszt's concertos. The recording is expertly balanced by Tony Kime.

Piano sonata in F sharp min., Op. 10; 8 Klavierstücke, Op. 5; Klavierstücke, Op. 16/2–3; 5 schliche Klavierstücke 9 (Capriolen), Op.32; Serenata.

(N) *** Hyperion Dig. CDA 66945 [id.]. Piers Lane.

Eugen d'Albert's solo keyboard music, of which there is a considerable quantity, is well worth exploring. Although it inhabits the worlds of Brahms and Liszt, there is much that can lay claim to a quiet individuality. Piers Lane plays it with total commitment, as if every bar is inspired, and almost persuades us that it is. No want of virtuosity and dedication here and very good recorded sound.

Die Abreise.

(M) **(*) CPO/EMI CPO 999 558-2 [id.]. Prey, Edda Moser, Schreier, Philh. Hung. O, Janos Kulka.

Eugen d'Albert wrote this charming one-acter, *Die Abreise* ('The Departure'), in 1898, five years before his most celebrated opera, *Tiefland*. Gilfen, bored with his wife Luise, plans to depart on a journey, but the machinations of his friend Trott alert him to the dangers, and it is Trott who departs. With delicate orchestral writing, it tells the story deftly in 20 brief sections of melodic conversation – though there are no separate tracks after the overture and their absence makes it harder to follow the synopsis which is provided instead of a libretto. Nevertheless this is a first-rate, highly enjoyable performance, recorded in 1978 with three outstanding and characterful soloists. Warm, clear EMI sound.

Tiefland (complete).

(N) (M) *** RCA 74321 40574 (2) [id.]. Strauss, Schock, Feldhoff, Sardi, RIAS Ch., BSO, Hans Zanotelli.

(N) ** Berlin Classics 0091082 BC (2) [id.]. Kuhse, Gutstein, Rönisch, Hoppe, Adam, Dresden Staatsoper Ch., Staatskapelle Dresden, Schmitz.

Often described as the German answer to Italian verismo, *Tiefland*, first heard in 1903, is generous with red-blooded melodrama, weaker on memorable melody. Nonetheless, the story of Pedro the simple shepherd, his love for Marta, and the wickedness of his landowner employer, Sebastiano, comes over strongly in the 1963 RCA version, thanks to d'Albert's warm, easygoing style and a full, upfront sound. Hans Zanotelli builds up the dramatic moments well, with Rudolf Schock as Pedro and Isabell Strauss as Marta singing powerfully. The German libretto is provided, but only a synopsis in English.

The Berlin Classics version is no match for the RCA set, also recorded in 1963. The sound is dim and relatively distant, and the Dresden casting is generally weaker, with Paul Schmitz's direction lacking bite. Heinz Hoppe is a strong Pedro, but he hardly matches Schock.

Albert, Stephen (1941–92)

Cello concerto.

*** Sony Dig. SK 57961 [id.]. Yo-Yo Ma, Baltimore SO, David Zinman – BARTOK: *Viola concerto;* BLOCH: *Schelomo.* ***

Stephen Albert's *Cello concerto* (1989–90) was written for Yo-Yo Ma. The idiom is both tonal and distinctive. Albert is very much his own man and his music is both inventive and imaginative. Yo-Yo Ma and the Baltimore orchestra give a passionately committed account of it and are superbly recorded.

Albicastro, Henricus (1661–*c.*1730)

Concerti à 4, Op. 7/2 & 12; Violin sonata with continuo (La Follia), Op. 9/12; Trio sonatas, Op. 8/9 & 11; (i) Motet: *Coelestes angelici chori*

(N) (B) *** HM Musique d'abord Dig. HMA 1905208 [id.]. Ens. 415, Chiara Banchini; (i) with Guy de Mey.

Swiss-born Henricus Albicastro, né Johannes Weysenbergh, himself a virtuoso violinist, may be placed among those Southern German composers who became almost totally influenced by the Italian style, notably that of Corelli, as the *La Folia* variations readily demonstrate. They are a shade conventional, but like the *Trio sonatas* (each in five brief movements), pleasingly assured and easily inventive. The two *Concerti* are even more striking in character, the *Allegros* vivacious and neatly imitative and the *Grave* slow movements rather fine. But the best work here is the cantata, which has both melodic appeal and genuine emotional eloquence. It is quite beautifully sung by Guy de Mey (and a translation is provided). Chiara Banchini and Ensemble 415 are on excellent form throughout and the whole concert is very well recorded. This is neither great nor highly individual music, but it is certainly rewarding when so well presented.

Albinoni, Tommaso (1671–1751)

Adagio in G min. for organ and strings (arr. Giazotto).

(M) *** Sony Theta SMK 60161. La Grand Ecurie et la Chambre du Roy, Jean-Claude Malgoire – Concert: ECO, Leppard: *'Music of the Baroque'*. ***

(B) *** Carlton Dig. PCD 2001 [(M) id.]. Scottish CO, Laredo (with String masterpieces ***).

(M) *** DG 449 724-2 [id.]. BPO, Karajan – RESPIGHI: *Ancient airs* etc. ***

Malgoire and his authentic string group (with a sonorously balanced organ contribution) give an impressively dignified account of a justly attractive piece that can too readily sound inflated. This comes as the final item in a generous concert of baroque lollipops, stylishly played on modern instruments by the ECO under Raymond Leppard.

The bargain-priced, digitally recorded Carlton account is strongly contoured and most responsively played by the Scottish Chamber Orchestra under Jaime Laredo.

Karajan's view is stately and measured, and the Berlin Philharmonic strings respond with dignity and sumptuous tone. The anachronism of Giazotto's arrangement is obviously relished.

12 Concerti a cinque, Op. 5.

(B) *** Ph. Dig. 442 688-2. Pina Carmirelli, I Musici.

This fine body of concertos has variety and resource to commend it. I Musici, with Pina Carmirelli as the solo player, are every bit as fresh as the music, and they are accorded altogether first-rate sound. This is one of the best sets of its kind among recent reissues; those prepared to explore these concertos will be well rewarded, and the disc (which plays for 76 minutes) is remarkably inexpensive.

12 Concerti, Op. 7; Sonatas for strings a 5: in D & G min., Op. 2/5–6.

*** Ph. (IMS) Dig. 432 115-2 (2). Heinz Holliger, Maurice Bourgue, I Musici.

Albinoni's Op. 7 consists of four each of solo oboe concertos, double oboe concertos and concertos for strings, with continuo. This recording by Heinz Holliger and Maurice Bourgue and I Musici is comparatively robust in using modern instruments but is eminently stylish, the effect sunny and lively by turns. The digital recording is fresh and naturally balanced. The two *String sonatas* from Op. 2 are particularly attractive works, and here the recording is slightly closer.

Concerti a cinque, Op. 7/1–6; Oboe concertos in G; G min.; G.

(N) **(*) Tactus Dig. TC 670103 [id.]. Paolo Pollastri, Simone Bensi, Sinf. Perusina, Pollastri.

Tactus is an enterprising new Italian label specializing in rare repertoire, distributed in the UK by Chandos. Here besides the familiar first six concertos (for one or two oboes) of Op.7 we are offered three more unpublished works preserved in German libraries. The *G minor Concerto* is quite a find, with an unusually wide-ranging solo part, and a brief *Adagio*, accompanied pizzicato throughout. The second of the two *G major* works is also one of the composer's best. The two soloists here play their period instruments with expert bonhomie; the strings are athletic but a bit raw on top. There are odd moments when intonation is suspect, but these are few and will not worry all listeners. The recording is forward, with good ambience.

Concerti a cinque, Op. 7/1, (i) *2; 3,* (i) *6; 8;* (i) *Sinfonia in G* (arr. Anthony Camden).

(BB) *** Naxos Dig. 8.553002 [id.]. Anthony Camden; (i) Alison Alty, L. Virtuosi, John Georgiadis.

Concerti a cinque, Op. 7/4, (i) *5; 6,* (i) *11; 12;* (i) *Op. 9/12.*

(BB) *** Naxos Dig. 8.553035 [id.]. Anthony Camden; (i) Alison Alty, L. Virtuosi, John Georgiadis.

Concerti a cinque, Op. 9/2, (i) *3; 5, 8,* (i) *9; 11.*

(BB) *** Naxos Dig. 8.550739; *4.550739* [id.]. Anthony Camden, (i) Julia Girdwood, L. Virtuosi, John Georgiadis.

Anthony Camden and the London Virtuosi conducted by John Georgiadis are working their way through the Albinoni concertos. The London Virtuosi use modern instruments, but their playing is fresh and refined and the digital recording is natural and beautifully balanced. The calibre of Anthony Camden's solo contribution is readily shown in slow movements, matched by Georgiadis's rapt, sensitive accompaniments. On the first disc Camden's excellent colleague is Julia Girdwood, but for the two other collections Alison Alty takes over and the partnership seems even more felicitous, with the two instruments quite perfectly blended. Also included is a *Sinfonia* arranged by Camden as a sinfonia concertante. This series can be strongly recommended on all counts.

Oboe concertos, Op. 7/3, 6, 9 & 12; Op. 9/2, 5, 8 & 11.
*** Unicorn Dig. DKPCD 9088 [id.]. Sarah Francis, L. Harpsichord Ens.
*** Chandos Dig. CHAN 0579 [id.]. Anthony Robson, Coll. Mus. 90, Simon Standage.

Those looking for a selection of *Oboe concertos* from both Opp. 7 and 9 will find that Sarah Francis is an immensely stylish and gifted soloist. She is accompanied with warmth and grace, and the recording is first class, transparent yet full and naturally balanced.

Anthony Robson also plays all eight solo concertos from Op. 7 and Op. 9, but using a period oboe. His tone is most appealing and his phrasing and musicianship are second to none. Simon Standage provides alert accompaniments, also using original instruments, and creates bright, athletic string-timbres. Authenticists need not hesitate.

(i) *Double oboe concertos, Op. 7/8 & 11; Op. 9/9 & 12. Concerto for strings, Op. 7/7 & 10; Op. 9/7 & 10.*
(N) *** Chandos Dig. CHAN 0610 [id.]. (i) Anthony Robson, Catherine Latham; Coll. Mus. 90, Simon Standage.

Here Catherine Latham joins Anthony Robson to complete the Collegium Musicum sets of Opp. 7 and 9, including the works for strings. Performances are well up to the standard and so is the excellent Chandos sound. The artistic results are very lively and refreshing, although the balance remains rather close.

(i) *Concerti a cinque, Op. 7/2–3, 5–6, 8–9, 11–12;* (ii) *Adagio in G min.* (arr. Giazotto).
(B) *** DG Classikon 439 509-2 [(M) id. import]. (i) Holliger, Elhorst, Bern Camerata; (ii) Lucerne Festival Strings, Baumgartner.

The playing of Heinz Holliger, Hans Elhorst and the Bern Camerata is refined, persuasive and vital, and the CD could hardly be more truthful or better detailed. This famous *Adagio* (in a perfectly acceptable performance under Baumgartner) has been added to tempt a wider public. Let us hope it does so.

Concerti a cinque, Op. 9/1–12.
(N) (B) *** Erato/Warmer Ultima 3984 25593-2 (2) [id.]. Pierlot, Toso, I Solisti Veneti, Scimone.

(i) *Concerti a cinque, Op. 9/1–12;* (ii) *Adagio in G min. for organ and strings* (arr. Giazotto).
(B) *** Ph. Duo 456 333-2 (2) [id.]. (i) Felix Ayo, Heinz Holliger, Maurice Bourgue; (i; ii) Maria Garatti (harpsichord or organ); I Musici.

Albinoni's set of 12 Opus 9 concertos are delightful and inspired throughout. They are played on this Philips Duo with much finesse and style, which comment also applies to the famous *Adagio*. Ayo, Holliger and Bourgue are on top form throughout, and so are the Philips engineers.

However (even though it does not include the ubiquitous *Adagio*) the Erato Ultima set is not upstaged. The slightly later analogue recording is particularly fresh and transparent, and vividly transferred. Pierre Pierlot with his elegant phrasing and lovely tone, Jacques Chambon (in the Double oboe concertos) and Piero Toso (in the two concertos for violin) all make very appealing contributions, Scimoni and I Solisti Veneti are also on top form and in the *F major Double concerto* they make the most of Albinoni's echo effects.

Concerti a cinque, Op. 9/2, 5, 8 & 11.
(M) *** Virgin/EMI Veritas (SIS) Dig. VER5 61152–2 [CDM 611522]. Hans de Vries, Alma Musica Amsterdam, Bob van Asperen – TELEMANN: *Oboe concertos.* ***

Hans de Vries plays a baroque oboe, made by Gottlob Crone in Leipzig around 1735, and produces a most appealing timbre, while his technique is remarkably assured and true. There is one cavil: the solo balance seems a shade too forward, even though the interaction with the strings (which are well in the picture) is effectively managed. The accompaniments are as alert and stylish as the solo playing.

12 Concerti, Op. 10.
(B) *** Erato/Warner Ultima 0630 18943-2 (2) [(M) id. import]. Piero Toso, Giuliano Carmignola, Sol. Ven., Claudio Scimone.

Although the existence of this set of concertos was long known and was listed by the Amsterdam publisher, Le Cène, their rediscovery is comparatively recent. Four of the set are violin concertos (Nos. 6, 8, 10 and 12) and three are concerti grossi with a small concertino group (2, 3 and 4), while the remainder are without soloists and have non-fugal last movements. They were composed in the mid-1730s, 13 years after Op. 9 and after the composer had been absorbed by operatic ventures. They radiate simple vitality and love of life and a youthful exuberance that belies the composer's age. The playing is warm and musical, and the recording is made in an ample acoustic. Some may prefer more sharply etched detail (particularly in the concerti grossi), but the resonant string-timbres are agreeably natural and immaculately transferred to CD.

6 Sonate da chiesa, Op. 4; 12 Trattenimenti armonici per camera, Op. 6.
*** Hyperion Dig. CDA 66831/2 [id.]. Locatelli Trio.

The set of '*Church*' *sonatas*, showing the composer at his most lyrically appealing, contrasts with Op.

6. *Trattenimento* indicates 'Entertainment', suggesting a more secular style; and certainly the allegros of Op. 6 are strikingly lively and infectiously dance-like in character. The slow movements are often more formal, although never dull. The excellent continuo player of the Locatelli Trio uses a discreet and often touchingly understated organ continuo to support the violin and cello in Op. 4 and a harpsichord in Op. 6. The performances, using original instruments, are of high quality, well paced, sensitive and fresh, and the recording is well balanced and vivid.

Il nascimento dell'Aurora (*festa pastorale*; complete).
(B) **(*) Erato/Warner Dig. 4509 96374-2 (2) [(M) id.]. Anderson, Zimmermann, Klare, Browne, Yamaj, Sol. Ven., Scimone.

Written as a court celebration, *Il nascimento dell'Aurora* makes a substantial and attractive two-hour stage entertainment. This well-balanced live recording, made in Vicenza, Italy, puts forward a persuasive case despite some roughness in the choral singing (which is particularly distracting in the first chorus) and some intrusive audience applause. Soloists are first rate and the orchestra generally stylish. The CD transfer is excellently managed. With full libretto and translation included, this is well worth exploring.

Alfvén, Hugo (1872–1960)

A Legend of the Skerries, Op. 20; Swedish rhapsodies Nos. 1 (Midsummer vigil), Op. 19; 2 (Uppsala rhapsody), Op. 24; 3 (Dala rhapsody), Op. 47; King Gustav II Adolf, Op. 49: Adagio.
*** Chandos Dig. CHAN 9313 [id.]. Iceland SO, Sakari.

Petri Sakari is a totally unaffected guide in this repertory and secures excellent playing from the Icelandic orchestra. *Midsummer vigil*, Alfvén's masterpiece, is quintessential Sweden and so, too, is the affecting *Elegy* from the incidental music to Ludwig Nordström's play about *Gustav II Adolf*. Sakari produces musically satisfying results, and this useful anthology can be warmly recommended. The Chandos sound is excellent.

Swedish rhapsody No. 1 (Midsummer vigil), Op. 19.
(N) *** Decca Dig. 452 482-2 [id.]. Montreal SO, Charles Dutoit. – ENESCU, DVORAK, GLAZUNOV, LISZT: *Rhapsodies etc.* ***

A first-class account of Alfvén's captivating score, recorded with great clarity and presence.

Symphony No. 1 in F min., Op. 7; Andante religioso; Drapa (Ballad for large orchestra); Uppsala rhapsody, Op. 24.
*** BIS Dig. CD 395 [id.]. Stockholm PO, Neeme Järvi.

Järvi's version of the *First Symphony* supersedes the earlier Westerberg version; it is superior both artistically and technically and leaves the listener more persuaded as to its merits. The *Uppsala rhapsody* is based on student songs but it is pretty thin stuff, and the *Andante religioso* is rather let down by its sugary closing pages. *Drapa* opens with some fanfares, full of sequential clichés and with a certain naïve pomp and splendour that verges on bombast.

Symphony No. 2 in D, Op. 11; Swedish rhapsody No. 1 (Midsummer vigil).
*** BIS Dig. CD 385 [id.]. Stockholm PO, Neeme Järvi.

Like those of its predecessor, the ideas of the *Second Symphony* are pleasing though they do not possess a particularly individual stamp. On the whole, Järvi is very persuasive in the symphony and gives a delightful performance of the popular *Midsummer vigil*.

(i) *Symphony No. 4 (Havsbandet – From the outermost skerries), Op. 29; A Legend of the Skerries, Op. 20.*
*** BIS Dig. CD 505 [id.]. Stockholm PO, Järvi, (i) with Christina Högman, Claes-Håkan Ahnsjö.

Alfvén's *Fourth Symphony* is perhaps his most ambitious work. There is a romantic programme relating to the emotions of two young lovers, whose wordless melisma is heard to excellent effect in this very fine recording. However, although Alfvén's scoring is eminently resourceful, the results are conventionally voluptuous rather than ethereal. The performance is sensitive and persuasive, the recording has a natural perspective and admirable detail.

Symphony No. 5 in A min.; The Mountain King (Bergakungen): suite; Gustav II Adolf: Elegy.
*** BIS Dig. CD 585 [id.]. Royal Stockholm PO, Neeme Järvi.

The *Fifth Symphony* is a late work; it draws freely on ideas from the ballet, *The Mountain King*, whose suite completes this CD. The first movement is by far the best, despite its echoes of Wagner and Sibelius. The second movement has some beautiful ideas but the last two movements, which became 'problem children' in his old age, are really rather feeble. *The Mountain King* is an inventive and attractive score; and both works, as well as the touching *Elegy* from the music to *Gustav II Adolf*, could hardly be presented more persuasively. The engineering is absolutely first class.

Choral music: (i) *Aftonen; Anders, han var en hurtiger dräng; Berceuse;* (ii) *Glädjens blomster.*

Gryning vid havet; Gustaf Frödings jordafärd; Hör I Orphei Drängar; Kulldansen; (ii) *Lindagull (Serenade). Min kära;* (ii) *Natt. Och jungfrun hon går i ringen; Oxbergsmarschen; Papillon;* (ii) *Prövningen. Roslagsvår; Stemning; Sveriges flagga; Trindskallarna; Uti vår hage; Vaggvisa;* (ii) *Vallgossens visa;* (ii) *Värmlandsvisan.* Songs (ii; iii) *Du är stilla ro; I stilla timmar; Jag längtar dig; Saa tag mit Hjerte; Skogen sofver; Sommardofter.* (i) SODERMAN, arr. ALFVEN: *I månans skimmer.*

*** BIS Dig. CD 633 [id.].(i) Orphei Drängar Ch., Robert Sund; (ii) with Claes-Håkan Ahnsjö; (iii) Folke Alin.

Some of the part-songs Alfvén composed for the Orphei Drängar (Sons of Orpheus) are collected here and are sung to the highest standards of tonal virtuosity. Recommended with enthusiasm even to those who find the symphonies inflated and self-indulgent.

Alkan, Charles (1813–88)

Concerti da camera Nos. 1 in A min; 2 in C sharp min. Op. 10/1–2.

(N) *** Hyp. Dig. CDA 66717 [id.]. Marc-André Hamelin, BBC Scotish SO, Martyn Brabbins – HENSELT: *Piano concerto; Variations de concert.* ***

These are early pieces, miniature concertos of no mean interest and individuality. Elegantly played by Marc-André Hamelin and the BBC Scottish Symphony under Martyn Brabbins, they make an excellent foil for the Henselt *F minor concerto.*

Piano concerto, Op. 39 (orch. Klindworth); *Concerti da camera Nos. 1 in A min., Op. 10; 2 in C sharp min.; 3 in C sharp min.* (reconstructed Hugh Macdonald).

(BB) *** Naxos Dig. 8.553702 [id.]. Dmitri Feofanov, Razumovsky SO, Robert Stankovsky.

Alkan's Op. 39 consists of twelve *Etudes*, of which Nos. 8–10 comprise the *Concerto for piano.* The first movement alone runs to 1,342 bars, more than in Beethoven's *Hammerklavier*, and (to quote Allan Ho's notes) 'poses special problems of endurance as well as myriad technical difficulties'. Performances of all three movements are rare nowadays and none was given in Alkan's lifetime. However, the first movement was orchestrated by the conductor and pianist, Karl Klindworth. A contemporary critic summed it up as 'a concert piece by Klindworth based on Alkan'. Alkan's work is only the core from which the rather long work developed. Earlier in his career, Alkan himself had composed three concertos for piano and orchestra, the *First* in 1831 when he was seventeen, and the *Second in C sharp minor* two years later for a visit to London. Feofanov does a heroic job in the Klindworth and shows a sympathy with Alkan that the Slovak-based Razumovsky Orchestra and Robert Stankovsky obviously share. Good recording makes this well worth anybody's money.

Barcarolle; Gigue, Op. 24; Marche, Op. 37/1; Nocturne No. 2, Op. 57/1; Saltarelle, Op. 23; Scherzo diabolico, Op. 39/3; Sonatine, Op. 61.

(B) *** HM HMA 190 927 [id.]. Bernard Ringeissen.

Bernard Ringeissen could be more flamboyant but he is fully equal to the cruel technical demands of this music. The recording, from the beginning of the 1970s, is first class.

12 Etudes in the minor keys, Op. 39/1–12. Etudes, Op. 3/5: Allegro barbaro. Chants: Assez vivement, Op. 38/1; Barcarolle, Op. 65/6. Esquisses: La staccatissimo; Les cloches; Les soupirs; En songe, Op. 63/2, 4, 11 & 48. Les Mois: Gros temps, Op. 74 (Suite 1: No. 2). Nocturne in B, Op. 22; Preludes: La chanson de la folle au bord de la mer; Le temps qui n'est plus; J'étais endormie, mais mon coeur veillait, Op. 31/8, 12 & 13.

*** ASV Dig. CDDCS 227 (2) [id.]. Jack Gibbons.

Liszt himself spoke of Alkan as having the finest piano technique he had ever known, and Alkan's music (like Medtner's and Scarlatti's) is almost exclusively for the keyboard but, unlike theirs, rarely finds its way into the modern concert hall – not surprisingly, given its fiendish, hair-raising difficulties and (to be fair) uneven quality. Jack Gibbons has obviously inherited the mantle of Ronald Smith, to whom his notes pay homage, and he rises to the challenge these pieces present with triumphant virtuosity. Good sound, too.

Grande sonate (Les quatre âges), Op. 33; Barcarolle; Le festin d'Esope; Sonatine, Op. 61.

*** Hyperion Dig. CDA 66794 [id.]. Marc-André Hamelin.

Under studio conditions, Marc-André Hamelin records works by Alkan with a virtuosity just as breathtaking as on his live Wigmore Hall disc, also for Hyperion (see our Recitals section, below). In his flair and brilliance he has rarely, if ever, been matched. Written six years before the Liszt *Sonata*, Alkan's *Grande sonate* over its four massive movements represents the hero at various ages, with the second, *quasi-Faust*, the key one. The *Sonatine*, the most approachable of Alkan's major works, is just as dazzlingly done, with the hauntingly poetic *Barcarolle* and the swaggering *Festin d'Esope* as valuable makeweights.

25 Preludes, Op. 31.

*** Decca (IMS) Dig. 433 055-2 [id.]. Olli Mustonen – SHOSTAKOVICH: *24 Preludes.* ***

The *Preludes* are more poetic than barnstorming and date from 1847. They go through all the major and minor keys, returning to C major in No. 25. The young Finnish pianist Olli Mustonen plays them supremely well. The recording is absolutely first class, though the pedal-stamping in the *Tenth Prelude, Dans le style fugué*, should have been curbed. Strongly recommended.

ORGAN MUSIC

8 Petits Préludes sur les huit gammes du plainchant; 13 Prières, Op. 64; Impromptu on Luther's 'Un fort rampart est notre Dieu', Op. 69.
*** Nimbus Dig. NI 5089 [id.]. Kevin Bowyer (organ of Salisbury Cathedral).

One does not think of Alkan as a composer for the organ, and indeed only the eight *Little preludes on the eight modes of plainchant* were actually conceived for this instrument. Kevin Bowyer is clearly a master of this repertoire and conveys his enjoyment in music which has personality and is readily melodic. Perhaps the mellow Salisbury Cathedral organ was not an ideal choice (a French instrument would have had more reedy bite), but this remains an attractive and generous (74 minutes) recital.

Allegri, Gregorio (1582–1652)

Miserere.
*** Gimell/Philips 454 939-2 [id.]. Tallis Scholars, Phillips – MUNDY: *Vox patris caelestis;* PALESTRINA: *Missa Papae Marcelli.* ***
(M) *** Decca Legends 466 373-2 [id.]. King's College Ch., Willcocks – PALESTRINA: *Collection.* ***

Mozart was so impressed with Allegri's *Miserere* when he heard it in the Sistine Chapel (which originally claimed exclusive rights to its performance) that he wrote the music out from memory so that it could be performed elsewhere. On the much-praised Gimell version, the soaring treble solo is taken by a girl, Alison Stamp, and her memorable contribution is enhanced by the recording itself.

The famous 1963 King's performance of Allegri's *Miserere*, with its equally arresting treble solo so beautifully and securely sung by Roy Goodman, is now reissued, impressively remastered in Decca's Legends series – coupled with Palestrina at mid-price.

Almeida, Francisco António de (*c.* 1702–55)

La Giuditta (oratorio).
(B) *** HM Dig. HMA 901411/12 [id.]. Lootens, Congiu, M. Hill, Köhler, Concerto Köln, Jacobs.

Here is a superb oratorio (based on the story from the Apocrypha of Judith's deception of Holofernes) by a virtually unknown Portuguese composer who studied Italian music in Rome between 1722 and 1726. His music keeps reminding one of Handel at his finest. Almeida is surely lucky that René Jacobs has assembled such a fine cast, with Lena Lootens singing freshly and appealingly as Giuditta, Martyn Hill a generally fine Holofernes (though perhaps not an entirely convincing seducer) and Alex Köhler most impressive of all as Ozia, Commander of Bethulia, a male alto role which he makes totally convincing. The work is brimful of melody, its invention of such consistently high quality that one hardly misses the choruses that Handel would surely have provided. The orchestral writing, using flutes, oboes, horns – which come through spectacularly – and strings, shows a true feeling for the orchestral palette and the way it can be used to sharpen and colour the narrative. Jacobs directs a performance that springs vividly to life, and everything about this production, including the recording, is first class. With excellent documentation this is very highly recommended.

Motets: *Beatus vir; O quam suavis.*
(M) *** DG Codex 453 182-2. Jennifer Smith, Magali, Schwartz, Fernando Serafim, Gulbenkian Chamber Ch. & O, Michel Corboz – CARVALHO: *Te Deum;* SEIXAS: *Adebat Vincentius* etc.; TEIXEIRA: *Gaudate, astra.* ***

These two beautiful (and beautifully sung) motets establish the Portuguese baroque composer, Francisco António de Almeida, as a composer of individuality. *Beatus vir* makes considerable florid demands on both soprano and tenor soloists, ending with an expansive *Amen* from the chorus. The recording is in every way excellent, fresh and clear within a warm acoustic.

Alonso-Crespo, Eduardo (born 1956)

Juana, la loca (overture and ballet music); *Putzi: Mephisto* (waltz); *Yubarta:* overture.
(N) *** Ocean Dig. OR101. Cincinnati CO, composer – GALBRAITH: *Piano concerto No. 1.* ***

The Argentinian-born Alonso-Crespo writes colourfully in a style which absorbs Latin-American rhythms and bright orchestral colours into a style of concert music which clearly reflects eclectic lyrical influences from his adopted North American homeland, not least from Copland. There is no shortage of melody. His operetta *Putzi* mixes Lisztian biography with the Faust legend, and if he begins the *Mephisto waltz* with a quotation, it is used as a springboard for a rather charming pastiche. The Cincinnati Chamber Orchestra responds to the composer's direction with considerable aplomb and the recording is excellent.

Alwyn, William (1905–85)

(i) *Autumn legend* (for cor anglais and string orchestra); (ii) *Lyra Angelica* (concerto for harp and string orchestra); (iii) *Pastoral fantasia* (for viola and string orchestra); *Tragic interlude*.
*** Chandos Dig. CHAN 9065 [id.]. (i) Nicholas Daniel; (ii) Rachel Masters; (iii) Stephen Tees; City of L. Sinfonia, Richard Hickox.

Autumn legend (1954) is a highly atmospheric tone-poem, very Sibelian in feeling. So too is the *Pastoral fantasia*. Yet the piece has its own developing individuality. A fine performance, with Stephen Tees highly sympathetic to the music's fluid poetic line. The *Tragic interlude* is a powerful lament for the dead of wars past, written on the eve of the Second World War. But the highlight of the disc is the *Lyra Angelica*, a radiantly beautiful, extended piece (just over half an hour in length), inspired by the metaphysical poet, Giles Fletcher's '*Christ's victorie and triumph*'. The performance here is very moving, and the recording has great richness of string-tone and a delicately balanced harp texture. Rachel Masters's contribution is distinguished. This is the record to start with for those beginning to explore the music of this highly rewarding composer.

Concerti grossi Nos. 1 in B flat for chamber orchestra; 2 in G for string orchestra; 3 for woodwind, brass and strings; (i) *Oboe concerto*.
*** Chandos Dig. CHAN 8866 [id.]. (i) Daniel; City of L. Sinfonia, Hickox.

The improvisatory feeling and changing moods of the *Oboe concerto* are beautifully caught by Nicholas Daniel, with Hickox and the Sinfonia players providing admirable support. They then turn to the more extrovert and strongly contrasted *Concerti grossi*, the first a miniature concerto for orchestra, the second in the ripest tradition of English string writing. The third is a fine *in memoriam* for Sir Henry Wood. Excellent Chandos sound, gaining from the warm ambience of St Jude's in north-west London, yet with textures unclouded.

(i) *Piano concerto No. 1. Symphony No. 1*.
*** Chandos Dig. CHAN 9155 [id.]. (i) Howard Shelley; LSO, Hickox.

Hickox's performance of the *First Symphony* is just as compelling as the composer's own version on Lyrita (coupled with No. 4 – SRCD 227). The *First Piano concerto* is also a flamboyant piece, in a single movement. Howard Shelley is a splendid soloist, fully up to the rhetoric and touching the listener when the passion subsides, creating a haunting stillness at the very end. Again splendid recording.

(i) *Piano concerto No. 2. Sinfonietta for strings; Symphony No. 5 (Hydriotaphia)*.
*** Chandos Dig. CHAN 9196 [id.]. (i) Howard Shelley; LSO, Richard Hickox.

The *Piano concerto No. 2* opens boldly and expansively and is romantically rhetorical, with sweeping use of the strings. The imaginative *Andante* is its highlight, but the jazzy 'fuoco' finale with its calm central section is overlong (13 minutes). Howard Shelley plays with brilliance and much sensitivity, and Alwyn admirers will be glad to have the work available on record, even if it is flawed.

The cogent *Fifth Symphony* (1973), with its dense argument distilled into one movement with four sub-sections, has a strange subtitle. It is called '*Hydriotaphia*' and the work is dedicated to the memory of physician/philosopher Sir Thomas Browne (1605–82), whose writings were always on the composer's bedside table.

The *Sinfonietta for strings*, a much more expansive piece, is almost twice as long as the symphony. The string writing, very much in the English tradition, is vigorous in the first movement and hauntingly atmospheric, especially in the beautiful *Adagio*, desperate in its melancholy. Hickox is consistently sympathetic, with the structure of the symphony held in a strong grip.

(i) *Violin concerto. Symphony No. 3*.
*** Chandos Dig. CHAN 9187 [id.]. (i) Lydia Mordkovitch; LSO, Hickox.

The *Violin concerto* – so sympathetically played here by Lydia Mordkovitch – is discursive but has moments of intense beauty, especially at the rapt closing section of the first movement, where Lydia Mordkovitch plays exquisitely. Hickox's reading of the *Third Symphony* is every bit as convincing as that of the composer on Lyrita, while the LSO again respond to a symphony that is strongly conceived, powerfully argued, consistently inventive and impressively laid out. The expansive Chandos recording suits both works admirably, and the *Violin concerto* is balanced most convincingly.

4 Elizabethan dances (from the set of 6); *Derby Day overture; Festival march; The Magic island* (symphonic prelude); *Sinfonietta for strings*.
*** Lyrita SRCS 229 [id.]. LPO, composer.

An exceptionally attractive compilation and one of the composer's most successful records. Alwyn's *Elizabethan dances* are extrovert and tuneful in the Malcolm Arnold tradition (if not quite so ebullient in orchestration). Alwyn is no less successful in *Derby Day* with its pithily rhythmic main theme, and he is both poetic and romantically expansive in the Shakespearean evocation of *The Magic island*. In the *Festival march*, while acknowledging his debt to Elgar and Walton, he brings an individual, restrained nobilmente to the main lyrical tune. But the most important work here is the *Sinfonietta for strings*. The Lyrita recordings were made between 1972 and 1979 and show the usual engineering flair which distinguishes all issues on this label.

Film scores: *The Fallen Idol; The History of Mr Polly; Odd Man Out; The Rake's Progress: Calypso* (all restored and arr. Christopher Palmer).
*** Chandos Dig. CHAN 9243 [id.]. LSO, Richard Hickox.

Alwyn made his name as a film composer in the days when the immediate post-war British films as often as not had a 'symphonic score'. Unfortunately the major scores were all inadvertently destroyed at Pinewood Studios, and Christopher Palmer has had to return to the composer's sketches for these recordings. The result is impressive. *Odd Man Out* (about the IRA) has the most compellingly poignant music, but the lightweight *History of Mr Polly* is charming and *The Fallen Idol* sophisticated in its delineation of action and character. The orchestral playing is both warmly committed and polished, and the recording is out of Chandos's top drawer.

Symphonies Nos. 1–4; 5 (Hydriotaphia); Sinfonietta for strings.
*** Chandos Dig. CHAN 9429 (3) [id.]. LSO, Richard Hickox.

William Alwyn's five symphonies plus the expansive *Sinfonietta for strings* are given outstanding performances from the LSO under Hickox to match the composer's own in natural understanding. Here they are separated from their various couplings and fitted snugly on to three CDs. The Chandos recordings are consistently up to the high house standard, and this set can be commended without reservation to all collectors interested in the twentieth-century English symphony which, on the evidence of this box, is alive and well.

Symphonies Nos. 1; 4.
*** Lyrita SRCD 227 [id.]. LPO, composer.

The first of Alwyn's symphonies dates from 1950 and is a work of considerable power and maturity. Its gestures are occasionally overblown, particularly in the finale, and offer obvious echoes of the film-scores of which Alwyn is so consummate a master. The LPO responds splendidly to the composer's direction and the Lyrita analogue recording has fine presence, body and clarity.

Symphony No. 2; Derby Day overture; Fanfare for a joyful occasion; The Magic island; Overture to a masque.
*** Chandos Dig. CHAN 9093 [id.]. LSO, Richard Hickox.

Hickox's account of the Sibelian *Second Symphony* is every bit as fine as the composer's own performance on Lyrita, and the modern Chandos digital recording provides even fuller and more expansive sound for brass and strings and a natural concert-hall balance. *The Magic island* is a fine piece, inspired by *The Tempest*, and Hickox's account is beautifully played and full of atmosphere. The pithy *Derby Day overture* has plenty of energy here, but the *Overture to a masque* with its 'pipe and tabor' Elizabethan flavour is comparatively slight. The brilliant *Fanfare*, appropriately dedicated to the percussion player, James Blades, ends the concert spectacularly with the bright, sonorous recording impressively wide in range.

Symphony No. 4; Elizabethan dances; Festival march.
*** Chandos Dig. CHAN 8902 [id.]. LSO, Richard Hickox.

Richard Hickox's conception of the *Fourth* is marginally more spacious than the composer's own – as the timings of the outer movements demonstrate. Yet he has a masterly grip on the score. The *Elizabethan suite* doesn't bridge the opposing styles of the times of the queens, Elizabeth I and II, too convincingly, but there is a graceful waltz, an engaging mock-morris dance and a pleasing pavane. The *Festival march* is agreeable enough, but its grand tune lacks the memorability of those by Elgar and Walton.

CHAMBER MUSIC

Concerto for flute and 8 wind instruments; Music for three players; Naiades fantasy (Sonata for flute and harp); Suite for oboe and harp; Trio for flute, cello and piano.
*** Chandos Dig. CHAN 9152 [id.]. Haffner Wind Ens. of L., Daniel, with Jones, Drake.

Alwyn's *Concerto for flute and eight wind instruments* is richly textured, yet the consistent inner movement fascinates the ear. The charmingly pastoral *Suite for oboe and harp* is most delectably played by Nicholas Daniel (oboe) and Ieuan Jones (harp). The *Naiades fantasy for flute and harp* is a chimerical piece in six movements (alas, not cued individually). The final work is an equally attractive two movement *Trio*. The Haffner Wind Ensemble are very impressive, both individually as solo personalities and as a team, expertly matching timbres in part-writing which always rewards their skill and musicianship. The recording is admirably balanced and very realistic.

Crépuscule for solo harp; Divertimento for solo flute; Clarinet sonata; Flute sonata; Oboe sonata; Sonata impromptu for violin and viola.
*** Chandos Dig. CHAN 9197 [id.]. L. Haffner Wind Ens. (members), Nicholas Daniel; Julius Drake (piano).

The *Oboe sonata* is an inspired work; it is beautifully played here by Nicholas Daniel and Julius Drake. The *Clarinet sonata* is a fantasy piece in which Joy Farrall combines extrovert freedom with a more thoughtful reserve, yet with wild excursions into the upper tessitura. By contrast the solo *Divertimento* for flute (the responsive Kate Hill) is neo-classical. The *Crépuscule* for solo harp (Ieuan Jones) is a quiet evocation of a cold, clear and frosty Christmas Eve. The *Sonata for flute and piano* and the *Sonata impromptu for violin and viola* are no less striking. Overall this programme is consistently rewarding and the recording is very real and immediate.

(i) *Rhapsody for piano quartet. String quartet No. 3; String trio*.
*** Chandos Dig. CHAN 8440 [id.]. (i) David Willison; Qt of London.

The *Third Quartet* is the most important work on this record; like its two predecessors, it is a concentrated and thoughtful piece of very considerable substance, elegiac in feeling. The playing of the Quartet of London throughout (and of David Willison in the *Rhapsody*) is both committed and persuasive. The recording brings the musicians vividly into one's living-room.

String quartets Nos. 1 in D min.; 2 (Spring waters).
**(*) Chandos Dig. CHAN 9219 [id.]. Qt of London.

Both quartets are works of substance. The *First* has a probing, deeply felt first movement, a dancing, gossamer Scherzo and a profound, yearning *Andante*. Its companion comes 20 years later and derives its subtitle, *Spring waters*, from Turgenev. Both works are well played and the performances are obviously felt and thoroughly committed. The digital recording from the early 1980s has clarity and presence and sounds admirably natural in its CD format. However, the playing time is too short for a full-priced record (45 minutes).

Fantasy-waltzes; 12 Preludes.
**(*) Chandos Dig. CHAN 8399 [id.]. John Ogdon.

This record has been restored to the catalogue at full price (even though it dates from 1985) and a price reduction might have been feasible. The *Fantasy-waltzes* are highly attractive and are excellently played by John Ogdon, who is also responsible for a perceptive insert-note. The *Twelve Preludes* are equally fluent and inventive pieces that ought to be better known and well repay investigation.

VOCAL MUSIC

(i) *Invocations;* (ii) *A Leave-taking* (song-cycles).
*** Chandos Dig. CHAN 9220 [id.]. (i) Jill Gomez, John Constable; (ii) Anthony Rolfe Johnson, Graham Johnson.

In each of these two song-cycles, with a distinctive and unexpected choice of poems, Alwyn shows a keen ear for matching word-movement in music with a free arioso style. Notable in the tenor cycle, *A Leave-taking*, is *The ocean wood*, subtly evocative in its sea inspirations. The soprano cycle is almost equally distinguished, leading to a beautiful *Invocation to the Queen of Moonlight*, which suits Jill Gomez's sensuous high soprano perfectly. Excellent performances, not least from the accompanists, and first-rate recording.

Miss Julie (complete).
*** Lyrita SRCD 2218 (2) [id.]. Jill Gomez, Benjamin Luxon, Della Jones, John Mitchinson, Philh. O, Tausky.

Alwyn's operatic gestures are big and, though the melodies hardly match Puccini's, the score is rich and confident, passionately performed by the Philharmonia under Tausky's direction. Jill Gomez sings ravishingly as Miss Julie and Benjamin Luxon gives a most convincing characterization of the manservant lover, with roughness a part of the mixture. Della Jones's mezzo is not contrasted enough with the heroine's soprano, but she sings warmly, and it is good to have as powerful a tenor as John Mitchinson in the incidental role of Ulrik. The 1983 Lyrita recording is well up to standard, beautifully clear as well as full, and it projects the narrative evocatively and involvingly.

Anderson, Leroy (1908–75)

Belle of the ball; Blue tango; Chicken reel; China doll; Fiddle-faddle; The first day of spring; The girl in satin; Horse and buggy; Jazz legato; Jazz pizzicato; The phantom regiment; Plink, plank, plunk!; Promenade; Saraband; Scottish suite: The bluebells of Scotland. Serenata; Sleigh ride; Song of the bells; Summer skies; The syncopated clock; The typewriter; The waltzing cat. Arr. of HANDEL: *Song of Jupiter*.
(M) *** Mercury 432 013-2 [id.]. Eastman-Rochester Pops O, or O, Frederick Fennell.

The reissue of Fennell's Mercury performances is most welcome; although certain key numbers such as *Bugler's holiday*, *Forgotten dreams* and *A Trumpeter's lullaby* are missing from this record, they do arrive on a later issue (see below). His performances have a witty precision which is most attractive. The sound throughout is truthful, if not opulent.

(i) *Carol suite:* excerpts. *A Christmas festival. Goldilocks: Pirate dance*. (ii) *Irish suite. Bugler's holiday; Forgotten dreams; Penny-whistle song; Sandpaper ballet; Trumpeter's lullaby*.
(M) *** Mercury 434 376-2 [id.]. (i) London Pops O; (ii) Eastman-Rochester Pops O, Frederick Fennell (with COATES: *Four ways; London suites*. **(*))

Here Mercury complete their reissues of the vintage Fennell recordings of Leroy Anderson, including the *Irish suite,* one of Anderson's more ambitious enterprises. Its highlight is a clever arrangement of *The Minstrel boy* in the form of a haunting little funeral march, advancing and retreating. The half-dozen orchestral lollipops include several favourites, notably *Bugler's holiday* and *Forgotten dreams*. Fennell also includes some arrangements of notable Christmas carols, and the vintage, rather dry and studio-ish recording suits the bright precision of the playing.

Antheil, George (1900–1959)

Symphony No. 4, '1942'.

(*) Everest EVC 9039 [id.]. LSO, Sir Eugene Goossens – COPLAND: *Statements for orchestra*. *

The American composer, George Antheil was born in Trenton, New Jersey, of Polish and German ancestry. There are influences of his East European background in this symphony, which is probably his best. The performance, from a famous advocate of contemporary music, could not be more convincing, and the Everest stereo (from 1959) entirely belies its age. This music is not deep but it readily communicates, and one's only real complaint is that this excellently remastered reissue should have been offered less expensively – the disc plays for only 49 minutes.

Antill, John (1904–86)

Corroboree (ballet suite).

(*) Everest EVC 9007 [id.]. LSO, Sir Eugene Goossens – GINASTERA: *Estancia; Panambi* *; VILLA-LOBOS: *Little train of the Caipira*. **(*)

The ballet-score *Corroboree*, the best-known work by the Australian composer, John Antill, is based on an aboriginal dance ceremony. Its primitivism generates imaginatively exotic invention, very colourfully scored, to include an enticing *Dance to the Evening Star*, a strongly rhythmic *Rain dance* and a boisterously frantic *Closing fire ceremony*. The performance here generates plenty of energy, and if the recording is over-resonant it is immensely vivid. It is a pity that this Everest series is not in the mid-priced range, although it costs slightly less than the highest premium-priced CDs.

Arensky, Anton (1861–1906)

Piano concerto in F min., Op. 2; Fantasia on Russian folksongs, Op. 48.

*** Hyperion Dig. CDA 66624 [id.]. Coombs, BBC Scottish SO, Maksymiuk – BORTKIEWICZ: *Piano concerto*. ***

Arensky's *Piano concerto in F minor* is an endearing piece, highly Chopinesque in feeling and with some very appealing ideas. Coombs is an artist of great sensitivity and effortless virtuosity, and he makes out the best possible case for both the *Concerto* and the much shorter *Fantasia on Russian folksongs*. Good orchestral support and recording.

Violin concerto in A min., Op. 54.

*** Chandos Dig. CHAN 9528 [id.]. Alexander Trostiansky, I Musici de Montréal, Yuli Turovsky – GLAZUNOV: *Concerto ballata* etc. ***

(N) **(*) Globe Dig. GLO 5174 [id.]. Mark Lubotsky, Estonian Nat. SO, Volmer – RIMSKY-KORSAKOV: *Concert fantasy;* TCHAIKOVSKY: *Violin concerto*. **(*)

Overshadowed by his mentor, Tchaikovsky, and his pupil, Rachmaninov – understandably so, for no one would claim that he is their peer – Arensky is still a composer to reckon with, and his neglect is our loss. The *Violin concerto in A minor* is a delightful piece that deserves to be every bit as popular as, say, the Glazunov. It has generosity of spirit and is brimming over with lyrical invention and memorable ideas. The concerto is beautifully played by Alexander Trostiansky, now in his early- to mid-twenties. He is not a larger-than-life showman who plays like a machine but a talented young artist from Novosibirsk, and he has refinement, musicianship and impeccable taste. He is perhaps balanced rather too reticently, but the case for this concerto, which is not generously represented in the present catalogue, is made very persuasively by orchestra and engineers alike.

Mark Lubotsky's fine recording is also one of the best we have had since Aaron Rosand's dazzling Luxembourg Radio account from the early 1970s. Like this, it is coupled with the Rimsky-Korsakov *Concert fantasy*. Good orchestral playing under Arvo Volmer and naturally balanced sound.

Symphonies Nos. 1 in B min., Op. 4; 2 in A, Op. 22; Dream on the Volga: Overture. Intermezzo in G min., Op. 13; Nal and Damayanty: Introduction. Suites Nos. 1 in G min., Op.7; 2 (Silhouettes), Op. 23; 3 in C (Variations), Op. 33.

(B) **(*) BMG/Melodiya Twofer Dig. 74321 53462-2 (2) [id.]. USSR SO, Svetlanov.

Arensky's *First Symphony*, composed shortly after his graduation in 1882, is a work of great fluency and charm. It is beautifully put together and has considerable melodic freshness. The *Second* is the more individual of the two and is full of highly attractive ideas: its four movements are linked together, the finale returning to the material of the opening movement; however, there is little serious attempt at organic cohesion. The *Overture* to the opera *Dream on the Volga* (1888) opens bombastically but also has its attractive moments, though its inspiration is less consistent than either. The *First Suite* (1885) opens with a characteristic miniature set of variations on a Russian folksong. The *Second suite* (*Silhouettes*) derives from a set of pieces for two pianos dating from 1892, and it is scored with great skill and, in the case of *La coquette* and *Polichinelle*, delicacy. The whole of the *Third Suite* (1894) is in itself a set of variations on a gracious theme and, like the *Second*, originates in music conceived for the piano. All this music is very vividly played and recorded and, if climaxes are just a little overwhelming at times, they are not really coarse. A thoroughly worthwhile set which greatly increases our knowledge of this composer, so admired by Tchaikovsky, who was his lifelong friend.

Variations on a theme of Tchaikovsky, Op. 35a.
(B) *** EMI forte CZS5 69361 (2) [CDFP 69361]. LSO, Barbirolli – RIMSKY-KORSAKOV: *Scheherazade* **; GLAZUNOV: *The Seasons; Concert waltzes.* ***
(B) *(*) Mercury Double 434 391-2 (2) [id.]. Philharmonia Hungarica, Dorati – TCHAIKOVSKY: *Symphonies Nos. 1–3.* ❁ ***

These delightful variations, arguably Arensky's best-known work, originally formed the slow movement of the *Second String quartet in A minor*, composed in 1894, a year after Tchaikovsky's death, and subsequently arranged for full strings. Sir John Barbirolli's recording, made in the Kingsway Hall in 1965 and first published in harness with the Tchaikovsky *Serenade for strings*, is warm and spacious. The playing of the LSO under this endearing conductor is suitably affectionate. It comes as part of a quite attractive two-CD Russian music package, let down a little by Svetlanov's rather idiosyncratic *Scheherazade*.

Dorati's performance is polished and elegantly turned, yet it is not easy to decide whether the fact that this recorded account conveys so little of the naïve charm of the music is altogether the conductor's fault or that of the engineers. The recording was made in the Grosse Saal of the Vienna Konzerthaus in 1958. The effect is curiously dry, and the string players are made to seem too close to the listener.

CHAMBER MUSIC

Piano trio No. 1 in D min., Op. 32.
(M *** CRD CRD 3409; *CRDC 3409* [id.]. Ian Brown, Nash Ens. – RIMSKY-KORSAKOV: *Quintet.* ***
*** Chandos Dig. CHAN 8477 [id.]. Borodin Trio – GLINKA: *Trio.* ***

Arensky's delightful *D minor Piano trio* was composed a year after Tchaikovsky's death and a decade after Tchaikovsky's own contribution to the genre. The account by members of the Nash Ensemble is first class in every way. These fine players capture the Slav melancholy of the *Elegia*, and in the delightful *Scherzo* Ian Brown is both delicate and nimble-fingered. The warm, resonant 1982 analogue recording has transferred naturally to CD.

The Borodins, too, give a lively and full-blooded account of the *Trio*. The *Scherzo* comes off well, and the whole does justice to the Borodins' genial playing.

Piano trios Nos. 1 in D min., Op. 32; 2 in F min., Op. 73.
*** Ph. Dig. 442 127-2 [id.]. Beaux Arts Trio.

The Beaux Arts offer the more logical coupling. While the *D minor Trio* is well represented in the catalogue, its later companion is neglected, and the Beaux Arts is a first recommendation now: lively playing, full of engagement and sparkle, and very well recorded.

String quartet No. 2 in A min., Op. 35.
(N) *** Hyperion Dig. CDA 66648 [id.]. Raphael Ens. – TCHAIKOVSKY: *Souvenir de Florence.* ***

The *A minor Quartet* is unusual in being for only one violin and two cellos. A charming three-movement work, it is dedicated to the memory of Tchaikovsky, the composer's mentor and friend. The second movement is a set of variations on Tchaikovsky's *Legend* from the *Children's songs*, Op. 54, much better known in its transcription for full strings. The short finale quotes from the folk-song associated with the coronation scene of *Boris Godunov* and also used by Beethoven in the second of the *Razumovsky* quartets. It is marvellously played by members of the Raphael Ensemble though the recording is a bit close, placing the listener in the front row of the hall.

Suites for 2 pianos Nos. 1, Op. 15; 2 (Silhouettes), Op. 23; 3 (Variations), Op. 33; 4, Op. 62.
*** Hyperion Dig. CDA 66755 [id.]. Stephen Coombs, Ian Munro.

Arensky was enormously fluent and all the music here is endearingly fresh. The *Polonaise*, which ends the *First suite*, would not disgrace a ballet by Tchaikovsky. *Suite No. 2*, written four years later, is subtitled *Silhouettes*, and each of its five movements represents a different character, *Le Savant* ('The Scholar'), *La Coquette*, and so on. *Suite No. 3* is a set of nine variations and is the most brilliant and pianistically resourceful of all four. *Suite No. 4* was written five years before the composer's death and is hardly less beguiling than its companions. Two pianos are difficult to record and the recording, though too resonant, reproduces them very truthfully. Altogether delightful music and captivating playing. Were it not so resonant, it would have a Rosette.

Egyptian Nights, Op. 50.
(N) **(*) Marco Polo Dig. 8.225028 [id.]. Moscow SO, Dmitry Yablonsky.

Egyptian Nights was composed in 1900 for Fokine and is based on Pushkin, albeit very loosely. The story is flimsy in the extreme: Amoun is so enamoured of Cleopatra that he offers his own life in exchange for just one kiss from her, a bargain she accepts. The emergence of Antony on the scene brings all concerned to their senses. The music cultivates a certain pallid exoticism with dances for Egyptian girls and although the invention is not top-drawer, it is often endearing. Arensky was a master of the orchestra and the ballet, which runs for 50 minutes, is far from unpleasing. Decent playing and recording.

Armstrong, Sir Thomas (1898–1994)

(iv) *Fantasy quintet*. (iii, iv) *Friends departed*. (iii) *Never weather-beaten sail; O mortal folk*. (ii–iv) *A passer-by*. (iii) *She is not fair to outward view*. (iv) *Sinfonietta*. (iii) *Sweet day; With Margerain Gentle*.
(N) *** Chandos Dig. CHAN 9657 [id.]. (i) Janice Watson; (ii) Stephen Varcoe; (iii) L Philh. Ch.; (iv) LPO. Paul Daniel.

As a distinguished academic, both at Oxford and finally as Principal of the Royal Academy of Music, Sir Thomas Armstrong was a key figure in British musical life, who early in his career submitted the three longest pieces in this selection of his music as part of his doctoral thesis. Sadly, he never heard them performed, for in their echoes of English choral music from Parry to Vaughan Williams, and Holst by way of Delius, both *A passer-by* (with baritone soloist) and *Friends departed* (with soprano) have an immediate impact, passionate not academic. The *Fantasy quintet* and the *Sinfonietta* are more sensuous still, amiable pieces, and the six part-songs are beautifully written too. As conductor, Paul Daniel is a most persuasive advocate in the big pieces, and the recording is warm and atmospheric. Lord Armstrong, the son of the composer, and a former cabinet secretary, writes a charmingly informative note.

Arne, Thomas (1710–78)

Keyboard concertos (played as listed): *Harpsichord concertos: in C; in G min.; Organ concertos: in B flat; in G; Piano concertos: in A; in B flat.*
*** Hyperion Dig. CDA 66509 [id.]. Paul Nicholson, Parley of Instruments, Holman.

The six keyboard concertos of Arne date from different periods in his career and have a wide variety of movement-structures. Holman varies the solo instrument according to the character of each work, with the earliest, *No. 2 in G major*, given on the organ, but the next oldest, *No. 5 in G minor*, played on the harpsichord, when the Scarlattian cross-hands writing is better suited to that instrument. As a sampler, try the delectable *No. 3 in A*, given here on a gentle-toned fortepiano. Exhilarating performances, the instrumental balances perfectly managed, achieving clarity without exaggeration.

Organ concertos Nos. 1 in C; 2 in G; 3 in A; 4 in B flat; 5 in G min.; 6 in B flat.
**(*) Chandos Dig. CHAN 8604/5; (2) [id.]. Roger Bevan Williams, Cantilena, Shepherd.

Though Arne's concertos are simpler in style and construction than those of Handel, their invention is consistently fresh. The performances here have admirable style and spirit, and the recording is ideally balanced – the organ seems perfectly chosen for this consistently engaging music. A recommendable set in every respect, except for the playing time (only 86 minutes).

Cymon and Iphigenia; Frolic and free (cantatas); Jenny; The Lover's recantation; The Morning (cantata); Sigh no more, ladies; Thou soft flowing Avon; What tho' his guilt.
*** Hyperion Dig. CDA 66237 (id.]. Emma Kirkby, Richard Morton, Parley of Instruments, Goodman.

The present collection admirably shows the ingenuous simplicity of Arne's vocal writing, very much in the mid-eighteenth-century English pastoral school with its 'Hey down derrys'. Excellent, warm recording, with the voices naturally projected. A most entertaining concert.

Artaxerxes (complete).
*** Hyperion Dig. CDA 67051/2 [id.]. Robson, Bott, Partridge, Spence, Edgar-Wilson, Hyde, Parley of Instruments, Roy Goodman.

This sparkling, lively performance impressively explains why Arne's opera was such a success when it was first produced at Covent Garden in February 1762, three years after Handel died. The one number that has latterly become popular – largely thanks to Joan Sutherland's brilliant recording – is *The soldier tir'd*, but that dazzling climactic number is only one of Mandane's formidable solos, whether expressive or vehement. Catherine Bott gives a masterly performance, with the counter-tenor, Christopher Robson, also impressive in the castrato title-role, and with Ian Partridge pure-toned and incisive in the role of the villain, Artabanes, even if his sweet tenor hardly conveys evil. With the mezzo-soprano, Patricia Spence, taking the castrato role of Arbaces, the others are first rate too. On two very well-filled

CDs the set owes much of its success to the inspired direction of Roy Goodman, who from the overture onwards electrifies the players and singers, bringing out the point and charm as well as the vigour of the writing. The reconstruction of the score – involving the recitatives which were separated from the original – has been most capably achieved by Peter Holman, who contributes an excellent note.

Arnell, Richard (born 1917)

Punch and the child (ballet), *Op. 49*.
(B) (***) Sony mono SBK 62748. RPO, Beecham – BERNERS: *Triumph of Neptune;* DELIUS: *Paris*. (***)

Richard Arnell enjoyed something of a vogue immediately after the war. His imaginative and inventive ballet, *Punch and the child*, was mounted by the New York City Ballet. Sir Thomas Beecham recorded the *Punch and the child suite*. Its musical inspiration is as fresh, individual and memorable as its neglect is unaccountable. We have relished this score over the years, and its attractions remain as strong as ever in this well-transferred set. The sound is amazingly good for 1950 – but then it was pretty much state-of-the-art at that time – and this is very attractive indeed at bargain price.

Arnold, Malcolm (born 1921)

Overture: *Beckus the Dandipratt, Op. 5; Commonwealth Christmas, Op. 64; The Fair field, Op. 110; The Smoke, Op. 21; A Sussex overture*.
*** Reference Dig. RR 48CD [id.]. LPO, composer.

This collection of overtures valuably fills in gaps in the Arnold discography, notably *Beckus the Dandipratt*, his very first orchestral work. If its scherzando rhythms owe much to Walton's *Scapino*, the fizzing energy and brilliant orchestration are very much Arnold's own. Arnold at seventy is perhaps a less exhilarating conductor than in his earlier recordings, but only *The Fair field* (celebrating the Croydon Fairfield Halls) lacks something in effervescence. *The Smoke* brings a contrasting sultry atmosphere in its central section and the Prokofievian *Sussex overture* is jauntily full of good spirits, as is the exuberant *Commonwealth Christmas overture*, with its injection of West Indian popular music, complete with steel band evocations. The LPO playing is strikingly alert throughout and the recording suitably brilliant. Christopher Palmer, the recording producer, provides excellent documentation.

Carnival of the animals, Op. 72; (i) *Concerto for 2 pianos, 3 hands (Concerto for Phyllis and Cyril), Op. 104; A Grand, grand overture, Op. 57; Symphony No. 2, Op. 40*.
*** Conifer Dig. 75605 51240-2 [id.]. (i) David Nettle and Richard Markham; RPO, Vernon Handley.

Malcolm Arnold's *Double piano concerto* was originally the *'Concerto for Phyllis and Cyril'*, written in 1969 for Phyllis Sellick and Cyril Smith when Cyril lost the use of his left hand and he and his wife continued as a highly successful piano duo. The piano duo here, Nettle and Markham, are obviously captivated by the piece, which they play with much flair and understanding. The *Second Symphony* is fresh and colourful, far more complex in structure than it may initially seem. Vernon Handley is a persuasive advocate, and the spectacular recording is especially effective in the moments of brassy flamboyance in the outer movements. The *Grand, grand overture* was written for the famous Hoffnung Festivals and comes up remarkably effectively here.

Concerto for 28 players, Op. 105; (i) *Viola concerto, Op. 108. Larch trees, Op. 3; Serenade for small orchestra, Op. 105*.
*** Conifer Dig. 75605 51211-2 [id.]. (i) Rivka Golani; L. Musici, Stephenson.

Following up his other excellent Conifer disc of Arnold concertos, Mark Stephenson here fills in more important gaps in the CD catalogue of Arnold's music. *Larch trees* dates from as early as 1943, written when he was only 21. It is his first orchestral work, a tone-poem that instantly reveals his natural feeling for effective, evocative instrumentation. The *Viola concerto* and the *Concerto for 28 players* both date from the period 1970–71. The *Viola concerto* is the more immediately approachable, with Arnold exploiting the lower register of the solo instrument more consistently than Walton did in his concerto. The most enigmatic work here is the *Concerto for 28 players*, chamber-music writ large, often abrasive in an almost Stravinskian way. Stephenson and his talented team are just as convincingly idiomatic in the charming *Serenade*.

Clarinet concertos Nos. 1, Op. 20; 2, Op. 115; Scherzetto.
*** Hyperion Dig. CDA 66634 [id.]. Thea King, ECO, Wordsworth – BRITTEN: *Clarinet concerto movement;* MACONCHY: *Concertinos*. ***

Designed in part as a tribute to the great clarinettist, Frederick Thurston, Thea King's collection of short concertante works for clarinet makes an exceptionally attractive disc, beautifully recorded and superbly performed. The *Scherzetto* is a delightfully jaunty piece adapted by Christopher Palmer from Arnold's music for the film, *You Know What Sailors Are*. Not only Thea King but the ECO (the orchestra in which she has been a distinguished principal for many years) under Barry Wordsworth bring out the warmth as well as the rhythmic drive.

Clarinet concertos Nos. 1, Op. 20; 2, Op. 115; Divertimento for flute, oboe and clarinet, Op. 37; Fantasy for B flat clarinet, Op. 87; Clarinet sonatina, Op. 29; 3 Shanties for wind quintet.
*** ASV Dig. CDDCA 922 [id.]. Emma Johnson, Jaime Martin, Jonathan Kelly, Claire Briggs, Susanna Cohen, Malcolm Martineau; ECO, Ivor Bolton.

With the characterful Emma Johnson as the central figure in all five works, this makes a delightful collection of what is labelled as Arnold's 'Complete Works for Clarinet'. Above all, these performances bring out the fun in Arnold's music, his bluff sense of humour set alongside a vein of warm lyricism matched by few of his contemporaries. Compared with Thea King on Hyperion, Emma Johnson has a rather reedier tone, less smooth, and her speeds tend to be a little more relaxed. Choice can safely be left to preference over coupling, though the recording of the orchestra is rather less transparent than in the rival versions. Otherwise first-rate sound.

(i) *Clarinet concerto No. 2, Op. 115;* (ii) *Flute concerto No. 2, Op. 111;* (iii) *Horn concerto No. 1, Op. 11;* (iv) *Concerto for piano duet and strings, Op. 32.*
*** Conifer Dig. 75605 51228-2 [id.]. (i) Michael Collins; (ii) Karen Jones; (iii) Richard Watkins; (iv) David Nettle & Richard Markham; L. Musici, Mark Stephenson.

In the *Second Clarinet concerto*, written for Benny Goodman in 1974, Michael Collins is equally sympathetic in the *Flute Concerto No. 2*. The *Concerto for piano duet* of 1950 should not be confused with the three-handed *Concerto for two pianos* that Arnold wrote for Cyril Smith and Phyllis Sellick. Nettle and Markham play as one at their single keyboard; and under Mark Stephenson the young musicians of London Musici perform throughout with the understanding and precision that have marked all their Conifer recordings.

(i) *Flute concertos Nos. 1–2;* (ii) *Serenade for small orchestra;* (iii) *5 Pieces for violin and piano;* (iv) *Children's suite.*
*** Koch Dig. 3-7607-2 [id.]. (i) Alexa Still, New Zealand CO, Nicholas Braithwaite; (ii) San Diego CO, Donald Barra; (iii) St Clair Trio (members); (iv) Benjamin Frith.

Koch seem to be offering collectors a choice in their Malcolm Arnold series, for the delightful performance of the *Serenade*, (both witty and ironic) by Donald Barra and the San Diego Chamber Orchestra is also available on another disc (Koch 3-7134-2), where it is accompanied by the pair of *Sinfoniettas* and the *Double violin concerto*. As the account of the latter isn't entirely successful, the present collection must be the preferable recommendation. Alexa Still gives memorable accounts of the two *Flute concertos*, full of dazzling virtuosity, while the central soliloquy of No. 1 is utterly haunting. For a sampler of this ever-stimulating composer, writing with equal skill in four different formats, the present collection is hard to beat.

(i) *Flute concerto, Op. 45;* (ii) *Oboe concerto, Op. 39. Sinfoniettas Nos. 1, Op. 48; 2, Op. 65; 3, Op. 81.*
(BB) *** Arte Nova/BMG Dig. 74321 46503-2 [id.]. (i) Anna Pyne; (ii) Malcolm Messiter; L. Festival O, Ross Pople.

This is the identical programme of three *Sinfoniettas* plus concertos which Ross Pople recorded earlier for Hyperion with his London Festival Orchestra. In between he has radically rethought his interpretations, often choosing quite different speeds, sometimes faster (as in the *Sinfonietta No. 1*), sometimes much slower (as in the first movements of the other two *Sinfoniettas*). The changes in whichever direction generally bring lighter textures and manner, with Anna Pyne a more warmly expressive flute soloist than her predecessor, and the oboist, Malcolm Messiter, lighter than before. Very well recorded, at super-bargain price it makes an excellent issue, bringing together charming, beautifully crafted works that are far too little heard in the concert hall.

Guitar concerto, Op. 67.
(M) *** RCA 09026 61598-2. Julian Bream, Melos Ens., composer – Richard Rodney BENNETT: *Concerto;* RODRIGO: *Concierto de Aranjuez.* ***
*** EMI (SIS) Dig. CDC7 54661-2 [id.]. Julian Bream, CBSO (members), Rattle – RODRIGO: *Concierto de Aranjuez.* TAKEMITSU: *To the Edge of Dream.* ***

There are few guitar concertos to match the effectiveness of this jazz-inflected piece, written in 1957 for Julian Bream, whose first recording, made two years later with the composer directing the Melos Ensemble, is surely definitive. It was recorded by Decca engineers, so the balance is exemplary and the sound has plenty of atmosphere and the most vivid colouring.

Bream's second recording, with Rattle, is also very successful indeed and gains from the modern digital sound, which is vividly focused. As with the earlier version, the work is recorded in its original chamber scoring, which is especially effective in the infectious finale.

(i) *4 Cornish dances; 8 English dances, Sets 1, Op. 27; 2, Op. 33; 4 Scottish dances, Op. 59* (all arr. Farr); *Fantasy for brass band, Op. 114; Little*

suites for brass band Nos. 1, Op. 80; 2, Op. 92; (ii) *The Padstow Lifeboat* (march), *Op. 94.*
*** Conifer Dig. 74321 16848-2 [id.]. Grimethorpe Colliery Band, (i) Elgar Howarth; (ii) composer.

Sir Malcolm Arnold, who was present at the recording sessions, gave high praise to Elgar Howarth's carefully prepared yet winningly spontaneous performances, unerringly paced. This is very much in the demonstration bracket and is also a most entertaining 66 minutes of good tunes and brilliant invention, very cleverly scored.

4 Cornish dances, Op. 91; 8 English dances, Set 1, Op. 27; Set 2, Op. 33; 4 Irish dances, Op. 126; 4 Scottish dances, Op. 59; 4 Welsh dances, Op. 138.
(B) *** Naxos Dig. 8.553526 [id.]. Queensland SO, Andrew Penny.

The advantage this Naxos disc has over its competitors – to say nothing of its price – is the inclusion of the four *Welsh dances*, the last to be written and closer in mood to the *Cornish* and *Irish dances* than to the cheerful ebullience of the masterly *English dances* of 1950–51. They remain perennial favourites, and Andrew Penny and the Queensland Orchestra present them with their colours gleaming. These performances have the composer's imprimatur (he was present at the recording sessions) and can be cordially recommended. Only Arnold's own Lyrita recordings surpass them, and then only marginally. The Naxos sound might be thought a shade over-resonant, but it does not lack brilliance.

Film music: *The Bridge on the River Kwai* (suite for large orchestra); *Hobson's Choice* (orchestral suite); *The Inn of the Sixth Happiness* (suite); *The Sound Barrier* (rhapsody), *Op. 38; Whistle Down the Wind* (small suite for small orchestra).
*** Chandos Dig. CHAN 9100 [id.]. LSO, Richard Hickox.

Malcolm Arnold wrote over 100 film scores, and it was the music for *The Bridge on the River Kwai* which – as the composer has acknowledged – put his name before the wider public. All this music is superbly played by Hickox and the LSO (who obviously relish the often virtuoso instrumental scoring), and the recording is as lavish as anyone could wish – very much in the Chandos demonstration bracket.

The Sound Barrier (rhapsody) after film score, *Op. 38.*
(M) *** ASV Dig. CDWHL 2058. RPO, Kenneth Alwyn – BAX: *Malta G.C.* etc. ***

Malcolm Arnold's *Rhapsody*, adapted in 1952 from his film score, shows the composer at his most characteristically inventive. Kenneth Alwyn and the RPO clearly relish the virtuosity demanded of them, and the recording is equally brilliant.

Symphonies Nos. 1, Op. 22; 2, Op. 40.
*** Chandos Dig. CHAN 9335 [id.]. LSO, Richard Hickox.
(N) (BB) **(*) Naxos Dig. 8.553406 [id.]. Nat. SO of Ireland, Andrew Penny.

Richard Hickox takes naturally to the Malcolm Arnold idiom and moves easily from geniality to angry intensity, as in the first movement of No. 1; and he is particularly impressive in the two slow movements, which are full of atmosphere, vividly coloured and strongly felt. The rumbustious finale of No. 2 brings a splendid release of tension, and throughout the LSO response is powerful and thoroughly committed. The recording is well up to the high standard we expect from this label and the spontaneity of the playing communicates the feeling of live music-making. A first-rate coupling.

Andrew Penny in his Naxos version matches Hickox closely, but the National Orchestra of Ireland cannot command the richness of sonority of the LSO, nor are their (otherwise excellent) wind soloists quite so strong in personality. The Dublin performances of both symphonies are fresh and spontaneous, but in the poignant *Lento* of the *Second*, with its plangent funeral march, Hickox's more spacious tempo is profoundly moving. Yet the composer was present at these sessions and undoubtedly Penny consulted him over questions of tempo and especially that for the slow movement of the *Second Symphony*, which certainly communicates strongly in the Dublin performance. The Naxos recording is excellent, full and spacious, but the Chandos is very much in the demonstration bracket.

Symphonies Nos. (i) *2, Op. 40;* (ii) *5, Op. 74;* (i) *Peterloo overture, Op. 97.*
(M) *** EMI CDM5 66324-2. (i) Bournemouth SO, Groves; (ii) CBSO, composer.

The recoupling of two of Arnold's most impressive symphonies can be warmly welcomed. Both recordings date from the 1970s. The composer secures an outstanding response from the Birmingham orchestra; in many ways his performance has not been surpassed, particularly in the expressive power of the slow movement. Groves, too, in Bournemouth is equally dedicated, and this is one of his finest recordings. The CD transfer is outstandingly successful, and the overture makes a highly effective encore. Splendid value at mid-price.

Symphony No. 3, Op. 63.
**(*) Everest EVC 9001 [id.]. LPO, composer – VAUGHAN WILLIAMS: *Symphony No. 9.* **(*)

Arnold made his first recording of the *Third Symphony* at Walthamstow in the late 1950s. In the outer movements the performance has a certain chimerical, spontaneous quality that balances out the deeper feelings which are beneath the music's surface. The result is uncommonly fresh, even if Hickox's later recording has more gravitas. The early stereo is remarkably spacious and the brass writing is given fine sonority, though the violins are less full-bodied than we would expect today.

Symphonies Nos. 3, Op. 63; 4, Op. 71.
*** Chandos Dig. CHAN 9290 [id.]. LSO, Hickox.
*** Conifer Dig. 75605 51258-2 [id.]. RLPO, Vernon Handley.
(BB) *** Naxos Dig. 8.553739 [id.]. Nat. SO of Ireland, Andrew Penny.

Arnold's immediately communicative *Third Symphony* is notable for the long, expressively austere string-melody in the opening movement and the desolation of its *Lento* slow movement, both played with great expressive intensity under Hickox. The first movement of the *Fourth Symphony* is dominated by one of those entirely winning, Arnoldian lyrical tunes, even though there is jagged dissonance in the central episode. The slow movement brings another long-breathed, almost Mahlerian, melodic flow, although with more overt sensuousness, and the finale, complete with fugue, has its bizarre, indeed raucous moments, including a curious march sequence. Richard Hickox has the work's full measure, and the Chandos recording is superb, full of colour and atmosphere.

As the Royal Liverpool Philharmonic Society commissioned the *Third Symphony* and the Liverpool orchestra gave its première, it is not surprising that they should play it with such sympathy, with most engagingly sensitive woodwind contributions to the opening movement and the strings at their most eloquent in the Mahlerian *Lento*. Handley's performances of both works are every bit the equal of the competing Chandos pairing from Hickox and the LSO. The sinuously seductive treatment of the swinging Arnoldian tune in the first movement of the *Fourth* is very engaging indeed and the rumbustious finale of this work, with its grotesque pastiche of a Sousa march, has irresistible vigour and impulse. The Conifer recording is in the demonstration class, spacious and vivid, with a most convincing hall ambience.

Andrew Penny and his Dublin orchestra also give finely played and spontaneous performances that can readily stand alongside the full-price competition, and this Naxos record understandably has the composer's imprimatur. Penny's pacing, overall shaping and concern for detail bring readings which are very persuasive in following the composer's quixotic mood-changes, while still holding the structures together. The recording, if not as rich as the Chandos, is of high quality, atmospheric and with the orchestral colours emerging vividly; the special percussion effects in the exuberantly fugal finale of the *Fourth* are also very telling.

Symphonies Nos. 5, Op. 74; 6, Op. 95.
*** Chandos Dig. CHAN 9385 [id.]. LSO, Richard Hickox.

Arnold's *Fifth Symphony* is a consciously elegiac work, written in memory of friends who died young; it contains some of his most intense and emotional music but remains easily approachable. While the first movement brings moments of valedictory evocation in Hickox's hands, it is also dramatically vibrant, and the *Andante* has a certain restrained warmth of feeling to balance its dejection. Whereas the jocularly brash Scherzo and finale are bursting with rhythmic life and colour, the work's ambivalent close is caught perceptively. The disconsolate *Sixth Symphony* is a good deal less comfortable than the *Fifth*, but Hickox handles the powerfully menacing climax of the *Lento* quite superbly, gripping the listener in the music's bleak despair, which then suddenly evaporates with the arrival of the joyous, syncopated brass fanfares of the rondo finale. In both symphonies the committed response of the LSO, together with the richly expansive Chandos recording, increases the weight and power of the readings, and this coupling stands out as a highly suitable point of entry for those collectors wanting to explore Arnold's symphonic canon.

Symphony No. 6, Op. 95; (i) *Fantasy on a theme of John Field for piano and orchestra, Op. 116. Sweeney Todd* (ballet): *concert suite, Op. 68a; Tam O'Shanter overture, Op. 51.*
*** Conifer Dig. 74321 16847-2 [id.]. RPO, Vernon Handley, (i) with John Lill.

Written in 1967 during his unhappy Cornish period, the powerfully bleak *Sixth Symphony* brings a striking example of the darker, more troubled side of Arnold's genius. The work finally resolves its enigmatic despondency in the up-beat *Con fuoco* finale, a rondo based on a characteristically ebullient Arnoldian trumpet-tune, a movement somewhat Shostakovich-like in its quirkiness. The *Fantasy on a theme of John Field*, written for John Lill during the composer's Irish period, is a splendid example of the more extrovert Arnold in the bravura of the piano writing. The *Sweeney Todd* music, drawn from a ballet score with the help of David Ellis, brings a contradiction between the grimness of the subject and the open jollity of the treatment, with cakewalks, polkas and other dance-rhythms freely used. The *Tam O'Shanter overture*, the best-known item, is an idiosyncratic, rumbustious showpiece characteristic of the early Arnold. Handley draws colourful and committed playing from the orchestra, with John Lill a masterful, flamboyant soloist in the music written for him. First-class recording.

Symphonies Nos. 7, Op. 113; 8, Op. 124.
*** Conifer 74321 15005-2 [id.]. RPO, Vernon Handley.

The bitterness in the *Seventh* is inescapable. Dedicated to the composer's three children, the writing is most strongly influenced by his son Edward, tragically autistic. The *Eighth* is emotionally hardly less pungent. Handley's performances of both symphonies generate great power and depth of feeling, with the most eloquent response from the RPO players, and the recording is outstandingly real and vivid. However, neither work offers an easy listening experience.

Symphony No. 9, Op. 128.
(BB) *** Naxos Dig. 8.553540 [id.]. Nat. SO of Ireland, Andrew Penny.

(i) *Symphony No. 9;* (i; ii) *Concertino for oboe and strings* (orch. Steptoe); (ii) *Fantasia for oboe solo, Op. 90.*
*** Conifer Classics Dig. 75605 51273-2. (i) Bournemouth SO, Handley; (ii) Nicholas Daniel.

Just ten years after Sir Malcolm Arnold wrote his *Ninth Symphony* this superb first Naxos recording arrived to confirm the work as a fitting culmination to his symphonic series. The baldness of the arguments, with two-part writing the general rule, might initially be thought disconcerting. But the music consistently speaks in a true Arnoldian accent, culminating in the long slow finale, almost as long as the other three movements together, registering a mood of tragedy and disillusion. The parallel with the final *Adagio* of Mahler's *Ninth Symphony* is clear, though without neurosis or self-pity. The symphony ends quietly on a major triad, a firm D major chord, a mere sop towards granting release. The other three movements are just as direct, bald in their arguments but pointful, not facile, built on instantly memorable material. As to Penny's performance, this is not just concentrated and consistently committed but warmly resonant, with the Dublin strings sounding glorious and the woodwind and brass consistently brilliant. The recording is rich and firmly focused.

The rival Handley version provides a different slant on Arnold's *Ninth*, equally valid, on what, for all its simplicity of texture, is an enigmatic work. With a unique coupling of two oboe pieces, superbly played by Nicholas Daniel, it makes a formidable alternative. The contrast of recording quality, with the Conifer issue presenting the orchestra much closer, with textures made warmer and beefier, matches the broad contrast of interpretation. Where the slight distancing of sound on the Naxos issue keeps the music at one remove, the weight of sound which Handley draws from the Bournemouth Symphony in his fuller-bodied recording goes with a rather more expressive style, so that unison string melodies, as in the Trio of the third-movement Scherzo or throughout the long, slow finale, sound more obviously Mahlerian. The result is that the Handley version is less desolate in its presentation of that extended slow finale. There is much to be said for Penny's balder, chillier treatment in music which, as the composer himself has explained, reflects a period when he had 'been through hell'. However thin the argument may look on the page, this is a masterly conclusion to Arnold's unique, keenly original symphony cycle.

CHAMBER MUSIC

Brass quintet.
*** Collins Dig. 1489-2 [id.]. Center City Brass Quintet (with Concert: *Brass quintets* ***).

Arnold's *Brass quintet* dates from the early, exuberant period in his career. The performance from a virtuoso group of American orchestral principals is superlative – they are especially happy with the jazzy inflexions – and the recording is in the demonstration bracket. The rest of the concert, too, proves highly stimulating.

Divertimento for flute, oboe and clarinet, Op. 37; Duo for flute and viola, Op. 10; Flute sonata, Op. 121; Oboe quartet, Op. 61; Quintet for flute, violin, viola, horn and piano, Op. 7; 3 Shanties for wind quintet, Op. 4.
*** Hyperion Dig. CDA 66173 [id.]. Nash Ens.

Duo for 2 cellos, Op. 85; Piano trio, Op. 54; Viola sonata No. 1, Op. 17; Violin sonatas Nos. 1, Op. 15; 2, Op. 43; Pieces for violin and piano, Op. 54.
*** Hyperion Dig. CDA 66171 [id.]. Nash Ens.

Clarinet sonatina, Op. 29; Fantasies for wind, Opp. 86–90; Flute sonatina, Op. 19; Oboe sonatina, Op. 28; Recorder sonatina, Op. 41; Trio for flute, bassoon and piano, Op. 6.
*** Hyperion Dig. CDA 66172 [id.]. Nash Ens.

There is much here that belies Malcolm Arnold's image as just an entertaining and genial tunesmith. All the pieces on the first disc show conspicuous resource in the handling of the instruments. The second disc includes two *Violin sonatas* which are cool, civilized and intelligent. The *Piano trio* of 1956 has a powerful sense of direction. The third listing concentrates on the wind music. This is perhaps more for admirers of Arnold's music than for the generality of collectors. The playing is brilliant and sympathetic throughout all three discs and the recording first rate.

PIANO MUSIC

Allegro in E min.; 2 Bagatelles, Op. 18; 8 Children's pieces, Op. 36; Children's suite, Op. 16; 3 Fantasies; 3 Pieces (1937); *2 Pieces* (1941); *3 Pieces* (1943); *Prelude; Serenade in G;*

Sonata; Variations on a Ukrainian folksong, Op. 9.
*** Koch Dig. 3-7162-2 [id.]. Benjamin Frith.

This splendid disc spans Malcolm Arnold's almost unknown piano output, from his earliest pieces (including the *Allegro in E minor*) from 1937, dedicated to his mother and firmly neo-classical in the manner of Bach, to the *Three Fantasies* of 1986, terse in structure and much more ambivalent in expressive mood. The *Sonata* (1942), succinct and strongly argued, brings motoric pungency and in the finale a reminder of Prokofiev; the slow movement, however, still has a popular ambience in its harmony and melodic style. The *Variations on a Ukrainian theme* (1948) makes a bold contrast, its complexities demonstrating the composer imaginatively stretched. The two groups of short pieces for children are very much in the spirit of Elgar's nursery music. The comparatively enigmatic, more sombrely coloured, *Ballades* provide further contrast. Benjamin Frith is clearly at home in all this music, presenting it discerningly and spontaneously in order of composition, to make a thoroughly rewarding 72-minute recital. Arnold communicates in every bar, and the piano recording is very fine indeed.

Arriaga, Juan (1806–26)

Symphony in D; Overture: Los esclavos felices.
*** Hyperion Dig. CDA 66800 [id.]. SCO, Sir Charles Mackerras – VORISEK: *Symphony in D.* ***

The *Overture*, which comes before the *Symphony*, is a real charmer, opening with a gracious melody that is almost Schubertian, and then carrying on very much in the style of Rossini, complete with crescendo. The *Symphony* (1824) is contemporary with the better-known string quartets – and indeed the Voříšek coupling as well. It could scarcely be played with more character, and the somewhat resonant but very well-balanced recording does not cloud detail. Highly recommended.

String quartets Nos. 1 in D min.; 2 in A; 3 in E flat.
*** CRD CRD 33123 (2) [id.]. Chilingirian Qt – WIKMANSON: *String quartet No. 2.* ***
*** Ph. Dig. 446 092-2 [id.]. Guarneri Qt.

These three *Quartets* are marvellous works of great warmth and spontaneity that can hold their own in the most exalted company. It is barely credible that a boy still in his teens could have produced them. The Chilingirians play with both conviction and feeling. But they involve a pair of CDs (admittedly with an interesting coupling) and many collectors will now be looking for a single disc containing the triptych.

Fortunately the newest set by the Guarneri Quartet, although too up-front as a recording, offers smoother quality, coupled with a truthful balance and a vivid presence. They play the *Adagio* of the *D minor Quartet* very beautifully, and the *Theme and variations* of the *A major* work is hardly less appealing. Their playing throughout is immaculate in ensemble yet has both warmth and ardour. But if the Chilingirians were to be reissued on a single disc, they would still take pride of place.

Atterberg, Kurt (1887–1974)

Symphony No. 6 in C, Op. 31; Ballad without words, Op. 56; A Värmland rhapsody, Op. 36.
** BIS Dig. CD 553 [id.]. Norrköping SO, Jun'ichi Hirokami.

Atterberg's *Sixth Symphony* is a colourful and inventive score which deserves wide popularity. *A Värmland rhapsody* is, appropriately enough, strongly folkloric. The *Ballad without words* has many imaginative touches. The Norrköping orchestra includes many sensitive players, but the string-tone lacks weight and opulence. The recording is very clean.

Symphonies Nos. 7, Op. 45 (Sinfonia romantica); 8, Op. 48.
(N) ** Sterling Dig. CDS 1026-2 [id.]. Malmö SO, Michail Jurowski.

Atterberg's first six symphonies have been recorded at one time or another but Nos. 7 and 8 are new to the catalogue. Of the two, No. 7 is the more impressive: it dates from the war years (1941–2) and was revised in 1972. Like, say, Prokofiev's *Third*, which draws on *Fiery Angel* or Vaughan Williams's *Fifth*, it draws on (or in this instance rescues) material from an earlier opera. It was in four movements, though Atterberg elected to drop the finale when he revised the score. It is romantic in feeling, a protest against the modernity of the times. The *Eighth* is less successful even if the slow movement has some characteristically beautiful ideas. The finale is insufferably folksy. Good playing from the Malmö Orchestra and well-detailed recording.

Auber, Daniel (1782–1871)

Overtures: The Bronze horse; Fra Diavolo; Masaniello.
❁ (M) *** Mercury 434 309-2 [id.]. Detroit SO, Paray – SUPPE: *Overtures.* ***

Dazzling performances, full of verve and style, which will surely never be surpassed. The present recordings, made in the suitably resonant acoustic of Detroit's Old Orchestra Hall, show Mercury engineering (1959 vintage) at its very finest.

(i) *Le domino noir* (complete); *Gustave III ou Le Bal masqué* (Overture & ballet music)
✿ *** Decca Dig. 440 646-2 (2) (i) Sumi Jo, Vernet, Ford, Power, Bastin, Olmeda, Cachemaille, L. Voices; ECO, Bonynge.

Richard Bonynge here fulfils a long-held ambition to record this enchanting opéra-comique about two novices in a convent illicitly attending a masked ball. To a libretto by Scribe – one of dozens he provided for Auber's many operas – Auber was inspired to write a sparkling score, full of delightful invention. So the opening number, after the Spanish-flavoured overture, has a passage in thirds for the heroine and her confidante, Brigitte, that directly anticipates the celebrated duet in Delibes's *Lakmé*, and other numbers bring clear anticipations of Gounod's *Faust* and of Verdi's *Il trovatore*, not to mention Gilbert and Sullivan. Three accompanied recitatives, written by Tchaikovsky for a planned performance in St Petersburg, are used very effectively in Act II. Otherwise dialogue is crisply tailored and is very well delivered. Bonynge makes the ideal advocate, moulding melodies, springing rhythms and aerating textures to make the music sparkle from first to last. The playing of the ECO is outstanding, not least from the wind soloists, and the casting is near-perfect. Sumi Jo takes on a role that is lower in tessitura than usual, but with elaborations devised by Bonynge leading her into dazzling coloratura. Bruce Ford as the hero and Patrick Power as his friend, Juliano, sing stylishly in well-contrasted tenor tones, while Isabelle Vernet is excellent as Brigitte. Martine Olmeda and Jules Bastin are both characterful in servant roles. The recording is among Decca's most vivid. On the second disc, after Act III, the fill-up aptly comes from another colourful but more serious opera of Auber, also involving a masked ball and a libretto by Scribe, the one which, translated into Italian, prompted Verdi's *Ballo in maschera*.

Fra Diavolo (complete).
*** EMI Dig. CDS7 54810-2 (2) [id.]. Gedda, Mesplé, Corazza, Berbié, Dran, Bastin, Jean Laforge Ch. Ens., Monte Carlo PO, Soustrot.

With a comic English milord and two comic bandits (played by Laurel and Hardy in the Hollywood film version of 1933), *Fra Diavolo* is a delightful piece, given a sparkling performance under Marc Soustrot. Some of the patter ensembles suggest that Sullivan and maybe Gilbert too knew this comic opera. The numbers are separated by spoken French dialogue but, with a cast very much in tune with the style of the piece, it adds to the dramatic point. Though Nicolai Gedda's voice has lost its youthful sweetness and often sounds strained, he is very characterful in the title, and similarly Mady Mesplé with her typically French, tinkly soprano is very idiomatic as Zerline. The others are all excellent, and the 1984 digital sound is well balanced.

Aubert, Jacques (1689–1753)

Concerts de simphonies for violins, flutes & oboes: Suites: Nos. 2 in D; 5 in F; Concertos for 4 violins, cello & bass continuo: in D & G min., Op. 17/1 & 6; in E min. (Le Carillon), Op. 26/4.
*** Chandos Dig. CHAN 0577 [id.]. Coll. Mus. 90, Simon Standage.

Aubert was a contemporary of Rameau and Leclair; he possessed much of the former's melodic flair and feeling for orchestral colour and shared the latter's interest in extending violin technique. The leader (here the inestimable Simon Standage, sounding much sweeter than he did in the earliest days of period performances on record) has most of the bravura; the other violin soloists are subservient, and sometimes the cello joins the solo team. The orchestral concertos are neatly scored and full of attractive ideas. They are each in eight sprightly movements with a brief overture or introduction and a closing chaconne. The performances here are polished, refreshingly alive and invigorating, and the recording is first class. Well worth investigating.

Aufschnaiter, Benedikt Anton
(1665–1742)

Concors discordia: Serenades 1–6.
(N) *** CPO Dig. CPO 999 457-2 [id.].L'Orfeo Bar. O, Michi Gaigg.

Benedikt Aufschnaiter (born in Kitzbühel) wrote his *Concors discordia* in 1695, a decade before he took up the appointment of Court Music Director in Passau, which was to be his lifetime career. The six *Serenades* are in essence elegant orchestral suites in the French style. They certainly celebrate instrumental discourse but are not dissonant. Originally scored for strings alone, the composer commended the use of oboes or shawms, and bassoons, if 'among your musicians a few do a fine job of playing them'. So Michi Gaigg has taken him at his word and included a recorder also, to double up the string parts. She also introduces wind solos, as in the charming *Air* of No. 4, and solo groupings, as in the *Ballo* second movement of No. 1, where a tambourine also brings added spice. The *Overture* of No. 6 (perhaps the finest of the series) is quite ambitious, and in this work an extended wind palette is introduced to excellent effect. These *serenades* are agreeably inventive and tuneful, often sounding rather like Telemann and certainly not inferior to all but the finest of his equivalent suites. They are given vigorous, polished performances. Although the somewhat edgy attack the Orfeo violins bring to allegros seems a shade overenthusiastic, rhythms are nicely bounced, and the ear soon adjusts when the contrasting dance movements are so graceful and amiable, and the wind playing excellent. The recording too is warm and the acoustic unconfined.

Auric, Georges (1899–1983)

L'éventail de Jeanne (complete ballet, including music by Delannoy, Ferroud, Ibert, Milhaud, Poulenc, Ravel, Roland-Manuel, Roussel, Florent Schmitt). *Les Mariés de la Tour Eiffel* (complete ballet, including music by Honegger, Milhaud, Poulenc, Tailleferre).

❁ *** Chandos Dig. CHAN 8356 [id.]. Philh. O, Simon.

A carefree spirit and captivating wit run through both these composite works. In fact these pieces are full of imagination and fun. Geoffrey Simon and the Philharmonia Orchestra give a very good account of themselves and the Chandos recording is little short of spectacular.

Overture.

(M) *** Mercury (IMS) 434 335-2 [id.]. LSO, Dorati – FETLER: *Contrasts;* FRANCAIX: *Piano concertino;* MILHAUD: *Le boeuf sur le toit;* SATIE: *Parade.* ***

Georges Auric's breezy *Overture* is irrepressibly high-spirited and its melodic freshness and Dorati's vivacious performance help to dispel the impression that it is a shade too long for its content. Vividly clear and transparent sound from near the end of the Mercury vintage era: 1965.

Avison, Charles (1709–70)

12 Concerti grossi after Scarlatti.

(B) *** Ph. Duo 438 806-2 (2) [id.]. ASMF, Marriner.

**(*) Hyperion CDA 66891/2 [id.]. Brandenburg Consort, Roy Goodman.

Marriner and the ASMF pioneered a complete recording of these works by the Newcastle-upon-Tyne composer, Charles Avison, which he ingeniously based on the keyboard sonatas of Domenico Scarlatti, and Marriner's fine set, with Iona Brown leading the solo group, has much grace and style. It makes a fine bargain on a Philips Duo two-discs-for-the-price-of-one.

Those seeking a period-instrument performance will find Roy Goodman's version has plenty of vitality. Fast movements fizz spiritedly, but the linear style of the slower movements, though not lacking expressive feeling, is altogether less smooth, and these performances are essentially for those totally converted to the authentic style. The recording is excellent.

Babadzhanian, Arno Harutyuni (1921–83)

Heroic ballade; Nocturne.

(N) *** ASV Dig. CD DCA 984 [id.]. Armen Babakhanian, Armenian PO, Tjeknavorian– TJEKNAVORIAN: *Piano concerto.* ***

Babadzhanian won a Stalin prize for the *Heroic ballade*, but after a flamboyant opening, it turns out to be a rather engaging set of concertante variations. The writing is eclectic (mixing Armenian influences with Rachmaninov and water), returning to populist flamboyance at the close, but not before giving the soloist a chance to be poetically expressive. The performance is excellent, the recording vivid.

(i–iii) *Piano trio in F sharp min.;* (ii; iii) *Violin sonata in B flat min.* (Piano) (i) *Impromptu.*

(N) *** Marco Polo Dig. 8.225030 [id.]. (i) Avo Kuyumjian; (ii) Ani Kavafian; (iii) Susan Bagratuni.

Rostropovich, who was a friend and admirer of the composer, declared that Babadzhanian 'made a significant contribution to the music of our time'. He was not prolific, but both major works here show a strong lyrical impulse, plenty of ideas, recognizably Armenian in colouring, and an ability to create a cogent whole out of a loosely structured form. The volatile *Violin sonata* (1959) has plenty of energy, but even the vibrant, syncopated finale gives way to a hauntingly nostalgic closing section – reminiscent of Shostakovich to whom the work is dedicated – although there is a sudden, passionate outburst in the closing few bars. The *Piano trio*, written seven years earlier, opens with a grave sustained *Largo* (whose theme is to dominate the work) and although it develops a passionate impetus of a very Russian kind, its *Andante* opens with a serene melisma from the solo violin, and is essentially ruminative. The catchy, syncopated finale has the energetic rhythmic drive we recognize in Khachaturian's better music, balanced by a warmly flowing secondary theme on the cello. The engaging *Impromptu* for piano acts as a cantabile encore. The performances here are fierily passionate, but the players relax naturally into tenderness whenever needed. The recording is bright, full and well balanced.

The Bach family, including Johann Sebastian

Georg Christoph (1642–1697) **Johann Christoph** (1642–1703) **Johann Michael** (1648–94) **Johann Bernhard** (1676–1749) **Johann Sebastian** (1685–1750) **Johann Lorenz** (1695–1773) **Wilhelm Friedmann** (1710–1784) **Johann Ernst** (1722–77)

'In the name of Bach': J. B. BACH: *Ouverture in D: Passepieds I & II; La Joye.* W. F. BACH: *Adagio and fugue in D min., F.65. Duet for 2 flutes in E min., F.54.* J. C. BACH: *Quartet in G for violin, 2 cellos and fortepiano, Op.2.* J. E.

BACH: *Violin sonata in F. Lieder from Sammlung auserlesener, F.1: Der Affe und die Schäferin; Der Hund; Die ungleichen Freunde; Die Unzufriedenheit.* G. C. BACH: *Geburstagskantate: Sie wie fein und lieblich ist es'.*
(N) *** Channel Classics Dig. CCS 9095 [id.]. Florilegium; with (i) Catherine Bott; (ii) J.Podger, R. Evans, M. McCarthy.

Florilegium, the enterprising and expert period-instrument group, provides here a diverting collection of variously scored instrumental and vocal works to show the extraordinary talents inherent in the genes of the Bach family, not only those of the sons of Johann Sebastian, but also of his predecessors, cousins, uncles and nephews. The fine *Fortepiano quartet* by J. C. Bach is by no means the most interesting work. The programme opens with an engaging bravura cantata for two tenors and bass by Georg Christoph, robust and jolly, and with a remarkable command of vocal polyphony. It is sung with aplomb. The excerpts from Johann Bernhard's *Ouverture* (a French suite for chamber orchestra) show him as a distinct musical personality, as do the works of Johann Ernst. His well-crafted *Violin sonata* brings closely interwoven part-writing and a slightly quirky central *Arioso*. This is very fresh, but expressively plain compared with his charming vocal fables about animals, written for high soprano and characterfully sung by Catherine Bott. But the highlight of the concert is the lovely *Adagio* and busy *fugue* of Wilhelm Friedmann, who is more and more emerging as a major figure. The serenely sustained interplay between two flutes, contrasts with a closing *Allegro*, when the two solo violins also enter, together with viola, cello, violone and harpsichord, to create a rich-textured final interplay, a little like a *Brandenburg* of J. S. B. Performances are full of life and sensitivity, and the recording is warm and naturally balanced. The one minus point is that only German texts are provided, without translations.

Bach, Carl Philipp Emanuel
(1714–88)

Cello concertos: in A min., Wq.170, H.432; in B flat, Wq.171, H.436; in A, Wq.172, H.439.
(N) ❁ *** BIS Dig. CD 807 [id.]. Hidemi Suzuki, Bach Collegium, Japan.
(M) *** Virgin/Veritas EMI Dig. VM5 61401-2. Anner Bylsma, OAE, Leonhardt.
(N) (BB) **(*) Naxos Dig. 8.553298 [id.]. Tim Hugh, Bournemouth Sinf., Richard Studt.

These concertos also have alternative versions for both keyboard and flute, but they suit the cello admirably. Bylsma's expressive intensity communicates strongly, without ever taking the music outside its boundaries of sensibility, and these artists convey their commitment to this music persuasively.

However, the Virgin reissue is upstaged by the splendid new triptych on BIS. Hidemi Suzuki creates a dashing flow of energy in the orchestral ritornellos of outer movements and the Bach Collegium play with great zest and commitment. In slow movements Suzuki's eloquent phrasing, warmth of feeling and breadth of tone is totally compelling. There is nothing meagre about the period instrumental sounds here. The glorious orchestral introduction to the beautiful slow movement of Bach's finest *concerto in A major* is followed by a cello line of heart-stopping intensity, and the finale brings thrilling virtuosity from all concerned. The recording is splendid.

Tim Hugh on Naxos is altogether more reticent. But he plays with a persuasive lyrical warmth, and Richard Studt's accompaniments are crisp and stylish. The effect is spontaneous, the recording is vividly natural, and these modern-instrument performances are alive and enjoyable in their less extrovert way. Tim Hugh does not wear his heart on his sleeve but there is certainly no lack of feeling in the memorable *Largo* of the *A major Concerto.*

Cello concerto (No. 2) in B flat, Wq. 171.
(N) *** Teldec/Warner Dig. 9031 77311-2 [id.]. Rostropovich, Saint Paul CO, Hugh Wolff – TARTINI; VIVALDI: *Concertos.* ***

All three of Carl Philipp Emanuel's concertos for the cello began life for the keyboard, and the present transcription has been edited by Hugh Wolff. It is played with commanding eloquence and authority not only by Rostropovich but the fine Saint Paul Orchestra. They produce great warmth along with the transparency of texture to which period-instrument ensembles aspire. The couplings too are worth having, particularly the lovely Tartini concerto which is something of a rarity. An excellently focused and fresh recording from 1993.

Koopman Edition

Flute concertos: in D min., Wq.22, H.425; in B flat, Wq.167. H.435; in A, Wq. 168, H.428 (with Konrad Hünteler; 0630 16183-2).

Flute concertos in A min., Wq.166, H.431; in G, Wq.169, H.445 (with Konrad Hünteler); *Double harpsichord concerto in F, Wq. 46, H.408* (with Ton Koopman, Tini Mathot; 0630 16184-2).

Oboe concertos: in B flat, Wq.164, H.466; in E flat, Wq.165, H.468; Sonata for oboe and continuo in G min., Wq.135, H.549 (with Ku Ebbinge; 0630 16182-2).

Double concerto for harpsichord and fortepiano in E flat, Wq.43, H.479 (with Ton Koopman, Tini Mathot); *4 Hamburg sinfonias, Wq.183/1–4, H.663-6* (0630 16181-2).

Koopman Edition (as above).
(N) (M) *** Warner/Erato 0630 16180-2 (4) Soloists, Amsterdam Bar. O, Ton Koopman.

If you want all the music in Koopman's somewhat abitrary collection, these performances can certainly be recommended. Konrad Hünteler's period flute sounds a shade pale, but he is a nimble and expressive player and fully responsive to the beautiful *Largo con sordine, mesto* of the *A major Concerto*, Wq. 168, while the sprightly *Allegretto* which opens the *B flat major*, Wq. 167 is pleasingly vivacious. The spirited and delightful *Concerto for harpsichord and fortepiano* comes from Bach's last year; the *F major Double harpsichord concerto* comes from a different world: it was composed half a century earlier for Frederick II's court. Both are persuasively presented (the sombre *Largo* of the latter is particularly fine) and the recording is deftly balanced. The two *Oboe concertos* are very ap-ng in their wide range of mood and the slow movement of Wq.164 is plaintively haunting in Ku Ebbinge's hands. Throughout accompaniments are gracefully alert and the recording balance is realistic. Koopman and his talented Amsterdam players (like their soloists) use period instruments, and while they tend to favour relatively relaxed speeds in the four *Hamburg sinfonias*, the music-making is very enjoyable in its easy-sounding spontaneity. The recording has a resonant bloom, yet detail remains well defined. At present these discs are not available separately.

Flute concertos: in D min., Wq.22; in A min., Wq.166; in B flat, Wq.167; in A, Wq.168; in G, Wq.169.
*** Capriccio Dig. 10 104 (Wq.22, 166, 168); 10 105 (Wq.167, 169) [id.]. Eckart Haupf, C. P. E. Bach CO, Haenchen.

Eckart Haupf gives lively, cleanly articulated performances of these concertos, written for the court of Frederick the Great, well supported by the strong, full-bodied and vigorous accompaniments of the C. P. E. Bach Chamber Orchestra under Hartmut Haenchen. Full, atmospheric recording from East German VEB engineers.

Flute concerto in D min., Wq.22.
(BB) **(*) ASV CDQS 6012. Dingfelder, ECO, Mackerras – HOFFMEISTER: *Concertos Nos. 6 & 9.* **(*)

Those who are interested in the Hoffmeister coupling will find Ingrid Dingfelder's playing both spirited and stylish.

(i) *Flute concertos: in A min., Wq.166; in B flat, Wq.167; in A, Wq.168; in G, Wq.169;* (ii; iii) *Oboe concertos: in B flat, Wq.164; in E flat, Wq.165;* (ii; iv; v) *Solo in G min., for oboe and continuo*; (v) *Solo in G for harp, Wq.139.*
(B) **(*) Ph. Duo 442 592-2 (2) [id.]. (i) Aurèle Nicolet, Netherlands CO, David Zinman; (ii) Heinz Holliger; (iii) ECO, Leppard; (iv) Rama Jucker; (v) Ursula Holliger.

Nicolet uses a modern instrument and plays very well, but the effect with a rather heavy string accompaniment (partly the result of the acoustic) makes less of the music than the rival versions on Capriccio. But those are at full price, and the Philips Duo set offers a great deal more music. Holliger's accounts of the *Oboe concertos* are masterly. In addition to the excellence of the support from the ECO under Leppard, the Philips engineering is distinguished. The bonuses for oboe and continuo (in this instance harp and cello) and Ursula Holliger's harp *Solo* also add to the attractions of this very generous set.

Flute concertos: in A, Wq.168; in G, Wq.169; in D min. (from *Harpsichord concerto*).
*** RCA Dig. RD 60244 [60244-2-RC]. James Galway, Württemberg CO, Joerg Faerber.

James Galway plays these three works with his customary musicianship, virtuosity and polish. Faerber and his Württemberg orchestra accompany persuasively, with no attempt made to create 'authentic' textures. Excellent recording. Recommended, except to authenticists.

Complete solo harpsichord concertos

Harpsichord concertos Nos. 1 in A min.; 2 in E flat; 3 in G, Wq.1–3 (H.403–5).
**(*) BIS Dig. CD 707 [id.]. Miklós Spányi (harpsichord), Concerto Armonico, Péter Szüts.

Harpsichord concertos Nos. 4 in G ; 7 in A; 12 in F, Wq.4, 7 & 12 (H.406, 410 & 415).
**(*) BIS Dig. CD 708 [id.]. Miklós Spányi (harpsichord), Concerto Armonico, Péter Szüts.

Harpsichord concertos Nos. 6 in G min.; 8 in A; 18 in D, Wq.6, 8 & 18 (H.409, 411 & 421).
**(*) BIS Dig. CD 767 [id.]. Miklós Spányi (harpsichord or fortepiano), Concerto Armonico, Péter Szüts.

Harpsichord concertos Nos. 9 in G; 13 in D; 17 in D min., Wq. 9, 13 & 17 (H.412, 416 & 420).
**(*) BIS Dig. CD 768 [id.]. Miklós Spányi (harpsichord), Concerto Armonico, Péter Szüts.

This is an ongoing project in which Miklós Spányi is planning to record all 52 keyboard concertos which Carl Philipp Emanuel wrote between 1733 and 1788, most of which date from the early years of his musical life at the court of Frederick the Great in Berlin. From the very beginning his style moves away from the baroque concerto principles of Vivaldi and Handel to a more clearly defined and always engaging dialogue between the soloist and ensemble, making a direct path to the piano concertos of Mozart.

The first concerto was written in Leipzig in 1733, the second in 1734; the third followed in 1737 (although all three were revised a decade later in Berlin). The early works are simply scored for strings and, although not without surprises, are free from the idiosyncrasies which the composer subsequently developed; instead they concentrate on display; lyrical lines often faintly pre-echo early Mozart, while allegros radiate energy. This is immediately striking in the bustling finale of the *A minor Concerto*, which is otherwise fairly conventionally *galant*, though with an appealing central *Andante* in which the responses between soloist and accompanying group are already becoming a cultivated conversation.

Miklós Spányi has chosen to play the early concertos on a harpsichord with a strong personality: a modern copy by Michael Walker of a 1734 Haas whose original maker lived in Hamburg. It is very well balanced with a period-instrument string-group (6;2;1;1), which is probably larger than the ensemble the composer would have expected, and the resonance of the recording (made in a Budapest church) also militates against a really intimate effect. But the playing has animation and elegance, and the soloist effectively improvises his own cadenzas at the recording sessions, which increases the sense of spontaneity. So, with spirited and sympathetic accompaniments one can readily warm to music-making which is polished and always alive, if not perhaps in the last resort distinctive.

The three concertos on the second disc all date from Carl Philipp's early years in Berlin, yet each has its own individuality. The *F major Concerto* (1744) opens gruffly, but the soloist takes a much more lyrical stance and refuses to be chastised by the strong orchestral chords. The *Largo e sostenuto* continues with the participants not wholly reconciled, but they join together to share the joyously vigorous finale; the orchestral comments remain strong, but more genially so. A wholly original and remarkable work, and one of the very best performances in the series so far. Indeed all three works here are strongly characterized.

On the third disc both the *G minor* (1740) and *A major* (1741) *Concertos* are among the more remarkable of the composer's early works: in the former the lively dialogue between orchestra and keyboard, each independent though sharing ideas, has great individuality, and the following serene *Largo* is quietly memorable, followed by a robust *Allegro molto* of the strongest character. The slow movement of the *A major* (here played just a little heavily) is very beguiling with its muted strings

In the first movements of both the *G major* and *D major Concertos*, Wq. 9 and 13, Bach establishes a pioneering principle of sonata form. The closing section of the opening movement of the *G major* (1742) repeats the material of the opening section but moving from the dominant key to which the first section has modulated, back to the tonic. The ruminative dialogue of the *Adagio* of the *G major* work is also forward-looking, as is the pensive *un poco Adagio* of the *D minor*, where the theme on the violins floats over a gentle stalking bass Spányi introduces a highly suitable fortepiano (built by Hemel after a 1749 Freiburg) for the *D major Concerto*, Wq. 13, which works especially well in the *un poco Andante* and offers contrast of colour and dynamic in the finale, where the string tuttis are so vigorously forthright. All these performances are impressive, and it is only in the opening of the *G major Concerto* that the resonance blurs the focus of the bold hustling ritornellos.

Keyboard concertos Nos. 11 in D; 14 in E; 19 in A, (H.414, 417 & 422).

(N) **(*) BIS Dig. CD 785 [id.]. Miklós Spányi (fortepiano), Concerto Armonico, Péter Szüts.

Keyboard concertos Nos. 15 in E min.; 25 in B flat; 32 in G min. (H.418, 442 & 492).

(N) **(*) BIS Dig. CD 786 [id.]. Miklós Spányi (tangent piano), Concerto Armonico, Péter Szüts.

Keyboard concertos Nos. 24 in E min.; 28 in B flat; 29 in A, (H. 428, 434 & 437).

(N) **(*) BIS Dig. CD 857 [id.]. Miklós Spányi (tangent piano), Concerto Armonico, Péter Szüts.

For the latest issues in Miklós Spányi's ongoing series he turns to the fortepiano (or the slightly more ambitious tangent piano). The *D major Concerto*, H.414 (which opens BIS 785) immediately brings an aural surprise in its spectacular and rhythmic use of trumpet and drum parts in the outer movements which here, within a reverberant acoustic serve to dwarf the fortepiano! On the other hand the opening ritornello of the *A major* (H.422) recalls Bach's *Brandenburg concerto No. 6*. The three concertos on BIS CD 786 are well contrasted. The outer movements of the *E minor* have an exhilarating driving momentum, whereas the *G minor* opens with an amiable *Allegretto*. The *Allegro di molto* of the *B flat major* work is boldly rhythmic, followed by a dramatically expressive *Largo mesto* before the exuberant *Prestissimo* finale. The *A major concerto* (H.437) which opens the third collection has a darkly memorable slow movement; this and the *B flat major* work (H.434) are perhaps better known in alternative versions for cello and flute, yet they are very effective on the fortepiano, even if here the balance is less than ideal, with the rather beefy string textures given added gruffness of attack by the period instruments.

Harpsichord concertos Nos. 3 in G (H.405); 32 in G min.(H.442); 44 in G (H.477); 45 in D (H.478).

(N) *(*) CPO Dig. CPO 999 566-2 [id.]. Ludger Rémy (harpsichord), Les Amis de Philippe.

It is good to have an alternative view of these vivid concertos, but alas, Ludger Rémy's versions are less than ideal. The harpsichord he favours has an attractively intimate sound and his solo playing is very musical. But the accompanying group is a bit too aggressive and favours bold accents. In H.477 and H.478, editions which include horns are used, and they tend to overwhelm the strings, and fortissimo tuttis sound coarse and congested by the resonance.

Harpsichord concerto in G min., Wq.6.
*** Capriccio Dig. 10 283 [id.]. Gerald Hambitzer, Concerto Köln – J. C. BACH: *Sinfonia;* J. C. F. BACH: *Sinfonias;* W. F. BACH: *Sinfonia* etc. ***

The *G minor Concerto*, Wq.6 (1740), is one of the most remarkable of C. P. E. Bach's early works. Gerald Hambitzer is an expert and persuasive soloist, and the performance has abundant vitality and imagination. The recording is very naturally balanced.

Double concerto for harpsichord and fortepiano in E flat.
(M) *** Teldec/Warner 0630 12326-2. Uittenbosch, Antonietti, Leonhardt Cons. – J. C. BACH: *Sinfonia concertante in F;* W. F. BACH: *Double concerto for 2 harpsichords.* **(*)

(i) *Double concerto in E flat for harpsichord & fortepiano, Wq.47;* (ii) *Double concerto in F, for 2 harpsichords, Wq.46;*(i) *Sonatina for 2 harpsichords & orchestra in D, Wq.109.*
(BB) *** DHM Baroque Esprit 05472 77410-2 [id.]. (i) Eric Lynn Kelley, Jos van Immersel (fortepiano or harpsichord); (ii) Alan Curtis, Gustav Leonhardt; Coll. Aur., Maier.

The spirited and delightful *E flat Concerto for harpsichord and fortepiano* comes from Bach's last year and ought to be far better known than it is. It has a chirpily inviting opening theme and is given a wholly persuasive account by Kelley and Immersel, with the solo instruments naturally balanced and a warm acoustic assisting a lively authentic accompaniment. The *Sonatina for two harpsichords and orchestra* is one of fifteen; it was written in 1762 and is ambitiously scored for three trumpets, two each of flutes, oboes and horns, bassoon and strings. The first movement (of two) is a free fantasia, characteristically quirky and diverse. There are surprises, too, towards the end of the second, which is a Minuet with variations. The *F major Concerto*, scored for strings with the addition of two horns, comes from a different world: it was composed much earlier (probably in 1740) for Frederick II's court, yet is still thoroughly representative of this composer, with a memorable *Largo* slow movement. It is also very well played and, at its very economical price, this is a reissue not to be missed.

A hardly less attractive account of the *Concerto for harpsichord and fortepiano* also comes on Teldec in a higher price-range. The orchestral balance is somewhat better here and the fortepiano has a slightly bolder, more tangible image. The interplay between the two soloists is felicitous, and choice between the two performances must depend on couplings.

Oboe concertos: in B flat, Wq.164; in E flat, Wq.165.
(N) *** Ph. Dig. 454 450-2 [id.]. Heinz Holliger, Camerata Bern – J. S. BACH: *Oboe d'amore concerto* etc. ***

Holliger's stylishly appealing accounts of these two delightful concertos tend to sweep the board, the more so as the accompaniments from the Camerata Bern, led by Thomas Zehetmair have all the lightness of touch one expects from period-instrument performances, yet an added fullness of timbre. The Philips recording is beautifully balanced.

Oboe concertos: in B flat, Wq.164; in E flat, Wq.165; (Unaccompanied) *Oboe sonata in A min., Wq.132.*
(BB) **(*) Naxos Dig. 8.550556 [id.]. József Kiss, Ferenc Erkel CO – MARCELLO: *Concerto.* **(*)

József Kiss's account of Bach's pair of *Oboe concertos* is sensitive and musical, if without quite the individuality of Ebbinge's versions on Erato, but they are very well accompanied and beautifully recorded. The solo *Sonata* is also worth having on disc, although one might have liked more dynamic light and shade here. But with an enjoyable Marcello coupling, this is well worth its modest cost.

Berlin Sinfonias: in G, C & F, Wq. 173/5; in E min., Wq.178; in G, Wq. 180.
(N) *(*) CPO Dig. CPO 999 418-2 [id.]. Les Amis de Philippe, Ludger Rémy.

Rémy's account of the symphonies are athletic and bursting with energy. Slow movements provide expressive contrast within a wide range of dynamic, but accents are strong and bring an aggressive element. Yet the real snag is that the resonance makes the loud tuttis of the more fully scored works, with horns and oboes, sound ugly and uncomfortable.

Berlin sinfonias: in C; in F, Wq.174/5; in E min.; in E flat, Wq.178/9; in F, Wq.181.
*** Capriccio Dig. 10 103 [id.]. C. P. E. Bach CO, Haenchen.

The playing of Haenchen's excellent C. P. E. Bach group is alert and vigorous, with airy textures and attractively sprung rhythms. Modern instruments are used in the best possible way. Excellent sound.

6 Hamburg sinfonias, Wq.182/1–6.
(BB) *** Naxos Dig. 8.553285 Capella Istropolitana, Christian Benda.

The six *Hamburg string sinfonias* are magnificent examples of Bach's later style when, after the years at the Berlin court, he had greater freedom in Hamburg. They are particularly striking in their unexpected twists of imagination and they contain some of his most inspired and original ideas.

Using modern instruments at higher modern pitch, Benda directs light, well-sprung accounts. With more varied textures and tonal contrasts than in most period performances, Benda's have extra light and shade. The darkly chromatic slow movement of No. 3, for example, has a hushed mystery rarely caught. The excellent sound is full and open as well as immediate. This makes an excellent bargain recommendation.

(i) *6 Hamburg Sinfonias, Wq. 182/1–6; Berlin Sinfonias: in C, Wq. 174; in D, Wq. 176;* (ii) *Quartets for flute, viola, fortepiano and* (optional) *cello: Nos. 1 in A min.; 2 in D; 3 in G, Wq. 93–5.* (iii) (Keyboard) *Fantasy in C, Wq. 59/6.*
(B) *** O-L Double 455 715-2 (2) [id.]. (i) AAM, Hogwood; (ii) McGegan, Mackintosh, Pleeth, Hogwood; (iii) Hogwood.

The abrasiveness of the writing comes out more sharply in the kind of authenticity favoured by Hogwood's Academy of Ancient Music in 1979. Indeed Hogwood continually has one responding as to new music, not least in the dark, bare slow movements. The two *Berlin symphonies* with wind are marginally less original, but still make refreshing listening. The three *Quartets* come from the last year of Bach's life and are all beautifully fashioned, civilized pieces with many of the expressive devices familiar from this composer. There is a highly chromatic slow movement for the D major work and some of the outer movements are characteristically unpredictable. Although the works were designated by Bach as *Quartets*, no bass part survives. In these Oiseau-Lyre performances the cello line is added judiciously where it seems useful to reinforce the texture. Christopher Hogwood uses a fortepiano rather than harpsichord and makes a good case for doing so (with documentary support in the notes). He secures a wide dynamic range and clean, intelligent articulation. The playing overall is absolutely first rate; the recording is most naturally balanced and could hardly be bettered. Moreover the keyboard *Fantasia in C* is a most remarkable work – it is roughly contemporary with Mozart's *C minor Fantasy* and is more than just a bonus. It is splendidly played by Hogwood. Altogether this is one of the most stimulating of Hogwood's Oiseau-Lyre Doubles.

4 Hamburg sinfonias, Wq.183/1–4.
(BB) **(*) Naxos Dig. 8.553289 [id.]. Salzburg CO, Yoon K. Lee – W. F. BACH: *Sinfonia in F.* **(*)

4 Hamburg sinfonias, Wq.183/1–4; String sinfonia in B min., Wq.182/5 (H661).
(M) *** Virgin Veritas/EMI (SIS) Dig. VER5 61182-2. OAE, Gustav Leonhardt.

Unlike the six *Hamburg sinfonias* which C. P. E. Bach wrote earlier for Baron von Swieten, these four later works involve wind as well as strings. The writing is just as refreshing in its unexpectedness and originality. Gustav Leonhardt's account of this second set, Wq.183, is the one to have if you want them on period instruments. They are lively and alert, and distinguished by fine musical intelligence. This Leonhardt set is to be preferred, albeit by a small margin, to that by Koopman on Erato and in any case includes an extra work.

The Naxos Salzburg versions are also freshly played, the results spick and span, with polished playing from strings and woodwind alike. Obviously Yoon K. Lee knows about period-performance styles and, though modern instruments are used here, textures are clear and clean. While there is plenty of dramatic contrast, by the side of Leonhardt the expressive music seems just a shade cool. But the results are certainly stimulating, and this disc is worth its modest cost.

CHAMBER AND INSTRUMENTAL MUSIC

Duo for flute and violin in E min., Wq.140; 12 Short pieces for 2 flutes, 2 violins & continuo, Wq.81; Sonata for flute & continuo in G (Hamburg Sonata), Wq.133; Trios for flute, violin & continuo: in B min., Wq.143; in C, Wq.147; (i) Cantata: *Phyllis and Thirsis, Wq.232.*
(BB) *** DHM Baroque Esprit Analogue/Dig. 05472 77435-2 [77188-2]. Soloists, Les Adieux, Schola Cantorum Basiliensis.

A wholly engaging anthology. The dozen pieces for two flutes, two violins and continuo deftly vary textures and the result is most attractive when the authentic timbres are so fresh. The following *Hamburg Flute sonata* needs to be played separately because there is a pitch change as it begins; but it is the *Trio sonatas* which form the kernel of the concert, and they each have touchingly nostalgic *Adagios* to contrast with their bright outer movements. The programme ends with a miniature (7-minute) pastoral cantata, *Phyllis and Thirsis*, obviously selected because it includes obbligatos for two flutes. Both soloists (Nigel Rogers and Rosmarie Hofmann) rise to the occasion. Excellent recording – a real bargain.

Flute sonatas: in C, Wq.73; in D, Wq.83; in E, Wq.84; in G, Wq.85; in G, Wq.86.
(BB) **(*) ASV Quicksilva Dig. CDQS 6205 [(M)

id.]. Christopher Hyde-Smith, Jane Dodd (harpsichord).

This collection is preferable to its Naxos competitor (8.550513). The ASV performances have plenty of life and feeling and, though again the recording is resonant and with the flute close-miked, the effect is very spirited. The collection includes one of the least predictable of these works, Wq.73 (*in C major*), written in 1745, with its striking *Allegro di molto* opening movement, alongside Wq. 84 (*in E major*) of four years later, which has an equally remarkable central *Adagio di molto*.

Flute sonatas: in G, Wq.86; in C, Wq.87; in E min., Wq.124; in D, Wq.129; (Solo) *Flute sonata in A min., Wq.132;* (i) *12 2- and 3-part kleine Stücke for 2 flutes, Wq.82.*
*** ASV Gaudeamus Dig. CDGAU 161 [id.]. Nancy Hadden, Lucy Carolan; Erin Headly; (i) Elizabeth Walker.

The most striking work here is the unaccompanied *Flute sonata in A minor*, written in 1747, with its remarkable opening *Adagio*, an improvisatory work of characteristic originality written for Frederick the Great, who, Bach said, 'could not play it'. Nancy Hadden certainly can (using a copy of a Dresden period transverse flute). The twelve *Little pieces* (1770) alternate trio and duo format and are very jolly and entertaining until the expressively wilting closing *Andante*. Bach favoured the clavichord rather than the harpsichord as appropriate in duo sonatas and Lucy Carolan proves a fine partner, and the balance is equally well judged in the works with additional viola da gamba. This is all most engaging music, and it is admirably presented here in a concert running for 74 minutes.

Flute sonatas: in E min., Wq.124; in G; in A min.; in D, Wq.127–9; in G, Wq.133; in G, Wq.134.
*** Capriccio Dig. 10 101 [id.]. Eckart Haupf, Siegfried Pank, Armin Thalheim.

Six more of the composer's eleven flute sonatas in fresh, lively performances, well recorded, ending with one written in Bach's Hamburg period, two years before he died, altogether lighter and more conventionally classical, presenting an interesting perspective on the rest.

Oboe sonata in G min., Wq.135.
(BB) **(*) DHM/BMG Baroque Esprit 05472 77440-2 [id.]. Michel Piguet, Colin Tilney – J. S. BACH: *Oboe sonatas* **(*); W. F. BACH: *Polonaise in E flat.* ***

C. P. E. Bach's '*Hoboe solo*', as it is described on the manuscript, was probably written around 1740. Opening with a brief *Adagio*, Bach moves on to a perky *Allegro* and concludes with a movement marked *vivace*, in effect a theme with three variations. Although always spirited, it is the expressive quality of the writing which makes this sonata so individual, especially in the finale. The performance is polished and responsive, but the resonant yet forward recording does reduce the effective dynamic range.

Quartet in D for flute, viola, cello & fortepiano, Wq.94; (Unaccompanied) *Flute sonata in A min., Wq.132: Sonata in G min. for viola da gamba and harpsichord, Wq.88: Larghetto. Trio sonatas: in C for flute, violin and continuo, Wq.147; in C min. for 2 violins and continuo (Sanguineus & Melancholicus), Wq.161.*
(N) ✿ *** Channel Classics Dig. CCS 11197 [id.]. Florilegium.

A wholly delightful collection. Ashley Solomon's exquisite flute playing dominates the *D major Quartet*, and the balance with Neal Peres da Costa's delicate fortepiano is quite perfect, registering subtle nuances of dynamic contrast. The *Larghetto* for viola da gamba and harpsichord then makes a melancholy interlude before Bach's highly imaginative dialogue between Sanguine and Melancholy brings quixotic changes of mood and tempo, even in the central *Adagio*, where Sanguineus eventually wins and makes way for a lighthearted finale. The haunting solo *Flute sonata* is recorded at a lower pitch to suit the period instrument used; the timbre has an almost alto sonority. Finally comes the diverting *Trio sonata in C major* which brings winningly imitative interchanges between flute and violin, particularly exuberant in the finale. The recording balance could hardly be bettered.

Sinfonia a tre voci in D; 12 Variations on La Folia, Wq.118/9; Trio sonatas: in B flat, Wq.158; in C min. (Sanguineus & Melancholicus), Wq.161/1; Viola da gamba sonata in D, Wq.137.
*** Hyperion Dig. CDA 66239 [id.]. Purcell Qt.

The *Variations on La Folia* are fresh and inventive, particularly in Robert Woolley's hands, but the remaining pieces are hardly less rewarding. The Purcell Quartet play with sensitivity and seem well attuned to the particularly individual sensibility of this composer. The Hyperion recording is well balanced, faithful and present.

Trio sonatas: (i) *for flute, violin and continuo, Wq.143, 146/7 & 150;* (ii) *for 2 flutes and continuo, Wq.162.*
(N) ** Globe Dig. GLO 5110 [id.]. Hazelzet, Ogg, Van der Meer; with (i) Stuurop; (ii) Clarke.

These are agreeable works and the performances are fluent, well integrated and pleasing. Wilbert Hazelzet dominates both aurally and artistically. There are two drawbacks: the timbre of Alda Stuurop's period violin is unseductively thin, and the forward balance of the recording not only does not flatter her, but irons out much of the dynamic contrast.

Viola da gamba sonatas (for viola da gamba and continuo): *in G min., Wq. 88; in C & D, Wq. 136/7; Harpsichord sonatas in A min. (Württemberg No. 1), Wq. 49/1; in E (Prussian No. 3), Wq.48/3.*

(B) *** HM Musique d'abord Dig. HMA 1901410 [id.]. London Baroque (Charles Medlam, William Hunt, Richard Egarr).

Carl Philipp Emanuel wrote his sonatas for viola da gamba during a period when all over Europe the instrument was being replaced by the cello. The solo line lies comparatively high and Charles Medlam achieves an impressively full singing cantilena. Of the three works the *G minor* is particularly fine and it is very beautifully played. So are the splendid keyboard sonatas, where the level of invention is more immediately striking than in the two other gamba works. They are played with eloquence and spirit by Richard Egarr. The recording throughout is most naturally balanced, and at such a modest price this is a reissue which should not be missed by admirers of this highly individual composer.

KEYBOARD MUSIC

Keyboard sonatas: in B flat, Wq.62/16; In G, Wq.65/22; in E min., Wq.65/30; in A, Wq.65/37; in G, Wq.65/48; in A, Wq.70/1; Rondo in E flat, Wq.61/1.

(BB) *** Naxos Dig. 8.5536450 [id.]. François Chaplin (piano).

François Chaplin plays these works freshly and confidently on the modern piano rather than on the clavichord (or harpsichord) which the composer would have expected, and he makes no attempt to imitate those instruments. The result demonstrates how foward-looking these sonatas are, especially the appealingly expressive slow movements of the later works. The closing *Rondo* of 1786 is particularly successful in using the piano's fuller sonority.

Keyboard sonatas: in C & A (Prussian sonatas), Wq.48/5–6; in E min., C and B flat, Wq.65/5, 8 & 9.

(N) ** BIS Dig. CD 879 [id.]. Miklós Spányi (clavichord).

Keyboard sonatinas Nos. 1–6, Wq.64/1–6; Sonata in D min., Wq.65/3.

(N) ** BIS Dig. CD 882 [id.]. Miklós Spányi (clavichord).

Miklós Spányi rightly choses a clavichord for his performances (a copy of a German instrument from about 1770). Its sound is comparatively full and robust (take care not to set the volume level too high). His playing is alive and sympathetic, but not everyone will respond to the eccentric little pauses with which he interrupts the melodic flow, especially in slow movements.

ORGAN MUSIC

Organ sonatas: in F; A min.; D; G min., Wq.70/3–6; Fantasia and fugue in C min., Wq.119/7; Fugue in D min.; Prelude in D, Wq.70/7; 6 Variations.

**(*) Meridian Dig. CDE 84313 [id.]. Gerald Gifford (Organ of the Chapel of Hull University).

Carl Philipp Emanuel's organ music is a far cry from the magisterial polyphony of his father's output. The *Prelude in D major* opens grandly, but its imitative passage-work is simplicity itself and rather jolly. The *Fantasia and fugue* is a little more aspiring, but not that ambitious, and neither is the *D minor Fugue*. However, while the four lightweight *Sonatas* make no great technical demands on the performer, they are engaging enough when freshly presented, as here, with a lively, 'orchestral' palette. The *Variations* are in much the same style. The chapel organ at Hull University has bright, glowing reeds and Gerald Gifford's playing is persuasive. The recording is excellent, but this music is not among the composer's most stimulating output.

VOCAL MUSIC

Anbetung dem Erbarmer (Easter cantata) Wq.243; Auf schicke dich recht feierlich (Christmas cantata), Wq.249; Heilig, Wq.217; Klopstocks Morgengesang am Schöpfungsfeste, Wq.239.

*** Capriccio Dig. 10 208 [id.]. Schlick, Lins, Prégardien, Elliott, Varcoe, Schwarz, Rheinische Kantorei, Kleine Konzert, Hermann Max.

Klopstocks Morgengesang am Schöpfungsfeste ('Klopstock's morning song on the celebration of creation') is a work of many beauties and is well performed by these artists. *Anbetung dem Erbarmer* ('Worship of the merciful') is another late work, full of modulatory surprises. *Auf schicke dich recht feierlich* ('Up, be reconciled') and *Heilig* ('Holy') (1779) are Christmas works. A record of unusual interest, very well performed and naturally recorded.

(i) *Die Auferstehung und Himmelfahrt Jesu (The Resurrection and Ascension of Jesus), Wq.240;* (ii) *Gott hat den Herrn auferweckt (Easter cantata), Wq.244.*

*** Capriccio Dig. 10 206/7 (2) [id.]. (i) Schlick, Lins, Prégardien; (ii) Elliott, Varcoe, Schwarz; Rheinische Kantorei, Kleine Konzert, Hermann Max.

Carl Philipp Emanuel numbered *Die Auferstehung und Himmelfahrt Jesu* among his finest works. This two-CD set offers good solo singing and generally very good playing; the choral singing for the most part is respectable without being distinguished.

Impressive music which no one with an interest in this composer should pass over.

Die Israeliten in der Wüste, Wq.238.
(N) **(B) HM Musique d'abord Dig. HMA 190 1321 [id.]. Schlick, Lootens, Meens, Varcoe, Corona & Capella Coloniensis, Christie.

This is something of a disappointment. Carl Philipp Emanuel's setting of the Old Testament story of the Israelites in the desert is singularly lacking in drama. The opening chorus '*The tongue cleaves to the dry palate*', although expressive, lacks any sense of desperation and the closing chorus of Part I, although the orchestra graphically describes the welcome 'cool silver streams', is vigorous but hardly overwhelming. Part II then becomes an anticlimax. After the acknowledgment of God's help, the remainder of the work is simply an extended acknowledgment of faith. Moses is portrayed musically as rather a flabby character (not really the fault of the tenor, Hein Meens), and almost all the finest lyrical music goes to the First and Second Israelite Women. Fortunately Barbara Schlick (especially) and Lena Lootens, whose voices are pleasingly contrasted, rise to the challenge, even if the chorus seldom really does so. William Christie is content to direct what is essentially an easygoing performance, atmospherically recorded, though with little real vocal bite.

Magnificat, Wq.215.
(N) (B) *** Decca Double 458 370-2 (2) [id.]. Palmer, Watts, Tear, Roberts, King's College Ch., ASMF, Ledger – J. S. BACH: *Magnificat;* A. SCARLATTI: *St. Cecilia mass.* ***

(i) *Magnificat, Wq.215*; (ii) *Cello concerto in B flat, Wq.171.*
(N) (BB) **(*) DHM Baroque Esprit 05472 77473-2 [id.]. (ii) Ameling, Lehane, Altmeyer, Hermann, Tölz Boys' Ch., (ii) Angelica May; Collegium Aureum, Maier.

With vividly atmospheric recording, the performance under Philip Ledger comes electrically to life, with choir, soloists and orchestra all in splendid form. Indeed the solo singing (notably the lovely contribution of Felicity Palmer) is striking for its stylish expressive feeling. Aptly coupled with Johann Sebastian's earlier setting, and now also with Alessandro Scarlatti's splendid *St Cecilia mass* added, this Decca Double can be strongly recommended.

The alternative Deutsche Harmonia Mundi recording is enjoyable too, even if the period-instrument playing at the introduction is robustly enthusiastic rather than immaculately tuned. Elly Ameling is outstanding among the soloists. The performance has plenty of life, if not quite the vitality of its Decca competitor, and although the closing *Sicut erat* comes over impressively, the resonant recording is not ideally clear on inner detail. Nevertheless, joined to one of Bach's finest cello concertos (with a particularly fine central *Adagio*), expressively and resonantly played by Angelica May, this is a bargain not to be dismissed.

Bach, Johann Christian (1735–82)

Bassoon concerto in E flat; Flute concerto in D; Oboe concerto No. 1 in F.
(N) *** CPO Dig. CPO 999 346-2 [id.]. Ward, Brown, Robson, Hanover Band, Halstead.

Bassoon concerto in B flat; Flute concerto in G; Oboe concerto No. 2 in F.
(N) *** CPO Dig. CPO 999 347-2 [id.]. Ward, Brown, Robson, Hanover Band, Halstead.

These six early concertos are all attractively melodic and nicely conceived in their individual instrumental terms. The orchestral ritornellos, richly filled out by the horns, add to their appeal. They had an obvious influence on Mozart's wind concertos (apart from the *Clarinet concerto* which is uniquely his own) and if you enjoy the Mozart works, you will surely enjoy those by J. C. Bach. The *First Oboe concerto* on the first disc is another version of the *G major* work for flute on the companion CD (Mozart did much the same thing with K.314), and it is difficult to say which is the more attractive. The so-described *D major Flute concerto* is a joining of two separate movements taken from independent manuscripts and how well they work together! The *Bassoon concerto in E flat* is an alternative version of the *Sinfonia concertante* in the same key for two violins and cello included below (in CPO 999 348): its fine central *Largo* sounds more effective on the bassoon. The *Bassoon concerto in B flat* is an even more winning piece, with a dignified *Adagio* set against a delectably frivolous finale. The six concertos are played with much felicity by Jeremy Ward, Rachael Brown and Anthony Robson, respectively, and Halstead's accompaniments are a model of elegance. The recording is full and natural. Most enjoyable.

Harpsichord concertos, Op. 1/1–6.
*** CPO Dig. 999 299-2 [id.]. Anthony Halstead, Hanover Band.

Bach composed three sets of *Clavier concertos*, each comprising six works. Those wanting a set of Op. 1 on period instruments could hardly better this CPO disc. These are all simple two-movement works, except for No. 4 with its wistful central *Andante* and No. 6 which closes with variations on *God save the King*. The performances are sprightly and perfectly in scale and the balance quite excellent.

5 Berlin harpsichord concertos: in B flat; F min.; D min., E and G. Concerto in F min. (attrib.).
(N) *** CPO Dig. CPO 999 393-2 & CPO 999

462-2 [id.]. (available separately) Anthony Halstead, Hanover Band.

According to the 'New Grove', Bach's early Berlin concertos (from the 1750s) 'exhibit the serious, somewhat angular style of the North German concerto of the time'. But in these splendid performances from Anthony Halstead, directing the Hanover Band from the keyboard, they are the opposite of severe, being appealingly fluent, full of flair and vitality. Slow movements are certainly thoughtful, but also deeply expressive, and outer movements bustle vigorously. The *D minor Concerto* which opens the first disc is a particularly fine work, but the *Andante* of the *B flat major* is also very touching. The *F minor* is the best known of the set: it is splendidly played here and one discovers that its warmly appealing *Andante e grazioso* has much in common with the *Adagio affettuoso* of the *D minor*; however the *Poco adagio* of the *G major* is in some ways the most searching of all, when the concentration of the hushed pianissimo playing is so compelling. The attributed *F minor Concerto* may or may not be by J. C. B. Its outer movements certainly have a fine energetic thrust. The recordings throughout are in the demonstration bracket, with the harpsichord – which has a most pleasing, unlattery sound image – in perfect balance and perspective with the accompanying string group.

Clavier concertos, Op. 1/1–6; Op. 7/1–6.
(B) *** Ph. Duo (IMS) 438 712-2 (2) [id.]. Ingrid Haebler (fortepiano), V. Capella Ac., Melkus.

(i) *Clavier concertos, Op. 13/1–6;* (ii) *6 Sinfonias, Op. 3.*
(B) *** Ph. Duo 456 064-2 (2) [id.]. (i) Ingrid Haebler (fortepiano), V. Capella Ac., Melkus; (ii) ASMF, Marriner.

All the concertos here are in major keys and are attractive, well-wrought compositions. It would be difficult to find a more suitable or persuasive advocate than Ingrid Haebler, who is excellently accompanied and most truthfully recorded. There is some delightful invention here and it is difficult to imagine it being better presented.

The coupled *Sinfonias* are beguilingly played by the Academy of St Martin-in-the-Fields under Sir Neville Marriner, and beautifully recorded. None of this can be called great music but it has an easy-going and fluent charm. Erik Smith, who has edited them, describes them as 'in essence Italian overtures, though with an unusual wealth of singing melody'.

Clavier concertos, Op. 7/1–6.
(N) *** CPO Dig. CPO 999 600-2 [id.]. Anthony Halstead, Hanover Band.

Using Bach's own published manuscripts, Anthony Halstead has recorded Opus 7 in chamber form with just an accompanying string trio. His solo playing is every bit as persuasive as Haebler's and the result is delightfully intimate. The first four concertos are each in two-movement form, but Nos. 5 and 6 subdivide into three. No. 5 in *E flat*, the finest of the set, surely anticipates Mozart from the very opening onwards; it has a touchingly expressive slow movement in C minor and a dancing finale. The disc is worth having for this performance alone. With recording of the highest quality, this is one of the most attractive CDs so far in Halstead's Hanover Band series.

Clavier concertos, Op. 13/1–3; Concerto in E flat.
(N) *** CPO Dig. CPO 999 601-2 [id.]. Anthony Halstead (piano), Hanover Band.

Bach's Op. 13 appeared in 1777 and shows him still developing in ideas and orchestration. These are most enjoyable concertos and are played here with great freshness by Halstead. The *Concerto in E flat* is almost identical with the *Sinfonia concertante* in the same key, but in the present version the soloist has a strongly dominant role. The slow movement is memorable, as is the *Andante* of Op. 13/2; the other two works only have two movements.

Sinfonia concertante in C for flute, oboe, violin, cello and orchestra; Sinfonia in G min., Op. 6/6; Sinfonia for double orchestra in E flat, Op. 18/1; Sinfonia in D, Op. 18/4; Overture: Adriano in Siria.
**(*) Chandos Dig. CHAN 0540 [id.]. AAM, Standage.

An enterprising and enjoyable programme. The *Sinfonia concertante* is perhaps the most conventional piece but it has a memorable finale. The *G minor Sinfonia* shows J. C. Bach's imagination at full stretch, lively and intense. The little overture is given three separate bands to show how its fast–slow–fast format was the basis of the symphony. Excellent, well-played 'authentic' performances, but the characteristic Chandos resonance prevents the crispest focus.

Sinfonia concertante in F for oboe, cello and orchestra, T.VIII/6.
(M) **(*) Teldec/Warner 0630 12326-2. Schaeftlein, Bylsma, Leonhardt Cons. – C. P. E. BACH: *Double concerto for harpsichord and fortepiano* ***; W. F. BACH: *Double concerto for 2 harpsichords.* **(*)

The *Sinfonia concertante in F* is a pleasing but not distinctive work in two movements, given a good rather than distinctive performance.

Sinfonia concertante in A for violin, cello and orchestra; Grand Overture in E flat.
(*) Sony MK 39964 [id.]. Yo-Yo Ma, Zukerman, St Paul CO – BOCCHERINI: *Cello concerto* (arr. Grützmacher). *

Generally this is an enjoyable pairing and the

playing of the soloists in the *Sinfonia concertante* establishes a fine musical interplay, although the cadenza is over-elaborated. Good sound, with excellent stereo effects.

Sinfonias concertantes in A for violin, cello and orchestra, SC 3; E flat for 2 violins, 2 violas, cello and orchestra (MSC E flat 1); E flat for 2 clarinets, bassoon and orchestra (MSC E flat 4); G for 2 violins, cello and orchestra, SC 1.
(BB) *** ASV CDQS 6138 [(M) id.]. London Festival O, Ross Pople.

The performances here are eminently vital and enthusiastic, and the recording is very bright and present. This is an invigorating disc which can be recommended strongly, especially at super-bargain price.

Sinfonias concertantes: in E flat for 2 violins, oboe and orchestra; in E flat and in G for 2 violins cello and orchestra.
(N) **(*) CPO Dig. CPO 999 348-2 [id.]. Soloists, Hanover Band, Anthony Halstead.

Sinfonias concertantes: in B flat for violin, cello and orchestra; in D for 2 violins and orchestra; in F for oboe, bassoon and orchestra.
(N) *** CPO Dig. CPO 999 347-2 [id.]. Soloists, Hanover Band, Anthony Halstead.

Sinfonias concertantes: in A for violin and cello; in E for 2 violins, cello, flute and orchestra; in E flat for 2 clarinets, bassoon, 2 horns and flute. Flute concerto in D; Andante.
(N) *** CPO Dig. CPO 999 538-2 [id.]. Soloists, Hanover Band, Anthony Halstead.

Johann Christian Bach might well be regarded as the true father of the sinfonia concertante, for (among others, including Karl Stamitz) he wrote over a dozen of them for various solo instruments, and they are of a consistently higher musical quality than those of most of his contemporaries. Even so these works have a certain conventionality, notably the energetic but rather long (some might feel too long) orchestral ritornellos with which each first movement opens. The solo writing, though seldom demanding extrovert bravura, is always effective; the orchestration (with flutes, horns, clarinets) adds to the interest of tuttis, and colours slow movements. Finales are usually robust minuets.

The piquant oboe solo in the *Andante* of *E flat* work on the first disc is ear-catching, the two works for violins and cello are more uneven. The *B flat concerto* on the second disc has an ambitious opening *Allegro maestoso* (almost Mozartean), which leads to a *Larghetto* dominated by a melancholy violin cantilena. Here the finale is an amiable rondo, featuring both soloists. The *F major* work for oboe and bassoon is also characterful. Although it has only two movements, the orchestral horns add some nice touches to the closing minuet. The *D major* work for a pair of violins is the exception in inviting virtuosity for its soloists and it includes a lengthy and striking written-out cadenza. The third disc opens with one of Bach's very finest works – in *E major* with four soloists. After an impressively individual opening movement featuring the three string players, the solo flute makes its only appearance in the plaintive *Larghetto*, but the string soloists return in the energetic closing *Allegro molto*. The *E flat* work for woodwind has charmingly interwoven solo parts against a busy orchestral backing; the doleful but delectable *Larghetto* gives prominence to the flute, while the bassoon embroiders in the bass. In the closing Minuet the soloists are reserved for the Trio. The two-movement *A major* work for violin and cello again shows Bach's invention at its most elegantly appealing. With the inclusion of the recently discovered slow movement for the *Flute concerto in D major* (see above on CPO 999 346-2), this (third) disc offers the most rewarding collection of the three listed above. Throughout the performances have warmth and proper finish and refinement: the string soloists are perhaps a shade reticent at times, but the balance and recording are excellent and the effect is undoubtedly authentic.

Sinfonias, Op. 3/1–6.
*** CPO Dig. 999268-2 [id.]. Hanover Band, Anthony Halstead.

This excellent CPO disc offers a lively group of six symphonies (or overtures), each in three brief movements, which were dedicated to the then Duke of York, the younger brother of George III, given at a concert series organized by Bach in 1765. These are all excellent examples of a fast-developing genre, offering arguments both pithy and imaginative, with the vigorous finales particularly enjoyable. Though the strings of the Hanover Band under Anthony Halstead are on the abrasive side, performances are fresh and alert. Enjoyment is much enhanced by the authoritative notes of Ernest Warburton.

Sinfonia (Huberty), Op. 6/1; Sinfonias (Markardt), Op. 8/2–4; Symphony in C (Venier No. 46; 2 versions); Symphony in F.
(N) *** CPO Dig. CPO Dig. CPO 999 382-2 [id.]. Hanover Band, Halstead.

J. C. Bach's most successful symphonies were often available from more than one publisher, and the music was seldom identical: hence the necessity of including the publishers' names in the documentation here. The Huberty edition of Op. 6/1, for instance, includes an added Minuet and trio (with an agreeable horn duet), an interpolation from the hand of an unknown composer. The three Op.8 *Sinfonias* are lively but comparatively conventional and most appealing for their elegant slow movements. However none is without interest and Op.8/4 is the finest, attention-seeking throughout all three movements and with a most engaging Minuet and trio for its finale. Halstead offers two versions of the work in *C major*, described as No. 46 by its Parisian publisher. The splendid first movement is common to both; the other movements are quite different in each edition. The *Symphony in F,* which is recorded from manuscript, is very striking, probably dating from around 1760. Its restless development certainly anticipates Mozart and the *Andante* (for flute and strings) is quite delightful. Altogether a splendid collection, made the more so by the vitality and elegance of the playing. The recording is first class: the stereo detail particularly striking.

Sinfonia in G min. Op. 6/6.
*** Capriccio Dig. 10 283 [id.]. Concerto Köln – C. P. E. BACH: *Harpsichord concerto;* J. C. F. BACH: *Sinfonias;* W. F. BACH: *Sinfonia* etc. ***

This remarkable symphony, written in 1770 when Johann Christian was at the height of his fame, is altogether darker than is usual with this most gracious and genial of composers, and the Concerto Köln discover greater dramatic intensity in it than do most ensembles. It is recorded as excellently as it is played.

6 Sinfonias, Op. 6; 6 Sinfonias, Op. 9; 6 Sinfonias, Op. 18; Overture, La calamità de cuori.
(B) *** Ph. Duo 442 275-2 (2) [id.]. Netherlands CO, David Zinman.

David Zinman secures good, lively playing from the Netherlanders and few (except dedicated authenticists) will quarrel with the results. A case could be made for giving some of the outer movements less elegance and greater weight. But if there are times when one feels that Zinman is too brisk, any newer versions using original instruments are likely to be brisker! Certainly Zinman gives stimulation and pleasure with the vigour of his presentation of the outer movements and the charm of the slower ones.

Sinfonias, Op. 9/1–2 (standard & original versions); Op.9/3; in E flat, Sieber collection, No. 2.
(N) *** CPO Dig. CPO 999 487-2 [id.]. Hanover Band, Halstead.

The Hanover Band are in their element in Op. 9, with crisp, dynamic allegros, and making the most of the sensuous element in slow movements, notably the delectable melody of No. 2. This work opens with an imaginative orchestral crescendo and closes with an elegant minuet. No. 3 has a galant central *Andante*, winningly scored and a brief, whirlwind finale. Halstead then gives us the opportunity of hearing the first two symphonies in different versions. These rediscovered original scores feature clarinets and a bassoon (in the place of oboes) which colour the music quite differently. The additional *Sinfonia in E flat* was published independently by several houses in an arranged format (with oboes), but is again heard here in its original scoring, making full use of clarinet dueting. Its *Andante* brings another charming cantilena, followed by a characterful Gavotte finale, where the bassoon chortles away in dialogue with his companions. With such lively, personable playing and excellent recording this is one of the best of the Halstead series so far.

Sinfonias, Op. 9/1–4; Sinfonia concertante in A for violin and cello; Sinfonia concertante in E flat, for 2 violins, oboe and orchestra.
(BB) **(*) Naxos 8.553085 [id.]. Camerata Budapest, Hanspeter Gmür.

This disc is of interest not so much for the symphonies as for the two *Sinfonias concertantes* which are beautifully played, with stylish and appealing contributions from the soloists, all drawn from the orchestra. The solo writing in the *A major Sinfonia concertante* is quite elaborate, and in the *Andante* of the E flat work there is a surprise when the two solo violins introduce Gluck's *Che farò senza Euridice*, which is then taken up by the oboe. The Op. 9 symphonies are not perhaps as interesting overall as Op. 6, but the second of the set of four has a real lollipop *Andante con sordini*, presented over a pizzicato accompaniment. The balance is excellent.

6 Sinfonias (Grand overtures), Op. 18.
(BB) **(*) Naxos Dig. 8.553367 [id.]. Failoni O, Hanspeter Gmür.

Gmür and the Failoni Orchestra give warm and graceful accounts of Op. 18. The spirited allegros are slightly cushioned by the resonance, but slow movements are phrased very musically (particularly the lovely, almost Handelian melody of Op. 18/2, which also has a fine oboe solo from Laszló Párkányi).

CHAMBER MUSIC

Flute quartets (for 2 flutes, viola and cello), *Op. 19/1–4.*
(N) ** CPO Dig. CPO 999 579-2 [id.]. Camerata Köln.

Bach's Op. 19 *Flute quartets* were dedicated to the Earl of Abingdon and probably date from around 1780. They are elegant enough but the scoring for two flutes means that the wind timbres, even using period instruments, tend to overwhelm the strings and the ear easily tires of the unvarying texture. The performances here are refined and polished.

KEYBOARD MUSIC

Duet in A (for harpsichord, 4 hands), *Op. 18/5.*
(N) (M) *** Mercury 434 395-2 [id.]. Rafael Puyana, Genoveva Galvez (Pleyel harpsichord)

– J. S. BACH: *Harpsichord music* **(*); W. F. BACH: *Concerto for2 harpsichords*. ***

A most engaging little two-movement work: the opening *Allegretto* immediately catchy. It is performed with flair, and well recorded; but don't set the volume level too high.

6 Sonatas for harpsichord or fortepiano, Op. 5; Arr. of Haydn's Symphony No. 53 (Impériale).
(N) ** CPO 999 530-2 [id.]. Harold Heoren (fortepiano).

The six *Sonatas Op. 5*, dedicated to the Duke of Mengelberg, were published commercially in 1766. They are comparatively simplistic works in two or more often three movements, popular in their day, as they are obviously not too difficult for gifted amateurs. Harold Heoren plays them straightforwardly, but does not make them sound distinctive. He is faithfully recorded. The attribution of the arrangement of the Haydn symphony carries a fair degree of doubt; it is not especially effective in this instance.

6 Sonatas for the harpsichord or pianoforte with an accompaniment for the violin or flute, Op. 16.
(N) ** CPO Dig. 999 494-3 [id.]. Salzburger Hofmusik.

These atttractive galant sonatas (from 1779) are given period performances with plenty of life. They are played alternately on the violin, by Christine Busch, whose timbre is rather thin and edgy, or flute (Karl Kaiser) where the smoothness of sound is nigh perfect. In both cases the balance cannot be faulted and Wolfgang Brunner's contribution (on a most pleasing Viennese fortepiano) is first class throughout. The music itself is lightweight, spontaneously spirited and tuneful.

Bach, Johann Christoph Friedrich (1732–95)

Sinfonias: in D min.; E flat, Wfv 1/3 & 10.
*** Capriccio Dig. 10 283 [id.]. Concerto Köln – C. P. E. BACH: *Harpsichord concerto;* J. C. BACH: *Sinfonia;* W. F. BACH: *Sinfonia* etc. ***

Both works recorded here are elegantly written and are well worth investigating, even if Johann Christoph Friedrich does not have the strong musical personality of his brothers. The playing of the Concerto Köln is enthusiastic, sprightly and sensitive, and they are excellently recorded.

Musikalisches Vielerley: Cello sonata in A.
*** Sony Dig. SK 45945 [id.]. Anner Bylsma, Bob van Asperen – J. S. BACH: *Viola da gamba sonatas Nos. 1–3.*

This *Sonata* is a work of slight but not negligible musical interest, and it is here played imaginatively by Anner Bylsma, using a piccolo cello, and by Bob van Asperen on a 'trunk' or chamber organ. Excellently recorded.

Bach, Johann Sebastian (1685–1750)

DG Bach Edition: *Masterworks.*
(B) ** DG Analogue/Dig. 463 000-2 (26) [id.]. Various artists.

Brandenburg concertos Nos. 1–6; Oboe d'amore concerto in A, BWV 1055; Double concerto for violin and oboe, in D min., BWV 1060; Triple violin concerto in D, BWV 1064.
(M) ** DG 463 011/2 (2) [id.]. Soloists, Munich Bach Orchestra, Karl Richter.

Harpsichord concerto No. 1 in D min., BWV 1052; (i) *Double harpsichord in C, BWV 1061;* (i; ii) *Triple harpsichord concerto in D min., BWV 1063;* (i; ii; iii) *Qudruple harpsichord concerto in A min., BWV 1065.*
(M) **(*) DG 463 015-2 [id.]. Karl Richter with (i) Hedwig Bilgram; (ii) Iwona Fütterer; (iii) Ulrik Schütt; Munich Bach O.

Violin concertos Nos. 1 in A min.; 2 in E; (i) *Double violin concerto in D min.,* (ii) *Triple concerto for flute, violin, and harpsichord, BWV 1044.*
(M) *** DG Dig. 463 014-2 [id.]. Simon Standage, E Concert, Pinnock, with (i) Elizabeth Wilcock; (ii) Lisa Beznosiuk.

Orchestral suites Nos. 1–4, BWV 1066/69.
(M) ** DG 463 013-2 [id.]. E. Concert, Trevor Pinnock.

The Art of fugue, BWV 1080.
(M) ** DG Dig. 463 027-2 [id.]. Musica Antiqua Köln, Reinhard Goebel.

The Musical offering, BWV 1079; Verschiedene (Diverse) Canons, BWV 1087.
(M) **(*) DG Dig. 463 026-2 [id.]. Musica Antiqua Köln, Reinhard Goebel.

(i) *Partita for solo flute in A min., BWV 1013;* (i; ii) *Flute sonata* (for flute & harpsichord) *in A, BWV 1032;* (iii; ii) *Viola da gamba sonata in G* (for viola da gamba & harpsichord); (iv; v) *Violin sonata* (for violin & harpsichord) *No. 1 in B min., BWV 1014;* (iv; ii; iii) *Violin sonata in G* (for violin and continuo), *BWV 1021.*
(M) *** DG Dig. 463 025–3 [id.]. (i) Wilbert Hazelzet; (ii) Henk Bouman; (iii) Jaap Ter Linden; (iv) Reinhard Goebel; (v) Robert Hill.

Lute suites: in G min.; E min., C min., BWV 995/997; Prelude in C min.; Fuge in G min., BWV 999/1000.
(M) ** DG Dig. 463 022-2 [id.]. Narciso Yepes (lute).

(Unaccompanied) *Cello suites Nos. 1 in G; 3 in C; 6 in D, BWV 1007, 1009, & 1012.*

(M) *** DG 463 024-2 [id.]. Pierre Fournier.

(Unaccompanied) *Violin Sonatas Nos. 1 in G min.; 2 in D min., BWV 1001 & 1004; Partita No. 2 in D min., BWV 1006.*
(M) ** DG Dig. 463 023-2 [id.]. Shlomo Mintz.

Chromatic fantasia and fugue, BWV 903; Partitas: Nos. 1 in B flat, BWV 825; in B min., BWV 831; Toccata in D min., BWV 913.
(M) **(*) DG Analogue/Dig. 463 018-2 Trevor Pinnock (harpsichord).

4 Duets, BWV 802/4; English suite No. 6 in D min., BWV 811; Italian concerto in F, BWV 971; Toccata in C min., BWV 911.
(M) *** DG Dig. 463 021-2 [id.]. Angela Hewitt (piano).

Goldberg variations, BWV 988.
(M) ** DG Dig. 463 019-2 [id.]. Andrei Gavrilov.

The Well-tempered Clavier, Book I, excerpts: *Preludes and fugues Nos. 1–3; 5–17; 21–22.*
(M) *** DG 463 020–2 [id.]. Wilhelm Kempff (piano).

Fantasia in G, BWV 572; Fantasia and fugue in G min., BWV 542; Preludes and fugue; in A, BWV 536; in C, BWV 545; in E min., BWV 548; Toccata and fugue in F, BWV 540.
(M) ** DG 463 017-2 [id.]. Helmut Walcha (organ).

(i) *Pastorale in F, BWV 590; Passacaglia in C min., BWV 582; 6 Schübler chorales, BWV 645/650;* (ii) *Toccata, adagio and fugue in C, BWV 564;* (i) *Toccatas and fugues: in D min., (Dorian), BWV 538;* (ii) *in D min., BWV 565.*
(M) *** DG 463 016-2 [id.]. (i) Ton Koopman & Simon Preston (organs).

Cantatas Nos. 4: Christ lag in Todesbanden; 51: Jauchzett Gott; 140: Wachet auf.
(M) *** DG 463 007-2 [id.]. Mathis, Schrier, Fischer-Dieskau, Munich Bach O, Karl Richter.

Cantatas Nos. 56: (i) *Ich will den Kreuzstab gerne tragen; 106:* (ii) *Gottes Zeit ist die allerbeste Zeit (Actus tragicus);* (iii) *147: Herz und Mund und Tat und Leben.*
(M) *** DG 463 006-2 [id.]. (i) Fischer-Dieskau, Chamber Ch., Lucerne Fest. Strings, Baumgartner; (ii) Haefliger; Adam; (i; iii) Töpper; (iii) Buckel, Van Kesteren, Engen; Munich Bach Ch. & O, Karl Richter.

Cantatas Nos. 11: Lobet Gott in seinen Reichen (Ascension oratorio); 67: Halt im Gedächtnis Jesum Christ; 80: Ein feste Burg ist unser Gott.
(M) *** DG 463 009-2 [id.] Mathis, Reynolds, Schmidt, Schreier, Fisher-Dieskau, Munich Bach Ch. & O, Karl Richter.

Christmas oratorio, BWV 248: Arias and choruses.
(M) **(*) DG 463 003-2 [id.]. Janowitz, Ludwig, Wunderlich, Crass, Munich Bach Ch. & O, Karl Richter.

(i) *Magnificat, BWV 243;* (ii) Motets: *Singet dem Herrn; Der Geist hilft unser Schwacheit auf; Jesu meine Freude, BWV 225/7.*
(M) ** DG 463 010-2 [id.]. (i) Tomowa-Sintow, Baltsa, Schreier, Luxon, German Op. Berlin Ch., BPO, Karajan; (ii) Regensburg Domspatzen, V. Capella, Academica, Schneidt.

Mass in B min., BWV 232 (complete).
(M) ** DG 463 004-2 (2) [id.]. Stader, Töpper, Haefliger, Fischer-Dieskau, Engen, Munich Bach Ch. & O, Karl Richter.

St John Passion, BWV 245: Arias and choruses.
(M) *** DG 463 002-2 [id.]. Argenta, Chance, Archer, Müller, Hauptmann, Monteverdi Ch., E. Bar. Soloists, Gardiner.

St Matthew Passion, BWV 244 (complete).
(M) ** DG 463 001-2 [id.]. Janowitz, Ludwig, BPO, Karajan.

Deutsche Grammophon's new Bach Edition, in supposedly making a fairly comprehensive survey of that master's output, poses as many questions as it answers. Why, for instance is the *Easter oratorio* omitted while, apart from the *Magnificat*, the *Mass in B minor* is the only major choral work to be included in a complete performance (and that in a version that pays little heed to modern Bach scholarship); and why is the selection from the *St John Passion* the single representation from the distinguished series of Bach recordings made by John Eliot Gardiner for DG's Archiv label? Pinnock is better represented, yet his key sets of the *Brandenburgs* and keyboard concertos are ignored in favour of dated versions from Karl Richter. Clearly the answer must be that this 26-disc collection is aimed primarily at the German market, which explains the high proportion of performances of the old school. Certainly, as a set – handsomely packaged as it is, and sound as the performances are of their kind – this will not have much appeal to the knowledgeable general collector, on either side of the Atlantic. Fortunately all the CDs are available separately and are each discussed individually below.

The Art of fugue, BWV 1080; A Musical offering, BWV 1079.
(B) *** Ph. Duo 442 556-2 (2) [id.]. ASMF, Marriner.

How to perform *The Art of fugue* has always presented problems, since Bach's own indications are so sparse. Sir Neville Marriner in the edition he prepared with Andrew Davis has varied the textures most intelligently, giving a fair proportion of the fugues and canons to keyboard instruments, organ as well as harpsichord. In each instance the instrumentation has been chosen as specially suitable to that particular movement. Marriner's style of performance is profoundly satisfying, with finely judged tempi, unmannered phrasing and resilient rhythms, and the 1974 recording is admirably refined. Similarly, in the *Musical offering* Marriner uses his own edition and instrumentation: strings with three solo violins, solo viola and a solo cello; flute, organ and harpsichord. The performance here is of high quality, though some of the playing is a trifle bland. It is excellently recorded and is among the most successful accounts of the work.

The Art of Fugue, BWV 1080; Brandenburg concertos Nos. 1–6, BWV 1046/51; Musical offering, BWV 1079; Cantata No. 147: Jesu joy of man's desiring. Cantata No. 208: Sheep may safely graze. Christmas oratorio: Sinfonia.; Fugues: in A min., BWV 947; in G min., BWV 542. Orchestral suites Nos. 1–4, BWV 1066/69.

(N) (B) ** Decca/London Analogue/Dig. 458 319-2 (5) [id.]. Stuttgart CO, Karl Münchinger.

In the earliest days of LP, Münchinger pioneered Bach played on an apt scale and his 1972 analogue set of the *Brandenburg concertos* still stands up well among the available versions on modern instruments. The performances have genuine style and plenty of warmth and vitality if not the detailed imagination of some of the finest rival versions. *The Art of Fugue* too cannot really be faulted and its essential sobriety has a cumulative effect. The instrumentation usually allots the fugues to the strings and the canons to solo woodwind, varied with solo strings. After the incomplete quadruple fugue, Münchinger rounds off the work with the choral prelude, *Vor deinen Thron*, in principle quite wrong, but moving in practice. *The Musical Offering* is comparably impressive; indeed there is playing of genuine breadth and eloquence here, particularly in the *Trio sonata*. The *Canons* are grouped together and come off well. Not that the playing is entirely free from the heavy-handedness that sometimes disfigures Münchinger's art, but the performance has many fine qualities. The selection of shorter works in orchestral dress is also pleasingly presented and throughout the recording comes from a vintage Decca period and is full, clear and well balanced. The snag is the set of *Orchestral suites* in Münchinger's later digital version from 1985. Although well played and brilliantly recorded, the conductor's manner is unattractively heavy, with rhythms unlifted.

Brandenburg concertos Nos. 1–6, BWV 1046–51.

(N) ***Teldec/Warner Dig.4509 98442-2 (2) [id.]. Il Giardino Armonico, Giovanni Antonini.

*** DG Dig. 410 500/1-2 [id.]. E. Concert, Trevor Pinnock.

(B) *** Hyperion Dyad Dig. CDD 22001 (2) [id.]. Brandenburg Consort, Roy Goodman.

(B) *** EMI Dig. CD-EMX 2200 (*Nos. 1, 3 & 4*); CD-EMX 2201 (*Nos. 2, 5 & 6*) [(M) id. import]. Hanover Band, Anthony Halstead.

*** Sony Dig. S2K 66289 (2) [id.]. Tafelmusik, Jeanne Lamon.

(N) (BB) *** Virgin Veritas/EMI Dig. VBD5 61552-2 (2) [id.]. OAE.

*** Telarc Dig. CD 80368 (*Nos. 1–3*), CD 80354 (*Nos. 4–6*) (2) [id.]. Boston Bar., Pearlman.

*** Ph. 400 076/7-2 (2) [id.]. ASMF, Marriner.

(B) *** Carlton Dig. PCD 2006 (*Nos. 1–3*); PCD 2009 (*Nos. 4–6*) [(M) id.]. ECO, Ledger.

(B) *** EMI forte CZS5 69749-2 (2) [CDFB 69749]. Polish CO, Jerzy Maksymiuk (with CORELLI: *Concerto grosso, Op. 6/8;* MANFREDINI: *Concerto grosso, Op. 3/12;* TORELLI: *Concerto a quattro, Op. 8/6;* LOCATELLI: *Concerto grosso, Op. 1/8* ***).

(N) (B) ** RCA Twofer Dig. 74321 49184-2 (2) [id.]. Paillard CO, Paillard.

The various competing versions of the *Brandenburg concertos* offer so much excellence in every price range that to make a primary recommendation seems almost impossible. Yet the exhilarating new set from the Milanese period-instrument group, Il Giardino Armonico, directed by Giovanni Antonini, seems to carry all before it. Tempi seem perfectly judged, buoyantly brisk but never exaggeratedly so. The playing is wonderfully alive and joyful; slow movements have a touching expressive warmth and serenity. The wind and brass soloists are first rate: the horns bray lustily in the outer movements of No. 1 and the trumpeter in No. 2 plays with keen bravura yet is perfectly balanced with his colleagues. The recorder, flute and oboe sounds are equally characterful, and the strings are bright and clean without edge; the recording is both warm and freshly transparent, so that one can hear the harpsichord coming through quite naturally.

Undoubtedly Pinnock's DG set of *Brandenburgs*, played on original instruments, represents the peak of his achievement as an advocate of authentic performance with sounds that are clear and refreshing but not too abrasive. After a period when a limited edition of this set was available at mid-price, this now reverts to DG's full-price Archiv label and the set now seems expensive. The recordings are, however, alternatively available on three mid-priced CDs (423 492-2) coupled with the *Orchestral Suites*, but the latter are somewhat controversial, bringing a distinct loss of breadth and grandeur.

In considering the other versions, that by the Linde Consort, coupled with the *Musical offering* (see below), can be spoken of in the same breath as Pinnock's set. However, the excellent Hyperion set of the *Brandenburgs* now re-emerges on a Dyad, with the two discs offered for the price of one. Roy

Goodman not only directs but also acts as a string soloist. The stylish, lively playing is another attractive example of authenticism, lacking something in polish (notably from the horns in No. 1) but not in spirit, with the last three concertos especially fresh. There is also fine trumpet-playing from Stephen Keavy in No. 2. Characterization is strong and slow movements are often appealingly expressive, especially the delicately managed *Affettuoso* of No. 5 which, like No. 4, gains from the fine flute contribution of Rachel Brown. Tempi of outer movements are very brisk, but often bring the lightest rhythmic touch. Very good sound.

Anthony Halstead and the Hanover Band make a good alternative. The playing is consistently fresh and tempi are admirably chosen to give a feeling of liveliness and a joyful alertness without pressing on too hard while, throughout, lyrical lines flow pleasingly and textures are clean and transparent. The recording was made in the Henry Wood Hall and its warm acoustic provides an admirable background ambience for the music-making.

Tafelmusik seldom disappoint, and their set of *Brandenburgs* is enjoyably robust and spontaneous, if inevitably not always as polished as the best versions on modern instruments. Many will find this more infectious than Pinnock, with the horn soloists in No.1, Ab Koster and Derek Conrod, playing mid-eighteenth-century hand horns with lustily extrovert vigour and bravura, so that one does not mind that intonation is not always exact. Crispian Steele-Perkins, the trumpet soloist in No. 2, plays a modern copy of a 1667 instrument with remarkable sophistication. Tempi are brisk (the finale of No. 3 is most invigorating) but never hurried, and slow movements relax warmly as they should, with bulges in phrasing fairly minimal. The recording is excellent.

With the direction shared among four violinists – Monica Huggett (Nos. 2, 4 and 6), Catherine Mackintosh (No. 1), Alison Bury (No. 3) and Elizabeth Wallfisch (No. 5) – the Orchestra of the Age of Enlightenment presents an amiable set of *Brandenburgs* on period instruments. These performances bring all the advantages of light, clear textures and no sense of haste, even when a movement is taken faster than has become traditional. With generally excellent recording, this makes a most inexpensive alternative to the outstanding version by Trevor Pinnock on DG; but the OAE ensemble cannot quite match that of the English Concert in crispness.

Another most enjoyable set on period instruments comes from the Boston Baroque under Martin Pearlman. He sets attractively lively and spirited tempi in outer movements, yet for once slow movements are not pressed on but are allowed space to expand. Solo playing is excellent, although Friedemann Immer's trumpet does have a few moments of ungainliness in No. 2. But there is no vinegar here in the string timbre, even in the *Sixth Concerto*, which is played with one instrument to a part and uses violas da gamba. Not quite a first choice but, with first-class Telarc sound and a feeling that the players are enjoying themselves, this is well worth considering.

Those wanting a first-class set using modern instruments can still rest content with Marriner – if paying a premium price is acceptable. With star soloists and beautifully sprung performances, this is very enjoyable indeed, with sound that is natural and lively.

On Carlton, Ledger also has the advantage of fresh and detailed digital recording. He directs resilient, well-paced readings of all six concertos on modern instruments, lively yet never overforced. The slow movements in particular are most beautifully done, persuasively and without mannerism. Flutes rather than recorders are used in No. 4.

If you enjoy brisk tempi, the Polish set is a first-class example of a stylish account on modern instruments. The crisp articulation and buoyancy of the playing are exhilarating. The orchestra is augmented with English recorder soloists who are obviously enjoying themselves, as does the trumpeter, who is called to flights of virtuosity in No. 2. No. 5 has a first-class contribution from the solo harpsichord player, Wladyslaw Klosiewicz. The analogue sound is first class, full and clear and very well balanced. What makes the set doubly attractive at its very modest price is the inclusion of a 1984 collection of key *concerti grossi* by Corelli, Manfredini, Torelli and Locatelli, each with a beautiful *Pastoral* slow movement to make a Christmas connection. They are very beautifully played and recorded.

Alas Jean-François Paillard's new digital RCA set with his own Chamber Orchestra is a non-starter. His easygoing style has been bypassed by musical history. Fine playing, of course, but one needs more sparkle than this.

(i) *Brandenburg concertos Nos. 1–6;* (ii) *Flute concerto in G min.* (from *BWV 1056*); *Double concerto for violin, oboe and strings in D min.* (from *BWV 1060*).
(B) *** Decca Double 443 847-2 (2) [id.]. (i) ECO, Britten; (ii) ASMF, Marriner.

Britten made his recordings in the Maltings concert-hall in 1968. The result is a fairly ample sound that in its way goes well with Britten's interpretations. There is some lack of textural delicacy in the slow movements of Nos. 1, 2, 4 and 6; but the bubbling high spirits of the outer movements are hard to resist, and the harpsichordist, Philip Ledger, follows the pattern he had set in live Britten performances, with Britten-inspired extra elaborations a continual delight. As a makeweight for the Double Decca reissue, two more of Marriner's stylish performances of reconstructions of Bach's harpsichord concertos for alternative instruments have been added. First-class (originally Argo) recording, too.

Brandenburg concertos Nos. 1–6; Oboe d'amore concerto in A, BWV 1055; Double concerto for violin and oboe in D min., BWV 1060; Triple violin concerto in D, BWV 1064.
(N) (M) ** DG 463 011/2 [id.]. Soloists, Munich Bach Orchestra, Karl Richter.

Richter undoubtedly draws superb playing from his orchestra in the *Brandenburgs*, and the recording is admirably clear. But rhythmically Richter, in his Germanic way, puts the music rather into a strait-jacket – witness the first movement of No. 6, which needs more persuasive handling. Fortunately in slow movement he allows a greater degree of expressive relaxation. Both the *Oboe d'amore concerto* and *Double concerto for violin and oboe* have fine soloists, and both here and in the *Triple concerto* Richter gives good support.

Brandenburg concertos Nos. 1–4.
(N) (M) *** Penguin Classics Decca 466 209-2 [460 601-2] ECO, Britten.

(i) *Brandenburg concertos Nos. 5 in D; 6 in B flat, BWV 1050/51;* (ii)*Violin concerto No. 1 in A min., BWV 1042.*
(N) (M) *** Penguin Classics Decca 460 627-2 [id.]. (i)ECO, Britten; (ii) Arthur Grumiaux, Soloistes Romands, Gerecz.

This first Penguin Classics disc will suit anyone wanting a single CD including the *Second concerto*, with its famous trumpet solos, and the popular *Third* for strings alone. But it was a pity that Penguin did not take the opportunity to be generous, and offer all six concertos on a pair of CDs for the price of one. The author's note is by Douglas Adams, better known for his *Hitch-hiker's Guide to the Galaxy*.

Penguin Classics then complete their set of *Brandenburgs* and no one could grumble about the coupling – Arthur Grumiaux's outstandingly fine version of the *A minor Violin concerto*. Douglas Adams again provides a personal commentary.

Brandenburg concertos Nos. 1–6; (i) *Oboe concertos: in A* (from *BWV 1055*); *in D min.* (from *BWV 1059*); *in F* (from *BWV 1053*).
(M) **(*) DG 445 578-2 (2). COE, (i) with Douglas Boyd.

A spirit of fun infects the COE version of the *Brandenburg concertos*. Using modern instruments, these are among the happiest performances ever, marked by easily bouncing rhythms and warmly affectionate – but never sentimental – slow movements. Unfortunately, the first movement of No. 1 – the movement which many will sample first – takes relaxation too far, becoming almost ragged; conversely, the first movement of No. 6 is uncharacteristically rigid. Otherwise these performances, well recorded, give pure joy. The three *Oboe concertos* are reconstructed from keyboard concertos and cantata movements. The soloist, Douglas Boyd, principal oboe of the COE from its foundation, directs his colleagues in delectable performances. First-rate sound.

Brandenburg concertos Nos. 1–3; (i) *Violin concertos Nos. 1 in A min.; 2 in E, BWV l041–2.*
(M) *** Ph. 442 386-2. ECO, Leppard; (i) with Arthur Grumiaux.

Brandenburg concertos Nos. 4–6; (i) *Triple concerto in A min. for violin, flute and harpsichord, BWV 1044.*
(M) *** Ph. 442 387-2. ECO, Leppard; (i) with Grumiaux, Garcia & Adeney.

Brandenburg concertos Nos. 1–6, BWV 1046–51; (i) *Violin concertos Nos. 1 in A min.; 2 in E;* (i–ii) *Double violin concerto in D min., BWV 1041–3.*
(BB) *** Virgin Classics Dig. Double VBD5 61403-2 (2) [CDVB 61403]. Scottish Ens., Jonathan Rees; with (i) J. Rees; (ii) Jane Murdoch.

Brandenburg concertos Nos. 1–6, BWV 1046–51; Brandenburg concerto No. 5 (early version), *BWV 1050a; Triple concerto in A min. for flute, violin and harpsichord, BWV 1044.*
(M) *** Virgin/EMI VCD5 45255-2 (2). La Stravaganza, Hamburg, Siegbert Rampe.

The La Stravaganza *Brandenburgs* are immensely vigorous and stimulating. Overall, the tempi must be among the fastest on record (disconcertingly so upon first hearing) and the throaty hand-horn playing in the outer movements of No. 1 brings the most extraordinary virtuosity – while the intonation is remarkably accurate. The buoyant outer movements of No. 2 are just as spirited, with the solo trumpet (Hans-Martin Kothe) admirably balanced with the baroque oboe (Alfredo Barnardini). Not to be outdone, the strings in No. 3 play with enormous zest, particularly in the finale, where the light buoyancy of rhythm and crispness of attack and ensemble are a joy. Yet throughout, slow movements bring the warmest expressive feeling: this is period-instrument playing with a smile of pleasure thrown in. No. 5 is offered not only in the 1719 version we know so well, but also in an earlier chamber version, probably written in Carlsbad a year earlier, when Bach only had five players at his disposal. It is refreshingly light-textured. Siegbert Rampe (his virtuosity ever impressive) directs from the harpsichord and plays as felicitously and involvingly here as he does throughout, in this instance using a smaller instrument to match what the composer himself had available, but which nevertheless comes through the texture quite admirably. The *Triple concerto* is played with comparable spirit and finesse. Outstandingly realistic recording.

The Jonathan Rees set is reissued as a Virgin Double, with the two discs offered in the UK at the cost of one mid-priced CD. These modern-instrument Scottish *Brandenburgs* are in every way competitive. Directed with much spirit, they are freshly played, with warm, clear recording and excellent internal balance. The tempi seem very apt when the players so convey their enjoyment and the sound has such a pleasing bloom. Rees then becomes the principal soloist in equally warm, buoyant performances of the *Violin concertos*, with Jane Murdoch matching his stylishness in the *Double concerto*. Allegros are sprung infectiously, while slow movements are allowed full expressiveness without sentimentality. In the clear, digital recording the harpsichord continuo of Sally Heath is prominent without being distracting.

The exhilaration of the mid-1970s Leppard set also brings much to enjoy and the soloists include John Wilbraham's trumpet in No. 2 and a piquant recorder contribution from David Munrow in No.4. The remastered sound is fresh and full. Grumiaux's accounts of the two solo concertos come from 1964, but the playing from one of the most musical soloists of our time is extremely satisfying. It has a purity of line and an expressive response that communicate very positively, and Leppard's stylish accompaniments have striking buoyancy. The *Triple concerto* (recorded two decades later) has plenty of vitality, too; although the balance is a little contrived, the effect is certainly vivid.

Brandenburg concertos Nos. 1–6; A Musical offering, BWV 1079.

(M) *** Virgin Veritas/EMI Dig./Analogue VED5 61154–2 (2) [CDMB 61154]. Linde Consort, Hans-Martin Linde.

Quite apart from the considerable bonus of the *Musical offering*, many will prefer the Linde version of the *Brandenburgs*, for the 1981 EMI recording is rather fuller than the Pinnock's DG Archiv sound, with the strings very slightly less immediate. In *Brandenburg No. 3* there is a distinct gain in body and warmth, and No. 6 (also for strings alone) again brings a slightly more ample texture, without loss of inner definition. In the *Musical offering* (recorded a year earlier) Linde is as stylish and accomplished as any of his rivals, and he and his six colleagues offer the preferred version of this work using original instruments. They are again warmly as well as clearly recorded; indeed the analogue to digital transfer is particularly natural, and this set offers remarkable value.

Harpsichord concertos Nos. 1–7, BWV 1052–8; Double harpsichord concertos Nos. 1–3, BWV 1060–62.

(B) *** Ph. Duo Analogue/Dig. 454 268-2 (2) [id.]. Raymond Leppard, Andrew Davis, Philip Ledger, ECO, Leppard.

Harpsichord concertos Nos. 1 in D min.; 2 in E; 3 in D; 4 in A; 5 in F min.; 6 in F; 7 in G min., BWV 1052–8; (i) *Double harpsichord concertos: Nos. 1 in C min.; 2 in C; 3 in C min., BWV 1060–62;* (i; ii) *Triple harpsichord concertos Nos. 1 in D min.; 2 in C, BWV 1063–4;* (i–iii) *Quadruple harpsichord concerto in A min., BWV 1065.*

(B) *** DG Analogue/Dig. 447 709-2 (3) [(M) id. import]. Pinnock with (i) Gilbert; (ii) Mortensen; (iii) Kraemer; E. Concert.

Pinnock's performances of the Bach *Harpsichord concertos* first appeared in 1981, and they have dominated the catalogue ever since. In the solo concertos he plays with real panache, his scholarship tempered with excellent musicianship. Pacing is brisk, but to today's ears, used to period performances, the effect is convincing when the playing is so spontaneous and the analogue sound bright and clean. The *Double*, *Triple* and *Quadruple concertos* are digital, and the combination of period instruments and playing of determined vigour certainly makes a bold effect. There is a bit more edge on the strings and everything is clearly laid out and forwardly projected. Outer movements emphasize the bravura of Bach's conceptions and, if slow movements could at times be more relaxed, those ears prepared to accept a hint of aggressiveness in the energetic musical flow will find this set as stimulating now as when it first appeared.

Leppard, Davis and Ledger provide a modern instrument alternative, playing with skill and flair; the ECO shows plenty of life and, if the performances overall are less incisive than the English Concert versions with Pinnock, they have resilience and communicate such joy in the music that criticism is disarmed. The Philips sound is very realistic, the harpsichords life-size and not too forward; one does reflect that modern strings, however refined, create a body of tone which tends slightly to outweigh the more slender keyboard timbres. However, in the works for two or more harpsichords there is a pleasing absence of jangle. Excellent value.

(i) *Harpsichord concertos Nos. 1 in D min., BWV 1052; 3 in D, BWV 1054; 5 in F min., BWV 1056; Violin concerto No. 2 in E, BWV 1042.*

(N) *** O/L (IMS) Dig. 448 178-2 [id.]. (i) Christophe Rousset; (ii) Jaap Schöder, AAM, Hogwood.

(i) *Harpsichord concertos Nos. 2 in E, BWV 1053; 4 in A, BWV 1055; 7 in G min., BWV 1058;* (ii) *Violin concerto No. 1 in A min., BWV 1041.*

(N) *** O/L (IMS) Dig. 443 326-2 [id.] (i) Christophe Rousset; (ii) Jaap Schröder, AAM, Hogwood.

The ongoing survey from Rousset and Hogwood mixes up keyboard and violin concertos, which is a less than ideal plan, as it looks as though the complete set will run to at least four premium-priced discs (each with about an hour's playing time). Rousset's performances of the *Harpsichord concertos* are very fine, the effect warmer, softer grained, than with Pinnock (although the harpsichord is not so sharply focused). Neat ornamentation and plenty of flair from Rousset, ample vigour and vitality from the string group, and the slow movement of the *F minor* is beautifully played. Jaap Schröder's accounts of the solo violin concertos are also first class, with expressive slow movements and no unwanted edge of the violin timbre.

Harpsichord concerto No.1 in D min., BWV 1052; (i) *Double harpsichord in C, BWV 1061;* (i; ii) *Triple harpsichord concerto in D min., BWV 1063;* (i; ii; iii) *Quadruple harpsichord concerto in A min., BWV 1065.*

(N) (M) **(*) DG 463 015-2 [id.]. Karl Richter with (i) Hedwig Bilgram; (ii) Iwona Fütterer; (iii) Ulrik Schütt; Munich Bach O.

In many ways these are attractive performances. The solo-playing here is all highly musical and quite persuasive, and these works are well recorded. But today's ears seek a lighter rhythmic touch and more transparent textures.

Clavier concertos Nos. 1 in D min.; 2 in E; 3 in D, 4 in A; 5 in F; 6 in F; 7 in G min., BWV 1052–8.

*** Decca Dig. 425 676-2 (2) [id.]. András Schiff (piano), COE.

Clavier concertos Nos. 1 in D min., BWV 1052; 2 in E, BWV 1053; 3 in D, BWV 1054.

(BB) *** Naxos Dig. 8.550422; *4.550422* [id.]. Hae-won Chang (piano), Camerata Cassovia, Stankovsky.

Clavier concertos Nos. 4 in A, BWV 1055; 5 in F min., BWV 1056; 6 in F, BWV 1057; 7 in G min., BWV 1058.

(BB) *** Naxos Dig. 8.550423; *4.550423* [id.]. Hae-won Chang (piano), Camerata Cassovia, Stankovsky.

As in his solo Bach records, Schiff's control of colour and articulation never seeks to present merely a harpsichord imitation, and his shaping of Bach's lovely slow movements brings fine sustained lines and a subtle variety of touch. He directs the Chamber Orchestra of Europe from the keyboard and chooses spirited, uncontroversial tempi for allegros, at the same time providing decoration that always adds to the joy and sparkle of the music-making. This makes a clear first choice for those who, like us, enjoy Bach on the piano.

Miss Chang is a highly sympathetic Bach exponent, playing flexibly yet with strong rhythmic feeling, decorating nimbly and not fussily. Robert Stankovsky directs freshly resilient accompaniments; and both artists understand the need for a subtle gradation of light and shade. The digital recording, made in the House of Arts, Kŏsice, is first class, with the piano balanced not too far forward. A fine super-bargain alternative.

Oboe d'amore concerto in D, BWV 1068; Sinfonia from Cantata No. 156; Canonic trio in F, BWV 1040.

(N) *** Ph. Dig. 454 450-2 [id.]. Heinz Holliger, Camerata Bern – C. P. E. BACH: *Oboe concertos: in B flat, Wq.164; in E flat, Wq.165.* ***

The *Oboe d'amore concerto* is better known in its harpsichord version, but Holliger is a highly convincing advocate and he plays the lovely cantilena from the cantata exquisitely. The brief *Canonic trio* is hardly less pleasing and here Zehetmair, Polidor and Erisman add their musicianship to make a well-balanced team. The recording is admirably natural.

Violin concertos Nos. (i) *1–2;* (ii) *Double violin concerto, BWV 1041–3;* (iii) *Double concerto for violin & oboe in C min., BWV 1060.*

✽ (M) *** Ph. 420 700-2. Grumiaux; (ii) Krebbers, (iii) Holliger; (i–ii) Les Solistes Romandes, Arpad Gerecz; (iii) New Philh. O, Edo de Waart.

(M) *** Nimbus Dig. NI 7031 [id.]. Oscar Shumsky, Scottish CO; with (ii) John Tunnell; (iii) Robin Miller.

(M) *** Classic fM Dig. 75605 57008-2. Joji Hattori, with (i) James Clark, (ii) Robin Williams; SCO, Hattori.

Arthur Grumiaux is joined in the *Double concerto* by Hermann Krebbers. The result is an outstanding success. The way Grumiaux responds to the challenge of working with another great artist comes over equally clearly in the concerto with oboe, reconstructed from the *Double harpsichord concerto in C minor*. Grumiaux's performances of the two solo concertos are equally satisfying.

One has only to sample the simple beauty of Shumsky's playing in the *Andante* of the *A minor Violin concerto* to be won over to his dedicated Bach style, which is not quite as pure as Grumiaux's but is seductive in its simplicity of line and tonal beauty. John Tunnell makes highly musical exchanges with him in the *Double violin concerto* and Robin Miller is a no less appealing partner in the work for violin and oboe. Shumsky directs the orchestra from the bow and, although the sound is full in the way of modern-instrument performances, rhythms are resilient and there is no excess weightiness in the bass. The recording is warm to match. A most enjoyable collection for those looking for (fairly) modern (1984) digital recordings of these works at mid-price.

The Classic fM disc is also outstanding in every way, not just offering performances which stand high among versions using modern instruments, but full, immediate recording and a generous measure of four concertos instead of the more usual three, with the *Violin and oboe concerto*, reconstructed from the *Double harpsichord concerto in C minor*, as well as the three great violin works. Joji Hattori, winner of the Menuhin International Competition in 1989, plays with a tone both sweet and pure, flawless in intonation and immaculate in crisply alert passage-work. As director, he draws from the orchestra playing both clear and well sprung, with the clarity enhanced by the recording, and he is well matched by both his duet partners.

(i) *Violin concertos Nos. 1 in A min.; 2 in E;* (i; ii) *Double violin concerto in D min., BWV 1041–3;* (i; iii) *Double concerto for violin and oboe in C min., BWV 1060. Orchestral Suites Nos. 1 in C;* (iv) *2 in B min.* (for flute and strings); *3 in D, BWV 1066–8.*

(BB) *** EMI Seraphim (SIS) CES5 68517-2 (2) [CDEB 685172]. (i) Y. Menuhin; (ii) Christian Ferras; (iii) Leon Goossens; (iv) Elaine Schaffer; Bath Festival CO, Sir Yehudi Menuhin.

Menuhin's set of the *Violin concertos* date from 1960 and, played as they are here, both the solo concertos take flight, for their balance of warmth, humanity and classical sympathy is very appealing. In the *Double violin concerto* Ferras matches his timbre beautifully to that of Menuhin and the duet is a real partnership, with the slow movement especially fine. Leon Goossens makes a ravishing contribution to the *Adagio* of the *Concerto for violin and oboe*, the only slight snag being that the oboe is too backwardly balanced in the outer movements. To complete this attractive Menuhin/Bach package, we are offered three of the four *Orchestral Suites*, where Menuhin finds an admirable balance between freshness and warmth, conveying the music's spirit and breadth without inflation. The current remastering brings sound which is quite full, yet clear. The documentation – or lack of it – is no credit to the famous old EMI trademark, but the music-making is of the highest order.

(i) *Violin concertos Nos. 1 in A min.; 2 in E;* (ii) *Double concerto, BWV 1041–3;* (iii) *Orchestral Suite No. 4 in D, BWV 1068.*

(B) **(*) DG Classikon 449 844-2 [(M) id. import]. (i–ii) D. Oistrakh, RPO, Goossens; (ii) with I. Oistrakh; (iii) Munich Bach O, Karl Richter.

It is good to have David Oistrakh's justly renowned performances back in the catalogue on DG's bargain Classikon label, since the playing is peerless and can be ranked alongside the Grumiaux versions. In the *Double concerto* father and son are suitably contrasted in timbre and the performance of the great slow movement is Elysian. The 1961 recording hardly sounds dated. Richter's account of the *Fourth Orchestral Suite* is rhythmically unstylish in the matter of double-dotting, but is otherwise alert – less heavy than we had remembered.

Violin concertos Nos. 1 in A min.; 2 in E; (i) *Double concerto, BWV 1041–3.*

(M) *** HM/BMG GD 77006 [77006-2-RG]. Sigiswald Kuijken; (i) Lucy van Dael; La Petite Bande.

Kuijken is a fine Bach player, and these performances of the *Violin concertos* are well worth considering by those who want period performances on original instruments. The slight edge on the solo timbre is painless and La Petite Bande provide lively, resilient allegros, the playing both polished and alert. Excellent, well-balanced, 1981 digital recording. But the measure is short.

Violin concertos Nos. 1 in A min.; 2 in E, BWV 1041-2; (i) *Double violin concertos: in D min., BWV 1043 and BWV 1060.*

(N) *(*) HM Dig. HMU 907155 [id.]. Andrew Manze; (i) Rachel Podger; AAM.

These period-instrument performances bring a fair amount of re-editing, notably in BWV 1042, but particularly in BWV 1060 which is heard in an alternative version in *D minor, for two violins*, instead of the more familar combination of violin and oboe. Andrew Manze and Rachel Podger fail to make a case for it. The solo-playing in the slow movement is little short of prosaic and in the familiar duo in the *Largo* of the more famous *Double violin concerto*, BWV 1043, their interchange brings a passage where one violin plays legato and the other separates the notes in an almost staccato manner. Although allegros have plenty of life, with thin solo timbres this is a disc for dedicated authenticists only.

Violin concertos Nos. 1 in A min.; 2 in E; (i) *Double violin concerto in D min.,* (ii) *Triple concerto for flute, violin, and harpsichord, BWV 1044.*

(N) (M) *** DG Dig. 463 014-2 [id.]. Simon Standage, E. Concert, Pinnock, with (i) Elizabeth Wilcock; (ii) Lisa Beznosiuk, Pinnock.

This collection of violin concertos, played on original instruments, is one of the finest reissues in the present collection, and is welcome back in the catalogue. Rhythms are crisp and lifted at nicely chosen speeds – not too fast for slow movements – and the solo playing is very stylish. The *Triple concerto* is also very successful. The only snag is the edge on violin timbre which will not please all ears.

Violin concerto No. 2 in E, BWV 1042.

(N) **(*) Simax Dig. PSC 1159 [id.]. Tellefsen, Oslo Chamber Music Festival Strings, Berglund – SHOSTAKOVICH: *Violin concerto No. 1.* **(*)

Good, stylish playing that should enjoy wide appeal. Arve Tellefsen has never enjoyed the international exposure to which his gifts entitle him but he is a fine musician who plays with great spirit, and is well recorded too.

(i) *Double violin concerto in D min., BWV 1043. Suite in D, BWV 1068: Air* (arr. Wilhelmj). (Unaccompanied) *Violin sonata No. 1 in G min., BWV 1001: Adagio*.
(M) (***) Biddulph mono LAB 056-7 [id.]. Arnold Rosé, (i) with Alma Rosé, O – BEETHOVEN: *String quartets Nos. 4, 10 & 14.* (***)

The issue is valuable in that it affords an insight into a style of playing that has long passed into history. Arnold Rosé's sonata-partner was Bruno Walter and his brother-in-law was Mahler. His daughter, Alma, with whom he is heard in a 1931 recording of the Bach *D minor Double concerto*, perished in Auschwitz. Interesting though these recordings are, the principal musical rewards in the set come from the three Beethoven quartets with which they are coupled.

A Musical offering, BWV 1079 (see also below under Chamber Music).
(BB) **(*) Naxos Dig. 8.553286 [id.]. Capella Istropolitana, Christian Benda.

Christian Benda uses a small chamber group. Strings alone, with a minimum of vibrato, play the framing *Ricercars*. The first group of canons add in flute, oboe, and bassoon; in the second group, the stringed instruments predominate. A harpsichord joins in the first, and the cor anglais and bassoon dolorously share the last (common) solution of the four offered alternative proposals for solving Bach's so-called 'puzzle canon'. The *Trio sonata*, at the centre, is given a pleasing performance, expressive and lively, and overall this seems a thoroughly musical interpretation of a work about which any performance is conjectural . The recording is excellent, clear yet with a pleasing bloom, and the result, if a little didactic at times, is undoubtedly fresh.

Orchestral suites Nos. 1–4, BWV 1066–9.
(M) *** Decca 430 378-2 [id.]. ASMF, Marriner.
(N) ** Ph. Dig. 442 151-2 (2) [id.]. OAE, Franz Brüggen.
(N) (M) ** DG 463 013-2 [id.]. E. Concert, Trevor Pinnock.

Orchestral suites Nos. 1–4; Violin concerto movement in D, BWV 1045; Sinfonias from Cantatas Nos. 29; 42; 209.
(B) *** Hyperion Dyad Dig. CDD 22002 (2) [id.]. Brandenburg Consort, Roy Goodman.

Orchestral suites Nos. 1–4, BWV 1066–9. Sinfonias from Cantatas Nos. 42; 174 & Easter Oratorio, BWV 249; (i) *Cantata No. 118: Chorus: Ich liebe den Höchsten von ganzem Gemüte.*
*** DG (IMS) Dig. 439 780-2 (2) [id.]. E. Concert, Pinnock; (i) with Ch.

With sound rather warmer and string-tone sweeter, Trevor Pinnock and the English Concert manage to improve on their benchmark readings of 16 years earlier. In the dance movements of the *Suite No. 2* Lisa Beznosiuk takes her flute solos faster and more brilliantly than her predecessor, Stephen Preston, but otherwise speeds are generally a fraction broader in all four suites, with allegros more jauntily sprung and phrasing a degree more espressivo. Above all, the great *Air* of the *Suite No. 3* sounds far warmer, persuasively phrased on multiple violins instead of on a single, acid-toned instrument. This time Pinnock also opts to observe the marked repeats not only in the slow introductions to the opening overtures but in the main allegros as well, making them substantially longer. The fill-ups are brief but make a fascinating bonus, winningly performed. The chorus from *Cantata No. 118* is a brilliant choral setting of the opening *Overture* of *Suite No. 4*, while the *Sinfonias* from *Cantatas Nos. 42* and *174* are re-orchestrations of the opening movements of the *First* and *Third Brandenburg Concertos* respectively, the latter with oboes and horns delightfully elaborating the original string textures.

Roy Goodman directs brisk and stylish readings of the four Bach *Orchestral Suites*, which are aptly supplemented by four *Sinfonias*, each following a suite in the same key. Though in the *Suites* Goodman in his eagerness occasionally chooses too breathless a tempo for fast movements, the lightness of rhythm and the crispness of ensemble are consistently persuasive, with textures cleanly caught in excellent, full-bodied sound. These are among the finest versions on a long list, with Rachel Brown an exceptionally warm-toned flautist in No. 2. Goodman observes all repeats, making the opening overtures longer than usual.

Marriner's 1970 recording of the Bach *Suites* with the ASMF comes on a single CD (77 minutes 48 seconds) and the remastering of the fine (originally Argo) recording is fresh and vivid. The playing throughout is expressive without being romantic, and always buoyant and vigorous. A fine bargain for those not insisting on original instruments; there is nothing remotely unstylish here.

The Orchestra of the Age of Enlightenment play warmly, but dotted rhythms are too often lacking in the necessary lift. Lisa Beznosiuk is the able soloist in the *Second suite*, but the performance is in no way memorable. The opening of the *Third* makes a bold impact and the famous *Air* is given more body than in some period performances but overall, Brüggen's set is a disappointment.

Pinnock's earlier analogue recording of the *Suites* (now neatly fitted on to a single CD), dates from 1979, when period instrument performances were still full of stylistic excesses, and the unprepared listener could find the bright edge on the squeezed vibratoless string-timbres disconcerting, even though the recording has a full ambience. Playing is alert, with rhythms refreshingly sprung – not least in the slow introductions which, as one would expect, are anything but ponderous. In the *B minor Suite*, although there could be more contrast in feeling, there is no sense that reverence for supposed authenticity is stifling musical spontaneity.

Orchestral suites Nos. 1–4; (i) *Double harpsichord concertos Nos. 1 & 3.*
(N) (B) *** Decca Double Dig. 458 069-2 (2) [id.]. AAM, Hogwood; (i) with Christoph Rousset, Christopher Hogwood.

Hogwood's set of the Bach orchestral *Suites* illustrates how the Academy of Ancient Music has developed in refinement and purity of sound, modifying earlier abrasiveness without losing period-instrument freshness. That comes out in the famous *Air* from *Suite No. 3* where, with multiple violins and an avoidance of the old squeezed style, the tone is sweet even with little or no vibrato – a movement which in the Pinnock version on DG Archiv, for example, sounds very sour. *Allegros* tend to be on the fast side but are well sprung, not breathless. The *Concertos for two harpsichords* added for the mid-priced reissue are imaginatively played by Christopher Hogwood and Christophe Rousset. Hogwood aficionados need not hesitate.

CHAMBER MUSIC

The Art of fugue, BWV 1080.
*** Sony Dig. S2K 45937 (2) [id.]. Juilliard Qt.
(N) **(*) ECM Dig. 1652 [id.]. Keller Quartet.
(N) (M) ** DG Dig. 463 027-2 [id.]. Musica Antiqua Köln, Reinhard Goebel.

The Juilliard Quartet's version has the field virtually to itself, and hearing it again in this medium gives undoubted pleasure. They play with far less vibrato than usual (at times one is tempted to feel that they are aspiring to the condition of a consort of viols) and they convey a feeling of intimacy and a clarity of the part-writing that is very satisfying. This is a very worthwhile alternative to the relatively abundant keyboard versions, and musically very satisfying.

The Hungarian Keller Quartet give the impression of using slightly more vibrato than the Juilliards, although it is varied and carefully controlled. Their perfectly matched tonal blend means that one is always aware of the harmonic implications of the polyphony, and this brings a more expressive style, so that the cello solo that opens Contrapunctus 3 is almost a lament. There is plenty of variety of both mood and tempo. Nevertheless keyboard versions delineate the part-writing more pointedly. The chosen layout places the canons together at the end of the work, which then closes with Bach's unfinished triple fugue, played very sparely, so that the sudden cessation is the more dramatic. The recording is full and naturally balanced.

Goebel's *Art of fugue* is very clearly recorded. In this Cologne performance, the movements are divided between strings and solo harpsichord. The two harpsichord players are often imaginative and expressive, to contrast with the rhythmic vigour of the playing of the strings. This has genuine vitality but the bite on the string tone, and also the expressive bulges which are at times exaggerated, will pose a listening problem for some listeners.

(Unaccompanied) *Cello suites Nos. 1–6, BWV 1007–12.*
✿ *** EMI Dig. CDS5 55363-2 (2) [id.]. Mstislav Rostropovich.
*** EMI (SIS) Dig. CDS7 47471-8 (2). Heinrich Schiff.
(M) *** DG 449 711-2 (2) [id.]. Pierre Fournier.
(M) *** Sony Dig. S2K 63203 (2) [id.]. Yo-Yo Ma.
*** Virgin/EMI Dig. VCD5 45086-2 (2) [id.]. Ralph Kirshbaum.
(B) *** Ph. Duo 442 293-2 (2) [id.]. Maurice Gendron.
(N) (B) *** Ph. Virtuoso 422 494-2 (1, 4 & 6); 422 495-2 (2–3 & 5) Maurice Gendron.
(M) (***) EMI mono CHS7 61027-2 (2) [Ang. CDH 61028/9]. Pablo Casals.

Rostropovich, the most intrepid of cellists, ever eager to tackle concertos by the score, has nevertheless approached these supreme masterpieces of the solo cello repertory with caution. He played them all in his teens but, until the 1990s, refrained from recording them as a complete cycle. The result is revelatory, in many ways the most powerful recording of all, positive and personal, full of individual perceptions. Rostropovich verbally characterizes each one of the series: 'No. 1, lightness; No. 2, sorrow and intensity; No. 3, brilliance; No. 4, majesty and opacity; No. 5, darkness; and No. 6, sunlight'. True to his word, more than usual he draws distinctions between each, also reflecting the point that the structure of each suite grows in complexity. The results are both moving and strong with the sound of the cello, as recorded in a warm acoustic, full and powerful. Dynamics are romantically free but always compelling, making one hear the music afresh, with pianissimo repeats magically achieved. Anyone who has ever been daunted by solo cello music will find its range of expression astonishingly expanded by Rostropovich.

Strong and positive, producing a consistent flow of beautiful tone at whatever dynamic level, Schiff here establishes his individual artistry very clearly, his rhythmic pointing a delight. He is treated to an excellent recording, with the cello given fine bloom against a warm but intimate acoustic.

Fournier's richly phrased and warm-toned performances carry an impressive musical conviction. Fournier can be profound and he can lift rhythms infectiously in dance movements, but above all he conveys the feeling that this is music to be enjoyed. This recording has been remastered splendidly for reissue in DG's 'Legendary Recordings' series and now has even greater presence and realism.

Yo-Yo Ma's playing has a characteristic rhythmic freedom and favours the widest range of dynamic. The improvisatory effect is seemingly spontaneous and these performances are very compelling indeed, for Ma seems right inside every bar of the music. The break betweeen the two CDs comes in the middle of the (*Fourth*) *E flat major Suite*, so the second disc opens with the *Sarabande*, played very freely and with inspired concentration, while the famous *Gavotte* of No. 6, boldly accented, is no less individual. The first-class recording is very real and natural, with the warm acoustic never blurring the focus. The set comes generously illustrated with photo images from the TV series and excellent documentation.

Ralph Kirshbaum's 'authentic' set of the Bach *Cello suites* is also very fine. He also has the advantage of an absolutely natural recording which displays his full timbre to great advantage. He plays a Domenico Montagnana Venetian cello of 1729 and gives it a warmly vivid personality. Articulation in the dance movements is clear; expressive playing is without bulges and does not shirk a degree of vibrato. The performances have intensity, dedication, spontaneity and an intimate thoughtfulness which is genuinely moving.

No one artist holds all the secrets in this repertoire, but few succeed in producing such consistent beauty of tone as Maurice Gendron, with the digital remastering firming up the focus of what was originally an excellent and truthful analogue recording. His phrasing is unfailingly musical, and although these readings have a certain sobriety (save, perhaps, for No. 6 which has distinct flair) their restraint and fine judgement command admiration. At Philips's Duo price, they can be given a warm welcome back to the catalogue. As can be seen, these performances are also available on two separate bargain CDs, costing about the same as the Duo.

It was Casals who restored these pieces to the repertory after long decades of neglect. Some of the playing is far from flawless; passage-work is rushed or articulation uneven, and he is often wayward. But he brought to the *Cello suites* insights that remain unrivalled. Casals brings one closer to this music than do most of his rivals. The sound is inevitably dated but still comes over well in this transfer.

(Unaccompanied) *Cello suites Nos. 1–6, BWV 1007–12;* (i) *Viola da gamba sonatas Nos. 1–2, BWV 1027–8.*

(M) **(*) Mercury (IMS) 432 756-2 (2) [id.].
Janos Starker, (i) with György Sebök.

The Mercury set is not to be confused with the incandescent set Janos Starker made in the early days of mono LP (issued in the UK on the old Nixa label). These later performances come from 1963 and 1965 and are of great integrity and dedication, without having quite the same electric communication of the earlier recording. The two *Viola da gamba sonatas* are not ideally balanced and favour György Sebök's piano; though there is no question of his artistry, the actual sound of his instrument is a bit shallow and wanting in colour. Recommended, but not in preference to Fournier.

(Unaccompanied) *Cello suites Nos. 1 in G, BWV 1007; 3 in C, BWV 1009; 6 in D, BWV 1012.*

(N) (M) *** DG 463 024-2 [id.]. Pierre Fournier.

Fournier's performances are very distinguished indeed, and truthfully recorded. But the collector would be better advised to get the complete set (see below).

Musical offering, BWV 1079 (see also above).

(N) *** HM/BMG Dig. 05472 77307-2 [id.].
Barthold, Sigiswald, & Wieland Kuijken,
Robert Kohnen.

The Kuijkens give a virtually ideal chamber account of the *Musical offering*. With four period instruments taking individual parts (and each creating a timbre which is never in the least edgy or anaemic) the polyphony is absolutely clear, yet because of the warm acoustic, never clinical. After the harpsichord plays the opening *Ricercar a 3* the group joins together for the *Canon perpetua* on the King's theme, and then again for the *Ricercar a 6* and the *Trio sonata*. In between, the other canons are shared out between the players, who come together again for the closing *Canon perpetua*. The recording is most natural.

The Musical offering, BWV, 1079; Verschiedene (Diverse) Canons, BWV 1087.

(N) (M) ** DG Dig. 463 026-2 [id.]. Musica
Antiqua Köln, Reinhard Goebel.

There are some very good things here. The *Ricercars* open and close the work, and are played on the harpsichord by Henk Boum, an impressive artist who is somewhat austere in making no registration changes, but has a strong grasp of the architecture. Goebel places the *Canons* (which are finely done) together and successfully follows them with the *Trio sonatas*. However, these sonatas are the musical centre-piece of the work and Goebel's reading is too mannered and self-conscious (particularly in the slow movement) to carry a strong recommendation.

(i) *Partita for solo flute in A min., BWV 1013;* (i; ii) *Flute sonata* (for flute & harpsichord) *in A,*

BWV 1032; (iii; ii) *Viola da gamba sonata in G* (for viola da gamba & harpsichord);(iv; v) *Violin sonata* (for violin & harpsichord) *No. 1 in B min., BWV 1014;* (iv; ii; iii) *Violin sonata in G* (for violin and continuo), *BWV 1021.*

(N) (M) *** DG Dig. 463 025-3 [id.]. (i) Wilbert Hazelzet; (ii) Henk Bouman; (iii) Jaap Ter Linden, (iv) Reinhard Goebel; (v) Robert Hill.

In the works for flute, Wilbert Hazelzet plays with a gentle authority and sensitivity that are most persuasive, and he and his accomplished partner Henk Bouman, also bring unobtrusive virtuosity to the allegros.The Goebel/Hill partnership in the *Violin sonatas* give vigorous performances, pleasantly abrasive in violin tone, bringing dance-based movements in particular, vividly to life. Slow movements do not lack expressive feeling, and the sound is first rate.

Flute sonatas Nos. 1–6, BWV 1030–35; in G min., BWV 1020; Partita in A min. (for solo flute), *BWV 1013.*

(M) *** CRD CRD 3314/5 (2) [id.]. Stephen Preston, Trevor Pinnock, Dordi Savall.

Two of these *Sonatas*, BWV 1031 and 1033, are unauthenticated, but still contain attractive music. Using an authentic one-key instrument, Stephen Preston plays all six with a rare delicacy. Throughout, the continuo playing, led by Trevor Pinnock, is of the highest standard; for those willing to stretch to the expense of two premium-priced records, this is a clear first choice for this repertoire. This set now comes handsomely repackaged in a box.

Flute sonatas Nos. 1 in B min.; 2 in E flat; 3 in A; 4 in C; 5 in E min.; 6 in E, BWV 1030–35.

(BB) *** ASV Quicksilva CDQS 6108 [(M) id.]. William Bennett, George Malcolm, Michael Evans.

Flute sonatas (for flute and harpsichord) *Nos. 1 in B min., BWV 1030; 3 in A, BWV 1032; 5 in E min., BWV 1034; 6 in E, BWV 1035.*

(M) *** HM Suite Dig. HMT 790065 [id.]. Marc Beaucoudray, William Christie.

William Bennett uses a modern flute, and in the first three sonatas he and George Malcolm manage without the nicety of including a viola da gamba in the continuo. In *Sonatas Nos. 4–6* the two players are joined by Michael Evans and the bass is subtly but tangibly reinforced and filled out, though the balance remains just as impressive. The playing, as might be expected of these artists, has superb character: it is strong in personality yet does not lack finesse. Moreover it is strikingly alive and spontaneous and, since the CD transfer brings the most vivid presence without the sound being in the least overblown, this can be enthusiastically recommended at super-bargain price to all but those who demand the finer points of authenticity above all else. Bennett himself has made the reconstruction of the first movement of BWV 1032.

Those looking for period performances will surely be delighted with the Harmonia Mundi disc. Marc Beaucoudray makes the most delightful sounds on his baroque flute (not in the least watery), and the balance with William Christie's (Dowd) harpsichord could not be improved on. They play beautifully together, with great sensitivity and a true sense of baroque style; the result is altogether captivating. The acoustic, too, is ideally judged.

Flute sonatas Nos. 1 in B min.; 2 in E flat; 4 in C; 5 in E min.; 6 in E, BWV 1030–31; 1033–35; in G min., BWV 1020.

(N) *** RCA Dig. 09026 62555-2 [id.]. James Galway, Philip Moll, Sarah Cunningham.

Flute sonata No. 3 in A, BWV 1032; Partita in A min. (for solo flute), *BWV 1013; Musical offering, BWV 1079: Trio sonata in C min.; Trio sonatas Nos. 3 & 4 in G, BWV 1038–9.*

(N) *** RCA Dig. 09026 68182-2 [id.]. James Galway, Monica Huggett, Sarah Cunningham, Philip Moll.

James Galway has now progressed to using period instrumentalists as partners. He is a superb artist (witness the unsurpassed account of the *Solo Partita*) and his line in slow movements is exquisite. Vibrato is sparing and the flute timbre is refined, if obviously richer than an eighteenth-century instrument. The balance in the *Trio sonatas* (which are full of life) is first class, but in the works with continuo Galway tends to dominate the sound picture aurally, as well as musically. But who will grumble when he plays so beautifully, and his companions give excellent support; moreover these two CDs contain considerably more music than the competing CRD set above.

Flute sonatas Nos. 1, 3, 5, & 6, BWV 1030, 1032, 1034–5; Partita in A min. (for unaccompanied flute), *BWV 1013* (2 versions); *Concerto in D min.* (fragment) *for strings* (arr. BRUGGEN from BWV 1030).

(N) (B) ** Sony Seon SB2K 60718 (2) [id.]. Brüggen, Leonhardt, Bylsma; Kuijken Ens.

Brüggen's RCA set is a curiosity. He plays those four *Sonatas* which he considers authentic very beautifully, and the flute timbre is nicely in scale with the continuo. Then come two versions of the *Partita*, one for solo flute, the second with the movements divided up between flute and various stringed instruments. Lastly we are offered Brüggen's own arrangement for strings of part of the *Sonata*, BWV 1031, which he admits is sketchy and 'still leaves much to be desired'. The 1975 sound is very good.

Music for lute and guitar

Sonatas for solo guitar (trans. from *Unaccompanied Violin sonatas Nos. 1 in G min.; 2 in A min.; 3 in C, BWV 1001, 1003 & 1005*, arr. Barrueco).
(M) *** EMI CDM5 56416-2 [id.]. Manuel Barrueco (guitar).

Manuel Barrueco's guitar transcriptions of Bach's three *Sonatas for Unaccompanied Violin* are astonishingly successful. He makes them entirely his own, and such is the magnetism of this playing that, while under his spell, one almost forgets their original provenance. His technical mastery is matched by his sense of line and colour. The thoughtful improvisational feeling is very compelling. The fugues are beautifully clear, and his crisp articulation shows extraordinary control and unexaggerated virtuosity, to say nothing of a remarkable use of light and shade. In short, Barrueco is a true Bach player, and these performances are a joy to the ear, for the guitar is beautifully recorded.

Lute suites: in G min.; E min., C min., BWV 995/997; Prelude in C min.; Fugue in G min., BWV 999/1000.
(N) (M) ** DG Dig. 463 022-2 [id.]. Narciso Yepes (lute).

Yepes uses a baroque lute. He plays very musically and there is a good deal to enjoy here as the early 1970s analogue recording is excellent. However, guitar players do not always take easily to the lute, which employs a wholly different technique, and this playing does not have the same degree of lively communication of Yepes's earlier recordings of Bach on the guitar.

Lute suites transcribed for guitar

Lute suites (arranged for guitar) *Nos. 1–3, BWV 995–7. Prelude in C min.; Fugue in G min., BWV 999–1000.*
(B) *** Sony SBK 62972 [id.]. John Williams (guitar).

Lute suite No. 4, BWV 1006a; Prelude, fugue and allegro in E flat, BWV 998. (Unaccompanied) *Cello suite No. 3, BWV 1009: Bourrées Nos. 1–2.* (i) arr. guitar and organ: *Cantata No. 140: Chorale: Wachet Auf!; Fugue à la gigue in G, BWV 877; Italian concerto, BWV 971: Allegro. Trio sonata No. 6 in G, BWV 530; Violin sonata No. 4, BWV 1017: Adagio.*
(B) **(*) Sony Analogue/Dig. SBK 62973 [id.]. John Williams (guitar); (i) with Peter Hurford (organ).

John Williams shows a natural response to Bach, and his performances of the four *Lute suites* are among his finest records. The first of these two discs can be recommended unreservedly: the flair of his playing, with its rhythmic vitality and sense of colour, is always telling. The guitar is closely balanced but, when the volume is turned down, its image has a believable presence and background noise is not a problem.

The second disc opens with a most winning account of the *Fourth Suite* which includes a famous and catchy *Gavotte en Rondeau*, beloved of all guitarists from Segovia onwards. The work overall is of course a transcription of the *Partita in E major for unaccompanied violin* (BWV 1006). The transcriptions of the *Bourrées* from the *Cello suite* are effective enough; but not all listeners will care for the rest of the programme of rather contrived duets for guitar and organ (an unlikely combination), in spite of the distinguished presence of Peter Hurford and skilful balancing by the Sony engineers.

(i) *Lute suites Nos. 1 in E min., BWV 996; 2 in C min., BWV 997;* (ii) *Trio sonatas Nos. 1 in E flat, BWV 525; 5 in C, BWV 529* (ed. Bream).
(M) *** RCA 09026 61603-2 [id.]. Julian Bream (i) (guitar); (ii) (lute), George Malcolm.

This RCA compilation comes from records made between 1965 and 1969. The two *Lute suites* are played with great subtlety and mastery on the guitar; the *Trio sonatas* were originally written for organ; here they are heard on lute and harpsichord and are elegantly played and cleanly recorded within a convincing ambience. Perhaps the harpsichord is a little less well defined in the bass register than is ideal, but the effect is pleasingly transparent and intimate.

(i) *Oboe sonatas* (for oboe and harpsichord) *in G min., BWV 1020; in G min., BWV 1030b. Fugue on a theme of Albinoni in B min., BWV 951.*
(BB) **(*) DHM/BMG Baroque Esprit 05472 77440-2 [id.]. Michel Piguet, Colin Tilney – C. P. E. BACH: *Oboe sonata* **(*); W. F. BACH: *Polonaise in E flat.* ***

As can be seen above and below, these two sonatas are better known in their versions for violin (BWV 1020) and flute (BWV 1030). But they are certainly pleasing on the baroque oboe (especially the *Siciliana* slow movement of the latter). Michel Piguet's timbre is appealing, and it is given an expansive bloom by the resonant recording, although the close microphones (one can hear the player take a breath) mean a reduction in the effective dynamic range. The *Fugue* is used as a central interlude and seems to have been recorded at a different time, since the pitch is fractionally different; however, there are sufficiently long pauses to make this relatively unimportant.

6 (organ) *Trio sonatas: Nos. 1 in E flat* (arr. for 2 violins & continuo); *2 in C min.* (for violin, viola & continuo); *3 in D min.* (for oboe, violin & continuo); *4 in E min.* (for oboe d'amore, viola &

continuo); *5 in C* (for oboe, viola & continuo); *6 in G* (for 2 violins & continuo), *BWV 525–30*.
*** Hyperion Dig. CDA 666843 [id.]. King's Consort, Robert King.

Bach's Organ sonatas readily invite transcription, and Robert King makes a good case for presenting them in such arrangements as are offered here, all retaining the original keys. The baroque oboe and oboe d'amore suit Bach's invention especially well and the resulting ranges of colour are very appealing, giving this music a completely new dimension. The playing is joyous and lighthearted and always warm in spirit. First-class recording, too.

6 (organ) *Trio sonatas: Nos. 1 in B flat; 2 in E min.; 3 in G min.; 4 in E min.; 5 in F; 6 in C, BWV 525–30.*
*** Virgin Veritas/EMI (SIS) Dig. VC5 45192-2. Musica Pacifica.

Musica Pacifica is an excellent period-instrument group which is part of the San Francisco Early Music Society. Their arrangements of Bach's organ *Trio sonatas* necessitate transcriptions in order to place the upper voices in a suitable range for the recorder, partnered by the violin, with the cello given the upper bass lines and the harpsichord filling in the continuo. The effect here is admirably fresh; Judith Linsenberg, the recorder player who leads the ensemble, plays with fine spirit, while the liveliness of the allegros is matched by striking, often melancholic, expressive feeling in slow movements. The recording is first class, and this ranks as a fine alternative to the (differently scored) King's versions on Hyperion above.

Viola da gamba sonatas Nos. 1–3, BWV 1027–9.
*** Sony Dig. MK 37794 [id.]. Yo-Yo Ma (cello), Kenneth Cooper.
*** DG Dig. 415 471-2 [id.]. Mischa Maisky (cello), Martha Argerich (piano).
*** Virgin Veritas/EMI (SIS) VER5 61291-2 [EMI CDM 61291]. Jordi Savall (viola da gamba), Ton Koopman (harpsichord).
(M) *** HM/BMG GD 77044 [77044-2-RG]. Wieland Kuijken (cello), Gustav Leonhardt.

Yo-Yo Ma plays with great eloquence and natural feeling. His tone is warm and refined and his technical command remains, as ever, irreproachable. Kenneth Cooper is a splendid partner.

Mischa Maisky is also a highly expressive cellist and he opts for the piano – successfully, for Martha Argerich is a Bach player of the first order. In fact the sonority of the cello and the modern piano seems a happier marriage than the compromise Ma and Cooper adopt. A most enjoyable account for collectors who do not care for period instruments.

It is good to have an outstanding version on period instruments. While the timbre of the viola da gamba may perhaps be an acquired taste, Jordi Savall certainly makes his instrument sing in slow movements, and Ton Koopman is an excellent partner. With allegros as lively as you could wish the added advantage here is the transparency of the contrapuntal lines, when the two instruments are so well and naturally balanced.

Kuijken and Leonhardt are both sensitive and scholarly musicians. This is the most authentic cello account to have appeared on the market in recent years and is among the most rewarding.

(Unaccompanied) *Violin sonatas Nos. 1–3, BWV 1001, 1003 & 1005; Violin partitas Nos. 1–3, BWV 1002, 1004 & 1006.*
(N) (M) *** Audivis Valois V 4477 (2) Sándor Végh.
✿ *** EMI Dig. CDS7 49483-2 (2) [id.]. Itzhak Perlman.
(M) *** DG 457 701-2 (2) [id.]. Nathan Milstein.
*** Testament SBT 2090 (2) [id.]. Ida Haendel.
(B) *** Ph. Duo 438 736-2 (2) [id.]. Arthur Grumiaux.
(B) *** DG Double 453 004-2 (2) [id.]. Henryk Szeryng.
(M) (***) Sony mono MP2K 46721 (2) [id.]. Henryk Szeryng.
(M) *** HM/BMG GD 77043 (2) [77043-2-RG]. Sigiswald Kuijken.
(N) *(*) Virgin Veritas/EMI Dig. VCD 5 45205-2 (2) [id.]. Monica Huggett.
(N) *(*) Hänssler Dig. 92.119 (2) [id.]. Dimitry Sitkovetsky.
(N) (BB) * Naxos Dig. 8.554422/23 (available separately) Lucy van Dael.

Sándor Végh's set ranks with the very finest. His playing has an improvisational feel from the very opening of the *First Sonata*, which is not to say that it is undisciplined in the swifter-running passages, or self-seeking in the reflective moments, but thoughtful and searching. The *D minor Partita* shows how deep Végh is inside this music, and in the great *Chaconne* his linear ebb and flow and subtle dynamic variations are made to sound seemingly spontaneous. The *Adagio* of the *C major* which follows is musingly withdrawn. The 1971 analogue recording is remarkable true and faithful, not too closely observed.

The range of tone in Perlman's playing adds to the power of these performances, infectiously rhythmic in dance movements but conveying the intensity of live performance in the great slow movements in hushed playing of great refinement. Some may still seek a greater sense of struggle conveyed in order to bring out the full depth of the writing, but the sense of spontaneity, of the player's own enjoyment in the music, make this set a unique, revelatory experience.

Milstein's set from the mid-1970s remains among the most satisfying of all versions. Every phrase is beautifully shaped, there is a highly developed feeling for line, and these performances have an aristocratic poise and a classical finesse which is very satisfying. This seems an admirable choice for reissue in DG's series of Originals.

Though Ida Haendel's speeds are exceptionally broad, her playing is magnetic, making one welcome her decision to observe all repeats. She takes a full 18 minutes over the great *Chaconne* of the *D minor Partita*, but the strong, steady pacing means that the build-up is all the more powerful, with counterpoint clearly defined, helped by vividly immediate recording.

Arthur Grumiaux strikes just the right balance between expressive feeling and purity of style. Some may prefer a rhythmically freer, more charismatic approach, as with Perlman and Milstein for instance; but Grumiaux's simplicity of manner, without exaggerated temperament, lets the music unfold naturally, and his readings of all six works are the product of superlative technique and a refined musical intellect. At bargain price this set is very tempting.

Henryk Szeryng's tone has never been caught before on record with such leonine fullness and beauty. The technical mastery and polish are quite remarkable, his intonation flawless. These performances are rhythmically free and full of subtle touches of baroque light and shade; there is a thoughtful, improvisatory feeling too, heard at its most impressive in Szeryng's imaginative and never predictable progress through the famous *Chaconne* which climaxes BWV 1004.

Szeryng's earlier set was recorded in mono in the mid-1960s. The recording is equally real and present and the performances are just as fresh, never identical but following the same general pattern of interpretation. One certainly would not say that generally one performance is finer than the other, both having much refreshment to offer, yet when one comes to the famous *Chaconne* of the *D minor Partita* there is no question that the earlier account is seemingly more spontaneous.

Kuijken's accounts are as little painful or scratchy as you are ever likely to get in the authentic field and are of the highest quality.

Monica Huggett plays her period instrument with skill and accuracy, but fails to communicate the inner world of this music. The result is curiously literal and uninvolving. Although a piece like the fourth movement *Double* of the *B minor Partita* offers a beautifully articulated stream of notes, which is technically very impressive, the famous *Chaconne* from the *D minor Partita* is made to sound didactic.

Sitkovetsky has a beautiful tone and his polished fluency in Bach's more virtuosic running passages is technically and musically admirable. But everything is too easygoing, there is no sense of grip, of difficulties being surmounted, of a strong forward pulse. The great *Chaconne* proceeds in a totally relaxed way and feeling of real concentration only appears near the end. The recording cannot be faulted in its naturalness.

Lucy van Dael plays a baroque instrument, but is not really any more successful. After opening the *Adagio* of the *G minor Sonata* impulsively, her style settles down, but the effect is too often angular, her timbre plangent, and there is a profusion of accents. The *Allemanda* which opens the *D minor Partita* brings more of an improvisational feeling, and the *Giga* is fluently appealing. The great *Chaconne* is presented boldly and accurately, and with no lack of light and shade. The performance is not without ongoing tension, but conveys the detail without a passionate impulse of the kind that made Heifetz's account unforgettable. The Naxos recording is faithful.

(Unaccompanied) *Violin partitas Nos. 2, BWV 1004* (complete); *3* (*Minuets I & II* only), *BWV 1006; Violin sonatas Nos. 1, BWV 1001; 3, BWV 1005* (complete); (i) *English suite No. 3 in E, BWV 808: Sarabande; Gavottes Nos. I & II.*
(***) EMI (SIS) mono CDH7 64492-2 [id.].
Heifetz, (i) with Arpad Sándor.

Heifetz's Bach was by no means romantic, indeed this is thoughtfully inspirational playing, but his chimerical bowing produces more variety of timbre and subtlety of dynamic shading in the *Allemanda* and *Giga* of the *D minor Partita* than would have been likely or possible in Bach's time, while the great *Chaconne* has wonderful detail, without losing strength. Such is the spontaneity of effect that the result gives enormous pleasure, with the *Giga* running like quicksilver. The transfer is bright but truthful: the violin image is real if the volume level is not set too high.

Violin sonatas (for violin and harpsichord) *Nos. 1–6, BWV 1014–19.*
(M) *** HM/BMG GD 77170 (2) [77170-2-RG].
Sigiswald Kuijken, Gustav Leonhardt.

Violin sonatas Nos. 1–6, BWV 1014–19; 1019a; Sonatas for violin and continuo, BWV 1020–24.
✿ (B) *** Ph. Duo 454 011-2 (2) [id.]. Arthur Grumiaux, Christiane Jaccottet, Philippe Mermoud (in *BWV 1021 & 1023*).
(N) *(*) Hänssler Dig. 92.122 [id.]. Dimitry Sitkovetsky, Robert Hill (harpsichord).

Violin sonatas (for violin and harpsichord) *Nos. 1–6, BWV 1014–19; Sonatas for violin and continuo, BWV 1021, 1023 & 1024; Fugue in G min., BWV 1021.*
(N) (M) **(*) Hyperion Dyad Dig. CDD 22025 (2) [id.]. Monica Huggett, Paul Nicholson.

Violin and harpsichord sonatas Nos. 1–6, BWV 1014–19; Alternative movements, *BWV 1019a*; (i) *Sonatas for violin and continuo, BWV 1021 & BWV 1023.*
*** Chandos Dig. CHAN 0603 (2) [id.].

Catherine Mackintosh, Maggie Cole; (i) with Jennifer Ward Clarke.

The Bach *Sonatas for violin and harpsichord* and for *violin and continuo* are marvellously played, with all the beauty of tone and line for which Grumiaux is renowned; they have great vitality too. His admirable partner is Christiane Jaccottet, and in BWV 1021 and 1023 Philippe Mermoud (cello) joins the continuo. There is endless treasure to be discovered here, particularly when the music-making is so serenely communicative.

However, it is good to welcome a superb modern recording of these consistently refreshing and melodically appealing works, authentically balanced and beautifully played on period instruments. Hitherto we have favoured Siegfried Kuijken and Gustav Leonhardt, and their analogue set remains highly recommendable at mid-price. But these Chandos versions are even more attractive. Catherine Mackintosh uses a baroque violin, but her timbre is full, her lyrical line flows with an affecting sensitivity, and she brings fine musicianship to her phrasing and much subtlety in the matter of light and shade. Articulation in allegros is exhilaratingly crisp and clean, and both players express their joy in the music. Maggie Cole's persuasive contribution is well in the picture, and the balance between violin and double-manual harpsichord could hardly be managed more adroitly, with the players set slightly back within a pleasingly resonant – but not too resonant – ambience. The first disc opens with one of Bach's two *Sonatas for violin and continuo* (BWV 1021), in which Jennifer Ward Clarke's cello contribution adds to the interest and sonority of the music. Our special allegiance to the Grumiaux performances of the same music on modern instruments remains undiminished, and their Philips Duo costs half as much as the Chandos set. But these new interpretations are very stimulating.

Sigiswald Kuijken uses a baroque violin, and both he and Gustav Leonhardt give us playing of rare eloquence. This reissue is an admirable example of the claims of authenticity and musical feeling pulling together rather than apart. This is a wholly delightful set and the transparency of the sound is especially appealing.

It was a pity that the Hyperion Dyad set had to begin with the *Fugue in G minor*, which is much less inviting a sound than the glorious opening *Adagio* of the *First Violin sonata* (BWV 1014), which Monica Huggett plays exquisitely, as she does the opening *Dolce* of No. 2 *in A major*. Clearly these marvellous works strike a chord in her sensibility and she gives a remarkably spirited display of bravura in the first movement *Allegro* of the *Sonata with continuo in E minor* (BWV 1023). One simply has to come to terms with her characteristic timbre, with its thinness (some would say edginess) on top. Yet in the dancing allegros she brings out all the music's joy. The violin is beautifully balanced with Paul Nicholson's sensitive harpsichord backing, and where appropriate, Richard Tunnicliffe's busy cello.

As in his set of the *Solo Violin sonatas* and *Partitas*, Sitkovetsky plays with great fluency and finish, and his tone is consistently easy on the ear. But his use of vibrato and indulgently relaxed, lyrical manner is out of style, and too often the musical flow is barely short of flabbiness. Robert Hill gives him fine support and the recording is truthful and well balanced, but this cannot compete with Grumiaux among modern instrument versions.

(Unaccompanied) *Violin Sonatas Nos. 1 in G min., BWV 1001; 2 in D min., BWV 1004; Partita No, 2 in D min., BWV 1006.*

(N) (M) ** DG Dig. 463 023-2 [id.]. Shlomo Mintz.

While Mintz takes all the technical difficulties in his stride, and his playing has youthful vitality and power, the famous *Chaconne* in the *D minor Partita* finds him wanting. Intonation is generally secure, but goes seriously awry in the middle of the *G minor Fugue*. The recording has a vivid presence, but the ear is conscious of the microphones.

KEYBOARD MUSIC

'Bach and Tureck at home' (A birthday offering): (i) *Adagio in G, BWV 968; Aria and 10 variations in the Italian style, BWV 989; Capriccio on the departure of a beloved brother, BWV 992; Chromatic fantasia and fugue, BWV 903; Fantasia, adagio and fugue in D, BWV 912; The Well-tempered clavier, Book 1: Prelude & fugue in B flat, BWV 866.* (ii) *English suite No. 3 in G min., BWV 808; Italian concerto, BWV 971; Sonata in D min., BWV 964* (trans. from Unaccompanied *Violin sonata No. 2 in A min., BWV 1003*); *Well-tempered clavier, Book 1: Preludes & fugues: in C min; in C, BWV 847–8; Book 2: Preludes & fugues in C sharp, BWV 872; in G, BWV 884.* (iii) *Goldberg variations, BWV 988;* (iv) *Partitas Nos. 1 in B flat, BWV 825; 2 in C min., BWV 826; 6 in E min., BWV 830.*

❁ *** (i) VAIA 1041; (ii) VAIA 1051; (iii) VAIA 1029; (iv) VAIA 1040 (available separately). Rosalyn Tureck (piano).

Rosalyn Tureck's Bach playing is legendary, and the performances here show that her keyboard command and fluent sense of Bach style are as remarkable as ever. Miss Tureck uses a wide dynamic and expressive range with consummate artistry, her decoration always adds to the musical effect, and she makes us feel that Bach's keyboard music could be played in no other way than this – the hallmark of a great artist.

English suite No. 3 in G min., BWV 808; 6 Preludes, BWV 933/938, Sonata in D min., BWV 964 (arr. of Unaccompanied Violin sonata, BWV 1003). Well-Tempered Clavier: Preludes and fugues, BWV 855, 880, & 849).
(N) (***) VAI mono VAIA 1085 [id.]. Rosalyn Tureck (piano).

Recorded (on 78s) at a live event in New York in 1948, this Bach recital shows the young Tureck as intimately discerning and already completely at home on the piano in Bach's keyboard world. She plays very intimately, and the recording is confined, but her thoughtfulness is magnetic throughout and one soon forgets the limited upper range of the sound. She plays the arrangement of the *Unaccompanied violin sonata* with a very personal improvisational freedom, making it sound like keyboard music; her account of the *Andante* is hauntingly other-worldly. Unfortunately the notes tell the collector little or nothing about the music.

Chromatic fantasia and fugue, BWV 903; Italian concerto, BWV 971; Well-tempered Clavier, Book I: Preludes and fugues: in D, BWV 850; in F sharp, BWV 858; in B flat, BWV 866; in C sharp, BWV 848. Book II: Preludes and fugues: in C min., BWV 871; in C sharp, BWV 872; in G, BWV 884; in G min., BWV 885; in A min., BWV 903. Encore: Goldberg variations: Variation No. 29.
*** VAI Audio VAIA 1139 [id.]. Rosalyn Tureck (harpsichord).

This superb harpsichord recital was recorded live in 1981 at the Metropolitan Museum of Art, New York. The balance is very close, but the sharp focus of the instrument suits Tureck's amazingly clean articulation. She opens with direct, considered performances of five *Preludes and fugues* from Book II of the *Well-tempered Clavier*; then, after a dazzling account of the *Chromatic fantasia* and a reflective fugue, she moves back to give us four *Preludes and fugues* from Book I, of which the opening *D major* brings the most remarkable bravura articulation, echoed in the equally sparkling *B flat major*; the fugues, however, unfold precisely. Then comes a buoyant *Italian concerto* with a touchingly thoughtful central Andante. The ear soon adjusts to the dry, close, slighty tinkly harpsichord image.

'*Live at St Petersburg*': *Adagio in G, BWV 968; Aria and 10 variations in the Italian style, BWV 989; Capriccio on the departure of a beloved brother, BWV 992; Chromatic fantasia and fugue in D min., BWV 903; Partita No. 2 in C min., BWV 826;Prelude in E flat min., BWV 853; Musette in D (S. Anh. 126).*
(N) **(*) VAI Dig. VAIA 1131 [id.]. Rosalyn Tureck (piano).

Although she was returning to the city where she gave her début recital at the age of nine and received a rapturous reception, there remains a slight element of disappointment about Tureck's 1995 Russian recital. She does not seem always to relax here as much as usual and, although the *Chromatic fantasia* is very commanding indeed, and the *Partita* is full of characteristic insights (as are the Italianate variations), the bold, truthful, but closely observed digital sound seems at times to bring an element of didacticism to her presentation, notably so in the lightweight *Capriccio*. However Tureck's full charisma returns in the closing *Prelude* and *Musette*, which are most movingly played. The documentation concentrates on the occasion and says little about the music.

(i) *The Art of Fugue, BWV 1080;* (ii) *Applicato in C, BWV 994; Aria & 10 Variations in the Italian style; Chorale: Joy and peace, BWV 512; Fantasia in G min., BWV 917; Invention in C, BWV 772 & 772a* (1720 & 1723 versions); *Italian concerto, BWV 971; Marches: in D and E flat, BWV Anh. 122 & 127; Musette in D, BWV Anh. 126; 2 Minuets in G, BWV Anh. 115–16; Polonaise in F, BWV Anh. 117a; Prelude and fugue in A min., BWV 895; Suite in F, BWV 623* (incomplete). TELEMANN: *Suite in A, BWV 824* (wrongly attributed to J. S. B.).
(B) *** Sony SB2K 63231 [S2K 63231]. (i) Charles Rosen; (ii) Rosalyn Tureck (piano).

Charles Rosen's superb account of *The Art of Fugue* is one of the great achievements of Bach keyboard recording. The use of a modern piano may appear controversial, but Rosen justifies his choice by his manner of playing, neutralizing any unwanted romantic overtones. The authority of his performance is remarkable and the depth of thought that lies behind the playing creates a satisfying sense of architecture. The 1967 recording is firm and clear, just right for such an exposition, and this performance has total mastery .

Miss Tureck's sound-world is firmly centred in the modern piano, and she makes a perfect foil for Rosen in offering an essentially lightweight programme, mainly of short keyboard vignettes in which we can hear Bach relaxing and enjoying himself. The little *F major Suite* with its thoughtful central *Sarabande* and joyous closing *Gigue* show the light and shade of this pianism at its most winning, as does its equally charming companion in A major. This was wrongly attributed, and is now thought to be by Telemann, and again it brings a delectable closing *Gigue*. One of the highlights of the recital is the slightly dolorous *Aria in the Italian style*, followed by ten crisply diverting variations, with the tenth magically reprising the gentle mood of the opening. Tureck's playing not only shows the utmost felicity but also sensitive control of dynamic contrast. The 1981 digital recording is rather forward but not shallow; the *Italian concerto* dates from 1979 and the sound is more clattery, less well focused. But this set is not to be missed by anyone who enjoys hearing Bach on the piano, and it is a great bargain.

The Art of fugue, BWV 1080 (see also string quartet and orchestral versions).
(N) *** Hänssler Dig. CD 92.134 (2) [id.]. Robert Hill.
*** HM HMC 901169/70 [id.]. Davitt Moroney (harpsichord).
(N) *** Collins Dig. 7043-2 (2) [id.]. Joanna MacGregor (piano) – NANCARROW: *Canons and studies*. ***
(N) *** MusicMasters Dig. 1612 67173-2 [id.]. Vladimir Feltsman.

Without being in the least didactic – indeed his ongoing progress has a relaxed flexibility – Robert Hill lays out Bach's fugal progression in front of the listener with admirable clarity and concern for the contrapuntal detail, and he varies tempi with excellent judgement to keep the music continually alive. He is particularly buoyant in each of the *Contrapuncti inversus*, then plays the *Canons* more deliberately, ending his sequence with the *Duet Fugue* in which he is joined by Michael Behringer. As an appendix he offers four contrapuncti and the *Augmented Canon in contrary motion* from Bach's early draft (BWV 1080a). The harpsichord itself has a fine, strong personality and is recorded in a warm acoustic, which yet never blurs the interplay of the part-writing.

Davitt Moroney's account commands not only the intellectual side of the work but also the aesthetic, and his musicianship is second to none.

Those preferring a piano version will find Joanna MacGregor's progress through Bach's great contrapuntal odyssey unerring in conveying the music's purpose, while using a wide pianistic expressive range, varying dynamics and timbre to convey what she sees as the work's underlying meditative nature. She uses the Henle Edition, which groups the canons together centrally, placing them after the extended climactic Contrapunctus 13. The closing four-handed mirror fugue is achieved by multi-tracking. With a piano image which is pleasingly full and natural, the result is very satisfying. Because the performance runs just beyond 80 minutes, it spreads on to a second disc; however, that means the set includes some of the dazzling contrapuntal and canonic excursions of Colin Nancarrow.

Although he begins gently, Vladimir Feltsman's articulation is at times bolder than MacGregor, although it is never hard-edged. He intersperses the canons individually within the body of the work and makes the very most of dynamic contrast. Yet he can be thoughtfully meditative, as in the triple fugue (which Bach left unfinished) which is very measured indeed, and is followed by a 54-second pause before the infectious closing mirror fugue, using the duet version. With an overall timing which is considerably longer than MacGregor's, Feltsman's interpretation is well thought-out and thoroughly convincing. He is very well recorded but offers no coupling.

The Art of fugue, BWV 1080; Italian concerto, BWV 971; Partita in B min., BWV 831; Prelude, fugue and allegro in E flat, BWV 998.
(M) *** HM/BMG GD 77013 (2) [77013-2-RG]. Gustav Leonhardt (harpsichord).

Under the fingers of Leonhardt every strand in the texture emerges with clarity and every phrase is allowed to speak for itself. This is a very impressive and rewarding set, well recorded and produced.

The Art of fugue, BWV 1080 (version for two harpsichords).
(M) *** Erato/Warner Dig. 0630 16173-2. Ton Koopman, Tini Mathot (harpsichords).

Koopman chooses a pair of instruments made by Willem Kroesbergen of Utrecht, himself leading with a copy of a Rückers, while his colleague, Tini Mathot, uses another modern copy, but of a Couchet. The partnership works well: pacing is well judged and contrapuntal detail is clear, yet within a not too dry acoustic. The approach is didactic, but by no means rigid.

Capriccio on the departure of a beloved brother in B flat, BWV 992. Chaconne in D min. (from Partita No. 2 for violin, BWV 1004); Choral preludes: Watchet auf, ruft uns die Stimme, BWV 645; Nun komm, der Heiden Heiland, BWV 659; Ich ruf zu dir, Herr, BWV 639; Jesu bleibet meine Freude (No. 10 from Cantata No. 147); Chromatic fantasia and fugue in D min., BWV 903; Four duets, BWV 802-805; Fantasia in C min., BWV 906. Fugue in G min., BWV 578; Inventions and sinfonias, BWV 772-801. Italian concerto in F, BWV 971. Siciliano in G min., (from flute sonata, BWV 1031); Toccata and fugue in D min., BWV 565.
(N) **(*) Olympia (i) Dig/Analogue OCD 627(3) [id.]. Tatiana Nikolayeva.

As is well known, it was Tatiana Nikolayeva's Bach playing that inspired Shostakovich to compose his *24 Preludes and fugues*, and this collection of her Bach performances recorded at various times gives a fairly representative picture of her artistry. Her Bach is commanding, old-fashioned perhaps, but undoubtedly masterly. She has poise, authority and an expressive quality that shines through. The sound, as one might expect, is variable in quality.

Chaconne in D min. (arr. Busoni from (unaccompanied) *Violin partita No. 2 in D min., BWV 1004*).
(M) *** RCA 09026 62590-2 [id.]. Artur Rubinstein – FRANCK: *Prelude, chorale and fugue* *** (with LISZT: *Piano sonata in B min.* **(*)).

Rubinstein recorded this performance in Rome in 1970, when he was already in his eighties, but the freshness and spirit are a delight. The transfer of the 1970 recording is just a little clangy, but not unpleasantly so.

Chorale preludes: Ich ruf' zu dir, BWV 639; Nun komm' der Heiden Heiland, BWV 659 (both arr. Busoni); *Chromatic fantasia and fugue in D min., BWV 903; Fantasia and fugue in A min., BWV 904; Italian concerto in F, BWV 971; Fantasia in A min., BWV 922.*
(M) *** Ph. 454 409-2; 442 400-2. Alfred Brendel (piano).

Brendel's performances are of the old school, with no attempt to strive after harpsichord effects, and with every piece creating a sound-world of its own. The *Italian concerto* is particularly imposing, with a finely sustained sense of line and beautifully articulated rhythms. The recording is in every way truthful and present, bringing the grand piano very much into the living-room before one's very eyes. Masterly. This disc is currently available on two different catalogue numbers.

Chromatic fantasia and fugue, BWV 903; 4 Duets, BWV 802–5; English suites Nos. 1–6, BWV 806–11; Goldberg variations, BWV 988; 2- & 3-Part Inventions, BWV 772a–786; French suites Nos. 1–6, BWV 812–17; Partitas Nos. 1–6 BWV 825–30; Partita in B min., BWV 831; Well-tempered Clavier, Books I–II, Preludes and fugues Nos. 1–48, BWV 846–93.
(B) *** Decca Dig. 452 279-2 (12) [(M) id. import]. András Schiff (piano).

András Schiff recorded Bach's major keyboard works for Decca over a decade between 1982 and 1991, and it is perhaps remarkable that, during an era when original instruments are all the rage, he has made such a convincing case for recording this music on the piano. Moreover he makes no apologies for the range of dynamic and colour that the modern keyboard can command and of which Bach can have had no inkling. Yet Schiff's playing is so stylish, his expressive phrasing and rubato so natural, the presentation so spontaneous, that the critical listener is disarmed and is encouraged to sit back and simply enjoy the music. Most of these recordings are available separately; only in the *Inventions* is there a suspicion that Schiff's expressive freedom approaches the outer boundaries of what is permissible, and even here the musical flow remains convincing. The Decca recording, natural and not too resonant, is surely ideal for such repertoire.

Chromatic fantasia and fugue, BWV 903; Goldberg variations, BWV 988; Italian concerto in F, BWV 971; Partita No. 1 in B flat, BWV 825; Prelude, fugue and allegro, BWV 998; Toccata, adagio and fugue, BWV 916.
(N) (BB) *** Virgin Veritas/EMI Dig. VBD5 61555-2 (2) [id.]. Maggie Cole (harpsichord).

Maggie Cole plays the *Goldberg variations* on a copy by Andrew Warlick of a harpsichord by J. C. Goujon of 1749. She is recorded with great clarity; as so often, the playback level needs to be reduced if a truthful and realistic effect is to be made. Her playing is completely straightforward and she holds the listener's interest throughout. The remaining items make up Maggie Cole's first solo recital, and very good it is too. She uses a Ruckers harpsichord of 1612 from the Royal Collection, tuned in unequal temperament. Again, her playing is splendidly unfussy, free from interpretative mannerisms and not bound by rigid rhythms; her virtuosity in the *Chromatic fantasia and fugue* seems effortless and unforced, and there is an agreeable naturalness about the whole recital. The recording is thoroughly faithful and the acoustic lively, if small.

Chromatic fantasia and fugue in D min., BWV 903; 4 Duets, BWV 802–5; Italian concerto in F, BWV 971; Partita in B min., BWV 831.
✽ *** O-L (IMS) Dig. 433 054-2 [id.]. Christophe Rousset (harpsichord).

Christophe Rousset's playing combines the selfless authority and scholarly dedication of such artists as Leonhardt and Gilbert with the flair and imagination of younger players, and all the performances here have a taste and musical vitality that reward the listener.

Chromatic fantasia and fugue in D min., BWV 903; Fantasia in C min., BWV 908; Fugue in A min., BWV 944; Italian concerto in F, BWV 971; Suites: in C min. (arr. from *Lute suite, BWV 995*); *in E flat* (arr. from *Cello suite No. 4, BWV 1010*); *Toccatas: in D, BWV 912; in D min., BWV 913.*
(N) (B) ** Sony/Seon SB2K 60375 [id.]. Gustav Leonhardt (harpsichord).

A good example of Leonhardt's playing from the late 1970s. He uses a highly suitable early eighteenth-century instrument made by Christian Zell, and is well balanced and recorded. But the two arranged suites are the least attractive performances here and all the rest could have been easily fitted on to a single CD. The pair of *Toccatas* is very successful, as on the whole is the *Italian concerto*, while the *Chromatic fantasia* shows him at his most digitally dextrous.

Chromatic fantasia and fugue in D min., BWV 903; French suite No. 5 in G, BWV 816; Italian concerto in F, BWV 971; A Musical offering, BWV 1079: Ricercar; Toccata in G, BWV 916.
(M) *** Erato/Warner Dig. 0630 16171-2. Ton Koopman (harpsichord).

Koopman is at his liveliest here, particularly in the brilliant *Chromatic fantasia*. The *French suite*, bright and brisk except for the thoughtful *Loure*, has plenty of character, and the *Italian Concerto* comes off equally vividly, helped by the clean projection of the Dutch harpsichord, built by Willem Kroesbergen of Utrecht, which Koopman is using for his Bach series.

Chromatic fantasia and fugue, BWV 903; Partitas: Nos. 1 in B flat, BWV 825; in B min., BWV 831; Toccata in D min., BWV 913.
(N) (M) **(*) DG Analogue/Dig. 463 018-2 Trevor Pinnock (harpsichord).

Trevor Pinnock's stylistic sensibility is matched by his technical expertise and there is no doubt that his explosive burst of bravura at the opening of the *Chromatic fantasia* is exciting. Sometimes his approach seems too literal, but at others he allows himself more expressive latitude, notably so in the *B minor Partita*, recorded. The playing is always rhythmically alive, but the close recording of the harpsichord and the high level combine to create a somewhat unrelenting dynamic level, without a great deal of light and shade, and the harpsichord timbre is metallic.

Concerto in G (arr. from music by an unknown composer), *BMV 597; Fantasia in C min., BWV 906; Partita in B min. (Overture in the French style), BWV; Toccata in F sharp min., BWV 910.*
(N) (M) **(*) Mercury 434 395-2 [id.]. Rafael Puyana (Pleyel harpsichord) – J. C. BACH: *Duet in A.*; W. F. BACH: *Concerto a dui cembali concertati.* **(*)

Rafael Puyana was a pupil of Landowska and under her influence he favoured a large-scale Pleyel harpsichord which produces a range of sound far beyond anything Bach would have known. But like his mentor, Puyana plays it with great panache and the great *B minor Partita* responds readily to his exuberant virtuosity, especially so in the paired *Bourrées*, where he so effectively changes registration. Some ears will find this kind of Bach playing too overwhelming, particular in his turbulent account of the *Fantasia in C minor*. But the *Concerto by an unknown composer* makes an engaging interlude before the *F sharp minor Toccata*, which readily yields to Puyana's spontaneous vigour, with full opportunities taken to include light and shade in the most imaginative way, only possible with an instrument of this kind. However, as ever, it is important not to set the volume control too high! The couplings are also of considerable interest.

4 Duets, BWV 802/4; English suite No. 6 in D min., BWV 811; Italian concerto in F, BWV 971; Toccata in C min., BWV 911.
(N) (M) *** DG Dig. 463 021-2 [id.]. Angela Hewitt (piano).

In both the *Italian concerto* and the *English suite*, Angela Hewitt's playing is enormously alive and stimulating. Textures are clean, with every strand in perfect focus and every phrase clearly articulated. She plays with vital imaginative resource, totally free from any idiosyncrasy and affectation. The piano is beautifully captured on this recording, which must be numbered as one of the most successful DG have given us, with fresh, lifelike sound and vivid presence.

English suites Nos. 1–6, BWV 806–11.
(N) *** Sony Dig. SK 60276 (Nos. 1, 3 & 6); SK 60277 (Nos.2, 4, & 5) [id.]. Murray Perahia (piano).
*** Decca Dig. 421 640-2 (2) [id.]. András Schiff (piano).
(B) *** Sony Seon S2BK 62949 [S2K 62949]. Gustav Leonhardt (harpsichord).

As can be seen Murray Perahia recorded the *English suites* in two groups, a year apart in La Chaux-de-Fonds, Switzerland in July 1997 and 1998. In his notes he comments on his response to Bach's polyphony as 'a coherent musical flow', with the 'horizontal and vertical elements of the music thus unified'. But in his hands the forward flow is never in the least didactic, but a living thing in itself, and the listener is always made conscious of the richness of the underlying harmony, especially in the *Sarabandes*, which are played very beautifully indeed. The lighter dance movements have a refreshing lightness of articulation, with the decoration made to seem integral. Perahia's mastery is such that while this is personalized Bach, using a full range of pianistic colour with a disarming naturalness, there is never any suggestion of self-awareness.

Schiff is straightforward, finely articulated, rhythmically supple and vital. Ornamentation is stylishly and sensibly observed. Everything is very alive, without being in the least over-projected or exaggerated in any way. The Decca recording is altogether natural and present.

Leonhardt uses a Skrowroneck harpsichord, vividly recorded, and if the volume level is set back a little the effect is very convincing, for the church acoustic is pleasing. At his best, Leonhardt combines scholarship and artistry, and his learning seldom inhibits his natural musical instincts. The music flows freshly and expansively, even if he is not equally inspired in every movement. He is inconsistent in the matter of repeats, sometimes observing them throughout, sometimes not. But this is a rewarding venture, well worth its modest price.

English suites Nos. 2 in A min.; 3 in G min., BWV 807–8.
(M) *** DG (IMS) Dig. 445 573-2. Ivo Pogorelich (piano) (with Domenico SCARLATTI: *Keyboard sonatas Kk. 87, 135, 380 & 450* ***).

The young Yugoslav pianist plays both *Suites* with a welcome absence of affectation. It is all beautifully articulate and fresh. Moreover, to make this reissue even more attractive, DG have added four well-chosen keyboard sonatas of Domenico Scarlatti, which also show this artist at his most perceptive. The recording is one of DG's best, with natural piano-sound and an excellent sense of presence.

English suite No. 2 in A min., BWV 807; Partita No. 2 in C min., BWV 826; Toccata in C min., BWV 911.
(M) *** DG 423 880-2. Martha Argerich (piano).

Martha Argerich's playing is alive and keenly rhythmic but also wonderfully flexible and rich in colour. She is very well recorded.

French suites Nos. 1–6, BWV 812–17.
*** Erato/Warner Dig. 0630 16172-2 [id.]. Ton Koopman (harpsichord).
*** DG Dig. 445 840-2 [id.]. Andrei Gavrilov (piano).
**(*) Collins Dig. 1371-2 [id.]. Joanna MacGregor (piano).
(N) (B) **(*) Sony Seon SBK 60717 [id.]. Gustav Leonhardt (harpsichord).

French suites Nos. 1–6, BWV 812–17 (including 3 additional movements); *18 Little Preludes, BWV 924–8; 930; 933–43; 999; Prelude and fugue in A min., BWV 894; Sonata in D min., BWV 964.*
*** Hyperion Dig. CDA 67121/2 [id.]. Angela Hewitt (piano).

Readers who enjoy Bach on the piano but who do not welcome a nineteenth-century approach will warm to Angela Hewitt's set of the *French suites*. We have had good accounts of them in recent years, most notably Gavrilov's excellent DG set. However, Angela Hewitt, who made her CD début on DG, need not fear any comparison. Her playing is informed by an intelligence and musicianship that are refreshing. Whether in the *Preludes*, written for Wilhelm Friedemann, or the suites themselves she displays an imaginative vitality of a high order. The recorded sound is very natural.

Ton Koopman fits all six *French suites* on to a single, 70-minute CD. He uses a copy of a Ruckers to admirable effect and these performances are stimulatingly rhythmic, exciting and thoughtful by turns. The best-known *Fifth suite* is especially spontaneous. The effect of the recording – not too closely balanced – is vivid and realistic. Ornaments are nicely handled and there is not a trace of pedantry here.

Andrei Gavrilov conveys the enormous inner vitality of these suites and makes this music vibrant. Such is the conviction he conveys that while he is playing one feels there is no other way to play this music and no other instrument to play it on. Very good sound.

Leonhardt's recordings were made in 1975. He uses a Rubio, modelled on a Taskin, and it sounds well, the recording only a shade close. The playing is generally flexible; perhaps the rhythmic French style is over-assertive at times, but the livelier dance movements, like the famous *Gavotte* in BWV 816, have plenty of character. Good value at bargain price, but not a primary choice.

Joanna MacGregor's style is relatively soft-grained to which the warm acoustics of The Maltings, Snape, contribute not a little. So the effect is mellow rather than incisive, quite unlike a clavichord or harpsichord. Indeed the characterization in both the *Fourth* and *Fifth suites* gives special pleasure. In spite of the hall resonance, MacGregor conveys intimacy of feeling alongside spontaneous joy in the music, and many will enjoy this playing a lot.

French suites Nos. 1–6; Italian concerto in F, BWV 971; Partita in B min., BWV 831.
*** Decca Dig. 433 313-2 (2). András Schiff (piano).

András Schiff has few peers in playing Bach on the piano. He continues his distinguished series with highly rewarding performances of the *French suites*, his expressive style entirely without personal indulgence, his freedom in slow movements seemingly improvisatory and spontaneous, and his faster dance movements an unqualified delight. The *Partita in B minor* is slightly more severe in style than the rest of the programme. As with the rest of his series, the Decca recording is appealingly realistic and an ideal acoustic has been chosen.

(i) *French suites Nos. 1–6, BWV 812–17;* (ii) *English suite No. 3 in G min., BWV 808; Italian concerto in F, BWV 971.*
(B) **(*) EMI forte Dig. CZS5 69479-2 (2) [CDFB 69479]. (i) Andrei Gavrilov (piano); (ii) Stanislav Bunin (piano).

Gavrilov's 1984 set of the *French suites* is full of interesting things, and there is some sophisticated, not to say masterly, pianism. He draws a wide range of tone-colour from the keyboard and employs a wider dynamic range than might be expected. There is an element of the self-conscious here, but there is much that is felicitous, too. To fill up the pair of discs, Stanislav Bunin's performances of the *Third English suite* and the *Italian concerto*, recorded six years later, have been added. His style is bold and direct, less flexible than Gavrilov's approach but totally unselfconscious. Both artists receive excellent recording.

Goldberg variations, BWV 988.
*** O-L Dig. 444 866-2 [id.]. Christophe Rousset (harpsichord).
(N) (M) *** Penguin Classics Decca Dig. 466 214-2 [460 611-2] [id.]. András Schiff (piano).
✿ *** VAI Audio VAIA 1029 [id.]. Rosalyn Tureck (piano).
*** DG 415 130-2 [id.]. Trevor Pinnock (harpsichord).

(N) (B) *** HM Musique d'abord Dig. HMA 190240 [(M) [id.].] Kenneth Gilbert (harpsichord).
(N) (M) *** DG. Double Dig. 459 599-2 [id.]. Rosalyn Tureck (piano).
(M) *** DG 439 978-2. Wilhelm Kempff (piano).
(M) *(**) Sony Dig. SMK 52619 [id.] (1981 recording). Glenn Gould (piano).
(N) (M) ** DG Dig. 463 019-2 [id.]. Andrei Gavrilov.

Goldberg variations, BWV 988; Fantasia in C min., BWV 906; Fantasia and fugue in F min., BWV 904; Italian concerto in F, BWV 971.
(B) **(*) DG 439 465-2. Ralph Kirkpatrick (harpsichord).

Goldberg variations; Fughetta in C min., BWV 961; Preludes and fugues: in A min., BWV 895; D min., BWV 899; E min., BWV 900; F, BWV 901; G, BWV 902.
**(*) Mer. CDA 84291 [id.]. Julia Cload (piano).

Goldberg variations; Well-tempered Clavier: Fugues in E, BWV 878; F sharp min., BWV 883.
(M) (**(*)) Sony mono SMK 52594 [id.] (1955 recording). Glenn Gould (piano).

Christophe Rousset takes his place fairly easily at the top of the list. He plays a 1751 Hemsch, which is superbly recorded within a generous but not too resonant acoustic, so that the harpsichord is very real and believable. His performance opens with an appealingly thoughtful account of the *Aria*, and the variations which follow are strong in character and consistently imaginative in presentation. A playing time of 77 minutes ensures that repeats can be fully observed, and the playing has great freshness and spontaneity.

For those who enjoy Bach on the piano, András Schiff's set can also receive the most enthusiastic advocacy. His recording carries the imprimatur of no less an authority than George Malcolm, who used to maintain that 'the *Goldberg variations* were the one work of Bach which positively demanded the two keyboards of the harpsichord in order to achieve the contrapuntal clarity in the numerous hand-crossing passages'. This performance changed his mind, and Schiff's much-admired dexterity and musicianship will go far in persuading sceptics that this not only can but does give profound satisfaction in the hands of a perceptive artist. The part-writing emerges with splendid definition and subtlety. Schiff does not play as if he is performing a holy ritual but with a keen sense of enjoyment of the piano's colour and sonority – and devoid of vocal obbligato. The Decca recording is excellent in every way, clean and realistic.

Rosalyn Tureck's recording is very special indeed – there is no other record of Bach played on the piano quite as compelling as this, and for I. M. it would be a desert island disc.

Trevor Pinnock retains repeats in more than half the variations – which seems a good compromise, in that variety is maintained yet there is no necessity for an additional disc. The playing is eminently vital and intelligent, with alert, finely articulated rhythm. The recording is very truthful and vivid.

Kenneth Gilbert gives a refreshingly natural performance. He uses a recent copy of a Ruckers-Taskin, and it makes a very pleasing sound. His is an aristocratic reading: he avoids excessive display and there is a quiet cultured quality about his playing that is very persuasive. An essentially introspective account, recorded in a rather less lively acoustic than is Pinnock, and he is a thoughtful and thought-provoking player.

We would not want to be without Rosalyn Tureck's newest, digital version of the *Goldberg*, which is overflowing with her characteristic insights and beautifully recorded. She has spread herself to two CDs to include repeats; each disc plays for about 45 minutes, but the two are offered for the price of one. The key to this latest reading is her statement, printed inside the jewel case: 'I play as a life experience'. Every variation bears evidence of this combination of scholarship and vision; each is sharply characterized, crystal clear in articulation, and deeply considered. (For profound inner feeling, sample Variation 15, the *Canone alla quinta*, which ends the first disc, or Variations 21 and 22 on the second.) Her reprise of the *Aria* at the close has an unforgettable poise and serenity. This is a set to return to for musical nourishment. But her earlier stereo version has a sense of being carried along and aloft by Bach's musical inspiration, with quicksilver fluidity, an impression shared by András Schiff's Decca account, so that detail is observed *en passant* rather than being deliberated upon.

Kempff's version is not for purists, but it has a special magic of its own. Ornaments are ignored altogether in the outlining of the theme and the instances of anachronisms of style are too numerous to mention. Yet, for all that, the sheer musicianship exhibited by this great artist fascinates and his playing is consistently refreshing. The 1969 recording is very natural.

Ralph Kirkpatrick is at his best in this work, providing light and subtle registration, and the music benefits both in clarity and in colour. The playing is lively when it should be, controlled and steady in the slow, stately, contrapuntal variations. He is a scholarly rather than an intuitive player and his thoughts are rarely without interest. Though not a first choice, this version includes three extra items where he uses his modern Neupert harpsichord to good effect, while sounding more pedantic, particularly in the *Italian concerto*.

Glenn Gould's famous (1955) mono recording enjoyed cult status in its day, and its return will occasion rejoicing among his admirers. He observes no repeats and in terms of sheer keyboard wizardry commands admiration, even if you do not respond to the results. There is too much that is wilful and eccentric for this to be a straightforward recommendation, but it is a remarkable performance nevertheless.

Julia Cload observes the repeats in the opening *Aria* but not elsewhere; she therefore finds room for the '*Little*' *Preludes and fugues*, which she plays appealingly and fluently. Her account of the *Goldberg variations* is strong and thoughtful; not as inspirational as Tureck's, but some may like its directness of manner. The piano is well recorded but the ear needs to adjust to the 'empty studio' acoustic.

Gould's later, stereo version was one of the last records he made. In his earlier record he made no repeats; now he repeats a section of almost half of them and also joins some pairs together (6 with 7 and 9 with 10, for example). Yet, even apart from his vocalise, he does a number of weird things – fierce staccatos, brutal accents, and so on – that inhibit one from suggesting this as a first recommendation even among piano versions. The recording is, as usual with this artist, inclined to be dry and forward, which aids clarity.

Andrei Gavrilov is a player of astonishing keyboard prowess and there is much that will prompt admiration for both his integrity and articulation. All the same, he makes heavy weather of some of the variations and is, more importantly, handicapped by a less than glamorous recording. There is not enough space round the sound and the instrument is too closely balanced.

15 2-Part Inventions, BWV 772–86; 15 3-Part Inventions, BWV 787–801.

*** Capriccio Dig. 10 210 [id.] (with *6 Little preludes, BWV 933–8*). Ton Koopman (harpsichord).

**(*) Decca Dig. 411 974-2 [id.]. András Schiff (piano).

Ton Koopman scores over rivals in offering the *Six Little preludes* in addition to the two sets of *Inventions*, and Koopman plays with spontaneity and sparkle.

András Schiff's playing is (for this repertoire) rather generous with rubato and other expressive touches, but elegant in the articulation of part-writing. Such is his musicianship and pianistic sensitivity, however, that the overall results are likely to persuade most listeners. The recording is excellent.

15 2-Part Inventions, BWV 772–86; 15 3-Part Inventions, BWV 787–801; Ornamented versions: *2-Part Invention No. 1 in C, BWV 772a* (ornamented in triplets); *3-Part Inventions Nos. 4, 5, 7, 9, 11 & 13, BWV 790–91, 793, 795, 797 & 799.*

*** Astrée Audivis Dig. E 8603 [id.]. Blandine Verlet (harpsichord).

Blandine Verlet uses a 1624 Ruckers which seems quite ideal for this repertoire, and it sounds very real when one achieves the right volume-control setting. She plays with great spirit and the imitation between the parts is admirably clear. Her passage-work is never inflexible and, when the writing is comparatively expressive, her minor hesitations in the flow prevent any sense of rigidity; this is more striking in the *Three-part* pieces. Having played through both sets, she then offers a selection with judicious ornamentation, strikingly effective in the very first of the *Two-part Inventions*.

Partitas Nos. 1–6, BWV 825–30.

*** O-L (IMS) Dig. 440 217-2 (2) [id.]. Christophe Rousset (harpsichord).

(N) *** Hyperion Dig. CDA 67191/2 [id.]. Angela Hewitt (piano).

(N) *** Chandos Dig. 0618 (2) [id.]. Robert Woolley (harpsichord).

*** Decca Dig. 411 732-2 (2) [id.]. András Schiff (piano).

(M) *** Virgin Veritas/EMI Dig. VED5 61292-2 (2) [ZDMB 61292]. Gustav Leonhardt (harpsichord).

Partitas Nos. 1–6, BWV 825–30; Partita in B min. (Overture in the French style), BWV 831.

(B) *** Ph. Duo 442 559-2 (2) [id.]. Blandine Verlet (harpsichord).

Bach playing doesn't come much better than it does in Christophe Rousset's two-CD set on Oiseau-Lyre. Here is an artist who wears his elegance and erudition lightly; there are none of the scholarly hang-ups that so often afflict performers of this repertoire. The playing has complete naturalness and is obviously the product of a vital musical imagination. This must now be the first recommendation in this repertoire.

Those wanting a set on the piano – and how well these works suit this instrument in the right hands – can safely turn to Angela Hewitt. Her performances are fluent, deeply musical and, while expressively flexible, are less personally wayward than Schiff in the *Sarabandes*, which she still plays very sensitively. Elsewhere, her style, always pianistic, can be bold and strongly articulated, or lighter in touch, as for instance in the fast trickling *Corrente* of the A minor work, BWV 829, while the closing *Gigues* have an engagingly rhythmic lift. The Hyperion recording is first class.

Robert Woolley's performances are also pleasingly fresh and musical, flowing naturally and spontaneously and with lively rhythmic feeling. He uses a particularly attractive harpsichord, a copy of a Mietke, an instrument of a kind which Bach would have known. It is beautifully recorded within a pleasing open acoustic. While Rousset remains first choice, this fine Chandos set could well be considered an alternative.

Schiff is a most persuasive advocate of Bach on the piano. Though few will cavil at his treatment of fast movements, some may find him a degree wayward in slow movements, though the freshness of his rubato and the sparkle of his ornamentation are always winning. The sound is outstandingly fine.

Gustav Leonhardt's set was recorded (in 1986) on a Dowd (modelled on an eighteenth-century German instrument by Michael Mietke). In terms of sheer sound it is among the most satisfactory available versions, and in terms of style it combines elegance, spontaneity and authority. There is nothing didactic about this playing, but it is never less than thought-provoking. In many respects it is musically among the most satisfying of current sets, save for the fact that Leonhardt observes no repeats. This will undoubtedly diminish its appeal – which is a great pity, since both illumination and pleasure are to be had from this set. It is offered at medium price, but the first disc plays for only 40 minutes 36 seconds and the second for 54 minutes 36 seconds.

Blandine Verlet's Philips Duo set is not only inexpensive, it is the only set of the *Partitas* to include the later *Overture in the French style*, BWV 831, which is played with much character. Indeed the performances throughout are direct and spontaneous, thoughtful and strongly characterized. Not an out-and-out first choice, which lies with Christophe Rousset on Oiseau-Lyre. But he does not give us the *B minor Partita* and, in its price range, Verlet can certainly be strongly recommended.

Partitas Nos. 2 in C min., BWV 826; 4 in D, BWV 828; 5 in G, BWV 829.

(N) *** Nonesuch/Warner Dig. 7559 79483-2 [id.]. Richard Goode (piano).

It is a pity that Richard Goode's recording is incomplete, for the performances are both stylish and appealing. The crisp rhythmic control of the *D major Partita* (which comes first) is arresting, as is the use of pianistic light and shade, and the thoughtful, ruminative playing in the *Sarabandes* is improvisational in feeling. In the *Courantes* and *Gigues*, tempi are brisk but articulation is clean, rhythms are lifted, and with piano tone that is clear, but never too dry, this is very stimulating.

8 Preludes for W. F. Bach, BWV 924–31; 6 Little Preludes, BWV 933–8; 5 Preludes, BWV 939–43; Prelude, BWV 999; Prelude, fugue and allegro in E flat, BWV 998; Preludes and fughettas: in F & G, BWV 901–2; Fantasia in C min., BWV 906; Fantasia and fugue in A min., BWV 904.

(M) **(*) DG (IMS) Dig. 447 278-2. Kenneth Gilbert (harpsichord).

Splendid artistry from this scholar-player; he is predictably stylish and authoritative. He uses a harpsichord by a Flemish maker, Jan Couchet, enlarged by Blanchet in 1759 and by Taskin in 1778, overhauled by Hubert Bédard. Even played at the lowest setting, the sound seems a bit unrelieved and overbright. This really has 'presence' with a vengeance. The excellence of the playing however is not in question.

Toccatas: in F sharp min.; C min.; D; D min.; E min.; G min.; G; BWV 910–16.

(M) ** Sony SM2K 52612 (2) [S2K 52612]. Glenn Gould (piano).

The seven *Toccatas* offer some of Glenn Gould's finest Bach playing. They are often quite complex in structure, but Gould has their full measure. The recording balance is close and rather dry but truthful and with rather more bloom than in previous incarnations. The one overriding snag is the vocalise.

The Well-tempered Clavier (48 Preludes & fugues), BWV 846–93.

*** DG Dig. 413 439-2 (4) [id.]. Kenneth Gilbert (harpsichord).

(N) *** Olympia Dig. OCD 703 ABCD (4) [id.]. Tatiana Nikolayeva (piano).

(B) *** HM Musique d'Abord HMA 1901285/8 [id.]. Davitt Moroney (harpsichord).

(N) ** Ph. Dig. 446 690-2 (4). Daniel Chorzempa (harpsichord, clavichord, organ or fortepiano).

Gilbert has made some superb harpsichord records, but his set of the 'Forty-eight' crowns them all. By a substantial margin it now supplants all existing harpsichord versions, with readings that are resilient and individual, yet totally unmannered, although some might feel that the acoustic is just a shade too resonant.

Tatiana Nikolayeva's set is totally pianistic, using a wide range of dynamic and articulation, sometimes lightly staccato, at others crisp and bold, or more gently sustained. No 8 in E flat, in Book I, is an extreme example, very measured indeed. She is at once authoritative, yet, like Schiff, highly individual in her approach to each prelude and fugue. She is clearly moved by the music and at times her inspirational, soft-grained manner reminds one of Kempff. Whatever she does, she does not forget the composer and is never self-aware to the apoint of agogic distortion of line. She is beautifully recorded, a true full, clear piano sound and the transfer to CD is impeccable. Collectors who already have her recording of Shostakovich's equivalent set (Op 87) will surely want this one – it is a consistent source of imaginative refreshment.

Davitt Moroney uses a modern harpsichord (built in 1980) which has a full-bodied yet cleanly focused image but which is rather too closely balanced. Yet the effect is certainly tangible and realistic, the perspective more convincing than with Leonhardt. His thoughtful, considered approach is satisfying in its way, stylistically impeccable, although the playing is less concentrated than with Gilbert. But it will suit those who like a thoughtful, unostentatious approach to Bach, yet one which does not lack rhythmic resilience. Moreover, with full documentation it is a very real bargain on Harmonia Mundi's Musique d'Abord budget label.

Daniel Chorzempa quite arbitrarily divides Book I of Bach's 48 between clavichord and harpsichord and more controversially allots four preludes and fugues to a Dutch cabinet organ. In Book II the fortepiano joins the other instruments and is allotted half-a-dozen items against the organ's three. For the listener the effect brings added variety but is a little unsettling. Chorzempa's style is on the whole fairly didactic, although always musically considered. This is not for everyone, but it's certainly a new approach.

The Well-tempered Clavier, Book I, Preludes and fugues Nos. 1–24, BWV 846–69.

(N) ✿ *** Hyperion Dig. CDA 67301/2 [id.]. Angela Hewitt (piano).

*** Decca Dig. 414 388-2 (2) [id.]. András Schiff (piano).

*** ECM Dig. 835246-2 (2) [id.]. Keith Jarrett (piano).

The Well-tempered Clavier, Book II, Preludes and fugues Nos. 25–48, BWV 870–93.

(N) ✿ *** Hyperion Dig. CDA 67303/4 [id.]. Angela Hewitt (piano).

*** Decca Dig. 417 236-2 (2) [id.]. András Schiff (piano).

*** ECM Dig. 847936-2 (2) [id.]. Keith Jarrett (harpsichord).

For a long time András Schiff has taken pride of place for the '48' played on the piano, and his Decca set remains highly recommendable. But now we feel the mantle (and Rosette) must pass on to Angela Hewitt, who is proving to be one of the finest Bach keyboard-players of our time. She uses all the resources of the modern piano (including crescendo and decrescendo) to turn these *Preludes and fugues* into ongoing concert music of great variety and interest. Her range of timbre and dynamic is wide, her articulation can be bold, lightweight or gently searching (as, for instance, in BWV. 849). But every bar is imaginatively alive, and her thoughtful expressiveness is never self-aware, nor does it obscure the clarity of the part writing. An inspirational set, most naturally recorded.

Schiff often takes a very individual view of particular preludes and fugues, but his unexpected readings regularly win one over long before the end. Consistently he translates this music into pianistic terms, rarely if ever imitating the harpsichord, and though his very choice of the piano will rule him out with those seeking authenticity, his voyage of discovery through this supreme keyboard collection is the more riveting, when the piano is an easier instrument to listen to over long periods. First-rate sound.

Keith Jarrett has recorded Book I on a modern piano, and we like it very much for its dedication, simplicity and integrity. In its way it is quite the equal of Schiff's recording. There is no attempt at any excessive indulgence in keyboard colour and the recording is very satisfying in its natural sonority. On the face of it, it seems a rather odd idea to revert to the harpsichord for Book II and, if his reasoning does not completely persuade us, his qualities of musicianship do. He is a highly intelligent and musical player whose readings and precise articulation can hold their own against the current competition.

The Well-tempered Clavier, Book I, excerpts: *Preludes and fugues Nos. 1–3; 5–17; 21–22.*

(N) (M) *** DG 463 020-2 [id.]. Wilhelm Kempff (piano).

Cool, clear and compelling, Kempff's performances from the first book of the *48* convey pianistic poetry as well as dedication to Bach. A splendid recital, with excellent sound, showing a great artist relaxed and enjoying himself. And so do we.

The Well-tempered Clavier, Book I, Preludes and fugues Nos. 1, 5–7, 11–13, 17–19, 23–24.

(N) *(*) RCA Dig. 74321 61446-2 (2) [id.]. Olli Mustonen – SHOSTAKOVICH: *Preludes and fugues.* *(*)

Olli Mustonen gives us a dozen of the *Preludes and fugues* of Book I of the *Well-Tempered Clavier*, interwoven with half of the Shostakovich Op. 87 set of *Preludes and Fugues*, composed for Tatyana Nikolaeva. This is an idea that might work well in the concert hall or in a broadcast but will not necessarily meet the needs of collectors. Mustonen's considerable technical prowess and command of part-writing are a vehicle for displaying his own insights and art. The eccentricities, exaggerated articulation and ugly staccatos pecked from the keyboard will not enjoy universal acclaim. In recent years this gifted artist (so it seems to us) has developed an unpleasing narcissism. He is very well recorded here by the RCA engineers.

ORGAN MUSIC

Complete organ music

Peter Hurford Complete Decca series

Disc 1: *Preludes & fugues, BWV 531–2, 548–50; Toccatas & fugues, BWV 540, 565* (444 411-2).

Disc 2: *Fantasias & fugues, BWV 542, 561; Kleines harmonisches Labyrinth, BWV 591; Preludes & fugues, BWV 533, 551; Toccata, adagio & fugue, BWV 564; Toccata & fugue, BWV 538; Trio, BWV 585* (444 412-2).

Disc 3: *Fantasias, BWV 562, 572; Fantasia & fugue, BWV 537; Fugues, BWV 575–7, 579, 581; Passacaglia & fugue, BWV 582; Pedal-Exercitium, BWV 598; Prelude & fugue, BWV 535; Trio, BWV 583* (444 413-2).

Disc 4: *Clavier-Ubung, Part 3* (beginning): *German organ Mass (Prelude & fugue in E flat, BWV 552, & Chorale preludes, BWV 669–71, 676, 678, 680, 682, 684, 686, 688)* (444 414-2).

Disc 5: *Clavier-Ubung, Part 3* (conclusion): *Chorale preludes, BWV 672–5, 677, 679, 681, 683, 685, 687, 689; 24 Kirnberger Chorale preludes, BWV 690–713* (444 415-2).

Disc 6: *6 Trio sonatas, BWV 525–30* (444 416-2).

Disc 7: *Canonic variations: Vom Himmel hoch, BWV 769; Chorale partitas: Christ, du bist der helle Tag; O Gott, du frommer Gott; Sei gegrüsset, Jesu gütig, BWV 766–8; Chorale variations: Ach, was soll ich Sünder machen, BWV 770* (444 417-2).

Disc 8: *Chorale preludes, BWV 730–40; Schübler chorale preludes, BWV 645–50; Chorale variations: Allein Gott in der Höh' sei Ehr, BWV 771* (444 418-2).

Disc 9: *Chorale preludes, BWV 726–9; Concertos Nos. 1–6, BWV 592–7* (444 419-2).

Disc 10: *Arnstadt chorale preludes, BWV 714, 719, 742 & 1090–1117* (from Yale manuscript, copied Neumeister) (444 420-2).

Disc 11: *Arnstadt chorale preludes, BWV 957, 1118–20* (from Yale manuscript, copied Neumeister); *Leipzig chorale preludes, BWV 651–62* (444 421-2).

Disc 12: *Leipzig chorale preludes, BWV 663–8. Chorale preludes, BWV 714–25* (444 422-2).

Disc 13: *Allabreve in D, BWV 589; Fugue, BWV 580; Prelude, BWV 568; Preludes & fugues, BWV 534, 536, 539, 541; 8 Short Preludes & fugues, BWV 553–60; Trios, BWV 584 & 586* (444 423-2).

Disc 14: *Aria in F, BWV 587; Canzona in D min., BWV 588; Fantasia, BWV 571; Fugues, BWV 574 & 578; Pastorale, BWV 590; Preludes, BWV 567 & 569; Preludes & fugues, BWV 546–7* (444 424-2).

Disc 15: *Fantasia, BWV 563; Musical offering: Ricercar, BWV 1079/5. Preludes & fugues, BWV 535a* (incomplete), *543–5; Prelude, trio & fugue, BWV 545b; Toccata & fugue in E, BWV 566; Trio, BWV 1027a* (444 425-2).

Disc 16: *Chorale preludes Nos. 1–41 (Orgelbüchlein), BWV 599–639* (444 426-2).

Disc 17: *Chorale preludes Nos. 42–6 (Orgelbüchlein), BWV 640–44. Chorale preludes, BWV 620a, BWV 741–8, BWV 751–2, BWV 754–5, BWV 757–63, BWV 765, BWV Anh. 55; Fugue in G min., BWV 131a* (444 427-2).

(B) *** Decca Analogue/Dig. 444 410-2 (17) [id.]. Peter Hurford (organs of Ratzeburg Cathedral, Germany; Church of Our Lady of Sorrows, Toronto, Canada; New College Chapel, Oxford; Knox Grammar School Chapel, Sydney, Australia; Eton College, Windsor; Stiftskirche, Melk, Austria; Augustinerkirche, Vienna, Austria; All Souls Unitarian Church, Washington, DC, USA; Domkirche, St Pölten, Austria; St Catharine's College Chapel, Cambridge).

With the exception of the 35 *Arnstadt chorale preludes*, as copied by Neumeister – discovered quite recently in the Music Library of Yale University – which were added in 1986, Peter Hurford recorded his unique survey of Bach's organ music for Decca's Argo label over a period of eight years, 1974–82. Following the example of Bach himself, who was renowned for trying out organs, Hurford uses ten different organs, moving from Ratzeburg in Germany to Toronto in Canada, back home to New College, Oxford, then to Sydney, Australia, and so on. Each organ is caught superbly by the recording engineers, and the registration features a range of baroque colour that is almost orchestral in its diversity. The digital recording of the Vienna Bach organ chosen for the *Neumeister chorales* is particularly beautiful.

It was Peter Hurford's achievement to influence a complete change in approach to this repertoire, moving away from an enduring and essentially pedagogic, German tradition (shown at its best by organists like Helmut Walcha on DG Archiv). Vigour and energy are the keynotes of his approach to the large-scale works and, without losing their majesty, he never lets the fugal momentum get bogged down by the the music's weight and scale. We hear Bach's organ writing with new ears, its human vitality revealed alongside its extraordinary architecture. The set is supported with very good notes by Clifford Bartlett which are both scholarly and readable; full specifications of all the organs used are included. The recordings are splendidly transferred to CD and while newer digital surveys are now appearing, from Kevin Bower, Christopher Herrick and Ton Koopman, among others this set of 17 bargain-price CDs remains a cornerstone among available recordings of this repertoire. Apart from several selections – see below – the discs are unfortunately, not available separatedly.

Wolfgang Rübsam Complete Philips series

Volume I, Disc 1: *Fantasia, BWV 572; Preludes and fugues, BWV 531–2; 535, 541, 544–5, 549–50; Toccata and fugue in D min., BWV 565* (438 172-2).

Disc 2: *Fugues, BWV 577–8; Fugue on a theme of Corelli, BWV 579; Prelude, BWV 568; Preludes and fugues, BWV 533–4; 536; 543; 546–7; Toccata and fugue in D min. (Dorian), BWV 538* (438 173-2).

Disc 3: *Canzona in D min., BWV 588; Preludes and fugues, BWV 537, 539–40, 542, 548; Prelude, Adagio-trio; Fantasia and fugue* (without BWV No.) (438 174-2).

Disc 4: *Allabreve in D, BWV 589; Fantasias: in C min.* (without BWV No.); *in C min., BWV 562; Fugues, BWV 575, 581; Passacaglia in C min., BWV 582; Pedal-Exercitium, BWV 598; Toccata, BWV 564; Toccata and fugue in E, BWV 566; Trios, BWV 583, 586, 1027a* (438 175-2).

Disc 5: *Fantasia in G, BWV 571; Trio sonatas for 2 keyboards and pedal, BWV 525–9* (438 177-2).

Disc 6: *Trio sonata No. 6, BWV 530; Chorales, BWV 691a, 717, 725; Chorale partitas, BWV 766–7; 770; Chorale preludes, 745, 747* (438 178-2).

Disc 7: *Canonic variations on 'Vom Himmel hoch', BWV 768; Chorale partita on 'Sei gegrüsset, Jesu gütig', BWV 768; Chorale variations on 'Allein Gott in der Höh' sei Ehr'', BWV 771; Chorale: 'Wie schön leuch't uns der Morgenstern', BWV 739; Fugue in C min. (Theme Legrenzianum, elaboratum cum subjecto pedaliter), BWV 574; Pastorale in D, BWV 590* (438 179-2).

Disc 8: *Orgelbüchlein: Chorales, BWV 599–644* (438 180-2).

Volume II, Disc 9: *Chorales, BWV 653b; O Lamm Gottes unschuldig* (without BWV No.); *Chorale preludes, BWV 748–50, 754, 756, 759; Fuga sopra il Magnificat, BWV 733; 6 Schübler chorales, BWV 645–50; Clavier-Ubung, Part 3: German organ Mass* (beginning): *Prelude in E flat, BWV 552, & Chorale preludes, BWV 669–74* (438 182-2).

Disc 10: *Clavier-Ubung, Part 3: German organ Mass* (cont.); *Chorale preludes, BWV 675–89; Fugue in E flat, BWV 552; Duets 1–4, BWV 802–5* (438 183-2).

Disc 11: *6 Concertos after various composers, BWV 592–7; Leipzig chorales Nos. 1–3, BWV 651–3* (438 184-2).

Disc 12: *18 Leipzig chorales, Nos.4–18* (438 185-2).

Disc 13: *Chorales and Chorale preludes, BWV 690, 692–4, 700, 703, 710, 715, 719, 722, 724, 729, 732, 734, 738, 746, 751, 755, 757–8, 763; Chorale fugues and fuguettas, BWV 699, 701–2, 716; Fantasia super 'Valet will ich dir geben', BWV 735; Fantasia in C, BWV 570; Fugues, BWV 570 & BWV 576; Kleines harmonisches Labyrinth, BWV 591; Prelude in C, BWV 567; Prelude and fugue in A min., BWV 551; Trio in G min., BWV 584* (438 187-2).

Disc 14: *Chorales and Chorale preludes, BWV 691, 695, 705–9, 711–12, 714, 718, 720, 723, 726, 730, 740–44, 752, 765; Chorale fantasia, BWV 713; Chorale fuguettas, BWV 696–8, 704* (438 188-2).

Disc 15: *Aria in F, BWV 587; Chorales and Chorale preludes, BWV 721, 760–62, 727–8, 731, 736–7; Fantasia con imitazione, BWV 563; Fantasia and fugue in A min., BWV 561; Fugue in D, BWV 580; Prelude in A min., BWV 569; Trio in C min., BWV 585; The Art of Fugue, BWV 1080* (beginning): *Contrapunctus 1–5* (438 189-2).

Disc 16: *The Art of Fugue* (conclusion): *Contrapunctus 6–11; Canon all'Ottava; Fura a 3 soggetti. Chorale: 'Wenn wir in Höchsten Nöten sein', BWV 668a* (438 190-2).

(B) *** Ph. 456 080-2 (16). Wolfgang Rübsam (organs of Frauenfeld & Freiburg).

Wolfgang Rübsam's magnificent survey of Bach's organ music, made at the beginning of the 1970s, is on 16 CDs, packaged in two boxes of 8 discs, contained within a sturdy slip case with excellent documentation. The bulk of the music was recorded on the fine instrument at St Nikolaus in Frauenfeld, Switzerland; for the chorale preludes and a few miscellaneous works, Rübsam turned to the Belgian Hockhois organ at Freiburg Münster. Sonically the results are highly stimulating, offering the widest range of colour, a rich overall blend without clouding of detail, and plenty of support from the pedals. The *Trio sonatas* are especially attractive in both their luminous palette and their liveliness. The six solo *Concertos*, based on music of others, principally Ernst and Vivaldi, are comparably successful, although here Rübsam adopts extreme tempi, with adagios very measured against sprightly allegros. But the key to the success of any Bach survey must lie with the way the performer approaches the large-scale concert pieces, notably the *Preludes and fugues* and *Toccatas and fugues*, and these are nearly all in the first volume. Certainly in these works Rübsam is consistently vital, and his registration often tickles the ear. The famous *Toccata, adagio and fugue*, BWV 564, is very well judged, a work that can easily become ponderous, while the *Passacaglia in C minor*, BWV 582, has a convincing forward momentum and plenty of imaginative detail. The so-called *German organ Mass* is split between CDs, which should not have been necessary, and the *Art of Fugue* is placed at the end; a suitable postlude is provided with a complete version of the *Chorale*, BWV 668a. There are many special insights here and, with such a spontaneous approach, Rübsam's distinguished and consistently enjoyable survey may readily be placed alongside that of Peter Hurford, while the remastered Philips analogue recording is often of comparable demonstration quality – a very major achievement. Again however, these discs are not available separately.

Marie-Claire Alain Erato series
(M) **(*) Erato/Warner Dig. 4509 96358-2 (14) [id.]. Marie-Claire Alain.

Marie-Claire Alain's series has much to offer the lover of Bach's organ music, and she plays to excellent effect on some splendid instruments. The complete set of fourteen records is available in a slip case at a small saving in cost, and admirers of this artist should not be disappointed with such an investment. But competition is strong, and for most collectors a choice from among the separate issues, all at mid-price, would seem more sensible.

Volume 1: *Leipzig chorale preludes: An Wasserflüssen Babylon, BWV 653; Schmücke dich, o liebe Seele, BWV 654; Von Gott will ich nicht lassen, BWV 658; Triple chorale (with Trio): Allein Gott in der Höh' sei Ehr', BWV 662–4; Preludes and fugues: in B min., BWV 544; in E min., BWV 548.*
(M) **(*) Erato/Warner Dig. 4509 96718-2 [id.]. Marie-Claire Alain (organ of Martinikerk, Groningen).

Volume 1 is recorded on the Martinikerk organ in Groningen and the results are not entirely satisfactory, for the engineers obtain a rich, weighty sound as in the opening *E minor Prelude and fugue*, but the resonance makes the result rather opaque, which does not enable Alain to clarify detail. The fugue, however, is measured and powerful. This whole programme bears out her comments about tempi, which are essentially relaxed.

Volume 2: *Orgelbüchlein: Chorale preludes, BWV 618–32; Prelude and fugue in G min., BWV 535; Toccatas and fugues: in D min. (Dorian), BWV 538; in C, BWV 566.*
(M) **(*) Erato/Warner Dig. 4509 96719-2 [id.]. Marie-Claire Alain (organ of Freiburg Cathedral).

Volume 2 was recorded in 1991 on the early eighteenth-century Silbermann organ at Freiburg, and the sound is immediately more vivid and clear. The opening *Dorian Toccata in D minor* is brightly registered and lively and, if the fugue is unhurried, the tension is well sustained. The *C major Toccata*, however, is one of the finest performances in the cycle. Alain presents the earlier chorales from the *Orgelbüchlein* gently and persuasively. Generally these simple pieces come off very well, although she does not always make the cantus firmus stand out. The second group of chorales, BWV 625–30, are richly textured until *Erschienen ist der herrliche Tag*, BWV 629, which makes an engaging lighter contrast.

Volume 3: *Allabreve in D, BWV 589; Canzona in D min., BWV 588; Fugues: in C min., BWV 575; in G, BWV 577; Fugue sopra 'Meine Seele erhebet den Herren'; Kirnberger chorale preludes: Wo soll ich fliehen hin, BWV 694; Wir Christenleut hab'n jetzund Freud, BWV 710; Kleines harmonisches Labyrinth, BWV 591; Partita sopra 'O Gott, du frommer Gott', BWV 767; Preludes and fugues: in D min., BWV 539; in C, BWV 545; in A min., BWV 551.*
(M) **(*) Erato/Warner Dig. 4509 96720-2 [id.]. Marie-Claire Alain (organ of Freiburg Cathedral).

The Freiburg organ is again used in Volume 3 (also recorded in 1991) and Alain uses its fullest sonority for her weighty presentation of the opening *Prelude and fugue in C*. However, the following *G major fugue* (better known as the *Fugue à la gigue* and of questionable authenticity) is impossibly slow and heavy. Alain is much more impressive in the *D minor fugue*, BWV 539, which is cleanly pointed and rhythmically positive. The splendid virtuoso *Fugue in C minor* (which reminds one of the more famous *D minor*, BWV 565) is fluent and quite dramatic at the end, while in the fugue, based on the *Magnificat*, Alain uses the pedals impressively to build a most powerful climax. The *Kleines harmonisches Labyrinth* has sounded more original in other hands, but here the registration is certainly interesting.

Volume 4: *Chorale preludes: BWV 711, 714–18, 722, 724–32, 734, 737–9, 765; Fantasia in B min., BWV 563; Preludes and fugues: in C, BWV 531; in E min., BWV 533.*
(M) **(*) Erato/Warner Dig. 4509 96721-2 [id.]. Marie-Claire Alain (organ of Georgenkirche, Rötha).

The Silbermann organ at Rötha (still 1991) proves ideal for this repertoire, and it stimulates Alain to some of her most spontaneous performances so far in this variable series. After a robust *Prelude and fugue in E minor*, Marie-Claire Alain is at her most chimerical in the Christmas chorale, *Nun freut euch, lieben Christen g'mein*, with the registration like tinkling bells. The two settings of *Liebster Jesu* then seem rather staid and solemn, and *In dulci jubilo* is very grand indeed. Alain clearly revels in the elaborate passage on the pedals which opens the *Prelude in C*, BWV 531, and even conveys exuberance (not a quality for which her Bach playing is notable), while the fugue is equally alive and vivid. The contrapuntally grand *Herr Gott, dich loben wir* ends the recital massively, and here one feels Alain could have moved the music on a bit. But there is no doubt that Alain is really enjoying this organ, which sounds as if it answers readily to her touch.

Volume 5: *Chorale preludes: BWV 690–91, 695, 700, 706, 709, 712, 721; Fantasia ('Jesu, meine*

Freude'), BWV 713; Fugue (on a theme of Corelli) in B min., BWV 579; Kirnberger chorale preludes for Christmas, BWV 696–704; Partita sopra 'Christ, der du bist der helle Tag', BWV 766; Preludes and fugues: in C min., BWV 537; in C min., BWV 549.

(M) **(*) Erato/Warner Dig. 4509 96722-2 [id.]. Marie-Claire Alain (organ of Georgenkirche, Rötha).

Alain opens Volume 5 with the early *Prelude and fugue in C minor* (1703/4) using the Rötha organ's pedals to bravura effect, following with a fairly spontaneous account of the jolly fugue. The first chorale, *Herr Jesus Christ, dich zu uns wend*, BWV 709, is full of gleaming sunshine, while *Erbarm' dich mein O Herre Gott* brings that dedicated feeling of repose which Alain manages so well. The *Partita sopra 'Christ, der du bist der helle Tag'* brings six variations and Alain finds an orchestral range of colour for them, with a gigue movement finally leading to a majestic close.

Volume 6: *Canonic variations: Vom Himmel hoch, BWV 769; Chorale preludes: BWV 669–79; Clavier-Ubung, Part 3: German organ Mass: Prelude in E flat, BWV 552; Prelude and fugue in C, BWV 547.*

(M) **(*) Erato/Warner Dig. 4509 96723-2 [id.]. Marie-Claire Alain (organ of Martinikerk, Groningen).

Volume 6 was one of the earlier sets of recordings, made in 1985 in Groningen, but the organ is beautifully focused and detail hardly ever clouds. If the *C major fugue*, BWV 547, proceeds on its way somewhat remorselessly, the *Canonic variations* (as with other similar, expansive sets of divisions) bring out the very best in Marie-Claire Alain, and the opening presentation, in which the Christmas chorale cantus firmus subtly creeps through the flowing decorative lines, is very cunningly managed, while the intricate contrapuntal writing remains clear throughout, and the chorales which follow have plenty of variety in presentation and mood.

Volume 7: *Chorale preludes: 'Herr Jesu Christ, dich zu uns wend', BWV 655; 'Vor Deinen Thron tret' ich', BWV 668; Clavier-Ubung, Part 3: German organ Mass: Chorale preludes, BWV 680–89; 4 Duets, BWV 802–5; Fugue in E flat, BWV 552.*

(M) *** Erato/Warner Dig. 4509 96724-2 [id.]. Marie-Claire Alain (organ of Martinikerk, Groningen).

Marie-Claire Alain returned to the Groningen organ in 1990, having decided that its range of colours was especially suitable for this collection of chorales, plus the four *Duets* and *Fugue in E flat* which make up the so-called 'German organ Mass'. (Its opening *Prelude in E flat* had already been included in the previous volume.) This is repertoire which finds Alain at her very finest, for her performances of the chorales clearly identify with their spiritual implications. Splendid recording: this can be strongly recommended.

Volume 8: *Chorale preludes: Orgelbüchlein Nos. 35–46, BWV 633–44; Fantasia in C, BWV 570; Partita sopra 'Sei gegrüsset, Jesu gütig', BWV 768; Preludes and fugues: in F min., BWV 534; in C min., BWV 546.*

(M) **(*) Erato/Warner Dig. 4509 96725-2 [id.]. Marie-Claire Alain (organ of St Laurentskerk, Alkmaar).

The famous Schnitger organ at Alkmaar has stimulated many Bach performers on record, but one has to say that Alain's opening *Prelude and fugue in C minor* is rather stoic, though it is certainly a powerful utterance. The dozen chorale preludes from the *Orgelbüchlein* bring the usual simplicity and variety, but it is the Partita on '*Sei gegrüsset, Jesu gütig*' which really excites Alain's imagination – not surprisingly, as it is one of Bach's very finest sets of keyboard variations; again one laments that there is no separate cueing for this expansive work (19 minutes 50 seconds) which reaches such a stunning apotheosis here. The recording dates from 1990.

Volume 9: *Chorale preludes: Orgelbüchlein Nos. 1–19, BWV 599–617; 'Valet will ich dir geben', BWV 735; Fantasias: in C min., BWV 562; in G, BWV 572; Fugue on a theme of Legrenzi in C min., BWV 574.*

(M) **(*) Erato/Warner Dig. 4509 96742-2 [id.]. Marie-Claire Alain (organ of St Laurentskerk, Alkmaar).

The *Très vitement* opening of the *G major Fantasia* is always appealing, and Alain plays it perkily enough, then returning to her full-bodied style for the *Gravement–Lentement*, which she takes very literally. The first of the Orgelbüchlein chorales included here, *Nunn komm' der Heiden Heiland*, BWV 599, is also very fully orchestrated, but in *Gottes Sohn ist kommen*, BWV 600, the balance between decoration and chorale is felicitous (something Alain does not always manage ideally). The host of ascending and descending angels in BWV 606 is evocatively pictured, but it is in a quietly reflective piece like *Das alte Jahr vergangen ist*, BWV 614, that Alain is at her finest.

Volume 10: *Leipzig chorale preludes: BWV 651–2, 656–7, 659–61, 665–7; Prelude and fugue in D, BWV 532; Trio in D min., BWV 583.*

(M) **(*) Erato/Warner Dig. 4509 96743-2 [id.]. Marie-Claire Alain (organ of St Laurentskerk, Alkmaar).

There is no denying the grandeur of Alain's opening *D major Prelude*, BWV 532, and the fugue is ebullient. The *Trio in D minor* provides a comparatively lightweight transition to a further extended grouping of Bach's splendid Leipzig chorales, including three different settings of *Nun komm der Heiden Heiland*, and two each of *Komm, heiliger Geist* and *Jesus Christus, unser Heiland*. They definitely suit the panoply of colour possible with the Alkmaar organ, and Alain is generally very persuasive. Recording date: again 1990.

Volume 11:*Concertos* (for solo organ): *Nos. 1 in G* (after ERNST); *2 in A min.* (after VIVALDI: *Concerto, Op. 3/8*); *3 in C* (after VIVALDI: *Concerto, Op. 7/11*); *4 in C* (after ERNST); *5 in D min.* (after VIVALDI: *Concerto, Op. 3/11*), *BWV 592/6; Aria in F, BWV 587; Chorale prelude 'An Wasserflüssen Babylon', BWV 653b; Preludes and fugues: in A, BWV 536; in G, BWV 550; Trio in G min., BWV 584.*
(M) *** Erato/Warner Dig. 4509 96744-2 [id.]. Marie-Claire Alain (organ of St Martin, Masevaux).

For Volume 11 (recorded in 1992) Marie-Claire Alain went to France, and this splendid Müller organ with its bright, sunny reeds sounds just right for Bach's vivacious Vivaldi transcriptions. Moreover the manuals and pedals have a compass sufficiently wide for these arrangements to be played as Bach conceived them, which is not possible on certain of the other organs in use for this series. The works by Johann Ernst are also most rewarding. Alain's tempi are apt; allegros are not raced, but they are certainly infectious. The *Aria in F* is a Couperin transcription (from *Les Nations*). The two *Preludes and fugues* are also comparatively lightweight, although still first-class Bach, from the early Weimar period. They are given attractively lively performances. A splendid disc and an ideal sampler to show this artist at her most perceptive.

Volume 12: *Pastorale, BWV 590; Prelude (Fantasia) and fugue in G min., BWV 542; Prelude and fugue in A min., BWV 543; Toccatas: in C, BWV 564; in D min., BWV 565; Toccata and fugue in F, BWV 540.*
✪ (M) *** Erato/Warner Dig. 4509 96745-2 [id.]. Marie-Claire Alain (organs of St Bavokerk, Haarlem; Jakobijnkerk, Leeuwarden).

Using a pair of magnificent Dutch organs, Marie-Claire Alain here (in 1992) surveys an ideally chosen group of Bach's organ works on the largest scale, and she is not found wanting. The pedal solo in the *Toccata in F* is spectacular indeed, while the *Fantasia and Fugue in G minor*, BWV 542, is particularly imposing, with the fugue given a thrilling impetus. The famous *Toccata and fugue in D minor* is a shade resonant – there have been clearer-focused versions – but the performance certainly does not lack panache. The *Prelude and fugue in A minor*, too, has unquestioned flair, while in the *Toccata, Adagio and fugue in C* the clarity of articulation (again with the pedals used spectacularly) is very commanding indeed, and the lyrical feeling in the *Adagio* provides fine contrast. This performance climaxes a recital of the very highest calibre, superbly recorded.

Volume 13: *6 Trio sonatas, BWV 525–30.*
(M) **(*)Erato/Warner Dig. 4509 96746-2 [id.]. Marie-Claire Alain (organ of Aa Kerk, Groningen).

Marie-Claire Alain decided to use the 'other' (Schnitger) organ in Groningen for the *Trio sonatas* and to our ears the organ sounds very good indeed and, if there is a criticism of the sound, it is its relative lack of intimacy as recorded. Alain plays these Italianate works with considerable flair, and she is particularly appealing in slow movements. Just occasionally the running passages of the outer movements seem almost too mellifluous but for the most part these are fresh and highly enjoyable performances that do justice to this splendid old instrument.

Volume 14: *Adagio (& Allegro), BWV 1027; Chorale prelude, 'Ein feste Burg ist unser Gott', BWV 720; Fugue in G min., BWV 578; Passacaglia and fugue in C min., BWV 582; Preludes: in G, BWV 568; in A min., BWV 569; Prelude and fugue in G, BWV 541; Ricercare a 6, BWV 1079; 6 Schübler chorale preludes, BWV 645–50.*
(M) **(*) Erato/Warner Dig. 4509 96747-2 [id.]. Marie-Claire Alain (organ of Stiftskirche, Goslar).

The famous *Schübler chorales* are the highlight of Marie-Claire Alain's final volume. They are particularly imaginative and pleasing. The action of the Goslar organ is more audible than in some of this series, but that is hardly a problem. Alain takes the famous *Passacaglia in C minor* very spaciously, and here she miscalculates slightly, for she does not quite generate a high enough degree of tension to carry it at such a slow speed. The *Fugue in G minor* is a little didactic, too – although again very effectively registered. On the other hand, the *Prelude and fugue in G major* is a considerable success, and the *Prelude in G major* is also a fine performance.

Kevin Bowyer Nimbus series

Volume 1: *Chorale preludes: Aus tiefster Not schrei ich zu dir, BWV 1099; Erbarm' dich mein, O Herre Gott, BWV 721; Concerto in G* (after Prince Johann Ernst), *BWV 592; Fantasia and fugue in G min., BWV 542; Trio sonata No. 1 in E flat, BWV 525.*
*** Nimbus Dig. NI 5280 [id.]. Kevin Bowyer (Marcussen organ of Sct. Hans Kirke, Odense, Denmark).

Volume 2: *Chorale preludes: Ein feste Burg ist*

unser Gott, BWV 720; Gelobet seist du, Jesu Christ, BWV 697 & BWV 722; In dulci jubilo, BWV 751 & BWV 729; Vom Himmel hoch, BWV 738; Fugue (Gigue) in G, BWV 577; Prelude and fugues: in D, BWV 532; in G, BWV 541; Trio sonata No. 5 in C, BWV 529.

*** Nimbus Dig. NI 5289 [id.]. Kevin Bowyer (Marcussen organ of Sct. Hans Kirke, Odense, Denmark).

Volume 3: *Chorale partita: Sei gegrüsset, Jesu gütig, BWV 768; Concerto in D min. after Vivaldi, BWV 596; Preludes and fugues: in F min., BWV 534; in F min., BWV 543.*

**(*) Nimbus Dig. NI 5290 [id.]. Kevin Bowyer (Marcussen organ of Sct. Hans Kirke, Odense, Denmark).

Volume 4: *Fantasia & imitatio in B min., BWV 563; Fugue in C min., BWV 575; 2 Fugues on themes of Albinoni: in A & B min., BWV 950–1; 8 Short Preludes and fugues, BWV 553–60; Toccatas: in G min., BWV 915; in G, BWV 915.*

❁ *** Nimbus Dig. NI 5377 [id.]. Kevin Bowyer (Marcussen organ of Sct. Hans Kirke, Odense, Denmark).

Volume 5: *Aria in F* (after COUPERIN), *BWV 587; Concerto in A min.* (after VIVALDI), *BWV 593; Fugue in G, BWV 576; Prelude and fugue in D min., BWV 539; Toccata and fugue in F, BWV 540.*

*** Nimbus Dig. NI 5400 [id.]. Kevin Bowyer (Marcussen organ of Sct. Hans Kirke, Odense, Denmark).

Volume 6: *Chorale partita 'Wenn wir in höchsten Nöten sein', BWV Anh. 78; Fantasias super 'Valet will ich dir geben', BWV 735–6; Prelude and fugues in E min., BWV 533; G min., BWV 535; Toccata in E, BWV 566; Toccata, adagio and fugue in C, BWV 564; Trio in G min., BWV 584; Trio sonata No. 6 in G, BWV 630.*

*** Nimbus Dig. NI 5423 [id.]. Kevin Bowyer (Marcussen organ of Sct. Hans Kirke, Odense, Denmark).

Volume 7: *Orgelbüchlein: Chorales and chorale preludes Nos. 1–46, BWV 599–644.*

**(*) Nimbus Dig. NI 5457/8 [id.]. Kevin Bowyer (organ of Sct Hans Kirke, Odense, Denmark); Fynske Chamber Ch., Alice Joensen.

Volume 8: *Chorale preludes: An Wasserflüssen Babylon, BWV 653; Herr Jesu Christ, BWV 709 & 726; Liebster Jesu, BWV 731; Wir glauben all' an einen Gott, BWV 765 (4 Neumeister chorales): Wir glauben all' an einen Gott, BWV 1098; Gott is mein Heil, BWV 1106; Herzlich lieb hab ich dich, O Herr, BWV 1115; Was Gott tut, das ist wohlgetan, BWV 1116. Concerto in F* (after Vivaldi's *Concerto, Op. 3/3*); *Fantasia and fugue in C min., BWV 537; Fugue in C min.* on a theme by Legrenzi, *BWV 574; Preludes and fugues: in C, BWV 531; in B min., BWV 544; in C, BWV 547; in A min., BWV 895* (attrib.); *6 Schübler chorales, BWV 645–50; Toccata and fugue in D min. (Dorian), BWV 538; Trio sonata in G, BWV 1039/1027a.*

(B) *** Nimbus Dig. Double NI 5500/1 [id.]. Kevin Bowyer (Marcussen organ of Sct. Hans Kirke, Odense, Denmark).

Volume 9: *Clavier-Ubung. Part 3: German organ Mass: Prelude in E, BWV 552; Chorale preludes, BWV 669–89; 4 Duets, BWV 802–5; Fugue in E flat (St Anne), BWV 552. Concerto in G* (after VIVALDI: *Violin concerto in G*) *BWV 973; Fugue in G min., BWV 578; Passacaglia and fugue in C min., BWV 582.*

❁ (B) *** Nimbus Dig. Double NI 5561/2 [id.]. Kevin Bowyer (Marcussen organ of Sct. Hans Kirke, Odense, Denmark).

Kevin Bowyer is another of the younger generation of organists who is embarking on a complete Bach survey, but he has chosen to produce a series of carefully planned recitals rather than grouping works together in their respective genres. For the collector this may bring the problem of duplication unless the intention is to acquire the whole series, but the advantage is that each CD can be enjoyed as an individual recital. Characteristically, the Nimbus engineeers produce a sound-image with plenty of ambience, with glowing, colourful pipings and throaty reeds, the effect often expansively grand.

The first volume in the series (NI 5280) sets the pattern by framing a collection of lighter pieces and chorale preludes with two ambitious major works. Bowyer's opening *Toccata and fugue in D minor* is second to none, the Toccata strong yet improvisational in feeling; then, after a solemn cadence, the fugue is vividly brilliant with a powerful apotheosis. The sound is magnificently rich in colour.

Volume 2 of Kevin Bowyer's survey (NI 5289), a predominantly cheerful programme, brings more examples of his lively rhythmic style and the appealing colours and husky reeds of this fine Danish organ.

Volume 3 (NI 5290) seems slightly less successful overall than some of Bowyer's collections, with a rather easy-going approach to the *Sei gegrüsset variations* and the Vivaldi concerto, too, not as sprightly as it might be. The framing *Preludes and fugues* are powerful and vigorous, especially the closing *A minor*, but the recording seems fractionally brighter than usual and the reeds just a trifle grainy.

Volume 4 (NI 5377) is much more stimulating, opening with the brilliantly flamboyant *Toccata in G minor* which, after its thoughtful centrepiece, encapsulates a bouncing, minor-key version of the '*Gigue*' *fugue*. This is marvellously played; yet the highlight of the recital is surely the set of *Short*

Preludes and fugues, BWV 553–60. Finally the three-part Weimar *G minor Toccata* closes the programme with sprightly, dancing 6/8 exuberance. The bright, clear recording seems ideally judged, cleaner in focus than the earlier Nimbus CDs in this fine series. There are few more invigorating Bach organ recitals than this.

Volume 5 (NI 5400) begins with Bach's arrangement of Vivaldi, the *Concerto in A minor*, opening jauntily, and almost immediately brings some engaging fluting in the glowing registration, as does the brightly extrovert *Fugue in G*. The colouring of the chorale preludes is nicely varied. The *Prelude and fugue in D minor* has an improvisational thoughtfulness, while the closing Weimar *Toccata and fugue in F* is vigorously articulated and suitably resplendent and weighty. The expansive recording provides a broad canvas but with the lighter detail bright and clear.

Volume 6 (NI 5423) is another well-planned and highly successful collection, that works well as an ongoing recital, on this superb Danish organ which is recorded most spectacularly. The powerful *Toccata, adagio and fugue in C* makes an arresting opener and Bowyer's virtuosity in the two contrasted Fantasias on '*Valet will ich dir geben*' is matched in the two often flamboyant *Preludes and fugues* which are among Bach's most interesting (and exciting). Then the flowing variants on the very attractive chorale, '*Wenn wir in höchsten Nöten sein*', make a perfect contrast before the powerful *Toccata in E*, which demands more and more bravura as it proceeds to its majestic denouement.

Volume 7 (NI 5457/8) is a double and presents the *Orgelbüchlein* with each organ chorale prelude immediately preceded by the sung chorale. While that is an admirable plan, its drawback is that there are no separate cues on the pair of CDs for each organ entry, and this is not even indicated by the overall times for each piece in the back-up documentation. The Danish choir sing admirably, but the choral focus is not as uniformly smooth as with the Amsterdam group on Koopman's set of the *Leipzig* and *Schübler chorales*.

Comparing Kevin Bowyer's performances of the *Orgelbüchlein* directly with Christopher Herrick's versions (which in general we find more satisfying) reveals an astonishing difference of sound and characterization. The Danish organ has much more plangent reeds and Bowyer's performances are less warmly mellifluous, more dramatic. This usually works very well, but at times the characterization seems almost too bold. Yet those who like a lively presentation will find this set very much to their taste, for Bowyer's tempi are usually brisker than Herrick's. He is recorded very vividly.

As with the previous single discs, the two recitals which are paired together in this second Nimbus double (Volume 8) are meant to be listened to separately. Both are highly enjoyable and bring plenty of contrast. On the first, after the vigorous *Fugue in C minor*, BWV 574, the arrangement of Vivaldi's concerto from *L'Estro armonico* for manuals only (no pedals) works extremely well, with the rich blending of colours in the *Largo* well contrasted with the framing allegros. Bowyer's choice of chorales is also intended to give maximum contrast, and sometimes he plays them in pairs to show Bach's imaginatively varied treatments of the same *cantus firmus*.

The *Trio sonata in G* is a conjectural reconstruction, but a very successful one. The *Preludes and fugues* have plenty of life and vigour. Bowyer also opens the famous first *Schübler chorale* with a bouncing rhythmic lift, and is equally enticing in his brilliant registration of the buoyant closing chorale of the set, *Kommst du nun, Jesu*, BWV 650. The recital ends with a superbly exuberant account of the *Dorian Toccata and fugue in D minor* which here proves quite as exciting as its more famous companion in the same key (BWV 565). The Nimbus recording of the magnificent Danish organ is superb in every respect, although the action sounds are also clearly picked up by the microphones.

Both discs of Kevin Bowyer's second Nimbus Double (Volume 9) are meant to be heard together, with the programme centring on Bach's so-called *German organ Mass*. This is music which can seem heavy and boring, but never so here; indeed, this account is unsurpassed on CD. Bowyer's approach is essentially more secular than some (notably that of Marie-Claire Alain), but that does not mean that the music is trivialized. After the powerful introductory *Prelude*, Bach presents each chorale in two contrasting versions, the first elaborate, then a simpler setting without pedals (although occasionally this order is reversed). Bowyer's imagination is inspired to use all the resources of the splendid organ to emphasize the contrapuntal and stylistic differences and create the widest variety of mood.

The fughettas are always pointed with rhythmic sharpness, but when Bowyer uses the organ's fullest resources the effect is weighty but not oppressive. Bowyer gives the four deceptively simple *Duets* sparkling registrations to make a foil for the weighty power of the closing *St Anne's fugue*, which holds the listener from the first bar to the last. Bowyer then continues his recital with a captivating account of Bach's transcription of one of Vivaldi's liveliest violin concertos and he ends with a superbly eloquent performance of the great *Passacaglia and fugue in C minor*, the pacing exactly right (with some remarkable detail at the centre of the work), and with the tension held at the highest level throughout.

Christopher Herrick Hyperion series

Trio sonatas Nos. 1–6, BWV 525–30.

*** Hyperion Dig. CDA 66390 [id.]. Christopher

Herrick (Metzler organ of St Nicholas Church, Bremgarten, Switzerland).

Christopher Herrick is very much of the new generation of organists, giving equal precedence to momentum and vitality and colourful registration, alongside a feeling for the musical architecture. These performances of the *Trio sonatas* may be comparatively relaxed, but the playing has plenty of lift and he produces colours in slow movements to charm the ear, with the lyrical lines flowing. He has an instrument well suited to this repertoire and he is in full command of its palette, with registration suited to the character of each movement and articulation that is precise without pedantry. The Hyperion recording, too, cannot be faulted, and even the order of works is chosen to make the most of their variety of style.

Passacaglia in C min., BWV 582; Toccatas and fugues: in D min. (Dorian), BWV 538; in D min., BWV 565; in F, BWV 540; Toccata, adagio and fugue in C, BWV 564.

*** Hyperion Dig. CDA 66434 [id.]. Christopher Herrick (Metzler organ of Stadkirche, Zofingen, Switzerland).

These are all powerfully structured yet attractively lively performances. The forward thrust is consistently impressive: the famous *D minor* work certainly sparkles yet does not lack power, while the *Fugue in C major* which follows on after the *Toccata and adagio*, BWV 564, is not too heavy. Similarly the *Passacaglia in C minor* has gravitas without seeming too sombre and is glowingly decorated. The recording has fine spectacle and realism.

Canonic variations: Vom Himmel hoch, BWV 769; Chorale partitas: Christ, der du bist der helle Tag, BWV 766; O Gott, du frommer Gott, BWV 767; Sei gegrüsset, Jesu gütig, BWV 767–8; Ach, was soll ich Sünder machen, BWV 770.

*** Hyperion Dig. CDA 66455 [id.]. Christopher Herrick (organ of St Nicholas Church, Bremgarten, Switzerland).

There is certainly no lack of momentum here, and in Christopher Herrick's hands the splendid Metzler organ at Bremgarten illuminates Bach's intricate divisions with a wide colouristic range. He always keeps the music moving and in the *Chorale partitas* this is to advantage. Certainly the recording does the organ justice in vivid palette and truthful balance, and the music-making is consistently alive.

Orgelbüchlein: Chorale preludes Nos. 1–46, BWV 599–644.

*** Hyperion Dig. CDA 66756 [id.]. Christopher Herrick (Metzler organ of Stadkirche, Rheinfelden, Switzerland).

Herrick's *Orgelbüchlein* is in every way recommendable and these performances can stand among the finest in the catalogue. The Swiss Metzler organ seem just right for these relatively simple yet sometimes florid pieces: it has a wide palette and an equal range of sonorities. The effect is never plangent, yet Herrick readily keeps the cantus firmus in front of the listener without exaggeration. His tempi invariably seem apt and his approach is obviously aware of the word-meaning of each chorale and its expressive implications. The recording is beautiful, smooth yet clear.

Fantasias: in C min., BWV 562; in G, BWV 572; in C min., BWV 537; in G min., BWV 542; Preludes and fugues: in A, BWV 536; in A min., BWV 543; in B min., BWV 544; in C, BWV 545; in C min., BWV 546; in C, BWV 547; in D, BWV 532; in E min. (Wedge), BWV 548; in E flat (St Anne), BWV 552; in F min., BWV 534; in G, BWV 541.

*** Hyperion Dig. CDA 66791/2 [id.]. Christopher Herrick (organ of Jesuits' Church, Lucerne).

Among all the individual mixed recitals, this very imposing two-disc set centres on some of the most powerfully structured and intellectually cogent of all Bach's major organ works. Christopher Herrick offers a presentation which is obviously built on a background of careful preparation, with a spontaneously vivid presentation that is as emotionally compelling as it is authoritative, with each fugue moving on to a gripping apotheosis. The chosen Swiss instrument seems ideal for the repertoire and it is superbly recorded, giving weight, amplitude and clarity in equal measure.

'*The Italian connection*': *Concertos* (for solo organ) *Nos. 1 in G, BWV 592* (after ERNST); *2 in A min.* (after VIVALDI: *Concerto in A min., Op. 3/8, RV 522*), *BWV 593; 3 in C* (after VIVALDI: *Concerto in D, Op. 7/11, RV 208*), *BWV 594; 4 in C* (after ERNST), *BWV 595; 5 in D min.* (after VIVALDI: *Concerto in D min., Op. 3/11, RV 565*), *BWV 596; Fugue on a theme of Corelli, BWV 579; Fugue on a theme of Legrenzi in C min., BWV 574.*

**(*) Hyperion Dig. CDA 66813 [id.]. Christopher Herrick (organ of St Peter and St Paul, Villmergen, Switzerland).

This is somewhat disappointing. The Metzler organ Christopher Herrick uses for these concerto transcriptions has a splendid range of colour – witness the delightful palette of the *Largo e spiccato* of Vivaldi's *D minor concerto* (which nevertheless could have been moved on just a fraction faster). But in the allegros Christopher Herrick is not helped by the lack of bite in the reeds, although the spirited finale of that same *D minor Concerto* still sounds splendid. The Corelli *Fugue* on the other hand tends to jog along and the *Concerto movement in C major* for Johann Ernst is quite heavy going.

19 Kirnberger chorales, BWV 690, 691, 694–713; 18 Leipzig chorales, BWV 645–650; 6 Schübler chorales, BWV 645–50.
(N) *** Hyperion CDA 67071/2 [id.]. Christopher Herrick (Metzler organ of Jesuitenkirche, Lucerne, Switzerland).

Christopher Herrick bounces along joyfully in the first two Schübler chorales which open this collection, and how beautifully he brings out the cantus firmus in No. 4 (*Meine seele erhebt den Herren*). These six chorales are among Bach's most masterly settings and these performances are unsurpassed. The eighteen *Leipzig chorales* offer considerable variety, with four texts bringing several contrasted settings of the same cantus firmus. Here at times Herrick is more withdrawn, even sombre, but the particularly fine *Kirnberger chorales* (which come from Bach's last years) are played and registered splendidly. They are all individual settings, which Herrick places in groups where the sources indicate Advent and Christmas, Easter and so on. As with the other recitals in this series the Lucerne organ is beautifully recorded.

'*Miniatures*': *Allabreve in D, BWV 589; Canzona in D min., BWV 588; Couperin Aria in F, BWV 587; 4 Duets, BWV 802/5; Fantasia in A min., BWV 561; in C, BWV 570; Fantasia con imitatione in B min., BWV 563; Fugues: in C min., BWV 575; in G, BWV 576; in G min., BWV 578; Fugue alla giga in G, BWV 577; Musical offering: 3 & 6 part Ricercares in C min., BWV 1079; Pastorale in F, BWV 590; Preludes: in A min., BWV 551 & BWV 569; in G, BWV 568; Preludes and fugues in E min., BWV 533; in G min., BWV 535; in D min., (Fiddle Fugue), BWV 539; in D min., BWV 549a; in G, BWV 550; in A min., BWV 569; Toccata in E, BWV 566; Trios: in D min., BWV 583; in C min. (Fasch), BWV 585; in G, (Telemann) BWV 586; in G (transcription),BWV 1027a.*
(N) *** CDA 67211/2 [id.]. Christopher Herrick (Metzler organ of Stadtkirche, Rheinfelden, Switzerland).

This is a curious mixture. Not all of these pieces are short (the *Pastorale* – a most attractive performance – is in four movements) and many of the *Preludes and fugues*, although not extended, are very considerable works and make a strong impression here. The very opening *Allabreve* is commanding as is the *Toccata in E major* with its weighty pedals. Of course the engaging *Gigue fugue*, the *Couperin Aria* and the *Telemann Trio* (all delightfully registered) are lightweight and serve well as interludes within the more substantial fare. The *4 Duets* properly belong with *Clavier-Ubung*, Part 3. But the set proves an attractive way of gathering up some of Bach's less obvious masterpieces, and they are all splendidly played, and recorded on a fine Swiss organ.

Clavier-Ubung, Part 3: Prelude and fugue in E flat, BWV 532; Chorale preludes, BWV 669/689. Chorale preludes, fantasias & fughettas, BWV 672/75; 677, 679, 681, 683, 685, 687, 715/718, 720/722, 724/727,728 729/736, 738/740.
(N) **(*) Hyperion Dig. CDA 67213/4 [id.]. Christopher Herrick (Metzler main and choir organs of Stadtkirche, Zofingen, Switzerland).

Unlike other recitalists Christopher Herrick does not present Part 3 of Bach's *Clavier-Ubung*, the so-called '*German organ mass*', as a complete entity. He has already given us the four *Duets* in the collection of 'Miniatures' above, so here (on the first disc) he frames just the ten large-scale chorale settings with the mighty *E flat St Anne Prelude and fugue*, using the church's large main organ. Then, on the second CD, turns to the beautiful (if much less spectacular), single manual choir organ for the remaining ten lightweight chorales. In principle this works well enough, but (without retracking) it robs the listener of the added stimulation of hearing Bach's simple and elaborate settings of the same chorale side by side. The other miscellaneous chorales are also played on the main organ. Herrick's performances are well up to standard, but we are inclined to choose Kevin Bowyer's version of Part 3 of the *Clavier-Ubung* which presents the music in the normal published sequence.

Ton Koopman Complete Teldec series

Volume 1: *Canzona in D min., BWV 588; Fantasias: in C min., BWV 562 ; in C, BWV 570; in G, BWV 572; Fantasia and fugue in G min., BWV 542; Fugue in G min., BWV 578; Passacaglia in C min., BWV 582; Preludes and fugues: in C, BWV 531; in A min., BWV 543; in B min., BWV 544.*
(N) *** Teldec/Warner Dig. 4509 94458-2 [id.]. Ton Koopman (Rudolph Garrels organ, Grote Kerk, Maassluis).

Ton Koopman gets his Teldec series off to a good start by choosing a superb early eighteenth-century Netherlands organ at Maassluis – weighty, yet with a glowing upper register. He opens with a richly upholstered *Fantasia in G minor* and yet he gives a nice lift to all the fugues which are aptly paced: his contrasts between prelude and fugue in each instance perceptively judged. The *Canzona* is effectively subdued but the flamboyant *Prelude in C*, BWV 531, and lighter, more buoyant *G major Fantasia* are splendidly done. The programme ends with a massive yet very clearly detailed account of the masterly *Passacaglia in C minor*, which progresses powerfully, yet never sounds leaden. A splendid disc.

Volume 2: *18 Leipzig chorale preludes, with chorales, BWV 651–68; 6 Schübler chorale preludes with chorales, BWV 645–50.*
(N) *** Teldec Warner Dig. 4509 94459-2 (2)

[id.]. Ton Koopman (Müller organ of Grote Kerk) with Amsterdam Baroque Ch.

For Volume 2, Ton Koopman has had the happy and useful idea of presenting two major sets of organ chorale preludes together with the vocal chorales on which they are based. These chorales are sung simply and very beautifully by the Amsterdam Baroque Choir, and the appropriate organ work follows. In the case of the famous *Schübler* set, with which he begins, there are (in all but *Kommst du nun, Jesu, vom Himmel herunter*, BWV 650) two different vocal chorales for each of the organ pieces, which here are played as concert pieces. The *Leipzig chorales* are played and registered very simply, so that the organ variants still carry the (usually) serene character of each hymn-like vocal setting. Both organ and choir are recorded most naturally.

Volume 3: *6 Trio sonatas, BWV 525/30.*
(N) *** Teldec/Warner 4509 94460-2 [id.]. Ton Koopman (Arp Schnitger organ of St Jacobi-Kirche, Hamburg).

These are engagingly sunny performances of beguiling music, Bach at his most lighthearted. There may be more ebullient accounts available on disc but none with more charm. Koopman's tempi are comparatively relaxed, but his concentration never lapses and the effect is consistently winning. The bright, mellow sounds he conjures from this Hamburg organ are a constant pleasure and his joy in the music comes over directly to the listener.

Volume 4: *Preludes and fugues: in D, BWV 532; in E, BWV 566; Toccata, adagio and fugue in D min., BWV 564; Toccatas and fugues: in F, BWV 540; in D min. (Dorian), BWV 538; in D min., BWV 565.*
(N) ❁ *** Teldec/Warner Dig. 4509 98443-2 [id.]. Ton Koopman (Arp Schnitger organ of St Jacobi-Kirche, Hamburg).

A magnificent record. What is so remarkable is the way Koopman uses the very same Arp Schnitger organ as for the *Trio sonatas* above, yet seems to create an entirely new sound world for these great, flamboyant masterpieces. The playing itself is strikingly more extrovert. Indeed these masterly works have never sounded more thrilling on record. The *Prelude in E major* is overwhelmingly massive, and while the fugue bounces along, the work's finale is powerfully expansive. Koopman revels in the nimble pedal-work of the *F major Toccata,* while the bravura scales for both keyboard and pedals at the opening of the *Toccata in C* are quite riveting; he then follows with a beautifully registered (and neatly ornamented) *Adagio* and buoyantly jolly *fugue*. He opens the most famous of all Bach organ *Toccatas – in D minor –* with a repeated trill on the opening phrase and then, with his bravura swirls of notes, creates gripping tension which is only finally resolved at the work's overwhelming cadential apotheosis. The recording is superb, and happily in almost all cases where the music is in more than one section, each is separately cued.

Volume 5: *Clavier-Ubung, Part 3: German organ mass (Prelude and fugue in E flat, BWV 532; Chorale preludes, BWV 669/689; 4 Duets, BWV 802/5). Canonic variations on Vom Himmel hoch, BWV 769a.*
(N) **(*) Teldec/Warner Dig. 4509 98464-2 (2) [id.]. Ton Koopman (organ of Dom St Marien, Freiberg).

The so-called German organ mass is not easy to bring off with its central extended collection of 21 chorales, each in two settings, a large-scale version with pedals, and a simpler presentation without. Koopman sets a serene mood for the earlier *Kyrie* chorales, but is soon extrending his palette and is especially impressive when he comes to contrast the two settings of *Allein Gott in derb Höh sei Ehr* with its following brief fughetta. The arrival of *Wir glauben all an einen Gott* makes an arrestingly powerful contrast. Later Koopman's presentation again becomes more sober. The ambitious *Canonic variations on Vom himmel hoch* make a fine pendant, and the recording is well up to standard. But overall we would not prefer Koopman's version of the *Clavier-Ubung* Part 3 to Kevin Bowyer's Nimbus account.

Volume 6: *Allabreve in D, BWV 589; Fantasia and fugue in C min., BWV 537; Fugue in C min., BWV 575; Prelude in A min., BWV 569; Preludes and fugues in E min., BWV 533; in G min., BWV 535; C min., BWV 546; in G, BWV 550; in C min., BWV 549.*
(N) *** Teldec/Warner Dig. 0630 13155-2 [id.]. Ton Koopman (Christian Muller organ, Waalse Kerk, Amsterdam).

As we know from many previous recordings, the Amsterdam Waalse Kerk organ, with its colourful baroque palette, is ideal for Bach, especially the chorales (see below) and shorter more lightweight pieces. The florid *Prelude in G*, amiable *Prelude in A minor,* busy *Prelude and fugue in G minor*, BWV 535, and the more virtuosic *Prelude in G, BWV 550* are all vividly played and the imitation is well observed in the *Fugue in E min.*, BWV 533, after the bravura flourishes of its lively Prelude. But Koopman opens imposingly with the *C minor Prelude* and its solemn fugue, BWV 546, dating from Bach's early Leipzig years; then he provides contrast with the following separate *Fugue* in the same key, which is a much earlier work and fluently appealing. We stay in *C minor* for yet another work from the same period, BWV 549, with its opening pedal solo, which reappears in the fugue; then aptly the closing Leipzig *Fantasia*, BWV 537, returns once more to this key. It begins over a pedal and has a fugue which is full of interest.

Volume 7: *Pastorale in F, BWV 590; Fugue in G, BWV 577; Pedal-exercitium in G min., BWV 598; Preludes and fugue: in F min., BWV 534; in D min., BWV 539; in G, BWV 541; in C, BWV 545 & BWV 547; Trio in D min., BWV 583.*

(N) **(*) Teldec/Warner Dig. 0630 17647-2 [id.]. Ton Koopman (Christian Muller organ, Waalse Kerk, Amsterdam).

For the *Prelude and fugue in C, BWV 545*, which opens this recital, Koopman uses the authentic earlier three-movement format (Bach borrowed the slow central movement from his *Trio sonata*, BWV 529). It works very well; but then Koopman disappoints with a very laid-back account of the *Gigue Fugue*, lacking rhythmic buoyancy. The *Trio in D minor* is a gentle piece, followed by the vigorous *Pedal-exercitium*, for which – as Bach left it unfinished – Koopman improvises his own ending. The *Prelude and fugue in G*, BWV 541 (which comes from Bach's Weimar period) is another most attractive performance, and the *D minor* work, BWV 539, makes a suitable contrast before the more floridly ambitious work in F minor. Then comes the engaging lightweight four-movement *Pastoral* before the catchy closing *Prelude and fugue in C major* work, with its scalic main subject, a splendid example of Bach's mature style. This is a very well-planned recital, and it is a pity it is slightly let down by BWV 577.

Volume 8: *Orgel-Büchlein: Choral preludes Nos. 1–46, BWV 599–644.*

(N) *** Teldec/Warner Dig. 3984 21466-2 [id.]. Ton Koopman (Riepp Dreifaltigkeitsorgel, Basilka of St Alexander and Theodor, Ottobeuren).

In surveying the chorale preludes in Bach's *Little Organ Book*, Ton Koopman revels in the kaleidescopic colour combinations possible with this splendid eighteenth-century organ at what was once the Benedictine Abbey at Ottobeuren. He varies dynamics imaginatively from piece to piece, interchanging intimacy with an occasional burst of splendour, and decorating the cantus firmus of the gentler pieces with affectionate subtlety. A mysterious, almost blurred effect surrounds *In dulci jubilo* and *Jesu meine Freude* with an acoustic halo, compared with a bright regal trumpety mixture for *Helft mir Gotts Güte preisen* and *Heut triumphieret Gottes Sohn*. There are already several fine sets of these delightful miniature chorales from other organists, but Koopman's certainly ranks with the very best. The recording is flawless.

Volume 9: *Chorale partitas (partite diverse):* (i) *Ach, was soll ich Sünder machen, BWV 770; Christ der du bist der helle Tag, BWV 766;* (ii) *O Gott, du frommer Gott, BWV 767; Sei gegrüsset, Jesu gütig, BWV 678; Chorale preludes, BWV 690–1; 705–8; 728–9; 764; Schmück Dich, o liebe Seele.*

(N) *** Teldec/Warner 3984 24829-2 [id.]. Ton Koopman (i) Riepp Dreifaltigkeitsorgel; (ii) Heilig-Geist-Orgel, both at the Basilika St Alexander & Theodor, Ottobeuren.

For one of the finest CDs of his series, Koopman has sought out the magnificent pair of Rieppe/Silbermann organs in Ottobeuren (named after the Trinity and Holy Ghost respectively) on which to play four of Bach's large-scale *Chorale partitas* in which the diverse variants have the widest range of styles and invite a rich palette of colour. He also choses two sets of chorale preludes as interludes. The first group, beginning with *In dulci jubilo*, BWV 729 is boldly and fully registered; the second, beginning with *Liebster Jesu*, BWV 706 more intimate and spiritual in feeling. The performances are of the highest order, imaginative in matters of registration and tempo, and the echo effects in the final variation of *O Gott du frommer Gott* are matched by *Ach, was soll ich Sünder machen*, with its even more brilliant, kaleidoscopic closing section. Superb recording.

Simon Preston DG series

Allabreve in D, BWV 589; Aria in F, BWV 586 (transcription of Couperin); *Fantasias: in C, BWV 570; Fantasia in G, BWV 571; Fantasias and fugues in A min., BWV 561; Fugues: in C min., on a theme by Legrenzi; in G, BWV 576; Fugue in B min. on a theme of Corelli, BWV 579; Preludes: in C, BWV 567; in G, BWV 568; in A min., BWV 569; in C, BWV 570; Kleines harmonisches Labyrinthe, BWV 591; Preludes and fugues: in A min., BWV 551; C min., BWV 549; Trio in C min. (Fasch), BWV 585.*

(N) **(*) DG Dig. 453 541-2 [id.]. Simon Preston (Klais organ, St John's, Smith Square).

This is Simon Preston's equivalent of Christopher Herrick's collection of miniatures. Not all the music is of equal interest, although the presentation is persuasive, and several pieces are not surely by Bach. But they give Preston a chance to show the wide range of colour of the rebuilt St John's organ, with which he is personally associated, notably the strange *Kleines harmonisches Labyrinth*. The restoration was completed in 1993 and the *Prelude and fugue in C minor* displays the full weight of this magnificent instrument. The St John's acoustic adds a pleasing resonant bloom to the sound yet the reeds are bright, quite like a continental organ, although the effect is slightly more mellow; however, Bach's polyphony is always clearly yet not clinically defined.

Canzona in D min., BWV 588; Fantasia con imitazione in B min., BWV 563; Fugue all giga in

G, BWV 577; Preludes and fugues: in C, BWV 548; in E min., BWV 548; in G, BW. 550; 8 Short Preludes and fugues, BWV 553/560; Toccata and fugue in E, BWV 566.
(N) *** DG Dig. 449 212-2 [id.]. Simon Preston.

This imposing recital includes music from Bach's Buxtehude-influenced early years, two fine *Preludes and Fugues* from his Leipzig period, very impressively played, and some enjoyable music which was probably not written by Bach at all. The *Gigue fugue* is irresistible just the same, and the lightweight *Short Preludes and fugues* are very agreeable listening. No 8, BWV 560 brings an astonishing burst of virtuosity from Preston in a bravura passage on the pedals. The recording is first class.

Concertos (for solo organ) *Nos. 1 in G* (after ERNST: *Concerto*); *2 in A min.* (after VIVALDI: *Concerto, Op. 3/8*); *3 in C* (after VIVALDI: *Concerto, Op. 7/11*); *4 in C* (after ERNST: *Concerto*); *5 in D min.* (after VIVALDI: *Concerto, Op. 3/11*), *BWV 592–6.*
*** DG (IMS) Dig. 423 087-2 [id.]. Simon Preston (organ of Lübeck Cathedral).

It was Prince Johann Ernst who introduced Bach to the Italian string concertos; these are Bach's arrangements, with the music for the most part left with little alteration or embellishment. The two Ernst works show a lively and inventive if not original musicianship. The performances are first class and the recording admirably lucid and clear, yet with an attractively resonant ambience. Again this set stands up well against the currrent competition.

Fantasia and fugue in G min., BWV 542; Passacaglia and fugue in C min., BWV 582; 6 Schübler chorales, BWV 645–50; Toccata, adagio and fugue in C, BWV 564; Toccata and fugue in F, BWV 540.
✿ *** DG Dig. 435 381-2 [id.]. Simon Preston (Sauer organ in St Peter's, Waltrop, near Dortmund).

Simon Preston's recital at St Peter's, Waltrop, is a magnificent demonstration of the splendour and power of Bach's more ambitious organ statements, admirably contrasted with music which is inherently less weighty, if not less inspired. The engaging *Schübler chorales* are used to provide contrast at the centre of the 71-minute recital, and Preston chooses a lighter, more pointed style than usual. The Sauer organ in Waltrop is a modern instrument (1984) of splendid range, with a diversity of colour that is ideal for baroque repertoire and Bach in particular. There is an enormous reserve of power in the pedals, and the richer sonorities elsewhere bring no attendant clouding. This is one of the very finest Bach collections of the digital CD era.

Other organ music

33 Arnstadt chorale preludes (from Yale manuscript).
(B) *** HM Dig. HMA 1905158 [id.]. Joseph Payne (organ of St Paul's, Brookline, Mass.).

Joseph Payne collects the complete set together on a single CD and is very economically priced. Now reissued on Harmonia Mundi's budget Musique d'Abord label, this is even more attractive.

Concertos (for solo organ) *Nos. 1 in G,* (after Ernst), *BWV 592; 2 in A min.* (after VIVALDI: *Concerto in A min., Op. 3/8, RV 522); BWV 593; 3 in C* (after VIVALDI: *Concerto in D, Op. 7/11, RV 208), BWV 594; 4 in C* (after ERNST), *BWV 595; 5 in D min.* (after VIVALDI: *Concerto in D min., Op. 3/11, RV 565*); *BWV 596; 6 in E flat* (arr. of Concerto by an unnamed composer), *BWV 597; Trio in C min.* (after FASCH), *BWV 585; Trio in G* (after TELEMANN), *BWV 586; Aria in F* (from COUPERIN: *Les Nations*), *BWV 587.*
(B) *** Naxos Dig. 8.550936 [id.]. Wolfgang Rübsam (Flenthrop organ of St Mark's Cathedral, Seattle, Washington).

Whereas Wolfgang Rübsam's new ongoing re-recording of Bach's organ music (discussed in detail in our companion *Penguin Guide to Bargain CDs*) has proved at times disappointingly heavygoing, this is a strikingly successful exception. Moreover it is very comprehensive in including the rarely played 'Anonymous' Concerto transcription, BWV 597. This is a most engaging piece, particularly the jaunty closing section, and it is nicely registered, as are the other individual movements here, by Couperin, Fasch and Telemann. Rübsam readily conveys his enjoyment of the Vivaldi concertos and he contrasts the difference between tutti and concertino most effectively. Rübsam's tempi for allegros remain buoyant throughout and the playing is always seemingly spontaneous. The recording is in the demonstration class.

Orgelbüchlein: 19 Chorale preludes for Advent, Christmas, New Year and the Purification, BWV 599–617; Fantasia in C, BWV 570; Fugue on a theme of Corelli in B min., BWV 579; Preludes and fugues in C, BWV 531; in F min., BWV 534; Prelude in G, BWV 568.
(B) *** Naxos Dig. 8.553031 [id.]. Wolfgang Rübsam (Flenthrop organ of Duke Chapel, Duke University, Durham, USA).

Orgelbüchlein: 27 Chorale preludes for Passiontide; Easter; Pentecost; and expressing Faith, BWV 618–44; Fantasia in C, BWV 570; Fugue in B min., BWV 579; Preludes and fugues: in C, BWV 531; in F min., BWV 534; Prelude in G, BWV 568.
(B) *** Naxos Dig. 8.553032 [id.]. Wolfgang

Rübsam (Flenthrop organ of Duke Chapel, Duke University, Durham, USA).

The *Orgelbüchlein* (or 'Little Organ book') includes 46 chorale preludes for the church year, written by Bach partly at Weimar and concluded later at Cöthen. Rübsam has obviously thought deeply about each chorale and its meditative character. His presentation here is very well planned, with preludes and fugues acting as introductions and postludes to the eight groupings, each of which centres on one of the key periods of the Church calendar. Rübsam finds great variety for his presentation of each chorale: *Herr Christ, der ein'ge Gottessohn* could hardly be more jubilant. The Christmas section is preceded by the flamboyant and joyous *Prelude and fugue in C*, with its resounding pedals, and the first recital is rounded off with a characteristically spacious account of the imposing *F minor Prelude and fugue*, BWV 534.

On the second disc Passiontide is heralded by the poignantly atmospheric *C minor Fantasy*. The Easter chorales are, not surprisingly, more robust and outward-giving, while the four Pentecost chorales are touchingly contemplative. There is infinite variety of mood and colour in the last group, opening with a piece symbolizing the ten commandments and showing Bach reflecting on various aspects of the Christian faith. The introduction of the closing *Prelude and Fugue in D minor*, BWV 539, is grave and dignified, but the fugue itself is optimistic and vital, ending the concert satisfyingly. The Duke University Chapel organ is a magnificent instrument, and the recording is superb throughout.

6 Trio sonatas, BWV 525–30 (see also arrangements under Chamber Music – above).
(M) **(*) DG (IMS) Dig. 447 277-2. Ton Koopman (organ of Waalse Kerk, Amsterdam).

Ton Koopman's earlier DG set comes from 1982 and is very well recorded on a highly suitable Dutch organ. The opening of the very first sonata promises well, with a buoyant rhythmic lift; the central *Adagio* is nicely coloured and the finale spirited. The *Adagio e dolce* of *No. 3 in D minor* again shows an apt choice of colouring, but the finale (marked *Vivace*) tends to jog along and the similarly indicated opening movement of No. 6 is also relaxed. Other versions of these works are that bit more spirited but not more glowing, and this is certainly enjoyable.

Organ recitals

Allabreve in D, BWV 589; Chorale prelude: Ach Gott und Herr, BWV 714; Preludes and fugues, BWV 532 and BWV 553–60; Toccata and fugue in D min., BWV 565.
*** Mer. ECD 84081 [id.]. David Sanger (organ of St Catharine's College, Cambridge).

The organ at St Catharine's College, Cambridge, was completely rebuilt in 1978–9. The result is a great success, and its reedy clarity and brightness of timbre are especially suitable for Bach. David Sanger's playing throughout is thoughtful and well structured; registration shows an excellent sense of colour without being flamboyant.

Canzona in D min., BWV 588; Fantasie in G, BWV 572; Passacaglia and fugue in C min., BWV 582; 6 Schübler chorales, BWV 645–50; Toccatas and fugues in F, BWV 540; in D min., BWV 565.
(B) **(*) DG Dig. 439 477-2 [(M) id. import]. Ton Koopman (various organs).

Ton Koopman uses two different organs here, principally that of the Grote Kerk, Maassluis, but the *Schübler chorales* are recorded on that of the Waalse Kerk, Amsterdam, whose reeds are brightly and colourfully projected. The recital opens with the famous *Toccata and fugue in D minor*, BWV 565, and Koopman (as is his wont) introduces decoration into the opening flourishes. The performance has an excitingly paced fugue and is superbly recorded. Contrast is provided by the *Canzona in D minor*, a slow and rather solemn contrapuntal exercise. Overall the performances are well structured and alive, if sometimes rather considered in feeling. The recital ends with the mighty *Passacaglia and fugue in C minor*, BWV 582.

Chorale preludes: Erbarm' dich mein, O Herre Gott, BWV 721; Herzlich tut mich verlangen, BWV 727; O Mensch, bewein' dein' Sünde gross, BWV 622; Wir gläuben all an einen Gott, BWV 680; Fugue in B min. on a theme of Corelli, BWV 579; Passacaglia and fugue in C min., BWV 582; Pastorale in F, BWV 590; Toccata and fugue in D min., BWV 565.
(B) *** EMI Dig. CD-EMX 2218 [(M) id. import]. Peter Hurford (organ of Martinkerk, Groningen, Holland).

Having left his complete Decca Bach series long behind him, Peter Hurford here sets off on his travels again to record a familiar programme on a remarkably fine Groningen organ. Perhaps the most famous *Toccata and fugue* is a fraction less flamboyant than before, and several of the chorale preludes are very relaxed and thoughtful. The *Pastorale*, too, is fairly static. But in the closing *Passacaglia and fugue* he demonstrates how he can hold and build tension when setting off at a very measured pace. What a masterpiece this is! The EMI engineers do him proud.

Chorale preludes: Herzlich tut mich verlangen, BWV 727; In dulci jubilo, BWV 729; Liebster Jesu, wir sind hier, BWV 730; Nun freut euch, lieben Christen g'mein, BWV 734; Nun komm, der Heiden Heiland, BWV 659; Wachet auf, ruft uns die Stimme, BWV 645; Wo soll ich fliehen hin, BWV 694; Fantasias: in C min., BWV 562; in G, BWV 572; Fantasia and fugues: in C min., BWV 537; in G min., BWV 542; Passacaglia and fugue in C min., BWV 582; Preludes and fugues: in A min., BWV 543; in D, BWV 532; in E flat (St Anne), BWV 552; Toccata, Adagio and fugue in C, BWV 564; Toccatas and fugues in D min. (Dorian), BWV 538; BWV 565.

(B) *** Decca Duo 443 485-2 (2) [id.]. Peter Hurford (organs of Ratzeburg Cathedral; Knox Grammar School, Sydney, Chapel; Church of Our Lady of Sorrows, Toronto; New College, Oxford, Chapel; All Souls' Unitarian Church, Washington, DC).

A generous 146-minute collection of major Bach organ works, taken from Peter Hurford's complete survey (see above), brings two separate recitals, each framed by major concert pieces, with the beautifully played chorales used in between the large-scale pieces to add contrast. The current bright transfers seem to have added an extra sharpness of outline to the sound of some of the big set pieces, but this is something which will be more noticeable on some reproducers than on others, and the various organs are caught with fine realism and plenty of depth.

Fantasia in G, BWV 572; Fantasia and fugue in G min., BWV 542; Preludes and fugue: in A, BWV 536; in C, BWV 545; in E min., BWV 548; Toccata and fugue in F, BWV 540.

(N) (M) ** DG 463 017-2 [id.]. Helmut Walcha (organ).

Helmut Walcha represents the older more circumspect German school of Bach playing which is essentially didactic, structurally impeccable, and with every detail laid out clearly before the listener. The famous Alkmaar organ is well focused in an excellent recording.

(i) *Pastorale in F, BWV 590; Passacaglia in C min., BWV 582; 6 Schübler chorales, BWV 645/650;* (ii) *Toccata, adagio and fugue in C, BWV 564;* (i) *Toccatas and fugues: in D min.(Dorian), BWV 538;* (ii) *in D min., BWV 565.*

(N) (M) *** DG 463 016-2 [id.]. (i) Ton Koopman & Simon Preston (organs).

This collection, representing a more modern approach to Bach playing, is divided between Simon Preston, on top form in his two contributions, and Ton Koopman, who has the lion's share and uses two different organs. The *Schübler chorales* are recorded on the organ of the Waalse Kerk, Amsterdam whose reeds are livelier, underscored by the emphatically rhythmic style of the playing. Excellent contrast is provided by the *Pastorale* where the registration features the organ's flute stops piquantly. The other performances are well structured and alive, if sometimes rather considered in feeling. Excellent recording throughout.

VOCAL MUSIC

Complete Cantatas Harnoncourt/Leonardt Teldec series

Cantatas Nos. 1–14; 16–52; 54–69; 69a; 70–117; 119–140; 143–159; 161–188; 192; 194–199 (complete).

(B) *** Teldec/Warner Analogue/Dig. 4509 91765-2 (60) [id.]. Treble Soloists from V. Boys' & Regensburg Choirs, Esswood, Equiluz, Van Altena, Van Egmond, Hampson, Nimsgern, Van der Meer, Jacobs, Iconomou, Holl, Immler, King's College, Cambridge, Ch., V. Boys' Ch., Tölz Boys' Ch., Ch. Viennensis, Ghent Coll. Vocale, VCM, Harnoncourt; Leonhardt Cons., Leonhardt.

Cantatas Nos. (i) *1: Wie schön leuchtet uns der Morgenstern; 2: Ach Gott, vom Himmel; 3: Ach Gott, wie manches Herzeleid; 4: Christ lag in Todesbanden; 5: Wo soll ich fliehen hin; 6: Bleib bei uns;* (ii) *7: Christ unser Herr zum Jordan kam; 8: Liebster Gott; 9: Es ist das Heil; 10: Meine Seele erhebt den Herrn;* (i) *11: Lobet Gott in seinen Reichen;* (ii) *12: Weinen, klagen, sorgen, zagen; 13: Meine Seufzer, meine Tränen; 14: Wär Gott nicht mit uns diese Zeit; 16: Herr Gott, dich loben wir;* (i) *17: Wer Dank opfert, der preiset mich; 18: Gleichwie der Regen und Schnee vom Himmel; 19: Es erhub sich ein Streit.*

(M) *** Teldec/Warner 4509 91755-2 (6) [id.]. Esswood, Equiluz, Van Altena, Van Egmond, treble soloists; (i) V. Boys' Ch., Ch. Viennensis, VCM, Harnoncourt; (ii) Tölz Boys' Ch., King's College Ch., Leonhardt Cons., Leonhardt.

Cantatas Nos. (i) *20: O Ewigkeit, du Donnerwort; 21: Ich hatte viel Bekümmernis;* (ii) *22: Jesus nahm zu sich die Zwölfe; 23: Du wahrer Gott und Davids Sohn;* (i) *24: Ein ungefärbt Gemüte; 25: Es ist nicht Gesundes an meinem Leibe; 26: Ach wie flüchtig, ach wie nichtig; 27: Wer weiss, wie nahe mir mein Ende!; 28: Gottlob! nun geht das Jahr zu Ende; 29: Wir danken dir, Gott; 30: Freue dich, erlöste Schar; 31: Der Himmel lacht! die Erde jubilieret;* (ii) *32: Liebster Jesu, mein Verlangen; 33: Allein zu dir, Herr Jesu Christ;* (i) *34: O ewiges Feuer, O Ursprung der Liebe; 35: Geist und Seele wird verwirret; 36: Schwingt freudig euch empor.*

(M) *** Teldec/Warner 4509 91756-2 (6) [id.]. Esswood, Jacobs, Van Altena, Equiluz, Van Egmond, Van der Meer, Nimsgern, Wyatt, (i) V. Boys' Ch., Ch. Viennensis, VCM, Harnoncourt; (ii) Hanover Boys' Ch., King's College Ch., Leonhardt Cons., Leonhardt.

Cantatas Nos. (i) *37: Wer da gläubet und getauft wird; 38: Aus tiefer Not schrei ich zu dir; 39: Brich dem Hungrigen dein Brot; 40: Dazu ist erschienen der Sohn Gottes;* (i) *41: Jesu, nun sei gepreiset; 42: Am Abend aber desselbigen Sabbats; 43: Gott fähret auf mit Jauchzen; 44: Sie werden euch in die Bann tun;* (ii) *45: Es ist dir gesagt, Mensch, was gut ist; 46: Schauet doch und sehet;* (i) *47: Wer sich selbst erhöhet; 48: Ich elender Mensch, wer wird mich erlösen; 49: Ich geh' und suche mit Verlangen; 50: Nun ist das Heil und die Kraft;* (ii) *51: Jauchzet Gott in allen Landen; 52: Falsche Welt, dir trau ihr nicht; 54: Widerstehe doch der Sünde; 55: Ich armer Mensch, ich Sündenknecht; 56: Ich will den Kreuzstab gerne tragen;* (i) *57: Selig ist der Mann; 58: Ach Gott, wie manches Herzeleid; 59: Wer mich liebet, der wird mein Wort halten; 60: O Ewigkeit, du Donnerwort.*

(M) *** Teldec/Warner 4509 91757-2 (6) [id.]. Kweksilber, Jelosits, Esswood, Jacobs, Van Altena, Equiluz, Van Egmond, Van der Meer, Kunz, Schopper, (i) V. Boys' Ch., Tölz Boys' Ch., Ch. Viennensis, VCM, Harnoncourt; (ii) Hanover Boys' Ch., Leonhardt Cons., Leonhardt.

Cantatas Nos. (i) *61: Nun komm, der Heiden Heiland; 62: Nun komm, der Heiden Heiland; 63: Christen, ätzet diesen Tag; 64: Sehet, welch eine Liebe; 65: Sie werden aus Saba alle kommen;* (ii) *66: Erfreut euch, ihr Herzen; 67: Halt im Gedächtnis Jesum Christ;* (i) *68: Also hat Gott die Welt geliebt; 69 & 69a: Lobe den Herrn, meine Seele; 70: Wachet! betet! betet! wachet!; 71: Gott ist mein König; 72: Alles nur nach Gottes Willen* (ii) *73: Herr, wie du willt, so schicks mit mir; 74: Wer mich liebet, der wird mein Wort halten; 75: Die Elenden sollen essen;* (i) *76: Die Himmel erzählen die Ehre Gottes;* (ii) *77: Du sollt Gott, deinen Herren, lieben; 78: Jesu, der du meine Seele.*

(M) **(*) Teldec/Warner 4509 91758-2 (6) [id.]. Esswood, Equiluz, Kraus, Van Egmond, Van der Meer, Visser, (i) Tölz Boys' Ch., VCM, Harnoncourt; (ii) Hanover Boys' Ch., Ghent Coll. Vocale, Leonhardt Cons., Leonhardt.

Cantatas Nos. (ii) *79: Gott der Herr ist Sonn' und Schild;* (i) *80: Ein feste Burg; 81: Jesus schläft, was soll ich hoffen?; 82: Ich habe genug; 83: Erfreute Zeit im neuen Bunde; 84: Ich bin vergnügt mit meinem Glücke; 85: Ich bin ein guter Hirt; 86: Wahrlich, wahrlich, ich sage euch; 87: Bisher habt ihr nichts gebeten;* (ii) *88: Siehe, ich will viel Fischer aussenden; 89: Was soll ich aus dir machen, Ephraim?; 90: Es reisset euch ein schrecklich Ende; 91: Gelobet seist du, Jesus Christ; 92: Ich habe in Gottes Herz und Sinn;* (i) *93: Wer nur den lieben Gott lässt walten; 94: Was frag' ich nach der Welt; 95: Christus, der ist mein Leben; 96: Herr Christ, der ein'ge Gottes-Sohn; 97: In allen meinen Taten;* (ii) *98: Was Gott tut, das ist wohlgetan; 99: Was Gott tut, das ist wohlgetan.*

(M) **(*) Teldec/Warner 4509 91759-2 (6) [id.]. Esswood, Equiluz, Van Egmond, Huttenlocher, Van der Meer, (i) Tölz Boys' Ch., V. Boys' Ch., Ch. Viennensis, VCM, Harnoncourt; (ii) Hanover Boys' Ch., Ghent Coll. Vocale, Leonhardt Cons., Leonhardt.

Cantatas Nos. (ii) *100: Was Gott tut, das ist wohlgetan;* (i) *101: Nimm von uns, Herr, du treuer Gott; 102: Herr, deine Augen sehen nach dem Glauben;* (ii) *103: Ihr werdet weinen und heulen;* (i) *104: Du Hirte Israel, höre; 105: Herr, gehe nicht ins Gericht;* (ii) *106: Gottes Zeit ist die allerbeste Zeit (Actus tragicus); 107: Wass willst du dich betrüben;* (i) *108: Es ist euch gut, dass ich hingehe; 109: Ich glaube, lieber Herr, hilf meinem Unglauben!; 110: Unser Mund sei voll Lachens; 111: Was mein Gott will, das g'scheh allzeit; 112: Der Herr ist mein getreuer Hirt;* (ii) *113: Herr Jesu Christ, du höchstes Gut; 114: Ach, lieben Christen, seid getrost;* (i) *115: Mache dich, mein Geist, bereit; 116: Du Friedefürst, Herr Jesu Christ;* (ii) *117: Sei Lob und Ehr dem höchsten Gut.*

(M) *** Teldec/Warner 4509 91760-2 (6) [id.]. Esswood, Jacobs, Van Altena, Equiluz, Van Egmond, Huttenlocher, Lorenz, Van der Meer, (i) Tölz Boys' Ch., VCM, Harnoncourt; (ii) Hanover Boys' Ch., Ghent Coll. Vocale, Leonhardt Cons., Leonhardt.

Cantatas Nos. (i) *119: Preise, Jerusalem, den Herrn; 120: Gott, mann lobet dich in der Stille; 121: Christum wir sollen loben; 122: Das neugebor'ne Kindelein; 123: Liebster Immanuel, Herzog der Frommen; 124: Meinen Jesum lass ich nicht; 125: Mit Fried und Freud ich fahr dahin; 126: Erhalt uns, Herr, bei deinem Wort;* (ii) *127: Herr Jesu Christ wahr' Mensch und Gott; 128: Auf Christi Himmelfahrt allein; 129: Gelobet sei der Herr, mein Gott;* (i) *130: Herr Gott, dich loben alle wir; 131: Aus der Tiefen rufe ich, Herr, zu dir;* (ii) *132: Bereitet die Wege, bereitet die Bahn; 133: Ich freue mich in dir; 134: Ein Herz, das seinen Jesum lebend weiss; 135: Ach Herr, mich armen Sünder;* (i) *136: Erforsche mich, Gott, und erfahre mein Herz; 137: Lobe den Herren, den mächtigen König der Ehren.*

(M) **(*) Teldec/Warner 4509 91761-2 (6) [id.]. Esswood, Jacobs, Van Altena, Equiluz, Van Egmond, Hartinger, Heldwein, Holl, Huttenlocher, Thomaschke, (i) Tölz Boys' Ch., VCM, Harnoncourt; (ii) Hanover Boys' Ch., Ghent Coll. Vocale, Leonhardt Cons., Leonhardt.

Cantatas Nos. (i) *138: Warum betrübst du dich, mein Herz?; 139: Wohl dem, der sich auf seinen Gott; 140: Wachet auf, ruft uns die Stimme;* (ii) *143: Lobe den Herrn, meine Seele; 144: Nimm, was dein ist, und gehe hin;* (i) *145: Ich lebe, mein*

Herze, zu deinem Ergötzen; 146: Wir müssen durch viel Trübsal; 147: Herz und Mund und Tat und Leben; 148: Bringet dem Herrn Ehre seines Namens; (ii) *149: Man singet mit Freuden vom Sieg; 150: Nach dir, Herr, verlanget mich; 151: Süsser Trost, mein Jesus kömmt;* (i) *152: Tritt auf die Glaubensahn; 153: Schau, lieber Gott, wie meine Feind; 154: Mein liebster Jesus ist verloren; 155: Mein Gott, wie lang, ach lange; 156: Ich steh' mit einem Fuss im Grabe* (ii) *157: Ich lasse dich nicht, du segnest mich denn; 158: Der Friede sei mit dir; 159: Sehet, wir gehn hinauf gen Jerusalem;* (i) *161: Komm, du süsse Todesstunde; 162: Ach! ich sehe, jetzt, da ich zur Hochzeit gehe.*

(M) **(*) Teldec/Warner Analogue/Dig. 4509 91762-2 (6) [id.]. Esswood, Equiluz, Van Egmond, Hampson, Holl, (i) Tölz Boys' Ch., VCM, Harnoncourt; (ii) Hanover Boys' Ch., Ghent Coll. Vocale, Leonhardt Cons., Leonhardt.

Cantatas Nos. (i) *163: Nur jedem das Seine;* (ii) *164: Ihr, die ihr euch von Christo nennet; 165: O heil'ges Geist und Wasserbad; 166: Wo gehest du hin?;* (i) *167: Ihr Menschen, rühmet Gottes Liebe; 168: Tue, Rechnung! Donnerwort; 169: Gott soll allein mein Herze haben;* (ii) *170: Vergnügte Ruh', beliebte Seelenlust;* (i) *171: Gott, wie dein Name, so ist auch dein Ruhm;* (ii) *172: Erschallet, ihr Lieder;* (i) *173: Erhöhtes Fleisch und Blut; 174: Ich liebe den Höchsten von ganzem Gemüte;* (ii) *175: Er rufet seinen Schafen mit Namen; 176: Es ist ein trotzig und verzagt Ding;* (i) *177: Ich ruf zu dir, Herr Jesu Christ; 178: Wo Gott der Herr nicht bei uns hält; 179: Siehe zu, dass deine Gottesfurcht.* (ii) *180: Schmücke dich, O liebe Seele; 181: Leichtgesinnte Flattergeister;* (i) *182: Himmelskönig, sei willkommen.*

(M) **(*) Teldec/Warner Dig. 4509 91763-2 (6) [id.]. Esswood, Equiluz, Van Altena, Van Egmond, Holl, (i) Tölz Boys' Ch., VCM, Harnoncourt; (ii) Hanover Boys' Ch., Ghent Coll. Vocale, Leonhardt Cons., Leonhardt.

Cantatas Nos. (i) *183: Sie werden euch in den Bann tun;* (ii) *184: Erwünschtes Freudenlicht;* (i) *185: Barmherziges Herze der ewigen Liebe; 186: Argre dich, O Seele, nicht;* (ii) *187: Es wartet alles auf dich;* (i) *188: Ich habe meine Zuversicht; 192: Nun danket alle Gott; 194: Höchsterwünschtes Freudenfest;* (ii) *195: Dem Gerechten muss das Licht immer wieder aufgehen;* (i) *196: Der Herr denket an uns;* (ii) *197: Gott ist unsrer Zuversicht; 198: Lass, Fürstin, lass noch einen Strahl;* (i) *199: Mein Herze schwimmt im Blut.*

(M) **(*) Teldec/Warner Dig. 4509 91764-2 (6) [id.]. Bonney, Esswood, Jacobs, Elwes, Equiluz, Van Egmond, Hampson, Holl, Van der Kamp, (i) Tölz Boys' Ch., VCM, Harnoncourt; (ii) Hanover Boys' Ch., Ghent Coll. Vocale, Leonhardt Cons., Leonhardt.

This pioneering Teldec project, a recording of all Bach's church cantatas begun in the 1970s, has reached completion. Now the whole series has been repackaged and is offered in two alternative choices: as a 60-CD box (with more music on each disc) at bargain price or as a series of ten separate collections, each of six CDs, at mid-price.

The recordings got off to a very good start but, later in the project, various flaws of intonation, and sometimes a feeling that the ensemble would have benefited from more rehearsal, plus occasionally sluggish direction, slightly undermined the overall excellence. However, the authentic character of the performances is in no doubt. Boys replace women not only in the choruses but also as soloists (which brings occasional minor lapses of security), and the size of the forces is confined to what we know Bach himself would have expected. The simplicity of the approach brings its own merits, for the imperfect yet otherworldly quality of some of the treble soloists refreshingly focuses the listener's attention on the music itself. Less appealing is the quality of the violins, which eschew vibrato and, it would sometimes seem, any kind of timbre! Generally speaking, there is a certain want of rhythmic freedom and some expressive caution. Rhythmic accents are underlined with some regularity and the grandeur of Bach's inspiration is at times lost to view. Nevertheless there is much glorious music here which, to do justice to Harnoncourt and Leonhardt, usually emerges freshly to give the listener much musical nourishment. The CD transfers recordings are first class. The acoustic is usually not too dry – and not too ecclesiastical, either – and the projection is realistic.

Cantatas Nos. (i) *208: Was mir behagt, ist nur die muntre Jagd! (Hunt). 212: Mer hahn en neue Oberkeet (Peasant).*

(M) *** Teldec/Warner Dig. 4509 97501-2 [2292 46151-2]. Angela Maria Blasi, Robert Holl; (i) with Yvonne Kenny, Kurt Equiluz; Arnold Schönberg Ch., VCM, Harnoncourt.

Harnoncourt tops off the complete Teldec set of Bach's church cantatas with admirably ebullient accounts of a pair of Bach's secular cantatas, celebrating the name-days of two local dignitaries. The solo contributions in both works are splendid, and Blasi and the robust Robert Holl both enjoy themselves hugely in the boisterous *Peasant cantata*. A lyrical eulogy from the soprano is introduced by a quotation of the famous *La Folia*, and the musical interest of this remarkably inspired cantata (considering its ragbag of a text) is Bach's use of various old melodies familiar to his audience. The exuberance of the performance carries over to Harnoncourt's accompaniments – no scholarly rectitude here – and the recording is first rate.

Complete cantatas Koopman Erato series

Volume I: *Cantatas Nos. 4* (with Appendix: Chorus: *Sie nun wieder zufrieden); 31; 71; 106 (Actus tragicus); 131; 150; 185; 196 (Wedding cantata).*

**(*) Erato/Warner Dig. 4509 98536-2 (3) [id.]. Barbara Schlick, Kai Wessel, Guy de Mey, Klaus Mertens, Amsterdam Bar. Ch. & O, Ton Koopman.

Volume II: *Cantatas Nos. 12; 18* (with Appendix); *61; 132; 152; 172; 182* (with Appendix); *199; 203: Amore traditore. Quodlibet, BWV 524.*

**(*) Erato/Warner Dig. 0630 12598-2 (3) [id.]. Schlick, Wessel; Christoph Prégardien, Mertens, Amsterdam Bar. Ch. & O, Koopman.

Volume III: *Cantatas Nos. 22; 23; 54; 63* (2 versions); *155; 161; 162* (2 versions)*; 163; 165; 208: Was mir behagt, ist nur die muntre Jagd (Hunt).*

**(*) Erato/Warner 0630 14336-2 (3) [id.]. Schlick, Caroline Stam, Ruth Holton, Els Bongers, Elisabeth von Magnus, Andreas Scholl, Paul Agnew, Amsterdam Bar. Ch. & O, Ton Koopman.

Ton Koopman has now embarked on a complete cycle which looks set to challenge the famous Leonhardt–Harnoncourt survey on Teldec. They differ in some important respects and readers will have to decide for themselves how these various factors weigh in their own balance-sheet. First, Koopman favours an intimate approach to choruses – namely one voice to a part – which seems to rob this repertory of some of the sheer majesty and breadth. Second, unlike Leonhardt–Harnoncourt, Koopman opts for female soloists rather than boys, as would have been the case in Bach's day, and he favours mixed rather than solely male choirs. For many this will be a plus point – and it is good news for fans of Barbara Schlick who is pretty well everywhere. Thirdly, and again unlike Leonhardt–Harnoncourt, he goes for a higher than normal pitch – a semitone above present-day pitch which, as Christoph Wolff's notes point out, is what Bach used in Mühlhausen and Weimar, brightening the sonority quite a lot. The singing in virtually all the cantatas is pretty impressive and the instrumental playing is of a high order of accomplishment. Those who set store by security of intonation and excellence of ensemble will probably prefer this new survey to the earlier set. Moreover Koopman offers the collector variants and alternative versions, which will again be an undoubted plus.

Koopman's survey is proceeding on largely chronological lines and Volume III includes the delightful secular cantata No. 208, *Was mir behagt, ist nur die muntre Jagd*, which includes '*Sheep may safely graze*'. All these works come from Bach's Weimar years. For the most part the singing here is of a high order of accomplishment – in particular Andreas Scholl and Elisabeth von Magnus, and the instrumental playing is certainly more finished than is often the case in the Teldec set, though here it is by no means always as fresh or secure as on the Japanese series now underway from BIS (see below). In No. 54, *Widerstehe doch der Sünde*, Suzuki surpasses Koopman in expressive power, and even when he doesn't, the string playing yields in vigour and polish and sonority to the Japanese. Besides offering various appendices, in No. 63, *Christen, ätzet diesen Tag* and in No. 162, *Ach! ich sehe, jetzt, da ich zur Hochzeit gehe*, Koopman gives alternative versions, giving him an undoubted advantage over the opposition.

Complete cantatas, Vol. IV: *Cantatas Nos.: 198: Lass Fürstin, lass noch einen Strahl; 201: Geschwinde, ihr wirbellnden Winde; 204: Ich bin in mir vergnügt; 209: Non sà che sia dolore; 211: Schweigt stille, plaudert nicht; 214: Tönet, ihr Pauken! Erschallet, Trompeten!; 215: Preise dein Glücke, gesegnetes Sachsen.*

(N) **(*) Erato/Warner Dig. 0630 15562-2(3) [id.]. Larsson, Bongers, Grimm, Stam, von Magnus, de Groot, Agnew, Ovenden, Mertens, Bentvelsen, Amsterdam Baroque O and Ch., Ton Koopman.

The fourth volume of Koopman's complete survey is given over to secular cantatas of the Leipzig period from 1726–34, most not included in the complete Teldec survey. Foremost among them is the 1727 Cantata, BWV198, *Lass Fürstin, lass noch einen Strahl* or the '*Funeral ode*' cantata, composed for the ceremonies to mark the death of Christiane Eberhardine, Queen of Poland and Electoral Princess of Saxony. The noble opening chorus is perhaps wanting in breadth (rhythms are often overaccentuated) – memories of Jürgen Jürgens's 1968 version, also with combined Amsterdam and Hamburg forces, are emphatically not erased (see below) – and Koopman's soloists are uneven, particularly Lisa Larsson whose confidence and intonation are occasionally vulnerable (she is better in BWV209, *Non sà che sia dolore*). Generally speaking the men are stronger. Koopman is rather breathless in the opening Sinfonia. All the same there are many felicities in the set and some expert and beautifully light wind-playing. The recording is absolutely first class.

Complete cantatas, Vol. V: *Cantatas Nos. 202: Weichet nur, betrübte Schatten; 205: Zerreisset, zersprenget, zertrümmert die Gruft; 206: Schleicht, spielende Wellen, und murmelt gelinde; 207a: Auf, schmetternde Töne der muntern*

Trompeten; 212: Mer hahn en neue Oberkeet; 213: Lasst uns sorgen, lasst uns wachen.
(N) **(*) Erato Dig. 0630 17578-2(4) [id.]. Larsson, Rubens, Grimm, Bongers, von Magnus, Prégardien, Mertens, The Amsterdam Baroque O and Ch., Ton Koopman.

The fifth volume completes the survey of the Leipzig secular cantatas up to the so-called *Peasant* cantata, *Mer hahn en neue Oberkeet*, BWV212. There is some distinguished singing from Klaus Mertens and Christian Prégardien and some highly accomplished and felicitous solo instrumental playing (there are some wonderfully poetic oboe obbligatos). Lisa Larsson seems far more at ease in BWV202, *Weichet nur, betrübte Schatten*, than she was in the earlier volume, though elsewhere intonation occasionally troubles Elisabeth von Magnus. Generally speaking this gives more consistent pleasure than earlier releases in the series, and the recordings are excellent.

Complete cantatas, Volume VI: *Cantatas Nos. 50; 59; 69; 69a; 75; 76; 104; 186 179; 190.*
(N) **(*) Erato/Warner Dig. 3984 21629-2 (3) [id.]. Ziesak, von Magnus, Agnew, Mertens, Amsterdam Bar. Ch. & O, Koopman.

With this sixth volume of his complete survey, Koopman inaugurates the long series of sacred cantatas from Bach's Leipzig years. With one exception the cantatas in the present set come from the first annual cycle and come from 1723–34. Admirers of Koopman's series will know what to expect from earlier issues, meticulously balanced but at times rather business-like tempi. However the singing of Ruth Ziesak, Paul Agnew and Klaus Mertens is eminently satisfying and the occasional lapses in intonation which marred earlier cantatas are absent. The standard of instrumental performance remains high and the recordings are refreshingly clean and well detailed.

Complete cantatas, Volume VII: *Cantatas Nos. 24; 25 ; 67; 95; 105; 136; 144; 147; 148; 173; 181; 184.*
(N) **(*) Erato/Warner Dig. 3984 23141-2 (3) [id.]. Larsson, Bartosz, von Magnus, Türk, Mertens, Amsterdam Bar. Ch. & O, Koopman.

This volume continues where its predecessor left off, in exploring the first annual cycle of cantatas that Bach composed in Leipzig in 1723–24 including the well-known *Herz und Mund und Tat und Leben*. The character of Koopman's survey is by now well known and admirers need not hesitate, and even if there is inevitably some unevenness in the individual cantatas, few performances disappoint either in accomplishment or the quality of sound the engineers produce.

Complete cantatas Richter DG Archiv series

Cantatas Nos. 4: Christ lag in Todesbanden; 51: Jauchzett Gott; 140: Wachet auf.
(N) (M) *** DG 463 007-2 [id.]. Mathis, Schrier, Fischer-Dieskau, Munich Bach O, Karl Richter.

Cantatas Nos. 56: (i) *Ich will den Kreuzstab gerne tragen; 106:* (ii) *Gottes Zeit ist die allerbeste Zeit (Actus tragicus);* (iii) *147: Herz und Mund und Tat und Leben.*
(N) (M) *** DG 463 006-2 [id.]. (i) Fischer-Dieskau, Chamber Ch., Lucerne Fest. Strings, Baumgartner; (ii) Haefliger; Adam; (i; iii) Töpper; (iii) Buckel, Van Kesteren, Engen; Munich Bach Ch. & O, Karl Richter.

Cantatas Nos. 11: Lobet Gott in seinen Reichen (Ascension oratorio); 67: Halt im Gedächtnis Jesum Christ; 80: Ein feste Burg ist unser Gott.
(N) (M) *** DG 463 009-2 [id.]. Mathis, Reynolds, Schmidt, Schreier, Fischer-Dieskau, Munich Bach Ch. & O, Karl Richter.

These cantata performances are discussed in more detail in the more extended collections below. But all three of these discs show Richter at his finest. Most of the solo singing is very distinguished, the choral contribution is always impressive, there is fine obbligato playing and, with rich orchestral textures, these performances often have a persuasive warmth and nobility. If at times Richter becomes a little earthbound, at others he can generate his own kind of dramatic vitality.

Cantatas (for the latter part of the Church year) *Nos. 5; 26; 38; 55; 56; 60; 70; 80; 96; 106: (Actus tragicus); 115; 116; 130 ;139; 140; 180.*
(B) **(*) DG 439 394-2 (5). Mathis, Buckel, Schmidt, Töpper, Schreier, Haefliger, Fischer-Dieskau, Adam, Engen, Munich Bach Ch. & O, Karl Richter.

This (fifth) Richter box collects cantatas that Bach composed for the last ten Sundays of Trinity, plus three others, a Reformation Festival piece (No. 80), a cantata for St Michael's Day (No. 130) and Bach's funeral cantata, *Gottes Zeit* – the so-called *Actus tragicus* (No. 106); it is given a first-rate performance, with fine solo singing and committed direction. Most of these cantatas are chorale-based and nearly all emerge with the dignity and majesty one expects from these forces. They were all recorded in the Munich Herkulessaal, for the most part in 1978, and the sound is warm and spacious. Karl Richter's heavy tread seems over the years to have moderated into a more flexible and human gait, though a certain inflexibility and lack of imagination still surface occasionally.

Cantatas (for the middle Sundays after Trinity) *Nos. 8; 9; 17; 27; 33; 45; 51; 78; 100; 102; 105; 137; 148; 178; 179; 187; 199.*

(B) **(*) DG 439 387-2 (6). Buckel, Mathis, Stader, Hamari, Töpper, Schreier, Haefliger, Van Kesteren, Fischer-Dieskau, Engen, Munich Bach Ch. & O, Karl Richter.

The fourth box in Richter's series runs to six CDs and offers the cantatas composed for the sixth Sunday after Trinity through to the seventeenth. Again the spacious venue is the Munich Herkulessaal. The chorus is probably larger than it should be, but the results are invariably musical, and Richter shows greater flexibility and imagination than often has been the case. Just occasionally his heavy touch is felt, but so much of this set is first rate that reservations can be all but overruled. The soloists are thoroughly dependable.

Cantatas (for Ascension Day; Whitsun; Trinity): *Nos. 10; 11; 21; 24; 30; 34; 39; 44; 68; 76; 93; 129; 135; 147; 175.*

(B) **(*) DG 439 380-2 (6). Edith Mathis, Ursula Buckel, Anna Reynolds, Hertha Töpper, Peter Schreier, Ernst Haefliger, John van Kesteren, Dietrich Fischer-Dieskau, Kurt Moll, Kieth Engen, Munich Bach Ch. & O, Karl Richter.

The first performance offered here (Volume 3 of the Richter series) is the glorious Ascension cantata, *Lobet Gott in seinen Reichen* (No. 11), which opens and closes joyfully with resplendent trumpets. All four soloists are first rate, and Anna Reynolds is especially memorable in her famous aria, *Ach, bleib doch, mein liebstes Leben*, warmly supported by the strings of the Munich ensemble. Richter's other performances have a breadth and sense of space that are really quite impressive. He makes heavy weather of *Ein ungefärbt Gemüte* (No. 24), but on the whole the dignity of these performances outweighs the occasional pedestrian moments. On the whole a successful box.

Complete cantatas BIS Suzuki series

Cantatas Nos. 4: Christ lag in Todes Banden; 150: Nach dir, Herr, verlanget mich; 196: Der Herr denket an uns.

*** BIS Dig. CD 751 [id.]. Kuriso, Tachikawa, Katano, Kooy, Japan Bach Coll., Masaaki Suzuki.

Although by now we are used to first-class Japanese orchestras and soloists, who could have possibly suspected that we should be embarking on a Bach cantata complete series on period instruments from Japanese singers and players – and recorded by a Swedish record company. The organist and harpsichordist, Masaaki Suzuki went to the Sweelinck Conservatoire in Amsterdam, where he became a pupil of Ton Koopman. Since 1990 he has directed the Bach Collegium Japan and teaches at the Tokyo National University of Fine Arts and Music, from which many of the soloists are drawn. The only European soloist in the first issues is Peter Kooy, also from the Sweelinck Conservatory. Like Koopman, Suzuki uses a higher pitch (A = 465) with its concomitant brighter sound, and he also favours female voices. This naturally places an additional hurdle before the soprano, Yumiko Kuriso, which she surmounts with conspicuous distinction. In many ways, the results of the pupil outstrip those of the master, for these performances radiate more joy in music-making and give more consistent pleasure than many European ones. The strings are clean, and the sense of inhibition – of excessive awareness of the constraints of period performance that occasionally mar the Harnoncourt–Leonhardt set – is refreshingly absent here. Knowing the problems European languages pose for the Japanese, their German diction is more than acceptable. The continuing evidence below suggests that the remainder of the series (which is also including the other major choral works) is going to be as enjoyable as this first instalment – and as well recorded – and this is obviously going to occupy a key contribution in the Bach discography. Recommended with enthusiasm.

Cantatas Nos. 12: Weinen, Klagen, Sorgen, Zagen; 54: Widerstehe doch der Sünde; 162: Ach! ich sehe, jetzt, da ich zur Hochzeit gehe; 182: Himmelskönig, sei willkommen.

*** BIS Dig. CD 791 [id.]. Yumiko Kurisu, Yoshikazu Mera, Makoro Sakurada, Peter Kooy, Bach Coll. Japan, Suzuki.

At almost 80 minutes, the second issue in the series offers splendid value for money and its artistic excellence is again not in dispute. Readers will recognize the opening of No. 12, *Weinen, Klagen, Sorgen, Zagen*, as a model for the *Crucifixus* of the *B minor Mass* and Suzuki gives it with feeling and gravitas, while his characterization elsewhere – both in No. 54, *Widerstehe doch der Sünde* and in No. 162, *Ach! ich sehe, jetzt, da ich zur Hochzeit gehe* – inspires confidence. No grumbles about the quality of the singing, the instrumental response or the present and pleasing sound, which is in the best traditions of the house.

Cantatas Nos. 18: Gleichwie der Regen und Schnee vom Himmel; 152: Tritt auf die Glaubensahn; 155: Mein Gott, wie lang, ach lange; ; 161: Komm, du süsse Todesstunde; 163.

(N) *** BIS Dig. CD 841 [id.]. Midori Suzuki, Schmithüsen, Mera, Sakurada, Kooij, Japan Bach Collegium, Masaaki Suzuki.

Cantatas Nos. 21: Ich hatte vie Bekämmernis (with 3 alternative movements)*; 31: Der Himmel lacht! die Erde jubilieret.*

(N) *** BIS Dig. CD 851 [id.]. Frimmer, Türk, Kooij, Japan Bach Collegium, Masaaki Suzuki.

Cantatas Nos. 22: Jesus nahm zu sich die Zwölfe; 23: Du wahrer Gott und Davids Sohn; 75: Die Elenden sollen essen.

(N) *** BIS Dig. CD 901 [id.]. Midori Suzuki, Mera, Türk, Kooij, Japan Bach Coll., Masaaki Suzuki.

Cantatas Nos. 24: Ein ungefärbt Gemüte; 76: Die Himmel erzählen die Ehre Gottes; 167: Ihr Menschen, rühmet Gottes Liebe.

(N) *** BIS Dig. CD 931 [id.]. Midori Suzuki, Blaze, Türk, Urano, Bach Collegium Japan, Masaaki Suzuki.

Cantatas Nos. 61: Nun komm, der Heiden Heiland; 63: Christen, ätzet diesen Tag; 132: Bereitet die Wege, bereitet die Bahn ; 172: Erschallet, ihr Lieder.

(N) *** BIS Dig. CD 881 [id.]. Ingrid Schmithüsen, Yoshikazu Mera, Makoto Sakurada, Peter Kooij, Japan Bach Coll., Masaaki Suzuki.

Taking stock of the most recent issues in the BIS Bach Cantata series, we can only echo the plaudits with which we have greeted earlier issues in the series. Turning to a Japanese group for the whole cantata cycle was a bold step which has been more than vindicated. As in the earlier issues the singers are uniformly excellent and can give many European soloists and choirs a lesson in diction; their German sounds immaculate. Yoshikazu Mera is a countertenor of the highest quality and the remaining soloists have nothing to fear from comparison with those in the Leonhardt–Harnoncourt set or the Koopman survey on Erato – quite the contrary. Above all the playing has sensitivity allied to vitality, and scholarship blended with imagination. The recordings are very well balanced and finely detailed, very much in the best traditions of BIS. If you find that any of the cantatas listed above fill gaps in your collection, there is no reason to hesitate – and if you are just starting out on a complete collection, this would be a viable first choice.

Cantatas Nos: 71: Gott ist mein König; 106: Gottes Zeit ist die allerbeste Zeit; 131: Aus der Tiefe rufe ich, Herr, zu dir.

*** BIS Dig. CD 781 [id.]. Midori Suzuki, Aki Yanagisawa, Yoshikazu Mera, Gerd Türk, Peter Kooy, Bach Coll. Japan, Masaaki Suzuki.

The present disc collects some of the earliest in the canon from Bach's time at Mühlhausen. Some may feel that Masaaki Suzuki's slow tempo at the opening of No. 106, the *Actus Tragicus* or *Gottes Zeit ist die allerbeste Zeit*, is a little too much of a good thing, but others (like us) may well be convinced by the breadth and space he brings to it. The singing is of a high standard throughout, and Midori Suzuki gives particular pleasure in No. 71, *Gott ist mein König*, with her freshness and expressiveness – as for that matter do Aki Yanagisawa and Gerd Türk. Freshness is what characterizes the chorus and instrumentalists too and what communicates a greater intensity of feeling than many rivals. The BIS sound is first class in terms of both clarity and ambience.

Cantatas Nos.(i) *163: Nur jedem das Seine; 165*: (ii) *O heiliges Geist - und Wasserbad; 185*: (iii) *Barmherziges Herze der ewigen Lieb; 199*: (iv) *Mein Herze schwimmt im Blut.*

(N) *** BIS Dig. CD 801 [id.]. (i–ii) Aki Yanagisawa; (i–iii) Akira Tachikawa, Makota Sakurada, Stephen Schreckenberger; (iii–iv) Midori Suzuki; Japan Bach Coll., Masaaki Suzuki.

Masaaki Suzuki has now at the time of writing reached the ninth volume of this undertaking. He treats this incomparable music with an appropriate sense of awe and at no time does one feel any trace of routine. The musical and technical standard of this BIS series is maintained at the highest level.

Complete cantatas Hänssler Rilling series

Cantatas Nos. (i; ii) *1: Wie schön leuchtet uns der Morgerstern*; (iii) *2: Ach Gott, vom Himmel*; (ii; iv) *3: Ach Gott, wie manches Herzeleid.*

(N) **(*) Hänssler CD 92.001 [id.]. (i) Nielsen, Kraus; (ii) Huttenlocher; (iii) Watts, Baldin, Heldwein; (iv) Augér, Schreckenbach, Harder, Gächinger Kantorei, Bach-Collegium Stuttgart, Rilling.

Cantatas Nos. 4: Christ lag in Todesbanden; 5: Wo soll ich fliehen hin; 6: Bleib bei uns, denn es will Abend werden.

(N) **(*) Hänssler CD 92.002 [id.]. Wiens, Augér, Watkinson, Schreier, Baldin, Kraus, Schöne, Heldwein, Gächinger Kantorei, Bach-Collegium, Stuttgart, Rilling.

Cantatas Nos. 7: Christ unser Herr zum Jordan kam; 8: Liebster Gott, wann werd ich sterben; 9: Es ist das Heil uns kommen her.

(N) **(*) Hänssler CD 92.003 [id.]. Augér, Sonntag, Watts, Schreckenbach, Kraus, Schöne, Huttenlocher, Gächinger Kantorei, Bach-Collegium Stuttgart, Rilling.

Cantatas Nos. 10: Meine Seel erhebt den Herren; 12: Weinen, Klagen, Sorgen, Zagen; 13: Meine Seufzer, meine Tränen.

(N) **(*) Hänssler CD 92.004 [id.]. Augér, Neubauer, Watts, Watkinson, Baldin, Kraus, Schöne, Heldwein, Gächinger Kantorei, Bach-Collegium Stuttgart, Rilling.

Cantatas Nos. 14: Wär Gott nicht mit uns diese Zeit; 16: Herr Gott, dich loben wir; 17: Wer Dank opfert, der preiset mich; 18: Gleichwie der Regen und Schnee vom Himmel fällt.

(N) **(*) Hänssler CD 92.005 [id.]. Laki, Augér, Csapò, Schreckenbach, Schnaut, Baldin, Schreier, Kraus, Huttenlocher, Heldwein, Schöne, Gächinger Kantorei, Bach-Collegium Stuttgart, Württemberg CO, Rilling.

Cantatas Nos. 19: Es erhub sich ein Streit; 20: O Ewigkeit, du Donnerwort.
(N) **(*) Hänssler CD 92.006 [id.]. Rondelli, Kessler, Gohl, Kraus, Altmeyer, Nimsgern, Schöne, Gächinger Kantorei, Frankfurter Kantorei, Bach-Collegium Stuttgart, Rilling.

Cantatas Nos. 21: Ich hatte viel Bekümmernis; 20: Jesus nahm zu sich die Zwölfe.
(N) **(*) Hänssler CD 92.007 [id.]. Augér, Amini, Watts, Hagerman, Kraus, Robinson, Schöne, Anderson, Gächinger Kantorei, Indiana Univ. Chamber Singers, Bach-Collegium Stuttgart, Rilling.

Cantatas Nos. 23: Du wahrer Gott und Davids Sohn; 24: Ein ungefärbt Gemüte; 25: Es ich nichts Gesundes an meinem Leibe; 26: Ach wie flüchtig, ach wie nightig.
(N) *** Hänssler CD 92.008 [id.]. Augèr, Watts, Soffel, Baldin, Kraus, Tüller, Heldwein, Gächinger Kantorei, Stuttgart Bach Collegium, Rilling.

Cantatas Nos. 27: Wer weiss, wie nahe mir mein Ende; 28: Gottlob! Nun geht das Jahr zu Ende; 29: Wir danken dir, Gott.
(N) *** Hänssler CD 92.009 [id.]. Wiens, Augèr, Watts, Sonntag, Schreckenbach, Graff, Harder, Baldin, Kraus, Tüller, Heldwein, Huttenlocher Gächinger Kantorei, Stuttgart Bach Collegium, Rilling.

Cantatas Nos. 30: Freue dich, erlöste Schar; 31: Der Himmel lacht! Die Erde jubilieret.
(N) *** Hänssler CD 92.0010 [id.]. Cuccaro, Augèr, Georg, Baldin, Kraus, Huttenlocher, Schöne, Gächinger Kantorei, Stuttgart Bach Collegium, Rilling.

Cantatas Nos. 32: Liebster Jesu, Mein Verlangen; 33: Allein zu dir, Herr Jesu Christ; 34: O ewiges Feuer, O Ursprung der Liebe.
(N) *** Hänssler CD 92.0011 [id.]. Augèr, Watts, Lang, Kraus, Heldwein, Huttenlocher, Schöne, Gächinger Kantorei, Stuttgart Bach Collegium, Rilling.

Cantatas Nos. 35: Geist und Seele wird verwirret; 36: Schwingt freudig euch empor; 37: Wer da gläubet und getauft wird.
(N) *** Hänssler CD 92.0012 [id.]. Augèr, Hamari, Schreckenbach, Watkinson, Kraus, Heldwein, Huttenlocher, Gächinger Kantorei, Stuttgart Bach Collegium, Rilling.

Cantatas Nos. 38: Aus tiefer Not Schrei ich zu dir; 39: Brich dem Hungrigen dein Brot; 40: Darzu ist erschienen der Sohn Gottes.
(N) *** Hänssler CD 92.0013 [id.]. Augèr, Watts, Schreckenbach, Gohl, Harder, Kraus, Huttenlocher, Nimsgern, Gächinger Kantorei, Stuttgart Bach Collegium, Rilling.

Cantatas Nos. 41: Jesu, nun sei gepreiset; 42: Am Abend aber desselbigen Sabbats.
(N) *** Hänssler CD 92.0014 [id.] Donath, Augèr, Hoeffgen, Hamari, Kraus, Nimsgern, Huttenlocher, Nimsgern, Gächinger Kantorei, Stuttgart Bach Collegium, Rilling.

Cantatas Nos. 43: Gott fähret auf mit Jauchzen; 44: Sie werden euch in den Bann tun; 45: Es ist dir gesagt, Mensch, was gut ist.
(N) *** Hänssler CD 92.0015 [id.]. Augèr, Hamari, Watts, Harder, Baldin, Huttenlocher, Schöne, Gächinger Kantorei, Stuttgart Bach Collegium, Rilling.

Cantatas Nos. 46: Schauet doch und sehet, ob irgendein Schmerz sei; 47: Wer sich selbst erhöhet, der soll erniedriget wernen; 48: ich elender Mensch, wer wird mich erlösen.
(N) *** Hänssler CD 92.0016 [id.]. Augèr, Watts, Hoeffgen, Kraus, Baldin, Huttenlocher, Schöne, Gächinger Kantorei, Stuttgart Bach Collegium, Rilling.

Cantatas Nos. 49: Ich geh und suche mit Verlangen; 50: Nun ist das Heil und die Kraft; 51: Jachzett Gott in allen Landen, 52: Falsche Welt, dir trau ich nicht.
(N) *** Hänssler CD 92.0017 [id.]. Augèr, Huttenlocher, Gächinger Kantorei, Stuttgart Bach Collegium, Rilling.

Cantatas Nos. 54: Widerstehe doch der Sünde; 55: Ich armer Mensch, ich Sündenknecht; 56: Ich will den Kreuzstab gerne tragen; 57: Selig ist der Mann.
(N) *** Hänssler CD 92.0018 [id.]. Augèr, Hamari, Kraus, Fischer-Dieskau, Heldwein, Gächinger Kantorei, Stuttgart Bach Collegium, Rilling.

Cantatas Nos. 58: Ach Gott, wie manches Herzleid; 59: Wer mich liebet, der wird mein Wort halten; 60: O Ewigkeit, du Donnerwort; 61: Nun komm, der Heiden Heiland.
(N) *** Hänssler CD 92.0019 [id.]. Reichelt, Augèr, Donath, Watts, Kraus, Schöne, Tüller, Gächinger Kantorei, Stuttgart Bach Collegium, Rilling.

Cantata No. 201: *Geschwinde, ihr wirbelden Winde (The contest between Pheobus and Pan).*
(N) **(*) Hänssler Dig. CD 98.162 [id.]. Rubens, Danz, Odinius, Taylor, Goerne, Henschel, Gächinger Kantorei, Stuttgart Bach Collegium, Rilling.

Cantatas Nos. 202: Weichet nur, betrübte Schatten; 203: Amore traditore; 204: Ich bin in mir vergnügt.
(N) **(*) Hänssler Dig. CD 92.062 [id.]. Rubens, Henschel; Behringer, Bach-Collegium Stuttgart, Rilling.

Cantatas Nos. 207a: Auf, schmetternde Töne der muntern Trompeten; 212 (Peasant cantata).

(N) **(*) Hänssler Dig. CD 98.163 [id.]. Schäfer, Danz, Olsen, Quasthoff, Volle, Gächinger Kantorei, Stuttgart Bach Collegium, Rilling.

Cantatas Nos. 208: Was mir hagt, ist nur die muntre Jagd (Hunt); 209: Non sa che sia dolore (Wedding).

(N) *** Hänssler CD 92.0065 [id.]. Rubens, Kirchner, Taylor, Goerne, Gächinger Kantorei, Stuttgart Bach Collegium, Rilling.

Cantatas Nos. 208: Was mir behagt, ist nur die muntre Jagd (Hunt); 211: Schweigt stille, plaudert nicht (Coffee).

(N) **(*) Hänssler Dig. CD 98.161 [id.]. Rubens, Schäfer, Kirchner, Taylor, Goerne, Quasthoff, Gächinger Kantorei, Stuttgart Bach Collegium, Rilling.

The Hänssler series looks as if it will be a godsend to all who rebel against the now mandatory period-instrument performances. The recordings were made in the 1970s and early 1980s, by a distinguished team of soloists under Helmuth Rilling. Those who want the warmth and depth of modern strings will not be disappointed. Rilling is an authoritative interpreter in this field whose merits are well known. He is oddly brisk in the heavenly opening of *Liebster Gott, wann werd ich sterben* (No.8) – and in some of the subsequent arias but on the whole his tempi are musically well judged. It is interesting to see that the secular cantatas have been included among the early releases, obviously because these are less well served in the catalogue than the ecclesiastical works. Altogether these readings hold up well and it is good news that the complete series is being restored to circulation in time for the Bach celebations in 2000.

Other Cantata groupings

Cantatas Nos. (i) *4, Christ Lag in Todesbanden;* (ii) *51, Jauchzet Gott in allen Landen!;* (i) *56, Ich will den Kreuzstab gerne tragen;* (i; iii) *140, Wachet auf, ruft uns die Stimme;* (iv) *147, Herz und Mund und Tet und Leben;* (ii) *202: (Wedding cantata).*

(B) *** DG Double 453 094-2. (i) Fischer-Dieskau; (ii) Maria Stader; (iii) Edith Mathis; Peter Schreier; (iv) Ursula Buckel, Hertha Töpper, John van Kesteren, Kieth Engen, Ansbach Festival Soloists; Munich Bach Ch. & O, Karl Richter.

Richter's stereo Bach cantata series for DG, which spanned two decades beginning in the late 1950s, is shown at its finest in this well-chosen half-dozen which are all among Bach's finest works in this form. *No. 4, Christ lag in Todesbanden* is early. Richter seems wholly in sympathy with the music and secures some splendid choral singing and dignified playing from the orchestra. Fischer-Dieskau is featured both here and in the solo cantata, *Ich will den Kreuzstab gerne tragen.* Some might feel that he is at times a little too expressive and over-sophisticated, but he pays characteristic attention to the text. Richter too, is at times a trifle heavy-handed, but this remains a memorable account. No. 51: *Jauchzet Gott* demands an abnormally high tessitura from the solo soprano, and Maria Stader is in splendid voice here (a virtuoso performance which is also most moving) and also in the Wedding cantata, *Weichet nur*, which is one of Bach's most immediately appealing works. Here the discipline of the choir is not always impeccable; but these performances truly belong to Stader, and her singing is firm and clear and shows no sense of strain. No. 140: *Wachet auf, ruft uns die Stimme* (which opens the programme) shows Richter's team at their most impressive throughout, with all the soloists on excellent form and the obbligato wind players, Manfred Clement (oboe) and Edgar Shann (cor anglais) making notable contributions, here as elsewhere. The gloriously heartwarming sound from the Munich orchestra is utterly different from what one would expect from a period-instrument performance today. *Herz und Mund und Tat und Leben* is another very successful performance, with both the soprano and contralto arias beautifully sung by Ursula Buckel and the rich-timbred contralto, Hertha Töpper, respectively. The tenor, John van Kesteren, is also impressive. This cantata contains the famous chorale, *Wohl mir, dass ich Jesum habe* (better-known as 'Jesu, joy of man's desiring') and this is spaciously and warmly presented. All in all, this set with its first-class CD transfers can be given the warmest welcome.

Cantatas (i) *Nos. 4, Christ lag in Todesbanden;* (ii) *56, Ich will den Kreuzstab gerne tragen; 82, Ich habe genug.*

(N) (M) (**(*)) DG mono 449 756-2 [id.]. (i & ii) Fischer-Dieskau, (i) Frankfurt Hochschule Ch., 1950 Bach Fest O, Fritz Lehman; (ii) Ristenpart CO, Karl Ristenpart.

These recordings, reissued as one of DG's 'Originals', come from 1950–51 when the 25-year-old Fischer-Dieskau was on the threshold of his international career. His artistry is heard to excellent effect nowhere more so than in *Ich habe genug*, which is exquisitely sung. Perhaps it is not as poignant as Hans Hotter, nor is Hermann Töttscher's oboe obbligato ideally expressive. The choral cantata, *Christ lag in Todesbanden* receives a dignified and expressive reading though we have heard more finely focused choral singing. Though the sound is not as vivid or present as one might expect, and as usual Fischer-Dieskau himself is forwardly balanced, it is eminently acceptable. A valuable issue, both as a reminder of an earlier Bach style and Fischer-Dieskau's consummate artistry. The CD reproduces the original covers, simple and dignified and a pleasure to behold.

Cantatas for the 1st, 2nd and 3rd days of Christmas, Nos. 40; 57; 63; 64; 91; 110; 121; 133; 151.

(N) (M) **(*) Teldec/ Warner 0630 17366-2 (3) [id.]. Soloists, Gent Collegium Vocale, Leonhardt Consort, Leonhardt; VCM, Harnoncourt.

A gathering of Bach's cantatas for the Christmas season seems an excellent idea, for they are among his finest. The performances are generally well up to the standard of this series. The ear has to accept moments of less than perfect intonation from the treble soloists of the Vienna Boys (notably Detlef Bratsch in No. 91), although on the plus side Peter Jelosits make a fine contribution to No. 53. Similarly among the original instruments, the horns are sometimes wildly astray in their upper harmonics (as in the introduction for the same cantata (*Gelobet seist du Jesu Christ*)). The Gent chorus are not always absolutely reliable either: they are not completely secure in No. 133; yet they are at their best in No. 151, a splendid cantata. But overall there is much to enjoy here and the music-making is appropriately spirited, if at times rhythmically rather didactic.

Cantatas Nos. 8: Liebster Gott, wann werd' ich sterben?; 51: Jauchzet Gott, in allen Landen; 78: Jesu, der du meine Seele; 80: Ein feste Burg ist unser Gott; 140: Wachet auf, ruft uns die Stimme; 147: Herz und Mund und Tat und Leben.

(B) **(*) O-L Double 455 706-2 (2) [id.]. Soloists, Bach Ens., Joshua Rifkin.

Rifkin's performances opt for the one-to-a-part principle not only in his instrumental ensemble but also as far as the choruses are concerned. He opts for female sopranos rather than boy trebles but uses adult male altos. Not all will find his solutions congenial and the use of one voice to a part in the chorales is not always convincing. But there is some good singing in this series, and the playing is lively enough. One feels the need for greater weight and a more full-blooded approach at times, but this is outweighed by the sensitivity and intelligence that inform these excellently balanced recordings. In *Jauchzet Gott* Julianne Baird is an excellent singer who possesses a pleasing voice and has commendable technique. The recording is excellent. *Jesu, der du meine Seele*, another fine work, shows all the four soloists (here Julianne Baird, Allan Fast, Frank Kelley and Jan Opalach) to good advantage.

Cantata Nos. (i) *11: Lobet Gott in seinen Reichen (Ascension oratorio);* (ii) *50: Chorus: Nun ist das Heil und die Kraft.*

(M) **(*) Virgin Veritas/EMI Dig. VM5 61340-2. (i) Kirkby, Tubb, Cable, Jochens, Charlesworth; (ii) Van Evera, Cable, Crook, Grant, Tubb, Trevor, Jochens, Charlesworth; Taverner Players, Parrott – *Magnificat.* **(*)

Bach's cantata, BWV 11, is also known as the 'Ascension oratorio' The first alto aria, *Ach, bleibe doch, mein liebstes Leben* is impressively sung here by Margaret Cable, and the other soloists do not disappoint either. As in the coupled *Magnificat*, the five soloists also economically provide the choruses, one voice to a part, and eight singers pit themselves antiphonally against Bach's spectacular orchestration (including three trumpets) for the chorus from the companion cantata, used as an encore. Some might feel that a larger group would have been more effective here, although the vocal detail is fairly clear. Parrott's performances are certainly refreshing, and very well recorded.

Cantatas Nos. 27: Wer weiss, wie nahe mir mein Ende!; 158: Der Friede sei mit dir; 198: Lass, Fürstin, lass noch einen Strahl (Trauer-Ode).

(M) *** Teldec/Warner 4509 93687-2. Rotraud Hansmann, Helen Watts, Kurt Equiluz, Max van Egmond, Hamburg Monteverdi Ch., Concerto Amsterdam, Jürgen Jürgens.

This is one of the most outstanding Bach cantata records on the market. Not only are the performances extremely sensitive yet vital, with excellent solo and choral singing as well as enthusiastic but disciplined instrumental support, but the cantatas themselves are among Bach's most inspired. The recording, from the mid-1960s, is also first rate.

Cantata No. 51: Jauchzet Gott in allen Landen.

*** Ph. Dig. 411 458-2 [id.]. Emma Kirkby, E. Bar. Soloists, Gardiner – *Magnificat.* ***

Jauchzet Gott is one of Bach's most joyful cantatas; Emma Kirkby follows the example of the opening trumpeting (Crispian Steele-Perkins – in excellent form) when she begins. It is a brilliantly responsive performance, admirably accompanied and very well recorded.

Cantatas Nos. (i) *51: Jauchzet Gott in allen Landen;* (ii) *202: Weichet nur (Wedding cantata);* (i) *209: Non sa che sia dolore.*

(M) *** Teldec/Warner 3984 21711-2. Agnes Giebel, André, Leonhardt, Concerto Amsterdam, Schroeder; or Leonhardt Consort.

Agnes Giebel gives a dazzling account of *Jauchzet Gott* – and so for that matter does the trumpeter, Maurice André. In the so-called *Wedding cantata* Giebel sings superlatively and Gustav Leonhardt's continuo support is beyond praise. *Non sa che sia dolore* is also sung excellently, and here she is most stylishly accompanied by the Leonhardt Consort.

Cantatas Nos. 54: Widerstehe doch der Sünde; 169: Gott soll allein; 170: Vergnügte Ruh'.

*** Hyperion Dig. CDA 66326 [id.]. James Bowman, King's Consort, King.

James Bowman is on impressive form and his admirers need not hesitate here. The present disc is very desirable and the King's Consort under Robert King give excellent support. Good recorded sound.

Cantatas Nos. 56; 82; 99; 106 (Actus tragicus); 131; 158.

(N) (B) *** Decca Double Dig 458 087-2 (2) [id.]. Soloists, Bach Ens., Joshua Rifkin.

Joshua Rifkin's series (where the soloists are one-to-a-part in the chorales) is somewhat uneven but this Oiseau-Lyre set, reissued as a Decca Double, challenges territory conquered in the past by Fischer-Dieskau, Haefliger and Souzay among others. In the two solo cantatas (Nos. 56 and 82), Jan Opalach is magnificent and is excellently supported by Rifkin and his group. Perhaps the marvellous opening ritornello of *Ich habe genug* could have been handled more imaginatively and held together better, though the individual instrumentalists are sensitive. *Der Friede sei mit dir* (No. 158) is much more of a rarity, but is hardly less rewarding. On the companion disc the performance of *Gottes Zeit* (the so-called Actus-tragicus) has considerable merit. Its opening, introduced by a solo recorder, is one of the most beautiful moments in all Bach and it is splendidly done. *Aus der Tiefen* (No. 131) is hardly less fine and the singers are all first class. As elsewhere in this series, one feels the need for greater weight but overall this is a worthwhile reissue.

Cantatas Nos. 57: Selig ist der Mann; 110: Unser Mund seil voll Lachens; 122: Das neugeborn Kindelein.

(N) **(*) HM Dig. HMC 901554 [id.]. Jezovsek, Connolly, Padmore, Kooy, Ghent Collegium Vocale, Herreweghe.

The three cantatas on this disc come from the Leipzig period and the Christmas services of 1724 and 1725. Readers will recognize the kinship of the introductory chorus of *Unser Mund seil voll Lachens* and the *Fourth Orchestral suite*. Much, though not all, of the singing gives pleasure, though the playing of the Collegium Vocale, Ghent, under Philippe Herreweghe is a trifle wanting in the joy that Christmas evokes.

Cantata No. 82: Ich habe genug.

✿ (***) EMI mono CDH7 63198-2 [id.]. Hans Hotter, Philh. O, Bernard – BRAHMS: *Lieder.* (***) ✿

One of the greatest cantata performances ever. Glorious singing from Hans Hotter and wonderfully stylish accompanying from Anthony Bernard and the Philharmonia. This 1950 mono recording was never reissued on LP, and it sounds eminently present in this fine transfer.

Cantatas Nos. (i; ii) *82: Ich habe genug;* (i; iii; iv) *159: Sehet, wir gehn hinauf gen Jerusalem;* (iii) *170: Vergnügte Ruh', beliebte Seelenlust.*

✿ (M) *** Decca 430 260-2 [id.]. (i) Shirley-Quirk; (ii) Lord; (iii) J. Baker; (iv) Tear, St Anthony Singers; ASMF, Marriner.

John Shirley-Quirk's performance of *Ich habe genug* is much to be admired, not only for the sensitive solo singing but also for the lovely oboe obbligato of Roger Lord. But this reissue is to be prized even more for the other two cantatas. Both Dame Janet Baker and Shirley-Quirk are in marvellous voice, and *Vergnügte Ruh'* makes a worthy companion. This is among the half-dozen or so cantata records that ought to be in every collection.

Cantatas Nos. 106: Gottes Zeit ist die allerbeste Zeit; 118: O Jesu Christ, mein Lebens Licht (2nd version); *198: Lass, Fürstin, lass noch einen Strahl.*

*** DG Dig. 429 782-2 [id.]. Argenta, Chance, Rolfe Johnson, Varcoe, Monteverdi Ch., E. Bar. Soloists, Gardiner.

Gardiner directs dedicated, intense performances of three of Bach's finest cantatas, all valedictory works. The new account of No. 118 is more intimate than the 1980 version, less grandly dramatic, more devotional; the whole record suggests a scale of performance apt for a small chapel.

Cantatas Nos. 140: Wachet auf, ruft uns die Stimme; 147: Herz und Mund und Tat und Leben.

*** DG Dig. 431 809-2 [id.]. Holton, Chance, Rolfe Johnson, Varcoe, Monteverdi Ch., E. Bar. Soloists, Gardiner.

Two popular Bach cantatas are coupled in highly accomplished performances under John Eliot Gardiner. The level of instrumental playing is generally more polished than in the celebrated Teldec series, and Ruth Holton, Anthony Rolfe Johnson, Michael Chance and Stephen Varcoe make equally satisfying contributions. The recordings are immediate and well balanced. A strong recommendation.

(i) *Cantatas Nos. 197: Gott ist unsre Zuversicht (Wedding cantata);* (ii) *205: Der Zufriedengestellte Aolus.*

(M) *** Teldec/Warner Dig. 0630 12321 [id.]. (i) Treble and alto soloists from V. Boys' Ch., Max von Egmond, Ch. Viennensis; (ii) Kenny, Lipovšek, Equiluz, Holl, Arnold Schönberg Ch.; VCM, Harnoncourt.

The performance of *Gott ist unsre Zuversicht* does not come from the complete Teldec set, above, but was recorded independently in 1969. It is a wedding cantata and an imposing work in two parts, the second of which was sung after the ceremony. On a large scale it is finely performanced, though the aria '*Schläfert aller Sorgen*' is a little sluggish. The use of boy treble and alto soloists may not be to all tastes but they put up a good showing and the recording is excellent. No. 205 is a much later recording (from 1983) and is digital. Bach describes this cantata as '*Dramma per musica*'. The performance is very good indeed, and the recording has a decently spacious acoustic and no lack of detail. Recommended.

Cantatas Nos. 199: Mein Herze schwimmt im Blut; 202: Weichet nur, betrübte Schatten (Wedding); 209: Non sa che sia dolore.
(B) *** Naxos Dig. 8.550431 [id.]. Friederike Wagner, Capella Istropolitana, Christian Brembeck.

Those who adjudge the meagre string-tone of some period-instrument groups unacceptable should find the sound-world favoured by Christian Brembeck and the Capella Istropolitana much more congenial. *Mein Herze schwimmt im Blut* comes from Bach's Weimar years, and Friederike Wagner proves both sympathetic and lively; and both *Weichet nur, betrübte Schatten*, popularly known as the '*Wedding cantata*', and No. 209, *Non sa che sia dolore* (both well represented in the catalogue), are given thoroughly enjoyable performances. Not for devotees of authentic performance practice, but enjoyable for those who prefer a more traditional approach. Decent recording too.

Cantatas Nos. 202: Weichet nur, Betrübte Schatten; 210: O holder Tag, erwüschte Zeit (Wedding cantatas). Cantata No. 82 (excerpt): Ich habe genug . . . Schlummert ein, ihr matten Augen. Arias (attrib.): *Bist du bei mir* (*BWV 508*, probably by Gottfried Stölzel); *Gedenke doch, mein Geist* (*BWV 509*, Anon.).
(N) *** O-L Dig. 455 972-2 [id.]. Emma Kirkby, AAM, Christopher Hogwood.

This is surely the most delightful of all the records of Bach's solo secular cantatas. Emma Kirkby, in her freshest voice, is ideally cast – as the lovely opening aria, *Weichet nur*, from the most famous of the two *Wedding cantatas*, immediately shows. Her singing is no less ravishing in *Schlummert ein* from BWV 82, *Schweigt, ihr Flöten* ('Hush, you flutes' – Bach here isn't meaning to be taken seriously) from BWV 210, or the most famous 'Bach aria' which is not written by Bach, *Bist du bei mir*. The accompaniments from Hogwood and his Academy of Ancient Music could not have a lighter touch or more finesse, and the obbligato playing (of which there is a great deal) from Frank de Bruine (oboe and oboe d'amore), Lisa Beznosiuk (flute) and Andrew Manze (lead violin) could not be more sensitive or more fluent. What a long way period-instrument playing has come towards beguiling the ear in the last decade! The recording is most natural and very well balanced indeed.

Cantata No. 208: Was mir behagt, ist nur die muntre Jagd! (Hunt cantata).
**(*) Hyperion Dig. CDA 66169 [id.]. Jennifer Smith, Emma Kirkby, Simon Davis, Michael George, Parley of Instruments, Goodman.

This is a cantata rich in melodic invention of the highest quality. The performance has the benefit of excellent soloists and first-class instrumental playing. However the measure is short compared with its competitors.

Secular cantatas Nos. 208: Was mir behagt, ist nur die muntre Jagd (Hunt); 215: Preise dein Glücke, Gesegnetes Sachsen.
(N) ** Ph. Dig. 454 467-2 [id.]. Frimmer, Dawson, Elwes, Wilson-Johnson, Ch. and OAE, Gustav Leonhardt.

Recordings of great clarity and presence with every detail clearly observed. Unfortunately, as is sometimes the case with this much-respected conductor, pleasure is diminished by over-emphatic heavy accents and a general air of earnestness. Good singing and the splendid sound quality do not really lift the spirits. This is resolutely businesslike, earth-bound Bach.

Cantatas Nos. 211: Schweigt stille, plaudert nicht (Coffee cantata); 212: Mer hahn en neue Oberkeet (Peasant cantata).
*** O-L Dig. 417 621-2 [id.]. Kirkby, Rogers, Covey-Crump, Thomas, AAM, Hogwood.

Emma Kirkby is particularly appealing in the *Coffee cantata* and her father is admirably portrayed by David Thomas. Hogwood opts for single strings, and some may find they sound thin. However, there is a corresponding gain in lightness and intimacy. The recording is altogether first class.

Major choral works

Christmas oratorio, BWV 248.
*** DG Dig. 423 232-2 (2) [id.]. Rolfe Johnson, Argenta, Von Otter, Blochwitz, Bär, Monteverdi Ch., E. Bar. Soloists, Gardiner.
(N) *** BIS Dig. CD 941/2 [id.]. Frimmer, Mera, Türk, Kooij, Bach Collegium, Japan, Masaaki Suzuki.
*** Erato/Warner Dig. 0630 14775-2 (2) [id.]. Larsson, Von Magnus, Prégardien, Mertens, Amsterdam Bar. Ch. & O, Ton Koopman.
(B) *** EMI forte CZS5 69503-2 (2). Elly Ameling, Janet Baker, Robert Tear, Dietrich Fischer-Dieskau, King's College, Cambridge, Ch., ASMF, Philip Ledger.
(N) ** EMI/Virgin (SIS) Dig. VCD7 59530-2 (2) [id.]. Schlick, Chance, Crook, Kooy, Ghent Collegium Vocale Ch. & O, Herreweghe.

The freshness of the singing and playing in the DG set is a constant pleasure. Far more than usual, one registers the joyfulness of the work, from the trumpets and timpani at the start onwards. Anthony Rolfe Johnson makes a pointful and expressive

Evangelist, and also outstanding is Anne Sofie von Otter with her natural gravity and exceptionally beautiful mezzo. Beauty of tone consistently marks the singing of Nancy Argenta, Hans-Peter Blochwitz and Olaf Bär. The whole oratorio is neatly contained on two discs, with three cantatas on each instead of two. The sound is full and atmospheric.

As in his recordings of the Bach cantatas, Masaaki Suzuki directs an exceptionally fresh and alert reading of the *Christmas oratorio*, bringing out the joy of Bach's inspiration, with outstandingly crisp singing from the chorus. Speeds are often fast, but when the music cries out for relaxation, as in the beautiful cradle-song, *Schlafe mein Liebster*, in the second of the six cantatas, relaxed pacing allows full expressiveness, here with Yoshikazu Mera as a characterful male alto soloist. Mera in florid writing does not always avoid the intrusive 'h', but that is one of the few blemishes in the solo singing, with Gerd Turk a fine Evangelist and Peter Kooij a firmly focused bass. Warm, atmospheric sound, though with the choir behind the instruments in the main choruses. This makes a fine alternative to the Gardiner version

Koopman with his superb choir and orchestra directs a relaxed and genial account of the *Christmas oratorio*, not as sharply focused as Gardiner's even more polished version on DG Archiv, currently our prime recommendation. It is partly a question of the Erato recording-balance, which favours instruments over voices, but most compellingly so, on a relatively intimate scale. The four soloists also sing the arias, and that includes the Evangelist, Christoph Prégardien, with his sweetly tuned tenor, who translates with no sense of strain from one role to the other. The others may not be as distinctive, but each voice is fresh and clear, well caught in the recording.

With generally brisk tempi (controversially so in Dame Janet's cradle-song, *Schlafe mein Liebster*, in Part II) Philip Ledger's 1976 King's performance anticipates more recent 'authentic' practice. The result is an intensely refreshing account which grows more winning the more one hears it, helped by four outstanding and stylish soloists. The King's acoustic gives a warm background to the nicely styled performance of choir and orchestra and, although in the CD transfer the choral focus is not absolutely clean, the sound overall is attractively balanced – certainly the timpani at the very start sound spectacularly impressive.

With a characterful line-up of soloists, notably Howard Crook as the Evangelist and Michael Chance as male alto, Herreweghe offers a lively reading, well-recorded, which yields to the finest rivals in the choral singing, not quite as crisply disciplined as it might be.

Christmas oratorio: Arias and choruses.
(N) (M) **(*) DG 463 003-2 [id.]. Janowitz, Ludwig, Wunderlich, Crass, Munich Bach Ch. & O, Karl Richter.

While Richter's complete recording would hardly be a top choice, this selection is worth considering. He takes an unvarying view of the chorales, but there is good choral work and the fine solo singing includes glowingly beautiful contributions from Christa Ludwig and the late Fritz Wunderlich, even if Franz Crass, the bass is coarse and unyielding.

Easter oratorio, BWV 249; Cantata No. 66: Erfreut euch, ihr Herzen.
(N) *** HM Dig. HMC 901513 [id.]. Schlick, Wessel, Taylor, Kooy, Collegium Vocale, Herreweghe.

Bach's *Easter oratorio* derives from a secular cantata, more than once revised. It opens with a joyful *Sinfonia* and an *Adagio* with oboe solo (very well played here) followed by a lively chorus ('*Come hasten, come running, ye swift feet*') with trumpets, but then depends very much on the soloists who blend beautifully together in their introductory recitativo before taking their individual roles with distinction – as Mary Magdalen, Peter and John respectively. The chorus and trumpets then return to end the work joyfully. The apt coupling of the *Easter cantata*, BWV 66 with its lovely closing *Alleluja* complete a disc which is fresh and vivid and will be hard to surpass.

Easter oratorio, BWV 249; Magnificat in D, BWV 243.
(N) (M) *** Decca 466 420-2 [id.]. Ameling, Watts, Krenn, Krause, V . Ac. Ch., Stuttgart CO, Münchinger.

This is one of Münchinger's very best records. The *Easter oratorio* and *Magnificat* share the same group of soloists and very impressive they are. Münchinger tends to stress the breadth and spaciousness of both works and the contribution of the Stuttgart Orchestra and the Vienna Academy Choir could hardly be finer, while the vintage Decca recordings have captured the detail with admirable clarity and naturalness.

Epiphany mass (1740) (includes *Cantatas BWV 65; BWV 180; Missa brevis in F, BWV 233*).
(N)*** DG Dig. 457 631-2 (2) [id.]. Monoyios, Davidson, Daniels, Harvey, Gabrieli Cons. & Players, Congregational Choirs of Freiberg & Dresden, McCreesh).

Paul McCreesh has made something of a corner in re-creating great ecclesiastical occasions, presenting church music in context instead of as concert material. Here he has assembled almost three hours of music to represent what might have been heard at Epiphany celebrations in the St Thomas church in Leipzig around 1740, when Bach was in charge. It transforms one's response to the *Missa brevis in F*, for example (in the Lutheran form of *Kyrie* and

Gloria alone) to hear it like this instead of comparing it unfavourably with the great *B minor Mass*. So too with the cantatas, carols, chorales and organ pieces which make up the varied sequence, all superbly performed.

Magnificat in E flat, BWV 243a.
(N) (B) *** Decca Double 458 370-2 (2) [id.]. Palmer, Watts, Tear, Roberts, King's College Ch., ASMF, Ledger – J. C. BACH: *Magnificat;* A. SCARLATTI: *St. Cecilia mass.* ***

Philip Ledger's account, recorded by Argo in the late 1970s, is also most attractive, highly recommendable if boys' voices are preferred in the chorus, and is excellent value. The soloists are first class. This now comes as a Decca Double with Alessandro Scarlatti's splendid *St Cecilia Mass* added, also performed with striking vigour and moving expressive feeling.

Magnificat in D, BWV 243.
*** Ph. Dig. 411 458-2 [id.]. Argenta, Kwella, Kirkby, Brett, Rolfe Johnson, David Thomas, E. Bar. Soloists, Gardiner – *Cantata No. 51.* ***
*** Chandos Dig. CHAN 0518 [id.]. Kirkby, Bonner, Chance, Ainsley, Varcoe, Coll. Mus. 90, Hickox – VIVALDI: *Gloria.* ***
*** EMI Dig. CDC7 54283-2 [id.]. Hendricks, Murray, Rigby, Heilmann, Hynninen, ASMF Ch. & O, Marriner – VIVALDI: *Gloria.* ***
(B) *** Naxos Dig. 8.554056 [id.]. Crookes, Whitaker, Trevor, Robinson, Gedge, Oxford Schola Cantorum, N. CO, Nicholas Ward – VIVALDI: *Gloria.* ***

The better-known, D major version of the *Magnificat* receives an exhilarating performance from Gardiner. Tempi are consistently brisk but the vigour and precision of the chorus are such that one never has the feeling that the pacing is hurried. A splendid team of soloists, and the accompaniment and recording are no less impressive.

Both Richard Hickox and Neville Marriner couple the *Magnificat* with the popular D major *Gloria*, RV 589, of Vivaldi, and for collectors seeking this coupling the clear choice is between period and modern instruments. Those who like the former will gravitate towards Hickox, who directs a most musical account and has the benefit of such fine singers as Emma Kirkby, Michael Chance and Stephen Varcoe, and good Chandos recording. Marriner's performance with the Academy is well paced and executed with precision and fine musical intelligence. No quarrel with the soloists either or the splendidly warm and present recording. Both can be recommended with confidence.

The fresh and lively Naxos version of the *Magnificat*, originally let down by its indifferent cantata coupling, is here attractively re-coupled with an outstanding version of Vivaldi's *Gloria*, also using modern instruments. None of the soloists from the choir, all of them stylish, is identified on the reissue; our listing of their names is retained from the original issue.

Magnificat in D, BWV 243; Masses (Missae breves): in F, BWV 233; in A, BWV 234; in G min., BWV 235; in G, BWV 236.
*** Ph. (IMS) Dig. 438 873-2 (2) [id.]. Bonney, Remmert, Trost, Bär, Berlin RIAS Chamber Ch., C. P. E. Bach CO, Peter Schreier.

Bach's *Short Masses* (sometimes described as 'Lutheran' – although they are sung in Latin) are comparatively little known. Taking their material from cantatas, they have considerable musical interest, with the *A major*, BWV 234 (which draws on *Cantata No. 67* for its *Gloria*), perhaps the most inspired. Yet all four offer many beauties and it is difficult to understand their neglect. This Schreier version can be warmly recommended, for he also includes a fine, fresh account of the *Magnificat*. He has excellent soloists, notably Barbara Bonney and Olaf Bär, and the Philips digital sound is first class. Schreier uses a chamber chorus and stylistically these modern-instrument performances show that he has absorbed much that is attractive from period-instrument practice, with his lively tempi and fresh orchestral textures. Moreover the ambience is particularly pleasing, bringing atmosphere without clouding detail.

(i) *Magnificat, BWV 243;* (ii) Motets: *Singet dem Herrn; Der Geist hilft unser Schwacheit auf; Jesu meine Freude, BWV 225/7.*
(N) (M) ** DG 463 010-2 [id.]. (i) Tomowa-Sintow, Baltsa, Schreier, Luxon, German Op. Berlin Ch., BPO, Karajan; (ii) Regensburg Domspatzen, V. Capella, Academica, Schneidt.

Karajan's reading of the *Magnificat* makes it an orchestral work with subsidiary chorus, and although the ingredients are polished and refined, the results are artificial even though the soloists are excellent. However, the three best-known Motets bring highly enjoyable performances which have a lusty freshness, enhanced by the brightness of the boy trebles of the Regensburger Domspatzen. The accompaniments by period instruments at lower pitch add to the bluffness, and though speeds are on the slow side, the resilience of the playing and singing makes them consistently convincing Excellent, atmospheric 1979 recording.

Mass in B min., BWV 232.
*** DG Dig. 415 514-2 [id.]. Argenta, Dawson, Fairfield, Knibbs, Kwella, Hall, Nichols, Chance, Collin, Stafford, Evans, Milner, Murgatroyd, Lloyd-Morgan, Varcoe, Monteverdi Ch., E. Bar. Soloists, Gardiner.
(N) (***) BBC Legends mono BBCL 4008-7

[id.]. Danco, Ferrier, Pears, Boyce, BBC Ch., Boyd Neel O, Georges Enescu.
*** Hyperion Dig. CDA 67201/2 (2) [id.]. Fritter, Mrasek, Schloderer, Fraas, Rolfe Johnson, George, Tölz Boys' Ch., King's Consort Ch., King's Consort, Robert King.
(B) *** EMI forte (SIS) Dig. CZS5 68640-2 (2) [CDFB 68640]. Donath, Fassbaender, Ahnsjö, Hermann, Holl, Bav. R. Ch. & O, Jochum.
(N) (BB) *** Arts Dig. 47525-2 (2) [id.]. Roberta Invernizzi, Lynne Dawson, Gloria Banditelli, Christoph Prégardien, Klaus Mertens, Swiss Radio Ch. Lugano, Sonatori de la Gioiosa Marca, Diego Fasolis.
(M) *** Virgin Veritas/EMI Dig. VMD5 61337-2 (2) [ZDCB 47292]. Kirkby, Van Evera, Iconomou, Immler, Kilian, Covey-Crump, David Thomas, Soloists from Tölz Boys' Ch., Taverner Cons. & Players, Parrott.
(N) (B) *** Nonesuch/Warner Dig. Ultima Double 7559 79563-2 (2) [id.]. Nelson, Baird, Dooley, Minter, Hoffmeister, Brownlees, Opalach, Bach Ens., Rifkin.
(N) **(*) HM Dig. 901614/5(2) [id.]. Zomer, Gens, Scholl, Prégardien, Kooy, Müller-Brachmann, Collegium Vocale Ch. and O, Herreweghe.
(N) (B) **(*) Naxos Dig. 8.550585/6 [id.]. Wagner, Schäfer-Subrata, Koppelstetter, Schäfer, Elbert, Slovak Philharmonic Ch., Cappella Istropolitana, Christian Bembreck.
(N) (B) * Arte Nova Dig. 74321 63632-2 (2) [id.]. Kwan, Fassbender, Straka, Newerla, Lika, Bach Ens. of Europe Choral Ac. Munich SO, Joshard Daus.
(N) (M) ** DG 463 004-2 (2) [id.]. Stader, Töpper, Haefliger, Fischer-Dieskau, Engen, Munich Bach Ch. & O, Karl Richter.

John Eliot Gardiner gives a magnificent account of the *B minor Mass*, one which attempts to keep within an authentic scale but which also triumphantly encompasses the work's grandeur. Gardiner masterfully conveys the majesty (with bells and censer-swinging evoked) simultaneously with a crisply resilient rhythmic pulse. The choral tone is luminous and powerfully projected. The regular solo numbers are taken by choir members making a cohesive whole. The recording is warmly atmospheric but not cloudy.

In the BBC series, the 1951 studio performance is indeed legendary. Even apart from the solo line-up, Suzanne Danco in her prime (a few months before recording her famous *Mélisande* with Ansermet) as was Kathleen Ferrier, Peter Pears and Bruce Boyce, Leslie Woodgate's BBC Chorus, and at the helm the incomparable Georges Enescu. Menuhin pays tribute to his mentor in a moving note. Robert Simpson spoke of this performance with awe and veneration, and was so inspired by his contact with the great musician and composer that he dedicated his *First String quartet* to him later the same year. The standards of the orchestral playing fall short of what one might expect in a modern commercial recording (the horn is somewhat tentative in the *Quoniam*) but the singing is glorious and the engineers have worked miracles on the sound, which though two-dimensional, is much better than you might expect. Even if you already have a modern stereo version of the *B minor Mass*, this is an essential supplement.

What distinguishes Robert King's vigorous and alert reading is the use of boy trebles not just for the upper parts of the choruses but as soloists too, both soprano and alto. With the distinctive continental tone of the Tölzer Boys, very different from their English counterparts, the performance has extra freshness, with 24 boys set brightly against 12 of the King's Consort tenors and basses. The individual finesse of the boy singers is impressively demonstrated in the solos. The interplay is charming between the treble of Matthias Ritter and the tenor of Anthony Rolfe Johnson in *Domine Deus*, and the direct, careful manner of Matthias Schloderer in the penultimate number, *Agnus Dei*, taken slowly, is most moving in its simplicity. This is a reading which consistently brings out the joy of Bach's inspiration, not least in the great celestial outbursts of the *Sanctus* or the final *Dona nobis pacem*. Warm, atmospheric recording.

Jochum's memorable, dedicated (1980) performance, marked by resilient rhythms, remains among the most completely satisfying versions even today. It makes a real bargain on EMI's forte label, with two discs offered for the cost of a single premium-priced CD. The choral singing – by far the most important element in this work – is superb and, though the soloists are variably balanced, they make a fine, clear-voiced team. Brigitte Fassbaender's *Agnus Dei* is very beautiful; coming as it does before the final choral *Donna nobis pacem*, it helps to leave Bach's inspired music resonating in the listener's memory. The digital recording is admirably spacious and clear. Presentation is attractive; documentation is just about adequate, but with no text.

The Arts label offers a first-rate version at super-bargain price using period instruments. The five soloists are excellent, all with fresh young voices, and with Lynne Dawson radiant in *Laudamus te*. The Lugano Choir of Swiss Radio is outstanding too, with the elaborate counterpoint clean and transparent, thanks also to the recording. Fasano favours fast speeds in period style, giving a joyful lightness to *Et resurrexit*, and making the *Sanctus* happy rather than weighty. The performance gains in freshness and immediacy what it may lack in devotional intensity.

Parrott, hoping to re-create even more closely the conditions Bach would have expected in Leipzig, adds to the soloists a ripieno group of five singers from the Taverner Consort for the choruses. The instrumental group is similarly augmented with the keenest discretion. Speeds are generally fast, with rhythms sprung to reflect the inspiration of dance; however, the inner darkness of the *Crucifixus*, for example, is conveyed intensely in its hushed tones, while the *Et resurrexit* promptly erupts with a power to compensate for any lack of traditional weight. Soloists are excellent, with reduction of vibrato still allowing sweetness as well as purity. If you want a performance on a reduced scale, the recording, made in St John's, Smith Square, is both realistic and atmospheric.

Whether or not you subscribe to the controversial theories behind the performance under Rifkin, the result is undeniably refreshing and often exhilarating. Rifkin here presents Bach's masterpiece in the improbable form of one voice to a part in the choruses; and the listener gets a totally new perspective when – at generally brisk speeds – the complex counterpoint is so crisp and clean, with original (relatively gentle) instruments in the orchestra adding to the freshness and intimacy. The soloists also sing with comparable brightness, freshness and precision, even if lack of choral weight means that dramatic contrasts are less sharp than usual. An exciting pioneering set, crisply and vividly recorded, which rightly won *Gramophone* magazine's Choral award in 1983, and is well worth exploring at Ultima price.

Following the pattern of his other Bach recordings, Herreweghe offers a period performance which thoughtfully avoids extremes, favouring moderate or even slow speeds by period-style standards. He is well served by his choir, though the recording has them placed behind the orchestra, not always cleanly focused on detail. The soloists are all first rate with Veronique Gens and Andreas Scholl outstanding.

The Naxos set offers a chamber-scale performance on modern instruments. The orchestral playing is first rate, very well recorded, with string playing finely detailed and with trumpets braying out superbly to bring out the joy of such numbers as the *Gloria*. The soloists are a reliable team, with the contralto, Martina Koppelstetter, outstanding in her two big solos, *Qui tollis* and *Agnus Dei*, the latter taken broadly with fine concentration. In this of all Bach's works the chorus is central to the success of any performance. In the big extrovert moments like the opening of the *Kyrie* and the *Sanctus*, the singers are bold and confident; at times elsewhere there is less bite, though one doesn't want to make too much of this; Brembeck's pacing is well judged, and this set is still very recommendable in the budget range.

Despite excellent women soloists and bright choral sound, the Arte Nova version cannot be recommended. From the ponderous account of the opening *Kyrie* onwards, Joshard Daus proves an uninspiring conductor, often choosing funereal speeds, with rhythms unsprung. In this price category the Arte Nova is far preferable for a period performance, the Naxos for one on modern instruments.

Richter's performance dates from the early 1970s and is obviously deeply felt. The choral work is well focused, firm and distinct; among the soloists Hertha Töpper is disappointing, but the others, Fischer-Dieskau in particular, are most impressive. But there are far finer versions in this price range.

Mass in B min. BWV 232; Magnificat in D, BWV 243.

(M) *** Erato/Warner 0630 13732-2 (2) [id.]. (i) Rachel Yakar, Jennifer Smith, Birgit Finnilä, Anthony Rolfe Johnson, Philippe Huttenlocher, José van Dam, Lausanne Vocal and Instrumental Ens., Corboz.

Corboz offers the *Mass in B minor* and the *Magnificat* together on a pair of mid-priced Erato discs, and they make a splendid bargain. The two works were recorded in Switzerland in 1979, and the analogue sound is first class in every way, very well balanced in a warm acoustic, yet the chorus has both body and clarity. The professional singers of the Lausanne choir are admirable in both works. In the *B minor Mass*, Corboz's performance has underlying concentration and the *Cum sancto spiritus* is splendidly incisive; like a live performance, as the work proceeds the music-making steadily increases in concentration and power. The *Magnificat* has comparable life and spontaneity, and in both works the soloists make an excellent team. If there are more urgent original-instrument versions of both works available at premium price, notably from Gardiner, this dedicated and inexpensive set should give great satisfaction, particularly as the coupling is so generous and the sound so pleasing.

Motets: *Singet dem Herrn ein Neues Lied; Der Geist hilft unser Schwachheit auf; Jesu, meine Freude; Fürchte dich nicht, ich bin bei dir; Komm, Jesu, komm!; Lobet den Herrn alle Heiden, BWV 225–30.*

(M) *** Teldec/Warner Dig. 0630 17430-2 [2292 42881-2]. Stockholm Bach Ch., VCM, Harnoncourt.

Motets: *Singet dem Herrn ein neues Lied, BWV 225; Der Geist hilft unser Schwachheit auf, BWV 226; Jesu, meine Freude, BWV 227; Fürchte dich nicht, BWV 228; Komm, Jesu, komm!, BWV 229; Lobet den Herrn alle Heiden, BWV 230.*

**(*) Hyperion Dig. CDA 66369 [id.]. The Sixteen, Harry Christophers.

To Bach's motets, which include some of the greatest music he ever wrote for chorus, went the honour of being the first of his vocal music to be issued digitally in 1980. The Teldec recording is very successful indeed, beautifully fresh and clear, the acoustic attractively resonant without clouding detail, and the accompanying instrumental group giving discreet yet telling support. The vigour and joy of the singing come over splendidly. This is one of Harnoncourt's most impressive Bach records, and the conductor's timing and use of pauses are finely judged, while the Stockholm chorus show stamina as well as sympathy; the spontaneity of their performance is impressive. At mid-price this must now be the prime recommendation for these six works.

Christophers and The Sixteen give elegant readings, beautifully tuned and balanced, of the six principal motets, not as strongly characterized as Harnoncourt's but consistently refreshing and satisfying.

St John Passion, BWV 245.

*** DG Dig. 419 324-2 (2) [id.]. Rolfe Johnson, Varcoe, Hauptmann, Argenta & soloists, Monteverdi Ch., E. Bar. Sol., Gardiner.

*** Erato/Warner Dig. 4509-94675-2 (2) [id.]. Barbara Schlick, Kai Wessel, Guy de Mey, Gerd Türk, Peter Kooy, Klaus Mertens, Netherlands Bach Soc. Ch., Amsterdam Bar. O, Koopman.

(N) *** BIS Dig. CD 921/22 [id.]. Schmithüsen, Mera, Türk, Sakurada, Hida, Urano, Kooij, Bach Collegium, Japan, Masaaki Suzuki.

*** Columns Dig. 290241 (2). John Mark Ainsley, Catherine Bott, Paul Agnew, Michael Chance, King's College, Cambridge, Ch., Brandenburg Consort, Stephen Cleobury.

*** Hänssler Dig. CD 98.170 [id.]. Juliane Banse, Ingelborg Danz, Michael Schade, James Taylor, Matthias Goerne, Andreas Schmidt, Helmuth Rilling, Stuttgart Gächinger Kantorei & Bach-Collegium, Rilling.

(N) (B) **(*) RCA Twofer 74321 49181-2 (2) [id.]. Arleen Augér, Peter Schreier, Armin Ude, Theo Adam, Siegfried Lorenz, Heidi Reiss, Leipzig Thomanerchor & Gewandhaus O, Hans/Joachim Rotzsch.

(N) ** Hänssler Dig. CD 98.968(2) [id.]. Schäfer, Jänicke, Kras, Hagen, Possemeyer, Stuttgarter Hymnus-Chorkknaben, Eckkkhard Weyand.

(i) *St John Passion;* (ii) *Cantata No. 140: Wachet auf.*

(N) (B) **(*) Ph. Duo 462 173-2 (2) [id.]. Giebel, Haefliger, Berry, Hoffgen, Young, Crass, Netherlands Radio Ch., Concg. O, Jochum; (ii) Ameling, Baldin, Ramey, London Voices, ECO, Leppard.

Gardiner conducts an exhilarating performance, so dramatic in its approach and so wide-ranging in the emotions conveyed it might be a religious opera. Speeds are regularly on the fast side but, characteristically, Gardiner consistently keeps a spring in the rhythm. Chorales are treated in contrasted ways, which may not please the more severe authenticists but, as with so much of Gardiner's work, here is a performance using authentic scale and period instruments which speaks in the most vivid way to anyone prepared to listen, not just to the specialist. Soloists – regular contributors to Gardiner's team – are all first rate. Warm and atmospheric, yet clear and detailed recording.

The great glory of the Koopman version is the vividly dramatic singing of the choir, very much a protagonist in the drama of the Passion, both in the virtuoso rendering of the turba choruses (one can really imagine an angry mob) and also in the meditative commentary of the big choruses and in the freshness of the chorales. The soprano, Barbara Schlick, is pure and silvery, setting the pattern for clear, fresh voices. The other soloists complete a fine team, with Guy de Mey an expressive Evangelist, well contrasted with the solo tenor in the arias, Gerd Türk, and with the Jesus of Peter Kooy contrasted against Klaus Mertens in the arias and incidental roles, though not everyone will like the hooty counter-tenor of Kai Wessel. This is a keen contender even against the Gardiner version, though the Erato recording is not as bright and clear, with the chorus set a little behind the orchestra.

Suzuki directs an urgently refreshing reading of the *St John Passion*, with fine singing from the chorus giving dramatic impact to the 'turba' choruses. The big choruses at beginning and end are beautifully sung too, though there the voices are set back behind the orchestra and are rather lightweight. Suzuki's feeling for the natural timing of numbers – generally on the fast side in the modern period manner – is impeccable, and the soloists make an excellent team, with Gerd Türk an outstanding Evangelist, light and clear.

Stephen Cleobury conducts a lively, well-paced reading using period instruments, with an excellent team of characterful soloists and with the fresh-toned choir of King's College Choir, including boy-trebles, adding dramatic bite. What specially distinguishes this set is that the alternative numbers which Bach wrote for the revival in 1725 are given in an appendix, including the chorale fantasy which he wrote in place of the opening chorus and the chorale postlude he wrote in place of the final chorale. John Mark Ainsley is a warmly expressive tenor Evangelist, nicely contrasted with the lighter-toned Paul Agnew, who sings the tenor arias. Among the others, Catherine Bott is warmer and more tenderly expressive than almost any latterday rival, very different from the usual light, bright sopranos used in most period performances; and the counter-tenor, Michael Chance, sounds in fuller, warmer voice here than in Gardiner's DG Archiv version, a question of recording-balance, with the Cleobury performance setting the soloists close so as to counteract the reverberant acoustic of King's College Chapel. Most enjoyable.

The Rilling version on Hänssler uses rather

larger forces than on most period versions and, paradoxically, modern instruments are used in period style, using today's higher pitch. Speeds in recitative tend to be broader in a relatively traditional way, but that allows the soloists, notably the superb Evangelist, Michael Schade, to bring out the meaning of the words most vividly, with an electrifying sense of drama, most important in this work. The other soloists are outstanding too, all of them young singers with firm, characterful voices, and they sound particularly well on record. The third disc comes as a (free) appendix, giving not just the five alternative numbers which Bach wrote for the 1725 revival but also detailed changes in various numbers, setting fragments from the original against the amended versions. These are explained in a spoken commentary between items, so that it is vital for English-speaking listeners to get the English-language version, instead of Hänssler's main German issue, which also has a single-language booklet of notes.

Rotzsch's version was recorded for Ariola in 1975–6, and, using modern instruments, presents a performance which in some ways anticipates period practice, with chorales and recitative generally brisk. The soloists make a strong and characterful team, with Peter Schreier as the Evangelist at his very peak, clear and true and more powerful than most, as well as deeply expressive. It is good too to hear Arleen Augér in the soprano arias. Full, warm sound. A good 'twofer' package.

Eugen Jochum's 1967 recording with the Concertgebouwe represents the old German tradition at its finest, with weighty choral singing, and with dedicated performances sustaining even the slowest speeds. The final chorale sung in crescendo, blazes in fervour, maybe unauthentic but deeply moving. Though Jochum's speeds are slow, this Philips Duo still generously adds to the *Passion* a fine performance of the cantata, *Wachet auf*, recorded in 1981 under Raymond Leppard.

The alternative Hänssler set under Eckhard Weyand offers a crisp and fresh reading using modern instruments, very well-recorded. The manner is plain, the speeds are well chosen, and it is interesting to hear Christine Schäfer at the very beginning of her career, recorded in 1990. Otherwise, at full-price hardly a first choice.

(i) *St. John Passion, BWV 245;* (ii) *Cantata No. 10: Meine Seele erhebt den Herren.*
(N) (B) **(*) Decca Double 460 223-2 (2) [id.]. (i) Watts, Krenn, Rintzler, (i–ii) Ameling, (i) V. Ac. Ch.; (ii) Ellenbeck, Berry, Hamari, Hollweg, Prey, Stuttgart Hymnus Ch.; Stuttgart CO, Münchinger.

Münchinger's reading matches his other recordings of Bach's choral works, with a superb line-up of soloists, all of them clear-toned and precise, and a fresh, young-sounding tenor as Evangelist, Dieter Ellenbeck. Though Münchinger does not equal a conductor like Britten in individuality of imagination, he points the musical balance of the score most satisfyingly without idiosyncrasy. For sound scholarly reasons he uses organ continuo with no harpsichord. The *Cantata* is very well performed too, and the recordings are excellent. Good value.

St John Passion, BWV 245 (sung in English).
✿ (B) *** Decca Double 443 859-2 (2) [id.]. Peter Pears, Heather Harper, Alfreda Hodgson, Robert Tear, Gwynne Howell, John Shirley-Quirk, Wandsworth School Boys' Ch., ECO, Britten.

Britten characteristically refuses to follow any set tradition, whether baroque, Victorian or whatever; and, with greater extremes of tempo than is common (often strikingly fast), the result makes one listen afresh. The soloists are all excellent, Heather Harper radiant, and the Wandsworth School Boys' Choir reinforces the freshness of the interpretation. A superb bargain.

St John Passion, BWV 245: Arias and choruses.
(N) (M) *** DG 463 002-2 [id.]. Argenta, Chance, Archer, Müller, Hauptmann, Monteverdi Ch., E. Bar. Soloists, Gardiner.

St Matthew Passion, BWV 244 (excerpts).
(N) (M) ** DG 463 001-2 [id.]. Janowitz, Ludwig, BPO, Karajan.

The selection from Gardiner's exhilarating performance of the *St John Passion*, combining high drama with deep expressive feeling, could hardly be more contrasted with the excerpts from Karajan's *St Matthew Passion*, which are above all polished and smooth, with excellent singing and recording moulded to the rather flat interpretation.

St Mark Passion (reconstructed Andor Gomme with recitatives and turbas by Reinhard Keiser).
(N) **(*) ASV Dig CDGAX 237 (2) [id.]. Jeremy Ovenden, Timothy Mirfin, Ruth Gomme, William Towers, James Gilchrist, Paul Thompson, Gonville & Caius College Ch., Cambridge, Cambridge Bar. Camerata, Geoffrey Webber (with KEISER: *Laudate pueri Domini* **(*)).

Of the five Passion settings that Bach is thought to have written, two are the masterpieces we know, the *St Matthew* and the *St John*, and two are completely lost. The fifth is the *St Mark Passion*, performed in Leipzig in 1731 at a difficult time for the composer. The libretto was unearthed last century, and it has been deduced that Bach simply used existing material. More specifically, there is strong evidence that he used the various movements of the *Cantata* No. 198 or *Trauer-Ode*, 'Ode of Mourning', to provide the opening and closing choruses and three of the six arias. The chorales, far more of them than in the other two Passions, are taken from the collection of Bach's chorales prepared by his son, Carl Philipp Emanuel. Andor Gomme, editor of the edition used here, explains the detective work required to fill in the rest, and his decision to adapt the recitatives from the *St Mark Passion* of Reinhard Keiser, Bach's senior by a decade, to fill in the narrative sections. That includes the turba choruses, even though they are far more conventional than Bach's. The result in no way rivals the two great Bach Passions we know, but it offers much fine music normally buried. This performance may not be ideal – with the period instruments of the Cambridge Baroque Camerata often rough – but the Caius Chorus is fresh and alert; as is the solo singing, with Jeremy Ovenden a clear-toned Evangelist, Ruth Gomme the bright, fresh soprano and the counter-tenor, William Towers, excellent in the alto arias and such roles as that of Judas. Keiser's ambitious setting of *Psalm 112* provides a welcome makeweight. Warmly atmospheric sound.

St Matthew Passion, BWV 244.

*** DG Dig. 427 648-2 (3) [id.]. Rolfe Johnson, Schmidt, Bonney, Monoyios, Von Otter, Chance, Crook, Bär, Hauptmann, Monteverdi Ch., E. Bar. Soloists, Gardiner.

(N) *** Channel Classics Dig. CCS 11397 (3) [id.]. Türk, Smits, Zomer, Scholl, Mammel, Kooy, St. Bavo Cathedral, Haarlem Boys' Ch., Netherlands Bach Society Baroque O and Ch., Jos van Veldhoven.

(M) *** EMI CMS7 63058-2 (3). Pears, Fischer-Dieskau, Schwarzkopf, Ludwig, Gedda, Berry, Hampstead Parish Church Ch., Philh. Ch. & O, Klemperer.

(B) *** Naxos Dig. 8.550832/34 [id.]. József Mukk, István Gáti, Judit Németh, Ibolya Verebits, Péter Köves, Péter Cser, Ferenc Korpás, Rózsa Kiss, Agnes Csenki, Hungarian R. Children's Ch., Hungarian Festival Ch. & State SO, Géza Oberfrank.

(N) **(*) Ph. Dig. 454 434-2(3) [id.]. Nico der Meel, Sigmundsson, Kiehr, Julsrud, Schubert, Brummelsroete, Bostridge, Spence, Kooy, der Kamp, St. Bavo Cathedral, Haarlem Boys' Ch., Netherlands Chamber Ch., O. of the 18th. Century, Frans Brüggen.

(N) ** Ph. Dig. 462 515-2 (3) [id.]. Mark Ainsley, Quasthoff, Oelze, Stutzmann, Olsen, Volle, Tokyo Opera Singers, SKF Matsumoto Children's Ch, Saito Kinen O., Ozawa.

Gardiner's version of the *St Matthew Passion*, the culminating issue in his Bach choral series for DG Archiv, brings an intense, dramatic reading which now makes a clear first choice, not just for period-performance devotees but for anyone not firmly set against the new authenticity. The result is an invigorating, intense telling of the story, with Gardiner favouring high dynamic contrasts and generally fast speeds which are still geared to the weighty purpose of the whole work. He and his performers were recorded in what proved an ideal venue, The Maltings at Snape, where the warm acoustic gives body and allows clarity to period textures.

The Channel Classics version with Jos van Veldhoven was recorded live in 1997, in the same Utrecht venue as Brüggen's (see below). You would never register that from the recording which is more spacious and balanced less close, though van Veldhoven's manner is lighter and more flexible. His team of soloists is also young and fresh, with Gerd Türk a fine Evangelist – as he is for Suzuki in Japan – and with Andreas Scholl singing the alto role beautifully, a real highlight of the set.

While it certainly will not appeal to the authentic lobby, Klemperer's 1962 Philharmonia recording of the *St Matthew Passion* represents one of his greatest achievements on record, an act of devotion of such intensity that points of style and interpretation seem insignificant. The whole cast clearly shared Klemperer's own intense feelings, and one can only sit back and share them too, whatever one's preconceptions.

At bargain price the new version from Naxos uses modern, not period, instruments but, following authentic trends, has brisk speeds and well-sprung rhythms. Though the performance takes no less than 35 minutes less than, say, Richter's, in its alertness it never seems rushed, with the Hungarian State Symphony Orchestra and Festival Choir on excellent form, conducted by Géza Oberfrank. A refreshingly lithe and young-sounding Evangelist, József Mukk, leads a team of Hungarian soloists with fresh, clear voices. The obbligato wind-playing is also attractive (if closely balanced) and the recording is spacious and full, and kind to voices.

Recorded live in Utrecht, a year earlier than van Veldhoven's set, in vivid, immediate sound, Frans Brüggen's reading is typically fresh and alert, with speeds generally fast but not invariably so, when Brüggen is consistently thoughtful. With a very light-toned Evangelist (Nico van der Meel) telling the story expressively, this is an intimate reading, with the freshness intensified by the singing of the soloists, mostly young.

Ozawa's speeds are mostly fast, but the results sound less period-like than balletic, with modern instruments tending to smooth lines. Ainsley as the Evangelist and Quasthoff as Jesus are splendid but all the soloists are first rate, as is the choral singing. Excellent recording, but even so this is far from a first choice.

St Matthew Passion: Arias and choruses.

(B) **(*) DG Classikon 439 447-2 (from complete recording with Schreier, Fischer-Dieskau, Mathis, J. Baker, Salminen, Regensburger Domspatzen, Munich Bach Ch. & O, Karl Richter).

(N) ** Ph. Dig. 462 626-2 [id.]. Ainsley,

Quasthoff, Oelze, Stutzmann, Olsen, Volle, Tokyo Opera Singers, SKF Matsumoto Children's Ch, Saito Kinen O., Ozawa.

Many collectors who have another complete set will be glad to have this 73-minute Classikon bargain selection from Richter's dedicated second (1979) stereo recording, particularly as Dame Janet Baker's *Erbarme dich* is included.

Ozawa offers 21 numbers out of the 68, including most of the favourites. Ainsley as the Evangelist and Quasthoff as Jesus have disappointingly little to do, but otherwise this makes a good sampler of an essentially lightweight performance

St. Matthew Passion, BWV 244.(in English).
(N) (B) (**(*)) Dutton 2CD AX2005 (3) [id.]. Eric Greene, Elsie Suddaby, Kathleen Ferrier, Henry Cummings, Bach Ch., Jacques O., Reginald Jacques – PERGOLESI: *Stabat Mater.* (**)

In 1947 Decca recorded highlights from the *St Matthew Passion* based on the annual performances conducted by Dr Reginald Jacques and at a time when even this masterpiece was neglected on disc, they were an immediate success. Decca, a year later, went on to record the rest and that is what Michael Dutton has here transferred immaculately to CD, with the bonus of the 1946 Decca recording of the Pergolesi *Stabat Mater*, also with Ferrier as soloist. The Bach is very much a performance of its time, with measured speeds and an expressively devotional manner, in the chorales and recitatives as well as in the big choruses. Only the 'turba' choruses commenting on the action are brisk in the way one would now expect. Eric Greene is the noble Evangelist and the sweet-toned Elsie Suddaby shines out in the soprano arias, but it is Ferrier who instantly on each entry conveys quite a different degree of intensity from the rest, immediately magnetic. Sadly Henry Cummings is too woolly-toned to give much pleasure, but the atmosphere of a performance at that time is vividly caught. Having an English text is well justified, when the words are so clear.

Schemelli's Musicalisches Songbook: 57 sacred songs.
(N) *** CPO Dig. CPO 99407-2 (2) [id.]. Barabara Schlick, Klaus Mertens, Bob van Asperen, Wouter Möller.

Bach was the principal contributor to the important collection of hymns published in Leipzig in 1736, when he was Kapellmeister there. Some are settings of traditional hymn-tunes, some with improvements by Bach and some are original. This is the biggest selection yet recorded of Bach's work on the *Songbook*, and though this is not a set to play from end to end, it is good to have these dedicated performances from two stylish soloists, very well recorded.

Vocal collections

Arias: *Bist du bei mir; Cantata 202: Weichet nur, Betrübte Schatten. Cantata 209: Ricetti gramezza. St Matthew Passion: Blute nur; Ich will dir mein Herze schenken.*
**(*) Delos Dig. D/CD 3026 [id.]. Arleen Augér, Mostly Mozart O, Schwarz – HANDEL: *Arias.* **(*)

Arleen Augér's pure, sweet soprano, effortlessly controlled, makes for bright performances of these Bach arias and songs, very recommendable for admirers of this delightful singer, well coupled with Handel arias.

Arias: *Mass in B min.: Agnus dei; Qui sedes. St John Passion: All is fulfilled. St Matthew Passion: Grief for sin.*
(M) (***) Decca mono 433 474-2. Kathleen Ferrier, LPO, Boult – HANDEL: *Arias.* (***) ✽

On 7th and 8th October 1952, Kathleen Ferrier made her last and perhaps greatest record in London's Kingsway Hall, coupling four arias each by Bach and Handel. The combined skill of John Culshaw and Kenneth Wilkinson ensured a recording of the utmost fidelity by the standards of that time. Now it re-emerges with extraordinary naturalness and presence.

Transcriptions

Chorales (arr. Koopman for cello and chamber ensemble): *Dein Blut, der edle Saft* (from *Cantata, BWV 136*); *Erbarme dich* (from *St Matthew Passion*); *Ertot' und durch deine'Güte* (from *Cantata, BWV 22*); *Ich ruf' zu dir, Herr Jesu Christ, BWV 639; Jesus, bleibet meine Freude (Jesu, joy of man's desiring;* from *Cantata, BWV 147*); *Kommst du nun, Jesu, vom Himmel herunter, BWV 650; Lass mein Herz die Münze sein* (from *Cantata, BWV 163*); *Sei Lob und Preis mit Ehren*, from *Cantata, BWV 167. Suite No. 3 in D, BWV 1056: Air.*
(N) ** Sony Dig. SK 60680 [id.]. Yo-Yo Ma, Amsterdam Bar. O, Ton Koopman – BOCCHERINI: *Cello concertos Nos. 5 & 7.* **

This CD is called 'Simply Baroque' and is obviously aimed at a crossover market. These chorales include some of Bach's best tunes, and they are played quite persuasively on a period instrument, but with a degree of vibrato that gives a romantic tinge to the colouring.

Chaconne (from *Partita No. 2 in D min., BWV 1004*) (arr. Busoni).
(M) *** Nimbus Dig. NI 8810 [id.]. Ferruccio Busoni (piano) – CHOPIN: *Preludes* ** (with LISZT: *Etudes d'exécution transcendante* etc. ***).

This is the nearest we shall ever come to hearing Busoni play and, as nearly always, the impression with a first-class modern recording taken from a piano-roll gives an uncanny feeling of the artist's presence. His famous transcription of the Bach *Chaconne* is almost as much Busoni as it is Bach, but it is none the less compelling for that. The prodigious account of it by its arranger projects powerfully in this splendid digital recording, in the Nimbus Duo-Art Grand Piano series. The recording dates from 1925, but the reproduction makes it sound as if it were made yesterday.

Transcriptions: arr. BUSONI: *Chaconne* (from *Violin Partita No. 2*); *Chorales: Ich ruf zu dir; Nun freut euch, lieben Christen; Nun komm der Heiden Heiland; Wachet auf; Toccata & fugue in D min.* arr. LISZT: *Prelude & fugue in A min.* arr. LORD BERNERS: *In dolci jubilo.* arr. MYRA HESS: *Jesu, joy of man's desiring.* arr. KEMPFF: *Siciliano.* arr. LE FLEMING: *Sheep may safely graze.* arr. RACHMANINOV: *Suite from Partita No. 3 in E.*
*** ASV Dig. CDDCA 759 [id.]. Gordon Fergus-Thompson (piano).

A highly entertaining collection, played with much flair and, in the case of the lyrical pieces at the centre of the recital (notably Wilhelm Kempff's delightful *Siciliano* and Dame Myra Hess's famous arrangement of *Jesu, joy of man's desiring*), stylish charm.

Arrangements: Bach–Stokowski

Adagio in C, BWV 564; Chorales: Jesus Christus Gottes Sohn (from *Easter cantata*); *Komm süsser Tod; Mein Jesu; Sheep may safely graze; Wir glauben all' an Einen Gott (Giant fugue), BWV 680. Fugue in G min. (Little), BWV 578; Passacaglia and fugue in C min., BWV 582; Suite No. 3 in D, BWV 1068: Air. Toccata and fugue in D min., BWV 565; Violin & harpsichord sonata No. 4, BWV 1017: Siciliano; Well-tempered Clavier, Book 1, Prelude No. 24.*
*** Chandos Dig. CHAN 9259 [id.]. BBC PO, Matthias Bamert.

This sumptuously recorded Chandos CD brings together the dozen published Stokowski Bach transcriptions. Bamert's warmly sympathetic readings obviously follow his mentor's way with this music, if without quite managing the naturally spontaneous rubato which was one of Stokowski's special gifts. Nor is the playing as vital and electrifying as the great conductor's own record. But the result is very enjoyable, and the Chandos stereo here is very much in the demonstration bracket.

Chorale prelude: Wir glauben all' an einen Gott ('Giant fugue'), BWV 680; Easter cantata, BWV 4: Chorale; Geistliches Lied No. 51: Mein Jesu, BWV 487; Passacaglia and fugue in C min., BWV 582; Toccata and fugue in D min., BWV 565; Well-tempered Clavier, Book 1: Prelude No. 8 in E flat min., BWV 853 (all orch. Stokowski).
(M) *** Decca Phase Four 448 946-2 [id.]. Czech PO, Stokowski (with Concert of miscellaneous orchestral transcriptions ***).

Stokowski's flamboyant arrangements of Bach organ works are presented here with spectacular, closely balanced but truthful Phase Four sound to match. Big, bold and reverberant, the results are massively compelling. Stokowski, over ninety at the time, challenges his players in expansive tempi, but the results are passionate in concentration. The famous *D minor Toccata and fugue* is a shade less vital here than in Stokowski's earlier, mono version with the Philadelphia Orchestra, but the stereo sumptuousness is ample compensation. Most remarkable of all is the mighty *Passacaglia and fugue in C minor*, highly romantic in its decorative detail, but moving steadily to an overwhelming climax.

Bach, Wilhelm Friedemann
(1710–84)

Harpsichord concertos: in D, F41; in F, F44; in A min., F45.
*** HM Dig. HMC 901558 [id.]. Richard Egarr, L. Bar., Charles Medlam.

These three concertos have plenty of interest. The often intricate solo writing always holds the listener's attention in these lively performances from Richard Egarr, more particularly as the harpsichord is very truthfully caught and is not made to seem larger than life-size. The earliest work here, in A minor, dates from 1733 and has a sunny *Cantabile* slow movement which brings an engaging interplay between soloist and orchestra. The *Molto adagio* of the F major work is more poignant in feeling and shows the composer at his most darkly expressive, while the *Presto* finale is quirky in its rhythmic high spirits. The London Baroque provide alert, polished accompaniments, but the sharp-edged timbre of leader Ingrid Seifert and her period style, with its swelling out on individual notes, may not appeal to all, although the ear does adjust to it.

(i) *Harpsichord concerto in D, F41; Sinfonias: in D, F64; D min., F65; F, F67; Suite in G min.* (attrib. also to J. S. BACH, BWV 1070).
(N) ** Sony Dig. SK 62720 [id.]. (i) Charlotte Nediger; Tafelmusik, Jeanne Lamon.

This would seem to make a useful compendium, but proves disappointing. The highlight is the *Harpsichord concerto* in which Charlotte Nediger is a nimble and appealing soloist and is placed in convincing perspective. However, in the *sinfonias* Tafelmusik's edgily thin string timbre, and rather fierce articulation is not very appealing. The *Suite* brings a more friendly style of playing, but is surely wrongly attributed.

Double concerto for 2 harpsichords in D, F46.
(N) (M) *** Mercury 434 395-2 [id.]. Rafael Puyana, Genoveva Galvez (Pleyel harpsichord) – J. C. BACH: *Duet in A* ***; J. S. BACH: *Harpsichord music.* **(*)
(M) **(*) Teldec/Warner 0630 12326-2 [id.]. Uittenbosch, Curtis, VCM, Harnoncourt – C. P. E. BACH: *Double concerto for harpsichord and fortepiano* ***; J. C. BACH: *Sinfonia concertante in F.* **(*)

This attractive little four-handed work makes a fine encore for an impressive recital of music by Johann Sebastian. It is in three movements and the central *Andante* is really quite memorable. The Mercury performance could hardly be more sympathetic.

The alternative orchestral version on Teldec is also well played, though tuttis are a bit gruff and rather heavily accented.

Sinfonia in F.
(B) **(*) Naxos Dig. 8.553289 [id.]. Salzburg CO, Yoon K. Lee – C. P. E. BACH: *Sinfonias.* **(*)

Wilhelm Friedemann Bach's *F major Sinfonia* is not really a match for those by his brother, Carl Philipp Emanuel, with which it is coupled. But it is agreeable enough and certainly not entirely conventional. It is given a lively account in Salzburg; modern instruments are used but textures are clean and fresh and the recording is faithful and well balanced.

Sinfonia in D, F64; Adagio & fugue in D min., F65.
*** Capriccio Dig. 10 283 [id.]. Concerto Köln – J. C. F. BACH: *Sinfonia;* C. P. E. BACH: *Harpsichord concerto;* J. C. BACH: *Sinfonia.* ***

Wilhelm Friedemann's three-movement *Sinfonia in D major* was intended for use as an introduction to the Whitsun cantata, *Dies ist der Tag*. The better-known *Adagio and fugue in D minor* may possibly have originally formed the last two movements of a symphony. It is a very extraordinary and expressive piece. It is played by this period group with great expressive vitality and is well recorded.

6 Sonatas for flute duet, Fk 54/59.
(N) *** MDG Dig. MDG 311 984402 [id.]. Konrad Hüteler, Michael Schmidt-Casdorf.

This is a well-crafted set of flute duets; not a CD to play all at one go, but distinctly appealing for those who enjoy the flute timbre, or who are amateur flautists. These works must be fun to play, especially when the two instruments chirrup together, as in the first-movement *Allegro* of No. 2, dance along graciously as in final *Gigue* of the same work, or chase each other's tails as in the *Presto* finale of No. 4. Slow movements are innocent, but yet have a thoughtful melancholy, notably in the *Adagio* of No. 3 and the *Lamentabile* of No. 4. Overall, the final work in *F minor* is the most individual of the six, but all are different, and it is a hallmark of the composer's skill that this simple polyphony stands up to repeated listenings. The performances here are technically immaculate, have a pleasing spontaneous simplicity, and are beautifully recorded. The only real criticism is that the documentation tries too hard to intellectualize the music.

Fantasia in C min., F2; 8 Fugues, F31; March, F30; Prelude, F29; Sonatas: in G, F7; F min., F8; Suite in G min., F24.
(B) *** HM Dig. HMA 1901305 [id.]. Christophe Rousset (harpsichord).

Here is another recital to confirm Wilhelm Friedemann's strong musical personality. The extraordinary *Fantasia in C minor* has a darkly dramatic opening, then immediately evokes memories of Johann Sebastian's *Chromatic fantasia* in its florid brilliance. The two sonatas are also impressive works. Christophe Rousset was nineteen when he recorded this recital and he plays with remarkable maturity and discernment throughout. He certainly brings out the diversity of the eight succinct miniature *Fugues* which readily demonstrate Wilhelm's contrapuntal mastery.

Polonaise in E flat, F 12/5.
(B) *** DHM/BMG Baroque Esprit 05472 77440-2 [id.]. Colin Tilney – J. S. BACH: *Oboe sonatas;* C. P. E. BACH: *Oboe sonata.* **(*)

Wilhelm Friedemann's *Polonaise* is not a lively dance form in the modern sense, but a fairly placid piece with a constantly repeated refrain. Played here very simply, it is rather engaging.

Baermann, Heinrich (1784–1847)

Adagio for clarinet and orchestra.
*** ASV Dig. CDDCA 559 [id.]. Emma Johnson, ECO, Groves – CRUSELL: *Concerto No. 2* *** ✿; ROSSINI: *Introduction, theme and variations* ***; WEBER: *Concertino.* ***

Heinrich Baermann's rather beautiful *Adagio*, once attributed to Wagner, is offered by a young clarinettist who plays the work warmly and sympathetically.

Baguer, Carlos (1768–1808)

Symphonies Nos. 12 in E flat; 13 in E flat; 16 in G; 18 in B flat.
(N) *** Chandos Dig. CHAN 9456 [id.]. LMP, Bamert.

The Catalan composer Carlos Baguer was born in Barcelona and spent his musical life there, centred on the cathedral of which he was organist from 1789 until his death. The orchestra of the Barcelona Opera gave evening concerts, to which symphonies were introduced in the 1780s, and those of Haydn were to dominate the musical scene from 1782 onwards. Baguer soon adopted the four-movement Haydn pattern, and these symphonies date from a decade later. In one way, they would have pleased his mentor, as he could write a very good minuet. Elsewhere the craftsmanship is sound but conventional, as is the scoring, although there is some pleasingly assured invention. The finale of No. 13 and the first movement of No. 16, which has a characteristic second subject, and the following *Adagio a solo con sordina*, an elegant set of variations, are all very much after the Haydn style. Although there is a certain warm graciousness to the writing, it is suprising that there is no local colour and no gypsy influences, not even in the finales. The performances here are nicely turned, and beautifully recorded in the best Chandos manner.

Baines, William (1899–1922)

The Chimes; Coloured leaves; Etude in F sharp min.; Idyll; The Naiad; Paradise gardens; 7 Preludes; Silverpoints; Tides; Twilight pieces.
(N) *** Priory Dig. PRCD 550 [id.]. Eric Parkin.

Born at Horbury, in the West Riding, William Baines spent his whole life in Yorkshire. Although he has written orchestral and vocal music, it is his piano music for which he is renowned, and this collection explains why. He had a natural feeling for keyboard colouring and his music shows cross-influences from many sources, including Cyril Scott, Scriabin and the twentieth-century French school: *Water-pearls*, the third of the *Silver points* might almost have been written by Poulenc, and *The Naiad* is unashamedly Debussian. However his rhapsodic melodic style is undoubtedly individual and his use of irregular rhythms is so smoothly employed, that they seem imperceptible. The second of the *Seven Preludes*, entitled *Slowly, with Serenity*, and the impressionistic *Fifth* number, *Poppies gleaming in the moonlight*, contrast with the four *Coloured leaves* which are much more English in feeling. The greater number of these pieces are pictorial and the harmonic progressions are often quite strikingly effective, as in the second of the *Tides*, *Goodnight to Flamboro*'. Baines was at his finest when writing reflectively and the three *Twilight pieces* are delightful, while the brief *Etude in F sharp minor*, which ends the recital somewhat abruptly, is melodically quite haunting. The versatile Eric Parkin proves an ideal advocate of this rewarding music and he is very naturally recorded.

Baird, Tadeusz (1928–81)

Colas Breugnon: suite.
(M) *** EMI CDMS5 65418-2 [id.]. Polish CO, Jerzy Maksymiuk (with SZYMANOWSKI: *Violin concertos Nos. 1–2.* **(*)).

Baird's delightful neo-classical suite (for flute and strings) has much in common with Warlock's *Capriol suite*. It is beautifully played and recorded.

Bairstow, Edward (1874–1946)

Organ sonata in E flat.
*** Priory Dig. PRCD 401 [id.]. John Scott (St Paul's Cathedral organ) (with William HARRIS: *Sonata* ***) – ELGAR: *Sonata No. 1.* ***

Bairstow's *Organ sonata* was written in 1937 and is Elgarian in feeling and the central Scherzo produces a blaze of orchestral sound unsurpassed by Elgar in either of his works for the instrument. The performance here is admirable and the St Paul's Cathedral organ is just right for it. The third work on the disc, a much more conventional sonata by William Harris (1883–1973), at least has a rather pleasing central *Adagio*.

Anthems and choral settings: *Blessed city, heavenly Salem; Blessed Virgin's cradle song; Evening Canticles in D; If the Lord had not helped me; Jesu, grant me this I pray; Jesu, the very thought; Lamentation* (from *Jeremiah*); *Let all mortal flesh keep silence; Lord I call upon Thee; Lord thou has been our refuge; Save us O Lord.*
*** Priory Dig. PRDC 365 [id.]. York Minster Ch., Philip Moore; John Scott Whiteley.

Bairstow is (rightly) best known for his moving and comparatively short anthem, *Let all mortal flesh keep silence*; but, as this collection shows, he wrote much else that gives full rein to his subtle understanding of choral blending and instinctive response to liturgical texts. The gloriously expansive *Blessed city, heavenly Salem*, which opens the concert, makes the firmest of Christian statements and the depth of the composer's religious feeling is expressed touchingly in the poignant *Jesu, the very thought of you*. The performances here are very well prepared and excitingly committed and spontaneous. The chorus is set back in the ample and resonant Minster acoustic, which provides plenty of space for climaxes to expand gloriously, while the balance with the excellent organ accompaniments could hardly be bettered.

Balakirev, Mily (1837–1910)

Piano concertos Nos. 1 in F sharp min., Op. 1; 2 in E flat, Op. posth.

*** Hyperion Dig. CDA 66640 [id.]. Malcolm Binns, E. N. Philh. O, Lloyd-Jones – RIMSKY-KORSAKOV: *Concerto*. ***

The one-movement *First Piano concerto* (*Youth*) was composed when Balakirev was eighteen and is modelled on his adored Chopin. All the same, there are some touches of individuality, and it is well served by Malcolm Binns's intelligent and sensitive performance, which also has the advantage of fine orchestral support and up-to-date recording. It also has the only available account of the more characteristic *Second Concerto*, which Balakirev started in 1861 but (like the *First Symphony*) put on one side. It was left incomplete and finished after his death by Lyapunov.

Symphony No. 1 in C.

(N) ✪ (M) *** EMI mono CDM5 66595-2 [id.]. Philh. O, Karajan – ROUSSEL: *Symphony No. 4*. (***) ✪

Symphony No. 1 in C; In Bohemia (symphonic poem); *King Lear overture.*

(N) **(*) Chandos Dig. CHAN 9667 [id.]. BBC PO, Vassily Sinaisky.

Symphonies Nos. (i) *1 in C;* (ii) *2 in D min.*

(M) *** Revelation RV 10038. (i) USSR State SO, Svetlanov; (ii) Grand SO of R. & TV, Rozhdestvensky.

Symphonies Nos. 1–2: Overture on Russian themes; Symphonic poems: Russia; Tamara.

(N) (B) **(*) Hyperion Dyad Dig. CDD 22030 (2) [id.]. Philh. O, Svetlanov.

We seem to be permanently at odds about the Balakirev symphonies, but there is no doubt that Karajan's pioneering version of No. 1, recorded in November 1949 remains unequalled as a performance, even by Beecham and Svetlanov. The *Symphony* is an endearing piece, finely wrought, melodious, brilliantly scored and memorable. The Scherzo sounds mercurial and effervescent in Karajan's hands, and the slow movement is done with great sensitivity. The present transfer is an improvement over its earlier LP and CD issues, and the coupling is equally superb.

The most recent challenge to Karajan's pre-eminence has come from Chandos and E. G.'s view is that not since that Philharmonia account has there been a version of this glorious Russian symphony quite so richly expressive, with outstanding playing from the BBC Philharmonic opulently recorded. However, I. M. finds this performance, for all its affectionate warmth, fine playing – especially the seductive clarinet solo which opens the languorous slow movement – lacks bite and a strong adrenalin flow. R. L.'s view lies in between, but he is less enthusiastic than E. G. We are all agreed that the two Balakirev rarities make strong and characterful fill-ups.

Hyperion have now paired their Svetlanov accounts as a Duo. The performances bring more beautiful playing from the Philharmonia Orchestra: the soaring clarinet solo at the beginning of the slow movement of No. 1 is again rapturously done and in the *Second Symphony* the effect is cultured, the sound pleasingly natural. However there is some disagreement concerning Svetlanov's grip on the proceedings, and especially so in the first three movements of the *First*, although in the finale the emotional thrust is undeniable. The reading of the *Second* also has a spacious breadth; however, while agreeing that it is tauter than that of the *First*, E. G. suggests that it does little to promote a symphony which inevitably runs the risk of seeming a repetition of the earlier work. *Tamara* too – almost as extended as a one-movement symphony – needs to be stronger and more purposeful, although *Russia* is more successful. But first choice, after Karajan in No. 1, now lies with the Russian Revelation disc pairing both symphonies at mid-price.

Rescued from the Soviet radio archive, these performances of the early 1970s have a passion and urgency, a natural feeling for idiomatic phrasing and rhythm, which make you forget any slight shortcoming in the recorded sound. This Russian performance from Svetlanov of No. 1 is altogether tauter and more urgent than the version he recorded in London for Hyperion. Rarely if ever has there been such a radiant account on disc of the lovely slow movement, surging warmly forward, with resonant strings and with a prominent harp, superbly played, adding flair. Though as a rule the *Second Symphony* seems rather pale after the powerful inspiration of No. 1, Rozhdestvensky convinces one that it is a worthy successor, rich and passionate in the dance rhythms of the first movement, furious and swaggering in the Scherzo, electrically alert in the slow movement and Polacca finale. An ideal coupling, strongly recommended.

Symphony No. 2 in D min.; (i) *Piano concerto No.1 in F sharp min.; Tamara* (symphonic poem).

(N) *** Chandos Dig. CHAN 9727 [id.]. (i) Howard Shelley, BBCPO, Sinaisky.

Though the *Second Symphony* cannot compare with the *First* in scale or memorability, Vassily Sinaisky (like Rozhdestvensky above) makes a most persuasive case for it in his warm and thrustful performance. He underlines the high dramatic contrasts, drawing playing from the BBC Philharmonic that is incisive and pointed in such a movement as the Cossack dance of the *Scherzo* as well as sweetly refined in the lyrical slow movement. *Tamara* is played with similar panache, and Howard Shelley is a powerful soloist in the single movement of the *Piano concerto*, relishing the bravuara writing. Warm, full Chandos sound.

Islamey (oriental fantasy).
❀ *** Teldec/Warner Dig. 4509 96516-2 [id.]. Boris Berezovsky – LIADOV: *Preludes, Opp. 39/4; 40/2; 57/1;* MEDTNER: *Fairy tales, Opp. 20/1; 34/2–3; 51/1;* RACHMANINOV: *Etudes-tableaux, Op. 39/3–4, 7 & 9* ***) – MUSSORGSKY: *Night on a bare mountain.* *** ❀
(M) *** EMI (IMS) CDM7 64329-2. Andrei Gavrilov – PROKOFIEV: *Concerto No. 1;* TCHAIKOVSKY: *Piano concerto No. 1* etc. ***

An amazing account of *Islamey* from Boris Berezovsky, the 1991 Tchaikovsky Competition prizewinner. Stunning, effortless virtuosity. Berezovsky makes an ideal Rachmaninov interpreter too, and it would be difficult to flaw these fine accounts of four of the Op. 39 set of *Etudes-tableaux*. Berezovsky is also a champion of Medtner and has an obvious affinity with his music. He has all the subtlety, poetic feeling and keyboard mastery that this music calls for. The Liadov *Preludes* too are played impeccably. This is in every respect an outstanding recital.

Gavrilov's dazzling account of Balakirev's fantasy is also outstandingly charismatic; it is well recorded, too. It comes in harness with an equally dazzling version of Prokofiev's *First Piano concerto* and a performance of the Tchaikovsky *B flat minor Concerto* which is rather less convincing.

Islamey (1902 version).
(N) * Sony Dig. SK60689 [id.]. Yefim Bronfman – TCHAIKOVSKY: *The Seasons* (**)

Yefim Bronfman takes the legendary difficulties of *Islamey* in his stride, but the recorded sound is horrible: shallow and closely miked in a claustrophobic studio. In climaxes it hovers very close to discoloration. A pity since the playing is undeniably impressive.

Piano sonata in B flat min.
**(*) Olympia OCD 354 [id.]. Donna Amato – DUTILLEUX: *Sonata.* **(*)
**(*) Kingdom Dig. KCLCD 2001 [id.]. Gordon Fergus-Thompson – SCRIABIN: *Sonata No. 3* etc. **(*)

The Balakirev is arguably the greatest Russian piano sonata of the pre-1914 era. Donna Amato gives a musicianly account of it, well paced and authoritative. The recording is very lifelike, and this is a most desirable issue, even if the playing time at 47 minutes is not particularly generous.

Gordon Fergus-Thompson, too, is fully equal to the considerable demands of this remarkable *Sonata* and offers excellent playing, though the recording is reverberant and the piano not always dead in tune. Fergus-Thompson also includes Balakirev's arrangement of Glinka's *The Lark* as an encore.

Banchieri, Adriano (1568–1634)

Barca di Venetia per Padova.
(B) *** HM Dig. HMC 90856.58 (3) [(M) id. import]. Ens. Clément Jannequin, Dominique Visse – MARENZIO: *Madrigals* **(*) ; LASSUS; VECCHI: *Madrigal comedies.* ***

Adriano Banchieri was a close contemporary of Monteverdi. His *Barca di Venetia per Padova* ('Boat from Venice to Padua') was published in 1605, the year following *Il Zabaione musicale* (see below). It is a similar and equally diverting kaleidoscope of short madrigals, but here linked – and at times dominated – by a robust (semi-parlando) tenor 'Argomento' which briefly but histrionically underlines the details of the voyage. With the passengers including lawyers, a student, a fisherman, a music-master and a bookseller, a drunken German and a pair of courtesans, the solos and ensembles are wildly contrasted and include a quintet in different dialects, a touching *madrigal affettuoso* ('provided' by the musician) and a no less charmingly lyrical *Madrigal cappriccioso*. The performance here has polish, vitality and style, and it is vividly recorded, too. It makes a highly stimulating and at times touching entertainment and, with its apt Marenzio coupling, comes as part of a Harmonia Mundi Bargain CD Trio of '*Comédies madrigalesques*' which is well worth exploring.

Festino nella sera del giovedi grasso avanti cena, Op. 18; Il Zabaione musicale.
(BB) *** Naxos Dig. 8.553785 [id.]. R. Svizzara (Lugano) Ch., Sonatori de la Gioiosa Marca, Treviso, Diego Fasolis.

Banchieri again here presents a pair of musical entertainments built on varied sequences of madrigals. *Il Zabaione musicale*, first published in 1604 and described as a 'sylvan invention', consists of an introduction and three Acts, made up of 17 very brief madrigals. Each Act is dramatically separate, representing – so one modern scholar suggests – the development of the madrigal as a form. The *Festino* – an 'Entertainment for the Eve of Carnival Thursday before Dinner' – is an even more relaxed entertainment. Published in Venice in 1608, it is a sequence of 21 very light-hearted madrigals, some of them involving animal and bird noises, as for example the memorable quartet for owl, cuckoo, cat and dog. Diego Fasolis draws superb singing from his Lugano choir, with incisively crisp ensemble, colourfully enhanced by brass and timpani. The intensity of the performance helps to bring out the genuine, rip-roaring humour, which in less taut performances might seem heavy or simply childish. Excellent recording made in the studios of Radio Lugano. A splendid example of Naxos enterprise, with documentation that other companies sometimes fail to match at higher prices. Full texts and an English translation are provided.

Bantock, Granville (1868–1946)

Celtic Symphony; Hebridean Symphony; The Sea reivers; The Witch of Atlas.
*** Hyperion Dig. CDA 66450 [id.]. RPO, Handley.

Vernon Handley conducts warmly atmospheric performances of four of Bantock's Hebridean inspirations. Most ambitious is the *Hebridean Symphony* of 1913, with nature music echoing Wagner and Delius as well as Sibelius, whose music Bantock introduced into Britain. The two tone-poems are attractive too, but best of all is the *Celtic Symphony*, a late work written in 1940, which uses strings and six harps. This is in the grand string tradition of Vaughan Williams's *Tallis fantasia* and Elgar's *Introduction and allegro*, a beautiful, colourful work that deserves to be far better known. With warm, atmospheric recording to match, Handley draws committed performances from the RPO.

Pagan Symphony; Fifine at the fair; 2 Heroic ballads.
*** Hyperion Dig. CDA 66630 [id.]. RPO, Handley.

A fine successor to Handley's earlier pairing of the *Celtic* and *Hebridean Symphonies*. The *Pagan Symphony* dates from 1928, so it comes mid-way between the others, and the writing brings touches of Elgar as well as German influences. It is tuneful and well crafted. Perhaps it isn't as individual a work as *Fifine at the fair*, with which Beecham understandably identified; but Handley is equally at home in this colourful tone-poem, and it is good to have it presented in stereo as vivid as this. The two *Ballads* are rather more conventional but still make a considerable impression.

The Pierrot of the minute: overture.
(M) *** Chandos CHAN 6566 [id.]. Bournemouth Sinf., Norman Del Mar – BRIDGE: *Summer* etc.; BUTTERWORTH: *Banks of Green Willow*. ***

Bantock's overture is concerned with Pierrot's dream, in which he falls in love with a Moon Maiden who tells him their love must die at dawn, but he will not listen. He wakes to realize that his dream of love lasted a mere minute. The writing is often delicate and at times Elgarian, and the piece is well worth investigating. The 1978 recording sounds remarkably fresh.

(i) *Sapphic poem for cello and orchestra*; (ii) *Sappho*.
(N) *** Hyperion Dig. CDA 66899 [id.]. RPO, Handley with (i) Julian Lloyd Webber; (ii) Susan Bickley.

Sappho, completed in 1905 – to a text from the Greek poetess, prepared by the composer's wife – is an hour-long song-cycle brimming with music of a sensuousness rare from an English composer. The passion behind each of the nine songs, introduced by an extended orchestral Prelude, is vividly brought out by the RPO under Vernon Handley and sumptuously recorded. The mezzo, Susan Bickley, sings radiantly with fresh clear tone, rapt and intense in the final song, *Music of the golden throne*. The concertante piece for cello and small orchestra, written in 1906, makes the perfect coupling – a warmly expressive meditation on the same theme, with Julian Lloyd Webber a dedicated soloist.

Symphony No. 3 (The Cyprian Goddess); Dante and Beatrice (poem for orchestra); *Helena (variations on the theme HFB).*
*** Hyperion Dig. CDA 66810 [id.]. RPO, Vernon Handley.

As in his previous Hyperion issues of Bantock, Vernon Handley draws from the RPO ripely persuasive performances of high romantic works that have been too long neglected. *The Cyprian Goddess*, completed in 1939 when the composer was seventy, echoes Strauss in its sumptuous orchestration and melodic writing, and in its refinement it has something of the elegiac tone of late Strauss. The *Helena variations*, written in tribute to his wife, echo the freshness and variety of Elgar's newly completed *Enigma*, while *Dante and Beatrice* is a free-ranging programme work which in its warmth and dramatic contrasts echoes Tchaikovsky's *Romeo and Juliet*. Whatever the echoes, in each piece Bantock establishes his own distinctive voice, here more tautly controlled than in his expansive, middle-period works. First-rate sound.

Barber, Samuel (1910–81)

Adagio for strings, Op. 11.
*** Argo 417 818-2 [id.]. ASMF, Marriner – COPLAND: *Quiet city;* COWELL: *Hymn;* CRESTON: *Rumor;* IVES: *Symphony No. 3*. ***
(N) (B) *** DG Classikon 445 129-2 [(M) [id.].import]. LAPO, Bernstein – BERNSTEIN: *Candide overture;* COPLAND: *Appalachian spring;* SCHUMAN: *American festival overture.* ***
(M) *** DG Dig. 427 806-2; *427 806-4*. LAPO, Bernstein – BERNSTEIN: *Overture Candide; West Side Story; On the Town* *** (with GERSHWIN: *Rhapsody in blue*. **(*)).
(M) *** DG Dig. 439 528-2 [id.]. LAPO, Bernstein – COPLAND: *Appalachian spring* ***; GERSHWIN: *Rhapsody in blue*. **(*)
*** Koch Schwann Dig. 3-7243-2 [id.]. New Zealand SO, James Sedares – DELLO JOIO: *The Triumph of St Joan* etc. ***

Marriner's 1976 performance of Barber's justly famous *Adagio* is arguably the most satisfying version we have had since the war, although Bernstein's alternative has the advantage of digital recording. The quality of sound on the remastered Argo CD retains most of the richness and body of the analogue LP, but at the climax the brighter lighting brings a slightly sparer violin texture than on the original LP.

Bernstein recorded the *Adagio* earlier for Sony, but the later DG recording (alternatively coupled), slow and intense, is just as deeply felt and has the advantage of modern digital sound.

The principal interest of this Koch CD is the coupled music by Norman Dello Joio, but the programme ends with a deeply felt account of Barber's *Adagio*, given in memory of Andrew Schenck who conducted many of the New Zealand orchestra's earlier records on this label.

(i) *Adagio for strings;* (i; ii) *Cello concerto, Op. 22;* (ii; iii) *Cello sonata, Op. 6.*
*** Virgin/EMI Dig. VC7 59565-2 [id.]. (i) SCO; Saraste; (ii) Ralph Kirshbaum; (iii) Roger Vignoles.

Kirshbaum's view of the Barber *Cello concerto*, with splendid support from Saraste and the Scottish Chamber Orchestra, is darker and spikier than those of his direct rivals, and rather more urgent in the outer movements, yet it is just as beautifully played. He is equally convincing in Barber's other, much rarer cello work, the *Cello sonata* of 1932. Roger Vignoles copes well with piano-writing unhelpful to a degree surprising from a pianist-composer. The celebrated *Adagio*, coolly done, makes a worthwhile fill-up. Spacious, well-focused recording.

Adagio for strings; (i) *Piano concerto, Op. 38; Medea's meditation and Dance of vengeance, Op. 23a.*
*** ASV Dig. CDDCA 534 [id.]. (i) Joselson; LSO, Schenck.

In Barber's *Concerto* Tedd Joselson is marvellously and dazzlingly brilliant, as well as being highly sensitive and poetic with an unforced and responsive orchestral contribution from the LSO under Andrew Schenck. The LSO also give a singularly fine account of the *Medea* excerpt (not to be confused with the Suite) and a restrained and noble one of the celebrated *Adagio*.

Adagio for strings, Op. 11; Essays Nos. 1, Op. 12; 2, Op. 17; Music for a scene from Shelley, Op. 7; Overture, The School for Scandal, Op. 5; Symphony No. 1, Op. 9.
*** Argo Dig. 436 288 [id.]. Baltimore SO, Zinman.

These performances are very alert and vital, particularly that of the *First Symphony,* which is as good as any now available; the recording has superb presence and detail. Apart from the first two *Essays* for orchestra, Zinman's disc includes the more rarely heard *Music for a scene from Shelley*, a sumptuously scored and gloriously atmospheric work inspired by lines from *Prometheus Unbound.* This adds greatly to the attractions of an already desirable issue, and Zinman and his excellent orchestra play the *Overture* to Sheridan's *The School for Scandal*, with equal commitment. Strongly recommended.

(i) *Adagio for strings;* (ii) *Essay No. 2 for orchestra; Music for a scene from Shelley; Serenade for strings, Op. 1;* (ii; iii) *A Stopwatch and an ordnance map, Op. 15;* (iv) Chorus: *Let down the bars, O Death!* (ii; v) *A Hand of bridge* (chamber opera), *Op. 35.*
(M) *** Van. 08.4016.71 [OVC 4016]. (i) I Solisti di Zagreb, Antonio Janigro; (ii) Symphony of the Air, Golschmann; (iii) with Robert De Cormier Chorale; (v) with Neway, Alberts, Lewis, Maero; (iv) Washington Cathedral Ch., Callaway.

An admirable and highly rewarding anthology of works by a composer whose *Adagio for strings* has wrongly overshadowed his achievement elsewhere. Excellent singing and playing throughout.

Adagio for strings, Op. 11; Knoxville, Summer of 1915; Songs, Op. 13: Nocturne; Sure on the shining night.
*** EMI Dig. CDC5 55358-2 [id.]. Barbara Hendricks, LSO, Tilson Thomas – COPLAND: *Quiet city* etc. ***

Between them, Tilson Thomas and Barbara Hendricks have devised a programme of Copland as well as Barber with both composers at their most radiantly inspired. *Knoxville*, to a poem by James Agee, is one of the most magically evocative pieces of its kind, and is the more magical here for the authentically American inflexions that Hendricks gives it, together with glowing string-tone. The two songs which Barber orchestrated from his Opus 13 are most beautifully done too, while the celebrated *Adagio* is taken at a flowing tempo with no self-indulgence or sentimentality at all. A radiant disc.

(i) *Adagio for strings, Op. 14;* (ii) *Piano concerto, Op. 38;* (iii) *Violin concerto, Op. 14;* (iv) *2nd Essay for orchestra, Op. 17; Overture: The School for Scandal, Op. 5.*
(M) **(*) Sony Theta SMK 6004 [id.]. (i) Phd. O, Ormandy; (ii) John Browning, Cleveland O, Szell; (iii) Isaac Stern, NYPO, Bernstein; (iv) NYPO, Schippers.

Barber's career has a number of parallels with that of William Walton: a vein of acid-tinged romanticism that can readily blossom, as in the *Adagio for strings*, or the *Violin concerto*; comparatively sparse output, mainly of major works; and a comparative failure to maintain full intensity in later work. His first popular success, the *School for Scandal* overture, has a Waltonesque orchestral brilliance and a most touching secondary theme. The *Piano concerto*, written for John Browning, is one of those later works and, though technically it is most impressive and the seriousness cannot be denied, it never quite adds up to the sum of its parts. However, although the performance here from its dedicatee and Szell is of superlative quality, it is not helped by the forward balance of the (originally CBS) recording or the shallowness of the fortissimo piano-tone and the fierceness of the tuttis. The *Violin concerto* is a different matter and Stern's performance with Bernstein is unsurpassed (see below). The famous *Adagio* is played with great eloquence by the Philadelphia strings under Ormandy and the early (1957) stereo is impressively spacious. The *Second Essay* is a highly concentrated piece about ten minutes in length with quixotic mood-changes and, like the light-hearted Overture, it is played superbly by the New York Philharmonic Orchestra under Schippers. The recording is brightly lit but acceptable.

Adagio for strings, Op. 11; (i) *Violin concerto, Op. 14.*
(M) *** Sony SMK 63088 [id.]. (i) Stern; NYPO, Bernstein – SCHUMAN: *In praise of Shahn; To thee old cause.* ***

Stern's performance of Barber's *Violin concerto* is full of conviction and feeling, with the soloist is in his element in the virtuosic finale. Bernstein secures as eloquent and expressive an orchestral accompaniment as one could wish for. This comes as part of the Sony 'Bernstein Century' series together with Bernstein's 1971 account of the *Adagio*, measured and intense. In both works the newly remastered recording sounds very good indeed, though in the concerto the soloist is fairly far forward. The latter is also available paired with Maxwell Davies, but many will count the two fine William Schuman works a more apt coupling.

(i) *Canzonetta;* (ii) *Souvenirs.*
** ASV Dig. CDDCA 737. (i) Julia Girdwood, SCO; (ii) LSO; Serebrier – BRITTEN: *Les Illuminations* etc. **

With Julia Girdwood a deeply moving oboe soloist, the *Canzonetta*, shortest item on this Barber/Britten disc, is the most valuable of all. It is a piece left incomplete at the composer's death, the slow movement of a projected oboe concerto, with the strings of the Scottish Chamber Orchestra sweetly expressive too. This is a 'three-star' performance; but in *Souvenirs*, by turns nostalgic and witty, the LSO playing boldly under Serebrier sound too heavy, missing the wit of the parodies. Full-blooded recording.

Cave of the heart (original version of *Medea*).
*** Koch Dig. 3-7019-2 [id.]. Atlantic Sinf., Schenck – COPLAND: *Appalachian spring.* ***

The original version of *Medea* was entitled *Cave of the heart*; in this original form it sounds much darker in feeling and harder-edged, and it has stronger Stravinskian overtones. The effect in this full-blooded, vividly present recording is, if anything, brawnier than the more sumptuous revision. A most interesting and stimulating score.

Cello concerto, Op. 22.
*** Chandos Dig. CHAN 8322 [id.]. Wallfisch, ECO, Simon – SHOSTAKOVICH: *Cello concerto No. 1.* ***

Wallfisch gives an impressive and eloquent reading, and the elegiac slow movement is especially fine. Wallfisch is forwardly balanced, but otherwise the recording is truthful; the orchestra is vividly detailed.

(i) *Piano concerto, Op. 38*; (ii) *Violin concerto, Op. 14. Souvenirs, Op. 28.*
(N)*** Telarc Dig. CD 80441 [id.]. (i) Jon Kimura Parker; (ii) McDuffie, Atlanta SO, Levi.

Robert McDuffie is a powerful violinist with a formidable technique, if not as individual an artist as many rivals in this warmly romantic *Violin concerto*. His reading makes an excellent coupling for Jon Kimura Parker's outstanding performance of the *Piano concerto* and the suite, *Souvenirs*, in its orchestral form. The Telarc recording opens out rather more in that later, more problematic concerto, with the solo piano caught with extra weight and presence. The performance is rather tauter and more purposeful than the fine one which John Browning recorded for RCA with Slatkin and the St Louis Orchestra. However, the latter offers a fine account of the *Symphony* and will suit collectors who already have the *Violin concerto*.

(i; ii) *Piano concerto, Op. 38;* (ii) *Symphony No. 1, Op. 9;* (i; iii) *Souvenirs, Op. 28* (arr. piano, 4 hands); *Canzone.*
*** RCA Dig. RD 60732 [60732-2-RC]. (i) John Browning; (ii) St Louis SO, Leonard Slatkin; (iii) Slatkin (piano).

It is good to have a new RCA recording of the *Piano concerto* by John Browning, the pianist for whom Barber originally wrote this formidable half-hour work, while in his version of Samuel Barber's *Symphony No. 1*, Slatkin has an obvious advantage. At the very start, the tautness of attack by the St Louis players immediately commands attention, while Järvi (see below) builds tension more gradually. Though Järvi's sense of spontaneity gives extra warmth at times, Slatkin secures ensemble a degree crisper. The coupling will be the decisive point for many, and an exceptionally generous makeweight Slatkin joins Browning in a piano duo playing Barber's two-piano piece, *Souvenirs*, as Browning points out a work of 'pure nostalgia', played here with winning lightness.

Violin concerto, Op. 14.

(N) *** Decca Dig. 452 051-2 [id.]. Joshua Bell, Baltimore SO, David Zinman – BLOCH: *Baal Shem*; WALTON: *Violin concerto*.***

(M) *** Sony Stern Edition II SMK 64506 [id.]. Stern, NYPO, Bernstein – MAXWELL DAVIES: *Violin concerto*. ***

*** DG Dig. 439 886-2 [id.]. Gil Shaham, LSO, Previn – KORNGOLD: *Violin concerto* etc. ***

*** EMI Dig. CDC5 55360-2 [id.]. Perlman, Boston SO, Ozawa – BERNSTEIN: *Serenade;* FOSS: *Three American pieces*. ***

**(*) Revelation RV 10058 [id.]. Kogan, Ukrainian SO, Pavel Kogan – BARSUKOV: *Violin concerto No. 2*; BUNIN: *Violin concerto*. **

Joshua Bell won the *Gramophone*'s Concerto Award in 1998 with this outstanding coupling of two works that in many ways are related – similarly romantic and lyrical, and written at the same period. Bell's passionate playing in the Barber, full of tender poetry, is well-matched by the excellent orchestra, ripely and brilliantly recorded, with the soloist well forward but not aggressively so. This now takes pride of place, but Stern and Shaham have their own insights to offer.

Isaac Stern gave the Barber *Violin concerto* its stereo première in 1964 and his performance, which is consistently inspired, is of superlative quality. It has warmth, freshness and humanity, and the slow movement is glorious. The CBS forward balance for the orchestra is less than ideal, but the recording is otherwise very good and has been impressively remastered. This is one of Stern's most important and most distinguished recordings: one feels that he realized that the work was a masterpiece from the very beautiful opening phrase.

Gil Shaham's performance of the Barber also has great virtuosity and is a reading of strong profile, with every moment of dramatic intensity properly characterized. The effect is warm and ripe, with the sound close and immediate, bringing out above all the work's bolder side. It is good to have a sharp distinction drawn between the purposeful lyricism of the first movement, marked *Allegro*, and the withdrawn, tender lyricism of the heavenly *Andante*. In the *moto perpetuo* finale Shaham brings out the fun behind the movement's manic energy, with Previn pointing the Waltonian wit. This really *is* good – and worthy to rank alongside the Stern/Bernstein (Sony). Indeed it is to be preferred to the richly extrovert Perlman account.

For Perlman the kernel of the Barber *Concerto* lies in the central slow movement. When the soloist enters after the extended orchestral introduction, he plays with a warmth and intensity that even he has rarely matched, making the return of the main theme on the G-string a wonderful resolution, with vibrato so perfectly controlled that there is no hint of soupiness. Weight, power and virtuoso brilliance then come together in Perlman's dazzling account of the finale. Though orchestral textures could be more open, the rich tapestry of the Boston sound is moulded beautifully to the fullness of Perlman's violin.

Leonid Kogan in this 1981 recording proves a passionately committed interpreter of this romantic American concerto, giving one of the most persuasive performances yet, with the Ukrainian orchestra matching his ardour with some brilliant playing. The balance seriously favours the soloist, though ample orchestral detail comes through. The two Soviet violin concertos, equally romantic in style, make an unexpected but attractive coupling.

Essays Nos. 1, Op. 12; 2, Op. 17; 3, Op. 47.

*** Chandos Dig. CHAN 9053 [id.]. Detroit SO, Järvi – IVES: *Symphony No. 1*. ***

Both in terms of sonority and approach, Neeme Järvi's account of these appealing works differs from their American predecessors. The strings have a lightness and subtlety and are highly responsive. The recording is very natural and present, and beautifully balanced.

Essay for orchestra No. 3, Op. 47; Fadograph of a Yestern Scene, Op. 44; Medea: suite, Op. 23.

*** Koch Dig. 3-7010-2 [id.]. New Zealand SO, Andrew Schenck.

A welcome recording of two Barber rarities from the 1970s in sympathetic performances by the New Zealand orchestra under Andrew Schenck. The recording has outstanding clarity and definition, but the acoustic has the very slightly dry quality of a studio rather than the expansiveness of a concert hall.

Medea (ballet): suite.

(M) *** Mercury (IMS) 432 016-2 [id.]. Eastman-Rochester O, Howard Hanson – GOULD: *Fall River legend* etc. ***

Hanson's performance is both polished and dramatic, and the brilliant 1959 Mercury recording has astonishing clarity and vivid presence.

Souvenirs.

*** Koch Dig. 3-7005-2 [id.]. New Zealand SO, Schenck – MENOTTI: *Amahl* etc. ***

Souvenirs is an absolutely enchanting score which has bags of charm and, unlike the delightful Menotti with which it is coupled, every idea is so memorable that it instantly replaces the one that came before. It is very well played here by the New Zealand Symphony Orchestra under Andrew Schenck and is eminently well recorded too. Strongly recommended.

Symphony No. 1 (in one movement), *Op. 9; Essays for Orchestra Nos. 1, Op. 12; 2, Op. 17; Night flight, Op. 19a.*
(M) *** Unicorn UKCD 2046 [id.]. LSO, David Measham.

David Measham proves a splendid advocate of Barber's *First Symphony*, securing a passionately committed performance and bringing out its (at times) somewhat Waltonian manner. The first two *Essays for orchestra* are also very well played, as is the hauntingly evocative movement, *Night flight*, all that the composer wanted to survive from his *Symphony No. 2*.

Symphonies Nos. 1, Op. 7; 2, Op. 19; Adagio for strings; Overture, A School for Scandal.
(N) *** Chandos Dig. CHAN 9684 [id.]. Detroit SO, Neeme Järvi.

By coupling the *First* and *Second Symphonies* together, Chandos enhance the appeal of this issue. The *First* (1937) with its glowing colours, rich and impassioned Sibelian rhetoric, comes off well in Neeme Järvi's hands as does the wartime *Second* (1943), commissioned by the US Army Airforce. Barber recorded the latter himself in the days of mono LP, but the subsequent neglect of the score by conductors prompted him to withdraw it in a moment of despondency – save only for the middle movement. The ubiquitous but none the less moving *Adagio* and the *Overture: The School for Scandal*, an astonishing graduation exercise if ever there was one, complete a disc that could well serve as an admirable entry point into Barber's world. Of the available performances of the symphonies, these Chandos version are the ones to have. The Detroit orchestra turn in polished playing and the recording is rich and vivid.

CHAMBER MUSIC

Canzone for violin and piano.
(N) *** DG Dig. 453 470-2 [id.]. Gil Shaham, André Previn – COPLAND: *Sonata; Nocturne.* GERSHWIN: *3 Preludes.* PREVIN: *Sonata.* ***

This brief songful piece, with material from the slow movement of Barber's *Piano concerto*, provides a valuable makeweight in Shaham and Previn's fine collection of American violin music.

(i) *Serenade for string quartet, Op.1; String quartet, Op. 11;* (i; ii) *Dover Beach, Op. 3;* (ii; iii) *3 Songs (The daisies; With rue my heart is laden; Bessie Bobtail), Op. 2; 3 Songs (Rain has fallen; Sleep now; I hear an army), Op. 10; Sure on this shining night; Nocturne, Op. 13/3–4; Solitary hotel; Despite and still, Op. 41/4–5; 3 Songs (Now I have fed and eaten up; A green lowland of pianos; O boundless, boundless evening), Op. 45.*
*** Virgin/EMI Dig. VC5 45033-2 [id.].(i) Endellion Qt; (ii) Thomas Allen; (iii) Roger Vignoles.

This imaginatively conceived collection is geared to the Endellion Quartet, both as accompanist in *Dover Beach* and in the two early string quartet works. The *Serenade*, Op. 1, was written when Barber was only nineteen, with the first two of its three brief movements belying any idea of a lightweight work, even bringing echoes of late Beethoven. The Endellion Quartet play with the hushed gravity and clear intensity that it deserves, and their reading of the Opus 11 *Quartet* has points of advantage over even the finest rivals, with more mystery and variety of expression, and with the *Adagio* kept flowing. With Thomas Allen a superb soloist, this account of *Dover Beach* not only conveys both mystery and a keen feeling for atmosphere, it builds to a thrilling climax on the poet's expression of love. In the solo songs Allen and Vignoles opt consistently for speeds on the fast side, so that the slow tango of the Joyce setting, *Solitary hotel*, is more clearly established.

String quartet, Op. 11.
(*) DG (IMS) Dig. 435 864-2 [id.]. Emerson Qt – IVES: *Quartets 1–2.* *

The Emerson Quartet play with all the brilliance and technical expertise with which one associates them, but there is something rather soulless about them. The tone is rich, their tonal blend immaculate and their ensemble impeccable – indeed nothing can be faulted; but their expressive eloquence sounds over-rehearsed as if the feeling is painted on afterwards. All the same it is in its way stunningly played, and those who admire their brilliance and tonal sheen will find it eminently well captured by the DG engineers. Given this level of accomplishment, it would be curmudgeonly to deny them a strong recommendation.

Summer music.
*** Crystal CD 750 [id.]. Westwood Wind Quintet – CARLSSON: *Nightwings;* LIGETI: *Bagatelles;* MATHIAS: *Quintet.* ***

Samuel Barber's *Summer music* is an evocative mood-picture of summer, a gloriously warm and lyrical piece whose neglect on record is difficult to understand. The Crystal CD offers superbly committed and sensitive playing and vivid, warm recording.

PIANO MUSIC

Ballade, Op. 46; 4 Excursions, Op. 20; Interlude, Op. posth.; Nocturne (Homage to John Field), Op. 33; Sonata, Op. 26; Souvenirs, Op. 28.
*** Virgin/EMI Dig. VC5 45270-2 [id.]. Leon McCawley.

This CD accommodates Barber's entire output for the piano – including the *Souvenirs*, which date from 1952 and which exist both as an orchestral (ballet) score and in alternative piano versions for two and four hands. Leon McCawley manages excellently with just two, even in the prodigiously difficult *Sonata*, written for Horowitz. McCawley's account is highly convincing, breathtakingly so in the dazzling Scherzo and the formidable closing *Fuga*, while his freely spontaneous approach suits the opening movement especially well. The *Souvenirs*, too, are brilliantly played; if the *Tango* seems a bit heavy-going, he makes a great deal of the *Pas de deux*. The posthumous *Interlude* is also well worth having; and this well-recorded survey displaces Angela Brownridge's Hyperion disc, which omits the latter piece as well as the *Souvenirs*.

Piano sonata, Op. 26.

(M) (***) RCA mono GD 60377 [60377-RG]. Vladimir Horowitz (with FAURE: *Nocturne No. 13;* POULENC: *Presto* ***) – KABALEVSKY; PROKOFIEV: *Sonatas* etc. (***)

(M) **(*) [RCA 60415-2-RG]. Van Cliburn (with DEBUSSY: *Estampes: Soirée dans Grenade; Jardins sous la pluie; Etude No. 5; Images, Book I: Reflets dans l'eau; Préludes, Book 2: La terrasse des audiences du clair de lune; Feux d'artifice* **; MOZART: *Piano sonata No. 10* **).

Horowitz gave the première of Barber's *Sonata* and his performance has never been surpassed. It is a remarkable work and, in Horowitz's hands, completely riveting: sample his playing in the quicksilver Scherzo or the articulation of the spirited closing *Fuga*. The 1950 sound is confined but fully acceptable. Of the encores, the scintillating Poulenc *Presto* shows the great pianist at his most dazzling, with a good (if not outstanding) supporting programme.

Van Cliburn's recording is pretty masterly and, although the sound could be more ingratiating and have a warmer ambience, it is still acceptable. This CD has been withdrawn in the UK.

VOCAL MUSIC

Agnus Dei.

*** Hyperion Dig. CDA 66219 [id.]. Corydon Singers, Matthew Best – BERNSTEIN: *Chichester Psalms;* COPLAND: *In the beginning* etc. ***

Barber's *Agnus Dei* is none other than our old friend the *Adagio*, arranged for voices by the composer in 1967. Matthew Best's fine performance moves spaciously and expansively to an impressive climax.

(i) *Andromache's farewell;* (ii) *Dover Beach;* (iii) *Hermit songs;* (iv) *Knoxville: summer of 1915.*

(M) (***) Sony mono/stereo MPK 46727 [id.]. (i) Arroyo, NYPO, Schippers; (ii) Fischer-Dieskau, Juilliard Qt; (iii) Leontyne Price, composer; (iv) Eleanor Steber, Dumbarton Oaks O, William Strickland.

This collection of vintage recordings makes a splendid mid-priced Barber compendium, representing four of his finest vocal works, all in superb performances. Excellent CD transfers. No texts are provided but words are exceptionally clear.

Despite and still (song-cycle), *Op. 41; 10 Hermit songs* (to poems translated from anonymous Irish texts of 8th to 13th centuries), *Op. 29; Mélodies passagères (Puisque tout passe; Un cygne; Tombeau dans un parc; Le clocher chante), Op. 27; 3 Songs (The daisies; With rue my heart is laden; Bessie Bobtail), Op. 2; 3 Songs (Rain has fallen; Sleep now; I hear an army), Op. 10; 4 Songs (A nun takes the veil; The secrets of the old; Sure on this shining night; Nocturne), Op. 13; 2 Songs (The Queen's face on a summery coin; Monks and raisins), Op. 18; 3 Songs (Now I have fed and eaten up the rose; A green lowland of pianos; O boundless, boundless evening), Op. 45; Beggar's song; Dover Beach; In the dark pinewood; Love at the door; Love's caution; Night wanderers; Nuvoletta; Of that so sweet imprisonment; Serenades; A slumber song of the Madonna; Strings in the earth and air; There's nae lark.*

*** DG Dig. 435 867-2 (2) [id.]. Cheryl Studer, Thomas Hampson, John Browning; Emerson Qt.

Samuel Barber wrote songs throughout his composing career. Barber's style, easily lyrical, sensitively responding to the cadences of English verse, remained remarkably consistent. Cheryl Studer sings beautifully in the *Hermit songs*, but it is Thomas Hampson who establishes the full flavour of the collection, which includes a sprinkling of vigorous, extrovert songs. He is particularly fine in Barber's best-known song, the extended *Dover Beach*. In that Hampson is accompanied immaculately by the Emerson Quartet. Otherwise it is John Browning – a pianist specially associated with Barber's music and the prime mover behind this recording project – who sharpens the focus and heightens the fantasy in deeply sympathetic accompaniments. Excellent, natural recording, first-class documentation and full texts.

(i) *Hermit songs, Op. 29;* (ii) *Knoxville: Summer of 1915* (cantata); (i) Songs: *The Daisies; Nocturne; Nuvoletta; Sleep now.* (ii) *Antony and Cleopatra* (opera): scenes: *Give me some music; Give me my robe.*

(M) (***) RCA mono/stereo 09026 61983-2 [id.]. Leontyne Price, with (i) composer (piano); (ii) New Philh. O, Schippers.

The evocative cantata to words by James Agee, *Knoxville: Summer of 1915*, has never been done more hauntingly and is well coupled with the heroine's arias from the opera, *Antony and Cleopatra*. Far rarer is the private recording of the *Hermit songs*, also specially written for her. Accompanied by the composer, she is more rugged than Studer in the collected song edition, but just as intense. The mono sound is very limited but conveys the atmosphere of a historic occasion. Otherwise good stereo sound.

The Lovers, Op. 43. Prayers of Kierkegaard, Op. 30.
*** Koch Dig. 3-7125-2. Dale Duesing, Sarah Reese, Chicago Ch. & SO, Andrew Schenck.

The Lovers, written in 1971, was Barber's last major work, a substantial choral cantata setting nine erotic poems by the Chilean, Pablo Neruda. It makes a moving sequence, with the soloist, Dale Duesing, matching the responsiveness of the outstanding Chicago Symphony Chorus. *The Prayers of Kierkegaard*, written in 1952, is a tougher, more uncompromising work, but approachable too, again with magnificent writing for chorus.

Vanessa (opera): complete.
(M) *** RCA GD 87899 (2) [7899-2-RG]. Steber, Elias, Resnik, Gedda, Tozzi, Met. Op. Ch. & O, Mitropoulos.

Vanessa inhabits much the same civilized world as Strauss or Henry James. Although it has not held the stage, its melodic freshness and warmth will ensure a reversal of its fortunes some day. This, its only recording so far, was made at the time of its first performance in 1958, but no apologies are needed for its quality; it stands the test of time as well as does the opera itself.

Bargiel, Woldemar (1828–97)

Octet in C min. for strings, Op. 15a.
*** Hyperion Dig. CDA 66356 [id.]. Divertimenti – MENDELSSOHN: *Octet.* ***

What strikes one about this music is its independence of outlook and dignity. Indeed it is something of a discovery; the delightful scherzo-like section embedded in the slow movement is particularly felicitous. Divertimenti play it with real feeling and conviction and are excellently recorded.

Barraud, Henry (born 1900)

Offrande à une ombre.
(M) **(*) Mercury 434 389-2 [id.]. Detroit SO, Paul Paray – CHAUSSON: *Symphony;* LALO: *Le rois d'Ys; Namouna.* **(*)

Henry Barraud was active in the French resistance, and his wartime *Offrande à une ombre* was dedicated jointly to a fellow-composer, Maurice Jaubert, who fell in 1940 during the retreat from Alsace, and to Barraud's brother, Jean, who was shot by the Gestapo. Barraud was a prolific composer whose style owes something to Dukas and Roussel. *Offrande à une ombre* is an effective ten-minute piece, which is eminently well played by the Detroit orchestra and Paray. The recording was made in 1957 and appears in stereo for the first time. It completes an excellent programme.

Barrios, Agustin (1885–1944)

Las abejas; Aconquija; Aire de zamba; La catedral; Choro de saudade; Cueca; Julia Florida; Una limosna por el amor de Dios; Medallon antiguo; Maxixa; Mazurka appassionata; Preludios: in C min.; in G min. Un sueño en la floresta; Valses Nos. 3–4; Villancico de navidad.
*** Sony Dig. SK 64396 [id.]. John Williams.

This duplicates almost all the music on John Williams's first (bargain-priced) recital of music by this fine Paraguayan composer and has the advantage of the complete background silence of digital recording. The playing is of the highest calibre and has both concentration and charisma. However, the earlier disc (see below) offers about 10 minutes' more music by including the Ponce *Variations* and it remains very attractive in its own right.

Aconquija; Aire de Zamba; Le catedral; Cueca; Estudio; Una limosna por el amor de Dios; Madrigal (Gavota); Maxixa; Mazurka appassionata; Minuet; Preludio; Un sueño en la floresta; Valse No. 3; Vallancico de Navidad.
(M) *** Sony SBK 47669; *SBT 47669* [id.]. John Williams – PONCE: *Folia de España.* ***

In the expert hands of John Williams this collection provides a very entertaining recital, ideal for late-evening listening. The recording is excellent. The remarkable extended set of Ponce *Variations* added for the CD reissue brings the total playing time up to 77 minutes.

Barsukov, Sergei (born 1912)

Violin concerto No. 2.
** Revelation RV 10058 [id.]. Kogan, Grand R. & TV SO, Rozhdestvensky – BARBER: *Violin concerto* **(*); BUNIN: *Violin concerto.* **

The Soviet composer, Sergei Barsukov, is here influenced more by the exotic world of Scriabin than by any Soviet model, and Kogan in this 1969 recording gives a warmly persuasive reading, rather better balanced in sound than the much later recording of the Barber.

Bartók, Béla (1881–1945)

Concerto for orchestra.
(M) *** Decca 417 754-2 [id.]. Chicago SO, Solti – MUSSORGSKY: *Pictures.* ***
(B) **(*) EMI forte CZS5 72664-2 (2) [(M) id. import]. Chicago SO, Seiji Ozawa – JANACEK: *Sinfonietta* ***; LUTOSLAWSKI: *Concerto for orchestra* **(*); STRAVINSKY: *Firebird ballet.* **(*)
(*) Chandos Dig. CHAN 8947 [id.]. RSNO, Järvi – ENESCU: *Romanian rhapsodies Nos. 1–2.* *
(M) **(*) Telarc Dig. CD 82010 [id.]. Los Angeles PO, André Previn – JANACEK: *Sinfonietta.* **(*)

Solti gave Bartók's *Concerto for orchestra* its compact disc début. The upper range is very brightly lit indeed, which brings an aggressive feeling to the upper strings. This undoubtedly suits the reading, fierce and biting on the one hand, exuberant on the other. Superlative playing from Solti's own Chicago orchestra, and given vivid sound.

Ozawa's EMI reissue produces dazzling playing from the Chicago orchestra. The performance is full of life and energy. There are more searching and more atmospheric accounts available, but this stands alongside the Solti version for brilliance. However, as with the Lutoslawski coupling, the CD transfer brings sound which, though most vivid, is rather two-dimensional.

Recorded in opulent sound with the Royal Scottish Orchestra, Järvi directs an amiable reading, not as brilliant or precise in ensemble as the finest but warm and convincing, with some fine solo playing. Anyone who also wants the Enescu *Rhapsodies*, the rare No. 2 as well as the popular No. 1, could well consider this.

Previn and the Los Angeles Philharmonic give a comfortable, relaxed reading of Bartók's *Concerto*. Previn is at his best in the fun of the couple-play in the second movement or the Shostakovich parody of the fourth movement. For him, it is above all a work of fun, although there is no lack of excitement in the finale. The Telarc recording captures the full bloom of the orchestra as few recordings from Los Angeles have. The coupling is unique.

(i) *Concerto for orchestra;* (ii) *Piano concertos Nos. 1–3*; (i; iii) *Violin concerto No. 2 in B min.*
(B) *** Ph. Duo 438 812-2 (2) [id.]. (i) Concg. O, Haitink; (ii) Kovacevich, LSO or BBC SO (in *No. 2*), Sir Colin Davis; (iii) Szeryng.

This is as enticing a bargain Bartók collection as you could find. Not unexpectedly in Haitink's 1960 *Concerto for orchestra*, the orchestral playing is of the highest quality and the recording is both atmospheric and clear. The performance is more subtle, less tense than Solti's mid-priced version, although the element of dramatic contrast is not missing. Szeryng joins Haitink for the *B minor Violin concerto* with equally satisfying artistic results. Haitink keeps a firm grip on proceedings and there is a genuine sense of momentum and impetus about the performance that is really exciting. The 1969 recording is vivid, and firmly and realistically focused. Kovacevich's direct, concentrated readings of the three *Piano concertos* are hardly less persuasive. Sir Colin Davis accompanies sensitively and vigorously. No complaints about the bright, full recording.

(i) *Concerto for orchestra;* (ii) *Dance suite; 2 Portraits, Op. 5; Mikrokosmos* (orch. Serly): *Bourrée; From the diary of a fly.*
(M) *** Mercury (IMS) 432 017-2 [id.]. (i) LSO; (ii) Philharmonia Hungarica, Dorati.

Dorati secures outstandingly brilliant and committed playing from the LSO. The recording, made in Wembley Town Hall, shows characteristic expertise of balance. The rest of the programme was recorded in 1958 in the Grosse Saal of the Vienna Konzerthaus, which affords Dorati's fine orchestra of Hungarian émigrés plenty of body without blurring outlines.

Concerto for orchestra; The Miraculous Mandarin (ballet suite).
*** EMI Dig. CDC5 55094-2 [id.]. CBSO, Sir Simon Rattle.

Even Sir Simon Rattle has rarely matched his achievement in his superb Bartók coupling, a brilliant studio recording of the violent *Miraculous Mandarin* ballet suite married to a live recording of the *Concerto for orchestra* which draws on an exceptionally wide emotional and expressive range. The ballet score is here as remarkable for the sensuousness of much of the playing as for the biting energy of the violent music. Rich, full and well-balanced recording, to match the brilliance of the performances. There are no finer readings of either work.

Concerto for orchestra; Music for strings, percussion and celesta.
*** EMI (SIS) Dig. CDC7 54070-2 [id.]. Oslo PO, Jansons.
(M) **(*) DG 457 890-2. BPO, Karajan.
**(*) Chant du Monde Praga PR 254047 [id.].(i) Czech PO, Lehel; (ii) Leningrad PO, Mravinsky.
(N) (M) ** Sony SMK 60730 [id.]. NYPO, Bernstein.

Jansons and the Oslo Philharmonic give outstanding performances of both works, making this a fine primary recommendation in this now-favourite coupling of two Bartók masterpieces. The Oslo orchestra plays with unfailingly crisp ensemble, and the sound is excellent too, full and open.

In the *Concerto* the Berlin Philharmonic, in superb form, give a performance that is rich, romantic and smooth – for some ears perhaps excessively so. Karajan is right in treating Bartók emotionally, but comparison with Solti points the contrast between Berlin romanticism and earthy Hungarian passion. Karajan's moulding of phrases is essentially of the German tradition. The *Music for strings, percussion and celesta* has well-upholstered timbre, and here Karajan's essentially romantic view combines with the recording to produce a certain urbanity. However, the playing of the Berlin strings is a pleasure in itself and the sound is impressive and full-bodied.

The Mravinsky version of the *Music for strings, percussion and celesta* was recorded at a concert during the Prague Spring in 1967. In this performance the slow movement has tremendous mystery and intensity, and it makes one regret the rather less than opulent sound. The *Concerto for orchestra*, conducted by György Lehel, is highly atmospheric and has both a magisterial sweep and a sensitive ear for detail. Though the recording is not quite comparable in quality with the very best, it is warm and spacious and truthfully balanced – and infinitely superior to that accorded Mravinsky.

Bernstein's coupling of Bartók's two most popular pieces brings gripping performances, typical of his work in New York at the end of the 1950s and beginning of the 1960s (the recording dates are 1959 and 1961 respectively). The performances are full of excitement and vitality (the finale of the *Concerto* is breathtaking) and although the recording is fairly forward, the dynamic range is surprisingly wide, and because of the drama of the playing there is still plenty of contrast. However, while the remastered sound does not lack atmosphere, there is an unattractive glare on the very brightly lit violins, which are thin above the stave. Yet for the animal energy which Bernstein finds in Bartók, this is still a record worth hearing.

Concerto for orchestra; Music for strings, percussion and celesta; Hungarian sketches.
(M) *** RCA 09026 61504-2 [id.]. Chicago SO, Fritz Reiner.

Reiner's version of the *Concerto for orchestra* was recorded in 1955 but in its latest CD format the sound approaches demonstration standard in its spacious warmth, clarity and impact. The performance is most satisfying, surprisingly straightforward from one brought up in central Europe, but with plenty of cutting edge. The *Music for strings, percussion and celesta*, recorded three years later, suffers from a forward balance which prevents a true pianissimo, yet the concentration of the playing all but overcomes this defect, and the folk-based set of five *Hungarian sketches*, which completes the programme, is utterly seductive when played and recorded with such vividness of colour and a natural understanding of the music's rhythmic impetus.

Concerto for orchestra; 4 Orchestral pieces, Op. 12.
**(*) DG (IMS) Dig. 437 826-2 [id.]. Chicago SO, Boulez.

Boulez's is a strong and perceptively detailed account of the *Concerto for orchestra*. He secures brilliant playing from the Chicago orchestra, but they are able to relax in the central movements – which is just as well, for the finale is very powerfully driven indeed. The *Four Orchestral Pieces* was the nearest Bartók came to writing a symphony, complete with Scherzo and melancholy slow movement.

Piano concertos Nos. 1–3.
*** Teldec/Warner Dig. 0630 13158-2 [id.]. Schiff, Budapest Festival O, Fischer.
*** Ph. (IMS) Dig. 446 366-2 [id.]. Kocsis, Budapest Festival O, Ivan Fischer.
*** EMI Dig. CDC7 54871-2 [id.]. Peter Donohoe, CBSO, Rattle.
(M) *** DG 447 399-2 [id.]. Géza Anda, Berlin RSO, Ferenc Fricsay.
(M)*** Decca Dig./Analogue 448 125-2. Ashkenazy, LPO, Solti.
(BB) **(*) Naxos Dig. 8.550771 [id.]. Jenö Jandó, Budapest SO, András Ligeti.

András Schiff has become so magnetic an interpreter of the central classics that his Hungarian roots are easily forgotten, yet his colourful, winning performances of Bartók's three piano concertos are totally idiomatic, brilliantly and warmly accompanied by the fine Budapest orchestra. Above all, Schiff gives the lie to the idea of Bartók as a mainly violent composer, bringing out point and sparkle even in aggressive music like the first movements of both No. 1 and No. 2. Equally his depth of meditation in the slow movements matches that which equally he brings to Bach or Schubert, while the *Third Concerto* has rarely sounded so exuberant in its outer movements.

The Kocsis performances, extracted from the Philips box listed below, remain a strong alternative choice for the three piano concertos, although one could be equally happy with the Donohoe/Rattle EMI disc.

Peter Donohoe and Sir Simon Rattle give first-class accounts of all three Bartók concertos and they have the advantage of equally impressive sound. Taken in isolation and purely on its own merits, this EMI CD is a highly recommendable issue which offers thoroughly idiomatic playing.

The Géza Anda recordings with Fricsay from the beginning of the 1960s are rather special. Both artists show a feeling for the music's inner world and its colouring, which is magnetic in the slow movements. The performances are refined yet urgent, incisive but red-blooded too. They make a worthy addition to DG's series of 'Originals'. The recording, from the beginning of the 1960s, is vivid and remarkably atmospheric, yet still tangible in detail.

The partnership of Ashkenazy and Solti, combined with vintage Decca sound, makes this Ovation mid-price reissue a further strong competitor. The *Second* and *Third Concertos* spark off the kind of energy and dash one would usually expect only at a live performance. Tempi tend to be fast, but the focus of the playing is superbly clear. The *First Concerto*, recorded digitally in 1981, is even tougher, urgent and biting, with the widest range of dynamics, never relaxing in the outer movements. The sound is slightly sharper but the Kingsway Hall aura remains, and the slow movements in all three works bring a hushed inner concentration, beautifully captured in warmly refined recording.

With an all-Hungarian cast, Naxos offers invigorating accounts of the three Bartók *Piano concertos* with Jandó on top form, playing with exciting bravura throughout. The energy of the motoric *First Concerto* is not brutalized; and in the slow movement with its important percussion parts and the haunting 'Night music' of the *Second* the resonance of the recording ensures that there is plenty of atmosphere, even if in outer movements the violent brass interjections could be more cleanly focused. Apart from the excess of resonance, the recording is vivid and well balanced.

(i) *Piano concertos Nos. 1–3. Allegro barbaro; 14 Bagatelles, Op. 6; 4 Dirges, Op. 9a; 2 Elegies, Op. 8b; First term at the piano; For Children, Books I–IV; 3 Hungarian folksongs from Csík; 3 Hungarian folk tunes; Rumanian Christmas carols; 6 Rumanian folk tunes; 2 Rumanian dances, Op. 8a; 3 Rondos on folk tunes; Sonatina; 3 Studies, Op. 18; Suite, Op. 14.*
*** Ph. Dig. 446 368-2 (4) [id.]. Zoltán Kocsis; (i) Budapest Festival O, Iván Fischer.

The calibre of this Philips set cannot be denied, but it is relatively expensive: four full-price CDs for the price of three. Kocsis's recordings of the three concertos are as idiomatic as they are vibrant, and the *Third* is superbly done, among the finest on record. The Philips recording is admirably bold and full-bodied. But there are other fine versions which cost less (notably Anda), and many may prefer to approach the solo piano music separately.

Piano concerto No. 3.
(M) *** DG 447 666-2. Géza Anda, Dresden State O, Karajan – SCHUMANN: *Symphony No. 4.* ***
(BB) *** Arte Nova Dig. 74321 52248-2 [id.]. Russell Sherman, SWF SO, Gielen – BERG: *3 Pieces from the Lyric suite;* CARTER: *Piano concerto* etc. ***
(N) **(*) EMI CDC5 56654-2 [id.]. Martha Argerich, Montreal SO, Charles Dutoit – PROKOFIEV: *Piano concertos Nos. 1 & 3.* **(*)

As in the Carter and Berg, Gielen directs an intense, crisply pointed account of the Bartók *Concerto*, matched by the sharply rhythmic, well-pointed playing of Russell Sherman. This makes a generous and unusual coupling of twentieth-century masterpieces, well recorded, and made the more attractive at super-budget price.

Elegant playing from Martha Argerich in the Bartók *Third concerto* which is new to discography. There is a wonderful improvisatory feel to much of it, though at times in the slow movement she caresses a phrase in a way which draws attention to her rather than Bartók. Very distinguished playing but not a first recommendation. Excellent support from the Montreal Orchestra under Dutoit and good recording.

Viola concerto (ed. Tibor Serly).
*** EMI Dig. CDC7 54101-2. Tabea Zimmermann, Bav. RSO, David Shallon – HINDEMITH: *Der Schwanendreher.* ***
*** Sony Dig. SK 57961 [id.]. Yo-Yo Ma, Baltimore SO, David Zinman – ALBERT: *Cello concerto;* BLOCH: *Schelomo.****

Tabea Zimmermann and the Orchestra of Bayerischen Rundfunk are strongly recommendable. This is playing of great eloquence and taste, and the balance is much finer than that offered by the DG engineers on their newest version – see below. The soloist is helped, but she is not so forward as to mask orchestral detail, which is wonderfully present and beautifully placed.

Yo-Yo Ma had originally intended to record the cello version of the Bartók concerto which Tibor Serly made at the instigation of the Bartók Estate; but eventually he discovered he could play it at the correct pitch on the alto violin or vertical viola, in which the instrument is fitted with a long end-pin and played upright like a cello. His performance has characteristic finesse and eloquence, and it gains from the transparent sound which Zinman draws from the Baltimore orchestra.

Viola concerto; Violin concerto No. 1; (i) *Rhapsodies Nos. 1–2.*
(M) *** EMI (SIS) CDM7 63985-2 [id.]. Sir Yehudi Menuhin, New Philh. O, Dorati; (i) BBC SO, Boulez.

Menuhin with his strongly creative imagination plays these concertos with characteristic nobility of feeling, and he and Dorati make much of the Hungarian dance rhythms. There is a comparably earthy, peasant manner in Menuhin's playing of the two *Rhapsodies*, and it is matched by Boulez's approach, warm and passionate rather than clinical. The soloist is rather close. However, the balance responds to the controls, and this remains one of Menuhin's most worthwhile reissues.

(i) *Viola concerto* (two versions; ed. Peter Bartók & ed. Serly); *Two pictures, Op. 10.*
(N) (BB) *** Naxos Dig. 8.554183 [id.]. Xiao, Budapest PO, Kovacs – SERLY: *Rhapsody for viola and orchestra.* ***

Having a première recording of Bartók on Naxos makes an unmissable bargain. His *Viola concerto* was the uncompleted work which, soon after his death, Tibor Serly put together from sketches. Now Bartók's son Peter, with the scholar Paul Neubauer, has re-edited those sketches. Though the differences are small, this first recording of the revised version, superbly played, proves fascinating, sounding closer to the *Concerto for orchestra*. With the rich-toned Chinese viola-player, Xiao, as soloist, that version is here presented alongside Serly's. The warmly atmospheric *Two Pictures* and a viola work by Serly make a good coupling.

Violin concertos Nos. (i) *1;* (ii) *2.*
(M) *** Sony Stern Edition II SMK 64502 [id.]. Stern; (i) Phd. O, Ormandy; (ii) NYPO, Bernstein.
(M) *** Decca Dig./Analogue 425 015-2 [id.]. Kyung Wha Chung, Chicago SO or LPO, Solti.
*** Nimbus Dig. NI 5333 [id.]. Gerhart Hetzel, Hungarian State SO, Adám Fischer.

Stern brings to the mature masterpiece an enviable combination of tautness and lyricism, steely strength and melting beauty of tone. The accompaniment is sensitive and subtle; Bernstein is evidently in complete sympathy with both the music and the soloist, and the overall impression is of understanding between these two inspirational artists. Stern's passionate playing suits the earlier concerto to perfection, his ardour readily surmounting the clash of styles in the second and final movement, with Debussy and Strauss – particularly the latter – alternating with the genuine Hungarian Bartók. The 1961 recording brings a balance which favours the soloist in a manner typical of CBS, but otherwise it sounds well in its successfully remastered format.

Though on Decca the soloist is rather forwardly balanced, the hushed intensity of the writing, as well as bitingly Hungarian flavours, is caught superbly, thanks to the conductor as well as to the soloist. The expressive warmth behind Bartók's writing is fully brought out, and there is no sentimental lingering. Among modern recordings, this leads the field in both works.

Gerhart Hetzel plays both concertos with great feeling and understanding. There is no want of virtuosity, but nor is there virtuosity for its own sake (or, rather, that of the soloist's ego). Ideas are fashioned with great sensitivity and, although dynamic nuances are scrupulously observed, there is none of the exaggeration which draws attention to the soloist rather than to Bartók. These are performances of strong but unintrusive personality. Both concertos are very well recorded, with a natural, excellent balance which helps the soloist to just the right extent, and it must rank among the very best now available.

Violin concerto No. 2 in B min.
(M) *** EMI (SIS) CDM5 66060-2. Perlman, LSO, Previn – CONUS: *Violin concerto;* SINDING: *Suite.* ***
(N) ** Ph. Dig. 456 542-2 [id.]. Viktoria Mullova, LAPO, Esa-Pekka Salonen – STRAVINSKY: *Violin concerto in D.* ***

Perlman's is a superb performance, totally committed and full of youthful urgency, with the sense of spontaneity that comes more readily when performers have already worked together on the music in the concert hall. The slow movement is deliberately understated by the soloist, with the fragmentation of the theme lightly touched in, but even there the orchestra has its passionate comments. The 1973 recording is full and gains much from the Kingsway Hall acoustics, though Perlman is balanced characteristically forward. With its interesting new couplings, this is one of the most stimulating reissues taken from EMI's 'Perlman Collection'.

Viktoria Mullova gives a brilliant enough account of Bartók's marvellous *concerto* and she is well supported by the Los Angeles Orchestra under Esa-Pekka Salonen. But there is all too little of the warmth or humanity that others from Menuhin onwards have found in this powerful score. Good recorded sound but not a first choice given the present abundance of versions. The Stravinsky coupling is more successful.

Violin concerto No. 2; 2 Rhapsodies for violin and orchestra.
*** EMI Dig. CDC7 54211-2. Kyung Wha Chung, CBSO, Rattle.
(N) *** DG Dig. 459 639-2 [id.]. Shaham, Chicago SO, Boulez.

Kyung Wha Chung in her EMI version gives a commanding, inspired performance, full of fire and imagination, helped by the inspirational accompaniment of Rattle and the Birmingham orchestra. The same qualities come out just as vividly in the two flamboyant *Rhapsodies*, each in two nicely contrasted movements.

Shaham's reading of the *Second Violin concerto* is also full of flair and imagination, taut and intense to justify speeds on the broad side, while Boulez draws superb playing from the Chicago orchestra, both warm and sharply focused. The hushed intensity of Shaham's playing in the slow movement has rarely been matched. The two *Rhapsodies*, each in two compact movements, make an ideal coupling, colourful medleys of folk-themes in Bartók's most approachable manner. Shaham may not be so impulsive as Chung in this same coupling, but he plays with a firm strength and precision that is just as satisfying. Full-bodied, well-detailed sound.

(i) *Violin concerto No. 2; Second Suite for orchestra* (revised, 1943 version).
(M) **(*) Mercury (IMS) 434 350-2 [id.]. (i) Sir Yehudi Menuhin; Minneapolis SO, Dorati.

Menuhin's third version of the *Second Violin concerto* dates from 1957. It is much better recorded than either of his earlier records, and (even taking into account the comments above) remains thoroughly worthwhile, with the solo playing demonstrating those special qualities of lyrical feeling and warmth for which he was justly famous. The rare coupling makes this Mercury reissue doubly attractive. The *Second Orchestral Suite* is a colourful, half-hour-long piece in four movements; the second introduces a vibrant fugue and the *Andante* opens with an unusual extended recitative from the bass clarinet. The energetic, folksy finale ends serenely (*molto quieto*). Dorati is a persuasive advocate, and the characteristically graphic Mercury recording has no lack of primary colours.

Dance suite; Divertimento; Hungarian sketches; 2 Pictures.
**(*) DG Dig. 445 825-2 [id.]. Chicago SO, Boulez.

As in their other Bartók recordings together, the partnership of Pierre Boulez and the Chicago orchestra makes for brilliant results, if here rather smoother and less sharply focused than usual. So the *Dance suite* has its Hungarian flavours muted and in the *Divertimento* the contrasts between solos and tutti are underplayed, though the hushed intensity of the slow movement is magical. The slower movements among the *Two Pictures* and the five *Hungarian sketches* are also done most poetically.

(i) *Dance suite;* (ii) *Music for strings, percussion and celesta;* (i) *The Wooden Prince* (complete), *Op. 13.*
(M) **(*) Sony SM2K 64100 (2) [id.]. (i) NYPO; (ii) BBC SO; Boulez – SCRIABIN: *Poème de l'exstase.* ***

In *The Wooden Prince* Boulez is the most compelling of advocates, maintaining his concentration throughout; the *Dance suite* brings a performance just as warm, but a degree less precise. The 1975 analogue recording, originally among CBS's best, emerges vividly on CD with plenty of atmosphere, although the upper strings could be more expansive. The *Music for strings, percussion and celesta* was made in Walthamstow two years later and was one of Boulez's finest records of that period. Unfortunately the recording suffers from the artificial balance sometimes favoured by CBS. However, for those who can overlook this there are genuine rewards in this magnetic music-making, and the Scriabin coupling is quite superb.

Divertimento for strings.
(N) *** MDG Dig. MDG 321 0180-2 [id.]. Polish CO, Jerzy Maksymiuk – BRITTEN: *Variations on a theme of Frank Bridge.* ***

Among recent (or rather recently issued, for the performance dates from 1985) accounts of Bartók's masterly score, this Polish version under Jerzy Maksymiuk is among the best. The playing is never less than distinguished and the recording very fine indeed. Rather short measure at 52 minutes but an issue of quality, and worth the money if the coupling is what you want.

Divertimento for strings; Music for strings, percussion and celesta.
(M) *** Decca 448 577-2 [id.]. ASMF, Marriner – SHOSTAKOVICH: *Piano concerto No. 1.* ***
(B) *** HM HMA Dig. 190 3052 [id.]. Liszt CO, Rolla.

A superlative coupling from Marriner, fully worthy of Decca's Classic Sound series, even though the recording originally appeared (in 1970) on the Argo label. Marriner follows the composer's intentions, like Sacher using a chamber-sized group, and his reading (helped by the superb Argo engineering) also reveals extra detail, extra expressiveness, extra care for tonal and dynamic nuances. The *Divertimento* is given a similarly vivid performance and the recording is again outstandingly good. With a generous and attractive Shostakovich bonus, this is a reissue not to be missed.

The Liszt Chamber Orchestra comprises seventeen players, including Janos Rolla who directs from the first desk, though they are augmented for the *Music for strings, percussion and celesta.* These are both expert performances and distil a powerful atmosphere in the slow movements of both pieces. They command beautifully rapt *pianissimo* tone and keen intensity. The sound is less reverberant than for some rivals, but there is no lack of ambience. Readers who want accounts of these works that would not have greatly differed from Sacher's at the first performance will not be disappointed.

(i) *Divertimento for strings;* (ii) *Music for strings, percussion and celesta;* (iii) *Sonata for 2 pianos & percussion.*
**(*) Oxford OOCD-CD2 ½ (2). (i–ii) Oxford O da Camera, Paul Sacher; (ii–iii) Tristan Fry, James Holland; (iii) Boris Berman, Stephane Lemin.

In September 1995, to commemorate the fiftieth

anniversary of Bartók's death and within months of his own ninetieth birthday, Paul Sacher recorded these live performances with the Oxford Orchestra da Camera and he here introduces each with his own unique commentary in English. At speeds generally broader than usual, these unique performances may lack the vitality and bite of the finest rivals, but they have a compelling warmth and concentration, along with fine playing from the professional band, and they are atmospherically recorded. The two discs may be obtained from the orchestra direct (2 Axtell Close, Kidlington, Oxford).

Divertimento for strings; Rumanian folk dances.
(M) **(*) DG (IMS) Dig. 445 541 [id.]. Orpheus CO – STRAVINSKY: *Dumbarton Oaks Concerto* etc. ***

The American Orpheus Chamber Orchestra give an eminently well-prepared account of the *Divertimento*. A good performance with a sense of mystery and intensity of feeling, if not entirely idiomatic. The recording is very clean and well balanced. The *Rumanian folk dances* are also attractively done, and the recording is fresh and immediate.

Hungarian folk-dance suite, Op. 18; Hungarian pictures.
(M) *** Chandos Dig. CHAN 7083 [id.]. Philh. O, Järvi (with ENESCU: *Romanian rhapsodies*. ***)

The *Folk-dance suite* and the *Hungarian pictures* (the latter also drawn from various folk-based pieces), originally written for piano, are lightweight Bartók but are vividly colourful here and are aptly coupled with Enescu's pair of *Romanian rhapsodies*. A lightweight but attractive disc, particularly when playing and recording are suitably red-blooded.

(i) *Hungarian pictures;* (ii) *The Miraculous Mandarin* (complete ballet); *Music for strings, percussion and celesta;* (iii) *Rhapsody for piano and orchestra;* (ii) *Suite No. 1, Op. 3; 2 Pictures, Op. 10.*
(B) **(*) Decca Double 448 276-2 (2) [id.]. (i) Israel PO, Mehta; (ii) Detroit SO, Dorati; (iii) Pascal Rogé, LSO, Weller.

Mehta gives a fine performance of the five *Hungarian pictures*. They have great charm, and the glowing orchestral colours are well realized here. The Israel Philharmonic, recorded in Kingsway Hall, sounds far finer than when it faces the microphones on home ground. Pascal Rogé shows genuine feeling for the keyboard colour of Bartók's *Rhapsody*: in his hands the music is far from abrasive, with an atmospheric recording to match. The rest of the programme is in the hands of Antal Dorati. In the *Suite No. 1*, Dorati's approach is strong and vigorous to match the music's character, as it is in the much more advanced *Pictures* of 1910. The two major works here, the complete *Miraculous Mandarin* ballet and the *Music for strings and percussion*, are recorded digitally, and the range and brilliance of the sound are spectacular. This makes up for any lessening of tension in the actual performances compared with Dorati's previous recordings of both works for Mercury.

Hungarian sketches; Rumanian folk dances.
(M) *** Mercury (IMS) 432 005-2 [id.]. Minneapolis SO, Dorati – KODALY: *Dances; Háry János*. ***

Dorati, himself a Hungarian, provided the pioneer stereo recording of these works, yet the 1956 sound is vivid and full and wears its years very lightly indeed. The Minneapolis orchestra, on top form, provides plenty of ethnic feeling and colour.

The Miraculous Mandarin (complete ballet), *Op. 19.*
(*) Chandos Dig. CHAN 9029 [id.]. L. Voices, Philh. O, Järvi – WEINER: *Hungarian folk-dance suite*. *
(*) Delos Dig. DE 3083 [id.]. Seattle SO, Gerard Schwarz – KODALY: *Háry János; Galánta dances*. *

The Miraculous Mandarin (complete); *Music for strings, percussion and celesta.*
** DG (IMS) Dig. 447 747-2 [id.]. Chicago SO, Boulez.

(i) *The Miraculous Mandarin* (complete); (ii) *2 Portraits, Op. 5.*
(M) *** DG (IMS) Dig. 445 501-2 [id.]. LSO, Abbado; (i) with Amb. S.; (ii) Shlomo Minz – JANACEK: *Sinfonietta*. ***

(i) *The Miraculous Mandarin* (complete). *4 Orchestral pieces, Op. 12;* (ii) *3 Village scenes.*
(M) *** Sony SMK 45837 [id.]. (i) Schola Cantorum; (ii) Camerata Singers; NYPO, Pierre Boulez.

Abbado directs a fiercely powerful performance of Bartók's barbarically furious ballet – including the wordless chorus in the finale – but one which, thanks to the refinement of the recording, makes the aggressiveness of the writing more acceptable while losing nothing in power. The Janácek coupling is highly appropriate and equally successful; before that, however, the ear is sweetened by Minz's warmth in the *Portraits*.

On Sony Boulez also proves a strong and sympathetic advocate in all this music, and his approach is surprisingly warm. This is even more striking in *The Miraculous Mandarin*. The New York orchestra responds with deeply expressive playing and, with spacious recording, many will prefer it on that account.

Neeme Järvi conducts a strong, rugged reading of *The Miraculous Mandarin*, opulently recorded.

There are more sharply focused versions than this, but the energy of this performance convincingly brings out the barbaric quality of the score, getting one vividly to visualize the gruesome plot as it develops. The amiable and colourful Weiner *Folk dances* make an unusual and attractive coupling.

Gerard Schwarz directs the Seattle orchestra in a powerfully atmospheric account of Bartók's malignant ballet score, not as idiomatically aggressive as some, but with plenty of grip and excitement at the climax. Aptly and generously coupled with Kodály, this can be strongly recommended.

In his later DG recording, Boulez takes a characteristically objective view of both works. The playing is brilliant and the recording full and detailed, but in the ballet the clinical approach means that there is a total absence of sensuousness, not to mention the other dramatic qualities which can make this violent piece so involving. With Boulez it is a musical tapestry and not much more. His objectivity works better in the *Music for strings, percussion and celesta*, which begins with the most refined pianissimo.

(i) *The Miraculous Mandarin* (complete); *Hungarian peasant songs; Hungarian sketches; Romanian Folk Dances; Transylvanian Dances.*
(N) *** Ph. Dig. 454 430-2 [id.]. (i) Hung. R. Ch.; Budapest Fest. O, Iván Fischer.

Iván Fischer's account of *The Miraculous Mandarin* is the best to have appeared for many years – indeed it is possibly the best ever committed to disc, and certainly the best recorded. The sound is certainly in the demonstration category, with enormous range and depth. It has vivid presence and impact, and the balance is both truthful and refined. The performance has collected golden opinions almost everywhere (it was voted as *Gramophone* magazine's 1998 orchestral award) for the performance has virtuosity, bite and real flair. No disrespect intended to Abbado, Dorati and Solti, but this now supersedes other recommendations.

The Miraculous Mandarin (suite); The Wooden Prince (suite, arr. Järvi).
**(*) Chandos Dig. CHAN 9133 [id.]. Philh. O, Järvi.

These suites from Bartók's two ballets are taken from Järvi's separate recordings of the complete ballet scores of each. It makes a useful and illuminating coupling of two works which could hardly be more sharply contrasted, though the suite versions simply involve the omission of some 15 minutes of music from each score – from the end of *The Miraculous Mandarin* and from the middle of *The Wooden Prince*.

Music for strings, percussion and celesta.
(M) (***) Mercury mono 434 378-2 [id.]. Chicago SO, Rafael Kubelik – MUSSORGSKY: *Pictures at an exhibition*. (***)

This was the second LP Mercury made in Chicago in 1951, following the coupled *Pictures at an exhibition*, and if the sound is not as spectacular as the Mussorgsky/Ravel score, that is partly because in those early LP days the timbre of the upper strings still remained somewhat illusive to the available microphones. But the balance is excellent, and the warmth and intensity at the work's opening are maintained throughout, and especially in the evocation of the *Adagio*, with subtly concentrated string-playing. The rhythmic freedom and energy of the second and fourth movements combine to make Kubelik's performance highly compelling overall.

2 Pictures, Op. 10.
*** Sony Dig. SK 58949 [id.] La Scala, Milan, PO, Muti – STRAVINSKY: *Le baiser de la fée.* ***

A puzzling coupling, as an all-Bartók or all-Stravinsky record would have made better sense. However, there is nothing wrong with either the playing or the recording here. Muti gets an orchestral response that stands up well to the competition from native Hungarians.

Rhapsodies for violin and orchestra: No. 1 in G min.; 2 in D min.
(B) *** [EMI Red Line Dig. CDR5 69806]. Kyung Wha Chung, CBSO, Rattle – DVORAK: *Violin concerto.* ***
(M) ** Sony Stern Edition II SMK 64503 [id.]. Stern, NYPO, Bernstein (with PROKOFIEV: *Violin concertos.* **(*)).

Kyung Wha Chung gives commanding, inspired performances, full of fire and imagination, helped by the inspirational accompaniment of Rattle and the Birmingham orchestra. The *Rhapsodies* are flamboyant works, each in two nicely contrasted movements.

Stern and Bernstein seem less happy with the *Rhapsodies* than with the mature *Concerto*. The first, a colourful and immediately attractive piece, is played well enough; however, the second, taut and pithily rhythmic, surely needs a drier acoustic. Neither Stern nor Bernstein seems comfortable, and the constant rhythmic thrusting becomes monotonous.

The Wooden prince (complete ballet), *Op. 13* (complete); *Hungarian pictures.*
*** Chandos Dig. CHAN 8895 [id.]. Philh. O, Järvi.

The Wooden prince (complete); *Music for strings, percussion and celesta.*
(M) **(*) Mercury (IMS) 434 357-2 [id.]. LSO, Dorati.

The Wooden prince (complete); (i) *Cantata profana.*

*** DG (IMS) Dig. 435 863-2 [id.]. Chicago SO Ch. & SO, Boulez; (i) with Aler, Tomlinson.

With the Chicago Symphony Orchestra Pierre Boulez gives a bitingly powerful reading of Bartók's often uncharacteristically mild ballet-score of 1914. Since he recorded it earlier with the New York Philharmonic (for CBS/Sony), Boulez's view has grown noticeably more expansive and a degree warmer, though at times the DG recording puts an edge on the sound to the point of abrasiveness. The enigmatic *Cantata profana* of 1930 is superbly done with the Chicago Symphony Chorus responding in total confidence to the challenge of the thorny choral writing, and with John Aler incisive in the taxing tenor role.

Järvi's red-blooded performance relates the work to romantic sources, even to Wagner's *Rheingold* at the very start. The drama of the fairy story is told in glowing colours and, unlike most rivals, Järvi ignores the many little cuts that the composer sanctioned, reluctantly or not, over the years. The opulent playing of the Philharmonia is greatly enhanced by the full, vivid Chandos recording. The suite, *Hungarian pictures*, drawn from various folk-based piano pieces, provides a colourful if trivial makeweight.

Dorati's performances of both works are brilliantly authentic. *The Wooden Prince* is given a fresh, dynamic reading, vivid in its detail, with the reminders of Stravinsky and the Debussian textures brilliantly caught. The *Music for strings, percussion and celesta* is comparably atmospheric, the playing full of tension, and Dorati brings out the Hungarian dance inflexions in the finale. The recordings, from 1964 and 1960 respectively, hardly sound their age except for a degree of rawness in the upper range of the strings in the more strident moments of the ballet.

CHAMBER AND INSTRUMENTAL MUSIC

(i) *Andante* (for violin and piano); (ii) *Piano quintet;* (iii) *Rhapsodies Nos. 1 & 2.*
(BB) *** Naxos Dig. 8.550886-2. (i; iii) Pauk; (i; ii) Jandó; (ii) Kodály Qt.

The *Piano quintet*, a substantial work in the received idiom over 40 minutes in length, is wholly uncharacteristic. The *Andante* for violin and piano is also early (1902) and is otherwise not recorded. It is slight but charming. The two *Rhapsodies* come from 1928, written respectively for Joseph Szigeti and Zoltán Székely, and are more popular in style than the *Fourth Quartet*, written the same year. Very good playing from György Pauk and alert playing from Jenö Jandó, whose humming is at times faintly audible. No quarrels with either recording or performances. Excellent value.

Contrasts for clarinet, violin and piano.
*** Delos Dig. D/CD 3043 [id.]. Shifrin, Bae, Lash – MESSIAEN: *Quatuor*. ***

(i) *Contrasts. Mikrokosmos:* excerpts.
(M) (***) Sony mono MPK 47676 [id.]. Composer; (i) with Joseph Szigeti, Benny Goodman.

Contrasts was commissioned by Benny Goodman. In 1940 Bartók added a further movement, and it was in this form that the three artists made their recording. That same year Bartók recorded 31 pieces from *Mikrokosmos* and these performances are indicative of the wide range and delicacy of keyboard colour that Bartók commanded. The sound is surprisingly good, given that it is over half a century old! An indispensable issue.

David Shifrin and his colleagues from Chamber Music Northwest admirably capture the diverse moods of Bartók's triptych, including the mordant wit and vitality of the outer sections and the dark colouring of the centrepiece. They are very well recorded in an agreeable acoustic.

(i; ii) *Contrasts;* (ii) *2 Rhapsodies; Rumanian folk dances.* (Solo) *Violin sonata.*
*** Hyperion Dig. CDA 66415 [id.]. Krysia Osostowicz; with (i) Michael Collins; (ii) Susan Tomes.

Hyperion's coupling of the Bartók *Contrasts*, *Rhapsodies* and the *Sonata for solo violin* is a distinguished and well-recorded issue which finds all these artists on excellent form. Krysia Osostowicz is as good as any of her rivals in the *Sonata for solo violin*, and the remainder of the programme is hardly less impressive.

(i) *Contrasts. Violin sonatas Nos. 1–2.*
(BB) *** Naxos Dig. 8.550749 [id.]. György Pauk, Jenö Jandó; (i) with Kálmán Berkes.

The Naxos collection offering both the *Violin sonatas*, together with *Contrasts* for clarinet, violin and piano, making 75 minutes of music for less than £5 (or its equivalent) is very highly recommendable, particularly when they are played by such experienced artists as György Pauk and his fellow Hungarian, Jenö Jandó. The refinement and subtlety of Pauk's playing here, is very persuasive, the only very small qualification being the balance, which favours the piano too much in both sonatas. In the superb account of *Contrasts*, in which Kálmán Berkes joins them, the balance is better. Outstanding value.

(i) *44 Duos. Solo Violin sonata.*
(BB) *** Naxos Dig. 8.550868 [id.]. György Pauk, (i) with Kazuki Sawa.

György Pauk's impressive recording of the remarkable *Solo Sonata* of 1944, commissioned by Menuhin, is alone worth the price of this Naxos

CD. His account is commanding and everywhere his pacing seems just right and his playing effortless. In the *44 Duos* Pauk, partnered by the Japanese violinist, Kazuki Sawa, offer expertly judged and splendidly characterful accounts of these pieces: there is an impressive rapport and spontaneous give-and-take between the two musicians. The Naxos recording is very good indeed and enhances the attractions of this super-bargain issue.

Sonata for 2 pianos and percussion.

*** Sony Dig. MK 42625 [id.]. Perahia, Solti, Corkhill, Glennie – BRAHMS: *Variations on a theme by Haydn.* ***

*** Chandos Dig. CHAN 9398 [id.]. Safri Duo & Slovak Piano Duo – LUTOSLAWSKI: *Paganini variations* ***; HELWEG: *American fantasy.* **

On Sony an unexpected and highly creative partnership produces a vivid and strongly characterized performance. The recording is vivid to match, giving the players great presence.

The Slovak Piano Duo was formed in 1986 while they were still students, and the Safri Duo, two Danish percussion players, came together two years later. They are all dazzlingly alive and vital. All the same, their CD labours under a handicap: it is not good value at full price, lasting about 50 minutes.

Piano quintet.

(B) **(*) ASV Quicksilva Dig. CDQS 6217 [(M) id.]. Suzanne Bradbury, Silvestri String Qt – SCHUMANN: *Piano quintet.* **(*)

(i–ii) *Piano quintet*; (i; iii) *Andante* (for violin and piano); *Rhapsodies Nos. 1 & 2.*

(BB) *** Naxos Dig. 8.550886-2. (i) Jenö Jandó; (ii) Kodály Qt; (iii) György Pauk.

Readers who enjoyed the *Contrasts* and the two *Violin sonatas* from Naxos (see above) will need no prompting to invest in this companion disc. The *Piano quintet* dates from 1903–4. A substantial work in the received idiom, over 40 minutes in length, it is wholly uncharacteristic. The *Andante* for violin and piano comes from 1902 and is otherwise not recorded. It is slight but charming. The two *Rhapsodies* come from 1928. They were written respectively for Joseph Szigeti and Zoltán Székely and are popular in style. Very good playing from György Pauk and alert playing from Jandó, whose humming is at times faintly audible. No quarrels with either recording or performances.

On ASV Quicksilva, these artists make a good case for this eclectic and predominantly romantic score in which traces of Brahms, Dohnányi, Liszt and Strauss mingle with Debussy. In the early years of the century, Bartók himself used to programme his quintet with the Schumann, so that the coupling is particularly apposite. The performances and recording are both recommendable – though not perhaps in preference to the Naxos coupling.

String quartets Nos. 1–6.

(N) *** Decca Dig. 455 297-2 (2) [id.]. Takács Qt.

(N) (B) *** Erato/Warner Ultima Dig. 3984 25594-2 (2) [id.]. Keller Qt.

*** RCA Dig. 09026 68286-2 (3) [id.]. Tokyo Qt – JANACEK: *Quartets Nos. 1–2.* ***

*** DG Dig. 423 657-2 (2) [id.]. Emerson Qt.

(B) *** Teldec/Warner 0630 12334-2 (2) [id.]. Eder Qt.

(M) *** Audivis Astrée V 4809 (3) [id.]. Végh Qt.

**(*) EMI (SIS) Dig. CDS7 47720-8 (3) [Ang. CDCC 47720]. Alban Berg Qt.

(**(*)) ASV Dig. CDDCS 301 (3) [id.]. Lindsay Qt.

(B) **(*) Ph. (SIS) Duo 442 284-2 (2) [id.]. Novák Qt.

(N) (M) **(*) DG 457 740-2 (2) [id.]. Hungarian Qt.

It is difficult to go far wrong among the available recordings of the Bartók *quartets*. The latest set comes from Decca and the Takács Quartet who, since the untimely death of their founder, are half-Hungarian half-English. Their recordings have been enthusiastically received and were the choice of *Gramophone* magazine as 1998's best chamber music set. This was fully deserved, for they bring to these masterpieces the requisite virtuosity, tonal sophistication and command of idiom. These are full-blooded accounts of enormous conviction, with that open-air quality which suggests the fragrance of the forests and lakes of Hungary. The recording is excellent and this Decca set now takes its place at the top of the list.

The Keller Quartet are another Hungarian group who have attracted international attention. They made their recordings of the Bartók cycle in 1993-4, and enjoyed the imprimatur of no less an authority than Sándor Végh. Indeed these recordings were made in the Salle de musique de la Chaux-de-Fonds, where the Végh recorded their second cycle. The performances are totally idiomatic; intense yet natural, and at their new and highly competitive price are among the best you can find.

The Tokyo Quartet's RCA version of the Bartók cycle encompasses a third disc, but it includes the two Janácek *Quartets* as well. These are on the first disc along with the *First Quartet*. Nos. 2, 3 and 4 occupy the second, and 5 and 6 the third. The same beauty of tone and finesse that mark the earlier set are everywhere in evidence, and the playing has intensity and authority.

The Emerson Quartet's set comes on only two CDs. They project very powerfully and, in terms of virtuosity, finesse and accuracy, outstrip most of their rivals. If at times their projection and expressive vehemence are a bit too much of a good thing, these are concentrated and brilliant performances that are very well recorded.

Considerable competition comes from the Eder Quartet, a much-respected Hungarian ensemble whose complete digital set now returns to the catalogue on a pair of budget-priced CDs. Their playing has great intensity and is full of insights. There is a sense of onward movement without any feeling that the music is over-projected or held on a tight rein; on the contrary, one is hardly aware of the bar-line. With such rapt tone and concentration of atmosphere, this version is very competitive. The recording too approaches the demonstration bracket.

The analogue Végh recordings date from 1972, but the CD transfers are splendidly managed: there is a fine sense of presence, but also the ambient fullness one associates with the best analogue recordings, and there is bite without edginess on top. The Végh players sometimes respond with more expressive warmth than some would expect to be applied to Bartók; but others will find this the very quality in their music-making which prevents the music from becoming too aggressive. On the whole they give very perceptive performances and, above all, they produce an effect of seeming spontaneity.

The Alban Berg Quartet's are very impressive performances indeed, technically almost in a class of their own. They are very well recorded too, but at times they appear to treat this music as a vehicle for their own supreme virtuosity.

The Lindsay performances, searching, powerful and expressive, are now reissued together. The digital recording, though first class, occupies three discs which, like the Alban Berg set, places it at a distinct disadvantage to the DG Emerson version.

The Novák Quartet, a fine Czech group, bring plenty of grip to their performances and there is certainly no lack of fire and expressive intensity. If not as polished as the Tokyo versions, they have the advantage of being complete on a pair of Duo CDs, which Philips offer for the cost of one premium-price disc. So there is no question of their bargain status, as the recording is firm and well balanced.

The DG set by the Hungarian Quartet has considerable authority: the Hungarians were the first to record Nos. 5 and 6, and their leader gave the première of the *Violin concerto*. But they do not quite convey the full intensity that distinguishes the best rival versions and this seems a curious choice for DG's Legendary 'Originals'. The recording is excellent for its age (1962).

String quartets Nos. 1, Op. 7; 5.
*** Collins Dig. 1279-2 [id.]. Talich Qt.

String quartets Nos. 2; 6.
*** Collins Dig. 1188-2 [id.]. Talich Qt.

No need for reservations about the Talich Quartet, who are completely inside this music, and the Talich pianissimo tone has a rapt quality that seems just right. These are finely argued, marvellously played and splendidly and truthfully recorded versions that can be recommended without any serious qualification.

Violin sonata No. 1.
*** DG (IMS) Dig. 427 351-2 [id.]. Gidon Kremer, Martha Argerich – JANACEK: *Sonata* **(*); MESSIAEN: *Theme and variations.* ***

The *First Violin sonata* is played with great expressive intensity, enormous range of colour and effortless virtuosity by Gidon Kremer and Martha Argerich; but the ASV alternative is more sensibly coupled.

Violin sonata No. 1; Sonatina (trans. André Gertler); *Rhapsody No. 2 for violin and piano; Hungarian folksongs* (trans. Tivadar Országh); *Hungarian folk-tunes* (trans. Jozsef Szigeti).
*** ASV Dig. CDDCA 883 [id.]. Susanne Stanzeleit, Gusztáv Fenyö.

Susanne Stanzeleit and her partner, Gusztáv Fenyö, are completely inside the idiom – as you might expect, since the latter is related to Jelly d'Arányi, for whom Bartók composed the sonatas. The *Violin sonata No. 1* and the *Rhapsody No. 2* are every bit as well played and recorded as on the companion disc (see below), and this makes a worthy successor. Strongly recommended.

(Solo) *Violin sonata; Violin sonata No. 2; Rhapsody No. 1; Rumanian folk dances.*
*** ASV Dig. CDDCA 852 [id.]. Susanne Stanzeleit, Gusztáv Fenyö.

The young German-born violinist Susanne Stanzeleit plays the *Solo sonata* and the *Second Sonata* for violin and piano (1922) with uncommon authority. This is totally committed playing – and the performances are as good as any you can find in the current catalogue. The recording, too, is altogether first rate.

PIANO MUSIC

Allegro barbaro; 6 Dances in Bulgarian rhythm; 3 Hungarian folksongs; 15 Hungarian peasant songs; Mikrokosmos: Vol. 2/37, 40 & 50; Vol. 3/ 73, 82 & 87; Vol. 4/100, 113, 115–16 & 120; Vol. 5/122, 126, 128–31, 133, 135 & 138; Vol. 6/ 140, 144, 146–7; 3 Rondos on Slovak folk tunes; Sonatina.
(BB) **(*) Naxos Dig. 8.550451-2. Balázs Szokolay.

Balázs Szokolay is a highly musical player. His performances are always vitally intelligent and perceptive, and he is acceptably recorded. This is a thoroughly recommendable recital and excellent value, though Szokolay is by no means as well recorded as Kocsis on Philips, nor does he quite have the latter's subtlety or distinction.

Allegro barbaro; 4 Dirges, Op. 9a; First term at the piano; 3 Hungarian folksongs from Csík; Romanian Christmas carols; 2 Romanian dances, Op. 8a; 3 Rondos on folk tunes; 3 Studies, Op. 18; Suite, Op. 14.
*** Ph. (IMS) Dig. 442 016-2 [id.]. Zoltán Kocsis.

14 Bagatelles, Op. 6; 2 Elegies, Op. 8b; 3 Hungarian folk tunes; 6 Rumanian folk tunes; Sonatina.
❀ *** Ph. (IMS) Dig. 434 104-2 [id.]. Zoltán Kocsis.

For Children, Books 1–4.
*** Ph. (IMS) Dig. 442 146-2 [id.]. Zoltán Kocsis.

Earlier records of Bartók's piano music by Andor Foldes in the 1950s and by György Sándor have carried the authenticity of close association with the composer, but this Philips survey has the advantage not only of state-of-the-art recording quality but of playing that is far more subtle and imaginative than Foldes'. Kocsis penetrates to the very centre or soul of this music more deeply than almost any other rival. He is scrupulously attentive to Bartók's own wishes as shown not only in autographs and revised editions of the published scores but as expressed on record. Kocsis can produce power and drama when required, but he also commands a wide-ranging palette and a marvellously controlled vitality. The sound is never beautified but is also never aggressive; indeed his playing calls to mind Bartók's own injunction that performances must be 'beautiful but true'. This is likely to be the classic set for a long time to come, and the recorded sound is altogether natural and realistic.

For Children (Books 1–4) complete; *Mikrokosmos (Books 1–6)* complete.
(M) *** Teldec/Warner 9031 76139-2 (3). Dezsö Ránki.

Dezsö Ránki here shows his musicianship and plays all 85 pieces with the utmost persuasion and with the art that conceals art, for the simplicity of some of these pieces is deceptive; darker currents lurk beneath their surface. He gives us the composer's original edition of 1908–9. Ránki also plays the *Mikrokosmos* with an effortless eloquence and a welcome straightforwardness. He is very clearly if forwardly recorded, and he is given a realistic presence.

Mikrokosmos (complete).
(N) **(*) Ph. Dig. 462 381-2 (2) [id.]. Zoltán Kocsis; (with Karoly Mocsári in Nos. 43, 44, 55, 68, 74 & 95; Martá Lukin in Nos. 65, 74, 95, 127).
(B) **(*) HM Musique d'abord HMA 190968/9 [id.]. Claude Helffer (with Haakon Austbö).

Bartók originally intended the piano pieces he began composing in 1926 as a pedagogic exercise with his young son, Péter, in mind and that is exactly the way Kocsis plays the first third of the 153 pieces. Indeed, his stoic approach is hardly inviting and makes the listener feel that to record the complete set may be taking comprehensiveness a bit too far. Most music-lovers will undoubtedly concentrate on the second half of the work, where the playing really begins to grip the ear, with greater colour and more flexibility of line to bring these brief pieces fully to life. Martá Luki seems an admirable choice for the four vocal settings, and Karoly Mocsári takes the second part in the pieces for piano duo. The recording is excellent.

Claude Helffer also gives an intelligent account of all six books, but his approach at times goes to the other extreme, as he tends to invest detail with rather more expressive emphasis than this most simple of music can bear. He too is naturally recorded. However, unlike the excellently documented and comprehensively banded Philips set, Harmonia Mundi's cueing is ungenerous (there are only twelve bands to cover the whole series!). If you don't mind that, this is good value in the bargain range.

VOCAL MUSIC

Cantata profana.
(N) *** Decca Dig. 458 929-2 [id.]. Daróczy, Agache, Hungarian Radio and TV Ch. and Children's Ch., Schola Cantorum Budapestiensis, Budapest Festival O, Sir Georg Solti – KODALY: *Psalmus hungaricus*; WEINER: *Serenade.****

Solti's very last recording sessions in Budapest, June 1997, resulted in inspired performances, designed as a tribute to his three teachers at the Liszt Academy – not just Bartók and Kodály, but Leo Weiner. This reading of the *Cantata profana* is both warm and idiomatic, marred only by the unsteadiness of the tenor soloist. Solti came finally to regard the cantata as symbolic of his own life, with the allegory of the stag returning home reflecting his own return to Hungary after almost sixty years of exile.

OPERA

Bluebeard's Castle (sung in Hungarian).
*** EMI Dig. CDC5 65162-2 [id.]. Tomlinson, Von Otter, Sandor Elès (nar.), BPO, Haitink.
(N) *** DG Dig. 447 040-2 [id.]. Jessye Norman, László Polgár, Chicago SO, Pierre Boulez.
*** Sony Dig. MK 44523 [id.]. Marton, Ramey, Hungarian State O, Adám Fischer.

(M) *** Decca Legends 466 377-2 [id.]. Berry, Ludwig, LSO, Kertész.
(M) *** Sony SMK 64110 [id.]. Nimsgern, Troyanos, BBC SO, Boulez.

Never before has Bartók's darkly intense one-acter been given such a beautiful performance on disc, intense and concentrated, as by Bernard Haitink in EMI's live recording of a concert performance with the Berlin Philharmonic. Rival versions by such Hungarian-born conductors as Kertész and Dorati may bite more sharply, but, guided by Haitink, Anne-Sofie von Otter conveys new tenderness in Judith, with John Tomlinson magisterially Wagnerian as the implacable Bluebeard, both singing superbly, naturally balanced, not spotlit. Most impressive of all, Haitink builds the performance to a terrifying climax, when Judith is consigned to darkness with her predecessors.

Boulez, in his tautly intense DG version, opts for marginally faster speeds than he did in his earlier Sony recording, with voices close to add to the involvement. László Polgár is superb as Bluebeard – firm, dark and incisive as well as idiomatic. Jessye Norman is a magisterial Judith, never girlish or vulnerable but nobly commanding. She may not be a believable victim, but this is still a glorious performance, matching the beauty of the Chicago orchestra's playing, weighty and rich on detail.

The glory of the Fischer version is the magnificent singing of Samuel Ramey in the title-role. Eva Marton, also Hungarian-born, may lack the vulnerability as well as the darker tone-colours of the ideal Judith but, with more than a touch of abrasiveness in the voice, she still gives a powerful reading. The recording brings full and brilliant sound, well balanced and clear. The single CD comes with libretto in a separate box.

In 1965 Kertész set new standards in his version of *Bluebeard's Castle* with Christa Ludwig and Walter Berry, not only in the playing of the LSO at its peak, in the firm sensitivity of the soloists and the brilliance of the recording, but also in the natural Hungarian inflexions inspired by the conductor. There is still a strong case for preferring the reading conducted by a Hungarian – especially as the Decca sound reaches demonstration standard in its remastering for Decca's Legends series – but on performance Haitink's later, EMI CD has the balance of advantage.

Boulez reveals himself as an impressively warm Bartókian, the soloists are vibrantly committed and the recording is outstandingly vivid, presenting the singers in a slightly contrasted acoustic as though on a separate stage. Boulez has rarely if ever made a finer Bartók record. A full libretto is provided.

Bax, Arnold (1883–1953)

(i) *The Bard of the Dimbovitza;* (ii) *Concertante for piano (left hand) and orchestra. In memoriam.*
(N) *** Chandos Dig. CHAN 9715 [id.]. BBC PO, Handley with (i) Jean Rigby; (ii) Margaret Fingerhut.

Chandos enrich the lists with three Bax works new to the catalogue. *In memoriam* – from 1916, the period of *The Garden of Fand* – was not performed in Bax's lifetime and was long thought not to have been scored. It is vintage Bax and its main theme was reused in his score for David Lean's *Oliver Twist*. The *Concertante for piano left hand* comes from 1949, and was written for Harriet Cohen who had injured her right hand the previous year, but after its première under Barbirolli and a Prom performance some weeks later, it languished unheard. It is a far finer piece than it was given credit for at the time. Margaret Fingerhut is a most persuasive advocate and that no doubt helps the positive impression it makes here. *The Bard of the Dimbovitza*, settings of Romanian peasant songs, comes from 1914 though Bax overhauled it in 1922. The poetry bears much the same relationship with Romania as Fitzgerald's 'Omar Khayyam' does with Persian verse, and its translator, Carmen Sylva, was in fact Queen Elisabeth of Romania. Exemplary performances from the BBC Philharmonic under Vernon Handley and state-of-the-art recording.

(i) *Christmas eve; Dance of Wild Irravel; Festival overture; Nympholept; Paean;* (ii) *Tintagel.*
**(*) Chandos Dig. CHAN 9168 [id.]. (i) LPO; (ii) Ulster O, Bryden Thomson.

These shorter works were originally used as fillers for the separate issues of the symphonies, and it might have been more generous of Chandos to reissue them at mid-price. Apart from *Tintagel*, *Nympholept* is probably the most interesting piece. The *Paean* and the *Dance of Wild Irravel* may strain the allegiance of some. Performances and recordings give absolutely no cause for complaint.

(i) *Cello concerto; Cortège; Mediterranean; Northern Ballad No. 3; Overture to a picaresque comedy.*
*** Chandos Dig. CHAN 8494 [id.]. (i) Wallfisch; LPO, Bryden Thomson.

The *Cello concerto* is rhapsodic in feeling and Raphael Wallfisch plays it with marvellous sensitivity and finesse, given splendid support by the LPO under Bryden Thomson. The other pieces are of mixed quality: in the *Overture to a picaresque comedy* Bryden Thomson sets rather too measured a pace for it to sparkle as it should. The recording maintains the high standards of the Bax Chandos series.

(i) *Violin concerto. Golden Eagle* (incidental music): *suite; A Legend; Romantic overture.*
*** Chandos Dig. CHAN 9003 [id.]. (i) Lydia Mordkovitch; LPO, Bryden Thomson.

The *Violin concerto* is full of good, easily remembered tunes, yet there is a plangent, bitter-sweet quality about many of its ideas and an easygoing Mediterranean-like warmth that is very appealing. Lydia Mordkovitch plays it with commitment and conviction. The *Romantic overture* is for chamber orchestra and has a prominent role for the piano. All this music is new to the catalogue and the concerto deserves to be popular.

The Garden of Fand; The happy forest; November woods; Summer music.
*** Chandos Dig. CHAN 8307 [id.]. Ulster O, Bryden Thomson.

The Celtic twilight in Bax's music is ripely and sympathetically caught in the first three items, while *Summer music*, dedicated to Sir Thomas Beecham and here given its first ever recording, brings an intriguing kinship with the music of Delius. The Chandos recording is superb.

The Garden of Fand (symphonic poem); *Mediterranean; Northern ballad No. 1; November Woods; Tintagel* (symphonic poems).
*** Lyrita SRCD 231 [id.]. LPO, Boult.

Sir Adrian Boult's recording of *The Garden of Fand* is full of poetry and almost erases memories of Beecham's magical account. *Tintagel* is no less involving and beguiling and, though not as uninhibited as Barbirolli's, is equally valid. The *Northern ballad No. 1*, though less memorable than either *Fand* or *Tintagel*, is well worth having, as is *November Woods*, a lush, romantic score. *Mediterranean*, a Spanish picture postcard and almost a waltz, has an endearing touch of vulgarity uncharacteristic of its composer. Excellent sound.

In the faery hills; Into the twilight; Rosc-Catha; The tale the pine-trees knew.
*** Chandos Dig. CHAN 8367 [id.]. Ulster O, Bryden Thomson.

The tale the pine-trees knew is here done with total sympathy. The other three tone-poems form an Irish trilogy. The performances and recording are well up to the high standard of this series.

Malta G.C. (complete); *Oliver Twist: suite* (film-scores).
(M) *** ASV Dig. CDWHL 2058. RPO, Kenneth Alwyn – ARNOLD: *The Sound Barrier.* ***

Both these film-scores are in the form of a series of miniatures; on the whole, *Oliver Twist* stands up more effectively without the visual imagery. Kenneth Alwyn conducts the RPO with fine flair and commitment.

On the sea-shore.
*** Chandos Dig. CHAN 8473 [id.]. Ulster O, Handley – BRIDGE: *The Sea* (with BRITTEN: *Sea interludes.* ***)

Bax's Prelude, *On the sea-shore*, makes a colourful and atmospheric companion to the masterly Bridge and Britten pieces on the disc, played and recorded with similar warmth and brilliance.

Overture to an Adventure; Symphony No. 6; Tintagel.
(N) (*) Classico Dig. CLASSCD 254 [id.]. Munich SO, Douglas Bostock.

Douglas Bostock, who studied with Bryden Thomson and Sir Adrian Boult, is doing good work in championing Bax's music in Munich. However his recording of all three pieces is simply not well enough played to be competitive or recommendable.

Spring fire; Northern ballad No. 2; Symphonic scherzo.
*** Chandos Dig. CHAN 8464 [id.]. RPO, Vernon Handley.

Highly idiomatic playing from Vernon Handley and the RPO, and a thoroughly lifelike and characteristically well-detailed recording from Chandos.

Symphonic variations for piano and orchestra; Morning Song (Maytime in Sussex).
*** Chandos Dig. CHAN 8516 [id.]. Margaret Fingerhut, LPO, Bryden Thomson.

Margaret Fingerhut reveals the *Symphonic variations* as a work of considerable substance with some sinewy, powerful writing in the more combative variations, thoughtful and purposeful elsewhere. This CD is in the demonstration class.

Symphonies 1–7.
(M) *** Chandos Dig. CHAN 8906/10 [id.]. LPO or Ulster O, Bryden Thomson.

Chandos have repackaged the cycle of seven symphonies and it makes better sense for those primarily interested in these richly imaginative symphonies to pay for five rather than seven CDs. The recordings continue to make a strong impression. For those who prefer to have the symphonies separately and with their original couplings, we list below full details.

Symphony No. 1 in E flat; Christmas Eve.
*** Chandos Dig. CHAN 8480 [id.]. LPO, Bryden Thomson.

Symphonies Nos. 1 in E flat; 7 in A flat.
*** Lyrita SRCD 232 [id.]. LPO, (i) Fredman; (ii) Leppard.

Symphony No. 2; Nympholept.
*** Chandos Dig. CHAN 8493 [id.]. LPO, Bryden Thomson.

Symphony No. 3; Paean; The Dance of Wild Irravel.
*** Chandos Dig. CHAN 8454 [id.]. LPO, Bryden Thomson.

Symphony No. 4; Tintagel.
*** Chandos Dig. CHAN 8312 [id.]. Ulster O, Bryden Thomson.

Symphony No. 5; Russian suite.
*** Chandos Dig. CHAN 8669 [id.]. LPO, Bryden Thomson.

Symphony No. 6; Festival overture.
*** Chandos Dig. CHAN 8586 [id.]. LPO, Bryden Thomson.

Symphony No. 7 in A flat; (i) *4 Songs: Eternity; Glamour; Lyke-wake; Slumber song.*
*** Chandos Dig. CHAN 8628 [id.]. (i) Martyn Hill; LPO, Bryden Thomson.

Bax's symphonies remain controversial and some listeners find their quality of invention and argument less intensely sustained than the composer's shorter orchestral tone-poems. Nevertheless they have a breadth of imagination which the smaller structures do not always carry. The Lyrita coupling is particularly generous (78 minutes) and the performances by Myer Fredman and Raymond Leppard respectively are powerful and finely shaped and can well hold their own with the later, Chandos digital versions. The Lyrita 1970s analogue sound, too, is vivid and clear.

The Chandos couplings have their own interest. *Christmas Eve* is an early work, coming from the Edwardian era, and it displays a less developed idiom than the symphonies. The four songs offer great contrasts of manner and style, and Martyn Hill presents them very sensitively.

Symphony No. 1; The Garden of Fand; In the faery hills.
(BB) *** Naxos Dig. 8.553525 [id.]. RSNO, David Lloyd-Jones.

This first disc in what Naxos plan to be a Bax series offers warmly idiomatic readings of two early symphonic poems as well as the *First Symphony*, dating from 1921. The refined originality of the orchestration is brought out in recording less weighty than in rival versions, such as that on Chandos at full price, but finely detailed. In the two symphonic poems, more specifically inspired by Irish themes, Lloyd-Jones draws equally warm and sympathetic performances from the Scottish orchestra, bringing inner clarity to the heaviest scoring. First-rate sound, though Bryden Thomson on Chandos has even richer recording.

The Truth about the Russian dancers (incidental music); *From dusk till dawn* (ballet).
*** Chandos Dig. CHAN 8863 [id.]. LPO, Bryden Thomson.

The Truth about the Russian dancers is vintage Bax, full of characteristic writing decked out in attractive orchestral colours. *From dusk till dawn* has many evocative ideas with some impressionistic orchestral touches. Not top-drawer Bax but often delightful, and very well played by the London Philharmonic under Bryden Thomson, and splendidly recorded.

Winter Legends; Saga fragment.
*** Chandos Dig. CHAN 8484 [id.]. Margaret Fingerhut, LPO, Bryden Thomson.

The *Winter Legends*, for piano and orchestra, comes from much the same time as the *Third Symphony*, to which at times its world seems spiritually related. The soloist proves an impressive and totally convincing advocate for the score and it would be difficult to imagine the balance between soloist and orchestra being more realistically judged. The companion piece is a transcription of his one-movement *Piano quartet* of 1922. A quite outstanding disc.

CHAMBER AND INSTRUMENTAL MUSIC

Concerto for flute, oboe, harp and string quartet; In memoriam, for cor anglais, harp and string quartet; Threnody and Scherzo for bassoon, harp and string sextet; (i) *Octet for horn, piano and string sextet*; *String quintet.*
(N) *** Chandos Dig. CHAN 9602 [id.]. (i) Margaret Fingerhut; ASMF Ch. Ens.

More Bax rarities. All are new to the catalogue though the *Concerto for flute, oboe, harp and string quartet* of 1936 may be more familiar to some in its 1928 form as a sonata for flute and harp. *In memoriam* is the earliest piece here (it comes from 1917 and originally bore the subtitle, 'An Irish Elegy' – an obvious allusion to the Easter uprising). The *Octet*, inspired by Aubrey Brain (the father of Dennis) and the pianist Harriet Cohen, is arguably the most appealing work in the collection. However the companion pieces, particularly the *Concerto* or *Septet*, are hardly less beguiling. Indeed most of this music is captivating; the performances are absolutley first class, and the recording in the best traditions of the house.

Cello sonata in E flat; Cello sonatina in D; Legend sonata in F sharp min.; Folk tale.
** ASV Dig. CDDCA 896 [id.]. Bernard Gregor-Smith, Yolande Wrigley.

The *Cello sonata* is a big piece, lasting over half an hour; it has many characteristic touches and an imaginative slow movement. Bernard Gregor-Smith and Yolande Wrigley are both highly sensitive and responsive players who command a wide dynamic range and variety of colour. In the *Sonata* the recording does not give quite enough back-to-front depth and there is a touch of glassiness about the sound. Things are a bit better in the *Folk*

Tale (1920), but the recording is sufficiently wanting in bloom to inhibit a three-star recommendation.

Clarinet sonata.
*** Chandos CHAN 8683 [id.]. Janet Hilton, Keith Swallow – BLISS: *Clarinet quintet;* VAUGHAN WILLIAMS: *6 Studies.* ***

Bax's *Clarinet sonata* opens most beguilingly, and Janet Hilton's phrasing is quite melting. Moreover the Bliss coupling is indispensable.

(i) *Clarinet sonata;* (ii) *Elegiac trio* (for flute, viola & harp); (iii) *Harp quintet;* (iv) *Nonet;* (v) *Oboe quintet.*
*** Hyperion Dig. CDA 66807 [id.]. (i; iv) Michael Collins; (i) Ian Brown (piano); (ii; iv) Philippa Davies; (ii–v) Roger Chase; (ii–iv) Skaila Kanga; (iii–v) Marcia Crayford, Christopher van Kampen; (iii; v) Iris Juda; (iv) Elizabeth Wexler, Duncan McTier, Ian Brown (cond.); (iv–v) Gareth Hulse.

These are performances of exemplary quality, ranging from the *Elegiac trio* of 1916 through to the *Clarinet sonata* of 1934. In the chamber-music field Bax wrote with a fantasy and sensibility that are no less captivating than in *The Garden of Fand* or *Tintagel*. This music is characterized by seductive and alluring sonorities and a haunting atmosphere which lends it strong appeal. The members of the Nash Ensemble, including Michael Collins in the *Clarinet sonata* and Gareth Hulse in the *Oboe quintet*, seem totally attuned to the idiom, and they play with their usual artistry and dedication. Excellent recording.

(i) *Harp quintet;* (ii) *Piano quartet; String quartet No. 1.*
*** Chandos Dig. CHAN 8391 [id.]. (i) Skaila Kanga, (ii) John McCabe; English Qt.

The *First String quartet* is music with a strong and immediate appeal. The *Harp quintet* is more fully characteristic and has some evocative writing to commend it, alongside the *Piano quartet*, with its winning lyricism. These may not be Bax's most important scores, but they are rewarding; and the performances are thoroughly idiomatic and eminently well recorded.

Oboe quintet.
*** Chandos Dig. CHAN 8392 [id.]. Sarah Francis, English Qt – HOLST: *Air & variations*, etc.; MOERAN: *Fantasy quartet;* JACOB: *Quartet.* ***

Bax's *Oboe quintet* is a confident, inventive piece. Sarah Francis proves a most responsive soloist – though she is balanced too close; in all other respects the recording is up to Chandos's usual high standards, and the playing of the English Quartet is admirable.

(i) *Piano quintet in G min.; String quartet No. 2.*
**(*) Chandos Dig. CHAN 8795 [id.]. Mistry Qt; (i) with David Owen Norris.

The *Piano quintet* is symphonic in scale. The playing of the Mistry Quartet is dedicated and David Owen Norris is the excellent and sensitive pianist. The *Second Quartet* is tauter and more powerful. The performance has plenty of feeling and the recording is excellent.

Rhapsodic Ballad (for solo cello).
*** Chandos Dig. CHAN 8499 [id.]. Raphael Wallfisch – BRIDGE: *Cello sonata;* DELIUS: *Cello sonata;* WALTON: *Passacaglia.* ***

The *Rhapsodic Ballad* for cello alone is a freely expressive piece, played with authority and dedication by Raphael Wallfisch. The recording has plenty of warmth and range.

Viola sonata in G.
(N) (***) Biddulph mono LAB 148 [id.]. William Primrose, Harriet Cohen – BLOCH: *Suite;* HINDEMITH: *Sonata.* (***)

The legendary William Primrose made this recording of the Bax *Viola sonata* with Harriet Cohen for the second volume of the English Music Society on 78s in the late 1930s. This was the first published recording of a fine piece (it also included the *Nonet* and *Mater ora filium*) and it serves as a reminder of his sumptuous tone and glorious musicianship.

Violin sonatas Nos. 1 in E; 2 in D.
*** Chandos Dig. CHAN 8845 [id.]. Erich Gruenberg, John McCabe.

The *Second* is the finer of the two sonatas and is thematically linked with *November woods*. Rhapsodic and impassioned, this is music full of temperament. Erich Gruenberg is a selfless and musicianly advocate and John McCabe makes an expert partner.

PIANO MUSIC

Apple-blossom time; Burlesque; The maiden with the daffodil; Nereid; O dame get up and bake your pies (Variations on a north country Christmas carol); On a May evening; The princess's rose-garden (Nocturne); Romance; 2 Russian tone pictures: Nocturne (May night in the Ukraine; Gopak); Sleepy-head.
**(*) Chandos Dig. CHAN 8732 [id.]. Eric Parkin.

The smaller pieces are not among Bax's most important works, but in Eric Parkin's hands they certainly sound pleasingly spontaneous.

Piano sonatas Nos. 1 in E flat; 2 in G; Legend.
*** Continuum Dig. CCD 1045 [id.]. John McCabe.

Both Bax's *Piano sonatas* are convincing in John McCabe's hands – in fact, more convincing than the *Legend*, written for an Australian pianist, John Simons, in the mid-1930s but not performed by its dedicatee until 1969. A thoroughly enterprising issue, excellently recorded.

Piano sonatas Nos. 1 & 2; Country Tune; Lullaby (Berceuse); Winter waters.
**(*) Chandos Dig. CHAN 8496 [id.]. Eric Parkin (piano).

Piano sonatas Nos. 3 in G sharp min.; 4 in G; A Hill tune; In a vodka shop; Water music.
**(*) Chandos Dig. CHAN 8497 [id.]. Eric Parkin.

These *Sonatas* are grievously neglected in the concert hall. Eric Parkin proves a sympathetic guide in this repertoire. The recording is on the resonant side, but the playing is outstandingly responsive.

VOCAL MUSIC

I sing of a maiden; Mater ora filium; This world's joie.
(M) *** EMI Dig. CDM5 65595-2. King's College, Cambridge, Ch., Cleobury – FINZI: *Choral music;* VAUGHAN WILLIAMS: *Mass.* ***

Bax's ambitious setting of a medieval carol, *Mater ora filium*, is one of the most difficult *a cappella* pieces in the choral repertory. Here under Stephen Cleobury the King's College choir gives it a virtuoso performance, with trebles performing wonders in the taxingly high passages. It is particularly apt too, when the original inspiration for the piece came from Bax's hearing Byrd's *Mass in five voices*. The other two Bax pieces, also setting medieval texts, are also done most beautifully, with the unaccompanied voices vividly recorded against the spacious acoustic of King's Chapel. Besides the original Finzi coupling, the reissue includes a splendid analogue performance of Vaughan Williams's beautiful *Mass in G minor*.

Beach, Amy (1867–1944)

Symphony in E min. (Gaelic).
*** Chandos Dig. CHAN 8958 [id.]. Detroit SO, Järvi (with BARBER: *Symphony No. 1* etc. ***).

Amy Beach is a rather more remarkable figure than she is given credit for. She was largely self-taught. Her *Symphony in E minor* operates at a high level of accomplishment and has a winning charm, particularly its delightful and inventive second movement. Once heard, this haunting movement is difficult to exorcize from one's memory. A very persuasive performance by the Detroit orchestra under Neeme Järvi, and good recorded sound.

Piano quintet in F sharp, Op. 67.
*** ASV Dig. CDDCA 932-2 [id.]. Martin Roscoe, Endellion Qt – CLARKE: *Piano trio; Viola sonata.* ***

The Boston composer, Amy Beach, composed this *Piano quintet* in 1908 during the period when, as the dutiful wife of a businessman, she gave up her career as a pianist, and composed instead. She uses a post-Brahmsian idiom in an individual and lyrical way, with the slow movement centred on a ravishing main theme, almost Elgarian. With Roscoe's characterful playing well matched by the masterly Endellion Quartet, the performance is magnetic and very well recorded.

PIANO MUSIC

By the still waters; Far awa'; Gavotte fantastique; A Humming bird; Trois morceaux caractéristiques, Op. 28; Out of the depths; Scherzino: A Peterboro chipmunk; Scottish legend; Variations on Balkan themes, Op. 60; Young birches.
(N) *** Arabesque Dig. Z 6693 [id.]. Joanne Polk.

Ballad, Op. 6; A Cradle song of the lonely mother; The Fair hills of Eire, O!; A Hermit thrush at eve; A Hermit thrush at morn; Prelude and fugue, Op. 81; Les rêves de Columbine: suite française, Op. 65; Valse-caprice, Op. 4.
(N) *** Arabesque Dig. Z 6704 [id.]. Joanne Polk.

Eskimos, four characteristic pieces, Op. 64; Fantasia fugata, Op. 87; From Grandmother's garden, Op. 97; Five improvisations, Op. 148; Nocturne, Op. 107; Four sketches, Op. 15; Tyrolean valse-fantaisie, Op. 116. Transcription: R. STRAUSS: *Serenade.*
(N) *** Arabesque Dig. Z 6721 [id.]. Joanne Polk.

Arabesque are now exploring Amy Beach's piano music in depth and confirming the consistency of its quality. The *Variations on Balkan themes* readily demonstrates her ability to sustain a major work: the many quixotic transformations of the theme, *Adagio malincolico* are appealingly inventive. The imaginative pictorial evocations from nature, the *Hermit thrush*, the *Humming bird* and the *Scherzino Chipmunk* are capped by the beautiful evocation of *Young birches*, while the nocturnal *Cradle song of the lonely mother* is quite haunting. Her ability to assimilate different styles in a single work is never better displayed than in the attractive *Four Sketches*, Op. 15, where at times Schumann, Beethoven, Mendelssohn and Liszt all look over her shoulder. The *Five Improvisations* show her at her most thoughfully ruminative, while the disarming simplicity of characterization in *Eskimos* and *From Grandmother's garden* is quite delightful, with the melodies of *Exiles* from the one, and *Heartease* from the other, delicately memorable. Joanne Polk is an understanding and persuasive advocate, capturing the music's special combination of sophistication and innocence with fine spontaneity. She is most truthfully recorded.

Ballad in D flat, Op. 6; Hermit thrush at eve; at morn, Op. 91/1–2; Nocturne, Op. 107; Prelude and fugue, Op. 81; 4 Sketches, Op. 15; (i) *Suite for 2 pianos on Irish melodies, Op. 104.*
*** Koch Dig. 3-7254-2 [id.]. Virginia Erskin, (i) with Kathleen Supove.

Amy Beach continues to surprise as we discover more of her music. Her piano writing has a number of eclectic influences, but they are all well absorbed. Her invention is always pleasing, and sometimes an apparently trivial piece becomes more than that – witness the *Valse caprice*. The *Four Sketches* (*In Autumn*; *Phantoms*; *Dreaming*; *Fireflies*) are charmingly evocative, as are the two pictures of the *Hermit thrush*, yet her imposing *Prelude and fugue* is impressively worked out. Virginia Erskin is thoroughly sympathetic, never undervaluing a piece, and Kathleen Supove makes a fine partner in the demanding but by no means predictable *Suite for two pianos on Irish melodies*.

Beck, Franz Ignaz (1734–1809)

Sinfonias: in B flat; D; G; in D, Op. 10/2; in E, Op. 13/1.
(N) (BB) *** Naxos 8.553790 [id.]. Northern CO, Nicholas Ward.

Franz Ignaz Beck, born in Mannheim, was a much-travelled composer, absorbing influences where he may. Leaving his hometown after a dual, he eloped in Italy with the daughter of his patron, Galuppi! His three-movement *Sinfonias* are concise and sharply characterized, even if they are little more than Italian overtures. The *D major Sinfonia* is the exception with a Haydnesque pattern of four movements. His writing is usually more resourceful, less predictable than many of his minor contemporaries. Ideas are fresh, scoring simple but felicitous. The graceful *Largo* of the *B flat major* work, with its string cantilena floating over a pizzicato bass, is worthy of Boccherini, and the *E major*, Op.13/1 is a winning little work with a diverting finale. The performances here could hardly be more persuasive, warmly elegant, full of vitality. The recording, too, is first class.

Beethoven, Ludwig van (1770–1827)

The Complete Beethoven edition

DG Complete Beethoven Edition
(B) **(*) DG Analogue/Dig. 453 700-2 (87) [id.] (with MOZART: *Piano concerto No. 20*).

DG's Complete Beethoven Edition, issued as a 20-volume, 87-CD set to celebrate the company's centenary, is packaged in a substantial, suitcase-like cardboard box with illustrated book. The performances are generally good, though not invariably. Most collectors would do better to concentrate on individual volumes, all available separately in the mid-price range.

Volume 1: *Symphonies: Nos. 1–9.*
(M) *** DG 453 701-2 (5) [id.]. BPO, Karajan (with Janowitz, Rössel-Majdan, Kmentt, Berry, V. Singverein in *No. 9*).

Karajan's second Beethoven symphony cycle, recorded in 1961 and 1962, and is generally the most successful of his four. His refinement is shown in every movement of the *First Symphony* yet this is very far from being Mozartian and small-scale, and he takes a similar approach in the *Second Symphony*. In the *Eroica* the refinement of detail never undermines the dramatic urgency of the whole performance, lacking a little in weight only in the *Funeral march*. He gives a splendid interpretation of *No. 4*, with the dynamic contrasts heavily underlined. The *Fifth Symphony* is strong and extrovert at fast speeds in the Toscanini tradition. The *Pastoral* is the one real failure of the set, hard-driven and unyielding. The *Seventh Symphony*, again hard-driven, yet tingles with excitement, and it is the same in the *Eighth Symphony*. The *Ninth Symphony* is strong and refined with an urgency that carries the argument through from first to last. The soloists are excellent, and the Vienna Singverein, taken specially to Berlin, sing with great passion, though the balance could be better. Only the slow movement lacks spiritual intensity, though the beauty of sound, particularly in the hushed playing, is magical. This set is also available in a separate bargain-price box – see below (DG 429 036-2).

Volume 2: *Complete concertos: Piano concertos Nos.* (i; ii) *1–2;* (i; iii) *3–5;* (iv) *in E flat, WoO 4;* (v) *in D, Op. 61* (arr. composer); *Violin concertos:* (vi) *in D, Op. 61;* (vii) *in C, WoO 5;* (viii) *Triple concerto in C, Op. 56;* (ix) *Romances Nos. 1–2;* (x) *Romance cantabile for piano, flute and bassoon in E min., H. 13;* (xi) *Rondo for piano and orchestra in B flat, WoO 6.*
(M) ** DG Analogue/Dig. 453 707-2 (5) [id.]. (i) Pollini, VPO; (ii) Jochum; (iii) Boehm; (iv) Ander, Berlin CO, Gülke; (v) ECO, Barenboim (piano and cond.); (vi; viii) Mutter, BPO, Karajan; (vii) Kremer, LSO, Tchakarov; (viii) with Zeltser, Ma; (ix) Shaham, Orpheus CO; (x) Patrick Gallois, Pascal Gallois, Philh. O, Myung-Whun Chung (piano and cond.); (xi) Richter, VSO, Sanderling.

The Concerto box in DG's Beethoven Edition, with the juvenilia and completed fragments included, is a mixed bag. The choice of Pollini's first piano concerto cycle is controversial, though the reserve in Pollini's playing is counterbalanced by the warmth of his accompanists: Karl Boehm in Nos. 3 to 5, Eugen Jochum in the first two.

Anne-Sophie Mutter's early and beautiful recording of the *Violin concerto* with Karajan makes an excellent choice. The first two movements have rarely been more expansively presented on record, but the purity of the solo playing and the concentration make the result entirely convincing. Karajan is the domineering conductor in the *Triple concerto*. His young trio of soloists – Yo-Yo Ma and Mark Zeltser, as well as Mutter – are full of imagination but not a well-matched team.

Gil Shaham in the two *Romances* is outstanding, sweetly lyrical on an intimate scale; but the problems of the compilers are displayed in the extra works: this account of the curious little *Romance cantabile* for piano, flute and bassoon soloists has never been available in Britain before. Like the other juvenilia, the *E flat Piano concerto* of 1784 (completed like the *Romance* by the Swiss musicologist, Willy Hess) and the first movement of a *C major Violin concerto* (probably 1790–92), it is attractive and fresh but not very individual.

The arrangement of the *Violin concerto* for piano and orchestra alters the character of the music entirely, substituting charm for spiritual depth, though Barenboim gives a dedicated performance.

Volume 3: *Orchestral works and music for the stage:* (i–ii) *12 Contredanses, WoO 14;* (iii) *12 German dances, WoO 8; Minuets: WoO 7;* (i; iv) *WoO 3; Ritterballett, WoO 1; Wellington's victory, Op. 91;* (v–vi) Overtures: *Coriolan, Op. 62; Zur Namensfeier, Op. 115;* (vii) Overture and ballet music: *The Creatures of Prometheus, Op. 43;* Overtures and incidental music: (i; vi; viii; x–xii) *The Consecration of the house, H.118 (Opp. 113–14, 124, WoO 98);* (with ix) *The Ruins of Athens, Op. 113;* (i; vi; xiii) *Egmont, Op. 84;* (xiv) *King Stephen, Op. 117;* Miscellaneous items: (xviii–xix; xxi) *Es ist vollbracht, WoO 97; Germania, WoO 94;* (i; vi; ix; xv) *Leonore Prohaska, WoO 96;* (xvi) *2 arias for The Beautiful shoemaker's wife, WoO 91; Tarpeja, WoO 2:* (xvii) *Entr'acte,* (xxi) *Triumphal march;* (xix–xxi) *Vestas feuer, H.115.*

(M) **(*) DG Analogue/Dig. 453 713-2 (5) [id.]. (i) BPO; (ii) Maazel; (iii) ASMF, Marriner; (iv) Karajan; (v) VPO; (vi) Abbado; (vii) Orpheus CO; (viii) Augér, Hirte, Crass; (ix) McNair; (x) RIAS Chamber Ch.; (xi) Berlin R. Ch.; (xii) Klee; (xiii) Studer, Ganz; (xiv) Fischer-Dieskau, Jackwerth, Rühl, Mende, Aljinovicz, Santa Cecilia Ch. & O, Myung-Whun Chung; (xv) Eichhorn; (xvi) Gedda, Rothenberger, Convivium Musicum München, Keller; (xvii) Gothenberg SO, Neeme Järvi; (xviii) BBC Singers; (xix) Finley; (xx) Kuebler, Leggate, Gritton; (xxi) BBC SO, A. Davis.

The Creatures of Prometheus, splendidly done by the Orpheus Chamber Orchestra, offers much to admire, anticipating later, greater works. The other incidental music is musically more variable. Abbado (who also directs the overtures) gives excellent accounts of the music for *The Consecration of the House* and *Egmont*; Klee is equally impressive in *The Ruins of Athens*, a recording made much earlier for DG's Beethoven Bicentenary Edition. *King Stephen*, conducted by Myung-Whun Chung, was newly recorded (in Rome) and includes spoken melodrama (Fischer-Dieskau). Other more striking rarities include *Germania*, Beethoven's commemoration of the Allies' entry into Paris in 1814, and an operatic trio, *Vestas Feuer*, dramatically sung by Susan Gritton, David Kuebler and Gerald Finley. Karajan's version of *Wellington's victory* is very well played, but there is no sense of occasion; he is happier with the much lighter *Ritterballet*, presenting these dance vignettes affectionately. Marriner and his Academy are equally felicitous in the *German dances* and *Minuets*. The recording is consistently excellent throughout.

Volume 4: (i) *Fidelio* (complete); (ii) *Leonore* (complete); *Overtures:* (iii) *Fidelio, Op. 72c; Leonora Nos.* (iv) *1, Op. 138;* (v) *2, Op. 72a;* (vi) *3, Op. 72b.*

(M) *** DG Analogue/Dig. 453 719-2 (4) [id.]. (i) Janowitz, Kollo, Jungwirth, Sotin, Popp, Dallapozza, Fischer-Dieskau, V. State Op. Ch.; (ii) Martinpelto, Begley, Hawlata, Best, Oelze, Schade, Miles, Bantzer, Monteverdi Ch.; (i; iii–iv) VPO; (i; iii) Bernstein; (iv) Abbado; (ii; v) ORR, Gardiner.

Gardiner prepared for his recording of *Leonore* with a series of live performances. More than ever before, he presents this first version of the opera *Fidelio* as a masterpiece in its own right. At white heat, with the same team as on tour he set down this recording, confirming his passionate belief that *Leonore* is the more spontaneous and immediate work, compared with the more considered *Fidelio* of ten years later. One misses in *Leonore* such dramatic moments as the heroine's *Abscheulicher!*, but the gentle start of the final scene in place of the fortissimo of *Fidelio* is even more evocative, as interpreted by Gardiner.

Hillevi Martinpelto in the title-role conveys youthful ardour as well as power, well contrasted with the sweetly expressive Marzelline of Christiane Oelze. The tenor, Kim Begley, emerges in sharply focused, heroic strength as Florestan, with Michael Schade providing an ideal lyric contrast as Jaquino. Franz Hawlata as Rocco and Alastair Miles as Don Fernando are both first rate. Matthew Best as Pizarro is disappointing.

Bernstein's reading of *Fidelio* is full of dramatic flair. The recording was made in conjunction with live performances by the same cast at the Vienna State Opera. Lucia Popp as Marzelline is particularly enchanting, and Gundula Janowitz sings most beautifully as Leonore. Kollo as Florestan is strong and intelligent, as is the rest of the cast.

Volume 5: *Piano sonatas Nos. 1–32.*
(M) *** DG 453 724-2 (8) [id.]. Wilhelm Kempff.

As in 1970, when DG issued their Beethoven Bicentenary Edition, Wilhelm Kempff's stereo cycle of the piano sonatas remains the choice, with the sound noticeably improved. More than any other pianist, Kempff has the power to make one appreciate and understand Beethoven in a new way, thanks to his magnetism, his unfailing sense of spontaneity, his ability to clarify textures and and his lyrical flow, with extreme speeds avoided. Kempff may be erratic over observing exposition repeats, but the sense of live communication is what matters, not least in the late sonatas with sharp, clean attack set against sublime lyricism.

Volume 6: *Piano works:* (i) *Allegrettos in B min., WoO 61; in C min., WoO 53; H.69; Allegretto quasi andante in G min., WoO 61a; Allemande in A, WoO 81;* (ii) *Andante favori, WoO 57; Bagatelles: Opp. 33; 119;* (iii) *126;* (ii) *WoO 52; WoO 56;* (iii) *'Für Elise', WoO 59;* (i) *WoO 60;* (viii) *Canons à 2 in A flat, G, H.274/5; Ecossaises:* (vi) *WoO 83;* (i) *WoO 86; Fantasia in G min. Op. 77; Fugue in C, H.64; 12 German dances, WoO 13; 7 Ländler in D, WoO 11; 'Lustig-traurig' in C min., WoO 54; 6 Minuets, WoO* (ii) *10;* (i) *82;* (ii) *Polonaise in C, Op. 89;* (i) *Prelude in F min., WoO 55;* (ii) *Rondos in A, WoO 49; in C, Op. 51/1; WoO 48; in G, Op. 51/2;* (i) *Rondo a capriccio in G ('Rage over the lost penny'), Op. 129;* (ix) *Sonatas, WoO 47, Nos. 1 in E flat; 2 in F min.; 3 in D;* (i) *in C, WoO 51; 2 Sonata movements in F, WoO 50;* (ii) *6 Variations in F, Op. 34; Variations in C min., WoO 63; in F, WoO 64; in D, WoO 65; in C, WoO 68; in G, WoO 70;* (i) *in A, WoO 66; in C, WoO 72; in B flat, WoO 73; in F, WoO 75, 76; in G, WoO 77;* (iv) *15 Variations and fugue on a theme from Prometheus (Eroica variations), Op. 35;* (vi) *32 Variations on an original theme in C min., WoO 80;* (vii) *33 Variations on a waltz by Diabelli, Op. 120;* (v) *12 Variations on a Russian dance, WoO 71; Variations on 'God save the King', WoO 78,* and *'Rule, Britannia', WoO 79; 9 Variations on 'Quant'è più bello', WoO 69;* (i) *Waltzes, WoO 84–5.* Works for piano duet: (ix, x) *Grosse Fuge in B flat, Op. 134; 3 Marches, Op. 45; Sonata in D, Op. 6.* Solo pieces for miscellaneous instruments: (xi) *Fugue in D, WoO 31. Grenadier march, H.107; 5 Pieces, WoO 33* (both works for mechanical clock). *2 Preludes through all twelve major keys, Op. 39.*
(M) ** DG Analogue/Dig. 453 733-2 (8) [id.]. (i) Gianluca Cascioli; (ii) Mikhael Pletnev; (iii) Anatol Ugorski; (iv) Emil Gilels; (v) Olli Mustonen; (vi) Wilhelm Kempff; (vii) Daniel Barenboim; (viii) Walter Olbertz; (ix) Jörg Demus; (x) Norman Shetler; (xi) Simon Preston (organ).

Gilels's magisterial account of the *Eroica variations* is well contrasted with Barenboim's is an intensely personal reading of the *Diabelli variations*, giving the illusion of an improvisation, full of dramatic contrasts. Outstanding among the other recordings is Pletnev's *Bagatelles*, Opp. 33 and 119, but Ugorsky is far less imaginative in Op. 126. Many of the lesser-known pieces are entrusted to Gianluca Cascioli, who often makes them seem more than just chips from the master's workbench, notably the *Fantasia*, Op. 77. Olli Mustonen's stylish recordings of the four lesser sets of *Variations* come from Decca.

Volume 7: (i) *Violin sonatas Nos. 1–10;* (ii) *6 German dances, WoO 42;* (iii) *Rondo in G, WoO 41; 12 Variations on Mozart's 'Se vuol ballare'* from *Le nozze di Figaro, WoO 40.*
(M) *** DG Analogue/Dig. 453 743-2 (4) [id.]. (i) Kremer, Argerich; (ii) Garrett, Canino; (iii) Menuhin, Kempff.

Having two such volatile artists as Kremer and Argerich in partnership for the Beethoven *Violin sonatas* makes for exciting results, spontaneous and fresh in the three early sonatas of Opus 12, taken at high speed. The openings of both the *Spring Sonata* and the *Kreutzer*, less plain than usual, convey a thoughtfulness that looks forward to the last, most enigmatic of the sonatas, *No. 10 in G*. In that final work the contrasts of mood are vividly caught, with rapt mystery at the very start giving way to lightness. The *German dances*, *Rondo* and *Variations* are slight but are stylishly presented.

Volume 8: *Cello sonatas: Nos. 1–5; 7 Variations on 'Bei Männern, welche Liebe fühlen', WoO 46; 12 Variations on 'Ein Mädchen oder Weibchen', Op. 66,* both from Mozart's *Die Zauberflöte. 12 Variations on 'See the conqu'ring hero comes'* from Handel's *Judas Maccabaeus, WoO 45.*
(M) *** DG Dig. 453 748-2 (2) [id.]. Mischa Maisky, Martha Argerich.

Mischa Maisky and Martha Argerich make a characterful partnership, giving exhilarating performances that yet are overconcerned at times on detail.

Volume 9: *Piano trios:* (i) *Nos. 1–9; 10 (14 Variations on an original theme in E flat), Op. 44; 11 (10 Variations on 'Ich bin der Schneider*

Kakadu'), Op. 121a; (ii) *Allegretto in E flat, H.48; Trio in E flat* (arr. of *Septet, Op. 20), Op. 38;* (iii) *Trio in D* (arr. of *Symphony No. 2*), *Op. 36.*

(M) **(*) DG Analogue/Dig. 453 751-2 (5) [id.]. (i) Kempff, Szeryng, Fournier; (ii) Beaux Arts Trio; (iii) Besch, Brandis, Boettcher.

The Kempff–Szeryng–Fournier set of trios is a distinguished one, most successful in the early trios, though the sound is dated. The other items are well done, if of limited interest.

Volume 10: *String trios: Nos. 1–4; Serenade in D, Op. 8.*

(M) **(*) DG Dig. 453 757-2 (2) [id.]. Anne-Sophie Mutter, Bruno Giuranna, Rostropovich.

This starry trio of soloists certainly offers splendid playing, but the recording is rather forward and dry, and not intimate enough.

Volume 11: The early quartets: *String quartets* (i) *Nos. 1–6, Op. 18/1–6;* (ii) *Fugue from Handel's Solomon overture, H.36; Minuet in A flat, H.33;* (iii) *Preludes and fugues in F, H.30; in C, H.31; String quartets in F,* (ii) *H.32* (*Op. 18/1* first version); (i) *H.34* (arr. of *Piano sonata, Op. 14/1*)

(M) **(*) DG Analogue/Dig. 453 760-2 (3) [id.]. (i) Amadeus Qt; (ii) Hagen Qt; (iii) Mendelssohn-Qt.

The Op. 18 quartets inspire the Amadeus to their finest playing. The character of the playing at once polished and intimate. The 1961 recording still sounds well. The other items are interesting rarities.

Volume 12: The middle quartets: *String quartets Nos. 7 in F; 8 in E min., 9 in C (Rasumovsky), Op.59/1–3; 10 in E flat (Harp), Op. 74; 11 in F. min., Op. 95.*

(M) **(*) DG Dig. 453 764-2 (2) [id.]. Emerson Qt.

We are at odds over the Emerson performances of the mid-period Beethoven quartets. E. G. finds them very compelling indeed, with pianissimos of breath-taking delicacy and vibrant attack of fortissimos. R. L. agrees that their playing is in a class of its own technically, but feels the thrust is inappropriate in music composed before the discovery of electricity. First choice generally choice remains with the Lindsays (at mid-price), with the Italians hardly less satisfying and offering marvellous value in the bargain range (see below).

Volume 13: The late quartets: *String quartets Nos. 12 in E flat, Op. 127; 13 in B flat, Op. 130; 14 in C sharp min., Op. 131; 15 in A min., Op. 132; 16 in F, Op. 135; Grosse Fuge, Op. 133.*

(M) ** DG 453 768-2 (3) [id.]. LaSalle Qt.

Technically, the LaSalle Quartet are impressive with their unanimity of ensemble and fine tonal blend, but there is no sense of mystery and little feeling of inwardness or depth. The recordings (made between 1972 and 1977) are of fine analogue quality.

Volume 14: *Chamber works:* (i) *Canon in A, WoO 35;* (ii–iii) *Duets, in G for 2 flutes, WoO 26;* (i) *in A for 2 violins, WoO 34; in E flat for viola & cello, WoO 32;* (iv) *Fugue in D for string quintet, Op. 137;* (v–vi) *Horn sonata in F, Op. 17;* (i) *6 Ländler for 2 violins & bass, WoO 15; 6 Minuets for 2 violins & bass, WoO 9;* (vii) *Piano & wind quintet, Op. 16;* (viii; xii) *Piano quartets Nos. 1–3;* (ix) *Pieces for mandolin & piano: Adagio, WoO 43b; Sonatinas in C, WoO 44a; in C min., WoO 43a; Variations in D, WoO 44b;* (i) *Prelude and fugue in E min. for 2 violins & cello, H.29;* (x) *Serenade in D for flute, violin & viola, Op. 25;* (iv) *Septet in E flat, Op. 20;* (xi) *Sextet in E flat, Op. 81b;* (xii–xiii) *String quintet in C, Op. 29;* (ii; xiv) *Themes with variations for piano & flute, Opp. 105 & 107;* (xv) *Trio in B flat for piano, clarinet & cello, Op. 11;* (v; xvi) *Trio in G for piano, flute & bassoon, WoO 37.*

(M) **(*) DG Analogue/Dig. 453 772-2 (6) [id.]. (i) Hagen Qt, Posch; (ii) Gallois; (iii) Rampal; (iv) VPO Ens.; (v) Barenboim; (vi) Bloom; (vii) Levine, Vienna–Berlin Ens.; (viii) Eschenbach; (ix) Fietz, Webersinke; (x) Zoeller, Brandis, Ueberschaer; (xi) Seifert, Klier, Drolc Qt; (xii) Amadeus Qt (members); (xiii) Aronowitz; (xiv) Licad; (xv) Kempff, Leister, Fournier; (xvi) Debost, Sennedat.

Best here are the early *Piano quartets* of 1785, written in Bonn, not great works but most persuasive as played here. Outstanding too are the *C major String quintet* with the Amadeus and Cecil Aronowitz (one of their finest recordings) and the *Septet.* Barenboim is an inspired pianist in both the *G major Trio*, for piano, flute and bassoon, with principals from the Orchestre de Paris and the *Horn sonata* with the brilliant Myron Bloom. The early *E flat Sextet*, Op. 81, was recorded for the 1970 Edition and sounds remarkably fresh. So does the 1970 Zoeller–Brandis–Ueberschaer set of the *Serenade*, Op. 25. The Levine Vienna–Berlin Ensemble version of the Op. 16 *E flat Quintet* for piano and wind, which was made in 1986, is less satisfactory, but the Op. 11 *Trio* with Karl Leister, Pierre Fournier and Wilhelm Kempff is a delight.

Volume 15: *Wind music:* (i–ii) *Ecossaise in D, WoO 22;* (iii) *3 Equale for four trombones, WoO 30;* (i–ii) *Marches, WoO 18-20, WoO 24, WoO 29;* (i) *Octet in E flat, Op. 103;* (i–ii) *Polonaise in D, WoO 21;* (iv) *Rondino in E flat, WoO 25;* (i) *Sextet in E flat, Op. 71;* (v) *Trio in C, Op. 87; Variations on Mozart's 'Là ci darem la mano',* both for 2 oboes and cor anglais.

(M) *** DG 453 779-2 (2) [id.]. (i) BPO (members); (ii) cond. Hans Priem-Bergrath;

(iii) Philip Jones Brass Ens.; (iv) Netherlands Wind Ens.; (v) Holliger, Elhorst, Bourgue.

For Beethoven's wind music, DG mostly draws on the Philips catalogue with Decca providing the Philip Jones Ensemble's recording of the three sonorous *Equali* for trombones. Belying its opus number, the *C major Trio*, Op. 87, for the unlikely combination of cor anglais and two oboes is an early work, dating from 1794 and impressive in scale. The *Là ci darem variations* in a similar scoring were not published until the present century. The attractive *Rondino for wind octet* is given a crisp, clean performance by the Netherlands Wind Ensemble (also from Philips); the *Wind Sextet,* Op. 71, and *Octet in E flat*, Op. 103, are DG recordings from 1970, played by members of the Berlin Philharmonic Orchestra, equally alert and civilized, while Hans Priem-Bergrath directs the Berlin ensemble in lively accounts of the marches and dances.

Volume 16: *Lieder:* (i) *Abendlied unterm gestirnten Himmel;* (iv; ix) *Abschiedsgesang an Wiens Bürger;* (i) *Adelaide; Als die Geliebte sich trennen wollte; Andenken; An die ferne Geliebte, Op. 98;* (iii; ix) *An den fernen Geliebten, Op. 75/5; An die Geliebte* (ii; ix) 2nd version; (i) 3rd version; *An die Hoffnung, Op. 32* (1st version), *Op. 94* (2nd version); (iii; ix) *An einen Säugling;* (ii; ix) *An Laura; An Minna;* (i) *4 Ariettas and a duet, Op. 82; Aus Goethes Faust, Op. 75/3; Der Bardengeist; Das Blümchen Wunderhold, Op. 52/8;* (vii; x) *Der edle Mensch;* (ii; ix) *Elegie auf den Tod eines Pudels; Erhebt das Glas mit froher Hand; Feuerfarb', Op. 52/2; Der freie Mann; Gedenke mein!;* (i) *Das Geheimnis; Gesang aus der Ferne* (vi; x) 1st version; (i) 2nd version; (iii; ix) *Der Gesàng der Nachtigall; Gretels Warnung, Op. 75/4;* (i) *In questa tomba oscura; Der Jüngling in der Fremde;* (iii; ix) *Kennst du das Land, Op. 75/1;* (ii; ix) *Klage;* (v; x) *Der Knabe auf dem Berge;* (ii; ix) *Des Kriegers Abschied;* (iv; ix) *Kriegslied der Österreicher;* (i) *Der Kuss; Die laute Klage; Die Liebe, Op. 52/6;* (viii; x) *Das liebe Kätzchen;* (i) *Der Liebende; Das Liedchen von der Ruhe, Op. 52/3; 6 Lieder, Op. 48; 3 Lieder, Op. 83; 2 Lieder, WoO 118; Maigesang, Op. 52/4;* (iii; ix) *Man strebt, die Flamme zu verhehlen;* (iv; ix) *Der Mann von Wort;* (i) *Marmotte, Op. 52/7; Merkenstein* (vi; x) *WoO 144* (1st version), (ii–iii; ix) *Op. 100* (2nd version); (iii; ix) *Mollys Abschied, Op. 52/5; Neue Liebe, neues Leben* (vi; x) *WoO 127* (1st version), (i) *Op. 75/2* (2nd version); (ii; ix) *Oh care selve, oh cara;* (i) *Opferlied; La partenza;* (ii; ix) *Plaisir d'aimer; Punschlied; Que le temps me dure* 1st version; (v; x) 2nd version; (i) *Resignation; Ruf vom Berge; Schilderung eines Mädchens; Sehnsucht, WoO 146;* (iii; ix) *Sehnsucht, WoO 134* (4 versions); (ii; ix) *Ein Selbstgespräch; So oder so; La tiranna;* (i) *Urians Reise um die Welt, Op. 52/1; Vita felice; Der Wachtelschlag; Zärtliche Liebe; Der Zufriedene, Op. 75/6.*

(M) **(*) DG Analogue/Dig. 453 782-2 (3) [id.]. (i) Fischer-Dieskau, Demus; (ii) Schreier; (iii) Stolte; (iv) Leib; (v) Helzel; (vi) Maus; (vii) Person; (viii) Horn; (ix) Olbertz; (x) Hilsdorf.

Fischer-Dieskau gives searching readings of the Beethoven songs, recorded 1966, revealing their mastery, too little appreciated. Demus is a sensitive accompanist and the recording is good. For much of the rest DG draw on Telefunken recordings dating mainly from the 1970s, with Peter Schreier in excellent form. However, his colleagues are less reliable, including Adele Stolte in the duets.

Volume 17: *Folksong arrangements: 7 British songs, WoO 158b; 25 Irish songs, WoO 152; 20 Irish songs, WoO 153; 12 Irish songs, WoO 154; 25 Scottish songs, WoO 108; 12 Scottish songs, WoO 156; 26 Welsh songs, WoO 155; Songs of various nationalities, WoO 157, 158a, c.*

(M) *** DG Dig. 453 786-2 (7) [id.]. Lott, Watson, Wyn-Davies, Philogene, Walker, Murray, Ainsley, Robinson, Spence, Allen, Maltman; Layton, Osostowicz, Blankestijn, Smith, Martineau.

Unlike most of the other volumes in DG's Complete Beethoven Edition, this one is entirely new, an enchanting kaleidoscopic collection of folksong arrangements, mainly British. So Beethoven's setting of *Auld lang syne* has a vigorous Scottish snap to it, and he treats *God save the King* canonically, while *Charlie is my darling* is in 2/4 time, and *The Miller of Dee* is made the darker by a stylized accompaniment that is almost the Beethovenian equivalent of Benjamin Britten's free-ranging folksong accompaniments.

Altogether 168 songs are included, ending with a disc of non-British settings just as fascinating, particularly the Spanish ones. Beethoven consistently gives the lie to those who have dismissed these songs as pot-boilers, regularly bringing surprises in his accompaniments for piano trio. Note that Beethoven occasionally gets the country wrong for a song, dubbing a setting of Robert Burns as Irish! Malcolm Martineau as accompanist is the lynchpin, regularly providing the sparkle needed, and almost all the singing is first rate. An outstanding set in every way.

Volume 18: *Secular vocal works:* (i) *Abschiedsgesang;* (ii) *Ah! perfido, Op. 65;* (iii) *Bundeslied, Op. 122; Elegischer gesang, Op. 118;* (i; iv–vi) *Cantata campestre; Hochzeitslied; Lobkowitz-Kantate;* (vii) *Chor auf die verbündeten Fürsten;* (i) *Gesang der Mönche;* (viii; xi) *Mit Mädeln sich vertragen; Prüfung des Küssens;* (ix–xi) *Ne' giorni tuoi felici;* (ix; xi) *No, non turbati; Primo amore;* (iii; xii) *Opferlied,*

Op. 121b; (viii–xi) *Tremate, empi, tremate, Op. 116;* (i; vi; xiii) *43 Canons and musical jokes;* (i) *18 Italian partsongs.*

(M) ** DG Analogue/Dig. 453 794-2 (2) [id.]. (i) Berlin soloists; (ii) Studer, BPO, Abbado; (iii) Amb. S., LSO, Tilson Thomas; (iv) Jehser; (v) Olbertz; (vi) Knothe; (vii) BBC Singers, BBC SO, A. Davis; (viii) Vogel; (ix) Kuhse; (x) Büchner; (xi) Berlin Staatskapelle, Apelt; (xii) Haywood; (xiii) Berlin Singakademie Ch.

This two-disc set contains much that will intrigue the dedicated Beethovenian – the 43 *Canons and musical jokes*, for instance. For three of the more important inclusions DG have drawn on the Sony catalogue for outstanding performances from Michael Tilson Thomas of the *Bundeslied*, *Opferlied* (with Lorna Haywood an impressive soloist) and the remarkable *Elegischer Gesang* ('Elegiac song'). Cheryl Studer's dramatic account of *Ah! perfido* is new, as are most of the more trivial items.

Volume 19: *Large choral works:* (i–iii) *Cantatas on the accession of Emperor Leopold II, WoO 88;* (iii–iv) *On the death of Emperor Joseph II, WoO 87;* (v) *Choral fantasia for piano, chorus and orchestra in C min., Op. 80;* (vi) *Christus am Oelberge, Op. 85;* (vii) *Der glorreiche Augenblick, Op. 136;* (i; viii–ix) *Mass in C, Op. 86;* (ix) *Meeresstille und glückliche Fahrt, Op. 112;* (x) *Missa solemnis in D, Op. 123.*

(M) *** DG Analogue/Dig. 453 798-2 (5) [id.]. (i) Margiono; (ii) Shimell; (iii) German Opera Ch. & O, Thielemann; (iv) Schäfer, Bieber, von Halem; (v) Kissin, RIAS Ch., BPO, Abbado; (vi) Harwood, King, Crass, V. Singverein, VSO, Klee; (vii) Orgonasova, Vermillion, Robinson, Hawlata, Ch. di voci bianche dell'Arcum, St Cecilia Ac. Ch. & O, Myung-Whun Chung; (viii) Robbin, Kendall, Miles; (ix) Monteverdi Ch., ORR, Gardiner; (x) Studer, Norman, Domingo, Moll, Leipzig R. Ch., Swedish R. Ch., VPO, Levine.

Levine's account of the *Missa solemnis*, recorded live in Salzburg as a memorial to Karajan is outstanding, reflecting a great occasion, with a starry quartet of soloists. Gardiner's period performance of the *Mass in C* is excellent too, revealing it as a masterpiece, with clean textures and sprung rhythms, married to an expressive warmth. Aptly clear-toned soloists match the freshness of the Monteverdi Choir.

Beethoven's oratorio, *Christus am Oelberge*, is an even more under-rated work. The Heldentenor, James King, underlines the operatic quality, and the radiance of Elizabeth Harwood's voice is powerfully caught, while Franz Crass comparably intense. Bernhard Klee draws lively playing from the Vienna Symphoniker, and the recording stands the test of time.

The two youthful cantatas from Beethoven's Bonn period commemorating regal death and accession bring fine new recordings directed by DG's young star conductor, Christian Thielemann, aptly combining vitality and gravitas. The Viennese celebration, *Der glorreiche Augenblick* conducted by the ever-perceptive Myung-Whun Chung, is equally telling, with Luba Orgonasova an outstanding solopist. An essential purchase particular for those who want the two *Masses*.

Volume 20: Historic recordings: *Piano concertos Nos.* (i) *3 in C min., Op 37;* (ii–iii) *5 in E flat (Emperor), Op. 73;* (iv) *Violin concerto in D, Op. 61. Symphonies Nos.* (v) *3 in E flat (Eroica), Op. 55;* (vi) *5 in C min., Op. 67;* (vii) *7 in A, Op. 92;* (viii) *9 in D min. (Choral), Op. 125. Overtures:* (ix) *Coriolan, Op. 62;* (x) *Egmont, Op. 84; Leonore No. 2, Op. 72;* (ix) *Leonore No. 3, Op. 72. Violin sonatas Nos.* (xii; ii) *5 in F, 'Spring', Op. 24;* (xiii; ii) *9 in A, 'Kreutzer', Op 47;* (ii) *Rondo a capriccio in G, Op. 129.* (xiv) *An die ferne Geliebte* (song-cycle), *Op. 98.* Lieder: *Andenken, WoO 136; In questa tomba oscura, WoO 133; Der Wachtelschlag WoO 129. Zärtliche Liebe, WoO 123* – (xiii) MOZART: *Piano concerto No. 20 in D min., K.466* (with cadenzas by BEETHOVEN).

(M) (***) DG mono/stereo 453 804-2 (6) [id.]. (i) Annie Fischer, Bav. RSO, Fricsay; (ii) Wilhelm Kempff; (iii) BPO, Peter Raabe; (iv) Josef Wolfsthal, BPO, Manfred Gurlitt; (v–ix) BPO; cond. (v) Carl Schuricht; (vi) Artur Nikisch; (vii) Ferenc Fricsay; (viii) Fritz Busch, with Kerstin Lindberg-Torlind, Else Jena, Erik Sjöberg, Holger Byrding, Danish R. Ch. & O; (ix) Furtwängler; (x) Berlin Op. O, Otto Klemperer; (xii) Wolfgang Schneiderhan; (xiii) Georg Kulenkampff; (xiv) Heinrich Schlusnus, Sebastian Peschko & Franz Rupp; (xiii) Sviatoslav Richter, Warsaw PO, Wislocki.

Earliest here is the 1913 Nikisch account of the *Fifth Symphony*, the first complete recording of any symphony. The wartime (1941) set of the *Eroica* from Carl Schuricht and the Berlin Philharmonic, not widely available outside Germany, brings a totally dedicated reading, vibrant and alive. Ferenc Fricsay's recording of the *Seventh Symphony*, omitted from DG's 1994 ten-CD compilation of his work, has a fire, a gravitas and an integrity that make a powerful impression. The *Ninth Symphony* was made in Copenhagen in the autumn of 1950 with the *Staatsradiofoniens Orkester* under Fritz Busch, an undistracting, classical account.

Among the concertos, Annie Fischer's 1957 account of the *Third* with the Bavarian Radio Orchestra under Ferenc Fricsay fully deserves resurrection, and Wilhelm Kempff's fine (1936) *Emperor Concerto* is most impressive too, it is not necessarily superior to either of his post-war versions. Josef

Wolfsthal's 1929 account of the *Violin concerto* (his second recording of the piece) offers breathtaking mastery, making one regret that this pupil of Carl Flesch died in his early thirties.

The 1959 account by Sviatoslav Richter of Mozart's *D minor Concerto*, K.466, made in Warsaw, is included because of the Beethoven cadenzas the great Russian pianist used. Memorable too are the 1942 Furtwängler Berlin Philharmonic *Coriolan overture*, dramatic and intense, the 1935 set of the *Kreutzer Sonata* with Georg Kulenkampff and Wilhelm Kempff, remarkable for its purity, and the pre-war *An die ferne Geliebte* with Heinrich Schlusnus. Handsome presentation.

Other recordings

Piano concertos Nos. 1–5.
*** Sony S3K 44575 (3) [id.]. Perahia, Concg. O, Haitink.
(N) *** Ph. Dig. 462 781-2 (3) [id.]. Alfred Brendel, VPO, Sir Simon Rattle.

(i) *Piano concertos Nos. 1–5;* (ii) *Triple concerto for violin, cello and piano, Op. 56.*
(M) *** Sony SB3K 48397 (3) [id.]. (i) Fleisher, Cleveland O, Szell; (ii) Stern, Rose, Istomin, Phd. O, Ormandy.

Piano concertos Nos. 1–5; Rondos, Op. 51/1–2.
(M) (***) DG mono 435 744-2 (3) [id.]. Wilhelm Kempff, BPO, Van Kempen.

(i) *Piano concertos Nos. 1–5. 6 Bagatelles, Op. 126; Für Elise.*
(B) **(*) Decca 443 723-2 (3) [id.]. Ashkenazy, (i) Chicago SO, Solti.

(i) *Piano concertos Nos. 1–5. Diabelli variations, Op. 120.*
(M) **(*) Decca 433 891-2 (3) [id.]. Wilhelm Backhaus; (i) VPO, Schmidt-Isserstedt.

Piano concertos Nos. 1–5; (i) *Choral Fantasia, Op. 80.*
(M) *** EMI CMS7 63360-2 (3) [Ang. CDMC 63360]. Daniel Barenboim, New Philh. O, Klemperer, (i) with John Alldis Ch.

Perahia, with Haitink a deeply sympathetic partner, gives masterly performances, as close to the heart of this music as any. The sound is full and well balanced. This set has now reverted to full price and is well worth it.

Alfred Brendel offers this new Philips set as his third and last recorded survey of the Beethoven concertos, made under ideal conditions in Vienna with his chosen collaborator, Sir Simon Rattle. It was a labour of love. With each concerto recorded immediately after live performances, the results have an extra spontaneity, usually at speeds marginally faster than in his previous recordings. The dynamic range is greater too, with hushed *pianissimos* more intense, and with Rattle encouraging lightness in his accompaniments. So the opening solo in the *Fourth concerto* has extra intimacy and the slow movements are gentler and more songful. The ambience of the Musikverein casts a warm natural glow over the proceedings and adds the necessary weight to the *Emperor*. A fine achievement.

Fleisher's 1961 cycle with Szell represents this unique musical partnership at its peak, in performances consistently fresh and intense. In the lively account of the *Triple concerto*, recorded in Philadelphia, the soloists placed unnaturally forward.

The combination of Barenboim and Klemperer, recording together in 1967/8, brings endless illumination, with Klemperer's measured weight set against Barenboim's youthful spontaneity, specially compelling in slow movements. The *Choral Fantasia* too is given an inspired performance. The remastered sound is clear and full.

Carefree delight runs through the earlier of Kempff's two cycles of the Beethoven *Piano concertos*. Even more than his stereo cycle, this one, recorded in mono in 1953, finds Kempff at his most individual, turning phrases and pointing ornamentation with rare sparkle and sense of fun. The CD transfer offers immediate, well-detailed sound.

The partnership of Ashkenazy and Solti is fascinating, with Solti's fiery intensity contrasted with Ashkenazy's introspective qualities. Ashkenazy brings a hushed, poetic quality to every slow movement, while Solti's urgency maintains a vivid forward impulse in outer movements. At times as in the *C minor Concerto*, the music-making may seem too tautly intense, but freshness dominates. On CD the sound is fierce at times, while the piano tone rather shallow.

Backhaus recorded the Beethoven concertos with Schmidt-Isserdtedt in 1958–9 when he was in his mid-seventies (the *Diabelli variations* date from 1955). Though his bold style is lacking in grace and wit, yet the authority is unassailable, and the early stereo recordings are remarkably fresh, even if the close balance prevents a real pianissimo.

Piano concerto No. 1 in C, Op. 15; (i) *Choral Fantasia* (for piano, chorus and orchestra), *Op. 80.*
(B) *** EMI CfP CD-CFP 6025 [(M) id. import]. John Lill, SNO; (i) with SNO Ch., Sir Alexander Gibson.

Piano concertos Nos. 2 in B flat, Op. 19; 4 in G, Op. 58.
(B) *** EMI CfP CD-CFP 6026 [(M) id. import]. Lill, SNO, Gibson.

Piano concertos Nos. 3 in C min., Op. 37; 5 in E flat (Emperor), Op. 73.
(B) *** EMI CfP CD-CFP 6027 [(M) id. import]. Lill, SNO, Gibson.

John Lill has never been more impressive on record

than in his set of the Beethoven concertos, recorded in 1974–5. In each work he conveys spontaneity and a vein of poetry that in the studio have too often eluded him. Gibson and the Scottish National Orchestra provide strong, direct support, helped by very good analogue recording using the spacious City Hall, Glasgow. Very competitive with other versions at whatever price.

Piano concertos Nos. 1–4.

(N) (B) *** DG Double 450 400-2 (2) [id.]. Wilhelm Kempff, BPO, Leitner.

(B) *** EMI forte CZS5 69506-2 (2). Gilels, Cleveland O, Szell.

Kempff's analogue stereo accounts from the early 1960s (also available with No. 5 in a 3-disc bargain box, 427 237-2) still sound remarkably good for their age, with a warm ambience and natural piano timbre; the wisdom Kempff dispensed is as fresh as ever. Leitner's contribution is distinguished, there is memorable orchestral playing throughout, and especially in slow movements. Here Kempff's profound sense of calm is remarkable, while finales sparkle joyously. His reading of the *Third concerto* is more measured and serious than his earlier mono version (available in another box – see above), but in its unforced way, happily lyrical, and diamond-bright in articulation it is eminently satisfying. The *Fourth* shows these artists at their finest: Kempff's imagination and his nuancing of colour are magical, and he is matched by the orchestral response. The famous dialogue of the *Andante* has never sounded more poised.

Gilels is an incomparable Beethoven player, unfailingly illuminating and poetic. Szell, tautly controlled, gives rhythms an exhilaraing lift has tremendous grip and that the playing of the Cleveland Orchestra is beyond reproach, with a rhythmical point that has an exhilarating lift. The recordings, made in Severance Hall in 1968, are dry and clear but with ample atmosphere.

(i) *Piano concertos Nos. 1–4;* (ii) *Romances for violin and orchestra Nos. 1–2, Opp. 40 & 50.*

(B) *** Ph. Duo 442 577-2 (2) [id.]. (i) Steven Kovacevich, BBC SO, Sir Colin Davis; (ii) Arthur Grumiaux, Concg. O, Haitink.

The first four concertos bring characteristically crisp and refreshing readings from Kovacevich and Davis which convey their conviction with no intrusive idiosyncrasy. These are model performances, with Kovacevich conveying a depth and thoughtful intensity that have rarely been matched. The recording, from the early 1970s, is refined and well balanced and has been admirably transferred to CD. Grumiaux's *Romances* date from a decade earlier, but the sound is full, and the solo playing is peerless.

Piano concertos Nos. 1 in C, Op. 15; 2 in B flat, Op. 19.

*** Sony Dig. SK 42177 [id.]. Perahia, Concg. O, Haitink.

(B) *** Ph. Virtuoso 422 968-2 [(M) id. import]. Stephen Kovacevich, BBC SO, Sir Colin Davis.

(B) *** Decca Eclipse Dig. 448 982-2; *448 982-4* [id.]. Alicia de Larrocha, Berlin RSO, Chailly (with SCHUBERT: *Moment musical No. 6 in A flat, D.780* ***).

(M) *** DG (IMS) Dig. 445 504-2 [id.]. Martha Argerich, Philh. O, Sinopoli.

(M) *** Virgin Veritas/EMI Dig. VER5 61296-2 [CDM 61296]. Tan (fortepiano), L. Classical Players, Norrington.

*** DG Dig. (IMS) 437 545-2 [id.]. Krystian Zimerman, VPO.

**(*) Sony Dig. SK 68250 [id.]. Jos van Immerseel, Tafelmusik, Bruno Weil.

Murray Perahia's coupling of Nos. 1 and 2 brings strong and thoughtful performances, which draw a sharp distinction between the two works. No. 2, the earlier, brings a near-Mozartian manner in the first movement, but then rightly a deep and measured account of the slow movement takes Beethoven into another world, hushed and intense. The *First Concerto* finds Perahia taking a fully Beethovenian view from the start. Bernard Haitink proves a lively and sympathetic partner, with the Concertgebouw playing superbly. Warm recording.

Philips have now restored to the catalogue Stephen Kovacevich's recordings of the Beethoven concertos separately on their Virtuoso label to make a clear first bargain choice for this coupling.

Alicia de Larrocha in an uneven cycle with the Berlin Radio Symphony Orchestra under Chailly, gives delightful performances, lightly pointed, on a Mozartian scale, with beautifully poised accounts of both slow movements. Full, vivid recording.

The conjunction of Martha Argerich and Giuseppe Sinopoli in Beethoven produces performances which give off electric sparks, daring and volatile. Argerich is jaunty in allegros, and slow movements are songful, not solemn. Vivid sound in a reverberant acoustic.

Melvyn Tan's coupling of the first two concertos, using a fortepiano, brings performances of natural, unselfconscious expressiveness. Even when Tan's speeds for slow movements are very fast indeed, his ease of expression makes them very persuasive, while conveying necessary gravity.

Zimerman, completing the cycle he began with Bernstein, directs the Vienna Philharmonic in bright, elegant, often witty performances that bring home the point that these are early works. Bright recording.

Jos van Immerseel gives lively and stylish performances on Sony, but his fortepiano convinces less readily than the instrument played by Melvyn Tan, whose coupling of these two concertos has more sparkle.

Piano concertos Nos. 1–2; Piano concerto No. 1 (2nd performance, with cadenzas by Glenn Gould).
*** EMI Dig. CDC5 56266-2 [id.]. Lars Vogt, CBSO, Rattle.

The curiosity of Vogt's EMI issue is that it comes with a bonus disc containing a repeat performance of the *First Concerto* using Glenn Gould's weirdly atonal cadenzas instead of Beethoven's. That is more than a gimmick, for the young German pianist combines magnetism with keen imagination. His crisp, clean articulation and preference for transparent textures (matched by Rattle's work with the orchestra) reminds one of Wilhelm Kempff, his extreme speeds reflect the example of Artur Schnabel. Excellent, transparent sound.

Piano concertos Nos. 1 in C, Op. 15; 4 in G, Op. 58.
(M) **(*) [RCA Basic 100 09026 68083-2; *68083-4*]. Rubinstein, Boston SO, Leinsdorf.

Rubinstein gives sparkling, spontaneous-sounding performances of both concertos, conveying joy in No. 1, rather than the stress of early Beethoven with no half-tones. In the opening solo of No. 4 the manner is easy and confidential rather than intense, and so are the exchanges of the slow movement. The 1960s recordings are bright and sharply focused.

Piano concertos Nos. 1 in C, Op. 15; 5 in E flat (Emperor).
(B) *** Tring Dig. TRP 075 [(M) id. import]. Michael Roll, RPO, Howard Shelley.

Michael Roll, the very first winner of the Leeds Competition in 1963, was for too long neglected by the record companies. Here he gives magnetic performances of both concertos, at once sparkling and powerful, marked by articulation of diamond clarity, with rhythms persuasively sprung in fast Allegros. In the *Emperor*, Roll adopts a daringly wide dynamic range, with pianissimos that hold the ear on a thread. Another outstanding pianist, Howard Shelley, draws from the RPO playing comparably incisive and intense. Full, transparent recording.

Piano concertos Nos. 2 in B flat, Op. 19; 3 in C min., Op. 37.
(BB) *** Tring Dig. TRP 076 [id.]. Michael Roll, RPO, Howard Shelley.

Michael Roll's excellent super-bargain disc, offers bright, fresh, spontaneous-sounding performances of Nos. 2 and 3, recorded in full and warm digital sound. The orchestral playing under a fine pianist-turned-conductor is equally compelling.

Piano concertos Nos. 2; 4.
(M) *** Sony SBK 48165 [id.]. Fleisher, Cleveland O, Szell.

Leon Fleisher, partnered by George Szell, is both powerful and intense in his spontaneous-sounding performance of No. 2, giving weight to early Beethoven. In No. 4 Fleisher and Szell are even more searching, with the soloist's refreshingly imaginative playing matched by glorious sounds from the Cleveland Orchestra. The bright, forward recordings have satisfying fullness and body.

Piano concertos Nos. 2 in B flat, Op. 19; 4 in G, Op. 58 (with the composer's final revisions).
*** Conifer Dig. 75605 51237-2 [id.]. Mikhail Kazakevich, ECO, Mackerras.

Kazakevich uses an edition prepared by Dr Barry Cooper (the scholar who reconstructed the fragmentary *Tenth Symphony* from sketches) which has amendments taken from a score the composer himself used for a public performance of the *Fourth Piano concerto*. The differences are relatively minor, though Beethoven regularly adds sparkling virtuoso figuration. Kazakevich's crisply articulated playing is intensified by the sharply dramatic conducting of Sir Charles Mackerras with the ECO. In the *Second Piano concerto* the amendments come only in the first movement – inked into the autograph too late to be included in the published score – with cuts of ten complete bars, tautening and clarifying the result.

Piano concertos Nos. 3 in C min., Op. 37; 4 in G, Op. 58.
*** DG Dig. 429 749-2 [id.]. Krystian Zimerman, VPO, Bernstein.
*** Sony Dig. SK 39814 [id.]. Murray Perahia, Concg. O, Haitink.
(B) *** Ph. Virtuoso 426 062-2 [(M) id. import]. Stephen Kovacevich, BBC SO, Sir Colin Davis.
*** Ph. Dig. 446 082-2 [id.]. Mitsuko Uchida, Concg. O, Sanderling.

Zimerman finds freshness and poetry in both Nos 3 and 4, very sympathetically accompanied by Bernstein, who exactly matches his soloist in the thoughtful dialogue of the central *Andante* of No. 4. Bright sound that yet does not allow a full pianissimo.

Perahia gives readings that are at once intensely poetic and individual, but also strong, with pointing and shading of passage-work that consistently convey the magic of the moment caught on the wing, helped by fine, spacious and open recorded sound.

The Philips versions of Nos. 3 and 4 from the searching partnership of Kovacevich and Sir Colin

Davis make an excellent bargain alternative to Perahia with well-focused transfers.

Uchida proves a strong interpreter in Beethoven's *C minor Concerto*, understandingly supported by Sanderling. The *Largo*, spaciously presented, has depth and serenity. Uchida's gently persuasive entry in *No. 4* is freely improvisational leading to a reading of the first movement both poetic and strongly held together. With superb Concertgebouw recording this is refreshingly individual with a feeling of live music-making.

(i) *Piano concerto No. 3. Coriolan overture* (with rehearsal sequence).

(N) (B) (***) Naxos mono 8.110804 [id.].(i) Dame Myra Hess; NBC SO, Toscanini (introduced: Ben Grauer) (with WAGNER: *Götterdämmerung: Siegfried's Rhine Journey.* (***))

Despite the dry sound and intrusive spoken introductions, this live recording of a 1946 broadcast offers an outstanding account of the *Third concerto*, with the piano cleanly focused. Dame Myra Hess gives a thrilling performance, one of her very finest on disc, with the outer movements crisply articulated and beautifully sprung at high speed, and the slow movement warmly expressive, bringing out a rare warmth in Toscanini too. *Coriolan* is high-powered, dry and incisive, and the Wagner makes a welcome fill-up.

(i) *Piano concerto No. 3 in C min., Op. 37;* (ii) *Piano trio No. 7 (Archduke), Op. 97.*

(M) (***) Dutton Lab. mono CDLX 7015 [id.]. Solomon; (i) BBC SO, Boult; (ii) Henry Holst, Anthony Pini.

Solomon's 1944 performance is one of the great interpretations of this concerto, with every phrase alive and sharply characterized. Exceptionally, he plays the Clara Schumann cadenza in the first movement. The Dutton CD, vividly transferred, brings another wartime performance, from 1943, of the *Archduke Trio* with Henry Holst and Anthony Pini not quite so inspired alongside Solomon.

Piano concerto No. 4 in G, Op. 58.

✽ (M) ** RCA/Melodiya 74321 40722-2 [id.]. Maria Grinburg, USSR SO, Neeme Järvi (with R. STRAUSS: *Don Juan; Till Eulenspiegel* (*)).

Maria Grinburg, born in 1908, gives a performance of No. 4 of Beethoven *G major Concerto* of unusual depth and beauty, particularly in the slow movement. The sound is flawed – hence the two stars – but artistically this is remarkable. (The Strauss couplings are marvellously played, but the recordings are very coarse.)

Piano concertos Nos. (i) *4 in G, Op. 58;* (ii) *5 in E flat (Emperor).*

(M) *** DG 447 402-2 [id.]. Wilhelm Kempff, BPO, Leitner.

(B) *** DG Classikon 439 483-2; *439 483-4* [(M) id. import]. Pollini, VPO, Boehm.

(BB) *** Belart 450 022-2. Friedrich Gulda, VPO, Horst Stein.

The Kempff/Leitner performances, now reissued in DG's 'Originals' series, bring an outstanding mid-priced recommendation with excellent digital remastering. In the *Fourth Concerto* Kempff's delicacy of fingerwork and his shading of tone-colour are unsurpassed. Though Kempff's version of the *Emperor* is not on an epic scale, his exceptionally wide range of tone and dynamic gives it power in plenty.

This bargain Classikon coupling offers two of the most strikingly individual performances from Pollini's earlier cycle, excellently transferred, with believable piano-timbre and a full orchestral tapestry well focused within the warm ambience of the Grosser Saal of the Vienna Musikverein. After the poised account of the *Fourth Concerto*, the distinction of Pollini's interpretation of the *Emperor* is never in doubt, with the slow movement is elegant and the finale is urgent and energetic.

Excellently recorded by Decca at the beginning of the 1970s, Gulda's performances, using a clean-toned Bösendorfer piano are strong, direct and spontaneous-sounding. No. 4 with its eloquent opening is particularly fine, with a memorable central *Andante*. At super-bargain price warmly recommended.

(i) *Piano concerto No. 4 in G, Op. 58;* (ii) *Triple concerto for violin, cello and piano in C, Op. 56.*

(B) *** Tring Dig. TRP 077 [(M) id.]. (i) Michael Roll; (ii) Jean-Jacques Kantorow, Raphael Wallfisch, Michael Roll; RPO, Howard Shelley.

As in his other Tring recordings of Beethoven concertos, Michael Roll is both dramatic and poetic in the *Fourth Concerto*, springing rhythms infectiously even when he adopts a speed on the fast side. The *Triple concerto* makes an ideal fill-up, with Roll joined by equally inspired partners in Jean-Jacques Kantorow and Raphael Wallfisch. An outstanding bargain.

Piano concerto No. 5 in E flat (Emperor), Op. 73.

*** Ph. (IMS) Dig. 416 215-2 [id.]. Arrau, Dresden State O, Sir Colin Davis.

*** DG (IMS) Dig. 429 748-2 [id.]. Krystian Zimerman, VPO, Bernstein.

*** Sony Dig. SK 42330 [id.]. Perahia, Concg. O, Haitink.

(M) *** RCA 09026 61961-2 [id.]. Van Cliburn, Chicago SO, Reiner – TCHAIKOVSKY: *Piano concerto No. 1.* ***

(i) *Piano concerto No. 5 (Emperor). Piano sonata No. 7 in D, Op. 10/3.*

(***) EMI (SIS) mono CDH7 61005-2 [id.]. Edwin Fischer, (i) with Philh. O, Furtwängler.

Piano concerto No. 5 (Emperor); Piano sonata No. 30 in E, Op. 109.
❀(B) *** Ph. Virtuoso 422 482-2 [(M) id. import]. Stephen Kovacevich, (i) LSO, Sir Colin Davis.

(i) *Piano concerto No. 5 in E flat (Emperor). Overtures: Coriolan, Op. 62; Creatures of Prometheus, Op. 43; Leonora No. 3.*
(M) *** Chandos Dig. CHAN 7028 [id.]. (i) John Lill; CBSO, Walter Weller.

Piano concerto No. 5 in E flat (Emperor); Grosse Fuge in B flat, Op. 133.
(B) *** EMI Eminence Dig. CD-EMX 2184 [id. import]. Stephen Kovacevich, Australian CO.

Kovacevich is unsurpassed as an interpreter of this most magnificent of concertos. His superb account for Philips, now on Virtuoso, has set a model for everyone, and with its late sonata coupling, remains the strongest recommendation, very well transferred. His Eminence version, with the soloist directing from the keyboard, is recognizably from the same inspired artist, though speeds are consistently faster and the manner is sharper and tauter. The piano-sound on the digital recording is brighter, if not so well-balanced. The *Grosse Fugue* on Eminence makes an unusual but apt coupling.

The wonder is that Arrau, for long an inhibited artist in the studio, should in his *Emperor* recording, made when he was over eighty, sound so carefree. There are technical flaws, and the digital recording is rather resonant in bass, but with Sir Colin Davis and the Dresden State Orchestra as electrifying partners, the voltage is even higher than in his earlier versions of the mid-1960s.

Zimerman reserves for the *Emperor* his most powerful playing, and Bernstein sensitively encourages him into spontaneous-sounding expressiveness, turning phrases with consistent imagination.

Perahia's account of the *Emperor*, strong and thoughtful yet with characteristic touches of poetry, rounds off an outstanding cycle of the Beethoven concertos. The approach is spacious, and with Bernard Haitink and the Concertgebouw Orchestra firm, responsive partners, each movement immediately takes wing.

Van Cliburn is intense and exciting in the outer movements, with powerful support from Reiner. It is an individual but satisfying reading, with the slow movement poised in its beauty. The remastered recording sounds very well.

On Chandos John Lill's bold, authoritative Beethoven style brings breadth and majesty to the opening movement, with the slow movement coolly serene and the finale vigorously joyful. Walter Weller's performances of the three overtures are splendidly alive. The CBSO is on top form throughout, and the full, resonant sound is of best Chandos vintage. A good alternative mid-priced choice.

Edwin Fischer's 1951 recording with Furtwängler and the Philharmonia Orchestra is one of the classics of the gramophone, an *Emperor* both imperious and imperial. The *D major Sonata*, recorded in 1954, is not to be missed either, made at Fischer's last recording session.

(i) *Piano concerto No. 5 in E flat (Emperor), Op. 73. 32 Variations on an original theme in C min., WoO 80; 12 Variations on a Russian dance from 'Das Waldmädchen' (Wranitzky), WoO 71; 6 Variations on a Turkish march from 'The Ruins of Athens', Op. 76.*
(B) *** EMI forte (SIS) CZS5 69509-2 (2) [CDFB 69509]. Emil Gilels; (i) Cleveland O, Szell – DVORAK: *Symphony No. 8.* **(*)

Of the many versions of the *Emperor Concerto* available, few are finer than Gilels's, with strength matched by poetry, and with Szell offering the strongest backing. The *C minor Variations* are superbly done, and the other two sets bring the strongest characterized too. Bright, full sound.

(i) *Piano concerto No. 5 (Emperor);* (ii) *Piano concerto in E flat, WoO 4* (arr. & orch. Willy Hess); (iii) *Violin concerto in D, Op. 61;* (iv) *Triple concerto for violin, cello and piano in C, Op. 56.*
(B) **(*) Ph. Duo 442 580-2 (2) [id.]. (i) Kovacevich, LSO, Sir Colin Davis; (ii) Lidia Grychtolowna, Folkwang CO, Heinz Dressel; (iii) Herman Krebbers, Concg. O, Haitink; (iv) Szeryng, Starker, Arrau, New Philh. O, Inbal.

Kovacevich's superb 1969 account of the *Emperor* is here part of an attractive Duo compilation which includes also the early *E flat Piano concerto* (WoO 4) which the composer wrote when he was only fourteen, here offered in a spirited performance in a reconstruction by Willy Hess. Krebbers's 1974 recording of the *Violin concerto* is outstanding. In his hands the slow movement has a tender simplicity which is irresistible. The companion account of the *Triple Concerto* with Arrau, Szeryng and Starker is less strongly projected, at very unhurried tempi losing concentration. Yet at 'two CDs for the price of one' the set remains highly recommendable.

(i) *Piano concerto No. 5 (Emperor)*; (ii) *Violin concerto* (iii) *Romances Nos. 1–2, Opp. 40 & 50*; (iv) *Triple concerto for piano, violin & cello, Op. 56.*
(N) (B) *** DG Double 459 403-2 (2) [id.]. (i) Kempff, BPO, Leitner; (ii) Schneiderhan, BPO, Jochum; (iii) D. Oistrakh, RPO, Goossens; (iv) Anda, Schneiderhan, Fournier, Berlin RSO, Fricsay.

These performances, all from the early 1960s, have stood the test of time. If Kempff's *Emperor* is not as imposing as some, its authority is in no doubt; strength there is in plenty and excitement too, while the slow movement brings a characteristic communication of combined repose and concentration. David Oistrakh's accounts of the two *Romances* are notable for their poise. Schneiderhan's classical serenity in the *Violin concerto* brings a reading of great intensity and beauty (see below) and he also contributes to a generally impressive account of the *Triple concerto* which is better balanced and integrated than many versions. The performance has breadth and a genuine sense of structure, with a fine contribution from all three soloists. Only in the first movement does one sense a slight want of spontaneity, but in all other respects it is very satisfactory, although the actual sound is a little dated. The transfers, however, are all of high quality, especially the *Emperor*.

(i) *Piano concerto No. 5 in E flat (Emperor);* (ii) *Triple concerto for violin, cello and piano in C, Op. 56.*

(M) *** Sony SBK 46549 [id.]. (i) Leon Fleisher, Cleveland O, Szell; (ii) Stern, Rose, Istomin, Phd. O, Ormandy.

Leon Fleisher, who worked with Szell with special understanding, gives a reading of the *Emperor* impressive for its dramatic vigour. Stern, Rose and Istomin make an inspired trio of soloists in the *Triple concerto*, sadly marred by by their close balance.

Piano concerto No. 5 (Emperor); (i) *Choral Fantasia, Op. 80.*

**(*) DG Dig. 447 771-2 [id.]. Robert Levin (fortepiano), ORR, Gardiner; (i) with Monteverdi Ch.

Gardiner here follows up his Beethoven symphony cycle in a concerto series, with Robert Levin as soloist, the fortepianist who earlier recorded Mozart concertos with Christopher Hogwood for Oiseau-Lyre. When Gardiner's orchestra is fuller-bodied than those on rival versions, the discrepancy with the solo fortpiano is underlined, and the 1812 instrument chosen is disconcertingly twangy at the top. Speeds are midway between Tan (faster) and Lubin (slower), with the finale given an exhilarating performance. The performance of the *Choral Fantasy* too has fine panache, treating the variations with wit. Gardiner crowns the piece with a superb choral section. As a supplement, Levin offers on separate tracks two alternative improvisations of his own, easily interchangeable with the one Beethoven published years after the first performance.

Violin concerto in D, Op. 61.

(N) (M) *** EMI Dig. CDM5 66900-2 [CDM 66952]. Perlman, Philh. O, Giulini.

✿ (M) *** DG 447 403-2 [id.]. Schneiderhan, BPO, Jochum – MOZART: *Violin concerto No. 5.* ***

*** EMI Dig. CDC7 54072-2 [id.]. Kyung-Wha Chung, Concg. O, Tennstedt – BRUCH: *Violin concerto No. 1.* ***

✿ (B) (***) Dutton Lab. mono CDEA 5018 [(M) id. import]. Georg Kulenkampff, BPO, Hans Schmidt-Isserstedt (with MOZART: *Adagio* from *Violin concerto in A, K.219* (***)); SCHUMANN: *Violin concerto.* ***

(N) (M) (***) EMI mono CDM5 66975-2 [CDM 66902]. Lord Menuhin, Philh. O, Furtwängler – MENDELSSOHN: *Violin concerto.* (***)

(B) *** DG Double 453 142-2 (2) [id.]. Pinchas Zukerman, Chicago SO, Barenboim – BRAHMS: *Concerto* **(*); MENDELSSOHN; TCHAIKOVSKY: *Concertos.* ***

(M) *** RCA 09026 61742-2 [id.]. Heifetz, Boston SO, Munch – BRAHMS: *Concerto.* ***

(N) (M) *** RCA 09026 68980-2 [id.]. Heifetz, Boston SO, Munch – MENDELSSOHN: *Violin concerto.* ***

(N) *** Sony Dig. SK 60584 [id.]. Hilary Hahn, Baltimore SO, David Zinman – BERNSTEIN: *Serenade.* ***

(*) EMI Dig. CDC7 54574-2 [id.]. Kennedy, N. German RSO, Tennstedt (with BACH: (Unaccompanied) *Violin Sonatas* and *Partitas* *).

(BB) *** Belart 461 355-2 [(M) id. import]. Campoli, LPO, Krips – MENDELSSOHN: *Violin concerto.* ***

(N) (BB) **(*) Virgin Classics Dig. Double VBD5 61504-2 [CDVB 61504] (2) Mayumi Seiler, City of L. Sinf., Hickox – HAYDN; MENDELSSOHN: *Concertos.* **(*)

(***) APR Signature mono APR 5506 [id.]. Bronislaw Huberman, VPO, Szell – LALO: *Symphonie espagnole.* (**(*))

(**(*)) Testament mono SBT 1083. Ida Haendel, Philh. O, Kubelik – BRUCH: *Violin concerto No. 1.* (**(*))

(M) ** Decca Dig. 460 014-2 [id.]. Kyung-Wha Chung, VPO, Kondrashin – WALTON: *Violin concerto.* ***

(i) *Violin concerto in D;* (ii) *Romances Nos. 1 in G, Op. 40; 2 in F, Op. 50.*

✿ *** Teldec/Warner Dig. 9031 74881-2 [id.]. Kremer, COE, Harnoncourt.

*** EMI Dig. CDC7 49567-2 [id.]. Perlman, BPO, Barenboim.

(N)(***) Testament mono SBT 1109 [id.]. Lord Menuhin; (i) Lucerne Festival O; (ii) Philh. O, Furtwängler.

(B) *** Ph. Virtuoso 420 348-2 [(M) id. import]. Arthur Grumiaux; (i) Concg. O, Sir Colin Davis; (ii) New Philh. O, Edo de Waart.

(BB) *** Naxos Dig. 8.550149; *4550149* [id.].

Takako Nishizaki, Slovak PO (Bratislava), Kenneth Jean.

(B) **(*) [EMI Red Line Dig. CDR5 69787]. Zimmermann, ECO, Tate.

Gidon Kremer's Teldec account of Beethoven's *Violin concerto* was taken from performances with Nikolaus Harnoncourt and the COE in Graz in July 1992, and offers one of his most commanding recordings, both polished and full of flair, with tone ravishingly pure. The controversial point is the cadenza in the first movement. It is described as by 'Beethoven/Kremer', for (like Wolfgang Schneiderhan in his classic DG recording) he uses a transcription of the big cadenza which Beethoven wrote for his piano arrangement of the work, but with added piano as well as timpani. He also plays violin versions of the other cadenzas and flourishes that punctuate Beethoven's piano version. One of the most refreshing versions of the concerto ever put on disc, backed up by crisp, unsentimental readings of the two *Romances*.

Perlman's outstanding first digital recording of Beethoven's *Violin concerto* is rightly reissued as one of EMI's 'Great recordings of the Century'. This is the finest of his two EMI versions. The violin emerges in the first movement almost imperceptibly, rising gently from the orchestra, but there and throughout the performance the element of slight understatement, the refusal to adopt too romantically expressive a style, makes for a compelling strength perfectly matched by Giulini's thoughtful, direct accompaniment. Steadiness of pulse is a hallmark of this version, but there is never a feeling of rigidity, and the lyrical power of the music-making is a vital element. The beautiful slow movement has a quality of gentle rapture, almost matching Schneiderhan's sense of stillness; and the finale, joyfully and exuberantly fast, is charged with the fullest excitement. The digital recording is satisfyingly full and spacious, yet admirably clear and the current remastering adds extra presence and refines detail, though emphasizing the forward balance of the soloist.

Wolfgang Schneiderhan's stereo version of the *Violin concerto* is among the greatest recordings of this work: the serene spiritual beauty of the slow movement has never been surpassed on record. Schneiderhan uses cadenzas transcribed from Beethoven's piano version of the concerto. In DG's 'Legendary recordings' series, the transfer of the well-balanced 1962 recording is fresh and realistic. The Mozart coupling is apt and generous.

Kulenkampff, born in 1899, recorded the Beethoven *Violin concerto* in 1936. In the days of 78-r.p.m. discs it was a sign of the gramophone connnoisseur to prefer the Kulenkampff Telefunken set to such popular versions as Heifetz's or Kreisler's. Kulenkampff brought thoughtfulness and relaxation to his spontaneous-sounding performance. There is a radiance that casts a strong spell: rarely has the slow movement been given a greater sense of repose.

Recorded only months before the conductor's death, Menuhin's version with Furtwängler is another classic which emerges with extraordinary freshness in the latest transfer, a companion issue for the Perlman CD in EMI's 'Great recordings of the Century' series. Here the bond between the conductor and his younger soloist brought an extra intensity to a natural musical alliance between two inspirational artists, both at their peak. Rarely has the Beethoven *concerto* been recorded with such sweetness and such tenderness, yet with firm underlying strength. With its distinguished coupling it is a compact disc which defies the years. One hardly registers that it is a mono recording.

Kyung-Wha Chung's EMI performance, recorded live in the Concertgebouw, is searching and intense. Next to Perlman on another live recording from EMI, Chung is lighter and more mercurial. The element of vulnerability adds to the emotional weight, above all in the wistfully tender slow movement, while the outer movements are full of flair. The recording is full and atmospheric.

Testament here offers a legendary recording that has been buried for almost fifty years. Recorded in August 1947, this was Menuhin's first version of the Beethoven concerto and his first inspired collaboration with Furtwängler. The visionary spaciousness of the reading defied the fashion of the time for a brisk approach (largely prompted by Heifetz and Toscanini). Five years later Menuhin and Furtwängler made their definitive LP recording (now also reissued), but here, there is extra poetry and tenderness, particularly in the slow movement, and the CD transfer is first-rate.

Grumiaux's beautiful account is both classical and deeply felt. Warmly recorded, this bargain disc stands high in the list of versions. The *Romances*, too, are most persusive. The *Concerto*, together with the *F major Romance*, is also available on a Duo issue, with the concertos of Brahms, Mendelssohn and Tchaikovsky (442 287-2).

Those looking for a super-bargain, digital version will find that Nishizaki's spontaneous performance is a match for many by more famous names. With excellent backing from the Slovak Philharmonic under Kenneth Jean, her playing is individual yet unselfconscious. The *Larghetto* is poised and serene, and the finale buoyant. The two *Romances* are also very well played. The digital recording is excellent with resonant, spacious orchestral sound.

Oddly, Zukerman's 1977 recording of the Beethoven *Violin concerto* comes on a DG Double with three key recordings by Milstein. With Barenboim Zukerman gives a spacious and concentratedly persuasive account of the first movement. The slow movement is rapt in both its simplicity. For anyone wanting these four key concertos this is an excellent recommendation.

Heifetz's unique coupling of the Beethoven and Brahms *Concertos* on a single disc is made possible by his refusal to linger. RCA's digital transfer of a recording originally made in the very earliest days of stereo has a fine sense of realism and presence, with the soloist only a little closer than is natural. The extra immediacy of CD reinforces the supreme mastery of a performance which may adopt fast speeds but never sounds rushed.

As can be seen, Heifetz's famous recording has now additionally been reissued, coupled with the Mendelssohn *concerto*. The remastering is if anything smoother and fuller than ever.

With pure, refined tone, Hilary Hahn gives a dedicated performance of the Beethoven, which belies her age in its depth of perception. The long first movement has sinew in the control of tension, with the poetry of the work never underplayed but without self-indulgence. The hushed beauty of the central *Larghetto* – taken on the slow side – leads on to a clean-cut, athletic account of the finale. Recommended to anyone who fancies the imaginative coupling. Clear, well-balanced sound.

Nigel Kennedy's version was recorded live at a single performance in Lubeck, presented complete with encores (movements from the solo Bach *Sonatas* and *Partitas*). The snag is that tuning up and applause have also been included. Like his interpretation of the Brahms, Kennedy's reading is wilfully slow but is always persuasive, even when, after the big Kreisler cadenza in the first movement, he and Tennstedt threaten to come to a dead halt. The cadenza in the finale brings the most controversial point: Kennedy's improvisation which lapses into quarter-tones. Whatever the hype, Kennedy still produces much magical playing.

Campoli's early stereo Decca version has an appealing, freshly spontaneous lyricism, and the slow movement has depth and a simple poetry. Krips is in obvious sympathy with his soloist, and the orchestra displays a pleasingly light touch in the finale. This Belart reissue is even more notable for the captivating Mendelssohn coupling. A splendid bargain.

Zimmermann's account is restrained and classically pure and fresh. Tate supports him with a chamber orchestra, offering clarity of detail. The slow movement is serene if without much intensity. The two *Romances* are nicely judged.

An impressive account of the *concerto* from Mayumi Seiler which stands up well against distinguished bargain-priced competition. Hickox is slightly below his finest form and is a bit stiff in the opening of the first movement, but his soloist soars lyrically and is movingly serene in the slow movement, creating an ethereal thread of sound for the secondary theme; she then dances away in the finale, even though the tempo is not brisk. Max Rostal's cadenzas are used, which include the timpani parts used in Beethoven's transcription of the work for piano and orchestra. The sound is good and the couplings include two concertos each by Haydn and Mendelssohn, all offered for the cost of a single medium-priced CD!

Huberman's 1934 performance is another classic version, raptly intense – as in a magical opening to the first-movement coda – but taken at speeds that flow easily, far faster overall than is now the rule. The APR transfer is first rate, with the violin immediate and full of presence. The Lalo (minus its central intermezzo), recorded with the same conductor and orchestra, makes an apt coupling.

Ida Haendel's 1951 recording originally appeared on 11 sides of short-playing 78-r.p.m. discs and was never issued on LP in Britain. This is an exceptionally powerful reading, commanding and concentrated even at spacious speeds. In a transfer of Testament's highest standard, it makes a welcome, if relatively expensive, reissue, coupled with an outstanding account of the Bruch concerto.

Kyung Wha Chung's 1979 Decca performance is superseded by her later, full-priced, EMI version with Tennstedt (CDC7 54072-2), for the earlier account, measured and thoughtful, lacks the compulsion thanks to prosaic conducting of Kondrashin. The odd Walton coupling is welcome, when it offers one of her very finest performances, otherwise unavailable.

(i) *Violin concerto in D, Op. 61;* (ii) *Triple concerto in C, Op. 56.*

(M) **(*) Sony Stern Edition I SM2K 66941 (2) [id.]. Isaac Stern, with (i) NYPO, Barenboim; (ii) Leonard Rose, Eugene Istomin, Phd. O, Ormandy – BRAHMS: *Concertos*. ***

Stern's recording of the *Violin concerto* with Barenboim, dates from 1975, not as imaginative as his earlier one with Bernstein. Stern is less spontaneous-sounding than in his earlier version, though the sound is fuller. The *Triple concerto*, recorded a decade earlier in 1964, brings a recording from three friends who reveal their personal joy in making music together, though the soloists are balanced too close.

Triple concerto for violin, cello and piano in C, Op. 56.

(N) (M) *** EMI CDM5 66902-2 [CDM 66954]. D. Oistrakh, Rostropovich, S. Richter, BPO, Karajan – BRAHMS: *Double concerto*. ***

(N) *** RCA Dig. 09026 68964-2 [id.]. John Browning, Pinchas Zukerman, Ralph Kirshbaum, LSO, Eschenbach – BRAHMS: *Double concerto*. ***

(B) *** EMI forte CZS5 69331-2 (2) [id.]. David Oistrakh, Lev Oborin, Sviatoslav Knushevitzky, Philh. O, Sargent – BRAHMS:

Double concerto; MOZART: *Violin concerto No. 3;* PROKOFIEV: *Violin concerto No. 2.* ***
(BB) *** CfP Silver Double Dig. CDCFPSD 4775 (2). Zimmermann, Cohen, Manz, ECO, Saraste – DVORAK: *Cello concerto;* ELGAR: *Cello concerto;* TCHAIKOVSKY: *Variations on a rococo theme.* ***
(B) *** Carlton IMP Classics Dig. 30367 0091-2 [id.]. Trio Zingara, ECO, Heath – BOCCHERINI: *Concerto No. 7.* ***

(i) *Triple concerto, Op. 56. Overtures: King Stephen, Op. 117; Leonora No. 3, Op. 72b; The Ruins of Athens, Op. 113.*
(M) **(*) DG 447 907-2 [id.]. (i) Mutter, Ma, Zeltser; BPO, Karajan.

(i) *Triple concerto, Op. 56;* (ii) *Symphony No. 10: First movement* (realized & completed Cooper).
(M) *** Chandos Dig. CHAN 6501 [id.]. (i) Kalichstein–Laredo–Robinson Trio, ECO, Gibson; (ii) CBSO, Weller.

The star-studded cast on the EMI recording makes a breathtaking line-up led by David Oistrakh. This is warm, expansive music-making that confirms even more clearly than before the strength of the piece. The resonant recording suffers from loss of focus in some climaxes, but this is not too serious. The new transfer is remarkably vivid and has firmed up the orchestral tuttis most satisfactorily. Now coupled in EMI's 'Great recordings of the century' with a similarly commanding account of the Brahms *Double concerto*, this is an irresistible mid-priced bargain.

With Eschenbach a sympathetic, relaxed accompanist, the three distinguished American artists form a winning team in the *Triple concerto*, particularly impressive in the central Largo, where Kirshbaum's opening cello solo is most subtly shaped from its hushed start. The finale is then light and sparkling. A good recommendation for anyone wanting a first-class recently recorded version of this apt and generous coupling with the Brahms.

On Carlton, Felix Schmidt, who is also the cello soloist in the Boccherini, plays with consistently beautiful, firm and clean tone, well matched by his two partners, creating the illusion of live performance, full of bounce and vigour. Sir Edward Heath is the understanding conductor. At bargain price, in full and vivid digital sound, it makes an excellent recommendation.

The earlier EMI recording, also featuring distinguished Russian soloists, dates from the early days of stereo, yet the sound is excellent for its period, the balance one of the most successful this concerto has received even now. Sargent does not direct with Karajan's flair, but he is authoritative, and his soloists make a good team. On EMI's two-for-the-price of one Forte label, this collection is highly recommendable.

On Classics for Pleasure, with first-rate modern digital recording and with Robert Cohen leading an excellent team of prize-winning young soloists (his solo in the slow movement is superb), this makes an outstanding bargain version, keenly competitive. Jukka-Pekka Saraste and the ECO provide a lively, understanding accompaniment and the performance has splendid spontaneity throughout, with the finale sparkling. Coupled with three outstanding performances by Cohen, this is among the finest of these very economically priced Silver Doubles.

The 1984 Chandos version of the *Triple concerto* with three young American soloists is exceptionally well recorded. Sharon Robinson, the cellist, takes the lead with pure tone and fine intonation, though both her partners are more forceful artists. A clean-cut, often refreshing view of the work, it is now reissued coupled with Weller's strong version of Barry Cooper's completion of the first movement of Beethoven's projected *Tenth Symphony*, also very well recorded.

After Karajan's very positive opening tutti, the soloists seem rather small-scale, but each of the young players makes a positive contribution. Yo-Yo Ma's playing is not immaculate, but his natural expressiveness makes for an enjoyable version, well recorded. The overtures bring superlative playing from the Berlin Philharmonic.

(i) *Triple concerto in C for violin, cello & piano. Piano concerto in D* (arr. from *Violin concerto*), *Op. 61a.*
(N) (BB) *** Naxos Dig. 8.554288 [id.]. Jenö Jandó; (i) with Dong-Suk Kang, Maria Kliegel; Nicolaus Esterházy O, Drahos.

Very well recorded in clear, immediate sound, the Naxos version of the *Triple concerto* rivals any in the catalogue, with three characterful, well-contrasted soloists. This partnership of Dong-Suk Kang, Maria Kliegel and Jenö Jandó may not be familiar, but it is none the less formidable. All three are accomplished soloists and are so good that it seems invidious to single any of them out. Bela Drahos draws clean-cut, consistently alert playing from the orchestra, more crisply detailed than in most versions. Beethoven's piano version of the *Violin concerto* makes an apt and exceptionally generous coupling. Jenö Jandó uses his artistry to minimize any ungainliness in the piano-writing, articulating as cleanly and crisply as he does in the *Triple concerto*. No less an authority on this repertoire, H. C. Robbins Landon chose this as his record of the year in the 1998 *BBC Music Magazine*.

(i; ii; iii) *Triple concerto for piano, violin, cello and orchestra in C, Op. 56*; (ii) *2 Romances for violin and orchestra, Opp. 40 & 50*; (i; iv) *Romance cantabile for piano, flute and bassoon with 2 oboes and strings in E min.*
(N) **(*) DG Dig. 453 488-2 [id.]. (i) Myung-Whun Chung, (ii) Kyung-Wha Chung,

(iii) Myung-Wha Chung; (iv) Patrick Gallois, Pascal Gallois; Philh. O, Myung-Whun Chung.

The Chungs make a characterful trio and give a very fine account of the *Triple concerto* that has much going for it – not least the natural, vibrant recording, even if Myung-Whun's piano seems to be in a slightly different acoustic from the others. This conveys a feeling of spontaneous chamber-playing, with the finale taken thrillingly fast, with sparkling results. However, when great performances from the 1960s come with other major Beethoven works – the two *Romances*, beautifully played though they are, and the short, insignificant *E minor* fragment completed by Willy Hess do not enhance the competitiveness of what is after all a premium-priced disc.

(i) *Triple concerto, Op. 56;* (ii) *Choral Fantasia* (for piano, chorus & orchestra), *Op. 80.*
*** EMI Dig. CDC5 55516-2 [id.]. Barenboim; (i) Perlman; Ma; (ii) German Op. Ch.; BPO, Barenboim.
*** Ph. Dig. 438 005-2 [id.]. (i) Beaux Arts Trio; (ii) Menahem Pressler, Mid-German R. Ch.; Leipzig GO, Masur.

With such starry soloists as Perlman, Ma and Barenboim it is not surprising that these are strongly characterized, spontaneous-sounding performances. Here are great musicians who challenge and respond to one another, phrase by phrase, just as Oistrakh, Rostropovich and Richter did (with Karajan conducting) on an earlier EMI recording. Barenboim as conductor here keeps tension taut, as soloist conveying in the opening cadenza of the *Choral Fantasia* the impression of a Beethovenian improvisation.

Not only does Menahem Pressler's playing in the later Beaux Arts recording of the *Triple concerto* with Masur sparkle brightly, he is an inspired soloist in the *Choral Fantasia*. He sets a pattern of joyfulness, taking the work less seriously than usual, with witty pointing of the variations.

12 Contredanses, WoO 14; 12 German dances, WoO 8; 12 Minuets, WoO 7; 11 Mödlinger dances, WoO 17.
(BB) *** Naxos 8.550433 [id.]. Capella Istropolitana, Oliver Dohnányi.

It is always a delight to catch Beethoven relaxing and showing how warmly he felt towards the Viennese background in which he lived. The excellent Capella Istropolitana group used for the recording is of exactly the right size, and they play the music with light rhythmic feeling, with plenty of spirit.

The Creatures of Prometheus: Overture and ballet music, Op. 43 (complete).
*** Hyperion Dig CDA 66748 [id.]. SCO, Sir Charles Mackerras.
(M) *** DG Dig. 447 911-2 [id.]. Orpheus CO.
(BB) *** Naxos Dig. 8.553404 [id.]. Melbourne SO, Michael Halász.

The eighteen numbers of Beethoven's early ballet about Prometheus, the bringer of fire, are recorded all too rarely. Here in fresh, vigorous performances Sir Charles Mackerras and the Scottish Chamber Orchestra bring out not only the drama of the piece but the colourful qualities which made Beethoven a great composer of light music. The ballet ends with the number that gave him one of his most fruitful themes, used for the finale of the *Eroica Symphony*. Highly recommended.

The talented conductorless Orpheus Chamber Orchestra plays most stylishly, helped by bright, clean recording, a highly recommendable alternative.

The Naxos issue provides an excellent version at bargain price of Beethoven's bright and original score. The playing is neat and fresh with rhythms well pointed. Though the string sound is at times a little cloudy, such dramatic passages as the military trumpets and timpani of the *Allegro con brio* (No. 8) are very well caught, bringing out the panache of the playing. In the big *Adagio* (No. 5) the important cello solo confirms the quality of the Melbourne players.

OVERTURES

Overtures: The Consecration of the house, Op. 124; Coriolan, Op. 62; The Creatures of Prometheus, Op. 43; Egmont, Op. 84; Fidelio, Op. 72c; King Stephen, Op. 117; Leonora Nos. 1–3, Opp. 138; 72a; 72b; The Ruins of Athens, Op. 113; Zur Namensfeier, Op. 115.
(M) *** DG (IMS) 427 256-2 (2) [id.]. BPO, Karajan.

Karajan's set of overtures, recorded in the 1960s, bring impressive performances that have stood the test of time, with a command of structure and detail as well as the virtuosity one expects from the Berlin Philharmonic. The sound is fresh and bright.

(i) Overtures: *The Consecration of the house, Op. 124; Coriolan, Op. 62; The Creatures of Prometheus, Op. 43; Egmont, Op. 84; Fidelio, Op. 72c; King Stephen, Op. 117; Leonora Nos. 1–3, Opp. 138, 72 a–b; The Ruins of Athens, Op. 113; Zur Namensfeier, Op. 115;* (ii) *12 Contredanses, WoO 14; 12 German dances, WoO 8; 12 Minuets, WoO 7.*
(B) *** Ph. Duo 438 706-2 (2) [id.]. (i) Leipzig GO, Masur; (ii) ASMF, Marriner.

Masur's performances of the *Overtures* are more direct than those of Karajan, satisfying in thir lack of mannerism. The Philips recording from the early 1970s is of high quality, and the remastering has enhanced its vividness and impact. To complete the second CD, Marriner and the Academy offer a splendid foil with the dance music. Even as a composer of light music Beethoven was a master.

Overtures: The Consecration of the house, Op. 124; Coriolan, Op. 62; The Creatures of Prometheus, Op. 43; Egmont, Op. 84; Fidelio, Op. 72c; King Stephen, Op. 117; Leonora No. 2, Op. 72a; The Ruins of Athens, Op. 113.
**(*) Nimbus NI 5205 [id.]. Hanover Band, Roy Goodman or Monica Huggett.

Recorded at various periods in conjunction with the Hanover Band's other Beethoven recordings for Nimbus, this compilation makes a generous and attractive collection. Anyone who wants the principal Beethoven overtures played on period instruments will be well pleased.

Overtures: *Coriolan; Creatures of Prometheus; Egmont; Fidelio; Leonora No. 1; Leonora No. 3; The Ruins of Athens.*
(BB) *** RCA Navigator 74321 21281-2. Bamberg SO, Eugen Jochum.

Jochum presents a superb collection of overtures, naturally spontaneous and full of warmth and drama. The finest performance is of *Leonora No. 3*, making a thrilling end to the programme. The Bamberg Symphony Orchestra are in excellent form and the recording has a full, spacious acoustic.

Overtures: *Coriolan, Op. 62; Leonore No. 2, Op. 72.*
(M) (***) EMI mono CHS5 65513-2 (3) [id.]. BPO or VPO, Furtwängler – BRAHMS: *Symphonies Nos. 1–4* etc. (**(*))

These studio recordings of Beethoven overtures, the one from Vienna in 1947, the other from Berlin in 1954, make a fine supplement to Furtwängler's Brahms cycle, with Vienna mellower-sounding than Berlin

SYMPHONIES

Symphonies Nos. 1–9.
(N) ❁ (BB) *** Arte Nova Dig. 74321 65410-2 (5) [id.]. Zurich Tonhalle O, David Zinman (with Ruth Ziesak, Birgit Remmert, Steve Davislim, Detlef Roth, Swiss Chamber Ch. in No. 9).

David Zinman's achievement with the Zurich Tonhalle Orchestra is all the more impressive when his Beethoven cycle is considered as whole. Even more so than Sir Charles Mackerras on Eminence, he has learnt from the example of period performance and has consistently presented performances of all the symphonies, early and late, which have a transparency not usually achieved with modern instruments, helped by the clear, fresh acoustic of the Zurich hall. There is an important advantage too that this is the first modern-instrument cycle to use the new edition prepared by Jonathan Del Mar, with important modifications in the text. Zinman also allows a degree of ornamentation beyond convention. What matters above all is that not only are the performances electrifying, with the players responding to the challenge of fast speeds in observance of Beethoven's metronome markings, there is a refinement and tenderness in slow movements, even in face of fast-flowing tempi. The sound is vivid and beautifully balanced, making this a front runner among recommendations for cycles using modern instruments. Apart from Mackerras, who remains very highly recommendable, there are other cycles from the past that have their own special insights to offer, from Klemperer and Bruno Walter (among others), to more recent surveys from John Eliot Gardiner, Harnoncourt and the warmly human approach of the Lord Menuhin. But for collectors coming fresh to Beethoven, or for those wanting a stimulatingly fresh approach, this inexpensive Arte Nova set is very much worth considering.

Symphonies Nos. 1–9; 10 (realized Dr Barry Cooper): *1st movt.*
(M) *** Chandos CHAN 7042 (5) [id.]. CBSO, Weller (with Barstow, Finnie, Rendall, Tomlinson, CBSO Ch. in *No. 9*).

Symphonies Nos. 1–9.
(B) *** EMI CfP Dig. CDBOXLVB 1 (5) [(M) id.]. RLPO, Sir Charles Mackerras (with Joan Rodgers, Della Jones, Peter Bronder, Bryn Terfel, RLPO Ch. in *No. 9*).
*** DG Dig. 439 900-2 (5) [id.]. ORR, Gardiner (with Orgonasova, Von Otter, Rolfe Johnson, Cachemaille, Monteverdi Ch. in *No. 9*).
(B) *** RCA Dig. 74321 20277-2 (5). N. German RSO, Günter Wand (with Wiens, Hartwig, Lewis, Hermann, combined Ch. from Hamburg State Op. and N. German R. in *No. 9*).
*** Teldec/Warner Dig. 2292 46452-2 (5) [id.]. COE, Harnoncourt (with Margiono, Remmert, Schasching, Holl, Arnold Schoenberg Ch. in *No. 9*).
(B) *** DG 429 036-2 (5) [id.]. BPO, Karajan (with Janowitz, Rössel-Majdan, Kmentt, Berry, V. Singverein in *No. 9*).
**(*) Ph. Dig. 446 067-2 (6) [id.]. Dresden State O, Sir Colin Davis (with Sharon Sweet, Jadwiga Rappé, Paul Frey, Franz Grundheber & Dresden State Op. Ch. in *No. 9*).
**(*) Everest EVC 901014 (5) [id.]. LSO, Krips (with Vyvyan, Verrett, Petrak, Bell, BBC Ch. in *No. 9*).
(M) (**(*)) EMI (SIS) mono CHS7 63606-2 (5) [CDHE 63606]. VPO or Stockholm PO, Furtwängler, (with soloists & Ch. in *No. 9*).

Symphonies Nos. 1–9; Coriolan overture.
(M) *** Carlton IMG Dig. 30368 00025 [id.]. Sinfonia Varsovia, Sir Yehudi Menuhin (with Jean Glennon, Dalia Schaechter, Algirdas

Janutas, Benno Schollum & Lithuanian Kaunas State Ch. in *No. 9*).

Symphonies Nos. 1-9; Overtures: Coriolan; Egmont.

(B) **(*) O-L Dig. 452 551-2 (5) [(M) id. import]. AAM, Hogwood (with Augér, Robbin, Rolfe Johnson, Reinhardt, London Symphony Ch. in *No. 9*).

Symphonies Nos. 1–9; Overtures: Coriolan; Egmont; Fidelio; Leonora No. 3.

** DG Dig. Gold 439 200-2 (6) [id.]. BPO, Karajan (with Perry, Baltsa, Cole, Van Dam, V. Singverein in *No. 9*).

Symphonies Nos. 1–9; Overtures: Egmont; Fidelio; King Stephen.

(M) **(*) Sony SB5K 48396 (5). Cleveland O, George Szell (with Addison, Hobson, Lewis, Bell, Cleveland Ch. in *No. 9*).

(M) **(*) Sony SX5K 64201 (5) [id.]. NYPO, Bernstein (with Arroyo, Sarfaty, de Virgilio, Scott & Juilliard Ch. in *No. 9*).

Symphonies Nos 1–9; Overtures: Coriolan; Egmont; Leonora No. 3.

(B) **(*) Decca 430 792-2 (6) [(M) id. import]. Chicago SO, Solti (with Lorengar, Minton, Burrows, Talvela, Chicago Ch. in *No. 9*).

Symphonies Nos. 1–9; Overtures: Creatures of Prometheus; Egmont; Fidelio.

(BB) *** Royal Classics HR 703732 (5) [(B) id.]. BPO, Cluytens (with Brouwenstijn, Kerstin Meyer, Nicolai Gedda, Frederick Guthrie, St Hedwig's Cathedral Ch. in *No. 9*).

Sir Charles Mackerras's Beethoven cycle is among the most recommendable of all at any price, beautifully recorded and interpretatively refreshing, in a refined way steering a satisfying mid-course between traditional and period performance. So the brass have a satisfying braying roundness and the timpani echo period practice not only in the sharp attack with hard sticks, but also in their prominent balance, as in the finale of No. 5. Speeds are on the fast side, but it is a measure of Mackerras's mastery that rhythms are always beautifully sprung without any hint of breathlessness and with consistently refined detail.

Gardiner's cycle makes a clear first choice for those wanting period performances. With sound that is warm and weighty yet still transparent, it can be recommended strongly to those who would normally opt for modern instruments. These are exhilarating performances which have bite and imagination and a sense of spontaneity. Like others, Gardiner observes Beethoven's own fast metronome markings, but not rigidly, allowing himself expansion in the slow movements of the *Eroica* and the *Ninth*. Significant among Gardiner's many corrections of traditional scores – with Jonathan Del Mar a scholarly helper – is his amendment of the marking for the Turkish March in the finale of the *Ninth*, twice as brisk as Norrington and leading logically into the fugue. The set comes in full, luminous sound, complete on only five discs, with a sixth containing an illustrated talk by Gardiner in three languages.

Yehudi Menuhin's cycle, issued to celebrate his eightieth birthday, represents the refreshing response to Beethoven of a great interpretative musician. As in his recordings of Mozart symphonies with this same orchestra, these are fresh and fiery performances, five of them recorded live, including the *Ninth*. Menuhin uses the chamber scale positively, not only clarifying textures but achieving hushed pianissimos of ravishing beauty, as in the *Allegretto* of the *Seventh* or in the broken close of the *Eroica* funeral march. The *Ninth*, often a disappointment in complete cycles, here brings a fitting culmination, thanks to the fresh, clear singing of the Lithuanian choir and a young, lightweight quartet of soloists. With recording that puts a fine bloom on the sound without obscuring detail, this is an excellent set for those wanting dedicated performances on a chamber scale, which yet never underplay the strength and power of these masterpieces.

Wand's digital set with the North German Radio Orchestra, recorded between 1985 and 1988, makes a first-class bargain choice, offering performances without idiosyncrasy yet full of character. In the finale of the *Ninth* the combined choruses of North German Radio and Hamburg State Opera, well-balanced, sing with fervour, with the closing pages bringing a thrilling culmination. RCA have now made Wand's discs available separately at mid-price: *Symphonies Nos. 1* and *6* (74321 20278-2); *Symphonies Nos. 2* and *7* (74321 20279-2); *Symphonies Nos. 3* and *8* (74321 20280-2); *Symphonies Nos. 4–5* (74321 20281-2); *Symphony No. 9* (74321 20282-2).

Reflecting his work as a period-performance pioneer, Harnoncourt makes rhythms light and textures clean, with sparing string vibrato. Periodically, as in the first movement of the *Eroica*, he adopts a hectically fast tempo, but that is the exception. Regularly, his choice of speeds is geared to bringing out the refined expressiveness of this brilliant young orchestra. The *Ninth*, recorded almost a year after the rest, makes a fine culmination, though the dry manner in the great *Adagio*, taken at a flowing speed, underplays the emotional depth. Excellent sound.

Recorded between 1957 and 1960, the Cluytens set offers excellent traditional readings, very well played and recorded in full, open recording. Cluytens's reading of the *Pastoral* has always been highly regarded, but the other performances are comparably impressive, weighty, often at relatively broad speeds, but with resilient rhythms. At super-bargain price an excellent recommendation.

Of Karajan's four recorded cycles, the 1961–2

set is the most compelling, combining high polish with a biting sense of urgency and spontaneity. There is one major disappointment, in the over-taut reading of the *Pastoral*, which in addition omits a vital repeat in the scherzo. Otherwise these are incandescent performances, superbly played. On CD the sound is still excellent. On five CDs at bargain price, this offers outstanding value.

Walter Weller's Beethoven cycle for Chandos is among his finest achievements on record. He draws from the City of Birmingham Symphony Orchestra a warm, refined, Viennese quality, to remind you that this conductor started his career as concertmaster of the Vienna Philharmonic. The Chandos sound is full and glowing to match. Now available at medium price, including Barry Cooper's realization of the *Tenth Symphony*.

While Gardiner remains the prime recommendation for a Beethoven cycle on period instruments, Hogwood's set makes the safest recommendation in the lower-price category. It is vividly recorded, with a keen sense of presence and ample weight in the *Ninth*, with the London Symphony Chorus full and vivid. Hogwood also has the finest quartet of soloists, though in the first movement he is too rigid. His pointing of rhythms is not always as alert or imaginative as that of his direct rivals, but with clean, well-disciplined playing, it is consistently satisfying.

Solti's first cycle with his own Chicago orchestra, has a firm centrality to it, following the outstandingly successful version of the *Ninth* with which he started the series. The performance of the *Eroica* has comparable qualities, with expansive, steady tempi and a dedicated, hushed account of the slow movement. The recordings were made between 1972 and 1974 in three different venues, but the CD transfers bring an admirable consistency, with plenty of weight in the bass balancing the bright top register. At bargain price Solti admirers should not miss this set, particularly as these performances are more satisfying than those in his later, digital series.

As a Beethoven interpreter Krips is in the central tradition, with speeds rather broader than has latterly become the rule. In the *Pastoral* or the *Eighth*, one registers that here is a great Schubertian, for Krips makes the music sing, yet in the great opening movements of the *Eroica* and No. 9, weight and incisiveness go together. He is helped by the sharp focus of the 1960 sound, transferred with fine presence but with an acid edge on high violins. Only No. 5 is a degree disappointing, well shaped and pointed but lacking some of the tensions needed. Not a prime recommendation until the price is reduced.

In opulent sound Sir Colin Davis takes a spacious view of the Beethoven symphonies, drawing beautiful playing from the Dresden State Orchestra. At broad speeds he gives each symphony a concentrated strength, though the grinding dissonances at the heart of the development section in the first movement of the *Eroica* are warm rather than violent. Reflecting the mature responses of a conductor in his late sixties, this is comfortable Beethoven. Anyone wanting a mellow view will be well pleased.

Szell takes a compellingly strong, direct view of Beethoven. The highly polished, keenly responsive Cleveland playing never brings a suspicion of routine, though the close CBS sound-balance irons out pianissimos, even though the ear readily senses when the orchestra is playing gently.

In Karajan's last, digital set, the recording seems to have been affected by the need to make a version on video at the same sessions. The gain is that these performances have keener spontaneity, the loss that they often lack the brilliant, knife-edged precision of ensemble one has come to regard as normal with Karajan. The six discs are now remastered to Digital Gold standards – for comments see the individual issues below – and are offered at a slightly reduced price for the set: six CDs for the price of five.

The *Eroica* in Bernstein's earlier, New York cycle of the Beethoven symphonies was a mould-breaking interpretation, with a fast speed for the first movement made to sound fresh and exhilarating. The other symphonies too are given high-voltage performances, strong and purposeful, if occasionally self-indulgent; but the recordings are relatively coarse and lacking in contrast. The finest performances are of No. 2, electrifying under Bernstein, and No. 8. The *Ninth* has a finely shaped first movement, a very fast Scherzo, a slow movement warm but lack in inwardness, and dramatic finale. The CD transfers make the most of the original masters, but the quality cannot match the later, DG recordings, which are discussed individually below.

By unearthing a live recording of No. 2, made in the Royal Albert Hall in 1948, and borrowing a radio recording of No. 8 made in Stockholm, EMI has put together a complete Furtwängler cycle, and very impressive it is interpretatively. The sound of those two ad hoc recordings may be rough, with heavy background noise, but the performances are electrifying. No. 9 comes in the dedicated performance given at Bayreuth in 1951, but the others are EMI's studio versions, not always as inspired as Furtwängler's live performances but still magnetic and, with well-balanced mono sound, well transferred.

Symphonies Nos. 1 in C, Op. 21; 2 in D, Op. 36; 3 in E flat (Eroica), Op. 55; 8 in F, Op. 93.
(N) (B) *** EMI double fforte Dig. CZS5 73323-2 (2). Concg. O, Sawallisch.

Symphonies Nos. 4 in B flat, Op. 60; 5 in C min., Op. 67; 6 in F (Pastoral), Op. 68; 7 in A, Op. 92.
(N) (B) *** EMI double fforte Dig. CZS5 73326-2 (2). Concg. O, Sawallisch.

Symphony No. 9 in D min. (Choral), Op. 125; (ii) *Piano concerto No. 5 in E flat (Emperor).*
(N) (B) **(*) EMI double fforte Dig. CZS5 73329-2 (2). (i) Price, Lipovsek, Seiffert, Rootering, Düsseldorf Städtischer Musikverein, Concg. O; (ii) Egorov, Philh. O; Sawallisch – MOZART: *Piano concerto No. 20.* **(*)

Much of Sawallisch's Concertgebouw set is greatly admired by R. L. but, as almost always with Beethoven cycles, it has its disappointments and undoubtedly, the first of these three Double forte reissues is the one to go for. Throughout, the orchestral playing is of a high standard and Sawallisch has a fine sense of proportion. The *First Symphony* immediately sounds fresh and vibrant; the *Second* and the *Eighth* receive lovely, alert accounts that give much pleasure, and textures are clean and transparent. The *Eroica* receives a performance of some stature and has great breadth and dignity; the orchestral playing is a joy in itself. However, the mellow acoustic of the Concertgebouw Hall must have encouraged Sawallisch into middle-aged spread for the *Fifth Symphony*. The performance unashamedly adopts old-fashioned manners – notably in a lethargic account of the slow movement – but blazing brass introduces an altogether more electrifying view of the finale. A relaxed view of the *Pastoral* is more sympathetic but, with sound not ideally clear, this performance cannot be recommended without reservations. Sawallisch's version of the *Choral Symphony* was recorded live in the Concertgebouw, taken from three separate performances, but its sense of occasion is surprisingly muted, with little to indicate a live event until the applause at the end. Interpretatively it is a middle-of-the-road reading, with admirably chosen speeds but with playing too relaxed, lacking dramatic tension. Even the finale, with its impressive soloists, is disappointing when the chorus is placed backwardly and the singing lacks sharpness of focus. To fill up the set, Egorov gives a refreshingly direct but still individual account of the *Emperor*, helped by Sawallisch's authoritative conducting. The slow movement is taken at a very measured *Adagio* which might have flowed better had Egorov adopted a more affectionate style of phrasing.

Symphonies Nos. 1–4.
(B) *** Ph. Duo 454 032-2 (2) [id.]. Leipzig GO, Kurt Masur.

Symphonies Nos. 5–8.
(B) ** Ph. Duo 454 035-2 (2) [id.]. Leipzig GO, Masur.

(i) *Symphony No. 9 (Choral);* (ii) *Overtures: Consecration of the house; Fidelio; Leonora Nos. 1–3;* (iii) *Choral Fantasia, Op. 80.*
(B) *(*) Ph. Duo 454 038-2 (2) [id.]. (i) Tomowa-Sintow, Burmeister, Schreier, Adam and Ch.; (i–ii) Leipzig GO, Masur; (iii) Brendel, LPO, Haitink.

Kurt Masur's earlier, analogue Beethoven cycle has much to recommend it in its natural, unforced expressiveness and finely disciplined playing. The *Eroica* is exceptionally fine, particularly its nobly paced slow movement, and the *Fourth Symphony* Masur is marvellously alert. The *Ninth* is spacious and well-proportioned, but not as strongly characterized as many, so that the third of the Duo sets is the least recommendable, despite the inclusion of Haitink's fine account with Brendel of the *Choral Fantasia*.

Symphonies Nos. 1–4; Overture Egmont, Op. 84.
(N) (M) (**(*)) RCA mono 74321 55835-2 (2) [id.]. NBC SO, Toscanini.

Symphonies Nos. 5–8.
(N) (M) (**(*)) RCA mono 74321 55836-2 (2) [id.]. NBC SO, Toscanini.

(i) *Symphony No. 9 (Choral)*; (ii) *Missa solemnis, Op. 123.*
(N) (M) (**(*)) RCA mono 74321 55837-2 (2) [id.]. Merriman, Robert Shaw Ch., NBC SO, Toscanini, with (i) Farrell, Peerce, Scott; (ii) Marshall, Conley, Hines.

The harshness of sound on Toscanini's late recordings has till now defied even the cleverest transfer engineers. But here in completely new transfers you have sound with more body and atmosphere than before, letting one appreciate in relative comfort the unique intensity of Toscanini in Beethoven, even in No. 7 where some harshness remains. Speeds are often hectic, with tensions built up to breaking point, but the thrill of a Toscanini event is consistently caught, particularly in the *Eroica* and in the inspired coupling of the *Ninth Symphony* with the *Missa Solemnis*. The three double-disc boxes, available separately, each come at mid-price.

(i) *Symphonies Nos. 1–9. Overtures: Consecration of the house; Coriolan; Creatures of Prometheus; Egmont; Fidelio; King Stephen; Leonora No. 2; The ruins of Athens;* (ii) *Missa solemnis.*
(BB) **(*) Nimbus Dig. NI 1760 (7) [(B) id.]. Hanover Band, (i) cond. Roy Goodman or Monica Huggett; with Eiddwen Harrhy, Jean Bailey, Andrew Murgatroyd, Michael George, Oslo Cathedral Ch. in *No. 9*; (ii) Marianne Hirsti, Carolyn Watkinson, Murgatroyd, George, Oslo Cathedral Ch., cond. Terje Kvam.

Those wanting period-instrument performances of this repertoire will find these pioneering Hanover Band performances well worth considering, when the Nimbus package is so inexpensive. These are all readings which convey the fire and exuberance of live performance, set in a reverberant acoustic which means that the woodwind sometimes appear disembodied. Monica Huggett directs Nos. 1, 2 and 5; Roy Goodman Nos. 3, 4 and 7–9. In the later recordings Goodman draws consistently fresh, individual readings from his team, with rhythms well sprung in exhilarating *allegros*. Consistently the feeling of spontaneity is most winning. The overtures (also shared by the two conductors) are just as characterful, and it is specially good to have the fresh and gripping account of the *Missa solemnis*, conducted by Terje Kvam, chorus-master of the Oslo Cathedral Choir.

Symphonies Nos. 1–9; Overtures: Consecration of the house; Fidelio.

(N) (M) ** EMI Dig. CMS5 60089-2 [CDCB 60089] (5) [id.]. SW German R SO, Michael Gielen (with Orsanic, Minutillo, Winslade, Titus & Berlin R Ch. in No.9). Available separately: (IMS) 1 & 3 (CDM5 60090-2); 2 & 8 and *Overture Fidelio* (CDM5 60091-2); 4 & 7 (CDM5 60092-2); 5 & 6 (CDM5 60093-2); 9 & *Consecration of the House overture* (CDM5 60094-2).

Very well played and recorded, Michael Gielen's cycle with the South West German Radio Orchestra offers fresh, direct and generally brisk readings, marked by few distracting idiosyncrasies. Intelligent as his approach invariably is, he does not always avoid sounding matter-of-fact, missing the element of mystery and suspense in key passages, even in the *Eroica Funeral march* or the slow movement of the *Ninth*. Excellent singing from choir and soloists in that culminating work. But when compared with the Arte Nova set this is a non-starter.

Symphonies Nos. 1–9; Overtures: Consecration of the House; Fidelio; Leonora No. 3.

(N) (B) ** EMI Dig. CZS5 72923-2 (6) [CDZF 72923]. Phd. O, Muti (with Studer, Ziegler, Seiffert, Morris & Westminster Ch. in No. 9).

With a fiery Italian conductor and a great American orchestra, Muti's set brings obvious echoes of the electric example of Arturo Toscanini in the great days of the NBC Symphony Orchestra. Alas for history, Muti's Beethoven cycle, like Toscanini's, is beset by problems of recorded sound which are serious, if obviously of a less extreme kind. The first version of the *Seventh* which he recorded with the Philadelphia Orchestra is here replaced, but the sound is still harsh and ill focused. Even this version of the *Ninth*, the last of the symphonies to be recorded, has sound almost as opaque as the earliest. Unlike Toscanini, Muti had never conducted the *Ninth* before he prepared his players and singers for this recording. His delay was a measure of the gravity with which he approached the project. This is a very serious *Ninth*; but where one expects a Toscaninian spark from Muti to ignite the music, too much of the performance here is rhythmically square and stolid. Even the sublime slow movement, beautifully played as it is, becomes leaden. However this set is now offered in a box at EMI's bargain-basement price (with a handsome portait of Muti on each of the six cardboard inner-sleeves), and admirers of the conductor may well come to terms with the recording which does not lack fullness.

Symphonies Nos. 1 in C, Op. 21; 3 in E flat (Eroica); 6 in F (Pastoral); 8 in F, Op. 93.

(B) **(*) Decca Double (IMS) 440 627-2 (2) [id.]. VPO, Pierre Monteux.

Symphonies Nos. 2 in D, Op. 36; 4 in B flat, Op. 60; 5 in C min., Op. 67; 7 in A, Op. 92; Overtures: Egmont; King Stephen.

(B) *** Decca Double (IMS) 443 479-2 (2) [id.]. LSO, Pierre Monteux.

Pierre Monteux in his last years recorded these distinguished readings of the first eight Beethoven symphonies, sadly prevented from including the *Ninth*. They are all remarkable for Monteux's imaginative phrasing and glowing treatment of the detail in slow movements. The series is capped by an unforgettable account of the *Seventh Symphony*, which culminates in a headlong, incandescent account of the finale. The Double Decca reissues have been sensibly divided into the performances with the VPO and those with the LSO.

Symphonies Nos. 1 in C, Op. 21; 2 in D, Op. 36.

*** DG Dig. 447 049-2 [id.]. ORR, Gardiner.

(N) (BB) *** Arte Nova Dig. 74321 63645-2 [id.]. Zurich Tonhalle O, David Zinman.

(N) (B) *** Ph. Virtuoso 432 274-2 [id.]. ASMF, Marriner.

**(*) DG Dig. Gold 439 001-2 [id.]. BPO, Karajan.

Symphonies Nos. 1 in C; 2 in D; Overture Coriolan.

(M) *** Bruno Walter Edition: Sony SMK 64460 [id.]. Columbia SO, Bruno Walter.

(i) *Symphonies Nos. 1 in C; 2 in D;* (ii) *Overture: Leonora No. 1.*

(M) *** Sony Dig. SMK 66927 [id.]. (i) ECO, Michael Tilson Thomas, (ii) Bav. RSO, Sir Colin Davis.

Rather than treating the two early symphonies as Mozartian in the way most period performers do, John Eliot Gardiner uses his sonorous but clean-textured forces to bring out the power and revolutionary bite of the young Beethoven, opting for speeds on the fast side. Vivid, immediate sound in both the live recording of No. 1 and the studio one of No. 2.

Using the Bärenreiter scores newly edited by Jonathan Del Mar, David Zinman conducts electrifying performances of the first two symphonies, with a rather smaller band of strings than in later works. With textures transparent and rhythms crisply sprung at generally fast speeds, the results consistently reflect the influence of period performance, providing an excellent halfway house. Fast as the speeds are for the *Andantes* in both symphonies, there is a hushed dedication in Zinman's approach to compel attention. The clean, beautifully balanced recording allows one to hear detail and elaborations that would normally be obscured.

Marriner presents the first two symphonies on modern instruments but on an authentic scale with a Mozart-sized orchestra, and the result is fresh and lithe, with plenty of character but with few, if any, quirks and mannerisms. Nor are the dramatic contrasts underplayed, for the chamber scale is most realistically captured in the fine 1970 analogue recording, admirably remastered. A first-class and highly enjoyable coupling.

Bruno Walter's CBS recordings of the Beethoven symphonies were recorded in 1958/9 in Hollywood in warm, well-balanced sound with the Columbia Symphony, a pick-up orchestra of outstanding musicians. The most controversial point about his interpretation of the *Second Symphony* is the slow movement, which is taken very slowly indeed, with much rubato.

Michael Tilson Thomas offers excellent accounts of the first two symphonies with the ECO, both apt in scale but with no loss of weight because of the reduced number of players. Pacing is admirable, with vigour and urgency never leading to aggressiveness in outer movements. Davis's fine account of *Leonora No. 1*, warmly recorded, is a welcome makeweight.

Karajan's digital Beethoven series brings some surprisingly slack ensemble in the recording of the first two symphonies. The performances are relaxed in good ways too, with Karajan's flair and control of rhythm never leading to breathless speeds.

Symphonies Nos. 1 and 2 (trans. Liszt).
(M) *** Teldec/Warner Dig. 4509 97952-2 [id.]. Cyprien Katsaris (piano).

Transcendental technique and a fine musical intelligence are the distinguishing features of these performances, which remain without peer in the Beethoven–Liszt discography. Well worth having at mid-price.

Symphonies Nos. 1 in C, Op. 21; 2 in D, Op. 36; 3 (Eroica); Overture Coriolan.
(BB) **(*) Carlton LSO Double 30368 001157 (2) [(B) id.]. LSO, Wyn Morris.

This is one of the first of a series of Carlton CD Doubles featuring the LSO. In this instance the conductor is also the same, and the results are undoubtedly stimulating. Wyn Morris draws a clear distinction between the two earliest symphonies: the *First*, brightly paced, resilient and strongly classical in feeling; the *Second* clearly looking forward, leading to a taut reading of the *Eroica*, dark and intense, with allegros consistently urgent, and the LSO responds with both bite and refinement. The *Coriolan overture* is also very successful. Excellent value.

Symphonies Nos. 1 in C; 3 in E flat (Eroica), Op. 55.
(B) *** Carlton IMP Dig. 30367 02382 [(M) id.]. Sinfonia Varsovia, Lord Menuhin.
(B) *** EMI CfP Dig. CD-CFP 6067 [id.]. RLPO, Mackerras.
*** Teldec/Warner Dig. 9031 75708-2 [id.]. COE, Harnoncourt.
(M) **(*) Virgin Veritas/EMI Dig. VM5 61374-2 [CDCFP 61374]. L. Classical Players, Norrington.
(M) (***) RCA mono GD 60252 [60252-2-RG]. NBC SO, Toscanini.

Symphonies Nos. 1 in C, Op. 21; 3 in E flat (Eroica), Op. 55; Fidelio Overture, Op. 72.
(N) (B) (**(*)) Naxos mono 8.110802-3 [id.]. NBC SO, Toscanini.

The one irritant to Menuhin's performances on Carlton is the welcoming applause that comes before the music begins and also at the close of No. 1, but not before the opening of No. 3. Otherwise these highly musical performances, strong but on a convincing chamber scale, are among the most satisfying available, with a dedicated reading of the *Eroica* Funeral March. Warm, well-balanced recording.

Sir Charles Mackerras, as in his other Beethoven readings on the Classics for Pleasure label, seeks to reconcile the new doctrines of period performance with traditional ones. The *First* is fresh and alert in a Haydnesque way, while the *Eroica* has ample power, with heightened dynamic contrasts and with the flowing speed for the *Funeral march* still conveying dedication. First-rate recording.

Harnoncourt's *Eroica* brings an extremely fast tempo in the first movement, and his austere view of the great *Funeral march* is chillingly intense. The result is as individual as it is powerful. No. 1, too, is splendidly alive.

Norrington's Beethoven cycle now reappears on the Virgin label at mid-price. No. 1 lacks the lively energy of the best of the series, but the *Eroica* is one of the most successful performances, exceptionally fast with rhythms well-sprung, yet with natural gravity in the *Funeral march*.

Toscanini's RCA performances convey breathtaking power, notably the magnificent account of the *Eroica*, never comfortable but far from rigid or unloving.

Though the Naxos transfer is variable – with drying-noises in part of the *Eroica* slow movement and, like most of the Naxos historic series, intrusive American radio announcers introducing the performances – Toscanini's 1939 account of the *Eroica* is one of the very greatest ever recorded, incandescent from first to last. The *First Symphony* too has a sparkle missing in later Toscanini.

Symphonies Nos. 1 in C; 4 in B flat, Op. 60; Egmont overture.
(M) *** DG 419 048-2; *419 048-4* [id.]. BPO, Karajan.

Symphonies Nos. 1 in C; 4 in B flat; Overture Leonora No. 1.
(B) (***) Dutton Lab. mono CDEA 5004 [id.]. BBC SO, Toscanini.

Karajan's 1977 version of No. 1 is exciting, polished and elegant; in No. 4 the balance is closer, exposing every flicker of tremolando, helped by recording with fine presence and body.

The Toscanini recordings were made in London's Queen's Hall in 1937 and 1939, and they remain among the most treasurable Beethoven performances in the Toscanini legacy. All the electricity and concentration are here, yet there is a degree of warmth not often present in his NBC records. The sound too is remarkably good, and the Dutton transfers betray the 78 shellac source only with the slight hint of wow on the woodwind.

Symphonies Nos. 1 in C; 6 in F (Pastoral), Op. 68.
(M) *** EMI CDM5 66792-2 [id.]. Philh. O, Klemperer.
(M) **(*) DG 447 901-2 [id.]. VPO, Bernstein.
(BB) **(*) Naxos Dig. 8.553474 [id.]. Nicolaus Esterházy Sinfonia, Béla Drahos.

Symphonies Nos. 1 in C; 6 in F (Pastoral), Op. 68; Overture Egmont, Op. 84.
(B) **(*) Sony SBK 46532; *SBT 46532* [id.]. Cleveland O, Szell.

Though Klemperer's slow speeds and heavyweight manner may seem inappropriate, he gives No. 1 a magnetic performance, and his account of the *Pastoral* is one of the very finest of all his recordings. The Scherzo may be eccentrically slow but, with superbly dancing rhythms, it could not be more bucolic, and it falls naturally into place within the reading as a whole. The exquisitely phrased slow movement and the final *Shepherd's hymn* bring peaks of beauty, made the more intense by the fine, digital transfer, reinforcing the clarity and fullness of the original sound.

Bernstein's cycle of the Beethoven symphonies for DG with the Vienna Philharmonic Orchestra, issued first in 1980, offers live recordings, tactfully edited. Balances are not always perfect, but results are undistracting. In No. 1 the allegros are fast but not hectic, the slow introductions and slow movements carefully moulded but not mannered. In this work the live recording is not ideally clear but is very acceptable. The reading of the *Pastoral* is most characterful, persuasively combining joy and serenity.

In his Beethoven series for Naxos Drahos offers fresh, spontaneous-sounding performances, beautifully played by a chamber-sized group from Budapest, with recording outstandingly vivid. Plainer and less subtle than the finest versions, these lively, well-sprung performances make excellent bargains.

Szell's dynamic performance of the *First Symphony* makes up for any absence of charm. In the *Pastoral* Szell is subtle in his control of phrasing, for all the firmness of his style. However, it is a pity that the close-up sound robs the slow movement of much of its gentleness and delicacy of atmosphere. The finale, by contrast, is attractively relaxed.

Symphonies Nos. 1; 7 in A, Op. 92.
(BB) **(*) ASV CDQS 6066. N. Sinfonia of England, Richard Hickox.

Hickox's view of both works is unaffected and direct, finely detailed yet substantial. The lack of idiosyncrasy makes for easy listening. The CD transfer is full with a resonant bass.

Symphonies Nos. 2 in D, Op. 36; 4 in B flat, Op. 60; Overture Leonora No. 3
(N) (B) (**) Naxos mono 8.110815/6 (2) [id.]. NBC SO, Toscanini; (with broadcast commentaries and interval talk by Samuel Chotzinoff).

Though the sound is often rough and crumbly, and the NBC radio announcements intrusive, it is good to have these CD versions taken from Toscanini's legendary Beethoven cycle of 1939. They represent him at his peak, incandescent and tense – arguably too much so for these symphonies – but less brittle than in his later NBC recordings, issued by RCA.

Symphonies Nos. 2 in D; 5 in C min., Op. 67.
*** Teldec/Warner Dig. 9031 75712-2 [id.]. COE, Harnoncourt.
(M) **(*) DG 447 902-2 [id.]. VPO, Bernstein.
(M) **(*) EMI CDM5 66794-2 [id.]. Philh. O, Klemperer.
(B) **(*) Sony SBK 47651; *SBT 47651* [id.]. Cleveland O, George Szell.
(BB) **(*) Naxos 8.553476 [id.]. Nicolaus Esterházy Sinfonia, Béla Drahos.

Harnoncourt's exuberance does not mean a lack of weight in the *Fifth*. The slow movement is particularly fine and the finale grows seamlessly out of the Scherzo. This Teldec record makes a clear first choice in this coupling. The playing has fine bite and lift, making this a clear first choice for this coupling.

In Bernstein's inspired performance of No. 2 the tension rises superbly at the end of the finale. He seems intent on emphasizing how much bigger a symphony this is than No. 1. For his Vienna version, Bernstein rethought his reading of the *Fifth*, giving it resonance and spaciousness as well as drama. Less tense than before, the warmth and conviction are most persuasive, up to the blazing account of the finale. Good, warm sound.

The new coupling in EMI's 'Klemperer Legacy' series underlines the consistency of Klemperer's approach to Beethoven, with the *Second Symphony*, like the *First*, sounding the more powerful through weighty treatment. Only in the finale is the result too gruff. The *Fifth* is less electric than his earlier, mono version but, with exposition repeats observed in both outer movements, this retains its epic quality. Clean, natural CD transers with ample weight.

With marvellously clean articulation from the strings in the first movement Szell's No. 2 has the adrenalin running free; yet here, as in the similarly brilliant account of No. 5, Szell understands the need to give full scope to the lyrical elements.

With the Esterházy Sinfonia, Béla Drahos on Naxos conducts clean-cut readings of both works, with the excellent, well-balanced recording capturing the chamber scale very effectively. No. 2, less dramatic than some, easy and sweet in the slow movement, leads a youthfully athletic account of the finale. In No. 5 the call of fate at the opening may seem lightweight, with a limited dynamic range there and later, but on a chamber scale this is refreshing in its clarity, easily flowing in the middle movements, taut in the outer movements.

Symphonies Nos. 2 in D, Op. 36; 6 in F (Pastoral).

(B) *** Carlton IMP Dig. 30367 02292 [(M) id.]. Sinfonia Varsovia, Lord Menuhin.

Menuhin's reading of the *Second Symphony* is weighty, mature-sounding, the first movement lacking a little in bite but not buoyancy. The *Larghetto* is nobly phrased, the finale vigorous and high-spirited. Alongside the *Choral Symphony*, Menuhin's performance of the *Pastoral* crowns his cycle. The chamber-scale and the combination of warmth and lightness of touch bring a joyous momentum. The storm bursts in dramatically, and the heartfelt *Shepherds' thanksgiving* brings a lyrical apotheosis. Satisfyingly full sound, with natural brilliance.

Symphonies Nos. 2 in D; 7 in A, Op. 92.

(M) *** DG 419 050-2 [id.]. BPO, Karajan.

In Karajan's *Second*, the firm lines give the necessary strength. The *Seventh* is tense and exciting, with the conductor emphasizing the work's drama rather than its dance-like qualities.

Symphonies Nos. 2; 8 in F, Op. 93.

(B) *** EMI CfP Dig. 6068 [(M) id.]. RLPO, Sir Charles Mackerras

(M) *** Virgin Veritas/EMI Dig. VM5 61375-2 [CDM 61375]. L. Classical Players, Norrington.

(BB) **(*) ASV CDQS 5067 [(M) id. import]. N. Sinfonia, Hickox.

**(*) Sony Dig. SK 48238 [id.]. La Scala PO, Giulini.

Mackerras rounded off his outstanding Beethoven cycle with performances of these two even-numbered works which bring out the dramatic bite in performances at once refined and full of sharp contrasts. In this music Mackerras uses modern instruments while taking account of period practice, with exhilarating results. Recorded sound a degree fuller and more immediate than in the earlier discs of the series.

The coupling of Nos. 2 and 8 was the first of Norrington's Beethoven series and showed the London Classical Players as an authentic group with a distinctive sound, sweeter and truer in the string section than most, generally easier on non-specialist ears. In following Beethoven's own metronome markings for both symphonies the results are exhilarating, never merely breathless.

Richard Hickox directs his chamber-scale orchestra in fresh, warm and relaxed readings of these two even-numbered symphonies. Playing is refined and rhythms resilient. The scale is well established by the slightly backward balance of the modest string section, with the focus sharper in No. 8 than in No. 2.

Spacious readings from Giulini of both symphonies, resulting in a glowing account of No. 2 but one of No. 8 that is strong but lacks mercurial qualities; yet the purposeful strength of this reading remains impressive. Sound in No. 8 is not as full as in No. 2.

Symphony No. 3 in E flat (Eroica), Op. 55.

(M) (***) RCA mono GD 60271 [60271-2-RG]. NBC SO, Toscanini – MOZART: *Symphony No. 40*. (**)

(M) **(*) DG 447 444-2 [id.]. LAPO, Giulini (with SCHUMANN: *Manfred overture* ***).

(N) (B) **(*) Ph. Virtuoso Dig. 410 044-2 [id.]. ASMF, Marriner.

(N) (M) **(*) Sony SMK 60692 [id.] NYPO, Bernstein (with talk by Bernstein).

Symphony No. 3 (Eroica); Grosse Fuge, Op. 133.

✽ (M) *** EMI CDM5 66793-2 [id.]. Philh. O, Klemperer.

Symphony No. 3 (Eroica); Overture Egmont, Op. 84.

**(*) DG Dig. Gold 439 002-2 [id.]. BPO, Karajan.

Symphony No. 3 (Eroica); Overture Fidelio.

(BB) *** Tring TRP 026 [id.]. RPO, Guenther Herbig.

Symphony No. 3 (Eroica); Overture: Leonora No. 3.

(M) **(*) DG 419 049-2 [id.]. BPO, Karajan.

The digital remastering of Klemperer's spacious 1961 version of the *Eroica* weightily reinforces its magnificence, keenly concentrated to sustain speeds slower than in his earlier, mono account. Like his earlier mono version with the Philharmonia this later stereo *Eroica* is one of his supreme achievements. *The Grosse Fuge* has monolithic strength.

Although he does not include the first-movement exposition repeat, Guenther Herbig's 1994 recording of the *Eroica* with the RPO is most compelling, strong, aptly paced and concentrated, with the *Funeral march* conveying deep emotional intensity. With full, brilliant, digital sound, naturally balanced in a concert-hall acoustic, this is highly recommendable in the lowest price-range.

In many respects Sir Neville Marriner's version is outstanding, for although the Academy may use fewer strings, the impression is of weight and strength, coupled with a rare transparency of texture and extraordinary resilience of rhythm. The dance-rhythms of the fast movements are brought out captivatingly with sforzandos made clean and sharp. The *Funeral march* may emerge as less grave and dark than it can be, but Marriner's unforced directness is most compelling and the recorded sound is among the best ever in this symphony. But without a coupling, even at bargain price, its appeal is diminished.

Bernstein's first challenge here is to set what initially seems an impossibly fast opening *Allegro*. The result has a tautness that at least matches Karajan's (though the playing is not quite so polished as that of the Berlin Philharmonic Orchestra) and reminds one of a Toscanini performance. Bernstein takes the exposition repeat, and there is no slackening of tension whatever. The speed for the *Funeral march* is also on the fast side, but in that respect he anticipates modern practice. Even so he takes care – as Toscanini always did – to give the final disintegration of the theme the right pauseful weight and emotional point. The *Scherzo* is slower than usual, almost a jolly country-dance, and the finale shows Bernstein at his most ebullient. The speed again is almost impossibly fast, but the dash and bravura take the listener along magnificently. The 1964 Manhattan Center recording is a bit harsh but that adds to similarity with Toscanini's version. Bernstein's comments about the work make a fascinating bonus.

Toscanini's version has a far keener emotional intensity than the studio recording which appeared earlier as part of his Beethoven cycle in the BMG Toscanini series. Toscanini had a special insight into this of all Beethoven's symphonies, making this disc a valuable addition to his discography.

Karajan's 1977 account brings fiery intensity at fast tempi in the outer movements of Karajan's 1977 performance, with the *Funeral march* more concentrated than in his earlier recordings. An exciting performance of *Leonora No. 3* makes a fair bonus. The sound is well defined and clean.

The gain in Karajan's digital version of the *Eroica* over his previous recordings lies most of all in the *Funeral march*, very spacious and intense, with high dynamic contrasts. The playing is marginally less polished than before, lacking something of the knife-edged bite associated with Karajan. The recording, remastered for the Karajan Gold series, is clean and firm, but there is still a degree of congestion in big tuttis. An epic reading.

Giulini's refined and individual reading, with its very measured view of the first movement, was an early product of his love affair with the Los Angeles orchestra. Though it only wins a qualified recommendation, its reissue in DG's series of 'Legendary' Originals, for it remains a striking example of a conductor transforming an orchestra. The coupling, an excellent performance of Schumann's *Manfred overture*, was originally offered as a makeweight for the *Rhenish Symphony*.

Symphony No. 3 (Eroica) (trans. Liszt); *Eroica variations, Op. 35.*
(M) ** Teldec/Warner Dig. 4509 97953-2 [id.].
Cyprien Katsaris (piano).

This is one of the less impressive of the Katsaris series of Liszt's remarkable transcriptions. The first movement of the *Eroica* is heavily rhetorical and the *Marcia funèbre* sounds comparatively uninvolved. The rest of the work is more impressive, as are the appropriately coupled *Variations*.

Symphonies Nos. 3 in E flat (Eroica), Op. 55; 4 in B flat, Op. 60.
(N) (BB) *** Arte Nova Dig. 74321 59214-2 [id.].
Zurich Tonhalle O, David Zinman.
*** DG Dig. 447 050-2 [id.]. ORR, Gardiner.

In his splendid Beethoven series, using the new Bärenreiter edition prepared by Jonathan Del Mar, David Zinman and the Tonhalle Orchestra give outstanding performances of both symphonies, a rare and generous coupling. With speeds close to Beethoven's very fast metronome markings, these are performances which bridge the gap between traditional and period performances, getting the best of both worlds. The string and wind articulation in both symphonies is phenomenally crisp and clear, so that there is no feeling of excessive haste. In the *Eroica*, even with exposition repeat observed, the first movement lasts barely 15 minutes, and the *Funeral march* at a flowing speed still conveys darkly tragic intensity, not least at the close. First-rate recording with ample bloom on the sound.

Gardiner's fast speeds mean that he too can fit Nos. 3 and 4 on the same disc. The *Eroica* first movement may for some be too fast, but the argument is presented purposefully with full weight and biting intensity, helped by vivid recording. The

Funeral march has natural gravity even at a flowing speed, with high dynamic contrasts. Gardiner's ability to spring rhythms has one quickly accepting fast tempi, not just in the *Eroica* but also in No. 4, where the sublime melody of the slow movement is sweeter than usual with period violins.

Symphonies Nos. 3 (Eroica); 8 in F, Op. 93.
(M) **(*) Bruno Walter Edition: Sony SMK 64461 [id.]. Columbia SO, Bruno Walter.
(M) (***) RCA mono GD 60269 [60269-2-RG]. NBC SO, Toscanini.
(B) **(*) Sony SBK 46328; *SBT 46328* [id.]. Cleveland O, Szell.
(M) **(*) DG 447 903-2 [id.]. VPO, Bernstein.
(BB) **(*) Naxos Dig. 8.553475 [id.]. Nicolaus Esterházy Sinfonia, Béla Drahos.

It is a pleasure to turn from other accounts of the *Eroica* and hear as beautiful and sympathetic a performance as Walter's. He is not monumental, as Klemperer and Toscanini were in different ways; but the ripeness harks back to pre-war Vienna years. The digitally remastered recording is aptly expansive with rich horns and full-bodied strings. The *Eighth* has comparatively slow speeds, an interesting and sympathetic rather than a compelling reading.

Toscanini's 1939 recording of the *Eroica*, made live, brings one of the most compelling recordings he ever made. Not only does he conduct at white heat, he is far more flexible in his musical manners than he became later, both moulding melodic lines with Italianate warmth and allowing himself far freer rubato. The *Eighth* is hard-driven and on the biggest scale (Toscanini, exceptionally for the days of 78s, observes the exposition repeat in the first movement). Yet this is a performance which has satisfying power.

Szell's is a fine performance in the Toscanini tradition, hard-driven and dramatic. The digital remastering is very successful: the sound is firm, full and brilliant. The performance of the *Eighth* is also a compelling one. The first-movement repeat is taken and the performance is not over-driven.

Bernstein's 1980 Vienna Philharmonic recording of the *Eroica* is strong and dramatic, but brings a degree of disappointment compared with his earlier (1964) Sony record (SMK 47514), which is electrically intense, most of all in the first movement. The *Eighth* is both strong (first-movement exposition repeat again included) and genial, not so much a 'little' symphony as a jovial and commanding one, culminating in a vigorous though not overdriven finale.

Drahos's performances on Naxos with his excellent chamber orchestra from Budapest benefit greatly from the superb sound, clearer and with more vivid presence than on many other recent discs. The performances have the same qualities of freshness and spontaneity that mark the other initial disc in the series, making a good bargain, even if there are more searching readings of the *Eroica*.

Symphonies Nos. 4 in B flat; 5 in C min.; Egmont: Overture.
(M) **(*) Sony SMK 63079 [id.]. NYPO, Bernstein.

Bernstein's earlier (1962) New York recording of the *Fourth Symphony* brings a powerful performance at urgent speeds urgently, but the playing has both polish and concentration and the slow movement has an appealingly relaxed *espressivo*. The *Fifth* (from a year earlier) is also one of the finest of the Bernstein cycle, strong and dramatic, concentrated and vital. The recording has been improved in the present transfers. Though the sound, harsh at times, lacks the widest dynamic range there is a convincing depth. *Egmont* is comparably dramatic and well-recorded.

Symphonies Nos. 4 in B flat, Op. 60; 5 in C min., Op. 67; 6 in F (Pastoral), Op. 68; Egmont: Overture, Op. 84.
(BB) **(*) Carlton LSO Double Dig. 30368 01197 (2) [(B) id.]. LSO, Wyn Morris.

In the *Fourth* and *Fifth Symphonies* Wyn Morris generally adopts speeds close to those of Karajan and, though he cannot match that master in sharpness of focus or pointed intensity, his urgency goes with fine, biting strength, helped by some first-rate playing from the LSO. Morris takes a characteristically fresh and direct view of the *Pastoral*, with a brisk speed for the first movement. The piece becomes less atmospheric – with the entry into the *Storm* hardly suggesting raindrops – but one appreciates the structural originality the more. A similarly taut account of the *Egmont overture* follows.

Symphonies Nos. 4 in B flat; 6 in F (Pastoral), Op. 68.
✿ (M) *** Bruno Walter Edition: Sony SMK 64462 [id.]. Columbia SO, Walter.
(B) *** EMI CfP Dig. CD-CFP 6069 [id.]. RLPO, Mackerras.
(M) (***) RCA mono GD 60254 [60254-2-RG]. NBC SO, Toscanini.

For those collectors wanting a sampler of Bruno Walter's Beethoven series of the late 1950s, the coupling of the *Fourth* and *Sixth Symphonies* is the one to go for. Walter's reading of the *Fourth* is splendid, the finest achievement of his whole cycle. There is intensity and a feeling of natural vigour in every bar. The recording is full, yet clear, sweet-toned with a firm bass. This version of the *Pastoral* dates from the beginning of the 1960s and, like his recording of the *Fourth*, it represents the peak of his Indian summer in the American recording studios, an affectionate, finely integrated performance from a master, with beautifully balanced sound.

Following the pattern of his other Classics for Pleasure recordings of Beethoven with the Liverpool orchestra, Sir Charles Mackerras adopts consistently fast speeds in both symphonies, except in the slow introduction to No. 4. Crisp, light articulation allows for superb definition from the strings in the outer movements of No. 4, with resilient rhythms, and Mackerras's subtle rubato ensures that the opening of the *Pastoral* avoids any feeling of rigidity. With hard sticks used by the timpanist, the Storm has rarely sounded so thrilling, resolving on an ecstatic, glowing finale.

The *Pastoral* was one of Toscanini's favourite Beethoven symphonies and the performance has a natural, unforced freshness which allows the most delicate shading and persuasive moulding between sections. No. 4 is more characteristic of the later Toscanini, though the fast, fierce manner in the first movement conveys joyful exuberance, and the slow movement brings fine moulding.

Symphonies Nos. 4 in B flat; 7 in A, Op. 92.
(M) *** EMI CDM5 66795-2 [id.]. Philh. O, Klemperer.
(M) *** Virgin Veritas/EMI Dig. VM5 61376-2 [CDM 61376]. L. Classical Players, Norrington.
*** Teldec/Warner Dig. 9031 75714-2 [id.]. COE, Harnoncourt.
(M) *** DG 447 904-2 [id.]. VPO, Bernstein.
(BB) *** Naxos Dig. 8.553477 [id.]. Nicolaus Esterházy Sinfonia, Béla Drahos.

Symphonies Nos. 4 in B flat; 7 in A; King Stephen overture, Op. 117.
(B) *** Sony SBK 48158; *SBT 48158* [id.]. Cleveland O, Szell.

This coupling is perhaps the most impressive of the new Beethoven symphony pairings offered in EMI's 'Klemperer Legacy'. The *Fourth* brings one of the most compelling performances of all, with Klemperer's measured but consistently sprung pulse allowing for persuasive lyricism alongside power. Klemperer's 1955 recording of the *Seventh* is among his very finest Beethoven interpretations on disc, and it sounds all the more vivid in its stereo version. Speeds are consistently faster, the tension more electric, with phrasing moulded more subtly than in the later version. The 1955 sound is remarkably full, with good inner detail.

The coupling of Nos. 4 and 7 also shows Norrington at his very best. In both symphonies he adopts fast speeds and in the *Seventh* sforzandos are sharply accented and rhythms lightly sprung. He follows Beethoven's metronome markings – as in the brisk second-movement Allegretto – but finds time for detail and fine moulding of phrase. The recording is warm, but not ideally clear on detail.

Brilliant, vital readings from Harnoncourt, with high contrasts in the slow movement of No. 4, bringing soaring lyricism over nagging rhythmic figures below. In the outer movements of No. 7 – wonderfully spirited – the horns shine out, adding to the joyous release after an *Allegretto* full of under-the-surface tension.

In No. 4, Bernstein's taut manner brings out the compactness of argument. The development is especially fine: one registers it as the message of No. 1 retold in the language of the *Fifth*. If the tensions in Bernstein's Vienna performance of the *Seventh* are less marked than in his earlier, New York recording, here that makes for extra spring and exhilaration in the lilting rhythms of the first movement, while the *Allegretto* is reposeful without falling into an ordinary *Andante*, and the last two movements have the adrenalin flowing with a sense of occasion. One almost regrets the lack of applause. The recordings are among the fullest and brightest in the series. An outstanding coupling.

The coupling of Nos. 4 and 7 is also one of the most successful of the Drahos Naxos series. No. 4 has a joyful vitality, while in No. 7 Drahos keeps a spring in the rhythms without forcing the pace, lifting the finale with bouncing accents, leading to a thrilling coda. First-class playing and sound of vivid clarity and atmospheric warmth. An excellent bargain.

Szell is at his finest in both symphonies. Along with powerful outer movements, tense and spontaneous-sounding, go exceptional accounts of the slow movements in both symphonies and in No. 7 Szell makes the second movement a genuine *Allegretto*, with keen concentration taking it almost as fast as a period specialist.

Symphonies Nos. 4 in B flat, Op. 60; 8 in F, Op. 93; Coriolan overture.
(B) *** Carlton IMP Dig. 30367 02392 [(M) id.]. Sinfonia Varsovia, Lord Menuhin.

On the Carlton disc the applause precedes not only Mehuhin's warmly lyrical but not undramatic *Coriolan* but also the *Fourth Symphony*. The opening of the symphony is immediately full of tension, the allegro joyful and vigorous without being overdriven, and the rapt *Adagio* is played most beautifully. The opening movement of the *Eighth* launches itself joyfully, leading to an elegant second subject. In the *Allegretto*, also elegant, Menuhin's pacing is rather too relaxed, but the finale erupts in buoyant energy. Fine playing, with spacious sound of wide dynamic range.

Symphonies Nos. 4; 5 in C min. (trans. Liszt).
(M) *** Teldec/Warner Dig. 4509 98954-2 [id.]. Cyprien Katsaris (piano).

A remarkable disc. Apart from his dazzling technique, Katsaris has keen musicianship, a great range of colour and a real sense of scale. It is as if one is encountering this music for the first time. Note that this mid-priced reissue is a recoupling.

Symphony No. 5 in C min., Op. 67.
(M) *** DG (IMS) Dig. 445 502-2 [id.]. LAPO, Giulini – SCHUMANN: *Symphony No. 3 (Rhenish)*. ***

Giulini's 1982 Los Angeles recording of Beethoven's *Fifth* brings an outstandingly fine performance, majestic and powerful. The slow movement is glorious; the horn entry in the Scherzo is thrilling and the finale overwhelming in its force and grandeur. Outstanding digital sound, clear, full and well-balanced, and the Schumann coupling is hardly less distinguished.

Symphonies Nos. 5 in C min.; 6 (Pastoral).
(BB) **(*) BMG Arte Nova Dig. 74321 49695-2 [id.]. Zürich Tonnhalle O, David Zinman.
**(*) DG Dig. 447 062-2 [id.]. ORR, Gardiner.
(B) **(*) DG 439 403-2 [id.]. BPO, Karajan.
**(*) DG Dig. Gold 439 004-2 [id.]. BPO, Karajan.
(M) **(*) Virgin Veritas/EMI Dig. VM5 61377-2 [CDM 61377]. L. Classical Players, Norrington.
(M) (**(*)) Avid mono AMSC 583 [id.]. (i) LPO, Weingartner; (ii) VPO, Walter.

With bright, immediate recording, David Zinman conducts the Tonnhalle Orchestra in unusually direct and incisive readings which suggest that his Beethoven sympathies were once roused by Toscanini's example. The use of Jonathan Del Mar's Bärenreiter edition in No. 5 brings a full repeat of the Scherzo and Trio before the usual partial and lightweight reprise of the Scherzo leading into the mysterious link to the finale. Though in No. 5 Zinman's approach works extremely well in an exceptionally powerful reading, the *Pastoral* is more problematical. The opening *allegro*, at a brisk speed, is rarely allowed to relax: it has plenty of energy but not much warmth. The slow movement by contrast is spaciously done and the *Storm* is biting rather than atmospheric, with the finale rather plain, strong and intense, rather than warmly persuasive. Excellent playing makes this a coupling to reckon with, offering a refreshing change from more traditional readings. The sound is fresh and clean, perhaps a little lacking in weight, although it suits the performances.

Gardiner's fast speeds in No. 5, recorded live, bring allegros of manic energy and thrust, pushing the music to the limit. The *Pastoral*, at comparably fast speeds, is crisp and light, with fine shading of phrase and dynamic, not least in the slow movement, though the big violin melody in the finale inevitably lacks the full sweetness of modern strings. Vivid, forward sound, full of presence.

Karajan's 1962 *Fifth* is thoroughly recommendable, if anything more intense than his later (1977) version, more spacious in the *Andante* and with blazing horns in the finale. The *Pastoral* is a brisk, lightweight performance, very well played, and marred only by the absence of the repeat in the Scherzo. The sound has freshness and body.

Karajan's digital versions of the *Fifth* and *Sixth* present characteristically strong and incisive readings, recorded in longer takes than previously. The sound may not be as cleanly focused as in his earlier Berlin versions, but the feeling of spontaneous performance is most compelling, so that the fast speed for the first movement of the *Pastoral* no longer sounds too tense.

No. 5 shows Norrington at his most exciting and inspired, relishing his fast speeds, while the finale has an infectious swagger. No. 6 is disappointing with the EMI sound not as refined or clear, with Norrington surprisingly fussy at times. The *Scene by the brook*, for example, fails to flow when the phrasing is so short-winded.

To many older collectors, Felix Weingartner's Beethoven had no rivals and few modern peers. In his hands the composer speaks to you as if without any interpretative mediator. The *Fifth Symphony*, recorded with the London Philharmonic in 1933, is Beethoven pure and true, straightforward and plain, there is no lack of character and fire. The recording sounds less dated than one might expect, though there is a curious touch of dryness, characteristic of these Avid transfers. Bruno Walter's 1936 account of the *Pastoral* with the Vienna Philharmonic, taut and brisk, yet feels expansive. This is a vintage performance, though the strings are not quite sweet enough above the stave.

Symphonies Nos. 5; 7 in A, Op. 92.
❁ (M) *** DG 447 400-2 [id.]. VPO, Carlos Kleiber.
(B) *** Carlton IMP Dig. 30367 02402 [(M) id.]. Sinfonia Varsovia, Lord Menuhin.
(B) *** EMI CfP Dig. CD-CFP 6070. RLPO, Sir Charles Mackerras.
*** DG Dig. 449 981-2 [id.]. Philh. O, Christian Thielemann.
(M) *** Decca Penguin Classics 466 211-2; [*460 603-2*]. Philh. O, Ashkenazy.
(M) **(*) Bruno Walter Edition: Sony SMK 64463 [id.]. Columbia SO, Bruno Walter.

Symphonies Nos. 5; 8; Fidelio: overture.
(M) *** DG 419 051-2 [id.]. BPO, Karajan.

If ever there was a legendary recording, it is Carlos Kleiber's version of the *Fifth* from the mid-1970s. In Kleiber's hands the first movement is electrifying but still has a hushed intensity. The slow movement is tender and delicate, with dynamic contrasts underlined but not exaggerated. In the Scherzo the horns, like the rest of the VPO, are in superb form; the finale then emerges into pure daylight. In Kleiber's *Seventh* symphonic argument never yields to the charm of the dance. Incisively dramatic, he relies approach on sharp dynamic contrasts and thrustful rhythms. A controversial point is that Kleiber, like his father, maintains the pizzicato for the strings on the final phrase of the *Allegretto*, a curious effect. The latest digital remastering has again greatly improved the sound.

Menuhin opens the *Fifth* unselfconsciously, immediately setting a brisk tempo for the allegro, played comparatively lightly. The *Andante* too begins with a sense of delicate lyricism, and the finale launches into what he describes as 'the "joyful illumination" of the fate theme'. In the first movement of the *Seventh* the allegro dances along, and the *Allegretto* is eloquent, with the finale leading to an exhilarating yet weighty conclusion. Playing and recording are well up to the high standard of the cycle.

Sir Charles Mackerras and the Royal Liverpool Philharmonic also give revelatory performances of both the *Fifth* and *Seventh*. The fast speed for the first movement of the *Fifth* initially takes one's breath away, but having learnt from period practice, he gives it clarity and rhythmic spring. Tempi are on the fast side in all four movements but, thanks to the rhythmic control, they never sound hectic. The superb recording is both weighty and atmospheric. The coupling is an equally refreshing account of the *Seventh Symphony*. Thanks to the fast speeds, they fit on a single disc even with exposition repeats are observed.

Karajan's 1977 version of the *Fifth* is magnificent in every way, tough and urgently incisive, with fast tempi bringing weight as well as excitement. The coupling is an electrically intense performance of the *Eighth* plus the *Fidelio overture*.

Still in his thirties, Christian Thielemann is an exceptionally positive interpreter, daring in these two Beethoven warhorses to fly boldly in the face of current fashion, opting for broad speeds and resonant textures to remind one of the weighty Klemperer with this same orchestra, yet with speeds fluctuating in a manner far nearer to Furtwängler. The results are magnetic, with outstanding playing from the Philharmonia and vivid digital recording, this is an excellent recommendation for anyone wanting a traditional view with modern sound.

On Penguin Classics, Ashkenazy's reading of the *Fifth*, urgent and vivid, is notable for its rich, Kingsway Hall recording. Well-adjusted speeds here, with joyful exuberance a fair substitute for grandeur. The reading of the *Seventh* is equally spontaneous. Highly recommended, especially for those for whom outstanding recording quality is a priority. The special literary essay is by Arthur Miller.

In Bruno Walter's reading of the *Fifth*, the first movement is taken very fast, but lacks a little in nervous tension. The middle two movements are slow by contrast, and the finale, taken at a spacious, natural pace, is joyful rather than dramatic. Walter's *Seventh* has a comparatively slow first-movement allegro, and the *Allegretto* also seems heavier than usual (partly because of the rich, weighty recording), but this still gives the illusion of an actual performance. Rich, full sound that defies its age.

Symphonies Nos. 5 in C min., Op. 67; 7 in A, Op. 92; Overtures: Coriolan; Fidelio.

(N) (M) **(*) RCA 09026 68976-2 [id.]. Chicago SO, Fritz Reiner.

The full-bodied new transfer gives Reiner's 1955 account of the *Fifth* added weight. His opening is measured, but then he spurts forward impulsively and excitingly. The slow movement is expansive, its principal melody flowing warmly to make a link with the *Pastoral Symphony*, and the finale, taken fast, caps a somewhat mannered interpretation exhilaratingly. The *Seventh*, recorded four years later, is particularly impressive in the first and third movements, where power is combined with fine rhythmic lift to confirm Wagner's 'apotheosis of the dance', while the fast tempo for the finale draws unscampering brilliance from the Chicago Orchestra. Marginally less impressive are the symphony's slow introduction and the *Allegretto* second movement, where Reiner's manner at fastish speeds is cooler. Both the overtures are impressively played, *Coriolan* boldly dramatic.

(i) *Symphony No. 5 in C min., Op. 67*; (ii) *Triple concerto, Op. 56.*

(N) (B) (**(*)) Naxos mono 8.110801 [id.]. NYPO, Toscanini (i) with Piastro, Schuster, Dorfman.

This 1933 account of the *Fifth Symphony* brings a Toscanini performance to treasure, warmer and more refined than his later readings with the NBC Symphony Orchestra, showing a degree of flexibility missing later. The *Triple concerto*, recorded in 1942, brings a tautly controlled performance with three of Toscanini's favourite players as soloists, with the cellist, Josef Schuster, allowed fair expressive freedom. The soloists are clearly recorded, but in both works the orchestral sound is very limited, not helped by often heavy surface noise.

Symphony No. 5 in C min., Op. 67; Overture: Egmont, Op. 84; Septet in E flat, Op. 20.

(N) (M) (***) RCA mono GD 60270 [id.]. NBC SO, Toscanini.

This RCA account of the *Fifth* is taken from Toscanini's legendary Beethoven cycle of 1939, not from his later NBC recording, and the result is marginally less brittle, though already more rigid than his 1933 reading with the Philharmonic. The *Septet*, recorded in 1951, finds Toscanini surprisingly relaxed, relishing the sparkle of early Beethoven, while keeping a taut control and drawing brilliant playing from the full strings of the NBC Orchestra. Dry but clear sound.

Symphony No. 6 in F (Pastoral), Op. 68.
(M) *** DG 447 433-2 [id.]. VPO, Boehm – SCHUBERT: *Symphony No. 5.* ***
(N) (***) Cala mono CACD 0523 [id.]. NY City SO, Stokowski – MOZART: *Sinfonia concertante, K.297b.* (***)

Symphonies No. 6 (Pastoral); Overtures: Coriolan; Creatures of Prometheus.
(BB) *** ASV CDQS 6053. N. Sinfonia, Richard Hickox.

Symphony No. 6 (Pastoral); Overtures: Coriolan; Egmont.
*** Sony Dig. SK 53974 [id.]. La Scala PO, Giulini.

Symphony No. 6 (Pastoral); Overtures: Egmont; Leonora No. 3.
(B) *** Decca Eclipse Dig. 448 986-2 [(M) id. import]. Philh. O, Ashkenazy.

Symphony No. 6 in F (Pastoral); Overture Leonora No. 3.
(B) **(*) [EMI Red Line Dig. CDR5 72551]. Phd. O, Muti.

Boehm's 1971 version of the *Pastoral* is as fine as any, a beautiful, unforced reading, one of the best played, and in its day one of the best recorded. It still sounds fresh in its current reissue in DG's 'Originals' series with a Schubert coupling.

Surprisingly, when one remembers that it was a star item (cleverly abridged) in Walt Disney's *Fantasia*, this was Stokowski's first commercial recording of the *Pastoral*, made in Carnegie Hall in 1945 with an orchestra which he founded, but only conducted for a single season. As Edward Johnson points out in his excellent notes, there is 'no want of rustic jollity in the opening movement', but 'Stokowski's *Scene by the brook* is certainly more *Adagio* than *Andante*'. However, he sustains this leisurely tempo with affectionate ease, and gives a radiant account of the finale. The ear notices that he is fully aware how important the bass part and lower strings are in this symphony and this is reflected in the balance. Yet the violins sing out freshly and radiantly, and the only real complaint about the sound is the restricted dynamic range. A memorable account just the same, and indispensable for those (like I. M.) for whom *Fantasia* played a key role in their early awareness of classical music.

Giulini's newest version of the *Pastoral*, measured, warm and relaxed, speaks of sunny Italy where it was recorded. The La Scala players are on their finest form throughout, radiant in the finale. The symphony is framed by the two overtures, *Coriolan* ruggedly powerful at the opening and *Egmont* dramatic.

Ashkenazy's warm performance thanks spacious tempi brings a feeling of lyrical ease and repose, with glowing playing from the Philharmonia rich Kingsway Hall recording. The two overtures make a good bonus. An excellent bargain.

With the first two movements youthfully urgent, Muti's is an exhilarating performance, fresh and direct. It is a strong, symphonic view, rather than a programmatic one. The recording is warm and wide-ranging, though the high violins do not always live up to the 'Philadelphia sound'. This is currently only available in the USA.

Hickox directs a persuasively paced reading, with a small orchestra used to give a performance of high contrasts, intimate in the lighter textures but expanding dramatically in the tuttis, while the finale, fresh and pure, brings a glowing climax. With warm, analogue recording, this is one of the best of the Hickox Beethoven series. The two *Overtures* come in vigorously dramatic readings.

Symphonies Nos. 6 in F (Pastoral); 8 in F, Op. 91.
*** Teldec/Warner Dig. 9031 75709-2 [id.]. COE, Harnoncourt.
(BB) *** Belart 450 058-2 [(M) id. import]. Concg. O, Eugen Jochum.

There is nothing over-tense about Harnoncourt's *Pastoral*, even though the brook flows freely; No. 8 has drama and bite and resilience too.

Jochum's Concertgebouw coupling on Belart (originally Philips), dating from the end of the 1960s, still sounds extremely well, resonantly full-bodied, vivid and clear. Like his newer EMI recording, this is a leisurely reading, the countryside relaxing in sunshine. The *Eighth* too is given an outstanding performance, with plenty of energy. A fine alternative view of two of Beethoven's friendliest symphonies.

Symphonies Nos. 6 (Pastoral); 8 in F (trans. Liszt).
(M) **(*) Teldec/Warner Dig. 4509 97955-2 [id.]. Cyprien Katsaris (piano).

Katsaris, using an instrument with the ideal combination of weight and clarity, makes an excellent exponent of Liszt's transcription of the *Pastoral Symphony*, direct and fresh. The *Eighth* is much more perceptive. Good if resonant recording.

Symphony No. 7 in A, Op. 92.
❁ (B) *** EMI forte CZS5 69364-2 (2) [id.]. RPO, Sir Colin Davis – SCHUBERT: *Symphony No. 9* ***; ROSSINI: *Overtures* **(*).
(N)*(**) BBC Legends BBCL 4005-2 [id.]. BBC SO, Stokowski – BRITTEN: *Young person's guide to the orchestra* **(*); FALLA: *El amor brujo* *** ❁.
**(*) DG (IMS) Dig. 431 768-2. Boston SO, Bernstein (with BRITTEN: *Peter Grimes: Sea interludes* **(*)).

Sir Colin Davis's early (1961) *Seventh* brings a great, electrifying performance. Originally issued as a bargain LP, it dominated the catalogue in the early stereo era. It sounds splendid in this digital remastering, with the horns coming through thrillingly in the codas of both outer movements.

Those who attended the 1962 Prom at which Stokowski conducted Beethoven's *Seventh Symphony* with the BBC Symphony Orchestra will recall the sheer high voltage of the occasion. His reading still sounds pretty breathtaking and has great power and concentration. It is a performance of high contrasts, with the first movement pressed hard, and the slow speed for the *Allegretto* made persuasive through subtle phrasing and rhythmic control. Stokowski then mutilates the Scherzo by eliminating the second reprise of the Trio and the third repeat of the Scherzo proper. None the less this is an exceptional performance. In the hall itself he played the finale again as an encore! The couplings are outstanding (the Falla in particular is stunning) and the sound very good for its age.

Leonard Bernstein, recorded live with the Boston Symphony Orchestra, at the very last concert he ever conducted in Tanglewood on 19 August 1990, takes an expansive view, quite different from his previous recordings, consistently conveying the joy of Beethoven's inspiration while springing rhythms infectiously. First-rate sound, despite the problems of live recording at Tanglewood, and an unusual coupling.

Symphony No. 7 (trans. Liszt).
(M) *** Teldec/Warner Dig. 4509 97956-2 [id.]. Cyprien Katsaris – SCHUMANN: *Exercises on Beethoven's Seventh Symphony* **).

Cyprien Katsaris does wonders in translating Liszt's transcription into orchestral terms, providing an unexpectedly illuminating listening experience. The sound is excellent. Well worth having at mid-price.

Symphonies Nos. 7 in A; 8 in F.
*** DG (IMS) Dig. 423 364-2 [id.]. VPO, Abbado.
*** DG Dig. 447 063-2 [id.]. ORR, Gardiner.
(BB) **(*) Arte Nova Dig. 74321 56341-2 [id.]. Zürich Tonhalle O, David Zinman.
(B) **(*) [EMI Red Line Dig. CDR5 69785]. Phd. O, Muti.

The *Seventh* has always been a favourite symphony with Abbado, and the main allegro of the first movement is beautifully managed, as also is the *Eighth*, which is instantly established as more than a little symphony. As in the *Seventh*, speeds are beautifully judged, giving the impression of live performance. A splendid coupling.

With Gardiner the first movements of both Nos. 7 and 8 are very highly charged, with textures and rhythms lightened. Though there is comparable thrust in the finale of No. 7, the speed is not extreme. The *Allegretto* and Scherzo are fast and light too, as are the comparable movements of No. 8, leading to a hectic finale. Firm, forward sound.

Zinman's coupling of Nos. 7 and 8 has similar qualities to his earlier less recommendable coupling of Nos. 5 and 6 (74321 49695-2), again with echoes of Toscanini. That works very well in No. 7, with speeds on the brisk side, which yet have rhythmic resilience, notably in the *Allegretto*. In No. 8 Zinman, like Toscanini, takes a rather fierce view of this most compact of the symphonies, with a clipped manner and a fast speed in the first movement and with little or no charm in the middle movements. With clean, crisp ensemble and vivid recording, the power of the piece is reinforced. Hihgly recommended at super-bargain price.

The vigour and drive of Muti's account of the *Seventh* are never in doubt – but, surprisingly, the ensemble of the Philadelphia Orchestra is not immaculate. There is spontaneity, but it is paid for by a lack of precision. The *Eighth* is also lively, and it brings greater polish. The recording is a fair example of EMI's 'new Philadelphia sound'. This CD is available only in the USA.

Symphony No. 8 in F, Op. 93; Overtures: Coriolan; Fidelio; Leonora No. 3.
**(*) DG Dig. Gold 439 005-2 [id.]. BPO, Karajan.

Karajan's more relaxed view of the *Eighth* (compared with his 1977 Berlin version) is almost always pure gain, a massive reading of Beethoven's 'little symphony', with fierceness part of the mixture in the outer movements. The three overtures are made Olympian too, with *Coriolan* specially impressive.

Symphony No. 8; Overtures: Coriolan; Leonora Nos. 1–3, Opp. 138; 72a; 72b.
(M) ** EMI CDM5 66796-2 [id.]. Philh. O, Klemperer.

Klemperer's approach to the *Eighth* is deliberate and heavy. He has his justification at the wonderful climax of the development in the first movement, leading over into the recapitulation, but the finale plods for much of its length. In the three *Leonora overtures* he is strong rather than volatile, but with high tension the result is neither dull nor heavy. Full-bodied transfers.

Symphony No. 9 in D min. (Choral), Op. 125.
(B) *** EMI CfP Dig. CD-CFP 6071 [id.]. Joan Rodgers, Della Jones, Peter Bronder, Bryn Terfel, RLPO Ch. & O, Sir Charles Mackerras.
(N) (BB) *** Arte Nova Dig. 74321 65411-2 [id.]. Ruth Ziesak, Birgit Remmert, Steve Davislim, Detlef Roth, Swiss Chamber Ch., Zurich Tonhalle O, David Zinman.
*** Sony Dig. SK 62634 [id.]. Jane Eaglen, Waltraud Meier, Ben Heppner, Bryn Terfel,

Swedish R. Ch., Ericson Chamber Ch., BPO, Abbado.

(M) *** DG 415 832-2 [id.]. Tomowa-Sintow, Baltsa, Schreier, Van Dam, V. Singverein, BPO, Karajan.

*** DG 429 861-2 [id.]. Anderson, Walker, König, Rootering, various Chs., Bav. RSO, Dresden State O, etc., Bernstein.

*** DG Dig. 447 074-2; *447 074-4* [id.]. Orgonasova, Von Otter, Rolfe Johnson, Cachemaille, Monteverdi Ch., ORR, Gardiner.

(N) (M) (***) EMI mono CDM5 66901-2 [CDM 66953]. Schwarzkopf, Höngen, Hopf, Edelmann, Bayreuth Fest. Ch. & P, Furtwängler.

(B) *** Carlton IMP Dig. 30367 02412 [(M) id. import]. Jean Glennon, Dalia Schaechter, Algirdas Janutas, Benno Schollum, Lithuania Kaunas State Ch., Sinfonia Varsovia, Menuhin.

(M) *** DG Dig. 445 503-2 [id.]. Norman, Fassbaender, Domingo, Berry, V. State Op. Ch. Soc., VPO, Karl Boehm.

(B) *** DG Classikon 439 495-2. G. Jones, Schwarz, Kollo, Moll, V. State Op. Ch., VPO, Bernstein.

(M) *** DG 447 905-2 [id.]. Gwyneth Jones, Schwarz, Kollo, Moll, V. State Op. Ch., VPO, Bernstein.

*** DG Dig. 453 423-2 [id.]. Solveig Kringelborn, Felicity Palmer, Thomas Moser, Alan Titus, Dresden State Op. Ch., Dresden State O, Sinopoli.

(B) *** Tring TRP 051 [(M) id. import]. Gillian Webster, Catherine Wyn-Rogers, Martyn Hill, Robert Hayward, Amb. S., RPO, Leppard.

*** Teldec/Warner Dig. 9031 75713-2 [id.]. Margiono, Remmert, Schasching, Holl, Schoenberg Ch., COE, Harnoncourt.

(BB) *** ASV CDQS 6069 [id.]. Harper, Hodgson, Tear, Howell, Sinfonia Ch., London Symphony Ch. (members), N. Sinfonia, Hickox.

(N) (M) *** Decca Penguin Classics 460 622-2 [id.]. Lorengar, Minton, Burrows, Talvela, Chicago Ch. & SO, Solti.

(BB) *** Naxos Dig. 8.553478 [id.]. Papian, Donose, Fink, Otelli, Nicolaus Esterházy Ch. & O, Drahos.

(M) **(*) RCA 09026 61795-2 [id.]. Curtin, Kopleff, McCollum, Gramm, Chicago SO & Ch., Fritz Reiner.

(BB) **(*) Discover Dig. DICD 920151 [id.]. Gauci, Van Deyck, George, Rosca, Cantores Oratorio Ch., Belgian Nat. R. & TV PO, Rahbari.

(N) (BB) **(*) Arts Dig. 47248-2 [id.]. Halgrimson, Engert, Vendersteene, Kunder, Athestis Chorus, O. di Padova e del Veneto, Peter Maag.

**(*) DG Dig. Gold 439 006-2 [id.]. Perry, Baltsa, Cole, Van Dam, V. Singverein, BPO, Karajan.

(M) (**(*)) RCA mono GD 60256; [60256-2-RG]. Farrell, Merriman, Peerce, Scott, Shaw Ch., NBC O, Toscanini.

(M) **(*) Virgin Veritas/EMI Dig. VM5 61378-2 [CDM 61378]. Kenny, Walker, Power, Salomaa, Schütz Ch., L. Classical Players, Norrington.

(M) (**(*)) Avid mono AMSC 591 [id.]. Helletsgruber, Anday, Maikl, Mayr, V. State Op. Ch., VPO, Weingartner.

(i) *Symphony No. 9 (Choral), Op. 125. Overture Fidelio.*

(B) **(*) Sony SBK 46533; *SBT 46533* [id.]. (i) Addison, Hobson, Lewis, Bell, Cleveland O Ch.; Cleveland O, Szell.

Symphony No. 9 (Choral); Overture: Coriolan.

(M) *** DG 447 401-2 [id.]. Janowitz, Rössl-Majdan, Kmentt, Berry, V. Singverein, BPO, Karajan.

Symphony No. 9 (Choral); Overture: The Creatures of Prometheus, Op. 43.

(M) ** EMI CDM5 66797 [id.]. Lövberg, Ludwig, Kmentt, Hotter, Philh. Ch. & O, Klemperer.

(i) *Symphony No. 9 (Choral). Overture Egmont, Op. 84.*

(M) *** Decca (IMS) Phase Four 452 487-2 [id.]. (i) Harper, Watts, Young, McIntyre, L. Symphony Ch.; LSO, Stokowski.

Sir Charles Mackerras conducts the Royal Liverpool Philharmonic in an inspired account of the *Ninth*, one which has learnt from the lessons of period performance. Articulation is light and clean, vibrato is used sparingly, making textures unusually clear; and, like period specialists, Sir Charles has taken careful note of Beethoven's controversial metronome markings. The recording is outstanding, warm yet transparent and with plenty of body; and the singing in the finale is fine, even if the tenor, Peter Bronder, is on the strenuous side. A refreshingly different version of the *Ninth*, strongly recommended.

David Zinman crowns his Beethoven cycle, using the new Bärenteiter Edition, with a magnificent account of the *Ninth*, opting for the fast speeds that have latterly come to be thought authentic. It is his gift never to make them sound breathless, always giving the music the deeper qualities needed, as in, for example, mystery in the tremolos at the very start and a sense of hushed dedication in the slow movement, even when taken at a flowing speed. The finale crowns his performance, with the chamber chorus, not only fresh and dramatic but deeply dedicated too in the prayerful sections. The soloists are an excellent team of young-sounding singers, and the sound is full and well balanced. On a separate track the last half of the finale is given in an alternative version with a pause included towards the end, representing Beethoven's first thoughts, later amended.

Just ten years after Claudio Abbado recorded Beethoven's *Ninth Symphony* with the Vienna Philharmonic, he returned to it in a recording made at the 1996 Salzburg Easter Festival, this time as Artistic Director of the Berlin Philharmonic, Karajan's successor. The contrasts are astonishing, notably over speeds (consistently faster) and performing style (lighter and crisper in articulation). So the opening with its string tremolos is fresh and clear rather than ominous. Throughout, it captures the electricity of a great occasion far more clearly. The finale with a superb quartet of soloists and fine Swedish choirs brings the feeling of climax too often missing in recordings of the *Ninth*. Highly recommended.

Of the three stereo recordings Karajan has made of the *Ninth*, his 1977 account (415 832-2) is the most inspired, above all in the *Adagio*, where he conveys spiritual intensity at a slower tempo than before. In the finale, the concluding eruption has an animal excitement rarely heard from this highly controlled conductor. The soloists make an excellent team. The sound has fine projection and drama.

Recorded live on the morning of Christmas Day 1989 after the fall of the Berlin Wall, Bernstein's Berlin version brings a historic performance that has something special to say, not only because Bernstein substitutes the word '*Freiheit*', 'Freedom', for '*Freude*', 'Joy', in the choral finale. The orchestra, drawn mainly from Germany, both East and West, the Bavarian RSO and Dresden Staatskapelle, also included players of the Kirov Theatre Orchestra in Leningrad, the New York Philharmonic, the Orchestre de Paris and the LSO. The choirs similarly came from East and West Germany, while the soloists represented four countries: America (June Anderson), Britain (Sarah Walker), Germany (Klaus König) and Holland (Jan-Hendrik Rootering). For many, the uniqueness of this version and the emotions it conveys will make it a first choice, despite obvious flaws.

With Gardiner and his period forces, recorded close, there is no mystery in the tremolos at the start of the *Ninth*, but the movement at its brisk speed builds up inexorably, and the Scherzo is well sprung at a relatively modest tempo. The slow movement is far faster than usual but still conveys repose. The finale, urgent and dramatic, gains from Gardiner's cunning as a choral conductor, drawing incandescent sounds from his own professional choir, and the quartet of fresh-voiced soloists is exceptionally strong. An exuberant conclusion confirms this as a clear first choice among period versions.

It is thrilling to have such a splendid new CD transfer of Furtwängler's historic recording, made at the reopening of the Festspielhause in Bayreuth in 1951. The chorus may not be ideally focused in the background, and the audience noises are the more apparent on CD, but the extra clarity and freshness impressively enhance a reading without parallel. The spacious, lovingly moulded account of the slow movement is among Furtwängler's finest achievements on record and, with an excellent quartet of soloists, the finale crowns a performance fully worthy of reissue among EMI's 'Great recordings of the century'.

Stokowski's 1967 version, recorded in Kingsway Hall, makes a fine mid-priced choice for the *Ninth*, tense as in a live performance. The Phase Four recording has been vividly remastered and retains its fullness, both vocally and orchestrally. The first movement is strong and dramatic, taken at a Toscanini pace; the Scherzo is light and pointed, with timpani cutting through; the slow movement has depth and *Innigkeit*. The finale is uneven, despite fine singing, yet ends resplendently. The *Egmont Overture*, recorded just over five years later, is a strong and exciting.

Though the first movement is less biting than the rest, the *Ninth Symphony*, often a disappointment in complete cycles, in Menuhin's hands brings a fitting culmination, thanks also to the fresh, clear singing of the Lithuanian choir and a young, rather lightweight quartet of soloists. As in the Gardiner thesis, the drum-and-fife sequence in the finale is taken very fast, like a French military march. With a deeply felt slow movement this is among the finest modern bargain versions.

Karl Boehm's reading is spacious and powerful. Overall there is a sense of a great occasion; the concentration is unfailing, reaching its peak in the glorious finale, rugged and strong. With a fine, characterful team of soloists and a freshly incisive chorus formed from singers of the Vienna State Opera, Strongly recommendable.

Karajan's 1962 version, reissued in DG's 'Originals' series, is less hushed and serene in the slow movement than either of his later versions, but the finale blazes even more intensely, with Janowitz's contribution radiant in its purity. This reflected the electricity of the Berlin sessions, when it rounded off a cycle recorded over two weeks. The *Coriolan* coupling is an added bonus.

Bernstein's characterful VPO account of the *Ninth* crowns his Beethoven series superbly. The very start conveys immediate electricity, reflecting the presence of an audience, and the first movement is presented at white heat from first to last. In the finale Gwyneth Jones's hard-edged soprano will not please everyone. Otherwise this is a superb account, sung and played with dedication. The recording is bright, full and immediate. This seems to be available both on DG's Classikon bargain label (with very limited documentation) and, at mid-price.

Sinopoli's powerful version was recorded live

in 1996 at the annual Palm Sunday performance of the *Ninth* in Dresden, giving a sense of occasion. The venue was the small Semper Opera House, with the sound full and immediate. Where in romantic music Sinopoli generally favours a moulded, flexible style, here in Beethoven he takes a rugged view, warmly sympathetic but largely without mannerism. The weight of the chorus is splendidly caught, with high dynamic contrasts and with the soloists an undistractingly well-matched team.

Raymond Leppard and the RPO offer a bright, incisive performance, enhanced by sharply focused, forward recording. The precise triplets in the opening tremolos may lack mystery but they lead to a well-terraced reading in which the entry of the recapitulation makes a shattering impact. Speeds, on the broad side in fast movements, never sound too slow, thanks to rhythmic lift and crisp ensemble, while the slow movement flows smoothly and songfully. The fresh, forward balance of voices, both chorus and soloists, adds to the impact of the finale, making this another excellent recommendation at bargain price.

For some listeners the fast pace of the slow movement of Harnoncourt's *Ninth* will seem a drawback, but otherwise the performance caps the cycle splendidly, with a very compelling account of the finale.

Hickox's performance, beautifully paced, using an orchestra of the size Beethoven originally had, brings some of the advantages of period performance: clarity of articulation and texture; otherwise one might not realize that the string band is any smaller than one on a regular recording of the *Ninth*. This is the most successful issue in his Beethoven series for ASV. The performance culminates in a glowing account of the choral finale with four excellent soloists. At super-bargain price this is very competitive indeed.

If you regard the sublime slow movement as the key to this epic work, then Solti is clearly with you in his earlier, analogue version. With spacious, measured tempi he leads the ear on, not only with his phrasing but also with his subtle shading of dynamic down to whispered *pianissimo*. Here is *Innigkeit* of a concentration rarely heard on record, even in the *Ninth*. Solti in the first movement is searing in his dynamic contrasts – maybe too brutally so – while the precision of the finale, with superb choral work and solo singing, confirms this as one of the finest *Ninths* on CD. The descriptive essay is written by Philip Ziegler.

As bitingly dramatic as Toscanini in the first movement and electrically intense all through, Szell directs a magnetic account of the *Ninth* which demonstrates the glories of the Cleveland Orchestra. The chorus sings with similarly knife-edged ensemble, set behind the orchestra. The performance of the *Fidelio overture* is electrifying.

Bela Drahos with his outstanding chamber orchestra from Budapest, gives a dramatic, refreshingly direct performance of the *Ninth* is typically dramatic, with the first movement brisk and intense, the Scherzo well-sprung and equally biting, and the Adagio following period practice in its flowing speed, sweet and beautifully moulded rather than hushed. With a superb chorus and well-matched soloists, the finale is urgently intense, working to a superb climax. Exceptionally vivid and full sound, well-detailed.

Reiner's 1961 reading conveys power rather than mystery. Ensembles have knife-edged precision, rhythms are beautifully sprung and speeds are relatively broad, not least in the slow movement which, like the first, is presented in the full light of day. Throughout he sustains tension magnetically, helped by the warm Chicago ambience.

Among versions at super-bargain price, Rahbari's Brussels version, digitally recorded, makes a good recommendation, vigorous and spontaneous. The first movement is strong and purposeful, the Scherzo excitingly fast, with the slow movement sustaining measured speeds well, and the finale is helped by confident choral and solo singing. The recording is reverberant, but not so as to muddle an involving performance.

Peter Maag favours a traditional reading of the *Ninth*, tense and dramatic but often warm and relaxed, with a spacious account of the great *Adagio*, lovingly moulded. The playing is not always ideally polished, and in the finale the baritone soloist is wobbly in his opening solo, but this is a weighty performance, well recorded and well worth its super-bargain price.

The high point of Karajan's digital version of the *Ninth* is the sublime slow movement, here exceptionally sweet and true, with the lyricism all the more persuasive in a performance recorded in a complete take. The power and dynamism of the first two movements are also striking, but the choral finale is flawed above all by the singing of the soprano, Janet Perry, far too thin of tone and unreliable. The sound of the choir has plenty of body, and definition has been improved in this remastered version.

Sharp, exhilarating intensity comes over in Norrington's reading of the *Ninth*, with many of his contentions over observing Beethoven's fast metronome markings justified in the results, even the fast-slowing speed for the Adagio. A serious snag is the singing of the male soloists, with the baritone, Petteri Salomaa, tremulous, and the plaintive-sounding tenor, Patrick Power, cruelly exposed in the drum-and-fife march passage, taken slowly. Reverberant recording still allows the bite of timpani and valveless horns to cut through the texture.

In the 1990 CD transfer for the Toscanini Edition the maestro's electrifying account of the *Ninth* is marred by the excessive treble emphasis, more noticeable than on the earlier, full-priced reissue.

Weingartner's 1935 account of the *Ninth Symphony* was a mainstay of the 78-r.p.m. catalogue. It remains impressive, as in his whole cycle presenting Beethoven truthfully without any intervening filter or interpretative veneer. Weingartner's soloists are good, too, in particular the magisterial Richard Mayr. Over sixty years old, it still ranks high among *Ninths*. The transfer is fair but not outstanding.

Klemperer's 1958 sound is amazingly good for its period, with the finale fresher and better balanced than in many recent recordings. However, his weighty vision is marred by a disappointing quartet of soloists; and the slow speeds for the first two movements come to sound ponderous. Yet the flowing account of the slow movement shows Klemperer at his finest. The new CD transfer offers extra refinement.

Symphony No. 9 in D min. (Choral) (conjectural version using Beethoven's metronome markings).
(N) (M) *** Carlton Dig. 30366 01022 [id.]. Labelle, Fortunato, Cresswell, Arnold Pro Musica Ch., Boston PO, Benjamin Zander.

Zander made this unique recording of the *Ninth Symphony* in 1992, after extensive research over many years into Beethoven's metronome markings. The question hinges on Beethoven's communication of the critical tempi indications to his publisher, which were not conveyed directly but through the composer's nephew, Karl. Zander argues that in certain instances Karl misunderstood his uncle's intentions, and the result has perpetuated a tradition of performance that is wholly incorrect. The very quick pacing for the *Scherzo* had already been approximated by Bernstein in his New York recording, but the other two principal differences are even more controversial. Taken at Zander's much faster tempo, the character of the slow movement is totally altered, becoming much nearer that of the *Pastoral symphony*. Zander also virtually doubles the usual tempo of the Alla marcia section of the finale, arguing that the exultant words of the tenor 'As gloriously his suns fly across the glorious landscape of the heavens' fit this exuberant pacing. Moreover, when it is adopted there is no need for any accelerando either during this part of the work or the fugato which follows. When the chorus returns overwhelmingly with '*Freude, schöner Götterfunken*', the theme is now only slightly faster than when it is first heard. Zander provides a vibrant account of the symphony to illustrate his ideas and the very well-rehearsed Boston Philharmonic Orchestra make a strong impression in a reading that is nothing if not full of conviction. In the finale the soloists are very good (there are many groups of starrier names on record that do not sing as well), and the chorus is resplendent in its fervour. The recording could be clearer in focus, but is fully acceptable and rises to the occasion in the last movement. There is no record of the *Choral Symphony* more generously cued, and each cue is linked both to Zander's accompanying essay and the Breitkopf score. You may not like everything in this performance, and you may not agree with Zander's conclusions, but you cannot ignore either. The result is uncommonly stimulating.

Symphony No. 9 (trans. Liszt).
(M) *** Teldec/Warner Dig. 4509 97957-2 [id.]. Cyprien Katsaris (piano).

Cyprien Katsaris's performance is a *tour de force*: his virtuosity is altogether remarkable and there is a demonic Beethovenian vehemence and drive. The piano is closely observed in a reverberant acoustic, making it sound jangly at times jangly quality. At mid-price this should not be missed.

Wellington's victory (Battle symphony), Op. 91.
✿ (M) *** Mercury 434 360-2 [id.]. Cannon & musket fire directed Gerard C. Stowe, LSO, Dorati (with separate descriptive commentary by Deems Taylor) – TCHAIKOVSKY: *1812; Capriccio italien*. *** ✿

This most famous of all Mercury records was one of the most successful classical LPs of all time, selling some two million copies in the analogue era. Remastered for CD, it sounds even more spectacular than it ever did in its vinyl format, with Beethoven's musical picture of armies clashing vividly caught. The presentation, with handsome colour reproductions of appropriate paintings (and excellent documentation), is a model of its kind.

CHAMBER MUSIC

Cello sonatas Nos. 1–5.
(N) (***) Testament mono SBT 2158 (20 [id.]. Piatigorsky, Solomon – BRAHMS: *Sonata No. 1*; WEBER *Sonata in A*. (***)
(N) (BB) ** ASV Quicksilva Dig. CDQSS 235 (2) [id.]. Richard Markson, Osorio.

(i) *Cello sonatas Nos. 1–5*; (ii) *7 Variations on 'Bei Männern, welche Liebe fühlen'* (from Mozart's *Die Zauberflöte), WoO 46; 12 Variations on 'Ein Mädchen oder Weibchen'* (from Mozart's *Die Zauberflöte), Op. 66; 12 Variations on 'See the conqu'ring hero comes'* (from Handel's *Judas Maccabaeus), WoO 45.*
(B) *** Ph. Duo 442 565-2 (2) [id.]. (i) Mstislav Rostropovich, Sviatoslav Richter; (ii) Maurice Gendron, Jean Françaix.
(M) *** EMI double fforte CZS5 7333-2 (2) [ZDMB 63015]. Jacqueline Du Pré, Daniel Barenboim.
(B) *** DG Double 453 013-2 (2) [id.]. Pierre Fournier, Wilhelm Kempff.
(M) *** DG (IMS) 437 352-2 (2) [id.]. Pierre Fournier, Friedrich Gulda.
(B) *** EMI Rouge et Noir CZS5 69422-2 (2)

[(M) id. import]. Paul Tortelier, Eric Heidsieck.
(B) **(*) Hyperion Dyad Dig. CDD 22004 (2) [id.]. Anthony Pleeth, Melvyn Tan (fortepiano).
(B) **(*) Teldec/Warner Ultima 0630 17368-2 (2). Janos Starker, Rudolph Buchbinder.

Cello sonatas Nos. 1 in F, Op. 5/1; 2 in G min., Op. 5/2; 7 Variations on 'Bei Männern', WoO 46; 12 Variations on 'Ein Mädchen', Op. 66.
*** DG (IMS) Dig. 431 801-2 [id.]. Mischa Maisky, Martha Argerich.

Cello sonatas Nos. 3 in A, Op. 69; 4 in C, Op. 102/1; 5 in D, Op. 102/2; 12 Variations on 'See the conqu'ring hero comes' (from Handel's *Judas Maccabaeus), WoO 45.*
*** DG (IMS) Dig. 437 514-2 [id.]. Mischa Maisky, Martha Argerich.

Made in the early 1960s, the classic Philips performances by Mstislav Rostropovich and Sviatoslav Richter, two of the instrumental giants of the day, have withstood the test of time astonishingly well and sound remarkably fresh in this transfer. The performances of the *Variations* by Maurice Gendron and Jean Françaix have an engagingly light touch and are beautifully recorded. At its new price this reissue is very tempting.

The set of performances by Jacqueline Du Pré with Daniel Barenboim, now inexpensively reissued on a double fforte, was recorded live for the BBC during the Edinburgh Festival of 1970. The playing may not have the final polish of a studio-made version, but the concentration and intensity of the playing are wonderfully caught.

Fournier and Kempff recorded their cycle of the sonatas at live festival performances. These fine artists were inspired by the occasion to produce unexaggeratedly expressive playing and to give performances which are marked by their light, clear textures and rippling scale-work, even in the slow introductions, taken relatively fast. If with Kempff leading, some of the weight is missing such a stylish spontaneity is irresistible. In this remastering as a DG Double, the sound is beautifully clear, with the cello timbre somewhat dry.

Fournier's earlier accounts, made in the Brahms-Saal of the Vienna Musikverein in 1959, though not less spontaneous have more gravitas. Gulda's contribution is strong: he is more than a passive partner. The *Variations* are slight pieces, but in Fournier's hands they assume a greater significance than one might expect. The recording of both instruments is close but full, natural and beautifully balanced.

Mischa Maisky and Martha Argerich make a strong, characterful partnership, offering strikingly detailed, exhilarating performances, vividly recorded. Also available in DG's Beethoven Edition.

The Tortelier set with Eric Heidsieck dates from the early 1970s and has the advantage of more modern and perhaps slightly better sound than the Philips set. The performances are distinguished and make a useful alternative, with a bolder style than that of Fournier and Kempff on DG. The variations have been added and make a bonus for the reissue, two CDs for the price of one. The CD transfer is natural and clean.

The Piatigorsky–Solomon set made at Abbey Road in 1954 has claims to classic status. The performances have an aristocratic poise and a patrician elegance that puts them in the highest class. The recordings are in mono and at the time were never heard at their best in the 1957 HMV LP pressings. Subsequent transfers were a great improvement but these transfers by Paul Bailey present them in the best possible light.

Though the cello is balanced rather forwardly in relation to the fortepiano, the Hyperion collection of Beethoven's music for cello and piano, including the Variations, makes an attractive issue for anyone wanting period versions. Tan recorded this set with Pleeth in 1987, not long before he began his Beethoven series for EMI, and his imagination is comparably keen here. Despite the balance it is Tan who easily dominates the set and makes the allegros sparkle, notably in the *Variations*.

Janos Starker's warmly inspirational style is immediately apparent at the *Adagio* opening of the first *F major Sonata* and again at the beginning of the *G minor*. The slow movements of the two later sonatas, Op. 102, also show him in eloquent voice. The bolder, more direct approach of his partner, Rudolph Buchbinder gives these readings a classical strength, at times a little unyielding but always attentive to the music's detail. The *Variations* have an attractive lightness of touch. The 1980 recording is truthful, with good presence. Not a first choice perhaps, but individual and rewarding, and good value.

On ASV's bargain Quicksilva label Richard Markson, pupil of both Paul Tortelier and Pierre Fournier, very well partnered by Osorio, gives full-toned, direct readings of the five Beethoven *Cello sonatas*. Allegros are fresh and lively, though such a deep movement as the great *Adagio* from the last sonata, No. 5, misses the mystery implied. Warm and immediate recording, made in Wigmore Hall, London. Particularly with no fill-up on this two-disc set, it does not quite compete even in this price category.

Cello sonatas Nos. 3 in A, Op. 69; 5 in D, Op. 102/2.
(M) *** EMI CDM7 69179-2. Jacqueline du Pré, Kovacevich.

The Du Pré/Bishop-Kovacevich recordings of Nos. 3 and 5 come from 1966, the year after Jacqueline had made her definitive record of the Elgar *Con-*

certo. They stand among her very finest recordings. Du Pré's tone ranges from full-blooded fortissimo to the mere whisper of a half-tone in performances using the most expressive rubato. With excellent recording, the CD transfer is crisp and fresh.

Clarinet trio in B flat, Op. 11.
*** Sony Dig SK 57499 [id.]. Stoltzman, Ax, Ma – BRAHMS: *Clarinet trio* ***; MOZART: *Clarinet trio (Kegelstatt)*. **

The early *Clarinet trio*, Op. 11, comes off well on Sony and is accorded excellent sound. Stoltzman plays with great sensitivity and Yo-Yo Ma with almost too much. All the same, this is well worth investigating, and Emanuel Ax is spirited and vibrant.

(i) *Horn sonata in F, Op. 1*; (ii) *Sextet for horn and strings, Op. 81b.*
(N) (B) *** EMI Debut Dig. CDZ5 72822-2 [id.]. Andrew Clark (Waldhorn) Govier (fortepiano); (ii) Ensemble Galant. Roger Montgomery (horn); – BRAHMS: *Horn trio*; MOZART: *Horn quintet; Duos K.487 & K. 496.* ***

This is an endlessly refreshing disc, bringing together superb performances of some of the most important horn works in the chamber repertory, using a natural horn. Andrew Clark consistently relishes the ripe, fruity, often tangy tone of the Waldhorn, demonstrating that although such a piece as the slow movement of the Beethoven sonata brings uncomfortable technical problems, the extra tensions involved can add to the intensity of a performance. There is a flamboyance in the playing which carries the day. Gerald Govier is a persuasive advocate of the fortepiano. On one of EMI's cheapest labels this makes a splendid and stimulating bargain, very well recorded.

Notturno, Op. 42.
*** EMI (SIS) Dig. CDC5 55166-2 [id.]. Caussé, Duchable – REINECKE: *Fantasiestücke* ***; SCHUBERT: *Arpeggione sonata*. **(*)

Beethoven's *Notturno* is an 1803 arrangement by Franz Xaver Kleinheinz of the *Serenade*, Op. 8, for string trio. It is a slight work, but Gérard Caussé and François-René Duchable give a nicely turned and musicianly account. Exemplary recording.

Piano quartets Nos. 1 in E flat; 2 in D; 3 in C, WoO 36.
(BB) **(*) Discover Dig. DICD 920254 [id.]. Scheuerer Qt.

The enterprising Discover label does it again by giving Beethoven's three early *Piano quartets* their CD début. Written in Bonn when the composer was fifteen, they are obviously Mozart-influenced, as the charming *Rondo* finales of Nos. 1 and 3 readily demonstrate – particularly the one in the *D major* (otherwise less interesting), which is a lollipop. The central *Adagio* of No. 3 hints at the mature Beethoven, and the opening *Adagio assai* of No. 1 even more so – beginning like the slow movement for a piano concerto. The four sibling performers play throughout with pleasing freshness and vitality. The excellent pianist leads strongly, but the principal violinist could have a more generous tone. The balance is good within a fairly resonant acoustic. This well worth its modest cost.

Piano trios Nos 1–9; 10 (Variations on an original theme in E flat), Op. 44; 11 (Variations on 'Ich bin der Schneider Kakadu'), Op. 121a; Allegretto in E flat, Hess 48.
*** EMI Dig. CDS7 47455-8 (4) [Ang. CDCD 47455]. Ashkenazy, Perlman, Harrell.

Piano trios Nos. 1–3, Op. 1; 4 in B flat, Op. 11; 5 in D (Ghost), Op. 70/1; 6 in E flat, Op. 70/2; 7 in B flat (Archduke), Op. 97; 14 Variations on an original theme in E flat, Op. 44; 10 Variations on 'Ich bin der Schneider Kakadu', Op. 121a.
(M) **(*) Teldec/Warner Dig. 9031 73281-2 (3) [id.]. Trio Fontenay.

Piano trios Nos. 1–11.
(M) *** Ph. 438 948-2 (3) [id.]. Beaux Arts Trio.

Piano trios Nos. 1–11 Trio in E flat (from Septet), Op. 38.
(BB) **(*) Arte Nova Dig. 74321 51621-2 (4) [id.]. Seraphim Trio.

Piano trios Nos. 1–3, Op. 1; 8 in E flat, WoO 38; 10 (Variations on an original theme in E flat), Op. 44.
(M) *** Sony Stern Edition III SM2K 64510 (2) [id.]. Stern, Rose, Istomin.

Piano trios Nos. 4 in B flat, Op. 11; 5 in D (Ghost), Op. 70/1; 6 in E flat, Op. 70/2; 7 in B flat (Archduke), Op. 97; 9 in B flat, WoO 39; 11 (Variations on 'Ich bin der Schneider Kakadu'), Op. 121a.
(M) *** Sony Stern Edition III SM2K 64513 (2) [id.]. Stern, Rose, Istomin.

Piano trios Nos. 1–11; Trio in E flat (from Septet), Op. 38; Trio in D (from *Symphony No. 2*); *Trio movement in E flat.*
(M) **(*) Ph. Analogue/Dig. 432 381-2 (5) [id.]. Beaux Arts Trio.

Piano trios Nos. 1–3; 5–7; 9–10 (Variations on an original theme in E flat); 11 (Variations on 'Ich bin der Schneider Kakadu'); Allegretto in E flat, Hess 48.
(M) **(*) EMI (SIS) CMS7 63124-2 (3) [Ang. CDMC 63124]. Daniel Barenboim, Pinchas Zukerman, Jacqueline du Pré.

Piano trios Nos. 7 (Archduke); 9 in B flat, WoO 39.
*** EMI Dig. CDC7 47010-2 [id.]. Ashkenazy, Perlman, Harrell.

Ashkenazy, Perlman and Harrell lead the field in this repertoire. The recordings, made over a period of five years and at various locations, offer sound consistently fresher, warmer and more richly detailed than with most other rivals. The playing is unfailingly perceptive and full of those musical insights that make one want to return to the set. The *Archduke*, coupled with *No. 9 in B flat*, is available separately.

The Stern/Rose/Istomin recordings were made between 1968 and 1970, though the *Archduke* is earlier and was recorded in Switzerland in 1965. The performances are outstanding: strong, polished and alive. Istomin is always thoughtful and imaginative in slow movements, while Rose, although a less extrovert artist than Stern, holds his own by the warmth and finesse of his lyrical phrasing. One of the highlights of the set is the *Archduke*, commandingly bold and immediate, with a glorious slow movement; the *Ghost trio* also shows these artists at their most communicative, while they do not miss the charm of the early, Op. 1 works. The recording, improved on CD, is characteristically forward, in the CBS manner of the late 1960s.

In their analogue set, dating from 1965, the Beaux Arts are let down by the ungenerous tone of their leader, Daniel Guilet, but it matters little, set against the refreshing spontaneity of the playing as a whole. Tempi are admirably chosen (save in the *Ghost Trio*, which is very brisk, though the work's drama is projected brilliantly) and phrasing is marvellously alive. They convey a sense of music-making in the home rather than in the concert hall, with the naturally balanced recording attractively combining warmth and intimacy.

The Arte Nova set is as complete as most collectors will want. It runs to four discs (averaging out at 76 minutes each) and remains the least expensive way to collect this highly rewarding music. The Seraphim Trio have a splendid pianist in Gottfried Hefele, who dominates musically, while conforming to an apt chamber scale. The playing is freshly spontaneous throughout – the group readily conveys joy and exhilaration, especially in the delightful early works on the second and third discs. The recording is well balanced and the acoustic pleasing but the string timbre is somewhat dry, especially that of the violinist, Wilhelm Walz; the tone of the fine cellist, Jörg Metzger, is not very expansive, but he plays Beethoven's lyrical lines with a pleasing, simple warmth. Though the *Archduke Trio* is given a rather lightweight reading, it does not lack repose in the slow movements, typically expressive. A first-rate bargain.

The Fontenay versions were recorded between 1990 and 1992 in the Teldec studios in Berlin. Alert and intelligent playing throughout, attentive phrasing and bright, well-lit recorded sound. The *Ghost* is rather closely balanced; the Op. 1 *Trios* are much better. Very good playing, without the last touch of humanity and depth, as found in the Beaux Arts performances – particularly in their earlier set from the 1960s.

The Barenboim/Zukerman/du Pré set (by omitting Nos. 4 and 8) is fitted economically on to three mid-priced CDs. Even more than usual, the individual takes involved long spans of music, often complete movements, sometimes even a complete work. The result is music-making of rare concentration, spontaneity and warmth. The excellent recording has been freshened on CD.

Unlike their earlier set, the later Beaux Arts box offers everything Beethoven composed (or arranged) for this grouping, so that five well-filled CDs are involved; four of the recordings are digital. The transfers are well up to the usual high Philips standard and the performances are most accomplished and musical, if not quite matching the earlier Beaux Arts set in freshness and sparkle.

Piano trios Nos. 1 in E flat; 2 in G, Op. 1/1–2.
(B) *** HM HMA Dig. 1901361 [id.]. Patrick Cohen, Erich Höbarth, Christophe Coin.
*** Hyperion Dig. CDA 66197 [id.]. L. Fortepiano Trio.

Even more than in the recordings by the Fortepiano Trio, Patrick Cohen's group shows how fresh, alive and clear-textured these engaging works can be made to sound on period instruments, and how effective is the fortepiano, not only in the vivacious allegros but also in the slow movement of the *E flat major* and the *Largo con espressione* of the *G major*. The recording is first class, and this is a real bargain in its new Musique d'Abord format.

The London Fortepiano Trio play with considerable virtuosity, particularly in the finales, which are taken at high speed with fine attack. The use of a fortepiano serves to enhance clarity of texture in this particular repertoire. Well worth sampling what one hopes will be a complete cycle.

Piano trios Nos. 5 in D (Ghost); 6 in E flat, Op. 70/1–2; 7 (Archduke); ll (Variations on 'Ich bin der Schneider Kakadu'); 12 (Allegretto in E flat).
(B) *** Carlton Double Dig. 30366 00107 (2). Solomon Trio.

Three of Beethoven's greatest trios played with fine dedication and intelligence by Yonty Solomon, Rodney Friend and Timothy Hugh in lively but not over-bright acoustics. These artists have an excellent rapport, and one is left in no doubt that it is Beethoven's muse they are trying to serve rather than any corporate ego. The only snag is the dominance in the aural picture of the pianist, although in the *Archduke* Timothy Hugh's rich cello is very much in the picture, suitably so in a comparatively mellow performance. The *Kakadu variations* are also done splendidly and the brief *Allegretto in E flat* makes a fresh bonus.

Piano trios Nos. 5 in D (Ghost), Op. 70/1; 7 in B flat (Archduke).

(B) **(*) Sony SBK 53514 [id.]. Eugene Istomin, Isaac Stern, Leonard Rose.

The playing from the Istomin/Stern/Rose trio is strong, polished and alive, with good teamwork and the individual personality of each player coming over forcefully. The *Archduke* is a very impressive performance indeed (preferable to the Beaux Arts), bold and traditional in approach and full of energy. One of the slight drawbacks of the transatlantic recording is the comparative shallowness of the piano tone and the touch of thinness on the violin timbre, but the basic sound is warm and the balance not too close to rob the music-making of its dynamic range. An impressive coupling.

Piano trio No. 7 in B flat (Archduke), Op. 97.

(B) *** EMI forte CZS5 69367-2 (2). David Oistrakh, Sviatoslav Knushevitzky, Lev Oborin – BRAHMS: *Violin sonatas Nos. 1–2* **(*); SCHUBERT: *Piano trio 1* *** (with KODALY: *Three Hungarian folksongs;* SUK: *Love song;* WIENIAWSKI: *Légende;* YSAYE: *Extase* ***).

On EMI forte a well-rounded, well-groomed yet thoroughly alive performance by three eminent soloists experienced enough as chamber-music players to allow the necessary blend of personalities, the give-and-take that is essential for a great performance. They are rugged and assured in the first movement, brilliant in the last, and only a shade less compelling in the intervening movements. The 1958 recording is smooth and well-balanced. The Schubert coupling is equally impressive, while the encores come from a concurrent recital disc. Oistrakh is placed rather near the microphones, but his tone is pure and exceptionally rich, with remarkable changes of tone-colour – listen to the little-known but seductive Ysaÿe work and the *Hungarian folksongs* by Kodály. Yampolski provides supportive accompaniments and the balance remains very good.

Piano and wind quintet in E flat, Op. 16.

(M) *** Sony Dig. SMK 42099 [id.]. Perahia, members of ECO – MOZART: *Quintet.* ***

✽ (***) Testament mono SBT 1091 [id.]. Gieseking, Philh. Wind Ens. – MOZART: *Quintet* etc. (***) ✽

First choice for Beethoven's *Piano and wind quintet* lies with Perahia's CBS version, recorded at The Maltings. The first movement is given more weight than usual, with a satisfying culmination. In the *Andante*, Perahia's playing is wonderfully poetic and serene, and the wind soloists are admirably responsive. With the recording most realistically balanced, this issue can be warmly recommended.

Ideal chamber music-making in this earlier version by Walter Gieseking and members of the Philharmonia Wind (Dennis Brain, Sidney Sutcliffe, Bernard Walton and Cecil James). Recorded in 1955, it has few rivals in tonal blend and perfection of balance and ensemble. The mono sound comes up wonderfully fresh in this Testament transfer. This is a full-price reissue worth every penny.

Septet in E flat, Op. 20.

(B) *** Decca Eclipse Dig. 448 232-2; *448 232-4* [id.]. Vienna Octet (members) – MOZART: *Clarinet quintet.* ***

**(*) Nimbus Dig. NI 5461 [id.]. BPO Octet – HINDEMITH: *Octet.* **(*)

The Vienna Octet have been justly famous for their recordings of Beethoven's *Septet* for Decca, and this newest version of 1991 is no disappointment. Brio and good humour mark the performance, with a warmly elegant account of the slow movement contrasted with the high spirits of the Minuet and the Scherzo. The finale is no less infectious. The recording is wonderfully warm and real; it was made as recently as 1991. The coupled Mozart *Clarinet quintet* is cooler but beautifully played and recorded, using a basset clarinet.

The Berlin Philharmonic Octet give a delightful, characterful account of the *Septet*, with playing polished and refined. The only snag is that the recording, made in the Teldec Studios, Berlin, is rather too closely balanced. Recommended none the less.

(i) *Septet in E flat, Op. 20;* (ii) *Wind sextet in E flat.*

*** Hyperion Dig. CDA 66513 [id.]. Gaudier Ens.

The young members of the Gaudier Ensemble give an exuberant performance of the *Septet*, bringing it home as one of the young Beethoven's most joyfully carefree inspirations. The rarer *Sextet* for two horns and string quartet makes a generous coupling. Excellent sound, with the wind well forward.

Septet in E flat, Op. 20; Clarinet trio, Op. 11.

(BB) *** Virgin Classics Dig. Double VBD5 64109-2 (2) [CDVB 64109]. Nash Ens. (with SCHUBERT: *Octet* **).

This two-for-the-price-of-one issue brings uneven quality in the coupling. There is pure magic in these Beethoven performances, with the members of the Nash Ensemble conveying their own enjoyment in the young Beethoven's exuberant inspiration. So the *Clarinet trio* finds each player, not just the fine clarinettist Michael Collins but also the pianist Ian Brown and the cellist Christopher van Kampen. An apt sense of fun also infects the *Septet*, with Allegros exhilaratingly fast. Good, atmospheric sound, but the coupled Schubert *Octet* is not so successful either technically or musically.

Serenade in D, Op. 8 (arr. Matiegka).

*** Mer. Dig. CDE 84199 [id.]. Clive Conway,

Paul Silverthorne, Gerald Garcia – KREUTZER; MOLINO: *Trios*. ***

Beethoven's early *Serenade* for string trio was arranged for violin, viola and guitar as early as 1807 by the Bohemian composer and guitarist, Wenceslaus Matiegka. Gerald Garcia has here rearranged it for the present delightful combination, offering the violin part to the flute, and giving the guitar a more taxing contribution. As a companion-piece for the rare Kreutzer and Molino items, it makes a charming oddity in its seven brief movements, very well played and warmly recorded.

Serenade for flute, clarinet and guitar, Op. 8 (arr. Matiegka).
(N) *** Koch Dig. 3-7404-2. Still, Alemany, Falletta – KREUTZER: *Grand trio;* SCHUBERT: *Quartet for flute, guitar, viola and cello*. ***

The Austrian composer Wenzel Matiegka is also associated with another piece included in this entertaining triptych, as it was his *Notturno* that Schubert transcribed to make his *Quartet* for a rather similar combination of instruments. Matiegka's Beethoven transcription is equally felicitous, and the result here, with fine playing and recording, consistently charms the ear.

String quartets

(i) *String quartets Nos.1–11*; (ii) *12–16; Grosse Fuge*.
(N) (B) ** Decca/London Analogue/Dig. 458 301-2 (8) [id.]. (i) Gabrieli Qt.; (ii) Aeolian Qt.

In the mid-to-late 1970s Decca began a complete Beethoven cycle with the Gabrieli Quartet and the series continued through to October 1981 when Opus 18, Nos. 3 and 6 were the last of the set to be (digitally) recorded. Yet for some reason the Aeolian Quartet had already been contracted to complete the cycle in 1978, when they recorded the five last quartets plus the *Grosse Fuge*. The Gabrielis are very successful in the early Op. 18 set, splendidly accomplished – better in tune than, say, the Lindsays and more polished than the Végh. Phrasing is alive, rhythmic articulation well defined and they are responsive to the overall shape of the architecture. In the three *Rasumovsky Quartets* they can hold their own with the best of their rivals: their playing is extremely impressive and often really distinguished. Opp. 74 and 95 are also well-shaped and sensibly conceived readings, which only fall short of the last ounce of polish when put alongside their major rivals (the Italians, for instance). But their playing has no lack of vitality or fire. The recording is consistently warm and vivid and on CD faithfully reproduces the fine-grained sound familiar in the concert hall at that time. However the present reissue is flawed by the inclusion of the Aeolian recordings of the late Quartets. These have considerable merit, but on most counts simply do not measure up to their main competitors (the Végh or Italians), and the readings have less character than the Lindsays. There are moments of untidy detail, and for all their commitment, not all will take to the overtly expressive style of the leader (Emanuel Hurwitz) in the slow movements of Op. 132 and 135, particularly the latter. Again the recording is truthful if rather reverberant.

String quartets Nos. 1–16; Grosse Fuge, Op. 133.
(M) *** Valois V 4400 (8) [id.]. Végh Qt.
*** Valois V 4401 (*Nos. 1 & 5*); V 4402 (*Nos. 2–4*); V 4403 (*Nos. 6–7*); V 4404 (*Nos. 8–9*); V 4405 (*Nos. 10 & 12*); V 4406 (*Nos. 11 & 15*); V 4407 (*Nos. 13 & Grosse Fugue*); V 4408 (*Nos. 14 & 16*) [id.]. Végh Qt.
(B) *** Ph. 454 062-2 (10) [id.]. Italian Qt.
(M) (***) EMI mono CZS7 67236-2 (7). Hungarian Qt.

String quartets Nos. 1, 3 & 4, Op. 18/1, 3 & 4; 7 (Rasumovsky No. 1), Op. 59/1; 10 (Harp), Op. 74; 12, Op. 127; 13, Op. 130; 14, Op. 131.
*** EMI (SIS) Dig. CDS7 54587-2 (4) [Ang. ZDCD 54587]. Alban Berg Qt.

String quartets Nos. 2, 5 & 6, Op. 18/2, 5 & 6; 8–9 (Rasumovsky Nos. 2–3), Op. 59/2–3; 11, Op. 95; 15, Op. 132; 16, Op. 135; Grosse Fuge, Op. 133; Cavatina from Op. 130.
*** EMI (SIS) Dig. CDS7 54592-2 (4) [Ang. ZDCD 54592]. Alban Berg Qt.

For long a first choice, the Végh performances, recorded in the mid-1970s, have rightly been acclaimed for their expressive depth. That intonation is not always immaculate matters little in relation to the wisdom and experience conveyed. There is no cultivation of surface polish though there is both elegance and finesse. The CD transfers have a far cleaner image than the original LPs. The eight discs are now available together at mid-price.

The Italian performances, superbly stylish, are now offered in a bargain box of unbeatable value. The Végh versions, in some ways even finer, are at mid-price, but on eight discs instead of ten, the difference in cost is relatively marginal. The latest Philips remastering is most impressive, with the sound much smoother than before, and very naturally balanced. In the *Rasumovsky Quartets* in particular their tempi are perfectly judged and every phrase is sensitively shaped, while the late quartets receive satisfyingly thoughtful and searching interpretations.

The Hungarian Quartet's first recorded cycle of the Beethoven *Quartets*, with the mono sound firm and full, is superb, with tonal beauty never an end in itself. Polished ensemble goes with a sense of spontaneity in readings fresher and direct. The spacious, unhurried playing of the great slow movements here has rarely been matched. Those primarily concerned with the music as opposed to sound-quality will quickly adjust to the recording.

The Alban Berg's second set, recorded at public concerts, seeks to ensure that the greater intensity and spontaneity generated in the presence of an audience. On balance, these performances are freer and more vital than those in the earlier set, but the differences are small. Though the very perfection of ensemble and sheer beauty of sound are not always helpful in this repertoire, these performances are not superficial or slick. Strongly recommended to admirers of this ensemble.

String quartets Nos. 1–2, Op. 18/1–2.
** Hyperion Dig. CDA 66401 [id.]. New Budapest Qt.

String quartets Nos. 3, 4 & 6, Op. 18/3, 4 & 6.
*** Hyperion Dig. CDA 66402 [id.]. New Budapest Qt.

String quartets Nos. 8–9 (Rasumovsky Nos. 2–3), Op. 59/2–3.
*** Hyperion Dig. CDA 66404 [id.]. New Budapest Qt.

String quartets Nos. 10 in E flat (Harp), Op. 74; 14 in C sharp min., Op. 131.
*** Hyperion Dig. CDA 66405 [id.]. New Budapest Qt.

String quartets Nos. 11 in F min., Op. 95; 15 in A min., Op. 132.
*** Hyperion Dig. CDA 66406 [id.]. New Budapest Qt.

String quartets Nos. 12 in E flat, Op. 127; 16 in F, Op. 135.
*** Hyperion Dig. CDA 66408 [id.]. New Budapest Qt.

String quartet No. 13 in B flat, Op. 130; Grosse Fuge, Op. 133.
*** Hyperion Dig. CDA 66407 [id.]. New Budapest Qt.

The New Budapest Quartet offer fine performances, always intelligent, with many considerable insights. Throughout the cycle their playing is distinguished by consistent (but not excessive) refinement of sonority, perfect intonation, excellent ensemble and tonal blend. With excellent Hyperion recording, they fully deserve three stars, except for the disc of Op. 18/1–2, lacking a little in vitality. Yet the fact remains that the temptation to return to them for pleasure is not strong. Is it because they are somehow too clean and occasionally a shade characterless? They are certainly less searching than the Talich, the Lindsays, and, above all, the Végh.

String quartets Nos. 1–6, Op. 18/1–6.
(M) (***) Sony mono M2K 52531 (2) [id.]. Budapest Qt.
(M) **(*) Ph. 426 046-2 (3) [id.]. Italian Qt.

The celebrated set by the Budapest Quartet first appeared in the UK on the Philips label in 1956. Unlike their 1960s re-make, the sonority is perfectly focused and the readings have weight, animation and dedication, commanding the music's architecture and of expressive detail that is captured in sound of outstanding fidelity, given the period. The Sony engineers have produced transfers of excellent quality.

The Italian performances are superb. The only reservations concern Nos. 2 and 4: the latter is perhaps a little wanting in forward movement, while the conventional exchanges at the opening of No. 2 seem a shade too deliberate. The balance is truthful but the digital remastering brings out a thinness in the treble.

String quartets Nos. 1–6, Op. 18/1–6; F (arr. of *Piano sonata in E, Op. 14/1);* (i) *String quintet in C, Op. 29.*
*** RCA Dig. 09026 61284-2 (3) [id.]. Tokyo Qt; (i) Zukerman.

The Tokyo Quartet, one of the finest in the world, produce a sumptuous, beautifully blended sonority and play with impeccable ensemble, in interpretations of great musical insight. Their account of the Op. 18 *Quartets* is more imaginative than the Talich, has greater finesse than the Lindsay and can match, though not surpass, the Végh in depth. First-movement exposition repeats are all observed. The three CDs offer an additional *bonne bouche* in the form of Beethoven's own transcription of the *E major Piano sonata* and the more substantial bonus of the *C major String quintet*, Op. 29. There is plenty of space round the sound and a good back-to-front perspective. Among modern recordings this must now be a first recommendation.

String quartets Nos. 1–6, Op. 18/1–6; 10 in E flat (Harp), Op. 74; 11 in F min., Op. 95.
(M) *** ASV CDDDCS 305 (3) [id.]. Lindsay Qt.

It is good to have the Lindsay recordings now reissued at mid-price (retaining their old catalogue numbers). Their great merit in Beethoven lies in the natural expressiveness of their playing, most strikingly in slow movements, which brings a hushed inner quality too rarely caught on record. The sense of spontaneity necessarily brings the obverse quality: these performances are not as precise as those in the finest rival sets; but there are few Beethoven quartet recordings that so convincingly bring out the humanity of the writing, its power to communicate. The recording, set in a fairly reverberant acoustic, is warm and realistic.

String quartets Nos. 1–3, Op. 18/1–3.
*** Nimbus Dig. NI 5173 [id.]. Medici Qt.

The Medici are not a jet-set ensemble; their playing is refreshingly unglamorous yet thoroughly polished in searching interpretations. With natural, well-balanced recording, and these are most satisfying performances.

String quartets Nos. 1 in F; 4 in C min.; 6 in B flat, Op. 18/1, 4 & 6; 9 in C (Rasumovsky), Op. 59/3; 11 in F min., Op. 95; (i) *String quintet in C, Op. 29.*
❀ (M) (***) Sony mono MH2K 62870 (2) [id.]. Budapest Qt, (i) with Milton Katims.

String quartets Nos. 12 in E flat, Op. 127; 14 in C sharp min., Op. 131; 15 in A min., Op. 132; 16 in F, Op. 135 (with *Minuet* from *Quartet No. 5 in A, Op. 18/5*).
❀ (M) (***) Sony mono MH2K 62873 (2) [id.]. Budapest Qt.

These two-CD Sony sets are of exceptional interest. It collects the 78-r.p.m. cycle on which this group embarked during the war years between 1940 and 1945, for the most part recorded in the agreeable and spacious acoustic of the Liederkranz Hall in New York (with the exception of Op. 18, No. 6, and the *C major Quintet*, Op. 29, which come from the 30th Street New York Studios). The careful CD transfers are clean at the top and tonally full-bodied, belying their age. Such is the calibre of the playing that they even invite comparison with the legendary Busch set, with the fugal opening of the Budapest Op. 131 just as searching and technically more secure than the Busch. Elegant presentation reproduces facsimiles of the original 78-r.p.m. albums and their handsome labels. An outstanding, highly treasurable reissue at upper-mid-price.

(i) *String quartets Nos. 1 in F, Op. 18/1; 9 in C, Op. 59/3; 11 in F min., Op. 95; 12 in E flat, Op. 127; 14 in C sharp min., Op. 131; 15 in A min., Op. 132; 16 in F, Op. 135.* (ii) *Violin sonata No. 3 in E flat, Op. 12/3.*
❀ (M) *** EMI mono CHS5 65308-2 (4) [id.]. (i) Busch Qt; (ii) Adolf Busch, Rudolf Serkin – SCHUBERT: *String quartet No. 8.* ***

Beethoven's greatest music, it is often rightly said, is better than any performance of it can ever be. Listening to the Busch Quartet's pre-war HMV accounts of the quartets, however, one is almost tempted to doubt this received wisdom. No group since has ever penetrated deeper into the heart of these scores. In addition to the Beethoven quartets there is a bonus in the form of the *Violin sonata in E flat*, Op. 12, No. 3, from Busch and Serkin, playing of warmth and humanity, and a sparkling account of the early *B flat Quartet*, D.112, of Schubert. These are classics of the gramophone and not to be missed, excellently remastered and transferred.

String quartets Nos. 1 in F, Op. 18/1; 14 in C sharp min., Op. 131.
*** Capriccio Dig. 10510 [id.]. Petersen Qt.

Quite easily the best account of the Op. 131 *Quartet* to have appeared in recent years. Both here and in the less successful *F major Quartet*, Op. 18, No. 1, the Petersen Quartet prove dedicated and characterful. For those who are unduly worried by odd blemishes in the Végh or the leader's intakes of breath, this is a satisfying alternative recommendation in digital sound.

String quartets Nos. 3 in D; 4 in C min., Op. 18/3–4.
(BB) *** Arte Nova Dig. 74321 39103-2 [id.]. Alexander Qt.

String quartets Nos. 8 in E min.; 9 in C (Rasumovsky), Op. 59/2–3.
(BB) *** Arte Nova Dig. 74321 46491-2 [id.]. Alexander Qt.

No one investing in the Arte Nova accounts of the Op. 18 *Quartets* listed above will be disappointed. The San Francisco-based Alexander Quartet won the London International String Quartet Competition in 1985. Although these are super-bargain discs, they are top-drawer performances with excellent recordings of interpretations of fine musical intelligence. The same goes for their accounts of two *Rasumovsky Quartets*. One hopes the Alexander will maintain the standard of these two issues in a continuing series.

String quartets Nos. 3 in D, Op. 18/3; 7 in F (Rasumovsky), Op. 59/1.
*** Channel Classics Dig. CCS 6094 [id.]. Orpheus Qt.

The Orpheus Quartet are first class in every way. Their account of the *First Rasumovsky quartet* is among the best in recent years. In genuine music-making, the finale of the *D major Quartet*, for example, is not rushed off its feet, as it so often is. This is very natural playing, well-attuned to the period; much felt without being over-intense. The recording has clarity and presence.

String quartets Nos. 4 in C min., Op. 18/4; 10 in E flat (Harp), Op. 74; 14 in C sharp min., Op. 131.
(M) (***) Biddulph mono LAB 056-7 [id.]. Rosé Qt – BACH: *Double concerto* etc. (***)

Music-making from another age. These performances bring us as close as we can possibly get to the kind of strongly characterized playing Brahms and Mahler would have heard, refreshing after the relative anonymity so often heard today. The recordings were made in 1930 and 1932, while the *C sharp minor Quartet* dates from 1927, accounts for rather primitive sound.

String quartets Nos. 4 in C min., Op. 18/4; 15 in A min., Op. 132.
*** Capriccio Dig. 10722 [id.]. Petersen Qt.

The Petersen Quartet here confirm the positive impression made by their first Beethoven recording (Opp. 18/1 and 131). The *Heiliger Dankgesang* inspires playing of great depth, even though at other points they press ahead very slightly. An outstanding recommendation.

String quartets Nos. 7 in F; 8 in E min.; 9 in C (Rasumovsky), Op. 59/1–3.
(M) *** ASV Dig. CDDCS 207 (2) [id.]. Lindsay Qt.

The Lindsay set offers superb performances. Their insights are not often rivalled let alone surpassed in modern recordings. As to the sound, this set is comparable with most of its competitors and superior to many; artistically, it can hold its own with the best. They are now reissued in a box, retaining the old catalogue number, but with a reduction to mid-price.

String quartets Nos. 7–9 (Rasumovsky Nos. 1–3), Op. 59/1–3; 10 in E flat (Harp), Op. 74; 11 in F min., Op. 95.
*** RCA Dig. RD 60462 (3) [60462-2-RC]. Tokyo Qt.
(M) *** Ph. 420 797-2 (3) [id.]. Italian Qt.

The Tokyo Quartet's account of *No. 7 in F major* is one of the very finest in the catalogue. The tempi throughout are splendidly judged and the performance is beautifully proportioned. As a minor reservation in Op. 59, No. 3 the fugal finale is rather too headlong in pace and there are some traces of slickness elsewhere. But this is a powerful set and its strengths far outweigh its weaknesses. The recording is excellent, rich in sonority yet completely truthful and unglamorized.

The remastered Italian set still sounds well: there is now only a slight thinness on top to betray their age, with no lack of body and warmth. Superb playing is marked purity of intonation, perfectly blended tone and immaculate ensemble and attack. With tempi are perfectly judged and every phrase sensitively shaped, these performances remain a strong recommendation at mid-price.

String quartets Nos. 7 in F, Op. 59/1; 9 in C, Op. 59/3 (Rasumovsky Nos. 1 & 3).
**(*) Nimbus Dig. NI 5382 [id.]. Brandis Qt.

There is much to admire in the Brandis Quartet's accounts of the *F major* and *C major Rasumovsky Quartets*, distinguished by musical phrasing, good ensemble and tonal blend, well-judged tempi and a feeling for the architecture of each piece. Very well played, they are refreshingly unconcerned with outward show, yet their virtuosity in, say, the fugal finale of Op. 59/3 is not in question. The recording is acceptable but a little hard.

String quartets Nos. 7 in F (Rasumovsky), Op. 59/1; 10 in E flat (Harp), Op. 74.
(B) *** DG 447 919-2 [id.]. Amadeus Qt.

The recording of Op. 59/1 is taken from the first *Rasumovsky* set to be issued in stereo, in 1960. The four instruments of the quartet are perfectly balanced and the stereo is warm yet remarkably clear. The *F major Quartet*, a tough nut to crack, comes off very successfully, not least because of the players' attention to Beethoven's dynamic and other markings, and the *Harp quartet* benefits from similarly lively, sensitive and deeply musical playing. This is one of the very finest of the Amadeus's early stereo records and can be recommended to all their admirers.

String quartet No. 10 in E flat (Harp), Op. 74.
(B) **(*) Discover Dig. DICD 920171 [id.]. Sharon Qt – MOZART: *Quartet No. 1* *** (with RAVEL: *Quartet* **(*)).

The Sharon Quartet give a most enjoyable account of the the *Harp Quartet*, very well-matched, expressive and sensitive in the *Adagio* and perceptive in the closing *Allegretto con variazioni*. They are recorded in a Cologne church, which means that the sound is a shade reverberant, but the blend is attractively full.

String quartets Nos. 12 in E flat, Op. 127; 13 in B flat, Op. 130; 14 in C sharp min., Op. 131; 15 in A min., Op. 132; 16 in F, Op. 135.
**(*) RCA Dig. RD 60975 (3) [09026 60975-2]. Tokyo Qt.

String quartets Nos. 12–16; Grosse Fuge in B flat, Op. 133.
(M) *** ASV Dig. CDDCS 403 (4) [id.]. Lindsay Qt.
(**(*)) Testament mono SBT 3082 (3) [id.]. Hollywood Qt.

String quartets Nos. 12 in E flat, Op. 127; 13 in B flat, Op. 130; 16 in F, Op. 135; Grosse Fuge in B flat, Op. 133.
(B) *** Ph. Duo 454 711-2 (2) [id.]. Italian Qt.

String quartets Nos. 12 in E flat, Op. 127; 16 in F, Op. 135.
(N) (B) *** Ph. Virtuoso 422 840-2 [id.]. Italian Qt.
(B) **(*) [EMI Red Line Dig. CDR5 69791]. Alban Berg Qt.

String quartet No. 13 in B flat, Op. 130; Grosse Fuge in B flat, Op. 133.
(B) **(*) [EMI Red Line Dig. CDR5 69792]. Alban Berg Qt.

String quartets Nos. 14 in C sharp min., Op. 131; 15 in A min., Op. 132.
(B) **(*) Ph. Duo 454 712-2 (2) [id.]. Italian Qt.
(B) **(*) [EMI Red Line Dig. CDR5 69793]. Alban Berg Qt.

The Lindsays get far closer to the essence of this great music than most of their rivals, with the benefit of very well-balanced recording. They regularly find tempi that feel completely right, conveying both the letter and the spirit of the music, in rich, strong characterization. These are among the very finest versions to have been made in recent years. They now reappear, their catalogue number unchanged, but at mid-price – excellent value.

The Tokyo Quartet are a joy to listen to. Even if they do not displace earlier recommendations (Lindsay, Végh, Quartetto Italiano, etc.), they are well worth considering as an alternative. They are superbly recorded too, and, although they are just too beautiful at times to be ideal in this challenging music, they have obviously thought deeply about it.

As we have suggested above in considering their complete set, the merits of the Italian Quartet's performances are very considerable and their separate reissue on a pair of Philips Duos is very competitive, even if the second of the two sets seems short measure at only 90 minutes. However there is an alternative bargain coupling of Op. 127 and Op. 135 which some collectors may find useful. The remastered sound is very satisfying.

It has been some years since the renowned (1957) Hollywood set of the late Beethoven *Quartets* appeared. This is one of the classic sets and – *pace* the Budapest and Hungarian sets which also appeared in the 1950s – ranks as the finest after the Busch. Technically, the Hollywood players are superior to the latter (though the Busch have the deeper musical insights), and their virtuosity in the *Grosse Fuge* has to be heard to be believed. But there is no playing to the gallery at any time: this is Beethoven perfectly played without any thought to display. The recordings are mono but have plenty of presence. They are accommodated on three CDs, not available separately, well worth the high-priced premium label.

Some listeners may find the sheer polish of the Alban Berg Quartet gets in the way. Others dig deeper into the soul of this music, and this tells in movements like the *Heilige Dankegesang* of Op. 132 or the *Cavatina* of Op. 130. The recordings do full justice to the magnificently burnished tone that the Alban Berg command and the perfection of blend they so consistently achieve. These discs are only available in the USA.

String quartet No. 13 in B flat, Op. 130; Grosse Fuge in B flat, Op. 133.
*** ASV CDDCA 602 [id.]. Lindsay Qt.
**(*) Nimbus Dig. NI 5465 [id.]. Brandis Qt.

The Lindsay's account of Op. 130 includes both the *Grosse Fuge* as an ending and also the finale Beethoven substituted, so that listeners can choose for themselves.

The Brandis also offer both finales to this great quartet. Theirs is a good performance, humane in its musical approach, with tempi well judged and refreshingly selfless in approach. The Nimbus recording is undistracting.

String quartet No. 14 in C sharp min., Op. 131.
*** ASV CDDCA 603 [id.]. Lindsay Qt.

The Lindsay's account of Op. 131 is as fine as any in the catalogue.

String quartets No. 14 in C sharp min., Op. 131; 16 in F, Op. 135 (versions for string orchestra).
*** DG (IMS) Dig. 435 779-2 [id.]. VPO, Bernstein.

Not long before he died, Bernstein nominated his string-orchestra version of Op. 131 as his personal favourite among his own recordings. Basing the adaptation on one prepared by his mentor, Dmitri Mitropoulos, he draws dedicated playing from the Vienna Philharmonic, finding a concentration and an inner quality too often missing in recordings by four players alone. The CD version adds a similar string version of Op. 135, a work which Toscanini presented in this form a generation earlier.

String trios Nos. 1 in E flat, Op. 3; 2 in G; 3 in D; 4 in C min., Op. 9/1–3; Serenade in D, Op. 8.
(B) *** Ph. Duo 456 317-2 (2). Grumiaux Trio.

String trios Nos. 1 in E flat, Op. 3; Serenade in D, Op. 8.
(N)*** Hyperion Dig. CDA 67253 [id.]. Leopold String Trio.
(M) *** Unicorn Kanchana Dig. UKCD 2082 [id.]. Cummings Trio.

String trios Nos. 2 in G; 3 in D; 4 in C min., Op. 9/1–3.
(N)*** Hyperion Dig. CDA 67254 [id.]. Leopold String Trio.
(M) *** Unicorn Kanchana Dig. UKCD 2081 [id.]. Cummings Trio.

The young Beethoven, in preparation for writing string quartets, composed the three Op. 9 *String trios* in 1798, spare in texture but never thin. They may not be as memorable as the Opus 18 Quartets, but like the Opus 10 Piano sonatas written at the same time, they have a winning originality, each well contrasted with the others. The first in G is the most expansive, the second in D the most amiable, while the third in C minor has a gritty intensity reflecting that key. The Op. 3 trio was composed three years earlier, but is hardly less spontaneous (with two charming minuets); the delightful seven-movement *Serenade* (including a splendid set of variations) was published in 1797. The performances by the prizewinning Leopold Trio are particularly alive and fresh, and the Hyperion recording is remarkably real and vivid.

Even so the Cummings Trio on Unicorn are not completely upstaged. They have the advantage of economy (the two Unicorn discs cost upper-mid-price). Their playing is cultured but not over-civilized; there is an unforced naturalness about it all. These players let Beethoven speak for himself, and in quieter moments there is a winning sense of repose. In short this is real chamber-music playing, slightly more intimate than their Hyperion competitors, and with excellent recording – again in the demonstration class.

The return of the fine performances by the Grumiaux Trio (Arthur Grumiaux, George Janzer and Eva Czako) on a Philips Duo is a cause for celebration. Their playing is supremely musical and marvellously effortless; these artists are content to let the music speak for itself. In addition, the recording is fresh and full-bodied in the best Philips chamber-music tradition. The *Serenade*, Op. 8, not quite so persuasively done (originally coupled with the charming companion work, Op. 25 for flute, violin and viola), has been added for good measure. This performance, though polished, is perhaps not quite as persuasive as the rest of the programme. Strongly recommended, although the Cummings Trio remain first choice.

VIOLIN SONATAS

Clara Haskil: The Legacy, Volume 1: Chamber music

Violin sonatas Nos. 1–10.
(M) (***) Ph. (IMS) mono 442 625-2 (5). Arthur Grumiaux, Clara Haskil – MOZART: *Violin sonatas*. (***)

Arthur Grumiaux and Clara Haskil made their celebrated recordings in 1956–7, still sounding remarkably well for their age. The performances are wonderfully civilized and aristocratic. All ten *Sonatas* are fitted on three CDs at mid-price, as opposed to the four of Perlman and Ashkenazy, but they come in harness with two further CDs (equally desirable) of Mozart's mature *Violin sonatas*, as part of the 'Clara Haskil Legacy'. The discs are not at present available separately.

Violin sonatas Nos. 1–10.
*** DG (IMS) Dig. 415 138-2 [id.]. Kremer, Argerich.
(M) *** Decca 421 453-2 (4); 436 892-2 (*Nos. 1–3*), 436 893-2 (*Nos. 4–5*), 436 894-2 (*Nos. 6–8*), 436 895-2 (*Nos. 9–10*). Itzhak Perlman, Vladimir Ashkenazy.
(M) *** Sony Stern Edition IV Dig./Analogue SM3K 64524 (3) [id.]. Isaac Stern, Eugene Istomin.

Violin sonatas Nos. 1–3, Op. 12/1–3; 4, Op. 23; 5 (Spring), Op. 24. 12 Variations on a theme of Mozart, WoO 40; Rondo, WoO 41.
(B) *** DG Double 459 433-2 (2). Menuhin, Kempff.

Violin sonatas Nos. 6–8, Op. 30/1–3; 9 (Kreutzer), Op. 47; 10, Op. 96.
(B) *** DG Double 459 436-2 (2). Menuhin, Kempff.

Violin sonatas Nos. 1 in D; 2 in A; 3 in E flat, Op. 12/1–3.
*** DG (IMS) Dig. 415 138-2 [id.]. Kremer, Argerich.

(i) *Violin sonatas Nos. 1 in D; 2 in A; 3 in E flat, Op. 12/1–3; 4 in A min., Op. 23; 5 in F (Spring), Op. 24;* (ii) *Romances for violin and orchestra Nos. 1–2, Opp. 40 & 50.*
(B) *** Ph. Duo 446 521-2 (2) [id.]. Henryk Szeryng; (i) Ingrid Haebler; (ii) Concg. O, Haitink.

Violin sonatas Nos. 6 in A; 7 in C min.; 8 in G, Op. 30/1–3; 9 in A (Kreutzer); 10 in G, Op. 96.
(B) *** Ph. Duo 446 524-2 (2) [id.]. Henryk Szeryng, Ingrid Haebler.

Violin sonatas No. 9 (Kreutzer); 10 in G, Op. 96.
*** DG Dig. 447 054-2; *447 054-4* (from above). Kremer, Argerich.

Having two such volatile artists as Kremer and Argerich in partnership for the Beethoven *Violin sonatas* makes for exciting, heart-warming results. Perlman and Ashkenazy may be more centrally recommendable for being just as communicative and less idiosyncratic, but Kremer and Argerich have one magnetized from first to last by their individuality in performances that consistently sound spontaneous and fresh. Note that all ten sonatas are squeezed on to only three discs. Also available in DG's Beethoven Edition.

Perlman and Ashkenazy's performances offer a blend of classical purity and spontaneous vitality that it is hard to resist; moreover the realism and presence of the recording in its CD format are very striking. They are also now available (in the UK only) on four separate mid-priced CDs.

Though Menuhin and Kempff do not always offer the most immaculate performances on disc, they consistently reflect the joy and sense of wonder of pianist and violinist alike, often relaxed in tempo, but magnetic from first to last.

Szeryng and Haebler made their recordings between January 1978 and December 1979, with the *Kreutzer* saved until the end of the cycle. Philips used a favourite venue, La Chaux-de-Fonds in Switzerland; with clear CD transfers, the effect is very realistic and the balance impressive. Szeryng's timbre is small and thin, much less ample than Perlman's, yet firmly focused, with the recording slightly more flattering in the later sonatas. There is always a poised line and a natural warmth in his phrasing of slow movements, and allegros often gain from this relative lack of opulence. With the two *Romances for violin and orchestra* included for good measure, this pair of Duos, taken together, make a very good bargain, though the Perlman/Ashkenazy Decca set remains a primary recommendation for these sonatas.

The performances by Stern and Istomin have striking rhythmic strengths as well as lyrical appeal:

how delightfully the lilting opening theme of *No. 2 in A major* dances along, and how superbly the great *Adagio* of the *C minor*, Op. 30/2, is sustained. This and the very first sonata are analogue and were recorded in 1969; the remainder are digital and date from 1982–3. The *Spring Sonata* is more intense than some versions; the *C minor*, Op. 30/2, has similar electricity and the *Kreutzer* is splendid. The recording has fine presence, with the close balance suiting the highly projected style of music-making.

Violin sonatas Nos. 1–10; Contredances in B flat; in E flat, WoO 14/4, 7 (arr. Hess); *Minuet in G, WoO 10/2* (arr. Elman); *Allegro in G for mechanical clock, WoO 33/3* (arr. Hess).
(N) ** DG Dig. 457 619-2 (4) [id.]. Anne-Sophie Mutter, Lambert Orkis. (CD-ROM facility).

Anne-Sophie Mutter and Lambert Orkis were recorded at live performances in Wiesbaden during the summer of 1998 and there is no want of liveliness, expressive intelligence and tonal finesse. At the same time and despite many felicities, these are probably performances that would be better enjoyed in the recital room than on disc. There are too many impulsive touches, holding up the flow of the musical argument, and other personal idiosyncracies. Mutter is not always scrupulous in following Beethoven's dynamic indications and there are some agogic distortions too. Her playing (and that of her distinguished partner) has much personality, is commanding, masterly and undeniably compelling. However the idiosyncracies are intrusive and Beethoven is more selflessly (and no less brilliantly) served by the Perlman–Ashkenazy, Kremen–Argerich and Menuhin–Kempff partnerships. For those who are appropriately equipped, there is a CD score facility that runs on PC but not on Apple Macintosh.

Violin sonatas Nos. 1 in D; 2 in A; 3 in E flat, Op. 12/1–3.
(BB) *** Naxos Dig. 8.550284 [id.]. Takako Nishizaki, Jenö Jandó.

Violin sonatas No. 4 in A min., Op. 23; 10 in G, Op. 96; 12 variations on Mozart's 'Se vuol ballare' from 'Le nozze di Figaro', WoO 40.
(BB) *** Naxos Dig. 8.550285 [id.]. Takako Nishizaki, Jenö Jandó.

Naxos offer a winning combination here, in performances wonderfully fresh and alive. Takako Nishizaki's timbre, not large, is admirably suited to Beethoven and she is in complete rapport with Jandó, who is in excellent form. The *Mozart variations*, too, are winningly done. The recording is most naturally balanced, the acoustic is spacious without clouding the focus.

Violin sonatas Nos. 2 in A, Op. 12/2; 4 in A min., Op. 23; 5 in F (Spring), Op. 24; 8 in G, Op. 30/3.
(M) **(*) Ph. 442 651-2 [id.]. Arthur Grumiaux, Claudio Arrau.

This CD brings together performances recorded in the mid-1970s. *No. 2 in A* is particularly fresh; *No. 4 in A minor*, if fractionally less spontaneous, also comes off well. But in the *Spring Sonata* and the *G major*, although the readings are sensitive, understatement and lack of tension go together to undermine a feeling of live performance. The recording is rather closely balanced but warmly refined and truthful.

Violin sonatas Nos. 5 in F (Spring), Op. 24; 7 in C min., Op. 30/2.
(***) EMI CDH7 63494-2. Adolf Busch, Rudolf Serkin (with BACH: *Violin partita No. 2* (***)).

Music-making from another age, unhurried, humane and of supreme integrity. Playing of such naturalness and artistry transcends the limited sound.

Violin sonatas Nos. 5 in F (Spring), Op. 24; 9 in A (Kreutzer), Op. 47.
(M) *** Decca Legends 458 618-2 [id.]. Itzak Perlman, Vladimir Ashkenazy.
(B) *** Tring Dig. TRP 082 [(M) id. import]. Jonathan Carney, Ronan O'Hora.
(BB) *** Naxos Dig. 8.550283; *4550283* [id.]. Takako Nishizaki, Jenö Jandó.
(N) (B) *** DG Classikon 459 356-2 [id.]. Lord Menuhin, Wilhelm Kempff.
(B) **(*) [EMI Red Line Dig. CDR5 69789]. Yehudi & Jeremy Menuhin.

Couplings of the *Spring* and *Kreutzer Sonatas* are legion, and the combination of Perlman and Ashkenazy in Decca's Legends series must take pride of place. But the stimulating partnership of Jonathan Carney (one-time leader of the RPO and more recently of the Bournemouth Symphony Orchestra) and Ronan O'Hora need not fear comparison with the finest. These highly dramatic performances have great concentration and spontaneity. After the well-sustained *Variations*, the finale of the *Kreutzer* bursts with joy. The recording is resonant, the balance excellent.

Takako Nishizaki does not produce a large sound but the balance with Jandó is expertly managed, and the result is very natural and real. The performances are delightful in their fresh spontaneity. An excellent bargain.

There is no doubt that Menuhin and Kempff give inspirational accounts of both works, and the current transfer of a recording dating from the beginning of the 1970s is well balanced and has good presence.

In 1986 Yehudi Menuhin re-recorded these works, this time with his son replacing his sister, Hephzibah. Jeremy plays remarkably well, if not quite matching Hephzibah in the slow movement of the *Kreutzer*. Menuhin's timbre may be less rounded than formerly and his technique less refined, but the nobility of line is still apparent, and the spontaneity and family chemistry are as potent as ever. The *Kreutzer* finale is joyfully spirited. Excellent recording in a resonant acoustic. This is only available in the USA.

Violin sonatas Nos. 6 in A; 7 in C min.; 8 in G, Op. 30/1–3.
(BB) *** Naxos Dig. 8.550286; *4.550286* [id.]. Takako Nishizaki, Jenö Jandó.

All three of the Op. 30 *Sonatas* on one CD represents very good value, particularly with playing of such quality.

Violin sonatas Nos. 8 in G, Op. 30/3; 9 in A, Op. 47; 10 in G, Op. 96.
(B) *** Cal. Approche CAL 6251 [(M) id.]. Petr Messiereur, Stanislav Bogunia.

Strong, direct accounts of Beethoven's last three sonatas, of striking spontaneity and recorded with great presence and vividness. This playing, if not always subtle, leaps out of the speakers. Slow movements are felt but never sentimentalized. The *Adagio* of No. 10 is appealingly serene, and the following Scherzo and *Poco allegretto* finale offer admirable contrast. This disc is well worth its modest cost.

Wind music

Chamber music for wind (complete).
N (M) **(*) CPO Dig. 999 658-2 (4). Consortium Classicum (as below).

Allegro and minuet for 2 flutes in G, WoO 26; Duo No. 1 in C for clarinet and bassoon, WoO 27/1; Septet in E flat, Op. 20.
(N) **(*) CPO Dig. CPO 999 162-2 [id.]. Consortium Classicum.

Duo No. 2 in F for clarinet and bassoon, WoO 27/2; Fidelio: Harmoniemusik: Overture, arias and scenes (arr. SEDLAK); *Variations on Mozart's Là ci darem la mano.*
(N) ** CPO Dig. CPO 999 437-2 [id.]. Consortium Classicum.

Wind octet in E flat, Op. 103; Rondino in E flat, WoO 25; Trio for 2 oboes and cor anglais in C, Op. 87.
(N) **(*) CPO Dig. CPO 999 438-2 [id.]. Consortium Classicum.

Duo No. 3 in B flat for clarinet and bassoon, WoO 27; Grenadier march in B flat, WoO 29; Quintet in E flat for oboe, 3 horns and bassoon; Wind sextet in E flat, Op. 71.
(N) **(*) CPO Dig. CPO 999 439-2 [id.]. Consortium Classicum.

The Consortium Classicum are a highly musical and eminently stylish group, and anyone wanting all Beethoven's important music for wind ensemble will find the CPO recordings well balanced and pleasing. The *Allegro and minuet for two flutes* and the *Clarinet and bassoon Duos* are played most winningly and have great charm, while the *Trio for oboes and cor anglais*, a little-known but thoroughly rewarding work in the composer's wind output, is most persuasively presented. The *Grenadier march* is an engaging lollipop. However, few will want to repeat the 38-minute selection (*Harmoniemusik*) from *Fidelio* very often, and while Druschetsky's wind octet arrangement of the *Septet*, Op. 20 comes off spontaneously here, most collectors will prefer to have the original scoring. The four key works are available together on ASV in rather more characterful performances (see below): their superiority is most apparent in the more imaginative response to slow movements.

(Wind) *Octet in E flat, Op. 103; Quintet in E flat for oboe, 3 horns & bassoon; Rondino in E flat for wind octet, WoO 25; Sextet in E flat, Op. 71.*
*** ASV Dig. CDCOE 807 [id.]. Wind Soloists of COE.

The wind soloists of the Chamber Orchestra of Europe give strong and stylish performances of this collection of Beethoven's wind music, marked by some outstanding solo work, notably from the first oboe, Douglas Boyd. They are recorded in warm but clear sound, with good presence.

SOLO PIANO MUSIC

Piano sonatas Nos. 1–32 (complete).
*** Elektra Nonesuch/Warner Dig. 7559 79328-2 (10). Richard Goode.
❁ (B) (***) DG mono 447 966-2 (8) [(M) id. import]. Wilhelm Kempff.
(BB) *** EMI CES5 72912-2 (10) [CDZJ 72919]. Daniel Barenboim.
(BB) *** Nimbus Dig. NI 1774 (11) [id.]. Bernard Roberts.
(B) *** Decca 443 706-2 (10) [425 590-2] (with *Andante favori*). Vladimir Ashkenazy.
❁ (M) (***) EMI mono CHS7 63765-2 (8) [Ang. CDHH 3765]. Artur Schnabel.
(M) **(*) Decca 433 882-2 (8). Wilhelm Backhaus.

Piano sonatas Nos. 1–32; 6 Variations in F, Op. 43; Variations and fugue in E flat on a theme from Prometheus (Eroica), Op. 35; 32 Variations in C min., WoO 80.
(M) *** Ph. 432 301-2 (11). Claudio Arrau.

In America, Goode has often been likened to Schnabel or Serkin, rugged Beethovenians, but that is misleading. It is not just the power of Goode's playing that singles him out, but the beauty, when he has such subtle control over a formidably wide tonal and dynamic range. Even at its weightiest, the sound is never clangorous. Particularly in the early sonatas Goode brings out the wit and parody, while slow movements regularly draw sensuously velvety legato. Helped by an unusually full and clear recording, with no haze of reverberation, the clarity of his articulation is breathtaking, as in the running semiquavers of the finale of the *Appassionata sonata*. Above all, Goode has a natural gravity which compels attention. One has to go back to the pre-digital era to find a Beethoven cycle of comparable command and intensity. A clear first choice for those wanting a modern digital cycle.

Those who have cherished Kempff's later, stereo cycle for its magical spontaneity will find his qualities even more intensely conveyed in this mono set, recorded between 1951 and 1956, and reissued to celebrate his centenary in November 1995. The interpretations are the more personal, the more individual, at times the more wilful; but for any listener who responds to Kempff's visionary concentration, this is a magical series. No other set of the sonatas so clearly gives the impression of new discovery. Amazingly, the sound has more body and warmth than the stereo set, with Kempff's unmatched transparency and clarity of articulation even more vividly caught, both in sparkling allegros and in deeply dedicated slow movements. A ninth disc comes free, celebrating Kempff's achievement in words and music, on the organ in Bach, on the piano in Brahms, Chopin and Beethoven (a masterly pre-war recording of the *Pathétique sonata*) and accompanying Fischer-Dieskau in four of his own songs. The discs are handsomely packaged with a portrait of Kempff on each CD jacket.

Barenboim's earlier set of the Beethoven *Sonatas*, recorded for EMI when he was in his late twenties, remains one of his very finest achievements on record. The readings often involve extreme tempi both fast and slow, but the spontaneous style is unfailingly compelling. At times Barenboim's way is mercurial, with an element of fantasy. But overall this is a keenly thoughtful musician living through Beethoven's great piano cycle with an individuality that puts him in the line of master pianists. This box has now reappeared at bargain-basement price, handsomely packaged with a portrait of the young Barenboim on each of the cardboard inners. The admirably balanced recordings were made at Abbey Road between 1967 and 1970, the remastered quality brings a most believably natural piano image, and there is no doubt about the calibre of this highly rewarding cycle.

Bernard Roberts's cycle – his second for Nimbus – can be warmly recommended, the more so when it comes at super-bargain price. These are dedicated, undistracting readings which consistently reflect Roberts's mastery as a chamber-music pianist, intent on presenting the composer's arguments as clearly as possible, not drawing attention to himself. Always spontaneous-sounding, Roberts's approach to Beethoven has an element of toughness, whether in the early works or the late, a point that comes out the more clearly when the individual discs mix works of different periods. The mature sonatas are marked by rugged power, with Roberts's virtuosity given full rein, as in the finale of the *Appassionata*. The digital sound is full-bodied, with the piano set in a helpful, quite intimate acoustic. This is the least expensive set of the Beethoven sonatas available, well worth its modest cost.

Ashkenazy's set occupied him over a decade from 1971 until 1980, with the *Andante favori* added on as an encore in 1981. In the early sonatas his manner is strong, direct and concentrated, rightly treating the young Beethoven as a fully mature composer, no imitator of Haydn and Mozart. His readings of the middle-period sonatas are as masterly and penetrating as anything he has given us, and he is impressive in the late sonatas too, with a rapt sense of repose in the slow movement of Op. 109 (*No. 30 in E major*) while the last two sonatas are played with a depth and spontaneity which put these readings among the finest available. The *Hammerklavier*, one of the last to be recorded, is not quite on this level, hardly monumental. Generally the sound is excellent, if not always quite as full and natural as Barenboim's alternative and highly recommendable bargain-priced EMI set.

Arrau's Beethoven cycle, recorded during the 1960s, is a survey of great distinction. The Chilean master possessed a quite distinctive keyboard sonority, richly aristocratic and refined. The late sonatas show his artistry at its most consummate: outstanding (one of the very finest records he ever made) is his *Hammerklavier*, which represents his art at its most fully realized. No apologies need be made for the recordings, which belie their age.

For many music-lovers and record collectors of an older generation, Schnabel was the voice of Beethoven; returning to this pioneering set again, one realizes that his insights were deeper than those of almost anyone who followed him, though his pianism has been surpassed. This is one of the towering classics of the gramophone and, whatever other individual Beethoven sonatas you may have, this is an indispensable reference point.

Backhaus recorded his survey over a decade, from 1958 to 1969 (with the exception of the *Hammerklavier*, which came much earlier, in 1953, and is mono). As it happens, the latter represents the peak of the cycle, offering playing of great power and concentration. Backhaus's direct, sometimes brusque, manner does not derive from any lack of feeling, rather from a determination to present Beethoven's thoughts adorned with no idiosyncratic excrescences. At his best, as in the *Waldstein* and *Appassionata sonatas*, the performances present a characteristic mixture of rugged spontaneity and wilfulness which can be remarkably compelling. His massive, rather gruff style naturally suits the later rather than the earlier sonatas, but even the powerful accounts of Op. 109 and Op. 111 do not always leave the music quite enough space to breathe. But overall the set is a formidable achievement, a reminder of a keyboard giant. The recording is remarkably faithful, but with a limited dynamic range.

Piano sonatas Nos. 1 in F min.; 2 in A; 3 in C, Op. 2/1–3.
*** Sony Dig. SK 64397 [id.]. Murray Perahia.
*** Ph. Dig. 442 124-2 [id.]. Alfred Brendel.
*** Chandos Dig. CHAN 9212 [id.]. Louis Lortie.
(BB) **(*) Naxos Dig. 8.550150; *4550150* [id.]. Jenö Jandó.

As his accounts of the concertos have shown, Murray Perahia is as authoritative and sensitive an interpreter of Beethoven as he is of Mozart. These are commanding accounts of the greatest elegance and freshness. The *C major Sonata* recalls the classic Solomon account and, along with the Gilels on DG, is arguably the best we have had since the days of Kempff.

In Brendel's third Beethoven cycle, these recordings were made early in 1994 at The Maltings, Snape, coupling the first three sonatas together. This is distinguished, highly characterful playing, marked by superb control. Too controlled, some might say, for one sometimes feels the need, not so much for the unexpected, since Brendel is full of surprises, but for the volatile, bad-tempered quality that one remembers from Schnabel's records. Vividly alive recording.

Louis Lortie has the benefit of an immediate and truthful recording, greatly enhancing his playing gives. He brings his usual refined musical intelligence to all three of the Op. 2 *Sonatas*, giving ample evidence of his instinctive musicianship and artistry, sustaining momentum well and characterizing each phrase strongly.

Jenö Jandó's complete recording of the Beethoven *Piano sonatas* is also available in two flimsy slip-cases, each comprising five CDs (8.505002 and 8.505003). This first CD (actually Volume 3) establishes Jandó's credentials as a strong, unidiosyncratic Beethovenian. If there is not the individuality of a Kempff or a Barenboim, the playing is always direct and satisfying. The piano sound is full and bold.

Piano sonatas Nos. 4 in E flat, Op. 7; 13 in E flat, Op. 27/1; 19 in G min., 20 in G, Op. 49/1–2; 22 in F, Op. 54.
(BB) **(*) Naxos Dig. 8.550167; *4550167* [id.]. Jenö Jandó.

The performances of both the *E flat Sonata*, Op. 7, and the *Sonata quasi una fantasia*, Op. 27/1, in which Jandó is totally responsive to Beethoven's wide expressive range, show the excellence of this series, and the three shorter works are also freshly presented.

Piano sonata Nos. 4 in E flat, Op. 7; 15 in D (Pastoral), Op. 28; 20 in G, Op. 49/2.
*** Ph. Dig. 446 624-2 [id.]. Alfred Brendel.

Spacious and majestic are the words that spring to mind when the *E flat Sonata*, Op. 7, gets under way, and Brendel takes a magisterial view of the whole sonata. The *Pastoral* is now more inward-looking and has more gravitas than the VoxBox account or the earlier Philips cycle, and some may find it less congenial. Few, however, will find it less than thought-provoking.

Piano sonatas Nos. 5 in C min.; 6 in F; 7 in D, Op. 10/1–3; 25 in G, Op. 79.
(BB) *** Naxos Dig. 8.550161; *4.550161* [id.]. Jenö Jandó.

The three splendid Op. 10 *Sonatas* show Jandó at his most perceptive and unselfconscious.

Piano sonatas Nos. 5 in C min, Op. 10/1; 32 in C min, Op. 111; 32 Variations in C min.
(N) *** EMI Dig. CDC5 65136-2 [id.]. Lars Vogt.

Lars Vogt is an artist of quality and there is no playing to the gallery in this recital, which explores three of the many facets of Beethoven writing in the key of C minor. The most demanding of all, Op. 111, finds him at his most concentrated and penetrating. Whether or not you play all this C minor at one sitting or space it out, this player's intelligence and musical insight shine through. The EMI recording is first class, natural and with good perspective.

Piano sonatas Nos. 7 in D, Op. 10/3; 14 in C sharp min. (Moonlight), Op. 27/2; 28 in A, Op. 101.
(**(*)) Testament mono SBT 1070 [id.]. Géza Anda.

These recordings come from 1955 (the *Moonlight*) and 1958 (Opp. 10/3 and 101) during the heyday of Géza Anda's years as a Columbia (EMI) artist. The outstanding performance is the other-worldly account of the *A major Sonata*, Op. 101. Only Arrau and Gilels could command a sound-world that was as distinctive. All three sonatas are played with a vibrant sense of line and impeccable taste, and the recordings are fresh and clean. The one drawback is the premium price.

Piano sonatas Nos. 7 in D; 23 in F min. (Appassionata), Op. 57.
(M) *** Sony Dig. SMK 39344 [id.]. Murray Perahia.
(N) (M) **(*) RCA 09026 68977-2 [id.]. Vladimir Horowitz.

Intense, vibrant playing from Perahia in the *D major Sonata*, with great range of colour and depth of thought, and the *Appassionata* brings a performance of comparable stature. With truthful recorded sound, the disc is made even more attractive by being offered at mid-price.

In both these sonatas, Horowitz's combination of drama, poetry and impulsive flair sounds no less spontaneous for also conveying a considerable depth of intellectual power. Unfortunately the dry recording is not fully worthy of the playing. Although it sounds somewhat less brittle than it did on LP, the piano itself does not seem to be in top condition. The playing time of the CD is only 47 minutes.

Piano sonatas Nos. 8 in C min. (Pathétique), Op. 13; 9 in E, Op. 14/1; 10 in G, Op. 14/2; 11 in B flat, Op. 22.

(N) *** EMI Dig. CDC5 56586-2 [id.]. Steven Kovacevich.

There are few pianists who approach familiar repertoire with such insight and freshness. Readers jaded by the surfeit of Beethoven, who feel reluctance to invest in yet another sonata recital, will be surprised at how compelling an experience this is. Playing of stature and excellent EMI recording (much better than earlier issues in this series).

Piano sonatas Nos. 8 (Pathétique), Op. 13; 14 (Moonlight), Op. 27/2; 15 (Pastoral), Op. 28; 17 (Tempest), Op. 31/2; 21 (Waldstein), Op. 53; 23 (Appassionata), Op. 57; 26 (Les Adieux), Op. 81a.

(B) *** Ph. Duo 438 730-2 (2) [id.]. Alfred Brendel.

(B) *** Decca Double 452 952-2 (2) [id.]. Vladimir Ashkenzay.

In offering seven of Beethoven's most popular named sonatas, this Duo set – two discs for the price of one – is in every way an outstanding bargain. All the performances, taken from Brendel's analogue cycle for Philips, are impressive and the recording consistently excellent. The *Tempest*, Op. 31/2, is finely conceived and thoroughly compelling, and the central movements of the *Pastoral* resonate in the memory, the performance radiant and beautifully shaped, with every detail fitting in harmoniously. Outstanding too is Brendel's account of the *Waldstein*.

The comparable Decca collection of named sonatas was compiled (in late 1997) to celebrate Ashkenazy's sixtieth birthday and shows him consistently as a penetrating and individual Beethovenian. The *Moonlight* is poetic and unforced, and he brings concentration together with spontaneity of feeling to the *Tempest*, with an impressive command of keyboard colour. Taking a broadly lyrical view, the *Waldstein* is splendidly structured, and the *Appassionata* is superb. The very good analogue recordings were made over a period of seven years between 1973 and 1980 and are excellently transferred to CD.

Piano sonatas Nos. 8 in C min. (Pathétique), Op. 13; 14 in C sharp min. (Moonlight), Op. 27/2; 21 in C (Waldstein), Op. 53; 23 in F min. (Appassionata).

(M) *** DG 447 404-2 [id.]. Wilhelm Kempff.

Kempff's masterly recordings make a fitting contribution to DG's series of 'Originals'. Each performance here shows so well his ability to rethink Beethoven's music within the recording studio. Everything he does has his individual stamp; above all, he never fails to convey the deep intensity of a master in communication with Beethoven, as in the magic of his measured reading of the finale of the *Waldstein*. The *Appassionata* is characteristically clear and classically straight. The recording has gained in firmness with the clean sound of the digital remastering.

Piano sonatas Nos. 8 in C min. (Pathétique), Op. 13; 14 in C sharp min. (Moonlight), Op. 27/2; 23 in F min. (Appassionata), Op. 57.

(B) **(*) EMI CDM5 66796-2 [CDM5 66991]. Daniel Barenboim.

(BB) **(*) Naxos Dig. 8.550045; *4550045* [id.]. Jenö Jandó.

Barenboim's earlier performances combine impetuosity with a confident control of line. There is a rhapsodic feel to his approach which is very convincing. The *Appassionata*, like the *Pathétique*, is rather wild and rhapsodic in the first movement, and the slow speed for the central variations brings a simple, natural intensity which contrasts well with the lightness and clarity of the finale. The sound is first class, with excellent sonority.

Jandó's clean, direct style and natural spontaneity are particularly admirable in the slow movements of the *Pathétique* and *Appassionata*, warmly lyrical in feeling, yet not a whit sentimental. Only in the coda of the finale of the *Appassionata* does one feel a loss of poise, when the closing *presto* becomes *prestissimo* and the exuberance of the music-making nearly gets out of control.

Piano sonatas Nos. 8 (Pathétique); 14 (Moonlight); 23 (Appassionata); 26 (Les Adieux).

❀ (M) *** RCA 09026 61443-2 [Basic 100 09026 62561-2; *09026 62561-4*]. Artur Rubinstein.

Artur Rubinstein, always spontaneous-sounding, is specially vivid here in conveying the feeling of live music-making. Not a Beethoven specialist, he had never previously recorded the *Moonlight*, and brings to it a combination of freshness and maturity to make it stand out even among many fine recorded versions, with an improvisatory feeling in the opening movement. The *Pathétique* has a youthful urgency in the outer movements, and the impulsive surge of feeling in the *Appassionata* is equally compelling. The recordings, made in the Manhattan Center, New York City, sound firmer and fuller than they did on LP and reflect great credit on John Pfeiffer's remastering for CD.

Piano sonatas Nos. 8 in C min. (Pathétique); 21 in C (Waldstein); 23 in F min. (Appassionata).
❁ (B) *** DG Analogue/Dig. 447 914-2 [id.]. Emil Gilels.
(M) **(*) Ph. Dig. 454 686-2 [422 970-2]. Claudio Arrau.

Piano sonatas Nos. 8 in C min. (Pathétique); 23 in F min. (Appassionata), Op. 57; 31 in A flat, Op. 110.
(B) *** DG Classikon Dig./Analogue 439 426-2 [(M) id. import]. Gilels.

Gilels's account of the *Appassionata* is among the finest ever made, and so is that of the *Waldstein*. He is technically perfect as well as searching and profound. If the *Pathétique* does not quite equal that, such are the strengths of his playing the reading still leaves a profound impression. In this sonata the 1980 digital recording is balanced too close, bringing a touch of hardness. The good analogue recordings of the other two sonatas are preferable.

The *Pathétique* and *Appassionata sonatas* are also available on Classikon, in a coupling with Op. 110, and this makes a formidable bargain alternative, for the *A flat Sonata*, too, is given a searching performance. Even when Gilels storms the greatest heights in the closing fugue, no fortissimo ever sounds percussive or strained. This was (digitally) recorded five years later than the *Pathétique* with balance better judged.

Arrau's performances, made between 1984 and 1987, are magnificently recorded, the image bold and realistic. This helps to make Arrau's *Appassionata* very commanding, with gloriously rich timbre in the central *Andante*, powerful and commanding in the same way as his *Emperor concerto*. The *Waldstein* is impressive too, though the *Pathétique* (recorded in 1986 when Arrau was eighty-three) is a little lacking in colour and vitality, with the Adagio cantabile expansive.

Piano sonatas Nos. 9 in E; 10 in G, Op. 14/1–2; 24 in F sharp, Op. 78; 27 in E min., Op. 90; 28 in A, Op. 101.
(BB) *** Naxos Dig. 8.550162; *4550162* [id.]. Jenö Jandó.

Opp. 90 and 101 show this artist at full stretch. These are demanding works and Jandó does not fall short, particularly in the slow movements, which are very eloquent indeed. The piano sound is most believable.

Piano sonatas Nos. 11 in B flat, Op. 22; 29 in B flat (Hammerklavier), Op. 106.
(BB) **(*) Naxos Dig. 8.550234; *4550234* [id.]. Jenö Jandó.

From its very opening bars, the *Hammerklavier* is commanding; there is rapt concentration in the slow movement, and the closing fugue runs its course with a powerful inevitability. Again, most realistic recording.

Piano sonatas Nos. 12 in A flat, Op. 26; 16 in G; 18 in E flat, Op. 31/1 & 3.
(BB) **(*) Naxos Dig. 8.550166 [id.]. Jenö Jandó.

Volume 7 with its trio of middle-period sonatas can be recommended with few reservations. No. 18 is a considerable success, and there is much to stimulate the listener's interest here. Excellent sound.

Piano sonatas Nos. 12 in A flat, Op. 26; 19 in G min., Op. 49/1; 20 in G, Op. 49/2; 30 in E, Op. 109.
(*) EMI (SIS) Dig. CDC5 56148-2 [id.]. Stephen Kovacevich.

Stephen Kovacevich's credentials as a Beethoven interpreter are well known; anyone who heard his 1970s Philips recording of Opp. 110 and 111 or who has had the good fortune to hear his Op. 109 in the concert hall will know that in this work he is second to none. Sadly this digital version for EMI brings sound that is shallow and wiry in fortissimos, remaining unpleasant even after adjustment of the tone controls. The playing itself is most distinguished.

Piano sonatas Nos. 13 in E flat; 14 in C sharp min. (Moonlight), Op. 27/1–2; 15 in D (Pastoral), Op. 28; 26 in E flat (Les Adieux), Op. 81a.
(M) *** DG Dig. 445 593-2 [id.]. Daniel Barenboim.

Spontaneity and electricity, extremes of expression in dynamic, tempo and phrasing, as well as mood, mark Barenboim's performances. The lyrical flow in the *Pastoral* is as evident as the spontaneity of the music-making.

Piano sonatas Nos. 14 in C sharp min. (Moonlight), Op. 27/2; 21 in C (Waldstein), Op. 53; 23 in F min. (Appassionata), Op. 57.
*** Virgin/EMI Dig. VC5 45131-2 [id.]. Mikhail Pletnev.
(M) **(*) RCA GD 60375 [60375-2-RG]. Vladimir Horowitz.
(N) (M) *** Penguin Classics 466 210-2 [460 602-2]. Vladimir Ashkenazy.

Some will find the Pletnev *Moonlight* rather mannered, but he has the capacity to make you listen intently, and he finds the right depths in the slow movement and finale of the *Waldstein*. The account of the *Appassionata* is masterly. The engineering is immaculate, conveying Pletnev's individual sound-world.

Horowitz was not thought of primarily as a Beethoven pianist, but these recordings, made in 1956 (the *Moonlight* and *Waldstein*) and 1959, show how powerful he could be in the music of this composer. His delicacy, too, is equally impressive.

The sound has been improved in the remastering process; there is some hardness on top but little shallowness, and the bass sonority is telling.

These three performances are included on Ashkenazy's Double Decca above, which is economically the better proposition. But anyone wanting just these three sonatas will not be disappointed with this disc on either musical or technical grounds. The *Moonlight sonata* is among the finest in the catalogue.

Piano sonatas Nos. 15–18; 30–32.
(M) (**) Sony mono SM3K 52642 [S3K 52642]. Glenn Gould.

Wilful yet charismatic are adjectives to which so many have recourse whenever Glenn Gould's name is mentioned. There are no doubts as to his pianism or control or the quality of his musicianship but his late Beethoven, for all its intelligence, is quirky and marred by his vocal contributions. It can be recommended only to his admirers.

Piano sonatas: No. 15 in D (Pastoral), Op. 28; (Kurfürstensonaten) in E flat, F min., D, WoO 47/1–3; in C (incomplete), *WoO 51; Sonatinas: in G, F, Anh. 5/1–2.*
(BB) **(*) Naxos Dig. 8.550255 [id.]. Jenö Jandó.

Jandó's playing is fresh, clean and intelligent and, if the two *Sonatinas* are not authentic, they make agreeable listening here. The *Pastoral sonata* is admirably done.

Piano sonatas Nos. 16 in G; 17 in D min. (Tempest); 18 in E flat, Op. 31/1–3.
*** EMI Dig. CDC5 55226-2 [id.]. Stephen Kovacevich.

Even in this highly competitive field Stephen Kovacevich brings some extra distinction which makes this set special. This is playing of insight and of unfailing artistry that illumines and delights the listener. It is in the same class as his Opp. 110 and 111. If this cycle continues as it has begun, the Kovacevich could well be to the 1990s what Schnabel was to the 1930s and '40s.

Piano sonata No. 17 in D min., Op. 31/2.
✿ (B) *** EMI forte CZS5 69340-2 (2). Sviatoslav Richter – HANDEL: *Suites Nos. 9–16.* *** ✿

Richter's classic 1961 account of the so-called *Tempest Sonata* returns to circulation as a fill-up to the sublime set of Handel suites he recorded with Andrei Gavrilov during the 1979 Tours Festival. Richter makes the most of possibilities of contrast. He plays the opening extremely slowly, and then when the allegro comes he takes it unusually fast. Far from being odd, this effect is breathtaking. Excellent Abbey Road sound.

Piano sonatas Nos. 17 in D min., Op. 31/2; 18 in E flat, Op. 31/3; 26 in E flat (Les Adieux), Op. 81a.
*** Sony Dig. MK 42319 [id.]. Murray Perahia.

Wonderfully concentrated performances. All these readings have the blend of authority, finesse and poetry that distinguishes this great artist at his best.

Piano sonatas Nos. 17 in D min. (Tempest), Op. 31/2; 21 in C (Waldstein), Op. 53; 26 in E flat (Les Adieux), Op. 81a.
(BB) **(*) Naxos Dig. 8.550054 [id.]. Jenö Jandó.

Jandó offers here three famous named sonatas, and very enjoyable they are in their direct manner.

Piano sonatas Nos. 17 in D min. (Tempest), Op. 31/2; 29 in B flat (Hammerklavier), Op. 106.
(M) *** DG (IMS) 419 857-2 [id.]. Wilhelm Kempff.

Kempff's preference for measured allegros and fastish andantes gives a different weighting to movements from the usual, but the results are profoundly thoughtful.

Piano sonatas Nos. 21 (Waldstein); 24 in F sharp, Op. 78; 31 in A flat, Op. 110.
*** EMI Dig. (SIS) CDC7 54896-2 [id.]. Stephen Kovacevich.

This disc in Stephen Kovacevich's projected Beethoven cycle for EMI brings revelatory performances from one of the deepest thinkers among Beethoven pianists. Compared with Richard Goode – whose cycle has appeared complete – Kovacevich allows himself a degree more expressive freedom, giving foretastes of romantic music to come. The *Waldstein* as well as Op. 110 has a visionary quality. As with others in the series, the piano is set at a distance in a reverberant acoustic, blurring the edges.

Piano sonatas Nos. 24 in F sharp, Op. 78; 29 in B flat (Hammerklavier), Op. 106.
*** Sony SMK 52645 [id.]. Glenn Gould.

Whether or not you are a Gould devotee, no one could miss his unique magnetism in this long-buried recording. The first movement of the *Hammerklavier* must be the slowest version ever. It is not just that his basic tempo is very measured indeed, but that he takes every opportunity to linger over linking passages, coming virtually to a halt at the start of the development section. By personal magnetism the result is compelling, aptly rugged and muscular. The other movements too have their Gouldian eccentricities. Unhelpfully dry, if full and immediate, recorded CBC sound of 1970. In the little Op. 78 *Sonata*, Gould, consciously avoiding lightness and charm, is again magnetic – weighty and muscular in the first movement, bright and sparky in the *Allegro vivace*.

Piano sonatas Nos. 27 in E min., Op. 90; 28 in A, Op. 101; 29 in B flat (Hammerklavier), Op. 106;

30 in E, Op. 109; 31 in A flat, Op. 110; 32 in C min., Op. 111.

❀ (B) *** DG Double 453 010-2 (2) [id.]. Wilhelm Kempff.

❀ (M) (***) EMI mono CHS7 64708-2 (2) [ZDBH 64708]. Solomon.

(B) *** Sony SB2K 53531 (2) [S2K 53531]. Charles Rosen.

(B) *** Ph. Duo 438 374-2 (2) [id.]. Alfred Brendel.

Kempff has never been more inspirationally revealing than in these performances of the last six Beethoven sonatas. These are all great performances, and the remastered recordings have been enhanced to an extraordinary degree to give an uncannily realistic piano-image, helped by the immediacy of Kempff's communication.

Solomon's classic performances of the late Beethoven *Sonatas* present Beethoven pure and unadulterated, with the *Hammerklavier sonata* one of the greatest recordings of the work ever made. Opp. 109 and 111 were recorded in 1951, the *Hammerklavier* a year later; Opp. 90 and 110 in 1956, not long before he was struck down. The engineers have done wonders with the transfers. The sound emerges in startling freshness and fullness. Magisterial, thoughtful, lyrical performances that make many later versions sound shallow.

Charles Rosen is one of the most commanding interpreters of Beethoven's longest and most taxing sonatas. The first movement of the *Hammerklavier* is magnificently strong at a tempo as near Beethoven's impossible metronome marking as is reasonable and the great *Adagio* is played with an inner depth that allows no sentimentality, and the finale has rarely if ever been played on record with such dynamic power and clarity. In the visionary last two sonatas, less searingly intense than those preceding them, some may resist the uningratiating manner, but Rosen's commanding toughness consistently compels attention. The recordings, made at the EMI studios between November 1968 and July 1970, are firm and realistic, and allow a wide range of dynamic.

Reissued in Philips's Duo series, this Brendel set of the late sonatas makes an excellent bargain. This is among the most distinguished Beethoven playing of the analogue era. The recordings, made in the 1970s, are most realistic and satisfying in the CD transfers. The documentation too is first rate.

Piano sonatas Nos. 27 in E min., Op. 90; 28 in A, Op. 101; 30 in E, Op. 109; 31 in A flat, Op. 110.

(N) (M) *** DG 457 900-2 [id.]. Gilels.

This generously full Galleria disc is self-recommending. As a Beethoven interpreter, Gilels is almost peerless and though his reading of the *E minor sonata*, Op. 90 has some idiosyncratic rubato in the glorious second movement, its sunny almost Schubertian atmosphere is very appealing. In the remaining three works he is at his most inspired. The elusive Op. 101 is given a superb reading, the first movement and the *Adagio* before the elaborate contrapuntal finale both deeply expressive. The two final sonatas bring performances of enormous authority and power. Even when Gilels storms the greatest heights in the closing fugue of Op. 110, no fortissimo ever sounds percussive or strained. These last two sonatas are digitally recorded; Nos. 27 and 28 come from the early 1970s and are excellently transferred, and the effect is vividly real.

Piano sonatas Nos. 27 in E min., Op. 90; 28 in A, Op. 101; 32 in C min., Op. 111.

*** EMI (SIS) Dig. CDC7 54599-2 [id.]. Stephen Kovacevich.

Stephen Kovacevich's Op. 90 is among the finest in the catalogue and in the *A major*, Op. 101, the serene first movement has a subtlety of colour and tone that long resonates with the listener, while the short slow movement seems to commune with another world. The *C minor*, Op. 111, is given a searching performance, free from any attempt to beautify. The recording is excellent.

Piano sonatas Nos. 28 in A, Op. 101; 29 in B flat (Hammerklavier), Op. 106; 30 in E, Op. 109; 31 in A flat, Op. 110; 32 in C min., Op. 111.

(B) *** Decca Double Analogue/Dig. 452 176-2 (2) [id.]. Vladimir Ashkenazy.

(M) **(*) DG Originals 449 740-2 (2) [id.]. Maurizio Pollini.

Distinguished performances from Ashkenazy, and an impressive sense of repose in the slow movement of Op. 109, while the account of No. 28 is searching and masterly. This was Ashkenazy's second recording of the *Hammerklavier*, the performance fresher, more spontaneous than the earlier version, but less monumental. The last two sonatas are played with a depth and spontaneity which put them among the finest available. The analogue recordings, well transferred, date from between 1971 and 1980, and the remastering is very successful. The *Hammerklavier* is a digital recording and has a touch of hardness on top. Highly recommendable at Double Decca price.

Pollini's recordings of the late *Sonatas*, which won the 1977 *Gramophone* Critics' award for instrumental music, contain playing of the highest mastery. The remastering for reissue as a DG 'Original' has brought no marked improvement, but the two discs are now packaged like a DG Double and offered at a special price.

Piano sonatas Nos. 30 in E min., Op. 109; 31 in A flat, Op. 110; 32 in C min., Op. 111.

*** Ph. Dig. 446 701-2 [id.]. Alfred Brendel.

Rounding off the latest Brendel Beethoven cycle these performances are searching and concentrated.

They draw one into Beethoven's world immediately, with an eloquence that is all the more potent for being selfless. The recordings, made at Henry Wood Hall and at The Maltings, Snape, are excellent, real and full of presence.

Piano sonatas Nos. 30 in E, Op. 109; 31 in A flat, Op. 110; 32 in C min., Op. 111.
*** MusicMasters Dig. 67098-2 [id.]. Vladimir Feltsman.
(M) *** Cal. Dig./Analogue CAL 6648 [id.]. Inger Södergren.
(BB) *** Naxos Dig. 8.550151 [id.]. Jenö Jandó.

Vladimir Feltsman, born in Moscow in 1952 and since 1987 established in the United States, demonstrates in the last three sonatas that age is not an essential even with the most searching Beethoven works. The sound underlines unexpected differences in Feltsman's approach to each of the sonatas. In the first movement of Op. 109 he is freely rhapsodic to the point of wildness, with the piano made to clatter. In Op. 110 Feltsman's fresh, simple account of the measured paragraphs of the final fugue happily tends to cancel out any disappointment over the bright forcefulness earlier. Opus 111 then comes as a culmination, for here his many qualities focus splendidly, not just in the drama of the compressed first movement but in the spaciousness of the final *Arietta*.

Inger Södergren, little known in her native country, is a Swedish pianist who lives in France, where she enjoys a considerable reputation. Her analogue accounts of Opp. 110 and 111 come from 1979, when they earned golden opinions. They are musically most impressive; she is obviously a pianist of keen musical insights. These performances are fit to keep exalted company and the earlier, analogue recordings are most naturally balanced. A first-class mid-priced recommendation.

The last three sonatas of Beethoven, offered in Naxos's Volume 4, are very imposing indeed in Jandó's hands. There is serenity and gravitas in these readings and a powerful control of structure.

Miscellaneous piano music

Allegretto in C min., WoO 53; Andanti favori, WoO 57; 'Für Elise', WoO 59; 6 Variations on an original theme in F, Op. 34.
(M) *** Virgin Veritas/EMI Dig. VER5 61161-2 [id.]. Melvyn Tan (fortepiano) – SCHUBERT: *Moments musicaux* etc. ***

Melvyn Tan is a spirited artist and a persuasive exponent of the fortepiano. The *F major Variations* come off splendidly; this is a thoroughly enjoyable recital and is recorded with great realism and presence in the Long Gallery, Doddington Hall, Lincolnshire.

7 Bagatelles, Op. 33; 11 Bagatelles, Op. 119; 6 Bagatelles, Op. 126.
(B) *** Ph. Virtuoso 426 976-2. Stephen Kovacevich.
(BB) **(*) Naxos Dig. 8.550474 [id.]. Jenö Jandó.

Bagatelles, Op. 33; 119; 126; WoO 52 & 56.
*** Chandos Dig. CHAN 9201 [id.]. John Lill.

Beethoven's *Bagatelles*, particularly those from Opp. 119 and 126, have often been described as chips from the master's workbench; but rarely if ever has that description seemed so apt as in these searchingly simple and completely spontaneous readings by Kovacevich.

John Lill's collection of Beethoven's *Bagatelles*, the fill-up for his fine *Concerto* cycle for Chandos, is here brought together. Characteristically he takes a serious view of these chips from the master's workbench, bringing out their relationship to some of the full masterpieces.

Jandó plays the early set of *Bagatelles*, which date from 1802, with a crisply rhythmic style, almost at times as if he was thinking of a fortepiano. Then in the later works he finds more depth of tone and is thoughtful as well as flamboyant. He has an excellent, modern, digital recording.

7 Bagatelles, Op. 33; 6 Bagatelles, Op. 126; 6 Variations in F, Op. 34; 15 Variations with fugue in E flat (Eroica), Op. 35; 32 Variations on an original theme in C min., WoO 80.
(M) *(**) Sony SM2K 52646 (2) [id.]. Glenn Gould (piano).

Glenn Gould's *Bagatelles* and *Variations* are better and less quirky than his Beethoven *Piano sonatas*, which are not competitive. Gould fanatics can invest in them; others who are not converted can be assured that any eccentricity is positive and thought-provoking. Not a first choice but deserving of a place in the catalogue.

6 Bagatelles, Op. 126; 6 Easy variations on an original theme, WoO 77; 6 Ecossaisen, WoO 83; Klavierstücke in B min., WoO 61; 7 Ländler, WoO 11; Minuet in E flat, WoO 82; Rondo in C, Op. 51/1; 6 Variations on national airs: The cottage maid (Wales); Of noble race was Shenkin (Scotland); A Schüsserl und a Reindl (Austria); The last rose of summer; Chiling O'Guiry; Paddy Whack (Ireland). 12 Variations on a minuet à la Viganò from Haibel's 'Le nozze disturbate', WoO 68.
*** Decca 452 206-2 [id.]. Olli Mustonen.

Olli Mustonen plays the Op. 126 *Bagatelles* and the *Klavierstücke* with appealing simplicity and he finds a surprising depth in their lyrical inspiration. By their side, most of the other music, although skilfully crafted, stops only just short of triviality, but in Mustonen's hands the programme becomes a string of jewelled miniatures of great charm. His deliciously pointed articulation is a joy, particularly in the *Ländler*, while the *Easy variations*, WoO 77, are captivating, and the *Ecossaisen* hop and gallop along. The recording is most natural and believable. An outstanding collection in every way.

6 Bagatelles, Op. 126; 6 Ecossaisen, WoO 83; 'Für Elise', WoO 59; 15 Variations and fugue on a theme from Prometheus (Eroica variations), Op. 35.
*** Ph. (IMS) 412 227-2 [id.]. Alfred Brendel.

In bravura Brendel may not quite match his own early playing in this collection of shorter pieces, but his consistent thoughtfulness and imagination bring out the truly Beethovenian qualities of even the most trivial pieces.

6 Bagatelles, Op. 126; Polonaise in C, Op. 89; Variations and fugue on a theme from Prometheus (Eroica variations), Op. 35.
*** Nimbus Dig. NIM 5017 [id.]. Bernard Roberts.

Bernard Roberts gives a characteristically fresh and forthright reading of the *Eroica variations*, recorded in exceptionally vivid sound. He may not have quite the flair of Brendel, but the crispness and clarity of his playing are most refreshing. The shorter pieces bring performances even more intense, with the *Bagatelles* for all their brevity given last-period intensity.

6 Variations in F, Op. 34; 6 Variations on 'Nel cor più non mi sento', WoO 70; 15 Variations and fugue on a theme from Prometheus in E flat (Eroica variations), Op. 35; 32 Variations in C min., WoO 80.
(BB) **(*) Naxos Dig. 8.550676 [id.]. Jenö Jandó.

Jandó essays the same strong, direct style in his performances of the two major sets of variations that he does in the sonatas. Occasionally his forceful manner in Op. 35 and the *C minor Variations* reaches the point of brusqueness, but no one could deny the strength of this playing. His approach is appropriately lighter in Op. 34 and the very agreeable short set based on the duet by Paisiello. Excellent recording, clear and vivid, to match the other issues in his Naxos series.

6 Variations in F, Op. 34; 15 Variations and fugue on a theme from Prometheus in E flat (Eroica variations), Op. 35; 2 Rondos, Op. 51; Bagatelle: 'Für Elise', WoO 59.
*** Chandos Dig. CHAN 8616 [id.]. Louis Lortie.

The Canadian pianist Louis Lortie is an artist of distinction; his readings have both grandeur and authority. This account of the *Eroica variations* belongs in exalted company and can be recommended alongside such magisterial accounts as that of Gilels.

33 Variations on a waltz by Diabelli, Op. 120.
*** Hyperion Dig. CDA 66763 [id.]. William Kinderman.
*** Ph. Dig. 426 232-2 [id.]. Alfred Brendel.
(B) *** Ph. Virtuoso 422 969-2 [(M) id. import]. Stephen Kovacevich.

33 Variations on a waltz by Diabelli, Op. 120; 32 Variations in C min., WoO 80.
(B) *** ASV Dig. CDQS 6155 [id.]. Benjamin Frith.

The *Diabelli* is the greatest set of variations ever written. William Kinderman's version on Hyperion is outstanding, fresh and well thought out, sparkling with life and character, and it is almost worth buying the present disc for the sake of his illuminating liner-notes. He is very well recorded, too.

Now reissued in the lowest price range and with an equally fine account of the *32 Variations on an original theme in C minor* thrown in for good measure, the ASV reissue otherwise tends to sweep the board. Benjamin Frith gives a fresh and clear reading; tense and dedicated, this conveys Beethoven's mastery without exaggeration or self-indulgence. Clear, realistic recording to match.

On Philips, Brendel, here working in the studio, captures the music's dynamism, the sense of an irresistible force building up this immense structure, section by section. It would be hard to imagine a more dramatic reading, sparked off by the cheeky wit of Brendel's treatment of the Diabelli theme itself. The whirlwind power of the whole performance is irresistible, and the piano sound is full and immediate.

Kovacevich gives one of the most deeply satisfying performances ever recorded. Avoiding the idiosyncrasies of most other interpreters, he may at times seem austere, but his concentration is magnetic from first to last, with fearless dynamic contrasts enhanced in the excellent CD transfer. The reading culminates in the most dedicated account of the concluding variations, hushed in meditation and with no hint of self-indulgence. On the cheapest Philips label, it is a bargain that no Beethovenian should miss.

VOCAL MUSIC

Adelaide; Der Kuss; Resignation; Zärtliche Liebe.
(M) *** DG Originals 449 747-2 [id.]. Fritz Wunderlich, Hubert Giesen – SCHUBERT: *Lieder;* SCHUMANN: *Dichterliebe.* ***

Wunderlich was thirty-five when he recorded these songs, and the unique bloom of the lovely voice is beautifully caught. Though the accompanist is too metrical at times, the freshness of Wunderlich's singing makes one grieve again over his untimely death.

An die ferne Geliebte, Op. 98; An die Geliebte; An die Hoffnung; Adelaide; Aus Goethes Faust; Klage; Der Liebende; Das Liedchen von der Ruhe; 6 Lieder aus Gellert; Mailied; Neue Liebe, neues Leben; Sehnsucht; Wonne der Wehmut.
(N)*** Hyperion Dig. CDA 67055 [id.]. Stephan Genz, Vignoles.

Still in his twenties, the German baritone, Stephan Genz, not only has a voice of warm, velvety beauty, but already shows a rare depth of understanding. In the very first song here, *An die Hoffnung*,'To Hope' – Beethoven's response to suffering – he sings with rapt concentration, using the widest range of expression, while songs like *Adelaide* bring out Genz's honeyed tone, allied to flawless legato. That contrasts with the youthful energy of the brisk songs, and the biting irony of Goethe's *Song of the Flea*, taken very fast. A disc to have one reassessing Beethoven as songwriter, with the mould-breaking cycle, *An die ferne Geliebte*, as a fine climax.

An die ferne Geliebte, Op. 98; Abendlied unter gestirntem Himmel; An die Hoffnung; Adelaide; Andenken; Aus Goethes Faust; Ich liebe dich; Der Kuss; Der Liebende; Lied aus der Ferne; Maillied; Mit einem gemalten Band; Neue Liebe, neues Leben; Resignation; Sehnsucht; Seufzer eines Ungeliebten und Gegenliebe; Der Wachteslschlag; Wonne der Wehmut.
(N)**(*) Decca Dig. 444 817-2 [id.]. Peter Schreier, András Schiff.

As in Schubert, the inspired partnership of Peter Schreier with András Schiff results in deeply felt, finely detailed readings of an excellent selection of Beethoven songs, notably in such songs as *An die Hoffnung*. Though the voice is at times gritty, and no longer sounds youthful, the depth of feeling is never underplayed, with high dramatic contrasts, yet again heightening one's estimate of Beethoven as songwriter. Well-balanced sound.

Bundeslied, Op. 122; Elegischer Gesang, Op. 118; King Stephen (incidental music), *Op. 117; Meeresstille und glückliche Fahrt (Calm sea and a prosperous voyage), Op. 112; Opferlied, Op. 121b.*
*** Sony Dig. MK 76404 [MK 33509]. Amb. S., LSO, Tilson Thomas.

Tilson Thomas's collection of Beethoven choral rarities plus the *King Stephen* incidental music makes an attractive out-of-the-way disc for Beethovenians. With excellent singing and playing, they are all enjoyable.

(i–iv) *Cantata on the death of Emperor Joseph II, WoO 87;* (ii–v) *Cantata on the accession of Emperor Leopold II, WoO 88. Meerestille und glückliche Fahrt, Op. 112;* (ii) *Opferlied.*
✿ *** Hyperion Dig. CDA 66880 [id]. (i) Janice Watson; (ii) Jean Rigby; (iii) John Mark Ainsley; (iv) José van Dam; (v) Judith Howarth; Corydon Singers & O, Matthew Best.

Beethoven was only nineteen when in Bonn in 1790 he was commissioned to write his 40-minute cantata on the Emperor's death. It was never performed, and remained buried for almost a century. Arguably Beethoven's first major masterpiece, it was one of his few early unpublished works of which he approved: when he came to write *Fidelio* he used the soaring theme from the first of the cantata's soprano arias for Leonore's sublime moment in the finale, *O Gott! Welch ein Augenblick*. The aria is radiantly sung here by Janice Watson. Relishing the tragic C minor power of the choruses, Matthew Best conducts a superb performance, incisive and deeply moving, with excellent soloists as well as a fine chorus. The second cantata, much shorter, written soon after, brings anticipations of the *Fifth Symphony* and of the choral finale of the *Ninth*, while the two shorter pieces – with Jean Rigby as soloist in the *Opferlied* – make a generous fill-up, equally well performed. The atmospheric recording combines weight and transparency.

Che fa il mio bene? (2 versions); *Dimmi, ben mio; Ecco quel fiero istante!; In questa tomba oscura; T'intendo, si, mio cor.*
*** Decca Dig. 440 297-2 [id.]. Cecilia Bartoli, András Schiff – HAYDN: *Arianna a Naxos;* MOZART: *Ridente la calma;* SCHUBERT: *Da quel sembiante appresi* etc. ***

These rare Italian songs come as part of a recital which has an outstanding account of Haydn's *Arianna a Naxos* as its highlight. *La Partenza* has a winningly ingenuous simplicity and the *Ariettas* (including two completely contrasting settings of *Che fa il mio bene?*) are also full of charm.

(i) *Choral Fantasia* (for piano, chorus & orchestra), *Op. 80;* (ii) *Missa solemnis in D, Op. 123.*
(M) *** Sony SM2K 47522 (2) [id.]. (i) Rudolf Serkin, (i; ii) Westminster Ch.; (ii) Farrell, Carol Smith, Lewis, Borg; NYPO, Bernstein (with HAYDN: *Mass No. 12.* ***)

Bernstein is at his most intense in this fine, dedicated account of Beethoven's supreme choral masterpiece. It is an inspirational performance, though it is a drawback that it overlaps on to a second disc when, with an overall playing time of about 77 minutes, it could have been accommodated on a single CD. However, the couplings are well worth having, especially the Haydn (digital) *Theresia Mass*. Serkin's *Choral Fantasia* opens with a solo cadenza almost to rival Brendel's.

Christus am Olberge, Op. 85.
(M) **(*) Sony MPK 45878 [id.]. Raskin, Lewis,

Herbert Beattie, Temple University Choirs, Phd. O, Ormandy.
**(*) HM HMC 905181 [id.]. Pick-Hieronimi, Anderson, Von Halem, Ch. & O Nat. de Lyon, Baudo.

Ormandy is at his most purposeful and warmly understanding, and the soloists are outstandingly fine, with the pure-toned Judith Raskin very aptly cast as the Seraph and with Richard Lewis at his freshest and most expressive as Jesus.

Monica Pick-Hieronimi brings powerful Leonore-like qualities to her role as Seraph. Baudo directs an energetic and lively account of it which, if lacking the utmost refinement of detail, generates urgency and breadth in the fine closing section.

(i) *Egmont: Overture and incidental music* (complete), *Op. 84;* (ii) *Leonora overture No. 3.*
(B) *** Discover Dig. DICD 920114. (i) Miriam Gauci, Dirk Schortemeier, Belgian R. & TV O; (ii) LPO; Rahbari.

On the bargain Discover label, Alexander Rahbari offers all ten movements of Beethoven's *Egmont* music, not just the selection made by Szell, whose 1969 version has been reissued in Decca's Classic Sound series below. Such rarities as the third and fourth entr'actes and the melodrama, *Süsse Schlaf*, with Schortemeier as the speaker, may not be important, but they provide an attractive supplement to the well-known items. Both in *Egmont* and in the *Leonora No. 3 overture* (with the LPO) Rahbari conducts crisp, well-sprung, often exciting performances, with Miriam Gauci the warm-toned soprano. Atmospheric recording, pleasantly reverberant.

Egmont (incidental music), *Op. 84:* excerpts with narration based on the text by Grillparzer, and melodrama from the play by Goethe.
(M) **(*) Decca 448 593-2 [id.]. Pilar Lorengar, Wussow (narrator), VPO, Szell.

The problem with performing Beethoven's incidental music for Goethe's *Egmont* is at least partially solved by using a text by the Austrian poet, Franz Grillparzer. The music is interspersed at the appropriate points, including dramatic drum-rolls in Egmont's final peroration, this last scene being from Goethe's original. The Decca presentation, with Klaus-Jürgen Wussow the admirably committed narrator, is most dramatic. Szell's conducting is superb, the music marvellously characterized, and the songs are movingly sung by Pilar Lorengar. This has, appropriately enough, been reissued in Decca's Classic Sound series, and the CD transfer is vivid. A full translation is included, but there are no separating bands for the spoken narrative, so that it is impossible to programme the CD to listen only to the music.

Mass in C, Op. 86.
(BB) *** Belart 461 317-2 [id.]. Palmer, Watts, Tear, Keyte, St John's College, Cambridge, Ch., ASMF, Guest – BRUCKNER: *Motets.* ***

(i) *Mass in C, Op. 86; Meeresstille und glückliche Fahrt (Calm sea and a prosperous voyage), Op. 112.*
*** DG Dig. 435 391-2 [id.]. Margiono, Robbin, Kendall, Miles, Monteverdi Ch., ORR, Gardiner.

In this long under-rated masterpiece, Gardiner gives just as refreshing a performance as his earlier, prize-winning account of the *Missa solemnis*. Aptly clear-toned soloists match the freshness of the Monteverdi Choir. As an imaginatively chosen coupling Gardiner offers the dramatic soprano scena, *Ah! perfido*, with Charlotte Margiono as soloist, and the brief choral cantata, *Meeresstille und glückliche Fahrt.*

George Guest's reading is intimate, and with boys' voices in the choir and a smaller band of singers, less dramatic; yet with splendid recording, the scale works admirably and the result is refreshing. Excellent value at super-bargain price.

(i) *Mass in C, Op. 86;* (ii) *Missa solemnis, Op. 123.*
(B) **(*) Ph. Duo 438 362-2 (2) [id.]. (i) Eda-Pierre, Moll; (ii) Tomowa-Sintow, Lloyd; (i; ii) Payne, Tear, L. Symphony Ch., LSO, C. Davis.

The freshness of the choral singing and the clarity of the sound make Sir Colin Davis's an outstandingly dramatic version of the *Mass in C*. The cry, *'Passus'* ('suffered'), in the *Credo* has rarely been so tellingly presented on record, and the quartet of soloists is first rate. The *Missa solemnis* too receives a fine performance, if not quite so intense. The 1977 recording, well focused, spacious and atmospheric, is given a natural, concert-hall balance and the CD transfer is first class. Good documentation.

Missa solemnis in D, Op. 123.
*** DG Dig. 435 770-2 (2) [id.]. Studer, Norman, Domingo, Moll, Leipzig R. Ch., Swedish R. Ch., VPO, Levine.
*** DG Dig. 429 779-2 [id.]. Margiono, Robbin, Kendall, Miles, Monteverdi Ch., E. Bar. Soloists, Eliot Gardiner.
*** HM Dig. HMC 901557 [id.]. Mannion, Remmert, Taylor, Hauptmann, La Chapelle Royale, Collegium Vocale, O des Champs Elysées, Herreweghe.
(B) *** DG Double 453 016-2 (2) [423 913-2]. Janowitz, Ludwig, Wunderlich, Berry, V. Singverein, BPO, Karajan – MOZART: *Coronation Mass.* **(*)
(M) *** Beethoven Edition DG 447 922-2 (2) [id.]. Moser, Schwarz, Kollo, Moll, Hilversum R. Ch., Concg. O, Bernstein.
(B) *** Sony SBK 53517; *SBT 53517* [id.]. Arroyo, Forrester, Lewis, Siepi, Singing City Choirs, Phd. O, Eugene Ormandy.

(M) **(*) DG (IMS) Dig. 445 543-2 (2) [id.]. Cuberli, Schmidt, Cole, Van Dam, V. Singverein, BPO, Karajan – MOZART: *Mass No. 16*. **(*)

(M) **(*) Teldec/Warner Dig. 9031 74884-2 (2). Mei, Lipovšek, Rolfe Johnson, Holl, Schoenberg Ch., COE, Harnoncourt.

(M) (**(*)) RCA mono GD 60272 (2) [60272-RG-2]. Marshall, Merriman, Conley, Hines, Robert Shaw Ch., NBC SO, Toscanini – CHERUBINI: *Requiem*. (**(*))

(i) *Missa solemnis in D;* (ii) *Choral Fantasia in C, Op. 80*.

(M) **(*) EMI CMS7 69538-2 (2) [Ang. CDMB 69538-2]. (i) Söderström, Höffgen, Kmentt, Talvela, New Philh. Ch.; (ii) Barenboim, Alldis Ch.; New Philh. O, Klemperer.

The 1991 Salzburg Festival honoured its late music director, Herbert von Karajan, in this performance of Beethoven's *Missa solemnis* conducted by James Levine. With a starry quartet of soloists the live recording has an incandescence that conveys the atmosphere of a great occasion, and the DG engineers have obtained rich, weighty sound. For such an intense visionary experience, defying the conventional view of Levine, this is a version not to be missed. Also available in DG's Beethoven Edition.

Gardiner's inspired reading matches even the greatest of traditional performances on record in dramatic weight and spiritual depth, while bringing out the white heat of Beethoven's inspiration with new intensity. Though the performers are fewer in number than in traditional accounts, the Monteverdi Choir sings with bright, luminous tone, and the four soloists are excellent. The recording is vivid too. Even those who normally resist period performance will find this compelling.

Philippe Herreweghe's live recording of the *Missa solemnis* (edited together from two performances) makes a good alternative to Gardiner's prize-winning version on DG Archiv for a period-scale reading. Even at the start, with its odd balance, there is no mistaking that we are on a visionary journey, with an inner quality intensely conveyed. Though the choir is distantly balanced, the sharpness of attack is refreshing, amply justifying a performance on a relatively intimate, period scale. The four young soloists make an excellent team, headed by the sweet, firm, Canadian soprano, Rosa Mannion, previously heard as Dorabella in the Gardiner *Così*.

On Karajan's earlier (1966) analogue recording, made in the Jesus-Christus-Kirche, both the chorus and, even more strikingly, the superbly matched quartet of soloists, convey the intensity and cohesion of Beethoven's deeply personal response to the liturgy, not the ill-fated Fritz Wunderlich, singing radiantly. Now on a DG Double, it is attractively coupled with Mozart's *Coronation Mass*.

Bernstein's DG recording was edited together from tapes of two live performances, and the result has a spiritual intensity matched by few rivals. Edda Moser is not an ideal soprano soloist, but the others are outstanding, and the *Benedictus* is made angelically beautiful by the radiant playing of the Concertgebouw concertmaster, Hermann Krebbers. The recording is a little light in bass but is outstandingly clear, as well as atmospheric.

The glory of Klemperer's set is the superb choral singing of the New Philharmonia Chorus. The soloists are less happily chosen: Waldemar Kmentt seems unpleasantly hard and Elisabeth Söderström does not sound as firm as she can be. It was, however, a happy idea to include the *Choral Fantasia* as a bonus.

On a single disc in Sony's Essential Classics series at budget price, Ormandy's 1967 Philadelphia recording makes an excellent bargain. Ormandy takes a bold and firm view of this masterpiece. It may not plumb all the spiritual depths of the work but, with four outstanding soloists and an excellent, well-focused choir, he takes you magnetically through the drama of the piece. The vintage recording gives plenty of body to the sound, both of voices and of orchestra.

In his later version for DG Karajan conducts a powerful reading marked by vivid and forward recording for orchestra and soloists, less satisfactory in rather cloudy choral sound. This was one of Karajan's recordings made in conjunction with a video film, and that brings both gains and losses. The sense of spontaneity, of a massive structure built dramatically with contrasts underlined, makes for extra magnetism, but there are flaws of ensemble and flaws of intonation in the singing of Lella Cuberli.

Like Levine's performance a year earlier, Harnoncourt's was recorded live at the Salzburg Festival but it represents the new, post-Karajan era at that grandest of music festivals. Like Harnoncourt's Beethoven symphony cycle, this performance conveys the dramatic tensions of a live occasion, with finely matched forces performing with freshness and clarity. The rather distanced sound makes the results marginally less involving than either the Levine version or John Eliot Gardiner's period-performance.

Toscanini's tensely dramatic account of the *Missa solemnis* leaves you in no doubt as to the work's magisterial power, even if the absence of a true pianissimo makes it less meditative than usual. Fine singing from choir and soloists alike, though the typical harshness of the recording is unappealing.

OPERA

Fidelio (complete).

❀*** EMI CDS5 56211-2 (2) [CDC 56211]. Ludwig, Vickers, Frick, Berry, Crass, Philh. Ch. & O, Klemperer.

*** Ph. Dig. 426 308-2 (2) [id.]. Jessye Norman, Goldberg, Moll, Wlaschiha, Coburn, Blochwitz, Dresden State Op. Ch. & O, Haitink.

*** Teldec/Warner Dig. 4509 94560-2 (2) [id.]. Margiono, Seiffert, Bonney, Skovhus, Leiferkus, Polgár, Van der Walt, Arnold Schönberg Ch., COE, Harnoncourt.

(M) *** EMI CMS7 69290-2 (2) [CDMB 769290]. Dernesch, Vickers, Kélémen, Ridderbusch, German Op. Ch., BPO, Karajan.

(B) *** DG Double 453 106-2 (2) (includes *Overture Leonora No. 3*). Leonie Rysanek, Ernst Haefliger, Dietrich Fischer-Dieskau, Gottlob Frick, Irmgard Seefried, Friedrich Lenz, Kieth Engen, Bav. State Op. Ch. & O, Fricsay.

(M) (***) EMI (SIS) mono CHS7 64496-2 (2) [id.]. Kirsten Flagstad, Julius Patzak, Paul Schoeffler, Josef Greindl, Elisabeth Schwarzkopf, Anton Dermota, V. State Op. Ch., VPO, Furtwängler.

(N) **(*) Telarc Dig. CD 80439 (2) [id.]. Gabriela Beňačková, Rolfe Johnson, Ildikó Raimondi, Siegfried Vogel, Kapellman, John Mark Ainsley, Edinburgh Fest. Ch., SCO, Mackerras.

(M) (**) RCA mono [09026 60273-2]. Bampton, Peerce, Laderoute, Steber, Belarsky, Janssen, Moscona, Ch., NBC SO, Toscanini.

Klemperer's great set of *Fidelio*, reissued at full price, has been superbly remastered. The sound has a depth, beauty and realism far beyond any previous incarnation of this splendid 1962 Kingsway Hall recording. The result is a technical triumph to match the unique incandescence and spiritual strength of the performance, superbly cast, which leads to a final scene in which, more than in any other recording, the parallel with the finale of the *Choral Symphony* is underlined. It remains first choice; but the price rise is a move in the wrong direction.

The unsurpassed nobility of Jessye Norman's voice is perfectly matched to this noblest of operas. In detail of characterization she may not outshine Christa Ludwig, Klemperer's firm and incisive Leonore, but her reading is consistently rich and beautiful, like those rivals bringing a new revelation. With excellent digital sound and with strong, forthright conducting from Haitink, this is the finest of modern versions, even if it does not replace Klemperer or Karajan.

As you would expect, Nikolaus Harnoncourt, tackling *Fidelio*, reflects the climate of period performance, even though – with the Chamber Orchestra of Europe as immaculate as ever – modern instruments are used. At chamber scale, textures are consistently clean, with crisply sprung rhythms at surprisingly relaxed speeds. The casting matches this approach, with the central role of Leonore given not to a dramatic soprano but to a singer best known till now for singing Mozart and Bach, Charlotte Margiono. The voice here is warmer than we have known it, with marked but unobtrusive vibrato, so that the *Abscheulicher* has a bite and clarity which make up for not pinning you back in your seat. The casting of the rest is similar, with the radiant Barbara Bonney well contrasted with Margiono. Peter Seiffert sings with unforced clarity as Florestan, and Deon van der Walt is a fresh Jaquino. Contrasts of character are well established among the lower voices too, with Sergei Leiferkus an aptly sinister Pizarro, László Polgár a darkly resonant Rocco and Boje Skovhus a noble Don Pedro. Highlights are available (70 minutes) on Teldec 0630 13800-9.

Comparison between Karajan's strong and heroic reading and Klemperer's version is fascinating. Both have very similar merits, underlining the symphonic character of the work with their weight. Even so, Karajan uses bass and baritone soloists lighter than usual, for both the Rocco (Ridderbusch) and the Don Fernando (Van Dam) lack heft in lower registers. Yet they sing dramatically and intelligently, while the Pizarro of Zoltan Kélémen is made to sound the more biting and powerful. Jon Vickers as Florestan is, if anything, even finer than he was for Klemperer, Helga Dernesch as Leonore giving a glorious, thrilling performance. The orchestral playing is superb.

The Fricsay set dates from 1957, yet the recording has responded superbly to the CD remastering, with clean, warm, well-focused sound that projects the voices naturally. The result is astonishingly modern-sounding, lacking little or nothing in body. This was the first recording of this opera to offer not just Beethoven's score but also a sprinkling of dialogue between numbers, which in DG's CD transfer are banded separately. As for Fricsay's clear, fresh direction, it matches the excitement and keen tension of a Toscanini performance. The principals sing with exceptional clarity and point. Ernst Haefliger is a fine, clear-cut Florestan, lyric in timbre rather than fully heroic, and Frick and Fischer-Dieskau offer strong, intense characterizations, with Pizarro's aria chilling in its villainy. Rysanek's Leonore is also impressive, and her *Abscheulicher* is both dramatic and beautifully shaded. As for Irmgard Seefried, she makes an enchanting Marzelline. In this bargain package no libretto translation is included, but there is a well-cued synopsis. The *Leonore No. 3 Overture* is included as a supplement after the opera, not before the final scene as used to be the custom.

Taken from performances at the Salzburg Festival in 1950, with Wilhelm Furtwängler conducting an incomparably starry cast, this should not be confused with the studio recording he made with some of the same cast two years later. This is an Austrian Radio recording, previously available in pirated versions, but here treated to sound which captures the voices on stage with astonishing vividness. The epic scale of Kirsten Flagstad's voice as Leonore sometimes blasts the microphone, but it is a joy to hear such forthright power and security in a role nowadays too often given to squally singers. Elisabeth Schwarzkopf is a delight as Marzelline, vivacious in the dialogue and masterfully sustaining Furtwängler's expansive speed for the Act I quartet. With dialogue included, this is even more compelling than Furtwängler's studio recording, also with Julius Patzak as a superb Florestan, but with Paul Schoeffler a powerful Pizarro and Josef Greindl as Rocco.

As in his fine set of the Beethoven symphonies, Mackerras adopts a manner which with modern instruments takes account of period practice. Clean-cut textures and alert rhythms make the results in both intensely refreshing. With the modestly sized Scottish Chamber Orchestra set in a warmly atmospheric acoustic, *Fidelio* is given extra dramatic point. Voices are closer than usual, making the storytelling both more intimate and more intense, most strikingly in the opening scenes. The sudden switch from genial domesticity to the world of the prison and Pizarro comes over with chilling force, not just when the villainous governor enters with his biting aria (the incisive Franz-Josef Kapellmann set back further than the others) but even earlier in the Trio, when his very name is mentioned. That is typical of Mackerras's response to the drama, so that the confrontation quartet of Act 2 makes one sit up afresh, with Gabriela Beňačková as Leonore bitingly defiant in the face of Pizarro. Beňačková's voice has grown a degree edgier and less predictable at the top, but this is still a warmly expressive as well as a powerful performance. More serious are the reservations over Anthony Rolfe Johnson as Florestan, responsive as he is, for the stress of the role too often brings out an unevenness in the voice intensified by close-up recording. Siegfried Vogel is a clean-cut Rocco, less elderly than usual, and Ildikó Raimondi is a charming Marzelline, well contrasted with Beňačkova.

Recorded in December 1944, towards the end of the Second World War, this was the first of the concert performances of complete operas that Toscanini conducted in New York. This is just Beethoven's score with no dialogue, but that makes one concentrate the more on the music. Typically his choice of soloists favours voices that are clean-cut and accurate rather than conventionally beautiful, and it is good to have Rose Bampton as a powerful Leonore, an American singer too little appreciated in Europe and too little recorded. Eleanor Steber is a weightier Marzelline than usual, but the clarity and precision are impressive, well matched by the Jaquino of Joseph Laderoute. Sidor Belarsky as Rocco is similarly clean of attack and, though Herbert Janssen is not as fresh-toned as he was earlier, this is a strong and characterful performance. As Florestan, Jan Peerce, Toscanini's favourite American tenor of the time, sings cleanly too if not with great imagination. The transfer follows the honest if unflattering pattern favoured in RCA's Toscanini Edition. It has been temporarily withdrawn in the U.K.

Fidelio: highlights.

(M) *** EMI (SIS) CDM7 63077-2. Dernesch, Vickers, Ridderbusch, Van Dam, Kélémen, German Op. Ch., BPO, Karajan.

(M) *** DG 445 461-2 [id.] (from complete set, with Janowitz, Kollo, Sotin, Jungirth, Fischer-Dieskau, Popp; cond. Bernstein).

Those who acquire Klemperer's classic set will welcome just under an hour of well-chosen highlights from the fine alternative Karajan recording, made in 1970.

It is also good to have a selection of highlights from the Bernstein set, recorded in conjunction with live performances at the Vienna State Opera and full of dramatic flair, yet which presents the drama on a human scale, less monumental than with Klemperer. Janowitz sings most beautifully as Leonore and, although Hans Sotin is not an especially villainous Pizarro, his vocal projection is impressive, Kollo is an intelligent and musicianly Florestan and Lucia Popp is at her delightful best as Marzelline. The selection is generous (71 minutes), including the *Overture* and the final scene, and contains a cued synopsis of the narrative.

Fidelio: Abscheulicher!.

(M) (***) RCA mono GD 60280 [id.]. Rose Bampton, NBC SO, Toscanini – GLUCK: *Iphigénie en Aulide: Overture; Orfeo ed Euridice, Act II.* (***)

Rose Bampton was the soprano chosen by Toscanini to take the role of Leonora in his concert performance and recording of the complete *Fidelio*, and here, a few months later in June 1945, he invited her to repeat her performance of the climactic *Abscheulicher* in concert. Again the performance is magnificent, firm, true and clear, a degree warmer than in the complete recording but just as heroic in attack. A welcome fill-up to the Gluck recordings on the disc.

Leonore (complete).

(N) *** DG Dig. 453 461-2 (2) [id.]. Hillevi Martinpelto, Kim Begley, Matthew Best, Alastair Miles, Christiane Oelze, Franz Hawlata, Monteverdi Ch., ORR, Gardiner.

(N) ** MDG Dig. MDG 337 0826-2 (2) [id.]. Pamela Coburn, Mark Baker, Jean-Philippe Lafont, Eric Martin-Bonnet, Christine Neithardt-Barbaux, Victor von Halem, Benedikt Kobel; Cologne R Ch.; O of Beethovenhalle, Bonn; Marc Soustrot.

After conducting a brilliant sequence of performances of *Leonore* in both America and Europe, Gardiner immediately went to the recording studio, and at white heat with the same team set down this recording, confirming his passionate belief in Beethoven's first thoughts as a powerful alternative, quite distinct in aim. Gardiner's argument, brilliantly expressed in a note, is that *Leonore* in 1804 is the more spontaneous and immediate work, while *Fidelio* of ten years later is retrospective and considered in its response to tyranny and injustice. As he says, 'What strikes me so forcibly about *Leonore* is its power and purity of emotion'. He goes on to claim that the portraits of both hero and heroine are more poignant in the earlier version, where later they are presented as more self-assured and certain, more universal.

Admittedly, one misses some dramatic moments such as the cry of '*Abscheulicher*' at the start of the heroine's big aria, but the tenderly reflective recitative you have instead is moving in a different way. One also misses the great fortissimo outburst from the chorus at the start of the final scene, but the *Leonore* solution is even more evocative, with the chorus getting closer and closer in its signalling of freedom.

Hillevi Martinpelto in the title role conveys youthful ardour as well as power, well contrasted with the sweetly expressive Marzelline of Christiane Oelze. The tenor, Kim Begley, emerges in sharply focused, heroic strength as Florestan, with Michael Schade providing an ideal lyric contrast as Jaquino. Franz Hawlata as Rocco, and Alastair Miles as Don Fernando are both first-rate, and if Matthew Best as Pizarro comes too close to sing-speech, he is certainly evil-sounding.

Where John Eliot Gardiner aimed to give us Beethoven's earliest text – white-hot with inspiration – while adopting some later revisions, Marc Soustrot here offers the première recording of Beethoven's first revision, made for performances in 1806, a year after the original. As in the Gardiner set, a number-by-number commentary is given on the differences, with the original three acts reduced to two and minor incidental cuts, but with some additional material. In practice, this 1806 text, enjoyable in its own right, lacks some of the freshness of 1805, while failing to match the final version of 1814. It does not help that Soustrot is far less dramatic than Gardiner. The performance, well recorded, is reliable rather than inspired, led by Pamela Coburn as a warm-toned Leonore, Mark Baker a lyrical Florestan, and Christine Neidhard-Barbaux a sweetly charming Marzelline, but with Jean-Pierre Lafont a wobbly Pizarro.

Bellini, Vincenzo (1801–35)

Oboe concerto in E flat.
(B) *** Decca Double 452 943-2 (2) [id.]. Roger Lord, ASMF, Marriner – HANDEL: *Oboe concertos* etc.; VIVALDI: *Miscellaneous concertos*. ***

Bellini's *Oboe concerto* is brief but delectable. Its operatic lyricism is well understood by Roger Lord and Marriner, and their performance is not surpassed, even by Holliger.

Beatrice di Tenda (complete).
(M) ** Sony Dig. SM3K 64539 (3) [id.]. Nicolesco, Cappuccilli, Toczyska, La Scola, Prague Philharmonic Ch., Monte Carlo O, Alberto Zedda.

Beatrice di Tenda (complete); Arias: *Norma: Casta diva. I Puritani: Son vergin vezzosa; Oh rendetemi la speme. La sonnambula: Ah, non credea mirarti.*
(M) *** Decca (IMS) 433 706-2 (3) [id.]. Sutherland, Pavarotti, Opthof, Veasey, Ward, Amb. Op. Ch., LSO, Bonynge.

Beatrice di Tenda was Bellini's last opera but one, coming after *La sonnambula* and *Norma* and before *I Puritani*. It may not be compelling dramatically, with a story involving a string of unrequited loves, but the piece is a splendid vehicle for an exceptional prima donna with a big enough voice and brilliant enough coloratura. Dame Joan Sutherland had made it her own, when this recording was made in 1966, a dazzling example of her art. The other star of the set is Richard Bonynge, a natural Bellini conductor. The supporting cast could hardly be better, with Pavarotti highly responsive. The recording, of Decca's best vintage, has been transferred to CD with vivid atmosphere and colour. Four famous arias are provided as a filler: one from Sutherland's 1964 *Norma*, two from her 1963 *I Puritani* and one from the 1962 *La sonnambula*.

Originally issued on the Ricordi label, the Sony set offers a live recording made in Monte Carlo in 1986. The scholar, Alberto Zedda, conducts most sympathetically, and Mariana Nicolesco in the title-role sings with strength and character, using exciting and distinctive tone-colours, but spoiling Bellinian legato lines with squeezing and gusting and sudden moments of edginess. Others in the cast sing stylishly; but the Sutherland/Bonynge set is far preferable, both for the fresher, more beautiful performance and for the bright Decca sound of good (1966) vintage.

I Capuleti ed i Montecchi (complete).
(N) *** RCA Dig. 09026 68899-2 (3) [id.]. Vesselina Kasarova, Eva Mei, Ramón Vargas, Umberto Chiummo, Simone Alberghini, Bav. R. Ch., Munich RO, Roberto Abbado.
(M) **(*) EMI (SIS) Dig. CMS7 64846-2 (2) [CDMB 64846]. Baltsa, Gruberová, Raffanti, Gwynne Howell, Tomlinson, ROHCG Ch. & O, Muti.

Taking three discs instead of the usual two, the RCA set offers an important bonus in an alternative version of the Tomb scene by Nicolai Vaccai, dating from five years before Bellini's version. In Paris in 1832 the prima donna, Maria Malibran insisted on it being used instead of Bellini's, which she felt did not give her the vocal opportunities she needed. There are also a couple of alternative versions of arias ornamented by Rossini. Quite apart from that, Roberto Abbado conducts a beautifully sprung, warmly sympathetic reading, less hard-driven than the EMI live recording conducted by Muti. The sound too is warm, full and well-balanced, preferable to the EMI. Vocally the principal glory of the set lies in Kasarova's characterful and stylish performance as Romeo, firmer and more consistent than Baltsa's on EMI. Eva Mei makes a sweet and girlish Giulietta, sensitive and true if lacking some of the deeper insights of Gruberova on EMI. The rest of the cast is first-rate, with Ramón Vargas outstanding in the tenor role of Tebaldo (Tybalt).

Muti's set was recorded live at a series of performances at Covent Garden when the production was new, in March 1984. With the Royal Opera House a difficult venue for recording, the sound is hard and close. Agnes Baltsa makes a passionately expressive Romeo and Edita Gruberová a Juliet who is not just brilliant in coloratura but also sweet and tender. Muti's conducting is masterly, specially striking at the end of Act I, when the five principals sing a hushed quintet. With excellent contributions from the refined tenor Dano Raffanti (as Tebaldo), Gwynne Howell and John Tomlinson, it is a performance to blow the cobwebs off this once-neglected opera.

Norma (complete).

(M) *** Decca 425 488-2 (3) [id.]. Sutherland, Horne, Alexander, Cross, Minton, Ward, London Symphony Ch., LSO, Bonynge.

(***) EMI mono CDS5 56271-2 (3). Callas, Stignani, Filippeschi, Rossi-Lemeni, La Scala, Milan, Ch. and O, Serafin.

**(*) Decca Dig. 414 476-2 (3) [id.]. Sutherland, Pavarotti, Caballé, Ramey, Welsh Nat. Op. Ch. & O, Bonynge.

(M) **(*) EMI CMS5 66428-2 (3) [Ang. CDMC 66428]. Callas, Corelli, Ludwig, Zaccharia, Ch. & O of La Scala, Milan, Serafin.

Norma: highlights.

(M) *** Decca 421 886-2 [id.] (from above complete recording with Sutherland, Horne; cond. Bonynge).

(M) **(*) EMI CDM5 66662-2 (from above complete recording with Callas, Corelli; cond. Serafin).

In her first, mid-1960s recording of *Norma*, Sutherland was joined by an Adalgisa in Marilyn Horne whose control of florid singing is just as remarkable as Sutherland's own. The other soloists are very good indeed. A most compelling performance, helped by the conducting of Richard Bonynge, and the Walthamstow recording is vivid but also atmospheric in its CD format.

In Callas's earlier, mono set, the mono recording may be flat, although it is opened out in the new transfer, but the sense of presence gives wonderful intensity to one of the diva's most powerful performances, recorded at the very peak of her powers, before the upper register acquired its distracting wobble. Balance of soloists is close, and the chorus could hardly be dimmer, but Callas justifies everything, even the cuts. The veteran, Ebe Stignani, as Adalgisa is a characterful partner in the sisters' duets, but Filippeschi is disappointingly thin-toned and strained, and Rossi-Lemeni is gruff.

Though Dame Joan Sutherland was fifty-eight when her second *Norma* recording was made, her singing is still impressive, but Pavarotti is in some ways the set's greatest strength, easily expressive as Pollione, Caballé as Adalgisa seems determined to outdo Sutherland in cooing self-indulgently. Full, brilliant, well-balanced recording of the complete score.

By the time Callas came to record her 1960 stereo version, the tendency to hardness and unsteadiness in the voice above the stave, always apparent, had grown serious, but the interpretation was as sharply illuminating as ever, a unique assumption, helped by Christa Ludwig as Adalgisa, while Corelli sings heroically. Serafin as ever is the most persuasive of Bellini conductors.

Il Pirata (complete).

(M) *(**) EMI mono CMS5 66432-2 (2) [CDMB 66432]. Callas, Ego, Miranda Ferraro, Peterson, Watson, Sarfaty, American Op. Soc. Ch. & O, Rescigno.

(M) ** EMI (SIS) CMS5 67121-2 [CDMB 67121]. Cappuccilli, Caballé, Martí, Raimondi, Rome R. & TV Ch. & O, Gavazzeni.

Recorded live at a concert performance in New York in January 1959, the Callas version is flawed, with harsh sound and intrusive audience noises. Though Callas herself shows signs of vocal deterioration, with top notes often raw and uneven, hers is a fire-eating performance, totally distinctive, instantly magnetic from the moment she utters her first word, '*Sorgete*', in Act I. The rest of the cast is indifferent, with Constantine Ego strenuous in the tenor role of Ernesto. The second disc offers an alternative recording of the final scene, made in Amsterdam six months later, with Rescigno conducting the Concertgebouw Orchestra and with Callas in smoother vocal form, helped by less raw recording.

Gavazzeni's is the first absolutely complete recording of *Il Pirata*, the composer's third opera, written for La Scala and first produced in 1827. In the best traditions of Italian opera, in the finale the pirate-hero is killed, his rival is condemned to death, and the heroine loses her mind. Caballé is well suited to the role of the heroine, though by her finest standards there is some carelessness in her singing, with clumsy changes of register. Nor is the conducting and presentation sparkling enough to mask the comparative poverty of Bellini's invention. Caballe's husband, Bernabé Martí, battles valiantly with the difficult part of the pirate. The 1970 recording flatters the voices and has plenty of atmosphere.

I Puritani (complete).

*** Decca 417 588-2 (3). Sutherland, Pavarotti, Ghiaurov, Luccardi, Caminada, Cappuccilli, ROHCG Ch. & O, Bonynge.

(***) EMI mono CDS5 56275-2 (2). Callas, Di Stefano, Panerai, Rossi-Lemeni, La Scala, Milan, Ch. & O, Serafin.

(M) **(*) Decca 448 969-2 (2). Sutherland, Duval, Capecchi, Flagello, Elkins, De Palma, Maggio Musicale Fiorentino Ch. & O, Bonynge.

(B) **(*) Millennium MCD 80356 (3). Sills, Gedda, Van Allan, Plishka, Quilico, Cassinelli, Begg, Ambrosian Op. Ch., LPO, Rudel.

(M) **(*) EMI CMS7 69663-2 (2). Caballé, Kraus, Manuguerra, Hamari, Ferrin, Amb. Op. Ch., Philh. O, Muti.

Whereas her earlier set was recorded when Sutherland had adopted a soft-grained style, with consonants largely eliminated, her singing brings fresh, bright singing, rich and agile. Pavarotti emerges as a Bellini stylist, with Ghiaurov and Cappuccilli making up an impressive cast, but with Anita Caminada disappointing as Enrichetta. Vivid, atmospheric recording.

Those who complain that this opera represents Bellini at his dramatically least compelling should hear Callas. In 1953, when she made the recording, her voice was already hard on top with some unsteadiness, but Callas's portrayal is uniquely compelling. None of the other soloists is ideal, though most of the singing is acceptable. The mono sound (now opened up) still has a restricted upper range, but the solo voices project well. Like other EMI/Callas recordings, this has been remastered and handsomely redocumented.

As in the recording of *La Sonnambula*, made a year earlier, Joan Sutherland slides about too freely in *portamento*, but the beauty and freshness of the sound, as well as the phenomenal agility, are what matter above all. The final *Ah, non giunge* is dazzling. Pierre Duval controls his ringing tenor well, powerful at the top, and Renato Capecchi is a strong Riccardo, if not always well-focused. Though Bonynge conducts most sympathetically, controlling ensembles well, the text has cuts, confirming this as less recommendable than Sutherland's later set.

Now issued at bargain price on the Millennium label, Beverly Sills's 1973 recording of *I Puritani* was originally made by EMI. The excellent CD transfer ensures that the edge on Sills's bright coloratura is kept in check, letting one appreciate more fully her fine technique and her expressiveness, with moods instantly established, though the singing is at times too strenuous. Nicolai Gedda as Arturo is more effective in bold, heroic music than he is in such Bellinian cantilena as *A te o cara* in Act I. The rest of the cast is strong and characterful, though Paul Plishka as Sir Giorgio is unsteady.

Riccardo Muti's attention to detail and pointing of rhythm make for refreshing results, and the warm, luminous recording is excellent. But both the principal soloists – here below form – indulge in distracting mannerisms, hardly allowing even a single bar to be presented straight in the big numbers, rarely sounding spontaneous. The big ensemble, *A te, o cara*, at slow speed loses the surge of exhilaration which Sutherland and Pavarotti show so strongly.

I Puritani: highlights.

(N) (M) (***) EMI mono CDM5 66665-2 (from above recording with Callas, di Stefano, cond. Serafin).

The Callas highlights offer an hour of music – a dozen excerpts, and Elvira features in all but four of them, so this will be a useful disc for those not wanting to stretch to the full-priced complete set. The remastered sound is now surprisingly good.

La Sonnambula (complete).

*** Decca Dig. 417 424-2 (2) [id.]. Sutherland, Pavarotti, Della Jones, Ghiaurov, L. Op. Ch., Nat. PO, Bonynge.

(***) EMI mono CDS5 56278-2 (2). Callas, Monti, Cossotto, Zaccaria, Ratti, La Scala, Milan, Ch. and O, Votto.

(B) **(*) Naxos Dig. 8.660042/3 [id.]. D'Artegna, Papadjiakou, Orgonasova, Giménez, Dilbèr, De Vries, Micu, Netherlands R. Ch. and CO, Zedda.

(M) **(*) Decca 448 966-2 (2) [id.]. Sutherland, Monti, Elkins, Stalman, Corena, Maggio Musicale Fiorentino Ch. & O, Bonynge.

Sutherland's singing in her later version is even more affecting and more stylish than before, generally purer and more forthright, if with diction still clouded at times. The challenge of singing opposite Pavarotti adds to the bite of the performance, crisply and resiliently controlled by Bonynge.

Substantially cut, the Callas version was recorded in mono in 1957, yet it gives a vivid picture of the diva at the peak of her powers. Nicola Monti makes a strong rather than a subtle contribution but blends well with Callas in the duets; and Fiorenza Cossotto is a good Teresa. Again, the remastered recording for the Callas Edition shows considerable improvement.

Recorded live in 1992 in a concert performance at the Concertgebouw in Amsterdam, the Naxos issue offers the finest version of the opera at any price since Joan Sutherland's. Luba Orgonasova is an expressive and characterful heroine, agile and pointed in her phrasing of coloratura, deeply affecting in the tender legato of *Ah non credea mirarti*, with tone delicately varied. Raul Giménez is equally stylish as Elvino, the rich landowner, using his light Rossinian tenor most sensitively, with Alberto Zedda, scholar as well as conductor, pointing the accompaniment lightly. The other principals are not quite on this level but they make an excellent team. As usual with Naxos opera issues, there is a libretto in Italian but only a detailed summary of plot in English.

Sutherland's earlier version, reissued at mid-price in Decca's Grand Opera series, brings beautiful singing. Though her use of *portamento* is often excessive, the freshness of the voice is a delight, Bonynge's direction is outstanding, and the casting is first rate too, with Nicola Monti a Bellini tenor. Both Sylvia Stahlman as Lisa and Margareta Elkins as Teresa sing beautifully and with keen accuracy. Even Fernando Corena's rather coarse, *buffo*-style Rodolfo has an attractive vitality. The recording has come up vividly on CD.

Scenes and arias from: *Bianca e Fernando; Norma* (including *Casta diva*); *Il Pirata*.
**(*) Sony Dig. SK 62032 [id.]. Jane Eaglen, OAE, Elder – WAGNER: Excerpts from: *Götterdämmerung* etc. **(*)

It shows the versatility of Jane Eaglen, a singer who has both Brünnhilde and Norma in her stage repertory, that she dares to couple Bellini and Wagner. With such a massive voice it is amazing in Bellini cabalettas that she can tackle coloratura divisions with such agility, even if the results can be ungainly, and the legato in Bellini's soaring melodies is not as seamless as it might be. The period instruments of the Orchestra of the Age of Enlightenment add attractive colour.

Benda, Jiří Antonín (1722–1795)

Sinfonias Nos. 1 in D; 2 in G; 3 in C; 4 in F; 5 in G; 6 in E flat.
(N) (BB) **(*) Naxos Dig. 8.553408 [id.]. Prague CO, Christian Benda.

Sinfonias Nos. 7 in D; 8 in D; 9 in A; 10 in G; 11 in F; 12 in A.
(N) (BB) **(*) Naxos Dig. 8.553409 [id.]. Prague CO, Christian Benda.

The Bohemian Benda family was something of a musical dynasty in Europe over a period of some 300 years. Jiří, who moved in 1742 to join his brother, Frantisek, in Potsdam, eventually became Kapellmeister at Sax-Gotha. Later he moved to Italy, but on his return became famous as a composer of melodramas (music with spoken dialogue), which were admired by Mozart. His twelve three-movement symphonies are conventional, but are kept alive by the rhythmic vigour of the allegros and the graceful, but uneventful *Andantes*. One of the most striking is in the very first work, in the minor key, with the theme punctuated with pizzicatos. Benda takes the opportunity of using the horns to light up his textures when they are crooked in higher keys, as in the *G major* and *A major* works, but even then their use, though texturally telling, is unenterprising. Occasionally he features a solo flute and (as in the *Larghetto* of No. 7) a pair of flutes, in No. 9 a songful oboe, or in No. 6, one of the finest of the series, a solo violin takes a concertante role; the scoring for woodwind and horns in the finale is very effective. But the orchestration is seldom a striking feature, and these are Sinfonias which are best approached singly, rather than in a group. They could hardly be presented with more élan. Christian Benda is a more recent member of the family clan, and he directs the excellent Prague Chamber Orchestra with vigour and spirit, shaping slow movements with affection. At times he makes the listener feel that the music is better than it is, and that is a high compliment. The Naxos recording is admirably fresh and truthful, and the ambience is most pleasing.

(i) *Ariadne auf Naxos. Pygmalion.*
(BB) **(*) Naxos Dig. 8.553345 [id.]. Quadlbauer, Uray; (i) Schell; Prague CO, Benda.

Though neither *Ariadne auf Naxos* nor *Pygmalion* can quite match the longer and more ambitious melodrama, *Medea*, in originality, they equally demonstrate Benda's ability to illuminate classical stories, making the central characters believable. *Pygmalion*, with libretto adapted from a French text of Jean-Jacques Rousseau, is the lighter piece, with a happy ending. Performances under Christian Benda are as impressive as that of *Medea* on the companion disc, but again texts and translations are separated, and no internal tracks are provided. First-rate sound and good acting, though as Pygmalion Peter Uray is not as clear in his delivery as the Ariadne, Brigitte Quadlbauer.

Medea (complete).
(BB) **(*) Naxos Dig. 8.553346 [id.]. Hertha Schell & speaking cast, Prague CO, Christian Benda (with J. J. BENDA: *Violin concerto in G: Grave*).

Christian Benda here presents a most characterful and compelling version of what may be counted as

Jĭrí Benda's masterpiece, the melodrama *Medea*. Rarely have works built on speech superimposed on music remained long in the repertory, yet this CD demonstrates why they have a place and why this one initially had such success. Not only is the playing of the Prague Chamber Orchestra tautly committed, the performance offers an impressive team of actors, led by Hertha Schell. Irritatingly the Naxos booklet gives the German text and English translation on different pages. The fill-up is a treasure. Christian Benda as solo cellist gives a most moving performance of a deeply expressive violin concerto slow movement, as arranged for cello. Excellent sound, with good balance between speaking voices and orchestra.

Benjamin, Arthur (1893–1960)

Concertino for piano and orchestra; Concerto quasi una fantasia for piano and orchestra.
** Everest EVC 9029 [id.]. Lamar Crowson, LSO, composer.

Benjamin's *Concertino* dates from 1929 and was inspired directly by Gershwin's *Rhapsody in blue*. The jazz influence is mainly rhythmic and is felt at its strongest in the work's closing pages. The writing is fluent, the style eclectic, similar in many ways to the *Concerto quasi una fantasia* of 1949, particularly in the scherzando sections. Lamar Crowson gives spirited accounts of them here and is well, if not impeccably, accompanied by the LSO under the composer's direction. The 1959 recording is rather dry.

Symphony No. 1; Ballad for string orchestra.
**(*) Marco Polo Dig. 8.223764 [id.]. Queensland SO, Christopher Lyndon-Gee.

Anyone familiar with Arthur Benjamin's inconsequentially tuneful *Jamaican rumba* will find his symphony very different. The composer had served in each World War, and when it was written, in 1944–5, he was surely reflecting his personal experience in both conflicts. The opening of the first movement with its violent drum-beats immediately creates a darkness of mood which is seldom to lift throughout the work. The *Ballad* is hardly less disconsolate in feeling, again expressing its melancholy through an ongoing string cantilena. Here the Queensland strings are especially impressive, and Christopher Lyndon-Gee always responds convincingly to the emotional intensity which all this music carries. The recording is spacious if a little two-dimensional.

Benjamin, George (born 1960)

(i) *Ringed by the flat horizon.* (ii) *At first light. A Mind of winter.*
*** Nimbus Dig. NI 5075 [id.]. (i) BBC SO, Elder; (ii) Penelope Walmsley-Clark, L. Sinf., composer.

Ringed by the flat horizon is a 20-minute orchestral piece, with the big climax masterfully built. *A Mind of winter* is a 9-minute setting of *The Snowman* by Wallace Stevens, beautifully sung by the soprano Penelope Walmsley-Clark. Sound of great warmth and refinement to match the music make this a collection well worth exploring.

Piano sonata.
** Nimbus Single NI 1415 [id.]. Composer.

George Benjamin is one of the most imaginative composers of the younger generation. His *Piano sonata* dates from 1978 when he was still a student at the Paris Conservatoire. The influences are predominantly Gallic, and in particular the music of Messiaen (hardly surprising, considering that he studied with both that master and Yvonne Loriod). Benjamin is also a very good pianist, but the recording, made in 1980, sounds rather synthetic. A 'single', this runs to 22 minutes 26 seconds.

Bennett, Richard Rodney (born 1936)

Guitar concerto (for guitar and chamber ensemble).
(M) *** RCA 09026 61598-2. Julian Bream, Melos Ens., Atherton – ARNOLD: *Concerto;* RODRIGO: *Concierto de Aranjuez.* ***

Bennett's concerto, written in 1970, is dedicated to Bream. It is imaginatively conceived, and its variety of texture, glittering and transparent, consistently intrigues the ear. If the work's idiom and language start out from the twelve-tone system, there is nothing difficult for the listener to assimilate. The performance, like its Arnold coupling, is definitive and the 1972 recording is first class in every way.

(i) *Violin concerto. Diversions; Symphony No. 3.*
*** Koch Dig. 3-7431-2 [id.]. (i) Vadim Gluzman; Monte Carlo PO, DePreist.

With non-British performers Koch here fills an important gap in the catalogue, offering excellent performances of three of Bennett's later works, recorded in very full, well-balanced sound. The earliest of the three, the *Violin concerto* of 1975, in two contemplative movements, was written when he was bringing his idiom closer to that of his highly successful film music, embracing tonality more firmly. The brilliant, young Ukrainian-born soloist, Vadim Gluzman, plays superbly. Joseph DePreist is also most persuasive, drawing well-drilled, strongly committed playing from the Monte Carlo Philharmonic. The *Symphony*, dating from 1987, is in three compact movements, is bleaker, but the *Diversions* of 1990 bring an attractive set of variations on a theme like an Irish jig.

Sonata after Syrinx; 6 Tunes for the instruction of singing-birds.

(N) *** Koch Dig. 37355-2H1 [id.]. Auréole Trio (members) – MAW: *Flute quartet; Night thoughts for solo flute; Roman canticle.* ***

Two slight pieces serve as a fill-up to a disc primarily devoted to Nicholas Maw. The *Sonata after Syrinx* takes Debussy's piece as the starting point for an appealing and civilized discourse for the same combination. The *Six Tunes for the Instruction of Singing-birds* are for solo flute and are brilliantly played by Laura Gilbert.

Benoit, Peter (1834–1901)

Hoogmis (High Mass).

(B) *(**) Discover Dig. DICD 920178 [id.]. Donald George, Belgian R. & TV Philharmonic Ch., Koninklijk Vlaams Antwerp Music Conservatoire Ch. & Caecilia Chorale, Gemengd Ars Musica Merksem Ch., Zingende Wandelkring Saint Norbertus Ch., Belgian R. & TV PO, Rahbari.

The bargain Discover label offers a fascinating rarity, the *Hoogmis* (*High Mass*), by the Belgian composer, Peter Benoit, a contemporary of Brahms. Alexander Rahbari's account with the BRTN Philharmonic Orchestra of Brussels and massed choirs, with the tenor, Donald George, taking the solos in the *Benedictus* and *Dona nobis pacem*, has all the thrust you need for an ambitious work lasting 55 minutes, with echoes of Beethoven. The live recording, though atmospheric and full of presence, brings washy sound.

Bentzon, Niels Viggo (born 1919)

Feature on René Descartes, Op. 357.

(*) BIS CD 79 [id.]. Danish Nat. R. O, Schmidt (with JORGENSON: *To love music;* NORBY: *The Rainbow snake.* *)

Krönik om René Descartes ('Feature on René Descartes') comes from 1975, and this recording was made at its première that year. The first movement gives a 'musical version of the Cartesian vortex which refers to a medieval notion of rotating heavenly bodies moving at enormous speed', and the final movement addresses Descartes' celebrated proposition, *Cogito ergo sum.* Though there are enough good things to make it worth investigating, it is not a recommended or even characteristic entry-point into his world. A well-prepared performance and good recording.

Symphonies Nos. 3, Op. 46 (1947); 4 (Metamorphoses), Op. 55 (1949).

*** Marco Polo DaCapo Dig. DCCD 9102 [id.]. Aarhus SO, Ole Schmidt.

Bentzon's music fuses something of the lean, rhythmic neo-classicism of Stravinsky, the contrapuntal vitality of Hindemith and the open-air diatonicism of Nielsen. Both the symphonies recorded here are teeming with invention: the pastoral opening of the *Third* unleashes a rich flow of ideas, all of memorable quality. The *Fourth* (*Metamorphoses*) is a most imaginative work, visionary music, powerful, concentrated and inventive. Along with the *Sixth* and *Seventh Symphonies* of Holmboe, this is arguably the finest Nordic symphony after Nielsen and Ole Schmidt, and the Aarhus orchestra play it with all the conviction and passion they can muster. Although the acoustic of the Aarhus hall is not quite ample enough for big climaxes, the recording is very good indeed, with plenty of detail and a good balance. Two remarkable works.

Berg, Alban (1885–1935)

Chamber concerto for piano, violin & 13 wind instruments, Op. 6.

(M) *** DG 447 405-2 [id.]. Barenboim, Zukerman, Ens. Intercontemporain, Boulez – STRAVINSKY: *Concerto in E flat* etc. ***

(i) *Chamber concerto;* (ii) *3 Pieces for orchestra;* (iii) *Violin concerto.*

(M) ** Sony SMK 68331 [id.]. (i) Barenboim, Gavrilov; (i–ii) BBC SO; (iii) Zukerman, LSO; (i–iii) Boulez.

(i) *Chamber concerto;* (ii) *Violin concerto.*

(M) ** Sony Stern Edition II Analogue/Dig. SMK 64504 [id.]. Isaac Stern, with (i) Peter Serkin, LSO members, Abbado; (ii) NYPO, Bernstein.

On DG, Boulez sets brisk tempi in the *Chamber concerto*, seeking to give the work classical incisiveness; but the strong and expressive personalities of the pianist and violinist tend towards a more romantic view. The result is characterful and convincing, and not at all intimidating. Sadly, Boulez omits the extended repeat in the finale. The recording is attractively atmospheric.

In the Stern Edition this Sony issue conveniently couples Berg's two concertante works with violin, featuring Isaac Stern in both. The yoking is uneven, when these are recordings made 26 years apart. The 1959 recording of the *Violin concerto* underlines the coarser side of the performance in which Stern takes a red-blooded, romantic view of the work, as does Bernstein, with finer points skated over. Though there is coarseness in the *Chamber concerto* too, this is a virtuoso performance. The digital sound is very immediate indeed.

Boulez's personality strongly dominates the sharply focused Sony performances of the *Chamber concerto* and Op. 6 *Orchestral pieces* from 1967. The *Violin concerto,* with Zukerman as soloist very close indeed, was recorded two decades later in 1984. His strong, urgent reading matches Boulez's toughness, a robust rather than a subtle or poetic reading, with the elegiac quality missing.

Violin concerto.

(M) *** DG 447 445-2 [id.]. Itzhak Perlman, Boston SO, Ozawa (with RAVEL: *Tzigane;* STRAVINSKY: *Concerto.* ***)

(M) *** Decca Dig. 460 005-2 [id.]. Kyung Wha Chung, Chicago SO, Sir Georg Solti (with BACH: *Violin partita No. 2 & sonata No. 3.* **)

*** DG Dig. 437 093-2 [id.]. Mutter, Chicago SO, Levine – RIHM: *Gesungene Zeit; Time chant.* ***

(BB) *** RCA Navigator 74321 29243-2. Hoelscher, Cologne RSO, Wakasugi – SCHOENBERG: *Verklerte Nacht;* WEBERN: *Passacaglia for orchestra.* ***

(M) *** Sup. SU 1939-2 011 [id.]. Josef Suk, Czech PO, Karel Ančerl (with BRUCH: *Concerto* **) – MENDELSSOHN: *Concerto.* **(*)

(M) *** EMI (SIS) CDM7 63989-2 [id.]. Lord Menuhin, BBC SO, Boulez – BLOCH: *Violin concerto.* ***

Among modern concertos there are more than twice as many versions of the berg than of the Bartók or the Walton, only the Prokofiev No. 1 comparably represented. Perlman's performance is commanding. The Boston orchestra accompanies superbly and, though the balance favours the soloist, the recording is excellent. In DG's series of 'Originals' at mid-price it offers the bonus of the Ravel *Tzigane* as well as the Stravinsky *Concerto*. The current transfer shows the Boston acoustic at its most seductive.

No one excels Chung in tenderness and poetry. The violin is placed well in front of the orchestra, but not aggressively so. The recording is brilliant in the Chicago manner, more spacious than some from this source, but not everyone will want the Bach coupling.

Anne-Sophie Mutter begins the *Concerto* with a pianissimo of such delicacy that it has one's ears pricking. She proceeds to give an intensely passionate reading, both freely expressive and intensely purposeful, with James Levine and the Chicago orchestra matching her in subtle shading. As an imaginative coupling, Mutter offers a concerto written for her by the 40-year-old German composer, Wolfgang Rihm.

Ulf Hoelscher, well balanced in this fine (1977) Cologne recording, gives a passionately dedicated account of Berg's concerto, splendidly supported by Wakasugi and the excellent Cologne Radio Orchestra. This comes at the lowest possible price with two other key twentieth-century works, both very well played and recorded, although the documentation is totally inadequate.

Suk's sweet, unforced style movingly brings out the work's lyrical side without ever exaggerating the romanticism. The arrival of the chorale theme (which Berg took from a Bach cantata) is achieved most delicately and the final coda has rarely sounded more tender and hushed on record. A most beautiful performance, with the excellent (1965) recording very firmly and naturally transferred to CD.

Menuhin's is a warm and vibrant performance and, though technically this is not as dashing or immaculate a performance as several others on record, it is one that compels admiration for great artistry. Well-coupled with the Bloch.

(i) *Violin concerto;* (ii) *Lyric suite: 3 Pieces; 3 Pieces for orchestra, Op. 6.*

(B) *** DG Classikon 439 435-2 [(M) id. import]. (i) Szeryng, Bav. RSO, Kubelik; (ii) BPO, Karajan.

(***) Testament mono SBT1004 [id.]. (i) Louis Krasner, BBC SO, Anton Webern; (ii) Galimir Qt.

Henryk Szeryng gives a persuasive, perceptive and sympathetic account of the Berg *Concerto*, and is very well accompanied by the Bavarian orchestra under Kubelik, with a first-rate CD transfer. As coupling in DG's Classikon series you have two of Karajan's key recordings of Berg's orchestral music, wonderfully pure and clear, bringing out the romantic overtones. A beautiful, refined recording, well-transferred.

The Testament CD is of great interest in bringing back to life a broadcast of the *Violin concerto* by Louis Krasner who commissioned it and gave its first performance. This is the second performance of the work ever, given only five months after Berg's death, laden with a unique intensity of feeling. The sound quality is poor (it comes from the soloist's own acetates) but the spirit is powerful and vibrant, and the BBC orchestra play superbly. It comes with another 1936 recording, the Galimir Quartet's pioneering Polydor 78s of the *Lyric suite* – impeccably played but recorded in a horribly dry acoustic.

Lyric suite: 3 Pieces.

(BB) *** Arte Nova Dig. 74321 52248-2 [id.]. SWF SO, Gielen – BARTOK: *Piano concerto No. 3;* CARTER: *Piano concerto* etc. ***

Michael Gielen's passionate devotion to this Berg work comes out in his warmly expressive, finely detailed reading, very well played and recorded. This may be an unexpected coupling, but it is a refreshing one, a bargain invaluable for anyone investigating twentieth-century music.

Lyric suite: 3 Pieces; 3 Pieces for orchestra, Op. 6.

(M) *** DG 427 424-2 (3) [id.]. BPO, Karajan – SCHOENBERG; WEBERN: *Orchestral pieces.* ***

Karajan's justly famous collection of music by the Second Viennese School is here available as a set of three mid-priced CDs. Beautiful, refined recording, admirably transferred to CD.

Lyric suite: 3 Pieces; (i) *5 Altenberglieder, Op. 4.*
(BB) *** Arte Nova Dig 74321 27768-2 [id.]. (i) Vlatka Orsanic; SWFSO, Gielen – ZEMLINSKY: *Lyric symphony.* ***

The three movements which Alban Berg arranged for orchestra from his *Lyric suite* for string quartet make an ideal coupling for the Zemlinsky *Lyric symphony*, the work which Berg quotes and which prompted his title. They are beautifully played and recorded here, as are the five settings of Altenberg poems, crisp and compact yet full of emotion, here sung superbly with fresh tone and clean attack by the soprano, Vlatka Orsanic. First-rate recording. One of the most remarkable bargains in a catalogue. A pity the documentation does not match the musical excellence.

3 Pieces for orchestra, Op. 6; 5 Orchestral songs, Op. 4; (i) *Lulu: symphonic suite.*
(M) *** DG 449 714-2 [id.]. (i) M. Price; LSO, Abbado.

Abbado makes it clear above all how beautiful Berg's writing is, not just in the *Lulu* excerpts but in the early Opus 4 *Songs* and the Opus 6 *Orchestral pieces*. Now remastered and reissued as part of DG's 'Legendary Recordings', this mid-priced 'Original' offers even better value.

Lyric suite (string quartet version).
(N) *** Sony Dig. SK 66840 [id.]. Juilliard Qt. – JANACEK: *Quartets Nos 1 & 2.* **

The Juilliard bring great intensity and expressive eloquence to the *Lyric Suite*, which has hardly been bettered. Unfortunately they are less successful in the Janáček, but the Berg cannot be flawed. Very good recorded sound.

Lyric suite for string quartet; String quartet, Op. 3.
(M) *** Teldec/Warner 3984 21967-2. Alban Berg Qt – URBANNER: *Quartet No. 3;* WEBERN: *6 Bagatelles* etc. ***

The Alban Berg at their finest, admirably recorded in the mid-1970s, provide here a generous grouping (77 minutes) of key works by Berg and Webern, with a less important *Quartet* by Urbanner thrown in for good measure. The *Lyric suite* is very accessible in its chamber-music format, while the Op. 3 *Quartet* is another of Berg's undoubted masterpieces. The performances are excellent, the recording bright but with plenty of ambience. This Quartet's later digital EMI version of the *Lyric suite* and *Third Quartet* (CDC5 55190-2) is arguably the best ever but now seems short measure at 47 minutes.

Piano sonata, Op. 1.
(B) **(*) Cal. Approche CAL 6203 [(M) id.]. Inger Södergren (with J. S. BACH: *Keyboard collection.* **(*))
** DG (IMS) Dig. 423 678-2 [id.]. Maurizio Pollini (with DEBUSSY: *Etudes.* **)

Inger Södergren's characterful performance of Berg's *Sonata* has real character, but she softens its angst. Those attracted to her enjoyably relaxed Bach coupling may well be converted to enjoying her Berg too. The recording is pleasingly full and unpercussive, and with plenty of keyboard colour.

Pollini gives an impressive account of Berg's one-movement *Sonata*, as powerful as any on disc, but it is not helped by a clinical, closely balanced recording, and the Debussy *Etudes* with which it is coupled are seriously wanting in atmosphere and poetry.

7 Early songs (1905–8 versions).
*** DG Dig. 437 515-2. Anne Sofie von Otter, Bengt Forsberg – KORNGOLD: *Lieder;* STRAUSS: *Lieder.* ***

In the seven early songs of Berg, Anne Sofie von Otter and Bengt Forsberg follow up the success of their prize-winning disc of Grieg songs with inspired playing and singing, drawing out the intensity of emotion to the full without exaggeration or sentimentality. Along with Strauss and Korngold songs, a fascinating programme, magnetically performed.

Lulu (with orchestration of Act III completed by Friedrich Cerha).
*** DG 415 489-2 (3) [id.]. Stratas, Minton, Schwarz, Mazura, Blankenheim, Riegel, Tear, Paris Op. O, Boulez.
(N)*** Chandos Dig. CHAN 9540 (3) [id.]. Constance Haupman, Monte Jaffe, Pete Straka, Julia Juan, Danish Nat. RSO, Ulf Schirmer.
(N) *(*) RCA 74321 57734-2 (2) [id.] (incomplete version). Julia Migenes, Theo Adam, Richard Karczykowski, Brigitte Fassbaender, V. State Op O., Maazel.

Boulez's pioneering recording of Berg's *Lulu* in its full three-act form, brings an intensely involving performance, very well cast. Teresa Stratas's bright, clear soprano, well-recorded, fits the ruthless heroine perfectly, and Yvonne Minton is most moving as Countess Geschwitz. Firm, clear recording.

Recorded at a series of live performances in the Palace of Christiansborg in Copenhagen, the Chandos version is strongly and purposefully conducted by Ulf Schirmer. The pacing vividly brings out the interplay of characters in the complex story, enhancing the characterful singing from first-rate soloists. Constance Haupman makes Lulu a girlish, vulnerable figure, as well as thrusting and selfish. Her singing is commendably precise, even if under pressure the tone grows shrill. As Dr Schön, Monte Jaffe relies too heavily on unpitched sing-speech, but his is a vividly characterful performance too, and among the others Peter Straka makes a fresh, clear Alwa and Julia Juan a touchingly mature Geschwitz. Though the balance of voices on stage is at times recessed, the warmth and clarity of the sound enhances the post-romantic qualities of the score. Boulez's studio version for DG may have a more immediate impact, but this provides an excellent alternative.

Maazel's performance was recorded live by Austrian Radio at a performance in the Vienna State Opera in 1983. With voices well in front of the orchestra, the sound (analogue) is very dry, allowing little bloom on the voices. Even under Maazel there is far too little tension in the orchestral playing, whether in interludes or accompanying the singers. Migenes is characterful in the title part, treating it in cabaret style, often using plain speech rather than sing-speech. A good cast is largely wasted.

Wozzeck (complete).

*** Decca Dig. 417 348-2 (2) [id.]. Waechter, Silja, Winkler, Laubenthal, Jahn, Malta, Sramek, VPO, Dohnányi – SCHOENBERG: *Erwartung.* ***

(M) (***) Sony mono MH2K 62759 (2) [id.]. Harrell, Farrell, Jagel, Mordino, Herbert, Music & Arts High School Ch., Schola Cantorum Ch., NYPO, Mitropoulos – KRENEK: *Symphonic elegy* (***); SCHOENBERG: *Erwartung.* (**(*))

**(*) Teldec/Warner Dig. 0630 14108-2 (2) [id.]. Grundheber, Meier, Baker, Wottrich, Clark, Von Kannen, German Opera, Berlin, Ch. & Children's Ch., Berlin State O, Barenboim.

**(*) DG (SIS) 423 587-2 (2) [id.]. Grundheber, Behrens, Haugland, Langridge, Zednik, V. State Op. Ch., VPO, Abbado.

Dohnányi, with refined textures and superb playing from the Vienna Philharmonic, presents an account of *Wozzeck* that not only is more accurate than any other on record but also is more beautiful.

No finer memorial to the genius of Dimitri Mitropoulos exists on disc than this electrifying recording of *Wozzeck*, a version that has never been surpassed for its biting intensity. It was recorded live at a concert performance in Carnegie Hall, New York, in April 1951, and though the sound is only mono the result in this transfer is extraordinarily vivid, with the voices clear and immediate in front of the orchestra. The cast is consistently fine, pitching the notes cleanly, resorting relatively little to vague sing-speech. In the title-role Mack Harrell not only characterizes well, but he brings out musical beauty in the writing. As for Eileen Farrell as Marie, the power and biting precision of her singing as well as the vividness of her characterization make the character central to the whole opera, not just an attendant figure. The Sony transfer is excellent, and the presentation good, with Acts I and II on the first disc, leaving room for generous fill-ups on the second disc. A full libretto with translations is provided in a separate booklet.

Barenboim's Teldec version of *Wozzeck* was recorded live at the Deutsche Staatsoper in Berlin in 1994 seven years after the Abbado's live DG recording, also with Franz Grundheber in the title-role. With Grundhever if anything even finer than before, Barenboim leads a warmly expressive performance. The cast is an outstanding one, with such characterful singers as Graham Clark (Captain) in incidental roles. Less successful is Waltraud Meier as Marie, with an uneven, grainy quality in the voice.

The Abbado version, recorded live in the opera house, is very compelling in its presentation of the drama, given extra thrust through the tensions of live performance. The cast is first-rate, but as a drawback not only do you get intrusive stage noises, the voices are set behind the orchestra, with the instrumental sound putting a gauze between listener and singers.

Berio, Luciano (born 1925)

Différences; 2 Pieces; (i) *Sequenza III;* (ii) *Sequenza VII;* (i) *Chamber music.*

(M) *** Ph. (IMS) 426 662-2. (i) Cathy Berberian; (ii) Heinz Holliger; Juilliard Ens. (members), composer.

The biggest work here is *Différences* for five instruments and tape; but the two virtuoso solos – *Sequenza III* for voice and *Sequenza VII* for oboe – are if anything even more striking in their extensions of technique and expressive range. First-rate sound, well transferred.

Eindrücke; Sinfonia.

*** Erato/Warner Dig. 2292 45228-2 [id.]. Pasquier, New Swingle Singers, O Nat. de France, Boulez.

It was in 1969 that Berio's *Sinfonia*, written for the New York Philharmonic, made a far wider impact on the music world than is common with an avant-garde composer. Boulez records the complete work for the first time in this fine Erato version. *Eindrücke* is another powerful work, much more compressed, bare and uncompromising in its layering of strings and wind.

(i) *Recital I (for Cathy);* (ii) *Folk-song suite;* (iii) *3 Songs by Kurt Weill* (arr. Berio).

(M) *** RCA 09026 62540-2 [id.]. Cathy Berberian, with (i) L. Sinf.; (ii, iii) Juilliard Ens.; all cond. composer.

Recital I is the most elaborate, colourful work that Berio ever wrote for Cathy Berberian. Against fragmentary accompaniment from the instrumental band, the soloist in this semi-dramatic piece thinks back through her repertoire as a concert-singer from Monteverdi to the present day, a brilliant collage of musical ideas. With Berberian at her most intense, the result is very compelling. Excellent recording. Also included is a sparkling collection of folksongs arranged for Berberian with twinkling ingenuity by Berio. The record concludes with three Kurt Weill songs, arranged by Berio, with Berberian relishing every word.

Berkeley, Lennox (1903–89)

Guitar concerto.
(M) *** RCA 09026 61605-2 [id.]. Julian Bream, Monteverdi O, Gardiner – BROUWER; RODRIGO: *Concertos.* ***

This is a memorably inventive concerto, elegantly constructed, which presents a serious as well as attractive argument and a stylish brand of guitar writing that never leans barrenly on Spanish models. The *Lento* is particularly atmospheric. Bream's performance is superb and the recording vivid. This, with the equally stimulating Brouwer, makes an attractive if out-of-the-way coupling for the most popular of all guitar concertos.

Divertimento in B flat, Op. 18; Partita for chamber orchestra, Op. 66; Serenade for strings, Op. 12; (i) *Sinfonia concertante for oboe and chamber orchestra, Op. 84: Canzonetta* (only). *Symphony No. 3 in one movement, Op. 74; Mont Juic.*
*** Lyrita SRCD 226 [id.]. LPO, composer; (i) with Roger Winfield – with BRITTEN, *Op. 9.*

This beautifully planned Lyrita collection introduces some of the most elegant and enjoyable music that Berkeley wrote. The *Divertimento* is enchanting, with its four stylish and highly inventive movements, while the *String serenade*, similarly in four sections, is hardly less attractive and brings a beautiful *Lento* closing movement. In its rather weightier tone of voice the *Partita* belies that it was written originally with a youth orchestra in mind, while the fourth movement from the *Sinfonia concertante* makes a splendid interlude before the closing *Symphony No. 3*, a concise, one-movement work, slightly more austere in its lyricism. The recording, too, from the early 1970s, is first class. The programme opens with the charmingly spontaneous *Mont Juic* suite which Berkeley wrote in collaboration with Benjamin Britten, two movements each.

Improvisation on a theme of Falla, Op. 55/2; Mazurka, Op. 101/2; 3 Mazurkas (Hommage à Chopin), Op. 32; Paysage; 3 Pieces; Polka, Op. 5a; 6 Preludes, Op. 23; 5 Short pieces, Op. 4; Sonata, Op. 20.
**(*) Kingdom KCLCD 2012 [id.]. Christopher Headington (piano).

With the exception of the *Sonata*, all these pieces are miniatures, some of considerable elegance. Christopher Headington is a sympathetic exponent and he is completely attuned to the idiom. The recording is eminently serviceable and truthful.

6 Preludes, Op. 23.
(N) **(*) Paradisum Dig. PDS-CD2 [id.]. John Clegg – RAWSTHORNE: *Complete piano music.* **(*)

BBC listeners will recall that John Clegg was frequently heard in the 1960s and 1970s, championing rare repertoire (such as Reger and Medtner), and this CD presents the whole of Rawsthorne's output for the piano. Lennox Berkeley's charming and accomplished miniatures complete a valuable disc: the only snag is the rather claustrophobic acoustic.

(i) *Music for piano four hands: Sonatina, Op. 39; Theme and variations, Op. 73; Palm Court waltz, Op. 81/2.* (Solo piano music): *5 Short pieces, Op. 4; 6 Preludes, Op. 23; Sonata, Op. 20.*
*** British Music Society Dig. BMS 416CD. Raphael Terroni, (i) with Norman Beedie.

The British Music Society here presents a generous selection of the cultivated and tuneful piano music of Lennox Berkeley: the fine *Sonata* with its sensuously coloured *Adagio*, the often witty *Preludes* and the five charming *Short pieces*, which often have a whiff of Poulenc, the *Sonatina* with another elegantly individual slow movement, the more complex *Theme and variations* is more complex, but rewarding, and the engagingly carefree *Palm Court waltz.* Raphael Terroni is an accomplished and sympathetic exponent, with Norman Beedle an admirable partner in the *Music for piano four hands.* The piano recording is most natural. The CD is available direct from the British Music Society, 7 Tudor Gardens, Upminster, Essex.

Berkeley, Michael (born 1948)

(i; ii) *Clarinet concerto;* (i) *Flighting;* (iii; ii) *Père du doux repos (Father of sweet sleep* from *Speaking silence).*
*** ASV Dig. Single CDDCB 1101 [id.]. (i) Emma Johnson; (ii) N. Sinfonia, Sian Edwards; (iii) Henry Herford.

The *Clarinet concerto*, written for Emma Johnson in 1991, represents a new generation in Michael Berkeley's work, less lyrical than before, more abrasive and, above all, concentrated. The soloist's concentration leads one magnetically through a thicket of virtuoso writing, often marked by stratospheric shrieks, which she consistently makes compelling, thanks also to the dedicated accompaniment under Sian Edwards. As 'fitting pendants' come two shorter works, a setting of a sonnet by the sixteenth-century French poet, Pontus de Tyard, leading to a solo clarinet piece built on related material.

Berlin, Irving (1888–1989)

Annie get your gun (musical).
❀ *** EMI Dig. CDC7 54206-2 [id.]. Criswell, Hampson, Graee, Luker, Amb. Ch., L. Sinf., John McGlinn.

John McGlinn follows up the pattern of his best-selling set of Jerome Kern's *Show Boat* with another performance that is at once scholarly and pulsing with life. Not only is the singing strong, characterful and idiomatic, the whole performance – not least from the players of the London Sinfonietta – is full of fun. Kim Criswell as Annie with her electric personality and bitingly bright voice here, a natural successor to Ethel Merman, the original Annie Oakley. Equally remarkably, Thomas Hampson makes an ideal hero, an opera-singer with an exceptionally rich and firm baritone who gets inside the idiom. First-rate, full-bodied sound.

Berlioz, Hector (1803–69)

Complete orchestral works

(i) *Grande Symphonie funèbre et triomphale, Op. 15;* (i–ii) *Harold in Italy, Op. 16;* (i; iii) *Lélio, Op. 14b; Overtures:* (i) *Béatrice et Bénédict;* (iv) *Benvenuto Cellini;* (i) *Le carnaval romain, Op. 9; Le Corsaire, Op. 21; Les Francs-juges, Op. 3; Le roi Lear, Op. 4; Waverley, Op. 1;* (v) *Rêverie et caprice* (for violin and orchestra), *Op. 8;* (vi–vii) *Symphonie fantastique, Op. 14;* (i; vii) *Tristia, Op. 18* (excerpt): *Marche funèbre pour la dernière scène d'Hamlet;* (i) *La Damnation de Faust, Op. 24* (excerpts): *Menuet des follets; Marche hongroise;* (i; viii) *Romeo and Juliet, Op. 17;* (i) *Les Troyens à Carthage, Part II, Prélude, Act III;* (ix) *Les Troyens, Act IV: Royal hunt and storm; Marche pour l'entrée de la reine; Ballet music.*
(B) *** Ph. 456 143-2 (6) [id.]. (i) LSO; (ii) with Nobuko Imai; (iii) with José Carreras, Thomas Allen, John Constable (piano), Roy Jowitt (clarinet), Renata Scheffel-Stein (harp); (iv) BBC SO; (v) Arthur Grumiaux, New Philh. O, Edo de Waart; (vi) Concg. O; (vii) with John Alldis Ch.; (viii) with Patricia Kern, John Shirley-Quirk, Robert Tear, L. Symphony Ch.; (ix) ROHCG O; all (except *Op. 8*) cond. Sir Colin Davis.

(i) *Harold in Italy, Op. 16. Overtures: Le Carnaval romain, Op. 9; Le Corsaire, Op. 21; Symphonie fantastique;* (ii) *Symphonie funèbre et triomphale, Op. 15.*
(M) ** Ph. Duo 442 290-2 (2) [id.]. (i) Nobuko Imai; (ii) John Alldis Ch.; LSO, Sir Colin Davis.

These Philips recordings, all of very high standard, made over a period of a decade and a half between 1965 and 1980, consistently reveal Davis to be a natural Berliozian. Even the overtures, which were the first works to be recorded show the Philips analogue sound at its most impressively full and atmospheric. Davis's Concertgebouw recording of the *Symphonie fantastique*, made a decade later, has long been a top recommendation; it has been matched but not surpassed. Its strange successor, *Lélio*, is given by Davis without the spoken dialogue, a well-sprung reading with excellent solo contributions. *Harold in Italy* (with Nobuko Imai) is also distinguished, and in *Romeo and Juliet*, also with excellent soloists, Davis brings a rare sympathy to the score and secures playing of great vitality and atmosphere from the LSO. Although his new Vienna Philharmonic account of *Roméo et Juliette* is undoubtedly the finer recording (and perhaps performance), this classic 1968 performance more than holds its own – and still offers very good sound. The *Symphonie funèbre et triomphale*, however, needs rather more persuasive handling than he achieves. Its *Apotheosis* can be made to sound grander and more effective, but the sonority of the recording remains impressive. Curiously, *Tristia* is not given complete, with only the third section included, the *Funeral march for the last scene of Hamlet*, but that is presented most evocatively, while among the other excerpts it is good to have Davis's fine choral version of the *Royal Hunt and storm*, taken from the complete set of *Les Troyens*. An outstanding bargain.

(i) *Harold in Italy, Op. 16; Symphonie fantastique, Op. 14; Damnation de Faust: Hungarian march. Roméo et Juliette, Op. 17:* orchestral excerpts: *Roméo seul . . . Grand fête chez Capulet; Scène d'amour; La reine Mab (scherzo). Les Troyens:* (ii) *Royal hunt and storm.*
(B) **(*) Decca Double Dig. 455 361-2 (2) [id.]. Montreal SO, Charles Dutoit; (i) with Pinchas Zukerman; (ii) with Montreal Ch.

Dutoit's version of *Harold in Italy*, with speeds on the broad side and Zukerman an individual, warmly expressive soloist, is very richly recorded. Again in the *Symphonie fantastique*, it is the spectacular, wide-ranging recorded sound that is the first point to note, and also the broad speeds. The four extended orchestral excerpts from *Roméo and Juliette* then follow, with Dutoit and his orchestra at their finest, playing warmly as well as brilliantly. The *Royal Hunt and storm* comes from the complete set of *Les Troyens* and includes the chorus.

Harold in Italy.
(N) (B) (**(*)) Dutton Lab. mono CDEA 5013

[id.]. Primrose, Boston SO, Koussevitzky – R. STRAUSS: *Till Eulenspiegel* (***).

(i) *Harold in Italy, Op. 16;* (ii) *La damnation de Faust, Op. 24: Hungarian march; Ballet des sylphes; Menuet des follets;* (iii) *Les Troyens: Trojan march;* (iv) *Royal Hunt & Storm.*
(B) **(*) Sony SBK 53255 [id.]. (i) Joseph de Pasquale; (i; iii) Phd. O, Ormandy; (ii) Phd. O, Munch; (iv) O de Paris, Barenboim.

(i) *Harold in Italy, Op. 16. Overtures: Benvenuto Cellini; Le Carnaval romain; Le Corsaire.*
*** DG Dig. 447 102-2 [id.]. (i) Laurent Verney; O de l'Opéra Bastille, Myung-Whun Chung.

(i) *Harold in Italy, Op. 16;* (ii) *La mort de Cléopâtre.*
(N) (M) **(*) Sony SMK 60696 [id.]. (i) William Lincer; (ii) Jennie Tourel; NYPO, Bernstein.

(i) *Harold in Italy;* (ii) *Tristia (Méditation religieuse; La mort d'Ophélie; March funèbre pour la dernière scène de Hamlet), Op. 18.*
*** Ph. Dig. 446 676-2 [id.]. (i) Gérard Caussé; (ii) Monteverdi Ch.; ORR, Gardiner.

(i) *Harold in Italy;* (ii) *Tristia (Méditation religieuse; La mort d'Ophélie; Marche funèbre pour la dernière scène de Hamlet), Op. 18; Les Troyens à Carthage: Prelude to Act II.*
*** Ph. 416 431-2 [id.]. (i) Imai; (ii) Alldis Ch.; LSO, C. Davis.

Gardiner's pioneering account of *Harold in Italy* on period instruments is searingly dramatic, the more biting in its impact with textures transparent yet with plenty of weight and high dynamic contrasts. Gérard Caussé, earlier the soloist in the Plasson version, here produces far sparer sounds than before, making the result more eerie. The three separate movements of *Tristia* are equally refreshing and dramatic, with sharp dynamic contrasts. Excellent sound.

A good and thoroughly idiomatic performance of Berlioz's ardent score, with plenty of warmth, from Myung-Whun Chung on DG, one of the finest digital versions. It makes a good modern-instrument alternative to the Gardiner account on Philips. Chung has already shown himself to be a born Berliozian in the *Symphonie fantastique*, and both *Harold* and the overtures reaffirm his credentials.

Davis's Philips account offers even better value. In addition to a noble account of *Harold* in which Nobuko Imai is on top form, this CD offers the *Tristia*, which includes the haunting *Funeral march for the last scene of Hamlet* given with chorus; this CD also offers the *Prelude* to the second Act of *Les Troyens*. The sound is natural and realistic, with impressive transparency and detail.

Ormandy's 1965 recording of *Harold in Italy* with the Philadelphia Orchestra is warmly recommendable, with Joseph de Pasquale a thoughtful and cultured soloist, even though the sound is not as transparent as some rivals. For all that, this is an impressive *Harold*, superbly played. The three excerpts from *La damnation de Faust* were recorded in 1963, when Munch was guest conductor in Philadelphia, and they have a Beecham-like elegance. Daniel Barenboim's recording of the *Royal Hunt and Storm* from *Les Troyens* with the Orchestre de Paris is less distinguished, but has the benefit of better sound. Good value.

In his earlier CBS/Sony recording Bernstein proved a forceful conductor in this elusive work, and plainly his soloist is only first among equals in the orchestra. Bernstein drives hard, but the dramatic excitement is justification and the result is undoubtedly thrilling, yet with plenty of warmth in the swinging *Pilgrims's march*. The reverberant recording is certainly atmospheric, but the top is fierce. The coupling is in every way memorable. Jennie Tourel sings with great eloquence in *La mort de Cléopâtre*, and Bernstein gives her splendid dramatic support: the result is very powerful and moving, the closing section especially so. This recording was also made in 1961, yet the sound is much fuller and more convincingly balanced than in the main work.

Koussevitzky's 1944 recording of *Harold in Italy* was the first-ever commercially available, an urgent, red-blooded, reading, and Primrose's reading reflects that – warmer and more colourful than his others on disc. Though the Dutton transfer has far more body than an earlier Biddulph issue, it still does not capture the full quality of the original 78s, with tuttis sounding rather opaque, damped-down in comparison with the Strauss. Even so, the disc – at bargain price in Dutton's Essential Archive series – brings a wonderful demonstration of the mastery of a supreme conductor who has still not had his full due.

(i) *Harold in Italy. Roméo et Juliette* (excerpts).
(M) (***) RCA mono [09026] 60275-2]. (i) Carlton Cooley; NBC SO, Toscanini.

Toscanini's famous 1953 recording of *Harold in Italy* is of very high voltage, with Carlton Cooley an excellent soloist. The demonic fires glow with great intensity in the *Orgy of the Brigands*; perhaps the *Pilgrims' march* is just a shade hard driven. In spite of the sonic limitations, the excitement of the performance still comes across the decades.

(i–ii) *Harold in Italy, Op. 16;* (ii) *Symphonie fantastique, Op. 14;* (iii) *Overtures: Béatrice et Bénédict; Benvenuto Cellini; Le Carnaval romain; Le Corsaire; Les Francs-juges.*
(N) (B) **(*) EMI double fforte CZS5 73338-2 (2). (i) McInnes; (ii) O Nat. de France, Bernstein; (iii) LSO, Previn.

Bernstein gives a performance of *Harold in Italy* that is both exciting and introspective. With French players, his slightly more relaxed manner than with the NYPO (see above) is in some ways more authentic, so that the galloping rhythms of the first and third movements are more lilting, if fractionally less precise. Donald McInnes is a violist with a superbly rich and even tone. He responds at all times to the conductor, yet has plenty of individuality. The 1976 recording of this work has an opulent spread and plenty of warmth, but the CD transfer has brought a degree of shrillness to the upper range of the violins, although the solo viola timbre seems unaffected. Bernstein also directs a brilliant and understanding performance of the *Symphonie fantastique* which captures more than most the wild, volatile quality of Berlioz's inspiration. His reading culminates in superb accounts of the *March to the scaffold* and the *Witches' sabbath*, full of rhythmic swagger and natural flair. Again there is a disconcerting tendency to shrillness in the upper strings. The overtures provide a rich bonus and are otherwise very well recorded, but it is a pity about the unnatural treble response, which was certainly not on the analogue LPs. Under Previn, the swing-along melody of *Les Francs-juges* swaggers boldly.

Overtures: Béatrice et Bénédict; Benvenuto Cellini; Le Carnaval romain; Le Corsaire; Les Francs-juges; Le Roi Lear; Waverley.

(N) ✿ *** RCA Dig. 09026 68790 [id.]. Dresden State O, Sir Colin Davis.

Mercurial, full of vitality and poetic feeling, wonderfully light in articulation, and superbly played and recorded. It completely supersedes Sir Colin's earlier recordings on Philips in every way. A glorious issue, outstanding in every way, and now the best Berlioz overtures disc in the catalogue.

Overtures: *Béatrice et Bénédict; Benvenuto Cellini; Le Carnaval romain; Le Corsaire; Les Francs-juges; Le Roi Lear; Les Troyens à Carthage (Prélude); Waverley.*

(N) **(*) Decca Dig. 452 480-2 [id.]. Montreal SO, Dutoit.

The performances on this compilation disc have all appeared in the late 1980s or early 1990s. The lively account of *Le Corsaire* was recorded first in 1984, and the rest followed a decade later. The very opening of *Le Carnaval romain* is less than electrifying but the performance gathers excitement as it proceeds, and there is some brilliant playing elsewhere. The Montreal brass are especially commanding at the opening of *Les Francs-juges*, and later the famous swinging melody has a proper ebullience, as indeed have the jaunty secondary themes of *Waverley* and *Béatrice et Bénédict*, while *Le Roi Lear* has plenty of weight. Brilliant recording and a fine ambient effect. But these performances do not capture the spirit of this composer anywhere near to the same extent as do the Davis and Munch discs.

Overtures: *Béatrice et Bénédict; Benvenuto Cellini; Le Carnaval romain; Le Corsaire. Roméo et Juliette: Queen Mab scherzo. Les Troyens: Royal hunt and storm.*

✿ (M) *** RCA 9026 61400-2 [id.]. Boston SO, Munch (with SAINT-SAENS: *Le rouet d'Omphale* ***).

Dazzlingly brilliant performances of four favourite overtures lead to a wonderfully poetic and thrilling account of the *Royal hunt and storm* from *Les Troyens*, earning this CD its Rosette. The horn solo is ravishing and the brass produce a riveting climax as the storm reaches its peak. The early stereo (1957/9) is remarkable: one really feels the hall ambience. The Saint-Saëns bonus is the earliest recording of all (1957), and is beautifully played.

Overtures: *Béatrice et Bénédict; Le Carnaval romain, Op. 9; Le Corsaire, Op. 21; Rob Roy; Le Roi Lear, Op. 4.*

**(*) Chandos Dig. CHAN 8316 [id.]. SNO, Gibson.

Rob Roy finds Gibson and the SNO at their most dashingly committed. *King Lear*, another rarity, also comes out most dramatically, and though *Béatrice et Bénédict* is not quite so polished, the playing is generally excellent. With first-rate digital recording, this can be warmly recommended.

Overtures: *Le Carnaval romain; Le Corsaire; Damnation de Faust: Hungarian march.*

(M) **(*) Decca (IMS) 448 571-2 [id.]. Paris Conservatoire O, Martinon – BIZET: *Jeux d'enfants;* IBERT: *Divertissement;* SAINT-SAENS: *Danse macabre* etc. ***

Martinon's Berlioz recordings have been added as a bonus for this reissue (in Decca's Classic Sound series) of his highly praised 1960 collection of French music. They were recorded two years earlier and, although the playing is both brilliant and exciting, it is not on the level of the later performances.

Rêverie et caprice, Op. 8.

(M) *** DG Dig. 445 549-2 [id.]. Perlman, O de Paris, Barenboim – LALO: *Symphonie espagnole*; SAINT-SAENS: *Concerto No. 3.* ***

Berlioz's short concertante work for violin and orchestra uses material originally intended for *Benvenuto Cellini*. Perlman's ripely romantic approach to the *Rêverie* brings out the individuality of the melody and, with a sympathetic accompaniment from Barenboim, the work as a whole is given considerable substance. First-rate digital recording.

Roméo et Juliette: Queen Mab scherzo.

(M) (**) RCA mono [60314-2-RG]. Phd. O, Toscanini – MENDELSSOHN: *Midsummer Night's Dream.* (***)

Toscanini's quicksilver reading of this fairy scherzo

has much in common with his fine Philadelphia recording of Mendelssohn's fairy music. The 1941 recording is clear.

Symphonie fantastique, Op. 14.
*** DG Dig. 445 878-2 [id.]. Paris Opéra-Bastille O, Myung-Whun Chung (with DUTILLEUX: *Métaboles* ***).
(M) *** Ph. 446 202-2 [id.]. Concg. O, LSO, Sir Colin Davis.
*** Ph. Dig. 434 402-2 [id.]. ORR, Gardiner.
(B) (***) Dutton Lab. mono CDEA 5504 [(M) id.]. Hallé O, Barbirolli – FAURE: *Shylock: Nocturne* (***) (with WAGNER: *Meistersinger: suite* (***)).
(B) *** [EMI Red Line Dig. CDR5 72552]. Phd. O, Muti.
(N) (M) **(*) EMI CDM5 67034-2. [id.]. Philh. O, Klemperer (with HUMPERDINCK: *Hänsel und Gretel*: *Overture and dream pantomime* (**(*)).
(M) **(*) Virgin Veritas/EMI (SIS) VM5 61379-2 [id.]. L. Classical Players, Norrington (with *Les Francs-juges*).
(M) **(*) Telarc Dig. CD 82014 [id.]. Cleveland O, Lorin Maazel.
(N) (M)** Decca 452 305-2 [id.]. Paris Conservatoire O, Argenta – LISZT: *Les Préludes*. *
(N) (BB) ** Arte Nova Dig. 74321 46492-2 [id.]. Gran Canaria PO, Leaper.

(i) *Symphonie fantastique;* (ii) *La damnation de Faust: Danse des sylphes.*
(M) *** Decca Phase Four 448 955-2 [id.]. (i) New Philh. O; (ii) LSO; Stokowski (with DVORAK: *Slavonic dance No. 10 in E min., Op. 72/2:* Czech PO ***).

(i) *Symphonie fantastique;* (ii) *Overtures: Béatrice et Bénédict; Le Carnaval romain; Le Corsaire.*
(M) **(*) EMI (SIS) CDM7 64630-2 [id.]. (i) O Nat. de France, Bernstein; (ii) LSO, Previn.
(BB) **(*) RCA Navigator 74321 21283-2 [Basic 100 09026 61721-2]. Boston SO, (i) Prêtre; (ii) Munch.

(i) *Symphonie fantastique;* (ii) *Overture: Benvenuto Cellini; Les Troyens: Royal hunt and storm.*
(M) **(*) Sony SMK 60135 [id.]. (i) LSO; (ii) NYPO; Pierre Boulez.

Symphonie fantastique; Overture: Le Carnaval romain, Op. 9.
(N) (BB) **(*) Virgin Classics Digital Double Dig. VBD5 61513-2 [CDVB 61513] (2). RPO, Lord Menuhin – BIZET; CHAUSSON: *Symphonies.* **(*)
(N) (B) ** Ph. Virtuoso 422 253-2 [id.]. LSO, Sir Colin Davis.

(i) *Symphonie fantastique;* (ii) *Overtures: Le Carnaval romain; Le Corsaire.*
(N) (BB) **(*) ASV CDQS 6090 [id.]. RPO, Bátiz.
(N) (M) *(**) Carlton Dig. 30366 01232 [id.]. (i) Philh. O; (ii) RPO, Bátiz.

Symphonie fantastique; Overtures: Le Carnaval romain; Le Corsaire; La damnation de Faust: Marche hongroise. Les Troyens: Trojan march.
(M) **(*) Mercury (IMS) 434 328-2 [id.]. Detroit SO, Paul Paray.

Symphonie fantastique; Overture: Le Corsaire, Op. 21.
(M) *** Carlton/RPO Dig. 3036 60022-2 [id.]. RPO, Previn.

Symphonie fantastique, Op. 14; Roméo et Juliette, Op. 17: Love scene.
(N) ** Delos Dig. DE 3229 [id.]. New Jersey SO, Zdenek Macal.

Symphonie fantastique; (i) *Tristia (Méditation religieuse).*
(N)** DG Dig. 453 432-2 [id.]. Cleveland O; (i) with Cleveland Ch., Boulez.

With Myung-Whun Chung and the Bastille Orchestra the *Symphonie fantastique* has rarely seemed so fantastic, for he conveys to a rare degree the nervously impulsive inspiration of a young composer. With speeds extreme the hints of hysteria and overtones of nightmare in Berlioz's programme are freshly brought out, the result is volatile rather than symphonically foursquare, and the originality of the inspiration seems all the greater. An outstanding, strongly characterized reading, very well recorded. Chung's unusual coupling adds to the disc's attractions – the set of five brief and brilliant pieces which Dutilleux wrote for Szell and the Cleveland Orchestra in 1964. Chung's view is both poetic and atmospheric.

Sir Colin Davis's 1974 Concertgebouw recording has dominated the catalogue for two decades. Now reissued at mid-price on Penguin Classics, with an accompanying personal essay by Alan Sillitoe, it still remains a primary recommendation. The performance has superb life and colour, the slow movement memorably atmospheric and the final two movements very exciting. If the sound does not quite match recent rivals in brilliance and definition, the overall balance is very satisfying and believable.

There is no more spectacular recording than Stokowski's, made in Phase Four in the Kingsway Hall in 1968 and multi-miked so that the brass has satanic impact in the *Marche au Supplice* and finale. The performance is as idiosyncratic as it is charismatic and thrilling in every way. Stokowski's warmth of phrasing is aptly romantic, but generally the surprising thing is his meticulous concern for markings. As welcome bonuses come the *Danse des sylphes* from *La Damnation de Faust*, exquisitely done and a seductive account of the *E minor Slavonic dance* beautifully played by the Czech Philharmonic Orchestra.

Instead of working in the studio, John Eliot Gardiner, with his Orchestre Révolutionnaire et Romantique opted for his period performance to go to the old hall of the Conservatoire in Paris, where the symphony was first heard in 1830. Gardiner uses the extra sharpness of focus to add to the dramatic bite. In his electrifying, warmly expressive performance, heightening Berlioz's wild syncopations, he is second to none in conveying the astonishing modernity of music written within three years of Beethoven's death.

With full-ranging digital sound, with fine presence and atmosphere, André Previn conducts the RPO on Carlton in a keenly dramatic reading marked by characteristically well-lifted rhythms, with dynamic contrasts powerfully underlined, heightening the sinister side of the composer's nightmare vision. An excellent, mid-priced, alternative recommendation.

The Dutton disc in the Concert Classics series offers superb CD transfers of three recordings which Barbirolli made for EMI in his early years with the Hallé Orchestra. This version of the *Symphonie fantastique* was recorded in 1947, just when Barbirolli had built the Hallé into what was widely counted the finest orchestra in the country. This is a spacious, beautifully moulded reading, taut and urgent in the last three movements. The Fauré *Nocturne* makes a fine if brief bonus.

Bernstein directs a brilliant and understanding performance which thrillingly captures the wild, volatile quality of Berlioz's inspiration. His reading culminates in superb accounts of the *March to the scaffold* and the *Witches' sabbath*, full of rhythmic swagger and natural flair, but the remastering of the late-1970s analogue recording brings shrillness in the upper strings. The three overtures make a fine bonus.

The balance of fierceness against romantic warmth in Muti's own personality works well in this symphony, so that he holds the thread of argument together firmly without ever underplaying excitement. The sound is among the best that Muti has had in Philadelphia. A strong bargain recommendation for American collectors.

Weight is the keynote of Klemperer's highly individual reading. If the gallic volatile element is unemphasized, the effect is always spontaneous and no one could be in any doubt that this was the work of a great conductor. From the first movement onwards, which is not without its impetuous feeling but far more clearly symphonic than usual, Klemperer conveys a rugged strength which, in the massiveness of the *Witches' sabbath* for example, brings you close to Satan himself. There is certainly no lack of adrenalin and the *March to the scaffold*, its rhythms clipped, is also given commanding power; the close is made the more impressive by a recording that is outstanding for its period (the early 1960s), sounding superbly expansive in this new transfer (reissued as part of the 'Klemperer Legacy') with rich, resonant strings and full, sonorous brass. The music from *Hänsel und Gretel* is also very successful within its expansive Klempererian mantle, with some superb horn-playing in the overture.

Boulez's account of the *Symphonie fantastique* is intensely individual, crisp and intense, with clarity the essential, as unatmospheric as could be. Boulez's accounts of the *Royal hunt and storm* and the *Benvenuto Cellini overture* are also exciting, but unevocative.

Paray's exciting, hard-pressed reading is passionate, mercurial. The first movement immediately spurts away, and it is only the conductor's firm grip that prevents the movement from getting out of hand. The other movements are fast too, great verve in the last two. Few performances combine such a high level of tension with a true understanding of the music's inner pulse. Brilliant recording, with a tendency to thinness in the violins. The encores are similarly exciting and vivid, and again one marvels that a stereo recording from as early as 1958/9 should sound so impressive today.

Although not a first choice, Menuhin's reading of the *Symphonie fantastique* is full of character and he brings his own humanistic insights. The neurosis is there but slightly tempered, the *Waltz* notably effective, and the bizarre power of the final two movements is relished. Yet in Menuhin's hands this is primarily a symphony. The RPO play very well for him and the recording is first class, brilliant, but with a satisfyingly full and resonant bass. The *overture* is enjoyable in a similar way, not just treated as a vehicle for orchestral virtuosity. The performance of the Bizet is enjoyable, the Chausson Symphony is particularly successful, and this very inexpensive Virgin Double is excellent value if you want all three works.

Sir Colin Davis's earlier LSO recording does not match his Concertgebouw performance of a decade later. The final two movements are very exciting but the tension is not consistently maintained in the first movement and the *Adagio* is a little detached.

Bátiz's ASV CD is fully competitive in the super-bargain range, with excellent digital recording, brilliant and well balanced. He brings the score vividly to life, consistently warm, intense persuasive. One has the feeling of live music-making, and the two overtures are equally strong and spontaneous.

In his second digital recording Bátiz really lets his hair down. He is clearly well in control and the Philharmonia respond with remarkable virtuosity; but not all will take to the frenetic neurosis of his opening movement, with its wild changes of tempi. The waltz is supercharged too, and after the idyllic calm of the *Scène aux champs* the *Marche au supplice* mordantly prepares the way for the grotesque satanic ritual of the finale, where the bells toll for a monstrous, doom-laden climax. The conductor builds and holds the tension at the highest level, and this is certainly among the most physically exciting versions on record, even if it is not wholly convincing. Brian Culverhouse's vivid recording balance certainly matches Bátiz's conception; but when one turns to the brilliant RPO performances of the pair of overtures (common to both CDs) one realizes that a little more poise is advantageous in Berlioz.

Karajan's mono account of the *Symphonie fantastique* with the Philharmonia Orchestra, made in July 1954, is kept on a firm rein, hardly at all volatile, but not lacking in temperament or poetry. The *Royal hunt and storm* is strongly done too. The playing of the Philharmonia is marvellous, and the recording is very good for the period.

Prêtre's exciting Boston version, recorded in 1969 in full, warm sound, brings a highly volatile performance, with the finale combining an element of the grotesque with high adrenalin flow. An individual and involving account. Munch's famous recordings of the three *Overtures* make a thrilling bonus, but the sound tends to shrillness.

Norrington does his utmost to observe the composer's metronome markings; but where his Beethoven is consistently fast, some of these speeds are more relaxed than we are used to – as in the *March to the scaffold* and the *Ronde du sabbat*. His lifting of rhythms prevents the music from dragging, with period instruments giving new transparency; *Les Francs-juges* Overture is disappointingly low-key.

Maazel's rather plain reading for Telarc compares with the finest rivals only in its spectacular recording of demonstration quality. With no fill-up, the disc has a playing time of only 49 minutes.

It is good to be reminded in Decca's Classic Sound series of the incisive brilliance of the short-lived Ataulfo Argenta, who died tragically at 44 only three years after this Berlioz recording was made in 1955. It is a direct, purposeful performance, enhanced by bright Decca sound, which has plenty of body but in this transfer has a cutting edge on top that needs taming. Though the recording of the Liszt – made with the Suisse Romande – is not quite so weighty or cleanly defined, that too brings an exceptionally powerful, thrusting performance.

The bargain issue from Arte Nova offers a performance from the Gran Canaria Philharmonic under Leaper that may lack something in power, but which is most persuasive in its subtle expressiveness and consistently well-paced. The recording is both atmospheric and commendably transparent.

There is something to be said for a sharply analytical version of the *Symphonie fantastique*, emphasizing that the work is not just colourful programme music, but original as a symphonic structure. Pierre Boulez, who might seem the ideal exponent of such an approach, directs a powerful, sure-footed and beautifully played reading which is lacking emotional thrust. With rhythms crisp but unsprung, the result is unpersuasive, out of tune with the inspiration of an arch-romantic. The first two sections of *Tristia* are far warmer, with an element of mystery heightened by the distantly placed chorus. The third of the *Tristia* pieces, the weirdly atmospheric *Funeral march for the last scene of Hamlet*, receives a disappointingly plain, detached reading.

Macal achieves some very fine playing from the excellent New Jersey Symphony Orchestra, especially in the slow movement, and in the excerpt from *Romeo and Juliet*, where the strings distinguish themselves. But the performance of the *Symphonie fantastique*, perceptively detailed as it is, although it is not without ongoing tension, ultimately refuses to catch fire. The recording is warm and natural but lacks the last degree of brilliance, and the end effect is studio-bound.

Symphonie fantastique, Op. 14; (i) *Lélio (Le retour à la vie), Op. 14b.*

(B) *** EMI Rouge et Noir CZS5 69550-2 (2). (i) Gedda, Burles, Van Gorp, Sendrez, Topart, Fr. R. Ch.; ORTF Nat. O, Martinon.

Berlioz intended *Lélio* as a sequel to the *Symphonie fantastique*, and Martinon conveniently offers the works paired at bargain price. His account of the *Symphonie* is uniquely seductive, for though he is brilliant, he never presses on too frenetically. The finale, with its tolling bells of doom, has a flamboyance and power to match any available, and the 1973 sound remains remarkably vivid. *Lélio* quotes the *idée fixe* from the *Symphonie*, which helps the listener to feel at home. It is difficult to imagine this performance being bettered, and the 1974 sound is suitably atmospheric.

Symphonie fantastique, Op. 14; (i) *Lélio, Op. 14b*: excerpts.

(N) ** RCA Dig. 09026 68930-2 [id.] San Francisco SO; (i) with San Francisco SO Ch., Michael Tilson Thomas.

Michael Tilson Thomas gets very good playing from his San Francisco forces and is a committed Berliozian, very much at home in the composer's world. Those who have been brought up with a more restrained and classical view of the score may find him a little histrionic at times. All the same, given the quantity and quality of the present competition, this is unlikely to disturb recommendations. The recording is decent without being in the least state-of-the-art.

(i) Symphonie fantastique; (ii) *Lélio, ou Le Retour à la vie, Op. 14b;* (iii; iv) *La Mort de Cléopâtre;* (iii–v) *Les Nuits d'été, Op. 7;* (vi) *Béatrice et Bénédict: Overture & Entr'acte; Overtures: Benvenuto Cellini; Le carnaval romain, Op. 9; Les Troyens: Royal hunt and storm.*

(M) *** Sony SM3K 64103 (3) (i) LSO; (ii) with Jean-Louis Barrault (narrator), John Mitchinson, John Shirley-Quirk, L. Symphony Ch.; (iii) Yvonne Minton; (iv) BBC SO; (v) Stuart Burrows; (vi) NYPO; all cond. Boulez.

A thoroughly worthwhile Berlioz anthology, spanning a decade of Boulez recordings for CBS from 1967 (the *Symphonie* and *Lélio*) to 1976 (the two song-cycles). Though the spoken dialogue outstays its welcome (even when spoken most beautifully by M. Barrault), the individual cueing on CD allows one access to the music itself. Coupled with a unique reading of the *Fantastique* (clear-headed and intense rather than atmospheric), it shows Boulez at his most searchingly convincing. The dramatic scena, *La Mort de Cléopâtre*, an early work which yet gives many hints of the mature Berlioz, makes a particularly suitable companion, as it offers specific quotations of material later used in the *Symphonie fantastique* (the *idée fixe*) and the *Roman carnival overture* (the melody of the introduction). Yvonne Minton's account is dramatically incisive and strongly committed. *Les nuits d'été* shared by Minton and Stuart Burrows, both at their finest. The 1972 New York collection of *Overtures* is warmer, less concerned with sharpness of detail than the earlier recordings, yet they still show toughness. Overall this is strongly recommended to Boulez admirers.

Symphonie fantastique, Op. 14. (i) *Roméo et Juliette, Op. 17* (complete).

(B) *** RCA Twofer 74321 34168-2 (2) [(M) id. import]. Boston SO, Charles Munch, (i) with Rosalind Elias, Cesare Valletti, Giorgio Tozzi and Ch.

Symphonie fantastique, Op. 14; Roméo et Juliette: Love scene (only).

(N) (M) *** RCA 09026 68979-2 [id.]. Boston SO, Munch.

One of the most valuable of recent 'Twofers'. Earlier RCA issued Munch's wonderful mono account of the *Roméo et Juliette Symphony* in harness with Victoria de los Angeles's 1955 *Les nuits d'été*, both sounding impressively fresh enough to merit a qualified three-star recommendation. The later *Roméo et Juliette* offers a near-ideal performance and Munch's approach is sharp and dramatic. The stabbing agony of the frenzied allegro following Juliet's death has a frightening impact, and the jollity of the Capulets' party is taut and brittle. Yet the romanticism of the love music shows the depth of Munch's sympathy. The virtuosity of singers and orchestra is matched by the brilliance of the early stereo. At their price, these performances should be snapped up, even if you have either of the Davis versions.

Collectors content with just the *Love scene* from *Roméo et Juliette* will find the single disc equally recommendable, and the transfers to CD just as impressive.

(i) *Grande symphonie funèbre et triomphale;* (ii; iii) *La mort de Cléopâtre;* (iv) *Overtures: Benvenuto Cellini, Op. 23; Le Carnaval romain, Op. 9; Le Corsaire, Op. 21; Les Francs-juges, Op. 3;* (iii) *Les Troyens: Royal hunt and storm; Ballet music; Trojan march.*

(N) (B) *** Erato/Warner Analogue/Dig. Ultima Double 3984 24229-2 (2) [id.]. (i) Chorale Populaire de Paris, Musique des Gardiens de la Paix, Désiré Dondeyne; (ii) Nadine Denize; (iii) New PO of Radio France, Gilbert Amy; (iv) Strasbourg PO, Alain Lombard.

Dondeyne's 1958 performance of the *Grande symphonie funèbre et triomphale*, spaciously recorded in Notre-Dame, is exciting and convincing in a specially French way. The wind and brass group (with a convincing solo trombone) has an authentic tang, and a few moments of slightly awry intonation add to the earthy style, with the chorus at the end producing the kind of exhilarated robust fervour that one associates with Parisian performances of the *Marseillaise*. The sound has plenty of spectacle and bite – indeed some of the plangent cymbal clashes make the listener jump! Nadine Denize is equally at home in *La mort de Cléopâtre*, which combines dramatic flair with a moving closing section. The four key overtures, recorded digitally two decades later, are also very well played and the programme ends with key excerpts from *Les Troyens*, the *Royal hunt and storm* without chorus, but still impressive. Excellent recording throughout, but the documentation is totally inadequate, with no texts.

VOCAL MUSIC

(i; ii) *La damnation de Faust; L'enfance du Christ, Op. 25; Herminie; Lélio; La mort de Cléopatre; Nuits d'été; Roméo et Juliette; Requiem Mass; Te Deum.* (i) Mélodies: *La belle voyageuse; Le captive; La chasseur danois; Le jeune pâtre breton; Zaïde.*

(N) (B) *** Ph. 462 252-2 (9) [id.]. (i) Soloists; (ii) John Alldis Ch., LSO Ch., Amb. S., Wandsworth School Boys' Ch.; LSO, Sir Colin Davis.

This impressive bargain box of Sir Colin Davis's recordings of the major Berlioz vocal works can be recommended with enthusiasm. Many of them are still available separately and are discussed below. *Roméo et Juliette* has great vitality and atmosphere. *Lélio* is presented without the spoken dialogue, and is convincing within its structural limitations. The *Te Deum* conveys massiveness without pomposity, drama without unwanted excesses of emotion, and Davis's massed forces with the LSO respond superbly. The expansive choral climaxes and Nicolas Kynaston's fine organ contribution are impressively contained. Dame Janet Baker sings with passionate intensity in the two dramatic scenes, *Herminie* and *La mort de Cléopâtre*, but *Nuits d'été* is presented with different singers singing different songs. This idea is less successful than it sounds, for the unity of the work is undermined and the contribution of the four singers involved is uneven, with Sheila Armstrong the finest of the group, especially in the final exhilarating *L'île inconnue*. In the other songs Josephine Veasey's contribution is also an individual one, but Frank Patterson, the weakest of the soloists lacks the necessary charm. Nevertheless this is a small blot on what is overall a splendid achievement.

La damnation de Faust (complete).
*** Decca Dig. 444 812-2 [id.]. Pollet, Leech, Cachemaille, Philippe, Montreal Ch. & SO, Charles Dutoit.
*** Ph. 416 395-2 (2) [id.]. Veasey, Gedda, Bastin, Amb. S., Wandsworth School Boys' Ch., London Symphony Ch., LSO, C. Davis.
*** Decca (IMS) Dig. 414 680-2 (2) [id.]. Riegel, Von Stade, Van Dam, King, Chicago Ch. & SO, Solti.
(B) **(*) DG Double 453 019-2 (2) [id.]. Mathis, Burrows, McIntyre, Paul, Tanglewood Festival Ch., Boston Boys' Ch. & SO, Ozawa.
(N) (**) BBC Legends mono BBCL 4006/7 (2) [id.]. Régine Crespin, André Turp, Michel Roux, John Shirley-Quirk, LSO Ch., LSO, Monteux.

(i) *La damnation de Faust, Op. 24;* (ii) *La mort de Cléopâtre*.
(B) **(*) EMI forte CZS5 68583-2 (2). Janet Baker; (i) Gedda, Bacquier, Thau, Paris Opera Ch., O de Paris, Prêtre; (ii) LSO, Gibson.

Dutoit follows up his epic recording of *Les Troyens* with an account of this unique work which brings out its fully operatic qualities. So the chorus, a key element, sings with biting dramatic point to heighten the plot, rather than singing with oratorio discipline as a commentary. The choice of mainly French-speaking soloists equally intensifies the storytelling element, with singers balanced so as to allow words to be heard, and with the atmospheric warmth of the Montreal sound adding to the illusion of a stage picture. Leech is not the most characterful Faust but, unlike many, he sings clearly and without strain. Françoise Pollet is a warm, expressive Marguerite, tenderly affecting in her two big solos, and Gilles Cachemaille, though not the most powerful Mephistopheles, is brilliant at pointing words and bringing out the wry humour.

Both Gedda as Faust and Bastin as Mephistopheles are impressive in the 1974 Philips set. The response of the chorus and orchestra is highly intelligent and sensitive and the recording perspective is outstandingly natural and realistic.

Solti's performance, searingly dramatic, is given stunning digital sound to make the *Ride to Hell* supremely exciting. But with Von Stade singing tenderly, this is a warmly expressive performance too; and the *Hungarian march* has rarely had such sparkle and swagger. The extra brightness matches the extrovert quality of the performance, less subtle than Davis's.

Most valuable in the EMI *Damnation de Faust* is Dame Janet Baker's Marguerite, sung most beautifully. Prêtre is not always perceptive, and though there are many dramatic touches, the set does not outshine either Markevitch or Ozawa in this price-range. Berlioz's early scena on the death of a famous classical heroine, *La mort de Cléopâtre*, is most movingly done.

Now offered, economically priced, on a DG Double (with translation and full documentation included), Ozawa's performance provides an alternative, in a much more moulded style. The relative softness of focus is underlined by the reverberant Boston acoustics, but with superb playing and generally fine singing, the results are seductively enjoyable. The digital remastering has improved definition without losing hall ambience.

The BBC recording is of a relay from the Royal Festival Hall on 8 March 1962, and conveys a real sense of occasion. The Monteux performance is a distinguished one with a first-rate cast, and the sound wears its years very lightly.

L'enfance du Christ, Op. 25.
*** Hyperion Dig. CDA 66991/2 [id.]. Rigby, Miles, Finley, Aler, Howell, Corydon Singers & O, Best.
**(*) Ph. 416 949-2 (2) [id.]. Baker, Tappy, Langridge, Allen, Herincx, Rouleau, Bastin, Alldis Ch., LSO, C. Davis.
(N) (B) *** Erato/Warner Ultima Dig. 3984 25595-2 (2) [id.]. Von Otter, Rolfe Johnson, Van Dam, Cachemaille, Bastin, Monteverdi Ch., Lyon Op. O, Gardiner.
(B) **(*) RCA Twofer 09026 61234-2 (2) [id.]. Valletti, Kopleff, Souzay, Tozzi, New England Conservatory Ch., Boston SO, Munch – *Nuits d'été*. *
(N) (BB) **(*) Naxos Dig. 8.553650/1 [id.]. Lagrange, Michel Piquemal, Fernand Bernardi, Ch. Regional Vittoria de l'Ille de France, Maîtrice de Radio-France, Lille Nat. O, Jean-Claude Casadesus.

Vividly recorded in beautifully balanced digital sound, immediate yet warm, Matthew Best's version offers a keenly dramatic view, with the story of the Flight into Egypt made vital and involving.

So Alastair Miles conveys pure evil in Herod's monologue at the start and, with words exceptionally clear, Joseph's pleas for shelter are movingly urgent. Jean Rigby is a fresh, young-sounding Mary, with Gerald Finley warm and expressive as Joseph. John Aler is a powerful Reciter, and Gwynne Howell a strong, benevolent-sounding Father of the family. Though Sir Colin Davis's vintage Philips version has a starrier team of soloists, this one is no less consistent vocally and makes an ideal choice for those who want a more intimate view and a superb modern recording.

In Sir Colin Davis's second version for Philips the beautifully balanced recording intensifies the colour and atmosphere of the writing, so that the *Nocturnal march* in the first part is wonderfully mysterious. There is a fine complement of soloists, and though Eric Tappy's tone as narrator is not always sweet, his sense of style is immaculate. Others are not always quite so idiomatic, but Dame Janet Baker and Thomas Allen both sing beautifully. Even so, Davis's earlier set remains very competitive – see below.

John Eliot Gardiner in his vivid reading has the advantage of fine modern recording, made in the Church of Sainte-Madeleine, Pérouges, very well balanced and atmospheric. Among the soloists Anne Sofie von Otter's Mary is outstanding, sung with rapt simplicity. Gardiner often – though not always – adopts brisker tempi than Davis, and his vibrancy brings a new dimension to some of the music. Now as a two-for-the-price-of-one Ultima, it is very competitive, even if Davis's choice of pacing is even more apt.

Charles Munch's account of *L'enfance du Christ*, dating from 1956, makes a welcome return to circulation in a two-disc box. Needless to say, the performance is thoroughly idiomatic and the playing of the Boston Symphony has a splendour and sonority that the dated recording still conveys. The line-up of soloists is impressive: Florence Kopleff as Mary and Gérard Souzay, then at the height of his powers, as Joseph. The chorus is a weakness; they do not have the tenderness and flexibility in either of Colin Davis's accounts. Leontyne Price is gloriously full-toned in her 1963 recording of *Nuits d'été*, if not as characterful as some. The transfers are excellently effected.

Casadesus and the Lille Orchestra follow up the success of their Naxos recording of Debussy's *Pelléas et Mélisande* with this fresh and direct account of Berlioz's sacred trilogy, the most charming of his works. As in the opera, young singers have been chosen as the main soloists, generally clear-toned and idiomatic. The tenor, Jean-Luc Viala, makes an excellent narrator and the mezzo, Michèle Lagrange, a touching Mary, and if the others are not so distinguished, they form a satisfying team. Casadesus's approach can be well assessed from the fresh, unsentimental manner he adopts, along with a flowing speed, for the most celebrated number, the *Shepherds' farewell*. Rather short measure for two discs, the set includes in the excellent booklet full French text with English translation. Clear, pleasing sound.

(i; ii) *L'enfance du Christ*; (ii; iii) *Méditation religieuse; La mort d'Ophélie; Sara la baigneuse*; (iii; iv) *La mort de Cléopâtre*.

(B) *** Double Decca 443 461-2 (2) [id.]. (i) Pears, Morison, Cameron, Rouleau, Frost, Fleet, Goldsbrough O; (ii) St Anthony Singers, (iii) ECO; (iv) Anne Pashley; Sir Colin Davis.

Davis's 1961 recording of *L'enfance du Christ* (originally made for L'Oiseau-Lyre) is by no means inferior to his later, Philips set. At times the earlier performance was fresher and more urgent, and Peter Pears was a sweeter-toned, more characterful narrator. Elsie Morison and John Cameron are perfectly cast as Mary and Joseph, and Joseph Rouleau makes an impressive contribution as the Ishmaelite Father. This Decca reissue in atmospheric sound offers (on a Double Decca set) the entire contents of a third LP, issued in 1968 and also sounding freshly minted. This is an invaluable collection of off-beat vocal works, with fine choral singing and a splendid contribution from Anne Pashley.

(i) *L'enfance du Christ, Op. 25;* (ii) *Roméo et Juliette, Op. 17* (orchestral music only).

(B) *** EMI forte CZS5 88586-2 (2). (i) De los Angeles, Gedda, Soyer, Blanc, Depraz, Cottret, René Duclos Ch., Paris Conservatoire O, Cluytens; (ii) Chicago SO, Giulini.

This Cluytens performance of *L'enfance du Christ* from the mid-1960s sounds remarkably fresh on CD, very well transferred on EMI's Forte label with its generous new coupling. Gedda may not be as sensitive as Pears on the first Davis version, but de los Angeles is superlative and so is Ernest Blanc as Herod. The orchestra gives sensitive support to the fresh choral singing. The coupling is one of Giulini's best records from the same period (1969). The Chicago orchestra responds with fine discipline and beauty of tone, and also with great conviction in an incandescent performance. Good recording quality, though the focus is not always absolutely clean.

'Chant d'amour': La Mort d'Ophélie; Zaïde.

*** Decca Dig. 452 667-2; *452 667-4* [id.]. Cecilia Bartoli, Myung-Whun Chung – BIZET; DELIBES; RAVEL: *Mélodies*. ***

Cecilia Bartoli's collection of French songs is one of the most ravishing of her records yet, and these Berlioz items are among the highlights. Chung's contribution is both imaginative and supportive (see below under Recitals).

Irlande, Op. 2: excerpts; Mélodies: *La belle voyageuse; Adieu, Bessy!; Le coucher du soleil; Elégie; L'origine de la harpe.*
✿ *** EMI (SIS) Dig. CDC5 55047-2 [id.]. Thomas Hampson, Geoffrey Parsons – LISZT; WAGNER: *Lieder.* *** ✿

Thomas Hampson gives glowing performances of five of the nine songs, using translations from English texts by the poet Thomas Moore, which Berlioz wrote very early in his career. In their expressive warmth they make a perfect match for the fascinating selections of songs by Wagner and Liszt, with Geoffrey Parsons adding to the impact. Warm, helpful sound.

Mélodies: *Adieu Bessy; Amitié, reprends ton empire; La belle Isabeau; La belle voyageuse; Boléro; Canon libre à la quinte; La captive; Les champs; Chanson à boire; Chansonette de M. Léon de Wailly; Le chant des bretons; Chant guerrier; Le chasseur danois; Je crois en vous; Elégie en prose; Hélène; Le jeune pâtre breton; Le matin; Le Maure jaloux; Le Montagnard exilé; La mort d'Ophélie; Nocturnes à deux voix; L'Origine de la harpe; Pleure, pauvre Colette; Prière du matin; Le roi de Thulé; Sara la baigneuse; Sérénade de Méphistophélès; Le Trébuchet; Zaïde.*
*** DG (IMS) Dig. 435 860-2 (2) [id.]. Françoise Pollet, Anne Sofie von Otter, John Aler, Thomas Allen, Cord Garben (with Bernd Schenk, Christine Mühlbach, Göran Söllscher, Torleif Thedéen, Thomas Lutz, Royal Op. Ch., Stockholm (members)).

Starting magically with a little duet for soprano and mezzo to guitar accompaniment, this collection of 29 of Berlioz's songs and ensembles includes many rarities previously unrecorded. With four outstanding soloists, it makes a unique and attractive collection, despite piano accompaniment from Cord Garben that is often rhythmically too square. Among the rarities such a witty little duet for tenor and baritone as *Le trébuchet* ('The snare') proves a charmer with its bird-like accompaniment, and so does the *Boléro*, with castanets as well as piano. *Le matin*, Berlioz's last song, was written as early as 1850, and it makes one regret that from then on he ignored the genre. Though the recordings were made in different venues over several years, they present a consistent series.

Mélodies: *Aubade; La belle voyageuse; La captive; Le chasseur danois; Le jeune pâtre breton; La mort d'Ophélie; Les nuits d'été; Zaïde.*
(M) *** Erato/Warner Dig. 2292 45517-2 [id.]. Montague, Robbin, Fournier, Crook, Cachemaille, Lyon Op. O, Gardiner.

John Eliot Gardiner here divides the six keenly atmospheric songs of *Les nuits d'été* between four singers, in some ways an ideal solution when each song demands such different timbre and different tessitura. His choice of singers is inspired and the presiding genius of the conductor makes this a memorable Berlioz disc.

Mélodies: (i) *La belle Isabeau; La belle voyageuse; La captive; Le matin; La mort d'Ophélie.* (ii) *Nuits d'été* (song-cycle); (ii; iii) *Roméo et Juliette:* Prologue: *Premiers transports* (*Strophes*).
*** DG Dig. 445 823-2 [id.]. Anne Sophie von Otter, with (i) Royal Stockholm Op. Ch.; Cord Garben; (ii) BPO, Levine; (iii) Berlin RIAS Chamber Ch.

This is a most attractive compilation, bringing together von Otter's outstanding contributions both to DG's Berlioz song collection and to the Levine set of *Roméo et Juliette*, which had *Nuits d'été* as a fill-up. The five solo songs here are among the most moving and individual of all, notably the longest, *La mort d'Ophélie*. In *Les nuits d'été* von Otter is fresh and radiant, bringing out the dramatic contrasts between the songs, and the poise and weight of *Strophes* from *Roméo* is magical.

Messe solennelle; Resurrexit (revised version).
*** Ph. Dig. 442 137-2 [id.]. Donna Brown, Jean-Luc Viala, Gilles Cachemaille, Monteverdi Ch., ORR, Gardiner.

This massive work, completed in 1824, was among the first that the young Berlioz wrote. Both the scale of the inspiration and its actual execution are remarkable for a composer only twenty and largely untrained. It is an uneven work, but the glow of inspiration shines out over any shortcomings. Especially illuminating are the passages where Berlioz draws on themes we know from other contexts – a *Roman carnival* theme in the vigorous *Gloria*, a *Fantastic Symphony* theme in the *Gratias*, used totally differently. Gardiner conducts with characteristic flair and sense of drama, bringing brilliant singing from the Monteverdi Choir, though the choral sound is backwardly balanced. A second, modified and slightly expanded version of the violent *Resurrexit* is included as a supplement, a revised version that Berlioz himself acknowledged.

Les nuits d'été (song-cycle), *Op. 7.*
(M) *(*) Sony Theta Dig. SMK 60031 [id.]. Frederica von Stade, Boston SO, Ozawa – DEBUSSY: *La Damoiselle élue* *(*); RAVEL: *Shéhérazade.* **(*)
(M) * RCA 09026 61234-2 (2) [id.]. Leontyne Price, Chicago SO, Reiner – *L'enfance du Christ.* **(*)

Les nuits d'été (song-cycle); Mélodies: *La belle voyageuse; La Captive; Zaïde.*
(BB) *** Virgin Classics Dig. Double VBD5 61469-2 (2) [CDVB 61469]. Dame Janet Baker, City of L. Sinf., Hickox – BRAHMS:

Alto rhapsody etc.; MENDELSSOHN: *Infelice* etc.; RESPIGHI: *La Sensitiva*. ***

(i) *Les nuits d'été* (song-cycle), *Op. 7;* (ii) *La mort de Cléopâtre.*

(M) *** DG Dig. 445 594-2 [id.]. O de Paris, Barenboim, with (i) Kiri Te Kanawa; (ii) Jessye Norman.

This Virgin two-for-one-at-mid-price is a treasure-chest of Dame Janet Baker's later recordings, made in the early 1990s, including Dame Janet's later recording of *Les nuits d'été* and other orchestral songs (see above). Her classic EMI reading with Barbirolli is now coupled on a forte double with *Roméo et Juliette* (see below).

The coupling of Jessye Norman in the scena and Dame Kiri Te Kanawa in the song-cycle makes for a ravishing Berlioz record, with each singer at her very finest. Norman has natural nobility and command as the Egyptian queen in this dramatic scena, while Te Kanawa encompasses the challenge of different moods and register in *Les nuits d'été* more completely and affectingly than any singer on record in recent years.

Frederica von Stade, always intelligent and naturally musical, yet sounds less spontaneous than usual in a disappointing version of this most magical of orchestral song-cycles, not helped by Ozawa's cool and uninvolved accompaniment. Good recording.

Leontyne Price's account suffers from generalized responses and little variety of colour or dynamics, though her voice is striking, and she is well supported by Reiner and the Chicago orchestra in its heyday.

(i) *Les nuits d'été* (song-cycle); (ii) *Te Deum.*

(B) ** Sony SBK 63043 [id.]. (i) Yvonne Minton, Stuart Burrows, BBC SO, Boulez; (ii) Jean Dupouy, Ch. d'Enfants de Paris, Maîtrisse de la Resurrection, Ch. & O. de Paris, Barenboim.

In the Boulez version of *Nuits d'été* the six songs are shared between male and female voices. Yvonne Minton brings an almost operatic flair to *Le spectre de la rose*, *Sur les lagunes* and especially *L'île inconnue*, and Burrows is hardly less ardent in his heady opening *Villanelle*, while both *Absence* and *Au cimetière* are touchingly done, although his wide vibrato is sometimes intrusive. But this performance certainly does not lack variety of characterization, and Boulez provides sympathetic support. The coupling is unexpected, but Barenboim's Paris version of the *Te Deum* brings a strong and characterful performance, occasionally exaggerated but with fine choral singing and a stylish tenor soloist, and fine playing fro the organist, Jean Guillou. The recording is full and vivid.

Les Nuits d'été, Op. 7. Arias: *Béatrice et Bénédict: Dieu! Que viens-je d'entendre?. Benvenuto Cellini: Mais qu'ai-je donc?. La Damnation de Faust: D'amour l'ardente flamme. Les Troyens: Ah! Ah! Je vais mourir; Adieu, fière cité.*

(N) ** Sony Dig. SK 62730 (id.). Susan Graham, ROHCG, John Nelson.

As anyone who has heard her in the flesh will know, Susan Graham has a voice of great radiance and freshness. Her account of *Les nuits d'été* show her to be thoroughly at home in Berlioz's sound world and idiom. None the less there are reservations – not so much about the performances but the sound. This is not the thrilling, glorious voice one remembers from the opera-house. She is closely observed by the microphone so that the voice occasionally has a slight edge that is not present in real life. The orchestral sound, though not unpleasing, is synthetic and unreal.

Requiem, Op. 5.

(N) (***) BBC Legends mono BBCL 4011-2 [id.]. Richard Lewis, RPO Ch., RPO, Sir Thomas Beecham.

(i) *Requiem Mass (Grande messe des morts). Overtures: Benvenuto Cellini; Le Carnaval romain; Le Corsaire.*

**(*) DG (IMS) Dig. 429 724-2 (2) [id.]. (i) Pavarotti, Ernst-Senff Ch.; BPO, Levine.

(i) *Requiem Mass;* (ii) *Symphonie funèbre et triomphale, Op. 15.*

**(*) Ph. 416 283-2 (2) [id.]. (i) Dowd, Wandsworth School Boys' Ch., London Symphony Ch.; (ii) John Alldis Ch.; LSO, Sir Colin Davis.

(i) *Requiem Mass (Grande Messe des Morts), Op. 5.* (ii) *Symphonie fantastique.*

(B) *** EMI forte Dig./Analogue CZS5 69512-2 (2). (i) Robert Tear, LPO Ch., LPO; (ii) LSO; Previn.

Previn's 1980 Walthamstow recording of Berlioz's great choral work offers spectacular digital sound, with the gradations of pianissimo breathtakingly caught, to make the great outbursts of the *Dies irae* and the *Tuba mirum* the more telling. There is a fine bloom on the voices, while the separation of sound gives a feeling of reality to the massed brass and multiple timpani. Previn's view is direct and incisive, not underlining expressiveness but concentrating on rhythmic qualities. If Previn misses animal excitement, the contrasts of the closing *Agnus Dei* are movingly captured. Robert Tear, balanced close, is a sensitive soloist. The *Symphonie fantastique* in Previn's dramatic strongly structured reading makes a generous fill-up, also very well-recorded.

Though Beecham's live recording, made at the Royal Albert Hall in December 1959, comes in mono only, the BBC sound is warm and full. The weight and intensity of the performance, the sense of a great occasion, are vividly caught, not least in the great outburst of brass bands, widely separated, in the *Tuba mirum*. One regularly registers Beecham's attention to fine detail and his concern for clarity. Although the professional choir takes a little time to settle down – with imprecisions exposed by the closeness of sound – the Beecham magic quickly works, to make this one of the most compelling performances on disc. The tenor, Richard Lewis, is in superb form in the *Sanctus*, his voice given a halo of reverberation. A most cherishable historic issue.

For Sir Colin Davis's recording of the *Requiem* Philips went to Westminster Cathedral and, though thanks to the closeness of the microphones, one can hear individual voices in the choir, the large-scale brass sound is formidably caught and the choral fortissimos are glorious, helped by the fresh cutting edge of the Wandsworth School Boys' Choir. The LSO provides finely incisive accompaniment. The *Symphonie funèbre et triomphale*, not always persuasive, makes a generous fill-up.

Levine's account of the *Requiem*, one of his Berlioz series with the Berlin Philharmonic, is the most recommendable of the modern, digitally recorded versions, though it cannot quite match the vintage Colin Davis and the Ernst-Senff Choir falls short of its usual standards in some ragged entries. Pavarotti is a characterful, imaginatively expressive soloist in the *Sanctus* is an advantage, and three of Berlioz's most popular overtures come in excellent performances.

Roméo et Juliette, Op. 17 (both original 1839 and standard 1846 versions of score).

(N) *** Ph. Dig. 454 454-2 (2) [id.]. Catherin Robbin, Jean-Paul Fouchécourt, Gilles Cachemaille, Monteverdi Ch., O.R.R., Gardiner.

Without usurping Sir Colin Davis's version – see below – this new Gardiner set will be a mandatory acquisition for all Berliozians. It enables you to make your own choice from among the discarded material reproduced in the Appendices of the New Berlioz Edition. You can chart your own way through the score, trying Berlioz's first or final thoughts or Gardiner's own recommended combination of the two. Incidentally, Oliver Knussen's realization of the second *Prologue*, which Berlioz left unscored, is done with uncommon flair. For those with an enquiring interest in the creative process, Gardiner's 'choose-it-yourself' set will be of enormous fascination and no mean pleasure. Gardiner has a good team of soloists and gets an expert response from his Orchestre Révolutionnaire et Romantique. He presses ahead with too unyielding a grip in the *Queen Mab scherzo*, and although there is eloquence at times, his phrasing is crisp rather than light – and phrases do not always unfold naturally and breathe as freely as they would if a Beecham were on the podium. Where, you may ask, is the sense of enchantment and rapture in the *Scène d'amoury*? However there is keen intelligence and imagination here and the recording is absolutely first-class, beautifully balanced and transparent in texture.

Roméo et Juliette, Op. 17.

✿ *** Ph. Dig. 442 134-2 [id.]. Borodina, Moser, Miles, Bav. R. Ch., VPO, Sir Colin Davis.

(B) *** Millennium MCD 80354 (2). Resnik, Turp, Ward, London Symphony Ch., LSO, Monteux.

(M) (***) RCA mono GD 60681 (2) [09026 60681-2]. Roggero, Chabay, Yi-Kwei-Sze, Harvard Glee Club, Radcliffe Ch. Soc., Boston SO, Munch – *Nuits d'été.* **(*)

(M) (**) RCA mono GD 60274 (2) [60274-2-RG]. Gladys Swarthout, John Garris, Nicola Moscona, NBC Ch. & SO, Toscanini (with BIZET: *L'Arlésienne & Carmen suites* **).

(i) *Roméo et Juliette. Symphonie funèbre et triomphale, Op. 15.*

*** Decca 417 302-2 (2) [id.]. (i) Quivar, Cupido, Krause, Tudor Singers, Montreal Ch. & SO, Dutoit.

Colin Davis's first recording of *Roméo et Juliette* for many years long reigned supreme in the catalogue, and its successor, recorded in Vienna, is likely to do the same. Sir Colin's interpretative approach remains basically unchanged, yet he now offers greater depth, colour and body. Olga Borodina has the full measure of the Berlioz style. Thomas Moser is no less ardent and idiomatic, and Alastair Miles is a fine Friar Laurence. Apart from its all-round artistic excellence, this scores over all comers in the sheer quality of the sound, which reproduces the whole range of Berlioz's fantastic score in all its subtle colourings in remarkable detail and naturalness.

Dutoit's is a masterly, heart-warming reading of Berlioz's curious mixture of symphony, cantata and opera, superbly recorded in richly atmospheric sound, with a triumphantly successful account of the *Symphonie funèbre et triomphale* as a generous coupling. Dutoit is here at his most uninhibited, brilliantly skirting the very edge of vulgarity in this outgoing ceremonial piece.

In June 1962, at the age of 87, Pierre Monteux recorded this glowing performance of Berlioz's great dramatic symphony in the helpful acoustic of Walthamstow Assembly Rooms. This CD transfer brings out its full range of beauty as never before, vivid and immediate in sound. Monteux's pacing seems so inevitable that, though the party music is very fast, it conveys exuberance in its light springing, and rarely has the love music seemed so sensuous in its hushed intensity, luscious yet refined. The finale, with David Ward strong and firm as

Friar Lawrence and with alert choral singing, makes a warmly satisfying conclusion. The other soloists too are excellent, the velvet-toned Regina Resnik and the headily clear André Turp agile in his scherzando solo. At bargain price not to be missed, though the text is not given.

Charles Munch's version dates from 1953. The RCA remastering has done wonders for the sound and in the three orchestral movements the playing of the Boston orchestra is superb. This was the first commercial recording of the whole work and the soloists, Margaret Roggero, Leslie Chabay and Yi-Kwei-Sze, are impressive. A valuable historical document, it comes with a lovely account of *Nuits d'été* from Victoria de los Angeles in her prime.

Toscanini's concert performance of February 1947 brings many electrifying moments, with the melodic lines often drawn out lovingly in a Verdian way and with the virtuoso passages delivered with panache. But the sound, recorded in the notorious Studio 8H, is dry and fizzy. The Bizet coupling offers brilliant playing, but Munch is a more idiomatic Berliozian and offers a more interesting coupling in *Les nuits d'été* with Victoria de los Angeles.

Roméo et Juliette (excerpts); *Les Troyens à Carthage: Prelude and Royal hunt and storm.*
(BB) **(*) Naxos Dig. 8.553195 [id.]. San Diego Ch. and SO, Yoav Talmi.

Talmi and the San Diego orchestra offer a far more generous selection from Berlioz's great dramatic symphony than usual, lasting well over an hour and including important sections with chorus, such as the atmospheric passages for the party-goers at the Capulets' Ball. Talmi secures brilliant playing from his orchestra, with admirably crisp ensemble in such show-pieces as the *Queen Mab scherzo*, and with satisfying warmth in the great Love scene. It is good too on this very well-filled disc to have the *Prelude* to *Les Troyens* and the *Royal hunt and storm* (complete with offstage chorus) as makeweights. The recording is clean and detailed, but lacks full weight.

Te Deum, Op. 22.
*** DG Dig. 410 696-2 [id.]. Araiza, London Symphony Ch., LPO Ch., Woburn Singers, Boys' Ch., European Community Youth O, Abbado.

The DG recording from Abbado is very impressive. The sound is wide-ranging, with striking dynamic contrasts: Abbado brings great tonal refinement and dignity to this performance, and the spacious sound helps. Francisco Araiza is the fine soloist.

OPERA

Complete operas

(i) *Béatrice et Bénédict;* (ii) *Benvenuto Cellini;* (iii) *Les Troyens, Parts 1 & 2.*
(B) *** Ph. 456 387-2 (9) [(M) id. import]. (i) J. Baker, Tear, Watts, Van Allan, Alldis Ch., LSO; (i–ii) Eda-Pierre, Bastin, Lloyd; (ii) Gedda, Massard, Blackwell, Herincx, Cuénod, Berbié, BBC SO; (ii–iii) Soyer, ROHCG Ch.; (iii) Veasey, Vickers, Lindholm, Glossop, Begg, Partridge, Wandsworth School Boys' Ch., ROHCG O; Sir Colin Davis.

Sir Colin Davis's recordings of the three Berlioz operas (with *Benvenuto Cellini* made first in 1969, *Béatrice et Bénédict* following in 1972 and the series crowned with *Les Troyens* in 1977) makes another superb bargain package, with consistently fine CD transfers. The one blot on the set is the omission of libretto translations, although the synopses are adequately cued. If Dame Janet Baker and Robert Tear understandably stand out in *Béatrice et Bénédict*, the rest of the cast is also first rate. Similarly, it is Nicolai Gedda in superb form who dominates *Benvenuto Cellini*, but his colleagues do not let him down. Even more than the other two operas, *Les Troyens* was an ambitious team-project, with singers, chorus and orchestra all inspired by Davis and with Josephine Veasey a superb Dido. The Philips engineers rise to the occasion in capturing the opera's spectacle with brilliance, atmosphere and refined detail.

Béatrice et Bénédict (complete).
*** Ph. 416 952-2 (2) [id.]. Baker, Tear, Eda-Pierre, Allen, Lloyd, Van Allan, Watts, Alldis Ch., LSO, C. Davis.
*** Erato/Warner Dig. 2292 45773-2 (2) [id.]. Graham, Viala, McNair, Robbin, Bacquier, Cachemaille, Le Texier, Lyon Opera Ch. & O, John Nelson.

(i) *Béatrice et Bénédict* (complete); (ii) *Chant de la Fête de Pâcques; Irlande (9 Mélodies), Op. 2; La Mort d'Ophélie, Op. 18/2; Le Trébuchet, Op. 13.*
(B) *** Decca Double 448 113-2 (2) [id.]. (i) Veasey, Mitchinson, Cantelo, Cameron, Watts, Shirley-Quirk, Shilling, St Anthony Singers, LSO, Sir Colin Davis; (ii) Cantelo, Watts, Tear, Salter, Monteverdi Ch., Gardiner; Tunnard (piano).

Béatrice et Bénédict presents not just witty and brilliant music for the heroine and hero (Dame Janet Baker and Robert Tear at their most pointed) but sensuously beautiful passages too. First-rate solo and choral singing, brilliant playing and sound refined and clear in texture, bright and fresh, even if minimal hiss betrays an analogue source.

The Lyon Opera version conducted by John Nelson makes an excellent alternative to the vintage Colin Davis recording. In spacious, modern, digital sound it offers substantially more of the French dialogue, well spoken by actors but more dryly recorded than the musical numbers. Susan Graham is a characterful Béatrice, lighter in the big aria than Janet Baker for Davis but aptly younger-sounding. Jean-Luc Viala is a comparably light Bénédict, pointing the fun in his big aria, and Sylvia McNair and Catherine Robbin are superb as Hero and Ursule.

It is good to have back the early (1962) Oiseau-Lyre set sounding so fresh and vivid. Above all it is a triumph for Sir Colin Davis, who readily responds to Berlioz's quirkiness, bringing out the delicacy and the humour. The singing is equally fresh and vigorous with April Cantelo coping splendidly with Héro's fearsome opening aria. Josephine Veasey as Béatrice presents an appropriately formidable figure, John Mitchinson is a distinctive Bénédict. To make the Double Decca reissue even more tempting, Decca have added the contents of a third LP of little-known vocal Berlioz, including the nine songs grouped together under the title *Irlande* were inspired by the words of Thomas Moore, set in translation. The performances are all of a high standard.

Les Troyens, Parts 1 & 2 (complete).
*** Ph. 416 432-2 (4) [id.]. Veasey, Vickers, Lindholm, Glossop, Soyer, Partridge, Wandsworth School Boys' Ch., ROHCG Ch. & O, C. Davis.
*** Decca Dig. 443 693-2 (4) [id.]. Lakes, Pollet, Voigt, Montreal Schubert Ch. & SO, Dutoit.

Throughout this long and apparently disjointed score Davis compels the listener to concentrate, to appreciate its epic logic. Only in the great love scene of *O nuit d'ivresse* would one have welcomed the more expansive hand of a Beecham. Veasey makes a splendid Dido, singing always with fine heroic strength, with Vickers a ringing Aeneas. The Covent Garden Chorus and Orchestra excel themselves in virtuoso singing and playing, while CD brings out the superb quality of sound all the more vividly.

The alternative Decca recording was linked to two concert performances of each of the parts of the opera, *La prise de Troie* and *Les Troyens à Carthage*, recorded in spectacular digital sound. Interpretatively, the contrasts between Dutoit and Davis are quickly established at the very start of *La prise de Troie*. Dutoit launches in at high voltage, more volatile than Davis, conveying exuberance, consistently preferring faster speeds. Davis may be marginally less exciting, but he often compensates in the extra crispness and clarity of the playing of the Covent Garden Orchestra. Dutoit's faster speeds – reflecting the metronome markings – bring not just thrilling allegros but lyrically flowing andantes. So Cassandra's first solo is more persuasively moulded at a flowing speed, with Deborah Voigt far warmer than Berit Lindholm for Davis. She crowns her performance at the end of Act II, impetuous in leading the final ensemble of defiant Trojan women. As Dido the soprano, Françoise Pollet, sings with rich, even tone, sensuously feminine, even though she lacks the weight of a mezzo. Though Gary Lakes as Dido is less heroic than Jon Vickers for Davis, he is more sensitive in the love duet. For completeness, Dutoit includes the brief prelude that Berlioz wrote in 1863 for separate performances of the second part of the opera. The other textual addition comes in Act I. After the Andromache scene there is an extra scene, lasting six minutes, which the Berlioz scholar, Hugh Macdonald, editor of the Bärenreiter score, has orchestrated from the surviving piano score.

Les Troyens: Grand scenes.
(M) *** Decca Dig. 458 208-2 [id.] (from complete recording, with Lakes, Pollet, Voigt, Montreal Ch. & SO; cond. Dutoit).

To assemble a single-CD selection from an opera as expansive as *Les Troyens* is an almost impossible task. Act II has been omitted altogether, but otherwise the scenes here have been judiciously chosen and include the spectacular *Trojan march* at the end of Act I, so powerfully dominated by the foreboding of Deborah Voigt's Cassandra. In the final solo, Pollet portrays the distraught Dido, all purpose gone in the disjointed recitative, a closing sequence of great dramatic power that alone makes this Opera Gala CD worth considering. It is well-packaged, with a full translation included.

Berners, Lord (1883–1950)

Luna Park; March; (i) *A Wedding bouquet.*
** Marco Polo Dig. 8.223716 [id.]. (i) RTE Chamber Ch.; RTE Sinf., Kenneth Alwyn.

Stravinsky spoke of Lord Berners as 'droll and delightful . . . an amateur, but in the best – literal – sense'. Apart from Constant Lambert, he was the only English composer taken up by Diaghilev. *Luna Park* (1930) was written for a C. B. Cochran revue, with choreography by Balanchine. *A Wedding bouquet*, here given its first complete recording, was choreographed by Frederick Ashton and mounted at Sadler's Wells in 1937 with décor and costumes as well as music by Berners. This is good light music. Performances are decent, as are the recordings, but the acoustic does not permit tuttis to open out.

Les Sirènes (ballet; complete); *Caprice péruvien; Cupid and Psyche* (ballet suite).
** Marco Polo Dig. 8.223780 [id.]. Miriam Blennerhassett, RTE Sinf., David Lloyd-Jones.

Les Sirènes was the first ballet Ashton mounted for the Sadler's Wells company in 1946, on taking up residence at Covent Garden. It was not a great success, and the music, despite some bright moments, does not sustain a high level of invention. The *Caprice péruvien* derives from Berners's one and only opera, *Le Carrosse du Saint-Sacrement*, a one-Acter which shared a triple-bill with Stravinsky and Sauguet at the Théâtre des Champs-Elysées in 1924. The *Caprice* itself was expertly put together by Constant Lambert with Berners's help. The ballet *Cupid and Psyche* was another Ashton work, mounted in 1939. Good performances, but not well-polished. Again the recordings, made at a different venue from the companion disc listed above, are wanting in bloom.

The Triumph of Neptune (ballet suite): excerpts.
(B) (***) Sony mono SBK 62748 [id.]. Phd. O, Beecham – ARNELL: *Punch and the child* (ballet); DELIUS: *Paris*. (***)

The Triumph of Neptune was a rare example of music by an English composer being commissioned and performed by Diaghilev's Ballets Russes. The composer has often been called the English Satie, and Satie's love of circus music was echoed by Berners's taste for the music hall.

Beecham recorded the nine excerpts with the Philadelphia Orchestra in 1952, with two extra items (the charming *Cloudland* and the delicately haunting evocation of *The frozen forest*) not included on his earlier (1937) recording of the suite for EMI (currently unavailable). Robert Grooter is the intoxicated sailor who makes a brave shot at singing 'The last rose of summer'. The Philadelphia Orchestra respond to this music in a brilliant if rather bemused fashion, though they obviously enjoy the music, and Sir Thomas ensures that there is no lack of suave polish and wit. The recording is remarkably good, and this disc is also a 'must' for the sake of the couplings.

Bernstein, Leonard (1918–90)

Bernstein Edition

(i) *Candide overture;* (ii) *On the Waterfront* (symphonic suite); (iii) *Prelude, fugue and riffs;* (i) *West Side Story:* symphonic dances.
(M) *** DG Dig. 447 952-2. (i) LAPO; (ii) Israel PO; (iii) Peter Schmidl, VPO; composer.

In his later, DG account of the *Overture* to *Candide* the composer still directs with tremendous flair, his speed a fraction slower than in his New York studio recording for CBS. The score for *On the Waterfront* is film music pure and simple, and expertly underlines the film's action. Bernstein's Israeli recording sounds fuller than his earlier version on Sony, and the same comment applies to the *West Side Story symphonic dances*. Bernstein, recorded live, is here at his most persuasive, conducting a highly idiomatic account of the orchestral confection devised from his most successful musical. The *Prelude, fugue and riffs* was also recorded live, vibrant and rhythmic, with Peter Schmidl a comparatively reticent soloist.

(i) *Concerto for orchestra (Jubilee Games);* (ii) *Dybbuk* (ballet): *suites Nos. 1–2.*
(M) *** DG Dig. 447 956-2. (i) Chama, Israel PO; (ii) Sperry, Fifer, NYPO; composer.

The *Concerto for orchestra* shows Bernstein in audacious yet searching mood. Originally planned as a two-movement work to celebrate the Jubilee of the Israel Philharmonic, it opens with the aleatory raucousness of *Free-style events*, featuring vociferous orchestral shouts. The final touching *Benediction* (which was added for the re-opening of a refurbished Carnegie Hall in 1986) is eloquently sung here by José Eduardo Chama. The live recording brings music-making of striking intensity, not always immaculate.

The two suites taken from *Dybbuk* are no shorter than the original ballet (one of Bernstein's toughest works on a sinister subject – see below), dividing the score broadly between passages involving vocal elements and those purely instrumental. The first suite is the longer and more dramatic, the second the more contemplative. Even the jazzy dance-sequences so typical of Bernstein acquire a bitter quality. Bernstein directs strong, colourful performances, cleanly and atmospherically recorded, with excellent vocal contributions from Paul Sperry and Bruce Fifer. The transfer to CD is first rate.

Facsimile (choreographic essay); (i) *Fancy free* (ballet); *On the Town* (3 dance episodes).
(M) *** DG Dig./Analogue 447 951-2. (i) Ruth Mense; Bernstein (vocals); Israel PO, composer.

Facsimile, written in 1946 for Jerome Robbins, tells of two boys and a girl and their balletic flirtations; its beach scenario recalls Poulenc's *Les biches*. It is an attractively inventive and at times charming score, and this live performance from 1981 shows the Israel Philharmonic at their finest. The companion ballet, *Fancy free*, one of Bernstein's early successes from 1944, is another attractive example of his freely eclectic style, here raiding Stravinsky, Copland and Gershwin. The Israel Philharmonic does not match the New York Philharmonic Orchestra (see below) in virtuosity, but it still plays with tremendous spirit and also enjoys excellent recording. What makes this version of *Fancy free* special is Bernstein's own performance of the blues number, *Big stuff*, as the ballet's epilogue. Together with the colourful and vigorous dances from *On the Town* they are given vivid if close-up digital sound.

Divertimento for orchestra; (i) *Halil* (Nocturne for solo flute, strings and percussion); (ii) *3 Meditations* (from *Mass*) for cello and orchestra; *A Musical toast.*
(M) *** DG Dig./Analogue 447 955-2. Israel PO, Bernstein; with (i) Rampal; (ii) Rostropovich.

The *Divertimento* (written for the Boston Symphony Orchestra), easily and cheekily moving from one idiom to another, is often jokey. *Halil*, for flute and strings, and the *Meditation* also beautifully reflect the individual poetry of the two artists for whom they were written and who perform in masterful fashion here. The other two party-pieces were recorded live in fizzing performances, *A Musical toast* for André Kostelanetz, and *Slava* (a 'political overture, fast and flamboyant') to celebrate Rostropovich in Washington. Excellent recording throughout.

Symphonies Nos. (i) *1 (Jeremiah);* (ii) *2 (The Age of anxiety)* for piano and orchestra.

(M) *** DG 447 953-2 (2). Israel PO, composer; with (i) Christa Ludwig; (ii) Lukas Foss.

(i) *Symphony No. 3 (Kaddish);* (ii) *Chichester Psalms.*

(M) *** DG 447 954-2. (i) Caballé, Wager, V. Boys' Ch.; (ii) Soloist from V. Boys' Ch.; (i;ii) Wiener Jeunnesse Ch., Israel PO, composer.

Bernstein's three symphonies have been undervalued because of his willingness to draw on popular influences, but their surface facility is deceptive. The *Jeremiah Symphony* dates from the composer's early twenties and ends with a moving passage from Lamentations for the mezzo soloist – here with Christa Ludwig responding sensitively. As the title suggests, the *Second Symphony* was inspired by the poem of W. H. Auden, and the work includes a concertante piano part, admirably played by Lukas Foss. The *Third Symphony*, written in memory of John F. Kennedy, is recorded here in its revised version (with a male speaker), which concentrates the original concept of a dialogue between man and God, a challenge from earth to heaven. The performances here are not always quite as polished or as forceful as those Bernstein recorded earlier for CBS in New York, but they never fail to reflect the warmth of Bernstein's writing, and the playing of the Israel Philharmonic is extremely vivid throughout. The *Chichester Psalms* were recorded live in 1977. With the Vienna Boys' Choir the music's warmth and vigour compellingly projected. So are the CD transfers throughout both discs of (1977/8) recordings.

(i) *Serenade after Plato's Symposium* (for solo violin, string orchestra, harp and percussion); (ii) *Songfest* (cycle of American poems).

(M) *** DG 447 957-2. (i) Gidon Kremer, Israel PO; (ii) Dale, Elias, Nancy Williams, Rosenheim, Reardon, Gramm Nat. SO of Washington; composer.

The *Serenade* ranks among Bernstein's most inspired creations, full of ideas, often thrilling and exciting, and equally often moving. Gidon Kremer has all the nervous intensity and vibrant energy to do justice to this powerful and inventive score. *Songfest*, too, is one of the composer's most richly varied works – a sequence of poems which ingeniously uses all six singers solo and in various combinations. Characteristically, Bernstein often chooses controversial words to set, and by his personal fervour welds a very disparate group of pieces together into a warmly satisfying whole. Both recordings (from the late 1970s) are of excellent quality, atmospheric and clear.

(i) *Candide* (final, revised version); (ii) *West Side story:* complete recording.

✽ *** DG Dig. 447 958-2 (3). (i) Hadley, Anderson, Green, Ludwig, Gedda, Della Jones, Ollmann, London Symphony Ch., LSO; (ii) Te Kanawa, Carreras, Troyanos, Horne, Ollmann, Ch. and O; composer.

The composer's complete recordings of *Candide* and *West Side story* have been coupled together on three mid-priced discs for the Bernstein Edition to make an irresistible bargain for those who have not already aquired one or the other of these inspired scores. The satirical humour of *Candide*, reflecting Voltaire, draws a ready parallel between the Spanish Inquisition and Bernstein's own experience during the witch-hunting McCarthy period in America. The result is a triumph, both in the studio recording (which Bernstein made immediately after concert performances in London) and in the video recording of the actual concert at the Barbican. It confirms *Candide* as a classic, bringing out not just the vigour, the wit and the tunefulness of the piece more than ever before, but also an extra emotional intensity. There is no weak link in the cast. Jerry Hadley is touchingly characterful as Candide, producing heady tone, and June Anderson as Cunegonde is not only brilliant in coloratura but also warmly dramatic. The character roles are also brilliantly cast. It was an inspired choice to have Christa Ludwig as the Old Woman, and equally original to choose Adolph Green, lyric writer for Broadway musicals as well as cabaret performer, for the dual role of Dr Pangloss and Martin. Nicolai Gedda also proves a winner in his series of cameo roles, and the full, incisive singing of the London Symphony Chorus adds to the weight of the performance without inflation.

What is missing in the CD set is the witty narration, prepared by John Wells and spoken by Adolph Green and Kurt Ollmann in the Barbican performance. As included on the video of the live concert (Laser disc DG 072 423-1; VHS DG 072 423-3), those links leaven the entertainment delightfully. Even those with the CDs should investigate the video version, which also includes Bernstein's own moving speeches of introduction before each Act.

Bernstein's recording of the complete score of *West Side Story* takes a frankly operatic approach in its casting, but the result is highly successful, for the great vocal melodies are worthy of voices of the highest calibre. Tatiana Troyanos, herself brought up on the West Side, spans the stylistic dichotomy to perfection in a superb portrayal of Anita. The clever production makes the best of both musical worlds, with Bernstein's son and daughter speaking the dialogue most affectingly. Bernstein conducts a superb instrumental group of musicians 'from on and off Broadway', and they are recorded with a bite and immediacy that is captivating. The power of the music is greatly enhanced by the spectacularly wide dynamic range of the recording.

A Quiet place (complete).
(M) *** DG Dig. 447 962-2 (2) [id.]. Wendy White, Chester Ludgin, Beverly Morgan, John Brandstetter, Peter Kazaras, Vocal Ens., Austrian RSO, composer.

In flashbacks in Act II of *A Quiet place*, Bernstein incorporates his 1951 score, *Trouble in Tahiti*, with its popular style set in relief against the more serious idiom adopted for the main body of the opera. Bernstein's score is full of thoughtful and warmly expressive music, but nothing quite matches the sharp, tongue-in-cheek jazz-influenced invention of *Trouble in Tahiti*. The recording was made in Vienna, with an excellent cast of American singers and with the Austrian Radio orchestra responding splendidly on its first visit to the Vienna State Opera.

Bernstein Century Edition

Candide: Overture; Fancy free (ballet); On the Waterfront: symphonic suite. West Side Story: Symphonic dances.
(M) *** Sony SMK 63085 [id.]. NYPO, Bernstein.

For many this compilation, issued under the 'Bernstein Century' logo, will be the ideal way of acquiring this orchestral theatre and film music. The fizzing account of the *Candide overture* has never been surpassed and the sparkling *Fancy free* ballet-score is hardly less rhythmically seductive. The *Symphonic dances* from *West Side Story* confirm Bernstein as a truly great tunesmith; apart from the music's life-enhancing vitality, the closing section is infinitely touching. The recordings, made between 1960 and 1963, have never sounded better: bright and free, with plenty of ambient space.

Dybbuk (ballet): complete.
(M) *** Sony SMK 63090 [id.]. David Johnson, John Ostendorf, NY City Ballet O, composer.

For this 'Bernstein Century' reissue, the 1974 recording of the complete ballet, *Dybbuk*, has been sensibly separated from the *Mass* with which it was previously paired. Bernstein wrote his ghoulish ballet on lost spirits for Jerome Robbins and the New York City Ballet in 1974, when this splendidly atmospheric recording was made. The score presents much the same happy and colourful amalgam of influences as you find in other Bernstein ballets, a touch of the *Rite of spring* here and a whiff of *West Side Story* there – although, at 48 minutes, it is less concentrated. The vocal parts, although fairly substantial (and very well done), are merely incidental. The recording is brightly lit but spacious.

(i) *Fancy free* (ballet) (ii) *On the Town (3 Dance episodes)*; (iii) *Prelude, fugue and riffs* (for solo clarinet and jazz combo); (ii;iv) *Serenade after Plato's Symposium* (for solo violin, string orchestra, harp & percussion).
(N) (M) (**(*)) Sony mono/stereo SMK 60559 [id.]. (i) Columbia SO; (ii) NYPO; (iii) Benny Goodman & Columbia Jazz Combo; (ii;iv) Zino Francescatti; all cond. composer.

Bernstein's pioneering 1956 mono recording of *Fancy free* is here joined with his exhilarating early New York performance of the *Dance episodes* from *On the Town*, together with the (stereo) *Prelude, fugue and riffs*, with its dedicatee as soloist, and the second recording of the *Serenade after Plato's Symposium*, where Francescatti's response brings out the Hebrew flavour of the lyrical writing. But, like Stern before him, he is closely balanced, as is the orchestra, and Bernstein's passionate climaxes are given an aggressive fierceness.

Symphonies Nos. (i) *1 (Jeremiah);* (ii) *2 (The Age of anxiety)* for piano and orchestra; (iii) *I hate music!; La bonne cuisine.*
(N) (M) *** Sony SMK 60697 [id.]. (i–ii) NYPO, composer with (i) Jennie Tourel; (ii) Philippe Entremont. (iii) Tourel, composer.

Bernstein is always a persuasive conductor, and never more so than when conducting his own serious music. He was in his early twenties when he wrote his *Jeremiah* symphony. It is a brilliant *tour de force*, the three movements – slow, fast, slow – cunningly integrated by the use of traditional Jewish material. With Jennie Tourel as soloist, not so steady as Christa Ludwig on DG (see above), there is a strong reminder of the lament Prokofiev included in his *Alexander Nevsky* music. The Auden-inspired *Second symphony* is a purely instrumental work with a piano obbligato (here impressively played by Entemont), reflecting moods and ideas rather than actually expressing them. There will be different views on how far Bernstein succeeds in matching Auden, but there is no doubt of his own committedness and that certainly comes over in these performances which are even more concentrated and gripping than the later DG versions; if the CBS/Sony Manhattan Center recording is not as well balanced, it is still exceptionally vivid. The reissue is made exceptionally valuable by the inclusion of the two engaging song-cycles, the first expressing the thoughts of a ten-year-old girl ('*I'm a person too, like you!*'), the second dwelling on cuisinary delights, from *Plum pudding* to how to prepare Rabbit stew in a hurry. They are charmingly sung by Jennie Tourel, whom Bernstein accompanies himself at the piano.

(i) *Symphony No. 2 (The Age of anxiety)* for piano and orchestra; (ii) *Serenade after Plato's Symposium.*
(N) (M) (**(*)) Sony mono SMK 60558 [id.]. (i) Lukas Foss, NYPO; (ii) Stern, Symphony of the Air; Composer.

As with *Fancy free* above, Sony are now reissuing the composer's earlier New York recordings of his symphonies in the Bernstein Century Edition. In the case of No. 2 this is his very first (1950) mono version with Lukas Foss. (In the 1960s he turned to Philippe Entremont, but went back for Foss for his third DG recording.) The clear, forward mono sound reinforces the work's eclecticism, with the *Dirge* stridently dissonant, and the jazz interjections of the *Masque* contrasting boldly with the closing *Epilogue*. Foss is by turns evocative and dazzling, but he is too forwardly recorded. The (1956) mono performance of the *Serenade* has Stern even more naturally attuned to the score than Francescatti in the later stereo version (see above), but the recording again suffers from the unnaturally forward balance.

(i) *Symphony No. 3 (Kaddish);* (ii) *Chichester psalms.*
(N) (M) *** Sony SMK 60595 [id.]. (i) Montealegre, Tourel, Columbus Boychoir; (ii) Bogart; (i; ii) Camerata Singers, NYPO, Composer.

These recordings were made in the Manhattan Center in the mid-1960s; the acoustic is agreeably spacious, and many may prefer them to the later Israeli DG versions. However, the spoken dialogue in the *Kaddish Symphony* is recited here with melodramatic fervour by Felicia Montealegre (Mrs Bernstein at the time) and this is a serious stumbling block. However, the performance of the *Chichester Psalms*, written in response to a commisssion from the Dean of Chichester is vividly projected by singers and players alike.

Other recordings

Candide overture.
(N) (B) *** DG Classikon 445 129-2 [(M) [id.]. import]. LAPO, composer – BARBER: *Adagio for strings*; COPLAND: *Appalachian spring;* SCHUMAN: *American festival overture.* ***

Bernstein's later live Los Angeles account of the sparkling *Candide overture* has tremendous flair, his speed a fraction slower than in the earlier New York studio recording for CBS/Sony. It is here part of an aptly chosen bargain collection of music by four key twentieth-century American composers.

Candide: overture; Facsimile (choreographic essay); *Fancy free* (ballet); *On the town (3 Dance episodes)*
(B) *** [EMI Red Line Dig. CDR5 72091]. St Louis SO, Slatkin.

Though Slatkin cannot quite match Bernstein himself in the flair he brings to his jazzier inspirations, this is a very attractive bargain collection. Next to Bernstein, Slatkin sounds a little metrical at times, but he directs a beautiful, refined reading of the extended choreographic essay, *Facsimile*. As a gimmick, the song '*Big stuff*', before *Fancy free*, is recorded in simulation of a juke-box, complete with 78-r.p.m. surface-hiss and a blues singer with a very heavy vibrato. The sound otherwise is full rather than brilliant, set in a helpful, believable acoustic. This disc is only available in the USA.

Candide overture; Facsimile; Fancy free (ballet); *West Side story: symphonic dances.*
(N) **(*) Decca Dig. 452 916-2 [id.]. Baltimore SO, David Zinman.

Alongside Järvi, Zinman's rather similar Baltimore programme comes up as very much second-best. The *Candide overture* is lively enough, but the orchestral discipline and ensemble, lacks the final degree of bite and polish, while *Facsimile* and the *West Side story dances*, although very well played, are less sharply characterized. *Fancy free* includes as a prologue '*Big stuff',* sung by Billie Holiday with a rhythm group, which was originally heard on a jukebox before the curtain went up. The relatively mellow performance is beautifully played, colourful, and enjoyable, but again lacks the degree of spontaneous combustion one expects from a transatlantic performance. The Decca recording, made in Baltimore's Symphony Hall is well up to house standards, indeed approaching demonstration standards.

(i) *Candide: overture;* (ii) *On the Town: 3 Dance episodes;* (i) *West Side Story: Symphonic dances;* (iii) *America.*
(M) *** DG Dig. 427 806-2 [id.]. (i) LAPO; (ii) Israel PO; (iii) Troyanos with O; composer – BARBER: *Adagio* ***; GERSHWIN: *Rhapsody in blue.* **(*)

This alternative collection offers the same performances as those included in the Bernstein Edition, and has the added attraction of including a characteristically intense account of Barber's *Adagio*. The other coupling of *Rhapsody in Blue* is, however, less successful than Bernstein's earlier, CBS/Sony account.

Divertimento for orchestra; (i) *Facsimile* (choreographic essay). (ii) *Prelude, fugue and riffs. West Side story: symphonic dances* (original version).

(N) *** Virgin/EMI VC5 45295-2. CBSO, Järvi with (i) Wayne Marschall; (ii) Sabine Meyer.

Although Bernstein himself is always special in this music, it is good to have first-class modern recordings. And Järvi and the CBSO clearly enjoy themselves, especially in the elegantly polished and very spirited account of the *Divertimento* where, in the exhilarating finale, Järvi makes a boisterous link with Ibert. There is some beautiful woodwind-playing in *Facsimile* and, not surprisingly, Wayne Marshall's contribution is glitteringly idiomatic. The same could be said for Sabine Meyer in the very jazzy account of the *Prelude, fugue and riffs*, while in the *West Side story dances* (which happily has ten individual cues), Järvi relishes the romantic melodies, which are exquisitely played, and find plenty of rhythmic venom for the *Rumble*.

3 Meditations for cello and orchestra (from *Mass*).

(B) *** DG Double 437 952-2 (2) [id.]. Rostropovich, Israel PO, composer – BOCCHERINI: *Cello concerto No. 2;* GLAZUNOV: *Chant du Ménestrel;* SHOSTAKOVICH: *Cello concerto No. 2;* TARTINI: *Cello concerto;* TCHAIKOVSKY: *Andante cantabile* etc.; VIVALDI: *Cello concertos*. ***

Bernstein's concertante piece, *Meditations for cello and orchestra*, is fully worthy of the subtlety of Rostropovich's art, and he plays it masterfully. This is part of a remarkably generous Double DG bargain anthology.

(i) *On the Town: suite;* (ii) *7 Anniversaries*.

(M) (***) RCA mono 09026 60915-2. (i) On the Town O, Bernstein; (ii) Bernstein (piano) – COPLAND: *Billy the Kid* etc. (***)

There is always something special about first recordings like these. There is great vitality and swagger here, and no apologies need be made for the mono recording which, though slightly shrill, has great vividness. The stage music is followed by *Seven anniversaries*, a set of vignettes composed in 1943, dedicated to family and musical friends, opening with Aaron Copland and closing with William Schuman.

Prelude, fugue and riffs.

*** RCA Dig. 09026 61350-2 [id.]. Stolzman, LSO, Leighton Smith – COPLAND: *Concerto;* CORIGLIANO: *Concerto;* STRAVINSKY: *Ebony concerto*.

Like Benny Goodman before him, Richard Stolzman couples Bernstein's *Prelude, fugue and riffs* with Copland's masterly concerto and Stravinsky's *Ebony concerto*, and he makes the most of its unbuttoned jazziness. He is better recorded than Goodman was, and his record can be recommended strongly on all counts.

Serenade after Plato's Symposium (for solo violin, string orchestra, harp & percussion).

*** EMI Dig. CDC5 55360-2 [id.]. Perlman, Boston SO, Ozawa – BARBER: *Violin concerto;* FOSS: *Three American pieces*. ***

(N) *** Sony Dig. SK 60584 [id.]. Hilary Hahn, Baltimore SO, David Zinman – BEETHOVEN: *Violin concerto in D, Op. 61*. ***

(M) *(**) Sony Stern Edition II SMK 64508 [id.]. Stern, Symphony of the Air, composer – DUTILLEUX: *Violin concerto*. ***

Perlman may initially seem almost too confident, missing an element of fantasy in Bernstein's personalized meditation on Plato's *Symposium*, where the more reticent view of Gidon Kremer with the composer conducting (see above) seems to delve deeper. Yet increasingly through the five contrasted movements the purposefulness as well as the masterful power of Perlman's playing adds to the work's impact. He brings home the more tellingly how each movement leads thematically out of the preceding one, until the final movement, much the longest, with its references back to the beginning. He makes it seem a warmer piece too, thanks to his range of rich tone-colours, set against the richness of the Boston string-sound.

Belying its title and the forces involved – solo violin, strings, harp and percussion – Bernstein's *Serenade* is one of his most searching works. As one commentator suggests, it can be regarded as a self-portrait reflecting the composer's sharply contrasting moods. As in the Beethoven, Hilary Hahn gives an intense, deeply felt performance, crowned by a rapt account of the big Adagio fourth section, *Agathon*. Excellent sound.

Stern's temperament makes him an ideal soloist and he plays very beautifully and with intense feeling. The snag is the balance of the early 1956 stereo, with the violin right out in front and climaxes unpleasantly coarse. There is no mistaking the adrenalin flow, but the lack of any kind of refinement in the orchestral tuttis is a severe drawback.

(i–iii) *Symphony No. 1 (Jeremiah);* (iv) *Anniversaries: In memoriam Nathalie Koussevitzky;* (ii; v) *Songfest*.

(M) (***) RCA stereo/mono 09026 61581-2 [id.]. (i) Nan Merriman; (ii) St Louis SO; (iii) composer; (iv) Leonard Slatkin (piano); (v)

Hohenfeld, White, Spence, Planté, Hartman, Cheek, cond. Slatkin.

Songfest, a cycle for six soloists and orchestra celebrating all things American, finds Bernstein's inspiration focused sharply within a limited frame, and the result is one of his finest works, with each poem perceptively chosen to illustrate the variegated strands of American society. Leonard Slatkin's recording hardly replaces Bernstein's own (see above) on DG, but it offers another fine performance, recorded in a more mellow acoustic and with a warmer ensemble. As fill-up comes Bernstein's own historic first recording of the *Jeremiah Symphony*, made for RCA in 1945, with Nan Merriman the clear-toned soloist. The mono sound is limited but conveys the high voltage of the performance. Between the two main works Slatkin plays the brief piano piece commemorating the first wife of Serge Koussevitzky, taken from the *Anniversaries suite*.

(i) *Symphony No. 2 (Age of anxiety); Overture: Candide; Fancy Free* (ballet).
(M) *** Virgin/EMI Dig. CUV5 61119-2 [id.]. (i) Kahane; Bournemouth SO, Andrew Litton.

Bernstein holds nothing back, but Litton in his less thrusting way is just as compelling and often more subtly expressive, helped by a poetic pianist, Jeffrey Kahane. Anyone fancying Litton's popular coupling need not hesitate.

(i) *Symphony No.3 (Kaddish);* (ii) *Chichester Psalms*.
(N) ***Erato 3984-21669-2 (i) Lord Menuhin, Marita Mattila, (ii) Joseph Mills; French R Ch. & PO, Yutaka Sado.

Yehudi Menuhin, with his thoughtful measured tones, is the opposite of most narrators in the *Kaddish Symphony* but the emotion is just as intensely conveyed, and projects the more movingly when one realizes that the disc appeared in the very month that Menuhin died, March 1999, with the words 'I want to say Kaddish, my own Kaddish,' right at the start. Marita Mattila is a radiant soprano soloist and the choir sings brilliantly, but at relatively measured speeds this does not have the dramatic bite of Bernstein's own recordings though the sound here is fuller and clearer. In the *Chichester Psalms* the choir and orchestra seem more at home in Bernstein's jazzy syncopations, giving a dazzling performance, vividly recorded, with Joseph Mills from New College choir, Oxford, as a fine treble soloist.

VOCAL MUSIC

Arias and Barcarolles. On the Town: Some other time; Lonely town; Carried away; I can cook. Peter Pan: Dream with me. Songfest: Storyette, H. M.; To what you said. Wonderful Town: A little bit in love.
*** Koch International Classics Dig. 37000-2 [id.]. Judy Kaye, William Sharp; Michael Barrett, Steven Blier.

Arias and Barcarolles for two soloists and piano duet is a family charade of a work. It is a charming piece, here given – with the composer himself approving the performance – in the original version with piano and excellent, characterful soloists. The bizarre title relates to a comment made by President Eisenhower, after he had heard Bernstein play a Mozart concerto: 'I like music with a theme, not all them arias and barcarolles.' It became a Bernstein family joke. That half-hour work, very well recorded, is coupled with an equivalent collection of eight of Bernstein's most haunting songs and duets.

(i) *Arias and Barcarolles* (orch. Coughlin). *A Quiet place: suite; West Side Story: symphonic dances.*
*** DG Dig. 439 926-2 [id.]. (i) Von Stade, Hampson; LSO, Tilson Thomas.

It was Michael Tilson Thomas who joined Leonard Bernstein himself at two pianos for the first performance of the original chamber version of *Arias and Barcarolles*, one of Bernstein's very last works. With colourful orchestration by Bruce Coughlin, Tilson Thomas here fully justifies the expansion, intensifying the impact of this wayward sequence of settings of texts, each glorifying the family in ways very personal to Bernstein. What is completely avoided here, a danger in this work, is the coyness which these texts can suggest; and that also has much to do with the superb singing of Frederica von Stade (not least in the baby-talk fairy story attributed to Bernstein's mother) and of Thomas Hampson. The result is both beautiful and moving, not least the fifth-movement *Greeting* from Bernstein to his new-born son and the final humming duet. Similarly, the suite drawn from Bernstein's big 1983 opera, *A Quiet place*, offers a symphonic synthesis which both brings out the freshness and power of this late inspiration, and intensifies the emotions of an opera which tends to sprawl dramatically. Brilliant and heartfelt playing from the LSO, both in those two works and in the *Symphonic dances* from *West Side Story*, here vividly recorded to pack even greater punch than the composer's own last recording.

Chichester Psalms.
(M) *** Carlton Dig. 30366 0009-2 [id.]. Aled Jones, London Symphony Ch., RPO, Hickox – FAURE: *Requiem.* ***

Chichester Psalms (reduced score).
*** Hyperion Dig. CDA 66219 [id.]. Martelli, Corydon Singers, Masters, Kettel, Trotter; Best – BARBER: *Agnus Dei;* COPLAND: *In the beginning* etc. ***

Bernstein's *Chichester Psalms* communicate

strongly in Richard Hickox's fresh and colourful reading, with Aled Jones bringing an ethereal contribution to the setting of the 23rd Psalm. The recorded sound is firm and well focused.

Martin Best uses the composer's alternative reduced orchestration. The treble soloist, Dominic Martelli, cannot match Aled Jones, but his chaste contribution is persuasive and the choir scales down its pianissimos to accommodate him. Excellent, atmospheric sound, set in a church acoustic.

Mass (for the death of President Kennedy).
(M) **(*) Sony SM2K 63089 (2) [S2K 63089]. Alan Titus (celebrant), Scribner Ch., Berkshire Boy Ch., Rock Band & O, composer.

Outrageously eclectic in its borrowings from pop and the avant garde, Bernstein's *Mass* presents an extraordinary example of the composer's irresistible creative energy. The recording is vividly present but has a convincing ambience.

Songs: *La bonne cuisine* (French and English versions); *I hate music* (cycle); *2 Love songs; Piccola serenata; Silhouette; So pretty; Mass: A simple song; I go on. Candide: It must be so; Candide's lament. 1600 Pennsylvania Ave: Take care of this house. Peter Pan: My house; Peter Pan; Who am I; Never-Never Land.*
*** Etcetera Dig. KTC 1037 [id.]. Roberta Alexander, Tan Crone.

A delightful collection, consistently bearing witness to Bernstein's flair for a snappy idea as well as his tunefulness. Roberta Alexander's rich, warm voice and winning personality are well supported by Tan Crone at the piano. The recording is lifelike and undistracting.

STAGE WORKS

Candide (musical: original Broadway production): *Overture and excerpts.*
(M) *** Sony SK 48017 [full price id.]. Adrian, Cook, Rounseville and original New York cast, Krachmalnick.

This exhilarating CBS record encapsulates the original 1956 Broadway production and has all the freshness of discovery inherent in a first recording, plus all the zing of the American musical theatre. The lyrics, by Richard Wilbur, give pleasure in themselves. Brilliantly lively sound.

Candide (final, revised version).
❀ *** DG Dig. 429 734-2 (2). Hadley, Anderson, Green, Ludwig, Gedda, Della Jones, Ollmann, London Symphony Ch., LSO, composer.

Candide: highlights.
*** DG Dig. 435 487-2 (from above set, cond. composer).

John Mauceri, dissatisfied with the results of his 1982 score of *Candide*, undertook a further revision in the mid-1980s, this time with Bernstein's collaboration, and the result was a triumphant success. The composer's splendid DG recording is now available at mid-price as part of the Bernstein Edition – see above – but the set also remains available separately, costing approximately the same price. For those who already have *West Side Story*, the highlights disc would seem a better buy.

On the Town (complete; with narration by Comden and Green).
*** DG Dig. 437 516-2 [id.]. Frederica von Stade, Tyne Daly, Marie McLaughlin, Thomas Hampson, David Garrison, Kurt Ollmann, Samuel Ramey, Evelyn Lear, Adolph Green, Cleo Laine, Meriel Dickinson, LSO, Tilson Thomas.

In this 1992 concert performance with the LSO at the Barbican of Bernstein's earliest musical, *On the Town*, with the librettists, Betty Comden and Adolph Green, as narrators, it is as though Bernstein himself was performing as well as providing the music, another triumph. If anything, the full score in the exuberance of youth is even richer in catchy tunes than *West Side Story* or *Candide*. A concert performance, bringing in some of the extra numbers that were originally cut from the Broadway show for lack of time, provides the perfect formula.

As in *Candide* (if not *West Side Story*), the mixing of opera stars with the Broadway tradition works like a charm. Thomas Hampson, rich and resonant, sings Gabey, the lead-sailor in search of Miss Turnstiles, with another fine American baritone, Kurt Ollmann, as Chip and David Garrison giving authentic point to the third sailor, Ozzie. Then in opulent casting Samuel Ramey sings a series of incidental roles, including the ever-understanding Pitkin, constantly pushed aside by his man-mad girlfriend, Claire. In that role Frederica von Stade firmly establishes herself as the central star, and anyone hesitating should hear the way she leads the ensemble in the climactic nostalgia of *Some other time*. Marie McLaughlin as Ivy, Miss Turnstiles, is slightly less at home, but Tyne Daly – the Cagney of TV's 'Cagney and Lacey' – as the predatory taxi-driver, Hildy, is winningly larger than life.

In contrast to *Candide*, the live recording has been used for both the CD and the video (072 197-3 [VHS], 072 197-1 [Laserdisc]), yet the results are startlingly different. With the CD, the numbers are presented dry, as though recorded in the studio, with no linking narration and no applause. Not only that, but two of the extra numbers and several encores are omitted to keep the result on a single, well-filled CD. In recompense, an extra number, omitted from the video, *The intermission's great*, is included on the CD. As with *Candide*, the video version, over half an hour longer, proves even more enjoyable, including narration as well as extra numbers. As narrators, Comden and Green are the most winning of guides, ending up by leading a final encore of the big weepy tune, *Some other time*, helping to convey the magic and electricity of a great occasion. The video not only shows Patricia Birch's clever staging of the story (uncostumed), but punctuates it with black-and-white newsreel clips of wartime New York. So it must be the video which earns the Rosette.

(i) *Trouble in Tahiti*. (ii) *Facsimile* (choreographic essay for orchestra).
(N) (M) **(*) SMK 60969 [id.]. (i) NYPO; (ii) Williams, Patrick, Butler, Clarke, Brown, Columbia Wind Ens.; composer.

Trouble in Tahiti (1952), for which Bernstein wrote both words and music, is a very successful precursor to *West Side story*; its style lies between the musical and the opera-house. It concerns a day in the life of a middle-class American couple who no longer communicate. There is no lack of good tunes and memorable rhythmic numbers, and the performance has great flair and theatrical adrenalin. The recording is remarkably vivid. The ballet score *Facsimile*, written in 1946 for Jerome Robbins, is inventive and colourful. It is very well played, but makes less than its fullest rhythmic effect here. The composer's later version for DG (see above) is clearly preferable.

West Side story (complete recording).
(N) *** DG Dig. 457 199-2 [415 963-2]. Te Kanawa, Carreras, Troyanos, Horne, Ollman, Ch. & O, composer.

The composer's own recording of *West Side story* is now reissued complete on a single disc, but is also available in the Bernstein Edition on three mid-priced CDs coupled with *Candide* which is also indispensable.

West Side Story (film soundtrack recording).
(M) **(*) Sony SK 48211 [id.]. Nixon, Bryant, Tamblyn, Wand, Chakaris, Ch. & O, Johnny Green.

Few musicals have been transferred to the screen with more success than *West Side Story*, and many will feel that, even though the principals' voices are ghosted, the soundtrack recording is preferable to Bernstein's own version using opera stars. The film was splendidly cast and the 'ghosts' were admirably chosen. In the romantic scenes, *Tonight* and *One hand, one heart*, the changes from sung to spoken words are completely convincing and the tragic (mostly spoken) final scene – here included on record for the first time – is very moving. Russ Tamblyn, who sings his own songs, is first class and Marni Nixon and Jim Bryant as the pair of lovers sing touchingly and with youthful freshness. The performance is vibrantly conducted by Johnny Green, and it is a pity that the CD gives an edge both to voices and to the brilliant orchestral playing.

Bertrand, Anthoine de (1540–81)

Amours de Ronsard, Book 1; *Amours de Cassandre:* excerpts.
(B) *** HM Dig. HMA 1431147 [id.]. Clément Janequin Ens.

Anthoine de Bertrand's chansons as recorded here by the Clément Janequin Ensemble show him to be, if not a great master, at least a composer of feeling and considerable resource. The performances are excellent throughout, and admirably recorded. At bargain price this is well worth trying.

Berwald, Franz (1796–1868)

(i; ii) *Piano concerto in D;* (i; iii) *Duo in D for violin and piano;* (i) *Musical Journal: Tempo di marcia in E flat; Piano piece No. 2: Presto feroce. Rondeau-bagatelle in B flat; Theme and variations in G min.*
(N) ** Genesis GCD 111 [id.]. (i) Greta Erikson; (ii) Swedish RSO, Stig Westerberg; (iii) Josef Grünfarb.

Greta Erikson's 1971 recording of the *Piano concerto* originally appeared on LP on the Caprice label with the piano pieces (all but the *Presto feroce* are much earlier than the *concerto*). The performance is serviceable; very nimble and cleanly articulated but somewhat wanting in poetry. Josef Grünfarb gives a finely turned account of the *D major Duo* but this partnership is less persuasive than Marieke Blankestijn and Susan Tomes on Hyperion.

Symphony in A (1820; fragment); Symphonies Nos. 1–4; Overtures: Estrella di Soria; The Queen of Golconda.
*** Hyperion Dig. CDA 67081/2 [id.] Swedish RSO, Roy Goodman.

Roy Goodman's set with the Swedish Radio Symphony Orchestra has the advantage of including the early fragment of the *Symphony in A major* which Berwald completed (it was performed in the same concert as the *Violin concerto* in 1821) but which survives only in fragmentary form. It has been completed – and very well, too – by Duncan Druce, and makes its début on records. It is distinctively Berwaldian, though there are touches of Weber in the opening introduction and of Schubert in the second group. Goodman is always alert and intelligent, though he tends to favour brisk tempi. He starts the *Sinfonie singulière* far too quickly and is forced to pull back when the brass enter. There is a certain loss of breadth here, and again in the *Sinfonie sérieuse*. The *Overture* to *The Queen of Golconda* comes off very well. Berwald's orchestration tends to be top-heavy and the cool acoustic of the Berwald Hall in Stockholm slightly accentuates that.

Symphonies Nos. 1 in G min. (Sérieuse); 2 in D (Capricieuse); 3 in C (Singulière); 4 in E flat.
(M) *** DG Dig. 445 581-2 (2). Gothenburg SO, Järvi.

Neeme Järvi's set of the Berwald *Symphonies* appeared in the mid-1980s and is still highly recommendable; this is music that is wholly in the life-stream of the Gothenburg orchestra. The only reservation one might make concerns the brisk opening movement to the *Sinfonie singulière*, but Järvi's most recent rival (Roy Goodman on Hyperion) is even faster. Järvi's account of the *E flat Symphony* has marginally greater sparkle and lightness of touch. The DG recording, balanced by Michael Bergek (more familiar on the BIS label), is excellent in every way, and the warmer acoustic of the Gothenburg Concert Hall may sway some readers in favour of this version, particularly in view of the much more modest outlay involved.

Symphonies Nos. 1 in G min. (Sérieuse); 2 (Capricieuse); 3 in C (Singulière); 4 in E flat; Overture: Estrella de Soria; Play of the elves (Elfenspiel); Racing; Reminiscences from the Norwegian mountains.
(N) (B) **(*) EMI double fforte CZS5 73335-2 (2). RPO, Björlin.

Björlin's performances here are thoroughly sympathetic and now represent excellent value. They sound warm and fresh, though the orchestral playing under the late Ulf Björlin is a little deficient in vitality; the recordings were made during a heat-wave. Others may be more vital and alert, and Björlin does not succeed in creating the same degree of tension in shaping melodic lines. The tone-poems are neglected, but their invention is often captivating. The *Reminiscences from the Norwegian mountains* is attractively atmospheric, while *Play of the elves* is a delightful piece under whose deceptively Mendelssohnian surface resides an inventive and original mind. The *Overture Estrella de Soria* is full of resourceful and finely drawn ideas. There are no alternatives at this very reasonable cost, so these CDs are by no means to be written off, as the EMI engineers have provided excellent recording, and the transfers are clear and quite full-bodied.

Symphonies Nos. 1 in G min. (Sérieuse); 2 in D (Capricieuse); 3 in C (Singulière); No. 4 in E flat; (i) *Konzertstück for bassoon and orchestra.*
*** BIS Dig. CD 795/6 [id.]. (i) Christian Davidsson; Malmö SO, Sixten Ehrling.

As his earlier recordings of Berwald demonstrate, Sixten Ehrling has a natural feeling for the classic Swedish symphonist. Tempi are all well judged and there is an admirable lightness of touch. There is plenty of breadth in the *Sérieuse* and no want of sparkle in the *E flat Symphony*. The *Konzertstück*, composed in 1827 (the year before the *Septet*), is a charming piece much in its manner. This could well be regarded as a first choice in this repertoire. Järvi's Gothenberg DG set (445 581-2) costs much less but has no coupling.

Symphony No. 1 (Sinfonie sérieuse); Overtures: Drottningen av Golconda; Estrella di Soria. Tone-poems: *Festival of the Bayadères; Play of the Elves; Reminiscences from the Norwegian Mountains.*
(N) *** Bluebell ABCD 047 [id.]. Swedish Radio SO, Sixten Ehrling.

The *Sinfonie sérieuse* was recorded in 1970 and issued on the Swedish Radio's own label. It is arguably the finest account of the work ever recorded (including Ehrling's later BIS version). It is classically proportioned, beautifully played and unerringly paced. The overtures and tone-poems were recorded in 1966 and appeared on Swedish EMI and then briefly on American Vox/Turnabout. Excellent performances, more vital and imaginative than the RPO versions from the 1970s by the late Ulf Björlin. Very well recorded too.

Symphonies Nos. 3 in C (Sinfonie singulière); 4 in E flat.
(M) (***) DG mono 457 705-2 [id.]. BPO, Igor Markevitch – SCHUBERT: *Symphony No. 4.* (***)

In the mid-1950s Markevitch pioneered this pair of Berwald symphonies internationally on LP and, as so often with recording premières, he gave superlative performances, with the Berlin Philharmonic proving outstandingly responsive. The DG recordings, made in the Berlin Jesus-Christus-Kirche, also come from a vintage period. Partly because of the warmly atmospheric mono sound, the remastering has been outstandingly successful, and these fine readings celebrate an underestimated conductor at the peak of his interpretative form. The Schubert coupling is also very fine indeed.

Grand septet in B flat.
*** CRD CRD 3344 [id.]. Nash Ens. – HUMMEL: *Septet.* ***
(M) *** EMI (SIS) CDM5 65995-2. Gervase de Peyer, Melos Ens. – SPOHR: *Double quartet* **; WEBER: *Clarinet quintet.* **(*)

Berwald's only *Septet* is an imaginative work, which deserves a secure place in the repertory instead of on its periphery. It is very well played by the Nash Ensemble, and finely recorded.

On EMI the Melos Ensemble give an immaculately polished account of the *Septet*, in vivid, well balanced recording.

Grand Septet in B flat; Piano and wind quartet in E flat; Piano trio in F min.

*** Hyperion Dig. CDA 66834 [id.]. Gaudier Ens.

The first in a series to mark the bicentenary of Berwald's birth. The *Quartet in E flat for piano and wind* of 1819 is the earliest piece here and is good but not vintage Berwald, though it could not sound more persuasive in this performance. The *Grand Septet* (1828) is a captivating piece, and so is the inventive *F minor Piano trio* of 1851. Delightful performances on which it would be difficult to improve, and excellent recording too. This augurs well for this enterprise.

Piano quintet No. 1 in C min.; Piano trio No. 4 in C; Duo in D for violin and piano.
**(*) Hyperion Dig. CDA 66835 [id.]. Susan Tomes, Gaudier Ens.

Unlike the earlier issue in this series, which spanned Berwald's output from 1819 to 1851, this concentrates on his music from the 1850s. The *Piano quintet* (1853) comes off marvellously and compares favourably with any performance on record, past or present. Susan Tomes is both sensitive and expert, and the Gaudier Ensemble are hardly less distinguished. No quarrels with Tomes in the *Piano trio No. 4*, composed the same year, or in the less inventive *D major Duo*, written in the latter half of the decade, but the balance makes her sound too dominant. True, the *Duo* is for piano and violin – not the other way round – but the violinist, Marieke Blankenstijn, an impeccable artist, sounds far too pale and reticent.

Piano trios Nos. 1 in E flat; 2 in F min.; 3 in D min.
*** Marco Polo Dig. 8.223170 [id.]. Prunyi, Kiss, Onczay.

These Hungarian players give spirited accounts of all three trios recorded here and make out a persuasive case for this music. The string players (András Kiss and Czaba Onczay) are both highly accomplished; perhaps the most demanding writing is for the piano and it is a pity that Ilona Prunyi proves at times to be a little less imaginative than her companions. The recording, made at the Italian Institute in Budapest, is very good indeed, fresh and present.

Piano trios: in C (1845); No. 4 in C (1853); in C (fragment); in E flat (fragment).
**(*) Marco Polo Dig. 8.223430 [id.]. Kalman Drafi, Jozsef Mondrian, György Kertész.

The *C major Trio*, like its companions and the fragments recorded here, is fresh and inventive. These performances by Kalman Drafi, Jozsef Mondrian and György Kertész are faithful and committed and are very well recorded at the Festetic Castle in Budapest.

String quartet in G min.
*** CRD CRD 3361; *CRDC 4061* [id.]. Chilingirian Qt – WIKMANSON: *Quartet*. ***

The *G minor Quartet* is, as one would expect from an accomplished violinist, a remarkably assured piece, and the first movement is full of audacious modulations, with themes both characterful and appealing. The Chilingirian players give a well-shaped and sensitive account of it. They are truthfully recorded, and the coupling – another Swedish quartet – enhances the attractions of this issue. The CD transfer is fresh and clear, and there is an excellent cassette equivalent. Strongly recommended.

String quartets Nos. 1 in G min.; 2 in A min.; 3 in E flat.
*** BIS Dig. CD 759 [id.]. Yggdrasil Qt.

First-rate performances by this young Swedish ensemble of their great compatriot's output in this medium. The *G minor Quartet* was one of two that Berwald composed in 1818 (the second, in B flat, was lost). The two remaining *Quartets* were both composed in 1849, four years after the completion of the *Sinfonie singulière* and are both original and rewarding. This gifted ensemble play them very well indeed and are splendidly recorded. Anyone who enjoys the Mendelssohn or Schumann *Quartets* should not delay in investigating this music.

Besozzi, Alessandro (1702–1793)

Sonatas for oboe and bassoon No. 1–6.
(N) ***Tactus Dig. TC 700210 [id.]. Alessandro Baccini, Franco Perfetti (with Stefano Celegbin).

The music of Besozzi is a delightful discovery. Alessandro was both a composer and outstanding oboeist from the age of twelve onwards, who lived in Turin with his brother, Girolami, a fine bassoonist. Their lives were so intertwined, both personally and musically, that they became a star act – even dressing alike, down to the smallest detail, according to Charles Burney (who was very taken by their demeanour as well as their playing). Mozart was another admirer. Alessandro's music has grace and charm and makes virtuoso demands on the oboe, while for the most part the bassoon trundles or scurries below. Yet at times he has much more than a continuo, playing with the oboe, or echoing a phrase. The last of these six works (published around 1760) is the most ambitious. It is in four rather than three movements, and has a slightly more serious mien, with a quite melancholy slow movement, although returning to amiability in the jaunty final Presto. The performances here are admirable, catching the music's galant charm and its underlying geniality; the two instruments are nicely balanced.

Biber, Heinrich (1644–1704)

Arien à 4; Balletti lamentabili à 4; Mensa sonora.
** Lyrichord Dig. LEMS 8017 [id.]. La Follia Strasburg.

The major work here is the *Mensa sonora*, a set of six suites from 1680, Biber's equivalent of Telemann's *Tafelmusik.* They are usually in six or seven movements, including an *Intrada* and various dances: *Balletto, Allemande, Gagliarda, Courante, Gigue,* and so on. But the invention here is less winning than with Telemann. However, Biber's writing is not helped by the (at times) heavy-handed approach of this period German group, who only occasionally lighten the pervading tutti string texture, which tends to be somewhat thick-textured and gruff.

Balletae à 4 violettae Nos. 1–7; Battalia in D; Peasants' churchgoing sonata in B flat à 6; Sonatas Nos. 1–2 à 8 for 2 clarini, 6 violae; 3–4 à 5 violae; Sonata à 7 for 6 trumpets, tramburin and organ (168).
(M) *** Teldec/Warner 4509 97914-2. VCM, Harnoncourt.

This is a good and varied introduction to Biber's music. His *Battle* evocation is as spectacular as any of the baroque era and Harnoncourt is just the man for it. The battle sequence itself has some hair-raising instrumental effects, including barbaric pizzicati representing the cannon. The picture of '*the dissolute company*' brings a half-minute of well-organized instrumental cacophony to suggest that Biber could even anticipate Charles Ives. In the *March* there is a bizarre fife-and-drum imitation by violin and double bass. The piece closes with a *Lament of the wounded musketeers*. The *Sonatas* for strings and clarini (and notably the *Peasants' churchgoing*) show this Bohemian-born Viennese Court Kapellmeister as a resourceful and inventive musician who knew how to manage lyrical pictorial effects as well as dramatic ones. His musical ideas are certainly attractive. The performances have great character – Nikolaus Harnoncourt was always good at explosive accents – and are very well recorded.

Ballettae a 4 Violettae; Battalia a 10; Sonata Sancti Polycarpi a 9. Sonatae tam aris quam aulis servientes: 1 a 8 & VII a 5. Sonata a 3 (for sackbut, violins & continuo); *Sonata a 6* (for trumpet, violins, viols & continuo); *Sonata a 6 (die Pauern Kirchfarth genandt); Sonata a 7* (for trumpets, timpani & continuo); *Sonata pro tabula* (for recorders, violins, viols & continuo). (i) *Requiem in F min.*; (ii) *Serenada (der Nachtwächter).*
(N) (B) *** Decca Double 458 081-2 (2) New L. Consort, Pickett; (i) with Bott, Bonner, Robson, Mark Ainsley, George; (ii) Simon Grant – SCHMELZER: *Balletti & Sonate.* ***

This Decca Double derives from the Oiseau-Lyre label and currently offers just about the best Biber anthology in the catalogue. Moreover Decca now throw in some attractive music by Schmelzer as a considerable bonus. Philip Pickett's *Battle* sequence is less explosive than Harnoncourt's but many will admire its greater musicality. Pickett calls the *Serenade* (in which Simon Grant participates characterfully) and the *Peasants' churchgoing sonata* 'a programmatic tour de force' and they are both not only astonishingly vivid but also include central instrumental Arias of real charm. The other instrumental sonatas are hardly less impressive. The *Sonata a 7 for trumpets and timpani* also includes an organ continuo, and the opening is imposingly sonorous, while the *Sonata Sancti Polycarpi* uses the eight brass instruments in two antiphonal groups. The style is simpler than the Renaissance writing of the Gabrielis and the effect is grand without being overwhelming. The *Sonata pro tabula* alternates recorders, violins and viols with considerable charm, and the *Sonata* No. 7 (*Tam Aris quam Aulis servientes*) offers a comparable interplay between trumpet duo, violi and viols; both these pieces also use a continuo of organ, theorbo and lute. The *Sonata a 3* is most remarkable of all, featuring sackbut and solo violins with comparable ingenuity. The acoustic, although not lacking space and resonance, gives a relatively intimate effect and throughout these pieces there is an agreeable feeling of a chamber group. The artists contributing are all experts, with Crispian Steele-Perkins and Michael Laird among the trumpeters, Annecke Boeke leading the recorder consort and Paul Nieman on sackbut. Original instruments are used to pleasing effect and the engineers have managed an almost perfect balance so that all the polyphonic lines are clear and well matched. In the *F minor Requiem* Pickett lays out his forces as they would have been positioned in Salzburg Cathedral in the 1690s, using three choral groups and 'recreating the spatial polychoral effects which the surviving performance parts suggest'. The piece is powerful and makes a stronger effect here than in the 1968 Harnoncourt performance. Fine singing, remarkable music and excellent recording make this a very desirable Double indeed.

Harmonia artificiosa-ariosa (7 Partitas), Nos. 1–3 & 5 for 2 scordatura violins & continuo; 4 for scordatura violin, viola di braccio & continuo; 6 for 2 violins & continuo; 7 for 2 violas d'amore & continuo (complete).
*** Sony Dig. SK 58920 [id.]. Tafelmusik, Jeanne Lamon.
(N) *** Auvidis Astrée Dig. E 8572 [id.]. The Rare Fruits Council.
(M) *** Chandos Dig. 0575/6 [id.]. Purcell Quartet with Elizabeth Wallfisch.

Three complete recordings of Biber's masterly *Harmonia artificosa-ariosa* show us the amazing range of these seven partitas (or suites), which were published posthumously in 1712. Each work consists of a very free opening *Prelude* or a more structured *Sonata* (slow–fast–slow), usually improvisational in feeling, and includes the usual dance forms of *Allemande* and *Sarabande*, plus an *Aria* with divisions, and often closes with a lighthearted *Gigue*, although the *Third* ends with a remarkable *Canon in uniso*, liberally decorated with violin cascades. In many ways the three sets of performances are alike, and they certainly share the spontaneity and scholarship of the very best period-instrument performances. Tempi are usually similar, although the Purcell Consort tend to bring a slightly more spacious espressivo to slower movements. Their extra weight (with use of organ continuo) is especially telling in the passacaglias. On the other hand, the airy sprightliness of Tafelmusik, especially in the *Gigues*, often more dashing, is very attractive. The curiously named Rare Fruits Council also play with great energy and virtuosity and again effectively use an organ to add colour and weight to the texture. They are rather forwardly balanced which somewhat reduces the dynamic range, but some of the solo passages have striking delicacy, and the chaconne-like variations of the closing *Seventh Partita* are very powerfully integrated. In short, you cannot go wrong with any of these recordings. We have listed Tafelmusik and the Rare Fruits Council first, as both Sony and Audivis manage to squeeze all seven partitas on to a single CD. Chandos have been forced to use a pair, playing for 43 minutes and 47 minutes respectively. But the cost of each has been reduced accordingly to upper-mid-price.

Harmonia artificiosa-ariosa (for 2 violins scordatura and continuo): *Partitas III & V. Rosenkranz sonata No. 10* (for violin scordatura and continuo); *Passacaglia No. 16 for solo violin; Sonata No. VI; Sonata representativa* (both for violin and continuo).
*** BIS Dig. CD 608 [id.]. Maria Lindal, Ens. Saga.

Heinrich Biber is fast emerging as a major personality, and the melancholy *Passacaglia* for solo violin is totally memorable. But the hit of the programme is the *Sonata representativa* with its bird evocations – they are more than just imitations – including the nightingale, thrush, cuckoo (a most striking approach) and cockerel. Maria Lindal is a splendid soloist, and the style of the playing here is vibrantly authentic: the ear quickly adjusts to the plangent (but in no way anaemic) timbres which suit this repertoire admirably.

Rosenkranz sonatas Nos. 1–16 (complete); *Passacaglia.*
(M) *** DG Codex 453 173-2 (2). Edward Melkus, Huguette Dreyfus, Lionel Roff, Karl Scheit.
(M) **(*) DHM/BMG Dig. GD 77102 [77102-RG] (2). Franzjosef Maier, Franz Lehrndorfer, Max Engel, Konrad Junghänel.

The *Sonatas of the Rosary* are among the finest instrumental pieces of their kind before Bach. The sequence follows the Passional narrative from the Annunciation and Nativity through to the Crucifixion and Ascension, and the Assumption and Coronation of Mary. The more one hears of them the greater they seem: the language is remarkable for its purity of style and achieves the kind of spirituality and nobility of inspiration one encounters in the greatest music of this period. Melkus ends with an impressive *Passacaglia in G minor*, intended for the feast of the Holy Guardian Angels (2nd October). He plays most beautifully, and care is taken to vary the quality and colour of the continuo instruments, with Lionel Rogg's organ contribution aptly filling out the sonority when necessary. The 1967 recording, if forwardly balanced, has impeccable clarity and a pleasing bloom.

The alternative version from Franzjosef Maier is also of high quality, displaying genuine poetic feeling and sensibility. However, the Deutsche Harmonia Mundi recording, although full and pleasing, could ideally provide better internal definition, and the DG set makes a clear first choice.

12 Sonatae tam aris, quam aulis servientes.
*** Chandos Dig. CHAN 0591 [id.]. Bennett, Laird, McGillivray, Cronin, Purcell Qt.

Sonatae tam aris, quam aulis servientes: Nos. 2 in D; 3 in G min.; 5 in E min.; 11 in A.
**(*) HM/BMG 05472 77303-2 [id.]. Freiburg Bar. Cons. (with MUFFAT: *Sonatas*. **(*))

Biber's *Sonatae tam aris, quam aulis servientes* were written in 1670, intended, as the title suggests, for use in church (at the altar) or court. Each is short (4–7 minutes) and structured in a single movement, yet each combines both expressive elements and a rhythmic vitality deriving from the dance. They are splendidly chimerical miniatures and confirm yet again the fecundity of the composer's imagination, with sleight-of-hand changes of tempo and apt use of contrapuntal devices. The result is wittily entertaining, yet retains its propriety, with the dance elements thoroughly absorbed so as not to offend the clergy with any vulgar associations. The new Chandos complete set from the augmented Purcell Quartet is excellent in every way, full of life and imaginative detail. The sound is first class.

Those wanting a selection only will find the Freiburg Baroque Consort equally persuasive. Their performances too are winningly vital (try No. 2 as a sampler as it is briefest of all) and the only drawback for some ears is the tendency in sustained, chordal writing for the well-blended 'authentic' string group to sound like a harmonium. Also the playing time of 59 minutes should have allowed two more sonatas to be included.

8 Violin sonatas (for violin and continuo) (1681); *Sonata pastorella; Sonata representativa in A* (for solo violin); *Passacaglia for solo violin; Passacaglia for lute.*
*** HM Dig. HMU 907134/5 (2) [id.]. Romanesca (Andrew Manze, Nigel North, John Toll).

As a performer, Biber was obviously a virtuoso of the highest order, for these phenomenally difficult *Sonatas*, with their high tessitura and bizarre effects, could be played only by a violinist of remarkable technical gifts. Such is Andrew Manze, whose baroque violin encompasses all the demands made on it with consummate mastery. He conveys to the full the tension which always springs from strong performances of technically demanding music, yet at the same time retains an essentially expressive style. What is remarkable in these superbly played performances is the conveyed improvisatory feeling in the writing, to say nothing of its sublimely volatile unpredictability. The recording has a fine, spacious acoustic, and only those who find the abrasiveness of authentic fiddling aurally difficult should stay away from this highly stimulating pair of discs.

Missa Salisburgensis
(N)*** DG Dig. 457 611-2. Gabrieli Cons. and Players, Cologne Musica Antiqua Cologne, McCreesh; Goebel.

Paul McCreesh is well-experienced in recreating the sound of historic occasions and here is in partnership with Reinhold Goebel of Musica Antiqua of Cologne. He turns to one of the grandest of all ecclesiastical events, when in Salzburg Cathedral in 1682 they celebrated the 1,100th anniversary of Salzburg as a centre of Christianity. Though the score survived, there is no specific mention of the composer – all was created for the glory of God alone – but shrewd detective work, described in the note, clearly points to Heinrich von Biber, who was soon to be appointed Kapellmeister to the Archbishop. The blaze of sound on the disc is magnificent, with widely spaced antiphonal groups, choirs and instrumentalists, thrillingly capturing massive contrasts of sound.

Requiem à 15 in A.
*** DHM Dig. 05472 77344-2 [id.]. Almajano, Van der Sluis, Elwes, Padmore, Huijts, Van der Kamp, Netherlands Bach Festival Ch. & O, Leonhardt (with STEFFANI: *Stabat Mater.* ***)

Requiem a 15 in A; Vesperae a 32.
*** Erato/Warner Dig.4509 91725-2 [id.]. Bongers, Grimm, Wessel, De Groot, Reyans, S. Davies, Steur, De Koning, Amsterdam Bar. Ch. & O, Koopman.

As might be expected from the major key (hardly a usual one for a post-Renaissance requiem) Biber's A major setting is more robust than its companion in F minor. It is a gloriously exultant piece. Here death has very little sting, with the promises of forgiveness and heaven to come, and Biber immediately in the opening *Introitus* uses rich brass sonorities and his combined forces of singers in the grandest manner. In the Salzburg Court Cathedral of his day it was possible to place soloists, brass and choral groups in five different places. Here the polyphonic and polychoral writing is spread across a wide proscenium with brass and voices echoing each other ambitiously in overlapping phrases. Although the *Vespers* is hardly less complex and its writing equally inventive, this work depends more on continual contrast to makes its effect, with the soloists consistently used in alternation with the more massive choral and brass outbursts. The *Magnificat* brings a fine flowing fugato and, after much interplay between the solo group and the others, ends with a very positive closing *Amen.* Under Koopman the performances here are inspired with the solo team matching voices and singing splendidly together.

Leonhardt's account is also very fine indeed. There is no lack of spectacle, but the acoustic of Pieterskerk, Utrecht, is ideally free from excess resonance so that the results are particularly fresh with remarkably clear detail, yet there is the right warmth of ambience and a bloom on the excellent soloists, choir and orchestra alike. The performance has plenty of vitality and, for those interested in having a beautiful setting of *Stabat Mater* by Biber's contemporary, Agostino Steffani, this is an excellent alternative recommendation.

Sonata St Polycarp à 9 (for 8 trumpets and bass); In festo trium regium muttetum Natale (Epiphany cantata); Laetatus sum à 7 (cantata); Requiem in F min.
(M) *** Teldec/Warner 3984 21798-2. Soloists, V. Boys' Ch., Ch. Viennensis, VCM, Harnoncourt.

The music of Heinrich Biber is more familiar now than when this recording was made, in 1968; it is one of Harnoncourt's most distinguished pioneering Das Alte Werk collections, much admired in its day. The *Polycarp sonata*, using eight trumpets, makes a thrilling sound, and the two cantatas contain music that is both beautiful and striking. The larger-scale *Requiem* has since been recorded with greater success by Philip Pickett, but that is a premium-priced disc. Alongside it Harnoncourt's version tends to lack consistency of musical purpose, despite fine moments. The sound is excellent.

Birtwistle, Harrison (born 1934)

Carmen Arcadiae mechanicae perpetuum; Secret theatre; Silbury air.
*** Etcetera Dig. KTC 1052 [id.]. L. Sinf., Elgar Howarth.

Silbury air is one of Birtwistle's 'musical landscapes', bringing ever-changing views and perspectives on the musical material and an increasing drawing-out of melody. With melody discarded, *Carmen Arcadiae mechanicae perpetuum* (*The perpetual song of Mechanical Arcady*) superimposes different musical mechanisms to bring a rhythmic kaleidoscope of textures and patterns. The title of *Secret theatre* is taken from a poem by Robert Graves which refers to 'an unforeseen and fiery entertainment', and there is no doubting the distinctive originality of the writing, utterly typical of the composer. Howarth and the Sinfonietta could hardly be more convincing advocates, recorded in vivid, immediate sound.

Earth dances.
*** Collins Dig. Single 2001-2. BBC SO, Eötvös.

This is a characteristically rugged and characterful piece by Birtwistle, recorded live at the Proms in 1991 in spectacular sound. It is a generally slow-moving ritual, brilliantly written for the orchestra. Unfortunately, there are no separate tracks for the individual sections.

(i; iii) *Melencolia I;* (ii; iii) *Meridian;* (iii) *Ritual Fragment.*
*** NMC Dig. NMCD 009 [id.]. (i) Antony Pay; (ii) Mary King, Michael Thompson, Christopher van Kampen; L. Sinf. Voices; (iii) L. Sinf. (members); Oliver Knussen.

The NMC Birtwistle disc has the London Sinfonietta under Oliver Knussen in three works revealing the composer at his most uncompromising. *Ritual Fragment* was inspired by the death of Michael Vyner, the dynamic and influential artistic director of London Sinfonietta. It was perhaps the most moving of the pieces specially written for the Vyner memorial concert at Covent Garden. Just as dark and even more obsessive are the two longer works on the disc, *Melencolia I* and *Meridian*, that last the grimmest of love-songs.

Secret theatre; Ritual fragment; (i) *Nenia: The Death of Orpheus.*
*** CPO Dig. CPO 9993602 [id.]. (i) Rosemary Hardy; Musikfabrik NRW, Johannes Kalitzke.

It is fascinating to compare this German reading of Birtwistle's impressive *Secret theatre* with Boulez's on DG. The playing of Musikfabrik may not seem so powerful, partly because of a less forward recording, but the concentration builds up with comparable intensity, and the final climax is if anything even more uninhibited. *Nenia: The Death of Orpheus*, the earliest work here, is an elegiac piece in which the soloist's vocalizing is punctuated by percussive sing-speech, an early example of the composer's obsession with the Orpheus legend which culminated in the large-scale opera, *The Mask of Orpheus*. *Ritual fragment*, dating from 1990, is a moving lament on the death of Michael Vyner, artistic director of London Sinfonietta, not just dark and intense but at times angry, demonstrating that, for all the brutality of expression, Birtwistle's emotions are fundamental.

The Triumph of Time; Gawain (opera): *Gawain's journey.*
*** Collins Dig. 1387-2 [id.]. Philh. O, Elgar Howarth.

In their unmistakable power and authority, the two major works on this Collins disc are typical of the mature Birtwistle. *The Triumph of Time*, inspired by the Breughel engraving, was the piece which – with Pierre Boulez responsible for its first recording – was influential in making Birtwistle an international figure. Its power is undiminished: a grim, relentless processional. Even more welcome is *Gawain's journey*, one of Birtwistle's richest and most approachable scores, which in its 25-minute span reworks salient passages from his unforgettable Covent Garden opera, *Gawain*, first heard in 1991. Under Elgar Howarth, both works are brilliantly played by the Philharmonia and stunningly recorded.

OPERA

Gawain (complete).
(N) *** Collins Dig. 7041-2 (2) (id.). Angel, Walmsley-Clark, Howells, Kevin Smith, Greager, Marsden, Ebrahim, Le Roux, Tomlinsin, Alan Ewing, ROHCG O and Ch, Elgar Howarth.

With the Arthurian story of Gawain and the Green Knight distilled into stylized ritual, *Gawain* is a massive opera in two intense and abrasive acts. As so often with Birtwistle, this uncompromising music, if at first disconcerting, quickly reveals its magnetism. The orchestral sound is unique and distinctive, with complex wind textures dominating, and the energy of the writing adds to the impact. This is in no way easy to listen to, but this recording of a live Covent Garden performance, taken from a BBC Radio 3 broadcast, vividly captures the atmosphere. The disc brings an important advantage that the words are far clearer than in the theatre. The cast is as near ideal as one could imagine, with John Tomlinson as the Green Knight darkly intense in his baleful challenge, Richard Greager in the tenor role of Arthur, Marie Angel as Morgan Le Fay, and the French baritone, Francois Le Rouz in the relatively small role of Gawain himself. As in other Birtwistle scores, Elgar Howarth is a masterly and deeply committed advocate, drawing vivid playing from the Covent Garden Orchestra. Excellent, immediate BBC sound. The revised version of the score is used, with the 'Turning of the seasons' episode at the end of Act I reduced in length.

The Mask of Orpheus (complete).
(M) *** NMC Dig. D 050 (3). Garrison, Bronder, Rigby, Owens, Opie, Ebrahim, BBC Singers & O, Andrew Davis.

Birtwistle's *The Mask of Orpheus* is one of the most challenging operas ever written. The idiom may not be as abrasive as in some of Birtwistle's other works, often with lyrical vocal lines, but the telling and retelling of the Orpheus legend, with one version superimposed on another and with music reflecting that, makes it hard to take in for the listener who is unprepared. Even so, one cannot miss the magnetic intensity of Birtwistle's score, magnificently achieved here in this live recording, edited from two concert performances given at the Royal Festival Hall in London in March 1996.

The libretto is by Peter Zinovieff, himself an electronics composer, who collaborated with Birtwistle on the important electronic effects. The words are fluid, so that the printed text gives only an outline of what is presented. Act I is the longest and most enigmatic of the three Acts, with dreamlike superimposition of images and text, broadly based on the death of Eurydice, poisoned by a snake. Act II, following Orpheus in his progress through the Underworld over 17 arches, is far more direct, with the text more clearly defined, with the music building up powerfully in crescendo over the longest span. Act III, with its structure echoing the movement of the tide on a beach, rounds off the epic scheme, ending in Orpheus' death at the hands of the Dionysiac women, and the final fading of the myth.

With Andrew Davis controlling his massed forces masterfully, helped by Martyn Brabbins as assistant conductor, the purposefulness of the writing, the intense originality of a score dotted with havens of sheer beauty, is never in doubt. Central to success is the thrilling performance of the American tenor, Jon Garrison, as Orpheus the man, well supported by Peter Bronder as Orpheus the myth. Jean Rigby and Anne-Marie Owens, less prominent in the story, similarly take on the divided and superimposed role of the heroine, Eurydice woman and myth. The recorded sound is superb, vivid in conveying the different musical layers, electronic as well as instrumental and vocal. The documentation is very full. It is good that NMC have issued this important set as 'three discs for the price of two'.

Punch and Judy (opera) complete.
*** Etcetera KTC 2014 (2) [id.]. Roberts, DeGaetani, Bryn-Julson, Langridge, Wilson-Johnson, Tomlinson, L. Sinf., David Atherton.

Punch and Judy is a brutal, ritualistic piece, 'the first modern English opera', as it was called when it first appeared at the Aldeburgh Festival in 1968. It may not make easy listening, but nor is it easy to forget for, behind the aggressiveness, Birtwistle's writing has a way of touching an emotional chord, just as Stravinsky's so often does. Stephen Roberts is outstanding as Punch, and among others there is not a single weak link. David Atherton, conductor from the first performances, excels himself with the Sinfonietta. The clear, vivid recording, originally made by Decca for their enterprising LP Headline series, has been licensed by Etcetera.

Bizet, Georges (1838–75)

L'Arlésienne (complete incidental music; ed. Riffauld).
*** EMI (SIS) Dig. CDC7 47460-2. Orféon Donstiarra, Toulouse Capitole O, Plasson.

The score of the complete incidental music that Michel Plasson and his excellent French forces have recorded is based on the 1872 autograph, and the singing of the Orféon Donstiarra is as excellent as the orchestral playing. The less familiar music is every bit as captivating as the suites so that the performance has great charm, and the EMI recording is very good indeed. Strongly recommended.

L'Arlésienne: suites Nos. 1–2; Symphony in C.
*** EMI CDC7 47794-2 [id.]. RPO, Beecham.
(B) **(*) [EMI Red Line Dig. CDR5 69881]. ASMF, Marriner.

L'Arlésienne: suites Nos. 1–2: excerpts; *Carmen: suites Nos. 1–2:* excerpts; *Symphony in C.*
(BB) *** RCA Navigator 74321 17901-2 [(M) id. import]. Bamberg SO, Georges Prêtre.

Beecham's magical set of the incidental music for *L'Arlésienne*, dating from 1957, still sounds remarkably well. Besides the beauty and unique character of the wind solos, Beecham's deliciously sprightly *Minuet* and his affectingly gentle sense of nostalgia in the *Adagietto* (both from the first suite) are as irresistibly persuasive as the swaggering brilliance of the closing *Farandole* of the second. Beecham's version of the *Symphony* above all brings out its spring-like qualities. The playing of the French orchestra is not quite as polished as that of Marriner's group, but Beecham's panache more than compensates. The remastered sound is bright on top, without glare.

From Prêtre a most enjoyable and generous super-bargain disc, originating from the Eurodisc catalogue, very warmly and naturally recorded, most elegantly played and offering 77 minutes of music.

Marriner's EMI account of Bizet's *Symphony*, which is generous with repeats in the outer movements, does not quite re-create the sparkling lightness of touch of his earlier Argo (Decca) version. In the first movement there is plenty of energy, but not the same sense of complete spontaneity. But it is still very enjoyable, and the two *L'Arlésienne suites* are beautifully played, the *Adagietto* given a gossamer delicacy. The Abbey Road recording is first class. This CD is only available in the USA.

L'Arlésienne: suites Nos. 1–2; Symphony in C; (i) *Carmen:* highlights.
(B) **(*) Erato/Warner Ultima 0630 18947-2 (2) [(M) id. import]. Strasbourg PO, Alain Lombard; (i) with Régine Crespin, Gilbert Ply, Jeannette Pilou, José van Dam, Nadine Denize, Maria Rosa Carminati, Ch. of Opéra du Rhin.

These Strasbourg performances under Alain Lombard date from the mid-1970s. The two *L'Arlésienne suites* are nicely turned, and the *Symphony* too is alive and well, with an elegant oboe solo in the *Adagio* and an infectiously spirited finale. The analogue sound is full and pleasing, rather than especially brilliant. What makes this Ultima Double especially tempting is the substantial set of highlights from what is obviously a spontaneously vivid, complete recording of *Carmen*, hitherto unfamiliar to us. It brings an all-French (or rather, in the case of José Van Dam, Belgian) cast of principals, with Régine Crespin in excellent voice, exuding a sexy sultriness, and she is well partnered by Gilbert Ply, a boldly romantic Don José who rises passionately to the occasion in the *Flower song*. Some will feel that van Dam's Escamillo isn't very Spanish-sounding, but his vigorous delivery of the *Toreador song* certainly carries the day. Lombard directs the proceedings with evident relish, helped by the enthusiasm of the Rhine Opera Chorus and warmly atmospheric recording with plenty of depth. Though the singing is not always refined, there are few more compelling sets of highlights from *Carmen* than this.

L'Arlésienne: suites Nos. 1–2; Carmen: suite No. 1.
(M) *** DG (IMS) 423 472-2. LSO, Abbado.

L'Arlésienne: suites Nos. 1–2; Carmen: suites Nos. 1–2.
(M)*** Decca Dig. 466 421-2 [id.]. Montreal SO, Dutoit.

(i) *L'Arlésienne: suites Nos. 1–2; Carmen: suites Nos. 1–2;* (ii) *Jeux d'enfants.*
(M) **(*) Ph. (IMS) 446 198-2. (i) ASMF, Marriner; (ii) Concg. O, Haitink.

With playing that is both elegant and vivid, and with superb, demonstration-worthy sound, Dutoit's polished yet affectionate coupling of the *L'Arlésienne* and *Carmen* suites makes a clear first choice.

Among analogue couplings of *L'Arlésienne* and *Carmen suites*, Abbado's 1981 DG recording also stands out. The orchestral playing is characteristically refined, the wind solos cultured and eloquent, especially in *L'Arlésienne*, where the pacing of the music is nicely judged.

Marriner's collection is generous, offering 11 items from *Carmen* and both *L'Arlésienne suites*, while Haitink's *Jeux d'enfants* is delectably played and superbly recorded in the Concertgebouw. The London recording, too, is attractively rich and naturally balanced. But the musical characterization – despite fine LSO playing, notably from the flautist, Peter Lloyd – is sometimes lacking in flair and the last degree of *brio*.

L'Arlésienne: suite No. 1 (with *Andante molto*); *Jeux d'enfants* (*suite*; including *Les quatre coins*); *Overture in A; Marche funèbre in B min.*
*** EMI (SIS) Dig. CDC7 54765-2. Toulouse Capitole O, Michel Plasson.

Plasson does not offer the second *L'Arlésienne* suite, although he includes the delicate *Andante molto* with its refined saxophone solo. He also offers an attractively busy extra movement (*Les quatre coins*) from *Jeux d'enfants* which the composer unaccountably discarded, even though he had reworked and extended the piano duet original. The other important novelty here is the delightful *Overture in A* which is contemporary with the *Symphony* and is equally felicitously scored. Plasson's performances are alive and persuasive throughout. The recording, made in the Hall-aux-Grains, Toulouse, is of best EMI quality.

Carmen: suites Nos. 1–2; Jeux d'enfants.
(B) **(*) [EMI Red Line Dig. CDR5 69861]. O Nat. de France, Ozawa – LALO: *Symphonie espagnole;* SARASATE: *Zigeunerweisen.* **(*)

Very good performances from the Orchestre National de France under Ozawa, and the recording is both vivid and atmospheric. If the couplings are suitable, this is worth considering, even if other accounts of this much-played repertoire have even more character.

Jeux d'enfants (Children's games), Op. 22.
(M) *** Decca (IMS) 448 571-2 [id.]. Paris Conservatoire O, Martinon – BERLIOZ: *Overtures* **(*); IBERT: *Divertissement* ***; SAINT-SAENS: *Danse macabre* etc. ***
(B) *** CfP CD-CFP 4086. SNO, Gibson – RAVEL: *Ma Mère l'Oye;* SAINT-SAENS: *Carnival.* ***
(B) ** Tring Dig. TRP046 [(M) id.]. RPO, Andrea Licata – PROKOFIEV: *Peter*; SAINT-SAENS; *Carnival* **(*).

Martinon's memorable account of *Jeux d'enfants* was part of a famous 1960 Decca anthology of French orchestral music, now reissued in the 'Classic Sound' series. The crisp trumpet fanfares in the opening piece set the seal on a performance notable for its vivid colour and delicacy of feeling. The sound is remarkably good.

From Classics for Pleasure a fresh approach, lively orchestral playing and excellent mid-1970s sound; with excellent couplings, this is highly recommendable.

On Tring, the RPO under the Italian conductor, Andrea Licata, play sympathetically and are well recorded.

Roma suite; Patrie overture, Op. 19; Symphony in C.
**(*) EMI Dig. CDC5 55057-2. Capitole Toulouse O, Michel Plasson.
(BB) **(*) ASV Dig. CDQS 6135 [id.] (without *Patrie*). RPO, Enrique Bátiz.

Roma, written over a period, some years after the *Symphony in C*. It has not the overall spontaneity of that earlier work, and is uneven in quality, but with its orchestral colourings it is most enjoyable. The warmth of the opening horn chorale and the gaiety of the finale are brought out well in Toulouse and the orchestral playing is excellent. *Patrie*, too, comes over with plenty of gusto, and again its lyrical theme is warmly presented. The *Symphony* is lively and well played (with an imaginative oboe soloist) and is certainly enjoyable if not distinctive. Martinon's version (see below) has more sheer *joie de vivre* and Prêtre's slightly more character. But the disc is worth considering for *Roma*.

Bátiz's performances are also attractive, with very good playing from the RPO. As with the Plasson account of *Roma*, it is the first and last movements which come off the most effectively. Although he omits *Patrie*, Bátiz has a considerable price advantage and he receives excellent (1990) digital recording. In the *Symphony* the sound is full and weighty, adding to the impression that the performance is less lighthearted than usual in the first movement (repeat included), though there is no lack of vitality and, with its more serious manner, it is still both effective and enjoyable.

Symphony in C.
*** DG Dig. 423 624-2 [id.]. Orpheus CO – BRITTEN: *Simple symphony;* PROKOFIEV: *Symphony No. 1.* ***
(B) *** Sony SBK 48264 [id.]. Nat. PO, Stokowski (with MENDELSSOHN: *A Mid-summer Night's Dream* ***); SMETANA: *Vltava.* ***
(N) (BB) **(*) Virgin Classics Dig. Double VBD5 61513-2 (2) [CDVB 61513]. SCO, Saraste – BERLIOZ: *Symphonie fantastique; Le Carnaval romain;* CHAUSSON: *Symphony.* **(*)

The freshness of the seventeen-year-old Bizet's *Symphony* is well caught by the Orpheus group who present it with all the flair and polished ensemble for which they are famous. First-rate sound, most realistic in effect.

Stokowski's exhilaratingly polished account of the Bizet *Symphony* was recorded at Abbey Road in May/June 1977, only three months before he died; it is a superb example of his last vintage recording period, as vital and alive as anything he recorded in his youth. David Theodore's oboe solo in the *Adagio* is very elegantly done and the *moto perpetuo* finale is wonderfully light and sparkling. A fine bargain coupling, ranking alongside the top recommendations of Beecham and the Orpheus version. The couplings, too, show Szell at his finest.

Saraste gives a distinctly purposeful account of the first movement, rhythmically strong and bold; the *Adagio* with a rich-timbred oboe solo blossoms romantically in the strings, and the *Scherzo* has striking impetus to lead to a high-spirited finale. The effect of the recording is fuller than that provided by the Orpheus group on DG, and the Scottish performance is enjoyable in its own way. Good value if you want all three works.

PIANO MUSIC

Chants du Rhin.
(N) ** RCA Dig. 74321 53730-2 [id.]. Jean-Marc Luisada. – FAURE: *Nocturnes.* **

Bizet's piano music is much neglected in the concert hall, though Glenn Gould championed it on records. It has great charm. The Tunisian-born Jean-Marc Luisada is a fluent and often sensitive artist though one can imagine even more persuasive advocacy. Good recording.

Jeux d'enfants, Op. 22.
*** Ph. (IMS) Dig. 420 159-2 [id.]. Katia and Marielle Labèque – FAURE: *Dolly;* RAVEL: *Ma Mère l'Oye.* ***

The Labèque sisters characterize Bizet's wonderfully inventive cycle of twelve pieces with vitality, great wit and delicacy of feeling and touch. Superb recording in the best Philips tradition.

VOCAL

'*Chant d'amour*': Mélodies: *Adieux de l'hôtesse arabe; Chant d'amour; La Coccinelle; Ouvre ton coeur; Tarantelle.*
*** Decca Dig. 452 667-2 [id.]. Cecilia Bartoli, Myung-Whun Chung – BERLIOZ; DELIBES; RAVEL: *Mélodies.* ***

These delightful Bizet songs come as part of an outstanding recital of French repertoire, readily demonstrating the versatility of Bartoli who is so sympathetically accompanied by Chung. One of the highlights is *La coccinelle* ('The Ladybird'), a witty fast waltz. Both voice and piano are recorded beautifully.

OPERA

Carmen (opera; complete).
*** DG Dig. 410 088-2 (3) [id.]. Baltsa, Carreras,

Van Dam, Ricciarelli, Barbaux, Paris Op. Ch., Schoenberg Boys' Ch., BPO, Karajan.

(M) *** DG 427 440-2 (3) [id.]. Horne, McCracken, Krause, Maliponte, Manhattan Op. Ch., Met. Op. O, Bernstein.

(M) *** RCA 74321 39495-2 (3) [6199-2-RG]. Leontyne Price, Corelli, Merrill, Freni, Linval, V. State Op. Ch., VPO, Karajan.

**(*) Decca 414 489-2 (2) [id.]. Troyanos, Domingo, Van Dam, Te Kanawa, John Alldis Ch., LPO, Solti.

(N) **(*) EMI CDS5 56214-2 [CDC 56214] (3). Los Angeles, Gedda, Micheau, Blanc, French R. Ch. & O, Beecham.

(B) **(*) DG 427 885-2 (3) [419 636-2]. Berganza, Domingo, Cotrubas, Milnes, Amb. S., LSO, Abbado.

** EMI CDS 56281-2 (3) [CDCB 56281]. Callas, Gedda, Guiot, Massard, René Duclos Ch., Children's Ch., Paris Nat. Op. O, Prêtre.

(N) ** Teldec/Warner Dig. 0630 12672-2 (3) [id.]. Jennifer Larmore, Thomas Moser, Angela Gheorghiu, Samuel Ramey, Bavarian State Op. Ch. & O, Sinopoli.

Karajan's DG set of *Carmen* makes a clear first choice. In Carreras he has a Don José, lyrical and generally sweet-toned. José van Dam is incisive and virile, the public hero-figure; which leaves Agnes Baltsa as a vividly compelling Carmen, tough and vibrant, yet with tenderness under the surface.

Bernstein's 1973 *Carmen* was recorded at the New York Metropolitan Opera. Some of his slow tempi are very controversial, but what really matters is the authentic tingle of dramatic tension which permeates the whole entertainment. Marilyn Horne – occasionally coarse in expression – gives a most fully satisfying reading of the heroine's role, a great vivid characterization. The rest of the cast similarly works to Bernstein's consistent overall plan. It is very well transferred.

Karajan's RCA version, made in Vienna in 1964, owes much to Leontyne Price's seductive, smoky-toned Carmen. Corelli has moments of coarseness, but his is still a heroic performance. Robert Merrill sings with gloriously firm tone, while Mirella Freni is enchanting as Micaëla. With recording full of atmosphere, and attractively re-packaged at mid-price in RCA's UK Opera Treasury series, this is a very strong contender, even if Karajan's later, premium-priced set, with Carreras and Baltsa a vibrant, vividly compelling Carmen, remains the primary recommendation (DG 410 088-2).

Solti's Decca performance is remarkable for its new illumination of characters. Tatiana Troyanos is one of the subtlest Carmens on record. Escamillo too is more readily sympathetic, not just the flashy matador who steals the hero's girl, whereas Don José is revealed as weak rather than just a victim. Troyanos's singing is delicately seductive too, with no hint of vulgarity, while the others make up a most consistent singing cast. Solti, like Karajan, uses spoken dialogue and a modification of the Oeser edition, deciding in each individual instance whether to accept amendments to Bizet's first thoughts. Though the CD transfer brings out the generally excellent balances of the original analogue recording, it exaggerates the bass, although the voices retain their fine realism and bloom.

Beecham's approach to Bizet's well-worn score is no less fresh and revealing. His speeds are not always conventional but they always *sound* right. And unlike so many strong-willed conductors in opera Beecham allows his singers room to breathe and to expand their characterizations. It seems he specially chose de los Angeles to be his Carmen although she had never sung the part on the stage before making the recording. He conceived the *femme fatale* not as the usual glad-eyed character, but as someone far more subtly seductive, winning her admirers not so much by direct assault and high voltage as by genuine charm and real femininity. De los Angeles suits this conception perfectly: her characterization of Carmen is absolutely bewitching, and when in the Quintet scene she says *Je suis amoureuse* one believes her absolutely. Naturally the other singers are not nearly so dominant as this, but they make admirable foils; Gedda is pleasantly light-voiced as ever, Janine Micheau is a sweet Micaela, and Ernest Blanc makes an attractive Escamillo. The stereo recording does not add to things in the way that the best Decca opera recordings do, and there seems to have been little attempt at stage production, but in the CD transfer the sound is certainly brilliant, and the recording does not too greatly show its age.

Superbly disciplined, Abbado's performance nails its colours to the mast at the very start with a breathtakingly fast account of the opening prelude. Conductor and orchestra can take a large share of credit for the performance's success for, though the singing is generally enjoyable too. Teresa Berganza is a seductive if somewhat unsmiling Carmen – sensual, but lacking some of the flair which makes for a three-dimensional portrait. Ileana Cotrubas as Micaëla is not always as sweetly steady as she can be, but Milnes makes a heroic matador. The spoken dialogue is excellently produced, and the sound is vivid and immediate. This makes a good bargain alternative to the Bernstein set, now again available on cassette as well as CD.

Though in so many ways the vibrant, flashing-eyed personality of Maria Callas was ideally suited to the role of Carmen, her complete recording is disappointing. One principal trouble is that the performance, apart from her, lacks a taut dramatic rein, with slack ensemble from singers and orchestra alike. The moment the heroine enters, the tension rises; but by Callas standards this is a performance rough-hewn, strong and characterful but lacking the full imaginative detail of her finest work. 'Callas is Carmen', said EMI's original advertisements, but in fact very clearly Callas remains Callas. The CD transfer clarifies textures but brings out the limitations of the Paris recording. The set has been remastered and a new booklet prepared for this latest reissue.

Sinopoli directs a thoughtful, clean-textured but generally unidiomatic reading of *Carmen.* He is matched by Jennifer Larmore in the title role, keenly intelligent, singing with clear, firm tone, but never sounding sensuous or earthy in the way one wants of the wilful gypsy. This is a disconcertingly chilly view of this red-blooded character. Thomas Moser as Don José sings cleanly, better served by the microphones than usual, and Samuel Ramey is a heroic Escamillo, though he is not helped in the 'Toreador's song' by Sinopoli's rather slow, detached manner. Most recommendable is the characterful Micaela of Angela Gheorghiu, but this remains a curiosity of a set. As with most latterday recordings, the Oeser edition is used.

Carmen: highlights.
(M) *** Decca 458 204-2 [id.] (from complete recording, with Tatiana Troyanos, Plácido Domingo, José van Dam, Kiri Te Kanawa, John Alldis Ch., LPO; cond. Solti).
(N) (M) *** DG 457 901-2 [id.]. (from above complete set with Horne, McCracken,Krause; cond. Bernstein).
(B) **(*) DG Classikon 439 496-2 [(M) 447 270-2] (from above set, with Berganza, Domingo; cond. Abbado).
(N) (M) ** EMI CDM5 66663-2 [id.]. (from above recording with Callas, Gedda; cond. Prêtre).

The reissued mid-priced set of highlights from Solti's sharply characterful set is generous (75 minutes) and handsomely repackaged in a slipcase. A full translation is included, and the remastered recording sounds both brilliant, full-bodied, and atmospheric, though still somewhat over-weighted in the bass.

The DG Galleria disc can also be recommended, offering 70 minutes of well-chosen excerpts from the Bernstein's set recorded at the Met, the only snag being that the synopsis is not linked to the fourteen different cues. However, *Carmen* is not a difficult opera to follow!

The bargain highlights selection on DG Classikon offers a fairly generous sampler of the Berganza/Domingo/Abbado set with some 69 minutes of well-chosen excerpts, including all the hits. The documentation relates the music to the narrative in a brief but succinct synopsis.

The Callas set of highlights returns to the original 1964 selection, offering 61 minutes of key items relevant to the narrative; so Callas only sings in about half of the excerpts.

Les Pêcheurs de perles (complete).
(M) (***) EMI (SIS) mono CMS5 652662 (2).
Angelici, Legay, Dens, Noguera, Théâtre Nat. de l'Opéra-Comique Ch. & O, Cluytens.

Unavailable since the early days of LP, this superb EMI Cluytens set of 1954 offers the finest, most warmly expressive performance on disc of this delectable opera. Ironically, its nearest rival is the Philips set of the previous year under Jean Fournet, also in mono, both of them outshining later stereo sets. Cluytens is an even more sensitive conductor than his Philips rival, less foursquare, getting the music to flow flexibly; and his cast, idiomatically French, has no weak link. Martha Angelici as the heroine, Leila, is both sweet and bright, with no Gallic shrillness, and Henry Legay has a degree of heroic timbre in the rounded, lyric quality of his tenor, while Michel Dens, as in other French opera recordings of the period, proves a firm, characterful baritone. With excellent choral and orchestral work, one gets the impression of a stage experience translated to the studio. The mono transfer is a little dull on orchestral sound, but it captures voices vividly.

Blacher, Boris (1903–75)

(i) *Alla marcia; Chiarina;* (ii) *Dance scenes (La Vie).*
(N) *** Largo Dig. 5142 [id.]. (i) Berlin Radio SO; (ii) LPO; Noam Shariff.

In addition to the early *Alla marcia* (1934), this CD couples two ballets: *Dance scenes*, composed in England for Colonel de Basil's *Ballets Russes* in 1938 but never performed because of the war (the score only came to light after Blacher's death), and *Chiarina* composed in 1946. There is some Stravinsky in the former, and its sophistication, irony and syncopation (it embraces tango and rumba, as had Milhaud's *Saudades do Bresil*) would not have found favour with the Nazi notion of 'culture'. An inventive but uneven score. The post-war ballet is more wholly successful and elegantly mingles sambas and polkas with the cool poised atmosphere of Stravinsky in *Baiser de la fée* mode. Very good performances under Noam Shariff, himself a Blacher pupil, and excellent recorded sound.

Variations on a theme of Paganini Op. 26.
*** Decca Dig. 452 853-2 [id.]. VPO, Solti – ELGAR: *Enigma variations;* KODALY: *Peacock variations.* ***

Attractively coupled with comparable sets by Elgar and Kodály, the Blacher *Paganini variations* make a delightful fill-up, a brilliant quarter-hour work not nearly as well known outside Germany as it should be. The performance is infectious in its pointing of rhythm. Jazzy syncopations are consistently interpreted with a sense of fun, and the element of fantasy in Blacher's sequence of 16 free variations is regularly brought out, ending with a breathtaking account of the final *moto perpetuo*. The Decca engineers have done wonders in capturing the unique acoustic of the Musikverein splendidly, with plenty of air round the sound.

Der Grossinquisitor (oratorio; complete).
(N) *** Berlin Classics Dig. 0093782 BC [id.]. Siegmund Nimsgern, Leipzig Radio Ch. Dresden PO, Herbert Kegel.

Blacher's music is inventive, full of wit and high spirits, but his oratorio, *The Grand Inquisitor* which comes from the period 1942–3, strikes a more serious note. Never popular with the Nazis, Blacher remained in Germany during the war though his music was proscribed when he was discovered to be a quarter Jewish. His oratorio draws for its inspiration on Dostoevsky's *The Brothers Karamazov*. Its opening half in which Christ returns to earth in sixteenth-century Seville to witness the Cardinal Grand Inquisitor burning some hundred heretics, struck obvious resonances. The musical idiom remains strongly neo-classical with Stravinsky and Hindemith closely in view. There is some powerful writing here and the composer is well served by the distinguished soloist and the fine Dresden Orchestra under Herbert Kegel. Very good, well-balanced recorded sound with fine definition and no lack of warmth.

Blake, Howard (born 1938)

Clarinet concerto.
*** Hyperion Dig. CDA 66215 [id.]. Thea King, ECO, composer – LUTOSLAWSKI: *Dance preludes;* SEIBER: *Concertino*. ***

Howard Blake provides a comparatively slight but endearing *Clarinet concerto*, which is played here with great sympathy by Thea King, who commissioned the work.

(i) *Violin concerto (Leeds); A Month in the Country* (film incidental music): *suite; Sinfonietta for brass*.
*** ASV Dig. CDDCA 905 [id.]. (i) Christiane Edlinger; E. N. Philh., Paul Daniel.

It was the success of his music for *The Snowman* that gave Howard Blake the encouragement and the artistic breathing-space to write his beautiful and stimulating *Violin concerto*. Christiane Edlinger, who gave its première, is the soloist in what proves to be an inspired performance, caught 'on the wing', with playing as intense and communicative as it is spontaneous. The only snag is the excessively wide dynamic range of the recording. Blake's suite of string music written for the film, *A Month in the Country*, brings moments of comparable bitter-sweet elegiac feeling. It is most sensitively played, as is the brass *Sinfonietta*, sonorous and jolly by turns. In terms of overall concert-hall realism the recording is impressive and this record is strongly recommended.

Bliss, Arthur (1891–1975)

Adam Zero (ballet; complete); *A Colour Symphony*.
(BB) *** Naxos Dig. 8.553460 [id.]. N. Philh. O, David Lloyd-Jones.

Naxos here offer the first of a planned series of Sir Arthur Bliss's music, including his best-known major work, the *Colour Symphony* of 1922. Full of striking ideas and effects to illustrate four heraldic colours, the symphony here receives a refined and idiomatic reading, marked by superb wind-playing. More valuable still is the first complete recording of the ballet, *Adam Zero*, in which the process of creating a ballet is presented as an allegory for the ongoing life-cycle. Lloyd-Jones directs a dramatically paced performance, amply confirming this as one of Bliss's most inventive, strongly coordinated scores, shamefully neglected. Full, well-balanced sound.

(i; ii) *Adam Zero* (ballet): *suite; Mêlée fantasque; Hymn to Apollo;* (i; ii; iii) *Rout for soprano and orchestra;* (i; iv; v) *Serenade for orchestra and baritone;* (i; vi; vii) *The World is charged with the grandeur of God*.
*** Lyrita SRCS 225 [id.]. (i) LSO; (ii) cond. composer; (iii) with Rae Woodland; (iv) John Shirley-Quirk; (v) cond. Brian Priestman; (vi) with Amb. S.; (vii) cond. Philip Ledger.

The ballet *Adam Zero* may not show Bliss at his finest but the four excerpts here contain some attractive moments. The *Mêlée fantasque* (well named) is even more striking with strong Stravinskian influences but with a characteristic elegiac section at its centre. After the *Hymn to Apollo*, although the rest of the programme is primarily vocal, it is in fact the orchestral writing that one remembers most vividly, for the *Serenade* has two purely orchestral movements out of three. The second, *Idyll*, shows Bliss's lyrical impulse at its most eloquent. The orchestra is almost more important than the voice in *Rout*. The solo vocal performances throughout this CD are of high quality, with John Shirley-Quirk giving a swashbuckling account of the finale of the *Serenade*. In *The World is charged with the grandeur of God*, the invention is less memorable, and it is again the orchestration that shows the composer's imagination at work, notably the atmospheric scoring for the flutes in the second section. The recordings date from the early 1970s and are of high quality.

(i) *Checkmate suite; Hymn to Apollo;* (ii) *Music for strings;* (iii) *Clarinet quintet;* (ii, iv) *Lie strewn the white flocks.*

(N) (B) *** Chandos 2-for-1 Dig. CHAN 241-1 (2) [id.]. (i) Ulster O, Handley; (ii) N. Sinfonia, Hickox; (iii) Hilton, Lindsay Qt; (iv) Della Jones and N. Sinfonia Ch.

The first of a new series of Chandos 2-for-1 Doubles makes an impressive Bliss survey. The *Music for strings* (1933) is surely the key work here and Hickox directs it spontaneously with deep expressive feeling: the playing of the Northern Sinfonia strings is deeply committed and the Chandos sound rich and refined in detail. Vernon Handley conducts with complete authority and evident enthusiasm both the *Checkmate suite* (1937) and the less familiar *Hymn to Apollo* (premièred in 1926 under Monteux). In the masterly *Clarinet quintet* (see below) Janet Hilton and the Lindsays are totally persuasive, and the recording is most naturally balanced. The Pastoral, *Lie strewn the white flock* (1928), is another of the composer's most memorable works. It is melodically inspired and most imaginatively scored (there is a distinct French colouring at times, notably in the delectable flute obbligatos) and is brought vividly to life by the passionate singing of the Northern Sinfonia Chorus. Della Jones sings the *Pigeon song* touchingly, and the recording is in the demonstration bracket. On the whole this is to be preferred to the Hyperion version (see below).

Checkmate (ballet): *5 dances.*

(M) *** Chandos CHAN 6576 [id.]. West Australian SO, Schönzeler – RUBBRA: *Symphony No. 5* ***; TIPPETT: *Little music.* **(*)

The idea of a ballet based on chess with all its opportunities for symbolism and heraldic splendour appealed to Bliss, and the score he produced remains one of his most inventive creations. The five dances on the Chandos issue are well played under Hans-Hubert Schönzeler and, with its valuable Rubbra coupling, this is welcome back in the catalogue at mid-price.

A Colour Symphony; (i) *Cello concerto;* (ii) *The Enchantress* (scena for contralto and orchestra).

(M) *** Chandos Enchant Dig. CHAN 7073 [id.]. (i) Raphael Wallfisch; (ii) Linda Finnie; Ulster O, Vernon Handley.

Raphael Wallfisch is a powerful soloist in the *Cello concerto*, which Bliss wrote for Rostropovich in 1970, launching into the piece with a bite and attack which are instantly compelling. This is a reading which brings out the red-blooded warmth of the writing, with the soloist strongly supported by the Ulster Orchestra under Handley. They are equally persuasive accompanying Linda Finnie in the extended scena which Bliss wrote for Kathleen Ferrier nearly 20 years earlier. There, similarly, Bliss was inspired by the individual artistry of a great musician, even though, as he himself said, he found it hard to reconcile the goodness of Ferrier with the character of Simaetha, the central figure in the passage of Theocritus which he chose to set. For this reissue Chandos have added Vernon Handley's authoritative and enthusiastic account of the *Colour Symphony* and throughout the recording is warm and atmospheric.

(i) *A Colour Symphony; Introduction and allegro;* (ii) *Men of Two Worlds: Baraza;* (i) *Things to come* (film music): *suite* and excerpts: *Ballet for children; Pestilence; Attack; The world in ruins.*

(M) (***) Dutton Lab. CDLXT 2501 [id.]. (i) LSO, composer; (ii) Eileen Joyce, Ch. & Nat. SO, Muir Mathieson.

A Colour Symphony was the work that brought Bliss fame as an *enfant terrible*, but nowadays its flavour seems more Elgarian than modern, with the merest hint that Bliss knew his early Stravinsky. The sounds are attractive and the recording (1956 vintage) captures them well. But, as with so much of this composer's output, in all honesty the thematic material is never very memorable. The *Introduction and allegro*, written for Stokowski (also in the early 1920s), is another well-constructed, completely professional but unmemorable work. For the film *Men of Two Worlds: Baraza* Eileen Joyce was recruited to the piano part of a score of which only a snippet survives, including a chorus and some touches of syncopation. Again, the 1946 recording in Dutton's vivid transfer sounds astonishingly vivid. But Bliss's masterpiece was his incidental music for Korda's H. G. Wells film, *Things to come*. Bliss rescued his material and recorded an early set of four excerpts for Decca on 78-r.p.m. discs in 1936. This included a section called *The world in ruins*, missing from the final orchestral suite, which the composer published and recorded later in stereo in 1957. In memorability, Bliss never surpassed this music, and the *March* is unforgettable in its gutsy, flamboyantly tuneful vitality.

A Colour Symphony; Metamorphic variations.

*** Nimbus Dig. NI 5294 [id.]. BBC Welsh SO, Wordsworth.

The title, *Metamorphic variations*, may be unattractive, but this is one of the most cogent of Bliss's mature works. In *A Colour Symphony* Wordsworth is a degree broader in his approach than Vernon Handley on the rival Chandos version, yet his control of rhythm and line makes his reading just as warm and sympathetic. As recorded, the Welsh string-tone is not quite so full and warm as that of Handley's Ulster Orchestra, but anyone who wants this apt coupling is unlikely to be disappointed.

(i) *Piano concerto; March of homage.*
(M) **(*) Unicorn Dig. UKCD 2029. (i) Philip Fowke; RLPO, David Atherton.

Bliss's concerto is a work which needs a passionately committed soloist, and that is what it finds in Philip Fowke, urgent and expressive, well matched by David Atherton and the Liverpool orchestra. The occasional piece is also given a lively performance. The digital recording is full and vivid.

Discourse for orchestra; Miracle in the Gorbals (complete ballet); *Things to come* (complete film score, reconstructed Christopher Palmer).
(N) (BB) **(*) Naxos Dig. 8.553698 [id.]. Queensland SO, Christopher Lyndon-Gee.

The Naxos issue is most valuable for offering not only a première recording of the *Discourse for orchestra*, a cleanly argued piece of nearly twenty minutes, but of the complete ballet score of *Miracle in the Gorbals*, colourful and vigorous in illustrating the sordid but moving tale of murder and salvation in the slums of Glasgow. The eighteen brief sections are strongly contrasted in mood and atmosphere, and are here given a warmly committed performance by the Queensland Orchestra, as is the *Discourse*, even though the strings are challenged by the violin writing. The five movements from *Things to come* are welcome too in Christopher Palmer's reconstruction of the original opulent scoring, though it is astonishing to find the famous *March* omitted. Good warm sound.

(i) *Introduction and allegro;* (ii) *Theme and cadenza for violin and orchestra.*
(BB) (***) Belart mono 461 353-2 [(M) id. import]. (i) LSO, composer; (ii) Alfredo Campoli, LPO, Boult – ELGAR: *Violin concerto.* (***)

The *Introduction and allegro* (for full orchestra) was written for Stokowski and is a well-constructed piece with good ideas; it sounds very impressive in this virile performance under the composer's direction. The *Theme and variations* is shorter but no less striking. It was originally written for a radio play written by the composer's wife. One could do with more short concertante pieces like this. The performance, with Campoli a first-rate soloist, is authentic and vividly alive. The excellent mid-1950s Decca recording is well transferred, to make this a very desirable coupling.

(i) *Music for strings;* (ii) *A Knot of riddles;* (iii) *Pastoral: Lie strewn the white flocks.*
(N) (M) *** EMI CDM5 67117-2 [id.]. (i) LPO, Boult; (ii) Shirley-Quirk, LCO (members), Morris; (iii) Michelow; Knight, Bruckner-Mahler Ch. of L., LCO, Wyn Morris.

Music for strings, which was written at the same time as another particularly memorable piece by Bliss – the music to the H. G. Wells film *Things to come* – represents one in the long series of successful works for strings by British composers. It was first heard in Salzburg in 1935, with Boult conducting the Vienna Philharmonic, and here it receives a glowing performance under the same understanding interpreter. The LPO relishes the beautifully judged virtuoso writing and the recording is first rate. The remaining works here are two attractive song-cycles that show Bliss's art at its least demanding. He conceived the *Pastoral (Lie strewn the white flocks)* as a classical fantasy, linking verse from widely different sources, and using mezzo-soprano, chorus, flute (beautifully played by Norman Knight), timpani and strings. *A Knot of riddles* is just as easy on the ear – arguably too easy – with English riddles translated from the Anglo-Saxon and provided with a solution by the soloist after each one. This is a much more recent work, written for the Cheltenham Festival in 1963. It is here sung with fine point by John Shirley-Quirk. Good recording.

Conversations; Madam Noy; (i; ii) *Rhapsody;* (ii) *Rout; The Women of Yueh; Oboe quintet.*
*** Hyperion CDA 66137 [id.]. Nash Ens., (i) Anthony Rolfe Johnson; (ii) Elizabeth Gale.

The predominant influence in *Rout*, for soprano and chamber orchestra, and in the *Rhapsody*, with its two wordless vocal parts, is Ravel. The *Oboe quintet* is a work of considerable quality. The music assembled here represents Bliss at his very best. A lovely disc, which can be warmly recommended, and eminently well engineered, too.

Clarinet quintet.
*** Redcliffe Dig. RR 010 [id.]. Nicholas Cox, Redcliffe Ens. – RAWSTHORNE: *Clarinet quartet;* ROUTH: *Clarinet quintet.* ***
*** Chandos Dig. CHAN 8683 [id.]. Hilton, Lindsay Qt – BAX: *Sonata* **(*); VAUGHAN WILLIAMS: *Studies.* ***

The *Clarinet quintet* is Bliss's masterpiece. The flowing lyricism of the opening movement is matched by the intense valedictory feeling of the *Adagietto*, in which the composer remembers his younger brother, Kennard, killed at the Somme in 1916. The work could not be better played than in this very beautiful performance by Nicholas Cox and members of the Redcliffe Ensemble. The recording, too, in the glowing acoustic of St George's, Brandon Hill, Bristol, is quite ideal to capture the music's radiance of texture, yet detail in the lively Scherzo and *energico* finale is well captured.

Janet Hilton and the Lindsays also have the measure of the *Clarinet quintet's* autumnal melancholy; the recording is natural and well focused.

String quartets Nos. 1 in B flat; 2 in F min.
*** Hyperion CDA 66178 [id.]. Delmé Qt.

These performances by the Delmé Quartet are not only thoroughly committed but enormously persuasive and can be recommended even to readers not normally sympathetic to this composer. Strongly recommended.

Piano sonata; Pieces: *Bliss (One-step); Miniature scherzo; Rout trot; Study. Suite; Triptych.* Arr. of BACH: *Das alte Jahr vergangen ist (The old year has ended).*
*** Chandos Dig. CHAN 8979 [id.]. Philip Fowke.

The biggest work on the disc is the *Sonata*. Its neo-romantic rhetoric is less convincing than some of the earlier pieces he composed, in particular the *Suite* (1925). There are some other lighter pieces like the *The Rout trot* and *Bliss* (*One-step*), written in the 1920s when his inspiration was at its freshest. Good performances and excellent recording, made in The Maltings, Snape.

VOCAL MUSIC

Lie strewn the white flocks.
*** Hyperion CDA 66175 [id.]. Shirley Minty, Judith Pierce (flute), Holst Singers & O, Hilary Davan Wetton – BRITTEN: *Gloriana: Choral dances;* HOLST: *Choral hymns from Rig Veda.* ***

Bliss's *Pastoral* is given a winning performance by the Holst Singers and Orchestra, with the choral sections (the greater part of the work) aptly modest in scale but powerful in impact. With glowing sound and very attractive works for coupling, this is an outstanding issue.

Bloch, Ernest (1880–1959)

Baal Shem.
*** Decca Dig. 452 051-2 [id.]. Joshua Bell; Baltimore SO/Davis Zinman – BARBER: *Violin concerto*; WALTON: *Violin concerto.****

Bloch's own 1939 orchestrations of his three popular Hasidic pieces for violin and piano, *Baal Shem*, offers a fine, unusual makeweight for Bell's prizewinning disc of the Barber and Walton concertos.

Violin concerto.
(M) *** EMI (SIS) CDM7 63989-2 [id.]. Lord Menuhin, Philh. O, Kletzki – BERG: *Violin concerto.* ***

(i) *Violin concerto. Baal Shem.*
*** ASV Dig. CDDCA 785. (i) Michael Guttman; RPO, Serebrier (with SEREBRIER: *Momento; Poema* **).

Menuhin's deeply felt and finely recorded 1963 account is passionate and committed from the very first note, and any weaknesses in the score are quite lost when the playing is so compelling. Paul Kletzki accompanies with equal distinction. The 1964 Kingsway Hall recording sounds very well indeed.

The newcomer from Michael Guttman has both fire and colour, and no attempt is made to rein in the freely rhapsodic flow of the piece. It also has well-balanced modern digital recording and an interesting bonus.

From Jewish life (orch. Palmer).
*** RCA Single 09026 61966-2 [id.]. Steven Isserlis, Moscow Virtuosi, Spivakov – TAVENER: *Eternal memory.* ***

Bloch's soliloquy, if more extrovert and tangible than the drifting mysticism of Tavener's *Eternal memory*, nevertheless makes an apt coupling, especially when played with poignant warmth of feeling in this judicious expansion by Christopher Palmer of the composer's original version (for cello and piano) to feature instead orchestral strings.

(i) *Israel Symphony;* (ii) *Schelomo.*
(M) **(*) Van. 08 4047.71 [OVC 4047]. (i) Christensen, Basinger, Fraenkel, Politis, Heder, Watts; (ii) Nelsova; Utah SO, Abravanel.

Bloch's *Israel Symphony* is a large-scale work, but its way of anticipating the style of Hollywood film composers means that the music has something in common with the soundtracks of Hollywood's biblical epics. The performance here has the vigour and spontaneity that are characteristic of Abravanel's Utah performances, and the only snag is that the soloists, who are introduced at the end of the work, are wobbly and not especially distinguished. *Schelomo* is an appropriate coupling. The recordings were made in 1967 and are transferred to CD with great success.

Schelomo (Hebraic rhapsody) for cello and orchestra.
(N) (BB) *** Virgin Classics Dig. VBD5 61490-2 [CDVB 61490] [id.]. Steven Isserlis, LSO, Hickox – ELGAR: *Cello concerto;* KABALEVSKY: *Cello concerto No. 2* R.STRAUSS: *Don Quixote;* TCHAIKOVSKY: *Rococo variations* etc. ***
*** RCA Dig. RD 60757 [60757-2-RC]. Ofra Harnoy, LPO, Mackerras – BRUCH: *Adagio on Celtic themes* etc. ***
*** Sony Dig. SK 57961 [id.]. Yo-Yo Ma, Baltimore SO, David Zinman – ALBERT: *Cello concerto;* BARTOK: *Viola concerto.* ***
(B) *** Sony SBK 48278 [id.]. Leonard Rose, Phd. O, Ormandy – FAURE: *Elégie* ***; LALO: *Concerto* **(*); TCHAIKOVSKY: *Rococo variations.* ***

The dark intensity of Isserlis's solo playing and the sharp, dramatic focus of Hickox in the big climactic orchestral tuttis are magnetic, preventing Bloch's youthful outpouring on Solomon and the Song of Songs from sounding self-indulgent. Warm, refined recording. This now comes as part of a highly recommendable and very generous Virgin bargain Double, which includes key cello works by five different composers, all in first-class performances.

Harnoy also catches the passionate, Hebraic feeling of the melodic line and in this is matched by Mackerras, whose central climax is riveting. Fine, well-balanced and expansive sound.

Yo-Yo Ma is more cultured and refined than many of his current rivals, but there are moments when Solomon drops his voice, as it were, and dispenses his wisdom in a whisper rather than in full-throated fervour. It comes with an interesting first recording of a rewarding *Cello concerto* by the New York composer, Stephen Albert.

A darkly passionate, rhapsodical account from Leonard Rose, with an equally strong accompaniment from Ormandy. The recording balance is close, which reduces the possible dynamic range, but the compelling power of the music-making triumphs – this very good 71-minute compilation is worthy of a fine (perhaps underrated) cellist.

Violin sonatas Nos. 1; 2 (Poème mystique); Baal Shem: Nigun. Nuit exotique.
(N) (M) *** Carlton Dig. 30366 00232. Lydia Mordkovitch, Julian Milford.

Lydia Mordkovitch, passionate and intense, with her rich range of tone-colours, is an ideal interpreter of this music. With Julian Milford an equally committed partner, she brings out a purposefulness behind Bloch's eager rhapsodizing, not least in the span of almost half an hour making up the single movement of the second sonata, subtitled *Poème mystique*. From the hushed opening through to the passionate close, she plays with rapt concentration, relishing the sensuous beauty drawn from an unexpected amalgam of Jewish music and plainchant. That was written in 1924, but four years earlier the *First sonata* found Bloch in a more violent mood, weighty in his demands on both violinist and pianist. The well-known *Nigun* from the *Baal Shem* sequence and the evocative *Nuit exotique* make up a generous collection of Bloch's violin music. Warm, well-balanced recording.

Suite in A min. for viola and piano
(N) (***) Biddulph mono LAB 148 [id.]. William Primrose, Fritz Kitzinger – BAX; HINDEMITH: *Sonatas* (***).

During the 1940s when Bloch's music enjoyed much exposure, Primrose's 1938 recording on four HMV red-label 78s of the *Suite for viola and piano* was one of the mainstays of the catalogue. At present it has fallen from the repertoire and one appreciates that its rather loose construction and garrulity are factors in its neglect. Primrose and his excellent partner make out the strongest case for this piece, and considering its provenance the sound is amazingly good.

Blomdahl, Karl-Birger (1916–68)

Symphonies Nos. 1–2; 3 (Facetter).
*** BIS Dig. CD 611 [id.]. Swedish RSO, Segerstam.

Karl-Birger Blomdahl's *First Symphony*, written in his mid-twenties during the war, is not particularly individual and, though more than student work, is less than a mature one. There is a certain debt to his master, Hilding Rosenberg, and, in the slow movement, Honegger. At the same time a strong symphonic impulse runs through it. Blomdahl is an eclectic figure: there are echoes of Bartók, Hindemith and serial composers in the *Second* and *Third Symphonies*. The *Third* is a dark and powerful piece and though it is, as one critic put it, 'deficient in thematic vitality', there is a powerful atmosphere. Good performances by the Swedish Radio Orchestra under Segerstam and excellent BIS recording.

Blow, John (1649–1708)

Ode on the death of Mr Henry Purcell; Amphion Anglicus (songs): *Cloë found Amintas lying all in tears; Why weeps Asteria; Loving above himself (Poor Celadon); Shepherds, deck your crooks; Ah Heav'n! What is't I hear?; Epilogue: Sing, sing ye muses.*
(B) *** Sony Seon SBK 60097 [id.]. René Jacobs, James Bowman, soloists, Leonhardt Consort, Gustav Leonhardt.

The *Ode on the death of Mr Henry Purcell* is a most welcome addition to the catalogue, particularly as it is performed so superbly here under Gustav Leonhardt. There are some striking chromaticisms and dissonances and some inventive and noble music. James Bowman is the only native singer (he is in good voice, too) but the others – notably René Jacobs – are no less intelligent and stylish. Both the performance and recording are fine for this short but rewarding disc.

Ode on the death of Mr Henry Purcell: Mark how the lark and linnet sing. Ah, heav'n! What is't I hear?.
*** Hyperion Dig. CDA 66253 [id.]. James Bowman, Michael Chance, King's Consort, King – PURCELL: *Collection.* ***

Where Leonhardt on Seon is spacious in his concept and more detailed in his concern for word-meanings, the result also more polished, Robert King's spontaneous style is infectious with the orchestral comments engagingly animated. Both performances are highly rewarding, and in the last resort couplings will dictate choice. The Hyperion disc is more expensive but includes a quarter of an hour more music.

Venus and Adonis.

*** O-L (IMS) Dig. 440 220-2. Bott, George, Crabtree, Gooding, King, Grant, Robson, Agnew, Westminster Abbey School Choristers, New L. Consort, Pickett.

(B) *** HM Dig. HMA 190 1276 [id.]. Argenta, Dawson, Varcoe, Covey-Crump, L. Bar. & Ch., Medlam.

Venus and Adonis is already represented on CD, at bargain price, but Pickett has a pair of trump cards to play: Catherine Bott's imaginative, enticing Venus and Michael George's strongly characterized Adonis. The result is that this simple drama springs to life with unexpected vividness. The supporting cast is excellent, and so is the recording, and we are made to realize that this is a far finer and deeper work than hitherto suspected.

Venus and Adonis is like a Lully opera in miniature. Charles Medlam with London Baroque gives a period performance and takes care that the early instruments are well blended rather than edgy and the choral sound is full, bright and clean. The soloists too are all remarkable for sweetness and freshness of tone. This record is now offered at bargain price in the Musique d'Abord series.

Boccherini, Luigi (1743–1805)

Cello concertos Nos. 1 in E flat, G.474; 2 in A, G.475; 3 in D, G.476; 4 in C, G.477.

(BB) **(*) Arte Nova Dig. 74321 34041-2 [id.]. Emil Klein, Hamburg Soloists.

Cello concertos Nos. 5 in D, G.478; 6 in D, G.479; 7 in G, G.480; 8 in C, G.481.

(BB) *** Arte Nova Dig. 74321 51632-2 [id.]. Emil Klein, Hamburg Soloists.

The Romanian musician, Emil Klein, successfully manages the joint roles of solo cellist and conductor of the Hamburg Soloists. He is now in process of recording all Boccherini's cello concertos for Arte Nova, and he proves to be an excellent player with a small, sweet, cleanly focused timbre. He is equal to the considerable technical demands of these works, his intonation secure in the instrument's upper range, as is readily shown in the demanding higher tessitura of the *Adagio* of G.479 (where he shares a luscious duet with the orchestra's principal violin), and before that in G.478. This same D major work produces some fizzing bursts of virtuosity in the closing Rondo, and there are nicely pointed rhythms in the finale of G.477. Comparable, sharply articulated bravura adds to the character of the first movement of G.480, while the famous slow movement of that same work is shaped with touching eloquence. The Hamburg Soloists are a somewhat larger chamber group than their name suggests, although their tonal spectrum is amplified by a rather too reverberant acoustic on the first disc. The resonance seems better contained on the second, and on both nicely alert playing from the orchestra adds to the listener's pleasure.

Cello concertos Nos. 1 in E flat, G.474; 7 in G, G.480; 9 in B flat, G.482.

(M) **(*) Virgin Veritas/EMI Dig. VER5 61239-2. Wouter Möller, Linde Consort, Linde.

The Linde Consort, renowned for their baroque repertoire, now venture equally authentically into the *galant* world of Boccherini. Here we have the original version of the *B flat Concerto* played freshly, if without strong individuality, by the excellent Wouter Möller. The orchestral group (4.2.2.1, with 2 oboes, 2 hand horns and harpsichord) plainly seeks a chamber style, but the resonant acoustic amplifies the effect of both the forwardly placed soloist and the accompanying group. Möller plays the fine slow movement of G.482 with restrained *espressivo*. The Linde Consort provide polished accompaniments, and intonation (so important when there is only the merest hint of vibrato) is excellent: the finale of the *B flat Concerto* has an attractively easy pacing. The other works are hardly less successful.

Cello concerto No. 2 in D, G.479.

(B) *** DG Double 437 952-2 (2) [id.]. Rostropovich, Zurich Coll. Mus., Sacher – BERNSTEIN: *3 Meditations;* GLAZUNOV: *Chant du Ménestrel;* SHOSTAKOVICH: *Cello concerto No. 2;* TARTINI: *Cello concerto;* TCHAIKOVSKY: *Andante cantabile* etc; VIVALDI: *Cello concertos.* ***

Although essentially a performance in the grand manner, Rostropovich is so compelling that reservations are swept aside. He is given an alert accompaniment by Sacher, and the recording has fine body and presence. This is now part of a self-recommending Double DG bargain anthology.

Cello concertos Nos. 3 in D, G.476; 7 in G, G.480; 9 in B flat, G.482. (i) *Aria accademica in B flat, G.557.*

**(*) Astrée Audivis Dig. E 8517 [id.]. Christophe Coin, Limoges Bar. Ens., Coin; (i) with Marta Almajano.

Christophe Coin directs this excellent Limoges period-instrument group from the cello, and they accompany most stylishly. With his small-toned baroque cello, his playing is subtle and fastidiously elegant, its expressive feeling never worn on the sleeve. He is the exact opposite of Rostropovich, and those who enjoy intimacy in these works will find this much to their taste. The *Aria accademica* is included for its cello obbligato, and indeed it opens as if it is going to be another concerto, but then makes even greater bravura demands on its soprano soloist. It is sung expertly though brightly rather than seductively.

Cello concertos Nos. 4 in C, G.477; 6 in D, G.479; 7 in G, G.480; 8 in C, G.481.
(M) *** Teldec/Warner 9031 77624-2 [(M) id. import]. Anner Bylsma, Concerto Amsterdam, Schröder.

These concertos were originally published as Nos. 1–4 but are numbered as above in the Gérard catalogue. They are scored for strings with the addition of simple horn parts in Nos. 4 and 8, and they are agreeable works which sit easily between the *galant* and classical styles. There are few moments of routine in the writing, and it is always elegant and pleasing. *No. 6 in D major* is a particularly fine work, while the finale of No. 8 is very jolly. Anner Bylsma is a fine player, well-suited to this repertoire, while Schröder's accompaniments are most stylish and full of vitality. The 1965 recording is first class and, like so many of Teldec's *Das alte Werk* series, the immaculate CD transfer makes the very most of the sound.

Cello concertos Nos. 5 in D, G.478; 7 in G, G.480.
(N) ** Sony Dig. SK 60680 [id.]. Yo-Yo Ma, Amsterdam Bar. O, Ton Koopman – BACH: Chorales. **

Yo-Yo Ma has now taken up a period cello and this coupling of Bach chorales (played somewhat romantically) with Boccherini (a composer not obviously in the baroque category), does not work out very well. Koopman directs with rhythmic point and finds plenty of orchestral colour, but Ma's at times somewhat recessive solo contribution, is stylistically insecure, the timbre rather dry, and the playing itself lacking in charm. Finales come off best, though the cadenzas are not a great asset.

(i) *Cello concertos Nos. 6 in D, G.479; 7 in G, G.480;* (ii) *9 in B flat, G.482; 10 in D, G.483.*
(B) *** Erato/Warner Ultima 3984 201040-2 (2) [(M) id. import]. Frédéric Lodéon; (i) Lausanne CO, Jordan; (ii) Bournemouth Sinf., Guschlbauer.

This set combines two sets of performances recorded four years apart. Lodéon was in his thirties at the time and plays splendidly throughout. His playing is stylish and eloquent, and in the *G major concerto*, G.480, originally unearthed by Maurice Gendron, he is wonderfully fresh and fervent; in his hands the better-known *D major Concerto*, G.479 (also recorded by Bylsma and Rostropovich), has tenderness and depth. He is well accompanied by both groups, but the two Lausanne performances (from 1981) have slightly superior sound. The snag to this pair of records is the playing time of only 85 minutes, whereas the competing Bylsma collection manages to get four concertos (including G.479 and G.480) on a single mid-priced CD.

Cello concerto No. 7 in G, G.480.
(B) *** Carlton IMP Classics Dig. 30367 00912 [id.]. Felix Schmidt, ECO, Heath – BEETHOVEN: *Triple concerto.* ***

This is the concerto from which Grützmacher extracted the slow movement in his phoney, cobbled-together 'Boccherini Concerto', the movement everyone remembers. It makes an unusual but apt and attractive coupling for the Trio Zingara's excellent version of the Beethoven *Triple concerto*.

(i) *Cello concerto No. 9 in B flat* (original version, revised Gendron); (ii; iii) *Flute concerto in D, Op. 27* (attrib.; now thought to be by Franz Pokorny); (iv) *Symphonies Nos. 3 in C; 5 in B flat, Op. 12/3 & 5;* (v) *Guitar quintets Nos. 4 in D (Fandango); 9 in C (La Ritirata di Madrid);* (vi) *String quartet in D, Op. 6/1;* (iii) *String quintet in E, Op. 13/5: Minuet* (only).
(B) *** Ph. Duo 438 377-2 (2) [id.]. (i) Gendron, LOP, Casals; (ii) Gazzelloni; (iii) I Musici; (iv) New Philh. O, Leppard; (v) Pepe Romero, ASMF Chamber Ens.; (vi) Italian Qt.

Entitled 'The best of Boccherini including the *Minuet*', this most attractive anthology was assembled especially for the Philips Duo series. It is well documented and the famous *Minuet* could hardly be presented more winningly, the one digital recording here. It is good, too, that Gendron's version of the *Cello concerto* is included, for he pioneered the return of the original version (without Grützmacher's reworking), and he plays it admirably. The *Flute concerto* is a galant piece, elegantly played by Gazzelloni, and one can see why it was mistakenly attributed; Boccherini is all too readily dismissed as *la femme de Haydn*, but underneath the surface charm and elegance that one associates with him there are deeper currents and an altogether special pathos to disturb the attentive listener. Both *Symphonies* are full of vitality in these excellent performances under Raymond Leppard and are very well recorded. The Italian Quartet's performance of the *D major Quartet* is notable for its freshness and refinement. The charming *Guitar quintets* were arranged by Boccherini for his Spanish patron, the Marquis Benavente. The performances are unfailingly warm and sensitive and they are well recorded too, although there is a touch of thinness on top. The set is supported with good documentation.

Cello concerto in B flat (arr. Grützmacher).
(N) (M) *** EMI CDM5 66896-2 [CDM5 66948]. Jacqueline du Pré, ECO, Barenboim – HAYDN: *Concertos: 1–2.* ***
*** Sony MK 39964 [id.]. Yo-Yo Ma, St Paul

CO, Zukerman – J. C. BACH: *Sinfonia concertante* etc. **(*)
(BB) *** Naxos Dig. 8.550059; *4550059* [id.]. Ludovít Kanta, Capella Istropolitana, Peter Breiner – HAYDN: *Cello concertos Nos. 1 & 2.* ***

Jacqueline du Pré chose to record the completely unauthentic Grützmacher version of this concerto, but as she said herself, 'The slow movement is so beautiful', much more beautiful in fact than the one Boccherini provided. Working for the first time in the recording studio with her husband, Daniel Barenboim, du Pré was inspired to some really heart-warming playing, broadly romantic in style, but then that is what Grützmacher plainly asks for. Perhaps occasionally, by musical instinct, interpreting musicians know better than scholars. The 1967 recording is very good, if not quite as well focused as the couplings, but the performance is endearing. Du Pré admirers will surely feel that this is an apt choice for reissue as one of EMI's 'Great recordings of the century', and the disc now offers two Haydn cello concertos instead of one.

Like Jacqueline du Pré before him, Yo-Yo Ma chooses the Grützmacher version. He plays it with taste and finesse, not wearing his heart on his sleeve as obviously as du Pré, but with his warm, if refined, timbre and style not missing the romanticism. The recording is first class.

Ludovít Kanta's playing is distinguished by imaginative and musicianly phrasing and a warm tone. The Slovak players under Peter Breiner give a good account of themselves, and this can hold its own against versions costing twice or three times as much.

Symphonies: in D, G.490; in D min. (La casa del diavolo), Op. 12/4; in A; in F, Op. 35/3–4.
(B) **(*) HM Dig. Musique d'Abord HMA 190121 [id.]. Ensemble 415, Chiara Banchini.

Boccherini could write sunny, three-movement symphonies with winning *Andantes*, like the attractive A major work here, Op. 35/3, in which the central movement is a serenade. The F major work, Op. 35/4, has an assertive opening movement but is most notable for its agreeable finale, which has a central Minuet. But Boccherini could also be both innovative and dramatic, as in the *D minor Symphony*, subtitled *La casa del diavolo*. These period-instrument performances by the excellent Ensemble 415, led by Chiara Banchini, are very enjoyable. The slight drawback is the resonance of the recording which tends to cloud the busier fortissimos.

Symphonies, Op. 12, Nos. 1 in D; 2 in E flat; 3 in C; 4 in D min.; 5 in B flat; 6 in A.
(B) *** Ph. Duo 456 067-2 (2) [id.]. New Philh. O, Leppard.

Boccherini's Op. 12 was published in 1776. The scoring is for the normal classical orchestra, including two flutes or oboes and horns; but the composer's individuality emerges in his writing for the strings – with divided cellos – which are always predominant in the main argument. Even so, there are many pleasing touches of woodwind colour. The *E flat Symphony* (No. 2) is a remarkably fine work, virtually a sinfonia concertante with important bravura duets, first for two violins, then for a pair of cellos (the composer's own instrument); there is even a cadenza. The other symphonies are all of comparable interest, with Boccherini's silken melancholy strongly featured in the lyrical writing. This set is well worth exploring, particularly as Leppard consistently secures playing from the highly alert New Philharmonia Orchestra that is polished, elegant and never superficial. The Philips 1971 recording is excellent and so is the CD transfer, losing nothing of the bloom but firming up the overall focus admirably.

Symphonies: in D; in E flat; in A; in F; in E flat; in B flat, Op. 35/1–6.
*** Hyperion Dig. CDA 66903 [id.]. L. Festival O, Ross Pople.

The Op. 35 symphonies date from 1782. They are each in the three-movement, Italian overture style and are scored for oboes and horns (often used tellingly, especially in the finales of the *A major* and *B flat* works). The standard of invention is high and the music has plenty of vitality. The elegant *Andante* of the *A major* has much wistful charm – but then all the slow movements here are very attractive, not least the *soave* central movement of the *E flat Symphony* and the gentle march of the *B flat*, which then ends the set with a jolly finale. The performances here could hardly be bettered: crisp and neat, warm yet vital, and the recording is excellent. Boccherini set out to entertain his listeners and he surely succeeds here.

CHAMBER MUSIC

Flute quartets (for flute, violin, viola, 2 cellos), *Op. 17/1–6, G.419/424).*
(N) (BB) *** Naxos Dig. 8.553719 [id.]. Alexandre Magnin, Janáček Qt.

Flute quartets (for flute, violin, viola, 2 cellos) (unpublished) *Nos. 1–6, G.437–42.*
(N) *** Sony SK 62679 [id.]. Rampal, R. & B Pasquier, Pidoux, Sternay.

The *Op. 17 Quintets* are comparatively familiar and certainly rewarding, and they are very well played and recorded here. This Naxos disc is excellent value.

Boccherini's final collection until now has been unknown – the manuscipt languishing in the archives of Madrid's Palacio Real. They are even more delightful, and are marvellously played by Rampal and his colleagues. The scoring for two cellos adds richness but the textures here, while sensuous at times, are beautifully fresh and transparent. This is one of the finest Boccherini discs in the catalogue.

Guitar quintets Nos. 1–7, G.445/51; 9 (La Ritirata di Madrid), G.453.
(B) *** Ph. Duo 438 769-2 (2) [id.]. Pepe Romero, ASMF Chamber Ens.

Boccherini wrote or arranged twelve *Guitar quintets*, but only the present eight have survived, plus another version of *No. 4 in D* (*Fandango*), G.448. Although some of the music is bland, it is nearly all agreeably tuneful in an unostentatious way, and there are some highly imaginative touches, with attractive hints of melancholy and underlying passion. These performances by Pepe Romero (often willing to take a relatively minor role) and members of the ASMF Chamber Ensemble are wholly admirable, and Philips are especially good at balancing textures of this kind in the most natural way, the guitar able to be assertive when required without overbalancing the ensemble.

Guitar quintets Nos. (i) *4 in D (Fandango), G. 448. 7 in E min., G. 451; 9 in C (La Ritirata di Madrid), G. 453.*
(B) *** DG Classikon 449 852-2 [(M) id. import]. Narciso Yepes, Melos Qt; (i) with Lucero Tena.

In the DG bargain compilation from 1971 the sound is very good, full yet lively, and well projected. The playing is expert and, in the boisterous *Fandango* finale of No. 4, Lucero Tena makes a glittering contribution with his castanets. '*La Ritirata di Madrid*', famous from a string quintet, Op. 30/6, is used as the finale of the C major work. This picturesque evocation is created with a set of 12 brief variations set in a long slow crescendo, followed by a similarly graduated decrescendo, a kind of Spanish patrol with the 'night watch' disappearing into the distance at the end.

Piano quintets: in E min., G.407; in F, G.408; in D, G.411, Op. 56/1.
*** Audivis Dig. E 8518 [id.]. Patrick Cohen, Mosaïques Qt.

Piano quintets: in B flat, G.414; in E min., G.415; in C, G.418, Op. 57/2, 3 & 6.
*** Audivis Dig. E 8721 [id.]. Patrick Cohen, Mosaïques Qt.

The scope of Boccherini's achievement in the field of chamber music is becoming more and more apparent. There are twelve piano quintets and Patrick Cohen and the Mosaïques Quartet are obviously embarking – so far with great success – on a complete set. There is drama and grace and warmth of feeling, balanced by elegance, in this music; and the playing here also emphasizes its vitality. Slow movements are particularly eloquent and the use of period instruments in no way inhibits the expressive range of the music.

Piano quintets: in A min., Op. 56/2, G.412; in E flat, Op. 56/3, G.410; in E min., Op. 57/3, G.415; in C, Op. 57/6, G.418.
(B) *** DHM 05472 77448-2 [id.]. Les Adieux.

This a particularly attractive group of Boccherini works, and it is made the more so by its reissue on the bargain Baroque Esprit label. The lovely *E minor* (Op. 57/3) which starts the disc and the *A minor* (Op. 56/2) both have those hints of beguiling, almost sultry melancholy that makes this composer's musical language so distinctive. This accomplished period-instrument group turn in performances of great finesse and charm, though the recording-balance places the listener very much in the front row of the salon.

String quartet in E flat, Op. 58/2.
(M) *** Cal. CAL 6698 [id.]. Talich Qt – HAYDN: *Quartet No. 74;* MENDELSSOHN: *Quartet No. 2;* MICA: *Quartet No. 6.* ***

Boccherini's tuneful *E flat major Quartet*, Op. 58/2, opens with a friendly *Allegro lento*, yet characteristically its *Larghetto* brings a touch of gentle melancholy. The finale is a spirited *Allegro vivo*, played here with much geniality. Indeed the Talich are on top form and are very naturally recorded, so that this well-planned collection amounts to more than the sum of its parts.

String quintet in E, Op. 13/5.
**(*) Sony Dig. SK 53983 [id.]. Stern, Lin, Laredo, Ma, Robinson (with SCHUBERT: *String quintet in C.* **)

Stern and his illustrious colleagues create a much more intimate effect in Boccherini than they do in the Schubert coupling. This is the quintet with the famous 'Boccherini Minuet' and it is exquisitely played. An enjoyable if not distinctive account overall, and the recording balance seems less upfront than the coupling.

3 String quintets (with double bass), Op. 39/1–3 (G.337–9); String quartet in G (La Tiranna), Op. 44/4 (G 223).
(M) *** HM Suite Dig. HMT 7901334. Ensemble 415.

Boccherini wrote only three (out of a total of 125) quintets using a double-bass to (lightly) carry the bottom line of the harmony. They date from 1787 and the device seems very effective, with the careful balance of Ensemble 415 ensuring that Boccherini's scheme works extremely well. All three works are very attractive and none is predictable. The performances here are first class, refined and sensitive, and using period instruments always to bring aural pleasure. The recording is excellent too. A highly recommendable bargain reissue.

String sextets Nos. 1 in E flat, G.454; 2 in B flat, G.455; 5 in D, G.458, Op. 23/1–2 & 5.

**(*) HM Dig. HMC 90 1478 [id.]. Ens. 415.

Boccherini's special vein of melancholy, which yet never suggests gloom and indeed refreshes the spirit, is heard at its most appealing in these works, which are played with refined polish and feeling by this sensitive ensemble who use original instruments with much finesse. However, it must be said that the overall texture produced here is somewhat meagre, and at times one feels the need for the fuller, more robust sound of modern instruments.

KEYBOARD MUSIC

6 Quartets, Op. 26; Fandango (from *Quintettino, Op. 40/2*) (arr. for two harpsichords).
(M) **(*) HM Suite Dig. HMT 7901233. William Christie, Christophe Rousset (harpsichords).

It is not known who made this arrangement for two harpsichords of Boccherini's six *Quartets*, published in 1781 as Op. 32, but in the hands of William Christie and Christophe Rousset – who are obviously enjoying themselves – the music is robustly jolly and communicative and made to sound as if written for the keyboard, especially the imitative opening of No. 3. Each sonata is in two movements, with the second a minuet. The *Fandango* from Op. 40/2 is, not surprisingly, the most striking movement of all; but there is plenty of verve throughout, even if the close balance of the two harpsichords means that the dynamic range is limited.

VOCAL MUSIC

(i) *Stabat Mater, G.532* (first version); *Concert arias: Ah, no! son io che parlo; Care luci. Symphonies: in D min. (La Casa del Diavolo), Op. 12/4 (G.506); in C, Op. 21/3 (G.523); in A, Op. 37/4 (G.518).*
(N) (B) *** Erato/Warner Ultima Dig. 3984 24230-2 (2) [id.]. (i) Cecilia Gasdia; I Solisti Veneti, Claudio Scimone.

Boccherini wrote comparatively little vocal music but his *Stabat Mater*, an extended solo setting for soprano, here gloriously sung by Cecilia Gasdia, must be counted among his most inspired works. The beautiful sequence of movements towards the close – *Ei mater fons amoris . . . Tui nati vulnerati . . . Virgo virginum praeclara*, most affectingly sung here – contains some exquisite music, and in the despairing closing *Quando corpus morietur* Gasdia is very moving indeed. The music has a Mozartean purity of line, and the two concert arias which follow also take Mozart as their model. They are brilliantly sung: Claudio Scimone provides highly sensitive support, then on the second disc (with his I Solisti Veneti) offers vital and expressive accounts of three Symphonies, including not only *La Casa del Diavolo*, but a most appealing concertante work in C major. This was the composer's last symphony to be published (in 1798) and has prominent obbligato parts for oboe, violin and guitar which are most sympathetically played here and especially effective in the gentle *Grave* slow movement. The digital sound is bright and immediate, but there is plenty of ambient warmth.

Boeck, August de (1865–1937)

Symphony in G.
(B) *** Discover Dig. DICD 920126 [id.]. Brussels BRT PO, Karl Anton Rickenbacher – GILSON: *De Zee.* ***

The *Symphony in G* of August de Boeck, like Paul Gilson's suite, *De Zee*, with which it is coupled, is a ripely exotic work, full of Russian echoes. You might describe it as the Borodin symphony that Borodin didn't write, sharply rhythmic in the fast movements and sensuous in the slow movement, brilliantly orchestrated and full of tunes that are only marginally less memorable than those of the Russian master. Well played and recorded and, at Discover International's bargain price, an ideal disc for experimenting with.

Boëllmann, Léon (1862–97)

Cello sonata in A min., Op. 40; 2 Pieces for cello and piano, Op. 31.
*** Hyperion Dig. CDA 66888 [id.]. Lidström, Forsberg – GODARD: *Cello sonata in D min.* etc. ***

Boëllmann was one of 14 children, who left his native Alsace after the Franco-Prussian war to study in Paris, where he made a considerable name for himself as a teacher and organist. He is best known for his organ music and in particular the *Suite gothique*, whose final Toccata is a familiar *cheval de bataille*. The *A minor Sonata* reveals him to be a cultured and imaginative musician, more individual in style than Godard, but no less a craftsman. As in the Godard, Mats Lidström and Bengt Forsberg play with such passion and conviction that they almost persuade you that this piece is worthy to rank alongside the Brahms *Sonatas*. The recording is very acceptable, if rather close. Strongly recommended.

Böhm, Georg (1661–1733)

Capriccio in D; Chorale partitas on 'Ach wie nichtig, ach wie flüchtig'; on 'Wer nur den lieben Gott lässt walten'; Overture in D; Praeludium in G min.; Suites in C min.; E flat; F min.
*** Sony Dig. SK 53114 [id.]. Gustav Leonhardt (harpsichord/clavichord).

Böhm was one of the most interesting and influential North German precursors of Bach, and this excellent recital by Gustav Leonhardt makes a useful introduction to his art. His chorale partitas exercised a strong influence on Bach himself and his suites are both resourceful and inventive. Leonhardt intersperses the suites with the other pieces and ensures variety of texture and colour by using both clavichord and harpsichord, the latter a copy of an early-eighteenth-century instrument from Berlin and the clavichord a modern instrument by Skowroneck of Bremen. Excellent recording.

Boieldieu, François (1775–1834)

Harp concerto in 3 tempi in C.

❁ (M) *** Decca 425 723-2; *425 723-4*. Marisa Robles, ASMF, Iona Brown – DITTERSDORF; HANDEL: *Harp concertos* etc. *** ❁

Boieldieu's *Harp concerto* has been recorded before but never more attractively. The (originally Argo) recording is still in the demonstration class and very sweet on the ear. To make the reissue even more attractive, three beguiling sets of *Variations* have been added, including music by Handel and Beethoven and a *Theme, variations and Rondo pastorale* attributed to Mozart.

La Dame blanche (complete).

(N) (M) *** EMI Classics Dig. CMS5 56355-2 (2). Rockwell Blake, Verzier, Naouri, Fouchécourt, Deletré, Massis, Delunsch, Brunet, Dehont, Vajou, Ch. de Radio France, Paris Ens. O, Marc Minkowski.

This is a delightful set in every way. Completed in 1826, this lighthearted adaptation of Walter Scott's novel, sparkles from first to last, helped by the inspired direction of Marc Minkowski with an excellent team of soloists, who all sing with a natural feeling for the idiom. This is a piece which with its many lively ensembles points directly forward to Donizetti's *Daughter of the regiment* and even to Offenbach's two gendarmes from *Geneviève de Brabant*. Good teamwork is more important here than great solo singing, but here the cast has no weak link, with the outstanding Rossinian tenor, Rockwell Blake, matched by the others, not least Annik Massis as Anna and Mireille Delunsch as Jenny. For some non-French speakers there may be rather too much dialogue, but that can easily be excised on CD. Warm, well-balanced sound.

Boismortier, Joseph Bodin de (1689–1755)

6 Flute sonatas, Op. 1.

(N) *** Analekta Fleur de lys Dig. FL2 3008 [id.]. Claire Guimond, Luc Beauséjour.

The notes provided with this very enjoyable Analekta disc include a quote from contemporary literature (1754) : 'The fertile Monsieur Boismortier composed light and pleasing things and all that he gave to the public quickly sold. He came at the right time; people were avid for these pleasant trifles, which have a very attractive effect on the flutes and musettes: he took advantage of the current fashion and made double use of his time.'

Boismortier's Op. 91 was published at the beginning of the 1740s. Its music is elegant and well crafted, and the sonatas nicely blend French and Italian influences. All except the first, which has an opening Sicilienne, are in the fast–slow–fast Italian tradition (*Gayement–Gracieusement–Gayment*). They are beautifully and stylishly played by this excellent French-Canadian duo: Claire Guimond, baroque flute (who studied under Barthold Kuijken) and Luc Beauséjour (who studied the harpsichord under Ton Koopman). They play with an appealing delicacy to charm the ear, yet there is an underlying robustness which makes movements like the finale of *No. 3 in G minor* or the opening *Gayement* of the *E minor* (No. 4) seem far from merely trivial, while the gentle *Gracieusement* of No. 5 in *A major* trips along with disarming sweetness. The recording (as one expects from this Canadian label) is expertly balanced and altogether natural.

(i) *Suites for solo flute Nos. 3, 5 & 6;* (ii) *Harpsichord suites Nos. 1–4.*

(B) *** Cal. Approche Analogue/Dig. CAL 6865 [(M) id.]. (i) Luc Urbain; (ii) Mireille Lagacé.

These four *Harpsichord suites* were Boismortier's only works for harpsichord, published as a set in Paris in 1731. They are very much in the style of the *Pièces de clavecin* of Rameau, and Boismortier follows his practice in giving each movement a colourful sobriquet. *La Cavernesque*, which begins the *First Suite*, is aptly titled. The invention is attractive, if perhaps not as individual as with Rameau, although the finale of the last suite shows Boismortier writing a very characterful set of variations. Mireille Lagacé is an excellent advocate and she uses a restored Hemsch, which is truthfully recorded and suits the repertoire admirably. Interleaved with the harpsichord works are three suites for unaccompanied flute, also made up with dance movements but each with an introductory *Prelude* which has an improvisatory feeling about it. Again the playing is highly responsive, to make this a rewarding concert.

Première suite de clavecin.

(B) ** Cal. Approche CAL 6838 [(M) id.]. Mireille Lagacé – RAMEAU: *6 Concerts en sextuor*. **

Bodin de Boismortier was a contemporary of Rameau, and his musical career was divided between Spain and France. His harpsichord pieces (each of which have sobriquets, like those of Rameau) have their individual flavours, as in the gentle melancholy of the sarabande (*La Valtudi-*

nière) and the rhythmically winning closing *Pièce en rondeau* (*La Décharnée*). They are expertly played by Mireille Lagacé, who uses a restored 1754 Hemsch, and the recording is realistic, provided you turn down the volume.

Boito, Arrigo (1842–1918)

Mefistofele (complete).

*** Decca Dig. 410 175-2 [id.]. Ghiaurov, Pavarotti, Freni, Caballé, L. Op. Ch., Trinity Boys' Ch., Nat. PO, Fabritiis.

(M) **(*) Decca 440 054-2 [id.]. Siepi, Del Monaco, Tebaldi, Cavalli, Santa Cecilia Academy, Rome, Ch. & O, Serafin.

The modern digital recording given to the Fabritiis set brings obvious benefits in the extra weight of brass and percussion – most importantly in the heavenly prologue. With the principal soloists all at their best – Pavarotti most seductive, Freni finely imaginative on detail, Caballé consistently sweet and mellifluous as Elena – this is a highly recommendable set.

On the earlier (1958) Decca Rome set, Serafin, the most persuasive Italian conductor of his day, draws glorious sounds from his performers, even from Mario del Monaco, who is here almost sensitive. Tebaldi is a rich-toned Margherita – almost too rich-toned for so frail a heroine – and Siepi makes an excellent Mefistofele. The Decca engineers came up trumps: the stereo remains remarkably spacious, particularly in the Prologue, making a good mid-priced alternative to the later Decca version.

Mephistofele: scenes.

(N) (M) **(*) Decca 458 242-2 [id.]. Cesare Siepi, Renata Tebaldi, Giuseppe di Stefano, St Cecilia, Rome Ch., & O, Serafin.

This selection disc is a curiosity. At about the same time, Decca recorded the opera complete with the same forces except for the tenor. This obviously represents the results of an unfinished project, and admirers of Giuseppe di Stefano – a subtler artist than Mario del Monaco, his Decca rival at that time – will be pleased to have this sample of his work in the late 1950s. His characterization is strong, and he gets good support from Siepi and Tebaldi. Excellent recording for its period.

Bononcini, Antonio (1677–1726)

La Decollazione de S. Giovanni Battista (oratorio; complete).

*** Tactus Dig. TC 675201 [id.]. Michael Van Göethen, Maurizio Barazzoni, Daniela Piccini, Fernanda Piccini, Virgilio Bianconi, Guastalla Bar. Op. O, Sandro Volta.

Antonio Bononcini's oratorio, *La Decollazione de S. Giovanni Battista* was first performed in Vienna during Lent in 1709, for Emperor Joseph I. It dramatizes the story of St John the Baptist's fatal encounter with Herod and Salome – using an Angel to make narrative comments – in a series of brief recitatives and often very beautiful da capo arias. If there is little or nothing in the way of red-blooded histrionics, Herod's central aria, *Nulla si nieghi* (with cello obbligato) is telling enough, and finely projected by the excellent bass, Virgilio Bianconi.

John the Baptist is a male alto role (Michael Van Goethen), and it is his soliloquy, *Bacio l'ombre e le catane*, movingly sung here, which is the emotional centre of the work. Salome's arias, and the interchanges with Herodias are essentially lyrical, and Bononcini's music portrays Salome herself as an almost ingenuous charmer, with Daniella Piccini here responding with ravishing tone and simplicity of line. It is the chorus (formed by the five soloists), which makes the touchingly tragic final comment on the outcome, *Morir il giusto*. The performance here is outstanding in every way, without a weak link in the cast, and Sandro Volta never presses too hard, yet keeps this often lovely music flowing forward most appealingly. The recording is first class. Alas, the libretto is in Italian only, with no translation; otherwise this might well have earned a Rosette.

Stabat Mater.

(B) *** Decca Double 443 868-2 (2) [id.]. Palmer, Langridge, Esswood, Keyte, St John's College, Cambridge, Ch., Philomusica, Guest – PERGOLESI: *Magnificat in C; Stabat Mater* **(*); D. SCARLATTI: *Stabat Mater;* A. SCARLATTI: *Domine, refugium factus es nobis; O magnum mysterium;* CALDARA: *Crucifixus;* LOTTI: *Crucifixus*. ***

This fascinating Double Decca collection centres on three different settings of the *Stabat Mater dolorosa*, a medieval poem describing the anguish of Mary during her son's crucifixion, an experience with which women, especially, have readily identified down through the ages. Although its origins date from the end of the thirteenth century, it was not until 1727 that it became part of the Roman liturgy.

Antonio Bononcini is not to be confused with Handel's rival, Giovanni, his older brother. Antonio's *Stabat Mater* is a work of genuine melodic distinction and affecting tenderness; there are some striking harmonies, even moments of drama, and in general a nobility and simple expressiveness that leave a strong impression. The St John's performance is wholly admirable and is very well recorded.

Bononcini, Giovanni (1670–1755)

Cello sonata in A min.; Trio sonata for 2 violins and continuo in D min. (i) Cantatas: *Già la stagion d'amore; Lasciami un sol momento; Misero pastorello; Siedi, Amarilli mia.*

*** Virgin/EMI Dig. VC5 45000-2. Gérard Lesne, Il Seminario Musicale.

Giovanni Bononcini's cantatas were popular and were published in London in 1721. They reveal their composer to be far more than a historical figure. *Lasciami un sol momento* stands out as a particularly moving work with its melancholy opening aria ('Leave me but for one moment, O bitter memory of my betrayed love') leading to a bravura finale, *Soffro in pace* ('I bear these chains in peace'). The instrumental works are also highly inventive and characterful: the *Lento* of the lively *Trio sonata* is gently touching and its finale wonderfully spirited. All this music is worth knowing, and the advocacy of these fine artists brings it fully to life. The expressive eloquence of Gérard Lesne's singing could not be more winning, using the most felicitous ornamentation. The recording too is first class.

Griselda (highlights).

(M) *** Decca (IMS) 448 977-2 (2) [id.]. Elms, Sutherland, M. Sinclair, Elkins, Malas, Amb. S., LPO, Bonynge – GRAUN: *Montezuma*. ***

Bononcini is remembered well enough as Handel's rival as an opera composer, but how rarely one has the chance to study his theatrical music. All credit to Richard Bonynge for resurrecting what by all accounts is his most impressive work, and providing a sample of a score of numbers. This music never matches Handel's in inspiration, but the numbers are nicely varied, with lovely arias for the patient Griselda (sung by Lauris Elms), simpler pastoral airs and a couple of jolly bass arias. Joan Sutherland's contribution in the castrato role of Ernesto is limited to four arias and a duet but, with bright, lively conducting from Richard Bonynge the whole performance is most enjoyable. Excellent (1966) Kingsway Hall recording and a full translation provided. Graun's *Montezuma* is also well worth having on CD.

Borodin, Alexander (1833–87)

'The World of Borodin': (i) *In the Steppes of Central Asia; Prince Igor:* (ii) *Overture;* (ii–iii) *Polovtsian dances;* (iv) *Symphony No. 2 in B min.;* (v) *String quartet No. 2: Nocturne;* (vi) *Scherzo in A flat;* (vii, viii) *Far from the shores of your native land;* (vii, ix) *Prince Igor: Galitzky's aria.*

(M) *** Decca Analogue/Dig. 444 389-2. (i) SRO, Ansermet; (ii) LSO, Solti; (iii) with London Symphony Ch.; (iv) LSO, Martinon; (v) Borodin Qt; (vi) Ashkenazy; (vii) Nicolai Ghiaurov; (viii) Zlatina Ghiaurov; (ix) London Symphony Ch. and LSO, Downes.

An extraordinarily successful disc. There can be few if any other collections of this kind that sum up a composer's achievement so succinctly or that make such a rewarding and enjoyable 76-minute concert. Solti's *Prince Igor overture* is unexpectedly romantic, and very exciting too; there is no finer account in the current catalogue, and the same can be said for the *Polovtsian dances*, with splendid choral singing. Both recordings date from 1966 and have vintage Decca sound. The *Nocturne* follows the *Overture* so effectively that one might have thought it the composer's own plan. Then comes *Galitzky's aria* (complete with chorus), where the sound is over-bright, but no matter, and the *Scherzo in A flat* follows – with Ashkenazy in fine form – before the choral *Polovtsian dances*. Ansermet's *In the Steppes of Central Asia* is warm and atmospheric, if the Suisse Romande violins fail to do its voluptuous main theme full justice, Ansermet's interpretation is spacious and vivid. After Nicolai Ghiaurov has reminded us of the melancholy side of the Russian spirit, we come finally to Martinon's unsurpassed 1960 LSO performance of the *B minor Symphony*, notable for its fast tempo for the famous opening theme. The strong rhythmic thrust suits the music admirably, the Scherzo has vibrant colouring and the slow movement, with a beautifully played horn solo, is most satisfying. The sound has remarkable presence and sparkle, and only in the massed violin tone is there a suggestion that the recording is not modern.

'Essential Borodin': Symphonies Nos. (i) *1 in E flat;* (ii) *2 in B min.;* (iii) *3 in A min.; In the Steppes of Central Asia;* (iv) *String quartet No. 2 in B min.;* (v–vi) Song: *From the shores of your far-off native land. Prince Igor:* (vii) *Overture;* (vii–viii) *Polovtsian dances;* (v; viii–ix) *Galitzky's aria; Konchak's aria.*

(B) *** Decca Double Analogue/Dig. 455 632-2 (2) [(M) id. import]. (i) RPO, Ashkenazy; (ii) LSO, Martinon; (iii) SRO, Ansermet; (iv) Borodin Qt; (v) Nicolai Ghiaurov; (vi) Zlatina Ghiaurov; (vii) LSO, Solti; (viii) L. Symphony Ch.; (ix) LSO, Edward Downes.

Decca have now happily expanded the programme contained on '*The World of Borodin*' (see above) to fit on a Double, and in doing so they represent the composer even more comprehensively for very little extra outlay. Ashkenazy's reading of the *First Symphony* is less high-powered than Martinon's superb account of No. 2, but its many delights come over richly, thanks not only to the quality of the RPO playing but also to the warm (1992) digital recording. Ansermet's touch in the unfinished *Third* is attractively alive and spontaneous, with some delightful moments from the SRO woodwind. The early stereo (1954) shows its age with distinct thinness in the upper range of the strings, but the warm ambience remains. What makes this extended programme especially attractive is the inclusion of the whole of the *Second String quartet*, rather than just the slow movement. The performance by the eponymous Borodin Quartet is masterly in every respect, and the new transfer of their 1961 recording is admirably full and gives a natural presence to the four players. In *Prince Igor* Ghiaurov now adds a second role by singing Konchak's aria from Act II in addition to Galitzky's aria from Act I.

In the Steppes of Central Asia; (i) *Nocturne* (from *String quartet No. 2*) arr. for violin & orchestra by Rimsky-Korsakov; *Petite suite* (orch. Glazunov); (ii; iii) *Requiem* (orch. Stokowski, arr. Simon). *Prince Igor: Overture;* (iii) *Chorus of Polovtsian maidens. Dance of Polovtsian maidens; Polovtsian march; Polovtsian dances.*
**(*) Cala Dig. CACD 1011 [id.]. Philh. O, Geoffrey Simon, with (i) Stephanie Chase; (ii) Ian Boughton; (iii) BBC SO Ch.

An interesting and valuable anthology that is recommendable, but for one curious and serious drawback. Borodin's 5-minute piano piece called *Requiem* is played in Stokowski's flamboyantly expansive orchestration, to which Geoffrey Simon has very effectively added solo tenor and male chorus. The piece is ingeniously based on 'Chopsticks'. It is in the form of a long crescendo and diminuendo, and the great double climax has been recorded with an exaggerated dynamic range which is far too wide. The other works are all given full-bodied sound, a shade lacking in sparkle, and a normal dynamic range. *In the Steppes of Central Asia*, rather forwardly recorded, would have been more effective with more dynamic contrast, a warmly languorous performance. The excerpts from *Prince Igor* include the sinuously seductive *Chorus of Polovtsian maidens* which opens Act II of the opera and also a version of the *Polovtsian march* which includes both chorus and off-stage band. In the march and the famous *Polovtsian dances*, the singing of the BBC Chorus is of a high standard, though Geoffrey Simon's direction is lively rather than electrifying, both here and in the Overture. Rimsky-Korsakov's concertante arrangement of the famous *Nocturne* for violin and orchestra – in spite of Stephanie Chase's pleasing advocacy – gives the piece the character of a salon encore, charming but insouciant. The *Petite suite*, a set of six piano miniatures orchestrated by Glazunov, comes off very engagingly.

In the steppes of Central Asia; Prince Igor: Overture; Polovtsian march and dances; Symphony No. 2 in B min.
(B) *** Tring Dig. TRP 104 [(M) id. import]. RPO, Ole Schmidt.

Too long neglected on disc, Ole Schmidt in the Royal Philharmonic Collection with ideal couplings offers an outstanding version at bargain price of the Borodin *Second Symphony*, beautifully played and recorded in vivid, open sound, one of the very finest at any price. In the first movement of the symphony Schmidt avoids the pitfall of adopting too slow a speed, thus avoiding any ponderousness while giving the music an idiomatically earthy tang, and from then on, rhythms are delectably sprung. After that brisk first movement Schmidt takes a relatively relaxed view of the *Prestissimo Scherzo*, again beautifully sprung. At a nicely flowing tempo the great horn solo of the slow movement is gloriously played by the RPO's long-time principal, Jeffrey Bryant. The crisply sprung finale is then full of panache. The *Prince Igor overture* again brings masterly horn-playing, while the *Polovtsian dances* and *March* also show off the brilliance of the RPO wind soloists. With performances like these it is all the more welcome to have the full complement of RPO players individually named.

Symphonies Nos. 1 in E flat; 2 in B min.; 3 in A min. (completed Glazunov); *In the Steppes of Central Asia; Nocturne* (orchestrated Nicolai Tcherepnin); *Petite suite* (arr. Glazunov); *Prince Igor: Overture;* (i) *Polovtsian dances.*
*** DG Dig. 435 757-2 (2). Gothenburg SO, Neeme Järvi; (i) with Gothenburg Ch.

For those wanting all three symphonies, the Järvi DG set remains recommendable. The alternative versions by Serebrier (ASV CDDCA 706) and Gunzenhauser (Naxos 8.550238) each have the advantage of being offered on a single CD, but Serebrier's performances – recorded in Rome – lack Russian feeling, and one needs a more sumptuous body of tone for this music than the Bratislava Radio Symphony Orchestra on Naxos can provide, with Gunzenhauser's accounts are fresh and pleasing, but undistinctive.

Järvi's *First* has plenty of individuality and colour; the slow movement is radiant, the Scherzo beautifully sprung and the finale made to anticipate the *Prince Igor overture* in its bright, rhythmic pointing. The *Second* is a strong, spacious reading; however, alongside Martinon and Ashkenazy, the first movement is somewhat lacking in bite and thrust. The *Third Symphony* (completed by Glazunov), comes off vividly, although it is not as strong a work as the other two. The other pieces are equally well played by the excellent Gothenburg orchestra, notably the *Petite suite*, although there are some reservations about Tcherepnin's very exotic orchestration of the famous *Nocturne* from the *D major String quartet*, and perhaps Järvi doesn't pull out all the stops in his undoubtedly vivid account of the *Polovtsian dances*. Yet the choral Swedish singing, if not uninhibited, is vital enough and even includes a brief solo interpolation representing the

Khan. The digital recording throughout is from DG's top drawer.

Symphonies Nos. 1 in E flat; 2 in B min.; In the Steppes of Central Asia.
*** Decca Dig. 436 651-2 [id.]. RPO, Ashkenazy.

With the opening in octaves brisk and dramatic and with speeds throughout that never drag, Ashkenazy's Decca reading of Borodin's *Second Symphony* is exceptionally warm and brilliant, helped by full-bodied Decca recording. The RPO wind soloists are outstanding, and the horn solo in the slow movement is satisfyingly opulent. The prestissimo Scherzo of the second movement is a special delight, not just brilliant but witty, and the dashing speed for the finale is thrilling. The coupling is both apt and generous. *In the Steppes of Central Asia* is a fine example of Borodin's genius, and it is given a warmly atmospheric performance here. If in the *Symphony No. 1* Ashkenazy's performance is less high-powered than in the *Second*, its many delights come over richly, thanks not only to the quality of the RPO's playing but also to the warm recording.

Symphony No. 1 in E flat.
(N) **(*) Finlandia Dig. 3984 228352-2 [id.]. Norwegian RO, Ari Rasilainen. – TCHAIKOVSKY: *Symphony No. 2.* **(*)

A very enjoyable and recommendable account of this delightful symphony from the Norwegian Radio Orchestra and their Finnish conductor. Not necessarily a first choice but it is spirited, and well enough played and recorded if you want the coupling. It certainly gives pleasure.

Symphony No. 2 in B min.
(***) Testament mono SBT 1048 [id.]. Philh. O, Paul Kletzki – TCHAIKOVSKY: *Manfred Symphony.* (***)
(N)(BB) *(*) Belair Dig. BAM 9724 [id.]. New Russian O, Oleg Poltevsky – RIMSKY-KORSAKOV: *Tsar Saltan – suite.****

Kletzki draws superb playing from the Philharmonia at a vintage period in the mid-1950s. The ravishing account of the slow movement has Dennis Brain at his peak in the big horn solo, backed by Bernard Walton on the clarinet and Sidney Sutcliffe on the oboe producing whispered pianissimos that caress the ear. The first movement is brisk and dramatic, while in the Scherzo the tonguing of the woodwind makes for phenomenal precision. As for the transfer, after a dull opening the bite and immediacy of the brass and woodwind are so vivid they give an illusion of stereo.

At super-bargain price on the Belair label, comes Poltevsky's version with an excellent orchestra drawn from a range of Moscow orchestras. Impossibly heavy at the start, the fluctuation of tempo in the first movement and the other three movements are taken broadly too. A disc worth hearing for an electrifying account of the *Tsar Saltan suite.*

Symphony No. 2 in B min.; Nocturne (orch. Tcherepnin).
(M) *** DG (IMS) Dig. 445 568-2 [id.]. Gothenburg SO, Järvi – RIMSKY-KORSAKOV: *Symphony No. 2 (Antar).* ***

In a surprisingly rare coupling, Järvi's expansive approach to both these Russian symphonies works well when the DG recording is so warm and full-bodied. His account of the Borodin *Second* is at its finest in the *Andante* in which the key melody, so beautifully introduced by the solo horn, returns on the full strings in a flood of romanticism. Tcherepnin's added orchestral colour in the *Nocturne* remains controversial, but this too is very well played and recorded.

Sextet (2 movements).
** Mer. Dig. CDE 84211 [id.]. Arienski Ens. – ARENSKY: *Quartet* ***; TCHAIKOVSKY: *Souvenir de Florence.* **

Borodin composed his *Sextet* on a visit to Heidelberg in 1860 but, unfortunately, only two of its movements survive. The Arienski Ensemble play with enthusiasm and conviction and are decently recorded.

String quartets Nos. 1 in A; 2 in D.
(BB) *** BMG/Arte Nova Dig. 74321 51633-2 [id.]. Russian Qt.

The popularity of Borodin's *Second Quartet*, using themes later made popular in the musical, *Kismet*, has tended to get in the way of appreciation of the equally delightful *First Quartet*, making this a very welcome coupling at bargain price. The Russian Quartet, a group of women players with exceptionally warm, fruity tone, make persuasive advocates of both works, with charm and tender lyricism brought out in the *First Quartet*, and with the sweetness and warmth in the *Second Quartet.* Warm, immediate sound to match.

String quartet No. 2 in D.
*** Decca Dig. 452 239-2 [id.]. Takács Qt – SMETANA: *String quartet No. 1.* ***
(***) Testament mono SBT 1061 [id.]. Hollywood Qt – GLAZUNOV: *5 Novelettes;* TCHAIKOVSKY: *String quartet No. 1.* (***)
(BB) *** CfP Silver Double CDCFPSD 4772 (2). Gabrieli String Qt – BRAHMS: *Clarinet quintet* **(*); DVORAK: *String quartet No. 12* ***; SCHUBERT: *String quartet No. 14.* ***
(M) *** Classic fM Dig. 75605 57027-2. Chilingirian Qt – DVORAK: *Quartet in F, Op. 96;* SHOSTAKOVICH: *Quartet No. 8.* ***
(M) **(*) Cal. CAL 6202 [id.]. Talich Qt – TCHAIKOVSKY: *Quartet No. 1.* ***
(M) **(*) Decca 425 541-2 [id.]. Borodin Qt –

SHOSTAKOVICH; TCHAIKOVSKY: *Quartets*. **(*)

An outstanding version of Borodin's *D major Quartet* comes from the Takács group, who play with fine ensemble and plenty of feeling, yet bring subtlety of colour and delicacy of texture, as well as warmth, to the famous *Notturno*. The recording has striking presence, and the Smetana coupling is hardly less impressive.

At the time when the Hollywood Quartet's version of the Borodin *Second Quartet* first appeared in 1953, there were complaints that the sound was steely and hard, and the work itself was in the doldrums. Although later recordings may match this Hollywood version, it is still a performance with persuasive freshness and ardour. The sound has been improved, and the addition of the Glazunov, which is new to the catalogue, enhances the disc's value. The playing-time runs to one second short of 80 minutes.

As part of an outstanding Classics for Pleasure Silver Double compilation of Romantic string quartets, the Gabrielis offer a finely wrought, sensitive and thoroughly polished performance of the Borodin, warm in feeling. At less than half the price of its main competitor, this is excellent value, for the recording is first class and beautifully transferred to CD.

On the Classic fM label the Chilingirian Quartet offer powerful, incisive performances of an apt and generous coupling, bringing together three of the most popular of Slavonic string quartets. With Levon Chilingirian an exceptionally alert leader whose violin-tone is given a slight edge by the full, immediate recording, rhythms in the Borodin are consistently well sprung, with no sentimentality in a warmly expressive account of the celebrated slow movement.

The Talich performance is characteristically refined and beautifully played; although there is no lack of warmth and the leader shapes the famous theme of the *Notturno* with ravishing purity of timbre and line, the performance lacks something in Slavonic voluptuousness compared with the Borodin Quartet. The digital recording is however first class, full and naturally balanced, and this is easily preferable to the Borodins' Decca alternative. Moreover the Tchaikovsky coupling is outstanding in every way.

The Borodins' version of the *Second Quartet* on Decca is very fine, though the forward recording, rich-textured, approaches fierceness in the CD transfer, and most will prefer a softer-grained effect.

Prince Igor (opera) complete.

*** Ph. Dig. 442 537-2 (3) [id.]. Kit, Gorchakova, Ognovienko, Minjelkiev, Borodina, Grigorian, Kirov Ch. & O, St Petersburg, Gergiev.

*** Sony Dig. S3K 44878 (3) [id.]. Martinovich, Evstatieva, Kaludov, Ghiuselev, Ghiaurov, Miltcheva, Sofia Nat. Op. Ch. & Festival O, Tchakarov.

(N) (M) **(*) EMI CMS5 66814-2 [CDMB 66814] (2). Chekerliiski, Christoff, Todorov, Sofia Nat. Theatre Op. Ch. & O, Jerzy Semkow.

Gergiev has been an inspired musical director of the Kirov company in St Petersburg, and this electrifying account of Borodin's epic opera reflects not only his own magnetic qualities as a conductor but also the way he has welded his principal singers as well as the chorus and orchestra into a powerful team. Textually the oddity of this version is that Acts I and II are given in reverse order from the usual, with the substantial Prologue here followed by the first Polovtsian scene and its spectacular dances. Only then do you get the scene at Prince Galitsky's court, normally Act I, leading up to Yaroslavna's great lament, here superbly sung by Galina Gorchakova. The reordering works well, with contrasting elements better separated. Otherwise Gergiev generally follows that well-established edition, but he has included material omitted from Borodin's copious sketches, notably an extended monologue of lament for Igor himself as a prisoner of Khan Konchak in Act III, '*Why did I not fall on the field of battle*'. It may not be as fine as the aria Igor sings in the first Polovtsian scene, using the great melody introduced in the overture, but that and other supplementary passages are very welcome. That alone puts this ahead of the fine rival Sony recording from Tchakarov with Bulgarian forces, and Gergiev is even more sharply dramatic, generally adopting faster speeds. The Philips recording too is weightier than the Sony, with the chorus in particular sounding satisfyingly large as well as incisive. On the solo casting, honours are much more even. The two principal women here, not just Gorchakova but Olga Borodina too as Konchak's daughter, Konchakovna, are both magnificent, even finer than their Bulgarian rivals, but neither principal bass, Vladimir Ognovienko as Galitsky and Bulat Minjelkiev as Konchak, can match the vocal richness or character of the Bulgarians, Ghiuselev and Ghiaurov, both older-sounding but still compelling. Gegam Grigorian in the tenor role of Igor's son gives a lusty performance, while Mikhail Kit as Igor himself, though often gritty and even fluttery of tone, sings thoughtfully and intelligently, making him a fair match for his Bulgarian rival.

On Sony, Nicola Ghiuselev as Galitzky is powerful but rather unsteady and Nicolai Ghiaurov makes a splendid Konchak. Boris Martinovich makes a firm, very virile Igor, and both the principal women have vibrantly Slavonic voices which still never distract in wobbling. The dramatic tension in this long work is held very well and its richness of invention over its very episodic span comes across vividly, notably in all its memorable melody and high colour.

In the colourful EMI recording, Act III is completely omitted, on the grounds that it was almost entirely the work of Rimsky-Korsakov and Glazunov. Boris Christoff as both Galitzky and Konchak easily outshines all rivals. Jerzy Semkow with his Sofia Opera forces is most sympathetic, but the other soloists are almost all disappointing, with the women sour-toned and the men often strained and unsteady. The sound is limited but agreeably atmospheric. The set has now been re-transferred from three discs onto a pair of very full CDs.

Prince Igor: Overture and Polovtsian dances.
(M)*** EMI CDM5 66983-2 [CDM5 66998]. Beecham Choral Soc., RPO, Beecham – RIMSKY-KORSAKOV: *Scheherazade.****

Prince Igor: Polovtsian dances.
(M) *** Penguin Classics DG 460 618-2 [id.]. BPO, Karajan – RIMSKY-KORSAKOV: *Scheherazade.* ***
(M) *** Decca Phase 4 443 896-2 [id.]. Welsh Nat. Op. Ch., RPO Ch., RPO, Stokowski – MUSSORGSKY: *Night on the bare mountain* etc. ** (with TCHAIKOVSKY: *1812 overture* etc. **(*))
(M) **(*) Mercury (IMS) 434 308-2 [id.]. London Symphony Ch., LSO, Dorati – RIMSKY-KORSAKOV: *Capriccio espagnol* etc. ***

Beecham's 1957 performance of the *Polovtsian dances* – now reissued as one of EMI's 'Great recordings of the Century' – sweeps the board, even though it omits the percussion-led opening *Dance of the Polovtsian maidens*. Beecham draws an almost Russian fervour from his choristers. The recorded sound is little short of astonishing in its fullness, vividness and clarity.

Karajan's Berlin Philharmonic version now on Penguin Classics has great flair and excitement, though it lacks a chorus.

Stokowski misses out the percussion-led opening dance, but there is no question about the excitement he creates at the climax, with the chorus singing their hearts out. The recording is sumptuous and spectacular. However, the coupled *1812 overture* is rather coarse.

Dorati's Mercury recording is not among the most refined from this source, but no one could say that effect lacks vividness or boisterous vitality.

Børresen, Hakon (1876–1954)

Symphonies Nos. 2 in A, (The Sea) Op. 7; 3 in C, Op. 21.
(N) *** CPO Dig. CPO 999 353-2 [id.]. Frankfurt Radio SO, Ole Schmidt.

Once hailed as the white hope of Danish music, Hakon Børresen has virtually disappeared from the repertoire. He enjoyed considerable fame and status during his lifetime; Nikisch conducted his *Violin concerto* and King Christian X even cycled unannounced to his home to consult Børreson about his son's musical aspirations. He was a pupil of Svendsen, who conducted the première of his *First Symphony* (as he had Nielsen's) and the orchestration of the *Second Symphony* (1904) is expert. It is not quite as fresh and individual as Svendsen but both symphonies have a lot going for them. The delightful scherzo of No. 1 is as transparent in its orchestration as Mendelssohn, and the first movement has a Dvořákian sense of openness and space. Attractive works, not the last word in originality, but very persuasively presented by Ole Schmidt and the Frankfurt Radio Orchestra, and well recorded.

Bortkiewicz, Sergei (1877–1952)

Piano concerto No. 1 in B flat min., Op. 16.
*** Hyperion Dig. CDA 66624 [id.]. Coombs, BBC Scottish SO, Maksymiuk – ARENSKY: *Piano concerto.* ***

Serge Bortkiewicz's concerto is conservative in idiom, a conventional, romantic, virtuoso offering without much individual flavour. Stephen Coombs takes its considerable difficulties in his stride and plays the work as if it is great music, and at times he almost persuades one that it is; and he receives excellent support from the BBC Scottish Orchestra under Jerzy Maksymiuk, and good recording quality.

Börtz, Daniel (born 1943)

Sinfonias Nos. 1; 7; Parados; Strindberg suite.
*** Chandos Dig. CHAN 9473 [id.]. Stockholm PO, Rozhdestvensky.

Daniel Börtz is a Swedish composer of the middle generation. A pupil first of Hilding Rosenberg then of Karl-Birger Blomdahl and Ingvar Lidholm, he also studied electronic music at Utrecht. He made his name with two church operas, then came to wider notice in 1991 with his opera, *The Bacchantes*, to a libretto by Ingmar Bergman. He is never boring, though his limited range of expressive devices makes it hard to listen to all these pieces straight off, despite the refined sense of orchestral colour. The music is too static, with extensive use of chord-clusters and strong dynamic contrasts, but both the *First* and *Seventh Symphonies* are powerfully atmospheric. The playing of the Stockholm orchestra is superb and the Chandos recording is of demonstration standard: marvellously present, well balanced and realistic.

Bottesini, Giovanni (1821–89)

(i) *Double-bass concertino in C min.;* (i; ii) *Duo concertante on themes from Bellini's 'I Puritani' for cello, double-bass and orchestra;* (i) *Elégie in D;* (i; iii) *Passioni amorose* (for 2 double-basses); *Ali Baba overture; Il Diavolo della notte; Ero e Leandro: Prelude.*

*** ASV Dig. CDDCA 907 [id.]. (i) Thomas Martin; (ii) Moray Welsh; (iii) Francesco Petracchi; LSO, Petracchi, or (iii) Matthew Gibson.

A contemporary said of Bottesini's virtuoso playing: 'Under his bow the double-bass sighed, cooed, sang, quivered,' and it does all those things here on the flamboyant bow of Thomas Martin, himself a musician of the strongest personality. He 'coos' mellifluously in the *Elégie*, a conventional piece but agreeably melodic; then he sings the yearning cantilena which forms the slow movement of the *Concertino* with a grace unexpected from his comparatively unwieldy instrument. In this work the composer resourcefully commands the soloist to tune his instrument a minor third above the orchestra, which increases the instrument's projection. For the *Passioni amorose* the conductor, Francesco Petracchi (professor of the double-bass at the Geneva Conservatoire), exchanges his baton for another bow to join his colleague, establishing a close, decisive partnership. Further contrast is provided when Moray Welsh successfully interweaves with his larger instrumental cousin in the *Duo concertante* on melodies of Bellini. For contrast, the programme is interspersed with colourful orchestral miniatures. The *Prelude to Ero e Leandro* has a Neapolitan flavour (and a nice oboe solo); the *Sinfonia, Il Diavolo della notte*, turns naturally from warm lyricism to galloping liveliness, and the brief *Ali Baba overture* brings a spirited whiff of Rossini. The recording engineers have done marvels to balance everything so convincingly; the persuasive Thomas Martin's intonation is remarkably true, and this programme is surprisingly rewarding and entertaining, far more than a specialist collection for the musically curious.

Gran duo concertante for violin, double-bass and orchestra; Gran concerto in F sharp min. for double-bass; Andante sostenuto for strings; Duetto for clarinet and double-bass.

**(*) ASV Dig. CDDCA 563 [id.]. Garcia, Martin, Emma Johnson, ECO, Andrew Litton.

The ASV recording combines the *Gran duo concertante* with another *Duetto for clarinet and double-bass* which Emma Johnson ensures has plenty of personality, though none of this amiable music is very distinctive. The recording is excellent, well balanced and truthful.

Capriccio di bravura; Elegia in Re; Fantasia on Beatrice di Tenda; Fantasia on Lucia di Lammermoor; Grand allegro di concerto; Introduzione e Bolero; Romanza drammatica; (i) *Romanza: Une bouche aimée.*

**(*) ASV Dig. CDDCA 626 [id.]. Thomas Martin, Anthony Halstead; (i) with J. Fugelle.

Thomas Martin is a superb virtuoso of the double-bass, and he obviously relishes these display pieces, but some of the high tessitura is inevitably uncomfortable. The recording is most realistic.

Boughton, Rutland (1878–1960)

(i) *Oboe concerto No. 1 in C; Symphony No. 3 in B min.*

(N) (B) *** Hyperion Helios Dig. CDH 55019 [id.]. (i) Sarah Francis, RPO, Vernon Handley.

Rutland Boughton's *Third Symphony* comes from 1937 and proves something of a surprise. It is old-fashioned in idiom; some of it would not be out of place in Dvořák or Borodin, and its debt to Elgar is above all overwhelming. However, it is expertly fashioned, often imaginative and, save in the rumbustious scherzo (where the closing pages are clumsily scored), hardly puts a foot wrong. The *Oboe concerto*, written the previous year, which Boyd Neel took to Salzburg in the same year as he presented Britten's *Variations on a theme of Frank Bridge*, is hardly less rewarding. It opens a little floridly, but its pastoralism soon asserts itself, blossoms in the *Adagio espressivo*, and colours the gaily dancing finale. The recording of the *Symphony* approaches the demonstration bracket (in the concerto, the soloist is rather too forward) and the performances are totally committed, even if the strings of the RPO are not quite on top form. A bargain well worth seeking out.

Pastoral.

(N) (B) *** Hyperion Helios Dig. CDH 55008 [id.]. Sarah Francis, Rasumovsky Qt – HARTY: *3 Pieces*. HOWELLS: *Sonata*; RUBBRA *Sonata*. ***

Boughton's enchanting *Pastoral* for oboe and string quartet, makes a delightful pendant for this fine collection of English music for oboe and piano. It has a disarmingly attractive folksy pastoral melody, which haunts the memory. The performance could hardly be more persuasive.

Bethlehem (choral drama, adapted from the Coventry Nativity Play).

*** Hyperion Dig. CDA 66690 [id.]. Field, Bryan, Bryson, R. Evans, Bowen, Peacock, Opie, MacDougall, Van Allan, Seaton, Campbell, I. Boughton, Matheson-Bruce, Holst Singers, New L. Children's Ch., City of L. Sinf., Alan Melville.

Rutland Boughton wrote this choral drama in 1915 for the festival he had founded the previous year at Glastonbury. Boughton's score, lyrical and undemanding, with carols punctuating the scenes as chorales punctuate the Bach Passions, is an aptly fresh and innocent setting of an edited version of the Coventry Nativity Play. The scenes start with the annunciation and carry on the nativity story in a direct, uncomplicated way which, within its limits, is most moving. The villainous role of Herod is unexpectedly consigned to a tenor (perhaps for a composer representing unreliability) but otherwise there are no more surprises than you would find in a church pageant. Alan G. Melville conducts a warm, fluent performance generally well sung, though for the central role of the Virgin Mary it would have been better to have a sweeter voice than Helen Field's. Alan Opie and the two other wise men are outstanding, and the three shepherds characterize well in their pastoral cavortings. The score has been discreetly cut to fit the two Acts on a single CD – mainly involving the removal of an incidental ballad for Herod – with little loss. First-rate, well-balanced sound.

The Immortal hour (opera): complete.
(B)*** Hyperion Dyad Dig. CDD 22040 (2) [id.]. Kennedy, Dawson, Wilson-Johnson, Davies, Geoffrey Mitchell Ch., ECO, Melville.

Analysed closely, much of *The Immortal hour* may seem like Vaughan Williams and water; but this fine performance, conducted by a lifelong Boughton devotee, brings out the hypnotic quality which had 1920s music-lovers attending performances many times over, entranced by its lyrical evocation of Celtic twilight. The simple tunefulness goes with a fine feeling for atmosphere. The excellent cast of young singers includes Anne Dawson as the heroine, Princess Etain, and Maldwyn Davies headily beautiful in the main tenor rendering of the *Faery song*. Warm, reverberant recording, enhanced in its CD format and this delightful opera is not to be missed at its new Dyad price.

Boulez, Pierre (born 1925)

Eclat-Multiples; Rituel: In memoriam Bruno Maderna.
(M) *** Sony SK 45839 [id.]. BBC SO, Ens. InterContemporain, composer.

Eclat-Multiples appeared first in 1964 simply as *Eclat*, a brilliant showpiece, an exuberant mosaic of sounds; but then, in 1970, it started developing from there in the pendant work, *Multiples*. *Rituel* is the most moving music that Boulez has ever written, inspired by the premature death of his friend and colleague, Bruno Maderna. This record, very well played and recorded, provides both a challenge and a reward.

(i) *Livre pour cordes;* (ii) *Pli selon pli.*
(M) *** Sony SMK 68335 [id.]. (i) New Philh. O. Strings; (ii) Halina Lukomska, Maria Bergman (piano), Paul Stingle (guitar), Hugo d'Alton (mandolin), BBC SO; composer.

Pli selon pli is a grandly conceived work to refute the idea that serialists and their progeny are necessarily cramped in their inspiration. The title (literally 'fold upon fold') comes from the poet Mallarmé, and Boulez's layers of invention are used to illuminate as centrepieces three Mallarmé sonnets. Neither these craggy vocalizations nor the purely instrumental passages are at all easy to understand in a conventional sense, but the luminous texture of Boulez's writing is endlessly fascinating and, for the listener with an open mind, this is a rewarding way of widening experience of the avant-garde. *Livre pour cordes*, adapted from an early string quartet, is a less demanding piece, but one equally worth studying. Definitive performances and excellent (late-1960s) recording under the composer's sharp-eared and electrifying direction.

(i) *Dialogue*; (ii) *Répons.*
(N) **(*) DG Dig. 457 605-2. (i) Alain Damiens; (ii) Soloists, Ens. Intercontemporain, Composer.

As well as being one of Boulez's most ambitious works, 42 minutes long, *Répons* is also the most physically involving. Boulez chose the title in reflection of the interplay of solo and ensemble voices in Gregorian chant. The argument is highly organized, but even an unprepared listener can appreciate the sensuous element in this work for six contrasted soloists, an instrumental ensemble of 24 players, and computerized sound developed from that of the soloists. The spatial element is crucial. In concert the ensemble is set in the middle of the auditorium, with the soloists stationed round it, and with the loudspeakers of the electronic system surrounding the audience. Though a two-channel stereo recording cannot convey the full impact, this is a powerful performance that gives a fair impression of the live event. *Dialogue* applies similar techniques to a solitary clarinet, with more limited but tonally revealing results.

Piano sonatas Nos. 1–3.
(BB) *** Naxos Dig. 8.553353 [id.]. Idil Biret.

The Boulez sonatas are well served by the gramophone – particularly No. 2, which Pollini has recorded for DG. Those with an interest in this repertoire will be well rewarded by Idil Biret on Naxos; she is more than equal to their technical demands and is given good sound.

Bouzignac, Guillaume
(*c.* 1590–*c.* 1640)

Te Deum. Motets: *Alleluia, venite amici; Ave Maria; Clamant clavi; Dum silentium; Ecce Aurora; Ecce festivitas; Ecce homo; Flos in flores; Ha! Plange; In pace, in idipsum; Jubilate Deo; Salve Jesu Piissime; Tota pulchra es; Unus ex vobis; Vulnerasti cor meum.*

❁ *** HM Dig. HMC 901471 [id.]. Les Pages de la Chapelle, Les Arts Florissants, William Christie.

❁ (B) *** HM Dig. HMX 290850.52 (3) [(M) id. import]. Les Pages de la Chapelle, Les Arts Florissants, William Christie – Marc-Antoine CHARPENTIER: *Missa Assumpta est Maria* etc. *** ❁; DELALANDE: *Confitebor tibi Domine* etc. ***

You might call Bouzignac the Charles Ives of the sixteenth century. His music was almost totally forgotten for 250 years until rediscovered by a scholar at the beginning of the twentieth century. On record he has continued to be neglected, and this pioneering disc brings a revelation. The great refreshing quality of Bouzignac for the modern ear is that consistently he responds vividly and unpredictably to the texts of each of these motets, so that often you would be unlikely to deduce which century the music came from, let alone which country. Vigour is the essence, as in the exuberantly light-hearted setting of *Jubilate Deo*, yet such a motet as *In pace, in idipsum* in its sustained lines has a rare meditative beauty, and the dialogue of *Unus ex vobis* even brings echoes of Russian Orthodox music. The response of William Christie, always a vivid interpreter of early music, brings out the colour in all its variety, for once with boy trebles (Les Pages de la Chapelle) added to the finely disciplined forces, vocal and instrumental, of Les Arts Florissants. This will be a thrilling discovery for many, helped by vividly immediate sound.

While the separate issue (HMC 901471) remains available at full price, this now comes in a very highly recommendable Harmonia Mundi Bargain CD Trio, linked to a pair of other splendid discs, including the *Te Deums* by Charpentier and Delalande and much other fine music besides.

Bowen, York (1884–1961)

Ballade No. 2, Op. 87; Berceuse, Op. 83; Moto perpetuo from Op. 39; Preludes, Op. 102, Nos. 1 in C; 2 in C min.; 6 in D min.; 7 in E flat; 8 in E flat min.; 10 in E min.; 15 in G; 16 in G min.; 18 in G sharp min.; 19 in A; 20 in A min.; 21 in B flat; 22 in B flat min. Romances Nos. 1, Op. 35/1; 2, Op. 45; Sonata No. 5 in F min., Op. 72. Toccata, Op. 155.

❁ *** Hyperion Dig. CDA 66838 [id.]. Stephen Hough.

Few new discs of piano music are as magical as this: magnetic performances that come as a revelation, demonstrating that this long-neglected composer was a master of keyboard writing. Hough, always compelling on disc, not only technically brilliant but spontaneously expressive, consistently conveys his love for Bowen's music, starting with 13 of the 24 *Preludes*. He puts them in his own, very effective order, bringing out the contrasted qualities of jewelled miniatures, reflecting Rachmaninov on the one hand, Ireland and Bax on the other, but with a flavour of their own. The most powerful, most ambitious work is the *Sonata No. 5*, with two weighty, wide-ranging movements separated by an *Andante* interlude. Vivid piano sound and illuminating notes by Francis Pott and Hough himself.

Boyce, William (1710–79)

Overtures Nos. 1–9.

(M) *** Chandos CHAN 6531 [id.]. Cantilena, Adrian Shepherd.

Overtures Nos. 10–12; Concerti grossi: in B flat; in B min.; in E min.

(M) *** Chandos CHAN 6541 [id.]. Cantilena, Adrian Shepherd.

This reissue offers Cantilena's complete set of the Boyce *Overtures* and includes the three *Concerti grossi*. Though these works do not quite have the consistent originality which makes the Boyce *Symphonies* so refreshing, the energy of the writing – splendidly conveyed in these performances – is recognizably the same, with fugal passages that turn in unexpected directions. Cantilena's performances readily convey the freshness of Boyce's inspiration. The recording is oddly balanced but is both atmospheric and vivid and provides a refreshing musical experience.

Symphonies Nos. 1–8, Op. 2.

*** DG (IMS) Dig. 419 631-2 [id.]. E. Concert, Pinnock.

*** CRD CRD 3356 [id.]. Bournemouth Sinf., Ronald Thomas.

Pinnock's disc of the Boyce *Symphonies* wears its scholarship very easily and in so doing brings not only lively, resilient playing but fresh revelation in the treatment of the *vivace* movements. Nicely scaled recording, bright but atmospheric.

Thomas's tempi are often brisk, and certainly swifter-paced than Pinnock's 'new look'. But even against such strong competition as this, the buoyant playing of the Bournemouth Sinfonietta still gives much pleasure by its sheer vitality. Bright, clear sound.

12 Trio Sonatas (1747); *Sonatas Nos. 13–15* (unpublished).
(N) *** Hyperion Dig. CDA 67151/2 [id.]. Parley of Instruments or Parley Baroque O, Peter Holman.

Boyce gave the English trio sonata a new lease of life at a time when the format was in danger of falling into neglect, and the works published in 1747, according to Charles Burney 'were longer and more generally purchased, performed and admired than any production of the kind [in England], except those of Corelli'. Praise indeed, and while these Sonatas are not as fine as those of Corelli, they are consistently inventive and a good example of baroque 'easy listening'. Not only that, but they seem to get more and more attractive, and the second disc is more enjoyable than the first. As an appendix, Peter Holman has discovered three extra Sonatas (here numbered 13–15) which survive in a manuscript in the Cambridge Fitzwilliam Museum. They are almost certainly by Boyce, and hardly less enjoyable than the earlier works in the set. There is evidence to suggest that these sonatas were sometimes played in orchestral form and so the Hyperion recording alternates orchestral and chamber performance, with Nos. 1, 3, 5, 7–9, 11 and 13 heard on a full string group. These period performances are vigorously alert and stylish, with slow movements refined, yet warmly relished, especially those that remind the listener a little of Handel. Excellent recording without edginess.

Solomon (serenata).
*** Hyperion Dig. CDA 66378 [id.]. Bronwen Mills, Howard Crook, Parley of Instruments, Goodman.

William Boyce's *Solomon* is a totally secular piece, a dialogue between She and He, with the verses freely based on the *Song of Solomon*. As this stylish and alert period performance using young, fresh-voiced soloists makes clear, it has some delightful inspirations, less influenced by Italian models than by popular English song. First-rate sound.

Brade, William (1560–1630)

Hamburger Ratsmusik: Allemandes, Canzonas, Courantes, Galliards, Intradas (1609, 1614 & 1617 collections).
(M) *** HM/BMG Dig. GD 77168 (2) [77168-2-RG]. Hespèrion XX, Jordi Savall.

This collection of dances is absolutely delightful, varied in both content and instrumental colour, and excellently played by Hespèrion XX under Jordi Savall, while the recording, from 1981, is very good indeed.

Hamburger Ratsmusik: excerpts.
(N) (BB) ***DHM/BMG Baroque Esprit Dig. 05472 77476-2 [id.]. (from above).

Those content with a shorter selection including music taken from just the 1609 and 1615 collections will find this bargain disc just as enjoyable as the complete set.

Bræin, Edvard Fliflet (1924–76)

Anne Pedersdotter (opera; complete).
*** Simax Dig. PSC3121 (2) [id.]. Ekeberg, Handssen, Carlsen, Sandve, Thorsen, Norwegian Nat. Op. Ch. & O, Per Ake Andersson.

Edvard Fliflet Bræin was a highly talented Norwegian composer who died in his early fifties. His opera, *Anne Pedersdotter* (1971), is based on the most famous of witchcraft trials in Norway, the burning of Anne Pedersdotter in Bergen in 1590. Fliflet Bræin called it 'a symphonic opera' and, like Schoeck's *Venus*, its invention unfolds in an effortlessly organic fashion; in other words, his is the art that conceals art. It is effective music-theatre, and many of its ideas, as so often with this composer, are memorable. It gets a fine performance, with good singing from Kjersti Ekeberg as the eponymous heroine, Svein Carlsen as her husband, Absolon Pedersøn-Beyer, and Kjell Magnus Sandve as his son by his first marriage. The Norwegian Opera forces under the baton of Per Ake Andersson are excellent, and the recording, produced by Michael Woolcock, is very good indeed. Strongly recommended.

Brahms, Johannes (1833–97)

CENTENARY COLLECTIONS

DG Complete Brahms Edition: Volume 1: Orchestral works: (i, ii) *Symphonies Nos. 1–4;* (i; iii) *Academic festival overture;* (iii; iv) *Hungarian dances Nos. 1–21;* (i; iii) *Serenades Nos. 1–2;* (i; ii) *Tragic overture; Variations on a theme of Haydn.*
(M) ** DG Dig./Analogue 449 601-2 (5). (i) BPO; (ii) Karajan; (iii) Abbado; (iv) VPO.

Sampler: *Hungarian dances Nos. 1–21.*
(B) *** DG Dig. 449 655. VPO, Abbado.

With variably focused recording, Karajan's last digital cycle (1986–8) of the Brahms *Symphonies* is not his finest, but he remained a natural Brahmsian to the last. The sound is full and weighty but tends to be thick and generalized in tuttis. Characteristically Karajan does not observe the first-movement exposition repeats. He draws a typically powerful and dramatic performance of the *First Symphony*, but his reading does not have the grip of his earlier account, made in the 1960s. The *Second Symphony* is far more impressive, suffering less from the thick, undifferentiated recording, when textures in this later work tend to be lighter. As a performance, it is the highlight of the cycle, a highly satisfying reading, at times warmer and more glowing than his previous versions, with consistently fine playing from the orchestra. The opening of the *Third Symphony* makes a massively bold impression, but again the ill-defined textures are a drawback, and here the omission of the exposition repeat may be counted much more serious. The *Fourth Symphony* sounds fresher, with the slow movement expansively lyrical, but the very purposeful finale is again heavily weighted. Overall this series lacks the spontaneous inspiration of Karajan's earlier recordings.

Abbado's performance of the *First Serenade* is vital, imaginative and sensitive, but the digital recording (1981) is rather dry and lacking in bloom, though clear enough. The *Second Serenade* was recorded much earlier (1967) and the sound is greatly to be preferred, with plenty of analogue bloom; the performance is very persuasive and marvellously held together, with dynamic nuances nicely observed. Again the Berlin Philharmonic play superbly both here and in the *Academic festival overture*, made at the same time. Karajan's *Tragic overture* is impressively done and, though one may criticize the recording balance, the result is powerful and immediate; he also gives an appealing performance of the *Haydn variations*. Abbado's account of the *Hungarian dances* has great sparkle and lightness, and this CD is additionally offered as a bargain sampler for the whole edition.

Volume 2: Concertos: *Piano concertos Nos.* (i; ii) *1 in D min., Op. 15;* (i; iii) *2 in B flat, Op. 83;* (iv) *Violin concerto in D, Op. 77;* (iv–v) *Double concerto for violin, cello and orchestra in A min., Op. 102.*

(M) **(*) DG Analogue/Dig. 449 607-2 (3). (i) Pollini, VPO; (ii) Boehm; (iii) Abbado; (iv) Mutter, BPO, Karajan; (v) with Meneses.

Although Pollini and the Vienna Philharmonic under Karl Boehm are given finely detailed recording, in the *First Piano concerto* other versions (notably Gilels) provide greater wisdom and humanity. Not that Pollini is wanting in keyboard command, but he is a little short on tenderness and poetry. All too often here he seems to have switched on the automatic pilot and, although the *B flat Concerto* under Abbado is much fresher and offers some masterly painism, there are warmer and more spontaneous accounts to be had. (Admirers of Pollini will note that his accounts of the two piano concertos are also available – less expensively – on a DG Double.) Anne-Sophie Mutter's strikingly fresh version of the *Violin concerto* (available separately, coupled with the Mendelssohn *Concerto* – DG 445 515-2; *445 515-4*) can hold its own with the best, and the *Double concerto*, too, is particularly successful. With two young soloists Karajan conducts an outstandingly spacious and strong performance. Mutter conveys a natural authority comparable to Karajan's own, and the precision and clarity of Meneses's cello as recorded make an excellent match. The central slow movement in its spacious way has a wonderfully Brahmsian glow.

DG Complete Brahms Edition: Volume 3: Chamber music: (i) *Cello sonatas Nos. 1–2;* (ii; iii) *Clarinet quintet, Op. 115;* (ii; iv) *Clarinet sonatas Nos. 1–2;* (ii; v; vi) *Clarinet trio, Op. 114;* (v; vii; viii) *Horn trio, Op. 40;* (v; vi; viii; ix) *Piano quartets Nos. 1–3;* (x) *Piano quintet, Op. 34;* (v; vi; viii) *Piano trios Nos. 1–3;* (xi) *String quartets Nos. 1–3;* (iii; xii) *String quintets Nos. 1–2;* (iii; xii; xiii) *String sextets Nos. 1–2;* (xiv) *Violin sonatas Nos. 1–3; F.A.E. Sonata: Scherzo.*

(B) **(*) DG Dig./Analogue 449 611-2 (11). (i) Rostropovich, Rudolf Serkin; (ii) Leister; (iii) Amadeus Qt; (iv) Demus; (v) Vásáry; (vi) Borwitzky; (vii) Hauptmann; (viii) Brandis; (ix) Christ; (x) Pollini, Italian Qt; (xi) LaSalle Qt; (xii) with Aronowitz; (xiii) Pleeth; (xiv) Zukerman, Barenboim.

The Rostropovich/Serkin partnership in the *Cello sonatas* proved an outstanding success and these performances, recorded digitally in 1982, are self-recommending. The *Piano quintet* also brings some very commanding playing from Pollini, and the Italian Quartet is eloquent too. The balance, however, is very much in the pianist's favour; he dominates the texture rather more than is desirable and occasionally masks the lower strings. There are also minor agogic exaggerations. Karl Leister is a fine soloist in the *Clarinet sonatas* and his 1968 analogue recording is more convincingly balanced. The *Clarinet* and *Horn trios* are from 1981 and, like the *Piano quartets*, are digital. The *Clarinet trio* again brings excellent playing, although Leister's individuality comes over less strongly here than in the *Clarinet quintet* and the forward balance is less flattering. The *Piano trios* also date from 1981 and, like the *Piano quartets* from the following year, are undoubtedly impressive. These artists have a thorough grasp of these unfailingly rich and inventive scores and penetrate their character completely. However, the microphones have been placed very close and the effect is artificial: the bright, forward timbre of the strings is achieved at the expense of a natural tonal bloom. The LaSalle Quartet give efficient, streamlined accounts of the *String quartets*, but they lack tenderness. The 1978–9 analogue recording is bright and immediate. The Amadeus performances of the *String quintets* and *Sextets* were recorded a decade earlier in 1967–8, yet the sound is full and pleasingly balanced and the music-making has plenty of life and warmth. Karl Leister plays with considerable sensitivity in the *Clarinet quintet*, and there is much to enjoy here. Zukerman and Barenboim take an expansive view of the *Violin sonatas*, producing songful, spontaneous-sounding performances that catch the inspiration of the moment. Their 1974 recording is basically ripe and warm, but the CD transfer does not entirely flatter the upper partials of the violin timbre.

Volume 4: Keyboard works: Piano duet: (i) *Hungarian dances Nos. 1–21; Sonata in F min., Op. 34b; Souvenir de la Russie; Variations on a theme of Haydn, Op. 56b; Variations on a theme of Schumann, Op. 23; 16 Waltzes, Op. 39;* (ii) *4 Ballades, Op. 10; Fantasias, Op. 116; 3 Intermezzi, Op. 117;* (iii) *Pieces, Op. 76;* (ii) *Pieces, Op. 118–19; 2 Rhapsodies, Op. 79; Scherzo, Op. 4;* (iv) *Sonatas Nos. 1–3;* (v) *Theme and variations in D min.* (from 2nd movement of *String sextet, Op. 18*); (iii) *Variations on an original theme, Op. 21/1; Variations on a Hungarian song, Op. 21/2;* (v) *Variations and fugue on a theme of Handel, Op. 24;* (iii) *Variations on a theme of Paganini, Op. 35;* (v) *Variations on a theme of Schumann, Op. 9;* (iv) Arr. of BACH: *Chaconne from Partita, BWV 1004* (for left hand). Organ: (vi) *11 Chorale preludes, Op. 122; Chorale prelude and fugue in A min.; Fugue in A flat min.; Preludes and fugues in A min., G min.*

(B) *(*) DG Analogue/Dig. 449 623-2 (9). (i) Alfons and Aloys Kontarsky; (ii) Wilhelm Kempff; (iii) Tamás Vásáry; (iv) Anatol Ugorski; (v) Daniel Barenboim; (vi) Peter Planyavsky.

The Kontarskys' four-handed set of the *Hungarian dances* is vivacious and recommendable, but the *Schumann variations* and the *Waltzes* are a little short of charm. The *Double piano sonata* began as a string quintet before migrating to the keyboard and then ending life as the *Piano quintet*. The Kontarskys make heavy weather of much of it and are too prone to point-making and to interrupting the rhythmic flow of the music to be wholly recommendable. The opening theme is treated in an extremely mannered fashion and, generally speaking, one feels the lack of a true inner tension. Much the same applies to the *Haydn variations*. The *Souvenir de la Russie* is very lightweight and Brahms did not publish it under his own name. In Kempff's hands the four *Ballades* emerge very much as a young man's music and, like Opp. 116–19, these are highly individual performances with the Kempff magic most striking in the *Intermezzi*, Op. 117, and the *Pieces* of Op. 119. The Op. 79 *Rhapsodies* perhaps suit his temperament less obviously, but he plays them with conviction. He is more than acceptably recorded. Barenboim is allotted the *Theme and variations in D minor*, transcribed from the *Sextet*, Op. 18, plus the *Schumann variations*, Op. 9, and the *Variations and fugue on a theme of Handel*, Op. 24, and he shows himself in inspirational form. Both the latter sets have received more cohesive performances on record, but Barenboim has a magical way of making the listener's attention perk up at the start of each variation, and he shares his own sense of discovery with you. He is afforded first-class sound. To Vásáry, alongside the eight *Pieces*, Op. 76, go the *Variations on an original theme*, the *Variations on a Hungarian song* and the *Paganini variations*, Op. 35, which sound marvellously fresh and sparkling. His virtuosity is effortless and unostentatious and, generally speaking, he is well recorded too. The three *Sonatas* are brand-new recordings and one wonders why DG did not choose to use Zimerman's highly concentrated accounts. Ugorsky is infinitely more wayward, impulsive and self-aware, and in the first two *Sonatas* he fails to hold the architecture together convincingly. The first movement of the *F minor Sonata* is then pulled about unmercifully, and this performance is so eccentrically wilful that it cannot be taken seriously. Ugorsky is also very free in his handling of Brahms's transcription of Bach's *D minor Chaconne* for the left hand, which is more austere than the familiar Busoni arrangement, but it does not sound so here. The recording is excellent. Overall, this set is too flawed for a general recommendation.

Volume 5: Lieder: *Gesäng, Opp. 3; 6; 7; 43; 69–72;* (i) *91; Gedich, Op. 19; Lieder. Opp. 46–9; 85–6; 94–7; 105–7; WoO post. 23; Lieder und Gesänge, Opp. 32; 57–9; 63; Lieder und Romanzen, Op. 14; Ophelia-Lieder, WoO post. 23; Romanzen und Lieder. Op. 84; Die schöne Magelone (Romanzen), Op. 33; Vier ernste Gesänge (4 Serious songs), Op. 121; Zigeunerlieder, Op. 103.*

(M) *** DG Analogue/Dig. 449 633-2 (7) [id.]. Jessye Norman, Dietrich Fischer-Dieskau, Daniel Barenboim; (i) with Wolfgang Christ.

Song-writing for Brahms was as natural as breathing, and this glorious collection, spanning the fullest breadth of his career, consistently bears witness to his unique genius. Fischer-Dieskau's 1972 recording of the culminating *Four Serious songs* provides a superb conclusion, but the rest of the recordings were made between 1978 and 1982. Jessye Norman, full and golden of tone, consistently reveals her art at its most persuasive, in most ways even matching the artistry imagination of Fischer-Dieskau, who is in ravishing voice. Not the least important element is the playing of Barenboim who, in accompanying Lieder, gives an impression almost of improvisation, of natural fluidity and pianistic sparkle to match every turn of the singer's expression. Beautiful, faithful recording, admirable transfers and first-class documentation.

Volume 6: Vocal ensembles: *Ballads and Romances, Op. 75; 14 Children's folksongs; 49 Deutsche Volkslieder; Duets, Opp. 20; 28; 61; 66; Liebeslieder, Op. 52; Neue Liebeslieder, Op. 65; Quartets, Opp. 31; 64; 92; 112; Zigeunerlieder, Op. 103.*

(M) *** DG Dig./Analogue 449 641-2 (4). Edith Mathis, Brigitte Fassbaender, Peter Schreier, Dietrich Fischer-Dieskau; Karl Engel, Wolfgang Sawallisch, Gernot Kahl; N. German R. Ch., Günter Jena.

This box includes all Brahms's vocal ensembles for solo voices with piano, and they receive fresh, brightly affectionate performances from an almost ideally chosen quartet of distinguished singers, accompanied by excellent, imaginative pianists. There is much treasure to be found throughout these four discs, recorded with a nice balance between intimacy and immediacy.

Volume 7: Choral works: Female chorus: *Ave Maria, Op. 12; 13 Canons, Op. 113; Psalm 13, Op. 27; 3 Geistliche Chöre, Op. 37; 4 Songs, Op. 17; 12 Songs and Romances, Op. 44.* Male chorus: *7 Canons; Little wedding cantata; Songs, Op. 41; 23 German folksongs.* Mixed chorus: *Begräbnisgesang, Op.13; 3 Fest- und Gedenksprüche, Op. 109; Marienlieder, Op. 22; Motets, Opp. 29; 74; 110; Geistliches Lied, Op. 30; Songs, Opp. 42; 62; 104; Songs and Romances, Op. 93a; Tafellied Dank der Damen, Op. 93b.*

(M) *** DG Dig. 449 646-2 (4). Mathis, Murray, Julia Raines Hahn, Gerhard Dickel, Gernot Kahl, Martin-Albrecht Rohde, Jan Schroeder, Hans-Ulrich Winkler; N. German R. Ch., Günter Jena.

This four-disc collection of Brahms's unaccompanied choral music ranges wide, representing all periods of his career in intimate, warmly characterful writing, whether in motets, part-songs, canons or folksong settings. It contains much buried treasure, not least the fine *Motets for double chorus*, Opp. 109 and 110. The Hamburg choir gives radiant performances, beautifully recorded with no hint of routine: the sound is both clear and pleasingly atmospheric. Highly recommended.

Volume 8: Choral works with orchestra: (i; ii) *Alto rhapsody, Op. 53;* (iii) *German requiem, Op. 45; Nänie, Op. 82;* (ii; iv) *Rinaldo, Op. 50;* (ii) *Song of destiny (Schicksalslied), Op. 54; Song of the Fates, Op. 89;* (ii; v) *Song of triumph, Op. 55.*

(M) **(*) DG Dig. 449 651-2 (3). (i) Fassbaender; (ii) Prague Philharmonic Ch., Czech PO, Sinopoli; (iii) Bonney, Schmidt, V. Op. Ch., VPO, Giulini; (iv) Kollo; (v) W. Brendel.

When this box was originally issued on LP, all the music was conducted by Sinopoli; now Giulini's performance of the *German Requiem* has been substituted for Sinopoli's version, not altogether an advantage. Giulini's account is deeply dedicated but one which at spacious speeds lacks rhythmic bite. Meditation is a necessary part of Brahms's scheme, but here, with phrasing smoothed over and the choral sound rather opaque, there is too little contrast. Fassbaender makes a strong, noble soloist in the *Alto rhapsody*, but it is the other works which command first attention in such a collection, not least the *Triumphlied* of 1870, to which Sinopoli, helped by incandescent singing from the Czech choir, brings an Handelian exhilaration. There is freshness and excitement too in the other rare works, with Sinopoli lightening the rhythms and textures. In *Rinaldo*, for example – the nearest that Brahms came to writing an opera – Sinopoli moulds the sequence of numbers very dramatically. René Kollo is the near-operatic soloist. The recordings, made in Prague, bring sound which is warm and sympathetic, with the orchestra incisively close and the chorus atmospherically behind, if sometimes a little confusingly so.

Decca '*Masterworks*'

Volume I: *Symphonies Nos. 1–2; Academic festival overture; Variations on a theme of Haydn, Op. 56a; Tragic overture.*

(B) **(*) Decca Double 452 329-2 (2). Chicago SO, Solti.

Volume II: (i) *Symphonies Nos. 3–4;* (ii) *Hungarian dances Nos. 1–21.*

(B) *** Decca Double Analogue/Dig. 452 332-2 (2). (i) Chicago SO, Solti; (ii) RPO, Weller.

Those who think of Solti as a conductor who always whips up excitement may be surprised at the sobriety of his approach here. These are important and thoughtful statements, lacking only a degree of the fantasy and idiosyncrasy which make fine performances great. However, it is the second of the two Doubles which offers the two finest performances: Solti's big-scale view of the *Third Symphony* is most compelling, and the *Fourth* shows him at his most vibrantly individual, with the *Andante moderato* second movement treated more like an Adagio, unfailingly pure and eloquent. This second box also includes Walter Weller's splendid, complete, digital set of the *Hungarian dances*.

Volume III: *Piano concertos Nos.* (i) *1;* (ii) *2;* (iii) *Violin concerto.*

(B) **(*) Decca Double Analogue/Dig. 452 335-2 (2). (i) Lupu, LPO, de Waart; (ii) Ashkenazy, LSO, Mehta; (iii) Belkin, LSO, Fischer.

Radu Lupu's approach to the *First Piano concerto* is that of the time when the piano was not the leonine monster it was to become later on in the century.

His is a deeply reflective and intelligent performance, full of masterly touches and an affecting poetry which falls short of the thrusting combative power of a Serkin or Curzon. Decca produce a particularly truthful sound-picture. This could be recommended enthusiastically to those who want a second, alternative view. However, Ashkenazy's account of the *Second Piano concerto* is less successful, its chief shortcoming being a lack of tension. With much beautiful detail and some wonderfully poetic playing, the performance still fails to come alive and one remains uninvolved. On the other hand, Boris Belkin's performance of the *Violin concerto* is direct and spontaneous, a spaciously warm reading that makes a strong impression. No complaints about the recorded sound.

Volume IV: *4 Ballades, Op. 10; Intermezzo, Op. 117/2; 6 Piano pieces, Op. 118; Piano sonata No. 3, Op. 5; 2 Rhapsodies, Op. 79; Variations and fugue on a theme by Handel, Op. 24; Variations on a theme by Paganini, Op. 35.*
(B) **(*) Decca Double 452 338-2 (2). Julius Katchen.

Julius Katchen's style in Brahms is distinctive; it sometimes has a slightly unyielding quality that suits some works better than others. In general the bigger, tougher pieces come off better than, for example, the gentle *Intermezzo*. But such pieces as the two *Rhapsodies* are splendidly done, and so are the *Ballades*. The *Sonata* receives a commanding performance. However, the two sets of *Variations*, for all their sheer pyrotechnical display, are rather less compelling.

Volume V: (i; ii) *Cello sonata No. 2 in F, Op. 99;* (iii) *Clarinet quintet in B min., Op. 115;* (iv) *Horn trio in E flat, Op. 40;* (i; ii; v) *Piano trio No. 1 in B, Op. 8;* (ii; v) *Violin sonata No. 3 in D min., Op. 108.*
(B) *** Decca Double 452 341-2 (2). (i) Starker; (ii) Katchen; (iii) Brymer & Allegri Qt; (iv) Tuckwell, Perlman, Ashkenazy; (v) Suk.

The recordings of the *Piano trio* and the *Cello sonata* represent the results of Julius Katchen's last recording sessions before his untimely death. They were held at The Maltings, and the results have much warmth. Katchen and his team judge the tempi of the Op. 8 *Piano trio* admirably and they resist the temptation to dwell too lovingly on detail. The *Cello sonata* is given a strong and characterful performance, while Jack Brymer gives a masterly and finely poised account of the *Clarinet quintet*, which in terms of polish and finesse can hold its own with the very best. The highlight of this set is the superbly passionate performance of Brahms's marvellous *Horn trio* from Tuckwell, Perlman and Ashkenazy. By contrast, Josef Suk's personal blend of romanticism and the classical tradition in the *Violin sonata* is warmly attractive but small in scale. An intimate performance but most enjoyable and well recorded.

Volume VI: (i; ii) *Alto rhapsody, Op. 53;* (iii) *German Requiem, Op. 45;* (iv) *Song of destiny (Schicksalslied), Op. 54;* (v) *Geistliches Lied, Op. 30;* (vi) *Vier ernste Gesänge (4 Serious songs), Op. 121;* (i; vii) *2 songs with viola, Op. 91.*
(B) **(*) Decca Double Analogue/Dig. 452 344-2 (2). (i) Watts; (ii) SRO, Ansermet; (iii) Te Kanawa, Weikl, Chicago Ch. & SO, Solti; (iv) Amb. Ch., New Philh. O, Abbado; (v) King's College, Cambridge, Ch., Cleobury; (vi) Holl, Schiff; (vii) Parsons, Aronowitz.

Solti favours very expansive tempi, smooth lines and refined textures in the *Requiem*. There is much that is beautiful, even if the result overall is not as involving as it might be. Dame Kiri Te Kanawa sings radiantly, but Bernd Weikl with his rather gritty baritone is not ideal. Fine recording, glowing and clear. Helen Watts gives a sensitive account of the *Alto Rhapsody*, while the *Song of destiny* brings a refined contribution from the Ambrosian Chorus with Abbado directing strongly. Helen Watts, too, is in good form in her sensitive performances of the two songs with viola as well as piano accompaniment. Cecil Aronowitz plays his obbligato with great finesse, and the combination of voice, viola and piano is particularly effective in *Gestillte Sehnsucht*, where the poet Rückert is in his most elegantly Petrarchan mood, telling of the soft evening sunlight on the woods, and the desire and longing of the solitary lover. The contributions of Robert Holl, accompanied by András Schiff, are slightly marred by the slow tempi chosen but are well sung, with due note taken of the texts.

ORCHESTRAL MUSIC

Piano concertos Nos. (i) *1 in D min., Op. 15;* (ii) *2 in B flat, Op. 83.*
(BB) *** Virgin Classics Dig. Double VBD5 61412-2 [CDVB 61412]. Stephen Hough, BBC SO, Andrew Davis.

(i) *Piano concertos Nos. 1–2.* (ii) *Academic festival overture; Tragic overture; Variations on a theme of Haydn, Op. 56a.*
(B) *** EMI forte CZS5 72649-2 (2) [CDFB 72649]. (i) Barenboim, Philh. O; (ii) VPO; Barbirolli.
(B) **(*) Ph. Duo 438 320-2 (2) [id.]. (i) Claudio Arrau; Concg. O, Haitink.

(i) *Piano concertos Nos. 1 in D min., Op. 15; 2 in B flat, Op. 83;* (ii) *Academic festival overture, Op. 80; Variations on a theme of Haydn, Op. 56a.*

Piano concertos Nos. 1–2; Tragic overture, Op. 81; Variations on a theme of Haydn, Op. 56a.
(B) **(*) DG Double 453 067 (2) [id.]. Pollini, VPO, Boehm (*No. 1*) or Abbado (*No. 2*).

Piano concertos Nos. (i) *1 in D min., Op. 15;* (ii) *2 in B flat, Op. 83. Variations and fugue on a theme of Handel, Op. 24; Variations on a theme of Paganini, Op. 35.*
(B) **(*) Decca Double 440 612-2 (2) [id.]. Julius Katchen; (i–ii) LSO; (i) Pierre Monteux; (ii) János Ferencsik.

(i) *Piano concertos Nos. 1–2; Tragic overture; Variations on a theme of Haydn.*
(B) *(*) EMI CZS5 72013-2 (2) [CDZB 72013]. Arrau, Philh. O, Carlo Maria Giulini.

(i) *Piano concertos Nos. 1–2. Variations and fugue on a theme of Handel, Op. 24; Waltzes, Op. 39.*
(M) *** Sony Heritage MH2K 63225 (2) [id.]. Leon Fleisher; (i) Cleveland O, Szell.

(i) *Piano concertos Nos. 1–2. 4 Ballades, Op. 10; 8 Pieces, Op. 76; Scherzo in E flat, Op. 4.*
(B) *** Ph. Duo 442 109-2 (2) [id.]. Steven Kovacevich; (i) LSO, Sir Colin Davis.

(i) *Piano concertos Nos. 1–2. 4 Ballades, Op. 10; Theme and variations in D min.* (from *String sextet, Op. 18*).
(M) *** Ph. Brendel Edition Dig. 446 925-2 (5) [id.]. Alfred Brendel, (i) BPO, Abbado – SCHUMANN: *Collection.* ***

(i) *Piano concertos Nos. 1–2. Capriccio in B min., Op. 76/2; Intermezzi: in E, Op. 116/6; in E flat, Op. 117/1; in E min.; in C, Op. 119/2–3; Rhapsody in B min., Op. 79/1; 6 Pieces, Op. 118.*
(M) **(*) Decca (IMS) 433 895-2 (2) [id.]. Wilhelm Backhaus; (i) VPO, Boehm.

Piano concerto No. 2 in B flat, Op. 83.
(M) *** Decca 448 600-2 [id.]. Backhaus, VPO, Boehm – MOZART: *Piano concerto No. 27.* **(*)

(i) *Piano concertos Nos. 1–2. Fantasias, Op. 116.*
(M) *** DG 447 446-2 (2) [id.]. Gilels; (i) BPO, Jochum.

The Gilels performances were an obvious candidate for DG's 'Originals' series and can still hold their own against virtually all the competition, but the two concertos are also available separately – see below. However, the present set is offered at a reduced price and the remastered recording is quite outstanding: for these 'Legendary Recordings' DG have improved the sound well beyond previous incarnations of these works.

Barenboim's performance of the *First Piano concerto* with Barbirolli is among the most inspired ever committed to disc. The playing is heroic and marvellously spacious. In the *Second Concerto* the first two movements remain grandly heroic and the slow movement has something of the awed intensity you find in the middle movement of the *First*, while the finale erupts gracefully into rib-tickling humour. This is a performance to love in its glowing spontaneity. Of the fill-ups, the *Tragic overture* is a performance of considerable distinction, the measured account of the *Academic festival overture* could do with more sparkle, while the *Haydn variations* again show the conductor at his finest. The late-1960s recordings have transferred splendidly to CD.

Stephen Hough, always an intense and imaginative recording artist, here gives keenly distinctive and deeply thoughtful readings of both Brahms *Concertos*. Clarity is regularly the keynote, so that with refined recording the transparency of textures may be disconcerting for those who insist on a fat Brahms sound. Far more than most in these works, however, Hough balances the contrasting claims of introspection and bravura in a refreshing and illuminating way. He adopts the widest range of tone and dynamic, with the recording beautifully capturing the hushed pianissimos in both works, not least in both slow movements. Both recordings were made in 1989, but inexplicably No. 1 has been held back until this outstanding double-disc set, which in this format works out at super-bargain price.

Though Leon Fleisher's concert career was cruelly cut short when he lost the full use of his right hand, he made some superb recordings in the late 1950s and 1960s, most strikingly those with George Szell and the Cleveland Orchestra, then at its peak. The two concerto recordings are both masterly examples of their joint inspiration, bringing out the point that these are in many ways symphonies with piano, when Szell's direction is so powerful and incisive, as well as warmly expressive. Not that Fleisher in any way lacks individuality, for the crisp confidence of his virtuosity has a sureness in its musical and emotional thrust that carries one magnetically on, not just in the bravura writing but also in the poetic moments, hushed and concentrated. The sound is among the best offered by CBS at that period, with the piano forwardly balanced but not aggressively so. Generously, this Heritage issue also includes solo recordings by Fleisher of the *Handel variations* and *Waltzes*, similarly crisp and concentrated, though the 1956 mono sound here is rather clattery. Nevertheless this is an outstanding set; if you already have Gilels playing the concertos, these Cleveland readings offer a stimulating and compelling alternative view. However, it costs rather more than the usual upper-mid-price.

In the *D minor concerto* Kovacevich plays with great tenderness and lyrical feeling. Similarly, No. 2 combines poetic feeling and intellectual strength and reflects an unforced naturalness that compels admiration. The accounts of the *Ballades* and the Op. 76 *Klavierstücke* have both fire and tenderness and are truthfully recorded.

Brendel's digital recordings of the two Brahms *Concertos* with Claudio Abbado and the Berlin Philharmonic show him at his finest. In the *D minor Concerto* the result is both strong and spontaneous. His control of Brahmsian rubato is masterly, easily flexible but totally unexaggerated, and the basic tempi are set well and steadily. The balance is not too forward and the effect is warmly satisfying. The account of the *B flat Concerto* is hardly less striking. The account of the Op. 10 *Ballades* is also a performance of distinction. There is some highlighting of subsidiary part-writing that may strike some as just a little self-conscious, but much else will delight the listener. The digital recording is first class.

In the *First Concerto* Katchen was not particularly well served by the balance provided by the Decca engineers, but he plays superbly, particularly in the first movement, and is sonorously matched by some fine playing by the LSO under Monteux. Again in No. 2 he gives an impassioned and exciting account of the solo piano part, combining great drive with the kind of ruminating delicacy Brahms so often calls for in his piano writing. The balance places the piano well within the orchestral framework and the sound is not too dated. The sets of solo variations, brilliant though they are, are not among the most compelling of Katchen's solo Brahms recordings for Decca. Oddly enough, for all their sheer pyrotechnical display, they sound comparatively unspontaneous.

Arrau's readings undoubtedly have vision and power, and the *D minor Concerto* is majestic and eloquent. There is some characteristic agogic distortion that will not convince all listeners, and, by the side of Gilels, Arrau seems idiosyncratic. In the *Second Concerto* his playing has a splendid combination of aristocratic finesse and warmth of feeling, and in both concertos Haitink and the Royal Concertgebouw Orchestra give excellent support. Excellent value, and the set is well documented.

Arrau's first stereo versions of the two Brahms concertos for EMI, made at the beginning of the 1960s, suffer from the feeling of a lack of affinity with the recording studio that has often afflicted him in the past. Nor is Giulini the ideal conductor for him, polished and weighty, without being really inspired. Arrau provides some delicious moments in the more graceful passages of the work but is never fiery in the way Curzon, for instance, is with Szell. The *Second Concerto* has a certain massive strength, helped by the full-bodied sound, but though the thought and sensitivity are there overall it hardly adds up to a very convincing performance.

Although Pollini and the Vienna Philharmonic under Karl Boehm are given finely detailed recording, in the *First Piano concerto* other versions (notably Gilels) provide greater wisdom and humanity. Not that Pollini is wanting in keyboard command, but he is a little short on tenderness and poetry. All too often here he seems to have switched on the automatic pilot and, although the *B flat Concerto* under Abbado is much fresher and offers some masterly pianism, there are warmer and more spontaneous accounts to be had.

Backhaus recorded the *First Concerto* in 1953 and no apologies need be made for the mono recording. The acoustics of the Musikverein ensure a fine spread of sound and the performance has great impetus and authority. The *Second Concerto* was made in the Sofiensaal in 1967 when Backhaus was in his eighties, and the rugged strength of his conception is matched by playing of remarkable power. His is a broad, magisterial account. The recording wears its years remarkably lightly: it sounds fresh, full-bodied and is finely detailed. (As can be seen above, this is also available separately in Decca's Classic Sound series, coupled with Mozart's *Piano concerto No. 27*.) The solo pieces date from 1956. Backhaus is again in excellent form, though the *Intermezzi*, which are played sensitively, come in for rather more subtle treatment than the *Capriccio* and *Rhapsody*.

Piano concerto No. 1 in D min., Op. 15.

*** Ph. Dig. 420 071-2. Brendel, BPO, Abbado.
(M) *** Decca Legends 466 376-2 [id.]. Clifford Curzon, LSO, Szell – FRANCK: *Symphonic variations* (with LITOLFF: *Scherzo*) ***.
(B) **(*) Sony SBK 48166 [id.]. Rudolf Serkin, Cleveland O, Szell – MENDELSSOHN: *Capriccio brillant* **; SCHUMANN: *Intro. and allegro appassionata.* **(*)
**(*) Decca Dig. 410 009-2 [id.]. Ashkenazy, Concg. O, Haitink.
(BB) **(*) ASV CDQS 6083. John Lill, Hallé O, Loughran.
(N) *(*) DG Dig. 447 041-2 [id.]. Maurizio Pollini, BPO, Claudio Abbado.
(N) (M) *(*) Sony SMK 60675 [id.]. Glenn Gould, NYPO, Leonard Bernstein.

(i) *Piano concerto No. 1. Variations and fugue on a theme of Handel, Op. 24.*

(***) Testament mono SBT1041 [id.]. Solomon, (i) Philh. O, Kubelik.

(i) *Piano concerto No. 1. 4 Ballades, Op. 10.*

(M) *** DG 439 979-2 [id.]. Gilels; (i) BPO, Jochum.

(i) *Piano concerto No. 1. 4 Ballades, Op. 10; Scherzo in E flat min., Op. 4.*

(B) *** Ph. Virtuoso 442 110-2 [(M) id. import]. Stephen Kovacevich; (i) LSO, Sir Colin Davis.

(i) *Piano concerto No. 1. Capriccio in B min., Op. 76/2; Intermezzo in E flat min., Op. 118/6; Rhapsody in B min., Op. 79/1.*

(M) **(*) RCA 09026 61263-2 [id.]. Artur Rubinstein; (i) Chicago SO, Reiner.

(i) *Piano concerto No. 1;* (ii) *2 Songs, Op. 91.*

✽ *** EMI Dig. CDC7 54578-2. (i) Stephen Kovacevich, LPO, Sawallisch; (ii) Anne Murray, Nobuko Imai.

Noble and dedicated, Stephen Kovacevich's account of the Brahms *D minor Concerto* is a performance of stature which belongs in the most exalted company. It can be recommended alongside such classic accounts as the Gilels/Jochum (DG); indeed, it must now take precedence. Moreover it is accorded fine digital sound which has all the warmth and spaciousness one could ask for, together with splendid presence and detail. There is a welcome fill-up in the form of the two Op. 91 *Songs* with viola, admirably presented by Anne Murray and Nobuko Imai.

Gilels's reading of the *D minor Concerto* has a magisterial strength blended with a warmth, humanity and depth that are altogether inspiring. The *Ballades* have never been played so marvellously on record, and the recording is very believable.

Among recent digital versions Brendel produces a consistently beautiful sound and balances the combative and lyrical elements of the work with well-nigh perfect judgement.

Clifford Curzon's 1962 recording, produced by John Culshaw in Kingsway Hall, returns to the catalogue, superbly remastered by the Decca engineers for the Legends series. The fierceness of attack in the upper strings, especially in the powerful opening tutti, sounds naturally focused on CD, adding a leonine power to Szell's orchestral contribution, and the piano tone is admirably natural. For this generous reissue, the Franck *Symphonic variations* and Litolff *Scherzo* have been added.

Kovacevich's earlier Philips account of the *D minor Concerto* is also available on a Duo, which pairs it with the *Second Concerto* and also includes the solo piano music (see above). Those who want the *First Concerto* alone should be well satisfied with this separate issue on the Philips Virtuoso bargain label.

Serkin's 1968 account with Szell, his third on LP, brought tremendous command and grandeur. This is undoubtedly a memorable performance and the support from Szell and the Cleveland Orchestra has great power. The CBS/Sony recording has been considerably improved, but the balance still lacks a natural perspective and the sound ideally needs more opulence and depth.

Ashkenazy gives a commanding and magisterial account of the solo part that is full of poetic imagination. The performance is very impressive indeed and there is superlative playing from the Concertgebouw Orchestra. The recording is enormously vivid.

Rubinstein's Chicago recording was made in stereo as early as 1954 and the sound remains remarkably good, thanks to the sympathetic Chicago acoustics. This is a poetic and essentially lyrical reading, a fine memento of a great artist, not the most profound version but a consistently enjoyable one.

Solomon's magisterial account with Rafael Kubelik and the Philharmonia Orchestra belongs among the greatest ever made. It has a majestic grandeur and blends the dramatic power of youth with the wisdom of old age. Of course the 1952 recording does not possess the range or bloom of subsequent versions, but the transfer succeeds in making it sound astonishingly present. Of his celebrated 1942 set of the Brahms *Handel variations* one is tempted to say the same.

John Lill has the measure of the work's fire and drama, yet his playing is fundamentally classical. He is given warm and spirited support from Loughran and the Hallé even though woodwind intonation in one or two places is not wholly above reproach. At times there is a slightly reserved quality that inhibits unqualified recommendation.

Like his account of the *Second Concerto* with the Berlin Philharmonic and Abbado, Pollini's digital version comes without any fill-up, which is hardly competitive at premium price. Recorded at a concert performance when the orchestra was visiting the Musikverein in Vienna, it is further handicapped by a balance which places the piano far too forward. The pianism impresses as always though the overall effect is marmoreal and ultimately uninvolving.

Glenn Gould's performance carries a prefatory disclaimer from Bernstein, something rarely encountered in the concert hall and unprecedented on disc. Recorded at a Carnegie Hall concert in New York in April 1962, the performance is new to the catalogue, it finds the Canadian pianist at his most wilful and self-conscious. Of course it offers moments of insight but for the most part, this is for Gould *aficionados* only. Others will be spectacularly underwhelmed.

(i) *Piano concerto No. 1 in D min. 4 Ballades Op. 10; 2 Capricci, Op. 76/1–2; Intermezzo in B flat, Op. 76/4; 2 Rhapsodies, Op. 79; Piano sonata No. 3 in F min., Op. 5; Scherzo in E flat, Op. 4.*
(B) *** DG Double mono/stereo 437 374-2 (2) [id.]. Wilhelm Kempff; (i) Dresden State O, Konwitschny.

Kempff was born in 1895, two years before the death of Brahms, and the great pianist himself died in 1991. This set spans his major solo Brahms recordings, made between 1957 and 1963, and includes the mono account of the Brahms *D minor Concerto* from 1956; no complaints about the DG recording of this work. Kempff entering thoughtfully is able immediately to create rapt inner tension, yet providing the necessary bravura while investing the *Adagio* with characteristic poetry and bringing joyfully articulated vigour to the finale. This version of the concerto is also available at mid-price on a single CD, coupled with Kempff's mono reading of the *Handel variations*, less desirable than the present coupling. In the solo items, mostly recorded in the early 1960s, poetry is emphasized rather than brilliance, and the absence of extrovert virtuosity in Op. 79 does not mean that the music is without a strong impulse. The four *Ballades* emerge very much as a young man's music, full of ardour, as does the *F minor Sonata* which could hardly be warmer or more sympathetic. The *Scherzo in E flat minor* – still comparatively rarely heard – makes a fine encore. We noted at the time of the LP issue that the recording was splendidly full and clear and that the acoustic of the studio seemed just about right.

Piano concerto No. 2 in B flat, Op. 83.
*** Ph. Dig. 432 975-2. Brendel, BPO, Abbado.
(BB) **(*) ASV CDQS 6088. John Lill, Hallé O, Loughran.
(M) **(*) RCA 09026 64820-2 [id.]. Van Cliburn, Chicago SO, Reiner – MACDOWELL: Piano concerto No. 2. **(*)
(B) **(*) Sony SBK 53262 [id.]. Rudolf Serkin, Cleveland SO, Szell – R. STRAUSS: *Burleske.* *(**)
(N) **(*) DG Dig. 453 505-2 [id.]. Maurizio Pollini, BPO, Claudio Abbado.

(i) *Piano concerto No. 2; 4 Ballades, Op. 10.*
(M) *** DG 439 466-2 [435 588-2]. Gilels; (i) BPO, Jochum.

(i) *Piano concerto No. 2. Intermezzi: in E min., Op. 116/5; in B flat min., Op. 117/2; Rhapsody in G min., Op. 79/2.*
(M) *** RCA 09026 61442-2 [id.]. Rubinstein, (i) RCA Victor SO, Krips.

(i) *Piano concerto No. 2. Intermezzo in B flat min., Op. 117/2; in C, Op. 119/3; Rhapsody in G min., Op. 79/2.*
(***) Testament mono SBT1042 [id.]. Solomon, (i) Philh. O, Dobrowen.

(i) *Piano concerto No. 2;* (ii) *5 Lieder, Op. 105.*
**(*) EMI (SIS) Dig. CDC5 55218-2. (i–ii) Stephen Kovacevich; (ii) Ann Murray; (i) LPO, Wolfgang Sawallisch.

(i) *Piano concerto No. 2 in B flat. Symphony No. 1 in C min., Op. 61; Serenade No. 1 in D: Allegro molto.*
(N) (B) (**(*)) Naxos mono 8.110805/6 [id.]. (i) Horowitz; NBC SO, Toscanini; (with broadcast commentary by Gene Hamilton).

The partnership of Gilels and Jochum produces music-making of rare magic and the digital remastering has improved definition: the sound is full in an appropriately Brahmsian way. Readers will note that this reissue is now recoupled with the *4 Ballades*, Op. 10 (instead of the *Fantasias*, Op. 116), which seems perverse when the Gilels version of the *First Concerto* has the same coupling.

Brendel is massive and concentrated, and has greater depth than in his earlier account with Haitink. It is a worthy successor to their *D minor*, though in terms of humanity and wisdom it does not displace the celebrated Gilels–Jochum version.

Barenboim's reading with Barbirolli is a performance to cherish in its glowing spontaneity. Of the fill-ups, the *Tragic overture* is a performance of considerable distinction; but the measured account of the *Academic festival overture* could do with more sparkle.

Rubinstein was at his peak in 1958, and his technical mastery brings a charismatic response to the changing moods of the first movement, while the finale is a delight with its deftness of articulation and rippling lyricism. This reading emphasizes the bright and luminous aspects of the work and is all the more refreshing for that.

The commanding Solomon version of the *B flat Concerto* with Issay Dobrowen and the Philharmonia Orchestra comes from 1947. There is a leonine nobility about this performance and an immediacy, spontaneity and dramatic fire that sweep all before it. Like his *D minor Concerto*, this is a classic account, which no admirer of this artist (or of Brahms, for that matter) should pass over.

After his noble and dedicated account of the *First Piano concerto* with Wolfgang Sawallisch and the LPO, Stephen Kovacevich's version of its successor brings admiration tinged with disappointment. It does not match this partnership's *First* and does not take wing in quite the same way.

John Lill's 1982 version with the Hallé Orchestra under James Loughran is in many ways a strong account, well thought out, finely paced and without the slightest trace of self-indulgence. It is the space and power of Brahms's conception that are given priority, rather than his poetry.

Van Cliburn had a really great Brahms conductor to accompany him. To hear van Cliburn at his finest, go to the finale, where the gypsy themes have an infectious gaiety such as only Rubinstein otherwise conveys. The Chicago acoustics ensure a full-bodied Brahmsian sound, better than ever in the current remastering.

Serkin achieves an ideal balance between straightforwardness and expressiveness, while the slow movement has a genuine 'inner' intensity. He chooses a comparatively slow speed for the finale, but the flow and energy of the music are not impaired. Unfortunately the piano tone is not as full as one would ideally like, but the remastering produces a firm orchestral image and the hall ambience contributes to a Brahmsian sonority.

Though, with announcements, this Naxos version spreads to a second disc, and the 1940 sound is rough, it offers not only a glowing account of the *First Symphony* but a performance of the *Second Concerto* which makes it a symphony with piano. Even the mighty virtuoso, Horowitz, Toscanini's son-in-law, is outshone. The first movement of the *Serenade No. 1* acts as a light-hearted overture.

Pollini's latest account was made at a live concerto in Berlin in 1996 and is as one might expect, a performance of commanding quality. The sound is very good indeed even if, judged by the very highest standards, the balance is just a little synthetic. All the same, 48 minutes' music for a premium-price disc seems uncompetitive, however distinguished the performance. Gilels and Böhm, Kovacevich and Sawallisch are to be preferred.

Violin concerto in D, Op. 77.

*** Decca Dig. 444 811-2 [id.]. Joshua Bell, Cleveland O, Christoph von Dohnányi – SCHUMANN: *Violin concerto.* ***

(B) *** EMI Dig. CD-EMX 2203 [id.]. Tasmin Little, RLPO, Handley – SIBELIUS: *Violin concerto.* ***

(M) *** RCA 09026 61742-2. Heifetz, Chicago SO, Reiner – BEETHOVEN: *Concerto.* ***

(M) *** DG Dig. 445 515-2 [415 565-2]. Anne-Sophie Mutter, BPO, Karajan – MENDELSSOHN: *Violin concerto.* ***

*** EMI (SIS) Dig. CDC7 54580-2 [id.]. Itzhak Perlman, BPO, Barenboim.

*** ASV CDDCA 748 [id.]. Xue-Wei, LPO, Ivor Bolton – MENDELSSOHN: *Violin concerto.* ***

(B) *** Decca Eclipse Dig. 448 988-2 [(M) id. import]. Boris Belkin, LSO, Ivan Fischer – R. STRAUSS: *Violin concerto.* **(*)

*** Chandos Dig. CHAN 8974 [id.]. Hideko Udagawa, LSO, Mackerras – BRUCH: *Concerto No. 1.* ***

(***) EMI mono CDH7 61011-2. Ginette Neveu, Philh. O, Issay Dobrowen – SIBELIUS: *Concerto.* (***)

(***) Testament mono SBT 1037 [id.]. Johanna Martzy, Philh. O, Kletzki – MENDELSSOHN: *Concerto.* (***)

(***) Testament mono SBT 1038 [id.]. Ida Haendel, LSO, Celibidache – TCHAIKOVSKY: *Concerto.* (***)

(N) (M) *** EMI CDM5 66977-2 [CDM5 66992]. Perlman, Chicago SO, Giulini.

**(*) EMI Dig. CDC7 54187-2 [id.]. Kennedy, LPO, Klaus Tennstedt.

(M) **(*) EMI CDM7 64632-2 [id.]. David Oistrakh, Fr. Nat. RSO, Klemperer – MOZART: *Sinfonia concertante.* **

(B) **(*) DG Double 453 142-2 (2) [id.]. Nathan Milstein, VPO, Jochum – BEETHOVEN; MENDELSSOHN; TCHAIKOVSKY: *Concertos.* ***

(N)**(*) DG Dig. 457 075-2 [id.]. Anne-Sofie Mutter, NYPO, Masur (with SCHUMANN: *Fantasy, Op. 131.* ***)

(*) EMI (SIS) Dig. CDC5 55426-2 [id.]. Frank Peter Zimmermann, BPO, Sawallisch – MOZART: *Violin concerto No. 3.* *

(BB) **(*) RCA/Navigator Dig. 74321 29245-2 [60479-2-TV]. Ughi, Philh. O, Sawallisch – BRUCH: *Violin concerto.* **(*)

(i) *Violin concerto in D; Tragic overture, Op. 81.*

(B) *** Ph. Virtuoso 422 972-2 [(M) id. import]. (i) Hermann Krebbers; Concg. O, Haitink.

Joshua Bell is an outstanding young soloist who, though very highly regarded in America, has only just begun to establish himself on this side of the Atlantic. This commanding performance of the Brahms *Concerto* will surely confirm his reputation as a major recording artist. The playing is full of flair, demonstrating not only his love of bravura display, but also his ready gift for turning a phrase individually in a way that catches the ear, always sounding spontaneous. Full, atmospheric recording and a no less outstanding coupling put this among the very finest versions.

Tasmin Little gives a warmly satisfying account of the Brahms, at once brilliant and deeply felt. At bargain-price the disc is even more recommendable, as it also contains an equally searching and exuberant account of the Sibelius *Violin concerto*.

Like the Beethoven with which it is coupled, the CD transfer of Heifetz's dazzling performance makes vivid and fresh what on LP was originally a rather harsh Chicago recording, more aggressive than the Boston sound in the Beethoven. With the CD, the excellent qualities of RCA's Chicago balance for Reiner come out in full, giving a fine three-dimensional focus.

Hermann Krebbers, concertmaster of the Concertgebouw Orchestra, here gives one of the most deeply satisfying readings of the Brahms *Violin concerto* ever recorded: strong and urgent yet at the same time tenderly poetic, and always full of spontaneous imagination. The 1973 recording has been successfully remastered: the effect, with the violin slightly forward but not too obtrusively so, is full and immediate. But instead of offering another major concerto, the Philips bargain reissue gives us just the *Tragic overture*.

In many ways the playing of Anne-Sophie Mutter combines the unforced lyrical feeling of Krebbers with the flair and individuality of Perlman. There is a lightness of touch, a gentleness in the slow movement that is highly appealing, while in the finale the incisiveness of the solo playing is well displayed by the clear (yet not clinical) digital recording. Needless to say, Karajan's accompaniment is strong in personality and the Berlin Philharmonic play beautifully; the performance represents a genuine musical partnership between youthful inspiration and eager experience. The recording balance places the soloist rather close, but on this newly remastered CD the orchestral sound, while retaining its vivid presence, is smoother on top. The coupling is hardly less attractive.

Perlman's newest digital account of the Brahms finds him at his most commanding, powerful and full of nonchalant flair to a degree that no rival today can quite match. With Perlman the advantage of a live recording is that, as here, there is an extra warmth of commitment, with no sense that the performance has been too easily achieved. There is no fill-up, but few will complain with a reading that is so strong and compelling.

Those looking for a bargain digital recording should be well pleased with Boris Belkin's 1983 Decca Eclipse reissue, particularly as it is now generously recoupled with the engaging Mendelssohnian concerto of Richard Strauss. This is far more than a routine performance and, with excellent sound and a good balance, it is very competitive.

Xue-Wei's version of the Brahms is fresh and well-mannered. There is a degree of emotional reticence here compared with more flamboyant performers but, with Ivor Bolton drawing first-rate playing from the LPO, it is a performance to live with and can be warmly recommended. The sound is first rate too.

Hideko Udagawa gives a powerful, persuasively spontaneous-sounding reading. Her biting attack on the most taxing passages is often thrilling, even if her violin-sound is not always the sweetest. The personality of the player and her magnetic temperament submerge reservations on detail, particularly when Mackerras draws comparably powerful playing from the LSO. Warm, full and well-balanced recording.

Ginette Neveu's is a magnificent performance, urgently electric, remarkable not just for sweetness of tone and her pinpoint intonation but also for the precision and clarity of even the most formidable passages of double stopping. The transfer from the original 78s brings satisfyingly full-bodied sound, surprisingly good on detail.

Johanna Martzy's warmth of temperament is also ideal. She always sounds spontaneous in her freely flexible rubato which never falls into wilfulness or sentimentality. Hers is an exceptionally warm and persuasive account of the Brahms, marked by a very wide range of dynamic and tone. Few versions of whatever period can match the hushed tenderness of Martzy in the coda of the first movement, and so it is too in the slow movement, while the finale is played with Hungarian point and flair. Kletzki proves an ideal accompanist. The Testament reissue, superbly transferred, ideally coupled with an equally inspired account of the Mendelssohn, at last does justice to a long-underappreciated artist.

With Sergiu Celibidache making a rare appearance as conductor on disc, Ida Haendel, too, gives a powerful, full-toned reading of the Brahms. Recorded in mono in 1953, it comes up very freshly and intensely in this superb CD transfer from Testament, and the clarity and bite of the playing, as well as its strength and nobility, are splendidly caught, confirming the mastery of a great violinist too little heard on disc.

EMI have chosen Perlman's distinguished earlier account of 1976 for reissue in their 'Great recordings of the century' series. He is finely supported by Giulini and the Chicago Symphony Orchestra, and gives a reading of a darker hue than is customary, with a thoughtful, searching slow movement, rather than the autumnal rhapsody which it so often becomes. Giulini could be tauter, perhaps, in the first movement, but the songful playing of Perlman always holds the listener. The spacious recording is warm and full-bodied. It places the soloist rather too forward, and the orchestral detail could be more transparent, but admirers of Perlman looking for an alternative performance need not hesitate, this is both impressive and convincing. However the general collector will probably prefer the newer digital version, unless economy is a deciding factor. Neither CD has a coupling.

Kennedy's version of the Brahms is by a fair margin the slowest ever put on disc, but his devotion to the work give an intensity to sustain all the eccentricities. Tennstedt draws concentrated playing from the LPO, the whole richly recorded.

The conjunction of two such positive artists as Oistrakh and Klemperer makes for a reading characterful to the point of idiosyncrasy, monumental and strong rather than sweetly lyrical. Oistrakh sounds superbly poised and confident, and in the finale, if the tempo is a shade deliberate, the total effect is one of clear gain. The 1961 recording seems smoother than in its most recent incarnation.

To praise Milstein's version for the refinement and beauty of the accompaniment may sound like a backhanded compliment, and so perhaps it is when, for all the beauty and brilliance of the playing, this is not quite the flawless Milstein reading of the Brahms that he had previously put on record for other companies. Jochum secures playing of great warmth and distinction from the Vienna Philharmonic, and the hint of unease in the soloist is only relative. Those who want to hear Milstein in fine (1974) analogue sound can be safely directed here, for there are no such reservations about the other three performances on this DG Double.

In her New York recording, Anne-Sofie Mutter cannot quite match the mastery of her early version with Karajan. Her tone, as recorded, is less evenly beautiful, and live performance brings idiosyncrasies and the occasional flaw. It remains an enjoyable, warm-hearted version, recommendable for the unusual Schumann coupling.

Uto Ughi's account has the advantage of a strong and passionate orchestral backing from Sawallisch and first-rate (1983) digital sound, with a good balance. As with the Bruch coupling, this is a fresh and direct reading, not as charismatic as some, but with moments of considerable lyrical intensity and by no means unimaginative in the control of light and shade. In the bargain basement it is well worth considering – and even at mid-price, as issued in the USA.

Violin concerto (with cadenzas by Busoni, Joachim, Singer, Hermann, Auer, Ysaÿe, Ondricek, Kneisel, Marteau, Kreisler, Tovey, Kubelik, Busch, Heifetz, Milstein, Ricci).
*** Biddulph Dig. LAW 002 [id.]. Ruggiero Ricci, Sinf. of London, Del Mar.

The veteran Ruggiero Ricci not only gives a strong, assured performance of the concerto, he adds no fewer than 16 cadenzas as well, any of which can be programmed into the main performance on CD. Though Ricci is no longer as fiery or incisive as he once was, his is an attractive performance of the concerto, well recorded.

(i) *Violin concerto in D, Op. 77;* (ii) *Double concerto for violin, cello and orchestra in A min., Op. 102.*
(B) **(*) Sony SBK 46335 [id.]. Stern, (ii) with Rose; Phd. O, Ormandy.
(M) **(*) Sony Stern Edition I SM2K 66941 (2) [id.]. Isaac Stern, with (i) NYPO, Mehta; (ii) Rose, Phd. O, Ormandy – BEETHOVEN: *Concertos.* **(*)

Stern's glorious 1959 account of the *Violin concerto* with Ormandy is now given a coupling that is both generous and suitable, the mid-1960s collaboration with Leonard Rose in the *Double concerto*. The two soloists unfailingly match each other's playing, with Ormandy always an understanding accompanist.

Once again a wrong choice has been made for the Sony Stern Edition: instead of the 1959 account of the *Violin concerto* with Ormandy, the later (1978) version has been selected. Here Stern certainly has the measure of the *Violin concerto*'s lyricism and also its rhetoric. There are many thoughtful touches, but the orchestral playing under Mehta is not particularly distinguished; it is a little undercharacterized, and the recording is not in the first flight either. The mid-1960s recording of the *Double concerto* is another matter. Here, each soloist has a creative ear in pointing a comment so that the response is made to sound like an unfolding conversation. The forward balance brings glorious tone, even if this means that there are no pianissimos (although one can tell when they are playing quietly from the tone-colour). The CD transfer is well managed; the sound overall is full and clear.

(i) *Violin concerto in D, Op. 77;* (ii) *Symphony No. 2 in D, Op. 73.*
(B) *** Millennium Universal UMD 80394. (i) Erica Morini, RPO, Rodzinski; (ii) Pittsburgh SO, Steinberg.

This coupling is a treasurable discovery – two very early Brahms stereo recordings, the *Violin concerto* made in London in September 1956. Erica Morini gives an inspirational performance. Her initial presentation of the main lyrical theme in the first movement is ravishingly gentle and when it reappears on the half-tone after the cadenza the effect is of total magic, drawing a parallel with a similar sequence in the Beethoven concerto. Her playing in the *Adagio* is exquisite, again using lower dynamic levels to bewitching effect, while the buoyant Hungarian finale dances away with vigour and strength, yet never becoming merely lightweight. Artur Rodzinski proves an ideal partner, strong in ritornello yet warmly flexible in phrasing and rubato, following the lead of his soloist and always taking care with detail, and with the RPO continually responsive. The recording is bright, the soloist rather too forward – her timbre is relatively slender – but there is plenty of contrasting weight in the orchestra. Steinberg then takes over for a splendidly shaped *Second Symphony*, warmly and passionately spontaneous and gripping. The Pittsburgh strings produce a rich body of tone in the slow movement (and indeed for the second subject of the finale). The *Allegretto* is taken a fraction faster than usual, but its grazioso feeling is not lost, and the finale has splendid impetus, with a thrilling coda. The recording is brightly lit, but the Pittsburgh Hall gives plenty of ambient weight. A most rewarding coupling, well worth its modest cost.

(i) *Violin concerto*; (ii) *Violin sonata No. 3 in D min., Op. 108.*
(N) **(*) Teldec/Warner 0630 17144-2 [id.]. Maxim Vengerov; (i) Chicago SO, Barenboim; (ii) Barenboim (piano).

For E. G. this is an outstanding coupling. Maxim Vengerov here triumphantly tackles one of the most formidable war-horses among violin concertos, playing not just for display but with far deeper insights. This is not a live recording but it has the feel of one in its tensions, the inspiration of the moment captured at white heat. Using the widest dynamic and tonal range, this is a performance of extremes, just as felicitous in bravura as in lyrical purity. It adds to the feeling of new discovery that Vengerov uses a formidable cadenza he has written himself. In the slow movement he is light and flexibly songful, and the finale is taken fast, with a joyful swagger underlining its folk-like quality. The account of the *Violin sonata* is inspired too, with Vengerov bringing out the mystery of this minor-key work, and with Barenboim at the piano freely spontaneous too. Excellent sound, with no spotlighting of the violin. R. L., while not denying that Vengerov's technique is dazzling and spectacular, and that he produces a wonderful sound, finds the performance of the *concerto* open to the charge of being a bit too gleaming and slick, a kind of 'Brahms on Madison Avenue', and no match for the classic accounts listed above.

(i) *Violin concerto in D, Op. 77;* (ii) *Violin sonata No. 3 in D min., Op. 108;* (iii) *Variations on a theme of Paganini, Op. 35.*
(***) EMI (SIS) mono CDH5 66421-2. (i–ii)

Joseph Szigeti; (i) Hallé O, Sir Hamilton Harty; (ii–iii) Egon Petri.

In the immediate post-war years Szigeti recorded the Brahms concerto with Bruno Walter and the New York Philharmonic and again in Philadelphia with Ormandy. As part of the Brahms centenary celebrations, EMI have restored to circulation Szigeti's 1928 recordings with the Hallé Orchestra and Sir Hamilton Harty. Szigeti somehow blends serenity with a nervous intensity that is quite distinctive, and the transfer engineers have managed to bring colour to the faded sound. He forged a strong bond with Harty, having given the première of the latter's *Violin concerto* in 1908. The *D minor Sonata*, which he recorded with Egon Petri in 1937, is a reminder of their distinguished partnership, while Petri himself is represented by his celebrated account of both books of the *Paganini variations*. Exemplary transfers by Andrew Walter and Simon Gibson.

Double concerto for violin, cello and orchestra in A min., Op. 102.

(N) (M) *** EMI CDM5 66902-2 [CDM5 66954]. D. Oistrakh, Rostropovich, Cleveland O, Szell – BEETHOVEN: *Triple concerto for violin, cello and piano in C, Op. 36.* ***

(B) *** EMI forte (SIS) CZS5 69331-2 (2) [CDFB 69331]. David Oistrakh, Pierre Fournier, Philh. O, Galliera – BEETHOVEN: *Triple concerto;* MOZART: *Violin concerto No. 3;* PROKOFIEV: *Violin concerto No. 2.* ***

(N) *** Teldec/Warner Dig. 0630-15870-2 [id.]. Perlman; Ma, Chicago SO, Barenboim – MENDELSSOHN: *Violin concerto.* ***

(N) *** RCA Dig. 09026 68964-2 [id.]. Pinchas Zukerman, Ralph Kirshbaum, LSO, Eschenbach – BEETHOVEN: *Triple concerto.* ***

(BB) *** Naxos 8.550938 [id.]. Ilya Kaler, Maria Kliegel, Nat. SO of Ireland, Andrew Constantine – SCHUMANN: *Cello concerto.* ***

This (1969) EMI recording of the *Double concerto* has claims to be regarded as one of the finest of all versions. The remastered sound is full and vivid and has great presence. If it places the soloists too far forward, few will grumble when the playing is so ripely, compellingly Brahmsian and the solo timbres so richly projected. The *Andante* is glorious. Szell's powerful tutti and warmly sympathetic backing keep the Cleveland Orchestra well in the picture. Coupled with an equally arresting version of Beethoven's *Triple concerto*, this reissue is a superb bargain of the first order, and is fully worthy of its reissue as one of EMI's 'Great recordings of the century'.

David Oistrakh's first stereo account with Fournier dates from 1959, but the recording was balanced by Walter Legge and the sound is remarkably satisfying. The performance is distinguished, strong and lyrical – the slow movement particularly fine – and, with Galliera and the Philharmonia providing excellent support, this version, coupled with three other outstanding concerto recordings, makes an ideal choice for bargain-hunters.

In the live Teldec recording conducted by Barenboim, Perlman, in collaboration with Yo-Yo Ma, is more volatile, more flexible than when his partners were Rostropovich and Haitink on the 1979 Concertgebouw recording on EMI. Although in the outer movements the speeds are noticeably faster than before, Perlman and Ma are both freer, broadening more markedly in moments of repose, while the finale dances with extra lightness. A great performance, well-recorded, and well-coupled with Perlman's 1993 Chicago version of the Mendelssohn.

Zukerman and Kirshbaum are even more persuasive in this Brahms performance than they are in the Beethoven *Triple concerto* with which it is coupled, helped by the warm, positive accompaniment from the LSO under Eschenbach. Speeds are on the broad side – arguably too much so in the central Andante, but this can safely be recommended to anyone wanting a recent recording of this apt and generous coupling.

The Brahms and Schumann concertos make an excellent and apt coupling, here presented on the Naxos super-budget label in warmly spontaneous-sounding recordings, very well recorded. There are not many versions of the Brahms more warmly appealing than this, for the violinist, Ilya Kaler, is as clean in attack and intonation as is Maria Kliegel, who earlier impressed with her Naxos coupling of the Dvořák and Elgar *Cello concertos*.

(i) *Double concerto in A min. for violin, cello and orchestra;* (ii) *Symphony No. 4 in E min.*

(B) (**(*)) Dutton Lab. mono CDEA 5006 [id.]. (i) Jacques Thibaud, Pablo Casals, Pau Casals O, Barcelona, Alfred Cortot; (ii) Dresden State O, Karl Boehm.

The Thibaud/Casals/Cortot recording of the *Double concerto* is a gramophone classic, with superb contributions from all concerned; and Mike Dutton's transfer (from 78 shellac pressings) is worthy of it. Sadly the sound-balance in Boehm's suberb 1939 account of the *Fourth Symphony* with the Dresden Staatskapelle is less convincing. The focus is admirably clear, but the strings lack body and there is not enough middle and bass (so essential in a Brahms symphony) to balance the clean, bright upper range. Both I. M. and R. L. grew up on this performance and still hold it in great esteem, but the results here are comparatively disappointing.

Hungarian dances Nos. 1–21 (complete).
✿ (BB) *** Naxos Dig. 8.550110; *4550110* (*Nos. 1–2; 4–21*). Budapest SO, István Bogár.
(B) *** Decca Eclipse Dig. 448 240-2 [(M) id. import]. RPO, Walter Weller (with DVORAK: *Slavonic dances, Op. 46/1–3 & 6–8*; cond. Dorati **(*)).
(M) **(*) Chandos Enchant Dig. CHAN 7072 [id.]. LSO, Neeme Järvi.

The Budapest recording of the Brahms *Hungarian dances* is sheer delight from beginning to end. The playing has warmth and sparkle, and the natural way the music unfolds brings a refreshing feeling of rhythmic freedom. Bogár's rubato is wholly spontaneous. The recording is warm and full, yet transparent, with just the right brilliance on top. This is an outright winner among the available versions.

The RPO also play with wonderful spirit, as if they were enjoying every moment, and Walter Weller secures excellent playing from every department of the orchestra. The Kingsway Hall recording is lively and bright, eminently truthful in timbre and with good natural perspective. Moreover the Decca Eclipse reissue offers six *Slavonic dances* from Dvořák's Op. 46 as a considerable bonus. Dorati's performances have comparable *brio*, and the recording (in the same venue) is just as vivid, if not quite so sweet on top.

The Chandos recording is characteristically sumptuous and Järvi is warmly affectionate, attractively coaxing the rubato of a dance like No. 7 in F major. There is plenty of spirit and flexibility elsewhere, and this set is certainly warmly enjoyable. Yet both Weller and (especially) Bogár are even more spontaneously Hungarian in spirit.

Hungarian dances Nos. 1–2, 4 & 7.
*** EMI (SIS) Dig. CDC7 54753-2 [id.]. Sarah Chang, Jonathan Feldman – TCHAIKOVSKY: *Violin concerto*. ***

It may be an ungenerous coupling for the Tchaikovsky *Concerto*, but Chang's performances of four of the Brahms *Hungarian dances* – recorded with Jonathan Feldman in New York – are delectable.

Hungarian dances Nos. 1, 3, 5–6, 17–20.
(M) *** DG 447 434-2 [id.]. BPO, Karajan – DVORAK: *Scherzo capriccioso; 5 Slavonic dances*. **(*)

Karajan's performances have great panache and brilliance. But the brightly lit (1959) recording, reissued in DG's 'Originals' series, is given added fullness in the current remastering, and the superlative orchestral playing is by turns warmly affectionate and dazzling. The coupling offers comparably virtuoso performances of Dvořák's *Slavonic dances* and the *Scherzo capriccioso*.

Piano quartet in G min. (orch. Schoenberg); *Variations and fugue on a theme by Handel, Op. 24* (orch. Rubbra).
*** Chandos Dig. CHAN 8825 [id.]. LSO, Järvi.

The current craze for Schoenberg's transcription of the Brahms *Piano quartet in G minor* is puzzling. Neeme Järvi's new version with the LSO is as good as any. It is performed with some enthusiasm and well recorded.

Serenades Nos. 1 in D, Op. 11; 2 in A, Op. 16.
(M) *** Sony Theta Dig. SMK 60134 [id.]. LSO, Michael Tilson Thomas.
(N) (B) **(*) Ph. Virtuoso 432 510-2 [id.]. Concg. O, Haitink.

Serenades Nos. 1–2; Hungarian dances Nos. 1, 3 & 10.
(BB) *** ASV Quicksilva Dig. CDQS 6216 [(M) id.]. Philh. O, Francesco D'Avalos.

The reissue of Michael Tilson Thomas's digital recordings of the two *Serenades* (originally issued separately) on Sony's new Theta label tends to sweep the board, irrespective of price. His account of the glorious D major work has a sunny geniality and a youthful radiance that are most persuasive, and the A major is equally fresh. He gets admirable results from the LSO, and these readings have both vitality and sensitivity. The Sony recordings are natural and well detailed.

D'Avalos, too, gets some splendid playing from the Philharmonia. A fine, inexpensive alternative to the Sony coupling, which remains first choice.

Haitink's account of the *D major Serenade* is finely proportioned, relaxed yet vital. The Concertgebouw wind-playing is particularly distinguished and, while the players obviously relish the many delights of this underrated score, the architecture is held together firmly and without the slightest trace of expressive indulgence. However the resonant Concertgebouw acoustic, while giving agreeably full textures, does not afford the same degree of freshness and transparency to the sound-picture as on the competing Sony and ASV versions: the effect is more symphonic, less light-hearted. The *A major Serenade* has lighter scoring (Brahms's string section omits violins altogether) and while the recording is warm, it is yet more lucid in detail. Haintink's performance is similarly sound in conception and well shaped, and the conductor's affection is obvious. But this is not a first choice.

(i) *Serenades Nos. 1 in D, Op. 11; 2 in A, Op. 16; Academic festival overture;* (ii) *Tragic overture, Op. 81;* (i) *Variations on a theme of Haydn, Op. 56a;* (i, iii) *Alto rhapsody, Op. 53.*
(B) **(*) EMI forte (SIS) CZS5 68655-2 (2) [CDFB 68655]. (i) LPO; (ii) LSO; (iii) with J. Baker, John Alldis Ch.; all cond. Boult.

Sir Adrian Boult's warmly lyrical approach to the two *Serenades* is less ebullient and sparkling than that of Tilson Thomas or D'Avalos, yet he gives pleasure in a different way. The mellow opening of No. 2 is particularly appealing and with excellent orchestral playing he produces ripe performances, glowing and fresh. His spacious tempi are not always conventional, but Boult's way with these delightful scores is engaging enough to blunt any criticism, when the late-1970s Abbey Road recording is suitably full. What makes this inexpensive forte reissue even more attractive is the inclusion of Dame Janet Baker's devoted account of the *Alto rhapsody*, the performance essentially meditative, even though Boult's style is unlingering and the manner totally unindulgent, supported by warm, Abbey Road sound. The *Academic festival overture* opens the programme in a rather more extrovert fashion, and the *Variations* are also vividly presented and strongly characterized, the sound here rather more lively. The eloquent *Tragic overture* also shows Boult as a true Brahmsian. In playing time (just under two hours), however, this is rather less generous than some forte doubles.

Tragic Overture, Op. 81.
(M) *** EMI (SIS) CMS5 66109-2 (2) [id.]. BPO, Karajan – BRUCKNER: *Symphony No. 8;* HINDEMITH: *Mathis der Maler* (symphony). ***

A strong and impulsive, yet highly sympathetic performance from Karajan, showing him at his most charismatic. It is very well played and excellently recorded in the Berlin Jesus-Christus-Kirche in 1970. This set is a highlight of EMI's Karajan Edition, for the couplings are equally fine.

SYMPHONIES

Symphonies Nos. 1–4.
(B) *** DG Double 453 097-2 (2) [(M) id. import]. BPO, Karajan.
(M) **(*) Mercury 434 380-2 (2) [id.]. LSO, or (*No. 2*) Minneapolis SO, Antal Dorati.
(M) **(*) DG 429 644-2 (3) [id.]. BPO, Karajan.
(B) **(*) RCA Dig. 74321 20283-2 (2). N. German RSO, Günter Wand.
(M) (**(*)) DG mono 449 715-2 (2) [id.]. BPO, Eugen Jochum.
(N) (B) (**(*)) RCA mono Twofer 74321 55838-2 (2) [id.]. NBC SO, Toscanini.
(N) ** DG 459 635-2(3) [id.]. SW German RO, Stuttgart, Sergiu Celibidache.

Symphonies Nos 1–4, Hungarian dances Nos. 1, 3 & 10; Variations on a theme of Haydn.
(M) (**(*)) EMI CHS5 65513-2 (3) [ZDHC 65513]. BPO or VPO, Furtwängler – BEETHOVEN: *Overtures.* (***)

Symphonies Nos. 1–4; Academic festival overture; Tragic overture; Variations on a theme of Haydn, Op. 56a.
**(*) Erato/Warner Dig. 4509 94817-2 (4). Chicago SO, Barenboim.

Symphonies Nos. 1–4; Academic festival overture; Tragic overture; Variations on a theme of Haydn; (i) *Hungarian dances Nos. 17–21.*
(B) **(*) Sony SB3K 48398 (3). Cleveland O, George Szell; (i) Phd. O, Ormandy.

Symphonies Nos. 1–4; Academic festival overture; Tragic overture; Variations on a theme of Haydn, Op. 56a; (i) *Alto rhapsody, Op. 53; Fragment from Goethe's Harz Journey in Winter;* (ii) *Gesang der Parzen (Song of the Fates), Op. 89; Nänie, Op. 82; Schicksalslied, Op. 54.*
*** DG Dig. 435 683-2 (4) [id.]. BPO, Abbado; (i) with Marjana Lipovšek, Ernest Senf Ch.; (ii) Berlin R. Ch.

Symphonies Nos. 1–4; Tragic overture; Variations on a theme by Haydn.
(BB) *** RCA Navigator 74321 30367-2 (3) [(M) id. import]. Dresden State O, Kurt Sanderling.
(N) *** Telarc Dig. CD-80450 (4) [id.]. Scottish CO, Sir Charles Mackerras.
(***) Testament mono/stereo SBT 3054 (3) [id.]. BPO, Rudolf Kempe.
**(*) DG Dig. 427 602-2 (3) [id.]. BPO, Karajan.

Symphonies Nos. 1–4; Tragic overture, Op. 81; Variations on a theme by Haydn, Op. 56a; (i) *Alto rhapsody, Op. 51;* (ii) *Nänie, Op. 82.*
(M) **(*) Ph. Dig. 456 030-2 (4). (i) Jard van Nes; (i–ii) Tanglewood Festival Ch.; Boston SO, Haitink.

Symphonies Nos. 1–4; Tragic overture; (i) *Alto rhapsody, Op. 53.*
**(*) DG Dig. 449 829-2 (3) [id.]. VPO, James Levine; (i) with Anne Sofie von Otter, Arnold Schoenberg Ch.

Abbado's remains the most successful of the modern, digital cycles and makes a clear first choice, with playing at once polished and intense, glowingly recorded. The set gains from having a generous collection of imaginatively chosen couplings: the rare, brief, choral works, as well as the usual supplements in the overtures and variations.

From Mackerras a very interesting set indeed – Brahms with a difference. Mackerras uses the same-sized forces that Brahms would have had at his disposal in Meiningen. Although when Brahms conducted the *Second Symphony* in Hamburg he had as many as 115 performers in the orchestra, his preferred ensemble was at Meiningen. (Indeed when he was offered reinforcements for the *Fourth Symphony* at Meiningen he turned them down.) The smaller forces remove some of the thick-textured, overweight quality that the strings can produce in Brahms while retaining their warmth and richness. The strings are often thinned out to single parts at times, and the effect is – strangely enough – enriching. The set includes the very first version of the slow movement of the *First Symphony* as it was originally performed at Karlsruhe and Cambridge. There are fascinating differences both in the order of the material and at times in the harmony. There are informative notes by Professor Robert Pascall the leading Brahms scholar of the day, and a bonus CD in which Mackerras discusses performance practice in Brahms' day. The playing is exemplary and has no lack of warmth and the same must be said of the recording. Well worth getting.

Anyone wanting Karajan's readings of the four Brahms symphonies should be well satisfied with this DG Double, which offers his recordings made in the late 1970s. The current remastering makes the most of the analogue sound: while textures remain fresh and clear there is now more weight in the middle and lower frequencies. The playing of the Berlin Philharmonic remains uniquely cultivated: the ensemble is finely polished yet can produce tremendous bravura at times, and there is no lack of warmth. Karajan's interpretations, with lyrical and dramatic elements finely balanced, changed little over the years. A very real bargain, hard to beat, but apparently available in the USA only as an import.

Otherwise Sanderling's 1971–2 Dresden recordings of the four Brahms symphonies make an excellent choice. They originally appeared on the Eurodisc label and enjoyed a brief life in the LP catalogues. They have a warmth and humanity that stand out from the general run of Brahms cycles, with the Dresden orchestra responding to Sanderling's direction with playing of an unaffected and natural eloquence, so that the performances can stand comparison with any in the catalogue at any price. These were for R. L. the touchstone of Brahms symphony records for many years during the 1970s and early 1980s, and their return to circulation is cause for celebration.

Kempe's magnetism in Brahms lies very much in his compelling ability to draw out the lyrical warmth of the writing. Like Furtwängler, Kempe is freely expressive, but his freedom is very different, with far less extreme tempo changes. Speeds and timings are often very similar, but results are strikingly different, with Kempe's Brahms above all glowing with warmth and beauty. This conductor also brought great fire to the quicker movements and a tremendous sense of breadth. First and foremost, Kempe has his finger on the natural flow and pulse of these symphonies in a way which calls to mind only the most exalted comparisons. The *First* and *Third* were recorded in 1959 and 1960 in stereo, and are accommodated on the first disc; the *Second* and the *Fourth* (from 1955 and 1956 respectively) are both mono, and the sound is less transparent and fresh – but, ironically, they are at least as vivid and are rather better focused. The *Tragic Overture* is one of the best ever committed to disc. The noble performance of the *St Anthony chorale variations* was never issued in the UK and comes from 1957. The recording venue is the same throughout, the Grünewaldkirche in Berlin. Excellent transfers.

While not an obvious first choice, Dorati's Mercury set of the Brahms symphonies, made between 1957 and 1963, is also a competitive proposition at mid-price, always vital and interesting. The recording throughout is brightly lit in the Mercury manner, a bit fierce at times, but there is supporting body (Watford Town Hall was the venue). No listener could fail to be stimulated by this musicianly, strongly involved and involving music-making.

As with his companion box of Beethoven symphonies, Günter Wand's Brahms set, reissued on a pair of CDs, is highly recommendable for providing spontaneously compelling readings of all four works, very well played. The snag is that the early digital recording (1982/3) brings a degree of fierceness on violin tone in all but No. 2 and verges on shrillness in No. 3. Wand's is a consistently direct view of Brahms, yet the reading of each symphony has its own individuality. In the *First* the extra unity is clear and the performance is made convincing by its spontaneity. Even though he does not observe the exposition repeat, Wand's reading of the *Second* is the pick of his Brahms series, a characteristically glowing but steady reading, recorded with a fullness and bloom that are missing in the companion issues. In the *Third Symphony* Wand does observe the exposition repeat and his wise way with Brahms, strong and easy and steadily paced, works beautifully here, bringing out the autumnal moods, ending with a sober view of the finale. By contrast, the reading of No. 4 initially seems understated. But it is quite a strong reading and provides a generally satisfying culmination to an inexpensive modern set of the four symphonies and is well worth considering. As we go to press, Wand's recordings have been made available separately at mid-price: *Symphonies Nos. 1* and *3* (74321 20284-2); *Symphonies Nos. 2* and *4* (74321 20285-2).

Szell's powerful view of Brahms is consistently revealed in this masterful series of performances, recorded in the 1960s when he had made the Cleveland Orchestra America's finest. His approach is generally plain and direct, crisp and detached rather than smooth and moulded. Speeds are broad, and in the manner of the time no exposition repeats are observed, not even in No. 3. Though the sound, as transferred, is not as full as on the original LPs, it is clear and bright, with superb detail.

With variably focused sound, Karajan's last cycle of the Brahms *Symphonies* is not his finest; but he remained a natural Brahmsian to the last, and this compilation, with Nos. 2 and 3 on the second disc, and No. 4 coupled with the *Variations*, makes a better investment than the original issues, for those who must have digital sound. However, this set is at full price.

Levine's new set of the Brahms *Symphonies* brings a certain lack of unanimity of view. For E. G. the special chemistry between Levine and the Vienna Philharmonic has rarely worked as tellingly as in these big and bold readings. These are interpretations, conceived on a large scale, which yet are full of refinement and detailed subtleties, with speeds generally on the fast side, but never with any hint of breathlessness, well illustrated in the powerful accounts of the outer movements of No. 4. The performances are made the more magnetic, when (except for the *Tragic overture*) they were recorded live in Vienna at the Musikverein between 1992 and 1995 with warm, well-focused sound that has plenty of air round it. The *Alto rhapsody* is a delight too, with the soloist, Anne Sofie von Otter, warm and intense.

R. L. agrees that Levine's interpretations are free from undue eccentricity but he also finds them pretty hard-driven and wanting in personality. Of course they have the benefit of modern, digital recording but, even so, that is less than transparent in detail or ideally balanced.

Jochum's mono DG recordings of the Brahms *Symphonies* are characteristically wayward and could hardly be regarded as a primary recommendation, even though the concentration of the playing generally holds the readings together. The Berlin Philharmonic playing is splendid throughout, and the mono recordings, made between 1951 and 1956, are amazingly good, full and clear, far more detailed and vivid than the original LPs. Jochum aficionados will certainly want this set, which is priced comparably to a Polygram Double.

Anyone who thinks of Toscanini as a rigid conductor should hear his Brahms; high-powered it is true, but full of lyricism of an Italianate warmth. The *First Symphony* starts very fast and intensely but often speeds are surprisingly broad, and the *Fourth Symphony*, Toscanini's favourite, brings a magnificent performance. Though RCA's new processing for this reissue has not transformed the original sound quite so well as it has in the Beethoven symphonies, harsh still on high violins, it now has ample body to let one enjoy these readings in rather more aural comfort.

Barenboim dons his Furtwänglerian mantle for his Erato accounts of the first two symphonies which, though very well played, suffer from his wilful flexibility and eccentric structural control: at one point in the finale of the *First Symphony*, the great Chicago orchestra is very nearly brought to a dead stop but subsequently recovers to end the work very positively. Barenboim's inspirational volatility works well in the *Third Symphony*, which does not lose its ongoing purpose and brings beautiful orchestral playing in the central movements. No. 4 is finest of all, a highly concentrated interpretation that moves forward powerfully; even though the tempo for the *Andante* is slow, it is ardently presented and capped by a gripping performance of the closing *Passacaglia*.

Furtwängler's EMI compilation brings together the live recording of the *First Symphony* that he made with the Vienna Philharmonic in 1952 and live recordings of the remaining three symphonies made with the Berlin Philharmonic in 1948 and 1952, presumably taken from radio sources. The performance of the *First* is perhaps the best and it has the best sound, which otherwise is disappointingly thin, lacking in body and with some harshness; but the electricity of Furtwängler in Brahms is vividly captured. Despite the limitations of the sound, lacking in body but with plenty of detail, and despite the bronchial audiences in Nos. 2, 3 and 4, this is an inspirational set, with the makeweights an added attraction.

Celibidache's dislike of recording is well known and these DG performances come from his appearances with the Stuttgart Radio (Südfunk) Orchestra in the 1970s. At the time *Die Welt* wrote that 'the South-West German Radio Symphony Orchestra has become, since Celibidache has been in charge of it, perhaps the best German orchestra after the Berlin Philharmonic'. It certainly produces tone of the utmost refinement and subtlety (since Celibidache had a small repertory and demanded ten rehearsals per concert, this was possible). All the same it is questionable whether it is the equal of the Bavarian Radio Orchestra. The sheer intentness of the playing and the tonal sheen produced by the Stuttgart group is nearly always in evidence, but there is a certain want of real forward momentum and of sinew. Beauty rather than truth is dominant. Celibidache is a cult figure, of course, and those who venerate him will need no promptings to buy this set. Others should proceed with caution. The 1974–6 recordings come up well and there is a bonus rehearsal disc devoted to the first movement of the *Fourth Symphony*.

Symphonies Nos. 1–3; Academic festival overture; Tragic overture.

❁ (B) *** EMI forte (SIS) CZS5 69515-2 (2) [CDFB 69515]. LPO, Eugen Jochum.

Jochum's EMI stereo versions of the Brahms symphonies were made in the Kingsway Hall in 1976; the analogue recordings, produced by Christopher Bishop, are outstandingly full and vivid, with a rich Brahmsian ambience which means that the strings are brilliant, without edge, the bass is ample yet clean, and the overall balance is very convincing indeed. These remastered discs indeed sound better than almost any of their mid- or bargain-priced competitors (they are smoother on top than Wand's RCA set, and the violin timbre is much more distinguished than with Sanderling). The DG engineers secured a remarkably fine mono balance with Jochum's earlier, DG set (which is admired by R. L.) and the playing of the BPO is rather more polished and sleekly integrated than the LPO. But the LPO playing is excellent too, the greater spontaneity of its performances carrying the listener along on a wave of inspiration, and this also applies to the exuberant *Academic festival overture* and the hardly less vibrant *Tragic overture*. Moreover the first-movement exposition repeats are included in the first three symphonies and in every case are made to seem essential to the structure. The high drama of the *First Symphony* immediately shows Jochum at his most persuasive, giving the feeling of live communication in the ebb and flow of tension and natural flexibility. He is not as free as Furtwängler was – a specially revered master with him – but the warmth and lyricism go with comparable inner fire. Equally, No. 2 is a warmly lyrical reading, expansive in the first movement – helped by the richness of the recording of the middle and lower strings, allowing extremes of expression – fast and exciting in the finale. The inner movements are beautifully played and the natural fervour of the orchestral response is most compelling, justifying the natural flexibility. The *Third Symphony* represents the peak of Jochum's cycle, and this is among the most rewarding versions of this work, irrespective of price. He conveys the full weight and warmth of the work with generally spacious speeds, finely moulded. The first movement is magnificent, leading to a passionate coda, and in the central movements there is an engaging autumnal feeling, while in the finale, starting from hushed expectancy in the opening pianissimo, he builds powerfully and exuberantly and then creates a feeling of elegy in the closing pages. For I. M. these performances are unsurpassed; at its very reasonable price, this forte reissue is an almost obligatory purchase for any dedicated Brahmsian.

Symphony No. 1 in C min., Op. 68; (i) *Alto rhapsody, Op. 53.*
(N) (B) **(*) CfP 573 4332. (i) Bernadette Greevy, Hallé Ch.; Hallé O, Loughran.

Symphony No. 2 in D, Op. 73; Academic festival overture.
(N) (B) **(*) CfP 573 4342. Hallé O, Loughran.

Symphony No. 3 in F, Op. 90; Tragic overture.
(N) (B) **(*) CfP 573 4352. Hallé O, Loughran.

Symphony No. 4 in E min., Op. 98; Variations on a theme of Haydn, Op. 56a.
(N) (B) **(*) CfP 573 4362. Hallé O, Loughran.

This James Loughran set of the Brahms symphonies, recorded at the end of the 1970s, crowned James Loughran's highly successful period as principal conductor of the Hallé Orchestra. These performances are justly renowned, for the whole orchestra shows a natural feeling for the Brahms style throughout all four symphonies. Loughran's readings of the first two, exposition repeats included, are notable for their lyrical strength, the *First* with a refreshing spring-like quality, the *Second* with a naturally warm flow, carrying the listener on, even while the basic approach is direct and unfussy. By contrast, the *Third Symphony* (also with the important exposition repeat included) is unexpectedly measured in tempo, yet on repetition this emerges as an unusually satisfying account. In the *Fourth* Loughran's approach is unobtrusively direct. Concentration grows after his deceptively gentle start, so one appreciates more and more the satisfying assurance with which he solves every problem. Overall the Hallé ensemble and string tone are not always quite as polished as in the versions from metropolitan orchestras, but the sense of spontaneity is ample compensation. Bernadette Greevy gives a forthright, warmly enjoyable account of the *Alto rhapsody* and the two overtures and *Variations* also come off very well. Full atmospheric recording, excellent for the period. Admirers of the Hallé will certainly want this set.

Symphony No. 1 in C min., Op. 68.
(M) *** DG 447 408-2 [id.]. BPO, Karajan – SCHUMANN: *Symphony No. 1.* ***
(BB) **(*) ASV Dig. CDQS 6101 [(B) id.]. RLPO, Marek Janowski.
(M) ** DG (IMS) Dig. 445 505-2 [id.]. VPO, Bernstein (with BEETHOVEN: *Overtures: Coriolan; Egmont* **).

Symphony No. 1; Academic festival overture, Op. 80.
(M) *** Carlton Dig. PCD 2014 [id.]. Hallé O, Skrowaczewski.

Symphony No. 1; Academic festival overture Op. 80; Variations on a theme of Haydn, Op. 56a.
(M) **(*) Bruno Walter Edition Sony SMK 64470 [id.]. Columbia SO, Walter.
(N) (M) (*) Avid mono AMSC603 [id.]. (i) VPO, Bruno Walter (ii) NYPO, Toscanini.

Symphony No. 1; Tragic overture; Variations on a theme of Haydn, Op. 56a.
(M) **(*) Ph. 454 133-2. Concg. O, Haitink.

Symphony No. 1; Serenade No. 2 in A, Op. 16.
(M) (**) RCA mono GD 60277 [60277-2-RG]. NBC SO, Toscanini.

Symphony No. 1; Variations on a theme of Haydn, Op. 56a.
(BB) **(*) Naxos Dig. 8.550278 [id.]. Belgian R. PO, Brussels, Alexander Rahbari.

(i) *Symphony No. 1; Variations on a theme of Haydn;* (ii) *Hungarian dances Nos. 17–21.*
(B) **(*) Sony SBK 46534 [id.]. (i) Cleveland O, Szell; (ii) Phd. O, Ormandy.

Symphony No. 1 in C min., Op. 68; Tragic overture, Op. 81; (i) *Alto rhapsody, Op. 53.*

(N) ❁ (M) *** EMI CDM5 67029-2. [id.]. Philh. O, Klemperer, with (i) Christa Ludwig, Philh. Ch.

Symphony No. 1; (i) *Gesang der Parzen (Song of the Fates), Op. 89.*

*** DG Dig. 431 790-2 [id.]. BPO, Abbado, (i) with Berlin R. Ch.

One of the outstanding highlights of EMI's 'Klemperer Legacy', Klemperer's 1956–7 Kingsway Hall recording remains among the greatest performance this *symphony* has ever received on disc. Its spacious opening with thundering, relentless timpani strokes is as compelling as ever, and the close of the work has a comparable majesty. This is Klemperer at his very finest, and his reading remains unique for its authority and power, supported by consistently superb Philharmonia playing. The sound is both clear and full-bodied. The *Alto rhapsody* also shows Klemperer at his most masterful and Ludwig on fine form: it is a beautifully expressive performance. She sings gloriously in the opening section, and later her voice blends naturally with the male chorus.

After a spacious introduction, Abbado launches into a warm, dramatic reading, rhythmically well sprung and finely shaded, with the full power of the great dramatic climaxes brought out in the finale, from the rapt pianissimo of the opening onwards. The *Gesang der Parzen* makes an unusual and warmly attractive coupling, very well sung. A clear first choice, among modern recordings.

Karajan's 1964 recording of Brahms's *First Symphony* (the conductor's third version of five – DG 447 408-2) seems by general consensus to be regarded as his finest. The control of tension in the first movement is masterly, the orchestral playing is of superlative quality and the result is very powerful, with the finale a fitting culmination. The remastering has restored the original full, well-balanced, analogue sound, with plenty of weight in the bass (as is obvious at the timpani-dominated opening), yet detail is firmer. The coupling with Schumann's *First Symphony* makes this a very desirable record indeed – an obvious candidate for inclusion in DG's set of 'Originals'.

Walter's recordings have been carefully remastered to emerge clearer than before but with very slight loss of bloom on the high violins; otherwise the sound is full and well balanced. Walter's first two movements of the *First Symphony* have a white-hot intensity that shows this conductor at his very finest. The third movement begins with a less than ravishing clarinet solo and, though the 6/8 section is lively enough, the playing is not as crisp as in the first two movements. In the finale the performance reasserts itself, although some might find the big string tune too slow. The performance of the *Variations* is relaxed and smiling, and the genial account of the *Academic festival overture* gains from the extra brightness on top.

Skrowaczewski conducts the Hallé in a powerful performance of No. 1, both warmly sympathetic and refined, with sound which is fresh, bright and clear and with a good, open atmosphere. An excellent bargain-price digital choice.

Szell's account of No. 1 is one of the most impressive of his set. His bold, direct thrust gives the outer movements plenty of power and impetus, and the inner movements bring relaxation and a fair degree of warmth.

Opening powerfully with thundering timpani in the manner of Klemperer, though with generally more relaxed tempi, Alexander Rahbari gives an account of Brahms's *First* that is certainly recommendable. It is a strong, direct reading, spacious yet with plenty of impetus. A very good choice for those with limited budgets.

Janowski's plain yet sympathetic reading is greatly enhanced on a CD which is full-bodied, clearly detailed and well balanced. The added fullness is much more flattering to the orchestral timbres and makes a very satisfying sound overall. Janowski, unlike most, does observe the exposition repeat in the first movement. At super-bargain price, this is excellent value.

As an interpretation, Haitink's performance with the Concertegebouw Orchestra from the early 1970s stands up well. It is a strong, well-argued reading of considerable power, supported by first-class orchestral playing. Haitink does not observe the first-movement exposition repeat, but not everyone will object to that. The lively and well-shaped *Variations* and the excitingly volatile *Tragic overture* are an asset, and the recording is spacious and well balanced, if now somewhat sounding its age.

The finale in Bernstein's version brings a highly idiosyncratic reading, with the great melody of the main theme presented at a speed very much slower than the main part of the movement. In the reprise it never comes back to the slow tempo, until the coda brings the most extreme slowing for the chorale motif. These two points are exaggerations of accepted tradition and, though Bernstein's electricity makes the results compelling, this is hardly a version for constant repetition. The remastered sound is fully acceptable.

The *First Symphony* is the performance Toscanini recorded in Carnegie Hall during 1941. It differs from the version he made ten years later with the same orchestra in the greater breadth of the first movement allegro, and in the tenderness he shows in the *Andante*, which at the same time remains completely unsentimental. The sound is not at all bad for the period. There is however little one can do with the 1942 broadcast – made in Studio 8-H – of the *Serenade*. The performance, too, is held together on a tight rein and sounds unrelaxed.

Two gripping accounts from the 1930s by two outstanding Brahmsians. Bruno Walter was recorded in 1937 and Toscanini in 1936, his last year with the New York Philharmonic Symphony. Transfers on this label are variable and the present issues are by no means as expert as those we are used to from the Dutton or Testament labels. Although the ear adjusts, the sound remains distinctly synthetic.

(i) *Symphonies Nos. 1 in C min.; 2 in D; Academic festival overture;* (ii) *Tragic overture;* (i) *Variations on a theme of Haydn; Variations and fugue on a theme by Handel* (arr. Rubbra).
(B) ** Sony Take 2 SB2K 63287 (2) [id.]. (i) Phd. O, Ormandy; (ii) Nat. PO, Stokowski.

Ormandy's insight as a Brahms interpreter in the concertos was always recognized, but not his understanding in this purely orchestral repertory. As in the concertos, his manner is direct and warmly purposeful, with speeds (on the broad side) which are generally kept steady, even in exciting codas. The glories of Philadelphia sound are resonantly exploited with close but not aggressive focus in these 1960s recordings. A rarity is the arrangement of the *Handel variations* by Edmund Rubbra, which – in a rather un-Brahmsian way – gives the principal soloists of the Philadelphia Orchestra marvellous opportunities to shine. The one item conducted by Stokowski brings a complete contrast, a 1977 recording which demonstrates what fire and energy the nonagenarian conductor had only six months before he died, with fast speeds and electric tension. This is very much a three-star performance and needs to be re-coupled.

Symphony No. 2 in D, Op. 73.
(***) Testament mono SBT 1015 [id.]. BBC SO, Toscanini – MENDELSSOHN: *Midsummer Night's Dream:* excerpt; ROSSINI: *Semiramide: Overture* (***).

Symphony No. 2 in D; Academic festival overture.
(M) ** DG (IMS) Dig. 445 506-2 [id.]. VPO, Bernstein.

Symphony No. 2 in D; Academic festival overture; Tragic overture.
(N) (M) **(*) Penguin Classics Decca 460 623-2 [id.]. Chicago SO, Solti.

Symphony No. 2; Tragic overture.
(M) *** Carlton Dig. 30367 00982-2 [id.]. Hallé O, Skrowaczewski.
(BB) **(*) ASV Dig. CDQS 6102 [(M) id.]. RLPO, Marek Janowski.

Symphony No. 2; Tragic overture, Op. 81; Variations an a theme of Haydn, Op. 56a.
(B) *** DG Classikon 439 478-2 [(M) id. import]. BPO, Karajan.

Symphony No. 2; Variations on a theme of Haydn, Op. 56a.
*** DG (IMS) Dig. 423 142-2 [id.]. BPO, Karajan.

Symphony No. 2; (i) *Alto rhapsody, Op. 53.*
*** DG Dig. 427 643-2 [id.]. (i) Lipovšek, Senff Ch.; BPO, Abbado.

Among modern versions Abbado's still stands as an easy first choice, particularly when, with Marjana Lipovšek a radiant soloist, it also contains a gravely beautiful account of the *Alto rhapsody*. Abbado's approach to Brahms is generally direct, but his control of rhythm and phrase makes the performance instantly compelling. He observes the exposition repeat in the first movement, while in the finale, through his rhythmic control, Abbado makes a relatively measured speed sound much more exciting than it does with any of the speed-merchants.

Karajan's digital reading of the *Second Symphony* suffers less than the *First* from the thick, undifferentiated recording. It is a magnificent reading, even warmer and more glowing than his previous versions, with consistently fine playing from the Berlin Philharmonic, who approach with striking freshness a symphony which they must have played countless times. As in the *First Symphony*, Karajan omits the first-movement exposition repeat, but compensates with an appealing performance of the *Haydn variations*.

Karajan's 1964 reading of the *Second* is also available coupled with the *Third Symphony* – see below. But anyone preferring his account of the *Haydn variations* from the same period and of the splendid *Tragic overture* from a decade later will find that the present Classikon alternative has been very well transferred.

With beautifully open and transparent sound, Skrowaczewski and the Hallé Orchestra give a measured and restrained reading of the *Second Symphony*, unsensational, fresh and thoughtful. The opening may seem sleepy, but Skrowaczewski's broad speeds and patient manner build up increasingly as the work progresses. With exposition repeat observed and a generous fill-up, plus excellent digital recording, luminous to match the performance, it is a good bargain-priced recommendation.

Toscanini's account with the BBC Symphony Orchestra on Testament, recorded in 1938, will come as a revelation to those who view the legendary Italian as a hard-driving, demonic maestro. Tempi are relaxed, the first movement is unhurried and the mood is sunny and smiling. There is none of the hard-driven momentum and over-drilled intensity that marked his final, NBC version. Gratitude is in order that this performance has been rescued for posterity: the sound calls for tolerance but the playing is worth it.

A powerful, weighty performance from Solti, its lyrical feeling passionately expressed in richly upholstered textures. The reading displays a broad nobility, but the charm and delicately gracious qualities are much less part of Solti's view. Yet the lyric power of the playing is hard to resist, especially when the recording is so full-blooded and brilliant. Solti includes the first-movement exposition repeat and offers in addition a lively *Academic festival overture* and a splendidly committed *Tragic overture*.

Janowski's plain style is least convincing in this most lyrical of symphonies, with rhythms tending to sound too rigid, whether in his metrical view of the slow movement or the rather charmless account of the third. The overture is much more successful, and the digital recording is excellently balanced: this is certainly worth considering at its super-bargain price.

Bernstein in his live recording directs a warm and expansive account, notably less free and idiosyncratic than the *C minor Symphony*, yet comparably rhythmic and spontaneous-sounding. Considering the limitations of a live concert, the recording sounds well. But this is by no means a first choice, even at mid-price.

Symphonies Nos. 2–3.

(M) *** Bruno Walter Edition Sony SMK 64471 [id.]. Columbia SO, Walter.

(N) (M) *** EMI CDM5 67030-2. [id.]. Philh. O, Klemperer.

(B) *** DG Classikon 429 153-2 [(M) id. import]. BPO, Karajan.

(B) *** Sony SBK 47652 [id.]. Cleveland O, George Szell.

(M) **(*) Ph. (IMS) 426 632-2. Concg. O, Haitink.

The new Bruno Walter coupling of the *Second and Third Symphonies* is very recommendable indeed. Walter's performance of the *Second* is wonderfully sympathetic, with an inevitability, a rightness which makes it hard to concentrate on the interpretation as such, so cogent is the musical argument. As though to balance the romanticism of his approach on detail, Walter keeps his basic speeds surprisingly constant, yet little of the passion is lost in consequence. It is a masterly conception overall and one very easy to live with. Walter's pacing of the *Third* is admirable and the vigour and sense of joy which imbues the opening of the first movement (exposition repeat included) dominates throughout, with the second subject eased in with wonderful naturalness.

Klemperer's accoount of No. 2 is also a great performance, the product of a strong and vital intelligence. Alongside Walter, he may seem a trifle severe and uncompromising, but he was at his peak in his Brahms cycle and he underlines the power of the *symphony* without diminishing its eloquence in any way. Again in No. 3 there is a severity about his approach, which may at first seem unappealing, but which comes to underline the strength of the architecture. The remastered recording made concurrently and in the same venue as No. 1, is very impressive.

Karajan's 1964 reading of the *Second* is among the sunniest and most lyrical accounts, and its sound is competitive even now. The companion performance of the *Third* is marginally less compelling, but still very fine. He takes the opening expansively and omits the exposition repeat. But clearly he sees the work as a whole: the third movement is also slow and perhaps slightly indulgent, but the closing pages of the finale have a memorable autumnal serenity. A bargain.

With the Cleveland Orchestra at its peak and on its toes throughout, this is an inexpensive reissue that should be in every comprehensive Brahms collection. The Severance recordings have been improved immeasurably. When the *Second* first appeared we were unimpressed by 'the characteristic Cleveland recording quality' and found that its unexpansiveness helped to give the feeling 'that Brahms's heart is being encased in a precision-made casket'. That impression all but disappears now. The orchestral virtuosity remains and at times Szell's care for detail does become predominant, but the underlying ardour and warmth are in no doubt, especially in the *Adagio*, while the *Allegretto grazioso* has an appealing simplicity. The *Third* is a magnificent performance. Overall this is a reading to set alongside that of Bruno Walter, even if (as in the *Second Symphony*), the exposition repeat is omitted.

Haitink's account of No. 2 opens soberly. The sunshine quickly breaks through, however, so that the gentle high entry of the violins is magically sweet. This is a thoughtful reading, marked by beautifully refined string playing, but in a way it is too controlled. The *Third* is much more impressive, and Haitink's firmness of grip and lyrical eloquence make this a very satisfying account. The sound is fresh yet full in the Philips manner.

Symphony No. 3 in F, Op. 90.

(M) *** RCA 09026 61793-2 [id.]. Chicago SO, Fritz Reiner – SCHUBERT: *Symphony No. 5.* ***

Symphony No. 3; Tragic overture; (i) *Song of Destiny (Schicksalslied), Op. 54.*

*** DG Dig. 429 765-2 [id.]. BPO, Abbado; (i) with Ernest Senff Ch.

Symphony No. 3; Variations on a theme of Haydn, Op. 56a.

*** Erato/Warner Dig. 4509 95193-2. Chicago SO, Daniel Barenboim.

(M) *** Carlton IMP Dig. PCD 2039 [id.]. Hallé O, Skrowaczewski.

(BB) *** ASV Dig. CDQS 6103. RLPO, Marek Janowski.

Abbado directs a glowing, affectionate performance of No. 3, adopting generally spacious speeds and finely moulded phrasing but never sounding self-conscious, thanks to the natural tension which gives the illusion of live, spontaneous music-making. The rich, well-balanced, clean-textured recording underlines the big dramatic contrasts. This still heads the list of modern digital recordings of this symphony.

Reiner's magnificent performance dates from 1956. It is a glowing, marvellously proportioned account, exposition repeat included, and prepared in masterly fashion, and with the close of the work given a touchingly gentle, valedictory feeling. Yet there is no want of momentum in the outer movements and the lyrical intensity and warmth in the slow movement are equally memorable. Here the Chicago ambience adds to the atmosphere and it is a pity that in tuttis there is some loss of refinement in the upper strings. This has been improved in the CD transfer and this is a reading of stature. Besides the estimable Schubert coupling there is an exciting account of Mendelssohn's *Fingal's Cave overture*.

Barenboim's volatile approach works well in the *Third Symphony* and, although there must be some minor reservations about his freely spacious treatment of both central movements, they are beautifully played and warmly lyrical. The first movement (exposition repeat very much part of the interpretation) has plenty of power and glowing lyrical feeling, ensuring that Barenboim's flexible style is convincing. The finale has exciting thrust and the valedictory ending is managed most sensitively. The *Variations*, too, are full of imaginative touches. Fine, committed orchestral playing and richly expansive sound suit the nature of the interpretation.

Skrowaczewski chooses consistently slow tempi for the central movements, yet with refined playing there is no hint of dragging. In the third movement he underlines the tender wistfulness, with a gorgeous horn solo in the reprise, full and spacious. The hush at the start of the finale then leads to a powerfully rhythmic performance, ending with a most refined account of the gentle coda. An excellent digital lower mid-price version, well coupled with a fresh reading of the *Haydn variations*.

The *Third* is the finest of Janowski's Brahms cycle, with surging outer movements (exposition repeat included) and the central *Andante* and *Poco allegretto* given an appealing, unforced Brahmsian lyricism. An exciting and satisfying performance, given bright, full, digital sound, not absolutely refined on top. The *Variations* also have plenty of impetus and are strongly characterized. In its price-range this is very recommendable.

Symphony No. 3 in F, Op. 90; Tragic Overture; (i) *Alto rhapsody, Op. 53.*
**(*) DG Dig. 439 887-2. (i) Anne Sofie von Otter, Arnold Schoenberg Ch.; VPO, Levine.

Where in Levine's complete cycle the *Symphony No. 3* is coupled with No. 4, this separate issue comes with the two fill-ups, equally warm and sympathetic. Levine's treatment of the first movement is strong and urgent, warmly expressive without lingering. It is characteristic that in the hushed opening of the finale he does not start slowly, as many conductors do, but sets the tempo he means to adopt for the whole movement, instantly establishing a mood of expectancy. Glowing sound in live recording, not perfectly balanced but capturing the atmosphere of the Musikverein.

Symphonies Nos. (i) *3 in F, Op. 90;* (ii) *4 in E min., Op. 98.*
(M) *** DG 437 645-2 [id.]. BPO, Karajan.
(M) **(*) Teldec/Warner Dig. 4509 92144-2 [id.]. Cleveland O, Dohnányi.

In his 1978 recording Karajan gives superb grandeur to the opening of the *Third Symphony* but then characteristically refuses to observe the exposition repeat. Comparing this reading with Karajan's earlier, 1964 version (coupled with No. 2), one finds him more direct and strikingly more dynamic and compelling. In the *Fourth Symphony* Karajan refuses to overstate the first movement, starting with deceptive reticence. His easy, lyrical style, less moulded in this 1978 reading than in his 1964 account, is fresh and unaffected and highly persuasive. The scherzo, fierce and strong, leads to a clean, weighty account of the finale.

Those for whom quality of sound is of the highest consideration will certainly find Dohnányi's mid-priced Cleveland coupling tempting. The performances are clean and direct and superbly played. The fine tonal blend and balance in the *Third* means that the often thick orchestration is made clear as well as naturally weighty in a version which (exposition repeat included) emphasizes classical values. In the second-movement *Andante*, taken on the slow side, Dohnányi does not entirely avoid squareness and, although the third-movement *Allegretto* flows warmly, the horn reprise of the main theme is forthright rather than affectionate. The opening of the finale lacks mystery and the hemiola rhythms of the second subject, for all the power of the performance, fail to leap aloft. These detailed criticisms are given merely to suggest why, with such superlative playing and an irreproachably direct manner, the result finally lacks something in Brahmsian magic. The *Fourth* opens simply and seductively, a strong and finely controlled reading, lacking only occasionally in a flow of adrenalin. The slow movement is hushed and thoughtful, the third clear and fresh in its crisp articulation, while the weight of the finale is well caught – even if it is not thrust home at the close as sharply as it might be.

Symphony No. 4 in E min., Op. 98.
(N) (M) *** DG Dig. 457 706-2 [id.]. VPO, Carlos Kleiber.
(N) **(*) BBC Legends BBCL 4003-2 [id.]. BBC

SO, Rudolf Kempe – SCHUBERT: *Symphony No. 5.* **(*)

Symphony No. 4; Hungarian dances Nos. 1, 3 & 10.
(M) *** Carlton Dig. 30367 00272 [id.]. Hallé O, Skrowaczewski.

Symphony No. 4; Academic festival overture.
*** Erato/Warner 4509 95194-2. Chicago SO, Barenboim.
(N) (M) *** EMI CDM5 67031-2. [id.]. Philh. O, Klemperer (with SCHUMANN: *Overtures: Genoveva, Op. 81; Manfred, Op. 115.* **
(M) *** Telarc Dig. CD 82006 [id.]. RPO, Previn.
(BB) **(*) ASV Dig. CDQS 6104. RLPO, Marek Janowski.

Symphony No 4; Tragic overture, Op. 81.
(M) *** DG Dig. 445 508-2 [id.]. VPO, Bernstein.

Symphony No. 4; Tragic overture; (i) *Song of Destiny (Schicksalslied), Op. 54.*
(M) *** Bruno Walter Edition Sony SMK 64472 [id.]. Columbia SO, Walter, (i) with Occidental College Concert Ch.

Symphony No. 4; Variations on a theme by Haydn, Op. 56a.
(BB) **(*) RCA/Navigator 74321 24206-2. Dresden State O, Kurt Sanderling.

Symphony No. 4; Variations on a theme of Haydn; (i) *Nänie, Op. 82.*
*** DG Dig. 435 349-2 [id.]. BPO, Abbado, (i) with Berlin R. Ch.

Symphony No. 4 in E min., Op. 98. (i) *Fest-und Gedenksprüche, Op. 109; 3 Motets, Op. 110; Warum ist das Licht gegeben, Op. 74/1.*
(N) *** Decca Dig. 455 510-2 [id.]. Leipzig Gewandhaus O. (i) MDR Ch., Leipzig; Herbert Blomstedt.

Of recent versions Herbert Blomstedt's account with his new orchestra, the Leipzig Gewandhaus, is the finest and it is also among the most satisfying accounts on disc. It offers cultured playing, a reading that blends a highly developed sense of classical proportion with finely controlled feeling. It combines the classicism of the pre-war accounts by Boehm and Weingartner with the warmth and fire of Bruno Walter. First-class recording too. As a fill-up Blomstedt directs some fine a cappella pieces which are sung with great eloquence and restraint. A distinguished record well worth acquiring.

Abbado rounds off his outstanding series with an incandescent performance of the *Fourth*, marked by strong, dramatic contrasts and finely moulded phrasing. The coupling is exceptionally generous, not just the *Haydn variations* but the rare choral piece to words by Schiller, *Nänie*.

Carlos Kleiber's famous version has now rightly been reissued as one of DG's Originals, the 100th reissue in this celebrated series, and is presented in a slip case with a complete catalogue of its companions. It is a performance of real stature and much strength, with the attention to detail one would expect from this great conductor. A gripping and compelling performance, at the opposite end of the scale from Walter's coaxingly lyrical approach. DG have successfully remastered the 1981 sound which now has more than sufficient weight in the bass and more bloom than before. The violins under pressure still sound somewhat shrill at fortissimo, but this adds to the edge of the performance and there is room for the strings to expand in the *Andante*. The finale has tremendous thrust. Even without a coupling this carries the strongest recommendation at mid-price.

Walter's opening is simple, even gentle, and the pervading lyricism is immediately apparent; yet power and authority are underlying. The conductor's refusal to linger by a wayside always painted in gently glowing colours adds strength and impetus, building up to an exciting coda, the unanimity and cutting edge of the strings bringing a cumulative effect. A beautifully moulded slow movement, intense at its central climax, is balanced by a vivacious, exhilarating Scherzo. The finale has an underlying impetus so that Walter is able to relax for the slow middle section. The new transfer is very successful: the recording has never sounded fresher or warmer and there is plenty of necessary weight in the bass. The *Tragic overture* has characteristic breadth and vigour, while the *Song of destiny*, both warm and dramatic, displays the capability of the chorus to good effect. The recording is excellent.

Klemperer's granite strength and his feeling for Brahmsian lyricism makes his version one of the most satisfying ever recorded. The finale may lack something in sheer excitement but the gravity of Klemperer's tone of voice, natural and unforced in this movement as in the others, makes for compelling results. Among the fill-ups the *Academic festival overture* is made to sound grand rather than high-spirited, but the Schumann couplings are muscularly massive and Germanic, rather than incandescent. Excellent transfers.

Barenboim's Chicago reading is grippingly compulsive. He opens the first movement gently and affectionately, but the performance soon develops a compulsive lyrical power. Barenboim takes the *Andante* more slowly than marked but, with a richly ardent response from the Chicago strings, the result is eloquently convincing, with much refined orchestral detail. After an excitingly ebullient Scherzo, the finale sets off with a powerful thrust that carries through to the final bar, though Barenboim's flexible style prevents any feeling of rigidity. There is a tremendous burst of energy in the coda to make the *Passacaglia*'s final apotheosis very gripping indeed. The *Academic festival overture* is unusually expansive, bringing superb playing from the Chicago brass. Throughout the sound is suitably full-bodied within the aptly resonant acoustics of Chicago's Orchestra Hall.

Kempe's account with the BBC Symphony Orchestra comes from 1974 and (according to the label information) the Festival Hall. Such is the warmth and openness of the acoustic that the Albert Hall would seem the more likely venue. In conception it does not significantly differ from his commercial recordings with the Berlin Philharmonic (EMI/Testament) or the RPO (RCA). It is a beautifully natural account, relaxed and yet well held together, and totally free from eccentricity. Kempe gets excellent playing from the BBC Symphony Orchestra and the CD captures all the atmosphere of a live occasion. On balance this is to be preferred, perhaps, to his Berlin account.

Bernstein's 1981 Vienna version of Brahms's *Fourth*, recorded live, is exhilaratingly dramatic in fast music, while the slow movement brings richly resonant playing from the Vienna strings, not least in the great cello melody at bar 41, which with its moulded rubato comes to sound surprisingly like Elgar. This is easily the finest of Bernstein's Vienna cycle and, with generally good sound, is well worth considering.

There is a Boultian directness about the opening of Previn's account, fresh and alert, which immediately commands attention, helped by naturally balanced Telarc sound, just a little distanced. The finale is similarly strong and energetic, well drawn together; only in the bold third movement does the distancing detract from the impact of the performance, while allowing some clouding of inner detail. With a good – if hardly generous – coupling and now reissued on Telarc's Bravo! mid-priced label, it is one of the best of the modern digital versions.

The refinement of the very opening in Skrowaczewski's Carlton version leads to an exceptionally satisfying reading, outstanding in the lower mid-price range and finer than many full-price versions. The phrasing is affectionate without ever sounding self-conscious, and the alertness as well as the refinement of the Hallé playing confirms the excellence; if the coupling of only three *Hungarian dances* is hardly generous, they are certainly attractively presented.

Sanderling's super-bargain Dresden version has genuine fire and eloquence. It is finely recorded (in 1971), beautifully played and splendidly shaped, with some of the classical strength that distinguished this orchestra's account of the work under Karl Boehm in the days of 78s. However, it has a warmth and sense of enjoyment that make it a very rewarding performance indeed, and the *Variations* are also very successful. The warmth of the Dresden acoustic means that the quality remains pleasingly full, although the violins sound a little thin on top.

Following the success of the *Third*, Janowski gives a refreshingly direct reading of the *Fourth*. Speeds are unexceptionable, with the second-movement *Andante*, introduced very gently, slower than usual, but certainly expressive. The recording sounds vivid and full on CD and the weight of the final *Passacaglia* is well established. The coda of the symphony, like the overture which follows, brings real excitement.

(i) *Symphony No. 4;* (ii) *German Requiem, Op. 45;* (iii) *Schicksalslied, Op. 54.*

(B) **(*) EMI forte (SIS) Analogue/Dig. CZS5 69518-2 (2) [CDFB 69518]. (i) LPO, Jochum; (ii) Jessye Norman, Jorma Hynninen; (ii–iii) BBC Symphony Ch., LPO Ch., LPO, Tennstedt.

In the *Fourth Symphony*, Jochum's very opening phrase establishes the reading as warmly affectionate and, as in Bruckner, he combines a high degree of expressive flexibility with a rapt concentration, which holds the symphonic structure strongly together. Though the orchestra is British and the LPO is in fine form, this represents the German tradition at its most communicative; more than that, however, it demonstrates Jochum's passionate feeling for Brahms, with its spirit of soaring lyricism and – in the finale especially – a strong, even irresistible forward momentum. Although the performance has its idiosyncrasies of tempo, it is highly compelling in every bar, and it is a great pity that the appeal of this inexpensive reissue is somewhat diluted by the performance of the coupling, which may not be to all tastes.

In the *Requiem* Tennstedt brings speeds slower than on any rival version. His dedication generally sustains them well, though the choir's ensemble is not always perfect. What does sound monumental rather than moving is Jessye Norman's solo, *Ihr habt nun Traurigkeit*, though the golden tone is glorious. The *Schicksalslied* is also given a spacious, strong performance, with the London Philharmonic Choir singing dedicatedly, and the 1984–5 digital recording is spacious to match.

Variations on a theme of Haydn (St Anthony chorale), Op. 56a.

(M) *** Decca 452 893-2 [id.]. LSO, Pierre Monteux – HAYDN: *Symphonies Nos. 94 & 101.* ***

** Teldec/Warner Dig. 9031 74007-2 [id.]. NYPO, Masur (with IVES: *Variations on America;* REGER: *Variations and fugue on a theme of Mozart.* **)

(N) (**) Sony mono MHK 63328 [id.]. NYPO, Walter – MAHLER: *Symphony No. 1.* (**)

Monteux's performance of a work that can readily seem too easy-going is quite riveting. The orchestral playing is excellent and the vigorous style gives the music a splendid forward impulse: the listener is gripped from first bar to last. The bright (1958)

Kingsway Hall recording reveals the depth of sonority of Brahms's scoring at the very opening, but is otherwise slightly less glowing than in the Haydn couplings.

Walter's mono account comes from 1953 and appeared in the UK in 1955. It is naturally not as fresh or open as his later stereo version but it has the warmth and fine musicianship that characterize everything Walter did.

CHAMBER MUSIC

Complete chamber music

(i; ii) *Cello sonatas Nos. 1–2;* (iii; iv) *Clarinet quintet in B min., Op. 115;* (v; vi) *Clarinet sonatas Nos. 1–2;* (v; vii) *Clarinet trio in A min., Op. 114;* (ii; viii; ix) *Horn trio in E flat, Op. 40;* (x; xi) *Piano quartets Nos. 1–3;* (iv; xii) *Piano quintet in F min., Op. 34;* (x) *Piano trios Nos. 1–4;* (xiii) *String quartets Nos. 1–3;* (iv) *String quintets Nos. 1–2; String sextets Nos. 1–2;* (ii; ix) *Violin sonatas Nos. 1–3.*

(B) *** Ph. 454 073-2 (11) [id.]. (i) Starker; (ii) Sebök; (iii) Stähr; (iv) BPO Octet (members); (v) Pieterson; (vi) H. Menuhin; (vii) Pressler, Greenhouse; (viii) Orval; (ix) Grumiaux; (x) Beaux Arts Trio; (xi) Trampler (viola); (xii) Haas; (xiii) Quartetto Italiano.

This Philips bargain box of Brahms's chamber music happily combines a series of warmly appealing recordings made in Germany with other distinguished contributions from the Beaux Arts Trio and the Quartetto Italiano. Grumiaux and Starker lead the instrumental duos with slightly less success, but Starker and Sebök compensate by their passionate and subtle response to the *Cello sonatas* (this is a Mercury recording and is discussed separately below). The Berlin performance of the *Clarinet quintet* (led by Herbert Stähr) is exceptionally beautiful, an outstanding version in every way. In the *Clarinet trio* George Pieterson is the soloist, and this account with members of the Beaux Arts group offers a very well-integrated recording. The balance in the *Horn trio* is managed even more adroitly. The fine horn player, Francis Orval, seeks not to dominate but to be one of the group. Arthur Grumiaux's contribution is a constant pleasure, and the pianist, György Sebök, is hardly less admirable. The Beaux Arts set of *Piano trios* includes the *A major Trio*, which may or may not be authentic but which is certainly rewarding. The performances are splendid, with strongly paced, dramatic allegros, consistently alert, and with thoughtful, sensitive playing in slow movements. Characterization is positive (yet not over-forceful), and structural considerations are well judged: each reading has its own special individuality. The sound is first class.

Cello sonata No. 1 in E min., Op. 38.

(N) (***) Testament mono SBT 2158 [id.]. Piatigorsky, Rubinstein – BEETHOVEN: *Cello sonatas;* WEBER *Sonata in A.* (***)

Piatigorsky's patrician account of the *E minor Sonata* with Artur Rubinstein was recorded in Paris in the summer of 1936. It has been out of the catalogue for nearly half a century and Testament has put us right with this exemplary transfer.

Cello sonatas Nos. 1 in E min., Op. 38; 2 in F, Op. 99.

*** DG Dig. 410 510-2 [id.]. Mstislav Rostropovich, Rudolf Serkin.

(M) *** Mercury 434 377-2 [id.]. Starker, Sebök – MENDELSSOHN: *Cello sonata No. 2.* ***

*** Channel Classics Dig. CCS 5483 [id.]. Pieter Wispelwey, Paul Komen.

*** Hyperion Dig. CDA 66159 [id.]. Steven Isserlis, Peter Evans.

(N) *(*) Ph. Dig. 456 402-2 [id.]. Heinrich Schiff, Gerhard Oppitz.

Cello sonatas Nos. 1 in E min., Op. 38; 2 in F, Op. 99; in D min., Op. 108 (arr. of *Violin sonata in D min.*).

*** Sony Dig. SK 48191 [id.]. Yo-Yo Ma, Emanuel Ax.

The partnership of the wild, inspirational Russian cellist and the veteran Brahmsian pianist on DG is a challenging one. It proves an outstanding success, with inspiration mutually enhanced, whether in the lyricism of Op. 38 or the heroic energy of Op. 99. Good if close recording.

Starker was on his finest form when he made his Mercury recordings, and he had a splendid and understanding partner in György Sebók. These highly spontaneous performances rank alongside those by Rostropovich and Serkin: they have ardour and subtlety and an impressive sense of line. The 1964 recording is very well balanced, the acoustic is warm, yet the focus is admirably clear.

The Dutch partnership, Pieter Wispelwey and Paul Komen, offer something rather different. The cellist plays a nineteenth-century Bohemian cello and the pianist a Viennese period instrument: thus theirs is the only version of the sonatas to approximate to the sound Brahms himself might have heard. There is nothing anaemic or academic about their playing and no sense of scholarly inhibition. These are full-blooded performances, vivid in feeling and passionate, at no time wanting in eloquence.

Although with the Rostropovich/Serkin account available, Yo-Yo Ma and Emanuel Ax may not be a first choice in the Brahms *Cello sonatas*, their performances on Sony are certainly among the finest in the current lists. Both are highly responsive artists and are of one mind concerning matters of phrasing.

As always, Ma produces tone of great beauty and refinement and Ax plays with great sensitivity, though there are times when he is in danger of overpowering his partner.

Using gut strings, Isserlis produces an exceptionally warm tone, here nicely balanced in the recording against the strong and sensitive playing of his regular piano partner. In every way these perceptive and well-detailed readings stand in competition with the finest.

Heinrich Schiff is also well recorded and gives a noble account of the two sonatas, with natural and warm recorded sound on Philips, but the attractions of his recording are diminished by his somewhat pedestrian partner.

(i; ii) *Cello sonatas Nos. 1 in E min., Op. 38; 2 in F, Op. 99.*(ii) *Variations and fugue on a theme by Handel, Op. 24.*

(N) *** EMI Dig. CDC5 56440-2 [id.] (i) Lynn Harrell; (ii) Stephen Kovacevich.

Two new performances that are both well worth considering. Lynn Harrell and Steven Kovacevich are magnificent and commanding, and this might well be a first choice for many, particularly in view of Kovacevich's finely judged and eloquent account of the *Handel variations and fugue.*

(i) *Cello sonatas Nos. 1 in E min., Op. 38; 2 in F, Op. 99;* (ii) *Violin sonatas Nos. 1 in G, Op. 78; 2 in A, Op. 100; 3 in D min., Op. 108; F.A.E. Sonata: Scherzo.*

(B) **(*) Virgin Classics Dig. Double VBD5 61415-2 (2) [CDVB 61415]. (i) Leonard Rose; (ii) Jaime Laredo; Jean-Bernard Pommier.

The special interest of this Virgin Double is that it includes the last recordings made by Leonard Rose – at the Château de Malesherbes, France, in the summer of 1982. The original full-priced issue was well documented and included a warm tribute from colleague Isaac Stern. The present reissue makes no mention of this; in fact the documentation is sparse and inadequate. However, Rose achieved a fine partnership with Pommier, with whom he is ideally balanced, and though the recording is a trifle too close, it is very truthful. Not surprisingly these are strong, searching performances, especially the passionate *F major Sonata*. The *Violin sonatas* used the same venue the previous year, but here Laredo is not flattered by the close microphones, and this makes his ardent Brahmsian response seem a bit fierce at times. Once that is said, these too are impressively committed performances.

Clarinet quintet in B min., Op. 115.

(N) *** RCA Dig. 09026 68033-2 [id.]. Richard Stolzman, Tokyo Qt. – WEBER: *Clarinet quintet.* ***

(N) *** Ph. Dig. 442 149-2 [id.]. Harold Wright, Boston SO Chamber Players – MOZART: *Clarinet quintet.* ***

(M) *** Carlton Dig. 3036 70097-2 [id.]. Keith Puddy, Delmé Qt – DVORAK: *Quartet No. 12.* ***

(N) (B) *** H M Dig. HMN 911 691 [id.]. Alessandro Carbonare, Luc Hery, Florence Binder, Nicolas Bone, Muriel Pouzenc – MOZART: *Clarinet quintet.* ***

(BB) **(*) CfP Silver Double CDCFPSD 4772 (2). Keith Puddy, Gabrieli String Qt – BORODIN: *String quartet No. 2;* DVORAK: *String quartet No. 12;* SCHUBERT: *String quartet No. 14.* ***

(i) *Clarinet quintet;* (ii) *Clarinet sonata No. 2 in E flat, Op. 120/2.*

(M) *** Chandos CHAN 6522 [id.]. Janet Hilton, (i) Lindsay Qt; (ii) Peter Frankl.

(i) *Clarinet quintet;* (ii) *Clarinet trio in A min., Op. 114.*

*** Hyperion CDA 66107 [id.]. King, (i) Gabrieli Qt; (ii) Georgian, Benson (piano).

(BB) **(*) Naxos Dig. 8.550391. József Balogh, with (i) Danubius Qt; (ii) Jenö Jandó, Csaba Onczay.

The two newest recordings of the Brahms *Clarinet quintet* go straight to the top of the list. Richard Stolzman is a wonderfully imaginative and poetic soloist, and – as the very opening shows – the Tokyo Quartet play with extraordinary delicacy of feeling, yet there is a warm underlying current. Textures are transparent, the *Adagio* seems to float in the air and the *quintet*'s very closing pages have a touchingly gentle grace.

Harold Wright too gives a highly sensitive account, hardly less subtle in feeling in the slow *movement* and with some delightful individual touches in the *Andantino*. The Boston string-playing is only very marginally less refined, many will like their warmth in the middle range, although the leader's timbre is thinner; and of course couplings come into it also. If you would prefer Mozart to Weber that might tip the balance of advantage: certainly the Philips sound balance is most natural.

Keith Puddy's warm tone is well suited to Brahms and, with spacious speeds in all four movements, this is a consistently sympathetic reading; the Carlton digital recording is equally fine, vivid and full. Excellent value.

In Harmonia Mundi's bargain series, Les nouveaux interprètes, the talented young performers, are led by Alessandro Carbonare, the principal clarinet of the Orchestre Nationale of France. He produces exceptionally beautiful, liquid tone-colours over the widest dynamic range, with ear-catching *pianissimos* making the slow movement the high point, but with his entries in all four movements magically gentle. The string players, also members of the Orchestre Nationale as well as soloists, are not quite so distinctive, but provide consistently sympathetic support.

Janet Hilton's essentially mellow performance of the *Clarinet quintet*, with the Lindsay Quartet playing with pleasing warmth and refinement, has a distinct individuality. Her lilting syncopations in the third movement are delightful. Hilton's partnership with Peter Frankl in the *E flat Clarinet sonata* is rather less idiosyncratic and individual; nevertheless this performance offers considerable artistic rewards, even if the resonance means that the aural focus is a little diffuse.

Thea King and the Gabrieli Quartet give a radiantly beautiful performance of the *Clarinet quintet*, expressive and spontaneous-sounding, with natural ebb and flow of tension as in a live performance. The recording of the strings is on the bright side, very vivid and real.

Although the CD transfer of the 1970 recording brings a certain thinness in the violin timbre, Keith Puddy's earlier, CfP account with the Gabrielis of this elusive work rises to fine, intense poetry in the slow movement and in the visionary closing pages of the finale. There is a spontaneity in the playing here which is a vital quality in this work, far more important than mechanical precision. Moreover all three couplings on this Silver Double are highly recommendable.

József Balogh, principal clarinet with both the Hungarian State Opera and Radio Orchestras, is a highly sensitive player with a lovely tone. He is well supported by the Danubius Quartet and their account of the *Clarinet quintet* is a rewarding one, with warmth and atmosphere, and rising to considerable heights of intensity in the *Adagio*. The *Clarinet trio* is an enjoyably fresh account, though not quite so memorable, except in the *Andantino grazioso* which is delightfully done. Nevertheless Balogh, Jandó and Onczay are thoroughly sympathetic and, with excellent recording, this is still a worthwhile disc and inexpensive to boot.

(i) *Clarinet quintet in B min., Op. 115;* (ii) *Piano quintet in F min., Op. 34; String quintets Nos. 1 in F, Op. 88; 2 in G, Op. 111.*
(B) *** Ph. Duo 446 172-2 (2) [id.]. (i) Herbert Stähr; (ii) Werner Haas; Berlin Philharmonic Octet (members).

The Berlin performance of the *Clarinet quintet* is both beautiful and faithful to Brahms's instructions. The delicacy with which the 'Hungarian' middle section of the great *Adagio* is interpreted gives some idea of the insight of these players. It is an autumnal reading, never overforced, and is recorded with comparable refinement. The two *String quintets* are also admirably served by these same players (with Dietrich Gerhard, viola, replacing the clarinettist, Herbert Stähr). The performances combine freshness and polish, warmth with well-integrated detail. For the *Piano quintet* Werner Haas joins the group, and they give a strongly motivated, spontaneous account of this splendid work that is in every way satisfying. The piano is most convincingly balanced. The recordings come from the early 1970s and the sound is remarkably full and warm, the richness of texture suiting the *String quintets* especially well. This is among the finest bargains in the Philips Duo list.

(i) *Clarinet quintet in B min., Op. 115; String quartet No. 1 in C min., Op. 51/1.*
(M) (**(*)) EMI mono CDH7 64932-2. (i) Reginald Kell; Busch Qt.

Reginald Kell's beauty of tone was legendary and his 1937 account of the *Clarinet quintet* with the Busch Quartet is among the greatest recordings of the piece. Kell's vibrato was not to all tastes, but his playing here is heard at its most refined and the Busch produce a splendidly autumnal feeling in the slow movement. The *C minor Quartet*, recorded in 1932, may not be as polished as in some more recent accounts (and certainly sounds its age), but the playing is full of imagination and vitality.

(i) *Clarinet quintet in B min., Op. 115. String quartet No. 2 in A min., Op. 51/2.*
*** MDG Dig. 307 079-2 [id.]. Karl Leister; Leipzig Qt.

These performances from the Leipzig Quartet, with Karl Leister in the *Clarinet quintet*, are second to none. The quartet and its distinguished soloist produce impressive results in what is surely Brahms's most serene utterance, and the *A minor Quartet* also receives an authoritative and musical performance. For those wanting this particular coupling, this disc can certainly be recommended.

(i) *Clarinet quintet in B min., Op. 115. String quintet No. 2 in G, Op. 111.*
*** Delos Dig. DE 3066 [id.]. (i) David Shifrin; Chamber Music NorthWest.

David Shifrin plays most beautifully in the *Clarinet quintet* and fully catches its serenity and autumnal nostalgia. He receives highly sympathetic support from Chamber Music NorthWest who find a parallel in the atmosphere of the *Adagio* of the *String quintet*, which is also played with a natural Brahmsian feeling.

Clarinet sonatas Nos. 1 in F min.; 2 in E flat, Op. 120/1–2.
*** Chandos Dig. CHAN 8563 [id.]. Gervase de Peyer, Gwenneth Prior.
(BB) *** Naxos Dig. 8.553121 [id.]. Kálmán Berkes, Jenö Jandó.

Superb performances from Gervase de Peyer and Gwenneth Prior, commanding, aristocratic, warm and full of subtleties of colour and detail. The recording too is outstandingly realistic.

No one buying the Naxos CD coupling the two

late *Clarinet sonatas* is likely to have any regrets. They are beautifully played and freshly recorded by this distinguished Hungarian duo, and they would be recommendable even in a higher price-bracket.

(i) *Clarinet sonatas Nos. 1 in F min.; 2 in E flat, Op. 120/1–2;* (ii) *String quartets Nos. 1 in C min.; 2 in A min., Op. 51/1-2; 3 in B flat, Op. 67.*
(B) *** Ph. Duo 456 320-2 (2) [(M) id. import].
(i) George Pieterson, Hephzibah Menuhin; (ii) Italian Qt.

The three *String quartets* are marvellously played by the Quartetto Italiano. As always with the Philips remastering of analogue recordings (here from 1967, 1970 and 1971 respectively), the CD transfers are admirably truthful in timbre and balance. The *Clarinet sonatas* are very well played by George Pieterson and Hephzibah Menuhin. The autumnal twilight of the lovely *Andante un poco adagio* of the *F minor* is appealingly caught, and the following *Allegretto grazioso* flows engagingly. The *E flat Sonata* is more direct, less coaxing but strongly characterized, with plenty of light and shade. Vivid recording from 1980 adds to the feeling of boldness.

Clarinet trio in A min., Op. 114.
*** Sony Dig SK 57499 [id.]. Stoltzman, Ax, Ma – BEETHOVEN: *Clarinet trio* ***; MOZART: *Clarinet trio (Kegelstatt).* **

With Stolzman, Ax and Ma, the *Clarinet trio* comes off well and finds this team in excellent form. This is now one of the most recommendable of current versions, with Stoltzman playing with great sensitivity.

(i) *Clarinet trio in A min., Op. 114;* (ii) *Horn trio in E flat, Op. 40; Piano trios Nos. 1–3, Opp. 8; 87 & 101.*
(N) *** Hyperion Dig. CDA 67251/2 [id.].
Florestan Trio with (i) Richard Hosford; (ii) Stephen Stirling.

(i; ii) *Clarinet trio in A min., Op. 114;* (iii) *Horn trio in E flat, Op. 40;* (ii) *Piano trios Nos. 1 in B, Op. 8; 2 in C, Op. 87; 3 in C min., Op. 101; 4 in A, Op. posth.*
(B) *** Ph. Duo 438 365-2 (2) [id.]. (i) George Pieterson; (ii) Beaux Arts Trio; (iii) Francis Orval, Arthur Grumiaux, Gyorgy Sebok.

Hyperion package the three *Piano trios* together with the *Clarinet* and *Horn trios* in a full-price two-CD set. The Florestan set is the finest since the Beaux Arts comparable grouping, both in terms of performance and recording. These players have thought deeply about the music yet their readings are not in the least studied. There is a freshness and spontaneity that rekindles one's own enthusiasm for this music, and such is its dedication that one is left marvelling at the richness and quality of Brahms's inventive resource. The same must be said of the *Horn trio* and the late *A minor Clarinet trio*. The recorded sound is very natural and lifelike and brings the players into your living room. Although the Beaux Arts remain a very strong recommendation, readers attracted to this distinguished newcomer need not hesitate.

The splendid Beaux Arts set of the *Piano trios* come on a pair of joined CDs at bargain price, with two other outstanding performances thrown in for good measure. George Pieterson is a first-rate artist and his account of the *Clarinet trio* with members of the Beaux Arts group offers masterly playing from all three participants. The balance in the *Horn trio* is perhaps the most successful on record. The fine horn player, Francis Orval, achieves this without any loss of personality in his playing (note the richness of his contribution to the Trio of the Scherzo). The performance is warmly lyrical and completely spontaneous, with a racy finale to round off a particularly satisfying reading, never forced but deeply felt.

As for the *Piano trios*, the performances are splendid, with strongly paced, dramatic allegros, consistently alert and thoughtful, and with sensitive playing in slow movements. The sound is first class and the resonance of Bernard Greenhouse's cello is warmly caught without any clouding of focus. The CD transfer has brightened the top a little, but not excessively. Excellent notes, too.

Horn trio in E flat, Op. 40 (see also above).
(M) **(*) Decca 452 887-2 [id.]. Barry Tuckwell, Itzhak Perlman, Vladimir Ashkenazy – FRANCK: *Violin sonata.* ***
(N) (B) *** EMI Debut Dig. CDZ5 72822-2 [id.]. Andrew Clark (Waldhorn), Catherine Martin, Gerald Govier – BEETHOVEN: *Horn sonata; Sextet, Op. 81b*; MOZART: *Horn quintet; Duos.****

A superb performance of Brahms's marvellous *Horn trio* from Tuckwell, Perlman and Ashkenazy. They realize to the full the music's passionate impulse, and the performance moves forward from the gentle opening, through the sparkling Scherzo and the more introspective but still outgiving *Adagio*, to the gay and spirited finale. The 1968 recording has been remastered for reissue in Decca's Classic Sound series, but the attempt to provide a more sharply defined sound-picture has brought a curious loss of focus at times, verging on distortion at climaxes.

Andrew Clark's performance using a period Waldhorn is most stimulating. As in the Beethoven couplings there is a flamboyance in the playing which makes such a movement as the finale of the Brahms trio thrilling, and Clark's virtuosity is well matched by his partners, also using period instruments. Govier, who uses a fortepiano in Beethoven, here choses a Bösendorfer piano, made in Vienna in 1871/2. On one of EMI's cheapest labels it makes a splendid bargain. Warm, full sound.

(i) *Horn trio in E flat;* (ii) *Piano quintet in F min., Op. 34.*

**(*) CRD Dig. CRD 3489 [id.]. Nash Ens.: (i) Frank Lloyd; (i; ii) Marcia Crayford, Ian Brown; (ii) Elizabeth Layton, Roger Chase, Christopher van Kampen.

The Nash Ensemble have extra expressive warmth at spacious speeds, firmly underpinned by the incisive playing of the pianist, Ian Brown, and this is heard at its best in the *Piano quintet*. The romanticism of the Nash approach also comes out in the *Horn trio*, but the horn soloist, Frank Lloyd, is rather too reticent here. He produces an exceptionally rich tone to remind one of Dennis Brain and helps the group to give a raptly beautiful account of the *Adagio*. Following these relaxed accounts of the first three movements, the galloping finale is then given with joyful panache, with the horn braying splendidly. Thanks partly to the CRD recording, the Nash performances are made to sound satisfyingly beefy, almost orchestral. Yet, with both performances undoubtedly characterful and enjoyable, the disc can be recommended, particularly when this is the only issue coupling these two works.

(i) *Horn trio in E flat;* (ii) *String sextet No. 2 in G, Op. 36.*

✿ (B) *** Sony SBK 63209 [id.]. (i) Bloom, Tree, Serkin; (ii) Carmirelli, Toth, Naegele, Caroline Levine, Arico, Reichenberger.

The performance of the *Horn trio*, recorded at the Marlboro Festival in 1960, is quite splendid. Myron Bloom's horn playing is superb, and Michael Tree matches his lyrical feeling, while Rudolf Serkin holds the performance together so that, when the fervour of the music-making brings a few slips in rhythmic precision, the listener is carried along by the exhilaration of the moment. The *Trio* comes paired with another Marlboro performance, of the *G major String sextet*, by a string group led by Pina Carmirelli. Recorded in 1967, this has been very effectively remastered and the players given a striking presence. There is a degree of thinness on the violin timbre but no lack of body, and the performance is both warm and refined: it seems to gather tension as it proceeds. The finale is particularly successful.

Piano quartets Nos. 1 in G min., Op. 25; 2 in A, Op. 26; 3 in C min., Op. 60.

*** Sony Dig.S2K 45846 (2) [id.]. Jaime Laredo, Isaac Stern, Yo-Yo Ma, Emanuel Ax.

(i) *Piano quartets Nos. 1–3;* (ii) *Piano trios Nos. 1 in B, Op. 8; 2 in C, Op. 87; 3 in C min., Op. 101.*

(M) *** Sony Stern Edition III Dig./Analogue SM3K 64520 (3) [id.]. Isaac Stern, with (i) Laredo, Yo-Yo Ma, Ax; (ii) Rose, Istomin.

The Stern–Laredo–Ma–Ax partnership produces some pretty high-voltage playing and a real sense of give-and-take. There is little sense of four stars just coming together for a recording session but more of a genuine musical rapport. The listener is placed rather closer to the artists than some readers might like. All the same, no one investing in the Sony set is likely to be in the least disappointed.

This set is still available separately on two premium-priced CDs, but the three-disc set (taken from Volume III of Sony's celebration of Stern's 'Life in Music') is the one to go for. This includes equally fine versions of the *Piano trios*, recorded in New York two decades earlier, in 1964 and 1966. Here Stern joins with Rose and Istomin to give committed, romantic performances of comparable magnetism. The remastering has improved the original recording almost out of recognition, especially in relation to the piano sonority. The balance is close, but one relishes the presence of these fine artists.

(i) *Piano quartets Nos. 1–3; Piano quintet in F min., Op. 34. String quartet in A min., Op. 51/2.*

(***) Testament mono SBT 3063 (3) [id.]. (i) Victor Aller; Hollywood Qt – SCHUMANN: *Piano quintet* (***).

For a brief period in the 1950s the Hollywood Quartet dominated the chamber-music scene. Their records were as eagerly awaited as were their rare visits to the concert hall. Their discography was not extensive and nearly all of it is self-recommending. Certainly the Brahms *Piano quartets* have hardly been surpassed since, and the *A minor Quartet* has tremendous grip and an ardent lyricism. At the time they seemed to be more or less ideal performances, and so they do now. Due to the microphone placement there is a strident quality in the upper register in the *A minor Quartet*, but it can easily be tamed. There was nothing in the least strident about their tone in the flesh. Desmond Shawe-Taylor and Edward Sackville-West's *The Record Guide* (1955) spoke of the *A minor Quartet* having 'a sensibility that reveals the romantic soul beneath the classical surface'. Performances of this integrity do not come often.

(i) *Piano quartets Nos. 1 in G min., Op. 25; 2 in A, Op. 26; 3 in C min., Op. 60. Piano trio in A, Op. posth.*

(B) *** Ph. Duo 454 017-2 (2) [id.]. Beaux Arts Trio, (i) with Walter Trampler.

The Beaux Arts set of *Piano quartets* is self-recommending at Duo price, with the *A major Piano trio* thrown in as a bonus. Thoughtful, sensitive playing in slow movements, lively tempi in allegros, characteristic musicianship plus spontaneity combine to make these recordings highly recommendable throughout, alongside the Stern Sony set (see above), which is in a higher price bracket.

Piano quartet No. 1 in G min.
*** Sony Dig. MK 42361 [id.]. Murray Perahia, Amadeus Qt (members).

Perahia's version of the *G minor Piano quartet* has an expressive power and eloquence that silence criticism. The sound has both warmth and presence in its CD format and this is arguably the finest account of the work since Gilels recorded it with the same ensemble (see below).

(i) *Piano quartet No. 1 in G min., Op. 25. 4 Ballades, Op. 10.*
(M) **(*) DG 447 407-2 [id.]. Gilels, (i) with Amadeus Qt.

As might be expected, Gilels's account of the *G minor Quartet* with members of the Amadeus has much to recommend it. The great Russian pianist is in impressive form, and most listeners will respond to the withdrawn delicacy of the Scherzo and the gypsy fire of the finale. The slow movement is perhaps somewhat wanting in ardour and the Amadeus do not sound as committed or as fresh as their keyboard partner. At medium price, however, this version enjoys an advantage, and the 1971 DG recording is well balanced and sounds very natural in its new transfer. Moreover in the *Ballades* Gilels offers artistry of an order that silences criticism. In terms of imaginative vitality and musical insight it would be difficult to surpass these readings, and the 1976 recording is also first class.

Piano quartet No. 2 in A.
(N) (BB) *** ASV Quicksilva Dig. CDQS 6199 [id.]. Schubert Ens. of London – MENDELSSOHN: *Piano quartet No. 1.* ***

Musicianly and well-recorded performances that will give satisfaction at this (or any other) price level. Sensible tempi and very well-articulated phrasing.

Piano quartet No. 3 in C min., Op. 60.
(BB) *** ASV Dig. Quicksilva CDQS 6198 [(M) id.]. Schubert Ens. of London – MENDELSSOHN: *Piano quartet No. 3.****
** Sony Dig. MK 42387 [id.]. Stern, Ma, Laredo, Ax – *Double concerto.* ***

The *C minor Piano quartet*, though well served on CD, is represented less than generously at the bargain end of the spectrum. The Schubert Ensemble of London, which includes the pianist, William Howard, give a commendable account of it, though they do not perhaps penetrate all its depths. The Beaux Arts plus Walter Trampler remain a first recommendation, but readers attracted by the coupling can be assured that the ASV version is well worth the modest outlay required.

Excellent playing from all concerned on the Sony/CBS disc, even if Emanuel Ax delivers too thick a fortissimo tone at times – though he can produce beautiful pianissimo tone as well. There are pianists more sensitive in this respect on rival recordings.

Piano quintet in F min., Op. 34.
(N) *** BBC Legends BBCL 4009-2 (2) [id.]. Clifford Curzon, Amadeus Qt – SCHUBERT: *Trout quintet.****
(BB) *** Naxos Dig. 8.550406; *4550406* [id.]. Jenö Jandó, Kodály Qt – SCHUMANN: *Piano quintet.* ***
(N) *** Philips Dig. 446 710-2 [id.]. Peter Serkin, Guarneri Qt. – HENZE: *Piano quintet.* ***

Clifford Curzon, never an easy recording artist, is captured at his most spontaneously expressive in his live performance with the Amadeus Quartet, recorded at the Royal Festival Hall in 1974. Similarly the Amadeus Quartet are at their most compelling in live performance. Ensemble may not be quite so polished as in a studio performance, but the warmth and power are ample compensation, and the bonus disc of Schubert's *Trout quintet* makes a very attractive package. Indeed this coupling documents a unique collaboration which can be recommended to all admirers of these artists.

This fine Naxos account has a great deal going for it, even though it does not include the first-movement exposition repeat. The playing is boldly spontaneous and has plenty of fire and expressive feeling. The opening of the finale has mystery too, and overall, with full-bodied recording and plenty of presence, this makes a strong impression. It is certainly a bargain.

Recorded in 1995, Peter Serkin and the Guarneri Quartet's account of the Brahms *quintet* must rank among the most thoughtful and penetrating of recent recordings. Naturally it is technically impeccable but there is no want of spontaneity and poetic feeling. Those who have found the Guarneris rather chromium-plated and streamlined in the past, will find a lot to surprise them in this challenging and powerfully conceived reading. The Philips recording is first class. However, no doubt the coupling will be a prime influence here.

(i) *Piano quintet in F min., Op. 34*; *String quartet No. 2 in A min., Op. 51/2.*
(N) *** Teldec Dig.4509 97461-2.(i) Elizo Virzaladze; Borodin Qt.

These performances were recorded at The Maltings, Snape and benefit from its warm and vibrant acoustic. The *Piano quintet* receives a commanding yet sensitive treatment with Elizo Virzaladze making a positive contribution to the proceedings. In the *A minor Quartet* the Borodins have an agreeably unforced sense of forward movement and it goes without saying that in questions of tonal blend and ensemble they are impeccable. A fine disc for those who find this pairing attractive.

(i) *Piano quintet in F min., Op. 34*; (ii) *String quintets Nos. 1 in F, Op. 88; 2 in G, Op. 111.*
(N) *(*) Audivis Valois V4799 (2) [id.]. Danish Qt. with (i) Noël Lee; (ii) Serge Collot.

These performances all appeared on the Valois label in the LP era and date from the 1960s. Neither of the string quintets was particularly memorable at the time; the Danish quartet give what one might call rough-and-ready performances, perfectly serviceable though intonation and blend are less than ideal. Noël Lee is an impressive player and the *Piano quintet* gets a very decent, serviceable performance even if the recorded sound here (as in the two string quintets) is distinctly subfusc. Even at mid-price this is not strongly competitive.

(i) *Piano quintet in F min., Op. 34; String sextet No 1 in B flat, Op. 18.*
(B) **(*) DG Classikon 439 490-2 [(M) id. import]. (i) Eschenbach, Amadeus Qt (augmented).

Christoph Eschenbach gives a powerful – sometimes over-projected – account of his part in the *Quintet*, yet this is undoubtedly a moving performance with plenty of vitality. Good piano quality and, although the piano dominates, the Amadeus players remain well in the picture. The performance of the *Sextet* lacks something in purity of style, but the obvious tonal warmth and the undoubted merits of the ensemble, coupled with very good late-1960s recording, make this a pretty good recommendation for those with limited budgets.

Piano trios Nos. 1 in B, Op. 8 (original, 1854 version); 1 in B, Op. 8 (1889 version); 2 in C, Op. 87; 3 in C min., Op. 101.
(BB) *** Arte Nova Dig. 74321 51641-2 (2) [id.]. Trio Opus 8.

The prize-winning Trio Opus 8 is so-named because the ensemble was formed (in 1985) while the players were studying Brahms's *First Piano trio*. Their interest in it is such that they have recorded not only Brahms's final, revised version of 1889 but also the twenty-year-old composer's original (1854) score, his first major chamber work for strings. They make a very good case for it, sustaining tension powerfully in resonant, well-matched playing through even the long first movement. It certainly does not sound immature, even if both outer movements are considerably more expansive than the revised version (the opening movement has 200 more bars of music). Throughout all three works speeds are on the broad side, but that helps to give even the most compressed of these *Trios*, Op. 101 *in C minor*, heroic power in the outer movements. All three *Trios* are played with great verve and commitment and excellently crisp ensemble (especially in the sparkling Scherzos), while slow movements have fine concentration and lyrical warmth. The account of the *C major Trio*, Op. 87, is particularly fine. The pianist, Michael Hauber, leads the ensemble vibrantly, yet the balance places him well within the group. The cellist, Mario de Secondi, is a strikingly songful player, and his warm tone helps to offset the digital brightness on the violin timbre. This may need taming on some reproducers, but the recording is otherwise vivid and full, and the ambience pleasing.

Piano trios Nos. 1 in B, Op. 8; 2 in C, Op. 87; 3 in C min., Op. 101; 4 in A, Op. posth.
*** Teldec/Warner Dig. 9031 76036-2 (2) [id.]. Trio Fontenay.
*** Ph. Dig. 416 838-2 (2) [id.]. Beaux Arts Trio.

Powerful, spontaneous playing with a real Brahmsian spirit, given excellent, modern recording, puts these admirable performances by the Trio Fontenay at the top of the list.

The new digital recordings by the Beaux Arts Trio were made in La Chaux-de-Fonds, Switzerland, and they bring one close to the artists. The playing is always highly vital and sensitive. There is a splendid, finely projected sense of line and the delicate, sensitive playing of Menahem Pressler is always a delight.

(i) *Piano trios Nos. 1 in B, Op. 8; 2 in C, Op. 87; 3 in C min., Op. 101;* (ii) *Piano quintet in F min., Op. 34.*
(N) (BB) ** EMI double fforte CZS5 73341-2 (2). (i) Frankl, Pauk, Kirshbaum; (ii) Previn, Yale Qt.

Workmanlike performances of the *Piano trios*, expertly played, that give pleasure and satisfaction, yet at the same time fall short of being memorable. All three players are unfailingly reliable musicians but Peter Frankl does not shed new light on these scores in the way that Menahem Pressler does in the Beaux Arts version. The sound quality needs to be fresher and more cleanly focused. Previn and his American colleagues recorded the *Piano quintet* at a few hours' notice, at the time when they were also giving the work in a South Bank Summer Music concert. The challenge of the occasion comes over strongly, particularly in the strongly rhythmic, infectiously pointed account of the piano part from Previn. There may be more polished versions, but this is among the most spontaneous-sounding. The recording is good, though some will find it too reverberant.

Piano trio No. 1 in B, Op. 8.
(M) (***) RCA mono 09026 61763-2 [id.]. Heifetz, Feuermann, Rubinstein – DOHNANYI: *Serenade in C;* R. STRAUSS: *Violin sonata.* (***)

A commanding performance of the *B major Trio* comes from the legendary partnership of Heifetz, Feuermann and Rubinstein. Recorded in 1941, the sound calls for considerable tolerance on the part of the listener but this is well worth extending, given the quality of the playing.

Piano trios Nos. 1 in B, Op. 8; 2 in C, Op. 87.
*** DG Dig. 447 055-2. Pires, Dumay, Wang.

Following their fine accounts of the violin sonatas, Augustin Dumay and Maria João Pires are joined by the young Chinese cellist, Jian Wang. His contribution is certainly eloquent here and the performances overall have authority and finesse. Though the recording is not absolutely ideal in every respect it has a pleasing warmth and amplitude. The performance has personality and earns three stars.

Piano trios Nos. 1 in B, Op. 8; 2 in C, Op. 87.
(M) *** Decca (IMS) 421 152-2 [id.]. Julius Katchen, Josef Suk, János Starker.

(i-ii) *Piano trios Nos. 1 in B; 2 in G; 3 in C min.;* (i) *Cello sonata No. 2 in F;* (ii) *F.A.E. Sonata: Scherzo.*
(B) *** Decca Double 448 092-2 (2) [(M) id. import]. Julius Katchen, with (i) János Starker; (ii) Josef Suk.

The Katchen/Suk/Starker recordings of the *Piano trios* and *Cello sonata* were made in The Maltings in July 1968; the *Scherzo* from the *F.A.E. Sonata* comes from the previous year and was recorded in the Kingsway Hall. The performances of the first two *Piano trios* are warm, strong and characterful, while the tough *C minor Trio* and the epic, thrustful *Cello sonata* bring a comparably spontaneous response. If the sound of the CD transfers is a little limited in the upper range, the ear is grateful that no artificial brightening has been applied, for it provides a real Brahmsian amplitude which is very satisfying. Highly recommended in either format.

String quartets Nos. 1–2, Op. 51/1–2; 3 in B flat, Op. 67.
(B) *** Teldec/Warner 4509 95503-2 (2) [id.]. Alban Berg Qt (with DVORAK: *String quartet No. 13.* ***)

String quartets Nos. 1 in C min.; 2 in A min., Op. 51/1–2; 3 in B flat, Op. 67.
*** EMI (SIS) Dig. CDS7 54829-2 (2) [ZDCB 54283]. Alban Berg Qt.
**(*) Claves Dig. 50-9404/5 (2) [id.]. Quartet Sine Nomine.

We have commented on the analogue Alban Berg performances in earlier editions. They were made in the mid-1970s when the quartet was on peak form, highly polished yet completely fresh in their musical responses. The Teldec performances have the inestimable advantage of being economical in price and also space; they are accommodated in the now-popular two-in-one jewel-case. This set is strongly recommended and can stand alongside the best in the catalogue, even if the Dvořák coupling is not quite as fine as the Brahms.

On EMI, the outer quartets, the *C minor*, Op. 51/1, and the *B flat*, Op. 67, were recorded in Switzerland (in a church) and are accommodated on the first CD; the *A minor*, Op. 51/2, is from a live performance given at the Palais Yusopov in St Petersburg and is on the second CD – rather short measure these days for a full-price CD. All the same there is nothing short-measured about the performances, which have all the finesse and attack one expects from the Alban Berg Quartet along with impeccable technical address. The *A minor* has just the right kind of dramatic intensity, and the range of colour and dynamics they produce in all three works is impressive. The EMI engineers produced well-detailed, truthful sound in the Swiss venue; the slightly greater freshness and spontaneity of the St Petersburg performance is offset by a slight loss in tonal radiance. All the same, these are all performances of quality and can be recommended even to those who find this ensemble at times a little too glossy.

The Sine Nomine Quartet are splendidly recorded in a helpful acoustic, and the effect here is just like a series of live performances. The playing, though well integrated and responsive with plenty of Brahmsian spirit, has not the degree of sophistication and finesse the Alban Berg Quartet displays, but it does have consistent vitality and spontaneity; the *Third, B flat major Quartet* is particularly alive: it leaps out of the speakers towards the listener, and again the closing variations are a highlight of the performance.

String quartets Nos. 1 in C min.; 2 in A min., Op. 51/1–2; 3 in B flat, Op. 67; (i) *Clarinet quintet in B min., Op. 115.*
(M) (***) EMI Rouge et Noir (SIS) mono CHS5 66422-2 (2) [CDHB 66422]. Léner Qt, (i) with Charles Draper.

The Léner ensemble offer music-making from another age: civilized, free from expressive exaggeration and with nothing over-projected or forced. Three of the quartet members were pupils of Hubay, who made a virtue of his portamento. The earliest of the recordings here, the *Clarinet quintet*, comes from 1928; the three quartets were made between 1929 (Op. 67) and 1933 (Op. 51/1). The quartets unfold in a totally natural way – well, not quite wholly natural, for Léner's portamenti, very much of its period, tend to date them. Those who find it difficult to come to terms with this stylistic idiosyncrasy should perhaps look elsewhere. Portamenti apart, there is much to savour here. Connoisseurs of the clarinet will find Charles Draper's account of the *B minor Quintet* of particular interest. Draper had heard Richard Mühlfeld, the dedicatee and first performer of the work, and his slow tempo at the very opening had Brahms's own imprimatur. The transfers and annotations are excellent.

String quartets Nos. 1–3; (i) *Piano quintet in F min., Op. 34.*
(M) *** Hyperion Dyad Dig. CDD 22018 (2) [id.]. (i) Piers Lane; New Budapest Qt.

The New Budapest Quartet bring warmth and spontaneity to all three scores, responding to their dramatic fervour and lyrical flow in equal measure. Their intonation is altogether impeccable and they are scrupulously attentive to Brahms's dynamic markings, with pleasing results in terms of clarity and transparency. They enjoy two further advantages over some earlier rivals in that, first, they also offer an excellently shaped and musicianly account of the *F minor Piano quintet* with responsive playing from Piers Lane and, secondly, they are among the best and most naturally recorded to have appeared in recent years. At mid-price on a Hyperion Dyad Double, this admirable set tends to sweep the board for those wanting all three quartets, plus the *Piano quintet*.

String quartets Nos. 1 in C min.; 2 in A min., Op. 51/1–2.
*** Chandos Dig. CHAN 8562 [id.]. Gabrieli Qt.
(N) **(*) Simax Dig. PSC1156 [id.]. Vertavo Qt.

Richly recorded in an agreeably expansive ambience, the Gabrielis give warm, eloquent performances of both the Op. 51 *Quartets*, deeply felt and full-textured without being heavy; the *Romanze* of Op. 51, No. 1, is delightfully songful. There are both tenderness and subtlety here, and the sound is first class.

The Vertavo are a young Norwegian quartet founded in the 1980s who have won golden opinions in the concert hall and in various international competitions. There is evident feeling in these well-prepared performances though a trace of self-consciousness can be discerned in the wide dynamic range they cultivate. When they play softly, they certainly let you know it. All the same these are thoroughly recommendable accounts even if they do not displace first recommendations.

String quartets Nos. 1 in C min., Op. 51/1; 3 in B flat, Op. 67.
**(*) Teldec/Warner Dig. 4509 90889-2 [id.]. Borodin Qt.

Marvellously sophisticated playing from the Borodins, with wonderful tonal blending, absolute security of intonation and immaculate ensemble. The first movement of No. 1 sets off with considerable impetus, but the thoughtfulness of the performance establishes itself within a few bars, and the inner movements of this *Quartet* have much grace and delicacy of feeling, while in Op. 67 the subtle treatment of the variations which make up the last movement is a high point of the record. The digital recording is firm and truthful, if a shade close and bright; but the main reservation here is that these performances, although they offer much to admire and enjoy, lack the kind of spontaneity that really grips the listener; moreover many listeners might like their Brahms to sound rather more robust.

String quartet No. 2 in A min., Op. 51/2.
(BB) **(*) ASV Quicksilva CDQS 6173 [(M) id.]. Lindsay Qt (with MENDELSSOHN: *String quartet No. 6.* **)

The Lindsays are in fine fettle here and, besides generating spontaneous excitement, the playing has much imagination and subtlety, notably in the *Andante* but especially in the *Quasi minuetto – Allegro vivace* third movement, which is articulated with superb precision. This was a live recording and the microphones are too close, but the ear adjusts to the fierceness given to the players' attack when the performance has such spontaneous thrust. The Mendelssohn coupling, however, is rather less successful

String quartet No. 2 in A min., Op. 51/2.
*** RCA Dig. [09026 61866-2]. Vogler Qt – SCHUMANN: *String quartet No. 3.* ***

String quartet No. 3 in B flat, Op. 67.
*** RCA Dig. 09026 61438-2 [id.]. Vogler Qt – SCHUMANN: *String quartet No. 1.* ***

The Vogler is an extremely fine ensemble who have been engaged on recording the Brahms and Schumann quartets, as the Quartetto Italiano did on LP in the 1970s. Tough luck if you already have one and want the other (though there is no lack of alternatives) but, if you do want both in modern, digital recordings, it would be difficult to improve on them. They have the advantage of a rich and beautifully blended sonority and refined musicianship. Moreover the RCA recording is very good indeed. Recommended with enthusiasm. Only the second CD is available in the UK.

String quintets Nos. 1 in F, Op. 88; 2 in G, Op. 111.
*** Hyperion Dig. CDA 66804 [id.]. Raphael Ens.
*** DG Dig. 453 420-2. Hagen Qt, Gérard Caussée.
(M) **(*) Ph. 426 094-2. BPO Octet (members).

With the *First Quintet* opening seductively, these are fine, vital performances of both works from the Raphael Ensemble, who show themselves particularly sensitive to the grave melancholy of the slow movement of the *F major* and the wistfully gentle mood of the *Intermezzo* in the *G major*. Indeed these performances are on the same level of distinction as their accounts of the *String sextets* and, like that companion Hyperion disc, the recording is very present indeed, which to some ears may seem a minor drawback.

The Hagen Quartet and Gérard Caussée give highly enjoyable accounts of the two *Quintets* and the DG engineers give them good recorded sound. No need to say more than that it can rank alongside the Raphael Ensemble on Hyperion.

Although the remastering has brought a thinner, more astringent treble response than the original LP, the performances by the Berlin Philharmonic group are searching and artistically satisfying, combining freshness with polish, warmth with well-integrated detail.

String quintet No. 2 in G, Op. 111.
*** Naim Dig. CD 010 [id.]. Augmented Allegri Qt – BRUCH: *String quintet.* ***
*** Nimbus Dig. NI 5488 [id.]. Brandis Qt, with Brett Dean – BRUCKNER: *String quintet.* ***

The second of the two string quintets that Brahms wrote late in his career makes the ideal coupling for the long-buried Bruch *Quintet*, which was also the product of old age. Very well played and recorded.

The Brandis version of the *G major Quintet* offers good value in being coupled with Bruckner's *F major Quintet* and, although it might well not be a first choice in the present work, it remains a very good performance. The Brandis are a fine quartet and they give a warm and sympathetic account of this lovely work; the Nimbus recording is natural and lifelike.

String sextets Nos. 1 in B flat, Op. 18; 2 in G, Op. 36.
*** Hyperion Dig. CDA 66276 [id.]. Raphael Ens.
*** Sony Dig. S2K 45820 (2) [id.]. Stern, Lin, Ma, Robinson, Laredo, Tree.
*** Chandos Dig. CHAN 9151 [id.]. ASMF Chamber Ens.

The *Sextets* are among Brahms's most immediately appealing chamber works. The Raphael Ensemble are fully responsive to all their subtleties as well as to their vitality and warmth. In short, these are superb performances; the recording is very vivid and immediate, although some ears might find it a shade too present.

Names alone are not in themselves enough to ensure success, even if they are as resplendent as those of Isaac Stern, Cho-Liang Lin, Yo-Yo Ma, Jaime Laredo and so on; but the rapport and interplay so vital in chamber-music playing is in ample evidence. There is a keen feeling for the warmth and generosity of feeling, as well as for the strength and architecture of these masterpieces, and the Sony engineering is impressive. This can be recommended alongside the Raphael Ensemble (Hyperion), which are accommodated on one CD, so many may feel that the Hyperion remains the 'best buy'.

The Chandos alternative is also highly recommendable, with both *Sextets* again accommodated on one CD without sacrificing the exposition repeats, so that at almost 78 minutes the Academy of St Martin-in-the-Fields offer excellent value for money. Moreover these well-prepared and musical performances are perceptive and intelligent, and receive finely detailed and present recording.

String sextet No. 1 in B flat, Op. 18.
(***) Biddulph mono LAB 093 [id.]. Pro Arte Qt, with Hobday, Pini – SCHUBERT: *String quintet in C.* (***)

Although they enjoyed much renown in the concert hall, the Pro Arte Quartet were rather overshadowed in the recording studios of the 1930s by the Busch and Budapest Quartets. True, they were allocated the task of recording what was to have been a complete cycle for the Haydn Quartet Society, but this was a subscription set. They made a handful of other discs, including some Mozart (K.428 and, with Alfred Hobday, the *G minor Quintet*, K.516), which were classics of their day. They also recorded Bartók's *First Quartet* and championed the new music of the time (Honegger, Roussel, Tansman and Milhaud). Their impeccable technical address shows here, and their warmth and finesse make their Brahms as satisfying as any account recorded since. Needless to say, some allowance has to be made for the 1935 recording, eminently well transferred though it is.

Viola sonatas Nos. 1 in F min.; 2 in E flat, Op. 120/1–2; Violin sonatas Nos. 1 in G, Op. 78; 2 in A, Op. 100; 3 in D min., Op. 108. F.A.E; Sonata: Scherzo.
(B) *** DG Double 453 121-2 (2) [id.]. Pinchas Zukerman, Daniel Barenboim.

It seems a very sensible idea to join up the Zukerman/Barenboim performances of the *Violin* and *Viola sonatas* economically on a DG Double since they were recorded at the same time (1974). The *Viola sonatas* may be a little sweet for some tastes, but they are easy to enjoy, spontaneous-sounding, with the expressiveness never sounding contrived, always buoyant. In the *Violin sonatas*, Zukerman and Barenboim are inspired to take an expansive view of Brahms, producing songful, spontaneous-sounding performances that catch the inspiration of the moment. The manner is warmer, less self-conscious than some – if at times less refined. The sound itself is very natural with good presence. The lively *Scherzo in C minor* from the *F.A.E. Sonata*, a work composed jointly with Schumann and Albert Dietrich, is thrown in for good measure.

Viola sonatas Nos. 1 in F min.; 2 in E flat, Op. 120/1–2.
✿ *** Virgin/EMI Dig. VC7 59309-2. Lars Anders Tomter, Leif Ove Andsnes – SCHUMANN: *Märchenbilder.* ***

Viola sonatas Nos. 1 in F min.; 2 in E flat, Op. 120/1–2; F.A.E. Sonata: Scherzo.
**(*) Chandos Dig. CHAN 8550 [id.]. Nobuko Imai, Roger Vignoles – SCHUMANN: *Märchenbilder.* **(*)

This young Norwegian partnership gives us the best account of these sonatas in their viola form now on CD. Theirs is playing of great sensitivity and imagination. Lars Anders Tomter and Leif Ove Andsnes bring a wide range of colour to this music and phrase with an unforced naturalness that is very persuasive. Very well balanced, though there is a slight bias in favour of the piano. Altogether rather special.

Nobuko Imai is an almost peerless violist and it is difficult to flaw her accounts of the two Op. 120 *Sonatas* with Roger Vignoles. The reverberant acoustic does not show the piano to good advantage but, apart from that, this is an impressive issue.

Violin sonatas Nos. 1 in G, Op. 78; 2 in A, Op. 100; 3 in D min., Op. 108.

*** Hyperion Dig. CDA 66465 [id.]. Krysia Osostowicz, Susan Tomes.

*** Sony Dig. SK 45819 [id.]. Itzhak Perlman, Daniel Barenboim.

(N) (M) *** EMI Dig. CDM5 66893-2 [CDM5 66945]. Itzak Perlman, Vladimir Ashkenazy.

*** DG (IMS) Dig. 435 800-2. Augustin Dumay, Maria João Pires.

(***) Testament mono SBT 1024 [id.]. Gioconda De Vito, Edwin Fischer; Tito Aprea (in *No. 2*).

(M) **(*) Ph. 446 570-2. Arthur Grumiaux, György Sebök.

Krysia Osostowicz and Susan Tomes give performances of such natural musicality that criticism is almost disarmed. They phrase with great spontaneity yet with apparently effortless care and artistry, and the interplay between the two partners is instinctive. The Hyperion engineers manage the sound and balance with their customary skill, and theirs is certainly to be preferred to some of the more glamorous rivals now on the market.

The Sony recording, made at a live recital in Chicago, finds Perlman in far more volatile form, more urgently persuasive with naturally flowing speeds and more spontaneous rubato than he adopts in his spacious readings with Ashkenazy on EMI. Barenboim too is less aggressive and more fanciful than he was with Zukerman on DG.

Perlman and Ashkenazy bring out the trouble-free happiness of these lyrical inspirations, fully involved yet avoiding underlying tensions. In their sureness and flawless confidence at generally spacious speeds, they are performances which carry you along, cocooned in rich sound. But not all will agree that this is a suitable candidate for EMI's 'Great recordings of the century'.

Augustin Dumay and Maria João Pires on DG are certainly among the most interesting of the other CD couplings. They bring temperament and finesse to all three sonatas and, though there are one or two interpretative touches that may not enjoy universal appeal, these are unlikely to inhibit pleasure. These are artists of strong personality: certainly those with a special admiration for this partnership need not hesitate.

Gioconda De Vito made all too few records. Her accounts of the *G major* and *D minor Sonatas* with Edwin Fischer come from 1954 and show her to excellent advantage. She possessed warmth and finesse in equal measure, and her playing conveys a sense of expressive freedom which makes one regret that her recording career was so short. Fischer's playing is characteristically magisterial and the *A major Sonata*, which she recorded with her normal partner, Tito Aprea, is hardly less beautiful. This is all rather special playing, and few allowances need be made for the excellent mono recording.

When they were issued on LP, we found these Grumiaux performances from the mid-1970s slightly disappointing, mellifluous rather than vital, with even an element of blandness. Returning to them in this superb CD transfer, we must revise our response. While other versions of these works may be more volatile and passionate, Grumiaux, expertly partnered by Sebök, is very persuasive, and never short of warmth and character. The recording too is beautifully balanced and natural.

Violin sonatas Nos. 1 in G, Op. 78; 2 in A, Op. 100.

(B) **(*) EMI forte CZS5 69367-2 (2) [CDFB 69367]. Igor Oistrakh, Ginzburg – BEETHOVEN: *Archduke trio;* SCHUBERT: *Piano trio No. 1.* ***

Igor Oistrakh finds a rich tone and a fine lyrical line for two essentially lyrical works, and he is accompanied sympathetically by Anton Ginzburg. The recording of both instruments is beautiful, but the piano is backwardly balanced in a resonant acoustic and the violin is well forward. This is not disastrous, but it may irritate those who rightly consider that these are works for violin *and* piano.

Violin sonata No. 1 in G, Op. 78.

(B) **(*) Tring Dig. TRP 081 [(M) id. import]. Jonathan Carney, Ronan O'Hora – FRANCK: *Violin sonata.* ***

As we have discovered from their Beethoven, Jonathan Carney and Ronan O'Hora have formed a finely integrated musical partnership. Some might feel that their reading of the Brahms *G major Sonata* is too ruminative, not bold enough, and this effect is heightened by the resonant, somewhat diffuse sound-picture. But there is no lack of warmth or poetic feeling, and the reading, seemingly spontaneous, certainly communicates readily.

Violin sonata No. 2 in A, Op. 100.

(N) *** Orfeo C489981B [id.]. David Oistrakh, Sviatoslav Richter – PROKOFIEV: *Sonata No. 1.* ***

This Orfeo discs is rather special. It records the

Oistrakh-Richter partnership in a live concert at the 1972 Salzburg Festival in the very top of their form. The playing silences criticism and the recording from ORF (Austrian Radio) is perfectly serviceable.

PIANO MUSIC

Piano music, 4 hands

Hungarian dances Nos. 1–21; 18 Liebeslieder waltzes, Op. 52a.
(BB) *** Naxos Dig. 8.553140 [id.]. Silke-Thora Matthies, Christian Köhn.

Though this second volume of the Naxos edition of Brahms piano duets was recorded simultaneously with the first, it brings much livelier and more winning performances. It makes a generous and very attractive coupling to have all 21 *Hungarian dances* in their original form, coupled with the piano-duet version of the first and more popular set of *Liebeslieder waltzes*. Crisp, clean ensemble, matched by well-focused sound.

Piano music, 4 hands: *Hungarian dances Nos. 1–21; Waltzes, Op. 39.*
**(*) Sony Dig. SK 53285 [id.]. Yaara Tal and Andreas Groethuysen.

The playing here has enormous verve and energy and is seemingly spontaneous in the way the two artists play as one, with considerable rubato flowing quite naturally. Their style, however, brings the very widest dynamic range and is very percussive at fortissimo level. So this is not intimate playing, although the *Waltzes* provide plenty of examples when the brilliance scintillates, and there is also some beguilingly gentle pianism at times, especially in the delightful closing *D minor Waltz*, better known as Brahms's *Lullaby*.

Serenades Nos 1 in D, Op.11; No.2 in A, Op.16 (arr. piano duet).
(N) (BB) *** Naxos Dig. 8.553726 [id.]. Silke-Thora Matthies, Christian Köhn.

Brahms's two *Serenades*, among his earliest orchestral works – the *Second* without violins – have an open innocence which translates well to the plainer medium of piano duet in Brahms's own arrangements. The duo of Matthies and Kohn, very well recorded, bring out an extra freshness and clarity. An attractive addition to their Naxos series.

Sonata for 2 pianos in F min., Op. 34b; Variations on a theme of Haydn, Op. 56b.
(N) (BB) *** Naxos Dig. 8.553654 [id.]. Silke-Thora Metthies, Christian Köhn

While the first volume in Naxos's series covering Brahms's four-hand piano music (including the *New Liebeslieder waltzes* and the *Variations on a theme of Schumann* (8.553139)) was unsuccessful, this third brings fresh and alert performances of two of the most important works, each of them better known in alternative forms. The *Sonata for two pianos*, adapted from an earlier string quintet, was later given its definitive form as the *Piano quintet*. What the German duo demonstrate is that the two-piano format brings formidable advantages in bite and attack, as well as some disadvantages. Speeds are sensibly chosen, as they are in Brahms's own piano duet version of the *Haydn Variations*, again clarified. Bright, clear sound to match.

Variations on a theme by Haydn, Op. 56a (arr. for piano duet).
*** Sony Dig. MK 42625 [id.]. Murray Perahia, Sir Georg Solti – BARTOK: *Sonata for 2 pianos and percussion.* ***

Murray Perahia and Solti bring out the fullest possible colouring in their performance, so that one hardly misses the orchestra.

Solo piano music

4 Ballades, Op. 10; 7 Fantasias, Op. 116; Hungarian dances Nos. 1–10; (i) *Nos. 11–21. 3 Intermezzi, Op. 117; 8 Piano pieces, Op. 76; 6 Piano pieces, Op. 118; 4 Piano pieces, Op. 119; Piano sonatas Nos. 1 in C, Op. 1; 2 in F sharp min., Op. 2; 3 in F min., Op. 5; 2 Rhapsodies, Op. 79; Variations on a Hungarian song, Op. 21/2; Variations on a theme by Paganini, Op. 35; Variations and fugue on a theme by Handel, Op. 24; Variations on a theme by Schumann, Op. 9; Variations on an original theme, Op. 21/1; Waltzes, Op. 39.*
(B) *** Decca stereo/mono 455 247-2 (6) [id.]. Julius Katchen, (i) with J.-P. Marty.

Katchen's magisterial survey of Brahms's keyboard music was made for Decca between 1962 and 1965, save for the last three *Ballades*, which come from the 1950s and are in mono. Although we would rank the Gilels *Ballades* and some of the Kempff recordings of the later pieces as being special (not to mention Solomon's mono account of the *F minor Sonata* (Testament) and, indeed, some of the other recordings of this work listed separately below), those wanting a comprehensive survey need look no further. Katchen is an eminently faithful and sound interpreter who brings refined musicianship and a natural authority to this repertoire; and he is given the benefit of Decca recording which was excellent for its period, and remains so. There are six CDs at a very low price and, although they are not available separately, they still make a tremendous bargain. In addition to the three *Ballades*, the following are mono recordings: the *Schumann variations*, Nos. 1, 5 and 7 of the *Fantasias* and Nos. 11–21 of the *Hungarian dances*.

4 Ballades, Op. 10; Scherzo in E flat, Op. 4; Piano sonatas Nos. 2 in F sharp min., Op. 2; 3 in F min., Op. 5; Variations and fugue on a theme

by Handel, Op. 24; Variations on a theme by Paganini, Op. 35.
(M) **(*) Ph. 432 302-2 (3). Claudio Arrau.

As part of Arrau's eightieth-birthday celebrations in 1984, Philips issued a five-LP set of his Brahms recordings made in the 1970s. Two of the LPs were of the concertos (now on a Philips Duo – see above) and the remainder were accommodated on this three-CD set. The 1970s sound does justice to the wonderful sonority this great pianist produced, although he is at times characteristically 'personal', notably so in the *F minor Sonata*, where he does indulge in some generous rubato. Yet his playing is always stamped by a kind of wisdom that holds the listener, and there is no want of virtuosity in the *Handel* and *Paganini variations*.

4 Ballades, Op. 10.
*** DG (IMS) Dig. 400 043-2. Michelangeli – SCHUBERT: *Sonata No. 4.* **

Michelangeli gives the *Ballades* a performance of the greatest distinction and without the slightly aloof quality that at times disturbs his readings. He is superbly recorded.

4 Ballades, Op. 10; Piano sonata No. 3 in F min., Op. 5.
(BB) **(*) Naxos Dig. 8.550352 [id.]. Idil Biret.

As a pupil of Kempff, Idil Biret has a fine understanding of this repertoire, although her approach is more muscular than Kempff's. Thus the first of the *Four Ballades* opens with enticing lyrical feeling but has the most powerfully dramatic climax, to match the feeling of the Scottish ballad, *Edward*, on which it is based. The *Fourth Ballade* is gravely beautiful and shows her at her finest. The *Sonata* opens commandingly and its lyrical side is well balanced. These performances are full of character. Good recording, made in the Heidelberg studio.

4 Ballades, Op. 10; Variations and fugue on a theme by Handel, Op. 24; Variations and fugue on a theme by Schumann, Op. 9.
(BB) *** ASV Dig. CDQS 6161 [id.]. Jorge Federico Osorio.

The Mexican pianist, Jorge Federico Osorio, has been winning golden opinions in recent years and his account of the *Variations and fugue on a theme by Handel* is tremendously impressive. The texture has plenty of warmth and colour and he balances the sonorities in a most musical way. He possesses an unfailing sense of the Brahms style, giving us playing that is selfless and with no hint of the idiosyncratic. The four *Ballades* are also played with fine sensitivity and character. On top of all this, ASV provide excellent, well-focused sound, with plenty of depth, and this now comes in the super-bargain category.

Fantasias, Op. 116.
*** Ottavio Dig. OTRC 39027 [id.]. Imogen Cooper – SCHUMANN: *Abegg variations* etc. ***
(M) **(*) DG Dig. 445 562-2 [id.]. Yevgeny Kissin – LISZT: *Concert paraphrases of Schubert Lieder* etc. ***; SCHUBERT: *Wanderer fantasia.* **(*)

The impulsively spontaneous flow of Imogen Cooper's stirring account of the *Capriccio* which opens the set captures the listener immediately and the variety of colour and mood gives enormous pleasure throughout. The gentle *Intermezzi* are most beautiful, for the recording does this memorable playing full justice. The listening experience here is as if one was present at a live recital.

The Kissin recording comes from 1991 and finds the young virtuoso in masterful form. There is perhaps more to these extraordinary pieces than he uncovers but his pianism is glorious, and he is beautifully recorded too.

7 Fantasias, Op. 116; 3 Intermezzi, Op. 117; 8 Piano pieces, Op. 76; 6 Piano pieces, Op. 118; 4 Piano pieces, Op. 119.
(B) *** EMI forte (SIS) CZS5 69521-2 (2) [CDFB 69521]. Alexeev – SCHUMANN: *Etudes symphoniques.* ***

Fantasias, Op. 116; 3 Intermezzi, Op. 117; 6 Pieces, Op. 118; 4 Pieces, Op. 119.
(M) **(*) DG 437 249-2 [id.]. Wilhelm Kempff.

Dmitri Alexeev enjoys the advantage of really first-class piano-sound, full-bodied and totally natural and truthful. The piano timbre is rich, slightly bass-orientated, but eminently suitable for Brahms. Alexeev's playing has authority and he produces an ideally weighted sonority with the correct blend of colour. He brings the right kind of tenderness and insight to the quieter pieces. His mastery of rubato is consummate, and these performances generally hold their own with any now before the public. With its excellent Schumann coupling this is very highly recommendable.

Kempff's style in Brahms is characteristically individual: poetry emphasized rather than brilliance, subtle timbres rather than virtuosity. It follows that Kempff shines in the gentle fancies of Brahms's last period, with his magic utterly beguiling in the *Intermezzi in A minor*, *E major* and *E minor* from Op. 116 and especially in the lovely *E flat major Andante* of Op. 117. Don't be put off by the opening *Capriccio in D minor* of Op. 116 which sounds rather hard, the piano timbre lacking sonority; at lower dynamic levels the piano colouring is exquisite.

(i) *Fantasias, Op. 116; Intermezzi, Op. 117;* (ii) *Pieces, Op. 76;* (i) *Pieces, Opp. 118/119;* (ii) *Rhapsodies Nos. 1 in B min.; 2 in G min., Op. 79/1–2;* (i) *Variations and fugue on a theme by*

Handel, Op. 24; (iii) *Variations on a theme by Paganini, Op. 35.*
(B) *(**) Ph. Duo Analogue/Dig. 442 589-2 (2). (i) Stephen Kovacevich; (ii) Dinorah Varsi; (iii) Adam Harasiewicz.

The performances by Stephen Kovacevich can receive the strongest recommendation. He finds the fullest range of emotional contrast in the Op. 116 *Fantasias*, but is at his finest in the Op. 117 *Intermezzi* and the four *Klavierstücke*, Op. 119, which contain some of Brahms's most beautiful lyrical inspirations for the keyboard. On the second CD the *Handel variations* are also impressive and it seems perverse that Philips then turned to recordings by Dinorah Varsi of the two *Rhapsodies* and eight *Klavierstücke*, Op. 76, when Kovacevich has also recorded them. However, these are already available, coupled with the two piano concertos, on another Duo. Varsi's playing is at times very impulsive (as in the Op. 79 *Rhapsody*) and her performances of the *Klavierstücke* also lack the necessary degree of poise. Adam Harasiewicz, however, plays the *Paganini variations* with some flair and towards the end produces some exciting bravura. Generally the recordings are very good; Kovacevich's Op. 116 and Op. 118 are digital.

7 Fantasias, Op. 116; 8 Pieces, Op. 76; 2 Rhapsodies, Op. 79.
(BB) **(*) Naxos Dig. 8.550353 [id.]. Idil Biret.

Biret opens her programme strongly with the agitato *Capriccio in F sharp minor* (the first of the Op. 76 group), and then articulates the second lightly and engagingly. She readily captures the graceful intimacy of the *A flat* and *B flat Intermezzi*. Of the two *Rhapsodies*, the first is very impulsive indeed, but the second is particularly fine, boldly spontaneous, its dark colouring caught well. The *Fantasias*, Op. 116, bring some beautifully reflective playing, notably in the three *Intermezzi* grouped together (in E major and E minor), while the framing *G minor* and *D minor Capriccios* are passionately felt, the latter ending the recital strongly. This is all impressively characterized Brahms playing, and the recording does not lack sonority.

3 Intermezzi, Op. 117; 6 Pieces, Op. 118; 4 Pieces, Op. 119; 2 Rhapsodies, Op. 79.
*** Decca 417 599-2 [id.]. Radu Lupu.
(B) **(*) Cal. Approche CAL 6679 [id.]. Inger Södergren.

Radu Lupu's late Brahms is quite outstanding in every way. There is great intensity and inwardness when these qualities are required and a keyboard mastery that is second to none. This is undoubtedly one of the most rewarding Brahms recitals currently before the public.

Inger Södergren's Brahms is imaginative and poetic: her performances of the three *Intermezzi* are enticingly intimate, while there is a commanding volatility and passion in the *Rhapsodies*. She brings out all the colour of the Op. 118 *Pieces* and captures their variety of mood and atmosphere. The analogue recording is truthful but with a touch of hardness at fortissimo levels.

Piano sonatas Nos. 1 in C, Op. 1; 2 in F sharp min., Op. 2.
*** Decca (IMS) Dig. 436 457-2 [id.]. Sviatoslav Richter.

Recorded in Mantua in February 1987, these performances show Richter at his most commanding. He makes the most heavily chordal piano writing sound totally pianistic and there is exquisite shading of tone and flawless legato. Both slow movements are most subtly coloured and the opening of the finale of the *F sharp minor Sonata* has a wonderful improvisational feeling. The playing throughout has the spontaneity of live music-making and the Decca engineers have secured most realistic sound.

Piano sonata No. 3 in F min., Op. 5; 4 Ballades, Op. 10.
(N) *** Teldec Dig. 0630-14338-2. Daniel Barenboim.

Piano sonata No. 3; 4 Ballades; Intermezzo in E, Op. 116/6; Romance in F, Op. 118/5.
(M) ** RCA 09026 61862-2 [id.]. Artur Rubinstein.

Piano sonata No. 3; Intermezzi: in E flat, Op. 117/1; in C, Op. 119/3.
(M) *** Decca 448 578-2 [id.]. Clifford Curzon – SCHUBERT: *Piano sonata No. 21.* ***

Piano sonata No. 3 in F min., Op. 5; Theme and variations in D min. (from *String sextet, Op. 18*).
(M) *** Decca 448 129-2. Radu Lupu – SCHUBERT: *Sonata No. 5* etc. ***

Curzon's account of the *F minor Sonata* is special. His approach is both perceptive and humane, and his playing has great intensity and freshness. Curzon was at his peak, powerful and sensitive and, above all, spontaneous-sounding, both in the *Sonata* and in the two *Intermezzi* which act as encores. The 1962 recording was among the finest of its day and is worthy to be reissued in Decca's 'Classic Sound' series. The generous coupling with Schubert (an equally fine performance) makes this CD very desirable indeed.

Noble, dignified and spacious are the adjectives that spring to mind when listening to Lupu's Op. 5. His view is inward, ruminative and always beautifully rounded. The arrangement of the slow-movement theme and variations from the *B flat major String sextet* was made by the composer and presented to Clara Schumann as a forty-first birthday present in 1860. In Lupu's hands the transcription seems tailor-made for the piano. The 1981 digital recording is most realistic, the piano set slightly back, the timbre fully coloured and the focus natural.

Barenboim recorded the *Sonata* and *Ballades* in Chicago in 1996, his first purely solo recital disc since becoming an exclusive Teldec artist. Both are distinguished by an effortless technical command and excellent musical characterization and insight. Although he is not necessarily a first choice, this generally well-recorded account (fortissimo passages become a little muddy) is certainly among the most impressive of recent Brahms recitals.

Rubinstein's impulsive way with Brahms is not always convincing. The rather hard, unexpansive (1959) recording does not help matters in the *Sonata*, but the two shorter pieces seem to have slightly more bloom. The *Ballades*, too, recorded in Rome in 1970, are fuller although the balance remains close and the acoustic cool. There are times when one feels the playing is somewhat shorn of mystery: one misses the extremes of both tension and repose.

Variations on a theme by Paganini, Op. 35.
(B) *** Koch Discovery Dig. DICD 920423 [id.]. Evelyne Brancart – LISZT: *Paganini études.* ***
**(*) Decca Dig. 444 338-2 [id.]. Jean-Yves Thibaudet – SCHUMANN: *Arabesque* etc. **(*)

Evelyne Brancart is a Belgian pianist who studied with Eduardo del Pueyo. She has superb technique, fine musicianship and sensitivity; the recording is rather bright and forward but yields pleasing results. An enjoyable recital – though, even at super-bargain price, rather short measure at 47 minutes 40 seconds.

Although Jean-Yves Thibaudet is a cultured player and has impressive technical address, his set of the *Paganini variations* lacks the very last ounce of fire. The Decca sound is good, and it goes without saying that there is much to admire in Thibaudet's playing.

ORGAN MUSIC

11 Chorale preludes, Op. 122. Chorale prelude and fugue on 'O Traurigkeit, O Herzeleid'; Fugue in A flat min. (original and published versions); *Preludes and fugues: in A min.; G min.*
*** Nimbus Dig. NI 5262 [id.]. Kevin Bowyer (organ of Odense Cathedral).

11 Chorale preludes, Op. 122; Chorale prelude and fugue on 'O Traurigkeit, O Herzeleid'; Fugue in A flat min.; Preludes and fugues: in A min.; G min.
(M) *** CRD Dig. CRD 3404; *CRDC 4104* [id.]. Nicholas Danby (organ).

Kevin Bowyer, already successful in the music of Bach, now provides an admirable Brahms survey. He has the advantage of the splendid Danish organ in Odense Cathedral which combines a full tone and a warmly coloured palette with a clear profile. Like Nicholas Danby, Bowyer is obviously at home both in the early *Preludes and fugues* in which he produces considerable bravura (helped by the fresh, bright sound of the organ) and in the very late set of *Chorale preludes*, from the period of the *Four Serious Songs*, and which are comparably mellow. He then closes the recital with Brahms's original manuscript forms of the two earliest pieces (which we have already heard in their published formats), the *Chorale prelude and fugue on 'O Traurigkeit'* and the unpolished *A flat minor fugue*. The disc is very well documented.

Nicholas Danby playing the organ of the Church of the Immaculate Conception in London, gives restrained, clean-cut readings which yet have a strong profile. Choice between these two discs might well depend on preference for the type of organ used. The effect on CRD is rather more incisive, yet has firmness and weight of tone and certainly does not lack amplitude.

VOCAL MUSIC

Lieder: *Ach, wende diesen Blick; Die Mainacht; Heimweh; Mädchenlied; Meine Liebe ist grün; O kühler Wald; Ständchen; Unbewegte laue Luft; Von ewiger Liebe; Wie rafft' ich mich auf; Wiegenlied.* (i) *2 Songs with viola (Gestilte Sehnsucht & Geistliches Wiegenlied), Op. 91. 3 Volkslieder: Dort in den Weiden; Sonntag; Vergebliches Ständchen. 8 Zigeunerlieder Op. 103/1–7 & 11.*
*** DG Dig. 429 727-2 [id.]. Anne Sofie von Otter, Bengt Forsberg, (i) with Nils-Erik Sparf.

Anne Sofie von Otter gives these Brahms Lieder the natural freshness of folksong, which so often they resemble, or even quote, as in the radiant melody of *Sonntag*. She phrases unerringly, holding and changing tension and mood as in a live recital. Compared with some, there is still a degree of expressive restraint, but there are few Brahms song-recital discs to match this one, and her accompanist is strongly supportive. In the Op. 91 settings they are joined by Nils-Erik Sparf, who plays with admirable taste.

Lieder: *An die Nachtigall; Bottschaft; Dein blaues Auge hält so still; Feldeinsamkeit; Der Gang zum Liebchen; Geheimnis; Im Waldeseinsamkeit; Komm bald; Die Kränze; Die Mainacht; Meine Liebe ist grün; Minnelied; Nachtigall; O wüsst ich doch den Weg zurück; Sah dem edlen Bildnis; Salamander; Die Schale der Vergessenheit; Serenade; Sonntag; Ständchen; Von ewiger Liebe; Von waldbekränzter Höhe; Wie bist du, Meine Königin; Wiegenlied; Wir Wandelten.*
(BB) *** Virgin Classics Dig. Double VBD5 61418-2 (2) [CVBD 61418]. Thomas Allen, Geoffrey Parsons – WOLF: *Lieder.* ***

Thomas Allen gives fresh, virile performances of a

particularly attractive collection of Brahms songs. There is less underlining of words than Fischer-Dieskau or Bär give us but still a keen and detailed feeling for meaning as well as mood. If one generally associates the great song, *Von ewiger Liebe*, with a woman's voice, Allen triumphantly shows what benefits there are from having a baritone, hushed and intimately confidential at the start and bitingly powerful at the climax in heightened contrast. There are many such felicities here, with Geoffrey Parsons an ever-sympathetic accompanist and with sound more cleanly focused than in earlier Lieder issues from this source. Now coupled with an equally desirable recital of Wolf songs, with the two CDs offered for the cost of one mid-priced disc, this is a set not to be missed by any lover of German Lied, even though no translations are provided.

Lieder: *An eine Aolsharfe; Auf dem See; Dein blaues Auge; Botschaft; Brauner bursche führt zum Tanze; Dämmrung senkte sich von oben; Feldeinsamkeit; Frühlingstrost; Immer leiser wird mein Schlummer; Juchhe; Kommt dir manchmal in den Sinn; Lerchengesang; Liebestreu; Mädchenlied; Das Mädchen spricht; Die Mainacht; Meine Liebe ist grün; Mein wundes Herz verlangt; O wüss ich doch den Weg zurück; Ständchen; Vergebliches Ständchen; Von Strande; Wiegenlied; Wie Melodien zieht es mir.*
(N) (BB) **(*) Arte Nova Dig. 74321 59216-2 [id.]. Lan Rao, Micaela Gelius.

Lan Rao has a fresh, pretty soprano which she uses most sensitively, if within a rather limited tonal range. The items which stand out are those like *Wiegenlied* or *Immer Leiser* which involve poised legato and the gentlest dynamics. Response to word meaning is good, even if such a witty number as *Vergebliches Ständchen* is rather undercharacterized. None the less, with well-balanced recording, the disc makes an attractive bargain on the Arte Nova label.

Alto rhapsody; 4 Gesänge, Op. 17.
(BB) *** Virgin Classics Dig. Double VBD5 61469-2 (2) [CDVB 61469]. Dame Janet Baker, London Symphony Ch., City of L. Sinf., Hickox – BERLIOZ: *Les Nuits d'été* etc.; MENDELSSOHN: *Infelice* etc.; RESPIGHI: *La Sensitiva*. ***

Though the Virgin recording of the *Alto rhapsody* was recorded after Dame Janet's retirement from the concert platform, the voice is in glorious condition, superbly controlled. This is a more openly expressive and spacious reading than her earlier, EMI one with Boult, matching her performances in the two Mendelssohn items. The four early Brahms songs, Opus 17, for women's chorus with two horns and harp accompaniment, are delightfully done.

(i–ii) *Alto rhapsody, Op. 53;* (ii) *Begrabnisgesang, Op. 13; Gesang der Parzen, Op. 89;* (iii) *Geistlicheslied, Op. 30;* (iv) *2 Motets, Op. 29;* (iii) *2 Motets, Op. 74; 3 Motets, Op. 110;* (ii) *Nänie, Op. 82;* (v) *Rinaldo, Op. 50;* (ii) *Song of Destiny (Schicksalslied), Op. 54.*
(B) *** Decca Double Dig./Analogue 452 582-2 (2) [(M) id. import]. (i) Jard van Nes; (ii) San Francisco Ch. and SO, Blomstedt; (iii) New English Singers, Preston; (iv) King's College, Cambridge, Ch., Cleobury; (v) James King, Ambrosian Ch., New Philh. O, Abbado.

The recordings of the five key choral works here, the *Alto Rhapsody*, *Begrabnisgesang* (Funeral hymn), *Gesang der Parzen* (*Song of the Fates*), *Nänie* and the *Song of Destiny* (*Schicksalslied*), come from an outstanding 1989 collection using the Davis Symphony Hall, San Francisco, where the Decca team have made many outstanding records. This is no exception and, with inspired singing from the splendid San Francisco Choir, it is darkly intense in the rare and memorable *Funeral hymn*, exultant at the opening of *Nänie* and reaching a glorious climax. The *Song of the Fates* invites a more subtle approach, especially in the matter of light and shade, but is also very dramatically expansive, and Blomstedt and his choristers are not found wanting. Jard van Nes's moving account of the *Alto rhapsody* can stand alongside the famous versions from Dame Janet Baker and Kathleen Ferrier, although it is different from either; again the choral contribution is splendid. The King's College Choir under Cleobury then follows on with the two lovely *a cappella* five-part Motets of Op. 29, the second of which, *Schaffe in mir, Gott, ein rein Herz* ('Create in me a clean heart, O God'), is a partial setting of Psalm 51. Both these earlier (1860) Brahms settings pay tribute to the Bach tradition, whereas the later motets of Op. 74 (1877) and especially the three of Op. 110 (1889) look forward as well as backward in style. The final item on the second disc is the most substantial and the least satisfactory. James King's rather coarse Heldentenor approach to the 40-minute cantata *Rinaldo* is less than ideal for music that is much more easily lyrical than Wagner. However, again this is rare repertoire, and there is excellent singing from the Ambrosian Chorus, and Abbado ensures that the performance overall is fairly convincing. In any case the rest of the content of this set is more than worth its asking price.

(i) *Alto rhapsody, Op. 53; Deutsche Volkslieder:* (ii) *Ach, englische Schäferin; All mein' Gedanken; Da unten im Tale; Dort in den Weiden;* (iii) *Es war einmal ein Zimmergesell;* (ii) *Es wohnet ein Fiedler; In stiller Nacht; Maria ging aus wandern; Mein Mädel hat einen Rosenmund; Schwesterlein; Die Sonne scheint nicht mehr;* (iii) *Verstohlen geht der Mond auf.*

(ii) *Wach auf, mein' Herzensschöne.* (iv) Lieder: *Am Sonntagmorgen; Botschaft; Heimweh II; Junge Lieder I; Die Mainacht; Minnelied; O liebche Wangen; Regenlied; Sonntag; Uber die Heide; Von ewiger Liebe.*

(B) *** DG Classikon 439 441-2 [(M) id. import]. (i) Christa Ludwig, V. Singverein, VPO, Boehm; (ii) Edith Mathis or Peter Schreier, Karl Engel; (iii) N. German R. Ch., Jena; Kahl; (iv) Fischer-Dieskau, Barenboim.

Although the initial attraction of this highly recommendable bargain collection may be Christa Ludwig's strong and eloquent account of the *Alto rhapsody* (recorded in 1977) or the Lieder recital from Fischer-Dieskau and Barenboim (both in superb form), taken from a comprehensive survey recorded in the early 1980s, the highlight is the well-chosen selection from Brahms's folksong arrangements. These are simple, glowing settings, published only three years before the composer's death, but the product of a lifetime's love-affair with the music. Edith Mathis and Peter Schreier capture their innocent spirit delightfully, never overplaying their hands (sample Schreier's charming *Mein Mädel hat einen Rosenmund* or Mathis's lovely *Maria ging aus wandern*). Karl Engel accompanies sympathetically and the Chorus of the North German Radio (digitally recorded) provides two of the attractive choral settings.

(i) *Alto rhapsody, Op. 53;* (ii) *German Requiem; Song of destiny (Schicksalslied), Op. 54. Academic festival overture; Tragic overture; Variations on a theme by Haydn.*

(B) **(*) Ph. Duo 438 760-2 (2) [id.]. (i) Aafjé Heynis; (ii) Wilma Lipp, Franz Crass; (i; ii) V. Singverein; VSO, Sawallisch.

In the *German Requiem* Sawallisch may not penetrate the spiritual depths as deeply as a conductor like Haitink but the music flows naturally. It is a deeply satisfying version, with an account of the final movements both dramatic and ethereal. Franz Crass's dark bass colouring makes his solos tonally distinctive, but the singing of Wilma Lipp in *Ihr habt nun Traurigkeit* is a blot, wobbly and plaintive-sounding. However, what makes this inexpensive set worth considering, even against the competition, is Aafje Heynis's lovely singing in the *Alto rhapsody*. It is even more dedicated and 'inner' than Kathleen Ferrier's, and the tonal shading is most beautiful. The emotionally more turbulent *Song of destiny* is also a considerable success. Not all collectors will need the overtures, but they are well enough played and recorded, although the early date (1959) of the *Variations* shows in the violin timbre.

49 Deutsche Volkslieder; 14 Folksongs for children.

(M) *** (IMS) DG 449 087-2 (2). Edith Mathis, Peter Schreier, Karl Engel; N. German R. Ch., Günter Jena.

The writing here represents Brahms at his most engagingly domestic in these lovely folksong settings and the *Volks-Kinderlieder*, originally designed for the family of Robert and Clara Schumann. There is much to treasure here and the performances are fresh and brightly affectionate. The sound is first class and the documentation includes full translations. Recommended.

German Requiem, Op. 45.

❁ *** Ph. Dig. 432 140-2 [id.]. Margiono, Gilfry, Monteverdi Ch., ORR, Eliot Gardiner.

(M) *** Ph. Dig. 462 059-2. Janowitz, Krause, V. State Op. Ch., VPO, Haitink.

(N) (M) *** EMI CDM5 66903-2 [CDM 66955]. Schwarzkopf, Fischer-Dieskau, Philh. Ch. & O, Klemperer.

(N) (B) *** DG Classikon Dig. 459 355-2. Lucia Popp, Wolfgang Brendel, Prague Philharmonic Ch., Czech PO, Sinopoli.

(M) (***) EMI (SIS) mono CDH7 64705-2 [id.]. Grümmer, Fischer-Dieskau, St Hedwig's Cathedral Ch., BPO, Kempe.

(M) **(*) RCA Dig. 09026 61349-2. Battle, Hagegård, Chicago Ch. & SO, Levine.

(B) **(*) EMI Dig. CZS7 67819-2 (2) [id.]. Jessye Norman, Jorma Hynninen, LPO Ch., LPO, Tennstedt – SCHUMANN: *Requiem.* ***

(i) *German requiem. Burial song, Op. 13.*

(N) (M) *** Virgin Veritas/EMI Dig. VM5 61605-2. (i) L. Dawson, Bär; L. Schütz Ch., LCP, Norrington.

Gardiner's 'revolutionary' account of the *German Requiem* brings a range of choral sound even more thrilling than in the concert hall. With period instruments and following Viennese practice of the time, speeds tend to be faster than usual, though the speed for the big fugue is surprisingly relaxed. Charlotte Margiono makes an ethereal soprano soloist, while Rodney Gilfry, despite a rapid vibrato, is aptly fresh and young-sounding. One could not ask for a more complete renovation of a masterpiece often made to sound stodgy and square.

Sir Roger Norrington, using period forces, comes into direct rivalry with John Eliot Gardiner in his Philips version recorded eighteen months earlier. At speeds even faster and taking a plainer view, but drawing equally fine singing from his choir, Norrington lacks some of Gardiner's dramatic flair, but Lynne Dawson sings with ravishing sweetness in her central solo and Olaf Bär brings a lieder-like intensity to the baritone solos, even if he lacks a degree of darkness. Unlike Gardiner and most other rivals, Norrington offers a brief coupling, the dark *Burial song* with wind accompaniment.

Haitink chooses very slow tempi, but there is a

rapt quality in this glowing performance that creates an atmosphere of simple dedication; at slow speed *Denn alles Fleisch* ('All flesh is as grass') is made the more relentless when, with total concentration, textures are so sharply clarified. The digital recording offers beautiful sound and, with outstanding soloists – Gundula Janowitz notably pure and poised – this is altogether a very persuasive account, an excellent alternative to Previn. The disc is very handsomely re-packaged as part of the Philips 'Choral Collection', but no texts are provided.

Klemperer's reading has been effectively remastered for reissue as one of EMI's 'Great recordings of the century'. Measured and monumental, the performance defies preconceived doubts. The speeds are consistently slow – too slow in the *vivace* of the sixth movement, where Death has little sting – but, with dynamic contrasts underlined, the result is uniquely powerful. The solo singing is superb and the Philharmonia Chorus were at the peak of their form. The new CD transfer is excellent.

Sinopoli's DG version brings a performance of extremes – generally measured but consistently positive and often dramatically thrilling – helped by the wide-ranging recording, excellent soloists, and an incisive contribution from the Prague Philharmonic Chorus. The 1983 digital recording is full, clear and realistically balanced.

Rudolf Kempe's mono recording of 1955 is incandescent, glowing with warmth, a characteristic example of his dedicated intensity in such a work. His view is flexibly expressive rather than rugged and, though the mono recording is limited on orchestral sound, the voices are caught vividly and atmospherically, with the choir the more involving for being forwardly balanced, something which modern digital recordings should heed more often. There is vintage singing too from both soloists, with the young Fischer-Dieskau darkly intense and with Elisabeth Grümmer sweetly radiant, superbly sustaining Kempe's exceptionally slow speed for *Ihr habt nun Traurigkeit*.

Levine's version features the Chicago Symphony Chorus, which is probably the finest in America, while his two soloists both prove excellent, Kathleen Battle pure and sweetly vulnerable-sounding, Hagegård clear-cut and firm. Levine is not the most illuminating conductor in this work and his pacing is not always convincing; yet the performance is alive, with power as well as impetus, and it undoubtedly gives pleasure. The recording is not ideal, with inner textures growing cloudy in tuttis.

Tennstedt's is an unusually spacious view of the *Requiem*, with a reverential manner always alert, never becoming merely monumental. Jorma Hynninen proves an excellent soloist. On CD, generally fine, spacious recording which matches the spaciousness of the interpretation.

Liebeslieder waltzes, Op. 52.

(N) *** BBC Legends BBCB 8001-2 [id.]. Heather Harper, Dame Janet Baker, Peter Pears, Thomas Hemsley, Benjamin Britten, Claudio Arrau (piano duet) – ROSSINI: *Soirées musicales*; TCHAIKOVSKY: *4 Duets*. ***

These BBC recordings vividly capture the relaxed atmosphere of the more informal concerts which Britten and Pears loved to devise for the Aldeburgh Festival. Britten was allergic to the music of Brahms, but you would never know that from this magic performance of the *Liebeslieder waltzes*. As an inspired accompanist he is joined by Claudio Arrau in a perfect partnership, devised at the very last minute when Rostropovich failed to arrive. The soloists, all Aldeburgh regulars, make an outstanding and characterful team, whoopsing away throughout, with Janet Baker striking a deeper note in the poignant seventh waltz. Full clear radio sound.

Liebeslieder waltzes, Op. 52; New Liebeslieder waltzes, Op. 65/15.

(M) (***) Decca (IMS) mono 425 995-2. Irmgaard Seefried, Kathleen Ferrier, Julius Patzak, Günter, Curzon, Gá – MAHLER: *Kindertotenlieder*. (**)

Liebeslieder waltzes, Op. 52; New Liebeslieder waltzes, Op. 65; 3 Quartets, Op. 64.

*** DG (IMS) Dig. 423 133-2 [id.]. Mathis, Fassbaender, Schreier, Fischer-Dieskau; Engel and Sawallisch (pianos).

On DG one of the most successful recordings yet of the two seductive but surprisingly difficult sets of *Liebeslieder waltzes*. The CD has fine realism and presence.

Recorded at the Edinburgh Festival in September 1952, the Decca historic performance brings a dazzling team together. Though it is not the most relaxed account, there are countless touches of imagination, not least from the very distinctive tenor, Julius Patzak, and the ever-responsive Clifford Curzon taking the upper piano part. Limited but clear sound.

(i–ii) *Liebeslieder waltzes, Op. 52* (two performances); (iii) *Waltzes, Op. 39. Waltzes for piano duet, Op. 39,* (iv) *Nos. 2, 6 & 15;* (v) *Nos. 1, 2, 5, 6, 10, 14 & 15.*

(***) EMI mono CDH5 66425-2. (i) Seefried, Höngen, Meyer-Welfing, Hotter; (i, iv) Wührer; Von Nordberg; (ii) De Polignac, Kedroff, Cuénod, Conrad; (ii, v) Lipatti, Boulanger; (iii) Backhaus.

This historic tribute to Brahms in waltz-time makes a fascinating study, with early recordings of the first *Liebeslieder waltzes* – one very Viennese, one very French – set in contrast and the Opus 39 *Waltzes* offered in a variety of performances, with the popular *Waltz in A flat*, as well as two others, appearing in no fewer than three versions each, from Backhaus solo, from Wührer and Von Nordberg in Vienna and from Lipatti and Boulanger in Paris, all very different and equally winning. The vocal teams in the *Liebeslieder waltzes* are strikingly different too, with the Viennese much slower and more inclined to linger, with voices beautifully blended, where the Parisian performances are brisk and incisive, with voices – not least Hugues Cuénod's high tenor – clearly separated, despite the limited mono recording of 1937. Good, smooth transfers.

Motets

Ave Maria, Op. 12; Fest- und Gedenksprüche, Op. 109; Geistliche Chöre, Op. 37; Geistliches Lied, Op. 30; 2 Motets, Op. 29; 2 Motets, Op. 74; 3 Motets, Op. 110; Psalm 13, Op. 27.

(N) *** Conifer Dig. 74321 15252-2 [id.]. Trinity College, Cambridge Ch., Richard Marlow.

Ave Maria, Op. 12; 3 Fest- und Gedenksprüche, Op. 109; Geistliches Lied, Op. 30; 2 Motets, Op. 29; 2 Motets, Op. 74; 3 Motets, Op. 110; Psalm 13, Op. 27.

(N) (BB) *** Naxos Dig. 8.553877 [id.]. St Bride's Ch., Robert Jones; Matthew Morley (organ).

Throughout his composing career, from his Hamburg days onwards, Brahms was devoted to writing choral music both religious and secular, superbly crafted. Richard Marlow and his excellent Cambridge Choir add to their distinguished list of records with this outstanding collection, bringing together all sixteen of the motets. With superb singing, recorded vividly this is an outstanding issue.

In their first recording, Robert Jones and the choir of St Bride's, Fleet Street, give fresh, clear performances of an almost identical range of pieces, omitting only the *Geistliche Chöre, Op. 37*. The performances are beautifully scaled to give the illusion of church performance, helped by warm, atmospheric recording. If not quite as distinctive as the Trinity College collection this is excellent value.

3 Fest- und Gedenksprüche, Op. 109; Marienlieder, Op. 22; 2 Motets, Op. 29; 2 Motets, Op. 74; 3 Motets, Op. 110.

(N) *** Chandos Dig. CHAN 9671 [id.]. Danish Nat. R.Ch., Stefan Parkman.

The programme from the Danish Radio Choir is made especially attractive by the inclusion of the seven *Marienlieder*, which include some of Brahms's simplest and most beautiful lyrical inspirations. He described these settings of sacred texts as 'somewhat in the manner of old German church chorales and folk songs'. They are gloriously sung by this justly famous Danish Choir who are on splendid form throughout the disc and are beautifully recorded. This Chandos disc is marked 'A capella, Volume 1' and augurs well for an ongoing series.

3 Fest-und Gedenksprüche, Op. 109; Missa canonica, Op. posth.; 2 Motets, Op. 29; 2 Motets, Op. 74; 3 Motets, Op. 110.

(N) *** HM Dig. HMC 901951 [id.]. Berlin RIAS Chamber Ch., Marcus Creed.

This collection of Brahms's a cappella choral music is slightly less comprehensive than Marlow's Cambridge coverage, but includes the rare fragments (*Sanctus*, *Benedictus*, and *Agnus Dei*, all set in German) from the *Missa canonica*. This dates from 1856, a difficult period of the young composer's life due to the death of his mentor Robert Schumann, when Brahms was exchanging exercises in counterpoint with Joachim. There is a distinctive advantage of having German-born singers in this repertoire and the performances here by the RIAS Chamber Choir directed by Marcus Creed could hardly be more eloquent, especially the four beautiful *Festal and commemorative sentences*, Op. 109. The recording is first class.

Die schöne Magelone (song-cycle).

(N) **(*) Orfeo C490 981B [id.]. Dietrich Fischer-Dieskau, Sviatoslav Richter.

(N) ** Auvidis Valois Dig. V 4800 [id.]. Bernard Kruysen, Noël Lee.

Dietrich Fischer-Dieskau has done more than any singer to bring this once-neglected song-cycle back into the repertory, a love-story from the age of chivalry. With Sviatoslav Richter, he gave a series of performances over the years, recording the cycle more than once with him. This Orfeo version offers a live Salzburg Festival recording made in July 1970, and though audience noises occasionally intrude, the thrust and impulse of the reading are irresistible. As a bonus come his three encores of other Brahms songs. No texts are given or even translations of titles.

The Dutch baritone, Bernard Kruysen, is a sensitive lieder-singer who, with Noël Lee in this 1967 performance, gives a thoughtful and concentrated reading of this song-cycle, well recorded, though there are other more compelling versions.

(i) *Vier ernste Gesänge, Op. 121; An die Nachtigall;* (ii) *Dein blaues Auge;* (i) *Erinnerung;* (ii) *Der Gang zum Liebchen; Geheimnis;* (i) *Die Mainacht;* (ii) *Meine Liebe ist grün; O kühler Wald;* (i) *O wüsst' ich doch den Weg zurück;* (ii) *Ruhe, Süssliebchen;* (i) *Sonntag; Ständchen; Vergebliches Ständchen; Verrat; Von ewige Liebe;* (ii) *Vor dem Fenster; Ein Wanderer; Wiegenlied; Wie Melodien zieht es mir; Wir wandelten.*

(***) EMI mono CDH5 66426-2. Alexander Kipnis, with (i) Gerald Moore, (ii) Ernst Victor Wolff.

This disc in EMI's historic Références series brings together the great majority of the recordings made by Alexander Kipnis for EMI's Brahms Song Society edition in 1936, with the project rounded off for RCA in New York. The performances are a revelation, with Kipnis using his firm, dark bass with its very Russian timbre to bring out word-meaning and dramatic point with an intensity rarely matched. So the *Four serious songs* are both incisively powerful and movingly poetic, with legato perfectly controlled, as it is in such a taxing song as *Von ewige Liebe*. It is fascinating to find Kipnis, very much a virile singer, tackling songs normally sung by women, such as *Vergebliches Ständchen*, *Wiegenlied* or *Sonntag*, with a point and charm rarely matched, so that at times with his head voice he sounds like a bass version of Richard Tauber. The transfers, focusing on the voice, retain some surface noise but not enough to be intrusive.

Vier ernste Gesänge, Op. 121; Lieder: *Auf dem Kirchhofe; Botschaft; Feldeinsamkeit; Im Waldeseinsamkeit; Minnelied III; Mondenschein; O wüsst ich doch den Weg zurück; Sapphische Ode; Sommerabend; Ständchen.*

❁ (***) EMI (SIS) CDH7 63198-2 [id.]. Hotter, Moore – BACH: *Cantata No. 82: Ich habe genug.* (***) ❁

Glorious singing from Hans Hotter, wonderfully accompanied by Gerald Moore. An excellent transfer.

Braunfels, Walter (1882–1954)

Die Vögel (complete).

*** Decca Dig. 448 679-2 (2) [id.]. Kwon, Wottrich, Kraus, Holzmair, Görne, Berlin R. Ch., German SO, Berlin, Lothar Zagrosek.

In contrast with most issues in Decca's 'Entartete Musik' series, this charming opera, based on Aristophanes' *The Birds*, brings warm, uncomplicated music, setting no problems. The idiom is from the late nineteenth century rather than the twentieth, yet the innocence of the writing and the clarity of the composer's own libretto avoid any feeling of sentimentality. Bruno Walter, who conducted the first performance in Munich in 1920, remembered it many years later as a work which had 'given value to life', and with its richness and beauty that sums it up. It had phenomenal success in the early 1920s but, with Braunfels condemned by the Nazis, it was totally neglected from the 1930s and was never revived until the 1970s, twenty years after the composer's death.

The very opening magically introduces the Nightingale, a coloratura role sung at the first performance by Maria Ivogun. Another ravishing sequence is the long duet, which opens Act II, between the Nightingale and Good Hope, a tenor role beautifully sung by Endrik Wottrich. Helen Kwon as the Nightingale sings not just brilliantly but with sensuous beauty and a formidable range of tone. The rest of the cast could hardly be bettered, with such outstanding singers as Wolfgang Holzmair and Matthias Görne in smaller roles. Zagrosek conducts a glowing performance, superbly played and recorded.

Brian, Havergal (1876–1972)

Symphony No. 1 (Gothic).

*** Marco Polo Dig. 8.223280/1; *4.223280/1* [id.]. Jenisová, Pecková, Dolezal, Mikulás, Slovak Philharmonic Ch., Slovak Nat. Theatre Op. Ch., Slovak Folk Ens. Ch., Lucnica Ch., Bratislava Chamber Ch. & Children's Ch., Youth Echo Ch., Czech RSO (Bratislava), Slovak PO, Ondrej Lenárd.

This first of the symphonies here receives a passionately committed performance from Slovak forces. Despite a few incidental flaws, it conveys surging excitement from first to last, helped by a rich recording which gives a thrilling impression of massed forces. The final *Te Deum*, alone lasting 72 minutes, brings fervent choral writing of formidable complexity, with the challenge superbly taken up by the Czech musicians.

Symphony No. 3 in C sharp min.

**(*) Hyperion Dig. CDA 66334. Ball, Jacobson, BBC SO, Friend.

The *Third Symphony* began life as a concerto for piano; this perhaps explains the prominent role given to two pianos in the score. The work is full of extraordinarily imaginative and original touches, but the overall lack of rhythmic variety is a handicap. The playing of the BBC Symphony Orchestra under Lionel Friend is well prepared and dedicated, but the recording does not open out sufficiently in climaxes.

Briccialdi, Giulio (1818–81)

Wind quintet in D, Op. 124.

(BB) *** Naxos Dig. 8.553410 [id.]. Avalon Wind Quintet – CAMBINI: *Wind quintets Nos. 1–3.* ***

Giulio Briccialdi was an Italian flautist of considerable fame during his lifetime. His *Wind quintet in D major* bears a high opus number, though the CD catalogues seem to have ignored the remaining 123 works! It is carefree, empty, lightweight – and utterly charming. It is expertly played by these young German musicians – and the recording is as delightfully natural as the playing. Well worth its three stars.

Bridge, Frank (1879–1941)

Berceuse; Canzonetta; Suite for strings; There is a willow grows aslant a brook; Serenade; The Two hunchbacks; Threads.
(N) *** Conifer Dig. 75605 51327-2 [id.]. Britten Sinfonia, Cleobury.

This delightful collection has much in common with similar compilations of the lighter miniatures of Elgar. The beautiful *Suite for strings* and the inspired Butterworth-like *There is a willow grows aslant a brook* are masterpieces, but the vignettes are charming, notably the *Intermezzi* from incidental music for a children's play, *The Two hunchbacks* and the gentle *Andante* and winning little *Waltz* from another play called *Threads*. The playing is warmly sympathetic and polished, and beautifully recorded.

Cherry Ripe; Enter Spring (rhapsody); *Lament; The Sea* (suite); *Summer* (tone-poem).
(M) *** EMI CDM5 66855-2. RLPO, Groves.

Writing in the early years of the century, the composer confidently produced a magnificent seascape in the wake of Debussy, *The Sea*, but already by 1914 his responses were subtler, more original. *Summer*, written in that fateful year, was free of conventional pastoral moods, while in the last and greatest of Bridge's tone-poems, *Enter Spring*, he was responding to still wider musical horizons in experimentation which matches that of European contemporaries. Groves's warm advocacy adds to the impressiveness. First-rate recording, most successfully remastered.

Cherry ripe; Sir Roger de Coverley; Suite for strings; There is a willow grows aslant a brook.
**(*) Koch Dig. 3-7139-2 [id.]. New Zealand CO, Nicholas Braithwaite – DELIUS: *Sonata for strings*. **(*)

A nicely played, pastel-shaded performance of Bridge's *Suite for string orchestra*, with the delicacy of feeling in the lovely, ethereal *Nocturne* making amends for any lack of robustness elsewhere. The folksong arrangements are also attractively done and, if Britten's old ECO recording of *Sir Roger de Coverley* was even wittier, the poignant 'impression' (the composer's own term) *There is a willow grows aslant a brook* is beautifully played. The modern digital recording is both fresh and transparent.

Phantasm for piano and orchestra.
*** Conifer Dig. 74321 15007-2. Kathryn Stott, RPO, Handley – IRELAND: *Piano concerto;* WALTON: *Sinfonia concertante*. ***

Bridge's curiously titled *Phantasm* is a large-scale piano concerto, some 26 minutes long, in a single, massive movement. Kathryn Stott, most sympathetically accompanied by Vernon Handley and the RPO, proves a persuasive, committed interpreter, matching her achievement in the other two works on the disc. Warm, generally well-balanced recording.

The Sea (suite).
*** Chandos Dig. CHAN 8473 [id.]. Ulster O, Handley – BAX: *On the sea-shore;* BRITTEN: *Sea interludes*. ***

The Sea receives a brilliant and deeply sympathetic performance from Handley and the Ulster Orchestra, recorded with a fullness and vividness to make this a demonstration disc.

Suite for strings.
*** Chandos Dig. CHAN 8390 [id.]. ECO, Garforth – IRELAND: *Downland suite; Holy Boy; Elegiac meditations*. ***
*** Nimbus Dig. NI 5068 [id.]. E. String O, Boughton – BUTTERWORTH: *Banks of green willow; Idylls; Shropshire lad;* PARRY: *Lady Radnor's suite*. ***

Suite for string orchestra; Summer; There is a willow grows aslant a brook.
(M) *** Chandos CHAN 6566 [id.]. Bournemouth Sinf., Norman Del Mar – BANTOCK: *Pierrot of the minute;* BUTTERWORTH: *Banks of green willow*. ***

Summer is beautifully played by the Bournemouth Sinfonietta under Norman Del Mar. The same images of nature permeate the miniature tone-poem, *There is a willow grows aslant a brook*, an inspired piece, very sensitively managed. The *Suite for strings* is equally individual. Its third movement, a *Nocturne*, is lovely. The CD transfer is excellent and one can relish its fine definition and presence.

The ECO also play well for David Garforth in the *Suite for strings*. This performance is extremely committed; it is certainly excellently recorded, with great clarity and presence.

The Nimbus collection is more generous and is certainly well chosen. Here Bridge's *Suite* again receives a lively and responsive performance, from William Boughton and his excellent Birmingham-based orchestra, treated to ample, sumptuously atmospheric recording, more resonant than its competitors.

CHAMBER MUSIC

Cello sonata.
(M) *** Decca 443 575-2 [id.]. Rostropovich, Britten – SCHUBERT: *Arpeggione sonata*. **(*)
*** Chandos Dig. CHAN 8499 [id.]. Raphael and Peter Wallfisch – BAX: *Rhapsodic ballad;* DELIUS: *Sonata;* WALTON: *Passacaglia*. ***

Cello sonata; 2 Pieces: Meditation; Spring song.
**(*) ASV Dig. CDDCA 796 [id.]. Bernard Gregor-Smith, Yolande Wrigley – DEBUSSY; DOHNANYI: *Sonatas*. **(*)

Bridge wrote his *Cello sonata* during the First World War. The craftsmanship is distinguished and the lines delicately traced, and the modulations are often personal. The playing on Decca is of an altogether rare order, even by the exalted standards of Rostropovich and Britten, and the recording, made at The Maltings in 1968, has immediacy, warmth and great response. The reissue features its original coupling in Decca's Classic Sound series.

It is a distinctive world that Bridge evokes in the *Cello sonata* and one to which Raphael Wallfisch and his father, Peter, are completely attuned, and they are beautifully recorded.

The ASV account by Bernard Gregor-Smith and Yolande Wrigley can hold its head high. It is played with intensity and sensitivity. The recording is a bit close, but those wanting the coupling (and the Dohnányi is an excellent piece) need not hesitate.

3 Idylls for string quartet.
*** Hyperion Dig. CDA 66718 [id.]. Coull Qt – ELGAR: *Quartet* **(*); WALTON: *Quartet.* ***
*** Conifer Dig. 74321 15006-2. Brindisi Qt – BRITTEN: *String quartet No. 2;* Imogen HOLST: *String quartet No. 1.* ***

The *Three Idylls* date from 1906, soon after Bridge's first regular quartet. As this superb, purposeful performance by the Coull Quartet shows, the separate pieces, each marked by sharp changes of mood as a phantasie-form, make up a satisfying whole, a quartet in all but name. They provide a superb bonus to a fine performance of the Elgar and an outstanding performance of the Walton *Quartet.* Excellent sound.

They are also well served by the Brindisi Quartet.

(i) *Phantasy (quartet) in F sharp min. Phantasy trio in C min.; Piano trio No. 2.*
*** Hyperion Dig. CDA 66279 [id.]. Dartington Trio; (i) with Patrick Ireland.

The playing of the *Phantasy trio* by the Dartington Trio is of exceptional eloquence and sensitivity. They are no less persuasive in the *F sharp minor Phantasy*. Their account of the visionary post-war *Piano trio No. 2* of 1929 is completely inside this score. The Hyperion recording is altogether superb, in the demonstration bracket, perfectly natural and beautifully proportioned.

String quartets Nos. 1 in E min.; 4 (1937).
(N) ** Meridian Dig. CDE 84369 [id.]. Bridge Qt.

The eponymous Bridge quartet give committed and dedicated accounts of the *First Quartet* of 1906 and the much darker, searching quartet Bridge completed four years before his death. The overall sound is lustreless and uninviting and to be frank the playing could have a little more finish. However we are not spoilt for choice in this interesting repertoire.

String quartets Nos. 2 in G min.; 3.
*** Mer. Dig. CDE 843111 [id.]. Bridge Qt.

As more of Bridge's music comes to be recorded, so his stature seems to grow. His series of four quartets may one day come to be seen as a landmark of English chamber music. No. 2, written in 1915, immediately captures the listener's attention and brings together a sequence of movements thematically linked, each of which has a wide range of moods and tempi, phantasy-style. The *Third Quartet*, written a decade later, marks a radical change in Bridge's compositional style. The writing, without being strictly atonal, shows affinities with the Second Viennese School, yet, after the intensity of the argument and a haunting central *Andante*, the work has a valedictory close. The two quartets are superbly played by this eponymous group, who are right inside the music and present it with an almost improvisational spontaneity. The recording is first class, with fine body to the sound as well as a convincing interplay of detail.

String sextet.
(N) *** Chandos Dig. CHAN 9472 [id.]. ASMF Chamber Ens. – GOOSSENS: *Concertino; Phantasy sextet.* ***

Frank Bridge's *Sextet* (1906–12) is new to the catalogue and a valuable addition to the Bridge discography. A substantial piece that fills in the picture of the pre-First-World-War development of the composer. The Academy of St Martin-in-the-Fields Chamber Ensemble plays with great eloquence.

PIANO MUSIC

Arabesque; Capriccios Nos. 1–2; Dedication; Fairy tale suite; Gargoyle; Hidden fires; In autumn; 3 Miniatures; Pastorals, Sets 1–2; Sea idyll; 3 Improvisations for the left hand; Winter pastoral.
*** Continuum Dig. CCD 1016 [id.]. Peter Jacobs.

Berceuse; Canzonetta; 4 Characteristic pieces; Dramatic fantasia; Etude rhapsodic; Lament; Pensées fugitives; 3 Pieces; 4 Pieces; 3 Poems; Scherzettino.
*** Continuum Dig. CCD 1018 [id.]. Peter Jacobs.

Piano sonata; Graziella; The Hour-glass; 3 Lyrics; Miniature pastorals, Set 3; Miniature suite (ed. Hindmarsh); *3 Sketches.* arr. of BACH: *Chorale: Komm, süsser Tod, BWV 478.*
*** Continuum Dig. CCD 1019 [id.]. Peter Jacobs.

Peter Jacobs provides a complete survey of the piano music of Frank Bridge, and it proves an invaluable enterprise. The recorded sound is very good indeed: clean, well defined and present, and the acoustic lively. Calum MacDonald's excellent notes tracking his development over these years are worth a mention too.

Piano sonata; Capriccios Nos. 1 & 2; Ecstasy; The Hour-glass; Sea idyll; Vignettes de Marseille.
*** Conifer Dig. 75605 51186-2 [id.]. Kathryn Stott.

Kathryn Stott provides a formidable and illuminating single-disc selection from the piano music of Frank Bridge, for those who are unable or unwilling to stretch to Peter Jacobs's indispensable complete survey. Kathryn Stott's recital culminates in the masterly large-scale *Sonata* that Bridge wrote in disillusion in the years after the First World War, and she gives it a powerfully concentrated account. It is arguably the greatest piano sonata ever written by a British composer. The short early pieces, brilliantly and imaginatively written, give little inkling of such a development. Kathryn Stott is responsive to every changing mood. Outstanding performances, very well recorded.

VOCAL MUSIC

Songs: Disc 1: *Adoration; Blow, blow, thou winter wind; Come to me in my dreams; Cradle song; Dawn and evening; A dead violet; The Devon maid; A dirge; E'en as a lovely flower; Fair daffodils; Far, far from each other; Go not, happy day; If I could choose; Lean close thy cheek; Music, when soft voices die; My pent-up tears oppress my brain; Night lies on the silent highways; So perverse; The Primrose; Tears, idle tears; The Violets blue; When most I wink; Where'er my bitter tear drops fall; Where is it that our soul doth go?.*
Disc 2: *All things that we clasp; Day after day; Dear, when I look into thine eyes; Dweller in my deathless dreams; Goldenhair; Into her keeping; Isobel; Journey's end; The Last invocation; Love is a rose; Love went a-riding; Mantle of the blue; O that it were so!; Speak to me my love; So early in the morning, O; Strew no more red roses; Thy hand in mine; 'Tis but a week; What shall I your true love tell?; When you are old and gray; Where she lies asleep.*
(N) *** Hyperion Dig. CDA 67181/2(2) [id.]. Janice Watson, Louise Winter, Jamie MacDougall, Gerald Finley, Roger Chase; Roger Vignoles.

Bridge's song output was extensive and of quality. The first disc covers the songs from 1901 through to 1908, ending with the *Three songs with viola* with Louise Winter and Roger Chase, and the second carries them through to the Tagore settings and Humbert Wolfe's *Journey's End* of 1925. By this time Bridge's musical language had undergone a complete change. Not that the early songs are ever mere Edwardian ballads but one would be hard put to guess that they were by the same composer as *Dweller in my deathless dreams*. All four singers give thoroughly committed performances, and it would be invidious to single any one of them out for special praise. Roger Vignoles is superb throughout and Hyperion's recording is expertly balanced. Special mention, too, for the informative and judicious presentation.

Britten, Benjamin (1913–76)

An American overture; Canadian carnival, Op. 19; Sinfonia da Requiem, Op. 20; Suite on English folksongs (A time there was . . .), Op. 90; The Young person's guide to the orchestra (Variations and fugue on a theme of Purcell), Op. 34.
*** EMI Dig. CDC5 55394-2 [id.]. CBSO, Rattle.

Although concentrating on early works, this collection spans Britten's composing career. Both the *Sinfonia da Requiem* (1940) and the *American overture* (1941) belong to the composer's wartime stay in the USA. The *Suite on English folksongs* was not completed until 1974, although one movement, the quirky *Hankin Booby* (for wind and drums), dates from 1966, a commission for the opening of the Queen Elizabeth Hall in London. The whole programme is splendidly played by the City of Birmingham orchestra under Simon Rattle. His passionate view of the *Sinfonia da Requiem* is purposefully extrovert, yet subtly detailed too. Unlike the rest, from the 1980s, *The Young person's guide to the orchestra* is a brand-new (1995) recording, and the performance has the freshness of new discovery – a performance to match and even surpass the composer's own Decca version. The closing fugue has fine impetus and, as Purcell's tune re-emerges majestically, Rattle ensures that the contrapuntal texture is not overwhelmed. The recording is admirably vivid throughout.

An American overture; (i) *King Arthur suite* (arr. Hindmarsh); (i–ii) *The World of the Spirit* (cantata).
*** Chandos Dig. CHAN 9487 [id.]. BBC PO, Hickox, with (i) Britten Singers; (ii) Hannah Gordon, Cormac Rigby, Donald Mitchell, Philip Reed.

Since Britten died, a whole range of his music has been brought out of the cupboard, mostly written in the 1930s. The two main works here both derive from music written for radio productions, an epic dramatization of the *King Arthur* story by D. G. Bridson in 1937 and the religious cantata, *The World of the Spirit*, in 1938, using a sequence of texts prepared by R. Ellis Roberts. Though the mature Britten style is identifiable only occasionally, the invention and imagination are characteristic from first to last, for these are the inspirations of a prolific young composer rising to early challenges. The fanfares which open the *King Arthur* music – here assembled into four self-contained movements by Paul Hindmarsh – have the flavour of the film music of the period, but with a clear, Britten-like slant. The religious cantata, *The World of the Spirit*, follows the pattern of *The Company of Heaven* of the previous year, but the wide range of texts prompts Britten to use an astonishing range of techniques, starting with plainsong (*Veni creator spiritus*) set in a diatonic frame and even continuing with a Bach-like chorale. The result is a fascinating mosaic of contrasting elements, culminating at the end of the second of the three parts in an open imitation of Walton's *Belshazzar's Feast*, a work which Britten admired on hearing the first performance in 1931. Full texts are given; but just as useful is the sharply perceptive musical commentary of Donald Mitchell and Philip Reed. *An American overture* was rediscovered in his lifetime but was not performed until 1983, a good companion-piece to the radio-inspired works. First-rate singing from soloists and choir alike in the cantata, helped by full and rich recording.

An American overture; Sinfonia da Requiem, Op. 20; Peter Grimes: 4 Sea interludes and Passacaglia, Op. 33.

(BB) **(*) Naxos Dig. 8.553107 [id.]. New Zealand SO, Fredman.

Myer Fredman conducts warm and purposeful performances of this group of orchestral works from early in Britten's career. Though the New Zealand strings are not as rich or as resonant as most, the purity of sound makes up for power in spontaneous-sounding performances. Dramatic and atmospheric points are well made with the help of a warm hall acoustic and full-ranging recording. Recommendable at super-budget price.

Clarinet concerto movement (orch. Colin Matthews).

*** Hyperion Dig. CDA 66634 [id.]. Thea King, ECO, Wordsworth – ARNOLD: *Clarinet concertos* etc.; MACONCHY: *Concertinos*. ***

Benny Goodman, having commissioned Bartók to write *Contrasts*, turned in 1942 to the young Benjamin Britten, then in the United States, to write a concerto for him. Sadly, just before Britten returned to England, Goodman suggested a delay, and the composer never even sorted out the sketches. Colin Matthews, who worked closely with Britten during his last three years, has here fathomed what Britten intended and has orchestrated the result to make a highly attractive short piece, alternately energetic and poetic. Thea King, as in the rest of the disc, plays the piece most persuasively, making one regret deeply that it was never completed.

Piano concerto in D, Op. 13.

(N) **(*) RCA Dig. 09026 68127-2 [id.]. Barry Douglas, O Philh. de Radio France, Marek Janowski – DEBUSSY: *Fantasie; Pour le piano*. **(*)

(M) **(*) Chandos CHAN 6580 [id.]. Gillian Lin, Melbourne SO, John Hopkins – COPLAND: *Concerto*. **(*)

(M) **(*) Hyperion Dig. CDA 66293 [id.]. Annette Servadei, LPO, Giunta – KHACHATURIAN: *Piano concerto*. **(*)

(i) *Piano concerto, Op. 13;* (ii) *Violin concerto, Op. 15.*

(M) *** Decca 417 308-2. (i) Sviatoslav Richter; (ii) Lubotsky; ECO, composer.

(i) *Piano concerto, Op. 13. Paul Bunyan overture.*

*** Collins Dig. 1102-2 [id.]. (i) Joanna MacGregor; ECO, Bedford (with SAXTON: *Music to celebrate the resurrection of Christ*. ***)

Britten wrote his formidable *Piano concerto* for a Prom in 1938. He later rejected the slow movement and replaced it in 1945 with an *Impromptu*, simpler and more obviously apt. The characterful young Joanna MacGregor gets the best of both worlds by recording both slow movements. With Steuart Bedford a deeply understanding conductor, this is a ripe and refreshing performance, well recorded. The brassy *Paul Bunyan overture*, never used with the operetta, has been orchestrated by Colin Matthews. The Saxton coupling makes a fascinating bonus.

Richter is incomparable in interpreting the *Piano concerto*, not only the thoughtful, introspective moments but the Liszt-like bravura passages. With its highly original sonorities the *Violin concerto* makes a splendid vehicle for another Soviet artist, Mark Lubotsky. Recorded in The Maltings, the playing of the ECO under the composer's direction matches the inspiration of the soloists.

An eminently expert account from Barry Douglas, whose fingers are well equipped to meet the challenges of this score. He is as much at home in the Prokofievian brilliance of the Toccata as he is in evoking the poetic feeling of the Impromptu. There is on the negative side, some brittle and ugly sound from him at the *fortissimo* end of the dynamic spectrum. The Orchestre Philharmonique under Marek Janowski provide excellent support and the RCA engineers produce good results.

Gillian Lin cannot match Richter in detailed imagination but, from her sharp attack on the opening motif onwards, she gives a strong and satisfying reading, well accompanied by Hopkins and the Melbourne orchestra. The 1978 recording is wide-ranging and well balanced, making a useful mid-priced alternative, with its Copland coupling.

With good, well-balanced digital recording, Annette Servadei gives a strong, dedicated, muscular performance. South-African born but trained mainly in Italy, Servadei is a devotee of British music. She is particularly impressive in the hushed and sustained passacaglia, entitled *Impromptu*, which provided Walton with the theme of his *Variations on an Impromptu of Britten*.

Violin concerto, Op. 15.
(M) *** EMI CDM7 64202-2. Ida Haendel, Bournemouth SO, Berglund – WALTON: *Violin concerto.* ***
(N) *** Classico CLASSCD 233. Sergej Azizjan, Copenhagen PO, Osmo Vanska – WALTON: *Violin concerto.* **(*)

(i) *Violin concerto, Op. 15. Canadian carnival overture, Op. 19; Mont Juic* (written with Lennox Berkeley).
❁ *** Collins Dig. 1123-2 [id.]. (i) Lorraine McAslan, ECO, Steuart Bedford.

(i) *Violin concerto in D min., Op. 15;* (ii) *Serenade for tenor, horn and strings, Op. 31.*
(BB) *** CfP Silver Double CDCFPSD 4754 (2). (i) Rodney Friend; (ii) Ian Partridge, Busch; LPO, Pritchard (with TIPPETT: *Concerto for double string orchestra* ***; VAUGHAN WILLIAMS: *Tallis fantasia* etc. ***; WALTON: *Belshazzar's feast.* **(*))

Lorraine McAslan's virtuosity is effortless, her artistic insights unusually keen and she brings to the *Concerto* a subtle imagination and great emotional intensity. Steuart Bedford gets first-class playing from the English Chamber Orchestra and emphasizes the pain and poignancy underlying much of this music. The recording is very well balanced, exceptionally wide-ranging and vivid. *Mont Juic* and the *Canadian carnival overture* are eminently well served by these splendid musicians and the engineers.

It was a happy idea to combine the most colourful of Britten's song-cycles with the *Violin concerto*, and an equally good idea to exploit the artistry of two outstanding performers. Rodney Friend, at the time (1974) leader of the LPO, later concertmaster of the New York Philharmonic, proves a masterful soloist, magnificently incisive and expansive. As for Ian Partridge – one of the most consistently stylish of recording tenors – he gives a reading often strikingly new in its illumination, more tenderly beautiful and purer than Peter Pears's classic reading, culminating in a heavenly performance of the final Keats sonnet setting. With vivid recording, this is part of a highly desirable Silver Double aptly entitled '*The Best of England*', with only James Loughran's account of Walton's *Belshazzar's Feast* below the high standard of the rest.

Ida Haendel's ravishing playing places the work firmly in the European tradition. She brings panache and brilliance to the music, as well as great expressive warmth. This is a reading very much in the grand manner and it finds Paavo Berglund in excellent form. His support is sensitive in matters of detail and full of atmosphere. The recording is full and realistic, though the soloist is balanced a little close.

Trained in Leningrad, Sergej Azizjan was chosen as concert master of the Copenhagen Philharmonic in 1993. His is a superb technique, marked by flawless intonation and a wide tonal range. Where in the Walton he is passionate in an aptly extrovert way, in the Britten he adopts a manner at once lighter in the quicksilver bravura passages and more intimate and poetic in lyrical writing, ending a deeply felt account of the closing pages, one of Britten's deepest inspirations up to that time. Though some will still prefer the bigger-boned approach of Ida Haendel, or the more subtly idiomatic reading of Lorraine McAslan, such a fine and illuminating performance as Azizjan's is equally welcome, as is the coupling. Both this concerto and the Walton were completed in 1939, each using a similar structure, making an apt pairing.

Violin concerto, Op. 15 (original version).
(M) (**) EMI mono CDM5 66053-2. Theo Olof, Hallé O, Barbirolli – HEMING: *Threnody;* RUBBRA: *Symphony No. 5; Improvisations.* (***)

Allowances have to be made for the quality of this première recording, made by the young Dutch virtuoso, Theo Olof, and the Hallé Orchestra under Barbirolli in 1948, which makes its first appearance on CD. At work on a revised version of the score, Britten never sanctioned its release, though he can hardly have entertained any doubts on the virtuosity and dedication of the soloist or of Sir John, who had championed the piece in his New York days. Well worth hearing. The limited sound is a handicap.

Diversions for piano (left hand) and orchestra.
*** Sony Dig. SK 47188 [id.]. Fleisher, Boston SO, Ozawa – PROKOFIEV: *Piano concerto No. 4;* RAVEL: *Left-hand concerto.* ***

Leon Fleisher lost the use of his right hand at the height of his career and is currently engaged on recording repertoire for the left hand. The present issue assembles three of the most brilliant and rewarding pieces for the medium, all commissioned by Paul Wittgenstein, brother of the philosopher, who lost his right hand during the First World War. The *Diversions* is a wartime work, highly inventive and resourceful, whose neglect over the years is puzzling. Fleisher gives a sensitive and intelligent account with great sympathy and skill. His playing has strong character and he receives fine support from Ozawa and the Boston orchestra and fine recording.

(i) *Diversions for piano (left hand) and orchestra, Op. 21;* (ii) *Sinfonia da Requiem, Op. 20;* (iii) *Young person's guide to the orchestra, Op. 34.*
(M) **(*) Sony Dig./Analogue SBK 62746: SBT 62746 [id.]. (i) Leon Fleisher, Boston SO, Ozawa; (ii) St Louis SO, Previn; (iii) LSO, Andrew Davis.

Fleisher's recording is also available with this alternative coupling. The St Louis orchestra plays with great spirit in the *Sinfonia da Requiem* and Previn's performance is deeply felt, if not quite a match for the composer's own. The 1963 recording is well detailed. Andrew Davis also directs an account of the *Young person's guide* that is bright and workmanlike, enjoyable enough, and the (1975) Abbey Road recording sounds well on CD.

(i) *Lachrymae, Op. 48a. Movement for wind sextet*; (ii) *Night Mail* (end sequence). *Sinfonietta; The Sword in the Stone* (concert suite for wind and percussion); (iii) *Phaedra, Op. 93.*
*** Hyperion Dig. CDA 66845 [id.]. (i) Roger Chase; (ii) Nigel Hawthorne; (iii) Jean Rigby; Nash Ens, Lionel Friend.

Using different groupings for each work, the Nash Ensemble here offers a fascinating collection of neglected Britten works, mostly from the 1930s but starting with his last piece for solo voice, the dramatic scena *Phaedra*, which he wrote for Dame Janet Baker. Jean Rigby sings beautifully but lacks the biting intensity of Dame Janet. *Lachrymae*, for viola with string accompaniment, also dates from Britten's very last years, when he adpated a piece written in 1950 for William Primrose, played here with the beauty intensified, thanks to the firm, true playing of Roger Chase. Both the *Sinfonietta* of 1932 (with hints of Schoenbergian influence) and the *Wind sextet* movement of 1930 are astonishingly accomplished for a teenage composer, reflecting the mature Britten style only occasionally. The concert suite for wind and percussion was drawn from music for a radio production of T. H. White's ironic Arthurian piece, *The Sword in the Stone*, and brings some delightful Wagner parodies. It is also good to have the final sequence from Britten's music for the GPO film documentary, *Night Mail*, with W. H. Auden's rattling verse spoken by Nigel Hawthorne. Excellent playing from the Nash Ensemble, and first-rate recording.

(i; ii) *Lachrymae (Reflections on a song by Dowland);* (i) *Prelude and fugue, Op. 29; Simple Symphony, Op. 4; Variations on a theme of Frank Bridge, Op. 10;* (ii) *Elegy for solo viola.*
✿ *** Virgin/EMI Dig. VC5 45121-2 [id.]. (i) Norwegian CO, Iona Brown; (ii) Lars Anders Tomter.

Iona Brown gives performances of the *Simple Symphony* and the *Frank Bridge variations* to match the composer's own. The *Simple Symphony* fizzes with youthful energy, yet Brown brings an unusually wide and expressive range to the poignant *Sentimental sarabande*, which elevates Britten's writing far beyond any suggestion of juvenilia. The *Frank Bridge variations* have never sounded more emotionally powerful on record and in the *Lachrymae* Lars Anders Tomter is an outstanding soloist, not least in the touching full presentation of Dowland's tune in the haunting coda. He follows the *Lachrymae* with an ardent account of the solo *Elegy*. The recording is of demonstration quality.

(i; ii) *Lachrymae, Op. 48a;* (ii) *Simple Symphony, Op. 4; Variations on a theme of Frank Bridge, Op. 10; Young Apollo, Op. 16.* (iii) *Death in Venice: suite* (arr. Bedford); (iv) *Peter Grimes: 4 Sea interludes and Passacaglia.*
(N) (B) *** Chandos Dig. 2-for-1 CHAN 241-2 (2) [id.]. (i) Montreal I Musici, Turovsky; (ii) Rivka Golani; (iii) ECO, Bedford; (iv) Ulster O, Handley.

Under Yuli Turovsky the Montreal players give passionate performances of an attractively chosen group of Britten works: two popular, two rare. *Young Apollo*, resurrected after Britten's death, is particularly successful, with vivid recording capturing the unusual textures with piano and string quartet as well as strings. Rivka Golani is a resonant soloist in *Lachrymae*, and the *Variations* and *Simple Symphony* have similar heft, helped by the rich, upfront recording. Representing Britten's operas, Steuart Bedford's *Death in Venice suite* is well worth having, and Handley's *Peter Grimes* excerpts are second only to Previn's splendid EMI recording, helped by richly atmospheric digital sound of demonstration quality. This is one of the most recommendable of Chandos's new two-for-one Doubles.

(i) *Matinées musicales; Soirées musicales;* (ii; iv) *Young person's guide to the orchestra;* (iii; iv) *Peter Grimes: 4 Sea interludes and Passacaglia.*
(M) *** Decca 425 659-2. (i) Nat. PO, Bonynge; (ii) LSO; (iii) ROHCG O; (iv) composer.

Bonynge's sparkling versions of the *Matinées* and *Soirées musicales* are here reissued, coupled with Britten's accounts of the *Young person's guide to the orchestra* and the *Sea interludes and Passacaglia.*

Prelude and fugue for 18 solo strings, Op. 29; Simple Symphony, Op. 4; Variations on a theme of Frank Bridge, Op. 10.
*** ASV Dig. CDDCA 591 [id.]. N. Sinfonia, Hickox.

The ASV issue is notable for an outstandingly fine account of the *Frank Bridge variations*, which stands up well alongside the composer's own version. Throughout, the string playing is committedly responsive, combining polish with eloquence, the rich sonorities resonating powerfully in a glowing church acoustic.

The Prince of the Pagodas (complete).
✪ *** Virgin/EMI Dig. VCD7 59578-2 (2). L. Sinf., Knussen.

The multicoloured instrumentation – much influenced by Britten's visit to Bali – is caught with glorious richness in Oliver Knussen's really complete version. Most importantly he opens out more than 40 cuts, most of them small, which Britten sanctioned to fit his own Decca recording on to four LP sides. The performance is outstanding and so is the sound.

Simple Symphony (for strings), Op. 4.
*** DG Dig. 423 624-2 [id.]. Orpheus CO – BIZET: *Symphony;* PROKOFIEV: *Symphony No. 1.* ***

(i) *Simple Symphony, Op. 4;* (ii; iii) *Les Illuminations, Op. 18*; (ii; iv) *Serenade for tenor, horn and strings, Op. 31.*
(N) (B) *** DG Classikon Dig./Analogue 459 358-2 [id.]. (i) Orpheus CO; (ii) Robert Tear; (iii) Philh. O; (iv) Dale Clevenger, Cleveland O; Giulini.

Simple Symphony, Op. 4; Prelude and fugue for 18-part string orchestra, Op. 29.
(M) *** Decca 448 569-2. ECO, composer – Concert of *English string music.* *** ✪

(i) *Simple Symphony, Op. 4; Variations on a theme of Frank Bridge;* (ii) *Young person's guide to the orchestra; Peter Grimes: 4 Sea interludes.*
(M) **(*) Nimbus NI 7017 [id.]. (i) E. String O; (ii) E. SO, Boughton.

(i) *Simple Symphony, Op. 4;* (ii) *The Young person's guide to the orchestra (Variations and fugue on a theme of Purcell), Op. 34; Peter Grimes: 4 Sea interludes.*
(B) *** [EMI Red Line Dig. CDR5 72564]. (i) ASMF; (ii) Minnesota O; Marriner.

The composer's own recording of the *Simple Symphony* was originally contained in an outstanding anthology called 'Britten conducts English music' – see the Concerts section – but is also here available in a different permutation. where it makes a splendid foil for the *Prelude and Fugue* with its charm and high spirits, aided by the glowing resonance of The Maltings where the recording was made.

In 1979 Robert Tear recorded these two favourite Britten cycles for DG with Giulini who has long been a persuasive advocate of Britten's music. The fact that these two excellent performances were recorded on opposite sides of the Atlantic adds to the attractions, for the Philharmonia produces playing of warmth and resonance to match that of the Chicago orchestra. Without apology Giulini presents both cycles as full-scale orchestral works, and though some detail may be lost, the strength of Britten's writing amply justifies it. Tear is at his finest in both cycles, more open than in his earlier recording of the *Serenade*. As we know from other records, Dale Clevenger is a superb horn player, and it is good to have a fresh view in such music. Soloists are balanced rather close, in an otherwise excellent, vivid recording. The engaging *Simple Symphony*, spick and span and sparkling in its Orpheus performance, makes a stimulating introduction for an excellent bargain programme.

The *Simple Symphony* goes well alongside the Bizet and Prokofiev works, especially when played as freshly and characterfully as here by the Orpheus group. Britten himself found more fun in the *Playful pizzicato*, but the reading is all-of-a-piece and enjoyably spontaneous. Excellent, realistic sound.

William Boughton offers an attractive and generous 75-minute Britten anthology, very well played and showing the sumptuous Nimbus recording style at its most effective. The *Simple Symphony* and *Frank Bridge variations* were recorded in the Great Hall of Birmingham University in 1985 and are most sympathetically played. The *Young person's guide* and *Sea interludes* were recorded in Birmingham's new Symphony Hall in 1991 and have even better definition. The *Variations* are amiably colourful, and Boughton responds with strong emotion to the *Sea interludes*.

Marriner's Minnesota account of the *Young person's guide* and the *Peter Grimes interludes* are very well played, and if his direct approach is a little stiff, the digital sound is first rate, clean and clear, yet warmly atmospheric. The youthful *Simple Symphony* is delightfully spirited and fresh. This is only available in the USA.

Sinfonia da Requiem, Op. 20.
(M) *** EMI Dig. CDM7 64870-2. CBSO, Simon Rattle – SHOSTAKOVICH: *Symphony No. 10.* **

Rattle's passionate view of the *Sinfonia da Requiem* is unashamedly extrovert, yet well detailed. The EMI recording is admirably vivid and clear, but the Shostakovich coupling is less convincing.

Sinfonia da Requiem; Gloriana: symphonic suite; Peter Grimes: 4 Sea interludes and Passacaglia.
*** Collins Dig. 1019-2 [id.]. LSO, Bedford.

In his Britten series for Collins, Steuart Bedford conducts strong, idiomatic performances of these works, helped by exceptionally vivid recording. The atmosphere of the *Peter Grimes interludes* is caught superbly, and the *Sinfonia da Requiem*, treated expansively, culminates in a radiant account of the final *Requiem aeternam*. Recommended.

(i) *Sinfonia da Requiem, Op. 20;* (ii) *Symphony for cello and orchestra, Op. 68;* (iii) *Cantata misericordium, Op. 69.*
(M) *** Decca 425 100-2. (i) New Philh. O; (ii)

Rostropovich, ECO; (iii) Pears, Fischer-Dieskau, London Symphony Ch., LSO; composer.

All the performances here are definitive, and Rostropovich's account of the *Cello Symphony* in particular is commanding. The CD transfers are admirably managed.

Sinfonia da Requiem, Op. 20; The Young person's guide to the orchestra, Op. 34; Peter Grimes: 4 Sea interludes & Passacaglia, Op. 33.
(M) **(*) Virgin/EMI (SIS) Dig. CUV5 61195-2 [id.]. RLPO, Libor Pěsek.

Though Pěsek fails to convey the full ominous weight of the first movement of the *Sinfonia da Requiem*, he then directs a dazzling account of the central *Dies Irae Scherzo*, taken breathtakingly fast, and finds an intense repose in the calm of the final *Requiem aeternam*. The *Sea interludes* sound literal and unatmospheric, and the *Young person's guide* lacks a degree of tension, with the fugue not dashing enough. The recording is comfortably reverberant.

Sinfonia da Requiem, Op. 20; Peter Grimes: 4 Sea interludes and passacaglia.
✿ (B) *** EMI forte CZS5 72658-2 (2) [(M) id.]. LSO, Previn – SHOSTAKOVICH: *Symphonies Nos. 4 & 5.* **(*)

In Previn gives a passionately intense reading of the *Sinfonia da Requiem*, the most ambitious of Britten's early orchestral works, written after the death of his parents. It is warmer than the composer's own, less sharply incisive but presenting a valid alternative. So too in the *Four Sea interludes*, with Previn springing the bouncing rhythms of the second interlude – the picture of *Sunday morning in the Borough* – even more infectiously than the composer himself. These superb performances are presented in expansive seventies recordings of demonstration quality. It is a pity that the Shostakovich coupling is only partly recommendable: the *Fourth Symphony* is very successful but the *Fifth* fails to take off. Nonetheless a good Forte Double.

Sinfonietta, Op. 1.
*** BIS Dig. CD 540 [id.]. Tapiola Sinf., Vänskä – *Nocturne; Serenade* etc. ***

The *Sinfonietta* (also available in a chamber performance – see below) is busier in its textures than mature Britten; it is here presented with rare strength and warmth to make it totally convincing. It is very well recorded and comes with an attractive collection of vocal music.

Suite on English folksongs (A time there was); Young person's guide to the orchestra, Op. 34; Peter Grimes: 4 Sea interludes and Passacaglia.
(M) **(*) Sony SMK 47541. NYPO, Leonard Bernstein.

Bernstein's charismatic account of the *Young person's guide to the orchestra* brings much exhilarating bravura from the New York soloists, notably the flutes, clarinets and trumpets. The 1961 recording, made in the New York Manhattan Center, is fuller than usual from this source. The performance of *A time there was* (its title quoting Hardy) reveals a darkness and weight of expression behind the seemingly trivial plan. Bernstein misses a little of the wit but is warmly sympathetic, and the dramatic account of the *Grimes interludes*, with a powerful *Passacaglia*, makes a good coupling.

Symphony for cello and orchestra, Op. 68.
(N) *** Ph. Dig. 454 442-2 [id.]. Julian Lloyd Webber, ASMF, Marriner – WALTON: *Cello concerto.****
(M) *** Sony Dig. SMK 58928 [id.]. Yo-Yo Ma, Baltimore SO, David Zinman – MAXWELL DAVIES: *Violin concerto.* ***
(*) Russian Disc RDCD 11108. Rostropovich, Moscow PO, composer – SAUGUET: *Mélodie concertante.* *

(i) *Symphony for cello and orchestra, Op. 68. Death in Venice: suite, Op. 88* (arr. Bedford).
*** Chandos Dig. CHAN 8363 [id.]. (i) Wallfisch; ECO, Bedford.

Julian Lloyd Webber, in his finest recording yet, offers a unique coupling of two works, very different in character but closely parallel in the careers of their composers, each reflecting the mastery of a great Russian cellist (respectively Rostropovich and Piatigorsky). In passionately committed readings he brings out the power of each work and also the beauty, remarkably so in the grittily taxing Britten piece. Helped by sumptuous Philips sound, he and Sir Neville Marriner also demonstrate the extraordinary originality of Britten's scoring in a way beyond any rival, but find an extra expressive warmth.

Sounding less improvisatory than Rostropovich, Wallfisch and Bedford are more purposeful, and the weight and range of the brilliant and full Chandos recording quality add to the impact, with Bedford's direction even more spacious than the composer's. Steuart Bedford's encapsulation of Britten's last opera into this rich and colourful suite makes a splendid coupling.

What predominates in Yo-Yo Ma's partnership with David Zinman is the wayward mystery in the first movement, rather than its more aggressive qualities, and in the Scherzo Ma is masterly in bringing out the lightness and fantasy. The third-movement *Adagio* is softer-grained than usual, with the soloist placed naturally, leading on to a purposeful account of the finale, which brings out the Copland-like swagger of the main passacaglia theme. The orchestra plays with brilliance and commitment in a full and well-balanced recording.

The special interest of the Russian Disc issue is

that it includes a recording of the very first performance of the *Cello Symphony* on 12 March 1964, given by its dedicatee and 'onlie begetter' with Britten himself conducting. It is not as well recorded as the version Rostropovich and Britten made for Decca not long afterwards, but there is great intensity and concentration here.

A time there was (suite on English folk tunes), *Op. 90; Johnson over Jordan* (suite, arr. P. Hindmarsh); *Young person's guide to the orchestra, Op. 34; Peter Grimes: 4 Sea interludes*.
*** Chandos Dig. CHAN 9221 [id.]. Bournemouth SO, Hickox.

Richard Hickox and the Bournemouth orchestra offer an attractive coupling, opulently recorded, of two of Britten's most popular works, both done with flair, set against two rarities. *A time there was* is the suite which Britten wrote at the very end of his life, characteristically original and with a new, elusive vein. The *Johnson over Jordan suite* is drawn from the incidental music which Britten wrote in 1939 for an experimental play of J. B. Priestley in which music and mime played an integral part. If the style is uncharacteristic of the later Britten, the colour and vitality are most winning, played here with verve.

Variations on a theme of Frank Bridge, Op. 10.
✿ (M) (***) EMI mono CDM5 66601-2 [id.]. Philh. O, Karajan – VAUGHAN WILLIAMS: *Fantasia on a theme by Thomas Tallis* (***) ✿; STRAVINSKY: *Jeu de cartes*. (**)
(N) *** MDG Dig. MDG 321 0180-2 [id.]. Polish CO, Jerzy Maksymiuk – BARTOK: *Divertimento*. ***

If all digital CDs of the 1990s sounded like this Karajan mono recording of the early 1950s, there would be no need for a *Penguin Guide*. The sound is astonishingly fresh and vivid, and the playing of the Philharmonia strings is of the highest distinction. They produce beautifully blended tone, rich and full-bodied, yet marvellously delicate at the pianissimo end of the dynamic spectrum. Karajan's reading is unaffected yet impassioned, electrifying in the *Funeral music*. This is an issue that should never be out of the catalogue, marking the peak of Karajan's achievement during his London years with EMI, between 1948 and 1960.

Among recent accounts of Britten's youthful masterpiece, this Polish version under Jerzy Maksymiuk is among the best. Each variation is expertly shaped and well characterized and the piece is very well held together by Maksymiuk. Rather short measure at 52 minutes but nonetheless an issue of quality.

Variations and fugue on a theme by Frank Bridge; Young person's guide to the orchestra; Peter Grimes: 4 Sea interludes & Passacaglia.
*** Teldec/Warner Dig. 9031 73126 [id.]. BBC SO, Andrew Davis.

In his admirable British music series for Teldec, Andrew Davis gives full weight as well as brilliance to these masterpieces from early in Britten's career, making a particularly attractive triptych. The *Frank Bridge variations*, set here against the more popular Purcell set, gain particularly from large-scale treatment, with each variation strongly characterized. Excellent recording.

Young Apollo, Op. 16; (i) *Les Illuminations, Op. 18*.
** ASV Dig. CDDCA 737 [id.]. (i) Carole Farley, SCO, Serebrier – BARBER: *Canzonetta; Souvenirs*. **

Carole Farley is a forceful soloist in *Les illuminations*, incisive in attack but missing the subtlety and beauty of the piece, with the voice raw under pressure. *Young Apollo* too needs a subtler, less square reading than this for its full originality to be appreciated.

Young person's guide to the orchestra (Variations and fugue on a theme of Purcell), Op. 34.
(N) **(*) BBC Legends BBCL 4005-2 [id.]. BBC SO, Stokowski – BEETHOVEN: *Symphony No. 7* *(**); FALLA: *El amor brujo*. *** ✿

Stokowski's 1962 Prom performance with the BBC Symphony Orchestra is pretty spectacular. The whole occasion was highly charged and the quality of the orchestral response pretty breathtaking. Even if the opening is very relaxed, almost lethargic, this is a reading of outstanding personality and intensity; the sound is very good for its age.

Young person's guide to the orchestra (with narration)
(BB) *** Naxos Dig. 8.554170 [id.]. Dame Edna Everage, Melbourne SO, John Lanchbery – POULENC: *The story of Babar* *** ✿; PROKOFIEV: *Peter and the wolf*. ***
(M) **(*) Decca Phase Four 444 104-2 [id.]. Sean Connery (nar.), RPO, Dorati – PROKOFIEV: *Peter and the wolf* etc. **(*)

Using her own enthusiastically expanded version of the original commentary, Dame Edna is sure to draw any young possum into the world of the orchestra. Her exuberance offsets any twee moments, and the Melbourne orchestra illustrate vivid instrumental descriptions with splendidly alive and colourful playing. The Naxos recording is excellent and, with its highly enjoyable couplings, this inexpensive triptych is warmly recommendable.

Sean Connery's voice is very familiar and his easy style is attractive. His narration should go down well with young people, even if some of the points are made heavily. The orchestral playing is first rate and the vivid, forwardly balanced recording – with a Decca Phase Four source – is effective enough. The performance has plenty of colour and vitality.

CHAMBER MUSIC

Alla marcia; 3 Divertimenti for string quartet; 2 Insect pieces; Phantasy oboe quartet, Op. 2; Phantasy in F min. for string quintet; Temporal variations for oboe and piano.
(M) *** Unicorn Dig. UKCD 2060 [id.]. Derek Wickens, John Constable, Augmented Gabrieli Qt.

Derek Wickens is heard at his finest in his contributions to the *Phantasy oboe quartet* (with its passages of seeming improvisation) as well as to the two rediscovered works, the *Temporal variations* and the evocatively etched *Insect pieces*, which are incisive and poised, restrained and lyrical. The Gabrieli Quartet too play with a degree of restraint which works especially well in the two works for strings. The *Phantasy in F minor* is a finely wrought piece but not as striking as the *Phantasy oboe quartet* in its material. There is much striking material too in the *Alla marcia* of 1933 and the three string *Divertimenti* of 1936, both pointing forward to the song cycle, *Les Illuminations*. A rewarding reissue.

Cello sonata in C, Op. 65.
(M) *** Decca 452 895-2 [id.]. Rostropovich, composer – DEBUSSY: *Sonata;* SCHUMANN: *5 Stücke in Volkston.* ***
**(*) Sony Dig. MK 44980 [id.]. Yo-Yo Ma, Emanuel Ax – R. STRAUSS: *Sonata.* **(*)

The current reissue in Decca's Classic Sound series restores the original (1961) couplings. The strange, five-movement *Cello sonata* was written specially for Rostropovich's appearance that year at the Aldeburgh Festival, and the recording was made soon after the first performance. The idiom itself is unexpected, sometimes recalling Soviet models, as in the spiky *March*, perhaps out of tribute to the dedicatee. Although technically it demands fantastic feats from the cellist, it is hardly a display piece. It is an excellent work to wrestle with on a record, particularly when the performance is never likely to be outshone. The recording is superb in every way.

Yo-Yo Ma and Emanuel Ax give an account of the *Cello sonata* carefully thought out, with exaggerated pianissimi and self-conscious phrasing. The recording is very truthful.

(i) *Cello sonata in C, Op. 65;* (Unaccompanied) *Cello suites Nos. 1, Op. 72; 2, Op. 80.*
(M) *** Decca 421 859-2. Rostropovich; (i) with composer.

The *Cello sonata* in Rostropovich and Britten's definitive recording is here aptly coupled with two of the *Suites for unaccompanied cello.*

Cello suites (Suites for unaccompanied cello) Nos. 1, Op. 72; 2, Op. 80; 3, Op. 87.
*** Decca Dig. 444 181-2. Robert Cohen.
*** BIS Dig. CD 446 [id.]. Torleif Thedéen.

The *Cello suites* were all written for Rostropovich, and his recording has special claims on the collector. He offers inspired accounts of the first two *Suites*, coupled with the *Cello sonata* (Decca 421 859-2), but has never done the third. Robert Cohen is a commanding performer and his version of all three *Suites* is satisfyingly musical and thoughtful. He has the advantage of superbly natural recorded sound, with plenty of air round the instrument and the balance not too close.

Torleif Thedéen has magnificent tonal warmth and eloquence, and he proves a masterly advocate of these *Suites*, which sound thoroughly convincing in his hands, if not quite so powerful as Rostropovich in the Concertos and Sonatas.

Cello suite No. 3.
*** Virgin/EMI Dig. VC7 59052-2 [id.]. Steven Isserlis – TAVENER: *The Protecting veil.* ***

Steven Isserlis brings out the spiritual element in a work which draws on traditional Russian themes, including Orthodox church music, and such a performance relates well to the Tavener work with which it is coupled.

Lachrymae, Op. 48.
(N) *(*) Olympia Dig. OCD 625 [id.]. Yuri Bashmet, Sviatoslav Richter – HINDEMITH: *Viola sonata, Op. 11/4;* SHOSTAKOVICH: *Viola sonata, Op. 147.* *(*)

Distinguished playing as you would expect from these artists who were recorded live in Germany in 1985. In forte passages, the recording is distinctly unappealing, close and airless.

(i) *6 Metamorphosen after Ovid;* (i; ii) *Phantasy quartet* (for oboe, violin, viola & cello), *Op. 2;* (i; iii) *2 Insect pieces; Temporal variations;* (iii) *Holiday diary, Op. 5; Night piece; 5 Waltzes.*
*** Hyperion Dig. CDA 66776 [id.]. (i) Sarah Francis; (ii) Delmé Qt (members); (iii) Michael Dussek.

Sarah Francis has long had a special association with Britten's oboe music, studying the *Ovid* pieces with the composer himself. She gives strong and distinctive characterizations not only to those six unaccompanied pieces but also to the early *Phantasy quartet* and to the pieces for oboe and piano as well. Michael Dussek proves a magnetic interpreter of the solo piano music, bringing out the sparkle of the boyhood waltzes (or 'Walztes' as the boy Britten called them) and the *Holiday diary*. He then finds intense poetry and magic in the *Night piece*, written for the first Leeds Piano Competition with deliberately awkward keyboard layout.

6 Metamorphoses after Ovid (for solo oboe), *Op. 49; Phantasy quartet* (for oboe and string trio), *Op. 2; 2 Insect pieces; Temporal variations* (both for oboe and piano).
(M) *** Carlton Classics Dig. 30366 00962 [id.]. Robin Canter, Medici Qt (members) or Simon Nicholls – FINZI: *Interlude*. ***

The oboist, Robin Canter, offers this complete collection of Britten's oboe music, using a ripe, sumptuous tone which in its warmth suggests the influence of Leon Goossens, whose playing inspired the first of the three early works here, the *Phantasy quartet*. It was one of the composer's first published pieces, dating from 1931 and belying the idea of a student work. The sharply inventive and varied *Temporal variations* of 1936 and the neatly pointed *Insect pieces* of 1935 were published only after the composer's death. The *Metamorphoses*, written for the 1951 Aldeburgh Festival in their brilliance and expressive range have proved favourites with oboe players, short of solo repertory. The Finzi piece makes an apt and attractive coupling, equally well recorded.

String quartets: in F (1928); *in D* (1931); *No. 2, Op. 36*.
(N) *** Chandos Dig. CHAN 9664 [id.]. Sorrel Qt.

It is a revelation to find Britten at fourteen strongly influenced by Beethoven. This première recording of the *F major* work of 1928, his first written under the tutelage of Frank Bridge, is strong and confident with hints of later Britten. The *D major Quartet* of 1931 was revised by the composer himself not long before he died, tonally equivocal, with hints of Bergian influence. Warmly performed, they make a fine coupling for the magnificent *Second Quartet*, here made to start waywardly, leading to a passionate, concentrated reading, helped by wide-ranging sound.

String quartets Nos. 1 in D, Op. 25; 2 in C, Op. 36; 3 Divertimenti.
(N) (BB) *** Naxos Dig. 8.553883 [id.]. Maggini Qt.

The Maggini give clean, direct performances of the first two numbered quartets, not as intense as some but fresh and thoughtful, well coupled with the three colourful *Divertimenti* of 1936. Clean, slightly distanced sound. This makes a formidable bargain as its competitors all involve more than one disc.

String quartet No. 3, Op. 94; Quartettino (1930); *Alla marcia* (1933); *Simple symphony*.
(N) (BB) *** Naxos Dig. 8.554360 [id.]. Maggini Qt.

The Maggini's second CD is even finer than their first. They give a strongly characterized reading of the *Third quartet*, Op. 94, with the ethereal serenity of the third movement 'Solo', matched by the concentration in the finale. The *Poco adagio* of the *Quartettino* is particularly searching, while the account of the *Simple symphony* (which opens the programme) is as sprightly and sparkling as you could wish, with the *Sarabande* intimate and touching. First-class recording. The almost Mahlerian *Alla marcia* is the musical source of the penultimate movement of the song-cycle, *Les illuminations*, written six years later. This pair of Naxos discs all but trumps the opposition.

String quartet No. 1 in D, Op. 25a.
(M) *** CRD CRD 3351 [id.]. Alberni Qt – SHOSTAKOVICH: *Piano quintet*. **(*)

String quartets Nos. 2 in C, Op. 36; 3, Op. 94.
(M) *** CRD CRD 3395 [id.]. Alberni Qt.

The Alberni Quartet have good ensemble and intonation, and they play with great feeling; moreover the CDs are available separately. The recording is vivid and clear.

String quartet No. 1 in D, Op. 25; String quartet in D (1931); Simple Symphony.
**(*) Collins Dig. 1115-2 [id.]. Britten Qt.

The Britten Quartet's warm and spacious treatment of Britten's quartet writing brings out the expressive imagination of the fully mature *Quartet No. 1* of 1940. Their similarly strong qualities in the early work of 1930 are very convincing, but lighter treatment would have brought out the Britten flavour more. Full-blooded, wide-ranging sound.

String quartet No. 2 in C.
*** Conifer Dig. 74321 15006-2. Brindisi Qt – BRIDGE: *3 Idylls;* Imogen HOLST: *String quartet No. 1*. ***

The Brindisi on Conifer give an excellent account of the *Second Quartet* which can hold its own with the best and comes with interesting, sensibly chosen couplings.

String quartets Nos. 2 in C, Op. 36; 3, Op. 94.
*** Collins Dig. 1025-2 [id.]. Britten Qt.

The Britten Quartet give exceptionally powerful readings of Britten's two best-known quartets, the magnificent No. 2 completed in 1945, with its rare example of Britten using sonata-form, and the very late No. 3 with its rarefied, elliptical thoughts. The brilliant young players treat both works with red-blooded intensity, concentratedly sustaining very broad speeds in slow movements, never letting you forget the emotion behind the writing.

String quartet No. 3, Op. 94.
❁ *** Koch Dig. 3-6436-2 [id.]. Medici Qt – JANACEK: *Quartet No. 1;* RAVEL: *Quartet;* SHOSTAKOVICH: *Quartet No. 8;* SMETANA: *Quartet No. 1.* *** ❁
*** ASV Dig. CDDCA 608 [id.]. Lindsay Qt – TIPPETT: *Quartet No. 4.* ***

The Medici Quartet, in inspired form, are totally involved in Britten's valedictory word, with its rarefied atmosphere and ethereal slow movement, where Paul Robertson's *Solo* creates a haunted atmosphere, at once austere and powerfully communicative. The *Burlesque* is splendidly robust and the long final *Passacaglia* is sustained with complete concentration. The recording, like the playing, gives the impression of live music-making.

The Lindsay performance also brings one of the most expansive and deeply expressive readings on record. The ASV recording is vivid, with fine presence; but extraneous sounds are intrusive at times: heavy breathing, snapping of strings on fingerboard, etc.

(i) *Suite for harp, Op. 83;* (ii) *2 Insect pieces, for oboe & piano; 6 Metamorphoses after Ovid (for oboe solo), Op. 49.*
*** Mer. CDE 84119 [id.]. (i) Osian Ellis; (ii) Sarah Watkins; Ledger – *Tit for Tat*, etc. ***.

It was for Osian Ellis that Britten wrote the *Harp suite*, and Ellis remains the ideal performer. Sarah Watkins gives biting and intense performances of the unaccompanied *Metamorphoses*, as well as the two early *Insect pieces*, with Philip Ledger. The sound is full and immediate, set convincingly in a small but helpful hall.

VOCAL MUSIC

Advance democracy; Antiphon; The ballad of Little Musgrave and Lady Barnard; Rejoice in the Lamb; Sacred and profane; The Sycamore tree; Te Deum; A Wedding anthem.
*** Collins Dig. 1343-2 [id.]. The Sixteen, Harry Christophers.

The two main works of this third of Christophers' Britten series represent two very different periods: the delightful cantata to words by Christopher Smart, *Rejoice in the Lamb*, dating from 1943, and *Sacred and profane*, setting medieval lyrics, his last work for unaccompanied voices. Among the rest are celebratory works like the *Te Deum* and the *Wedding anthem* for Lord Harewood and Marion Stein. Even the anthem, *Advance democracy*, written during Britten's actively left-wing phase before the war, transcends Randall Swingler's propagandist words in its musical imagination. Bright, clear singing from The Sixteen with their boyish-sounding sopranos.

Advance Democracy; (i) *A Boy was born, Op. 3; 5 Flower songs, Op. 47; Sacred and profane, Op. 91.*
(N) *** Chandos Dig. CHAN 9701 [id.]. Finzi Singers; (i) Lichfield Cathedral Choristers, Paul Spicer.

The little propaganda piece of 1938, *Advance Democracy*, with its adventurous choral writing, sets the seal on a wide-ranging group of works representing Britten: both early (the nativity cantata, *A Boy was born*, written at the age of 19) and late (*Sacred and profane*, dating from 1975, the year before Britten died, which poignantly sets death-obsessed medieval lyrics). The *Five Flower songs*, written in 1949 for the 25th wedding anniversary of friends, demonstrate Britten's gift of writing occasional music which transcends the occasion, pointful and elegant. Under Paul Spicer the Finzi Singers give virtuoso performances, vividly caught in the warm and atmospheric Chandos recording.

Cabaret songs (to words of W. H. Auden): *As it is, plenty; Calypso; Funeral blues; O tell me the truth about love; Johnny; When you're feeling like expressing your affection.* Blues: *Blues; Boogie-Woogie; The Clock on the wall; The Spider and the fly.*
*** Unicorn Dig. DKPCD 9138 [id.]. Jill Gomez, Martin Jones, Instrumental Ens. – PORTER: *Songs.* **(*)

Jill Gomez finds a winning compromise between art-song and cabaret proper. These are all fun-pieces, and as a bonus she includes the jazzy song, *As it is, plenty*, from the cycle *On this Island*. The accompanist, Martin Jones, is far less helpful and more deadpan in five classic Cole Porter songs which Jill Gomez also sings. To fill the disc, an instrumental ensemble plays Daryl Runswick's inventive arrangements of four blues numbers by Britten, drawn from the operetta *Paul Bunyan* as well as his early incidental music for plays.

A Boy was born; A Ceremony of carols; Rejoice in the Lamb.
**(*) Argo Dig. 433 215-2 [id.]. Masters, Barley, King's College, Cambridge, Ch., Stephen Cleobury.

Stephen Cleobury conducts refined, beautifully controlled readings of three works from early in Britten's career, all with the sound of boy-trebles as a source of inspiration. These performances, set against a reverberant acoustic, may lack the bite and earthiness of the readings Britten is known to have preferred (including those he himself conducted), but they still have plenty of energy and can be recommended to those who fancy this very apt coupling.

A Boy was born; Christ's nativity; Hymn to the Virgin; Jubilate in C; Shepherd's carol; Te Deum in C.
*** Hyperion Dig. CDA 66285 [id.]. Gritton, Wyn-Rogers, Holst Singers, St Paul's Cathedral Choristers, Steven Layton; David Goode (organ).

Here is a disc to illustrate Britten's special fascination with the Christmas story, including the first ever recording of the Christmas suite for chorus, *Christ's nativity*. It was written early in 1931 when Britten was a first-year student at the Royal College of Music; but it was not performed complete until 60 years later, well after his death. The writing has many bold and original touches typical of the mature composer, not least in the opening cries of *Awake!*. Steven Layton conducts a finely controlled performance, full of sharp dynamic and rhythmic contrasts. Despite speeds slower than usual, the performance of the cantata, *A Boy was born* of 1934 has similar merits, with the *Jubilate* and *Te Deum* made the more vigorous by the organ accompaniment of David Goode. Atmospheric, spacious choral sound.

A Boy was born; 5 Flower songs; Hymn to St Cecilia; Gloriana: Choral dances.
*** Collins Dig. 1286-2 [id.]. The Sixteen, Harry Christophers.

This first of Harry Christophers' Britten series for Collins sets the fine pattern for the following issues, starting with the early cantata, *A Boy was born*, and including the brilliant Auden setting, *Hymn to St Cecilia*, and the choral dances taken from the opera, *Gloriana*. Bright, fresh soprano tone, atmospherically recorded, puts these among the finest versions of these works; if this particular grouping is wanted, this is very recommendable.

A Boy was born, Op. 3; Festival Te Deum, Op. 32; Rejoice in the Lamb, Op. 30; A Wedding anthem, Op. 46.
*** Hyperion CDA 66126 [id.]. Corydon Singers, Westminster Cathedral Ch., Best; Trotter (organ).

All the works included here are sharply inspired. The refinement and tonal range of the choirs could hardly be more impressive, and the recording is refined and atmospheric to match.

5 Canticles.
(*) Hyperion Dig. CDA 66498 [id.]. Rolfe Johnson, Chance, Opie, Vignoles, Williams, Thompson – PURCELL, arr. BRITTEN: *An evening hymn; In the black dismal dungeon of despair; Let the dreadful engines* *.

Canticles Nos. 1, My beloved is mine, Op. 40; 2, Abraham and Isaac, Op. 51; 3, Still falls the rain, Op. 55; 4, Journey of the Magi, Op. 86; 5, Death of St Narcissus, Op. 89. A birthday hansel. Arr. of PURCELL: *Sweeter than roses.*
(M) *** Decca 425 716-2. Peter Pears, Hahessy, Bowman, Shirley-Quirk, Tuckwell, Ellis, composer.

This Decca CD brings together on a single record all five of the miniature cantatas to which Britten gave the title 'Canticle', plus the *Birthday hansel*, written in honour of the 75th birthday of Queen Elizabeth the Queen Mother, and a Purcell song-arrangement. A beautiful collection as well as a historical document, with recording that still sounds well.

Though even Vignoles cannot always match the magic of Britten himself as accompanist, and the original Decca recordings are even more characterful and intense than these, yet the newer Hyperion versions make an excellent alternative. Rolfe Johnson's tenor is sweeter even than Pears's, most of all in the fifth of the *Canticles*, *The Death of St Narcissus*, written with harp accompaniment at the very end of Britten's life. Like the fourth, *The journey of the Magi*, it sets a T. S. Eliot poem. The three Purcell realizations are shared among the soloists, one apiece, all representing Purcell at his most beautiful and intense.

A Ceremony of carols; Deus in adjutorium meum; Hymn of St Columba; Hymn to the Virgin; Jubilate Deo in E flat; Missa brevis, Op. 63.
*** Hyperion Dig. CDA 66220 [id.]. Westminster Cathedral Ch., David Hill; (i) with S. Williams; J. O'Donnell (organ).

Particularly impressive here is the boys' singing in the *Ceremony of carols*, where the ensemble is superb, the solo work amazingly mature, and the range of tonal colouring a delight. Along with the other, rarer pieces, this is an outstanding collection, beautifully and atmospherically recorded.

A Ceremony of carols; Festival Te Deum; Jubilate Deo!; A Hymn of Saint Columba; Hymn to Saint Peter; Hymn to the Virgin; Missa brevis in D; A New Year carol; A Shepherd's carol; Sweet was the sound.
*** Collins Dig. 1370-2 [id.]. The Sixteen, Harry Christophers.

With bright-toned sopranos taking the place of boy trebles, Harry Christophers in his Britten series for Collins directs superbly incisive, refreshingly dramatic performances of all these works, giving extra bite even to so well-known a piece as the *Ceremony of carols*. The delightful *Missa brevis*, written for the boys of Westminster Cathedral, has never been more telling, and the shorter pieces all confirm Britten's mastery in choral writing, with Christophers terracing the dynamic contrasts with fine precision. Excellent sound, both warm and well detailed. Highly recommended.

(i; ii) *Ceremony of carols, Op. 28;* (i; iii) *Friday afternoons, Op. 7; Francie; King Herod and the*

cock; The oxen; (i) *Sweet was the song;* (iv) Song: *The Birds;* (iv; v; iii) *3 2-part settings of Walter de la Mare: The Ride-by-nights; The Rainbow; The Ship of Rio. A Wealden trio.*
(BB) *** Naxos Dig. 8.553183 [id.]. (i) New L. Children's Ch., Ronald Corp; (ii) Skaila Kanga; (iii) Alexander Wells; (iv) Catherine Hopper; (v) Emily Attree; Anna Kenyon.

Ronald Corp directs bright, refreshing performances of a delightful collection of Britten choral pieces written for children's voices. The New London Children's Choir is relatively large and is recorded against a lively hall acoustic, but there is no lack of impact, and the tenderness of expression as well as the liveliness is consistently refreshing. Though the *Processional* is recorded statically, losing in atmosphere, the *Ceremony of carols* brings ensemble remarkably crisp for a biggish choir, and these performances justify the decision to have full ensemble treatment for all of the *Friday afternoons* sequence. A splendid bargain.

(i) *A Ceremony of carols, Op. 28; Hymn to St Cecilia, Op. 27;* (ii) *Jubilate Deo;* (i) *Missa brevis in D, Op. 63;* (ii) *Rejoice in the Lamb* (Festival cantata), *Op. 30; Te Deum in C.*
(M) *** EMI CDM7 64653-2. King's College, Cambridge, Ch.; (i) Osian Ellis, Willcocks; (ii) James Bowman, Ledger.

The King's trebles may have less edge in the *Ceremony of carols* than their Cambridge rivals at St John's College, and the *Missa brevis* can certainly benefit from a throatier sound, but the results here are dramatic as well as beautiful. To make a generous reissue EMI have added Philip Ledger's 1974 version of the cantata, *Rejoice in the Lamb*, with timpani and percussion added to the original organ part. Here the biting climaxes are sung with passionate incisiveness, while James Bowman is in his element in the delightful passage which tells you that 'the mouse is a creature of great personal valour'. The *Te Deum* setting and *Jubilate* make an additional bonus and are no less well sung and recorded.

(i) *A ceremony of carols;* (ii) *Shepherd's carol; A Boy was born; Jesus, as Thou art our Saviour.*
(M) *** ASV CDWHL 2097 [id.]. Christ Church Cathedral Ch., Francis Grier; (i) with Frances Kelly; (ii) Harry Bicket (with Collection: '*Carols from Christ Church*' ***).

A first-class account of Britten's *Ceremony of carols*, attractively vigorous, full of rhythmic energy. There is an earthy quality which reflects the composer's own rejection of over-refined choirboy tone, yet the two treble solos, the delicate *That yongë child* (Andrew Olleson) and *Balulalow* (Edward Harris), are both delicate, and the latter soloist is radiantly assured, as he is in *Jesus, as Thou art our Saviour*. The dialogue *Shepherd's carol* is also sung most effectively. The reissue is combined with a dozen other carols by various composers, mostly English, making for an enticing Christmas CD.

Orchestral song-cycles: (i) *4 Chansons françaises (1928);* (ii) *Our Hunting Fathers, Op. 8;* (i) *Les illuminations, Op. 18;* (iii) *Nocturne, Op. 60;* (iv) *Phaedra, Op. 93;* (iii;v) *Serenade for tenor, horn and strings, Op. 31.*
*** Collins Dig. 7037-2 (2) [id.]. (i) Felicity Lott; (ii) Phyllis Bryn-Julson; (iii) Philip Langridge; (iv) Ann Murray; (v) Frank Lloyd; ECO or (in *Nocturne*) N. Sinf., Steuart Bedford.

Steuart Bedford, successor to Britten himself as conductor in Aldeburgh performances, here offers fresh, clear readings of the five orchestral song-cycles, plus the scena, *Phaedra*, written in 1975 long after the rest. In that Ann Murray may not match the dedicatee, Janet Baker, but the dramatic bite is intense. Similarly in the anti-blood-sports cantata, *Our Hunting Fathers*, Phyllis Bryn-Julson is refreshingly fluent and agile. In the even earlier cycle, *Quatre chansons françaises*, Felicity Lott could be warmer, but she is masterly in the Baudelaire cycle, *Les illuminations*. Best of all, with Philip Langridge the characterful, heady-toned tenor, are the two most popular cycles, the *Serenade* (horn soloist Frank Lloyd) and the *Nocturne*. Bright, forward sound.

4 Chansons françaises; Les illuminations; Serenade for tenor, horn and strings.
(N) (M) **(*) Chandos Enchant CHAN 7112 [id.]. Felicity Lott, Anthony Rolfe-Johnson, Michael Thompson, SNO, Bryden Thomson.

The *Four French songs* were written when Britten was only 14. Felicity Lott gives a strong and sensitive performance, as she does of the other early French cycle on the disc, *Les illuminations*, bringing out the tough and biting element rather than the sensuousness. Anthony Rolfe Johnson, soloist in the *Serenade*, gives a finely controlled performance, but Michael Thompson is not as evocative in the horn solo as his most distinguished predecessors. Bryden Thomson draws crisp, responsive playing from the SNO.

(i) *Children's crusade;* (ii) *The Little Sweep (Let's make an opera);* (iii) *Gemini variations.*
(M) (***) Decca (IMS) stereo/mono 436 393-2. (i) Hartnett, Purcell Singers, English Op. Group Boys' Ch.; Choristers of All Saints', Margaret St, composer; (ii) Soloists, Wandsworth School Boys' Ch., Burgess; composer (piano); (iii) G. & Z. Jeney.

Britten's own mono recording of *The Little Sweep* sounds amazingly vivid, with voices full and immediate. As a performance it has never been surpassed in its vigour and freshness, with David Hemmings here impressive in the title-role for treble. Others in the cast, like Jennifer Vyvyan and

April Cantelo, represent the accomplished group of singers that Britten gathered for his Aldeburgh Festival performances. The choruses, usually sung by the audience, are here done by the school choir. The *Children's crusade*, written for the Save the Children Fund, is darker but equally vivid. The *Gemini variations* (interchanging flute, violin and piano) was written for the Jeney twins, who play it here.

Curlew River (1st parable for church performance).
*** Koch-Schwann 3-1397-2 [id.]. Milhofer, Hargreaves, Hughes-Jones, M. Evans, Guildhall Chamber Ens., David Angus.
(M) *** Decca 421 858-2. Pears, Shirley-Quirk, Blackburn, soloists, Instrumental Ens., composer and Viola Tunnard.
(N) **(*) Ph. Dig. 454 469-2. Philip Langridge, Thomas Allen, Simon Keenlyside, Gidon Saks, Charles Richardson, L. Voices, ASMF (members), Sir Neville Marriner.

Recorded at a single performance in St Giles', Cripplegate, in February 1993, directed by David Angus with students of the Guildhall School of Music, this superb Koch version of *Curlew River* is in many ways even more involving than the original recording of almost 30 years earlier. Britten's daringly original concept of transferring the story of a Japanese Noh play to a mystery play in a medieval monastery can seem cold and detached, but having fresh, firm voices makes the drama much more compelling, with a live performance, often at broader speeds, conveying dramatic tension hypnotically. In particular the predicament of the madwoman searching for her child becomes more touching when the voice is as young and clear as Mark Milhofer's. The on-stage voices are set at a distance but words are commendably clear, and the bite of the chorus and of the instrumental ensemble (notably horn and percussion) makes this a moving experience, with stage and audience noises at a minimum.

In Britten's own version, which has its own special character, Harold Blackburn plays the Abbot of the monastery who introduces the drama, while John Shirley-Quirk plays the ferryman who takes people over the Curlew River and Peter Pears sings the part of the madwoman who, distracted, searches fruitlessly for her abducted child. The recording is outstanding even by Decca standards.

With an outstanding cast and a sharply focused digital recording, Marriner conducts a fresh, clean-cut reading of the first of Britten's church parables. Philip Langridge gives a sensitive account of the central role of the Madwoman, but neither he nor the others can quite match the example of Britten's own original recording. When the 1960s analogue recording is more atmospheric than the new one, and Britten's direction is more intense, this new account cannot match the old in mystery or warmth, while Pears is unique in conveying the tender vulnerability of the Madwoman.

Folksong arrangements (complete): Volume 1: *British Isles; Unpublished folksongs;* Volume 2: *France;* Volume 3: *British Isles; Unpublished folksongs;* Volume 4: *Moore's Irish melodies;* Volume 5: *British Isles;* Volume 6: *England; Unpublished folksongs; 8 Folksong arrangements for high voice and harp; Miscellaneous published and unpublished folksongs; Orchestral arrangements.*
*** Collins Dig. 7039-2 (3). Felicity Lott, Philip Langridge, Thomas Allen, Carlos Bonell, Osian Ellis, Graham Johnson, Wenhaston Boys' Ch., BBC Singers, N. Sinf., Steuart Bedford.

This three-disc collection follows closely on Hyperion's two-disc set, including as important extras ten unpublished settings as well as 14 orchestral arrangements. With Philip Langridge, Felicity Lott and Thomas Allen more positively characterful than their opposite numbers, and with Graham Johnson grippingly imaginative at the piano, one appreciates far more here that Britten's folksongs were not simple settings but original art-songs. Among the extra ten *I wonder as I wander* (unaccompanied except for interstanza commentary on the piano) is specially moving, a song that Pears often performed with Britten but which was never included in the regular collections. Tantalizingly, no one has yet identified the words for one tenderly beautiful setting, superbly performed here on the cello by Christopher van Kampen.

Folksong arrangements: *The ash grove; Avenging and bright; La belle est au jardin d'amour; The bonny Earl o' Moray; The brisk young widow; Ca' the yowes; Come you not from Newcastle?; Early one morning; The foggy, foggy dew; How sweet the answer; The last rose of summer; The Lincolnshire poacher; The miller of Dee; The minstrel boy; Oft in the stilly night; O Waly, Waly; The plough boy; Le roi s'en va-t'en chasse; Sally in our alley; Sweet Polly Oliver; Tom Bowling.*
(M) *** Decca 430 063-2 [id.]. Peter Pears, Benjamin Britten.

It is good to have the definitive Pears/Britten collaboration in the folksong arrangements. Excellent, faithful recording, well transferred to CD.

(i) *The Golden Vanity;* (ii) *Noye's Fludde.*
(M) *** Decca 436 397-2. (i) Wandsworth School Boys' Ch., Burgess, composer (piano); (ii) Brannigan, Rex, Anthony, East Suffolk Children's Ch. & O, E. Op. Group O, Del Mar.

Britten originally wrote his 'vaudeville', *The*

Golden Vanity, for the Vienna Boys, who wanted a piece in which they would not have to take the roles of girls, and they give a performance at once superbly controlled and lusty. The Wandsworth boys are completely at home in the music and sing with pleasing freshness. The coupling was recorded during the 1961 Aldeburgh Festival, and not only the professional choristers but the children too have the time of their lives to the greater glory of God. All the effects have been captured miraculously here, most strikingly the entry into the Ark, while a bugle band blares out fanfares, with the stereo readily catching the sense of occasion and particularly the sound of *Eternal Father* rising above the storm at the climax of *Noye's Fludde*.

The Holy Sonnets of John Donne, Op. 35; Harmonia Sacra (realizations of Pelham HUMFREY): *Hymn to God the Father; Lord I have sinned* (realization of William CROFT): *A Hymn on Divine Musick. The Way to the Tomb* (incidental music for Ronald Duncan's masque): *Evening; Morning; Night*. W. H. Auden settings: *Fish in the unruffled lakes; Night covers up the rigid land; To lie flat on the back with the knees flexed*. Songs: *Birthday song for Erwin; Cradle song for Eleanor; If thou wilt ease thine heart; Not even summer yet; The Red cockatoo; Um Mitternacht. When you're feeling like expressing your affection; Wild with passion*.

✿ *** Hyperion Dig. CDA 66823 [id.]. Ian Bostridge, Graham Johnson.

In his first solo recital disc, Ian Bostridge makes one forget the example of Peter Pears in songs inspired and performed by him. In the Donne *Sonnet* cycle, written when the composer returned in deep shock after playing at the death camp of Belsen at the end of the war, Bostridge makes one concentrate afresh on Britten's powerful response to Donne's grittily uncompromising poems. His voice may be lighter than that of Pears on either of his two recordings (1949 and 1967), but in its lyrical beauty it can encompass a wider range of tone and dynamic. So in the opening sonnet one registers the anger of the words even more bitingly than with Pears, thanks also to the inspired accompaniment of Graham Johnson.

The disc also offers inspired performances of 18 of the Britten songs which earlier fell by the wayside. It is astonishing that Britten could allow such jewels to be forgotten: the four Auden settings here, which include a provocatively sexual one, a dreamily atmospheric setting of *Fish in the unruffled lakes*, and a jolly cabaret song. The evocative title given to this CD collection '*The Red Cockatoo*' refers to the shortest song of all, a striking setting of Arthur Waley.

The Holy Sonnets of John Donne, Op. 35; 7 Sonnets of Michelangelo, Op. 22; Winter words, Op. 52; The children and Sir Nameless; If it's ever spring again.

*** Collins Dig. 1468-2 [id.]. Philip Langridge, Steuart Bedford.

Following up his inspired portrayals in the principal tenor roles in the Britten operas – not least as Peter Grimes and as Aschenbach in *Death in Venice* – Philip Langridge here gives intense and dramatic performances of the three most important Britten song-cycles with piano, also originally written with Peter Pears in mind. With Steuart Bedford, Britten's long-time collaborator, as accompanist, this reading of the Donne sonnet-cycle is marked by high contrasts of dynamic and tone, so that one hears echoes of Grimes's music. In the other two cycles Langridge is just as expressive but is generally lighter in manner. Valuably, Langridge adds two more Hardy settings, originally intended for *Winter words* but which neither fit the main pattern nor quite match the rest in imagination. Well-balanced sound.

(i) *Les Illuminations* (song-cycle), *Op. 18;* (ii) *Nocturne;* (iii) *Serenade for tenor, horn and strings, Op. 31.*

(M) *** Decca 436 395-2 [417 153-2]. (i–iii) Peter Pears; (i) ECO; (ii) wind soloists; (ii; iii) LSO strings, composer; (iii) with Barry Tuckwell.

(B) *** EMI Dig. CD-EMX 2247 [(M) CDM 65899]. John Mark Ainsley, David Pyatt, Britten Sinfonia, Cleobury.

(N) (BB) ** Naxos Dig. 8.553834 [id.]. Adrian Thompson, Michael Thompson, Bournemouth Sinf., David Lloyd-Jones.

With dedicated accompaniments under the composer's direction, these classic Pears versions of *Les Illuminations* and the *Serenade* (with its horn obbligato superbly played by Barry Tuckwell) make a perfect coupling, with the *Nocturne* from 1960 making an ideal addition on CD. It is a work full of memorable moments. Each song has a different obbligato instrument (with the ensemble unified for the final Shakespeare song) and each instrument gives the song it is associated with its own individual character. Pears, as always, is the ideal interpreter, the composer a most efficient conductor, and the fiendishly difficult obbligato parts are played superbly. The recording is brilliant and clear, with just the right degree of atmosphere althoug the transfer of *Les Illuminations* is brighter than the other two works.

This ideal coupling of Britten's three great orchestral song-cycles finds Ainsley echoing the example of the inspirer, Peter Pears, in the shading and moulding of each phrase, above all in the *Serenade*, where the brilliant horn-playing of David Pyatt provides an extra reason for recommending the disc. Ainsley's range of expression is wide and under pressure the voice grows a little rough, as in the final Shakespeare setting of the *Nocturne*. But that is contrasted with an exceptionally beautiful use of the head-voice, with total freedom in the upper register, as in the *Lyke-Wake dirge* from the *Serenade*. Warm, immediate recording.

This same coupling is welcome at super-bargain price, and David Lloyd-Jones draws vivid and responsive playing from the Bournemouth Sinfonietta, with Michael Thompson an outstanding horn soloist. Adrian Thompson is a sensitive and characterful singer who understands the idiom, unafraid of high tessitura, but the microphone brings out the heavy vibrato in the voice, often as a disagreeable wobble.

Nocturne, Op. 60; Now sleeps the crimson petal; Serenade, Op. 31 (both for tenor, horn & strings).
*** BIS Dig. CD 540 [id.]. Prégardien, Lanzky-Otto, Tapiola Sinf., Vänskä – *Sinfonietta*. ***

Drawing brilliant, expressive and purposeful playing from the Tapiola Sinfonietta, the players totally at home in this music, Osmo Vänskä brings together not only the two best-loved orchestral song-cycles but also the supplementary Tennyson setting intended for the *Serenade* and the elusive work, the *Sinfonietta*, which Britten honoured as his Opus 1. Christoph Prégardien has an ideally light and sweet tenor which, even in the high tessitura of the *Lyke-Wake dirge* from the *Serenade*, shows no strain whatever. Though one detects that he is not English, that is a tribute to his articulation, and he is totally in tune with the idiom. Excellent, spacious sound, if with the tenor soloist slightly backward.

(i) *Noye's Fludde, Op. 59. A Ceremony of carols, Op. 28.*
(N) *** Somm Dig. SOMMCD 212 [id.]. (i) Catherine Wyn-Rogers, Benjamin Luxon, David Wilson-Johnson; Finchley Children's Music Group, Nicholas Wilks.

Recordings of *Noye's Fludde* are surprisingly rare and this one – recorded to celebrate the 40th anniversary of the Finchley Children's Music Group – is delightfully fresh and energetic, capturing the atmosphere of a live performance very well, with its processions of birds and animals and the off-stage Voice of God. With Benjamin Luxon providing a sonorous Voice of God, David Wilson-Johnson a characterful Noye and Catherine Wyn-Rogers a fruity Mrs Noye, all the other roles are performed sharply and incisively by members of the group. *A Ceremony of carols*, given with comparable freshness and confidence, makes an ideal coupling, also well recorded.

(i) *Noye's Fludde;* (ii) *Serenade for tenor, horn & strings, Op. 31.*
(M) **(*) Virgin/EMI Dig. CUV5 61122-2. (i) Maxwell, Ormiston, Pasco, Salisbury & Chester Schools Ch. & O, Coull Qt, Alley, Watson, Harwood, Endymion Ens. (members); (ii) Martyn Hill, Frank Lloyd, City of L. Sinfonia, Hickox.

On the Virgin disc the instrumental forces, including a schools' orchestra as well as professional soloists, are relatively recessed. In the storm sequence the distancing undermines any feeling of threat so that the entry of the hymn, *Eternal Father*, instantly submerges the orchestral sound, instead of battling against it. Not even Donald Maxwell as Noah, strong and virile, can efface memories of Owen Brannigan on Britten's own version.

The Prodigal Son (3rd parable), Op. 81.
(M) *** Decca 425 713-2. Pears, Tear, Shirley-Quirk, Drake, E. Op. Group Ch. & O, composer and Viola Tunnard.

The last of the parables is the sunniest and most heart-warming. Britten cleverly avoids the charge of oversweetness by introducing the Abbot, even before the play starts, in the role of Tempter, confessing he represents evil and aims to destroy contentment in the family he describes: 'See how I break it up' – a marvellous line for Peter Pears. An ideal performance is given here with a characteristically real and atmospheric Decca recording.

Purcell realizations: *Orpheus Britannicus: The Knotting song; 7 Songs* (1947); *6 Songs* (1948); *O Solitude; 5 Songs* (1960); *Celemene; 6 Duets* (1961). *Harmonia Sacra: The Blessed Virgin's expostulation; The Queen's Epicedium; Saul and the Witch of Endor; 3 Divine hymns* (1947); *2 Divine hymns & Alleluia* (1960). Miscellaneous songs (1971): *Dulcibella; When Myra sings.*
*** Hyperion Dig. CDA 67061/2 [id.]. Lott, Gritton, S. Walker, Bowman, Ainsley, Bostridge, Rolfe Johnson, Jackson, Keenlyside; Johnson.

As a result of giving recitals with Peter Pears during and after the war, Britten was encouraged to make a series of realizations using the figured basses Purcell provided in his big collections, *Orpheus Britannicus* and *Harmonia Sacra*. Most of the arrangements date from the immediate post-war period, but Britten made more in about 1960 and again towards the very end of his life in 1971. The accompaniments for piano may defy latterday ideas of authenticity but Britten imaginatively follows the harmonic indications given, to produce entirely distinctive results, introducing a lyricism rare in keyboard continuo. With an outstanding team of soloists and with Graham Johnson as the inspired pianist, this collection stands as a monument to the devotion of one English master to another. The first disc, drawn from the *Orpheus Britannicus* collection, includes songs like *Fairest isle*, better known in the context of *King Arthur* or other entertainments. The second, from *Harmonia Sacra*, has darker, weightier and more extended items, notably the magnificent scena, *Saul and the Witch of Endor*, involving three singers and with side-slipping chromatics as daring as any Purcell ever imagined. The tenor Ian Bostridge confirms the high mastery he also displays in the *Red Cockatoo* collection of Britten songs, and Simon Keenlyside sings magnificently in the dark, bass items like *Job's curse* and the late *Let the dreadful engines*. Excellent, well-balanced sound.

St Nicholas; Hymn to St Cecilia.
*** Hyperion Dig. CDA 66333 [id.]. Rolfe Johnson, Corydon Singers, St George's Chapel, Windsor, Ch., Girls of Warwick University Chamber Ch., Ch. of Christ Church, Southgate, Sevenoaks School, Tonbridge School, Penshurst Ch. Soc., Occasional Ch., Edwards, Alley, Scott, ECO, Best.

For the first time in a recording, the congregational hymns are included in Matthew Best's fresh and atmospheric account of *St Nicholas*, adding greatly to the emotional impact of the whole cantata. Though the chorus is distanced slightly, the contrasts of timbre are caught well, with the waltz-setting of *The birth of Nicholas* and its bath-tub sequence delightfully sung by boy-trebles alone. The *Hymn to St Cecilia* is also beautifully sung, with gentle pointing of the jazzy syncopations in crisp, agile ensemble and with sweet matching among the voices.

(i) *St Nicholas, Op. 42;* (ii) *Rejoice in the Lamb, Op. 30.*
(M) (***) Decca mono 425 714-2. (i) Hemmings, Pears, St John Leman School, Beccles, Girls' Ch., Ipswich School Boys' Ch., Aldeburgh Festival Ch. & O; R. Downes; (ii) Hartnett, Steele, Todd, Francke, Purcell Singers, G. Malcolm; composer.

With rare exceptions, Britten's first recordings of his own works have a freshness and vigour unsurpassed since. Britten's performances capture the element of vulnerability, not least in the touching setting of words by the deranged poet, Christopher Smart, *Rejoice in the Lamb*.

Serenade for tenor, horn and strings.
(B) *** DG 439 464-2. Robert Tear, Dale Clevenger, Chicago SO, Giulini – DELIUS: *On hearing the first cuckoo; Summer night on the river*; VAUGHAN WILLIAMS: *Greensleeves; Lark ascending*. ***
(N) **(*) EMI Dig. CDC5 56183-2 [id.]. Ian Bostridge, Neunecker, Bamberg SO, Metzmacher – R. STRAUSS: *Horn concertos Nos 1 & 2*. **(*)

Robert Tear's 1977 interpretation of the *Serenade* is very much in the Aldeburgh tradition set by Pears, and Giulini has long been a persuasive advocate of Britten's music. He presents the cycle as a full-scale orchestral work and Tear is at his finest, more open than in his earlier, EMI recording. Dale Clevenger is a superb horn player. It is good to have a fresh view of the music, especially when inexpensively coupled with fine performances of music by Delius and Vaughan Williams.

Ian Bostridge gives an intensely characterful reading of the *Serenade*, providing many new insights, but it seems a pity that EMI had to record this most popular of Britten's song-cycles with its young star tenor as part of a disc centred on the horn-player. The recording reflects that, with the horn occasionally masking the singer, and with Bostridge at his most persuasive in the one song without horn, the final sonnet. The orchestra sounds rather thin behind.

(i) *Serenade for tenor, horn and strings, Op. 31;* (ii) *7 Sonnets of Michelangelo, Op. 22; Winter words, Op. 52.*
(M) (***) Decca mono 425 996-2. Peter Pears, (i) Dennis Brain, Boyd Neel String O, composer; (ii) composer (piano).

This compilation brings together some of Britten's historic early recordings for Decca. This first recording of the *Serenade*, though not helped by unatmospheric sound, is wonderfully intense, with Dennis Brain uniquely magnetic on the horn. The first recording of the Hardy song-cycle, *Winter words*, has never been matched by more recent recordings, an evocative performance with Britten drawing magical sounds from the piano in support of Pears. This version of the *Michelangelo sonnets* is not quite as fresh-toned as the even earlier EMI one, but it still offers a searching performance. Limited but clear mono sound.

Songs and proverbs of William Blake, Op. 74; Tit for Tat; 3 Early songs: Beware that I'd ne'er been married; Epitaph; The clerk. Folksong arrangements: Bonny at morn; I was lonely; Lemady; Lord! I married me a wife!; O Waly, Waly; The Salley Gardens; She's like the swallow; Sweet Polly Oliver.
**(*) Chandos Dig. CHAN 8514 [id.]. Benjamin Luxon, David Williamson.

Benjamin Luxon's lusty baritone gives an abrasive edge whether to early songs, folksong settings or the Blake cycle. Only rarely does he become too emphatic. Excellent, sensitive accompaniment and first-rate recording.

(i) *Songs from the Chinese, Op. 58;* Folksong arrangements: *I will give my love an apple; Master Kilby; Sailor boy; The shooting of his dear; The soldier and the sailor. Gloriana: Second lute song of the Earl of Essex. Nocturnal* (for solo guitar), *Op. 70.*

(M) *** RCA 09026 61601-2 [id.]. Julian Bream (guitar); (i) Peter Pears (with FRICKER: *O Mistress mine*) – SEIBER: *French folksongs*; WALTON: *Anon in love*. ***

Nearly all the music on this record was written with Julian Bream in mind, and the *Nocturnal*, based on a tune by Dowland, was dedicated to him. Characteristically Britten exploits every nuance of expression that Bream's virtuosity makes possible. The haunting lute song from *Gloriana* by contrast brings an Elizabethan feeling. The *Songs from the Chinese* are based on Arthur Waley's translations of Chinese poetry. Of the folksong arrangements, it is *I will give my love an apple* where Pears's tender vocal-line is particularly memorable, while the closing *Soldier and the sailor* brings a witty pay-off. Peter Racine Fricker's soaring setting of *O Mistress mine* seems tailor-made for Pears, his voice at its freshest throughout. With Seiber and Walton couplings equally rewarding, this (Volume 18) is outstanding among the reissues in the Julian Bream Edition where he is joined by other artists.

Spring Symphony, Op. 44.
(M) **(*) Revelation RV 10010 [id.]. Yakovenko, Postavnicheva, Mahov, Ch. & Grand USSR State SO, Rozhdestvensky (with WALTON: *Viola concerto* *).

Rozhdestvensky's Russian version of the *Spring Symphony* comes from the long-hidden archives of Moscow Radio, and it is fascinating to hear the work in Russian in a live recording made in 1963, not long after the composer's own version, for this is an invigoratingly fresh, high-voltage performance. Soloists and choirs are presented in sharp focus with no Slavonic wobbles. The boys' choir is wonderfully earthy but, sadly, is drowned by the horns in the final *Sumer is icumen in*. Though the Walton concerto suffers badly from having the viola far too close, it makes an interesting coupling, with a superstar viola player, Yuri Bashmet.

(i) *Spring symphony, Op. 44;* (ii) *Cantata academica;* (iii) *Hymn to St Cecilia*.
(M) *** Decca 436 396-2. (i; ii) Vyvyan, Pears; (i) Procter, Emanuel School, Wandsworth, Boys' Ch., ROHCG O, composer; (ii) Watts, Brannigan; (ii; iii) L. Symphony Ch.; (ii) LSO; (ii; iii) Malcolm.

(i; ii) *Spring Symphony, Op. 44;* (ii) *5 Flower songs* (for mixed chorus), *Op. 47;* (ii; iii) *Hymn to St Cecilia, Op. 27*.
*** DG Dig. 453 433-2 [id.]. (i) Alison Hagley, Catherine Robbin, John Mark Ainsley, Boy and Girl Choristers of Salisbury Cathedral, Philh. O; (ii) Monteverdi Ch.; (iii) with Preston-Dunlop, Ross, Vickers, Mitchell, Savage; Philh. O, Gardiner.

(i) *Spring symphony, Op. 44; Peter Grimes: 4 Sea interludes*.
(M) *** EMI CDM7 64736-2. (i) Armstrong, J. Baker, Tear, St Clement Dane's School Boys' Ch., L. Symphony Ch.; LSO, Previn.

(i) *Spring Symphony, Op. 44;* (ii) *Welcome ode, Op. 95;* (iii) *Psalm 150, Op. 67*.
**(*) Chandos Dig. CHAN 8855 [id.]. (i) Gale, Hodgson, Hill, Southend Boys' Ch., LSO; (ii) City of London Schools' Ch., LSO; (iii) City of London Schools' Ch. and O; Hickox.

It is the freshness of Britten's imagination in dozens of moments that makes this work as memorable as it is joyous. Thanks to the Decca engineers, one hears more than is usually possible in a live performance. Jennifer Vyvyan and Peter Pears are both outstanding, and Britten shows that no conductor is more vital in his music than he himself. The Decca reissue couples the work to the *Cantata academica*, with its deft use of a 12-note row, written for Basel, and the *Hymn to St Cecilia*, an ambitious piece written just before the war, when Britten's technique was already prodigious. The setting exactly matches the imaginative, capricious words of Auden. Performances are first class and so is the CD transfer.

In his version of the *Spring Symphony* John Eliot Gardiner provides a striking contrast with Britten himself. Never before on disc has there been a performance of this colourful anthology-work that so clarifies the complex textures at speeds generally flowing more briskly than usual. With Gardiner's Monteverdi Choir achieving wonders of precision both in ensemble and in shading of dynamic, this reading is more refined than those on rival discs, including Britten's. Gardiner draws equally refined playing from the Philharmonia, to make one appreciate afresh how often Britten marked pianissimos in the score; though the result is less wild and rustic-sounding in the bluff final chorus, the sharpness of focus makes it intensely refreshing. The soloists equally are fresh-toned, while the two fill-ups also demonstrate the Monteverdi Choir's astonishing virtuosity, with the syncopated rhythms of another Auden setting, the *Hymn to St Cecilia*, superbly sprung, and with the rare *Flower Songs* just as fresh.

Like Britten, Previn makes this above all a work of exultation, a genuine celebration of spring; but here, more than in Britten's recording, the kernel of what the work has to say comes out in the longest of the solo settings, using W. H. Auden's poem *Out on the lawn I lie in bed*. With Dame Janet Baker as soloist it rises above the lazily atmospheric mood of the opening to evoke the threat of war and darkness. The *Four Sea interludes*, which make a generous bonus, are presented in their concert form, with tailored endings. Previn springs the bouncing rhythms of the second interlude – the picture of Sunday morning in the Borough – even more infectiously than the composer himself in his complete recording of the opera.

With more variable soloists – the tenor Martyn Hill outstandingly fine, the soprano Elizabeth Gale often too edgy – Hickox's version of the *Spring Symphony* does not quite match the composer's own in gutsy urgency. But this CD brings the advantage of a first recording of Britten's last completed work, the *Welcome ode*. The third work, equally apt, is the boisterous setting of *Psalm 150*.

(i) *Tit for Tat;* (ii) Folksong arrangements: *Bird scarer's song; Bonny at morn; David of the White Rock; Lemady; Lord! I married me a wife!; She's like the swallow.*
*** Mer. CDE 84119 [id.]. Shirley-Quirk; (i) Ledger; (ii) Ellis – *Suite for harp*, etc. ***

John Shirley-Quirk was the baritone who first sang the cycle, *Tit for Tat*, with the composer at the piano, and he is still unrivalled in the sharp yet subtle way he brings out the irony in these boyhood settings of De la Mare poems. It is also good to have him singing the six late folk-settings with harp accompaniment, here played by Osian Ellis for whom (with Peter Pears) they were originally written.

War Requiem, Op. 66.
(N) *** Decca 414 383-2 [id.]. Vishnevskaya, Pears, Fischer-Dieskau, Bach Ch., London Symphony Ch., Highgate School Ch., Melos Ens., LSO, composer.
*** EMI Dig. CDS7 47034-8. Söderström, Tear, Allen, Trebles of Christ Church Cathedral Ch., Oxford, CBSO Ch., CBSO, Rattle.
**(*) DG Dig. 437 801-2 (2) [id.]. Orgonasova, Rolfe Johnson, Skovhus, Monteverdi Ch., Tölz Boys' Ch., N. German R. Ch. & SO, Gardiner.
(BB) ** Naxos Dig. 8.553558/9 [id.]. Russell, Randle, Volle, Scottish Festival Ch., St Mary's Episcopal Cathedral, Edinburgh, Ch., BBC Scottish SO, Brabbins (with Boddice).
(N) ** Teldec/Warner Dig. 0630-17115-2 [id.]. Vaness, Hadley, Hampson, American Boychoir, Westminster Symphonic Ch., NY Philh. Ch., Kurt Masur.

(i) *War Requiem;* (ii) *Ballad of heroes, Op. 14; Sinfonia da requiem, Op. 20.*
*** Chandos Dig. CHAN 8983/4 [id.]. (i) Harper, Langridge, Shirley-Quirk, (ii) Hill; St Paul's Cathedral Choristers, London Symphony Ch., LSO & CO, Richard Hickox.

Richard Hickox's Chandos version rivals even the composer's own definitive account in its passion and perception. Hickox thrusts home the big dramatic moments with unrivalled force, helped by the weight of the Chandos sound. The boys' chorus from St Paul's Cathedral is exceptionally fresh. Heather Harper is as golden-toned as she was at the very first Coventry performance, fearless in attack. Philip Langridge has never sung more sensitively on disc, and both he and John Shirley-Quirk bring many subtleties to their interpretations. Adding to the attractions of the set come two substantial choral works, also in outstanding performances.

Britten's own 1963 recording of the *War Requiem* comes near to the ideal, with the three soloists, British, German and Russian, for whom he wrote it. Though Vishnevskaya is abrasive in the soprano solos, she sings with incomparable emotional intensity. The 1963 recording has now been carefully and lovingly remastered under the supervision of the distinguished Decca sound engineer, Jimmy Lock, with the Cedar process used to absorb some but not all of the background hiss. It also now includes a rehearsal sequence The vivid realism of the sound balance (originally achieved by Kenneth Wilkinson – 'Wilkie' to Britten) now comes over the more strikingly, with uncannily precise placing and balancing of the many different voices and instruments, and John Culshaw's contribution as producer is the more apparent. A remarkable achievement.

With Elisabeth Söderström a more warmly expressive soloist than the oracular Vishnevskaya, the human emotions behind the Latin text come out strongly. If Tear does not always match the subtlety of Pears on the original recording, Allen sounds more idiomatic than Fischer-Dieskau. Rattle's approach is warm, dedicated and dramatic, with fine choral singing (not least from the Christ Church Cathedral trebles). The various layers of sound are well managed on the digital recording, if not quite with the definition of the finest rivals.

Recorded live in Lübeck by the North German Radio Orchestra and Choir under their chief conductor, John Eliot Gardiner, this is a thoughtful rather than a dramatic reading. It is intense and compelling, but it is seriously undermined by dim, inconsistent recording, with soloists and chorus often ill-focused. Richard Hickox's Chandos version is warmer and more powerful as an interpretation, as well as far better recorded.

What works far better than Gardiner's CD is the video version of the same performance (LaserDisc 072 198-1; VHS 072 198-3), set in the beautiful Marienkirche in Lübeck. With the singers in close-up, the ear tends to ignore bad balances to have one appreciating the firm Slavonic tang of Luba Orgonasova, the intimate intensity of Anthony Rolfe Johnson and the youthful ardour of the baritone, Boje Skovhus. Another advantage is that on a single VHS cassette there is no break in the middle.

The glory of the Naxos version, on two bargain discs, is the sound, with spatial contrasts caught thrillingly and atmospherically, thanks to the recording venue. Surprisingly, Naxos chose the former engine-shed of the Harland & Wolff shipyard, now converted into a media centre. With the benefit of a cathedral-like acoustic, it was able to cope with very large forces better than any available church, and the boys' choir in particular is beautifully caught, clear but at a distance. The choral singing generally is excellent, vivid and immediate in the big climaxes of such sections as *Dies irae*. Under Martyn Brabbins for the full orchestral sections, and under Nigel Boddice for the chamber orchestra settings of Wilfred Owen poems, the BBC Scottish Symphony Orchestra plays with fine point and precision, underlining the drama of the piece. The weakness is the solo singing with Thomas Randle sounding strained and Michael Volle unidiomatic, with Lynda Russell's fruity soprano too often edgy and uneven.

It is always revealing to have non-British performances of British music, and Kurt Masur directs a thoughtful, dedicated reading of the *War Requiem* with three first-rate American soloists. The virtuoso chamber group accompanying the Owen poems is made up of excellent players from the New York Philharmonic, and the choirs cannot be faulted, with the off-stage boys precisely placed. That said, this does not have the dramatic intensity of the finest versions, and the soloists are not helped by a relatively dry acoustic. With no fill-up it makes an expensive buy.

Winter words (song-cycle), *Op. 52*.
(BB) *** ASV CDQS 6172 [id.]. Ian Partridge, Jennifer Partridge – PURCELL: '*Sweeter than Roses*' (songs). ***

Ian Partridge with his heady, fresh tenor gives keenly sensitive performances of atmospheric Hardy settings dating from 1953. He is admirably supported by sister Jennifer, who makes the very most of the imaginative piano-writing, whether in simulating railway noises in *Midnight on the Great Western*, or the creaks of *The little old table*. Excellent late-1970s recording. A worthy coupling for a warmly sympathetic collection of favourite Purcell songs.

OPERA

Albert Herring (complete).
*** Collins Dig. 7042-2 (3) [id.]. Gillett, Barstow, Palmer, Della Jones, Taylor, Finley, Lloyd, Savidge, N. Sinfonia, Bedford.
**(*) Decca 421 849-2 (2) [id.]. Pears, Fisher, Noble, Brannigan, Cantelo, ECO, Ward, composer.

Britten's own 33-year-old Decca recording of the comic opera, *Albert Herring*, has long seemed as definitive as could be, but here Steuart Bedford – whom Britten chose to follow him in conducting operas at Aldeburgh – presents a brilliant recording, fuller and more immediate than the still vivid Decca original, which offers a performance that brings out the fun of the piece even more infectiously than Britten himself. It consistently gives the illusion of a stage comedy rather than a studio recording. Bedford has long made a speciality of conducting this opera in the theatre, a very English piece which yet amazingly has been among the most widely appreciated of Britten operas throughout the world. It helps that Christopher Gillett in the title-role has a clear, youthful-sounding tenor, whereas Pears, recording in his mid-fifties, 17 years after the first performance, inevitably sounds old as the gawky hero, however inspired his vocal acting. As Lady Billows, Josephine Barstow, with rasp in the voice, is every bit as formidable as Sylvia Fisher was before, and Felicity Palmer is wonderfully characterful as her prim housekeeper, Florence Pike. The other village worthies are also strongly cast, while the lower orders in this class-conscious story, Albert's Mum (Della Jones), Sid the butcher's boy (Gerald Finley) and Nancy (Ann Taylor), are earthier and lustier than their predecessors, with Sid and Nancy's love duets tenderly touched in. What seals the set's success is the way that in the ensembles – whether the fast chattering ones or the great Threnody when they think that Albert is dead – Bedford secures such crispness, wittily lifting rhythms, making the music swagger.

Britten's own 1964 recording of the comic opera, *Albert Herring*, remains a delight. Peter Pears's portrait of the innocent Albert was caught only just before he grew too old for the role, but it is full of unique touches. Sylvia Fisher is a magnificent Lady Billows, and it is good to have so wide a range of British singers of the 1960s so characterfully presented. The recording, made in Jubilee Hall, remains astonishingly vivid.

Billy Budd (original four-act version; complete).
(N) *** Erato/Warner Dig. 3984 21631-2 (2) [id.]. Thomas Hampson, Anthony Rolfe Johnson, Eric Halfvarson, Manchester Boys' Ch., Hallé Ch. & O, Kent Nagano.
(**) VAIA mono 1034-3 (3) [id.]. Pears, Uppman, Dalberg, Alan, G. Evans, Langdon, ROHCG Ch. & O, Britten.

Here at last we have a complete recording of Britten's original four-act version of his opera, *Billy Budd*, and very fine it is. This live recording made at Bridgewater Hall in Manchester in excellent open sound, is above all urgent and intense, more dramatic, less reflective than Britten's own recording for Decca of the revised two-act version (see below). Not only that, Thomas Hampson brings to the title role an extra beauty alongside heroic power.

On disc there is much to be said for the four-act version rather than the revision. It includes the important assembly scene on the deck of HMS *Indomitable* – removed in the revision – when the crew greet Captain Starry Vere, establishing his character. It also provides a thrilling fortissimo close to the original Act I, superbly achieved in Kent

Nagano's powerful performance with the Hallé Orchestra and Choir. Set against the velvet-toned Hampson, Anthony Rolfe Johnson as Vere has some grit in his voice, creating a believable character at once rugged and introspective. Eric Halfvarson as the evil Claggart is not as sinister as some of his predecessors, but apart from some roughness in the upper register it is a forceful, incisive performance, matching the urgency of Nagano's approach. Among the others Gidon Saks is superb as the Sailing Master, Mr Flint; Martyn Hill is most characterful as the whining Red Whiskers, and the veteran, Richard Van Allan, is ideally cast as old Dansker, with Andrew Burden clear-toned as the victimized Novice. Though Chandos promises a new recording of the two-act version conducted by Richard Hickox, this one, coming on two discs instead of three, has a clear advantage over existing sets.

Though the sound is very scrubby, disconcertingly so at the very start, the historic recording of the very first performance of the opera in December 1951 is doubly valuable: not only does it let us hear the fresh, youthful-sounding performance of Theodor Uppman in the title-role, as well as Peter Pears as Captain Vere, clearer and more flexible than in his studio recording of 16 years later; it also presents the original, four-Act text, with its substantial muster scene at the end of the original Act I, later cut. Other passages were also elided. Philip Reed provides a brief but informative comment on the text and the recording, but there is no libretto. It is interesting that, though the orchestra sounds dim and limp at the start, Britten as conductor whips up searing tension through the opera.

Billy Budd (revised version: complete).
*** Decca 417 428-2 (3) [id.]. Glossop, Pears, Langdon, Shirley-Quirk, Wandsworth School Boys' Ch., Amb. Op. Ch., LSO, composer (with *Holy Sonnets of John Donne; Songs and Proverbs of William Blake* ***).

Britten himself has an outstanding cast, with Glossop a bluff, heroic Billy, and Langdon a sharply dark-toned Claggart, making these symbol-figures believable. Magnificent sound, and the many richly imaginative strokes – atmospheric as well as dramatic – are superbly managed. The extravagant layout on three CDs begins with the *John Donne Holy Sonnets* (sung by Pears) and the *Songs and Proverbs of William Blake* (sung by Fischer-Dieskau), with the Prologue and Act I of the opera beginning thereafter. They are equally ideal performances.

Death in Venice (complete).
*** Decca 425 669-2 (2). Pears, Shirley-Quirk, Bowman, Bowen, Leeming, E. Op. Group Ch., ECO, Bedford.

Thomas Mann's novella, which made an expansively atmospheric film, far removed from the world of Mann, here makes a surprisingly successful opera. Pears's searching performance in the central role of Aschenbach is set against the darkly sardonic singing of John Shirley-Quirk in a sequence of roles as the Dionysiac figure who draws Aschenbach to his destruction and, though Steuart Bedford's assured conducting lacks some of the punch that Britten would have brought, the whole presentation makes this a set to establish the work outside the opera house.

Gloriana (complete).
*** Decca Dig. 440 213-2 (2). Josephine Barstow, Philip Langridge, Della Jones, Jonathan Summers, WNO Ch. & O, Mackerras.

Gloriana is a portrait of a lonely monarch forced to do her duty and condemn to the scaffold a man, the Earl of Essex, whom she loved more than anyone, but who had rebelled against her. Without effacing memories of earlier interpreters, Josephine Barstow gives a splendid performance as the Virgin Queen, tough and incisive, with the slight unevenness in the voice adding to the abrasiveness. Only in the final scene when, after the execution of Essex, the queen muses to herself in fragments of spoken monologue does her reading lack weight, but, just before that, the final confrontation between Elizabeth and Essex brings a thrilling climax, when Elizabeth attacks her lover not for infidelity but for treason.

Philip Langridge's portrait of Essex is just as striking, consistently bringing out the character's arrogant bravado. Though Langridge's voice is mellifluous and flexible in the lute songs, its bright, cutting quality helps to enhance that characterization. The rest of the cast is equally starry, with Alan Opie as the queen's principal adviser, Sir Robert Cecil, balefully dark rather than sinister, with the warm-toned Della Jones as Essex's wife and the abrasive Yvonne Kenny as his sister, Lady Penelope Rich, equally well cast. Sir Charles Mackerras directs his Welsh National Opera forces in a performance that brings out the full splendour of this rich score. The Decca recording is comparably splendid, a crowning achievement in the complete cycle of Britten operas begun by the composer himself.

Gloriana: Choral dances.
*** Hyperion CDA 66175 [id.]. Martyn Hill, Thelma Owen, Holst Singers & O, Hilary Davan Wetton – BLISS: *Lie strewn the white flocks;* HOLST: *Choral hymns from the Rig Veda.* ***

The composer's own choral suite, made up of unaccompanied choral dances linked by passages for solo tenor and harp, makes an excellent coupling for the equally attractive Bliss and Holst items. Excellent, atmospheric recording.

A Midsummer Night's Dream (complete).
*** Decca 425 663-2 (2) [id.]. Deller, Harwood, Harper, Veasey, Watts, Shirley-Quirk, Brannigan, Downside and Emmanuel School Ch., LSO, composer.
** Ph. Dig. 454 122-2 (2) [id.]. McNair, Asawa, Lloyd, Bostridge, Janice Watson, John Mark Ainsley, LSO, Sir Colin Davis.

The beauty of the instrumental writing comes out in this recording even more than in the opera house, for John Culshaw, the recording manager, put an extra halo round the fairy music to act as a substitute for visual atmosphere. Britten again proves himself an ideal interpreter of his own music and draws virtuoso playing from the LSO. Peter Pears has shifted to the straight role of Lysander. The mechanicals are admirably led by Owen Brannigan as Bottom; and among the lovers Josephine Veasey (Hermia) is outstanding. Deller, with his magical male alto singing, is the eerily effective Oberon.

Following on a brilliantly successful concert performance at the Barbican, Sir Colin Davis made his recording of *A Midsummer Night's Dream* in the same venue. The cast is a strong one, with the lovers aptly taken by generally younger, if less characterful, singers than in rival sets. The LSO play brilliantly but, thanks to a rather dry acoustic, there is little of the atmospheric magic which makes both Hickox's Virgin set and the composer's own original so compelling. Davis is also a more metrical, more literal, less freely expressive interpreter. In the casting there are incidental points of advantage, as in the choice of Sylvia McNair as Tytania with her pure, silver tone, and Ian Bostridge masterly in the tenor role of Flute. As Bottom the dark-toned Robert Lloyd responds strongly, with fine feeling for words, but a serious snag is the choice of the counter-tenor, Brian Asawa, as Oberon, with a marked vibrato which makes him sound too womanly.

(i) *Owen Wingrave* (complete); (ii) *6 Hölderlin fragments, Op. 61;* (iii) *The Poet's echo, Op. 76.*
*** Decca 433 200-2 (2) [id.]. (i) Pears, Fisher, Harper, Vyvyan, J. Baker, Luxon, Shirley-Quirk, ECO, composer; (ii) Pears, composer; (iii) Vishnevskaya, Rostropovich.

Britten's television opera marked a return after the *Church parables* to the mainstream pattern of his operatic style, with a central character isolated from society. Each of the seven characters is strongly conceived, with the composer writing specially for the individual singers in the cast. The performance is definitive and the recording very atmospheric. The set is filled out with the *Six Hölderlin fragments* and *The Poet's echo*, Russian settings of Pushkin, written for Vishnevskaya who performs them with her husband at the piano.

Paul Bunyan (complete).
✿ *** Virgin/EMI Dig. VCD7 59249-2 (2). James Lawless, Dan Dressen, Elisabeth Comeaux Nelson, soloists, Ch. & O of Plymouth Music Series, Minnesota, Philip Brunelle.

Aptly, this first recording of Britten's choral operetta comes from the state of Minnesota, where the story is set. When the principal character is a giant who can appear only as a disembodied voice, the piece works rather better on record or radio than on stage. Musically, Britten's conscious assumption of popular American mannerisms does not prevent his invention from showing characteristic originality. Recorded in clean, vivid sound, with Philip Brunelle a vigorous conductor, it is an excellent first recording.

Peter Grimes (complete).
*** Chandos Dig. CHAN 9447/8 (2) [id.]. Langridge, Watson, Opie, Connell, Harrison, Opera London, L. Symphony Ch., City of L. Sinf., Hickox.
✿ *** Decca 414 577-2 (3) [id.]. Pears, Claire Watson, Pease, Jean Watson, Nilsson, Brannigan, Evans, Ch. and O of ROHCG, composer.
*** EMI (SIS) Dig. CDC7 54832-2 (2). Anthony Rolfe Johnson, Felicity Lott, Thomas Allen, Ch. & O of ROHCG, Bernard Haitink.
(N) (B) *** Ph. Duo 462 847-2 (2) [id.]. Vickers, Harper, Summers, Bainbridge, Cahill, Robinson, Allen, ROHCG Ch. & O, C. Davis.

On Chandos, Richard Hickox follows up the success of his award-winning sets of the *War requiem* and of Walton's *Troilus and Cressida* with a comparably warm and involving performance, more atmospheric than any since the composer's own original version. The rhythmic spring which Hickox gives this colourful score harks back to that classic set, and Chandos backs him up with an exceptionally rich recording, with bloom on the voices and full, immediate orchestral sound. The casting of Philip Langridge in the title-role is central to the set's success. As on stage, he is unrivalled at conveying the character's mounting hysteria. The result is chilling. Janice Watson makes a most touching Ellen Orford, younger and less maternal than her rivals, but all the more tender, with the golden tones of the voice well caught. The others make a superb team, with Alan Opie an outstanding Bulstrode and John Connell commanding as lawyer Swallow at the start. Warmly recorded, this is a more atmospheric performance than the only digital rival, from Haitink on EMI, and is just as powerful, with choral singing even more sharply disciplined.

The Decca recording of *Peter Grimes* was one of the first great achievements of the stereo era. Few opera recordings can claim to be so definitive, with

Peter Pears, for whom it was written, in the name-part, Owen Brannigan (another member of the original team) and a first-rate cast. Britten conducts superbly and secures splendidly incisive playing, with the whole orchestra on its toes throughout. The recording, superbly atmospheric, has so many felicities that it would be hard to enumerate them, and the Decca engineers have done wonders in making up aurally for the lack of visual effects. Unlike later versions, this comes extravagantly on three CDs instead of two.

Bernard Haitink's reading of *Grimes*, helped by one of EMI's most spectacular recordings yet, finds more light and shade in this extraordinarily atmospheric score. Anthony Rolfe Johnson brings out the inward intensity of Grimes and is the most inward of the three, singing most beautifully, hardly more troubled than Pears by the high tessitura. Felicity Lott makes a tenderly sympathetic Ellen Orford, Sarah Walker is unforgettable as Mrs Sedley, the laudanum-taking gossip, and Thomas Allen is a wise and powerful Balstrode, making the Act III duet with Ellen an emotional resolution. The Covent Garden Chorus and Orchestra benefit from the extra range and vividness of EMI's digital recording adding to the impact.

Sir Colin Davis takes a fundamentally darker, tougher view of *Peter Grimes* than the composer himself. Jon Vickers's powerful, heroic interpretation sheds keen new illumination on what arguably remains the greatest of Britten's operas. Heather Harper as Ellen Orford is most moving, and there are fine contributions from Jonathan Summers as Captain Balstrode and Thomas Allen as Ned Keene. The recording is full and vivid, with fine balancing. Now reissued as a Duo, this is a genuine bargain.

(i, ii) *Peter Grimes* (scenes); (i, iii) *The Rape of Lucretia* (abridged); (iv) French folksong arrangements: *La belle est au jardin d'amour; La fileuse; Quand j'étais chez mon père; Le roi s'en va-t'en chasse; Voici le printemps;* (v) English folksongs: *The Ash grove; The Bonny Earl o' Moray; Come you not from Newcastle?; The Foggy, foggy dew; Heigh ho, heigh hi!; The King is gone a-hunting; Little Sir William; O, Waly, Waly; Oliver Cromwell; The Plough boy; The Salley Gardens; Sweet Polly Oliver; There's none to soothe.*

(M) (***) EMI mono CMS7 64727-2 (2). (i) Joan Cross, Peter Pears; (ii) Nancy Evans, E. Op. Group Chamber O; (iii) BBC Theatre Ch., ROHCG O, Reginald Goodall; (iv) Sophie Wyss, composer; (v) Peter Pears, composer.

Both of these abridged recordings of Britten's earliest operas, made in the 1940s, have a freshness and energy that reflect the excitement they aroused at their first appearance, transforming the British musical scene. They equally illustrate the resilient energy of Peter Pears at this early stage, lighter and fresher of voice than later, and the urgent intensity of Reginald Goodall, conducting Britten in a way very different from his later, solidly weighty manner in Wagner. Though the recordings, transferred from 78s, are boxy in sound, the closeness adds to the bite and impact. They are particularly valuable for demonstrating the character and point of Joan Cross as Ellen Orford. It was a role written for her, as was the Female Chorus part in *Lucretia*. In the latter opera it is good to have Nancy Evans in the title-role, tenderly affecting, with the contrasts between the heroine's tragic grief and the beauty of the serving maids' Flower duet superbly brought out.

The recordings of folksong settings are delightful, made not just by Peter Pears for both Decca and EMI, but by Sophie Wyss (for whom *Les illuminations* was written). The wit and point of such songs as *The foggy, foggy dew* and *Little Sir William* come out even more charmingly than in later recordings, with Britten as accompanist at his most inspired.

Peter Grimes: 4 Sea interludes and Passacaglia.

*** Chandos Dig. CHAN 8473 [id.]. Ulster O, Handley – BAX: *On the Sea-shore;* BRIDGE: *The Sea.* ***

Handley draws brilliant, responsive playing from the Ulster Orchestra in readings that fully capture the atmospheric beauty of the writing, helped by vivid recording of demonstration quality.

The Rape of Lucretia (complete).

*** Chandos Dig. CHAN 9254/5 [id.]. Rigby, Robson, Pierard, Maxwell, Miles, Rozario, Gunson, City of L. Sinf., Hickox.

(i) *The Rape of Lucretia* (complete); (ii) *Phaedra, Op. 93.*

*** Decca 425 666-2 (2) [id.]. (i) Pears, Harper, Shirley-Quirk, J. Baker, Luxon, ECO, composer; (ii) J. Baker, ECO, Bedford.

In combining on CD *The Rape of Lucretia* with *Phaedra*, Decca celebrates two outstanding performances by Dame Janet Baker, recorded at the peak of her career. Among other distinguished vocal contributions to the opera, Peter Pears and Heather Harper stand out, while Benjamin Luxon makes the selfish Tarquinius into a living character. The seductive beauty of the writing – Britten then at his early peak – is splendidly caught, the melodies and tone-colours as ravishing as any that he ever conceived.

Richard Hickox reinforces his claims as a Britten interpreter with this Chandos version, strongly cast and vividly recorded. Though the soloists in the Britten recording – notably Janet Baker in the title-role – are more sharply characterful and well-contrasted, the alternative views presented here are comparably convincing. Jean Rigby as Lucretia may lack the warmth and weight of Baker, but she gains from having a younger-sounding voice. Equally the timbre of Nigel Robson as the Male Chorus, rather darker than Peter Pears's, adds to the dramatic bite of his characterization, virile in attack. Catherine Pierard as the Female Chorus has a more sensuous voice than most sopranos taking this role, making it a more involved commentary. The digital sound is warm and glowing, fully revealing the sensuous beauty of Britten's chamber orchestration. Quite apart from its unique authority, Britten's Decca set (also at full price) comes with a valuable fill-up in *Phaedra*, the work he wrote for Janet Baker; but the Chandos rival gives an equally strong, in some ways more dramatic view of a masterly opera.

The Turn of the screw.
*** Collins Dig. 7030-2 (2) [id.]. Langridge, Lott, Pay, Hulse, Cannan, Secunde, Aldeburgh Festival Ens., Bedford.
(M) (***) Decca mono 425 672-2 (2) [id.]. Pears, Vyvyan, Hemmings, Dyer, Cross, Mandikian, E. Op. Group O, composer.
**(*) Ph. 446 325-2 (2). Helen Donath, Robert Tear, Heather Harper, Ava June, Lillian Watson, Michael Ginn, ROHCG O (members), Sir Colin Davis.

Steuart Bedford here presents a keenly idiomatic performance of *The Turn of the screw* with a sharpness and magnetism which, thanks to the spacious recording, brings out the eerie atmosphere of the piece. The singers too have been chosen to follow the pattern set by the original performers. Langridge here, like Pears before him, takes the double role of narrator and Peter Quint, echoing Pears's inflexions but putting his own stamp on the characterization. Felicity Lott is both powerful and vulnerable as the Governess, rising superbly to the big climaxes which, thanks to the recording quality, have a chilling impact. Sam Pay is a fresh-voiced Miles, less knowing than David Hemmings in the Britten set, with Eileen Hulse bright and girlish as Flora. Nadine Secunde is a strong Miss Jessel, and Phyllis Cannan even matches up to the strength of her predecessor, Joan Cross. An outstanding set.

Though the recording is in mono only, the very dryness and the sharpness of focus give an extra intensity to the composer's own incomparable reading of his most compressed opera. Peter Pears as Peter Quint is superbly matched by Jennifer Vyvyan as the governess and by Joan Cross as the housekeeper, Mrs Grose. It is also fascinating to hear David Hemmings as a boy treble, already a confident actor. Excellent CD transfer.

Sir Colin Davis's 1981 Covent Garden recording has the benefit of spacious and atmospheric sound, and Davis's ability to relax, to vary the expression, brings many dividends. There is no weak link in the singing cast, with Tear underlining the devilish side of Peter Quint's character, more forcefully sinister than was Peter Pears, but at times too melodramatic. Helen Donath sings feelingly as the Governess, making her a neurotic character; but she hardly erases memories of Jennifer Vyvyan. The treble, Michael Ginn, as Miles, is excellent, and Heather Harper as Miss Jessel is a warmly persuasive ghost. The playing of the Covent Garden orchestra is superb, bringing out the formidable compassion of the piece, and the transfer to CD is first class.

Collection

'*The World of Britten*': (i; ii) *Simple Symphony;* (iii; ii) *Young person's guide to the orchestra.* (iv; v) *Folksong arrangements: Early one morning; The plough boy.* (vi) *Hymn to the Virgin.* (iv; vii; iii; ii) *Serenade for tenor, horn & strings: Nocturne.* Excerpts from: *Ceremony of carols; Noye's Fludde; Spring Symphony; Billy Budd; Peter Grimes.*
(M) *** Decca 436 990-2. (i) ECO; (ii) cond. composer; (iii) LSO; (iv) Pears; (v) composer (piano); (vi) St John's College Ch., Guest; (vii) Tuckwell; & var. artists.

The Britten sampler is well worth having for the composer's own vibrant account of the *Variations on a theme of Purcell* and the *Simple Symphony*, where the *Playful pizzicato* emerges with wonderful rhythmic spring and resonance (in the warm Maltings acoustics). The Pears contributions are very enjoyable too, notably the haunting *Nocturne* from the *Serenade*, with Barry Tuckwell in splendid form. Excellent sound throughout, although the tuttis in the *Young person's guide to the orchestra* could with advantage have had a more expansive sonority.

Brossard, Sébastien de (1655–1730)

Elévations et motets (for 1, 2, or 3 voices): *Festis laeta sonent; O Domine quia refugium; Oratorio seu Dialogus poenitentis animae cum Deo; Psallite superi; Qui non diliget te; Salve Rex Christe; Templa nunc fumet.*
(N) (B) **(*) Opus 111 Invitation Dig. OPS 10-002 [id.]. Rime, Fouchécourt, Honeyman, Delétré, Parlement de Musique,Martin Gester.

Sébastien de Brossard came from Normandy to take a position as Chapel Master at Strasbourg Cathedral. He was most famous as a compiler and publisher of a musical dictionary. These motets are mostly dialogue cantatas. *O Domine quia refugium* is a fine example although the expressive and touching *Qui non diliget te* (for which the composer wrote the text) is a solo work, and very beautifully sung by Noémi Rime. The pervading atmosphere is melancholy, but a cantata often ends, as in the latter case, with a joyful *Alleluya. The Dialogue of the repentant soul with God* is shared by soprano and tenor: it is not especially dramatic, but the pace quickens as forgiveness is given. The final work *Festis laeta sonent cantibus organa* (*May the organ ring out with solemn songs*) begins and ends spiritedly, but most of the central sections are reflective. It is very well sung by the tenor, Jean-Paul Fouchécourt, but Brossard's weakness is the lack of a more robust spirit to many of these interchanges, surprising from a musician who was an advocate of the introduction of Italian styles into French music. Just the same these are works that grow on one with re-hearing. Although Le Parlement de Musique does not seek high polish, the singing here is very responsive, and the period-instrument accompaniments are stylish and pleasingly supportive. Excellent recording and full texts.

Brouwer, Leo (born 1939)

Concerto elegiaco (Guitar concerto No. 3).

(M) *** RCA 09026 61605-2 [id.]. Julian Bream, RCA Victor CO, composer – LENNOX BERKELEY; RODRIGO: *Concertos.* ***

Leo Brouwer has blended earlier Afro-Cuban and Javanese influences with romantic feeling, even adopting a cyclic structure as 'a homage to César Franck or the leitmotif of the nineteenth century'. The result is a piece with a short but haunting central *Lento* and a brilliant *Toccata*-like finale which sums up the earlier lyrical ideas. Bream's performance draws the music's threads together, displaying much bravura. He is very well recorded.

Bruch, Max (1838–1920)

Adagio on Celtic themes, Op. 56; Ave Maria, Op. 61; Canzone, Op. 55; Kol Nidrei, Op. 55.

*** RCA Dig. RD 60757 [60757-2-RC]. Ofra Harnoy, LPO, Mackerras – BLOCH: *Schelomo* etc. ***

Ofra Harnoy has the full measure of Bruch's sombre, Hebraic lyricism in the best-known piece here, *Kol Nidrei*, and she receives warm support from Mackerras. The rest of the programme creates a lighter mood, with the engaging *Adagio on Celtic themes* recalling the *Scottish fantasia*. An excellent recording, made in Watford Town Hall.

Double concerto in E min., for clarinet, viola and orchestra, Op. 88.

(B) *** Hyperion Dyad Dig. CDD 22017 (2) [id.]. Thea King, Nobuko Imai, LSO, Francis (with Concert – see below ***).

Bruch's *Double concerto* is a delightful work with genuinely memorable inspiration in its first two lyrical movements and a roistering finale making a fine contrast. Clarinet and viola are blended beautifully, with the more penetrating wind instrument dominating naturally and with melting phrasing from Thea King. The recording is excellent. This is part of a marvellous two-disc set including other attractive concertante works by Mendelssohn, Crusell, Spohr and other less familar names.

Double piano concerto in A flat min., Op. 88a.

**(*) Ph. Dig. 432 095-2. Katia and Marielle Labèque, Philh. O, Bychkov – MENDELSSOHN: *Double concerto.* **(*)

In Bruch's long-buried *Double piano concerto* Bychkov is heavy-handed at the start, but the contrapuntal writing for the pianos that follows is agreeable; in a Reger-like way. After a second movement which moves from *Andante* to *Allegro molto*, there is a romantic *Adagio* more typical of the composer. The Labèques play with bravura and panache and are given good solid support. The recording is full and resonant but lacks transparency, and the effect is surely heavier than need be.

Violin concertos Nos. 1 in G min.; 2 in D min., Op. 44; 3 in D min., Op. 58; Serenade for violin and orchestra, Op 75; Scottish fantasy, Op. 46.

(B) *** Ph. Duo 462 167-2 (2) [id.]. Salvatore Accardo, Leipzig GO, Masur.

This Philips Duo gathers together Bruch's three *Violin concertos*, plus two other major concertante works. Although no other piece quite matches the famous *G minor Concerto* in inventive concentration, the delightful *Scottish fantasia*, with its profusion of good tunes, comes near to doing so, and the first movement of the *Second Concerto* has two soaringly lyrical themes. The *Third Concerto* brings another striking lyrical idea in the first movement and has an endearing *Adagio* and a jolly finale. The engagingly insubstantial *Serenade* was originally intended to be a fourth violin concerto. Throughout the set Accardo's playing is so persuasive in its restrained passion that even the less inspired moments bring pleasure. With Accardo balanced rather close, the orchestral recording is full and spacious.

Violin concerto No. 1 in G min., Op. 26.

(M) *** Sony Dig. SMK 64250 [id.]. Cho-Liang Lin, Chicago SO, Slatkin – MENDELSSOHN: *Concerto;* VIEUXTEMPS: *Concerto No. 5.* ***

*** EMI Dig. CDC7 54072-2 [id.]. Kyung-Wha Chung, LPO, Tennstedt – BEETHOVEN: *Concerto.* ***

*** ASV Dig. CDDCA 680. Xue Wei, Philh. O, Bakels – SAINT-SAENS: *Concerto No. 3.* ***

(B) *** CfP Dig. CD-CFP 4566; [(M) id. import]. Tasmin Little, RLPO, Handley – DVORAK: *Concerto.* ***

(M) *** EMI CDM5 66906-2 [CDM5 66958]. Lord Menuhin, Philh. O, Susskind – MENDELSSOHN: *Concerto.* ***

(B) *** [EMI Red Line CDR5 69863]. Itzhak Perlman, LSO, Previn – MENDELSSOHN: *Violin concerto.* ***

(M) *** Carlton Dig. PCD 2005 [id.]. Jaime Laredo, SCO – MENDELSSOHN: *Concerto*. ***

(M) *** DG 449 091-2. Shlomo Mintz, Chicago SO, Abbado – DVORAK: *Concerto*. ***

(**(*)) Testament mono SBT 1083. Haendel, Philh. O, Kubelik – BEETHOVEN: *Violin concerto*. (**(*))

*** Chandos Dig. CHAN 8974 [id.]. Hideko Udagawa, LSO, Mackerras – BRAHMS: *Concerto*. ***

(BB) *** EMI Seraphim CES5 68524-2 (2) [CEDB 68524]. Lord Menuhin, LSO, Boult – MENDELSSOHN: *Violin concerto* etc. ***

*** EMI Dig. CDC7 49663-2 [id.]. Kennedy, ECO, Tate – MENDELSSOHN: *Concerto;* SCHUBERT: *Rondo*. ***

(BB) **(*) RCA/Navigator Dig. 74321 29245-2 [60479-2-TV]. Uto Ughi, LSO, Prêtre – BRAHMS: *Violin concerto*. **(*)

(M) **(*) Sony Stern Edition I SMK 66830 [id.]. Stern, Phd. O, Ormandy – TCHAIKOVSKY: *Méditation; Sérénade mélancolique* ***; WIENIAWSKI: *Violin concerto No. 2*. **(*)

(M) **(*) Sony SBK 48274 [id.]. Zukerman, LAPO, Mehta – LALO: *Symphonie espagnole;* VIEUXTEMPS: *Concerto No. 5*. **(*)

There have been few accounts on record of Bruch's slow movement that begin to match the raptness of Lin. He is accompanied most sensitively by Slatkin and the Chicago orchestra, and this reading is totally compelling in its combination of passion and purity, strength and dark, hushed intensity. The addition of the attractive *Fifth Concerto* of Henri Vieuxtemps makes this CD more attractive than ever. The recording is excellent.

Compared with her earlier Decca recording, Chung's expressive rubato in her EMI version is more marked, with her freedom vividly conveying magic such as you find in her live performances. The slow movement brings extreme contrasts of dynamic and expression from orchestra as well as soloist, and the finale is again impulsive in its bravura. An exceptionally attractive version, generously coupled with Chung's fine account of the Beethoven.

Xue Wei's approach to the concerto is at once passionately committed and refined in its delicacy of detail. He is accompanied superbly by Kees Bakels, while Wei can equally seduce the listener with a most magical *pianissimo*. The slow movement is ravishing in its poetic flair, and the finale is full of fire.

The movement in the Bruch where Tasmin Little's individuality comes out most clearly is the central *Adagio*, raptly done with a deceptive simplicity of phrasing, totally unselfconscious, that matches the purity of her sound. Her speeds in the outer movements are broader than those of such rivals as Lin. At full price this would be a first-rate recommendation: on CfP it is an outstanding bargain.

Menuhin's performance (with Susskind), now re-issued as one of EMI's 'Great recordings of the century', has long held an honoured place in the catalogue. The performance has a fine spontaneity, the work's improvisatory quality very much part of the interpretation, and there is no doubting the poetry Menuhin finds in the slow movement or the sparkle in the finale. The bright, forward sound of the 1960 recording has transferred vividly and naturally to CD.

Perlman gives a glowing, powerful account that is almost too sure of itself. With Previn and the LSO backing him up richly, this is a strong, confident interpretation, forthrightly masculine. The opulent, full recording suits the performance. This is only available in the USA.

Jaime Laredo with consistently fresh and sweet tone gives a delightfully direct reading, warmly expressive but never for a moment self-indulgent. The orchestral ensemble is particularly impressive, when no conductor is involved. With first-rate modern digital recording, this is a highlight of the Carlton mid-price catalogue.

Shlomo Mintz makes the listener hang on to every phrase, with his compelling playing. The vibrato is wide, but his approach is so distinctive and interesting that few listeners will resist. The Chicago Symphony Orchestra plays with great brilliance and enthusiasm, and Abbado's direction is most sympathetic. The vivid recording has transferred splendidly to CD.

It is good to have some of Ida Haendel's magnificent violin recordings restored to the catalogue, when – being in mono – they had an unfairly short life in the regular catalogue. Her 1948 reading of the Bruch, rather like her accounts of the Brahms and Tchaikovsky, reissued earlier by Testament, combines power and great warmth, with the first movement strong and purposeful, the second passionate in its lyricism and the third brilliant and sparkling. Excellent transfer, but it is a pity this is offered at full price.

Full of temperament, Hideko Udagawa gives a persuasively passionate performance of the Bruch, very well recorded, and with strong, colourful playing from the orchestra the hushed opening of the slow movement is caught beautifully.

Menuhin's second stereo recording of the Bruch *Concerto* was made in the early 1970s. While he is obviously on familiar ground, there is no sign of over-familiarity and the lovely slow movement is given a performance of great warmth and humanity. Boult accompanies admirably, and the recording is fuller and more modern than the earlier version with Susskind, even if the solo playing is technically less immaculate. On EMI's super-bargain Seraphim label, this coupling with Mendelssohn remains very attractive.

Nigel Kennedy's masculine strength goes with a totally unsentimental view of Bruch's lyricism, as in the central slow movement. This may not have quite the individual poetry of the very finest versions; but, coupled with an outstanding account of the Mendelssohn and the rare Schubert *Rondo*, it makes an excellent recommendation. The recording is full, warm and well balanced.

Those looking for a bargain coupling with the Brahms *Concerto* (though this CD is at mid-price in the USA), and very good (1982) digital recording, might well choose Ughi on RCA Navigator. His is a fresh, direct reading. There are more individual versions, but it is still a fine performance and excellent value.

Stern's vintage account from 1966 with Ormandy is one of the classic recordings of the work, warm-hearted and passionate, with a very involving account of the slow movement. The finale, too, has wonderful fire and spirit. Ormandy's accompaniment is first class and triumphs over the unrealistic balance, with the violin far too far in front.

Zukerman's reissued Sony triptych shows him at his finest, and it is a pity that the close-up balance brings inevitable reservations. His Bruch is a passionately extrovert performance, tempered by genuine tenderness in the slow movement. The brilliantly lit recording increases the sense of fiery energy in the outer sections and, with the excitement of the solo playing and the strongly committed accompaniment, the larger-than-life effect is overwhelming.

(i) *Violin concerto No. 1 in G min.;* (ii) *Kol Nidrei;* (iii) *Scottish fantasy, Op. 46.*

(N) (**(*)) Pearl GEM 0051 (i) Milstein, NYPO, Barbirolli; (ii) Casals, LSO, Landon Ronald; (iii) Heifetz, RCA Victor SO, Steinberg.

Neither the Milstein nor the Heifetz recordings have ever appeared in Britain. Aided by Barbirolli at his most passionate, Milstein gives a most moving account of the Bruch *G minor Concerto*, most remarkable for a hushed, tender reading of the slow movement. Heifetz in the *Scottish fantasy*, always a favourite work of his, is even richer and warmer than he is in the stereo recording he made later with Sargent in London, a complete answer to those who find him cold. Both are well transferred, though with the high surface characteristic of Pearl. The disappointment is the Casals reading of *Kol Nidrei*, in its caution lacking the prayerful intensity needed.

Violin concerto No. 1 in G min., Op. 26; Scottish fantasy, Op. 46.

(N) (M) *** Decca Legends 460 976-2 [id.]. Kyung Wha Chung, RPO, Kempe – MENDELSSOHN Concerto. ***

(N) (M) *** Decca Penguin Classics 460 620-2 [id.]. Kyung-Wha Chung, RPO, Kempe.

(M) *** RCA 09026 61745-2 [id.]. Heifetz, New SO of L., Sargent – VIEUXTEMPS: *Concerto No. 5.* ***

(B) **(*) Tring Dig. TRP 108. Yuzuko Horigome, RPO, Yuri Simonov.

The magic of Kyung-Wha Chung, always a spontaneously inspired violinist, comes over beguilingly in this very desirable Penguin Classics Bruch coupling from 1972, with the notes including a fascinating personal reminiscence from Louis de Bernières (author of the amazingly successful *Captain Corelli's Mandolin*). However, Decca have upstaged the Penguin Classics issue by reissuing the recordings on their Legends label, including also the Mendelssohn *Concerto*. Chung goes straight to the heart of the famous *G minor Concerto*, finding mystery and fantasy as well as more extrovert qualities. Just as strikingly in the *Scottish fantasy* she transcends the episodic nature of the writing to give the music a genuine depth and concentration, above all in the lovely slow movement. Kempe and the RPO accompany sympathetically, well caught in a glowing recording.

Heifetz plays with supreme assurance, and the slow movement shows this fine artist in masterly form. All lovers of great violin playing should at least hear this coupling, for Heifetz's panache and the subtlety of his bowing and colour bring a wonderful freshness to Bruch's charming Scottish whimsy. Sargent accompanies sympathetically, and though the soloist is balanced much too closely, there is never any doubt that Heifetz can still produce a true pianissimo.

Yuzuko Horigome's coupling of Bruch's two most popular concertante violin works is most welcome in Tring's RPO series and, very well played and recorded, makes an excellent recommendation at bargain price. Yuzuko Horigome was the first prize-winner in the Queen Elizabeth Competition in Belgium in 1980. She plays here with rich, pure tone, using an aptly wide dynamic range, taking a relatively expansive view of both works, not always quite impulsive enough, tending at times to sound too deliberate. Nevertheless these are warmly enjoyable performances, and the recording is full and immediate, with the important harp solo in the *Scottish fantasy* clearly focused.

Violin concerto No. 2 in D min., Op. 44.

❀ *** Delos Dig. DE 3156 [id.]. Nai-Yan Hu, Seattle SO, Schwarz – GOLDMARK: *Violin concerto.* *** ❀

As with the Goldmark coupling, Nai-Yan Hu is ideally balanced and well accompanied by Schwarz and the Seattle orchestra. The composer could not understand why this tuneful concerto was so dwarfed by the earlier, G minor work, and Hu's soaring lyrical lines underline its warmth and consistent melodic inspiration. Though Perlman strikes a high profile in his EMI version, the sympathetic warmth of this Hu/Schwarz partnership and the concert-hall fullness of the Delos recording is preferable.

Violin concerto No. 2 in D min., Op. 44; Scottish fantasy, Op. 46.

**(*) EMI Dig. CDC7 49071-2 [id.]. Perlman, Israel PO, Mehta.

Perlman may be less intimately reflective in both works than he was when he recorded this coupling before with the New Philharmonia, but in the fast movements there are ample compensations in the sharp concentration from first to last.

(i) *Double concerto for violin and viola, Op. 88; Kol Nidrei, Op. 47; Romance for viola and orchestra, Op. 85.*

(N) *** RCA Dig. 09026 63292-2 [id.]. Yuri Bashmet, LSO, Neeme Järvi; with (i) Victor Tretiakov – WALTON: *Viola concerto*.***

Bruch's fund of melodic invention, usually a youthful gift, stayed with him well into his seventies, as the *Double concerto* and the *Romance* winningly demonstrate. The latter work for viola and orchestra of 1912 harks straight back to the slow movement of the *G minor Violin concerto*. It is a radiant piece which draws a heartfelt performance from Bashmet, as does the well-known *Kol Nidrei*, the more poignant with viola taking the place of cello. The *Double concerto*, written just before the *Romance*, is better known in its version for clarinet and viola, but works just as well here, when the solo instruments meld together tonally rather than contrasting. That brings extra sensuousness, thanks also to the pure-toned playing of Viktor Tretyakov, a perfect foil for the resonant Bashmet. An unexpected coupling for the Walton Concerto but an attractive one.

Kol Nidrei, Op. 47.

*** EMI (SIS) Dig. CDC5 56126-2 [id.]. Han-Na Chang, LSO, Rostropovich – FAURE: *Elégie* ***; SAINT-SAENS: *Cello concerto No. 1* ***; TCHAIKOVSKY: *Rococo variations*. *** ❀

*** DG Dig. 427 323-2. Matt Haimovitz, Chicago SO, Levine (with LALO: *Concerto*; SAINT-SAENS: *Concerto No. 1*. ***)

(M) (***) Sony mono MHK 62876 [id.]. Gregor Piatigorsky, Phd. O, Ormandy – DVORAK: *Cello concerto* (***); SAINT-SAENS: *Cello concerto No. 1*. (***) ❀

The phenomenally gifted 13-year-old Korean-born cellist, Han-Na Chang, catches the intense atmosphere of Bruch's Hebrew melody with a natural sensitivity, spontaneous in her dynamic contrasts. Rostropovich has said, 'I did not play as well as her at that age,' and indeed the extraordinary poise and assurance of this playing, matched by her ability to touch the listener, reminds one of the young Yehudi Menuhin. Her mentor accompanies her with great sympathy and the Abbey Road recording is beautifully balanced. The other items in this recital are equally appealing, and her account of Tchaikovsky's *Rococo variations* is unsurpassed among modern versions. A collection not to be missed.

Matt Haimovitz, born in Israel, has a natural feeling for the piece and his performance, balancing restraint with expressive intensity, is serenely moving. The Lalo concerto is equally distinguished.

Piatigorsky's account comes from 1947 and has a keen eloquence that is as potent today as it was when it was made, just after the war. The Dvŏrák *Concerto* and, more especially, the Saint-Saëns under Frederick Stock are superb.

Scottish fantasy (for violin and orchestra), *Op. 46*.

(B) *** EMI Eminence Dig. CD-EMX 2277 [(M) id. import]. Tasmin Little, Royal SNO, Vernon Handley – LALO: *Symphonie espagnole*. ***

*** RCA Dig. RD 60942. Anne Akiko Meyers, RPO, López-Cobos – LALO: *Symphonie espagnole*. **(*)

(B) **(*) Revelation RV 10051 [id.]. David Oistrakh, USSR State SO, Rozhdestvensky (with BERLIOZ: *Harold in Italy*. (*))

It is an excellent idea to couple Bruch's evocation of Scotland with Lalo's of Spain, both works in unconventional, five-movement, concertante form. Tasmin Little takes a ripe, robust and passionate view of both works, projecting them strongly, as she would in the concert hall. In this she is greatly helped by the fine, polished playing of the Scottish orchestra under Vernon Handley, a most sympathetic partner. The recording is superb, with brass in particular vividly caught. Unlike Meyers on RCA, Little plays the Guerriero finale absolutely complete. An outstanding bargain on the Eminence label.

Anne Akiko Meyers is admirably partnered by López-Cobos and the RPO. The very opening, with its melancholy, sonorous brass, is unforgettable, and the hushed violin entry is to be matched later by most tender playing in the *Andante*, where the response of the RPO is equally warm. First-class Abbey Road recording, expansive and very well balanced.

It is sad that as inspired a version as David Oistrakh's of the Bruch *Scottish fantasy* should be coupled on Revelation with so seriously flawed a recording of *Harold in Italy*. The irony is that where the sound for the Bruch, dating from 1960, is full-bodied and generally well balanced, if limited in range, the 1974 recording of the Berlioz is very dim. With Rozhdestvensky drawing fine playing from the orchestra, Oistrakh gives the fast movements a rare sparkle, always spontaneous in his expressiveness, and in the *Andante* he builds from heartfelt meditation to the most passionate climax.

Symphonies Nos. 1 in E flat, Op. 28; 2 in F min., Op. 36; 3 in E, Op. 51.
**(*) EMI (SIS) CDS5 550 046-2 (3). Gürzenich O; Cologne PO, James Conlon.

In James Conlon's convincing performances both orchestras (it is not clear which plays which work) emphasize the music's Brahmsian and Schumannesque derivations. A good case is made for the *Third Symphony* here, with the romantic opening richly done, the slow-movement variations warmly effective and the Scherzo (which the composer regarded as the finest movement in each of works) made to sound original in its scoring. Only the finale lets the piece down. The orchestral playing is committed throughout, even if at times greater drive is needed from the conductor. There is no fill-up, and the second CD plays for only 36 minutes.

Symphonies Nos. 1 in E flat, Op. 28; 2 in F min., Op. 36; 3 in E, Op. 51; (i) *Adagio appassionato, Op. 57; Konzertstück, Op. 84; In memoriam, Op. 65; Romanze, Op. 42* (all for violin and orchestra).
(B) *** Ph. Duo 462 164-2 (2) [id.]. (i) Salvatore Accardo; Leipzig GO, Kurt Masur.

When the first of Bruch's three symphonies is the one that is most striking in its invention and each has its weaknesses, one has to deduce that he was a symphonist more by default than by nature. Yet this collected edition contains much attractive music, beautifully played and recorded, guaranteed to delight anyone wanting undemanding symphonies as alternatives to those of Brahms and Schumann. Masur's performances with the Leipzig Gewandhaus Orchestra are characteristically warm and refined, with smooth recording to match, but sparkle is largely missing. Room has also been found for the remaining works in Accardo's complete survey of Bruch's major works for violin and orchestra. The two-movement *Konzertstück* dates from 1911 and is one of Bruch's last works. *In Memoriam* is finer still and the *Adagio appassionato* and *Romanze* are strongly characterized pieces. Accardo's advocacy is just as persuasive here as in the concertos.

String quintet in A min., Op. posth.
*** Naim Dig. CD 010 [id.]. Augmented Allegri Qt – BRAHMS: *String quintet No. 2.* ***

Written in 1918, two years before he died, Bruch's *A minor Quintet* was one of two he wrote for sheer joy at the age of 80. The scores were lost by the publisher at the end of the First World War, and we owe the rediscovery of this one to the fact that Bruch's daughter-in-law made a copy of her own. Though it was in the BBC Music Library and two broadcasts were given over the years, this is its first recording. It is an unashamed throwback in idiom to Beethoven and Brahms, but the freshness of ideas and argument is most winning. Starting with what sounds like late Beethoven updated, the strongly constructed outer movements frame a jolly Scherzo full of cross-rhythms and a sweetly lyrical interlude. Like the Brahms *G major Quintet*, with which it is ideally coupled, it is very well performed and vividly recorded.

VOCAL MUSIC

Odysseus (Scenes from the Odyssey), Op. 41.
(N) **(*) Koch Schwann Dig. 3-6557-2 (2) [id.]. Jeffrey Kneebone, Nancy Maultsby, Camilla Nylund, Stephanie Lange, Xenia-Maria Mann, Bernhard Gärtner, Robert Holzer, NDR R Ch., Hanover RPO, Leon Botstein.

Best known for his orchestral works, Bruch wrote many choral works too, of which this oratorio, a series of self-contained scenes loosely based on Homer, was among the most popular in the last century. Written in 1872, when the composer was in his mid 30s, it is far less adventurous than the concertos that have remained in the repertory, regularly echoing the example of Mendelssohn, most strikingly in the writing for chorus. It is all easy on the ear, but there is a blandness not only in the musical invention but in the treatment of the text, which is static and undramatic, even in the scene of Odysseus's return to his wife, Penelope, when the banquet starts with a very conventional chorus. Even the joyful concluding chorus seems to imitate *Elijah*. Nonetheless, with a cast led by two American singers, Jeffrey Kneebone and Nancy Maultsby, it is an amiable piece, well presented and freshly recorded.

Bruckner, Anton (1824–96)

Symphonies Nos. '0'; 1–9; in F min.
(B **(*) Teldec/Warner Dig. 0630 14192-2 (11) [(M) 2292 46068-2]. Frankfurt RSO, Eliahu Inbal.

Eliahu Inbal has strong Brucknerian instincts and his survey of the first versions of all the Bruckner *Symphonies*, which includes the fascinating early *Study Symphony*, is of great interest to Brucknerians, especially as Nos. 3, 4 and 8 had never been recorded before in their original versions. The Frankfurt Radio Orchestra responds well to Inbal's advocacy, always producing very acceptable results, often with playing of concentration and power. The recordings are spacious, bold and clear. The 11 discs are offered in a slip-case at bargain price, and the set can be recommended with little reservation. Sadly the documentation is inadequate, when each CD contains only a folded insert leaflet which gives the date of the edition used and the date and location of the recording.

Symphonies Nos. '0'; 1–9.
(B) **(*) Ph. 442 040-2 (9) [(M) id. import]. Concg. O, Haitink.
(B) **(*) Decca Dig. 448 910-2 (10) [id.]. Chicago SO, Solti.

Haitink's set of Bruckner symphonies (reissued as part of the Haitink Edition) has all the classic virtues: they are well shaped and free from affectation or any kind of rhythmic distortion. Haitink's grasp of the architecture is strong and his feeling for beauty of detail refined, though he only hints at the spiritual dimension in these works. With the Haas editions preferred, Haitink's judgements on matters of text are as sound as his approach is dedicated, and he secures consistently fine playing from the Concertebouw Orchestra. Only the *Eighth* with its generally brisk tempi is at all controversial. The CD transfers bring much more vivid sound than on LP, yet the overall balance is always convincing. The set also has the additional advantage of economy, with only No. 1 split between CDs; the other symphonies each occupy a single CD.

Solti had previously recorded the *Eighth* with the VPO for John Culshaw in the Sofiensaal as early as 1966 (see below). With the Chicago Symphony Orchestra he recorded the whole cycle between 1979 (No. 6) and 1995 (No. 5). The two early symphonies are very impressive, but the *Third* is the one failure, relatively crude and coarse. Otherwise, the *Seventh*, with refined playing, lacks tension in the outer movements, but the series culminates in an inspired account of the *Eighth*, and the *Ninth*, similarly spacious, with the music given full time to breathe. Other performances may be more deeply meditative, but the power of Solti and the brilliance of the playing and the digital recording are formidable.

Symphonies Nos. 1–9.
(M) *** DG 429 648-2 (9). BPO, Karajan.
(B) *** DG 429 079-2 (9) [id.]. BPO or Bav. RSO, Jochum.

The reappearance of Karajan's magnificent cycle, long a yardstick by which others were measured – and at mid-price (if only in the UK) – must be warmly welcomed. We have sung the praises of these recordings loud and long, and in their new format they are outstanding value.

Jochum's DG cycle was recorded between 1958 (No. 5) and 1967 (No. 2), all but four (Nos. 2, 3, 5 and 6) with the Berlin Philharmonic. It enjoys the advantage of accommodating one symphony per disc. No apology need be made for either the performances or the quality of the recorded sound, which wears its years lightly. One of the finest is the 1957 *Fifth*, to which Jochum brought a unique sense of mystery and atmosphere to Bruckner, and it more than compensates for the occasional freedom he permitted himself. His was the first overview of Bruckner on record, and he still has special claims as a guide in this terrain. He communicates a lofty inspiration to his players, and many of these readings can more than hold their own with later rivals.

Symphony No. 00 in F min. (Study Symphony).
(B) *** Teldec/Warner Dig. 0630 14193-2 [id.]. Frankfurt RSO, Inbal.
(N) *** Ondine Dig. ODE 920-2 [id.]. Deutsches SO, Ashkenazy.

Bruckner's *Study Symphony*, a student work, was written in 1863. The composer, a late starter, was just turning 40 and at the very beginning of his composing career. The surprise is the way the music has distinct pre-echoes of what was to come, especially the *Andante*, a remarkable piece of writing with brief tuttis stabbing into the lyrical flow, well brought off here. The Scherzo, too, is entirely typical, with a delightful, flowing trio on the woodwind. The finale, however, is Schumannesque, with lyrical influences from Wagner. Inbal and his orchestra are in excellent form and they approach the music with total freshness as if it were a mature work. They are very well recorded, and this is well worth considering at budget price.

Ashkenazy conducts his Berlin orchestra in a strong and purposeful reading. His speeds are consistently faster than those of Inbal on the rival recording; his manner more direct but still expressive, so that he brings out the inner intensity of the fine slow movement. The lovely *Adagio* of the *String quintet* in string orchestra format brings just as dedicated a performance, an excellent bonus. Full, warm sound. However the Inbal version has a considerable price advantage.

Symphony No. 0 in D min.
(B) *** Teldec/Warner Dig. 0630 14194-2 [id.]. Frankfurt RSO, Inbal.
*(**) Decca Dig. 452 160-2 [id.]. Chicago SO, Solti.

Symphony No. 0 in D min.; Overture in G min.
**(*) Decca (IMS) Dig. 421 593-2. Berlin RSO, Chailly.

Die Nullte is a work of striking quality that at times portends the greatness to come. Although it may not be ideally proportioned, some of its ideas have all the innocence and purity that distinguishes the finest early Bruckner. Inbal and his Frankfurt orchestra are again in impressive form here, giving a performance of undoubted spontaneity. The character of the first movement is immediately caught at the atmospheric opening. This is not an easy movement to hold together, but Inbal succeeds both in retaining tension and in creating a natural forward flow, as he does in his powerful and exciting account of the finale. This is one of the most impressive of Inbal's series and is well worth its modest price.

Riccardo Chailly's account of the unnumbered *D minor* (the so-called *Die Nullte*) is very acceptable. The Berlin Radio Orchestra respond well to his direction, Recommended both as a recording and as a performance. The *Overture in G minor* makes a welcome bonus.

Solti's version was the last of his cycle to be recorded (in 1995) and one of the most successful. His affection shows immediately at the jaunty opening and his pacing is admirable throughout, and the concentration is never in doubt. Decca's planners, however, should have known better than to issue this without any fill-up. Who these days will want to pay premium price for 38 minutes?

Symphonies Nos. 0 in D min. (Die Nulte); 8 in C min. (1887 Nowak edition).
(N) (BB) *** Naxos Dig. 8.554215/6 [id.]. Nat. SO of Ireland, Georg Tintner.

There are few Bruckner interpreters more persuasive than Georg Tintner. In a moving note, he passionately argues the case for Bruckner's original 1887 version of No. 8, fresh and spontaneous, written at white heat in the wake of the success of No.7. (This was the form in which Bruckner sent the score to Hermann Levi.) Most conductors opt for the 1889–90 revision, edited either by Haas or Nowak. The differences are major and there is much that will take you completely by surprise. The result is an intense, keenly concentrated reading, with total dedication in the playing, which rises to supreme heights in the long *Adagio* slow movement, where the refined *pianissimo* playing of the Irish Orchestra is magically caught by the Naxos engineers. Even for those with rival versions this makes a very necessary recommendation, particularly when the two-disc package brings so generous and revealing a coupling as the the *D minor Symphony (Die Nullte)* in a very good performance. Tintner powerfully brings out the Brucknerian qualities in embryo, and is again very well served by the Irish orchestra, even if the weight of big tuttis is less than in some others of this series. Overall, the recording could be richer particularly in the bass, but this should not put you off a set that is of exceptional interest and unfailingly illuminating.

Symphony No. 1 in C min. (original, Linz version).
*** Decca Dig. 448 898-2 [id.]. Chicago SO, Solti.
(B) ** Teldec/Warner Dig. 0630 14195-2 [id.]. Frankfurt RSO, Inbal.

Bruckner's *First* is a rather intractable symphony. The composer's restless alternations of heavy tuttis, energetic passages more lightly scored, and lyrical blossoming are less well knit together than in his mature works. Solti, on top form, as in the '*Nullte*', again creates a sweeping forward momentum, especially in the finale, which disguises the weaknesses. Excellent, atmospheric recording.

Inbal's direct, comparatively brisk approach – with the tempo changes in the first movement convincingly handled – makes quite a good case for Bruckner's earlier (1866) Linz version of No. 1, although the lack of opulence in the recording adds to the impression that the end result is lightweight.

Symphony No. 1 in C min.
(N) (BB) *** Arte Nova Dig. 74321 59226-2 [id.]. Saarbrücken RSO, Skrowaczewski.

Symphony No. 1 in C min.; (i) *Helgoland.*
(N) *(*) Teldec/Warner Dig. 0630 16646-2 [id.]. BPO, Barenboim with (i) Male voices of Berlin Radio Ch. and Ernst-Senff Ch.

Symphony No. 1 in C min.; (i) *Te Deum.*
(M) **(*) DG (IMS) Dig. 435 068-2. Chicago SO, Barenboim; (i) with Jessye Norman, Minton, Rendall, Ramey, Chicago Symphony Ch.

Skrowaczewski draws dedicated, tautly sprung playing from the Saarbrucken orchestra in what remains a problematic work. At speeds on the fast side, this is a fresh and urgent reading, which yet brings out the hushed intensity of the spacious second movement *Adagio*. Beautifully recorded in a helpful acoustic, it is a match for any version at whatever price.

Barenboim's version of the *Symphony No. 1* comes with the *Te Deum* with its starry quartet of soloists and the magnificent Chicago Symphony Chorus. In both works he directs beautifully played, spontaneous-sounding performances that mould Brucknerian lines persuasively, but in the *Symphony* the dramatic tension is less keen, lacking something in concentration. The early digital recording is good but not ideally clear, with a brightness that needs a little taming.

Barenboim's later Teldec version also has a welcome fill-up in the symphonic chorus, *Helgoland*, but that is one of its few advantanges. This is a warm, weighty reading, at times heavy-handed, which does not reveal the Berlin Philharmonic at its polished best. The recording is rather cloudy in tuttis.

Symphony No. 2 in C min. (original, 1872 score).
(BB) *** Naxos Dig. 8.554006 [id.]. Nat. SO of Ireland, Georg Tintner.
(B) ** Teldec/Warner Dig. 0630 14196-2 [id.]. Frankfurt RSO, Inbal.

In his Bruckner series for Naxos, Georg Tintner here firmly favours the composer's first thoughts, arguing that later revisions are not improvements. He therefore opts for the edition of the original (1872) score, published in 1991 by Dr William Carragan, presenting the work at its most expansive and with the middle two movements in reverse order from usual, the Scherzo coming before the slow movement. The Scherzo has an extra repeat, but more important is the expansion of both the slow movement and finale, here presented in concentrated performances that feel not a moment too long. The coda of the *Andante* brings a horn solo at the very end (substituted by Herbeck in 1876), challenging to the player, which is more strikingly beautiful than the clarinet solo with which Bruckner replaced it. Excellent, refined playing from the Irish orchestra and full, rich sound, with the brass gloriously caught.

In his Frankfurt performance, so the Teldec label tells us, Inbal offers the revised version of 1877, but what we get is something much closer to the 1872 Haas edition which, like the Naxos recording, retains the Scherzo and trio with all repeats and uses the original horn, instead of the clarinet, at the end of the slow movement. The closing string chords are missing here, which brings one up with a start. For the most part the playing is good without being outstanding, and the recording, made at the Frankfurt Opera, is very good. However, Tintner's account remains first choice for Brucknerians seeking the composer's first thoughts.

Symphony No. 2 in C min.
*** Decca Dig. 436 154-2 [id.]. Concg. O, Chailly.
*** Decca Dig. 436 844-2. Chicago SO, Solti.
*** DG Dig. 415 988-2. BPO, Karajan.
(N) *(*) Teldec 3984-21485-2 [id.]. Berlin PO, Daniel Barenboim.

Bruckner's *Second Symphony* is very long. Chailly uses the complete, Haas edition and his laid-back performance does not shirk that problem. It is a beautifully simple reading, with the slow-movement climax nobly graduated, a strong Scherzo without repeats (the Trio has a tuneful charm) and a finale that is not pressed forward ruthlessly but generates a positive and exciting closing section. The Decca recording is spacious and luminous. A first choice for the most elusive work in the Bruckner canon.

Solti, too, follows Haas. He is more urgent than Chailly but with no sense of too much emotional pressure. Strongly recommended to those who may feel Chailly is too relaxed with his spaciously moulded paragraphs. The effect of the Chicago recording, too, is more robust and full-blooded.

Karajan modifies the Nowak edition by opening out some of the cuts, but by no means all. He starts reticently, only later expanding in grandeur. The scherzo at a fast speed is surprisingly lightweight, the finale relatively slow and spacious. It is a noble reading, not always helped by rather bright digital recording.

Barenboim's latest version of the *Second* recorded at concerts in the Philharmonie in 1997 comes as something of a disappointment. He opts for the Nowak version of Bruckner's score and the playing is curiously routine and uninspired. The recording, too, is nothing to write home about.

Symphony No. 3 in D min. (original, 1873 version).
(B) *** Teldec/Warner Dig. 0630 14197-2 [id.]. Frankfurt RSO, Inbal.

There are in all three versions of the *Third Symphony*: the first, completed on the last day of 1873; a second, which Bruckner undertook immediately after completion of the *Fifth Symphony* in 1877; and then, after this second version proved unsuccessful, a third which he completed in 1889. The 1873 version is by far the longest, running to nearly 66 minutes (the first movement alone lasts 24 minutes), and for those who have either of the others it will make far more than a fascinating appendix. The playing of the Frankfurt Radio Orchestra under Eliahu Inbal has keen feeling for atmosphere and refined dynamic contrasts; the recording is most acceptable.

Symphony No. 3 in D min. (1877 version).
*** Ph. Dig. 422 411-2. VPO, Bernard Haitink.

Haitink gives us the 1877 version, favoured by many Bruckner scholars. Questions of edition apart, this is a performance of great breadth and majesty, and Philips give it a recording to match. The playing of the Vienna Philharmonic is glorious throughout, and even collectors who have alternative versions should acquire this magnificent issue.

Symphony No. 3 in D min. (Nowak edition).
**(*) RCA Dig. 09026 61374-2. N. German RSO, Hamburg, Wand.

As in his earlier version from 1981, made with the Cologne orchestra, Günter Wand opts for the 1889 version. This recording was compiled from public performances given at the Hamburg Musikhalle in January 1992, with a keen feeling of a live occasion. The new version is better played and more sumptuously recorded, while Wand's overall conception of the work is largely unchanged. The only flaw in a most compelling account is the slow movement, which some Brucknerians may find a shade brisk.

Symphonies Nos. 3 in D min.; 4 in E flat (Romantic) (Nowak editions).
(B) *** Decca Double 448 098-2 (2) [id.]. VPO, Karl Boehm.

There are many who admire Boehm's Bruckner, and he certainly controls the lyrical flow of these two symphonies convincingly, helped by first-rate playing from the VPO. Both recordings offer vintage Decca sound from 1970 and 1973 respectively; each has the advantage of the spacious acoustics of the Sofiensaal, and the balance provides splendid detail and a firm sonority. Boehm's sobriety was also his strength. In every bar he gives the impression that he knows exactly where he is going and, choosing the Nowak edition, he shapes each structure compellingly.

Symphonies Nos. 3 in D min; 4 in E flat; 5 in B flat; 6 in A; 7 in E, 8 in C min; 9 in D min; (i) *Mass No. 3 in F min*; (ii) *Te Deum*.

(N) ** EMI Dig. CDS5 56688-2 [id.]. (i) Margaret Price, Doris Soffel, Peter Straka, Matthis Hölle; (i; ii) Munich Philharmonic Ch.; (ii) Price, Christel Borchers; Claes Ahnsjö, Karl Helm, Munich Bach Ch.; Munich PO, Sergiu Celibidache.

Celibidache's strengths are well attested: he had a highly refined ear and achieved an orchestral sonority of great subtlety and polish. He was a conductor who divided orchestras and audiences alike, inspiring the strongest allegiance among his admirers and an equally strong reaction from others who found his eccentricities difficult to accommodate. A cult figure, he was an undoubted idealist who proceeded from a sense of total conviction and was always a controversial interpreter. With his keen ear, care for detail and fastidious sense of colour and texture, Celibidache transformed the sound of the orchestras he conducted, such as the Swedish Radio Orchestra in the 1960s and the Munich Philharmonic in the 1980s and 1990s. But sceptics note that he rarely conducted any of the great orchestras. Some good judges have been persuaded by Celibidache's sense of texture and his obvious dedication, but for others the eccentricities place an insurmountable obstacle between the composer and the listener. He manages to take over 100 minutes over the *Eighth Symphony* as opposed to Jochum's or Karajan's 83, and he takes 20 minutes longer than Furtwängler. Likewise his *Ninth* is 68 minutes whereas most interpreters are under the hour. These performances are difficult to grade: for Celibidache devotees they will rate three stars no doubt, for both the orchestral response and the recorded sound are not to be faulted; others exasperated by his funereal tempi may not wish to accord them any at all!

Symphonies Nos. 3 in D min.; 7 in E.

(B) *** EMI forte (SIS) CZS5 68652-2 (2) [CDFB 68652]. Dresden State O, Jochum.

As a Brucknerian, Eugen Jochum has a special magnetism. Whatever the reservations that may be made on detailed points of style – Jochum believes in a free variation of tempo within a movement – his natural affinity of temperament with the saintly, innocent Austrian gives these massive structures an easy, warm, unforced concentration which brings out their lyricism as well as their architectural grandeur. So it is in these fine performances with the Dresden orchestra, made at the beginning of the 1980s. As in his earlier cycle with the Berlin Philharmonic and Bavarian Radio orchestras, he uses the Nowak edition. With his understanding of Bruckner developing towards a more direct and monumental approach, the authority is never in doubt, and this is matched by splendid playing from the Dresden orchestra.

Symphonies Nos. 3 in D min.; 8 in C min.

(B) **(*) Sony SB2K 53519 (2) [id.]. Cleveland O, Szell.

** Decca Dig. 443 753-2. Cleveland O, Dohnányi.

Szell is not a gentle Brucknerian, and in No. 3 the close-up Cleveland recording adds to the tangibility of his reading. But this outstanding American orchestra – here at its peak in 1966 – under the most incisive of conductors is hard to resist. Szell also uses the 1889 Nowak Edition and this reissue presents a marvellously strong interpretation. In No. 8 Szell again uses a revised text, but here the differences between this and the Nowak edition favoured by Jochum are relatively minor. Szell's interpretation as a whole is masterly, and the Cleveland Orchestra produces glorious playing, recorded, like No. 3, in the spacious acoustics of Severance Hall (in 1969). In the CD transfers the sound remains brightly lit but the dynamic range in No. 8 is wide.

There is also much magnificent playing from the Clevelanders in Dohnányi's similar coupling, particularly in slow movements. But Dohnányi (who uses the Oeser Edition in No. 3 and Haas in No. 8) fails to exert the same grip on the proceedings that makes the Szell performances so compelling: while there are moments of high drama, the tension ebbs and flows unevenly. Wide-ranging Decca sound.

Symphony No. 4 in E flat (Romantic) (original, 1874 version).

(B) **(*) Teldec/Warner 0630 14198-2 [id.]. Frankfurt RSO, Inbal.

Like the *Third*, there are three versions of the *Romantic Symphony*, and no one has recorded the original before. The Scherzo here is a completely different and more fiery movement, and the opening of the finale is also totally different. Inbal's performance is good, with a genuine feeling for the Bruckner idiom, paying scrupulous attention to dynamic refinements. The recording is well detailed, though the climaxes almost (but not quite) reach congestion. An indispensable and fascinating issue, especially attractive at bargain price.

Symphony No. 4 in E flat (Romantic).

(N) *** RCA Dig. 09026 68839-2 [id.]. Berlin PO, Günter Wand.

(M) *** DG 449 718-2 [id.]. BPO, Jochum (with SIBELIUS: *Night ride and sunrise, Op. 55* with Bav. RSO (***)).

(M) *** DG 439 522-2. BPO, Karajan.

(N) (BB) *** Naxos Dig. 8.554128 [id.]. RSNO, Georg Tintner.

(B) *** Ph. Virtuoso 442 044-2 [(M) id. import]. Concg. O, Haitink.

(N) (M) *** Decca Legends 466 374-2 [id.]. VPO, Karl Boehm.

(M) **(*) Sony Bruno Walter Edition SMK 64481 [id.]. Columbia SO, Bruno Walter.

(B) **(*) [EMI Red Line Dig. CDR5 69795]. BPO, Muti.

(M) **(*) EMI CDM5 66094-2 [id.]. BPO, Karajan.

(BB) **(*) RCA Navigator 74321 17895-2. Leipzig GO, Kurt Masur.

(M) **(*) Carlton IMP Dig. 30367 00282 [id.]. Hallé O, Skrowaczewski.

(N) ** Teldec/Warner Dig. 0630 17126-2 [id.]. Concg. O, Harnoncourt.

(N) *(*) Sony Dig. SK63301 [id.]. LAPO, Esa-Pekka Salonen.

Symphony No. 4 in E flat; Overture in G min.
(***) Testament mono/stereo SBT 1050 [id.]. Philh. O, Lovro von Matăcić.

Gunther Wand's Berlin version of the *Fourth Symphony* crowns his achievement as one of our greatest Bruckner conductors. The recording derives from a concert at the Philharmonie in Berlin and conveys a sense of occasion so often missing in the studio. Wand knows what this music is about and has the command of its architecture and space. One feels immediately comfortable in his hands, dedicated and purposeful, with consistently warm textures from the Berlin Philharmonic. Speeds are perfectly judged. Rubato is more extreme than in most studio readings, but the massive structure is lucidly held together in total concentration. Keenly dramatic, capped by towering climaxes, it offers full, rich sound, if with *pianissimos* not quite as hushed as they might be. This is much more successful than Wand's earlier recordings with the NDR Cologne Orchestra, and must rank alongside the finest now in the catalogue; for collectors wanting a premium-priced version this will probably be first choice.

Jochum's way with Bruckner is unique. So gentle is his hand that the opening of each movement or even the beginning of each theme emerges into the consciousness rather than starting normally. The purist may object that, in order to do this, Jochum reduces the speed far below what is marked, but Jochum is for the listener who wants above all to love Bruckner. The recording has been enhanced in this reissue in DG's 'Originals' series, and a fascinating mono recording of Sibelius's *Night ride and sunrise* has been added. Jochum was not thought of as a Sibelian, but this performance is most impressive.

Karajan's opening (on his DG version) also has more beauty and a greater feeling of mystery than almost anyone else on CD. As in his earlier, EMI record, Karajan brings a keen sense of forward movement to this music as well as showing a firm grip on its architecture. His slow movement is magnificent. The current remastering of the 1975 analogue recording, made in the Philharmonie, is very impressive. The sound may lack the transparency and detail of the very finest of his records, but it is full and firmly focused.

There are not many versions as fine as Georg Tintner's on Naxos, at whatever price. With extreme *pianissimos* magically caught, full of mystery, this is an exceptionally spacious reading, deeply reflective and poetic, which brings out the Schubertian qualities in Bruckner, sweet and songful as well as dramatic. The playing of the Scottish National Orchestra is as refined as the recording, with subtly terraced dynamics beautifully clear.

Haitink's performance is noble and unmannered; the opening horn solo is arresting and the orchestral playing is eloquent. The new CD transfer is excellent, and this is good value and a primary bargain choice, although Jochum on DG is worth the extra cost.

Boehm's fine 1973 version with the VPO, here reissued on Decca's Legends label is discussed above in its coupling with No. 3.

Although not quite as impressive as his Bruckner *Ninth*, Bruno Walter's 1960 recording is transformed by its CD remastering, with textures clearer, strings full and brass sonorous. The superbly played 'hunting horn' Scherzo is wonderfully vivid. Walter makes his recording orchestra sound remarkably European in style and timbre. The reading is characteristically spacious. Walter's special feeling for Bruckner means that he can relax over long musical paragraphs and retain his control of the structure, while the playing has fine atmosphere and no want of mystery.

With warm, slightly distanced sound, the sensuous beauty of the Berlin Philharmonic string section has rarely been caught so beautifully. Muti as a Brucknerian has a fine feeling for climax, building over the longest span, and his flexible phrase-shaping of Brucknerian melody, very different from traditional rugged treatment, reflects a vocal style of expressiveness. With that extra warmth and high dramatic contrasts, Muti takes Bruckner further south than usual.

Karajan's 1970 recording for EMI, made in the Berlin Jesus-Christus Kirche and now reissued in the Karajan Edition, at high voltage combines simplicity and strength. The playing of the Berlin Philharmonic is very fine. The resonance means that there is a touch of harshness on the considerable *fortissimos*, while *pianissimos* are relatively diffuse. However, at mid-price this remains well worth considering.

Lovro von Matăcić's Philharmonia account of the *Fourth Symphony* dates from 1954 and used the Franz Schalk–Karl Loewe edition of 1889, with cuts in the Scherzo and finale. This fine Testament transfer pays tribute to the fine ears of the Walter

Legge/Douglas Larter recording team, with the sound beautifully blended. When it was issued in the USA, the *Overture in G minor* was added two years later, and this was also recorded in stereo. The performance has both lucidity and majesty, with Dennis Brain's horn-playing outstanding.

In RCA's super-bargain Navigator series, Masur with the Leipzig orchestra, after opening poetically, shapes individual movements spaciously and convincingly. The resonant Leipzig recording has brought some problems with the digital remastering, with some coarseness in *fortissimos*. Still very recommendable at super-bargain price, when the interpretation is so instinctively sympathetic.

Stanislav Skrowaczewski's reading with the Hallé Orchestra is straightforward and well shaped. As one would expect from this conductor, the tempi are well judged and the concept spacious and majestic, with scrupulous attention to detail in matters of both phrasing and dynamics. The playing from the Hallé is responsive and sensitive, and there is no idiosyncrasy or self-indulgence. Overall this is a fine performance, full of perceptive touches. The recording has depth and atmosphere, but lacks warmth.

Harnoncourt's is a relatively objective view of Bruckner, rugged and purposeful, less emotional than most. Dynamic shading is precisely caught, and the Concertgebouw Orchestra plays with typical refinement, with refined recording to match. But there are many more compelling versions than this.

From Salonen on Sony, beautiful orchestral sound, and the unaffected opening paragraphs give promise of a fine performance, but there is soon an abrupt lurch forwards which is convincing at no level. The playing of the Los Angeles Philharmonic and the Sony recording are of the highest order and one only wishes that they were at the service of a selfless interpreter. Recommended to this conductor's admirers rather than Bruckner's.

Symphony No. 5 in B flat (original version).
(B) *(*) Teldec/Warner Dig. 0630 14199-2 [id.]. Frankfurt RSO, Inbal.

Eliahu Inbal makes a promising start to the *Fifth Symphony* and gets good playing from the Frankfurt Radio forces. Unfortunately his slow movement is far too brisk to be convincing - lasting 14 minutes, as against Jochum's 19 and Karajan's 21.

Symphony No. 5 in B flat.
*** Decca Dig. 433 819-2 [id.]. Concg. O, Chailly.
*** EMI Dig. CDC5 55125-2 [id.]. LPO, Franz Welser-Möst.
*** RCA Dig. 09026 68503-2 [id.]. BPO, Günter Wand.
(***) EMI (SIS) mono CDH5 56750-2 [id.]. VPO, Furtwängler.

Chailly gave us an outstanding Bruckner *Seventh* with the Berlin Radio Symphony Orchestra in the early days of CD which still ranks high among all the competition (see below), and this version of the *Fifth* is, if anything, even finer. The Royal Concertgebouw Orchestra play with sumptuous magnificence, and Chailly's overall control of a work that is notable for its diversive episodes is unerring, moving towards an overwhelming final apotheosis. The *Adagio* is very beautiful and never sounds hurried. The Decca recording is superb, with the brass attacking brilliantly. An easy first choice.

The London Philharmonic play eloquently for Franz Welser-Möst in their live recording, made in the Konzerthaus, Vienna, in late May–early June 1993 before an attentive and silent audience. There are some potentially disruptive agogic touches, but Welser-Möst succeeds in persuading you that they have logical motivation. The wide-ranging dynamics are well captured by the engineers.

In his later version Günter Wand forsakes the Cologne and Hamburg orchestras (with which he made his earlier recordings) in favour of the Berlin Philharmonic. The present disc was put together from three concert performances given in January 1996. Wand, an experienced and selfless interpreter, gives a noble reading, magnificently played.

Furtwängler's account of the *Fifth Symphony* comes from the invaluable Salzburg Archives and was recorded at the 1951 Salzburg Festival. (The remainder of the concert included Mendelssohn's *Fingal's Cave* and Mahler's *Lieder eines fahrenden Gesellen* with the 26-year-old Fischer-Dieskau.) Considering its age, the sound is remarkably good; the EMI engineers have done wonders in restoring its colours, and the performance has that blend of warmth, majesty and radiance which distinguishes the best Furtwängler.

Symphonies Nos. 5 in B flat (1878 edition); *6 in A* (original version).
(B) **(*) EMI (SIS) forte CZS5 72661-2 (2) [CDFB 72661]. Dresden State O, Jochum.

Jochum's DG account of the *Fifth Symphony* (with the Bavarian Radio Orchestra) was one of the earliest and one of the finest of his first cycle, and DG should consider issuing it as one of their 'Originals'. However, the Dresden version also has a very impressive slow movement, and the *Sixth* is similarly compelling. The CD transfers are admirably spacious, and the Dresden strings have plenty of depth. But the brass is rather too brightly lit, and, especially in the climaxes of the *Sixth Symphony*, the effect is brash.

Symphony No. 6 in A (original version).
(B) ** Teldec/Warner Dig. 0630 14200-2 [(M) id. import]. Frankfurt RSO, Inbal.

Again Inbal secures good playing from the Frankfurt Radio Orchestra, and he is well served by the engineers. The recording is full-bodied and spacious and has a dramatically wide dynamic range. Nevertheless the performance, even taking into account some fine string playing in the slow movement (the best part of the performance), is a little short on personality. After the *Fifth*, the *Sixth* is probably the least well served of Inbal's cycle.

Symphony No. 6 in A.
*** Decca (IMS) Dig. 436 129-2 [id.]. San Francisco SO, Blomstedt (with WAGNER: *Siegfried Idyll* ***).
(N) (M) *** EMI CDM5 67037-2 [id.]. New Philh. O, Klemperer – WAGNER: *Wesendonk Lieder.* **
(M) **(*) DG 447 525-2 [id.]. BPO, Karajan.
(BB) **(*) Arte Nova Dig. 74321 54456-2 [id.]. Saarbrücken RSO, Skrowaczewski.

Blomstedt uses the Nowak edition, and in warmth and intensity the San Francisco strings readily match those of any rival, even Karajan's Berlin Philharmonic. The performance is splendidly shaped and the broad-spanned slow movement is particularly fine. Quite apart from providing a generous and beautifully played coupling in Wagner's *Siegfried Idyll*, Decca's recording is also outstanding, at once full-bodied and warm but cleanly defined.

Klemperer directs a characteristically strong and direct reading. It is disarmingly simple rather than overly expressive in the slow movement (faster than usual), but is always concentrated and strong, and the finale is particularly well held together. Splendid playing from the orchestra, with the mid 1960s recording clear, bright, yet full-bodied in this remastering for 'The Klemperer Legacy'.

Karajan is not as commanding here as in his other Bruckner recordings, yet this is still a compelling performance, tonally very beautiful and with a glowing account of the slow movement that keeps it in proportion. The 1979 analogue recording might ideally have been more expansive.

Stanislaw Skrowaczewski has proved himself an impressive Bruckner interpreter. This Arte Nova recording, made in the Saarbrücken Congress Hall in 1997, is very serviceable indeed and Skrowaczewski guides his forces with unerring purpose and nobility. Tempi are well judged throughout and phrases shaped with refinement. The string-tone needs perhaps to be weightier, but this is a very good performance, recommendable alongside Tintner on Naxos, whose account has slightly less gravitas but still has its own appealing individuality.

Symphony No. 7 in E (original edition).
(B) ** Teldec/Warner Dig. 0630 14201-2 [(M) 4509 97437-2]. Frankfurt RSO, Inbal.

For excellence of orchestral playing and vividness of recording, Inbal's *Seventh* is well up to the standard of his Bruckner series, using the original scores; but the performance itself, although it does not lack an overall structural grip, is without the full flow of adrenalin that can make this symphony so compulsive. The orgasmic climax of the slow movement is much less telling without the two famous cymbal-crashes.

Symphony No. 7 in E.
(B) *** Decca Eclipse Dig. 448 710-2. Berlin RSO, Chailly (with MAHLER: *Des Knaben Wunderhorn: Des Antonius von Padua Fischpredigt; Das irdische Leben* – with Brigitte Fassbaender ***).
(N) (BB) *** Naxos Dig. 8.554269 [id.]. RSNO, Tintner
(M) *** Ph. 446 580-2 [id.]. Concg. O, Haitink.
(M) *** EMI CDM5 66095-2 [id.]. BPO, Karajan.
*** DG (IMS) Dig. 437 518-2 [id.]. VPO, Abbado.
*** EMI Dig. CDC7 54434-2 [id.]. LPO, Welser-Möst.
(N) (M) (***) Dutton Lab. mono CDK 1205 [id.]. Concg. O, Eduard van Beinum (with TCHAIKOVSKY: *Waltz* from *Serenade for strings.* (***)).
(M) **(*) DG Dig. 445 553-2 [id.]. VPO, Carlo Maria Giulini.
(M) ** Sony Bruno Walter Edition SMK 64481 [id.]. Columbia SO, Bruno Walter.
(N) ** EMI Dig. CMS5 56425-2 [id.]. CBSO, Rattle.

Chailly's account, with its superb Decca digital recording, makes an obvious first choice. He obtains some excellent playing from the Berlin Radio Symphony Orchestra and, though he may not attain the spirituality of Karajan and Jochum, his is a committed and very moving performance, and the apparent lack of weight soon proves deceptive. He has a considerable command of the work's architecture and controls its sonorities expertly. The recording, made in the Jesus-Christus Kirche, Berlin, is outstanding in every way. Reissued on Eclipse with the bonus of two delightful songs from Mahler's *Des Knaben Wunderhorn* sung by Brigitte Fassbaender, this is an unbeatable bargain.

Like his other Bruckner recordings for Naxos, Tintner's account of No. 7 brings a performance both subtle and refined, concentrated from first to last, often at spacious speeds. The glow of Brucknerian sound is beautifully caught, with the full nobility of the slow movement brought out. The *Scherzo* is not as rugged as it can be, but with sprung rhythms the dance element is infectious. An outstanding bargain to rival any version.

Haitink's 1978 version offers a fine alternative at mid-price. The recording is wide in range and refined in detail, yet retains the ambient warmth of the Concertgebouw. Haitink's reading is more searching than his earlier version, made in the 1960s. The Concertgebouw Orchestra play with their accustomed breadth of tone and marvellously blended ensemble.

Karajan's outstanding EMI version (recorded in the Berlin Jesus-Christus Kirche in 1970–71) also shows a superb feeling for the work's architecture and the playing of the Berlin Philharmonic is gorgeous. The recording has striking resonance and amplitude. This EMI reading, generally preferable to his later, digital recording for DG, has a special sense of mystery. The transfer for the Karajan Edition enhances the quality, and this recording has never sounded better.

It is difficult to fault Claudio Abbado's DG account, which brings playing of great eloquence from the Vienna Philharmonic. The sound has splendid lustre and the architecture is impressively realized. No one listening to it is likely to feel short-changed – but at the same time one comes away from it with the sense that, despite its tonal finesse and opulent recording, there are depths undiscovered and terrain unexplored.

EMI's version with the LPO conducted by Franz Welser-Möst comes from a 1991 Prom and so enjoys a warmer ambience than most studio performances. The LPO are responsive and produce a fine Bruckner sound, save perhaps at the bottom end of the aural spectrum. As one would expect from a native Austrian, Welser-Möst has a natural feel for Bruckner's spacious lyricism. Audience noise is minimal, save in the wild applause at the end

Eduard van Beinum's reading brings a wonderfully persuasive response from the Concertgebouw Orchestra, not only rich in sonority, but refined and often surprisingly transparent in texture, so that the effect of Bruckner's scoring is lighter than usual, especially in the lilting Scherzo. The great *Adagio* has superb concentration and if van Beinum does not manage the cymbal-capped climax quite as deftly as Chailly, the brass-playing which follows is wonderfully eloquent, and the end of the movement, like the apotheosis of the finale, is superbly managed. Given another of Dutton's miraculous transfers, the 1947 Decca recording sounds both spacious and full-bodied; one forgets almost immediately one is listening to a mono recording transferred from 78s. The Tchaikovsky *Waltz*, which acts as encore, is sheer delight. Edward Sackville West and Desmond Shawe Taylor's *Record Guide* described the original 78s of the symphony as 'a performance of extraordinary magnificence', and so it still is!

Giulini secures playing of the utmost refinement from the Vienna Philharmonic and shapes each paragraph lovingly – indeed, at times some might think too lovingly: the Vienna strings are occasionally prone to a little too much sweetness. All the same, here are some wonderful things and music-making of affecting eloquence, even though there is a lack of consistent forward movement. The DG recording has splendid warmth, with sumptuous sounds from the Vienna Philharmonic.

Walter's reading concentrates on detail at the expense of structure. The outer movements bring many illuminating touches and the final climax of the first is imposingly built, but overall the tension is loosely held, and in the *Adagio*, which is kept moving fairly convincingly, the climax is disappointing. The 1963 recording has been opened up in its remastering for CD and sounds fuller and more spacious than the original LPs.

Rattle's reading of No. 7 brings opulent sound from the Birmingham Orchestra, with exceptionally spacious speeds well sustained, and with subtle terracing of dynamics. Even so, this is not the most tensely dramatic of Rattle's recorded performances,. Recommended for those who value Bruckner for his heavenly length.

Symphonies Nos. 7 in E; 9 in D min.
(B) (**(*)) DG Double mono 445 418-2 (2).
BPO, Furtwängler.

These are both historic accounts, conveniently packaged as a Double; but the *Seventh Symphony*, recorded when the Berlin Philharmonic were on tour in Cairo in 1951, offers less appealing sound than the *Ninth*, which emanates from the closing months of the war, October 1944, not long before Furtwängler fled from the Nazis. The terrible times through which Europe was passing lent a special intensity to music-making, and this is a performance of vision. The *Seventh* is not quite so special; but the set is well worth acquiring for the sake of the *Ninth*.

Symphony No. 8 in C min. (original, 1887 version).
(B) **(*) Teldec/Warner Dig. 0630 14202-2 [id.].
Frankfurt RSO, Inbal.

Eliahu Inbal continues his stimulating series with a generally impressive and well-played first version of No. 8. There are considerable divergences here from the versions we know, and readers will undoubtedly derive much satisfaction from comparing them. The recording is very good.

Symphony No. 8 in C min.
✿ *** DG Dig. 427 611-2 (2) [id.]. VPO, Karajan.
*** Ph. Dig 446 659-2. VPO, Haitink.
*** DG Dig. 447 744-2. Dresden State O, Sinopoli – STRAUSS: *Metamorphosen*. ***
(M) *** EMI (SIS) CMS5 66109-2 (2). BPO, Karajan – BRAHMS: *Tragic Overture;* HINDEMITH: *Mathis der Maler* (symphony). ***
(M) *** EMI CDM7 64849-2. LPO, Tennstedt.
*** RCA Dig. 09026 68047-2 (2) [id.]. N. German RSO, Wand.

Karajan's last version of the *Eighth Symphony* is with the Vienna Philharmonic Orchestra and is the most impressive of them all. The sheer beauty of sound and opulence of texture are awe-inspiring but never draw attention to themselves: this is a performance in which beauty and truth go hand in hand. The recording is superior to either of its predecessors in terms of naturalness of detail and depth of perspective.

Bernard Haitink and the Vienna Philharmonic are a formidable combination; add to them the doyen of Philips engineers, Volker Strauss, and the results are outstanding. The performance is magnificent in its breadth and nobility. Not only does it possess great dramatic sweep, its slow movement has a greater depth than his earlier reading. The Vienna Philharmonic play with great fervour and warmth, and the recorded sound is sumptuous.

The newest transfer of Karajan's 1958 Berlin Philharmonic recording is remarkably successful. The EMI sound is spacious and, if the sonorities are not quite as sumptuous as we would expect today, the strings do not lack body and the brass makes a thrilling impact. Like Karajan's later versions for DG this has compelling power, with the slow movement concentratedly conveying dark and tragic feelings. As well as the advantage of economy, it offers outstanding couplings of Brahms and Hindemith.

Sinopoli in the *Eighth Symphony* is refreshingly straightforward and untouched by exaggeration. The playing of the Staatskapelle, Dresden, has an expressive power and beauty that are greatly enhanced by sumptuous recorded sound of outstanding quality.

The plainness and honesty of Tennstedt in Bruckner are heard at their finest in this impressive account of the *Eighth*. The inwardness and hushed beauty of the great *Adagio* in particular are superbly projected in unforced concentration. Though Karajan conveys more of the work's visionary power, Tennstedt in his comparative reticence carries similar conviction. Where generally in the other symphonies he prefers the Haas editions to those of Nowak, here he is in favour of Nowak without the additional material in the recapitulation. Fine, well-balanced recording, with the CD clarity filled out by the fullness of ambience. EMI's No. 1 Studio is made to sound like a concert hall.

Günter Wand is as far removed from the jet-set maestro as it is possible to get, and his later recording of the *Eighth Symphony* has patrician eloquence. It is the product of three live concerts from December 1993, and is a straightforward, selfless reading of integrity and vision. This comes on two CDs, packaged as one and costing as much. Given its artistic claims and the very truthful sound, it is certainly worth considering.

Symphony No. 8 in C min. (*Scherzo; Adagio; Finale* only).
(***) Koch Schwann mono/stereo 314482 [id.]. Prussian State O, Karajan.

Who would ever have thought that a Bruckner symphony *without its first movement* would ever score so resounding a success? Karajan's 1944 recording, made at a time when the war was at so crucial a stage, was among those which were spirited off to the then Soviet Union after the Nazi collapse. Technically the sound is quite astonishing – and in the finale, an early example of stereo, is little short of incredible. Not only is it extraordinary in terms of sound, it is also of exceptional artistic interest. The finale has a breadth and spaciousness, a grandeur and, above all, a sense of repose, that Karajan does not surpass in his later recordings.

Symphonies Nos. (i) *8 in C min;* (ii) *9 in D min.*
(N) *** BBC Legends BBCL 4017-2 (2) [id.]. (i) LSO; (ii) BBCSO, Jascha Horenstein.
(M) (***) DG mono 449 758-2 (2) [id.]. (i) Hamburg PO, (ii) Bav. RSO; Eugen Jochum.
(M) (***) Ph. mono 442 730-2; (IMS) 430 731-2 (available separately). Concg. O, van Beinum.

These BBC recordings of performances at the Royal Albert Hall in 1970 reveal the genius of Jascha Horenstein more tellingly than almost any of his studio recordings. With a Ukrainian father and an Austrian mother, he brings to these massive symphonies not just a rare concentration, devotional in its intensity, but an underlying passion. Though he draws out the warm expressiveness in Bruckner's lyrical writing, moulding phrases, he takes a rugged view of the overall structure, not least in his rapt account of the great *Adagio* in *Symphony No. 8*. Fine as the LSO is in that symphony with its brighter string tone, the performance of the *Ninth* with the BBC Symphony brings even finer playing – warm, strong and purposeful in the outer movements, relishing the contrasts in the central Scherzo, both witty and rugged. Warm, atmospheric radio sound.

Jochum's mono recordings of the *Eighth* and *Ninth Symphonies* date from 1949 and 1954. The DG sound is technically of astonishingly fine quality, particularly in the gloriously played *Adagio* of the *Eighth* which has a remarkably wide dynamic range. Jochum gives a feeling of total spontaneity as the music ebbs and flows foward. The conductor's sense of vision and unique understanding of Bruckner's spiritual base comes over as strongly here as in his later, stereo versions, if not more so.

Although van Beinum's *Ninth* has been reissued on LP, the *Eighth* makes its first appearance since the 1950s. It is a performance of considerable stature and sounds astonishingly good. In the *Eighth Symphony* tempi are on the brisk side and the musical argument proceeds with an impressive and compelling logic. And what a glorious sound the Concertgebouw Orchestra makes! These are performances of commanding integrity, well worth adding to any collection, and to be preferred to many full-price versions of the 1990s.

Symphony No. 9 in D min. (1896 original version).
(B) **(*) Teldec/Warner Dig. 0630 14203-2 [id.]. Frankfurt RSO, Eliahu Inbal.

Eliahu Inbal's reading of the *Ninth* with the Frankfurt Radio Orchestra in the original version is far from negligible. The playing is often very fine, and Inbal is scrupulously attentive to detail; however, there is not the sense of scale that is to be found in the best of his rivals.

Symphony No. 9 in D min.
✪ (M) *** Sony Bruno Walter Edition SMK 64483 [id.]. Columbia SO, Bruno Walter.
(M) *** DG 429 904-2 [id.]. BPO, Karajan.
*** Teldec/Warner Dig. 9031 72140-2 [id.]. BPO, Barenboim.
*** DG Dig. 427 345-2 [id.]. VPO, Giulini.
(B) **(*) DG Classikon 445 126 [(M) [id.]. import]. BPO, Jochum.
(N) **(*) DG Dig. 457 587-2 [id.]. Staatskapelle Dresden, Sinopoli.
(N) **(*) Decca Dig. 455 506-2 [id.]. Concg.O, Riccardo Chailly (with BACH, Orch. WEBERN: *Musical Offering: Fuga ricercata à 6.* ***)
(N) ** Nicone ICN9412-2 [id.]. Leningrad PO, Yevgeni Mravinsky.

Bruno Walter's 1959 account of Bruckner's *Ninth Symphony* represents the peak of his achievement during his Indian summer in the CBS recording studios just before he died. His mellow, persuasive reading leads one on through the leisurely paragraphs so that the logic and coherence seem obvious where other performances can sound aimless. Some may not find the Scherzo vigorous enough to provide the fullest contrast, but the final slow movement has a nobility which suggests that after this, anything would have been an anticlimax.

The DG Galleria reissue of Karajan's 1966 recording offers a glorious performance of Bruckner's last and uncompleted symphony, characteristically moulded and displaying a simple, direct nobility that is sometimes missing in this work. Even in a competitive field, this 1966 disc stands out at mid-price, to rank alongside Bruno Walter's noble 1959 version.

Daniel Barenboim's Berlin account has depth and strength, with the advantage of superb orchestral playing, and the recorded sound has splendid body and transparency. One of the strongest of newer recommendations.

Giulini's *Ninth*, too, is a great performance, the product of deep thought. There is the keenest feeling for texture and beauty of contour, and he distils a powerful sense of mystery from the first and third movements. The DG recording is spacious and transparent.

Jochum's reading has greater mystery than any other and the orchestral playing reaches a degree of eloquence that disarms criticism. If at times Jochum tends to phrase too affectionately, he is still magnetic in everything he does. The 1966 recording sounds remarkably fine. An excellent bargain version.

There is some disagreement about Sinopoli's live recording of the *Ninth*. E. G.'s view is that he conducts a passionate, intense reading, with its impact enhanced by superb playing and full, immediate sound. The freely expressive phrasing and rhythmic pointing, owing much to the inspiration of the moment, goes with fine control of structure and a sense of dedication, making this disc a top recommendation among modern digital recordings. For R. L. there is a lot to admire, not least the magnificence of the orchestral playing. But the recording venue is the Semperoper and not the Lukaskirche in which his earlier Bruckner recordings have been made and the acoustic, though not dry, is by no means as expansive as other Dresden recordings. The sound is impressively detailed and the performance goes well until the slow movement when Sinopoli's tendency to italicize and underline detail gets the better of him. At about 19 minutes into the movement, he loses impetus and the whole movement sags. Generally he allows the music to speak for itself in the first two movements – the *Scherzo* is particularly impressive. However this is not a reading to which R. L. would return in preference to, say, Walter's account.

Chailly conducts a soberly dedicated reading of the *Ninth*, with the Concertgebouw playing superbly. If in his spacious view of the finale, he lacks the concentration of the finest versions, this is still worth considering by those who prefer an objective reading. Excellent sound, rather less full-bodied than some from this source. The Webern arrangement of Bach makes an imaginative fill-up.

Mravinsky's account of the *Ninth Symphony* comes from 1982 and naturally sounds much better than his 1960 account included in the RCA/BMG box. He brings great breadth to the score and draws playing of intensity and warmth from his great orchestra. Not a first choice, given the abundance of recordings now in the catalogue, but highly recommendable – and not just to Mravinsky *aficionados* but to all who care about Bruckner.

CHAMBER MUSIC

String quintet in F.
*** Nimbus NI 5488 [id.] Brandis Qt, with Brett Dean – BRAHMS: *String quintet No. 2.* ***
String quintet in F; Intermezzo for string quintet.
(*) Hyperion Dig. CDA 66704 [id.]. Raphael Ens. – R. STRAUSS: *Capriccio: Sextet.* *
(M) **(*) CRD Dig. CRD 3456 [id.]. Alberni Qt.

This Brandis version of the *Quintet* offers a splendid coupling in Brahms's *G major Quintet*, Op. 111, and their playing stands up well alongside the current competition. They are well recorded and have a natural feeling for the space and pacing of this piece.

For those attracted by the coupling, this could well be a first choice.

The Raphael Ensemble, coupling their performance with the *Intermezzo in D minor* and the opening *Sextet* from Strauss's *Capriccio*, are ardently full-blooded in an eloquent account, and have the benefit of rich recorded sound.

The Alberni version comes from the early 1980s without any additional fill-up. It is well played without affectation and, taken in isolation, is most satisfying. Hardly a first choice.

VOCAL MUSIC

Masses Nos. (i) *1 in D min*. (for soloists, chorus and orchestra); *2 in E min*. (for 8-part chorus and wind ensemble); (ii) *3 in F min*. (for soloists, chorus and orchestra).

❁ (M) *** DG 447 409-2 (2) [id.]. (i) Mathis, Schiml, Ochman, Ridderbusch; (ii) Stader, Hellman, Haefliger, Borg; Bav. R. Ch. & O, Jochum.

Bruckner composed his three *Masses* between 1864 and 1868, although all three works were revised two decades later. Each contains magnificent music; Eugen Jochum is surely an ideal interpreter, finding their mystery as well as their eloquence, breadth and humanity. The *Kyrie* of the *E minor* swelling out gloriously from its gentle opening is breathtaking, while the fervour of the passionate *F minor* work is extraordinarily compelling, with the intensity and drive of an inspirational live performance. Throughout all three works the scale and drama of Bruckner's inspiration are fully conveyed. In these outstanding new transfers, the warmly atmospheric analogue recordings from the early 1970s are given remarkable vividness and presence. A splendid choice for DG's 'Original' series of Legendary Recordings.

Masses Nos. 1 in D min.; 2 in E min.; 3 in F min. Aequalis Nos. 1 & 2. Motets: Afferentur regi virgines; Ave Maria; Christus factus est; Ecce sacardos magnus; Inveni David; Locus iste; Os justi; Pange lingua; Tota pulchra es, Maria; Vexilla regis; Virga Jesse; Libera me; Psalm 150; Te Deum.

*** Hyperion Dig. CDS 4407 (3) [id.]. Soloists, Corydon Singers and O; ECO Wind Ens., Matthew Best; T. Trotter (organ).

It makes good sense to assemble all of the Bruckner choral music that the Corydon Singers and Matthew Best have done during the last few years in one three-CD set. They are very fine indeed and make a splendid modern alternative to the Jochum, when eloquent and natural, Best's direction is imaginative and he achieves a wide tonal range.

Missa solemnis in B flat min.; Psalms 112, 150.

(N) (BB) *** Virgin Classics Dig. Double VBD5 61501-2 [CDVB 61501] (2). Oelze, Schubert, Dürmüller, Hagen, Bamberg Ch. & SO, Rickenbacher – MOZART: *Requiem*. ***

Bruckner's *Missa solemnis* is a comparatively early work (1854) written a decade before the *D major Mass*. In most respects it is derivative yet clearly the work of a major composer – its invention confident, its construction sound, its orchestration vivid. It is given a strong, fresh performance here, with a good solo team, although the soprano, Christiane Oelze, sounds a bit hard at times. The two psalm settings are 30 years apart, with *Psalm 150* (1892) obviously the more mature: both are eloquently sung. The chorus, as in the Mozart coupling, are set back in a spacious acoustic. Altogether this makes a thoroughly worthwhile bargain Double, unexpectedly pairing early Bruckner with late Mozart.

Motets: *Afferentur regi; Ave Maria; Christus factus est; Ecce sacerdos; Iam lucis orto sidere; Inveni David; Libera me; Locus iste; Os justi; Pange lingua; Salvum fac populum tuum; Tantum ergo; Tota pulchra es; Vexilla regis; Virga Jesse.*

(BB) *** Naxos Dig. 8.550956 [id.]. St Bride's Church Ch., Robert Jones.

St Bride's Church in Fleet Street in London has since its post-war restoration in 1958 boasted a choir of 12 professional singers, providing an excellent example of the Anglican cathedral and collegiate tradition being extended to key parish churches. This Naxos disc is their first commercial recording, and very impressive it is, for with crisp, clear ensemble and fresh tone from boyish-sounding sopranos they give warmly sympathetic performances of these fine Bruckner motets, an excellent selection covering most of the best known. The recording is full and vivid, set against a helpful church acoustic which does not obscure detail.

(i) *Motets: Afferentur regi; Ave Maria; Christus factus est pro nobis; Ecce sacerdos magnus; Locus iste; Os justi; Pange lingua; Tota pulchra es; Vexilla regis; Virga Jesse.* (ii) *Psalm 150; Te Deum.*

(N) (M) *** DG 457 743-2 (2) [id.]. (i) Bav. R. Ch.; (ii) Stader, Wagner, Haefliger, Lagger, German Op. Ch., Berlin, BPO; Jochum.

Bruckner's choral music, like the symphonies, spans his musical career. The ten motets are among Bruckner's most beautiful music, they are superbly sung and among Jochum's most distinguished recordings. With excellent soloists, the performances of the two larger-scale works here have admirable breadth and humanity and no lack of drama, although the *Te Deum*, for instance, has had more blazing intensity and, with some fine singing from Maria Stader and Ernst Haefliger as well as superbly loving orchestral support from the Berliners, this has a special eloquence. The original recordings tended to be distanced; in making the sound more present and clear, the remastering is undoubtedly fresher and brighter. Another fine candidate for DG's 'Originals'.

Motets: Afferentur regi virgines; Ecce sacerdos magnus; Inveni David; Os justi; Pange lingua gloriosa.
(BB) *** Belart 461 317-2 [(M) id. import]. St John's College, Cambridge, Ch., ASMF, Guest – BEETHOVEN: *Mass in C.* ***

The St John's performances are of the highest quality and the recording is marvellously spacious. They come in the lowest price range, coupled with a fine account of Beethoven's *C major Mass.*

Requiem in D min.; Psalms 112 and 114.
**(*) Hyperion CDA 66245 [id.]. Rodgers, Denley, Maldwyn Davies, George, Corydon Singers, ECO, Best; T. Trotter (organ).

Matthew Best here tackles the very early setting of the *Requiem* which Bruckner wrote at the age of 25. The quality of the writing in the Psalm settings also varies; but with fine, strong performances from singers and players alike, including an excellent team of soloists, this is well worth investigating by Brucknerians. First-rate recording.

Te Deum.
(B) **(*) DG Double 453 091-2 (2). Tomowa-Sintow, Baltsa, Schreier, Van Dam, V. Singverein, VPO, Karajan (with VERDI: *Requiem Mass.* **(*))

Karajan's analogue account of the *Te Deum* is spacious and strong, bringing out the score's breadth and drama. This is very satisfying and, if the Verdi coupling is acceptable, this is self-recommending.

Bruhns, Nicolaus (1665–97)

2 Preludes in E min.; Preludes: in G ; G min.; (i) Fantasia on '*Nun komm der Heiden Heiland*'.
*** Chandos Dig. CHAN 0539 [id.]. Piet Kee (organ of Roskilde Cathedral, Denmark), (i) with Elisabeth Rehling – BUXTEHUDE: *Chorale preludes.* ***

Just five Bruhns organ works survive (all included in this recital). Though he uses the term '*Praeludium*', each consists of an introduction and one or two fugues, written with an eager flair that recalls the early organ works of the young Bach, who certainly knew of this music. The spirited opening *Prelude in E minor* is striking enough, but most remarkable of all is the flamboyant G major work with its bravura writing for the pedals. It also has a jolly fugue subject. The *Fantasia on 'Nun komm der Heiden Heiland'* has its *cantus firmus* introduced by a soprano voice, and she returns to repeat the chorale (undecorated) at a central point, after three variants. Piet Kee presents all this music with splendid life and colour, and his Danish organ, recently restored, brings vivid registration which is a pleasure to the ear. The recording is in the demonstration bracket.

Brüll, Ignaz (1846–1907)

Piano concertos Nos. 1 in F, Op. 10; 2 in C, Op. 24; Andante and allegro, Op. 88.
(N) *** Hyperion Dig. CDA 67069 [id.]. Roscoe, BBC Scottish SO, Brabbins.

Ignaz Brüll was an Austrian prodigy pianist and composer, best known these days (if at all) for his opera, *Das goldene kreuz*. From the start there is a winning directness in the first of his two piano concertos, and if the themes do not always avoid banality, that is hardly surprising, as the composer was only 14 when he wrote it. Like so many issues in Hyperion's admirable romantic piano concerto series, this brings real revelation about a composer who till now has seemed a shadowy figure, one of a Viennese group associated with Brahms. Both the concertos are early works, the second built on rather more distinguished material than the first, and their innocent flamboyance is superbly caught in these brilliant performances, with Martin Roscoe excelling himself in his dazzling virtuosity. The *Andante and allegro*, a much later work, provides a warmly expressive makeweight. Full, well-balanced sound of best Hyperion quality.

Brumel, Antoine (*c.* 1460–*c.* 1520)

Missa: Et ecce terrae motus; Sequentia: Dies irae, dies illa.
❁ *** Sony/Vivarte Dig. SK 46348 [id.]. Huelgas Ens., Paul van Nevel.

Missa: Et ecce terrae motus; Lamentations. Magnificat secundi toni.
*** Gimell/Ph. Dig. 454 926-2 [id.]. Tallis Scholars, Peter Phillips.

Brumel succeeded Josquin as *maestro di cappella* at Ferrara. Lassus himself prepared and took part in a performance of the 12-part Mass, *Et ecce terrae motus*, in Munich in the 1570s, and this is the only copy of the work that survives. It is not just the contrapuntal ingenuity of Brumel's music that impresses but the sheer beauty of sound with which we are presented. Brumel was not only one of the first to write a polyphonic *Requiem* but the very first to make a polyphonic setting of the sequence, *Dies irae, dies illa*. This is a more severe work than the glorious 12-part Mass which occupies the bulk of this CD, and it is written in a more medieval tonal language. The performances by the Huelgas Ensemble under their founder-director, Paul van Nevel, are fervent and eloquent and vividly bring this music back to life. This recording, made in the ample acoustic of the Irish Chapel in Liège, is resplendent.

The Tallis Scholars are hardly less impressive than the Huelgas Ensemble. In some respects their disc is complementary in that they opt for a different solution to the *Agnus Dei*, which is incomplete in the Munich manuscript. Nevel favours a Danish source that Phillips and his editor reject on the grounds that it uses six voices and voices of different range. The texture in their performance has greater transparency and clarity than the richer, darker sonority of the Nevel. Both can be recommended.

Bunin, Revol Samuilovich
(1924–76)

Violin concerto.

(B) ** Revelation RV 10058 [id.]. Kogan, USSR State Academic SO, Lazarev – BARBER: *Violin concerto* **(*); BARSUKOV: *Violin concerto No. 2.* **

Like the other concertos on this disc, Bunin's is an unashamedly romantic work, in places reflecting the idiom of his teacher, Shostakovich, but generally following a more conservative style. In a committed performance like Leonid Kogan's, it makes an attractive novelty, coupled with the Barber as well as the Barsukov. Curiously, the disc fails to insert tracks between the movements in this long, 32-minute work, and the live recording is marred by audience noise.

Burgon, Geoffrey (born 1941)

Acquainted with night; Cançiones del Alma; Lunar beauty; Nunc dimittis; This ean night; Worldës blissë.

(M) *** EMI Dig. CDM5 66527-2. James Bowman, Charles Brett, City of L. Sinf., Hickox.

This collection of Geoffrey Burgon's music for counter-tenor makes a hauntingly unusual record. Appropriately, it has at the centre his most celebrated piece, the setting of the *Nunc dimittis* used as theme-music in the television adaptation of John Le Carré's *Tinker, Tailor, Soldier, Spy*, originally for treble but well within counter-tenor range. Some of the other works are just as striking. In the three settings of St John of the Cross, *Cançiones del Alma*, Burgon was consciously seeking to get away from Anglican church-choir associations of the counter-tenor voice, and some of the bell-like effects are most beautiful. *Worldës blissë* was prompted by a dream of a counter-tenor and oboe in duet; while in *This ean night* he dared to set the same text as Britten and Stravinsky in the *Lyke-Wake Dirge*, producing distinctive results in the tangy duetting of counter-tenors. The performances are strongly committed, with James Bowman taking the lion's share of solos. The recording gives an aptly ecclesiastical glow to the sound while keeping essential clarity.

At the round earth's imagined corners; But have been found again; Laudate Dominum; Magnificat; Nunc dimittis; A prayer to the Trinity; Short mass; This world; Two hymns to Mary.

**(*) Hyperion Dig. CDA 66123 [id.]. Chichester Cathedral Ch., Alan Thurlow.

Burgon's famous *Nunc dimittis* is well matched here with the *Magnificat* that he later wrote to complement it and a series of his shorter choral pieces, all of them revealing his flair for immediate, direct communication, and well performed. First-rate recording.

Bush, Geoffrey (born 1920)

Symphonies Nos. (i) *1;* (ii) *2 (Guildford);* (iii) *Music for orchestra;* (iv) *Overture Yorick.*

*** Lyrita Analogue/Dig. SRCD 252. (i) LSO, Nicholas Braithwaite; (ii) RPO, Barry Wordsworth; (iii) LPO, or (iv) Philh. O, Vernon Handley.

Full of colourful and striking thematic material, with occasional echoes of Walton and Lambert, Geoffrey Bush's music is consistently warm and appealing. This very well-filled disc brings together fine Lyrita recordings made between 1972 and 1982, and adds a superb, completely new recording of the *Symphony No. 2*. The vigorous *Yorick overture* (1949), written in memory of the comedian, Tommy Handley, has all the exuberance of a Walton overture, with wit and warm lyricism nicely balanced. Geoffrey Bush was a pupil of John Ireland and he belongs to the lost generation of fine English composers whose music was upstaged by the new avant-garde. The first of his two symphonies dates from 1954 and is a positive, three-movement structure centring on an elegiac slow movement with blues overtones, written in memory of Constant Lambert, quoting from *The Rio Grande*. Bush does not shrink from the notion that music should entertain, and the main body of the first movement, as well as the finale, is much lighter in character than those of many contemporary British symphonists. The *Second Symphony* is outgoing, too, no formal exercise but a warm statement of personal feeling, built on a strong and complex structure in four linked sections. Its four clearly defined sections are played without a break, the first and last suitably genial and festive. *Music for orchestra* (1967), commissioned by the Shropshire Schools Symphony Orchestra, is 'a miniature symphony', with the string parts carefully written so that they are not beyond the reach of inexperienced players. All the performances and recordings are outstandingly good, notably that of the *Symphony No. 2*, conducted by Barry Wordsworth.

Farewell, earth's bliss; 4 Hesperides songs; A Menagerie; (i) *A Summer serenade.*
*** Chandos Dig. CHAN 8864 [id.]. Varcoe, Thompson, Westminster Singers, City of London Sinfonia, Hickox, (i) with Eric Parkin.

The delightful *Summer serenade* of seven song-settings, written in 1948, five years after Britten's very comparable *Serenade*, has long been Bush's most frequently performed work, and this first recording glowingly brings out the sharp contrasts of mood within and between the songs, with instrumentation just as felicitous as the choral writing. It is well coupled with a solo song-cycle of comparable length, *Farewell, earth's bliss*, with Stephen Varcoe the baritone soloist; four songs from Herrick's *Hesperides*, also for baritone and strings; and three for unaccompanied voices, including an insistently menacing setting of Blake's *Tyger*. The tenor, Adrian Thompson, not ideally pure-toned, contributes to only two of the *Serenade* songs; otherwise these are near-ideal performances in warm, open sound.

Busoni, Ferruccio (1866–1924)

Piano concerto, Op. 39.
(M) *** Telarc Dig. CD 82012 [id.]. Garrick Ohlsson, Cleveland Men's Ch., Cleveland O, Dohnányi.

Busoni's marathon *Piano concerto* is unique, running to 70 minutes, roughly the same time as Beethoven's *Choral Symphony*, with which it has another parallel in its choral finale. Garrick Ohlsson's bravura display is very exciting, and the pianist's own enjoyment in virtuosity enhances his electricity and flair, even if the first-rate modern digital sound brings fewer advantages than expected, other than highlighting the solo piano.

(i) *Piano concerto. Fantasia contrappuntistica.*
(N) (B) ** Erato/Warner Ultima Dig. 3984 24248-2 (2) [id.]. Viktoria Postnikova; (i) French R. Ch. & Nat. O, Rozhdestvensky.

Postnikova's version of Busoni's ambitious *concerto* is a curiosity. Her characteristic magic and that of Rozhdestvensky keep tension sustained for much of the time, despite speeds that by most standards are grotesquely slow, but the result is eccentric. The *Fantasia contrappuntistica* makes a valuable fill-up, but all other CD versions fit the whole of the *concerto* on to a single disc. Recording is good, but the choir in the finale sounds dim.

Turandot suite, Op. 41.
*** Sony Dig. SK 53280 [id.]. La Scala PO, Muti – CASELLA: *Paganiniana;* MARTUCCI: *Giga* etc. ***

Busoni's *Turandot suite* has all the ingredients of popularity: colour, a captivating lightness of spirit and vivid musical ideas presented with wonderful imagination. It is good that its CD première is so successful in every respect; with excellent playing from the La Scala Orchestra under Muti, its wit and character are splendidly conveyed. Muti conducts the 1905 version of the suite. Good, well-detailed recording in a slightly dryish acoustic.

Violin sonatas Nos. 1 in E min., Op. 29; 2 in E min., Op. 36a.
*** Chandos Dig. CHAN 8868 [id.]. Lydia Mordkovitch, Victoria Postnikova.

Busoni's two *Violin sonatas* are rarities in the concert hall. There is no current alternative to the *First*, and Lydia Mordkovitch and Victoria Postnikova are impressive advocates of this somewhat uneven piece. The *Second* is a one-movement piece, dating from 1898, with a *langsam* opening, a *Presto* and a most beautiful *Andante* section leading to a set of variations. Mordkovitch and her partner give a sympathetic reading and, with excellent recording, this disc should be sought out by admirers of this composer.

Fantasia contrappuntistica; Fantasia after J. S. Bach; Toccata.
**(*) Altarus AIR-2-9074. John Ogdon.

Ronald Stevenson calls Busoni's remarkable *Fantasia contrappuntistica* a masterpiece and, listening to John Ogdon's performance, one is tempted to agree. The *Fantasia after J. S. Bach* was written a year earlier and is among Busoni's most concentrated and powerful piano works. The balance places Ogdon rather far back and, as the acoustic is somewhat reverberant, the piano sounds a little clangy.

An die Jugend: Giga bolero e variazione. Elegies: All'Italia; Berceuse; Turandots Frauengemach. Exeunt omnes; Fantasia nach J. S. Bach; Indianisches Tagebuch (Red Indian Diary), Book I; Sonatinas Nos. 2; 6 (Kammerfantasie on Carmen); Toccata. Transcription of Bach: *Prelude and fugue in D, BWV 532.*
*** Chandos Dig. CHAN 9394 [id.]. Geoffrey Tozer.

Elegies Nos. 1 (Nach der Wendung); 7 (Elegy); Fantasia in modo antico, Op. 33b/4; Macchiette medioevali; Sonatinas Nos. 4 (In diem navitatis Christi MCMXVII); 6 (Kammerfantasie on Bizet's Carmen); Suite campestre. arr. of BACH: *Choral preludes: Ich ruf' zu dir Herr Jesu Christ; Non komm, der Heiden Heiland.*
*** Olympia Dig. OCD 461 [id.]. William Stephenson.

Both these collections are thoroughly worthwhile and they overlap very little. William Stephenson is possibly the more natural Busoni interpreter, and his programme is very stimulating. Yet the Chandos disc assembles nearly 80 minutes of Busoni's piano music and makes an admirable and well-chosen introduction to it. Most pieces come off very well indeed, and often brilliantly, from the *Exeunt omnes* and the *Elegien* to the *Indianisches Tagebuch* and the attractive *Turandots Frauengemach*. This is an excellent CD, very well recorded and thoroughly recommendable, but not in preference to the Olympia selection, if one has to make an outright choice between them.

OPERA

(i) *Arlecchino* (complete); (ii) *Turandot* (complete).
*** Virgin/EMI Dig. VCD7 59313-2 (2). (i) Ernst Theo Richter, Mohr, Holzmair, Huttenlocher, Dahlberg, Mentzer; (ii) Gessendorf, Selig, Dahlberg, Schäfer, Kraus, Holzmair, Struckmann, Sima, Rodde; Lyon Op. Ch. & O, Nagano.

Kent Nagano follows up the success of his previous Lyon Opéra recordings with a set which vividly illustrates the elusive genius of Busoni. *Arlecchino* ('Harlequin') is a sparkling comedy that builds on *commedia dell'arte* conventions with a point rarely matched in opera, though for the non-German-speaking listener a snag of the piece is that the title-role is a speaking part. On disc, prolonged passages of spoken German, not at all frothy, provide a deterrent to frequent repetition. Even so, it would be hard to imagine a finer performance than this, with the conductor's finesse matched by a brilliant German cast with no weak link.

Busoni's *Turandot* evokes a fantasy fairy-tale atmosphere in a piece that is light in texture, with motivation aptly quirky rather than realistic. In place of Puccini's Liù you have Adelma, Turandot's maidservant, and the *commedia dell'arte* element is more central than with Puccini's Ping, Pang and Pong. The surreal atmosphere is enhanced when the improbable theme for the evocative interlude before Act II is not Chinese but English – *Greensleeves*. Again Nagano's conducting gives a thrusting intensity to a piece that might seem wayward, and the casting is comparably brilliant, with Mechthild Gessendorf masterly as Turandot and Stefan Dahlberg heady-toned as Kalaf. The recording is vividly atmospheric, with plenty of presence.

Doktor Faust (opera) complete.
(M) *** DG (IMS) 427 413-2 (3) [id.].
Fischer-Dieskau, Kohn, Cochran, Hillebrecht, Bav. Op. Ch. & R. O, Leitner.

Busoni's epic *Doktor Faust* was left incomplete at the composer's death. Unfortunately, this recording is full of small cuts; however, with superb, fierily intense conducting from Leitner, it fully conveys the work's wayward mastery, the magnetic quality which establishes it as Busoni's supreme masterpiece, even though it was finished by another hand. The cast is dominated by Fischer-Dieskau, here in 1969 at his very finest; and the only weak link among the others is Hildegard Hillebrecht as the Duchess of Parma. Though this is a mid-priced set, the documentation is generous.

Butterworth, Arthur (born 1923)

Symphony No. 1, Op. 15.
(N) *** Classico Dig. CLASSCD 274 [id.].
Munich SO, Douglas Bostock – GIBBS: *Symphony No. 2.* ***

This CD serves to introduce not only some stimulating new music, but also an important new label (based at present in the North of England) which is funding première recordings of symphonies by British composers which are new to the record catalogue. Dennis Bostock is the musical force behind this enterprise and it is he who directs first-class performances of the two highly rewarding symphonies paired here. Arthur Butterworth (like Sir Malcolm Arnold, a professional trumpet player) is Manchester-born, and studied at the Royal Manchester College of Music, before it became the Royal Northern College, at the same time as your Editor, who makes no apology for his enthusiasm for and advocacy of his music. Butterworth has written four symphonies and a violin concerto (played by Nigel Kennedy).

The brooding *First Symphony* is clearly influenced by the bleak Pennine moorlands which are so near to Manchester, but also by Sibelius's *Sixth Symphony*, and the opening of the work uses a theme derived from that source. The slow movement, however, is a contemplation of the loneliness of the Scottish Highlands, in and around Rothiemurchus Forest (not far from Aviemore) and the third evokes the 'solitariness of the dark sea shore, the remorseless rumble of the surf' on the Eastern side of Scotland, near Aberdeen. The riotous moto perpetuo finale was initially stimulated by an 'exciting' train journey (in 1953) during the fin de siècle days of steam. The Royal Scot from Glasgow to London was headed by a Duchess-class locomotive, and on the subsequent return journey, the 'New Elizabethan' express travelled non-stop from King's Cross to Edinburgh – 'even over the maze of complex points and crossings outside Newcastle Central'. It is a powerful and evocative work that resonates in the memory, and Bostock and the Munich Orchestra capture both its sombre mood and its stormy climaxes: the composer had the desolate Cape Wrath in mind in the last movement where the music's whirlwind energy is splendidly conveyed. The recording is excellent, spacious and full-bodied.

Butterworth, George (1885–1916)

The banks of green willow.
(M) *** Chandos CHAN 6566 [id.]. Bournemouth Sinf., Norman Del Mar – BANTOCK: *The Pierrot of the minute: overture;* BRIDGE: *Summer* etc. ***

The banks of green willow; 2 English idylls; A Shropshire lad (rhapsody).
*** Nimbus Dig. NI 5068 [id.]. E. String O, Boughton – BRIDGE: *Suite;* PARRY: *Lady Radnor's suite.* ***

Boughton secures from his Birmingham-based orchestra warm and refined playing in well-paced readings. In an ample acoustic, woodwind is placed rather behind the strings.

On Chandos, Del Mar gives a glowingly persuasive performance of *The banks of green willow*, which comes as part of another highly interesting programme of English music, devoted also to Butterworth's somewhat older contemporaries, Bantock and Frank Bridge. The digital transfer of a 1979 analogue recording has the benefit of even greater clarity without loss of atmosphere.

Love blows as the wind (3 songs).
(M) *** EMI CDM7 64731-2. Robert Tear, CBSO, Vernon Handley – ELGAR; VAUGHAN WILLIAMS: *Songs.* ***

These three charming songs (*In the year that's come and gone, Life in her creaking shoes, Coming up from Richmond*), to words by W. E. Henley, provide an excellent makeweight for a mixed bag of orchestral songs based on the first recording of Vaughan Williams's *On Wenlock Edge* in its orchestral form. The sound is clear yet enjoyably warm and atmospheric.

A Shropshire Lad (cycle of 6 songs); *Bredon Hill* and other songs: *O fair enough are sky and plain; When the lad for longing sighs; On the idle hill of summer; With rue my heart is laden.*
(BB) *** Belart 461 491-2 [(M) id. import]. Benjamin Luxon, David Willison – FINZI: *Earth and air and rain.* ***

While Luxon can project his tone and words with great power, his delicate half-tones are equally impressive, and this applies especially to the best-known song here, *Is my team ploughing?*, which is full of touching contrasts. Both in the six songs of the regular *Shropshire Lad* cycle and in the other Housman settings (which make an ideal companion set), Luxon underlines the aptness of the music to words that have often been set by British composers, but never more understandingly than here. David Willison's accompaniments are wholly sympathetic and the mid-1970s Decca recording is strikingly real and vivid, and very well balanced.

Buxtehude, Diderik (*c.* 1637–1707)

Trio sonatas: in G; B flat and D min., Op. 1/2, 4 & 6 (BuxWV 253, 255 & 257); in D and G min., Op. 2/2–3, (BuxWV 260–1).
*** ASV/Gaudeamus CDGAU 110. Trio Sonnerie.

This is music of high quality: its invention is fertile and distinguished by a lightness of touch and colour that is quite individual; the melodic lines are vivacious and engaging, and their virtuosity inspiriting. The Trio Sonnerie show enthusiasm and expertise, and their virtuosity is agreeably effortless and unostentatious.

Trio sonatas for violin, viola da gamba and harpsichord: in A min., Op. 1/3; in B flat, Op. 1/4; in G min., Op. 2/3; in E, Op. 2/6 (BuxWV 254–5, 261; 264).
(B) *** HM HMA 901089 [id.]. Boston Museum Trio.

The Boston Museum Trio are a highly accomplished group and display an exemplary feeling for style. The music is unfailingly inventive and, despite the obvious Italianate elements, distinctive. Not only are the playing, recording and presentation of high quality, but the cost is modest.

Canzona in E min., BuxWV 169; Canzonetta in G, BuxWV 171; Ciacona in E min., BuxWV 160; Chorales: *Ach Herr, mich armen Sünder, BuxWV 178; In dulci jubilo, BuxWV 197; Komm, Heiliger Geist, Herre Gott, BuxWV 199; Vater unser im Himmelreich, BuxWV 219; Magnificat primi toni, BuxWV 203; Preludes: in C, BuxWV 137; in D, BuxWV 139.*
(*) Chandos Dig. CHAN 0514 [id.]. Piet Kee (organ of St Laurent Church, Alkmaar) – SWEELINCK: *Collection.* *

Kee's performance of the opening *Magnificat primi toni* is magnificent. The closing *Ciacona in E minor* is impressive too, while the *Canzonetta in G* is deliciously registered, with piping flute colouring. One's reservations concern the presentation of the chorales, which, Kee suggests, 'require poetic expression'. Perhaps they do, but they also need to be moved on rather faster. The Chandos recording is superb.

Canzonetta in G, BuxWV 171; Ciaconas: in C min., BuxWV 159; in E min., BuxWV 160. Chorales: *Ach, Herr, mich armen Sünder, BuxWV 178; Der Tag der ist so freudenreich, BuxWV 182; Durch Adams Fall ist ganz verderbt, BuxWV 183; In dulci jubilo, BuxWV 197; Komm, heiliger Geist, Herr Gott, BuxWV 199; Nimm von uns, BuxWV 207; Nun komm der Heiden Heiland, BuxWV 211; Wie schön leuchtet der Morgenstern, BuxWV 223. Fugue in C, BuxWV 174; Magnificat primi toni, BuxWV 203; Passacaglia in D min., BuxWV 161; Preludes: in A min., BuxWv 153; in*

C, BuxWV 137; in D, BuxWV 139; in D min., BuxWV 140; E min., BuxWV 142; F, BuxWV 145; F sharp min., BuxWV 146; G min., BuxWV 149. Te Deum laudamus, BuxWV 218; Toccatas: in D min., BuxWV 155; in F, BuxWV 156.

(M) *** Erato/Warner Dig. 0630 12979-2 (2). Marie-Claire Alain (Schnitger-Ahrend organ, Groningen).

Marie-Claire Alain's admirable mid-priced, two-disc set on Erato currently seems just about the best buy for those wanting a comprehensive survey of Buxtehude's splendid organ music. The magnificent opening *Prelude in C* shows not only how ideally the Groningen organ suits this repertoire, weighty yet never clouding sonorities, but also the full calibre of Buxtehude's music. Beginning floridly and thrillingly over massive pedals, Marie-Claire Alain presents it powerfully and spontaneously, and she is equally impressive in registering the chorales, using a wide palette of colour: they are gently paced but never drag. The second disc opens with the ebullient *Fugue in C* which is so like the *Fugue à la gigue* attributed to Bach (BWV 577). Then, after the impressive chaconnes, the *Canzonetta in G* is piped deliciously. The complex *Magnificat primi toni* and the large-scale chorale fantasia on the *Te Deum* (in which Buxtehude and Alain always ensure that the cantus firmus emerges clearly) make one understand why Bach so admired this music. The arresting *Toccata in D minor*, with its dramatic pauses, undoubtedly influenced Bach's most famous organ work in the same key. Superb playing throughout, and demonstration-standard recording.

Chorales: *Auf meinen lieben Gott, BuxWV 179; Gott der Vater wohn uns bei, BuxWV 190; Nimm von uns, Herr du treuer Gott, BuxVW 207; Nun komm der Heiden Heiland, BuxWV 211; Puer natus in Bethlehem, BuxWV 217; Von Gott will ich nicht lassen* (2 settings), *BuxWV 220/221.*

*** Chandos Dig. CHAN 0539 [id.]. Piet Kee (organ of Roskilde Cathedral, Denmark) – BRUHNS: *Preludes*. ***

The restored baroque organ at Roskilde Cathedral has a palette to tempt the most jaded listener and, although Piet Kee still persists in playing these chorales and their variants rather slowly, his piquant registration is very effective, so that they serve as attractively serene interludes between the remarkably flamboyant *Preludes* by Buxtehude's precociously inspired pupil, Nicolaus Bruhns, whose genius was sadly cut short when he died before his mentor, at the early age of 32. The recording is of demonstration quality.

Chorales: *Christ unser Herr zum Jordan kam; Durch Adams Fall ist ganz verderbt; Ein feste Burg ist unser Gott; Erhalt uns, Herr, bei deinem Wort; Es ist das Heil uns kommen her; Es spricht der unweisen Mund wohl; Gelobet seist du, Jesu Christ; Gott der Vater, wohn uns bei; Magnificat primi toni; 2 Preludes and fugues in A min.; Preludes and fugues: in C; F sharp min.*

(B) *** HM HMA 190942 [id.]. René Saorgin (Schnitger organ of the Church of St Michel de Zwolle, Holland).

The Schnitger organ is sensitively and colourfully registered by Saorgin: he is particularly impressive in the serene, reflective chorales, *Durch Adams Fall* and *Es spricht der unweisen Mund wohl*, while the elaborations of the *Magnificat* are finely made. Excellent recording, vividly transferred.

Ciaconas: in C min.; E min., BuxWV 159–60; Passacaglia in D min., BuxWV 161; Preludes and fugues: in D; D min.; E; E min., BuxWV 139–42; in F; F sharp min., BuxWV 145–6; in G min., BuxWV 149.

(M) *** DG (IMS) 427 133-2. Helmut Walcha (organ of Church of SS Peter and Paul, Cappel, West Germany).

Helmut Walcha has the full measure of this repertoire and these performances on the highly suitable Arp Schnitger organ in Cappel, Lower Saxony, are authoritative and spontaneous. The 1978 recording is excellent and the disc comprises generous measure: 73 minutes.

(i) *Preludes and fugues: in G min.; F.* Chorales: *Herr Christ, der einig Gottes Sohn; In dulci jubilo; Lobt Gott, ihr Christen allzugleich; Chorale fantasy: Gelobet seist du, Jesu Christ.* Cantatas: (ii) *In dulci jubilo; Jubilate Domino.*

(B) *** HM HMA 190700 [id.]. (i) René Saorgin (organ of St Laurent Church, Alkmaar); (ii) Alfred Deller, Deller Cons., Perulli, Chapuis.

A good, inexpensive sampler of Buxtehude, dating from 1971. The opening *Prelude and fugue in G minor* is fully worthy of the young J. S. Bach and, like its companion, is splendidly played by René Saorgin. The chorales are more static and less interesting than Bach's treatment of the same ideas. Of the cantatas, *In dulci jubilo* is a florid piece for four voices with instrumental accompaniment, while *Jubilate Domino* is a solo cantata accompanied by viola da gamba and organ continuo. Deller is in good form throughout.

Cantatas: *An Filius non est Dei, BuxWV 6; Cantate Domino, BuxWV12; Frohlocket mit Händen, BuxWV 29; Gott fähret auf mit Jauchzen, BuxWV 33; Herr, wenn ich nur Dich habe, Bux WV 39; Heut triumphieret Gottes Sohn, BuxWV 43; Ich bin die Auferstehung, BuxWV 44; Ich habe Lust absuzcheiden, BuxWV 46; Ihr lieben Christen, BuxWV 51; In dulci Jubilo, BuxWV 52; Jesus dulcis memoria, BuxWV 56; Jesu meines Lebens Leben, BuxWV 62; Jubilate Deo, BuxWV 64; Mein Gemüt erfreuet sich, BuxWV 72; Nichts soll uns scheiden, BuxWV 77;*

Nun danket alle Gott, BuxWV 79; Wie wird erneuet, wie ird erfreuet, BuxWV 110 (0630 17759-2 (3)).
Membra Jesu nostri, BuxWV 75 (0630 17760-2).
(N) (M) *** Erato/Warner Dig. 0630 17758-2 (4) Schlick, Frimmer, Chance, Jacobs, Prégardien, Kooy, Hannover Boys' Ch.,, Amsterdam Bar. O, Koopman.

This set of four discs comes in a slip case as part of the Ton Koopman Edition. All the works in the main three-disc collection are of a pietist religious character, although the music readily expands into joyously extrovert expressions of praise. The usual pre-Bach layout is observed: a short instrumental sonata followed by a short vocal concerto, an aria with interspersed instrumental interpolations and a final ensemble. Some attractively combine the form of a concerto grosso, with alternating solos and tuttis, and a few are more ambitious, including chorus, trumpets and cornetts, and even trombones, and drums too. The brass-writing is inevitably primitive but highly effective in its stylized way. The solo singing is excellent, and the soloists match pleasingly when they sing in duet or trio. There is plenty to discover here for any collector who enjoys the pre-Bach era, Accompaniments are alive, textures transparent, and the recording balance is altogether excellent. The collection is capped by the inclusion of a moving and beautifully sung version of *Membra, Jesu nostri*, a cycle of seven short cantatas, each addressed to a different member of the body of Christ crucified. Sufficient to say that the performances are of the highest quality, beautifully sung by the same group of soloists, and choir. His admirers will know what to expect from Koopman's direction: good taste, refined musicianship but a generally brisk, business-like approach. The recording is both spacious and clear, the style is expressively reverential, yet conveys the music's humanity.

Cantatas: Befiehl dem Engel, BuxWV 10; Fürwahr, er trug unsere Krankhelt, BuxWV 31; Gott hilf mir, BuxWV 34; Herzlich lieb hab ich Dich, O Herr, BuxWV 41; Ich suchte des Nachts, BuxWV 50; Nun danket alle Gott, BuxWV 79.
(N) *** HM Dig. HMC 901629 [id.]. Cantus Kölln, Konrad Junghänel.

This eminent German group give eminently stylish and cultured accounts of these lovely pieces and no one wanting a representative anthology of Buxtehude cantatas is likely to be unpersuaded by this splendid recording.

Membra Jesu nostri, BuxWV 75.
(M) *** DG Dig. 447 298-2. Monteverdi Ch., E. Bar. Soloists, Gardiner – SCHUTZ: *O bone Jesu.* ***
(N) *** BIS Dig. CD 871 [id.]. Yoshie Hida, Midori Suzuki, Aki Yanagisawa, Yuko Anazawa, Yoshikazu Mera, Makato Sakurada, Yoshitaka Ogasawara, Bach Collegium, Japan, Maasaaki Suzuki.
(BB) *** Naxos Dig. 8.553787 [id.]. Trogu, Invernizzi, Balconi, Cecchetti, Carnovich, R. Svizzera (Lugano) Ch., Sonatori de la Gioiosa Marca, Treviso, Accademia Strumentale Italiana, Verona, Fasolis (with ROSENMULLER: *Sinfonia XI* ***).

Membra Jesu nostri, BuxWV 75; Heut triumphieret Gottes Sohn, BuxWV 43.
**(*) HM Dig. HMC 901333 [id.]. Concerto Vocale & Instrumental Ens., Jacobs.

The *Membra Jesu nostri* is a cycle of seven cantatas, each addressed to different parts of the body of the crucified Christ, all of a simple, dignified, expressive power that make a strong impression. John Eliot Gardiner's is the most searching and devotional; the Concerto Vocale, though beautifully sung, is less atmospheric both as a performance and as a recording. The Harmonia Mundi is more forwardly balanced; the Gardiner has more space and the sense of one of Buxtehude's own Abendmusik. Compare the sixth of the cantatas, *Ad cor*, and the more reverential approach and feeling of the Gardiner tells. But both issues can be recommended; the impressive *Heut triumphieret Gottes Sohn* comes with the Harmonia Mundi disc and a Schütz *Geistliches Konzert*, *O bone Jesu*, related in spirit, comes on the Archiv recording, which is now offered at mid-price.

On BIS, Suzuki's Japanese ensemble bring a remarkably authentic feeling for period to this lovely work (Maasaaki Susuki worked with Ton Koopman for many years) and although the recording is made in a rather reverberant acoustic environment, this does not seriously diminish the pleasure this set gives. However, unlike both its competitors, it is without a coupling.

The performance from the Swiss-Italian Radio and ensembles from Verona and Treviso under Diego Fasolis is marginally less polished and accomplished vocally than those under John Eliot Gardiner and René Jacobs but it has feeling and depth. They are most expertly balanced and the sound is excellent in every way. Those wanting a bargain need not hesitate.

Byrd, William (1543–1623)

The Byrd Complete Edition, Volume I:(i) *Alma redemptoris mater a 4; Audivi vocem de caelo a 5; Christe qui lux es a 5; Christe redemptor omnium a 4; De lamentorum Jerimiae prophetae a 5; Domine quis habitat a 9; Ne perduas cum impiis a 5; Omni tempore benedic Deum a 5; Peccavi super numerum a 5; Vide Dominum quoniam tribulor a 5. Propers for the Lady Mass in Advent a 5: (Rorate caeli; Tollite portas/Ave*

Maria; Ecce virgo). Consort pieces:(i) *Christe qui es lux a 4; Miserere a 4; Sanctus a 3; Sermone blando a 4.*

(N) *** ASV Gaudeamus Dig. CDGAU 170 [id.]. Cardinall's Musick, Andrew Carwood; (ii) Friedeswide Consort.

Cardinall's Musick are putting us in their debt by preparing (in new editions by David Skinner) a complete recorded survey of one of the greatest Elizabethan English composers, William Byrd. Although not all of it is of equal quality the overall standard is very high, and most of it was published during the composer's lifetime, though not the superb *Peccavi super numerum*, which closes the recital. Volume I commences the series with a programme of the early manuscript works, which are used to frame the three Gradualia for the Lady Mass in Advent. At a centre point in each group of motets, a recorder consort provides two contrasting instrumental pieces. In some of the settings the polyphony is rich and complex, like the remarkable opening *Domine quis habitat* in nine interweaving parts or imaginatively quixotic like the lovely *Alma redemptoris mater*; at other times it is simpler and harmonic, as in the very touching *Christe qui lux es* a 5. Most of this music is virtually unknown: it is all sung with great conviction, richly blended and convincingly paced. The recording was made in the Fitzalan Chapel at Arundel Castle, which provides an ideal acoustic, resonant yet never blurring detail.

The Byrd Complete Edition, Volume II: *Ad Dominum, cum tribularer a 8 Alleluya – Confitemi Domino a 3; Alleluya – Laudate pueri Dominum a 3; Ave regina caelorum a 5; Decantabat populus a 5; Deus in adjutorium a 6; Hodie Christus natus est a 4/6; O admirable commertium a 4/7; O magnum mysterium a 4/8–9; O salutaris hostia a 6. 5 Propers for the Nativity a 4* (1607). BYRD/SHEPPARD/MUNDY: *In exitu Israel a 4.*

(N) ❁ *** ASV Gaudeamus Dig. CDGAU 178 [id.]. Cardinall's Musick, Andrew Carwood.

Volume 2 is, if anything, even more stimulating than Volume 1, including as it does *O salutarisis hostia* with its extraordinarily plangent harmonic clashes – the most musically daring work in the composer's whole output. Also harmonically striking is the extended psalm-setting, *In exitu Israel*, which was a composite work shared by Byrd with William Mundy and John Sheppard, who wrote the lion's share, setting seven of the fourteen verses. The Propers for Christmas and the three associated Gradualia, *Hodie Christus natus est, O admirabile commertium* and *O magnum mysterium*, all full of character, provide the central core of the recital. But the exultant *Decantabat populus* and the two closing motets – the noble and melancholy *Deus in adjutorium* (here reconstructed), and the heartfelt and passionate *Ad Dominum cum tribularer* – are among the composer's finest, most individual and most passionate works. Both reflect the frustrations of the Catholic-faithful living in Protestant England. The eloquent performances truly reflect this anguish, and again this group are superbly recorded.

Complete consort music: *Christe qui lux a 4, Nos. 1–3; Christe redemptor a 4; Fantasia a 3, Nos. 1–3; Fantasia a 4, No. 1; Fantasia a 5 (Two in one); Fantasia a 6, Nos. 2–3; In nomine a 4, Nos. 1–2; In nomine a 4, Nos. 1–5; Miserere a 4; Pavan & Galliard a 5; Pavan & Galliard a 6; Prelude & Ground a 5; Sermon blande blando a 3; Sermon blando a 4, No. 1; Te lucis a 4, No. 2, verse 2.*

*** Virgin/EMI (SIS) Dig. VC5 45031-2. Fretwork, with Christopher Wilson (lute).

Fretwork have now completed their survey of Byrd's consort music – part of which was originally issued coupled with Dowland's *Lachrimae* – and the complete consort music (76 minutes) is now fitted on to a single CD. The combination with Dowland is also additionally available on a Virgin Double (VBD5 61151-2). The grave feeling of much of this music is apparent in the opening *Prelude and Ground a 5*; then the mood quickly lightens as the texture is woven in more swiftly moving configurations to make a typically satisfying whole. *Browning* has the alternative title of *The leaves be green* and consists of divisions on a popular song, while the *Fantasia a 6* which closes the concert is a masterly compression of ideas into a fluid structure as powerful as Purcell's famous *Chaconne*. Performances have consistent authority and freshness and, although the recording seems rather close, it is vivid and realistic.

Music for Consorts and Virginals: *Browning; The Carman's whistle; A fancie; Fantasia à 6; French Corantos; The Irish March; My Lord of Oxenford's Maske; Pavan; Pavan à 5; Pavan: Belle qui tiens ma vie; Pavan: Mille Regretz; 2 Pavan and Galliards; Pavan and Galliard à 6; Pavan and Galliard: Kinbourough Good; Praeludium and Ground; The Queen's Alman.*

(N) *** Auvidis/Astrée Dig. E 8611 [id.]. Capriccio Stravagante, Skip Sempé.

Skip Sempé and his colleagues play every note with that authenticity of feeling that is so often missing from period performance. Sempé has poetic feeling, an astonishing keyboard flair and rare artistry. The sound of his Skowroneck harpsichord is vividly reproduced. One of the best CDs of its kind and a splendid introduction to the composer.

Music for viols: *Browning; 2 Fantasias a 3 in C; Fantasias a 4 in D and G; Prelude and voluntary;* (i) *Prelude (Pavana, Gagliarda Ph. Tregian); Ut re mi fa sol la* (for harpsichord); (ii; iii) *Delight is dead;* (ii) *Farewell false love;* (iii) *My mistress*

had a little dog; Rejoice unto the Lord; (ii; iii) *Who made thee, Hob, forsake the plough?* (ii) *Ye sacred muses.*
*** Lyrichord Dig. LEMS 8015 [id.]. (i) Louis Bagger; (ii) Tamara Crout; (iii) Lawrence Lipnik; NY Cons. of Viols.

Those who know only Byrd's church music – and in particular the Latin Masses – will find this concert a refreshing experience. The New York Consort of Viols play with an attractive blend of timbre, and everything they play is thoroughly alive. The harpsichordist, Louis Bagger, plays with great bravura when *Ut re mi fa sol* becomes more and more florid as it proceeds. The two vocal soloists work well together, especially in the rustic dialogue song, *Who made thee, Hob, forsake the plough?* Tamara Crout sings with great charm in her solo numbers – with the lightest touch in the charming song about the 'murdered' pet dog, and very expressively in *Rejoice unto the Lord* and the touching *Ye sacred muses*. In every way this is a most rewarding programme, excellently balanced and recorded.

Consort, keyboard music, anthems and songs: *Fantasia for 4 viols; Fantasia No. 2 for 6 viols; Fantasia No. 3 for 6 viols; Galliard; Have mercy upon me, O God; In nomine No. 2 for 4 viols; In Nomine No. 5 for 5 viols; Pavane;* (i) (Keyboard) *John, come kiss me now; Pavan in A min.; Qui passe (for my Lady Nevell);* (Vocal) (ii) *Christ rising again; Fair Britain isle; In angel's weed; Rejoice unto the Lord; Susanna fair; Triumph with pleasant melody.*
(BB) *** Naxos Dig. 8.550604 [id.]. Rose Consort, Red Byrd; (i) Timothy Roberts (harpsichord or virginals); (ii) Tessa Bonner.

Here is a useful and inexpensive cross-section of Byrd's secular output that gives a good idea not only of its artistic riches but its sheer variety. Both the ensembles recorded here, the Rose Consort of viols and Red Byrd, are in good form and Timothy Roberts and Tessa Bonner are sensitive and expert exponents of this repertoire. The recorded sound is eminently clean and well balanced, and there is plenty of space round the aural image, which greatly enhances the undoubted attractions of an attractive anthology.

VOCAL MUSIC

Motets in paired settings: *Ave verum corpus* (with PHILIPS: *Ave verum corpus*); *Haec dies* (with PALESTRINA: *Haec Dies*); *Iustorum animae* (with LASSUS: *Iustorum animae*); *Miserere mei* (with G. GABRIELI: *Miserere mei*); *O quam gloriosum* (with VICTORIA: *O quam gloriosum*); *Tu es Petrus* (with PALESTRINA: *Tu es Petrus*).
(B) *** CfP CD-CFP 4481. King's College, Cambridge, Ch., Sir David Willcocks.

This is an imaginatively devised programme of motets in which settings of Latin texts by Byrd are directly contrasted with settings of the same words by some of his greatest contemporaries. As was the intention, quite apart from adding variety to the programme, the juxtaposition makes one listen to the individual qualities of these polyphonic masters the more keenly, and register their individuality. The recording emerges with remarkable freshness on CD, and the singing is most beautiful.

Cantiones sacrae, Book I (1575): *Laudate pueri; O lux beata trinitas; Tribue Domine*. Book II (1589): *In resurrectione tua; Laetentur coeli; Ne irascaris; O quam gloriosum; Tribulationes civitatum*. Book III (1591): *Cantate Domino; Esurge Domine; Haec dies; Recordare Domine; Salve Regina.*
(BB) *** ASV Quicksilva Dig. CDQS 6211 [(M) id.]. Sarum Consort, Andrew Mackay.

Cantiones sacrae, Book 1: Aspice Domine; Domine secundum multitudinem; Domine tu iurasti; In resurrectione tua; Ne irascaris Domine; O quam gloriosum; Tristitia et anxiestas; Vide Domine afflictionem; Virgilate.
**(*) CRD Dig. CRD 3420; *CRDC 4120* [id.]. New College, Oxford, Ch., Higginbottom.

Cantiones sacrae, Book 2: Circumdederunt me; Cunctis diebus; Domine, non sum dignus; Domine, salva nos; Fac sum servo tuo; Exsurge, Domine; Haec dicit Dominus; Haec dies; Laudibus in sanctis Dominum; Miserere mei, Deus; Tribulatio proxima est.
**(*) CRD Dig. CRD 3439; *CRDC 4139* [id.]. New College, Oxford, Ch., Higginbottom.

Byrd published the first of his three Books of *Cantiones sacrae* in conjunction with his teacher and mentor, Thomas Tallis, contributing 17 motets to this initial collection; he went on to publish two further Books alone. Although all were written to be sung in Latin, some of the more successful were translated and sung in English. Their musical range is wide: the extended *Ne irascaris* opens sombrely and is for the most part serene, while the similarly extended *Tribulationes civitatum* generates great intensity. *O quam gloriosam* is justly renowned and the closing *Haec Dies* (the closing motet of the Third Book) moves along swiftly to climax with an exultant string of polyphonic *Allelujas*. The Sarum Consort is a finely balanced and blended group, admirably directed by Andrew Mackay, whose pacing and control of light and shade cannot be faulted. The recording, made in the ideal acoustic of Milton Abbey, is clear, yet rich in choral ambience. Excellent documentation, with full texts and translations makes this a first-rate bargain.

Though the New College Choir under its choirmaster Edward Higginbottom does not sing with the variety of expression or dynamic which marks its finest Oxbridge rivals, it is impossible not to respond to the freshness of its music-making. The robust, throaty style suggests a Latin feeling in its forthright vigour, and the directness of approach in these magnificent *Cantiones sacrae* is most attractive, helped by recording which is vividly projected, yet at once richly atmospheric.

The Great Service (with anthems).
*** Gimell/Ph. Dig. 454 911-2PH [id.]. Tallis Scholars, Phillips.

Peter Phillips and the Tallis Scholars give a lucid and sensitively shaped account of Byrd's *Great Service*. Theirs is a more intimate performance than one might expect to encounter in one of the great English cathedrals; they are fewer in number and thus achieve greater clarity of texture. The recording is quite excellent: it is made in a church acoustic (the Church of St John, Hackney) and captures detail perfectly. It includes three other anthems, two of which (*O Lord make thy servant Elizabeth* and *Sing joyfully unto God our strength*) are included on the rival EMI disc.

Mass for 3 voices; Mass for 4 voices; Mass for 5 voices.
✿ (M) *** Decca 433 675-2. King's College, Cambridge, Ch., Willcocks.
(B) **(*) HM HMA 90211[id.]. Deller Cons.

Masses for 3, 4 and 5 voices; Ave verum corpus.
*** Gimell/Ph. Dig. 454 945-2PH [id.]. Tallis Scholars, Phillips.

Masses for 3, 4 and 5 voices; Ave verum corpus; Magnificat; Nunc dimittis.
(B) *** Decca Double 452 170-2 (2) [(M) id. import]. King's College, Cambridge, Ch., Willcocks – TAVERNER: *Western Wynde Mass.* ***

Although later versions of the *Mass for 5 voices* have produced singing that is more dramatic and more ardent, the King's Choir versions of the *Masses for 3* and *4 voices*, dating from 1963, remain classics. Under Willcocks there is an inevitability of phrasing and effortless control of sonority and dynamic that completely capture the music's spiritual and emotional feeling. On Double Decca the 1959 recordings of the *Ave verum*, *Magnificat* and *Nunc dimittis* have been added, representing a more reticent, less forceful style than some might expect. But the singing is still affectingly beautiful and the sound comparably spacious, and the coupled Taverner programme shows the choir on top form.

Peter Phillips is also a master of this repertoire; undoubtedly these performances have more variety and great eloquence so that, when the drama is varied with a gentler mood, the contrast is the more striking. The sound made by the Scholars in Merton College Chapel is most beautiful, both warm and fresh.

Whether or not it is historically correct for Byrd's Masses to be sung by solo voices, the great merit of the Deller Consort's French Harmonia Mundi performances is their clarity, exposing the miracle of Byrd's polyphony, even though the tonal matching is not always flawless. The 1968 recording is clean and truthful, although it lacks something in ecclesiastical atmosphere.

Mass for 4 voices; Mass for 5 voices; Infelix ego.
(BB) *** Naxos Dig. 8.550574; *4.550574* [id.]. Oxford Camerata, Jeremy Summerly.

This coupling from the Oxford Camerata represents one of Naxos's most enticing bargains. The full-throated singing has spontaneous ardour but no lack of repose in the music's more serene moments. Summerly offers the motet, *Infelix ego*, as a bonus. These readings are distinctive in a different way from those by the Tallis Scholars. The recording is outstandingly vivid.

Mass for five voices.
(M) *** EMI CDM5 65211-2. King's College, Cambridge, Ch., Ledger – TALLIS: *Mass: Puer natus est nobis;* TYE: *Mass: Euge Bone.* ***

Ledger in his last two years (1980–81) as choirmaster at King's made a series of superb recordings with what must still be counted the premier collegiate/cathedral choir. The richest and most complex of Byrd's settings of the Mass here receives a superbly poised yet deeply expressive reading, atmospherically set against a warm, reverberant acoustic. Ledger combines the contemplative intensity that his predecessor, Sir David Willcocks, with an extra rhythmic urgency. The apt couplings of music by Tallis and Tye make this a particularly desirable and generous reissue, with first-class analogue sound impressively transferred to CD.

Mass for 5 voices with the Propers for the Feast of All Saints; Motets: *Ad Dominum cum tribularer; Diliges Dominum.*
**(*) Virgin Veritas/EMI Dig. VER5 61297-2. The Sixteen, Harry Christophers.

The *Mass for 5 voices* comes here in its ecclesiastical context together with the *Propers for the Feast of All Saints*, which are from the *Gradualia* of 1605. The disc also includes a pair of eight-part motets, *Ad Dominum cum tribularer*, notable for its rich-textured, poignant false relations, and the shorter *Diliges Dominum* (another early work). The latter is an ingenious eight-part canon in which the voices are paired and at the half-way point each then performs the music first sung by its partner, only backwards. The effect is above all expressively serene. The singing is very impressive, the recording excellently focused and the acoustic appropriately spacious; but this reissue now seems rather short measure at 55 minutes.

Masses a 5: In assumptione beau mari virginis; In tempore Paschali (Propers). Antiphons: *Ave Regina clorum; Salve Regina*. Motet: *Regina cli*.
(M) *** HM Suite Dig. HMT 7905182 [id.]. Chanticleer.

Byrd's three beautiful Masses in three, four and five parts – see above – were written between 1593 and 1595, but the composer later wrote more music that could be used for private Mass celebration by Roman Catholics living in Protestant England. This later music was published in two volumes of *Gradualia* in 1605 and 1607. Besides a great many motets, Byrd left sequences of Mass Propers which could be used for certain key feast days of the church year. Propers, of course, are the variable texts that relate to specific days in the Church calendar and they are used in conjunction with the Mass Ordinary. They can quite effectively be grouped and sung independently, and that is what the dozen singers of Chanticleer do here. They have chosen two main sequences, the first connected with Easter (the Mass *In tempore Paschali*) and the second for the *Assumption of the Blessed Virgin Mary*. Intonation is not always absolutely immaculate, but the singing always has expressive conviction; one finds oneself carried along by the very spontaneous flow, with very little pause between movements. A well-documented collection, including translated texts.

Anthems: *Praise our Lord, all ye Gentiles; Sing joyfully; Turn our captivity*. Motets: *Attolite portas; Ave verum corpus; Christus resurgens; Emendemus in melius; Gaudeamus omnes; Justorum animae; Laudibus in sanctis Dominum; Non vos relinquam; O magnum mysterium; O quam suavis; Plorans plorabit; Siderum rector; Solve iubente Deo; Veni, Sancte Spiritus; Visita quaesumus Domine*.
*** Coll. Dig. COLCD 110. Cambridge Singers, John Rutter.

John Rutter brings a composer's understanding to these readings, which have a simple, direct eloquence, the music's serene spirituality movingly caught; and the atmospheric recording is very faithful, even if detail could be sharper. The programme is divided into four groups: Anthems; then Motets: of penitence and prayer; of praise and rejoicing; and for the Church year.

Byström, Oscar (1821–1909)

Symphony in D min; Andantino; Concert Waltzes Nos. 1 & 3 Overture in D, Overture to Herman Vimpel.
(N) ** Sterling Dig. CDS 1025-2 [id.]. Gävle SO, Carlos Spierer.

Oscar Byström is an interesting figure. He was an accomplished pianist and conductor who, like his fellow Swede Berwald, pursued a career outside music alongside his work as a composer. He entered the military and also invented the hydropyrometer, a device for measuring the pressure in blast furnaces, which won a prize in London. At one time the Berwald family were convinced that he purloined the autograph of the *Sinfonie capricieuse*, which disappeared after his death, and that his *Symphony in D minor* (1872–4) drew on its material. Although it is clearly influenced by Berwald, it is equally clearly not by him. The second group of the first movement is delightful and the work as a whole has much to commend it. The overtures all come from much the same period and are pleasing, though no one would make great claims for them. They are well served on this CD.

Caldara, Antonio (*c.* 1670–1736)

Christmas cantata (Vaticini di Pace); Sinfonias Nos. 5 & 6.
(BB) *** Naxos 8.553772 [id.]. Mary Enid Haines, Linda Dayiantis-Straub, Jennifer Lane, David Arnot, Aradia Baroque Ens., Kevin Mallon.

Caldara, an Italian contemporary of Bach and Handel, wrote this rare and delightful cantata for the Christmas celebrations in Rome in 1712. Preceded by an overture, it is a free-running sequence of 14 arias for the allegorical characters of Peace, Human Heart and Divine Love, with Justice initially representing Old Testament values. Peace, in the longest and most beautiful of the arias, a siciliano, then woos Justice to mercy through a vision of the Infant Christ. This Canadian performance is fresh and lively, with four excellent soloists (notably Mary Enid Haines as Peace) and a good period-instrument ensemble. A rarity made doubly enticing at Naxos super-bargain price.

Crucifixus.
(B) *** Decca Double 443 868-2 (2) [id.]. Palmer, Langridge, Esswood, Keyte, St John's College, Cambridge, Ch., Philomusica, Guest – BONONCINI: *Stabat Mater* ***; PERGOLESI: *Magnificat in C; Stabat Mater* **(*); D. SCARLATTI: *Stabat Mater;* A. SCARLATTI: *Domine, refugium factus es nobis; O magnum mysterium;* LOTTI: *Crucifixus*. ***

The *Crucifixus* is an elaborate 16-part setting of great eloquence, texturally rich and concentrated into a few seconds short of five minutes. It follows on naturally after Bononcini's beautiful *Stabat Mater*.

Maddalena ai piedi di Cristo (oratorio; complete).
*** HM Dig. HMC 905221/22 (2) [id.]. Kiehr, Dominguez, Fink, Scholl, Messthaler, Türk, Schola Cantorum Basiliensis O, René Jacobs.

This oratorio about Mary Magdalene at the feet of Christ, an early work dating from around 1700, inspired Caldara to an astonishing sequence of *da capo* arias, most of them brief, but with several longer ones given to Maddalena herself, notably the heartfelt *Pompo inutile*, inspiring Maria Cristina Kiehr to warm, golden tone, or the agonized *In lagrime stemprato*, depicting falling tears. In contrasting characterization, her sister Marta has such jolly numbers as *Vattene, corri, vola*, with Rosa Dominguez bright and agile. The role of Christ is given to a tenor, but neither of his two arias is reflective, and the biggest proportion of arias go to the counterpart characters of Earthly Love (a mezzo, Bernarda Fink) and Heavenly Love (a counter-tenor, Andreas Scholl), both of them singing superbly, subtly contrasted in tone. René Jacobs draws fresh and alert playing from the Schola Basiliensis Orchestra, with the instruments, including varied continuo, set in a warm acoustic slightly behind the singers.

Cambini, Giuseppe Maria
(1746–1825)

Wind quintets Nos. 1 in B; 2 in D min.; 3 in F.
(BB) *** Naxos Dig. 8.553410 [id.]. Avalon Wind Quintet – BRICCIALDI: *Wind quintet in D.* ***

These *Wind quintets* are doubtless inconsequential but they are charming, particularly when played so superbly and elegantly by these fine young German musicians. The recording is expertly balanced and very natural. Slight music, but so well served that it will give much pleasure.

Camilleri, Charles (born 1931)

Piano concertos Nos. 1 (Mediterranean); 2 (Maqam); 3 (Leningrad).
**(*) Unicorn Dig. DKPCD 9150 [id.]. André de Grotte, Bournemouth SO, Michael Laus.

Charles Camirelli was born in Malta and there is an Italianate, sunny good nature about the *First Piano concerto* (1948), unashamedly popular and agreeably slight when presented with such sparkle. The *Second concerto* (1967/8) came from what is described as the composer's 'Afro-Arabic-Hindu period'. The even thornier *Leningrad Concerto* dates from a Russian visit in 1985 and has a political inspiration and a philosophical basis. Performances of all three works are full of vitality and the recording sharply observes and vividly details yet has plenty of atmosphere.

Campra, André (1660–1744)

Cantatas: *Arion; La dispute de l'Amour et de l'Hymen; Enée et Didon; Les femmes.*
(B) *** HM Musique d'Abord Dig. HMA 1901238 [id.]. Jill Feldman, Dominique Visse, Jean-François Gardeil, Les Arts Florissants, William Christie.

Jill Feldman is at her most spirited and eloquent in the dramatic narrative of *Arion* and Dominique Visse's tangy alto is equally telling in the altercation of the conflicting interests of Marriage and Love which need to be resolved harmoniously. In *Les Femmes* there is disillusion from a male lover who laments the vagaries of the fair sex; his final conclusions are far from optimistic. This is sung with both feeling and sparkle by Jean-François Gardeil. The most ambitious of the four works is a brilliant duet celebrating the nuptials of Aeneas and Dido. With sensitive and strongly paced accompaniments from Christie and Les Arts Florissants, it is difficult to imagine that these works could be re-created more tellingly, helped by the presence and atmosphere of the excellent recording.

Requiem Mass.
**(*) HM HMC 901251 [id.]. [id.]. Baudry, Zanetti, Benet, Elwes, Varcoe, Chapelle Royale Ch. & O, Herreweghe.

This *Requiem* is a lovely work, with luminous textures and often beguiling harmonies, and its neglect is difficult to understand. Herreweghe's performance, with refined solo and choral singing, is pleasing and sympathetic if comparatively cool. The recording is refined, to match the performance.

L'Europe galante (opera-ballet): suite.
(M) *** DHM/BMG GD 77059 (2) [77059-2-RG]. Yakar, Kweksilber, René Jacobs, La Petite Bande, Leonhardt – LULLY: *Bourgeois gentilhomme.* ***

Like Couperin's *Les Nations*, though in a very different fashion, this enchanting divertissement attempts to portray various national characteristics: French, Spanish, Italian and Turkish. The three soloists all shine and the instrumentalists, directed by Leonhardt, are both expert and spirited. The recording too is well balanced and sounds very fresh on CD.

OPERA

Idoménée (tragédie lyrique).
**(*) HM HMC 901396/8 [id.]. Delétré, Piau, Zanetti, Fouchécourt, Boyer, Les Arts Florissants, Christie.

In the manner of the time, Campra's *Idoménée* relies on free cantilena rather than formal numbers, with set-pieces kept short and with the chorus often contributing to such brief arias as there are. Christie with his talented Les Arts Florissants team presents the whole work with a taut feeling for its dramatic qualities. The matching of voices to character is close, and in the breadth of its span, this is a fascinating work, vividly recorded.

Idoménée: highlights.
(B) *** HM Dig. HMX 290844/46 (3) [(M) id.] (from complete recording, with Delétré, Piau, Zanetti, Fouchécourt, Les Arts Florissants; cond. Christie) – LULLY: *Atys:* highlights; RAMEAU: *Castor et Pollux:* highlights. ***

This 70-minute selection, with items well balanced to include the Overture, a brief reminder of the Prologue and excerpts from all five Acts, is inexpensive if taken in harness with its companion selections. It comes as part of one of Harmonia Mundi's 'Trios', compiling three discs of operatic highlights at bargain price, with full documentation, including translations.

Cannabich, Johann Christian
(1731–98)

Flute quintets, Op. 7/3–6.
(N) *** CPO Dig. CPO 999 544-2 [id.]. Camerata Köln.

Cannabich was born in Mannheim, and after studying in Italy, at the end of the 1750s he became leader of the famous court orchestra, and in the mid 1770s succeeded Johann Stamitz as the orchestra's Director. Later he counted Mozart among his friends. The *Flute quintets* are for one (or usually two) flutes, violin, viola and cello, and sometimes have optional keyboard parts. They were published in Paris (curiously labelled 'sinfonie concertante') around 1768/9. The music is elegant, well crafted and charming, if very lightweight, with the 'concertante' flute parts always dominant. Excellent performances here and natural recording within a pleasing ambience.

Canning, Thomas (born 1911)

Fantasy on a hymn tune by Justin Morgan (for double string quartet and string orchestra).
*** Everest EVC 9004 [id.]. Houston SO, Stokowski – R. STRAUSS: *Don Juan* etc. ***

The Pennsylvanian composer, Thomas Canning, has clearly modelled his *Fantasy* on the Vaughan Williams *Tallis fantasia*. Although the contrast with the secondary string group is less ethereal, in Stokowski's hands the work reaches a thrilling climax, and this fine if derivative piece is well worth having on disc when the recording is so rich and well focused. This CD is offered at slightly under premium price.

Canteloube, Marie-Joseph
(1879–1957)

Songs of the Auvergne: Series 1–5 (complete).
(B) *** Decca Double Dig. 444 995-2 (2) [id.]; *444 995-4*. Kiri Te Kanawa, ECO, Jeffrey Tate – VILLA-LOBOS: *Bachianas brasileiras No. 5*. ***

(i) *Chants d'Auvergne: Series 1–5* (complete); (ii) Appendix: *Chants d'Auvergne et Quercy: La Mère Antoine; Lorsque le meunier; Oh! Madelon, je dois partir; Réveillez-vous, belle endormie. Chants paysans Béarn: Rossignolet qui chants. Chants du Languedoc: La fille d'un paysan; Moi j'ai un homme; Mon père m'a plasée; O up!; Quand Marion va au moulin. Chants des Pays Basques: Allons, beau rossignol; Comment donc Savoir; Dans le tombeau; J'ai une douce amie; Le premier de tous les oiseaux.*
✿ (M) *** Van. 08.8002.72 [OVC 8001/2]. Netania Davrath, O, (i) Pierre de la Roche; (ii) Gershon Kingsley.

It was Netania Davrath who in 1963 and 1966 – a decade before the De los Angeles selection – pioneered a complete recording of Canteloube's delightful song-settings from the Auvergne region of France, plus an important appendix of 15 more, collected by Canteloube and admirably scored by Gershon Kingsley, very much in the seductive manner of the others. While her voice has a lovely, sweet purity and freedom in the upper range, she also brings a special kind of colour and life to these infinitely varied settings. The accompaniments are freshly idiomatic, warm but not over-upholstered, and the CD transfers retain all the sparkle and atmosphere of the original recordings.

In Dame Kiri Te Kanawa's recital the warmly atmospheric Decca recording brings an often languorous opulence to the music-making. In such an atmosphere the quick songs lose a little in bite, and *Baïlèro*, the most famous, is taken extremely slowly. With the sound so sumptuous, this hardly registers and the result remains compelling, thanks in large measure to sympathetic accompaniment from the ECO under Jeffrey Tate. At Double Decca price, this now makes a formidable bargain, for Dame Kiri's voice was at its freshest and most beautiful when she made these recordings in 1983/4.

Chants d'Auvergne: L'Aio dè rotso; L'Antouèno; Baïlèro; Brezairola; Malurous qu'o uno fenno; Passo pel prat; Pastourelle.
(M) *** RCA 09026 62600-2 [id.]. Anna Moffo, American SO, Stokowski – RACHMANINOV: *Vocalise;* VILLA-LOBOS: *Bachianas brasileiras No. 5*. ***

Moffo gives radiant performances, helped by the sumptuous accompaniment which Stokowski provides. The result is sweet, seductively so. The recording, from the early 1960s, is opulent to match.

Chants d'Auvergne: L'Antouèno; Baïlèro; 3 Bourrées; Lou Boussu; Brezairola; Lou coucut; Chut, chut; La Déläissádo; Lo Fïolairé; Jou l'pount d'o Mirabel; Malurous qu'o uno fenno; Passo pel prat; Pastourelle; Postouro, sé tu m'aymo; Tè, l'co, tè.

❀ (B) *** EMI Dig. CD-EMX 9500 [(M) id. import]. Jill Gomez, RLPO, Handley.

Jill Gomez's selection of these increasingly popular songs, attractively presented on a mid-price label, makes for a memorably characterful record which, as well as bringing out the sensuous beauty of Canteloube's arrangements, keeps reminding us, in the echoes of rustic band music, of the genuine folk base. An ideal purchase for the collector who wants just a selection.

Chants d'Auvergne: Baïlèro; 3 Bourrées; Brezairola; Lou Boussu; Lou coucut; Chut, chut; La Délaïssádo; Lo Fïolairé; Jou l'pount d'o Mirabel; Malurous qu'o uno fenno; Oï ayaï; Pastourelle; La pastrouletta; Postouro, sé tu m'aymo; Tè, l'co, tè; Uno jionto postouro.

(M) *** Virgin/EMI Dig. CUV5 61120-2. Arleen Augér, ECO, Yan Pascal Tortelier.

Arleen Augér's lovely soprano is ravishing in the haunting, lyrical songs like the ever-popular *Baïlèro*. In the playful items she conveys plenty of fun, and in the more boisterous numbers the recording has vivid presence.

Caplet, André (1878–1925)

La Masque de la mort rouge (Conte fantastique); Divertissements for harp; (i) *Les prières*, for soprano, harp & string quartet; (ii) *2 Sonnets*, for soprano & harp; (i–iii) *Septet à cordes vocales et instrumentales.*

(B) *** HM Musique d'Abord Dig. HMA 1901417 [id.]. Laurence Cabel, Ens. Musique Oblique; with (i) Sharon Coste; (ii) Sandrine Piau; (iii) Sylvie Deguy.

This bargain-priced Harmonia Mundi reissue is highly recommendable, offering the more intimate, chamber version of the *Conte fantastique* for harp and strings, based on Edgar Allen Poe's *Masque of the Red Death*. In the other three major works, female voices are richly integrated with the string quartet, and the composer makes a great success of this combination of voices and strings, especially in the *Septet*, using a trio of two sopranos and a mezzo. Beautiful singing, sensitive playing and warmly atmospheric sound add to the listener's aural pleasure. Two solo *Divertissements* for harp make an agreeable central interlude.

Cardoso, Frei Manuel (*c.* 1566–1650)

Lamentatio; Magnificat secundi toni.

(BB) *** Naxos Dig. 8.553310 [id.]. Ars Nova, Bo Holten – LOBO: *Motets;* MAGALHAES: *Missa O Soberana luz* etc. *** (with Concert of Portuguese polyphony ***).

Cardoso's serene, flowing polyphony with its forward-looking use of augmented chords is heard at its most striking in the *Magnificat*, while his *Lamentatio* for six voices is touchingly beautiful. Remarkably eloquent singing from this fine Danish choir and good recording in a suitably ecclesiastical acoustic. The rest of the programme is hardly less stimulating.

Missa Miserere mihi Domine; Magnificat secundi toni.

*** HM Dig. HMC 901543 [id.]. European Vocal Ens., Philippe Herreweghe.

Once again in the *Missa Miserere mihi Domine* we are aware of the extraordinary individuality of Cardoso's polyphony and its powerful and sumptuous expressive content. The composer's forward-looking use of harmonic relationships is also a striking feature of the *Magnificat*, a shorter but no less impressive work. The performers here really sound as if they believe both in the music and in the words they are singing, and the recording, made in L'Abbaye aux Dames de Saintes, is fully worthy of their richly sonorous blend of tone.

Requiem (Missa pro defunctis).

(BB) *** Naxos Dig. 8.550682 [id.]. Oxford Schola Cantorum, Jeremy Summerly – LOBO: *Missa pro defunctis.* ***

Requiem: Magnificat; Motets, Mulier quae erat; Non mortui; Nos autem gloriari; Sitivit anima mea.

❀ *** Gimell/Ph. 454 921-2 [id.]. Tallis Scholars, Phillips.

Cardoso's *Requiem* opens in striking and original fashion. The polyphony unfolds in long-breathed phrases of unusual length and eloquence, and both the motets, *Mulier quae erat* ('A woman, a sinner in that city') and the short *Nos autem gloriari* ('Yet should we glory'), are rich in texture and have great expressive resplendence. Cardoso's use of the augmented chord at the opening of the *Requiem* gives his music some of its distinctive stamp. The Tallis Scholars sing with characteristic purity of tone and intonation, and they are splendidly recorded. A glorious issue.

In Summerly's Naxos account, Cardoso's *Missa pro defunctis* is not as dramatic in its contrasts as the coupled setting of Duarte Lôbo. As with the Lôbo coupling, a solo treble makes a brief but effective introduction for each movement, a device which works very touchingly. The performance by Oxford Schola Cantorun is beautifully paced and the calibre of the singing itself is very impressive indeed, as is the Naxos recording.

Carissimi, Giacomo (1605–74)

Duos & cantatas: *A piè d'un verde alloro; Bel tempo per me; Così volete, così sarà; Deh, memoria è che più chiedi; Hor che si Sirio; Il mio cor è un mar; Lungi homai deh spiega; Peregrin d'ignote sponde; Rimati in pace homai; Scrivete, occhi dolente (Lettera amorosa); Tu m'hai preso à consumare; Vaghi rai, pupille ardenti.*
(B) *** HM Musique d'Abord Dig. HMA 1901262. Concerto Vocale, René Jacobs.

Carissimi's achievement as a sacred composer has long overshadowed his secular music, whose riches are generously displayed here and whose inspiration and mastery are immediately evident. These are performances of great style and are beautifully recorded. A bargain.

Abraham et Isaac; Ezecha (Hezekiah); Jephte (oratorios); *Missa septimi toni* (for unaccompanied double choir); Motets: *O quam pulchra es; O vulnera doloris; Salve, salve puellule; Tolle sponsa.*
(N) (B) **(*) Erato/Warner Ultima Duo 3984 24231 (2) [id.]. J. Smith, Serafim, Huttenlocher, Rosat, Elwes, Silva, Rossier, Dufour, Lisbon Gulbenkian Foundation Ch. & O, Corboz.

This Ultima Double further extends our knowledge of Carissimi's oratorios, and in itself makes a fine introduction to this gifted composer. The soloists are excellent throughout, with Philip Huttenlocher standing out, particularly as Jephtha. The three-movement choral *Mass* (*Kyrie–Gloria–Credo*) is also well sung, although here the recording aims at sonority, rather than aiming to separate the two choral groups. The other snag is the lack of full documentation and texts. But the four solo cantatas (given in turn to soprano, bass, tenor, and in the case of *Tolle sponsa*, soprano, bass and chorus) are so freshly sung and offer such enjoyable music that criticism is all but disarmed. No complaints about the vivid projection of the sound here.

(i) *Jephte;* (ii) *Jonas;* (iii) *Judicium Salomonis (The Judgement of Solomon)* (oratorios).
*** Mer. Dig. CDE 84132 [id.]. Coxwell, Hemington Jones, Harvey, Ainsley, Gabrieli Cons. 8 Players, Paul McCreesh.

No opening sinfonia survives for *Jephte*, and Paul McCreech chooses to preface this oratorio with a Frescobaldi *Toccata*, which works well. *Jephte* is affectingly presented, and the McCreesh performance brings overt expressive feeling, despite some vocal insecurities at the very top. Overall these are well-prepared and intelligent accounts. The continuo part is imaginatively realized with some pleasing sonorities (organ, double harp, chitarrone, etc.) and, despite some undoubted minor shortcomings, these are most convincing accounts of all three works, if on a fairly intimate scale. However, the back-up documentation is inadequate.

Carlsson, Mark (born 1952)

Nightwings.
*** Crystal Dig. CD 750 [id.]. Westwood Wind Quintet – BARBER: *Summer music;* LIGETI: *Bagatelles;* MATHIAS: *Quintet.* ***

In *Nightwings* the flute assumes the persona of a dreamer, the taped music may be perceived as a dream-world, and the other four instruments appear as characters in a dream. On this evidence, however, the conception is in some respects more interesting than the piece itself. Excellent playing and recording.

Carmina Burana (*c.* 1300)

Carmina Burana – songs from the original manuscript.
**(*) HM HMC 90335 [id.]. Clemencic Cons., René Clemencic.

This was the collection on which Carl Orff drew for his popular cantata. The original manuscript comprises more than 200 pieces from many countries, dating from the late eleventh to the thirteenth century, organized according to subject-matter: love songs, moralizing and satirical songs, eating, drinking, gambling and religious texts. René Clemencic's performances, recorded in 1977, have immense spirit and liveliness, and there is much character. The presentation suffers slightly from over-reverberant sound, though this at times brings a gain in atmosphere.

Cartellieri, Casimir Anton (1772–1807)

Clarinet concertos Nos. 1 in B flat; 2 – Adagio pastorale; 3 in E flat.
*** MDG Dig. MDG 301 0527-2 [id.]. Dieter Klöcker, Prague CO.

Hardly a household name, Casimir Anton Cartellieri was born in Danzig and eventually found his way to Vienna. His three *Clarinet concertos* (only the slow movement of the second survives) are expertly laid out for the instrument. While they are not searching or profound, they are astonishingly inventive and full of both charm and wit. Dieter Klöcker and the Prague Chamber Orchestra give thoroughly committed accounts of these delightful pieces, and the MDG recording is immaculate.

Carter, Elliott (born 1908)

(i) *Piano concerto. Variations for orchestra.*
*** New World NW 347 [id.]. (i) Ursula Oppens; Cincinnati SO, Gielen.

The *Concerto* is a densely argued piece, complex in its structure, with a concertino of seven instruments, surrounding the piano, who act as 'a well-meaning but impotent intermediary'. The *Variations* is an inventive and fascinating work, splendidly played by these Cincinnati forces. The recording was made at concert performances and is excellent.

Piano concerto; Concerto for orchestra; 3 Occasions for orchestra.
(BB) *** Arte Nova Dig. 74321 27773-2 [id.]. Oppens, SWF SO, Gielen.

Piano concerto; 3 Occasions for orchestra.
(BB) *** Arte Nova Dig. 74321 52248-2. Oppens, SWF SO, Gielen – BARTOK: *Piano concerto No. 3;* BERG: *3 Pieces from the Lyric suite.* ***

Michael Gielen directs strong, purposeful readings, very well played, of this taxing music, clarifying the thornily complex arguments with the help of vivid, sharply focused sound. Even with Ursula Oppens a powerful soloist, the *Piano concerto,* dating from 1964–5, is the most formidable piece for the unprepared listener. That leads naturally on to the *Concerto for orchestra* of 1969. More approachable than either is the third work, a collection of three pieces, written between 1986 and 1989, which display to the full the astonishing vitality and questing originality of a composer of rising 80. In performances like these, recorded live, the tension is magnetic and this makes an inexpensive introduction to one of the most intractable of twentieth-century composers.

The alternative disc brings together two of Gielen's outstanding Carter performances but offering the generous alternative coupling of Bartók and Berg works.

Concerto for orchestra.
(M) *** Sony SMK 60203 [id.]. NYPO, Bernstein – IVES: *Central Park in the dark* etc. ***

It is apt that on the Bernstein CD, Elliott Carter's key avant-garde orchestral work from 1969 should follow on after Ives, for its writing seems naturally to derive from that earlier master in its complexity. However, the argument here is much more thorny, the texture densely interwoven and prismatic; its energy is unquestioned, but its linear fragmentation is daunting. Certainly it could hardly be played with more expertise or display more conviction; and the close (1970) recording-balance ensures that every detail is well defined.

Carulli, Ferdinando (1770–1841)

Guitar concerto in A.
(M) **(*) DG (IMS) 439 984-2. Siegfried Behrend, I Musici – GIULIANI: *Concerto in A* ***; VIVALDI: *Guitar concertos* **(*).

The Italian virtuoso Ferdinando Carulli made his reputation in Paris, where this innocent post-Mozartian one-movement piece was written. It is elegantly played by Behrend and I Musici and immaculately recorded. A touch more vitality would have been welcome, but this is enjoyable enough.

Carvalho, João De Sousa (1745–98)

Te Deum.
(M) *** DG Codex 453 182-2. Luisa Bosabalian, Elsa Saque, Carmen Gonzales, John Mitchinson, Alvaro Malta, Gulbenkian Chamber Ch. & O, Pierre Salzmann – ALMEIDA: *Beatus vir* etc.; SEIXAS: *Adebat Vincentius* etc.; TEIXEIRA: *Gaudate, astra.* ***

The Portuguese composer João De Sousa Carvalho was a contemporary of Mozart, and there is a Mozartian impression within the extended (nine-minute) overture for two orchestras which opens his ambitious 1792 *Te Deum* (his third setting). During the course of this splendid and powerfully expressive work there is much thrilling writing for double chorus, and the florid arias – like Mozart's – are often semi-operatic in style, making great demands on the soloists, who generally rise to the occasion here, especially the fine mezzo, Carmen Gonzales, and the tenor, John Mitchinson. The performance here is eloquently moving and spaciously recorded (in 1970). Even if the double chorus at times could be more sharply defined, the overall focus and balance are very good. The reissue is made the more attractive by the substantial couplings from three major Portuguese baroque composers, all little known.

Carver, Robert (*c.* 1484–*c.* 1568)

Mass: Cantate Domino for 6 voices.
*** Gaudeamus/ASV Dig. CDGAU 136 [id.]. (i) Graham Lovett; David Hamilton, Cappella Nova, Alan Tavener (with ANGUS: *All my belief;* (i) *The Song of Simeon.* ANON.: *Descendi in hortum meum.* BLACK: *Ane lesson upone the feiftie psalme; Lytill Blak.* PEEBLES: *Psalms 107; 124; Si quis diligit me* ***).

This anthology celebrates the music heard in the 1560s after the return from France of Mary, Queen of Scots. Most of the pieces, by David Peebles (who flourished 1530–76), John Black (*c.* 1520–87) and

John Angus (fl. 1562–90), come from *Musica Britannica* Vol. XV ('Music of Scotland, 1500–1700') and appear on record for the first time. Though the authorship of the *Mass: Cantate Domino* is not definitely established, it is related to the five-part *Fera pessima* by Robert Carver and is almost certainly a re-working, possibly by Carver himself, of the earlier, five-part piece for six voices. In any event, this is a record of much interest, well sung and recorded.

Mass Dum sacrum mysterium in 10 parts; Motets: *Gaude flore Virginali; O bone Jesu.*
*** Gaudeamus Dig. CDGAU 124 [id.]. Cappella Nova, Alan Tavener.

The opening piece here, the motet *O bone Jesu*, is in 19 parts and is of exceptional luminosity and richness. The ten-part *Mass*, *Dum sacrum mysterium*, was written at the beginning of the sixteenth century, and it is thought that in its final form it was performed at the coronation of the infant James V at Stirling in 1513. As the note puts it, among Carver's *Masses* this is 'undoubtedly the grandest in scope, the most extended in development and the richest in detail'. The motet, *Gaude flore Virginali* for five voices, though less sumptuous, has some adventurous modulations. The Cappella Nova under Alan Tavener give a thoroughly dedicated account of all three pieces, though the pitch drops very slightly in the *Gaude flore Virginali*. The recording is very good indeed.

Masses: Fera pessima for 5 voices; Pater creator omnium for 4 voices.
*** Gaudeamus/ASV Dig. CDGAU 127 [id.]. Cappella Nova, Alan Tavener.

Missa: L'Homme armé for 4 voices; Mass for 6 voices.
*** Gaudeamus/ASV Dig. CDGAU 126 [id.]. Cappella Nova, Alan Tavener.

These two CDs, together with his ten-part *Missa Dum sacrum mysterium* (and probably the *Cantata Domino* listed above), represent the complete sacred music of the early-sixteenth-century Scottish composer, Robert Carver. In the *L'Homme armé Mass* of 1520, Carver is the only British composer to make use of the French popular song which inspired so many Mass settings by continental composers, from Josquin onwards. The six-part *Mass* of 1515 is cyclic (each Mass section opens with similar music), and the presence of other common material suggests that it is a parody Mass, possibly based, it is thought, on an earlier Carver motet.

Like the *L'Homme armé*, the *Fera pessima* is another *cantus firmus* Mass and dates from 1525; its companion, the four-part *Pater creator omnium*, comes from 1546 and reflects the changing style of the period. It survives only in incomplete form; the two missing parts in the *Kyrie* and *Gloria* have been added by Kenneth Elliott. Committed singing from the Cappella Nova and Alan Tavener, and very well recorded too.

Carwithen, Doreen (born 1922)

(i) *Concerto for piano and strings. Overtures: ODTAA, ('One damn thing after another'); Bishop Rock; Suffolk suite.*
*** Chandos Dig. CHAN 9524 [id.]. (i) Howard Shelley; LSO, Hickox.

Doreen Carwithen here emerges as a warmly communicative composer in her own right, owing rather more to Walton's style than that of her husband (William Alwyn), but always writing purposefully with strong, sometimes syncopated rhythms, and stirring melodies, all enhanced with brilliant and inventive orchestration. The two overtures in their vigour and atmospheric colour relate readily to her film music, the one inspired by John Masefield's novel, *ODTAA*, the other inspired by the rock in the Atlantic that marks the last contact with mainland Britain, stormy in places, gently sinister in others. The charming *Suffolk suite* uses melodies originally written for a film on East Anglia. Much the most ambitious work is the *Concerto for piano and strings*, with powerful virtuoso writing for the piano set against rich-textured strings. A deeply melancholy slow movement – in which the piano is joined by solo violin – leads to a strong finale which in places echoes the Ireland *Piano concerto*. Howard Shelley is the persuasive soloist, with Richard Hickox and the LSO equally convincing in their advocacy of all four works. Warm, atmospheric sound.

(i) *Violin sonata*; (ii) *String quartets Nos. 1 and 2.*
(N) *** Chandos Dig. CHAN 9596 [id.]. (i) Lydia Mordkovitch, Julian Milford; (ii) Sorrel Quartet.

This fine disc of Doreen Carwithen's chamber music follows up the success of the earlier Chandos issue of her orchestral music, with all three works offering most sensitive string writing. The *First Quartet*, written in 1948 when she was still a student, firmly establishes her personal idiom, tautly constructed in three movements, fast–slow–fast, with the open intervals of pentatonic melody set in contrast with semitone motifs. The result, identifably English, yet points forward, though it is only in the *Second Quartet* of 1952, in two extended movements, that one detects a hint that she may have been studying the quartets of Bartók; with warmly expressive performances from the well-matched Sorrel Quartet. The *Violin sonata*, written later, brings high dramatic contrasts, most strikingly in the central *Vivace*, a moto perpetuo in 9/8 rhythm. Lydia Mordkovitch, as ever, proves a passionate advocate, finding a depth and poignancy in the lyrical writing that may reflect her Russian roots. Julian Milford makes an ideal partner, though the piano is rather backwardly balanced. Otherwise the recording is first-rate.

Casella, Alfredo (1883–1947)

La Giara (symphonic suite), Op. 41 bis; Paganiniana (Divertimento for orchestra), Op. 65; Serenata for chamber orchestra, Op. 46 bis.
(N) (BB) Naxos Dig. 8.553706 [id.]. Italian Swiss RSO, Benda.

So far, the only work of Alfredo Casella to have entered and held its place in the recorded repertoire is *Paganiniana* and the performance here by the Italian Swiss Radio under Christian Benda is as bright-eyed, polished and sympathetic as its competitors below. Now this enterprising Naxos disc gives us an opportunity to savour two other equally enticing (and it must be admitted idiomatically similar) orchestral works by this attractive Turinese composer. Both the *Serenata*, which is precociously good humoured (it opens with a drole bassoon solo) and touchingly nostalgic by turns, and the ballet *La Giara*, are unashamedly eclectic. There are various influences from the French school and even a touch of neoclassical Stravinsky. But Casella has a ready fund of good tunes and they are delectably scored. He favours vivacious Neapolitan tarantellas, although the finale of *La Giara* is more like Ibert. The ballet also includes a melancholy vocal interlude, *The Story of the girl seized by pirates*, sensitively sung by Marco Beasley, affecting, but not in the least sentimental. The recording is first class, vividly atmospheric. This collection is well worth having, but don't play all three works at once.

Paganiniana, Op. 65.
*** Sony Dig. SK 53280 [id.]. La Scala PO, Muti – BUSONI: *Turandot suite;* MARTUCCI: *Giga* etc. ***
(***) Testament mono SBT 1017 [id.]. St Cecilia, Rome, O, Cantelli – DUKAS: *L'apprenti sorcier;* FALLA: *Three-cornered hat;* RAVEL: *Daphnis et Chloé: suite No. 2.* (***)

Paganiniana was commissioned by the Vienna Philharmonic to mark its centenary in 1942. It is a delightful, effervescent score whose sparkling yet dry wit and exuberance fare well in Muti's hands (as they did in Ormandy's celebrated recording with the Philadelphia Orchestra). It also has the advantage of an enterprising and imaginative coupling.

Cantelli's pioneering record dates from 1949 and comes up sounding very well in a marvellously transferred Testament issue which also offers his 1955–6 Philharmonia recording of the *Daphnis* suite and his 1954 *Three-cornered hat*. Elegant playing.

Casken, John (born 1949)

Cello concerto.
*** Collins Dig. CD single 2006-2 [id.]. N. Sinfonia, Heinrich Schiff.

John Casken wrote this 20-minute *Cello concerto* for Schiff and the Northern Sinfonia. On the Collins recording, as in his live performances, Schiff directs the orchestra from the cello, and the result is one of the richest, most powerful accounts of a new work on any recent disc. Collins has issued it in its twentieth-century-plus series as a CD 'single', costing about £6, the sort of price to encourage anyone to experiment.

Castelnuovo-Tedesco, Mario (1895–1968)

Guitar concerto No. 1 in D, Op. 99.
(BB) *** Naxos Dig. 8.550729 [id.]. Norbert Kraft, N. CO, Nicholas Ward – RODRIGO; VILLA-LOBOS: *Concertos.* ***
(M) **(*) DG (IMS) 449 098-2. Narciso Yepes, LSO, Navarro (with HALFFTER: *Concerto;* RODRIGO: *Fantasía.* **)

On Naxos a first-class version of this slight but attractive concerto, which is well suited by the relatively intimate scale of the performance. The recording is well balanced and vivid, and this is happily coupled with enjoyable versions of two other favourite concertos. The soloist, Norbert Kraft, has plenty of personality and the accompaniment is fresh and polished. Typically excellent Naxos value.

Narciso Yepes's plays this concerto admirably, receiving attentive support from Navarro and the LSO and fresh, vivid recording from DG; for the two coupled works, however, his partner was Odón Alonso and the results are less impressive, with a dry studio acoustic not flattering the music-making. The Naxos CD is a far more attractive proposition.

Cello sonata, Op. 50; Notturna sull'acqua, Op. 82a ;Scherzino, Op. 82b; I Nottambui (Variazione fantastiche), Op. 47; Paraphrase on Rossini's Largo al factotum; Toccata, Op. 83; Valse on the name of Gregor Piatigorsky.
(N) *** Biddulph Dig. LAW 024 [id.]. Nancy Green, Frederick Moyer.

For most collectors Castelnuovo-Tedesco is known as the composer of a single rather pleasing *Guitar concerto* (although he also achieved success with a number of film scores). But his range was much wider than that comparatively slight work would suggest. His *Cello sonata* is a splendid work, opening with a striking main theme (marked *Arioso e sereno*) followed by a highly inventive *Aria with variations* to act as slow movement and finale combined. The fairy-light *Scherzino* which follows, although written seven years later, might have been an additional movement. The two nocturnal pieces are full of Mediterranean atmosphere, the sultry principal theme of the extended *I Nottambuli* (*Night walk*) is soon to be spiced with habanera rhythms. Serenity and passion are interchanged and whirling Spanish dance rhythms follow, but the perfumes of the night return to end the work gently. The two witty encores sparkle, with Tchaikovsky's *Sleeping Beauty waltz* making a surprise entry in the Piatigorsky tribute. Nancy Green (a pupil of Leonard Rose and Lynn Harrell) is in full sympathy with this repertoire and she plays very persuasively indeed, with excellent support from her partner, Frerick Moyer. Biddulph are famous for resurrecting historic recordings but there is nothing dated about the excellent digital sound balance afforded to these artists. Recommended to all lovers of the cello.

Catalani, Alfredo (1854–93)

A Sera; Serenatella; String quartet in A.
(N) *** ASV Dig. CDDCA 909 [id.]. Puccini Qt. – PUCCINI: *Crisantemi; Fugues; Quartet* etc. ***

This disc brings together all the string quartet music written by the young Puccini and his Tuscan friend, Catalani, telling a fascinating story about the way that each developed. Though the three examples of Catalani's work are, like most of those of Puccini here, early works, they reveal a more formed style. The elegant *Serenatella* and the romantically melancholy *A Sera*, were arranged by the composer from piano originals, and Catalani understandably thought well enough of the latter to use it for the prelude to Act III of his most famous opera, *La Wally*. The *String quartet in A* is less consistent, but its scale is impressive, with the extended slow movement providing a moving expressive climax, confidently handled. A delightful disc, warmly played and atmospherically recorded.

La Wally (opera): complete.
(N) (B) *** Decca Double 460 744-2 (2) [id.]. Tebaldi, Del Monaco, Diaz, Cappuccilli, Marimpietri, Turin Lyric Ch., Monte Carlo Op. O, Fausto Cleva.

The title-role of *La Wally* prompts Renata Tebaldi to give one of her most tenderly affecting performances on record, a glorious example of her singing late in her career. Mario del Monaco begins coarsely, but the heroic power and intensity of his singing are formidable, and it is good to have the young Cappuccilli in the baritone role of Gellner. The sound in this late-1960s recording is superbly focused and vividly real. Reissued as a Double this is now one of Decca's prime operatic bargain sets. The new-style synopsis should prove attractive to newcomers to the opera.

Cavalli, Francesco (1602–76)

La Calisto (complete).
**(*) HM Dig. HMC 1901515/17 (3) [id.]. Bayo, Lippi, Keenlyside, Pushee, Mantovani, Concerto Vocale, René Jacobs.

La Calisto (complete version – freely arranged by Raymond Leppard).
(M) *** Decca 436 216-2 (2). Cotrubas, Trama, J. Baker, Bowman, Gottlieb, Cuénod, Hughes, Glyndebourne Festival Op. Ch., LPO, Leppard.

No more perfect Glyndebourne entertainment has been devised than Leppard's freely adapted version of an opera written for Venice in the 1650s but never heard since. It is the more delectable because of the brilliant part given to the goddess, Diana, taken by Dame Janet Baker. In this version she has the dual task of portraying first the chaste goddess herself, then in the same costume switching immediately to the randy Jupiter disguised as Diana, quite a different character. The opera is splendidly cast. Parts for such singers as James Bowman draw out their finest qualities, and the result is magic. Linfea, a bad-tempered, lecherous, ageing nymph, is portrayed hilariously by Hugues Cuénod. The recording, made at Glyndebourne, is gloriously rich and atmospheric, with the Prologue in a different, more ethereal acoustic than the rest of the opera. A full libretto is provided.

Jacobs directs a lively account, recorded in vivid, immediate sound, helped by some characterful, generally well-sung solo performances. In the title-role Maria Bayo is sweet and fresh, and Alessandra Mantovani as Diana sings warmly, though with some unsteadiness. The disappointment is that when Jove is disguised as Diana, the part is sung by the weighty baritone, Marcello Lippi, taking the role of Jove, in a piping falsetto. Graham Pushee, a reliable but hooty counter-tenor, takes the role of Endimione and the comic role of the nymph, Linfea, is taken by a male singer, Gilles Ragon, capable but nowhere near as characterful as Hugues Cuénod at Glyndebourne. However inauthentic the Leppard version is, it conveys more intense enjoyment than this and, though the vigour and variety of Cavalli's inspiration are brought out well by Jacobs and his team, the Decca mid-priced reissue is the one to go for.

La Didone (ed. Hengelbrock & Bratschke).
(N) *** DHM/BMG Dig. 05472 77354-2 (2)

[id.]. Kenny, Howarth, Dale, Balthasar Neumann Ens., Thomas Hengelbrock.

La Didone, one of Cavalli's earliest operas, tells the story of Dido and Aeneas, starting apocalytically with the fall of Troy. In this recording, taken from live performances at the Schwetzingen Festival, the conductor, Thomas Hengelbrock, has edited and cut the original score, with Detlef Bratschke filling out the spare treble and bass lines. The result has nothing like the lusciousness of Leppard's arrangements of Cavalli, but with lavish continuo avoids the bleakness of some realizations. Yvonne Kenny as Dido and Laurence Dale as Aeneas are both excellent in strongly characterized performances, standing out from most of the others, though Judith Howarth sings powerfully as Aeneas's doomed wife, Creusa. Not a magnetic performance but a valuable one. Atmospheric sound disturbed by stage noises.

Giasone (complete).
*** HM Dig. HMC 1901282/4. Chance, Schopper, Dubosc, Deletré, Mellon, Banditelli, Visse, De Mey, Concerto Vocale, Jacobs.

With the brilliant and sensitive counter-tenor, Michael Chance, in the title-role, René Jacobs's recording of Cavalli's opera is a remarkable achievement. The admixture of comedy that can be embarrassing in operas of this period is here handled splendidly. The vividly characterful Dominique Visse in particular scores a huge success in the drag-role of the nurse, Delfa, very much in the tradition of Hugues Cuénod's performances for Raymond Leppard in Cavalli at Glyndebourne. It is a pity that none of the others characterize like Visse, beautifully as they sing. Clean, well-balanced sound.

Xerse (complete).
*** HM HMC 1901175/8. René Jacobs, Nelson, Gall, Poulenard, Mellon, Feldman, Elwes, De Mey, Visse, Instrumental Ens., Jacobs.

Ombra mai fù, sings King Xerxes in the opening scene, addressing a plane tree, more famously set later by Handel. As well as directing his talented team, Jacobs sings the title-role, only one of the four counter-tenors, nicely contrasted, who take the castrato roles. The fruity alto of Dominique Visse in a comic servant role is particularly striking, and among the women – some of them shrill at times – the outstanding singer, Agnès Mellon, takes the other servant role, singing delightfully in a tiny laughing song. Excelllent recording.

Certon, Pierre (died 1572)

Chansons: *Amour a tort; Ce n'est a vous; C'est grand pityé; De tout le mal; En espérant; Entre vous gentilz hommes; Heilas ne fringuerons nous; Je l'ay aymé; Je neveulx poinct; Martin s'en alla; Plus nu suys; Que n'est auprès de moy; Si ta beaulté; Ung jour que Madame dormait.* Mass: *Sur le pont d'Avignon.*
(B) *** HM Musique d'Abord HMA 190 1034 [id.]. Boston Camerata, Joel Cohen.

The Mass, *Sur le pont d'Avignon*, has genuine appeal, and the chansons also exercise a real charm over the listener. The Mass is performed *a cappella*, and the chansons enjoy instrumental support. In both sacred and secular works the Boston Camerata bring freshness, musical accomplishment and stylistic understanding to bear; the recording, made in a spacious acoustic, creates the most beautiful sounds.

Cesti, Antonio (1623–69)

Cantatas: *Amanti, io vi disfido; Pria ch'adori.*
(B) **(*) HM Musique d'Abord HMA 1901011 [id.]. Concerto Vocale – D'INDIA: *Duets, Laments & Madrigals.* **(*)

Cesti's 17-minute cantata, *Pria ch'adori*, is a serenata for two voices, after the Monteverdi style, including even a *Lamento d'Arianna* in duet form. *Amanti, io vi disfido* is a much shorter, bravura piece. The performances by Judith Nelson and René Jacobs are certainly pleasingly fresh, and the distinguished instrumental group includes William Christie providing the continuo.

Chabrier, Emmanuel (1841–94)

Bourrée fantasque; España (rhapsody); *Joyeuse marche; Menuet pompeux; Prélude pastorale; Suite pastorale; Le Roi malgré lui: Danse slave; Fête polonaise.*
*** EMI (SIS) Dig. CDC7 49652-2. Capitole Toulouse O, Plasson.

Bourrée fantasque; España (rhapsody); *Joyeuse marche; Suite pastorale; Gwendoline: Overture. Le Roi malgré lui: Danse slave; Fête polonaise.*
(M) *** Mercury 434 303-2 [id.]. Detroit SO, Paray – ROUSSEL: *Suite.* **(*)

Chabrier is Beecham territory and he calls for playing of elegance and charm. Michel Plasson and his excellent Toulouse forces bring just the right note of exuberance and *joie de vivre* to this delightful music. The recording is eminently satisfactory, though it is a shade resonant and, as a result, lacks the last ounce of transparency. Even so, the effect suits the music, and the elegant performance of the delightful *Suite pastorale* ensures a strong recommendation for this EMI CD.

The return of the finely played and idiomatically conducted Mercury collection of Chabrier's best orchestral pieces does not disappoint. Paray's whimsically relaxed and sparkling account of

España gives great pleasure and his rubato in the *Fête polonaise* is equally winning. The *Suite pastorale* is a wholly delightful account, given playing that is at once warm and polished, neat and perfectly in scale, with the orchestra beautifully balanced. The *Marche joyeuse* was recorded in Detroit's Old Orchestral Hall a year before the rest of the programme.

España; Fête polonaise; Gwendoline overture; Habanera; (i) *Larghetto for horn and orchestra. Marche joyeuse; Prélude pastorale; Suite pastorale.*
*(**) DG Dig. 447 751-2 [id.]. (i) Janezic; VPO, Gardiner.

Gardiner's DG collection is disappointing. The *fortissimos* bring coarseness into the music-making and readily become tiring to listen to. Easily the most attractive and refined playing comes in the charming *Suite pastorale*, with the rustling leaves in *Sous-bois* delicately caught. The performances certainly do not lack vigour but are hardly subtle in rhythmic feeling. Clearly the VPO are not at home in this repertoire and, for all the brilliance of Gardiner's approach, *España* becomes heavy-going, with its over-enthusiastic bass drum, while the orchestra is not very seductive either in nudging the rhythms of the *Habanera*.

España (rhapsody).
❁ (B) *** Dutton Lab. mono CDEA 5017 [(M) id.]. LPO, Sir Thomas Beecham (with Concert: *'Beecham favourites'* *** ❁).

Beecham's fizzing 1939 recording has never been surpassed and is unsurpassable. The superb Dutton transfer restores all the warmth and bloom of the original 78-r.p.m. disc, made in the Kingsway Hall, where the glowing ambience adds to the lustre of a sparkling recording often used for demonstration in its day. The rest of this concert is hardly less enticing for Beecham aficionados.

España (rhapsody).
(M) **(*) Decca (IMS) 448 576-2. SRO, Ansermet – DUKAS: *L'apprenti sorcier* ***; DEBUSSY: *La Mer* **(*); HONEGGER: *Pacific 231* ***; RAVEL: *Boléro; La Valse.* ***

España (rhapsody); *Joyeuse marche; Suite pastorale; Le Roi malgré lui: Danse slave; Fête polonaise.*
(M) *** Decca 452 890-2 [id.]. SRO, Ansermet – FRANCK: *La chasseur maudit* etc. **

Extremely brilliant recording, typical of Decca's vintage sessions in the Geneva Victoria Hall during the 1960s. *España* (also available differently coupled) perhaps lacks the uninhibited exuberance that Beecham brought to it but is by no means lacking in flair. The *Suite pastorale* has appealing delicacy, with the orchestra at their best, and plenty of atmosphere. The *Joyeuse marche*, the *Danse slave*, and the *Fête polonaise* all have a good measure of high spirits. Excellent remastering means that this shows off the Ansermet charisma to fullest effect. A reissue worthy of Decca's Classic Sound logo.

España (rhapsody); *Suite pastorale.*
*** Chandos Dig. CHAN 8852 [id.]. Ulster O, Yan Pascal Tortelier – DUKAS: *L'apprenti sorcier; La Péri.* **(*)

Yan Pascal Tortelier and the excellent Ulster Orchestra give an altogether first-rate account of Chabrier's delightful *Suite pastorale*, distinguished by an appealing charm and lightness of touch. There is a spirited account of *España*, too.

PIANO MUSIC

Aubade; Ballabile; Caprice; Feuillet d'album; Impromptu; Pièces pittoresques; Ronde champêtre; (i) *3 Valses romantiques.*
*** Unicorn-Kanchana DKPCD 9158 [id.]. Kathryn Stott, (i) with Elizabeth Burley.

For those wanting a representative single-CD selection, Kathryn Stott provides the ideal answer. She plays this long-neglected but rewarding repertoire with intelligence, wit and elegance. Perhaps the very last ounce of charm is missing, but there is enough of it to provide delight. She is moreover recorded with great presence and fidelity; the piano sound is very alive, natural and fresh.

Bourrée fantasque; 5 Pièces posthumes; 10 Pièces pittoresques; Suite de valses.
(BB) **(*) ASV Dig. CDQS 6166 [id.]. Alan Schiller.

ASV provide an alternative, inexpensive entry into the world of Chabrier's piano music. Alan Schiller, if not quite as sympathetic as Kathleen Stott on Unicorn-Kanchana, can play tenderly (as in the *Feuillet d'album* from the *Pièces posthumes*) as well as brilliantly, and he is only occasionally percussive. He lifts rhythms nicely in the *Bourrée fantasque* and characterizes strongly. On the whole tempi are well chosen and his rubato is convincing. Good, clear piano recording.

OPERA

Briseis (complete).
❁ *** Hyperion Dig. CDA 66803 [id.]. Rodgers, Padmore, Keenlyside, Harries, George, BBC Scottish SO, Jean-Yves Ossonce.

Starting with a ripely seductive sailors' chorus, few operas are as sensuous as *Briseis*, subtitled 'The Lovers of Corinth', which the composer failed to complete. This passionate performance was recorded live at the 1994 Edinburgh Festival, the first-ever hearing in Britain. On disc it matters little that this is a torso. The writing is not just sensuous but urgent, a warm bath of sound that is also exhilarating. Casting is near ideal, with Joan Rodgers in the title-role rich and distinctive, and with Mark Padmore as the sailor, Hylas, equally warm, producing heady, clear tenor tone. Symbolizing the forces of Christian good, Simon Keenlyside as the Catechist and Kathryn Harries as the mother of Briseis, cured through faith, both sing with character and apt resonance. Full, atmospheric sound.

Gwendoline (complete).
*(**) HM Dig. ED 13059 (2) [id.]. Kohutková, Henry, Garino, Brno Philharmonic Ch., Slovak PO, Penin.

Like the unfinished *Briseis*, recorded by Hyperion, *Gwendoline* is a high romantic opera written in the shadow of Wagner – there are echoes of both *Tristan* and the *Ring*. Set in England in the dark ages,and with few direct echoes of Wagner, the score is yet vigorously red-blooded to match the story's blood and thunder, with many sensuous sequences, not just the love-duets but such evocative choral passages as the *Epithalamium*. The final love-death brings more echoes of the final trio of Gounod's *Faust* than it does of Wagner, with the idiom identifiably French throughout. This live recording, made in Bratislava in January 1996, offers a performance flawed vocally but with Jean-Paul Penin drawing playing that is both sensitive and passionate from the Slovak Philharmonic. In the title-role Adriana Kohutková sings sympathetically but with bright tone that leads to shrillness on top. Didier Henry's grainy baritone grows rough under pressure, hardly heroic-sounding, and Gérard Garino's fine, clear tenor sounds far too youthful for the aged Armel. Nevertheless, a very enjoyable first recording, with first-rate sound.

L'Etoile (complete).
✿ *** EMI Dig. CDS7 47889-8 (2). Alliot-Lugaz, Gautier, Bacquier, Raphanel, Damonte, Le Roux, David, Lyon Opéra Ch. and O, Gardiner.

This fizzing operetta is a winner: the subtlety and refinement of Chabrier's score go well beyond the usual realm of operetta, and Gardiner directs a performance that from first to last makes the piece sparkle bewitchingly. Colette Alliot-Lugaz and Gabriel Bacquier are first rate and numbers such as the drunken duet between King and Astrologer are hilarious. Outstandingly good recording, with excellent access.

Le roi malgré lui (complete).
(M) **(*) Erato/Warner 2292 45792-2 (2). Hendricks, Garcisanz, Quilico, Jeffes, Lafont, French R. Ch. & New PO, Dutoit.

This long-neglected opera is another Chabrier masterpiece, a modified Cinderella story, ending happily, which prompts a series of superb numbers, some *España*-like in brilliance (the well-known Waltz of Act II transformed in its choral form) and some hauntingly romantic, with even one sextet suggesting a translation of Wagner's Rhinemaiden music into waltz-time. The pity is that the linking recitatives have been completely omitted from this recording, and in addition the score has been seriously cut. But Charles Dutoit is a most persuasive advocate. Star among the singers is Barbara Hendricks as the slave-girl Cinderella figure, Minka. The recording is naturally balanced and has plenty of atmosphere.

Chadwick, George (1854–1931)

Overtures: Melpomene; Rip van Winkle. Tam O'Shanter (symphonic ballad).
(N) *** Chandos Dig. CHAN 9439 [id.]. Detroit SO, Neeme Järvi – Randall THOMPSON: *Symphony No. 2*. **

The *Rip van Winkle* overture, new to the catalogue, is an early work written in 1879 when Chadwick, still studying with Rheinberger, was living in Munich. An accomplished piece, it is well laid out for the orchestra, as for that matter are the other two pieces. *Melpomene* comes from 1887, the year after the delightful *Second Symphony*; it derives its title from the muse of tragedy and has been compared by some commentators to the symphonic poems of Franck or Dukas. *Tam O'Shanter* (1915) is brilliantly scored and enormously vital and rumbustious. Good playing from the Detroit Orchestra under Neeme Järvi and natural, lifelike recording.

Serenade for strings.
*** Albany Dig. TROY 033-2 [id.]. V. American Music Ens., Hobart Earle – GILBERT: *Suite*. ***

Chadwick's *Serenade*, written in 1890, is here given its European première. This very well-crafted piece by the so-called 'Boston classicist' gives much pleasure. It is quite beautifully played by this excellent Viennese group, drawn from younger members of the Vienna Symphony Orchestra. The sound too is first rate, a successful example of a 'live recording' bringing no loss in realism and a gain in spontaneity.

Symphonies Nos. 2 in B flat; 3 in F.
(N) *** Chandos Dig. CHAN 9685 [id.]. Detroit SO, Neeme Järvi.

This Chandos recoupling can be strongly recommended. Chadwick's *Second Symphony* dates from the early 1880s, though its delightful *Scherzo* was premièred two years ahead of the rest of the work. When this was first heard it had to be encored, which is hardly surprising. It has an engaging, cheeky quality (one contemporary review in the Boston Transcript wrote that 'it positively winks at you') and Järvi makes the very most of it. The *Third Symphony* is hardly less fresh and appealing, written in the received idiom of the day. In 1894 it won first prize in a competition whose jury was chaired by Dvořák, and it breathes much the same air as Brahms, Dvořák and Svendsen; although its musical language is not strongly individual, it is very compelling in so persuasive a performance as given here by Järvi and his Detroit Orchestra. The *Largo* is beautifully shaped and the Scherzo delightfully light and piquant. Absolutely first-class recording too.

Chambonnières, Jacques Champion de (*c*. 1602–72)

Pièces de clavecin, Livres I & II: Suites in A, C, D & G.
*** HM/BMG Dig. 05472 77210-2. Skip Sempé (harpsichord).

Chambonnières is spoken of as the father of the French harpsichord school, but Sempé speaks of his music as 'a keyboard synthesis of the *Air de cour* and Italian recitative, the declamation and rhetoric of Italian monody'. While retaining a feeling of dance, Sempé is able to convey an improvisatory touch that brings every piece alive. He plays a Flemish instrument of about 1680, and in four of them he is joined by Brian Feehan as theorbo continuo. Very good recording.

Chaminade, Cécile (1857–1944)

Piano trios Nos. 1 in G min., Op. 11; 2 in A min., Op. 34; Pastorale enfantine, Op. 12; Ritournelle; Serenade, Op. 29 (all 3 arr. Marcus); *Serenade espagnole* (arr. Kreisler).
*** ASV Dig. CDDCA 965 [id.]. Tzigane Piano Trio.

In these two *Piano trios* Chaminade confidently controls larger forms, building on a fund of melody. The two central movements of the *Piano trio No. 1* are charming, a passionately lyrical *Andante* and a sparkling, Mendelssohnian Scherzo. The *Piano trio No. 2*, in three movements, without a Scherzo, is weightier, almost Brahmsian, with themes rather more positive. Three of the four miniatures which come as fill-ups have been arranged for trio by the Tzigane's pianist, Elizabeth Marcus.

PIANO MUSIC

Air à danser, Op. 164; Air de ballet, Op. 30; Automne; Autrefois; Contes bleus No. 2, Op. 122; Danse créole, Op. 94; Guitare, Op. 32; La Lisonjera, Op. 50; Lolita, Op. 54; Minuetto, Op. 23; Pas des écharpes, Op. 37; Pas des sylphes: Intermezzo; Pierette, Op. 41; 3 Romances sans paroles, Op. 76/1, 3 & 6; Sérénade, Op. 29; Sous la masque, Op. 116; Toccata, Op. 39; Valse arabesque.
*** Chandos Dig. CHAN 8888 [id.]. Eric Parkin.

Album des enfants, Op. 123/4, 5, 9 & 10; Op. 126/1, 2, 9 & 10; Arabesque, Op. 61; Cortège, Op. 143; Inquiétude, Op. 87/3; Le Passé; Prelude in D min., Op. 84/3; Rigaudon, Op. 55/6; Sérénade espagnole; Sonata in C min., Op. 21; Les Sylvains, Op. 60; Valse-ballet, Op. 112; Valse brillante No. 3, Op. 80; Valse No. 4, Op. 91.
*** Hyperion Dig. CDA 66846 [id.]. Peter Jacobs.

Arlequine, Op. 53; Au pays dévasté, Op. 155; Chanson Brétonne; Divertissement, Op. 105; Etudes de concert, Op. 35: Impromptu; Tarantella. Etude symphonique, Op. 28; Feuillets d'album, Op. 98: Elégie. Gigue in D, Op. 43; Libellules, Op. 24; Pastorale, Op. 114; Pièces humoristiques Op. 87: Sous bois; Consolation. Nocturne, Op. 165; Passacaille in E, Op. 130; Poème romantique, Op. 7; Tristesse, Op. 104; Valse tendre, Op. 119; Scherzo-valse, Op. 148.
*** Hyperion Dig. CDA 66706 [id.]. Peter Jacobs.

Autrefois; Callirhoë; Elévation in E; Etude mélodique in G flat; Etude pathétique in B min.; Etude scholastique; La Lisonjera; L'Ondine; Pêcheurs de nuit; Romance; Scherzo in C; Sérénade in D; Solitude; Souvenance; Thème varié in A; Valse romantique; Waltz No. 2.
*** Hyperion Dig. CDA 66584 [id.]. Peter Jacobs.

Artistically these pieces are rather stronger than one had suspected and, although they are by no means the equal of Grieg or early Fauré, they can hold their own with Saint-Saëns and are more inventive than the *Brises d'orient* of Félicien David. There is a quality of gentility that has lent a certain pallor to Chaminade's charms, but both pianists here make out a stronger case for her than most people would imagine possible. Both are well recorded and in this respect there is little to choose between the two. Nor is there much to choose as far as the performances are concerned; both are persuasive, though Parkin has a slight edge over his colleague in terms of elegance and finesse. If you want a single disc collection you might choose the Chandos disc. If you seek a complete survey stay with Jacobs.

Charpentier, Gustave (1860–1956)

Louise (gramophone version conceived and realized by the composer).
(M) (***) Nimbus mono NI 7829 [id.]. Vallin, Thill, Pernet, Lecouvreur, Gaudel, Ch. Raugel & O, Eugène Bigot.

These substantial excerpts from *Louise* were

recorded in 1935 under the 75-year-old composer's supervision; they feature two ideally cast French singers as the two principals, Ninon Vallin enchanting in the title-role and the tenor, Georges Thill, heady-toned as the hero, Julien. France has produced few singers to rival them since. The original eight 78-r.p.m. records are fitted neatly on to a single CD, and – in the selection of items, made by the composer himself – just the delights and none of the *longueurs* of this nostalgically atmospheric opera are included. The voices are caught superbly in the Nimbus transfers, but with an early electrical recording like this the orchestral sound becomes muddled. Yet even Nimbus has rarely presented voices as vividly as here.

Louise (opera): complete.
(M) *** Sony S3K 46429 (3) [id.]. Cotrubas, Berbié, Domingo, Sénéchal, Bacquier, Amb. Op. Ch., New Philh. O, Prêtre.

This fine, atmospheric Sony recording, the first in stereo, explains why *Louise* has long been a favourite opera in Paris. The love-duets are enchanting and Ileana Cotrubas makes a delightful heroine, not always flawless technically but charmingly girlish. Plácido Domingo is a relatively heavyweight Julien, and Jane Berbié and Gabriel Bacquier are excellent as the parents. Under Georges Prêtre, far warmer than usual on record, the ensemble is rich and clear, with refined recording every bit as atmospheric as one could want. A set which splendidly fills an obvious gap in the catalogue.

Charpentier, Marc-Antoine
(1643–1704)

Concert à 4 (for viols), H.545; Musique de théâtre pour Circé et Andromède; Sonata à 8 (for 2 flutes & strings), H.548.
**(*) HM Dig. HMC 1901244 [id.]. London Baroque, Medlam.

These pieces are most expertly played here by the members of London Baroque (though the string sound still does not entirely escape the faint suspicion that it has been marinaded in vinegar) and will reward investigation. The sound is excellent.

Le malade imaginaire (incidental music).
*** HM Dig. HMC 90-1336 [id.]. Zanetti, Rime, Brua, Visse, Crook, Gardeil, Les Arts Florissants, Christie.

This sequence of extended prologue and three *intermèdes* tingles with energy, and is superbly realized on this first recording of the complete incidental music, much of which was lost for three centuries. With well-balanced, warmly refined sound, Christie – though he uses percussion dramatically – is light in his textures and rhythms, often opting for fast speeds. The format is cumbersome, with a single disc contained in a double jewel-case, but the libretto is very readable.

Motets: *Alma redemptoris; Amicus meus; Ave regina; Dialogus inter Magdalenam et Jesum; Egredimini filiae Sion; Elevations; O pretiosum; O vere, o bone; Magdalena lugens; Motet du saint sacrement; O vos omnes; Pour la Passion de notre Seigneur* (2 settings); *Salve regina; Solva vivebat in antris Magdalena lugens.*
*** HM HMC 1901149 [id.]. Concerto Vocale.

Half of the motets on this record are for solo voice and the others are duets. Among the best and most moving things here are *O vos omnes* and *Amicus meus*, which are beautifully done. Another motet to note is *Magdalena lugens*, in which Mary Magdalene laments Christ's death at the foot of the Cross. Expressive singing from Judith Nelson and René Jacobs, and excellent continuo support. Worth a strong recommendation.

Ave Maris stella, H.63; Domine salvum sine organo in C, H. 290; Messe pour le Port-Royal, H.5; Motet: *Flores o Gallia, H.342; Magnificat pour le Port-Royale, H.81; O salutaris hostia, H.261; Psaume Laudate Dominum, H. 182; Veni creator pour un dessus sel au catechisme, H. 69.*
(N) *** Auvidis/Astrée Dig. E 8598 [id.]. Les Demoiselles de Saint-Cyr, Emmanuel Mandrin.

In the mid 1680s, Charpentier composed several works 'for Port Royale'. There were two convents: one in the Chevreuse valley, south of Versailles, which was situated on a low-lying, marshy site; and the second, to which many of the nuns repaired, in the Faubourg, Saint-Jacques in Paris, for which most of this repertoire was written. The music is scored for female voices only and is generally austere in style. The main work, after which the record is titled, is the *Messe pour le Port-Royale* for three soloists, chorus and organ. This is supplemented by various other pieces, psalm settings and the fine *Magnifcat* also written for the convent. This is reposeful music, predominantly meditative in character, and very persuasively performed by Les Demoiselles de Saint-Cyr under Emmanuel Mandrin with Michel Chapuis providing the solo organ interludes. A rewarding issue.

Caecilia, virgo et martyr; Filius prodigus (oratorios); *Magnificat.*
*** HM Dig. HMC 90066 [id.]. Grenat, Benet, Laplenie, Reinhard, Studer, Les Arts Florissants, Christie.

The music's stature and nobility are fully conveyed here. The *Magnificat* is a short piece for three voices and has an almost Purcellian flavour. One thing that will immediately strike the listener is the delicacy and finesse of the scoring. All this music is beautifully recorded; the present issues can be recommended with enthusiasm.

(i) *Caecilia, virgo et martyr, H.397; De profundis, H.189;* (ii) *Elévation; In obitum augustissimae nec son piissimae gallorum Reginae lamentum; Luctus de morte augustissimae Mariae Theresiae Galliae.*
(N) (B) *** Erato/Warner Dig. Ultima 3984 24232-2 (2) [id.]. (i) Degelin, Reyghere, Mols, James, Meens, Van Croonenborgh, Ghent Madrigal Ch. & Cantabile; (ii) Degelin, Verdoodt, Smolders, Crook, Vandersteene, Widmer, Namur Chamber Ch.; (i; ii) Musica Polyphonica, Devos.

Charpentier composed seven settings of the *De profundis* (Psalm 179 in the Roman Psalter), only one of which is part of the *Requiem Mass*; the others are in all probability separate pieces. The one recorded here is the most elaborate; it is lavishly scored (soloists, double-chorus, two orchestras with flutes and continuo) and was composed in 1683 for the funeral of Louis XIV's first Queen, Marie Thérèse. It is an impressive and moving piece, and this somewhat restrained performance catches its gravitas, even if some of the grandeur and power eludes Devos, although he uses considerable forces. *Caecilia virgo et martyr* fares much better, although collectors will find some textual differences from William Christie's earlier recording (see below). All three works on the second disc further lament the death of the Queen. Clearly the event moved Charpentier deeply, and each reflects the paradox of the Christian faith in contrasting grief with joy and hope in the life hereafter. Here Devos's performances could hardly be bettered, bringing out all the music's drama, joy, and depth of feeling. The recordings, both made in spacious acoustics, are also first class and this Erato Ultima Double is highly recommended, for all the reservations expressed about the account of the *De profundis*. Such a collection can only further enhance the growing recognition of Charpentier's stature.

In navitatem Domini nostri Jésus Christi (canticum), H.414; Pastorale sur la naissance de notre Seigneur Jésus Christ, H.483.
*** HM HMC 901082. Les Arts Florissants Vocal & Instrumental Ens., Christie.

This *Canticum* has much of the character of an oratorio. The invention has great appeal and variety. The *Pastorale* is a most rewarding piece, and the grace and charm of the writing continue to win one over to this eminently resourceful composer. This collection by William Christie is self-recommending, so high are the standards of performance and recording, and so fertile is Charpentier's imagination.

In navitatem Domini nostri Jésus Christi, H.416; Pastorale sur la naissance de notre Seigneur Jésus Christ, H.482.
*** HM HMC 905130 [id.]. Les Arts Florissants Vocal & Instrumental Ens., Christie.

The cantata is one of Charpentier's grandest, a finely balanced edifice in two complementary halves, separated by an instrumental section, an eloquent evocation of the night. The little pastorale was written in the tradition of the ballet de cour or divertissement. This is enchanting music, elegantly played and excellently recorded.

Leçons de ténèbres.
*** HM HMC 901005 [id.]. Jacobs, Nelson, Verkinderen, Kuijken, Christie, Junghänel.

These *Leçons de ténèbres* are eloquent and moving pieces, worthy of comparison with Purcell. René Jacobs's performance, like that of his colleagues, is so authentic in every respect that it is difficult to imagine it being surpassed. The recording is as distinguished as the performances.

Leçons de ténèbres for Wednesday in Holy Week.
*** Virgin/EMI (SIS) VC5 45107-2. Catherine Greuillet, Caroline Pelon, Gérard Lesne, Christopher Purves, Il Seminario Musicale.

Leçons de ténèbres for Maundy Thursday.
*** Virgin/EMI VC5 45075-2. Sandrine Piau, Gérard Lesne, Ian Honeyman, Peter Harvey, Il Seminario Musicale.

Leçons de ténèbres for Good Friday.
*** Virgin/EMI (SIS) Dig. VC7 59295-2. Gérard Lesne, Agnès Mellon, Ian Honeyman, Jacques Bona, Il Seminario Musicale.

Leçons de ténèbres for Wednesday in Holy Week, Maundy Thursday and Good Friday.
(M) *** Virgin Veritas EMI Dig. VMT5 61483-2 (3). Gérard Lesne & soloists, Il Seminario Musicale, Lesne.

This series of Charpentier's *Leçons de ténèbres* from Il Seminario Musicale offers music of great variety and beauty, featuring soloists who are naturally attuned to this repertoire. The accompaniment is provided by a varied instrumental group, and their use is consistently imaginative and refreshing to the ear. The Psalms are sung by a small choral group. The effect is warm yet refined and the lyrical melancholy of much of this music is quite haunting, and the acoustic of L'Abbaye Royale de Fontevraud is ideal for the music. The documentation is first class. Charpentier's settings were enormously admired in his own time, and rightly so. Charpentier's music has a quiet and affecting directness as well as spirituality. Although these three CDs are individually in the premium price-range (and well worth every penny), they are now issued as a medium-price set in a slipcase, and any collector attracted to this remarkable and inspired composer should consider them.

Litanies de la Vierge; Missa Assumpta est Maria; Te Deum.
(N) *** HM Dig. HMC 901298 [id.]. Soloists, Les Arts Florissants, William Christie.

Marc-Antoine Charpentier's best-known choral work, the *Te Deum*, is introduced not only by the famous fanfare 'Prélude' but before that by Philidor's *Marche des timbales*. The performance of the *Te Deum* is almost certainly the finest in the catalogue, and the CD includes also the much less familiar but no less beautiful *Missa Assumpta est Maria* and the more restrained *Litanies de la Vierge*. Framed by a *Kyrie* and closing *Agnus Dei*, the seven movements each radiantly describe one of the Virgin's mystical attributes, followed by an intercessionary prayer. This is a deeply devotional work for eight singers, two viols and continuo, and the composer himself participated in its first performance. An outstanding disc in every way, beautifully recorded.

Magnificat, H.74 Te Deum, H.146.
(N) **(*) EMI (SIS) Dig. CDC7 54284-2. Upshaw, Murray, Robinson, Aler, Moll, Ch. & ASMF, Marriner.

These spirited accounts come from the early 1990s and are what one might call mainstream performances, very expert and accomplished in every way, and very well recorded into the bargain. A useful coupling, although Christie's account of the *Te Deum* is even finer.

Méditations pour le Carême; Le reniement de St Pierre.
(B) *** HM Musique d'Abord Dig. HMC 1905151 [id.]. Les Arts Florissants, William Christie.

The *Méditations pour le Carême* are a sequence of three-voice motets for Lent with continuo accompaniment (organ, theorbo and bass viol) that may not have quite the same imaginative or expressive resource as the coupling, but which are full of nobility and interest. *Le reniement de Saint Pierre* is one of Charpentier's most inspired and expressive works and its text draws on the account in all four Gospels of St Peter's denial of Christ. The performances maintain the high standards of this ensemble, and the same compliment can be paid to the recording.

(i) *Messe de minuit pour Noël (Midnight Mass for Christmas Eve);* (ii) *Te Deum.*
(M) **(*) EMI CDM7 63135-2. (i) Cantelo, Gelmar, Partridge, Bowman, Keyte, King's College Ch., ECO, Willcocks; (ii) Lott, Harrhy, Brett, Partridge, Roberts, King's College Ch., ASMF, Ledger.

There is a kinship between Charpentier's lovely *Christmas Mass* and Czech settings of the Mass that incorporate folk material, even the *Kyrie* having a jolly quality about it. The King's performance is warm and musical, but there isn't much Gallic flavour. The recording comes from the late 1960s and certainly now has more bite than it did; but reservations remain about the basic style of the singing. The coupling is the best known of the *Te Deum* settings, and this time the King's performance has a vitality and boldness to match the music and catches also its *douceur* and freshness.

Miserere, H.219; Motets: *pour la seconde fois que le Saint Sacrament vien au même reposoir, H.372; pour le Saint Sacrement au reposoir, H.346. Motet pour une longue offrande, H.434.*
*** HM Dig. HMC 901185 [id.]. Mellon, Poulenard, Ledroit, Kendall, Kooy, Chapelle Royale, Herreweghe.

Charpentier's *Motet pour une longue offrande* is one of his most splendid and eloquent works. The *Miserere* was written for the Jesuit Church on Rue Saint-Antoine, whose ceremonies were particularly sumptuous. All four works on the disc are powerfully expressive and beautifully performed. The recording, made in collaboration with Radio France, is most expertly balanced.

Missa Assumpta est Maria; Litanies de la Vierge; Te Deum.
✿ (B) *** HM Dig. HMX 290850.52 (3) [(M) id. import]. Soloists, Les Arts Florissants, William Christie – BOUZIGNAC: *Te Deum* etc. *** ✿; DELALANDE: *Confitebor tibi Domine* etc. ***

This CD remains available at full price, but now comes in a very highly recommendable bargain-priced triptych, linked to the *Te Deums* of Bouzignac and Delalande.

Les quatre saisons (Quatuor anni tempestates). Psalms of David Nos. 41: Quemadmodum desiderat cervus; 75: Notus in Judaea Deus; 126: Nisi Dominus.
(N) (B) **(*) Opus 111 Invitation Dig. OPS 10-004 [id.]. Noémi Rimi, Bernard Delétré, Parlement de Musique, Martin Gester.

Charpentier's *Four Seasons* is a group of four motets for two voices, drawing its inspiration from the 'Song of Songs', but it is a comparably routine inspiration. In the celebration of *Spring*, the two soprano voices here (the second unnamed) are not ideally matched and their vibratos clash. But in *Summer* and *Autumn*, their dialogue interchanges are much more pleasing and in *Winter*, the bravura scales (suggesting the gales, perhaps) come off quite effectively. With the Psalm settings, the vocal writing is of an altogether different order and the three singers respond to Charpentier's stimulating variety of colour and mood. *Nisi Dominus* brings some lovely solo work from Noémi Rimi and the vocal blending is often impressive. After a charming 'piping' instrumental introduction, the bass opens Psalm 75 rather gruffly, but the agreeable vigour of this opening makes way for a very touching centrepiece, before the buoyant close. The style of Le Parlement de Music is robust rather than refined, and while the recording is vivid, the focus is not always quite clean. But this inexpensive disc is still worth trying. Full texts and translations are provided.

Le Reniement de Saint Pierre – histoire sacrée.
(M) **(*) Erato/Warner 4509 97409-2. Robin, Chamonin, Maurant, Richez, Lesueur, Veyron-Lacroix, Ch. Philippe Caillard – COUPERIN: *Audite omnes et expanescite* etc. **

Charpentier's *Le Reniement de Saint Pierre* is a deeply expressive work and the performance, which presumably comes from the early 1960s, is also deeply felt. Both the singing and playing give pleasure, and the poignant dissonances of the final chorus make a strong impression. In some ways Christie's Harmonia Mundi performance (see above) is even finer, but it is not more moving. There are minor reservations about the Erato coupling, but on the whole this is a valuable reissue.

OPERA

Actéon (complete).
(B) *** HM Musique d'Abord HMA 1901095 [id.]. Visse, Mellon, Laurens, Feldman, Paut, Les Arts Florissants Vocal & Instrumental Ens., Christie.

Actéon is particularly well portrayed by Dominique Visse; his transformation in the fourth tableau and his feelings of horror are almost as effective as anything in nineteenth-century opera! The other singers are first rate, in particular the Diane of Agnès Mellon. Alert playing and an altogether natural recording, as well as excellent presentation, make this a most desirable issue and a real bargain.

Les Arts Florissants (opéra et idylle en musique).
(B) *** HM Musique d'Abord HMA 1901083 [id.]. Les Arts Florissants Vocal & Instrumental Ens., William Christie.

Les Arts Florissants is a short entertainment in five scenes; the libretto tells of a conflict between the Arts, who flourish under the rule of Peace, and the forces of War, personified by Discord and the Furies. This and the little Interlude that completes the music include some invigorating and fresh invention, performed very pleasingly indeed by this eponymous group under the expert direction of William Christie. Period instruments are used, but intonation is always good and the sounds often charm the ear. The recording is excellent. A bargain.

David et Jonathas (complete).
(B) **(*) HM Musique d'Abord Dig. HMA 190 1289/90 [id.]. Lesne, Zanetti, Gardeil, Visse, Les Arts Florissants, Christie.

David et Jonathas confirms the impression, made by many other Charpentier records during the last few years, that in him France has one of her most inspired Baroque masters. Christie's version on Harmonia Mundi may not always be especially dramatic, but it has a notably sure sense of authentic Baroque style and scale, as well as fine choral singing. However, only one of Christie's soloists is really outstanding: the characterfully distinctive counter-tenor, Dominique Visse, who gives a vivid, highly theatrical performance. Those who relish authenticity above all else will clearly take to this version, very well recorded.

La descente d'Orphée aux Enfers (chamber opera; complete).
*** Erato/Warner Dig. 0630 11913-2. Agnew, Daneman, Zanetti, Petibon, Károlyi, Gardeil, Les Arts Florissants, William Christie.

Charpentier's compact setting of this famous story starts with lightweight, sparkling movements in dance rhythms, but then dramatically changes tone with the death of Euridice, a moment superbly interpreted by Sophie Daneman. The following lament of Orphée is just the first of his moving and expressive solos, each of them brief but intense and beautifully sung by Paul Agnew. They culminate in a sequence when he seeks to charm Pluton in the Underworld, finally succeeding. The piece ends with the lamenting of Pluton's subjects at losing Orphée and his musical magic. With Christie drawing superb playing and singing from his well-chosen team, it is good to have such a delightful rarity revived, probably given once at the time and no more.

Médée (complete).
❁ *** Erato/Warner Dig. 4509 96558-2 (3) [id.]. Hunt, Padmore, Delétré, Zanetti, Salzmann, Les Arts Florissants, William Christie.

In his second recording of this rare opera, again with his group, Les Arts Florissants, Christie was glad to be able to open out the small cuts that were made before so as to fit the LP format. The success of his new interpretation is readily borne out in the finished performance, which easily surpasses the previous one in its extra brightness and vigour, with consistently crisper and more alert ensembles, often at brisker speeds, with the drama more clearly established. The casting is first rate, with Lorraine Hunt outstanding in the tragic title-role. Her soprano has satisfying weight and richness, as well as the purity and precision needed in such classical opera; and Mark Padmore's clear, high tenor copes superbly with the role of Jason, with no strain and with cleanly enunciated diction and sharp concern for word-meaning. The others follow Christie's pattern of choosing cleanly focused voices, even if the tone is occasionally gritty.

Chausson, Ernest (1855–99)

Poème for violin and orchestra.
*** EMI (SIS) Dig. CDC7 47725-2 [id.]. Perlman, O de Paris, Martinon – RAVEL: *Tzigane;* SAINT-SAENS: *Havanaise* etc. ***
(M) *** Decca 460 006-2. Kyung Wha Chung, RPO, Charles Dutoit – DEBUSSY; FRANCK: *Violin sonatas.* *** ❁
(M) **(*) RCA Heifetz Collection 09026 61753-2 [id.]. Heifetz, RCA Victor SO, Izler Solomon – LALO: *Symphonie espagnole* (**(*)); SAINT-SAENS: *Havanaise* etc.; SARASATE: *Zigeunerweisen.* (***)

Perlman's 1975 recording, with the Orchestre de Paris under Jean Martinon, of Chausson's beautiful *Poème* is a classic account by which newcomers are measured. What a glorious and inspired piece it is when played with such feeling! The digital transfer exchanges some of the opulence of the original for a gain in presence, but Perlman's glorious tone is undiminished, even if now the ear perceives a slightly sharper outline to the timbre.

Chung's performance of Chausson's beautiful *Poème* is deeply emotional, if not as opulent as Perlman's; but, with committed accompaniment from the RPO and excellent (1977) recording, this makes an apt bonus for superb performances of the Debussy and Franck *Violin sonatas.*

Heifetz is recorded very closely, as if in the glare of a spotlight, and the performance is robbed of much of its subtlety. Even so, the playing itself is quite remarkable.

(i) *Poème for violin & orchestra;* (ii) *Poème de l'amour et de la mer.*
*** Chandos Dig. CHAN 8952. (i) Yan Pascal Tortelier; (ii) Linda Finnie; Ulster O, Tortelier – FAURE: *Pavane* etc. ***

No quarrels with Yan Pascal Tortelier's playing in the *Poème*, which he directs from the bow. There is consistent beauty of timbre and, what is more important, refinement of feeling. In the *Poème de l'amour et de la mer* Linda Finnie can hold her own with the very best; her feeling for the idiom is completely natural and her voice is beautifully coloured; among newer recordings this has very strong claims. Indeed in rapport between singer and orchestra none is better.

Symphony in B flat, Op. 20.
(M) **(*) Mercury 434 389-2 [id.]. Detroit SO, Paul Paray – BARRAUD: *Offrande à une ombre;* LALO: *Le rois d'Ys; Namouna.* **(*)
(N) (BB) **(*) Virgin Classics Dig. Double VBD5 61513-2 [CDVB 61513] (2). French R. PO, Janowski – BERLIOZ: *Symphonie fantastique; Le Carnaval romain;* BIZET: *Symphony.* **(*)

Paul Paray's 1956 performance of the Chausson *Symphony* is first class and the recording is much better than we remembered from its mono version. Indeed its only serious rival in terms of style is the Munch. It is splendidly held together and commanding in its eloquence and authority. It can be recommended alongside the Munch and in preference to most modern accounts.

In many ways Janowski's highly idiomatic reading of the Chausson *Symphony* is the finest of the three performances on this inexpensive Virgin Double. It is very well played, and the performance has a strong impetus, particularly in the passionate finale, with the Franckian undertones well brought out throughout the work. The recording is obviously more modern than Paray's and is very good, if not absolutely top drawer. If you want the couplings this is well worth considering.

Symphony in B flat; Soir de fête, Op. 32; The Tempest, Op. 18: 2 Scenes.
**(*) Chandos Dig. CHAN 8369 [id.]. Radio-Télévision Belge SO, Serebrier.

Serebrier's account is more logically coupled with other Chausson pieces, *Soir de fête* plus two scenes from the incidental music for *The Tempest.* Serebrier's account of the *Symphony* has real conviction and receives good recording, but on balance Paray is first choice.

Symphony in B flat, Op. 20; Soir de fête, Op. 32; La tempête, Op. 18; Viviane, Op. 5.
(N) *** Chandos Dig. CHAN 9650 [id.]. BBC PO, Yan Pascal Tortelier.

Yan Pascal Tortelier and the BBC Philharmonic give thoroughly idiomatic and well-played accounts of all these Chausson pieces. They more than hold their own against any of the competitors and, given the excellence of the sound, may well be a first choice for collectors wanting an up-to-date recording of the *Symphony.*

CHAMBER MUSIC

Andante & allegro (for clarinet and piano); *Piano trio in G min., Op. 3; Pièce for cello and piano, Op. 39; Poème Op. 25* (arr. for violin, string quartet & piano).
(N) *** Hyperion Dig. CDA 67028 [id.]. Charles Neidlich, Pascal Devoyon, Gary Hoffman, Philippe Graffin; Chiligirian Qt.

Interest here focuses on the *Poème*, which appears in a newly discovered arrangement by the composer for violin, string quartet and piano, which came to light in 1996. There is an excellent note by Philippe Graffin which tells how the work was inspired by Turgenev's *Le chant de l'amour triomphant*, with its tale of a magic violin. Although Chausson never met Turgenev himself, he often met his neighbours, Louis and Pauline Garcia-Vardot. There is a complete naturalness and conviction about this performance in which Graffin is a wonderfully persuasive soloist. The remaining pieces including the early *Piano trio* come off well and can hold their own against any rival. The rich acoustic environment enhances the appeal of these dedicated performances.

Concert in D for violin, piano and string quartet, Op. 21.
*** Essex CDS 6044. Accardo, Canino, Levin, Batjer, Hoffman, Wiley – SAINT-SAENS: *Violin sonata No. 1.* ***

Salvatore Accardo and Bruno Canino and their four colleagues convey a sense of effortless music-making and of pleasure in making music in domestic surroundings. Accardo is particularly songful in the third movement, light and delicate elsewhere. It is a thoroughly enjoyable account, recorded in a warm acoustic.

Piano quartet in A, Op. 30; Piano trio in G min., Op. 3.
(B) **(*) HM Musique d'Abord HMA 1901115 [id.]. Les Musiciens.

The Op. 30 *Piano quartet* of 1896 is one of Chausson's finest works. Les Musiciens comprise the Pasquier Trio and Jean-Claude Pennetier, but they are recorded rather closely, and their performance is lacking some of the subtlety and colour one knows this ensemble can command. The effect both here and in the early *G minor Trio*, Op. 3, is somewhat monochrome. However, the playing is both warm and spontaneous, and the ambience of the acoustic is pleasing.

Piano trio in G min., Op. 3.
*** Ph. (IMS) Dig. 411 141-2. Beaux Arts Trio – RAVEL: *Trio in A min.* ***

The early *G minor Trio* will come as a pleasant surprise to most collectors, for its beauties far outweigh any weaknesses. The playing of the Beaux Arts Trio is superbly eloquent and the recording is very impressive on CD.

String quartet in C min., Op. 35 (completed Vincent d'Indy).
(BB) *** Naxos Dig. 8.553645 [id.]. Quatuor Ludwig – FRANCK: *Piano quintet.* ***

The success of the first movement, *Grave*, of the *String quartet in C minor* when it was first performed at Ysaÿe's house in Brussels in 1898, encouraged Chausson to go on, and he was revising the third movement when he died. Vincent d'Indy put the finishing touches to the score after Chausson's death. It is a rarity in the concert hall and on CD. The music is powerfully argued and the Quatuor Ludwig play it with conviction and aplomb. The recording is excellent.

VOCAL MUSIC

(i) *La Légende de Sainte Cécile, Op. 22;* (ii) *La Tempête, Op. 18.*
*** EMI Dig. CDC5 55323-2 (2). (i) Isabelle Verner, Choeur de Femmes de Radio France; (ii) Laurence Dale, Raphaëlle Farman, Marie-Ange Todorovitch, François le Roux, Jean-Philippe Lafont, Ens. O de Paris, Jean-Jacques Kantorow.

La Tempête comprises a dozen or so settings and is scored for unusual forces: three strings, flute, harp and celeste. In *La Légende de Sainte Cécile*, the shades of Wagner and Franck are never far away but, as always with this composer, the invention is fluent, the music often imaginative and always rewarding. The performances are expert and persuasive and the recording very natural. This is something of a find.

Chávez, Carlos (1899–1978)

Sinfonia de Antigona (Symphony No. 1); Sinfonia India (Symphony No. 2); Sinfonia Romantica (Symphony No. 4).
**(*) Everest EVC 9041 [id.]. New York Stadium SO, composer.

These Everest performances carry the authority of the composer's direction and include the best known, *Sinfonia India*, which is based on true Indian melodies. It has a savage, primitive character which is very attractive. The 1958 recording is detailed and bright, if not absolutely sharp in focus because of the resonance, and is somewhat wanting in real depth and weight. Nevertheless this is a valuable reissue, and it is a pity that it is not offered in a lower price range.

Cherubini, Luigi (1760–1842)

Symphony in D; Overtures: Ali-Baba; Anacréon; Médée.
(M) (***) RCA mono GD 60278 [60278-2-RG]. NBC SO, Toscanini (with CIMAROSA: *Overtures: Il matrimonio per raggiro; Il matrimonio segreto* (**)).

The Cherubini *Symphony* is rightly one of Toscanini's most famous records. It was made in the Carnegie Hall, so even the sound is good. The overtures are just as characterful, *Anacréon* taken from a broadcast concert, again using Carnegie Hall. The other performances, including the brilliant – some might say hard-driven – Cimarosa items, were done in the famously dry Studio 8-H. The sheer incandescent energy of *Il matrimonio per raggiro* is remarkable and *Ali-Baba*, too, is very brisk indeed. With its 'Turkish' percussion, it sounds very piquant and the end is very like the 'chase' music in a silent movie. The transfers are first class.

String quartet No. 1 in E flat.
*** Collins Dig. 1267-2 [id.]. Britten Qt – VERDI: *Quartet;* TURINA: *La Oración del Torero.* ***

Cherubini's early *First Quartet* (1814) apparently uses ideas borrowed from the symphonies of Méhul, but they are thoroughly absorbed, so that all four movements spring from the same basic material. This is a highly rewarding work and one cannot imagine it being better played or recorded.

String quartets Nos. 1 in E flat; 6 in A min.
(N) *** CPO Dig. CPO 999 463-2 [id.]. Hausmusik.

Hausmusik offer the first and last quartets in superb period-instrument performances. This is music of substance and deserves a more secure place in the repertory. Their account of the *Larghetto* of No. 1 is both searching and dramatic; the opening of the *A minor* is similarly perceptive, and both finales are full of zest and energy. In short this leads the field, as the recording is vivid and present.

Requiem in C min.
(B) *** EMI forte Dig. CZS5 68613-2 (2) [*CDFB 68613*]. Ambrosian Ch., Philh. O, Muti – VERDI: *Requiem.* ***
(M) (**(*)) RCA mono GD 60272 (2) [*60272-RG-2*]. Marshall, Merriman, Conley, Hines, Robert Shaw Ch., NBC SO, Toscanini – BEETHOVEN: *Missa solemnis.* (**(*))

The *C minor Requiem*, the best known, was called by Berlioz 'the greatest of the greatest of his [Cherubini's] works'. Muti directs a tough, incisive reading, underlining the drama. The digital recording is excellent.

Toscanini was an admirer of Cherubini's choral music, and though the start of this live performance of 1950 lacks the full Toscanini electricity, the Shaw Chorale, superbly disciplined, quickly responds to the maestro, to produce searingly incisive singing in such movements as the *Dies irae*. Characteristically dry recording.

Requiem Mass No. 2 in D min.
(N) (M) *** DG 457 744-2 [id.]. Czech PO & Ch., Markevitch – MOZART: *Coronation Mass.* ***
(M) ** BMG/Melodiya 74321 40723-2 [id.]. Estonian State Ac. Male Ch. Estonian RSO, Neeme Järvi (with SHOSTAKOVICH: *Loyalty.* **(*)).

Beethoven, too, revered Cherubini and listening to the *D minor Requiem* one can see why. Cherubini's inspiration is always dignified and fluent, and there is a nobility about his music that is imposing. It was the second of two this composer wrote and uses men's voices only – the ecclesiastical authorities of the time not allowing women in church choirs. It is perhaps this that gives the declamatory passages an almost revolutionary (in the secular sense) fervour, an effect helped by the stirring singing of the Czech chorus on this disc. Indeed the *Hosanna in excelsis* has the flavour of a call to arms. Another unusual aspect of the writing is the almost Berliozian use of the brass, to tremendous effect. One tends to think of Cherubini as one of those 'historical personages', but this original and often exciting work shows that in his old age (he was 76 when he wrote it) he was looking to the future and not the past. The performance is an outstandingly alive one and the recording has a wide dynamic range, making a remarkable impact in the climaxes. It becomes less immediate in the quieter passages and is notably withdrawn at the very beginning. But DG's current remastering has improved this considerably and this reissue is fully worthy to be one of DG's 'Originals'.

The BMG/Melodiya performance, given in Tallinn in 1967, has great eloquence and the Estonian forces give of their best. The disc is of special interest in that it brings a Shostakovich rarity, *Loyalty* (not conducted by Järvi), which is not otherwise available. Apart from a touch of rawness about the string-tone, the recording – if hardly state of the art – is very satisfactory.

OPERA

Lodoïska (complete).
**(*) Sony Dig. S2K 47290 (2) [id.]. Devia, Lombardo, Moser, Corbelli, Shimell, Luperi, La Scala, Milan, Ch. & O, Muti.

Muti's conviction in this live recording brings much to enjoy. The British baritone, William Shimell, is a splendid Dourlinski. As Lodoïska herself, the soprano Mariella Devia sounds sweeter and purer than when heard live, and so does Thomas Moser in the heavyweight tenor role of the Tartar chief, Titzikan. In the high tenor role of the hero, Floreski, Bernard Lombardo copes well with the high tessitura, but the voice bleats disagreeably. In the dry acoustic of La Scala the voices have been recorded close, so that there is a lack of atmosphere, and stage noises keep intruding, though the Sony engineers have done well to get such body in the sound.

Medea (complete).
(M) ** EMI CMS5 66435-2 (2) [Ang. CDMB 66435]. Callas, Scotto, Pirazzini, Picchi, La Scala Ch. & O, Serafin (with BEETHOVEN: *Ah! perfido* **).

The 1957 studio recording of *Medea* is a magnificent example of the fire-eating Callas. She completely outshines any rival. A cut text is used and Italian instead of the original French, with Serafin less imaginative than he usually was; but, with a cast more than competent – including the young Renata

Scotto – it is an enjoyable set. Callas's recording of the Beethoven scena, *Ah! perfido*, makes a powerful fill-up, even though in this late recording (1963/4) vocal flaws emerge the more.

Chopin, Frédéric (1810–49)

Idil Biret Complete Chopin Edition

Piano concerto No. 1, Op. 11; Andante spianato et Grande Polonaise brillante, Op. 22; Fantasia on Polish airs, Op. 13.
(BB) **(*) Naxos Dig. 8.550368; *4.550368* [id.] (with Slovak State PO, Stankovsky).

Piano concerto No. 2, Op. 21; Krakowiak, Op. 14; Variations on Mozart's 'Là ci darem la mano', Op. 2.
(BB) ** Naxos Dig. 8.550369; *4.550369* [id.] (with Slovak State PO, Stankovsky).

Ballades Nos. 1–4; Berceuse, Op. 57; Cantabile; Fantaisie, Op. 49; Gallop marquis; Largo; Marche funèbre; 3 Nouvelles Etudes.
(BB)** Naxos Dig. 8.550508; *4.550084* [id.].

Mazurkas, Op. posth: in D; A flat; B flat; G; C; B flat; Rondos, Op. 1, Op. 16 & Op. 73; Rondo à la Mazurka, Op. 5; Souvenir de Paganini; Variations brillantes; (i) *Variations for four hands; Variations on a German theme; Variations on themes from 'I Puritani' of Bellini.*
(BB) *** Naxos Dig. 8.550367 [id.] ((i) with Martin Sauer).

Nocturnes Nos. 1–21.
(BB) *** Naxos Dig. 8.550356/7 [id.] (available separately).

Polonaises Nos. 1–6; 7 (Polonaise fantaisie).
(BB) **(*) Naxos Dig. 8.550360 [id.].

Polonaises Nos. 8–10, Op. 71; in G min.; B flat; A flat; G sharp min.; B flat min. (Adieu); G flat, all Op. posth.; Andante spianato et Grande Polonaise in E flat, Op. 22 (solo piano version).
(BB) **(*) Naxos Dig. 8.550361 [id.].

Piano sonatas Nos. 1, Op. 4; 2 (Funeral march); 3, Op. 58.
(BB) *** Naxos Dig. 8.550363; *4.550363* [id.].

Waltzes Nos. 1–19; Contredanse in G flat; 3 Ecossaises, Op. 72; Tarantelle, Op. 43.
(BB) ** Naxos Dig. 8.550365; *4.550365* [id.].

The Turkish pianist, Idil Biret, has all the credentials for recording Chopin. Among others, she studied with both Cortot and Wilhelm Kempff. She has a prodigious technique and the recordings we have heard so far suggest that overall her Chopin survey is an impressive achievement.

Her impetuous style and chimerical handling of phrasing and rubato are immediately obvious in the *First Concerto*, and she makes a commanding entry in the *F minor Concerto*; in the *Larghetto*, too, the solo playing brings a gently improvisational manner, and the finale really gathers pace only at the entry of the orchestra (which is recorded rather resonantly throughout). Of the other short concertante pieces, the opening of the *Andante spianato* is very delicate and there is some scintillating playing in the following *Grande Polonaise* and *Fantasia on Polish airs* – and a touch of heaviness, too, in the former.The introductory *Largo* of the *Mozart variations* is a bit too dreamy and diffuse but, once the famous tune arrives, the performance springs to life. Similarly, the introduction to the charming *Krakowiak Rondo* hangs fire, but again the *Rondo* sparkles, with the rhythmic rubato nicely handled, though the orchestral tuttis could ideally be firmer.

The first of the solo recordings were made in the Clara Wieck Auditorium, Heidelberg; the sound is studio-ish but truthful. The *Ballades* brings impetuously romantic interpretations where the rubato at times seems mannered; the *Berceuse* is tender and tractable, the *Fantaisie in F minor* begins rather deliberately but opens up excitingly later; though the playing is rather Schumannesque, it is also imaginative; the three *Nouvelles Etudes*, too, are attractively individual.

The disc called '*Rondos and variations*' (8.550367) is worth anyone's money, showing Biret's technique at its most prodigious and glittering. Much of the music here is little known and none of it second rate. The *Nocturnes* are a great success in a quite different way, the rubato simple, the playing free and often thoughtful, sometimes dark in timbre, but always spontaneous. The recording venue has now changed to the Tonstudio van Geest in Heidelberg and throughout is pleasingly full in timbre. The *Polonaises* demonstrate Biret's sinewy strength: the famous *A major* is a little measured, but the *A flat* is fresh and exciting and the whole set commanding, while the *Polonaise fantaisie* shows imaginative preparation yet comes off spontaneously like the others. The recital ends with a fine account of the solo piano version of the *Andante spianato* (quite lovely) and *Grande Polonaise*, which is more appealing than the concertante version.

The three *Sonatas* are fitted comfortably on to one CD (75 minutes) and, irrespective of cost, this represents one of the finest achievements in Biret's series so far. The *Waltzes* brought another change of venue, to the Tonstudio in Sandhausen. The recording is bright, somewhat more resonant. This is charismatic playing, giving opportunities for exciting bravura, but too many of these pieces are pressed on without respite. The *Ecossaises* and *Tarantelle* are also thrown off at almost breakneck speed.

CONCERTOS AND CONCERTANTE MUSIC

Andante spianato et Grande Polonaise brillante (for piano and orchestra), *Op. 22.*

(M) *** RCA 09026 68886-2 [id.]. Rubinstein, Symphony of the Air, Wallenstein – FALLA: *Nights in the gardens of Spain;* RACHMANINOV: *Rhapsody on a theme of Paganini.* ***

Rubinstein gives an interpretation to the manner born, at once showy and emotional, yet sensitive. Wallenstein gives good if unostentatious support, and the recording is naturally balanced.

(i) *Piano concertos Nos. 1–2. Andante spianato et Grande polonaise brillante; Ballades Nos. 1–4; Barcarolle* (1946 & 1962 recordings); *Berceuse* (1946 & 1962 recordings); *Boléro; Fantaisie in F min.; Impromptus Nos. 1–4; 51 Mazurkas; 19 Nocturnes; 3 Nouvelles-études; 6 Polonaises; Polonaise-Fantaisie; 24 Préludes; Scherzi Nos. 1–4; Sonata No. 2* (1946 & 1961 recordings); *Sonata No. 3; Tarantelle; 14 Waltzes.*

(M) *** RCA GD 60822 [60822-2-RG] (11). Artur Rubinstein, (i) with London New SO, Skrowaczewski; or Symphony of the Air, Wallenstein.

Rubinstein's principal Chopin oeuvre is offered here on 11 CDs at mid-price. His achievement was unique in this repertoire, and for the most part the remastered recordings are almost worthy of the playing. Alternative versions are offered of several pieces, but most of the recordings listed are discussed below as individual issues, many still at full price.

(i) *Piano concertos Nos. 1–2. Nocturnes Nos. 1–19; Waltz, Op. 64/2.*

(M) (***) EMI (SIS) CHS7 64491-2 (2) [ZDHB 64491]. Rubinstein, (i) with LSO, Barbirolli.

(i) *Piano concertos Nos. 1 in E min., Op. 11; 2 in F min., Op. 21. Andante spianato et Grande Polonaise brillante, Op. 22; Barcarolle, Op. 60; Berceuse, Op. 57; Mazurkas Nos. 1–51; Nocturnes Nos. 1–19; Polonaises Nos. 1–7; Scherzi Nos. 1–4; Waltz in C sharp min., Op. 64/2.*

(M) (***) EMI (SIS) mono CHS7 64933-2 (5). Rubinstein, (i) with LSO, Barbirolli.

Andante spianato et Grande Polonaise brillante, Op. 22; Barcarolle, Op. 60; Berceuse, Op. 57; Mazurkas Nos. 1–51; Polonaises Nos. 1–7; Scherzi Nos. 1–4; Waltz in C sharp min., Op. 64/1.

(M) (***) EMI (SIS) mono CHS7 64697-2 (3). Artur Rubinstein.

The five-CD set listed above falls into two parts, the first consisting of the two piano concertos, recorded with Barbirolli and the LSO in 1937 (*E minor*) and 1931 (*F minor*), the *C sharp minor Waltz*, recorded in 1930, and the celebrated set of the *Nocturnes* from 1936–7. This is additionally available on a two-CD Références set. The second set of three CDs comprises the *Mazurkas* (recorded in 1938), some of the most totally idiomatic Chopin playing ever committed to record, the 1932 *Scherzi* and the *Polonaises* (1934) and various other pieces. They can be bought in two separate packages or together. Rubinstein was at the height of his powers when he made these recordings and he rarely equalled and never surpassed them in the post-war, LP era. The *Mazurkas* and *Nocturnes* have a poetic spontaneity and aristocratic finesse that are totally convincing. The transfers are excellent.

Piano concertos Nos. (i) *1 in E min., Op. 11;* (ii) *2 in F min., Op. 21.*

*** DG 415 970-2 [id.]. Zimerman, LAPO, Giulini.

**(*) Sony Dig. SK44922 [id.]. Perahia, Israel PO, Mehta.

*** Conifer Dig. 76505 51247-2 [id.]. Martino Tirimo, Philh. O, Fedor Glushchenko.

(N) *** EMI Dig. CDC5 56798-2 [id.]. Martha Argerich, Montreal SO, Charles Dutoit.

(M) *** Mercury 434 374-2 [id.]. Gina Bachauer, LSO, Dorati.

(BB) *** RCA Navigator 74321 17892-2 [Basic 100 09026 68023-2]. Emanuel Ax, Phd. O, Ormandy.

(BB) *** Naxos Dig. 8.550123; *4550123* [id.]. István Székely, Budapest SO, Gyula Németh.

(B) *** DG Classikon 429 515-2 [(M) id. import]. Tamás Vásáry, BPO, (i) Semkow; (ii) Kulka.

** Hyperion Dig. CDA 66647 [id.]. Nikolai Demidenko, Philh. O, Heinrich Schiff.

(N) (M) ** Carlton Dig. 30366 01152 [id.]. Fou Ts'ong, Sinf. Varsovia, Mu Hai Tang.

The CD coupling of Zimerman's performances of the two Chopin concertos with Giulini is hard to beat. Elegant, aristocratic, sparkling, it has youthful spontaneity and at the same time a magisterial authority, combining sensibility with effortless pianism. Both recordings are cleanly detailed.

Perahia's effortless brilliance and refinement of touch recall artists like Hofmann and Lipatti. Mehta provides a highly sensitive accompaniment once the soloist enters but is curiously offhand and matter-of-fact (indeed almost brutal) in the orchestral ritornelli. The sound is dryish and far from ideal. The three stars are for Perahia's playing, not the sound!

Martino Tirimo's performances are worthy to rank alongside those of Perahia and Zimerman. Poetic feeling is paramount: Tirimo's readings often bring exquisite delicacy and they are totally without barnstorming, yet there is spontaneity in every bar, and both slow movements bring playing where one has an impression of musing reverie. In outer movements passage-work is scintillatingly alive, and finales have a beguiling rhythmic lift. There is strong orchestral support and sparkling dance rhythms.

Martha Argerich's newest EMI coupling arrives over 30 years since she recorded the *E minor concerto* in Berlin with Abbado conducting, and 20 since she recorded the *F minor* in Washington with Rostropovich at the helm. There is no doubt that her pianism remains as mercurial and her virtuosity as incandescent as ever; indeed she has rarely sounded as captivating or characterful. Charles Dutoit gets good playing from the Montreal Orchestra but their contribution is not quite at the same level as their soloist though it is a good deal more sensitive than, say, Mehta's accompanying for Murray Perahia on Sony. Admirers of Argerich (and we might add Chopin) need not hesitate.

Gina Bachauer obviously sees these as full-bloodedly romantic concertos and Dorati gives her every support and the orchestral playing is first class. Passage-work scintillates and her phrasing and rubato have fine sensitivity. Both slow movements bring appealing delicacy, and finales have a lilting panache, while the central episode of the *Larghetto* of the *F minor* work can seldom have sounded more dramatic. With Mercury's spaciously realistic Watford Town Hall recording of orchestra and piano alike, and an excellent balance, this is very enjoyable indeed.

Emanuel Ax offers fine performances of both concertos at super-bargain price. This is genuinely poetic playing and the finale of the *F minor*, with its light, chimerical touch is particularly pleasing. The digital recording is not quite top-drawer in the matter of transparency. Yet it provides a fuller and more flattering sound for the Philadelphia Orchestra than on many of their recent records, and Ormandy is a highly sensitive accompanist in both works.

István Székely is particularly impressive in the *E minor Concerto*, but in both works he finds atmosphere and poetry in slow movements and an engaging dance spirit for the finales, with rhythms given plenty of character. Németh accompanies sympathetically; the orchestral contribution here is quite refined. The recording is resonantly full in the Hungarian manner, not absolutely clear on detail; but the piano image is bold and realistic. A splendid bargain in every sense of the word.

Vásáry's approach is much more self-effacing: his gentle poetry is in clear contrast with the opulent orchestral sound (especially in No. 1, where the recording is more resonantly expansive than in No. 2). Yet soloist and orchestra match their styles perfectly in both slow movements, which are played most beautifully, and the finales have no lack of character and sparkle. In their way, these performances will give considerable pleasure and, with recording that retains its depth and bloom, this makes a fine bargain coupling.

Nikolai Demidenko's recording of the two concertos can only be recommended to his admirers. He produces consistent beauty of sound but his rubati can be disruptive, influenced by moments of disturbing self-consciousness. Probably the best things are in the middle movements, though even these are not always allowed to speak for themselves. Heinrich Schiff gets an excellent response from the Philharmonia Orchestra throughout and the recording, though not top-drawer, is perfectly acceptable. For the dedicated admirer of the pianist rather than of the composer.

Fou Ts'ong made his recordings in Warsaw in 1989 and has now licensed them to Carlton Classics. The performances have much to commend them although there is some intrusive rubato at the beginning of the development of the first movement of the *E minor Concerto* which may worry some listeners more than others. More unpleasing is the reverbant acoustic, and the slightly unfocused, clamorous piano tone.

(i) *Piano concertos Nos. 1 in E min., Op. 11; 2 in F min., Op. 21. 2 Mazurkas in F min., Opp. 63/2 & 68/4; Waltz in E min., Op. posth.*
*** RCA 09026 68378-2 [id.]. Evgeny Kissin, Moscow PO, Dmitri Kitaenko.

Evgeny Kissin's programme was recorded at the Moscow Conservatory in 1984 when he was a boy of 12, though he sounds like a seasoned master. His later recitals have shown greater depth and poetic feeling, though there is no lack of either here and this still remains a pretty extraordinary feat. Kissin follows the concertos with three encores, again proclaiming his mastery of this repertoire, with the closing waltz thrown away with captivating insouciance. The applause is well justified and the recording is excellent.

Piano concerto No. 1 in E min., Op. 11.
(M) *** DG 449 719-2 [id.]. Martha Argerich, LSO, Abbado – LISZT: *Piano concerto No. 1.* ***

(BB) **(*) Naxos Dig. 8.550292 [id.]. Székely, Budapest SO, Németh – LISZT: *Concerto No. 1.* **(*)

(N) ** Decca Dig. 460 019-2. Ashkenazy, Deutsches SO, Berlin – GLAZUNOV: *Chopiniana.* **

(i) *Piano concerto No. 1. Barcarolle in F sharp, Op. 60; Preludes, Op. 28/1, 3, 6, 10, 15–17, 20–21 & 24; Scherzo No. 3, Op. 39.*
(B) **(*) DG Classikon 439 459-2 [(M) id. import]. Argerich; (i) LSO, Abbado.

(i) *Piano concerto No. 1 in E min., Op. 11. Berceuse in D flat, Op. 57; Fantaisie in F min., Op. 49; Fantasie-impromptu in C sharp min., Op. 66.*
(N) *** DG Dig. 457 585-2. Maria João Pires; (i) COE, Emmanuel Krivine.

(i) *Piano concerto No. 1. Etudes: in E, Op. 10/3;*

A flat, Op. 25/1; Fantaisie-impromptu in C sharp min., Op. 66; Impromptu No. 3 in G flat, Op. 51; Mazurkas: in A min., Op. 68/2; B flat, Op. 7/1; Nocturne No. 2 in E flat, Op. 9; Waltz No. 12 in F min., Op. 70/2.

(BB) **(*) Belart 461 149-2 [(M) id. import]. Tamás Vásáry; (i) BPO, Jerzy Semkow.

(*) Chesky CD 93 [id.]. Earl Wild, RPO, Sargent – FAURE: *Ballade;* LISZT: *Concerto No. 1.* *

(i) *Piano concerto No. 1. Ballade No. 1, Op. 23; Nocturnes Nos. 4 & 5, Op. 15/1–2; 7, Op. 27/1; Polonaise No. 6, Op. 53.*

(M) *** EMI CDM5 66221-2 [CDM 66221]. Pollini, (i) Philh. O, Kletzki.

Piano concerto No. 1 in E min., Op. 11; Variations on 'La ci darem', Op.2. Waltz in A min, Op.34/2.

(N) *** Sony SK 60771 [id.]. Emanuel Ax, OAE, Mackerras.

Pollini's classic recording still remains among the best available of the *E minor Concerto*. This is playing of such total spontaneity, poetic feeling and refined judgement that criticism is silenced. The digital remastering has been generally successful. The additional items come from Pollini's first EMI solo recital, and the playing is equally distinguished, the recording truthful.

Admirers of Maria João Pires need not hesitate in acquiring the DG version of the *E minor concerto*. The slip case speaks of her 'grace and eloquence' and it might well have added 'poetic feeling'. Her concerns centre on the more inward-looking side of Chopin rather than its incandescence or brilliance, but this is a performance of substance and she is given eminently responsive support from the Chamber Orchestra of Europe and Emmanuel Krivine. The solo pieces are thoughtful, sensitive accounts and there are no quarrels with the DG recording.

As with the companion version of No. 2 this Sony disc from Emanuel Ax offers period performances unlikely to be outshone for their imagination and poetry. Using a full-toned Erard piano of 1851, Ax produces warm, full tone which yet allows extra agility, thanks to the light action. Only the clattery quality in the topmost register betrays the age of the instrument. The transparency of textures is a delight, with the writing for left hand brilliantly articulated. Mackerras enhances the drama of these readings by drawing out a wide range of dynamics from the OAE, equally defying the idea of period performance as lacking in weight. The Opus 2 variations are relatively trivial, but Ax gives them both wit and poetry, and solo piano encore again finds Ax tenderly poetic. Excellent sound.

Martha Argerich's recording dates from 1968 and helped to establish her international reputation. With persuasive support from Abbado, she provides some lovely playing, especially in the slow movement. Perhaps in the passage-work she is rather too intense, but this is far preferable to the rambling style we are sometimes offered. This version is now reissued in two different formats. The first comes as one of DG's 'Originals' in a coupling with an equally individual and charismatic account of Liszt's *First Concerto*; for the bargain Classikon alternative a miscellaneous programme of encores has been added, showing well the impulsive qualities of her solo playing.

Earl Wild offers a flamboyantly romantic account, well supported by Sargent and the RPO. This was one of the RCA recordings produced for *Reader*'s *Digest* in the mid-1960s and engineered by Decca. The vintage recording hardly sounds dated at all. A pity this has to be at full-price.

Returning to Vásáry's fine mid-1960s Belart (originally DG) recording of the *E minor Concerto* gave us great pleasure. He is beautifully recorded with a good balance and fine piano-tone. The recital which follows is rather more uneven. The pianist's self-effacing style is at its most effective in the *E major Etude* and the justly famous *E flat Nocturne*. However, he finds plenty of brilliance for the closing *Fantaisie-impromptu*. Again good recording.

István Székely's account is also available with the *F minor Concerto* (see above), but those preferring a Liszt coupling should find this alternative coupling equally satisfactory.

Ashkenazy's recording of the *E minor concerto* is strangely enough his first, though he is not (*pace* Decca's publicity) the first also to direct from the keyboard (Tamás Vásáry did that on ASV in the early 1980s). While his pianism is elegant, there is little real magic here. Excellent Decca sound.

(i) *Piano concerto No. 2 in F min., Op. 21* (complete). *Ballade No. 1 in G min., Op. 23; Barcarolle in F sharp min., Op. 60; Berceuse in D flat, Op. 57; Fantaisie-impromptu in C sharp min., Op. 66; Mazurkas: in B flat, Op. 7/1; in D, Op. 33/2; in A min., Op. 68/2; Nocturnes: in E flat, Op. 9/2; in G min., Op. 37/1; Polonaises Nos. 3 in A (Military), Op. 40/1; 6 in A flat, Op. 53; Scherzo No. 2 in B flat min., Op. 31; Sonata No. 2 in B flat min. (Funeral march), Op. 35* (complete). *Waltzes: in A flat, Op. 34/1; in D flat (Minute), Op. 64/1; in E min., Op. posth.*

(B) *** RCA Twofer 74321 34175-2 (2) [(M) id. import]. Artur Rubinstein, (i) Symphony of the Air, Alfred Wallenstein.

Including,as it does,complete performances of the *F minor Piano concerto* and an unsurpassed *Funeral march Sonata*, this RCA Twofer must be counted a top choice among all the bargain collections of Chopin's piano music. Rubinstein's playing was in a class of its own. Adjectives like 'miraculous', 'inspired', 'magical' fail to do justice to the creative imagination of this pianism. The orchestral tuttis in the *Concerto* are dry and studio-ish, but the piano timbre and colouring are unimpaired, especially in the delicate filigree of the slow movement. Otherwise the sound is always good, and often very good.

Piano concerto No. 2 in F min., Op. 21.
(M) *** Decca 448 598-2 [id.]. Vladimir Ashkenazy, LSO, Zinman – BACH: *Clavier concerto No. 1;* MOZART: *Piano concerto No. 6.* **(*)

(i) *Piano concerto No. 2 in F min., Op. 21. 24 Preludes, Op. 24.*
(BB) **(*) Belart 461 055-2 [(M) id. import]. Alicia de Larrocha; (i) SRO, Sergiu Comissiona.

Ashkenazy's 1965 recording is a distinguished performance: obviously in full rapport with their soloist and the vintage recording has been remastered most satisfactorily. This is now reissued in Decca's Classic Sound series with new couplings, which are less than ideally chosen, although enjoyable enough.

Alicia de Larrocha is an artist of personality and temperament, and her performance of the concerto is highly poetic. It is supported by a strongly characterful accompaniment from Comissiona. Her *rubati* carry total conviction, whereas in the *Preludes* they sometimes seem more idiosyncratic. There is, however, much to admire here, including fine Decca engineering from the 1970s.

Piano concerto No. 2; Andante spianato et Grande polonaise brillante, Op. 22; Grand fantasia on Polish airs for piano and orchestra in A, Op. 13.
(N) *** Sony Dig. SK 63371 [id.]. Emanuel Ax (fortepiano), OAE, Mackerras.

It sounds unpromising to have a Chopin concerto played on an 1851 Erard piano, but Emanuel Ax, helped by Mackerras and this outstanding period orchestra, completely allays any doubts. The sound is full and firm, and Ax uses the extra clarity of an early instrument – with none of the twang associated with fortepianos – to intensify the poetry of the writing. The two other, more trivial concertante works are equally made the more winning by the freshness of approach from both soloist and conductor, with witty pointing and moments of pure magic. Well worth exploring.

(i) *Piano concerto No. 2. Ballades Nos. 1–4; Barcarolle, Op. 60; Berceuse, Op. 57* (2 versions); *Chants polonais, Op. 74* (trans. Liszt); *Etudes, Op. 10/1–12* (2 versions); *Op. 25/1–12* (2 versions); *Nouvelles Etudes; Impromptus, Opp. 29, 36; Nocturnes Opp. 9/2; 15/1–2; 27/1; 55/1–2; 24 Preludes, Op. 28; Prelude in C sharp min., Op. 45; Piano sonatas Nos. 2, Op. 35; 3, Op. 58; Waltzes Nos. 1–14.*
(M) (***) EMI (SIS) CZS7 67359-2 (6). Alfred Cortot, (i) with O, Barbirolli.

This Cortot compilation encompasses most (but not all) of the recordings he made between 1920 and 1949, arranged in roughly chronological order. The quality of the performances is such that they would need several pages to do them justice; Cortot's spontaneity, poetic feeling and keyboard refinement are heard to prodigal effect on these six CDs. Several alternative versions (for example, both sets of the Opp. 10 and 25 *Etudes* from 1934 and 1942 are included) offer food for thought. But in any event this is playing of a quite special quality: aristocratic yet full of fire and spontaneity. The transfers are strikingly good and bring Cortot very much before one's eyes.

Les Sylphides (ballet; orch. Douglas).
❁ (B) *** DG 429 163-2. BPO, Karajan – DELIBES: *Coppélia*: suite; OFFENBACH: *Gaîté parisienne:* excerpts. ***
(B) *** Sony SBK 46550 [id.]. Phd. O, Ormandy – DELIBES: *Coppélia; Sylvia: suites* ***; TCHAIKOVSKY: *Nutcracker suite.* **(*)
(B) **(*) Ph. Duo 438 763-2 (2) [id.]. Rotterdam PO, David Zinman – DELIBES: *Coppélia;* GOUNOD: *Faust: ballet music.* **(*)
(B) **(*) Decca Eclipse Dig. 448 984-2. Nat. PO, Bonynge (with MASSENET: *Thaïs: Méditation* with Nigel Kennedy). ROSSINI; RESPIGHI: *La Boutique fantasque.* **(*)

Karajan conjures consistently beautiful playing from the Berlin Philharmonic Orchestra, and he evokes a delicacy of texture which delights the ear throughout. The sound is full and atmospheric, and this is one of Karajan's very finest recordings. At bargain price it is unbeatable, coupled on CD not only with *Coppélia* (although the suite is not complete) but also with Offenbach's *Gaîté parisienne.*

The Philadelphia strings are perfectly cast in this score and, although the CBS sound is less svelte than the DG quality for Karajan, it is still very good. Ormandy begins gently and persuasively. Later the lively sections are played with irrepressible brilliance.

David Zinman's approach is less suavely characterful than Karajan's, but he secures smoothly beautiful playing from his Rotterdam orchestra and there is no lack of vitality. Most enjoyable, when the 1980 recording is so natural and resonantly full (obviously more modern than the DG).

Bonynge's performance shows a strong feeling for the dance rhythms of the ballet, and the orchestral playing is polished and lively. Bonynge also has the advantage of excellent (1982) digital recording, made in the Kingsway Hall. Nigel Kennedy plays very appealingly in the Massenet lollipop which acts as an encore. Even so, Karajan remains unsurpassed in this beautiful score.

CHAMBER MUSIC

Cello sonata in G min., Op. 65.
(M) **(*) EMI CMS7 63184-2 [id.]. Du Pré, Barenboim – FRANCK: *Cello sonata.* **(*)

The easy romanticism of the *Cello sonata* is beautifully caught by Jacqueline du Pré and Daniel Barenboim. Though the cellist phrases with all her usual spontaneous-sounding imagination, this is one of her more reticent records, while still bringing an autumnal quality to the writing which is very appealing. The recording is excellently balanced.

Cello sonata in G min., Op. 65; Grand duo concertante in E on themes from Meyerbeer's 'Robert le Diable'; Nocturne in C sharp min., Op. posth (arr. Piatigorsky); *Etudes: in E min., Op. 25/7; D min., Op. 10/6* (arr. Glazunov; ed. Feuermann); *Waltz in A min., Op. 34/3* (arr. Ginsburg).
(BB) *** Naxos 8.553159 [id.]. Maria Kliegel, Bernd Glemser.

Fresh and ardent performances of the *Sonata* and the remaining two pieces that comprise Chopin's complete output for cello and piano. The Naxos collection also throws in some cello arrangements for good measure. These gifted and accomplished young artists are also very well recorded indeed and, at the price, this is a bargain.

SOLO PIANO MUSIC

Vladimir Ashkenazy Chopin Edition

Albumblatt in E; Allegro de concert in A, Op. 46; Barcarolle in F sharp, Op. 60; Berceuse in D flat, Op. 57; Boléro in A min., Op. 19; 2 Bourrées; Cantabile in B flat; Fugue in A min.; Galop marquis; Hexameron: Variation in E min.; Largo in E flat; 3 Nouvelles études; Rondo in E flat, Op. 16; Souvenir de Paganini (Variations in A); Tarantelle in A flat, Op. 43; Variations brillantes in B flat, Op. 12; Wiosna (Spring) from Op. 74/2 (443 7512). *Ballades Nos. 1–4; Scherzi Nos. 1–4* (443 740-2). *12 Etudes, Op. 10; 12 Etudes, Op. 25* (443 743-2). *Impromptus Nos. 1–3; 4 (Fantaisie-impromptu); 24 Preludes, Op. 28; Preludes: in C sharp min., Op. 45; in A flat* (443 739-2). *Mazurkas Nos. 1–29* (443 747-2); *Nos. 30–68 (including 2 versions of Op. 68/4)* (443 748-2). *Nocturnes Nos. 1–12* (443 741-2); *Nos. 13–21* (443 742-2). *Polonaises Nos. 1–6; No. 7, Polonaise-fantaisie* (443 744-2); *Nos. 8–16* (443 745-2). *Sonata No. 1; Contredanse in G flat; 3 Ecossaises; Marche funèbre in C min., Op. 72/2; Rondo in C min., Op. 1; Rondo à la Mazur in F, Op. 5; Rondo in C, Op. 73; Variations on a German national air;* (i) *Variations in D* (for piano duet – with Vovka Ashkenazy) (443 750-2). *Sonatas Nos. 2–3; Fantaisie in F min., Op. 49* (443 749-2). *Waltzes Nos. 1–19* (443 746-2).
(B) *** Decca Analogue/ Dig. 443 738-2 (13) [id.].

Ashkenazy made his Chopin recordings for Decca over a decade from 1974 to 1984, using seven different locations, yet the recorded sound is remarkably consistent, always natural in colour and balance and with a good presence, whether from an analogue or a digital source. Consistently persuasive, these readings combine poetry with flair and (as in the *Ballades*) often bring a highly communicated warmth. The bravura brings genuine panache, whether in the large-scale, virtuoso pieces like the *Scherzi* or in the chimerical approach to a miniature like the *Souvenir de Paganini*. At bargain price this set makes an unbeatable investment.

Andante spianato et Grande polonaise brillante, Op. 22; Barcarolle in F sharp min., Op. 60; Berceuse in D flat, Op. 57; Boléro in C, Op. 19; Impromptus Nos. 1–4; Fantaisie-impromptu, Op. 66; 3 Nouvelles études, Op. posth.; Tarantelle in A flat, Op. 43.
*** RCA RD 89911 [RCA 5617-2-RC]. Artur Rubinstein.

In Chopin piano music generally, Rubinstein has no superior. The *Andante spianato et Grande polonaise* obviously inspires him, and his clear and relaxed accounts of the *Impromptus* make most other interpretations sound forced by comparison. The magnificent *Barcarolle* and *Berceuse* contain some of Chopin's finest inspirations – and if the *Tarantelle* may appear musically less interesting and not very characteristic, in Rubinstein's hands it is a glorious piece, full of bravura.

Ballades Nos. 1–4; Allegro de concert, Op. 45; Introduction and variations on 'Je vends des scapulaires', Op. 12.
(M)*** CRD CRD 3360. Hamish Milne.

Hamish Milne gives thoughtful and individual performances of the *Ballades*. They may initially sound understated, but in their freshness and concentration they prove poetic and compelling. Similarly he plays the two rarities with total conviction, suggesting that the *Allegro de concert* at least (originally a sketch for a third piano concerto) is most unjustly neglected. The recorded sound is first rate.

Ballades Nos. 1-4; Barcarolle, Op. 60; Berceuse, Op. 57; Scherzo No. 4 in E, Op. 54.
(N) **(*) RCA Dig. 09026 63259 [id.]. Evgeny Kissin.

Evgeny Kissin is a pianist of consummate artistry whose command of colour and keyboard authority are phenomenal. But this is not one of his best recitals. The *Four Ballades* are recorded in the Sudwestfunk studios in Freiburg and although the sound is natural enough, climaxes tend to be muddy in the reverberant acoustic. The *G minor Ballade* is curiously wayward and wanting in momentum. Of course, there are many beautiful things – particularly the *Barcarolle* – but at other times Kissin is intrusive and not content to leave Chopin to speak for himself. No challenge to Perahia and Zimerman.

Ballades Nos. 1–4; Barcarolle, Op. 60; Fantaisie in F min., Op. 49.
*** DG (IMS) Dig. 423 090-2 [id.]. Krystian Zimerman.

Ballades Nos. 1–4; Etudes: in E; C sharp min., Op. 10/3–4; Mazurkas: in F min., Op. 7/4; in A min., Op. 17/4; in D, Op. 33/2; Nocturne in F, Op. 15/1; Waltzes: in E flat (Grande valse brillante), Op. 18; in A flat, Op. 42.
✿ *** Sony Dig. SK 64399 [id.]. Murray Perahia.

Ballades Nos. 1–4; Scherzi Nos. 1–4.
*** RCA RD 89651 [RCD1 7156]. Artur Rubinstein.

Murray Perahia's set of the *Ballades* is unlikely to be surpassed. One has to go back to Hofmann, recorded in 1937, to find a more searching or poetic account of the *G minor Ballade*, and the *Waltzes* not only prompt thoughts to turn to the classic post-war Lipatti set, but comparison does not find Perahia less poetic. Moreover the Sony engineers do him justice. In every respect a masterly recital that is in a class of its own and which readers should not miss.

Krystian Zimerman's impressive set of the *Ballades* and the other two works on this disc are also touched by distinction throughout and have spontaneity as well as tremendous concentration to commend them, and the modern digital recording is of fine DG quality.

Rubinstein's readings are unique and the digital remastering has been highly successful. The performances of the *Ballades* are a miracle of creative imagination, with Rubinstein at his most inspired. The *Scherzi*, which gain most of all from the improved sound (they were originally very dry), are both powerful and charismatic.

Ballades Nos. 1–4; Nocturnes Nos. 1–21 (complete).
(B) *** Decca Double 452 579-2 (2) [id.]. Vladimir Ashkenazy.

Ashkenazy's readings of the *Ballades* are thoughtful and essentially unflashy; the rubato arises naturally from his personal approach to the music. The intimacy of the recording allows him to share this with the listener. The recording is admirably natural and satisfying. The *Nocturnes* were recorded over a decade, from 1975 to 1984. The disparity in dates seems not to have affected the consistency of sound that the Decca engineers have achieved. The playing is splendidly imaginative and atmospheric. As always, Ashkenazy is completely attuned to Chopin's unique sound-world, and the CD transfers are impeccable.

Barcarolle, Op. 60; Berceuse, Op. 57; Cantabile in B flat; Contredanse in G flat; Fantaisie in F min., Op. 49; Feuille d'album in E; Fugue in A min.; Funeral march in C min., Op. 72/2; Largo in E flat; 3 Nouvelles-Etudes, Op. posth; Polonaise-Fantaisie, Op. 61; Souvenir de Paganini in A (Variations).
(B) *** Sony Analogue/Dig. SBK 53515 [id.]. Fou Ts'ong.

Fou Ts'ong is a pianist of intelligence and sensibility and his admirers need not hesitate here. The programme is enterprising – how many readers, we wonder, have heard Chopin's succinct little *Fugue in A minor*? The smaller pieces are played with a distinction and dedication that completely win one over, and the closing *Paganini variations* are disarmingly attractive. The recording, partly analogue, partly digital, is good but not quite top-drawer: in general the analogue items sound best. But this 66-minute bargain recital is well worth exploring.

Barcarolle, Op. 60; Berceuse, Op. 57; Fantaisie in F min., Op. 49; Impromptus Nos. 1–3, Opp. 29, 36 & 51
*** Sony Dig. MK 39708 [id.]. Murray Perahia.

Perahia is a Chopin interpreter of the highest order. There is an impressive range of colour and an imposing sense of order. This is highly poetic playing and an indispensable acquisition for any Chopin collection. The CBS recording does him justice.

Barcarolle, Op. 60; Berceuse, Op. 57; Scherzi Nos. 1–4.
**(*) DG (IMS) Dig. 431 623-2 [id.]. Maurizio Pollini.

Berceuse, Op. 57; Fantaisie in F min., Op. 49; Scherzi Nos. 1–4.
*** Chandos Dig. CHAN 9018 [id.]. Howard Shelley.

Howard Shelley offers much the same programme as Maurizio Pollini on DG. He emerges unscathed from any comparison; he has the advantage of a more sympathetic recording. But there is a greater freshness and tenderness about his approach and though he is obviously totally inside this music, he manages to convey the feeling that he is discovering it for the first time. These are performances of no mean quality.

There is no want of intellectual power or command of keyboard colour in Maurizio Pollini's accounts of the Chopin *Scherzi*. This is eminently magisterial playing with powerfully etched contours and hard surfaces that inspires more admiration than pleasure.

Etudes, Op. 10/1–12; Op. 25/1–12; 3 Nouvelles études.
*** Chandos Dig. CHAN 8482 [id.]. Louis Lortie.

Etudes, Op. 10/1–12; Op. 25/1–12.
*** DG 413 794-2. Maurizio Pollini.

Etudes, Op. 10/1–12; Op. 25/1–12; Ballades Nos. 1 & 3.
(B) *** [EMI Red Line Dig. CDR5 69799]. Andrei Gavrilov.

Louis Lortie's set of the 24 *Etudes* can hold its own with the best. His playing has a strong poetic feeling and an effortless virtuosity. He is beautifully recorded at The Maltings, Snape (whose acoustic occasionally clouds the texture).

Pollini's record also comes from 1975 and sounds splendidly fresh in its digitally remastered form. These are vividly characterized accounts, masterly and with the sound eminently present, although not as full in sonority as the more recent versions.

Andrei Gavrilov's performances of the *Etudes* bring an exuberant virtuosity that is impossible to resist. Even if some of the tempi are breathtakingly fast, the sustained legato and his poetic feeling are indisputable. The impulsive bravura is often engulfing, so that one feels the need to take a breath on the soloist's behalf after the furious account of the *Revolutionary study*; but this is prodigious playing, given a bold, forward recording to match. The *Ballades* are also impulsive but full of romantic feeling too.

Mazurkas Nos. 1–59, Op. 6/1–4; Op. 7/1–5; Op. 17/1–4; Op. 24/1–4; Op. 30/1–4; Op. 33/1–4; Op. 41/1–4; Op. 50/1–3; Op.56/1–3; Op. 59/1–3; Op. 63/1–3; Op. 67/1–4; Op. 68/1–4; & Op. 68/4 (revised version); *Nos. 60–68, Op. posth.*
(B) *** Decca Double Dig./Analogue 448 086-2 (2) [id.]. Vladimir Ashkenazy.

Mazurkas Nos. 1–57.
(B) **(*) Sony Dig. SB2K 53246 (2) [id.]. Fou Ts'ong.

Mazurkas Nos. 1–51.
*** RCA RD 85171 (2) [RCA 5614-2-RC]. Artur Rubinstein.

As can be seen, Ashkenazy's survey of Chopin's *Mazurkas* is the most comprehensive available and as such must take pride of place over Rubinstein's set (irrespective of its extremely modest cost). Ashkenazy's are finely articulated, aristocratic accounts and he includes all the posthumously published *Mazurkas*. The Decca recordings (often digital) are more modern and more natural than that afforded to Rubinstein.

Rubinstein could never play in a dull way to save his life, and in his hands these fifty-one pieces are endlessly fascinating, though on occasion in such unpretentious music one would welcome a completely straight approach. As with the *Ballades* and *Scherzi*, the digital remastering has brought a much more pleasing piano timbre.

After recording the *Nocturnes*, Fou Ts'ong went on to record virtually all the *Mazurkas*. Sometimes the rubato seems a shade too impulsive, but for the most part the playing is compelling. The digital recording from 1984 is bold and clear.

Nocturnes Nos. 1–19 (see also under *Ballades*).
*** RCA RD 89563 (2) [RCA 5613-2-RC]. Artur Rubinstein.

Nocturnes Nos. 1–21.
*** DG Dig. 447 096-2 (2). Maria João Pires.
(BB) *** Arte Nova Dig. 74321 30494-2 (*Nos. 1–10*); 74321 54451-2 (*Nos. 11–21*) (available separately) [id.]. Ricardo Castro.
(B) *** DG Dig. 453 022-2 (2) [437 464-2]. Daniel Barenboim.
(BB) **(*) Carlton IMP Double 30367 02357 [(M) id. import]. Peter Katin.
(B) **(*) Sony SB2K 53249 (2) [S2K 53249]. Fou Ts'ong.
**(*) Hyperion Dig. CDA 66341/2 [id.]. Lívia Rév.

Nocturnes Nos. 1–21; Barcarolle; Fantaisie-impromptu.
**(*) Unicorn Dig. DKPCD 9147/8 [id.]. Kathryn Stott.

Nocturnes Nos. 1–21; Impromptus Nos. 1–4 (Fantaisie-impromptu).
(B) **(*) Ph. Duo 456 336-2 [id.]. Claudio Arrau.

Rubinstein in Chopin is a magician in matters of colour; his unerring sense of nuance and the seeming inevitability of his rubato demonstrate a very special musical imagination in this repertoire. The recordings were the best he received in his Chopin series for RCA.

However, from Pires comes quite the best set of *Nocturnes* we have had from any pianist in recent years. She gives performances of great character, her playing often bold as well as meltingly romantic, and brings the right poetic feel to this music. Hers is the art that conceals art, and that serves the composer to perfection. She uses the widest dynamic range and is recorded with a brilliant presence as well as a basically warm sonority.

To have an outstanding set of the *Nocturnes*, digitally recorded and in the lowest possible price-range, seems almost too good to be true, but the Brazilian pianist, Ricardo Castro, winner of the Leeds International Piano Competition in 1993, offers a series of performances to compete with almost any in the catalogue. They were recorded in two groups, in 1995 and 1997 respectively, but the degree of concentration and thoughtful simplicity of approach is consistent throughout both discs, his nuancing and rubato managed with convincing spontaneity. The recording, made in two quite different venues, is of high quality, clear and natural.

Barenboim recorded the *Nocturnes* in 1981 in DG's Berlin studio, and he was very beautifully recorded. His playing gives much pleasure. Phrasing is beautifully moulded, seemingly spontaneous, thoughtful and poetic, and becoming really impetuous only in the music's more passionate moments. There is an excellent, well-chosen, single-disc selection on DG's bargain label which offer 72 minutes of music and scores 13 out of a total of 21. But the complete set is surely worth the extra outlay.

Arrau's approach clearly reflects his boyhood training in Germany, creating tonal warmth coupled with inner tensions of the kind one expects in Beethoven. With the *Nocturnes* it can be apt to have an element of seriousness, and this is a very compelling cycle, full of poetry, the rubato showing an individual but very communicable sensibility. The *Impromptus* have been added for the present reissue. Although Arrau's Chopin is seldom mercurial, it is never inflexible, and it has its own special insights. The *Fantasie-impromptu* with its finely contoured central melody is a highlight. As always, the Philips piano recording is of the highest standard

Peter Katin's set dates from 1971. He has chosen not to present the *Nocturnes* in their usual, numbered sequence, but in their order of composition, so that the pieces which were published posthumously are placed in their natural position, a scheme which works very well. His approach is serene and civilized, essentially relaxed. Only occasionally does he not penetrate to the very heart of the music; almost always the playing is highly sensitive, with subtle rubato, delicate runs and exquisite shading in the gentle music. This set is inexpensive and naturally recorded: admirers of this fine artist need not hesitate.

As is immediately apparent in the *Fantaisie-impromptu* which acts as an introduction to her survey, Kathryn Stott's Chopin is very romantic, seldom understated and uses the widest dynamic range. Yet at times she touches the listener by her very calmness. Rubato is convincingly managed and overall her playing has a stronger profile than that of Lívia Rév. She is most realistically recorded.

Fou Ts'ong sometimes reminds one of Solomon – and there can surely be no higher tribute. He is at his very best in the gentle, poetic pieces; in the more robust *Nocturnes* his rubato is less subtle, the style not so relaxed. But this is undoubtedly distinguished and, with good transfers of well-balanced recording from the late 1970s, this is competitive at budget price.

Lívia Rév is an artist of refined musicianship and impeccable taste, selfless and unconcerned with display or self-projection. Indeed there are times when she comes too close to understatement. But still these are lovely performances and the recording has great warmth.

Nocturnes Nos. 2 in E flat, Op. 9/2; 5 in F sharp min., Op. 15; 7 in C sharp min.; 8 in D flat, Op. 27/1–2; 9 in B; 10 in A flat, Op. 32/1–2; 12 in G, Op. 37/2; Waltzes Nos. 1 in E flat (Grande Valse brillante), Op. 18; 3 in A min.; 4 in F, Op. 34/2–3; 5 in A flat, Op. 42; 9 in A flat; 10 in E min., Op. 69/1–2; 11 in G flat; 12 in F min.; 13 in D flat Op. 70/1–3.

(M) *** Decca Dig. 430 751-2 [id.]. Vladimir Ashkenazy.

Ashkenazy's selection of waltzes and nocturnes is aptly chosen and felicitously arranged to make a most satisfying programme of two groups in each genre. The *Nocturnes* are mostly reflective and poetically create a magical atmosphere in Ashkenazy's hands. The famous *E flat*, the very beautiful *D flat* and *B major* and the *Sylphides Nocturne in A flat*, Op. 32/2, are highlights. First-class digital sound ensures a welcome for this reissue.

Polonaises Nos. 1–6; 7 (Polonaise-fantaisie); 8–9, 10 (2 versions), *Op. 71; in G min.; B flat; A flat; G sharp min.; B flat min. (Adieu); G flat,* all *Op. posth.; Andante spianato et Grande Polonaise in E flat, Op. 22; Marche funèbre in C min., Op. 72/2* (3 versions).

*** Sony Dig. S2K 53967 [id.]. Cyprien Katsaris.

Cyprien Katsaris provides a fine new survey of the Chopin *Polonaises*, excellently recorded. We know he can sometimes rush his fences, but for the most part there is a strong sense of structure in these readings, a wide range of colour and plenty of flexibility. The *Andante spianato* is gentle and poetic and the posthumously published early works are presented with flair. Katsaris's virtuosity, one need hardly say, is never in doubt; indeed it is often breathtaking. A stimulating set. To tidy up properly, he includes both the autograph and an edited version by Julian Fontana of Op. 71/3 and three different versions of the *Marche funèbre* which the composer never finalized and which exists in a number of differing editions.

Polonaises Nos. 1–16, Op. 26/1–2; Op. 40/1–2; Op. 44; Op. 53; Polonaise-Fantaisie, Op. 61; Op. 71/1–3; Op. Posth./1–6. Albumblatt in E; Allegro de concert, Op. 46; Barcarolle in F sharp, Op. 60; Berceuse in D flat, Op. 57; 2 Bourrées; 3 Nouvelles Etudes; Fugue in A min.; Galop marquis; Tarantelle in A flat, Op. 43; Wiosna (arr. from *Op. 74/2*).

(B) *** Decca Double Analogue/Dig. 452 167-2 (2) [id.]. Vladimir Ashkenazy.

Ashkenazy's performances of the *Polonaises* have been out of the catalogue for some time, but the playing is of the highest calibre and the recording is of Decca's best. The second CD contains some items that are quite short (the piano transcription of Chopin's song *Wiosna* lasts for barely a minute, but it is very fetching). But there are substantial works too: the *Barcarolle* and *Berceuse*, the latter meltingly done, and the *Allegro de Concert* and *Nouvelles Etudes* also show Ashkenazy at his finest. At Double Decca price this pair of CDs is self-recommending.

Polonaises Nos. 1–7.
*** RCA RD 89814 [RCA 5615-2]. Artur Rubinstein.
(N) (M) *** DG 457 711-2 [id.]. Maurizio Pollini.

Master pianist that he was, Rubinstein seems actually to be rethinking and re-creating each piece, even the hackneyed '*Military*' and *A flat* works, at the very moment of performance in this recording, made in Carnegie Hall. His easy majesty and natural sense of spontaneous phrasing give this collection a special place in the catalogue.

Pollini's set is a justifiable candidate for DG's series of 'Legendary Originals'. It offers playing of outstanding mastery as well as subtle poetry, and the DG engineers have made a satisfactory job of the new transfer, although the hardness on top (immediately striking at the opening *C sharp minor Polonaise*) remains something to which the ear must adjust. Nevertheless this is magisterial playing, in some ways more commanding than Rubinstein (and rather more tangibly recorded), though not more memorable.

24 Preludes, Op. 28; Prelude in C sharp min., Op. 45. Andante spianato et Grande polonaise in E flat, Op. 22; Polonaise-fantaisie in A flat, Op. 61.
(N) *** Chandos Dig. CHAN 9597 [id.]. Louis Lortie.

Louis Lortie's expertly recorded account of the *Preludes* is among the best we have had in recent years. He has poetic feeling, character and finesse in equal measure. Not all his interpretative decisions will convince everyone, but on the whole this is enjoyable and distinguished Chopin playing.

24 Preludes, Op. 28; Etudes, Op. 10/4–6; Op. 25/ 1–2; 6 & 12.
**(*) Erato/Warner Dig. 0630 11726-2 [id.]. Moura Lympany.

24 Preludes, Op. 28; Preludes Nos. 25–26; Barcarolle, Op. 60; Polonaise No. 6 in A flat, Op. 53; Scherzo No. 2 in B flat min., Op. 31.
(M) **(*) DG 415 836-2 [id.]. Martha Argerich.

24 Preludes, Op. 28; Preludes Nos. 25–26; Berceuse, Op. 57; Fantasy in F min., Op. 4.
*** Hyperion Dig. CDA 66324 [id.]. Lívia Rév.

24 Preludes, Op. 28; Preludes Nos. 25–26; Scherzi Nos. 1–4; Waltzes Nos. 1–19.
(N) (B) *** Decca Double 460 991-2 (2) [id.]. Vladimir Ashkenazy.

The *Preludes* show Martha Argerich at her finest, spontaneous and inspirational, though her moments of impetuosity may not appeal to all tastes. But her instinct is sure, with many poetic, individual touches. The other pieces are splendidly played.

Lívia Rév's playing has an unforced naturalness that is most persuasive. She is an artist to her fingertips and, though she may not have the outsize musical personality of some great pianists, she does not have the outsize ego either. She includes not only the extra *Preludes*, but two other substantial pieces as well.

Dame Moura Lympany seldom disappoints on record. Hers may not be the most dazzling version of the Op. 28 *Preludes*, but she is often technically impressive and her feeling for keyboard colour is matched by the natural spontaneity of her rubato. She plays the whole set as an ongoing sequence and then adds a baker's halfdozen hand-selected *Etudes* for good measure in which her pedalling covers the not always quite precise articulation (in Op. 25/12, for instance). The piano recording is truthful, warm rather than brilliant.

This Duo represents splendid value. Ashkenazy's 1979 set of the *Preludes* combines drama and power with finesse and much poetic delicacy when called for. The *Waltzes* were recorded over the best part of a decade (1977–85) but despite the time-span, the sound is expertly matched by the engineers. There is an impressive feeling for line throughout, an ability to make each *Waltz* seem spontaneous and yet as carefully wrought as a tone-poem. The *Scherzi* have characteristic panache, the playing imbued with imaginative insights and spontaneity. Again excellent recording.

Preludes, Op. 28, Nos. 1–11; 14–16; 20 & 23.
(M) ** Nimbus Dig. NI 8810 [id.]. Ferruccio Busoni (piano) – BACH: *Chaconne;* LISZT: *Etudes d'exécution transcendante* etc. ***

There is no reason to believe that Busoni's Duo-Art piano-roll recordings (from 1923) do not project his Chopin manner truthfully, and he proves no stylist in this music. Indeed much of his playing, if strong in character, is heavy going. The opening *C major Etude* is gabbled, and the famous *E minor* is quite wilful, while *No. 9 in E major*, played sombrely, hardly sounds like Chopin at all. *No. 7 in A* bounces along, and in the *D flat major* (No. 15) the control of rubato is unconvincing. *No. 20 in C minor* opens very stolidly indeed, but the closing *F major* (No. 23), recorded four years after the rest of the sequence, brings a much lighter touch. Excellent sound.

Scherzos Nos. 1–4.
(N) ** DG 439 947-2. Ivo Pogorelich.

Scherzos Nos. 1–4; Introduction and variations on a German air; Variations on 'La ci darem la mano', Op. 2.

**(*) Hyperion Dig. CDA 66514 [id.]. Nikolai Demidenko.

Scherzos Nos. 1–4; Polonaise-fantaisie, Op. 61.
(M) *** Ph. (IMS) Dig. 442 407-2. Claudio Arrau.

Arrau's last recording of the four *Scherzi* was made in Munich, just after the artist's eightieth birthday. There is little sign of age, even if he would have produced a greater weight of sonority at the height of his powers. However, these accounts are full of wise and thoughtful perceptions and remarkable pianism, recorded with great presence and clarity. The Philips engineers seem to produce piano quality of exceptional realism. However, this is short measure (55 minutes).

Nikolai Demidenko plays with magisterial keyboard authority and command of colour. There are narcissistic and idiosyncratic touches to which not all listeners will respond; all the same, there is still much that will (and does) give pleasure, but this artist does not offer the 100 per cent Chopin we get, for instance, from Rubinstein or Ashkenazy.

As pianism, Pogorelich's set of the four *Scherzi* is quite dazzling in its delicacy, command of keyboard colour, dynamic range and keyboard authority. Interpretatively it is another matter: no nonsense here about the artist being the servant of the music. Phrases are pulled out of shape in the most egotistic and grotesque fashion. Superb recording though DG really have a nerve to ask full price for a mere 41 minutes.

Piano sonatas Nos. 1 in C min., Op. 4; 2 in B flat min. (Funeral march), Op. 35; 3 in B min., Op. 58.
(M) *** Decca 448 123-2. Vladimir Ashkenazy.
*** Sony Dig. SK 48483 [id.]. Cyprien Katsaris.

Piano sonatas Nos. 1–3; Etudes, Op. 10/6; Op. 25/3, 4, 10 & 11; Mazurkas, Op. 17/1–4.
(B) *** Virgin Classics Dig. Double VBD 5 61618 (2) [id.]. Leif Ove Andsnes.

The *C minor Sonata*, Op. 4, is a comparative rarity; it comes from 1827 and is not deeply characteristic; it is of greater interest to students of Chopin's style and budding pianists than to the wider musical public. Ashkenazy's account (like the finest of its rivals) enjoys classic status, and it is certainly well recorded, with very vivid sound. The *Third (B minor) Sonata* is almost as distinguished and is certainly memorable. Some might not like the accelerando treatment of the finale, but it is undoubtedly exciting. The recording throughout is well up to the high standard set by this series.

The young Norwegian pianist, Leif Ove Andsnes, has the advantage of state-of-the-art piano-sound and his recital comes in a slim, two-for-the-price-of-one CD pack. As such it is splendid value. Andsnes proves as idiomatic an interpreter of Chopin as he has done of Grieg. He also makes out a very good case for the early *C minor Sonata*, Op. 4, which is less well represented on disc and which he plays with real conviction and flair. The other pieces generally come off well and collectors can invest in this set with complete confidence.

Cyprien Katsaris gives highly characterized and well-thought-out readings of all three *Sonatas* and he is often challenging and thought-provoking. Ultimately, however, though less outwardly virtuosic, both Ashkenazy and Leif Ove Andsnes are more musically satisfying.

Piano sonata No. 2 in B flat min., Op. 35.
(***) Testament mono SBT 1089 [id.]. Emil Gilels – MOZART: *Sonata No. 17;* SHOSTAKOVICH: *Preludes and fugues Nos. 1, 5 & 24.* (***)

The *B flat minor Sonata* was recorded in New York and first appeared in 1984. The present reissue is more than welcome. The passage of time has not dimmed its classic status or its poetic intensity and, although some allowances have to be made for the recorded sound, they are few. Performances of this stature are rare indeed.

Piano sonatas Nos. 2 in B flat min. (Funeral march), Op. 35; 3 in B min., Op. 58.
*** DG Dig. 415 346-2 [id.]. Maurizio Pollini.
*** Sony MK 76242 [MK 37280]. Murray Perahia.

Piano sonatas Nos. 2 (Funeral march); 3 in B min., Op. 58; Fantaisie in F min., Op. 49.
*** RCA RD 89812 [RCA 5616-2-RC]. Artur Rubinstein.

Rubinstein's readings of the two finest *Sonatas* are unsurpassed, with a poetic impulse that springs directly from the music and a control of rubato to bring many moments of magic. The sound is improved, too, though Pollini gains in this respect.

Pollini's performances are enormously commanding; his mastery of mood and structure gives these much-played *Sonatas* added stature. The slow movement of Op. 35 has tremendous drama and atmosphere, so that the contrast of the magical central section is all the more telling. Both works are played with great distinction, but the balance is just a shade close.

Murray Perahia's technique is remarkable, but it is so natural to the player that he never uses it for mere display; always there is an underlying sense of structural purpose. The dry, unrushed account of the finale of the *B flat Sonata* is typical of Perahia's freshness, and the only pity is that the recording of the piano is rather clattery and close.

Piano sonata No. 3 in B min., Op. 58.
(B) ** EMI forte CZS5 69527-2 (2) [CDFB 68664]. Anievas – LISZT: *Sonata* *** (with RACHMANINOV: *24 Preludes* etc. **(*))

Agustin Anievas gives a strong if not absolutely

distinctive performance of the lesser-known *B minor Sonata*. However, the slow movement has the same thoughtfulness and sensitivity that distinguish his performance of the Liszt *Sonata*, and the bravura of the finale is striking. Good recording. If the couplings are suitable, this is worth considering.

Piano sonata No. 3 in B min., Op. 58; Barcarolle, Op. 60; Fantaisie-impromptu, Op. 66; Impromptus Nos. 1–3, Opp. 29, 36 & 51.
*** Chandos Dig. CHAN 9175 [id.]. Howard Shelley.

An outstanding Chopin recital from Howard Shelley whose interpretative powers continue to grow in stature. His playing has poetic feeling and ardent but well-controlled temperament. Very good sound.

Piano sonata No. 3 in B min., Op. 58; Mazurkas, in A min., Op. 17/4; in B flat min., Op. 24/4; in D flat, Op. 30/3; in D, Op. 33/2; in G; in C sharp min., Op. 50/ 1 & 3; in C, Op. 56/2; in F sharp min., Op. 59/3; in B; in F min.; in C sharp min., Op. 63/1–3; in F min., Op. 68/4.
*** RCA Dig. 09026 62542-2 [id.]. Evgeny Kissin.

Evgeny Kissin plays not only with an effortless mastery but with a naturalness and freshness that silence criticism. His sense of poetry and his idiomatic rubato are combined with impressive technical address and impeccable taste.

Waltzes Nos. 1–14.
*** RCA RD 89564 [RCD1-5492]. Artur Rubinstein.

Waltzes Nos. 1–14; Barcarolle, Op. 60; Mazurka in C sharp min., Op. 50/3; Nocturne in D flat, Op. 27/2.
(N) ❁ (M) (***) EMI mono CDM5 66904-2 [CDM 66956]. Dinu Lipatti.

Waltzes Nos. 1–17; Polonaises: in G min.; in B flat, Op. posth.
(BB) *** ASV Dig. CDQS 6149 [(M) id.]. Allan Schiller.

Lipatti's classic performances were recorded by Walter Legge in the rather dry acoustic of a Swiss Radio studio at Geneva in the last year of Lipatti's short life, and with each LP reincarnation they seem to have grown in wisdom and subtlety. The reputation of these meticulous performances is fully deserved, and they are rightly reissued as part of EMI's 'Great Recordings of the Century' series.

Rubinstein's performances have a chiselled perfection, suggesting the metaphor of finely cut and polished diamonds, emphasized by the crystal-clear quality of the RCA recording. The digital remastering has softened the edges of the sound-image, and there is an illusion of added warmth.

Allan Schiller's playing of the *Waltzes* is always musical and often very sensitive, though there are one or two in which he could have allowed his imagination freer rein. Very good recording quality. Not a first recommendation when artists like Rubinstein and Lipatti are around, but well worth its modest asking price.

RECITAL COLLECTIONS

Andante spianato et Grande polonaise brillante, Op. 22; Ballades Nos. 1, Op. 23; 4, Op. 52; Barcarolle, Op. 60; Etudes: in G flat, Op. 10/5; in C sharp min., Op. 25/7; Polonaise-fantaisie, Op. 61; Waltz in A flat, Op. 69/1.
(M) *** RCA GD 87752 [7752-2-RG]. Vladimir Horowitz.

All these performances derive from live recitals. The performances are fabulous; to the end of his career Horowitz's technique was transcendental and his insights remarkable. There is much excitement – but even more that is unforgettably poetic, and not a bar is predictable. With the sound so realistic, his presence is very tangible.

'*Favourite piano works*': *Ballades Nos. 1 in G min., Op. 23; 3 in A flat, Op. 47; Barcarolle, Op. 60; Etudes: in E; in G flat (Black keys); in C min. (Revolutionary), Op. 10/3, 5 & 12; in A min. (Winter wind), Op. 25/11; Fantaisie-impromptu, Op. 66; Mazurkas: in B flat, Op. 7/1; in D, Op. 33/1; Nocturnes: in E flat, Op. 9/2; in F sharp min., Op. 15/2; in B, Op. 32/1; in F min., Op. 55/ 1; Polonaises: in A (Military), Op. 40/1; in A flat, Op. 53; Preludes: in D flat (Raindrop), Op. 28/ 15; in C sharp min., Op. 45; Scherzos Nos. 1 in B flat min., Op. 31; 3 in C sharp min., Op. 39; Waltzes: in E flat (Grande valse brillante), Op. 18; in A min., Op. 34/2; in D flat (Minute); in C sharp min., Op. 64/1-2; in A flat, Op. 69/1; in B min., Op. 69/2; in G flat, Op. 70/1.*
(B) *** Decca Double 444 830-2 (2) [id.]. Vladimir Ashkenazy.

Most music-lovers would count themselves lucky to attend a recital offering the above programme, as effectively laid out as it is on these two discs and with a total playing time of 130 minutes. The first CD, which is an all-digital programme, opens commandingly with the *Grande valse brillante* and closes with the *Polonaise in A flat*; the second (an analogue collection, but of excellent technical quality) begins with the *A flat Ballade* and ends with the *Scherzo in C sharp minor*. Overall the recordings date from between 1972 and 1984. The two discs are offered for the price of one within a standard-width jewel case, centrally hinged.

Ballade No. 1 in G min., Op. 23; Barcarolle, Op. 60; Fantaisie-impromptu, Op. 66; Mazurkas: in B flat, Op. 7/1; in D, Op. 33/2; Nocturnes: in E flat, Op. 9/2; in F sharp, Op. 15/2; in D flat, Op. 27/2; in G min., Op. 37/1; Polonaises: in A (Military), Op. 40/1; in A flat, Op. 53; Waltzes: in A flat, Op.

34/1; in D flat (Minute); in C sharp min., Op. 64/1–2.
(M) *** RCA GD 87725 [Basic 100 09026 61717-2]. Artur Rubinstein.

An outstanding mid-priced recital – there is no more distinguished miscellaneous Chopin collection in the catalogue – with 14 contrasted pieces, well programmed. The recording is surprisingly consistent and Rubinstein's inimitable touch gives great pleasure. Particularly memorable is the *G minor Ballade*, coaxing and dazzling by turns.

Ballade No. 1 in G min.; Berceuse in D flat; Etudes, Op. 10/1, 5, 6, & 12 (Revolutionary); Impromptu No. 1 in A flat, Op. 29; Mazurkas: in B flat, Op. 7/1; in C, Op. 67/3; in A min., Op. 68/2; in A flat, Op. posth.; Polonaise No. 6 in A flat, Op. 53; Scherzos No. 3 in C sharp min.; 4 in E, Op. 54; Waltzes Nos. 3 in A min., Op. 34/2; 14 in E min., Op. posth.
(B) **(*) DG Classikon 439 406-2 [(M) id. import]. Tamás Vásáry.

An excellent bargain recital, compiled for DG's Classikon label from Vásáry's mid-1960s recordings. The layout is attractive, opening poetically with the *G minor Ballade* and *Berceuse*, ranging through the *Waltzes*, *Etudes*, *Scherzos* (very well done) and *Mazurkas*, and ending with the *A flat Polonaise*. But why no *Nocturnes*? The sound is a fraction dry but firm and believable. The documentation – which begins on the front of the liner-leaflet – is impressive.

'*Favourites*': *Ballade No. 1 in G min., Op. 23; Fantaisie-impromptu, Op. 66; Mazurkas: in B flat, Op. 7/1; in D, Op. 33/2; Nocturnes: in E flat, Op. 9/2; in F sharp, Op. 15/2; in B, Op. 32/1; Polonaise in A flat, Op. 53; Scherzo in B flat min., Op. 31; Waltzes: in E flat (Grande valse brillante), Op. 18; in A min., Op. 34/2; in A flat; B min., Op. 69/1–2; in G flat, Op. 70/1.*
(M) *** Penguin Classics Decca Dig. 460 614-2 [id.]. Vladimir Ashkenazy.

On Penguin Classics, another attractive recital, with many favourites, played with Ashkenazy's customary poetic flair and easy brilliance. The digital recordings were made at various times during the early 1980s but match surprisingly well: the sound has striking realism and presence. The special note is by Kazuo Ishiguro, author of *The Remains of the Day*. But the Decca Double above is even more enticing.

Ballade No. 1 in G min., Op. 23; Mazurkas Nos. 19 in B min., 20 in D flat, Op. 30/2–3; 22 in G sharp min., 25 in B min., Op. 33/1 and 4; 34 in C, Op. 56/2; 43 in G min., 45 in A min., Op. 67/2 and 4; 46 in C; 47 in A min., 49 in F min., Op. 68/1–2 and 4; Prelude No. 25 in C sharp min., Op. 45; Scherzo No. 2 in B flat min., Op. 31.
**(*) DG (IMS) 413 449-2 [id.]. Arturo Benedetti Michelangeli.

Although this recital somehow does not quite add up as a whole, the performances are highly distinguished. Michelangeli's individuality comes out especially in the *Ballade* and is again felt in the *Mazurkas*, which show a wide range of mood and dynamic. The *Scherzo* is extremely brilliant, yet without any suggestion of superficiality. The piano tone is real and lifelike.

Ballade No. 3 in A flat, Op. 47; Barcarolle in F sharp, Op. 60; Fantaisie in F min., Op. 49; Fantaisie-impromptu, Op. 66; Nocturnes Nos. 2 in E flat, Op. 9/2; 5 in F sharp, Op. 15/2; Prelude in D flat, Op. 28/15; Waltzes Nos. 7 in C sharp min., Op. 64/2; 9 in A flat, Op. 69/1.
(M) *** Ph. (IMS) 420 655-2. Claudio Arrau.

A fine recital, showing both poetry and the thoughtful seriousness which distinguishes Arrau's Chopin, which is West rather than East European in spirit. The CD is admirably transferred.

Ballade No. 4 in F min., Op. 54; Barcarolle, Op. 60; Nocturne in C min., Op. 48/1; Polonaise-fantaisie in A flat, Op. 61; Scherzo No. 4 in E, Op. 54; Piano sonata No. 3 in B min., Op. 58.
(B) *** EMI Debut CDZ5 69701-2. Nelson Goerner.

A valuable release in the welcome EMI Debut series. Nelson Goerner, still in his twenties, comes from Argentina and is a pianist of enormous talent and flair. This is playing of strong personality and poetic feeling. In every way a distinguished recital, and very well recorded too.

Ballade No. 4 in F min., Op. 52; Berceuse, Op. 57; Etudes, Opp. 10/3, 8 & 9; 25/1–3; Fantaisie in F min., Op. 49; Mazurka in A min., Op. 68/2; Nocturnes in E flat, Op. 9/2; D flat, Op. 27/2; Polonaise in A, Op. 40/1; A flat, Op. 53; Waltzes in A flat, Op. 42; E min., Op. posth.
(**(*)) Testament mono SBT 1030 [id.]. Solomon.

Although he was thought of primarily as a master of the central Viennese repertoire (and particularly Beethoven) rather than a Chopin interpreter, this anthology affords ample proof of Solomon's power to distil magic in pretty well whatever composer he touched. Most of these 78 recordings were made between 1942 and 1946; the F minor *Fantaisie* is pre-war (1932), a wonderfully searching account, and the sheer delicacy and poetry of the playing shine through the often frail recorded sound. Good transfers.

Ballade No. 4 in F min., Op. 52; Fantaisie in F min., Op. 49; Mazurkas: in G; in A flat; in C sharp min., Op. 50/1–3; Nocturnes: in D flat, Op.

27/2; in E, Op. 62/2; Polonaise in A flat, Op. 53; Scherzo No. 4 in E, Op. 54; Waltz in C sharp min., Op. 64/2.
(M) *** Van. Dig. 99122 [id.]. Nikolai Lugansky.

Nikolai Lugansky, a pupil of Tatiana Nikolaieva, won first prize at the 1994 Tchaikovsky Competition. His playing is selfless, full of character and unfailingly musical throughout this recital. There is nothing ostentatious or in the least sensational about him; he is a refined and natural artist whose playing gives much pleasure and at its best is touched by distinction.

Etudes: in G flat, Op. 10/5; in G sharp min.; in C sharp min., Op. 25/6–7; 3 Ecossaises, Op. posth. 72/3; Fantasy in F min., Op. 49; Impromptu in A flat, Op. 29; Sonata No. 3 in B min., Op. 58; Waltzes: in A flat; A min., Op. 34/1–2; in E min, Op. posth.
(N) *** DG Dig. 453 456-2 [id.]. Mikhail Pletnev.

This Chopin recital marked Mikhail Pletnev's debut on the DG label as a pianist. Opening with the great *F minor Fantasy* and closing with the *B Minor Sonata*, both superbly done, Pletnev's well-planned recital has all the hallmarks of a live recital, notably an electrical spontaneity plus the technical advantage of studio recording, for the piano image is very real and vivid. As piano-playing, it is almost in a league of its own. As always with this artist, there is marvellous articulation, subtlety of voicing and tonal finesse. At times, in the *A minor Waltz*, for example, his tone can be almost veiled and disembodied. Such is his command of tonal colour elsewhere that one is scarcely aware of the piano's hammers even in fortissimo passages. But interpretatively things are less straightforward and he is often wilful. His rubato in the *B minor Sonata* is at times intrusive. The *G flat* and *G sharp minor Etudes* are dazzling, as is the famous *E minor Waltz* (written when the composer was 20) and the *Ecossaises*, which are even earlier, are deliciously frothy. Yet the *C sharp minor Etude* takes the listener into a wholly different world and is very touching, as is the slow movement of the *sonata*. For all one's reservations about the personal element, this is very distinguished playing indeed.

Fantaisie in F min., Op. 49; Nocturnes in C sharp min., Op. 27/1; in D flat, Op. 27/2; in A flat, Op. 32/2 ; Polonaise in F sharp min., Op. 44; Scherzo No. 2 in B flat min., Op. 31; Waltzes: in A flat, Op. 34/1; in A min., Op. 34/2; in A flat, Op. 42.
❀ *** RCA Dig. 09026 60445-2 [id.]. Evgeny Kissin.

Evgeny Kissin's Chopin anthology comes from a Carnegie Hall recital given early in 1993 when he was still only 21. His playing remains remarkably unaffected and, in the *F minor Fantasy* for example, touchingly direct. His virtuosity and brilliance are always harnessed to musical ends and there is total dedication to Chopin and no indulgence in the narcissistic idiosyncrasies that at times have afflicted such young talents as Demidenko and Pogorelich. Chopin playing of real quality and well recorded, though the sound is a bit thick in the bass.

Mazurkas in A min, A flat, F sharp min, Op. 59/1–3; Nocturne in F, Op. 15/1; Polonaise in A flat, Op. 53; Scherzo No. 3 in C sharp min., Op. 39; Sonata No. 3 in B min. Op. 58.
(N) ** EMI CDC5 56805-2 [id.]. Martha Argerich.

Argerich's recital is called '*The Legendary 1965 Recording*' and carries a fetching photo of the then young artist. It was made at the Abbey Road Studios in June of that year, just before Argerich won the Warsaw Competition and was snapped up by Deutsche Grammophon. Hence EMI were never able to issue it for contractual reasons. There are numerous felicities in the *Mazurkas* and the *Nocturne* but – despite the producer Suvi Raj Grubb's assertion to the contrary – Argerich went on to make a finer account of the *B minor Sonata* for DG. Grubb's assertion (taken from his autobiography) is reproduced in the notes, which otherwise offer no information whatsoever about the composer or the repertoire. The sound is surprisingly shallow and hard.

Cilea, Francesco (1866–1950)

Adriana Lecouvreur (complete).
*** Decca (IMS) Dig. 425 815-2 (2) [id.]. Sutherland, Bergonzi, Nucci, d'Artegna, Ciurca, Welsh Nat. Op. Ch. & O, Bonynge.
(M) **(*) Decca IMS 430 256-2 (2) [id.]. Tebaldi, Simionato, Del Monaco, Fioravanti, St Cecilia, Rome, Ac. Ch. & O, Capuana.

Sutherland's performance in the role of a great tragic actress could not be warmer-hearted. She impresses with her richness and opulence in the biggest test, the aria *Io son l'umile ancella*, an actress's credo, and her formidable performance is warmly backed up by the other principals, and equally by Richard Bonynge's conducting, not just warmly expressive amid the wealth of rich tunes, but light and sparkling where needed, easily idiomatic.

Tebaldi's consistently rich singing misses some of the flamboyance of Adriana's personality but in her characterization both *Io son l'umile ancella* and *Poveri fiori* are lyrically very beautiful. One wishes that Del Monaco had been as reliable as Tebaldi but, alas, there are some coarse moments among the fine, plangent top notes. Simionato is a little more variable than usual but a tower of strength nevertheless. The recording is outstanding for its time (early 1960s), brilliant and atmospheric.

L'arlesiana (complete).
(M) ** EMI CMS5 66762-3 (2). Elena Zilio, Péter Kelen, Maria Spacagna, Barry Anderson, Hungarian State Ch. & O, Charles Rosekrans.

As an opera story the oddity of *L'arlesiana* is that the girl from Arles herself, who wreaks such havoc on the life of the innocent Federico, is never seen or heard. The principal female role is for Federico's mother, Rosa, warmly sung in this performance by Elena Zilio, and Barry Anderson is equally strong and firm in the role of Baldassare, the old shepherd who acts as the understanding adviser to all the others. The role of the hero, Federico, originally created by the young Caruso, is taken by Péter Kelen, a tenor inclined to overdo the histrionics, often using his tenor with restraint, as in the most celebrated aria, *E la solita storia*, but then indulging in excessively emotional outbursts. The conductor, Charles Rosekrans, brings out the warmth of the lyricism, but the dramatic thrust is not always strong enough. A useful stop-gap at mid-price.

Cimarosa, Domenico (1749–1801)

Requiem (rev. Negri).
(N) (B) *** Ph. Virtuoso 422 489-2. Ameling, Finnila, Van Vrooman, Widmer, Montreux Fest. Ch., Lausanne CO, Negri.

The choral writing in Cimarosa's *Requiem* is most assured, whether in the big contrapuntal numbers or in the more homophonic passages with solo interpolations, and the Montreux Festival Chorus conveys a feeling of spacious eloquence. It is a pity that the recording is too reverberant to produce an incisive edge to the choral sound; its warm atmosphere, however, adds to the feeling of weight and serenity. The soloists are very good, notably Elly Ameling and Kurt Widmer. Vittorio Negri secures excellent playing from the Lausanne orchestra and the CD transfer enhances the 1969 recording, which does not seem too dated. A recommendable bargain reissue.

Il maestro di cappella (complete).
(M) *** Decca 433 036-2 (2). Fernando Corena, ROHCG O, Argeo Quadri – DONIZETTI: *Don Pasquale*. ***

Corena's classic assumption of the role of incompetent Kapellmeister has been out of the catalogue for too long. Corena shows complete mastery of the buffo bass style, and he is so little troubled by the florid passages that he can relax in the good humour. The vintage 1960 recording is clear and atmospheric, with the directional effects naturally conveyed.

Clarke, Rebecca (1886–1979)

(i) *Piano trio*; (ii) *Viola sonata*.
✿ *** ASV Dig. CDDCA 932 [id.]. Martin Roscoe, with (i) Andrew Watkinson, David Waterman; (ii) Garfield Jackson – BEACH: *Piano quintet*. ***

Born and educated in Britain, Rebecca Clarke was a frequent visitor to the United States and lived there permanently from the Second World War onwards. She played the viola herself, and the bitingly romantic *Sonata*, superbly written for the instrument, is here given a warm and purposeful performance. The *Piano trio* of two years later (1921) is, if anything, even more striking, with clean-cut, thrusting themes bringing echoes of Bartók and Bloch which never submerge Clarke's individual voice. The performances by Roscoe with members of the Endellion Quartet are masterly, with full-bodied, well-balanced recording.

Clemens non Papa, Jacob
(*c*. 1510/15–*c*. 1555/6)

Missa Pastores quidnam vidistis; Motets: *Pastores quidnam vidistis; Ego flos campi; Pater peccavi; Tribulationes civitatum.*
✿ *** Gimell/Ph. Dig. 454 913-2 [id.]. Tallis Scholars, Peter Phillips.

This admirable disc serves as an introduction to the music of Jacob Clement or Clemens non Papa (who was jokingly known as Clemens-not-the-Pope, so as to distinguish him from either Pope Clement VII or the Flemish poet, Jacobus Papa). The beauty of line and richness of texture in the masterly *Missa Pastores quidnam vidistis* are unforgettable in this superb performance by the Tallis Scholars. The programme opens with the parody motet associated with the Mass, which has a glorious eloquence. Of the other motets, *Pater peccavi*, solemnly rich-textured, is especially memorable; but the whole programme is designed to reveal to twentieth-century ears another name hitherto known only to scholars. The recording is uncannily real and superbly balanced. It was made in the ideal acoustics of the Church of St Peter and St Paul, Salle, Norfolk.

Clementi, Muzio (1752–1832)

(i) *Piano concerto in C. Symphonies: in B flat & D, Op. 18; Nos. 1 in C; 2 in D; 3 (Great National) in G; 4 in D; Minuetto pastorale; Overtures in C & D.*
(M) ** ASV Dig. CDDCS 322 (3) [id.]. (i) Pietro Spada; Philh. O, Francesco D'Avalos.

Six of Clementi's 20 symphonies survive, and these are here made available thanks to the researches of Pietro Spada. The four numbered works are all scored for much larger forces than the Op. 18 set and even include trombones. Their musical content explains Clementi's high reputation in his lifetime as a composer for the orchestra, not just the piano. If the *Great National Symphony* is the most immediately striking, with *God save the King* ingeniously worked into the third movement so that its presence does not emerge until the very end, the other works are all boldly individual. The *Fourth* is a remarkably powerful symphonic statement which brings some striking modulations, and there is some unexpected chromatic writing (unexpected, that is, to those who are not familiar with the famous set of the piano sonatas that Horowitz recorded). Moreover Clementi's use of the orchestra is often very imaginative, though his indebtedness to the Haydn of the *London Symphonies* is very striking.

Symphonies: No. 1 in C; in B flat and D, Op. 18/1–2 (1787).
*** Chandos Dig. CHAN 9234 [id.]. LMP, Matthias Bamert.

Bamert's performances are on a chamber scale and are refreshingly alive and polished. They are given top-class Chandos sound. If you want just one CD of Clementi symphonies, this is the one to have, and indeed the music here is rather engaging.

Symphonies Nos. 1 in C; 2 in D; 3 in G (Great National); 4 in D.
(B) *** Erato/Warner Ultima 3984 21039-2 (2) [(M) id. import]. Philh. O, Claudio Scimone.

The performances by Claudio Scimone and the Philharmonia Orchestra are strong and sympathetic, and the recording (made in London's Henry Wood Hall in 1978) is full, resonant and natural, bringing weight as well as freshness. Now that Erato have accommodated these so economically both in price and in space on the shelf, they deserve a warm recommendation.

Piano sonatas in G min., Op. 7/3; in F min., Op. 13/6; in B flat, Op. 24/2; in F sharp min.; in D; Op. 25/5–6.
**(*) D & J Athene Dig. ATH CD 4 [id.]. Peter Katin.

Peter Katin plays a square piano, built by Clementi and Company in 1832 (the year of the composer's death), which has subsequently been restored. So the sounds he creates are as authentic as one could find. The work which comes off best in his recital is the *G minor Sonata*, Op. 7/3, which sounds so effective on the fortepiano. The slow movement of the *F sharp minor*, Op. 25/5, sounds utterly different here from Maria Tipo's version, the playing altogether more direct, seeking no romantic overtones; generally, Peter Katin's approach is plainspun to suit the somewhat dry sonority of his instrument. He is very realistically recorded.

Piano sonatas: in F min., Op. 13/6; in B flat, Op. 24/2; in F sharp min., Op. 25/5; in G, Op. 37/1.
*** Accent ACC 67911D [id.]. Jos van Immerseel (fortepiano).

Very fleet and brilliant performances from Jos van Immerseel. The slow movements of these sonatas have some considerable expressive depth, and the outer ones are full of a brilliance that is well served by this eminently skilful and excellent artist.

Piano sonatas: in F min., Op. 14/3; in F sharp min., Op. 26/2; in C (quasi concerto), Op. 33/3; in G min., Op. 34/2; Rondo (from Sonata, Op. 47/2).
(M) *** RCA GD 87753 [7753-2-RC]. Vladimir Horowitz (piano).

These electrifying performances from the 1950s show a Clementi of greater substance and sterner mettle than the composer we thought we knew and, though the piano sound is shallow by the side of most up-to-date recordings, the quality is a great improvement upon either of the vinyl transfers with which we have compared it.

Piano sonatas: in B flat, Op. 24/2; in G; in F sharp min., Op. 25/2 & 5; in D, Op. 37/2; 6 Progressive sonatinas, Op. 36.
(BB) *** Naxos Dig. 8.550452 [id.]. Balázs Szokolay.

Balázs Szokolay made a strong impression at the Leeds Piano Competition some years back and we have much admired his Naxos records of some of the Grieg *Lyric pieces* (see below). This Clementi anthology is hardly less successful and his playing inspires enthusiasm. Let us hope he will go on to record some more of this master's underrated keyboard work. Decent recording; excellent value.

Coates, Eric (1886–1958)

Ballad; By the sleepy lagoon; London suite; The Three Bears (phantasy); *The Three Elizabeths* (suite).
(M) *** ASV Dig. CDWHL 2053. East of England O, Malcolm Nabarro.

Nabarro has the full measure of Coates's leaping allegros and he plays the famous marches with crisp buoyancy. *The Three Bears* sparkles humorously, as it should; only in *By the sleepy lagoon* does one really miss a richer, more languorous string-texture. Excellent, bright recording, and the price is right.

By the sleepy lagoon; London suite; London again suite; London Bridge march.
(B) *** Millennium UMD 80395. Eric Johnson and his O (with SULLIVAN: *The Gondoliers* etc.: excerpts. **)

Eric Johnson presents all the marches here with proper panache and a nice broadening for the final reprise, and he finds plenty of life in the evocations of *Covent Garden* and *Oxford Street*. But what is the more striking is the degree of romantic expansiveness he brings to the central slow movements of the two *London suites*: *Westminster*, with its famous chimes, and the unexpectedly romantic *Langham Place*. He is helped by an ardent orchestral response and a fullness of string-sound rare in recordings of Coates's music, plus plenty of weight from the brass. Most enjoyable, as are the coupled Sullivan selections.

The Four Centuries: suite; The Jester at the wedding: ballet suite; The 7 Dwarfs.
(M) **(*) ASV Dig. CDWHL 2075 [id.]. East of England O, Malcolm Nabarro.

For their second anthology of music by Eric Coates, the orchestra based in Nottinghamshire (where the composer was born) offer a particularly delectable account of *The Jester at the wedding ballet suite*. *The Four Centuries* is a masterly and engaging pastiche of styles from four different periods, and again it receives a performance of some subtlety, although at times one wishes for a more opulent sound from the violins, and the closing jazzy evocation of the 1930s and 1940s could be more uninhibitedly rumbustious. *The Seven Dwarfs* is an early work (1930), a ballet written for a short-lived London revue.

The Three Elizabeths (suite).
(M) **(*) Mercury 434 330-2 [id.]. London Pops O, Fennell – GRAINGER: *Country gardens* etc. **

Fennell's performance is notable for its spirit and polish: the closing march, *The Youth of Britain*, sounds particularly fresh and alert, while the slow movement is nicely expressive. But the 1965 Mercury recording, made in Watford Town Hall, though fuller and with a more attractive ambience than the coupled Grainger items, still lacks something in expansiveness, though not clarity of detail.

VOCAL MUSIC

Songs: *Always as I close my eyes; At sunset; Bird songs at eventide; Brown eyes I love; Dinder courtship; Doubt; Dreams of London; Green hills o'Somerset; Homeward to you; I heard you singing; I'm lonely; I pitch my lonely caravan; Little lady of the moon; Reuben Ranzo; Song of summer; A song remembered; Stonecracker John; Through all the ages; Today is ours.*
(M) *** ASV Dig. CDWHL 2081. Brian Rayner Cook, Raphael Terroni.

Eric Coates, as well as writing skilful orchestral music, also produced fine Edwardian ballads which in many instances transcended the limitations of the genre, with melodies of genuine refinement and imagination. Most date from earlier in his career, prior to the Second World War. Brian Rayner Cook, with his rich baritone beautifully controlled, is a superb advocate and makes a persuasive case for every one of the 19 songs included in this recital. His immaculate diction is infectiously demonstrated in the opening *Reuben Ranzo* (a would-be sailor/tailor), in which he breezily recalls the spirited projection of another famous singer of this kind of repertoire in the early days of the gramophone, Peter Dawson. The recording is admirably clear.

Colding-Jørgenson, Henrik
(born 1944)

To love music.
** BIS CD 79 [id.]. Danish Nat. RO, Schmidt (with BENTZON: *Feature on René Descartes* **); NORBY: *The Rainbow snake*. ***

At elske musikken ('To love music') falls into two parts: 'To love music with the head' and, secondly, '. . . with the heart'. Its musical language is eclectic and far from inaccessible; indeed, during the course of its 26 minutes there are many moments of beauty. But while it is undeniably imaginative, it is difficult to discern any strong sense of musical purpose and organic growth. One feels that the music could stop or start anywhere and, given the thinness of some of the musical substance, it outstays its welcome. Dedicated playing from the Danish orchestra under Ole Schmidt, and a good analogue recording.

Coleridge-Taylor, Samuel
(1875–1912)

Scenes from The Song of Hiawatha (complete).
(B) *** Decca Dig. 458 591-2 (2). Helen Field, Arthur Davies, Bryn Terfel, WNO Ch. & O, Kenneth Alwyn.

Part One of Coleridge-Taylor's choral trilogy based on Longfellow's epic poem is still regularly performed by choral societies in the north of England. The reasons for the neglect of Parts Two and Three, *The Death of Minnehaha* and *Hiawatha's Departure*, are made only too clear by this complete recording: there is a distinct falling-off in the composer's inspiration, so fresh and spontaneously tuneful in Part One. Indeed, when the main theme of *Hiawatha's Wedding Feast* returns in Part Three with the words 'From his place rose Hiawatha', one realizes how memorable it is, compared with what surrounds it. Of course the choral writing is always pleasingly lyrical and makes enjoyable listening. Part Two has plenty of drama, and towards the end Helen Field has a memorably beautiful solo passage, which she sings radiantly, echoed by the chorus, 'Wahonomin! Wahonomin! Would that I had perished for you.' There is also an almost Wagnerian apotheosis at the actual moment of the Farewell, which is sung and played here with compelling grandiloquence. Kenneth Alwyn directs a freshly spontaneous account and has the advantage of excellent soloists (including an early appearance on CD by Bryn Terfel as Hiawatha, now featured prominently on the front of the reissue), though the Welsh Opera Choir do not seem at home in the idiom. The recording was made in the rather intractable Brangwyn Hall, Swansea, and the engineers have put their microphones fairly close to the performers. The result, while vivid, lacks the glowing ambient effect of the Royal Albert Hall, which would have been a much better venue.

(i) *Hiawatha's wedding feast. The Bamboula* (rhapsodic dance).
(B) *** EMI Eminence Dig. CD-EMX 2276. (i) Rolfe Johnson, Bournemouth Ch.; Bournemouth SO, Alwyn.

Hiawatha's wedding feast blew a fresh breeze through a turgid British Victorian choral tradition. This reissue is first class in every way, and Kenneth Alwyn secures a vigorous and committed contribution from his Bournemouth forces, with Anthony Rolfe Johnson an excellent soloist in the famous *Onaway! Awake, beloved!* The music throughout is delightfully melodious and extremely well written for the voices. *The Bamboula* makes an agreeable if inconsequential encore.

Confrey, Edward (1895–1971)

African suite; Amazonia; Blue tornado; Coaxing the piano; Dizzy fingers; Fourth dimension; Jay walk; Kitten on the keys; Meandering; Moods of a New Yorker (suite); Rhythm venture; Sparkling waters; Stumbling paraphrase; Three little oddities; Wisecracker suite.
(N) *** Marco Polo Dig. 8.223826 [id.]. Eteri Andjaparidze.

The name Edward 'Zez' Confrey will not strike a chord with most readers, but older collectors will surely remember *Kitten on the keys* and perhaps *Dizzy fingers* and *Coaxing the piano* (all dazzlingly played here). Confrey established his international fame as a precocious virtuso pianist/composer in the early 1920s. He had much in common with his British contemporary, Billy Mayerl, and he too (by writing a best-selling book) established a method for 'Novelty piano playing'. His music has a witty charm and is clearly influenced by French impressionism as well as Gershwin and the Scott Joplin rags. The Georgian pianist, Eteri Andjaparidze, gives engagingly sparkling performances of the bravura pieces including the ingenious closing *Fourth dimension*, with its amazingly virtuosic cross-hand accents, and is equally at home in the more relaxed ragtime of *Jay walk*, *Stumbling* and the sauntering gait of *Meandering*. But she also relishes the atmosphere and charm of the gentler pieces among the *Oddities* and the suites (two of the *Moods of a New Yorker* recall the tranquil simplicity of MacDowell's *To a wild rose*). A most entertaining collection given excellent piano recording.

Constantinescu, Paul (1909–63)

The Nativity (Byzantine Christmas oratorio).
**(*) Olympia OCD 402 (2) [id.]. Emelia Petrescu, Martha Kessler, Valentin Teodorian, Helge Bömches, Bucharest Georges Enescu Ch. & PO, Mircea Basarab.

Paul Constantinescu's *Byzantine Christmas oratorio* is an extended work of some quality in three parts: *Annunciation*, *Nativity* and *The Three Magi*. This impressive performance comes from the late 1970s. Constantinescu writes effectively both for the chorus and for solo voices, and his orchestration too is expert. The soloists are excellent (and in different circumstances might well have made names for themselves outside their native country) and the analogue recording is very good indeed. Readers with an interest in the exotic and a touch of enterprise are recommended to investigate this set.

Conus, Julius (1869–1942)

Violin concerto in E min.
(M) *** EMI (SIS) CDM5 66060-2 [id.]. Perlman, Pittsburgh O, Previn – BARTOK: *Violin concerto No. 2;* SINDING: *Suite.* ***
(N) **(*) Chandos Dig. CHAN 9622 [id.]. L. Edwin Csüry, I Musici de Montréal, Yuli Turovsky – DAVIDOV: *Cello concerto No. 2 in A min., Op. 14.* GLAZUNOV: *Piano concerto No. 2.* **(*)

Julius Conus, of French extraction from a family of musicians, wrote his *Violin concerto* in Moscow in 1896–7, a ripely romantic piece in one continuous movement with only a few memorable ideas but with luscious violin writing, while the lyrical theme of the opening movement blossoms persuasively. Here the opening is very commanding and Perlman's first entry quite magical; he shows his supreme mastery in giving the piece new intensity, helped by fine playing from Previn and the Pittsburgh orchestra. The 1979 recording is vivid and, if the violin is very close, Perlman's tone is honeyed; the Pittsburgh hall ensures orchestral weight and provides an attractive background warmth.

This Chandos record brings together prize-winners at the Turovsky Orford Festival and very good they are. The composer Conus is variously transliterated as Konius and Konyus. Csüry is a most musical player and he plays this concerto very sympathetically, even if he is no match for Perlman. Turovsky's Montreal band give him admirable support.

Cooke, Arnold (born 1906)

Clarinet concerto.
*** Hyperion CDA 66031 [id.]. Thea King, NW CO of Seattle, Alun Francis – JACOB: *Mini-concerto;* RAWSTHORNE: *Concerto.* ***

Arnold Cooke's music contains an element of Hindemithian formalism, carefully crafted, but the slow movement of this concerto soars well beyond. Thea King makes a passionate advocate, brilliantly accompanied by the Seattle Orchestra in excellent 1982 analogue sound, faithfully transferred.

Copland, Aaron (1900–90)

Appalachian spring (ballet; complete original version)
*** Koch Dig. 3-7019-2; 2-7019-4 [id.]. Atlantic Sinf., Schenck – BARBER: *Cave of the heart.* ***

This Koch International issue offers a welcome chance to hear a modern digital recording of *Appalachian spring* in its original form for 13 instruments and the bright, upfront recording presents the chamber version in the best possible light. This is a most interesting and stimulating issue.

Appalachian spring (ballet) *suite.*
*** Everest EVC 9003 [id.]. LSO, Walter Susskind – GOULD: *Spirituals* ***; GERSHWIN: *American in Paris.* **(*)
(N) (B) *** DG Classikon 445 129-2 [(M) [id.].import]. LAPO, Bernstein – BARBER: *Adagio for strings.* BERNSTEIN: *Candide overture;* SCHUMAN: *American festival overture.* ***
(M) *** DG Dig. 439 528-2 [431 048-2]. LAPO, Bernstein – BARBER: *Adagio for strings* ***; GERSHWIN: *Rhapsody in blue.* **(*)

Susskind's dramatic and sympathetic reading of what is perhaps Copland's finest orchestral score is most spaciously and vividly recorded. Although it is an English performance, it compares very favourably indeed with the composer's own – see below – and the American-style engineering with wide dynamics adds plenty of drama, but not at the expense of amplitude. With its apt Gould coupling – no less well done – this is an outstanding reissue. It is a pity that it is offered at only slightly less than full price, but it is worth its cost.

Bernstein's DG version of *Appalachian spring* was recorded at a live performance, and the conductor communicates his love for the score in a strong yet richly lyrical reading, and the compulsion of the music-making is obvious. The recording is close but not lacking in atmosphere, and it sounds extremely vivid. It is offered in alternative couplings, a recommendable bargain Classikon compilation of four key twentieth-century American works, or at mid-price, with Bernstein at the piano in his rather less recommendable second recording of Gershwin's *Rhapsody in blue.*

(i) *Appalachian spring* (ballet) *suite; Billy the Kid: ballet suite;* (ii) *Clarinet concerto;* (i) *Danzón Cubano; Fanfare for the common man; John Henry; Letter from home;* (i; iv) *Lincoln portrait;* (iii) *Music for movies;* (i) *Our Town; An Outdoor overture; Quiet city; Rodeo (4 Dance episodes);* (iii) *El Salón México;* (i) *Symphony No. 3;* (v) *Las agachadas.*
(M) *** Sony SM3K 46559 (3) [id.]. (i) LSO; (ii) Benny Goodman, Columbia Symphony Strings; (iii) New Philh. O; (iv) with Henry Fonda; (v) New England Conservatory Ch.; composer.

Sony here offer a comprehensive anthology of the major orchestral works, ballet suites and film scores dating from Copland's vintage period, 1936–48. The composer directs with unrivalled insight throughout. The remastering for CD is done most skilfully, retaining the ambience of the originals, while achieving more refined detail.

(i) *Appalachian spring* (ballet) *suite; Billy the Kid* (ballet) complete; (ii) *Danzón cubano; El salón México.*
(M) *** Mercury 434 301-2 [id.]. (i) LSO; (ii) Minneapolis SO, Antal Dorati.

Dorati pioneered the first stereo recording of the complete *Billy the Kid* ballet, and the 1961 Mercury LP caused a sensation on its first appearance for its precision of detail and brilliance of colour, while the generous acoustics of Watford Town Hall added ambient warmth. The gunshots (track 13) were and remain electrifying, with their clean percussive transients, while the LSO playing combines tremendous vitality and rhythmic power with genuine atmospheric tension. For the CD, earlier (1957) Minneapolis versions of the *Danzón cubano* and *El salón México* have been added. The recording is crisp and clean to suit his approach.

Appalachian spring (ballet): *suite; Billy the Kid* (ballet) *suite; Fanfare for the common man; Rodeo (four dance episodes).*
(BB) **(*) Naxos Dig. 8.550282 [id.]. Slovak RSO (Bratislava), Gunzenhauser.

The Bratislava Orchestra play with such spontaneous enjoyment in *Rodeo* and *Billy the Kid* that one cannot help but respond. Gunzenhauser, a fine conductor of Czech music, is equally at home in Copland's folksy, cowboy idiom and all this music has plenty of colour and atmosphere. If some of the detail in *Appalachian spring* is less sharply etched than with Bernstein, the closing pages are tenderly responsive. The recording is admirably colourful and vivid with a fine hall ambience, and the spectacle of the *Fanfare for the common man* is worth anybody's money. A bargain.

(i) *Appalachian spring;* (ii) *Billy the Kid* (suite); *Rodeo* (suite).
(BB) *** RCA Navigator 74321 21297-2. (i) Boston SO, composer; (ii) Morton Gould and his Orchestra.

Copland's first recording of *Appalachian spring*, recorded in Boston in 1959, has an appealing breadth and warmth of humanity, helped by the Symphony Hall resonance: the Shaker climax is wonderfully expansive. Morton Gould conducts the other two ballets with enormous zest and vitality, and 'his' orchestra play as if their very lives depended on it. The early (1957) stereo is a little dated but remains arrestingly spectacular and the quieter, evocative writing is haunting, distilling a special combination of tender warmth and underlying tension. The *Corral Nocturne* and wistful *Saturday night waltz* in *Rodeo* are especially fine, and here Gould also includes the *Honky-tonky interlude* on an appropriate piano. The closing *Hoe-down* is refreshingly folksy and has great rhythmic energy.

(i) *Appalachian spring* (ballet) *suite;* (ii) *Ceremonial fanfare;* (iii) *Dance symphony; El salón México;* (i) *Fanfare for the common man;* (i; iv) *Lincoln portrait;* (v) *Music for movies;* (vi) *Quiet city;* (iii) *Rodeo: 4 Dance episodes;* (vii) *Old American songs* (excerpts): *Simple gifts; Ching-a-ring-chaw; Long time ago; I bought me a cat; At the river.*
(B) *** Decca Double Analogue/Dig. 448 261-2 (2) [id.]. (i) LAPO, Mehta; (ii) Philip Jones Brass Ens.; (iii) Detroit SO, Dorati; (iv) Gregory Peck; (v) L. Sinf., Elgar Howarth; (vi) ASMF, Marriner; (vii) Marilyn Horne, ECO, Carl Davis.

Mehta's performance of *Appalachian spring* is one of the most distinguished of several fine recordings he made for Decca in the late 1970s, which also included the spectacular *Fanfare for the common man* and the *Lincoln portrait*, with Gregory Peck a comparatively laid-back narrator who speaks Lincoln's prose with dignity and restraint. Dorati's performances of the *Dance symphony*, *El salón México* and *Rodeo* were digitally recorded in 1981. They are notable for their bright, extrovert brilliance, having evidently been chosen for their immediate, cheerful qualities, and the only reservation is that, somewhat surprisingly, Dorati's treatment of jazzy syncopations is rather literal. But as sound this is very impressive, and the performances have much vitality. The evocative opening picture of the *New England Countryside* occupies the same musical world as *Appalachian spring*. Again fine playing from the London Sinfonietta under Elgar Howarth and vivid recording. Marriner's account of *Quiet city* is second to none, but the highlight of the second CD is Marilyn Horne's delightful performances of five *Old American songs*: the rhythmic sparkle of *Ching-a-ring-raw* and the charm of *I bought me a cat* contrasting with the moving simplicity of the closing *At the river*. Excellent value.

Appalachian spring (ballet) *suite;* (i) *Piano concerto. Symphonic ode.*
**(*) Delos Dig. DE 3154 [id.]. (i) Lorin Hollander; Seattle SO, Gerard Schwarz.

The glowing acoustics of the Seattle Opera House smooth some of the abrasiveness away from Lorin Hollander's impressive account of Copland's *Piano concerto* and also filter out some of the glitter from the jazzy piano-writing. Similarly, *Appalachian spring* loses some of the bite in the dance rhythms, although the glowing woodwind detail and the richly expansive closing variations on *A gift to be simple* are more than compensation. The exultantly monumental close of the pungently flamboyant *Symphonic ode* is given similar weight and breadth. The Seattle orchestra plays splendidly throughout and Schwarz is a master of all this repertoire.

(i) *Appalachian spring* (ballet): *suite; Fanfare for the common man; An outdoor overture;* (ii) *3 Latin-American sketches;* (i) *Rodeo (4 Dance episodes);* (ii) *El Salón México.*
(M) *** Sony Theta SMK 60133 [id.]. (i) LSO; (ii) New Philh. O; composer.

This generously filled (79 minutes) CD is drawn from the composer's more comprehensive anthology above. It is eminently recommendable. Copland's own account of *Appalachian spring* is particularly evocative and beautifully recorded.

Appalachian spring (ballet) *suite; Short symphony.*
*** Pro Arte Dig. CDD 140 [id.]. St Paul CO, Russell Davies – IVES: *Symphony No. 3.* ***

On Pro Arte, using a smaller ensemble than is usual, Russell Davies conducts fresh and immediate performances of both the *Short symphony* and the well-known suite from *Appalachian spring*, which was originally conceived for chamber orchestra. The recording is bright and forward to match the performances. An excellent and recommendable anthology.

Appalachian spring (ballet) *suite; The Tender Land* (opera): *suite.*
(M) *** RCA 09026 61505-2 [id.]. Boston SO, composer – GOULD: *Fall River legend* etc. ***

(i) *Appalachian spring* (ballet) *suite; The Tender Land* (excerpts); (ii) *Billy the Kid* (ballet) *suite;* (iii) *El salón México;* (ii) *Fanfare for the common man;* (iii) *Rodeo: Hoe-down.*
(M) *** [RCA Basic 100 09026 68020-2]. (i) Boston SO, composer; (ii) Phd. O, Ormandy; (iii) Boston Pops O, Fiedler.

The composer's first (1959) Boston recording of the *Appalachian spring suite* (also available less expensively, differently coupled – see above) has moments of special resonance, its atmospheric feeling at times quite profound, helped by splendid orchestral playing and the warm Boston acoustic. The suite from *The Tender Land* is also well worth having. We are given the *Love duet* virtually complete, the Party music from Act II and the quintet, *The promise of living* (all, of course, without voices). As can be seen, these two recordings are also available (in the USA only) in RCA's Basic 100 series, more aptly coupled with excellent versions of more of Copland's music.

(i) *Billy the Kid* (ballet suite); (ii) *Piano sonata.*
(M) (***) RCA mono GD 60915 [60915-2]. (i) RCA Victor SO, Bernstein; (ii) Bernstein (piano) – BERNSTEIN: *On the Town: suite* etc. (***)

Bernstein got to know the music of *Billy the Kid* by sitting with the composer and playing the full score on the piano. He also learned the formidable *Sonata* as it was being written in 1941. Both performances are full of nervous energy and must be regarded as definitive.

Billy the Kid: ballet suite and Waltz; Rodeo: 4 Dance episodes.
(B) *** Millennium Universal UMD 80396 [id.]. Utah SO, Maurice Abravanel – GROFE: *Grand Canyon suite.* ***

Abravanel's 1958 pioneering recordings of Copland's *Billy the Kid* and *Rodeo* ballet suites predate Bernstein's versions. The Utah performances are full of character and colour, with the woodwind playing often quite memorable, helped by the warmly atmospheric sound. If the *Gun Battle* in *Billy the Kid* does not quite match the famous Dorati Mercury version in sheer spectacle, and Bernstein achieves greater virtuosity with the NYPO in *Buckaroo holiday* and *Hoedown*, Abravanel's performances are still to be reckoned with and they include as a bonus the engaging *Waltz* from *Billy the Kid*, with its witty bassoon and trombone solos.

Ceremonial fanfare; John Henry (A railroad ballad); Jubilee variations; (i) *Lincoln portrait;* (ii) *Old American songs, set 1; An Outdoor overture; The Tender Land: The promise of living.*
*** Telarc Dig. CD 80117 [id.]. Cincinnati Pops O, Kunzel; (i) with Katharine Hepburn (nar.); (ii) Sherrill Milnes.

Katharine Hepburn's remarkable delivery of Abraham Lincoln's words quite transcends any limitations in Copland's *Lincoln portrait* and makes it an undeniably moving experience, and Kunzel, clearly inspired by the authority of her reading, punctuates the text with orchestral comments of singular power. The shorter pieces are also given splendid life. Sherrill Milnes's highly infectious performance of the first set of *Old American songs* shows a spirited boisterousness that recalls Howard Keel in *Seven Brides for Seven Brothers*. Altogether a collection that is more than the sum of its parts, given superlative Telarc recording, highly spectacular and realistic, yet with natural balance.

Clarinet concerto.
*** RCA Dig. 09026 61350-2. Stoltzman, LSO, Leighton Smith – BERNSTEIN: *Prelude, fugue and riffs.* CORIGLIANO: *Concerto;* STRAVINSKY: *Ebony concerto.* ***
*** Chandos Dig. CHAN 8618 [id.]. Janet Hilton, SNO, Bamert – NIELSEN: *Concerto;* LUTOSLAWSKI: *Dance preludes.* ***
*** ASV Dig. CDDCA 568 [id.]. MacDonald, N. Sinfonia, Bedford – FINZI: *Concerto;* MOURANT: *Pied Piper.* ***

Copland's splendid *Clarinet concerto* is at last coming into its own, on record at least. Stoltzman is effectively cool in the serene opening and catches the work's later quirky jazz elements to perfection; in this he is well matched by Lawrence Leighton Smith and the LSO players, who let their hair down without losing rhythmic sharpness or crispness of ensemble. The finale's flair is exhilarating and, with first-rate RCA recording, this bids to upstage even Benny Goodman in its combination of idiomatic understanding, natural virtuosity and superior sound. Now reissued with Stravinsky's *Ebony concerto* added to the original programme, this CD is even more attractive.

Janet Hilton's performance is softer-grained and has a lighter touch than Stolzman's, yet she finds plenty of sparkle for the finale and her rhythmic felicity is infectious. She is at her very finest, however, in the gloriously serene opening, where her tender poetic line is ravishing.

George MacDonald gives a virtuoso performance, not quite as dramatic and full of flair as that of the dedicatee, Benny Goodman, but in many ways subtler in expression and particularly impressive in the long lyrical paragraphs of the first of the two movements.

(i; ii) *Piano concerto;* (iii) *Dance symphony;* (ii) *Music for the theatre;* (iii) *2 Pieces for string orchestra; Short symphony (Symphony No. 2); Statements; Symphonic ode;* (iv; ii) *Symphony for organ and orchestra.*

(M) *** Sony SM2K 47232 (2) [id.]. (i) Composer (piano); (ii) NYPO, Bernstein; (iii) LSO, composer; (iv) with E. Power Biggs.

This second Sony Copland collection covers early orchestral and concertante music written between 1922 and 1935 and is, if anything, more valuable than the first box. The 1923 *Rondino*, the second of his *Two Pieces for string orchestra*, is the earliest work here. The *Lento* is a totally memorable piece. The *Symphony for organ and orchestra* is a powerful and strikingly innovative work, dating from 1924. It is given an extremely idiomatic and responsive performance by Power Biggs, who is fully sensitive to its atmosphere, and Bernstein balances the overall sounds with great skill and a marvellous feeling for colour. The pungently flamboyant *Symphonic ode*, commissioned by the Boston Symphony, helped the orchestra to celebrate its fiftieth anniversary: it was written between 1927 and 1929. All these performances have a definitive authority combined with total spontaneity of response from the participants which makes them compelling listening, and the recordings – dating from between 1964 and 1967 – are very well engineered, extremely vivid in the excellent CD transfers.

Piano concerto.

(M) *** Van. 08.4029.71 [OVC 4029]. Earl Wild, Symphony of the Air, composer – MENOTTI: *Piano concerto.* **(*)

(M) **(*) Chandos CHAN 6580 [id.]. Gillian Lin, Melbourne SO, John Hopkins – BRITTEN: *Piano concerto.* **(*)

This Vanguard record, with a supreme piano virtuoso providing a glittering account of the piano part, is very recommendable. The 1961 recording is first rate.

Gillian Lin too, is undoubtedly successful in the Copland *Concerto*, bringing out the jazz element in this syncopated music. The 1978 stereo recording is well balanced and realistically transferred to CD.

(i–ii) *Piano concerto; Connotations for orchestra;* (iii) *El salón México;* (ii) *Music for the theatre* (suite).

(M) *** Sony SMK 60177 [id.]. (i) Composer (piano); (ii) NYPO; (iii) (mono) Columbia SO; Bernstein.

The present collection is drawn from the two sets listed above and below – except for *El salón México*, which was Bernstein's earlier mono recording and was made with the Columbia Symphony in 1951. It has great vitality and bite: no one coaxes that sleazy dance-hall rhythm quite like Bernstein. The programme opens with the suite of *Music for the theatre*, with its spaciously atmospheric *Prologue*, unmistakably and uniquely by Copland (few composers have such indelible harmonic fingerprints); the poignant *Interlude*, shared by cor anglais and trumpet, is very reminiscent of *Quiet city*. If you already have Bernstein's disc of the ballet scores, this would be a splendid way to continue an exploration of Copland's music: the opening of the *Piano concerto* is utterly haunting. *Connotations* (which also includes the piano within the orchestra) is less obviously popular in appeal but is undoubtedly magnetic. The present transfers are first class.

(i) *Connotations;* (ii) *Dance panels; Down a country lane;* (i) *Inscape;* (ii) *3 Latin-American sketches; Music for a great city; Orchestral variations; Preamble for a solemn occasion; The Red Pony* (film score).

(M) *(**) Sony SM2K 47236 (2) [id.]. (i) NYPO, Bernstein; (ii) LSO or New Philh. O, composer.

This third Copland box from Sony is something of a disappointment – not the music, which is even rarer than before and of great interest. *The Red Pony* is vintage Copland, and the *Orchestral variations*, though strictly an orchestral version of the *Piano variations* of 1930, make a unique and impressive contribution to Copland's oeuvre. *Connotations* and to a lesser extent *Inscape*, the major work of the composer's final period, are serially orientated. *Dance panels* is an abstract ballet without a narrative line, and *Music for a great city*, with its jazz influences and nocturnal scene, derives from another film-score (*Something Wild*). The performances are all extremely successful, but the CD transfers are over-bright and, for all their vividness of detail, tiring to the ear, particularly the thin violins and the more pungent climaxes of the later works.

Quiet city.

*** Argo 417 818-2 [id.]. ASMF, Marriner – BARBER: *Adagio;* COWELL: *Hymn;* CRESTON: *Rumor;* IVES: *Symphony No. 3.* ***

Marriner's 1976 version is both poetic and evocative, and the playing of the trumpet and cor anglais soloists is of the highest order. The digital remastering has brought added clarity without loss of atmosphere.

Quiet city; (i) *8 Poems of Emily Dickinson.*

*** EMI Dig. CDC5 55358-2 [id.]. (i) Barbara Hendricks; LSO, Tilson Thomas – BARBER: *Adagio for strings*, etc. ***

Tilson Thomas and Barbara Hendricks have between them devised a programme of Copland as well as Barber, with both composers at their most radiantly inspired. This is an intensely beautiful disc, especially *Quiet city*, with solo trumpet and cor anglais (superbly played by Maurice Murphy and Christine Pendrill) creating great atmospheric intensity. The freshness and sharp imagination of the accompaniments are enhanced in support of vocal lines lovingly matched to Dickinson's distinctive poetic style. Radiant singing from

Hendricks, and equally sensuous sounds from the orchestra.

Statements for orchestra.
*** Everest EVC 9039 [id.]. LSO, Sir Eugene Goossens – ANTHEIL: *Symphony No. 4.* **(*)

Statements for orchestra (1934–5), as the bald title suggests, is one of Copland's less expansive works, but its six vignettes, *Militant*, *Cryptic* (hauntingly scored for brass and flute alone), *Dogmatic* (but disconsolate), *Subjective* (an elegiac soliloquy for strings), the witty *Jingo* and the thoughtfully *Prophetic* conclusion, reveal a compression of material and sharpness of ideas that are most stimulating. Goossens's performance is first rate in every way; so is the LSO playing, and the atmospheric (1959) recording sounds hardly dated at all.

Symphony No. 3; Billy the Kid (ballet): *suite.*
** Everest EVC 9040 [id.]. LSO, Copland.

Symphony No. 3; Quiet city.
*** DG Dig. 419 170-2 [id.]. NYPO, Bernstein.

Symphony No. 3; (i) *Symphony for organ and orchestra.*
(M) **(*) Sony SMK 63155 [id.]. (i) E. Power Biggs; NYPO, Bernstein.

Dating from 1959, the composer's first recordings of *Billy the Kid* and his *Third Symphony* (made at Walthamstow) are presented in stereo of sharp clarity with inner detail remarkable clear; the violins, however, are distinctly thin, which makes *fortissimos* sharp-edged, in spite of the basically warm ambience. The LSO are obviously coming fresh to *Billy the Kid*, and clearly they are enjoying the music's colour, playing with plenty of rhythmic bite. They give a far less virtuoso performance of the *Symphony*, which is convincing as an expression of emotion in the opening movement and the *Andantino*, but less than perfect in the playing of the brilliant Scherzo.

With Bernstein conducting Copland's *Third Symphony*, you appreciate more than with rival interpreters that this is one of the great symphonic statements of American music. The electricity of the DG performance is irresistible. The recording is full-bodied and bright, but its brashness is apt for the performance. The hushed tranquillity of *Quiet city*, another of Copland's finest scores, is superbly caught by Bernstein in the valuable fill-up.

In his earlier CBS/Sony recording Bernstein built the music up in a manner that the material will not quite stand and the result does not always avoid a feeling of inflation. Copland marks the very opening 'with simple expression', and in the folk-like trio of the second movement he puts the request '*cantando semplice*', yet at such points the New York players sound too smooth and polished. The account of the work for organ and orchestra is discussed above. The Avery Fisher Hall recordings, from 1966 and 1967 respectively, sound suitably spacious in these fine new transfers, although the organ balance is close, and in this latter work tuttis have an element of harshness.

Violin sonata; Nocturne for violin and piano.
(N) *** DG Dig. 453 470-2 [id.]. Gil Shaham, André Previn – BARBER: *Canzone for violin and piano*; GERSHWIN: *3 Preludes;* PREVIN: *Sonata.* ***

The *Violin sonata* of 1944 represents the Copland of 'wide-open spaces', with broad intervals and open harmonies as in the ballets *Rodeo* and *Billy the Kid*. Shaham with his wide and beautiful contrasts of tone is an ideal interpreter, with Previn the thoughtful partner. The *Nocturne* dates from Copland's Paris period, charming in 1920s style.

PIANO MUSIC

Down a country lane; In the evening air; Midday thoughts; Midsummer nocturne; 3 Moods; Night thoughts (Homage to Ives); Passacaglia; Petite portrait; 4 Piano blues; Piano fantasy; Proclamation; Piano variations; Scherzo humoristique: The cat and the mouse; Sentimental melody (Slow dance); Sonata; Sunday afternoon music; The Young Pioneers.
(M) *** Sony Analogue/Dig. SM2K 66345 (2) [id.]. Leo Smit.

The sound-quality here may not be ideal – the piano is recorded in a rather small acoustic – but this is nevertheless an important and valuable set, containing a collection of all Copland's important piano music from the very earliest pre-Boulanger days – the abrasively impressionistic *Scherzo*, *The cat and the mouse* (1920) – right down to his most recent works, *Midday thoughts* and *Proclamation* completed in November 1982. The three most important works, the *Variations* (1930), the *Sonata* (1941) and the *Fantasy* (1957), are by the composer's own description, lean, percussive and rather harmonically severe. But of course not all this writing is uncompromising. Apart from the bluesy and jazzy pieces, the wistful *In the evening air* and *Midday thoughts* have something of the evocation of the atmospheric writing in the three great ballets, and *Down a country lane* brings a comparable brand of pastoralism. Both are played very sympathetically. Leo Smit has been closely associated with Copland's music over the years, and he recorded the *Sonata* in the days of 78s. It would be difficult to find anyone who is more inside the idiom and whose command of nervous energy so well matches the needs of this vital music. Authoritative, stimulating and vivid performances.

VOCAL MUSIC

(i) *In the Beginning. Help us, O Lord; Have mercy on us, O my Lord; Sing ye praises to our King.*
*** Hyperion Dig. CDA 66219 [id.]. (i) Catherine Denley; Corydon Singers, Best – BARBER: *Agnus Dei;* BERNSTEIN: *Chichester Psalms.* ***

In the Beginning is a large-scale, 15-minute motet for unaccompanied chorus and soprano solo, written in 1947, and the long span of the work is well structured with the help of the soprano soloist, here the fresh-toned Catherine Denley. The chorus is just as clear and alert in its singing, not only in the big motet but also in the three delightful little pieces which come as an appendix. Vivid recording, full of presence.

Old American songs: Sets 1 and 2 (original versions).
*** Chandos Dig. CHAN 8960 [id.]. Willard White, Graeme McNaught (with collection: '*American spirituals; Folk-songs from Barbados and Jamaica*' ***).

Characteristically White's opulent bass comes with a pronounced vibrato which on disc tends to get exaggerated. Yet with its helpful acoustic the Chandos recording captures the richness of his voice most attractively, very characterfully black in its evocations.

Corelli, Arcangelo (1653–1713)

Concerti grossi, Op. 6/1–12.
(B) *** Hyperion Dyad Dig. CDD 22011 (2) [id.]. Brandenburg Consort, Roy Goodman.
*** HM Dig. HMC90 1406/7 [id.]. Ensemble 415, Banchini.
(B) *** DG Dig. Double 459 451-2 (2) [id.]. E. Concert, Pinnock.
(BB) *** Naxos Dig. 8.550402/3 [id.]. Capella Istropolitana, Jaroslav Krechek.
(B) **(*) Ph. Duo 456 326-2 (2) [(M) id. import]. I Musici.
(B) **(*) Decca Double 443 862-2 [id.]. ASMF, Marriner.

Concerti grossi, Op. 6/1–6.
*** HM Opus 111 Dig. OPS 30-147 [id.]. Europa Galante, Fabio Biondi.

Concerti grossi, Op. 6/7–12.
*** HM Opus 111 Dig. OPS 30-155 [id.]. Europa Galante, Fabio Biondi.

Corelli's glorious set of *Concerti grossi*, Op. 6, is now very well represented in the catalogue in all price-ranges. In fact one cannot go wrong with any of the three-star listings here. For those who prefer period performances there is plenty of choice, with the Goodman set now available as a two-for-the-price-of-one Hyperion Dyad. However, although a clear-cut recommendation is difficult, the balance of advantage in authenticity seems to lie between Goodman and Banchini. One can invest in either with confidence. Roy Goodman and the Brandenburg Consort use the smaller forces (17 string players) plus harpsichord continuo, archlute and organ; Harmonia Mundi's Ensemble 415, with Chiara Banchini and Jesper Christensen, number 32 strings and a comparably larger continuo section with several archlutes, chitarrone, harpsichords and organ. The richer bass and altogether fuller sonority may cause some readers to prefer it (and we would incline towards it for its greater splendour and imaginative use of continuo instruments, whereas at times Goodman's textures sound just a little meagre). However, there is a sense of style and a freshness of approach in the Goodman version that is very persuasive. In both instances the recorded sound is first class.

The newest set, from the appropriately named Europa Galante, is as fine as any. The chamber-sized ripieno of period instruments (2,2,2,1,1) offers crisp detail yet no feeling of any lack of sonority, and the elegant playing is alert and vital yet smiles pleasingly: these musicians are obviously enjoying the music and so do we. The soloists are excellent, as is the recording.

The DG performances bring not only an enthusiasm for this music but a sense of its spacious grandeur. The English Concert are entirely inside its sensibility, and the playing of the concertino group (Simon Standage, Micaela Comberti and Jaap Ter Linden) is wonderfully fresh-eyed and alert, yet full of colour.

At super-bargain price, the Naxos set by the Capella Istropolitana under Jaroslav Krechek represents very good value indeed. The players are drawn from the Slovak Philharmonic and have great vitality and, when necessary, virtuosity to commend them. The digital recording is clean and well lit, but not over-bright, and makes their version strongly competitive.

I Musici bring a full sonority and expert musicianship to these *Concertos*. They are especially good in slow movements, where the playing has an agreeable lightness of touch and often creates delicately radiant textures. In allegros, rhythms are less bouncy than with Goodman, and the effect is less exhilarating. Yet there is an appealing warmth here, and certainly the Philips recording provides beautifully rich string-sound. Good value as a Duo, but not a first choice.

The reissued ASMF version uses a performing edition by Christopher Hogwood and has been prepared with evident thought and care; if one cavils it is only at two small points: some fussy continuo playing here and there, and a certain want of breadth and nobility of feeling in some of the slow movements. These are perhaps small points when weighed alongside the liveliness and intelligence of these performances, so expertly played. Yet compared to the issues mentioned above, there is at times a hint of blandness

Concerti grossi, Op. 6/1, 3, 7, 8 (Christmas), 11 & 12.
(M) *** DG Dig. 447 289-2 [431 706-2].
E. Concert, Pinnock.

At mid-price, with the *Christmas Concerto* included, this will admirably suit those collectors who want an original-instrument version and who are content with a single-disc selection.

Concerti grossi, Op. 6/1–12 (complete; with wind and brass, arr. Sardelli).
(N) ✿ *** Tactus Dig. TC 650307 (Nos. 1–6); TC 650308 (Nos. 7–12). Modo Antiquo, Federico Sardelli.

Of all the discoveries made so far by the enterprising Tactus label, this is the most fascinating. Modern scholarship has revealed that it was not unusual in Corelli's time to have fully scored performances of baroque concerti grossi, doubling the strings with wind and brass as available, and that is what happens in these thoroughly stimulating period performances by Modo Antiquo.

Their conductor, Federico Sardelli, has obviously given much thought to his choice of instrumentation. For instance, trumpets are only used in Nos. 1, 4 and 7 (all in D major) and then only where appropriate. In the last-named they open the work as if they had been originally chosen to do so! Oboes are featured with equal discernment in Nos. 3, 7 and 10; recorders are used most sparingly, but always to felicitous effect. For the most part the wind are only added to the ripieno, but just occasionally they play phrases drawn from the concertino, and there is a splendid baroque interplay of colours.

At times the listener is reminded of Vivaldi, but as Corelli's original string textures (and style) predominate, the listener need not worry that the music's essential character is lost. Especially in slow movements, which have genuine expressive nobility, for the group's string textures, although transparent, are never in the least anaemic, and their phrasing is both warm and refined. Allegros are alert and vivacious and the excellent recording ensures that this music is given an entirely fresh lease of life. Not a replacement for the originals, but a most valid alternative.

CHAMBER MUSIC

Sonate da camera (Trio sonatas), Op. 2/1–11.
(N) ** Tactus Dig. TC 650306 [id.]. Il Ruggiero.

Sonate da camera (Trio sonatas), Op. 2/1–12; Op. 4/1–12.
(N) (B) *** HM Musique d'abord Dig. HMA 1901342/3 [id.]. L. Baroque, Medlam.

Corelli's *Sonate da camera*, Opp. 2 and 4 appeared in print in 1685 and 1694 respectively. The twenty-four sonatas are usually written in a four-movement form with a stately opening prelude followed by four light and graceful dance movements, very much influenced by the French 'courtly' style. In essence they are more lighthearted than the *Sonate da chiesa*, Op. 1 and Op. 3, and yet it is not possible to draw clear distinctions between the different formats. Corelli was incapable of writing trivially, and of the earlier chamber sonatas of Op. 2, the *Second* and *Sixth* both have extended slow opening *Allemandes* while the remarkable No. 4 *in E minor* has a very touching central *Adagio* in addition to its solemn opening *Prelude*. Throughout, these *Preludes* are deeply expressive and in some of the later sonatas the opening movement becomes the longest, creating a mood of seriousness, which is then dispelled by the following dances – correntes, faster and usually rhythmically dotted allemandes, gavottes and gigues. The final work of Op. 2 (omitted on the Tactus disc) is a single-movement *Ciacona* which deserves to be better known. London Baroque under Charles Medlam catch the varying moods of these rewarding works to perfection, and they are beautifully recorded.

Il Ruggiero, the alternative period-instrument group on Tactus, play rather soberly for Italians. Although dance movements are deft and vigorous, the overall texture is close-grained so that although the opening *Preludes* and slow movements have a sombre dignity, the serious mood predominates and there is an absence of elegant, lighthearted contrast.

Trio sonatas, Op. 1/9, 10 & 12 (Ciacona); Op. 2/4; Op. 3/5; Op. 4/1; Violin sonata, Op. 5/3; Concerto grosso in B flat, Op. 6/5.
(M) *** Virgin Veritas/EMI Dig. VER5 61210-2. L. Baroque, Medlam.

Trio sonatas, Op. 1/9; Op. 2/4 & 12 (Ciacona); Op. 3/12; Op. 4/3; Op. 5/3, 11 & 12 (La Folia).
*** Hyperion Dig. CDA 66226 [id.]. Purcell Qt.

The quality of invention in these pieces underlines the injustice of their neglect. Though not lacking vitality, the London Baroque performances here are graceful and comparatively restrained. Reissued on Virgin Veritas, they also now have a price advantage.

The Hyperion disc is one of six designed to illustrate the widespread use in the eighteenth century of the famous *La Folia* theme. It includes a varied collection of sonate da chiesa and sonate da camera. Excellent performances from all concerned, and recording to match.

Trio sonatas, Op. 5/1–6.
(B) *** HM Dig. HMX 290853.55 (3) [(M) id.].
Chiara Banchieri, Jesper Christensen, Luciano

Contini, Käthi Gohl – TARTINI: *Concerti grossi*; VIVALDI: *Chamber sonatas*. ***

Corelli's Op. 5, of which the first six sonatas are offered here, were published in 1700. Like his *Concerti grossi*, they were enormously influential throughout Europe. Their invention is of the highest quality, and Chiara Banchieri and her colleagues present them with vitality, warmth and finesse. Their period-instrument manners are not excessive, and the acoustic resonance adds to the body of the sound without impairing clarity. In this Harmonia Mundi bargain-priced Trio presentation, Corelli's music is aptly linked with sonatas of Vivaldi and – rather less obviously – with concertos of Tartini.

Trio sonatas, Op. 5/1, 3, 6, 11 and 12 (La Follia).
*** Accent Dig. ACC 48433D [id.]. Sigiswald & Wieland Kuijken, Robert Kohnen.

When authenticity of spirit goes hand in hand with fine musical feeling and accomplishment, the results can be impressive, as they undoubtedy are here, drawing one into the sensibility of the period. This is a thoroughly recommendable issue which deserves to reach a wider audience than early-music specialists; the recording is natural and the musicianship refined and totally at the service of Corelli.

12 Violin sonatas, Op. 5; Sonata in A, Op.5/9 (elaborated Geminiani).
(N) *** Hyperion Dig. CDA 66381/2 [id.]. Locatelli Trio.
(N) (B) **(*) Ph. Duo 462 306-2 (2) [id.]. (with Geminiani elaboration) Arthur Grumiaux, Riccardo Castogne (harpsichord).

Corelli's Opus 5 was published in 1700 as *Twelve Sonate a violino e violone o cimbalo*. Though not now as familiar as his concerti grossi, they were enormously popular and influential in their day and were even used by his contemporaries as vehicles for improvised or written elaboration and ornamentation. The Hyperion set includes Geminiani's elaborated version of No. 9, using a manuscript in the latter's own handwriting. Needless to say, the originals stand up perfectly well without such accretions. They are in essence suites of usually five (sometimes four) movements and the later works incorporate dance forms – Corrente, Sarabanda, Giga, etc. No. 12 is a set of variations on the famous *La Folia*. These period performances by the Locatelli Trio are eminently alive and stylish. Allegros sparkle, decoration seems entirely apt and Adagios have a sympathetic expressive line and there is imaginative use of dynamic contrast. The recording balance cannot be faulted. These versions make an obvious first choice, yet it has to be admitted that Elizabeth Wallfisch's period violin does not produce such a beautiful timbre as Arthur Grumiaux's.

Indeed Grumiaux has a glorious tone, and on his bow Corelli's beautiful slow movements are phrased simply and with an appealingly warm lyricism. At times he gives the impression of echoing a phrase to striking effect. Moreover, he and Riccardo Castagnone are eminently well recorded – although the violin balance is close. But Grumiaux has no cello continuo; at times he plays in a more nineteenth-century fashion than we are accustomed to nowadays, and his vibrato is distinctly apparent. While it is difficult to resist playing of such tonal beauty and warmth, there is just a hint of blandness which slightly diminishes the appeal of this reissue. The transfer of the mid 1970s recording is immaculate.

Corigliano, John (born 1938)

Clarinet concerto.
*** RCA Dig. 09026 61350-2 [id.]. Stoltzman, LSO, Leighton Smith – BERNSTEIN: *Prelude, fugue and riffs;* COPLAND: *Concerto;* STRAVINSKY: *Ebony concerto*. ***

Stoltzman gives an outstanding performance of John Corigliano's attractive *Concerto*, his richly expressive treatment of the slow movement balanced by superb flair and virtuosity in the finale. Moreover his reissued CD sweeps the board in including three equally outstanding couplings.

Flute concerto (Pied Piper fantasy); Voyage.
**(*) RCA Dig. RD 86602 [6602-2-RC]. James Galway, Eastman Philh. O, David Effron.

Galway is at his inimitable best in Corigliano's *Flute concerto*. The picaresque qualities of its invention in detailing the Pied Piper narrative are spread thinly in memorability of material, although the closing section when the children are led away into the distance is right up Galway's street. The serene *Voyage* is shorter and more memorable.

(i) *Oboe concerto;* (ii; iii) *3 Irish folksong settings: The Sally Gardens; The foggy dew; She moved thro' the fair;* (ii; iv) *Poem in October*.
(M) *** BMG Analogue/Dig. GD 60395 [60395-2-RG]. (i) Humbert Lucarelli, American SO, Kazuyoshi Akiyama; (ii) Robert White; (iii) Ransom Wilson; (iv) Nyfenger, Lucarelli, Rabbai, American Qt, Peress (cond. from harpsichord).

John Corigliano's highly imaginative *Oboe concerto* opens ingeniously with the orchestra tuning up, and the music springs fairly naturally from this familiar aleatory pattern of sound. The performance here is outstanding, expert and spontaneous and very well recorded. The three *Folksong settings*are for tenor and flute; Robert White's headily distinctive light tenor gives much pleasure, as he does in the Dylan Thomas setting, *Poem in October*.

(i) *Piano concerto. Elegy; Fantasia on an ostinato; Tournaments.*
*** RCA Dig. 09026 68100-2 [id.]. (i) Barry Douglas; St Louis SO, Slatkin.

Corigliano's *Piano concerto* is a powerful and ambitious work in four sharply contrasted movements which communicates with great immediacy. If Corigliano unashamedly uses a freely eclectic style, his writing is consistently positive and energetic, never merely conventional. The *Elegy* and the showpiece, *Tournaments*, were his first full orchestral works – the one developed from the love scene in incidental music Corigliano wrote for a play about Helen of Troy, the other a virtuoso piece, substantially monothematic, that tests the orchestra to the limit in its three clearly defined sections, fast–slow–fast. Slatkin draws outstanding playing from the St Louis orchestra, and Barry Douglas proves the most powerful advocate, using a daringly wide dynamic range and tonal palette.

Symphony No. 1; Of rage and remembrance (Chaconne).
*** RCA Dig. 09026 68450-2 [id.]. Choral Arts and Oratorio Soc. of Washington Ch., Nat SO, Slatkin.

John Corigliano's *Symphony No. 1*, first heard in 1990, is an elegy in memory of the composer's friends who have died of AIDS – deeply felt, vitally communicative, directly challenging the listener to respond in an openly emotive way. The result is made the more intense by those specific references, venturing, Tchaikovsky-like, to the very verge of sentimentality. This superb new recording outshines Barenboim's previous Chicago one (Erato 2292 45601-2) not only in its brilliant, clean-focused sound, but also in having as supplement the choral piece which reworks the symphony's beautiful slow movement, restoring the words which provided the original inspiration.

Troubadours (variations for guitar and orchestra).
(*) EMI Dig. CDC5 55083-2 [id.]. Sharon Isbin, St Paul CO, Hugo Wolff – SCHWANTNER: *From afar* **; FOSS: *American landscapes.* *

Corigliano's very free set of variations is an elliptical work, beginning and ending in the mists of time. Two-thirds of the basic theme is Corigliano's own, but the final cadence comes from an actual twelfth-century song. When the troubadours enter, they do so boisterously to dance rhythms from a raucously exuberant 'shawm band', and it has to be said that the climax becomes rather ugly. However, the work's reflective passages, notably the melancholy final section, communicate readily. Like the companion *Fantasy* by Joseph Schwantner, this is a piece that undoubtedly makes a strong impression in live performance, although the playing and recording by its dedicatee do it full justice.

Cornelius, Peter (1824–74)

6 Weihnachtslieder, Op. 8: Christbaum; Die Hirten; Die Könige; Simeon; Christus der Kinderfreud; Christkind.
❀ *** EMI Dig. CDC5 56204-2. Bär, Deutsch (with Recital: '*Christmas Lieder*' *** ❀).

Peter Cornelius was born on Christmas Eve, so perhaps it is not surprising that his set of *Weihnachtslieder* so readily captures the seasonal mood with such charm and spontaneity. Cornelius's settings have a winningly tender simplicity, and the final *Christkind* turns the mood into light-hearted happiness. Olaf Bär sings with a natural beauty of line and phrase and much affection, and his accompanist, Helmut Deutsch, is wonderfully supportive.

Cornysh, William (*c.* 1468–1523)

Adieu, adieu my heartes lust; Adieu, courage; Ah Robin; Ave Maria, mater Dei; Gaude, virgo, mater Christi; Magnificat; Salve regina; Stabat Mater; Woefully arrayed.
❀ *** Gimell/Ph. 454914-2 [id.]. Tallis Scholars, Phillips.

Cornysh's music is quite unlike much other polyphony of the time and is florid, wild, complex and, at times, grave. The Tallis Scholars give a magnificent, totally committed account of these glorious pieces – as usual their attack, ensemble and true intonation and blend are remarkable. Excellent recording.

Ave Maria mater Dei; Gaudi virgo mater Christi (motets); *Magnificat; Salve Regina.*
(N) *** ASV Gaudeamus Dig. CDGAU 164 [id.]. Cardinall's Musick, Andrew Carwood (with TURGES: *Magnificat*; PRENTES: *Magnificat.* ***)

In his survey of early Tudor polyphony, Andrew Carwood, with his keenly responsive group, Cardinall's Musick, here matches his prizewinning issues of Ludford and Fayrfax with a disc centred on the Latin church music of William Cornysh senior. All four of Cornysh's surviving liturgical works, including a fine *Magnificat* and a radiant *Salve Regina*, are presented alongside even more elaborate *Magnificats* by two composers far less well-known but just as inspired. Complex and beautiful, the *Magnificat* of Turges is the most expansive of all, while Prentes's *Magnificat*, closely following Cornysh's, even outshines that model both in scale and sublimity.

Corrette, Michel (1709–95)

6 Organ concertos, Op. 26.
(B) *** HM Musique d'Abord HMA 190 5148

[id.]. René Saorgin (organ of L'Eglise de l'Escarène, Nice), Bar. Ens., Gilbert Bezzina.

These lively and amiable concertos are here given admirably spirited and buoyant performances, splendidly recorded using period instruments. The orchestral detail is well observed and René Saorgin plays vividly on an attractive organ. Michel Corrette's invention has genuine spontaneity and this makes an enjoyable collection to dip into, though not to play all at one go.

Sonatas: for bassoon and continuo: in F & G (Les Délices de la Solitude), Op. 20/1 & 5; for flute and continuo: in E min.; D min., Op. 13/2 & 4; for harpsichord and flute in E min., Op. 15/4; for oboe and continuo in D min. (L'école d'Orphée). Suite for recorder and continuo in C min. (from Les Pièces, Op. 5). (Harpsichord): *Les Amusements du Parnasse: La Furstemberg and variations; Le Sabotier Hollandois and variations; Première Livre de Pièces de Clavecin: Suite in D* (complete); *Suite No. 3 (Les Etoiles): Rondeau, Op. 12* (both from *Op. 12*).

*** Mer. Dig. CDE 84325 [id.]. Paul Carroll, David Rowland, Sally Civil.

These attractive instrumental works were written with an eye to maximum sales, so Corrette's designated instrumentation was interchangeable. The rather agreeable *Oboe sonata*, for instance, comes from *L'école d'Orphée*, a violin tutor, and the Op. 5 *Pièces*, from which the *Suite for recorder and continuo* is taken, were primarily designated for the musette (an aristocratic set of bagpipes). However, the composer suggested a whole range of alternatives (including vielle, oboe and viola d'amore) as well as the recorder, which they suit rather well. The versatile and expert Paul Carroll has mastered all the baroque instruments featured in these works and plays each of them with spirit and character. But it is perhaps his harpsichord music for which Corrette is best remembered – and justly so. The *D major Suite* is strikingly inventive and the final two movements, the *Faste milannoise* and the hurdy-gurdy-like *Bal*, are real lollipops. David Rowland plays them on excellent modern copies of two different period instruments, and he is beautifully recorded. The instrumental works, too, are naturally balanced. An entertaining 73 minutes – but not necessarily to be taken all at once.

Couperin, Armand-Louis

(1725–1789)

Pièces de clavecin, Books I–II: excerpts.

** CPO Dig. CPO 999 312-2 [id.]. Harald Hoeren (harpsichord).

Armand-Louis Couperin was distantly related to both François and Louis. His *Pièces de clavecin* were published in 1751 in two books, and here we are offered a good selection of 19 pieces – about 74 minutes of music. Some of the music is unadventurous but he could write a good Minuet. *L'Arlequin*, for instance, is quite engagingly spirited and the closing piece, *Les tendres sentiments*, has a pleasingly ingenuous melodic line. In short this is not great music but it is very much of its period. Harald Hoeren plays expertly, he does not over-decorate and is obviously sympathetic. He plays a German copy of a Flemish harpsichord which has plenty of character and is well caught, if just a shade close.

Couperin, François (1668–1733)

Concerts Royaux Nos. 1 in G; 2 in D; 3 in A; 4 in E min.

(N) (B) *** Sony Seon SBK 60370 [id.]. Kuijken Ens.

*** ASV Gaudeamus CDGAU 101 [id.]. Trio Sonnerie.

The *Concerts Royaux* can be performed in a variety of forms. Kuijken and his distinguished colleagues (Franz Brüggen, flute, Jürg Schaeftlein, oboe, Milan Turkovic, bassoon, with continuo) feature a variety of wind-colouring to pleasing effect, and the 1971 recording is well balanced if forward. This reissue also has the advantage of economy.

On the alternative ASV Gaudeamus disc the Trio Sonnerie give them in the most economical fashion (violin, viola da gamba and harpsichord) and the contribution of all three musicians is unfailingly imaginative. Excellent recording.

Les Goûts réunis: Nouveaux concerts Nos. 5–7; 9 (Ritratto dell'amore); 10–11; 12 (à deux violes); 14.

(N) (B) **(*) Sony Seon SB2K 60714 (2) [id.]. Kuijken Ens.

Couperin followed his four initial *Concerts royaux* of 1722 with eight more, published two years later. He acknowledged that the music combined the French and Italian styles with his title *Les Goûts réunis*. The Kuijken Ensemble use period instruments and one only has to sample the opening *Prélude* (*gracieusement*) of the Fifth concert, the central *Sarabande* (*grave*), or the closing *Musette* (*dans le goût de Carillon*) to find how attractive is their sound world. The *Ninth concert* has a linking programme and its eight dance movements contrast the many facets of love. The first, *Le charme*, has all the delicacy one would expect, and the mood of *La douceur* (*amoureusement*) is perfectly caught by Kuijken's melancholy flute. But all these vignettes are engaging in their different ways. *Concert* No. 12 is effectively scored for a pair of violes, but in general Couperin left the instrumentation up to the performers, and Kuijken has researched and followed Couperin's own practice. The playing too is idiomatic and pleasing and the balance is excellent. This is most rewarding but why were Nos. 8 and 13 omitted – there is plenty of room on the second disc, which only plays for 50 minutes?

KEYBOARD MUSIC

L'Art de toucher le clavecin: Harpsichord suites, Books 1–4, Ordres 1–27 (complete); (i) *L'apothéose de Lulli. La Paix du Parnasse; Le Parnasse ou l'Apothéose de Corelli; Pièces de clavecin: 9e Ordre: Allemand à deux. 14e Ordre: La Juilliet. 15e Ordere: Musète de Choisi; Musète de Taverni; 16e Ordre: La Létiville.*

(B) *** HM Dig. HMX 901442–52 (& HMC 901269) (12) [id.]. Christophe Rousset (harpsichord); (i) with William Christie; with Blandine Rannou (in Book 3); with Kaori Uemura (in Book 4).

L'Art de toucher le clavecin: Harpsichord suites, Book 1, Ordres 1–5.

*** HM Dig. HMC 901450/2 [id.]. Christophe Rousset (harpsichord).

(i) *Harpsichord suites, Book 2, Ordres 6–12. L'Art de toucher le clavecin.*

*** HM Dig. HMC 901447/9 [id.]. Christophe Rousset (harpsichord), (i) with William Christie.

Harpsichord suites, Book 3, Ordres 13–19; Concerts royaux Nos. 1–4.

*** HM Dig. HMC 901442/4 [id.]. Christophe Rousset (with Blandine Rannou).

Harpsichord suites, Book 4, Ordres 20–27.

*** HM Dig. HMC 901445/6 [id.]. Christophe Rousset (with Kaori Uemura).

Rousset's distinguished series of the *Pièces de clavecin* includes *L'Art de toucher le clavecin*, using appropriate instruments. Apart from his inherent sense of style and feeling for decoration, Rousset well understands terms like *gracieusement*, *gayement*, *très tendrement* and *agréable, sans lenteur*, which he realizes to perfection. The *Concerts royaux* were of course written for a small chamber group, but the composer also encouraged their performance on the keyboard alone. In Book 2, Rousset is joined in certain pieces (the *Allemande* which opens Ordre No. 9 is for two harpsichords) by the estimable William Christie. In Book 3, he is joined in a very few items by Blandine Rannou on a second harpsichord; and in *La Croûilli ou la Couperinète*, from Book 4, Ordre 20, Kaori Uemura provides a vigorous basso continuo for the closing section. One could carp here and there about choice of tempi and so on, but Couperin wanted his music to be played creatively and flexibly, and that is what Christophe Rousset does – and with total spontaneity, too. He is beautifully recorded within an open but not too resonant acoustic, and this series can be welcomed very cordially indeed. This whole set now comes as a special offer at bargain price and throws in as a bonus the extra disc in which Rousset is joined by William Christie and which includes *L'apothéose de Lulli* and *Le Parnasse ou l'apothéose de Corelli* among other pieces (see below). The four books of *Suites* are also still available separately at premium price, but the lover of this repertoire will surely want to opt for the whole series when this bargain offer is so tempting.

L'Art de toucher le clavecin: Harpsichord suites, Book 1, Ordres 1–5.

(B) *** HM Musique d'Abord HMA 190351/3 [id.]. Kenneth Gilbert.

Harpsichord suites, Book 2, Ordres 6–12.

(B) *** HM Musique d'Abord HMA 190354/6 [id.]. Kenneth Gilbert.

Harpsichord suites, Book 3, Ordres 13–19.

(B) *** HM Musique d'Abord HMA 190357/8 [id.]. Kenneth Gilbert.

Harpsichord suites, Book 4, Ordres 20–27.

(B) *** HM Musique d'Abord HMA 190359/60 [id.]. Kenneth Gilbert.

Professor Gilbert's performances are scrupulous in matters of registration, following what is known of eighteenth-century practice in France. There is no want of expressive range throughout the series and Gilbert plays with authority and taste – and, more to the point, artistry. He is also well served by the engineers. Gilbert's survey is offered at bargain price spead over ten CDs, but there are no extra items.

L'apothéose de Lulli; La Parnasse ou l'apothéose de Corelli; Pièces de clavecin: 9e Ordre: Allemande à deux; 14e Ordre: La Juilliet; 15e Ordre: Musète de Choisi; Musète de Taverni; 16e Ordre: La Létiville.

(B) *** HM Musique d'Abord Dig. HMA 190 1269 [id.]. William Christie, Christophe Rousset (harpsichords).

Couperin's preface explains that he himself played these works on two harpsichords with members of his family and pupils; and William Christie has chosen to follow his example. Surprisingly, they sound rather more exciting in this form than in the more familiar instrumental versions, largely perhaps because of the sheer sparkle and vitality of these performers.

Harpsichord suites, Book 1, Ordre 1; Concerts Royaux Nos. 1–2.

(BB) *** Naxos Dig. 8.550961 [id.]. Laurence Cummings.

Laurence Cummings has already won golden opinions from us for his admirable and idiomatic earlier recital of Louis Couperin (see below), and his account of the *Premier Ordre* of François is hardly less fine. Cummings plays a modern instrument by Michael Johnson modelled on a Taskin, and he produces pleasing and musical results. The disc bears the legend, Harpsichord Music Vol. 1, and if the remaining issues maintain the standard achieved here, both artistically and in terms of recorded sound, it will be a valuable addition to the catalogue.

ORGAN MUSIC

Messe à l'usage ordinaire des Paroisses; Messe propre pour les Couvents de religieux et religieuses (reconstructed by Jean Saint-Arromen to include Plainchant and Motets: *Domine salvum fac Regem* (2 versions); *Quid retribuam tibi dominum*).

(M) *** Virgin Veritas/EMI (SIS) Dig. VED5 61298-2 (2). Jean-Patrice Brosse (organ of Saint-Bertrand, Saint-Bertrand de Comminges), with Isabel Poulenard, Jacques des Longchamps, François Le Roux, Val-de-Grâce Gregorian Ch.

(i) *Messe à l'usage ordinaire des Paroisses;* (ii) *Messe propre pour les Couvents de religieuses* (reconstructed by Edward Higginbottom to include plainchant, taken from Nivers's *Graduale romanaomonasticum* of 1658).

(B) *** Decca Double 455 026-2. Peter Hurford (organ of St-Pierre, Toulouse), with (i) Gentlemen of Ch. of New College, Oxford; (ii) Ladies of Oxford Chamber Ch.; Edward Higginbottom.

There have been a number of fine solo recordings of the organ scores of the two Couperin Masses in the past, but until now none has given us these pieces with the plainsong framework in which they were intended to be heard. Jean-Patrice Brosse has the full measure of this music and the Saint-Bertrand organ brings the necessary plangent French timbre. In the *Mass for Parishes* the plainsong interpolations are mostly brief and always simple, although the *Credo* is an obvious exception with the organ spectacularly framing this declaration of faith with the elaborately registered *Dialogue sur les grands jeux* and the *Offertoire sur les grands jeux*. Brosse faithfully follows the composer's indicated registrations, and there are many piquant sounds throughout both works, using solo stops or combinations. In reconstructing his conjectural performances, Jean Saint-Arromen has added short motets within the Elévation for the *Benedictus* and *Agnus Dei*, and these are sung effectively enough by Jacques des Longchamps (alto) and François Le Roux (baritone); although to have a vocal ending for each Mass does bring something of an anticlimax after the organ's final *Deo gratias, petit plein jeu*, it emphasizes the dedicated spiritual nature of Couperin's overall conception. These beautifully recorded performances give a splendid illusion of being in the cathedral and participating in an occasion which is alternately solemn and lively, evocative and vividly colourful.

Peter Hurford plays the two organ Masses on the restored organ, designed by Robert Delaunay in 1683, of Saint-Pierre des Chartreux. The Decca engineers have made an excellent job of marrying the acoustic with that of the Chapel of New College, Oxford, and they capture the atmosphere of both to splendid effect. Edward Higginbottom's reconstruction is less elaborate that that of Jean Saint-Arromen, using plainchant economically to follow on simply after the organ dialogues. Male voices of the New College, Oxford, Choir are used in the *Messe des Paroisses*, while in the *Messe des Couvents* women's voices are an obvious choice. They sing very beautifully and the effect is memorable, particularly when Hurford is such an obvious master of Couperin's organ writing, which is again superbly recorded. It cannot be denied that the French voices used in the Virgin Veritas alternative recording do bring an added feeling of vocal authenticity. But both versions have their own merits.

VOCAL MUSIC

Leçons de ténèbres pour Mercredy.

(B) *** HM Musique d'Abord HMA 190210 [id.]. Deller, Todd, Perulli, Chapuis.

(N) *(*) HM Dig. HMC 901133 [id.]. René Jacobs, Darras, Concerto Vocale, Jacobs (with PURCELL: *Divine hymn; Evening hymn.* CLARKE: *Blest be those sweet regions.* **(*)).

Couperin wrote a complete set of *Leçons ténèbres* for performance during Holy week, but only the three for Wednesday (Mercredy) have survived; they were actually intended for performance just after midnight in the first hours of Maunday Thursday morning. Neither Jacobs's nor Deller's versions are authentic, since this music, written for a convent, did not envisage performances by male voices. In every other respect, however, Deller's account has a wonderful authenticity of feeling, and a blend of scholarship and artistry that gives it a special claim on the attention of collectors.

On the other hand René Jacobs's singing seems emotionally overloaded and over-dramatized. Although his phrasing and intonation cannot be faulted, the result is curiously unmoving. He is joined in the *Third lesson* by Vincent Darras. The other pieces on the disc are much more successful. Purcell's *Divine and Evening Hymn* (the latter doubtfully attributed) is quite eloquently sung, and a remarkably fine *Hymn* from Jeremiah Clarke (of *Trumpet voluntary* fame) is most successful of all.

Motets: *Audite omnes et expanescite; Pour le jour de Pâques. 3 Leçons de ténèbres.*

(M) ** Erato/Warner 4509 97409-2. Nadine Sautereau, Janine Collard, Ens., Laurence

Boulay – CHARPENTIER: *La Reniement de Saint Pierre.* **(*)

Boulay's performances come from the period 1954–69 and are none the worse for that. Both Nadine Sautereau and Janine Collard show themselves to be thoroughly at home in this idiom, and the instrumental ensemble under Laurence Boulay is admirably discreet. In the first of the *Leçons de ténèbres* Mme Sautereau sings occasionally on the flat side of the note, but for the most part both the singing and playing give pleasure.

Motets: *Domine salvum fac regem; Jacunda vox ecclesiae; Laetentur coeli; Lauda Sion salvatorem; Magnificat; O misterium ineffabile; Regina coeli; Tantum ergo sacramentum; Venite exultemus Domine; Victoria! Christo resurgenti.*
(B) *** HM Musique d'Abord HMA 1901150 [id.]. Feldman, Poulenard, Reinhart, Linden, Moroney.

The motets on this record cover a wider spectrum of feeling and range of expressive devices than might at first be imagined. The performances are eminently acceptable, with some particularly good singing from Jill Feldman; the recording is made in a spacious and warm acoustic.

Couperin, Louis (*c.* 1626–61)

Suites de pièces and complete harpsichord music.
(B) *** HM HMX 901124/27 (4) [(M) id. import]. Davitt Moroney (harpsichord).

Louis Couperin was a pupil of Chambonnières, and his keyboard output comprises enough individual dance pieces to make 16 suites, as well as other pieces. This comprehensive survey makes out a strong case for this repertoire; readers expecting it to be greatly inferior in quality to the clavecin music of François-le-Grand will be pleasantly surprised – though, of course, there is less of the poetic fantasy of his nephew at his best. The recording is eminently truthful and the CD transfer wholly natural.

Harpsichord suites: in A min.;in C; in D; in F (including *Le Tombeau de M. de Blancrocher*).
(BB) *** Naxos Dig. 8.550922 [id.]. Laurence Cummings.

Harpsichord suites: in A min.; in C; in F; Pavane in F sharp min.
(M) *** HM/BMG GD 77058 [77058-2-RG]. Gustav Leonhardt (harpsichord).

Laurence Cummings was an organ scholar at Christ Church, Oxford, and he seems quite as much at home in this repertoire as Leonhardt. He plays a modern copy of a Ruckers, which is very well recorded by Naxos. His selection is rather more generous than Leonhardt's and he arranges his own groupings. His decoration is convincing and he plays with more spontaneity and flair than his illustrious colleague. The CD offers some 75 minutes of music and is one of Naxos's best bargains.

Leonhardt has much subtlety and panache, and he makes the most of the grandeur and refinement of music to whose sensibility he seems wholly attuned. But the Naxos disc now offers the best single-disc introduction to this repertoire.

Coward, Noël (1899–1973)

After the ball: I knew that you would be my love. Bitter Sweet: I'll see you again; Zigeuner. Conversation piece: I'll follow my secret heart; Never more; Melanie's aria (sung in French); *Charming. Operette: Dearest love; Where are the songs we sung? Countess Mitzi. Pacific 1860: Bright was the day; This is a changing world.*
(BB) *** Belart 450 014-2. Dame Joan Sutherland, Noël Coward, soloists, Ch. & O, Richard Bonynge.

It is fairly easy to criticize this disc on the grounds that a full operatic style does not always suit Noël Coward and that Joan Sutherland does not always get right inside the characters Coward created (she tries very hard with Countess Mitzi). But all this is swept aside in the sheer pleasure of hearing such a wonderful voice sing such delightful music. Dame Joan Sutherland's tonal lustre and sense of line in *I'll see you again* are incomparable, as is her display of fireworks in *Zigeuner*, and her gentle delicacy in *I knew that you would be my love*, with its ravishing final cadence. Noël Coward's own vocal contributions are quite small but they magically create atmosphere, and Richard Bonynge's affectionate and stylish conducting is a model.

Cowell, Henry (1897–1965)

Hymn and fuguing tune No. 10 for oboe and strings.
*** Argo 417 818-2 [id.]. Nicklin, ASMF, Marriner – BARBER: *Adagio;* COPLAND: *Quiet city;* CRESTON: *Rumor;* IVES: *Symphony No. 3.* ***

This likeable *Hymn and fuguing tune*, by a composer otherwise little known, is well worth having and is expertly played and recorded here. The digital remastering has slightly clarified an already excellent recording.

Cowen, Frederick (1852–1935)

Symphony No. 3 in C min. (Scandinavian); The Butterfly's ball: concert overture; Indian rhapsody.
** Marco Polo Dig. 8.220308 [id.]. Czechoslovak State PO (Kŏsice), Adrian Leaper.

The *Symphony No. 3* (1880) shows (to borrow Hanslick's judgement) 'good schooling, a lively sense of tone painting and much skill in orchestration, if not striking originality'. But what Cowen lacks in individuality he makes up for in natural musicianship and charm. His best-known work is the *Concert overture, The Butterfly's ball* (1901), which is scored with Mendelssohnian delicacy and skill. The *Indian rhapsody* (1903) with its naïve orientalisms carries a good deal less conviction. The performances are eminently lively. The recording is pleasingly reverberant but somewhat lacking in body.

Creston, Paul (1906–85)

A Rumor.
*** Argo 417 818-2 [id.]. ASMF, Marriner – BARBER: *Adagio;* COPLAND: *Quiet city;* COWELL: *Hymn;* IVES: *Symphony No. 3.* ***

A Rumor is a witty and engaging piece and is played here with plenty of character by the Academy under Sir Neville Marriner. It completes a thoroughly rewarding and approachable disc of twentieth-century American music that deserves the widest currency. The sound is first class.

Symphony No. 2, Op. 35.
*** Chandos Dig. CHAN 9390. Detroit SO, Järvi – IVES: *Symphony No. 2.* ***

Symphony No. 2, Op. 35; Corinthians XIII, Op. 82; Walt Whitman, Op. 53.
*** Koch Dig. 37036-2 or KI 7036 [id.]. Krakow PO, David Amos.

Paul Creston's *Second* is one of the most inventive of American symphonies and it is good to see it getting the attention it deserves. It has lush orchestral textures and a refreshing, exhilarating vitality. Järvi's well-recorded and excellently performed Chandos version makes a viable first choice and can be recommended to all with an interest in the American symphony.

The *Second Symphony* is also played with real enthusiasm and affection by these Polish forces and is very well recorded, even though the sound could do with greater transparency in the upper range. This should enjoy wide appeal.

Symphony No. 3 (Three Mysteries), Op. 48; Invocation and Dance; Out of the cradle; Partita for flute, violin and strings.
*** Delos Dig. DEL 3114 [id.]. Seattle SO, Schwarz.

Creston's work is uneven, but the idiom is approachable, nowhere more so than in the *Third Symphony*, a work of strong invention and lyrical impulse. Incidentally, the *Three Mysteries* of the subtitle allude to the Nativity, Crucifixion and Resurrection. Gerard Schwarz gives a fervent and committed account, drawing excellent playing from his Seattle orchestra. The exhilarating *Invocation and Dance*, the *Partita*, which is somewhat more austere, and the less successful *Out of the cradle,* benefit not only from Schwarz's committed advocacy but also from superb engineering. The sound is in the demonstration class.

String quartet, Op. 8.
(***) Testament mono SBT 1053 [id.]. Hollywood Qt – DEBUSSY: *Danse sacrée* etc. RAVEL: *Intro & allegro;* TURINA: *La Oración del torero;* VILLA-LOBOS: *Quartet No. 6.* (***)

The *String quartet*, Op. 8, is a pleasing, well-fashioned piece, slightly Gallic in feeling but not possessed of strong individuality. The *Adagio* is perhaps the most memorable of the four movements, and its argument unfolds with eloquence. It could not be better served than it is by the Hollywood Quartet, recorded in 1953: the playing is stunning, and the recording, too, is very good for its period, even if the acoustic is on the dry side.

Crusell, Bernhard (1775–1838)

Clarinet concertos Nos. 1 in E flat, Op. 1; 2 in F min., Op. 5; 3 in E flat, Op. 11.
❀ *** ASV Dig. CDDCA 784 [id.]. Emma Johnson, RPO/ECO, Herbig; Groves; or Schwarz.
(N) (BB) *** Virgin Veritas/EMI Dig. VBD5 61585-2 (2) [id.]. Antony Pay, OAE – WEBER: *Clarinet concertos.* ***
*** Hyperion CDA 66708 [id.]. Thea King, LSO, Alun Francis.

Crusell, born in Finland but working in Stockholm most of his career, was himself a clarinettist and these delightful concertos demonstrate his complete understanding of the instrument. There are echoes of Mozart, Weber and Rossini in the music, with a hint of Beethoven.

No one brings out the fun in the writing quite as infectiously as Emma Johnson, and this generous recoupling (74 minutes) bringing all three concertos together is a delight. With well-structured first movements, sensuous slow movements and exuberant finales, Johnson establishes her disc as a first choice above all others.

Pay's is the first period performance of these works. As well as directing the Orchestra of the Age of Enlightenment himself, he uses a reproduction of a nine-key clarinet as made around 1810 by Heinrich Grenser; Crusell himself is known to have used a ten-key Grenser clarinet. The slight edginess of the sound goes well with Pay's preference for fastish – often very fast – speeds which yet never get in the way of his imaginative rhythmic pointing. The results in outer movements are exhilarating, with phenomenal articulation of rapid passage-work. They sparkle with wit, while slow movements have a flowing songfulness that is comparably persuasive. The Virgin recording, made at Abbey Road studio, is clear, well balanced and atmospheric.

Thea King with her beautiful, liquid tone also makes an outstanding soloist. Her approach is often more serious, especially in the *Second Concerto*, where she brings out the Beethovenian character of the first movement, while the *Andante pastorale* slow movement is played with the widest range of tone-colour. Throughout, she is well accompanied by Alun Francis; and the resonant Hyperion recording, with the soloist balanced forward, emphasizes the feeling of added gravitas.

Clarinet concerto No. 1 in E flat, Op. 1.
*** ASV Dig. CDDCA 763 [id.]. Emma Johnson, RPO, Herbig – KOZELUCH; KROMMER: *Concertos.* ***

Even though many collectors may prefer the CD containing all three of the Crusell concertos, Emma Johnson's version of the *First Clarinet concerto* makes a highly attractive compilation with lesser-known but enticing works by Kozeluch and Krommer, especially when her warm-toned playing is magnetically individual, and the ASV recording brings out the great range of sensuously beautiful tone-colours she produces.

Clarinet concerto No. 2 in F min., Op. 5.
✿ *** ASV Dig. CDDCA 559 [id.]. Emma Johnson, ECO, Groves – BAERMANN: *Adagio;* ROSSINI: *Introduction, theme and variations;* WEBER: *Concertino.* ***

Crusell's *Second Clarinet concerto* made Emma Johnson a star, and in return she put Crusell's engagingly lightweight piece firmly on the map. Her delectably spontaneous performance is now caught on the wing and this recording sounds very like a live occasion.

Concertino for bassoon and orchestra in B flat; Introduction et air suédois for clarinet and orchestra, Op. 12; Sinfonia concertante for clarinet, horn, bassoon and orchestra, Op. 3.
*** BIS Dig. BIS CD 495 [id.]. Hara, Korsimaa-Hursti, Lanski-Otto, Tapiola Sinf., Vänskä.

The most substantial piece here is the *Sinfonia concertante for clarinet, horn, bassoon and orchestra.* The finale is a set of variations on a chorus from Cherubini's opera, *Les deux journées*. The much later *Concertino for bassoon and orchestra* is an altogether delightful piece, which quotes at one point from Boïeldieu. It is played with appropriate freshness and virtuosity by László Hara. The *Introduction et air suédois for clarinet and orchestra* is nicely done by Anna-Maija Korsimaa-Hursti. The Tapiola Sinfonietta, the orchestra of Esspoo, play with enthusiasm and spirit for Osmo Vänskä, and the BIS recording has lightness, presence and body.

Clarinet quartets Nos. 1 in E flat, Op. 2; 2 in C min., Op. 4; 3 in D, Op. 7.
*** Hyperion CDA 66077 [id.]. Thea King, Allegri Qt (members).

These are captivatingly sunny works, given superb performances, vivacious and warmly sympathetic. Thea King's tone is positively luscious, as recorded, and the sound is generally excellent. The CD transfer is highly successful.

Divertimento in C, Op. 9.
*** Hyperion CDA 66143 [id.]. Francis, Allegri Qt (with KREUTZER: *Grand quintet*); REICHA: *Quintet.* ***

No one wanting this slight but charming piece and its companions need look further than this nicely played and well-recorded account.

Introduction and variations on a Swedish air (for clarinet and orchestra), *Op. 12.*
(B) *** Hyperion Dyad Dig. CDD 22017 (2) [id.]. Thea King, LSO, Francis (with Concert – see below ***).

The Weberian Crusell *Variations* show Thea King's bravura at its most sparkling. It is far from being an empty piece; its twists and turns are consistently inventive. This is part of an excellent two-disc set including other attractive concertante works by Max Bruch, Mendelssohn, Spohr and other less familiar names.

Cui, César (1835–1918)

(i) *Suite concertante* (for violin & orchestra), *Op. 25. Suite miniature No. 1, Op. 20; Suite No. 3 (In modo populari), Op. 43.*
**(*) Marco Polo Dig. 8.220308 [id.]. (i) Nishizaki; Hong Kong PO, Schermerhorn.

These pieces have a faded period charm that is very appealing (try the *Petite Marche* and the equally likeable *Impromptu à la Schumann* from the *Suite miniature*) and are very well played by the Hong Kong Philharmonic. Takako Nishizaki is the expert soloist in the *Suite concertante*. An interesting issue that fills a gap in the repertoire, and very decently recorded too.

Curzon, Frederick (1899–1973)

The Boulevardier; Bravada (Paso doble); Capricante (Spanish caprice); Cascade (Waltz); Galavant; In Malaga (Spanish suite); Punchinello: Miniature overture; Pasquinade; La Peineta; Robin Hood suite; (i) *Saltarello for piano and orchestra; Simionetta (Serenade).*

*** Marco Polo Dig. 8.223425 [id.]. (i) Silvia Cápová; Slovak RSO (Bratislava), Leaper.

The best-known piece here is *Dance of an ostracised imp*, a droll little scherzando, much played on the radio during the Second World War. But the *Galavant* is hardly less piquant and charming, the delicious *Punchinello* sparkles with miniature vitality, and the *Simionetta* serenade is sleekly beguiling. Curzon liked to write mock Spanishry, and several pieces here have such a Mediterranean influence. Yet their slight elegance and economical scoring come from cooler climes farther north. Both *In Malaga* and the jolly *Robin Hood suite* are more frequently heard on the (military) bandstand, but their delicate central movements gain much from the more subtle orchestral scoring. The performances throughout are played with the finesse and light touch we expect from this fine Slovak series, so ably and sympathetically conducted by Adrian Leaper. The recording is admirable.

Czerny, Karl (1791–1857)

Andante e polacca in E for horn and piano, Op. posth.; 3 Fantasias brillantes on themes of Schubert for horn and piano, Op. 339.

*** Etcetera Dig. KTC 1121 [id.]. Barry Tuckwell, David Blumenthal.

The *Andante and polacca* is a characteristically ripe piece which is enjoyable enough when played with such aplomb, but the real interest of this recital lies with the three Schubertian *Fantasias*. In effect they are pot-pourris of favourite Schubert songs, with the horn given the vocal melody against a background of glittering piano cascades. The performances could hardly be bettered; if you want Schubert Lieder without the words, then the present recording is most pleasing, the resonance flattering to both artists but the focus realistically firm.

Da Crema, Giovanni Maria
(died *c.* 1550)

Con lagrime e sospiri (Philippe Verdelot); De vous servir (Claudin de Sermisy); Lasciar il velo (Jacques Arcadelt); O felici occhi mieie (Arcadelt); Pass'e mezo ala bolognesa; Ricercars quinto, sexto, decimoquarto, decimoquinto, duodecimo, tredecimo; Saltarello ditto Bel fior; Saltarello ditto El Giorgio; Saltarello ditto El Maton.

(BB) *** Naxos Dig. 8.550778 [id.]. Christopher Wilson (lute) – DALL'AQUILA – *Lute pieces.* ***

The pieces here are taken from a First Lute Book which Da Crema published in 1546. The inclusion of the dance movements alongside reflective pieces like *Con lagrime e sospiri* gives variety to an attractive programme, and the *Pass'e mezo ala bolognesa* is rather catchy. The performances are of the highest order, and Christopher Wilson is recorded most naturally. Well worth exploring, especially at such a modest cost.

Dall'Abaco, Evaristo Felice
(1675–1742)

Concerti a quattro de chiesa, Op. 2/1, 4, 5, & 7; Concerti a più instrumenti, Op. 5/3, 5, & 6; Op.6/ 5 & 11.

(N) *** Teldec/Warner Dig. 3984 22166-2. Concerto Köln.

Evaristo Felice Dall'Abaco was born in Verona but spent the greater part of his career with the Elector Maximillian's Bavarian Court Orchestra, which subsequently (for local political reasons) moved to Brussels in 1705, and then on to France, and finally back home to Munich in 1715, where the composer reigned as Konzertmeister until 1726, when his employer died. Dall'Abaco's foreign travels exposed him to both French and Italian influences and he draws on them just as it suits him. We also find him astutely keeping up with public taste and subtly modifying his style over the years. Of the four *Concerti a quattro da chiesa*, taken from his Opus 2 (1712), No. 5 *in G minor* is a particularly fine work, worthy of Corelli. The Op. 5 set of *Concerti a più instrumenti* (*c.*1719) brings predominantly French influences and very appealing they are. No. 3 *in E minor* includes a pair of flutes and No. 5 brings an oboe soloist. No. 6 *in D* includes both an engaging *Aria* slow movement, a spiccato ciaconna, and a gallumphing finale. Opus 6 (c.1734) is more forward-looking, galant in style, with amiable allegros and nicely expressive cantabiles. All in all this is a most stimulating collection. The Concerto Köln's virtuosity brings a sparkling response, with the group's somewhat abrasive string timbres infectiously bending to the composer's force of personality. They are splendidly recorded. A real find.

Dall'Aquila, Marco (*c.* 1480–1538)

Amy souffrez (Pierre Moulu); La cara cosa; Priambolo; Ricercars Nos. 15, 16, 18, 19, 22, 24, 28, 33, 70, 101; 3 Ricercar/Fantasias; La Traditora.

(BB) *** Naxos Dig. 8.550778 [id.]. Christopher Wilson (lute) – DA CREMA – *Lute pieces.* ***

Marco dall'Aquila was a much-admired Venetian composer/lutenist in his day. These are relatively simple pieces, rhythmically active but often dolorous; *Amy souffrez* and *La cara cosa* are among the more striking, but the *Ricercars* can be haunting too. They are beautifully played by Christopher Wilson and the recording is admirably balanced.

Damase, Jean-Michel (born 1928)

Quintet for flute, harp, violin, viola & cello (1948); *Sonata for flute & harp* (1964); *Trio for flute, harp & cello* (1946); *Variations 'Early Music' for flute & harp* (1980).
*** ASV Dig. CDDCA 898 [id.]. Noakes, Tingay, Friedman, Atkins, Szucs.

Jean-Michel Damase was a pupil of Alfred Cortot and Henri Büsser, and his chamber music (and in particular the *Trio for flute, harp and cello* and the *Quintet*) has a fluent, cool charm. It is beautifully fashioned and those coming to it for the first time will find it very attractive. It is nicely played and very well recorded.

Danzi, Franz (1763–1826)

(i; ii) *Concertante for flute and clarinet in B; Op. 41*; (i) *Flute concerto No. 2 in D min., Op. 31;* (ii) *Fantasia on Mozart's 'La ci darem la mano' for clarinet and orchestra.*
*** RCA Dig. 09026 61976-2 [id.]. (i) James Galway; (ii) Sabine Meyer, Württemberg CO, Joerg Faerber.

Danzi wrote four flute concertos. The dramatic minor key opening of No 2, included here, is remarkably like Mozart's *D minor Piano concerto*, but James Galway's entry immediately lightens the mood; he also plays the charming *Larghetto* very persuasively, and the finale trips along delightfully. His partnership with Sabine Meyer affords equal felicity in the *Concertante*, and in Danzi's *Fantasia*, Meyer clearly enjoys all the bravura roulades with which Mozart's famous theme is decorated, after its delectably gentle entry. The accompaniments are stylishly supportive and the recording is both full and well balanced.

Horn concerto in E.
(M) **(*) Teldec/Warner 0630 12324-2 [id.]. Hermann Baumann, Concerto Amsterdam, Jaap Schröder – HAYDN, ROSETTI: *Horn concertos*. **(*)

Danzi's *Horn concerto* is a straightforward affair. Baumann plays the piece sympathetically and is well accompanied.

Bassoon quartets Nos. 1 in C; 2 in D min.; 3 in B flat.
*** CRD Dig. CRD 3503 [id.]. Robert Thompson, Coull Qt.

These three charming *Quartets* have a *galant* innocence and a gentle lyrical feeling. Danzi seeks primarily to capture the bassoon's doleful, lyrical character; its lighter side is not dismissed, but he never becomes too jocular. In short, these are slight but appealing works, presented here with affectionate warmth and spirit, and they are beautifully recorded.

(i) *Piano quintet in F, Op. 53. Wind quintets, Op. 67/1–3.*
*** BIS Dig. CD 539 [id.]. (i) Love Derwinger; BPO Wind Qt.

Danzi was one of the first composers to cultivate the wind quintet and these diverting pieces, played with much distinction and recorded with great clarity and presence, offer unexpected pleasure. The *Piano quintet* is insubstantial, but rather delightful all the same.

Da Ponte, Lorenzo (1749–1838)

L'ape musicale.
**(*) Nuova Era Dig. 6845/6 (2). Scarabelli, Matteuzzi, Dara, Comencini, Teatro la Fenice Ch. & O, Vittorio Parisi.

This greatest of librettists was no composer, but he was musical enough to devise a pasticcio like *L'ape musicale* ('The musical bee') from the works of others, notably Rossini and Mozart. The first Act – full of Rossinian passages one keeps recognizing – leads up to a complete performance of Tamino's aria, *Dies Bildnis*, sung in German at the end of the Act. Similarly, Act II culminates in an adapted version of the final cabaletta from Rossini's *Cenerentola*. The sound is dry, with the voices slightly distanced. The stage and audience noises hardly detract from the fun of the performance.

Dauvergne, Antoine (1713–97)

Concerts de simphonies: Premier Concert in B flat, Op. 3/1; Deuxième Concert in F, Op. 3/2; Quatrième concert in A, Op. 4/2.
(N) (M) *** Virgin Veritas/EMI VM5 61542-2 [id.]. Concerto Köln.

The catalogue of Dauvergne's instrumental output contains only four publications, of which the *Concerts de simphonies*, Op. 3 and Op. 4 represent exactly half. They are a real find, full of attractive ideas and catchy rhythms. Each begins with an Overture and ends with a Chaconne. The *F major* work (included also below) has five movements in between; the *B flat Simphonie* appears to have only two, but each is subdivided; the *A major* work has five, but again two are subdivided. One has only to sample the skipping *Andantino* of Op. 3/2, the engaging *Minuetto grazioso* or the penultimate *Presto* (with its fizzing groups of double triplets and double quadruplets) to confirm that Dauvergne is a composer of individuality. The performances here have both grace and much vigour: the period-instrument playing is polished, aurally pleasing, and often has real bravura. The recording too is first-class. Well worth seeking out.

(i) *Les Troqueurs* (opéra-bouffon et ballet; complete). *Concerts de simphonies in F, Op. 3/2.*
(N) (B) *** HM Musique d'abord Dig. HMA 1901454 [id.].(i) Mary Saint-Palais, Sophie Marin-Degor, Nicholas Rivenq, Jean-Marc Salzmann; Cappella Coloniensis.

This disc is a splendid find and sheer delight. Historically important as a pioneering French opéra-comique, and clearly influenced by Pergolesi's *La serva padrona*, *Les Troqueurs* ('The Barterers') is a splendid little work in its own right. Two pairs of engaged lovers decide to exchange partners until the temperamental explosions of one of the ladies (Margot) makes her substitute paramour quickly change his mind; all is resolved when the original relationships are resumed. To have such a frothy Italianate conception given a French accent doubles the listener's pleasure. The two pairs of singers are not individually outstanding (indeed their voices are very alike), but their repartee is ever-vivacious, and Christie deftly keeps the pot boiling with his excellent and stylish *Cappella Coloniensis*. At the close of the opéra-comique, the orchestra then entertains us with a *Concert of symphonies*, in essence an elegant little suite, with bouncing rhythms, and a gracious chaconne as a closing movement, altogether very winning. The recording is excellent, and with full translation included, this is a bargain not to be missed.

Davydov, Karl (1838–89)

Cello concerto No. 2 in A min., Op. 14.
(N) **(*) Chandos Dig. CHAN 9622 [id.]. Alexander Ziumbrovsky, I Musici de Montréal, Yuli Turovsky – CONUS: *Violin concerto*; GLAZUNOV: *Piano concerto No. 2.* **(*).

Davydov (or Davïdov) was one of the greatest cellists of his day – Tchaikovsky described him as 'the king of cellists'. His *A minor concerto* is rather bland, almost Mendelssohnian, but it is an excellent visiting card for the soloist, Alexander Ziumbrovsky, who plays with a fine and natural musicianship.

Dawson, William (1899–1990)

Negro Folk Symphony.
*** Chandos Dig. CHAN 9226 [id.]. Detroit SO, Neeme Järvi – STILL: *Symphony No. 2;* ELLINGTON: *Harlem.* ***

William Dawson began life the son of a poor Alabama labourer, yet he worked his way up to become Director of Music at the Tuskegee Institute. His *Negro Folk Symphony* is designed to combine European influences and Negro folk themes. All three movements are chimerical. The music is rhapsodic and has plenty of energy and ideas, but they are inclined to run away with their composer. Järvi, however, is persuasive and has the advantage of excellent orchestral playing and first-class Chandos sound.

Debussy, Claude (1862–1918)

Complete orchestral music (as below).
(M) **(*) Chandos Dig. CHAN 7019 (4) [id.]. Soloists, Ulster O, Yan Pascal Tortelier.

La boîte à joujoux; Children's corner (orch. Caplet); *Danse (Tarantelle styrienne*, orch. Ravel); *Marche écossaise sur un thème populaire; Petite suite* (orch. Büsser).
(M) *** Chandos Dig. CHAN 7017 [id.]. Ulster O, Y. P. Tortelier.

(i) *Fantaisie for piano and orchestra;* (ii) *Danse sacrée et danse profane for harp and strings; L'Isle joyeuse* (orch. Molinari); (iii) *La plus que lente;* (iv) *Première rapsodie for clarinet and orchestra;* (v) *Rapsodie for alto saxophone and orchestra* (orch. Roger-Ducasse); *Sarabande* (orch.Ravel); *Suite bergamasque: Clair de lune* (orch. Caplet).
(M) *** Chandos Dig. CHAN 7018 [id.]. Ulster O, Y. P. Tortelier, with (i) Anne Queffélec; (ii) Rachel Masters; (iii) Derek Bell (cimbalom); (iv) Christopher King; (v) Gerard McChrystal.

Images; Jeux; Khamma.
(M) **(*) Chandos Dig. CHAN 7016 [id.]. Ulster O, Y. P. Tortelier.

La Mer; Nocturnes; Printemps; Prélude à l'après-midi d'un faune.
** Chandos Dig. CHAN 7015 [id.]. Ulster O, Y. P. Tortelier.

As can be seen, Chandos have now assembled Debussy's orchestral music (previously coupled with Ravel) in an upper-mid-priced box in recordings which generally represent the state of the art. There are excellent soloists in the concertante works. The subtlety and atmosphere of *La boîte à joujoux* are captured splendidly, and the concertante works are equally sensitive. Not all the performances are a first choice, but the shorter works come off particularly well. CHAN 7017 and 7018, now available separately, are very desirable indeed.

2 Arabesques (orch. Mouton); (i) *La cathédrale engloutie* (orch. Stokowski); *La mer; Petite suite* (orch. Henri Büsser); *Pagodes* (orch. Grainger). *Première rapsodie for clarinet and orchestra; Suite bergamasque: Clair de lune* (orch. Caplet).

*** Cala Dig. CACD 1001 [id.]. (i) James Campbell; Philh. O, Geoffrey Simon.

Geoffrey Simon's warm, urgent reading of *La Mer*, very well recorded, comes in coupling with six items originally involving piano. Debussy did his own arrangement of the *Clarinet rhapsody* and approved André Caplet's arrangement of *Clair de lune* as well as Henri Büsser's of the *Petite suite*. Stokowski's freely imagined orchestral version of *La cathédrale engloutie* is effectively opulent, and the most fascinating instrumentation of all comes in Percy Grainger's transcription of *Pagodes*, with an elaborate percussion section simulating a Balinese gamelan.

(i) *Berceuse héroïque;* (ii; iii) *Danses sacrée et profane* (for harp and strings); (ii) *Images; Jeux; Marche écossaise; La Mer;* (ii; iv) *Nocturnes;* (ii) *Prélude à l'après-midi d'un faune;* (ii; v) *Première rapsodie for clarinet and orchestra.*
❀ (B) *** Ph. Duo 438 742-2 (2) [id.]. Concg. O, (i) Eduard van Beinum; (ii) Bernard Haitink; with (iii) Vera Badings; (iv) Women's Ch. of Coll. Mus.; (v) George Pieterson.

This Duo must now rank as the finest Debussy collection in the CD catalogue. Although the programme as a whole is directed by Haitink, it is good that his distinguished predecessor, Eduard van Beinum, is remembered by the opening *Berceuse héroïque*, played with great delicacy and a real sense of mystery, with the early stereo (1957) highly effective. For the *Danses sacrée et profane* Haitink takes over, with elegant playing from the harpist, Vera Badings, who is excellently balanced. Haitink's reading of *Images* is second to none and is beautifully played by the wonderful Dutch orchestra; this applies equally to *Jeux*, while in the *Nocturnes* the choral balance is perfectly judged, and few versions are quite as beguiling and seductive as Haitink's. His *La Mer* is comparable with Karajan's 1964 recording. The hazily sensuous *Prélude à l'après-midi d'un faune* and the undervalued *Clarinet rhapsody* are also played atmospherically, although the former is more overtly languorous in Karajan's hands. Again the Philips recording is truthful and natural, with beautiful perspectives and realistic colour, a marvellously refined sound.

Berceuse héroïque; Images; Jeux; Marche écossaise; La Mer; Musiques pour le Roi Lear; Nocturnes; Prélude à l'après-midi d'un faune; Printemps.
(B) *** EMI forte CZS5 72667-2 (2) [CDFP 72667]. Fr. R. & TV Ch. & O, Martinon.

Martinon's is a very good *Images*, beautifully played, with the orchestral detail vivid and glowing. *Jeux* is also very fine, with the sound attractively spacious. *La Mer* enjoys the idiomatic advantage of fine French orchestral playing, even if it does not quite match Karajan or Haitink. The *Musiques pour le Roi Lear* is a real rarity; the colourful *Fanfare* remains impressive, and *Le sommeil de Lear* is highly evocative. The *Nocturnes* are beautifully played, as indeed is *Printemps*, with Martinon penetrating its charm. At bargain price these are competitive recommendations, and the current transfers are warmly atmospheric; even if the upper end of the range is rather brightly lit, there is plenty of depth in the sound.

La boîte à joujoux; Children's corner (orch. Caplet); *Danse* (orch. Ravel); (i) *Danses sacrée et profane.* (ii) *Fantaisie for piano and orchestra. La plus que lente; Khamma; Petite suite* (orch. Büsser); (iii) *Première rhapsodie for clarinet and orchestra.* (iv) *Rhapsodie for saxophone.*
(B) *** EMI forte CZS5 72673-2 (2) [CDFB 72673]. Fr. R. & TV O, Martinon; with (i) Marie-Claire Jamet; (ii) Aldo Ciccolini; (iii) Guy Dangain; (iv) Londe.

Children's corner and *La boîte à joujoux* contain much to enchant the ear, as does the tuneful *Petite suite*. The rarity here is *Khamma*. This and the two *Rhapsodies* are underrated and, although there are alternative versions of all these pieces, none is more economically priced. The performances are sympathetic and authoritative, and the recordings have been remastered successfully. The sound is full and spacious with an attractive ambient glow.

La boîte à joujoux; Jeux; Prélude à l'après-midi d'un faune.
*** Sony Dig. SK 48231 [id.]. LSO, Tilson Thomas.

La boîte à joujoux is ideally suited to Michael Tilson Thomas's talents. His account is second to none and has the right lightness of touch and wistful charm. Nor will collectors be disappointed with his account of *Jeux*, which is admirably unhurried and atmospheric, or his dreamy, languorous *Prélude à l'après-midi d'un faune*. *Jeux* does not displace the Haitink Duo version on Philips but can be recommended alongside it and has the advantage of modern digital sound of the first order, very natural and spacious.

Children's corner; Danse (Tarantelle styrienne) (arr. Ravel); *Estampes: La soirée dans Grenade* (arr. Stokowski). *L'isle joyeuse; Nocturnes; Préludes: Bruyères; La fille aux cheveux de lin.*
*** Cala CACD 1002 [id.]. Philh. O, Geoffrey Simon.

Geoffrey Simon's version of the three *Nocturnes* is colourful and atmospheric, with nothing vague in *Fêtes*. The orchestrations of piano music include Stokowski's vivid realization of *La soirée dans Grenade*, as well as Ravel's magical reinterpretation of *Danse* and André Caplet's sensitive orchestration of *Children's corner*. Full, vivid recorded sound.

Danse; Images: Ibéria, Marche écossaise; La Mer; Nocturnes: Nuages; Fêtes (only); (i) *La damoiselle élue*.

(N) (B) (***) Naxos mono 8.110811-2 [id.]. NBC SO, Toscanini; (i) with Jarmila Novotna, Hertha Glaz, Schola Cantorum Women's Ch.

This is one of the most valuable of the Naxos historic issues of Toscanini, bringing revelations both predictable and unpredictable. These are incandescent, sharply focused performances quite unlike any others, and offering the longest of the irascible rehearsals which are a fascinating feature of the series. It is specially valuable to have the three rare works – the *Marche écossaise* of 1908; the *Danse*, an early piano piece orchestrated by Ravel; and the early lyric poem, *La damoiselle élue* – with clean-cut soloists.

Danse (Tarantelle styrienne); Sarabande (orch. Ravel).

(M) *** Virgin/EMI Dig. CUV5 61206-2. Lausanne CO, Zedda – MILHAUD: *Création du monde;* PROKOFIEV: *Sinfonietta*. ***

Zedda's performances with the Lausanne Chamber Orchestra are neat and polished, full of character and well recorded. But it is the couplings that make this disc especially attractive.

Danse sacrée et danse profane (for harp and string orchestra).

(***) Testament mono SBT 1053 [id.]. Anne Mason Stockton, Concert Arts Strings, Slatkin – CRESTON: *Quartet;* RAVEL: *Intro & allegro;* TURINA: *La Oración del torero;* VILLA-LOBOS: *Quartet No. 6*. (***)

Felix Slatkin and his Hollywood colleagues give as atmospheric an account of the *Danse sacrée et danse profane* as any on record, and Anne Mason Stockton is the excellent harpist. The mono recording dates from 1951 but is uncommonly good. This comes as part of a remarkably fine anthology of Hollywood Quartet recordings.

(i) *Danses sacrée et profane; Images. Jeux; La Mer;* (ii) *Nocturnes; Printemps;* (iii) *Première rapsodie for clarinet and orchestra*.

(M) **(*) Sony SM2K 68327 (2) [id.]. New Philh. O or (i) Cleveland O; Boulez; with (i) Alice Chalifoux; (ii) John Alldis Ch.; (iii) Gervase de Peyer.

Jeux, a work of seminal importance in Boulez's development, is here given very persuasively. The *Images* are carefully shaped and balanced, and like the coolly distinctive *Danses sacrée et profane*, were recorded in Cleveland and gain from the ambience of Severance Hall, even if the balance is close. *La Mer* and the *Prélude à l'après-midi d'un faune* (which certainly does not lack passionate feeling) are a good deal better than some accounts, but *La Mer* cannot compare with the Karajan version from the same era in subtly conveying the briny marine atmosphere. Needless to say, Gervase de Peyer gives a distinguished account of the lovely *Clarinet rhapsody*, and the contribution of the John Alldis Choir to *Sirènes*, the third of the *Nocturnes*, is poised, even if the effect overall is cool rather than ethereal. But those who respond to Boulez's clarity of vision in this repertoire will find that the Sony engineers have made a marvellous job of these transfers to CD, maximizing the ambient effect and retaining the sharply defined detail.

Fantaisie for piano and orchestra.

*** Ph. Dig. 446 713-2. Zoltán Kocsis, Budapest Festival O, Iván Fischer – RAVEL: *Concertos*. **

Zoltán Kocsis's credentials as a Debussy interpreter scarcely need asserting. His account of the *Fantaisie* is both lucid and delicate and can be recommended with confidence. This would be a clear first choice, but the two Ravel concertos with which it is coupled are not.

(i) *Fantaisie for piano and orchestra. Pour le piano*.

(N) **(*) RCA 09026 68127-2 [id.]. Barry Douglas with (i) O Philh. de Radio France – BRITTEN: *Piano concerto*. **(*)

Debussy never heard his early *Fantaisie* for piano and orchestra and never carried out his projected revision of the score. Barry Douglas gives a very straightforward account of it without commanding perhaps the degree of tonal finesse that distinguishes Gieseking's version. His *Pour le piano* is very good without being touched by distinction; the *Toccata* is a little wanting in refinement of colour and there is some ugly tone in its fortissimos.

Images.

**(*) Sony Dig. SK 53284 [id.]. BPO, Levine – ELGAR: *Enigma variations*. **(*)

Images; Jeux; Le Roi Lear (incidental music).

(B) *** [EMI Red Line CDR5 72095]. CBSO, Rattle.

Images; Nocturnes; (i) *Le Martyre de Saint Sébastien:* (symphonic fragments); *La Mer; Prélude à l'après-midi d'un faune; Printemps* (orch. Büusser).

(N) (B) *** Decca Double Dig. 460 217-2 (2) [id.]. Montreal SO, Dutoit (i) with chorus.

In *Images* Rattle is memorably atmospheric, while in *Jeux* he is just a touch more expansive than most rivals, and also more evocative, though he does not depart from the basic metronome markings. Haitink probably remains a first choice in this score, for he has atmosphere and a tauter grip on the music's flow. The *King Lear* excerpts sound splendid. First-rate recording, very vivid but beautifully balanced. This CD is only available in the USA.

Images is hardly central repertory for the Berlin

Philharmonic and it brings a degree of controversy among us. For EG, Levine draws thrilling, intense performances from the players, clear-cut rather than atmospheric, making an unexpected but exciting coupling, and offering sound as full and immediate as has ever been achieved in the Philharmonie. RL feels that the sonority produced by the Berlin Philharmonic is much changed since Karajan's days, and the orchestra's corporate personality of the previous era is here replaced by a general-purpose sound such as any orchestra of the first rank might produce. The recording is very good indeed, with fine definition and dynamic range.

In *Images* and the *Nocturnes* Dutoit is freer than some with rubato, as well as in his warm, espressivo moulding of phrase. His sharp pointing of rhythm, as in the Spanish dances of *Ibéria* or the processional march in *Fêtes*, is also highly characteristic of his approach to French music. By contrast Dutoit conducts taut and powerful readings of the remaining works. They are strong on purposeful strength rather than evocative magic, though few versions of *L'après-midi* match this one in the seductive beauty of Timothy Hutchins' flute playing. For those who like these impressionistic masterpieces to be presented in full colour, with a vivid feeling for atmosphere, this is an ideal choice.

Images: Ibéria (only).
❁ (M) *** RCA GD 60179 [60179-2-RG]. Chicago SO, Fritz Reiner – RAVEL: *Alborada* etc. *** ❁

Fritz Reiner and the Chicago orchestra give a reading that is immaculate in execution and magical in atmosphere. This marvellously evocative performance, and the Ravel with which it is coupled, should not be overlooked, for the recorded sound with its natural concert-hall balance is greatly improved in terms of body and definition. It is amazingly realistic even without considering its vintage.

Images: Ibéria. La Mer; Nocturnes: Nuages; Fêtes. Prélude à l'après-midi d'un faune.
(M) (**(*)) RCA mono GD 60265 [60265-2-RG]. NBC SO, Toscanini.

By emphasizing clarity, Toscanini with his electric intensity and sense of purpose consistently compels attention. One thinks of these supreme examples of musical impressionism, not as colour pieces but as masterly structures of great originality in purely musical terms. Clean, bright transfers.

Images: Ibéria. La Mer; Prélude à l'après-midi d'un faune.
(M) *** Mercury (IMS) 434 343-2 [id.]. Detroit SO, Paray – RAVEL: *Ma Mère l'oye*. ***

Paray, in 1955, gave us the first stereo recording of *La Mer* which is very exciting, balancing powerful evocation and firm overall control. The balance is slightly recessed, which provides plenty of atmosphere and a hazy warm luminosity to the glowingly voluptuous account of *L'après-midi* with its ardently beautiful string climax. The recording is without sharply delineated detail, yet for body, natural concert-hall balance and richness of orchestral colour there are few stereo recordings made in the mid- to late-1950s to match this.

Jeux; La Mer; Nocturnes: Nuages, Fêtes (only).
(N) (***) Testament mono SBT 1108 [id.]. St Cecilia Ac., Rome O, Victor de Sabata. – RESPIGHI: *Fountains of Rome*. (***)

Victor de Sabata's 1947 account with his Rome Orchestra of *Jeux* brings great character and atmosphere to this wonderful score. Although the two purely orchestral *Nocturnes* first appeared on record in 1948, de Sabata's account of *La Mer* did not and makes its first appearance now. He presumably did not pass it and it is not without blemish, but it is still music-making of quality that deserves a place in any Debussy collection.

Jeux; La Mer; Nocturnes; Prélude à l'après-midi d'un faune.
(N) (M) ** Sony SMK 60972 [id.]. NYPO, Bernstein.

There is plenty to admire in the orchestral playing under Bernstein, which is of considerable virtuosity but these performances, notably of *La Mer* and the *Prélude* are very personal readings indeed. The atmosphere, and Bernstein has undoubted feeling for atmosphere, is at a stage removed from the experience itself and the resulting performance has an air of self-indulgence, magnetic as it is. The phrasing in *Prélude à l'après-midi d'un faune* is very self-conscious in places and *Jeux* too lacks a consistent forward pulse. The recording is atmospheric, but the woodwind is too forward in balance.

La Mer.
(M) *** DG 447 426-2 [id.]. BPO, Karajan – MUSSORGSKY: *Pictures;* RAVEL: *Boléro*. ***
(M) *** RCA 0926 68079-2 [id.]. Chicago SO, Fritz Reiner – RESPIGHI: *Fountains & Pines of Rome*. *** ❁
(M) *** RCA 09026 60875 [id.]. Chicago SO, Reiner – RIMSKY-KORSAKOV: *Scheherazade*. ***
(M) **(*) RCA 09026 61500-2 [id.]. Boston SO, Munch – IBERT: *Escales* ***; SAINT-SAENS: *Symphony No. 3*. *** ❁
(M) **(*) Decca (IMS) 448 576-2 [id.]. SRO, Ansermet – CHABRIER: *España* **(*); DUKAS: *L'apprenti sorcier* ***; HONEGGER: *Pacific 231* ***; RAVEL: *Boléro; La Valse*. ***
(N) (**) Orfeo C 488 981 B [id.]. BPO, Mitropoulos – MENDELSSOHN: *Symphony No. 3*; SCHOENBERG: *Variations*. (**)

La Mer; Danse (Tarantelle styrienne); (i) *Nocturnes. Prélude à l'après-midi d'un faune.*

(B) *** Sony SBK 53266 [id.]. Phd. O, Ormandy, (i) with Temple University Womens' Ch.

La Mer; Images: Iberia. Nocturnes: Nuages; Fêtes (only); *Prélude à l'après-midi d'un faune.*

(M) *** [RCA Basic 100 09026 61556-2]. Boston SO, Munch.

La Mer; (i) *Nocturnes.*

(BB) *** EMI Seraphim Dig. CES5 68539-2 (2) (i) Amb. S.; LSO, Previn – MUSSORGSKY: *Pictures*; RAVEL: *Alborada* etc. **(*)

La Mer; (i) *Nocturnes. Prélude à l'après-midi d'un faune.*

(M) *** Penguin Classics DG 460 636-2 [id.]. O de Paris, Barenboim, (i) with Ch.

La Mer; (i) *Nocturnes. Prélude à l'après-midi d'un faune.*

(BB) *** Carlton LSO Double Dig. 30368 01187 (2) [(B) id. import]. LSO, Frühbeck de Burgos, (i) with L. Symphony women's chorus – BIZET: *Jeux d'enfants* **; (with RAVEL: *Ma Mère l'Oye* **(*)); SAINT-SAENS: *Carnival of the animals.* **

La Mer; Nocturnes: Nuages; Fêtes (only). *Prélude à l'après-midi d'un faune. Printemps* (symphonic suite).

(BB) *** RCA Navigator 74321 21293-2 [(M) 6179-2-RG]. Boston SO, Munch.

La Mer; Prélude à l'après-midi d'un faune.

(M) *** DG 427 250-2. BPO, Karajan – RAVEL: *Boléro; Daphnis et Chloé.* ***

(i) *La Mer; Prélude à l'après-midi d'un faune;* (ii) *Prélude: La cathédrale engloutie* (orch. Stokowski).

(M) *** Decca Phase Four 455 152-2 [id.]. (i) LSO; (ii) New Philh. O; Stokowski – RAVEL: *Daphnis et Chloé: suite No. 2.* ***

After three decades, Karajan's 1964 account of *La Mer* is still very much in a class of its own. It enshrines the spirit of the work as effectively as it observes the letter, and the superb playing of the Berlin orchestra, for all its virtuosity and sound, is totally self-effacing. It is now available coupled with Karajan's outstanding (1966) record of Mussorgsky's *Pictures at an exhibition* and a gripping account of Ravel's *Boléro*, but we prefer the original coupling of the *Prélude à l'après-midi d'un faune* and Ravel's *Daphnis et Chloé*, which are equally unforgettable.

Reiner's 1960 recording is available coupled with either Rimsky-Korsakov's *Scheherazade* or Respighi's *Fountains* and *Pines of Rome*. It has great warmth and atmosphere, while the *pianissimo* opening has enormous evocative feeling and the *Jeux des vagues* has a haunting sense of colour. Of course the marvellous acoustics of the Chicago Hall contribute to the appeal of this superbly played account: the effect is richer and fuller than in Karajan's remastered DG version, and Reiner's record gives no less pleasure.

Stokowski's version of *La Mer* is a Phase Four recording, using multi-microphones to most brilliant effect, but the effect is breathtaking in its vividness and impact. The performance has surprisingly slow basic tempi, even for Stokowski, and the *Prélude à l'après-midi d'un faune* is comparably languorous. But the playing has a wonderful intensity. Stokowski's spectacular arrangement of *La cathédrale engloutie* presents the music in wholly orchestral terms and is quite different from the piano original.

Previn's ocean, like Reiner's, is clearly in the southern hemisphere, with Debussy's orchestral colours made to sound more vividly sunlit. The playing of the LSO is extremely impressive, particularly the ardour of the strings. The recording has glittering detail and expands brilliantly at climaxes (though there is a slight loss of refinement at the very loudest peaks). The *Nocturnes* have even greater spontaneity.

The new CD transfers have completely transformed the Munch recordings, the Boston acoustic now casting a wonderfully warm aura over the orchestra, and the sound is gloriously expansive and translucent. There is marvellous Boston playing here, especially from the violins. Munch's inclination to go over the top may not appeal to all listeners, but the results are very compelling when the orchestral bravura is so thrilling. The *Prélude* makes a ravishing interlude, expanding to a rapturous climax. The permutation of music is slightly different on the RCA Basic 100 reissue.

In Ormandy's 1964 set of *Nocturnes* the orchestral playing has the superb subtlety of timbre we expect from a Philadelphia performance, although in *Sirènes* the female chorus refuses to sound quite ethereal enough. *La Mer* dates from 1959 and is relatively closely balanced, though not impossibly so. The orchestral playing in *Jeux de vagues* has thrilling virtuosity. The *Prélude à l'après-midi d'un faune* (with a fine flute solo from William Kincaid) is sensuous but refined; the *Danse* is stunningly played, yet the conductor's touch is as light as anyone could wish. Indeed this is one of Ormandy's most impressive Sony reissues.

Barenboim's 1978 coupling of *La Mer* and *Nocturnes*, reissued on the Penguin Classics label, offers not only first-class analogue recording but performances which, although highly individual in their control of tempo, have great electricity and ardour. The *Prélude à l'après-midi d'un faune* has comparable languor to *Sirènes*, the last of the *Nocturnes*, if not quite the same refinement of feeling. Excellent sound for its period. The accompanying essay is by Marina Warner.

Although strong in Mediterranean atmosphere, Frühbeck de Burgos's account of *La Mer* has an underlying grip, so he can concentrate on evocation at the opening and continue to lead the ear on spontaneously. Overall there is plenty of excitement and much subtlety of detail, both here and in the *Nocturnes*, where textures again have the sensuousness of southern climes, and no lack of glitter. The *Prélude à l'après-midi d'un faune* brings lovely, delicate flute-playing from Paul Edmund-Davies and a richly moulded string climax. If these are not conventional readings, they are full of impulse and are superbly recorded.

Karajan's 1978 analogue re-recording of *La Mer* for EMI may not have quite the supreme refinement of his earlier DG version – partly a question of the warmer, vaguer recording – but it has a comparable concentration, with the structure persuasively and inevitably built. The *Prélude* has an appropriate languor, and there is a persuasive warmth about this performance, beautifully moulded; but again the earlier version distilled greater atmosphere and magic.

Ansermet's 1964 *La Mer*, although characteristically vibrant and vividly detailed, did not match his earlier recordings in the quality of the orchestral playing, with moments of suspect intonation. The rest of this concert, however, shows the Swiss conductor on top form.

The Orfeo *La Mer* was recorded at the Salzburg Festival in 1960 and is a magical and atmospheric performance. Mitropoulos casts a strong spell but the frequency range is narrow and the sound of the strings above the stave is shrill and strident.

La Mer; Nocturnes: Nuages; Fêtes (only); *Le Martyre de Saint-Sébastien* (symphonic fragments); *Prélude à l'après-midi d'un faune.*
(***) Testament mono SBT 1011. Philh. O, Guido Cantelli.

Cantelli's account of the four symphonic fragments from *Le Martyre de Saint-Sébastien* is one of the most beautiful performances he ever committed to vinyl; the textures are impeccably balanced and phrases flawlessly shaped. Its atmosphere is as concentrated as that of the legendary first recording under Coppola. *La Mer* and the *Prélude à l'après-midi d'un faune* are hardly less perfect and the transfers are excellent.

Petite suite (orch. Büsser).
(B) *** Sony SBK 63056 [id.]. Cleveland O, Louis Lane – RAVEL: *Introduction and allegro*, etc.; SATIE: *Gymnopédies Nos. 1 & 3.* ***

It is good to have a first-class performance of Debussy's *Petite suite* in Büsser's charming orchestration on bargain label. The warmly atmospheric recording dates from the late 1960s when Louis Lane was a colleague of George Szell at Cleveland and the orchestra was still at the peak of its form.

CHAMBER MUSIC

Cello sonata; Petite pièce for clarinet and piano; Première rapsodie for clarinet and piano; Sonata for flute, viola and harp; Violin sonata; Syrinx for solo flute.
*** Chandos CHAN 8385 [id.]. Athena Ens.

The most ethereal of these pieces is the *Sonata for flute, viola and harp*, whose other-worldly quality is beautifully conveyed here. In the case of the other sonatas, there are strong competitors but, as a collection, this is certainly recommendable.

Cello sonata in D min.
(M) *** Decca 452 895-2. Rostropovich, Britten – BRITTEN: *Sonata;* SCHUMANN: *5 Stücke in Volkston.* ***
(N) (M) *** Decca Legends 460 974-2 [id.]. Rostropovich, Britten – SCHUBERT: *Arpeggione sonata* **(*); SCHUMANN: *5 Stücke in Volkston.* ***
**(*) ASV Dig. CDDCA 796 [id.]. Bernard Gregor-Smith, Yolande Wrigley – BRIDGE; DOHNANYI: *Sonatas.* **(*)

(i) *Cello sonata;* (ii) *Violin sonata.*
(*) Chandos Dig. CHAN 8458 [id.]. (i) Yuli Turovsky; (ii) Rostislav Dubinsky; Luba Edlina – RAVEL: *Piano trio.* *

Like Debussy's other late chamber works, the *Cello sonata* is a concentrated piece, quirkily original. The classic version by Rostropovich and Britten has a clarity and point which suit the music perfectly. The recording is first class and, if the couplings are suitable, this holds its place as first choice. It is fully worthy of reissue in Decca's Classic Sound series, and also comes with slightly different couplings in Decca's latest Legends series.

Bernard Gregor-Smith and Yolande Wrigley play with great refinement and authority, as well as much sensitivity. They are perhaps too closely balanced but this does not prevent their record being a highly desirable one.

Turovsky gives a well-delineated, powerful account with Luba Edlina. In the *Violin sonata*, Rostislav Dubinsky and Luba Edlina (his wife) are in excellent form, though this is red-blooded Slavonic Debussy rather than the more ethereal, subtle playing of a Grumiaux.

Le petit nègre; Petite pièce; Première rapsodie; Rapsodie for cor anglais; Rapsodie for saxophone; Sonata for flute, viola and harp; (i) *Syrinx.*
(B) *** Cala Dig. CACD 1017 (2) [id.]. William Bennett, Nicholas Daniel, James Campbell, Rachael Gough, (i) Simon Haram & Ens. – SAINT-SAENS: *Chamber music.* ***

The *Rapsodie for cor anglais* with which this Cala Duo opens is more familiar in its form for alto saxophone, which was originally to have been called

Rapsodie Mauresque. Daniel plays it with great sensitivity. It is also heard in its alternative form, splendidly played by Simon Haram. The performance of the *Sonata for flute, viola and harp* is highly sensitive.

Piano trio in G (1880).

(*) Arabeske. Dig. Z 6643 [id.]. Golub Kaplan Carr Trio – FAURE: *Piano trio* *; SAINT-SAENS: *Piano trio*. **(*)

(BB) **(*) Naxos Dig. 8.550934 [id.]. Joachim Trio – RAVEL: *Piano trio;* SCHMITT: *Piano trio: Très lent*. **(*)

The *G major Trio* is an early work and is not very characteristic. The Golub–Kaplan–Carr Trio give a very good account of this slender piece, and they are decently recorded.

The Joachim Trio also play with consistent sensitivity and finesse. This is a thoroughly musical account and beautifully recorded; but it would not necessarily be a first choice, though the attractive price-tag (and the agreeable Schmitt bonus) makes it competitive.

Sonata for flute, viola and harp.

❁ (M) *** Decca 452 891-2 [id.]. Osian Ellis, Melos Ens. (members) – RAVEL: *Introduction and allegro*; ROUSSEL: *Sérénade for flute, violin, viola, cello & harp;* ROPARTZ: *Prélude, marine et chansons*. *** ❁

*** Koch Dig. 3-7016-2 [id.]. Atlantic Sinf. – JOLIVET: *Chant de Linos;* JONGEN: *Concert*. ***

The delectable *Sonata for flute, viola and harp* is ravishingly played by members of the Melos Ensemble, and it brings a hauntingly magical atmosphere to compare with its sublime Ravel coupling.

The three members of the Atlantic Sinfonietta are well balanced and achieve a feeling of repose and mystery. This is the best of the recent recordings of this enormously civilized and ethereal music, but the Melos version remains special.

String quartet in G min.

*** DG (IMS) Dig. 437 836-2 (id.]. Hagen Qt – RAVEL; WEBERN: *Quartets*. ***

*** RCA Dig. 09026 61816-2 [id.]. Vogler Qt – JANACEK *Quartet* (with SHOSTAKOVICH: *Quartet No. 11*. ***)

*** Sony Dig. SK 52554 [id.]. Juilliard Qt – DUTILLEUX; RAVEL: *Quartets*. ***

(B) *** Ph. 420 894-2. Italian Qt – RAVEL: *Quartet*. ***

(B) *** CfP Dig. CD-CFP 4652. Chilingirian Qt – RAVEL: *Quartet*. ***

(BB) **(*) Naxos Dig. 8.550249 [id.]. Kodály Qt – RAVEL: *Quartet* etc. ***

**(*) ASV Dig. CDDCA 930 [id.]. Lindsay Qt – RAVEL: *String quartet* **(*); STRAVINSKY: *3 Pieces*. **(*)

**(*) RCA Dig. 09026 62552-2 [id.]. Tokyo Qt – RAVEL: *Introduction and allegro; Quartet*. **(*)

The Debussy and Ravel quartets are an almost mandatory coupling these days and even Dover Scores reprint the two together! The Hagen Quartet on DG produce the greatest refinement of sound without beautifying the score; they also enjoy the benefit of superb engineering. Indeed, this might well be a first choice among recent issues.

The Vogler on RCA offer a more unusual combination. This is an exceptionally fine account of the Debussy, fiery when required, highly sensitive to dynamic nuance and keenly atmospheric; it is as good as any now before the public. Put the Vogler slow movement, say, alongside the Juilliard, and comparison is very much to their advantage. The Janáček and Shostakovich couplings are equally fine.

The Juilliard performance is impressive all the same, in spite of the wider vibrato these players employ, which one barely notices except when making a direct comparison. Their first movement is not as fresh and ardent as the Vogler, but overall this is very satisfying and they are well recorded.

Turning now to the bargain-priced versions, it need hardly be said that the playing of the Quartetto Italiano is outstanding. Perfectly judged ensemble, weight and tone still make this a most satisfying choice and, even if it is rather short measure, the Philips recording engineers have produced a vivid and truthful sound-picture.

Also at bargain price, the Chilingirian coupling is in every way competitive. They give a thoroughly committed account with well-judged tempi and very musical phrasing. The Scherzo is vital and spirited, and there is no want of poetry in the slow movement. The recording has plenty of body and presence and has the benefit of a warm acoustic: the sound is fuller than on the competing version by the Italian Quartet.

As we know from their Haydn recordings, the Kodály Quartet are an excellent ensemble and they too give a thoroughly enjoyable account . There are moments here (in the slow movement, for example) when the Kodály are touched by distinction. This music-making has the feel of a live performance: these players also have the benefit of a generous fill-up and very good recorded sound. Excellent value.

The Lindsays play with their usual aplomb and panache. There are splendid things here, notably the youthful fire of the opening movement and the finely etched finale. They do not always match the *douceur* and *tendresse* which the Quartetto Italiano, the Hagen and the Tokyo find, but they are always stimulating. Fine recording.

The Tokyo Quartet play with great beauty and sweetness of tone. Their tonal refinement and perfect ensemble are a joy in themselves and are heard to great advantage in the inner movements. Unfortunately the first movement is pulled around rather more than is acceptable on a disc designed for repeated hearing, and some listeners will find this problematic.

Violin sonata.

❀ (M) *** Decca 460 006-2. Kyung-Wha Chung, Radu Lupu – FRANCK: *Violin sonata* *** ❀; CHAUSSON: *Poème.* ***

*** DG Dig. 445 880-2. Dumay, Pires – FRANCK: *Violin sonata in A*; RAVEL: *Berceuse*, etc. ***

*** Virgin/EMI Dig. VC5 45122-2. Tetzlaff, Andsnes – JANACEK: *Sonata;* RAVEL: *Sonata;* NIELSEN: *Sonata No. 2.* ***

(B) *** EMI Eminence Dig. CD-EMX 2244 [(M) id. import]. Tasmin Little, Piers Lane – POULENC: *Violin sonata;* RAVEL: *Violin sonata; Tzigane.* ***

(N) (BB) *** Arte Nova Dig. 74321 59233-2 [id.]. Miriam Contner, Valéry Rogatchev – FRANCK, SAINT-SAENS: *Violin sonatas.* ***

*** Sony Dig. SK 66839 [id.]. Cho-Liang Lin, Paul Crossley – POULENC: *Violin sonata;* RAVEL: *Sonatas; Tzigane.* ***

(N) ** Ph. Dig. 446 091-2 [id.]. Viktoria Mullova, Piotr Anderszewski – JANACEK; PROKOFIEV: *Violin sonatas.* **

Kyung-Wha Chung plays with marvellous character and penetration, and her partnership with Radu Lupu could hardly be more fruitful. Nothing is pushed to extremes, and everything is in perfect perspective. The recording sounds admirably real.

Augustin Dumay and Maria João Pires give as idiomatic and sensitive an account of the Debussy *Sonata* as one could wish for, and those wanting their particular coupling with Franck and Ravel need not really hesitate.

However, Christian Tetzlaff and Leif Ove Andsnes provide as expert and imaginative a partnership as any of their rivals. The sheer interest of their couplings, not least the Nielsen *G minor Sonata*, and the quality of the performances make this also one of the strongest contenders in the current catalogue.

Tasmin Little and Piers Lane also give a highly dedicated performance which tautly holds together the often fragmentary argument, making the result sound spontaneous in its total concentration. Excellent sound and a first-rate coupling.

Born in Germany in 1976, Mirijam Contner is a superb young violinist with plenty of fire and temperament, one who plays the elusive Debussy *Sonata* from the heart, as though improvising the music, helped by the understanding pianist. Full tone and immaculate technique. Well-balanced sound ensures a warm welcome for this excellent CD in the lowest price.

Cho-Liang Lin and Paul Crossley give a vibrant, well-argued account of the Debussy *Sonata* to which Sony accord excellent recording, and the strength of the present issue is the generous programme on offer. In addition to the Ravel *G major Sonata* (1922), they include the poignant and touching earlier essay Ravel made in this medium.

Mullova and Anderszewski give a well-projected account of the *Sonata* and receive a finely detailed recording which will give pleasure. However, despite the sound this is not as sympathetic or responsive in mood as the very best versions.

PIANO MUSIC

Piano duet

Danses sacrée et profane; En blanc et noir; Lindaraja; Nocturnes (trans. RAVEL); *Prélude à l'après-midi d'un faune.*

(N) (B) *** Hyperion Helios Dig. CDH 55014 [id.]. Stephen Coombs and Christopher Scott.

Stephen Coombs and Christopher Scott made an outstanding début with this fine recording, which leads the field in this repertoire. It has now transferred to Hyperion's bargain label, having first appeared on LDR. Very highly recommended.

En blanc et noir; 6 épigraphes antiques; Lindaraja; Petite suite; Nocturnes: Nuages, Fêtes (arr Ravel).

(N) *** Ph. Dig. 454 471-2 [id.]. Katia and Marielle Labèque.

The Labèque sisters focus on brilliance and sparkle, and their performances will stimulate and astonish. Martha Argerich and Stephen Kovacevich found more repose in their classic version of *En blanc et noir* but the Labèques' virtuosity is not in question, nor the excellence and presence of the Philips recording.

(i) *En blanc et noir; Lindaraja.* (Piano): *Estampes; Images I & II; L'isle joyeuse; Masques.*

(B) *** EMI CZS5 72376-2 (3) [(M) id. import]. Jean-Philippe Collard, (i) with Michel Béroff – RAVEL: *Piano music.* ***

Distinguished playing from Jean-Philippe Collard in the *Estampes* and the two sets of *Images*, and his collaboration with Michel Béroff in *En blanc et noir* is hardly less successful. The recording, made in the early 1970s at the Salle Wagram, is less satisfactory but good enough to warrant a full three-star recommendation on artistic grounds.

(i) *En blanc et noir; 6 Epigraphes antiques; Lindaraja; Marche écossaise; Petite suite.* (Solo piano): *Ballade slave; Berceuse héroïque; Danse (Tarantelle styrienne); Danse bohémienne; D'un cahier d'esquisses; 12 Etudes; Hommage à Haydn; Masques; Nocturne; Le petit nègre; La*

plus que lente; Rêverie; Suite bergamasque; Valse romantique.
(B) *** Ph. Duo 438 721-2 (2) [id.]. Werner Haas, (i) with Noël Lee.

2 Arabesques; Children's corner; Estampes; Images, Books 1–2; L'isle joyeuse; Mazurka; Pour le piano; Préludes, Books 1–2.
(B) **(*) Ph. Duo 438 718-2 (2) [(M) id. import]. Werner Haas.

The playing of Werner Haas is rarely routine. Book II of the *Préludes* and many of the pieces from Book 1 are very well worth having; the *Images* are pretty good too, and many of the shorter pieces in the second listed volume are neatly and sensitively characterized. What makes its companion pair of CDs indispensable is the splendid collection of Debussy's music for piano duet (four hands or two pianos), recorded a decade later, in which Haas is joined by Noël Lee. The *Petite suite* is delightfully fresh, and *En blanc et noir* and the *Six épigraphes antiques* are very distinguished indeed. The (early 1960s) piano recording throughout is well up to Philips's high standard.

Solo piano music

2 Arabesques; Ballade; Berceuse héroïque; Children's corner; Danse; Danse bohémienne; D'un cahier d'esquisses; Estampes; 12 Etudes; Hommage à Haydn; Images 1–2; L'isle joyeuse; Masques; Mazurka; Nocturne; Le petit nègre; La plus que lente; Pour le piano; Préludes, Books 1–2; Rêverie; Suite bergamasque; Valse romantique. (i) *Fantaisie for piano and orchestra.*
(M) (***) EMI mono CHS5 65855-2 (4) [CDHD 65855]. Walter Gieseking; (i) with Hessischen R. O, Schröder.

Gieseking's Debussy enjoyed legendary status in the 1930s and '40s, and EMI are to be congratulated for not only restoring to circulation the famous recordings he then made but also even adding to them. The two sets of *Préludes* date from 1953 and 1954, as indeed do most of the recordings collected here. The earliest is *Children's corner* from 1951, which is also the date of the Frankfurt recording of the *Fantaisie*. The latter calls for some (albeit not great) tolerance, but the remaining performances sound better than ever. Gieseking's artistry is too well known to need further exegesis or advocacy. As Bryce Morrison puts it in the accompanying notes, 'Deeply sensitive and personal, virtuosic in the truest sense, Gieseking's performances are quite without preening mannerisms or idiosyncrasy and are, from this point of view alone, instantly recognizable.' A marvellous set which all pianists should investigate.

2 Arabesques; Ballade slave; Berceuse héroïque; Children's corner; Danse (Tarantelle styrienne); Danse bohémienne; D'un cahier d'esquisses; Elégie; Estampes; Etudes, Books I–II; Hommage à Haydn; Images, Books I–II; Images oubliées; L'isle joyeuse; Masques; Mazurka; Morceau de concours; Nocturne; Page d'album; Le petit nègre; La plus que lente; Pour le piano; Préludes, Books I–II; Suite bergamasque; Valse romantique.
❁ (BB) *** ASV Dig. CDQS 432 (4) [(B) id.]. Gordon Fergus-Thompson.

This ASV set represents an extraordinary bargain in offering distinguished performances of Debussy's complete piano music, admirably recorded, for quite a lot less than the cost of two premium-priced CDs. Gordon Fergus-Thompson's survey maintains a consistently high standard of artistry. His set of the elusive *Etudes* is altogether excellent, and so is *Pour le piano*. He finds the full charm and character of *Children's corner*, while the shorter pieces, the *Arabesques*, the quirky *Le petit nègre* and *Rêverie* for instance, are beguilingly presented. The evocation of this unique repertoire is perceptively caught throughout, not least in the *Images*. If one places his sets of *Préludes* alongside those of Gieseking or Arrau, they are less individually distinctive, yet the characterization remains telling. Throughout, this playing shows a genuine feeling for the Debussy palette and, with fine, modern, digital recording, the piano-image mellow and true, these records will give great satisfaction.

2 Arabesques; Berceuse héroïque; D'un cahier d'esquisses; Hommage à Haydn; Images, Books 1–2; L'isle joyeuse; Page d'album; Rêverie.
*** Ph. Dig. 422 404-2 Zoltán Kocsis.

Artistically, this new recital is if anything even more distinguished in terms of pianistic finesse, sensitivity and tonal refinement than Kocsis's earlier (1983) Debussy collection – see below.

2 Arabesques; Children's corner; Estampes; Images, Books 1–2; L'Isle joyeuse; Pour le piano; Préludes, Book 1; Rêverie; Suite bergamasque.
(B) *** Decca Double 443 021-2 (2). Pascal Rogé.

Pascal Rogé's playing is distinguished by a keen musical intelligence and sympathy, as well as by a subtle command of keyboard colour, and this Double Decca set must receive the warmest welcome. *Children's corner* is played with neat elegance and the characterization has both charm and perception, while the *Suite bergamasque* and *Pour le piano* and the *Images* are no less distinguished. In *Estampes* there are occasional moments when the listener senses the need for more dramatic projection, but Rogé brings genuine poetic feeling to the first book of the *Préludes* communicating atmosphere and character in no small measure, partly the effect of the 1978 recording, which has a slightly fuller bass than the rest of the programme. The other recordings were made in 1977 and 1979 and the CD transfers are clear and firm.

2 Arabesques; Children's corner; Estampes; Images, Books I & II; Masques; Préludes, Books I & II.
(N) (M) (***) Sony mono SM2K 60795 (2) [id.]. Robert Casadesus.

Robert Casadesus's accounts of the *Préludes* are (like Gieseking's before him) legendary. They were made in 1953–4 and the other works followed (except for the appealing account of *Children's corner* which came first in 1950, yet sounds extremely good, if closely balanced). The new transfers are impressive, and there is now very little difference in quality between the two Books of *Préludes*. There is some marvellous playing in *Estampes* and in both Books of *Images* (notably *Mouvement*, *Cloches à travers les feuilles* and *Poissons d'or*), while the performances of *Book II* of the *Préludes* show the pianist at his finest: *Brouillards* and *Feuilles mortes*, for instance, are superbly atmospheric, and *Feux d'artifice* repeats the ready virtuosity we have already encountered in *Images*, glittering with fiery brilliance. The reissue is handsomely packaged and offered at mid-price, rather than in Sony's more expensive Heritage series.

(i) *2 Arabesques; Danse; L'isle joyeuse; Masque; La plus que lente; Pour le piano;* (ii) *Préludes, Books I–II* (complete); (i) *Suite bergamasque.*
(B) *** DG 453 070-2 (2). (i) Tamás Vásáry; (ii) Dino Ciani.

Vásáry is at his finest in the *Suite bergamasque*, and *Clair de lune* is beautifully played, as are the *Arabesques*. Diano Ciani has a fine technique (witness *Feux d'artifice*) and plays both Books of *Préludes* with intelligence and taste. Both artists are very well recorded indeed. There is a good deal of Debussy's best-known piano music here, offered inexpensively, and this is a very satisfying pair of discs in its own right.

2 Arabesques; Danse bohémienne; D'un cahier d'esquisses; Estampes; Images oubliées; L'isle joyeuse; Morceau de concours; Nocturne; Pour le piano; Préludes, Books 1–2 (complete); *Masques; Rêverie.*
*** Decca Dig. 452 022-2 (2) [id.]. Jean-Yves Thibaudet.

Beautifully recorded, Thibaudet's wide range of tone and dynamic is used with great imagination, and his playing often suggests an improvisatory quality. The music's subtlety of colour, with half-lights as well as sudden blazes of light (as in the stunning *Feux d'artifice*), is fully understood by this fine artist, and there is no question as to the spontaneity of his playing. The *Préludes* are among the finest on record.

Ballade; Children's Corner; Elégie; Le petit nègre; La plus que lente; Mazurka; Morceau de concours; Nocturne; Préludes: Books 1 & 2; Valse romantique.
(N) * Ph. Dig. 456 568-2 (2) [id.]. Zoltán Kocsis.

The appearance of the two books of *Préludes* from Kocsis naturally aroused high expectations but surprisingly and sadly these were soon dashed. Indeed this set proves a major disappointment. Dynamic markings always scrupulously observed in his previous Debussy CDs, are disregarded in the most cavalier fashion. There are explosive whirlwinds, capricious sforzati and little sense that he really cares about this music. Of course, there are good things but they are too few to redeem this set.

Children's corner; Images, Books 1–2; Préludes, Books 1–2.
**(*) DG 449 438-2 (2) [id.]. Michelangeli.

'Immaculate' is one of the words that spring to mind when one hears Michelangeli's Debussy. There is no doubt that his performances of *Children's corner* and the two sets of *Images* are very distinguished. The *Préludes* undoubtedly bring piano playing which is pretty flawless. At the same time, it is very cool and detached and, although Book II excited enormous enthusiasm in some quarters, both Books here will strike many as somewhat glacial and curiously unatmospheric. Moreover the set is uncompetitively priced.

Estampes; Images, Books 1–2; Préludes, Books 1–2.
(M) *** Ph. (IMS) 432 304-2 (2). Claudio Arrau.

Claudio Arrau's versions of these solo piano works by Debussy are very distinguished. The piano timbre in these 1978/9 analogue recordings has a consistent body and realism typical of this company's finest work.

Estampes; Préludes, Books 1–2 (complete); *Images: Reflets dans l'eau.*
(BB) *** CfP Dig. Silver Double CDCFPSD 4805 (2) [id.]. Youri Egorov.

The Classics for Pleasure Silver Double has the advantage of considerable economy since it brings us the *Estampes* and the first of the *Images*, *Reflets dans l'eau*, as well as the two Books of *Préludes*, at the cost of a single medium-priced CD. Youri Egorov is a very fine player indeed; he gives performances of commanding keyboard technique, exquisite refinement and atmosphere. The recording is very good, a shade too reverberant perhaps, but this must rank high in current CD sets of the complete *Préludes*.

Etudes, Books 1–2.
❁ *** Ph. Dig. 422 412-2 [id.]. Mitsuko Uchida.

12 Etudes; Estampes; L'isle joyeuse.

(M) **(*) Carlton Dig. 30367 0018-2 [id.]. Martino Tirimo.

Mitsuko Uchida's remarkable account of the *Etudes* on Philips is not only one of the best Debussy piano records in the catalogue and arguably her finest recording, but also one of the best ever recordings of the instrument.

Martino Tirimo offers not only the *Etudes*, played with imagination and much subtlety of colour, but also a set of *Estampes* and *L'isle joyeuse*, neither quite as impressive but still worth having. He is very well recorded. But first choice for the *Etudes* remains with Uchida.

Images: Poissons d'or. Préludes: La fille aux cheveux de lin; Général Lavine – eccentric; Feux d'artifice. La Plus que lente; Rêverie.
(M) (***) EMI (SIS) mono CDM5 66069-2 [id.]. Rudolf Firkŭsny – SMETANA: *Polkas & dances*. (***)

This record is of special interest for the sparkling Smetana items which are Firkŭsny's special province. But his Debussy is also distinguished and, if the sound is limited, it is perfectly acceptable.

Préludes, Books 1–2 (complete).
❁ (M) *** EMI mono CDH7 61004-2 [id.]. Walter Gieseking.
(M) *** Carlton IMP Classics Dig. 30367 0079-2. Martino Tirimo.
*** DG Dig. 435 773-2 (2) [id.]. Krystian Zimerman.
(B) **(*) RCA Dig. Twofer 74321 49185-2 (2) [id.]. Catherine Collard.
(B) **(*) Nonesuch/Warner Ultima 7559 79474-2 (2) [(M) id. import]. Paul Jacobs.

Gieseking penetrates the atmosphere of the *Préludes* more deeply than almost any other artist. This is playing of rare distinction and great evocative quality. However, the documentation is concerned solely with the artist and gives no information about the music save the titles and the cues. The *Préludes* are also included in Gieseking's complete (four-disc) survey of Debussy's piano music – see above under *Fantaisie for piano and orchestra*.

Like Gieseking, Martino Tirimo accommodates both Books on the same disc. His playing is very fine indeed and can withstand comparison with most of his rivals – and, apart from the sensitivity of the playing, the recording is most realistic and natural. This is probably a first choice for those wanting a modern digital record offering the complete set, although Egorov's CfP Silver Double (see above) offers more music.

There is no want of atmosphere or poetic feeling in Krystian Zimerman's account of the *Préludes*. This is a very distinguished performance indeed, though some may find the level of intensity too much to live with. Yet his playing is imaginative and concentrated. The DG recording is sensitively balanced, but there is more than a hint of hardness in climaxes.

Catherine Collard's RCA set brings the problem that the reflective qualities of her playing mean that her total timing is 85 minutes – too long for a single CD. But this is a very distinguished set, and her playing has superb technical command and flair, matched by her evocative imagination. She brings a penetrating understanding to this many-faceted music. The recording is first class, cleanly focused and fully coloured, the ambience virtually ideal.

As with Collard on RCA, Paul Jacobs's choice of occasionally slower tempi means that his complete set of *Préludes* stretches over a pair of CDs, although offered as an Ultima Double,they cost more than Gieseking or Tirimo. Jacobs's playing is highly evocative, and he can be quirky too, as in the engagingly lighthearted account of *La danse de Puck*. There is much to appeal here, but in the last resort this Nonesuch set cannot be a top recommendation.

Préludes, Book 1; Images oubliées (1894).
(M) **(*) Channel Classics Dig. CCS 4892 [id.]. Jos van Immerseel.

The special interest of Jos van Immerseel's recording of the first book of *Préludes* lies in his instrument, an Erard of 1897, of the kind which Debussy would have known and played. The sonority is gentle and veiled and curiously seductive except in *forte* passages; the timbre, particularly in the upper register of the instrument, is monochrome and dry, and this tells in a piece such as *La sérénade interrompue*. There is a real turn-of-the-century feel to the shadowy sound-world of *Des pas sur la neige* and the first of the *Images oubliées*. An interesting appendix for a Debussy discography, but essentially this is an issue for specialist collections.

VOCAL MUSIC

3 Ballades de François Villon; 3 Chansons de France; Fêtes galantes (2nd series); Noël des enfants qui n'ont plus de maison; 3 Poèmes de Stéphane Mallarmé; Le promenoir des deux amants.
(M) **(*) Auvidis Valois V 4803. Bernard Kruysen, Noël Lee.

Bernard Kruysen was perhaps the most distinguished Dutch baritone of his day and arguably the finest exponent of French song after Souzay. The present recital comprises the contents of one 1971 LP which, at just under 40 minutes, is distinctly poor value even at mid-price. Artistically these are strong performances, aristocratic in demeanour and well characterized. Kruysen is sensitively and perceptively accompanied by Noël Lee, and well recorded too.

Mélodies: *Beau soir; 3 Chansons de Bilitis; 3 Chansons de France; Les cloches; Fêtes galantes* (2nd group); *Mandoline*.

(M) *** Unicorn-Kanchana Dig. UKCD 2078 [id.]. Sarah Walker, Roger Vignoles – ENESCU: *Chansons* ***; ROUSSEL: *Mélodies*. **(*)

Sarah Walker's Debussy collection makes an outstandingly fine disc of French songs. With deeply sympathetic accompaniment from Roger Vignoles, Sarah Walker's positive and characterful personality comes over vividly, well tuned to the often elusive idiom. Excellent recording in a warm acoustic.

3 Chansons de Charles d'Orléans.

*** Ph. Dig. 438 149-2 [id.]. Monteverdi Ch., O Révolutionnaire et Romantique, Gardiner – FAURE: *Requiem;* RAVEL; SAINT-SAENS: *Choral works*. ***

With Gardiner and his period forces bringing out the medieval flavour of these charming choral settings, this adds to a generous and unusual coupling for Gardiner's expressive reading of the Fauré *Requiem*.

Le Martyre de Saint-Sébastien (incidental music): complete.

*** Sony Dig. SK 48240 [id.]. Leslie Caron; McNair, Murray, L. Symphony Ch., LSO, Tilson Thomas.

Michael Tilson Thomas here records the complete incidental music in a form that the composer approved, using a narrator, Leslie Caron, to provide the spoken links between sections. What it shows is how much richer and more varied the complete score is than the usual symphonic fragments. This is as near an ideal performance as could be imagined, with Sylvia McNair singing radiantly in the principal soprano roles, with brilliant playing from the LSO, and glorious recording which brings out the full atmospheric beauty of the choral singing, often off-stage.

Le Martyre de Saint Sébastien (symphonic fragments); (i) *Nocturnes;* (ii) *La Damoiselle élue*.

(N) *(*) Sony Dig. SK 58952 [id.]. (ii) Dawn Upshaw, Paula Rasmussen. (i, ii) Women of the Los Angeles Master Ch., Los Angeles PO, Esa-Pekka Salonen.

Salonen is very well recorded but very mannered. No doubt these performances are effective in its their way and Dawn Upshaw's contribution is impressive. But although often atmospheric, this does not belong up there with the best.

OPERA

Pelléas et Mélisande (complete).

*** DG Dig. 435 344-2 (2) [id.]. Ewing, Le Roux, Van Dam, Courtis, Ludwig, Pace, Mazzola, Vienna Konzertvereingung, VPO, Abbado.

*** Decca Dig. 430 502-2 (2) [id.]. Alliot-Lugaz, Henry, Cachemaille, Thau, Carlson, Golfier, Montreal Ch. & SO, Dutoit.

(B) *** Naxos 8.660047-9 (3) [id.]. Mireille Delusch, Gérard Theruel, Armand Arapian, Gabriel Bacquier, Hélène Jessoud, Ch. Regional Nord/Pas de Calais, O Nat. de Lille, Jean-Claude Casadesus.

*** EMI Dig. CMS5 67057-2 (3) [CM15 67168]. Stilwell, Von Stade, Van Dam, Raimondi, Ch. of German Op., Berlin, BPO, Karajan.

(M) **(*) Sony SM3K 47265 (3) [id.]. Shirley, Söderström, McIntyre, Ward, Minton, ROHCG Ch. & O, Boulez.

(***) EMI mono CHS7 61038-2 (3). Joachim, Jansen, Etcheverry, Paris CO, Désormière (with *Mélodies*).

(***) Testament mono SBT 3051 (3) [id.]. Jansen, De los Angeles, Souzay, Froumenty, Collard, French Nat. R. O, Cluytens.

Abbado's outstanding version broadly resolves the problem of a first recommendation in this opera, which has always been lucky on record. If among modern versions the choice has been hard to make between Karajan's sumptuously romantic account, almost Wagnerian, and Dutoit's clean-cut, direct one, Abbado satisfyingly presents a performance more sharply focused than the one and more freely flexible than the other, altogether more urgently dramatic. The casting is excellent, with no weak link.

Charles Dutoit brings out the magic of Debussy's score with an involving richness typical of that venue which has played so important a part in the emergence of the Montreal orchestra into the world of international recording. This is not the dreamy reading which some Debussians might prefer, but one which sets the characters very specifically before us as creatures of flesh and blood, not mistily at one remove.

Though the spaciousness of Casadesus's sensitive and poetic reading means that the Naxos set stretches to three discs rather than two, the result is most compelling, with fresh, young voices helping to make the drama more involving. Mireille Delusch is a bright and girlish Mélisande, well matched against the high baritone of Gérard Theruel as a boyish Pelléas, and it provides a convincing slant on the story that the young and virile Golaud of Armand Arapian is a more credible lover-figure than is usually presented. The others are first rate too, including the veteran, Gabriel Bacquier, aptly sounding old as Arkel. The voices are to the fore in the recording, with every word made clear, and the orchestra, with a modest band of strings, adds to the chamber-scale intimacy. The libretto comes in

French only, but with good notes and a synopsis in English – though it would have made it easier for the non-French speaker to follow, had there been more than a minimal number of cue-points provided. An outstanding bargain nevertheless.

EMI have restored the rich and passionate Karajan set to the catalogue as one of the 'Great Recordings of the Century'. It is a performance that sets Debussy's masterpiece as a natural successor to Wagner's *Tristan*, with the orchestral tapestry at the centre and the singers providing a verbal obbligato, but Karajan's concentration carries one in total involvement through a story that can seem inconsequential. Frederica von Stade is a tenderly affecting heroine and Richard Stilwell a youthful and upstanding hero, set against the dark, incisive Golaud of Van Dam. The playing of the Berlin Philharmonic is both polished and deeply committed.

Boulez's sharply dramatic view of Debussy's atmospheric score is a performance which will probably not please the dedicated Francophile – for one thing there is not a single French-born singer in the cast – but it rescues Debussy from the languid half-tone approach which for too long has been accepted as authentic. He is supported by a strong cast; the singing is not always very idiomatic but it has the musical and dramatic momentum which stems from sustained experience on the stage. In almost every way this has the tension of a live performance.

In Roger Désormière's wartime recording, Etcheverry is arguably the most strongly characterized Golaud committed to disc, and neither Joachim's Mélisande nor Jansen's Pelléas has been readily surpassed. A *Pelléas* without atmosphere is no *Pelléas*, and this classic reading puts you under its spell immediately. A further inducement for collectors is a generous selection of Debussy songs from Maggie Teyte and the celebrated recording of *Mes longs cheveux* by the original Mélisande, Mary Garden, accompanied on the piano by Debussy himself in 1904. A very special set.

It is good to see the Cluytens (1956) recording return to currency. Victoria de los Angeles as Mélisande is often affecting and always sings the role exquisitely, and readers will obviously want the set for her. Souzay's Golaud is also magnificent vocally. André Cluytens gets superior playing from the Orchestre National de la Radiodiffusion Française and casts a strong spell even if he does not always distil as powerful an atmosphere. The transfer is altogether exemplary, a model of its kind, and the well-focused mono sound gives unalloyed pleasure.

Rodrigue et Chimène (opera; completed Langham Smith; orch. Denisov).
*** Erato/Warner Dig. 4509 98508-2 (2). Donna Brown, Dale, Jossoud, Van Dam, Bastin, Le Texier, Lyon Op. Ch. & O, Nagano.

In the years immediately before he started work on his masterpiece, *Pelléas et Mélisande*, Debussy all but completed this opera to a much more conventional libretto, telling the story of El Cid, and the manuscript was virtually complete, mainly in well-detailed short-score. Richard Langham Smith reconstructed the rest, and Edison Denisov did the inspired orchestration, adding music from other sections to fill in a few gaps. The best comes first, with radiant singing from Laurence Dale, ideal as Rodrigue, and the fresh and expressive soprano, Donna Brown, as Chimène. Atmospheric off-stage choruses are distinctive too, but little of Act III gives much clue as to the identity of the composer, enjoyable though it is. Kent Nagano's superb recording brings vividly atmospheric sound. José van Dam sings strongly and clearly as the heroine's father, Don Diègue, with the veteran, Jules Bastin, in splendid voice as Don Gomez.

Delage, Maurice (1879–1961)

4 Poèmes hindous.
(N) *** Testament mono SBT 1135 [id.]. Janine Micheau, O. Radiodiffusion Française, André Cluytens – STRAVINSKY: *Le rossignol.* *** ❁

The *Quatre Poèmes hindous* make an ideal coupling for *Le rossignol*. They were both composed at about the same time, when the two composers were close friends, at a time when the East fascinated the French musical world. Delage came late to composition, but thanks to the encouragement of Ravel, proved a fastidious craftsman. These four songs are very much in the received post-Debussian tradition and are exquisitely sung by Janine Micheau. While the mono sound is less transparent than is ideal, the recording is expertly transferred and gives great pleasure.

Delalande, Michel-Richard (1657–1726)

Symphonies pour les soupers du roy (complete).
*** HM Dig. HMC 901337/40 (4) [id.]. Ensemble La Simphonie du Marais, Reyne.

In the last years of his life, Louis XIV could choose from among a dozen suites to accompany his meal. This is the first time all have been committed to disc. Each of these four CDs contains between 36 and 45 individual movements, much of it as charming and inventive as the familiar excerpts. The young members of the Ensemble La Simphonie du Marais, led by Hugo Reyne, give thoroughly fresh and stylish accounts of them.

Cantate Domino; De profundis; Regina coeli.
*** ASV/Gaudeamus Dig. CDGAU 141 [id.]. Ex Cathedra Chamber Ch. & Bar. O, Skidmore.

Jeffrey Skidmore with his fine, Birmingham-based choir and orchestra presents vividly characterized performances of three of Delalande's '*grands motets*', written to be performed simultaneously with the daily celebration of Mass at Louis XIV's court. *De profundis* is a magnificent piece, as are the two lighter, joyful motets. As the title indicates, *Regina coeli* has a Marian text, while *Cantate Domino* represents the peak of Delalande's long career. With their sequences of brief, sharply contrasted movements, these motets, in performances as lively and sensitive as these, can be warmly recommended to many more than baroque specialists. Warm, full sound.

Confitebor tibi Domine; Super flumina Babilonis; Te Deum.
*** HM Dig. HMC 901351 [id.]. Gens, Piau, Steyer, Fouchécourt, Piolino, Corréas, Les Arts Florissants, Christie.
(B) *** HM Dig. HMX 290850.52 (3) [(M) id. import]. Gens, Piau, Steyer, Fouchécourt, Piolino, Corréas, Les Arts Florissants, William Christie – BOUZIGNAC: *Te Deum* etc.; Marc-Antoine CHARPENTIER: *Missa Assumpta est Maria* etc. *** ❁

Confitebor tibi Domine (1699) and *Super flumina Babilonis* (1687) have much expressive writing, and the performances under William Christie are light and airy but not wanting in expressive feeling. The more familiar *Te Deum* is given as good a performance as any that has appeared in recent years. The sound is airy and spacious, and the performances combine lightness and breadth. While this CD remains available at premium price, it also comes in a slip-case as part of a highly recommendable bargain triptych, linked with the *Te Deum* settings of Bouzignac and Charpentier. This is a superb set in every way.

3 Leçons de ténèbres.
(M) *** Erato/Warner 4509 98528-2. Etcheverry, Charbonnier, Boulay.

Delalande brings a distinctive personal stamp to these settings and is no less a master of the ariosa style than his contemporaries; indeed, in melodic richness some of this is even finer than the Couperin version. And the continuo realization (viola da gamba; harpsichord; chamber organ) was spontaneous and not prepared in every detail beforehand; it sounds fresh and immediate. Micaëla Etcheverry is an excellent soloist; she sings with considerable lyrical beauty, and the artists are eminently well balanced and recorded. A welcome reissue.

De la Rue, Pierre (*c.* 1460–1518)

Missa l'homme armé; Missa pro defunctis (Requiem).
(M) *** HM Suite Dig. HMT 7901296. Clement Janequin Ens., Dominique Visse.

Pierre de la Rue was Flemish. His music is extraordinarily expressive, and this *Mass*, based on the chanson *L'homme armé*, exploits that famous tune with great resourcefulness: the music is outgoing and affirmative in spirit and full of imagination. He composed his *Requiem* before its liturgical sequence was fixed, and its format is: *Introitus* (*Requiem*); a brief *Kyrie*; *Psalmus* (No. 41); *Offertorium*; *Sanctus et Benedictus*; *Agnus Dei* and *Communio*. The lyrical melancholy of its lines is most affecting, with the harmony often resting sonorously on its firm bass. The *Sanctus et Benedictus* is simple yet remarkably diverse and powerful. The closing *Communio* is compressed, but none the less telling for that. Marvellous music, beautifully sung and recorded. A real find.

Delden, Lex van (1919–88)

(i) *Concerto for double string orchestra, Op. 71; Piccolo concerto, Op. 67*; (ii) *Musica sinfonica, Op. 93*; (iii) *Symphony No. 3 (Facets), Op. 45.*
*(**) Etcetera stereo/mono KTC 1156 [id.]. Concg. O; (i) Eugen Jochum; (ii) Bernard Haitink; (iii) George Szell.

The idiom of the Dutch composer, Lex van Delden, is predominantly tonal and his style offers occasional reminders of Roussel, Honegger and Stravinsky. The strongest of the works here are the *Third Symphony* and the brilliant *Piccolo concerto* for 12 wind instruments, timpani, percussion and piano. Van Delden is inventive and intelligent, and these four pieces leave you wanting to hear more. The recordings were made at various times and are of varying quality, all in the Concertgebouw Hall and taken from various broadcast tapes, the two concertos conducted by Jochum in 1968 and 1964 respectively (the latter is mono), the *Musica sinfonica* with Haitink in 1969, and the *Third Symphony* with Szell, again mono, in 1957.

Delibes, Léo (1836–91)

Coppélia (ballet): complete.
*** Erato/Warner Dig. 4509 91730-2 (2). Lyon Opéra O, Kent Nagano.
*** Decca (IMS) Dig. 414 502-2 (2) [id.]. Nat. PO, Richard Bonynge.
(B) *** Decca Double 444 836-2 [425 472-2]. SRO, Bonynge – MASSENET: *Le Carillon.* ***
(B) **(*) Ph. Duo 438 763-2 [id.]. Rotterdam PO, David Zinman – CHOPIN: *Les Sylphides;* GOUNOD: *Faust: ballet music.* **(*)

Delibes's delightful score for *Coppélia*, which Tchaikovsky admired so much, is available in a number of different formats, but Kent Nagano's new complete set rises fairly easily to the top of the current list of recommendations. The performance has many felicities and the Orchestre de L'Opéra de Lyon bring a sure sense of style to this elegantly crafted and engagingly tuneful music. Their playing is polished, yet warm and graceful and, under the lively yet nicely detailed direction of Kent Nagano, the spontaneity of the music-making seems to grow as the ballet proceeds. The recording has a nicely judged acoustic, warm yet clear.

The only slight drawback to Bonynge's digital recording is the relatively modest number of violins which the clarity of the digital recording makes apparent. In all other respects the recording is praiseworthy, not only for its vividness of colour but for the balance within a concert-hall acoustic (Walthamstow Assembly Hall).

On the Double Decca reissue of his earlier (1969) analogue set, Bonynge secures a high degree of polish from the Suisse Romande Orchestra, with sparkling string and wind textures, and with sonority and bite from the brass. The Decca recording sounds freshly minted and, with its generous Massenet bonus, little-known music of great charm, this set remains very competitive.

David Zinman's performance of *Coppélia* is beautifully played and most naturally recorded. The warm acoustic of the Rotterdam concert hall certainly suits Delibes's colourful scoring and the gracefully delicate string-playing is nicely flattered. The performance has no want of vigour or refinement and, if it is without the sheer character of Kent Nagano's performance, it is still very enjoyable in its own right. The Chopin and Gounod couplings are similarly smooth and elegant, and all are offered at the cost of one premium-priced CD.

Coppélia (ballet; complete); (ii) *La Source: suites Nos. 2 & 3; Intermezzo: Pas de fleurs.*
(BB) *** Naxos Dig. 8.553356/7 [id.]. Slovak RSO (Bratislava), Mogrelia.

The Bratislava orchestra plays with characteristic finesse and grace and with glowing lyrical feeling. There is both drama and vitality. The recording is warm and spacious, with the orchestra set slightly back. Other versions may have more surface brilliance, but most lovers of ballet music will enjoy the naturalness of perspective and the attractively smooth string-quality. *La Source* somes off equally well. The *Pas de fleurs Grande valse* is a real lollipop and in the two suites the music (selected rather arbitrarily) has plenty of colour and rhythmic life.

(i) *Coppélia* (ballet): complete; (ii) *Sylvia* (ballet): complete.
(M) *** Mercury 434 313-2 (3) [id.]. (i) Minneapolis SO, Dorati; (ii) LSO, Fistoulari.

Both Mercury recordings are very early stereo (*Coppélia* 1957, *Sylvia* 1958), but neither sounds its age and *Sylvia*, using the expansive acoustics of Watford Town Hall, approaches the demonstration bracket. Fistoulari was among the very greatest of ballet interpreters and this shows him at his most inspired. The LSO play superbly for him, the woodwind ensemble is outstanding and the solo playing most beautiful. Dorati's recording of *Coppélia* makes a lively contrast. This Minneapolis recording is rather more confined at the bottom end, but the conductor's vivid combination of energy and grace is appealing in a score that teems with bright melodies and piquant orchestral effects.

Coppélia: extended excerpts; *Sylvia:* extended excerpts.
(B) *** EMI Rouge et Noir (SIS) CZS5 69659-2 (2) [CDZB 67208]. Paris Op. O, Mari.

Jean-Baptiste Mari uses ballet tempi throughout, yet there is never any loss of momentum, and the long-breathed string-phrasing and the felicitous wind solos are a continual source of delight. Mari's natural sympathy and warmth make the very most of the less memorable parts of the score for *Sylvia* (and they are only slightly less memorable). Seventy-five minutes are offered from each ballet.

Coppélia (ballet): suite.
(B) *** DG 429 163-2. BPO, Karajan – CHOPIN: *Les Sylphides* *** ✿; OFFENBACH: *Gaîté parisienne:* excerpts. ***

Karajan secures some wonderfully elegant playing from the Berlin Philharmonic Orchestra, and generally his lightness of touch is sure. The *Csárdás*, however, is played very slowly and heavily, and its curiously studied tempo may spoil the performance for some. The recording is very impressive; but it is a pity that in assembling the CD the suite had to be truncated (with only 71 minutes' playing time, at least one more number could have been included). As it is, the *Scène et valse de la poupée*, *Ballade de l'épi* and the *Thème slave varié*, all present on the original analogue LP, are omitted here. The complete suite is available in a Berlin Philharmonic compilation of Ballet music (DG 459 445-2).

(i) *Coppélia* (ballet) suite; (ii) *Sylvia* (ballet) suite.
(B) *** Sony SBK 46550 [id.]. Phd. O, Ormandy – CHOPIN: *Les Sylphides* ***; TCHAIKOVSKY: *Nutcracker suite.* **(*)

Ormandy and the Philadelphia Orchestra are on top form here. The playing sparkles and has a fine sense of style. Both suites are done in a continuous presentation but are, unfortunately, not banded. The recording is notably full and brilliant.

Coppélia: suite; *Kassya: Trepak; Le roi s'amuse:* suite; *La Source:* suite; *Sylvia:* suite.
(BB) **(*) Naxos Dig. 8.550080 [id.]. Slovak RSO (Bratislava), Ondrej Lenárd.

An attractive hour of Delibes, with five key items from *Coppélia*, including the *Music for the Automatons* and *Waltz*, four from *Sylvia*, not forgetting the *Pizzicato*, and four from *La Source*. Perhaps most enjoyable of all are the six pastiche ancient airs de danse, provided for a ballroom scene in Victor Hugo's play, *Le roi s'amuse*. They are played most gracefully, and the excerpts from the major ballets are spirited and nicely turned. Vivid sound.

Sylvia (ballet): complete.

(B) *** Decca Double 448 095-2 (2) [id.]. New Philh. O, Richard Bonynge – MASSENET: *Le Cid*. ***

(BB) *** Naxos Dig. 8.553338/9 [id.]. Razumovsky Sinfonia, Mogrelia – SAINT-SAENS: *Henry VIII ballet music*. ***

Sylvia is played by Richard Bonynge with wonderful polish and affection, and the recording is full, brilliant and sparkling in Decca's best manner. The CDs offer a splendid Massenet bonus, another recording out of Decca's top drawer, and this is even more attractive as a Double Decca.

Mogrelia's performance of *Sylvia* is above all spacious, bringing out the music's pastel-shaded lyricism yet finding plenty of weight for the more vigorous music depicting the hunters. The *Divertissement* of Act III (which includes some of the best numbers, including the famous *Pizzicato*) is vividly done. However, in the performance as a whole, glowing sentience takes precedence over vitality, and some might find the atmosphere at times a little sleepy. Excellent, naturally balanced recording.

VOCAL MUSIC

Les filles de Cadiz.

*** Decca Dig. 452 667-2 [id.]. Cecilia Bartoli, Myung-Whun Chung (with VIARDOT: *Les filles de Cadiz; Hai Luli!; Havanaise*) – BIZET; BERLIOZ; RAVEL: *Mélodies*. ***

Cecilia Bartoli could hardly be more seductive or more Carmen-like than she is here in Delibes's most famous song, *Les filles de Cadiz*; here, within a delectable recital of French songs, it is placed alongside the setting of the same poem made by the great prima donna, Pauline Viardot, giving a refreshingly different view. The other Viardot items too are highly engaging in this memorable collection of French mélodies.

OPERA

Lakmé (complete).

(N) *** EMI Dig. CDC5 56569-2 (2) [id.]. Natalie Dessay, Gregory Kunde, José van Dam, Haidan, Toulouse Capitole Ch. & O, Plasson.

(N) (B) *** Decca Double 460 741-2 (2) [id.]. Sutherland, Berbié, Vanzo, Bacquier, Monte Carlo Op. Ch. & O, Bonynge.

Lakmé is a strange work, not at all the piece one would expect knowing simply the famous *Bell song*. This performance on Decca seizes its opportunities with both hands. Sutherland swallows her consonants, but the beauty of her singing, with its ravishing ease and purity up to the highest register, is what matters; and she has opposite her one of the most pleasing and intelligent of French tenors, Alain Vanzo. Excellent contributions from the others too, spirited conducting and brilliant, atmospheric recording. The reissue as a Decca Double makes a splendid bargain and the new-style synopsis will prove especially helpful for newcomers to this opera.

The glory of the EMI set is the fresh, girlish portrayal of the heroine by Natalie Dessay, starrily seductive with her silvery, girlish tone, first heard ravishingly from afar. Technically, she is superb too, and the *Bell song* becomes a narrative, not just a coloratura display piece. As Gerald, Gregory Kunde has an appealingly light and heady tenor, sounding totally idiomatic. José van Dam as the vengeful Nilakantha is not as menacing as some, but he sings with satisfying firmness. Delphine Haldan's fruity mezzo contrasts rather than blends with Dessay's soprano in the popular Flower duet but with Plasson warmly expressive, generally taking an expansive view, the sensuousness of the score is well brought out, helped by atmospheric Toulouse recording; though not as sharply focused as the vintage Decca recording, with Bonynge more bitingly dramatic. That is now very tempting, offered inexpensively as a Decca Double, but the new set is very fine indeed.

Delius, Frederick (1862–1934)

The Delius Collection

With many of the performances directed by the composer's devoted amanuensis and dedicated interpreter, Eric Fenby, the Unicorn Delius Collection can be given the strongest recommendation. Quite apart from the consistent quality of the music-making, the warm and spacious digital sound seems ideally suited to music which depends on atmosphere and evocation to make its fullest effect.

Volume 1: (i–ii) *Dance rhapsody No. 1* (ed. Beecham); (i; iii) *Dance rhapsody No. 2; Fantastic dance;* (iv) (Piano) *Preludes Nos. 1–3; Zum carnival* (polka); (v; i; iii) *Song of the high hills*.

❁ (M) *** Unicorn Dig. UKCD 2071 [id.]. (i) RPO; (ii) Del Mar; (iii) Fenby; (iv) Parkin; (v) Amb. S.

Norman Del Mar and Eric Fenby, both natural Delians, give spontaneously volatile performances of the *Dance rhapsodies*, and the spacious recording with its wide dynamic range captures well the music's sudden mood-changes. The *Fantastic dance* is an agreeable late miniature. Eric Parkin also breathes Delian air naturally. The *Preludes* for piano are typical miniatures, the *Polka* an oddity. The piano is naturally caught. But the highlight of this well-planned programme is the *Song of the high hills*, written in 1911. Fenby draws a richly atmospheric performance, here finely balanced within an evocative sound-picture, ideally warm yet with the most delicate *pianissimo* detail.

Volume 2: (i–ii) *Piano concerto;* (iii–iv) *Violin concerto;* (v) *Irmelin: Prelude; A Late lark; A Song of summer.*

(M) *** Unicorn Dig. UKCD 2072 [id.]. RPO; (i) Fowke; (ii) Del Mar; (iii) Holmes; (iv) Handley; (v) Fenby.

Philip Fowke, in partnership with Del Mar, rides confidently over the orchestra in this impassioned account of the one-movement *Piano concerto*; Ralph Holmes and Vernon Handley form a comparable symbiosis in their strong and beautiful account of the *Violin concerto. A Late lark* was the last composition which Delius was able to finish, except for a few bars, before the arrival of Eric Fenby; while *A Song of summer* is the finest of the works which Fenby subsequently took down from the composer's dictation; the performance is loving and dedicated. The programme opens with a ravishingly atmospheric account of the *Irmelin Prelude*.

Volume 3: (i) *Koanga: La Calinda;* (i–iii) *Idyll;* (i–iv) *Songs of sunset;* (v) *A Village Romeo and Juliet: Walk to the Paradise Garden.*

(M) *** Unicorn Dig. UKCD 2073 [id.]. RPO; (i) Fenby; with (ii) Felicity Lott, (iii) Thomas Allen; (iv) Sarah Walker, Amb. S.; (v) Del Mar.

The love scene entitled *Idyll* was rescued from an abortive opera project (*Margot la rouge*). It becomes a beautiful, extended duet in this impressive performance by Felicity Lott and Thomas Allen. Allen is no less persuasive in the *Songs of sunset*, where he is joined by Sarah Walker, and this fine recording brings ravishing sounds from the Ambrosians, with both soloists deeply expressive. The concert opens with Norman Del Mar's languorously brooding yet passionate account of the *Walk to the Paradise Garden* and ends with Fenby's expansive performance of *La Calinda*, which begins with deceptive delicacy. First-class digital sound throughout.

Volume 4: (i) *Cello sonata;* (ii) *Violin sonatas Nos. 1–3.*

(M) *** Unicorn Dig./Analogue UKCD 2074 [id.]. (i) Julian Lloyd Webber; (ii) Ralph Holmes; Eric Fenby.

Lloyd Webber is a warmly persuasive advocate of the *Cello sonata* and Fenby partners him admirably. The three *Violin sonatas*, particularly the last, are also among the finest of Delius's chamber works. Though Fenby as pianist may not be a virtuoso, the natural affinity of his playing and that of Ralph Holmes makes this one of the most treasurable and moving of Delius recordings. The *Cello sonata* was recorded digitally in 1981 and is set in a natural and pleasing acoustic. The *Violin sonatas*, dating from a decade earlier, are also atmospheric in ambience, but the violin timbre has just a hint of thinness on top.

Volume 5: Orchestral songs: (i) *The bird's story;* (ii) *I-Brasil;* (i) *Le ciel est par-dessus le toit;* (ii) *La lune blanche;* (i) *Let springtime come;* (ii) *Il pleure dans mon coeur;* (iii) *To daffodils; Twilight fancies; Wine roses.* Songs with piano: (iii) *Autumn;* (i) *Avant que tu ne t'en ailles;* (iii) *Chanson d'automne;* (i) *Le ciel est par-dessus le toit;* (ii) *I-Brasil;* (i) *In the garden of the Seraglio; Irmelin Rose;* (iii) *Let springtime come;* (ii) *La lune blanche; Il pleure dans mon coeur; Silken shoes; So white, so soft, so sweet is she;* (i) *Sweet Venevil;* (iii) *To daffodils; Twilight fancies;* (i) *The violet.*

(M) *** Unicorn Dig. UKCD 2075 [id.]. (i) Felicity Lott; (ii) Anthony Rolfe Johnson; (iii) Sarah Walker; RPO, Eric Fenby; or Fenby (piano).

All the orchestral songs here are sung in the original language, whereas in the larger collection of English, French and Scandinavian songs – in which Eric Fenby accompanies on Delius's own piano – except for three in German, the Scandinavian settings are sung in English. Apart from the early *Twilight fancies* they are little known, but they consistently reflect the composer's feeling for words. The duplications in both versions are particularly welcome. All three soloists sing most understandingly and characterfully. Excellent recording.

Volume 6: (i) *Fennimore and Gerda: intermezzo;* (ii) *Paris* (*the song of a great city*; ed. Beecham); (iii; iv) *Suite for violin and orchestra;* (i; v) *An Arabesque.*

(M) *** Unicorn Dig. UKCD 2076 [id.]. RPO, cond. (i) Eric Fenby; (ii) Norman Del Mar; (iii) Vernon Handley; with (iv) Ralph Holmes; (v) Thomas Allen, Amb. S.

Paris is spaciously conceived by Norman Del Mar, and the splendidly atmospheric Unicorn sound-picture suits this evocatively leisurely reading. In Fenby's hands, *An Arabesque* emerges as a masterpiece. The emotional thrust of the opening sequence, superbly sung by Thomas Allen and with passionate singing from the chorus too, subsides into characteristic Delius reflectiveness. The early *Suite for violin and orchestra* is played with much understanding;

and Fenby closes the programme with a warmly evocative account of the best-known piece here, the lovely *Intermezzo* from *Fennimore and Gerda*.

Volume 7: (i) *2 Aquarelles;* (i; iv) *Caprice and elegy;* (ii; v) *Légende;* (iii) *Life's dance;* (i; vi) *Cynara;* (i; vii) *Songs of farewell.*
(M) *** Unicorn Dig. UKCD 2077 [id.]. RPO, cond. (i) Eric Fenby; (ii) Vernon Handley; (iii) Norman Del Mar; with (iv) Julian Lloyd Webber; (v) Ralph Holmes; (vi) Thomas Allen; (vii) Amb. S.

Once again Eric Fenby draws loving and dedicated performances from the RPO and the Ambrosian Singers: the *Songs of farewell* are most beautiful; and Thomas Allen is very impressive in *Cynara. Life's dance* certainly does not lack ebullience in Norman Del Mar's hands, and Ralph Holmes and Handley again find an admirable partnership in the *Légende*. The two gentle *Aquarelles* for strings, together with the *Caprice and elegy* (dedicated to Fenby) for cello and small orchestra, make an attractive central interlude in the programme. Julian Lloyd Webber is very persuasive as soloist in the latter piece. As throughout this series, the recording is warmly atmospheric and beautifully balanced.

Other orchestral recordings

Air and dance; Fennimore and Gerda: Intermezzo. Hassan: Intermezzo and Serenade; Koanga: La Calinda. On hearing the first cuckoo in spring; A Song before sunrise; Summer night on the river; A Village Romeo and Juliet: The Walk to the Paradise Garden. (i) *Sea drift.*
(M) *** Decca 440 323-2. ASMF, Marriner; (i) John Shirley-Quirk, L. Symphony Ch., RPO, Hickox.

These are lovely performances, warm, tender and eloquent. They are played superbly and recorded (in 1977) in a flattering acoustic though, with a relatively small band of strings, the sound inevitably has less body than with a full orchestral group. *Sea drift* was recorded three years later in 1980 and is a total success. Rather than lingering, Richard Hickox is urgent in his expressiveness, but there is plenty of evocative atmosphere. John Shirley-Quirk sings with characteristic sensitivity and the chorus – trained by Hickox – is outstanding. The effect of the CD transfer is most real and tangible, the chorus set back within a warm ambience.

American rhapsody (Appalachia); Norwegian suite (Folkeraadet: The Council of the people); Paa Vidderne (On the heights); Spring morning.
** Marco Polo 8.220452 [id.]. Slovak PO, Bratislava, John Hopkins.

Paa Vidderne, the most substantial piece here, is rather melodramatic but has a distinct melodic interest. *Spring morning* is shorter and similarly picaresque, but the *Folkeraadet suite* displays a sure orchestral touch and is most attractive in its diversity of invention. The *American rhapsody* is a concise version of *Appalachia* without the chorus, given here in its original 1896 format. John Hopkins brings a strong sympathy and understanding to this repertoire and secures a committed and flexible response from his Czech players in music which must have been wholly unknown to them.

2 Aquarelles (arr. Fenby); *Brigg Fair; Dance Rhapsodies Nos. 1–2* (ed. Beecham); *Florida suite; In a summer garden; North Country sketches. On hearing the first cuckoo in spring; Summer night on the river* (both ed. Beecham); *The Walk to the Paradise Garden.*
(N) (B) **(*) Decca Double Dig. 460 290-2 (2) [id.]. WNO O, Mackerras.

Mackerras is just as warmly sympathetic in these Delius orchestral pieces as in his complete opera recording, *A Village Romeo and Juliet*. The contrast between the two performances of the interlude, *The Walk to the Paradise Garden*, reflects the contrast between the orchestras, the Welsh more direct and passionate. The *Dance rhapsodies*, music which is far from rhapsodic, here receive fresh, taut performances. In the shorter works Mackerras is warmly sympathetic, with the woodwind playing in particular quite excellent. But the recording, made in the Brangwyn Hall, Swansea is less spacious, less sensuous than the Austrian-made one of the opera, lacking Delian mystery. The massed strings in particular have too much brightness; one requires more lambent textures in this music.

2 Aquarelles (arr. FENBY); *Fennimore and Gerda: Intermezzo. Hassan: Intermezzo and serenade* (all arr. BEECHAM); *Irmelin: Prelude. Late swallows* (arr. FENBY); *On hearing the first cuckoo in spring; A Song before sunrise; Summer night on the river.*
(M) *** Chandos CHAN 6502 [id.]. Bournemouth Sinf., Norman Del Mar.

The 49-minute concert creates a mood of serene, atmospheric evocation – into which Eric Fenby's arrangement of *Late swallows* from the *String quartet* fits admirably – and the beauty of the 1977 analogue recording has been transferred very well to CD, with all its warmth and bloom retained.

2 Aquarelles; Fennimore and Gerda: Intermezzo. On hearing the first cuckoo in spring; Summer night on the river.
(M) *** DG 439 529-2. ECO, Barenboim – VAUGHAN WILLIAMS: *Lark ascending* etc.; WALTON: *Henry V*. ***

Barenboim's luxuriant performances have a voluptuous sensuousness and their warm, sleepy atmosphere should seduce many normally resistant to Delius's pastoralism. The couplings are no less enticing.

Brigg Fair; Dance rhapsodies Nos. 1–2; Hassan: Intermezzo and Serenade. On hearing the first cuckoo in spring; A Song before sunrise; Summer night on the river; Danish songs: (i) *Whither (Autumn); The violet.* Norwegian songs: (ii) *Heimkehr (The homeward journey);* (i) *Twilight fancies. Irmelin: Prelude.*

(N) (M) (***) Dutton Lab. mono CDLX 7028 [id.]. RPO, Beecham, with (i) Elsie Suddaby; (ii) Majorie Thomas.

The wonderfully translucent orchestral textures Beecham achieved in these unsurpassed mono recordings, made at Abbey Road between 1946 and 1952, make one understand why he was not especially enthusiastic about early stereo experiments. The warmth of atmosphere achieved is remarkable, and thanks to the miraculous Dutton transfers, these performances are just as enjoyable as the later ones (see below), and if anything even more beautifully played. David McCallum presents the violin solo in the *Hassan serenade* as vocally as one could wish, and the two Norwegian songs are ravishingly sung by Elsie Suddaby and Marjorie Thomas (with all the words clear), while the Danish songs are hardly less beautiful. The sheer loveliness of the sound here is breathtaking.

Brigg Fair; Dance rhapsody No. 2; Fennimore and Gerda: Intermezzo. Florida suite; Irmelin: Prelude. Marche-caprice; On hearing the first cuckoo in spring; Over the hills and far away; Sleigh ride; Song before sunrise; Summer evening; Summer night on the river; (i) *Songs of sunset.*

✿ *** EMI CDS7 47509-8 (2) [CDCB 47509]. RPO, Beecham; (i) with Forrester, Cameron, Beecham Ch. Soc.

The remastering of the complete stereo orchestral recordings of Delius's music, plus the choral *Songs of sunset*, is something of a technological miracle. Beecham's fine-spun magic, his ability to lift a phrase, is apparent throughout. In the *Songs of sunset* the choral focus is soft-grained, but the words are surprisingly audible, and the backward balance of the soloists is made to sound natural against the rich orchestral textures. The gramophone here offers music-making which is every bit as rewarding as the finest live performances.

Brigg Fair; Dance rhapsody No. 2; On hearing the first cuckoo in spring; In a summer garden.

(B) *** Sony SBK 62645 [id.]. Phd. O, Ormandy – VAUGHAN WILLIAMS: *Fantasias*, etc. ***

Ormandy and his great orchestra, on peak form in the early 1960s, give warm, stirring and highly romantic performances of these four masterpieces. Ormandy and his engineers do not seek the fragility, the evanescence of Delius's visions; for that one can turn to Beecham. But this music responds well to a riper approach and there is no danger here of Delius sounding faded. The sound is remarkably full and expansive, far more convincing than the original LP. With its equally involving coupling, this is a true bargain.

(i) *Brigg Fair; La Calinda* (arr. Fenby); *In a summer garden; Fennimore and Gerda: Intermezzo. Hassan: Intermezzo* and (iii) *Serenade* (arr. Beecham); (ii) *Irmelin prelude;* (i) *Late swallows* (arr. Fenby); *On hearing the first cuckoo in spring; A song before sunrise;* (ii) *A song of summer;* (i) *Summer night on the river;* (ii) *A Village Romeo and Juliet: Walk to the Paradise Garden* (arr. Beecham); (i; iv) *Appalachia* (with brief rehearsal sequence).

(M) *** EMI CMS5 65119-2 [Ang. ZDMB 65119]. (i) Hallé O; (ii) LSO; Sir John Barbirolli; (iii) with Robert Tear; (iv) Balun Jenkins, Amb. S.

Sir John shows an admirable feeling for the sense of light Delius conjures up and for the luxuriance of texture his music possesses. The gentle evocation of *La Calinda* contrasts with the surge of passionate Italianate romanticism at the climax of *The walk to the Paradise Garden*. Barbirolli's style is evanescent in repose and more romantic than the Beecham versions but, with lovely playing from both the Hallé and the LSO, the first-rate analogue sound from the mid to late 1960s adds to the listener's pleasure. *Appalachia* is given an admirably atmospheric reading that conveys the work's exotic and vivid colouring.

Caprice and Elegy (for cello and chamber orchestra).

(N) *** RCA 09026 61695-2 [id.]. Janos Starker, Philh. O, Slatkin – ELGAR: *Cello concerto*; WALTON: *Cello concerto*.**(*)

As a bonus to the apt coupling of the Elgar and Walton concertos Janos Starker offers these two tender and evocative Delius miniatures, originally dictated to Eric Fenby, with chamber orchestra accompaniment. The reserve which marks his view of the major works, here evaporates in warm, sweet playing.

(i) *Caprice & elegy;* (ii; iii) *Piano concerto;* (iv; v) *Violin concerto;* (vi; iii) *Hassan: Intermezzo and serenade; Koanga: La Calinda;* (v) *On hearing the first cuckoo in spring;* (vii) *Legend for violin and piano.*

(***) Testament mono SBT 1014 [id.]. (i) Beatrice Harrison, CO, Eric Fenby; (ii) Moiseiwitsch, Philh. O; (iii) Constant Lambert; (iv) Albert Sammons; (v) Liverpool PO, Sargent; (vi) Hallé O; (vii) Henry Holst, Gerald Moore.

The greatest treasure here is the first ever recording of the *Violin concerto*, made in 1944 and featuring the original soloist, Albert Sammons, arguably the most eloquent and moving account of the work ever committed to disc. Moiseiwitsch's recording of the *Piano concerto*, also the first ever, is hardly less powerful, making a very good case for this warm but less cogent piece. The other items range from the 1930 recording of the *Caprice and elegy* by Beatrice Harrison, the dedicatee, with suspect intonation and plentiful portamento, to Sargent's 1947 recording of the *First cuckoo*, very warm and free in its rubato. Constant Lambert is also a first-rate interpreter of Delius, as the *Hassan* and *Koanga* excerpts show. This transfer has higher surface-hiss than later issues on this label, but the disc must be strongly recommended.

Cello concerto.
*** EMI Dig. CDC5 55529-2. Jacqueline du Pré, RPO, Sir Malcolm Sargent – Recital. ***

The EMI disc offers what was du Pré's first concerto recording and this recital is a transfer of the material, mainly from her very first EMI sessions in 1962 which gave such clear promise of glories to come. Most recommendable, although readers will note that it remains at full price.

(i) *Cello concerto;* (ii) *Double concerto for violin and cello. Paris (the song of a great city).*
(N) (B) *** CfP Dig. 573 1132. (i; ii) Rafael Wallfisch; (ii) Tasmin Little; RLPO, Mackerras.

This superb CfP recording of the *Double concerto*, with soloists who easily outshine their predecessors on record (however distinguished), confirms the strength of a piece which establishes its own logic, with each theme developing naturally out of the preceding one. Wallfisch is just as persuasive in the *Cello concerto*, and Mackerras proves an understanding interpreter of the composer in the big tone-poem, *Paris, the song of a great city*. The recording is comparably full and atmospheric.

Piano concerto in C min.
(B) *** EMI Dig. CD-EMX 2239 [id.]. Piers Lane, RLPO, Handley – FINZI: *Eclogue;* VAUGHAN WILLIAMS: *Piano concerto.* ***

Piers Lane gives a masterly performance of the Delius *Piano concerto*, weighty without pomposity, which effectively counters ideas of this being 'sub-Grieg', early as it is. Lane's measured, concentrated reading of the slow movement is particularly compelling.

Violin concerto.
(M) **(*) EMI CDM7 64725-2. Lord Menuhin, RPO, Meredith Davies – ELGAR: *Violin concerto.* ***

Menuhin's account, well accompanied and recorded in 1976, does not show the polish of his playing in earlier years, and the timbre is not always ideally sweet; but he gives a heartfelt performance, and the semi-improvisational freedom and radiant beauty of the writing above the stave are superbly caught. The Abbey Road recording is truthful, warmly atmospheric and well balanced, to make this an indispensable coupling for lovers of English music.

Dance rhapsodies Nos. 1–2; In a summer garden; North Country sketches; A Village Romeo and Juliet: Walk to the Paradise Garden.
**(*) Chandos Dig. CHAN 9355 [id.]. Bournemouth SO, Richard Hickox.

Hickox is a sensitive and flexible Delian and the Bournemouth orchestra play passionately for him, especially in the *Walk to the Paradise Garden*. The *Dance rhapsodies* are not held together quite so persuasively as by Eric Fenby, who also has the advantage of smoother and more natural string recording. *In a summer garden* is both ardent and luxuriant in its shimmering summer heat-haze, while the wintry landscape of the *North Country sketches* brings almost crystalline iciness from the violins. But the recording, made in the Winter Gardens, Bournemouth, although basically full and spacious, brings a somewhat two-dimensional effect in catching the fervent sweep of violin-tone, as if the microphones were a little too close.

Eventyr; North country sketches; Over the hills and far away; (i) *Koanga: Closing scene.*
(B) (***) Sony mono SBK 62747. RPO, Beecham; (i) with RPO Ch. (members).

A particularly valuable bargain reissue offering very successful transfers of Beecham recordings which have not been available for some time and which have never seemed as firm and realistic as this. The orchestral playing is memorably fine, and the *North country sketches* that are especially valuable, with translucent sounds from the high violins in *Winter landscape* that are almost Sibelian in feeling. The woodwind shine in the capricious *Eventyr* (*Once upon a time*), where Beecham handles the rhapsodic changes of impetus and dynamic with characteristic passion and subtlety. The closing scene from *Koanga*, full of evocative feeling, makes a fascinating coda with its brief solo and choral sequence. No apologies need be made for the mono recordings – made in 1950–51 – for Beecham was a master of orchestral balance.

Fennimore and Gerda: Intermezzo. Irmelin: Prelude. Koanga: La Calinda (arr. Fenby). *On hearing the first cuckoo in spring; Sleigh ride; A Song before sunrise; Summer night on the river; A Village Romeo and Juliet: The Walk to the Paradise Garden.*
(B) *** CfP CD-CFP 4304 [id.]. LPO, Vernon Handley.

Those looking for a bargain collection of Delius should find this very good value; Handley's approach to *The Walk to the Paradise Garden* is strongly emotional, closer to Barbirolli than to Beecham.

Florida suite; North Country sketches.
*** Chandos Dig. CHAN 8413 [id.]. Ulster O, Handley.

Handley's choice of tempi is always apt and it is fascinating that in the *North Country sketches* which evoke the seasons on the Yorkshire moors a Debussian influence is revealed. Handley's refined approach clearly links the *Florida suite* with later masterpieces. The recording is superbly balanced within the very suitable acoustics of the Ulster Hall.

On hearing the first cuckoo in spring; Summer night on the river.
(B) *** DG 439 464-2. ECO, Barenboim – (with BRITTEN: *Serenade*); VAUGHAN WILLIAMS: *Greensleeves; Lark ascending.* ***

Hazily sensuous in the summer sunshine, Barenboim's performances are warmly and enticingly recorded, and here offered as part of a fine bargain collection of English music.

Paris (The song of a great city).
(B) (***) Sony mono SBK 62748. RPO, Beecham – ARNELL: *Punch and the child;* BERNERS: *Triumph of Neptune.* (***)

Many Delius connoisseurs prefer Sir Thomas's 1934 account of *Paris*, but to our ears there is nothing much wrong and a lot right about this 1955 version. There is plenty of atmosphere and the old Beecham magic still casts a strong spell. The new transfer is really very good, clear and well balanced, if lacking amplitude at the climax.

Sonata for strings (arr. from *String quartet* by Eric Fenby).
**(*) Koch Dig. 3-7139 [id.]. New Zealand CO, Nicholas Braithwaite – BRIDGE: *Suite* etc. **(*)

It was Sir John Barbirolli who in 1963 commissioned Delius's amanuensis, Eric Fenby, to score the 'Late swallows' slow movement of the *String quartet* for full orchestral strings, and in 1977 he completed the arrangement of the whole work. It is arguable whether the other movements transcribe as effectively as the third (marked by the composer 'Slow and wistfully') but the performance here is persuasive, and the warm yet transparently natural sound seems right for the music.

CHAMBER MUSIC

Cello sonata.
*** Chandos Dig. CHAN 8499 [id.]. Raphael and Peter Wallfisch – BAX: *Rhapsodic ballad;* BRIDGE: *Cello sonata;* WALTON: *Passacaglia.* ***

In this alternative version of the *Cello sonata* these Chandos performers give as strong and sympathetic an account as is to be found. They are also excellently recorded.

Cello sonata (in one movement); *2 Pieces for cello and piano; Romance; Hassan: Serenade.*
(N) *** Ph. Dig. 454 458-2 [id.]. Julian Lloyd Webber, Bengt Forsberg – GRIEG: *Cello sonata.* ***

Julian Lloyd Webber offers a most attractive coupling of the complete cello and piano music of both Delius and Grieg, composers closely linked both in musical style and as personal friends. Since he last recorded the Delius *Cello sonata* (for Unicorn in 1981) Lloyd Webber has refined and deepened his reading, making it tauter than before. He is just as warmly sympathetic in the shorter pieces.

Violin sonatas Nos. 1–3; in B Op. Posth.
(N) ❀ *** Conifer Dig. 75605 51315-2 [id.]. Tasmin Little, Piers Lane.

This is the first disc to bring together all four of Delius's *Violin sonatas*, here magnetically performed, with Tasmin Little's deeply felt playing superbly matched by Piers Lane; these are works that find Delius at his most meltingly lyrical. The rarity is the earliest and longest, written in 1892 but not published until 1977, less distinctive than the three numbered works, but already very characteristic. The others are tauter and more compact than one expects of Delius, culminating in the haunting masterpiece that, when blind and paralysed, he dictated to his amanuensis, Eric Fenby.

String quartet.
*** ASV Dig. CDDCA 526 [id.]. Brodsky Qt – ELGAR: *Quartet.* ***

In this music, the ebb and flow of tension and a natural feeling for persuasive but unexaggerated rubato is vital; with fine ensemble but seeming spontaneity, the Brodsky players consistently produce that. First-rate recording.

VOCAL MUSIC

(i) *Appalachia: Chorus* (arr. B. SUCHOFF) Songs: *An den Sonnenschein; Ave Maria; Durch den Wald; Frühlingsabruch; Her ute skai gildet saa; Little birdie; On Craig Ddu. Two songs to be sung of a summer night on the water:* No. 1, without words; No. 2, with tenor solo; *Sonnenscheinlied; The splendour falls on Castle Walls; The streamlet's slumber song. Hassan*, Act I: *Chorus*; Act II: *Chorus of beggars and dancing girls*; *Irmelin*, Act I (arr. E. LUBIN): (i) *Chorus. A Village Romeo and Juliet: Wanderer's song* (male voices); *Wedding music.*

(N) *** Somm Dig. SOMMCD 210. Stephen Douse, Andrew Ball, Elysian Singers of London, Matthew Greenhall with (i) Joanna Nolan.

Though you would hardly recognize the early part-songs of 1887 as the work of Delius, their Englishness is attractive, making a delightful prelude to an evocative sequence freshly performed. In chronological order, it follows the composer's development through his early operas, with appropriate sequences turned into separate numbers – those from *A Village Romeo and Juliet* and *Appalachia* involving accompaniments for organ and piano respectively. The climax comes with the two haunting *Songs to be sung of a summer night on the water*. The *Hassan* items too are vintage Delius, before the final Tennyson setting rather pales in face of Britten's far more vivid setting in the *Serenade*. Warm, atmospheric sound.

(i) *An Arabesque;* (ii) *Hassan* (incidental music); (iii) *Sea drift*.

(B) (**(*)) Sony mono SBK 62752. (i) Einar Nørby; (ii) Lesley Fry; (iii) Bruce Boyce; (i–iii) BBC Ch., RPO, Beecham.

It is sad that these three Delius recordings, though made between December 1954 and February 1958 (after the advent of stereo), were done in mono only. Once that is said, the results are persuasive in a way unsurpassed by any rival Delius interpreter, with the lyrical line of each passage, central to the argument, lovingly drawn out. The transfers are clear but have some roughness from the original recording.

Florida suite; Idylle de printemps; Over the hills and far away; La Quadroone; Scherzo; (i) *Koanga: closing scene.*

(BB) *** Naxos Dig. 8.553535 [id.]. E. N. Philh. O, Lloyd-Jones; (i) with Susannah Glanville, Susan Lees, Irene Evans, Sandra Francis, Sue Peerce, Shirley Thomas.

This richly enjoyable collection of early Delius works, is seductively played and beautifully recorded in full and atmospheric sound. Several of the works are new to disc, including the *Idylle de printemps*, fresh and charming, leading to an ecstatic climax. *La Quadroone* and *Scherzo* were originally planned as movements in a suite. Lloyd-Jones has clearly learnt from Beecham's example in his glowing and intense readings of the other three works, with the orchestra's woodwind soloists excelling themselves in delicate pointing, not least in the haunting *La Calinda*, included in the *Florida suite*. *Over the hills and far away*, raptly done, is richly evocative too, and the epilogue to the opera, *Koanga*, rounds off a generously filled disc with music both sensuous and passionate, featuring six female vocal soloists from Opera North, three sopranos and three mezzos.

(i) *Irmelin suite*; (ii) *Two pieces for strings*; (i) *7 Danish songs*.

(N) *(*) Dinemic Dig. DCCD 019 [id.]. (i) Carol Farley, Rhein PO, (ii) Philh. O; José Serebrier.

Delians will welcome this issue which brings rare repertoire: the Danish songs have not been recorded before. However the value of these performances is diminished by the recording which is far too reverberant and by no means well focused.

(i) *A Mass of Life* (sung in German); (ii) *Requiem*.

*** Chandos CHAN 9515 (2) [id.]. (i) Joan Rodgers, Jean Rigby, Nigel Robson; (ii) Rebecca Evans; (i–ii) Peter Coleman-Wright; Waynflete Singers, Bournemouth Ch. & SO, Hickox.

Hickox gives a glowing account of this ambitious setting of a German text drawn from Nietzsche's *Also sprach Zarathustra*. He is helped by excellent singing and playing from his Bournemouth forces, and by fine solo singing, notably from the soprano, Joan Rodgers. The full and atmospheric Chandos recording confirms the primacy of this version even over the excellent previous recordings. The *Requiem*, half an hour long, makes the ideal coupling, emerging as a fine example of Delius's later work, not as distinctive in its material as the *Mass*, but with an element of bleakness tempering the lushness of the choral writing. Here too – with Rebecca Evans this time as soprano soloist – Hickox conducts a most persuasive performance, ripely recorded.

4 Old English lyrics. Songs: *I-Brasil; Indian love song; Love's philosophy; The nightingale; The nightingale has a lyre of gold; Secret love; Sweet Venevil; Twilight fancies*.

**(*) Chandos Dig. CHAN 8539 [id.]. Benjamin Luxon, David Willison – ELGAR: *Songs*. **(*)

This group of Delius songs draws most persuasive performances from Luxon and Willison, sadly marred by the rough tone which has latterly afflicted this fine baritone. Excellent, well-balanced recording.

Sea drift.

(M) ** EMI CDM5 65113-2. John Noble, RLPO Ch. & O, Groves – STANFORD: *Songs of the Fleet* etc. **(*)

Sir Charles Groves could be a persuasive Delian, but his 1973 recording of *Sea drift* is rather too matter-of-fact, failing to convey the surge of inspiration that so exactly matches the evocative colours of Walt Whitman's poem about the seagull, a solitary guest from Alabama. The recording is very good.

(i) *Sea drift; Songs of farewell;* (i; ii) *Songs of sunset*.

*** Chandos Dig. CHAN 9214 [id.]. (i) Bryn Terfel; (ii) Sally Burgess; Bournemouth

Symphony Ch., Waynflete Singers, Southern Voices, Bournemouth SO, Hickox.

Having earlier recorded *Sea drift* for Decca (see above), Hickox in this second recording of Delius's masterpiece finds even more magic, again taking a spacious view – which keeps the flow of the music going magnetically. Bryn Terfel adds to the glory of the performance, the finest since Beecham, as he does in the *Songs of sunset*, with Sally Burgess the other characterful soloist. The *Songs of farewell*, helped by incandescent choral singing, complete an ideal triptych, presented in full and rich Chandos sound.

OPERA

Fennimore and Gerda (complete).
(N) *** Chandos Dig. CHAN 9589 [id.]. Randi Stene, Judith Howarth, Mark Tucker, Peter Coleman-Wright, Danish Nat. R. Ch. & SO, Hickox.

Fennimore and Gerda, the sixth and last of Delius's operas, may suffer from a lopsided libretto – based on a Danish novel by Jens Peter Jacobsen, with a German text by the composer – but it has some of his most inspired vocal music. Fennimore, the first heroine, dominates the first nine of the eleven scenes, with Gerda, the second heroine, introduced only at the end to provide an idyllic conclusion. Using the original German, Hickox's reading is aptly sensuous – far warmer than the only previous recording on EMI conducted by Meredith Davis (CDM5 66314-2) – with fresh-voiced principals headed by Randi Stene as Fennimore, Judith Howarth as Gerda, and Peter Coleman-Wright and Mark Tucker as rivals in this very Scandinavian love-tangle.

Dello Joio, Norman (born 1913)

The Triumph of St Joan (Symphony); Variations, chaconne and finale.
*** Koch Schwann Dig. 3-7243-2 [id.]. New Zealand SO, James Sedares – BARBER: *Adagio for strings.* ***

Norman Dello Joio is little played outside America, and his *Triumph of St Joan Symphony* makes a welcome CD début here and has worn well. For those who do not know it, the idiom relates loosely to early Bernstein and more closely to Hindemith, Piston and Honegger; the music is spacious, dignified and imaginative. The *Variations, chaconne and finale* is a little earlier and a good deal less convincing. However, the disc is well worth investigating for the sake of the symphony (and there are good things in the companion work).

Denisov, Edison (born 1929)

Variations on Haydn's Canon, 'Tod ist ein langer Schlaf' (Death is a long sleep).
*** RCA Dig. 09026 68061-2 [id.]. Moscow Virtuosi, Vladimir Spivakov – SHOSTAKOVICH: *Chamber symphony No. 2;* PART: *Collage on B-A-C-H* etc.; SHCHEDRIN: *Stalin cocktail.* ***

The Soviet composer Edison Denisov's *Variations* celebrated the 250th anniversary of Haydn's birth in 1982, and one wonders what Haydn would have made of this 13-minute concertante cello piece. The soloist's eloquent soliloquy reaches a climax against weird slithers and oscillations from the strings and woodwind, then finally vanquishes their intrusions and breaks free into a touching unaccompanied elegy. The piece closes with three gentle bell-strokes, thus preparing the way for the Arvo Pärt *Cantus*, which follows in this well-planned, very well-played and admirably recorded concert.

Dering, Richard (*c.* 1580–1630)

Motets: *Ardens est cor meum; Ave Maria gratia plena: Ave verum corpus; Factum est silentium; Gaudent in coelis; O crux ave spes unica; O bone Jesu; O quam suavis; Quem vidistis, pastores?.*
(M) **(*) EMI Dig. CDM5 66788-2 [id.]. King's College, Cambridge, Ch., Cleobury – PHILIPS: *Motets.* **(*)

Richard Dering and his older contemporary, Peter Philips, were Catholic expatriates who lived in the Spanish-dominated southern Netherlands. This CD contrasts and compares the two composers' settings of the same texts, drawing on Dering's *Cantiones sacrae* of 1617 and the *Cantica sacra* of 1618 and the posthumously published set of 1662. The performances are faithful, though sometimes a bit stiff; the actual sound, though good, is not ideal in focus or blend, partly perhaps but not solely due to the recording. Very recommendable all the same.

Dett, R. Nathaniel (1882–1943)

8 Bible vignettes; In the bottoms; Magnolia suite.
**(*) New World Dig. NW 367 [id.]. Denver Oldham.

Robert Nathaniel Dett graduated from Oberlin Conservatory in 1908, the first African American to gain a Bachelor of Music degree. His writing is at times colourful and, though limited in its range of expressive devices, is attractive, particularly so in the suite *In the bottoms*, which evokes the moods and atmosphere of life in the 'river bottoms' of the Deep South. However, this is not a disc to be taken all at once. Denver Oldham is a persuasive enough player and he is decently recorded.

Devreese, Godfried (1893–1972)

(i) *Cello concertino;* (ii) *Violin concerto No. 1. Tombelène* (choreographic suite).
*** Marco Polo Dig. 8.223680 [id.]. (i) Viviane Spanoghe, (ii) Guido de Neve. Belgian R. & TV PO (Brussels), Frédéric Devreese.

Godfried Devreese, a Belgian composer, is imaginative as well as a gifted and colourful orchestrator, and this suite from *Tombelène* gives pleasure. His *Violin concerto No. 1* also sounds balletic in inspiration, and if you respond to the Bloch and Delius concertos, you would find much here to engage your sympathies. The *Cello concertino* (1930) originally appeared scored for 15 wind instruments, celesta, harp, six double-basses and variously tuned side-drums. The present version is rescored by his son for more practical forces; it, too, is imaginative without possessing a strong individual voice. Very good performances and vivid, well-detailed recording.

Diabelli, Anton (1781–1858)

Guitar sonata in A (ed. Bream).
(M) **(*) RCA 09026 61593-2. Julian Bream (guitar) – GIULIANI: *Grand overture* etc.; SOR: *Grand solo Sonata in C.* **(*)

Bream combined the first two movements of Diabelli's (guitar) *Sonata in F* with the two final movements of his *Sonata in A* into a single composite work with appropriate transpositions. The result makes a quite strong (if conventional) piece, which Bream brings fully to life, even if it is perhaps a shade long for its material at 18 minutes.

Diamond, David (born 1915)

(i) *Concert piece for flute and harp. Concert piece for orchestra.* (i) *Elegy in memory of Ravel. Rounds for string orchestra; Symphony No. 11: Adagio.*
*** Delos Dig. DE 3189 [id.]. Seattle SO, Gerard Schwarz, (i) with Glorian Duo.

The *Rounds for string orchestra* (1944) is a masterpiece and ought to be part of the international repertoire. It conjures up the vastness of the American continent but suggests also the presence of humanity, while the vigorous closing movement encapsulates barn-dance energy within a neoclassical structure, with a really memorable secondary idea. The *Concert piece for orchestra* is also snappily rhythmic, more jagged, with a cool, elegiac counterpart and a sudden resolution. The *Elegy for Ravel* is unexpectedly troubled and dissonant, but the delicately evoked *Concert piece for flute and harp* is far closer to Ravel's world. The eloquent *Adagio* from the *Eleventh Symphony* has been described as Brucknerian, although Bruckner would not have acknowledged the degree of dissonance at its somewhat inflated climax. All this music is played superbly by the fine Seattle orchestra and the disc is worth considering for the *Rounds* alone.

(i) *oncerto for small orchestra;* (ii) *Symphonies Nos 2; 4.*
*** Delos Dig. D/CD 3093 [id.]. (i) NY CO; (ii) Seattle SO, Gerard Schwarz.

The *Second Symphony* is a large-scale work, and it has great sweep and power. The music unfolds with a sense of inevitability and purpose. The *Concerto for small orchestra* is original in form; there are two parts which open and conclude with a Fanfare with two preludes and fugues in between. The Mediterranean-like *Fourth Symphony* with its glowing, luminous textures sounds even more relaxed and lyrical in this performance than in Bernstein's account from the 1960s. Dedicated and expert performances from the Seattle Orchestra under Gerard Schwarz. The acoustic is spacious and the balance is very well judged.

(i) *Violin concerto No. 2. The Enormous room; Symphony No. 1.*
*** Delos Dig. DE 3119 [id.]. (i) Ilkka Talvi; Seattle SO, Gerard Schwarz.

A further addition to Diamond's growing representation in the catalogue brings the *First Symphony*, an urbane and intelligently wrought piece which has a strong sense of both purpose and direction. The *Second Violin concerto* is a bit Stravinskian with a dash of Walton and keeps the excellent soloist fully stretched. Not perhaps top-drawer Diamond, though *The Enormous room* shows the composer at his most imaginative. It derives its title from e. e. cummings's 'high and clear adventure'. It is rhapsodic in feeling, with orchestral textures of great luxuriance. Excellent performances from Gerard Schwarz and the Seattle orchestra, and outstanding recording.

(i) *Kaddish for cello and orchestra. Psalm; Romeo and Juliet; Symphony No. 3.*
*** Delos Dig. DE 3103 [id.]. (i) Starker; Seattle SO, Gerard Schwarz.

The *Third Symphony* is a four-movement work of no mean power. The *Romeo and Juliet* music is an inventive score, full of character and atmosphere, which shows Diamond as a real man of the orchestra; and the Seattle orchestra proves an eloquent advocate. *Kaddish* is a more recent piece and is played here by its dedicatee, János Starker.

Symphony No. 4.
(N) (M) **(*) Sony SMK 60594 [id.]. NYPO, Bernstein – HARRIS: *Symphony No. 3;***(*) THOMPSON: *Symphony No. 2.* **(*)

Bernstein recorded David Diamond's *Fourth Symphony* way back in 1958. He obviously has great feeling for this euphonious and beautifully shaped work, and in his hands every note means something. Wonderfully eloquent and even though the recorded sound cannot match the recent account from Gerard Schwarz on Delos, it is a rather special record.

Symphony No. 8; Suite No. 1 from the ballet, Tom; (i) *This sacred ground.*
*** Delos Dig. DE 3141 [id.]. (i) Erich Parce, Seattle Ch., Seattle Girls' Ch., NorthWest Boys' Ch.; Seattle SO, Gerard Schwarz.

The *First Suite from the ballet, Tom* is often powerful and inventive, and inhabits much the same musical world as Aaron Copland, Diamond's mentor and friend, for whose sixtieth birthday the *Eighth Symphony* was composed. Although it makes use of serial technique, it will still present few problems to those familiar with Diamond's earlier music, for it remains lyrical and thought-provoking. It culminates in a double fugue of considerable ingenuity. *This sacred ground* is a short setting for soloist, choirs and orchestra of the Gettysburg Address, which may not travel so well. Well worth investigating for the ballet and the symphony. Committed performances and excellent, natural, recorded sound.

Dibdin, Charles (1745–1814)

(i) *The Brickdust man* (musical dialogue); (ii) *The Ephesian Matron* (comic serenata); (iii) *The Grenadier* (musical dialogue).
*** Hyperion Dig. CDA 66608 [id.]. (i) Barclay, West; (ii) Mills, Streeton, Padmore, Knight; (iii) Bisatt, West, Mayor; Opera Restor'd, Parley of Instruments, Holman.

Dibdin, best known as the composer of *Tom Bowling*, the song heard every year at the Last Night of the Proms, here provides three delightful pocket operas, the shorter ones officially described as musical dialogues and *The Ephesian Matron* as a comic serenata. *The Grenadier* – dating from 1773 – lasts well under a quarter of an hour, using a text that is possibly by David Garrick. The brief numbers – duets and solos – are linked by equally brief recitatives, then rounded off with a final trio. The other two pieces are just as delightful in these performances by a group that specializes in presenting just such dramatic works of this period in public. Excellent Hyperion sound.

Diepenbrock, Alphons (1862–1921)

Elektra suite; (i) *Hymn for violin & orchestra. Marsyas suite; Overture: The Birds.*
*** Chandos Dig. CHAN 8821 [id.]. (i) Emmy Verhey; Hague Residentie O, Vonk.

The *Birds Overture*, written for a student production of Aristophanes, is rather delightful if very Straussian, with some vaguely Impressionist touches. The *Marsyas music* (1910) is expertly and delicately scored with touches of Strauss, Reger and Debussy. Good performances from the Residentie Orchestra under Hans Vonk and eminently truthful recording quality. Recommended.

(i) *Hymne an die Nacht;* (ii) *Hymne;* (i) *Die Nacht;* (iii) *Im grossen Schweigen.*
*** Chandos Dig. CHAN 8878 [id.]. (i) Linda Finnie; (ii) Christoph Homberger; (iii) Robert Holl; Hague Residentie O, Hans Vonk.

This second volume brings four symphonic songs, all of great beauty and with an almost Straussian melancholy. There are touches of Reger and Debussy as well as Strauss, and all four pieces are expertly and delicately scored. Good performances from all three soloists and the Residentie Orchestra under Hans Vonk, and very good recording indeed.

Dittersdorf, Carl Ditters von (1739–99)

(i) *Double-bass concerto in E;* (ii) *Flute concerto in E min.;* (iii) *Symphonies in C & D.*
** Olympia OCD 405 [id.]. (i) Stefan Thomas, Arad PO, Boboc; (ii) Gavril Costea, Cluj-Napoca PO, Cristescu; (iii) Oradea Philharmonic CO, Ratiu.

The *C major* is an agreeably conventional three-movement symphony, but the *D major* is more elaborate, with an infectious opening movement, an engaging *Chanson populaire d'Elsass* for its *Andante*, a minuet with two trios and a set of variations for its modestly paced finale. Both the concertos are attractive and require considerable bravura from their soloists. The recorded sound varies somewhat but is always fully acceptable and quite well balanced.

Harp concerto in A (arr. Pilley).
❁ (M) *** Decca 425 723-2 [id.]. Marisa Robles, ASMF, Iona Brown – BOIELDIEU; HANDEL: *Harp concertos* etc. *** ❁

Dittersdorf's *Harp concerto* is a transcription of an unfinished keyboard concerto with additional wind parts. It is an elegant piece, thematically not quite as memorable as the Boieldieu coupling, but captivating when played with such style.

6 Symphonies after Ovid's Metamorphoses.
**(*) Chandos Dig. CHAN 8564/5 (2). Cantilena, Shepherd.

All the *Ovid symphonies* have a programmatic inspiration and relate episodes from the *Metamorphoses* of Ovid, such as *The fall of Phaeton*, which are vividly portrayed. *The rescue of Andromeda by Perseus* is a particularly effective work (it has an inspired *Adagio*) and the slow movement of the *D major, The petrification of Phineus and his friends*, is a delight. One well appreciates the contemporary verdict that Dittersdorf 'spoke to the heart'. *The transformation of the Lycian peasants into frogs* could hardly be more graphic and is full of wit. This is inventive and charming music that will give much pleasure, and it is generally well served by Cantilena under Adrian Shepherd. There is also a set on Naxos (8.553368/9) acceptably performed by the Failoni Symphoy Orchestra under Hanspeter Gmür, but the Chandos versions have much more character and are worth the extra cost.

Dodgson, Stephen (born 1924)

(i) Flute concerto (for flute and strings); (ii) *Duo concertant for violin, guitar and strings;* (iii) *Last of the leaves* (cantata for bass, clarinet and strings)
*** Biddulph Dig. LAW 015 [id.]. (i) Robert Stallman; (ii) Jean-Jacques Kantorow, Anthea Gifford; (iii) Michael George, John Bradbury, N. Sinfonia, Zollman.

Dodgson wrote his *Flute concerto* for the American flautist, Robert Stallman, who is also the fine soloist on this disc. Dodgson wanted to draw not only on Stallman's agility and rhythmic flair, but on his tonal bloom and subtlety, and the performance bears that out. The *Duo concertant* also receives a persuasive performance. With its hints of an English Stravinsky, this is another work that is at once thoughtful and charming. *Last of the leaves* is a cantata for bass soloist accompanied by clarinet and strings, more consistently autumnal and elegiac. Framing the work are settings of poems by poets now neglected, Austin Dobson and Harold Monro, with the necessary contrast provided by the best-known poem, G. K. Chesterton's *The Donkey*, light-hearted, leading up to its surprise reference at the end to Christ's entry into Jerusalem. Though Michael George's noble bass voice is not as sweetly caught as it might be, it is a tenderly moving performance, with John Bradbury equally expressive and with the Belgian conductor, Ronald Zollman, as in the other works, a sympathetic accompanist.

Dohnányi, Ernst von (1877–1960)

Piano concertos Nos. 1 in E min., Op. 5; 2 in B min., Op. 42.
*** Hyperion Dig. CDA 66684 [id.]. Martin Roscoe, BBC Scottish SO, Fedor Glushchenko.

These concertos are well wrought, with a melodic warmth that fails to be indelible, but they provide bravura for the soloist and contrast for the orchestra. The present performances are surely unlikely to be surpassed for their commitment, and the playing is finished as well as ardent; the recording, too, is excellent.

Konzertstück for cello and orchestra, Op. 12.
*** Chandos Dig. CHAN 8662 [id.]. Wallfisch, LSO, Mackerras – DVORAK: *Cello concerto.* ***

Dohnányi's *Konzertstück* has many rich, warm ideas, not least a theme in the slow movement all too close to *Pale hands I loved beside the Shalimar*, and none the worse for that. Wallfisch's performance, as in the Dvŏrák, is strong, warm and committed, and the Chandos sound is first rate.

Symphony No. 1 in D min, Op. 9.
(N) *** Telarc Dig. CD 80511 [id.]. LPO, Leon Botstein.

Symphony No. 1 in D min, Op. 9; American Rhapsody, Op. 47.
(N) *** Chandos Dig. CHAN 9647 [id.]. BBC PO, Bamert.

Dohnányi's *First Symphony* is something of a find. He was 23 when he composed it, and already possessed an astonishing command of the orchestra. Indeed it is not just accomplished, the scoring shows real flair. A large-scale piece, some 55 minutes in duration, it reveals a strong sense of form. It is a measure of its quality that Bartók committed it to memory and played it by heart on the piano! Having languished in obscurity since 1900, it suddenly appears in two new recordings. Telarc's account with the LPO under Leon Botstein has grip and fervour, and benefits from first-rate recorded sound.

Mathias Bamert offers the *American rhapsody* which comes from the other end of Dohnányi's career, though it is not anywhere as interesting as the early piece. He has the advantage of the BBC Philharmonic and excellent engineering from the BBC/Chandos team. There is surprisingly little to choose between the two performances; the Telarc sound is brighter, the Chandos richer. Both have plenty of body and presence. Whichever you opt for, you will find this most rewarding music.

Symphony No. 2, Op. 40; Symphonic minutes, Op. 36.
*** Chandos Dig. CHAN 9455 [id.]. BBC PO, Bamert.

Dohnányi's *Symphonic minutes* are richly inventive and have enormous charm. Like the enchanting *Suite in F sharp minor*, they are close in idiom to Richard Strauss, Kodály and Rachmaninov. The *Second Symphony* is a generally well-argued and finely crafted piece which betrays none of the trauma of its genesis. It is well worth getting to know, even if (at nearly 50 minutes) it rather outstays its welcome. The playing of the BBC Philharmonic under Mathias Bamert is vital and sensitive, and the Chandos recording in the best traditions of the house.

Variations on a nursery tune (for piano and orchestra), *Op. 25.*
(M) *** Decca 448 604-2. Julius Katchen, LPO, Boult – RACHMANINOV: *Piano concerto No. 2* etc. ***

(i) *Variations on a nursery tune, Op. 25. Capriccio in F min., Op. 28.*
*** Chesky CD-13 [id.]. Earl Wild, (i) New Philh. O, Christoph von Dohnányi – TCHAIKOVSKY: *Piano concerto No. 1.* ***

Katchen's 1959 remake of the *Nursery variations* has the advantage of Decca's finest vintage stereo. The performance is both perceptive and spontaneous, as full of wit as it is of lilt and flair. While the earlier account of 1954 by the same artists was a dazzling example of Decca's mono recording at its most electrifying, collectors should not miss this more modern version which is otherwise unsurpassed and very beautifully balanced and recorded – indeed, in the demonstration bracket for its period. The generous couplings are hardly less recommendable.

A scintillating account of the piano part from Earl Wild is matched by a witty accompaniment directed by the composer's grandson, who doesn't miss a thing. Splendid vintage analogue recording from the early 1960s. The *Capriccio*, brilliantly played, acts as an encore (before the Tchaikovsky coupling), but the recording is rather recessed.

Cello sonata in B flat min., Op. 8.
**(*) ASV Dig. CDDCA 796[id.]. Bernard Gregor-Smith, Yolande Wrigley – BRIDGE; DEBUSSY: *Sonatas.* **(*)

Like so much of Dohnányi's early music, the *Cello sonata* (1899) is very Brahmsian in feeling. There is a marvellously inventive scherzo, which leaves no doubt that it is the work of a great pianist-composer. The finale is a theme and variations and what a superb theme it is too. It is played with great expertise and fine musicianship by this excellent duo partnership. The recording is just a bit too bright and forward to be ideal but, with that proviso, the disc can be cordially recommended.

Piano quintets Nos. 1 in C min., Op. 1; 2 in E flat min., Op. 26; Serenade in C, Op. 10.
*** Hyperion Dig. CDA 66786 [id.]. Schubert Ens. of London.

The Schubert Ensemble also give us the *Serenade for string trio.* Good though this newcomer is, both artistically and in terms of recording, readers should not forget the amazing 1941 set with Heifetz, Primrose and Feuermann, which is now back in circulation after many years (see below). Still, a clear three-star recommendation to the Hyperion disc and their excellent pianist, William Howard.

(i) *Piano quintet No. 1 in C min., Op. 1. String quartet No. 2 in D flat, Op. 15.*
**(*) Chandos Dig. CHAN 8718 [id.]. (i) Wolfgang Manz; Gabrieli Qt.

(i; ii) *Piano quintets Nos. 1 in C min., Op. 1; 2 in E flat min., Op. 28;* (i) *Suite in the old style, Op. 24.*
*** ASV Dig. CDDCA 915 [id.]. (i) Martin Roscoe; (ii) Vanbrugh Qt.

Dohnányi wrote the first of his two *Piano quintets* when still in his teens, ripely Brahmsian, built strongly on memorable themes. The *Second quintet*, dating from 20 years later, just after the *Nursery variations*, is sharper and more compact, with Hungarian flavours more pronounced, if never Bartókian. The *Suite in the old style*, for piano alone, is an amiable example of pre-Stravinsky neo-classicism, again beautifully written for the instrument. The Vanbrugh Quartet is well matched by Martin Roscoe in keen, alert performances, warmly recorded.

Manz's performance of Dohnányi's *First Piano quintet* lacks something in fantasy and lightness of touch. But the bigger-boned, somewhat Brahmsian effect of this performance is certainly compelling, if less strong on charm. The scherzo of the *Second String quartet* is reminiscent of the opening of *Die Walküre* and there are reminders of Dvõrák and Reger as well as Brahms. It is a strong piece, splendidly played by the Gabrielis and beautifully recorded.

Serenade in C for string trio, Op. 10.
(M) (***) RCA mono 09026 61763-2 [id.]. Heifetz, Primrose, Feuermann – BRAHMS: *Piano trio No. 1;* R. STRAUSS: *Violin sonata.* (***)

Quite sublime playing from Heifetz, Primrose and Feuermann, recorded in 1941. This performance has never been surpassed, though the recorded sound has! However, its deficiencies do not diminish the artistic impact of the performance.

Sextet in C for piano, clarinet, horn, violin, viola and cello, Op. 37.
*** ASV Dig. CDDCA 943 [id.]. Endymion Ens. – FIBICH: *Piano quintet.* ***

The Endymions play with great feeling and panache, they are splendidly recorded and can be strongly recommended.

String quartets Nos. 1 in A, Op. 7; 2 in D flat, Op. 15.
(N) (M) *** Koch/Treasure CD 316352 [id.]. Artis Qt, Vienna.

The *First Quartet* comes from Dohnányi's mid 20s and though not the equal of the *Second* in the quality of its ideas, is still well worth investigation. The idiom is still heavily indebted to Brahms and Strauss but none the worse for that. The playing of the Artis

Quartet of Vienna is persuasive, and the recordings, which come from the 1980s, very present.

String quartets Nos. 2 in D flat, Op. 15; 3 in A min., Op. 33.
(N) *** ASV Dig. CDDCA 985 [id.]. Lyric Qt. – KODALY: *Intermezzo for string trio*. ***

These two quartets are separated by two decades, the *D flat, Op. 15* comes from 1906 and the *A minor, Op. 33* from 1926. Dohnányi's emerging personality is already much in evidence. The scherzo has an astonishing affinity with the opening of *Die Walküre*, and this idea resurfaces in the third and final movement, the *Adagio*. The *Third quartet* is a finely crafted and richly inventive score, conservative in idiom. The Lyric Quartet play with commitment and conviction that more than outweighs the odd moment of inelegance.

Donizetti, Gaetano (1797–1848)

Ballet music from: *L'assedio di Calais; Dom Sébastien; La favorita; Les martyres.*
(B) *** Ph. (IMS) Duo 442 553-2 (2) [id.]. Philh. O, Antonio de Almeida – ROSSINI: *Ballet music*. **(*)

Music from the baroque period has given us dozens of records which are validly used for aural wallpaper. The ballet music from four of Donizetti's operas which were presented in Paris provides a nineteenth-century equivalent, sparkling, refreshing dances of no great originality, delivered here with great zest and resilience and fine solo playing, and excellently recorded. The Rossini coupling offers even more characterful music, and if the playing of the Monte Carlo Orchestra cannot match that of the Philharmonia, this is still very enjoyable.

Sinfonias (String quartets): in A; D min. (both arr. Benedek); *D* (arr. Angerer).
**(*) Marco Polo Dig. 8.223577 [id.]. Failoni CO, Géza Oberfrank.

We have had the *D major Sinfonia* (arranged here by Paul Angerer) from the ASMF under Marriner (see below). It is a delightfully spontaneous piece with a graciously beautiful *Larghetto*. The D minor work opens darkly, but the sun soon comes out and at times we are reminded of Rossini. The *Larghetto* is pensive. The *A major* has a fine, siciliano-like *Larghetto cantabile*. All this is warmly appealing music, well played and flatteringly recorded; a touch more wit and sparkle would not have come amiss, but the music is well worth having. A pity that this was not issued on the Naxos label.

String quartet in D (arr. for string orchestra).
(B) *** Decca Double 443 838-2 (2) [id.]. ASMF, Marriner – ROSSINI: *String sonatas Nos. 1–6* (with CHERUBINI: *Etude No. 2 for French horn and strings* (with Barry Tuckwell); BELLINI: *Oboe concerto in E flat* (with Roger Lord) ***).

This delightful 'prentice work has a sunny lyricism and a melodic freshness that speak of youthful genius. The composer's craftsmanship is obvious and the writing is such that (unlike Verdi's *String quartet*) it lends itself readily to performance by a string orchestra, especially when the playing is so warm-hearted and polished and the recording transferred so immaculately to CD. A fine bonus for the irresistible Rossini *String sonatas*.

Il Barcaiolo; Cor anglais concerto in G; Oboe sonata in F; (Piano) Waltz in C.
*** Mer. CDE 84147 [id.]. Jeremy Polmear, Diana Ambache (with PASCULLI: *Concerto on themes from La Favorita; Fantasia on Poliuto;* LISZT: *Réminscences de Lucia di Lammermoor*).

The *Sonata in F* is an agreeable piece with a fluent *Andante* and a catchy finale; and the vignette, *Il Barcaiolo*, is even more engaging. The *Cor anglais concerto* centres on a set of variations which are not unlike the fantasias on themes from his operas by Pasculli. However, these demand the utmost bravura from the soloist. Diana Ambache proves a sympathetic partner and gives a suitably flamboyant account of Liszt's famous *Lucia* paraphrase.

String quartet No. 13 in A.
(M) *** CRD CRD 3366; *CRDC 4066* [id.]. Alberni Qt – PUCCINI: *Crisantemi;* VERDI: *Quartet*. ***

This is an endearing work, with a scherzo echoing that in Beethoven's *Eroica*, and with many twists of argument that are attractively unpredictable. It is given a strong, committed performance and is well recorded.

Requiem.
(M) ** Decca (IMS) 425 043-2 [id.]. Cortez, Pavarotti, Bruson, Washington, Arena di Verona Lyric Ch. & O, Fackler.

There are many passages in Donizetti's *Requiem* which may well have influenced Verdi when he came to write his masterpiece. Donizetti's setting lasts for 65 minutes, but its inspiration is short-winded and it is not helped here by limited performance and recording, deriving from the Cime label. The singing and playing are generally indifferent. Pavarotti, recorded in 1979, is the obvious star, singing flamboyantly in his big solo, *Ingemisco*. Of curiosity value only.

OPERA

Anna Bolena (complete).
*** Decca (IMS) Dig. 421 096-2 (3) [id.]. Sutherland, Ramey, Hadley, Mentzer, Welsh Nat. Op. Ch. & O, Bonynge.

(B) **(*) Millennium MCD 80355 (3). Sills, Burrowes, Verrett, Plishka, Lloyd, Kern, Tear, John Alldis Ch., LSO, Rudel.

(M) (**(*)) EMI mono CMS5 66471-2 (2) [CDMB 66471]. Callas, Simionato, Rossi-Lemeni, G. Raimondi, Carturan, La Scala, Milan, Ch. & O, Gavazzeni.

In this 1987 recording of *Anna Bolena*, Sutherland crowns her long recording career with a commanding performance. Dazzling as ever in coloratura, above all exuberant in the defiant final cabaletta, she poignantly conveys the tragedy of the wronged queen's fate with rare weight and gravity. Ramey as the king is outstanding in a fine, consistent cast. Excellent recording.

Sills, lacking only a little in weight, here gives one of her finest, most characterful performances on disc. Anna's final scene before her execution is poignantly beautiful, prayerful, with lovely, poised singing, though the final cabaletta brings some edginess at the top. Sills is well matched by the heady tenor of Stuart Burrowes as Riccardo, with Shirley Verrett characterful as Giovanna Seymour and smaller roles excellently cast. Paul Plishka as the king sings powerfully, in firmer voice than usual. Ensembles are first rate, not least the Act I *Quintet* which finds Sills at her finest. As usual with operas on the Millennium label, no libretto is provided.

The Callas recording was made live at La Scala in 1957, with the great diva at her most searingly magnetic. This is a performance which, despite the occasional sour note, has one marvelling at the imaginative phrasing and subtlety of dynamic shading, with top notes firm and clear if characteristically edgy. Gavazzeni proves a most sympathetic conductor and, though the rest of the cast is no match for Callas, there is characterful if rather inflexible singing from Simionato as Giovanna and a fresh, clear contribution from Gianni Raimondi in the relatively small tenor role of Percy, here made the smaller by cuts. Nicola Rossi-Lemeni as Henry VIII is positive but gritty of tone in a less than convincing characterization. The radio sound is dry and limited with occasional interference, but for Callas fans this is well worth hearing.

L'assedio di Calais (complete).

*** Opera Rara OR 9 (2) [id.]. Du Plessis, Della Jones, Focile, Serbo, Nilon, Platt, Glanville, Smythe, Treleaven, Harrhy, Bailey, Geoffrey Mitchell Ch., Philh. O, David Parry.

The Opera Rara set is one of the most invigorating of all the complete opera recordings made over the years by that enterprising organization. With Della Jones and Christian du Plessis in the cast, as well as a newcomer, Nuccia Focile, as Queen Eleanor, David Parry conducts the Philharmonia in a fresh, well-sprung performance which gives a satisfying thrust to the big ensembles. The one which ends Act II, including a magnificent sextet and a patriotic prayer for the chorus, brings the opera's emotional high-point. When, in Act III, Edward III's big aria turns into a sort of jolly waltz song, the music seems less apt.

Il Campanello (complete).

*** Sony Dig. MK 38450 [id.]. Baltsa, Dara, Casoni, Romero, Gaifa, V. State Op. Ch., VSO, Bertini.

This sparkling one-Act piece is based on something like the same story which Donizetti developed later in *Don Pasquale*. Enzo Dara as the apothecary, Don Annibale, and Angelo Romero as the wag, Enrico, are delightful in their patter duet, and Agnes Baltsa is a formidable but sparkling Serafina. Gary Bertini is a sympathetic conductor who paces things well, and the *secco* recitatives – taking up rather a large proportion of the disc – are well accompanied on the fortepiano. Generally well-balanced recording.

Don Pasquale (complete).

*** RCA Dig. 09026 61924-2 (2) [id.]. Bruson, Mei, Allen, Lopardo, Bav. R. Ch., Munich R. O, Roberto Abbado.

*** EMI Dig. (SIS) CDS7 47068-2 (2) [Ang. CDCB 47068]. Bruscantini, Freni, Nucci, Winbergh, Amb. Op. Ch., Philh. O, Muti.

(M) *** Decca 433 036-2 (2). Corena, Sciutti, Oncina, Krause, V. State Op. Ch. & O, Kertész – CIMAROSA: *Il maestro di cappella*. ***

In vivid, immediate sound and with voices balanced well forward, Roberto Abbado's Munich set for RCA is on balance the finest modern version of Donizetti's sparkling comedy. Not only does Abbado spring rhythms cleanly and lightly, they are made the more infectious by the clarity of focus. The cast has no weak link. Renato Bruson may accentuate Pasquale's comic lines with little explosions of underlining, but that helps to distinguish him sharply as a *buffo* character from his opposite number, Malatesta, here sung with rare style and beauty by Thomas Allen, as well as with a nicely timed feeling for the comedy. Frank Lopardo as Ernesto shades his clear tenor most sensitively, singing his *Serenade* with far more refinement than most latterday rivals. Eva Mei sings the role of Norina with an apt brightness and precision (including an excellent trill), even if others have presented a more characterful heroine.

Muti's is a delectably idiomatic-sounding reading, one which consistently captures the fun of the piece. Freni is a natural in the role of Norina, both sweet and bright-eyed in characterization, excellent in coloratura. The *buffo* baritones, the veteran Bruscantini as Pasquale and the darker-toned Leo Nucci as Dr Malatesta, steer a nice course between vocal comedy and purely musical values. Muti is helped by the beautifully poised and shaded singing of Gösta Winbergh, honey-toned and stylish as Ernesto. Responsive and polished playing from the Philharmonia and excellent studio sound.

Under Kertész, Corena is an attractive *buffo*, even if his voice is not always focused well enough to sing semiquavers accurately. Juan Oncina, as often on record, sounds rather strained, but the tenor part is very small; and Krause makes an incisive Malatesta. Graziella Sciutti is charming from beginning to end, bright-toned and vivacious, and remarkably agile in the most difficult passages. The 1964 Decca recording is excellent, with plenty of atmosphere as well as sparkle.

Don Pasquale (complete in English).

(N) [M] *** Chandos Dig. CHAN 3011 (2) [id.]. Andrew Shore, Lynn Dawson, Barry Banks, Jason Howard, Geoffrey Mitchell Ch., LPO, David Parry.

There are obvious benefits from having a comic opera in English rather than the original language, and David Parry with a lively team of soloists, using Parry's own translation, deliver a jolly and amiable performance, well-paced. The interplay of characters is well caught, but the celebrated patter duet between Don Pasquale and Dr Malatesta, wonderfully articulated, brings none of the traditional comic wheezing at the end – on the whole an advantage. Shore and Howard are good buffo singers, characterful if a little gruff, with Howard's Malatesta rather younger-sounding than usual, a believable brother of Norina. Lynne Dawson is fresh, sweet and agile as the heroine, and Barry Banks is a clear and unstrained Ernesto. Full sound, atmospheric enough to give warmth to the voices without obscuring words. If your preference is for opera in English you can't go wrong with this.

L'elisir d'amore (complete).

(N) *** Decca Dig. 455 691-2 (2) [id.]. Angela Gheorghiu, Roberto Alagna, Roberto Scaltriti, Simone Alaimo, Lyon Opera Ch. & O, Evelino Pidò.

(M) *** Erato/Warner Dig. 4509 98483-2 (2) [4509 91701-2]. Devia, Alagna, Spagnoli, Praticò, Tallis Chamber Ch., ECO, Viotti.

*** Decca 414 461-2 (2) [id.]. Sutherland, Pavarotti, Cossa, Malas, Amb. S., ECO, Bonynge.

(M) *** Sony M2K 79210 (2) [M2K 34585]. Cotrubas, Domingo, Evans, Wixell, ROHCG Ch. & O, Pritchard.

(B) **(*) Decca Double 443 542-2 (2). Gueden, Di Stefano, Corena, Capecchi, Mandelli, Maggio Musicale Fiorentino Ch. & O, Molinari-Pradelli.

(M) **(*) RCA Dig. 74321 25280-2 (2). Popp, Dvorsk'y, Weikl, Nesterenko, Munich R. Ch. & O, Wallberg.

(M) **(*) EMI CMS5 65658-2 [CDMB 65658] (2). Carteri, Alva, Panerai, Taddei, La Scala, Milan, Ch. & O, Serafin.

The prizewinning husband-and-wife team of Angela Gheorghiu and Roberto Alagna helps to make this a winning version of Donizetti's sparkling comedy. Alagna's voice is weightier and recorded closer than in his earlier Erato version, a portrait of the innocent Nemorino on the hefty side, with a newly unearthed variant of the great aria, *Una furtive lagrima*, which proves no advantage, neither tender nor subtle. Otherwise the new set is excellent all round, with Gheorghiu an enchanting Adina, tenderly poignant in her final solo. Roberto Scaltriti as Belcore and Simone Alaimo as Dulcamara are both firm and characterful. A formidable rival for the outstanding earlier Decca set with Pavarotti and Sutherland, although that still holds its place alongside this as a top recommendation.

This mid-priced Erato set presents an exceptionally winning performance, in many ways the finest of all on record, with no weak leak. This is a light, generally brisk account of the score that provides another modern alternative to Richard Bonynge's version with Joan Sutherland as Adina and with the young Pavarotti. Mariella Devia cannot match Sutherland for beauty of tone in the warmly lyrical solos, but she sparkles more, bringing out what a minx of a heroine this is. At the time of making this recording Roberto Alagna's tenor timbre was not unlike Pavarotti's, lighter if not quite so firm, and, like Devia, he delectably brings out the lightness of the writing. His performance culminates in a winningly hushed and inner account of the soaring aria, *Una furtiva lagrima*. Rounding off an excellent cast, Pietro Spagnoli is a fresh, virile Belcore, and Bruno Praticò a clear, characterful Dr Dulcamara, an excellent *buffo* baritone, making the very most of a voice on the light side. The sound is first rate, if not as forwardly focused as the analogue Decca.

Joan Sutherland makes Adina a more substantial figure than usual, full-throatedly serious at times, at others jolly like the rumbustious Marie; and in the key role of Nemorino Luciano Pavarotti proves ideal, vividly portraying the wounded innocent. Spiro Malas is a superb Dulcamara, while Dominic Cossa is a younger-sounding Belcore, more of a genuine lover than usual. Bonynge points the skipping rhythms delectably, and the recording is sparkling to match, with striking presence.

On the Sony reissue delight centres very much on the delectable Adina of Ileana Cotrubas. Plácido Domingo by contrast is a more conventional hero and less the world's fool that Nemorino should be. Sir Geraint Evans gives a vivid characterization of Dr Dulcamara, though the microphone sometimes brings out roughness of tone, and Ingvar Wixell is an upstanding Belcore. The stereo staging is effective and the remastered recording bright and immediate. This set remains at full price in the USA.

With Hilde Gueden at her most seductive – an enchanting, provocative Adina, characterfully using her golden tone to bring out the minx-like qualities of the heroine – the very early (1955) Decca stereo recording offers a delightful, spontaneous-sounding performance. Not just Gueden but also the other soloists are strikingly characterful, with Giuseppe di Stefano at his most headily sweet-toned, singing with youthful ardour, Fernando Corena a strong and vehement Dulcamara and Renato Capecchi well contrasted as Sergeant Belcore, though not quite so firm of tone, but both splendidly comic. Even without a libretto it makes a good bargain, with two CDs offered for the price of one.

Wallberg conducts a lightly sprung performance of Donizetti's sparkling comic opera, well recorded and marked by a charming performance of the role of Adina from Lucia Popp, bright-eyed and with delicious detail both verbal and musical. Nesterenko makes a splendidly resonant Dr Dulcamara with more comic sparkle than you would expect from a great Russian bass. Dvorsk'y and Weikl, both sensitive artists, sound much less idiomatic, with Dvorsk'y's tight tenor growing harsh under pressure, not at all Italianate, and Weikl failing similarly to give necessary roundness to the role of Belcore. Like other sets recorded in association with Bavarian Radio, the 1982 sound is excellent.

Although reissued at mid- rather than bargain price (it last appeared on Classics for Pleasure), the La Scala set of *L'elisir d'amore* now comes with a full translation instead of a synopsis. It is still worth considering: it was a fine cast in its day (1959). Alva is a pleasantly light-voiced and engaging Nemorino. Carteri's Adina ideally should be more of a minx than this, but the part is nicely sung all the same. Panerai as Belcore once again shows what a fine and musical artist he is, and Taddei is magnificent, stealing the show as any Dulcamara can and should. The drawback is Serafin's direction. The La Scala Chorus is lively enough, and it is not that the orchestral playing is slipshod, but they provide less sparkle than they should.

L'elisir d'amore: highlights.

(N) (M) *** Erato/Warner Dig. 0630 15731-9 [id.]. (from above recording with Devia, Alagna, Spagnoli; cond. Viotti).

(N) *** Decca Dig. 466 064-2 [id.]. (from above recording with Gheorghiu, Alagna, Scaltriti; cond. Pidò).

There is very little to choose between these sets of highlights, except price. Both include full translations; the Erato's playing time is 72 minutes against Decca's 76 minutes, but the latter costs far more. However, the cast lists will be the prime consideration for most collectors.

Emelia di Liverpool (complete). *L'eremitaggio di Liwerpool* (complete).

*** Opera Rara OR 8 (3) [id.]. Kenny, Bruscantini, Merritt, Dolton, George Mitchell Ch., Philh. O, David Parry.

The very name, *Emelia di Liverpool*, makes it hard to take this early opera of Donizetti seriously. In this set, sponsored by the Peter Moores Foundation, we have not only the original version of 1824 but also the complete reworking of four years later, which was given the revised title noted above. Such a veteran as Sesto Bruscantini makes an enormous difference in the *buffo* role of Don Romualdo in *Emelia*, a character who speaks in Neapolitan dialect. His fizzing duet with Federico (the principal tenor role, superbly sung by Chris Merritt) sets the pattern for much vigorous invention. With fresh, direct conducting from David Parry, this is a highly enjoyable set for all who respond to this composer.

La Favorita (complete).

(M) **(*) Decca (IMS) 430 038-2 (3) [id.]. Cossotto, Pavarotti, Bacquier, Ghiaurov, Cotrubas, Teatro Comunale Bologna Ch. & O, Bonynge.

La Favorita may not have as many memorable tunes as the finest Donizetti operas, but red-blooded drama provides ample compensation. Fernando is strongly and imaginatively sung here by Pavarotti. The mezzo role of the heroine is taken by Fiorenza Cossotto, formidably powerful if not quite at her finest, while Ileana Cotrubas is comparably imaginative as her confidante Ines, but not quite at her peak. Bacquier and Ghiaurov make up a team which should have been even better but which will still give much satisfaction. Bright recording.

La Fille du régiment (complete).

*** Decca 414 520-2 (2) [id.]. Sutherland, Pavarotti, Sinclair, Malas, Coates, ROHCG Ch. & O, Bonynge.

It was with this cast that *La Fille du régiment* was revived at Covent Garden, and Sutherland immediately showed how naturally she takes to the role of Marie, a vivandière in the army of Napoleon. Sutherland is in turn brilliantly comic and pathetically affecting, and Pavarotti makes an engaging hero. Monica Sinclair is a formidable Countess in a fizzing performance of a delightful Donizetti romp that can be confidently recommended both for comedy and for fine singing. Recorded in Kingsway Hall, the CD sound has wonderful presence and clarity of focus.

(i) *Gabriella di Vergy* (1838 version); (ii) Scenes from 1826 version.

**(*) Opera Rara Dig. ORC 3 (2) [id.]. (i) Andrew, Du Plessis, Arthur, Tomlinson, J. Davies, Winfield; (ii) Harrhy, Della Jones, RPO, Alun Francis.

Dating from 1979 and transferred well to CD, this Opera Rara set of *Gabriella di Vergy* (not to be confused with *Gemma di Vergy*) presents the rediscovered score, written in the composer's hand, of a piece which Donizetti himself never heard. It was unearthed by Don White and Patric Schmid, and makes one wonder how this inventive score with its many sparkling cabalettas and superb Act II finale could have been neglected for so long. The cast is a capable one with Alun Francis, as ever, a sympathetic conductor; it is interesting to hear John Tomlinson early in his career, slightly miscast. It is fascinating to have as appendix three excerpts from the original, 1836 score, with Della Jones taking the role of the hero, Raoul, later rewritten for tenor.

Lucia di Lammermoor (complete).

*** Decca 410 193-2 (2) [id.]. Sutherland, Pavarotti, Milnes, Ghiaurov, Ryland Davies, Tourangeau, ROHCG Ch. & O, Bonynge.

(N) (B) *** Decca Double 460 747-2 (2) [id.]. Sutherland, Cioni, Merrill, Siepi, St Cecilia Ac., Rome, Ch. & O, Pritchard.

(M) (***) EMI mono CMS5 66641-2 (2) [CDMB 66641]. Callas, Di Stefano, Panerai, Zaccaria, La Scala Ch. & O, Karajan.

*** DG Dig. 435 309-2 (2) [id.]. Studer, Domingo, Pons, Ramey, Amb. Op. Ch., LSO, Marin.

(M) (***) EMI mono CMS5 66438-2 (2) [CDMB 66438]. Callas, Di Stefano, Gobbi, Arie, Ch. & O of Maggio Musicale Fiorentino, Serafin.

(B) **(*) Ph. Duo 446 551-2 (2) [id.]. Caballé, Carreras, Sardinero, Ramey, Murray, Ahnsjö, Amb. S., New Philh. O, López-Cobos.

**(*) EMI CDS5 56284-2 (2) [CDCB 56284]. Callas, Tagliavini, Cappuccilli, Ladysz, Philh. Ch. & O, Serafin.

(N) *(*) Sony Dig. S2K 63174 (2) [id.]. Andrea Rost, Bruce Ford, Anthony Michaels-Moore, Alistair Miles, L. Voices, Hanover Band, Sir Charles Mackerras.

Though some of the girlish freshness of voice which marked the 1961 recording disappeared in the 1971 set, Sutherland's detailed understanding was intensified. Power is there as well as delicacy, and the rest of the cast is first rate. Pavarotti, through much of the opera not as sensitive as he can be, proves magnificent in his final scene. The sound-quality is superb on CD. In this set, unlike the earlier one, the text is absolutely complete.

The 1961 Sutherland version of Lucia now reappears as a splendid bargain in Decca Double format. Though consonants were being smoothed over, the voice is obviously that of a young singer and dramatically the performance was close to Sutherland's famous stage appearances of that time, full of fresh innocence. Sutherland's coloratura virtuosity remains breathtaking, and the cast is a strong one, with Pritchard a most understanding conductor. The reissue has Decca's new-style synopsis, with a 'listening guide' for newcomers to the opera.

Recorded live in 1955, when Karajan took the company of La Scala to Berlin, for years this finest of Callas's recordings of *Lucia* was available only on pirate issues. Despite the limited sound, Callas's voice is caught with fine immediacy. Her singing is less steely than in the 1953 studio recording, and far firmer than in the 1959 one (now withdrawn).

On DG, Cheryl Studer makes an affecting heroine, singing both brilliantly and richly, and Plácido Domingo rebuts any idea that his tenor is too cumbersome for Donizetti. This is the finest version yet in digital sound, with the young Romanian, Ion Marin, drawing fresh, urgent playing from the LSO. The rest of the cast is outstandingly strong too, with Juan Pons as Lucia's brother, Enrico, and Samuel Ramey as the teacher and confidant, Raimondo, Bide-the-Bent.

Callas's earlier mono set dates from 1953. The diva is vocally better controlled than in her later stereo set (indeed some of the coloratura is excitingly brilliant in its own right), and there are memorable if not always perfectly stylish contributions from Di Stefano and Gobbi. As in the later set, the text has the usual stage cuts, but the remastered sound is impresssive.

The idea behind the set with Caballé is fascinating: a return to what the conductor, Jésus López-Cobos, believes is Donizetti's original concept, an opera for a dramatic soprano, not a light coloratura. Compared with the text we know, transpositions paradoxically are for the most part upwards (made possible when no stratospheric coloratura additions are needed); but López-Cobos's direction hardly compensates for the lack of brilliance and, José Carreras apart, the singing, even that of Caballé, is not very persuasive. Certainly this is good value as a Philips Duo reissue and, although only a synopsis of the plot is included, it is generously cued.

The Callas stereo version was recorded in Kingsway Hall in 1959. The sound is very good for its period and comes over the more freshly on CD, with Callas's edgy top notes cleanly caught. Her flashing-eyed interpretation of the role of Lucia remains unique, though the voice has its unsteady moments. One instance is at the end of the Act I duet with Edgardo, where Callas on the final phrase moves sharpwards and Tagliavini – here past his best – flatwards. Serafin's conducting is ideal, though the score, as in Callas's other recordings, still has the cuts which used to be conventional in the theatre.

The Sony set under Mackerras benefits textually from the conductor's new edition of the score, absolutely complete with illicit transpositions removed. Yet it is not substantially different from others like Jesus Lopez-Cobos on EMI who have similarly sought authenticity. Unlike his rivals, Mackerras uses a period orchestra but the benefits of that are very limited, when the players seem out of tune with the idiom, too often sounding square, failing to lift rhythms. Anthony Michaels-Moore is excellent as Enrico, and Alistair Miles a strong Raimondo. Bruce Ford is a fluent and stylish Edgardo, but the tone as recorded is often gritty, while Andrea Rost, bright and flexible in coloratura, yet sings with too sour a tone to give much pleasure, the final blot on a disappointing set.

Lucia di Lammermoor: highlights.
(M) *** Decca 421 885-2 [id.] (from above complete recording, with Sutherland, Pavarotti; cond. Bonynge).
(M) **(*) EMI CDM5 66664-2 [id.]. Callas, Tagliavini, Cappuccilli, Ladysz, Philh. Ch. & O, Serafin.

For those who have chosen Callas or Sutherland's earlier, complete set, this 63-minute selection from her later (1971) version should be ideal.

A satisfactory hour-long selection from Callas's 1959 Kingsway Hall stereo recording, with Callas not as completely in vocal control as she was in her earlier, mono sets.

Lucrezia Borgia (complete).
(M) *** Decca (IMS) 421 497-2 (2). Sutherland, Aragall, Horne, Wixell, London Op. Voices, Nat. PO, Bonynge.

Sutherland is in her element here. Aragall sings stylishly too, and though Wixell's timbre is hardly Italianate he is a commanding Alfonso. Marilyn Horne in the breeches role of Orsini is impressive in the brilliant *Brindisi* of the last Act, but earlier she has moments of unsteadiness. The recording is characteristically full and brilliant.

Maria Padilla (complete).
**(*) Opera Rara ORC 6 (3) [id.]. McDonall, Della Jones, Clark, Du Plessis, Earle, Caley, Kennedy, Joan Davies, Geoffrey Mitchell Ch., LSO, Francis.

Maria Padilla marks a return to Donizetti's Italian manner, a piece based on strong situations. It even matches *Lucia di Lammermoor* in places, with the heroine ill-used by the prince she loves, Pedro the Cruel. When the obligatory mad scene is given not to the heroine but to her father, even a tenor such as Graham Clark – future star in Bayreuth – can hardly compensate, however red-blooded the writing and strong the singing. In the title-role Lois McDonall is brightly agile, if at times a little raw. Alun Francis directs the LSO in a fresh, well-disciplined performance and, as ever with Opera Rara sets, the notes and commentary contained in the libretto are both readable and scholarly.

Maria Stuarda (complete).
(M) *** Decca 425 410-2 (2) [id.]. Sutherland, Tourangeau, Pavarotti, Ch. & O of Teatro Comunale, Bologna, Bonynge.

In Donizetti's tellingly dramatic opera on the conflict of Elizabeth I and Mary Queen of Scots, the contrast between the full soprano Maria and the dark mezzo Elisabetta is underlined by some transpositions, with Tourangeau emerging as a powerful villainess in this slanted version of the story. Pavarotti turns Leicester into a passionate Italian lover, not at all an Elizabethan gentleman. As for Sutherland, she is at her most fully dramatic too, and the great moment when she flings the insult *Vil bastarda!* at her cousin brings a superb snarl; Richard Bonynge directs an urgent account of an unfailingly enjoyable opera. Unusually for Decca, the score is slightly cut. The recording is characteristically bright and full.

Mary Stuart (complete in English).
(N) (M) **(*) Chandos Dig. CHAN 3017 (2) [id.]. Dame Janet Baker, Plowright, Rendall, Opie, Tomlinson, E. Nat. Op. Ch. & O, Mackerras.

Mary Stuart was the opera chosen at the ENO just before Dame Janet Baker decided to retire from the opera stage in 1982; happily, EMI took the opportunity to make live recordings of a series of performances at the Coliseum. Though far from ideal, the result is strong and memorable, with Dame Janet herself rising nobly to the demands of the role, snorting fire superbly in her condemnation of Elizabeth as a royal bastard and above all, making the closing scenes before Mary's execution deeply moving. Her performance is splendidly matched by that of Rosalind Plowright, though the closeness of the recording of the singers makes the voices sound rather hard. The singing of the rest of the cast is less distinguished, with chorus ensemble often disappointingly ragged, a point shown up by the recording balance. The acoustic has the listener almost on stage, with the orchestra relatively distant. Now reissued by Chandos under the auspices of the Peter Moore Foundation, it is a valuable and historic set, but the Decca version (in Italian) with Sutherland gives a fuller idea of the work's power.

Poliuto (complete).
(M) (***) EMI mono CMS5 65448-2 (2) [Ang. CDMB 65448 2]. Callas, Corelli, Bastianini, Zaccaria, La Scala Ch. and O, Votto.
*** Sony Dig. M2K 44821 (2) [id.]. Carreras, Ricciarelli, Pons, Polgar, V. Singakademie Ch., VSO, Oleg Caetani.

In 1960 Maria Callas returned to La Scala, having missed the two previous seasons, and had a triumph. This live recording, made at the time, demonstrates the scale of that triumph, with Callas's musical imagination and intensity of communication at their very peak. Corelli gives a heroic performance, noticeably subtler and more sensitive in scenes opposite Callas than when he is on his own. Callas herself consistently shows why this role inspired her, both in her natural gravity and poised intensity in slow music and in her biting brilliance in coloratura, marred slightly by the characteristic edge on the voice. Bastianini and Zaccaria complete the top Scala team of principals and, though the chorus is often rough, Votto heightens the dramatic impact in his conducting, right up to the improbable march at the end as hero and heroine bravely face martyrdom. Variable and limited mono sound, dry in the orchestra, but with voices generally well caught, now effectively remastered.

Carreras's voice is in splendid form. Ricciarelli as Paolina lacks something in dramatic bite, but she gives the heroine an inward warmth and tenderness. Pons and Polgar are also excellent and the piece is well worth investigating for one of Donizetti's most inspired ensembles in the Act II finale. The recording is clear and vivid, hardly betraying the fact that it was made live at a concert performance.

Ugo, conte di Parigi (complete).
*** Opera Rara ORC1 (3) [id.]. Della Jones, Harrhy, J. Price, Kenny, Arthur, Du Plessis, Geoffrey Mitchell Ch., New Philh. O, Francis.

The 1977 recording of *Ugo, conte di Parigi* was the result of formidable detective work, revealing in this early opera of 1832 a strong plot and some fine numbers, including excellent duets. Matching such singers as Janet Price and Yvonne Kenny, Maurice Arthur sings stylishly in the title-role, with a clear-cut tenor that records well. Della Jones and Christian du Plessis, regular stalwarts of Opera Rara sets, complete a stylish cast. Reissued on CD, thanks to the Peter Moores Foundation, it offers a fresh and intelligent performance under Alun Francis, and the scholarly, readable notes and commentary, as well as libretto and translation, are models of their kind.

Arias: *Don Pasquale: Com'è gentil. Don Sebastiano: Deserto in terra. Il Duca d'Alba: Inosservato, penetrava . . . Angelo casto e bel. La Fille du régiment: Ah! mes amis . . . Pour mon âme; Pour me rapprocher de Marie. L'elisir d'amore: Quanto è bella; Una furtiva lagrima. La Favorita: Una vergine, un' angelo di Dio; Si, che un solo accento; Favorita del re! . . . Spirto gentil. Lucia di Lammermoor: Tombe degli avi miei; Tu che a Dio spigasti l'ali. Maria Stuarda: Ah! rimiro il bel sembiante.*
(M) *** Decca 458 203-2 [id.]. Pavarotti, with various orchestras & conductors.

A cleverly chosen compilation of Pavarotti recordings of Donizetti from various sources – not just complete sets but previous recital discs. It is good to have one or two rarities along with the favourite numbers, including Tonio's celebrated 'High-C's' solo from the Act I finale of *La Fille du régiment*. Sound from different sources is well co-ordinated. In all, 13 items are included, and this makes an attractive reissue in Decca's Opera Gala series, rather handsomely presented with an additional outer slip-case. Full translations are included.

Arias: *L'elisir d'amore: Prendi, prendi per me sei libero. La Figlia del reggimento: Convien partir. Lucrezia Borgia: Tranquillo ei posa! . . . Come'è bello!.*
(M) ** EMI CDM5 66464-2 [id.]. Callas, Paris Conservatoire O, Rescigno – ROSSINI: *Arias.* **(*)

Reissued as part of EMI's Callas Edition, and very well recorded in 1963–4, this is a good example of the latter-day Callas, not always sweet-toned, and at times demonstrating less than the usual fire. If the singing rarely shows her at her most imaginative, and if there are fewer phrases that stick in the memory by their sheer individuality, that is not Donizetti's fault. Yet there is still much to admire, and the remastering flatters the voice by providing a warmly atmospheric orchestral backing. Excellent documentation: full translations are provided.

Dowland, John (1563–1626)

The Collected Works (complete).
(B) *** O-L 452 563-2 (12) [(M) id. import]. Emma Kirkby, Glenda Simpson, John York Skinner, Martyn Hill, David Thomas, Consort of Musicke, Anthony Rooley.

Volume 1: *First Booke of Songes 1597* (452 564-2).

Volume 2: *Second Booke of Songs 1600* (452 565-2).

Volume 3: *Third Booke of Songs 1603* (452 566-2).

Volume 4: *A Pilgrimes Solace 1612* (beginning) *(Fourth Booke of Songs)* (452 567-2).

Volume 5: *A Pilgrimes Solace 1612* (conclusion) *(Fourth Booke of Songs)*. Keyboard transcriptions of Dowland's music: ANON.: *Can she excuse* (2 versions); *Dowland's almayne; Frogs' galliard; Pavion solus cum sola;* BYRD: *Pavana lachrymae.* FARNABY: *Lachrimae pavan.* MORLEY: *Pavana and Galiarda.* PEERSON and BULL: *Piper's Paven and Galliard.* SCHILDT: *Paduana lachrymae.* SIEFERT: *Paduana (la mia Barbara).* WILBYE: *The Frogge* (Colin Tilney (harpsichord)) (452 568-2).

Volume 6: *Mr Henry Noell Lamentations 1597; Lachrimae 1604* (452 569-2).

Volume 7: Sacred songs: *An heart that's broken and contrite; I shame at mine unworthiness; Sorrow, come!.* Psalms: *All people that on earth do dwell* (2 versions); *Behold and have regard; Lord to thee I make my moan; My soul praise the Lord; Put me not to rebuke O Lord. A Prayer for the Queen's most excellent Majesty.* Instrumental music (mainly anon. arrangements): *Comagain (Comagain sweet love); Pavan lachrymae* (both arr. VAN EYCK); *Earl of Essex galliard; Galliard; If my complaints; Lachrimae; Lachrimae; Lachrimae Doolande; Lady Rich galliard; Lord Willoughbie's welcome home; My Lord Chamberlaine his galliard; Pipers Pavan; Solus cum sola pavan; Sorrow stay* (452 570-2).

Volume 8: Lute music: (i) *Almain; Almain; Can she excuse; Coranto; Dr Case's Pavan; A Dream; Fantasia; Fantasia; Lachrimae; Loth to depart; Melancholy galliard; Mr Dowland's midnight; Mrs Vaux galliard; Preludium; The Queen's galliard; Resolution; Sir John Smith, his almain;* (ii) *Aloe; Come away; Fancy (Fantasia); Galliard; John Dowland's galliard; Mr Giles Hobie's galliard; Pavan; The Earl of Essex, his galliard; The Lady Clifton's spirit (Galliard); The Most Sacred Queen Elizabeth, her galliard; What if a day.* (i) Anthony Bailes; (ii) Jakob Lindberg (452 571-2).

Volume 9: Lute music: (i) *Complaint; A Fancy (Fantasia); The Frog galliard; Galliard on 'Walsingham'; Galliard to Lachrimae; Jig; Lachrimae; Mignarda; Semper Dowland semper dolens;* (ii) *Captain Dogorie Piper's galliard; Dowland's first galliard; Dowland's galliard; 2 Fancies (Fantasias); 2 Galliards; Go from my window; Lady Hunsdon's puffe; Lady Laiton's almain; Lord Willoughbie's welcome home; Mr Langton's galliard; Mrs Clifton's almain; Pavan; Piper's pavan; Sir Henry Guilforde, his almain; Tarleton's jig; Walsingham.* (i) Jakob Lindberg; (ii) Nigel North (452 572-2).

Volume 10: Lute music: (i) *Pavana Johan Douland;* (ii) *Can she excuse; Farewell Fancy; Farewell (on the 'In nomine' theme); The Frog galliard; 2 Galliards; The King of Denmark's galliard; Lachrimae; La mia Barbara; Lord Strang's march; Mrs Brigide Fleetwood's pavan; Mrs Nichol's almain; Mrs Norrish's delight; Mrs Vaux's jig; Mrs White's nothing; Mrs White's thing; Mrs Winter's jump; The Shoemaker's wife, a toy; Sir Henry Umpton's funeral;* (iii) *Forlorn hope fancy; Galliard; Orlando sleepeth; Robin; Solus cum sola; The Lord Viscount Lisle, his galliard.* (i) Nigel North; (ii) Anthony Rooley; (iii) Christopher Wilson (452 573-2).

Volume 11: Lute music: *A Coy toy; Almain; Earl of Derby, his galliard; Fancy (Fantasia); Fortune my foe; Mr Knight's galliard; Sir John Langton's pavan; Sir John Souch his galliard; Tarletone's riserrectione; The Lady Rich, her galliard; The Lady Russell's pavan.* Consort music (arrangements): *Almain à 2; Can she excuse galliard; Captain Piper's pavan and galliard; Dowland's first galliard; Fortune my foe; The Frog galliard; Katherine Darcie's galliard; Lachrimae antiquae novae pavan and galliard; Lachrimae pavan; La mia Barbara pavan and galliard; Mistress Nichols alman à 2; à 5; Mr John Langton pavan and galliard; Round Battell galliard; Susanna fair; Tarleton's jigge* (452 574-2).

Volume 12: Consort music: *Lady if you so spite me; Mistress Nichols alman; Pavan à 4; Volta à 4; Were every thought an eye. A Musicall Banquet 1610: works collected by Robert Dowland* (452 575-2).

This set, recorded over half a decade in the late 1970s, is a remarkable achievement. The discs originally appeared separately, but are now available only in a bargain box, well documented and with full texts provided. However, it seems useful to make a comment about each collection individually. The contents of the *First Booke of Songes* of 1597 were recorded in the order in which they are published, varying the accompaniment between viols, lute with bass viol, voices and viols, and even voices alone. There is hardly any need to stress the beauties of the music itself, which is eminently well served by this stylish ensemble and is beautifully recorded.

The *Second Booke* contains many of Dowland's best-known songs, such as *Fine knacks for ladies, I saw my lady weep* and *Flow my tears*. Incidentally, the latter are performed on lute and two voices, the bass line being sung by David Thomas; this is quite authentic, though many listeners will retain an affection for its solo treatment. The solo songs are given with great restraint and good musical judgement, while the consort pieces receive expressive treatment. Emma Kirkby is at her freshest and most appealing in *Come, ye heavy states of night* and *Clear or cloudy*. Perhaps it is invidious to single her out, as the standard of performance throughout is distinguished. Refined intelligence is shown throughout by all taking part. The recording is of the highest quality.

In the *Third Booke* David Thomas gives an excellent account of himself in *What poor astronomers they are*, and Emma Kirkby's voice is again a delight. Apart from a certain reluctance to characterize, this disc also commands admiration.

A Pilgrimes Solace (1612), Dowland's *Fourth Booke of Songs*, appeared when he was 50, and here it spreads over more than a single CD. In a collection pervaded by melancholy, variety has been achieved here by using contrasts of texture: some of the songs are performed in consort, others are given to different singers. Emma Kirkby sings with great purity and beauty of tone, and the disc also offers some perceptive singing from Martyn Hill. Anthony Rooley's playing is accomplished, and so is his direction of the proceedings. The second of the two CDs also includes some interesting 'transcriptions', but they are less 'transcriptions for the keyboard of Dowland', rather pieces composed 'after' Dowland.

In any event, these performances are elegant and have plenty of body, and the recording, if cut at a high level, is faithful and vivid.

Volumes 6 and 7 offer a superb collection of motets and sacred songs, an invaluable counterpart to the better-known secular works, instrumental and vocal. The recording is first rate. The *Lachrimae* are most beautiful pieces and are played with splendid taste. The instrumental music which closes Volume 7 is an anthology of arrangements of Dowland's music, presented not as second-best (as we today think of arrangements) but as a genuine illumination, a heightening of the original inspiration. Particularly attractive are the items for two or more lutes.

Volumes 8, 9, 10 and 11 concentrate on Dowland's huge output of lute music. This impressive survey is entrusted to more than one player and contains a number of surprises. Though Dowland is best known for his melancholy – *semper dolens*, etc. – he has far greater range than the popular imagination would give him credit for. Of particular note are some of the *Fantasias* from Jakob Lindberg (who uses a bandora as well as a lute); their chromatic boldness and fantasy place them among the greatest music for this instrument. Both Christopher Wilson and Anthony Bailes play very freely and expressively (some may feel they could do with a tauter sense of rhythm), but they and their colleagues give performances that are dedicated and highly accomplished.

The second half of Volume 11 and the first part of Volume 12 concentrate on the consort music. Three of the *Pavans* and *Galliards* come from Thomas Simpson's *Opusculum* (1610) and two of the *Pavans* are direct recompositions of Dowland's *Lachrimae*. Marvellous playing comes in the pieces from Simpson's *Taffel-consort* (1621). Although the forward balance brings a comparatively limited dynamic range, in all other respects the sound is first class.

The final Volume concludes with '*A Musicall banquet*' (1610) which Robert Dowland, the great lutenist's son, compiled and published but which he did not compose. The composers range from his celebrated father to lesser-known masters such as Holborne and Tessier, or more familiar ones such as Caccini. Not all the performances are equally satisfying, but overall this box cannot be recommended too highly – although essentially it is meant to be dipped into rather than taken a whole CD at a time. The CD transfers are of the very highest quality. The discs are not available separately and, so far as we can determine, the set is available in the USA also.

CONSORT MUSIC

Consort music: *Captain Digorie Piper, his pavan and galliard; Fortune my foe; Lachrimae; Lady Hunsdon's almain; Lord Souche's galliard; Mistress Winter's jump; The shoemaker's wife (a toy); Sir George Whitehead's almain; Sir Henry Guildford's almain; Sir Henry Umpton's funeral; Sir John Smith's almain; Sir Thomas Collier's galliard; Suzanna.*
*** Hyperion Dig. CDA 66010 [id.]. Extempore String Ens.

The Extempore Ensemble's technique of improvising and elaborating in Elizabethan consort music is aptly exploited here in an attractively varied selection of pieces by Dowland, and on record, as in concert, the result sounds the more spontaneous. Excellent recording.

'*Treasures from my mind*': Instrumental pieces: *Captaine Digorie Piper his galliard; The Earl of Essex galliard; Fine knacks for ladies; Frog galliard; Lord Strangs march; M. Bucton's galliard; Mistress Nichols almand; M. Thomas Collier his galliard with two trebles*. Lute pieces: *Fantaisie; Pavane: La mia Barbara*. Songs: *Awake sweet love, thou art returned; Come again, sweet love doth now invite; Come away, come sweet love; Flow my teares, fall from your springs; From silent night, true register of moanes; Go nightly cares, the enemy to rest; If my complaints could passions move; In darknesse let mee dwell; Lasso vita mia, mi fa morire; Sorrow, sorrow stay; Time stands still.*
(N) *** Virgin Veritas/EMI Dig. VC5 45288-2 Catherine King, Virelai.

Virelai is a quintet, led by the fine mezzo, Catherine King, with a group of four instrumentalists who between them can offer a considerable variety of instrumental textures, including viols, various lutes and cittern, and tenor or bass flutes. Indeed, two of the more fascinating instrumental items here are *Captaine Digorie Piper his galiard* and the *Frog galiard* played as duets on the uniquely sonorous bass flute and bass lute. *Lord Strangs march* and *Fine knacks for ladies*, however, use tenor flute, viol and cittern in the freshest, most jolly fashion. The songs, with their characteristic melancholy, are movingly sung, sometimes lute accompanied (*In darkness let me dwell*), sometimes using lute and bass viol (*Flow my teares*) or alternatively the rich textures of the full ensemble (*From silent night*). The two famous opening songs, *Come again* and *Goe nightly cares* also use an abundant tapestry to great effect. And a pair of lute solos are thrown in for good measure. Beautifully recorded, this is a satisfyingly diverse collection.

Consort music, lute solos and songs: *Captain Digorie Piper his galliard; The King of Denmark's galliard; M. Buctons galliard; The Earle of Essex galliard; M. George Whitehead his galliard; M. Giles Hobies galliard; M. Henry Noel his galliard; M. Nicholas Gryffith his galliard; Mistress Nichols almand; Mr John*

Langton's pavan; M. Thomas Collier his galliard; Semper Dowland semper dolens; Sir Henry Umpton's funerall; Sir John Such his galliard. Lute: *A Fancy; Farewell (In nomine).* Lute and bass viol: *Dowlands adieu for Master Oliver Cromwell.* Songs: *All ye who love or fortune; Burst forth my tears; Can she excuse my wrongs; Lasso vita mia; A shepherd in a shade; Stay sweet awhile.*

(BB) *** Naxos Dig. 8.553326 [id.]. Rose Consort of Viols, with Jacob Heringman & Catherine King.

There is little vocal duplication here, but in any case Catherine King's fresh voice and simplicity of line are all her own and she is very touching in the melancholy songs. The Rose Consort, lively enough in the galliards, also show their sensitivity to Dowland's doleful moods, notably in the famous *Semper Dowland semper dolens*, but also in the lament for Oliver Cromwell, played sombrely on bass viol and lute. The programme ends with a moving account of *Sir John Umpton's funerall* music, darkly resonant, which would lose much of its grave poignancy without the viol colouring. The two lute solos, very well played by Jacob Heringman, offer further contrast, and the whole programme is recorded most naturally.

Lachrimae, or Seaven Teares.

*** BIS Dig. CD 315 [id.]. Dowland Consort, Jakob Lindberg.

Lachrimae, or Seaven Teares; Semper Dowland semper dolens (Pavane à 5) Pavane in C à 4).

(N) (M) *(*) Vanguard Dig. 99175 [id.]. Musica Antiqua Köln, Reinhard Goebel (with SCHNEIDEMANN: *Pavana lachrimae.* SCHOP: *Pavana lachrimae.* HOLBORNE: *The image of melancholy (Pavane).* FARINA: *Pavane in A min. à 4.* ***).

Jakob Lindberg and his consort of viols give a highly persuasive account of Dowland's masterpiece. The texture is always clean and the lute clearly present.

The Cologne Musica Antiqua seem unable to identify easily with Dowland's special world of melancholy. They play with considerable intensity, but plod steadily forward, and the effect eventually becomes rather monotonous. They are much more convincing in the lively *C major Pavane* which closes the concert, and even more so in the North German repertoire, especially the *Pavanas* of Schneidemann (a harpsichord solo) and Schop (violin with continuo).

Lachrimae: Seven passionate pavans. Consort settings: *Captain Piper his galiard; The Earl of Essex galiard; The King of Denmarks galiard; M. Bucton his galiard; M. George Whitehead his almand. M. Giles Hoby his galiard; M. Henry Noell his galiard; M. John Langtons pavane; M. Nicholas Gryffith his galiard; M. Thomas Collier his galliard with two trebles; Mrs Nichols Almand; Semper Dowland, semper dolens; Sir Henry Umptons funerall; Sir John Souch his galiard.*

*** Virgin/EMI Dig. VC5 45005-2. Fretwork, with Christopher Wilson.

This is a reissue of Fretwork's 1989 recording of excerpts from the *Lachrimae*, for which the 'passionate' pavans serve as introduction. Structurally they form a variation sequence, linked by a falling fourth at the opening of the first *Lachrimae antiquae* and by other common motifs of melodic line and harmony, followed by a newly recorded collection of Dowland's own galliards, so one can choose to move over to more cheerful music at any time. All the performances are of undoubted merit and are well recorded. The original two-disc set with music of Byrd is now available on a Virgin Double (VBD5 61561-2).

COMPLETE LUTE MUSIC

Complete lute works, Volume 1: *Almain, P 49; Dr Cases Pauen; A Dream (Lady Leighton's paven); A Fancy, P 5; Farwell; Frogg galliard; Galliards, P 27; P 30; P 35; P 104; Go from my windowe; The Lady Laitons Almone; Mellancoly galliard; M. Giles Hobies galliard; Mistris Whittes thinge; Mr Knights galliard; Mrs whites nothing; Mrs Winters jumpp; My Ladie Riches galyerd; My lord willobies wellcome home; Orlando sleepeth; Pavan P 18; Pavana (Mylius 1622); Piece without a title, P 51; What if a day.*

*** HM Dig. HMU 907160 [id.]. Paul O'Dette (lute and orpharion).

Dowland wrote about 100 lute solos, using every musical form familiar at the time. Where either divisions (variations) or ornaments are obviously missing, Paul O'Dette has supplied his own – and very convincing they are. The music on this first disc is particularly rich in ideas. *Orlando sleepeth* is a hauntingly delicate miniature and it is played, like *Mrs Winters Jumpp* and *Go from my window*, on the orpharion, a wire-strung instrument very like the lute but with a softer focus in sound because 'the fingers must be easily drawn over the strings, and not sharply gripped or stroken, as the lute is'. Paul O'Dette is an acknowledged master of this repertoire: his playing, which can be robust or with the most subtle nuance, is permeated with a natural and unexaggerated expressive feeling.

Complete lute works, Volume 2: *Aloe; As I went to Walsingham; Can she excuse; Captain Candishe his galyard; Captain Digorie Piper his galliard; A coye joye; Dowlands first galliard; Dowland's galliard; Farwell (An 'In nomine'); Fantasia; Lachrimae; Mayster Pypers pavyn; Mignarda; Mounsieur's almaine; Mrs Brigide*

fleetwoods paven alias Solus sine sola; Mrs vauxes galliarde; Mrs vauxes gigge; My lady hunnsdons puffe; Sir Henry Guilforde his almaine; Sir John Smith his almain; Sir John Souche his galliard; Solus cum sola; Suzanna galliard; Sweet Robyne.
*** HM Dig. HMU 907161 [id.]. Paul O'Dette (lute).

Dowland's use of other composers' music is very prevalent in this programme, and several of the works are not certainly his but are of such a quality that the attribution is just. There is a good deal of melancholy music here, even the *Galliard* named after *Captain Digorie Piper*. Of course there is robust writing too. The opening *My lady hunnsdons puffe* is very catchy, as is *Can she excuse* with its sharp cross-rhythms. Once again Paul O'Dette constantly beguiles the ear, with his feeling for the special mood and colour of Dowland's writing, and the recording is impeccable.

Complete lute works, Volume 3: *Dowlands adew for Master Oliver Cromwell; A Fancy, P 7; Forlorne hope fancye; Fortune my foe; Lord Strangs march; Mistresse Nichols almand; The most high and mightie Christianus, the fourth King of Denmark, his galliard; The most Sacred Queene Elizabeth, her galliard; Mr Dowlands midnight; Mr Langtons galliard; Mrs Cliftons allmaine; A Pavan, P 16; The Queenes galliard; The Right Honourable Ferdinando Earle of Darby, his galliard; The Right Honourable the Lady Cliftons spirit; Semper Dowland semper dolens; Sir John Langton, his pavin; Tarletones riserrectione; Tarletons Willy; Wallsingham & A galliard on Wallsingham.*
*** HM Dig. HMU 907162 [id.]. Paul O'Dette.

Dowland was never satisfied with his music; he was always revising and rethinking earlier works. The exotic *King of Denmark's galliard*, the opening item here, was originally called the 'Battle galliard' because of its bugle-calls, so engagingly portrayed on the lute. *Queen Elizabeth's* not dissimilar *galliard* was originally written for someone else. Generally the third volume of this excellent series has more extrovert music, but there are still interludes of melancholy. The closing *Semper Dowland semper dolens* (extended to seven minutes) speaks for itself.

Complete lute works, Volume 4: *Almand, P 96; Awake sweet love – Galliard; Come away; Coranto, P 100; Fancy, P 6; Fantasia, P 71; Frog Galliard; Galliard, P 82; Galliard on a galliard by Daniel Bachelar; Galliard to Lachrimae; Lachrimae, P 15; The Lady Russells pavane; La mia Barbara; Loth to depart; My Lord Wilobies welcome home; Pavana; Preludium; The Right Honourable the Lord Viscount Lisle, his galliard; The Right Honourable Robert, Earl of Essex, his galliard; The shoemaker's wife – A Toy.*
**(*) HM Dig. HMU 907163 [id.]. Paul O'Dette.

For his fourth volume, Paul O'Dette uses two different lutes as appropriate, an 8-course and a 10-course, both after Hans Frei. For the most part this is a low-key programme, very much in the '*semper dolens*' mood. Of course there are highlights, like the famous *Fantasia*, P 71, and the mood perks up for the galliard written for the Earl of Essex, while the galliard after Daniel Bachelar is also very striking and the penultimate piece, *La mia Barbara*, is very charmingly presented. But overall this is not one of the more memorable of the O'Dette collections.

Complete lute works, Volume 5: *Almande; Captain Pipers galliard; Doulands rounde battell galyarde; Earl of Darbies Galliard; Earl of Essex Galliard; 2 Fancies; A Fantasie; Gagliarda; Galliard; Hasellwoods galliard; A Jig; Mistris Norrishis delight; Pavana Dowland Angli; Pavana lachrimae; Pavin; Sir Henry Umpton's funerall; Sir Thomas Monson his Pavin and Galliard; Squires galliard; Une jeune fillette.*
(**N**) *** HM Dig. HMU 907164 [id.].

Volume 5 includes a fascinating mixture of genuine Dowland, and music written by other composers very much in the Dowland manner. Paul O'Dette considers it unlikely that many of the pieces here written by Dowland were conceived by the composer in their present form. The *Pavana lachrimae* and the striking *Earl of Essex Galliard* are both solo arrangements by others. *Une jeune fillette* (with its extended divisions) is probably by Bachelar. The sombrely memorable *Sir Henry Upton's Funeral* is certainly by Dowland, but was originally conceived as a consort piece, as was *Haselwood's Galliard. Mistress Norris's delight* is most engaging, using an inversion of the opening of the *Early of Derby's Galliard*, but was almost certainly put together by other hands. Three items are probably by Dowland's son, Robert, including the rather fine *Pavin and galliard for Sir Thomas Monson* and the very characterful *Almande*, which appears to be derived from a piece by Robert Johnson. Some of the items with simple titles (*Fancies*, *Galliards* and the *Jig*) are very personable. Dowland's own splendid closing *Fantasie* comes from a late manuscript, but in a profusely ornamented version which suggests that it is not completely authentic. Dowland was known not to favour excess ornamentation, which he called 'blind divisions'. Yet it makes a lively ending to a fine concert which is full of good things.

Complete Lute works: Volumes 1–5.
(**N**) (M) *** HM Dig.HMX 2907160.64 (5) [id.].

This set collects all the above five discs together in a slip case at lower-medium-price. An excellent booklet collects together the extended notes provided with the original issues, so this is excellent value for the collector of lute music and Dowland in particular.

Music for lute and (i) orpharion: (i) *Can she excuse me; A Dream. Fancies, P 6 & P 73; Fantasie, P 1a; Farwell; Frog galliard; Lachrimae, P 15; Lady Hunsdon's puffe; Melancholy galliard; Mignarda; The most high and mightie Christianus, the fourth King of Denmark, his galliard; Mr Knights galliard; Mrs Brigide Fleetwood's pavan alias Solus sine sola; Mrs Vaux Jig;* (i) *Mrs Winters jump; My Lord Willoughby's welcome home;* (i) *Orlando sleepeth; Resolution; The Right Honourable The Lord Viscount Lisle, his galliard; Semper Dowland semper dolens; The Shoemaker's wife; Sir John Smith his almain; Tarleton's riserrection; Walsingham.*
*** BIS Dig CD 824 [id.]. Jacob Lindberg (lute), or (i) orpharion.

Those not collecting Paul O'Dette's complete series will find this BIS CD offers a cross-section of many of the finest of Dowland's lute pieces. The programme is generous (75 minutes) and Jacob Lindberg is no less at home in this repertoire than his colleague on Harmonia Mundi. He is particularly successful in the lively (battle) galliard written for the King of Denmark, which is full of personality, as is the gentle piece called *Resolution*. The orpharion is used to atmospheric effect in the four works for which it was intended. *Semper Dowland, semper dolens* is most eloquently presented, as is the remarkable *Farwell*; and the divisions on *Walsingham* are played with a nice flow and an unexaggerated bravura. The recording is first class.

VOCAL MUSIC

Ayres and Lute-lessons: *All ye whom love; Away with these self-loving lads; Come again sweet love; Come heavy sleep; Go Christal teares; If my complaints; My thoughts are winged; Rest awhile;* (Lute): *Semper Dowland, semper dolens. A shepherd in a shade; Stay sweet awhile; Tell me, true love; What if I never speede; When Phoebus first did Daphne love; Wilt thou unkind.*(Lute)*Prelude and Galliard.*
(B) **(*) HM Musique d'abord HMA 901076 [id.]. Deller Consort, Mark Deller; Robert Spencer.

Dowland's 'ayres' were designed for a consort of singers as well as for solo singer and lute, and it is good to hear them in this form. Two of the Lute Lessons are excellently played by Robert Spencer. The performances for the most part give consistent pleasure. The sound is excellent.

Can she excuse my wrongs?; Come again! Sweet love doth now invite; Come, heavy sleep; Fine knacks for ladies; Flow my tears; His golden locks; If my complaints could passions move; In darkness let me dwell; I saw my lady weep; Lady, if you so spite me; Me, me and none but me; Now, O now I needs must part; Say love if ever thou did'st find; Sorrow stay; Stay awhile thy flying; Think'st thou then by feigning?; Time stands still; When Phoebus first did Daphne love; Wilt thou unkind thus reave me?. Lute solos: *Fortune my foe; Melancholy galliard.* (With *Galliards* by Mary, Queen of Scots. Attrib. Francis CUTTING: *Greensleeves (Divisions)*. ANON.: *Bonny Sweet Robin; Callino; Kemp's Jig.*)
(BB) *** Naxos Dig. 8.553381 [id.]. Steven Rickards, Dorothy Linell (lute).

Steven Rickards has a light, precise counter-tenor voice which he uses very imaginatively in this sequence of 19 madrigals, including many of Dowland's finest. So a lively number like *Fine knacks for ladies* has a crispness and spring to bring out its lightness; even more impressively Rickards, with tone rock-steady and little or no hooting, superbly sustains the long legato lines of such great madrigals as *Flow my tears*, *I saw my lady weep* and *Come, heavy sleep*. There are also well-chosen lute solos from Dorothy Linell supplementing her excellent accompaniments. The recording, made in New York, is clear and well balanced. Full texts and good notes are provided.

Can she excuse my wrongs?; Come again! Sweet love doth now invite; Far from triumphing court; Flow so fast, ye fountain; In darkness let me dwell; I saw my lady weep; Lady, if you so spite me; Thou almighty God; Shall I sue?; Weep you no more, sad fountains. Lute solos: *Lachrimae antiquae pavane; Semper Dowland, semper dolens.*
*** Lyrichord LEMS 8011 [id.]. Russell Oberlin, Joseph Iadone (lute).

One can hardly believe this recital was recorded in 1958, so fresh and vivid is the sound. Russell Oberlin's very special counter-tenor timbre is beautifully caught. The very free rhythmic style of *Can she excuse my wrongs?* is confidently handled and *Shall I sue?* also brings a lively element into what is essentially a melancholy selection. *I saw my lady weep* is most moving, while *Flow my tears* soars; but most touching of all is the closing *In darkness let me dwell.* Joseph Iadone contributes two of Dowland's most famous instrumental pieces. He affects a very mellow style which is believed to be authentic. The only drawback to this disc is the comparatively short playing-time of 48 minutes.

Ayres: *Can she excuse my wrongs?; Come again, sweet love; Come heavy sleep; Flow not so fast, ye fountains; From silent night; Go nightly cares; In darkness let me dwell; I saw my lady weep; Shall I sue?*. Consort pieces: *Captain Digory*

Piper's pavane and galliard; The First galliard. Lute lessons: *Melancholy galliard; Mistress White's nothing; Mistress Winter's jump; My Lady Hunsdon's puff.* Lute duets: *My Lord Chamberlain's galliard; My Lord Willoughby's welcome home.* Lute lessons: *Orlando sleepeth; Sir John Smith's almain; Tarlton's resurrection.*
*** HM HMC 90245 [id.]. Alfred Deller, Consort of Six, Robert Spencer.

Ayres: *Come away, come away sweet love; Flow my tears; If my complaints could passions move; If that a sinner's sighs be angel's food; Lasso, vita mia; Me, me and none but me; O gentle Death; Say, love, if ever thou didst find; Sorrow stay; Weep you no more sad fountain; What if I never speed?; Wilt thou unkind, thus leave me.* Consort pieces: *Can she excuse galliard; Fortune my foe; The Frog galliard; Katherine Darcy's galliard; Lachrimae pavane; The Round battle galliard.* Lute lessons: *Can she excuse galliard; Galliard; The Lady Laiton's almain; Midnight; Mistress White's thing; The shoemaker's wife (a toy).*
*** HM HMC 90244. Alfred Deller, Consort of Six, Robert Spencer.

Deller's two collections are admirably planned and beautifully recorded. He is in excellent voice, while variety is provided by interweaving his solos with lute pieces and music for Elizabethan consort of six instruments (two viols, flute, lute, cittern and bandora). The recording is naturally balanced and neither of these recitals outstays its welcome.

'*Earth, water, air and fire*': Lute songs: *Come again, sweet love doth now invite; Shall I strive; Sleep, wayward thoughts; Woeful heart; Would my conceits. Pilgrims Solace: Toss not my soul; From silent night; Go nightly cares; Sorrow stay; In darkness let me dwell; Though mighty God.*
(N) *** ASV Gaudeamus Dig. CDGAU 187 [id.]. Consort of Musicke, Rooley (with LOCKE: *Break, distracted heart.* MORLEY: *Deep lamenting; Leave now mine eyes.* TOMKINS: *O let me live for true love; Weep no more*; WEELKES: *Cease sorrows now*; DE SERMISY: *Las, je m'y plains*).

The note accompanying this stimulating concert suggests that the four elements were 'everywhere in English lyrics' during Dowland's time, 'celebrating England as a veritable Arcadia'. Like the collection from Virelai (see above) the programme opens with *Come again*, only here not sung by a single voice with instrumental accompaniment, but madrigal-like, by a vocal quartet led by Evelyn Tubb. The word 'laugh' unexpectedly delivered with sharp attack at the very end of Dowland's song typifies the way that Anthony Rooley and the Consort of Musicke have rethought this Elizabethan repertory. Fresh response to word-meaning is the keynote, not just in Dowland but in items by his friends, Tomkins, Morley and Weelkes, and notably, Matthew Locke's melodramatic *Break, distracted heart*, sung by 'Two despairing men and two despairing women', ending with a spoken dialogue between the two principal characters, before they make away with themselves! The closing sequence, in complete contrast, brings the most intense illumination of all, Dowland's five devotional songs, *The Pilgrimes Solace*, crowned by an extended motet, *Thou Mighty God*, visionary and uplifting.

Du Fay, Guillaume (*c.* 1400–1474)

Secular music (complete).
(B) *** O-L 452 557-2 (5) [id.]. Timothy Penrose, Rogers Covey-Crump, John Elwes, Paul Elliott, Paul Hillier, Michael George, Medieval Ens. of London, Peter & Timothy Davies.

Volume 1: *Belle, que vous ay ie mesfait; Ce jour de l'an voudray joye mener; Entre vous, gentils amoureux; Helas, et quant vous veray?; Invidia nimica; J'ay mis mon cueur et ma pensée; Je donne a tous les amoureux; Je requier a tous amoureux; Je veuil chanter de cuer joyeux; L'alta belleza tua, virtute, valore; Ma belle dame, je vous pri; Mon chier amy, qu'aves vous empensé; Mon cuer me fait tous dis penser; Navré je sui d'un dart penetratif; Par droit je puis bien complaindre et gemir; Passato è il tempo omaj di quei pensieri; Pour ce que veoir je ne puis; Resvellies vous et faites chiere lye; Resvelons nous, resvelons, amoureux; Se madame je puis veir* (452 558-2).

Volume 2: *Adieu ces bon vins de Lannoys; Belle plaissant et gracieuse; Belle, veullies moy retenir; Belle, vueillies vostre mercy donner; Bien veignes vous, amoureuse liesse; Bon jour, bon mois, bon an et bonne estraine; Ce moys de may soyons lies et joyeux; Dona i aredenti ray; Estrines moy, je vous estrineray; He, compaignons, resvelons nous; Helas, ma dame, par amours; J'atendray tant qu'il vous playra; J'ay grant (dolour); Je me complains piteusement; Je ne puis plus ce que y'ai peu; Je ne suy plus tel que souloye; La belle se siet au piet de la tour; La dolce uista; Ma belle dame souveraine; Portugaler; Pour l'amour de ma doulce amye* (2 versions); *Quel fronte signorille in paradiso; Vergene bella, che di sol vestita* (452 559-2).

Volume 3: *Bien doy servir de volente entiere; Ce jour le doibt, aussi fait la saison; C'est bien raison de devoir essaucier; Craindre vous vueil, doulce dame de pris; Dona gentile, bella come l'oro; Donnes l'assault a la fortresse; Entre les plus plaines danoy; Hic iocundus sumit mundus; Je prens congie de vous, amours; Las, que feray?*

Ne que je devenray?; Mille bonjours je vous presente; Mon bien, m'amour et ma maistresse; Pouray je avoir vostre mercy?; Qu'est devenue leaulte?; Seigneur Leon, vous soyes bienvenus; Se la face ay pale (452 560-2).

Volume 4: *Adieu m'amour, adieu ma joye; Adieu, quitte le demeurant de ma vie; Belle, vueilles moy vangier; J'ayme bien celui qui s'en va; Je languis en piteux martire; Je n'ai doubté fors que des envieux; Juvenis qui puellam; Lamentatio sanctae matris ecclesiae constantinopolitanae; Ne je ne dors ne je ne veille; Or pleust a dieu qu'a son plaisir; Par le regart de vos beaux yeux; Puisque celle qui me tient en prison; Puisque vous estez campieur; Se la face ay pale* (2 versions); *S'il est plaisir que je vous puisse faire; Trop lonc temps ai esté en desplaisir; Va t'en, mon cuer, jour et nuitie; Vo regard et doulce maniere* (452 561-2).

Volume 5: *De ma haulte et bonne aventure; Departes vous, male bouche et envie; Dieu gard la bone sans reprise; Du tout m'estoie abandonné; En triumphant de Cruel Dueil; Franc cuer gentil, sur toutes gracieuse; Helas mon dueil, a ce cop sui ie mort; Je ne vis onques la pareille; Je vous pri, mon tres doulx ami; Les douleurs, dont me sens tel somme; Le serviteur hault guerdonné; Malheureulx cueur, que vieulx tu faire?; Ma plus mignonne de mon cueur; Mon seul plaisir, ma doulce joye; O flos florum virginum; Resistera . . .; Vostre bruit et vostre grant fame* (452 562-2).

The collector with special interests in this period will naturally acquire this handsomely produced and lovingly prepared set, but the non-specialist might well be deterred by the sheer scale of the enterprise: 96 songs are quite a lot. What will surprise those who dip into these discs is the range, beauty and accessibility of this music. There is nothing really specialized about this art beyond the conventions within which the sensibility works. The documentation is thorough and the performances have great commitment and sympathy to commend them. The actual sound-quality is of the first order, and readers who investigate the contents of this box will be rewarded with much delight. The discs are not available separately, but we are glad to see that the box is available on both sides of the Atlantic.

Ceremonial and Liturgical motets; Recollectio Festorum Beate Marie Virginis.
(N) *** DG Dig. 447 773-2 [id.]. Pomerium, Alexander Blachly.

This is a set of plainchants that Du Fay composed in 1458 when he was 60, for the Recollection of the Feasts of the Virgin Mary. It was recently authenticated by the American scholar Barbara Haggh and is one of the very few instances of chant being composed by a major composer. Pomerium perform the *First Vespers* in their entirety with *Psalms* (not all by Dufay). They add two motets. The singing and recording are clean and clear. Recommended.

Chansons: *Adieu ces bons vins de Lannoys; Belle, que vous ay je mesfait; Bon jour, bon mois; Ce jour de l'an; Donnes l'assault à la fortress; Helas mon dueil; J'ay mis mon cuer; Mon chier amy; Par droit je puis bien complaindre; Pas le regard de vos beaux yeux; Pour l'amour de ma doulce amye; Puisque vous estez campieur; Quel fronte signorille La doce vita; Resvelliés vous et faites chiere lye; Resvelons nous; Se la face ay pale; Vergene Bella.*
(BB) ** Naxos Dig. 8.553458 [id.]. Bernhard Landauer, Unicorn Ens., Michael Posch.

This Naxos anthology with the counter-tenor Bernhard Landauer and the Ensemble Unicorn under the direction of Michael Posch offers some 17 items. They are freely interpreted, taking the text as a guideline rather than a rigid musical framework, and are given with some panache. There is an improvisatory freedom that would doubtless delight in the concert hall but is perhaps less satisfying on repetition. Well recorded by the Viennese engineers, but ultimately not as rewarding as the performances in the more authoritative Oiseau-Lyre set.

Missa: Ecce ancilla Domini; Mass Propers De angelis Dei officium.
(N) *** Virgin/EMI Dig. VC5 45050-2. Gilles Binchois, Dominique Vellard.

Dufay's four-part mass *Ecce ancilla Domini* comes most probably from the 1460s and the three-part *Mass Propers* were composed 20 years earlier. The sound of this group is mellifluous and euphonious without any expressive or dynamic exaggeration. They adopt generally leisurely tempi but they are convincing.

Missa L'homme armé; Motet: *Supremum est mortalibus bonum.*
(BB) *** Naxos Dig. 8.553087 [id.]. Oxford Camerata, Jeremy Summerly.

Jeremy Summerly and his Oxford Camerata give a powerfully expressive and wholly convincing account of Du Fay's masterly cyclic Mass using a Burgundian chanson as its basis. We hear this sung first in its original format as an introduction, and its message, 'The armed man should be feared', makes a dramatically appropriate contrast with the motet, *Supremum est mortalibus*, which is a peace song. The latter was written some 30 years earlier, yet shows just as readily the remarkable inventiveness and eloquence of this fifteenth-century French composer. The Mass movements are interspersed with plainchant in the same Dorian mode. With vivid yet atmospheric recording, this can be given the strongest recommendation.

Chanson and Mass: *Se la face ay pale;* Motet: *Gloria ad modum tubae.*
(M) *** Virgin Veritas/EMI VER5 61283-2 [CDM 61283]. Early Music Cons. of L., David Munrow.

David Munrow's pioneering recording of Du Fay's austere yet moving Mass is superb in every way. The Mass itself is prefaced by the chanson on which it is based, first in its original three-part version, then in two keyboard versions from the Buxheimer Organ Book, and finally in a four-part instrumental version scored for alto cornett, alto shawm and alto and tenor sackbutts, attributed to the great Burgundian master himself. The performance is controversially but effectively accompanied by tenor and bass viols in the solo sections of the *Gloria* and *Credo*, cornetts and sackbutts in the full sections. The soloists are all distinguished (they include James Bowman), and David Munrow himself plays the alto shawm. As a curtain-raiser before the Mass, we are offered the catchy motet, *Gloria ad modum tubae*, written in a lively canonic form, with the effect of a round. An indispensable reissue.

Missa Santi Anthoni de Padua. Hymnus: *Veni creator spiritus.*
*** DG Dig. 447 772-2. Pomerium, Alexander Blachly.

Missa Santi Anthoni de Padua. Motet: *O proles Hispaniae/O sidus Hispaniae.*
*** Hyperion Dig. CDA 66854 [id.]. Binchois Cons., Andrew Kirkman.

It was long thought that Du Fay's *Mass for St Anthony of Padua* was lost but, at the beginning of the 1980s, the British musicologist, Dr David Fallows, produced evidence to suggest that two separate groups of manuscripts held at Trent, Italy could convincingly be linked to make a whole, and that is what is recorded here. Moreover we have a choice of style of performance for this beautiful music. The Binchois Consort is a small, intimate, all-male group, while Alexander Blachly's Pomerium is a much larger choir, drawing on four sopranos, three altos, four tenors and four basses, although the whole ensemble is used only in the Ordinary movements. This makes for greater dynamic contrast; moreover the two recording acoustics are different, the DG Archiv recording being made in the richly resonant Grotto Church of Notre Dame in New York, whereas the Hyperion ambience is drier and the inner detail emerges with much greater clarity. Pomerium offer as a bonus Du Fay's setting of the hymn, *Veni creator spiritus*, while the Binchois Consort performs a motet with two texts also associated with St Anthony. Both recordings are first class.

Dukas, Paul (1865–1935)

L'apprenti sorcier (The sorcerer's apprentice).
*** DG Dig. 419 617-2 [id.]. BPO, Levine – SAINT-SAENS: *Symphony No. 3.* ***
(M) *** Decca (IMS) 448 576-2 [id.]. SRO, Ansermet – CHABRIER: *España* **(*); DEBUSSY: *La Mer* **(*); HONEGGER: *Pacific 231* ***; RAVEL: *Boléro; La Valse.* ***
(*) Decca Dig. 421 527-2. Montreal SO, Dutoit (with Concert: '*Fête à la française*' *).
(M) **(*) Chandos CHAN 6503 [id.]. RSNO, Gibson – ROSSINI: *La boutique fantasque* (arr. RESPIGHI); (with SAINT-SAENS: *Danse macabre.* **(*))
(***) Testament mono SBT1017 [id.]. Philh O, Cantelli – CASELLA: *Paganiniana;* FALLA: *Three-cornered hat;* RAVEL: *Daphnis et Chloé: suite No. 2.* (***)

Levine chooses a fast basic tempo, though not as fast as Toscanini (who managed with only two 78 sides), but achieves a deft, light and rhythmic touch to make this a real orchestral scherzo. Yet the climax is thrilling, helped by superb playing from the Berlin Philharmonic. The CD has an amplitude and sparkle which are especially telling.

Ansermet's performance is more relaxed, yet it has a cumulative effect. There is plenty of atmosphere here and the detail of the recording shows the Swiss conductor at his finest. This was originally part of a very successful 1963 collection (with music by Honegger and Ravel) to which the Chabrier and Debussy works have been added for this reissue in Decca's 'Classic Sound' series.

Dutoit does not quite match Levine's zest (nor indeed achieves the sense of calamity at the climax that the latter does), but he is genially enjoyable and is featured within a desirable collection, given demonstration-worthy recording – see our Concerts section.

Gibson secures excellent playing from the SNO, if without the sheer panache of some of his competitors. The recording (made in City Hall, Glasgow, in 1972) is less overtly brilliant than Ormandy's but has plenty of atmosphere. The Chandos disc, however, is ungenerous in playing time (37 minutes).

Cantelli's 1954 mono account still remains one of the very best performances ever recorded, and it is splendidly transferred.

L'apprenti sorcier (The Sorcerer's apprentice) (with spoken introduction).
(N) (BB) **(*) Naxos Dig. 8.554463 [id.]. Johnny Morris (nar.), Slovak RSO, Jenneth Jean – RAVEL: *Ma Mère l'Oye* ***. SAINT-SAENS: *Carnival of the animals.* **(*)

In this Naxos triptych clearly aimed at young children, Johnny Morris provides a concise and effective narrative introduction. The performance is alive and well paced. It takes a while to generate the fullest tension, but the re-emerging chopped-up broomstick creaks picaresquely, and the waters swirl around spectacularly at the climax – any child should respond to this imagery. The recording is excellent, spacious and vivid.

L'apprenti sorcier; La péri (with *Fanfare*); *Polyeucte: overture.*
❁ (M) *** Ph. 454 127-2. Rotterdam PO, David Zinman (with D'INDY: *Symphonie sur un chant montagnard.* **)

L'apprenti sorcier; La péri.
(*) Chandos Dig. CHAN 8852 [id.]. Ulster O, Yan Pascal Tortelier – CHABRIER: *España* etc. *

Dukas's *La péri* was written for Diaghilev in 1912. David Zinman's 1978 recording is arguably the finest account of Dukas's colourful score ever to have been put on record. Here is a conductor acutely sensitive to the most delicate colourings and the hushed atmosphere of this evocative score, with its colours drawn as much from Rimsky-Korsakov as from Debussian impressionism. Only in the introductory *Fanfare* could some ears crave more sonic brilliance from the well-balanced recording, and that comment might also be applied to *L'apprenti sorcier*. Certainly no one should be disappointed with either the climax or the tale's rueful dénouement. The *Polyeucte overture* is not dissimilar in style to *La péri* but has less interesting material; it is presented equally effectively. The coupled d'Indy *Symphonie* is enjoyable if not distinctive and may be regarded as a bonus. Marie-Française Bucquet is a strong and personable soloist.

Yan Pascal Tortelier gives a very good performance indeed of *La péri*, with plenty of atmosphere and feeling, and *L'apprenti sorcier* is equally successful as a performance.

(i) *L'apprenti sorcier (The sorcerer's apprentice);* (ii) *Ariane et Barbe-bleue: Act III Prelude; La péri;* (iii) *Symphony in C.*
(M) **(*) EMI CDM7 63160-2. (i) (mono) Philh. O, Markevitch; (ii) (stereo) Paris Op. O, Dervaux; (iii) (stereo) ORTF, Martinon.

Martinon brings real vigour and feeling to the *Symphony in C*, and the (slightly but not excessively reverberant) 1974 recording comes up well. *La péri* was recorded in 1957 and wears its years well, though the orchestral playing is not first class (the wind intonation is not always true). Markevitch's 1953 Philharmonia account of *L'apprenti sorcier* (mono, of course) is brilliantly played, but there is an ugly edit (cut-off reverberation) halfway through. Still, this is worth having.

Symphony in C; l'apprenti sorcier; La Péri: poème dansé (with *Fanfare*).
(N) *** RCA Dig. 09026 88022-2 [id.]. O. Nat de France, Leonard Slatkin.

Symphony in C; Polyeucte Overture.
(N) *** Chandos Dig. CHAN 9225 [id.]. BBC PO, Tortelier.

Very fine playing from the Orchestre National under Leonard Slatkin and a very well-shaped account of Dukas's fine *Symphony* plus a highly persuasive and atmospheric account of *La Péri*. Extremely well recorded too. This can be warmly recommended alongside Yan Pascal Tortelier on Chandos; the different choice of couplings will no doubt be a decisive factor but there is not a great deal to choose between them if it is just the *Symphony* you are after.

Ariane et Barbe-bleue (opera): complete.
(M) *** Erato/Warner Dig. 2292 45663-2 (2). Ciesinski, Bacquier, Paunova, Schauer, Blanzat, Chamonin, Command, Fr. R. Ch. & O, Jordan.

Ariane et Barbe-bleue is, like Debussy's *Pelléas*, set to a Maeterlinck text, but there is none of the half-lights and the dream-like atmosphere of the latter. The performance derives from a French Radio production and is, with one exception, well cast; its direction under the baton of Armin Jordan is sensitive and often powerful; the recording is eminently acceptable. The complete libretto is included, and this most enterprising and valuable reissue is strongly recommended.

Dunstable, John (d. 1453)

Missa Rex seculorum. Motets: *Albanus roseo rutilat – Quoque ferundus eras – Albanus domini Laudus; Ave maris stella; Descendi in ortum meum; Gloria in canon; Preco preheminence – Precursor premittur – textless – Inter natos mulierum; Salve regina mater mire; Specialis Virgo; Speciosa facta es; Sub tuam protectionem; Veni sancte spiritus – Veni creator spiritus.*
*** Metronome Dig. METCD 1009 [id.]. Orlando Con.

The Orlando Consort present their generous, 74-minute survey with an impressive combination of direct, impassioned feeling and style. If the splendid *Missa Rex seculorum* is of doubtful attribution, every piece here, motets and antiphons alike, is clearly by a major composer with a highly individual voice. The recording is excellent in every way, and this CD, which won the *Gramophone*'s Early Music Award in 1996, offers the collector an admirable and highly rewarding entry into this composer's sound-world.

Motets: *Agnus Dei; Alma redemptoris Mater; Credo super; Da gaudiorum premia; Gaude virgo salutata; Preco preheminenciae; Quam pulcra es; Salve regina misericordiae; Salve sceme sanctitatis; Veni creator; Veni sancte spiritus.*

*** Virgin Veritas/EMI Dig. VER5 61342-2. Hilliard Ens., Hillier.

These motets give a very good idea of Dunstable's range, and they are sung with impeccable style. The Hilliard Ensemble have perfectly blended tone and impeccable intonation, and their musicianship is of the highest order. Some collectors may find the unrelieved absence of vibrato a little tiring on the ear when taken in large doses, but most will find this a small price to pay for music-making of such excellence, so well recorded.

Duparc, Henri (1848–1933)

Mélodies (complete): *Au pays où se fait la guerre; Chanson triste; Elégie; Extase; La fuite (duet); Le galop; L'invitation au voyage; Lamento; Le Manoir de Rosamonde; Phidylé; Romance de Mignon; Sérénade; Sérénade florentine; Soupir; Testament; La vague et la cloche; La vie antérieure.*
*** Hyperion Dig. CDA 66323 [id.]. Sarah Walker, Thomas Allen, Roger Vignoles.

The Hyperion issue is as near an ideal Duparc record as could be. Here are not only the 13 recognized songs but also four early works – three songs and a duet – which have been rescued from the composer's own unwarranted suppression. Roger Vignoles is the ever-sensitive accompanist; and the recording captures voices and piano beautifully, bringing out the tang and occasional rasp of Walker's mezzo and the glorious tonal range of Allen's baritone.

Duphly, Jacques (1715–89)

Pièces pour clavecin: La Bouchon; Courante; La Félix; La Forqueray; Les Graces; La d'Héricourt; Légèrement; Menuets; Rondo in D; Rondeau in D min.; La Vanlo; La Victoire; La de Villeneuve.
*** Gaudeamus/ASV Dig. CDGAU 108 [id.]. Mitzi Meyerson (harpsichord).

These performances come from the mid-1980s (still analogue, and none the worse for that) and are very spirited and characterful. Though none of this music can lay a claim to greatness, it has undoubted charm and grace. Mitzi Meyerson plays a Goble harpsichord and uses no fewer than four tunings during the course of the recital. There are excellent notes by Nicholas Anderson. Recommended.

Dupré, Marcel (1886–1971)

Symphony in G minor for organ and orchestra, Op. 25.
*** Telarc Dig. CD 80136 [id.]. Michael Murray, RPO, Ling – RHEINBERGER: *Organ concerto No. 1.* ***

If you enjoy Saint-Saëns's *Organ Symphony* you'll probably enjoy this. The organ's contribution is greater, though it is not a concerto. It is a genial, extrovert piece, consistently inventive if not as memorably tuneful as its predecessor. The performance has warmth, spontaneity and plenty of flair, and the recording has all the spectacle one associates with Telarc in this kind of repertoire.

ORGAN MUSIC

Chorale and fugue, Op. 57; 3 Esquisses, Op. 41; Preludes and fugues: in B; G min., Op. 7/1 & 3; Le tombeau de Titelouse: Te lucis ante terminum; Placare Christe servulis, Op. 38/6 & 16; Variations sur un vieux Noël, Op. 20.
*** Hyperion Dig. CDA 66205 [id.]. John Scott (St Paul's Cathedral organ).

An outstandingly successful recital, more spontaneous and convincing than many of the composer's own recordings in the past. Dupré's music is revealed as reliably inventive and with an atmosphere and palette all its own. John Scott is a splendid advocate and the St Paul's Cathedral organ is unexpectedly successful in this repertoire.

6 Chorales, Op. 28; 2 Chorales, Op. 59; 24 Inventions, Op. 50; 4 Modal fugues, Op. 63.
(BB) *** Naxos Dig. 8.553862 [id.]. James Biery.

The 24 *Inventions*, Op. 50, which are divided to begin and end this CD, are, like Bach's *Well-Tempered Clavier*, composed in all the major and minor keys. They are distinguished by fastidious craftsmanship and considerable imagination as are the 79 *Chorales*, Op. 28 (1930). The *Chorales*, Op. 59, and the *Four Modal Fugues* come from the 1960s. James Biery is an excellent advocate and the recording, made on the Casavant organ of the Cathedral of Saints Peter and Paul, in Providence, Rhode Island, is splendidly lifelike and has great clarity and definition. A rewarding issue.

Duruflé, Maurice (1902–86)

Fugue sur le thème du Carillon des heures de la Cathédrale de Soissons; Prélude, adagio et choral varié sur la thème du Veni Creator; Prélude sur l'Introit de l'Epiphanie; Prélude et fugue sur le nom d'Alain, Op. 7; Scherzo, Op. 2; Suite, Op. 5.
**(*) Delos Dig. D/CD 3047 [id.]. Todd Wilson (Schudi organ of St Thomas Aquinas, Dallas, Texas).

The producer of this record, which contains all Duruflé's organ music, consulted the composer before choosing the present organ, and the performances of Duruflé's often powerful and always engagingly inventive music are of the highest quality. The account of the closing *Toccata* of the *Suite*, Op. 5, has breathtaking bravura and if here, as elsewhere, detail is not sharply registered, the spontaneity and power of the playing are compulsive.

Messe Cum jubilo, Op. 11; 4 Motets, Op. 10.
*** Conifer Dig. 74321 15351-2 [id.]. Griffiths, Trinity College, Cambridge, Ch., Marlow – FAURE: *Requiem.* ***

Duruflé's *Requiem*, echoing Fauré's, is deservedly well known, but these four *a cappella* motets and the *Messe Cum jubilo* of 1966 equally reveal his feeling for evocative choral sound. The *Mass* here comes in its version for organ alone, with the highly distinctive organ-writing adding to the beauty and drama of the piece. An apt and attractive coupling, strongly performed, for a fine version of Fauré's *Requiem*.

Requiem, Op. 9.
*** Teldec/Warner Dig. 4509 90879-2 [id.]. Jennifer Larmore, Thomas Hampson, Amb. S., Philh. O, Legrand – FAURE: *Requiem.* ***
(B) *** Sony SBK 67182 [id.]. Kiri Te Kanawa, Siegmund Nimsgern, Amb. S., Desborough School Ch., New Philh. O, Andrew Davis – FAURE: *Requiem.* ***
(B) *** Decca Eclipse Dig. 448 711-2. Palmer, Shirley-Quirk, Boys of Westminster Cathedral Ch., L. Symphony Ch., LSO, Hickox – FAURE: *Pavane;* POULENC: *Gloria.* ***

(i; ii; iii) *Requiem. Op. 9;* (ii) *4 Motets (Ubi Caritas et Amor; Tota pulchra es; Tu es Petrus; Tantum ergo), Op. 10;* (iii) (Organ) *Prélude et fugue sur le nom d'Alain.*
(B) *** Decca Double 436 486-2 [id.]. (i) Robert King, Christopher Keyte; (ii) St John's College, Cambridge, Ch.; (iii) Stephen Cleobury (organ); George Guest – FAURE: *Requiem* etc.; POULENC: *Messe* etc. ***
(N) *(*) DG Dig. 459 365-2 [id.]. Cecilia Bartoli, Bryn Terfel, Santa Cecilia Nat. Ac. Ch. & O, Myung-Whun Chung – FAURE: *Requiem.* *(*)

Duruflé wrote his *Requiem* in 1947, overtly basing its layout and even the cut of its themes on the Fauré masterpiece. The result is far more than an imitation for (as it seems in innocence) Duruflé's inspiration is passionately committed. Michel Legrand uses the full orchestral version and makes the most of the passionate orchestral eruptions in the *Sanctus* and *Libera me*. He strikes a perfect balance between these sudden outbursts of agitation and the work's mysticism and warmth. The Ambrosian Choir sing ardently yet find a treble-like purity for the *Agnus Dei* and *In Paradisum*, while Jennifer Larmore gives the *Pie Jesu more plangent feeling than its counterpart in the Fauré Requiem.* The recording, made in Watford Town Hall, is spacious and most realistically balanced. A clear first choice in the premium price range.

However Andrew Davis directs a warm and atmospheric reading of Duruflé's beautiful setting with the Desborough School Choir which makes an excellent bargain alternative. He too uses the full orchestral version with its richer colourings. Kiri Te Kanawa sings radiantly in the *Pie Jesu*, and the darkness of Siegmund Nimsgern's voice is well caught. In such a performance Duruflé establishes his claims for individuality, even in the face of Fauré's setting. The recording is nicely atmospheric.

Hickox tempers the richness of the orchestral version by using boys' voices in the choir. He relishes the extra drama of orchestral accompaniment with biting brass at the few moments of high climax. Felicity Palmer and John Shirley-Quirk sing with deep feeling and fine imagination, if not always with ideally pure tone. The recording has a pleasantly ecclesiastical ambience, which adds to the ethereal purity of the trebles, and the stereo spread is wide.

The (originally Argo) St John's version also uses boy trebles instead of women singers, even in the solo of the *Pie Jesu* – exactly parallel to Fauré's setting of those words, which was indeed first sung by a treble. The alternative organ accompaniment is used here, not so warmly colourful as the orchestral version, but very beautiful nevertheless. The 1974 recording is vividly atmospheric. To this have been added the *Four Motets* on plainsong themes which are also finely sung. The organ piece, another sensitive example of Duruflé's withdrawn genius, makes a further bonus, especially when one realizes that this generous pair of CDs includes also the *Mass* and *Salve Regina* of Poulenc.

The characterful contributions of Cecilia Bartoli and Bryn Terfel add to the point of the newest DG coupling with Fauré. Memorably, Terfel gives the *Dies Irae* section of the *Libera me* an apt violence. Sadly, the chorus is so dim and distant, with the dynamic range of the recording uncomfortably extreme, that the disc cannot be recommended.

(i; ii) *Requiem, Op. 9;* (ii; iii; iv) *Mass Cum jubilo, Op. 11;* (ii) *4 Motets on Gregorian themes, Op. 10;* (iv) *3 Dances for orchestra, Op. 10;* (Organ) (v) *Prélude, adagio et choral varié sur Veni Creator, Op. 4;* (vi) *Prélude et fugue sur le nom d'Alain, Op. 7; Scherzo, Op.2;* (v) *Suite, Op. 5: Prelude in E flat min.; Sicilienne.*
(N) ❁ (B) *** Erato/Warner Ultima 3984 24235-2 (2) [id.]. (i) Bouvier, Depraz, Philippe Caillard Ch., LAP, (ii) Stéphane Caillat Ch.; (iii) Soyer; (iv) French RO; all cond. Composer; (v) The Composer or (vi) Marie-Madeleine Duruflé-Chevalier (organ).

This is a particularly valuable set as it gathers together two-thirds of Duruflé's entire output. It centres on the now familiar *Requiem*, given a spontaneously dedicated performance which blossoms into great ardour at emotional peaks. The less familiar but not less beautiful *Mass Cum jubilo* receives a comparatively inspirational account, its gentler passages sustained with rapt concentration, with beautiful playing from the French Radio Orchestra. And surprisingly, the ravishing horn solo in the *Agnus Dei* is played without vibrato. The soloists in both works rise to the occasion and the choral singing combines passionate feeling with subtle colouring: the Chorale Stéphane Caillat are at their finest in the four brief a cappella motets which are no less memorable. The three orchestral *Dances* are impressionistic in feeling and the French Radio Orchestra play with appealing delicacy in the central *Danse lente* and an ecstatic vigour in the closing *Tambourin*, which recalls the Dukas of *L'apprenti sorcier*. The colourful organ works are shared between the composer and his daughter, using organs at Soissons Cathedral and L'Eglise Saint Etienne-du-Mont, Paris. The excellent recordings, spaciously atmospheric, date from between 1959 and 1963. Not to be missed.

Requiem, Op. 9 (3rd version); *4 Motets, Op. 10.*
*** Hyperion Dig. CDA 66191 [id.]. Ann Murray, Thomas Allen, Corydon Singers, ECO, Best; Trotter (organ).

Using the chamber-accompanied version, with strings, harp and trumpet – a halfway house between the full orchestral score and plain organ accompaniment – Best conducts a deeply expressive and sensitive performance of Duruflé's lovely setting of the *Requiem*. With two superb soloists and an outstandingly refined chorus, it makes an excellent recommendation, well coupled with motets, done with similar freshness, clarity and feeling for tonal contrast. The recording is attractively atmospheric yet quite clearly focused.

Dussek (Dusik), Jan Ladislav
(1760–1812)

Keyboard sonatas: in D, Op. 31/2; in B flat; in G; in C min., Op. 35/1–3.
*** HM/BMG Dig. 05472 77286-2. Andreas Staier (fortepiano).

Staier's exhilarating recital is recorded on a Broadwood of 1806, restored by Christopher Clarke, who describes it as 'loud, sonorous, dramatic, a little vulgar'. It has all the weight to cope with the dramatic flair which Staier brings to these highly interesting and occasionally prophetic sonatas. At one point the *B flat Sonata*, Op. 35/1, anticipates Schubert, and the *C minor*, Op. 35/3, has often been compared with the Beethoven *Pathétique*.

Elégie harmonique, Op. 61; Fantasia and fugue (composed and inscribed to J. B. Cramer by his friend, J. S. Dussek), Op. 55; Sonata (Le retour à Paris), Op. 64.
*** HM/BMG 05472 77334-2 [id.]. Andreas Staier (fortepiano).

After his recital of works from Dussek's London years Andreas Staier follows him to France, celebrating appropriately with the remarkably romantic *Sonata, Le retour à Paris* (1806). But before that, in 1804 Dussek was engaged by Louis Ferdinand, Prince of Prussia, and wrote his striking, elegiac memorial. The recital opens by looking back towards London with the flamboyantly improvisational *Fantasia* and simpler *fugue*, dedicated to the composer's friend, J. B. Cramer, publisher and piano manufacturer. Once again the playing throughout has great impetus and all the panache needed to bring these remarkable works back to life on the same Broadwood fortepiano that was used for the earlier disc. First-class recording.

Dutilleux, Henri (born 1916)

Cello concerto (Tout un monde lointain).
*** EMI (SIS) CDC7 49304-2. Rostropovich, O de Paris, Baudo – LUTOSLAWSKI: *Cello concerto.* ***

Dutilleux's *Cello concerto* (whose subtitle translates as 'A whole distant world') is a most imaginative and colourful score which exerts an immediate appeal and sustains it over many hearings. Rostropovich plays it with enormous virtuosity and feeling, the Orchestre de Paris under Serge Baudo gives splendid support, while the 1975 recording is immensely vivid, with Rostropovich looming larger than life but given great presence.

(i) *Cello concerto (Tout un monde lointain);* (ii) *Violin concerto (L'Arbre des songes).*
*** Decca (IMS) Dig. 444 398-2. (i) Harrell; (ii) Amoyal; Fr. Nat. O, Dutoit.

Both Pierre Amoyal and Lynn Harrell are first class and withstand the exalted comparisons they confront. The Decca recording is finer than that of rivals, clean, well detailed and with great presence and refinement. What imaginative music this is.

(i) *Cello concerto (Tout un monde lointain); Métaboles; Mystères de l'instant.*
(N) *** Chandos Dig. CHAN9565 [id.].(i) Boris Pergamenschikov; BBC PO, Yan-Pascal Tortelier.

There would have been more recordings of Dutilleux's concerto, *Tout un monde lointain,* had Rostropovich's premier account with the composer conducting not been so marvellous. Boris Pergamenschikov rises to the challenge and although Rostropovich's remains an almost mandatory recommendation, thanks to the composer's authority, the excellence of the orchestral playing under Yan-Pascal Tortelier and the Chandos recording earn it a three-star grading. The *Métaboles* and the *Mystères de l'instant* are expertly and persuasively played.

Violin concerto (L'Arbre des songes).
(M) *** Sony Stern Edition II SMK 64508 [id.]. Stern, O Nat. de France, Maazel – BERNSTEIN: *Serenade.* *(**))

Dutilleux's *Violin concerto*, written for Isaac Stern, is a beautiful work. Always the perfect craftsman and consistently writing with refinement, Dutilleux shows how taut self-discipline can go with natural expressive warmth, and the underlying romantic fervour finds Stern playing with warm commitment, strongly accompanied by Maazel and the Orchestre National. First-rate recording.

(i) *Violin concerto (L'arbre des songes); Timbres, espaces, mouvement;* (ii) *2 Sonnets de Jean Cassou.*
*** Chandos Dig. CHAN 9504 [id.]. (i) Olivier Charlier; (ii) Neal Davies; BBC PO, Yan Pascal Tortelier – ALAIN: *Prière.* ***

In terms of artistry and musicianship Charlier yields nothing to his rivals, and Tortelier gives us the *Timbres, espaces, mouvement* (*La nuit étoilée*) from 1979 as a makeweight. This is its fourth recording and suffice it to say that this newcomer can hold its own even in terms of recorded quality. The *Deux Sonnets de Jean Cassou* come in Dutilleux's own orchestral transcription, in which Martyn Hill and Neal Davies are effective soloists.

Le Loup (ballet): *symphonic fragments.*
(M) *** EMI (SIS) CDM7 63945-2. Paris Conservatoire O, Prêtre – MILHAUD: *Création du monde*; POULENC: *Les Biches.* ***

Dutilleux's score for *Le Loup*, with its 'Beauty and the Beast' storyline bringing a tragic ending, is dominated by a haunting, bitter-sweet waltz theme of the kind that, once heard, refuses to budge from the memory. But the invention throughout has plenty of colour and variety, and Dutilleux's orchestral palette is used individually to great effect. Prêtre makes a persuasive case for the suite, and this vivid recording is part of a highly attractive triptych of French ballet scores.

(i) *Symphonies Nos. 1–2 (Le Double);* (ii) *Métaboles;* (iii) *Mystère de l'instant* (for 24 strings, cymbalum and percussion); (ii) *Timbres, espace, mouvement (La nuit étoilée);* (iv) *Ainsi la nuit (String quartet);* (v) *Les citations* (Diptych for oboe, harpsichord, double-bass & percussion); (vi) *3 Strophes sure le nom de Sacher* (for unaccompanied cello); (vii; viii) *Figures de résonances* (for 2 pianos); (vii) *Piano sonata; 3 Préludes Nos. 1–3;* (ix; viii) *2 Sonnets de Jean Cassou.*
(M) *** Erato/Warner Dig./Analogue 0630 14068-2 (3). (i) O de Paris, Barenboim; (ii) O Nat. de France, Rostropovich; (iii) Zurich Coll. Mus., Paul Sacher; (iv) Sine Nomine Qt; (v) Bourgue, Dreyfus, Cazauran, Balet; (vi) David Geringas; (vii) Geneviève Joy; (viii) composer; (ix) Gilles Chachemaille.

These three Erato CDs afford an excellent survey of Dutilleux's orchestral, chamber and instrumental music. The symphonies are well played, and the recording of both is eminently serviceable. *Métaboles* is otherwise the best-known orchestral work here, alongside *Timbres, Espace, Mouvement*, and it is good to have both under the baton of Rostropovich. *Mystère de l'instant* is a set of ten miniatures, splendidly played by the Collegium Musicum under Sacher and digitally recorded. The *Sonata* is played by Geneviève Joy with great zest and panache. Joy is no less excellent in the *Préludes*. Both *Les Citations* and *Ainsi la nuit* are equally successful. The recordings are very fine and the documentation is excellent and is illustrated with photographs of the composer and major participants.

Symphonies Nos. 1–2.
✪ *** Chandos Dig. CHAN 9194 [id.]. BBC PO, Tortelier.

Marvellously resourceful and inventive scores which are given vivid and persuasive performances by Tortelier and the BBC Philharmonic Orchestra. The engineers give us a splendidly detailed and refined portrayal of these complex textures – the sound is really state-of-the-art. This issue supersedes Serge Baudo's version with the Orchestre National de Lyon of the *First Symphony*, coupled with *Timbres, espace, mouvement.*

Symphony No. 1; Timbres, espace, mouvement.
(M) *** HM Suite Dig. HMT 7905159 [id.]. O. Nat. de Lyon, Serge Baudo.

In Dutilleux's *First Symphony* there is a sense of forward movement: you feel that the music is taking you somewhere. *Timbres, espace, mouvement* is a more recent work, dating from 1978. Serge Baudo is an authoritative interpreter of this composer, and the Lyon orchestra also serve him well. The engineering is superb and the balance is thoroughly realistic. At mid-price this reissue makes an admirable sampler for those unfamiliar with this very distinctive composer.

Symphony No. 2; Timbres, espace, mouvement (La nuit étoilée); Métaboles.
*** Ph. 438 008-2 [id.]. O de Paris, Bychkov.

Bychkov's performance has all the virtuosity and brilliance you could want, and has real fire. All the same, Tortelier and the BBC Philharmonic on Chandos have greater atmosphere and their disc of the two symphonies remains the preferred recommendation. The *Timbres, espaces, mouvement* (*La nuit étoilée*) is very successful and those who do not have that or Munch's disc of the *Métaboles* might do well to consider this vividly recorded account.

Ainsi la nuit (String quartet).
*** Sony Dig. SK 52554 [id.]. Juilliard Qt – DEBUSSY; RAVEL: *Quartets.* ***

There have been other versions of Dutilleux's fascinating quartet, *Ainsi la nuit*, but this impressive account from the Juilliard Quartet is the finest yet, offering superb playing and recording. The music conjures up the moods and impressions surrounding the idea of 'night' – not night itself so much as its aura.

Piano sonata.
**(*) Olympia Dig. OCD 354 [id.]; Archduke MARC 2. Donna Amato – BALAKIREV: *Sonata.* **(*)

Donna Amato gives a totally committed and persuasive account of this brilliant sonata, and the recording is very truthful.

Dvořák, Antonín (1841–1904)

(i) *American suite in A, Op. 98b;* (ii) *Serenade for strings in E, Op. 22; Serenade for wind in D min., Op. 44.*
(B) *** Decca Eclipse Dig. 448 981-2 [id.]. (i) RPO, Dorati; (ii) LPO, Hogwood.

Dvořák's *American suite* has clear influences from the New World. Dorati has its measure and finds its charm: the RPO are very responsive, while the Kingsway Hall recording-balance seems to suit the scoring rather well. The two *Serenades* also receive fresh, bright, spring-like accounts from Hogwood and the LPO in clean, slightly recessed sound. Textually this version of the *String serenade* is unique on record when it uses the original score, newly published, in which two sections (one of 34 bars in the Scherzo and the other of 79 bars in the finale), missing in the normal printed edition, are now included.

Cello concerto in B min., Op. 104.
❁ (M) *** DG 447 413-2 [id.]. Rostropovich, BPO, Karajan – TCHAIKOVSKY: *Variations on a rococo theme.* *** ❁
*** Sony Dig. SK 67173 [id.]. Ma, NYPO, Masur – HERBERT: *Cello concerto No. 2.* ***
*** Chandos Dig. CHAN 8662 [id.]. Wallfisch, LSO, Mackerras – DOHNANYI: *Konzertstück.* ***
(M) *** [RCA Basic 100 09026 68086-2; *68086-4*]. Lynn Harrell, LSO, Levine – TCHAIKOVSKY: *Rococo variations.* ***
(M) *** Sony Dig. SMK 60151 [id.]. Yo-Yo Ma, BPO, Maazel – SCHUMANN: *Cello concerto.* ***
(BB) *** CfP Silver Double CDCFPSD 4775 (2). Robert Cohen, LPO, Macal – BEETHOVEN: *Triple concerto;* ELGAR: *Cello concerto;* TCHAIKOVSKY: *Variations on a rococo theme.* ***
(M) (***) EMI CDH7 63498-2 [id.]. Casals, Czech PO, Szell – ELGAR: *Concerto* (**(*)) (with BRUCH: *Kol Nidrei* (***)).
(*) EMI CDC5 55527-2 [id.]. Jacqueline du Pré, Chicago SO, Barenboim – ELGAR: *Concerto.* *
**(*) Finlandia Dig. 4509 98886-2 [id.]. Arto Noras, Finnish RSO, Sakari Oramo (with SCHUMANN: *Cello concerto.* **)
(M) **(*) RCA 09026 61498-2 [id.]. Piatigorsky, Boston SO, Munch – WALTON: *Concerto.* ***

The intensity of lyrical feeling and the spontaneity of the partnership between Karajan and Rostropovich ensures the position of their DG disc at the top of the list of recommendations for this peer among nineteenth century cello concertos. The orchestral playing is glorious. Moreover the analogue recording, made in the Jesus-Christus Kirche in September 1969, is as near perfect as any made in that vintage analogue era, and the CD transfer has freshened the original.

Yo-Yo Ma's partnership with Masur brings an extra weight of expression, and a firmer control, making for a performance that is both more commanding and more spontaneous-sounding than his earlier version with Maazel. Ma's expressiveness is simpler and nobler in such great lyrical passages as the second-subject melody, and the result is one of the finest versions available, ideal if one wants for coupling the Victor Herbert concerto which sparked off Dvořák's inspiration.

Rafael Wallfisch's is also an outstanding version, strong and warmly sympathetic, masterfully played. The excitement as well as the warmth of the piece comes over as in a live performance, and Wallfisch's tone remains rich and firm in even the most taxing passages. The orchestral playing, the quality of sound and the delightful, generous and unusual coupling all make it a recommendation which must be given the strongest advocacy.

In Lynn Harrell's first RCA recording, made in the mid 1970s, his collaboration with James Levine in Dvořák's *Cello concerto* proved a powerful and sympathetic one. Richly satisfying accounts of the first and second movements culminate in a reading of the finale which proves the most distinctive of all. The recording is bright and full and has been remastered most successfully for CD. This has been withdrawn in the UK, but in the USA it is attractively coupled with Ofra Harnoy's highly individual account of Tchaikovsky's *Rococo variations.*

Ma's rapt concentration and refined control of colour at times bring an elegiac dimension to his earlier reading, and Maazel accompanies with understanding and great sensitivity, fining down the orchestral textures so that he never masks his often gentle soloist, yet providing exuberant contrast in orchestral *fortissimos*. The solo cello is most skilfully balanced – and ensures that the *pianissimo* detail of the *Adagio* registers naturally.

Robert Cohen is strong and forthright, very secure technically, with poetry never impaired by his preference for keeping steady speeds. The result is most satisfying, helped by a comparably incisive and understanding accompaniment from the Czech conductor, Zdenek Macal. With first-class recording, orchestrally full-bodied and with a truthful balance, this is part of an outstanding quartet of works featuring this fine cellist.

Casals plays with astonishing fire and the performance seems to spring to life in a way that eludes many modern artists; the rather dry acoustic of the Deutsches Haus, Prague, and the limitations of the 1937 recording are of little consequence. This disc is one of the classics of the gramophone.

Jacqueline du Pré's version is newly transferred for a so-called 'dream coupling' with her unique Elgar performance. The original harshness of the Chicago Dvořák recording has been tamed and, though the exaggeratedly forward balance of the cello is still very noticeable, the sound has filled out nicely and is clearly detailed; the inspirational result is very rewarding.

The excellent Finnish cellist, Arto Noras – well remembered for making the first recording of the Bliss *Cello concerto* – gives a sensitive reading of the Dvořák, not helped by the backward balance of the soloist. Most impressive are the tender moments, not least the epilogue, raptly done. However, the coupled Schumann has far less vitality.

Piatigorsky's recording has been improved remarkably for this CD, although the balance is still too close and not always flattering to the soloist. The performance is the very opposite of routine, with Piatigorsky and Munch in complete rapport, producing a consistently spontaneous melodic flow.

(i) *Cello concerto;* (ii) *Rondo in G min., Op. 94;* (iii) *Silent woods, Op. 68/5.*
**(*) Channel Classics Dig. CCS 8695 [id.]. Pieter Wispelwey; (i) Netherlands PO, Lawrence Renes; (ii–iii) Paulo Giacometti (piano or harmonium) (with ARENSKY: *Chant triste, Op. 56/3;* DAVIDOV: *Am Springbrunnen, Op. 20/2;* TCHAIKOVSKY: *Andante cantabile, from Op. 11* **(*)).

(i) *Cello concerto;* (ii) *Rondo in G min., Op. 94; Silent woods, Op. 68/5; Slavonic dance in G min., Op. 46/8.*
*** Ph. Dig. 434 914-2. Heinrich Schiff, (i) VPO, Previn; (ii) Previn (piano).

Heinrich Schiff's newest recording of Dvořák's *Cello concerto*, at once fresh, direct and warm, is commanding and spontaneous-sounding, as well as urgent. The finale has more fun in it than before, bringing a more dramatic contrast with the meditation of the epilogue. Previn, drawing ravishing sounds from the Vienna Philharmonic, particularly the brass, gives an extra lift to the Slavonic rhythms. Then at the piano Previn similarly adds sparkle to the shorter Dvořák pieces that come as encore, all of them better-known in orchestral form, but here more winning still. An ungenerous coupling, but an attractive one.

The Dutch cellist, Pieter Wispelwey, equally at home in period or modern style, here gives a more intimate reading than most on disc, with rather more *portamento* than usual, bringing out autumnal tone-colours, as he does in the shorter pieces which come as fill-up. The performance may be less bitingly dramatic than most, but the concentration and expressive warmth make it extremely compelling. Three of the shorter pieces – in all of which Wispelwey uses gut strings – have harmonium accompaniment. That is most effective in the Tchaikovsky and the Arensky (which sounds as though it is about to turn into Tchaikovsky's song, *None but the lonely heart*), but then sounds muddled in Dvořák's *Silent woods*. Happily the *Rondo* comes with piano accompaniment, as does the Davidov. Excellent sound.

(i) *Cello concerto in B min., Op. 104;* (ii) *Symphony No. 8 in G, Op. 88.*
(B) *** DG Classikon 439 484-2. (i) Fournier; (i–ii) BPO; (i) Szell; (ii) Kubelik.
(BB) **(*) RCA Navigator 74321 21289-2. (i) Piatigorsky; Boston SO, Munch.

Pierre Fournier's reading of the *Cello concerto* has a sweep of conception and a richness of tone and phrasing which carry the melodic lines along with exactly that mixture of nobility and tension the work demands. DG's recording, dating from 1962, is forward and vivid, with a broad, warm tone for the soloist. Kubelik's *Eighth* is appealingly direct and the polished, responsive playing of the Berlin Philharmonic adds to the joy and refinement of the performance, making for a highly recommendable bargain coupling.

Piatigorsky's 1960 recording (see above) is here also available coupled with Munch's account of the *G major Symphony*, recorded a year later. As in the *Concerto*, the improvement in the recorded sound is remarkable and the work is made to sound extremely vivid against the spacious Boston acoustic. Munch's reading is strongly characterized and, though he occasionally presses hard, the thrust comes from a natural ardour.

(i) *Cello concerto;* (ii) *Symphony No.9 (New World).*
(M) *** Ph. 442 401-2. (i) Heinrich Schiff; Concg. O; (i) Sir Colin Davis; (ii) Antal Dorati.

(i) *Cello concerto;* (ii) *Symphony No. 9 (New World); Carnival overture, Op. 92; Scherzo capriccioso, Op. 66.*
(BB) *** EMI Seraphim CES5 68521-2 (2) [CEDB 68521]. (i) Paul Tortelier, LSO, Previn; (ii) Philh. O, Giulini – TCHAIKOVSKY: *Variations on a Rococo theme.* ***

The two Philips performances are fascinatingly different in character. Schiff's earlier reading of the *Concerto* (from the beginning of the 1980s) brings an unexaggerated vein of poetry akin to the approach of Yo-Yo Ma's first recording – its range of emotion is on a relatively small scale, though satisfying in its intimacy. This performance sounds extremely well in its CD transfer. Dorati's *New World* is characteristically vibrant and extrovert; indeed the level of tension is high in the outer movements and the finale ends with a thrilling surge of adrenalin. The rich Concertgebouw acoustic, from the late 1950s, does not sound too dated; indeed the woodwind glow attractively in the *Largo.*

Tortelier's 1978 recording with Previn has a satisfying centrality, not as passionately romantic as Rostropovich's recording on DG, but with the tenderness as well as the power of the work held in perfect equilibrium, even if the microphones are obviously rather too near the soloist. Giulini's recording of the *New World Symphony* has a refinement, coupled to an attractive directness, which for some will make it an ideal reading. The remastering gives the sound plenty of warmth and projection and with two attractive bonuses, this is a bargain on EMI's Seraphim series, offering two discs for the cost of one medium-priced CD.

Piano concerto in G min., Op. 33 (original version).
(N) (M) *** EMI CDM5 66895-2 [CDM5 66947]. Sviatoslav Richter, Bav. State O, Carlos Kleiber – SCHUBERT: *Wanderer fantasia.* ***

Dvořák's *Piano concerto* comes from a vintage period which also saw the completion of the *F major Symphony*. The quality of the inspiration falls below that of the *Violin concerto*, but it still has many striking beauties, notably in the fine slow movement which has never before sounded so moving as it does in Richter's hands. Much has been made of the concerto's pianistic deficiencies, but Richter plays the solo part in its original form (and not the more pianistically 'effective' revision by Wilém Kurz which is published in the Complete Edition), and his judgement is triumphantly vindicated. This is the most persuasive and masterly account of the work ever committed to disc; its ideas emerge with an engaging freshness and warmth, while the greater simplicity of Dvořák's own keyboard writing proves in Richter's hands to be more telling and profound. Carlos Kleiber secures excellent results from the Bavarian orchestra, and the 1977 recording has clarity and good definition to recommend it. The current remastering for EMI's 'Great recordings of the century' series is infinitely smoother and fuller than the original CD transfer and the quality now is most impressive.

Piano concerto in G min., Op. 33.
*** RCA Dig. RD 60781 [60781-2]. Rudolf Firkušný, Czech PO, Václav Neumann – JANACEK: *Concertino; Capriccio.* ***

(i) *Piano concerto in G min., Op. 33; The Water Goblin (symphonic poem), Op. 107.*
(BB) *** Naxos Dig. 8.550896 [id.]. (i) Jenö Jandó; Polish Nat. RSO, Antoni Wit.

Firkušný has played the Dvořák *Piano concerto* in both the original version and that by Vilém Kurz, as well as this, a *mélange* of the two. The present recording conveys its sunny geniality to good effect, and although the great pianist was 79 when this record was made, the playing still sounds both youthful and aristocratic. Firkušný now makes an admirable first choice among modern recordings , and his claims are enhanced by the value of the coupling (as well as the 73 minutes' playing time of the CD).

An infectiously fresh and warmly lyrical account from Jandó and the highly supportive Polish National Radio Orchestra under Antoni Wit. Jandó conveys his own pleasure, and Wit's accompaniment glows with colour; he then offers a splendidly vibrant and colourful portrayal of *The Water Goblin*, one of the composer's most vividly melodramatic symphonic poems. The recording is spacious and realistically balanced. The violins are a shade overbright, but otherwise the sound is excellent. Very enjoyable and well worth its modest cost.

Violin concerto in A min., Op. 53.
(B) *** CfP Dig. CD-CFP 4566. Tasmin Little, RLPO, Handley – BRUCH: *Concerto No. 1.* ***
*** EMI (SIS) Dig. CDC7 54872-2. Zimmermann, LPO, Welser-Möst – GLAZUNOV: *Concerto.* ***
(M) *** DG Dig. 449 091-2 [id.]. Shlomo Mintz, BPO, Levine – BRUCH: *Concerto No. 1.* ***
(M) *** Ph. 420 895-2. Accardo, Concg. O, C. Davis – SIBELIUS: *Violin concerto.* ***
(N) (M) (***) Dutton Lab. mono CDK 1204 [id.]. Ida Haendel, Nat.SO, Karl Rankl – SAINT-SAENS: *Introduction and rondo capriccioso*; TCHAIKOVSKY: *Violin concerto in D, Op. 35.* (***) ✿

Violin concerto in A min., Op. 53; Romance in F min., Op. 11.
(B) *** [EMI Red Line Dig. CDR5 69806]. Kyung-Wha Chung, Phd. O, Muti – BARTOK: *Rhapsodies.* ***
**(*) EMI (SIS) CDC7 47168-2 [id.]. Perlman, LPO, Barenboim.
(BB) *** Naxos Dig. 8.550758 [id.]. Ilya Kaler,

Polish Nat. RSO (Katowice), Camilla Kolchinsky – GLAZUNOV: *Concerto*. ***

(M) *** Sup. SU 1928-2 011 [id.]. Josef Suk, Czech PO, Karel Ančerl – SUK: *Fantasy*. ***

(N) ** Decca Dig. 460 316-2. Pamela Frank, Czech PO, Mackerras – SUK: *Fantasy in G min*. ***

Tasmin Little brings to this concerto an open freshness and sweetness, very apt for this composer, that are extremely winning. The firm richness of her sound, totally secure on intonation up to the topmost register, goes with an unflustered ease of manner, and the recording brings little or no spotlighting of the soloist; she establishes her place firmly with full-ranging, well-balanced sound that co-ordinates the soloist along with the orchestra.

Frank Peter Zimmermann's account of the Dvořák concerto is full of spirit. His rhythms are lightly sprung and he conveys great delight in this genial yet underrated score. This performance also is highly recommendable. Certainly the LPO under Franz Welser-Möst are supportive, and the EMI recording is first class.

There is dazzling playing from Shlomo Mintz, whose virtuosity is effortless and his intonation astonishingly true. There is good rapport between soloist and conductor, and the performance has the sense of joy and relaxation that this radiant score needs. The digital sound is warm and natural in its upper range.

In his Philips recording, Accardo is beautifully natural and unforced, with eloquent playing from both soloist and orchestra. The engineering is altogether excellent, and in a competitive field this must also rank high.

Kyung-Wha Chung gives a heartfelt reading of a work that can sound wayward. The partnership with Muti and the Philadelphia Orchestra is a happy one, with the sound warmer and more open than it has usually been in the orchestra's recording venue. She finds similar concentration in the *Romance*. This CD is only available in the USA.

Perlman and Barenboim still sound pretty marvellous and show all the warmth and virtuosity one could desire. This CD also has the eloquent and touching *F minor Romance*. Perlman is absolutely superb in both pieces: the digital remastering undoubtedly clarifies and cleans the texture, though there is a less glowing aura about the sound above the stave. However, this EMI record remains at premium price and offers no other music.

The performance of the Russian violinist, Ilya Kaler, has great romantic warmth and natural Slavonic feeling, and he is given excellent support by Kolchinsky and the Polish orchestra. The very resonant acoustics of the recording, made in the Concert Hall of Polish Radio, give the soloist a somewhat larger-than-life image against a widely resonant orchestral backcloth. But the effect is easy to enjoy when the playing is so ardent; moreover these artists offer (besides the Glazunov) the *Romance in F minor*, and that is also beautifully played.

Suk's earlier performance is back in the catalogue at mid-price, effectively remastered, recoupled with the Suk *Fantasy*. Its lyrical eloquence is endearing, the work is played in the simplest possible way and Añcerl accompanies glowingly. Readers will note that, since its last appearance, the *Romance* has been restored, an equally delightful performance. This is one of Suk's very finest records.

The Dutton Lab. transfer offers the last recording Ida Haendel made for Decca in July 1947 before she moved to EMI. While it is slightly less successful than her Tchaikovsky, and Karl Rankl was perhaps a less than ideal partner, it is still a memorable and endearing performance, with some really lovely playing in the *Adagio* and an engagingly spirited finale. The recording is less successful too, with the bass resonance a little cavernous, but the expert transfer brings sound which is full and atmospheric, the violin timbre sweet and natural, and one soon adjusts to the mono sound picture, even if tuttis are not ideally clear.

Pamela Frank plays the *Concerto* with virtuoso assurance, but is a degree more reticent than her finest rivals on disc. Where she scores is in the light, lilting account of the Furiant finale. The *Romance* is persuasively done at a flowing speed, but neither Dvořák work is helped by the backward balance of the orchestra. By far the most compelling performance on the disc is of the Suk fill-up.

Czech suite, Op. 39; A Hero's song, Op. 111; Festival march, Op. 54; Hussite overture, Op. 67.

(BB) **(*) Naxos Dig. 8.553005 [id.]. Polish Nat. RSO (Katowice), Antoni Wit.

Antoni Wit, who has already given us a memorable performance of Smetana's *Má Vlast*, is almost equally impressive in *A Hero's song*. There is an outburst of patriotic hyperbole towards the close (with thundering trombones), which is considerably inflated by the resonant acoustics of the Concert Hall of Polish Radio, which have a similar effect on the *Hussite overture* and *Festival march*; however Wit generates excitement without letting things get out of hand. The performance of the *Czech suite* is warm and relaxed, nicely rustic in feeling, but again is affected by the resonance.

Czech suite, Op. 39; Nocturne for strings, Op. 40; Prague waltzes.
(B) *** Decca Double Dig. 443 015-2 (2) [id.]. Detroit SO, Dorati – SMETANA: *Má Vlast* etc. **

The *Czech suite* can sometimes outstay its welcome, but not here; and the charming set of waltzes, written for balls in Prague – Viennese music with a Czech accent – is complemented by the lovely *Nocturne* with its subtle drone bass. The recording has an attractive warmth and bloom to balance its brightness. However, the principal Smetana coupling is less readily recommendable. Readers will note that the *Czech suite* and *Prague waltzes* are also available on Eclipse, coupled with the *New World Symphony* – see below.

Overtures: *Carnival, Op. 92; Hussite, Op. 67; In nature's realm, Op. 91; My home, Op. 62; Othello, Op. 93; Scherzo capriccioso, Op. 66.* Symphonic poems: *The golden spinning wheel, Op. 109; The Noonday Witch, Op. 108; The Water Goblin, Op. 107; Symphonic variations, Op. 78.*
(B) *** Decca Double 452 946-2 (2). LSO, István Kertész.

Kertész's collection comes into direct competition with Kubelik's DG set, which has slightly more modern recording; but the vintage Decca sound from the 1960s and 1970s stands up well, and Kertész was very much at home in this repertoire. He makes the very most of the brilliant *Carnaval overture* and also offers an outstanding version of the *Scherzo capriccioso*. *Carnaval* forms a triptych with *Othello* and *In nature's realm*, linked by a recurring main theme. These pieces like the melodramatic symphonic poems are also handled most evocatively: all have the most vivid colouring. So has the *Hussite overture*, where the drama is comparably red-blooded. *My home*, a more spontaneously inspired work, is even more successful, while the Brahmsian derivations of the *Symphonic variations* are all but submerged, when the playing has such spirit and freshness.

Overtures: *Carnival, Op. 92; Hussite, Op. 67; In nature's realm, Op. 91; My home, Op. 62; Othello, Op. 93.* Symphonic poems: *The Golden spinning wheel, Op. 109; The Noonday witch, Op. 108; The Water goblin, Op. 107; The Wood dove, Op. 110. Symphonic variations, Op. 78.*
(M) *** DG 435 074-2 (2) [id.]. Bav. RSO, Rafael Kubelik.

Kubelik's performances are among his finest on record and they are superbly played. He is splendidly dashing in *Carnival*; in the two companion pieces there is magic and lustre in the orchestra, and the atmospheric tension is striking. Among the dramatic accounts of the symphonic poems, he also includes *The Wood dove*, omitted by Kertesz, but misses out the *Scherzo capriccioso*. The *Symphonic variations* opens warmly and graciously, yet, like Kertesz, he is obviously determined to minimize the Brahmsian associations; his light touch and apt pacing lead on to the lively finale. The recordings, made in the Munich Hercules-Saal between 1973 and 1977, are freshly transferred to CD and generally sound excellent.

Overtures: *Carnival, Op. 92; In Nature's realm, Op. 91; Othello, Op. 93. Scherzo capriccioso, Op. 66.*
**(*) Chandos Dig. CHAN 8453 [id.]. Ulster O, Handley.

Overtures: *Carnival, Op. 92; In Nature's realm, Op. 91; Othello, Op. 93. Scherzo capriccioso, Op. 66; Symphonic variations, Op. 78.*
**(*) ASV Dig. CDDCA 794 [id.]. RPO, Farrer.

Dvořák wrote this triptych immediately before his first visit to America in 1892. Handley's excellent performances put the three works in perspective. Superbly recorded, this now seems short measure at premium price.

John Farrer scores over Handley by including also the *Symphonic variations*, here given a performance of great freshness. The three linked overtures have comparable warmth and delicacy of colouring. There is plenty of drama too, and the only slight disappointment is that *Carnival*, while vigorous enough and with a richly hued central section, could have been even more exuberant. The *Scherzo capriccioso* is brightly vivacious. The recording, made at St Barnabas Church, Mitcham, is wide-ranging and naturally balanced.

Overture: *My home, Op. 62*. Symphonic poems: *The Golden spinning-wheel, Op. 109; The Hero's song, Op. 111; The Noon witch, Op. 108; The Water goblin, Op. 107; The Wood dove, Op. 110.*
(N) (B) Chandos Dig. 2-for-1 CHAN 241-3 (2) [id.]. RSNO, Neeme Järvi.

Many will be attracted to Järvi's collection on a Chandos 2-for-1 Double for the modern digital sound, warmly atmospheric in typical Chandos style, not always clean on detail but firmly focused. These recordings were all fill-ups for Järvi's integral set of the symphonies. The real rarity here is *The Hero's song*, Dvořák's very last orchestral work. It has no specific programme, though the journey from darkness to light in the unspecified hero's life is established clearly enough. Järvi's strongly committed, red-blooded performance minimizes any weaknesses. *My home* is given an exuberant performance, bringing out the lilt of the dance rhythms, and Järvi is a dramatic advocate of *The Water goblin*, a piece based on a gruesome little fairy-story, full of sharp dramatic contrasts. He also brings out the storytelling vividly in *The Noon Witch*, with tremolando strings breathtakingly delicate on the entry of the witch herself, while the most memorable of all the symphonic poems, *The Golden spinning wheel*, has plenty of drama and atmosphere, helped by the fine bloom of the recording. The only snag here is the relatively short measure. Both Kertesz and Kubelik are more generous, and one wonders why Chandos did not include *Carnaval*, or the *Symphonic variations*, recorded in the same series.

The Golden spinning-wheel, Op. 109; The Noonday Witch, Op. 108; The Wood dove, Op. 110 (symphonic poems).
(BB) *** Naxos Dig. 8.550598 [id.]. Polish Nat. RSO (Katowice), Stephen Gunzenhauser.

The Polish orchestra seem thoroughly at home in Dvořák's sound-world and Gunzenhauser gives warm, vivid performances and is especially evocative in the masterly *Golden spinning wheel*. There is shapely string phrasing and a fine, sonorous contribution from the brass. The concert hall of Polish Radio in Katowice has expansive acoustics – just right for the composer's colourful effects.

Rondo in G min. (for cello and orchestra), *Op. 94*.
(M) *** Carlton Dig. 30366 0011-2 [id.]. Tortelier, RPO, Groves – ELGAR: *Cello concerto* **(*); TCHAIKOVSKY: *Rococo variations*. ***

The Dvořák *Rondo* is one of Tortelier's party pieces, and its point and humour are beautifully caught here.

Scherzo capriccioso, Op. 66; Slavonic dances, Opp. 46/1, 3 & 7; 72/2 & 8.
(M) **(*) DG 447 434-2 [id.]. BPO, Karajan – BRAHMS: *8 Hungarian dances*. ***

Virtuoso performances from Karajan which remain stylish because of the superbly polished ensemble. The 1959 recording, originally very brightly lit, sounds better balanced in this remastered reissue in DG's 'Originals'. The *Scherzo capriccioso* is exhilarating, but the lilt of the lyrical secondary tune does seem a trifle calculated. However, coupled with eight of the Brahms *Hungarian dances*, this reissue certainly shows the Karajan/BPO combination in dazzling form.

Scherzo capriccioso, Op. 66; Slavonic rhapsody No. 3, Op. 45/3.
(B) *** EMI (SIS) forte CZS5 68649-2 (2) [CDFB 68649]. Dresden State O, Berglund – GRIEG: *Old Norwegian romance* etc.; SMETANA: *Má vlast*. ***

Berglund's *Scherzo capriccioso* is warmly engaging, not the most brilliantly exciting version on record, but with plenty of impetus and a seductively lilting second subject. The *Slavonic rhapsody* is superbly done, and the recording is pleasingly warm and full.

Serenade for strings in E, Op. 22.
(M) *** EMI CDM5 66760-2. RPO, Stokowski – VAUGHAN WILLIAMS: *Fantasia on a theme by Thomas Tallis;* PURCELL: *Dido and Aeneas: Dido's lament*. ***
(M) **(*) Virgin/EMI Dig. CUV5 61144-2. LCO, Warren-Green – SUK: *Serenade* ***
(BB) **(*) Naxos Dig. 8.550419 [id.]. Capella Istropolitana, Krček – SUK: *Serenade*. ***

Serenade for strings; Romance, Op. 11.
(B) *** Carlton IMP Classics Dig. 30367 0029-2. Laredo, SCO, Laredo – WAGNER: *Siegfried idyll*. ***

Serenade for strings; Serenade for wind in D min., Op. 44.
*** ASV Dig. CDCOE 801 [id.]. COE, Alexander Schneider.
*** Ph. 400 020-2 [id.]. ASMF, Marriner.

Serenade for strings; Serenade for wind; Miniatures, Op. 74a.
(BB) *** Discover Dig. DICD 920135 [id.]. Virtuosi di Praga, Oldrich Vlček.

The Stokowskian magic is very apparent in his 1975 EMI recording of the *String serenade*, not only in the ripeness of the string playing but also in the masterly control of tension. Thus the opening is slow and affectionate, but there is concentration in every bar and the lyrical flow is highly engaging. In the second movement Stokowski's delicacy at a quick tempo is exhilarating, and the lilting Scherzo is matched by the warmth of the *Larghetto*. The RPO strings are kept on their toes throughout, and the wide-ranging Abbey Road recording offers the most beautiful string-sound.

The young players of the Chamber Orchestra of Europe give winningly warm and fresh performances of Dvořák's *Serenades*, vividly caught in the ASV recording.

Marriner's Philips performances are direct without loss of warmth, with speeds ideally chosen, refined yet spontaneous-sounding; in the *Wind serenade* the Academy produce beautifully sprung rhythms, and the recording has a fine sense of immediacy.

Laredo's performance of Dvořák's lovely *Serenade* is volatile, full of spontaneous lyrical feeling. The recording, made in City Hall, Glasgow, is admirably balanced to give a true concert-hall effect and add ambient lustre to the string timbre. As an encore Laredo takes the solo role in the *F minor Romance*, which he plays with appealing simplicity.

The wind players of the Virtuosi di Praga give a bright, idiomatic performance of Opus 44, using characteristically reedy tones. The *String serenade* is done with equal understanding, though the recording catches an edge on high violins. The rare *Miniatures* for string trio provide an attractive makeweight. An excellent bargain in full, bright sound.

Warren-Green and his excellent London Chamber Orchestra bring their characteristically fresh, spontaneous approach to the Dvořák *Serenade*. If without the winning individuality of the outstanding COE version under Schneider, this is still very enjoyable, and the Suk coupling is outstanding. Excellent sound.

Fine playing from the Capella Istropolitana on Naxos, and flexible direction from Jaroslav Krček. His pacing is not quite as sure as in the delightful Suk coupling, and the *Adagio* could flow with a stronger current, but this is still an enjoyable and well-recorded performance.

Serenade in D min. for wind, Op. 44.

(M) *** CRD CRD 3410; *CRDC 4110* [id.]. Nash Ens. (with KROMMER: *Octet-Partita.* ***)

**(*) EMI Dig. CDC5 55512-2 [id.]. Sabine Meyer Wind Ens. – MYSLIVECEK: *Octets Nos. 1–3.* **(*)

The Nash Ensemble can hold their own with the competition in the *D minor Serenade*, and their special claim tends to be the coupling, a Krommer rarity that is well worth hearing. The CRD version of the Dvořák is very well recorded and the playing is very fine indeed, robust yet sensitive to colour, and admirably spirited.

The Sabine Meyer Ensemble have elegance but are perhaps a little laid back by comparison with some current rivals. Yet they give undoubted pleasure, and the EMI recording is excellent.

Slavonic dances Nos. 1–16, Op. 46/1–8; Op. 72/1–8.

*** Decca Dig. 430 171-2 [id.]. Cleveland O, Christoph von Dohnányi.

(M) *** DG 457 712-2 [id.]. Bav. RSO, Kubelik.

✿ (M) *** Sony SBK 48161 [id.]. Cleveland O, George Szell.

*** Ph. Dig. 442 125-2. VPO, André Previn.

(N) *** Telarc Dig. 80497 [id.]. Atlanta SO, Yoel Levi.

(M) *(**) Mercury 434 384-2 [id.]. Minneapolis (Minnesota) SO, Antal Dorati.

**(*) DG Dig. 447 056-2. Russian Nat. O, Pletnev.

Dohnányi's rhythmic flexibility and the ebb and flow of his rubato are a constant delight. The recording is superb, very much in the demonstration bracket, with the warm acoustics of the Cleveland Hall ideal in providing rich textures and brilliance without edge. A delightful disc.

Kubelik's set, now issued as one of DG's Originals, offers polished, sparkling orchestral playing. The sound has greater refinement and a rather wider range of dynamic than the competing Sony disc and for that reason many will choose it in preference to Szell, for Kubelik has a very special feeling for Dvořák and the playing of the Bavarian orchestra brings a thrilling virtuosity and a special panache of its own.

In Szell's exuberant, elegant and marvellously played set of the *Slavonic dances* the balance is close (which means *pianissimos* fail to register) but the charisma of the playing is unforgettable and, for all the racy exuberance, one senses a predominant feeling of affection and elegance. The warm acoustics of Severance Hall ensure the consistency of the orchestral sound.

Previn with his rhythmic flair brings out the playfulness of the *Slavonic dances* as few others do. One is regularly reminded of the closeness of Dvořák's Bohemia to Vienna, when in the warm Musikverein acoustic these dances become first cousins to the waltzes and polkas of the Strauss family. Helped by the Vienna ambience, however, Previn has more light and shade than Szell. Whatever the contrasts, all three are outstanding versions, with Previn's the most genial.

The Atlanta Symphony Orchestra enter a hotly competitive field and emerge with flying colours. The playing has exhilaration, warmth and flexibility, helped by the pleasing ambience of Symphony Hall and Levi's easygoing rubato. The strings have plenty of bloom, indeed the sound is richly blended rather than sharply detailed. Perhaps the cymbals (as in the very first dance) could emerge with more transient bite, but better this than artificial brightness: the brilliance comes from the orchestra's response, with the conductor at his affectionate best in the second set (Opus 72).

Dorati's performances have splendid brio and Slavonic flair. They are also very well played, and the gentler, lyrical sections are often quite delightful. The snag is the curiously confined recording, full-bodied but somehow unable to expand properly.

Refinement and crispness of ensemble are the keynotes of Mikhail Pletnev's distinctive reading. The approach is at times almost Mozartian in its elegance, with little of the earthier Slavonic qualities and with even the wildest furiants kept under control, and the extrovert joy of the music rather underplayed. Yet consistently Pletnev and his Russian players make one marvel at the beauty of the instrumentation, and this is a disc to give a fresh view of well-loved music. However, the acoustic of the Concert Hall of Moscow Conservatory is not particularly flattering, and competition is strong.

Slavonic dances, Op. 72, Nos. 9–16.

(B) *** Decca Eclipse Dig. 448 991-2. RPO, Dorati – GOLDMARK: *Rustic Wedding Symphony.* **(*)

Anyone wanting just the second set of the Dvořák *Slavonic dances* will find that Dorati's performances have characteristic brio. Sparkle is the keynote, and the Kingsway Hall recording adds suitable atmosphere. The 1983 recording sounds very good in this Eclipse reissue.

Slavonic rhapsody No. 3 in A flat min.
(N) *** Decca Dig. 452 482-2 [id.]. Montreal SO, Charles Dutoit. – ALFVEN, ENESCU, GLAZUNOV, LISZT: *Rhapsodies etc.* ***

A very enjoyable account of the *Slavonic Rhapsody No. 3* from Montreal and Dutoit which has much going for it, particularly the spectacularly realistic sound.

SYMPHONIES

Symphonies Nos. 1–9.
(M) *** Chandos Dig. CHAN 9008/13. RSNO, Neeme Järvi.

Symphonies Nos. 1–9; Overtures: Carnival; In nature's realm; My home. Scherzo capriccioso.
❁ (B) *** Decca 430 046-2 (6). LSO, István Kertész.

Järvi has the advantage of outstanding, modern, digital recording, full and naturally balanced. The set is offered at upper mid-price, six CDs for the price of four. Only the *Fourth Symphony* is split centrally between discs; all the others can be heard uninterrupted. But there are no fillers, as with Kertész on Decca.

For those not wanting to go to the expense of the digital Chandos Järvi set, Kertész's bargain box is an easy first choice among the remaining collections of Dvořák symphonies. The CD transfers are of Decca's best quality, full-bodied and vivid with a fine ambient effect. It was Kertész who first revealed the full potential of the early symphonies, and his readings gave us fresh insights into these often inspired works. To fit the symphonies and orchestral works on to six CDs some mid-work breaks have proved unavoidable; but the set remains a magnificent memorial to a conductor who died sadly young.

Symphony No. 1 in C min. (The Bells of Zlonice), Op. 3; A Hero's song, Op. 111.
*** Chandos Dig. CHAN 8597 [id.]. RSNO, Järvi.

Symphony No. 1 in C min. (The Bells of Zlonice), Op. 3; Legends, Op. 59/1–5.
(BB) *** Naxos Dig. 8.550266 [id.]. Slovak PO, Czecho-Slovak RSO, Gunzenhauser.

The first of Dvořák's nine symphonies is on the long-winded side. Yet whatever its structural weaknesses, it is full of colourful and memorable ideas, often characteristic of the mature composer. Järvi directs a warm, often impetuous performance, with rhythms invigoratingly sprung in the fast movements and with the slow movement more persuasive than in previous recordings. The recording is warmly atmospheric in typical Chandos style.

Though on a super-bargain label, the competing Bratislava version rivals Järvi's Chandos disc both as a performance and in sound. The ensemble of the Slovak Philharmonic is rather crisper, and the recording, full and atmospheric, has detail less obscured by reverberation. The first five of Dvořák's ten *Legends* make a generous coupling: colourful miniatures, colourfully played.

Symphony No. 2 in B flat, Op. 4; Legends, Op. 59/6–10.
(BB) *** Naxos Dig. 8.550267 [id.]. Slovak PO, Czecho-Slovak RSO, Gunzenhauser.

Symphony No. 2 in B flat, Op. 4; Slavonic rhapsody No.3 in A flat, Op. 45.
**(*) Chandos Dig. CHAN 8589 [id.]. RSNO, Järvi.

With speeds more expansive than those of his Chandos rival, Neeme Järvi, Gunzenhauser gives a taut, beautifully textured account, very well played and recorded, clearly preferable in every way, even making no allowance for price. The completion of the set of *Legends* makes a very generous coupling (73 minutes).

Järvi's performance, characteristically warm and urgent, is let down by the reverberant Chandos sound, here missing the necessary sharpness of focus, so that the tangy Czech flavour of the music loses some of its bite. The *Slavonic rhapsody* is done with delicious point and humour, with the sound back to Chandos's normally high standard.

Symphony No. 3 in E flat, Op. 10; Carnival overture, Op. 92; Symphonic variations, Op. 78.
*** Chandos Dig. CHAN 8575 [id.]. RSNO, Järvi.

Järvi's is a highly persuasive reading, not ideally sharp of rhythm in the first movement but totally sympathetic. The recording is well up to the standards of the house and the fill-ups are particularly generous.

Symphonies Nos. 3 in E flat, Op. 10; 6 in D, Op. 60.
(BB) *** Naxos Dig. 8.550268; *4.550268* [id.]. Slovak PO, Stephen Gunzenhauser.

These exhilarating performances of the *Third* and *Sixth Symphonies* are well up to the standard of earlier records in this splendid Naxos series. Gunzenhauser's pacing is admirably judged through both works, and rhythms are always lifted. Excellent, vivid recording in the warm acoustics of the Bratislava Concert Hall.

Symphonies Nos. 3 in E flat, Op. 10; 7 in D min., Op. 70.
*** DG Dig. 449 207-2. VPO, Myung-Whun Chung.

Myung-Whun Chung has the full measure of both the *E flat* and especially the the *D minor Symphony*. His approach is well considered and finely shaped, and yet he manages to make everything sound as fresh and as spontaneous as Dvořák must. The playing in both symphonies is impressive and they deserve – but do not receive – state-of-the-art recorded sound. There needs to be a better-ventilated, more spacious orchestral texture, such as Chandos provide for Bělohlávek (in No. 7). All the same, the stature of the performances is such as to warrant a full three-star recommendation.

Symphony No. 4 in D min., Op. 13; (i) *Biblical songs, Op. 99.*
*** Chandos Dig. CHAN 8608 [id.]. RSNO, Järvi, (i) with Brian Rayner Cook.

Järvi's affectionate reading of this early work brings out the Czech flavours in Dvořák's inspiration and makes light of the continuing Wagner influences, notably the echoes of *Tannhäuser* in the slow movement. This is a performance to win converts to an often underrated work. The recording is well up to the Chandos standard.

Symphonies Nos. 4 in D min., Op. 13; 8 in G, Op. 33.
(BB) **(*) Naxos Dig. 8.550269; *4550269* [id.]. Slovak PO, Stephen Gunzenhauser.

Gunzenhauser's *Fourth* is very convincing. In his hands the fine lyrical theme of the first movement certainly blossoms and the relative lack of weight in the orchestral textures brings distinct benefit in the Scherzo. The slow movement, too, is lyrical without too much Wagnerian emphasis. The naturally sympathetic orchestral playing helps to make the *Eighth* a refreshing experience, even though the first two movements are rather relaxed and without the impetus of the finest versions. The digital sound is excellent, vivid and full, with a natural concert-hall ambience.

(i) *Symphony No. 5 in F, Op. 76;* (ii) *Carnival overture, Op. 92;* (iii) *The American Flag* (cantata), *Op. 102.*
(B) **(*) Sony Dig./Analogue SBK 60297 [id.]. (i) Philh. O, Andrew Davis; (ii) NYPO, Mehta; (iii) Joseph Evans, Barry McDaniel, St Hedwig's Cathedral Choir, Berlin RIAS Chamber Ch., Berlin RSO, Tilson Thomas.

Andrew Davis's account of the *Fifth Symphony*, freshly played but somewhat undercharacterized, is rather more successful than his *Sixth*, but there is nothing special about Mehta's *Carnival overture*. Yet what makes this bargain CD well worth considering is *The American Flag*. It was commissioned for the composer's visit to the New World in 1892, and Dvořák's setting has real flair. The opening sections addressing the American Eagle are spirited enough, but when the tenor (as the Foot Soldier) presents the *First address to the flag*, Dvořák produces an infectiously jigging tune which is then taken up enthusiastically by the chorus; the work continues in this vein until its effective closing apotheosis. The singing of both soloists is first rate and the combined choruses are magnificent. The analogue recording could not be bettered, and this surely needs to be more aptly re-coupled with Tilson Thomas's account of the *American suite* (see below).

Symphony No. 5 in F, Op. 76; Othello overture, Op. 93; Scherzo capriccioso, Op. 66.
✿ *** EMI (SIS) Dig. CDC7 49995-2. Oslo PO, Jansons.

Symphony No. 5 in F, Op. 75; The Water goblin, Op. 107.
*** Chandos Dig. CHAN 8552 [id.]. RSNO, Järvi.

Jansons directs a radiant account of this delectable symphony and the EMI engineers put a fine bloom on the Oslo sound. With its splendid encores, equally exuberant in performance, this is one of the finest Dvořák records in the catalogue.

Järvi is also most effective in moulding the structure, subtly varying tempo between sections to smooth over the often abrupt links. His persuasiveness in the slow movement, relaxed but never sentimental, brings radiant playing from the SNO, and Czech dance-rhythms are sprung most infectiously, leading to an exhilarating close to the whole work, simulating the excitement of a live performance.

Symphonies Nos. 5 in F, Op. 76; 7 in D min., Op. 70.
(BB) *** Naxos Dig. 8.550270; *4550270* [id.]. Slovak PO, Stephen Gunzenhauser.

Gunzenhauser's coupling is recommendable even without the price advantage. The beguiling opening of the *Fifth*, with its engaging Slovak wind solos, has plenty of atmosphere, and the reading generates a natural lyrical impulse. The *Seventh*, spontaneous throughout, brings an eloquent *Poco adagio*, a lilting Scherzo, and a finale that combines an expansive secondary theme with plenty of excitement and impetus.

Symphony No. 6 in D, Op. 60; The Wood dove, Op. 110.
*** Chandos Dig. CHAN 9170 [id.]. Czech PO, Jiří Bělohlávek.

Bělohlávek conducts a glowing performance of No. 6, rich in Brahmsian and Czech pastoral overtones, helped by satisfyingly full and immediate Chandos sound. This easily takes precedence over the Järvi version (CHAN 8350). His reading of the late symphonic poem is comparably warm and idiomatic in a relaxed way.

Symphonies Nos. 6 in D, Op. 60; 7 in D min., Op. 70; 8 in G, Op. 88; 9 (New World); Scherzo capriccioso, Op. 66.
(M) **(*) EMI (SIS) CMS5 65705-2 (3). LPO, Rostropovich.

Rostropovich's *Sixth Symphony* opens freshly. The slow movement is leisurely and romantic but has an imposing climax and coda. The Scherzo brings an accent on forceful vigour and the finale certainly does not lack impetus and power: its forceful close is characteristic of Rostropovich's weighty approach throughout the set. The *Seventh* is a big, thrustful reading which underplays the genial Dvořák, who now becomes biting and unrelenting. The Scherzo is emphatic rather than urgent, the most controversial point of an unconventional interpretation. The *Eighth* produces slow tempi throughout and a consciously *espressivo* manner, and the performance overall disappointingly refuses to catch fire. Rostropovich's very opening chords for the *New World* suggest an epic view, and from then on, with generally expansive tempi, the reading clearly follows this weighty conception, though in all four movements Rostropovich contrasts the big tuttis with light pointing in woodwind solos. The *Scherzo capriccioso* is incisive and energetic, lilting yet essentially symphonic in feeling. With all reservations taken into account, these readings are all full of character and only the *Eighth* lacks the fullest concentration. The Kingsway Hall recording is bright and fresh on top, yet remains full and expansive.

Symphony No. 7 in D min., Op. 70; Nocturne for strings, Op. 40; The Water goblin, Op. 107.
*** Chandos Dig. CHAN 9391 [id.]. Czech PO, Bělohlávek.

Bělohlávek knows better than his direct rivals how to draw out idiomatic warmth from the Czech Philharmonic, and he is helped by satisfyingly full and glowing Chandos sound. Fresh, well paced and intelligently shaped, this is a thoroughly recommendable reading paired with an excellent account of *The Water goblin*, and the eloquent, poignant *Nocturne for strings*. In this spacious reading of the *Nocturne* the Czech strings produce ravishing sounds, and *The Water goblin* is similarly relaxed and warm rather than sharply dramatic.

Symphonies Nos. 7 in D min., Op. 70; 8 in G, Op. 88.
*** EMI (SIS) Dig. CDC7 54663-2. Oslo PO, Jansons.
(M) *** Mercury 434 312-2 [id.]. LSO, Antal Dorati.
(N) (M) *** DG 457 902-2. BPO, Kubelik.
(M) **(*) Telarc Dig. CD 82018 [id.]. LAPO, André Previn.
(B) **(*) Sony SBK 67174 [id.]. Philh. O, Andrew Davis.

Mariss Jansons's readings of both works are outstandingly fine, with the dramatic tensions of the *D minor* work bitingly conveyed, yet with detail affectionately treated, and with rhythms exhilaratingly sprung. No. 8 is given a performance of high contrasts too, with the slow movement warmly expansive and the whole crowned by a winningly spontaneous-sounding account of the finale, rarely matched in its exuberance. Excellent sound. This makes a new first choice for this coupling, although at mid-price there are strongly recommendable alternatives, notably Dorati on Mercury.

Dorati's coupling brings an extraordinary successful account of No. 7, with the spontaneous feel of a live performance enhanced by the vividly realistic concert hall balance of the (1963) Mercury recording – one of their very finest. The interpretation is free, the *Poco Adagio* is impulsive and the Scherzo lifts off with a sparkle. The finale has enormous energy and bite, and an exuberant thrust, leading on to a thrilling coda. The *Eighth Symphony* was recorded four years earlier, with the acoustic of Watford Town Hall again providing a highly convincing ambience. Dorati's reading proves comparably vibrant.

Kubelik's splendid performances are also available on a DG Double, including also the *New World Symphony* and *The Wood dove* (see below), which is better value; those wanting just Nos. 7 and 8 will find the present Galleria disc eminently satisfactory.

Andrew Davis's coupling with the Philharmonia was recorded at EMI's Abbey Road studios. Yet, with the violins given a bright sheen, the sound is more like a CBS recording than a mellower, EMI offering. Davis's comparatively lightweight account of the *Seventh* has an attractive lyrical freshness; the *Eighth* is much more compulsive and dramatically spontaneous, making the most of the music's dynamic contrasts, with high drama in the climaxes of the *Adagio*, which also has plenty of expressive feeling, and a sense of vibrant energy throughout the outer movements. The finale is thrilling (although there is some raucous tone from the brass) and there is no doubt about the individuality of the reading as a whole.

Previn directs a tautly rhythmic account of the *Seventh Symphony*. Rather than developing Slavonic atmosphere, he tends to bring out the symphonic cohesion. The slow movement is warmly done, with fine horn solos; but some of the lightness of the last two movements is lost – notably in the lilting Scherzo – with such rhythmic emphasis. The *Eighth*, too, is sharply rhythmic but rather more idiomatic in feeling. Warmth and freshness here go with the finest orchestral sound yet achieved by this orchestra in Royce Hall, full and with a vivid sense of presence that allows fine inner quality. In the *Seventh Symphony* the upper range has marginally less bloom.

Symphonies Nos. (i) *7 in D min., Op. 70;* (ii) *8 in G, Op. 88; 9 (New World); Overture: Carnival, Op. 92; Scherzo capriccioso, Op. 66.*
(B) **(*) EMI forte CZS5 68628-2 (2). (i) LPO; (ii) Philh. O; Giulini.

Symphonies Nos. 7 in D min., Op. 70; 8 in G, Op. 88; 9 (New World); Scherzo capriccioso, Op. 66.
(B) *** Decca Double 452 182-2 (2) [id.]. Cleveland O, Christoph von Dohnányi.

(i) *Symphonies Nos. 7 in D min., Op. 70; 8 in G, Op. 88;* (ii) *9 (New World);* (i) *Symphonic variations, Op. 78.*
(B) *** Ph. Duo 438 347-2 (2) [id.]. (i) LSO; (ii) Concg. O, Sir Colin Davis.

(i) *Symphonies Nos. 7 in D min., Op. 70; 8 in G, Op. 88; 9 in E min. (From the New World), Op. 95;* (ii) *The Wood dove, Op. 110.*
(B) *** DG Double 439 663-2 (2) [id.]. (i) BPO; (ii) Bav. RSO; Kubelik (with SMETANA: *Vltava* (with Boston SO) ***).

Symphonies Nos. 8 in G, Op. 88; 9 in E min. (From the New World), Op. 95.
(M) *** DG 447 412-2 [id.]. BPO, Kubelik.

Rafael Kubelik's performances of the last Dvořák symphonies are among the finest ever recorded. They are superbly played, and the recordings sound admirably fresh, full yet well detailed, the ambience attractive. Kubelik's glowing approach to the *Seventh* is essentially expressive, but his romanticism never obscures the overall structural plan and there is no lack of vitality and sparkle. The account of the *Eighth* is a shade straighter, without personal idiosyncrasy, except for a minor indulgence for the phrasing of the glowingly lyrical string-theme in the trio of the Scherzo. The orchestral balance in the *G major Symphony* is particularly well judged. Kubelik's marvellously fresh *New World*, recorded in the Jesus-Christus Kirche, also remains among the top recommendations, providing one does not mind the omission of the first movement's exposition repeat. There is a choice of formats. The best buy is surely the DG Double, which includes a comparably fine Bavarian Radio Orchestra performance of *The Wood dove*, plus Smetana's *Vltava*, recorded in Boston. However, the *Eighth* and *Ninth Symphonies* are also reissued as 'Legendary Recordings' in DG's 'Originals' series at mid-price, and the *New World* is additionally available on a DG Classikon bargain CD (439 436-2), coupled with five sparkling *Slavonic dances* (see below).

Dohnányi's Cleveland performances of the last three Dvořák symphonies from the mid 1980s are among his very finest recordings, and they make an admirable Double Decca triptych. However Dohnányi's *New World*, superbly played and recorded, like the companion recordings of Nos. 7 and 8 (see above), like Kubelik's, fails to observe the first-movement exposition repeat. That said, there is much to praise in this grippingly spontaneous performance, generally direct and unmannered but glowing with warmth. The great cor anglais melody in the *Largo* and the big clarinet solo in the finale are both richly done, with the ripe and very well-balanced Decca recording adding to their opulence. The sound is spectacularly full and rich. In the *Scherzo capriccioso* Dohnányi brings out the Slavonic dance sparkle and moulds the lyrical secondary theme with comparable affectionate flair.

Giulini is at his finest in both the *Seventh* and the *New World*. In the *D minor Symphony* he and the LPO players really make the music sing, and the Dvořákian sunshine keeps breaking out. The glowing (1976) recording encourages rounded textures and rounded phrases. No. 8 (like the *New World*), recorded with the Philharmonia 14 years earlier, brings a similar mellow approach, but the result is comparatively disappointing. Giulini's speeds are on the slow side, especially in the *Adagio* and rather bland *Allegretto*, while the finale opens in a somewhat subdued fashion. Frankly this does not altogether come off. The *New World* is a different matter, refreshingly direct. It is discussed above in its alternative, Seraphim coupling with the *Cello concerto*.

Sir Colin Davis's performances of Nos. 7 and 8, with their bracing rhythmic flow and natural feeling for Dvořákian lyricism, are appealingly direct yet have plenty of life and urgency. In the *New World*, however, the very directness has its drawbacks. The cor anglais solo in the slow movement brings an appealing simplicity. The reading is completely free from egotistical eccentricity and, with beautiful orchestral playing throughout, this is enjoyable in its way. The set is made the more attractive by the inclusion of the *Symphonic variations* – one of Dvořák's finest works, much underrated by the public – and here Davis's performance has striking freshness. The remastering of all the recordings is very successful.

Symphonies Nos. 7–9 (New World); Legends, Op. 59/4, 6 & 7; Scherzo capriccioso; Serenade in D min., Op. 44.
(N) (BB) *** Royal Classics HR 703992 (3) [id.]. Hallé O, Barbirolli (with BRAHMS: *Double concerto*: 1st movt.; with Campoli & Navarra).

Barbirolli's red-blooded performances of Dvořák's last three symphonies (which derive from the Pye/ Nixa label, were recorded between 1957 and 1959, and have been remastered by EMI) are offered here with other works on three CDs, in separate jewel cases, within a slip case at the lowest possible price. They make a very remarkable bargain. The *Seventh* and *Eighth Symphonies* sustain characteristically high adrenalin levels and splendidly warm lyrical feeling. The *Eighth* (engineered by the Mercury team) is especially fine, sounding like a live performance, rather than a studio account: it received a ✿ from us on its individual issue. The *New World* is comparably spontaneous and exciting with a ravishingly warm slow movement (beautiful wind and string playing) and a thrilling finale. This also is Barbirolli at his revelatory finest and the sound is remarkably full-bodied (splendid timpani). The other works come off well too, the *Legends* affectionately lyrical, while the *Scherzo capriccioso* bounces buoyantly. The *Wind Serenade* is an unexpected bonus, an intimate performance of persuasive charm. The playing is good too, and the recording limited, but satisfactory. For some curious reason, only the first movement of the Brahms *Double concerto* is included. No matter, the rest is not to be missed.

Symphonies Nos. 7 in D min., Op. 70; 9 in E min. (New World), Op. 95.
(B) *** EMI Eminence Dig. CD-EMX 2202. LPO, Mackerras.

At mid-price, Mackerras's coupling offers performances of both works which are among the finest ever. With Mackerras, tragedy is not uppermost in the *D minor Symphony* but rather Dvořákian openness. After a hushed, mysterious opening it is the lilting joy of the inspiration which makes the performance so winning. In the *New World* he takes a warmly expansive view, remarkable for a hushed and intense account of the slow movement and superb playing from the LPO, treated to warm, atmospheric recording.

Symphony No. 8 in G; The Golden spinning-wheel, Op. 109.
**(*) Chandos Dig. CHAN 9048 [id.]. Czech PO, Bělohlávek.

Symphony No. 8 in G, Op. 88; Slavonic dances Nos. 3, Op. 46/3; 10, Op. 72/2.
(B) **(*) EMI forte CZS5 69509-2 (2) [CDFB 69509]. Cleveland O, Szell – BEETHOVEN: *Piano concerto No. 5* etc. ***

Symphony No. 8 in G; Symphonic variations, Op. 78.
(B) *** EMI Dig. CD-EMX 2216. LPO, Mackerras.

Symphony No. 8 in G; The wood dove, Op. 110.
*** Chandos Dig. CHAN 8666 [id.]. RSNO, Järvi.

Mackerras's version of No. 8 matches in its effervescence his outstanding accounts of Nos. 7 and 9, also on Eminence. The colour and atmosphere of the piece are brought out vividly and with a lightness of touch that makes most rivals seem heavy-handed. In the *Symphonic variations* too, his relaxed treatment is consistently winning, helped by fine playing and recording. While Barbirolli's interpretation of the symphony remains very special, Mackerras has the advantage of first-rate digital recording.

Järvi's highly sympathetic account of the *Eighth* underlines the expressive lyricism of the piece, the rhapsodic freedom of invention rather than any symphonic tautness, with the SNO players reacting to his free rubato and affectionate moulding of phrase with collective spontaneity. The warm Chandos sound has plenty of bloom, with detail kept clear, and is very well balanced.

Szell's reading of the *Eighth Symphony* is strong and committed, consistent from first to last, and marvellously played. With full-bodied 1970 sound, it remains both distinctive and very enjoyable. The pair of *Slavonic dances* are mellower than the earlier complete set on Sony but are still a fine example of Cleveland orchestral bravura. The transfers are first class – this is a richer sound than on many records from this source.

Bělohlávek directs the Czech Philharmonic in a warmly idiomatic reading of No. 8. He is helped by a satisfyingly beefy recording with plenty of bloom that yet focuses the players more sharply than most recordings with this orchestra. Though basic speeds are on the fast side, Bělohlávek is never reticent over giving full expansiveness to linking passages, so adding to the warmth. The longest and richest of Dvořák's late symphonic poems is given similarly idiomatic treatment but in a version with cuts, a considerable drawback.

Symphonies Nos. 8 in G; 9 in E min. (New World).
(M) *** Sony Bruno Walter Edition SMK 64484 [id.]. Columbia SO, Bruno Walter.

Walter's account of Dvořák's *Eighth* was one of the last recordings he made (in 1962), but the overall lyricism never takes the place of virility and Walter's mellowness is most effective in the *Adagio*. His pacing is uncontroversial until the finale, which is steadier than usual, more symphonic, though never heavy. The *New World* was recorded two years earlier. Once more, this is not a conventional reading, but it is one to fall in love with. Its recognizably Viennese roots lead to a more relaxed view of the outer movements than usual. Nevertheless, as so often with Walter, there is an underlying tension to knit the structure together and the result is more involving and satisfying than some other rivals which have greater surface excitement. The new transfers are admirable.

Symphony No. 9 in E min. (From the New World), Op. 95.
(M) *** Decca Phase Four 448 947-2 [id.]. New Philh. O, Dorati – KODALY: *Háry János suite.* ***
(M) *** Mercury [434 317-2]. Detroit SO, Paray – SIBELIUS: *Symphony No. 2.* **
(M) (***) RCA mono GD 60279 [60279-2-RG]. NBC SO, Toscanini – KODALY: *Háry János*: suite (***); SMETANA: *Má Vlast: Vltava.* (**)

(M) (***) Mercury mono 434 387-2 [id.]. Chicago SO, Kubelik – MOZART: *Symphony No. 38 in D (Prague)*. (**)
**(*) DG Dig. 439 009-2 [id.]. VPO, Karajan – SMETANA: *Vltava*. **(*)
(M) **(*) Teldec/Warner CD 82007 [id.]. St Louis SO, Leonard Slatkin.
(N) (M) ** EMI CDM5 67033-2. [id.]. Philh. O, Klemperer – HAYDN: *Symphony No. 101*.

Symphony No. 9 (New World); Carnival overture, Op. 92.
(M) *** RCA 09026 62587-2 [id.]. Chicago SO, Fritz Reiner – SMETANA: *Bartered Bride overture;* WEINBERGER: *Schwanda polka and fugue*. ***

Symphony No. 9 (New World); Overtures: Carnival; Othello.
(M) *** Penguin Classics Decca 466 212-2 [460 604-2]. LSO, Istvan Kertész.

Symphony No. 9 (New World); Carnival overture; (ii) Scherzo capriccioso, Op. 66.
(M) *** [RCA Basic 100 09026 61716-2]. Chicago SO; (i) Reiner; (ii) Levine.

Symphony No. 9 (New World); (ii) *Czech suite; Prague waltzes.*
(B) *** Decca Eclipse Dig. 448 245-2. (i) VPO, Kondrashin; (ii) Detoit SO, Dorati.

Symphony No. 9 (New World); My home overture, Op. 62.
*** Chandos Dig. CHAN 8510 [id.]. RSNO, Järvi.

(i) *Symphony No. 9 (New World);* (ii) *Serenade for strings.*
(M) **(*) Sony SBK 46331 [id.]. (i) LSO, Ormandy; (ii) Munich PO, Kempe.

(i) *Symphony No.9 in E min. (New World);* (ii) *Slavonic dances Nos. 1, 2, 7 & 8, Op. 46/1, 2, 7 & 8; 16, Op. 72/8.*
(B) *** DG Classikon 439 436-2. (i) BPO; (ii) Bav. RSO; Rafael Kubelik.

Symphony No. 9 (New World); Slavonic dances Nos. 1, 3 and 7, Op. 46/1, 3 & 7; 10 and 15, Op. 72/2 & 7.
(M) *** DG 435 590-2. BPO, Karajan.

Symphony No. 9 (New World); Symphonic variations, Op. 78.
(B) *** CfP Dig. CD-CFP 9006. LPO, Macal.

Kondrashin's Vienna performance of the *New World Symphony* was one of Decca's first demonstration CDs. Recorded in the Sofiensaal, every detail of Dvořák's orchestration is revealed within a highly convincing perspective. Other performances may exhibit a higher level of tension but there is a natural spontaneity here. The cor anglais solo in the *Largo* is easy and songful, and the finale is especially satisfying, with the wide dynamic range adding drama and the refinement and transparency of the texture noticeably effective as the composer recalls ideas from earlier movements. Previously available in a mid-priced coupling with Dorati's RPO version of the engaging *American suite*, the new budget-priced Eclipse CD is enhanced by Dorati's bright, fresh Detroit versions of the *Czech suite* and the even rarer *Prague waltzes* (Viennese music with a Czech accent).

Among earlier analogue accounts, Kertész's LSO version (now on Penguin Classics) stands out. It remains one of the finest performances ever committed to record, with a most exciting first movement (exposition repeat included) in which the introduction of the second subject group is eased in with considerable subtlety; the *Largo* brings playing of hushed intensity to make one hear the music with new ears. Tempi in the last two movements are perfectly judged. Reissued, very successfully remastered, with equally fine accounts of *Othello* and the *Carnival overture*, this remains very competitive, but for most collectors the Kondrashin version is even more attractive. In the UK, the special note is by Paul Bailey; in the USA by Wendy Wasserstein.

Reiner's 1957 *New World* is an essentially lyrical performance without idiosyncratic disturbances. There is no first-movement exposition repeat, but how well the music flows, both here and in the *Largo*, with consistently lovely playing, especially in the rapt closing section. The Scherzo sparkles, while there is no lack of excitement in the finale. Typically warm Chicago sound. What makes this disc the more attractive are the fill-ups, not just the brilliant *Carnival overture*, but the other items too. Reiner's recording is also available in the USA with an alternative coupling as part of RCA's Basic 100 series.

Macal as a Czech takes a fresh and unsentimental view of the *New World Symphony*. His inclusion of the repeat balances the structure convincingly. With idiomatic insights there is no feeling of rigidity, with the beauty of the slow movement purified, the Scherzo crisp and energetic, set against pastoral freshness in the episodes, and the finale again strong and direct, bringing a ravishing clarinet solo. The *Symphonic variations*, which acts as coupling, is less distinctive but is well characterized. A fine bargain recommendation.

Karajan's 1964 DG analogue recording is preferable to his digital version. It has a powerful lyrical feeling and an exciting build-up of power in the outer movements. The *Largo* is played most beautifully, and Karajan lets the orchestra speak for itself, which it does, gloriously. The rustic qualities of the Scherzo are affectionately brought out, and altogether this is very rewarding. The recording is full, bright and open. This is now reissued, sounding as good as ever, coupled with five favourite *Slavonic dances*, given virtuoso performances.

Kubelik's *New World* (see above) remains

among the top recommendations. It is brightly transferred in this Classikon reissue, where it is recoupled with five sparkling *Slavonic dances*.

Järvi's opening introduction establishes the spaciousness of his view, with lyrical, persuasive phrasing and a very slow speed, leading into an *Allegro* which starts relaxedly, but then develops in big dramatic contrasts. The expansiveness is underlined, when the exposition repeat is observed. The *Largo* too is exceptionally spacious, with the cor anglais player taxed to the limit but effectively supported over ravishingly beautiful string-playing. The Scherzo is lilting rather than fierce, and the finale is bold and swaggering.

Dorati's performance is immediate and direct, with bold primary colours heightening the drama throughout. Rarely have the Phase Four techniques been used to better artistic effect, and the recording is extremely vivid, without loss of warmth. Not a first choice, perhaps, but eminently recommendable if the excellent Kodály coupling is suitable.

Paray's 1960 *New World* is uncommonly fresh. In the first-movement *Allegro* he is airy and graceful; the exposition repeat is not observed. The *Largo*, with its poised cor anglais melody, makes a gentle contrast, and the Scherzo is admirably vivacious. The finale goes furiously and its spontaneity leaves the listener with that rare feeling that the music really has been made while he or she was listening. The recording, made in Detroit's Cass Technical High School auditorium, is well balanced in a typically natural Mercury way and adds to the freshness of effect.

With speeds consistently fast and the manner clipped, Toscanini's reading of the *New World* is anything but idiomatic, but it still tells us something unique about Dvořák and his perennial masterpiece, presenting a fiery, thrilling experience. The sound is fuller than most from this source and the transfer brings that out, despite the usual dryness.

Kubelik's Mercury recording of the *New World Symphony* was almost as celebrated in its day (1951) as his *Pictures from an exhibition*. The Chicago players are kept consistently on their toes. There is no first-movement exposition repeat, but the *Largo* is played most beautifully, with the one proviso that the cor anglais soloist is not ripe-toned and has what comes across as a rather nervous vibrato. The sparkling Scherzo, crisply rhythmic and full of idiomatic character, then leads to a thrilling finale, where the tension is held at the highest level until the very last bar. Here the sound, hitherto remarkably good, tends to become a bit shrill.

Under Ormandy the playing of the LSO has life and spontaneity, and the rhythmic freshness of the Scherzo (achieved by unforced precision) is matched by the lyrical beauty of the *Largo* and the breadth and vigour of the finale. Perhaps the reading has not the individuality of the finest versions; but the sound is full and firm in the bass to support the upper range's brilliance. For coupling, we are offered an essentially mellow account of the *String serenade*, directed by Kempe with affectionate warmth.

Karajan's digital recording of the *New World Symphony* is enjoyably alive and does not lack spontaneity, although the VPO playing is less refined than on either of Karajan's analogue versions with the BPO, especially in the *Largo*. However, those wanting a Karajan performance in modern digital sound could be well satisfied with this.

The St Louis Symphony plays for Slatkin with polish and refinement; the cor anglais solo of the slow movement is so velvety it hardly sounds like a reed instrument, and the brass which introduces the *Largo* is characteristically rich in sonority. One or two mannerisms apart, the reading is both enjoyably direct and vital, and the recording, full-bodied and naturally balanced, brings out the sweetness of the strings, even in the gentlest *pianissimos*. This is most enjoyable but even at mid-price (with a playing-time of only 44 minutes) remains uncompetitive without a coupling.

Klemperer is given good recording for its date of 1963, and fine playing from the Philharmonia Orchestra. The *Largo* is very beautiful but, although the conductor's deliberation in the first movement brings a well-detailed account of the score, the scherzo and finale are too solid to be totally convincing. Admirers of this conductor's style will probably not be disappointed.

CHAMBER AND INSTRUMENTAL MUSIC

Piano quartets Nos. 1 in D, Op. 23; 2 in E flat, Op. 87.

❁ *** Hyperion Dig. CDA 66287 [id.]. Domus.

The Dvořák *Piano quartets* are glorious pieces, and the playing of Domus is little short of inspired. This is real chamber-music-playing: intimate, unforced and distinguished by both vitality and sensitivity. Domus are recorded in an ideal acoustic and in perfect perspective; they sound wonderfully alive and warm.

Piano quartet No. 2 in E flat, Op. 87; Piano quintet in A, Op. 81.

(BB) *** ASV Dig. CDQS 6200 [(M) id.]. Clementi Ens.

A very enjoyable account of the *A major Piano quintet* given by an accomplished and musical group new to records. The Clementi may not be celebrated and glamorous but they are none the worse for that. The quintet is refreshingly unmannered and pleasingly musical and this modestly priced and well-engineered ASV disc will give a lot of pleasure in both works and can be especially recommended to those wanting modern digital sound.

Piano quintet in A, Op. 81.
*** ASV Dig. CDDCA 889 [id.]. Peter Frankl, Lindsay Qt – MARTINU: *Piano quintet No. 2.* ***
(M) *** Decca 448 602-2 [id.]. Clifford Curzon, VPO Qt – SCHUBERT: *Trout quintet.* ***

This ASV account of Dvořák's glorious *Piano quintet* by the Lindsays with Peter Frankl is the finest of modern versions and can readily stand comparison with the famous early Decca account with Clifford Curzon. Apart from Peter Frankl's fine contribution, one especially responds to Bernard Gregor-Smith's rich cello-line. Because of the resonance, the recording is full and warm and, if there is just a hint of thinness on the violin timbre, the balance with the piano is particularly well managed.

This wonderfully warm and lyrical (1962) performance of Dvořák's *Piano quintet* by Clifford Curzon is a classic record, one by which all later versions have come to be judged, and the CD transfer retains the richness and ambient glow of the original analogue master, yet has improved definition and presence. The piano timbre remains full and real. This performance is now available coupled with Schubert's *Trout quintet* in Decca's Classic Sound series.

Piano quintet in A, Op. 81; Piano quartet No. 2 in E flat, Op 87.
**(*) DG (IMS) Dig. 439 868-2 [id.]. Menahem Pressler, Emerson Quartet (augmented).

Menahem Pressler joins the Emerson Quartet in powerful, intense accounts of these two magnificent works, and they demonstrate how the *Second Piano quartet* is just as rich in its thematic material. The *Lento* is given with a rapt, hushed concentration to put it among the very finest of Dvořák inspirations. The performance of the *Quintet* is comparably positive in its characterization, but the DG New York recording gives an unpleasant edge to high violins, making the full ensemble abrasive.

Piano quintet in A, Op. 81; Piano trio No. 4 in E min. (Dumky), Op. 90.
(N) (BB) *** Virgin Classics Double Dig. VBD5 61516-2 [CDVB 61516] (2) Nash Ens. – SAINT-SAENS: *Carnival of the animals* (chamber version); *Piano trio; Septet.* ***

It is surprising that the coupling of the *A major Piano quintet* and the *Dumky trio* has not been chosen more often. The Nash Ensemble offer warmly enjoyable performances of both, with genuine intimacy of feeling and no lack of vitality. They are eminently well recorded and give considerable satisfaction without being as memorable as such classic accounts of the quintet as that by Clifford Curzon. The Saint-Saëns couplings are delightful, particularly the chamber version of the *Carnival of the animals*, and this inexpensive Virgin Double is splendid value for money.

(i) *Piano quintet in A, Op. 81; String quartet No. 12 in F (American), Op. 96.*
*** Testament SBT 1074 [id.]. (i) Pavel Stepán; Smetana Qt – JANACEK: *String quartet No. 1.* ***
*** RCA RD 86263 [6263-2-RC]. (i) Rubinstein; Guarneri Qt.

In terms of tonal finesse and bloom the Smetana Quartet had few peers, and their ensemble is perfect. Moreover the quality of the mid-1960s recorded sound is as good as many being produced today. The *Piano quintet*, in which they are joined by Pavel Stepán, is glorious even if the acoustic is slightly drier than is ideal. No quarrels with the *F major Quartet* either. The sound is analogue and has great warmth.

Both the RCA performances are memorably warm and spontaneous; tempi tend to be brisk, but the lyrical element always underlies the music and the playing has both great vitality and warmth. Needless to say, Rubinstein's contribution to the *Quintet* is highly distinguished. The recordings, made in April 1971 and 1972 respectively, are well balanced, detailed and fairly full, helped by the attractive studio ambience.

(i) *Piano quintet in A, Op. 81. String quintet in G, Op. 77.*
*** Hyperion Dig. CDA 66796 [id.]. Gaudier Ensemble, (i) with Susan Tomes.

With Susan Tomes (also of Domus) the inspired pianist, the Gaudier Ensemble gives a sparkling performance of the *Piano quintet*, full of mercurial contrasts that seem entirely apt and with rhythms superbly sprung. The *G major String quintet* is lighter than most rival versions, with speeds on the brisk side and with Marieke Blankestun's violin pure rather than rich in tone. Very well recorded, this makes an excellent recommendation if you fancy the coupling. In neither work are the exposition repeats observed.

(i) *Piano quintet in A, Op. 81. String quintets Nos. 1–3, Opp. 1, 77 & 97; String sextets in A, Op. 46.*
(N) (B) *** Ph. Duo 462 284-2 (2). (i) Stephen Kovacevich; Berlin PO Octet (members).

This is the first time these works have been gathered together on CD and they make up a very enticing Duo. The Opus 1 *String quintet in A minor* was written in 1861 when the composer was twenty; it is classical in feeling, but has a fine slow movement; and despite its much later opus number (77) the *G major String quintet* is also an early work. Its inspiration is uneven but the first movement is jolly enough and there is plenty to be found in the beautiful *Poco andante* and the vital finale. The masterly and endearingly characteristic Opus 97 *quintet* (1893) dates from the composer's American years. The Berlin Philharmonic soloists play most eloquently; these performances are both musical and polished. Both here and in the glorious *A major Sextet* there is freshness and an easy warmth which never develops into sentimentality. In that they are splendidly matched in the *Piano quintet* by Stephen Kovacevich, who at times is perhaps a little over-reticent, but whose clarity of articulation is a marvel. The recordings, from 1968 and 1972, occasionally show their age just a little in the upper range of the string timbre in *fortissimos*. But there is a pleasing ambient fullness and the sound is generally well balanced, although the piano quintet is not as weighty as it might be, lacking a little in bass.

Piano trios Nos. 1 in B flat, Op. 21; 2 in G min., Op. 26; 3 in F min., Op. 65; 4 in E min. (Dumky), Op. 90.
(M) *** Carlton Dig. 30366 00247-2 (2) [id.]. Solomon Trio.
(M) *** Teldec/Warner Dig. 9031 76458-2 (2) [id.]. Trio Fontenay.
(B) **(*) Ph. Duo 454 259-2 (2) [id.]. Beaux Arts Trio.

The Solomon Trio (Daniel Adni, Rodney Friend and Raphael Sommer) have the advantage of an outstandingly realistic and well-balanced recording. This is a different group of players from the performers in the earlier, excellent, two-disc set of Beethoven *Piano trios* (Carlton 30366 00107), with only the violinist, Rodney Friend, common to both. But, if anything, these Dvořák performances are even more successful. It is good to welcome the pianist, Daniel Adni, back to the recording studio: it is he who holds the performances together so naturally, so that the players can relax yet bring the music fully to life. The warm tone and musical phrasing of Raphael Sommer, the cellist, is a rewarding feature of the *Adagios* of Opp. 21 and 65; the latter is a performance which brings much subtlety as well as drama and brilliance. The *Dumky* is flexibly quixotic in its spontaneous mood-changes and it combines freshness with communicated affection. This set is at upper-mid-price.

First-class playing and expertly balanced modern recording combine to make the version by the Trio Fontenay very attractive indeed. Wolf Harden, the pianist, dominates – but only marginally so: his colleagues match him in lyrical ardour, and they are as sympathetic to Dvořák's warm lyricism as to the Czech dance characteristics of the livelier allegros.

The Beaux Arts versions of the *Piano trios* come from the end of the 1960s. The *F minor*, arguably the most magnificent and certainly the most concentrated of the four, is played with great eloquence and vitality. And what sparkling virtuosity there is in the Scherzo of the *G minor*, Op. 26. The splendours of the *Dumky* are well realized in an account of great spontaneity and freshness. The recording is naturally balanced and splendidly vivid; only a degree of thinness on the violin timbre, most noticeable on the first disc but also at the first *fortissimo* of the *Dumky*, gives any grounds for reservation. At Duo price this is excellent value.

Piano trios Nos. 1 in B flat min., Op. 21; 2 in G min., Op. 26.
*** Chandos Dig. CHAN 9172 [id.]. Borodin Trio.

We liked the Borodins' earlier recording of the *F minor Piano trio* (see below) and find much to admire in the present disc: these are spontaneous yet finely shaped performances, very well recorded.

Piano trio No. 3 in F min., Op. 65.
**(*) Chandos Dig. CHAN 8320 [id.]. Borodin Trio.

Piano trios No. 3 in F min., Op. 65; 4 in E min. (Dumky), Op. 90.
*** Sony Dig. MK 44527 [id.]. Emanuel Ax, Young-Uck Kim, Yo-Yo Ma.
*** Hyperion Dig. CDA 66895 [id.]. Florestan Trio.
(B) *** HM Musique d'Abord Dig. HMA 901404 [id.]. Trio de Barcelona.
(M) **(*) Ph. 426 095-2. Beaux Arts Trio.

Piano trio No. 4 in E min. (Dumky), Op. 90.
*** Chandos Dig. CHAN 8445 [id.]. Borodin Trio – SMETANA: *Piano trio*. ***

The performances by the Ax/Kim/Ma trio have warmth and freshness. The *F minor Trio* is given a powerful yet sensitive reading and the recording is faithful and natural. A marginal first choice for this coupling.

However the Hyperion disc offers an eminently satisfying alternative. These are musicianly and refined performances that will give much pleasure, and the recording, too, is excellent.

The accounts of both *Trios* from the Trio de Barcelona are also first rate and hold up well against the competition, including the Beaux Arts Trio – which is no mean compliment. They really have the measure of this music and portray its changing moods, dramatic fire and lyrical repose, bringing both poetic feeling and refined musicianship to both pieces. Warm, well-defined, excellent sound. A fine bargain.

The Beaux Arts' 1969 performances of Op. 65 and the *Dumky* still sound fresh and sparkling, though the recording on CD is a little dry in violin timbre; the *F minor*, arguably the finer and certainly the more concentrated of the two, is played with great eloquence and vitality.

The playing of the Borodin Trio in the *F minor Trio* has characteristic ardour and fire; such imperfections as there are arise from the natural spontaneity of a live performance; however, this now seems short measure. But in the *Dumky trio* it is the spontaneous flexibility of approach to the constant mood-changes that makes the splendid Borodin performance so involving. The recording here is naturally balanced and the illusion of a live occasion is striking.

String quartets Nos. 1–14; Cypresses, B.152; Fragment in F, B.120; 2 Waltzes, Op. 54, B.105.
(M) *** DG 429 193-2 (9). Prague Qt.

Dvõrák's *Quartets* span the whole of his creative life. The glories of the mature *Quartets* are well known, though it is only the so-called *American* which has achieved real popularity. The beauty of the present set, made in 1973–7, is that it offers more *Quartets* (not otherwise available) plus two *Quartet movements*, in *A minor* (1873) and *F major* (1881), plus two *Waltzes* and *Cypresses* for good measure, all in eminently respectable performances and decent recordings.

String quartet No. 7 in A min., Op. 16; Cypresses.
**(*) Chandos Dig. CHAN 8826 [id.]. Chilingirian Qt.

String quartets Nos. 8 in E, Op. 80; 9 in D min., Op. 34.
**(*) Chandos Dig. CHAN 8755 [id.]. Chilingirian Qt.

String quartets Nos. 10 in E flat, Op. 51; 11 in C, Op. 61.
**(*) Chandos Dig. CHAN 8837 [id.]. Chilingirian Qt.

Chandos provide very fine recorded sound for the Chilingirians, who play with sensitivity in all five *Quartets*. These are straightforward, well-paced readings that are eminently serviceable. Some collectors may feel, perhaps, that they fall short of the very highest distinction, but they are unfailingly musicianly and vital.

String quartets Nos. 8 in E., Op. 80; 11 in C, Op. 61.
(BB) *** Naxos 8.553372 [id.]. Vlach Qt.

String quartet No. 9 in D min., Op. 34; Terzetto in C (for 2 violins and viola), Op. 74.
(BB) *** Naxos 8.553373 [id.]. Vlach Qt.

String quartets Nos. 10 in E flat, Op. 51; 14 in A flat, Op. 105.
(BB) *** Naxos 8.553374 [id.]. Vlach Qt.

The tonal matching of the Vlach Quartet seals their claims to be an outstanding international group and there is nothing 'bargain basement' about these Vlach performances except their price. The playing is cultured and has warmth and vitality, and there can be no grumbles as far as the quality of the recorded sound is concerned. It is natural, well focused and warm. The dark intensity on a whispered *pianissimo* which marks the hushed opening of Op. 105, one of Dvořák's masterpieces, leads on to performances of exceptional strength and refinement, and throughout the series the vigorous movements bring exhilaratingly sprung rhythms and slow movements that are deeply expressive. So far this has been one of Naxos's success stories, and we are inclined to think the series strongly competitive even alongside most of the full-priced alternatives.

String quartet No. 12 in F (American), Op. 96.
(M) *** Carlton IMP Dig. 3036 70097-2 [id.]. Delmé Qt – BRAHMS: *Clarinet quintet.* ***
(BB) *** CfP Silver Double CDCFPSD 4772 (2) [id.]. Gabrieli String Qt – BORODIN: *String quartet No. 2* ***; BRAHMS: *Clarinet quintet* **(*); SCHUBERT: *String quartet No. 14.* ***
*** EMI (SIS) Dig. CDC7 54215-2. Alban Berg Qt – SMETANA: *Quartet.* ***
(M) *** Classic fM 75605 57027-2. Chilingirian Qt – BORODIN: *Quartet No. 2;* SHOSTAKOVICH: *Quartet No. 8.* ***
(***) Testament mono SBT 1072 [id.]. Hollywood Qt – KODALY; SMETANA: *Quartets.* (***)
(M) **(*) DG (IMS) 437 251-2. Amadeus Qt. – SMETANA: *String quartet No. 1.* **(*)
**(*) Collins Dig. 1386-2 [id.]. Duke Qt (with BARBER: *Quartet;* GLASS: *Quartet No. 1.* **)

String quartet No. 12 (American); Cypresses.
*** DG Dig. (IMS) 419 601-2. Hagen Qt – KODALY: *Quartet No. 2.* ***

The Delmé Quartet on a superbly recorded Carlton IMP disc at bargain price give a winningly spontaneous-sounding performance, marked by unusually sweet matching of timbre between the players, which brings out the total joyfulness of Dvořák's American inspiration.

The Hagen Quartet make an uncommonly beautiful sound and their account of this masterly score is very persuasive indeed. Their playing is superbly polished, musical and satisfying, and they play the enchanting *Cypresses*, which Dvořák transcribed from the eponymous song-cycle, with great tenderness. The recording is altogether superb, very present and full-bodied.

Another thoroughly satisfying account of the *American quartet* from the Gabrielis, notable for its warmth, vitality and polish, and a touching account of the slow movement. As part of a Classics for Pleasure Silver Double it makes an outstanding reissue, given first-class 1973 sound, smoothly yet vividly transferred to CD.

The Alban Berg also give a very fine account of the *F major*, Op. 96. They have their finger on the vital current that carries its musical argument forward. Phrasing is dextrously shaped and the polish and elegance of their playing are never in danger of diminishing the spontaneous-seeming character of this music. In this respect they are perhaps less successful in the Smetana coupling. Very good recording, and thoroughly recommendable to admirers of this ensemble.

On Classic fM an excellent and generous coupling of three of the most popular Slavonic quartets in the repertory, with the Chilingirian Quartet giving powerful, incisive performances, though they are recorded a bit too forward. Levon Chilingirian's violin-tone is given a slight edge by the full, immediate recording. In the Dvořák the big contrasts of mood and atmosphere are brought out, with the slow movement yearningly beautiful and the fast movements given an infectious spring.

The Hollywood Quartet is pretty well self-recommending, and their account of the *F major Quartet*, Op. 96, is everything one would expect: impeccable in terms of execution, ensemble and taste. This was a quartet which brought real artistry to everything they played.

Although we have some reservations about Norbert Brainin's vibrato, which at times sounds self-conscious (especially in the slow movement), admirers of the Amadeus will certainly want their 1977 coupling of Dvořák and Smetana, recorded in Finland. This is a strongly conceived performance, full of ardour. The Scherzo and exhilarating finale show their brilliance of ensemble at its most appealing and infectious. The sound is vivid, full and immediate.

The Duke Quartet is handicapped by a curiously hybrid coupling: two American works, though it would have been better to have had a Schumann or Piston quartet along with Barber's celebrated piece rather than the empty Glass. They play the *F major Quartet* well, but not better than many rivals in the catalogue: they are very well recorded, though the balance is a bit forward.

String quartets Nos. 12 in F (American), Op. 96; 13 in G, Op. 106.
*** ASV Dig. CDDCA 797. Lindsay Qt.

In the *F major Quartet* (*American*) the Lindsays' account is certainly among the very best in terms of both performance and recording. The *G major*, Op. 106, is also very well played, with much the same dedication and sensitivity. An outstanding coupling.

String quartets Nos. 12 in F (American), Op. 96; 14 in A flat, Op. 105.
**(*) Chandos Dig. CHAN 8919 [id.].
Chilingirian Qt.

These Chilingirian performances are well up to the standard of their fine series, even if their version of the *American Quartet* would not be a first choice. The recording is first class and those needing this coupling will not be disappointed.

String quartet No. 12 in F (American), Op. 96; (i) *String quintet in E flat, Op. 97.*
*** Erato/Warner Dig. 4509 96968-2. Keller Qt; (i) with Anna Deeva.

Dvořák wrote the second of his string quintets, the one with extra viola, at the same period as the popular Opus 96 *Quartet*, similarly using thematic material with American inflexions, so that the two works make an apt and attractive coupling. The Keller Quartet give outstanding readings of both works, crisp and fanciful, with light, clear textures and with speeds generally on the fast side. The tenderness of the lyricism is beautifully caught in consistently imaginative phrasing, and the Erato recording is beautifully balanced.

String quartet No. 13 in G, Op. 106; Quartet movement in F, B.120; 2 Waltzes, Op. 54.
**(*) Chandos Dig. CHAN 8874 [id.].
Chilingirian Qt.

The playing of the Chilingirians has momentum and vitality and, though there are moments when they could make more of dynamic nuance, these are sympathetic and well-recorded performances. They include the *Quartet movement in F major* that Dvořák had originally intended for the piece, as well as two of the *Waltzes* he arranged from the Op. 54 piano pieces.

String quartet No. 14 in A flat, Op. 105.
*** Sony Dig. SK 53282 [id.]. Artis Qt –
SMETANA: *String quartet.* ***

String quartet No. 14 in A flat, Op. 105; Terzetto in C, Op. 74.
*** Testament SBT 1075 [id.]. Smetana Qt –
JANACEK: *String quartet No. 2.* ***

The Artis Quartet give one of the best accounts of the *A flat Quartet*, Op. 105, to have reached the catalogue since the Smetana Quartet recorded it in the early 1970s. It is ardent and expressive without being in the least overstated, and is compelling throughout. The Sony recording is in every way first class.

The Smetanas observe the traditional cut in the finale of Op. 105, from 11 bars before fig. 11 until 4 bars after fig. 12. This is a wonderful performance. Moreover it comes with the *Terzetto in C* for two violins and viola, a rarity in the concert hall, played freshly and elegantly , and their outstanding account of Janácek's *Intimate letters* which is new to the British catalogues.

String quintets: (i) *in G, Op. 77;* (ii) *in E flat, Op. 97.*
*** Bayer Dig. BR 100 184CD [id.]. Stamitz Qt, with (i) Jĩrí Hudec; (ii) Jan Talich.

String quintets in G, Op. 77; in E flat, Op. 97; Intermezzo in B, Op. 40.
*** Chandos Dig. CHAN 9046 [id.]. Chilingirian Qt with D. McTier.

Artistically, honours are pretty evenly divided between the Stamitz Quartet and the Chilingirians in the quintets. The Stamitz Quartet is perhaps balanced more forwardly but is pleasantly recorded, and the Chilingirian set on Chandos has more air round the sound but without any loss of focus. Both performances have the warmth and humanity that Dvořák exudes, but the Chilingirians undoubtedly score in including the beautiful *B major Intermezzo* that the composer had originally intended for the *G major Quintet* and which he subsequently expanded into an independent work for full strings, the *Nocturne*, Op. 40. This tips the balance in its favour.

String quintet in E flat, Op. 97; String sextet in A, Op. 48.

*** Hyperion Dig. CDA 66308 [id.]. Raphael Ens.

The *E flat major Quintet*, Op. 97, is one of the masterpieces of Dvořák's American years, and it is most persuasively given by the Raphael Ensemble, as is the coupled Sextet. It is also very well recorded, though we are placed fairly forward in the aural picture.

Piano duet

Slavonic dances Nos. 1–16, Op. 46/1–8; Op. 72/1–8.

(M) *** DG (IMS) 449 550-2. Alfons and Aloys Kontarsky.

(BB) *** Naxos Dig. 8.553138 [id.]. Silke-Thora Matthies, Christian Köhn.

Characteristically the excellent Kontarsky brothers offer crisp, clean performances and, more than usually, allow themselves the necessary rubato, conveying affection and joy along with their freshness (sample Nos. 4 and 5 of Op. 46, delightfully contrasted, or for sheer élan the *Furiant* of No. 8). The recording was made in the Berlin Jesus-Christus Kirche, where the engineers put their microphones in exactly the right place: there is just the right degree of resonance, yet no feeling that they are too near.

The brilliant piano duo of Matthies and Köhn are also most persuasive performers, radiating their own enjoyment, bringing out inner parts, giving transparency to even the thickest textures, subtly shading their tone and, above all, consistently springing rhythms infectiously, with an idiomatic feeling for Czech dance music. The forwardly balanced recording brings out the brightness of the piano while letting warmth of tone come forward in such gentler dances as No. 3 in D. An excellent bargain.

VOCAL AND CHORAL MUSIC

(i) *Requiem, Op. 89;* (ii) *6 Biblical songs from Op. 99.*

✿ (B) *** DG Double 453 073-2 (2) [437 377-2]. (i) Maria Stader, Sieglinde Wagner, Ernst Haefliger, Kim Borg, Czech PO & Ch., Karel Ančerl; (ii) Dietrich Fischer-Dieskau, Joerg Demus.

This superb DG set from 1959 brings an inspired performance of a work that can sound relatively conventional but which here emerges with fiery intensity, helped by a recording made in an appropriately spacious acoustic that gives an illusion of an electrifying live performance, without flaw. The passionate singing of the chorus is unforgettable, and the German soloists not only make fine individual contributions but blend together superbly in ensembles. Ančerl controls his forces with expert precision and the Czech chorus responds to the manner born. The balance between soloists, chorus and orchestra is particularly well handled in DG's best analogue manner. DG have added Fischer-Dieskau's 1960 recordings of six excerpts from Op. 99. He is at his superb best in these lovely songs. (The numbers included are: *Rings an den Herrn*; *Gott, erhöre meine inniges Flahen*; *Gott ist mein Hirte*; *An den Wassern zu Babylon*; *Wende dich zu mir*; and *Singet ein neues Lied.*) Joerg Demus accompanies sensitively, and the recording balance is most convincing.

(i) *Requiem, Op. 89;* (ii) *Mass in D, Op. 86.*

(B) *** Decca Double 448 089-2 (2) [id.]. (i) Lorengar, Komlóssy, Isofalvy, Krause, Amb. S., LSO, Kertész; (ii) Ritchie, Giles, Byers, Morton, Christ Church Cathedral Ch., Oxford, Cleobury (organ), Preston.

Kertész's fine (1968) account of Dvořák's *Requiem* acted as a distinguished pendant to his pioneering set of the symphonies, and it has comparable freshness. Kertész conducts with a total commitment to the score and secures from singers and orchestra an alert and sensitive response. The recording, which has the advantage of the Kingsway Hall ambience, has a lifelike balance, and for this Double Decca reissue the work has been sensibly recoupled with Simon Preston's beautifully shaped Christ Church account of the *Mass in D*, recorded six years later. In both works the CD remastering shows how good were the original recordings.

(i) *Stabat Mater, Op. 58*; (ii) *Legends Nos. 1–10, Op 59.*

(B) *** DG Double 453 025-2 (2) [id.]. (i) Mathis, Reynolds, Ochman, Shirley-Quirk, Bav. R. Ch. & SO; (ii) ECO; Kubelik.

Dvořák's devout Catholicism led him to treat this tragic religious theme with an open innocence that avoids sentimentality. Kubelik is consistently responsive and this is a work which benefits from his imaginative approach. The recording, made in the Munich Herkules-Saal, is of very good quality. The ten *Legends* are beautifully played by the ECO. This music ought to be better known, with its colourful scoring and folksy inspiration of a high order. One is often reminded of the *Slavonic dances*; although the prevailing mood is more amiable, there is no lack of sparkle. Again very good recording.

OPERA

Dimitrij (complete).

**(*) Sup. Dig. 11 1259-2 (3) [id.]. Vodĭcka, Drobková, Hajossyová, Aghová, Mikulas, Prague R. Ch., Czech PO Ch. and O, Albrecht.

Dimitrij, Dvořák's attempt to write a really grand opera, might be regarded as a sequel to *Boris Godunov*. As in Mussorgsky but in a less rugged way, Dvořák contrasts large-scale ensemble scenes with intimate ones full of lyrical ideas as ripely inspired as he ever conceived for an opera. The title-role is taken by the tenor, Leon Marian Vodĭcka, whose Slavonic timbre is very apt for the music, even if he is strained at times. Drahomira Drobková as Marfa and Magdalena Hajossyová as Marina sing strongly, but it is Livia Aghová as Xenia who with sweet, pure tone brings out the beauty of Dvořák's melodies more than anyone. Gerd Albrecht draws brilliant playing from the Czech Philharmonic, though the choral singing is less well disciplined. This recording follows a reconstruction of Dvořák's original score of 1882 and contains sections of the score never previously heard this century.

The Jacobin.

*** Sup. 11 2190-2 (2) [id.]. Zítek, Sounová, Přibyl, Machotková, Blachut, Prusa, Tŭcek, Berman, Katilena Children's Ch., Kuhn Ch., Brno State PO, Pinkas.

The background to *The Jacobin* is one of revolt and political turmoil, but Dvořák was more interested in individuals, so this is more a village comedy than a tract for the times. The sequence of exuberant, tuneful numbers, dances and choruses as well as arias, is more than enough to make the piece a delight on disc. Jĭri Pinkas draws lively and idiomatic performances from a first-rate cast, including such stalwarts as Vilem Přibyl as the hero (a little old-sounding but stylish) and the veteran tenor Beno Blachut giving a charming portrait of the heroine's father. Václav Zítek sings the heroic part of the Jacobin himself with incisive strength and Daniela Sounová is bright and clear as the heroine. The analogue sound is clear and firmly focused. A full libretto/translation is included.

The Jacobin: highlights.

(M) **(*) Sup. 11 2250-2 [id.] (from above complete recording, cond. Pinkas).

The highlights disc is at medium price and, with 62 minutes' playing time, makes a good sampler. However, there is no libretto included, not even a synopsis, which is unhelpful in an unfamiliar work of this kind.

Kate and the Devil (complete).

**(*) Sup. 11 1800-2 (2). Barová, Jĕzil, Novák, Sulcová, Suryová, Horácek, Brno Janácek Op. Ch. & O, Pinkas.

Attracted by the combination of folk element and fairy-tale, Dvořák began composing this opera in 1898, a charming comic fantasy about the girl who literally makes life hell for the devil who abducts her. It inspired a score that might almost be counted an operatic equivalent of his *Slavonic dances*, full of sharply rhythmic ideas, colourfully orchestrated. The role of Kate is very well taken by Anna Barová, firm and full-toned, with Jirka sung attractively by Milŏs Jĕzil, though his Slavonic tones are strained on top. The snag is the ill-focused singing of Richard Novák as the Devil, characterful enough but wobbly. Jĭri Pinkas persuasively brings out the fun and colour of the score, drawing excellent singing from the chorus; and the 1979 recording has plenty of space, agreeably warm and atmospheric. The libretto is well produced and clear, but assumes that the set is on three CDs instead of two with Acts II and III together on the second.

Rusalka (complete).

(N) ✿ *** Decca Dig. 460 568-2 (3) [id.]. Renée Fleming, Ben Heppner, Franz Hawlata, Dolora Zajick, Eva Urbanová, Ivan Kusnjer, Zdena Kloubová, Kühn Mixed Ch., Czech PO, Mackerras.

*** Sup. Dig. 10 3641-2 (3) [id.]. Bĕnăcková-Cápová, Novák, Soukupová, Ochman, Drobková, Prague Ch. & Czech PO, Neumann.

Dvořák's late masterpiece, *Rusalka*, is rapidly overtaking Smetana's *Bartered Bride* as the world's favourite Czech opera, and rightly so. Yet till now the only complete recordings have been domestic Czech ones, always idiomatic but indifferently recorded and vocally variable, with few international names. Here Decca offers not only ripely atmospheric sound but what in almost every way is the ideal cast, with the Czech Philharmonic incandescent under one of the world's leading Czech specialists, Sir Charles Mackerras.

The role of the lovelorn water-nymph, Rusalka, is one which has long held a special place in the affections of Renée Fleming, and she gives a heartfelt performance, having performed it on stage many times. That experience is reflected in the intensity of her sharply detailed performance, with the voice consistently beautiful over the widest range. Both the pathos and the vulnerability of the heroine are movingly brought out. Ben Heppner too, with his powerful tenor at once lyrical and heroic, is ideally cast, also a singer with long stage experience of his role as the Prince. Franz Hawlata as the Watergnome, Rusalka's father, and Dolora Zajick as the witch, Ježibaba, are both outstanding too, with even the smaller roles cast from strength, using leading singers from the Prague Opera. In his inspired conducting Mackerras does not resist the obvious Wagnerian overtones, bringing out in the love music the sensuous echoes of the *Tristan* love duet. Yet Czech flavours are never underplayed in the many colourful dance rhythms.

Dvořák's fairy-tale opera is also given a magical performance by Neumann and his Czech forces, helped by full, brilliant and atmospheric recording. The title-role is superbly taken by Gabriela Běnačková-Cápová, and the famous *Invocation to the Moon* is enchanting. Vera Soukupová as the Witch is just as characterfully Slavonic in a lower register, though not so even; while Wieslaw Ochman sings with fine, clean, heroic tone as the Prince, with timbre made distinctive by tight vibrato. Richard Novák brings out some of the Alberich-like overtones as the Watersprite, though the voice is not always steady. The banding could be more generous, but a full translation is included. However the Decca set makes a clear first choice.

Rusalka: highlights.
(M) **(*) Sup. Dig. 11 2252-2 [id.] (from above complete recording; cond. Neumann).

This is a first-class selection, including, of course, the famous *Invocation to the moon* and offering an hour of music. But the current mid-priced reissue has neither libretto nor synopsis, merely a list of the excerpts.

Dyson, George (1883–1964)

(i)*Violin concerto. Children's suite* (after Walter De La Mare).
❀ *** Chandos Dig. CHAN 9369 [id.]. (i) Mordkovitch; City of L. Sinfonia, Hickox.

Completed in 1941, Dyson's *Violin concerto* is a richly inspired, warmly lyrical work that readily sustains its 43-minute span. Not that the extended first movement, *Molto moderato*, lacks dark undercurrents and the third-movement *Andante* for violin and muted strings, divided into variations, brings a rare hushed beauty, superbly achieved in this dedicated performance. Lydia Mordkovitch gives a reading both passionate and deeply expressive. The *Children's suite* of 1924 has four sharply characterized movements, inspired by De La Mare poems. In its lighter way it reflects similar qualities to those in the concerto, not least a tendency to switch into waltz-time and a masterly ability to create rich and transparent orchestral textures, beautifully caught in the opulent Chandos recording. Two rarities to treasure.

(i) *Concierto leggiero* (for piano & strings); *Concerto da camera; Concerto da chiesa* (both for string orchestra).
*** Chandos Dig. CHAN 9076 [id.]. (i) Eric Parkin; City of L. Sinfonia, Hickox.

Until now we have been inclined to think of Dyson as essentially a composer of vocal music, but this splendid Chandos CD rights the balance and brings not only an engagingly light-textured concertante item for piano but also two powerful and eloquent works in the great tradition of English string music. All these pieces belong to the composer's last composing years and date from 1949/51. The writing shows both a strongly burning creative flame as well as new influences from outside. The performances here are wonderfully fresh and committed and the string recording has plenty of bite and full sonority, while the balance with the piano is quite admirable. Highly recommended.

Symphony in D.
*** Chandos Dig. CHAN 9200 [id.]. City of L. Sinfonia, Richard Hickox.

Dyson's *Symphony*, composed in 1937, was played in the 1940s and then forgotten. Its best movement by far is the third, an attractive and diverse theme and variations. The finale is confident in its use of ideas from *The Canterbury Pilgrims* with majestic scoring for the brass, but the charming second-movement *Andante* is rather slight and the first movement, marked *Energico*, flags . An enjoyable piece, nevertheless, very well played and resonantly and realistically recorded, in the way of Chandos, but not an essential acquisition, except for those especially attracted to this composer.

(Organ) *Fantasia and Ground bass. 3 Choral hymns; Hierusalem; Psalm 150; 3 Songs of praise.*
*** Hyperion CDA 66150 [id.]. Valery Hill, St Michael's Singers, Thomas Trotter, RPO, Jonathan Rennert.

Where the organ piece unashamedly builds on an academic model, *Hierusalem* reveals the inner man more surprisingly, a richly sensuous setting of a medieval poem inspired by the thought of the Holy City, building to a jubilant climax. It is a splendid work, and is backed here by the six hymns and the Psalm setting, all of them heartwarming products of the Anglican tradition. Performances are outstanding, with Rennert drawing radiant singing and playing from his team, richly and atmospherically recorded.

(i; ii) *The Canterbury Pilgrims. Overture at the Tabard Inn;* (i) *In honour of the city.*
*** Chandos Dig. CHAN 9531 (2) [id.]. (i) Yvonne Kenny, Robert Tear, Stephen Roberts; (ii) London Symphony Ch.; LSO, Hickox.

At last Chandos provide us with the long-awaited recording of Dyson's best-known work, preceded by the Overture based on its themes. Here the soloists all have major contributions to make, for Dyson's characterization of the individual pilgrims is strong; but the glory of the piece is the choruses, which are splendidly sung here. The recording was made soon after a live performance at the Barbican in September 1996 and carries through the spontaneity of that occasion. *In honour of the city*, Dyson's setting of William Dunbar, appeared in 1928, nine years before Walton's version of the same text; Dyson, however, unlike Walton, uses a modern version of the text, as he does in *The Canterbury Tales*, and to fine direct effect. The splendid Chandos recording is fully worthy of the vibrant music-making here.

Eckhard, Johann Gottfried
(1735–1809)

Keyboard sonatas, Op. 1/1–3; Op. 2/1–2; in G; Menuet d'Exaudet with variations.
(B) *** Koch Discovery Dig. DICD 920392 [id.]. Brigitte Haudebourg (fortepiano).

Johann Gottfried Eckhard's published keyboard sonatas included on this disc are forward-looking and embody expressive and dynamic markings characteristic of the piano. His music is often inventive and, although of no great originality, is persuasively played by Brigitte Haudebourg, and decently recorded. Not an issue that will set the pulse racing but nevertheless quite rewarding in its way.

Egk, Werner (1901–83)

The Temptation of St Anthony (cantata).
(M) *** DG (IMS) 449 097-2. Dame Janet Baker, Koeckert Qt, Bav. RSO (strings), composer – ORFF: *Catulli Carmina.* ***

Egk's *Temptation of St Anthony* shows him at his best: it is in effect a song-cycle, and Dame Janet Baker who was in particularly good voice at this period of her career (the mid 1960s), sings it with great beauty. The recording, too, is good, and this can be recommended as a good sampler for those who want to investigate Egk's music for themselves.

Eisler, Hanns (1898–1962)

Deutsche Sinfonie, Op. 50.
(N) *** Decca Dig. 448 389-2 [id.]. Hendrijke Wangemann, Annette Markert, Matthias Görne, Peter Lika, Gert Gütschow, Volker Schwarz, Ernst Senff Ch. Leipzig Gewandhaus O, Lothar Zagrosek.

More talked about than played, the *Deutsche Sinfonie* is hailed as Eisler's most important work. Subtitled 'An anti-fascist cantata', it consists of 11 disparate movements mostly composed during Eisler's period of exile after the Nazis came to power. The first two (comprising 'an Anti-Hitler Symphony') were ready for performance in 1936, and all the vocal movements of the symphony (save for the Epilogue) were ready by the following year. The *Étude* for orchestra that constitutes the third was written in 1930 and used in the first Orchestral suite, while the *Epilogue* (1957) was subtracted from the *Bilder aus der Kriegsfibel* inspired by Brecht. In all seven of the movements are Brecht settings. Despite its unusual provenance, the work seems to hang together and for all the reminders of Shostakovich, Hindemith and Mahler, it makes a strong impression. Eisler's is not a strongly individual voice but this piece is worth getting to know. The various soloists and the two speaking roles are as impressive as the orchestral playing, which is scrupulously prepared. The recording is state-of-the-art.

Prelude and fugue on B-A-C-H for string trio, Op. 46; String quartet, Op. 75.
(N) *** CPO Dig. CPO 999 341-2 [id.]. Leipzig Qt – ADORNO: *String quartet; 2 Pieces, Op. 2; 6 Studies.* ***

Hanns Eisler wrote relatively little chamber music. The *Prelude and fugue on B-A-C-H* comes from 1934, the year after he left Berlin for the United States, and the *String quartet* was written four years later. Rather anonymous music, composed at the time he was renewing his faith in his teacher Schoenberg.

'The Hollywood Songbook': Anakreontische Fragmente; An den kleinen Radioapparat; Auf der Flucht; Automne californian; 5 Elegien; Epitaph aud einen in der Flandernschlacht Gefallenen; Erinnerung an Eichendorff und Schumann; Die Flucht; Frühling; Gedenktafel für 4000 Soldaten; Die Heimkehr; Hollywood-Elégie No. 7; Hölderlin-Fragmente; Hotelzimmer 1942; In den Weiden; Der Kirschdieb; Die Landschaft des Exils; Die letzte Elégie; 2 Lieder nach Wofrten von Pascal; Die Maske des Bösen; Der Mensch; Nightmare; Ostersonntag; Panzerschlacht; Der Schatzgräber; Der Sohn; Speisekammer 1942; Spruch; Uber den Selbstmond; Vom Sprengen des Gartens; Winterspruch.
(N) Decca Dig. 460 582-2 [id.]. Matthias Gorne, Erich Schneider.

Like many other German composers fleeing from the Nazis, Hanns Eisler went to Los Angeles, but unlike many reacted violently against the culture of Hollywood. So it is that the 'Hollywood Songbook', far from being a celebration, is a collection of Lieder reflecting bitterness, cynicism and disillusion. This disc offers a mixed group of 46 brief songs, mainly to words by Bertolt Brecht who, like Eisler, returned after the war to live in Communist East Germany. These songs both reflect Eisler's studies with Schoenberg and a desire to communicate directly, standing very much in the central tradition of the German Lied, which Eisler felt was in direct conflict with everything that Hollywood represented. Matthias Goerne is an ideal interpreter with his incisive baritone and feeling for words, very well accompanied by Eric Schneider.

Elgar, Edward (1857–1934)

(i–ii) *Adieu; Beau Brummel: Minuet;* (i; iii) *3 Bavarian dances, Op. 27; Caractacus, Op. 35: Woodland interlude. Chanson de matin; Chanson de nuit, Op. 15/1–2; Contrasts, Op. 10/3; Dream children, Op. 43;* (iv) *Enigma variations, Op. 36;* (i; iii) *Falstaff, Op. 68: 2 Interludes.* (iv) *Pomp and circumstance marches Nos. 1–5, Op. 39;* (i; iii) *Salut d'amour; Sérénade lyrique;* (i; iii; v) *Soliloquy for oboe* (orch. Gordon Jacob); (i–ii) *Sospiri, Op. 70; The Spanish Lady: Burlesco. The Starlight Express: Waltz. Sursum corda, Op. 11.*
(N) (B) *** Chandos 2-for-1 Dig. CHAN 241-4 (2) [id.]. (i) Bournemouth Sinf.; (ii) George Hurst; (iii) Norman Del Mar; (iv) RSNO, Gibson; (v) with Leon Goossens.

At the centre of this Chandos Double is Sir Alexander Gibson's reading of *Enigma*, which has stood the test of time and remains very satisfying, warm and spontaneous in feeling, with a memorable climax in *Nimrod*. The 1978 recording, made in Glasgow's City Hall, remains outstanding, with the organ sonorously filling out the bass in the finale, which has real splendour. The *Pomp and circumstance marches*, too, have fine *nobilmente* and swagger. The rest of the programme is a collection of miniatures directed either by George Hurst or Norman Del Mar – both understanding Elgarians. The special treasure is the *Soliloquy* which Elgar wrote right at the end of his life for Leon Goossens. Here the dedicatee plays it with his long-recognizable tone-colour and feeling for phrase, in an orchestration by Gordon Jacob. Most of the other pieces in Norman Del Mar's programme are well known, but they come up with new warmth and commitment here, and the 1976 recording made in the Guildhall, Southampton, has an appealing ambient warmth and naturalness. George Hurst recorded his Elgar rarities a year earlier in Christchurch Priory and again the recording has plenty of body, but there is more thinness in the sound of the violins in these items than with Del Mar.

'*A portrait of Elgar': 3 Bavarian dances, Op. 27; Carissima; Chanson de matin; Chanson de nuit, Op. 15/1–2; Cockaigne overture, Op. 40; Dream children, Op. 43; Enigma variations, Op. 36; Froissart overture, Op. 19; Gavotte (Contrasts), Op. 10/3; Introduction and allegro for strings, Op. 47; May song; Mazurka, Op. 10/1; Nursery suite; Pomp and circumstance marches Nos. 1–5, Op. 39; Rosemary ('That's for remembrance'); Sérénade lyrique; Serenade for strings, Op. 20; Salut d'amour, Op. 12; Spanish Lady (suite); The Wand of youth suite No. 2, Op. 1b.*
(B) **(*) Nimbus Dig. NI 1769 (4) [id.]. E. SO or E. String O, William Boughton.

This very inexpensive four-disc set is made up of four separate Elgar collections, and Disc 3 duplicates the *Chanson de matin* and *Chanson de nuit*, already included on Disc 2. However, the latter collection (including the *Nursery suite* plus the *Dream children* and most of the miniatures) is particularly attractive, for William Boughton's performances are graceful and sympathetic and have plenty of character. The *Introduction and allegro* has a ripely overwhelming climax, but the fugal argument is not lost. The *Enigma variations* have many pleasingly delicate touches of colour with the brass and organ making a fine effect in the finale. There is an easy swagger about the *Pomp and circumstance marches*. The warmly reverberant acoustic of the Great Hall of Birmingham University gives the performances of these larger-scale works a spacious scale that is entirely apt. What is more questionable is the scale conveyed by the recording (in the same acoustic) for the other lighter and more intimate pieces. The manner is sparkling, the playing refined and well detailed, with rhythms nicely sprung, but the large scale implied tends to inflate the music, particularly in the *Wand of youth* excerpts.

3 Bavarian dances, Op. 27; 3 Characteristic pieces, Op. 10; Chanson de nuit; Chanson de matin, Op. 15/1–2; (i) *Violin concerto in B min., Op. 61. Crown of India (suite), Op. 66; Enigma variations, Op. 36; Nursery suite; Severn suite; Wand of youth suites 1–2, Op. 1a/b; The Light of Life: Meditation.* arr. of Bach: *Fantasia & fugue in C min., Op. 86;* (ii) (Choral) *The Banner of St George: It comes from the misty ages. Land of hope and glory.* Arrangements of Croft: *O God, our help in ages past. National anthem.*
(***) EMI mono CDS7 54564-2 (3). LSO, Royal Albert Hall O, New SO or LPO, composer, with (i) Y. Menuhin; (ii) Philharmonic Ch.

Volume 2 of the Elgar Edition centres on the two masterpieces which make up the first of the three discs: the *Enigma variations* in the 1926 recording with the Royal Albert Hall Orchestra, volatile and passionate, and the 16-year-old Menuhin's classic reading of the *Violin concerto*, as fresh and intense as ever. The *Wand of Youth*, *Nursery* and *Severn suites* make up the second disc, with Elgar sparkling as a conductor. The third disc of shorter works includes a number of rarities, all of them revealing. Excellent transfers and background notes.

Beau Brummel: minuet (2 versions); (i) *Caractacus: Woodland interlude and Triumphal march, Op. 35; Carissima;* (ii) *Cello concerto in*

E min, Op. 85; Cockaigne: concert overture, Op. 40 (2 versions); (iii) *Coronation march, Op. 65; Elegy, Op. 58; Falstaff: interludes, Op. 68; Froissart: concert overture, Op. 19; In the South: concert overture, Op. 50; Land of hope and glory; The Kingdom: prelude, Op. 51; May song;* (iv) *Mina* (2 versions); *Minuet, Op. 21; Pomp and circumstance marches Nos. 1–5, Op. 39* (2 versions); *Rosemary; Salut d'amour, Op. 12; Sérénade in E min., Op. 20; Sérénade lyrique;* (v) *5 Piano Improvisations.*

(***) EMI mono CDS7 54568-2 (3). LPO, Royal Albert Hall O, LSO or New SO, composer, with (i) Collingwood; (ii) Beatrice Harrison; (iii) Ronald; (iv) Murray, Wood; (v) composer (piano).

This third and last issue of EMI's Elgar Edition centres on the *Cello concerto* (with Beatrice Harrison as soloist in another urgent performance) and the overtures, *Froissart* and *In the South* as well as *Cockaigne*. The most fascinating contrast is between the two versions of the overture, *Cockaigne*. His remake in 1933 with the recently founded BBC Symphony Orchestra is far more polished; but the earlier (1926) performance has a more intense emotional thrust. The incidental items are fascinating too, including multiple versions of the *Pomp and circumstance marches* and two *Caractacus* excerpts conducted by Lawrance Collingwood, which Elgar supervised by telephone from his sick-bed only a month before he died. Yet the items which give the most intimate portrait of Elgar are the five improvisations that he recorded at the piano in 1929. It is also good to have the soundtrack recording from the Pathé newsreel covering the opening of the Abbey Road studio. Preparing to conduct *Land of hope and glory*, Elgar asks the LSO to 'play this tune as though you've never heard it before'. Transfers are astonishingly clear and full, though at times the background hiss is higher than in previous volumes.

'*The lighter Elgar*': (i) *Beau Brummel: Minuet;* (ii) *Carissima;* (i) *Chanson de matin, Op. 15/2;* (ii) *3 Characteristic pieces, Op. 10: Mazurka; Sérénade mauresque; Contrasts: The Gavottes AD 1700 & 1900;* (i) *Dream children, Op. 43/1–2;* (ii) *May song; Mina; Minuet, Op. 21; Rosemary (That's for remembrance);* (ii; iii) *Romance for bassoon and orchestra, Op. 62;* (i) *Salut d'amour, Op. 12;* (ii) *Sevillana, Op. 7; Sérénade lyrique;* (i; iv) *The Starlight Express, Op. 78:* Organ grinder's songs: *My old tunes; To the children.* (i) *The Wand of Youth suite No. 1:* excerpt: *Sun dance.*

❁ (M) *** EMI CDM5 65593-2. (i) RPO, Lawrance Collingwood; (ii) N. Sinfonia, Marriner; with (iii) Michael Chapman; (iv) Frederick Harvey.

This beautifully recorded CD combines almost all the contents of two LPs. In the first (originally called '*The Miniature Elgar*') the orchestral playing under Lawrance Collingwood is especially sympathetic. Frederick Harvey joins the orchestra for two organ grinder's songs from the incidental music for *The Starlight Express*, and they have seldom been sung more winningly on record. It is these items one remembers most, but the second collection under Sir Neville Marriner is hardly less successful. All the music is pleasingly delightful in its tender moods and restrained scoring, favouring flute, bassoon and the clarinet in middle or lower register. A boisterous piece like *Sevillana* may be rather conventional but it has Elgar's characteristic exuberance, which represents the other side of the coin. Very much worth having is the rhapsodic *Romance for bassoon and orchestra* with Michael Chapman the elegant soloist. The Northern Sinfonia play with style and affection. Throughout, EMI have provided that warm, glowing sound that is their special province in recording Elgar's music, and the CD transfers bring out all the bloom one remembers on the analogue LPs. Not to be missed.

(i) *Chanson de matin; Chanson de nuit, Op. 15;* (iii; iv) *Enigma variations;* (iii; ii) *In the South (Alassio), Op. 50;* (iii; iv) *Pomp and circumstance march No. 5;* (iii) *The Starlight Express, Op. 78;* Songs: *My old tunes; To the children.*

(N) (M) *** Dutton Lab. mono CDK 1203 [id.] (i) Boyd Neel String O; (ii) Boyd Neel; (iii) National SO; (iv) Sir Malcolm Sargeant; (v) with Henry Cummings, cond Sir Charles Groves.

Boyd Neel's account of *In the South* has a fine thrusting impetus, and in that respect is only surpassed (if it is), by Silvestri's famous Bournemouth version. More than that, it is most perceptively characterized, with the gentle central interludes warmly delicate and tender, and the Roman juggernaut section as powerful as you could wish. It sounds totally spontaneous, as does Sargent's *Enigma*, full of Elgarian character, warmth and colour – his finest performance on disc. The playing of the National Symphony Orchestra is most responsive. There is much romantic delicacy of feeling, yet the cello variation has great ardour, and the powerful climax of *Nimrod* is superbly controlled. The finale makes a thrilling culmination, and it is followed by the ripest, most *nobilmente* account of the underrated *Fifth Pomp and circumstance march* on record (which was the fill-up, side 8 of the 78 r.p.m. set). The *Chansons* are played with affectionate finesse, and the disc ends with the two charming (and inspired) *Organ grinders' songs* from *The Starlight Express*, sung with great character (and splendid diction) by Henry Cummings in a style of received pronunciation that belongs to a bygone era. Those original 1945 *ffrr* 78s of *Enigma* and the march were astonishingly real (at times almost like stereo), and as always the Dutton transfers are marvellously full and vivid). Sargeant was recorded in the Kingsway Hall, Boyd Neel's *In the South* a month later, at Wembley Town Hall, where the balance brings less body to the strings, and less weight in the bass. But the sound is still pretty impressive. The *Chansons* and songs were recorded in the drier acoustic of Broadhurst Gardens, but still sound fresh and clear.

(i) *Cockaigne overture;* (ii) *Cello concerto in E min.;* (iii) *Violin concerto;* (i) *Enigma variations, Op. 36;* (iv) *Pomp and circumstance marches Nos. 1–5, Op. 39.*

(B) *** Sony Take 2 SB2K 63247 (2) [S2K 63247]. (i) Phd. O, Ormandy; (ii) Jacqueline du Pré, Phd. O, Barenboim; (iii) Zukerman, LPO, Barenboim; (iv) Philh. O, Andrew Davis.

Jacqueline du Pré's outstanding second recording of the Elgar *Cello concerto* is discussed below, as is Zukerman's ardent account of the *Violin concerto*, recorded six years later – also with Barenboim. Andrew Davis brings plenty of imaginative flair to the five *Pomp and circumstance marches* and is sumptuously recorded. Ormandy's view of *Enigma* is characteristically forthright, lacking some Elgarian nuance – although *Nimrod* is finely shaped – but, with the help of glorious Philadelphia string-playing, urgently convincing just the same. Ormandy paints his picture of Edwardian London with even broader strokes of the brush in vivid primary colours and the Philadelphia players rise to his exultant direction. Again the expansively resonant sound adds to the sense of spectacle.

Cockaigne overture, Op. 40; Enigma variations, Op. 36; Introduction and allegro for strings; Serenade for strings, Op. 20.

✿ *** Teldec/Warner Dig. 9031 73279-2 [id.]. BBC SO, Andrew Davis.

Andrew Davis's collection of favourite Elgar works is electrifying. The very opening of *Cockaigne* has rarely been so light and sprightly, and it leads on to the most powerful characterization of each contrasted section. The two string works are richly and sensitively done. Similarly the big tonal contrasts in *Enigma* are dramatically brought out, notably in Davis's rapt and spacious reading of *Nimrod*, helped by the spectacular Teldec recording. This is surely a worthy successor to Barbirolli in this repertoire and is an outstanding disc in every way.

(i) *Cockaigne overture, Op. 40;* (ii) *Froissart overture, Op. 19; Pomp and circumstance marches, Op. 39, Nos* (i) *1 in D;* (ii) *2 in A min.; 3 in C min.;* (i) *4 in G;* (ii) *5 in C.*

(M) *** EMI CDM5 66323-2. (i) Philh. O; (ii) New Philh. O; Barbirolli.

It is good to have *Cockaigne*, Barbirolli's ripe yet wonderfully vital portrait of Edwardian London, back in the catalogue – one of the finest of all his Elgar records. *Froissart* is very compelling too (though the CD transfer is slightly less flattering here), and Barbirolli makes a fine suite of the five *Pomp and circumstance marches*. The lesser-known Nos. 2 and 5 are particularly gripping, with plenty of contrast in No. 4 to offset the swagger elsewhere. Here the sound is as expansive as you could wish.

Cockaigne overture, Op. 40; Introduction and allegro for strings, Op. 47; Serenade for strings, Op. 20.

(N) (M) (***) EMI mono CMS5 66543-2 (2). Hallé O, Barbirolli – VAUGHAN WILLIAMS: *Oboe concerto; Tuba concerto; Sinfonia antartica;* etc. (***)

Barbirolli later recorded all three of these works in stereo, but these mono versions from the early postwar period have an immediacy and positive strength rarely matched. Transfers are vivid and clear, with fine detail, only rarely thin or edgy. With the important Vaughan Williams recordings, an outstanding double-disc issue.

Cello concerto in E min., Op. 85.

✿ *** EMI CDC5 56219-2 [CDC 56219]. Du Pré, LSO, Barbirolli – *Sea Pictures*. *** ✿

*** EMI CDC5 55527-2 [id.]. Jacqueline du Pré, LSO, Barbirolli – DVORAK: *Cello concerto*. **(*)

(M) *** Sony Dig. SMK 53333 [id.]. Yo-Yo Ma, LSO, Previn – WALTON: *Cello concerto*. ***

(M) (***) Revelation mono RV 10100 [id.]. Rostropovich, Moscow PO, Rakhlin – BRITTEN: *Cello symphony*. (***)

(BB) *** CfP Silver Double CDCFPSD 4775 (2) [id.]. Robert Cohen, LPO, Del Mar – BEETHOVEN: *Triple concerto;* DVORAK: *Cello concerto;* TCHAIKOVSKY: *Variations on a rococo theme*. ***

*** BIS Dig. CD 486 [id.]. Torleif Thedéen, Malmö SO, Markiz – SCHUMANN: *Concerto*. ***

*** Finlandia Dig. 4509 95768-2 [id.]. Arto Noras, Finnish RSO, Saraste – LALO: *Cello concerto*. ***

(M) **(*) Carlton Dig. 30366 0011-2 [id.]. Tortelier, RPO, Groves – DVORAK: *Rondo;* TCHAIKOVSKY: *Rococo variations*. ***

(N) **(*) RCA 09026 61695-2 [id.]. János Starker, Philharmonia Orch, Slatkin – DELIUS: *Caprice & Elegy* ***; WALTON: *Cello concerto*. **(*)

(N) (BB) *** Virgin Classics Dig. VBD5 61490-2 [CDVB 61490] [id.]. Steven Isserlis, LSO, Hickox – BLOCH: *Schelomo;* KABALEVSKY: *Cello concerto No. 2;* R. STRAUSS: *Don*

Quixote; TCHAIKOVSKY: *Rococo variations*, etc. ***

(**(*)) EMI mono CDH7 63498-2 [id.]. Casals, BBC SO, Boult – DVORAK: *Concerto* (***) (with BRUCH: *Kol Nidrei* (***)).

(i) *Cello concerto;* (ii) *Cockaigne overture, Op. 40; Enigma variations, Op. 36.*

*** Sony SK 76529. (i) Du Pré, Phd. O; (ii) LPO; Barenboim.

(i) *Cello concerto. Enigma variations, Op. 36.*

*** Ph. Dig. 416 354-2. (i) Julian Lloyd Webber; RPO, Menuhin.

Jacqueline du Pré was essentially a spontaneous artist. Her style is freely rhapsodic, but the result produced a very special kind of meditative feeling; in the very beautiful slow movement, brief and concentrated, her inner intensity conveys a depth of espressivo rarely achieved by any cellist on record. Brilliant virtuoso playing too in the Scherzo and finale. CD brings a subtle extra definition to heighten the excellent qualities of the 1965 recording, with the solo instrument firmly placed.

Alongside the original pairing with Dame Janet Baker's *Sea pictures*, EMI have now given an alternative coupling with the Dvořák *Concerto*, and this much-loved recording is given extra warmth and clarity in the new transfer. However, we retain our allegiance to the original pairing, which was earlier revamped when it won a platinum disc award.

In its rapt concentration Yo-Yo Ma's recording with Previn is second only to Du Pré. The first movement is lighter, a shade more urgent than the Du Pré/Barbirolli version, and in the Scherzo he finds more fun, just as he finds extra sparkle in the main theme of the finale. The key movement with Ma, as it is with du Pré, is the *Adagio*, echoed later in the raptness of the slow epilogue, poised in its intensity. Warm, fully detailed recording, finely balanced, with understanding conducting from Previn. At mid-price a splendid bargain.

The Philips coupling of the *Cello concerto* and the *Enigma variations*, the two most popular of Elgar's big orchestral works, featuring two artists inseparably associated with Elgar's music, made the disc an immediate bestseller, and rightly so. These are both warmly expressive and unusually faithful readings, the more satisfying for fidelity to the score, and Julian Lloyd Webber in his playing has never sounded warmer or more relaxed on record, well focused in the stereo spectrum.

Jacqueline du Pré's second recording of the Elgar *Cello concerto* was taken from live performances in Philadelphia in November 1970, and this is a superb picture of an artist in full flight, setting her sights on the moment in the Epilogue where the slow-movement theme returns, the work's innermost sanctuary of repose. Barenboim's most distinctive point in *Enigma* is in giving the delicate variations sparkle and emotional point, while the big variations have full weight, and the finale brings extra fierceness at a fast tempo. *Cockaigne* is comparably lively and colourful. The sound of the CBS transfer lacks something in body and amplitude.

The mid-priced Revelation disc offers an early account from Rostropovich, made 40 years ago, which demonstrates that his inspirational style regularly sounds like a concentrated improvisation. In the main arguments of each movement Rostropovich uses the widest dynamic range, conveying a raptly reflective intensity, full of poignancy, to match even du Pré. Rakhlin proves a most sensitive Elgarian and has great feeling for the reticence and longing that this music conveys. The cello is far too forwardly balanced, making the orchestra sound dim by comparison, but the warmth of the reading is powerfully conveyed. It is in mono, though nowhere on the label or sleeve do Revelation say so.

Robert Cohen's performance is strong and intense, with steady tempi, the colouring more positive and less autumnal than usual. The ethereal half-tones at the close of the first movement are matched by the gently elegiac poignancy of the *Adagio*. Del Mar's accompaniment is wholly sympathetic, underlining the soloist's approach and his songful line. The 1978 Walthamstow recording is wide-ranging and brilliant but shows Cohen's tone as bright and well focused rather than especially resonant in the bass.

Two Nordic views of the Elgar *Cello concerto* come from BIS and Finlandia. The former offer the young Swedish virtuoso, Torleif Thedéen, splendidly recorded with the Malmö orchestra, and the latter brings his Finnish colleague, Arto Noras, with Finnish Radio forces; both artists seem completely attuned to the Elgar sensibility. Thedéen has a nobility and reticence that are strongly appealing and Noras is hardly less impressive. Neither will disappoint; both enrich and do justice to the Elgar discography.

Tortelier's latest version of the Elgar, now reappearing on Carlton, was originally issued to celebrate the cellist's 75th birthday in March 1989. It may not be as firm and powerful as his earlier account with Boult: in the finale the septuagenarian shows signs of strain; but the performance has a spontaneity and a new tenderness which make it very compelling.

János Starker in his seventies here turns to English repertory not previously associated with him, offering performances which reflect both the understanding and intellectual strength that has always marked his playing. In the Elgar his tough, slightly wiry tone goes with a relatively objective approach, with flowing speeds generally kept steady, and Slatkin, as in his other Elgar recordings, shows his natural feeling for the idiom. Well-balanced sound.

The most distinctive point about Steven

Isserlis's version of Elgar's *Cello concerto* on Virgin is his treatment of the slow movement, not so much elegiac as songful. Using a mere thread of tone, with vibrato unstressed, the simplicity of line and the unforced beauty are brought out. The very placing of the solo instrument goes with that, rather more distant than is usual, with the refinement of Elgar's orchestration beautifully caught by both conductor and engineers. Now reissued as part of a Virgin Double covering concertante cello works by five different composers, this is an almost irresistible bargain.

Casals recorded the Elgar *Cello concerto* in London in 1946, and the fervour of his playing caused some raised eyebrows. A powerful account, not least for Sir Adrian's contribution, even though its eloquence would have been even more telling were the emotion recollected in greater tranquillity. A landmark of the gramophone all the same, and the strongly characterized Max Bruch *Kol Nidrei* makes a fine encore.

(i) *Cello concerto in E min., Op. 85;* (ii) *Violin concerto in B min., Op. 61.*
(B) (***) Avid mono AMSC 587 [id.]. (i) Pablo Casals, BBC SO, Sir Adrian Boult; (ii) Albert Sammons, New Queen's Hall O, Sir Henry Wood.

In some ways Albert Sammons's 1929 recording of the *Violin concerto* has never been surpassed, though of course Menuhin's with the composer himself is also very special. The first Avid CD transfer of these recordings was singularly unsuccessful. But the second, current version is infinitely superior. The sound in both works is now excellent, the *Cello concerto* full and with the soloist firmly focused, the *Violin concerto* even more remarkable in its warmth and natural clarity, with the solo violin vividly and cleanly caught. Sammons's high level of concentration and atmospheric magnetism generated in the unsurpassed account of the finale comes over very directly to complete a remarkably compelling listening experience.

(i) *Cello concerto in E min., Op. 85. Elegy, Op. 58. Enigma variations, Op. 36; Introduction and allegro, Op. 47.*
❁ (M) *** EMI stereo/mono CDM7 63955-2 [id.]. (i) Navarra, Hallé O, Barbirolli.

This Hallé version of the *Enigma variations* was recorded in the Manchester Free Trade Hall in 1956 by the Mercury team: the sound is extraordinarily good, and the performance is revealed as Barbirolli's finest account ever on record. He generates powerful fervour and an irresistible momentum: at the very end, the organ entry brings an unforgettable, tummy-wobbling effect which engulfs the listener thrillingly. The *Introduction and allegro* is mono and, though not quite so impressively recorded, has comparable passion. The concert closes with a moving account of the *Elegy*, simple and affectionate. In between comes Navarra's strong and firm view of the *Cello concerto*. With his control of phrasing and wide range of tone-colour this 1957 performance culminates in a most moving account of the Epilogue.

(i) *Cello concerto in E min., Op. 85. Enigma variations, Op. 36; Serenade for strings, Op. 20.*
(N) (M) *** Penguin Classics DG Dig. 460 624-2 [id.]. (i) Mischa Maisky; Philh. O, Sinopoli.

Maisky is highly persuasive in the *Cello concerto* and, with Sinopoli a willing partner, gives a warmly nostalgic performance, essentially valedictory in feeling. The slow movement is deeply felt, but not in an extrovert way, and the soloist's dedication is mirrored in the finale. The mood of the *Concerto* is carried over into the other works here. The lyrical variations of *Enigma* are expressively relaxed and *Nimrod* has a simple direct nobility. Though Sinopoli avoids the usual speeding-up at the end of the finale, the thrust of that and the other vigorous climaxes is pressed home passionately. The *Serenade* is similarly expansive, and some may feel that the *Larghetto*, for all its sympathetic feeling, is too measured. The rich recording adds to the character of the readings, with the Philharmonia strings on particular playing superbly. The descriptive essay is written by Rosamund Pilcher.

Violin concerto in B min., Op. 61.
(N) *** EMI Dig. CDC5 56413-2 [id.]. Kennedy, CBSO, Rattle – VAUGHAN WILLIAMS: *The lark ascending.* ***
(M) *** EMI CDM7 64725-2. Lord Menuhin, New Philh. O, Boult – DELIUS: *Violin concerto.* **(*)
(M) *** Decca 460 015-2. Kyung Wha Chung, LPO, Solti – MENDELSSOHN: *Violin concerto in E min.* ***
(***) Beulah mono 1PD 10. Campoli, LPO, Boult – MENDELSSOHN: *Violin concerto.* (***)
(BB) (***) Belart mono 461 353-2. Alfredo Campoli, LPO, Boult – BLISS: *Introduction and allegro* etc. (***)

(i) *Violin concerto in B min.; Cockaigne overture,* Op. 40.
(BB) *** Naxos Dig. 8.550489; *4.550489* [id.]. Dong-Suk Kang, Polish Nat. RSO (Katowice), Adrian Leaper.

(i) *Violin concerto; In the South (Alassio)* (concert overture).
(B) *** Sony SBK 62745 [id.]. (i) Pinchas Zukerman; LPO, Barenboim.

With this impressive remake of the Elgar *concerto*, Kennedy launched masterfully into his new career, refreshed after years of self-imposed exile from the regular concert platform. He made this new recording in Birmingham immediately after giving his first live concerto performance in years, and the reading has extra thrust and passion compared with his earlier recording of this epic work. The outer movements are faster and more freely expressive than before, the slow movement more expansive, with *pianissimos* of magical intensity, qualities equally impressive in the evocative Vaughan Williams piece.

Menuhin's second stereo recording, in partnership with Sir Adrian Boult, is hardly less moving and inspirational than his first. There is an added maturity in Menuhin's contribution to compensate for any slight loss of poise or sweetness of tone, and the finale – the most difficult movement to keep together – is stronger and more confident than it was. The (1966) Kingsway Hall recording is characteristically warm and atmospheric, yet vividly focused by the CD transfer. A record indispensable for its documentary value as well as for its musical insights.

Chung's deeply felt performance is also available (see above) coupled with Lynn Harrell's similarly moving account of the *Cello concerto*, altogether a more apt coupling. However, those collectors for whom the Mendelssohn *Violin concerto* is more suitable will find Chung again on her finest form.

Zukerman, coming fresh to the Elgar *Violin concerto* in 1976, was inspired to give a reading which gloriously combined the virtuoso swagger of a Heifetz with the tender, heartfelt warmth of the young Menuhin, plus much individual responsiveness, and culminating in a deeply felt rendering of the long accompanied cadenza. Barenboim is a splendid partner, and with full but clearly defined recording, naturally balanced, at EMI's Abbey Road studios, this is a version which all Elgarians should seek out, especially at its new bargain price (with cassette equivalent). The coupling is an exciting and virile account of *In the South*, not quite as remarkable as the *Concerto* but a worthwhile bonus, even if the sound is marginally less full.

Dong-Suk Kang, immaculate in his intonation, plays the Elgar with fire and urgency. This is very different from most latterday performances, with markedly faster speeds; yet those speeds relate more closely than usual to the metronome markings in the score, and they never get in the way of Kang's ability to feel Elgarian rubato naturally, guided by the warmly understanding conducting of Adrian Leaper. Irrespective of price, this is a keenly competitive version, with excellent, wide-ranging digital sound, if with rather too forward a balance for the soloist.

Campoli gives a deeply felt but highly individual account of Elgar's great concerto. One can judge one's reaction to this performance by the control of vibrato on the opening phrase of his first entry. This is an essentially romantic approach, full of warmth, but Campoli applies himself here with dedication to a work he obviously loves, and the result – with Boult securely and compellingly at the helm – is most rewarding. The 1954 Kingsway Hall recording has been impeccably transferred from the *ffrr* master tape by Tony Hawkins at the Decca studios. With its outstanding Mendelssohn coupling this is a fully worthy memento of a strikingly fine soloist.

With its alternative equally valuable Bliss coupling this is one of the most valuable mono reissues in Belart's 'Boult Historic Collection', although the Bliss couplings are not conducted by Boult, but by the composer.

(i) *Violin concerto in B min., Op. 64*; (ii) *Enigma variations, Op. 36.*

(N) (M) (***) EMI mono CDM5 66979-2 [CD5 66994]. (i) Lord Menuhin, LSO; (ii) Royal Albert Hall O, Composer.

The 1932 Menuhin/Elgar recording of the *Violin concerto* emerges on this newly remastered CD with a fine sense of presence and plenty of body to the sound. As for the performance, its classic status is amply confirmed; in many ways no one has ever matched – let alone surpassed – the 16-year old Menuhin in this work, even if the first part of the finale lacks something in fire. Elgar's own 1926 recording of *Enigma* is too well known for much further comment. But his accelerando surge just before he broadens the climax of *Nimrod*, and the hustle and bustle of *G.R.S.* emphasize the spontaneous individuality of the reading. Although allowances have to be made for the sound, which is somewhat recessed at lower dynamic levels, the engineers have done wonders with the current remastering, and this coupling is surely worthy to take its place among EMI's 'Great recordings of the century'.

Coronation march, Op. 65; Froissart: concert overture, Op. 19; In the South (Alassio) (concert overture), *Op. 50; The Light of life: Meditation, Op. 29.*

*** ASV Dig. CDDCA 619 [id.]. RPO, Yondani Butt.

Yondani Butt draws warm and opulent performances from the RPO. Both overtures have splendid panache. Rich, atmospheric recording, yet with plenty of brilliance – an excellent Elgar sound, in fact.

Crown of India: suite, Op. 66; Enigma variations, Op. 36; Pomp and circumstance marches Nos. 1–5.

(M) **(*) Sony SBK 48265 [id.]. LPO, Barenboim.

Barenboim's view of *Enigma* is full of fantasy. Its most distinctive point is its concern for the miniature element, while the big variations have full weight, and the finale brings the fierceness of added adrenalin at a fast tempo. Tempi are surprisingly fast in the *Pomp and circumstance marches* (though Elgar's tended to be fast too) and not all Elgarians will approve of the updating of Elgarian majesty. The rumbustious approach to the *Crown of India suite* brings this patriotic celebration of the Raj vividly to life, though here the lack of opulence in the recording is a drawback. The marches, too, could do with a more expansive middle range, though *Enigma* is fully acceptable.

Elegy for strings, Op. 58; Sospiri, Op. 70; Serenade for strings in E min., Op. 58.

(M) *** EMI Dig. CDM5 66541-2. City of L. Sinfonia, Hickox – PARRY: *English suite; Lady Radnor's suite.* ***

Hickox draws beautifully refined string-playing from his City of London Sinfonia, notably in the three elegiac movements, the slow movement of the *Serenade* as well as the two separate pieces. An excellent coupling for the rare Parry items, excellently recorded.

Enigma variations (Variations on an original theme), Op. 36.

*** Decca Dig. 452 853-2 [id.]. VPO, Solti – BLACHER: *Paganini variations;* KODALY: *Peacock variations.* ***

(M) *** Decca 452 303-2 [id.]. LSO, Monteux (with HOLST: *Planets.* ***)

(B) *** DG Classikon 439 446-2. LSO, Jochum – HOLST: *Planets.* ***

(N) **(*) Cala CACD 0524 [id.]. LSO, Stokowski (with BRAHMS: *Symphony No. 1 in C min., Op. 68.* **(*))

(M) *** EMI CDM7 64748-2 [id.]. LSO, Boult – HOLST: *Planets.* ***

*** Sony Dig. SK 53284 [id.]. BPO, Levine – DEBUSSY: *Images.* ***

(M) (***) RCA mono GD 60287 [60287-2-RG]. NBC SO, Toscanini – MUSSORGSKY: *Pictures.* (**)

Celebrating his half-century as a Decca artist in 1997, Sir Georg Solti finally paid a tribute to his unique Britishness in Elgar's *Enigma variations*. In contrast to Solti's brittle Chicago version of 1974, this warmly spontaneous-sounding account of the *Enigma variations* reflects not just the special qualities of this great Viennese orchestra but the way in which Solti has mellowed over the last two decades. This is a heartfelt, incandescent performance, delicate and subtle on detail, and it is the more moving when Solti refuses to over-emote, for example, in the great climax of *Nimrod*, taking it at a flowing speed. The Decca engineers place the orchestra vividly within the unique acoustics of the Musikverein, with close balance avoided and fine sense of spaciousness.

Monteux's *Enigma* remains among the freshest versions ever put on disc and the music is obviously deeply felt. The reading is famous for the real *pianissimo* which Monteux secures at the beginning of Nimrod, the tension electric, and the superb climax is more effective in consequence. Differences from traditional tempi elsewhere are marginal and add to one's enjoyment. The vintage Kingsway Hall stereo was outstanding in its day and it is almost impossible to believe that this dates from 1958 and, with its stunning Holst coupling, this is one of the very finest (and most generous – 78 minutes) reissues in Decca's Classic Sound series.

Like others – including Elgar himself – Jochum sets a very slow *Adagio* at the start of *Nimrod*, slower than the metronome marking in the score; unlike others, he maintains that measured tempo and, with the subtlest gradations, builds an even bigger, nobler climax than you find in *accelerando* readings. It is like a Bruckner slow movement in microcosm around which the other variations revolve, all of them delicately detailed, with a natural feeling for Elgarian rubato. The playing matches the strength and refinement of the performance.

Stokowski adroitly guides the players of the Czech Philharmonic through Elgar's masterpiece, illuminating every bar with his special affection, and they readily respond to his warmth. Phrases are moulded in the most flexible (and sometimes unidiomatic) way, but the result is gloriously rich in spontaneous feeling, casting an entirely new slant on a work which one felt to have known very well indeed. Stokowski's insights are special to himself. This reissue (the recording comes from the Decca Phase 4 archives and is extremely full and vivid) was sponsored by the Rt. Hon. David Mellor, a noted Stokowskian and Elgarian, who knows a special performance when he hears one. The coupling is a splendid version of Brahms's *First Symphony* recorded live with the LSO at the Royal Festival Hall in 1972.

Boult's *Enigma* comes from the beginning of the 1970s, but the recording has lost some of its amplitude in its transfer to CD: the effect is fresh, but the violins sound thinner. The reading shows this conductor's long experience of the work, with each variation growing naturally and seamlessly out of the music that has gone before. Yet the livelier variations bring exciting orchestral bravura and there is an underlying intensity of feeling that carries the performance forward.

Levine and the Berlin Philharmonic may not be idiomatic but their live recording has a thrust and passion that are hard to resist, least convincing at the start, but spacious and unhurried in *Nimrod* and thrillingly powerful in the final variation, which draws cheers from the Berlin audience. However, this is not a first choice.

It is a pity that Toscanini's sharply focused but warmly expressive NBC reading of *Enigma* should come in a coupling with his severe account of the Mussorgsky. The Elgar, often expansive as well as affectionately phrased, as in the statement of the theme, gives a much more sympathetic view of the taskmaster conductor than most of his late recordings. Though traditionalist Elgarians may not always approve, it makes for an electrifying experience. The transfer is clean but not too aggressive.

Enigma variations; Coronation march, Op. 65; In the South overture, Op. 50.
(BB) *** Naxos Dig. 8.553564 [id.].
Bournemouth SO, Hurst.

George Hurst, with the Bournemouth orchestra, inspires richly expressive playing, full of subtle rubato which consistently sounds natural and idiomatic, never self-conscious. Like Elgar himself, he tends to press ahead rather than linger, as in the great climactic variation in *Enigma*, *Nimrod*, as well as in the finale. Similarly in the Overture, *In the South*, he reminds one that it was the Bournemouth orchestra under Silvestri which, many years ago, made a recording that brought a new assessment of what was till then an underrated work. The *Coronation march* also inspires an opulent, red-blooded performance and the recording thoughout is rich and sumptuous.

(i) *Enigma variations;* (ii) *Falstaff, Op.68.*
(M) *** EMI CDM5 66322-2. (i) Philh. O; (ii) Hallé O; Barbirolli.
(B) **(*) [EMI Red Line CDR5 72553]. LPO, Mackerras.

Ripe and expansive, Barbirolli's view of *Falstaff* is colourful and convincing; it has fine atmospheric feeling too, and the interludes are more magical here than in the Boult version. *Enigma*, too, was a work that Barbirolli, himself a cellist, made especially his own, with wonderfully expansive string-playing and much imaginative detail; the recording was made when he was at the very peak of his interpretative powers. The massed strings have lost some of their amplitude, but detail is clearer and the overall balance is convincing, with the Kingsway Hall ambience ensuring a pleasing bloom.

With recorded sound far more reverberant than is common in EMI recordings of Elgar, Mackerras's powerful readings of the composer's own favourite among his orchestral works, together with the most popular, are given a comfortable glow, while losing some inner clarity. The reading of *Falstaff* is superb, among the most electrically compelling put on disc; but *Enigma* is marred by mannered and self-conscious phrasing in the opening statement of the theme and the first variation, as well as in *Nimrod*. *Falstaff* is indexed very generously.

Enigma variations, Op. 36; Falstaff, Op. 68; Grania and Diarmid: Funeral march.
*** EMI CDC5 55001-2 [id.]. CBSO, Simon Rattle.

In *Enigma*, Rattle and the CBSO are both powerful and refined, overwhelming at the close, and they offer a generous and ideal coupling. *Falstaff* is given new transparency in a spacious reading, deeply moving in the hush of the final death scene, with the *Grania and Diarmid* excerpts as a valuable makeweight.

Enigma variations, Op. 36; Falstaff, Op. 68; Introduction and allegro for strings, Op. 47.
(M) *** Carlton Dig. 30366 00922 [(M) id.]. Nat. Youth O of Great Britain, Christopher Seaman.

These works have rarely been given such heartfelt performances as those by Christopher Seaman and the National Youth Orchestra. The weight of string-sound, combined with the fervour behind the playing, makes this an exceptionally satisfying reading of the *Introduction and allegro*, while *Falstaff* demonstrates even more strikingly how, working together intensively, these youngsters have learnt to keep a precise ensemble through the most complex variations of expressive rubato. The orchestra then goes on to give a wonderfully rich and ardent account of *Enigma*, yet one which opens with persuasively gentle lyricism and produces the most delicate portrayals of *Ysobel* and *Dorabella*, while *Nimrod* explores the widest gradation of dynamic to reach its climax. The finale is engulfing in its excitement, and Seaman does not forget to add the 'tummy-wobbling' organ reinforcement to the closing pages. The recording is fully worthy of an account which has all the hallmarks of a live performance, even though it was recorded in Watford Town Hall under studio conditions.

(i) *Enigma variations;* (ii) *Pomp and circumstance marches Nos. 1–5, Op. 39.*
(M) *** DG 429 713-2. RPO, Norman Del Mar.
(M) *** EMI CDM7 64015-2. (i) LSO; (ii) LPO, Sir Adrian Boult.

In the *Enigma variations* Del Mar comes closer than any other conductor to the responsive rubato style of Elgar himself, using fluctuations to point the emotional message of the work with wonderful power and spontaneity. The RPO plays superbly, both here and in the *Pomp and circumstance marches*, given Proms-style flair and urgency – although some might feel that the fast speeds miss some of the *nobilmente*. The reverberant sound here adds something of an aggressive edge to the music-making.

Boult's *Enigma* (also available coupled with Holst's *Planets* – see above) is self-recommending. Boult's approach to the *Pomp and circumstance marches* is brisk and direct, with an almost no-nonsense manner in places. There is not a hint of vulgarity and the freshness is most attractive, though it is a pity he omits the repeats in the Dvořák-like No. 2. The brightened sound brings a degree of abrasiveness to the brass.

(i) *Enigma variations;* (ii) *Pomp and circumstance marches Nos. 1–5;* (iii) *Serenade for strings.*

(B) *** Decca 433 629-2. (i) LAPO, Mehta; (ii), LSO, Bliss; (iii) ASMF, Marriner.

Mehta proves a strong and sensitive Elgarian, and this is a highly enjoyable performance. If there are no special revelations, the transition from the nobly conceived and spacious climax of *Nimrod* to a delightfully graceful *Dorabella* is particularly felicitous. The vintage Decca recording, with the organ entering spectacularly in the finale, is outstanding in its CD transfer, and this is one of Mehta's very finest records. Marriner's elegantly played yet highly sensitive account of the *String serenade* makes a fine bonus, and Sir Arthur Bliss's rumbustiously vigorous accounts of the *Pomp and circumstance marches* are worth anyone's money.

(i) *Enigma variations; Pomp and circumstance marches Nos. 1 & 4; Salut d'amour, Op. 12;* (ii) *Serenade for strings in E min., Op. 20.*

(BB) *** Naxos Dig. 8.554161 [id.]. (i) Czecho-Slovak RSO; (ii) Capella Istropolitana; Leaper.

Though Leaper's slow account of the 'Enigma' theme makes an unpromising start, his reading of the *Variations* is most beautiful, with ripely resonant string-playing and with warmly expressive rubato in *Nimrod* suggesting that the Slovak players had been won over to Elgar by Leaper's advocacy. In the march the '*Land of Hope and Glory*' tune is played by them, as Elgar himself instructed, 'as though they had never heard it before'. *Salut d'amour* is not sentimentalized. Most refined of all is the Capella Istropolitana's account of the *Serenade*, with the slow movement specially beautiful, finely shaded. An excellent compilation of Elgar's most popular orchestral pieces, brilliantly recorded.

Falstaff, Op. 68; Elegy, Op. 58; The Sanguine Fan (ballet), Op. 81.

(N) (BB) *** Naxos Dig. 8553879 [id.]. Northern Philh., David Lloyd-Jones

Rich, full Naxos sound with high dynamic contrasts adds satisfying weight to David Lloyd-Jones's taut and dramatic account of Elgar's elaborate Shakespearean portrait. Speeds are often on the fast side, but idiomatically so, with a natural feeling for Elgarian rubato and sprung rhythms. Both in *Falstaff* and *The Sanguine Fan*, Lloyd-Jones draws fragmented structures warmly and persuasively together, so that the late ballet-score emerges strongly, not just a trivial occasional piece. The beautiful *Elegy* is most tenderly done, modest in length but no miniature. An outstanding bargain, competing with all premium-price rivals.

Falstaff, Op. 68; Imperial march, Op. 32; (i) *Sea pictures, Op. 37.*

(B) *** Sony SBK 63020 [id.]. LPO, Barenboim; (i) with Yvonne Minton.

Barenboim's habit of moulding the music of Elgar in flexible tempi, of underlining romantic expressiveness, has never been as convincing on record as here in *Falstaff.* Rarely has the story-telling element in Elgar's symphonic study been presented so captivatingly. Yvonne Minton uses her rich tone sensitively in Elgar's orchestral song-cycle. There is perhaps less subtlety in her reading than in Janet Baker's, but she responds to this music richly and ardently. Barenboim is a persuasive Elgarian and this makes a most welcome bargain reissue, with his ripe account of the *Imperial march* thrown in for good measure. The CD transfers are excellent, with the warmly atmospheric sound in the *Sea pictures* particularly appealing.

Falstaff; Symphonies Nos. 1–2; (i) *Dream of Gerontius: Prelude* and excerpts. *The Music makers*: excerpts. *Civic fanfare and National anthem.*

*** EMI mono CDS7 54560-2 (3). (i) Margaret Balfour, Steuart Wilston, Herbert Heyner, Tudor Davies, Horace Stevens, Royal Ch. Soc., Three Choirs Festival Ch., LSO or Royal Albert Hall O, composer.

It is thrilling in this first volume of EMI's Elgar Edition to find that the recordings, made between 1927 and 1932, have a body and immediacy that give the most astonishing sense of presence. Consistently these are tough performances, with rhythms pressed sharply home and with speeds generally faster than has become normal today. In addition, Elgar's sense of line, his ability to mould rhythms with natural flexibility, regularly brings an extra emotional thrust and an extra intensity and poignancy. Most thrilling of all is the *First Symphony*, where Elgar modifies some of the markings in the score on speed-changes; and this reading of *Falstaff*, too, has never been surpassed. *Symphony No. 2* comes with fascinating supplements, including a rehearsal of the Scherzo and an alternative take of the first part of the movement. Most atmospheric of all are the live recordings of *Gerontius* and *The Music makers* on the third disc, all recorded live at a time when recording on wax discs in short spans of under five minutes presented almost insoluble problems. The brief *Civic fanfare* is a curiosity, the only Elgar first performance preserved on record.

Introduction and allegro for strings.

(N) *** Arabesque Dig. Z 6723 [id.]. San Francisco Ballet O, Lark Qt., Jean-Louis Le Roux – HANDEL: *Concerto grosso in B flat,*

Op. 6/7. SCHOENBERG: *Concerto for string quartet and orchestra after Handel's Concerto grosso, Op. 6/7.* SPOHR: *Concerto for string quartet and orchestra.* ***
(N) (M) **(*) EMI Dig. CDM5 66761-2. City of L. Sinfonia, Hickox – VAUGHAN WILLIAMS: *Fantasia on a theme by Tallis* **(*). WALTON: *Sonata for strings.* ***

A passionately committed performance from these excellent San Francisco string players, with a warmly tender contribution from the solo group. They are not entirely idiomatic – they do not quite let rip in the striding unison string tune in the way that British players would – but their slower tempo remains convincing when the underlying fervour is in no doubt. The final climax is superb. Splendidly vivid recording.

Hickox's account of the *Introduction and allegro* is slightly disappointing. The athleticism is exhilarating but lacks ripeness, especially in the great surging tune on unison strings, where the playing conveys forceful brilliance rather than ripeness of feeling (like Barbirolli). The recording, made in St Augustine's Church, Kilburn, is brightly lit by the close microphone placing, but does not lack weight.

Introduction and allegro for strings, Op. 47; Serenade for strings in E min., Op. 20.
(M) *** Virgin/EMI Dig. CUV5 61126-2 [id.]. LCO, Christopher Warren-Green – VAUGHAN WILLIAMS: *Tallis fantasia,* etc. ***

(i; ii) *Introduction and allegro for strings, Op. 47;* (i) *Serenade for strings in E min., Op. 20;* (iii) *Elegy, Op. 58; Sospiri, Op. 70.*
✿ *** EMI CDC7 47537-2 [id.]. (i) Sinfonia of L.; (ii) Allegri Qt; (iii) New Philh. O; Barbirolli – VAUGHAN WILLIAMS: *Greensleeves & Tallis fantasias.* *** ✿

Barbirolli brings an Italianate ardour and warmth to this music without in any way robbing it of its Englishness, and the response of the string players, full-throated or subtle as the music demands, was matched by superb analogue recording, notable for its combination of clarity and ambient richness. For CD, the *Elegy* (like the *Serenade*, showing Barbirolli in more gentle and beguiling mood) and the passionate *Sospiri* have been added for good measure. The new CD transfer has retained the fullness, amplitude and analogue ambience and has refocused the upper range most believably. A triumph!

Christopher Warren-Green, directing and leading his London Chamber Orchestra, directs the *Introduction and allegro* with tremendous ardour. The whole work moves forward in a single sweep and the sense of a live performance, tingling with electricity and immediacy, is thrillingly tangible. It is very difficult to believe that the group contains only 17 players (6-5-2-3-1), with the resonant but never clouding acoustics of All Saints' Church, Petersham, helping to create an engulfingly rich body of tone. Appropriately, the *Serenade* is a more relaxed reading yet has plenty of affectionate warmth, with the beauty of the *Larghetto* expressively rich but not overstated.

King Arthur: suite; (i) *The Starlight Express* (suite), *Op. 78.*
(M) **(*) Chandos CHAN 6582 [id.]. (i) Cynthia Glover, John Lawrenson; Bournemouth Sinf., George Hurst.

The *King Arthur suite* is full of surging, enjoyable ideas and makes an interesting novelty on record. *The Starlight Express suite* is taken from music Elgar wrote for a children's play, with a song or two included. Though the singers here are not ideal interpreters, the enthusiasm of Hurst and the Sinfonietta is conveyed well, particularly in the *King Arthur suite*. The recording is atmospheric if rather over-reverberant, but the added firmness of the CD and its refinement of detail almost make this an extra asset in providing a most agreeable ambience for Elgar's music.

Nursery suite; Wand of Youth suites Nos. 1 and 2, Op. 1a and 1b.
*** Chandos Dig. CHAN 8318 [id.]. Ulster O, Bryden Thomson.

The playing in Ulster is attractively spirited; in the gentle pieces (the *Sun dance*, *Fairy pipers* and *Slumber dance*) which show the composer at his most magically evocative, the music-making engagingly combines refinement and warmth. The *Nursery suite* is strikingly well characterized, and with first-class digital sound this is highly recommendable.

Romance for cello and orchestra, Op. 62.
(M) *** EMI Dig. CDM7 64726-2. Julian Lloyd Webber, LSO, Mackerras (with SULLIVAN: *Cello concerto*, etc. ***)

Julian Lloyd Webber has rescued the composer's own version of the *Romance* for cello (originally for bassoon) and it provides a delightful makeweight for the Sullivan reissue, beautifully played and warmly recorded.

Serenade for strings in E min., Op. 20.
(B) *** Carlton IMP Dig. 30367 02242 [(M) id.]. Serenata of London – GRIEG: *Holberg suite;* MOZART: *Eine kleine Nachtmusik*, etc. ***

A particularly appealing account of Elgar's *Serenade*, with unforced tempi in the outer movements admirably catching its mood and atmosphere. The Serenata of London is led rather than conducted by Barry Wilde, and it is recorded with remarkable realism and naturalness.

Symphonies Nos. 1–2; In the South overture, Op. 50; Pomp and circumstance marches, Op. 39, Nos. 1 in D; 3 in C min.; 4 in G.
(B) **(*) Teldec/Warner Ultima Dig. 0630 18951-2 (2) [(M) id. import]. BBC SO, Andrew Davis.

Symphonies Nos. 1–2; Overtures: Cockaigne; In the South.
(B) *** Decca Double 443 856-2 (2) [id.]. LPO, Solti.

Symphonies Nos.1–2; Cockaigne overture; Pomp and circumstance marches Nos. 1–5.
(B) **(*) Ph. Duo Dig. 454 250-2 (2). RPO or LSO, André Previn.

Symphonies Nos. 1–2; Pomp and circumstance march No. 5.
(B) **(*) EMI forte CZS5 69761-2 (2) [CDFB 69761]. Philh. O, Haitink.

In the *First Symphony* Solti's thrusting manner will give the traditional Elgarian the occasional jolt, but his clearing away of the cobwebs stems from the composer's own 78-r.p.m. recording, here with very much the same rich, committed qualities that mark out the Elgar performance. Again modelled closely on the composer's own surprisingly clipped and urgent reading, the *Second Symphony* benefits from virtuoso playing from the LPO and full, well-balanced sound. Fast tempi bring searing concentration, yet the *nobilmente* element is not missed and the account of the finale presents a true climax. The effect is magnificent. The CD transfers bring out the fullness satisfyingly as well as the brilliance of the excellent 1970s sound, and this applies also to the sharply dramatic account of *Cockaigne*. *In the South*, recorded in 1979, is less successful, overtense if still exciting. Here Solti is not helped by Decca recording in which the brilliance is not quite matched by weight or body (an essential in Elgar).

Previn's performances find the conductor as idiomatic and understanding in Elgar as he is in Walton and Vaughan Williams. His view of the opening movement of the *First Symphony* is spacious, with moulding of phrase and lifting of rhythm beautifully judged, to bring natural flexibility within a strongly controlled structure, steadier than usual in basic tempo. The syncopations of the scherzo/march theme have an almost jazzy swagger, and the reading is crowned by a flowing account of the finale. There Previn confirms his ability to point Elgarian climaxes with the necessary heart-tug, above all in the lovely passage where the main theme is augmented in minims on high violins, here achingly beautiful, neither too reticent nor too heavy-handed. The opening movement of the *Second* has a similar Elgarian ebb and flow, but here one senses an absence of thrust and he does not display as tight a grip on the structure as Solti, although the *Larghetto* is deeply felt and is eloquently played by the LSO. Nevertheless, many will warm to Previn's expansive approach, which is again apparent in the bold, purposeful finale. *Cockaigne* is in a similar mould, though attractively affectionate and spirited. The five *Pomp and circumstance marches* are not quite as flamboyant as some versions but are beautifully sprung. The recordings were made at Abbey Road and the Philips sound certainly does not lack opulence.

With consistently slow tempi – far slower than Boult or Barbirolli used to adopt – Haitink's is a spacious reading of No. 1. The result is hardly idiomatic but, with superb playing from the Philharmonia under Haitink's concentrated direction, it is profound and moving, elegiacally glowing with genuine Elgarian warmth. Splendid (1983) Walthamstow analogue sound to match. The *Second Symphony*, recorded a year later at Abbey Road, is more controversial, and here the CD transfer remains just a little disappointing. The ear notices more readily that the sound of the strings (middle and upper) is not as expansively opulent as expected. The opening movement in particular is very volatile, and throughout there are many wayward touches that fail to convince entirely on repeated hearing. It is a reading which clearly relates Elgar, on the one hand, to Richard Strauss but also – and more significantly – to Bruckner. Elgarians will miss some of the usual spring in the 12/8 compound time of the first movement. But for many the performance will be a revelation in its strength and depth of feeling.

With sound of demonstration quality Andrew Davis conducts a broad, rather plain reading of the *First Symphony* which is yet highly idiomatic and is beautifully played. With one important reservation this is as fine as any of its bargain-price competitors. Sadly, the performance falls short at the very end, where the brassy coda fails to blaze as it should. However, Davis provides a strong and passionate account of the *Second*. It is an impetuous performance, but convincingly so, and the slow movement has great eloquence. The finale has splendid impetus, and one can only lament that Davis did not insist on the organ reinforcement at the climax. But Davis offers an exuberant *In the South* as a bonus, catching the music's Straussian surge, yet tenderly depicting the melancholy moonlight of the central section. The recording is first class, with fine range and amplitude.

Symphony No. 1 in A flat, Op. 55.
❁ (B) *** Carlton IMP Dig. PCD 2019 [(M) id.]. Hallé O, James Judd.
(B) *** CfP CD-CFP 9018 [id.]. LPO, Vernon Handley.

Symphony No. 1 in A flat; Chanson de matin; Chanson de nuit; Serenade for strings, Op. 20.
(M) *** EMI CDM7 64013-2. LPO, Sir Adrian Boult.

(i) *Symphony No. 1 in A flat;* (ii) *Cockaigne overture.*
(M) **(*) EMI CDM7 64511-2. Philh. O, Barbirolli.
(N) (B) *** Ph. Virtuoso 416 612-2. RPO or LSO, André Previn.

Symphony No. 1 in A flat; Imperial march, Op. 32.
(BB) *** Naxos Dig. 8.550634 [id.]. BBC PO, George Hurst.

(i) *Symphony No. 1 in A flat;* (ii) *Introduction and allegro, Op. 47;* (iii) *Pomp and circumstance march No. 1.*
(BB) *** RCA Navigator Dig./Analogue 74321 24217-2 [(M) id. import]. (i) BBC SO, Sir Colin Davis; (ii) Boston SO, Charles Munch; (iii) Boston Pops O, Arthur Fiedler.

James Judd, more than any rival on disc, has learnt directly from Elgar's own recording of this magnificent symphony. So the reading has extra authenticity in the many complex speed-changes (sometimes indicated confusingly in the score), in the precise placing of climaxes and in the textural balances. Above all, Judd outshines others in the pacing and phrasing of the lovely slow movement which in its natural flowing rubato has melting tenderness behind the passion, a throat-catching poignancy not fully conveyed elsewhere but very much a quality of Elgar's own reading. The refinement of the strings down to the most hushed *pianissimo* confirms this as the Hallé's most beautiful disc in recent years, recorded with warmth and opulence.

Vernon Handley directs a beautifully paced reading which can also be counted in every way outstanding. The LPO has performed this symphony many times before but never with more poise and refinement than here. It is in the slow movement above all that Handley scores, spacious and movingly expressive. With very good sound, well transferred to CD, this is a highly recommendable alternative version.

On the bargain Naxos label comes a warmly sympathetic version from the BBC Philharmonic under George Hurst. Masterly with Elgarian rubato, he refreshingly chooses speeds faster than have become the norm, closer to those of Elgar himself. James Judd's even warmer, more tender, more ripely recorded version on Carlton is still preferable, but no one will be disappointed with Hurst's powerful reading, well coupled with the *Imperial march*.

Boult clearly presents the *First Symphony* as a counterpart to the *Second*, with hints of reflective nostalgia amid the triumph. His EMI disc contains a radiantly beautiful performance, with no extreme tempi, richly spaced in the first movement, invigorating in the syncopated march rhythms of the Scherzo, and similarly bouncing in the Brahmsian rhythms of the finale.

Previn's account is also available coupled to No. 2 on a Duo (see above) but as that is a marginally successful reading, many collectors may prefer to have the *A flat Symphony* with this bargain *Cockaigne* coupling.

The lyrical spontaneity of Sir Colin Davis's version of the *First Symphony* with the BBC Symphony Orchestra is very winning, an evocatively atmospheric live recording, made at the Royal Albert Hall during a Concertaid event in May 1985. Though in the finale ensemble is not as crisp as earlier in the performance, and audience noises intrude in all four movements, this is persuasive in a way hard to achieve without an audience. Munch's vibrant if unidiomatic account of the *Introduction and allegro* makes a good bonus, and Fiedler is ebullient in *Pomp and circumstance*, which is also very well recorded. Worthwhile considering in the lowest price-range.

In Barbirolli's later (1962) Philharmonia account on EMI there is a hint of heaviness where, after the march introduction, the music should surge along. The slow movement, too, is very slow: it is done more affectionately in the earlier, Pye version, which we hope will reappear in due course. The present transfer of a Kingsway Hall recording has lost some of the fullness in the violins; otherwise, it sounds very well. The *Cockaigne overture* is one of Barbirolli's most notable Elgar recordings.

Symphony No. 2 in E flat, Op. 63.
(B) *** CfP CD-CFP 4544. LPO, Vernon Handley.
(BB) *** Naxos Dig. 8.550635 [id.]. BBC PO, Downes.

Symphony No. 2; Cockaigne overture, Op. 40.
(M) *** EMI CDM7 64014-2. LPO, Sir Adrian Boult.

Symphony No. 2; The Crown of India (suite), *Op. 66.*
(M) *** Chandos CHAN 6523 [id.]. RSNO, Gibson.

(i) *Symphony No. 2;* (ii) *Elegy, Op. 58; Sospiri, Op. 70.*
(M) **(*) EMI CDM7 64724-2. (i) Hallé O; New Philh. O, Barbirolli.

(i) *Symphony No. 2;* (ii) *Serenade for strings, Op. 20.*
*** RCA Dig. 09026 60072 [60072-2-RC]. LPO, Slatkin.

Handley's remains the most satisfying modern version of a work which has latterly been much recorded. What Handley conveys superbly is the sense of Elgarian ebb and flow, building climaxes like a master and drawing excellent, spontaneous-sounding playing from an orchestra which, more than any other, has specialized in performing this symphony. The sound is warmly atmospheric and vividly conveys the added organ part in the bass, just at the climax of the finale, which Elgar himself suggested 'if available': a tummy-wobbling effect. This would be a first choice at full price, but as a bargain CD there are few records to match it.

Downes uses an expansive speed in the first movement to give the writing its full emotional thrust, and the hushed tension of the slow movements leads up to towering climaxes, well controlled. The Scherzo is brilliant, delicate and witty, and the finale with its sequential writing is perfectly paced. Although it has not quite the bite and thrust of Handley's version (partly the effect of the recording-balance), its valedictory feeling at the close is very moving. Indeed the only reservation is that the sound, though warm and refined, is a degree too distanced, so that the noble opening of the work does not have its full impact. This does not displace Vernon Handley, except for those needing digital recording, but it can be recommended alongside it.

For his fifth recording of the *Second Symphony* Sir Adrian Boult, incomparable Elgarian, drew from the LPO the most richly satisfying performance of all. Over the years Sir Adrian's view of the glorious nobility of the first movement had mellowed a degree, but the pointing of climaxes is unrivalled. With Boult more than anyone else the architecture is clearly and strongly established, with tempo changes less exaggerated than usual. This is a version to convert new listeners to a love of Elgar, although, even more than in the *First Symphony*, the ear notices a loss of opulence compared with the original LP. This is also very striking in *Cockaigne*, which opens the disc.

Slatkin's account of the *Second Symphony* is splendid, timed beautifully to deliver authentic frissons, and it too has extra power in the finale from the addition of pedal notes on the organ, just before the epilogue – as Elgar once suggested to Sir Adrian Boult. Previously, only Vernon Handley had included them on his equally outstanding version for CfP. Though the new Slatkin is much more expensive than that, it also includes a strong account of the *Serenade for strings*. Those looking for a first-class modern digital recording of the symphony should be well satisfied.

Gibson's recording shows his partnership with the RSNO at its peak, and this performance captures all the opulent nostalgia of Elgar's masterly score. The reading of the first movement is more relaxed in its grip than Handley's, but its spaciousness is appealing and, both here and in the beautifully sustained *Larghetto*, the richly resonant acoustics of Glasgow City Hall bring out the full panoply of Elgarian sound. The finale has splendid *nobilmente*. In the *Crown of India* suite Gibson is consistently imaginative in his attention to detail, and the playing of the Scottish orchestra is again warmly responsive.

Barbirolli's 1964 Kingsway Hall recording shows its age a little in the massed violins (especially by comparison with the richer tapestry for the two short string-pieces, beautifully played, which were recorded two years later). Barbirolli's ardour is never in doubt – witness the exuberant horn-playing in the first movement and the passion of the finale – but his interpretation is a very personal one, deeply felt but with the pace of the music often excessively varied, sometimes coarsening effects which Elgar's score specifies very precisely and weakening the structure.

Symphony No. 3: sketches and commentary by Anthony Payne.

(N) (B) *** NMC Dig. NMCD 052 [id.]. Robert Gibbs, David Owen Norris, BBC SO, Andrew Davis.

Symphony No. 3 (completed from sketches, elaborated by Anthony Payne).

(N) ✿ *** NMC Dig. NMCD 053 [id.]. BBC SO, Andrew Davis.

It is well known that in 1932 the BBC commissioned a third symphony from Elgar, which he did not complete, and equally well known that on his deathbed, the composer begged his friend Willy Reed not to let anyone tinker with the sketches he had left. The sketches were deposited in the British Museum after Elgar's death. In the late 1960s Roger Fiske had planned a talk on the sketches which R. L. was to have produced for the Third Programme. It would have been illustrated by the BBC Symphony Orchestra and Sir Adrian Boult, who also would have given the first performance had Elgar completed it. Elgar's daughter, Carice Elgar Blake, and the Elgar Estate finally gave their approval for one transmission and everything was in place when Sir Adrian had second thoughts. By one of those strange ironies of fate, the orchestral material was sent for copying to Maurice Johnston, a former BBC head of music, who was much opposed to the project on ethical grounds, and it was he who persuaded Sir Adrian not to proceed and pull out of the project.

Anthony Payne's illustrated talk on the sketches comes very close to the talk Dr Fiske had in mind, and those who have marvelled at the strength and coherence of Payne's completion of Elgar's copious sketches will find it most illuminating. Payne here gives precise details of his thinking and procedures. He discusses in exactly what state Elgar left the sketches, many of which were in full score, and what problems any conjectural completion would encounter, confirming that whatever extra inspiration Elgar himself would have added to a finished score, this remains a wonderful bonus to our knowledge of the composer. The majority of the sketches were written out for violin and keyboard, and (on NMCD 052) Robert Gibbs plays the very instrument on which Elgar himself ran through the fragments with Reed. This bargain-price CD makes a splendid supplement to Andrew Davis's outstanding recording of the complete work (NMCD 53).

As the expiry of copyright protection approached, the Elgar Estate finally decided to entrust the composer Payne with the job of making a conjectural 'elaboration' of the sketches. Payne steeped himself in these sketches over a very long period. Although misgivings are natural, the fact remains that Payne has brought before the wider musical public Elgar's last symphonic thoughts; he has elaborated them with insight and orchestrated them with extraordinary mastery.

The success of Payne's loving and inspired re-creation makes one profoundly grateful that the composer's injunction was finally disregarded. On any count it demonstrates how Elgar's creative powers, far from fading, remained at full strength to the end. This now has to be judged, not as the work which Elgar himself would have completed, but in its own right as a deeply satisfying symphony, most of all in the powerful first movement, for which Elgar himself substantially completed the exposition and recapitulation. One may regret the absence of a big Elgarian tune in the slow movement, but so much that Payne has inferred from the sketches seems so right, not least the close of the finale, fading away. Andrew Davis gives an inspired performance, and the playing of the BBC Symphony Orchestra is thoroughly committed. The symphony is very well recorded. One now looks forward to rival readings.

CHAMBER AND INSTRUMENTAL MUSIC

(i) *Piano quintet in A min., Op. 84. String quartet in E min., Op. 83.*

(BB) *** Naxos Dig. 8.553737 [id.]. Maggini Qt, (i) with Peter Donohoe.

(BB) *** Discover Dig. DICD 920485. Aura Ens., (i) with Hans Joerg Fink.

(i–ii) *Piano quintet in A min.;* (i) *String quartet in E min.;* (ii–iii) *In moonlight (Canto popolare for viola and piano).*

(M) *** EMI Dig. CD-EMX 2229. (i) Vellinger Qt; (ii) Piers Lane; (iii) James Boyd.

The Vellinger approach to Elgar is impulsive, with allegros taken faster than in rival versions, to make the finale of the *Quintet* bold and thrusting and the finale of the *Quartet* light and volatile. The middle movement of the *Quartet* is light and flowing too, like an interlude rather than a meditation; but the central *Adagio* of the *Quintet* is by contrast very slow and weighty, not as thoughtful as in other versions. What crowns the disc is the little fill-up, a ravishing performance of the magical interlude which Elgar arranged for viola and piano from the central *Nocturne* passage from his *Overture In the South*. James Boyd, the Vellinger viola, plays with a richness and firmness of intonation that make one long to hear him in more solo work.

The Naxos and Discover versions appeared simultaneously, both at super-bargain price, both very recommendable. The Naxos issue with the young British Maggini Quartet, joined by Peter Donohoe, promptly won an important record prize in France, stylish, nicely pointed, slightly understated readings. Yet it is the Aura Ensemble of Switzerland which, perhaps surprisingly, offers even more red-blooded, urgently expressive readings, helped by rich, forward sound. One hopes it is a sign that rare Elgar is at last communicating outside Britain.

Piano quintet in A min., Op. 84; Violin sonata in E min., Op. 82.

*** Hyperion Dig. CDA 66645 [id.]. Nash Ens. (members).

With the violinist, Marcia Crayford, and the pianist, Ian Brown, as both the duo in the *Sonata* and the key players in the *Quintet*, these are performances more volatile than usual, but the slow movements above all are what mark these performances as exceptional. The central *Adagio* of the *Quintet*, far slower than usual, then brings the most dedicated playing of all, making this not just a lyrical outpouring but an inner meditation. Warm, immediate recording.

String quartet in E min., Op. 83.

*** Collins Dig. 1280-2 [id.]. Britten Qt – WALTON: *Quartet.* ***

*** ASV Dig. CDDCA 526 [id.]. Brodsky Qt – DELIUS: *Quartet.* ***

(*) Hyperion Dig. CDA 66718 [id.]. Coull Qt – BRIDGE: *3 Idylls;* WALTON: *Quartet.* *

There is a poignancy in this late work which the beautifully matched members of the Britten Quartet capture to perfection. Not only do they bring out the emotional intensity, they play with a refinement and sharpness of focus that give superb point to the outer movements. With more portamento than one would normally expect today, the result is totally in style, and the Brittens are even more searching than their main competitors.

The young players of the Brodsky Quartet take a weightier view than usual of the central, interlude-like slow movement but amply justify it. The power of the outer movements, too, gives the lie to the idea of this as a lesser piece than Elgar's other chamber works. First-rate recording.

Though in the Elgar the Coulls sound almost too comfortable, less successful at conveying the volatile mood-changes than the Vellinger Quartet on EMI Eminence (see above), their relaxed warmth is still very persuasive; and the Walton performance, with the melancholy of the slow movement intensified, compares very favourably even with that of the Brittens. Excellent sound.

Violin sonata in E min., Op. 82.
(BB) *** ASV Quicksilva CDQS 6191 [id.]. Lorraine McAslan, John Blakely – WALTON: *Violin sonata.* ***
(M) **(*) EMI CDM5 66122-2. Lord Menuhin, Hephzibah Menuhin – VAUGHAN WILLIAMS: *Sonata* **(*); WALTON: *Sonata.* (**)

Though Lorraine McAslan's performance of Elgar's inspired sonata cannot quite match the virtuoso command and body of tone of Nigel Kennedy's on Chandos, hers is an impressive and warm-hearted version, full of natural imagination and bringing some rapt *pianissimo* playing in the outer movements. She is helped by the sympathetic partnership of John Blakely, who is attractively incisive. The digital recording is faithful but rather forward, which gives the violin-tone less bloom than it might have. But this coupling with Walton is more than worth its modest cost.

The Menuhins present a large-scale view of this sonata. Unfortunately, though slow speeds bring their moments of insight and revelation at the hands of a Menuhin, the result overall is too heavy, and it is marred too by imperfect intonation. The recording is first rate.

Violin sonata in E min., Op. 82; Canto popolare; La capricieuse, Op. 17; Chanson de matin, Op. 15/2; Chanson de nuit, Op. 15/1; Mot d'amour, Op. 13/1; Offertoire, Op. 11 (arr. Schneider); *Salut d'amour, Op. 12; Sospiri, Op. 70; Sursum corda, Op. 11.*
(N) ❁ *** Chandos Dig. CHAN 9624 [id.]. Lydia Mordkovich, Julian Milford.

Violin sonata in E min., Op. 82; Canto popolare; Chanson de matin, Op. 15/2; Chanson de nuit, Op. 15/1; Mot d'amour, Op. 13/1; Salut d'amour, Op. 12; Sospiri, Op. 70; 6 Easy pieces in the first position.
*** Chandos Dig. CHAN 8380 [id.]. Nigel Kennedy, Peter Pettinger.

Lydia Mordkovich, always a warmly responsive interpreter of English music, here transforms the elusive Elgar *Violin sonata*. In rapt and concentrated playing she gives it new mystery, with the subtlest pointing and shading down to whispered *pianissimos*. The shorter works include not only popular pieces like *Salut d'amour, Chanson de matin* and *Sospiri*, but rarities like a version of *Sursum corda* never previously recorded and a little salon piece of 1893 which Elgar inexplicably published under the pseudonym Gustav Francke. On this same label the young Nigel Kennedy has covered most of the same works, but less subtly than Mordkovitch.

At the start of the *Sonata*, Kennedy establishes a concerto-like scale, which he then reinforces in a fiery, volatile reading of the first movement, rich and biting in its bravura. The elusive slow movement, *Romance*, is sharply rhythmic in its weird Spanishry, while in the finale Kennedy colours the tone seductively. As a coupling, Kennedy has a delightful collection of shorter pieces, not just *Salut d'amour* and *Chanson de matin* but other rare chips off the master's bench. Kennedy is matched beautifully throughout the recital by his understanding piano partner, Peter Pettinger, and the recording is excellent.

Music for wind

Adagio cantabile (Mrs Winslow's soothing syrup); Andante con variazione (Evesham Andante); 5 Intermezzos; Harmony music No. 1.
(M) *** Chandos CHAN 6553 [id.]. Athena Ens.

4 Dances; Harmony music Nos. 2–4; 6 Promenades.
(M) *** Chandos CHAN 6554 [id.]. Athena Ens.

As a budding musician, playing not only the violin but also the bassoon, Elgar wrote a quantity of brief, lightweight pieces in a traditional style for himself and four other wind-players to perform. He called it 'Shed Music'; though there are few real signs of the Elgar style to come, the energy and inventiveness are very winning, particularly when (as here) the pieces – often with comic names – are treated to bright and lively performances. Excellent recording, with the CD transfers sounding as fresh as new paint.

PIANO MUSIC

Adieu; Carissima; Chantant; Concert allegro; Dream children, Op. 43; Griffinesque; In Smyrna; May song; Minuet; Pastorale; Presto; Rosemary; Serenade; Skizze; Sonatina.
**(*) Chandos Dig. CHAN 8438 [id.]. Peter Pettinger.

This record includes all of Elgar's piano music. It has not established itself in the piano repertoire but, as Peter Pettinger shows, there are interesting things in this byway of English music (such as the *Skizze* and *In Smyrna*). We get both the 1889 version of the *Sonatina* and its much later revision. Committed playing from this accomplished artist, and a pleasing recording too, with fine presence on CD.

ORGAN MUSIC

Organ sonata No. 1 in G, Op. 28.
*** Priory Dig. PRDC 401 [id.]. John Scott (organ of St Paul's Cathedral) (with HARRIS: *Sonata* ***) – BAIRSTOW: *Organ sonata.* ***

(BB) **(*) ASV CDQS 6160 [id.]. Jennifer Bate (Royal Albert Hall organ) – with Recital: *British organ music*. **(*)

(i) *Organ sonata No. 1 in G, Op. 28;* (ii) *Vesper voluntaries, Op. 14: Introduction; Andante.*
(M) *** EMI CDM5 65594-2. (i) Herbert Sumsion (organ of Gloucester Cathedral); (ii) Christopher Robinson (organ of Worcester Cathedral) – *Choral music*. **(*)

Elgar's *Organ sonata* is a ripely expansive piece dating from 1895, written in the period leading up to the *Enigma variations*, a richly inspired work, more of a symphony than a sonata. John Scott gives an excitingly spontaneous performance and the St Paul's Cathedral organ seems an ideal choice, although some of the *pianissimo* passages become rather recessed (a feature of organ playing that works better 'live' than on a record, heard domestically). The recording has plenty of spectacle and the widest dynamic range.

It was a pity that Herbert Sumsion's recording of the *Organ sonata* was not made on the organ at Worcester, for which it was written, but the Gloucester instrument makes a splendidly expansive sound and the gentler pages, glowingly registered, are not as recessed as in some other versions. Sumsion opens grandly and rises to the work's closing climax. His performance is sympathetically idiomatic, though it could perhaps be more flamboyantly extrovert. He is very well recorded, as is Christopher Robinson (who does play at Worcester) in the relatively slight *Voluntaries*, used to make an interlude within the concert of choral music for which the *Sonata* acts as a pendant.

Jennifer Bate plays with all the necessary flair, with her rubato only occasionally sounding unidiomatic, bringing out the dramatic contrasts of dynamic encouraged by the vast Royal Albert Hall organ in its massive setting – emphasized by its facility for causing the sound-image to recede in quieter passages. The analogue recording brings good detail, even if the very wide dynamic range means that Bate's *piano* registers as *pianissimo* because of the distancing.

VOCAL AND CHORAL MUSIC

Vocal and dramatic music, Volume 1: (1912–1948): (i) *The Apostles: By the wayside.* (ii) *Caractacus: Sword song; O my warriors!* (iii) *Crown of India: Imperial masque. Dream of Gerontius:* (iv) closing scene; (v) *My work is done.* (vi) *Saga of King Olaf: And King Olaf heard the cry!* (vii) *The Starlight Express:* excerpts. (viii) Songs (arranged for orchestra by Haydn Wood): *Like to the damask rose; Rondel; Queen Mary's song; Shepherd's song.* (ix) Motet: *O hearken thou, Op. 64.* Chorus: (x) *The shower, Op. 71/1.*
(***) Elgar Soc./Dutton Lab. mono CDAX 8019 [id.]. (i) Dora Labette, Hubert Eisdell, Dennis Noble, Harold Williams, Robert Easton, Hallé Ch. & O, Harty; (ii) Peter Dawson, O, Barbirolli; (iii) Black Diamonds Band; (iv) Maurice D'Oisly, Clara Butt, Queen's Hall Ch. & O, Sir Henry Wood; (v) Kathleen Ferrier, Gerald Moore; (vi) Tudor Davies, SO, Goossens; (vii) Alice Moxton, Stuart Robinson, O; (viii) Light SO, Haydn Wood; (ix) St George's Chapel Ch., Windsor, Sir Walford Davies; (x) Glasgow Orpheus Ch., Sir Hugh Roberton.

This is a fascinating anthology, including some of the earliest recordings of Elgar's music, opening with the Black Diamonds Band (1912) making the first and only recording of the *March* from *Crown of India*, called *Imperial masque*. The excerpts from the *Dream of Gerontius* conducted by Sir Henry Wood (1916) are revelatory, with Dame Clara Butt a rich-voiced but not fruity Angel and the tiny chorus making a most convincing impression. Kathleen Ferrier's radiant 1944 performance of the Angel's soliloquy, accompanied by Gerald Moore, is no less treasurable. Peter Dawson projects the *Sword song* from *Caractacus* with typical charisma and makes it sound surprisingly like the *Floral dance*, while no one has ever sung the delightful *Organ grinder's songs* from *The Starlight Express* with such endearing warmth and charm as Stuart Robertson; his colleague, Alice Moxton, has a pretty soubrette delivery that one would not hear today. Finally the famous prewar Glasgow Orpheus Choir sing *The shower* gently and touchingly, a 1948 recording never before published. Throughout Mike Dutton waves his magic spell over the transfers and, within seconds of starting to listen, one quite forgets any recording inadequacies. This disc is available directly from The Elgar Society, 2 Marriott's Close, Haddenham, Bucks, HP17 8BT.

Choral music: *Angelus, Op. 56/1; Ave Maria, Op. 2/2; Ave maris stella, Op. 2/3; Ave verum, Op. 2/1; Give unto the Lord, Op. 74; O hearken thou, Op. 64; Te Deum and Benedictus, Op. 34.*
(M) **(*) EMI CDM5 65594-2. Worcester Cathedral Ch., Christopher Robinson (with BRAHMS *Organ sonata No. 1*, etc. ***)

Elgar was one of a handful of Roman Catholics among our major English composers (Byrd was another). Like Byrd, he wrote much of his early sacred music within a Protestant tradition. *O hearken thou* is a coronation anthem, written in the composer's official capacity for the coronation of George V. The genuinely Catholic works were written during Elgar's apprenticeship at St George's Church, Worcester. Both the *Ave verum* and the *Ave*

Maria have a gentle, romantic colouring; but most memorable is the *Angelus*, with its repeated figure like an echoing bell. There is much in this programme to show an emerging musical individuality. Performances are sympathetic and alive, and the cathedral ambience is highly suitable for the music. The 1969 recording has been transferred admirably to CD. The coupled organ music increases the interest of this generously full reissue (76 minutes).

Songs: *After; Arabian serenade; Is she not passing fair; Like to the damask rose; Oh, soft was the song; Pleading; Poet's life; Queen Mary's song; Rondel; Shepherd's song; Song of autumn; Song of flight; Through the long days; Twilight; Was it some golden star?*
**(*) Chandos Dig. CHAN 8539 [id.]. Benjamin Luxon, David Willison – DELIUS: *Songs*. **(*)

Benjamin Luxon seemingly cannot avoid the roughness of production which has marred some of his later recordings, but gives charming freshness to this delightful selection. Brilliant and sensitive accompaniment, and a very fine recording balance.

Angelus, Op. 56/1; Ave Maria; Ave maris stella; Ave verum corpus, Op. 2; Ecce sacerdos magnus; Fear not, O land; Give unto the Lord, Op. 74; Great is the Lord, Op. 67; I sing the birth; Lo! Christ the Lord is born; O hearken thou, Op. 64; O salutaris hostia Nos. 1–3.
*** Hyperion Dig. CDA 66313 [id.]. Worcester Cathedral Ch., Donald Hunt; Adrian Partington.

Though one misses the impact of a big choir in the *Coronation anthem, O hearken thou*, and in the grand setting of Psalm 48, *Great is the Lord*, the refinement of Dr Hunt's singers, their freshness and bloom as recorded against a helpful acoustic, are ample compensation, particularly when the feeling for Elgarian phrasing and rubato is unerring. Vividly atmospheric recording, which still allows full detail to emerge.

The Apostles, Op. 49.
*** Chandos Dig. CHAN 8875/6 [id.]. Hargan, Hodgson, Rendall, Roberts, Terfel, Lloyd, London Symphony Ch., LSO, Hickox.
(M) *** EMI CMS7 64206-2 (2) [CDMB 64206]. Armstrong, Watts, Tear, Luxon, Grant, Carol Case, Downe House School Ch., LPO Ch., LPO, Boult.

Where Boult's reading has four-square nobility, Hickox is far more flexible in his expressiveness, drawing singing from his chorus which far outshines that on the earlier reading. Most of his soloists are preferable too, for example Stephen Roberts as a light-toned Jesus and Robert Lloyd characterful as Judas. Only the tenor, David Rendall, falls short, with vibrato exaggerated by the microphone. The recording, made in St Jude's, Hampstead, is among Chandos's finest, both warm and incandescent, with plenty of detail.

Boult's performance gives the closing scene great power and a wonderful sense of apotheosis, with the spacious sound-balance rising to the occasion. Generally fine singing – notably from Sheila Armstrong and Helen Watts – and a 1973/4 Kingsway Hall recording as rich and faithful as anyone could wish for. The powerfully lyrical *Meditation* from *The Light of Life* makes a suitable postlude without producing an anticlimax, again showing Boult at his most inspirational.

The Banner of St George, Op. 33; (i) *Great is the Lord (Psalm 48), Op. 67; Te Deum and Benedictus, Op. 34.*
(M) *** EMI Dig. CDM5 65108-2. L. Symphony Ch., N. Sinfonia, Hickox; (i) with Stephen Roberts.

In telling the story of St George slaying the dragon and saving the Lady Sylene, Elgar is at his most colourful, with the battle sequence leading to beautifully tender farewell music (bringing one of Elgar's most yearningly memorable melodies) and a final rousing chorus. The three motets, written at the same period, bring 'Pomp and circumstance' into church and, like the cantata, stir the blood in Hickox's strong, unapologetic performances, richly recorded.

(i) *The Black Knight* (symphony for chorus and orchestra); Part-songs: *Fly singing bird; The snow; Spanish serenade;* (ii) *Scenes from the Saga of King Olaf, Op. 30.*
(M) *** EMI Dig. CMS5 65104-2 (2). (i) RLPO Ch. & O, Groves; (ii) Cahill, Langridge, Rayner Cook, LPO Ch., LPO, Handley.

Charles Groves conducts a strong, fresh performance of *The Black Knight*, not always perfectly polished in its ensemble but with bright, enthusiastic singing from the chorus, and the happiness and confidence of the writing are what come over with winning freshness, even though Elgarians must inevitably miss the deeper, darker and more melancholy overtones. The emotional thrust in Handley's reading confirms *King Olaf* as the very finest of the big works Elgar wrote before the *Enigma variations* in 1899. In its big choruses its style keeps anticipating the later masterpieces, equally reflecting the influence of Wagner's *Parsifal*. The wonder is that Elgar's inspiration rises high above the doggerel of the text (Longfellow, adapted by Harry Acworth) and, though the episodic dramatic plan eventually tails off, the opposite is the case with Elgar's music, which grows even richer towards the end, with the exciting, dramatic chorus, *The Death of Olaf* (very Wagnerian) followed by an epilogue which transcends everything, building to a heart-tugging climax on the return of the 'Heroic Beauty' theme.

Though strained at times by the high writing, Philip Langridge makes a fine, intelligent Olaf, Teresa Cahill sings with ravishing silver purity and Brian Rayner Cook brings out words with fine clarity; but it is the incandescent singing of the London Philharmonic Chorus that sets the seal on this superb set, ripely recorded, one of the finest in EMI's long Elgar history.

The Black Knight, Op. 3; Scenes from the Bavarian Highlands, Op. 27.
✿ *** Chandos Dig. CHAN 9436 [id.]. L. Symphony Ch., LSO, Richard Hickox.

These two choral works, strongly contrasted, both here receive incandescent performances, easily outshining previous recordings. The cantata, *The Black Knight*, is based on a similar story to that of Mahler's early cantata, *Das klagende Lied*, but Elgar's inspiration is more open and less tortured, with the orchestration already showing the mastery which was to bloom in *Enigma*. Hickox, helped by exceptionally rich and full recording, with vivid presence, consistently brings out the dramatic tensions of the piece as well as the refinement and beauty of the poetic sequences, to make the previous recording under Sir Charles Groves sound too easy-going, enjoyable as it is. The part-songs inspired by the composer's visit to Bavaria then add even more exhilaration, with the vigour and joy of the outer movements – better-known in Elgar's orchestral versions – winningly brought out, and with the London Symphony Chorus at its freshest and most incisive. A disc to win new admirers for two seriously neglected works.

(i) *Caractacus* (complete). *Coronation march; Enigma variations; Imperial march.*
(N) (M) *** EMI CMS7 63707-2 (2). (i) Peter Glossop, Sheila Armstrong, Robert Tear, Bryan Rayner Cook, Malcolm King, Richard Suart, R. Liverpool PO Ch., RLPO, Groves.

Groves's is a very fine performance of *Caractacus*, which with ripe recording brings out all the Elgarian atmosphere (even if it does not manage a clear projection of the words). The soloists are excellent and this is a work that gives a rich insight into the happy Elgar early in his career, a composer still limited, but delightfully approachable. Such passages as the duet between Caractacus's daughter and her lover are as tender as anything Elgar wrote before *Enigma*. The two marches are also welcome in context, and the coupled account of *Enigma* brings a straightforward reading with comparatively slow tempi throughout. Some ears may find Groves's manner staid, but others will respond to the warmth. *Nimrod* is characteristic of the whole: there is no hushed *pianissimo* at the beginning; rather the climax is allowed to unfold simply, but with undoubted eloquence, and then fall away again with a natural ebb and flow. There is some rich orchestral tone which compensates for the occasional less-than-crisp ensemble. The finale has real nobilmente.

(i) *Caractacus, Op. 35. Severn suite* (full orchestral version).
*** Chandos Dig. CHAN 9156/7 [id.]. (i) Howarth, Wilson-Johnson, Davies, Roberts, Miles, London Symphony Ch.; LSO, Hickox.

Elgar's *Caractacus* draws from Hickox and his splendid LSO forces a fresh, sympathetic reading, generally very well sung, with David Wilson-Johnson in the title-role, recorded in opulent Chandos sound. Much the most memorable item is the well-known *Imperial march*, introducing the final scene in Rome, made the more exciting with chorus. One even forgives the embarrassment of the concluding chorus which predicts that 'The nations all shall stand, and hymn the praise of Britain hand in hand.' The only reservation is that the earlier, EMI recording conducted by Sir Charles Groves, a sure candidate for CD, was crisper in ensemble and even better sung, with even more seductive pointing of rhythm. For coupling, Hickox has the full orchestral arrangement of Elgar's very last work, originally for brass band, the *Severn suite*.

(i) *Coronation ode, Op. 44; The Spirit of England, Op. 80.*
(M) *** Chandos CHAN 6574 [id.]. Cahill, SNO Ch. and O, Gibson; (i) with Anne Collins, Rolfe Johnson, Howell.

Gibson's performances combine fire and panache, and the recorded sound has an ideal Elgarian expansiveness, the choral tone rich and well focused, the orchestral brass given plenty of weight, and the overall perspective highly convincing. He is helped by excellent soloists, with Anne Collins movingly eloquent in her dignified restraint when she introduces the famous words of *Land of hope and glory* in the finale; and the choral entry which follows is truly glorious in its power and amplitude. *The Spirit of England*, a wartime cantata to words of Laurence Binyon, is in some ways even finer, with the final setting of *For the fallen* rising well above the level of his occasional music.

The Dream of Gerontius, Op. 38.
*** Chandos Dig. CHAN 8641/2 [id.]. Palmer, Davies, Howell, London Symphony Ch. & LSO, Hickox – PARRY: *Anthems.* ***
(B) *** EMI CZS5 73579-2 (2) [CDFB 73579]. Dame Janet Baker, Richard Lewis, Kim Borg, Hallé & Sheffield Philharmonic Ch., Amb. S. Hallé O, Barbirolli.

(i) *The Dream of Gerontius;* (ii) *Cello concerto.*
(***) Testament mono SBT 2025 (2) [id.]. (i) Heddle Nash, Gladys Ripley, Dennis Noble, Norman Walker, Huddersfield Ch. Soc.,

Liverpool PO; (ii) Tortelier, BBC SO; Sargent.

Sir Malcolm Sargent, never finer on disc, in 1945 paced the score perfectly, drawing incandescent singing from the Huddersfield Choral Society. The soloists too, led superbly by Heddle Nash as Gerontius, have a freshness and clarity rarely matched, with Nash's ringing tenor consistently clean in attack. Though Gladys Ripley's fine contralto is caught with a hint of rapid flutter, she matches the others in forthright clarity, with Dennis Noble as the Priest and Norman Walker as the Angel of the Agony, both strong and direct. The mono recording captures detail excellently, even if inevitably the dynamic range is limited. Having the soloists balanced relatively close allows every word to be heard; in the present transfer, though the chorus lacks something in body, such a climax as *Praise to the Holiest* has thrilling bite. The first and finest of Tortelier's three recordings of the Elgar *Cello concerto* makes an ideal coupling, emotionally intense within a disciplined frame. The 1953 recording is transferred very clearly and vividly. Like all the Testament transfers of EMI material, it comes with excellent background notes.

Barbirolli's red-blooded reading of *Gerontius* is the most heart-warmingly dramatic ever recorded; here it is offered, in a first-rate CD transfer. No one on record can match Dame Janet in this version of *Gerontius* for the fervent intensity and glorious tonal range of her singing as the Angel, one of her supreme recorded performances; and the clarity of CD intensifies the experience. In pure dedication the emotional thrust of Barbirolli's reading conveys the deepest spiritual intensity, making most other versions (though not Boult's) seem cool by comparison. The recording may have its hints of distortion, but the sound is overwhelming. Richard Lewis gives one of his finest recorded performances, searching and intense, and, though Kim Borg is unidiomatic in the bass role, his bass tones are rich in timbre, even if his projection lacks the dramatic edge of Robert Lloyd on the re-issued Boult set.

Hickox's version outshines almost all rivals in the range and quality of its sound. Quite apart from the fullness and fidelity of the recording, Hickox's performance is deeply understanding, not always ideally powerful in the big climaxes but most sympathetically paced, with natural understanding of Elgarian rubato. The soloists make a characterful team. Arthur Davies is a strong and fresh-toned Gerontius; Gwynne Howell in the bass roles is powerful if not always ideally steady; and Felicity Palmer, though untraditionally bright of tone with her characterful vibrato, is strong and illuminating. Though on balance Boult's soloists are even finer, Hickox's reading in its expressive warmth conveys much love for this score, and the last pages with their finely sustained closing *Amen* are genuinely moving.

(i) *The Dream of Gerontius, Op. 38;* (ii) *The Music Makers, Op. 69.*

(N) ❁(M) *** EMI CMS5 66540-2 (2) [CDMB 66540]. (i) Nicolai Gedda, Helen Watts, Robert Lloyd, Alldis Ch., LPO Ch., New Philh. O; (ii) Dame Janet Baker, LPO Ch., LPO; Boult.

Boult was 86 when in 1975 he made his recording of *Gerontius*. He was very determined to do so, for in a letter to Michael Kennedy earlier in the year he had written '. . . *my "Gerontius" was generally thought boring beside those of J. B. and Malcolm and therefore I was left out* . . .' The inspired result is the very opposite of boring: Boult's total dedication is matched by his powerful sense of drama. Indeed it is difficult to conceive of a more powerful conclusion to Part I when Robert Lloyd (a magnificent Priest and Angel of Agony) and the chorus send Gerontius's soul on its way: '*Proficisecere, anima Christiana* . . . *Go in the name of Angels.*' The spiritual feeling is intense throughout, but the human qualities of the narrative are also fully realized. Boult's controversial choice of Nicolai Gedda in the role of Gerontius brings a new dimension to this characterization, and he brings the sort of echoes of Italian opera that Elgar himself – perhaps surprisingly – asked for. He is perfectly matched by Helen Watts as the Angel. It is a fascinating vocal partnership, and is equalled by the commanding manner which Robert Lloyd finds for both his roles. The orchestral playing is always responsive, and often, like the choral singing, very beautiful, while the dramatic passages bring splendid incisiveness and bold assurance from the singers. The 1976 Kingsway Hall recording (produced by Christopher Bishop) is extremely well balanced by Christopher Parker and has been quite stunningly remastered – especially at the bass end of the spectrum: the sound has great presence as well as ideal ambient warmth and atmosphere. It is technically, as well as musically, a truly great recording.

The performance and recording of *The Music Makers*, made at Abbey Road a decade earlier, is also very successful. It is not one of the composer's greatest works, and it is some measure of its musical material that the passages which stand out are those where Elgar used themes from his earlier works. If only the whole piece lived up to the uninhibited choral setting of the *Nimrod* variation from *Enigma*, it would be another Elgar masterpiece. Neverthless Boult's dedication, matched by Dame Janet Baker's masterly eloquence, holds the listener throughout, and the current transfer has brought a new vividness to the choral contribution. The CD layout has now been improved from the original issue. Disc

1 includes the whole of *The Music Makers* and Part I of *Gerontius* (both generously cued). Part II is then complete on the second disc.

(i) *The Kingdom, Op. 51;* (ii) *Coronation Ode, Op. 34.*
(M) *** EMI CMS7 64209-2 [ZDMB 64209]. (i) Margaret Price, Yvonne Minton, Alexander Young, John Shirley-Quirk, LPO Ch., LPO, Boult; (ii) Felicity Lott, Alfreda Hodgson, Richard Morton, Cambridge University Music Soc., King's College, Cambridge, Ch., New Philh. O, Band of Royal Military School of Music, Kneller Hall, Philip Ledger.

(i) *The Kingdom* (with BACH, arr. ELGAR: *Fantasia and fugue in C min.(BWV 537), Op. 86;* HANDEL, arr. ELGAR: *Overture in D min.* from *Chandos anthem No. 2*).
**(*) RCA Dig. 07863 57862-2 (2) [id.]. (i) Kenny, Hodgson, Gillett, Luxon, LPO Ch.; LPO, Slatkin.

The Kingdom; Sursum corda; Sospiri.
*** Chandos Dig. CHAN 8788/9 [id.]. Marshall, Palmer, Davies, Wilson-Johnson, London Symphony Ch., LSO, Hickox.

Boult was devoted to *The Kingdom*, identifying with its comparative reticence, openly preferring it even to *Gerontius*, and his dedication emerges clearly throughout a glorious performance. The melody which Elgar wrote to represent the Holy Spirit is one of the noblest that even he created, and the soprano aria *The sun goeth down* (beautifully sung by Margaret Price) leads to a deeply affecting climax. The other soloists also sing splendidly, and the only reservation concerns the chorus, which is not quite as disciplined as it might be and sounds a little too backward for some of the massive effects which cap the power of the work. The coupling of the *Coronation ode* is handy and certainly welcome, rather than particularly appropriate. It is far more than a jingoistic occasional piece, though it was indeed the work which first featured *Land of hope and glory*. All told, the work contains much Elgarian treasure, and Ledger is superb in capturing the necessary swagger and panache, flouting all thought of potential bad taste. With recording of outstanding quality – among the finest made in King's College Chapel during the analogue era – and with extra brass bands, it presents a glorious experience. Excellent singing and playing, too, although the male soloists do not quite match their female colleagues. Both works are generously cued.

Hickox proves a warmly understanding Elgarian and his manner is more ripely idiomatic. His soloists make a characterful quartet. Margaret Marshall is the sweet, tender soprano, rising superbly to a passionate climax in her big solo, *The sun goeth down*, and Felicity Palmer is a strong and positive – if not ideally warm-toned – Mary Magdalene. David Wilson-Johnson points the words of St Peter most dramatically, and Arthur Davies is the radiant tenor. The fill-ups are not generous: the intense little string adagio, *Sospiri*, and the early *Sursum corda*.

Slatkin sometimes jumps the gun in unleashing his forces, but he makes nonsense of any suggestion that this is an undramatic, merely meditative piece. Urgent as his view of Elgar is, Slatkin has a natural feeling for Elgarian rubato and is never rigid or breathless. When it comes to the gentler moments, he conveys a hushed dedication. The choral singing is incandescent; but sadly the set falls short in the choice of soloists. All four in varying degrees (Alfreda Hodgson less than the others) sing with uneven production and with noticeable flutter or vibrato amounting to wobble. The sound is full, rich and atmospheric, as it also is in the two ripely characteristic transcriptions of Bach and Handel that come as fill-ups.

The Light of Life (Lux Christi), Op. 29.
*** Chandos Dig. CHAN 9208 [id.]. Judith Howarth, Linda Finnie, Arthur Davies, John Shirley-Quirk, LSO Ch., LSO, Hickox.
(M) **(*) EMI CDM7 64732-2. Marshall, Watts, Leggate, Shirley-Quirk, RLPO Ch. & O, Groves.

Notably more than Sir Charles Groves in the earlier, EMI recording, Hickox conveys the warmth of inspiration of *The Light of Life* in glowing sound, with the chorus incandescent. The solo singing is richly characterful, even if the microphone catches an unevenness in the singing of the mezzo, Linda Finnie, and of John Shirley-Quirk; nevertheless he sings nobly as Jesus in the climactic Good Shepherd solo. Arthur Davies as the blind man and the soprano, Judith Howarth, are both excellent, singing with clear, fresh tone.

Sir Charles Groves's understanding performance features four first-rate soloists and strongly involving, if not always flawless, playing and singing from the Liverpool orchestra and choir. The recording is vivid and full in EMI's recognizable Elgar manner and has been admirably transferred, with cleaner focus and no appreciable loss of amplitude.

(i) *The Music Makers, Op. 69. Chanson de matin; Chanson de nuit, Op. 15/1–2; Dream children, Op. 43; Elegy, Op. 58; Salut d'amour, Op. 12; Sospiri, Op. 70; Sursum corda, Op. 11.*
**(*) Teldec/Warner Dig. 4509 92374-2 [id.]. (i) Jean Rigby, BBC Symphony Ch.; BBC SO, Andrew Davis.

The Music Makers, Op. 69; Sea pictures, Op. 37.
*** Chandos Dig. CHAN 9022 [id.]. Linda Finnie, LPO Ch., LPO, Bryden Thomson.
(M) **(*) EMI Dig. CDM5 65126-2. Felicity Palmer, L. Symphony Ch., LSO, Hickox.

On Chandos, the song-cycle and the neglected

cantata make a good coupling, with a contralto soloist as the key figure in each work. Bryden Thomson directs warmly expressive, spontaneous-sounding performances of both works, easily flexible in an idiomatic way, and this now makes a first choice among modern recordings. The recording, full and atmospheric, with the chorus well balanced and with the organ obbligatos richly caught in both works, yet brings out an unevenness in Linda Finnie's strong, forthright voice, giving a hint of flutter.

Hickox's coupling of *Sea pictures* and the big cantata, *The Music Makers*, brings strong, powerful performances, very individual in the song-cycle thanks to the urgent, tough and indeed characterful singing of Felicity Palmer. Hickox gives a convincing, red-blooded reading of the cantata, atmospherically recorded and with the voices well caught, but with reverberation masking some of the orchestral detail.

Andrew Davis conducts a dedicated, refined reading of *The Music Makers*, giving a rare intensity to the quotations from such earlier works as the symphonies and the *Enigma variations*, making one catch the breath. Jean Rigby sings with clear, firm focus. The rather backward balance of the chorus prevents the performance from having the full impact it deserves; but the sound, both refined and atmospheric, consistently brings out the beauty of Elgar's orchestration, both in the cantata and in the very generous and imaginative selection of shorter pieces which come as coupling. Among the encores, the early *Sursum corda*, Op. 11, for brass, organ and strings, stands well between the two masterly elegiac pieces of his high maturity, *Elegy* and *Sospiri*.

3 Partsongs, Op. 18; 4 Partsongs, Op. 53; 2 Partsongs, Op. 71; 2 Partsongs, Op. 73; 5 Partsongs from the Greek Anthology, Op. 45; Death on the hills; Evening scene; Go song of mine; How calmly the evening; The Prince of Sleep; Weary wind of the West.

*** Chandos Dig. CHAN 9269 [id.]. Finzi Singers, Paul Spicer.

Elgar's part-songs span virtually the whole of his creative career, and the 22 examples on the Finzi Singers' disc range from one of the most famous, *My love dwelt in a Northern land*, of 1889 to settings of Russian poems (in English translation) written during the First World War. *Death on the hills*, to words by Maikov, presents a chilling narrative about villagers on the hills being visited by the figure of Death. The basses in unison sing menacingly, representing Death, while the remaining voices sing a nagging ostinato to represent the villagers. The Finzi Singers under Paul Spicer give finely tuned, crisp and intense readings of all the pieces. The Hyperion two-disc collection also includes Elgar's ecclesiastical motets, but for the secular part-songs the Chandos performances are even finer.

4 Partsongs, Op. 53; 5 Partsongs from the Greek anthology, Op. 45. Choral songs: *Christmas greeting; Death on the hills; Evening scene; The fountain; Fly, singing bird; Goodmorrow; Go, song of mine; The herald; How calmly the evening; Love's tempest; My love dwelt; Prince of sleep; Rapid stream; Reveille; Serenade; The shower; Snow; Spanish serenade; They are at rest; The wanderer; Weary wind of the West; When swallows fly; Woodland stream; Zut! zut! zut!*

*** Hyperion Dig. CDA 66271/2 [id.]. Worcester Cathedral Ch.; Donald Hunt Singers, Hunt; K. Swallow, J. Ballard; R. Thurlby.

The finest item on the Hyperion CD is the last, in which both choirs join, the eight-part setting of *Cavalcanti* in translation by Rossetti, *Go, song of mine*. It is also fascinating to find Elgar in 1922, with all his major works completed, writing three charming songs for boys' voices to words by Charles Mackay, as refreshing as anything in the whole collection. Atmospherically recorded – the secular singers rather more cleanly than the cathedral choir – it is a delightful collection for anyone fascinated by Elgar outside the big works.

5 Partsongs from the Greek anthology, Op. 45: Yea, cast me from heights of the mountains; Whether I find thee; After many a dusty mile; It's oh! to be a wild wind; Feasting I watch. The Wanderer; The Reveille.

(M) *** EMI CMS5 65123-2 (2). Baccholian Singers; Jennifer Partridge (with HOWELLS: *A Dirge;* BAX: *The Boar's Head;* DELIUS: *Wanderer's song;* WARLOCK: *The Shrouding of the Duchess of Malfi; The Lady's birthday;* BRITTEN: *The ballad of Little Musgrave and Lady Barnard* *** HOLST: *Choral songs;* VAUGHAN WILLIAMS: *Folksong arrangements.* ***)

Elgar's *Part songs*, Op. 45, for male voices date from 1902 and are settings of Greek translations by English poets. They are all brief but vivid, and the miscellaneous group of choral songs by various other English composers brings great variety. Perhaps the most striking is Britten's extended *Ballad of Little Musgrave*, with piano accompaniment, a macabre piece presented with great drama. Here Jennifer Partridge provides a telling accompaniment, and she also contributes to the success of Peter Warlock's rollicking third 'Sociable song', *The Lady's birthday*. Excellent, truthful recording.

Songs: *Pleading; 3 Songs (Was it some golden star?; Oh, soft was the song; Twilight), Op. 59; 2 Songs (The torch; The river), Op. 60.*

*** (M) EMI CDM7 64731-2. Robert Tear,

CBSO, Vernon Handley – BUTTERWORTH: *Songs;* VAUGHAN WILLIAMS: *On Wenlock Edge*, etc. ***

At his most creative period in the early years of the century, Elgar planned another song-cycle to follow *Sea pictures*, but he completed only three of the songs, his Op. 59. The other three songs here are even more individual, a fine coupling for Vaughan Williams and Butterworth. Incisive and characterful, yet expressively sympathetic performances from Tear. The recording, well focused, is appropriately warm and atmospheric.

Scenes from the Bavarian Highlands, Op. 27; Ecce sacerdos magnus; O salutaris Hostia (3 settings); *Tantum ergo. The Light of Life: Doubt not thy Father's care; Light of the World.*
(M) **(*) Chandos CHAN 6601 [id.]. Worcester Cathedral Ch., Christopher Robinson; Frank Wibaut; Harry Bramma.

It is good to have a fine mid-priced performance of the original piano-accompanied version of the charmingly tuneful *Bavarian scenes*. Even without the orchestra, the music lifts up with remarkable freshness when the singing in Worcester is appropriately committed and spontaneous. The three versions of *O salutaris Hostia* are also worth having, and the strong performances of *Tantum ergo* and *Ecce sacerdos magnus* add to the interest of this reissue.

Scenes from the Bavarian Highlands, Op. 27 (orchestral version).
(M) *** EMI CDM5 65129-2 [id.]. Bournemouth Ch. & SO, Del Mar – STANFORD: *Symphony No. 3.* ***

The EMI recording uses the orchestral version of the score; although the choral recording is agreeably full, balances are not always ideal, with the choral descant in the *Lullaby* outweighing the attractive orchestral detail. However, the performances are infectiously spirited, conveying warmth as well as vigour – Del Mar is a natural Elgarian. Moreover the EMI coupling of the Stanford *Third Symphony* was a happy and generous choice.

Sea pictures (song-cycle), *Op. 37.*
✿ *** EMI CDC5 56219 [CDC 56219]. Dame Janet Baker, LSO, Barbirolli – *Cello concerto.* *** ✿

(i) *Sea pictures, Op. 37. Pomp and circumstance marches Nos. 1–5, Op. 39.*
(B) *** CfP CD-CFP 9004 [id.]. (i) Bernadette Greevy; LPO, Handley.

Like du Pré, Baker is an artist who has the power to convey on record the vividness of a live performance. With the help of Barbirolli she makes the cycle far more convincing than it usually seems, with often trite words clothed in music that seems to transform them. On CD, the voice is caught with extra bloom, and the beauty of Elgar's orchestration is enhanced by the subtle added definition.

Bernadette Greevy – in glorious voice – gives the performance of her recording career in an inspired partnership with Vernon Handley, whose accompaniments are no less memorable, and with the LPO players finding a wonderful rapport with the voice. In the last song Handley uses a telling *ad lib.* organ part to underline the climaxes of each final stanza. The coupled *Marches* are exhilarating, and if Nos. 2 and (especially) 3 strike some ears as too vigorously paced, comparison with the composer's own tempi reveals an authentic precedent.

(i) *Sea pictures, Op. 37;* (ii; iii) *The Starlight Express: Songs: O children, open your arms to me; There's a fairy that hides; I'm everywhere; Wake up, you little night winds; O stars, shine brightly; We shall meet the morning spiders; My old tunes are rather broken; O think beauty; Dustman, Laughter, Tramp and busy Sweep.* (iii) *Dream children, Op. 43.*
(M) **(*) Decca Dig. 452 324-2. (i) Della Jones, RPO; (ii) Alison Hagley, Bryn Terfel; (iii) Welsh Nat. Op. O; all cond. Mackerras – LAMBERT: *The Rio Grande.* **(*)

There has never been a more dramatic presentation of the *Sea pictures* than under Mackerras. The opening of the *Sea slumber-song* is simple and touching but he creates a big climax for *Sabbath morning at sea*, and Della Jones brings even more histrionic feeling to the final climax of *The swimmer*. She sings richly throughout and the performance could not be more vivid; however, although *Where corals lie* is obviously deeply felt, one feels that not all the secrets of this music are fully revealed. The vocal numbers from *The Starlight Express* are well sung by Alison Hagley and Bryn Terfel, but why divorce them from the rest of the score? Mackerras is as warmly affectionate in the delicately scored *Dream children* as he is dramatic in the *Sea pictures*, and the recording throughout, made in Brangwyn Hall, Swansea, has plenty of atmosphere and presence.

The Spirit of England, Op. 80; O give unto the Lord (Psalm 29); Land of hope and glory; O hearten Thou (Offertory); *The Snow.*
(M) *** EMI Dig. CDM5 65586-2. Felicity Lott, L. Symphony Ch., N. Sinfonia, Hickox.

In his series of lesser Elgar choral works for EMI, Hickox conducts a rousing performance of *The Spirit of England*, adding three short choral pieces, including a setting of Psalm 29, and ending with *Land of hope and glory* in all its splendour. The London Symphony Chorus is in radiant form and Felicity Lott is a strong soloist in the main work. First-rate EMI digital sound, made at Abbey Road in 1987.

The Starlight Express (incidental music), *Op. 78*.
(B) *** EMI CD-EMX 2267 [id.]. Masterson, Hammond-Stroud, LPO, Handley.

It has been left to latterday Elgarians to revive a 1916 score (incidental music for a children's play) which was not a success in its day but which reveals the composer at his most charming. On CD in this dedicated reconstruction (without the spoken dialogue) one is conscious of the element of repetition. But the ear is constantly beguiled and the key sequences suggest that this procedure would have won the composer's approval. Much of the orchestral music has that nostalgically luminous quality which Elgarians will instantly recognize. Both soloists are excellent and the LPO plays with warmth and sympathy. The 1976 recording is excellent and it matters little that, in order to fit the piece complete on to a single CD, some minor cuts have had to be made.

Eller, Heino (1887–1970)

Dawn (tone poem); (i) *Elegia for harp & strings; 5 pieces for strings*.
*** Chandos Dig. CHAN 8525 [id.]. (i) Pierce; SNO, Järvi – RAID: *Symphony No. 1*. ***

Dawn is frankly romantic – with touches of Grieg and early Sibelius as well as the Russian nationalists – and the *Five Pieces for strings* have a wistful, Grieg-like charm. The *Elegia for harp and strings* of 1931 strikes a deeper vein of feeling and has nobility and eloquence, tempered by quiet restraint; there is a beautiful dialogue involving solo viola and harp which is quite haunting. Excellent performances and recording, too. Strongly recommended.

Ellington, Edward Kennedy 'Duke' (1899–1974)

Harlem.
*** Chandos Dig. CHAN 9226 [id.]. Detroit SO, Neeme Järvi – DAWSON: *Negro Folk Symphony;* STILL: *Symphony No. 2*. ***

Duke Ellington wrote *Harlem* on board the *Ile de France* in 1950, a wildly exuberant but essentially optimistic picture of Harlem as it used to be before the drug age. Ellington's own programme says, 'We are strolling from 110th Street up Seventh Avenue. Everybody is nicely dressed and in a friendly mood and on their way to or from church.' He pictures a parade and a funeral, and ends with riotous exuberance. This is true written-down orchestral jazz, more authentic than Gershwin and marvellously played by musicians who know all about the Afro-American musical tradition. The trumpets are terrific. Superb recording.

Emmanuel, Maurice (1862–1938)

Sonatine bourguignonne; Sonatine pastorale; Sonatines Nos. 3–4; Sonatine No. 5 (Alla francese); Sonatine No. 6.
✿ *** Continuum CCD 1048 [id.]. Peter Jacobs.

Maurice Emmanuel was born in Burgundy and celebrated his native province in the *Sonatine bourguignonne* (1893), drawing on folk tunes as well as featuring the carillon and chimes of the cathedral at Beaune where he was a boy chorister. Later in his career he was to number Messiaen among his pupils and his *Sonatine pastorale* (1897) is inspired by the birdsong which fascinated his more famous contemporary. The later works are impressionistic, the *Third* (1920) very Debussian, then erupting into a Messiaen-like cascade of brilliance for the finale. The sinuous charms of the *Sonatine Hindous*, written in the same year, contrast with the elegant pastiche of the masterly *Sonatine alla francese* (1926), a 'French suite' in six dance movements of considerable appeal, not so far removed from Ravel's *Tombeau de Couperin*. All this music is superbly played by Peter Jacobs, whose clean articulation and vitality throughout the series afford as much pleasure as his feeling for the music's lyricism and atmosphere. Not to be missed.

Enescu, Georges (1881–1955)

Roumanian rhapsody No. 1.
(N) *** Decca Dig. 452 482-2 [id.]. Montreal SO, Charles Dutoit. – ALFVEN, DVORAK, GLAZUNOV, LISZT: *Rhapsodies, etc*. ***
(M) *** Mercury 432 015-2 [id.]. LSO, Dorati – LISZT: *Hungarian rhapsodies Nos. 1–6*. **(*)
(M) **(*) Sony SMK 47572 [id.]. NYPO, Bernstein – LISZT: *Hungarian rhapsodies; Les Préludes*. **(*)

Enescu's chimerical and exhilarating *Roumanian rhapsody* is played with appropriate high spirits and panache by the Montreal Orchestra under Dutoit, while the Decca engineers produce vivid, brightly lit sound. This is part of a successful orchestral spectacular which collects various rhapsodies – Slavonic, Hungarian and Swedish.

Dorati too finds both flair and exhilaration in this enticing piece, especially in the closing pages, and the Mercury sound from the early 1960s is of a vintage standard. The coupling with the Liszt *Hungarian rhapsodies* is entirely appropriate.

Not surprisingly, Bernstein's charisma comes well to the fore in Enescu's chimerical *First Rhapsody*, a vividly individual performance gathering excitement as it proceeds. The recording does not match Dorati's Mercury version in richness of colour, but it has been effectively remastered. The Liszt couplings are impressive too, and the CD also includes a pair of Brahms *Hungarian dances*.

Roumanian rhapsodies Nos. 1–2, Op. 11/1–2.
*** Chandos Dig. CHAN 8947 [id.]. RSNO, Järvi – BARTOK: *Concerto for orchestra.* **(*)

Järvi has a warmly idiomatic feeling for these amiable, peasant-inspired rhapsodies, moulding phrases and linking sections with spontaneity, drawing committed playing from the Royal Scottish National Orchestra, ripely recorded. Though the first of the two rhapsodies is much the more popular, the second is also lively and colourful. Together they make an unusual coupling for Järvi's warmly sympathetic version of the much-recorded Bartók *Concerto for orchestra*.

Roumanian rhapsodies Nos. 1–2, Op. 11; (i) *Symphonie concertante for cello and orchestra, Op.8; Suites for orchestra Nos. 1 in C, Op. 9; 2 in C, Op. 20; 3 (Villageoise), Op. 27;* (ii) *Poème roumaine, Op. 1.*
(N) (B) **(*) Erato/Warner Ultima Double Dig. 3984 24247-2 (2) [id.]. Monte Carlo PO, Lawrence Foster; with (i) Franco Maggio-Ormezowski; (ii) Male Ch. of Colonne O, & Ensemble Audita Nova de Paris.

The *First Roumanian rhapsody* (easily the most memorable piece here) combines a string of glowing folk-derived melodies with glittering scoring; the *Second*, though still attractive, is not so indelible in its melodies as the *First*. The *Poème Roumain*, written when its composer was 16, is given by Lawrence Foster in its original form. Although it is overlong, it has lyrical appeal, and uses an evocative, wordless male chorus with bells at the opening, and later a solo violin; it features the Roumanian national anthem as its finale, yet surprisingly this does not have a choral contribution. The *Symphonie concertante* is contemporary with the *Rhapsodies* and is an attractively written piece again using national dances. The cello soloist is excellent. The first two of the three *Suites* are well crafted without being in the very first rank; they are expertly laid out for the orchestra and have a charm and appeal that ought to ensure them a wider following. Enescu conducted the première of the *First* when he was only 21, and its successor followed more than a dozen years later in 1915. The idiom is overtly nationalist, though in the *Second* there is something of the delicacy of Reger in the *Gigue*. The *Air* is a richly imaginative piece which shows that the example of such contemporaries as Debussy, Strauss and Florent Schmitt was not lost on its developing composer. The *Third (Village) suite* brings a series of pastoral scenes: children at play, an extended sunset tableau, which contains the most imaginative invention; followed by an evocation of the river in the moonlight and more national dances to conclude. All this is well enough served by the Monte Carlo Orchestra under Lawrence Foster and given the benefit of natural, spacious recording. The offering is generous and this is worth a recommendation for the sake of the little-known repertoire.

(i) *Symphony No. 3; Roumanian Rhapsody No. 1, Op. 11.*
(N) ** Chan. Dig. CHAN 9633 [id.]. (i) Leeds Fest. Ch.; BBC PO, Gennady Rozhdestvensky.

Enescu's creative accomplishments were long overshadowed by his career as a violinist, teacher and conductor; a fate not dissimilar to Busoni, whose pianistic career eclipsed his music. A further handicap was that both composers divided their allegiance between two cultures: Romanian and French in Enescu's case, and German and Italian in Busoni's. The *Third Symphony* dates from the middle of the First World War and is a long, loosely constructed piece, scored for large forces including six horns, organ, piano, two harps and wordless chorus. Rozhdestvensky conducts with much sympathy, though he could perhaps have adopted a brisker tempo for the first movement. The performance lacks the last ounce of urgency and the same goes for the popular *Roumanian Rhapsody No. 1*. Good Chandos sound.

Cello sonatas Nos. 1 in F min.; 2 in C, Op. 26/1–2.
(N) (BB) *** Arte Nova Dig. 74321 54461-2 [id.]. Gerhard Zank, Donald Sulzen.

Despite the identical opus number, Enescu's two cello sonatas are separated by over three decades. The *First sonata in F minor* comes from 1898, when he was 17, and the *Second in C major* is a much later piece, composed in the 1930s when Enescu was in his 50s. The *F minor sonata* is very much in the received tradition, inventive and well constructed, muscular in character and Brahmsian in feeling. Though it is still conservative in approach, the *Second sonata* of 1935 is far more individual and searching in its musical language, a thoughtful piece with the occasional reminiscence of the *Third violin sonata*. It deserves a firmer place in the repertory; there can be no greater praise to say that it is worthy of its dedicatee, Casals. Gerhard Zank has impressive musical credentials (he studied with Menahem Pressler and Norbert Brainin) and founded the Munich Piano Trio. He is a masterly and eloquent cellist and he is well partnered by the Kansas-born Donald Sulzen. Very clean, bright (perhaps overbright) recording with plenty of presence. We are glad to see that the sleeve note thanks Rainer Schmidt 'for the wonderful tuning and work he did on the Steinway Concert Grand'. It is not always that you can rely on such a beautifully conditioned and consistently true instrument on record. A rewarding disc and well worth the modest asking price.

Octet in C, Op. 7.
(N) *** Chandos Dig. CHAN 9131 [id.]. ACMF Chamber Ens. – SHOSTAKOVICH: *2 Pieces for string octet, Op. 11.* STRAUSS: *Capriccio: Sextet.* ***

(i) *Octuor in C, Op. 7;* (ii) *Dixtuor in D for winds, Op. 14.*
(N) (BB) *** Arte Nova Dig. 74321 63634-2 [id.]. Georges Enescu Ens. from Bucharest PO with Cristian Mandeal.
(N) ** Marco Polo Dig. 8.223147 [id.]. (i) Voces and Euterpe String Quartets; (ii) Winds of Iasi Moldava PO, Ion Baciu.

Enescu's *C major Octet* for strings (1900) is an amazingly accomplished piece for a 19-year-old and its contrapuntal mastery says much for his studies with André Gédalge to whom the piece is dedicated. It is a masterly and inventive score, whose inspiration flows with wonderful naturalness. From the Academy of St Martin-in-the-Fields Chamber Ensemble comes a very good performance and recording.

On both Marco Polo and the Pro Arte super-bargain label it is paired with a most valuable coupling, the *Dixtuor* (or Decet) for wind instruments of 1906, one of Enescu's best pieces. Both are impressively presented by the eponymous Bucharest group.

No quarrels either with the response of the Romanian strings, and the *Dixtuor* is very well played by the winds of the Iasi Moldova Philharmonic under Ion Baciu. But the Marco Polo recording is far less impressive than the Chandos, or the excellent quality offered by the Pro Arte bargain label. That is the one to go for, on both artistic and price grounds.

Violin sonatas Nos. 2–3; Torso.
**(*) Hyperion Dig. CDA 66484 [id.]. Adelina Oprean, Justin Oprean.

Enescu's *Second Violin sonata* is an early work. The *Third* (1926) is masterly and shows an altogether different personality; the difference in stylistic development could hardly be more striking. Adelina Oprean is thoroughly inside the idiom and deals with its subtle rubati and quarter-tones to the manner born; her partner (and brother) is somewhat less scrupulous in his observance of dynamic nuance. The additional *Torso* is a sonata movement from 1911, which was published only in the 1980s.

7 Chansons de Clément Marot, Op. 15.
(M) *** Unicorn-Kanchana Dig. UKCD 2078 [id.]. Sarah Walker, Roger Vignoles – ROUSSEL: *Mélodies* **(*); DEBUSSY: *Mélodies.* ***

The set of Enescu songs, written in 1908, makes a rare, attractive and apt addition to Sarah Walker's recital of French song. As a Romanian working largely in Paris, Enescu was thinking very much in a French idiom, charming and witty as well as sweetly romantic. Ideal accompaniments and excellent recording.

Oedipe (opera) complete.
*** EMI (SIS) Dig. CDS7 54011-2 (2) [Ang. CDCB 54011]. Van Dam, Hendricks, Fassbaender, Lipovšek, Bacquier, Gedda, Hauptmann, Quilico, Aler, Vanaud, Albert, Taillon, Orfeon Donostiarra, Monte Carlo PO, Lawrence Foster.

This is an almost ideal recording of a rare, long-neglected masterpiece, with a breathtaking cast of stars backing up a supremely fine performance by José van Dam in the central role of Oedipus. The idiom is tough and adventurous, as well as warmly exotic, with vivid choral effects, a revelation to anyone who knows Enescu only from his *Roumanian rhapsody*. The only reservation is that the pace tends to be on the slow side, but the incandescence of the playing of the Monte Carlo Philharmonic under Lawrence Foster and the richness of the singing and recorded sound amply compensate for that, making this a musical feast.

Englund, Einar (born 1916)

Symphonies Nos. 1 (War) (1946); *2 ('Blackbird')* (1948).
**(*) Ondine Dig. ODE 751-2 [id.]. Estonian SO, Peeter Lilje.

Einar Englund's *First Symphony* is in his own words 'an expression of euphoric joy'. He has a spontaneous and natural gift, and his musical language is probably closer to Shostakovich than to anyone else. The *Second Symphony* presumably acquired its nickname from the apparent evocation of birdsong at the very opening. Good performances and very acceptable (though not outstanding) recorded sound.

Eyck, Jakob van (1590–1657)

Der Fluyten Lust-hof (excerpts).
*** Astrée Audivis E 8588 [id.]. Jill Feldman, Sébastien Marq, Rolf Lislevand.

Jakob van Eyck was blind but, as his tombstone stated, 'What God took from his eyes he gave back in his ear'. He began his career as Utrecht's town carilloneur (engineer and tuner, as well as performer); he also played the recorder 'like a bird' in the local park to the delight of the weekend promenaders. *Der Fluyten Lust-hof*, published in two volumes, dates from the middle of the seventeenth century. Van Eyck wrote divisions and improvisations on famous tunes of the time, most of which came from France and England – half a dozen of

Dowland's most famous numbers are featured. Jill Feldman sings with engaging purity of line and tone, and she has a knack for simple embellishment. The intimacy of the performances is nicely reflected in the recording, which is refined yet with a most natural presence. A pleasing recital for a summer evening.

Falla, Manuel de (1876–1946)

El amor brujo (Love the magician; ballet) (original version, complete with dialogue); (i) (Piano) *Serenata; Serenata andaluza; 7 Canciones populares Españolas.*
*** Nuova Era Dig. 6809. Martha Senn, Carme Ens., Luis Izquierdo; (i) Maria Rosa Bodini.

(i) *El amor brujo* (original version); (ii) *El corregidor y la molinara.*
(M) *** Virgin/EMI Dig. CUV5 61138-2. (i) Claire Powell; (ii) Jill Gomez; Aquarius, Cleobury.

By including the dialogue, spoken over music, the Nuova Era issue provides the complete original conception of *El amor brujo*, rather like a one-act zarzuela, with chamber scoring. Martha Senn is perfectly cast in the role of the gypsy heroine. She sings flamboyantly and often ravishingly, both here and in the delectable *Canciones populares* and the other two songs offered as coupling, and she is accompanied very sympathetically. Luis Izquierdo directs the main work atmospherically and finds plenty of gusto for the piece we know as the *Ritual fire dance*; and the recording is suitably atmospheric and vivid.

The Virgin alternative, by omitting the dialogue, finds room for the original version of the *Three-cornered hat*, also conceived for chamber orchestra, which first appeared as a mime play with music. Much is missing from the ballet we know today. Claire Powell makes an admirable gypsy in *El amor brujo*, while Jill Gomez is equally vibrant in her contributions to the companion work. Nicholas Cleobury concentrates on atmosphere rather than drama and, helped by the translucent textures of the outstanding Virgin Classics recording, certainly seduces the ear.

El amor brujo: complete.
(N) ✿ *** BBC Legends BBCL 4005-2 [id.]. Gloria Lane, BBC SO, Stokowski – BEETHOVEN: *Symphony No. 7* *(**). BRITTEN: *Young person's guide to the orchestra.***(*)
(M) *** Decca 448 601-2. Nati Mistral, New Philh. O, Frühbeck de Burgos – ALBENIZ: *Suite española.* ***

(i) *El amor brujo* (complete); (ii) *Nights in the gardens of Spain.*
✿ (M) *** Decca Dig. 430 703-2 [id.]. (i) Tourangeau, Montreal SO, Dutoit; (ii) De Larrocha, LPO, Frühbeck de Burgos – RODRIGO: *Concierto.* *** ✿
(B) **(*) DG Classikon 439 458-2 [(M) id. import]. (i) Teresa Berganza, LSO, Navarro; (ii) Margrit Weber, Bav. RSO, Kubelik (with RODRIGO: *Concierto de Aranjuez.* **)

Stokowski's account of Falla's *El amor brujo* was given at a Prom in 1964 and has all the electricity of a live occasion. Indeed it has tremendous atmosphere and personality, and can hold its own against any commercial recording of the period – or later. This is an outstanding and thrilling performance and one can hardly believe that an 82-year-old is responsible. In almost every movement Stokowski opts for fast speeds, with the players of the BBC Symphony Orchestra challenged to the limit, as in the *Ritual fire dance* which is electrifying. Consistently Stokowski finds toughness in the score as well as colour and atmosphere, and his soloist, Gloria Lane, with her fruity mezzo tone-colours, sounds comparably idiomatic.In short this is the most gripping and hypnotic performance on or off record, and the recording quality, is very good indeed.

Dutoit's brilliantly played *El amor brujo* has long been praised by us. With recording in the demonstration class, the performance has characteristic flexibility over phrasing and rhythm and is hauntingly atmospheric. The sound in the coupled *Nights in the gardens of Spain* is equally superb, rich and lustrous and with vivid detail. Miss de Larrocha's lambent feeling for the work's poetic evocation is matched by her brilliance in the nocturnal dance-rhythms.

Raphael Frühbeck de Burgos provides us with another excellent mid-priced version of *El amor brujo*, attractively coupled with Albéniz. The score's evocative atmosphere is hauntingly captured and, to make the most striking contrast, the famous *Ritual fire dance* blazes brilliantly. Nati Mistral has the vibrant open-throated projection of the real flamenco artist, and the whole performance is idiomatically authentic and compelling. Brilliant Decca sound to match. Well worthy of reissue in Decca's Classic Sound series.

Navarro conducts a vibrantly atmospheric account of *El amor brujo* and Teresa Berganza is a strong, dark-throated soloist. The LSO are on top form.

The performance of *Nights in the gardens of Spain* is similarly compelling. With Margrit Weber giving a brilliant account of the solo part, particularly in the latter movements, the effect is both sparkling and exhilarating. De Larrocha on Decca (430 703-2) is gentler, but the DG performance, with its strong sense of drama, is certainly not without its evocative qualities. A stimulating pairing; a pity the Rodrigo coupling is less recommendable.

(i; ii) *El amor brujo* (complete); (iii) *Nights in the gardens of Spain;* (ii) *The Three-cornered hat* (ballet): suite.
(M) **(*) EMI CDM7 64746-2 [id.].
(i) De los Angeles; (ii) Philh. O, Giulini; (iii) Soriano, Paris Conservatoire O, Frühbeck de Burgos.

(i) *El amor brujo* (complete); (ii) *Nights in the gardens of Spain; The Three-cornered hat: Dance of the Neighbours; Dance of the Miller; Finale (Jota).*
(BB) **(*) RCA Navigator 74321 24215-2 [(M) id. import]. (i) Mistral; (ii) Achucarro; LSO, Mata.

(i) *El amor brujo* (complete); (ii) *Nights in the gardens of Spain; La vida breve: Interlude and dance.*
*** Chandos Dig. CHAN 8457 [id.]. (i) Sarah Walker; (ii) Fingerhut, LSO, Simon.

Giulini's performances come from the early 1960s, and the disc also includes Soriano's excellent account of *Nights in the gardens of Spain*. The Philharmonia playing is polished and responsive and Giulini produces civilized, colourful performances. The recording, too, is brightly coloured and, although noticeably resonant in *The Three-cornered hat*, the present transfers offer vivid and full-bodied sound. *El amor brujo* is not as red-blooded here as it is in the hands of Dutoit, but Victoria de los Angeles's contribution is an undoubted point in its favour.

The late Eduardo Mata's account of *El amor brujo* is much more exciting than Giulini's; although the famous *Ritual fire dance* is measured, it does not lack rhythmic force. Mata, too, has an uninhibited vocal soloist in Nancy Mistral and her singing is, if anything, more earthy than Los Angeles's. *Nights in the gardens of Spain* brings a highly sympathetic contribution from Joaquin Achucarro, and the performance is both evocative and exciting, if not as delicately refined as the Soriano/Giulini account. The sound throughout is warmly atmospheric and vivid. The dances from the *Three-cornered hat* are more rhythmically subtle than usual, although here the LSO violin timbre sounds thinner. A good superbargain triptych, nevertheless.

The brightly lit Chandos recording emphasizes the vigour of Geoffrey Simon's very vital account of *El amor brujo*, and Sarah Walker's powerful vocal contribution is another asset, her vibrantly earthy singing highly involving. The Simon/Fingerhut version of *Nights in the gardens of Spain* also makes a strongly contrasted alternative to Alicia de Larrocha's much-praised reading and the effect is more dramatic, with the soloist responding chimerically to the changes of mood, playing with brilliance and power, yet not missing the music's delicacy. The *Interlude and Dance* from *La vida breve* make a very attractive encore.

(i) *El amor brujo (Love, the magician);* (ii) *The Three-cornered Hat* (ballets; both complete).
✪ (M)*** Decca Legends Dig. 466 231-2 [id.]. Boky, Tourangeau, Montreal SO, Dutoit.
(B) *** DG Classikon 457 878-2 [(M) id. import]. Teresa Berganza, (i) LSO, García Navarro; (ii) Boston SO, Ozawa.

Dutoit is in his element in this apt but surprisingly rare coupling of Falla's two popular and colourful ballets, each complete with vocal parts. Few more atmospheric records have ever been made. Performances are not just colourful and brilliantly played, they have an idiomatic feeling in their degree of flexibility over phrasing and rhythm. The ideal instance comes in the tango-like seven-in-a-bar rhythms of the Pantomime section of *El amor brujo* which is lusciously seductive. The sound is among the most vivid ever; this remains in the demonstration class for its vividness and tangibility. This is now reissued in Decca's Legends series.

Teresa Berganza links the comparable DG pairing. Both the recordings date from the late 1970s, and at that time Ozawa's highly colourful *Three-cornered Hat* was counted by us the best version on the market in its complete form. The Boston sound is vividly alive, even more so on CD, and has a wide dynamic range yet an admirable presence without distorting perspectives. *El amor brujo*, recorded in London's Henry Wood Hall, brings a slightly more recessed effect and the score's magical moments of evocation are beautifully done, while Berganza's contribution is vibrantly idiomatic, and the responsive LSO playing (wind and strings alike) is comparably seductive in the *Pantomime* sequence.

(i) *El amor brujo* (complete); *Three-cornered hat* (ballet): *3 dances. La vida breve: Interlude and dance.*
(M) *** RCA 09026 62586-2 [id.]. (i) Leontyne Price; Chicago SO, Reiner – ALBENIZ: *Iberia* etc.; GRANADOS: *Goyescas: Intermezzo.* ***

Reiner's complete *El amor brujo*, from a vintage period with the Chicago orchestra, is a fiery and colourful account, yet totally seductive in its nudging of rhythms in *The magic circle* and in the languorous *Pantomime*. Leontyne Price's contribution has all the dark, guttural fire you could ask for, flamenco singing to the manner born. The excerpts from *La vida breve* and three dances from *The Three-cornered hat* are both sultry and gripping; they have far more sparkle than many recordings made since: the final dance brings really exciting orchestral virtuosity. The recording (from 1958) still sounds amazingly good.

'*Música española*': (i; ii) *El amor brujo* (ballet; complete); (iii; iv) *Harpsichord concerto* (for harpsichord, flute, oboe, clarinet, violin & cello); (v) *Nights in the gardens of Spain;* (vi; ii) *The*

Three-cornered hat (ballet; complete); (ii) *La vida breve: Interlude and dance;* (vii; iv) *Psyché;* (vii; viii; iv) *El retablo de Maese Pedro (Master Peter's puppet show).*

(N) (M) *** Decca Double 433 908-2 (2) [id.]. (i) Marina de Gabarain; (ii) SRO, Ansermet; (iii) John Constable; (iv) L. Sinfonia, Rattle; (v) De Larrocha, LPO, Frühbeck de Burgos; (vi) Teresa Berganza; (vii) Jennifer Smith; (viii) with Oliver, Knapp.

Reissued as a Double in Decca's '*Música española*' series, this is a wholly recommendable set offering 140 minutes of top-quality Falla; it is worth investigating even if some duplication is involved. Ansermet's vivaciously spirited complete *Three-cornered hat* is also available coupled with Alicia de Larrocha's distinguished earlier, analogue version of *Nights in the gardens of Spain* (see below); here we are offered her later, digital account which is finer still. The surprise is the Ansermet mid-1960s *El amor brujo*, glittering with flamenco colour and with a particularly appealing soloist in the vibrant Marina de Gabarain. John Constable proves an admirable interpreter of the *Concierto* and there is no doubting the truth and subtlety of the balance or the excellence of the performance. *Psyché* is a setting of words by Jean Aubry for voice and a small instrumental grouping of the size used in the *Harpsichord concerto*. Jennifer Smith is an excellent soloist and the orchestral response in both works is thoroughly alive and characterful. *Master Peter's Puppet show* is not really an opera but a play within a play, both audience and performers being puppets. A series of tableaux is presented with The Boy (Jennifer Smith) as MC. It would be difficult to imagine The Boy being better done than it is here, and the other singers are also excellent. Simon Rattle shows himself completely at home in the Spanish sunshine and the orchestral playing and recording are matchingly vivid.

(i) *Harpsichord concerto;* (ii) *Soneto a Córdoba; 7 Spanish popular songs; El amor brujo: Canción del fuego fátuo.*

(M) (***) EMI mono CDC7 54836-2. (i) Composer (harpsichord), Moyse, Bonneau, Godeau, Darrieux, Cruque; (ii) Maria Barrientos, composer (piano) – GRANADOS: *Danzas españolas* etc.; MOMPOU: *Piano pieces;* NIN: *Cantos populares españolas.* (***)

Maria Barrientos' account of the *Siete canciones populares españolas* was made in 1928 and 1930 in Paris, and it is marvellously intense from both singer and pianist; the *Asturiana* is particularly moving, as indeed are the *Canción del fuego fátuo* from *El amor brujo* ('Love, the magician') and the *Sonnet to Córdoba*. The *Harpsichord concerto* was recorded in Paris in 1930 with a group of distinguished soloists, including the incomparable Marcel Moyse; and again, though one would not mistake it for a modern recording, it sounds remarkably good.

Nights in the gardens of Spain.

(M) (***) Ph. (IMS) mono 442 751-2 (2). Eduardo del Pueyo, LAP, Jean Martinon – GRANADOS: *Danzas españolas*, etc. ***

(M) *** RCA 09026 68886-2 [id.]. Rubinstein, San Francisco SO, Enrique Jorda – CHOPIN: *Andante spianato & Grande Polonaise;* RACHMANINOV: *Rhapsody on a theme of Paganini.* ***

(i) *Nights in the gardens of Spain. El amor brujo: Ritual fire dance.*

(M) **(*) RCA 09026 61863-2 [id.]. Rubinstein; (i) Phd. O, Ormandy – FRANCK: *Symphonic variations* ***; SAINT-SAENS: *Concerto No. 2.* **(*)

(i) *Nights in the gardens of Spain;* (ii) *The Three-cornered hat* (ballet): complete; *La vida breve: Interlude and dance.*

(M) *** Decca (IMS) 417 771-2. (i) De Larrocha, SRO, Comissiona; (ii) SRO, Ansermet.

Dating from 1955, Del Pueyo's *Nights in the gardens of Spain* has never been surpassed. Martinon's magically evocative orchestral opening is matched by the delicacy of the solo entry, and the continuing dialogue between piano and the Paris orchestra brings incandescent subtlety of colour. The slightly diffuse orchestral tapestry presented by the warmly atmospheric recording, which sounds for all the world like stereo, suits the music admirably. Unforgettable.

Alicia de Larrocha's earlier (1971) recording makes an excellent alternative mid-priced recommendation, coupled with Ansermet's lively and vividly recorded complete *Three-cornered hat*; she receives admirable support from Comissiona. The Decca analogue recording entirely belies its age. The *La vida breve* excerpts make an agreeable bonus.

Rubinstein and Jorda make an excellent team and they give a glittering performance, full of evocation and colour. Jorda sustains great tension in the orchestra, yet he creates a basically warm and sultry atmosphere. John Pfeiffer's remastering of the 1957 recording is admirable in all respects, and the disc is equally worth having for the superb account of the Rachmaninov *Rhapsody*, splendidly recorded with Reiner in Chicago a year earlier.

Rubinstein's later Philadelphia version dates from 1969. It is an aristocratic reading, treating the work as a brilliantly coloured and mercurial concert-piece rather than a misty evocation, with flamenco rhythms glittering in the finale. The two encores which follow are even more arresting.

The Three-cornered hat (ballet; complete).

*** Chandos Dig. CHAN 8904 [id.]. Jill Gomez,

Philh. O, Yan Pascal Tortelier – ALBENIZ: *Iberia*. ***

Yan Pascal Tortelier is hardly less seductive than Dutoit in handling Falla's beguiling dance-rhythms, bringing out the score's humour as well as its colour. The fine Chandos recording is full and vivid, if rather reverberant, and Jill Gomez's contribution floats within the resonance; but the acoustic warmth adds to the woodwind bloom and the strings are beguilingly rich. The closing *Jota* is joyfully vigorous.

The Three-cornered hat (ballet): *3 Dances*.
(***) Testament mono SBT1017 [id.]. Philh O, Cantelli – CASELLA: *Paganiniana;* DUKAS: *L'apprenti sorcier;* RAVEL: *Daphnis et Chloé: suite No. 2*. (***)

It is good that Cantelli's excellent (1954) performances of these vivid dances are back in such fine transfers. Elegant, polished accounts, given very good mono sound.

GUITAR MUSIC

7 Spanish popular songs (*Suite populaire españolas;* arr. for guitar).
(B) *** [EMI Red Line Dig. CDR5 69850]. Manuel Barrueco – GRANADOS: *Danzas españolas*. ***

Barrueco is a magician among the new school of guitarists, and his delicate nuances of colouring in these song transcriptions are matched by his seemingly spontaneous rhythmic freedom. Excellent recording too.

PIANO MUSIC

Fantasía bética.
(BB) **(*) ASV CDQS 6079 [(M) id.]. Alma Petchersky – ALBENIZ: *Suite española*. **(*)

Falla's masterly *Fantasía bética* calls for more dramatic fire and projection than Alma Petchersky commands. But she is a musical and neat player, the recording is very acceptable and this recital (which also includes Granados's *Allegro de concierto*) is competitively priced.

Fantasia bética; 4 Piezas españolas.
(N) (B) *** Decca Double 433 926-2 (2) [id.]. Alicia de Larrocha – ALBENIZ: *Iberia; Navarra* etc. ***

These welcome and attractive couplings for Albéniz's *Iberia* are given exemplary performances and most realistic recording.

OPERA

La vida breve (complete).
(M) *** EMI CDM7 69590-2. De los Angeles, Higueras, Rivadeneyra, Cossutta, Moreno, Orfeon Donostiarra Ch., Nat. O of Spain, Frühbeck de Burgos.

La vida breve is a kind of Spanish *Cavalleria rusticana* without the melodrama, and the final scene is weakened by a fundamental lack of drama in the plot. Victoria de los Angeles deepened her interpretation over the years and her imaginative colouring of the words gives a unique authority and evocation to her performance. The flamenco singer in Act II (Gabriel Moreno) also matches the realism of the idiom with an authentic 'folk' style. The other members of the cast are good without being memorable; but when this is primarily a solo vehicle for de los Angeles, and the orchestral interludes are managed so colloquially, this is readily recommendable. The recording remains atmospheric, as well as having increased vividness and presence. It now fits conveniently on a single CD.

Farnon, Robert (born 1917)

A la claire fontaine; Colditz march; Derby Day; Gateway to the West; How beautiful is night; 3 Impressions for orchestra: 2, In a calm; 3, Manhattan playboy. Jumping bean; Lake in the woods; Little Miss Molly; Melody fair; Peanut polka; Pictures in the fire; Portrait of a flirt; A Star is born; State occasion; Westminster waltz.
*** Marco Polo Dig. 8.223401 [id.]. Slovak RSO (Bratislava), Adrian Leaper.

Farnon's quirky rhythmic numbers, *Portrait of a flirt, Peanut polka* and *Jumping bean* have much in common with Leroy Anderson in their instant memorability; their counterpart is a series of gentler orchestral watercolours, usually featuring a wistful flute solo amid gentle washes of violins. *A la claire fontaine* is the most familiar. Then there is the film music, of which the *Colditz march* is rightly famous, and the very British genre pieces, written in the 1950s. All this is played by this excellent Slovak orchestra with warmth, polish and a remarkable naturalness of idiomatic feeling. The recording is splendid, vivid with the orchestra set back convincingly in a concert hall acoustic.

Fasch, Johann (1688–1758)

Chalumeau concerto in B flat, FWV L:B1; Concerto in C min. for bassoon and 2 oboes, FWV L:C2; Concerto in D for 2 horns, 2 oboes & 2 bassoons, FWV L:D14; Trumpet concerto in D, FWV L:D1.
*** DG Dig. 449 210-2. Soloists, E. Concert, Pinnock.

Fasch's *Suite in G minor* is attractively inventive and colourful, very much in the manner of Telemann. The *Trumpet concerto* is a short, unambitious work, but Mark Bennett makes a fairly good case for it. The *Concerto for chalumeau*, an early clarinet, is altogether more individual. Colin Lawson is completely in command of his period instrument, his tone is succulent, his performance winning. This work is a real find. The *Concerto* which features a pair of horns makes considerable demands on the players in the jolly allegros which frame a *Largo*, where the sustained upper tessitura brings trills and other ornamentation. The *C minor Concerto for bassoon and two oboes* is more of a concerto grosso and agreeable rather than distinctive. However, the excellence of the performances here and the fine recording make this a collection well worth exploring.

Fauré, Gabriel (1845–1924)

Ballade for piano and orchestra, Op. 19.
*** Chandos Dig. CHAN 8773 [id.]. Louis Lortie, LSO, Frühbeck de Burgos – RAVEL: *Piano concertos.* **(*)
*** Chesky CD 93 [id.]. Earl Wild, Nat. PO, Gerhardt – CHOPIN: *Concerto No. 1* **(*); LISZT: *Concerto No. 1.* ***
(BB) **(*) Naxos 8.550754 [id.]. Thiollier, Nat. SO of Ireland, Antonio de Almeida – FRANCK: *Symphonic variations*; D'INDY: *Symphonie sur un air montagnard français.* **(*)

Louis Lortie is a thoughtful artist and his playing has both sensitivity and strength. This is as penetrating and well recorded an account of Fauré's lovely piece as any now available; however, the coupling is not one of the preferred versions of the Ravel concertos.

A comparatively extrovert account from Earl Wild, but spontaneous and not lacking in finesse or warmth. Gerhardt accompanies positively and is also responsible for the excellent (1967) recorded quality. Admirers of this fine pianist will find this triptych very successful.

Naxos offer an intelligently planned triptych. François-Joël Thiollier shows some imagination and sensitivity in Fauré's lovely *Ballade*, which is not represented as generously on CD as it should be. The orchestral playing is perfectly acceptable, without being in any way out of the ordinary; likewise the recording. All the same, it is worth the money.

(i) *Ballade for piano and orchestra, Op. 19. Dolly suite;* (ii) *Elégie for cello and orchestra;* (iii) *Fantaisie for flute and orchestra* (orch. I. Aubert). *Masques et bergamasques, Pavane* (orch. H. Rabaud); *Pénélope: Prelude.*
*** Chandos Dig. CHAN 9416. (i) Kathryn Stott; (ii) Peter Dixon; (iii) Richard Davis; BBC PO, Yan-Pascal Tortelier.

Beautifully played and richly recorded, with Yan-Pascal Tortelier a most understanding interpreter, this neatly brings together the most popular orchestral pieces of Fauré, miniatures which often convey surprising weight of feeling as well as charm, as for example the celebrated *Elégie*, here tenderly played by Peter Dixon. Kathryn Stott brings out not only the poetry in the *Ballade for piano and orchestra*, but the scherzando sparkle of the virtuoso passages. Just as convincing are the *Fantaisie* for flute (soloist Richard Davis) and the ever-popular *Dolly suite*, both arranged by other hands. The four brief movements of *Masques et bergamasques* are charmingly done and Tortelier's account of the *Overture* to *Masques et bergamasques* is second to none. Indeed he has the measure of all the music on this disc, be it the poignancy of the *Pénélope Prelude* or the delicacy of the *Dolly* suite.

(i) *Ballade for piano and orchestra, Op. 19.* (ii) *Piano quartet No. 2 in G min., Op. 45.* (iii) *Les berceaux, Op. 23/1. Barcarolle No. 6 in E flat, Op. 70; Impromptus Nos. 2 in F min., Op. 31; 5 in F sharp min., Op. 102; Nocturnes Nos. 4 in E flat, Op. 36; 6 in D flat, Op. 63.*
(N) (**) Biddulph mono LHW 035 [id.]. Marguerite Long with (i) O. Société des Concerts, Philippe Gaubert; (ii) Jacques Thibaud, Maurice Vieux, Pierre Fournier; (iii) Ninon Vallin.

Marguerite Long studied with Debussy and enjoyed the friendship of both Fauré and Ravel. Indeed she claimed to be the torch-bearer of *the* Fauré tradition, much to the chagrin of some of her contemporaries. The *G minor Piano quartet* was recorded in 1940 as the German invaders were approaching Paris. There is some less than subtle pianism and although it is obviously good to have a recording by an artist close to the composer, later recordings have surpassed this as much artistically as they have technically. There is greater elegance to be found in the 1931 recording of the *Ballade*, and some of the solo pieces. In the *F sharp minor Impromptu, Op. 102*, Long's technique is in good repair but elsewhere there is the odd absence of the finish one finds in the generation of Collard and Rogé. Good transfers.

(i) *Berceuse, Op. 116. Dolly* (suite), *Op. 56; Masques et bargamasques, Op. 112; Pelléas et Mélisande* (suite), *Op. 80;* (ii) *Shylock* (suite), *Op. 57.*
(BB) *** Naxos Dig. 8.553360 [id.]. Dublin RTE Sinf., John Giorgiadis; with (i) Michael Healy; (ii) Lynda Russell.

John Georgiadis and the RTE Sinfonietta consistently produce polished and cultured playing and present an ideal collection of his orchestral music. Georgiadis with his rhythmic flair not only brings out the colour and vigour of the fast movements but, as a fine violinist himself, persuades his Irish players to draw out the expressive warmth of such numbers as *Tendresse* in the *Dolly suite*. *Masques et bergamasques*, the *Dolly suite* and the incidental music to *Pelléas et Mélisande* are all among Fauré's best-loved works, and it is good too to have the rarer music for the Shakespeare-based play, *Shylock*, complete with two vocal movements sweetly sung by Lynda Russell. Michael Healy is the expressive violin soloist in the lovely *Berceuse*. Warm, atmospheric recording, transferred at rather a low level.

Elégie in C min. (for cello and orchestra), *Op. 24*.
*** EMI Dig. CDC5 56126-2 [id.]. Han-Na Chang, LSO, Rostropovich – BRUCH: *Kol Nidrei* ***; SAINT-SAENS: *Cello concerto No. 1* ***; TCHAIKOVSKY: *Rococo variations*. *** ✿
(B) *** Sony SBK 48278 [id.]. Leonard Rose, Phd. O, Ormandy – BLOCH: *Schelomo* ***; LALO: *Concerto* **(*); TCHAIKOVSKY: *Rococo variations*. ***
(B) *** DG 431 166-2. Heinrich Schiff, New Philh. O, Mackerras – LALO: *Cello concerto;* SAINT-SAENS: *Cello concerto No. 1*. ***
** Ph. Dig. 432 084-2. Julian Lloyd Webber, ECO, Yan Pascal Tortelier – D'INDY: *Lied;* HONEGGER: *Concerto*; SAINT-SAENS: *Concerto* etc. **(*)

Chang is a naturally inspirational artist, and on her sensitive bow the lovely and sometimes elusive *Elégie* is made to sound like a vocal aria, the shaping and use of light and shade unerring, with a dedicated accompaniment from her mentor, Rostropovich. The recorded sound is very beautiful.

An ardent yet not over-pressed account from Leonard Rose of Fauré's lovely *Elégie* which admirably captures its idiom and its feeling of burgeoning yet restrained ecstasy. The recording is close, but the cello image is natural and firm. The rest of this collection is also highly recommendable.

Heinrich Schiff also gives an eloquent account of the *Elégie*, and he is finely accompanied and superbly recorded.

Julian Lloyd Webber certainly plays Fauré's *Elégie* sensitively enough. His account comes, however, on a disc of much interest in that it includes rarities by Honegger and Vincent d'Indy.

(i) *Fantaisie for flute and orchestra, Op. 79* (orch. Aubert); *Masques et bergamasques, Op. 112; Pavane, Op. 50; Pelléas et Mélisande suite, Op. 80.*
*** Decca Dig. 410 552-2. (i) Bennett; ASMF, Marriner.

Marriner's Fauré programme was among Decca's earlier CD collections, and it has first-class sound; detail is well defined and there is atmosphere and excellent body. *Masques et bergamasques* is among the finest versions available. William Bennett, too, is most sensitive in the *Fantaisie*, and the *Pelléas* suite is also played with characteristic Academy finesse and warmth.

Pavane, Op. 60.
(B) *** Decca Eclipse Dig. 448 711-2. ASMF, Marriner – DURUFLE: *Requiem;* POULENC: *Gloria*. ***

Marriner's warmly elegant account of the famous *Pavane* is used effectively on this Decca disc as an interlude between Duruflé's *Requiem* and Poulenc's *Gloria*, both fine performances.

(i) *Pelléas et Mélisande (incidental music), Op. 80*; (ii) *Pavane, Op. 50.*
(N) (B) *** Ph. Double 462 309-2 [id.]. Rotterdam PO, Zinman, with Jill Gomez; (ii) Jean Fournet – SCHOENBERG: *Pelleas and Melisande; Verklaerte Nacht*. SIBELIUS: *Pelléas et Mélisande; Swan of Tuonela*. **(*)

To couple together three different works inspired by Maeterlinck's drama is a stimulating idea, although not everyone who responds to Fauré and Sibelius will be drawn to the more inflated symphonic poem of Schoenberg, warmly luscious as the Rotterdam textures are. Fauré's incidental music is beautifully played and to make the selection complete, Jill Gomez gives a delightful account of the song *The Three blind daughters*, not previously recorded. David Zinman's refined approach suits Fauré admirably and there is a pervasive tenderness and delicacy (the *Sicilienne* is memorable). The 1979 analogue recording too is naturally balanced and of high quality. Fournet's account of the famous *Pavane* is also very sensitive.

Pelléas et Mélisande (suite), Op. 80; (i) *Pavane, Op. 50.*
*** Chandos Dig. CHAN 8952 [id.]. (i) Renaissance Singers; Ulster O, Y. P. Tortelier – CHAUSSON: *Poème*, etc. ***

These finely finished and atmospheric performances come in harness with a fine account from the soloist-conductor of Chausson's *Poème* and a perceptive and idiomatic performance of the *Poème de la mer et de l'amour*. Very good orchestral playing and exemplary recording.

CHAMBER MUSIC

(i) *Andante in B flat, Op. 75; Berceuse, Op. 16;* (ii) *Cello sonatas Nos. 1 in D min., Op. 109; 2 in G min., Op. 117; Elégie, Op. 24;* (iii) *Fantaisie, Op. 79; Morceau de concours;* (i) *Morceau de lecture;* (ii) *Papillon, Op. 77;* (i–ii) *Piano trio in D min., Op. 120.* (i) *Romance, Op. 28;* (ii) *Serenade in B min., Op. 98; Sicilienne, Op. 78;* (i) *Violin sonatas Nos. 1 in A, Op. 15; 2 in E m in., Op. 108;*
(B) *** EMI (SIS) Rouge et Noir CZS5 69261-2 (2). Jean-Philippe Collard; (i) Augustin

Dumay; (ii) Frédéric Lodéon; (iii) Michel Debost.

Piano quartets Nos. (i; ii) *1 in C min., Op. 15;* (i; iii) *2 in G min., Op. 45; Piano quintets Nos. 1 in D min., Op. 89; 2 in C min., Op. 115;* (iii) *String quartet in E min., Op. 121.*
(B) **(*) EMI (SIS) Rouge et Noir CZS5 69264-2 (2) [(M) id. import]. (i) Jean-Philippe Collard; (ii) Augustin Dumay, Bruno Pasquier, Frédéric Lodéon; (iii) Parrenin Qt.

Dumay and Collard bring different and equally valuable insights, and the performances of the *Piano quartets* are masterly. In addition, there are authoritative and idiomatic readings of the two *Piano quintets*, the enigmatic and other-worldly *Quartet*, and on the first set above, the *Piano trio*, the two *Cello sonatas* (what a fine player Lodéon is!), plus all the smaller pieces. True there are excellent accounts of the *Violin sonatas* elsewhere, from Grumiaux/Crossley and Amoyal/Rogé, and the *Cello sonatas* are well served by both Ingloi and Isserlis (see below); but many of the smaller pieces are more elusive, and they are presented here with a generally admirable standard of performance and recording. This is enormously civilized music whose rewards grow with each hearing; however, one has to accept that, because the Paris Salle Wagram was employed for the recordings (made between 1975 and 1978), close microphones have been used to counteract the hall's resonance. The remastering has both increased the sense of presence and brought a certain dryness to the ambient effect, although the string timbres are fresh.

Piano quartet No. 1 in C min., Op. 15; Piano quintet No. 1 in D min., Op. 89.
(N) *** Decca Dig. 455 149-2. Pascal Rogé, Ysaÿe Qt.

No other artists couple the *C minor quartet* and the *D minor quintet*. It goes without saying that Pascal Rogé and the Ysaÿe Quartet give performances of great finesse and sensitivity. They are perhaps more successful in the *quintet* than in the earlier piece, where they must yield to Domus (Hyperion) who find greater delight and high spirits in the scherzo. The recording is very good though there is the occasional moment when the reverberant acoustic affects the focus. This is scarcely worth mentioning and there is no cause to withhold a full three-star rating.

(i) *Allegretto moderato for two cellos;* (ii) *Andante. Elégie, Op. 24; Papillon, Op. 77; Romance, Op. 69; Sérénade, Op. 98; Sicilienne, Op. 78; Sonatas Nos. 1 in D min. Op. 109; 2 in G min., Op. 117.*
**(*) RCA Dig. 09026 68049-2 [id.]. Steven Isserlis, Pascal Devoyon; with (i) David Waterman; (ii) Francis Greer.

Steven Isserlis understands the essential reticence and refinement of Fauré's art. Perhaps he is at times a shade too reticent in the music and could allow himself to produce a more ardent and songful tone. The balance, which slightly favours his partner, contributes to this impression. Pascal Devoyon is a no less perceptive and sensitive artist. A welcome, then, for the artistry of these performances, but tinged with slight disappointment at the less than ideal balance.

Cello sonatas Nos. 1 in D min., Op. 109; 2 in G min., Op. 117; Elégie, Op. 24; Sicilienne, Op. 78.
(M) **(*) CRD CRD 3316; *CRDC 4016* [id.].
Thomas Igloi, Clifford Benson.

Noble performances from the late Thomas Igloi and Clifford Benson that do full justice to these elusive and rewarding Fauré sonatas, and the recording is clear, if not one of CRD's finest in terms of ambient effect.

Piano quartets Nos. 1 in C min., Op. 15; 2 in G min., Op. 45.
✿ *** Hyperion CDA 66166 [id.]. Domus.
*** Sony Dig. SK 48066 [id.]. Ax, Stern, Laredo, Ma.

Domus have the requisite lightness of touch and subtlety, and just the right sense of scale and grasp of tempi. Their nimble and sensitive pianist, Susan Tomes, can hold her own in the most exalted company. The recording is excellent, too, though the balance is a little close, but the sound is not airless.

Sony's starry version of the two *Piano quartets* with Emanuel Ax, Isaac Stern, Jaime Laredo and Yo-Yo Ma offers the first serious challenge to the Domus account on Hyperion. The performances are of high quality and anyone could rest happy with them. But Domus convey the more idiomatic feel; theirs is domestic music-making at the highest level of accomplishment and conveys an altogether special freshness and spontaneity.

Piano quintets Nos. 1 in D min., Op. 89; 2 in C min., Op. 115.
✿ *** Hyperion Dig. CDA 66766 [id.]. Domus, with Anthony Marwood.
*** Claves Dig. CD 50-8603 [id.]. Quintetto Fauré di Roma.

The playing of Domus in these two masterpieces is as light, delicate and full of insight as one would expect. They make one fall for this music all over again. The second is among the masterpieces of Fauré's Indian summer as he approached his eighties. As this concentrated performance suggests, its autumnal lyricism brings likenesses to late Elgar, with the pianist, Susan Tomes, at her most sparkling in the mercurial Scherzo. Excellent sound.

The Quintetto Fauré di Roma also have the measure of Fauré's subtle phrasing and his wonderfully plastic melodic lines, and their performances are hard to fault. The recording, made in a Swiss church, is warm and splendidly realistic. This music, once you get inside it, has a hypnotic effect and puts you completely under its spell.

Piano trio in D min., Op. 120.
*** Ara. Dig. Z 6643 [id.]. Golub Kaplan Carr Trio – DEBUSSY: *Piano trio* **(*); SAINT-SAENS: *Piano trio.* **(*)

Piano trio in D min., Op. 120; (i) *La bonne chanson, Op. 61.*
(M) *** CRD CRD 3389; *CRDC 4089* [id.]. Nash Ens., (i) with Sarah Walker.

David Golub, Mark Kaplan and Colin Carr give as understanding and idiomatic a performance of the sublime Fauré *Trio* as is to be found. They convey its understatement and subtlety of nuance to perfection, and the interplay among them is a model of the finest chamber-music-making. The recording is very good indeed, with plenty of warmth.

The members of the Nash Ensemble also give a dedicated performance of the late, rarefied *Piano trio*, capturing both the elegance and the restrained concentration. They are hardly less persuasive in the song cycle where the characterful warmth and vibrancy of Sarah Walker's voice, not to mention her positive artistry, come out strongly in this beautiful reading of Fauré's early settings of Verlaine, music both tender and ardent. The atmospheric recording is well up to CRD's high standard in chamber music.

String quartet in E min., Op. 121.
(N) *** Conifer Dig. 75605 51291-2 [id.]. Miami Qt. – SAINT-SAENS: *String quartets Nos. 1 & 2.* ***

Fauré's only quartet is among his most elusive scores and is very difficult to bring off. The Miami Quartet are equipped both with great understanding and refined musicianship, but are richly endowed with technical finesse and musical insight. Theirs is the finest account of the quartet to have appeared for many years. The claims of their set are further enhanced by the interest of the coupling, the two string quartets of Saint-Saëns.

Violin sonatas Nos. 1 in A, Op. 13; 2 in E min., Op. 108.
(M) *** Ph. 426 384-2. Arthur Grumiaux, Paul Crossley – FRANCK: *Sonata.* **(*)
*** Hyperion Dig. CDA 66277 [id.]. Krysia Osostowicz, Susan Tomes.

Violin sonatas Nos. 1–2; Andante, Op. 75; Berceuse, Op. 16.
(BB) **(*) ASV Dig. CDQS 6170 [id.]. Fujikawa, Osorio.

Violin sonatas Nos. 1 in A, Op. 13; 2 in E min., Op. 108; Andante in B flat, Op. 75; Berceuse, Op. 16; Romance in B flat, Op. 28.
✿ *** Decca Dig. 436 866-2. Pierre Amoyal, Pascal Rogé.
(BB) *** Naxos Dig. 8.550906 [id.]. Dong-Suk Kang, Pascal Devoyon.

Readers wanting a modern recording of the two Fauré *Violin sonatas* need look no further. Pierre Amoyal and Pascal Rogé play them as to the manner born. As one would expect, they are totally inside the idiom and convey its subtlety and refinement with freshness and mastery. There are admirable alternatives from Grumiaux and Crossley at mid-price and from Krysia Osostowicz and Susan Tomes, but Amoyal and Rogé more than hold their own against them and throw new light on the three slight miniatures that they offer as a bonus. Impeccable recording, too. A lovely disc.

Dong-Suk Kang, splendidly partnered by another French pianist, Pascal Devoyon, gives us performances which are hardly less fine and which cost only a third as much as the Decca CD. Without disturbing our allegiance to other earlier issues, this is a welcome newcomer – and very good value for money.

These *Sonatas* are beautifully played and recorded on the Philips reissue. Moreover the two artists sound as if they are in the living-room; the acoustic is warm, lively and well balanced. An excellent mid-priced recommendation.

Krysia Osostowicz and Susan Tomes bring an appealingly natural, unforced quality to their playing and they are completely persuasive, particularly in the elusive *Second Sonata*. The acoustic is a shade resonant but, such is the eloquence of these artists, the ear quickly adjusts.

Mayumi Fujikawa and Jorge Federico Osorio produce playing of the highest accomplishment and finesse. There is genuine passion here and real commitment. They are recorded in a resonant hall, and the fairly close microphones are not always flattering to the violin's upper range under stress, although not too much need be made of this: Fujikawa often makes a beautiful sound, and particularly so in the lovely *Berceuse*.

PIANO MUSIC

Ballade in F sharp, Op. 19; Barcarolles Nos. 1–13; (i) *Dolly, Op. 56. Impromptus Nos. 1–5; Impromptu, Op. 86; Mazurka in B flat, Op. 32; 13 Nocturnes; Pièces brèves Nos. 1–8, Op. 84; 9 Préludes, Op. 103; Romances sans paroles Nos. 1–3;* (i) *Souvenirs de Bayreuth. Theme & variations in C sharp min., Op. 73; Valses-caprices Nos. 1–4.*
✿ *** Hyperion CDA 66911/4 (4) [id.]. Kathryn Stott, (i) with Martin Roscoe.

Both the *13 Barcarolles*, written between 1880 and 1921, and the *13 Nocturnes*, from an even wider period between 1875 and 1921, give a most illuminating view of Fauré's career, gentle and unsensational like the music itself, but with the subtlest of developments towards a sparer, more rarefied style. That comes out all the more tellingly when, as here, they are given in succession and are played with such poetry and spontaneous-sounding freshness. Stott earlier recorded for Conifer a generous selection of Fauré piano music (see below) but, quite apart from the warmer, clearer and more immediate sound on the Hyperion issue, allowing for velvet tone-colours, the later performances are more winningly relaxed, ranging wider in expression. Each of the four discs contains well over 70 minutes of music, logically presented, with the *Nocturnes* spread between the third and fourth discs, framing the lighter pieces, including such duets as the witty Wagner quadrille, *Souvenirs de Bayreuth*, and the ever-fresh *Dolly suite*, both with Stott ideally partnered by Martin Roscoe. A masterly set.

Ballade in F sharp, Op. 19; Mazurka in B flat, Op. 32; 3 Songs without words, Op. 17; Valses-caprices Nos. 1–4.
(M) *** CRD Dig. CRD 3426; *CRDC 4126* [id.]. Paul Crossley.

Crossley is especially good in the quirky *Valses-caprices*, fully equal to their many subtleties and chimerical changes of mood. He is extremely well recorded too.

Ballade in F sharp, Op. 19; Nocturnes Nos. 1–13 (complete); *9 Préludes, Op. 103; Theme and variations in C sharp min., Op. 73.*
(B) *** EMI Rouge et Noir CZS5 69437-2 (2). Jean-Philippe Collard.

This is glorious music which ranges from the gently reflective to the profoundly searching. The *Nocturnes* offer a glimpse of Fauré's art at its most inward and subtle. The *Préludes* are comparably intimate, and this is all music to which Jean-Philippe Collard is wholly attuned. His account of the *Theme and variations* is no less masterly, combining the utmost tonal refinement and sensitivity with striking keyboard authority. The recording is good, though it has not the bloom and body of the very finest piano records.

Barcarolles Nos. 1–13 (complete).
(M) *** CRD CRD 3422; *CRDC 4122* [id.]. Paul Crossley.

Paul Crossley has a highly sensitive response to the subtleties of this repertoire and is fully equal to its shifting moods. The CRD version was made in the somewhat reverberant acoustic of Rosslyn Hill Chapel, and is more vivid than the 1971 EMI recording of Jean-Philippe Collard.

Barcarolles Nos. 1–13; (i) *Dolly. Impromptus Nos. 1–5; Mazurka, Op. 32; Pièces brèves Nos. 1–8, Op. 84; Romances sans paroles Nos. 1–3;* (i) *Souvenir de Bayreuth. Valses-caprices Nos. 1–4.*
(B) **(*) EMI Rouge et Noir CZS5 69431-2 (2). Jean-Philippe Collard, (i) with Rigutto.

Jean-Philippe Collard has the qualities of reticence yet ardour, subtlety and poetic feeling to penetrate Fauré's intimate world but, while Collard has exceptional beauty and refinement of tone at all dynamic levels, the only regret is that full justice is not done to it by the French engineers.

Barcarolles Nos. 1, 2, 4, Opp. 26, 41, 44; Impromptus Nos. 2 & 3, Opp. 31, 34; Nocturnes Nos. 4 & 5, Opp. 36–7; 3 Romances sans paroles, Op. 17; Valse-caprice, Op. 30.
*** Decca Dig. 425 606-2. Pascal Rogé.

This CD makes an ideal single-CD introduction to Fauré's piano music. Rogé brings warmth and charm as well as all his pianistic finesse to this anthology, and his artistry is well served by the Decca engineers.

Dolly, Op. 56.
*** Ph. Dig. 420 159-2. Katia and Marielle Labèque – BIZET: *Jeux d'enfants;* RAVEL: *Ma Mère l'Oye.* ***

The Labèque sisters give a beautiful account of Fauré's touching suite, their playing distinguished by great sensitivity and delicacy. The recording is altogether first class.

Impromptus Nos. 1–5; 9 Préludes, Op. 103; Theme and variations in C sharp min., Op. 73.
(M) *** CRD CRD 3423; *CRDC 4123* [id.]. Paul Crossley.

The *Theme and variations in C sharp minor* is one of Fauré's most immediately attractive works; Paul Crossley plays it with splendid sensitivity and panache, so this might be a good place to start for a collector wanting to explore Fauré's special pianistic world. The recorded sound, too, is extremely well judged.

Nocturnes Nos. 1 in E flat min., Op. 33/1; 2 in B, Op. 33/2; 6 in D flat, Op. 63; 7 in C sharp min., Op. 74; 12 in E min., Op. 107; 13 in B min., Op. 119.
(N) ** RCA Dig. 74321 53730-2 [id.]. Jean-Marc Luisada. – BIZET: *Chants du Rhin.* **

The Tunisian-born Jean-Marc Luisada produces some beautiful sounds, though he plays with an appropriate reticence and understatement – too much so! He is a little unimaginative. He does not have the full measure of this elusive and subtle music as do Jean-Philippe Collard and Pascal Rogé. Good RCA recording.

Nocturnes (complete); *Pièces brèves, Op. 84.*
(M) **(*) CRD CRD 3406/7; *CRDC 4106/7* [id.]. Paul Crossley.

Here the recording is rather closely balanced, albeit in an ample acoustic, but the result tends to emphasize a percussive element that one does not normally encounter in this artist's playing. There is much understanding and finesse, however, and the *Pièces brèves* are a valuable fill-up.

Collections

Barcarolles Nos. 1 in A min., Op. 26; 6 in E flat, Op. 70; Impromptus Nos. 2 in F min., Op. 31; 3 in A flat, Op. 34; Nocturnes Nos. 1 in E flat min.; 3 in A flat min., Op. 33/1 & 3; 4 in E flat, Op. 36; 6 in D flat, Op. 63; 13 in B min., Op. 13; 8 Pièces brèves, Op. 84; Romances sans paroles No. 3, Op. 17/3.

(N) *** Hyperion Dig. CDA 67074 [id.]. Kathryn Stott.

An admirably chosen collection, arranged in the form of a recital taken from Kathryn Stott's complete survey. The opening *Romance without words* is inviting and *A minor Barcarolle* and *E flat major* and *minor Nocturnes* are particularly winning, as are the charming eight miniatures of Op. 84. A pity the *C sharp minor Theme and variations* was not included, but what is (69 minutes) is well worth having when played and recorded so persuasively.

VOCAL MUSIC

Mélodies (complete): (i) *L'Absent;* (ii) *Accompagnement; Après un rêve; Arpège; Aubade;* (i) *Au bord de l'eau;* (ii) *Au cimetière; Aurore;* (i) *L'aurore; Automne;* (ii) *Barcarolle; Les berceaux; La bonne chanson* (song-cycle), *Op. 61;* (i) *2 Cantiques (En prière; Noël); C'est la paix!; Chanson;* (ii) *Chanson d'amour;* (i) *La chanson d'Eve* (song-cycle), *Op. 95;* (ii) *Chanson du pêcheur; Chanson de Shylock; Chant d'automne; Clair de lune; Dans la forêt de septembre;* (i) *Dans les ruines d'une abbaye;* (ii) *Le Don silencieux;* (i) *2 Duos for 2 sopranos (Puisqu'ici-bas; Tarantelle); La Fée aux chansons; Fleur jetée;* (ii) *La fleur qui va sur l'eau; L'horizon chimérique* (song-cycle), *Op. 118; Hymne; Ici-bas!;* (i) *Les jardins clos* (song-cycle), *Op. 106;* (ii) *Larmes; Lydia; Madrigal de Shylock; Mai; Les matelots;* (i) *Mélisande's song; 5 Mélodies de Venise;* (ii) *Mirages* (song-cycle), *Op. 113;* (i) *Nell;* (ii) *Nocturne;* (i) *Notre amour; Le papillon et la fleur; Le parfum impérissable; Le pays des rêves;* (ii) *Pleurs d'or; Le plus doux chemin; 3 Poèmes de jour; Les présents; Prison; Le ramier; La rançon;* (i) *Rêve d'amour; La rose; Les roses d'Ispahan; Le secret;* (ii) *Sérénade du bourgeois gentilhomme; Sérénade toscane;* (i) *Seule; Soir;* (ii) *Spleen; Sylvie; Tristesse;* (i) *Vocalise-étude;* (ii) *Le voyageur.*

(M) *** EMI (SIS) CMS7 64079-2 (4) [ZDMD 64079]. (i) Elly Ameling; (ii) Gérard Souzay; Dalton Baldwin.

The songs were written over the fullest span of Fauré's life, during a period of no less than 60 years, starting with a jolly waltz-song written when the composer was 16. The most striking melodies tend to come in the earlier songs – with the second of the four CDs offering many favourite items like *Chanson d'amour*, winningly done by Souzay, and *Les roses d'Ispahan* bringing a ravishing example of Ameling at her most radiant. Even so, the style is astonishingly consistent throughout. In the late cycles, *La chanson d'Eve*, *Les jardins clos*, *Mirages* and *L'horizon chimérique*, there is an extra subtlety in the composer's restraint; but even in that last period Fauré allowed himself one extrovert return to an earlier style, a simple, jaunty song for soprano celebrating the Armistice of 1918, *C'est la paix!*. Souzay is not quite as even in his vocal production as at the beginning of his career, but no baritone of recent years has surpassed him in this repertory, and Ameling is at her very peak throughout, fresh and even in line, with beautiful colourings. The texts of the songs are given only in French.

Mélodies: *Après un rêve; Au bord de l'eau; Aurore; Clair de lune; Dans les ruines d'une abbaye; En sourdine; Fleur; Green; Ici-bas; Mai; Mandoline; Nell; Nocturne; Notre amour; Le papillon et la fleur; Le pays des rêves; Les présents; Prison; Les roses d'Ispahan; Le secret; Soir.*

(BB) *** Virgin Classics Dig. Double VBS5 61433-2 (2) [CDVB 61433]. Rachel Yakar, Claude Lavoix (with BIZET: *Pastorale; Rose d'amour; Sonnet;* CHABRIER: *Chanson pour Jeanne; L'île heureuse; Lied* ***) – HAHN: *Mélodies.* ***

Rachel Yakar with her warm, very French-sounding timbre is an ideal interpreter of French *mélodie*, bringing out the subtleties of word-meaning, though it is a pity that in this super-bargain double-disc issue no texts are provided, only a cursory survey of the genre. The selection of 22 songs could hardly be more attractive, with settings of individual poets grouped together, so that early and late settings of Verlaine can be compared and contrasted. Excellent (1991) recording from Radio France. Coupled with an equally imaginative collection of Hahn songs, plus extra cherishable items from Bizet and Chabrier, it is a delightful issue.

La chanson d'Eve, Op. 95; Mélodies: Après un rêve; Aubade; Barcarolle; Les berceaux; Chanson du pêcheur; En prière; En sourdine; Green; Hymne; Des jardins de la nuit; Mandoline; Le papillon et la fleur; Les présents; Rêve d'amour; Les roses d'Ispahan; Le secret; Spleen; Toujours!.

✽ *** Hyperion Dig. CDA 66320 [id.]. Dame Janet Baker, Geoffrey Parsons.

Dame Janet Baker gives magical performances of

a generous collection of 28 songs, representing the composer throughout his long composing career, including many of his most winning songs. Geoffrey Parsons is at his most compellingly sympathetic, matching every mood. Many will be surprised at Fauré's variety of expression over this extended span of songs.

Requiem, Op. 48.
*** Teldec/Warner Dig. 4509 90879-2 [id.]. Barbara Bonney, Thomas Hampson, Amb. S., Philh. O, Michel Legrand – DURUFLE: *Requiem.* ***
(B) *** Sony SBK 67182 [id.]. Lucia Popp, Siegmund Nimsgern, Amb. S., New Philh. O, Andrew Davis – DURUFLE: *Requiem.* ***
(N) (M) *** EMI CDM5 66894-2 [COM5 66946]. Victoria de los Angeles, Dietrich Fischer-Dieskau, Elisabeth Brasseur Ch., Paris Conservatoire O, Cluytens.
(B) **(*) EMI (SIS) CZS5 69647-2 (2). Rayner Cook, Burrowes, CBSO Ch., CBSO, Frémaux (with BERLIOZ: *Requiem.* **)
(N) *(*) DG Dig. 459 365-2 [id.]. Cecilia Bartoli, Bryn Terfel, Santa Cecilia Nat. Ac. Ch. & O, Myung-Whun Chung – DURUFLE: *Requiem.* *(*)

Requiem; Pavane, Op. 50.
(M) *** Carlton Classics Dig. 30366 0009-2 [id.]. Aled Jones, Stephen Roberts, London Symphony Ch., RPO, Hickox – BERNSTEIN: *Chichester Psalms.* ***
(M) *** EMI CDM7 64634-2 [id.]. Sheila Armstrong, Fischer-Dieskau, Edinburgh Festival Ch., O de Paris, Barenboim (with BACH: *Magnificat.* **)
*** Ph. Dig. 446 084-2 [id.]. (i) McNair, Allen; ASMF Ch. & O, Marriner (with KOECHLIN: *Choral sur le nom de Fauré;* SCHMITT: *In Memoriam No. 2: Scherzo sur le nom de Gabriel Fauré;* RAVEL: *Pavane pour une infante défunte* ***).
(B) **(*) [EMI Red Line CDR5 69858]. Chilcott, Carol Case, King's College, Cambridge, Ch., New Philh. O, Willcocks (with PALESTRINA: *Missa Papae Marcelli.* **)

(i; ii) *Requiem, Op. 48;* (i) *Pavane; Pelléas et Mélisande: suite, Op. 80.*
*** Decca Dig. 421 440-2 [id.]. (i) Kiri Te Kanawa, Sherrill Milnes; (ii) Montreal Philharmonic Ch.; Montreal SO, Dutoit.

(i) *Requiem, Op. 48. Masques et bergamasques; Pelléas et Mélisande (suite), Op. 80; Pénélope: Prélude.*
(M) *(*) Decca 452 304-2 [id.]. SRO, Ansermet; (i) with Danco, Souzay, L'Union Chorale de la Tour de Peitz.

(i) *Requiem, Op. 48;* (ii) *Messe basse.*
(B) **(*) EMI CfP Dig. CDCFP 6072 [id.]. (i) Arleen Augér, Benjamin Luxon; (ii) Paul Smy; King's College, Cambridge. Ch., Ledger.

Requiem, Op. 48 (1893 version). *Ave Maria, Op. 67/2; Ave verum corpus, Op. 65/1; Cantique de Jean Racine, Op. 11; Maria, Mater gratiae, Op. 47/2; Messe basse; Tantum ergo, Op. 65/2.*
*** Collegium COLCD 109 [id.]. Ashton, Varcoe, Cambridge Singers, L. Sinfonia (members), Rutter.

Requiem, Op. 48 (1893 version); *Ave verum corpus, Op. 65/1; Cantique de Jean Racine, Op. 11; Messe basse; Tantum ergo, Op. 65/2.*
*** Hyperion Dig. CDA 66292 [id.]. Mary Seers, Isabelle Poulenard, Michael George, Corydon Singers, ECO, Matthew Best.

Requiem, Op. 48; Cantique de Jean Racine, Op. 11.
*** Conifer Dig. 74321 15351-2 [id.]. Otaki, Griffiths, Trinity College, Cambridge, Ch., London Musici, Marlow (with MESSIAEN: *O sacrum convivium* ***) – DURUFLE: *Messe Cum jubilo* etc. ***

(i) *Requiem, Op. 48;* (ii) *Cantique de Jean Racine, Op. 11;* (ii; iii) *Messe basse.*
(BB) *** Naxos Dig. 8.550765 [id.]. Beckley, Gedge, Schola Cantorum of Oxford, Oxford Camerata, Summerly (with DE SEVERAC: *Tantum ergo;* VIERNE: *Andantino;* with Colm Carey, organ ***).
(B) *** Decca Double 436 486-2 (2). (i) Jonathon Bond, Benjamin Luxon; (ii) Stephen Cleobury; (iii) Andrew Brunt; (i–iii) St John's College, Cambridge, Ch., Guest (i) with ASMF – DURUFLE: *Requiem;* POULENC: *Mass* etc. ***

(i; ii; iv) *Requiem, Op. 48;* (ii; iii) *Les Djinns, Op. 12;* (ii) *Madrigal, Op. 35.*
*** Ph. Dig. 438 149-2 [id.]. (i) Catherine Bott, Gilles Cachemaille; (ii) Monteverdi Ch., Salisbury Cathedral Boy Choristers; (iii) Sabine Vatin; (iv) ORR, Gardiner – DEBUSSY: *3 Chansons de Charles d'Orléans;* RAVEL: *3 Chansons;* SAINT-SAENS: *3 songs.* ***

Requiem, Op. 48 (1894 version); *Messe des pêcheurs de Villerville.*
*** HM Dig. HMC 90 1292 [id.]. Mellon, Kooy, Audoli, Petits Chanteurs de Saint-Louis, Paris Chapelle Royale Ch., Musique Oblique Ens., Herreweghe.

John Rutter's inspired reconstruction of Fauré's original 1893 score, using only lower strings and no woodwind, opened our ears to the extra freshness of the composer's first thoughts. Rutter's fine, bright recording includes the *Messe basse* and four motets, of which the *Ave Maria* setting and *Ave verum corpus* are particularly memorable. The recording is first rate but places the choir and instruments relatively close.

The directness and clarity of Andrew Davis's reading go with a concentrated, dedicated manner and a masterly control of texture to bring out the purity and beauty of Fauré's orchestration to the full. Moreover the fresh vigour of the choral singing achieves an admirable balance between ecstasy and restraint in this most elusive of Requiem settings, culminating in a wonderfully measured and intense account of the final *In Paradisum*. Lucia Popp is both rich and pure, and Siegmund Nimsgern (if less memorable) is refined in tone and detailed in his pointing. The recording, made in a church, matches the intimate manner and, with its equally fine Duruflé coupling, this is a very highly recommendable bargain version.

It is good that the de Los Angeles/Fischer-Dieskau version, made under the late André Cluytens in the early 1960s, has been restored to the catalogue as one of EMI's 'Great recordings of the century'. If this claim is perhaps a little overstated, the performance has great expressive eloquence and the choir, if not as fine as Rutter's or Gardiner's (to name but two) has a certain idiomatic advantage. It has always been a highly recommendable version with dedicated contributions from both soloists and the full, warmly atmospheric recording sounds very beautiful. However it has no coupling.

Richard Hickox opts for the regular full-scale text of the *Requiem*, yet at speeds rather faster than usual – no faster than those marked – he presents a fresh, easily flowing view, rather akin to John Rutter's using the original chamber scoring on his full-price Collegium issue. Aled Jones sings very sweetly in *Pie Jesu*. With its generous and equally successful coupling, this makes a strong alternative recommendation.

John Eliot Gardiner with period forces also chooses the version of the *Requiem* with the original instrumentation. The darkness matches Gardiner's view of the work which he makes more dramatic than it often is. The mellow recording takes away some of the bite but, with excellent soloists – Catherine Bott radiantly beautiful in the *Pie Jesu*, Gilles Cachemaille vividly bringing out word-meaning – and a generous, unusual coupling, it makes an excellent choice. *Les Djinns* is specially welcome, with piano accompaniment on a gentle-toned Erard of 1874; and all the other pieces, including Fauré's enchanting *Madrigal*, are in various ways inspired by early French part-songs, with the medieval overtones brought out in the Debussy and with the humour of the Ravel nicely underlined.

Like Gardiner on Philips, Richard Marlow uses the Nectoux-Delage edition, but he gives the *Requiem* a more liturgical flavour, helped by a chapel acoustic, with an emphasis on fresh, young voices, soloists included. It is a strong, purposeful performance, warmly expressive. The disc can be strongly recommended to those who fancy the coupling of Messiaen's one motet and four of Duruflé, as well as the latter's superb *Messe Cum jubilo* of 1966 in its version with inspired organ accompaniment.

Matthew Best's performance with the Corydon Singers uses the Rutter edition but presents a choral and orchestral sound that is more refined, set against a helpful church acoustic. *In paradisum* is ethereally beautiful. Best's soloists are even finer than Rutter's, and he too provides a generous fill-up in the *Messe basse* and other motets, though two fewer than Rutter.

Barenboim's 1975 recording has been splendidly remastered. The sound is firmer and better focused without loss of atmosphere. The Edinburgh Festival Chorus is freshly responsive so that, although their tone is beefier than in some versions, the effect is never heavy and the performance is given a strong dimension of drama. Sheila Armstrong's *Pie Jesu* is even more successful here than with de los Angeles. Fischer-Dieskau is not quite as mellifluous as in his earlier account with Cluytens, but he brings a greater sense of drama. A first-rate version, including a sensitive account of the *Pavane*.

The Naxos version makes an excellent bargain choice for the *Requiem* in its original orchestration. The fresh, forward choral tone goes with a direct, unmannered interpretation from Jeremy Summerly, with soloists comparably fresh-toned and English-sounding. The recording brings out the colourings of the orchestra in sharp detail, with the organ and brass vividly caught. The performance of the *Messe basse* is comparably direct, made to sound a little square at times, but *Le cantique de Jean Racine* is most winningly done. The little meditative organ piece by Vierne and the unaccompanied motet by de Severac are pleasing makeweights.

Philippe Herreweghe, unlike Rutter and Best, tends to adopt speeds that are a degree slower than those marked. His soloists are more sophisticated than their British rivals, tonally very beautiful but not quite so fresh in expression. The recording has chorus and orchestra relatively close, but there is a pleasant ambience round the sound.

Michel Legrand uses the full orchestral version of 1900 in the most dramatic way possible, yet the delicacy of the *In Paradisum* reflects an equally sympathetic response to the gentler, mystical side of the music. Barbara Bonney's *Pie Jesu* with its simplicity and innocence is very touching. Thomas Hampson makes an eloquent contribution to the *Libera me*, and after the climax the flowing choral line shows the subtle range of colour and dynamic commanded by the Ambrosian Singers (as well as the orchestra). With superb, spacious recording this performance is very compelling indeed, and it is coupled with an equally fine account of the Duruflé work which was inspired by Fauré's masterpiece.

Not surprisingly, the acoustics of St Eustache, Montreal, are highly suitable for recording the regular full orchestral score of Fauré's *Requiem*, and the Decca sound is superb. Dutoit's is an essentially weighty reading, matched by the style of his fine soloists, yet the performance has both freshness and warmth and does not lack transparency. There are attractive bonuses.

The St John's account has a magic that works from the opening bars onwards. Jonathon Bond and Benjamin Luxon are highly sympathetic soloists and the 1975 (originally Argo) recording is every bit as impressive as its digital competitors, while the smaller scale of the conception is probably nearer to Fauré's original conception. The Double Decca reissue offers exceptionally generous couplings, not only the Duruflé *Requiem* but other fine music by both Duruflé and Poulenc.

Marriner in his 1993 recording for Philips returns to the fuller re-orchestration. But where many larger forces encourage expansive speeds, Marriner's pacing is ideal, and the clean choral attack is matched by superb singing from Sylvia McNair and Thomas Allen. Though other versions convey even more magic, Marriner can be warmly recommended, particularly for those who fancy the instrumental pieces offered as coupling, including charming rarities by Koechlin and Schmitt.

Frémaux has a moulded style which does not spill over into too much expressiveness, and there is a natural warmth about this performance that is highly persuasive. Norma Burrowes sings beautifully, her innocent style most engaging. However, this is coupled with a much less recommendable set of the Berlioz *Requiem*.

On the earlier (1967) King's version under Willcocks, the solo soprano role is taken appealingly by a boy treble, Robert Chilcott. The recording is very fine and splendidly remastered. The performance is eloquent and warmly moving, although some may feel its Anglican accents unidiomatic. The modest coupling is a melting version of the famous *Pavane*, with Gareth Morris playing the flute solo, given lovely, rich sound. As can be seen, this recording (with the *Pavane*) is available only in the USA, on EMI's budget Red Line label, including also a moderately effective account of Palestrina's most famous Mass.

In the later (1982) digital King's College recording, Ledger presents the *Requiem* on a small scale, with considerable restraint. The singing is refreshingly direct, but anyone who warms to the touch of sensuousness in the work, its Gallic quality, may well find a degree of disappointment, though the *Sanctus* conveys drama. This is less beautiful a performance than the earlier one, now also reissued, which was made with the same choir by Sir David Willcocks. On the Classics for Pleasure reissue the comparatively brief *Messe basse*, also sweetly melodic, makes a rather more apt but still not generous alternative coupling.

It was tempting for Decca to reissue this Ansermet repertoire in the Classic Sound series. The *Requiem* is very early stereo indeed (1955), but the vividly clear recording only serves to emphasize the rather thin-toned contribution of the chorus. The solo singing is good, but this CD is most notable for the orchestral items, recorded six years later: sympathetic and stylish performances, highly regarded in their day and still sounding well.

On the latest DG coupling with Fauré, Chung's speeds are often excessively slow, challenging even Bartoli's control in the *Pie Jesu*. The characterful singing of both soloists has to be balanced against dim and distant choral sound and an excessively wide dynamic range in the recording. Not recommended.

Fayrfax, Robert (1464–1521)

Albanus Domini laudans; Ave lumen gratie; Missa Albanus; Antiphons: *Eterne laudis lilium; O Maria Deo grata.*

*** ASV Gaudeamus Dig. CDGAU 160 [id.].
Cardinall's Musick, Andrew Carwood.

The magnificent *Missa Albanus*, written for St Alban's Abbey (where Fayrfax was finally buried) is aptly coupled with two extended antiphons, just as elaborate in their polyphonic complexity. *O Maria Deo grata* is directly associated with this particular Mass, having also been written for St Alban's. *Eterne laudis lilium* won for Fayrfax the sum of 20 shillings from the much-loved Queen Elizabeth of York, wife of Henry VII, and is a dedicated tribute to St Elizabeth, mother of John the Baptist. Fresh and intense performances, beautifully balanced.

Antiphona Regali ex progenie; Magnificat Regali; Missa Regali ex progenie; Alas for the lak of her presens; Lauda vivi alpha et O; That was my woo.

(N) *** ASV Gaudeamus CDGAU 185 [id.].
Cardinall's Musick, Andrew Carwood.

The final instalment of the Cardinall's Musick's distinguished survey of the music of Fayrfax is centred around the *Mass* and *Magnificat Regali ex progenie*, but opens with the extended votive antiphon *Lauda vivi Alpha et O*. The collection also includes two rare songs, including the plangent duet, *That was my woo*. The performances are very fine and if the Mass itself is not among the composer's most ambitious works, its textures are as strongly individual as ever. Splendid recording.

Antiphon: Tecum principium (plainsong); *Missa Tecum principium;* Motet: *Maria plena virtute;* Music for recorders: *Mese tenor; O lux beata trinitas; Parames tenor.*

*** ASV Gaudeamus Dig. CDGAU 145 [id.]. Cardinall's Musick, Andrew Carwood; Frideswide Cons.

Though the *Missa Tecum principium* is less complex than the brilliant Mass *O quam glorifica*, the argument is not just more direct but even more extended, with the four big sections lasting almost 50 minutes. The final sublime *Agnus Dei* is followed by three tiny instrumental pieces played on recorders by the Frideswide Consort. An extended votive antiphon, *Maria plena virtute*, then rounds off the disc with the most moving music of all, a narrative on the Virgin Mary at the Cross, full of deeply personal responses immediately to involve the modern listener.

Ave Dei patris filia; Missa O quam glorifica; O quam glorifica (hymnus); Orbis factor (Kyrie). 3 secular songs: *Sumwat musyng; That was joy; To complayne me, alas.*

❁ *** ASV/Gaudeamus Dig. CDGAU 142 [id.]. Cardinall's Musick, Andrew Carwood.

This first ASV disc to be issued of Robert Fayrfax's music won the *Gramophone* Award for early vocal music. Cardinall's Musick, directed by Andrew Carwood, used editions specially prepared by David Skinner, and as Skinner's notes explain, the Mass, *O quam glorifica*, is the most complex that Fayrfax ever wrote. The rhythmic complexities too, sound wonderfully fresh to the modern ear, with conflicting speeds often involving bold cross-rhythms, parading the composer's closely controlled freedom, before bar-lines applied their tyranny. Above all this is music immediately to involve one in its radiant beauty. The separate antiphon or motet, *Ave Dei patris filia*, is comparably adventurous and beautiful, and is well supplemented by three secular part-songs for male voices. They even anticipate the Elizabethan madrigal, notably the third and most poignant, *To complayne me, alas*. Carwood draws inspired performances from his singers, crisp and dramatic as well as beautifully blended, and most atmospherically recorded in the Fitzalan Chapel at Arundel Castle.

Ferguson, Howard (born 1908)

(i) *Concerto for piano and string orchestra;* (ii) *Amore langueo, Op. 18.*

(M) *** EMI Dig. CDM7 64738-2 [id.]. (i) Howard Shelley; (ii) Martyn Hill, L. Symphony Ch.; City of L. Sinfonia, Hickox – FINZI: *Eclogue.* ***

Ferguson's concerto has something in common with the lyrical feeling of John Ireland's comparable work, and as with Ireland, the finale is gay and melodically carefree. Howard Shelley's performance is admirable and Hickox secures highly sympathetic response from the City of London Sinfonia string section. *Amore langueo* is an extended cantata, lasting just over half an hour. The setting, for tenor solo and semi-chorus, with a strong contribution from Martyn Hill, brings a powerful response in the present performance, and Ferguson's music moves with remarkable ease from the depiction of Christ's suffering on the Cross to the sometimes even playful atmosphere of lovers in the bedchamber. An unusual and rewarding piece, recorded with great vividness on CD.

Overture for an occasion, Op. 16; Partita, Op. 5a; (i) *2 Ballads, Op. 1;* (ii) *The Dream of the Rood, Op. 19.*

*** Chandos Dig. CHAN 9082 [id.]. (i) Rayner Cook; (ii) Dawson, London Symphony Ch.; LSO, Hickox.

This collection offers a splendid cross-section of Ferguson's music, starting with his Opus 1 – which includes a striking setting of the *Lyke-Wake dirge*, written in 1928 long before Britten. The *Partita* of 1935–6 is a compact, four-movement symphonic structure, surprisingly dark until the last movement, with a weirdly enigmatic second movement and a lamenting slow movement. The *Overture for an occasion*, written for the Queen's coronation, has the warmth and colour of comparable Walton works, and further echoes of Walton flavour the *Dream of the Rood*, a setting of an Anglo-Saxon poem with a radiant soprano solo introducing a sequence of richly atmospheric choruses. Hickox proves an ideal advocate, drawing incandescent singing and playing from his performers, with rich and clear Chandos sound to match.

(i) *Octet;* (ii; iii) *Violin sonata No. 2, Op. 10;* (iii) *5 Bagatelles.*

*** Hyperion Dig. CDA 66192 [id.]. (i) Nash Ens.; (ii) Levon Chilingirian; (iii) Clifford Benson – FINZI: *Elegy.* ***

Ferguson's *Octet* is written for the same instruments as Schubert's masterpiece, a delightful counterpart. Those seeking a first-class modern version will find that the Nash Ensemble fill the bill admirably. The other works on the Hyperion disc display the same gift of easy, warm communication, including the darker *Violin sonata* and Finzi's haunting *Elegy for violin and piano*.

(i) *Violin sonatas Nos. 1, Op. 2; 2, Op. 10;* (ii) *4 Short pieces;* (iii) *Three sketches, Op. 14;* (iv) *Discovery* (song-cycle), *Op. 13;* (v) *5 Irish folksongs, Op. 17;* (vi) *Love and reason;* (iv) *3 Mediaeval Carols, Op. 3.*

*** Chandos Dig. CHAN 9316-2 [id.]. (i) Lydia Mordkovitch; (ii) Jane Hilton; (iii) David Butt; (iv) John Mark Ainsley; (v) Sally Burgess; (vi) Schneider-Waterberg; all with Clifford Benson.

This generous collection of Ferguson's chamber

music, beautifully performed, provides a fine counterpart to Hickox's choral and orchestral disc. It is framed by the two *Violin sonatas* (1931 and 1946), both powerful works, with Lydia Mordkovitch a rich and persuasive interpreter. Clifford Benson is the lynchpin among the performers, contributing to all the works here. The *Four Short pieces* for clarinet and the *Three Sketches* for flute are delightful miniatures, as is the counter-tenor song, *Love and reason*, and the *Carols* and the *Discovery* cycle for tenor. Best of all is the colourful cycle of Irish folksongs for mezzo, vividly performed by Sally Burgess. Excellent, well-balanced sound.

(i) *Partita for 2 pianos, Op. 56. Piano sonata in F min., Op. 8.*
*** Hyperion CDA 66130 [id.]. Howard Shelley, (i) Hilary Macnamara.

Ferguson's *Sonata* is a dark, formidable piece in three substantial movements, here given a powerful and intense performance, a work which, for all its echoes of Rachmaninov, is quite individual. The *Partita* is also a large-scale work, full of good ideas, in which Howard Shelley is joined for this two-piano version by his wife, Hilary Macnamara. Excellent, committed performances and first-rate recording, vividly transferred to CD.

Ferranti, Marco Aurelio Zani de (1801–78)

Exercice, Op. 50/14; Fantaisie variée sur le romance d'Otello (Assisa à piè), Op. 7; 4 Mélodies nocturnes originales, Op. 41a/1–4; Nocturne sur la dernière pensée de Weber, Op. 40; Ronde des fées, Op. 2.
*** Chandos Dig. CHAN 8512 [id.]. Simon Wynberg (guitar) – FERRER: *Collection.* ***

Simon Wynberg's playing fully enters the innocently compelling sound-world of this Bolognese composer; it is wholly spontaneous and has the most subtle control of light and shade. Ferranti's invention is most appealing, and this makes ideal music for late-evening reverie; moreover the guitar is most realistically recorded.

Ferrer, José (1835–1916)

Belle (Gavotte); La danse de naïades; L'étudiant de Salamanque (Tango); Vals.
*** Chandos Dig. CHAN 8512 [id.]. Simon Wynberg (guitar) – FERRANTI: *Collection.* ***

José Ferrer is a less substantial figure than Ferranti, but these four vignettes are almost as winning as that composer's music. The recording has striking realism and presence.

Fesch, Willem de (1687–1761)

Concerti grossi, Op. 2/6; Op. 3/3–4; Op. 5/2; Op. 10/4–5; (i) *Violin concertos, Op. 2/2 & 5; Op. 3/6; Op. 5/5.*
*** Olympia Dig. OCD 450. (i) Gordon Nikolitch; O d'Auvergne, Arie van Beek.

De Fesch was born in Alkmaar, but his career took him to Amsterdam, Antwerp and finally (in 1732) to London; his writing reflects influences absorbed from Italy and France, and also from Handel, of whom he was an almost exact contemporary. His melodic inspiration in slow movements often falls little short of that master and he must have been a pretty impressive fiddler himself, judging from the bravura demanded of the soloist in his violin concertos. The *Concerti grossi* are first rate. Op.3/4 is very like a sinfonia concertante in the way de Fesch uses his solo group of two oboes plus genial bassoon. The five-movement *G minor* work, Op. 5/2, features a pair of flutes with equal felicity, its undoubted charm coming from delicate scoring and a melancholy atmosphere. The Orchestre d'Auvergne are an excellent chamber group and Gordon Nikolitch an estimable soloist. Although modern instruments are used, the light textures and resilient rhythms suggest a thorough knowledge of authentic practices, though melodic lines are mercifully unsqueezed. Excellent recording too. A strong recommendation for this pioneering CD.

Fetler, Paul (born 1920)

Contrasts for orchestra.
(M) *** Mercury (IMS) 434 335-2 [id.]. Minneapolis SO, Dorati – AURIC: *Overture;* FRANCAIX: *Piano concertino;* MILHAUD: *Le boeuf sur le toit;* SATIE: *Parade.* ***

Paul Fetler's four-movement sinfonietta, *Contrasts*, is based on four notes (B flat, F, C, A flat), yet it is as impressive for its fine use of brass sonorities in the slow movement as for the neo-classical athleticism of the opening *Allegro* and the pervading energy of the finale where everything comes together. It is an eclectic work yet has distinct character. The performance is first rate, and so is the Mercury recording.

Fibich, Zdeněk (1850–1900)

Symphonies Nos. 1 in F, Op. 17; 2 in E flat, Op. 38; 3 in E min., Op. 53.
(N) (B) *** Chandos Dig. Double CHAN 9682 (2) [id.]. Detroit SO, Neeme Järvi.

Anyone who has ever responded to Dvořák should hear the symphonies of his contemporary, Fibich – similarly echoing the cadences of Czech folk music, but with touches of Mendelssohn, no doubt developed by the composer's studies in Leipzig. The grouping together of the three works in a single jewel-case is sensible enough, and while the *Third* (alone on the second disc) plays for barely 38 minutes, the set is most attractive when reissued as a Double, rather than as two discs at mid price. There is a strong Bohemian feel to these works, and if, like so much of Fibich's music, the *First Symphony* which opens so invitingly is a little square, such is the excellence of Neeme Järvi's performance that it does not feel so. It is the best account so far on record. The performances of the *Second* and *Third* come into competition with a Supraphon issue from the Brno Orchestra under Jiři Walddans and Bělohlávek (11 0657-2) respectively. But on Chandos, opulent sound adds to the rustic charm of much of the writing, as well as heightening the warmth and drama of the playing. Moreover the Chandos recording scores in terms of fidelity and space, and the Detroit Orchestra respond with enthusiam to these scores. The thematic substance of both latter works derives from the *Moods, impressions and reminiscences,* the product of the composer's infatuation with Anežka Schulzová. In the *Third Symphony* the invention is fresher than that of its predecessor, and the Scherzo with its catchy syncopations has great charm. Overall this set is well worth exploring.

Symphonies Nos 1 in F, Op. 17; 2 in E flat, Op. 38.
(N) (BB) ** Naxos Dig. 8.553699 [id.]. Razumovsky SO, Mogrelia.

The Naxos issue of the first two symphonies offers fresh, clean-cut performances with transparent textures, making an attractive bargain issue, though they are pale beside Järvi's Chandos performances.

Piano quartet in E min. Op. 11; Quintet for violin, clarinet, horn, cello and piano, Op. 42.
(N) *** MDG Dig. MDG 304 0775-2 [id.]. Villa Musica Ens.

The *E minor Piano Quartet* is an early piece, which enjoyed the approval of Hanslick, while its companion comes from 1893. The ideas though pleasing are a little square; they do not have the fresh, outdoor quality of Fibich's great compatriots. This is well-wrought music and beautifully played by these accomplished artists and excellently recorded.

Piano quintet, Op. 42.
*** ASV Dig. CDDCA 943 [id.]. Endymion Ens. – DOHNANYI: *Sextet.* ***

Fibich's *Piano quintet* is a relatively late piece; it comes from the last decade of his life and has much lively invention and no mean charm. Like the two symphonies listed above, it incorporates some of the thematic ideas which originated from the book of nearly 400 piano miniatures inspired by his infatuation with Anězka Schulzová. She must have been an enchanting young lady. The Endymions give a first-rate account of it and are excellently recorded.

Moods, impressions and reminiscences, Opp. 41, 44, 47 & 57.
*** Chandos Dig. CHAN 9381. [id.]. William Howard.

A generally preferable alternative to Rudoslav Kvapil's thoughtful and perceptive recital on Unicorn-Kanchana (DKPCD 9149). William Howard is equally sensitive to the varying moods of these pieces, and he is much more convincingly recorded.

Sárka (opera; complete).
*** Sup. SU 0036-2 612 (2) [id.]. Ďepoltová, Zítek, Přibyl, Randová, Brno Janácek Ch., Brno State PO, Jan Stych.

Sárka is Fibich's sixth opera. Some of the invention is predictable, but there is much that is both endearing and fresh, while the choral writing is distinctly appealing. In addition to the nationalist element, there is also a strong awareness of Wagner. Fibich, though a composer of the second order, is nevertheless far from unrewarding and there are many colourful and melodically appealing episodes here, even if the quality of inspiration is not consistent. The cast here is a fine one, and readers who enjoy Czech music will find this set well worth investigation. The transfer to CD is admirably managed – the atmospheric warmth is immediately apparent in the evocative Overture. A full translation is included.

Field, John (1782–1837)

Piano concertos Nos. 1 in E flat; 2 in A flat.
*** Chandos Dig. CHAN 9368 [id.]. Míceál O'Rourke, LMP, Bamert.

Míceál O'Rourke embarks on what appears to be a complete cycle of the Field concertos with hardly less success than with his first disc of solo piano music (see below). The music of the present pair of concertos is uneven, but the Scottish slow movement of No. 1 features the folk tune '*Within a mile of Edinburgh town*' rather winningly. No. 2 brings a characteristic Field Rondo with an engaging principal theme which becomes catchier as it is given more rhythmic treatment. The soloist is very persuasive, and he receives admirable support from Bamert and the London Mozart Players. First-class, naturally balanced recording.

Piano concertos Nos. 1 in E flat, H.27; 3 in E flat, H.32.
(BB) *** Naxos Dig. 8.553770 [id.]. Benjamin Frith, Northern Sinfonia, David Haslam.

Piano concertos Nos. 2 in A flat, H.31; 4 in E flat, H.28.
(N) (BB) *** Naxos Dig. 8.553771 [id.]. Benjamin Frith, Northern Sinfonia, David Haslam.

Benjamin Frith has already given us the Mendelssohn and Weber concertos, and the Field concertos are not a far call from them. This talented young artist has the bargain field to himself. His playing is characteristically sensitive and fresh, and he is well supported by the Northern Sinfonia and David Haslam. Very good, warm recording, in a decent acoustic. The second disc is particularly attractive.

Piano concertos Nos. 2 in A flat; 3 in E flat.
*** Telarc Dig. CD 80370 [id.]. John O'Conor, SCO, Mackerras.

John O'Conor has recorded all the John Field concertos before with the New Irish Chamber Orchestra (Onyx CD 101/3) but these Telarc versions are distinctly superior. They are beautifully recorded and the warm, naturally balanced sound gives the music the elegance it needs. The *Andantino* of No. 3 (not a part of the original concerto) brings a nicely rhapsodical feeling and uses one of the composer's daintiest *Nocturnes*, orchestrated to have a gentle string accompaniment. It is played with much grace and delicacy and is then followed by a Rondo, with a catchy, hopping main theme which is also one of Field's very best finales. O'Conor plays throughout with great distinction and always displays the lightest touch and Mackerras accompanies with warmth and character. The recording has a somewhat resonant bass but the violins sing in an atmosphere of pleasing bloom.

Piano concertos Nos. 3 in E flat; 5 in C (L'incendie par l'orage).
*** Chandos Dig. CHAN 9495 [id.]. Míceál O'Rourke, LMP, Matthias Bamert.

Míceál O'Rourke is well up to form in the *Third concerto* and readily matches the poetry found by O'Conor. The coupling (No. 5) is notable mainly for its histrionic storm effects in the middle of the first movement, which climax with a bold stroke on the tam-tam. After this, the weather breaks and we are ready for the songful *Andante*, before the comparatively robust and spirited finale which brings delicacy as well as brilliance of articulation from the soloist. Excellent support throughout from Bamert, and first-class recording.

Piano concertos Nos. 4 in E flat; 6 in C.
*** Chandos Dig. CHAN 9442 [id.]. Míceál O'Rourke, LMP, Bamert.

O'Rourke continues his Chandos series with highly persuasive accounts of Nos. 4 and 6, with both works providing delightful slow movements. The *C major Concerto* is the more interesting of the two, giving the soloist some scintillating passage-work in the first movement and a lolloping Rondo finale. Excellent, sympathetic accompaniments and first-rate recording.

(i) *Piano concerto No. 7 in C; Divertissements Nos. 1–2; Nocturne No. 16 in F; Rondeau in A flat.* (ii) *Quintetto.*
(N) *** Chandos Dig. CHAN 9534 [id.]. Míceál O'Rorke, (i) L. Mozart Players, Bamert (ii) Juritz, Godson, Bradley, Desbruslais.

Field's *Seventh Piano concerto* is not one of his very best, for the first movement is rather long, and although the finale is characteristically chirpy, in both movements some of the passagework is a shade garrulous (not the fault of the soloist, who is well on form). However, the opening movement has a beautiful central *Lento* section which the composer later extracted and published as one of the nocturnes. What makes this disc treasurable is the series of lollipops which follow – the two *Divertissements*, *Rondeau* and *Nocturne*, every one of which has a really good tune. The serene single-movement *Piano quintet* is also delicately charming. Performances and recordings are well up to the high standard of this excellent Chandos series.

Air du bon roi Henri IV; 2 Album leaves in C min.; Andante inédit in E flat; Fantaisie sur un air russe, 'In the garden'; Fantaisie sur l'air de Martini; Irish dance: 'Go to the devil'; Marche triomphale; Nocturne in B flat; Nouvelle fantaisie in G; Polonaise en rondeau; Rondeau d'écossais; Rondo in A flat; Sehnsuchtswalzer; Variations in D min. on a Russian song, 'My dear bosom friend'; Variations in B flat on a Russian air: Kamarinskaya.
*** Chandos Dig. CHAN 9315 [id.]. Míceál O'Rourke.

Míceál O'Rourke is as sympathetic and sensitive an advocate of these rarities as one could wish for. He presents this (nearly 80-minute) recital with intelligence and taste. Most of this repertory is not otherwise available, and much of it has the quiet charm one expects from this delightful composer. Míceál O'Rourke proves a dedicated interpreter of real artistry. Recorded at The Maltings, Snape, he is admirably served by the Chandos team.

Nocturnes Nos. 1–16.
**(*) Athene ATH CD 1. Joanna Leach (fortepiano).

Joanna Leach uses three 'square' fortepianos, by Stodart and Broadwood (both from the 1820s) and a D'Almain from a decade later. The latter instrument most closely approaches the quality of a modern piano, though the Broadwood is not far behind. Joanna Leach coaxes poetic sounds from these comparatively recalcitrant instruments and plays this repertoire very sensitively. However, it cannot be denied that for most ears this music (with its remarkable anticipations of Chopin) sounds even better on a modern concert grand.

Nocturnes 1, 2, 4–6, 8–16, 18.
*** Telarc Dig. CD-80199 [id.]. John O'Conor.

It would be difficult to better John O'Conor's sensitive and beautifully recorded accounts of his countryman's pioneering essays in the *Nocturnes*. He captures their character to perfection, and his tonal finesse is remarkable but never self-regarding. Strongly recommended.

Piano sonatas: Nos. 1 in E flat; 2 in A; 3 in C min., Op. 1/1–3; 4 in B.
**(*) Chandos Dig. CHAN 8787 [id.]. Míceál O'Rourke.

Míceál O'Rourke plays these two-movement *Sonatas* written by his countryman with some flair. He is particularly good in the famous Rondo finale of the *First Sonata*, which he plays with real Irish whimsy and sparkling touch. The *Allegretto scherzando* of No. 3 also has hit potential.

Finzi, Gerald (1901–56)

Cello concerto in A min., Op. 40.
*** Chandos Dig. CHAN 8471 [id.]. Wallfisch, RLPO, Handley – K. LEIGHTON: *Veris gratia.* ***

Finzi's *Cello concerto* is perhaps the most searching of all his works. Wallfisch finds all the dark eloquence of the central movement, and the performance overall has splendid impetus, with Handley providing the most sympathetic backing. The Chandos recording has an attractively natural balance.

Clarinet concerto, Op. 31.
*** Hyperion CDA 66001 [id.]. Thea King, Philh. O, Francis – STANFORD: *Concerto.* ***
*** ASV Dig. CDDCA 568 [id.]. MacDonald, N. Sinfonia, Bedford – COPLAND: *Concerto;* MOURANT: *Pied Piper.* ***

(i) *Clarinet concerto, Op. 31;* (ii) *5 Bagatelles for clarinet and piano.*
*** ASV CDDCA 787 [id.]. Emma Johnson; (i) RPO, Groves; (ii) Malcolm Martineau – STANFORD: *Clarinet concerto* etc. ***

(i) *Clarinet concerto, Op. 31; 5 Bagatelles for clarinet and strings* (arr. Ashmore), *Op. 23a; Love's Labour Lost: 3 Soliloquies, Op. 28.* (ii) *Introit in F for solo violin and small orchestra, Op. 6. Romance in E flat for String orchestra, Op. 11*; *A Severn rhapsody, Op. 3.*
(N) (BB) *** Naxos Dig. 8.553566 [id.]. (i) Robert Plane; (ii) Lesley Hatfield; Northern Sinf., Howard Griffiths.

(i) *Clarinet concerto. New Year music: Nocturne. Romance for string orchestra.* (ii) *Dies Natalis.*
(N) *** Ph. Dig. 454 438-2. (i) Andrew Marriner; (ii) Ian Bostridge.

Emma Johnson is even more warmly expressive in the concertos than Thea King on her Hyperion disc, and with Sir Charles Groves and the RPO ideally sympathetic accompanists. Finzi's sinuous melodies for the solo instrument are made to sound as though the soloist is improvising them, and with extreme daring she uses the widest possible dynamic, ranging down to a whispered *pianissimo* that might be inaudible in a concert-hall.

Andrew Marriner gives a particularly sensitive account of the *Clarinet concerto* in which simplicity is the keynote. Marriner is an admirable partner and secures some ravishingly gentle playing from the ASMF in the *Adagio*. The finale lilts engagingly. If memories of Emma Johnson's account are not entirely banished, the present version is very seductive as are the performances of the two endearingly lyrical orchestral pieces, flowing on in the finest English pastoral tradition. But it is the coupling with *Die Natalis*, perhaps the composer's best-known work, which makes this Philips disc so enticing. Ian Bostridge's ravishing account of an inspired song-cycle that occupies a midway point between the vocal music of Elgar and Britten, but yet has the stamp of the composer's personality set firmly on every bar, is unsurpassed. His exultant response to the third song, *Rapture*, and the gentle radiance of the fourth, *Wonder* is unforgettable. Marriner accompanies with comparable warmth and subtlety of line and the atmospheric sound adds to the magic, when the orchestral playing is of such high quality.

Robert Plane's highly responsive performance of the concerto also uses a wide range of dynamic, and movingly brings out the work's sense of improvisatory lyricism. Not to be outdone, the Naxos collection offers the *3 Soliloquies*, plus an orchestration of the five lovely *Bagatelles*, which is even more evocative than the original version with piano. The virtually unknown *Introit* for violin and orchestra brings another memorable theme and is well worth having; it originally formed the middle movement of a larger work whose outer movements Finzi withdrew. Meditative and thoughtful, it is most sensitively played by Lesley Hatfield. The *Romance* is hardly less engaging, while *Severn rhapsody* shows its composer spinning his pastoral evocation in the manner of Butterworth. All this music is most persuasively presented by the Northern Sinfonia under Howard Griffiths and the Naxos recording has plenty of warmth and atmosphere.

On the Hyperion label, Thea King also gives a definitive performance, strong and clean-cut. Her characterful timbre, using little or no vibrato, is highly telling against a resonant orchestral backcloth. The accompaniment of the Philharmonia under Alun Francis is most sympathetic. With Stanford's even rarer concerto, this makes a most attractive issue, and the sound is excellent.

The coupling of Finzi and Copland makes an unexpected but attractive mix, with the Canadian clarinettist, George MacDonald, giving a brilliant and thoughtful performance, particularly impressive in the spacious, melismatic writing of the slow movement. Refined recording, with the instruments set slightly at a distance.

(i) *Clarinet concerto. Love's Labour's Lost: suite; Prelude for string orchestra; Romance for strings.*
*** Nimbus Dig. NI 5101 [id.]. (i) Alan Hacker; E. String O, Boughton.

Alan Hacker's reading of the *Concerto* is improvisatory in style and freely flexible in tempi, with the slow movement at once introspective and rhapsodic. The concert suite of incidental music for Shakespeare's *Love's Labour's Lost* is amiably atmospheric and pleasing in invention and in the colour of its scoring. The two string pieces are by no means slight and are played most expressively; the *Romance* is particularly eloquent in William Boughton's hands.

Eclogue for piano and string orchestra.
(M) *** EMI Dig. CDM7 64738-2. Howard Shelley, City of L. Sinfonia, Hickox – FERGUSON: *Piano concerto No. 2* etc. ***
(M) *** EMI Dig. CD-EMX 2239 [id.]. Piers Lane, RLPO, Handley – DELIUS: *Piano concerto*; VAUGHAN WILLIAMS: *Piano concerto.* ***

This is the central movement of an uncompleted piano concerto which the composer decided could stand on its own. It was Howard Ferguson who edited the final manuscript and set the title, and it is appropriate that this essentially valedictory piece should be coupled with his own concerto. The mood is tranquil yet haunting, and Shelley's performance brings out all its serene lyricism. The recording is admirably realistic.

This haunting work makes a valuable makeweight for the Eminence coupling of the Delius and Vaughan Williams *Piano concertos*. Piers Lane gives it a tenderly sympathetic reading, even if this does not quite match in magic the Howard Shelley version on EMI.

Grand Fantasia and Toccata (for piano and orchestra), *Op. 38;* (ii) *Intimations of Immortality, Op. 29.*
(M) *** EMI Dig. CDM7 64720-2. (i) Philip Fowke; (ii) Philip Langridge, RLPO Ch.; RLPO, Hickox.

Finzi's setting of Wordsworth, with its rich, lyrical cantilena, brings constant reminders of the Elgar of *Gerontius*, while the writing remains essentially within the pastoral tradition of English song-setting. The performance here is wholly committed, with the fervour of the chorus echoing the dedication of the soloist. The choral recording is both spacious and brilliant. The coupling, a Bachian *Grand fantasia*, is followed by a genial *Toccata*, fugal in style. The piece is played compellingly by Philip Fowke, and Hickox is a fine partner. Again vividly realistic sound. Highly recommended.

Interlude in A min.
(M) *** Carlton Dig. 30366 00962 [id.]. Robin Canter, Medici Qt (members) – BRITTEN: *6 Metamorphoses after Ovid* etc. ***

Finzi's *Interlude* for oboe quartet is a warmly evocative piece in his characteristic pastoral style, subtly different from that of his friend and mentor, Vaughan Williams. Canter and the Medici Quartet play it with the same warmth and sympathy as in the Britten *Phantasy* for the same combination.

Elegy for violin and piano.
*** Hyperion Dig. CDA 66192 [id.]. Chilingirian, Benson – FERGUSON: *Octet* etc. ***

Finzi's moving little *Elegy for violin and piano* makes an apt fill-up for the record of chamber music by his friend, Howard Ferguson.

Dies natalis.
(M) *** EMI CDM5 65588-2. Wilfred Brown, ECO, Christopher Finzi – HOLST: *Choral fantasia; Psalm 86;* VAUGHAN WILLIAMS: *5 Mystical songs*, etc. ***

Dies natalis is one of Finzi's most sensitive and deeply felt works, using meditative texts by the seventeenth-century writer, Thomas Traherne, on the theme of Christ's nativity. Finzi's setting is very well sung here by Wilfred Brown, and this record must be recommended to all interested in modern English song setting. The remastered recording sounds wonderfully fresh and is naturally balanced within a glowing acoustic.

Dies natalis; Intimations of immortality.
**(*) Hyperion Dig. CDA 66876 [id.]. John Mark Ainsley, Corydon Singers & O, Matthew Best.

Matthew Best, with John Mark Ainsley as soloist in both works, offers the ideal Finzi coupling. Using a relatively small orchestra, this is a more intimate reading of the latter work than on the earlier, EMI recording from Richard Hickox, yet it conveys an almost comparable concentration. Ainsley has a sweeter if smaller voice than his EMI rival, Philip Langridge, very apt for both works, even if under pressure there is some unevenness. The chorus sings with feeling, though the recording is not as vividly immediate as the analogue EMI recording which features the Royal Liverpool Philharmonic Choir and Orchestra. That performance is exceptionally committed, and it remains a marginally stronger recommendation at mid-price. Nevertheless, it is very welcome to have new digital recordings of both choral works.

Earth and air and rain (song-cycle to words by Thomas Hardy).

(BB) *** Belart 461 491-2 [(M) id. import]. Benjamin Luxon, David Williamson – BUTTERWORTH: *A Shropshire Lad*, etc. ***

These distinctive Finzi settings of Hardy make an ideal coupling for the outstanding performances of Butterworth on the same disc. There is sometimes a flavour of Vaughan Williams and, in *When I set out for Lyonnesse*, a distinct reminder of Stanford's *Songs of the sea*. But in the touching *Waiting both* and the dramatic *Clock of the years*, Luxon demonstrates the versatility of Finzi's word-settings. Excellent accompaniments from David Williamson – his gentle postlude for the final song, *Proud songsters*, ends the cycle movingly. Fine mid-1970s (originally Argo) recording.

God is gone up; Lo, the full, final sacrifice; Magnificat.

(M) *** EMI Dig. CDM5 65595-2. King's College, Cambridge, Ch., Cleobury; Farnes – BAX: *Choral music;* VAUGHAN WILLIAMS: *Mass.* ***

Both the extended anthem, *Lo, the full, final sacrifice*, setting Richard Crashaw's version of an Aquinas hymn, and the *Magnificat* were commissioned works, the one for St Matthew's, Northampton, the other for Massachusetts; in their rich climaxes they bring out a dramatic side in Finzi along with his gentle beauty, splendidly conveyed by the King's choir. The recording, made in the Chapel, is so nicely balanced that part-writing is clear even against the ample acoustic.

Fiorillo, Federigo (1755– after 1823)

Violin concerto No. 1 in F.

*** Hyperion Dig. CDA 66210 [id.]. Oprean, European Community CO, Faerber – VIOTTI: *Violin concerto No. 13.* ***

Fiorillo's *Concerto* is charmingly romantic. Adelina Oprean's playing can only be described as quicksilver: her lightness of bow and firm, clean focus of timbre are most appealing. She is given a warm, polished accompaniment and the recording is eminently truthful and well balanced.

Flotow, Friedrich (1812–83)

Martha (complete).

(M) *** RCA 74321 32231-2 (2). Popp, Soffel, Jerusalem, Nimsgern, Ridderbusch, Bav. R. Ch. and O, Wallberg.

Martha is a charming opera, and the cast of this 1978 recording (originating with Eurodisc) is as near perfect as could be imagined. Lucia Popp is a splendid Lady Harriet, the voice rich and full yet riding the ensembles with jewelled accuracy. Doris Soffel is no less characterful as Nancy, and Siegfried Jerusalem is in his element as the hero, Lionel, singing ardently throughout. Siegmund Nimsgern is an excellent Lord Tristan, and Karl Ridderbusch matches his genial gusto. Wallberg's direction is marvellously spirited and the opera gathers pace as it proceeds. The Bavarian Radio Chorus sings with joyous precision and the orchestral playing sparkles. The first-class recording has been vividly tranferred, though there is a touch of edge on the voices of Lady Harriet and Nancy. The libretto promised on the back of the box is in German only, but the story of this opera is very easy to follow.

Floyd, Carlisle (born 1926)

Susannah (opera; complete).

*** Virgin/EMI Dig. VCD5 45039-2 (2) [CDCB 45039]. Cheryl Studer, Samuel Ramey, Jerry Hadley, Lyon Op. Ch. & O, Kent Nagano.

This is an updating of the story of Susanna and the Elders in the Apocrypha, which readily adapts to the background of a traditional community in the Appalachian mountains. The idiom is tuneful and unashamedly tonal, influenced by American folk-music. With echoes of Puccini on the one hand, of the American musical on the other, you might describe it as a cross between *Fanciulla del West* and *Carousel*. It is a pity that the musical invention is not more distinguished and that the words of the libretto are too often banal. Most effective are the two big solos for the heroine, one in each of the compact Acts, both gloriously sung by Cheryl Studer, who as a native American sounds easily in character, taking to the idiom naturally. Samuel Ramey is similarly at home in this music, singing strongly with his richest tone, even if one can hardly believe in him as a vile hypocrite. With Jerry Hadley ideally cast as the tenor hero, Sam, Susannah's brother, who finally murders the predatory Blitch, the rest of the cast is first rate. The chorus and orchestra of the Lyon Opera are also inspired by their American conductor to give heartfelt, idiomatic performances. Excellent sound, as in previous Lyon Opera recordings with Nagano.

Foerster, Josef Bohuslav (1859–1951)

Symphony No. 4 in C min. (Easter), Op. 54; Springtime and desire, Op. 93.

*** Sup. Analogue/Dig. 111 822-2 [id.]. Prague SO, Smetácek.

This beautiful if overlong symphony is both dignified and noble; its Scherzo is infectiously memorable and could be as popular as any of the *Slavonic dances* if only it were known. The idiom is best described as being close to that of Josef Suk. Above all, Foerster has a feeling for architecture and there is a sweep to the first movement that is most impressive. The finale is the least successful of the four movements, and here attention flags. All the same, the symphony wears well and it is good to have it on CD. To this analogue recording Supraphon add a 1985 account, digitally recorded, of his *Springtime and desire*, a symphonic poem with a strong emphasis on the symphonic, and this, like the symphony, is a most welcome addition to the catalogue. Good performances, decent recording.

Forqueray, Antoine (1671–1745)

Harpsichord suites Nos. 1 in D min.; 3 in D; 5 in C min.

(BB) *** Naxos 8.553407 [id.]. Luc Beauséjour (harpsichord).

These suites are transcriptions of music for the viol of uncertain provenance. They were long thought to be by Forqueray's son, Jean-Baptiste, taking advantage of his father's posthumous reputation and the fact that Antoine's music remained unpublished in his lifetime. But they could possibly be the work of his second wife, who was an accomplished musician. Whatever the case may be, the music itself is of quality and originality, and it is well served by the Canadian harpsichordist, Luc Beauséjour, as recorded at the Church of St Alphonse-de-Rodriguez in Quebec. He plays with great flair and zest, and the sound is first class.

(i) *Pièces de viole;* (ii) *Pièces de clavecin.*

*** HM/BMG Dig. RD 77262 [77262-2]. (i) Jay Bernfeld; (ii) Skip Sempé.

Antoine Forqueray was a younger contemporary of Marin Marais and enjoyed a reputation as one of the greatest gamba players of his day. Skip Sempé's performances have all the expressive freedom and poetic feeling that the music calls for. The music has an intimacy and character that is beguiling, and Jay Bernfeld's playing has a comparable instinctive artistry. Both players are well served by the engineers who do not attempt to make either instrument larger than life.

Foss, Lucas (born 1922)

American landscapes for guitar and orchestra.

*** Virgin/EMI Dig. CDC5 55083-2 [id.]. Sharon Isbin, St Paul CO, Hugo Wolff – CORIGLIANO: *Troubadours* **(*) (with SCHWANTNER: *From afar.* **)

Lucas Foss's winning three-movement concertante evocation, written in 1989, has plenty of attractive invention and a vivid orchestral palette. The haunting central variations on '*The wayfaring stranger*' are framed by a quirky *mélange* of folksy ideas, and the whimsical finale dances along joyfully to tunes like '*Stay a little longer*' and '*Cotton-eyed Joe*'. The performance could hardly be more spontaneous and readily displays Sharon Isbin's virtuosity and range, although a great deal happens in the orchestra too (with violin and piano solos in the finale offering the guitar a little competition). The piece ends suddenly, immediately following the introduction of '*America the beautiful*'.

3 American pieces.

*** EMI Dig. CDC5 55360-2 [id.]. Perlman, Boston SO, Ozawa – BARBER: *Violin concerto;* BERNSTEIN: *Serenade.* ***

As the title suggests,Foss's *Three American pieces* have a strong element of Copland-like folksiness, married to sweet, easy lyricism and with some Stravinskian echoes. Skilfully orchestrated for a small orchestra with prominent piano, all three of the pieces, not just the final allegro, *Composer's holiday*, but the first two, *Early song* and *Dedication*, have a way of gravitating into hoe-down rhythms, often with a surprising suddenness.

Song of Songs.

(M) *** Sony SM2K 47533 [id.]. Jennie Tourel, NYPO, Bernstein (with BLOCH: *Sacred service* ***; BEN-HAIM: *Sweet Psalmist of Israel.* **(*))

This highly imaginative cantata is an attractive mixture of Copland-flavoured sonorities and a wider folk influence, not unlike that found in Canteloube's *Songs of the Auvergne*. Jennie Tourel is a strong and compelling soloist, suitably histrionic, but her lyrical singing, especially in the final song which becomes more darkly intense as it unfolds, is memorable. Bernstein secures a bravura accompaniment from his New York players, strongly involved and at their peak in 1958. Like the coupled Bloch *Sacred service*, the remastered sound is surprisingly full and graphic.

Foulds, John (1880–1939)

Dynamic triptych for piano and orchestra.

*** Lyrita SRCD 211 [id.]. Howard Shelley, RPO, Handley – VAUGHAN WILLIAMS: *Piano concerto.* ***

John Foulds's ambitious concerto brings a profusion of memorable ideas, not always well disciplined; but it makes for an attractive piece, particularly so in the last of the three movements, *Dynamic rhythm*, with its extrovert references to Latin-American rhythms and the American musical. Played with dedication and beautifully recorded, it makes an interesting coupling for the masterly and underestimated Vaughan Williams *Piano concerto.*

String quartets Nos. 9 (Quartetto intimo), Op. 89; 10 (Quartetto geniale), Op. 97. Aquarelles, Op. 32.
❁ *** Pearl SHECD 9564. Endellion Qt.

The *Quartetto intimo*, written in 1931, is a powerful five-movement work in a distinctive idiom more advanced than that of Foulds's British contemporaries, with echoes of Scriabin and Bartók. Also on the disc is the one surviving movement of his tenth and last quartet, a dedicated hymn-like piece, as well as three slighter pieces which are earlier. Passionate performances and excellent recording, which is enhanced by the CD transfer. A uniquely valuable issue.

Françaix, Jean (born 1912)

Piano concertino.
*** Decca Dig. 452 448-2 [id.]. Jean-Yves Thibaudet, Montreal SO, Dutoit – HONEGGER: *Concertino*; RAVEL: *Concertos.* **
(M) *** Mercury (IMS) 434 335-2 [id.]. Claude Françaix, LSO, Dorati – AURIC: *Overture;* FETLER: *Contrasts;* MILHAUD: *Le boeuf sur le toit;* SATIE: *Parade.* ***

Claude Françaix, the composer's daughter, made the first recommendable stereo recording of this delectable, miniature, four-movement *Concertino* in 1965. The conductor's touch is deliciously light in the outer movements and the pianist's touch is neat and accomplished.

Jean Françaix's delightful *Concertino* also comes off well in Thibaudet's hands. However, the two Ravel *Concertos*, the main works, while very well played and recorded, do not present a strong challenge to existing recommendations.

L'horloge de flore.
*** Nimbus Dig. NI 5330 [id.]. John Anderson, Philh. O, Simon Wright – MARTINU; R. STRAUSS: *Concertos.* ***

Inspired by the Linnaeus Flower Clock, *L'horloge de flore* is music of real memorability and much charm. John Anderson's performance is most enjoyable; the Nimbus recording is digital and has each movement separately cued.

A huit (Octet); Clarinet quintet; Divertissement for bassoon and string quintet; (i) *l'heure du berger.*
(N) *** Hyperion Dig. CDA 67036 [id.]. Gaudier Ens. (i) Susan Tomes.

A huit (Octet); Clarinet quintet; Divertissement for bassoon and string quintet.
(N) **(*) MDG Dig. MDGL 3300 [id.]. Charis Ens.

Jean Françaix's music is always elegant and high-spirited, never more so than in the four works collected on this disc. *A huit*, written for the Vienna Octet in 1972 and dedicated to the memory of Schubert, is a delight. The *Clarinet quintet* is a relatively late work (1977) but full of the beguiling charm that distinguishes so much of Françaix's invention. Despite its wartime provenance, the *Divertissement for bassoon and string quintet* manages to smile, while *L'heure du berger*, background music for a brasserie – familiar from a recording made in the early 1990s by Pascal Rogé – comes off equally well. Highly polished and characterful playing from all concerned and excellent recording.

Highly accomplished playing from the Charis Ensemble and eminently acceptable recording. But the Gaudier Ensemble offer the same repertoire as well as an elegant performance of *L'heure du berger*. Though the Charis are very good, the Gaudier have the competitive edge over them.

Wind quintets Nos. 1 & 2; (i) *L'heure du berger.*
*** MDG Dig. 603 0557-2 [id.]. Kammervereinigung Berlin; (i) Frank-Immo Zichner.

These Berliners put over Françaix's delightful *Wind quintets* with great charm and delicacy. These are performances that radiate freshness and fun and, apart from the virtuosity of the performances, the naturalness of the recording and the balance are a continuing source of delight. *L'heure du berger* is a piano and wind sextet, but this is as good in its different way. Delicious playing and enchantingly light-hearted music.

Franchomme, Auguste (1808–84)

(i) *Air auvergnat varié, Op. 26; Air russe varié No. 2; Grande valse: Morceau de concert* (all for cello and strings); (ii) *Caprices, Op. 7/2, 4 & 7* (for 2 cellos); (iii) *Nocturne in A flat, Op. 15/2* (for cello and piano). arr. of CHOPIN: *Nocturne in G, Op. 15/1 & Op. 37/1.* FRANCHOMME/CHOPIN: *Grand duo concertante on themes from Robert le Diable* (for cello and piano).
*** Sony Dig. SK 53980 [id.]. Anner Bylsma, with (i) L'Archibudelli & Smithsonian Chamber Players; (ii) Kenneth Slowik; (iii) Lamber Orkis (piano).

Auguste Franchomme became famous when, as a personal friend of Chopin, they collaborated in this rather jolly *Grand duo concertante*. His own variations are effective enough when using folk themes, though his melodic facility was not really distinguished. But Anner Bylsma is a superb advocate and the pieces for two cellos are made attractive by his fine partnership with Kenneth Slowik. The back-up group for the amiable concertante pieces (of which the *Air auvergnat* and – especially – the

Grande valse are the most winning) enjoy themselves playing splendid original instruments from the Smithsonian collection in Washington, DC. The result is both authentic and entertaining, and the recording could hardly be bettered. It is very well balanced and has vividness, warmth and transparency.

Franck, César (1822–90)

Symphonic poems: *La chasseur maudit; Les Eolides*.

(M) ** Decca 452 890-2 [id.]. SRO, Ansermet – CHABRIER: *España* etc. ***

Ansermet's narrative detail, not achieved at the expense of drama or momentum, means that these two symphonic poems communicate strongly, even if the string-playing in *Les Eolides* is lacking in allure. The remastering flatters these brilliantly wide-ranging recordings from 1964 and 1967, reissued in Decca's Classic Sound series.

Symphonic variations for piano and orchestra.

❀ (B) *** Decca 433 628-2 [(M) id. import]. Clifford Curzon, LPO, Boult – GRIEG: *Concerto* ***; SCHUMANN: *Concerto.* **(*)

(M) *** Decca Legends 466 376-2 [id.]. Curzon, LPO, Boult – BRAHMS: *Piano concerto No. 1* (with LITOLFF: *Scherzo.* ***)

(M) *** RCA 09026 61863-2 [id.]. Rubinstein; Symphony of the Air, Wallenstein (with PROKOFIEV: *Love for 3 oranges: March* ***) – FALLA: *Nights in the gardens of Spain*, etc. SAINT-SAENS: *Concerto No. 2.* **(*)

(M) (**(*)) EMI mono CDM5 66597-2 [id.]. Walter Gieseking, Philh. O, Karajan – GRIEG: *Piano concerto;* SCHUMANN: *Piano concerto.* (**(*))

(BB) **(*) ASV Dig. CDQS 6092 [(M) id.]. Osorio, RPO, Bátiz – RAVEL: *Left-hand concerto* ***; SAINT-SAENS: *Wedding-cake* ***; SCHUMANN: *Concerto.* **(*)

(BB) **(*) Naxos 8.550754 [id.]. Thiollier, Nat. SO of Ireland, Antonio de Almeida – FAURE: *Ballade;* D'INDY: *Symphonie sur un chant montagnard français.* **(*)

Clifford Curzon's 1959 recording of the Franck *Variations* has stood the test of time; even after four decades there is no finer version. It is an engagingly fresh reading, as notable for its impulse and rhythmic felicity as for its poetry. The vintage Decca recording is naturally balanced and has been transferred to CD without loss of bloom. The Grieg *Concerto* coupling is hardly less desirable, and there is also an alternative coupling with Brahms and Litolff, reissued in Decca's Legends series.

Rubinstein's recording of the *Symphonic variations* was the first to appear in stereo. There is refinement and charm, yet his bravura tautens the structure while his warmth and freedom prevent it from seeming hard or in any way aggressive. The 1958 recording was made in the Manhattan Center, New York City, and has a warm atmosphere. The two solo encores are marvellously done, particularly the Prokofiev *March*.

Gieseking's performance dates from 1951 and appears now for the first time. Artistically it belongs among the very finest accounts of the work that were made in the 1950s, given its many beauties and the wonderful orchestral support from Karajan. The piano has one or two notes that are not in perfect condition, but this is a small price to pay for playing of such distinction and poetic feeling.

The ASV super-bargain disc offers fine performances of four concertante works including a really outstanding version of the Ravel *Left-hand concerto* and it adds up to more than the sum of its parts. It can receive a strong recommendation, for reservations about the Franck performance are minor. It has both poetry and impulse and lacks only a little in sparkle at the very end. It is very well recorded.

François-Joël Thiollier shows imagination, and the orchestral playing is perfectly acceptable without being in any way distinguished. All the same, many will find it tempting at this price.

(i) *Symphonic variations for piano and orchestra;* (ii) *Symphony in D min.; Les Eolides;* (iii) *Violin sonata in A;* (iv) (Piano) *Prélude, choral et fugue;* (v) (Organ) *Cantabile in B; Choral No. 2; Pièce héroïque in B min.;* (vi) *Panis angelicus*.

(B) **(*) Ph. Duo 442 296-2 (2). (i) Bucquet, Monte Carlo Op. O, Capolongo; (ii) Concg. O, Otterloo; (iii) Arthur Grumiaux, István Hajdu; (iv) Eduardo del Pueyo; (v) Pierre Cocherau (organ of Notre-Dame de Paris); (vi) José Carreras.

Although the performances are variable, this Philips Duo set is certainly worth its asking price. Its highlights are Otterloo's splendid (1964) account of the *Symphony* (plus *Les Eolides*) and the Grumiaux/Hajdu performance of the *Violin sonata* (see below). Otterloo's reading of the *Symphony* has tremendous thrust and its romantic urgency is impossible to resist when the orchestral playing is so assured. *Les Eolides* is a welcome bonus. Marie-Françoise Bucquet gives a perfectly satisfactory account of the *Symphonic variations*, and Carreras sings his heart out in *Panis angelicus*. But del Pueyo's piano contribution is a routine one and Cochereau's organ pieces are also unmemorable, not helped by wheezily unflattering sound.

Symphony in D min.

(N) ❀ (M) *** 09026 63303-2 [id.]. Chicago SO, Monteux – STRAVINSKY: *Petrushka.* ***

(M) *** DG 449 720-2 [id.]. Berlin RSO, Maazel – MENDELSSOHN: *Symphony No. 5.* ***

(M) **(*) DG (IMS) Dig. 445 512-2 [id.]. O Nat.

de France, Bernstein – ROUSSEL: *Symphony No. 3*. **(*)

**(*) Teldec/Warner Dig. 4509 98416-2. BPO, Mehta – SAINT-SAENS: *Symphony No. 3*. **(*)

(B) *(*) DG 439 494-2. Chicago SO, Barenboim – SAINT-SAENS: *Symphony No. 3*. **(*)

(i) *Symphony in D min.;* (iii) *Le chasseur maudit;* (iv) *Psyché: Psyché and Eros;* (ii; iii) *Symphonic variations for piano and orchestra.*

*** Chesky CD 87 [id.]. (i) London O, Boult; (ii) Earl Wild; (iii) RCA Victor SO, Freccia; (iv) RPO, Prêtre.

(i) *Symphony in D min.;* (ii) *Le chasseur maudit;* (iii) *Symphonic variations for piano and orchestra.*

(BB) **(*) RCA Navigator 74321 29256-2 [(M) id. import]. (i–ii) Boston SO, Munch; (iii) Leonard Pennario, Boston Pops O, Fiedler.

(M) **(*) EMI CDM7 64747-2 [id.].(i; iii) BPO, Karajan; (iii) with Alexis Weissenberg; (ii) Phd. O, Muti.

(i) *Symphony in D min.;* (ii) *Pièce héroïque* (orch. Charles O'Connell).

✪ (M) *** RCA 09026 61967-2 [id.]. (i) Chicago SO; (ii) San Francisco SO; Monteux (with (ii): d'Indy: *Istar* (***)).

Monteux exerts a unique grip on this highly charged Romantic symphony, and his control of the continuous ebb and flow of tempo and tension is masterly, so that any weaknesses of structure in the outer movements are disguised. The splendid playing of the Chicago orchestra is ever responsive to the changes of mood, and the most recent remastering by John Pfeifer for the Monteux Edition brings a further improvement; indeed, now the quality reflects the acoustics of Chicago's Orchestra Hall in the same way as the Reiner recordings, with textures full-bodied and glowing without loss of detail. Vincent d'Indy's *Istar* is a colourful and increasingly energetic piece. Although the 1945 mono sound is boxy, the strings have plenty of middle sonority, and the vivid performance is unlikely to be bettered.

However, many collectors will undoubtedly choose the alternative coupling – Monteux's uniquely authoritative 1962 Boston recording of *Petrushka*, for he conducted the première of Stravinsky's ballet.

Maazel's account is beautifully shaped, both in its overall structure and in incidental details. He adopts a fairly brisk tempo in the slow movement, which, surprisingly enough, greatly enhances its poetry and dignity; his finale is also splendidly vital. The work gains enormously from strong control and deliberate understatement, as well as from the refinement of tone and phrasing which mark this reading, for there is no lack of excitement. The recording, admirably well blended and balanced, is enhanced in this new CD transfer for DG's 'Originals'.

Boult's manner is brisk, urgent and direct, with crisply pointed rhythms and with all sentimentality and vulgarity completely removed. This is as compelling as Monteux's famous version, yet in Sir Adrian's hands much of this music might almost be by Elgar, with nobility one of the elements. The recording is bright, clean and well balanced. Fortunately Earl Wild's account of the *Symphonic variations* is memorable for its gentle lyricism and poetic feeling, while Freccia ensures a vigorously buoyant closing section. He also directs a thrilling account of *The accursed huntsman*. Prêtre's *Psyché and Eros* is idiomatic but nothing special as either a performance or recording. But no matter, this record is highly recommendable, even at full price.

Bernstein conducts a powerful, warmly expressive performance which, thanks in part to a live recording, carries conviction in its flexible spontaneity. It has its moments of vulgarity, but that is part of the work; the reservations are of less importance next to the glowing, positive qualities of the performance. The recording is vivid and opulent, but with the brass apt to sound strident.

Munch's 1957 performance of the *Symphony in D minor* was always among the finest ever recorded, a performance of great élan, but it suffered – as it still does – from the internal balance of the orchestra, which lets the trumpets (with a nasal edge to their tone) coarsen the texture of the loud moments. Otherwise the warm Boston acoustics are heard to good effect. *Le chasseur maudit* (recorded five years later) also sounds spectacular: Franck's horn-calls come over arrestingly. The *Symphonic variations* are brilliantly played by Leonard Pennario. Altogether this Navigator compilation is well worth its modest cost.

Karajan's tempi are all on the slow side, but his control of rhythm prevents any feeling of sluggishness or heaviness. There is always energy underlying the performance, and by facing the obvious problems squarely Karajan avoids the perils. Weissenberg's account of the *Symphonic variations* has less distinction, but the poetry of the lyrical sections is not missed and Karajan ensures that the orchestral contribution is a strong one.

Mehta's live performance brings an individual and powerful reading with highly responsive playing from the BPO, whose playing style has a strong influence over the interpretation. Resolutely controlled, the outer movements have consistent thrust and generate plenty of adrenalin. The *Allegretto*, taken slowly, is gentle. In the finale Mehta maintains his grip firmly, so that the closing peroration is the more forceful. A compelling version, given full-bodied if not always refined sound, which is worth considering if the coupling is suitable.

Barenboim adopts a surprisingly plodding tempo in the first movement, the first subject lacking bite. There are also places where the reading is self-indulgent (Barenboim putting on his Furtwänglerian mantle) and, in an otherwise fine account of the slow movement, the cor anglais solo is disappointingly wooden. The 1976 sound, however, is firmer than the original and very acceptable.

(i) *Symphony in D min.;* (i; ii) *Symphonic variations for piano and orchestra;* (iii; v) *Piano quintet in F min.;* (iii; iv) *Violin sonata;* (vi) *Prelude, choral et fugue.*
(N) (B) **(*) Erato/Warner Ultima Double Analogue/Digital 3984 24234-2 (2) [id.]. (i) O. Nat. de l'O.R.T.F, Martinon; (ii) with Philippe Entremont; (iii) Jean Hubeau, (iv) Olivier Charlier; (v) Viotti Qt; (vi) Pascal Devoyon.

Not surprisingly Jean Martinon's volatile acccount of the *D minor Symphony* is exciting, idiomatic and well held together, and Philippe Entremont makes a warm and sensitive contribution to the *Symphonic variations*. The late 1960s stereo is full-bodied and is otherwise well balanced, with warmly coloured piano timbre. It is amazing how rarely the *Piano quintet* has been recorded in recent years and Jean Hubeau's performance with the Viotti Quartet is faithful and committed, as is the ardent and sensitive account of the *Violin sonata,* where he is joined by Olivier Charlier. These are digital recordings and in the *Quintet* the string timbre could be more sweetly focused, although there is no lack of ambience. No complaints about Pascal Devoyan's admirably sensitive response to the *Prélude, choral et fugue*, and here the sound is very good. At its modest cost this package is worth considering, even if the documentation is inadequate.

CHAMBER MUSIC

Cello sonata in A (trans. of *Violin sonata*).
(M) **(*) EMI CDM7 63184-2. Du Pré, Barenboim – CHOPIN: *Sonata.* **(*)
**(*) CRD CRD 3391; *CRDC 4091* [id.]. Robert Cohen, Roger Vignoles (with DVORAK: *Rondo*) – GRIEG: *Cello sonata.* **(*)

Du Pré and Barenboim give a fine, mature, deeply expressive reading of a richly satisfying work. They are well balanced, but the effect of the music when transferred to the cello is inevitably mellower, less vibrant.

Cohen gives a firm and strong rendering of the Franck *Sonata* in its cello version, splendidly incisive and dashing in the second-movement *Allegro*, but the recording is more limited than one expects from CRD, a little shallow. The addition of the Dvŏrák *G minor Rondo*, Op. 94, makes a pleasing bonus.

Flute sonata in A (trans. of *Violin sonata*).
(M) *** RCA 09026 61615-2 [id.]. James Galway, Martha Argerich – PROKOFIEV; REINECKE: *Flute sonatas.* ***

Although the prospect of hearing the Franck *Violin sonata* arranged for flute may strike you as unappealing, it is surprising how well this music responds to James Galway's transcription and his sweet-toned virtuosity. Argerich is in absolutely superb form here and the recording, if just a trifle close, is truthful, pleasingly fresh and well defined. An outstanding reissue.

Piano quintet in F min.
(BB) *** Naxos Dig. 8.553645 [id.]. Michaël Levinas, Quatuor Ludwig – CHAUSSON: *Quartet in C min.* ***
(***) Testament mono SBT 1077 [id.] Victor Aller, Hollywood Qt – SHOSTAKOVICH: *Piano quintet.* (***)

Michaël Levinas and the Quatuor Ludwig give a very impressive account of 'the king of piano quintets' (the phrase is Tournemire's). This is a very competitive account which is well worth its modest asking price. Michaël Levinas is a sensitive player, and those who are attracted by the enterprising Chausson coupling should consider the present disc. Both the playing and the recorded sound are of a high standard.

Edward Sackville-West and Desmond Shawe-Taylor, the authors of *The Record Guide*, spoke of the Aller/Hollywood version four decades ago as a 'clean-limbed performance . . . the players' attack is extraordinarily vivid and the instrumental balance beautifully maintained'. Even if there is no mistaking the (1953) mono sound as being of its time, the performance has such eloquence and power that the music leaps out of the speakers with a vibrant intensity.

Viola sonata in A (transcription of *Violin sonata).*
(N) *** Chandos Dig. 8873 [id.]. Nobuko Imai, Roger Vignoles – VIEUXTEMPS: *Viola sonata* etc. ***
(N) *** Simax Dig. PSC 1126 [id.]. Lars Anders Tomter, Håvard Gimse – VIEUXTEMPS: *Viola sonata* etc. ***

An all-Belgian coupling from these two violists, Imai and Tomter. The Franck loses a certain amount of its flamboyance and passion, and gains in a kind of measured dignity. Both performances listed above are exemplary if you want it in this form. There is absolutely nothing to choose between them; both are commanding performances and have an impressive eloquence.

Violin sonata in A.
✿ (M) *** Decca 460 006-2. Kyung Wha Chung, Radu Lupu – DEBUSSY: *Violin sonata* *** ✿; CHAUSSON: *Poème.* ***

(M) *** Decca 452 887-2 [id.]. Itzhak Perlman, Vladimir Ashkenazy – BRAHMS: *Horn trio*. **(*)
*** DG Dig. 445 880-2. Dumay, Pires – DEBUSSY: *Violin sonata in G min.;* RAVEL: *Berceuse*, etc. ***
(M) *** DG 431 469-2. Kaja Danczowska, Krystian Zimerman – SZYMANOWSKI: *Mythes*, etc. *** ❁
(N) (BB) *** Arte Nova Dig. 74321 59233-2 [id.]. Miriam Contner, Valéry Rogatchev – DEBUSSY; SAINT-SAENS: *Violin sonatas*. ***
(B) *** Tring Dig. TRP 081 [(M) id. import]. Jonathan Carney, Ronan O'Hora – BRAHMS: *Violin sonata No. 1*. **(*)
(M) **(*) Ph. 426 384-2. Arthur Grumiaux, György Sebok – FAURE: *Sonatas*. ***

Kyung Wha Chung and Radu Lupu give a glorious account, full of natural and not over-projected eloquence, and most beautifully recorded. The slow movement has marvellous repose and the other movements have a natural exuberance and sense of line that carry the listener with them. The 1977 recording is enhanced on CD and, with an apt Chausson coupling, this reissue remains very desirable indeed.

How beautifully and simply Perlman and Ashkenazy open the first movement and how poetically Ashkenazy responds to the melody on Perlman's bow. Yet the second movement catches the listener by the ears with the thrust of its forward impulse and the intensity of its lyrical flow. There is no lack of flexibility, and the sheer ardour of the interpretation makes it a genuine alternative to the Chung/ Lupu account. The fine (1980) recording was understandably chosen for inclusion in Decca's Classic Sound series.

The distinguished partnership of Augustin Dumay and Maria João Pires offers as assured and powerful an interpretation of Franck's indestructible *Sonata* as any now in the catalogue. They have a firm grip on line and combine both intellectual conviction and tenderness of feeling. The DG recording is more than acceptable, and readers wanting this particular coupling need not hold back. It is a pity that the opportunity was not taken to record the Ravel *Sonata*, for which there is room, which would have further enhanced the claims of this issue.

Kaja Danczowska's account of the Franck is distinguished by a natural sense of line and great sweetness of tone, and she is partnered superbly by Krystian Zimerman. Indeed, in terms of dramatic fire and strength of line, this version can hold its own alongside the finest, and it is perhaps marginally better balanced than the Kyung Wha Chung and Radu Lupu recording.

The brilliant young German violinist, Mirijam Contner, naturally responding to the French idiom, gives a passionate, warmly intense performance of the Franck *Sonata* not just in the extrovert passages but also as compellingly in the hushed musing at the very start, or the improvisatory sequence of the third movement. Very well partnered, this makes up an outstanding disc of French violin sonatas, with excellent sound – an outstanding bargain.

The delicately poised opening of the Carney/ O'Hora performance sets the mood for a poetically evocative reading, which certainly does not lack impulse in the second movement or passion in the finale. The recording is truthful if rather resonant, but this serves to add romantic warmth and gives an appealing glow to the third movement, where both artists create a sense of thoughtful improvisation. A fine bargain version.

Grumiaux's account, if less fresh than Chung's, has nobility and warmth to commend it. He is slightly let down by his partner, who is not as imaginative as Lupu in the more poetic moments, including the hushed opening bars.

ORGAN MUSIC

Andantino in E (arr. Vierne); *Cantabile; Chorales Nos. 2–3; Pièce héroïque; Prélude, fugue et variation, Op. 18.*
*** Chandos Dig. CHAN 8891 [id.]. Piet Kee (Cavaillé-Coll organ of Basilica de Santa Maria del Coro, San Sebastian).

The Dutch composer-organist Piet Kee omits the *Chorale No. 1*, for which room could surely have been found, as the playing-time is only 61 minutes 43 seconds, but, apart from this, there can be few grumbles about his record. His interpretations strike an excellent balance between expressive freedom and scholarly rectitude.

Fantaisie in A; Pastorale.
*** Telarc Dig. CD 80096 [id.]. Michael Murray (organ of Symphony Hall, San Francisco) – JONGEN: *Symphonie concertante*. ***

Michael Murray plays these pieces very well, although the San Francisco organ is not tailor-made for them. The Telarc recording is well up to standard.

PIANO MUSIC

Choral No. 3; Danse lente; Grand caprice; Les plaintes d'une poupée; Prélude, aria et final; Prélude, choral et fugue.
*** Hyperion Dig. CDA 66918 [id.]. Stephen Hough.

Stephen Hough's impressive recital must now take pride of place among recordings of this repertoire. The *Prélude, choral et fugue* is worthy to rank alongside Murray Perahia's account (see below), and no praise could be higher. In addition to the piano music, Hough gives us his own transcription of the *Third* of the Organ *Chorals*, which in his hands sounds as if it had been written for the piano, so splendidly is it played. A most distinguished record in every way.

Prélude, choral et fugue.
*** Sony Dig. SK 47180 [id.]. Murray Perahia – LISZT: *Années de pèlerinage*, etc. ***
(M) *** RCA 09026 62590-2 [id.]. Artur Rubinstein – BACH: *Chaconne* ***; LISZT: *Sonata.* **(*)

Murray Perahia's recording of the *Prélude, choral et fugue* is in a class of its own, carefully thought out yet apparently spontaneous and highly poetic.

In music like this, strangely poised between classical form and Romantic expression, between the piano and the organ-loft, Rubinstein is also very persuasive. This performance, recorded in 1970, has fire and spontaneity. The piano-tone is firm and clear: its brightness suits the music.

VOCAL MUSIC

Les Béatitudes.
(N) (B) **(*) Erato/Warner Dig. Ultima Double 3984 24233-2 (2). Lousie Lebrun, Jane Berbié, Nathalie Stutzmann, David Rendall, Marcel Vanaud, François Loup, Daniel Ottevaere, French R. Ch. & Nouvel PO, Jordan.

Les Béatitudes has been out of circulation for some years: the Schwann Musica Sacra version conducted by Jean Alain was made as long ago as 1962. The oratorio occupied Franck through the 1870s, but despite the revival of interest in his work in recent years, it has never really established itself. There is much writing of quality as one would expect, but also much that is pedestrian by the standards of the *Symphony*, the *Sonata* or *Psyché*. Also on such a canvas – the score runs to two hours – the invention is curiously deficient in character and in rhythmic variety. The recording was made at a live performance in Paris in 1985 and is sensitively shaped under the baton of Armin Jordan. The solo singers are more than adequate, the choral and orchestral contributions are also admirable, and the sound-picture is very natural.

Psyché (symphonic fragments).
(N) (***) Testament mono SBT1128 [id.]. René Duclos Ch., Paris Conservatoire O, André Cluytens – RAVEL: *Daphnis et Chloë.* ***

It is logical that André Cluytens's sensitive account of *Daphnis* should be coupled with Franck's most sumptuous and imaginative score. Both are inspired by classical mythology. For though Ravel's admiration for Debussy, Mozart and Saint-Saëns is well known, his regard for César Franck is not. True, he was critical of the symphony and in particular its orchestration, but in 1932, while he was being interviewed in the Amsterdam Concertgebouw, Mengelberg was rehearsing the *Symphonic variations for piano and orchestra* in the background; Ravel broke off at one point to say 'How wonderful that sounds!'. He also spoke of much of Franck being 'beautifully orchestrated', second only to Saint-Saëns in that respect. The 1954 recording is mono but the transfer is of high quality and no collector will fail to respond.

Frankel, Benjamin (1916–71)

(i) *The Aftermath, Op. 17. Concertante lirico, Op. 27; 3 Sketches for strings, Op. 2; Solemn speech and discussion, Op. 11; Youth music, Op. 12.*
*** CPO Dig. CPO 999 221-2 [id.]. (i) Robert Dan; Northwest CO, Seattle, Alun Francis.

All the works recorded here are for string orchestra. While the *Concertante lirico* is very attractive, one of the strongest pieces is *The Aftermath*, a song-cycle for tenor, strings and off-stage trumpet and timpani, to words of Robert Nichols. It is an evocative and imaginative piece. Frankel's craftsmanship is always of the highest order and his invention and imagination are more often impressive than not. This issue, like others in this series, is recommended to all with an interest in contemporary music that has real individuality and eschews trendiness like the plague. The notes are exceptionally helpful and informative.

(i) *Viola concerto, Op. 45;* (ii) *Violin concerto (In memory of the six million), Op. 24;* (iii) *Serenade concertante for piano trio and orchestra, Op. 37.*
(N) *** CPO Dig. CPO 999 422-2 [id.]. (i)Brett Dean; (ii) Ulf Hoelscher; (iii) Alan Smith, David Lale, Stephen Emmerson; Queensland SO, Werner Albert.

The *Violin concerto* comes from 1951 when the holocaust was still a vivid and horrific memory. Its emotional core is the expressive and eloquent slow movement. Yet apart from its elegiac centre, the overwhelming impression the work leaves is powerful and positive, free from any trace of bitterness or emotional self-indulgence, a testament to the strength of the human spirit. The *Viola concerto* is much later and was composed in 1967, between the *Fourth* and *Fifth Symphonies*, and is hardly less memorable. Frankel's lyricism and his musical ingenuity are always in evidence, but the latter is never intrusive. His is the art of concealing art. The composer describes the *Serenata concertante,* which is for piano trio and orchestra, as 'a street scene' in which passing traffic, a distant jazz band, lovers dancing and much else besides can be heard. It was composed between the *First* and *Second Symphonies* and wears its serial organization lightly. Both Ulf Hoelscher and Brett Dean are impressive soloists in the two concertos and the Queensland Orchestra respond with supportive playing. The recording engineers serve these fine players faithfully and produce an impressive and wide-ranging sound. Strongly recommended.

Symphonies Nos. 1, Op. 33; 5, Op. 46; May Day overture, Op. 22.
*** CPO Dig. CPO 999 240-2 [id.]. Queensland SO, Werner Andreas Albert.

Benjamin Frankel is a master of the orchestra and the *First Symphony* (1959) leaves no doubt that he was also a master symphonist. It is a powerfully concentrated and finely argued piece which has a constant feeling of onward movement. The music develops organically; Frankel has something of the strength of Sibelius combined with a Mahlerian anguish, and his serialism, like that of Frank Martin, never undermines tonal principles. The *Fifth Symphony*, too, is a well-argued and impressive score. The Queensland orchestra play with dedication, and the performances of both symphonies and the inventive *May Day Overture* are very well recorded too.

Symphonies Nos. 2, Op. 38 (1962); *3, Op. 40* (1964).
❀ *** CPO Dig. CPO 999 241-2 [id.]. Queensland SO, Werner Andreas Albert.

Like the *First*, his *Second Symphony* is a powerfully concentrated and finely argued piece which has a constant feeling of onward movement. While the *Second* springs from painful emotions, the *Third Symphony* with its almost Stravinskian opening is a compact one-movement work, predominantly positive in expression and compelling in its sense of purpose. Each symphony is prefaced by a paragraph or so of spoken introduction that the composer recorded at the time he conducted the first performance of these symphonies on the Third Programme. Once more the playing of the Queensland Orchestra is excellent, and so, too, is the recording.

Symphonies Nos. 4, Op. 44; 6, Op. 49; Mephistopheles' Serenade and dance, Op. 25.
*** CPO Dig. CPO 999 242-2 [id.]. Queensland SO, Werner Andreas Albert.

The *Fourth Symphony* is arguably one of the very finest of Frankel's works. It has a more restrained palette than its predecessors, yet its invention is both powerful and distinctive. The Scherzo has a memorable delicacy and the elegiac finale has great eloquence. The *Sixth* is dark and powerfully argued and gets very persuasive advocacy from the Queensland orchestra under Werner Andreas Albert, and very fine recording. Readers might well start either with this latest issue or with the coupling of Nos. 2 and 3.

Bagatelles for 11 instruments (Cinque pezzi notturni), Op. 35; Clarinet quintet, Op. 28; Clarinet trio, Op. 10; Pezzi pianissimi, Op. 41 (for clarinet, cello & piano); *Early morning music.*
*** CPO Dig. CPO 999 384-2 [id.]. Paul Dean, Australian String Qt (members); Queensland Symphony Chamber Players.

The *Clarinet quintet* is beautifully crafted and is expertly played by these Australian artists. The *Clarinet trio* was composed in 1940, but Frankel's musical language and fluent invention are already in place. The short but disturbing *Pezzi pianissimi* are thoughtful, gentle pieces which resonate in the memory afterwards, as do the *Bagatelles for eleven instruments* of 1959. This work is serial but not 'atonal' – much in the same way as Frank Martin is. Excellent playing and recording make this another most desirable introduction to a much-neglected and underrated composer whose work is at last gaining ground.

Frescobaldi, Girolamo (1583–1643)

Il Primo Libro de' Madrigale a 5 (1608).
*** Opus 111 Dig. OPS 30-133 [id.]. Concerto Italiano, Rinaldo Alessandrini.

Frescobaldi, born in Ferrara, was 25 when his first book of madrigals was published in 1608. They are songs about lovers, longing, admiring, often not daring to speak directly, about parting and loss, and always about passions unrequited. They produced a glorious stream of lyrical invention and a skill in construction remarkable in a composer at the outset of his career. Rinaldo Alessandrini and the Concerto Italiano have been winning golden opinions in this repertoire, and these delightful performances bear out their reputation for fine tuning and blending, and a richly expressive line. They not only give pleasure but should at last put this composer's name firmly in front of the public.

Primo Libro di Toccate (1616): excerpts. *Il Secondo Libro di Toccata, Canzoni, Versi d'hinni; Magnificat; Gagliarde, Corrente*: excerpts. *Partite sopra l'aria della romanesca* (1624); *Aria di balletto* (1637).
(M) *** Virgin/Veritas EMI Dig. VM5 61398-2. Scott Ross (harpsichord).

Scott Ross here surveys the keyboard music of a composer whose music demands a free, improvisatory style of performance, of which he is obviously a master. Indeed he presents this repertoire in a most appealing way, opening with four (very free) *Toccatas* from Book I. The excerpts from the Second Book which, alongside three more *Toccatas*, include four *Correnti*, a pair of *Canzoni* and three *Gagliarde*, are framed by two highly inventive sets of variations. The second is a rather engaging *Aria di balletto*, not unlike Handel's variations known as *The Harmonious blacksmith*. Ross's easy bravura is particularly attractive here, and his Jean-Louis Val harpsichord is very vividly recorded.

Froberger, Johann (1616–67)

Canzon No. 2; Capriccio No. 10; Fantasia No. 4 sopra sollare; Lamentation faîte sur la mort très douloureuse de Sa Majesté Imperiale, Ferdinand le troisième; Ricercar No. 5; Suites Nos. 2 & 3; Suite No. 14: Lamentation sur ce que j'ay été volé. Toccatas Nos. 9, 10 & 114; Tombeau faict à Paris sur la mort de M. Blancrocher.

*** HM/BMG Dig. RD 77923. Gustav Leonhardt (harpsichord).

Froberger's music is highly exploratory in idiom and, in works such as the *Tombeau faict à Paris sur la mort de M. Blancrocher* and the *Plainte faite à Londres pour passer la Melancholie*, from the *Suite No. 3*, he reveals great expressive poignancy. There is space round the instrument and, heard at a low level-setting, this well-played recital produces very good results. Recommended with enthusiasm.

Capriccio in C, FbWV 632; Lamentation sur la mort de Ferdinand III in F, FbWV 633; Partitas: in C, FbWV 612; C min., FbWV 619; D, FbWV 611a; E flat, FbWV 631; in G (auff Die Maÿerin), FbWV 606; Toccatas: in A min., FbWV 101; D, FbWV 121; G, FbWV 103; Tombeau sur la mort de M. Blancheroche in C min., FbWV 632.

*** Virgin Veritas/EMI VC5 45259-2. Siegbert Rampe (various harpsichords and virginals).

Lamentation sur la mort de Ferdinand III in F, FbWV 633; Partitas (Suites) Nos. XVIII in G min.; XIX in C min., FbWV 619; XX in D, FbWV 611a; XXX in A min.; Toccatas Nos. II in D min., IX in C; XIV in G, FbWV 103; XVIII in F; Tombeau sur la mort de M. Blancheroche in C min., FbWV 632.

(M) *** HMT Dig. 1901372 [id.]. Christophe Rousset (harpsichord).

Siegbert Rampe brings this rewarding repertoire vividly to life on four different period instruments, each admirably chosen; bearing in mind that slight pitch changes are involved as well as the changing character of the instrument, Rampe is immediately commanding in the opening *Tombeau sur la mort de M. Blancheroche*, who was a celebrated lutenist and who died after falling down the stairs (the fall is reputedly included in the music), and the similarly meditative *Lamentation for the death of Ferdinand III*. Both these extended valedictions and the intervening *C minor Partita* are played on a double-manual 1628 Ruckers harpsichord, rebuilt a century later in Paris, which produces a satisfying body of tone. The first two *Partitas* are played on a Miklis Czech harpsichord, made in Prague in 1671, which gives an appropriately more lightweight effect; its pitch, too, is slightly higher. The three bold *Toccatas* are heard on a tangy Spanish instrument made in 1629, which is in splendid condition. In between comes the reflective and touching *Capriccio in C*, which seems ideally suited to the chosen (1587) virginal, made in Venice by Giovanni Celestini. The performances here are outstanding in every way and the recording is very real and believable, but – as always with the harpsichord – it is important not to set the volume control too high.

Needless to say, Christophe Rousset is hardly less impressive in this repertoire. He uses a restored (1652) Couchet double-manual harpsichord which suits all these works admirably in his hands. Its pitch (A392) is the same as Rampe's Prague instrument; in the two *Partitas* which are played by both artists (FbWV 611a and FbWV 619), the effect of Rousset's instrument is brighter than Rampe's Ruckers, which is tuned at A370. This is very effective in the *Gigues*, but some may prefer Rampe's slightly more sonorous effect in the *Allemandes*. If Rousset is often slightly brisker than Rampe, he takes the closing *Sarabande* of the meditative *D major Suite* considerably more slowly. Like Rampe, he is very well recorded and, although he includes slightly less music, his disc is offered at mid-price.

Frohlich, Johannes (1806–1860)

Symphony in E flat, Op. 33.

(N) *** Chandos Dig. CHAN 9609 [id.]. Danish Nat. RSO, Christopher Hogwood – GADE: *Symphony No. 4*. ***

This delightful disc resurrects a long-buried work which proves far more than just a curiosity. Johannes Frederik Frohlich, born in 1806, was one of the fathers of Danish music. A pupil of Kuhlau, he was an accomplished instrumentalist playing the flute, violin and the piano. As a young man Frohlich composed violin concertos and quartets, before going abroad to study in the 1830s when he met both Cherubini and Spohr, whose violin concertos he knew (he made his Copenhagen debut in one of them). He wrote his *Symphony* in 1833, but it was so poorly played it sank without trace, and was never given again. The score disappeared, and was discovered only long after Frohlich's death, failing either to get published or be performed. Yet this is a totally refreshing, beautifully written work, not unlike the symphonies of another Scandinavian, Berwald; it also owes much to Weber. The writing is inventive and full of character, and the Danish Radio Orchestra under Christopher Hogwood play it with both spirit and conviction. It is well coupled here in splendid performances with the best-known symphony by another Dane, Niels Gade, devoted follower of Mendelssohn. Good recording too, if not Chandos's very finest.

Fuchs, Robert (1847–1927)

Cello sonatas Nos. 1 in D min., Op. 29; 2 in E flat min., Op. 83; Phantasiestücke, Op. 78.

*** Marco Polo Dig. 8.223423 [id.]. Mark Drobinsky, Daniel Blumenthal.

*** Biddulph Dig. LAW005 [id.]. Nancy Green, Caroline Palmer.

The *Cello sonatas*, like the more Schumannesque *Phantasiestücke*, offer well-fashioned, cultured and civilized music (no mean virtues) which may not have a strongly original profile but is well worth investigating for all that. After long neglect these works are available in two different versions. To be frank, there is not much to choose between them; both offer very good performances; both are very well recorded and deserve their three stars, so no agonies of choice are required: you can safely invest in one or the other.

Clarinet quintet, Op. 102.

*** Marco Polo Dig. 8.223282 [id.]. Rodenhäuser, Ens. Villa Musica – LACHNER: *Septet.* ***

This is beautifully crafted and speaks with the accents of Schubert and Brahms rather than with any strong individuality. It is nicely played by the Mainz-based Ensemble Villa Musica whose excellent clarinettist, Ulf Rodenhäuser, is worth a mention. A curiosity rather than a revelation then, but eminently well recorded.

Piano sonatas Nos. 1, Op. 19; 2, Op. 88.

*** Marco Polo Dig. 8.223377 [id.]. Daniel Blumenthal.

The early *F minor Sonata*, Op. 19 (1877), is indeed heavily indebted to Brahms, and the Rondo finale with which it concludes seems heavily indebted to the latter's *Ballades*, Op. 10. All the same it has a certain breadth and lyrical fertility that impress. The *Second Sonata*, Op. 88, is mature Fuchs. Its invention is more chromatic and there are hints of Reger and even of Debussy and Fauré. Although Fuchs may lack a strong individual voice, his musical thinking has the merit of breadth and span and these are both rewarding works, given such masterly and persuasive advocacy as they receive at the hands of Daniel Blumenthal.

String trio in A, Op. 94.

(N) *** MDG Dig. MDG 634 0841-2 [id.]. Belcanto Strings – REINECKE: *Trio in C min, Op. 249.* ***

In his day Robert Fuchs was a much admired teacher whose pupils included Mahler, Sibelius, Wolf, Franz Schmidt, Schreker and Zemlinsky! He was also a prolific composer, even if none of his works to reach the catalogues reveals evidence of a strong or original voice. He was a friend of Brahms whose art casts its shadow over much of his work, including the present *Trio*. Finely crafted and cultured music, very conservative for its date of composition (1910), but superbly played and recorded.

Furtwängler, Wilhelm (1886–1954)

Symphony No. 2 in E min.

(M) (***) DG mono 457 722-2 (2) [id.]. BPO, Furtwängler – SCHUMANN: *Symphony No. 4.* (***) ✪

Furtwängler spoke of his *Second Symphony* as his spiritual testament. It is Brucknerian in its dimensions and sense of space: it runs to 82 minutes, and the finale alone is as long as most performances of Schumann's *Fourth Symphony*. It is Brucknerian, too, in its nobility. The first movement, lasting 24 minutes, is accommodated on the first CD, and the remaining three on the second. Furtwängler himself thought the present studio recording, made in the Jesus-Christus Kirche, Berlin, in 1950 'stilted', but it sounds amazingly clear and warm in this transfer and readers should not be put off acquiring it. The Schumann coupling – one of Furtwängler's very finest mono records – makes a superb coupling.

Fux, Johann Joseph (1650–1741)

Il Concentus musico instrumentalis: Overtures (Suites) Nos. 2 in B flat; 4 in G min. Overtures (Suites) in B flat; D min.

(M) *** Van. Dig. 99705 [id.]. Il Fondamento, Paul Dombrecht.

Fux wrote a great many overtures or suites which combine the French and Italian styles, of which the present four are lively and quite colourful examples. They have a good deal in common with similar works of Telemann, even if not nearly so skilfully scored. Il Fondamento, a period-instrument group under Paul Dombrecht bring these works to life quite vividly. They are agreeably recorded; though the sound could ideally be more transparent. But the thickness of texture is partly caused by the doubling up in the scoring, with the wind playing in tutti with the strings. Perhaps this was an influence from Dresden, where tutti unisons were very fashionable.

Gabrieli, Andrea (1520–86)

Aria della battaglia a 8.

(B) ** Decca Eclipse Dig. 448 993-2. Philip Jones Brass Ens., Jones – Giovanni GABRIELI: *Collection.* **(*)

The *Aria della battaglia* is a rambling piece lasting over ten minutes, rather too long to retain the listener's interest – at least in the present performance. It is very well played, without any dramatic dynamic contrasts, and tends to jog along rather than create any great degree of tension. The recording is clear and nicely resonant.

Gabrieli, Giovanni (1557–1612)

Music for brass, Vol. 1: *Canzon à 12 in double eco; Canzon septimi toni à 8 No. 2; Canzon septimi e octavi toni à 12; Canzon noni toni à 8; Canzon noni toni à 12; Canzoni duodecimi toni à 10, Nos. 1 & 3; Canzoni VII; VIII; IX; XI; XIII; XIV; XVII; XXVIII; Sonata pian' e forte alla quarta bassa à 8.*
(BB) *** Naxos Dig. 8.553609 [id.]. LSO Brass, Eric Crees.

Starting with the *Canzon XVII* of 1615 in 12 parts, involving three choirs of instruments, Eric Crees and his brilliant players from the brass section of the LSO demonstrate at once what variety of tone they can produce, with the finest shading of timbre and texture. In the great *Sonata pian' e forte* of 1597 in eight parts and the even more striking *Double echo Canzon* in 12 parts, the playing is remarkable as much for its restraint and point as for its dramatic impact. Beautiful sound, both clear and atmospheric, not aggressive. Naxos could not have chosen better for the first volume of what promises to be an exciting series.

Symphoniae sacrae II (1615): Buccinate in neomania (a 19); In ecclesiis (a 14); Jubilate Deo (a 10); Magnificat a 14; Magnificat a 17; Misericordia (a 12); Quem vidistis pastores (a 14); Suscipe a 12; Surrexit Christus (a 11).
*** O-L 436 860-2. Taverner Ch., L. Cornett and Sackbutt Ens., Parrott.

As principal composer of ceremonial music at St Mark's, Venice, the younger Gabrieli had to write all kinds of appropriate church music, and this fine collection contains some of the pieces of his later years, when – relying on instrumentalists rather than choristers – he came to include elaborate accompaniments for cornetts and sackbutts. Here, for example, six sackbutts accompany the six-part setting of *Suscipe* with glowing results; after hearing modern brass instruments and without the benefits of the St Mark's acoustics, these more authentic instruments may seem on the gentle side, with Gabrielian panoply underplayed, but the singing and playing are most stylish, helped by first-rate 1977 recording, smoothly transferred to CD.

(i) *Canzon a 6; Canzon primi toni a 8; Canzon, La Spiritata, a 4; Canzon vigesimasettima a 8; Sonata a 3.* (i; ii) *Canzon per sonar a 4; Canzoni Nos. 4 a 6; 12 a 8; In ecclesiis; Jubilate Deo; O Jesu mi dulcissime; O magnum mysterium; Quem vidistis pastores?; Timor et tremor.*
(B) **(*) Decca Eclipse Dig. 448 993-2. (i) Philip Jones Brass Ens., Jones; (ii) Soloists, King's College, Cambridge, Ch., Cleobury – Andrea GABRIELI: *Aria della battaglia.* **

The first group of *Canzoni* here is played immaculately on modern brass instruments, skilfully balanced and recorded in the Kingsway Hall which gives a nicely resonant bloom, good detail and excellent antiphony. Yet the result is curiously bland. The *Sonata a 3* comes off best; otherwise there seems to be a lack of tension and not the widest range of dynamic. In the rest of the programme, recorded four years later in 1986, the widely resonant acoustics of King's College Chapel make an admirable alternative to St Mark's for this repertoire. In the festive motet, *In ecclesiis*, with its three choirs plus organ and instrumental accompaniment, the complex layout is thrilling, and the Christmas motet, *Quem vidistis pastores?*, with its solo voices from the choir representing the shepherds, is very well managed. The canzoni for brass alone, which act as interludes, are undoubtedly enhanced by the King's ambience, and climaxes have real impact. At Eclipse price this is well worth having for the choral music alone.

Angelus ad pastores ait; Buccante in neomenia tuba; Canzon septimi toni à 8; Hodie Christus natus est; Hodie completi sunt; O Domine Jesu Christe; O magnum mysterium; Omnes gentes, plaudite manibus.
(B) **(*) EMI forte CZS5 68631-2 (2) [CDFB 68631]. Cambridge University Musical Soc., Bach Ch., King's College Ch., Wilbraham Brass Soloists, Willcocks (with SCHEIDT: *In dulci jubilo* ***) – SCHUTZ: *Psalm 150* **(*); MONTEVERDI: *Vespers.* *(*)

Originally recorded in King's College Chapel, using quadraphonic sound, the CD transfer brings stereo which is notable for the opulent richness of brass and choral textures rather than inner clarity, yet is resonantly resplendent. There is an impressively wide dynamic range, as is shown by the serene motet, *O Domine Jesu Christe*. Added to the Gabrieli works is Scheidt's setting in eight parts of the famous *In dulci jubilo*, which is particularly successful. It is a pity that the principal Monteverdi coupling is not more recommendable.

Gade, Niels (1817–90)

Andante and allegro (arr. Rachlevsky); *Novelettes, Opp. 53 & 58.*
*** Claves Dig. CD 50-9607 [id.]. Kremlin CO, Misha Rachlevsky.

The *Andante and allegro* is a transcription for full strings of a quartet movement. The two sets of *Novelettes* also have great allure. This is eminently civilized writing, inventive and intelligent, full of charm, and the performances by the Kremlin Chamber Orchestra under Misha Rachlevsky are beyond praise. It is a joy to hear such natural and beautifully shaped phrasing and the recording is pleasingly natural and warm.

Novellettes in F, Op. 53; in E, Op. 58.
(N) *** CPO Dig. CPO 999 516-2 [id.]. German Chamber Academy Neuss, Goritzki – HAMERIK: *Symphony No. 6.* ***

These miniatures for strings, like most of Gade's music, are full of charm, and are excellently played by the Deutsche Kammerakademie with their splendid cellist-conductor Johannes Goritski. They have great lightness of touch and vital rhythmic articulation. First-rate sound.

Symphony No. 1 in C min. (On Sjølund's fair plains), Op. 5; Overture, Echoes from Ossian, Op. 1; Hamlet Overture, Op. 37.
*** Chandos Dig. CHAN 9422 [id.]. Danish Nat. RSO, Dmitri Kitaenko.

This performance of the engaging, folksong-inspired *First Symphony* has an unaffected quality and an unforced eloquence that give much delight. The two shorter works, *Hamlet* and the *Echoes from Ossian overture*, are also very well played. The recording, made in the fine concert hall of Danish Radio, is absolutely first rate, natural in perspective, with plenty of presence and detail. An excellent introduction to the composer and a first choice unless the coupling with the *Eighth* is preferred.

Symphonies Nos. 1 in C min. (On Sjøland's fair plains), Op. 5; 8 in B min., Op. 47.
*** BIS Dig. CD 339 [id.]. Stockholm Sinf., Järvi.

Thirty years separate the *First Symphony* from his *Eighth* and last symphony, like the *First* much indebted to Mendelssohn. Despite this debt, there is still a sense of real mastery and a command of pace. The Stockholm Sinfonietta and Neeme Järvi give very fresh and lively performances, and the recording is natural and truthful.

Symphonies Nos. 2 in E, Op. 10; 7 in F, Op. 45.
**(*) BIS Dig. CD 355 [id.]. Stockholm Sinf., Järvi.

Schumann thought No. 2 'reminiscent of Denmark's beautiful beechwoods'. The debt to Mendelssohn is still enormous here, but it is very likeable, more spontaneous than the *Seventh*, though this work has a delightful Scherzo. Splendid playing from the Stockholm Sinfonietta under Järvi, and good recording too.

Symphonies Nos. 3 in A min., Op. 15; 4 in B flat, Op. 20.
*** BIS Dig. CD 338 [id.]. Stockholm Sinf., Järvi.

Gade's *Third* has great freshness and a seemingly effortless flow of ideas and pace, and a fine sense of musical proportion. No. 4 was more generally admired in Gade's lifetime, but its companion here is the more winning. It is beautifully played and recorded.

Symphonies Nos. 3 in A min., Op. 15; (i) *5 in D min., Op. 25.*
**(*) Dacapo Dig. DCCD 9004 [id.]. (i) Amalie Malling, Coll. Mus., Copenhagen, Schønwandt.

Michael Schønwandt's performances of these two Gade symphonies are most musical, and distinguished by sensitive phrasing and a fine feeling for line. In the *Fifth Symphony*, the piano is less closely observed than it is in the BIS recording. Amalie Malling is the more reticent player, too, and plays with taste and grace. However, the 1988 recording though perfectly acceptable is not as good or as fresh sounding as its BIS rival which is on balance to be preferred.

Symphony No. 4 in B flat, Op. 20.
(N) *** Chandos Dig. CHAN 9609 [id.]. Danish Nat. RSO, Christopher Hogwood– FROLICH: *Symphony.****

Niels Gade, devoted follower of Mendelssohn, became a key figure in nineteenth-century Danish music. In this best known of his eight symphonies, as in most of his works, he charmingly echoes that master. Very well played and recorded, it makes an excellent coupling for the delightful, long-buried Frohlich symphony. The performance does not supplant Neeme Järvi, coupled with the *Third* which has more transparent, better balanced recorded sound. All the same, a very recommendable disc, for the coupling is delightful.

Symphonies Nos. (i) *5 in D min., Op. 25; 6 in G min., Op. 32.*
*** BIS Dig. CD 356 [id.]. Stockholm Sinf., Järvi; (i) with Roland Pöntinen.

The *Fifth Symphony* is a delightfully sunny piece which lifts one's spirits; its melodies are instantly memorable, and there is a lively concertante part for the piano, splendidly played by the young Roland Pöntinen. The *Sixth Symphony* is rather more thickly scored and more academic. The recording is very good and, given the charm of the *Fifth Symphony* and the persuasiveness of the performance, this coupling must be warmly recommended.

CHAMBER MUSIC

Allegro in A min., for string quartet; (i) *Andante and Allegro molto in F min., for string quintet. String quartet in F (Wilkommen und Abschied);* (ii) *Octet in F, Op. 17.*
**(*) BIS Dig. CD 545 [id.]. Kontra Qt, with (i–ii) Hans Nygaard; (ii) Anne Egendal, Per Lund Madsen, Sune Ranmo.

All this music is youthful and has charm and freshness of invention. The influence of Mendelssohn had not become stultifying and, though Gade's work belongs to that tradition, it has a spontaneity – particularly the *F minor Quintet* – which is quite captivating. This is a useful supplement to the Kontra's recording of the three later *Quartets* discussed below, and in many ways it is to be preferred. The Kontra performance of the *Octet* is more persuasive than the Sony version discussed below. The excellent performances are well recorded, but there is a slightly strident edge in tutti passages which inhibits a full three-star recommendation.

String quartets Nos. 1 in F min., 2 in E min., 3 in D, Op. 63.
*** BIS Dig. CD 516 [id.]. Kontra Qt.

These are pleasing works of great facility and are worth hearing, particularly in such good performances and recordings as we are given here. However, the fact remains that they show too strong a gravitational pull of Mendelssohn. Nevertheless, in terms of invention and craftsmanship, they give a certain pleasure.

VOCAL MUSIC

(i) *Efterklange af Ossian (Echoes from Ossian), Op. 1;* (ii) *Elverskud (The Elf-King's daughter), Op. 30*; (iii) *5 Partsongs, Op. 13.*
*** Chandos Dig. CHAN 9075 [id.]. (ii) Johansson, Gjevang, Elming, Danish Nat. R. Ch.; (iii) Danish Nat. R. Chamber Ch., Parkman; (i; ii) Danish Nat. RSO, Kitaienko.

(i) *Elverskud Op. 30;* (ii) *Forårs-fantasi (Spring fantasy), Op. 23.*
*** Marco Polo DaCapo Dig. 8.224051 [id.]. (i) Susanne Elmark, Guido Paëvatalu; (i; ii) Kirsten Dolberg; (ii) Anne-Margarethe Dahl, Gert Henning-Jensen, Sten Byriel, Elisabeth Westenholz; (i) Tivoli Concert Ch.; Tivoli SO, Michael Schønwandt.

Forårs-fantasi (Spring fantasy), Op. 23.
(M) ** EMI (SIS) CDM5 66000-2. Bodil Gøbil, Minna Nyhus, Ole Jensen, Mogens Schmidt Johansen, Eyvind Møller, Danish RSO, Frandsen – NIELSEN: *Hymnus Amoris; Sleep.* **

Gade's *Elverskud*, variously translated as *The Elf-King's daughter*, *The Erl-King's daughter*, *The Fairy spell* or *The Elf-shot*, is a work of great appeal and the opening of the second half – an evocation of the moonlit world of the fairy hill – is much more than that: it is little short of inspired. Michael Schønwandt's account has a good deal to recommend it. In some ways this Marco Polo disc scores over its Chandos rival: the solo singers are generally more satisfying and the conductor keeps a firmer grip on proceedings without any loss of poetic feeling or atmosphere. It also has the advantage of the more adventurous coupling, the *Forårs-fantasi* (*Spring fantasy*) another of Gade's most delightful inspirations, radiant in its happiness and full of sun. Excellent soloists and very good playing from all concerned. Slightly close recording, but there is still plenty of space round the artists and the texture is reasonably transparent.

On Chandos *Elverskud* comes with Gade's very first opus, the delightful *Ossian Overture*. A further bonus is the set of *Five Partsongs*, Op. 13, beautifully sung by the Danish Radio Chamber Choir; the fourth, *Autumn song*, is particularly memorable and haunting. Gade never escapes the embrace of Mendelssohn for long; if his world is urbane, well ordered and free from any hint of tragedy, *Elverskud* again gives unfailing pleasure, particularly in such a persuasive performance and excellent recording.

John Frandsen's performance of the charming *Spring fantasy* first appeared on the Danish Music Anthology label in the 1970s and is now transferred to the EMI catalogue. It is a good performance, fresh, well shaped and decently recorded. Not superior to the newer version under Schønwandt, but still eminently worthwhile at mid-price, and attractively coupled.

Korsfarerne (The Crusaders), Op. 50.
**(*) BIS Dig. CD 465 [id.]. Rorholm, Westi, Cold, Canzone Ch., Da Camera, Kor 72, Music Students' Chamber Ch., Aarhus SO, Frans Rasmussen.

Gade's *Korsfarerne* is in three sections, *In the desert*, *Armida* and *Towards Jerusalem*, and lasts the best part of an hour. The Danish forces assembled here do it proud, as do the BIS recording team, but the debt to Mendelssohn, say in the *Chorus of the Spirits of Darkness* which opens the second section, overwhelms any feeling of originality.

Galbraith, Nancy (born 1951)

Piano concerto No. 1.
(N) *** Ocean Dig. OR101. Ralph Zitterbart, Cincinnati CO, Keith Lockhart – ALONSO-CRESPO: *Overtures and dances from operas.* ***

The first movement of Nancy Galbraith's attractively colourful concerto uses what she calls 'sensuous rhythmic pulses' in the orchestra, minimalist style, from which the piano regularly surfaces in a concertante manner. A high string tremolando leads into the atmospherically lyrical slow movement, and a delicate woodwind dialogue. The piano then achieves an essentially reflective solo role, before the orchestra reasserts its dominance in a driving, energetic toccata-like finale, which has quite haunting lyrical interludes. It is the longest and most individual part of the work. This is writing that communicates directly to the listener. The performance here is persuasively full of life and colour and the recording excellent.

Galuppi, Baldassare (1706–1785)

Motets: (i) *Arripe alpestri ad vallem;* (ii) *Confitebor tibi, Domine.*
❁ *** Virgin/EMI (SIS) Dig. VC5 45030-2. (i) Gérard Lesne, (ii) with Véronique Gens, Peter Harvey; Il Seminario Musicale.

These two very beautiful motets show Galuppi at his most inspired, and they are performed superbly by Gérard Lesne, who is joined by Véronique Gens and Peter Harvey in *Confitebor tibi* (praising God for His munificence) which brings a skill in its overlapping part-writing worthy of Mozart. The accompaniments from Il Seminario Musicale are refreshingly sensitive, alive and polished, while the recording has a natural presence.

Gardiner, Henry Balfour (1877–1950)

Humoresque; The joyful homecoming; Michaelchurch; Noel; 5 Pieces; Prelude; Salamanca; Shenandoah and other pieces (suite).
*** Continuum CCD 1049 [id.]. Peter Jacobs.

Balfour Gardiner was a musical contemporary of Cyril Scott, Roger Quilter and Percy Grainger. Like his musical friends he was at his finest in miniatures, and his writing has an attractive simplicity and innocence. Most of this music is slight, but its appeal is undeniable when it is presented with such authority and sympathy. It is very well recorded indeed. The source is analogue, but there is no background worth mentioning and the piano image is absolutely real, with a natural presence.

Gaubert, Philippe (1879–1941)

Music for flute and piano: *Sonatas Nos. 1–3; Sonatine. Ballade; Berceuse; 2 Esquisses; Fantaisie; Nocturne et allegro scherzando; Romance; Sicilienne; Suite; Sur l'eau.*
*** Chandos Dig. CHAN 8981/2 [id.]. Susan Milan, Ian Brown.

Gaubert had a genuine lyrical gift and his music has an elegance and allure that will captivate. He is eminently well served by Susan Milan and Ian Brown, and they are all well balanced by the Chandos engineers. Truthful sound; civilized and refreshing music, not to be taken all at one draught but full of delight. Edward Blakeman's notes are particularly informative and interesting and there are two charming illustrations.

Gay, John (1685–1732)

The Beggar's opera (arr. Pepusch and Austin).
❁ (BB) *** CfP Silver Double CDCFPSD 4778 (2). Morison, Cameron, M. Sinclair, Wallace, Brannigan, Pro Arte Ch. & O, Sargent.

The Beggar's Opera was the eighteenth-century equivalent of the modern American musical. It was first produced in 1728 and caused a sensation with audiences used to the stylized Italian opera favoured by Handel. This performance under Sargent is in every way first class and the soloists here could hardly be bettered, with Elsie Morison as Polly and Owen Brannigan a splendid Peachum. The linking dialogue is spoken by actors to make the result most dramatic, with every word crystal clear. The chorus is no less effective, and the recording has a most appealing ambience. Its sense of presence and atmosphere is remarkable, yet it was made at Abbey Road – astonishingly – as long ago as 1955.

Geminiani, Francesco (1687–1762)

Concerti grossi, Op. 2/1–6; Op. 3/1–4.
(BB) *** Naxos Dig. 8.553019 [id.]. Capella Istropolitana, Jaroslav Krĕcek.

This is part of an ongoing Naxos project to record all Geminiani's concerti grossi using modern instruments but in a style which clearly reflects the freshness and vitality of period-instrument practice. The Capella Istropolitana offer excellent accounts of the whole of Op. 2 and the first four concertos of Op. 3 (with the remainder to follow). Not perhaps quite as characterful as Tafelmusik's version of Op. 2 (Sony SK 48043) but invigoratingly enjoyable and very well recorded.

Concerti grossi, Op. 2/1–6; Concerti grossi after Corelli, Op. 5/3 & 5.
*** Sony Dig. SK 48043 [id.]. Tafelmusik, Jeanne Lamon.

Although these works are essentially concerti grossi, the frequent dominance of the solo violin in the concertino points the way to the solo concertos of Vivaldi. Jeanne Lamon takes this solo role and directs the performances with plenty of vitality, and the recording produces clean, full, yet transparent textures. The recording is bright and immediately balanced within the warm acoustic of Notre Dame Convent in Waterdown, Ontario, Canada.

Concerti grossi, Op. 2/5–6; Op. 3/3; Op. 7/2; in G min. (after Corelli, *Op. 5/5*); *in D min.* (after Corelli, *Op. 5/12*); *Theme & variations (La Folia).*
(M) *** RCA Dig. GD 77010 [77010-2-RG]. La Petite Bande, Sigiswald Kuijken.

The quality of invention in the Geminiani concertos consistently rises high above the routine. There is considerable expressive depth in some of the slow movements too. La Petite Bande is incomparably superior to many of the period-instrument ensembles. Those who are normally allergic to the vinegary offerings of some rivals will find this record a joy. It is beautifully recorded too, and makes an admirable and economical introduction to this underrated and genial composer.

12 Concerti grossi, Op. 5 (after Corelli).
(B) *** Ph. Duo 438 766-2 (2) [id.]. Michelucci, Gallozzi, Bennici, Centurione, I Musici.

The music on which Geminiani based his Op. 5 is drawn from the splendid *Sonatas for violin and continuo* of Corelli with the same opus number. Their skilful adaptation to concerto grosso form features a viola in the solo group as well as violins and cello. The performances by I Musici – at their very finest – are admirable in all respects, spirited and responsive, polished yet never bland. The recording is first class too, wide-ranging, full and clearly detailed. Highly recommended: if you enjoy Handel's Op. 6, this inexpensive reissue is not to be missed.

Concerti grossi, Op. 7/1–6.
(N) *** ASV Dig. CDDCA 724 [id.]. ASMF, Iona Brown.

The striking textural richness of Geminiani's Op. 7 is achieved by the composer's inclusion of *two* violas, one in the concertino and one in the ripieno, and to increase the colour range he adds a pair of flutes in Nos. 3, 4, and 5 and a solo bassoon in No.6 (which comes first on this CD). The music itself is equally rich, imaginative and vital and nobly expressive, aligning these works with the achievement of Handel and Corelli. There is a sense of scale and breadth too in these splendid ASMF performances under Iona Brown who gave us a superb set of Handel's Op. 6. The leonine string sound has body and transparency, and the concertino is well focused and naturally separated from the main group. A splendid disc.

Concerti grossi: in D min. (*La Folia,* from CORELLI: *Sonata in D min., Op. 5/12*); *in G min., Op. 7/2; Trio sonatas Nos. 3 in F* (from *Op. 1/9*); *5 in A min.* (from *Op. 1/11*); *6 in D min.* (from *Op. 1/12*); *Violin sonatas: in E min., Op. 1/3; in A, Op. 4/12.*
*** Hyperion Dig. CDA 66264 [id.]. Purcell Band & Qt.

This record comes from Hyperion's '*La Folia*' series, though the only piece here using that celebrated theme is the arrangement Geminiani made of Corelli's *D minor Sonata*. Apart from the *G minor Concerto*, Op. 7, No. 2, the remainder of the disc is given over to chamber works. The Purcell Quartet play with dedication and spirit and convey their own enthusiasm for this admirably inventive music to the listener.

Gerhard, Roberto (1896–1970)

(i) *Harpsichord concerto. Symphony (Homenaje a Pedrell).*
(N) *** Chandos Dig. CHAN 9693 [id.]. (i) Geoffrey Tozer; BBC SO, Bamert.

Gerhard's unnumbered *Symphony* of 1941, written in homage to his teacher, Felipe Pedrell, is a far more approachable, less radical piece than his later works. Based on themes from an opera by Pedrell, it is openly tonal, with a Dvořák-like first movement, a warmly elegiac central slow movement and a jolly finale, with Spanish flavours increasingly emerging. The *Harpsichord concerto*, written for Thurston Dart, is altogether grittier, revealing Gerhard's increasing confidence in handling serial argument. Excellent performances and full-ranging sound.

Concerto for orchestra; Symphony No. 2 (original version).
(N) *** Chandos Dig. CHAN 9694 [id.]. BBC SO, Bamert.

Gerhard's *Concerto for orchestra*, the best known of the orchestral works he wrote in his Indian-summer period in the 1960s, provides an excellent introduction to this fascinating composer. In its colour and energy, it reflects a mood of controlled wildness, with the composer's exuberant enjoyment of exotic sound exploited to the full. It receives a warm, incisive performance from Bamert and the BBC Orchestra, who are comparably persuasive in the grittier arguments of the *Second Symphony*. This is the first recording which, ignoring his incomplete revision (edited and performed under the title *Metamorphosis*) goes back to his original score of 1959. It is a powerful work, in two long movements, each subdivided in two, with the pent-up energy of the first giving way to the stillness and concentration of the second. Oustanding rich and full recording.

(i) *Piano concerto. Epithalamion; Symphony No. 3 (Collages).*
(N) *** Chandos Dig. CHAN 9556 [id.]. BBCSO, Matthias Bamert with (i) Geoffrey Tozer.

The key work here is the *Third Symphony* of 1960, which brings out Gerhard's fascination with electronic sounds, set in contrast with a large orchestra, hence the subtitle, *Collages*. The visual inspiration here was seeing a sunrise from a high-flying aircraft, with the physical element vital in Gerhard's ever-inventive, thornily complex writing. That is vividly captured in Bamert's powerful performance, which easily outshines those on earlier recordings. The *Piano concerto* of 1951 is complex too in its thought, but readily approachable, and the *Epithalamion*, written for the wedding of friends, using a very large orchestra, represents the composer at his wildest. Full, rich sound.

(i) *Violin concerto. Symphony No. 1.*
(N) *** Chandos Dig. CHAN 9588 [id.]. BBC SO, Matthias Bamert (i) with Olivier Charlier.

It was the belated first performance in 1955 of the *Symphony No. 1* that sparked off the surge of creativity which marked Gerhard's last years. The work's athematicism makes it initially less approachable than the coupled *Violin concerto*, but it is a brilliant and rewarding piece. Though written a decade earlier than the concerto, it sets the pattern for Gerhard's sharply disciplined writing, the exuberant expression of joy in complex and original sound. It is a work which richly repays repeated listening, and here under Bamert receives a powerful performance. The *Violin concerto* is more immediately inviting, a neo-Romantic and haunting score with a strong sense of atmosphere: its slow movement has a sultry langour that recalls the Mediterranean. Some commentators have compared it with Szymanowksi. It is also a bravura work and the piece includes Spanish references, very like those in the opera *The Duenna*, written soon afterwards. Olivier Charlier is a brilliant advocate, not least in the dazzling finale. Rich, full-bodied sound. A fascinating and highly recommendable issue.

Concert for 8; Gemini; Leo; Libra. (i) *Three Impromptus.*
(N) *** Largo Dig. LARGO 5134 [id.]. Nieuw Ens., Spanjaard. (i) John Snijders.

'I have a certain weakness for astrology in general and for horoscopes in particular' wrote Gerhard in 1968, having just completed the third of his three astrological pieces for chamber ensemble. It is specially valuable to have all three on a single disc. With contrasted instrumental groups in each, this is Gerhard at his most personal: taut and abrasive, thornily inventive. The strongest and boldest of the three, as well as the longest, is *Leo*, his last completed work, a celebration of the star sign of his wife, Poldi. That association makes the close, written in the face of serious illness, specially poignant. The *Concerto for 8* – with an accordion among the instruments – is an apt extra, as are the three little piano *Impromptus*, written in 1950 as a wedding present for Lord and Lady Harewood. Clean-cut performances and recording.

The Duenna (opera; complete).
*** Chandos Dig. CHAN 9520 (2) [id.]. Van Allan, Clark, Glanville, Powell, Archer, Taylor, Roberts, Wade, Opera North Ch., E. N. Philh. O, Antoni Ros Marbá.

Sheridan's play, *The Duenna*, was originally presented with music by Thomas Linley. But Gerhard resolved to turn it into an opera, being attracted not just by the wit of the dialogue but by its setting in Seville. The work which resulted was the culmination of a period during the 1940s when the Spanish influence was strongest in his music and here the characteristic hints of atonality simply add extra spice to the Spanish flavours, with sensuously colourful instrumentation and lively dance rhythms to produce a superbly crafted, consistently inspired work, even if there is rather too much reliance on speech over music to fill gaps in the story. This recording was made in connection with the 1996 revival of the 1992 Opera North production, and the teamwork – so important in a lively and fast-moving comedy like this – is what matters, with generally fresh, young voices well contrasted and defined. As the heroine, Donna Luisa, Susannah Glanville sings charmingly, rising to the challenge of her big monologue in Act II, one of the most tenderly lyrical passages in the whole opera, where Gerhard touches deeper emotions than one expects in an eighteenth-century comedy. Richard Van Allan makes an aptly gruff and characterful Don Jerome, the heavy father, and Neill Archer is an ardent hero. In the title-role of the Duenna, Claire Powell is firm and fruity, delightful in her duet with Don Isaac, the rich Jew who is tricked into marrying her. The recording, made in the Royal Concert Hall, Nottingham, is vivid and immediate, with fine presence, letting words be heard with commendable clarity even over the richest orchestral background.

German, Edward (1862–1936)

The Conqueror: Berceuse. Gipsy suite. Henry VII: 3 Dances. Nell Gwyn: Overture & 3 Dances. Romeo and Juliet (incidental music): *Pavane; Nocturne; Pastorale. Merrie England: 4 Dances. Tom Jones: Waltz song.*
**(*) Marco Polo Dig. 8.223419 [id.]. Slovak RSO (Bratislava), Leaper.

The Edward German collection in Marco Polo's enterprising series of English light music is just a little disappointing. The Slovak Radio Orchestra play with their usual verve and Adrian Leaper is ever sympathetic. But in the series of pieces offered here, the 'Hey nonny nonny' English country-dance style becomes rhythmically rather repetitive. It is a pity that the *Merrie England* excerpts could not have included vocalists – the *Minuet* delivers up the glorious 'With sword and buckler by my side' which cries out for a voice, as does *Sophia's waltz song* from *Tom Jones*. The most rewarding numbers are the *Berceuse* from *The Conquerer* and the three pieces written for the Forbes-Robertson production of *Romeo and Juliet* at the London Lyceum in 1895. All are charming and very nicely scored. Excellent recording.

Welsh rhapsody.
(B) *** CfP CD-CFP 4635. RSNO, Gibson – HARTY: *With the wild geese;* MACCUNN: *Land of mountain and flood;* SMYTH: *Wreckers overture.* ***

Edward German is content not to interfere with the traditional melodies he uses in his rhapsody, relying on his orchestral skill to retain the listener's interest, and in this he is very successful. The closing pages, based on *Men of Harlech*, are prepared in a Tchaikovskian manner to provide a rousing conclusion. The CD transfer is very well managed, though the ear perceives a slight limitation in the upper range.

Merrie England (complete; without dialogue).
(BB) (**) CfP Silver Double CDCFPSD 4796 (2). McAlpine, Bronhill, Glossop, M. Sinclair, Kern, Williams Singers, O, Michael Collins.

Although this recording dates from 1960, it cannot compare in stereo sophistication with EMI's *Beggar's Opera* of five years earlier. While all the present soloists came from Sadler's Wells, the production team was obviously drawn from EMI's popular department; the result, technically speaking, is a near disaster. All the solo voices are close-miked, usually in a most unflattering way, and too often they sound edgy, while the chorus is made artificially bright; the orchestra is lively enough, but the violins are thin. However, it must be said that Michael Collins directs the proceedings in an attractively spirited fashion. But there is much pleasing lyricism in German's music and one or two really outstanding tunes which will ensure that the score survives. Among the soloists Howell Glynne is splendid as King Neptune, and Monica Sinclair sings with her usual richness and makes *O peaceful England* more moving than usual. Patricia Kern's mezzo is firm and forward, while McAlpine as Sir Walter Raleigh sings with fine, ringing voice. The Rita Williams Singers are thoroughly professional even if just occasionally their style is suspect. However, another recording seems unlikely so this is acceptable, *faute de mieux*.

Gershwin, George (1898–1937)

An American in Paris.
(*) Everest EVC 9003 [id.]. Pittsburgh SO, Steinberg – COPLAND: *Appalachian spring*; GOULD: *Spirituals*. *

The recorded sound is rather dry and unexpansive, but otherwise vivid. Steinberg's performance is lively, idiomatic and convincing. The central blues tune is pleasingly sultry. Incidentally, the sleeve-note points out that the Parisian taxi horns that Gershwin took home with him to use in the orchestra and which Steinberg adopts now date the piece irretrievably, as horn-tooting is now forbidden in Paris by law.

An American in Paris; Catfish Row (suite from *Porgy and Bess*); *Cuban overture; Lullaby.*
(B) *** [EMI Red Line CDR5 72554]. St Louis SO, Slatkin.

Slatkin is clearly at home in *Catfish Row*, and he relishes the sophistication of Gershwin's own suite from *Porgy and Bess*, while still bringing out the special effects (bell and wind simulator in *Hurricane*). In the brash *Cuban overture* some of the gutsy feeling of the piece is lost; while for *American in Paris*, although he often disguises the seams, he could at times be more extrovert. It is partly the gloriously ample acoustics of the Lovell Hall, St Louis, that makes everything seem opulent, and certainly on sonic grounds no American collector should be disappointed with this concert, especially the *Lullaby* (which derives from *Blue Monday*) in which the St Louis strings sound richly seductive. This CD is only available in the USA.

(i) *An American in Paris; Cuban overture*; (ii) *Funny Face: overture* (orch. Don Rose); *Girl Crazy: suite* (orch. Leroy Anderson); *Oh, Kay!: overture* (orch. Rose); (i; iii) *Rhapsody in blue*; (iv) *Porgy and Bess: suite* (arr. Roland Shaw).
(N) (M) *** Penguin Classics 460 612-2 [id.]. Cleveland O, Maazel; (ii) Boston Pops O, Fiedler; (iii) with Ivan Davis; (iv) Frank Chacksfield and his Orchestra.

Maazel's Penguin Classics triptych of three key Gershwin orchestral works dates from 1974. The performances are all strikingly energetic. Ivan Davis is both a brilliant and sophisticated soloist in the *Rhapsody*; the boisterous account of *Cuban overture* is immensely spirited, and *An American in Paris* is given an upbeat reading, well held together. There are more sumptuous versions (the great blues tune in the latter piece could be more sensuous) but with superb Cleveland playing, these performances are easy to enjoy. The original CD has been nicely expanded with characteristically lively Boston Pops performances of the series of marvellous show tunes which make up the theatre overtures, and Leroy Anderson's similarly brief pot-pourri from *Girl Crazy*. Frank Chacksfield's account of Roland Shaw's brilliantly scored selection from *Porgy and Bess* lacks nothing in panache, and the luscious Decca sound here is outstanding of its kind. An exhilarating compilation. The author's note is by Humphrey Carpenter.

(i) *An American in Paris;* (ii) *Cuban overture;* (ii–iii) *'I got rhythm' variations;* (i; iii) *Rhapsody in blue;* (ii–iii) *Second Rhapsody; Porgy and Bess:* medley.
(M) *** EMI/Angel CDM5 66086-2 [id.]. Hollywood Bowl SO; (i) Felix Slatkin; (ii) Alfred Newman; with (iii) Leonard Pennario.

This reissued programme, taken from two Capitol LPs of the early stereo era, is among the most attractive and idiomatically authentic collection of Gershwin's shorter orchestral and concertante works in the catalogue. Of course Bernstein's CBS/ Sony *Rhapsody in blue* is special, but Pennario's version has hardly less rhythmic verve, and his irresistible performance of the *Second Rhapsody* has a pulsing vitality, well supported by the exuberant orchestral accompaniment. Alfred Newman directs this, the dazzling *'I got rhythm' variations* and a sparkling account of the *Cuban overture*, played with comparable Latin zest. His concertante selection from *Porgy and Bess* is equally brilliant and seductive. The young Felix Slatkin directs *An American in Paris* with audacious flair, not missing out the taxi horns, and the performance is made the more memorable by the panache of the violins in this remarkable orchestra of virtuosi. With close microphones, the stereo effect is both spacious and brash, and the bright sound-picture, like the somewhat shallow piano-timbre, adds to the character of the occasion – a wonderful memento of Hollywood top musicians playing music they know so well with enormous spirit and enthusiastic relish.

(i) *An American in Paris;* (ii) *Piano concerto in F;* (iii) *Rhapsody in blue.*
(N) (M) *** EMI Dig. CDM5 66891-2 [CDM5 66943]. André Previn with LSO.
(BB) *** Carlton LSO Double Dig. 30368 01257 (2) [(B) id.]. (ii–iii) Gwenneth Pryor; LSO, Richard Williams – Concert: LSO, Roderick Dunk: *'That's entertainment'*. **(*)
(M) *** Ph. (IMS) 442 395-2. (ii–iii) Werner Haas; Monte Carlo Op. O, De Waart.

An American in Paris; (i) *Piano concerto in F; Rhapsody in blue; Variations on 'I got rhythm'.*
(M) *** RCA 09026 68792-2 [id.]. (i) Earl Wild; Boston Pops O, Arthur Fiedler.

The digital remastering of Previn's EMI set, made at the beginning of the 1970s, has brought a striking enhancement of the recording itself. There is now much more sparkle, and the extra vividness comes without loss of body; indeed, in the *Concerto* the strings sound particularly full and fresh and the piano timbre clean and natural. The performance of the *Concerto* was always a fine one by any standards, but now in the *Rhapsody* one senses many affinities with the famous Bernstein account. *An American in Paris* is exuberantly volatile, and the entry of the great blues tune on the trumpet has a memorable rhythmic lift. This now returns to the catalogue at mid-price in EMI's 'Great recordings of the century series'.

From the opening glissando swirl on the clarinet, the performance of the *Rhapsody in blue* by Gwenneth Pryor and the LSO under Richard Williams tingles with adrenalin, and the other performances are comparable. The *Rhapsody* has splendid rhythmic energy, yet the performers can relax to allow the big expressive blossoming at the centre really to expand. Similarly in the *Concerto*, the combination of vitality and flair and an almost voluptuous response to the lyrical melodies is very involving. *An American in Paris*, briskly paced, moves forward in an exhilarating sweep, with the big blues tune vibrant and the closing section managed to perfection. The performances are helped by superb recording, made in the EMI No. 1 Studio. This was an outstanding disc in its own right, but as a Double it is joined to a series of selections of Show music which are much less repeatable than the Gershwin works.

The reissued CD on RCA's mid-price Living Stereo label is particularly generous (70 minutes) in including, besides the usual triptych, the *'I got rhythm' variations*, given plenty of rhythmic panache. Indeed these are essentially jazzy performances: Earl Wild's playing is full of energy and brio, and he inspires Arthur Fiedler to a similarly infectious response. The outer movements of the *Concerto* are comparably volatile and the blues feeling of the slow movement is strong. At the end of *An American in Paris* Fiedler (like Steinberg and slatkin) adds to the exuberance by bringing in a bevy of motor horns. The brightly remastered recording suits the music-making. This is also available in the USA as one of RCA's 'Basic 100' series (09026 61724-2) but, according to Schwann, this disc does not include the *Variations*.

In Monte Carlo the lyrical moments of the *Concerto* have a quality of nostalgia which is very attractive. Werner Haas is a volatile and sympathetic soloist, and his rhythmic verve is refreshing. Edo de Waart's *An American in Paris* is not only buoyant but glamorous too – the big blues melody is highly seductive and, as with all the best accounts of this piece, the episodic nature of the writing is hidden. There is a cultured, European flavour to this music-making that does not detract from its vitality, and the jazz inflexions are not missed, with plenty of verve in the *Rhapsody*. Very good sound.

An American in Paris; (i) *Rhapsody in blue.*
✿ (M) *** Sony SMK 63086 [id.]. NYPO, Bernstein, (i) Bernstein (piano) – GROFE: *Grand Canyon suite.* ***

Bernstein's 1958–9 CBS (now Sony) coupling was recorded when (at the beginning of his forties) he was at the peak of his creativity, with *West Side Story* only two years behind him. This record set the standard by which all subsequent pairings of *An American in Paris* and *Rhapsody in blue* came to be judged. It still sounds astonishingly well as a recording, and the current remastering for the Bernstein Century Edition has restored all the bloom of the original. Bernstein's approach is inspirational, exceptionally flexible but completely spontaneous. The performance of *An American in Paris* is vividly characterized, brash and episodic; an unashamedly American view, with the great blues tune marvellously timed and phrased as only a great American orchestra can do it.

An American in Paris (revised F. Cambell-Watson); (i) *Rhapsody in blue; Girl Crazy*: excerpts (arr. Leroy Anderson); *Porgy and Bess* (suite, arr. R. R. Bennett & A. Courage).
*** Ph. Dig. 426 404-2 [id.]. (i) Misha Dichter; Boston Pops O, John Williams.

John Williams is just the man for a programme like this. His touch is light and *An American in Paris* is relaxed in a most appealing way. So is the *Rhapsody in blue*, yet Misha Dichter provides plenty of bravura. The selections from *Girl Crazy* (with its two big hits, *Embraceable you*, and *I got rhythm*) is infectious, and each of the eight numbers from *Porgy and Bess* is given its full individual character, rather than being streamlined into an ongoing pot-pourri. The Boston sound is first class.

Broadway and film music: *A Damsel in distress:* suite, arr. McGlinn. *Stiff upper lip: Funhouse sequence*. Overtures: *Girl Crazy; Of thee I sing; Oh, Kay!; Primrose; Tip-Toes*.
(B) **(*) EMI forte Dig. CZS5 68589-2 (2) [CDFB 68589]. New Princess Theatre O, McGlinn – KERN: *Overtures* **; PORTER: *Overtures and film music*. ***

This inexpensive two-disc forte set makes a pretty good collection for those who enjoy authentic re-creations of Broadway music composed by three of its greatest names. John McGlinn has recorded his selections using the original scores. The extended dance-sequence, *Stiff upper lip*, comes from a 1937 movie and has some good tunes. So has *Oh Kay!* (half a dozen) while *Girl Crazy* offers the irresistible *I got rhythm*. Elsewhere the famous melodies are more thinly spread, but the marvellous playing of the New York pick-up orchestra (gorgeous saxes and brass) has splendid pep. The lively, close-miked sound gives an authentic theatre-pit brashness, with very bright violins, although the backgound ambience is warm enough.

Catfish Row (suite from *Porgy and Bess*).
*** Telarc Dig. CD 80086 [id.]. Tritt, Cincinnati Pops O, Kunzel – GROFE: *Grand Canyon suite*. ***

Catfish Row was arranged by the composer after the initial failure of his opera. It includes a brief piano solo, played with fine style by William Tritt in the highly sympathetic Telarc performance which is very well recorded.

Piano concerto in F; Rhapsody in blue; Second Rhapsody for piano and orchestra; Variations on 'I got rhythm'.
❁ (M) *** Classic fM Dig. 76505 57012-2 [id.]. Michael Boriskin, Eos O, Jonathan Sheffer.

This is the most seductive pairing of the *Rhapsody in blue* and the *Concerto in F* to have come our way for a long time. The performances have a superb sense of style, and are for the 1990s what Bernstein's famous versions were for the 1950s and '60s. Michael Boriskin is a native New Yorker, and he and Jonathan Sheffer immediately establish a partnership which brings an idiomatic and freshly individual approach to these two concertante masterpieces, which uniquely span the jazz world and the ethos of the concert hall. The keenly sophisticated and inventive *'I got rhythm' variations* are no less glittering and are wonderfully infectious. The Eos Orchestra is a group of first-class freelance musicians from the New York area: the individuality of their response is immediately set by Todd Levy's naughtily provocative clarinet glissando at the opening of the *Rhapsody*. The orchestral detail throughout is a joy (especially illuminating in the less inspired *Second rhapsody*), while in the concerto the big climaxes open out to engulf the listener expansively and ardently. Boriskin's brilliant pianism is wittily skittish in the most infectious way, both in the *Rhapsody* and in the delectably played central section of the concerto's slow movement, which Neil Balm has opened so languorously with his trumpet. The finale brings dazzling yet totally unforced bravura from ever nimble fingers, matched by sparkling orchestral rhythms. The recording is first rate. This is not to be missed.

3 Preludes (transcribed Heifetz for violin & piano).
(N) *** DG Dig. 453 470-2. Gil Shaham, André Previn – BARBER: *Canzone for violin and piano*; COPLAND *Violin sonata; Nocturne;* PREVIN: *Violin sonata*. ***

Heifetz's evocative transcriptions of the three little Gershwin *Preludes*, brilliantly done, make a pointful addition to Shaham and Previn's fine recital, '*The American connection*'.

Rhapsody in blue (see also above, under *An American in Paris*).
(M) **(*) DG Dig. 439 528-2 [431 048-2]. Bernstein with LAPO – BARBER: *Adagio for strings;* COPLAND: *Appalachian spring*. ***
(M) **(*) Decca Dig. 430 726-2. Katia & Marielle Labèque, Cleveland O, Chailly – ADDINSELL: *Warsaw concerto;* GOTTSCHALK: *Grand fantasia;* LISZT: *Hungarian fantasia;* LITOLFF: *Scherzo*. ***

In his last recording of this work for DG, Bernstein rather goes over the top with his jazzing of the solos in Gershwin. Such rhythmic freedom was clearly the result of a live rather than a studio performance. This does not match Bernstein's inspired 1959 analogue coupling for CBS.

There seems no special reason for preferring the two-piano version of the *Rhapsody in blue*, and although the Labèque duo play charismatically their account is made somewhat controversial by the addition of an improvisatory element (more decorative than structural). However, the playing does not lack sparkle and the recording is first class.

Song arrangements for orchestra: *Bidin' my time; But not for me; Embraceable you; Fascinating rhythm; I got rhythm; Liza; Love is sweeping the country; Love walked in; The man I love; Oh, Lady be good; Someone to watch over me; 'S wonderful* (all arr. Ray Wright).
(M) **(*) Mercury (IMS) 434 327-2 [id.]. O, Frederick Fennell – PORTER: *Song arrangements.* **(*)

This is reputed to be Fennell's favourite record, and he directs every one of these famous tunes with affectionate style and a sparkling rhythmic lift. Unusually for this label, the smooth (1961) Mercury sound is multi-miked, yet it has plenty of ambience as well as both a silky lustre and a natural clarity. The orchestral playing is fully worthy of the sophistication of the scoring, and Gershwin's songs with their ripe tunefulness respond more easily than Cole Porter's to presentation without the lyrics.

'*The Piano rolls*' Vol. 1: (i) *An American in Paris*; (ii) *Idle dreams; Kicking the clouds away; Novelette in fourths; On my mind the whole night long; Rhapsody in blue; Scandal walk; So am I; Swanee; Sweet and lowdown; That certain feeling; When you want 'em you can't get 'em, when you've got 'em you don't want 'em.*
*** Nonesuch Dig. 7559 79287-2 [id.]. (i) Milne and Leith; (ii) composer.

This series, recorded by the composer between 1916 and 1926 using the Welte-Mignon and Duo-Art piano-roll systems, was reproduced through a 1911 pianola (operated by Artis Wodehouse) on a Yamaha Disklavier player-piano with computer links, and then recorded in digital stereo – with the umost realism. The result is as if Gershwin himself was playing in the studio. The four-handed arrangement of *An American in Paris*, attributed to Milne and Leith, dates from 1933. It seems, however, that Leith was one of Frank Milne's pseudonyms and that he was responsible for both parts. It is a marvellous 'orchestral' performance and matches the composer in its flamboyance and breadth of style. *Rhapsody in blue* is the composer's special arrangement which Michael Tilson Thomas used later for his recording with full orchestra by editing out Gershwin's transcription of the orchestral parts. But it sounds pretty good here, with the composer filling in. The sound is first class and admirably present.

'*The Piano rolls*' Vol. 2: FREY: *Havanola.* CONRAD/ROBINSON: *Singin' the blues.* GERSHWIN: *From now on.* AKST: *Jaz-o-mine.* SILVERS: *Just snap your fingers at care.* KERN: *Whip-poor-will.* GERSHWIN/DONALDSON: *Rialto ripples.* PINKARD: *Waitin' for me.* WENDLING/WILLS: *Buzzin' the bee.* C. SCHONBERG: *Darling.* BERLIN: *For your country and my country.* MORRIS: *Kangaroo hop.* MATTHEWS: *Pastime rag No. 3.* GARDNER: *Chinese blues.* SCHONBERGER: *Whispering.* GRANT: *Arrah go on I'm gonna go back to Oregon.*
** Nonesuch Dig. 7559 79370-2 [id.]. George Gershwin.

As can be seen, Volume II includes music by others, and few of these numbers even approach the quality of Gershwin's own output. But it is all played in good, lively style, although one senses that Gershwin was doing a professional job rather than acting as an enthusiastic advocate, and some pieces come off more appealingly than others. Frankly, much of this is cocktail bar music, although Chris Schonberg's *Darling* is a rather effective exception. Again the recording cannot be faulted.

'*The authentic George Gershwin*' (Piano arrangements of songs)

Volume 1 (1918–25): *Come to the moon; Drifting along with the tide; Fascinatin' rhythm; The half of it, Dearie, blues; Hang on to me; I'd rather Charleston; I was so young; Kicking the clouds away; Limehouse nights; The man I love; Nobody but you; Oh Lady be good; So am I; Swanee; Tee-Oodle-Um-Bum-Bo. Piano concerto in F: slow movt. Rhapsody in blue.*
(M) **(*) ASV Dig. CDWHL 2074 [id.]. Jack Gibbons.

Volume 2 (1925–30): *Clap yo' hands; Do, do, do; Embraceable you; He loves and she loves; I got rhythm* (2 versions); *Liza; Looking for a boy; Maybe; Meadow serenade; My one and only; Someone to watch over me; Sweet and low-down* (2 versions); *'S Wonderful; Funny face; That certain feeling; When do we dance? An American in Paris (overture); Strike up the band (overture); Irish waltz (Three-quarter blues); 3 Piano preludes.*
(M) **(*) ASV Dig. CDWHL 2077 [id.]. Jack Gibbons.

Volume 3 (1931–37): *For you, for me, for evermore; Isn't it a pity; Jilted; Let's call the whole thing off; Our love is here to stay; They can't take that away from me. Cuban overture; Second rhapsody; Porgy and Bess: suite. Good morning, Brother: excerpts. Variations on 'I got rhythm'.*
(M) **(*) ASV Dig. CDWHL 2082 [id.]. Jack Gibbons.

Volumes 1–3 (complete).
(M) **(*) ASV Dig. CDWLS 328 (3) [id.].

Jack Gibbons has transcribed Gershwin's own piano transcriptions from the records and piano rolls made by the composer himself, and in certain cases from recorded radio programmes and film sound-tracks. His playing is brightly idiomatic, fresh and spontaneous, and has received much praise for its closeness to the composer's own keyboard style. The modern digital recording adds to the appeal of this set. But the arrangements of the orchestral works and the solo piano versions of the *Rhapsody in blue*, the *Second Rhapsody* and the '*I got rhythm*' *variations* (drawn from the composer's four-handed versions) often sound rather prolix and are much less effective and enjoyable than the songs, although played with the same sense of style. There are also more impressive versions on disc of the three *Piano preludes*.

Piano arrangements of songs: *Bidin' my time; But not for me; Clap yo' hands; Do, do, do; Embraceable you; Fascinating rhythm; A foggy day; Funny face; He loves and she loves; How long has this been going on; I got rhythm; I'll build a stairway to paradise; I've got a crush on you; Let's call the whole thing off; Liza; Love is here to stay; Love is sweeping the country; Love walked in; The man I love; Maybe; Mine; Of thee I sing; Oh, Lady be good; Somebody loves me; Someone to watch over me; Soon; Strike up the band; Swanee!; 'S Wonderful; That certain feeling; They can't take that away from me; Who cares;* Excerpts from: *An American in Paris;* Themes from *Concerto in F; Piano prelude No. 2; Rhapsody in blue*: excerpts.
(M) *** Van. 08.6002.71 [OVC 6002]. George Feyer (with Tommy Lucas, George Mell, Sy Salzberg, Edward Caccavate).

The American Hungarian émigré pianist, George Feyer, is unsurpassed in this repertory, playing all these tunes with a rhythmic lift and naturally lilting inflexions that make one almost forget that most of them also had lyrics! The rhythmic backing is first class and the 1974 recording very real. Offering some 64 minutes of marvellous melody, this CD is in a class of its own. An ideal disc to titillate the ear and senses on a late summer evening.

VOCAL MUSIC

'Kiri sings Gershwin': Boy wanted; But not for me; By Strauss; Embraceable you; I got rhythm; Love is here to stay; Love walked in; Meadow serenade; The man I love; Nice work if you can get it; Somebody loves me; Someone to watch over me; Soon; Things are looking up. Porgy and Bess: Summertime.
**(*) EMI Dig. CDC7 47454-2 [id.]. Kiri Te Kanawa, New Theatre O, McGlinn (with Chorus).

In Dame Kiri's gorgeously sung *Summertime* from *Porgy and Bess*, the distanced heavenly chorus creates the purest kitsch. But most of the numbers are done in an upbeat style. Dame Kiri is at her most relaxed and ideally there should be more variety of pacing: *The man I love* is thrown away at the chosen tempo. But for the most part the ear is seduced; however, the pop microphone techniques bring excessive sibilants on CD.

OPERA AND MUSICALS

Girl Crazy (musical).
*** Elektra-Nonesuch/Warner Dig. 7559 79250-2. Judy Blazer, Lorna Luft, David Carroll, Eddie Korbich, O, John Mauceri.

Girl Crazy with its hit numbers (*Embraceable you, I got rhythm* and *Bidin' my time*) is an escapist piece, typical of the early 1930s. Judy Blazer takes the Ginger Rogers role of Kate, the post-girl, while Judy Garland's less well-known daughter, Lorna Luft, is delightful in the Ethel Merman part of the gambler's wife hired to sing in the saloon. David Carroll is the New Yorker hero, and Frank Gorshin takes the comic role of the cab-driver, Gieber Goldfarb. The whole score, 73 minutes long, is squeezed on to a single disc. The only serious reservation is that the recording is dry and brassy, aggressively so – but that could be counted typical of the period too.

Lady Be Good (musical).
*** Elektra Nonesuch/Warner Dig. 7559 79308-2 [id.]. Teeter, Morrison, Alexander, Pizzarelli, Blier, Musto, Ch. & O, Stern.

This charming score, dating from 1924 (just after *Rhapsody in blue*), emerges as one of the composer's freshest. Such numbers as the title-song, as well as *Fascinatin' rhythm* and the witty *Half of it, dearie, blues*, are set against such duets as *Hang on to me* and *So am I*, directly reflecting the 1920s world that Sandy Wilson parodied so affectionately in *The Boy Friend*. *Lady Be Good* was the piece originally written for the brother-and-sister team of Fred and Adele Astaire, and the casting of the principals on the disc is first rate. These are not concert-singers but ones whose clearly projected voices are ideally suited to the repertory, including Lara Teeter and Ann Morrison in the Astaires' roles and Michael Maguire as the young millionaire whom the heroine finally marries. The score has been restored by Tommy Krasker, and an orchestra of first-rate sessions musicians is conducted by Eric Stern.

Let 'em Eat Cake; Of Thee I Sing (musicals).
*** Sony Dig. M2K 42522 (2) [id.]. Jack Gilford, Larry Kert, Maureen McGovern, Paige O'Hara, David Garrison, NY Choral Artists, St Luke's O, Tilson Thomas.

Of Thee I Sing and *Let 'em Eat Cake* are the two operettas that George Gershwin wrote in the early 1930s on a political theme, the one a sequel to the other. What the British listener will immediately register is the powerful underlying influence of Gilbert and Sullivan, not just in the plot – with Gilbertian situations exploited – but also in the music, with patter-songs and choral descants used in a very Sullivan-like manner. In every way these two very well-filled discs are a delight, offering warm and energetic performances by excellent artists under Michael Tilson Thomas. Both Larry Kert and Maureen McGovern as his wife make a strong partnership. With the recording on the dry side and well forward – very apt for a musical – the words are crystal clear.

Oh Kay!
*** Nonesuch/Warner Dig. 7559 79361-2 [id.]. Dawn Upshaw, Kurt Ollman, Adam Arkin, Patrick Cassidy, Robert Westenberg, Liz Larsen, Ch. & O of St Luke's, Eric Stern.

The last in this splendid Nonesuch series of Gershwin musicals is in many ways the finest of all. With the music (including hits like *Someone to watch over me*, *Clap yo' hands*, *Do, do do* and the very catchy *Fidgety feet*) fitting neatly on to one CD, this is a fizzing entertainment. Dawn Upshaw is a highly enticing Kay, and she gets vivid support from Kurt Ollman as Jimmy, Adam Arkin as Shorty McGee and Patrick Cassidy as Larry. The cast could hardly be more naturally at home in Gershwin's sparkling score. Eric Stern directs with great flair and the recording is admirably vivid. Not to be missed.

Porgy and Bess (complete).
✿ *** EMI Dig. CDS7 49568-2 (3) [Ang. CDCC 49568]. Willard White, Cynthia Haymon, Harolyn Blackwell, Cynthia Clarey, Damon Evans, Glyndebourne Ch., LPO, Rattle.

Simon Rattle here conducts the same cast and orchestra as in the opera house, and the EMI engineers have done wonders in re-creating what was so powerful at Glyndebourne, establishing more clearly than ever the status of *Porgy* as grand opera, not a mere jumped-up musical or operetta. By comparison, Lorin Maazel's Decca version (414 559-2) sounds a degree too literal, and John DeMain's RCA set (RD 82109 [RCD3 2109]) is less subtle. More than their rivals, Rattle and the LPO capture Gershwin's rhythmic exuberance with the degree of freedom essential if jazz-based inspirations are to sound idiomatic. The chorus is the finest and most responsive of any on the three sets, and the bass line-up is the strongest. Willard White is superbly matched by the magnificent Jake of Bruce Hubbard and by the dark and resonant Crown of Gregg Baker. As Sportin' Life, Damon Evans gets nearer than any of his rivals to the original scat-song inspiration without ever short-changing on musical values. Cynthia Haymon as Bess is movingly convincing in conveying equivocal emotions, Harolyn Blackwell as Clara sensuously relishes Rattle's slow speed for *Summertime*, and Cynthia Clarey is an intense and characterful Serena. EMI's digital sound is exceptionally full and spacious.

Porgy and Bess: highlights.
*** EMI Dig. CDC7 54325-2 [id.] (from above recording, with White, Haymon; cond. Rattle).
(BB) ** RCA Navigator 74321 24218-2 [RCA (M) High Performance 09026 633/2-2]. Price, Warfield, Bubbles, Boatwright, Henson, Webb, Burton, Alonzo Jones, Berneice Hall, Stewart, RCA Victor O, Skitch Henderson (with BERNSTEIN: *West Side Story: Symphonic dances*. **)
(N) **(*) Decca Dig. 436 306-2 [id.]. (from complete recording with Willard White, Leona Mitchell, McHenry Boatwright, François Clemmons, Cleveland Ch. & O, Maazel).

Rattle's highlights disc is most generous (74 minutes) and most comprehensive. However, not all the tailoring is clean: *Summertime* ends rather abruptly and there is at least one fade.

The RCA studio compilation was recorded in 1963. Both Price and Warfield sing magnificently, and the supporting group is given lively direction by Skitch Henderson. The rest of the cast comes from the opera house rather than the musical theatre, which underlined the claims of Gershwin's work to be regarded as being in the mainstream of opera, some 25 years before this was confirmed by Rattle's complete recording. (N.B.: In the USA this appears to be still available at mid-price on the new RCA 'High Performance' label.)

Decca offer a generous set of highlights (76 minutes) from their Maazel set from the mid 1970s. As he was to confirm in the later Rattle set for EMI, Willard White proved a magnificent Porgy, while in Cleveland Leona Mitchell's vibrant Bess has a moving streak of vulnerability. François Clemmons as Sportin' Life achieves the near-impossible by singing the role and actually making one forget Cab Calloway. Maazel too brings dazzling playing from the Cleveland Orchestra and the Decca recording is as brilliant as you would expect. But good as it is, why is this selection from a 20-year-old recording offered at full price?

Strike up the Band (musical).
**(*) Nonesuch/Warner Dig. 7559 79273-2; *7559 79273-4* [id.]. Barrett, Luker, Chastain, Graae, Fowler, Goff, Lambert, Lyons, Sandish, Rocco, Ch. & O, Mauceri.

Strike up the Band was the nearest that George and Ira Gershwin ever came to imitating Gilbert and Sullivan although its two hit numbers, *The man I love* and *Strike up the band* are entirely characteristic. For all its vigour, the performance lacks something of the exuberance which marks the recordings of musicals conducted by John McGlinn for EMI. It may be correct to observe the dotted rhythms of *The man I love* as precisely as this performance does, but something is lost in the flow of the music, and to latterday ears the result is less haunting than the customary reading. The singers are first rate, but they would have been helped by having at least one of their number with a more charismatic personality. The second disc includes an appendix containing seven numbers used in the abortive 1930 revival.

Gesualdo, Carlo (*c.* 1561–1613)

Ave, dulcissima Maria; Ave, regina coelorum; Maria mater gratiae; Precibus et meritus beatae Mariae (motets). *Tenebrae responsories for Holy Saturday.*
*** Gimell Dig. Ph. 454 915-2 [id.]. Tallis Scholars, Peter Phillips.

The astonishing dissonances and chromaticisms may not be as extreme here as in some of Gesualdo's secular music but, as elaborate as madrigals, they still have a sharp, refreshing impact on the modern ear which recognizes music leaping the centuries. The Tallis Scholars give superb performances, finely finished and beautifully blended, with women's voices made to sound boyish, singing with freshness and bite to bring home the total originality of the writing with its awkward leaps and intervals. Beautifully recorded, this is another of the Tallis Scholars' ear-catching discs, powerful as well as polished.

Leçons de Ténèbres: Responsories for Maundy Thursday.
(B) *** HM HMA Musique d'Abord 190220 [id.]. Deller Cons., Deller.

The Responses for Holy Week of 1611 are as remarkable and passionately expressive as any of Gesualdo's madrigals, and in depth of feeling they should be compared only with the finest music of the age. The Deller Consort bring to this music much the same approach that distinguishes their handling of the madrigal literature. The colouring of the words is a high priority, yet it never oversteps the bounds of good taste. The consort blends remarkably well and intonation is excellent. This is temptingly inexpensive.

Getty, Gordon (20th century)

The White election (song-cycle).
*** Delos Dig. D/CD 3057 [id.]. Kaaren Erickson, Armen Guzelimian.

The simple, even primitive, yet deeply allusive poetry of Emily Dickinson is sensitively matched in the music of Gordon Getty. Here he tackles a sequence of 32 songs, building them into an extended cycle in four linked parts to tell Emily's story 'in her own words'. If at times the tinkly tunes seem to be an inadequate response to profound emotions, the total honesty of the writing disarms criticism, particularly in a performance as dedicated and sensitive as this, with Kaaren Erickson a highly expressive artist with a naturally beautiful voice. The pianist too is very responsive.

Gibbons, Christopher (1615–76)

Cupid and Death (with Matthew Locke).
(B) *** DHM Baroque Esprit 0542 77428-2. Kirkby, Tubb, Holden, Nichols, King, Cornwell, D. Thomas, Wistreich, Consort of Musicke, Rooley.

Cupid and Death, 'a masque in four entries', dates from 1653. Christopher Gibbons, the son of Orlando, seems to have been the lesser partner in the project, with Matthew Locke providing the bulk of the music for this rustic fantasy on an ancient fable. Each of the five 'entries' or Acts is formally laid out in a set sequence of items – a suite of dances, a dialogue, a song and a chorus – and Rooley's team consistently brings out the fresh charm of the music. The spoken sections have been edited out for this welcome reissue, and now the music fits neatly on to a single CD (71 minutes).

Gibbons, Orlando (1583–1625)

Fantasia in 2 Parts; 4 Fantasias in 3 parts; 3 Fantasias in 6 Parts; Go from my window in 6 parts. Galliard in 3 parts; 2 Fantasias in 3 parts; Fantasia in 4 parts (all 4 '*for the Great Dooble Bass*'); *In nomine in 4 parts; In nomine in 5 parts; Fantasia, Prelude and Ground* (for organ). (i) *The Cries of London:* Parts I & II.
(M) **(*) Virgin/EMI Dig. VC5 45144-2. Fretwork, with Paul Nicholson (organ); (i) with Red Byrd.

Easily the most interesting items here are the *Fantasias* (and *Galliard*) which feature – not too ostentatiously – 'the Great Dooble Bass' (in fact an oversized viol – pictured on the back of the excellent accompanying booklet). Its inclusion seemed to have inspired Gibbons to produce a sequence of his more attractive ideas. *Go from my window in 6 parts* is a set of divisions on a popular ballad which tends to outstay its welcome because of the lack of dynamic range in the music-making – a criticism which applies also to the simpler *Fantasias*. Paul Nicholson provides variety with his organ solos, but the most memorably expressive pieces are the pair of *In nomine* settings. In between come the two charming brief selections from the *Cries of London*, sung by the members of Red Byrd with a nice feeling for their popular declamatory style, yet with musical sophistication and good tuning.

Madrigals and motets (1612): *Ah dear heart; Dainty fine bird; Fair is the rose; Fair ladies that*

to love; Farewell all joys; How art thou thralled; I feign not friendship; I see ambition never pleased; I tremble not at the noise of war; I weigh not fortune's frown; Lais now old; 'Mongst thousands good; Nay let me weep; Ne'er let the sun; Now each flowery bank of May; O that the learned poets; The silver swan; Trust not too much fair youth; What is our life?; Yet if that age.
(N) (B) *** Decca Double 458 093-2 (2) Consort of Musicke, Anthony Rooley – MORLEY; WILBYE: *Madrigals.* ***

Gibbons left only one book of madrigalian pieces and the Consort of Musicke here present it complete. The vocal group includes well-known names like Martyn Hill, Rogers Covey-Crump and David Thomas and is led by the young Emma Kirkby, who opens the 1975 programme with a delightfully fresh, young-voiced solo performance of *The Silver swan* (which is used as the title of the collection). She is accompanied by a quartet of viols and half the pieces here are sung *and* played with viols, and sensitive attention is paid to phrasing and colour. Performances are eminently thoughtful; diction is not always first class, though Rooley is at some pains to avoid obtrusive or explosive consonants. But it would be curmudgeonly to dwell on minor criticisms in so enjoyable an enterprise, for the set (which derives from the Oiseau-Lyre catalogue), is expertly recorded and beautifully produced. It is not only a welcome addition to Gibbons's representation on record, but is equally valuable for the coupled repertoire by Morley and Wilbye. Full texts are included.

Almighty and everlasting God; Blessed are all they; Glorious and powerful God; Lord, grant grace; O Lord, how do my woes increase; Sing unto the Lord; This is the record of John; We praise Thee, O Father.
(B) *** Cal. Approche CAL 6621 [id.]. Clerkes of Oxenford, David Wulstan – SHEPPARD: *Mass 'Cantate'; Respond: 'Spiritus Sanctus'.* ***

This collection of eight verse-anthems of Orlando Gibbons makes an admirable coupling for some lesser-known music of John Sheppard. They are written for solo groups as well as for the full choir, and often with instrumental accompaniments, and their style obviously recalls similar music by Purcell. By comparison they are not found wanting. They are splendidly sung and recorded, and this is a genuine bargain.

Anthems & Verse anthems: *Almighty and everlasting God; Hosanna to the Son of David; Lift up your heads; O Thou the central orb; See, see the word is incarnate; This is the record of John. Canticles: Short service: Magnificat and Nunc dimittis. 2nd Service; Magnificat and Nunc dimittis. Hymnes & Songs of the church: Come kiss me with those lips of thine; Now shall the praises of the Lord be sung; A song of joy unto the Lord. Organ fantasia: Fantasia for double organ; Voluntary.*
*** ASV Gaudeamus CDGAU 123 [id.]. King's College Ch., L. Early Music Group, Ledger; John Butt.

This invaluable anthology was the first serious survey of Gibbons's music to appear on CD. It contains many of his greatest pieces. Not only are the performances touched with distinction, the recording too is in the highest flight and the analogue sound has been transferred to CD with complete naturalness. Strongly recommended.

Gibbs, Ruth (1921–1999)

Symphony No. 2 (in one movement), Op. 30.
(N) *** Classico Dig. CLASSCD 274 [id.]. Munich SO, Douglas Bostock – BUTTERWORTH: *Symphony No. 1.* ***

Ruth Gibbs was born in Bexhill-on-Sea and entered the Royal College of Music in 1937 on a Caird Scholarship; later (1967) she was to succeed her teacher, Gordon Jacob, as Professor of Composition. Her *First Symphony* was premièred by the CBSO under George Weldon in 1945, where she spent the war years playing the oboe and cor anglais. Back in London (alongside other traditional composers, who had no time for serialism, and wrote tunes) she found it almost impossible to get her orchestral music performed, and turned her attention to chamber repertory. She began her *Second Symphony* in Cornwall in 1945, and its fine slow movement surely captures similar seascapes to those of Bax's *Tintagel* (if without the Arthurian evocations). The work is immediately and attractively melodic and approachable, with her own instrument providing the secondary theme of the lyrical first section. The Scherzo/march is a fife-and-drum patrol, which approaches and recedes, and the finale begins as a touching elegy, perhaps looking back to the war years. But a reprise of earlier material finally leads to an exultant, life-enhancing close, reflecting the hopeful mood of the immediate post-war era. Bostock and his fine Munich players have the work's full measure, and present it warmly and at times flamboyantly, yet readily capture its underlying idyllic English atmosphere. The recording is excellent and the coupling (quite a different work) is equally stimulating.

Gilbert, Henry (1868–1928)

Suite for chamber orchestra.
*** Albany Dig. TROY 033-2 [id.]. V. American Music Ens., Hobart Earle – CHADWICK: *Serenade for strings.* ***

Henry Gilbert belonged to a time when almost all musical influences came from Europe and the

American public did not value the output of its indigenous composers. This *Suite*, which harmonically is innocuous but which has an agreeable nostalgic languor, has something in common with Delius's *Florida suite*, although Gilbert's invention is less indelible. An excellent performance here from members of the Vienna American Ensemble, who are completely at home in the music, as well they might be. The recording is excellent.

Gilles, Jean (1668–1705)

Messe des morts (Requiem Mass).
(M) *** DG (IMS) 437 087-2. Rodde, Nirouët, Hill, U. Studer, Kooy, Ghent Coll. Voc., Col. Mus. Ant., Herreweghe (with CORRETTE: *Carillon des morts* ***).

The Gilles *Requiem*, which for many years was a favourite work in France, was rejected by the two families who originally commissioned it, so Gilles decreed that it should be used for his own funeral. Gilles's rhythmic and harmonic vigour (with plentiful false relations to add tang) is well caught in this performance on original instruments, and the singers find the music's expressive style admirably. The *Carillon* was included by Michel Corrette in his own edition of the Gilles *Requiem*, printed in 1764, and is appropriately included here as a postlude.

Gilson, Paul (1865–1942)

De Zee (suite).
(B) *** Discover Dig. DICD 920126 [id.]. Brussels BRT PO, Karl Anton Rickenbacher – DE BOECK: *Symphony in G.* ***

Like August de Boeck, also represented on this disc, Paul Gilson was a Belgian composer, born in 1865. His suite, *De Zee*, like de Boeck's *Symphony* is full of Russian echoes. It is a series of four seascapes half-way between Wagner's *Flying Dutchman* and Debussy's *La Mer*, with Rimsky-Korsakov's *Scheherazade* mixed in. Well played and recorded and, at Discover International's bargain price, an ideal disc for experimenting with.

Ginastera, Alberto (1916–83)

Harp concerto, Op. 25.
*** Chandos Dig. CHAN 9094 [id.]. Rachel Masters, City of L. Sinfonia, Hickox – GLIERE: *Concertos.* ***

Ginastera's 1956 *Harp concerto*, full of vivid colours and snappy, incisive rhythms also has a highly atmospheric slow movement. All its kaleidoscopic moods are keenly projected by Rachel Masters in this refreshing and invigorating performance. Alert playing, too, from the City of London Sinfonia under Richard Hickox. Strongly recommended, as are the two Glière concertos with which it is coupled.

(i) *Harp concerto, Op. 25;* (ii) *Piano concerto No. 1; Estancia* (ballet suite), *Op. 89.*
*** ASV Dig. CDDCA 654 [id.]. (i) Nancy Allen; (ii) Oscar Tarrago; Mexico City PO, Bátiz.

The *Harp concerto* is brought fully to life here by Nancy Allen and the Mexican orchestra. *Estancia* is a comparably vivid piece of Coplandesque machismo, its character also very successfully realized. The *First Piano concerto* is mildly serial but far from unattractive – and very brilliantly (and sensitively) played by Oscar Tarrago. An excellent introduction to this composer.

Estancia (ballet suite); *Panambi* (choreographic legend).
*** Everest EVC 9007 [id.]. LSO, Sir Eugene Goossens – ANTILL: *Corroboree*; VILLA-LOBOS: *Little train of the Caipira.* **(*)

Both these brightly hued scores bring a high standard of invention. *Panambi* is the earlier – written when the composer was only twenty. It opens with a haunting picture of *Moonlight on the Panama* and the *Lament of the Maidens* is gently touching, while the *Invocations of the Powerful Spirits* and *Dance of the Warriors* are powerfully primitive. *Estancia* dates from a slightly later period. Again the scoring is exotic and impressive, and the lively dances are full of primeval energy, notably the closing *Malambo*, while the lovely *Wheat dance* brings another nostalgic interlude. The performances are in every way first class and the atmospheric recording brilliantly captures the composer's imaginatively varied sound-world.

(i) *Cello sonata, Op. 49. Danzas argentinas, Op. 2; Estancia, Op. 8:* (i) *Pampeana No. 2, Op. 21* (rhapsody for cello and piano). *Pequeña danza; Piano sonata No. 1, Op. 22; 5 Canciones populares argentinas:* (i) *Triste.* (arr. Fournier)
*** ASV Dig. CDDCA 865 [id.]. Alberto Portugheis, (i) with Aurora Natola-Ginastera.

The four-movement *Cello sonata*, ardently rhapsodic, chimerical and full of atmosphere, is dedicated to Ginastera's wife, who is the soloist here, while *Pampeana* is a rhapsody which has an Argentinian flavour without using folk melodies. The *Piano sonata No. 1* (1952) is a powerful, integrated piece with a desolate *Adagio* and a brilliant, rhythmically chimerical folk-dance finale. Alberto Portugheis is thoroughly at home in this repertoire and plays compellingly throughout. He is well recorded.

Canciones, Op. 3: Milonga. Malambo, Op. 7; 3 Piezas, Op. 6; Piezas infantiles; Rondo sobre

temas infantiles argentinos, Op. 19; Sonatas Nos. 1, Op. 53; 3, Op. 58; Toccata.
*** ASV Dig. CDDCA 880 [id.]. Alberto Portugheis.

The pieces for children are most welcoming and are delightfully varied and intimate: the *Milonga* is seductive in a Latin-American way, as are the *Three Pieces*, Op. 6. The *Sonatas* are harder nuts to crack: the first has a formidable opening movement and a ferocious closing toccata, and the *Toccata*, written for the organ and played with great bravura here, is also a piece to make one sit up. Alberto Portugheis is a first-rate artist and his natural sympathies for the music's idiom are apparent throughout. He is very well recorded.

Giordano, Umberto (1867–1948)

Andrea Chénier (complete).
(M) *** RCA 74321 39499-2 (2) [2046-2-RG]. Domingo, Scotto, Milnes, Alldis Ch., Nat. PO, Levine.
**(*) Decca Dig. 410 117-2 (2) [id.]. Pavarotti, Caballé, Nucci, Kuhlmann, Welsh Nat. Op. Ch., Nat. PO, Chailly.
(M) **(*) EMI (SIS) CMS5 65287-2 (2) [Ang. CDMB 65287]. Corelli, Stella, Sereni, Rome Op. Ch. & O, Santini.

Andrea Chénier with its defiant poet hero provides a splendid role for Domingo at his most heroic and the former servant, later revolutionary leader, Gérard, is a character well appreciated by Milnes. Scotto gives one of her most eloquent and beautiful performances, and Levine has rarely displayed his powers as an urgent and dramatic opera conductor more potently on record, with the bright recording intensifying the dramatic thrust of playing and singing. This set is at premium price in the USA.

Pavarotti may motor through the role of the poet-hero, singing with his usual fine diction; nevertheless, the red-blooded melodrama of the piece comes over powerfully, thanks to Chailly's sympathetic conducting, incisive but never exaggerated. Caballé, like Pavarotti, is not strong on characterization but produces beautiful sounds, while Leo Nucci makes a superbly dark-toned Gérard. Though this cannot replace the Levine set, it is a colourful substitute with its demonstration sound.

The glory of the 1964 EMI version is the Chénier of Franco Corelli, one of his most satisfying performances on record with heroic tone gloriously exploited. The other singing is less distinguished. Though Antonietta Stella was never sweeter of voice than here, she hardly matches such rivals as Scotto or Caballé. The 1960s recording is vivid, with plenty of atmosphere, and has been transferred to CD most naturally, but the RCA set in the same price range, with Domingo and Scotto, remains a clear first choice.

Fedora (complete).
(M) **(*) Decca 433 033-2 (2) [id.]. Olivero, Del Monaco, Gobbi, Monte Carlo Nat. Op. Ch. & O, Gardelli – ZANDONAI: *Francesca da Rimini*. **(*)
(M) ** Sony Dig. M2K 42181 (2). Marton, Carreras, Hungarian R. & TV Ch. & O, Patanè.

Fedora will always be remembered for one brief aria, the hero's *Amor ti vieta*; but, as this highly enjoyable recording confirms, there is much that is memorable in the score, even if nothing else quite approaches it. Meaty stuff, which brings some splendid singing from Magda Olivero and (more intermittently) from Del Monaco, with Gobbi in a light comedy part. Fine, vintage (1969), atmospheric recording.

On Sony, Eva Marton as Fedora, the Romanov princess, is aptly cast, with José Carreras taking the role of hero. In a work that should sound sumptuous it is not a help that the voices are placed forwardly, with the orchestra distanced well behind. That balance exaggerates the vibrato in Marton's voice, but it is a strong, sympathetic performance; Carreras, too, responds warmly to the lyricism of the role of the hero, Loris, giving a satisfyingly forthright account of *Amor ti vieta*. The rest of the cast is unremarkable, and Patanè's direction lacks bite, again partly a question of orchestral balance.

Giuliani, Mauro (1781–1828)

(i; ii) *Guitar concertos Nos. 1 in A, Op. 30; 2 in A, Op. 36; 3 in F, Op. 70; Introduction, theme with variations and polonaise (for guitar and orchestra), Op. 65.* (i) *Grande ouverture, Op. 61; Gran Sonata Eroica in A; La Melanchonia; Variations on 'Ich bin a Kohlbauern Bub', Op. 49; Variations on a theme by Handel, Op. 107;* (i; iii) *Variazioni concertanti, Op. 130.*
(B) *** Ph. Duo 454 262-2 (2) [id.]. (i) Pepe Romero, (ii) with ASMF, Marriner; (iii) with Celedonio Romero.

Romero is a first-rate player, and his relaxed music-making and easy bravura bring an attractive, smiling quality. But what makes these concertos so distinctive are the splendid accompaniments provided by the Academy of St Martin-in-the-Fields under Marriner. The shaping of the naïf contours of Giuliani's orchestral ritornello for the *First Concerto* is deliciously judged, and throughout there are many delightful touches from the orchestra. The *F major Concerto* has comparable charm. Its first movement begins with an engaging little march theme whose dotted contour reminds one of Hummel (the two composers were almost exact contemporaries), and the amiable *Siciliano* which forms the slow movement is matched by an unforceful closing Polonaise. Hummel again comes rhythmically to mind in the first movement of the *Second concerto*, which is for strings alone. The *Introduction, theme with variations and polonaise* is like a mini-concerto and, if the basic idea of the variations only just rises above the trivial, it is redeemed by a performance of vitality and charm. The Op. 49 *Variations* are agreeable but slight, but the *Sonata Eroica*, although effectively conceived and impressively presented, hardly merits its grand sobriquet as provided by Ricordi when it was published posthumously. The *Variations concertanti* for two guitars, in which Pepe is joined by Celedonio, is a more ambitious late work which exploits the duet variation form with much skill. It is played with affection and ready virtuosity. The mid 1960s recording throughout is warm and refined, very easy on the ear.

Guitar concerto in A, Op. 30.
(M) *** DG (IMS) 439 984-2. Siegfried Behrend, I Musici – CARULLI: *Concerto in A* **(*); VIVALDI: *Guitar concertos.* **(*)
(B) **(*) Decca Eclipse 448 709-2. Eduardo Fernández, ECO, Malcolm – PAGANINI: *Sonata* (with VIVALDI: *Concertos.* **(*))

Giuliani's *A major Concerto* is presented by Behrend with much elegance and finesse and is immaculately recorded. Its catchy main theme is endearing; though the music overall is slight, it is nicely crafted.

A rather low-key, essentially chamber performance from the highly musical Fernández, who refuses to show off. He is accompanied elegantly by Malcolm and the ECO and is most naturally recorded.

Duo concertante for violin & guitar, Op. 25; Gran duetto concertante for flute & guitar, Op. 52; Serenade for violin, cello & guitar in A, Op. 19.
**(*) RCA 09026 60237-2 [id.]. Swensen, Galway, Anderson, Yamashita.

Giuliani is an elegant purveyor of ingenuous, pleasing phrases, and these three works show him at his most gallantly generous. These four artists do the composer proud, playing with warmth and elegance – Joseph Swensen's timbre in the *Duo concertante* is sumptuous (almost too lush) and only in the *Serenade* is the penchant of American engineering – the recordings were made in New York City – for close balancing disturbing, when the violin catches the microphone in the galloping Scherzo. Even so, this concert is easy to enjoy.

Sonata for violin and guitar.
*** Sony MK 34508 [id.]. Itzhak Perlman, John Williams – PAGANINI: *Cantabile*, etc.***

Giuliani's *Sonata* is amiable enough but hardly substantial fare; but it is played with such artistry here that it appears better music than it is. The recording is in need of more ambience, but sound is invariably a matter of taste, and there is no reason to withhold a strong recommendation. The CD transfer is admirably managed.

Grand overture, Op. 61; Rossiniana No. 3, Op. 121.
(M) **(*) RCA 09026 61593-2. Julian Bream (guitar) – SOR: *Grand solo sonata* etc.; DIABELLI: *Sonata in A*. **(*)

The *Grand Overture* is a rather imposing piece which Bream despatches with panache, whereas Giulini's six *Rossinianae* were, as the title suggests, based on the operas of Rossini, and one might expect the music of No. 3 to be witty and memorably tuneful, but that is not so. Bream makes cuts, but the music outstays its welcome. The playing is first class, of course, and the recording exemplary.

Variations on a theme by Handel, Op. 107.
(B) *** Sony SBK 62425 [id.]. John Williams (guitar) – PAGANINI: *Caprice 24; Grand sonata;* D. SCARLATTI: *Sonatas;* VILLA-LOBOS: *5 Preludes*. ***

The *Variations* are on Handel's famous *Harmonious blacksmith* theme. Their construction is guileless but agreeable, and they are expertly played and well recorded. This is only a small part of a well-planned and exceptionally generous collection devoted mainly to Paganini and Domenico Scarlatti.

Glass, Philip (born 1937)

Company; Façades.
(M) *** Virgin/EMI Dig. CUV5 61121-2. LCO, Warren-Green – ADAMS: *Shaker loops* *** ✪; REICH: *8 Lines* ***; HEATH: *Frontier*. ***

Company consists of four brief but sharply contrasted movements for strings; *Façades* offers a haunting cantilena for soprano saxophone, suspended over atmospherically undulating strings. The performances are full of intensity and are expertly played, and the recording is excellent.

Dance Pieces: Glasspieces; In the Upper Room: Dances Nos. 1, 2, 5, 8 & 9.
*** CBS Dig. MK 39539 [id.]. Ens., dir. Michael Riesman.

These two ballet scores bring typical and easily attractive examples of Glass's minimalist technique. Heard away from the stage, the music seems to have a subliminally hypnotic effect, even though rhythmic patterns often repeat themselves almost endlessly.

String quartets Nos. 2 (Company); 3 (Mishima); 4 (Buczak); 5.
*** Elektra-Nonesuch/Warner Dig. 7559 79356-2 [id.]. Kronos Quartet.

Happily, the quartets here are presented in reverse order, for the last of the four, No. 5, dating from 1991, presents Glass at his most warmly expressive and intense. Textures are luminous, shimmering in their repetitions rather than thrusting them home relentlessly. The Kronos Quartet, for whom the work was written, give a heartfelt performance, as they do of the *Quartet No. 4* (1990), written in memory of Brian Buczak, who died of AIDS. The valedictory mood is intensified by a lyrical and poignantly beautiful middle movement, leading to a noble finale. The *Quartet No. 2* (1983) consists of four brief movements originally written to accompany the staged soliloquy of a dying man, entitled *Company*. Again it is valedictory in tone but is far less tender. The *Quartet No. 3* (1985) is repetitive in the characteristic Glass manner, this time with six brief movements. Though Nos. 4 and 5 most clearly reveal the hand of a master, the earlier works also represent Glass at his most approachable, the more so when they are treated to magnetic performances by the Kronos Quartet, superbly recorded.

OPERA

Akhnaten (complete).
*** CBS M2K 42457 (2) [id.]. Esswood, Vargas, Liebermann, Hannula, Holzapfel, Hauptmann, Stuttgart State Op. Ch. & O, Russell Davies.

Akhnaten, Glass's powerful third opera, is set in the time of Ancient Egypt. Paul Esswood in the title-role is reserved, strong and statuesque; this is an opera of historical ghosts, and its life-flow lies in the hypnotic background provided by the orchestra; indeed the work's haunting closing scene with its wordless melismas is like nothing else in music. It offers a theatrical experience appealing to a far wider public than usual in the opera house; and here the Stuttgart chorus and orchestra give the piece impressively committed advocacy.

La Belle et la Bête (opera based on the film of Jean Cocteau): complete.
*** Nonesuch-Elektra/Warner Dig 7559 794347 [id.]. Felty, Purnhagen, Kuether, Martinez, Neill, Zhou, Philip Glass Ens., Michael Riesman.

What Glass has done here is to provide a new musical accompaniment to a showing of Cocteau's 90-minute film, *La Belle et la Bête*, dispensing with Auric's original film-music and synchronizing the singing-parts with the speech of the actors in the film. In the opening scenes the music is far lighter and more conventionally beautiful than most Glass, but then the poignancy of the story is more and more reflected in the score, both tender and mellifluous. The hypnotic quality of Glass's repetitions helps to enhance the magical atmosphere, while the use of the original French film-script prompts Glass to be more warmly melodic than usual. Glass's justification lies in the intensity of the score overall, with Janice Felty and Gregory Purnhagen both clearly focused in the central roles, though Purnhagen's baritone suggests from the start a heroic, not a bestial, figure. Vividly atmospheric sound.

Einstein on the Beach (complete).
*** Teldec/Warner Dig. 7559 79323-2 (3) [id.]. Soloists, Philip Glass Ens., Riesman.

Glass himself explains the need for a new recording of this bizarre and relentless opera – as the surreal title implies, more dream than drama. Where the earlier recording had an abrasive edge, this new one is more refined, melding the different elements, electronic alongside acoustic, more subtly and persuasively than before. Even so, the first train episode, over 20 minutes long, remains mind-blowing in its relentlessness. The impact is heightened by the vividness of the recording, with spoken voices in particular given such presence that they startle you as if someone had burst into your room. The vision remains an odd one, but with a formidable group of vocalists and instrumentalists brilliantly directed, often from the keyboard, by Michael Riesman, the new recording certainly justifies itself.

Satyagraha (complete).
*** Sony Dig. M3K 39672 (3) [id.]. Perry, NY City Op. Ch. & O, Keene.

The subject here is the early life of Mahatma Gandhi and the text is a selection of verses from the *Bhagavadgita*, sung in the original Sanskrit and used as another strand in the complex repetitive web of sound. The result is undeniably powerful. Where much minimalist music in its shimmering repetitiveness becomes static, a good deal of this conveys energy as well as power. The writing for chorus is often thrilling, and individual characters emerge in only a shadowy way. The recording, using the device of overdubbing, is spectacular.

Glazunov, Alexander (1865–1936)

Carnaval overture, Op. 45; Concert waltzes Nos. 1–2, Opp. 47 & 51; Spring, Op. 34; Salomé (incidental music), Op. 90: Introduction; Dance.
(BB) **(*) Naxos Dig. 8.553838 [id.]. Moscow SO, Igor Golovschin.

This collection of shorter pieces by Glazunov makes up a delightful disc, bringing out the composer's amiable side. The *Carnaval overture* is a jaunty, sparkling piece with first-rate tunes. There are also some attractive ideas in *Spring* (*Vesna*), a charming work and similarly refined and transparent in its orchestration, playing on birdsong, and building to a sensuous climax. The more familiar *Concert waltzes* contain some of Glazunov's most winning tunes, the one Tchaikovskian in flavour, the other Viennese. They are played decently enough, though the last ounce of finish is missing. The novelty most likely to excite curiosity here is Glazunov's music for Oscar Wilde's *Salomé*, written in 1908, three years after Richard Strauss's celebrated opera, with Salome's dance leading to a Polovtsian climax. It is surprisingly conventional and tame, and Salome sheds her veils in a most unerotic fashion. But this cannot be blamed on the conductor, and generally these are warm, idiomatic performances, richly recorded.

Chant du ménestrel (for cello and orchestra), Op. 71.

(B) *** DG Double 437 952-2 (2) [id.]. Rostropovich, Boston SO, Ozawa – BERNSTEIN: *3 Meditations;* BOCCHERINI: *Cello concerto No. 2;* SHOSTAKOVICH: *Cello concerto No. 2;* TARTINI: *Cello concerto;* TCHAIKOVSKY: *Andante cantabile* etc.; VIVALDI: *Cello concertos.* ***

*** Chandos Dig. CHAN 8579 [id.]. Wallfisch, LPO, Bryden Thomson – KABALEVSKY; KHACHATURIAN: *Cello concertos.* ***

Glazunov's *Chant du ménestrel* shows the nostalgic appeal of 'things long ago and far away'. It is a short but appealing piece and is splendidly played by Rostropovich within a highly recommendable Double DG anthology. Alternatively, it becomes a welcome makeweight on the Chandos CD.

Chopiniana, Op. 46.

(N) ** Decca Dig. 460 019-2. Deutsches SO, Berlin, Ashkenazy – CHOPIN: *Piano concerto No. 1.* **

Glazunov's scoring of various piano pieces, made in 1893, is at times rather thick but it makes a satisfactory fill-up to Ashkenazy's less than special account of the Chopin *E minor concerto.*

(i) *Concerto ballata for cello and orchestra, Op. 108;* (ii) *Piano concerto No. 1, Op. 92.*

*** Chandos Dig. CHAN 9528 [id.]. (i) Dyachkov; (ii) Pirzadeh; I Musici de Montréal, Turovsky – ARENSKY: *Violin concerto.* ***

The highly romantic *First Piano Concerto* is already well served by Stephen Coombs (see below). The *Concerto ballata* is more of a rarity and, like the *Saxophone concerto*, is the product of the composer's last years in Paris. Apart from Pergamenschikow on Koch, there is no other version of the *Concerto ballata*, and it is a far from negligible piece. Yegor Dyachkov is a fine soloist, and the young Iranian-born Canadian pianist, Maneli Pirzadeh, proves a most poetic and brilliant exponent of the *Piano concerto*. All in all this makes a highly recommendable coupling.

Piano concertos Nos. 1 in F min., Op. 92; 2 in B flat, Op. 100.

**(*) Hyperion Dig. CDA 66877 [id.]. Stephen Coombs, BBC Scottish SO, Martyn Brabbins – GOEDICKE: *Concertstück.* **(*)

These two piano concertos are ripely lyrical, like a mixture of Brahms and Rachmaninov, but the inspiration is anything but tired or faded. In the *First Concerto*, an extended first movement – with echoes of Rachmaninov's *Second Symphony* – is followed by a long and elaborate set of variations, while the Liszt-like structure of the *Second Concerto* includes the most beautiful slow movement. As in his survey of Glazunov's piano music for the same label, Stephen Coombs is a persuasive advocate, and he always leaves one with the feeling that this music means more than it does. The BBC Scottish Symphony Orchestra under Martyn Brabbins give sympathetic support, and the only serious reservation one might make concerns the over-resonant recording acoustic.

Piano concerto No. 2 in B, Op. 100.

(N) **(*) Chandos Dig. CHAN 9622 [id.]. Matthew Herskowitz, I Musici de Montréal, Yuli Turovsky – DAVIDOV: *Cello concerto No. 2 in A min., Op. 14.* **(*) CONUS: *Violin concerto.* **(*)

The *Second Piano Concerto* is not strong Glazunov and Matthew Herskowitz is not quite as persuasive an artist as, say, Stephen Coombs on Hyperion. However, the merit of this record, which serves as a showcase for the winners of Turovsky's Orford Competition, is to explore Russian concertos of the second rank which deserve a place in your library.

Violin concerto in A min., Op. 82.

*** Teldec/Warner Dig. 4509-90881-2 [id.]. Vengerov, BPO, Abbado – TCHAIKOVSKY: *Violin concerto.* ***

(N) *** DG Dig. 457 064-2 [id.]. Gil Shaham, Russian Nat. O, Pletnev – KABALEVSKY: *Concerto*; TCHAIKOVSKY: *Souvenir d'un lieu cher* etc. ***

(N) *** Erato/Warner Dig. 0630 17722-2. Anne-Sophie Mutter, Nat.SO, Rostropovich – PROKOFIEV: *Violin concerto No. 1;* SHCHEDRIN: *Stihira.* ***

*** EMI (SIS) Dig. CDC7 54872-2. Zimmermann, LPO, Welser-Möst – DVORAK: *Violin concerto.* ***

✿ (***) EMI (SIS) mono CDH7 64030-2 [id.]. Heifetz, LPO, Barbirolli – SIBELIUS: *Violin* *concerto* (**); TCHAIKOVSKY: *Violin concerto*. (***)

(M) *** RCA 09026 61744-2 [61744-2-RG]. Heifetz, RCA Victor SO, Hendl – PROKOFIEV: *Violin concerto No. 2;* SIBELIUS: *Concerto*. ***

*** EMI (IMS) Dig. CDC7 49814-2 [id.]. Perlman, Israel PO, Mehta – SHOSTAKOVICH: *Violin concerto No. 1*. ***

(BB) *** Naxos Dig. 8.550758 [id.]. Ilya Kaler, Polish Nat. RSO (Katowice), Kolchinsky – DVORAK: *Concerto* etc. ***

(M) *** Carlton Dig. 30367 0031-2 [id.]. Udagawa, LPO, Klein – Concert ***.

Outstanding as Vengerov's Tchaikovsky performance is, his Glazunov is even more exceptional, for he gives a familiar concerto extra dimensions, turning it from a display piece into a work of far wider-ranging emotions. Above all he makes one appreciate afresh what a wonderful sequence of melodies the composer here offers, when in each he contrasts and shades the tone-colours so magically, keeping his richest tone in reserve for the third theme. Predictably, the dashing final section is breathtaking in its brilliance.

Gil Shaham gives a pretty dazzling account of the concerto with Mikhail Pletnev and the Russian National Orchestra, which can well hold its own with the current opposition. It reminds us what a superb (and often touching) piece it is. The coupling is unusual and readers attracted by it need not hesitate. Good, ample sound.

The collaboration of the firmly disciplined Anne-Sophie Mutter and the warmly inspirational Rostropovich produces some magical results. Mutter is here more volatile and more freely expressive than she has usually been on disc, sounding totally spontaneous, and that is particularly impressive in the Glazunov. The only complaint is that Erato provide only a single track for the whole work, 20 minutes long. The recording, made in the Kennedy Center, Washington, DC is more airy and spacious than many from this venue, with the soloist forwardly balanced.

The Glazunov also comes up sounding delightfully fresh in Frank Peter Zimmermann's hands. Among recent versions this can hold its head high: Zimmermann plays with effortless virtuosity, great polish and great beauty of tone. Franz Welser-Möst provides excellent support, and the recording is outstandingly natural and realistic.

Heifetz's recording of the Glazunov *Violin concerto* with Barbirolli was made in 1934 when the composer was still alive. It has greater expressive breadth and spaciousness than his later record with Walter Hendl and the Chicago orchestra and there is great warmth. Intonation is incredibly sure and the tone sweet; generally speaking, this first Heifetz version of the concerto has never been surpassed. For those who want more modern, stereo sound, Heifetz is again incomparable; his account is the strongest and most passionate (as well as the most perfectly played) in the catalogue. The RCA orchestra under Hendl gives splendid support.

The command and panache of Perlman are irresistible in this showpiece concerto, and the whole performance, recorded live, erupts into a glorious account of the galloping final section, in playing to match that even of the supreme master in this work, Heifetz.

The Russian violinist Ilya Kaler gives a rapturously lyrical performance, and Camilla Kolchinsky's accompaniment is equally warm and supportive. The resonant acoustic of the Concert Hall of Polish Radio gives a big, spacious orchestral sound, but Ilya Kaler's tone is full to match, and the violin playing can certainly accommodate the scrutiny of the fairly close microphones. The Dvořák *Concerto* is hardly less successful, and the delightful *Romance* is thrown in for good measure.

The Glazunov also receives a heartfelt performance from Udagawa which is just as compelling as the virtuoso stereo accounts from such master violinists as Heifetz and Perlman. In the finale she may not offer quite such bravura fireworks as they do but, with more open sound, the result is very persuasive in its lilting way.

(i) *Violin concerto. The Seasons* (ballet), *Op. 67*.

*** Chandos Dig. CHAN 8596 [id.]. (i) Oscar Shumsky; RSNO, Järvi.

Neeme Järvi obtains good results from the Scottish National Orchestra in *The Seasons*, though tempi tend to be brisk. The Chandos acoustic is reverberant and the balance recessed. In the *Violin concerto*, Oscar Shumsky is perhaps wanting the purity and effortless virtuosity of Heifetz, but the disc as a whole still carries a three-star recommendation.

From the Middle Ages, Op. 79; Scènes de ballet, Op. 52.

*** Chandos Dig. CHAN 8804 [id.]. RSNO, Järvi (with LIADOV: *A Musical snuffbox* ***).

From the Middle Ages (suite), *Op. 79; The Sea, Op. 28; Spring, Op. 34; Stenka Razin, Op. 13.*

(M) *** Chandos Dig. CHAN 7049 [id.]. RSNO, Järvi.

Järvi makes out an excellent case for these charming Glazunov suites. Although this music is obviously inferior to Tchaikovsky, Järvi has the knack of making you think it is better than it is and the Chandos recording is up to the best standards of the house. The first disc also includes a fine account of Liadov's delightful *A Musical snuffbox*.

The tone-poem *Spring* was written two years after *The Sea* and is infinitely more imaginative; in fact it is as fresh and delightful as its companion is cliché-ridden. At one point Glazunov even looks forward to *The Seasons*. *Stenka Razin* makes a colourful enough opening item for this alternative collection which offers persuasive and very well-recorded performances from the Royal Scottish National Orchestra.

Oriental rhapsody in G, Op. 29.
(N) *** Decca Dig. 452 482-2 [id.]. Montreal SO, Charles Dutoit. – ALFVEN, DVORAK, ENESCU, LISZT: *Rhapsodies etc.* ***

A very enjoyable account of the *Oriental rhapsody* comes from Montreal and Dutroit, recorded with great clarity and presence. It is not great music but will give pleasure nonetheless.

Raymonda (complete ballet).
(BB) **(*) Naxos 8.553503/4 [id.]. Moscow SO, Alexander Anissimov.

This Naxos version is played elegantly and affectionately, and the Moscow upper strings are full and warm as recorded. It does not lack life. But in seeking atmosphere, the playing creates a less than vibrant effect, although this is partly caused by Anissimov's tendency to luxuriant tempi. That is not to say it is not very enjoyable in its sumptuously spacious manner, for the orchestral playing is very sympathetic.

Raymonda (ballet), *Op. 57:* extended excerpts from Acts I & II.
**(*) Chandos Dig. CHAN 8447 [id.]. RSNO, Järvi.

Järvi chooses some 56 minutes of music from the first two Acts, omitting entirely the Slavic/Hungarian Wedding *Divertissement* of the closing Act, and this contributes to the slight feeling of lassitude. But with rich Chandos recording this is a record for any balletomane to wallow in.

Les ruses d'amore (ballet), Op. 61; Scènes de ballet (suite), Op. 52; Suite caractèristique, Op. 9; Triumphal march, Op. 40. Chopiniana (suite arr. from Chopin's works), *Op. 46.*
(N) (B) *** BMG/Melodiya Dig. Twofer 74321 59055-2 (2) [id.]. USSR SO, Svetlanov.

Les ruses d'amore (with the appropriate subtitle *Pastorale after Watteau*) was written in 1900, following the success of *Raymonda*. Opening with a beguiling Russian folk melody it offers 55 minutes of music, not unlike *Raymonda*, though not perhaps quite as fine as *The Seasons*. Glazunov had prepared the way in 1893 with his earlier *Scènes de ballet*, another engaging score, and he took over its most delectable number, *Marionnettes*, into the later work. The eight-movement *Suite caractèristique* is even earlier (1883–4), and is an orchestral transcription of various piano variations, composed several years before. So the work has linking thematic material, but still sounds very like a ballet score. All this music is warmly and elegantly played, and directed with affectionate understanding by Svetlanov. *Chopiniana* consists of transcriptions of four major Chopin piano pieces, opening with the famous *Polonaise in A major* and closing with a lively *Tarantella* in the same key. It is agreeable enough, but not in the same class as the Roy Douglas score for *Les Sylphides*. The *Triumphal march* seems at first surprisingly lyrical for a work written for an 1893 celebration (in Chicago) of the 400th anniversary of Columbus's discovery of America, but it ends with a rumbustious climax, introducing and repeating ad lib the *Battle Hymn of the Republic*. The 1989–90 digital recording is excellent in every respect, full, vivid, and with plenty of ambient warmth.

The Seasons (ballet; complete) *Op. 67.*
*** Decca Dig. 433 000-2 (2) [id.]. RPO, Ashkenazy – TCHAIKOVSKY: *Nutcracker.* ***
(N) (B)*** Decca Double Dig. 455 349-2 (2) [id.]. RPO, Ashkenazy – PROKOFIEV: *Cinderella.* ***
(M) *** EMI CDM5 65911-2. Concert Arts O, Robert Irving – SCARLATTI/TOMMASINI: *Good humoured ladies;* WALTON: *Wise virgins.* ***
(BB) **(*) Naxos Dig. 8.550079; *4550079* [id.]. Czech RSO (Bratislava), Ondrej Lenárd (with TCHAIKOVSKY: *Sleeping Beauty suite.* **)

The Seasons (ballet), *Op. 67; Concert waltzes Nos. 1 in D, Op. 47; 2 in F, Op. 51.*
(B) *** EMI forte CZS5 69361-2 (2) [CDFB 69361]. Philh. O, Svetlanov – ARENSKY: *Variations on a theme of Tchaikovsky* ***; RIMSKY-KORSAKOV: *Scheherazade.* **

The Seasons (ballet) complete; *Scènes de ballet, Op. 52.*
*** Telarc CD Dig. CD 80347 [id.]. Minnesota O, Edo de Waart.

Ashkenazy's account of Glazunov's delightful ballet is the finest it has ever received. The RPO playing is dainty and elegant, refined and sumptuous, yet the strings respond vigorously to the thrusting vitality of the Autumnal *Bacchanale*. The Decca engineers, working in Watford Town Hall, provide digital sound of great allure and warmth, very much in the demonstration bracket. As can be seen this recording is also available less expensively on a Decca Double coupled with Prokofiev's *Cinderella* ballet.

But if you want *The Seasons* separately on a single CD, you will be hard put to better the Minnesota performance, elegant, polished, warm and alive, and given Telarc's top-drawer sound. The famous thrusting tune of *Autumn* is only marginally less athletic than with Ashkenazy. The *Scènes de ballet* make an ideal coupling, not quite as melodically distinctive but still very enjoyable and cosily tuneful, although the second-movement *Marionnettes* matches Delibes at his most piquant.

In many ways Robert Irving's 1960 account has never been surpassed, and the recording, made at New York's Manhattan Center Ballroom, still sounds astonishingly fresh, while the resonant ambience prevents the quality from being too dated. The Concert Arts Orchestra is a pseudonym for a much better-known British combination, and they play with wit, warmth and astonishing precision. Irving shapes and points the melodies with consummate balletic feeling and his reading is delightfully evocative. The stirring tune of *Autumn* is taken very fast and has strikingly more vitality than with Svetlanov.

Svetlanov's account is played most beautifully. His approach is engagingly affectionate; he caresses the lyrical melodies persuasively so that, if the big tune of the *Bacchanale* has slightly less thrust than usual, it fits readily into the overall conception. The glowing Abbey Road recording is excellent and vividly remastered. It comes in harness with a very Russian *Scheherazade*, which he recorded with the LSO but about which we have some reservations (see below), and Barbirolli's highly persuasive version of the endearing Arensky *Variations* for strings.

Ondrej Lenárd gives a pleasing bargain account of Glazunov's delightful score, finding plenty of delicacy, while the entry of Glazunov's most famous tune at the opening of the *Autumn Bacchanale* is very virile indeed. The sound is atmospheric, yet with plenty of fullness.

Stenka Razin (symphonic poem), *Op. 13.*
*** Chandos Dig. CHAN 8479 [id.]. RSNO, Järvi

Stenka Razin has its moments of vulgarity – how otherwise with the *Song of the Volga Boatmen* a recurrent theme? The recording is splendid.

Symphonies Nos. 1 in E (Slavyanskaya), Op. 5; 4 in E flat, Op. 48.
(BB) **(*) Naxos Dig. 8.553561 [id.]. Moscow SO, Alexander Anissimov.

What a remarkable and delightful work the Glazunov *First Symphony* is! – not only on account of the composer's youth (he was a mere sixteen at the time) but also for the quality and fertility of its invention and its expert craftsmanship! Both here and in the *Fourth*, Alexander Anissimov gets an eminently sympathetic performance from the Moscow orchestra, though one can imagine livelier and lighter playing.

Symphony No. 2 in F sharp min., Op. 16. (i) *Coronation cantata, Op. 56.*
(N) *** Chandos CHAN 9709 [id.]. Russian State SO, Valeri Polyansky (i) with Olga Lutiv-Ternovskaya, Ludmila Kuznetsova, Vsevolod Grivnov, Dmitri Stepanovich, Russian State Symphonic Cappella.

Glazunov wrote his amiably lyrical *Symphony No. 2* when he was still only 21. It is full of very Russian themes that echo Borodin's *Prince Igor*, which Glazunov himself helped to complete after the composer's death. Though Polyansky's performance loses some concentration in the finale, it is warmly expressive and colourful, helped by rich, full recording. What makes the disc specially attractive is the substantial fill-up, the premiere recording of the *Coronation cantata* which Glazunov wrote almost ten years later, commissioned to celebrate the coronation of the last Tsar, Nicolas II. Framed by forthright choruses, the opening one in a swinging triple time, the middle five movements feature the four soloists in turn, culminating in an exhilarating movement, *Heaven and earth*, enriched with sensuously beautiful orchestration. A winning rarity, very well performed, with a strong team of soloists, all attractively slavonic in timbre, even if the soprano grows edgy under pressure.

Symphonies Nos. 2 in F sharp min., Op. 16; 7 in F (Pastoral), Op. 77.
(BB) ** Naxos Dig. 8.553769 [id.]. Moscow SO, Alexander Anissimov.

The slow movement of Glazunov's *Second Symphony* has a sinuous, Borodin-like melody of genuine memorability and here Anissimov and the Moscow Symphony Orchestra respond to the music's Slavonic feeling, but overall without quite the degree of passion and drama the work demands, and the violins, as recorded, lack allure. However, the 'Pastoral' *Seventh* of 1902 (which makes a distinct melodic reference to Beethoven's work in the same key) is rather more successful. The recording is well balanced and full, if not top-drawer. With any reservations noted, this is fair value.

(i) *Symphony No. 3;* (ii) *Serenades Nos. 1 in A, Op. 7; 2 in F, Op. 11;* (i) *Stenka Razin, Op. 13.*
**(*) ASV Dig. CDDCA 903 [id.]. (i) LSO; (ii) RPO; Yondani Butt.

Yondani Butt's performance of the symphony is a good one and very well played. One would have liked a greater sense of soaring (over the throbbing wind chords) at the opening, but the response of the LSO catches the colour and melancholy of the slow movement, and the Scherzo (easily the best movement) has sparkle. But it is the two charming early *Serenades* that catch the ear, seductively played by the RPO.

Symphonies Nos.4 in E flat, Op. 48; 5 in B flat, Op. 55.
(N) *** Chandos Dig. CHAN 9739 [id.]. Russian State SO, Valeri Polyansky.
(N) *** ASV Dig. CDDCA 1051 [id.]. Philh. O, Yondani Butt.

Yondani Butt continues his cycle for ASV with fine performances of the *Fourth* and *Fifth Symphonies*. The *Fourth* dates from the year of Tchaikovsky's death (1893) and is a charming and well-composed work, full of good things including a sparkling Scherzo. It is distinctly Russian in outlook and held together structurally by a theme which Glazunov uses in all three movements. The *Fifth*, written two years later, is more imposing, but not so very different really, although the first movement is more vigorous. There is another delectable Scherzo which the Philharmonia woodwind again relish. The *Andante* opens atmospherically on the horns and woodwind, but the strings soon take over, with a burst of Russian ardour. The spirited, outgoing finale, with rollicking brass, comes off buoyantly: Butt lifts the rhythm of the main theme infectiously. Throughout both works the Philharmonia playing is persuasuively warm and sympathetic, helped by the spacious, well-balanced recording.

However, the Chandos competitor has the advantage of a fine Russian orchestra who immediately establish a richly Slavic atmosphere of melancholy for the languorous opening theme of No. 4; and Polyansky is able to relax and recreate this mood at the very end of the first movement without losing concentration. The Chandos recording is glowingly warm in capturing string and woodwind timbres alike, yet the scherzos of both symphonies sparkle translucently. However, the resonance means that the finales have less bite than with the ASV recording, and while they are played with robust Russian-dance vigour, Butt is exceptionally spirited in the finale of No. 5. It is a case of swings and roundabouts, for the ASV recording is clearer, if not more lustrous.

(i) *Symphony No. 6; Raymonda* (ballet), *Op. 57a: suite;* (ii) *Triumphal march, Op. 40.*
*** ASV Dig. CDDCA 904 [id.]. (i) LSO; (ii) RPO; Yondani Butt.

Taken overall, Yondani Butt's is the preferred choice for Glazunov's *Sixth*, helped by the open sound of the ASV recording, and the fine wind and brass contributions from the LSO; the brass chorale at the end of the *Variations* is effectively sonorous. The selection from *Raymonda* concentrates on the first two Acts and offers only a brief *Entr'acte* from Act III; most of the music in fact comes from Act I, some 21 minutes out of a selection lasting just over half an hour. The playing is both graceful and lively, and the recording has plenty of amplitude and warmth.

CHAMBER MUSIC

5 Novelettes, Op. 15.
(***) Testament mono SBT1061 [id.]. Hollywood Qt – BORODIN: *String quartet No. 2;* TCHAIKOVSKY: *String quartet No. 1.* (***)

The Hollywood Quartet bring a freshness and ardour to these charming compositions that is most persuasive. The *Novelettes* last a little under half an hour, and as a result the disc is only one second short of 80 minutes long. The sleeve warns that some CD players may have difficulty in tracking it. We have not found this to be the case, but some caution may be necessary on the part of readers with older players.

String quartets Nos. 3 in G (Slavonic), Op. 26; 5 in D min., Op. 70; The Fridays, Book 2: Kuranta; Prelude and fugue in D min.
**(*) Olympia OCD 525 [id.]. Shostakovich Qt.

The appeal of the *Third Quartet* is immediate and the thematic inspiration folk-like and of the highest level. The *Fifth Quartet* (1898) opens with a noble and expressive fugue, and on hearing it one is tempted to agree with Calvocoressi that this is the finest of the seven. Very good performances, though they are not the last word in polish; but they are rather too closely balanced for complete comfort.

String quartets Nos. 6 in B flat, Op. 106; 7 in C, Op. 107.
** Olympia OCD 526 [id.]. Shostakovich Qt.

The turbulence of the 1910s and '20s seems not to have cast any shadows here; the *Fifth* and *Sixth Quartets* have all the sad charm of old Russia. The Shostakovich Quartet generally play with conviction, though their performances are by no means as polished as those of Nos. 3 and 5. The recording is rather up-front and has some roughness on climaxes, but there is no alternative version of either work.

String quintet in A, Op. 39.
*** Chandos Dig. CHAN 9878 [id.] ASMF Chamber Ens. – TCHAIKOVSKY: *Souvenir de Florence.* ***

Glazunov's *String quintet* (with second cello) is a work of characteristic warmth and lyricism. The performance is thoroughly committed and persuasive, and very well recorded too. There is no alternative version in the catalogue – but, even if there were, this would be hard to beat.

Complete piano music

Piano sonata No. 1 in B flat min., Op. 74; Grande valse de concert, Op. 41; 3 Miniatures, Op. 42; Petite valse, Op. 36; Suite on the name 'Sacha'; Valse de salon, Op. 43; Waltzes on the theme 'Sabela', Op. 23.
*** Hyperion Dig. CDA 66833 [id.]. Stephen Coombs.

Easy Sonata; 3 Etudes, Op. 31; Miniature in C; 3 Morceaux, Op. 49; Nocturne, Op. 37; 2 Pieces, Op. 22; 2 Poèmes-improvisations; Sonatina; Theme and variations, Op. 72.

*** Hyperion Dig. CDA 66844 [id.]. Stephen Coombs.

Marking the start of a new Russian series, each of these two discs contains a major work, the *Piano sonata No. 1* on the first and the *Theme and variations*, Op. 72, on the second. For the rest, you have a dazzling series of salon and genre pieces, full of the easy charm and winning tunefulness that mark Glazunov's ballet, *The Seasons*. Stephen Coombs proves a most persuasive advocate, consistently conveying sheer joy in keyboard virtuosity to a degree rare in British pianists. Coombs plays with a natural warmth and a spontaneous feeling for line which give magic to pieces which otherwise might seem trivial. Leading up to the sonata, the first disc starts with the *Suite on the name 'Sacha'*, the work of a keenly confident 18-year-old. The three *Miniatures*, Op. 42, brilliantly exploit the piano's upper registers, ending with a waltz, and that leads to a whole sequence of attractive waltzes. As well as the engaging *Variations*, Op. 72, simple in outline but elaborate and colourful in texture, the second disc offers what might be counted Glazunov's most assured piano work, the set of three *Etudes*, Op. 31.

(i) *Piano sonata No. 2 in E min., Op. 75; Barcarolle sur les touches noires; Idyll, Op. 103. 2 Impromptus, Op. 54; In modo religioso, Op. 38; Prelude and 2 Mazurkas, Op. 25; Song of the Volga boatmen, Op. 97* (arr. Siloti); (ii) *Triumphal march, Op 40.*
*** Hyperion Dig. CDA 66866 [id.]. (i) Stephen Coombs; (ii) Holst Singers, Stephen Layton.

The most substantial work here is the *Second Sonata* of 1901, which is better played than by any of its rivals we have heard. The most unusual piece is the transcription of a Wagnerian *Triumphal march*, written for the Chicago Exposition, which eventually introduces *Hail Columbus*, sung in Russian! Not all the music on this generously filled CD is of equal merit but most of it is rewarding, and the recording serves the music well. Admittedly it is slightly over-reverberant so that climaxes in the *Sonata* are opaque, but this should not stand in the way of a strong recommendation.

4 Preludes and fugues, Op. 101; Prelude and fugue in D min., Op. 62; in E min. (1926).
*** Hyperion Dig. CDA 66855 [id.]. Stephen Coombs.

The prelude-and-fugue format has attracted relatively few major twentieth-century keyboard composers, apart from Shostakovich. Glazunov's examples are rarely heard but, as Stephen Coombs shows us, their neglect is unjustified. The *D minor Prelude and fugue* is not just a powerful essay in Bachian counterpoint, but a dramatic and compelling piece. The set of four, Op. 101, are not only intellectually rewarding but they are also artistically most satisfying and inventive pieces. The *E minor* from 1926 opens dramatically and is another impressive piece. The recording is eminently satisfactory, without any excessive reverberance.

Piano sonatas Nos. 1 in B flat min., Op. 74; 2 in E min., Op. 75; Grande valse de concert in E flat, Op. 41.
**(*) Pearl SHECD 9538. Leslie Howard.

As we have observed above, the Glazunov *Sonatas* are well worth investigating, and the Pearl disc has the advantage of grouping them together in performances which are both committed and just as well recorded. Admirers of Glazunov's art not following the Hyperion series, should investigate this issue which sounds extremely impressive.

VOCAL MUSIC

Tsar Iedesyskiy (King of the Jews).
*** Chandos Dig. CHAN 9467 [id.]. Russian State Symphony Ch. & SO, Rozhdestvensky.

Glazunov's incidental music to Konstantin Romanov's *Tsar Iedesyskiy* (*King of the Jews*), is new to the catalogue and, although its invention is not always consistent in quality, the score offers considerable artistic rewards. There is an unaffected simplicity that is quite touching, and the naturalness of the musical inspiration outweighs any of its longueurs or miscalculations. Rozhdestvensky shapes each phrase with feeling and imagination, and he gets good results from his chorus and orchestra. Moreover the quality of the recorded sound is first rate in every respect, with well-balanced choral and orchestral forces and a lifelike perspective. There are informative and helpful notes by David Nice.

Glière, Reinhold (1875–1956)

The Bronze Horseman: suite; (i) *Horn concerto, Op. 91.*
** Chandos Dig. CHAN 9379 [id.]. (i) Richard Watkins; BBC PO, Sir Edward Downes.

The Bronze Horseman is not great music – nor, for that matter, is the *Horn concerto*. Richard Watkins is a fine soloist in the latter; Downes gets good rather than really distinguished playing from the BBC Philharmonic, though the recording is excellent.

(i) *Concerto for coloratura soprano, Op. 82;* (ii) *Harp concerto, Op. 74.*
*** Chandos Dig. CHAN 9094 [id.]. (i) Eileen Hulse; (ii) Rachel Masters; City of L. Sinfonia, Hickox – GINASTERA: *Harp concerto.* ***

This digital recording of Glière's lush concertos is highly competitive in both works. The recording is suitably rich and opulent, yet every detail is audibly in place. Eileen Hulse is an impressive soloist with excellent control, well-focused tone and a good sense of line, and she is excellently supported by the City of London Sinfonia and Richard Hickox. Nor need Rachel Masters fear comparison with her predecessor, Osian Ellis; so, given such excellent sound, this is all highly self-indulgent and sybaritic.

Symphony No. 2 in C min, Op. 25; Zaporozhy Cossacks, Op. 64.
**(*) Chandos Dig. CHAN 9071 [id.]. BBC PO, Downes.

Not even the advocacy of Sir Edward Downes with his magnificent Manchester orchestra can conceal the banality of some of the writing in this early Glière symphony – it cannot compare with Glière's later and grander *Symphony No. 3*. *Zaporozhy Cossacks* is less ambitious but also contains banalities. Excellent performances and outstanding recording.

Symphony No. 3 in B min. (Ilya Murometz), Op. 42.
*** Chandos Dig. CHAN 9041 [id.]. BBC PO, Sir Edward Downes.

Downes and the BBC Philharmonic in magnificent form give an urgently passionate performance of this colourful programme piece, more convincing than any rival in what can easily seem too cumbersome a work. Downes, taut and intense, relates the writing very much to the world of Glière's close contemporary, Rachmaninov. The recording, made in the concert hall of New Broadcasting House, Manchester, is one of Chandos's finest, combining clarity and sumptuousness.

Glinka, Mikhail (1805–57)

(i) *Andante cantabile and Rondo in D min.; Jota aragonesa (Spanish overture No. 1); Polka No. 1* (orch. Balakirev); *Prince Kholmsky* (incidental music): *Overture and Entr'actes to Acts II–V. Recollections of a summer night in Madrid (Spanish overture No. 2); Symphony on two Russian themes* (orch. Shebalin); *Waltz fantasia; A Life for the Tsar (Ivan Susanin): Overture and dances. Ruslan and Ludmilla:* (ii) *Overture; Dances; Tchernomor's march.*
(B) *** BMG/Melodiya Twofer 74321 53461-2 (2) [id.]. (i) USSR SO; (ii) Bolshoi Theatre O; Svetlanov.

An eminently recommendable survey of Glinka's orchestral output. Apart from the *Ruslan and Ludmilla* overture and the *Jota aragonesa*, little of Glinka's music is heard in the concert hall, and these recordings are most useful in filling a gap. The performances embrace a considerable time-span (1963–90) though the majoriy are from the 1970s and 1980s, and some have been available before on LP on HMV Melodiya. The playing of the USSR Symphony Orchestra is nothing if not expert and idiomatic; and the recordings, though variable in quality, are generally very good indeed.

Ruslan and Ludmilla: Overture.
(M) *** RCA GD 60176 [Basic 100 09026 683-2]. Chicago SO, Fritz Reiner – PROKOFIEV: *Alexander Nevsky*, etc. ***

Reiner's performance is highly infectious and the (1959) Chicago sound brings plenty of colour and warmth. Solti's famous Decca/LSO performance is currently awaiting reissue as part of a collection of Russian music, and should be well worth waiting for.

Grand sextet in E flat.
*** Hyperion CDA 66163 [id.]. Capricorn – RIMSKY-KORSAKOV: *Quintet*. ***

Glinka's *Sextet* is rather engaging, particularly when played with such aplomb as it is here. The contribution of the pianist, Julian Jacobson, is brilliantly nimble and felicitous. The balance places the piano rather backwardly, but the CD provides good detail and presence.

Trio pathétique in D min.
*** Chandos Dig. CHAN 8477 [id.]. Borodin Trio – ARENSKY: *Piano trio*. ***

Glinka's *Trio* is prefaced by a superscription: '*Je n'ai connu l'amour que par les peines qu'il cause*' ('I have known love only through the misery it causes'). It is no masterpiece – but the Borodins almost persuade one that it is. The recording is vivid and has excellent presence.

Variations on an original theme in F; Variations on the romance 'Benedetta sia la madre'; Variations on two themes from the ballet, Chao-Kang; Variations on The Nightingale (by Alabyev)*; Variations on a theme from Anna Bolena* (by Donizetti); *Variations and Rondino brillante on a theme from the opera, I Capuleti e i Montecchi* (by Bellini); *Variations on a theme from Faniska* (by Cherubini); *Variations on the Russian folk-song 'In the shallow valley'.*
(N) ** BIS Dig. CD 980 [id.]. Victor Ryabchikov.

All these variations were written when the composer was in his twenties. Most of them have been fodder for music schools and have not held the concert platform. Ryabchikov suggests in his thorough and authoritative notes, that 'the music is full of tenderness and expression, elegant simplicity and nobility'. Although he plays with evident feeling, he is handicapped by a rather forward recording. When he is playing above *forte* there is a touch of glare. The recording was made in Moscow, not by the familiar BIS team, and produced by the pianist himself.

A Farewell to St Petersburg (song-cycle); *Doubt; Elegy; The fire of longing burns in my heart; How sweet it is to be with you; I recall a wonderful moment; Mary; Say not that it grieves the heart.*
*** Conifer Dig. 75605 51264-2 [id.]. Sergei Leiferkus, Simeon Skigin.

This is the only version of *A Farewell to St Petersburg*, the collection of 12 songs published in 1840. Our own authority on Glinka and all things Russian, David Brown, speaks in his sleeve-notes of their 'instant and direct appeal' that transcends any language barrier, and he describes them as having 'a quiet magic of their own, a subtlety and distinctiveness greater than might have been suspected at first hearing'. The aristocrat of Russian baritones, Sergei Leiferkus, is on prime form here and is superbly accompanied by Simeon Skigin. Very natural recorded sound sets the seal on a most distinguished and thoroughly rewarding issue.

A Life for the Tsar (complete).
**(*) Sony Dig. S3K 46487 (3) [id.]. Martinovich, Pendachanska, Merritt, Toczyska, Sofia Nat. O Ch. & O, Tchakarov.

When this opera was first given in St Petersburg in November 1836 it marked a breakthrough in Russian music. Glinka introduced Russian themes far more than his predecessors, and the subject itself reflected the nationalist fervour behind his inspiration. There are many delightful sequences in the opera, not least the many choruses and dances, which regularly inspire the late Emil Tchakarov to spring rhythms infectiously, bringing out the peasant flavour. Against the background of a good ensemble performance the soloists are more than reliable, with Boris Martinovich singing characterfully, if not always steadily. Aleksandrina Pendachanska is bright and fresh as his daughter, only occasionally edgy in a Slavonic way, and Stefania Toczyaska sings beautifully as Vanya, singing this character's two arias delightfully. From outside the Slavonic area the American tenor Chris Merritt is well attuned, singing without strain. Though in its clear recording this gives little idea of a staged rather than a studio performance, it is more than a stop-gap for an essential work in the repertory.

Ruslan and Ludmilla (complete).
*** Ph. 446 746-2 (3) [456 248-2]. Ognovienko, Netrebko, Diadkova, Bezzubenkov, Gorchakova, Kirov Op. Ch. & O, Gergiev.
(M) **(*) RCA/Melodiya 74321 29348 (3) [id.]. Nesterenko, Rudenko, Yaroslavtsev, Sinyavskaya, Morozov, Fomina, Bolshoi Theatre, Moscow, Ch. & O, Yuri Simonov.

Gergiev in his Kirov recording, done live on stage, launches into this classic Russian opera with a hair-raisingly fast and brilliant account of the overture, and then characteristically brings out the subtlety of much of the writing, as well as the colour. The voices come over well, with Vladimir Ognovienko characterful as Ruslan, bringing out word-meaning, most impressively in his big Act II aria. Anna Netrebko is fresh and bright as Ludmilla, as well as agile, not as shrill as many Russian sopranos; but it is Galina Gorchakova as Gorislava who takes first honours, rich and firm, as is Larissa Diadkova in the travesti role of Ratmir, especially impressive in the delightful duet with Finn (Konstantin Pluzhnikov). A video recording is also available.

The Bolshoi recording on BMG/Melodiya at mid-price brings a warm and convincing account, typical of Bolshoi standards in the late 1970s, with Yevgeni Nesterenko magnificent as Ruslan, rich, firm and heroic. Another outstanding performance comes from Boris Morozov as the braggart, Farlaf, with his comic patter Rondo in Act II, not just brilliantly agile but resonant too and full of fun, reminding one of Chaliapin's famous recording. Alexei Maslennikov is most affecting in Finn's Ballad, and Nina Fomina is a rich, firm Gorislava. One snag is that Bela Rudenko as Ludmilla is shrill under pressure, and a few cuts are made in Act V; but it is still an enjoyable if uneven set.

Gluck, Christophe (1714–87)

Alceste (Vienna version 1767; complete).
(N) (B) *** Naxos Dig. 8.660066/68 (3) [id.]. Teresa Ringholz, Justin Lavender, Jonas Degerfeldt, Miriam Treichl, Lars Martinsson, Drottningholm Theatre Ch. & O, Arnold Ostmann.

When previously Ostman has recorded operas with the Drottningholm company, stars have been specially imported, but this presents the company as you would hear it in the perfectly restored 18th-century theatre. This is the first recording of the Vienna version of *Alceste*, rather simpler and more direct in manner than the far better-known French version of 1776. Here Alceste's powerful aria, 'Divinites du Styx', becomes 'Ombre, larve', less imposing, and the intimate scale of the Drottningholm presentation reflects that, with a cast of young singers remarkable for their freshness rather than for power.

Where the self-sacrificing heroine usually emerges as a formidable figure, here she is more girlish, more vulnerable as portrayed by the American, Teresa Ringholz, who is consistently pure and sweet, clear and true in every register, if a little lacking in variety. Her sweetness and purity are matched by the young Swedish soprano, Miriam Treichl, in the role of Ismene, Alceste's confidante – a most promising singer, even if it is at times confusing here to have such similar singers juxtaposed. The clear-toned British tenor, Justin Lavender, sings stylishly in the relatively small role of Admeto, husband of Alceste, with Jonas Degerfeldt, aptly lighter and more youthful as his confidant, Evandro.

After a dull start the chorus warm up well in Act II, with the period orchestra a little edgy but always alert under Ostman's direction. At Naxos price one can hardly complain that the opera is rather extravagantly laid out on three discs, when in any case that brings the advantage of one disc per act. Well-balanced sound with voices well to the fore. Full libretto, synopsis and translation are provided.

Armide (complete).
(N) *** DG Dig. 459 616-2 [id.]. Mireille Delunsch, Charles Workman, Ewa Podles, Laurent Naouri, Ch. & Musiciens du Louvre, Minkowski.

Armide, the fifth of Gluck's 'reform' operas, written for Paris in 1777, has remained unjustly neglected, and this electrifying performance under Minkowski, recorded live, makes one wonder why. In five compact Acts, it is both passionate and dramatic in telling the story of the sorceress, Armide, and her unwilling love for the knight Renaud. It leads to a sensuous love duet in Act V before Renaud finally rejects her love. Using a libretto set by Lully almost a century earlier, Gluck develops a compellingly flexible structure, with arias, duets and recitatives merging in quick succession, Minkowski's treatment could not be more dramatic, persuasively leading one on at speeds on the brisk side. The cast is strong, powerfully led by Mireille Delunsch in the title role, singing with rich firm tone, and with Charles Workman fresh and clean cut as the tenor hero, Renaud. In the brief but important role of La Haine, Ewa Podles sings with commanding intensity, and the minor roles are also well taken. The live recording gives weight and bite to the substantial instrumental band.

Der betrogene Kadi (complete).
(M) *** CPO/EMI CPO 999 552-2. Rothenberger, Donath, Gedda, Berry, Hirte, Marheineke, Bav. State Op. Ch. & O, Suitner.

Gluck wrote this light-hearted *Singspiel*, *Die betrogene Kadi* ('The cheated Cadi'), in the year before he completed his first version of *Orfeo*, providing an astonishing contrast with that masterpiece. Unlike Mozart in *Entführung*, Gluck generally avoids the exotic, preferring a gentler style. Even so, he gives the Kadi a vigorous aria which may have given Mozart the idea for some of Osmin's music. The cast is a strong one, with Helen Donath providing a sweet contrast to the ever-bright Anneliese Rothenberger, and with Walter Berry as the Kadi and Nicolai Gedda as the hero, Nuradin, characterizing well. The 1978 EMI recording still sounds full and vivid.

Le Cinesi (The Chinese women).
(M) *** HM/BMG Dig. GD 77174 [77174-2-RG]. Poulenard, Von Otter, Banditelli, De Mey, Schola Cantorum Basiliensis O, Jacobs.

Gluck's hour-long opera-serenade provides a fascinating view of the composer's lighter side and, rather like Mozart in *Entführung*, Gluck uses jangling and tinkling percussion instruments in the overture to indicate an exotic setting. Otherwise the formal attitudes in Metastasio's libretto – written some 20 years before Gluck set it – are pure eighteenth century.

Don Juan (ballet): complete.
(M) *** Erato/Warner 2292 45980-2 [id.]. E. Bar. Soloists, Gardiner.

Reissued as part of the Gardiner Collection, this has much to recommend it. The 1981 recording is full and modern. The performance too has a clean and dramatic profile.

Iphigénie en Aulide (complete).
(M) *** Erato/Warner Dig. 2292 45003-2 (2) [id.]. Van Dam, Von Otter, Dawson, Aler, Monteverdi Ch., Lyon Op. O, Gardiner.

Iphigénie en Aulide was Gluck's first piece in French and it anticipated the *Tauride* opera in its speed and directness of treatment, so different from the leisurely and expansive traditions of *opera seria*. Gardiner here reconstructs the score as presented in the first revival of 1775; the recording conveys the tensions of a live performance without the distractions of intrusive stage noise. The darkness of the piece is established at the very start, with men's voices eliminated, and a moving portrait built up of Agamemnon, here sung superbly by José van Dam. In the title-role Lynne Dawson builds up a touching portrait of the heroine. Her sweet, pure singing is well contrasted with the positive strength of Anne Sofie von Otter as Clytemnestra, and John Aler brings clear, heroic attack to the tenor role of Achille. The performance is crowned by the superb ensemble-singing of the Monteverdi Choir in the many choruses.

Iphigénie en Aulide (complete in German; arr. Wagner).
(M) **(*) RCA 74321 32236-2 (2). Moffo, Fischer-Dieskau, Schmidt, Spiess, Stewart, Augér, Bav. R Ch., Munich R. O, Eichhorn.

Wagner's arrangement used here is, by the standards of modern purism, a total travesty and the use of German instead of French only reinforces the stylistic conflict. But with an urgently dramatic performance, with a formidable list of soloists, excellent choral singing and fine playing, this is enjoyable entertainment in its own right. Maybe, as the scholars tell us, we shall come to regard Raymond Leppard's arrangements of Cavalli in the same light as this realization, with its enriched orchestration and harmony, its cuts and additions and its amended plot. But, compact as it is, Gluck/Wagner is every bit as effective as Cavalli/Leppard, and Wagnerians at least need not hesitate. Good stage atmosphere in the recording. The German libretto comes without a translation.

Iphigénie en Tauride (complete).
✪ *** Ph. Dig. 416 148-2 (2). Montague, Aler, Thomas Allen, Argenta, Massis, Monteverdi Ch., Lyon Op. O, Gardiner.

Gardiner's electrifying reading of *Iphigénie en Tauride* is a revelation. Though his Lyon orchestra does not use period instruments, its clarity and resilience and, where necessary, grace and delicacy are admirable. Diana Montague in the name-part sings with admirable bite and freshness, Thomas Allen is an outstanding Oreste, characterizing strongly but singing with classical precision. John Aler is a similarly strong and stylish singer, taking the tenor role of Pylade. The recording is bright and full.

Orfeo ed Euridice (complete).
*** Ph. Dig. 434 093-2 (2) [id.]. Ragin, McNair, Sieden, Monteverdi Ch., E. Bar. Soloists, Gardiner.
*** EMI Dig. CDS7 49834-2 (2). Hendricks, Von Otter, Fournier, Monteverdi Ch., Lyon Opera O, Gardiner.
(M) *** Erato/Warner Dig. 2292 45864-2 (2). J. Baker, Speiser, Gale, Glyndebourne Ch., LPO, Leppard.
*** Teldec/Warner Dig. 4509 98418-2 (2). Larmore, Upshaw, Hagley, San Francisco Op. Ch. & O, Runnicles.
(M) **(*) RCA GD 87896 (2) [7896-2-RG]. Verrett, Moffo, Raskin, Rome Polyphonic Ch., Virtuosi di Roma, Fasano.
(M) **(*) RCA Dig. 74321 32238-2 (2). Lipovšek, Popp, Kaufmann, Bav. R. Ch., Munich R. O, Hager.

Gardiner's newest set for Philips could not be more sharply contrasted with the earlier recording he made for EMI in 1989. Then he was persuaded at the Lyon Opéra to record the Berlioz edition, in French. But all along Gardiner has much preferred the tautness of the original, Vienna version in Italian, which here on Philips he presents with a bite and sense of drama both totally in period and deeply expressive. The element of sensuousness, not least in the beautiful singing of the counter-tenor, Derek Lee Ragin, in the title-role, complements the Elysian beauty Gardiner finds in such passages as the introduction to *Che puro ciel*. Sylvia McNair as Euridice and Cyndia Sieden as Amor complete Gardiner's outstanding solo team. One's only regret is that the set does not provide as a supplement such numbers written for Paris as *The Dance of the Blessed Spirits*.

Many will be glad to have the Berlioz edition, sung in French, which aimed at combining the best of both the Vienna and Paris versions, although once again Gardiner omits the celebratory ballet at the end of the opera. Anne Sofie von Otter is a superb Orfeo, dramatically most convincing. The masculine forthrightness of her singing matches the extra urgency of Gardiner's direction; and both Barbara Hendricks as Eurydice and Brigitte Fournier as Amour are also excellent. The chorus is Gardiner's own Monteverdi Choir, superbly clean and stylish. The recording is full and well balanced.

The Erato version of *Orfeo ed Euridice*, directly based on the Glyndebourne production in which Dame Janet Baker made her very last stage appearance in opera, was recorded in 1982. Leppard presents the score with freshness and power, indeed with toughness. Nowhere is that clearer than in the great scene leading up to the aria, *Che farò*, where Dame Janet commandingly conveys the genuine bitterness and anger of Orpheus at Eurydice's death. Elisabeth Speiser as Eurydice and Elizabeth Gale as Amor are both disappointing but, as in the theatre, the result is a complete and moving experience centring round a great performance from Dame Janet. The complete ballet-postlude is included, delightful celebration music. The recording has been enhanced in the CD transfer, bright and vivid without edginess. At mid-price this makes a clear first choice. Highlights (74 minutes) are available on Erato (0630 13805-9).

Donald Runnicles also conducts a performance based on the 1869 Berlioz edition, generally adopting speeds a degree broader than those preferred by Gardiner in his EMI set, and with a smoother style. Jennifer Larmore makes a strong and positive Orphée, brilliant in the aria which in this edition ends Act I, rich and warm in rather broad treatment of the big aria, *J'ai perdu mon Eurydice*. Next to von Otter for Gardiner she sounds very feminine, and not quite as flexible. Dawn Upshaw is a charming Eurydice, and Alison Hagley a sweet-toned L'Amour, though she is balanced very backwardly, as is the chorus at times in what is otherwise a good recording. Unlike Gardiner, but like Leppard on Erato, Runnicles includes ballet music at the end.

Clearly, if you have a mezzo as firm and sensitive as Shirley Verrett, then everything is in favour of your using the original Italian version. Fasano also uses the right-sized orchestra (of modern instruments) and adopts an appropriately classical style. Anna Moffo and Judith Raskin match Verrett in clean, strong singing, and the Rome Polyphonic Chorus is far more incisive than most Italian choirs. The recording is vivid and atmospheric but emphasizes the music's dramatic qualities rather than its tenderness. However, this makes a good alternative mid-priced recommendation.

Hager's Munich version brings a good, enjoyable, middle-of-the-road performance. Marjana Lipovšek has a beautiful, rich mezzo inclined to fruitiness, which yet in this breeches role is well able to characterize Orfeo strongly and positively. So *Che farò* is warm and direct in its expressiveness. Lucia Popp makes a delightful Euridice and Julie Kaufman, though less distinctive, is fresh and bright as Amor. The chorus, on the heavyweight side, adds to the power of the performance, which uses the 1762 Vienna version of the score, though with instrumental numbers added from the Paris version. The libretto has the full Italian text without translation.

Orfeo ed Euridice (abridged version).
(B) (***) Dutton Lab. mono CDEA 5015 [(M) id.]. Kathleen Ferrier, Ann Ayars, Zoë Vlachopoulos, Glyndebourne Festival Ch., Southern PO, Fritz Stiedry.

Recorded in 1947 after the early post-war staging of the opera at Glyndebourne, this hour-long collection of excerpts concentrates on the contribution of Kathleen Ferrier in the title-role, giving a very vivid idea of her darkly intense reading. Stiedry keeps a taut rein on the performance while letting Ferrier emerge in full expressiveness. So the climactic aria, *Che faro*, is much faster than in Ferrier's later recording in English, but no less moving in context. In their brief contributions, Ann Ayars as Euridice and Zoë Vlachopoulos as Amor sing with clean precision. No text is provided; otherwise, this is an outstanding disc. The Dutton transfers are superb, offering astonishingly vivid and immediate sound.

Orfeo ed Euridice: highlights.
(M) *** Decca 452 735-2 (from complete recording, with Marilyn Horne, Pilar Lorengar, Helen Donath, ROHCG Ch. & O, Solti).

Solti's recording of *Orfeo ed Euridice* was made in the Kingsway Hall in 1969. His conducting combines his characteristic brilliance and dramatic bite with warm sympathy for the eighteenth-century idiom. Marilyn Horne makes a formidably strong Orfeo, wonderfully secure, with fine control of tone. Pilar Lorengar sings sweetly and appealingly, but is not always quite steady, while Helen Donath is charming in the role of Amor. The 62-minute selection is well made, including Solti's dramatic accounts of the *Dance of the Furies* and the winningly gracious *Dance of the Blessed Spirits*. The recording quality is excellent. A cued synopsis is included.

Godard, Benjamin (1849–95)

Cello sonata in D min., Op. 104; 2 pieces for cello and piano, Op. 61.
*** Hyperion Dig. CDA 66888 [id.]. Lidström, Forsberg – BOELLMANN: *Cello sonata in A min.*, etc. ***

An interesting and compellingly played disc of offbeat repertoire. Benjamin Godard was a pupil of Vieuxtemps and his *D minor Sonata* is very much in the Schumann–Brahms tradition and is beautifully crafted and powerfully shaped, as are the *Aubade and Scherzo*. Mats Lidström and Bengt Forsberg play with such passion and conviction that they almost persuade you that this piece is worthy to rank alongside the Brahms sonatas. The recording is just a trifle on the close side, but it produces eminently satisfactory results. Strongly recommended.

Goedicke, Alexander (1877–1957)

Concertstück in D (for piano and orchestra), *Op. 11.*
**(*) Hyperion Dig. CDA 66877 [id.]. Stephen Coombs, BBC Scottish SO, Martyn Brabbins – GLAZUNOV: *Piano concertos Nos. 1 & 2.* **(*)

Alexander Goedicke's *Concertstück* is far from negligible, both in its melodic invention and in its musical structure. Stephen Coombs is a brilliant and sympathetic interpreter of this music and the BBC Scottish Symphony Orchestra under Martyn Brabbins give every support. The recording is too reverberant – and this perhaps inhibits a full three-star recommendation.

Goehr, Alexander (born 1932)

Metamorphosis/Dance, Op. 36; (i) *Romanza for cello and orchestra, Op. 24.*
(M) *** Unicorn Dig. UKCD 2039. (i) Moray Welsh; RLPO, Atherton.

Moray Welsh plays the *Romanza* warmly and stylishly. *Metamorphosis/Dance*, inspired by the Circe episode in the *Odyssey*, is a sequence of elaborate variations, full of strong rhythmic interest. The performance is excellent.

Goetz, Hermann (1840–76)

Francesca da Rimini: Overture; Spring overture, Op. 15; (i) *Nenie, Op. 10;* (i–ii) *Psalm 137, Op. 14.*
** CPO Dig. CPO 999 316-2 [id.]. (i) N. German R. Ch.; (ii) Stephane Stiller; N. German R. PO, Hanover, Werner Andreas Albert.

Hermann Goetz was born in the same year as Tchaikovsky. The best piece here is *Nenie*, which has a strong sense of purpose and a genuine lyrical flow. The *Francesca da Rimini overture* comes from an opera its composer left unfinished. The musical language is very much in the tradition of Mendelssohn and Spohr, but the invention is of some quality, even if a little bland. Good performances from all concerned and decently balanced, well-rounded sound.

Goldmark, Karl (1830–1915)

Violin concerto in A min., Op. 28.

❁ *** Delos Dig. DE 3156 [id.]. Nai-Yuan Hu, Seattle SO, Schwarz – BRUCH: *Violin concerto No. 2.* *** ❁

*** EMI (SIS) Dig. CDC7 47846-2 [id.]. Perlman, Pittsburgh SO, Previn – KORNGOLD: *Violin concerto.* ***

(BB) *** Naxos Dig. 8.553579 [id.]. Vera Tsu, Razumovsky Sinfonia, Yu Long – KORNGOLD: *Violin concerto.* ***

The Taiwanese soloist Nai-Yuan Hu (pronounced Nigh-Yen Who) makes an outstanding début on CD with a coupling of two underrated concertos which on his responsively lyrical bow are made to sound like undiscovered masterpieces. The Goldmark is a tuneful and warm-hearted concerto that needs just this kind of songful, inspirational approach: Hu shapes the melodies so that they ravishingly take wing and soar. Moreover Schwarz and the Seattle orchestra share a real partnership with their soloist, and provide a full, detailed backcloth in a natural concert-hall framework.

Not surprisingly, the concerto is also beautifully played by Perlman, whose effortless virtuosity and strong profile in the bravura passage-work are combined with striking lyrical poise. In the first-movement cadenza he is unsurpassed. However, the EMI balance places the violin in a forward spotlight so that orchestral detail does not always register as it should: in this respect the Delos alternative is in almost every way preferable.

Vera Tsu, born in Shanghai and then discovered by Isaac Stern and trained in America, is another outstanding soloist. Her tone is rich, bringing out to the full the ripe romanticism of the Goldmark *Concerto*. Her attack is fearless in the many bravura passages, so that the dance rhythms of the dance-finale have a rare sparkle, and her hushed playing in the central slow movement at a very broad speed movingly demonstrates her inner concentration, helped by the equally beautiful, finely varied playing of the Razumovsky Sinfonia of Bratislava. Rich, full, open sound.

Rustic Wedding Symphony, Op. 26.

(M) *** Van. 08 6151 71 [OVC 5002]. Utah SO, Abavanel (with ENESCU: *Romanian rhapsodies Nos. 1–2.* **)

(B) **(*) Decca Eclipse Dig. 448 991-2. LAPO, López-Cobos – DVORAK: *Slavonic dances Nos. 9–16.* ***

Rustic Wedding Symphony, Op. 26; Overtures: In Italy, Op. 49; In the Spring, Op. 36.

(BB) **(*) Naxos Dig. 8.550745 [id.]. Nat. SO of Ireland, Stephen Gunzenhauser.

Rustic Wedding Symphony, Op. 26; Sakuntala overture, Op. 13.

*** ASV Dig. CDDCA 791 [id.]. RPO, Yondani Butt.

Goldmark's *Rustic Wedding Symphony* opens with a distinctly rustic theme on the lower strings, which when taken up by the horns (with woodwind bird-song overhead) is as magical as any passage in the romantic symphonic repertory, not forgetting the beginning of Mahler's *First*. The hazily romantic evocation of a summer garden which forms the slow movement leads to a boisterous dance finale, with genial injections of fugato. Yondani Butt and the RPO clearly enjoy themselves. The recording has brightly lit violins, but plenty of bloom on the woodwind, and the only miscalculation of balance concerns the trombone entry in the first movement which is too blatant and too loud. Otherwise this is in every way enjoyable. The *Overture Sakuntala* opens impressively but does not quite sustain its 18 minutes. Butt presents it with persuasive vigour and lyrical feeling, and does not shirk the melodrama.

The Vanguard recording from the late 1960s sounds splendid in its new CD transfer. The Utah acoustic is expansive and the music certainly blossoms here, for the playing has a pleasing freshness and spontaneity. Abravanel's approach is direct. There is plenty of warmth and the woodwind bring a Beechamesque charm to the inner movements. *In the garden* is as deeply felt as anyone could want, and altogether, with its attractive Enescu coupling (recorded not quite so glowingly), this stands high in the list of recommendations, irrespective of price.

Gunzenhauser gives a fresh, bright-eyed account. He takes both the opening movement and the Andante (*In the garden*) appreciably faster than does Butt, and he loses something in poise and spacious eloquence in consequence. But the overall performance is spontaneous and enjoyable. It is well recorded and, although the violins sound thin, that is almost certainly not the fault of the engineers. Of the two jaunty overtures, *In Italy* is especially vivacious and sparkling.

López-Cobos directs a refreshing and attractive reading. In the first movement the generally fast tempi again detract from the charm of the piece, but the horns sound as magical as ever and there is sympathetic playing from the Los Angeles orchestra in the central movements. With a lively finale this is easy to enjoy when the digital recording is vivid but naturally balanced. Moreover, this inexpensive reissue offers a considerable Dvořák bonus.

Symphony No. 2 in E, Op. 35; In Italy overture, Op. 49; Prometheus bound, Op. 38.

*** ASV Dig. CDDCA 934 [id.]. Philh. O, Yondani Butt

Goldmark's *Second Symphony* is a highly confident piece with a strong opening movement possessing the symphonic impulse of Brahms and a flavour of Mendelssohn, an ambivalent but appealing *Andante*. After a vivaciously delicate Scherzo which is Mendelssohn undiluted, Goldmark concludes with a characteristically folksy, dance-like finale. Butt has the work's full measure.

The Lisztian *Promtheus bound* on the other hand is overlong and melodramatic, and the main allegro is routine in its working out. Yet it has some winning lyrical ideas and Butt does his very best for it. The *Italian overture* is genuinely vivacious, though not especially Italianate: it has a rather beautiful nocturnal sequence as a central episode. The ASV recording is in every way excellent.

Goldschmidt, Berthold (born 1903)

(i) *String quartets Nos. 2–3;* (ii) *Letzte Kapitel*; *Belsatzar.*

*** Largo Dig. LC 5115 [id.]. (i) Mandelring Qt; (ii) Marks; Ars-Nova Ens., Berlin, Schwarz.

Berthold Goldschmidt was hounded from Nazi Germany in 1935 and settled in London. This disc collects his *Letzte Kapitel* for speaker and an instrumental ensemble, very much in the style of Kurt Weill, and the *Second Quartet*, which has something of the fluency of Hindemith. It is an excellently fashioned piece with a rather powerful slow movement, an elegy subtitled *Folia*. The CD is completed by *Belsatzar*, an *a cappella* setting of Heine, and the *Third Quartet*, a remarkable achievement for an 86-year-old, the product of a cultured and thoughtful musical mind. The performances are dedicated, the recordings satisfactory.

OPERA

(i) *Beatrice Cenci* (opera; complete). (ii) Songs: *Clouds; Nebelweben; Ein Rosenzweig.*

*** Sony Dig. S2K 66836 (2) [id.]. Estes, Della Jones, Alexander, Kimm, Rose, Wottrich, Berlin R. Ch., German SO, Berlin, Zagrosek; (ii) Iris Vermillion, composer.

Commissioned to write an opera for the Festival of Britain in 1951, Berthold Goldschmidt responded with this richly imaginative rendering of a melodramatic play of Shelley, in which Beatrice is portrayed not as a murderess but as the victim of an evil father. Much of the most moving music involves the relationship of Beatrice and her mother, Lucia, with Della Jones strongly cast against Roberta Alexander in the title-role, singing radiantly. Her big final aria brings the most moving moment of all. Simon Estes sings well, but is not evil-sounding enough to convey the full villainy of the father. Vividly recorded and powerfully conducted by Lothar Zagrosek, the set makes generous amends for the work's long neglect. The songs, with Iris Vermillion accompanied by the nonagenarian composer, make a delightful bonus.

Goossens, Eugene (1893–1962)

Concertino for double string orchestra, Op. 47; Fantasy for nine wind instruments, Op. 36; Symphony No. 2, Op. 62.

(N) *** ABC Dig. 8.770013 [id.]. Sydney SO, Handley.

The *Second Symphony* is an important work – and something of a discovery. A substantial piece of some 40 minutes, it occupied Goossens between 1942 and 1945; its material is strong and the imaginative landscape it inhabits quite individual. In his breadth he has something of Bax (whose *Second Symphony* Goossens conducted with the BBC Symphony Orchestra in the mid 1950s), yet he is undoubtedly his own man. There is a dark, Nordic feeling about the opening and a fertility of invention in the Scherzo that recalls Prokofiev. If you are at home in Bax, Honegger, Tubin or Prokofiev, you will respond to this score. The *Concertino* is more effective for full strings than in its chamber form (see below), and the *Fantasy for wind instruments* (1924) has a touch of Stravinsky and Les Six. Expert playing from the ABC Sydney Orchestra of which Goossens was conductor in the 1950s, and well-prepared and meticulously shaped readings from Vernon Handley. Recommended with enthusiasm.

Concertino for string octet, Op. 47; Phantasy sextet, Op. 37.

(N) *** Chandos Dig. CHAN 9472 [id.]. ASMF Chamber Ens. – BRIDGE: *String sextet.* ***

The *Concertino for string octet, Op. 47*, comes from 1928 and was subsequently scored for double string orchestra (see above). It has brightness and vitality, and is expertly laid out for the instruments, as is the 1923 *Phantasy sextet, Op. 37*, commissioned by Elisabeth Sprague Coolidge. Intelligent and inventive music, well played by the Academy of St Martin-in-the-Fields and eminently well recorded by the ever enterprising Chandos.

Górecki, Henryk (born 1933)

(i) *Harpsichord concerto;* (ii) *Little Requiem for a polka (Kleines Requiem für eine Polka);* (iii) *Good night (In Memoriam Michael Vyner)* for soprano, alto flute, 3 tam-tams and piano.

*** Nonesuch/Warner Dig. 7559 79362-2 [id.]. L. Sinf.; (i) David Zinman; (ii) Ezbieta Chojnacka, cond. Markus Stenz; (iii) Dawn Upshaw, Sebastian Bell, John Constable, David Hockings.

Those listeners who have encountered the *Third Symphony* and who are looking for further Górecki to explore might well start here. The *Little Requiem* (1993) opens with a single quiet bell-stroke; a piano (John Constable) then engages in a tranquil dialogue with the violins, to be rudely interrupted by a burst of bell-ringing; the energetic, marcato *Allegro impetutoso* follows. The piece ends with a raptly sustained elegiac *Adagio*, still dominated by the quietly assertive tolling bells.The two-movement *Harpsichord concerto*, written a decade earlier, combines soloist and strings in a vibrant, jangly ménage. *Good night* is nocturnally serene. The soprano voice enters only in the third movement, with a cantilena to Shakespeare's words from *Hamlet*: 'Good night . . . and flights of angels sing thee to thy rest!' Both here and in the *Little Requiem* the very atmospheric recording brings an added dimension to the communication from performers who are obviously totally committed to the composer's cause.

Symphony No. 3 (Symphony of sorrowful songs), Op. 36.
*** Elektra Nonesuch Dig. 7559 79282-2 [id.]. Dawn Upshaw, London Sinf., David Zinman.

Symphony No. 3 (Symphony of sorrowful songs), Op. 36; 3 Pieces in the olden style.
(BB) *** Naxos Dig. 8.550822 [id.]. Zofia Kilanowicz, Polish Nat. RSO, Antoni Wit.
**(*) Koch Schwann 311041 [id.]. Stefania Woytowicz, Berlin RSO, Kamirski; or Warsaw CO, Karol Teutsch.

Scored for strings and piano with soprano solo in each of the three movements, all predominantly slow, Górecki's *Symphony No. 3* sets three laments taking the theme of motherhood. The first movement, nearly half an hour long, resolves on the central setting of a fifteenth-century text from a monastic collection. The second movement incongruously brings a switch to a sensuously beautiful idiom, with the soprano solo soaring radiantly. The third movement is the setting of a folksong with a two-chord ostinato as accompaniment, concluding in a passage of total peace. The Sinfonietta's fine performance, beautifully recorded, is crowned by the radiant singing of Dawn Upshaw.

Zofia Kilanowicz on Naxos has also obviously become immersed in the word-settings. In the work's closing section, with its hint of a gentle but remorseless tolling bell, Wit achieves a mood of simple serenity, even forgiveness. The *Three Pieces in olden style* make a fine postlude, the second with its dance figurations, the third with its fierce tremolando violins, like shafts of bright light, suddenly resolving to a very positive ending. All in all, this seems in many ways a 'best buy'.

The Koch performance is also most eloquent, with Woytowicz again completely at home in her solo role, but it is no more moving than either of the other versions and the analogue recording is not appreciably finer than that offered on Naxos.

Genesis I (Elementi per tre archi); Sonata for 2 violins, Op. 10; String quartets Nos. 1 (Already it is dusk), Op. 62; 2 (Quasi una fantasia), Op. 64.
*** Olympia OCD 375 [id.]. Silesian Qt.

This record (74 minutes) contains all Górecki's chamber music written so far. The opening of the *Double violin sonata* is harsh and spiky and, although calm soon descends, it is an uneasy calm and the restlessness soon reasserts itself. *Genesis* is full of extraordinary effects: if this is the beginning of life, the bubblings and glissandi suggest a volatile primeval melting pot. The *First Quartet* opens with an emphatic chord which diminuendos; then mysticism takes over, with emphatic chordal interruptions; later there is a nagging ostinato which produces a climax of considerable power. The *Second Quartet* begins in an atmosphere of utter desolation; the effect is of a desperate plodding journey to nowhere. The *Arioso* slow movement begins in a mood of piercing despair. The finale moves on with a remorseless, toccata-like insistence, then the slow plodding of the work's opening reappears and, gradually becoming less insistent, returns the music to infinity. The playing throughout this collection combines power and intensity. The recording is of very high quality. The composer was present and there is something special about these performances.

VOCAL MUSIC

(i) *Miserere, Op. 44; Amen, Op. 35; Euntes ibant et flebant, Op. 32;* (ii) *Wuslo moja (My Vistula, grey Vistula), Op. 46; Szeroka woda (Broad waters): choral suite of folksongs, Op. 39 (Oh, our River Narew; Oh, when in Powistle; Oh, Johnny, Johnny; She picked wild roses; Broad waters).*
*** Nonesuch/Warner 7559 79348-2 [id.]. (i) Chicago Symphony Ch. & Lyric Op. Ch., Nelson; (ii) Lyra Chamber Ch., Lucy Ding.

Górecki's powerful *Miserere* was prompted by the political upheaval in Poland in 1981. Górecki set a text of only five words: *Domine Deus noster, Miserere nobis*; although the work's span is ambitious, it is sustained by profound intensity of feeling. The combined Chicago choirs maintain the sombrely atmospheric opening *pianissimo* with impressive concentration, and the dynamic climax of the piece, when the combined choirs sing in ten parts, is very compelling. The following *Euntes ibant et flebant* (for unaccompanied chorus) is simpler, more serene. The five folksong settings are also essentially expressive (even *Oh, Johnny, Johnny* is marked *Molto lento – dolce cantabile*) and all are harmonically rich. They are beautifully sung by the smaller group. The recording, made in the Church of St Mary of the Angels in Chicago, is admirable.

Gottschalk, Louis (1829–69)

Grand fantasia triumfal for piano and orchestra.
(M) *** Decca Dig. 430 726-2. Ortiz, RPO, Atzmon – ADDINSELL: *Warsaw concerto* ***; GERSHWIN: *Rhapsody* **(*); LISZT: *Hungarian fantasia* ***; LITOLFF: *Scherzo.* ***

Gottschalk's *Grand fantasia* has naïvety, and a touch of vulgarity too, but the performers here give it an account which nicely combines flair and a certain elegance, and the result is a distinct success.

(i; ii) *Grande tarantelle for piano and orchestra;* (ii) *Symphony No. 1 (A Night in the tropics);* (iii) Music for one piano, four hands: *L'étincelle; La gallina; La jota aragonesa; Marche de nuit; Orfa; Printemps d'amour; Radieuse; Réponds-moi; Ses yeux; Souvenirs d'Andalousie; Tremolo.* (2 pianos): *The Union* (concert paraphrase on national airs).
(M) *** Van. 08.4051 71. (i) Reid Nibley; (ii) Utah SO, Abravanel; (iii) Eugene List with Cary Lewis or Joseph Werner.

With nearly 77 minutes of music this well-recorded Vanguard reissue makes an ideal introduction to Gottschalk's music. The *Grande tarantelle* has a very catchy main theme; the two-movement *Night in the tropics* uses its title of 'symphony' very loosely. The second movement is a kind of samba, rhythmically very winning. The music for piano, four hands, is played with flair and scintillating upper tessitura. The opening arrangement of *La jota aragonesa* heads an ear-tickling programme, with a touch of wit in the piece called *Tremolo*. When the participants move to two pianos for *The Union* concert paraphrase, the acoustic expands and the effect is properly grand. The orchestral recordings date from 1962, the piano pieces from 1976, and the sound is excellent throughout.

PIANO MUSIC

Piano music for four hands

Le Bananier (Chanson nègre), Op. 5; La Gallina (Danse cubaine), Op. 53; Grande Tarantelle, Op. 67; La jota aragonesa (Caprice espagnol), Op. 14; Marche de nuit, Op. 17; Ojos criollos (Danse cubaine – Caprice brillante), Op. 37; Orfa (Grande polka), Op. 71; Printemps d'amour (Mazurka-caprice de concert), Op. 40; Réponds moi (Danse cubaine), Op. 50; Radieuse (Grand valse de concert), Op. 72; La Scintilla (L'Etincelle – Mazurka sentimentale), Op. 21; Ses yeux (Célébre polka de concert), Op. 66.
**(*) Nimbus Dig. NI 5324 [id.]. Alan Marks & Nerine Barrett (piano, 4 hands).

Alan Marks and Nerine Barrett make an effervescent Gottschalk partnership, playing this repertoire to the manner born. *La jota aragonesa* shimmers with twinkling light, while the *Grande tarantelle* makes a splendid finale. The slight snag is that they are – very realistically – recorded in an empty, resonant hall.

Solo piano music

Bamboula; Le Bananier; Le Banjo; The Dying Poet; The Last hope; The Maiden's blush; Ojos criollos; Pasquinade; La Savane; Souvenir de Porto Rico; Suis-moi!; Tournament galop.
(M) *** Van. 08.4050.71 [OVC 4050]. Eugene List.

Eugene List made this repertoire very much his own in the USA in the late 1950s and early '60s, and his performances are second to none. The glittering roulades in *Le Bananier* and *Ojos criollos* are brought off with unaffected brilliance, and the plucking imitations at the close of *The Banjo* are equally successful. The pieces with sentimental titles are more appealing than their names might suggest, and the *Tournament galop* closes the recital at an infectious canter. The recording dates from 1956 but doesn't sound its age at all: it is very well balanced and realistic.

Le Banjo; Berceuse (cradle song); *The dying poet* (meditation); *Grand Scherzo; The last hope* (religious meditation); *Mazurka; Le Mancenillier* (West Indian serenade); *Pasquinade caprice; Scherzo romantique; Souvenirs d'Andalousie; Tournament galop; The Union: Concert paraphrase on national airs (The Star-spangled banner; Yankee Doodle; Hail Columbia).*
*** Nimbus Dig. NI 5014 [id.]. Alan Marks.

Alan Marks plays with unassuming panache: his *Souvenirs d'Andalousie* glitter with bravura, his felicity of touch and crisp articulation bring much sparkle to the *Grand scherzo* and *Scherzo romantique*, while he sounds like a full orchestra in the *Tournament galop*. Most importantly, he finds simplicity and charm in the delightful *Berceuse* and *Le Mancenillier*, while there is not a hint of sentimentality in *The last hope* or *The dying poet*. He is most realistically recorded in a fairly reverberant acoustic, which suits the flair of his playing.

Gould, Morton (1913–96)

Fall River legend (ballet; complete).
*** Albany Dig. TROY 035 [id.]. Brock Peters, National PO, Milton Rosenstock (with recorded conversation between Agnes de Mille and Morton Gould).

This complete recording of *Fall River legend* opens dramatically with the Speaker for the Jury reading out the Indictment at the trial, and then the ballet tells the story of Lizzie Borden in flashback. Gould's music has a good deal in common with the folksy writing in Copland's *Appalachian spring*, and it is given a splendidly atmospheric performance and recording by the New York orchestra under Rosenstock. There is also a 26-minute discussion on the creation of the ballet between Agnes de Mille and the composer.

Fall River legend (ballet): *suite. Latin-American symphonette: Tango and Guaracha.*
(M) *** RCA 09026 61505-2. O, composer – COPLAND: *Appalachian spring* etc. ***

Morton Gould's own recording of the suite from *Fall River legend* is so vivid and atmospheric that at times one almost thinks this could be Copland. The two movements from the engaging *Latin-American symphonette* are also splendidly done. With astonishingly full and vivid recording (made in the New York Manhattan Center in 1960), triumphantly remastered by John Pfeiffer, the irresistibly catchy *Guaracha* is demonstration-worthy.

Fall River legend: suite; Spirituals for string choir and orchestra.
(M) *** Mercury (IMS) 432 016-2 [id.]. Eastman-Rochester SO, Howard Hanson – BARBER: *Medea: suite.* ***

The composer's orchestral suite from the ballet is brightly played by the Eastman-Rochester Orchestra under the highly sympathetic Howard Hanson, who also gives an outstandingly vibrant account of the *Spirituals*. The 1959/60 Mercury recording has astonishing clarity, range and presence.

Spirituals for string choir and orchestra.
*** Everest EVC 9003 [id.]. LSO, Walter Susskind – COPLAND: *Appalachian spring* ***; GERSHWIN: *American in Paris.* **(*)

It is unexpected to find an English performance of this essentially American piece, the more so as it has never been bettered, not even by the composer himself. The slow movement is really moving and *A little bit of sin* is wittily pungent, while the wide-ranging recording (brightly lit in a transatlantic way) looks after the dramatic needs of *Protest* and the ambivalent exuberance of *Jubilee*. The couplings are hardly less welcome.

Gounod, Charles (1818–93)

Faust: ballet music and Waltz.
(B) **(*) Ph. Duo 438 763-2 [id.]. Rotterdam PO, David Zinman – DELIBES: *Coppélia;* CHOPIN: *Les Sylphides.* **(*)

If without quite the panache of a Beecham, David Zinman's account of the *Faust ballet music* springs readily to life: it has polish and elegance. Very good (1980) recording in a warm acoustic ensures the listener's aural pleasure, making this collection a genuine bargain.

Symphonies Nos. 1 in D; 2 in E flat.
*** ASV Dig. CDDCA 981 [id.]. O of St John's, Smith Square, John Lubbock.

Symphonies Nos. 1 in D; 2 in E flat; Faust (ballet music): suite.
(N) *** Ph. Dig. 462 125-2 [id.]. ASMF, Sir Neville Marriner.

Gounod's two symphonies – delightful, lyrical works full of sparkling invention – were written in quick succession when he was in his mid thirties, his only extended orchestral works. In No. 1 the effortless flow of first-rate ideas, both of the orchestra and of symphonic form, is very striking, and the Bizet *Symphony* immediately springs to mind, while No. 2 brings an unmistakable reminder of early Beethoven.

They make an outstanding coupling in these splendid performances from Marriner and the Academy of St Martin-in-the-Fields, which – as the Philips disc also aptly includes the *Faust* ballet music, so beloved of Sir Thomas Beecham – is now a clear leader in the field. The ASMF playing has sparkle, elegance and style, the recordings have clarity and presence.

Until now we have recommended the beautifully sprung and subtly phrased performances from John Lubbock and the Orchestra of St John's. In their lightness and transparency they too bring out the charm of the writing; Lubbock's care for detail and the refreshingly polished playing are matched by a pervading warmth, repeating the success he achieved earlier with his splendid coupling of Mendelssohn's *Scottish* and *Italian Symphonies* (now in the bargain Quicksilva series). We hope, in view of the latest competition, ASV will decide to reissue the Gounod pairing on the same label, when it would again be fully competitive.

Michel Plasson's mid-price coupling with the Orchestre du Capitole de Toulouse (on EMI CDM7 63949-2) remains eminently satisfactory. But the best is the enemy of the good, and both in terms of artistry and sound quality, it is no match for the Marriner and Lubbock discs.

Petite symphonie in B flat (for 9 wind instruments).
(M) *** Chandos CHAN 6543 [id.]. Athena Ens. – IBERT: *3 Pièces brèves;* POULENC: *Sextet.* ***

An astonishingly fresh and youthful work, the *Petite symphonie* in fact has impeccable craftsmanship and is witty and civilized. It makes ideal listening at the end of the day, and its charm is irresistible in a performance as full of *joie de vivre* as that provided by the Athena group, who are particularly light-hearted in the finale.

String quartet Nos. 1 in D (Le petit quatuor); 2 in A; 3 in F.

(N) *** Auvidis/Valois Dig. V 4798 [id.]. Daniel Qt.

In his last years, having finally abandoned opera, Gounod turned to the string quartet, yet – as Saint-Saëns found on visiting him – he was secretive about the results. He did allow the first of these three finely crafted quartets to be published, but it was quickly forgotten, while the other two were not discovered at all until 1993. They are really quite a find, and provide (though in a very different way) almost as much delight as the early symphonies. There are Mendelssohnian echoes in all three works, not least in the scherzos, but this is more than just charming music, with Beethoven among the composer's models, most strikingly in slow movements (though there is a whiff of Franck in the *D major*). The slow movement of the *A major* is quite captivating but then so are most of the movements. Outstanding performances from the Daniel Quartet and truthful recording.

Mélodies and songs: *L'absent; The arrow and the song; Au rossignol; Ave Maria; Boléro; Ma belle amie est morte; La Biondina* (song-cycle); *Ce que je suis sans toi; Chanson de printemps; Clos ta paupière; Envoi de fleurs; The fountain mingles with the river; If thou art sleeping, maiden; Ilala; A lay of the early spring; Loin du pays; Maid of Athens; Mignon; My true love hath my heart; Oh happy home! o blessed flower!; Où voulez-vous aller?; La Pâquerette; Prière; Rêverie; Sérénade; Le soir; Le temps des roses; Trust her not!; Venise; The worker.*

*** Hyperion Dig. CDA 66801/2 [id.]. Felicity Lott, Ann Murray, Anthony Rolfe Johnson, Graham Johnson.

Graham Johnson here devises an enchanting programme of 41 songs presenting the full span of Gounod's achievement not just in French *mélodie* (on the first of the two discs) but also in songs Gounod wrote during his extended stay in England. The soloists here are at their very finest. So on the first disc, after charming performances of the opening items from Felicity Lott, Ann Murray enters magically, totally transforming the hackneyed lines of *Ave Maria*, before tackling the most joyous of Gounod songs, the barcarolle-like *Serenade*. Rolfe Johnson is comparably perceptive in *Biondina*, bringing out the Neapolitan-song overtones, as well as in six of the English settings. As in the Schubert series, Johnson's notes are a model of scholarship, both informed and fascinating.

Messe solennelle de Saint Cécile.

*** EMI Dig. CDC7 47094-2 [id.]. Hendricks, Dale, Lafont, Ch. and Nouvel O Philharmonique of R. France, Prêtre.

Gounod's *Messe solennelle*, with its blatant march setting of the *Credo* and sugar-sweet choral writing, may not be for sensitive souls, but Prêtre here directs an almost ideal performance, vividly recorded, with glowing singing from the choir as well as the three soloists.

Faust (complete).

✿ *** Teldec/Warner Dig. 4509 90872-2 (3) [id.]. Hadley, Gasdia, Ramey, Mentzer, Agache, Fassbaender, Welsh Nat. Op. Ch. & O, Rizzi.

*** EMI (SIS) Dig. CDS5 56224-2 [CDCC 56224]. Leech, Studer, Van Dam, Hampson, Ch. & O of Capitole de Toulouse, Plasson.

(M) **(*) EMI (SIS) CMS7 69983-2 (3) [Ang. CDMC 69983]. De los Angeles, Gedda, Blanc, Christoff, Paris Nat. Op. Ch. and O, Cluytens.

(M) (***) EMI (SIS) mono CMS5 65256-2 (3). De los Angeles, Gedda, Christoff, Borthayre, Angelici, Paris Opéra Ch. & O, Cluytens.

Rizzi, with an outstanding cast and vividly clear recording, makes the whole score seem totally fresh and new. Jerry Hadley as Faust has lyrical freshness rather than heroic power, brought out in his headily beautiful performance of *Salut! demeure* and, like Rizzi's conducting, his singing has more light and shade in it than that of rivals. The tenderness as well as the bright agility of Cecilia Gasdia's singing as Marguerite brings comparable variety of expression, with the *Roi de Thulé* song deliberately drained of colour to contrast with the brilliance of the *Jewel song* which follows. Her performance culminates in an angelic contribution to the final duet, with Rizzi's slow speed encouraging refinement, leading up to a shattering moment of judgement and a fine apotheosis. Alexander Agache as Valentin may be less characterful than Hampson on the EMI set, but his voice is caught more richly; but it is the commandingly demonic performance of Samuel Ramey as Mephistopheles that sets the seal on the whole set, far more sinister than José van Dam on EMI. Like the EMI set, the Teldec offers a valuable appendix, not just the full ballet music but numbers cut from the definitive score – a drinking song for Faust and a charming aria for Siebel. EMI's supplementary items, four, all different, are more generous, but musically less interesting.

On EMI, Plasson comes near to providing another recommendable *Faust*, even if José van Dam's gloriously dark, finely focused bass-baritone does not have the heft of a full-blooded bass voice such as is associated with the role of Mephistopheles.

Cheryl Studer conveys the girlishness of Marguerite, using the widest range of dynamic and colour. If Richard Leech's voice might in principle seem too lightweight for the role of Faust, the lyrical flow and absence of strain make his singing consistently enjoyable. As Valentin, Thomas Hampson is strongly cast, with his firm, heroic baritone. The sound has a good sense of presence, set in a pleasantly reverberant acoustic which does not obscure necessary detail. In addition to supplementary numbers, the appendix offers the complete ballet music.

In the reissued Cluytens set, the seductiveness of de los Angeles's singing is a dream and it is a pity that the recording hardens the natural timbre slightly. Christoff is magnificently Mephistophelian. Gedda, though showing some signs of strain, sings intelligently, and among the other soloists Ernest Blanc has a pleasing, firm voice, which he uses to make Valentin into a sympathetic character. Cluytens's approach is competent but somewhat workaday. The set has been attractively repackaged and the libretto has strikingly clear print, to make a good mid-priced choice for this popular opera.

Not to be confused with the stereo remake of this opera with the same three principals (and conductor), this mono set of 1953 offers an advantage in the extra freshness of Victoria de los Angeles as Marguerite, sparkling and girlish, with Gedda also in fresher voice. Christoff is more uninhibited here, which makes his French even less idiomatic, but the result is thrilling; Jean Borthayre as Valentin and Martha Angelici as Siebel sing beautifully. The mono sound, less dry than others from this source, captures the voices well, and Cluytens proves a persuasive interpreter.

Faust (complete in English).
(N) (M) *** Chandos Dig. CHAN 3014 (3) [id.]. Faust (Paul Charles Clarke), Marguerite (Mary Plazas), Mephistopheles (Alistair Miles), Valentin (Garry Magee) Siebel (Diana Montague), Sarah Walker. Geoffrey Mitchell Ch., Philh. O, David Parry.

Faust, in a good English translation by Christopher Cowell, works brilliantly. The dramatic intensity is consistently heightened by David Parry's lively conducting, with the music paced to bring out the full impact of the big climaxes, and with freshness and sparkle given to such familiar numbers as the *Soldier's chorus*. Not often has the beauty and refinement of Gounod's orchestration been so vividly caught on disc, thanks both to the fine playing of the Philharmonia and to the rich, weighty Chandos recording. The chorus too is electrifying, and the cast of principals is first-rate. Paul Charles Clarke sings strongly in the title role (if not always sweetly), well experienced from appearing in the Welsh National Opera production. Alastair Miles also sang with WNO, outstanding in every way as Mephistopheles, dark, firm and incisive, if not always sinister. Mary Plazas brings out the girlish innocence in Marguerite, sweet and pure, making light of the vocal challenges, above all giving joy to the *Jewel song*. With singers as characterful as Diana Montague and Sarah Walker in smaller roles, this is the finest issue yet in the excellent Opera in English series promoted by the Peter Moores Foundation. The third disc includes the complete ballet music as a supplement.

Faust (abridged version).
(B) (**(*)) Naxos mono 8.110016/7 [id.]. Jepson, Crooks, Pinza, Warren, Olheim, NY Met. Op. Ch. & O, Pelletier.

Naxos offers a performance broadcast from the Boston Opera House in April 1940. Richard Crooks's ringing tenor sounds more Italianate than French, but he makes an ardent Faust, and Ezio Pinza gives a vividly dynamic and characterful portrait of Mephistopheles, singing superbly and offering what must be the fastest account of the *Calf of gold* aria on disc. Leonard Warren even in 1940 did not sound youthful enough for Valentin, with vibrato already obtrusive, and though Helen Jepson as Marguerite is a little shrill at times under pressure, it is a winning performance. Wilfred Pelletier proves an inspired conductor. Pacing the music very well, he draws excellent ensemble from the whole company, even if the radio recording has the orchestra presented rather dimly, well behind the singers. Applause and stage noises tend to be obtrusive, with the performance preceded and punctuated by an announcer summarizing the plot.

Faust: highlights.
(M) *** Teldec/Warner Dig. 4509 97959-2 (from above complete recording, with Hadley, Gasdia, Ramey; cond. Rizzi).
(M) *** EMI CD-EMX 2215 (from above stereo complete set, with de los Angeles, Gedda; cond. Cluytens).

The Teldec CD makes an obvious first choice for highlights from this ever-tuneful opera. The 76-minute selection is well made to include both the finale and the ballet music. No translations are offered but there is a cued synopsis.

In the EMI (75-minute) set of excerpts the singing gives much pleasure, particularly that of de los Angeles and Christoff, and the choral contribution is spirited. Excellent value and an ideal way of sampling a performance which has many virtues.

Faust (abridged version sung in English with ballet music; introduced by Sir Thomas Beecham).
(M) *** Dutton mono 2CDAX 2001 (2) [id.] Nash, Licette, Easton, Williams, Vane, Brunskill, Carr, BBC Ch. & SO, LPO, Sir Thomas Beecham.

Beecham's 1929 recording, superbly transferred on the Dutton label, gives a vivid and refreshing idea of British opera performance in the 1920s. The old Chorley translation is used, stilted and creaking but memorable – 'What rubbishy wine!' says Mephistopheles. Voices are firm and cleanly projected, with the bright-toned Miriam Licette as Marguerite delivering a splendid trill at the start of the *Jewel song*. Heddle Nash sings with heady tone as Faust, Harold Williams is a youthfully fresh Valentine and the distinctive flicker in Robert Easton's bass never gets in the way of clean focus in the role of Mephistopheles. Beecham himself is inspired, pointing rhythms and phrases infectiously, though, curiously, four of the 32 sides of the original 78s were conducted by Clarence Raybould. A supplement on the second CD includes a brief spoken introduction by Beecham, as well as the *Nubian dance* and *Adagio* from the ballet music – otherwise omitted, like the *Walpurgisnacht* scene.

Roméo et Juliette (complete).

(N) *** EMI Dig. CDS5 56123-2 [CDCC 56123] (2). Roberto Alagna, Angela Gheorghiu, Daniel Galvez Vallejo, José Van Dam, Simon Keenlyside, Capitole de Toulouse Ch. & O, Michel Plasson.

(N) **(*) RCA Dig. 09026 68440-2 (2) [id.]. Placido Domingo, Ruth Ann Swenson, Paul Charles Clarke, Kurt Ollmann, Alastair Miles, Bav. R Ch., Munich R O, Slatkin.

(B) (**(*)) Decca Double mono 443 539-2 (2) [id.]. Jobin, Micheau, Mollet, Rialland, Rehfuss, Opéra Nat. Ch. & O, Erede.

With Gheorghiu and Alagna inspired as the lovers, with Plasson masterly in his timing for dramatic and musical effect, totally idiomatic, the EMI Toulouse set offers the finest performance on disc yet, in almost every way. Gheorghiu does not just sing sweetly without strain, the subtlety of her expression and her ability to rise to the demands of tragedy set her apart, and Alagna – who made such an impact in this role at Covent Garden early in his career – is youthfully ardent and unstrained. The rest of the cast is generally excellent too, with José van Dam as Frère Laurent and Simon Keenlyside as Mercutio both outstanding, though Marie-Ange Todorovitch, bright and agile as Stephano, is rather shrill. Given absolutely complete with the Act IV ballet music – not a dramatic gain – the set takes three discs instead of two, but is well worth it. Warm, atmospheric sound.

Leonard Slatkin directs a strong account of Gounod's Shakespearean opera, lacking a little in Gallic point but generally well cast. Domingo may seem rather old for the role of Roméo, but he brings to it all of his characteristic finesse. Ruth Ann Swenson sings with warm, full tone as Juliette, but the waltz song lacks sparkle, and elsewhere too she sounds too mature. Alastair Miles is a very good Frère Laurent, and Susan Graham is charming as Stephano, but otherwise the cast does not match that in the EMI set, its one advantage being that it is offered on a pair of CDs. Full, well-focused recording.

It is an interesting comment that in 1953 Paris could offer a far finer team of singers than latterly, with the tenor Pierre Mollet, for example, light and airy as Mercutio, not least in the *Queen Mab aria*, and Charles Cambon a fine Capulet. The only non-French singer, Heinz Rehfuss, projects with the clearest focus as Frère Laurent, while the roles of the two lovers are both warmly characterful. Janine Micheau is tenderly charming as a vulnerably girlish Juliette and, as Roméo, Raoul Jobin sings stylishly and with little of the pinched tone that too often has afflicted French tenors. The transfer is more than full-bodied enough to compensate for the slightly edgy top.

Gouvy, Louis Théodore (1819–98)

Aubade, Op. 77/2; Ghiribizzi, Op. 83; 6 Morceaux, Op. 59; Scherzo, P77/1; Sonatas: in D min., Op. 36; in C min., Op. 49; in F, Op. 51.

✿ *** Sony Dig. SK 53110 [id.]. Yaara Tal, Andreas Groethuysen.

Louis Théodore Gouvy was born near Saarbrücken and was equally at home with French and German cultures. In the notes, these artists speak of falling in love with this music at first sight, and this is how the playing sounds: beautifully shaped without being in the slightest bit beautified, every shading of colour and dynamic scrupulously observed without the slightest exaggeration. As piano duet playing, it is absolutely outstanding; so, too, is the recording.

Grainger, Percy (1882–1961)

Blithe bells; Colonial song; English dance; Duke of Marlborough's fanfare; Fisher's boarding house; Green bushes; Harvest hymn; In a nutshell (suite); Shepherd's hey; There were three friends; Walking tune (symphonic wind band version); *We were dreamers.*

*** Chandos Dig. CHAN 9493 [id.]. BBC PO, Richard Hickox.

This first disc in Chandos's projected series covering Grainger's complete works could not be more enticing. Hickox is masterly, with rhythms always resilient, both in bringing out the freshness of well-known numbers like *Shepherd's hey* and in presenting the originality and charm of such little-known numbers as *Walking tune*. The BBC Philharmonic is in superb form, warmly and atmospherically recorded. By far the longest item is the suite, *In a nutshell*, which includes pieces like the *Arrival platform humlet*, well known on their own, and which has as its core a powerful and elaborate piece, *Pastoral*, which with its disturbing undertow belies its title.

Blithe bells (Free ramble on a theme by Bach: Sheep may safely graze): Country gardens; Green bushes (Passacaglia); Handel in the Strand; Mock morris; Molly on the shore; My Robin is to the greenwood gone; Shepherd's hey; Spoon River; Walking tune; Youthful rapture.
(M) *** Chandos CHAN 6542 [id.]. Bournemouth Sinf., Montgomery.

For those wanting only a single Grainger orchestral collection, this could be first choice. Among the expressive pieces, the arrangement of *My Robin is to the greenwood gone* is highly attractive, but the cello solo in *Youthful rapture* is perhaps less effective. Favourites such as *Country gardens*, *Shepherd's hey*, *Molly on the shore* and *Handel in the Strand* all sound as fresh as new paint. The 1978 recording, made in Christchurch Priory, has retained all its ambient character in its CD transfer.

Children's march; Colonial song; Country gardens; Handel in the Strand; The immovable 'Do'; Irish tune from County Derry; Mock Morris; Molly on the shore; My Robin is to the greenwood gone; Shepherd's hey; Spoon River.
(M) ** Mercury 434 330-2 [id.]. Eastman-Rochester Pops O, Fennell – COATES: *Three Elizabeths suite.* **(*)

Lively and sympathetic performances from Fennell, and good playing. But the 1959 Mercury sound here is more dated than most CDs from this source: the acoustics of the Eastman Theatre in Rochester are too dry for Grainger's more expansive string writing in the *Colonial song* and the *Irish tune from County Derry*. The pithily rhythmic pieces like *Mock Morris* come off best as the sound is always clear and clean.

Country gardens; In a nutshell (suite); Lincolnshire posy; Train music (ed. Rathburn); *The Warriors*.
(N) *** EMI Dig. CDC5 56412-2 [id.]. CBSO, Rattle (with DEBUSSY (orch. Grainger): *Pagodes*; RAVEL (orch. Grainger): *La vallée des cloches*).

'*Grainger in a Nutshell*' is the title of this EMI issue, a collection that in Rattle's dazzling, exhilaratingly wild performances aptly sums up this idiosyncratic composer's genius, echoing the title of the four-movement suite with which the disc opens. That charming piece starts with the *Arrival platform Humlet* and ends with the equally characterful *Gum-suckers' march*. The *Lincolnshire posy* is a similar compilation of folk-based pieces brilliantly scored, and the disc ends with Grainger's most ambitious work, his thrillingly varied 'Music to an imaginary ballet', *The Warriors*, for huge orchestra. There are also idiosyncratic arrangements of Debussy and Ravel piano pieces and a spectacular version of Grainger's own *Country gardens* specially written for Stokowski. Brilliant sound to match.

Irish tune from County Derry; Lincolnshire Posy (suite); *Molly on the shore; Shepherd's hey.*
(M) *** ASV CDWHL 2067. L. Wind O, Wick – MILHAUD; POULENC: *Suite française.* ***

First-class playing and vivid recording, with the additional attraction of delightful couplings, make this very highly recommendable.

The Warriors (music for an imaginary ballet).
*** DG Dig. 445 860-2 [id.]. Philh. O, Gardiner – HOLST: *The Planets.* ***

Colourful and vigorous, *The Warriors* is described as 'an imaginary ballet for orchestra and three pianos'. With richly scored echoes of *Rosenkavalier* and *Petrushka* brought improbably together at the start, the piece throbs with energy, at one point – in a gentler interlude – involving an offstage orchestra in Ivesian superimpositions. The result is hugely enjoyable in such a fine performance as Gardiner's. It makes an unexpected and valuable coupling for his brilliant account of the favourite Holst work. Dazzling sound.

(i) *Ye banks and braes o' Bonnie Doon.* (ii) *Colonial song; Country gardens.* (i) *The Gum-suckers' march; Faeroe Island dance; Hill song No. 2.* (ii) *Irish tune from County Derry.* (i) *The lads of Wamphray march.* (ii) *Lincolnshire posy.* (i) *The merry King; Molly on the shore.* (ii) *Shepherd's Hey.*
(N) *** Chandos Dig. CHAN 9549 (id.). Royal Northern College of Music Wind O, with (i) Clark Rundell, (ii) Timothy Reynish.

Even more than most issues in the Chandos Grainger series, this is a fun disc, with the brilliant young players of the Royal Northern College relishing the jaunty rhythms. Many of the pieces are well known in Grainger's alternative arrangements, but this version of Grainger's most popular piece, *Country gardens*, is not just an arrangement of the piano version, but as he explained himself 'a new piece in every way'. The *Faeroe Island dance* in this late band version of 1954 has a pivoting ostinato for horns that echoes the opening of Vaughan Williams's *Fifth Symphony*, before launching into the dance proper with echoes of *The Rite of spring*.

PIANO MUSIC

Colonial song; Country gardens; Handel in the Strand; Harvest hymn; The hunter in his career; In a nutshell (suite): Gum-suckers' march; In Dahomey (Cakewalk smasher); Irish tune from County Derry; Jutish medley; A march-jig; The merry king; Mock morris; Molly on the shore; Ramble on the last love-duet from Richard's

Strauss's *Der Rosenkavalier; A Reel; Scotch strathspey and reel; Shepherd's hey; Spoon river; Walking tune.*
**(*) Hyperion Dig. CDA 66884 [id]. Marc-André Hamelin.

Hamelin's articulation is phenomenally crisp, and the recording is excellent, but he misses the charm of some of these pieces, when he is often too metrical, pushing ahead a shade too fast in such pieces as *Country gardens* or *Shepherd's hey*, so that rhythms fail to spring infectiously as they should. Yet the choice of items is generous and apt.

Country gardens; In a nutshell (suite); *Gay but wistful; The Gum-suckers' march; Jutish medley; March-jog (Maguire's kick); Molly on the shore; One more day my John; Ramble on the last love-duet in Strauss's 'Der Rosenkavalier'; Sheep and goat walkin' to the pasture; Shepherd's hey; Spoon river; Sussex mummers' Christmas carol; Turkey in the straw; The Warriors.* STANFORD: *Irish dances* arr. GRAINGER: *Leprechaun's dance; A reel.*
*** Nimbus NI 8809 [id]. Percy Grainger (from Duo-Art piano rolls).

We have always been admirers of the Duo-Art player-piano recording system, and here is another remarkably convincing example of modern stereo reproduction from such a source. Grainger's personality leaps out from between the speakers: it is just as if the composer were there in person, yet the original rolls were cut between 1915 and 1929! It is good to have such a winningly vigorous *Country gardens* and such a characterful *Shepherd's hey*, while *Sheep and goat walkin' to the pasture* has rhythmical character of the kind that makes one smile. *Gay but wistful* is neither – nonchalant, rather – but endearing. The lyrical numbers like the touching *Sussex mummers' Christmas carol, One more day my John* and the lilting Zanzibar boat song have a winningly relaxed flair, and Grainger makes his arrangement of the Richard Strauss love-duet from *Der Rosenkavalier* sound intimately luscious and deliciously idiomatic. The recording is first class.

Complete: *'Dished up for piano', Volumes 1–5.*
(B) *** Nimbus Dig. NI 1767 (5) [id.]. Martin Jones.

'Dished up for piano', Volume 1: Andante con moto; Bridal lullaby; Children's march; Colonial song; English waltz; Handel in the Strand; Harvest hymn; The immovable 'Do'; In a Nutshell (suite) *(Arrival platform humlet; Gay but wistful; The Gum-suckers' march; Pastoral); In Dahomey; Mock morris; Peace; Sailor's song; Saxon twi-play; To a Nordic princess; Walking tune.*
*** Nimbus Dig. NI 5220 [id.]. Martin Jones.

'Dished up for piano', Volume 2: Arrangements: BACH: *Blithe bells; Fugue in A min.* BRAHMS: *Cradle song.* Chinese TRAD.: *Beautiful fresh flower.* DOWLAND: *Now, o now, I needs must part.* ELGAR: *Enigma variations: Nimrod.* Stephen FOSTER: *Lullaby; The rag-time girl.* GERSHWIN: *Love walked in; The man I love.* RACHMANINOV: *Piano concerto No. 2: Finale* (abridged). R. STRAUSS: *Der Rosenkavalier: Ramble on the last love-duet.* TCHAIKOVSKY: *Piano concerto No. 1* (opening); *Paraphrase on the Flower waltz.*
**(*) Nimbus Dig. NI 5232 [id.]. Martin Jones.

'Dished up for piano', Volume 3: Folksong arrangements: *The brisk young sailor; Bristol Town; Country gardens; Died for love; Hard-hearted Barb'ra Helen; The hunter in his career; Irish tune from County Derry; Jutish medley; Knight and shepherd's daughter; Lisbon (Dublin Bay); The merry king; Mo Ninghean Dhu; Molly on the shore; My Robin is to the greenwood gone; One more day my John* (2 versions, easy and complex); *Near Woodstock Town; The nightingale and the two sisters; O gin I were where Gowrie rins; Rimmer and goldcastle; The rival brothers; Scotch Strathspey; Shepherd's hey; Spoon River; Stalt vesselil; Sussex mummers' Christmas carol; The widow's party; Will ye gang to the Hielands, Lizzie Lindsay?.*
*** Nimbus Dig. NI 5244 [id.]. Martin Jones.

Volume 4: Arrangements: ANON.: *Angelus ad Virginem.* BACH: *Toccata and fugue in D min.* DELIUS: *Air and dance.* FAURE: *Après un rêve; Nell.* Stephen FOSTER: *Lullaby* (Easy: Grainger). GRIEG: *Piano concerto* (first movement). HANDEL: *Water music: Hornpipe.* SCHUMANN: *Piano concerto* (first movement). STANFORD: *Four Irish dances.* GRAINGER: *At twilight; The Bigelow march; Eastern intermezzo; Tiger-tiger; Klavierstücke in A min., B flat, D & E.*
*** Nimbus Dig. NI 5255 [id.]. Martin Jones.

Volume 5: Original works for up to six hands: BRAHMS: *Paganini variation No. 12.* BYRD: *The Carman's whistle.* (i) *Children's march;* DELIUS: *A Dance rhapsody.* (i–ii) *English dance.* (i) GERSHWIN: *Girl crazy: Embraceable you.* (i–ii) *Green bushes; Spoon River. Train music; Up-country song.* (i–ii) *The Warriors* (music to an imaginary ballet); *Ye banks and braes o' bonnie Doon; Zanzibar boat-song.*
*** Nimbus Dig. NI 5286 [id.]. Martin Jones; with (i) Richard McMahon; (ii) Philip Martin.

Martin Jones's splendid Nimbus survey of Grainger's piano music is available on five separate, full-priced CDs, but they now come together in a slip-case at bargain price. The playing is refreshingly alive and spontaneous. Volume 1 is particularly attractive, and that is the place to start, for there is not a dull item here. There is plenty of dash in the folksong arrangements, and charm too, and they display a much greater range than one might have expected. The transcriptions are fascinating. Martin Jones is especially good in the freely composed pastiche on Bach's *Sheep may safely graze* (*Blithe bells*). But he plays *Nimrod* and the *Der Rosenkavalier* excerpts too slowly; such a degree of languor might come off with the orchestra, but on the piano the effect is enervating. The fourth and fifth volumes are the most enjoyable of all. Grainger's arrangements in Volume 4 are often very free, but Jones plays them with such spontaneity that they are freshly enjoyable in their own right. The opening *Four Irish dances* of Stanford are attractively spiced, yet Grainger is careful to treat Fauré with discretion. His 'concert version' of Bach's most famous *Toccata and fugue* in based on the arrangements by Tausig and (mainly) Busoni, with whom Grainger briefly studied in 1903: Jones excitingly gives it the full bravura treatment. But there are gentle, original pieces too, and the *Eastern intermezzo* features peals of bells. *Tiger-tiger* is simplicity itself, as is *At Twilight*, but this piece then ends with a bluesy 'added sixth' chord. The programme is rounded off with three early *Klavierstücke* (1897–8), eclectic but already full of personality.

Volume 5 offers the original works for up to six hands, and the opening *Children's march*, in which Jones is joined on one piano by Richard McMahon, could not be more rumbustiously attactive. In *Ye banks and braes* (prolix but effective) and the lilting *Zanzibar boat-song* three players share a single piano. But in the intricate *Passacagalia on green bushes* (a *tour de force* which steadily increases in pace and excitement), Philip Martin joins the other two to make up the six hands, on three pianos, and this is the complex scoring of both the 'rambling' *English dance*, which is very diverting, and the closing *Warriors* ballet (which is complete). Martin Jones also has four solo pieces, including the comparatively elaborate and very pianistic *Byrd variations*. All the playing here is splendidly secure technically, and the performances not only have panache but readily convey the enjoyment of the participants. The pianos are recorded reverberantly in the Nimbus manner – but it rather suits this repertoire, and the image is absolutely truthful.

VOCAL MUSIC

Anchor song (setting of Rudyard Kipling); *Thou gracious power* (setting of Oliver Wendell Holmes); Arrangements of folk songs: *Afterword; Air from County Derry; Brigg Fair; Early one morning; Handel in the Strand; I'm seventeen come Sunday; The lonely desert-man sees the tents of the Happy Tribes; Marching time; Molly on the shore; 2 Sea chanties; Shallow Brown; Six dukes went a-fishing; There was a pig went out to dig; Ye banks and braes o' bonnie Doon.*

*** Chandos Dig. CHAN 9499 [id.]. Mark Padmore, Stephen Varcoe, Joyful Company of Singers, City of L. Sinf., Hickox; Penelope Thwaites.

In this third infectiously enjoyable disc in Chandos's Grainger series, Richard Hickox is particularly successful in capturing the exuberance of the composer's inspiration, his joy in sound, his delight in taking you by surprise. In the darkly intense *Shallow Brown*, Hickox has less prominent janglings than Gardiner (see below) in the accompaniment, but he has a clear advantage in opting for an excellent baritone soloist (Stephen Varcoe) instead of a rather uncertain soprano, with an equally fine choral ensemble. Hickox's version of the *County Derry* (the 'Londonderry air') is quite different from Gardiner's, for he has chosen a more extended, much more elaborate setting. *Ye banks and braes* is another item given in a version previously unrecorded, with a whistled descant. Among the pieces completely new to disc are the *Marching tune* (a Lincolnshire folk-tune made to sound like a lusty Salvation Army chorus with brass accompaniment), and *Early one morning* (with a minor-key cello solo as introduction, before dawn comes up with the tune in the major, when baritone and chorus enter). Also most striking is the brief, keenly original choral piece, *The lonely desert-man sees the tents of the Happy Tribes*, here given a dedicated performance, with the tenor intoning a theme from Grainger's orchestral piece, *The Warriors*, and the distant chorus chattering a chant borrowed from his *Tribute to Foster*.

(i) *Bell piece. Blithe bells*; (ii) *Children's march; Hill songs I & II; The immovable Do. Irish tune from County Derry; Marching song of democracy; The Power of Rome and the Christian heart.*

(N) *** Chandos Dig. CHAN 9630 [id.]. Royal Northern College Music Wind O, Timothy Reynish or Clark Rundell; with (i) James Gilchrist; (ii) vocal group from the band.

Where in their first collection (above) the splendid players of the Royal Northern College of Music Wind Orchestra clearly so enjoy Grainger's rhythmic buoyancy, here they equally relish his feeling for wind colour (as in the engaging *Hill songs*) and rich sonorities, as in the powerful and remarkable tone poem, *The Power of Rome and the Christian heart*, and equally so in this characteristically imaginative arrangement of the *Londonderry air* for band and pipe organ. It opens sombrely with an expansive bass line, then lightens just a little before the hugely powerful climax, superbly graduated here. *Bell piece* (a 'ramble' on Dowland's melancholy air, *Now, O now I needs must part*), begins with a tenor solo with piano, before the wind players gently steal in. In the *Children's march*, members of the band are invited twice to sing a vocalise when they are not playing. Altogether a fascinating and greatly enjoyable programme, strikingly well directed by Timothy Reynish and Clark Rundell.

Folksong arrangements: *The Bride's tragedy* (for chorus & orchestra); *Brigg Fair* (for tenor & chorus); *Danny Deever* (for baritone, chorus & orchestra); *Father and daughter* (*A Faeroe Island dancing ballad;* for 5 solo narrators, double chorus, & 3 instrumental groups); *I'm seventeen come Sunday* (for chorus, brass & percussion); *Irish tune from County Derry* (*Londonderry air;* for wordless chorus); *The Lost lady found; Love verses from The Song of Solomon* (for tenor & chamber orchestra); *The merry wedding* (*Bridal dances;* for 9 soloists, chorus, brass, percussion, strings & organ); *My dark-haired maiden* (*Mi nighean dhu;* for mixed voices); *Scotch strathspey and reel – inlaid with several Irish and Scotch tunes and a sea shanty* (orchestral version); *Shallow Brown* (for solo voice or unison chorus, with an orchestra of 13 or more instruments); *The Three ravens* (for baritone solo, mixed chorus & 5 clarinets); *Tribute to Foster* (for vocal quintet, male chorus & instrumental ensemble).
❁ *** Ph. Dig. 446 657-2 [id.]. Soloists, Monteverdi Ch., English Country Gardiner O, Gardiner.

It would be hard to imagine a more exhilarating disc of Grainger's music than this collection of 'songs and dancing ballads'. The variety is astonishing even among the folksong settings, which often use melodies transcribed from original sources by Grainger himself. Gardiner singles out the hypnotically measured sea-shanty, *Shallow Brown*, as the most 'searingly original' of Grainger's works and the most haunting. The performance here backs that up, with furious tremolandos from guitars and banjos, which Grainger called 'wogglings'. The richest, most exotic piece is the setting of *Love verses* from *The Song of Solomon*, while the longest and most elaborate items bring astonishingly original effects for both voices and orchestra, the richly evocative *Tribute to Stephen Foster* and the setting of a mock Scottish ballad by Swinburne, *The Bride's tragedy*. Even if the choir's attempts at various dialects, from Mummerset onwards, may not be to everyone's taste, the virtuosity of the singing is breathtaking. The bitter element in some of the numbers provides a clue to the inspiration which fired Grainger, as in the grim setting of Kipling's *Danny Deever*, with its refrain, 'Oh they're hanging Danny Deever in the morning'. Superb sound, though (because of the complexity of textures) words are often inaudible. Full text and really outstanding notes – a model of what documentation should be with a full-priced CD.

Folksong arrangements: *Songs of the North (4 Scottish settings); 6 settings of Rudyard Kipling; The Secret of the sea; Sailor's chanty*. Traditional folksong settings: *Bold William Taylor; British Waterside; Creepin' Jane; Hard hearted Barb'ra; The lost lady found; The pretty maid milking her cow; Shallow Brown; Six Dukes went afishin'; Willow willow.*
(N) **(*) Chandos Dig. CHAN 9503 [id.]. Stephen Varcoe, Penelope Thwaites.

Stephen Varcoe is obviously at home in these folksongs (Grainger himself had collected many of them on his early countryside explorations). Most of them are set fairly simply, as in the lovely opening *Willow willow*, or the bold, jiggy narrative of *The lost lady found*, while *The pretty maid milking her cow* is very touching. These are essentially concert performances and Varcoe does not have the artless quality in the Scottish songs which Kenneth McKellar finds for his wonderful recital of Kennedy Fraser's Hebridean songs (Australian Decca 844 840-2). However Varcoe's vernacular account of Kipling's *Soldier soldier come from the wars* is especially successful and *Hard hearted Barb'ra* is delightfully done, as is Grainger's own setting of Longfellow's *The secret of the sea*. *Shallow Brown*, which ends the programme, is very dramatic indeed, although some might feel Varcoe goes over the top here, helped by Penelope Thwaites's strong accompaniment; indeed she makes an admirable contribution throughout this well-recorded recital.

Granados, Enrique (1867–1916)

Piano trio; Violin sonata. Intermezzo (from *Goyescas); Madrigal; Rondo aragonesa* (from *Danzas españolas No. 6*) all for cello and piano.
(N) **(*) CPO Dig. CPO 999 365-2 [id.]. Salzburg Piano Trio.

Granados's *Piano trio* is an early work and uncharacteristic. But it is still very enjoyable, with a memorable secondary theme in the first movement, a sparkling *Scherzetto* and a charming *Andante con molto expressione*. It is played here with considerable warmth and the cyclic, somewhat Franckian, *Violin sonata* is volatile and paasionate. The two transcriptions are perhaps a little over-accented, but the *Madrigal*, written for Casals, makes a pleasing encore. Good if rather resonant recording.

12 Danzas españolas; Escenas poeticas, Book II (arr. for guitar and orchestra).
(BB) *** Naxos Dig. 8.855037 [id.]. Norbert Kraft, Razumovsky Sinf., Peter Breiner.

These are attractive transcriptions for guitar and orchestra of Granados's piano pieces. The Canadian guitarist Norbert Kraft is a brilliant and effective player. If you want to try Granados in this orchestral garb rather than in its original keyboard form, you can invest in this with confidence.

Goyescas: Intermezzo.
(M) *** RCA 09026 62586-2 [id.]. Chicago SO, Reiner – ALBENIZ: *Iberia* etc.; FALLA: *El amor brujo* etc. ***

A totally memorable performance of the *Goyescas intermezzo* from Reiner, seductively sultry and vibrant by turns. The 1958 Chicago recording sounds amazingly rich and vivid.

GUITAR MUSIC

Cuentos para la juventud, Op. 1: Dedicatoria. Danzas españolas Nos. 4 & 5, Op. 37/4–5; Tonadillas al estilo antiguo: La maja de Goya. Valses poéticos.
❀ (BB) *** RCA Navigator Dig. 74321 17903-2. Julian Bream (guitar) – ALBENIZ: *Collection;* RODRIGO: *3 Piezas españolas.* *** ❀

Like the Albéniz items with which these Granados pieces are coupled, these performances show Julian Bream at his most inspirational. The illusion of the guitar being in the room is especially electrifying in the middle section of the famous *Spanish dance No. 5*, when Bream achieves the most subtle *pianissimo*. Heard against the background silence, the effect is quite magical. But all the playing here is wonderfully spontaneous. This is one of the most impressive guitar recitals ever recorded, and for this super-bargain reissue RCA have generously added the *Tres Piezas españolas* of Rodrigo, recorded a year later and no less distinguished.

12 Danzas españolas (trans. for guitar).
(B) *** [EMI Red Line Dig. CDR5 69850]. Manuel Barrueco – FALLA: *Spanish popular songs.* ***

As in the Falla coupling, this is masterly playing, warmly coloured, subtly nuanced, and naturally idiomatic in its rhythms, so that one might think that these piano pieces had been orginally intended for the guitar.

PIANO MUSIC

Allegro de concierto; Escenas románticas; Goyescas (complete); *Goyescas: Intermezzo. Goyesca (El pele); Oriental, canción, variada, intermedio y final Rapsodia aragonesa; Valse de concert; Reverie* (Improvisation; transcribed from a Duo Art piano roll).
(N) (BB) *** Nimbus Dig. NI 5595/8 (4) [id.]. Martin Jones – ALBENIZ: *Iberia* etc. ***

As in the coupled collection of the major piano works of Albéniz, Martin Jones's instinctive sympathy with the Spanish idiom brings a remarkable freshness of approach to music which until now seems to have been the sole province on record of Alicia de Larrocha. His imaginative spontaneity throughout shows very personal insights; the playing, with its wide range of colour and dynamic, sparkles and glimmers and is full of poetry. He is at his most beguiling in the flowing contrasts of the *Oriental, canción, variada, intermedio y final*, and the delightful *Escenas Romanticas*. Granados marks the *Epilogue* of the latter suite '*con exaltacion poética*', and Jones's playing here is exquisitely touching. Yet in the comparatively flimsy *Valse de concert* he has a deliciously light touch. The familiar *Goyescas* are vividly and warmly characterized, and the most famous number *Quejas, o La maja y el ruiseñor* is just as memorable here as in the hands of de Larrocha. The Nimbus recording is pleasingly real and natural and this set is highly recommendable.

Allegro de concierto; 12 Danzas españolas; El Pelele.
(N) (B) *** Decca Double Analogue/Dig. 433 923-2 (2) [id.]. Alicia de Larrocha – ALBENIZ: *Cantos de España; Suite española.* ***

Escenas románticas; Goyescas; 6 Piezas sobre cantos populares españoles.
(N) (B) *** Decca Double Analogue/Dig. 433 920-2 (2) [id.]. Alicia de Larrocha – M. ALBENIZ: *Sonata;* SOLER: *Sonatas.* ***

These two Double Deccas are reissued as part of Decca's 'Música española' series. Alicia de Larrocha has an aristocratic poise to which it is difficult not to respond, and she plays with great flair and temperament in the *Danzas españolas. El Pelele* is an appendix to the Goyescas collection and is brilliantly played as is the *Allegro de concierto*. The subtle, expressively ambitious *Escenas románticas* again show the amazingly wide range of Granados's piano music. They were recorded digitally as were the *6 Piezas sobre cantos populares*. However many collectors may opt for the alternative coupling of Goyescas with Albéniz's Iberia (see below).

12 Danzas españolas; Goyescas.
(M) *** Ph. (IMS) mono 442 751-2 (2). Eduardo del Pueyo – FALLA: *Nights in the gardens of Spain.* ***

Eduardo del Pueyo, born in Aragon, made these recordings in 1956 (although the ear would hardly guess, so natural is the mono piano recording). His playing of the colourful *Spanish dances* has much flair and poetic delicacy – sample *No. 2 in C minor*, so beautifully articulated – and the magical *pianissimo* at the centre of No. 5 makes one wonder if Julian Bream listened to Del Pueyo before making his equally memorable account of this famous piece. But it is in the *Goyescas* that Del Pueyo's evocation so immediately captures the Spanish atmosphere and especially in the haunting *Quejas o la maja y el ruiseñor*. The Falla coupling is perhaps even more remarkable.

Danzas españolas: Valenciana; Danza triste. Goyescas; El pelele.
(M) (***) EMI mono CDC7 54836-2. (i)
Composer – FALLA: *Harpsichord concerto* etc.; MOMPOU: *Piano pieces;* NIN: *Cantos populares españolas.* (***)

Granados was a formidable pianist and it was a pity that he did not live long enough to make electric recordings. The two *Danzas españolas* and *El pelele* from the *Goyescas* were recorded in Barcelona around 1912 but the engineers have done a marvellous job in restoring them, thoughthey have not been able to remove all the surface noise in *El pelele* and the sound remains somewhat watery but gives a good idea of what an impressive and sensitive player Granados must have been.

12 Danzas españolas; Valses poéticos.
(N) *** RCA Dig. 09026 68184-2 [id.]. Alicia de Larrocha.

Alicia de Larrocha has already recorded the *Danzas españolas* definitively for Decca. Yet her newest version is every bit as perceptive, and her Spanish temperament remains naturally attuned to this repertoire. The spontaneity of feeling is there too, and the *Valses poéticos* are a delightful bonus. The RCA recording is very natural, fully coloured and with fine sonority. However the Decca set offers a great deal more music for the same outlay.

Goyescas (complete).
❁ (B) *** Decca Double 448 191-2 (2) [id.]. Alicia de Larrocha – ALBENIZ: *Iberia* etc. ***

Goyescas (complete); *Escenas románticas; 6 Piezas sobre cantos populares españoles; Valses poéticos.*
(M) *** EMI (IMS) CMS7 64524-2 (2). Alicia de Larrocha.

Alicia de Larrocha brings special insights and sympathy to the *Goyescas* (given top-drawer Decca sound in 1977); her playing has the crisp articulation and rhythmic vitality that these pieces call for, while she is hauntingly evocative in *Quejas o la maja y el ruiseñor.* The overall impression could hardly be more idiomatic in flavour nor more realistic as a recording. This Double Decca coupling with Albéniz's *Iberia* is very distinguished.

Alicia de Larrocha's EMI set of *Goyescas* derives from the Spanish Hispavox catalogue and was made in 1963, a decade before her first Decca set. The performance is more impulsive, at times more intensely expressive, if less subtle in feeling than the later version, and the recording, if not as fine as the Decca, is eminently realistic. The closing *Zapateado* of the *Cantos populares españoles* has a fire and sparkle characteristic of her playing at this stage of her career.

Goyescas (complete); *El pelele.*
(N) **(*) Chandos Dig. CHAN 9412 [id.]. Eric Parkin.

Eric Parkin is obviously comfortable in the balmy Spanish climate and his performance of *Quejas ó la maja y el Ruiseñor* is as seductive as any. His approach to the gentler music is thoughtfully intimate, yet the brilliantly played *El pelele* brings plenty of extrovert sparkle. However in the two more extended pieces of *Goyescas*, *Los requiebros* ('Flatteries') and, especially *El amore y la muerte*, Alicia de Larrocha's combination of impulsiveness with ruminative evocation is that bit more temperamentally spontaneous. The Chandos recording cannot be faulted, but this is not a first choice.

Graun, Karl Heinrich (1704–1759)

Cleopatra e Cesare (opera): 'Great arias'.
(M) *** HM Suite Dig. HMT 7901602 [id.]. Janet Williams, Iris Vermillion, Lynne Dawson, Robert Gambill, RIAS Chamber Ch., Concerto Köln, René Jacobs.

Taken from a complete three-disc set, recorded in Berlin in 1995, this generous, 77-minute selection from *Cleopatra e Cesare*, very well performed, gives a most welcome insight into the work of the Kapellmeister of Frederick the Great of Prussia. Graun may not match in imagination such contemporaries of his in Berlin as C. P. E. Bach, but this collection of overture and ten arias plus two ensembles is consistently refreshing. In this selection, fast arias predominate – no doubt a wise choice – with all the principals singing most stylishly, with clean, agile attack, not least Janet Williams and Iris Vermillion in the twin title-roles, as well as Lynne Dawson, singing most beautifully as Cornelia, widow of Pompey. Janet Williams is sweetly affecting in her big Act III aria, and Iris Vermillion with her firm, strong mezzo makes a most characterful Caesar. Under René Jacobs, a sensitive director, there is no weak link in the rest of the cast either, and recorded sound is nicely balanced to convey an apt scale for this music.

Montezuma: highlights.
(M) *** Decca (IMS) 448 977-2 (2). Elms, Sutherland, M. Sinclair, Ward, Woodland, Harwood, Amb. S., LPO, Bonynge – BONONCINI: *Griselda.* ***

Montezuma is based on the conquest of Mexico as portrayed in a play by Voltaire and it was the Emperor, Frederick the Great, who provided the very professional libretto for this work. One serious shortcoming of the full work is the wordiness of the recitatives between numbers (presumably Graun jibbed at cutting any of the royal text) but here the selection, while giving the flavour of recitatives, omits its longueurs. Besides Sutherland who, in the role of Princess Eupaforice, has a stunning aria to sing, Monica Sinclair in the breeches role of the Conquistador, Cortes, is especially impressive. Good singing from the others, too. Richard Bonynge conducts briskly, with a real sense of style, and this tuneful piece is every bit as attractive as the Bononcini opera with which it is coupled. The recording, too, is excellent. A full translation is provided.

Gray, Steve (born 1947)

Guitar concerto (for guitar and small orchestra).
❁ *** Sony Dig. SK 68337 [id.]. John Williams, LSO, Paul Daniel – HARVEY: *Concerto antico*. *** ❁

The kernel of Steve Gray's *Guitar concerto* (1987), written for its performer here, John Williams, is the long, expressively atmospheric slow movement, which reaches a bold expansive climax. The effect is haunting, but the jocular finale also brings loudly vociferous, even vulgar, orchestral outbursts – reflecting the composer's jazz-orientated background – and these probably come off better at a concert than on disc. However, the work ends with music of the utmost delicacy. The performance here is surely definitive and the recording first class.

Grechaninov, Alexander
(1864–1956)

(i) *Cello concerto, Op. 8. Symphony No. 4, Op. 102.* (ii) *Missa festiva, Op. 154.*
(N) *** Chandos Dig. CHAN 9559 [id.]. Russian State SO, Valeri Polyansky with (i) Alexander Ivashkin. (ii) Russian State Symphonic Cappella, with Ludmila Golub (organ).

A contemporary of Glazunov and a fellow exile of Rachmaninov, Grechaninov was immensely prolific and lived into his early nineties. The *Cello concerto* is an early work, rather pale and conventional, but the *Fourth Symphony*, which bears the high opus number of 102, was composed when he had left Russia and was living in St. Jean-de-Luz in France, close to the Spanish border. It is intensely Russian and its idiom more reminiscent of the 1880s than the 1920s. It is no masterpiece but if you feel at home in the world of Glière and Glazunov, it is worth investigating. Decent performances.

Symphony No. 1 in B min., Op. 6; (i) *Snowflakes, Op. 47; Missa Sancti Spiritus, Op. 169.*
*** Chandos Dig. CHAN 9397 [id.] (i) Russian State Symphony Cappella; Russian State SO, Valery Polyansky.

As its opus number indicates, the *First Symphony* is a student work, and it is not particularly individual, and the debt to Borodin is striking. Even so, it is well-schooled music and, like so much Russian music of the period, its craftsmanship is not in question. *Snowflakes* is a middle-period work, written before Grechaninov moved to America after the revolution; and it has charm. The *Missa Sancti Spiritus* comes from the other end of Grechaninov's long career, when he was living in America. Good performances and excellent recording.

Symphony No. 3, Op. 100; (i) *Cantata, Kvalite Boga (Praise the Lord), Op. 65.*
(N) *** Chandos Dig. CHAN 9698 [id.]. (i) Ludmila Kuznetsova, Russian State Symphonic Cappella: Russian State SO, Valeri Polyanski.

The *Third Symphony* comes from 1923, before Grechaninov left the Soviet Union to settle temporarily in France. It is said to be the composer's own favourite among his five essays in the genre. It has some of the pastoral charm of Glazunov's *Seventh* though Grechaninov's scoring is not as thick. While the ideas fall short of melodic distinction, they are sunny and genial, and the theme and variations that comprise the third movement have a delightful fairy-tale atmosphere. The cantata *Kvalite Boga* ('Praise the Lord') is earlier (1915) and if the ideas in themselves are not strong, the overall effect of the piece is. It is endearing and quite touching. The performances are very good, as is the recording. A very enjoyable disc.

Gregorian chant

'Gregorian chant': Responsories; Hymns; Antiphons; Gospel tone: Vos estis sal terrae; Laudes seu Acclamationes; Gradual: Flores apparuerunt; Alleluia: Justus germinabit; Communions; Antiphon: Montes Gilboe; Ave verum corpus; Antiphonal Psalmody; Marian antiphons.
❁ (M) *** Decca Penguin Classics 460 641-2. L. Carmelite Priory Ch., John McCarthy.

Mass Propers for Good Friday and Easter.
(M) *** DG 447 299-2. Abteikirche Münsterschwarzach, Pater Godehard Joppich.
(BB) **(*) Naxos Dig. 8.550951. Nova Schola Gregoriana, Alberto Turco.

Mass Propers for the Church Year.
(BB) *** Naxos Dig. 8.550711. Nova Schola Gregoriana, Alberto Turco.

'Gregorian chant according to the Aquitaine tradition': Mass for St John the Baptist; Mass for the Nativity of Jesus Christ.

❁ (B) *** HM Musique d'Abord HMA 190 3031 [id.]. Schola Hungarica, László Dobszay or Janka Szendrei.

'Christmas Eve' (Gregorian chant and simple polyphony from the Middle Ages): *Noel settings; Alleluia and sequence; Antiphons; Chants; Graduals; Hymns; Responses and Tropes.*

(B) *** HM Musique d'Abord Dig. HMA 190 3037 [id.]. Schola Hungarica, László Dobszay & Janka Szendrei.

The liturgy of the Catholic Church has the Mass as its central focus. The Ordinary of the Mass – those elements that are unchanging through the Church year – have been set by countless composers and include the *Kyrie* ('Lord have mercy'), the *Gloria*, *Credo* and *Sanctus* ('Holy, holy, holy') and the *Agnus Dei* ('Lamb of God, who takes away the sins of the world, have mercy on us and grant us peace'). The Mass Propers are chants which change with the seasons of the year or the occasion of the celebration; they consist of Introit, Gradual, Alleluia, Tract, Offertory and Communion. These are amplified by Sequences (accretions to the liturgy) and Tropes (additions which amplify and heighten the meaning of the biblical text in prose or poetry). The changes brought about by the reforming Council of Trent in the sixteenth century removed many of these additions, but they are at the heart of medieval Church music.

To evaluate Gregorian Chant in a volume of this kind is hazardous and essentially subjective. However, for the general collector, there is one collection that stands out from all the others. Planned by the late Alec Robertson, who also provided the fascinating detailed notes describing the music's ecclesiastical and spiritual background, the beautifully sung and excellently recorded anthology now reissued on Penguin Classics as '*Gregoran chant*' is the finest possible introduction to plainsong. Extra variety of tone is provided by the use of female voices as well as male. Edgar Fleet acts as cantor and John McCarthy directs the singing with dedication and authority, using a wide dynamic range and sometimes crescendos and diminuendos to simulate a processional effect. The recording, made in Brompton Little Oratory, London, in January 1961 is absolutely natural. The accompanying essay is by Richard Mabey.

DG's Archiv label offers a number of seasonal discs, such as the Gregorian chant for Good Friday and Easter from the Abteikirche Münsterschwarzach, led by Pater Godehard Joppich and recorded in 1981–2, while an inexpensive Naxos disc (with full texts provided, though no translations) by the Nova Schola Gregoriana, directed by the Italian scholar, Alberto Turco, covers this same area very effectively, and this choir is recorded in the Parish Church of Quatrelle, Mantua, which provides a suitably atmospheric setting.

However, this fine choral group are heard to even better effect in an excellently chosen 75-minute compilation of chants taken from different Sundays in the Church year. The singing has a firm profile and is well recorded, not seeking to create a purely atmospheric effect. It is a pity that texts and translations are not provided, but the back-up notes are very helpful.

The Chant of the Aquitaine tradition is quite different from anything else previously discussed, not least because it moves forward at a much faster pace, but also because the performances here use a choir which includes not only men but also both boy trebles and women's voices. While the men's voices remain dark-timbred and sonorous when singing alone, the soprano line is sweet, and the trebles are frequently plangent. The performances by the Schola Hungarica have remarkable feeling and rich, clean textures. The result is totally refreshing, and the choir is beautifully recorded within an ideal ambience: the Parish Church of Sainte Famille, Zugliget, Budapest.

Those who have enjoyed the Schola Hungarica's recording of chant according to the Aquitaine tradition will surely want to move on to their equally stimulating collection of chant and polyphony centring on Christmas, drawing on both English and Hungarian sources. Men's and women's voices are again used to create a rich tapestry, and the opening *Noel* polyphonic settings, first for two and then three voices, are memorable. There is, of course, soaring monody, and another fine example of an early *Alleluja* and sequence (*Dominus dixit/Grates nunc*). Tempi are kept moving onwards so that the music never drags, and the recording is full and expansive. This is much more enjoyable than many more famous recordings of such repertoire.

'Liturgia defuntorum': Gregorian chant for the dead (from the Order of Burial and for All Souls' Day).

(BB) **(*) Naxos Dig. 8.553192 [id.]. Aurora Surgit, Alessio Randon.

To use a group of female voices in this repertoire (but with a male cantor) may not be completely authentic but the soaring monody gains a special character from the use of female trebles, and the added element of contrast in the responsories is also attractive. By no means all this music is solemn or dark in feeling: the closing group of chants, the *Libera me*, and especially the soaring *In paradisum – Chorus angelorum*, followed by the *Ego sum Resurrectio*, are intended to give the Christian soul an eloquent send-off. Fine singing and atmospheric yet clear recording.

Grétry, André-Ernest-Modeste
(1741–1813)

Zémire et Azor: Air de ballet.
❁ (B) *** Dutton Lab. mono CDEA 5017 [(M) id.]. LPO, Sir Thomas Beecham (with Concert: *'Beecham favourites'* *** ❁).

The orchestral suite which Beecham fashioned from music from Grétry's opera produced this famous lollipop which *The Record Guide* (of Edward Sackville West and Desmond Shawe-Taylor) described as 'one of the most captivating morsels in the gramophone repertory'. It is exquisitely played here, especially the immensely delicate closing *pianissimo* reprise, where the Dutton transfer is wonderfully refined. This Beecham anthology, which includes also his justly renowned account of Chabrier's *España*, is an essential purchase, for every conceivable reason.

Grieg, Edvard (1843–1907)

At the cradle, Op. 68/5; Country dance; 2 Elegiac melodies, Op. 34; Holberg suite, Op. 40; 2 Melodies, Op. 53.
*** Virgin/EMI Dig. VC5 45224-2. Norwegian CO, Iona Brown – NIELSEN: *At the bier of a young artist*, etc. ***

The Norwegian Chamber Orchestra are an excellent group and they collect all of Grieg's music for strings, together with Nielsen's first opus, the *Little Suite* for strings, and his elegiac threnody, *Andante lamentoso* (*At the bier of a young artist*). Very alert and responsive playing, though some may feel that some accents in the opening movement of the *Suite from Holberg's time* are a bit too marked. But this is hardly worth mentioning in a programme that offers such lovely music-making of great feeling and sensitivity. The recording, made in the glorious acoustic of Eidsvoll Church in Norway, is in the demonstration bracket.

Piano concerto in A min. (original 1868/72 version); *Larvikspolka* (1858); *23 Small pieces* (1859).
*** BIS Dig. CD 585 [id.]. Love Derwinger, Norrköping SO, Hirokami.

All his life Grieg tinkered with his orchestration of the *Piano concerto* and in the first version many of the familiar orchestral landmarks are absent. This CD offers us a fascinating glimpse of how the concerto must have sounded to its contemporaries. Love Derwinger is the intelligent and accomplished soloist with the Norrköping orchestra, and he proves a sensitive guide in the collection of juvenilia that completes the disc. The *Larvikspolka*, written when Grieg was 15, is probably the very earliest of his piano pieces to survive, and the *Nine Children's Pieces* included in the set of *23 Small pieces* were written during his first months at the Leipzig conservatory. They are all very slight in substance, but they fill out the picture of the young composer and the world in which he grew up. The concerto is well balanced and Love Derwinger's solo pieces are well recorded too.

Historic recordings:

Disc 1: (i) *Piano concerto in A min., Op. 16. Album leaf, Op. 28/4; Ballade in G min., Op. 24; Lyric pieces: Op. 12/4, 5; Op. 38/1, 2, 5; Op. 43/1, 4; Op. 47/6; Op. 54/1, 3; Op. 68/5.*
(*(*)) RCA mono 09026 61883-2 [id.]. Rubinstein, (i) with Phd. O, Ormandy.

Disc 2: (i) *String quartet in G min., Op. 27;* (ii) *Violin sonata No. 3 in C min., Op. 45;* (iii) *Album leaf, Op. 28/2;* (iv) *The last spring.*
(***) RCA mono 09026 61826-2. (i) Budapest Qt; (ii) Kreisler, Rachmaninov; (iii) Elman; (iv) Boston SO, Koussevitzky.

Disc 3: Songs: *And I shall have a true love; At the brook; Bilberry slopes; A Dream* (3 versions); *Eros; Good morning; Greeting; I love thee* (5 versions); *In the boat; The mother sings; The Norse people; To Norway; A swan* (3 versions); *With a primrose; With a water lily* (2 versions); *Peer Gynt: Solveig's lullaby; Solveig's song.*
(**(*)) RCA mono 09026 61827-2. Björling; Crooks; Farrar; Flagstad; Frijsh; Galli-Curci; Kline; Krogh; Marsh; Melchior; Nilsson; Schumann-Heink; Traubel.
(**) (M) RCA mono 09026 61879-2 (3) [id.]: Discs 1–3 complete.

The three-CD RCA set has the great advantage of being available singly. The first disc couples Rubinstein's 1942 recording of the *Piano concerto* with the Philadelphia Orchestra under Ormandy with the 1953 recordings he made in Hollywood of the *G minor Ballade* and some of the *Lyric pieces*. This account of the *Concerto* has brilliance and sensitivity but is a little wanting in spontaneity. The 78 surface-noise, while not disturbing, is probably more discernible than some collectors would like, and the end of the second side of the 78-r.p.m. set used for this transfer is excessively busy. Nor are the solo pieces distinguished by the poetry and freshness one might expect. The *Lyric pieces* do not begin to compare with Gilels, and both they and the *Ballade*, arguably Grieg's most deeply felt piano work, are recorded in a shallow and claustrophobic acoustic environment.

The second CD brings the famous 1928 Kreisler–Rachmaninov set of the Op. 45 *C minor Sonata*, already available in RCA's ten-CD Rachmaninov retrospective. The superb (1937) Budapest version of the *G minor String quartet* is a masterly performance, with splendid grip but at the same time great lyrical warmth and freshness. The eloquence of the Boston Symphony Orchestra's strings in the days of Koussevitzky was legendary and their seamless phrasing and glorious tone shine vibrantly through the years.

With such celebrated singers as Björling, Farrar, Flagstad, Galli-Curci and Melchior represented on the generously filled last disc, RCA's song compilation is self-recommending. One might regret the absence of Flagstad's earliest *Haugtussa*, particularly when there are several duplications, but no doubt it will appear in subsequent reissues. Given the quality and interest of the singing, this CD will no doubt be eagerly sought by collectors. The transfers are acceptable, though not in any way superior to the specialist issues one encounters of this repertoire on the Danacord label.

Piano concerto in A min., Op. 16.

*** Sony Dig. SK 44899 [id.]. Perahia, Bav. RSO, Sir Colin Davis – SCHUMANN: *Concerto.* ***

(B) *** Decca 433 628-2. Curzon, LSO, Fjeldstad – FRANCK: *Symphonic variations* *** ✿; SCHUMANN: *Concerto.* **(*)

*** EMI Dig. CDC7 54746-2. Lars Vogt, CBSO, Rattle – SCHUMANN: *Concerto.* ***

(B) **(*) [EMI Red Line Dig. CDR5 69859]. Cécile Ousset, LSO, Marriner – SCHUMANN: *Piano concerto.* **(*)

(M) **(*) Decca Legends 466 383-2 [id.]. Radu Lupu, LSO, Previn – SCHUMANN: *Concerto.* **(*)

(***) EMI mono CDH7 63497-2 [id.]. Lipatti, Philh. O, Galliera (with CHOPIN: *Piano concerto No. 1.* (**))

(M) (**(*)) EMI mono CDM5 66597-2 [id.]. Walter Gieseking, Philh. O, Karajan – FRANCK: *Symphonic variations;* SCHUMANN: *Piano concerto.* (**(*))

(N) * Chandos Dig. CHAN 9699 [id.]. Amalie Malling, Danish Nat. RSO, Michael Schønwandt – KUHLAU: *Piano concerto.* **

(i) *Piano concerto in A min. 6 Lyric pieces, Op. 65.*

*** Virgin/EMI (SIS) Dig. VC7 59613-2. Leif Ove Andsnes, (i) Bergen PO, Dmitri Kitaenko – LISZT: *Piano concerto No. 2.* ***

(i) *Piano concerto in A min. Lyric pieces: Arietta; Elves' dance; Folk melody, Op. 12/1, 4 & 5; Butterfly; Little bird; To spring, Op. 43/1, 4 & 6; Notturno, Op. 54/4; Gade, Op. 57/2; Sylph; French serenade, Op. 62/1 & 3; Salon, Op. 65/4; Summer evening, Op. 71/2.*

✿ (B) *** Tring Dig. TRPO 24 [id.]. Ronan O'Hora, (i) with RPO, James Judd.

(i) *Piano concerto in A min.;* (ii) *Peer Gynt: suites Nos. 1 and 2; Prelude; Dance of the Mountain King's Daughter.*

(M) *** Decca 448 599-2 [id.]. (i) Clifford Curzon, LPO; (ii) LSO; Fjeldstad.

(i) *Piano concerto in A min.;* (ii) *Piano sonata in E min., Op. 7.*

(M) *** Ph. 446 192-2. (i) Kovacevich, BBC SO, Sir Colin Davis; (ii) Zoltan Kocsis – SCHUMANN: *Concerto.* ***

Whether in the clarity of virtuoso fingerwork or the shading of half-tone, Kovacevich is among the most illuminating of the many great pianists who have recorded the Grieg *Concerto*. He plays with bravura and refinement, the spontaneity of the music-making bringing a sparkle throughout, to balance the underlying poetry. The 1972 recording has been freshened most successfully and, for the mid-priced reissue, Philips have added a characterfully impulsive performance by Zoltán Kocsis of the *Piano sonata*, recorded digitally at the beginning of the 1980s. The recording is bright and immediate and suits his style. With its new addition as a supplement to the Schumann coupling, this reissue has a playing time of 78 minutes.

Perahia revels in the bravura as well as bringing out the lyrical beauty in radiantly poetic playing. He is commanding and authoritative when required, with the blend of spontaneity, poetic feeling and virtuoso display this music calls for. He is given sympathetic support by Sir Colin Davis and the fine Bavarian Radio Symphony Orchestra, and there is no finer version of the Grieg recorded in the digital age than this.

Curzon's approach to Grieg is wonderfully poetic and this is a performance with strength and power as well as lyrical tenderness. This reading is second to none in distilling the music's special atmosphere and is available coupled either with Franck and Schumann at bargain price or with more music by Grieg at mid-price in the 'Classic Sound' series. In its original format Fjeldstad's *Peer Gynt* was counted to be one of the really outstanding early Decca stereo LPs. The LSO is very sensitive, and the tender string-playing in *Solveig's song* is quite lovely. Fjeldstad's persuasive direction is comparable with that of Beecham, making the listener feel he or she is experiencing this familiar music in a new way. The conductor builds up a blaze of excitement during *In the Hall of the Mountain King*. The early (1958) Kingsway Hall recording retains its glowing lustre, and only when the violins are under pressure above the stave is there some loss of sweetness.

The young Manchester pianist, Ronan O'Hora, with a totally sympathetic partner in James Judd, now provides us with a recorded performance which is for the 1990s what Solomon and Clifford Curzon were for the later 1950s, Steven Kovacevich for the 1970s, and Perahia for the end of the 1980s. Indeed in imagination and delicacy of feeling, combined with natural, authoritative brilliance, this new performance is unsurpassed. The piano is rather forwardly balanced and some listeners may find it a little bright, but in the music's gentler pages the piano's timbre is beautifully coloured. The programme is completed by a wholly delightful selection of a dozen of Grieg's most cherishable *Lyric pieces*, in which the pianist's simplicity of approach is consistently disarming.

Lars Vogt never allows his personality to obtrude; he colours the familiar phrases with great subtlety yet without the slightest trace of narcissism. He is very well supported by Rattle and the CBSO, and excellently recorded. An unusually sensitive player, his version, with the inevitable Schumann coupling, is eminently satisfying. Curzon, Kovacevich and O'Hora are top recommendations, but among newcomers this has strong claims to be put among them.

Andsnes wears his brilliance lightly. There is no lack of display and bravura here, but no ostentation. Indeed he has great poetic feeling and delicacy of colour, and Grieg's familiar warhorse comes up with great freshness. His piano is in perfect condition (not always the case on records) and is excellently balanced in relation to the orchestra. This is one of the best modern accounts.

Ousset's is a strong, dramatic reading, not lacking in warmth and poetry but, paradoxically, bringing out what we would generally think of as the masculine qualities of power and drive. Marriner gives persuasive support, the sound is full, firm and clear, and this reading gives a refreshingly individual slant on a much-played work.

Radu Lupu's recording dates from 1974 and is now even more brightly lit than it was originally, not entirely to advantage. But the performance is a fine one; there is both warmth and poetry in the slow movement; the hushed opening is particularly telling. The orchestral contribution under Previn is a strong one. This is now reissued in Decca's Legends series.

The famous 1947 Lipatti performance remains eternally fresh, and its return to the catalogue is a cause for rejoicing, although the ear now notices a slightly drier quality and a marginal loss of bloom.

Gieseking's 1951 recording with Karajan and the Philharmonia was overshadowed at the time by Lipatti and Curzon, understandably so. It was compared unfavourably with his pre-war account; but nevertheless, although some of the passagework is open to the charge of being cursory, there is a great deal that gives delight – not least Gieseking's beautiful and poetic tone.

Chandos and Amelie Malling depart from tradition and couple their Grieg with the Kuhlau *Concerto in C major* instead of the usual and more logical Schumann. Their recording made in collaboration with Danish Radio is excellent technically and their soloist, Amalie Malling, is a capable artist. However in terms of poetic feeling, and refinement and subtlety of tone, she does not begin to outshine the many great performances in the catalogue.

(i) *Piano concerto in A min.;* (ii) *Peer Gynt suites Nos. 1–2.*

(B) **(*) DG Classikon 439 427-2. (i) Géza Anda, BPO, Kubelik; (ii) BPO, Karajan.

Anda's account of the *Piano concerto* is more wayward than some but is strong in personality and has plenty of life. Kubelik's accompaniment is good too, and the 1963 recording sounds well. However, Karajan's analogue *Peer Gynt suites* are in a class of their own. They were also recorded – a decade later – in the Berlin Jesus-Christus Kirche but, for some reason, the CD transfer seems very brightly lit, although the fullness and analogue ambience are retained.

2 Elegiac melodies, Op. 34; Erotik; 2 Melodies, Op. 53; 2 Norwegian airs, Op. 63.

(BB) **(*) Naxos Dig. 8.550330; *4550330* [id.]. Capella Istropolitana, Adrian Leaper (with SIBELIUS: *Andante festivo* etc. **)

Adrian Leaper secures responsive and sensitive playing from the Capella Istropolitana in this Grieg collection, and the recording is very good indeed and the balance natural.

2 Elegiac melodies; Holberg suite, Op. 40.

(BB) **(*) ASV Quicksilva CDQS 6094 [id.]. Swiss CO – SUK: *String serenade*; TCHAIKOVSKY *String serenade*. ***

The Swiss Chamber Orchestra take the first movement of the *Holberg suite* very briskly, but it is an enjoyably spick-and-span account, with good lyrical contrast; although the *Elegiac melodies* lack opulence, these brightly recorded performances make a good bonus for outstanding versions of the Suk and Tchaikovsky *Serenades*.

2 Elegiac melodies (Heart's wounds; The last spring), Op. 34; Holberg suite, Op. 40; 2 Lyric pieces (Evening in the mountains; At the cradle); 2 Melodies (Norwegian; The first meeting), Op. 53; 2 Nordic melodies (In folk style; Cow-call), Op. 63.

*** DG (IMS) Dig. 437 520-2 [id.]. Gothenburg SO, Neeme Järvi.

A most attractive and well-designed anthology. The *Holberg suite* is presented with much character, and the other folk melodies bring some beautiful playing from the Gothenburg strings. The two lovely *Elegiac melodies* sound freshly minted and the innocent appeal of the much less familiar *Nordic melodies* is fully captured. In the *Evening in the mountains* the effect of oboe solo – backwardly placed as the composer intended – is piquantly and engagingly managed. The following *Cradle song* is very touching. Excellent, bright, modern recording with a good ambient effect.

(i) *2 Elegiac melodies, Op. 34; Lyric suite, Op. 54: Norwegian march and Nocturne. Norwegian dance, Op. 35/2;* (i) *Peer Gynt suites Nos. 1–2* (including *Solveig's lullaby*); (i) *Sigurd Jorsalfar: Homage march, Op. 56/3.*
(B) *** Sony SBK 53257 [id.]. (i) Phd. O, Ormandy; (ii) Elisabeth Söderström, New Philh. O, Andrew Davis.

Andrew Davis offers freshly thought performances of the two *Peer Gynt suites*, beautifully played and warmly recorded at Abbey Road in 1976. A special attraction is the singing of Elisabeth Söderström, not only in *Solveig's song* but also in *Solveig's lullaby*, which has been added to the second suite. The Ormandy recordings date from a decade earlier but they make up a most attractive anthology. The orchestral playing is very good indeed and Ormandy's warmth is obvious. The transfers are well managed.

Holberg suite, Op. 40.
(B) *** Carlton Dig. IMP 30367 02242 [(M) id.]. Serenata of London – ELGAR: *Serenade;* MOZART: *Eine kleine Nachtmusik*, etc. ***

The performance by the Serenata of London is first class in every way, spontaneous, naturally paced, and played with considerable eloquence. The digital recording is most realistic and very naturally balanced.

Holberg suite, Op. 40; Lyric suite, Op. 54; 4 Norwegian dances, Op. 35; Old Norwegian romance with variations, Op. 51; Peer Gynt (incidental music): *suites Nos. 1, Op. 46; 2, Op. 55; Sigurd Jorsalfar (suite), Op. 56; Symphonic dances, Op. 64.*
(N) (B) ** Ph. Duo 462 290-2 (2) ECO, or Philh. O, Raymond Leppard.

Leppard's performances included in the alternative Philips Duo above (the so-called '*Best of Grieg*' which offers also the *Piano concerto*) are here extended to include instead more orchestral music. Leppard is at his very best in the *Old Norwegian romance with variations*. But the performances from Barbirolli – see below– have far more character.

Holberg suite, Op. 40; Peer Gynt suites Nos. 1 & 2.
*** DG Gold Dig. 439 010-2. BPO, Karajan – SIBELIUS: *Finlandia; Valse triste; Swan of Tuonela.* ***

Karajan's performance of the *Holberg suite* is the finest currently available. The playing has wonderful lightness and delicacy, with cultured phrasing not robbing the music of its immediacy, while in *Peer Gynt* many subtleties of colour and texture are revealed by the vividly present recording, clear and full and with a firm bass-line, especially in the thrillingly gutsy *In the hall of the Mountain King*. Grieg's perennially fresh score is marvellously played. *Anitra* dances with elegance, and the *Death of Aase* is movingly eloquent. The digital recording now proves to be one of the best to have emerged from the Philharmonie in the early 1980s.

In Autumn overture, Op. 11; Lyric piece: Erotik, Op. 43/5; Norwegian dances, Op. 35; Old Norwegian romance with variations, Op. 51.
*** Chandos Dig. CHAN 9028 [id.]. Iceland SO, Sakari (with SVENDSEN: *2 Icelandic melodies* for strings ***).

The Iceland orchestra play very responsively for their Finnish conductor, Petri Sakari, who gives very natural and straightforward accounts of this endearing music. Highly musical performances, with no lack of personality, truthfully recorded. Very recommendable.

Lyric suite, Op. 54; Norwegian dances, Op. 35/1–4; Symphonic dances, Op. 64. Sigurd Jorsalfor (incidental music)*: Homage march, Op.56/3.*
(N) *** Barbirolli Society/ Dutton Lab. CDSJB 1012. Hallé O, Sir John Barbirolli.

In this Barbirolli Society issue, Dutton Laboratories have neatly brought together Grieg recordings made originally for both HMV and Pye. The set of four *Symphonic dances* is the earliest recording here, with a Pye source dating from 1957. With Harold Lawrence leading a team of Mercury engineers, the sound is if anything even cleaner and brighter than the first-rate EMI quality for the rest, recorded in 1969–70. Sir John brings out all their drama and colour, and the orchestral wind soloists make an often memorable contribution. There are characteristic touches too in the rest of the programme, notably in the expressive warmth of the *Nocturne* in the *Lyric suite*, and in the *Homage march* from *Sigurd Jorsalfar*. The *Norwegian dances*, too, are affectionately done and very positively presented. It makes a splendid compilation, not only because of the expressive warmth of the conducting, but because of the quality of the excellent Dutton CD transfers. As ever, Mike Dutton gives the sound plenty of body and weight, not least in the *Symphonic dances* and finally in the *Homage march*, which rounds the selection off.

Lyric suite, Op. 54; Sigurd Jorsalfar (suite), Op. 56; Symphonic dances, Op. 64.
**(*) ASV Dig. CDDCA 722 [id.]. RPO, Yondani Butt.

The *Symphonic dances* are particularly successful here. They are not easy to bring off, yet Butt and the RPO capture their charm and energy without succumbing to melodrama in No. 4. The *Lyric suite*, too, is fresh and the trolls in the finale have an earthy pungency. However, the outer movements of *Sigurd*

Jorsalfar bring an element of ponderousness. Excellent, vivid recording.

Old Norwegian romance with variations, Op. 51; 4 Symphonic dances, Op. 64.
(B) *** EMI (SIS) forte Dig. CZS5 68649-2 (2) [CDFB 68649]. Bournemouth SO, Berglund – DVORAK: *Scherzo capriccioso* etc.; SMETANA: *Má vlast.* ***

Berglund's performances of the *Symphonic dances* are both fresh and volatile – as fine as any in the catalogue. They have a strong sense of drama, yet Berglund's beautifully moulded shaping of the lovely oboe solo (exquisitely delicate) in No. 2 gives a personal imprint to the music-making. The *Old Norwegian romance* is introduced persuasively, and the variations are sympathetically and imaginatively done. The digital recording, made in the Southampton Guildhall, is first class, warmly atmospheric yet with just the right degree of brilliance. On all counts this EMI forte double is highly recommendable.

CHAMBER MUSIC

(i) *Album leaf, Op. 27/3*; (ii) *Elegiac melody: The Last spring*; (iii) *String quartet in G min., Op. 27.*(iv) *Violin sonata No. 3 in C min., Op. 45.*
(N) (M) (***) BMG/RCA mono 09026 61826-2 [id.]. (i) Elman; (ii) Boston SO, Koussevitsky; (iii) Budapest String Qt; (iv) Kreisler, Rachmaninoff.

These performances have already appeared as part of an historic three-CD set at the time of the 150th anniversary celebrations of Grieg's birth. The famous 1928 Kreisler–Rachmaninov set of the *Violin sonata No. 3 in C minor*, is already available in RCA's ten-CD Rachmaninov retrospective and is too well known to need further discussion. The 1937 Budapest version of the *String Quartet in G minor* is masterly in every way with splendid grip but at the same time great lyrical warmth and freshness. An alternative and highly competitive transfer is now on offer (see below). The eloquence of the Boston Symphony Orchestra's strings in *The Last spring* and their seamless phrasing under Koussevitzky still shines vibrantly down the years.

Cello sonata in A min., Op. 36.
*** RCA Dig. 09026 68290-2 [id.]. Steven Isserlis, Stephen Hough – RUBINSTEIN: *Cello sonata No. 1;* LISZT: *Elégies* etc. ***
**(*) CRD CRD 3391; *CRDC 4091* [id.]. Robert Cohen, Roger Vignoles – FRANCK: *Cello sonata.* **(*)

Cello sonata in A min., Op. 36; Intermezzo.
(N) *** Ph. Dig. 454 458-2 [id.]. Julian Lloyd Webber, Bengt Forsberg – DELIUS: *Cello sonata; 2 Pieces; Romance; Hassan: Serenade.* ***

Cello sonata in A min.; Intermezzo in A min.; Piano sonata, Op. 7.
(BB) *** Naxos Dig. 8.550878 [id.]. Oystein Birkeland, Håvard Gimse.

The *Cello sonata* very much reflects the *A minor Concerto* in manner and material, with Grieg at his most richly distinctive. With Steven Isserlis and Stephen Hough an inspired duo, natural recording artists both, these are outstanding performances of high romantic works that deserve to be better known. In an exhilarating performance Isserlis and Hough are consistently spontaneous-sounding and imaginative. Never running the risk of sounding sentimental, they give full emotional weight to each movement at speeds that flow easily and naturally. An outstanding cello disc in every way, very well recorded.

Oystein Birkeland and Håvard Gimse also give the sonata an alive and sensitive account, coupled with the early and unrepresentative *Intermezzo in A minor*. They are both imaginative players and are decently recorded. Given the modest outlay involved, this competes very strongly with its rivals, but even if it were at mid- or full-price it would be highly recommendable. Håvard Gimse's performance of the early *Piano sonata*, Op. 7, is also very good indeed. Altogether a first-rate bargain.

In the folk element Cohen might have adopted a more persuasive style, bringing out the charm of the music more, but certainly he sustains the sonata structures well. The recording presents the cello very convincingly. It has been most naturally transferred to CD.

In their apt coupling of the complete cello and piano music of both Delius and Grieg, Julian Lloyd Webber and Bengt Forsberg give a magnetic performance of the Grieg *sonata*, among the most inspired and intense of his longer works. With plenty of light and shade, the *pianissimos* from both cellist and pianist are daringly extreme, magically so in the central slow movement with its haunting quotation from Grieg's *Homage march.*

String quartet No. 1 in G min., Op. 27.
(N) *** Finlandia/Warner Dig. 3984 21445-2 [id.]. New Helsinki Qt. – SIBELIUS: *Quartet in D min. Op. 56.* ***
(M) (***) Biddulph mono LAB 098 [id.]. Budapest Qt – SIBELIUS: *Quartet;* WOLF: *Italian serenade.* (***)

String quartets Nos. 1 in G min., Op. 27; 2 in F (unfinished).
(BB) *** Naxos Dig. 8.550879 [id.]. Oslo String Qt – JOHANSEN: *String quartet.* ***

String quartets Nos. 1–2; (i) *Andante con moto for piano trio. Fugue in F min.*
*** Olympia Dig. OCD 432 [id.]. Raphael Qt, (i) with Jet Röling.

String quartets Nos. 1–2; Fugue (1861).
*** Victoria Dig. VCD 19048 [id.]. Norwegian Qt.
**(*) BIS Dig. CD 543 [id.]. Kontra Qt.

The Naxos account of the quartets from the Oslo String Quartet, a relatively new group, proves the best of the lot – indeed it is the best version we have had since the Budapest. They would easily sweep the board even at full price, on account of their sensitivity, tonal finesse and blend, and the keenness of their artistic responses. They (rightly) play only the first two movements of the *F major Quartet*, leaving room for a fine quartet by Grieg's biographer, David Monrad Johansen. The recording balance, made in the Norwegian Radio studios, is excellent, neither too forward nor too recessed. Three stars – and indeed verging on a Rosette.

The most recent version of the *First Quartet* from the New Helsinki Quartet couples it with the Sibelius *Quartet*. It is dramatic, well shaped and vital, yet full of sensitivity and can be strongly recommended among modern recordings, assuming price is no consideration. Apart from the excellence of the playing, the recording is also very present and well detailed. But the Naxos coupling makes a a more obvious primary recommendation.

The Budapest Quartet's recording, dating from 1936, has already appeared on RCA, as part of a three-CD Historic Grieg anthology (see above). There is no difference in cost between this and the Biddulph transfer, both being at mid-price, but its attractions in terms of coupling here are even stronger. The Sibelius *Voces intimae* and the Hugo Wolf *Italian serenade* are both superb performances and still remain unsurpassed. The Biddulph transfer has a slight edge over the RCA.

The Raphael Quartet do not give quite as spirited an account of the *F major Quartet* as the Oslo Quartet, but their CD enjoys two points of special interest: they give us Julius Röntgen's conjectural realization of the sketches to the remaining two movements Grieg had planned for the *F major Quartet*; and they also include another rarity in the shape of the *Andante con moto* for piano trio.

The Norwegian Quartet may not be immaculate in terms of tonal blend or ensemble but the performances are decent and have plenty of spirit, and the recorded sound is excellent.

The Kontras play with much dramatic power and invest the music with great feeling; one would hesitate to speak of unforced eloquence. In this respect the Norwegians score, for their playing is somehow truer in scale. The BIS recording is excellent and, though not perhaps a first choice artistically, the disc is perfectly recommendable.

Violin sonatas Nos. 1 in F, Op. 8; 2 in G, Op. 13; 3 in C min., Op. 45.
*** DG (IMS) Dig. 437 525-2. Augustin Dumay, Maria João Pires.
*** Chandos Dig. CHAN 9184 [id.]. Lydia Mordkovitch, Elena Mordkovitch.

Like the *Piano concerto*, the *Violin sonata* works possess extraordinary resilience and survive countless repetition. The French violinist, Augustin Dumay, and his distinguished partner, Maria João Pires, give poised, animated accounts of all three sonatas, and their CD is available both separately and as part of the six-CD Grieg Edition on DG. Their performances are exemplary in every way, and the recorded sound is also excellent in terms of both balance and realism.

Yet the same goes for Lydia and Elena Mordkovitch (*mère et fille*) on an admirably recorded Chandos CD. They, too, give splendidly fresh and well-shaped accounts of all three sonatas which give much pleasure in music-making. Affectionate yet virile performances – thoroughly recommendable.

PIANO MUSIC

Einar Steen-Nøkleberg Complete Naxos series

Einar Steen-Nøkleberg has recorded every note of music Grieg composed for the piano so that his survey, running to 14 CDs, is the most comprehensive ever to appear either on CD or on any other medium. He has impressive musical credentials and is, among other things, the author of a book on Grieg's piano music and its interpretation. His survey displaces earlier sets in quality: he is responsive to mood and is searchingly imaginative in his approach.

Volume 1: *Funeral March in memory of Rikard Nordraak; Humoresques, Op. 6; I love you (Jeg elsker dig), Op. 41/3; Melodies of Norway: The Sirens' enticement. Moods (Stimmungen), Op. 73; 4 Piano pieces, Op. 1; Sonata in E min., Op. 7.*
(BB) *** Naxos Dig. 8.550881 [id.]. Steen-Nøkleberg.

Steen-Nøkleberg does not proceed chronologically: the first disc couples early and late Grieg – the very earliest of his published pieces, written while he was still studying at Leipzig, the *Humoresques*, Op. 6, and the *E minor Piano sonata*, Op. 7, alongside the *Stimmungen* ('Moods'), Op. 73, composed in the early years of the present century (1901–5). Whether the music is early or late, Steen-Nøkleberg plays with total sympathy and dedication, and he is beautifully recorded throughout in the Lindeman Hall of the Norwegian State Academy of Music. Only in the *Sonata* does he suffer a trace of self-consciousness.

Volume 2: *The first meeting, Op. 52/2; Improvisations on 2 Norwegian folksongs, Op. 29; Melodies of Norway: Ballad to St Olaf. 25 Norwegian folksongs and dances, Op. 17; 19 Norwegian folksongs, Op. 66.*

(BB) *** Naxos Dig. 8.550882 [id.].
Steen-Nøkleberg.

The second disc includes the remarkable *Nineteen Norwegian folksongs*, Op. 66, which are contemporaneous with what many would see as Grieg's masterpiece, the song-cycle *Haugtussa*, which the composer himself spoke of as full of 'hair-raising' chromatic harmonies. (One of the folksongs appears in Delius's *On hearing the first cuckoo in spring*.) But the earlier set, Op. 17, written not long after the first version of the *Piano concerto*, is also full of delights.

Volume 3: *4 Album Leaves, Op. 28; Ballade, Op. 24; Melodies of Norway: Iceland. Pictures from everyday life (Humoresques), Op. 19; Poetic Tone-pictures, Op. 3; Sigurd Jorsalfar: Prayer, Op. 56/1.*
(BB) *** Naxos Dig. 8.550883 [id.].
Steen-Nøkleberg.

Volume 4: *Holberg suite, Op. 40; Melodies of Norway: I went to bed so late. 6 Norwegian mountain melodies; Peer Gynt suite No. 1, Op. 46/1: Morning. Norwegian peasant dances (Slåtter) Op. 72.*
(BB) *** Naxos Dig. 8.550884 [id.].
Steen-Nøkleberg.

The third CD includes the poignant *Ballade in G min.*, Op. 24, composed by Grieg on the death of his parents, Steen-Nøkleberg is highly imaginative and, even if some may find his rubato a little extreme, the keyboard colouring is subtle and rich. He conveys a splendidly rhapsodic spontaneity and there is much feeling. This and the companion disc, with the *Seventeen Norwegian peasant dances* (*Slåtter*), Op. 72, deserve a particularly strong recommendation. These extraordinary pieces with their quasi-Bartókian clashes are most characterful in Steen-Nøkleberg's hands.

Volume 5: *Norway's melodies Nos. 1–63.*
(BB) **(*) Naxos Dig. 8.553391 [id.].
Steen-Nøkleberg.

Volume 6: *Norway's melodies Nos. 64–117.*
(BB) **(*) Naxos Dig. 8.553392 [id.].
Steen-Nøkleberg.

Volume 7: *Norway's Melodies Nos. 118–152 (EG 108).*
(BB) **(*) Naxos Dig. 8.553393 [id.].
Steen-Nøkleberg.

The next three discs are devoted to *Norges Melodier* ('Norway's Melody'), an anthology Grieg made in the mid-1870s for a Danish publisher, of 'easy to play' arrangements of tunes, some of them charming, others less so Steen-Nøkleberg plays some on the house-organ or harmonium, some on the clavichord, some on a Graf piano to match those sonorities which would have been familiar in Norwegian homes in the 1870s, and some on a Steinway.

Volume 8: *Lyric pieces: Book I, Op. 12; Book II, Op. 38; Book III, Op. 43; Book IV, Op. 47.*
(BB) *** Naxos Dig. 8.553394 [id.].
Steen-Nøkleberg.

Volume 9: *Lyric pieces: Book V, Op. 54; Book VI, Op. 57; Book VII, Op. 62.*
(BB) *** Naxos Dig. 8.553395 [id.].
Steen-Nøkleberg.

Volume 10: *Lyric pieces: Book VIII, Op. 65; Book IX, Op. 68; Book X, Op. 71.*
(BB) *** Naxos Dig. 8.553396 [id.].
Steen-Nøkleberg.

Volumes 8–10 survey the delightful *Lyric pieces*. They are admirably fresh and are presented with the utmost simplicity, yet are obviously felt. These performances come into direct competition with Daniel Adni's not quite complete but otherwise excellent set on an EMI forte double CD. Many will like to have the coverage absolutely complete, and the three Naxos discs cost about the same. The EMI piano-sound is perhaps very slightly warmer and fuller, but the Naxos recording is wholly natural and believable. Einar Steen-Nøkleberg is totally idiomatic and authoritative, and readers wanting a complete set need not hesitate.

Volume 11: *Bergliot, Op. 42; Peer Gynt suites Nos. 1, Op. 46; 2, Op. 55; Sigurd Jorsalfar (suite), Op. 22;* (i) *Olav Trygvason, Op. 50: 2 Pieces.*
(BB) *** Naxos Dig. 8.553397 [id.]. Einar Steen-Nøkleberg; (i) Norwegian State Institute of Music Chamber Ch., Schiøll.

Volume 12: *Agitato, EG 106; Albumblad, EG 109; Norwegian dances, Op. 35;* (i) *Peer Gynt: excerpts, Op. 23* including *Dance of the Mountain King's daughter, Op. 55/5 (Op. 23/9);* 3 piano transcriptions from *Sigurd Jorsalfar. Waltz caprices, Op. 37.* arr. of HALVORSEN: *Entry of the Boyards.*
(BB) *** Naxos Dig. 8.553398 [id.]. Einar Steen-Nøkleberg; (i) Norwegian State Instute of Music Chamber Ch., Schiøll.

With the remaining four volumes we enter the realm of Grieg's transcriptions of his orchestral works and his juvenilia, as well as sketches for works that did not materialize. Most valuable are the *Waltz caprices*, Op. 37, and the early *Agitato*, EG 106, and *Albumblad*, EG 109. Both these issues are recommendable but dispensable.

Volume 13: *2 Elegiac melodies, Op. 34; 2 Melodies, Op. 53; 2 Nordic melodies, Op. 63; Norwegian melodies Nos. 6 & 22; 3 Piano pieces, EG 105; 3 Piano pieces, EG 110/112;* Piano transcriptions of *Songs, Op. 41.*

(BB) *** Naxos Dig. 8.553399 [id.]. Einar Steen-Nøkleberg.

Volume 14: *At the Halfdan Kjerulf Statue, EG 167; Canon à 4 voci for organ, EG 179; Piano concerto in B min.* (fragments), *EG 120; Larsvikspola, EG 101; Mountain song, Norwegian melodies Nos. 87 & 146, EG 108; 23 Small pieces for piano, EG 104; Piano sonata Op. 7* (1st version: mvts 2 and 4); Piano transcriptions of *Songs, Op. 52.*
(BB) *** Naxos Dig. 8.553400 [id.]. Einar Steen-Nøkleberg.

The last two volumes are another matter. Volume 13 brings rarities in the shape of the *Three Piano pieces*, EG 105, and a further three, EG 110–112, all of which are otherwise available only on Love Dervinger's full-priced BIS record of the 1874 version of the *Piano concerto*. The last volume is of particular interest in that it brings – in addition to various juvenilia – the sketches for a *Second Piano concerto* – very Lisztian – and the first versions of the slow movement and finale of the Op. 7 *Sonata.*

Agitato; Album leaves, Op. 28/1 & 4; Lyric pieces, Opp. 43 & 54; Piano sonata in E min., Op. 7; Poetic tone pieces, Op. 3/4–6.
❀ *** Virgin/EMI (SIS) Dig. VC7 59300-2 [id.]. Leif Ove Andsnes.

A notable recital by Grieg's countryman, Leif Ove Andsnes, which has won golden opinions – and rightly so! He includes two sets of the *Lyric pieces*, the Op. 43 which begins with the famous *Butterfly*, and the Op. 54 which Grieg later scored; there are various other short pieces, as well as the *Sonata in E minor*, Op. 7. Andsnes's virtuosity is always at the service of the composer and he plays with real imagination and lightness of touch.

Ballade in G min., Op. 24; Holberg Suite, Op. 40; Lyric Pieces: Arietta, Op. 12/1; Nocturne & Scherzo, Op. 54/4–5; At your feet, Op. 68/3; Puck, Op. 71/3, Remembrances, Op. 71/7. Piano sonata in E min., Op. 7.
(N) ** Decca Dig. 455 631-2. Peter Jablonski.

This accomplished young Swedish pianist proves a more persuasive advocative of Grieg than he did of Chopin. He is refreshingly direct throughout this recital even if he does not fully penetrate the plangent core of the *G minor Ballade*. There is much that gives pleasure, not least the good recorded sound the Decca engineers provide him, but by the side of Andsnes in the *Sonata* (Virgin) or Steen-Nøkleberg (Naxos), he strikes a less personal response.

Ballade, Op. 24; 4 Lyric pieces: March of the dwarfs; Notturno, Op. 54/3–4; Wedding day at Troldhaugen, Op. 65/6; Peace of the woods, Op. 71/4. Sonata in E min., Op. 7; arr. of songs: *Cradle song; I love thee; The princess; You cannot grasp the wave's eternal course. Peer Gynt: Solveig's song.*
**(*) Olympia OCD 197 [id.]. Peter Katin.

The *Sonata* is not one of Grieg's finest works, but it has a touching *Andante* and is agreeably inventive, if perhaps conventionally so. Katin gives it a clean, direct performance, and he is impressive in the rather dolorous set of variations which forms the *Ballade*. The song arrangements, too, come off well, and the four *Lyric pieces* are presented very appealingly.

Lyric pieces: Opp. 12; 38; 43; 47; 54; 57; 62; 65; 68 & 71 (complete).
(M) **(*) Unicorn Dig. UKCD 2033, *UKC 2033* (1–4); UKCD 2034, *UKC 2034* (5–7); UKCD 2035, *UKC 2035* (8–10) [id.]. Peter Katin.

Lyric pieces: Op. 12/3, 5, 7 & 8; Op. 38/1, 3 & 6; Opp. 43, 47 & 54; Op. 57; Opp. 62, 65, 68 & 71.
(B) *** EMI forte CZS5 68634-2 (2) [CDFB 68634]. Daniel Adni.

Peter Katin is a persuasive and sensitive exponent of this repertoire, and he has the benefit of a recording of exceptional presence and clarity (though very occasionally it seems to harden in climaxes, when one notices that the microphone is perhaps a shade close). Katin has the measure of Grieg's sensibility and characterizes these pieces with real poetic feeling.

Daniel Adni has also made a complete recording but, in order to fit the majority of the works on to two CDs (with a total playing time of 155 minutes), some of the earlier pieces from Books I and II have been omitted. Adni plays with genuine feeling for their character and a strong sense of atmosphere, and the 1973 EMI recording is very good indeed.

Lyric pieces: Opp. 12/2, 7; 38/1, 3; 43/1-6 (1, 2, 4, 6 two versions); *47/2, 3, 4; 54/1, 3, 4, 6; 57/6; 62/3, 5, 6; 65/1, 2, 6* (6 two versions); *68/2, 3, 5; 71/2, 3, 4, 7; Norwegian bridal procession, Op. 19/2.*
(N) (BB) **(*) EMI mono CHS5 66775-2 (2) [CDHB 66775]. Walter Gieseking – MENDELSSOHN: *Songs without words.* **(*)

Gieseking was a distinguished interpreter of the *Lyric pieces* as his pre-war 78s testify. However these recordings made towards the end of his life are not really his most inspired. Of course, some are touched by his special poetry but others sound a little as if he is on automatic pilot. The recorded sound too, is a little studio-bound.

Lyric pieces: Op. 12/1; Op. 38/1; Op. 43/1–2; Op. 47/2–4; Op. 54/4–5; Op. 57/6; Op. 62/4 and 6; Op. 68/2, 3 and 5; Op. 71/1, 3 and 6–7.
❀ (M) *** DG 449 721-2 [id.]. Emil Gilels.

With Gilels we are in the presence of a great keyboard master whose characterization and control of colour and articulation are wholly remarkable. An altogether outstanding record in every way. This recording has been admirably remastered for reissue in DG's 'Originals' series and now sounds better than ever.

Lyric pieces, Op. 12/1, 4 & 5; Op. 38/1–2, 5 & 7; Op. 43/1, 4 & 6; Op. 47, 1–4; Op. 54/1–4; Op. 57/6; Op. 62/3, 4 & 6; Op. 65/5–6; Op. 68/9; Op. 71/3 & 7.
(BB) *** Naxos Dig. 8.554051 [id.]. Einar Steen-Nøkleberg.

A compilation disc for those who do not want to invest in all three of this artist's discs of the *Lyric pieces*. Very distinguished playing, though not to be preferred to Gilels's anthology in the DG Originals series.

Lyric pieces: Op. 12/1, 6; Op. 38/5; Op. 54/1, 4 & 5; Op. 57/4, 6; Op. 62/3, 4 & 6; Op. 65/1–4; Op. 68/2, 4 & 5; Op. 71/1.
(BB) **(*) Naxos Dig. 8.550650 [id.]. Balázs Szokolay.

Lyric pieces: Op. 12/3, 8; Op. 38/1; Op. 43/1, 3 & 6; Op. 47/3–7; Op. 54/3, 5–6; Op. 57/1–3; Op. 62/1–2, 5; Op. 65/6; Op. 71/7.
(BB) **(*) Naxos Dig. 8.550557 [id.]. Balázs Szokolay.

Naxos are not always lucky with their piano recordings, but the two CDs Balázs Szokolay has recorded are very good. Szokolay's playing is not as consistently subtle in colouring or as poetic in feeling as Leif Ove Andsnes, but it is pretty idiomatic. However, at super-bargain price it is really very good value indeed and the balance, though very slightly close, is not oppressively so. Both CDs give pleasure.

'The long, long winter night': Norwegian Folksongs and Slåtter Opp. 66 & 73.
*** EMI CDC5 56541-2 [id.]. Leif Ove Andsnes – David Monrad JOHANSEN: *Portraits, Op. 5*; SAEVERUD: *Slåtter og stev fra Siljastøl*; Geirr TVEITT: Hardanger folk tunes, Op. 150; Farlein VALEN: *Variations, Op. 23*.

Here is a second unforgettable recital by Grieg's countryman, Leif Ove Andsnes, made the more attractive by the rarity of the repertoire included. His playing, ever sensitive and full of special insights, is a joy, and he is given EMI's best quality piano sound.

VOCAL MUSIC

A cappella choral music: (i) *At the Halvdan Kjerulf monument; Ave maris stella; Dona nobis pacem*; (ii) *Four Psalms, Op. 74; Holberg Cantata*; *Male-voice choruses: Election song; Impromptu; Inga Litamor; The late rose; Westerly Wind.*
(N) *** Simax Dig. PSC 1187 [id.]. (i) Kjell Magnus Sandve; (ii) Per Vollestad; Oslo Ph. Ch., Stefan Skiöld.

Popular though *Peer Gynt*, the *Piano concerto* and his piano works are, Grieg's *a cappella* output is among the least known. This disc by the Oslo Philharmonic Choir offers a generous helping of it and presents it persuasively. Although Grieg was not a conventional believer, he was influenced by his encounter in Birmingham in 1888 with Unitarianism. His last work, the *Four Psalms, Op. 74* dates from 1906 and is based on traditional tunes of popular Norwegian origin. Writing just after the Second World War, Edmund Rubbra had 'no hesitation in placing the *Psalms* among the finest choral music of the century'. The Oslo Philharmonic Choir produce a beautiful and well-blended sound. Good recording.

Orchestral songs: *Album lines, Departed; En svane (The swan); Eros* (orch. Reger) *Fra Monte pincio* (orch. Grieg); *Spillemnd (Fiddlers)*; *The Mountain Thrall, Op. 26; The Princess; 4 songs, Op. 60; 6 Songs, Op. 48; To the Motherland. A Vision* (orch Byl); *With a water-lily. Peer Gynt: Solveig's cradle song.*
(N) *** Dinemec Dig. DCCD022 [id.]. Carole Farley, LPO or Philh. O, José Serebrier.

This anthology collects 23 Grieg songs, three in the composer's own orchestrations but the vast majority in transcriptions by the conductor, José Serebrier. Some of them, like *Princessan (The Princess)* do not gain in the process, but the vast majority do, and Serebrier's orchestrations are both expert and idiomatic. Carole Farley does not use the white-toned, vibrato-free style favoured by some of the younger generation of Norwegian singers, but her disc is none the worse for that. Only occasionally is her vibrato obtrusive. For the most part she commands a wide expressive range and exhibits considerable feeling for the character of each of the songs. Moreover the orchestral support is sensitive and the recording well balanced.

Songs in historic performances (1888–1924): *Den første møte (First meeting); Dulgte kjaerlighed (Hidden love); En fuglevis (A Bird-Song); Eros; Fra Monte Pincio; Den gamle vise (The old song); God Morgen; Jag elsker Dig (I love thee); Jag reiste en deilig sommerkvaeld (I walked one balmy summer evening); Killingdans (Kids' dance); Kongekvadet (The King's Song); Margretas Vuggesang (Margreta's cradle song); Mens jeg venter (On the water); Moderen synger (The mother's lament); Norønnafolket (The Northland folk); Og jeg vil ha mig en Hjertenskaer (Midsummer Eve); Ragnhild; Solveig's Song; Solveigs vuggevise (Solveig's lullaby); Stambogsrim (Album Lines); En Svane (A swan); Takk for dit råd (Say what you will); Eine Traume (A dream); Trudom (Faith); Våren*

(Spring); Vaer hilset I Damer (Greetings, fair ladies).

(*(**)) SIMAX mono PSC 1810 (3). Aino Ackté, Giuseppe Anselmi, Maria Barrientos, Borghild Bryhn-Landgaard, Otta Bronnum, Robert Burg, Eugenia Burzio, Erik Bye, Feodor Chaliapin, Edmund Clément, Peter Cornelius, Emmy Destinn, Kaia Eide, Gervase Elwes, Elisa Elizza, Geraldine Farrar, Kirsten Flagstad, John Forsell, Amelita Galli-Curci, Lucy Gates, Elena Gerhardt, Gunnar Graarud, Ellen Gulbranson, Nina Grieg, Hans Hedemark, Melitta Heim, Frida Hempel, Vilhelm Herold, Clara Hultgren, Hermann Jadlowker, Beatrice Kernic, Olive Kline, Salomea Kruszelnicka, Lilli Lehmann, Augusta Lütken, Magna Lykseth-Schjerven, Cally Monrad, Carl-Martin Ohman, Rosa Olitzka, Elisabeth Rethberg, Ernestine Schumann-Heink, Karl Scheidemantel, Leo Slezak, Greta Stückgold, Joseph Schwarz, Richard Tauber, Luisa Tetrazzini (various pianists).

As the cast-list shows, this is a veritable treasure-house of singing at the turn of the century, not only in northern Europe but elsewhere. Naturally in the early years of the gramophone singers tended to gravitate towards a handful of songs so that familiar numbers such as *Jag elsker Dig* and *En Svane* turn up in several versions, the former 11 times and the latter seven. There are no fewer than 16 different versions of *Solveig's song*, including a few bars sung without accompaniment by Nina Grieg in 1889 when she would have been 44. (She stopped singing in public in the 1890s.) Grieg himself declared her to be the finest interpreter of his songs and, although she is barely audible through the deluge of background noise, the voice is obviously of great purity. Listening to her across a divide of over a century is a curiously moving experience. The roll-call is pretty dazzling, ranging as it does from big names such as Aino Ackté (for whom Sibelius composed *Luonnotar*), to Chaliapin and Emmy Destinn (the copy of her *Mens jeg venter* is unfortunately pretty rough) and there are 47 singers in all, but the less familiar names also offer valuable insights into performance practice. There are nearly 80 performances altogether, and the quality of the recordings which have been subjected to the NoNoise system of reduction calls for more tolerance than many listeners will feel able to extend. This is a set for libraries, specialist collectors and students of song, and it is an invaluable resource into which to dip.

4 Songs, Op. 14; 6 Songs, Op. 49; Songs from Peer Gynt, Op. 55.

**(*) Victoria Dig. VCD 19038. Marianne Hirsti, Kjell Magnus Sandve, Knut Skram, Rudolf Jansen.

Marianne Hirsti possesses a voice of great purity; her intonation is spot-on, and the overall sound radiates a childlike innocence. She is heard at her best in, say, *Margaret's Cradle song*, one of the four songs of Op. 15 and Grieg's very first setting of Ibsen. Characterization, on the other hand, is not always her strong suit; all the same, it's a beautiful voice. Knut Skram has lost some of the bloom his voice once possessed – though none of his artistry or musical intelligence. Good recordings throughout. This should prove a rewarding series, and when it comes Hirsti's set of *Haugtussa* will be of special interest in that it will include five songs Grieg suppressed on grounds of length.

Songs: *At Rodane; A bird song; The first primrose; From Monte Pincio; Hope; I love but thee; I walked one balmy summer evening; Last spring; Margaret's cradle song; On the water; The princess; Spring showers; A Swan; To her II; Two brown eyes; Upon a grassy hillside. 4 Poems from Bjørnstjerne Bjørnson's Fishermaiden, Op. 21; 6 Songs, Op. 48; Peer Gynt: Solveig's song; Solveig's cradle song.*

(BB) **(*) Naxos Dig. 8.553781 [id.]. Bodil Arnesen, Erling Eriksen.

An inexpensive and, at 70 minutes, well-filled CD, beautifully recorded and pleasingly sung. Bodil Arnesen has a voice of great purity and radiance. She sings marvellously in tune, though some may find that in this repertoire she has something of a 'little-girl', innocent quality that does not give the whole picture. This perhaps is troubling when you are listening to all the songs straight off. Taken a group at a time, she will touch most hearts, particularly in the setting of Bjørnson's *Prinsessen* and *Det første møte*. Erling Eriksen is an excellent pianist.

(i) *Bergliot, Op. 42;* (ii) *Den Bergtekne (The mountain thrall), Op. 32;* (iii & iv) *Foran sydens kloster (Before a southern convent);* (ii & iii) *7 Songs with orchestra: Den første møde; Solveigs sang; Solveigs vuggesang; Fra Monte Pincio; En svane; Våren; Henrik Wegeland.*

*** DG (IMS) Dig. 437 519-2. (i) Rut Tellefsen, (ii) Håkan Hagegård; (iii & iv) Barbara Bonney; (iii) Randi Stene; Gothenburg SO, Neeme Järvi.

Before a southern convent is based on a Bjørnson poem which tells how Ingigerd, the daughter of a chieftain, has seen her father murdered by the villainous brigand, Arnljot. He was on the verge of raping her but relented and let her go; she seeks expiation by entering a foreign convent, and the piece ends with a chorus of nuns who admit her to their number. It's not great Grieg but it's well worth investigating, and is very naturally balanced. Generally speaking, the quality on all these DG recordings is excellent – which is not surprising, as they're made by the same Gothenburg team who have recorded for the BIS label.

Haugtussa (song-cycle), *Op. 67; 6 Songs, Op. 48. Songs: Beside the stream; Farmyard song; From Monte Pincio; Hope; I love but thee; Spring; Spring showers; A Swan; Two brown eyes; While I wait; With a waterlily* (sung in Norwegian).
❁ *** DG Dig. 437 521-2 [id.]. Anne Sofie von Otter, Bengt Forsberg.

This recital of Grieg's songs by Anne Sofie von Otter and Bengt Forsberg is rather special. Von Otter commands an exceptionally wide range of colour and quality and in Bengt Forsberg has a highly responsive partner. Altogether a captivating recital, and beautifully recorded too.

(i) *Landkjenning (Land-sighting), Op. 31;* (i & ii) *Olav Trygvason, Op. 50; Peer Gynt Suites Nos. 1 & 2.*
*** DG (IMS) Dig. 437 523-2. (i) Anne Gjevang; (ii) Randi Stene; (i; ii) Håkan Hagegård; Gothenburg SO, Neeme Järvi.

The three scenes that survive from the opera, *Olav Trygvason* and *Landkjenning* ('Land-sighting') are on DG, coupled together with the two *Peer Gynt* suites. In the second tableau, the role of the priestess is sung by Anne Gjevang, the Erda in the Haitink *Ring* on EMI. Some may find her vibrato a bit excessive. The other soloists, Randi Stene and Håkan Hagegård, acquit themselves well, as does the Gothenburg Orchestra and Chorus under Neeme Järvi. The *Peer Gynt* suites are not new, though two of the numbers have been re-recorded. Recommended.

Melodies of the heart, Op. 5; 9 Songs, Op. 18; 6 Songs, Op. 25; The last spring, Op. 33/2; The Mountain thrall, Op. 32; Rocking, rocking on the gentles waves, Op. 49/2; Henrik Wergeland, Op. 58/3.
**(*) RCA Dig. 09026 61518-2. Håkan Hagegård, Warren Jones.

Songs and ballads, Op. 9; 4 Songs, Op. 21; 5 Songs, Op. 26; Romances & songs, Op. 39; Reminiscences from mountain and fjord, Op. 44.
**(*) RCA Dig. 09026 61629-2. Håkan Hagegård, Warren Jones.

Håkan Hagegård's two CDs with Warren Jones find the great Swedish baritone less than wholly persuasive. Here there is a certain uniformity of colour and approach in many of these songs, and an occasional hardness at the tenor end of the voice. However, these discs have been widely admired and Hagegård's artistry and musical intelligence are always in evidence.

6 songs, Op. 25: Spillemnd (Fiddlers), En svane (A swan), Stambogsrim (Album lines), Med en vadnlilje (With a waterlily), Borte (Departed), En fuglevis (A birdsong).
(N) *** Virgin/EMI Dig. VC5 45273-2. Solveig Kringelborn, Malcolm Martineau (with NIELSEN, RANGSTROM, SIBELIUS: *Songs.* ***)

Solveig Kringelborn's anthology is called '*Black roses*' after the famous Sibelius song she includes. The Op. 25 songs of Grieg including the famous *Swan*, are beautifully sung: she sets great store by a smooth legato and purity of tone, which she commands in abundance. Her characterization could perhaps be stronger; the overall effect when one listens to her record straight off is just a shade uniform. But she is possessed of a lovely voice and her pianist is quite superb. Excellent recording.

Peer Gynt (incidental music), *Op. 23* (complete).
(M) *** Unicorn UKCD 2003/4 [id.]. Carlson, Hanssen, Bjørkøy, Hansli, Oslo PO Ch., LSO, Dreier.

Per Dreier achieves very spirited results from his soloists, the Oslo Philharmonic Chorus and our own LSO, with some especially beautiful playing from the woodwind; the recording is generally first class, with a natural perspective between soloists, chorus and orchestra. The Unicorn set includes 32 numbers in all, including Robert Henrique's scoring of the *Three Norwegian dances*, following the revised version of the score Grieg prepared for the 1886 production in Copenhagen. This music, whether familiar or unfamiliar, continues to astonish by its freshness and inexhaustibility.

Peer Gynt (incidental music), *Op. 23* (complete); *Sigurd Jorsalfar* (incidental music), *Op. 56* (complete).
*** DG Dig. 423 079-2 (2) [id.]. Bonney, Eklöf, Sandve, Malmberg, Holmgren; Foss, Maurstad, Stokke (speakers); Gösta Ohlin's Vocal Ens., Pro Musica Chamber Ch., Gothenburg SO, Järvi.

Neeme Järvi's recording differs from its predecessor by Per Dreier in offering the Grieg Gesamtausgabe *Peer Gynt*, which bases itself primarily on the 26 pieces he included in the 1875 production rather than the final published score, prepared after Grieg's death by Halvorsen. This well-documented set comes closer to the original by including spoken dialogue, as one would have expected in the theatre. The CDs also offer the complete *Sigurd Jorsalfar* score, which includes some splendid music. The performances by actors, singers (solo and choral) and orchestra alike are exceptionally vivid, with the warm Gothenburg ambience used to creative effect; the vibrant histrionics of the spoken words undoubtedly add to the drama.

Peer Gynt: extended excerpts.
*** DG (IMS) Dig. 427 325-2. Bonney, Eklöf, Malmberg, Maurstad, Foss, Gothenburg Ch. & SO, Järvi.
*** Decca (IMS) Dig. 425 448-2. Urban Malmberg, Mari-Ann Haeggander, San Francisco Ch. & SO, Blomstedt.
(BB) *** Belart 450 018-2. VPO, Karajan – SIBELIUS: *En Saga* etc. ***

Neeme Järvi's disc offers more than two-thirds of the 1875 score, and the performance has special claims on the collector who wants one CD rather than two (half the second CD of the set is taken up by *Sigurd Jorsalfar*).

Decca's set of excerpts makes a useful alternative to the Järvi disc. All but about 15 minutes of the complete score is here and the spoken text is included too, all admirably performed. Perhaps the Gothenburg acoustic is to be preferred to the Davies Hall, San Francisco. However, the Decca recording approaches the demonstration class.

Karajan's shorter set of excerpts (from 1962) makes a first-class super-bargain alternative on Belart, with a particularly fresh response from the VPO. It includes a beautiful account of *Solveig's song*, and the sound is warm and atmospheric. The Sibelius couplings are equally recommendable.

(i) *Peer Gynt*: excerpts. *In Autumn* (overture), *Op. 11; An Old Norwegian song with variations, Op. 51; Symphonic dance No. 2.*
❁ (M) *** EMI CDM5 66914-2 [CDM5 66966]. (i) Ilse Hollweg, Beecham Ch. Soc.; RPO, Beecham.

Beecham showed a very special feeling for this score and to hear *Morning*, the gently textured *Anitra's dance* or the eloquent portrayal of the *Death of Aase* under his baton is a uniquely rewarding experience. Ilse Hollweg makes an excellent soloist. The recording dates from 1957 and, like most earlier Beecham reissues, has been enhanced by the remastering process. The most delectable of the *Symphonic dances*, very beautifully played, makes an ideal encore after *Solveig's lullaby*, affectingly sung by Hollweg. The *In Autumn* overture, not one of Grieg's finest works, is most enjoyable when Sir Thomas is so persuasive, not shirking the melodramatic moments. Finally for the present reissue, we are offered *An Old Norwegian folksong with variations* (not previously released in its stereo format). It is a piece of much colour and charm, which is fully realized here.

Peer Gynt (incidental music): *Overture; Suites 1–2. Lyric pieces: Evening in the mountain; Cradle song, Op. 68/5; Sigurd Jorsalfar: suite, Op. 56; Wedding day at Troldhaugen, Op. 65/6.*
(BB) **(*) Naxos Dig. 8.550140; *4550140* [id.]. CSSR State PO, Kŏsice, Stephen Gunzenhauser.

A generous Grieg anthology on Naxos (70 minutes, all but 3 seconds) and the performances by the Slovak State Philharmonic Orchestra in Kŏsice (in eastern Slovakia) are very fresh and lively and thoroughly enjoyable. There is wide dynamic range both in the playing and in the recording, and sensitivity in matters of phrasing.

Peer Gynt Suites Nos. 1 & 2, Opp. 46 & 55.
(N) *** Finlandia/Warner Dig. 0630 17675-2. Norwegian Radio O, Ari Rasilainen. – SAEVERUD: *Peer Gynt suites.* ***

The thinking behind this disc is to contrast the two sets of incidental music for Ibsen's *Peer Gynt*; Grieg's romantic setting of 1874 on which he later based his two orchestral suites, and Harald Sæverud's anti-romantic incidental music of 1947. The idea is so obvious that it is surprising no one has done it before, though it has been done more than once in London concert halls, and on the radio. The Norwegian Radio Orchestra under their Finnish conductor, Ari Rasilainen give fresh, well-characterized accounts of the familiar suites and are very well recorded. They may not enjoy the same ranking as the Oslo Philharmonic (their strings do not possess the same tonal opulence or weight) but they are a good orchestra in their own right and these performances give pleasure.

Peer Gynt: suites Nos. 1, Op. 46; 2, Op. 55. Sigurd Jorsalfar: suite.
(B) *** DG Double 447 358-2 (2). BPO, Karajan – SIBELIUS: *The Bard* etc. ***

Karajan's earlier analogue performances from the early 1970s reappear here on a DG Double, coupled with a very generous and enticing Sibelius programme. The Grieg performances are highly expressive and superbly played. Anitra dances with allure and there is contrasting simplicity and repose in *Aase's death*. The current transfers are rather brightly lit, but there is no lack of body.

(i) *Peer Gynt: suites Nos. 1–2. Lyric suite, Op. 54; Sigurd Jorsalfar: suite.*
(M) *** DG Dig. 427 807-2 [id.]. (i) Soloists, Ch.; Gothenburg SO, Järvi.

Järvi's excerpts from *Peer Gynt* and *Sigurd Jorsalfar* are extracted from his complete sets, so the editing inevitably produces a less tidy effect than normal recordings of the *Suites*. However, the performances are first class and so is the recording, and this comment applies also to the *Lyric suite*, taken from an earlier, digital orchestral collection.

4 Psalms, Op. 74.
**(*) Nimbus Dig. NI 5171 [id.]. Håkan Hagegård, Oslo Cathedral Ch., Terje Kvam – MENDELSSOHN: *3 Psalms.* **(*)

The *Four Psalms* are dignified, beautiful pieces, very well sung here by the choir and the Swedish baritone, Håkan Hagegård. The recording is eminently faithful, though the pauses between the Psalms are not long enough.

Grigny, Nicolas de (1672–1703)

Organ Mass.
(M) *** Cal. CAL 6911 [id.]. André Isoir (Cliquot organ at the Cathedral of Saint-Pierre de Poitiers).

Nicolas de Grigny's fame as a composer rests upon one book, including 49 pieces of music, and the present Couperin-influenced *Organ Mass* which was very influential in its own right. Although the *Mass* is presented here as a solo work, when it was performed in its own time the organ undoubtedly alternated with the sung sections of the Mass. The variety of the writing is remarkable, and certainly André Isoir's performance on the Cliquot organ at Poitiers Cathedral (with its characteristically pungent reeds but full underlying sonority) readily demonstrates the music's imaginative range. As a double encore we are offered an *Elévation en sol* and a *Symphonie* by Nicolas LeBegue, both strong pieces. The analogue recording is of fine quality and, while this reissue has specialist rather than general appeal, it is a fine example of the contrapuntal church organ music being written in France before the later domination of this field by Bach.

Grofé, Ferde (1892–1972)

Grand Canyon suite.
*** Telarc Dig. CD 80086 [id.] (with additional cloudburst, including real thunder). Cincinnati Pops O, Kunzel – GERSHWIN: *Catfish Row.* ***
(M) *** Sony SMK 63086 [id.]. NYPO, Bernstein – GERSHWIN: *An American in Paris*, etc. *** ❁
(B) *** Millennium Universal UMD 80396 [id.]. Utah SO, Maurice Abravanel – COPLAND: *Billy the Kid: suite and Waltz*, etc. ***
(M) *(*) Decca Phase Four 448 956-2 [id.]. L. Festival O, Stanley Black – IVES: *Orchestral Set No. 2.* ***

The Cincinnati performance is played with great commitment and fine pictorial splendour. What gives the Telarc CD its special edge is the inclusion of a second performance of *Cloudburst* as an appendix with a genuine thunderstorm laminated on to the orchestral recording. The result is overwhelmingly thrilling, except that in the final thunderclap God quite upstages the orchestra.

Bernstein treats the music as if it was a masterpiece of orchestral impressionism, while the famous *On the trail* (John Corigliano the solo fiddler) has never sounded more infectiously witty. The closing storm has real spectacle, powerfully generated by the orchestral playing itself. The recording has never sounded half as good as it does here.

If Abravanel does not quite match Bernstein's wit in *On the trail*, in all other respects his account is highly recommendable, with the Utah orchestra playing with great conviction and the resonant acoustic expansively spectacular throughout, and especially so in *Cloudburst*.

Stanley Black is thoroughly at home in Grofé's picaresque spectacular, but the exaggeratedly forward balance is unrealistic. Yet the performance is a colourful one and easy to enjoy.

Grand Canyon suite; Mississippi suite.
(M) **(*) Mercury (IMS) 434 355-2 [id.]. Eastman-Rochester O, Hanson – HERBERT: *Cello concerto No. 2.* **

It is impossible not to respond to the pictorial vividness and gusto of Hanson's performances and, even if the studio-ish acoustic of the Eastman Theater is not ideally expansive, the 1958 Mercury stereo is brilliantly detailed in the *Grand Canyon suite*. The *Mississippi suite*, a much lesser piece, is also persuasively presented, especially the exuberant portrait of *Huckleberry Finn*. But the canyon storms rage much more spectacularly on the rival versions.

Grosz, Wilhelm (1894–1939)

7 Afrika songs, Op. 29; Bänkel und Balladen, Op. 31; Rondels, Op. 11. Hit songs (arr. Robert Ziegler): *Along the Sante Fe Trail; Harbour lights; Isle of Capri; Red sails in the sunset.*
*** Decca Dig. 455 116-2 [id.]. Cynthia Clarey, Kelly Hunter, Jake Gardner, Andrew Shore, Matrix Ens., Ziegler.

It is astonishing to find that the writer of such hit songs of the 1930s as *Isle of Capri* and *Red Sails in the sunset* was a very serious, Vienna-trained composer with a remarkable melodic gift. He is credited with being the first Austrian composer to use a jazz element in his music, and the *Afrika songs* reflect that in settings of poems by black writers, translated into German. The accompaniment has a jazz grouping complementing classical strings and woodwind, with the eight songs linked by imaginative interludes and – last and longest – a haunting, sensuous duet. The three *Rondels* are charming mixtures, similarly sensuous, while the *Ballades* strike a sharper note in their satirical flavour, with echoes of Mahler. Robert Ziegler's arrangements of the hit songs do not precisely imitate the 1930s manner but introduce a Viennese flavour, with hints of Weill. A first-rate team of soloists, as well as fine playing from the Matrix Ensemble.

Gubaidulina, Sofia (born 1931)

(i) *Bassoon concerto* (for bassoon and low strings); (ii) *Detto II* (for cello and chamber orchestra); (iii) *Misterioso* (for 7 percussion); (iv) *Rubaiyat* (cantata).
(M) *** BMG/Melodiya Analogue/Dig. 74321 49957-2 [id.]. (i) Valeri Popov, Chamber Ens., Meshchaninov; (ii) Ivan Monighetti, Chamber Ens., Nikolaevsky; (iii) Bolshoi Theatre O percussion, Grishkin; (iv) Sergei Yakovenko, Chambe Ens., Rozhdestvensky.

Sofia Gubaidulina belongs to the same generation as Alfred Schnittke and Edison Denisov. The *Rubaiyat*, a cantata for baritone and chamber orchestra, and the *Detto II* for cello and chamber forces were both recorded in the 1970s, as was the *Concerto for bassoon and low strings*. *Misterioso* for seven percussion instruments is later (from 1990). Her music is unlikely to enjoy wide popular appeal – no harm in that – but readers who have become interested in this composer need not hesitate.

In croce for bayan and cello; Seven last words for cello, bayan and strings; Silenzio for bayan, violin and cello.
(BB) *** Naxos Dig. 8.553557 [id.]. Elsbeth Moser, Maria Kliegel, Kathrin Rabus, Camerata Transsylvanica, György Selmeczi.

In croce is an arrangement of a work for cello and organ, composed in 1979 and arranged for bayan or push-button accordion in 1993. The *Seven last words*, composed in 1982 for cello, accordion and strings, is probably the best entry-point into Gubaidulina's strange world, mesmerizing for some, boring for others. Maria Kliegel is an intense and powerful cellist, and Elsbeth Moser is a dedicated player long associated with this repertoire. Good recorded sound.

Guerrero, Francisco (1528–99)

Missa de la batalla escoutez; Conditor alme siderum; Duo Seraphim clamabant (motet); *In exitus Israel; Magnificat octavi toni; Pange lingua gloriosi; Regina caeli laetari, Alleluia* (instrumental version).
(N) *** Hyperion Dig. CDA 67075 [id.]. Westminster Cathedral Ch., His Majestys Sackbutts and Cornetts, James O'Donell.

The celebration of the quatrocentenary of Guerrero's death is at last bringing another important, but hitherto little-known Spanish composer before the public. A boy chorister and brilliant instrumentalist in his youth, he spent virtually his entire career as maestro at Seville Cathedral. But he also travelled widely, visiting Rome and Venice, and the Holy Land (writing a best-selling description of his *Journey to Jerusalem*). His music was printed both in Italy and France but mainly exists in manuscripts in Spain. The performances here (even in the *Mass*) use brass instruments as well as voices, following a well-documented (and here pictured) Sevillean tradition of *ministrilles*. At times these musicians played as a concerted group without singers (as they do here in the *Regina caeli laetari*), but were also used as part of the *alternatim* style, which was a particular feature of Guerrero's music, where plainchant regularly alternates with polyphony (notably so here in the splendid *Magnificat* and the psalm setting, *In exitu Israel)*. The Trinity motet, *Duo seraphim*, opening descriptively with two solo trebles, uses 12 voices in three choirs to create wide contrasts of dynamic and texture. The *Missa de la batalla*, for five voices, has something in common with *L'homme armé* in using a chanson of Jannequin, *La guerra*, as its basis, indicated by including the French word '*escoutez*' in its title. It is a comparatively restrained, sombre work, but the radiant closing *Agnus Dei*, which moves into eight parts, is particularly beautiful. *Pange lingua gloriosi* uses a popular melody, a gently swinging Iberian song, ornamented with counterpoint, and moving from voice to voice, in many ways like a primitive theme and variations. Throughout the disc, the eloquent singing, and very well-balanced, never overwhelming brass choir makes this a varied and highly enjoyable introduction to a remarkable composer, of whom we shall surely discover much more.

Missa Sancta et immaculata; Hei mihi, Domine; Lauda mater ecclesia; Magnificat septimi toni; O lux beata Trinitas; Trahe me post te, Virgo Maria; Vexilla Regis.
(N) *** Hyperion Dig. CDA66910 [id.]. Westminster Cathedral Ch., James O'Donnell.

Guerrero's *Missa Sancta et immaculata* is based on the celebrated four-part motet of that name by his one-time master Christóbal de Morales. It comes from his *Liber primus missarum* which was published in Paris in 1566. The two serene motets *Hei mihi, Domine* and *Trahe me post te, Virgo Maria* come from the second book of masses (1582) and the three hymns, *Vexilla Regis*, composed for Passion Sunday, *O lux beata Trinitas* and the spirited *Lauda mater ecclesia* are of striking quality and character. The Westminster Cathedral Choir and James O'Donnell give performances of quite outstanding eloquence and purity. The recording is first-class and there are exemplary notes by Bruno Turner.

Guilmant, Félix Alexandre (1837–1911)

Symphony No. 1 for organ and orchestra, Op. 42.
*** Chandos Dig. CHAN 9271 [id.]. Ian Tracey (organ of Liverpool Cathedral), BBC PO, Yan

Pascal Tortelier – WIDOR: *Symphony No. 5* ***; POULENC: *Organ concerto*. **(*)

This Guilmant *Symphony* (the composer's own arrangement of his *First Organ sonata*) is a real find, with all the genial vigour of the famous work of Saint-Saëns. The first movement has a galumphing main theme and an equally pleasing secondary idea. It is followed by a tunefully idyllic *Pastorale* (with some delicious registration from Ian Tracey) and a rumbustiously grandiloquent finale. All great fun, and well suited to the larger-than-life resonance of Liverpool Cathedral with its long reverberation period.

Haas, Joseph (1879–1960)

Krippenlieder (6 Songs of the Crib), Op. 49.
❀ *** EMI (SIS) Dig. CDC5 56204-2. Bär, Deutsch (with Recital: '*Christmas Lieder*' *** ❀).

Joseph Haas was professor of composition at both Stuttgart and Munich, but his own output has been sadly neglected. These delightful strophic songs help to make Olaf Bär's collection of German Christmas Lieder most treasurable. Their romantic melodic style also features a strong folk element. In the lovely opening *Weihnachtslegende* the 'Hosianna! Alleluja!' is very winning indeed, while the somewhat graver closing *Die Heiligen drei König* brings a charming repeated 'Eia Christkindelein, eia'. Marvellously warm and subtle performances from Bär and Deutsch alike, and splendidly natural recording.

Haas, Pavel (1899–1944)

String quartets Nos. 2 (From the Monkey Mountains), Op. 7; 3, Op. 15.
*** Decca Dig. 440 853-2 [id.]. Hawthorne Qt – KRASA: *Quartet*. ***

Pavel Haas, like Hans Krása, was one of the many Jewish musicians who were murdered by the Nazis at the Terezín (Teresienstadt) camp. Haas's *String quartet No. 2* dates from 1925 and its sub-title, *From the Monkey Mountains*, alludes to the Czech–Moravian highlands, which are so known in Brno. It is a highly imaginative and often beautiful score, with the strong, open-air feeling that one recognizes in Janáček. The *String quartet No. 3* (1938) comes after the lapse of a decade which had seen the rise of Nazism and the Munich treaty which led to the dismemberment and occupation of Czechoslovakia. It is a strong piece, more astringent in character than its predecessor, but it is well-argued and likeable music. The Hawthorne Quartet, members of the Boston Symphony Orchestra who have devoted themselves to music by victims of Nazi persecution, give dedicated performances. Excellent recording.

Hadley, Patrick (1899–1973)

(i–ii) *The Hills;* (ii–iii) *I sing of a maiden;* (iii–iv) *My beloved spake.*
(N) (M) *** EMI CDM5 67118-2 [id.]. (i) Palmer, Tear, Lloyd, Cambridge University Musical Society Ch.; (ii) Ledger; (iii) King's College, Cambridge, Ch.; (iv) Willcocks.

Once settled in Cambridge as a don (finally Professor of Music), Patrick Hadley became too contented to be a very active composer. But the richly enjoyable cantata *The Hills*, written on the unlikely subject of his parents' love-affair, showed what warmth and vitality lay behind his creative reticence. The style is attractively conservative, not unlike the music of Constant Lambert (whom Hadley in some respects resembled) but with echoes of Delius and Vaughan Williams. The writing is obviously grateful to all the performers, who here respond to Philip Ledger's dedicated direction with a ripe, committed performance, atmospherically recorded.

(i) *Lenten cantata. The cup of blessing; I sing of a maiden; My beloved spake; A Song for Easter.*
*** ASV Dig. CDDCA 881 [id.]. (i) John Mark Ainsley, Donald Sweeney; Ch. of Gonville & Caius College, Cambridge, Geoffrey Webber; Hill or Phillips (organ) – RUBBRA: *Choral music*. ***

The most substantial piece here is the *Lenten cantata* or *Lenten meditations* for two soloists, choir and orchestra (here given in an organ transcription), composed in 1963. Not a strongly individual voice, Hadley is nevertheless a refined craftsman whose feeling for line and texture is highly developed. The performances are of high quality, and so is the recording.

Hahn, Reynaldo (1875–1947)

Le bal de Béatrice d'Este (ballet suite).
*** Hyperion Dig. CDA 66347. New London O, Ronald Corp – POULENC: *Aubade; Sinfonietta*. ***

Le bal de Béatrice d'Este is a charming pastiche, dating from the early years of the century and scored for the unusual combination of wind instruments, two harps, piano and timpani. Ronald Corp and the New London Orchestra play it with real panache and sensitivity.

Piano concerto in E.
*** Hyperion Dig. CDA 66897 [id.]. Stephen Coombs, BBC Scottish SO, Ossonce – MASSENET: *Piano concerto*. ***

Entitled *Improvisation*, the opening movement of this charming work starts with a theme which surprisingly has an English flavour, easily lyrical, leading on to variations full of sharp, sparkling contrasts. A brief, light-hearted Scherzo leads to a combined slow movement (*Reverie*) and finale (*Toccata*). What Coombs's inspired performance demonstrates, most sympathetically supported by Jean-Yves Ossonce with the BBC Scottish Symphony, is that, though no deep emotions are touched, this is a delightful piece, well worth reviving, here perfectly coupled with another concerto also uncharacteristic of its composer and written late in his career.

Songs: *L'Air; A Chloris; L'Automne; 7 Chansons grises; La chère blessure; D'une prison; L'enamourée; Les étoiles; Fêtes galantes; Les fontaines; L'Incrédule; Infidélité; Offrande; Quand je fus pris au pavillon; Si mes vers avaient des ailes; Tyndaris.*
**(*) Hyperion CDA 66045 [id.]. Hill, Johnson.

If Hahn never quite matched the supreme inspiration of his most famous song, *Si mes vers avaient des ailes*, the delights here are many, the charm great. Martyn Hill, ideally accompanied by Graham Johnson, gives delicate and stylish performances, well recorded.

Mélodies: *L'air; Chansons grises; D'une prison; L'énamourée; Les fontaines; L'incrédule; Je me metz en vostre mercy; La nuit; Quand je fus pris au pavillon; Le rossignol des lilas; Seule; Si mes vers avaient des ailes; Le souvenir d'avoir chanté.*
(BB) *** Virgin Classics Dig. Double VBD5 61433-2 [CDVB 61433]. Rachel Yakar, Claude Lavoix – FAURE: *Mélodies.* ***

Rachel Yakar with her warm, very French-sounding timbre is an ideal interpreter of the songs of Hahn, Bizet and Chabrier on this second disc of this well-conceived bargain-priced Double. It is a pity that in this reissue no texts are given, but Yakar's way of bringing out the subtleties of word-meaning goes with beautifully clear diction. Though Hahn cannot match the other composers in depth or imagination, his facile genius in 19 songs, including the seven *Chansons grises*, setting Verlaine, and the most popular of all, a teenage inspiration, *Si mes vers avaient des ailes*, brings many delights. Excellent (1988) recording from Radio France.

Mélodies: *A Chloris; Au rossignol; Les cygnes; D'une prison; Fêtes galantes; L'heure exquise; Infidélité; Je me souviens; Mai; Ma jeunesse; Nocturne; La Nymphe de la Source; Offrande; Paysage; Le plus beau présent; Puisque j'ai mis ma lèvre; Quand la nuit n'est pas étoilée; Rêverie; Le rossignol des lilas; Séraphine; Seule; Si mes vers avaient des ailes; Sur l'eau; Trois jours de vendange. Ciboulette: C'est sa banlieue (Y a des arbres); Non avons fait un beau voyage. O mon bel inconnu: C'est très vilain d'être infidèle. 10 Etudes Latines; 12 Rondels. Mozart* (musical comedy): *Air de la lettre. Une Revue: La dernière* (valse).
(N) *** Hyperion Dig. CDA 67141/2 [id.]. Felicity Lott, Susan Bickley, Ian Bostridge, Stephen Varcoe, L. Schubert Chorale, Stephen Layton, Graham Johnson.

This is the most comprehensive collection of Hahn songs ever recorded, including a number of items never available before and even items from stage works. As in his Schubert edition for Hyperion, Graham Johnson masterminds the project to give endless new insights, whether in his ideal choice of soloists, his inspired playing or his illuminating notes. Specially valuable are the ten *Etudes latines*, both pure and sensuous in their classical evocation. Fine, atmospheric sound.

'La belle epoque': Mélodies: *A Chloris; L'Automne; D'une prison; L'enamorée; Dans la nuit; Fêtes galantes; Les fontaines; Fumée; L'heure exquise; Infidélité; Je me souviens; Mai; Nocturne; Offrande; Paysage; Le printemps; Quand je fus pris au pavillon; Quand la nuit n'est pas étoilée; Le rossignol des lilas; Si mes vers avaient des ailes; Trois jours de vendange. Etudes Latines: Lydé; Phyllis; Tyndaris.*
(N) *** Sony SK 60168 [id.]. Susan Graham, Roger Vignoles.

The solemnity of Susan Graham's first song, *A Chloris*, with its Bachian pastiche, may surprise those who think of Hahn as merely a dilettante tunesmith, and Graham finds the fullest range of expression in this charming collection. Hahn may fail to bring out the poignancy behind the Verlaine poem, *D'une prison*, but within his limited range he is a master. A good single-disc choice, made the more attractive by the glowing beauty of Graham's voice, sensuous in the most famous song, *Si mes vers avait des ailes*. Fine, sensitive accompaniment from Roger Vignoles.

Halévy, Jacques Fromental

(1799–1862)

La juive (opera): complete.
*** Ph. Dig. 420 190-2 (3). Varady, Anderson, Carreras, Gonzalez, Furlanetto, Amb. Op. Ch., Philh. O, Almeida.

La juive ('The Jewess') was the piece which, along with the vast works of Meyerbeer, set the pattern for the epic French opera, so popular last century. Eléazar was the last role that the great tenor, Enrico Caruso, tackled. The greater part of the recording was completed in 1986, but that was just at the time when José Carreras was diagnosed as having leukaemia, and it was only in 1989 that he contributed his performance through 'overdubbing'. He sings astonishingly well, but the role of the old

Jewish father really needs a weightier, darker voice, such as Caruso had in his last years. Julia Varady as Rachel makes that role both the emotional and the musical centre of the opera, responding both tenderly and positively. In the other soprano role, that of the Princess Eudoxia, June Anderson is not so full or sweet in tone, but she is impressive in the dramatic coloratura passages. Ferruccio Furlanetto makes a splendidly resonant Cardinal in his two big solos, and the Ambrosian Opera Chorus brings comparable bite to the powerful ensembles. Antonio de Almeida proves a dedicated advocate.

Halvorsen, Johan (1864–1935)

Air norvégien, Op. 7; Danses norvégiennes.

(BB) *** Naxos Dig. 8.550329 [id.]. Dong-Suk Kang, Slovak (Bratislava) RSO, Adrian Leaper – SIBELIUS: *Violin concerto;* SINDING: *Légende;* SVENDSEN: *Romance.* ***

Dong-Suk Kang plays the attractive *Danses norvégiennes* with great panache, character and effortless virtuosity, and delivers an equally impeccable performance of the earlier *Air norvégien*.

Hamerik, Asger (1843–1923)

Symphony No. 6 in G minor (Symphonie spirituelle), Op. 38.

(N) *** CPO Dig CPO 999 516-2 [id.]. German Chamber Academy, Neuss, Johannes Goritski – GADE: *Novelletter, Opp. 53 & 58.* ***

Asger Hamerik belongs to the generation of Danish symphonists between Gade and Nielsen. He was briefly a pupil of Berlioz and in 1867 composed a *Hymn à la Paix* whose scoring called for no fewer than twelve harps! On Berlioz's death he left France and went to Baltimore as the director of the Peabody Institute. His *Sixth Symphony (Symphonie spirituelle)* for strings comes from 1897 and is in the Gade–Schumann tradition. There is a *Seventh* and *choral symphony*, composed the following year, after which he gave up America and composing altogether, returning to retire in Copenhagen. No. 6 is quite an appealing work and this is its first modern recording. (Boyd Neel recorded it for Decca in the days of 78s.) First-class playing and recording.

Handel, George Frideric
(1685–1759)

The Alchymist: suite; Concerti a due cori Nos. 1–3; 2 Arias for wind band; Royal Fireworks music; Water music: suites Nos. 1–3 (complete).

(B) **(*) O-L Double Analogue/Dig. 455 709-2 (2) [id.]. AAM, Hogwood.

A useful and attractive two-CD collection, bringing together rarities as well as the complete Fireworks and Water music. *The Alchymist* suite is made up of 'act tunes' used for a revival of Ben Jonson's play at the Queen's Theatre, Haymarket in 1710. It is jolly music but, presented here spiritedly, is much more conventional than the consistently inspired invention for the two great royal occasions. It was the *Water music* with which Hogwood's Academy of Ancient Music made its début at the Proms in 1978, and the joy of that occasion is matched by this performance. While it may still seem disconcerting to hear the well-known *Air* taken so fast – like a minuet – the sparkle and airiness of the invention have rarely been caught on record so endearingly. Hogwood's account of the *Fireworks music*, recorded two years later, can also be counted among the best available. The *Concerti a due cori*, sharing musical material taken from familiar works (including *Messiah*), are scored for two groups of wind instruments with an accompanying string orchestra plus continuo. Horns are strongly featured in the *F major Concertos* (Nos. 1 and 3). The present (1983) performances are lively enough, but the recording is thinner. The two *Arias for wind band* include an arrangement of an actual operatic aria (from *Teseo*) and again are rather spoilt by the inaccurate tuning of the period horns.

Ballet music: *Alcina: overture; Acts I & III: suites. Il pastor fido: suite. Terpsichore: suite.*

(M) *** Erato/Warner 2292-45378-2 [id.]. E. Bar. Soloists, Gardiner.

John Eliot Gardiner is just the man for such a programme. He is not afraid to charm the ear, yet allegros are vigorous and rhythmically infectious. The bright and clean recorded sound adds to the sparkle, and the quality is first class. A delightful collection, and very tuneful too.

Amaryllis: suite; *The Faithful shepherd:* suite; *The Gods go a-begging:* suite; *The Great elopement:* suite; *The Origin of design:* suite (all arr. Beecham).

(M) (***) Dutton mono CDAX 8018 [id.]. LPO, Sir Thomas Beecham.

Superbly transferred by Dutton, these colourful, ever-charming transcriptions come in vintage performances from the magician himself, made in his LPO days. No one will ever quite match him in bringing out the colour and sparkle of arrangements which boldly fly in the face of all that the purists tell us. As Lyndon Jenkins's admirable note says, the first of the Handel–Beecham suites appeared in 1928: *The Gods go a-begging*, designed as ballet, with movements drawn from various operas, *Alcina*, *Rodrigo*, *Admeto* and *Teseo*, and adding the *Hornpipe* from the *Concerto grosso*, Op. 6/7. After that, Beecham's purloinings are rather harder to identify, and his modifications include a burst of *Rule Britannia* on the final cadence of the *Hornpipe* in

The Great elopement, hilariously timed. The Dutton transfers let one appreciate the extra frequency-range of the 1945 recording of *The Great elopement*. Otherwise, rather surprisingly, the earliest recordings, dating from January 1933 – *The Origin of design* and two movements from *The Gods go-abegging* – are the most sharply focused, with astonishing body and presence.

Concerti a due cori Nos. 1 in B flat; 2 in F; 3 in F; Overture in D; Solomon: Arrival of the Queen of Sheba; Concerto grosso in C (Alexander's Feast).
(M) *** Ph. 454 131-2 [id.]. ASMF, Marriner.

The *Concerti a due cori* were almost certainly written for performance with the three patriotic oratorios (No. 1 with *Joshua*, No. 2 with *Alexander Babus* and No. 3 with *Judas Maccabaeus*). They are full of good tunes (some very familiar, as they are drawn from the *Messiah*). The performances here are rich-timbred and stylish, full of warmth, with modern instruments conveying the grandeur of Handel's inspiration. This applies equally to the *Overture in D* and the better-known *Concerto grosso* associated with *Alexander's Feast*. Only in the *Arrival of the Queen of Sheba* would a lighter touch have been beneficial.

Concerti a due cori Nos. 1 in B flat; 2–3 in F, HWV 332–4; Music for the Royal Fireworks.
(N) *** Sony Dig. SK 63073 [id.]. Tafelmusik, Lamon.

The Tafelmusic *Fireworks music* is both boldly expansive and crisply rhythmic, with fine clean drums underpinning the brassily full textures of the outer sections, and plenty of character elsewhere. The *Concerti a due cori* are better played and much better tuned than Hogwood's set, and there are some fascinating sonorities here (familiar tunes emerge in new instrumental costume). The playing of the baroque horns is spectacular. This stands alongside Marriner's fine modern-instrument recording coupled with the *Alexander's Feast concerto grosso* (see above).

(i) *Concerti grossi, Op. 3/1–6; Op. 6/1–12*; (ii) *in C (Alexander's Feast)*. (iii) *Concerti a due cori Nos. 1–3*; (i; iv) *Oboe concertos Nos. 1–3*; (i; v) *Organ concertos Nos 1–6, Op. 4/1–6; 7–12, Op. 7/1–6; 13–16.*(i) *Music for the Royal Fireworks; Sonata: Il trionfo del tempo e del disinganno; Solomon: Arrival of the Queen of Sheba. Water music: suites 1–3* (complete).
(N) (B) *** Decca Analogue/Dig. 458 333–2 (8) [id.]. (i) ASMF, Marriner; (ii) L. Philomusica O, Granville Jones; (iii) AAM, Hogwood; (iv) Roger Lord; (v) George Malcolm.

An outstanding collection. The great majority of the performances are from Marriner and his Academy on peak form. The *Concerti grossi*, Opp. 3 and 6, the *Fireworks* and *Water music* remain among the finest performances ever committed to disc. Hogwood steps in for the *Concerti a due cori* and makes a less than ideal case for period instruments when directly contrasted with the greater sophistication (and incomparably precise intonation) which one takes for granted with the ASMF. Never mind, the effect is still stimulating and with first class Decca (originally Argo) sound throughout, this box is worth any collector's consideration. Incidentally the Sonata: *Il trionfo del tempo e del disinganno* is short and sweet: it lasts for just under three minutes.

Concerti grossi, Op. 3/1–6; Op. 6/1–12.
❁ (M) *** Decca 444 532-2 (3). ASMF, Marriner.

Concerti grossi, Op. 3/1–6 (including *No. 4b*); *Concerti grossi, Op. 6/1–12.*
(M) **(*) Teldec/Warner Analogue/Dig. 4509 95500-2 (4) [id.]. VCM, Harnoncourt.

This integral Decca recording of the Handel *Concerti grossi* makes a permanent memorial of the partnership formed by the inspired scholarship of Thurston Dart and the interpretative skill and musicianship of (then plain Mr) Neville Marriner and his superb ensemble, at their peak in the late 1960s. Dart planned a double continuo of both organ and harpsichord, used judiciously to vary textural colour and weight. Flutes and oboes are employed (with delightful effect) where Handel suggested in Op. 3, and in Op. 6 the optional oboe parts are used in concertos 1, 2, 5 and 6. The final concerto of Op. 3 features the organ as a solo instrument, a choice questioned by Christopher Hogwood in his researches. The three records come at a special lower-mid-price. But, alas, the superb CD transfer brings no separate cues for individual movements, only one band for each work.

The Teldec set is the most endearing of Harnoncourt's earlier authentic performances of baroque music. In Op. 3, tempi tend to be relaxed, but the performances are very enjoyable in their easy-going way, the ripe, fresh colouring of the baroque oboes, played expressively, is most attractive to the ear, and the string-sound is unaggressive. Tuttis are curiously dry, suggesting that the microphones were close to the violins; otherwise the sound is very good and the whole effect quite distinctive. So it is in Op. 6, where the recording is much more ample. Unfortunately Op. 3 (with its extra concerto) plays for 71 minutes at Harnoncourt's chosen tempi and Teldec have spread Op. 6 uneconomically over three more CDs, an expensive way of obtaining this music, even at mid-price.

Concerti grossi, Op. 3/1–6.
(M) **(*) Erato/Warner 2292 459981-2 [id.]. E. Bar. Soloists, Gardiner.

Gardiner's analogue set from 1980 has transferred

well to CD. Recorded in the Henry Wood Hall, textures are slightly more ample but still clear and admirably balanced. The starry cast-list includes Simon Standage and Roy Goodman among the violins, and the playing is both lively and stylish. There is a slight lack of finish in one or two places and some poor intonation in *No. 2 in B flat* – yet one also notes the imaginative treatment of the *Largo e staccato* of Op. 3/3 and its following *Adagio*, with Lisa Beznosiuk the engaging flute soloist.

Concerti grossi, Op. 3/1–6.
*** Sony Dig. SK 52553 [id.]. Tafelmusik, Jeanne Lamon.
*** DG (IMS) 413 727-2. E. Concert, Pinnock.
*** Ph. (IMS) Dig. 411 482-2 [id.]. ASMF, Marriner.

Those looking for a fine, digital recording of Op. 3, with its woodwind complement added to the strings and a concertante organ in No. 6, will find the Tafelmusik disc very satisfactory. The playing is fresh and unfussy – plainer than with Gardiner. It is alert, elegant and with plenty of warmth, and tempi are admirably judged. Original instruments are used but not flaunted too abrasively and the sound is first class, clear as well as full.

The six Op. 3 concertos with their sequences of brief jewels of movements also find Pinnock and the English Concert at their freshest and liveliest, with plenty of sparkle and little of the abrasiveness associated with 'authentic' performance.

In Sir Neville Marriner's latest version with the Academy, tempi tend to be brisk, but the results are inspiriting and enjoyable. Predictably, textures are fuller here than on Pinnock's competing Archiv recording, and the CD quality is admirably fresh.

(i) *Concerti grossi, Op. 3/1–6;* (ii) *Organ concertos Nos. 1–6, Op. 4/1–6.*
(B) **(*) Ph. Duo (IMS) 442 263-2 (2) (i) ECO, Leppard; (ii) Daniel Chorzempa, Concerto Amsterdam, Schröder.

Among versions of Handel's Op. 3, Leppard's set stands high. The playing is lively and fresh, and the remastered recording sounds very good. Leppard includes oboes and bassoons and secures excellent playing all round. In general this reissue offers one of the best versions of Op. 3 on modern instruments. In this Duo pairing we are also offered Daniel Chorzempa's set of Handel's Op. 4 *Organ concertos*, and here we move over to period instruments. The Concerto Amsterdam, with their robustly substantial sound, bring plenty of rhythmic buoyancy and life to the accompaniments. Chorzempa uses an appropriate Dutch organ and the balance is admirable. Regarding ornamentation, Chorzempa's approach is fairly elaborate and he interpolates a sonata movement from Op. 1 after the *Adagio* of the *Third Concerto*. The recording is again excellent, and those for whom the coupling is suitable will find this is good value.

(i) *Concerti grossi, Op. 3/1–6;* (ii) *Water music: suites 1–3* (complete).
(N) (B) ** Erato/Warner Ultima Dig. 3984 24243-2 (2) [id.]. (i) Les Musiciens du Louvre, Minowski; (ii) Amsterdam Bar. O, Koopman.

In Minowski's set of the *Concerti grossi* the original wind instruments alter the character of the tuttis, with the oboe or oboes bringing a reedy quality, and at times the wind instruments steal so much of the limelight from the strings that one has the impression that these are solo concertos for oboe or, in the case of No. 3, recorder and flute. In No. 6 the organ dominates. String textures are bright and transparent, with the lightest possible sonority, and the continuo comes through intimately. With brisk allegros that are always alert and vivacious, the effect here is of hearing a completely new series of concertos.

Koopman's approach to the *Water music*, again using period instruments, also brings an individual approach. In the first, *F major Suite*, he starts almost gingerly, as if he were dipping his toes in the water, and it is not until the third movement *Allegro*, with the entry of the horns, that the music becomes more robust. The second suite places elegance of style first and foremost, and the effect, engaging as it is in its way, seems more like eighteenth-century French court music. The opening of the third *D major suite* has a ceremonial feeling, but overall this has the character of a chamber performance: even the famous *Hornpipe* brings a crisp small-scale approach. The result in both performances is undoubtedly refreshing, but some Handelians will miss a fuller sound.

Concerti grossi, Op. 6/1–12.
*** Chandos Dig. CHAN 9004/6 [id.]. I Musici de Montréal, Yuli Turovsky.
(N) (B) *** Decca Double Dig. 458 817-2 (2) [id.]. Handel & Haydn Soc. of Boston, Hogwood.
(BB) *** Belart 461 329-2 (*Nos. 1–4*); 461 330-2 (*Nos. 5–8*); 461 331-2 (*Nos. 9–12*) (available separately). ECO, Leppard.
**(*) DG Dig. 410 897-2 (*1–4*); 410 898-2 (*5–8*); 410 899-2 (*9–12*) [id.]. E. Concert, Pinnock.
(N) (BB) *(*) Arte Nova Dig. 74321 34020-2 *(Nos. 1–2, 5–6)*; 30470-2 *(Nos. 3–4, 7–8)*; 30497-2 *(Nos. 9–12)* (available separately) [id.]. Hamburg Soloists, Emil Klein.
(B) (***) Millennium mono MCD 80078 (*Nos. 1–4*); MCD 80123 (*Nos. 5–8*); MCD 80131 (*Nos. 9–12*). E. Bar. O, Hermann Scherchen.

12 Concerti grossi, Op. 6/1–12; Concerto grosso in C (Alexander's feast).

(N) **(*) Chandos Dig. CHAN 0600 *(Nos. 1–5)*; 0616 *(Nos. 6–9)*; 0622 *(Nos. 10–12); Alexander's feast)* (available separately) [id.]. Coll. Musicum 90, Standage.

I Musici de Montréal offer a refreshing and stimulating set of Handel's Opus 6. The group uses modern instruments and Yuli Turovsky aims to seek a compromise between modern and authentic practice, by paring down vibrato in some of the expressive music, with just a hint of squeezing on the melodic line, as when the solo group make their restrained entry in slow movements. The concertino, Eleonora and Natalya Turovsky and Alain Aubut, play impressively, while the main group (6.3.1.1) produces full, well-balanced tone and Handel's joyous fugues are particularly fresh and buoyant. Turovsky paces convincingly, not missing Handel's breadth of sonority and moments of expressive grandeur. This is now our first choice for this wonderful music.

Admirers of Hogwood's characteristically astringent rhythmic style will be well satisfied with his Op. 6. The playing has enormous vitality, with bracingly brisk tempi and emphasis on refinement and transparency of texture rather than sonority. Two harpsichords and an arch-lute are used as continuo. The playing is heard at its finest in the masterly *Fifth Concerto in D major*, with the allegros sparkling with vivacity. The sound of the solo original instruments in the lyrical writing almost suggests viols rather than violins, although the forward balance gives the concertino soloists a strikingly firm presence. Listening to this exhilarating music-making is certainly a refreshing experience, and Hogwood is undoubtedly preferable to Pinnock, helped by the fuller, more naturally focused, Decca sound. However, the great tune of No. 12 (*Larghetto e piano*) is without the feeling of noble breadth achieved in Marriner's modern-instrument performance.

Simon Standage's Chandos set with Collegium Musicum 90 has been much admired and indeed, for its combination of delicately crisp rhythmic vitality and airy grace, it has much to offer. Yet anyone looking for weight of Handelian sonority in the ripieno will not find it here. Even though the main orchestral group is not small in numbers (5, 5, 3, 3, 1) and includes Handel's optional oboes and bassoon, the tutti is very much that of a small chamber group. Clearly, robustness is not part of Standage's conception: fresh, refined transparency is his hallmark and this means no bold, full contrasts with the concertino. The playing is of high calibre, though there is a complete absence of geniality, notably in the fugal writing, where Handel is so different from Bach. The Chandos recording is first-class.

Leppard's 1967 Philips set is now offered on Universal Classics' Belart label for little more than the cost of just one of the Chandos CDs. Moreover it sounds splendid in its newly remastered format, not in the least dated. The main group is comparatively full-bodied, which means that Leppard's soloists stand out in greater relief, graceful and elegant. These performances, too, have plenty of spirit and lively rhythmic feeling, while the richer orchestral texture brings added breadth in slow movements. How beautiful is the famous melody from the very last concerto, marked *Larghetto e piano*, when played so smoothly and lyrically on modern instruments.

For all its 'authenticity', Pinnock's is never unresponsive music-making, with fine solo playing set against an attractively atmospheric acoustic. Ornamentation is often elaborate – but never at the expense of line. These are performances to admire and to sample, but not everyone will warm to them. If listened through, the sharp-edged sound eventually tends to tire the ear, and there is comparatively little sense of grandeur and few hints of tonally expansive beauty. The recording is first class.

If Standage's set of Handel's masterpiece is distinguished by its lightness of touch, Emil Klein's Hamburg version, using modern instruments, goes to the opposite extreme. There is certainly no lack of sonority, but the music's progress is too often marked by its lack of resilience and sparkle. The soloists are very good and the orchestral playing itself is finished, but the rhythmic weightiness and sporadic lack of vitality are enervating. The plodding opening of Op.5/6 is matched by the leaden progress of the famous *Larghetto e piano* melody of the third movement of No.12, which in Standage's hands is feather-light.

Recorded in September 1954, Scherchen's warm and affectionate performances are sheer joy. He presents the music on the grandest scale, bringing out the full richness of the lyrical invention (the famous *Largo* from the last of the set is even more graciously beautiful than with Leppard). Indeed the playing of the English Baroque Orchestra (the ECO under a pseudonym perhaps?) is full of grace, while allegros, although leisurely paced, have a balancing rhythmic spring. At cadences Scherchen endearingly produces weighty rallentandos. The recording is fresh and clear, although the upper range of the violins is made characteristically thin by the microphones of the time.

Concerti grossi, Op. 6/1–10.

(N) (B) **(*) EMI double fforte CZS5 73344-2 (2) [id.]. Bath Festival CO, Lord Menuhin.

(i) *Concerti grossi, Op. 6/11–12; Water music* (suites 1–3; complete); (ii) *Violin sonatas, Op. 1/3, 10, 12–15.*

(N) (B) **(*) EMI double fforte CZS5 73347-2

(2) [id.]. (i) Bath Festival CO, Lord Menuhin (ii) Menuhin, Malcolm, Gauntlet.

It was Boyd Neel who pioneered the first complete recording of Handel's Opus 6 on six early Decca mono 10″ LPs, later to be transferred (less successfully) to three 12″ LPs, and we hope Mike Dutton has his sights on these superbly played versions for transfer to CD. Scherchen then provided the very enjoyable mono version mentioned above, but it was Menuhin who gave us the first complete stereo set in the early 1960s, recording the later concertos first and working backwards. Seeking authenticity he used a modest body of strings, and during the sessions it was suggested to the artists that a double continuo might be used, as was Handel's practice. But this does not appear to happen until what was originally the third LP, containing Nos. 1, 2, 4, and 5 (in this reissue the works are presented in a straightforward numerical sequence). In these four works, a chamber organ fills out the sonority of the ripieno, and George Malcolm plays a harpsichord with the soloists. In consequence, the performances of the first two concertos – the last to be recorded – are the finest of the set, both buoyant and rich in expressive feeling; the harpsichord contribution comes through splendidly, and the result (recorded in the Kingsway Hall) is sonically glorious. In the later concertos the harpsichord continuo is too backwardly balanced. But they are still very enjoyable. Even if tempi are slower than we would expect today, *allegros* are spirited and have an agreeable lift, while Menuhin takes care not to sentimentalize the famous *Larghetto e piano* of No. 12, presenting it with an appealing combination of warmth and delicacy. For the *Water music* he used a new edition especially prepared by Neville Boyling, and his genial approach again demonstrates the humanity and freshness which always informed his music-making, with excellent playing and lively spontaneity throughout. Both recordings have been admirably transferred to CD. The Opus 1 *Violin sonatas* were pioneering authentic versions, vital and stylish, using a well-balanced continuo (Ambrose Gauntlet, viola da gamba and George Malcolm, harpsichord). But here the CD transfer makes Menuhin's violin timbre sound slightly edgy. The 1963 Abbey Road recording is warm, fresh and clear in its new CD transfer.

Concerti grossi, Op. 6/1–4; Concerto grosso in C (Alexander's feast).

(N) *** Virgin Veritas/EMI Dig. OAE, Nicholas McGegan.

McGegan's Virgin Veritas disc is the first instalment of a most enjoyable new set which promises to be among the top recommendations for period-instrument versions. Above all, the playing appealingly combines rhythmic vitality with a graceful warmth in slow movements, while Handel's fugal passages are spirited and joyous. This is a chamber performance in character, yet the ripieno (6, 6, 4, 4, 2) plus 2 oboes and 2 bassoons, while refined, also has weight: the bold rhythmic focus prevents the bass spreading and becoming too opulent. The concertino (Elizabeth Wallfisch, Catherine Mackintosh, Alison Bury and Susan Sheppard) play most beautifully, without a suspicion of edginess. In the infectious account of the *Alexander's Feast concerto*, the ripieno is further augmented, but textures remain fresh. The Abbey Road recording has just the right degree of resonance.

Concerto grosso in B flat, Op. 6/7.

(N) *** Arabesque Dig. Z 6723 [id.]. San Francisco Ballet O, Lark Qt., Jean-Louis Le Roux – SCHOENBERG: *Concerto for string quartet and orchestra after Handel's Op. 6/7*; ELGAR: *Introduction and allegro for strings*; SPOHR: *Concerto for string quartet and orchestra*. ***

What a pleasure to hear a Handel *concerto grosso* played for once on a full body of modern strings, emphasizing its warmth of sonority. But this is included as part of an imaginative concert of string music so that the listener can compare the original with Schoenberg's bizarre but aurally fascinating recomposed pastiche.

(i) *Flute concerto in D* (attrib.); (ii) *Double cello concerto in G min.;* (iii) *Harp concerto in B flat, Op. 4/6;* (iv) *Oboe concertos Nos. 1–3.*

(BB) **(*) Arte Nova Dig. 74321 51634-2 [id.]. (i) Edward Beckett; (ii) Ferenc Szucs; (iii) Lucy Wakeford; (iv) Malcolm Messiter; L. Festival O, Ross Pople.

An enjoyable collection of Handelian concertos, not all of them authentic. The *Harp concerto* sounds as delectable as ever, and Malcolm Messiter is a neatly stylish soloist in the three works for oboe, although Pople's accompaniments have not quite the degree of finesse which Marriner finds for Roger Lord. The agreeable *Flute concerto* is almost certainly not by Handel (the CD notes suggest that it was commissioned by an aristocratic amateur flautist in about 1737) but it is well played. The other novelty is the amiable work for a pair of cellos (although only one player is credited), arranged most effectively from a *Sonata in G minor* (HWV 393). The recording is truthful and pleasingly balanced.

(i) *Harp concerto, Op. 4/6. Variations for harp.*

✿ (M) *** Decca 425 723-2. Marisa Robles, (i) ASMF, Iona Brown – BOIELDIEU; DITTERSDORF: *Harp concertos* etc. ***✿

Handel's Op. 4/6 is well known in both organ and harp versions. Marisa Robles and Iona Brown make an unforgettable case for the latter by creating the most delightful textures, while never letting the work sound insubstantial. The ASMF accompaniment, so stylish and beautifully balanced, is a treat in itself, and the recording is well-nigh perfect.

Oboe concertos Nos. 1–3; Air and Rondo (ed. Camden); (i) *Suite in G min.* (ed. Camden); *Otho: overture.*

(BB) *** Naxos Dig. 8.553430 [id.]. Anthony Camden, (i) Julia Girdwood; City of London Sinfonia, Ward.

Oboe concertos Nos 1–3; Concerto grosso, Op. 3/3; Hornpipe in D, HWV 356; Overture in D, HWV 337/8; Sonata à 5 in B flat, HWV 288.

(M) **(*) Ph. 426 082-2 [id.]. Heinz Holliger, ECO, Raymond Leppard.

Oboe concertos Nos. 1 in B flat, HWV 301; 2 in B flat, HWV 302a; 3 in G min., HWV 287; Largo in F, HWV 302b. Solomon: Arrival of the Queen of Sheba.

(B) *** Decca Double 452 943-2 (2). Roger Lord, ASMF, Marriner – BELLINI: *Oboe concerto in E flat;* – VIVALDI: *Miscellaneous concertos.* ***

Handel's three *Oboe concertos* have an immediate appeal, their style predominantly lyrical, and they are given sensitive, polished performances by Roger Lord and the Academy. Incidentally, the *Largo in F* uses the same musical material as the first movement of the *Second Concerto*, but with quite spectacular horn parts added to the accompaniment. With Bellini's brief but delightful concerto added for good measure, this makes a fine coupling for the Academy's generous programme of miscellaneous Vivaldi concertos, which are in every way recommendable. The vintage (originally Argo) sound is first class.

Anthony Camden, for years principal oboe of the LSO, here makes a very welcome solo appearance on disc, playing with typical point and style, using his attractively reedy tone. The regular oboe concertos are well supplemented by the *Suite in G minor* as edited by Camden, where he is joined by the prize-winning Julia Girdwood on the second oboe. The *Otho Overture* too features prominent roles for oboes in duet. Ward and the City of London Sinfonia are sympathetic accompanists using modern instruments. First-rate sound from All Saints, East Finchley. A fine alternative to Roger Lord with the ASMF.

Holliger, a masterly interpreter, does not hesitate to embellish repeats; his ornamentation may overstep the boundaries some listeners are prepared to accept. His playing and that of the other artists in this collection is exquisite, and the recording is naturally balanced.

Oboe concertos Nos. 1 in B flat, HWV 301; 2, HWV 302a; 3, HWV 287; Sonatas for oboe and continuo in B flat, HWV 357; in F, HWV 363a; in G min., Op. 1/6, HWV 364a; in C min., Op. 1/8, HWV 366; Sonata in G min. for oboe, violins and continuo, HWV 404.

(N) *** Unicorn Dig. DKP 9153 [id.]. Sarah Francis, L. Harpsichord Ens.

Sarah Francis has already recorded oboe concertos by Telemann and she is a superb baroque oboeist, at the same time directing the members of the London Baroque Ensemble with spirit and finesse. These performances are not only delightful, but a model of style, and make an unanswerable case for playing this music on modern instruments when the recording is really well balanced, as it is here. In the *sonatas*, Handel's ever-engaging contrapuntal interplay is beautifully clear (the harpsichord comes through in perfect balance with the continuo), so that for sheer pleasure, these performances almost upstage the more familiar concertos. Apart from the nimble articulation in allegros, Miss Francis's playing is memorable both for her appealing timbre and her sensitive, lyrical phrasing, where she varies her vibrato with the utmost subtlety. A collection which easily leads the field, not least for its excellent sound.

Organ concertos

Organ concertos Nos. 1–6, Op. 4/1–6.

(N) *** Virgin Veritas EMI Dig. VC5 45174-2 [id.]. Bob van Asperen, OAE.

Organ concertos Nos. 7–12; Op. 7/7–6; 13 in F (Cuckoo and nightingale), HWV 295; 14 in A, HWV 296; 15 in D min., BWV 304; 16 in D, BWV 305a.

(N) *** Vergin Veritas/EMI Dig. VCD5 45256-2 (2) [id.]. Bob van Asperen, OAE.

Bob van Asperen's survey is absolutely complete and its combination of musicianship and scholarship gives this Virgin set a special feeling of authenticity. Although the accompanying group is comparatively modest (the orchestra includes four violins, two each of violas and cellos, double bass, plus oboes, bassoons and continuo) there is no feeling that the scale of the music is minimized. The recording could hardly be bettered. In Opus 4, van Asperen chooses an organ built by Goetz and Gwynne in 1985 using seventeenth-century models, and he directs the Orchestra of the Age of Enlightenment from the keyboard, as Handel would have done. The results are refreshingly alert and buoyant. From the orchestra there is expressive warmth as well as vitality, and no lack of weight when called for. For Op.7 he turns to an equally appealing four-stop continuo organ by N. P. Mander Ltd. Also included here are the pair of concertos known as the '*Second set*' (one is the famous *Cuckoo and nightingale*) and the two final works, as published by Arnold in 1797. No. 15, HWV 304 is reworked from a flute sonata in Telemann's *Musique de table*, linked by an ad lib *Adagio and fugue* to be provided by the performer (here transcribed movements from the *Violin sonata, Op. 1/3*). No. 16 is an eight-movement concerto in F, robustly orchestrated and closely based on the *Concerto a due cori No. 3*, ending grandly with the *March* from *Judas Maccabaeus* with horns braying exuberantly. Throughout, in the places where Handel would have improvised, extra Handelian movements are interpolated (mainly from the keyboard suites and solo sonatas, and all listed in the synopsis), but van Asperen improvises shorter linking passages himself. A considerable achievement.

Organ concertos, Op. 4/1–6; Op. 7/1–6; in F (The cuckoo and the nightingale), HVW 295; in A, HWV 296; in D min., HWV 304.

(M) *** DG Dig. 435 037-2 (3). Simon Preston, E. Concert, Pinnock.

Simon Preston's set of the Handel *Organ concertos* now comes on three discs. On the first, containing the six Op. 4 works, plus the *A major*, though the balance of the solo instrument is not perfect, the playing of both Preston and the English Concert is admirably fresh and lively. Ursula Holliger is outstanding on a baroque harp (taking the place of the organ) in Op. 4, No. 6, and she creates some delicious sounds. The second and third discs, containing the six Op. 7 works, plus *The cuckoo and the nightingale* and the *D minor*, were recorded on the organ at St John's, Armitage, in Staffordshire, and are even more attractive for the warmth and assurance of the playing, which comes near the ideal for a period performance. The *A major* which completes the set was recorded earlier with Op. 4. For those wanting a complete set of the *Organ concertos* this is also strongly recommended.

Organ concertos: Op. 4/1–6; Op. 7/1–6.

(N) ❁ Erato/Warner Dig. 0630 17871-2 (2) [id.]. Ton Koopman, Amsterdam Bar. O.

(B) **(*) Decca Double 452 235-2 (2) [id.]. George Malcolm (organ or harpsichord), ASMF, Marriner.

(M) **(*) Teldec/Warner 4509 91188-2 (2) [id.]. Herbert Tachezi, VCM, Harnoncourt.

Organ concertos Op. 4/1–3; (i) *Op. 4/4*; (ii) *Op. 4/6. Op. 7/1–6.*

(N) ** Hyperion Dig. CDA 67291/2 [id.]. Paul Nicholson, Brandenburg Consort, Roy Goodman; (i) with Clare College Ch., Cambridge; (ii) Frances Kelly (harp).

Ton Koopman's combined sets of Opp. 4 and 7 lead the field, complete on a pair of mid-priced CDs taken from the Koopman Handel Edition. They take precedence over all the competition except Bob van Asperen's set above, both as performances and as recordings. The playing has wonderful life and warmth, tempi are always aptly judged and, although original instruments are used, this is authenticity with a kindly presence, for the warm acoustic ambience of St Bartholomew's Church, Beek-Ubbergen, Holland, gives the orchestra a glowingly vivid coloration and the string timbre is particularly attractive. So is the organ itself, which is just right for the music. Ton Koopman plays imaginatively throughout and he is obviously enjoying himself: no single movement sounds tired and the orchestral fugues emerge with genial clarity. Koopman directs the accompanying group from the keyboard, as Handel would have done, and the interplay between soloist and ripieno is a delight. The sound is first class and the balance could hardly be better.

In his ornamentation and interpolations Malcolm is both imaginative and stylistically impeccable. He plays two of the concertos on the harpsichord (Op. 4/3 and Op. 7/6) and here achieves a near-perfect balance so that the harpsichord is in proper scale with the orchestra without being larger than life. Malcolm's registrations (using the organ of Merton College Chapel for Op. 4, and the instrument at St John the Evangelist, Islington, for Op. 7) are always colourful (notably in Op. 4/4). The lithe, resilient orchestral textures are vigorous in allegros, but in slow movements warmly refined and often subtly shaded. The vintage 1972–3 (originally Argo) recording is warm and full, and this music-making is easy to enjoy.

Herbert Tachezi also concentrates on the twelve concertos which make up Opp. 4 and 7. The ornamentation provided by the soloist was achieved spontaneously at the actual recording sessions, but Harnoncourt's accompaniments are straightforward, at times even seeming unadventurous and rhythmically positive. But Tachezi's registration and flourishes give constant pleasure, and the chest organ (made by Jürgen Ahrend) is very well chosen for this repertoire. Although Handel's more robust and grander qualities are rather played down, the recording is fresh, full, transparent and cleanly transferred, and there is much to enjoy here.

Besides using Handel's own organ (still in excellent condition) in St Lawrence, Whitchurch, at Canons, near Edgware, north of London, the Nicholson/Goodman set offers a novelty in including Op.4/4 in a 1737 version where Handel concluded the finale with an *Alleluia* chorus from *Athalia*, an eccentric idea which in the event is effective enough. Op.4/6 is heard in the arrangement for harp, which seems less sensible, when there are plenty of separate recordings of the *harp concerto*, and the performance lacks charm. In any case the performances here are at times curiously didactic. The crisp rhythms with which these works abound, and which should sound amiably jaunty, are often here just that bit too rigid. Both playing and recording are otherwise fresh, but the competition is fierce and this is far from a first choice.

Organ concertos, Op. 4/1–6.
(N) (BB) *** Naxos Dig. 8.553835 [id.]. Simon Lindley, N. Sinf., Bradley Creswick.

A most enjoyable and inexpensive modern instrument performance of Op. 4, rhythmically jaunty and warmly expressive by turns. Simon Lindley is an excellent soloist and the piping reeds of the organ at Holy Cross Church, Fenham, seem very apt for the music. Op. 4/6 is played and registered with appealing delicacy to remind us of the alternative version for harp. The recording balance is admirable. Not a first choice overall but an undoubted bargain.

Organ concertos, Op. 4/1, 2 & 4; Op. 7/1 & 4.
(N) *** Erato/Warner Dig. 3984 25486-2 [id.]. Marie-Claire Alain, Freiburg Baroque O, Gottfried Von Der Goltz.

This is perhaps a first instalment of a new digital recording of Handel's Op. 4 and Op. 7, but even if it were not, the disc includes five of Handel's most attractive concertos splendidly played on a Cavaillé-Coll organ with a superb baroque personality at Saint-Pierre des Chartreux, Toulouse. Although the Freiburg Orchestra uses period instruments, the effect is more robust than with Bob van Asperen's recordings, partly because of the larger personality of the organ. But Marie-Claire Alain's performances, too, are more extrovert and vivid. Goltz's orchestral support is stylish and refined, but never meagre (sample the fullness of the opening Adagio of Op. 7/4 with bassoons), and allegros have exhilarating buoyancy. The documentation includes a detailed plan of the registrations used. Most enjoyable.

Organ concertos, Op. 4/2; Op. 7/3–5; in F (The cuckoo and the nightingale).
(M) *** DG Dig. 447 300-2. Simon Preston, E. Concert, Pinnock.

This is more generous than the previous (full-price) sampler from Preston's series with Pinnock. Both performances and sound are admirably fresh.

Music for the Royal Fireworks (original wind scoring).
*** Telarc Dig. CD 80038 [id.]. Cleveland Symphonic Winds, Fennell – HOLST: *Military band suites.* ***✿

Music for the Royal Fireworks; Concerto grosso in C (Alexander's Feast); Overtures: Alceste; Belshazzar; Samson; Saul. Solomon: Arrival of the Queen of Sheba.
(M) *** DG Dig. 447 279-2. E. Concert, Trevor Pinnock.

Music for the Royal Fireworks (original version); (i) *Coronation anthems* (see also below).
*** Hyperion Dig. CDA 66350 [id.]. (i) New College, Oxford, Ch.; augmented King's Consort, Robert King.

In 1978, in Severance Hall, Cleveland, Ohio, Frederick Fennell gathered together the wind and brass from the Cleveland Symphony Orchestra and recorded a performance to demonstrate spectacularly what fine playing and digital sound could do for Handel's open-air score. The overall sound-balance tends to favour the brass (and the drums), but few will grumble when the result is as overwhelming as it is on the CD, with the sharpness of focus matched by the presence and amplitude of the sound-image.

Pinnock's performance of the *Fireworks music* has tremendous zest; this is not only the safest but the best recommendation for those wanting a period-instrument version. The account of the *Alexander's Feast concerto* has both vitality and imagination and is no less recommendable. The vigorous and exhilarating performances of five *Overtures*, most of them hardly known at all but full of original ideas, are all freshly and cleanly recorded.

King provides the first ever period performance of Handel's *Royal fireworks music* to use the full complement of instruments Handel demanded, assembling no fewer than 24 baroque oboists and 12 baroque bassoonists, 9 trumpeters, 9 exponents of the hand horn and 4 timpanists. It all makes for a glorious noise. King's Handel style has plenty of rhythmic bounce, and the recording in its warmly atmospheric way gives ample scale. The coupled performances of the four *Coronation anthems* are not as incisively dramatic as some but still convey the joy of the inspiration.

Music for the Royal Fireworks, HWV 351 (original wind scoring); *Concertos in D* (arr. from *Fireworks music, HWV 335a*); *in F* (arr. from *Water music, HWV 331/316*); *Occasional suite in D* (arr. Pinnock); *Passacaille, gigue et menuet* (arr. from *Trio sonata, Op. 5/4*).
(N) *** DG Dig. 453 451-2 [id.]. E. Concert, Pinnock.

Pinnock's newest (1996) recording of the *Royal Fireworks music* adds grandeur to vitality. It is superbly played, although fascinatingly the period horns do not quite produce the exciting edge that made Mackerras's early stereo Pye recording so memorable. The rest of the programme is agreeable occasional music, played with warmth and the new elegance which original-instrument performances have discovered recently, and the *Passacaglia, Gigue and Minuet* has the warmth of timbre one would expect from modern instruments. The two *concertos* have interpolated slow movements from other sources; the *Occasional suite* (a pastiche in the manner of Beecham) draws on the *Overture* from the *Occasional oratorio* (with a particularly beautiful oboe solo) plus excerpts from *Ariodante, Joshua*, and *Alessandro Severo*. All most enjoyable in a most unexpected way, almost old-fashioned in its colour and popular appeal.

Music for the Royal Fireworks; Water music (complete).
❀ *** DG Dig. 435 390-2 [id.]. Orpheus CO.
(N) *** Virgin Classics Dig. VC5 45265-2 [id.]. L. Classical Players, Norrington.
(N) (M) *** Classic fM Dig. 75605 570442. Scottish CO, McGegan.
*** Argo 414 596-2 [id.]. ASMF, Marriner.
(BB) *** Naxos Dig. 8.550109; *4550109* [id.]. Capella Istropolitana, Bohdan Warchal.

The conductorless Orpheus Chamber Orchestra are always impressive, but here their playing and ensemble are little short of superlative in polished and alive performances that sweep the board. Although modern instruments are used, such is the Orpheus sense of baroque style, so crisp and buoyant are the rhythms, that the effect has much in common with a period performance without any of the snags. How warmly and elegantly they play the colourful and more intimate dances in the central *G major Suite* of the *Water music*, and they begin with a riveting account of the *Royal Fireworks music*, catching its sense of spectacle. Strings are used as Handel wished, but the wind and brass dominate. The recording is in the demonstration bracket, and these performances are so fresh that it is like listening to this marvellous music for the very first time.

Norrington uses a full orchestra but highlights the bright trumpets and braying horns to give both works a vividly robust open-air flavour. The dance movements have grace, but a lively grace, and it is the consistent vitality that makes these performances so stimulating. The overtures of both works bring the crispest double-dotting, while the outer movements of the *Fireworks music* are as strong and rugged as you could want, without loss of polish or tuning.

McGegan and his excellent Scottish players, very well recorded in the Caird Hall, Dundee, use modern instruments but seek a style deriving from period-instrument experience, with brisk tempi and lifted rhythms, though somewhat more easygoing than Norrington. The Overture and finale of the *Royal Fireworks music* are boldly expansive and in the *Water music* textures are attractively light, phrasing neat and stylish. At mid-price this Classic fM pairing is very competitive.

Marriner, using modern instruments, directs a sparkling account of the complete *Water music* plus the *Fireworks music*. Here Marriner deliberately avoids a weighty manner, even at the magisterial opening of the overture. But with full, resonant recording, this coupling makes sound sense and the remastered Argo recording still sounds both full and fresh. However, it remains at full price.

Bohdan Warchal directs the Capella Istropolitana in bright and lively performances of the complete *Water music* as well as the *Fireworks music*, well paced and well scaled, with woodwind and brass aptly abrasive, and with such points as double-dotting faithfully observed. Textures are clean, with an attractive bloom on the full and immediate sound, to provide a strong bargain recommendation.

Music for the Royal Fireworks; Water music (complete); (i) *Oboe concerto No. 2 in B flat*.
(B) **(*) Decca Eclipse Dig. 448 227-2 [417 743-2]. Stuttgart CO, Karl Münchinger, (i) with Lothar Koch.

Here is a much better way of remembering Münchinger's expertise in baroque repertoire than in the Bach *Orchestral Suites*. His style is a compromise between authenticity and the German tradition. In the complete *Water music* he uses recorders most effectively; the balance, helped by Decca's very transparent sound, is often attractively lightweight. If occasionally tempi seem a shade on the slow side, there is much to enjoy both here and in the *Fireworks music*. First-class digital recording, vivid and well focused, and with an oboe concerto (well played by Lothar Koch) thrown in for good measure.

Music for the Royal Fireworks; Water music suite (arr. Harty).
(N) (M) **(*) Mercury 434 398-2 [id.]. LSO, Dorati – MOZART: *Serenade: Eine kleine Nachtmusik; Dances; Marches*. **

Dorati takes us back to the pioneering Harty suites, vividly adapted for modern orchestra, and very good they sound too in the glowing resonance of Watford Town Hall. The 1957 recording hardly sounds at all dated. They could hardly be better played, mixing elegance and warmth, although the leisured tempi in the *Fireworks music* (particularly the *Alla siciliana*) now seem out of style.

Music for the Royal Fireworks: suite; Water music: suite (arr. Harty and Szell); *The Faithful shepherd: Minuet* (ed. Beecham); *Xerxes: Largo* (arr. Reinhardt).
(BB) *** Belart 450 001-2. LSO, Szell.

Many readers will, like us, have a nostalgic feeling for the Handel–Harty suites from which earlier generations got to know these two marvellous scores. George Szell and the LSO offer a highly recommendable coupling of them on a Belart super-bargain issue, with Handel's *Largo* and the *Minuet* from Beecham's *Faithful shepherd suite* thrown in for good measure. The orchestral playing from the early 1970s is outstanding, and the strings are wonderfully expressive in the slower pieces. The horns excel, and the crisp new transfer seems to add to the sheer zest of the music-making. A splendid bargain.

Overtures:(i) *Agrippina; Alcina; Belshazzar; Deidamia; Jephtha; Messiah; Radamisto; Rinaldo; Rodelinda; Susanna;* (ii) *Samson*.
(N) (M) **(*) DG 457 903-2 [id.]. (i) LPO, (ii) Munich Bach O; Karl Richter.

While today's ears are used to much lighter Handelian textures, and Richter (recorded in 1969) is weighty, his broadness of style is tempered by brilliantly alert playing from the LPO, with allegros taken exhilaratingly fast. Those who enjoy the German tradition in Handel will find this partnership with a British orchestra fruitful and rewarding. The *Messiah Sinfonia* is particularly fine. Richter's own Munich Bach Orchestra is used for *Samson*, the closing item, which has been added for the present reissue. They play most impressively, with a strikingly fine contribution from the horns.

Water music: Suites Nos. 1–3 (complete).
(BB) *** ASV Quicksilva Dig. CDQS 6152 [id.]. ECO, George Malcolm.
(M) *** Vanguard/Passacaille Dig. 99713. Il Fondamento, Paul Dombrecht – TELEMANN: *Water music*. ***
(N) *** Hyperion Dig. CDA 66967 [id.]. King's Cons., Robert King – TELEMANN: *Water music*. ***
*** Ph. Dig. 434 122. E. Bar. Soloists, Gardiner.
(B) *** [EMI Red Line Dig. CDR5 69809]. BPO, Muti.
*** DG Dig. 410 525-2 [id.]. E. Concert, Pinnock.
(M) **(*) Virgin Veritas/EMI VER5 61240-2. Linde Consort, Linde.

This super-bargain set of the complete *Water music* on the ASV Quicksilva label from George Malcolm and the English Chamber Orchestra makes an outstanding recommendation, except for those insisting on period instruments. This is a most stylish realization of Handel's intentions, with the closing dances of the *Third Suite in G* particularly elegant, while the digital recording approaches demonstration standard. The playing is first class, articulation is deft and detail admirable.

Il Fondamento is an excellent Belgian period-instrument group; under the lively direction of Paul Dombrecht they present Handel's *Water music* with a nice mixture of verve and elegance. The throaty reeds and robust brass ensure a vigorous response, but the more graceful numbers in the centre of the work have pleasing colour and much character. This ranks high among the 'authentic' versions and is made doubly attractive by being coupled at mid-price with Telemann's *Wassermusik*, not as inspired as Handel's but engagingly inventive and entertaining.

Robert King's is above all a performance of contrasts – between the elegant lighter dance movement, the playing warmly refined, and the set-piece allegros where the baroque horns and trumpets burst forth exuberantly. They always play with joyful vigour, with as much weight and more brightness and bite than with modern instruments. The strings are never edgy and often quite mellow as in the famous *Air*. The coupling with Telemann's *Water music* works well.

The playing of the Berlin Philharmonic under Muti is polished and elegant. In the *Overture* of the first suite, a small instrumental group is featured as a neat counterpoint to the main ripieno: throughout there is a strong emphasis on contrast, with instrumental solos often treated in a concertante manner. The playing is very responsive and the strings generally display a light touch, but the horns are almost aggressive in their spirited vigour in the famous fanfare tune. With a full, vivid, yet clear sound-picture, this is very easy to enjoy. This is only available in the USA.

Gardiner's set of the *Water music* (with the *F major Suite* played first) brings a characteristically bright and resilient performance, full of vitality and colour – period-intrument playing at its most stimulating. With first-class recording, this is an obvious first choice in its field; but with only 53 minutes on the disc, why did Philips not add the *Royal Fireworks music*?

To offer the *Water music* without the *Fireworks music* at full price now seems ungenerous, but Pinnock's version on DG Archiv remains very enticing. Speeds are consistently well chosen and are generally uncontroversial. One test is the famous *Air*, which here remains an engagingly gentle piece. The recording is beautifully balanced and clear.

Using period instruments, the Linde Consort provides a gentler, more intimate alternative to the outstanding versions of Pinnock and Hogwood. The ensemble is not always so polished, but the easy warmth of the playing is most attractive, not least in the G major movements for flute, recorder, bassoon and strings which Linde (himself the flute- and recorder-player) turns into a separate suite after the groups in F major and D major. First-rate sound backs up bright but unabrasive performances.

CHAMBER MUSIC

Complete chamber music

Volume 1: *Flute sonatas: in E min., Op. 1a/b; in G, Op. 1/5; in B min., Op. 1/9; in D (HWV 378); Halle sonatas Nos. 1–3.*
(M) *** CRD CRD 3373; *CRDC 4073* [id.]. L'Ecole d'Orphée (Stephen Preston, Susan Sheppard, John Toll, Lucy Carolan).

Volume 2: *Oboe sonatas Nos. 1 in B flat (HWV 357); in F (HWV 363a); in C min., Op. 1/8 (HWV 366); Violin sonatas: in D min.* (original version of *Op. 1/1) (HWV 359a); in A, Op. 1/3 (HWV 361); in G min., Op. 1/6 (HWV 364a); in D, Op. 1/13 (HWV 371); Allegros for violin and continuo: in A min. (HWV 408); in C min. (HWV 412).*
(M) *** CRD CRD 3374; *CRDC 4074* [id.].

L'Ecole d'Orphée (David Reichenberg, John Holloway, Susan Sheppard, Lucy Carolan).

The first pair of CDs in CRD's complete survey are very well recorded. The date is given as 1991, but they are analogue and from the early 1980s. Volume 1 contains the seven sonatas for flute (three are the so-called 'Halle' *Trio sonatas*, published in 1730 and thought to be the product of Handel's youth) as well as a sonata recently discovered in Brussels, for flute and continuo in D major (HWV 378). The question of the authenticity and provenance of some of the other music in this set is clearly set out in the insert notes. The playing itself is always spirited and intelligent, and if Stephen Preston's eighteenth-century flute timbre sounds a little watery, his phrasing is often beguiling. David Reichenberg's Hailperin oboe is full of ripe colour, and the playing of both artists is immaculate.

Volume 3: *Trio sonatas, Op. 2: Nos. 1 for flute, violin and continuo in B min.; 2 in G min.; 3 in B flat for 2 violins and continuo; 4 in F for recorder, violin and continuo; 5 in G min.; 6 in G min. for 2 violins and continuo.*

(M) *** CRD CRD 3375; *CRDC 4075* [id.]. L'Ecole d'Orphée (John Holloway, Micaela Comberti, Stephen Preston, Philip Pickett, Susan Sheppard, Robert Woolley, John Toll).

Volume 4: *Trio sonatas, Op. 5 for 2 violins and continuo: Nos. 1 in A; 2 in D; 3 in E min.; 4 in G; 5 in G min.; 6 in F; 7 in B flat.*

(M) *** CRD 3376; *CRDC 4076* [id.]. L'Ecole d'Orphée (John Holloway, Micaela Comberti, Susan Sheppard, Lucy Carolan).

Volume 5: *Sinfonia in B flat (HWV 338); Trio sonatas: in C min., Op. 2/1a; in F (HWV 392); in G min.(HWV 393); in E (HWV 394); in C (HWV 403).*

(M) *** CRD 3377; *CRDC 4077* [id.]. L'Ecole d'Orphée (John Holloway, Micaela Comberti, Susan Sheppard, Lucy Carolan).

The *Trio sonatas* recorded by L'Ecole d'Orphée include the complete Op. 2 set, an alternative version of another sonata of Op. 2 (namely *No. 1 in C minor*, which also appears in its B minor guise for flute, violin and continuo), the seven sonatas of Op. 5, and the three so-called 'Dresden' *Sonatas* (HWV 392–4). Only one of them (in F) is totally authentic, though whoever composed the remaining two was no mean figure. In addition there is a very attractive *Sinfonia in B flat* (HWV 338), which is written in trio sonata form. It is given a splendidly alert and sympathetic performance. There are many musical riches here and no want of accomplishment in the performances. The two violins in use by John Holloway and Micaela Comberti have markedly different tone-quality.

As with the flute and oboe sonatas, those who want to make a start on these wonderful works in which Handel's invention seems inexhaustible might begin with Volume 4 of the CRD set, which includes Op. 5. Here Handel frequently borrows from himself, and much of this material is also found in the overtures for the *Chandos anthems* or in the dance music for his operas. The flowing opening theme of the very first *A major Sonata* (HWV 396) has fine Handelian character. No. 6 is familiar, as Handel himself re-used the material of the first and fourth movements for the '*Cuckoo and the Nightingale' Organ concerto*. But one of the most exasperating features of these CD transfers, and one which makes them less easy to use than the original LPs, is that individual movements are uncued, only each complete work.

Volume 6: *Recorder sonatas, Op. 1: Nos. 2 in G min. (HWV 360); 4 in A min. (HWV 362); 7 in C (HWV 365); 11 in F (HWV 369); in G (HWV 358); in B flat (HWV 377); in D min. (HWV 367a); Trio sonata in F (HWV 405).*

(M) *** CRD 3378; *CRDC 4078* [id.]. L'Ecole d'Orphée (Philip Pickett, Rachel Beckett, Susan Sheppard, Lucy Carolan).

These much-praised CRD performances bring elegant and finished playing from the two recorder players and, besides the Op.1 *Sonatas*, the programme includes a *G major Sonata*, first published in 1974, and the original D minor version of the *Flute sonata*, Op. 9/1, which has an engaging second movement based on a minor-key variant of a famous allegro in the *Water music*. The *Trio Sonata in F* for two recorders and continuo also represents a recent discovery – by Christopher Hogwood in the Library of Congress – of the second and third movements of a recorder duo and a bass line to go with all three. Excellent, intimate recording, but again with the irritating drawback that individual movements are not cued, and the *D minor Sonata* has seven of them.

Sonatas, Op. 1: Nos. 1 in D min. (HWV 359a) (for violin & continuo); *1a in E min. (HWV 379); 1b in E min. (HWV 359b)* (both for flute & continuo); *2 in G min. (HWV 360)* (for recorder & continuo); *3 in A (HWV 361)* (for violin & continuo); *4 in A min. (HWV 362)* (for recorder & continuo); *5 in G (HWV 363b)* (for flute & continuo); *6 in G min. (HWV 364a)* (for violin & continuo); *7 in C (HWV 365)* (for recorder & continuo); *8 in C min. (HWV 366)* (for oboe & continuo); *9a in D min. (HWV 367a)* (for recorder & continuo); *9b in B min. (HWV 367b)* (for flute & continuo); *11 in F (HWV 369)* (for recorder & continuo); *13 in D (HWV 371)* (for violin & continuo); *Halle sonatas Nos. 1–3* (for flute & continuo) *(HWV 374–6); Sonata for oboe & continuo in B flat (HWV 357); Sonata for recorder & continuo in B flat (HWV 377); Sonata for violin & continuo in G (HWV 358).*

*** Hyperion Dig. CDA 66921/3 [id.]. Elizabeth Wallfisch, Lisa Beznosiuk, Rachel Beckett, Richard Tunnicliffe, Paul Nicholson.

The Hyperion set concentrates on Op. 1, although illogically four of the violin sonatas, previously counted as being part of Handel's opus, have been omitted as spurious (HWV 368, 370 and 372–3), which seems unnecessary when there would have been plenty of room for them (all three discs have a playing time of under an hour). The fine *Halle sonatas* have been included, plus some other miscellaneous works now considered to be authentic. The performances use period instruments and have the advantage of current practice, so both flute and oboe timbres have a strong baroque flavour but the violins are less raw-timbred than the quality offered by L'Ecole d'Orphée; on the other hand the playing itself is mellower and perhaps at times slightly less vital than on the more comprehensive CRD set.

Flute sonatas (for flute and continuo): *in E min., Op. 1/1a; in D, HWV 378; Halle sonatas* (for flute and continuo) *Nos. 1–3; Oboe sonatas* (for oboe and continuo): *No. 1 in B flat (HWV 357); in F (HWV 363a), Op. 1/5; in C min. (HWV 366), Op. 1/8; Recorder sonatas* (for recorder and continuo): *in G min. (HWV 360); in A min. (HWV 362); in C (HWV 365); in F (HWV 369), Op. 1/2, 4, 7 & 11; in B flat (HWV 377); in D min. (HWV 367a); Sinfonia in B flat for 2 violins and continuo (HWV 338); Trio sonatas: in E min. for 2 flutes and continuo (HWV 395); in F for 2 recorders and continuo (HWV 405).*

(B) *** Ph. Duo 446 563-2 (2). ASMF Chamber Ens.

This superb Philips set assembles virtually all the important wind sonatas, plus a single *Trio sonata* for two violins and continuo, on a pair of discs offered for the price of one. William Bennett uses a modern flute very persuasively in the *Flute sonatas* and includes, besides the work from Op. 1 and the three *Halle sonatas*, a more recent discovery from a Brussels manuscript. Nicholas Kraemer and Denis Vigay provide admirable support, and the recording is most realistic and present. In the *Recorder sonatas* Michala Petri plays with her customary virtuosity and flair, and Neil Black is marvellously accomplished in the *Oboe sonatas*. Both artists share an excellent rapport with their continuo players, who include George Malcolm (harpsichord), Denis Vigay (cello) and Graham Sheen (bassoon), and again the sound is exemplary, natural and spacious. Only those seeking original instruments need look elsewhere.

Flute sonatas (for flute and continuo): *in E min., HWV 359b; in G, HWV 363b; in B min., HWV 367b* (6th movt); *in A min., HWV 374; in E min., HWV 375* (4th movt); *in B min., HWV 376; Oboe sonatas* (for oboe and continuo): *in C min., HWV 366; in B flat, HWV 357; in F, HWV 363a* (2nd movt); *Recorder sonatas* (for recorder and continuo): *in G min., HWV 360; in A min., HWV 362; in C, HWV 365; in D min., HWV 367a* (movts 1-5, 7); *in F, HWV 369; in B flat, HWV 377; Andante in D min., HWV 409.*

(B) *** Sony Seon Double SBK 60100 (2) [id.]. Frans Brüggen, Bruce Haynes, Hans Jürg Lange, Anner Bylsma, Bob van Asperen (harpsichord and organ).

These performances, on period instruments, are most accomplished: Brüggen plays with characteristic mastery and so do his companions. There are some mannerisms: he swells all too predictably on sustained notes and is generous with stress accents. However, Handelians will want to consider the set for its scholarship and expertise, even though the flute is balanced rather close. This makes a clear alternative to the ASMF set, although it is not so complete, including only key movements from some works; and the documentation, by leaving out the opus numbers, is less clear.

Sonatas for flute or alto recorder: Op. 1/2, 4, 7, 9 & 11; in B flat.

*** HM Dig. HMU 907151 [id.]. Marion Verbruggen, Ton Koopman, Jaap ter Linden.

Marion Verbruggen uses modern copies of two alto recorders from the early eighteenth century and a similar voice flute in D; the sounds here are appealingly mellow, with the continuo featuring cello, harpsichord and chest organ. The effect is intimate, expressive and lively by turns, but with no attempt at self-conscious bravura. The recording is beautifully balanced.

Recorder sonatas, Op. 1/2, 4, 7, 11; in D min (Fitzwilliam), HWV 367a; Trio sonata in F, HWV 405; Favourite air (Lelio's Aria from Scipio); Gavotte, HWV 604; Gigue, HWV 599; Minuet, HWV 603.

(N) (BB) *** Naxos Dig. 8.550700 [id.]. László Czidra, Zsolt Harsányi, Zsuzsa Pertis, Pál Keleman.

A particularly attractive and generous anthology. These Hungarian musicians are first-class players and their accounts of the *sonatas* from Op.1 and the *Trio sonata* (for two recorders and continuo) are second to none. The encores (for various combinations) are most engaging, especially the *Gavotte* and *Gigue*. The recording is excellent.

(i) *Trio sonatas, Opp. 2/5; 5/4 & 7 for 2 violins and continuo*; Italian cantatas: (i; ii) *Notte placida e cheta;* (i; ii; iii) *Tra la fiamme.*

(N) *** Chandos Dig. CHAN 0620 [id.]. (i) Purcell Qt (members); (ii) Catherine Bott; (iii) with Kershaw, Downer, Amherst, Manson.

An entirely delightful recital of the kind one might hear at the Wigmore Hall. (Overseas readers please note: this is an experience not to miss if you are visiting London.) The *Trio sonatas* are full of attractive invention, notably an impressive passacaglia in Op. 5/4, and they are used to frame and act as an interlude between the two Italian cantatas, ravishingly sung by Catherine Bott. It is difficult to decide which of the two – *Tra la fiamme* (about Daedalus and Icarus) with its descriptive aria '*Among the flames*', or *Notte placida e cheta* ('Calm and quiet night') – is the more enchanting. The recording is ideally balanced.

KEYBOARD MUSIC

Capriccio in F; Chaconne in G, HWV 435; Fantaisie in C; Prelude in D min.; Prelude and allegro in G min.; Sonata in C; Suites Nos. 1 in A, HWV 426; 4 in D min., HMW 429; 7 in G min., HWV 432.
(N) *** Erato/Warner Dig. 0630 14886-2 [id.]. Olivier Baumont.

Olivier Baumont uses three different harpsichords for his well devised programme: a 1707 Dumont for the *Chaconne* and *G minor Suite*, a 1652 Couchet for the other two *Suites*, and an anonymous Italian instrument from 1677 for the shorter works (the one-movement *Sonata*, the *Capriccio*, the contrasting *G minor Prelude and allegro* and *Fantaisie*), all particularly appealing pieces from the composer's 'early youth'. Baumont plays the more extended final version of the *Chaconne* and his own version of the *Suite No. 4*, omitting the *Prelude*, 'as it represents a preliminary sketch for the opening movement of the *Third suite*', and including instead a very beautiful *Sarabande* with variations (which you might recognize) taken from an autograph manuscript in the Fitzwilliam Museum at Cambridge. All in all this is a very stimulating and enjoyable collection, played with great vitality and splendidly recorded.

Chaconne in G, HWV 435; Harpsichord suites Nos. 2 in F, HWV 427; 5 in E, HWV 430; 12 in F min., BWV 433; 13 in B flat, HWV 434. Passacaglia in G min., HWV 432 (from *Suite No.7*).
(N) **(*) Sony Dig. SK 68260 [id.]. Bob van Asperen (harpsichord).

Bob van Asperen chooses four of Handel's finest suites, including No. 5, with *The Harmonious blacksmith* as finale, and *No. 13 in B flat* which includes the *Air* which Brahms used for his piano *Variations and fugue* and a *Minuet* which Handel also featured in the *Water music*. The suites are framed by the *Passacaglia in G minor* (normally the last movement of the *Suite No. 7*) and the early *G major Chaconne*, which makes a splendid end-piece. It is most impressively presented, as is all the music here, on a modern copy of a 1764 Pascal Taskin harpsichord which has a strong personality. No doubt this is to be part of an overall survey and while it is distinguished by both scholarship and spontaneity; it is also rather short measure (59 minutes). However, as van Asperen plays a different version of the *Chaconne*, it is conveniently complementary to Baumont's collection above.

Suites Nos. (i) *1 in A;* (ii) *2 in F; 3 in D min.;* (i) *4 in E min.;* (ii) *5 in E;* (i) *6 in F sharp min.; 7 in G min.;* (ii) *8 in F min.*
❁ (B) *** EMI forte CZS5 69337-2 [CDFB 69337] (2). (i) Gavrilov; (ii) Richter.

Suites (i) *Nos. 9 in G min.;* (ii) *10 in D min.; 11 in D min.;* (i) *12 in E min.;* (ii) *13 in B flat;* (i) *14 in G;* (ii) *15 in D min.;* (i) *16 in G min.*
❁ (B) *** EMI forte CZS5 69340-2 [CDFB 69340] (2). (i) Richter; (ii) Gavrilov – BEETHOVEN: *Piano sonata No. 17.* *** ❁

These superb recordings of the Handel *Keyboard suites* were recorded by Sviatoslav Richter and Andrei Gavrilov at the Château de Marcilly-sur-Maulne during the 1979 Tours Festival, and first appeared in 1983 in a handsome five-LP box, but were never reissued as single- or double-pack LPs in the UK. They have been slow to reach CD, but EMI have made amends by issuing the set in first-class transfers, and in an economical format – two twin-CDs packaged as one, available separately, and competitively priced – and with Richter's famous 1961 account of Beethoven's *D minor Sonata*, Op. 31, No. 2, thrown in for good measure. The serenity and tranquillity of the slow movements and the radiance of the faster movements have never before been so fully realized. Not to be missed.

Harpsichord suites Nos. 1–8, HWV 426/433; 6 Fugues or Voluntarys for organ or harpsichord, HWV 605/10; Fugues: in F; E, HWV 611/12.
*** Hyperion Dig. CDA 66931/2 [id.]. Paul Nicholson (harpsichord).

Paul Nicholson gives us not only the eight splendidly diverse suites of 1720, but also the contrapuntal *Voluntaries*. They are simple, four-part baroque fugal pieces, varied in mood and style according to the key. As an appendix we are offered two miniature fugues, the *F major* from around 1705 and the *E major* from the time of the *Voluntaries*. Paul Nicholson's playing is admirable, full of life yet with a degree of intimacy that is very appealing. He has an ideal (unnamed) harpsichord, which is perfect for this repertoire and which is superbly recorded. Nicholson's crisp and stylish ornamentation is never fussy, and he is generous with repeats. His playing can seem to be improvisational in the preludes, fugues are crystal clear yet never stiff, and the closing *Gigues* have a joyful rhythmic lift. The most famous of the eight is, of course, No. 5, which has the variations known as '*The harmonious black-*

smith' as its finale, here ending in a blaze of bravura. Highly recommended, and unlikely to be surpassed in the near future.

Harpsichord suites Nos. 1–8.
(B) *** HM Musique d'Abord HMA 190447/48 [id.]. Kenneth Gilbert (harpsichord).
*** Erato/Warner Dig. 2292 45452-2 (2). Scott Ross (harpsichord).

Gilbert is a scholar as well as a distinguished player, and his version of the suites, recorded on a copy of a Taskin harpsichord by Bédard, is well worth seeking out, making a fine bargain alternative to Paul Nicholson's more comprehensive (and more expensive) set. Gilbert observes most first-half repeats but not those of the second, and he is as imaginative in the handling of decoration and ornamentation as one would expect. The recording is natural and very well balanced.

Scott Ross plays a copy of a 1733 Blanchet, which suits this repertoire very well, and his performances are in exemplary style. He plays most repeats, but not all – and one wonders why, when the overall playing time is short of two hours. Still, this is a fine set, well though closely recorded.

Suite No. 5 in E (includes *The Harmonious blacksmith*).
(B) *** Decca Eclipse Dig. 448 992-2. Alicia de Larrocha, VSO, Uri Segal – MOZART: *Piano concertos Nos. 19 & 22.* ***

Alicia de Larrocha's performance was recorded in the Henry Wood Hall; she gives a robust and vital account of the best-known of Handel's *Suites*, with its famous variations, and again fully justifies the use of the piano for this repertoire. Her performance may not banish memories of Richter (his Touraine performance is now available on an EMI forte re-issue) but it is thoroughly enjoyable. There is plenty of warmth, and the recording is most realistic. This makes a splendid bonus for an outstanding bargain Mozart coupling.

VOCAL MUSIC

(i) *Aci, Galatea e Polifemo;* (ii) *Recorder sonatas in F; C & G* (transposed to *F*).
(B) *** HM Musique d'abord Dig. HMA 901253/4 [id.]. (i) Kirkby, Watkinson, Thomas, L. Bar., Medlam; (ii) Michel Piquet, John Toll.

Aci, Galatea e Polifemo proves to be quite a different work from the always popular English masque, *Acis and Galatea*, with only one item even partially borrowed. Charles Medlam directs London Baroque in a beautifully sprung performance with three excellent soloists, the brightly characterful Emma Kirkby as Aci, Carolyn Watkinson in the lower-pitched role of Galatea, and David Thomas coping manfully with the impossibly wide range of Polifemo's part. The three recorder sonatas are comparably delightful, a welcome makeweight. Excellent sound, full of presence. Particularly enticing at bargain price.

Acis and Galatea (masque).
*** DG 423 406-2 (2). Burrowes, Rolfe Johnson, Martyn Hill, Willard White, E. Bar. Soloists, Gardiner.
(N) (BB) ** Naxos Dig. 8.553188 [id.]. Kym Amps, Robin Doveton, Angus Davidson, David van Asch, Scholars Bar. Ens., David van Asch.

Acis and Galatea; *Il pastor fido: Hunting scene.*
(B) *** Decca Double 452 973-2 (2). Robert Tear, Jill Gomez, Philip Langridge, Benjamin Luxon, Ch. & ASMF, Marriner – Robert Tear: *'Baroque recital'.* ***

(i) *Acis and Galatea;* (ii) *Cantata: Look down, harmonious saint.*
*** Hyperion Dig. CDA 66361/2; *KA 66361/2.* (i; ii) Ainsley; (i) McFadden, Covey-Crump, George, Harre-Jones; King's Cons., Robert King.

Robert King directs a bluff, beautifully sprung reading of *Acis and Galatea* that brings out its domestic jollity. Using the original version for five solo singers and no chorus, this may be less delicate in its treatment than John Eliot Gardiner's reading but it is, if anything, even more winning. The soloists are first rate, with John Mark Ainsley among the most stylish of the younger generation of Handel tenors, and the bass, Michael George, characterizing strongly. Claron McFadden's vibrant soprano is girlishly distinctive. This Hyperion issue provides a valuable makeweight in the florid solo cantata, thought to be originally conceived as part of *Alexander's Feast*, nimbly sung by Ainsley.

The refinement and rhythmic lift of the Academy's playing under Marriner make for a lively, engaging performance of *Acis and Galatea*, marked by characterful solo singing from a strong team. The choruses are sung by a quartet drawn from a distinguished vocal sextet (Jennifer Smith, Margaret Cable, Paul Esswood, Wynford Evans, Neil Jenkins and Richard Jackson) and, with warmly atmospheric recording, the result is a sparkling entertainment. Robert Tear's tone is not always ideally mellifluous (for instance in *Love in her eyes sits playing*) but, like the others, he has a good feeling for Handelian style; the sweetness of Jill Gomez's contribution is a delight. The 1977 (originally Argo) recording is of vintage quality and this Double Decca reissue is made the more attractive by the inclusion of a further solo recital from Robert Tear of rare English baroque repertoire – music by Arne, Boyce and Hook, as well as Handel. Before this, as an interlude, comes a sprightly (orchestral) *Hunting scene* from *Il pastor fido* consisting of a *March* and a pair of *Airs pour les chasseurs*.

Some of John Eliot Gardiner's tempi are idiosyncratic (some too fast, some too slow), but the scale of the performance, using period instruments, is beautifully judged, with the vocal soloists banding together for the choruses. Willard White is a fine Polyphemus. The authentic sounds of the English Baroque Soloists are finely controlled and the vibrato-less string timbre is clear and clean without being abrasive. A thoroughly rewarding pair of CDs.

On a single disc at super-bargain price, the Naxos version is well worth hearing. David van Asch, leading the Scholars Baroque Ensemble, directs a brisk and light reading with Kym Amps as Galatea, sweeter and purer than she has sometimes been on disc, and Robin Doveton a light-toned Acis, stylish if not always firm in his legato singing. The counter-tenor, Angus Davidson, is rather unsteady as Damon, and though David van Asch as Polyphemus copes well with the with the wide range required, he is unresonant as the giant. Clear, well-balanced sound.

Acis and Galatea (complete; arr. Mozart in German).
(M) *** DG (IMS) Dig. 447 700-2 (2). MacDougall, Bonney, Schaefer, Tomlinson, E. Concert Ch. & O, Pinnock.

It may seem perverse for three English-speaking principals to choose to do *Acis and Galatea* in German, but Mozart's arrangement with added woodwind is most interesting, comparable with the more radical one he prepared of *Messiah*. Pinnock's performance, well recorded, is as persuasive as one could imagine, with Barbara Bonney an enchanting Galatea and John Tomlinson a characterful Polyphemus, clear and precise. Jamie MacDougall as Acis sounds gusty at times but makes an attractively ardent hero.

Agrippina condotta a morire; Armeda abbandonata; Lucrezia (Italian cantatas).
(N) **(*) Virgin Veritas/EMI VC5 45283-2. Véronique Gens, Les Basses Réunies.

The only really well-known piece here is *Lucrezia,* which Dame Janet Baker has also recorded with distinction and whom Véronique Gens does not quite match. Nevertheless, she is convincingly and powerfully indignant at her violation, and in her closing suicidal aria, although at first touchingly vulnerable, she becomes really vehement as she determines on vengeance '*nell'inferno*'. The abandoned Armida, against a bare accompaniment, laments her fate (*Ah crudele!*) to a particularly lovely melisma, and at the close she reveals her deep distress in a simple siciliana, movingly sung here. Agrippina, at her son Nero's mercy, contemplates her coming execution with all the volatile anger of her tempestuous character. She too has a moving lyrical aria (*Se infelice*) and her closing recitativo also begins poignantly and then ends in mid-air as she leaves the scene (and the listener) abruptly. Véronique Gens is here in her element, revelling in the dramatic mood changes, and in the vocal bravura, where she is always in control. Her decoration is apt and she is persuasively accompanied. This is perhaps a specialist record but good of its kind.

Marian arias and cantatas: *Ah! Che troppo inequale; Donna, che in ciel; Haec est Regina;* G. B. FERRANDINI (attrib. HANDEL): *Il pianto di Maria.*
*** DG Dig. 439 866-2 [id.]. Von Otter, Col. Mus. Ant., Goebel.

Dating from his years in Italy, these Handel works, directly linked to the worship of the Virgin Mary, inspire von Otter to give radiant performances. Ironically, the longest work, *Il pianto di Maria*, long attributed to Handel, has been found to be by G. B. Ferrandini; but it has many beauties, not least in a measured cavatina, *Se d'un Dio*. Both *Haec est Regina* and *Ah! che inequale* are strong, imaginative arias, and *Donna, che in ciel* is a superb, full-scale cantata with a fine overture and four splendid arias. Reinhard Goebel and his team give sympathetic support, though the period string-playing is on the abrasive side. Warm, immediate recording, which captures von Otter's firm mezzo superbly.

(i) *Alexander's Feast* (complete). (ii) *Harp concerto, Op. 4/6;* (iii) *Organ concerto, Op. 4/1.*
*** Collins Dig. 7016-2 (2). (i) Argenta, Partridge, George, The Sixteen Ch.; (ii) Lawrence-King, Tragicomedia; (iii) Nicholson; (i; iii) The Sixteen O, Christophers.

Alexander's Feast; Concerto grosso in C (Alexander's Feast).
**(*) Ph. Dig. 422 053-2 (2). Carolyn Watkinson, Robson, Donna Brown, Stafford, Varcoe, Monteverdi Ch., E. Bar. Soloists, Gardiner.

Alexander's Feast was the first and greatest of the odes by Dryden which Handel set to celebrate St Cecilia's Day. It was written in 1736 (three years before the less ambitious work he called the *Ode for St Cecilia's Day*) and was one of the composer's London successes. The invention is consistently on the highest level, without a single poor number. Not only are the vocal solos and choruses among Handel's finest, but the orchestration shows many imaginative touches. Handel holds his brass in reserve and the horns must have made something of a sensation in their colourful entry in praise of Bacchus. The trumpets, too, make a commanding entry in the opening chorus of Part 2: '*Break his bonds of sleep asunder*'. In no other work are they used with greater brilliance.

Harry Christophers directs a lively, sympathetic account of Handel's extended cantata, very well sung and recorded. The three soloists – Nancy Argenta, Ian Partridge and Michael George – are all first rate, making a more consistent team than the quintet used by Gardiner. The bass, Michael George, is satisfyingly firm and dark in the two big bass arias. Christophers also provides two of the related Opus 4 concertos instead of Gardiner's one.

Gardiner's version of *Alexander's Feast* was recorded live at performances given at the Göttingen Festival, with sound that takes away some of the bloom on voices and instruments. What matters is the vigour and concentration of Gardiner's performance. Stephen Varcoe may lack the dark resonance of a traditional bass, but he projects his voice well. Nigel Robson's tenor suffers more than do the others from the dryness of the acoustic. The soprano, Donna Brown, sings with boyish freshness, and the alto numbers are divided very effectively between Carolyn Watkinson and the soft-grained counter-tenor, Ashley Stafford. The *Concerto grosso in C* was given with the oratorio at its first performance.

L'allegro, il penseroso, il moderato.
(M) *** Erato/Warner 2292 45377-2 [id.]. Kwella, McLaughlin, Jennifer Smith, Ginn, Davies, Hill, Varcoe, Monteverdi Ch., E. Bar. Soloists, Gardiner.

(i) *L'Allegro ed il penseroso* (complete); (ii) *Ode for St Cecilia's Day.*
(N) (B) *(*) Decca Double 460 287-2 (2). (i) Morison, Delman, Harwood, Watts, Pears, Alan, St Anthony Singers, Philomusica of L.; (ii) Cantelo, Partridge, King's Coll., Cambridge, Ch., ASMF; Willcocks.

Taking Milton as his starting point, Handel illustrated in music the contrasts of mood and character between the cheerful and the thoughtful. Then, prompted by his librettist, Charles Jennens, he added compromise in *Il moderato*, the moderate man. The sequence of brief numbers is a delight, particularly in a performance as exhilarating as this, with excellent soloists, choir and orchestra. The recording is first rate.

Somehow the Willcocks performance of *L'Allegro ed il penseroso* does not quite come to life, perhaps because it tries too hard. Pace is all-important in Handel, and at times the impression is too leisurely, at others too hurried for comfort. Pears sings intelligently as ever, but the other soloists are uneven in quality and seem unable to offer sufficient variety of tone colour and phrasing. The performance of the *Ode* is also disappointing. It is not the fault of the Academy of St Martin-in-the Fields, for the Overture is one of the highlights, and there is superb solo playing throughout, and a notably warm contribution from the cellos. April Cantelo phrases sensitively and accurately, if with rather a white tone, but her singing seldom beguiles, and it is the tenor who brings the performance fully to life with *The Trumpet's loud clangour*. The sound is excellent, but this set is altogether a non-starter.

Alpestre monte; Mi palpita il cor; Tra le fiamme; Tu fedel? Tu costante? (Italian cantatas).
*** O-L (IMS) Dig. 414 473-2 [id.]. Emma Kirkby, AAM, Hogwood.

The four cantatas here, all for solo voice with modest instrumental forces, are nicely contrasted; they offer a spirited sequence of little arias rejecting a lover. Even 'A heart full of cares' in *Mi palpita il cor* inspires Handel to a charming, pastoral aria, with a delectable oboe obbligato, and even those limited cares quickly disperse. Light-hearted and sparkling performances to match.

Aminta e Fillide (cantata).
*** Hyperion CDA 66118 [id.]. Fisher, Kwella, L. Handel O, Darlow.

In writing for two voices and strings, Handel presents a simple encounter in the pastoral tradition over a span of ten brief arias which, together with recitatives and final duet, last almost an hour. The music is as charming and undemanding for the listener as it is taxing for the soloists. This lively performance, beautifully recorded with two nicely contrasted singers, delightfully blows the cobwebs off a Handel work till now totally neglected.

(i) *Apollo e Daphne* (cantata); (ii) *Oboe concerto in G min.*
(B) *** HM Musique d'Abord HMA 1905157 [id.]. (i) Judith Nelson, David Thomas; (ii) Haynes; San Francisco Bar. O; McGegan.

Apollo e Daphne, one of Handel's most delightful cantatas, tells how the determinedly chaste heroine, after an unwelcome and persistent pursuit by her godly suitor, finally escapes a fate worse than death by being transformed into a laurel bush. It has two strikingly memorable numbers, a lovely siciliano for Dafne with oboe obbligato and an aria for Apollo, *Come rosa in su la spina*, with unison violins and a solo cello. Both soloists are first rate, and Nicholas McGegan is a lively Handelian, though the playing of the orchestra could be more polished. The sound is over-resonant but has plenty of atmosphere. For the bargain-priced reissue (retaining the full documentation plus translation) a neat account of Handel's *G minor Oboe concerto* has been added.

Athalia (oratorio; complete).
*** O-L Dig. 417 126-2 (2). Sutherland, Kirkby, Bowman, Aled Jones, Rolfe Johnson, David Thomas, New College, Oxford, Ch., AAM, Hogwood.
(N) (BB) *** Naxos Dig. 8.554364/5 [id.]. Elisabeth Scholl, Barbara Schlick, Friederike Holzhausen, Annette Reinhold, Markus Brutscher, Stephan MacLeod, Junge Kantorei, Frankfurt Bar. O, Martini.

As Queen Athalia, Dame Joan Sutherland sings boldly with a richness and vibrancy to contrast superbly with the pure silver of Emma Kirkby, not to mention the celestial treble of Aled Jones, in the role of the boy-king, Joas. That casting is perfectly designed to set the Queen aptly apart from the good Israelite characters led by the Priest, Joad (James Bowman in a castrato role), and Josabeth (Kirkby). Christopher Hogwood with the Academy brings out the speed and variety of the score that has been described as Handel's first great English oratorio. The recording is bright and clean, giving sharp focus to voices and instruments alike.

Very well cast and stylishly performed, using period instruments, the Naxos set of the third of Handel's English oratorios, based on Racine, makes an excellent bargain. Even if the playing is not quite so crisp or purposeful as on the rival (full-priced) set from Hogwood, the result is compellingly dramatic. Outstanding among the singers is Barbara Schlick as Josabeth, pure, sweet and expressive, and though Elisabeth Scholl in the title role provides rather too little contrast, with her rather boyish tone not really apt for this 'Jewish Clytemnestra', her attack is clean and fresh. The castrato role of Joad is taken by Annette Reinhold, who sounds uncannily like a low counter-tenor, firm and secure, with little vibrato. Good, undistracting recording.

Belshazzar (complete).
(M) **(*) Teldec/Warner 0630 10275-2 (3) [id.]. Felicity Palmer, Maureen Lehane, Robert Tear, Paul Esswood, Peter van der Bilt, Stockholm Chamber Ch., VCM, Harnoncourt.

With authentic style and instruments set against a relatively intimate acoustic, Harnoncourt's opening of the fine overture to *Belshazzar* on this Teldec recording may initially seem gruff. The drama is the more pointed when the soloists, led by Felicity Palmer and Robert Tear, keep the story-line clearly in mind with their expressive enunciation of the words. The other soloists, too, are excellent, notably Paul Esswood with his fresh counter-tenor tone, and the bass, Peter van der Bilt. Most enjoyable of all is the singing of the fine Stockholm choir, delectably light and pointed in some of the end-of-scene choruses. Harnoncourt is at his best when given the chance to point a brisk number with lifted rhythms, but he is less effective in warmer music.

Carmelite Vespers.
(N) (BB) *** Virgin Classics Dig. Double VBD5 61579-2 (2) [id.]. Feldman, Kirkby, Van Evera, Cable, Nichols, Cornwell, David Thomas, Taverner Ch. & Players, Parrott.

What Andrew Parrott has recorded here is a reconstruction by Graham Dixon of what might have been heard in July 1707 at the church of the Carmelite Order in Rome for the Festival of Our Lady of Mount Carmel. Dixon has put the motets and Psalm settings in an order appropriate for the service of Second Vespers, noting that it is not the only possible reconstruction. So *Dixit Dominus* is introduced by plainchant and a chanted antiphon, with similar liturgical links between the other Handel settings – in turn *Laudete pueri, Te decus Virgineum, Nisi Dominus, Haec est Regina Virginum, Saeviat Tellus* and *Salve Regina*. Of these, the only unfamiliar Handel piece is *Te decus Virgineum* – which makes this not quite the new experience promised but a nevertheless enjoyable way of hearing a magnificent collection of Handel's choral music. In a liturgical setting in 1707, women's voices would not have been used, but the sopranos and altos of the Taverner Choir produce an aptly fresh sound, as does the fine group of soloists, headed by an outstanding trio of sopranos: Emma Kirkby, Jill Feldman and Emily Van Evera. The recording, made in St Augustine's, Kilburn, London, has a pleasant and apt ambience, which however does not obscure detail. At its modest price this reissue is well worth having.

Chandos anthems Nos. 1–11 (complete).
*** Chandos Dig. CHAN 0554/7 [id.]. Dawson, Kwella, Partridge, Bowman, George, The Sixteen Ch. & O, Harry Christophers.

It is appropriate that a record label named Chandos should record a complete set of Handel's *Chandos anthems*. This is now available on four CDs in a box (still at full price) and marks one of the most successful and worthwhile achievements of The Sixteen on CD. From the first of these fine works, which Handel based on his *Utrecht Te Deum*, to the last with its exuberant closing *Alleluja*, the music is consistently inspired; it has great variety of invention and resourceful vocal scoring. The recordings are well up to the house standard.

Chandos anthems Nos. 1: O be joyful in the Lord; 2: In the Lord put I my trust; 3: Have mercy on me, HWV 246/8.
*** Chandos Dig. CHAN 8600 [id.]. Lynne Dawson, Ian Partridge, The Sixteen Ch. & O, Christophers.

The impact of these performances is affected strongly by the recorded sound, set in a warm acoustic but with rather a close balance; that makes the choir sound bigger. Ian Partridge is the radiant-voiced linchpin of these performances and is superbly matched by Lynne Dawson with her gloriously pure, silvery soprano. The closeness of sound makes the instrumental sonatas which start each *Anthem* more abrasive than they might be, but not uncomfortably so.

Chandos anthems Nos. 4: O sing unto the Lord a new song; 5: I will magnify thee; 6: As pants the hart for cooling streams.
*** Chandos Dig. CHAN 0504 [id.]. Lynne Dawson, Ian Partridge, The Sixteen Ch. & O, Christophers.

The second volume of the Chandos series is hardly

less appealing than the first. There are some splendidly vigorous choruses, while in No. 6 there is an equally memorable soprano aria, beautifully sung by Lynne Dawson.

Chandos anthems Nos. 7: My song shall be alway; 8: O come let us sing unto the Lord; 9: O praise the Lord.
*** Chandos Dig. CHAN 0505 [id.]. Patrizia Kwella, James Bowman, Ian Partridge, Michael George, The Sixteeen Ch. & O, Christophers.

Again in this third volume there is splendid singing from the soloists, with Patrizia Kwella joining the team, and there is plenty of interest in the solo writing in these fine, contrasted works, while the choral contribution is well up to standard.

Chandos anthems Nos. 10: The Lord is my light; 11: Let God arise.
*** Chandos Dig. CHAN 0509. Lynne Dawson, Ian Partridge, The Sixteen Ch. & O, Christophers.

The tenor soloist dominates No. 10, and Ian Partridge sings with his customary style and sweetness of timbre. Lynne Dawson makes her entry on the penultimate number. The chorus is again in exhilarating form, especially in the closing *Alleluja*. The recording is spacious while continuing to preserve the music's intimate feeling.

(i) *Coronation anthems* (complete); (ii) *Concerti a due cori Nos. 2–3, HWV 333/4.*
(M) *** DG Dig. 447 280-2. (i) Westminster Abbey Ch., Preston; (i–ii) E. Concert; (ii) Pinnock.

Coronation anthems (complete); *Judas Maccabaeus; See the conqu'ring hero comes; March; Sing unto God.*
*** Ph. Dig. 412 733-2 [id.]. ASMF Ch., ASMF, Marriner.

The extra weight of the Academy of St Martin-in-the-Fields Chorus compared with the Pinnock version seems appropriate for the splendour of music intended for the pomp of royal ceremonial occasions, and the commanding choral entry in *Zadok the Priest* is gloriously rich in amplitude, without in any way lacking incisiveness. The excerpts from *Solomon* are delightful.

Those who like sparer, period textures will favour Preston in the *Coronation anthems*, where, although the result is less grand, the element of contrast is even more telling. To have the choir enter with such bite and impact underlines the freshness and immediacy, with characterful period playing. An exhilarating version. The new coupling of the two *Concerti a due cori* is welcome, with the performances full of rhythmic vitality.

Dettingen Te Deum; Dettingen anthem.
*** DG Dig. 410 647-2 [id.]. Westminster Abbey Ch., E. Concert, Preston.

The *Dettingen Te Deum* is a splendid work, continually reminding one of *Messiah*, written the previous year. Preston's Archiv performance with the English Concert makes an ideal recommendation, with its splendid singing, crisp but strong, excellent recording and a generous, apt coupling. This setting of *The King shall rejoice* should not be confused with the *Coronation anthem* of that name. It is less inspired, but has a magnificent double fugue for finale. The recording is first class.

Dixit Dominus; Coronation anthem: Zadok the Priest.
(M) *** Erato/Warner 2292 45136-2 [id.]. Palmer, Marshall, Brett, Messana, Morton, Thomson, Wilson-Johnson, Monteverdi Ch. & O, Gardiner.

Handel's *Dixit Dominus* dates from 1707 and was completed during his prolonged stay in Italy from 1706 to 1710. It divides into eight sections, and the setting, while showing signs of Handel's mature style in embryo, reflects also the Baroque tradition of contrasts between small and large groups. The writing is extremely florid and requires bravura from soloists and chorus alike. John Eliot Gardiner catches all its brilliance and directs an exhilarating performance, marked by strongly accented, sharply incisive singing from the choir and outstanding solo contributions. In high contrast with the dramatic choruses, the duet for two sopranos, *De torrente*, here beautifully sung by Felicity Palmer and Margaret Marshall, is languorously expressive, but stylishly so. Other soloists match that, and the analogue recording is first rate, proving ideal for CD remastering.

Dixit Dominus; Nisi Dominus; Salve Regina.
*** DG Dig. 423 594-2 [id.]. Augér, Lynne Dawson, Montague, Nixon, Birchall, Westminster Abbey Ch. & O, Simon Preston.

Dixit dominus; Nisi dominus; Silete venti.
*** Chandos Dig. CHAN 0517 [id.]. Dawson, Russell, Brett, Partridge, George, The Sixteen Choir & O, Harry Christophers.

On DG Archiv *Dixit Dominus* is very aptly coupled with fine performances of another – less ambitious – Psalm setting, *Nisi Dominus*, and a votive antiphon, *Salve Regina*, which Handel composed between the two. Preston here draws ideally luminous and resilient singing from the Westminster Abbey Choir, with a fine team of soloists in which Arleen Augér and Diana Montague are outstanding. The playing of the period orchestra, led by Roy Goodman, in every way matches the fine qualities of the singing.

Christophers' speeds tend to be more extreme, slow as well as fast, and the recorded sound, though full and well detailed, is less immediate. On balance Preston with his rather more bouncy rhythms remains the first choice, but the Chandos issue gains significantly from a much more generous third item. *Silete venti* allows the silver-toned Lynne Dawson to shine even more than in the other items, ending with a brilliant *Alleluia* in galloping compound time.

Esther (1718 version).
*** Collins Dig. 7040-2 (2). Russell, Randle, Padmore, Argenta, Chance, George, Sixteen Ch. & O, Christophers.
**(*) O-L Dig. 414 423-2 (2) [id.]. Kwella, Rolfe Johnson, Partridge, Thomas, Kirkby, Elliott, Westminster Cathedral Boys' Ch., Ch. and AAM, Hogwood.

Esther was the first of Handel's oratorios with a substantial role for the chorus and, like the Hogwood recording on L'Oiseau-Lyre, this period performance opts for the 1718 version of the oratorio. That was originally designed, like the so-called Chandos anthems, for performance at the Duke of Chandos's mansion, Canons. It may be odd structurally compared with later revisions – with Esther appearing only after the half-way point – but the six compact scenes in a single Act are crisper, so suiting modern taste. Christophers with a small choir of 18 singers offers an aptly intimate view, light and fresh, helped by bright, immediate recording. Lynda Russell and Nancy Argenta are exceptionally sweet and pure in the soprano roles, with the two tenors sharply contrasted – Thomas Randle more heroic, Mark Padmore purer and more refined. Michael George gives fine Handelian thrust to the bass solos.

Like Christophers, Hogwood has opted for the original, 1718 score, and his rather abrasive brand of authenticity goes well with the bright, full recorded sound which unfortunately exaggerates the choir's sibilants. The elaborate passage-work is far too heavily aspirated, at times almost as though the singers are laughing. The vigour of the performance is unaffected and the team of soloists is strong and consistent, with the sweet-toned Patrizia Kwella sounding purposeful in the name-part, and Anthony Rolfe Johnson and Ian Partridge both outstanding in the tenor roles.

Funeral anthem for Queen Caroline: The ways of Zion do mourn.
(M) **(*) Erato/Warner 4509 96954-2. Norma Burrowes, Charles Brett, Martyn Hill, Stephen Varcoe, Monteverdi Ch. & O, Gardiner.

Queen Caroline – whom Handel had known earlier as a princess in Hannover – was the most cultivated of the royal family of the Georges, and when she died in 1737 he was inspired to write a superb cantata in an overture and eleven numbers including the splendid chorus, *How are the mighty fall'n*. He later used the material for the first Act of *Israel in Egypt*. Gardiner directs a stirring performance which brings out the high contrasts implicit in the music, making the piece energetic rather than elegiac. Excellent work from soloists, chorus and orchestra alike, all very well recorded. The only snag is the playing time of 44 minutes.

Israel in Egypt (oratorio).
(M) **(*) DG (IMS) 429 530-2 (2) [id.]. Harper, Clark, Esswood, Young, Rippon, Keyte, Leeds Festival Ch., ECO, Mackerras.

Israel in Egypt (oratorio; with *The Lamentations of the Israelites for the Death of Joseph*).
(M) **(*) Virgin/Veritas EMI (SIS) Dig. VMD5 61350-2 (2) [CDCB 54019]. Argenta, Van Evera, Wilson, Rolfe Johnson, Thomas, White, Taverner Ch. & Players, Parrott.

(i) *Israel in Egypt;* (ii) *Organ concerto in F (The cuckoo and the nightingale), HWV 295.*
*(**) Collins Dig. 7035-2 (2) [id.]. (i) Nicola Jenkin, Sally Dunkley, Caroline Trevor, Neil MacKenzie, Robert Evans, Simon Birchall, The Sixteen; (ii) Paul Nicholson; O of The Sixteen; Harry Christophers.

(i) *Israel in Egypt*; (ii) *Chandos anthem No. 10: The Lord is my light. Organ concerto in F (The cuckoo and the nightingale).*
(B) *** Decca Double 443 470-2 (2) [id.]. (i) Gale, Watson, Bowman, Partridge, McDonnell, Watts, Christ Church Cathedral, Oxford, Ch., ECO, Preston; (ii) Cantelo, Partridge, King's College, Cambridge, Ch., ASMF, Willcocks.

(i) *Israel in Egypt. Coronation anthems: Zadok the Priest; The King shall rejoice.*
(M) *** Ph. Dig. 432 110-2 (2) [id.]. (i) Holton, Priday, Deam, Stafford, Chance, Collin, Kenny, Robertson, Salmon, Tindall, Tusa, Clarkson, Purves; Monteverdi Ch., E. Bar. Soloists, Gardiner.

(i) *Israel in Egypt: Lamentations of the Israelites for the Death of Joseph;* (ii) *The Ways of Zion do mourn* (Funeral anthem).
(M) *** Erato/Warner 2292 45399-2 (2) [id.]. (i) Knibbs, Troth, Greene, Priday, Royall, Stafford, Gordon, Clarkson, Elliott, Kendall, Varcoe, Stewart; (ii) Burrowes, Brett, Hill, Varcoe; Monteverdi Ch. & O, Gardiner.

In his Philips digital version of *Israel in Egypt* Gardiner secures subtler playing from his period instruments, not just more stylish and generally more lightly sprung than in the earlier, Erato version, but conveying more clearly the emotional and dramatic thrust. So the start is more mysterious, and such illustrative numbers as the hopping of the frogs during the plague choruses is even more delightfully pointed than before. As before, first-rate soloists have been chosen from the chorus, and the digital recording is full and well balanced. The *Coronation anthems*, though relatively brief, are also winningly performed.

Using the modern instruments of his Monteverdi Orchestra, Gardiner made his Erato recording in 1978, not long before he decided to adopt period instruments instead. His style here, crisply rhythmic, superbly sprung, with dozens of detailed insights in bringing out word-meaning, is very much what has since become his forte in period performances of Handel and others. The singing both of the chorus and of the twelve soloists chosen from its members is excellent, though, like all other modern recordings, this one slightly falls down in resonance on the most famous number, the duet for basses, *The Lord is a Man of War*. In almost every way Gardiner gains by presenting the *Lamentations* not as an introduction to the main oratorio, but as a supplement, with the same music given in its original form, with text unamended: the funeral cantata for Queen Caroline. Excellent, full-bodied, analogue sound.

Simon Preston, using a small choir with boy trebles and an authentically sized orchestra, directs a performance of this great dramatic oratorio, vigorous and resilient, which is beautifully in scale. He starts with *The cuckoo and the nightingale organ concerto* – a procedure sanctioned by Handel himself at the first performance. Though Elizabeth Gale is not as firm a soprano as Heather Harper on Mackerras's alternative mid-priced Archiv set, the band of soloists is an impressive one and the ECO is in splendid form. The 1975 recording (originally Argo), vividly transferred, is warmly atmospheric. This Double Decca set generously includes the tenth Chandos anthem, *The Lord is my light*, remarkable for magnificent fugal writing, freshly performed by King's Choir under Sir David Willcocks.

Parrott directs a clean-cut, well-paced reading which wears its period manners easily. This may lack the distinctive insights of Gardiner's more sharply rhythmic versions, but with excellent choral and solo singing the performance is unlikely to offend anyone. Good, warm sound. Parrott follows the precedent of Handel's very first performance in using as the first part of the oratorio the cantata written on the death of Queen Caroline, *The Lamentations of the Israelites for the Death of Joseph*, with text duly adapted.

Mackerras's performance represents a dichotomy of styles, using the English Chamber Orchestra sounding crisp, stylish and lightweight and a fairly large amateur choir, impressively weighty rather than incisive. Thus the work makes its effect by breadth and grandiloquence rather than athletic vigour. The solo singing is distinguished, but its style is refined rather than earthy.

Christophers uses the *Lamentations* as a first part to the oratorio, and also – another nod towards Handelian performance-practice – adds the best-known of Handel's organ concertos, the *Cuckoo and the Nightingale*, between Parts One and Two. The playing and singing are bright, but sadly the Collins recording is so reverberant that there is a serious loss of inner detail.

Jephtha.

*** Ph. Dig. 422 351-2 (3). Robson, Dawson, Von Otter, Chance, Varcoe, Holton, Monteverdi Ch., E. Bar. Soloists, Gardiner.

(M) *** Van. 08 5091 73 (3) [id.]. Young, Forrester, Grist, Watts, Lawrenson, Amor Artis Chorale, ECO, Somary.

John Eliot Gardiner's recording was made live at the Göttingen Festival in 1988 and, though the sound does not have quite the bloom of his finest studio recordings of Handel, the exhilaration and intensity of the performance come over vividly, with superb singing from both chorus and an almost ideal line-up of soloists. Nigel Robson's tenor may be on the light side for the title-role, but the sensitivity of expression is very satisfying. Lynne Dawson, with her bell-like soprano, sings radiantly as Iphis; and the counter-tenor, Michael Chance, as her beloved, Hamor, is also outstanding. Anne Sofie von Otter is powerful as Storge, and Stephen Varcoe with his clear baritone, again on the light side, is a stylish Zebul. As for the Monteverdi Choir, their clarity, incisiveness and beauty are a constant delight.

The Vanguard set was the first ever recording of *Jephtha*, made in 1969. It stands up surprisingly well against period performances so that anyone preferring modern instruments need not hesitate. The analogue sound, full, forward and bright, is well transferred, and the freshness and liveliness of Somary's direction, with brisk speeds lightly sprung, are worlds away from the old oratorio tradition. The singers make a formidably starry team with no weak link. Alexander Young, a superb Handel singer, recorded far too little; here he sings most beautifully as Jephtha, not least in *Waft her, angels*. The Canadian mezzo, Maureen Forrester, is caught richly and firmly as Hamor, and the others are first rate too. The small professional chorus is equally assured, producing bright, fresh tone, firmly and forwardly focused.

Joshua (complete).

✿ *** Hyperion Dig. CDA 66461/2 [id.]. Kirkby, Bowman, Ainsley, George, Oliver, New College, Oxford, Ch., King's Consort, King.

Emma Kirkby is here ideally sparkling and light in the role of Achsa, daughter of the patriarchal leader, Caleb (taken here by the bass, Michael George). Her love for Othniel, superbly sung by James Bowman, provides the romantic interest in what is otherwise a grandly military oratorio, based on the Book of Joshua. The brisk sequence of generally brief arias is punctuated by splendid choruses, with solo numbers often inspiring choral comment. The singing is consistently strong and stylish, with the clear, precise tenor, John Mark Ainsley, in the title-role. Robert

King and his Consort crown their achievement in other Hyperion issues, notably their Purcell series, with polished, resilient playing, and the choir of New College, Oxford, sings with ideal freshness. Warm, full sound.

Judas Maccabaeus (complete).

(M) *** DG 447 692-2 (3). Felicity Palmer, Janet Baker, Esswood, Ryland Davies, Shirley-Quirk, Keyte, Wandsworth School Ch., ECO, Mackerras.

**(*) Hyperion Dig. CDA 66641/2 (2) [id.]. Kirkby, Denley, Bowman, MacDougall, George, Birchall, Ch. of New College, Oxford, King's Consort, King.

(M) **(*) Van. 08 4072 72 (2) [id.]. Harper, Watts, Young, Shirley-Quirk, Amor Artis Ch., Wandsworth School Boys' Ch., ECO, Somary.

** HM Dig. HMU 907077/8 [id.] (with appendix). De Mey, Saffer, Spence, D. Thomas, UCLA, Berkeley, Chamber Ch., Philh. Bar. O, McGegan.

Judas Maccabaeus may have a lopsided story, with a high proportion of the finest music given to the anonymous soprano and contralto roles, Israelitish Woman and Israelitish Man; but the sequence of Handelian gems is irresistible, the more so in a performance as sparkling as DG's reissued 1976 recording under Sir Charles Mackerras. Though not everyone will approve of the use of boys' voices in the choir (inevitably the tone and intonation are not flawless) it gives an extra bite of character. Hearing even so hackneyed a number as *See, the conqu'ring hero* in its true scale is a delightful surprise. The orchestral group and continuo sound splendidly crisp. Ryland Davies and John Shirley-Quirk are most stylish, while both Felicity Palmer and Dame Janet crown the whole set with glorious singing, not least in a delectable sequence, towards the end of Act I, on the subject of liberty. The recording quality is outstanding, fresh, vivid and clear.

With some superb solo singing and refined instrumental textures, Robert King's performance of what was once Handel's most popular oratorio can be recommended warmly, even though it is not as lively as some of his Purcell recordings. It is partly that the chorus is not as forward or as bright-toned as one wants in Handel; but there is much to enjoy, with Jamie MacDougall clean and bright if not always ideally firm in the title-role, and with the pure-toned Emma Kirkby well contrasted with the much warmer mezzo of Catherine Denley. Michael George gives splendid weight to the bass arias so central to Handel oratorio.

On Vanguard the solo singing is excellent, with Alexander Young a ringing tenor, and Helen Watts singing the opening aria in Act III exquisitely. Very good recording – the choruses could ideally have a crisper focus, but the effect is wholly natural – and a sense of commitment throughout from all departments.

Like Robert King's Hyperion version, McGegan's rival period performance lacks something of the grandeur which, like other late Handel choral works, this oratorio seems to require. This two-disc set generously offers an appendix, including two arias which Handel added after the first performance in 1747. In a first-rate line-up of soloists Lisa Saffer is outstanding in the key role of the Israelite Woman and, though Guy de Mey in the title-role is hardly idiomatic, his singing is clean and stylish. McGegan is rather more dramatic and incisive than King, but that advantage is offset by the dryness of the recording, typical of the venue in Berkeley, California.

Lucrezia (cantata). Arias: *Ariodante: Oh, felice mio core ... Con l'ali do constanza; E vivo ancore? ... Scherza infida in grembo al drudo; Dopo notte. Atalanta: Care selve. Hercules: Where shall I fly? Joshua: O had I Jubal's lyre. Rodelinda: Pompe vane di morte! ... Dove sei, amato bene? Serse: Frondi tenere e belle ... Ombra mai fù (Largo).*

(M) *** Ph. 426 450-2. Dame Janet Baker, ECO, Leppard.

Even among Dame Janet's most impressive records this Handel recital stands out, ranging as it does from the pure gravity of *Ombra mai fù* to the passionate virtuosity in *Dopo notte* from *Ariodante*. Leppard gives sparkling support and the whole is recorded with natural and refined balance. An outstanding disc, with admirable documentation.

Messiah (complete).

*** DG Dig. 423 630-2 (2). Augér, Von Otter, Chance, Crook, J. Tomlinson, E. Concert Ch., E. Concert, Pinnock.

(N) ✿ *** BIS Dig. CD 891/892 (2) [id.]. Midori Suzuki, Yoshikazu Mera, John Elwes, David Thomas, Bach Collegium Japan, Masaaki Suzuki.

(B) *** Hyperion Dyad Dig. CDD 22019 (2) [id.]. Lynne Dawson, Denley, Maldwyn Davies, Michael George, The Sixteen Ch. & O, Christophers.

*** HM Dig. HMC 901498.99-2 (2) [id.]. Schlick, Piau, Scholl, Padmore, Berg, Les Arts Florissants, Christie.

(N) *** DG Dig. 453 464-2 (2). Dorothea Röschmann, Susan Gritton, Bernarda Fink, Charles Daniels, Neal Davies, Gabrieli Consort & Players, Paul McCreesh.

*** Ph. Dig. 434 297-2 (2). Marshall, Robbin, Rolfe Johnson, Brett, Hale, Shirley-Quirk, Monteverdi Ch., E. Bar. Soloists, Gardiner.

(B) *** Ph. Duo 438 356-2 (2) [id.]. Harper, Watts, Wakefield, Shirley-Quirk, L. Symphony Ch., LSO, Sir Colin Davis.

(B) *** EMI CZS7 62748-2 (2) [Ang. CDMB 62748]. Harwood, J. Baker, Esswood, Tear, Herincx, Amb. S., ECO, Mackerras.

*** Decca Dig. 414 396-2 (2) [id.]. Te Kanawa, Gjevang, Keith Lewis, Howell, Chicago Ch. & SO, Solti.

(N) (M) **(*) IMG/ISS Classics Dig. 691112 (2) [id.]. Susan Roberts, Liliana Bizeneche-Eisinger, Algirdas Janutas, Benno Schollum, Staatscho Kaunas, Lithuanian CO, Menuhin

(B) **(*) CfP CD-CFPD 4718 (2) [id.]. Morison, Thomas, Lewis, Milligan, Huddersfield Ch. Soc., RLPO, Sargent.

(M) **(*) EMI CMS7 63784-2 (2) Trebles from King's, Bowman, Tear, Luxon, King's College, Cambridge, Ch., ASMF, Willcocks.

(BB) **(*) Naxos Dig. 8.550667/8 [id.]. Amps, Davidson, Doveton, Van Asch, Scholars Bar. Ens.

(M) **(*) Van. 08.4019 72 (2) [id.]. Margaret Price, Yvonne Minton, Alexander Young, Justino Diaz, Amor Artis Chorale, ECO, Somary.

(N) (M) *(*) SM2K 60205 (2) [id.]. Adele Addison, Russell Oberlin, David Lloyd, William Warfield, Westminster Ch., NYPO, Bernstein.

Pinnock presents a performance using authentically scaled forces which, without inflation, rise to grandeur and magnificence, qualities Handel himself would have relished. The fast contrapuntal choruses, such as *For unto us a Child is born*, are done lightly and resiliently in the modern manner, but there is no hint of breathlessness, and Pinnock (more than his main rivals) balances his period instruments to give a satisfying body to the sound. There is weight too in the singing of the bass soloist, John Tomlinson, firm, dark and powerful, yet marvellously agile in divisions. Arleen Augér's range of tone and dynamic is daringly wide, with radiant purity in *I know that my Redeemer liveth*. Anne Sofie von Otter sustains *He was despised* superbly with her firm, steady voice. Some alto arias are taken just as beaituflly by the outstanding counter-tenor, Michael Chance. The tenor, Howard Crook, is less distinctive but still sings freshly and attractively. With full, atmospheric and well-balanced recording, this is a set not to be missed.

With his excellent Japanese singers and players, Masaaki Suzuki has produced a series of intensely refreshing readings of baroque choral works, and here he excels himself. His crisp, sharp manner goes with transparent textures and sprung rhythms, and though modest forces are used the result has natural dramatic weight. The consistent alertness of the chorus is a delight but the fast speeds he tends to prefer never sound breathless, and he is never afraid to choose a spacious tempo, if the mood of the music demands it – as in the aria, *He was despised*, sung with seamless beauty by the male alto, Yoshikazu Mera. The soprano Midori Suzuki sings with radiant purity, notably in *I know that my Redeemer liveth*, and the two British soloists are excellent too, with John Elwes bright and eager, and David Thomas caught at his warmest. This can readily be recommended alongside Pinnock, Christophers, and Christie and is a special favourite of I. M.'s

Christophers consistently adopts speeds more relaxed than those we have grown used to in modern performances, and the effect is fresh, clear and resilient. Alto lines in the chorus are taken by male singers; a counter-tenor, David James, is also used for the *Refiner's fire*, but *He was despised* is rightly given to the contralto, Catherine Denley, warm and grave at a very measured tempo. The team of five soloists is as fine as that on any rival set, with the soprano, Lynne Dawson, singing with silvery purity. The band of 13 strings sounds as clean and fresh as the choir. Even the *Hallelujah chorus* – always a big test in a small-scale performance – works well, with Christophers in his chosen scale, through dramatic timpani and trumpets conveying necessary weight. The sound has all the bloom one associates with St John's recordings. Now offered as a two-for-one Dyad, this is first-class value.

William Christie and Les Arts Florissants offer yet another outstanding account of *Messiah*. More than most period performances – but like Trevor Pinnock's – it gives the impression of a live performance caught on the wing, even though it was recorded in the studio. Christie's preference for fast, resilient speeds and light textures, not least in choruses, never prevents him from giving due emotional weight to such key numbers as *He was despised*. That is superbly sung, with touching simplicity, firm tone and flawless intonation, by the counter-tenor, Andreas Scholl. The other singers too sound fresh and young, with the two sopranos, Barbara Schlick and Sandrine Piau, delectably counterpointed, both pure and true, making light of the elaborate divisions in such a number as *Rejoice greatly*. The treble, Tommy Williams, also sings with beautiful, firm clarity in the Angel's narration, *There were shepherds abiding in the fields*. The tenor, Mark Padmore, and the bass, Nathan Berg, complete the pattern, light by old-fashioned standards but fresh and cleanly focused. Christie in his text opts for Handel's later versions of numbers. Excellent sound, though the chorus is placed a little backwardly. At the time of going to press, this set is available at bargain price (HMX 2901 498.99) in a slip case with a complete Harmonia Mundi catalogue. It is a limited edition, but copies may still be available in the shops.

Using the Foundling Hospital version of the score, Paul McCreesh, in recreating the sort of performance Handel supervised there in 1754, seeks to present a 'thoroughly modern performance – A

Messiah for the Millennium', as he puts it. If he has not quite achieved that, this is still a bright and individual reading, bringing out the drama of the music, with extreme speeds in both directions. The chorus copes well with some tempi that run the risk of breathlessness, and the soloists make an excellent team with their fresh, young voices. Good, warm sound.

Gardiner chooses bright-toned sopranos instead of boys for the chorus and he uses, very affectingly, a solo treble to sing *There were shepherds abiding*. Speeds are fast and light, and the rhythmic buoyancy in the choruses is very striking, though idiosyncratically Gardiner begins *Hallelujah!* on a pianissimo. *Why do the nations* and *The trumpet shall sound* (both sung with great authority) come over dramatically, and the soloists are all first class, with the soprano Margaret Marshall finest of all, especially in *I know that my Redeemer liveth*. Other highlights include Margaret Marshall's angelic version of *Rejoice greatly*, skipping along in compound time.

Reissued at bargain price on Philips's Duo label, the LSO recording conducted by Sir Colin Davis, in the sixties the first of a new generation of *Messiah* recordings, fresh and urgent, has not lost its impact, remastered in bright sound. Textures are beautifully clear and, thanks to Davis, the rhythmic bounce of such choruses as *For unto us* is really infectious. Even *Hallelujah* loses little and gains much from being performed by a chorus of this size. Excellent singing from all four soloists, particularly Helen Watts, who, following early precedent, is given *For He is like a refiner's fire* to sing, instead of the bass, and produces a glorious chest register. Excellent value at its new price.

With Mackerras in another 'new generation' recording of the sixties, the chorus is not so fresh as Davis's LSO Choir, but has a compensating breadth and body. More than Davis, Mackerras adopts Handel's alternative versions, so the soprano aria *Rejoice greatly* is given in its optional 12/8 version. A male alto is also included, Paul Esswood, and he is given some of the bass arias as well as some of the regular alto passages. Among the soloists, Dame Janet Baker is outstanding. Her intense, slow account of *He was despised* – with decorations on the reprise – is sung with profound feeling. The recording is warm and full in ambience and, with the added brightness of CD, sounds extremely vivid.

Sir Georg Solti inspires a vital, exciting reading. The Chicago Symphony Orchestra and Chorus respond to some challengingly fast but never breathless speeds, showing what lessons can be learnt from authentic performance in clarity and crispness. Yet the joyful power of *Hallelujah* and the *Amen chorus* is overwhelming. Dame Kiri Te Kanawa matches anyone on record in beauty of tone and detailed expressiveness, while the other soloists are first rate too, though Anne Gjevang has rather too fruity a timbre. Brilliant, full sound.

The performance under Menuhin was recorded live in 1996 as part of his 80th birthday celebrations. Using modern instruments, it finds him adopting consistently fast speeds, often faster than those in period performances. Though the chorus is relatively large, the manner is light and transparent, and with generally good soloists this is an attractive memento of what plainly was a moving occasion, helped by warm, atmospheric sound.

It is good to have Sir Malcolm Sargent's 1959 recording now restored to the catalogue in full for, apart from the pleasure given by a performance that brings out the breadth of Handel's inspiration, it provides an important corrective to misconceptions about pre-authentic practice. Sargent unashamedly fills out the orchestration, and though, by the side of Davis, his tempi are very measured, his pacing is natural, and, with a hundred-strong Huddersfield group, he gives weight and vigour to the choruses. There is some splendid singing from all four soloists, and Marjorie Thomas's *He was despised* is memorable in its moving simplicity. Remarkably clear CD transfer.

Often though *Messiah* may have been recorded, there is always room for alternative versions, particularly those which show a new and illuminating view of the work. Willcocks's recording, made in the Chapel at King's in 1971/2, has been described as the 'all-male *Messiah*', since a counter-tenor takes over the contralto solos, and the full complement of the trebles of King's College Choir sings the soprano solos, even the florid ones like *Rejoice greatly*; the result is enchanting, often light and airy. The bigger choruses do not lack robust qualities. The sound is vivid and atmospheric. A gimmicky version, perhaps, but one that many will find refreshing and involving.

On the bargain Naxos label comes a period performance with a difference. With fresh, immediate sound adding to the impact, the Scholars Baroque Ensemble presents the oratorio on the smallest possible scale, with individual singers from the small chorus coming forward to sing the arias. In keeping with this approach, the performance is directed by one of the basses, David van Asch, and characteristically the booklet seeks as far as possible not to highlight individual contributions but to emphasize teamwork. At brisk speeds, with rhythms well sprung, this will please those who fancy such an approach, though the instrumental sound is abrasive, and none of the singers has a voice of star quality. By their own definition, these are good choristers rather than great soloists.

Somary directs a crisp, small-scale performance that features sparkling orchestral playing (on modern instruments) and first-rate singing from soloists and chorus alike. His direction is not always consistent but it is never dull, and the recording is first class, warm yet bright and natural. An excellent choice for those wanting a relatively traditional approach and who have a special fondness for all or any of the soloists. The chorus is excellent, its size nicely judged.

Bernstein's *Messiah* was recorded in 1956, and has come up well on CD; indeed the style of singing sounds more dated than the sound quality. Handel's masterpiece cannot fail to make an impact when conducted with such conviction and vigour (even if Bernstein indulges himself expressively in the *Pastoral symphony,* and the *Hallelujah chorus* now sounds too slow and solid). He has the advantage of two outstanding soloists: Adele Addison's soprano arias, especially *I know that my Redeemer liveth*, are sung with ravishing purity of line, and Russell Oberlin's contribution is very distinguished indeed. His is a unique voice, and the plangent bite of the middle section of *He was despised* is unforgettable. The tenor and baritone have strong voices but are more conventional; the real snag is the chorus. They sing with conviction (especially in the lively *For unto us a child is born*) but the quavery soprano line is uningratiating and today we are used to crisper accuracy in the running passages.

Messiah (completely reorchestrated).
❁ (M) *** RCA 09026 61266-2 (3) [id.].
Vyvyan, Sinclair, Vickers, Tozzi, RPO Ch. & O, Sir Thomas Beecham.

This is a performance flamboyantly reorchestrated, both dramatic and moving, which at every point radiates the natural flair of the conductor. The use of the cymbals to cap the choruses *For unto us a child is born* and *Glory to God* is unforgettable. Many of Beecham's tempi are slower than we expect today, but not the *Hallelujah chorus*, which is fast and resilient. Jennifer Vyvyan and Monica Sinclair both sing freshly. Jon Vickers brings to his tenor arias a heroic quality that is often welcome and effective. Giorgio Tozzi's English is sound and his management of the tricky bass arias (especially *Why do the nations*) compels admiration. The 1959 recording of the chorus and orchestra is full and expansive in its CD transfer and the soloists have remarkable presence and immediacy. The third disc with its 17-minute appendix of eight items – normally cut at the time this recording was made – comes as a bonus, as the set is priced as for two mid-range CDs.

(i) *Messiah* (complete).(ii) *Israel in Egypt* 3 Choruses: *But for His people; Moses and the children of Israel; The Lord is a man of war. Amaryllis suite* (arr. Beecham): *Gavotte; Scherzo.*
(N) (***) Biddulph mono WHL 059/61(3) [id.].
(i) Elsie Suddaby, Marjorie Thomas, Heddle Nash, Trevor Antony, Luton Choral Society; (ii) Leeds Festival Chorus; RPO, Beecham (with BACH: *Christmas Oratorio: Sinfonia.* (***)).

Issued only in the United States, never in Britain, this recording of 1947 is one of Beecham's rarest, an oddity but a fascinating one. Unlike his later RCA version of *Messiah* this one has no percussion trimmings in the orchestra, but as he explains in a spoken introduction, he uses choirs of different sizes for different numbers. Speeds are often extreme, commendably so in brisk numbers, while his expansive slow speeds bring persuasive Beechamesque moulding. A fine quartet of soloists includes the great tenor Heddle Nash. The *Israel in Egypt* excerpts date from 1934, celebrating Beecham's work at the Leeds Festival, the instrumental pieces from 1947.

Beecham rarely conducted Bach, and in this brief bonus he makes the *Sinfonia* sound like one of his arrangements of Handel.

Messiah (slightly abridged).
❁ (B) (***) Dutton Lab. mono 2CDEA 5010 (2) [id.]. Isobel Baillie, Gladys Ripley, James Johnson, Norman Walker, Huddersfield Ch. Soc., Liverpool PO, Malcolm Sargent.

Sargent's first recording of Handel's *Messiah* is not complete. Following his usual performance practice, three numbers are cut from Part II and four from Part III. The recording venue was Huddersfield Town Hall in 1946, when that great Choral Society was still at its peak, and Handel's masterpiece is here brought vividly to life in a brilliant Dutton transfer from the 78s. What is so involving is the way this remarkably realistic and present recording (in many ways more vivid than the later stereo set), made in a series of four-minute takes, comes over with the tension of a live performance. There may be strictures about the style, not least the slow tempi (especially in Part II) and the orchestration (Prout's edition, plus additions from Mozart's version) and of course its weight and scale. But the chorus sings throughout with enormous conviction and the four fine soloists obviously live their parts, with their enunciation making every word clear. The star of the performance is Isobel Baillie. Her first entry in *There were shepherds* is a moment of the utmost magic, and what follows is utterly ravishing, while her gloriously beautiful *I know that my Redeemer liveth* has never been surpassed on record. Gladys Ripley sings *He was despised* with moving simplicity and restraint, and she warmly introduces *He shall feed his flock*, sharing it with Baillie, who re-enters exquisitely. At bargain price this is an essential investment for anyone who loves the English amateur choral tradition.

Der Messias (sung in German, arr. Mozart): complete.
(M) **(*) DG (IMS) 427 173-2 (2). Mathis,

Finnilä, Schreier, Adam, Austrian R. Ch. & O, Vienna, Mackerras.

Mozart's arrangement of *Messiah* is fascinating. It is not simply a question of trombones being added but of elaborate woodwind parts too – most engaging in a number such as *All we like sheep*, which even has a touch of humour. *The trumpet shall sound* is considerably modified and shortened. To avoid the use of a baroque instrument, Mozart shares the obbligato between trumpet and horn. Mackerras leads his fine team through a performance that is vital, not academic in the heavy sense. The remastered recording is excellent and a translation is provided.

Messiah (sung in English): highlights.

*** Ph. (IMS) Dig. 412 267-2 (from above set, cond. Gardiner).

(M) *** Penguin Classics Decca Dig. 466 215-2 [460 605-2] (from above set, cond. Solti).

(N) (M) **(*) Classic FM Dig. 75605 57057-2. Kwella, Denley, Ainsley, Terfel, London Musici & Chamber Ch., Mark Stephenson.

(M) *** [EMI Red Line CDR5 72431] (from above set, cond. Mackerras).

(B) **(*) CfP CD-CFP 9007 (from above stereo set, cond. Sargent).

(BB) **(*) ASV Quicksilva Dig. CDQS 6001 [(M) id. import]. Kwella, Cable, Kendal, Drew, Jackson, Winchester Cathedral Ch., L. Handel O, Neary.

(BB) **(*) Belart 450 045-2 (from above Philips Duo set, cond. Sir Colin Davis).

(M) **(*) Ph. 462 055-2. Margaret Marshall, Catherine Robbins, Charles Brett, Robin Hale, Monteverdi Ch., E. Bar. Soloists, John Eliot Gardiner.

Here Gardiner's collection reigns supreme, with the single caveat that *The trumpet shall sound* is missing.

Solti's selection on Penguin Classics is undoubtedly generous, including all the key numbers and much else besides. The sound is thrillingly vivid and full. The note is provided by Garrison Keillor.

Recorded for Conifer in 1989, Mark Stephenson's disc of favourite numbers offers fresh, bright performances vividly recorded in full, atmospheric sound. In style this follows the example of Colin Davis's vintage recording, using modern instruments but with choruses challengingly fast and with bright, crisp choral singing. It was recorded before Bryn Terfel became an international star, and his voice is gloriously dark and firm in his two solo passages. Sadly, *The trumpet shall sound* is not included. The others are impressive too, notably Patricia Kwella at her most golden. A pity this is not the complete oratorio.

Otherwise Mackerras is first choice (although available in the USA only), while the great and pleasant surprise among the bargain selections is the Classics for Pleasure CD of highlights from Sir Malcolm Sargent's 1959 recording; no one will be disappointed with *Hallelujah*, while the closing *Amen* brings a powerful apotheosis.

Brightly if reverberantly recorded in Winchester Cathedral, Martin Neary's collection of excerpts gives a pleasant reminder of the work of one of our finest cathedral choirs. In its authentic manner Neary's style is rather too clipped to convey deep involvement, but the freshness is attractive, with some very good solo singing.

Although it is not generous, the Belart set of highlights from Sir Colin Davis's mid-1960s recording is the least expensive high-quality selection currently available. It offers a dozen key items, including most of the favourites, but not *He was despised*.

The second mid-priced selection from Gardiner's set centres on the choruses (which feature bright-toned sopranos). Some arias are included, notably *The trumpet shall sound*, sung with great authority by Robin Hale; but too much is missing here: any selection from *Messiah* which omits *I know that my Redeemer liveth* can receive only a limited recommendation, even though the selection runs to 76 minutes. The presentation in Philips's 'Choral Collection' is handsome, but the notes are sparse and no texts are included.

The Occasional oratorio.

*** Hyperion Dig. CDA 66961/2 [id.]. Gritton, Milne, Bowman, Ainsley, George, New College, Oxford, Ch., King's Consort Ch. & Ens., Robert King.

Handel's *Occasional oratorio* may have a slack dramatic structure but, with plentiful borrowings from such works as *Israel in Egypt*, it offers a wonderful showcase of Handel at his most inspired and vigorous. The lively choruses in particular, some only a few seconds long, regularly punctuate the work to heighten the effect of the arias, whether lively or beautiful, with some of the solo numbers leading directly into a related chorus with exhilarating effect. The piece culminates in an adaptation of Handel's great coronation anthem, *Zadok the Priest*, with loyal cries of *God save the King* ringing out at the end. The whole performance is fresh and electrifying, with excellent singing from all the soloists. Susan Gritton and Lisa Milne, the clear-toned sopranos, are set against the increasingly dark counter-tenor tones of James Bowman, with John Mark Ainsley and Michael George both clear and fresh Handelian stylists. The chorus fares rather less well in a generally excellent recording for, though the ensemble is first rate, the backward balance takes some of the edge off the more dramatic choruses.

Ode for the birthday of Queen Anne (Eternal source of light divine); Sing unto God (Wedding anthem); Te Deum in D (for Queen Caroline).
*** Hyperion Dig. CDA 66315 [id.]. Fisher, Bowman, Ainsley, George, New College, Oxford, Ch., King's Consort, Robert King.

Handel's *Birthday ode for Queen Anne* combines Purcellian influences with Italianate writing to make a rich mixture. King's performance is richly enjoyable, with warm, well-tuned playing from the King's Consort and with James Bowman in radiant form in the opening movement. The other two items are far rarer. Warmly atmospheric recording, not ideally clear on detail.

Ode for St Cecilia's Day.
*** DG Dig. 419 220-2 [id.]. Lott, Rolfe Johnson, Ch. & E. Concert, Pinnock.
*** ASV Dig. CDDCA 512 [id.]. Gomez, Tear, King's College Ch., ECO, Ledger.
(M) *** Teldec/Warner 0630 12319-2. Palmer, Rolfe Johnson, Stockholm Bach Ch., VCM, Harnoncourt.

Trevor Pinnock's account of Handel's magnificent setting of Dryden's *Ode* comes near the ideal for a performance using period instruments. Not only is it crisp and lively, it has deep tenderness too, as in the lovely soprano aria, *The complaining flute*, with Lisa Beznosiuk playing the flute obbligato most delicately in support of Felicity Lott's clear singing. Anthony Rolfe Johnson gives a robust yet stylish account of *The trumpet's loud clangour*, and the choir is excellent, very crisp of ensemble. Full, clear recording with voices vivid and immediate.

Those seeking a version with modern instruments will find Ledger's ASV version a splendid alternative. With superb soloists – Jill Gomez radiantly beautiful and Robert Tear dramatically riveting in his call to arms – this delightful music emerges with an admirable combination of freshness and weight. Ledger uses an all-male chorus; the style of the performance is totally convincing without being self-consciously authentic. The recording is first rate, rich, vivid and clear.

Harnoncourt's Teldec version of the *Ode*, recorded in 1979, is only slightly less recommendable than Trevor Pinnock's Archiv version, though the non-British choir, for all its fluency, sounds less comfortable than its rival and sings less crisply. Anthony Rolfe Johnson is excellent on both versions, while Felicity Palmer as soprano sings most characterfully. One special point in favour of Harnoncourt is his own striking cello playing in the beautiful setting of Dryden's second stanza, *What Passion cannot Musick raise and quell!* Now reissued in Teldec's Das Alte Werk mid-priced series.

La Resurrezione.
*** O-L Dig. 421 132-2 (2). Kirkby, Kwella, C. Watkinson, Partridge, Thomas, AAM, Hogwood.
(B) *** HM Musique d'Abord HMA 1907027/8 [id.]. Saffer, George, Nelson, Spence, Thomas, Phil. Bar. O, Nicholas McGegan.
(N) *** DG Dig. 447 767-2(2) [id.]. Massis, Jennifer Smith, Maguire, Ainsley, Naouri, Les Musiciens du Louvre, Marc Minkowski.

In 1708, halfway through his four-year stay in Italy, the young Handel wrote this refreshingly dramatic oratorio. With opera as such prohibited in Rome, it served as a substitute, not solemn at all, but with dramatic and moving exchanges between the central characters. There is no chorus until the close, but Handel makes up for this with a wonderful palette of orchestra colour in his accompaniments, liberally featuring trumpets, recorders and oboes.

Hogwood directs a clean-cut, vigorous performance with an excellent cast. Emma Kirkby is at her most brilliant in the coloratura for the Angel, Patrizia Kwella sings movingly as Mary Magdalene and Carolyn Watkinson as Cleophas adopts an almost counter-tenor-like tone. Ian Partridge's tenor has a heady lightness as St John, and though David Thomas's Lucifer could have more weight he too sings stylishly. Excellent recording.

McGegan's performance is as lively as one could wish and is excellently cast. Lisa Saffer is an appealing Angel, nimble (in breathtakingly florid coloratura) and touching, especially good in her dialogues with the boldly resonant Lucifer (Michael George). But Judith Nelson is equally affecting as Mary Magdelene, whereas Patricia Spence's dark contralto (as Cleophas) and Jeffrey Thomas's fresh tenor St John bring plenty of dramatic contrast. The sounds from the period instruments of the Philharmonia Baroque Orchestra are ear-tickling, and the soloists join together for the life-assertive closing chorus. Excellent recording, both atmospheric and vivid, makes for a fine bargain alternative to Hogwood.

Marc Minkowski brings out the dramatic bite of this early Handel oratorio, often opting for extreme speeds, particularly fast ones, challenging his excellent soprano Annick Massis to the limit in the Angel's brilliant first aria. He may rarely relax in the way that Ton Koopman did on his earlier Erato version (currently withdrawn), but in this episodic piece there is much to be said for such a taut approach, with fine, clean-textured playing from Les Musiciens du Louvre. However, Hogwood remains first choice and the enjoyable alternative from McGegan is in the bargain price-range.

Samson (complete).
(M) *** Erato/Warner 2292 45994-2 (3). Tear, J. Baker, Lott, Watts, Shirley-Quirk, Luxon, L. Voices, ECO, Leppard.
*** Teldec/Warner Dig. 9031 74871-2 (2) [id.]. Rolfe Johnson, Alexander, Kowalski,

Scharinger, Venuti, Blasi, Arnold Schoenberg Ch., VCM, Harnoncourt.

Leppard directs a highly dramatic account of Handel's most dramatic oratorio; its culmination, the exultant aria *Let the bright seraphim*, is here beautifully sung by Felicity Lott, but for long was associated with Joan Sutherland. The moment when the orchestra interrupts a soloist in mid-sentence to indicate the collapse of the temple is more vividly dramatic than anything in a Handel opera, and Leppard handles that and much else with total conviction. Robert Tear as Samson produces his most heroic tones – rather too aggressively so in *Total eclipse* – and the rest of the cast could hardly be more distinguished. Dame Janet Baker – not by nature a seductress in the Dalila sense – yet sings with a lightness totally apt for such an aria as *With plaintive notes*, and the others are in excellent voice. The recording is outstanding, atmospheric and well balanced.

Harnoncourt here conducts a Handel performance where Handelian grandeur shines out from the opening overture with its braying horns and genially strutting dotted rhythms. He is altogether warmer than before, and a fine team of singers, led by Anthony Rolfe Johnson in the title-role, is allowed full expressiveness, with speeds in slow numbers broader than one might expect. So the blind Samson's first aria, *Total eclipse*, is very measured, with Rolfe Johnson using the widest tonal and dynamic range. Though the recording catches some flutter in Roberta Alexander's voice as Dalila, she gives a characterful performance, well contrasted with Angela Maria Blasi, her attendant, who sings the lovely aria, *With plaintive note*, most beautifully. Maria Venuti in the climactic *Let the bright seraphim* at the end is not ideally pure-toned, but she sings strongly and flexibly. Other fine singers include Alastair Miles, magnificent in the bass role of the giant, Harapha, not least in *Honour and arms*, as well as the rich-toned counter-tenor, Jochen Kowalski as Micah and Christoph Prégardien in the tenor role of the Philistine. With the Schoenberg choir singing incisively, Harnoncourt presents the work not only with period instruments but on an authentic scale.

Saul (complete).

*** Ph. Dig. 426 265-2 (3). Miles, Dawson, Ragin, Ainslie, Mackie, Monteverdi Ch., E. Bar. Soloists, Gardiner.

(M) *** DG 447 696-2. Armstrong, M. Price, Bowman, Ryland Davies, English, Dean, McIntyre, Winfield, Leeds Festival Ch., ECO, Sir Charles Mackerras.

(N) (BB) **(*) Naxos 8.554361/63 (3) Stephan McLeod, David Cordier, Knut Schuch, Barbara Schlick, Claron McFadden, Marcel Beekman, Junge Kantorei, Frankfurt Baroque O., Joachim Carlos Martini.

Gardiner's performance is typically vigorous in what represents Handel's full emergence as a great oratorio composer, with the widest range of emotions conveyed. The alternation of mourning and joy in the final sequence of numbers is startlingly effective. With Derek Lee Ragin in the counter-tenor role of David, with Alastair Miles as Saul, Lynne Dawson as Michal and John Mark Ainslie as Jonathan, it is not likely to be surpassed on disc for a long time.

With an excellent combination of soloists Mackerras steers an exhilarating course in a work that naturally needs to be presented with authenticity but equally needs to have dramatic edge, and the result is powerful on one hand, moving on another. The contrast of timbre between Armstrong and Price is beautifully exploited, and Donald McIntyre as Saul, Ryland Davies as Jonathan and James Bowman as a counter-tenor David are all outstanding, while the chorus willingly contributes to the drama. An outstanding set, beautifully recorded (at the Leeds Triennial Music Festival in 1972) and vividly transferred to CD.

Joachim Carlos Martini on Naxos offers a clear, fresh, lively reading using period instruments, very well recorded, making an excellent bargain version. Outstanding among the soloists is the creamy-toned Barbara Schlick, who sings the role of Michal, Saul's daughter and David's wife. Singers with fresh, young voices fill the other roles effectively, if not always very characterfully. Stephan McLeod as Saul is a clear, firm baritone, rather than the dark bass the role ideally requires, and David Cordier as David is a very English-sounding counter-tenor, clean and cultivated. Claron McFadden in the dual role of Merab and the Witch of Endor is rather edgy, better suited to the second of those roles. The chorus sing well, but are not ideally focused. Otherwise the sound is fresh and clear.

Solomon (complete).

✿ *** Ph. Dig. 412 612-2 (2) [id]. C. Watkinson, Argenta, Hendricks, Rolfe Johnson, Monteverdi Ch., E. Bar. Soloists, Gardiner.

(N) *** DG Dig. 439 688-2 (3) [id.]. Andreas Scholl, Inger Dam-Jensen, Alison Hagley, Susan Bickley, Susan Gritton, Paul Agnew, Gabrieli Cons. & Players, Paul McCreesh.

(M) **(*) Van. 08 5086 72 (2) [id.]. Diaz, Armstrong, Tear, Rippon, Palmer, Amore Artis Chorale, ECO, Somary.

This Philips set is among the very finest of all Handel oratorio recordings. With panache, Gardiner shows how authentic-sized forces can convey Handelian grandeur even with clean-focused textures and fast speeds. The choruses and even more magnificent double-choruses stand as cornerstones of a structure which may have less of a story-line than some other Handel oratorios – the Judgement apart – but which Gardiner shows has consistent human warmth. The Act III scenes between Solomon and the Queen of Sheba are given extra warmth by having in the latter role a singer who is sensuous in tone, Barbara Hendricks. Carolyn Watkinson's pure mezzo is very apt for Solomon himself, while Nancy Argenta is clear and sweet as his Queen, but the overriding glory of the set is the radiant singing of Gardiner's Monteverdi Choir. Its clean, crisp articulation matches the brilliant playing of the English Baroque Soloists, regularly challenged by Gardiner's fast speeds, as in *The arrival of the Queen of Sheba*; and the sound is superb, coping thrillingly with the problems of the double choruses.

The great merit of Paul McCreesh's version of Solomon is that he includes every item that Handel wrote for the 1749 première, where even John Eliot Gardiner in his Philips version, one of his very finest recordings, omits five arias. McCreesh and his team, taking a more relaxed view than Gardiner, though equally dramatic, are lighter in texture, though the recording, made in All Saints, Tooting, is a degree more reverberant. A controversial point is that where Handel originally wrote the title role for a woman singer, not a castrato, McCreesh opts for a counter-tenor, arguing that had Handel heard such an outstanding falsettist as Scholl, he would have been amply convinced. Scholl sings magnificently, and the rest of the team is strong too, with no weak link. The extra items, involving almost half an hour of music, mean that the work spreads on to three discs instead of two.

Somary in this and other recordings for Vanguard did impressive work in the 1960s and 1970s in helping to establish a new, fresher approach to Handel oratorio, well before period performance took over. With a crisp professional chorus and a formidable line-up of soloists, this offers an enjoyable, infectiously sprung performance, marred by the choice of voice for the title-role. Handel himself opted for a mezzo rather than a castrato or a tenor, but here Somary, following now-discredited tradition, has a bass, singing an octave lower than written. Admittedly Justino Diaz sings with satisfyingly dark, firm tone to make the result dramatically very convincing, and the other soloists, drawn from among the finest British singers of the time, are all excellent. For this pageant of an oratorio, John Eliot Gardiner's period performance remains a firm first choice, but it is good to have this too, at mid-price.

Susanna.

**(*) HM Dig. HMU 907030/2 [id.]. Hunt, Minter, Feldman, Parker, J & D. Thomas, U. C. Berkeley Chamber Ch., Philh. Bar. O, McGegan.

The wealth of arias and the refreshing treatment of the Apocrypha story of Susanna and the Elders make it ideal for records. McGegan's performance does not quite match those of his earlier Handel recordings, made in Budapest. This one was done live with a talented period group from Los Angeles. The main snag is that the dry acoustic brings an abrasive edge to the instrumental sound and takes away bloom from the voices. Yet with fine soloists including Lorraine Hunt (Susanna), Drew Minter (Joacim) and Jill Feldman (Daniel), this is far more than a mere stop-gap.

Susanna: highlights.

(M) **(*) HM Suite Dig. HMT 7907168 [id.] (from complete recording, with Lorraine Hunt, Drew Minter, Jill Feldman, William Parker, Jeffrey and David Thomas, Philh. Bar. O, Nicholas McGegan).

Many collectors who might not want to stretch to the complete work on three full-priced CDs will welcome this 72-minute selection of highlights, particularly as it comes with full text and good documentation.

Theodora (complete).

*** HM Dig. HMU 907060/62 (3) [id.]. D. Thomas, Minter, J. Thomas, Hunt, Lane, Rogers, University of California (Berkeley) Chamber Ch., Philh. Baroque O, McGegan.

(M) **(*) Van. 08.4075.72 (2). Harper, Forrester, Lehane, Young, Lawrenson, Amor Artis Ch., ECO, Somary.

**(*) Teldec/Warner Dig. 2292 46447-2 (2). Alexander, Blochwitz, Kowalski, Van Nes, Scharinger, Schönberg Ch., VCM, Harnoncourt.

Theodora was a favourite with Handel himself among his oratorios, and McGegan's spirited, exuberant performance makes one realize why, so many fine numbers does it contain. Unlike previous recordings, this one not only gives the text absolutely complete but also offers alternative numbers not included in the regular Handel edition. The fine team of soloists is impressively headed by Lorraine Hunt, who also shone in McGegan's earlier, prize-winning recording of *Susanna*, with the counter-tenor, Drew Minter, the tenor, Jeffrey Thomas, and the bass, David Thomas, again singing stylishly. They are not helped by the dry acoustic, but the sound is less aggressive than in the earlier set, and it means that words are crystal clear.

The reissued Vanguard account is traditional in style and is directed by an understanding and intelligent Handelian, Johannes Somary. With fresh and sympathetic singing from soloists who are stylistically at home in Handel, the result is most enjoyable. Maureen Forrester in particular sings superbly, but all the singing is at least reliable, and the recording has transferred warmly and vividly to CD.

There is much to enjoy in this lively Teldec account, with fresh, clean textures typical of the Concentus Musicus, and with Harnoncourt thrusting in manner, occasionally to the point of being heavy-handed. The solo casting is strong, though this team of international singers does not always sound at home, either stylistically or in singing English. Roberta Alexander is the finest of the soloists, with the counter-tenor Jochen Kowalski exceptionally warm of tone but hardly sounding Handelian in the role of Didymus. Jard van Nes is warm and fruity as Irene and Hans Peter Blochwitz is light and fresh as Septimius. Bright, full recording.

The Triumph of time and truth.
*** Hyperion CDA 66071/2 [id.]. Fisher, Kirkby, Brett, Partridge, Varcoe, L. Handel Ch. and O, Darlow.

Darlow's performance of Handel's very last oratorio is broad and strong and very enjoyable. The soloists have all been chosen for the clarity of their pitching – Emma Kirkby, Gillian Fisher, Charles Brett and Stephen Varcoe, with the honey-toned Ian Partridge singing even more beautifully than the others, but with a timbre too pure quite to characterize 'Pleasure'. Good atmospheric recording.

OPERA

Admeto, re di Tessaglia (complete).
(M) *** Virgin Veritas/EMI VMT5 61369-2 [CDMC 61369] (3). René Jacobs, Rachel Yakar, Jill Gomez, James Bowman, Ulrik Cold, Rita Dams, Max van Egmont, Il Complesso Barocco, Alan Curtis.

Admeto is among the very greatest of Handel's operas, probably the most successful of all in his lifetime, and it is surprising that this recording, made in 1977 in Holland, has not appeared earlier on CD. Under Alan Curtis it was one of the first complete recordings of a Handel opera to attempt an authentic approach, and the most successful up to that time. Though recitatives are on the slow side, it stands the test of time, a fine performance, very well cast, played with refinement on period instruments and excellently recorded. The original five LPs here conveniently become three CDs, one per Act. Handel wrote *Admeto* at the end of his years presenting opera at the Royal Academy (at the King's Theatre in the Haymarket), with the three greatest singers of the time in mind, the castrato, Senesino, in the title-role, and the rival prima donnas, Cuzzoni and Bordoni, as Antigona and Alceste. Here the counter-tenor René Jacobs gives an understanding and characterful performance in the title-role, but it is Jill Gomez as Antigona who steals first honours, with magnificent singing, sweet, pure and strong of tone, with ornamentation beautifully crisp. Rachel Yakar is not so sweetly caught by the microphones, but hers is a stylish performance too, and the rest of the cast has no weak link, with James Bowman outstanding as Admeto's brother, Trasimede.

Agrippina (complete).
*** Ph. Dig. 438 009-2 (3) [id.]. Della Jones, Miles, Lee Ragin, Donna Brown, Chance, Von Otter, Mosley, E. Bar. Soloists, Gardiner.
*** HM Dig. HMU 907063/65 [id.] (3). Bradshaw, Saffer, Minter, Hill, Isherwood, Popken, Dean, Banditelli, Szilági, Capella Savaria, McGegan.

Agrippina was the second and last of the operas that Handel wrote during his stay in Italy between 1706 and 1710. His libretto was specially written for him by Cardinal Vincenzo Grimani, using historical characters from the time of the Emperor Claudius, in which the immoral goings-on in the court are treated with a lightness and vein of irony that marked operas in the previous century by Monteverdi and Cavalli. Handel responded with a delightful work in which the characters are colourfully drawn, not least Agrippina, the Emperor's scheming wife, here superbly taken by Della Jones, strong and characterful, bringing out the necessary fire and sparkle.

This Gardiner recording comes into direct rivalry with the fine Harmonia Mundi version of 1991 under Nicholas McGegan, fresh and immediate with a generally youthful cast. Not just Della Jones, but most of the other principals are a degree more characterful than their opposite numbers – Derek Lee Ragin as Nero (a counter-tenor clearly preferable to McGegan's soprano), Alastair Miles as the Emperor and Michael Chance as Ottone among them. The Philips sound is warmer and more spacious, with the period instruments sounding sweeter and less abrasive. Gardiner also has an extra ballet movement at the very end after the goddess Juno's epilogue aria, superbly sung here by Anne Sofie von Otter.

McGegan's version is delightfully light-hearted, markedly sympathetic and, with a fine bloom on voices and instruments, notably the brass, the performance is exhilaratingly fresh and alert. The cast is first rate, led by the silvery Sally Bradshaw as Agrippina, the bright Nero of Wendy Hill and the seductive Poppea of Lisa Saffer, all well contrasted in their equally stylish ways.

(i) *Alceste: Overture and incidental music*; (ii) *Anthem for the Foundling Hospital; Ode for the birthday of Queen Anne*; (iii) *Utrecht Te Deum and Jubilate in D.*
(N) (B) *** Decca Double Dig. 458 072-2 (2). (i; ii; iii) Kirkby, Nelson, Thomas, AAM; (i) Cable, Thomas, Elliott, Ch., Hogwood; (ii) Minty, Bowman, Hill; (ii; iii) Christ Church Cathedral Ch., Preston; (iii) with Brett, Covey-Crump, Elliott.

Handel left us much to enjoy in the impressively dramatic *Alceste overture* in D minor and the *Grand entrée* for Admetus, Alceste and their wedding guests which get the proceedings off to a fine start. There follows a series not just of solo items but also some simple tuneful choruses in which a small secondary vocal group participates. There is nearly an hour of freshly enjoyable music and Hogwood draws lively, sympathetic performances from his team. The *Ode* has its Italianate attractions and opens with a splendid counter-tenor aria from James Bowman, with an elaborate trumpet obbligato, superbly played here. But it is the much later *Foundling Hospital anthem* which is the more memorable, not just because it concludes with an alternative version of the *Hallelujah chorus*, but also because the other borrowed numbers are also superb. The Utrecht pieces were written just before Handel came to London and were intended as a sample of his work. Preston directs performances which are characteristically alert and vigorous, particularly impressive in the superb closing *Glory be to the Father* with its massive eight-part chords. Throughout the team of soloists regularly associated with the Academy give of their best, and the recordings, made in 1977 and 1979, are splendidly transferred, clean and clear yet not losing their analogue atmosphere.

Alcina (complete).
*** EMI (IMS) Dig. CDS7 49771-2 (3) [Ang. CDCB 49771]. Augér, Della Jones, Kuhlmann, Harrhy, Kwella, Maldwyn Davies, Tomlinson, Opera Stage Ch., City of L. Bar. Sinfonia, Hickox.

(i) *Alcina* (complete); (ii) *Giulio Cesare (Julius Caesar)*: highlights.
(M) **(*) Decca 433 723-2 (3) [id.]. Sutherland, M. Sinclair; (i) Berganza, Alva, Sciutti, Freni, Flagello, LSO; (ii) Elkins, M. Horne, Conrad, New SO; Bonynge.

It would be hard to devise a septet of Handelian singers more stylish than the soloists in Hickox's version. Though the American, Arleen Augér, may not have the weight of Joan Sutherland, she is just as brilliant and pure-toned, singing warmly in the great expansive arias. Even next to her, Della Jones stands out in the breeches role of Ruggiero, with an extraordinary range of memorable arias, bold as well as tender. Eiddwen Harrhy as Morgana is just as brilliant in the aria, *Tornami a vagheggiar*, usually 'borrowed' by Alcina, while Kathleen Kuhlmann, Patrizia Kwella, Maldwyn Davies and John Tomlinson all sing with a clarity and beauty to make the music sparkle. Hickox underlines the contrasts of mood and speed, conveying the full range of emotion, with warm, spacious sound, recorded at EMI's Abbey Road studio.

Although the 1962 Decca *Alcina* is less complete than the newer EMI set, it has the advantage of including some 50 minutes of highlights from *Giulio Cesare*, made a year later, which Sutherland did not undertake in a complete version. *Alcina*, however, represents the extreme point of what can be described as Sutherland's dreamy, droopy period. The fast arias are stupendous. But anything slow and reflective, whether in recitative or aria, has Sutherland mooning about the notes, with no consonants audible. Of the others, Teresa Berganza is completely charming in the castrato part of Ruggiero, even if she does not manage trills very well. Monica Sinclair shows everyone up with the strength and forthrightness of her singing. Both Graziella Sciutti and Mirella Freni are delicate and clear in their two smaller parts. Richard Bonynge draws crisp, vigorous playing from the LSO. The 37-year-old Walthamstow recording is vintage Decca, and the CD transfer hints at its age only in the orchestral string sound.

Not surprisingly, the *Giulio Cesare* highlights are used as a vehicle for Sutherland, and her florid elaborations of melodies turn *da capo* recitatives into things of delight and wonder. There is some marvellous singing from Marilyn Horne and Monica Sinclair too, and Bonynge conducts with a splendid sense of style. As a sample, try *V'adoro pupile* – Cleopatra's seduction aria. Full translations are provided in both works.

Alessandro (complete).
(M) **(*) HM/BMG GD 77110 (3) [77110-2-RG]. Jacobs, Boulin, Poulenard, Nirouët, Varcoe, Guy de Mey, La Petite Bande, Kuijken.

Sigiswald Kuijken directs his team of period-performance specialists in an urgently refreshing, at times sharply abrasive, reading of one of Handel's key operas. As a high counter-tenor, René Jacobs copes brilliantly with the taxing role of Alexander himself. His singing is astonishingly free and agile, if too heavily aspirated. Among the others, Isabelle Poulenard at her best sounds a little like a French Emma Kirkby, though the production is not quite so pure and at times comes over more edgily. The others make a fine, consistent team, the more effective when the recording so vividly conveys a sense of presence with sharply defined directional focus.

Almira (complete).
(M) **(*) CPO Dig. CPO 999 275-2 (3). Monoyios, Rozario, Gerrard, Thomas, Nasrawi, MacDougall, Elsner, Fiori Musicale, Andrew Lawrence-King.

Almira was Handel's first opera, written in Hamburg in 1704 and first given just before his twentieth birthday. Setting a libretto partly in German, partly in Italian and with a plot involving the loves of Almira, Queen of Castile, it is a long piece lasting almost four hours. The arias are generally more compact than in the mature Handel, with argument more constrained, less developed. Even so, one regularly detects a genuine Handelian flavour in the themes, and he himself borrowed a fair measure of the material here in later works. This recording, with three discs offered for the price of two, was made after a staging presented in both Halle and Bremen in 1994. Lawrence-King secures a fresh and well-paced – if rather plain – performance, with deft playing from the German period orchestra. Ann Monoyios is a light, bright Almira, with Patricia Rozario, taxed a little by the high tessitura. equally stylish as Edilia. The two principal tenor roles are very well taken by Jamie MacDougall and Douglas Nasrawi, with the third tenor, Christian Elsner, taking the comic servant role. David Thomas sings with clean attack in the bass role of the Prince of Segovia. Good, undistracting and well scaled in an intimate acoustic.

Amadigi di Gaula (complete).
*** Erato/Warner Dig. 2292 45490-2 (2) [id.]. Stutzmann, Jennifer Smith, Harrhy, Fink, Musiciens du Louvre, Minkowski.

Minkowski's electrifying performance is one of his sharpest, dominated vocally by the magnificent young French contralto (no mere mezzo) of Nathalie Stutzmann in the title-role. She sings Amadigi's gentle arias most affectingly, notably the lovely *Sussurrate, onde vezzose*, and the two women characters, Amadigi's lover Melissa and Princess Oriana, are well taken by Eiddwen Harrhy and Jennifer Smith, with the brilliant arias for Prince Dardano of Thrace superbly sung by Bernarda Fink. It is a performance on an intimate scale, and the more involving for that.

Ariodante (complete).
*** HM Dig. HMC 907146/48 (3) [id.]. Hunt, Gondek, Saffer, Lane, Cavallier, Muller, Wilhelmshaven Vocal Ens., Freiburger Bar. O, McGegan.
(N) *** DG 457 271-2 (3) [id.]. Ann Sophie von Otter, Lynne Dawson, Ewa Podles, Croft, Musiciens du Louvre, Minkowski.
(M) *** Ph. 442 096-2 (3). J. Baker, Mathis, N. Burrowes, Bowman, Rendall, Ramey, L. Voices, ECO, Leppard.

Ariodante, dating from 1735, the same year as *Alcina*, is among the most richly inspired of Handel's operas, as the Raymond Leppard recording with Dame Janet Baker has long borne witness. McGegan's performance on Harmonia Mundi, recorded in Göttingen in 1995 immediately after festival performances on stage, brings clear advantages. Not only is there an exceptionally strong and consistent cast, the text is far fuller and the period-instrument orchestra is full-bodied and sweetly tuned, with the experience of live performing adding to the dramatic bite. McGegan springs rhythms infectiously, making speeds that are faster than Leppard's seem natural, never breathless, letting the music relax where necessary, again influenced by live experience. In the castrato title-role Lorraine Hunt may not have the emotional weight of Janet Baker, but hers is a fresh, clear and firm mezzo, which she uses most characterfully and imaginatively. Her big Act II aria, *Scherza infida*, in its positive strength even brings unexpected echoes of Kathleen Ferrier. The others too, mainly American singers, all have fresh, clean delivery and free flexibility, notably Juliana Gondek as the heroine, Ginevra, Lisa Saffer as Dalinda and Jennifer Lane as Polinesso. Nicolas Cavallier as the King may not have the richness of Samuel Ramey in Leppard's set, but his attack too is clean, and Rufus Muller in the tenor role of Lucanio, clear and firm, like the women sings elaborate divisions with ideal precision. Excellent recording with bloom on the voices, aptly intimate and full of presence.

On DG Archiv, with an outstanding starry team of soloists, Marc Minkowski conducts a high-powered reading of *Ariodante*, urgently dramatic and a compelling set in every way. Though von Otter in the title role is not quite at her freshest, and Lorraine Hunt and Dame Janet Baker on rival sets give even more moving performances, her characterization is as strong as ever. Among the others Lynne Dawson and Ewa Podles are outstandingly fine, though by a very narrow margin the Harmonia Mundi set with Hunt remains first choice.

Ariodante has a story which inspired Handel to write an amazing sequence of memorable and intensely inventive arias and duets, with not a single weak link in the chain, a point superbly conveyed in this colourful, urgent performance under Raymond Leppard. The castrato role of Ariodante is a challenge for Dame Janet Baker, who responds with singing of enormous expressive range, from the dark, agonized moments of the C minor aria early in Act III to the brilliance of the most spectacular of the three display arias later in the Act. Dame Janet's duets with Edith Mathis as Princess Ginevra, destined to marry Prince Ariodante, are enchanting too, and there is not a single weak member of the cast, though James Bowman as Duke Polinesso is not as precise as usual, with words often unclear. Consistently resilient playing from the English Chamber Orchestra and refined, beautifully balanced (1978) analogue recording, vividly transferred to CD.

Flavio (complete).
*** HM Dig. HMC 901312/13 (2) [id.]. Gall, Ragin, Lootens, Fink, *et al.*, Ens. 415, Jacobs.

Based on a staging of this unjustly neglected Handel opera at the 1989 Innsbruck Festival, René Jacobs' recording vividly captures the consistent vigour of Handel's inspiration. Handel's score was brilliantly written for some of the most celebrated singers of the time, including the castrato, Senesino. His four arias are among the highspots of the opera, all sung superbly here by the warm-toned and characterful counter-tenor, Derek Lee Ragin; almost every other aria is open and vigorous, with the whole sequence rounded off in a rousing ensemble. René Jacobs' team of eight soloists is a strong one, with only the strenuous tenor of Gianpaolo Fagotto occasionally falling short of the general stylishness. Full, clear sound.

Giulio Cesare (complete).
*** HM Dig. HMC 901385/7 [id.]. Larmore, Schlick, Fink, Rorholm, Ragin, Zanasi, Visse, Concerto Köln, Jacobs.
*** Astree Auvidis E 8558 (3) [id.]. Bowman, Dawson, Laurens, James, Visse, La Grande Ecurie et la Chambre du Roy, Jean-Claude Malgoire.

The counter-tenor, René Jacobs, conducting the German group, Concerto Köln, is a warmly expressive rather than a severe period performer. With a cast of consistently fresh voices, with rhythms sprung infectiously, he also allows the broadest expansion on the great reflective moments. The casting of the pure, golden-toned Barbara Schlick as Cleopatra proves outstandingly successful. Jennifer Larmore too, a fine, firm mezzo, with a touch of masculine toughness in the tone, makes a splendid Caesar. Together they crown the whole performance with the most seductive account of their final duet. Derek Lee Ragin is excellent in the sinister role of Tolomeo (Ptolemy); so are Bernarda Fink as Cornelia and Marianne Rorholm as Sesto, with the bass, Furio Zanasi, as Achille. Jacobs' expansive speeds mean that the whole opera will not fit on three CDs, but the fourth disc, at 18 minutes merely supplementary, comes free as part of the package, and includes an extra aria for the servant, Nireno, delightfully sung by the French counter-tenor, Dominique Visse. Firm, well-balanced sound.

Jean-Claude Malgoire, taking a lighter, less abrasive view of Handel than in his earlier recordings, directs his outstanding cast in a fresh, free-running performance of Handel's most frequently performed opera. The direct rival here is the Harmonia Mundi set directed by René Jacobs with an equally fine cast, and choice may well depend on preference over the central singer, the counter-tenor, James Bowman, in the Malgoire set strongly contrasted against the firm and purposeful mezzo, Jennifer Larmore. Bowman cannot quite match Larmore in the brilliance of his florid singing, but the timbre is firm and rich at less demanding speeds, and the portrait of a hero is conveyed convincingly. The contrast between Lynne Dawson as Cleopatra and Barbara Schlick is a key one too, for Dawson, following Malgoire's general approach, concentrates on beauty and classical poise, whereas Schlick brings out greater depth of expression. The contrast is similar over Giullemette Laurens as Cornelia as against Bernarda Fink, the one poised, the other more deeply expressive, often at broader speeds. By contrast the counter-tenor, Dominique Visse, is the more actively characterful as the villainous Tolomeo, where Derek Lee Ragin for Jacobs combines sharp characterization with cleaner vocalization. Malgoire's text is not quite as complete as Jacobs', with cuts in recitative.

Julius Caesar (complete in English).
(N) (M) *** Chandos Dig. CHAN 3019 (3) [id.]. Baker, Masterson, Walker, Della Jones, Bowman, Tomlinson, E. Nat. Op. Ch. & O, Mackerras.

Dame Janet is in glorious voice and draws on the widest range of expressive tone-colours, and Valerie Masterson makes a charming and seductive Cleopatra, fresh and girlish, though the voice is caught a little too brightly for caressing such radiant melodies as those for *V'adoro pupille ('Lamenting, complaining')* and *Piangero ('Flow my tears')*. Sarah Walker sings with powerful intensity as Pompey's widow; James Bowman is a characterful counter-tenor Ptolemy and John Tomlinson a firm, resonant Achillas, the other nasty character. The ravishing accompaniments to the two big Cleopatra arias amply justify the use by the excellent ENO Orchestra of modern, not period instruments. The full, vivid studio sound makes this one of the very finest of the invaluable series of ENO opera recordings in English, now being made available again by Chandos, sponsored by the Peter Moores Foundation.

Giustino (complete).
*** HM Dig. HMU 907130/32 [id.]. Chance, Röschmann, Kotoski, Gondek, Lane, Padmore, Minter, Cantamus Halle Chamber Ch., Freiburg Baroque O, McGegan.

First heard in 1737 and never revived until 1967, the opera *Giustino* has been consistently underestimated. Based loosely on Roman history, the plot follows the career of the self-made man among emperors, Justinian (or Justin), described in the notes as 'a baroque Dick Whittington'. This splendid, lively set should do much to bring a full reassessment, for McGegan with his fast, crisp manner and fondness for extra decoration in *da capo* repeats brings out the element of sparkle and irony implied in the improbable story, treated refreshingly in dozens of brief arias. The recording was made in studio conditions immediately after a sequence of stage performances at the Göttingen Festival in 1994. Michael Chance is outstanding in the title-role originally written for a castrato, and Dorothea Röschmann sings most movingly in the key role of Arianna, who in each of the three Acts has the most important and substantial arias. The counter-tenor, Drew Minter, stylish and intelligent as he is, fails to give enough bite to the villainous role of Amanzio; but there are few other disappointments, and the tenor, Mark Padmore, sings with virtuoso flair in the military role of Vitaliano. The German string-players are less sweet-toned and more abrasive than one expects nowadays, but, with clear, well-balanced sound, this is a set to delight all Handelians, filling in an important gap. The three substantial Acts – the middle one much shorter than the other two – are each complete on a single CD.

Hercules (complete).
(M) *** DG Dig. 447 689-2 (2). Tomlinson, Sarah Walker, Rolfe Johnson, Jennifer Smith, Denley, Savidge, Monteverdi Ch., E. Bar. Soloists, Gardiner.

Gardiner's brisk performance of *Hercules* using authentic forces may at times lack Handelian grandeur in the big choruses, but it conveys superbly the vigour of the writing, its natural drama; and the fire of this performance is typified by the outstanding singing of Sarah Walker as Dejanira. John Tomlinson makes an excellent, dark-toned Hercules. Fresh voices consistently help in the clarity of the attack – Jennifer Smith as Iole, Catherine Denley as Lichas, Anthony Rolfe Johnson as Hyllus and Peter Savidge as the Priest of Jupiter. Refined playing and outstanding recording quality make this most welcome at mid-price.

Orlando (complete).
*** O-L Dig. 430 845-2 (3) [id.]. Bowman, Augér, Robbin, Kirkby, D. Thomas, AAM, Hogwood.
*** Erato/Warner Dig. 0630 14636-2 (3). Bardon, Mannion, Summers, Joshua, Van der Kamp, Les Arts Florissants, Christie.

Handel's *Orlando* was radically modified to provide suitable material for individual singers, as for example the bass role of the magician, Zoroastro, specially created for a member of Handel's company. Even so, the title-role seems to have failed to please the celebrated castrato, Senesino, for whom it was intended, probably because of Handel's breaks with tradition, notably in the magnificent mad scene which ends Act II on the aria, *Vaghe pupille*. That number, superbly done here by James Bowman, with appropriate sound effects, is only one of the virtuoso vehicles for the counter-tenor. For the jewelled sequences of arias and duets, Hogwood has assembled a near-ideal cast, with Arleen Augér at her most radiant as the queen, Angelica, and Emma Kirkby characteristically bright and fresh in the lighter, semi-comic role of the shepherdess, Dorinda. Catherine Robbin assumes the role of Prince Medoro strongly and David Thomas sings stylishly as Zoroastro. This is one of Hogwood's finest achievements on record, taut, dramatic and rhythmically resilient. Vivid, open sound.

William Christie's Erato recording of *Orlando* makes a valuable alternative to the outstanding version recorded earlier by Christopher Hogwood for Oiseau-Lyre. The most obvious difference is that where Hogwood has a male alto singing the title-role, Christie here opts for a fine mezzo, Patricia Bardon. Her approach is more overtly dramatic than James Bowman's for Hogwood, with moods and passions more positively characterized. The celebrated mad scene ending Act II illustrates the point perfectly, with Christie and Bardon more violent, using bigger contrasts, ending in a scurrying *accelerando*, whereas the Bowman/Hogwood approach keeps some classical restraint to the end, pointing the drama of the moment in thunder effects. The Erato recording is warm and full, but is not as transparent or well separated as the earlier one, with Christie often opting for marginally broader speeds. His other soloists are all excellent, readily matching their rivals, not least the contralto, Hilary Summers, as Prince Medoro.

Ottone, re di Germania (complete).
*** Hyperion Dig. CDA 66751/3 [id.]. Bowman, McFadden, Jennifer Smith, Denley, Visse, George, King's Consort, Robert King.
**(*) HM Dig. HMU 907073/5 [id.]. Minter, Saffer, Gondek, Spence, Popken, Dean, Freiburg Bar. O, McGegan.

Previously unrecorded, *Ottone* simultaneously prompted these two versions, both of which have their points of advantage. Nicholas McGegan continues his impressive Handel series for Harmonia Mundi in a recording with the Freiburg Baroque Orchestra and with Drew Minter taking the title-role, while Robert King and his King's Consort offer a version on Hyperion with James Bowman as Ottone. When the women principals in McGegan's version have purer, firmer voices than their rivals, there is a strong case for preferring his set. As the heroine, Teofane, Lisa Saffer for McGegan is markedly sweeter and clearer than Claron McFadden for King. When it comes to the key castrato roles taken by counter-tenors, it is quite different. For McGegan, Drew Minter, a stylish singer, no longer has the power to give the many bravura arias the thrust they need, whereas for King, Bowman with his far richer tone continues to sing with enormous panache and virtuoso agility. Dominique Visse as the duplicitous Adalberto on King's set tends to overcharacterize, but the singing makes the rival version seem colourless. Add to that the extra richness and bloom on the instrumental sound in the Hyperion version, and the balance clearly goes in its favour. This may not be as distinctive as some of Handel's later Italian operas, but the sequence of brief numbers has an irresistible freshness.

Partenope (complete).
(M) *** HM/BMG GD 77109 (3) [77109-2-RG].

Laki, Jacobs, York, Skinner, Varcoe, Müller-Molinari, Hill, La Petite Bande, Kuijken.

With the exception of René Jacobs, rather too mannered for Handel, the roster of soloists here is outstanding, with Krisztina Laki and Helga Müller-Molinari welcome additions to the team. Though ornamentation is sparse, the direction of Sigiswald Kuijken is consistently invigorating, as is immediately apparent in the *Overture*; the 1979 recording sounds splendid in its CD format.

Radamisto (complete).
**(*) HM Dig. HMU 907111/13 [id.]. Popken, Gondek, Saffer, Hanchard, Dean, Cavallier, Freiburger Bar. O, McGegan.

Radamisto is a magnificent work. The best-known aria, the plaintive *Ombra cara*, sung by Radamisto, leads on to a whole sequence of magnificent minor-key numbers in Act II, with some of the arias given to Zenobia, Radamisto's wife, marked by strange, sudden switches of mood. This first complete recording is very welcome in revealing much superb material, even if the period-performance manners are less sympathetic, with the strings of the Freiburg orchestra very abrasive. Even under the direction of McGegan rhythms are too often square, not sprung as winningly as they might be, while recitative is on the heavy side. Yet there is some first-rate singing, with the title-role – originally written for the castrato, Senesino – strongly taken by the firm-toned counter-tenor, Ralf Popken, even if he is occasionally hooty. It is not his fault that *Ombra cara* sounds rather stodgy, for he shades his tone most beautifully for the reprise. Juliana Gondek sings with full, warm tone as Zenobia, producing crisp trills and ornaments, though most of the others are not quite so successful. The recording, made in Göttingen after a festival production, is on the dry side but has plenty of presence.

Riccardo Primo (Richard the Lionheart).
*** O-L Dig. 452 201-2 (3) [id.]. Mingardo, Piau, Lallouette, Scaltriti, Brua, Bertin, Les Talens Lyriques, Christophe Rousset.

Recorded in the Abbaye Royale de Fontevrault, where Richard the Lionheart is buried, Christophe Rousset conducts a lively, well-characterized performance of one of the rarest of Handel operas. It was the last but two of the 13 operas which Handel wrote for the Royal Academy of Music in London, and one which aimed to cater for the rival claims of the two leading prima donnas of the day, Francesca Cuzzoni and Faustina Bordoni, as well as for the leading castrato, Senesino. It is one of the most elaborately scored of Handel's operas, even using a sopranino recorder for a delightful bird aria in Act III, for the princess of Navarre, Costanza, Richard's betrothed, Cuzzoni's role. It is a long opera, and you have to wait until Act III for many of the jewels in the score, which then round the piece off with great flair.

Vocally, the principal glory of this recorded performance is the singing of Sara Mingardo in the title-role, gloriously firm and true. The richness of the sound never gets in the way of flexibility, so that such a showpiece as Richard's Act III aria, *All'orror delle procelle*, has one readily registering what must have been the impact of Senesino in the first performances. In quite a different mood, the duet between Richard and Costanza which ends Act II is enchantingly poetic, later adapted for Handel's last oratorio, *Jephtha*. Sandrine Piau as Costanza is tenderly expressive, even though (as recorded) the voice, sweet in tone, is not perfectly even, and Claire Brua in the Bordoni role of Pulcheria tends to be too gusty to enunciate elaborate divisions clearly, but the contrast between the rival ladies is well established. The counter-tenor, Pascal Bertin, is excellent as Oronte, and the two baritone roles are well taken by Roberto Scaltriti (aptly villainous-sounding) and Olivier Lallouette. First-rate, well-balanced sound.

Rinaldo (complete).
(M) *** Sony SM3K 34592 (3) [id.]. Carolyn Watkinson, Cotrubas, Scovotti, Esswood, Brett, Cold, La Grande Ecurie et la Chambre du Roy, Malgoire.

The vigour of Malgoire's direction of an opera which plainly for him is very much alive makes this a very attractive set, with the one caveat that it has been reissued without a translation (the full libretto is in Italian only). The elaborate decorations on *da capo* arias are imaginatively done, but most effectively the famous *Cara sposa* is left without ornamentation, beautifully sung by the contralto Rinaldo, Carolyn Watkinson. The finest singing comes from Ileana Cotrubas, but the whole team is convincing. The bright but spacious recording adds to the projection, and the magic sounds associated with the sorceress, Armida, such as the arrival of her airborne chariot, are well conveyed, and throughout Handel's invention is a delight.

Rodelinda, Regina de Langobardi (complete).
(N) *** Virgin/Veritas Dig. VCT5 45277-2(3) [CDCC 45277]. Daneman, Taylor, Thompson, Robbin, Blaze, Purves, Raglan Bar. Players, Kraemer.

Rodelinda, dating from 1725, has a plot typically involving disguises and forced coincidences, together with rapidly switching loves, hatreds and misunderstandings, which may be hard for the modern listener to accept. Yet the variety of Handel's invention triumphs over all complication in clearly defining each character, not least the two villains, tenor and bass respectively. Nicholas Kraemer, drawing refined playing from the Raglan Baroque Players, has a winningly light touch, making this first choice. The singers in this live recording work very effectively as a team, characterizing sharply. Sophie Daneman as Rodelinda, with vibrato stilled, produces sound of bell-like purity and crisp ornamentation. Daniel Taylor, as the hero, Bertarido, uses his refined counter-tenor with subtlety and point, not least in the most famous aria, *Dove sei*, while the mezzo, Catherine Robbin, is superb as his disappointed sister, Eduige.

Rodrigo (complete).

(N) *** Virgin Veritas/EMI Dig. VCD5 45897-2 (2) [id.]. Gloria Banditelli, Sandrine Piau, Elena Cecci Fedi, Rufus Müller, Roberta Invernizzi, Caterina Calvi, Il Complesso Barocco, Alan Curtis.

Rodrigo was Handel's very first Italian opera, written for the Medici court in Florence in 1707. It was not heard again until 1984, when Alan Curtis (the conductor here) directed a performance using a score he himself had prepared, with newly rediscovered material restored. This spirited performance has been neatly tailored to fit on two generously filled CDs, with cuts mainly of the *secco* recitatives. The freshness of the performance matches the freshness of Handel's youthful inspiration, with numbers generally more compact than in later Handel operas. Gloria Banditelli sings richly and firmly in the castrato role of Rodrigo, King of Spain, with Sandrine Piau sweet and bright as his wife Esilena, who is given many of the most memorable arias. Elena Cecchi Fedi sings edgily as Florinda but is well in character, and Rufus Müller is a strong Giuliano. A valuable first recording, with bright, fresh sound.

Semele (complete).

*** DG Dig. 435 782-2 (3) [id.]. Battle, M. Horne, Ramey, Aler, McNair, Chance, Mackie, Amb. Op. Ch., ECO, John Nelson.

(M) *** Van. 08.5082 72 (2) [id.]. Armstrong, Watts, Palmer, Tear, Diaz, Deller, Fleet, Amor Artis Chorale, ECO, Somary.

(M) **(*) Erato/Warner 2292 45982-2 (2) [id.]. Burrowes, Della Jones, Lloyd, D. Thomas, Rolfe Johnson, Kwella, Penrose, M. Davies, Monteverdi Ch., E. Bar. Soloists, Gardiner.

With its English words, *Semele*, using a libretto of 1708 by Congreve based on Ovid's *Metamorphoses*, stands equivocally between the genres of opera and oratorio, presenting even more interpretative problems than usual. DG's digital recording turns away from current fashion in using modern rather than period instruments, but the balance of advantage lies very much in its favour, compared with the Erato set of Gardiner; even period fanatics may well find it the better choice. Surprisingly, the Nelson performance is generally crisper and faster than Gardiner's, with rhythms sprung just as infectiously. Most importantly, he opens out the serious cuts made by Gardiner, following the old, bad tradition. If *Semele* – dating from 1744, three years after *Messiah* – is known as a rule only by its most celebrated aria, *Where'er you walk*, it contains many other superb numbers. Handel was aiming to satirize George II's mistress, Lady Yarmouth, in his portrayal of the central character of Semele – a self-regarding princess seduced by Jupiter who through him seeks to become immortal, just as Lady Yarmouth wanted to become queen.

Though at times he favours slow, oratorio-like tempi, Somary still keeps in mind an operatic flavour and the Amor Artis Chorale (a pseudonym for a well-known professional recording choir) sings splendidly, often with great vigour, and even attempts some attractive if inauthentic corporate ornamentation. Overall the performance has much charm and spirit with superb soloists. Like the rest of this Vanguard series from the 1970s, the fine recording allows excellent detail, yet is full and expansive.

The Erato reissue in the Libretto series of John Eliot Gardiner's 1981 version of *Semele* offers a period performance with the English Baroque Soloists using an excellent cast of British singers. Very well recorded, it has the very practical advantage of coming on only two mid-priced discs. The extensive cuts which make that possible are the traditional ones, some of them sanctioned by Handel himself. Though this was an early EBS recording, not quite as polished as later ones, Gardiner's ability to use period performance with warmth and imagination makes it consistently compelling. Norma Burrowes is a sweet, pure Semele, and Anthony Rolfe Johnson is outstanding as Jupiter, singing *Where'er you walk* with a fine sense of line and excellent pacing.

Semele: highlights.

(N) (M) *** Erato/Warner Dig. 0630 15734-9. (from above complete recording with Rolfe Johnson, Burrowes, Della Jones, cond. Gardiner).

Gardiner's Erato set is not first choice for *Semele*, but this well produced and excellently documented highlights disc (74 minutes) is worth having. The booklet includes a full text of the excerpts.

Serse (*Xerxes;* complete).

(N) *** Conifer Dig. 75605 52312-2 (3) [id.]. Judith Malafronte, Jennifer Smith, Lisa Milne, Susan Bickley, Brian Asawa, David Thomas, Dean Ely, Ch. & Hanover Band, Nicholas McGegan.

(M) **(*) Sony SM3K 36941 (3) [id.]. Carolyn Watkinson, Esswood, Wenkel, Hendricks, Rodde, Cold, Bridier Vocal Ens., La Grand Ecurie et la Chambre du Roy, Malgoire.

Recorded in the studio following a series of live performances at the Gottingen Festival of 1997, McGegan's crisp and fresh reading of this most sparkling of Handel's later operas is most welcome, making it a clear first choice. Following Venetian fashion, Handel here wrote a piece built on dozens of short numbers, which has humour and irony as part of the mixture. Even the most celebrated number, Xerxes' aria, *Ombra mai fù*, addressed to a plane tree, is hardly serious, rather illustrating the central character's quirky tastes. McGegan, with light textures and generally brisk speeds, gives necessary momentum, while allowing his principals full expressiveness in such deeper numbers as the hero's Act II aria, *Il core spera e teme*, warmly sung by Judith Malafronte, as is *Ombra mai fù*. The counter-tenor, Brian Asawa, in the role of Xerxes' brother, Arsamene, is equally expressive with rich even tone and fine agility, and Jennifer Smith as the heroine, Romilda, is particularly effective in her dramatic arias. Lisa Milne as her sister, Atalanta, nicely catches an ironic tone, with Susan Bickley fresh and agile as Amastre. Characterful baritone contributions from David Thomas (as a comic servant) and Dean Ely, with the chorus's brief interjections adding brightness and sparkle. Full, open sound.

Malgoire's vigorous, often abrasive style in baroque music makes for a lively, convincing performance of one of Handel's richest operas, helped by a fine complement of soloists. Carolyn Watkinson may not be the most characterful of singers in the high castrato role of Xerxes himself, but it is good to have the elaborate roulades so accurately sung. The celebrated *Ombra mai fù* is most beautiful. Paul Esswood is similarly reliable in the role of Arsamene (originally taken by a woman) and the counter-tenor tone is pure and true. Barbara Hendricks and Anne-Marie Rodde are both outstanding in smaller roles, and the comic episodes (most unexpected in Handel) are excellently done. There are detailed stylistic points one might criticize in his rendering (for instance the squeeze effects on sustained string notes) but the vitality is never in doubt, and the close recording is vivid too. As in the rest of this series of Sony reissues, the snag is the absence of an English translation.

The Sorceress (pasticcio).
**(*) Ph. Dig. 434 992-2 [id.]. Kiri Te Kanawa, AAM, Hogwood.

This pasticcio, with items drawn from a whole range of Handel operas (*Rinaldo*, *Alcina*, *Giulio Cesare*, *Ariodante*, *Agrippina*, *Admeto* and *Giustino*), was devised for a Dutch television programme. The CD – like the video version, complete with ballet interludes – is taken from the soundtrack, providing in effect a sequence of seven arias, sung with characteristic poise and sumptuous tone by Dame Kiri, spiced with instrumental pieces, mostly brief. Though the plot is broadly based on the situation in *Alcina*, only one aria is taken from that opera, *Ombre pallide*, which, preceded by an accompanied recitative, makes up by far the longest item. It seems even longer thanks to Dame Kiri's somewhat languid performance. Otherwise, even with speeds on the slow side, Dame Kiri sings gloriously, with four of Cleopatra's arias from *Giulio Cesare* – including the seduction aria, *V'adoro pupille* – providing the cornerstones. Hogwood draws fresh sounds from the Academy but he might have sounded even sharper at faster speeds. Clear, well-balanced sound.

Tamerlano (complete).
(M) *** Erato/Warner Dig. 2292 45408-2. Ragin, Robson, Argenta, Chance, Findlay, Schirrer, E. Bar. Soloists, Gardiner.
(M) **(*) Sony Dig. SM3K 37893-2 (3) [S3K 37893-2]. Ledroit, Elwes, Van der Sluis, Jacobs, Poulenard, Reinhart, La Grande Ecurie et la Chambre du Roy, Malgoire.

John Eliot Gardiner's live concert performance of *Tamerlano* presents a strikingly dramatic and immediate experience. The pacing of numbers and of the recitative is beautifully thought out and the result is electrifying. Leading the cast are two outstanding counter-tenors whose encounters provide some of the most exciting moments: Michael Chance as Andronicus, firm and clear, Derek Lee Ragin in the name-part equally agile and more distinctive of timbre, with a rich, warm tone that avoids womanliness. Nigel Robson in the tenor role of Bajazet conveys the necessary gravity, not least in the difficult, highly original G minor aria before the character's suicide; and Nancy Argenta sings with starry purity as Asteria. The only snag is the dryness of the sound, which makes voices and instruments sound more aggressive on CD than they usually do in Gardiner's recordings with the English Baroque Soloists.

Malgoire's performance style here is less abrasive than it has been on some other opera sets, but one looks in vain for an element of elegance or charm, despite consistently excellent contributions from a good band of soloists. The two counter-tenors are well contrasted – René Jacobs as ever a tower of strength – and Mieke van der Sluis is outstanding among the women. Some arias have been cut, but one has been added in Act I (*Nel mondo e nell'abisso*), well sung by the bass, Gregory Reinhardt. Good, clear, but not too dry sound gives a comparatively intimate effect, and the CD transfer is first class. The snag is that, like the other reissues in this series, the full Italian libretto includes no translation.

Teseo (opera; complete).
*** Erato/Warner Dig. 2292 45806-2 (2) [id.]. James, Della Jones, Gooding, Lee Ragin, Napoli, Gall, Les Musiciens du Louvre, Minkowski.

Dating from December 1712, *Teseo* was only the second opera that Handel wrote for London, and the first after he had established himself here. Using an Italian translation of a French libretto originally written for Lully 40 years earlier, Handel uniquely produced a hybrid between an Italian *opera seria* and a French *tragédie lyrique*, with the classical story of Theseus and Medea told in a brisk sequence of short arias. Sadly, after its initial run of 13 performances *Teseo* was never produced again until the present century. The score may not contain great Handel melodies, but it is characteristically fresh and imaginative. Marc Minkowski, among the liveliest of period performance specialists, brings out the inventiveness, helped by an excellent cast, dominated by British and American singers. These include Della Jones as Medea, Eirian James in the castrato role of Teseo, Julia Gooding as Agilea and characterful counter-tenors, Derek Lee Ragin and Jeffrey Gall, as Egeo and Arcane.

COLLECTIONS

Airs, 'scènes célèbres', sinfonias and instrumental music from: *Alcina; Admeto; Giulio Cesare; Radamisto; Rodelinda; Serse. Concerto grosso (Alexander's Feast).*

(N) ✿ *** HM Dig. HMC 901685 [id.]. Andreas Scholl, Berlin Akademie for Alte Musik.

Andreas Scholl created something of a sensation at the *Gramophone* Awards ceremony in 1997 with a magical performance of Handel's most celebrated aria, *Ombra mai fù*. It is radiantly sung here, with firm golden tone, alongside the equally lovely *Chiudetevi, miei lumi* from *Admeto*, and the glorious *Dove sei* from *Rodelinda*, with the programme capped by an unforgettably beautiful *Verdi prati* from *Alcina*. There are lively moments too, notably the genial *Va tacito* ('Silently and stealthily the cunning hunter moves, when he is eager for his prey'), which has a jolly horn obbligato, confidently played on a hand-horn by Christian-Friedrich Dallman. Indeed, the splendid period-instrument accompaniments by the Berlin Akademie for Alte Musik are a real bonus, and they make the 76-minute programme doubly diverting by playing sinfonias and dance movements (including an engaging suite from *Radamisto*) in between the arias. They end the programme with a superb account of the *Alexander's Feast concerto grosso*, light and airy, yet with the slow movement truly worthy of Handel's gently expressive melodic line. But it is the unique voice and Scholl's wonderfully stylish and moving singing (with superbly managed cadential trills) which makes this record indispensable. His simplicity of presentation, combined with deep feeling, recalls the art of Kathleen Ferrier. The playing of the Berlin period ensemble is fresh and lively, the recording full and immediate, in some ways more flattering to the voice than the Decca miscellaneous recital which followed '*Heroes*' (Decca Dig. 466 196-2).

Arias: *Aci, Galatea e Polifemo: Qui l'augel di pianta in pianta. Floridante: Bramo te sola; Se dolce m'era già. Giulio Cesare in Egitto: Se in fiorito ameno prato; Va tacito. Orlando: Ah stigie larve / Vaghe pupille; Fammi combattere. Partenope: Furibondo spira il vento. Radamisto: Ombra cara di mi sposa. Rinaldo: Cara sposa, amante cara.*

*** RCA Dig. 09026 61205-2 [id.]. Nathalie Stutzmann, Hanover Band, Goodman.

Nathalie Stutzmann is both characterful and brilliant in this valuable collection of arias from ten Handel operas, recorded in London with Roy Goodman and the Hanover Band. With Stutzmann so positive a singer, each item emerges as a winner, strikingly memorable. Military rhythms are a feature in several, including the opening item, *Fammi combattere* from *Orlando*, which is like a trial run for *Let the bright Seraphim* from *Samson*. The sequence ends with the most tragic of the arias, *Ombra cara* from *Radamisto*, in which Stutzmann and her accompanists give the darkly chromatic writing the fullest expressive weight.

Arias: (i) *Agrippina: Pur ritorno a rimimiravi. Alexander's Feast: Revenge, Timotheus cries. Belshazzar: Oh, memory still bitter to my soul ... Oppress'd with never-ceasing grief. Berenice: Si, tra i ceppi.* (ii) *Giulio Cesare: Va tacito e nascosto; Dall'ondoso periglio; Aure, deh per pietà.* (i) *Ottone: Con gelosi sospetti? ... Dopo l'orrore. Samson: Honour and arms. Saul: To him ten thousands! ... With rage I shall burst. Serse: Frondi tenere e belle? ... Ombra mai fù. Solomon: Prais'd be the Lord ... When the sun o'er yonder hills. Susanna: Down my old cheeks ... Peace, crown'd with roses.*

(M) **(*) DG (IMS) 449 551-2. Dietrich Fischer-Dieskau; Munich Bach O; (i) Stadlmair; (ii) Karl Richter.

Opening with an arresting performance of *Revenge, Timotheus cries* from *Alexander's Feast*, this 1977 collection then goes on to emphasize Handel's lyricism rather than the drama. Fischer-Dieskau is at his finest in *Ombra mai fù* from *Serse* (Handel's '*Largo*') with its beautifully controlled opening single-note crescendo. The voice is forwardly balanced and naturally caught; the orchestra is set in a resonant acoustic with modern-instrument textures which are full rather than detailed, especially the two *Giulio Cesare* items now added, which were recorded much earlier (in 1969).

Arias: *Alexander's Feast: The Prince, unable to conceal his pain; Softly sweet in Lydian measures. Atalanta: Care selve. Giulio Cesare: Piangerò. Messiah: Rejoice greatly; He shall feed his flock. Rinaldo: Lascia ch'io pianga. Samson: Let the bright Seraphim.*

**(*) Delos Dig. D/CD 3026 [id.]. Arleen Augér,

Mostly Mozart O, Schwarz – BACH: *Arias*. **(*)

Arleen Augér's bright, clean, flexible soprano is even more naturally suited to these Handel arias than to the Bach items with which they are coupled. The delicacy with which she tackles the most elaborate divisions and points the words is a delight.

Arias from: *Giulio Cesare; Rinaldo; Rodelinda; Serse; Tamerlano*.
(N) *** Virgin/Veritas EMI Dig. VC5 45326-2 [id.]. David Daniels, OAE, Norrington

Even in a generation that has produced a fine crop of counter-tenors, David Daniels stands out for the evenness and beauty of his voice, with an exceptionally rich lower register. Though the orchestra is not always as alert as it might be, his singing in this challenging group of arias, starting with *Ombra mai fù* from *Serse*, is warmly expressive in slow numbers and brilliantly dramatic in fast ones like *Al lampo dell'armi* from *Giulio Cesare*. Well-balanced sound.

Arias: *Judas Maccabaeus: Father of heaven. Messiah: O Thou that tellest; He was despised. Samson: Return O God of Hosts*.
✿ (M) (***) Decca 433 474-2. Kathleen Ferrier, LPO, Boult – BACH: Arias. (***)

Kathleen Ferrier had a unique feeling for Handel; these performances are unforgettable for their communicative intensity and nobility of timbre and line. She receives highly sympathetic accompaniments from Boult, another natural Handelian.

Overtures and excerpts from *Jephtha; Joseph and his brethren; Joshua; Solomon. Belshazzar: Let festival joy reign!*
(N) **(*) Arabesque Dig. Z 6720 [id.]. John Elwes, St Lukes CO.

An enjoyable if slightly old-fashioned collection, vividly played on modern instruments by this excellent conductor-less ensemble. There are lots of good tunes here and each selection includes a key aria strongly and dramatically sung by John Elwes. His manner is direct and forward, and he sings Handel's runs with gusto, using his vibrato with individuality. He tends to over-phrase in the lyrical music, yet can produce lovely tone in a number like *Waft her angels* (from *Jephtha*), which he does not attempt to decorate. Excellent recording, lively but with a nice degree of resonance.

Hanson, Howard (1896–1981)

(i) *Piano concerto, Op. 36. For the first time (suite); Merry Mount suite; Mosaics* (with composer's spoken analyses of all three orchestral works, concerning orchestral colour, pitch spectrum, musical form, and 'tone relationships').
(M) *** Mercury 434 370-2 (2) [id.]. Eastman-Rochester O or Philh. O, composer (cond. & narrator); (i) with Alfred Mouledous.

Mercury not only pioneered many of Hanson's major works on record, with the composer conducting the Eastman-Rochester Orchestra, but also invited him to talk about his music. The three orchestral works here seem ideal for the purpose and his 'guide to the instruments of the orchestra' (directly related to the scoring of the *Merry Mount suite*) is particularly instructive, the more so as the microphones have been set up to project solo instruments and groupings of woodwind, brass and strings with extraordinary realism and presence. The four-movement *Piano concerto* is brilliantly played by Alfred Mouledous, especially in the Scherzo, marked *Allegro molto ritmico* (though they are not jazzy rhythms) and the *giocoso* finale, while the slow movement is eloquently expressive. The recordings here were made between 1957 and 1965 (the *Concerto*) and are characteristically vivid, though occasionally very bright on top.

Symphonies Nos. 1–7; (i) *Piano concerto in G. Elegy in memory of Koussvitzky;* (i) *Fantasy variations on a theme of Youth, Op. 40. Mosaics; Merry Mount suite, Op. 31; Pastorale for oboe, harp and strings, Op. 38; Serenade for flute, harp and strings, Op. 38;* (ii) *Lament for Beowulf, Op. 25; Song of democracy*.
(M) *** Delos Dig. DE 3150 (4) [id.]. Seattle SO, Gerard Schwarz; with (i) Carol Rosenberger; (ii) Ch.

Gerard Schwarz has proved himself a master of Hanson's Nordic idiom and a consistently convincing interpreter of his symphonies, in which he secures high commitment and playing of the highest quality from the excellent Seattle orchestra. Carol Rosenberger is an excellent soloist in the two concertante piano works; the other soloists are drawn from the orchestra, and all make admirable contributions. This is all music which is easy to enjoy, and these artists are afforded full, brilliant recording from the Delos engineers within an expansive acoustic.

Symphonies Nos. 1 in E min. (Nordic), Op. 21; 2 (Romantic), Op. 30; (i) *Song of democracy*.
(M) *** Mercury 432 008-2 [id.]. Eastman-Rochester O, composer; (i) with Eastman School of Music Ch.

Hanson's own pioneering stereo recordings of his two best-known symphonies have a unique thrust and ardour. The *Song of democracy* has plenty of dramatic impact and is also very well recorded.

Symphonies Nos. 1 in E min. (Nordic); 3; 5 (Sinfonia sacra), Op. 43; (i) *Piano concerto in G, Op. 36;* (ii) *Lament for Beowulf, Op. 25; Merry Mount: suite, Op. 31*.
(N) (B) *** Delos Dig. Double DE 3709 (2) [id.].

Seattle SO, Gerard Schwarz; (i) with Carol Rosenberger; (ii) with Symphony Ch.

It was a splendid idea for Delos to reissue Hanson's symphonies and other key works on a pair of two-for-the-price-of-one Delos Doubles. We hope it will tempt many collectors to explore this highly rewarding music who would not otherwise have done so. Hanson is of Swedish descent and his music has a strong individuality of idiom and colour. The *First Symphony* is very like the more famous *Second* – warmly appealing, held together with indelible ideas which appear in all three movements. After getting to know these two works (which are also available coupled together on D/CD 3073) the musical terrain of the *Third* will seem familiar. The single movement *Sinfonia sacra* – inspired by Christ's Passion – is also very succinct, again showing the composer's Nordic inheritance. The four-movement *Piano concerto* (1948) is also compressed. It has no want of ideas and has a memorable slow movement. Carol Rosenberger is a brilliant and responsive soloist. The *Lament for Beowolf* is an eloquent, elegiac piece with chorus which does not outstay its welcome. These Seattle performances have plenty of breadth and ardour, and Schwarz's feeling for the ebb and flow of the musical paragraphs is very satisfying. The recording, made in Seattle Opera House, is gloriously expansive and the balance convincingly natural.

Symphonies Nos. 2 (Romantic), Op. 30; 4 (Requiem), Op. 34. Elegy (to the memory of my friend, Serge Koussevitsky), Op. 44.
(BB) **(*) Arte Nova Dig. 74321 43306-2 [id.]. Jena PO, David Montgomery.

David Montgomery, who studied under René Leibowitz before his career took him across the Atlantic, has the full measure of the haunting, nostalgic feeling which permeates Hanson's symphonies, and especially No. 2 – which is I. M.'s favourite American symphony. The lovely lilting central *Andante con tenerezza* is radiantly done. The Jena Philharmonic cannot quite produce the body of tone which Schwarz has at his disposal with the superb Seattle orchestra on Delos, but there is no lack of vigour and spontaneity, with excellent brass playing. Montgomery is thoroughly at home in shaping the spacious string paragraphs which are the hallmark of this composer's writing in both works, and in No. 4 he does not miss the Sibelian influences, especially in the sombre *Requiescat*. The touching tribute to Koussevitzky, who originally helped to put Hanson's music in front of the American public, is eloquently played. The Arte Nova recording is spacious and well balanced.

Symphonies Nos. (i) *2 (Romantic); 4 (Requiem); 6;* (i–ii) *7 (Sea Symphony after Walt Whitman);* (i) *Elegy in memory of Serge Koussevitzky;* (i; iii) *Fantasy variations on a theme of youth* (for piano and orchestra); (i) *Mosaics;* (iv) *Serenade for flute, harp and strings.*
(B) *** Delos Dig. Double DE 3705 (2) [id.]. (i) Seattle SO; (ii) Seattle Chorale; (iii) Carol Rosenberger; (iv) Judith Meredith, Susan Jollies, NY Chamber Ens.; all cond. Gerard Schwarz.

A warm welcome for this comprehensive introduction to the highly rewarding music of Howard Hanson, which includes his *Second Symphony*, melodically so memorable. Like this symphony, the *Fourth* has strong Nordic influences, and the *Sea Symphony* brings stirring choral writing to words of Walt Whitman. All three are superbly played in Seattle and Schwarz's powerful direction is thoroughly idiomatic and committed. The *Fantasy variations* have a fine piano soloist in Carol Rosenberger, who catches the noble serenity of the work's opening and closing sections and enters fully into the fray of the energetic central variations. *Mosaics* is another set of variations, written in 1957 for Szell and the Cleveland Orchestra and inspired by a visit to Taormina Cathedral, near Rome. The even briefer and delicately scored *Serenade* makes a delightful contrast, finely crafted. All this music is well worth getting to know, and much of it is very rewarding indeed. The recordings are in the demonstration bracket.

Symphony No. 3.
(***) Biddulph mono WHL 044 [id.]. Boston SO, Koussevitzky (with MUSSORGSKY: *Khovanshchina: Prelude.* LIADOV: *The enchanted lake.* RIMSKY-KORSAKOV: *Legend of the invisible city of Kitezh: Entr'acte. Dubinushka.* FAURE: *Pelléas et Mélisande: Prélude; La Fileuse; Mort de Mélisande* (**(*)).

The composer himself directed the first public performance of the *Third* in Boston in 1930, and Koussevitzky later performed it a number of times, before making this recording in 1940. Sibelius's influence is obvious, but the construction and Nordic atmosphere are the composer's own, and so too is the rich stream of lyrical melody. Indeed the *Andante tranquillo* brings one of the composer's most memorable themes, which returns to provide an apotheosis for the finale. With passionate playing from the Boston Orchestra, Koussevitzky's reading is powerfully committed, immediately establishing the northern atmosphere of Hanson's sound-world and building the finale steadily to its final climax with gripping concentration. The Biddulph transfer is very good, with sonic inadequacies easily forgotten. The other pieces, which come before the symphony, are all played superbly, but the sound is more variable. Highlights include the Mussorgsky *Khovanshchina Prelude*, sombrely paced, and the Liadov *Enchanted lake*, both highly evocative and the latter remarkably full and atmospheric. The excerpts from Fauré's *Pelléas et Mélisande* are delicately done, although here climaxes are less refined.

Symphony No. 3; Elegy in memory of my friend Serge Koussevitzky, Op. 44; (i) *Lament for Beowulf.*
(M) *** Mercury [434 302-2]. Eastman-Rochester O, composer, (i) with Eastman School of Music Ch.

In the *Third Symphony* the string threnodies surge purposefully forward, there are similar rhythmic patterns and confident rhetorical gestures. This is highly accessible music. This applies also to the *Elegy*, while the cantata also makes an immediate impression and is very well sung. Here as in the orchestral works the 1958 Mercury sound is first rate. This disc is available only in the USA.

Harbison, John (born 1938)

(i) *Concerto for double brass choir and orchestra;* (ii) *The Flight into Egypt;* (iii) *The Natural world.*
*** New World Dig. NW 80395-2 [id.]. (i) LAPO, Previn; (ii) Roberta Anderson, Sanford Sylvan, Cantata Singers & Ens., David Hoose; (iii) Janice Felty, Los Angeles Philharmonic New Music Group, Harbison.

These three fine works provide an illuminating survey of the recent work of one of the most communicative of American composers today. The most striking and vigorous is the concerto he wrote as resident composer for Previn and the Los Angeles Philharmonic, and for the orchestra's brass section in particular. The other two works reveal the more thoughtful Harbison, the one a collection of three songs to nature poems by Wallace Stevens, Robert Bly and James Wright. *The Flight into Egypt* is a measured and easily lyrical setting of the story of the Holy Family fleeing from King Herod. Sanford Sylvan and the choir sing the main text, with Roberta Anderson interjecting as the Angel. Excellent performances and recording.

Harris, Roy (1898–1979)

(i) *Violin concerto; Symphonies Nos. 1; 5.*
** Albany AR012 [id.]. (i) Gregory Fulkerston; Louisville O, Leighton Smith; Mester or Whitney.

The *First Symphony* is strong stuff, hardly less impressive than No. 3, but neither No. 5 nor the *Violin concerto* adds greatly to our picture of its composer. Gregory Fulkerston gives a persuasive account of the solo part, but the strings of the enterprising Louisville Orchestra are wanting in body and lustre. The recordings are serviceable rather than distinguished.

Symphony No. 3.
(N) (M) **(*) Sony SMK 60594 [id.]. NYPO, Bernstein – DIAMOND: *Symphony No. 4*; THOMPSON: *Symphony No. 2.* **(*)

Bernstein has recorded the *Third Symphony* twice – his later 1985 version, coupled with William Schuman's *Third* on DG, is currently withdrawn. This Sony account comes from 1961 and is quite simply the best LP/CD version artistically; only his mentor Koussevitzky's pioneering 78s have greater concentration and fire, and Bernstein runs him pretty close, even if the forwardly balanced recording is less than ideal. It comes with another classic of the American discography, the Diamond *Fourth Symphony*.

Harty, Hamilton (1879–1941)

A Comedy overture; (i) *Piano concerto;* (ii) *Violin concerto;* (iii) *In Ireland (Fantasy). An Irish symphony;* (ii) *Variations on a Dublin air. With the wild geese.* (iv) *The Children of Lir; Ode to a nightingale.* Arrangement: *Londonderry Air.*
(M) *** Chandos Dig. CHAN 7035 (3) [id.]. (i) Binns; (ii) Holmes; (iii) Fleming, Kelly; (iv) Harper; Ulster O, Thomson.

Bryden Thomson's box gathers together Harty's major orchestral and concertante works with great success, and each disc is also available separately – see below.

(i) *Piano concerto in B min.;* (ii) *Violin concerto in D.*
(M) *** Chandos Dig. CHAN 7032 [id.]. (i) Malcolm Binns, (ii) Ralph Holmes; Ulster O, Thomson.

Harty's *Piano concerto*, written in 1922, has strong Rachmaninovian influences, but the melodic freshness remains individual in this highly sympathetic performance. Though the *Violin concerto* has no strongly individual idiom, the invention is fresh and often touched with genuine poetry. Ralph Holmes gives a thoroughly committed account of the solo part and is well supported by an augmented Ulster Orchestra under Bryden Thomson.

An Irish symphony; A Comedy overture; (i) *In Ireland* (fantasy for flute, harp and orchestra). *With the wild geese.*
(M) *** Chandos Dig. CHAN 7034 [id.]. Ulster O, Thomson, (i) with Fleming, Kelly.

The *Irish symphony* has won great acclaim for its brilliant scoring and craftsmanship, with the Scherzo particularly engaging. It is extremely well played by the Ulster Orchestra under Bryden Thomson, while the *In Ireland fantasy* is full of delightful Irish melodic whimsy. Melodrama enters the scene in the symphonic poem, *With the wild geese*, but its Irishry asserts itself immediately in the opening theme. Again a splendid performance and a high standard of digital sound.

With the wild geese (symphonic poem).
(B) *** CfP CD-CFP 4635. RSNO, Gibson – GERMAN: *Welsh rhapsody;* MACCUNN: *Land of Mountain and flood;* SMYTH: *Wreckers overture.* ***

With the wild geese is a melodramatic piece about the Irish soldiers fighting on the French side in the Battle of Fontenoy. The ingredients – a jolly Irish theme and a call to arms among them – are effectively deployed; although the music does not reveal a strong individual personality, it is carried by a romantic sweep which is well exploited here. The 1968 recording still sounds most vivid, and this anthology makes a first-rate bargain.

3 Pieces for oboe and piano.
(N) (B) *** Hyperion Helios Dig. CDH 55008 [id.]. Sarah Francis, Peter Dickenson – BOUGHTON: *Pastorale*; HOWELLS: *Sonata*; RUBBRA: *Sonata.* ***

Harty's three oboe *Pieces*, played here with piano, were written for Henry Wood's 1911 Proms with an orchestral accompaniment. They are utterly charming in this more intimate version, and both artists respond to their disarming melodiousness, especially in the very Irish tune of the closing *A la Campagne*. The balance is too forward but the playing has delicacy of feeling and, if you turn the volume down, the effect is very pleasing.

VOCAL MUSIC

(i) *The Children of Lir; Ode to a nightingale.* (ii) *Variations on a Dublin air.* Arrangement: *Londonderry Air.*
(M) *** Chandos Dig. CHAN 7033 [id.]. Ulster O, Thomson, with (i) Heather Harper; (ii) Holmes.

Harty's setting of Keats's *Ode to a nightingale* is richly convincing, a piece written for his future wife, the soprano, Agnes Nicholls. The other work, directly Irish in its inspiration, evocative in an almost Sibelian way, uses the soprano in wordless melisma, here beautifully sung by Heather Harper. The performances are excellent, warmly committed and superbly recorded. The *Variations on a Dublin air*, for violin and orchestra, and Harty's arrangement of the *Londonderry Air* have been added for the reissue.

Harvey, Richard (born 1953)

Concerto antico (for guitar and small orchestra).
❁ *** Sony Dig. SK 68337 [id.]. John Williams, LSO, Paul Daniel – GRAY: *Concerto.* *** ❁

Richard Harvey's highly atmospheric *Concerto antico* flows over with colour and attractive invention, in heartwarming melodies. It is easily the best concerto for the guitar since the work by Malcolm Arnold of several decades earlier, admirably written for the soloist and most imaginatively scored in the orchestra. As much a five-movement suite as a concerto, the piece uses old song- and dance-forms, but the composer's ideas are his own – and very tuneful they are, with an element of pastiche in their settings, yet nicely spiced with modern harmonic touches. The brilliant *Lavolta* finale opens with Stravinskian syncopated accents and then introduces a most winning lyricism that alternates lusciously with the rushing *con fuoco* forward momentum. In every way this is a masterly work, and it is played superbly by its commissioner and dedicatee, John Williams, splendidly accompanied by the LSO under Paul Daniel. The recording, ideally balanced, is of demonstration quality.

Hasse, Johann (1699–1783)

Sinfonias: in D, Op. 3/3; in F, Op. 3/5; Fugue in G min. (i) *Motette: Chori angelici laetantes; Salve Regina in A;* (ii) *Salve Regina in E flat.*
(N) *** DG Dig. 453 435-2 [id.]. Musica Antiqua Köln, Reinhard Goebel with (i) Bernarda Fink; (ii) Barbara Bonney, Bernarda Fink.

Given the commanding position he occupied in his lifetime, it is surprising that Hasse enjoys relatively little exposure on record. But doubtless this, his tercentenary year, will confirm that Hasse was a truly international figure, beginning life in the Hamburg and Brunswick operas, and then, after studying with Alessandro Scarlatti in Naples, working in Venice before going to Dresden as Kapellmeister to the Saxon Court (1734–64). Burney visited him in 1772 when he was living in Vienna, and it was for him that Hasse's daughters sang the *Salve Regina in E flat*. Bernarda Fink and Barbara Bonney share it with obvious delight. It is a lovely piece and the level of inspiration of its companions is high. The *Sinfonia in D* is the overture to *Cleofide*, the opera that put him on the map in Dresden in 1731. Quite apart from his work directing these performances, Reinhard Goebel has written richly informative notes: he calls the three vocal pieces here 'sublime in anyone's language' – and he is absolutely right. First-rate sound, very clean and well balanced.

(i; ii) *Aria 'Ah Dio, ritornate'* from *La conversione di San'Agostino* for viola da gamba and harpsichord; (iii; i–ii) *Flute sonata in B min., Op. 2/6;* (ii) *Harpsichord sonata in C min. Op. 7/6;* (iv; i–iii) Cantatas: *Fille, dolce mio bene; Quel vago seno, O Fille;* Venetian ballads: *Cos e' sta Cossa?; Grazie agli inganni tuoi; No ste' a condanare; Si' la gondola avere', non crie'.*

*** CRD Dig. CRD 3488 [id.]. (i) Erin Headley; (ii) Malcolm Proud; (iii) Nancy Hadden; (iv) Julianne Baird.

Johann Hasse was a remarkable example of a composer who outlived his times and was left behind by the musical course of events – the penalty of surviving until his 85th year. A member of the group of composers centred round the court of Frederick the Great at Potsdam, his career peaked in the 1730s, although his success as an operatic composer continued on and off for another three decades. Finally in his seventies he graciously acknowledged Mozart's superiority; nevertheless he went on producing operas. The cantatas here are written in a pastoral style, with important flute obbligatos (a legacy from Frederick). They show much charm and distinct expressive feeling, and Julianne Baird has exactly the right voice for them, with a freshness of tone and purity of line matched by the right degree of ardour. The *Harpsichord sonata*, alternating fast and slow movements, is inventive and good-humoured and the *Aria* for viola da gamba readily shows the composer's operatic style, while the Venetian ballads which close this elegantly performed and very well-recorded concert are also full of character, cultivated rather than folksy in their more popular idiom.

Haydn, Josef (1732–1809)

Cassation in D for 4 horns, violin, viola & bass, Hob deest; Horn concerto No. 1 in D, Hob VII/d3; Divertimenti: in E flat for 2 horns & string quartet, Hob II/21; in D for 2 horns & string quartet, Hob II/22; in E flat for horn, violin & cello, Hob IV/5.

**(*) Sony Dig. SK 68253 [id.]. Abe Koster, soloists, L'Archibudelli.

After Abe Koster demonstrated his prowess so effectively in the Mozart *Horn concertos*, this collection is something of a disappointment. For one thing, apart from the concerto, the music – in spite of H. C. Robbins Landon's enthusiastic advocacy in the accompanying notes – is far from top-quality Haydn; both the *Divertimenti*, Hob II/21–2, are pre-Esterházy. The performances are very robust, and in at least one instance the horn players are content to play their upper-harmonics with bad tuning rather than lip them (or hand-stop them) into a more exact pitch. Abe Koster manages the high tessitura of the *Concerto* confidently, and he even manages to play every note of the very difficult solo line of the trio which Haydn called his '*Divertimenti a tre*', Hob IV/5. The horn part immediately travels right up into the stratosphere and the listener is very aware of the continual technical challenge. The result resembles a musical obstacle race for the soloist, with the string players tagging along in the background.

Cello concertos in C & D, Hob XVIIb/1–2.

*** Ph. Dig. 420 923-2. Heinrich Schiff, ASMF, Marriner.

(N) (M) *** EMI CDM5 66896-2 [CDM5 66948]. Jacqueline du Pré, ECO, Barenboim – BOCCHERINI: *Cello concerto in B flat* (arr. GRUTZMACHER). ***

*** O-L Dig. 414 615-2. Christophe Coin, AAM, Hogwood.

(BB) *** Naxos Dig. 8.550059; *4550059* [id.]. Ludovít Kanta, Capella Istropolitana, Peter Breiner – BOCCHERINI: *Cello concerto*. ***

(N) **(*) Virgin/EMI Dig. VC5 45014-2 [id.]. Truls Mørk, Norwegian CO, Iona Brown.

(M) **(*) EMI (SIS) Dig. CDM7 64326-2 [id.]. Lynn Harrell, ASMF, Marriner – VIVALDI: *Concertos*. **(*)

Heinrich Schiff produces a beautiful sound, as indeed do the Academy under Marriner. These are impressively fresh-sounding performances with lyrical and affectionate playing from all concerned. The recording has the realistic timbre, balance and bloom one associates with Philips.

Jacqueline du Pré's recording of the *C major Concerto* in April 1967 was the first she made with her husband, Daniel Barenboim, and she gives a performance of characteristic warmth and intensity. Her style is sometimes romantic in a way that is, strictly speaking, inappropriate in this music, yet when the very power of her personality is strongly conveyed, even through rhythmic distortions, one can but marvel – and Barenboim ensures that the orchestra follows every nuance. Equally, with Barbirolli scaling his accompaniment to match the inspirational approach of his young soloist, the performance of the better-known *D major concerto* is just as warm and expressive. Again the conviction and flair of the playing are extraordinarily compelling, and the romantic feeling is matched by an attractively full, well-balanced sound-picture. An apt choice for EMI's 'Great recordings of the century' series.

Christophe Coin, too, is a superb soloist and, provided the listener has no reservations about the use of original instruments, Hogwood's accompaniments are equally impressive. Excellent sound.

Kanta is a fine soloist. The excellent Naxos recording is made in a bright, resonant acoustic in which every detail is clearly registered, though the players are perhaps forwardly placed. The accompaniments are alert and fresh. Kanta plays contemporary cadenzas. An excellent bargain.

Truls Mørk gives characterful readings of both concertos, full of individual touches. The outer movements of the *C major* are daringly fast, though the opening movement of the *D major* brings a surprisingly relaxed approach. Both the slow movements are romantically spacious. Well recorded, though at premium price, with no extra work included, it is hardly a first recommendation.

The attractions of Harrell's coupling are enhanced by the inclusion of two Vivaldi concertos interspersed with Haydn (although the recorded sound is strikingly different). Harrell, rather after the manner of Rostropovich, seeks to turn these elegant concertos into big, virtuoso pieces, helped by Marriner's beautifully played accompaniments. Although touches of romantic expressiveness tend to intrude, the result is enjoyable, even if cadenzas are distractingly long. The digital recording is full and vivid (the analogue Vivaldi transfers are brighter and less smooth).

(i) *Cello concertos in C; D, Hob. VIIb/1–2. Overture in G (Lo speziale).*
(N) **(*) EMI Dig. CDC5 56535-2. (i) Han-Na Chang; Dresden State O, Sinopoli.

(i) *Cello concertos in C; D, Hob. VIIb/1–2. Sinfonia concertante in B flat for violin, cello, oboe, bassoon and orchestra, Hob I/105.*
(N) *** DHM/BMG Dig. 05472 77506-2 [id.]. (i) Hidemi Suzuki; La Petite Bande, Sigiswald Kuijken.

(i) *Cello concertos in C & D, Hob VIIb/1–2*; (ii) *Sinfonia concertante in B flat. Symphony No. 13: Adagio cantabile in G.*
(N) *** RCA Dig. 09026 68578-2 (i) Steven Isserlis; (ii) Blakenstijn, Boyd, Wilkie, COE, Norrington.

Cello concertos in C & D, Hob VIIb/1–2; Symphony No.104. (arr. Salomon)
(N) *** Channel Classics Dig. CCS 7395 [id.]. Pieter Wispelwey, Florilegium.

Steven Isserlis is a commanding soloist in both cello concertos, and unlike many rivals he does not linger in slow movements, preferring flowing speeds. Nor does he race breathlessly in finales. Particularly with such a generous coupling, this makes a first choice among modern versions, if the *Sinfonia concertante* is wanted also. Here the other soloists are distinguished principals from the COE, playing just as pointedly as Isserlis. Vivid and immediate sound.

Hidemi Suzuki is second only to Isserlis as a soloist in these two concertos, playing with fine tone, sensibility and refinement, and producing electrifying bravura in the finales – especially the *C major*, which Kuijken takes exhilaratingly briskly. La Petite Bande provides the stylish soloists for the engaging *Sinfonia concertante*, and the balance is again just right.

Pieter Wispelwey is also an inspired soloist in the period performance with Florilegium, at times abrasive but always transparent in texture with the soloist's clean articulation allowing fast speeds in outer movements with no feeling of rush. The central *Adagios* by contrast are surprisingly slow, not as elegant as some, but deeply felt. Salomon's arrangement of Haydn's last symphony for flute, string quartet and piano makes an unusual if lightweight coupling.

The young Korean cellist Han-Na Chang is only fourteen and exhibits remarkable prowess and accomplishment – not just for her age either! She enjoys the imprimatur of Rostropovich, no less. With her natural tonal delicacy, she gives warm but essentially refined readings of both concertos and in the beautiful slow movement of the *D major* she draws out the melodic line exquisitely on a half-tone, and she conveys pleasure in what she does. Sinopoli affectionately fines down the orchestral accompaniment to match his soloist's delicacy. The finale then flows along buoyantly. Chang is a splendidly musical soloist; her musicality and abundant gifts are not in question, but some may prefer a more robust, more mature approach in eighteenth-century concertos. The Italian *overture* (in effect a miniature sinfonia) is most deftly played and makes an engaging interlude between the two works. The recording is clear yet full.

(i) *Cello concerto in C, Hob VIIb/1;* (ii; iv) *Horn concertos Nos. 1–2;* (iii; iv) *Trumpet concerto in D.*
(M) *** Decca 430 633-2 [id.]. (i) Rostropovich, ECO, Britten; (ii) Tuckwell; (iii) Alan Stringer; (iv) ASMF, Marriner.

Rostropovich's earlier (1964) stereo recording of the *C major Cello concerto* for Decca is warmly romantic, and some may feel he takes too many liberties in the slow movement, but with Britten accompaying it is magnetic throughout. A first-rate coupling in excellent 1966 versions of both the *Horn concertos* by Tuckwell in peak form and Stringer's 1967 account of the *Trumpet concerto.*

Cello concerto No. 2 in D, Hob VIIb/2.
(M) **(*) BMG/Melodiya 74321 40724 [id.]. Daniil Shafran, USSR SO, Neeme Järvi – TCHAIKOVSKY: *Andante cantabile* etc. **(*)

Daniil Shafran enjoys cult status among cellists – understandably so, you may think, on hearing this 1962 account of the Haydn *D major Concerto*, made when Järvi was twenty-five. Shafran had a wonderfully rich, singing tone and an intensity that is always held within the right limits. He obviously inspired both the USSR Symphony Orchestra and Neeme Järvi. By the side of the finest recordings of the period, the sound is two-dimensional, but it is more than adequate, and playing like this is very special.

(i) *Cello concertos: in C, Hob VIIb/1; in D, Hob VIIb/2;* (ii) *Violin concertos: in C; in A; in G, Hob VIIa/1, 3 & 4;* (ii; iii) *Double concerto for violin and harpsichord in F, Hob XVIII/6.*
(B) *** Ph. Duo 438 797-2 (2) [id.]. ECO with (i)

Walevska, De Waart; (ii) Accardo; (iii) Canino.

The three *Violin concertos* are all early; the *C major*, written for Tomasini, is probably the best. The other two have come into the limelight fairly recently. Accardo plays with great elegance and charm. It would be idle to pretend that either they or the *Double Concerto for violin and harpsichord* are great music, in that the soloists are rather forward, but the 1980 recording has been well transferred. The two *Cello concertos* are much better known; Christine Walevska presents them freshly, well partnered by Edo de Waart and the ECO. She is balanced almost within the orchestra, to give an agreeable chamber-like quality to the music-making.

(i) *Harpsichord concertos: in F, Hob XVIII/3; in G, Hob XVIII/4; in D, Hob XVIII/11;* (i; ii) *Double concerto in F for harpsichord and violin, Hob XVIII/6;* (iii) *Concertini: in C, Hob XIV/3; in C, Hob XIV/11; in C, Hob XIV/12; Concertino (Divertimento) in G, Hob XIV/13; Concertino in F, Hob XIV/F2; Divertimenti in C, Hob XIV/4; in C, Hob XIV/7; in C, Hob XIV/8; in F, Hob XIV/9; in C, Hob XIV/C2.*

(B) *** Ph. Duo 446 542-2 (2) [id.]. Ton Koopman; (i) Amsterdam Musica Antiqua or Amsterdam Bar. O; (ii) with Huggett; (iii) Goebel, Stuurop, Medlam.

Ton Koopman's admirable Philips Duo set covers the 14 concertante Haydn keyboard works listed in the Hoboken catalogue now thought to be authentic. (He has recorded the *Organ concertos*, Hob XVIII/1, 2, 7, 7, 8 and 10 separately, and no doubt these will reappear during the lifetime of this book.) The present coverage includes the ten small concertos from the 1760s called either *Divertimenti* or *Concertini* which are of little real substance but which still make attractive, undemanding listening. Here the accompanying group is made up of Reinhard Goebel and Alda Stuurop (violins) and Charles Medlam (cello), all playing on period instruments. The four longer concertos, including the rightly famous *D major* (scored for oboes and horns) and the *Double concerto for violin, keyboard and strings*, Hob XVIII/6, use a larger accompanying group, which Koopman directs from the keyboard. As sound, these recordings could hardly be bettered: the balance is finely judged and the acoustic warm, with detail registered perfectly. The performances are alive and highly accomplished. Though occasionally Koopman might have allowed the music to unfold at a more leisurely pace, this invites the strongest recommendation.

Horn concerto No. 1 in D, Hob. VII/d3.

(M) **(*) Teldec/Warner 0630 12324-2 [id.]. Hermann Baumann, Concerto Amsterdam, Jaap Schröder – DANZI: *Horn concerto in E;* ROSETTI: *Horn concerto in D min.* **(*)

Baumann's 1969 account has crisp, clean, classical lines, emphasized by the rather dry sound of the remastered recording, which gives a bold, open horn-timbre and unexpansive string-timbre. The *Adagio* is rather sombre here (it has some splendidly resonating low notes from the soloist), but the finale is spirited enough.

(i) *Horn concertos Nos. 1–2;* (ii) *Trumpet concerto in E flat;* (i) *Divertimento a 3 in E flat.*

**(*) Nimbus NI 5010 [id.]. (i) Thompson; (ii) Wallace; Philh. O, Warren-Green.

Michael Thompson gives bold, confident accounts of the two *Horn concertos*, with a sprinkling of decoration. John Wallace's trumpet timbre is strikingly brilliant, and his playing in the *Trumpet concerto* is full of personality. He too likes to decorate and there are some attractive surprises in the finale. The recording was made in the resonant ambience of All Saints', Tooting.

Piano concertos: in F, Hob. XVIII/3; in G, Hob. XVIII/4; in D, Hob. XVIII/11.

*** Sony Dig. SK 48383 [id.]. Emanuel Ax, Franz Liszt CO.

(BB) *** Arte Nova Dig. 74321 51635-2 [id.]. Lisa Smirnova, Sinfonia Varsovia, Volker Schmidt-Gertenbach.

The popular *D major Concerto* comes with the *F major*, from Haydn's first years at Esterháza, and the *G major*, which is somewhat later but still written with the harpsichord in mind. Emanuel Ax gives them on the modern grand piano and he does so with great elegance and finesse. He evidently enjoys a good rapport with the Franz Liszt Chamber Orchestra, who respond warmly to his direction, and throughout all three concertos the music sounds fresh and sparkling. The quality of the recording is outstanding; the piano sounds real and lifelike, and the balance is well struck.

These works are also played with freshness and point by Lisa Smirnova and admirably accompanied with a sure sense of style and a nice feeling for light and shade by Schmidt-Gertenbach and the excellent Sinfonia Varsovia. The recording is beautifully balanced.

Piano concertos in G, Hob XVIII/4; F, Hob XVIII/7; D, Hob XVIII/11.

*** Virgin/EMI Dig. VC5 45196-2. Mikhail Pletnev, Deutsche Kammerphilharmonie.

The keyboard concertos are by general consent not the greatest Haydn and, of the three recorded here, one is of doubtful authenticity: the *F major* (XVIII/7 in the Hoboken catalogue) is probably by Wagenseil; and not very much is known about the *G major*, which is very early. In both pieces, as well as in the well-known *D major Concerto*, Mikhail Pletnev offers playing of great character and personality. He is not frightened of being anachronistic, as in the cadenza of the *G major*, yet nor is he out to draw attention to himself. He obviously enjoys a splendid rapport with the Deutsche Kammerphilharmonie, with whom he has recently recorded some Mozart concertos. The recording is very alive and present without bringing the players too close, and the colour and feeling Pletnev discovers in these pieces is a source of wonder, both distinctive and distinguished.

(i) *Piano concerto in D, Hob XVIII/11;* (ii) *Violin concertos: in C; in G; Hob VIIa/1 & 4;* (ii–iii) *Double concerto for violin and harpsichord in F, Hob XVIII/6.*

*** Sup. Dig. SU 3265-2 [id.]. (i) Bella Davidovich; (ii) Dmitry Sitkovetsky; (iii) Václav Hudeček; Prague CO, Sitkovetsky.

Here is the most winning of Haydn's solo keyboard concertos together with two of the violin concertos, including the *C major* with its engaging, serenade-like, cantabile slow movement. They are impeccably played, with just the right degree of expressive feeling. The piano used by Davidovich has a crisp, clean timbre, rather like a fortepiano, only with more colour, and it suits the dancing outer movements of the *D major* keyboard work admirably. What clinches the appeal of this attractive collection is the delightful account of the *Double concerto*. Here the interplay of piano and violin in Haydn's shared cadenza at the end of the first movement, and in the fine *Largo* with its walking bass followed by solo entries over pizzicatos, is perfectly balanced. This disc makes a splendid case for the use of modern instruments in this repertoire when Sitkovetsky directs the accompanying group so stylishly, with the overall effect pleasingly intimate.

Trumpet concerto in E flat.

❁ *** Ph. Dig. 420 203-2 [id.]. Håkan Hardenberger, ASMF, Marriner – HERTEL ***; HUMMEL *** ❁; STAMITZ: *Concertos.* ***

*** Sony CD 37846 [id.]. Marsalis, Nat. PO, Leppard – HUMMEL: *Concerto* *** (with L. MOZART: *Concerto* ***).

(N) (B) *** CfP Dig. 573 4392. Ian Balmain, RLPO, Kovacevich – MOZART: *Horn concertos.* ***

(N) *** EMI Dig. CDC5 55231-2 [id.]. Maurice André, Franz Liszt O, Budapest, János Rolla – HERTEL; HUMMEL: *Trumpet concertos* *** (with MARCELLO: *Concerto in D min.* **(*)).

Hardenberger's playing of the noble line of the *Andante* is no less telling than his fireworks in the finale and, with Marriner providing warm, elegant and polished accompaniments throughout, this is probably the finest single collection of trumpet concertos in the catalogue.

Marsalis is splendid too, his bravura no less spectacular, with the finale a tour de force, yet never aggressive in its brilliance. His way with Haydn is eminently stylish, as is Leppard's lively and polished accompaniment.

With Stephen Kovacevich as conductor, Ian Balmain favours extreme speeds for Haydn's delectable *Trumpet concerto*, playing brilliantly. It makes an apt and attractive coupling for Claire Briggs's fine recordings of all four Mozart *Horn concertos*, very well recorded.

Maurice André has recorded this work a number of times over the years and his latest 1994 version has the advantage of a warm, stylish accompaniment from Rolla. André's touch is as sure as ever, his phrasing if anything even more elegant. The Hertel and Hummel concertos are equally enjoyable, but the Marcello concerto was written for the oboe, and although André manages the high tessitura of the Adagio with skill and taste, such a transcription seems superfluous.

Violin concertos Nos. 1 in C; 4 in G, HobVIIa/1 & 4; (i) *Double concerto for violin and piano, HobVIII/6.*

(N) (BB) *** Hyperion Helios Dig. CDH 55007 [id.]. Adelina Oprean, European CO; (i) with Justin Oprean.

Violin concertos Nos. 1 in C; 4 in G, Hob VIIa/1 & 4; (i) *Sinfonia concertante in B flat for violin, cello, oboe, bassoon & orchestra, Hob I/105.*

*** Virgin/Veritas EMI Dig. VER5 61301-2. Elizabeth Wallfisch, O of Age of Enlightenment; (i) with Watkin, Robson, Warnock.

Haydn's *Violin concertos* are early works; the *C major* with its winding, serenade-like melody is probably the finer, but the *G major* too has an eloquent *Adagio* and a bustling finale. Wallfisch leads the Orchestra of the Age of Enlightenment from her bow and proves a highly sensitive soloist – these performances are if anything even more impressive than those of the Mozart concertos by the same soloist. Her serenely reflective account of the *Adagio molto* of the *C major* is memorable. In the *Sinfonia concertante* the smiling interplay of the various wind and string soloists has never been bettered on record and the use of period instruments brings a pleasing intimacy and plenty of spirit. The recording is truthfully balanced and vivid.

The Helios disc makes a good modern-instrument alternative for those interested in the well-crafted (and very well-played) *Double concerto for violin and piano*, which has a particularly striking dialogue between the two soloists in the central *Largo*. In the two solo concertos, Adelina Oprean proves a persuasive soloist with a dulcet but not over-opulent timbre. The central cantilena of the *G major Concerto*, with its pizzicato accompaniment, is delightful and she directs the orchestra in outer movements with vigour and point. The sound is good too.

Violin concertos Nos. 3 in A; 4 in G, HobVIIa/ 3–4.

(N) (BB) **(*) Virgin Classics Dig. Double VBD5 61504-2 (2) [CDVB 61504]. Mayumi Seiler, City of L. Sinf. – BEETHOVEN; MENDELSSOHN: *Concertos*. **(*)

Unlike in the coupled Beethoven and Mendelssohn concertos on this generous Virgin bargain Double, the soloist Mayumi Seiler also directs the orchestra. The effect is very much of chamber performances – warm, polished and comparatively intimate. The result is musically enjoyable, if not distinctive, but this inexpensive two-disc set offers five concertos, all very well played and recorded, for the cost of a single medium-priced CD.

Sinfonia concertante in B flat for violin, cello, oboe, bassoon and orchestra, Hob I/105.

(BB) **(*) ASV Quicksilva Dig CDQS 6140 [id.]. Frieman, Pople, Anderson, Gambold, L. Festival O, Ross Pople – STAMITZ: *Sinfonias concertantes*. **(*)

Directing the players from the solo cello, Ross Pople draws a strong and alert rather than an elegant performance from his London Festival Orchestra, well recorded in bright, firmly focused sound. Though the solo playing is not always ideally refined, there is a winning sense of musicians acting out a drama, at speeds that are comfortable, never exaggerated. The coupling of *Sinfonias concertantes* by Stamitz is very apt and attractive.

SYMPHONIES

Symphonies Nos. 1–104; Symphonies A; B. Alternative versions: *Symphony Nos. 22 in E flat (Philosopher),* 2nd version. *Symphony No. 63 in C (La Roxelane)*, 1st version. *Symphony No. 53 (L'Impériale):* 3 alternative Finales: (i) *A (Capriccio)*; (ii) *C* (Paris version, attrib. Haydn); *D: Overture in D* (Milanese version). *Symphony No. 103:* Finale (alternative ending). (i) *Sinfonia concertante in B flat for oboe, bassoon, violin and cello.*

❁ (B) *** Decca 448 531-2 (33) [id.]. Philh. Hungarica, Antal Dorati; (i) with István Engl, László Baranyai, Igor Ozim, Zóltán Rácz.

Dorati was ahead of his time as a Haydn interpreter when, in the early 1970s, he made this pioneering integral recording of the symphonies. Superbly transferred to CD in full, bright and immediate sound, the performances are a consistent delight, with brisk allegros and fast-flowing *Andantes*, with textures remarkably clean. The slow, rustic-sounding accounts of Minuets are more controversial, but the rhythmic bounce makes them attractive too. The set remains as yet the only complete survey. It includes not only the *Symphonies A* and *B* (Hoboken Nos. 106 and 108) but also the *Sinfonia concertante in B flat*, a splendidly imaginative piece with wonderful unexpected touches. Dorati's account – not surprisingly – presents the work as a symphony with unusual scoring, rather than as a concerto. As H. C. Robbins Landon tells us in the accompanying notes, the *Symphonies A* and *B* were omitted from the list of 104 authentic symphonies by error, as the first was considered to be a quartet – wind parts were discovered later – and the second a divertimento. Dorati also includes as an appendix completely different versions of *Symphony No. 22* (*The Philosopher*), where Haydn altered the orchestration (a pair of flutes substituted for the cor anglais), entirely removed the first movement and introduced a new *Andante grazioso*; plus an earlier version of No. 63, to some extent conjectural in its orchestration, for the original score is lost. Of the three alternative finales for *L'Impériale* (No. 53), the first (A) contains a melody which Robbins Landon suggests 'sounds extraordinarily like Schubert'; the second (C) seems unlikely to be authentic; but the third (D) uses an overture which was first published in Vienna. 'In some respects,' Robbins Landon suggests, 'this is the most successful of the three concluding movements.' He feels the same about the more extended finale of the *Drum Roll Symphony*, which originally included 'a modulation to C flat, preceded by two whole bars of rests'. But Haydn thought that this made the movement too long and crossed out the whole section. Robbins Landon continues: 'Perhaps Haydn was for once in his life too ruthless here.'

Symphonies Nos. 1 in D min.; 2 in C; 4 in D; 5 in A; 10 in D; 11 in E flat; 18 in G; 27 in G; 32 in C; 37 in C; Symphony A (Partita) in B flat.

**(*) O-L Dig. 436 428-2 (3). AAM, Hogwood.

Symphonies Nos. 3 in G; 14 in A; 15 in D; 17 in F; 19 in D; 20 in C; 25 in C; 33 in C; 36 in E flat; 108 (Partita) in B flat.

**(*) O-L Dig. 436 592-2 (3) [id.]. AAM, Hogwood.

Symphonies Nos. 6 in D (Le Matin); 7 in C (Le Midi); 8 in G (Le Soir); 9 in C; 12 in E; 13 in D; 16 in B flat; 40 in F; 72 in D.

**(*) O-L Dig. 433 661-2 [id.]. AAM, Hogwood.

Symphonies Nos. 21 in A; 22 in E flat (Philosopher); 23 in G; 24 in D; 28 in A; 29 in E; 30 in C (Allelujah); 31 in D (Horn signal); 34 in D min.

**(*) O-L Dig. 430 082-2 (3) [id.]. AAM, Hogwood.

Symphonies Nos. 26 in D; 42 in D; 43 in E flat (Mercury); 44 in E min. (Trauer); 48 in C (Maria Theresia); 49 in F min. (La Passione).

**(*) O-L Dig. 440 222-2 (3) [id.]. AAM, Hogwood.

Symphonies Nos. 35 in B flat; 38 in C; 39 in G min.; 41 in C; 58 in F; 59 in A (Fire); 65 in A.
**(*) O-L Dig. 433 012-2 (3) [id.]. AAM, Hogwood.

Symphonies Nos. 45 in F sharp min.; 46 in B; 47 in G; 51 in B flat; 52 in C min.; 64 in A.
*** O-L Dig. 443 777-2 (3) [id.]. AAM, Hogwood.

In his Haydn series Hogwood has mellowed in period-performance manners, compared with his pioneering set of the Mozart *Symphonies*. The playing, too, is now more polished. He uses a small group of strings (about half the size of that chosen by Tafelmusik, who have the benefit of H. C. Robbins Landon's advice in this matter). In particular he avoids abrasiveness in slow movements, which, though much leaner than with modern instruments, are sympathetically phrased though sometimes a little stiff. In general his direct, crisply rhythmic approach to these works tends not to convey the charm of Haydn. He offers all repeats, but for scholarly reasons no harpsichord continuo is employed. The finely detailed, firmly focused recording perfectly brings out the transparency of textures, while giving body to the sound. If you are a Hogwood aficionado, these boxes can be acquired with confidence, particularly the collection appropriately subtitled 'Climax of the *Sturm und Drang*'.

Symphonies Nos. 50 in C; 54 in G (1st. version); 55 in E flat (Schoolmaster); 56 in C; 57 in D; 60 in C (Il distratto).
(N) *** O-L Dig. 443 781-2 (3) [id.]. AAM, Hogwood.

In this group of symphonies from 1773–4, following the *Sturm und Drang* sequence, Hogwood's speeds are generally brisk, with typically crisp, transparent textures, but he occasionally allows himself to luxuriate in broader tempi, generally effectively. With second-half repeats regularly observed, these period performances come in pairs, only two per disc. As with the earlier issues in this Haydn series, the style of the AAM has softened a degree more than in their pioneering set of the Mozart symphonies on the same label, with a warmer approach to slow movements. A scholarly note explains Hogwood's continuing avoidance of harpsichord continuo. Clean, undistracting sound.

Symphonies Nos. 53 in D (L'Impériale); 54 in G (second version)*; 61 in D; 66 in B flat; 67 in F; 68 in B flat; 69 in C (Laudon).*
*** O-L Dig. 460 776-2 [id.]. AAM, Hogwood.

The ninth volume of Christopher Hogwood's Haydn series vividly demonstrates the merits of presenting these symphonies in chronological order, rather than in the old (sometimes misleading) numerical sequence. These works, all presumed to date from 1775/6, are here dubbed as 'theatrical and popular symphonies', simpler and less demanding than the *Sturm und Drang* masterpieces which preceded them. What these refreshing, clean-cut performances demonstrate is that Haydn was here turning his increasing technical command towards entertainment. Speeds for fast movements are characteristically brisk, but slow movements – exceptionally long with all repeats observed – are again taken broadly. With recording that heightens the transparency of texture, all the usual qualities of the Hogwood series are here, with braying natural horns, sharply percussive timpani, and no harpsichord continuo.

Symphonies Nos. 1 in D; 2 in C; 3 in G; 4 in D; 5 in A.
*** Hyperion Dig. CDA 66524 [id.]. Hanover Band, Roy Goodman.

Symphonies Nos. 6 in D (Le Matin); 7 in C (Le Midi); 8 in G (Le Soir).
*** Hyperion Dig. CDA 66523 [id.]. Hanover Band, Roy Goodman.

Symphonies Nos. 9 in C; 10 in D; 11 in E flat; 12 in E.
*** Hyperion Dig. CDA 66529 [id.]. Hanover Band, Goodman.

Symphonies Nos. 13 in D; 14 in A; 15 in D; 16 in B flat.
*** Hyperion Dig. CDA 66534 [id.]. Hanover Band, Goodman.

Symphonies Nos. 17 in F; 18 in G; 19 in D; 20 in C; 21 in A.
*** Hyperion Dig. CDA 66533 [id.]. Hanover Band, Goodman.

Symphonies Nos. 22 in E flat (Philosopher); 23 in G; 24 in D; 25 in C.
*** Hyperion Dig. CDA 66536 [id.]. Hanover Band, Goodman.

Symphonies Nos. 42 in D; 43 in E flat (Mercury); 44 in E min. (Trauer).
**(*) Hyperion Dig. CDA 66530 [id.]. Hanover Band, Goodman.

Symphonies Nos. 45 in F sharp min. (Farewell); 46 in B; 47 in G.
**(*) Hyperion Dig. CDA 66522 [id.]. Hanover Band, Goodman.

Symphonies Nos. 48 in C (Maria Theresia); 49 in F min. (Passione); 50 in C.
**(*) Hyperion Dig. CDA 66531 [id.]. Hanover Band, Goodman.

Symphonies Nos. 70 in D; 71 in B flat; 72 in D.
*** Hyperion Dig. CDA 66526 [id.]. Hanover Band, Roy Goodman.

Symphonies Nos. 73 in D (La chasse); 74 in E flat; 75 in D.
*** Hyperion Dig. CDA 66520 [id.]. Hanover Band, Roy Goodman.

Symphonies Nos. 76 in E flat; 77 in B flat; 78 in C min.
*** Hyperion Dig. CDA 66525 [id.]. Hanover Band, Roy Goodman.

Symphonies Nos. 82 in C (The Bear); 83 in G min. (The Hen); 84 in E flat.
*** Hyperion Dig. CDA 66527; *KA 66527* [id.]. Hanover Band, Goodman.

Symphonies Nos. 90 in C; 91 in E flat; 92 in G (Oxford).
*** Hyperion Dig. CDA 66521; *KA 66521* [id.]. Hanover Band, Goodman.

Symphonies Nos. 93 in D; 94 in G (Surprise); 95 in C min.
*** Hyperion Dig. CDA 66532 [id.]. Hanover Band, Goodman.

Symphonies Nos. 101 in D (Clock); 102 in B flat; Overture: Windsor Castle.
*** Hyperion Dig. CDA 66528 [id.]. Hanover Band, Goodman.

From the very outset of his Hyperion project, Goodman, who began at the beginning with the low-numbered symphonies, established a winning manner in early Haydn and, as the series progressed, he showed that his dramatic approach (tougher than Kuijken, for instance, in his COE recordings for Virgin) was being fruitful in the middle-period and later works. The performances offer consistently alert and well-sprung readings, which generally favour fast Allegros and relatively spacious slow movements which, more than in most period performances, give expressive warmth to Haydn's melodies, without overstepping the mark into romanticism. That Goodman is very much the positive director of the group is brought out by the generally close balance given to the harpsichord continuo, which is far more audible than in most versions. The recording is resonant, giving bloom to the strings, yet oboes and horns (and other wind and brass, when used) come through vividly. This Hyperion series is achieving a balance of style somewhere between the Hogwood approach and the fuller scale of Dorati, using modern instruments.

Symphonies Nos. 1–20.
(M) **(*) Nimbus Dig. NI 5426/30 [id.]. Austro-Hungarian Haydn O, Adám Fischer.

The Nimbus project of recording all the Haydn symphonies on modern instruments in the Haydnsaal of the Esterházy Palace brings playing which is fresh yet warm, with the considerable reverberation adding to the weight and scale of the earlier symphonies, in a manner that some ears will relish but others will find too opulent. In the accompanying notes the conductor, Adám Fischer, comments that the chosen orchestra, which is made up of players from Vienna and Budapest, carries forward the tradition of Austro-Hungarian music-making. The playing itself is warm and elegant, and again and again in these early symphonies the ear enjoys the finesse of this music-making and its ripeness of texture, with the rich-toned Viennese horns soaring out over the strings when given an opportunity to do so. The woodwind are sprightly and offer plenty of colour, and in Nos. 6–8 the various orchestral solos are taken with distinction. The conductor's speeds are moderate. Slow movements are gracious and phrasing is cultivated; minuets are courtly and finales lively and resilient, without being rushed. The sound itself is rich in ambience and easy to enjoy, for it does not cloud.

Symphonies Nos. 40 in F; 41 in C; 42 in D; 43 in E flat (Mercury); 44 in E min. (Trauer); 45 in F sharp min. (Farewell);46 in B flat; 47 in G; 48 in C (Maria Theresia); 49 in F min.(La Passione); 50 in C; 51 in B flat; 52 in C min.; 53 in D (L'Impériale); 54 in G.
(N) (M) *** Nimbus Dig. NI 5530/4 [id.]. Austro-Hungarian Haydn O., Adám Fischer.

In Volume 3 of his ongoing series, Adám Fischer, like Brüggen (see below), homes in on the *Sturm und Drang* works, but he is working in numerical order, so includes one or two other symphonies, though none that is not full of stimulating ideas (the theme and variations which forms the *Andante* of *L'Impériale* is sheer delight). The orchestral playing is consistently warm and committed and of course there is none of the astringency of texture one expects with Hogwood, or squeezed violin phrasing that Brüggen and others insist is authentic. The result is richly enjoyable and slow movements in particular consistently gain from such a dedicated orchestral response. The *Adagios* of the *Mercury* and *Trauersymphonie* are both very beautiful indeed, and the contrasting finale of the latter shares the same rhythmic energy with the bold, striding opening movement of the *Farewell*. Pungent, trumpet-enforced rhythmic accenting in the first movement of *Maria Theresia* is most arresting and again the slow movement is very fair in contour. The *Adagio* opening of *La Passione* is gentle yet is intensely concentrated in feeling and the following *Allegro di molto* is crisp, fast and biting. Minuets are faster and racier than with Dorati, with plenty of dynamic contrasts – and finales, if helter-skelter, still retain an elegant poise. The unnamed *C major Symphony* (No. 50) and the following *B flat major* work are among the finest performances here, splendidly characterful – and in the *Adagio* of the latter there is a glorious horn solo, followed by the graceful *Allegretto* finale. The Viennese elegance of phasing, and polish combined with sparkle, often remind one of Beecham in their friendly listener-appeal. The recording is first-class, full and warm with a natural concert-hall ambience. I. M. reflects that if he had to choose a complete set of the Haydn symphonies for a desert island, he would be very tempted towards this Nimbus series.

Symphonies Nos. 55 in E flat (Schoolmaster); 56 in C min.; 57 in D; 58 in F; 59 in A (Fire); 60 in C (Il distratto); 61 in D; 62 in D; 63 in C (La Roxelane); 64 in A (Tempora mutantur); 65 in A; 66 in B flat; 67 in F; 68 in B flat; 69 in C (Laudon).

(N) (M) *** Nimbus Dig. NI 5590/4 (5) [id.].
Austro-Hungarian Haydn O., Adám Fischer.

With Adám Fischer a dedicated advocate, inspiring fresh, persuasive playing from his hand-picked orchestra, there is no slackening of standards in this fourth volume of Nimbus's projected Haydn cycle. This group of works follows up the *Sturm und Drang* sequence with symphonies regularly related to Haydn's theatre music, at times with eccentric effects, as in the six-movement *Il distratto*, No.60, or No. 67 with its *col legno* and hurdy-gurdy effects. In the helpful acoustic of the Haydnsaal of the Esterhazy Palace at Eisenstadt, the sound is at once warmly atmospheric and intimate, with high contrasts of dynamic and texture. Continuing to use modern, not period instruments, but with limited string vibrato, and Viennese oboes and horns standing out distinctively, these are recordings to challenge the long-time supremacy of Dorati's pioneering Decca set. In important ways, not just in the extra fullness of the digital sound, the new performances improve on the old, notably in the brisker speeds for Minuets. Fischer generally tends to prefer speeds in slow movements a fraction more flowing than those of Dorati, while outer movements are regularly a degree more relaxed. Thanks to Fischer's springing of rhythm, speeds never drag, even if those dedicated to period practice might well prefer the more hectic Prestos and Prestissimos of the earlier set. These are performances which register Haydn's humour more clearly, even in the *Sturm und Drang* symphonies here, Nos 58 and 59 (*The Fire*).

Symphonies Nos. 82 in C (The Bear); 83 in G min. (The Hen); 84 in E flat; 85 in B flat (La Reine); 86 in D; 87 in A (Paris Symphonies).

(M) *** Nimbus Dig. NI 5419/20 [id.].
Austro-Hungarian Haydn O, Adám Fischer.

The expansive sound of the Austro-Hungarian Orchestra suits the *Paris Symphonies*. *La Poule* and *La Reine* (with its rhythmically powerful opening movement) both show Fischer and his players at their best, and finest of all is one of the least known, *Symphony No. 84 in E flat*, with another remarkably original first movement. Slow movements are warm and poised: the *Largo* of No. 86 is particularly successful, as is the light-hearted trio of its Minuet, with a vigorous finale, lightly articulated, to round the work off. The sound is always satisfyingly full-bodied, with the violins resonantly rich. The weighty bass is not always absolutely clean, but generally the effect is very believable.

Symphonies Nos. 88 in G; 89 in F; 90 in C; 91 in E flat; 92 in G (Oxford); Sinfonia concertante in B flat for violin, cello, oboe, bassoon and orchestra.

(M) ** Nimbus Dig. NI 5417/8 [id.].
Austro-Hungarian Haydn O, Adám Fischer.

When so much trouble has been taken to record this specially assembled orchestra in the authentic venue of the old Haydnsaal in the Esterházy Palace, it is surprising that in this second volume Fischer's readings are apparently little influenced by the example of period performances. As with the other issues in this Nimbus series the recording is full and pleasing, but the warm resonance prevents sharpness of detail and also has the effect of blunting the string articulation. Too often one feels the need for more bite in allegros. Tempi are almost always relaxed, so that the famous slow movement of No. 88 in G, warmly expressive as it is, very nearly drags, although Fischer brings off the *Adagio* of the *Oxford symphony* beautifully. Throughout Minuets are very stately indeed but finales dance gracefully and opening Adagios are warmly expressive; yet in the end there is an absence of conveyed exhilaration. The *Sinfonia concertante* included on the second disc is a particularly pleasing performance, with most sympathetic solo playing.

Symphonies Nos. 93–104.

(M) **(*) Nimbus Dig. NI 5200/4 [id.].
Austro-Hungarian Haydn O, Adám Fischer.

With three symphonies apiece on the first two discs of the five-disc Nimbus set, Fischer's cycle of all twelve *London Symphonies* makes a neat and attractive package, with consistently fresh, resilient and refined performances. Though these works were first given in the intimate surroundings of the Hanover Square Rooms in London, they were very quickly heard in this much grander setting, and the performances reflect the fact, with broad speeds and weighty tuttis made weightier by the reverberant Nimbus recording. Such a movement as the lovely *Adagio* of No. 102 with its soaring melody is given added beauty by the ambience and slow speed. The set can be warmly recommended to most who resist period performance when, even at broad speeds, rhythms are light and resilient. Never sounding breathless, Fischer's Haydn consistently brings out the happiness of the inspiration. These are very much performances to relax with.

Symphonies Nos. 93 in D; 99 in E flat; 100 in G (Military).

(N) **(*) RCA 09026 68425-2 [id.]. Philh. O, Leonard Slatkin.

Symphonies Nos. 94 (Surprise); 98 in B flat; 104 in D (London).

(N) **(*) BMG/RCA Dig. 09026 62549-2 [id.]. Philh. O, Leonard Slatkin.

Symphonies Nos. 96 in D (Miracle);102 in B flat; 103 in E flat (Drum Roll).
(N) **(*) RCA Dig. 09026 68424-2 [id.]. Philh. O, Leonard Slatkin.

Leonard Slatkin's series of Haydn's *London Symphonies* brings fresh, refined readings at speeds that never sound breathless on the fast side. The pity is that the first work on what was the third disc to appear, No. 93, comes in a recording noticeably less full-bodied than the rest, where the quality is generally excellent. The tripping *Allegretto* that Slatkin adopts for the second movement of No. 100 in G brings even more swagger than usual to the military incursions that give the symphony its nickname. But especially when compared with Sir Colin Davis (see below) there is a certain urbane quality about these readings which puts polish and eighteenth-century elegance before an earthier gusto. There is wit from the Philharmonia woodwind and the string phrasing always gives pleasure (especially as Slatkin likes to divide his first and second violins on either side of the stereo spectrum). But Davis finds an added tension, a more searching emotional dimension, especially in No. 98, and this applies to nearly all the later symphonies: No. 104 is a work that can readily sound too easygoing, and with Davis there is more bite. It is worth noting that all twelve of the late Haydn symphonies are included in Sir Colin Davis's Concertgebouw series on a pair of Philips Duos – two CDs for the price of one. So you get three extra symphonies, Nos 94, 97 and 101 as well, for the price of only two of the RCA discs, making a clear first choice among modern-instrument versions of the *London Symphonies*.

Other miscellaneous symphonies

Symphonies Nos. 6 in D (Le Matin); 7 in C (Le Midi); 8 in G (Le Soir).
(N) (B) *** DG Classikon Dig. 459 357-2 [id.]. E. Concert, Pinnock.
(BB) *** Naxos Dig. 8.550722 [id.]. N. CO, Ward.
(M) **(*) Teldec/Warner Dig. 2292 46018-2. VCM, Harnoncourt.

These were almost certainly the first works that Haydn composed on taking up his appointment as Kapellmeister to the Esterházys. Pinnock's performances are polished and refined, yet highly spirited, with infectious allegros and quite generous *espressivo*. There is certainly weight here, yet essentially this is a bracing musical experience, with the genius of these early works fully displayed.

The Northern Chamber Orchestra under Nicholas Ward has wind players who relish their solos, so that the flute chirps merrily and the bassoon immediately has a chance to shine in the Trio of the Minuet of No. 6. In the *Andante* of *Le Soir* the strings create a chamber-music atmosphere, and it is the intimate scale of these performances that is so attractive. Modern instruments are used, but textures are fresh and the ambience of the Concert Hall of New Broadcasting House, Manchester, adds the right degree of warmth.

Harnoncourt is nothing if not dramatic. He opens No. 6 with an impressively controlled crescendo, beginning from an almost inaudible pianissimo, while the opening of the main allegro is characteristically gruff. But this music-making bursts with vitality, and a soothing flute solo soon appears to calm the listener. The very opening of Harnoncourt's slow movement (of No. 6) is austere but the atmosphere lightens, and it is again a flute which gaily introduces the lively finale. So it is throughout, with tuttis edgily bold and with plenty of accents, yet with balancing passages of delicacy. The recording is as vivid as the playing; if Harnoncourt's eccentricities prevent an unreserved period-instrument recommendation, this will be welcomed by his admirers.

(i) *Symphonies Nos. 6 in D (Le Matin); 7 in C (Le Midi); 8 in G (Le Soir); 22 in E flat (Philosopher);* (ii) *26 in D min. (Lamentatione);* (i) *31 in D (Horn signal); 43 in E flat (Mercury); 44 in E min. (Trauer-symphonie); 45 in F sharp min. (Farewell);* (ii) *47 in G (Palindrome);* (i) *48 in C (Maria Theresia); 49 in F min. (La Passione); 53 in D (L'Impériale); 55 in E flat (Schoolmaster); 59 in A (Fire); 60 in C (Il distratto); 63 in C (La Roxelane); 69 in C (Laudon); 73 in D (La Chasse); 82 in C (L'ours); 83 in G min. (La poule); 85 in B flat (La Reine); 92 in G (Oxford); 94 in G (Surprise); 96 in D (Miracle); 100 in G (Military); 101 in D (Clock); 103 in E flat (Drum Roll); 104 in D (London).*
(B) **(*) Ph. Analogue/Dig. 454 335-2 (10) [id.]. (i) ASMF, Marriner; (ii) ECO, Leppard (directed from harpsichord).

This fine collection, recorded between 1968 and 1981, is beautifully transferred to CD and offers Philips's most natural sound-quality. Opening with characterful accounts of the three symphonies Haydn composed not long after taking up his appointment at the Esterházy court in 1761, Marriner and Leppard between them offer consistently elegant performances of 29 'named' symphonies, not all of them well known. Marriner has the lion's share; Leppard, conducting from the harpsichord, is in excellent form in the *Lamentatione* and the so-called *Palindrome*, with its set of slow-movement variations on a pair of invertible themes. Under Marriner the Academy playing is more polished and urbane than in the rival accounts under Dorati. Although ultimately there is an earthier quality in the music than Marriner perceives, these are most enjoyable performances, and they often have a compensating charm which Dorati misses (the *Schoolmaster*, for instance). Nos. 44 and 49 are among the highlights, and here Marriner follows Leppard by featuring a discreet harpsichord continuo. Haydn chose No. 44 for performance at his funeral (hence the title) and Marriner shapes the radiantly elegiac slow movement with much tenderness. The richly expressive string phrasing of the opening *Adagio* of the *Farewell Symphony* is superbly contrasted with the genial and buoyant rhythms of the second-movement Allegro. There is some excellent horn playing in both works. On the other hand the *Horn signal* seems curiously undercharacterized. *Il Distratto* and *La Roxelane* both have theatrical connections, and in the former Dorati's account has the greater sense of theatre, while the Academy orchestral playing is more finished. The 'named' *Paris Symphonies* are distinguished by excellent ensemble and keen articulation; they have a winning charm, yet are lively and musical, again offering a distinct alternative to Dorati. No. 94 has a particularly fine performance of the variations which form the slow movement (the 'surprise' itself most effective) and there is most delightful woodwind detail in No. 96 – the oboe solo in the trio of the Minuet is a joy. The playing in the *Clock* is very spruce and clean, and the atmosphere at the opening of the *Drum Roll* is wonderfully caught. At bargain price the set offers excellent value, and if at times there is just a hint of blandness Marriner has set himself high standards and there is much to admire in each of these performances, which always rise above the routine.

Symphonies Nos. 22 in E flat (Philosopher); 86 in D; 102 in B flat.
*** EMI Dig. CDC5 55509-2. CBSO, Sir Simon Rattle.

More than other Haydn symphony recordings on modern instruments, Rattle establishes a middle path between traditional and period styles of performance. It is also refreshing to have a coupling of symphonies from different periods of Haydn's career. One of the most striking of the early works, the *Philosopher*, with its trudging chorale on two cor anglais, comes with one of the *Paris Symphonies*, No. 86, and one of the final *London* set. If only No. 102 had a nickname, it would be even more widely appreciated as a supreme masterpiece with its exhilarating outer movements and the most beautiful of all Haydn slow movements. Rattle's speeds are on the fast side but not extreme. Only in the final *Presto* of No. 86 does Rattle opt for a hectic speed, making one marvel at the agility of the Birmingham horns in repeated triplets.

Symphonies Nos. 26 in D min. (Lamentatione); 35 in B flat; 38 in C; 39 in G min.; 41 in C; 42 in D; 43 in E flat (Mercury); 44 in E min. (Mourning); 45 in F sharp min. (Farewell); 46 in B; 47 in G; 48 in C (Maria Theresia); 49 in F min. (La Passione); 50 in C; 51 in B flat; 52 in C min.; 58 in F; 59 in A (Fire); 65 in A.
(N) **(*) Ph. Dig. 462 177-2 (5) [id.]. OAE, Franz Brüggen.

With four of the five discs containing four symphonies each instead of the usual two or three, Brüggen offers an attractive package of all the *Sturm und Drang* works, presented in what is deduced as chronological order. It makes an impressive series, with a relatively small group of OAE players crisply responsive, even though Brüggen's preference for minimal vibrato brings much edgy and squeezed violin tone, the more obtrusive with so few instruments. Speeds are impeccably chosen, rarely if ever sounding rushed, with dynamic contrasts dramatically brought out. Aptly the sequence ends with the *Farewell Symphony*. The recordings, made in the Blackheath Concert Halls over a period of nearly three years, are both warm and intimate.

Symphonies Nos. 23 in G; 24 in D; 61 in D.
(BB) *** Naxos Dig. 8.550723 [id.]. N. CO, Nicholas Ward.

The fresh, stylish approach of the Northern Chamber Orchestra is entirely suited to these three symphonies, and here Nicholas Ward makes a persuasive case for the use of modern instruments. No. 24 includes a leading semi-concertante flute part (nicely managed) and the *G major* has a wistful *Andante* for strings alone, and a vital *Presto* finale, well sprinkled with strongly accented quadruplets. The opening movement of No. 61 is obviously more mature and is presented with both character and charm. Excellent recording.

Symphonies Nos. 26 in D min. (Lamentatione); 35 in B flat; 49 in F min. (La Passione).
(BB) **(*) Naxos Dig. 8.550721 [id.]. N. CO, Ward.

Although enjoyable, this disc from Nicholas Ward and his Northern Chamber Orchestra is not quite as fresh-sounding as his first. The playing remains elegant and the horns (in B flat alto) are splendid in the Minuet of No. 35. But the opening *Allegro assai con spirito* of the *Lamentatione* could do with a shade more bite, and in the *Adagio* the warm resonance makes the finely played oboe solo almost a cor anglais and the melodic line like a Handel aria. The opening slow movement of No. 49 is not as intense as it might be, though the *Allegro di molto* which follows has plenty of energy. The resonance of the BBC's Studio 7 in Manchester brings a pleasingly mellow sound-picture, but the string detail is not sharply defined.

Symphonies Nos. 26 (Lamentatione), 35, 38–9, 41–2, 43 (Mercury), 44 (Trauer), 45 (Farewell), 46–7, 48 (Maria Theresia), 49 (La passione), 50–52, 58, 59 (Fire), 65.

(M) *** DG Dig. 435 001-2 (6). E. Concert, Trevor Pinnock.

Pinnock's forces are modest (with 6.5.2.2.1 strings), but the panache of the playing conveys any necessary grandeur. It is a new experience to have Haydn symphonies of this period recorded in relatively dry and close sound, with inner detail crystal clear (harpsichord never obscured) and made the more dramatic by the intimate sense of presence, yet with a fine bloom on the instruments. Some may find a certain lack of charm at times, and others may quarrel with the very brisk one-in-a-bar minuets and even find finales a little rushed.

Symphonies Nos. 26 in D min. (Lamentatione); 52 in C min.; 53 in D (L'Impériale).
(M) *** Virgin Veritas/EMI Dig. VER5 61212-2. La Petite Bande, Sigiswald Kuijken.

These are fresh, vital, cleanly articulated performances which wear their authenticity lightly and even indulge in speeds for slow movements that are more expansive and affectionate than many purists would allow.

Symphonies Nos. 30 in C (Alleluja); 55 in E flat (Schoolmaster); 63 in C (La Roxelane).
(BB) *** Naxos Dig. 8.550757 [id.]. Northern CO, Nicholas Ward.

An entirely winning triptych of named Haydn symphonies, spanning a highly creative period from the three-movement *Alleluja* (1765), with its delightful woodwind contribution in the *Andante*, to *La Roxelane* (1780), where the *Allegretto* paints an engaging portrait of a flirtatious character in a play and the finale fizzes with energy. In between comes *The Schoolmaster*, whose Adagio brings a theme and variations of disarming simplicity. Alert and vivacious playing from all concerned; admirable pacing and first-class sound ensure a welcome for a disc that would be just as recommendable if it cost far more.

Symphonies Nos. 31 in D (Horn signal); 59 in A (Fire); 73 in D (La chasse).
*** Teldec/Warner Dig. 4509 90843-2 [id.]. VCM, Nikolaus Harnoncourt.

This is one of Harnoncourt's very best records. All three symphonies are notable for their spectacular horn parts. The playing here – using natural horns – is superb, with throatily exuberant braying at the opening of the *Horn signal*, an equally striking contribution throughout the *Fire Symphony* (where the horns are crooked in A), and more cheerful hunting-calls in the spirited finale of *La chasse*. The playing is not only extremely vital and polished but even has an element of charm (not something one can always count on from this source). The orchestra communicate their involvement throughout.

Symphonies Nos. 39 in G min.; 70 in D; 73 in D (La Chasse); 75 in D.
❁ (M) *** Van. 08 6152 71. Esterházy O, David Blum.

David Blum pioneered authentic chamber-orchestra performances of the mid-period Haydn symphonies (using modern instruments) in the early 1960s with his aptly named Esterhazy Orchestra, some time before Dorati began his integral Haydn cycle for Decca. There are few CDs which offer first-class accounts of four major Haydn symphonies, so this fine Vanguard reissue makes a splendid reminder of his achievement. His alert stylishness is matched by the warmth of the slow movements, which are beautifully played and are made the expressive centrepiece of each symphony. Blum's gentle pointing of the *Andante* of No. 39, with its striding forward motion, is never too heavy, while the virtuosity in the tremolos and passionate scales of the finale is exhilarating. One could make similar comments about No. 70, and the finale brings a tantalizing, witty introduction, which returns at the close. Throughout all four symphonies Blum takes the Minuets at a spirited tempo, in that way anticipating modern practice. Outstanding among Haydn symphony issues.

Symphonies Nos. 41 in C; 42 in D; 43 in E flat (Mercury).
*** Sony Dig. SK 48370 [id.]. Tafelmusik, Weil.

Symphonies Nos. 44 in E min. (Trauer); 51 in F sharp min.; 52 in C min.
*** Sony Dig. SK 48371 [id.]. Tafelmusik, Weil.

Symphonies Nos. 45 in F sharp min. (Farewell); 46 in B; 47 in G.
*** Sony Dig. SK 53986 [id.]. Tafelmusik, Weil.

Symphonies Nos. 50 in C; 64 in A; 65 in A.
*** Sony Dig. SK 53985 [id.]. Tafelmusik, Weil.

This series from Sony is produced with the estimable H. C. Robbins Landon as musicological and artistic consultant, who has expressed his pleasure in performances which set new standards in this repertoire. The size of the group seems just about ideal with 20 strings, 7.6.3.2.2, against which oboes and horns and sometimes trumpets are vividly balanced. There is no harpsichord continuo. All four of these discs are a great success. Bruno Weil's tempi are apt and Tafelmusik is sensitive to details of phrasing and dynamics and they obviously love Haydn. The effect is admirably spontaneous. The group are very well recorded, too. The sound is full yet admirably transparent. The notes are exemplary and, although competing authentic performances offer different insights, the present series is surpassed by none of them.

Symphonies Nos. 42 in D; 45 in F sharp min. (Farewell); 46 in B.
(M) *** DG (IMS) 447 281-2 [id.]. E. Concert, Pinnock.

Haydn's famous *Farewell Symphony*, given a vibrant and characterful performance with a very beautiful slow movement, is here coupled with two apparently straightforward but still forward-looking works, No. 42 with its memorably solemn *Andantino e cantabile* and *No. 46 in B major*. Here the ethereal 6/8 *Poco Adagio* contrasts with an invigorating scherzando finale where the high horns (crooked in B alto) produce repeated bursts of hair-raising virtuosity. And Haydn has a characteristic trick up his sleeve for, just before the end, the Minuet returns, only to be swept away by a final rally from the horns.

Symphony No. 44 in E min. (Trauer).
(B) *** Carlton Dig. 30367 02372 [(M) id.]. O of St John's, Smith Square, Lubbock – MOZART: *Symphony No. 40.* **(*)

The Orchestra of St John's are on their toes throughout their splendidly committed account of the *Trauersymphonie*. Outer movements are alert and vivacious – the finale has striking buoyancy and spring – and there is some lovely espressivo playing in the beautiful *Adagio* slow movement, which brings out the forward-looking qualities of the writing. The recording too is in the demonstration class.

Symphonies Nos. 44 in E min. (Trauer); 88 in G; 104 in D (London).
(BB) *** Naxos Dig. 8.550287; *4550287* [id.]. Capella Istropolitana, Barry Wordsworth.

Symphonies Nos. 45 in F sharp min. (Farewell); 48 in C (Maria Theresia); 102 in B flat.
(BB) *** Naxos Dig. 8.550382; *4550382* [id.]. Capella Istropolitana, Barry Wordsworth.

Symphonies Nos. 82 in C (The Bear); 96 in D (Miracle); 100 in G (Military).
(BB) *** Naxos Dig. 8.550139; *4550139* [id.]. Capella Istropolitana, Barry Wordsworth.

Symphonies Nos. 83 in G min. (The Hen); 94 in G (Surprise); 101 in D (The Clock).
(BB) *** Naxos Dig. 8.550114; *4550114* [id.]. Capella Istropolitana, Barry Wordsworth.

Symphonies Nos. 85 in B flat (La Reine); 92 in G (Oxford); 103 in E flat (Drum roll).
(BB) *** Naxos Dig. 8.550387 [id.]. Capella Istropolitana, Barry Wordsworth.

Like Barry Wordsworth's recordings of Mozart symphonies, also with the Capella Istropolitana on the Naxos label, this Haydn collection provides a series of outstanding bargains at the lowest budget price. The sound is not quite as clean and immediate as in the Mozart series, a little boomy at times in fact, and Wordsworth's preference for relatively relaxed speeds is a little more marked here than in Mozart, but the varied choice of works on each disc is most attractive. At their modest cost, these are well worth collecting.

Symphonies Nos. (i) *45 in F sharp min. (Farewell);* (ii) *88 in G;* (iii) *104 in D (London).*
(B) *** DG Classikon 439 428-2. (i) ECO, Barenboim; (ii) VPO, Boehm; (iii) LPO, Jochum.

A stimulating triptych of Haydn performances by three different conductors, all of whom have something positive to say about this repertoire. Barenboim's *Farewell Symphony* has much vitality and there is sensitive playing in the remarkable *Adagio*, one of Haydn's finest. Boehm and the VPO are at their very best in No. 88, with the slow movement gravely expansive. The playing has great polish and refinement, and Boehm's touch instantly charms in the spirited finale. Jochum's is among the most musically satisfying accounts of No. 104 in the catalogue; and all three recordings (from the 1970s) sound first class in their remastered form. A genuine bargain, playing for 77 minutes.

Symphonies Nos. 54 in G; 56 in C; 57 in D.
(BB) *** Naxos Dig. 8.554108 [id.]. Cologne CO, Müller-Brühl.

In vivid, full-ranging recordings made by German Radio, Müller-Brühl conducts lively performances with his excellent chamber orchestra of three symphonies from around 1774. Unlike the *Sturm und Drang* symphonies of the years immediately preceding, these present few problems, with winningly fresh and vigorous outer movements. Müller-Brühl, using modern instruments, yet reflects period practice in asking for very limited vibrato and light articulation from the strings.

Symphonies Nos. 69 in C (Laudon); 89 in F; 91 in E flat.
(BB) **(*) Naxos Dig. 8.550769 [id.]. Budapest Nicolaus Esterházy Sinfonia, Béla Drahos.

The resonance of the Reformed Church, Budapest, prevents the sharpest definition here. The orchestra is set back and the internal balance is natural: the strings have bloom without edginess. This is alert, thoroughly musical playing with apt tempi. The *Andante con moto* of No. 89 is elegantly done, and the variations of the *Andante* of No. 91 are neatly handled (with an elegant bassoon solo). All in all this gives pleasure, but more brightness on top would have been welcome.

Symphonies Nos. 72 in D; 93 in D; 95 in C min.
(BB) *** Naxos 8.550797 [id.]. Nicolaus Esterházy Sinfonia, Béla Drahos.

These performances are polished, warm and spirited and, if the Naxos recording is on the reverberant side, it does not cloud textures. Four horns are featured prominently in No. 72 and provide many bravura flourishes and virtuoso scales in the opening movement; the playing here is first class. This engaging work is fully worthy to stand alongside its mature companions when played as seductively as this. The orchestral response is equally impressive in the fine slow movements of these later works, and throughout Béla Drahos's pacing is matched by the overall sense of spontaneity and style.

Symphonies Nos. 74 in E flat; 75 in D; 76 in E flat.
(BB) *** Naxos Dig. 8.554109 [id.]. Cologne CO, Müller-Brühl.

As in the other Haydn issues from this fine chamber orchestra, the recorded sound, engineered by German Radio, is full and vivid, both immediate and with fine bloom. The three symphonies, dating from the early 1780s, make an attractive group, characteristically lively in outer movements but each with slow movements involving the use of mysterious muted strings. Müller-Brühl, as in his other Haydn recordings, favours broad Adagios and Minuets that retain the idea of a stately dance. Yet the freshness and rhythmic resilience never fail to bring the performances to life. Like its companions, an excellent recommendation.

Symphonies Nos. 77 in B flat; 78 in C min.; 79 in F.
(N) (BB) *** Naxos Dig. 8.553363 [id.]. Northern CO, Nicholas Ward.

For these three little-known but most engaging symphonies, written in 1782–3, Naxos turn back to the Northern Chamber Orchestra, under Nicholas Ward, who could hardly be more persuasive. The colourful charm of Haydn's scoring in the *B flat Symphony* is most sensitively caught, the *Vivace* opening of *No. 78 in C minor* is highly dramatic, while both slow movements are eminently graceful. The Minuets, though not rushed, are suitably spirited and finales are deft and lively, especially the winning monothematic *Presto* of the *C minor* work, which includes some of the composer's genial pauses. In short these chamber-style performances, using modern instruments, are very enjoyable indeed, and they are most beautifully recorded.

Symphonies Nos. 80 in D min.; 81 in G; 99 in E flat.
(BB) *** Naxos Dig. 8.554110 [id.]. Cologne CO, Müller-Brühl.

Müller-Brühl, with his excellent chamber orchestra brilliantly recorded by German Radio, here couples two symphonies of 1783–4 with the first of the masterpieces which Haydn wrote for Salomon for the second of his two visits to London. No. 80 is remarkable for the dark intensity of the minor-key opening with its dramatic use of tremolo. Chromatic touches break in later too. In these later symphonies, unlike the earlier ones, Müller-Brühl does allow Minuets to acquire a hint of the Scherzo at brisker speeds. No. 99 is remarkable for Haydn's inclusion for the first time in a symphony of a pair of clarinets. Even in this more ambitious symphony the chamber scale brings out the grandeur of the inspiration.

Symphonies Nos. 80 in D min.; 87 in A; 89 in F.
(BB) *** ASV Quicksilva Dig. CDQS 6156 [(M) id.]. LMP, Jane Glover.

Jane Glover conducts the London Mozart Players in strong and energetic performances of these three relatively rare symphonies. No. 87 is the least known of the *Paris symphonies*; but all three of these works show Haydn at his most inventive. *No. 80 in D minor* begins as though it were a throwback to the *Sturm und Drang* period, but then at the end of the exposition Haydn gives a winning smile. No. 89 ends with a dance movement which contains delectable *strascinando* (dragging) passages. Though textures are not as transparent as we are beginning to demand in an age of period performance – largely a question of the ambient recorded sound – these modern-instrument performances are both winning and lively.

Symphonies Nos. 82–87 (Paris); 93–104 (London Symphonies).
(B) **(*) Sony SX7K 64202 (7). NYPO, Leonard Bernstein.

Bernstein obviously enjoys the music, and the playing of the New York Philharmonic is very alive. The rhythmic jokiness of the finale of *The Bear* is attractively managed and the witty string writing in the first movement, which led to the christening of No. 83 as *The Hen*, is nicely pointed. The account of *No. 84 in E flat* is particularly impressive. The recordings were made in the Manhattan Center or Avery Fisher Hall between 1962 and 1967, and the CD transfers bring rather shrill violins, which at times make the allegros sound fierce.

Bernstein offers comparably large-scale performances of the *London Symphonies*, mainly recorded between 1970 and 1975. The sound is full but again with some fierceness on the violins. The performances show Bernstein's warmth and the spirited NYPO response to the conductor's often grand manner. But while there are many fine individual moments, like the *Andante* of No. 96 or the *vivace* finale of No. 99, often the phrasing is rather heavily expressive, and this especially applies to the Minuets. The last five symphonies are among the most successful, particularly the *Drum roll*, with slow movements always individual. The *Andante* of *The Clock* is particularly engaging, and the *Allegretto* of the *Military* brings spectacular percussion. No. 104 was the earliest to be recorded (in 1958) and sounds thinner than the others. Music-making full of personality and always committed.

(Paris) Symphonies Nos. 82 in C (The Bear); 83 in G min. (The Hen); 84 in E flat.
✪ *** Virgin/EMI Dig. VC7 59537-2. O of Age of Enlightenment, Kuijken.
*** Sony Dig. SK 66295 [id.]. Tafelmusik, Bruno Weil.

(Paris) Symphonies Nos. 85 in B flat (La Reine); 86 in D; 87 in A.
✪ *** Virgin/EMI Dig. VC7 59557-2. O of Age of Enlightenment, Kuijken.
*** Sony Dig. SK 66296 [id.]. Tafelmusik, Bruno Weil.

Symphonies Nos. 82 in C (The Bear); 83 in G min. (The Hen); 84 in E flat; 85 in B flat (La Reine); 86 in D; 87 in A (Paris Symphonies).
(B) *** Decca Double 448 194-2 (2) [id.]. Philharmonia Hungarica, Antal Dorati.
(B) *** Ph. Duo 438 727-2 (2) [id.]. ASMF, Sir Neville Marriner.
(B) **(*) RCA Twofer 74321 34169-2 (2) [id.]. BSO, Kurt Sanderling.

Kuijken's two Virgin discs present an outstanding set of Haydn's six *Paris Symphonies*, between them offering some of the most enjoyable period performances of Haydn ever. The players of the OAE wear their authenticity lightly, and often allow themselves spacious speeds in slow movements. Textures are airily transparent, yet there is a warm bloom on the sound. Above all Kuijken conveys the full joy of Haydn's inspiration in every movement.

However, notwithstanding their excellence, the newer Sony Tafelmusik recordings also continue to set new standards in this repertoire. The texture is at once full, yet hardly less transparent than on Virgin, and detail is exceptionally vivid. The performances are brim full of character, pacing is rhythmically energetic, and finales have irrepressible spirit without being rushed.

Dorati's set of *Paris Symphonies* makes a fine Double Decca bargain. These performances are well up to the high standard of his integral Haydn series, freshly stylish performances with plenty of vigour. The sinewy strength of the G minor opening of No. 83 for a moment brings a hint of *Sturm und Drang*, then yields its surprise as it gives way to the clucking of its titular *Hen*, while the variations which form its slow movement are matched in charm by those based on the French folksong ('*La gentille et jeune Lisette*') which make up the *Romance: Allegretto* of No. 85. No. 84 has a first movement of the most delicate fantasy, while No. 87, after its sublime *Adagio*, ends in a mood of lithe high spirits. The only point of controversy here is Dorati's consistently slow tempi for the Minuets, nicely pointed as they are.

From Marriner, spirited and well-played accounts of the *Paris Symphonies*, distinguished by excellent ensemble and keen articulation. Nos. 86 and 87 (and perhaps 84) are digital recordings, the remainder being analogue, though this is not indicated in the documentation. The playing has that touch of charm which is so essential in Haydn. It is possible to imagine performances of greater character and personality than these (in the slow movements there is a tendency to blandness) but they are lively and musical and a good alternative to the Dorati recordings, economically priced.

Kurt Sanderling's account of the *Paris symphonies* with the Berlin orchestra are straightforward and unfussy, belonging to the big-band type which has gone out of fashion in recent years, at times with measured tempi. They were recorded in 1972 and sound very good, with plenty of warmth and body to commend them. The East Berlin orchestra is first class.

Symphonies Nos. 83 in G min. (The Hen); 84 in E flat; 88 in G.
(N) (BB) *** ASV Quicksilva Dig. CDQS 6167 [id.]. L. Mozart Players, Jane Glover.

A very winning companion for Jane Glover's earlier Haydn triptych – see above. Once again there is a lesser-known symphony, No. 84, with its shapely Theme and Variations slow movement (elegantly played here), alongside two favourites. Jane Glover neatly enunciates the 'clucking' second subject which gives No. 83 its nickname, and finds a warm serenity for the noble slow movement of No. 88. Outer movements are as lively as you could wish and the recording is excellent. A genuine bargain.

Symphonies Nos. 83 in G min. (La Poule); 88 in G; 96 in D (Miracle).
(***) Dutton mono CDSJB 1003 [id.]. Hallé O, Sir John Barbirolli.

Barbirolli's recording of No. 83 (*The Hen*), made in 1949, was the very first in the catalogue, originally appearing on three 78-r.p.m. records. Characteristically, he gives it an energetic reading full of fun and high dramatic contrasts. So the clucking of the second subject has rarely been pointed with more wit. By latter-day standards this is a rugged rather than an elegant performance, but the magnetism and vigour are irresistible. No. 96, with which *The Hen* was originally coupled on LP, has freer, more open sound. The playing is a degree more polished and elegant, with no diminution of energy or wit, and again the flute and oboe emerge as stars in the Hallé team. No. 88 was recorded in 1953 but was never issued, maybe for lack of a coupling. He sustains the great melody of the *Largo* at a slow speed with elegance as well as warmth, and the fun of the finale is delightfully caught.

Symphony No. 88 in G.
✪ (M) (***) DG mono 447 439-2 [id.]. BPO, Furtwängler – SCHUBERT: *Symphony No. 9.* (***)

Even those who usually find Furtwängler's interpretations too idiosyncratic will be drawn to this glowing performance. The beauty of his shaping of the main theme of the slow movement is totally disarming, and the detail of the finale, lightly sprung and vivacious, is a constant pleasure. The Berlin Philharmonic plays marvellously well for him, and the 1951 recording in its remastered form sounds admirably fresh, yet has plenty of body. Here it is coupled with Schubert's *Ninth Symphony*, an ideal candidate for reissue in DG's 'Originals' series of legendary recordings.

Symphonies Nos. 88 in G; 89 in F; 90 in G.
*** Sony Dig. SK 66253-2 [id.]. Tafelmusik, Weil.

Continuing on after the *Paris Symphonies*, Bruno Weil and Tafelmusik offer here another stimulating triptych from 1787/8. The first movement of No. 88 is not rushed and the noble tune of the slow movement is unerringly paced, so that the energetic Minuet with its robust drone trio is the more telling, and the finale sparkles. No 89 in F is particularly winning, with vivacious outer movements and plenty of charm in the *Andante*. For all the strength and vigour of these performances Weil never misses the touches of humour and the joke false ending of the G major work, and its continuation after four bars of silence, is neatly managed.

Symphonies Nos. 88 in G; 89 in F; 90 in C; 91 in E flat; 92 in G (Oxford).
(N) (BB) ** Virgin Classics Dig. Double VBD5 61567-2 (2) [id.]. La Petite Bande, Kuijken.

Kuijken's performances of this nicely balanced group of key Haydn symphonies have many of the qualities that made his set of the *Paris Symphonies* also on Virgin (see above) so winning. Yet with a gap of two years, and a change of orchestra to La Petite Bande, come differences which weigh significantly against this reissue. For these rather later symphonies, Kuijken has abandoned the use of harpsichord continuo, and his preference for very measured speeds in slow movements leads him to at least one serious miscalculation. At a funereal pace he makes the heavenly *Largo* of No. 88 far too heavy, seriously holding up the flow of the great melody with over-emphasis and exaggerated pauses. The sound is warm and well balanced, though violins could be better defined in tuttis; but overall this is something of a disappointment when compared with Kuijken's earlier achievement.

Symphonies Nos. 88 in G; 92 in G (Oxford); 94 in G (Surprise).
(M) **(*) DG (IMS) Dig. 445 554-2. VPO, Bernstein.

All three G major symphonies emanate from concerts at the Musikvereinsaal in the mid-1980s, using the full strings of the Vienna Philharmonic and given a richly upholstered recording. For all his idiosyncrasies, Bernstein is never more winning than in Haydn, with a romantic, beautiful account of the *Largo* of No. 88. The slow movement of the *Surprise* is also taken relaxedly, and the speed of the finale is challengingly fast. Good sound.

Symphonies Nos. 88 in G; 104 in D (London).
*** CRD CRD 3370; *CRDC 4070* [id.].
Bournemouth Sinf., Ronald Thomas.

With an orchestra on a chamber scale, the playing has great freshness and vitality; indeed it is the urgency of musical feeling that Ronald Thomas conveys which makes up for the last ounce of finesse.

Symphony No. 92 in G (Oxford).
(M) (***) Dutton Lab. mono CDEA 5003 [id.] Paris Conservatoire O, Walter – SCHUBERT: *Symphony No. 9.* (***)

Only three months after the Anschluss, Bruno Walter made this Haydn recording in Paris, where he had taken refuge with the Paris Conservatoire Orchestra. These magnetic performances have one marvelling at the whirlwind energy and resilience of allegros in both the Schubert and the Haydn symphonies. Even Walter's broad tempos and expressive phrasing in slow movements are firmly controlled. Despite one or two blips, Dutton's transfer, coupled with the classic account of the *Great C major Symphony* of Schubert (made in London later the same year), is infinitely superior in terms of focus, body and smoothness to the Canadian alternative, which is coupled with Berlioz's *Symphonie fantastique*.

Symphonies Nos. 92 in G (Oxford); 104 in D (London).
(B) *** Carlton IMP Classics Dig. 30367 0035-2 [(M) id.]. E. Sinfonia, Groves.
(M) (***) DG mono 457 720-2 [id.]. BPO, Hans Rosbaud – MOZART: *Violin concerto No. 4.* (***)

Sir Charles Groves's performances are robust yet elegant as well; both slow movements are beautifully shaped, with Haydn's characteristic contrasts unfolding spontaneously. In the last movement of the *Oxford*, the dancing violins are a special delight in what is one of the composer's most infectious finales.

Hans Rosbaud is heard at his finest here, particularly in the beautifully shaped *Andante* of the *London Symphony*. Throughout, the playing of the Berlin Philharmonic has remarkable finesse and polish, and they are again at their most winning in both the Minuet of the *Oxford Symphony* and its sparkling finale. Rosbaud's tempi never languish, and the recording, clear and fresh, is impressively remastered.

Symphonies Nos. 93 in D; 94 in G (Surprise); 97 in C; 99 in E flat; 100 in G (Military); 101 in D (Clock) (London Symphonies).
✿ (B) *** Ph. Duo Analogue/Dig. 442 614-2 (2). Concg. O, Sir Colin Davis.

Symphonies Nos. 95 in C min.; 96 in D (Miracle); 98 in B flat; 102 in B flat; 103 in E flat (Drum Roll); 104 in D (London) (London Symphonies).
✿ (B) *** Ph. Duo Analogue/Dig. 442 611-2 (2). Concg. O, Sir Colin Davis.

Symphonies Nos. 93 in D; 94 in G (Surprise); 97 in C; 100 in G (Military); 103 in E flat (Drum Roll); 104 in D (London).
(B) *** Decca Double 452 256-2 (2) [(M) id. import]. Philharmonia Hungarica, Antal Dorati.

Symphonies Nos. 94 in G (Surprise); 100 in G (Military); 104 in D (London).
(N) (M) *** Penguin Classics Decca 460 628-2 [id.]. Philharmonia Hungarica, Dorati.

Symphonies Nos. 95 in C min.; 96 in D (Miracle); 98 in B flat; 99 in E flat; 101 in D (Clock); 102 in B flat.
(B) *** Decca Double 452 259-2 (2) [(M) id. import]. Philharmonia Hungarica, Antal Dorati.

Symphonies Nos. 93–104.
(M) *** DG 437 201-2 (4) [id.]. LPO, Jochum.

Sir Colin Davis's Haydn series (recorded between 1975 and 1981) is one of the most distinguished sets he has given us over his long recording career, and its blend of brilliance and sensitivity, wit and humanity gives these two-for-the-price-of-one Duo reissues a special claim on the collector. There is no trace of routine in this music-making and no failure of imagination. The excellence of the playing is matched by Philips's best recording quality, whether analogue or digital. The Concertgebouw sound is resonant and at times weighty but has good definition. The *Allegretto* of the *Military Symphony* is properly grand and expansive, balanced by vital, sparkling outer movements. Excellent notes from Robin Golding. A bargain in every sense of the word.

Dorati and the Philharmonia Hungarica, working in comparative isolation in Marl in Germany, carried through their monumental project of recording all the Haydn symphonies with consistent zeal and dedication. These final masterpieces are performed with a glowing sense of commitment; and Dorati, doubtless taking his cue from the editor, H. C. Robbins Landon, generally chooses rather relaxed tempi for the first movements – as in No. 93, which is just as deliciously lilting as in Szell's masterly version (SBK 67175 – see below). In slow movements his tempi are on the fast side, but only in No. 94, the *Surprise*, is the result controversial. Though an extra desk of strings has been added to each section, the results are authentically in scale, with individual solos emerging unforcedly against the glowing acoustic, and with intimacy comes extra dramatic force in sforzandos. A magnificent conclusion to a magnificent project and all the more desirable, now that this series is being economically reissued in Duo format. There is adequate new documentation by Lindsay Kemp.

The Penguin Classics disc joins the *Surprise*, with its briskly paced slow movement, with two of the most popular named London Symphonies, which are equally finely played and recorded. The personal comments about the music are from Bamber Gascoigne.

Jochum secures fine, stylish playing from the LPO, challenging them with often very fast tempi in outer movements. Those fast tempi sometimes prevent the music from having quite the lilt it has with Beecham or the gravitas of Sir Colin Davis; but the athletic exuberance of Jochum in Haydn, his ability to mould slow movements with tenderness that never spills over into unstylish mannerism (and to handle the sets of themes and variations to bring great diversity of atmosphere and mood), makes these wonderfully satisfying readings of Haydn's greatest symphonies. In the finale of No. 98 Jochum adds a harpsichord to the texture so that Haydn's charming little joke at the end can make its point all the better. The recording is naturally balanced and clear, with its warm reverberation presenting these works on a somewhat bigger scale, yet with rather less weight than Davis brings.

Symphonies Nos. 93 in D; 95 in C min.; 97 in C (London Symphonies).
(B) *** Sony SBK 67175 [id.]. Cleveland O, George Szell.

With superb polish in the playing and precise phrasing it would be easy for performances such as these to sound superficial, but Haydn's music obviously struck a deep chord in Szell's sensibility and there is humanity underlying the technical perfection. Indeed there are many little musical touches from Szell to show that his perfectionist approach is a dedicated and affectionate one. There is also the most delectable pointing and a fine judgement of the inner balance. The recordings have been splendidly remastered and the sound is fuller and firmer than it ever was on LP. A highly recommendable reissue.

Symphonies Nos. 94 in G (Surprise); 101 in D (Clock).
(M) *** Decca 452 893-2 [id.]. VPO, Pierre Monteux – BRAHMS: *Variations on a theme of Haydn.* ***
**(*) HM/BMG Dig. 05472 77351-2 [id.]. La Petite Bande, Sigiswald Kuijken.

A captivating pair of performances from Monteux. Both he and the VPO are on top form and there are no more wittily enjoyable performances of these two symphonies in the catalogue. Monteux turns a genial eye on a genial composer and secures very polished playing throughout, with many a turn of phrase to delight the ear. The recordings still sound remarkably fine, well worth including in Decca's Classic Sound series. The exciting account of the Brahms coupling makes this disc doubly attractive.

Kuijken is in fine form for this coupling of two of the *London Symphonies*. The *Andante* of the *Clock* is ideally paced, and indeed tempi throughout are apt, with allegros full of life, especially the exuberant finale of No. 102. Here the *Adagio* is presented thoughtfully and with a slight degree of detachment but remains pleasingly spontaneous. Excellent recording, but the 53 minutes' content is ungenerous.

Symphonies Nos. 96 in D (Miracle); 97 in C; 98 in B flat; 99 in E flat.

(B) **(*)Teldec/Warner Ultima Dig. 3484 21337-2 (2) [(M) id. import]. Concg. O, Harnoncourt.

Harnoncourt is nothing if not wide-ranging in his Haydn interpretations; the vigorous and polished Concertgebouw playing, with hard-driven allegros and contrasting moments of great delicacy, is certainly never dull. If one accepts the gruffness of manner, the fierce accenting and the weight of the orchestral tuttis, the *Miracle* is an impressive reading, with the secondary theme of the opening movement elegant enough, and No. 97 is similarly compelling. The recording is first class throughout.

Symphonies Nos. 96 in D (Miracle); 100 in G (Military); 103 in E flat (Drum roll).

(B) *** [EMI Red Line Dig. CDR5 69810]. ECO, Tate.

Consistently Tate chooses speeds that allow the wit and sparkle of Haydn's writing to come out naturally, as in the second subject of the *Military* or in the joyful lilt of the 6/8 rhythms of the first-movement allegro in the *Drum roll*. Tate's speeds bring out Haydn's humour far more than anything faster and fiercer would do. And always, with his slow speeds, crisp articulation ensures that the music sounds light and springy, never too heavy. Warm, well-balanced sound. A most attractive triptych.

Symphony No. 97 in C.

(B) (***) Dutton Lab. mono CDLX 7019 [id. full price]. LPO, Beecham – MOZART: *Piano concerto No. 12* etc. (***)

This Haydn symphony was one of the very first recordings that Beecham made in 1944 after his wartime return from the United States. The characteristic point and elegance reflect the delight of everyone at the reunion, giving little idea of the frustrations that Beecham was beginning to feel over working with an orchestra by then self-governing. The performance is sparkling in the outer movements (the bassoon clearly audible against the strings in the finale), with a slow, moulded *Andante* and a bold Minuet marked by high contrasts. Beecham was later to record the same symphony with the RPO with the benefit of stereo, though the Dutton transfer is excellent, making this a valuable supplement to the Mozart items on the disc.

Symphonies Nos. 97 in C; 98 in B flat; 99 in E flat.

(N) *** Sony MHK 62979 [id.]. Cleveland O, George Szell.

This is one of George Szell's very finest records, perhaps even finer than the later triptych of Nos. 93, 95 and 97 (see above). It is fully worthy of reissue in Sony's (comparatively expensive) Heritage series, with 97 and 99 – recorded in 1957 – appearing in stereo for the first time. The remastering is superb: this is demonstration Cleveland quality, full and glowing, with splendid inner detail. The performances have great strength without heaviness, with Szell clearly anticipating Beethoven, yet never missing Haydn's geniality and touches of wit. The slow movements of all three symphonies have heart-warming beauty of line: Szell's dedication comes over in every bar and especially so in the *Adagio* of No. 98. Minuets are sturdy but are given fine rhythmic lift. The consistently deft Cleveland playing brings finales which fizz with energy yet have some of the weight of early Beethoven.

Symphony No. 98 in B flat.

(N) (M) ** EMI CDM5 67032-2. Philh. O, Klemperer – TCHAIKOVSKY: *Symphony No. 5.* **(*)

Symphony No. 101 in D (Clock).

(N) (M) ** EMI CDM5 67033-2. Philh. O, Klemperer – DVORAK: *Symphony No. 9.* **

Klemperer is not the first conductor one thinks of in relation to Haydn, and his approach is characteristically broad and measured. Although he shows his mastery in structuring and rhythmic pointing, these readings (for all their integrity) could not be further removed from modern rethinking about the way this music should be performed.

Symphonies Nos. 101 in D (Clock); 102 in B flat; 103 in E flat (Drum Roll); 104 in D (London).

(B) *(**) Teldec/Warner Ultima Dig. 0630 18953-2 (2) [(M) id. import]. Concg. O, Harnoncourt.

As these recordings of Haydn's last four symphonies readily demonstrate, Harnoncourt can at times be an exasperatingly unpredictable conductor. These performances with the Concertebouw Orchestra, recorded in 1987–8, bring a curious stylistic mixture and bizarre eccentricities. In period-performance manner, first movements are fierce and emphatic and slow movements are clipped and short-winded (disastrously so in the glorious *Adagio* of No. 102). But there are occasional lapses into a smooth, modern manner. This is powerfully persuasive music-making, very well played and impressively recorded.

Symphonies Nos. 103 in E flat; 104 in D.
(N) *** HM/BMG Dig. 05472 77362-2 [id.]. La Petite Bande, Sigiswald Kuijken.

La Petite Bande are fully back on form in this highly stimulating coupling of Haydn's last two *London symphonies*. After an arresting opening, the *Drum Roll* has a delightfully frisky opening *Allegro*, with delectably nimble oboe-playing at the second subject yet in no way lacking rhythmic weight. The *Andante* brings an appealing gravity, and after a dynamic Minuet the even more vigorous finale is played with winning dynamic subtlety. No. 104, too, opens very dramatically. It is a work which in its ready tunefulness can easily sound bland – but not here. The song-like slow movement brings a touching, ethereal delicacy from the strings, echoed later by the woodwind, so that the first *fortissimo* creates a true burst of passion, more dramatic than Haydn's more famous 'Surprise'. After the jolly, swinging Minuet, the finale, for all its geniality, makes a brilliantly compelling conclusion, the closing bars given a superb sense of finality. The orchestral sound is full, yet clean and fresh, with the powerful impact of the timpani never made over-resonant.

CHAMBER MUSIC

Cassations (Divertimenti): in G, Hob II/1; in G, Hob II/G1; in C (Birthday), Hob II/11; in F, Hob II/20.
(M) **(*) Virgin Veritas/EMI Dig. VER5 61163-2. Linde Consort, Hans-Martin Linde.

Haydn's *Cassations* and *Divertimenti* have not the finesse of the best works of Mozart, but they have plenty of imaginative touches, particularly in their instrumentation. Two of those offered here are fairly ambitious (Hob II, Nos. G1 and 20), scored for a nonet (including a pair each of oboes and horns); the remaining two, written around 1765, are scored for a sextet (including flute and oboe), often used with charm and effectively demonstrating the special timbres of the early instruments played here. Overall the performances have plenty of character. The recording, made in a fairly reverberant acoustic, has a quite large-scale effect.

Divertimenti Nos. 1–12, Hob III/1–4; Hob II/6; Hob III/6–12.
(BB) *** Arte Nova Dig. 74321 31682-2 (4). Hamburg Soloists, Emil Klein.

These string *Divertimenti* (given that name by Haydn himself) are in fact his earliest string quartets (including Op. 1 and Op. 2). Legend has it that Haydn informed his publisher that he wished the term 'string quartet' to be used only from No. 19 (Op. 9) onwards, in which he finally established a four-movement format. The present works are all symmetrically structured in five movements. Each is framed by two outer *Prestos* within which there is an inner frame of two Minuets and at the centre an *Adagio*, the musical heart of each work, almost always containing the finest music. The other movements are well crafted but relatively conventional, although every so often there is something to catch the ear, for instance the hunting style of the opening movement of the very first work (which recurs in No. 6). Inexpensive, with excellent recording.

Flute trios for 2 flutes and cello (bassoon) Nos. 1–4 (London), Hob IV/1–4; Duo for 2 flutes (arr. of *String quartet in D, Op. 76/5*); *Echo for 2 flutes* (arr. of *Divertimento for 2 string trios in E flat*).
**(*) Sony Dig. SK 48061 [id.]. Rampal, Schulz, Audin.

(i) *Flute trios for 2 flutes & cello Nos. 1–4 (London), Hob IV/1–4;* (ii) *Flute quartets, Op. 5, Nos. 1 in D, Hob II/D9; 2 in G, Hob II/G4; 3 in D, Hob II/D10; 4 in G, Hob II/1; 5 in D, Hob II/D11; 6 in C, Hob II/11.*
*** Accent Dig. ACC 9283/4 (2) [id.]. (i) Bernard Kuijken, Mark Hantaï, Wieland Kuijken; (ii) Bernard, Siegfried & Wieland Kuijken, François Fernandez.

The *London Trios* date from 1794 during Haydn's visit to England and the first two include variations on the song, '*Trust not too much*'. They are delightful works and receive felicitous performances from this authentic group on Accent who make the most winning sounds. The *Flute quartets*, Op. 5, in the view of H. C. Robbins Landon may not all be by Haydn. It seems fairly certain, however, that the first two, also known as *Divertimenti*, are authentic, very early works from the 1750s. All the music is engaging when played with such finesse and warmth, although this is a set to be dipped into rather than taken in large doses. The recording is admirably fresh and realistic.

The arrangement of the *String quartet*, Op. 76/5, for two flutes was the work of a London musician, Samuel Arnold. This is essentially for collectors with a very sweet musical tooth indeed, although undoubtedly the *Presto* finale heard by itself is captivating. On Sony come equally fine performances and excellent recording.

8 Notturni for the King of Naples, Hob II/25–32 (originally for lira organizzata, woodwind, horn and strings, arranged by Haydn for instrumental ensemble).
(N) *** Sony Dig. SK 62878 [id.]. Mozzafiato & L'Archibudello.

(N) (B) *(*) Decca Double 458 075-2 (2) [id.]. Music Party, Alan Hacker.

These eight divertimenti, in three or four movements (although No. 6 has only two), were commissioned by King Ferdinand IV of Naples and written for the lira organizzata. Or rather a pair of them, for the King played in duet with his friend Norbert Hadrava, an Austrian diplomat. The lira comprised a keyboard and a revolving wheel and was really a modified hurdy-gurdy. It seems a pity that someone could not have managed a reconstruction of this seemingly fascinating instrument. Haydn's original scoring was for two lire, two horns, two clarinets (or later, violins), two violas, and cello (later with double bass added). He thought sufficiently well of the works and brought them to London with him to play at the Salomon Concerts in 1791, with the lira parts given to flutes, or flute and oboe, and the clarinet parts for practical reasons allotted to violins, which also have independent solo roles in Nos. 7 and 8. This is the nearest Haydn came to writing wind divertimenti of the calibre of those by Mozart, and although this music is slight, it has much charm with particularly sprightly finales, including a jolly fugue for No. 5. (The last movement of No. 6 is lost, although the engaging *Andante* makes up for it.) No. 8 with a slow introduction before the first movement *Allegro* is like a miniature symphony without a minuet, and H. C. Robbins Landon has declared the touching *Adagio* as being the greatest single movement of the whole set. It is eloquently played here and these fresh, dedicated performances by the combined period instrument groups, Mozzafiato (woodwind, horns and double bass) and L'Archibudelli, are very winning, with the clarinet parts restored. They are beautifully recorded.

The competing performances by Alan Hacker's Music Party stretch to a pair of discs (though costing approximately the same) but fail to take off in the same way; they are not helped by a resonant acoustic which slightly deadens the focus. Only the finales are really vivacious.

Piano trios Nos. 1–46, Hob XV:1–41; Hob XIV:C1 in C; Hob XV:C1 in C; Hob XIV6/ XVI6 in G; Hob XV:fl in F min.; Hob deest in D (complete).

❁ (B) *** Ph. 454 098-2 (9) [id.]. Beaux Arts Trio.

It is not often possible to hail one set of records as a 'classic' in quite the way that Schnabel's Beethoven sonatas can be so described. Yet this set can be described in those terms, for the playing of the Beaux Arts Trio is of the very highest musical distinction. The contribution of the pianist, Menahem Pressler, is inspired, and the recorded sound on CD is astonishingly lifelike. The CD transfer has enhanced detail without losing the warmth of ambience or sense of intimacy. Now offered in a bargain box of nine CDs, this is a set no Haydn lover should miss: it is desert island music.

Piano trios, Hob XV, Nos. 24–27.

(B) *** Ph. 422 831-2 [(M) id.]. Beaux Arts Trio.

These are all splendid works. No. 25 with its *Gypsy rondos* is the most famous, but each has a character of its own, showing the mature Haydn working at full stretch. The playing here is peerless and the recording truthful and refined.

Piano trios in A, Hob. XV18; Nos. 38 in D; 39 in G (Gypsy), Hob XV24–25; in E flat, Hob XV29.

(N) *** Nimbus Dig. NI 5535 [id.]. Vienna Piano Trio.

Piano trios in A, Hob XV 18; in C, Hob XV 21; Nos. 39 in G (Gypsy), HobXV 25; in E flat, Hob XV 29.

(N) *** Teldec/Warner 0630 15857-2. Trio Fontenay.

There is little to choose here between the Nimbus and Teldec performances: both are polished, warm and spirited, and both are beautifully recorded. Each collection is delightful, and both discs include the best-known *Gypsy Trio* with its sparkling closing rondo. It has to be said, too, that a modern piano adds much colour to these works, which are for the most part light-hearted, and even more in gentle, expressive moments like the finale of the *D major Trio*, which is marked *Allegro, ma dolce*, to which Stefan Mendl, the fine pianist in the Vienna Trio, makes an appropriate response. Yet his colleague in the Fontenay group, Wolf Harden, is an equally fine ensemble player.

Piano trios No. 38 in D; 39 in G (Gypsy); 40 in F sharp min., Hob. XV 24–26.

(N) **(*) HM Dig. HMC 901514 [id.]. Patrick Cohen, Erich Höbarth, Christopher Coin.

The Cohen Trio are in good form here and for those wanting period instrument performances their playing is pleasingly musical and the recording well balanced. However they only provide three works, which is short measure (47 minutes).

Piano trios Nos. 42 in E flat, Hob XV/30; 43 in C, Hob XV/27; 44 in E, Hob XV/28; 45 in E flat, Hob XV/29.

❁ *** Sony Dig. SK 53120 [id.]. Vera Beths, Anner Bylsma, Robert Levin.

Piano trios Nos. 43–45.

(B) **(*) HM HMC Dig. 901572 [id.]. Patrick Cohen, Erich Höbarth, Christophe Coin.

Outstanding performances in every way. This Sony group plays with immense flair and spirit and conveys the exhilaration of the finale of the *C major Trio* (No. 43, Hob. XV/27) superbly well and the depth and poetry of the middle movements. Infectious in its high spirits and delight in music-making, and very well recorded! It is good to have modern digital alternatives to the justly famous Beaux Arts versions. Strongly recommended.

The Cohen Trio are not quite so successful in Haydn as they were in early Beethoven but their playing is still refreshing. In the *C major Trio* there are a few over-strong accents and an occasional touch of abrasiveness, brought by the close microphones. The players capture the *innocentement* of the *Andantino* and are at their finest in the robust vigour of the rustic dance which ends the piece boisterously. However, the competing Sony disc offers an extra work and makes an obvious first choice.

String quartets

String quartets Nos. 1–12; 19–83; String quartet fragments in D min. (Andante grazioso & Minuet), Op. 103 (includes *The Seven Last Words of Christ on the Cross, Op. 51/1–7,* with readings selected by Reginald Barrett-Ayres).
(B) *** Decca 455 261-2 (22). Aeolian Qt.

The first complete recording of the Haydn *String quartets* in stereo was Decca's project parallel to Dorati's integral recording of the symphonies, and in most ways it was equally successful. The performances were recorded over a period of four years between December 1972 and December 1976, using the critical edition by Reginald Barrett-Ayres and H. C. Robbins Landon. The recordings were made in two London churches, beginning in St George the Martyr with Opp. 71 and 74, followed by Op. 2. Though the performances of these late works are vigorously enjoyable, the engineers let the ecclesiastical acoustic provide the four players with a degree of 'helpful' reverberation which in Opp. 71 and 74 made them sound a little like a string orchestra. This is not as detrimental as a similar effect in some of the recordings by the Kodály Quartet for Naxos, for the microphone placing ensures clarity of part-writing as well as warmth. No. 69 has a magnificent slow movement, surprisingly romantic, and No. 70 is remarkably original from first to last: both are well projected here. By the time Decca came to record Op. 2, the problem was solved, and for the remaining sessions the recording team moved to St John's, Smith Square, where an excellent and realistic presence was consistently achieved, the profile of the leader (Emanuel Hurwitz) bright without being edgy.

It is not always an advantage in the early quartets of Opp. 1 and 2 that the Aeolian players are wedded to repeats. Nevertheless, on their own unpretentious level these are charming works, and Hurwitz readily takes his chances in such a *Quartet* as Op. 2/1, which includes stylish cadenzas. Though they were recorded at the time, the Op.3 *Quartets* are now claimed to be by Romanus Hofstetter, not by Haydn, and they have understandably been omitted from the present box. This is a pity for, whatever their provenance, the *Andante cantabile* of Op. 3/2 – the so-called '*Serenade*' – is understandably a popular favourite.

Though few of the quartets of Opp. 9 and 17 are consistently inspired from beginning to end (the *G major*, No. 29, is a marvellous exception), they all contain their moments of magic and every one of them has a superb finale, showing the young Haydn at full stretch. Even at this period Haydn had developed his quartet-writing beyond the stage of giving all the interesting writing to the first violin, and by now the Aeolian group, having settled into their task, play with consistent freshness and imagination.

After he had consolidated his style and technique in the fine Op. 20 set, given here in well-prepared and musical accounts, Haydn sought to expand his musical boundaries. 'Written in a new and special way,' he said of his six Op. 33 *Quartets*. Tovey describes them as 'the lightest of all Haydn's mature comedies', for by the time he wrote them, in 1781, many years after the Op. 20 group, he was learning from the young Mozart. Mozart returned the compliment in the six masterpieces he dedicated to Haydn; in his turn, Haydn responded with his Op. 50 group, cogent in their monothematic form. The Aeolians came to these marvellous works fairly late on in their complete cycle, but the players' perception and energy are, if anything, keener than ever. Not all their tempi are beyond question, but the wonder is how consistently enjoyable their playing is.

The set is crowned by their admirable performances of the consistently inspired last *Quartets*, Opp. 77 and 76. The straight, unmannered approach disguises consistent imaginative thoughtfulness, and the warmth of the interplay of ideas among the instruments is engagingly spontaneous. The music's characteristic touches of humour (as in the genial bouncing opening Allegro of Op. 77/1) are not missed. The recording is in the demonstration bracket and we hope Decca may make these masterpieces available separately as a Double. *The Seven Last Words of Jesus Christ* (Nos. 50–56, Op. 51) are treated as an appendix. They were originally composed as orchestral pieces, commissioned in 1787 by the ecclesiastical authorities of Cádiz Cathedral for performance at a Good Friday service. However, it is in their string quartet format that they have become most familiar. Haydn confessed that it was 'no easy task to compose seven adagios, lasting approximately ten minutes each, and to succeed one another, without fatiguing the listener'. But the result is profound, and the magnificent performances here avoid any risk of monotony by inserting poetry readings between movements. The texts (from John Donne, George Herbert, Robert Herrick and Edith Sitwell, among others) are aptly chosen and are beautifully read by Sir Peter Pears. All told, this is a remarkable achievement: many of these performances are unsurpassed. The documentation consists of an excellent essay by Lindsay Kemp, but analysis is confined to Opus number groupings.

String quartets: Nos. 1 in B flat (La chasse), Op. 1/1; 32 in C, Op. 20/2; 35 in F min., Op. 20/5; 46 in E flat, Op. 50/3; 57 in G; 58 in C; 59 in E, Op. 54/1–3; 65 in B flat; 66 in G, Op. 64/3–4; 74 in G min. (Rider), Op. 74/3; 77 in C (Emperor), Op. 76/3; 78 in B flat (Sunrise), Op. 77/2.
(**(*)) Testament mono SBT 3055 (3) [id.]. Pro Arte Qt.

String quartets: Nos. 6 in C, Op. 1/6; 16 in B flat; 17 in F (Serenade), Op. 3/4–5 (Hoffstetter); 31 in E flat; 34 in D, Op. 20/1 & 4; 38 in E flat (Joke); 39 in C (Bird); 42 in D (How do you do?), Op. 33/2, 3 & 6; 49 in D (Frog), Op. 50/6; 60 in A; 62 in B flat, Op. 55/1 & 3; 68 in E flat, Op. 64/6; 69 in B flat, Op. 71/1; 72 in C; 73 in F, Op. 74/1–2; 81 in G, Op. 77/1.
(**(*)) Testament mono SBT 4056 (4) [id.]. Pro Arte Qt.

While LP and CD reissues have kept the name of the Busch Quartet alive, the Pro Arte (for whom, incidentally, Bartók composed his *Fourth Quartet*) is a less familiar one to modern collectors. All the players were from the Brussels Conservatoire and enjoyed international repute in the 1920s and '30s, not only for their Viennese classics but for their advocacy of contemporary music. In their hands the Haydn *Quartets* bring us a world of delight, wisdom and sanity, and few groups are better guides. They have great purity of style and an immaculate intonation and technique, while they seem always to hit on exactly the right tempo, which in turn enables phrasing to speak naturally. The interplay between each of the musicians could hardly be more subtle in its responsiveness. However, the actual sound of these recordings calls for a little tolerance. The violin timbre, particularly above the stave, is wanting in bloom, and one would welcome more space between movements. Less than perfect sound, perhaps, as might be expected from their recording dates (1931–8), but impeccable Haydn playing.

String quartets: in E flat, Op. 1/0; Nos. 43 in D min., Op. 42; 83 in B flat, Op. 103.
**(*) Mer. ECD 88117 [id.]. English Qt.

These fine players rise to all the challenges posed by this music, and the recorded sound is eminently truthful. There would have been room for another quartet on this disc, which offers rather short measure at 43 minutes.

String quartets Nos. 1 in B flat; 2 in E flat; 3 in D; 4 in G, Op. 1/1–4.
(BB) **(*) Naxos Dig. 8.550398 [id.]. Kodály Qt.

String quartets Nos. 5 in E flat; 6 in C, Op. 1/5–6; 7 in A; 8 in E, Op. 2/1–2.
(BB) **(*) Naxos Dig. 8.550399 [id.]. Kodály Qt.

Haydn is credited with 'inventing' the string quartet, but he claimed that he had come across the form by accident. The Op. 1 and Op. 2 quartets are in essence five-movement divertimenti scored for four string players. The first four were published in Paris in 1764, together with two other works, under the collective title, '*Six Simphonies ou Quatuors dialogués*'. These earliest works have not quite the unquenchable flow of original ideas that the early symphonies have but, in such fresh performances as these, they make easy and enjoyable listening even if, with the performances generous in observing repeats, some movements outstay their welcome. The resonant ambience of the Unitarian Church in Budapest seems not unsuitable for works which lie midway between divertimenti and quartets, and the focus seems brighter and sharper on the second CD, recorded in June 1991, two months after the first.

String quartets Nos. 1 in B flat, Op. 1/1; 67 in D (Lark), Op. 64/5; 74 in G min., Op. 74/3 (Rider).
*** DG (IMS) Dig. 423 622-2. Hagen Qt.

The Hagen are supple, cultured and at times perhaps a little overcivilized, but in these three Haydn quartets they play flawlessly and are wonderfully alert and intelligent.

String quartets Nos. 9 in F; 10 in B flat, Op. 2/4 & 6; 35 in D min., Op. 42.
(BB) **(*) Naxos Dig. 8.550732 [id.]. Kodály Qt.

The Unitarian Church, Budapest, continues to provide a warm, flattering tonal blend of much aural beauty, but a texture that is a little too ample, while the fairly close microphones reduce the dynamic range. However, the Kodály's friendly style and elegant finish suit early Haydn. (Both Op. 2 quartets are simple five-movement works, each with a pair of minuets.) These performers find exactly the right degree of expressiveness for the *Adagio* of Op. 2/4 and are equally at home in the engaging *Andante ed innocentemente* which opens the first movement of Op. 42, a splendid work, written a quarter of a century later.

String quartets Nos. 17 in F (Serenade), Op. 3/5; 38 in E flat (Joke), Op. 33/2; 76 in D min. (Fifths), Op. 76/2.
(B) **(*) Discover Dig. DIDCD 920172 [id.]. Sharon Qt.

The Sharon Quartet are an excellent group and they give warm and spirited accounts of these three favourite quartets. They are recorded in the resonant acoustics of St John's Church in Cologne and, like some of the recordings made for Naxos by the Kodály Quartet, the resonance expands the texture, although not seriously enough to prevent enjoyment, for they make a bright, clean sound. They find charm in Hofstetter's famous '*Serenade*' of Op. 3 and are equally good in the *Variations* which form the slow movement of the *Fifths*; at the same time, they find the right approach to the '*Joke*' in the finale of Op. 33/2.

String quartets Nos. 17 in F (Serenade), Op. 3/5; 63 in D (Lark), Op. 64/5; 76 in D min. (Fifths), Op. 76/2.
(M) *** Ph. 426 097-2. Italian Qt.

First-class playing here; although the first movement of the *Lark* is a bit measured in feeling, the *Serenade quartet* is made to sound inspired, its famous slow movement played with exquisite gentleness. The *D minor Quartet* is admirably poised and classical in feeling.

String quartets Nos. 19 in C; 21 in G; 22 in D min., Op. 9/1, 3 & 4.
(BB) *** Naxos Dig. 8.550786 [id.]. Kodály Qt.

String quartets Nos. 20 in E flat; 23 in B flat; 24 in A, Op. 9/2, 5 & 6.
(BB) *** Naxos Dig. 8.550787 [id.]. Kodály Qt.

The Kodály Quartet are in excellent form throughout Opus 9. Their simple eloquence in all three slow movements on the first disc serves Haydn well: the *Largo* of Op. 9/3 is ideally paced and beautifully poised. The players then go on to give a captivating account of the finale. Indeed, all the finales here are superb, showing Haydn at full stretch. The last of the set in A major opens with a very attractive *Presto* in 6/8, which is delightfully buoyant here. Fortunately the Naxos recording team (in December 1992 and January 1993) have mastered the acoustics of the Unitarian Church in Budapest. The microphones are in the right place, the sound is not inflated.

String quartets Nos. 25 in E; 26 in F; 28 in C min., Op. 17/1, 2 & 4.
(N) (BB) *** Naxos Dig. 8.550853 [id.]. Kodály Qt.

The Kodály Quartet seem very much at home in this music, which they approach with affection, yet with an appealing directness which leads to playing which is perfectly integrated, yet fresh. The recording could hardly be bettered: the balance is most natural.

String quartets Nos. 27 in E flat; 29 in G; 30 in D, Op. 17/3, 5 & 6.
(N) (BB) *** Naxos Dig. 8.550854-2 [id.]. Kodály Qt.

While the other works here are also played with pleasing warmth and finesse, the highlight of the second Naxos disc of Op.17 is the *D major Quartet*, which has a searching, aria-like slow movement, dominated by the principal violin, which is played most eloquently here. This is the last of the set, and appropriately the last recording in this highly distinguished Naxos series. The recording balance is quite admirable.

String quartets Nos. 31 in E flat; 32 in C; 33 in G min.; 34 in D; 35 in F min.; 36 in A, Op. 20/1–6.
✿ *** Astrée Dig. E 8784 (2) [id.]. Mosaïques Qt.

String quartets Nos. 31 in E flat; 32 in C; 33 in G min., Op. 20/1–3.
(BB) ** Naxos Dig. 8.550701 [id.]. Kodály Qt.

String quartets Nos. 34 in D; 35 in F min.; 36 in A (Sun quartets), Op. 20/4–6.
(BB) ** Naxos Dig. 8.550702 [id.]. Kodály Qt.

Using period instruments, the four players of the Mosaïques Quartet create individual timbres which are pleasing to the ear without any overt opulence, textures which have body and transparency, are perfectly matched and never edgy. There is no squeezed phrasing, and the use of vibrato is as subtle as the control of colour and dynamic. Intonation and ensemble are remarkably exact. The effect, not as genially friendly or casual as the Kodály series on Naxos, is often breathtaking in its rapt concentration. Such is the calibre of this music-making and the strength of insight of these players that the character of these fine, relatively early works is communicated with seemingly total spontaneity. This is playing of rare distinction which is immensely revealing and rewarding, helped by state-of-the-art recording of complete realism and presence within an acoustic that provides the necessary intimacy of ambience.

The Naxos Kodály series brings polished, sympathetic playing of considerable warmth. Allegros are lively, but the acoustics of the Unitarian Church, Budapest, though providing beautifully rich string-textures, here make the effect almost orchestral and bring an element of blandness to the fine *Adagio* slow movements; throughout, the dynamic range of the playing is reduced by the microphone positioning. The *Adagio* of Op. 20/2 brings some fine playing, and the theme and variations of the *Poco adagio e affettuoso* of the *D major Quartet*, Op. 20/4, are attractively characterized but badly need a wider dynamic contrast. This is even more striking in the *Fuga a quattro soggetti* which forms the finale of Op. 20/2.

String quartets Nos. 31 in E flat; 33 in G min.; 34 in D (Sun), Op. 20/1, 3, & 4.
(N) **(*) ASV Dig. CDDCA 1027 [id.]. Lindsay Qt.

The Lindsays are at their finest in the *D major* work and make much of its theme and variations slow movement, brief Gypsy Minuet, and scherzando finale. These recordings were apparently made under studio conditions and the playing in the slow movements of the other two quartets has slightly less concentration than one has come to expect from their 'live' recordings. The sound is first-class, and the extra finish of the ensemble brings its own rewards.

String quartets Nos. 32 in C; 34 in F min.; 35 in A, Op. 20/2, 5 & 6.
(N) *** ASV Dig. CDDCA 1057 [id.]. Lindsay Qt.

These are three of Haydn's very greatest mid-period Quartets and the Lindsays have their full measure, with the feeling of 'live' music-making persisting throughout. The rich-textured opening of the *C major* is immediately inviting, and the *Capriccio* second movement is most sensitively done, as is the lovely, rocking siciliano *Adagio* of the *F minor*. The *Allegro di molto e scherzando* character of the first movement of the *A major* is perfectly caught. All three finales are fugal, and the lightness and keeness of articulation here is a joy. Excellent truthful recording. Very highly recommended.

String quartets Nos. 32 in C, Op. 20/2; 44 in B flat, Op. 50/1; 76 in D min. (Fifths), Op. 76/2.
(BB) *** ASV Quicksilva Dig. CDQS 6144 [id.]. Lindsay Qt.

Since these are public performances, one has to accept music-making reflecting the heat of the occasion, the odd sense of roughness (the finale of Op. 76, No. 2), for these artists take risks – and this is perhaps a shade faster than it would be in a studio. There is splendid character in these performances and plenty of musical imagination. These readings have a spontaneity which is refreshing in these days of retakes! The recordings are eminently truthful and audience noise is minimal. An excellent bargain.

String quartets Nos. 34 in D (Sun), Op. 20/4; 38 in E flat (Joke), Op. 33/2; 39 in C (Bird), Op. 33/3; 61 in F min. (Razor), Op. 55/2; 67 in D (Lark), Op. 64/5; 77 in C (Emperor), Op. 76/3.
(N) (M) *** ASV Dig. CDDCS 236 (2) [id.]. Lindsay Qt.

All these performances show the Lindsays on top form; indeed the *Sun Quartet* is the finest performance on the full-priced CD from which it comes. Anyone wanting a grouping of these named quartets (all masterpieces) cannot go wrong here as the recordings are all vividly real: the *Emperor*, for instance, which was recorded live, is very present indeed. The only snag is that a compilation like this cuts across other collections which group together works of a single Opus number.

String quartets Nos. 34 in D, Op. 20/4; 47 in C sharp min., Op. 50/4; 77 in C (Emperor), Op. 76/3.
*** ASV Dig. CDDCA 731 [id.]. Lindsay Qt.

The Lindsay performances were again recorded at public performances, on this occasion in London's Wigmore Hall. The advantages this brings are twofold: higher spontaneity and a greater propensity to take risks. In all three performances the gains outweigh any loss, though the balance tends to cause some coarse-sounding tone in fortissimo passages.

String quartets Nos. 35 in F min., Op. 20/5; 40 in B flat, Op. 33/4; 70 in D, Op. 71/2.
(BB) *** ASV Quicksilva Dig. CDQS 6146 [id.]. Lindsay Qt.

The immediacy of the Lindsays' playing here is just as striking as before, yet at the rather serious opening of the *F minor*, Op. 20/5, the approach is appropriately sober and considered as well as spontaneous. This quartet also has a tender *Siciliano* slow movement which is played with affecting simplicity and grace. The account of the *B flat Quartet*, Op. 33/4, brings a burst of applause at the end, as well it might, with its deeply thoughtful *Largo* and engaging finale. Three marvellous works, recorded with striking presence.

String quartets Nos. 37–42, Op. 33/1–6; 43 in D min., Op. 42.
(B) *** HM Dig. HMA 1903002/3. Festetics Qt.

String quartets Nos. 37 in B min.; 38 in E flat (Joke); 39 in C (Bird), Op. 33/1–3.
*** Kingdom KCLCD 2014 [id.]. Bingham Qt.

String quartets Nos. 37 in B min.; 38 in E flat (Joke); 40 in B flat, Op. 33/1–2 & 4.
**(*) ASV Dig. CDDCA 937 [id.]. Lindsay Qt.

String quartets Nos. 37 in B min.; 40 in B flat; 42 in D, Op. 33/1, 4 & 6.
(N) *** Audivis Astrée Dig. E 8570 [id.]. Mosaïques Qt.

String quartets Nos. 38 in E flat (Joke); 39 in C (Bird); 41 in G, Op. 33/2, 3 & 5.
*** Audivis Astrée Dig. E 8569 [id.]. Mosaïques Qt.

String quartets Nos. 37–38 & 41, Op. 33/1–2 & 5.
(BB) **(*) Naxos 8.550788 [id.]. Kodály Qt.

String quartets Nos. 39–40 & 42, Op. 33/3–4 & 6.
(BB) **(*) Naxos 8.550789 [id.]. Kodály Qt.

String quartets Nos. 39 in C (Bird); 41 in G; 42 in D, Op. 33/3, 5 & 6.
*** ASV Dig. CDDCA 938 [id.]. Lindsay Qt.

String quartets Nos. 40 in B flat; 41 in G; 42 in D (How do you do), Op. 33/4–6.
*** Kingdom KCLCD 2015 [id.]. Bingham Qt.

Although Haydn had written some fine quartets before these were published in 1782, this Op. 33 set proved a watermark. Here he finally established himself as complete master of a new medium with such skill, musical fecundity and wit that he never surpassed them in terms of cultivated musical pleasure, even if later works, Op. 76 for instance, embrace a somewhat wider range of mood and feeling.

Those wanting Op. 33 on period instruments can be recommended without reservation to the Mosaïques Quartet, whose performances are more penetrating than any of their competitors. Indeed the intensity of the playing is remarkable, with concentration held throughout the widest range of dynamic, and constantly uncovering hidden depths in these works, even in the *Joke Quartet*. There are touches of darkness, as well as serenity, in adagios; and finales dance with fairy lightness, while the crisply pointed *Allegretto* which ends Op. 33/6 has a Beechamesque rhythmic panache. Marvellous playing throughout, with every detail revealed in sound which is both transparent, yet never in the least textually meagre. The superb recording is perfectly balanced.

Those wanting Op. 33 plus Op. 42 on period instruments will be delighted with this Musique d'Abord set from the Quatuor Festetics. These Hungarians play with great spirit (the finale of the *Joke* has the requisite sense of fun), and their overall lightness of touch and the transparency of texture are very appealing. Slow movements have freshness and just the right combination of gravitas and expressive feeling: the phrasing is smoothly linear without those unattractive bulges that seem to haunt performances on original instruments. Almost every movement has the kind of sparkle and spontaneity that make one want to return to it, and the recording is most naturally balanced in the much-used Unitarian Church of Budapest.

The tonal matching and ensemble of the Bingham Quartet are most impressive, with the leader, Stephen Bingham, a remarkably stylish player who really understands how to shape a Haydn phrase. Above all the Binghams convey their pleasure in the music, and every performance here sounds fresh. The recording was made at the Conway Hall, London, in 1990. The balance is a shade close, but the instruments are naturally focused, individually and as a group. Even if the range of dynamic is a little affected, the playing itself is full of light and shade so that if the volume level is carefully set one soon forgets this reservation in the sheer pleasure this music affords.

The Kodály Quartet play Op. 33 with an easy relaxed warmth. Their style is low-key so that the 'Joke' finale of Op. 33/2 is rather gentle and muted; on the other hand, the reason for the sobriquet of the *Bird Quartet* is affectionately conveyed and the finale is delightfully light-hearted. Slow movements are serene and quietly musical. Minuets are generally full of character, with the trios nicely realized, and this applies especially to the charming middle section of the Scherzo in the *Joke Quartet*. In short these are performances which convey the players' affection for this wonderful music with no possible desire to put their own personalities between composer and listener. The Naxos recording is wholly natural, with the acoustics of the Budapest Unitarian Church beautifully caught without any textural inflation.

If the Kodály Quartet are exceptionally relaxed in Op. 33, the Lindsays are at the opposite end of the scale: vividly alert and with the playing full of tension. This effect is emphasized by the recording, made in Trinity Church, Wentworth, where the microphones are close, giving striking presence and emphasizing the bite on the timbre of the leader, Peter Cropper, the effect only just short of edginess. Fortunately the superb ensemble stands up to such scrutiny. No one could say that the Lindsays miss the wit inherent in the finale of the *Joke*; yet, in spite of the gentle ending, the smile is weakened by the vibrant purposefulness. The performances here use the Henle Urtext edition, which differs quite substantially in phrasing and, in places, even in notes from the more familiar Peters Edition, especially at the opening of Op. 33/1. The second disc includes a Rosette-worthy account of Op. 33/3 with Haydn's birdsong exquisitely simulated.

String quartets Nos. 43 in D min., Op.42; 67 in D (Lark), Op. 64/5; 79 in D, Op. 76/5.
(BB) *** ASV Quicksilva Dig. CDQS 6145 [id.]. Lindsay Qt.

The Lindsays are given a striking presence here and the spontaneity of their playing is gripping. The presto finales (particularly the moto perpetuo of *The Lark*, which overall is most strikingly done) offer fizzing bravura and the beautiful slow movement of Op. 76/5 is rapt in its quiet intensity. There are remarkably few moments of roughness of ensemble arising from the impetuosity of the playing.

String quartets Nos. 44–49, Op. 50/1–6 (Prussian).
(N) (BB) *** Naxos Dig. 8.553983 *(Nos. 44–46)*; 8.553984 *(Nos. 47–49)* (available separately) [id.]. Kodály Qt.

The Kodály Quartet are back to their finest form in Op. 50 and they are most naturally recorded. Dedicated to the King of Prussia (hence the sobriquet), the set dates from 1787, and was reputedly influenced by Mozart: the writing certainly shows Haydn at his most imaginatively cultivated. These are mellow performances, warm and polished, with perfect blending of timbre, yet refined detail. Slow movements are beautifully shaped, with the leader Attila Falway frequently distinguishing himself with the graceful finish of his phrasing. Allegros are spirited but unforced, Minuets have an affectionate modicum of wit, and finales are never rushed.

String quartets Nos. 50–56 (The Seven Last Words of our Saviour on the Cross), Op. 51.
✿ *** ASV Dig. CDDCA 853 [id.]. Lindsay Quartet.

String quartets Nos. 50–56 (The Seven Last Words of our Saviour on the Cross), Op. 51; 83 in B flat, Op. 103.
(BB) *** Naxos Dig. 8.550346 [id.]. Kodály Qt.

No work for string quartet, not even late Beethoven, presents more taxing interpretative problems than Haydn's *Seven Last Words of our Saviour on the Cross*. The recording by the Lindsay Quartet, while offering all the devotional gravity that Haydn demands, brings not just an illuminating variety but also a sense of drama. In concert the Lindsays have performed it, as Haydn wanted, with a brief spoken address between movements explaining the title of each. The CD booklet provides the text of just such a commentary by Dr John Taylor, formerly Bishop of Winchester, and the performance makes no compromise for, unlike some others, the Lindsays observe the first-half repeats in each movement, extending the work to a full 70 minutes, instead of under an hour. Their range of expression, in dynamic, tempo and phrasing, is extremely wide, and they intensify the fundamental darkness of Haydn's minor-key inspirations with magical contrasts into the major mode. After the long sequence of slow movements, the Lindsays' account of the final, brief Presto, *Il terremoto*, then conveys the full, elemental force of the earthquake. It is thrilling with so elusive a work to have so complete an answer in a single recording, with sound both well defined and glowingly beautiful, set against an apt church acoustic.

The Kodály Quartet give a memorable performance, strongly characterized and beautifully played, with subtle contrasts of expressive tension between the seven inner slow movements. They also offer an appropriate bonus in Haydn's last, unfinished, two-movement *Quartet*. The recording is first rate, vividly present yet naturally balanced, like the other issues in this attractive Naxos series.

String quartets Nos. 57 in G; 58 in C; 59 in E, Op. 54/1–3.
*** ASV Dig. CDDCA 582 [id.]. Lindsay Qt.
(BB) *** Naxos Dig. 8.550395; *4550395* [id.]. Kodály Qt.
*** Hyperion Dig. CDA 66971 [id.]. Salomon Qt.

The present works show Haydn at his most inventive. The playing of the Lindsay Quartet is splendidly poised and vital, and the recording is very fine indeed.

The Kodály players enter animatedly into the spirit of the music; the leader, Attila Falvay, shows himself fully equal to Haydn's bravura embellishments in the demanding first violin writing. The Naxos sound is fresh and truthful.

The Salomon Quartet, led by Simon Standage, play on period instruments, but there is nothing anaemic or edgy about the body of tone they command, and the pervading feeling here is of freshness, with finales spirited without being rushed off their feet. This is one of the very best records from these excellent players and the recording is first class.

String quartets Nos. 57 in G; 58 in C; 59 in E, Op. 54/1–3; 71 in C; 73 in F; 74 in G min., Op. 74/1–3.
(BB) *** Virgin Classics Dig. Double VBD5 61436-2 (2) [CDVB 61436]. Endellion Qt.

The Endellion Quartet were recorded in The Maltings, Snape (in 1988 and 1990 respectively), which provides an ideal acoustic environment. The playing is bright-eyed, fresh and vital, and in both sets they prove a sound guide to this repertoire. The sound is strikingly immediate but is beautifully integrated, and there are many moments of musical insight. With the two discs offered for the cost of a single mid-priced CD, this set is very competitive.

String quartets Nos. 60 in A; 61 in F min. (Razor); 62 in B flat, Op. 55/1–3 (Tost Quartets).
*** ASV Dig. CDDCA 906 [id.]. Lindsay Qt.
(BB) **(*) Naxos Dig. 8.550397. Kodály Qt.
**(*) Hyperion Dig. CDA 66972 [id.]. Salomon Qt.

Here the Lindsays are heard under studio conditions, but in Holy Trinity Church, Wentworth, and the results, on the second set of *Tost Quartets*, are marginally less chimerical than in their live recordings, but not less dedicated or less vital. There is of course greater polish, as the fizzing finale of Op. 55/3 readily demonstrates. The recording is lifelike and vivid without excessive resonance.

Opus 55 brings playing from the Kodály Quartet which is undoubtedly spirited and generally polished, but the music-making at times seems plainer than usual in the Naxos series. The recording is bright and clear, with a realistic presence.

Generally fine playing from the Salomon Quartet in Op. 55, although this record is not quite as memorable as was Op. 54. The *Razor*, the second of the set, comes off very well indeed; but the slow movements in the two works on either side of it sound a shade too precise. The recording is truthful but rather close.

String quartets Nos. 63–8, Op. 64/1–6.
(B) *** HM Dig. HMA 1903040/1 [id.]. Festetics Qt.

String quartets Nos. 63 in C; 64 in B min.; 65 in B flat, Op. 64/1–3.
*** Hyperion Dig. CDA 67011 [id.]. Salomon Qt.
(BB) *** Naxos Dig. 8.550673 [id.]. Kodály Qt.

String quartets Nos. 66 in G; 67 in D (Lark); 68 in E flat, Op. 64/4–6.
*** Hyperion Dig. CDA 67012 [id.]. Salomon Qt.
(BB) *** Naxos Dig. 8.550674 [id.]. Kodály Qt.

Like Opp. 54 and 55, Haydn's Op. 64 set was dedicated to the violinist and businessman Johann Tost, who had led the second violins in the Eszterházy orchestra, and they show Haydn at his most inspired. The Salomon performances are well up to the standard of their versions of those earlier works. Their timbre is leaner than that of the estimable Kodály Quartet on Naxos but they blend beautifully and have their own insights to offer: their precise ensemble in no way inhibits commitment and feeling. The second of the two discs is particularly rewarding, with the famous opening movement of the *Lark* readily taking flight and the *Adagio* poised and intense. The Hyperion recording is admirably truthful, but those wanting period performances of these fine works will surely be tempted by the Festetics Harmonia Mundi bargain versions, which are in some ways even more perceptive.

The excellent Hungarian Festetics Quartet follow their esteemed recording of Haydn's Op. 33 with an equally perceptive and animated set of Op. 64. Again their readings are very positive, yet the lightness of touch is balanced by buoyant rhythmic feeling and spontaneous impetus. Slow movements are played with a restrained vibrato and nicely judged espressivo, the line not spoilt by exaggerated bulges. Minuets are infectious and finales sparkle. The last three quartets of the set continually demonstrate not only the high quality of this music-making, but how much these works can gain from performance on period instruments when the authentic style is unexaggerated and the ensemble and tonal matching are so precise. The recording, made in the Budapest Unitarian Church, is fairly close but could hardly be more beautifully balanced.

These Kodály performances are all enjoyable, but the set seems to get better and better as it progresses. Op. 64/1–3 were recorded on 25–29 April 1992; the last to be done, the *B flat major*, is remarkably successful, with a vigorous opening *Vivace assai* and a rapt *Adagio*. The other three works were taped on 1–3 May, and clearly the group had found its top form. The *Adagio – cantabile e sostenuto* of No. 4 finds them at their most concentrated: the *Lark* has never soared aloft more spontaneously and the Minuet and finale of No. 6 close the set in a winningly spirited fashion. The warm acoustics of the Budapest Unitarian Church provide a mellow and expansive sound-image, but not an orchestral one, and detail remains clear. A most enjoyable set.

String quartets Nos. 67 in D (Lark), Op. 64/5; 74 in G min. (Rider), Op. 74/3; 77 in C (Emperor), Op. 76/3.
(B) *** DG Classikon 439 479-2. Amadeus Qt.

Here is a worthwhile triptych of named quartets for those seeking to sample the Amadeus Quartet in Haydn. Their superb ensemble is immediately noticeable at the opening of the *Lark Quartet*, as is Norbert Brainin's vibrato, giving the Amadeus sound its special stamp. The finale brings spiccato precision that dazzles the ear. The *Largo* of the *Rider Quartet* sounds just a little deliberate but its intensity is in no doubt, and the gutsy vibrancy of the playing in the finale is equally remarkable. These date from the 1970s; the *Emperor* was made a decade earlier and the recording is a trifle thinner. The performance shows these fine musicians in the best possible light. The CD transfers are expertly done, and this Classikon reissue is excellent value.

String quartets Nos. 69 in B flat; 70 in D; 71 in E flat (Apponyi Quartets), Op. 71/1–3; 72 in C; 73 in F; 74 in G min. (Rider), Op. 74/1–3.
(BB) *** Naxos Dig. 8.550394 (*Nos. 69–71*); 8.550396 (*Nos. 72–74*) [id.]. Kodály Qt.
(M) *** Arcana Dig. A 918 (2) [id.]. Festetics Qt.

The *Apponyi Quartets* are among the composer's finest. The Naxos recordings by the Kodály Quartet are outstanding in every way and would be highly recommendable even without their considerable price advantage. The digital recording has vivid presence and just the right amount of ambience: the effect is entirely natural.

The Festetics Quartet continue their period-instrument Haydn series with beautifully judged performances of Opp. 71 and 74. The playing has the customary animation and finish, with detail perceptively observed, and well-blended yet beautifully transparent textures. As before, there is nothing vinegary here, and phrasing and line are impeccably musical. Minuets are pleasing, without heaviness (sample the Trio of Op. 71/3 for delectable articulation), and finales sparkle. These are three-star performances without a doubt, and the recording could hardly be better judged. One's only reservation concerns slow movements, sometimes a little solemn.

String quartets Nos. 69 in B flat; 70 in D; 71 in E flat, Op. 71/1–3 (Apponyi).
**(*) Chandos Dig. CHAN 9416 [id.]. Chilingirian Qt.

The Chilingirians' opening of the first of the *Apponyi Quartets* (so named because their 'onlie begetter' was Count Antal Apponyi) is very positive. This is spick-and-span playing, highly musical and full of character. Slow movements are well shaped and expressive and there are moments of wit, notably in the Minuet and Trio of No. 3. The recording is truthful. Yet this playing, although by no means plain, lacks something of the sunny quality the Kodály Quartet brings to this music.

String quartets Nos. 71 in E flat, Op. 71/3; 72 in C, Op. 74/1.
**(*) Hyperion CDA 66098 [id.]. Salomon Qt.

String quartets Nos. 73 in F; 74 in G min., Op. 74/2–3.
**(*) Hyperion CDA 66124 [id.]. Salomon Qt.

The appropriately named Salomon Quartet use period instruments. They are vibrato-less but vibrant; the sonorities, far from being nasal and unpleasing, are clean and transparent. There is imagination and vitality here, and the Hyperion recording is splendidly truthful. However, each disc offers short measure.

String quartets Nos. 72 in C; 73 in F; 74 in G min. (Rider), Op. 74/1–3.
(BB) *** Naxos Dig. 8.550396 [id.]. Kodály Qt.

The Kodály Quartet are on top form here and give refreshing accounts of these three splendid quartets. Their simplicity of approach to the slow movement of the F major is particularly appealing, and the finale is sheer delight. The *Rider* is another of their most striking performances, including another memorable slow movement and a closing movement combining grace and refined ensemble with plentiful energy. The recording could hardly be bettered, completely natural and with the acoustic perfectly handled.

String quartet No. 74 in G min., Op. 74/3.
(M) *** Cal. CAL 6698 [id.]. Talich Qt – BOCCHERINI: *Quartet, Op. 58/2;* MENDELSSOHN: *Quartet No. 2;* MICA: *Quartet No. 6.* ***

The *Quartet in G minor*, Opus 74, No. 3 (dedicated to Count Apponyi), is one of Haydn's greatest quartets. It brings a very beautiful, serenely introspective *Largo assai* in which, in this searching Talich performance, one has the feeling of eavesdropping on private music-making. After the blithe Minuet, the finale is engagingly light and spirited. Superb playing and most natural recording, and the rest of the performances on this generously filled mid-priced CD (76 minutes) are equally distinguished.

String quartets Nos. 74 in G min. (Rider), Op. 74/3; 77 in C (Emperor), Op. 76/3.
(B) *** Teldec/Warner 3984 21849-2 [(M) id. import]. Alban Berg Qt.

A superb disc in every way. Back in the early 1970s, the Alban Berg Quartet displayed admirable polish, but the end-result was without that hint of glossy perfection which poses a problem with some of their more recent, digital recordings. The playing here has wonderful resilience and sparkle. The famous slow movement of the *Emperor Quartet* has seldom been put on record with such warmth and eloquence, and the slow movement of No. 74 is even more beautiful. Indeed the performance of this quartet is masterly, with the rhythmic figure in the first movement which gives the work its title admirably managed. The recording too is first class, full and clear, and this is one of the most rewarding of all Haydn quartet couplings. The playing time is only 45 minutes, but every one of them is treasurable and this disc is inexpensive.

String quartets Nos. 75 in G; 76 in D min. (Fifths); 77 in C (Emperor); 78 in B flat (Sunrise); 79 in D; 80 in E flat, Op. 76/1–6 (Erdödy Quartets).
❁ (BB) *** Naxos Dig. 8.550314; *4550314* (*Nos. 75–77*); 8.550315; *4550315* (*Nos. 78–80*). Kodály Qt.
(B) **(*) Sony SB2K 53522 (2) [S2K 53522]. Tokyo Qt.

String quartets Nos. 76 in D min. (Fifths); 77 in C (Emperor); 78 in B flat (Sunrise), Op. 76/2–4.
❁ (BB) *** Naxos Dig. 8.550129; *4550129* [id.]. Kodály Qt.

Haydn's six *Erdödy Quartets*, Op. 76, contain some of his very greatest music, and these performances by the Kodály Quartet are fully worthy of the composer's inexhaustible invention. Their playing brings a joyful pleasure in Haydn's inspiration and there is not the slightest suspicion of over-rehearsal or of routine: every bar of the music springs to life spontaneously, and these musicians' insights bring an ideal combination of authority and warmth, emotional balance and structural awareness.

The Tokyo Quartet offer superb playing and an immaculate tonal blend, and they are unfailingly intelligent. Yet it is a pity that they do not relax a little more and allow the music to unfold at greater leisure, as do the Kodály players, for they do not convey the humanity and charm that distinguish the Naxos set. The recording is faithful, but they are not as well served by the engineers as they were by DG for their prize-winning Bartók cycle; the sound, though fresh, is a little lacking in bloom at upper dynamic levels.

String quartet No. 76 in D min., Op. 76/2.
**(*) Testament mono SBT 1085 [id.]. Hollywood Qt – HUMMEL: *Quartet in G* *(*); MOZART: *Quartet No. 17.* **(*)

The Hollywood Quartet were recorded at a memorable concert in London's Royal Festival Hall in September 1957, which also included the Mozart coupling and, in the second half of the programme, the Schubert *C major Quintet*. These recordings have never been available before. The playing can only be described as impeccable, not surprisingly so, given the tonal beauty and musical sophistication these artists commanded; and the sound is astonishingly good for the period. There are a couple of minutes of balance test and a brief exchange among the players.

String quartets Nos. 76 in D min. (Fifths); 77 in C (Emperor); 78 in B flat, Op. 76/2–4.
*** EMI (SIS) Dig. CDC5 56166-2 [id.]. Alban Berg Qt.

The Alban Berg Quartet present the first movement of the *Fifths Quartet* with great energy and vigour.

Perhaps they could smile a little more here. Nevertheless this is playing of distinction, bringing impeccable blending and ensemble. They are more relaxed for the opening movement of the *Emperor* and beguilingly pensive at the beginning of the *Sunrise*, although they can be vehemently dramatic too, as in the *Emperor*'s finale. But the three slow movements are played very beautifully, with much delicacy of feeling and sophistication of light and shade, and the rapt pianissimo for the *Adagio* of Op. 76/4 is affectingly intimate. Although the recording is brightly lit and the effect a shade too up-front, it is realistic and admirably balanced.

String quartets Nos. 77 in C (Emperor); 78 in B flat (Sunrise), Op. 76/3–4.
(M) *** DG 449 092-2. Amadeus Qt – MOZART: *String quartet No. 17.* ***

The Amadeus's 1963 version of the *Emperor*, coupled with Mozart's *Hunt quartet*, was always one of their very best records: it has breadth and warmth, to say nothing of immaculate ensemble. The famous slow movement is particularly successful. The *Sunrise*, which was recorded seven years later, is another finely blended performance, somewhat suaver but still with plenty of vitality in outer movements. Both recordings were truthfully balanced and emerge very successfully on CD.

String quartets Nos. 81 in G; 82 in F, Op. 77/1–2; 83 in D min., Op. 103.
*** Astrée Dig. E 8799 [id.]. Mosaïques Qt.
*** Hyperion Dig. CDA 66348 [id.]. Salomon Qt.
(B) **(*) HM Dig. HMA 1903001 [id.]. Festetics Qt.

String quartets Nos. 81 in G; 82 in F, Op. 77/1–2; 83 in D min., Op. 103; Quartettsatz (Der Greis), Hob XXVc/5.
(N) **(*) Sony Dig. SK 62731 [id.]. L'Archibudelli.

String quartets Nos. 81 in G; 82 in F, Op. 77/1–2.
(BB) ** Naxos Dig. 8.553146 [id.]. Kodály Qt.

Using period instruments to totally convincing effect, the Mosaïques Quartet give outstanding performances of Haydn's last three quartets. They play with much subtlety of colour and dynamic and bring total concentration to every bar of the music. The crisp, bouncing rhythm of the first movement of Op. 77/1 is engagingly arresting, and the *Adagio* is ideally paced and extremely eloquent; the *presto* Minuet of Op. 77/2 is bracingly crisp in articulation, followed by a rapt *sotto voce* introduction for the following *Andante*. The *E flat Quartet*, Haydn's last, is beautifully judged. The recording is absolutely real: the sound is transparent as well as immediate. This is among the finest of all Haydn quartet records.

The Salomon, recorded in a less ample acoustic, produce an altogether leaner sound but one that is thoroughly responsive to every shift in Haydn's thought. They seem to have great inner vitality and feeling.

L'Archibudelli play with plenty of life (appealingly so in the bouncing opening rhythms of Op. 77/1) and finesse. Yet they do not match the Mosaïques in subtlety of colour or expressive warmth. Their blended tone includes a full cello sound, but the timbre of the leader, Vera Beths, is comparatively thin. There is a short bonus in the *Quartettsatz*, but this Sony disc would not be a first choice.

Although the opening of Op. 77/1 has a pleasing rhythmic character, there is a coolness about the playing of the Festetics Quartet that lends itself less well to Haydn's expressive slow movement. They are at their best in the last quartet; and the transparency of texture from the use of original instruments brings some refreshing textures elsewhere, but in the last resort the effect is too austere.

The Kodály Quartet give comparatively robust performances of both works, made to seem even more robust by the close balance which reduces the dynamic range – not that the playing is notable for pianissimo contrast. This is warm, friendly music-making and in that respect (and in that respect only) preferable to the Festetics; but the latter's playing has considerably more subtlety, and they offer an extra work.

KEYBOARD MUSIC

Piano sonatas Nos. 1–16; 17–19 (Hob deest); 20; 28, Hob XIV/5; 29–62, Hob XVI/1–52 & G1; XVII/D1; The Seven Last Words on the Cross; Adagio in F; Capriccio in G on the song 'Acht Sauschneider müssen sein'; Fantasia in C; 7 Minuets from 'Kleine Tänz für die Jugend'; Variations in F min.; 5 Variations in D; 6 Variations in C; 12 Variations in E flat; 20 Variations in A.
(B) *** Decca 443 785-2 (12) [id.]. John McCabe.

John McCabe made the first successful complete survey of the Haydn *Sonatas* for Argo between 1974 and 1977, including also *The Seven Last Words on the Cross*, an arrangement not made by the composer but approved by him. It is remarkably successful here. Indeed two things shine through John McCabe's performances: their complete musicianship and their fine imagination. In presenting them as he does on a modern piano, McCabe makes the most of the colour and subtlety of the music, and in that respect his style is more expressive, less overtly classical than Jandó's (see below) while the recording is made to sound somewhat softer-grained by the acoustic of All Saints' Church, Petersham. Given phrasing so clearly articulated and alertly phrased, and such varied, intelligently thought-out and wholly responsive presentation, this set can be recommended very enthusiastically. The recordings are of the very highest quality, truthful in timbre and firmly refined in detail, and they must be numbered among the most successful of this repertoire ever to be put on disc, for the piano is notoriously difficult to balance in eighteenth-century music. The set is most reasonably priced and the pianist provides his own extensive and illuminating notes. To sample the calibre of this enterprise, begin with *The Seven Last Words* – playing of unexaggerated expressive feeling that almost makes one believe this was a work conceived in pianistic terms.

Adagios: in F, Hob XVII/9; in G, Hob XV/22 (II); Allegrettos: in G after Hob III/41 (IV); in G, Hob XVII/10; Arietta with 12 variations in A, Hob XVII/2; Fantasia in C (Capriccio), Hob XVII/4; Piano sonatas Nos. 17 in E flat, Hob deest; 19 in E min., Hob XVI/47bis; 28 in D, Hob XVI/5a (incomplete).

(N) (BB) *** Naxos Dig. 8.553826 [id.]. Jenö Jandó.

Jandó is at his best in the simple *Adagios* and *Allegrettos* (that in G, Hob III/41, is an arrangement of the engaging variations from the '*How do you do?' Quartet, Op. 33/5*). He gives a strongly impulsive and exciting account of the *Fantasia in C*, which ends the recital boldly. The two complete sonatas are a shade on the literal side, but still fresh, however he does not make much of the unfinished fragment of the first movement of *No. 28 in D*, where he tends to rush his fences. The good things here outweigh reservations, and there is much to enjoy, and the recording is up to standard.

Andante with variations in F min., Hob. XVII/6; Piano sonatas Nos. 59 in E flat, Hob. XVI/49; 60 in C, Hob. XVI/50; 62 in E flat, Hob. XVI/52.

(B) *** Ph. Brendel Edition Dig./Analogue 446 921-2. Alfred Brendel – MOZART: *Piano concertos and sonatas.* **(*)

This disc acts as a mere sampler of Brendel's outstanding Haydn recordings. In Hob. XVI/49 (analogue), the first to be recorded, he observes all the repeats and the sound is first class. The rest of the programme is digital. His playing throughout is most distinguished, aristocratic without being aloof, concentrated without being too intense. Everything is cleanly articulated and finely characterized. Vivid, lifelike recording.

Piano sonatas Nos. 11 in B flat, Hob XVI/2; 12 in A, Hob XVI/12; 13 in G, Hob XVI/6; 14 in C, Hob XVI/3; 15 in E, Hob XVI/13; 16 in D, Hob XVI/14; 18 in E flat, Hob XVI deest.

(N) (BB) *** Naxos Dig. 8.553825 [id.]. Jenö Jandó.

These early sonatas are all played freshly in Jandó's pleasingly direct style. All but one are simple three-movement works; the exception isNo. *13 in G*, which has an attractive additional *Adagio* which Jandö treats simply but appealingly. The recording is truthful and this issue, Volume 8 in the series, cannot be faulted.

Piano sonatas Nos. 11 in B flat, Hob XVI/2; 31 in A flat, Hob XVI/46; 39 in D min., Hob XVI/24; 47 in B min., Hob XVI/32.

*** Decca (IMS) Dig. 436 455-2 [id.]. Sviatoslav Richter.

Richter's crisp, classical style, with sparing use of the pedal and strong rhythmic feeling, is immediately noticeable at the opening of the *B minor* work, bringing a feeling almost of a *moto perpetuo*, although the variations of colour and dynamic prevent any hint of monotony. The *Andante* is cool and gentle and the finale brings toccata-like brilliance of execution. So it is with the others here, though the *Adagios* of both the *D minor* and (especially) the *A flat major* are gentle and touching, while the two closing movements of the early *B flat Sonata* have an engaging simplicity. Clear, realistic 1986 sound and not too much applause.

Piano sonatas Nos. 20 in B flat, Hob XVI/18; 30 in D, Hob XVI/19; 31 in A flat, Hob XVI/46; 32 in G min., Hob XVI/44.

(BB) **(*) Naxos Dig. 8.553364 [id.]. Jenö Jandó.

Jandó continues his Haydn sonata series in his clean, direct style. The first movement of the *G minor Sonata* is particularly appealing, with its neat articulation and tight little runs, and the same might be said of the opening movement of the *A flat major* (No. 31), while its finale is similarly bright and sparkling. But first prize goes to the closing movement of the *D major*, which skips along delightfully and brings quite dazzling dexterity. The thoughtful *Adagio* of the *B flat major*, however, is just a little too studied; but this is not enough of a disadvantage to prevent a recommendation. The piano recording is very realistic.

Piano sonatas No. 24 in A (Hob. XVI/26); 30 in D (Hob. XVI/32); 32 in C sharp min. (Hob. XVI/36); 33 in D (Hob. XVI/37); 44 in E flat (Hob. XVI/49).

(N) ❁ *** EMI Dig. CDC5 56756-2. Leif Ove Andsnes.

Playing of great elegance and and consummate artistry, the finest Haydn sonata record to have appeared for a long time. Very different in approach from Pletnev's 1989 recital (see below) – the repertoire does not overlap – but no less individual or persuasive. The young Norwegian pianist plays with rare imagination and keyboard colour, and the EMI sound is first-class. The recordings are all made in Abbey Road, save for the *E flat* (No. 44), which was recorded in Oslo.

Piano sonatas Nos. 29 in E flat, Hob. XVI/45; 33 in C min., Hob. XVI/20; 34 in D, Hob. XVI/33; 35 in A flat, Hob. XVI/43.
(BB) *** Naxos Dig. 8.553800 [id.]. Jenö Jandó.

Jandó is on very good form here. His style is a little plain and classical but never insensitive, and he is well recorded. A useful addition to a fine series.

Piano sonatas Nos. 32 in G min., Hob XVI/44; 54 in G, Hob XVI/40; 55 in B flat, Hob XVI/41; 58 in C, Hob XVI/48; 62 in E flat, Hob XVI/52.
*** Decca (IMS) Dig. 436 454-2 [id.]. Sviatoslav Richter.

Richter's second Decca Haydn CD, made in Mantua in 1987, is undoubtedly the more attractive of the two, the playing no less direct but with less of a sense of classical austerity. The opening of the *G minor Sonata* is very winning indeed, and his softness of approach is carried over to the following *G major* work. Both the *C major* (Hob XVI/48) and the well-known *E flat major* (Hob XVI/52) are among Haydn's finest works for the piano – and that means very fine indeed – and Richter's playing is fully worthy of this marvellous music. Again the sound is vivid and immediate.

Piano sonatas Nos. 33 in C min., Hob XVI/20; 47 in B min., Hob XVI/32; 53 in E min., Hob XVI/34; 50 in D, Hob XVI/37; 54 in G, Hob XVI/40; 56 in D, Hob XVI/42; 58 in C; 59 in E flat; 60 in C; 61 in D; 62 in E flat, Hob XVI/48–52; Adagio in F, Hob XVII/9; Andante with variations in F min., Hob XVII/6; Fantasia in C, Hob XVII/4.
*** Ph. 416 643-2 (4). Alfred Brendel.

This collection offers some of the best Haydn playing on record – and some of the best Brendel, too. The eleven sonatas, together with the *F minor Variations* and the *C major Fantasia*, have been recorded over a number of years and are splendidly characterized and superbly recorded. The first is analogue, the remainder digital.

Piano sonatas: 33 in C min., Hob XVI/20; 60 in C, Hob XVI/50; 62 in E flat, Hob XVI/52; Andante & Variations in F min., Hob XVII/6.
*** Virgin/EMI Dig. VC5 45254-2 [CDC 45254]. Mikhail Pletnev.

Pletnev's reading of the *Sonatas* is full of personality and character. The *C major* is given with great elegance and wit, and the great *E flat Sonata* is magisterial. This playing has a masterly authority, and Pletnev is very well recorded.

Piano sonatas Nos. 36 in C, Hob XVI/21; 37 in E, Hob XVI/22; 38 in F, Hob XVI/23; 39 in D, Hob XVI/24; 40 in E flat, Hob XVI/25; 41 in A, Hob XVI/26.
(BB) **(*) Naxos Dig. 8.553127 [id.]. Jenö Jandó.

Piano sonatas Nos. 48 in C, Hob XVI/35; 49 in C sharp min., Hob XVI/36; 50 in D, Hob XVI/37; 51 in E flat, Hob XVI/38; 52 in G, Hob XVI/39.
(BB) *** Naxos Dig. 8.553128 [id.]. Jenö Jandó.

Jandó seems to have been very slightly below par when he recorded Volume 4 (8.553127) of his ongoing set of Haydn sonatas in May 1993. The playing is as bright and clear as before and the interpretations are well thought out, but just occasionally there is a hint of stiffness and overall there is not always the degree of spontaneity we expect from this artist.

A month later, in June of the same year, he was back on form with all the freshness that marked his earlier records in the series, as the opening of *No. 36 in C* immediately shows. The finale of *No. 37 in E major* is beautifully played, and the following two sonatas with their fine slow movements will not disappoint his admirers. Excellent piano sound, crisp but not too dry.

Piano sonatas Nos. 38 in F, Hob XVI/23; 51 in E flat, Hob XVI/38; 52 in G, Hob XVI/39.
*** Mer. CDE 84155. Julia Cload.

Julia Cload's cool, unidiosyncratic style is heard at its best in her second group of sonatas. The piano image is bright and clear, with just a touch of hardness on *fortes*.

Piano sonatas Nos. 42 in G, Hob XVI/27; 43 in E flat, Hob XVI/28; 44 in F, Hob XVI/29; 45 in A, Hob XVI/30; 46 in E, Hob XVI/31; 47 in B min., Hob XVI/32.
(BB) *** Naxos Dig. 8.550844 [id.]. Jenö Jandó (piano).

The six sonatas offered here (in what is Volume II of Jenö Jandó's ongoing series) were written between 1774 and 1776 and were later grouped together and published by Hummel as Haydn's Op. 14. Although they are all comparatively straightforward three-movement classical sonatas, such a comment is deceptive for Haydn consistently has something individual to contribute. The last work of the set, in B minor, opens with perhaps the most striking idea of all and, after the gracious central Minuet, ends in a flurry of precocious virtuosity, with Jandó clearly in his element. He shows himself a complete master of this repertoire, and the recording, crisp and clean but not too dry, is first class.

Piano sonatas Nos. 50 in D, Hob XVI/37; 54 in G, Hob XVI/40; 55 in B flat, Hob XVI/41; Adagio in F, Hob XVII/9.
*** Mer. ECD 84083 [id.]. Julia Cload.

Julia Cload's playing is fresh, characterful and intelligent, and will give considerable pleasure. She has the advantage of very truthful recorded sound.

Piano sonatas Nos. 53 in E min., Hob XVI/34; 54 in G, Hob XVI/40; 55 in B flat, Hob XVI/41;

56 in D, Hob XVI/42; 58 in C, Hob XVI/48; Variations in F min. (Sonata, un piccolo divertimento), Hob XVII/6.
(BB) *** Naxos Dig. 8.550845 [id.]. Jenö Jandó (piano).

These are appealing performances of the three *Sonatas*, Hob XVI/40–42, dedicated to Princess Marie Esterházy, who had married the grandson of Haydn's princely patron. They are each in two movements, and in the case of the *G major* the first is marked *Allegretto e innocente*, an obvious tribute to feminine charm. But all three are fine works and not as simple as they at first appear. Jandó also gives a splendid account of the more ambitious three-movement *Sonata in E minor*, Hob XVI/34. He is a true Haydn player and this (Volume III of his projected series) is in every way recommendable, particularly as the recording is so vivid and clean: just right for the repertoire.

Piano sonatas Nos. 56 in D, Hob XVI/42; 58 in C; 59 in E flat; 60 in C; 61 in D; 62 in E flat, Hob XVI/48–52.
(M) *(**) Sony Dig. SM2K 52623 [id.]. Glenn Gould.

Gould's classical style in Haydn is often refreshing, but after a while the squeaky-clean articulation, although quite remarkably crisp, becomes a little wearing and the ear craves a less staccato, less percussive approach to allegros. This is not a fortepiano imitation but a pianoforte played with the most sparing sonority. Gould undoubtedly makes a sensitively expressive response to slow movements, but an air of eccentricity remains in the overall shaping of phrases. The digital recording is clear, to match the playing.

Piano sonatas Nos. 58 in C; 59 in E flat; 60 in C; 61 in D; 62 in E flat, Hob XVI/48–52.
*** RCA Dig. RD 77160 [77160-2-RC]. Andreas Staier (fortepiano).

Andreas Staier plays a recent copy by Christopher Clarke of a fortepiano from around 1790 by the Viennese maker, Anton Walter, and proves a highly sensitive and imaginative interpreter. He brings a surprisingly wide dynamic range as well as a diversity of keyboard colour to these pieces and holds the listener throughout. He is very well recorded indeed.

Piano sonatas Nos. 59 in E flat; 60 in C; 61 in D; 62 in E flat, Hob XVI/49–52.
(BB) *** Naxos Dig. 8.550657 [id.]. Jenö Jandó.

Jenö Jandó here shows himself as strong and sympathetic in Haydn as in Beethoven. Without allowing himself stylistic idiosyncrasies, Jandó shows himself a thoughtfully imaginative player as well as a bold one, and the finale of the great *E flat Sonata* has splendid, unforced bravura. The recording, made in the Unitarian Church, Budapest, provides an attractive ambience without an excess of ecclesiastical resonance.

VOCAL MUSIC

Arianna a Naxos (cantata).
*** Decca Dig. 440 297-2 [id.]. Cecilia Bartoli, András Schiff – BEETHOVEN: *Che fa il mio bene?* etc.; MOZART: *Ridente la calma;* SCHUBERT: *Da quel sembiante appresi* etc. ***

Arianna a Naxos; Fidelity; The mermaid's song; Pastoral song; Sailor's song; She never told her love; Spirit's song; Der verdienstvolle Sylvius.
*** DG Dig. 447 106-2 [id.]. Anne Sofie von Otter, Melvyn Tan (fortepiano) – MOZART: *Lieder.* ***

To declare a preference between Cecilia Bartoli and Anne Sofie von Otter in Haydn's extended scena is virtually impossible. With its double alternating recitative and aria, the first doubtful concerning a lover's faithfulness, the second expressing the despair and anger of known betrayal, Haydn's setting demands the widest range of mood and identification with the words; both singers rise to the occasion with passion and consummate artistry. Bartoli has the inestimable András Schiff as partner; Von Otter has Melvyn Tan's eloquent fortepiano. So in the end it depends on the couplings: the other Haydn songs on the DG disc are happily varied in mood, to bring either innocent simplicity (*A Pastoral song*), histrionics (*Fidelity*) – with Tan very much rising to the occasion – or touching, unexaggerated pathos (*She never told her love* and *Der verdienstvolle Sylvius*). By comparison, the *Sailor's song* is suitably robust and the melancholy *Spirit's song*, which ends the recital, pensively nostalgic. The recording balance is just about ideal.

The Creation (complete; in English).
*** EMI Dig. CDS7 54159-2 (2). Augér, Langridge, David Thomas, CBSO & Ch., Simon Rattle.
*** Decca Dig. 430 397-2 (2) [id.]. Kirkby, Rolfe Johnson, George, New College, Oxford, Ch., AAM Ch. & O, Hogwood.
**(*) Telarc Dig. CD 80298 (2) [id.]. Upshaw, Humphrey, Cheek, Murphy, McGuire, Chamber Ch. & SO, Shaw.

The English version may have its oddities – like the 'flexible tiger' leaping – but it is above all colourful, and Rattle brings out that illustrative colour with exceptional vividness: birdsong, lion-roars and the like. He has plainly learnt from period performance, not only concerning speeds – often surprisingly brisk, as in the great soprano aria, *With verdure clad* – but as regards style too. The male soloists sound none too sweet as recorded, but they characterize positively; and there is no finer account of the soprano's music than that of Arleen Augér. The weight of the Birmingham chorus is impressive, achieved without loss of clarity or detail in a full, well-balanced recording.

Hogwood defies what has become the custom in period performance and opts for large forces. The result, for all its weight, retains fine clarity of detail and an attractive freshness. The choir of New College, Oxford, with its trebles adds to the brightness of choral sound, and the trio of soloists is admirably consistent – Emma Kirkby brightly distinctive, and Anthony Rolfe Johnson sweet-toned. Hogwood may lack some of the flair and imagination of Rattle, but it would be hard to find a period performance to match this. The sound has fine presence and immediacy.

Robert Shaw with his keenly disciplined chamber choir conducts a strong, clean-cut performance, using an English translation modified from the traditional one. Though Shaw's generally broad speeds show little influence from period performance, his concern for clarity of texture is very different from old-style performances, and the Telarc engineers help with full, immediate sound, bringing out sharp dynamic contrasts. Dawn Upshaw adopts too romantically expressive a manner, but the solo singing is good, with Heidi Grant Murphy and James Michael McGuire brought in for the Adam and Eve numbers of Part 3.

The Creation (*Die Schöpfung;* in German).
(M) *** DG 449 761-2 (2) [id.]. Janowitz, Ludwig, Wunderlich, Krenn, Fischer-Dieskau, Berry, V. Singverein, BPO, Karajan.
*** DG Dig. 449 217-2 (2). McNair, Brown, Schade, Finley, Gilfry, Monteverdi Ch., E. Bar. Soloists, Gardiner.
*** Sony SX2K 57965 (2) [id.]. Monoyios, Hering, Van der Kamp, Tölz Boys' Ch., Tafelmusik, Bruno Weil.
(B) *** DG Double 453 031-2. Blegen, Popp, Moser, Ollman, Moll, Bav. R. Ch. & SO, Bernstein.
*** Decca (IMS) 443 445-2 (2) [id.]. Ziesak, Lippert, Pape, Scharinger, Chicago Ch. & SO, Solti.
(M) **(*) DG (IMS) Dig. 445 584-2 (2) [427 629-2]. Battle, Winbergh, Moll, Stockholm R. Ch. and Chamber Ch., BPO, Levine.
(B) **(*) EMI forte (SIS) CZS5 69343-2 (2) [CDFB 69343]. Donath, Tear, Van Dam, Philh. Ch. & O, Frühbeck de Burgos.

(i) *The Creation (Die Schöpfung):* complete (in German); (ii) *Salve regina.*
(B) *** Double Decca 443 027-2 (2) [id.]. (i) Lucia Popp, Werner Hollweg, Kurt Moll, Helena Döse, Benjamin Luxon, Brighton Festival Ch., RPO, Dorati; (ii) Arleen Augér, Alfreda Hodgson, Anthony Rolfe Johnson, Gwynne Howell, L. Chamber Ch., Argo CO, László Heltay.

Among versions of *The Creation* sung in German, Karajan's 1969 set remains unsurpassed and, now reissued as one of DG's 'Originals' at mid-price, is a clear first choice despite two small cuts (in Nos. 30 and 32). The combination of the Berlin Philharmonic at its most intense and the great Viennese choir makes for a performance that is not only polished but warm and dramatically strong too. The soloists are an extraordinarily fine team, more consistent in quality than those on almost any rival version.

Issued to celebrate the 50th anniversary of the DG Archiv label, Gardiner's version brings the benefit of a period performance on a relatively large scale, involving speeds broader than in direct rival versions, yet with clearer, more detailed recording. Characteristically, Gardiner takes a dramatic view, overtly expressive, vividly pointing the highlights of the Creation story. Gardiner may not always convey the relaxed joy of Weil's fresh and brisk version on Sony, but the exhilaration and power of Haydn's inspiration, as well as its lyrical beauty, have never been conveyed more tellingly in a period performance on disc, with the Monteverdi Choir singing with virtuoso clarity and phenomenal precision of ensemble. The soloists are outstanding too, though the silvery soprano, Sylvia McNair, does not always sing full out. A first choice among period performances.

Bruno Weil conducts a brisk, clean-cut reading, using the period instruments of Tafelmusik and a bright-toned chorus, augmented by the Tölz Boys' Choir. If the intimacy at times seems to reduce the scale of this masterpiece, and Weil at times is fussy over detail, the urgent exuberance of the performance is most winning, with an outstanding trio of cleanly focused soloists. The chorus is finely focused too, providing sharp, dramatic contrasts, and the orchestral sound is so clean that one can hear the fortepiano continuo even in tuttis. A good contrasting approach to Christopher Hogwood's on his large-scale period performance in English.

Dorati, as one would expect, directs a lively and well-sprung account. The very opening is magnetic and its imaginative touches and joyfulness of spirit more than compensate for any minor lapses in crispness of ensemble. The soloists are a splendid team. The chorus is as gutsy as you like in *Die Himmel erzählen*, with the soloists nicely balanced. While Karajan is not superseded, Dorati's enjoyably spontaneous 1976 account is certainly well worth considering, especially as it is offered for the cost of a single premium-priced CD. The set opens gloriously with Heltay's lovely 1979 recording of the *Salve regina*, an early work dating from 1771, comparable in its depth of feeling with his finest vocal music. The recording is most realistic and the CD transfer of *The Creation* is strikingly vivid and immediate.

Bernstein's DG version, recorded at a live performance in Munich, uses a relatively large chorus, encouraging him to adopt rather slow speeds at times. What matters is the joy conveyed in the story-telling, with the finely disciplined chorus and orchestra producing incandescent tone, blazing away in the big set-numbers, and the performance is compulsive from the very opening bars. Five soloists are used instead of three, with the parts of Adam and Eve sung by nicely contrasted singers, confirming this as an unusually persuasive version, well recorded in atmospheric sound. This appears not to be available in the USA but is preferable to his earlier, New York version.

Recorded live in the autumn of 1993, Sir Georg Solti's second recording, made (like the first) with Chicago forces, presents a striking difference. The influence of period performance means that not only does he adopt fast speeds, but his very choice of soloists reflects the new generation of light, clear singers, all excellent. Ornamentation and the use of a fortepiano continuo also give further indication of Sir Georg's new stance on this work, which results in a crisp, buoyant reading, full of dramatic contrasts, which nevertheless is not out of scale with Haydn's vision. Splendid choral singing, captured in full, bright sound.

Though James Levine with his weighty forces is occasionally heavy-handed over both dynamics and rhythm, lacking rather in elegance, he conveys the joy of inspiration in this work with characteristic boldness. He is helped not just by the highly polished playing of the orchestra but by characterful singing from all three soloists and fresh, finely disciplined choral singing. The recording, made not in the Philharmonie but in the Jesus-Christus Kirche, is weighty and satisfyingly full, with ample bloom.

Rafael Frühbeck de Burgos directs a genial performance, recorded with richness and immediacy. The soloists are all excellent and, though Helen Donath has a hint of flutter in her voice, she is wonderfully agile in ornamentation, as in the bird-like quality she gives to the aria, *On mighty pens*. The chorus might gain from a more forward balance but their singing is impressive. An enjoyable set.

The Creation: highlights.
(B) *** DG Classikon 439 454-2 (from above recording; cond. Karajan).

Anyone whose budget will not stretch to a complete version of Haydn's masterpiece will find that this 70-minute bargain Classikon highlights disc includes the key solos and choruses.

Masses

Masses Nos. (i–iii) *1 in F (Missa brevis), Hob XXII/1;* (i; iii–vi) *1a in G (Rorate coeli desuper), Hob XXII/3; 3 in C: Missa Cellensis in honorem Beatissimae Virginis Mariae (Missa Santae Caecilae), Hob XXII/5;* (i; iii; v–viii) *4 in E flat: Missa in honorem Beatissimae Virginis Mariae (Great organ Mass), Hob XXII/4;* (i; iii; vi; ix; x) *6 in G (Missa Sancti Nicolai), Hob XXII/6;* (xi–xv) *7 in B flat: Missa brevis Sancti Joannis de Deo (Little organ Mass);* (xi; xiii–xviii) *8 in C: Mariazeller Messe, Hob XXII/8;* (xiii–xvii; xix; xx) *9 in B flat: Missa Sancti Bernardi de Offida (Heiligmesse), Hob XXII/10;* (ix; xiii–xv; xix; xxi; xxii) *10 in C: Missa in tempore belli (Paukenmesse), Hob XXII/9;* (xvi; xxiii–xxvi) *11 in D min.: Missa in augustiis (Nelson Mass), Hob XXII/11;* (xiii–xv; xxv; xxvii–xxviii) *12 in B flat: Theresienmesse, Hob XXII/12;* (xiii–xvii; xix; xxix) *13 in B flat: Schöpfungsmesse (Creation Mass), Hob XXII/13;* (xiii–xvi; xxvii; xxx) *14 in B flat (Harmoniemesse), Hob XXII/14.*
(B) *** Decca 448 518-2 (7) [id.]. (i) Nelson; (ii) Kirkby; (iii) Christ Church Cathedral Ch., AAM, Preston; (iv) Cable; (v) Hill; (vi) Thomas; (vii) Watkinson; (viii) Hogwood (organ); (ix) Minty; (x) Covey-Crump; (xi) Jennifer Smith; (xii) Scott (organ); (xiii) St John's College, Cambridge, Ch.; (xiv) ASMF; (xv) George Guest; (xvi) Watts; (xvii) Tear; (xviii) Luxon; (xix) Cantelo; (xx) McDaniel; (xxi) Partridge; (xxii) Keyte; (xxiii) Stahlman; (xxiv) Wilfred Brown; (xxv) Krause; (xxvi) King's College, Cambridge, Ch., LSO, Willcocks; (xxvii) Spoorenberg; (xxviii) Greevy; Mitchinson; (xxix) Forbes Robinson; (xxx) Young, Rouleau.

Decca's survey of the complete Masses of Haydn, which appeared originally on the Argo and Oiseau-Lyre labels, omits only the newly discovered fragmentary *Missa Sunt bona mixta malis*, Hob XXII/2, of 1768. Overall this achievement stands alongside Dorati's complete recording of the symphonies (and the Beaux Arts' *Piano trios*) as one of the landmarks of the gramophone during the analogue LP era.

Starting in 1962 with Sir David Willcocks's King's version of the *Nelson Mass*, the production team then moved down the road to St John's for the five remaining magnificent Mass settings which Haydn wrote between 1796 and 1802 for his patron, Prince Esterházy, after his return from London. With changing soloists, of generally consistent quality, George Guest directed a series of performances notable for their fresh directness and vigour, with his St John's Choir showing itself a ready match for the more famous choir at King's College and the sound even more vivid. The recordings were made between 1965 and 1969, with the *Little organ Mass* and *Mariazellermesse* following in 1977. The project was completed over the next two years with the early Masses. But the 'authentic' era had arrived and the orchestra changed from the Academy of St Martin-in-the-Fields to the Academy of Ancient Music. Simon Preston took over, and he directed his

Christ Church Cathedral Choir with a comparable freshness and spontaneity to that established at St John's. The engineering team excelled themselves throughout, to produce a well-balanced and spacious yet clearly detailed sound, boldly projected against a nicely resonant acoustic. As with the companion Decca box of the symphonies, H. C. Robbins Landon has provided the notes with his usual spirited scholarship.

Masses Nos. (i) *1 in F (Missa brevis), Hob XXII/1;* (ii) *3 in C: Missa Cellensis in honorem Beatissimae Virginis Mariae (Missa Sanctae Caecilia), Hob XXII/5;* (iii) *4 in E flat: Missa in honorem Beatissimae Virginis Mariae (Great organ mass), Hob XXII/4;* (iv) *6 in G (Missa Sanctae Nicolai), Hob XXII/6.*

(B) *** O-L Double 455 712-2 (2) [id.]. (i) Emma Kirkby; (i–iv) Judith Nelson; (ii) Margaret Cable; (ii–iii) Martyn Hill; (ii–iv) David Thomas; (iii) Carolyn Watkinson; (iv) Shirley Minty, Rogers Covey-Crump; Christ Church, Oxford, Cathedral Ch., AAM, Simon Preston.

Haydn wrote the early *Missa brevis* when he was seventeen. The setting is engagingly unpretentious, some of its sections last for under two minutes and only the *Credo* takes slightly more than three and a half. The two soprano soloists, Judith Nelson and Emma Kirkby, match their voices admirably and the effect is delightful. By contrast the *Missa Cellensis* (which is split between the two discs, after the *Gloria*), at 68 minutes, is Haydn's longest setting of the liturgy. Preston directs an excellent performance with fine contributions from choir and soloists, set against a warm acoustic. In the early *E flat Mass* Haydn followed the rococo conventions of his time, generally adopting a style featuring Italianate melody which to modern ears inevitably sounds operatic. The *Missa Sanctae Nicolai* has a comparable freshness of inspiration and the performance is first rate in every way, even finer than that of the earlier *Great organ mass*, beautifully sung, with spontaneity in every bar and a highly characterized accompaniment. Both are admirably recorded, and the CD transfers are first class.

Masses Nos. (i) *1a in G (Rorate coeli desuper), Hob XXII/3*; (ii) *8 in C: Mariazellermesse, Hob XXII/8*; (iii) *9 in B flat: Missa Sancti Bernardi de Offida (Heiligmesse), Hob XXII/10*; (iv) *13 in B flat: Schöpfungsmesse, Hob XXII/13.*

(N) (B) *** Decca Double 458 376-2 (2) [id.]. (i) Christ Church Cathedral Ch., Oxford, AAM, Preston; (ii) J. Smith, Watts, Tear, Luxon; (iii) Cantelo, Minty, Partridge, Keyte; (iv) Cantelo, Watts, Tear, Forbes Robinson; (ii–iv) St John's College, Cambridge Ch., ASMF, Guest – Michael HAYDN: *Ave Regina.* ***

The little *Missa rorate coeli desuper* was written by Haydn when he was still a choirboy in Vienna, and it may well be his earliest surviving work, while the *Schöpfungsmesse* or *Creation Mass* was the last but one of this magnificent series that Haydn wrote for his patron, Prince Esterházy, after his return from London. The *Mariazellermesse* of 1782 was described by H. C. Robbins Landon as 'the most perfect large-scale work Haydn achieved', and the later *Heiligmesse* is one of the most human and direct in appeal of his religious works. The performances and recordings are all well up to the high standard of the Guest series, with Simon Preston directing a freshly authentic account of the earliest work.

Masses No. 2a (1768): *Sunt bona mixta malis* (fragment), *Hob XXII/2; 7 in B flat (Little organ mass): Missa brevis Sancti Joannis de Deo, Hob XXII/7; Ave Regina, Hob XXIIIb/3; Offertorium: Non nobis, Domine, Hob XXIIIa/1; Responsorium ad absolutionem: Libera me, Hob XXIIb/1; 4 Responsoria de Venerabili, Hob XXIIIc/4 a–d; Salve Regina, Hob XXIIIb/1.*

❁ *** Sony Dig. SK 53368 [id.]. Marie-Claude Vallin, Ann Monoyios, Tölz Boys' Ch., L'Archibudelli, Tafelmusik, Bruno Weil.

The Mass fragment, *Sunt bona mixta malis* (consisting of a *Kyrie* and part of the *Gloria* of an incomplete mass in D minor), was recently discovered in the attic of a country house in Northern Ireland and establishes that at that time Haydn was composing vocal music in an austere, antique, contrapuntal style, looking back towards Palestrina. The four *Responsoria de Venerabili* are more extrovert in feeling, but the second is again in the older style. Other works on this record – the *Responsorium ad absolutionem, Libera me*, and the *Offertorium, Non nobis, Domine* – reflect this same grave contrapuntal idiom and have had to be re-dated in consequence. The collection is completed with a later Mass and two fine early works from the 1750s, the *Ave Regina*, in which Marie-Claude Vallin sings with the purity of a boy treble, and the poignant *Salve Regina in E*. Here the soprano solo is superbly and touchingly sung by Ann Monoyios. It is undoubtedly a profoundly felt work, certainly the finest of Haydn's youthful period. The *Missa brevis: Sancti Joannis de Deo* features a solo organ which delightfully accompanies the boy treble soloist in the *Benedictus* (sung here by a member of the Tölz Boys' Choir). This fascinating record cannot be recommended too highly. The performances are admirably stylish and very fresh and alive.

Masses Nos. (i) *7 in B flat (Little organ mass): Missa brevis Sancti Joannis de Deo;* (ii) *10 in C (Paukenmesse): Missa in tempore belli;* (iii) *11 in D min. (Nelson);* (iv) *14 in B flat (Harmoniemesse).*

(B) *** Decca Double 455 020-2 (2) [id.]. (i) Jennifer Smith, John Scott (organ); (ii) April

Cantelo, Helen Watts, Robert Tear, Barry McDaniel; (iii) Sylvia Stahlman, Watts, Wilfred Brown, Tom Krause; (iv) Erna Spoorenberg, Watts, Alexander Young, Joseph Rouleau; (i–ii; iv) St John's College, Cambridge, Ch., ASMF, George Guest; (iii) King's College Ch., LSO, Sir David Willcocks.

Three major Masses and one shorter work are combined here to make a very tempting Decca Double for those not wanting the complete set listed above.

Mass No. 11 in D min. (Nelson); Te Deum in C, Hob XXIIIc/2.

*** DG Dig. 423 097-2 [id.]. Lott, C. Watkinson, Maldwyn Davies, Wilson-Johnson, Ch. & E. Concert, Pinnock.

Mass No. 11 in D min. (Nelson): Missa in angustiis.

(M) *** Decca 421 146-2 [id.]. Stahlman, Watts, Wilfred Brown, Krause, King's College, Cambridge, Ch., LSO, Willcocks – VIVALDI: *Gloria.* ***

(i) *Mass No. 11 in D min. (Nelson): Missa in augustiis, Hob XXII/11;* (ii) *Arianna a Naxos* (orchestral version), *Hob XXVIb/2; Scena di Berenice (Berenice che fai?), Hob XXIVa/10.*

(M) *** Decca Eclipse Dig. 448 983-2. (i) Bonney, Howells, Rolfe Johnson, Roberts, L. Symphony Ch., Hickox; (ii) Arleen Augér, Handel & Haydn Society, Hogwood.

The *Nelson Mass* (*Missa in angustiis*: 'Mass in times of fear') brings a superb choral offering from Trevor Pinnock and the English Concert. With incandescent singing from the chorus and fine matching from excellent soloists, Pinnock brings home the high drama of Haydn's autumnal inspiration. Similarly, the *Te Deum* leaps forward from the eighteenth century all the more excitingly in an authentic performance such as this. Excellent, full-blooded sound, with good definition.

The CD of the famous Willcocks account of the *Nelson Mass* (*Missa in angustiis*: 'Mass in times of War') is admirably full-bodied and vivid; those not wanting to stretch to Pinnock's full-priced digital CD will find this a satisfactory alternative with its very generous Vivaldi coupling.

Hickox conducts a lively, well-sung reading of the most celebrated of Haydn's late Masses, most impressive in the vigorous, outward-going music which – with Haydn – makes up the greater part of the service; here the choral singing is little short of glorious. In serene moments the choral sound is slightly recessed, with inner parts less well defined than they might be. The soloists are very good, and Barbara Bonney's purity of line is impressive, although tonally she is a little thin. While in some ways the Willcocks version of 20 years earlier is even finer, in the work's more resplendent moments the London Symphony's choral focus is given greater impact by the more modern digital sound.

What makes Hogwood's version almost indispensable is the inclusion of Haydn's two major solo cantatas (a full half-hour of wonderful music) which he wrote for his two London visits in the 1790s. The first was written with fortepiano accompaniment (which Haydn himself played in London), and the effective string arrangement had been made by an anonymous hand. Arleen Augér was never more impressive in the recording studio than here. She is superbly dramatic in the cantata which tells of Ariadne abandoned by Theseus on Naxos, and – in melting voice – infinitely touching in the *Scena di Berenice.* Hogwood accompanies most sympathetically and the recording is perfectly balanced. Not to be missed.

(i) *Mass No. 12 in B flat (Theresienmesse), Hob XXII/12;* (ii) *Salve Regina in G min., Hob XXIIb/2*; (ii; iii) *Stabat Mater, Hob XX/bis.*

(N) (B) *** Decca Double 458 373-2 (2) [id.]. (i) Spoorenberg, Greevy, Mitchinson, Krause, St John's College, Cambridge, Ch., ASMF, Guest; (ii) L. Chamber Ch., Argo CO, László Heltay; (iii) with Augér, Hodgson, Rolfe-Johnson, Howell.

The *Theresienmesse* followed on a year after the *Nelson Mass.* It may be less famous, but the inspiration is hardly less memorable, and Haydn's balancing of chorus against soloists, contrapuntal writing set against chordal passages, was never more masterly than here. George Guest injects tremendous vigour into the music and the St John's Choir is on top form throughout. The *Stabat Mater* is scandalously neglected. It was written in his early years at Esterháza. Scored for strings with oboes, the work is far bigger than that scale might suggest, and it is good that Heltay's reading conveys its essential greatness, helped by excellent soloists and vivid recording. The *Salve Regina* – another early work, comparable in its depth of feeling – is here given with full chorus; although solo voices were originally intended, the weight of the piece is better conveyed in this way. Excellent transfers throughout.

(i; ii) *Mass No. 9 in B flat (Heiligmesse): Missa Sancti Bernardi von Offida, Hob XXII/10;* (ii) *Mare Clausum* (fragment), *Hob XXIVa/9*; Motet: *Insanae et vanae curae, Hob XXI/1:13c; Motetti de Venerabili sacramento, Hob XXIIIc/5a–d; Te Deum for the Empress Marie Thérèse, Hob XXIIIc/2.*

(N) ✿ *** Sony SK 66260 [id.]. (i) Jörg Hering, (ii) Harry van de Kamp, Soloists from Tölz Boys' Ch., Tölz Ch., Tafelmusik, Weil.

Enjoyable as are the Guest and Hogwood recordings on Decca, it is good that Bruno Weil is continuing his inspired and inspiring new period-instrument series, under the guidance of H. C. Robbins Landon, who provides the excellent notes. There could be no more thrilling example than this. The choral singing in the magnificent *Heiligmesse* has overwhelming momentum, yet is radiantly rich in expressive intensity, and the listener is carried through on a tide of exultant spiritual energy to a closing *Agnus Dei* of real grandeur. And in the *Credo* how touchingly the soloists from the Tölz Boys Choir enter, one by one, at the *Et incarnatus est*, with just a simple clarinet accompaniment. Then comes a surprise. The *Mare Clausum* brings a jolly patriot bass solo, sung in English, followed by a rousing chorus (all about preserving Britain's marine power!). The two affirmative sacred motets are hardly less vigorous, with the second using a solo group of trebles in alternation with the full chorus, and the programme ends with the even more dramatic Marie Thérèse *Te Deum*, which concludes with a thrilling, trumpet-laden climax. This is a superb collection, and the bright, spaciously resonant recording, with the words always clear, is in every way outstanding.

Mass No. 10 in C (Paukenmesse): Missa in tempore belli, Hob XXII/9; Salve Regina, HobXXIIIb:2.

(N) **(*) Teldec/Warner Dig. 0630 13146-2. Röschmann, Von Magnus, Lippert, Widmer, Arnold Schoenberg Ch., Harnoncourt.

(i) *Mass No. 10 in C (Paukenmesse): Missa in tempore belli, Hob XXII/9;* (ii) Motet: *O Coelitum beata, Hob XXIIIa:G9*; (ii) *Salve Regina, HobXXIIIb: 2.*

(N) *** Sony Dig. SK 68255 [id.]. (i; ii) Monoyios, (i) Groop, Hering, Van der Kamp; (i; ii) Tölz Boys' Ch., (ii) Soloists from Ch., Tafelmusik, Bruno Weil.

Once again in the dramatic *Paukenmesse*, the bite and exuberance of Bruno Weil's Tölz Choir (not just boys) and the excellent Tafelmusik are very stimulating indeed; the soloists are also excellent, notably Ann Monoyios, who sings equally beautifully in the short additional Latin motet, and also leads soloists from the choir in the rightly admired *Salve Regina*. Excellent, fresh, yet resonant sound. This makes the strongest possible case for period-instrument performances of this music. A superb disc that will be hard to surpass.

Harnoncourt comes near to matching it. He has the advantage of the gleaming-voiced Barbara Bonney and a really excellent tenor (Jörg Hering). The four soloists also show their fine tonal matching in the *Salve Regina*. The choral singing in the mass is excellent too and as it is a live recording there is an added dimension of concentration, so that Harnoncourt can afford to be more relaxed in his tempi. Yet compare his *Gloria* with the vibrant Weil version, and the extra lift and bite in the Viennese performance is striking. But on its own terms, Harnoncourt's reading is satisfying, and at its finest in the *Agnus Dei*. The recording is spacious but the chorus, although vivid, lacks something in edge. In any case this is upstaged by the Sony disc, which offers an extra work and a very attractive one too.

Mass No. 14 in B flat (Harmoniemesse), Hob XXII/14; Te Deum for Maria Theresia, XXIIIc/2.

(N) **(*)BMG/DHM Dig. 05472 77337-2 [id.]. Piau, Groop, Prégardien, Van der Kamp, Namur Chamber Ch., La Petite Bande, Sigiswald Kuijken.

The *Harmoniemesse* sounds pleasingly fresh in this smaller-scale, chamber-styled performance from Kuijken. He has a good team of soloists and they bring out the music's devotional nature in the more intimate moments. The Namur Choir (about two dozen strong) certainly sings with conviction in both works, and is given a clear projection by the recording. This is enjoyable and authentic, but less than overwhelming.

The Seasons (*Die Jahreszeiten;* complete; in German).

*** DG Dig. 431 818-2 (2). Bonney, Rolfe Johnson, Schmidt, Monteverdi Ch., E. Bar. Soloists, Gardiner.

(B) *** Ph. Dig. 438 715-2 (2) [id.]. Edith Mathis, Siegfried Jerusalem, Dietrich Fischer-Dieskau, Ch. & ASMF, Marriner.

(M) *** DG 457 713-2 (2) [id.]. Janowitz, Schreier, Talvela, V. Singverein, VSO, Karl Boehm.

(B) *** Decca Double 448 101-2 (2) [id.]. Cotrubas, Krenn, Sotin, Brighton Festival Ch., RPO, Dorati.

(M) **(*) EMI (SIS) CMS7 69224-2 (2). Janowitz, Hollweg, Berry, Ch. of German Op., BPO, Karajan.

As in so many of his choral recordings, Gardiner brushes away any cobwebs from the music in Haydn's last oratorio. Gardiner here more than ever rejects the idea prevalent among period performers that slow, measured speeds should be avoided, and almost always gets the best of both worlds in intensity of communication, whatever the purists may say. Even more than usual, this studio performance conveys the electricity of a live event. The silver-toned Barbara Bonney and Anthony Rolfe Johnson at his most sensitive are outstanding soloists, and though the baritone, Andreas Schmidt, is less sweet on the ear, he winningly captures the bluff jollity of the role of Simon.

Sir Neville Marriner directs a superbly joyful performance of Haydn's last oratorio, effervescent with the optimism of old age. Edith Mathis and Dietrich Fischer-Dieskau are as stylish and characterful as one would expect, pointing the words as narrative. The tenor too is magnificent: Siegfried

Jerusalem is both heroic of timbre and yet delicate enough for Haydn's most elegant and genial passages. The chorus and orchestra, of authentic size, add to the freshness. The recording, made in St John's, Smith Square, is warmly reverberant without losing detail. The CD transforms the sound, with added definition for both chorus and soloists. Highly recommended – a remarkable bargain by any standards.

Boehm's performance enters totally into the spirit of the music and is fully worthy of its reissue as one of DG's 'Originals'. The soloists are excellent and characterize the music fully; the chorus sing enthusiastically and are well recorded. But it is Boehm's set. He secures fine orchestral playing throughout, an excellent overall musical balance and real spontaneity in music that needs this above all else. The CD transfer of the 1967 recording is admirably managed; the sound overall is warmly expansive, the chorus have plenty of body, if not the sharpest focus, and there is an excellent sense of presence.

Dorati brings to the work an innocent dedication, at times pointing to the folk-like inspiration, which is most compelling. This is not as polished an account as Boehm's but, with excellent solo singing and bright chorus work, is enjoyable in its own right. The choruses of peasants in Part 3, for instance, are boisterously robust. Textually there is an important difference in that Dorati has returned to the original version and restored the cuts in the introductions to *Autumn* and *Winter*, the latter with some wonderfully adventurous harmonies. With Dorati, this is above all a happy work, a point made all the more telling by the immediacy of the new transfer. This is all the more welcome at Double Decca price and competes strongly with the Boehm set now at mid-price.

Karajan's 1973 recording of *The Seasons* offers a fine, polished performance which is often very dramatic too. The characterization is strong, and in Karajan's hands the exciting Hunting chorus of Autumn (*Hört! Hört! Hört das laute Getön*) with its lusty horns anticipates *Der Freischütz*. The remastered sound is drier than the original but is vividly wide in dynamic range. Choruses are still a little opaque, but the soloists are all caught well and are on good form; and the overall balance is satisfactory. Those drawn to Karajan might try the fairly generous (53 minutes) highlights CD (CDM7 69010-2).

Stabat mater.

(N) **(*) Teldec/Warner Dig. 4509 95085-2. Bonney, von Magnus, Lippert, Miles, Arnold Schoenberg Ch., VCM, Harnoncourt.

Harnoncourt's is a spacious and eloquent account of the *Stabat mater*, with a good solo team (although the tenor has moments of insecurity). But when the splendid bass, Alastair Miles, enters arrestingly at the *Pro peccatis* and the *Flammis orci ne succedar*, there are bursts of energy from Harnoncourt and the orchestra too, and one realizes that the overall tension has been lower than one expects with this conductor. Yet the penultimate *Quando corpus morietur* brings lovely singing from soprano and mezzo together, and the closing contrapuntal *Paradisi gloria* makes a telling close, even if here the soloists are not entirely comfortable in their sudden bravura entries.

Te Deum in C, Hob XXIIIc/2.

(BB) *** RCA Navigator 74321 29238-2. V. Boys' Ch., Ch. Viennensis, VCO, Gillesberger – MOZART: *Requiem mass.* ***

A fine, vigorous account of the *Te Deum* by these Viennese forces, very vividly recorded, coupled to a not inconsiderable account of Mozart's *Requiem*. At super-bargain price it makes excellent value.

OPERA

L'Anima del filosofo (Orfeo ed Euridice) (complete).

*** O-L Dig. 452 668-2 (2) [id.]. Bartoli, Heilmann, D'Arcangelo, Silvestrelli, AAM Ch., AAM, Hogwood.

Haydn wrote his last and grandest opera for London in 1791 but, when the king refused to give the theatre a licence, it was never performed. In 1806 Breitkopf published 11 numbers from the score, but it was not until 1950 that the opera was performed complete, and then with Erich Kleiber conducting and Maria Callas as Euridice. It is a curious piece, quite different in treatment from most operatic versions of the story, with Euridice very much the central figure at the start, leading to her death in Act II.

Impressed by Handel oratorios and the English choral tradition, Haydn includes many choruses of comment. He also takes the opportunity of writing for a large orchestra, far beyond what he had been used to in Esterháza. The result has many impressive moments, even though Haydn would clearly have modified, and possibly expanded, what he wrote in the light of experience, had it been staged. As it is, a first-rate recording has long been needed, and this one fills the bill very well indeed. Hogwood uses an enlarged Academy, with 12 first violins, and though at times his manner is severe, he paces the piece very effectively, making the most of the drama.

The very opening brings one of the most telling passages, a monologue when Euridice in distress flees into the forest. Cecilia Bartoli is in her element, passionately expressive, creating a larger-than-life character, as Maria Callas no doubt did too. Euridice's death scene, Orfeo's agony of lament (agitated, and very different from Gluck's *Orfeo* aria, *Che farò*), and a brilliant coloratura aria for the Sybil (dazzlingly done by Bartoli) bring other high points. Though Orfeo's death comes as an anticlimax, the final chorus for the Bacchantes is most memorable, in a minor key, dark and agitated, then fading away to the close, suggesting that Haydn may have had the end of Act II of Mozart's *Idomeneo* in mind. Uwe Heilmann is a most sympathetic Orfeo, musically stylish, even if the microphone catches the hint of a flutter, as it does too with the well-contrasted voices of Ildebrando d'Arcangelo as King Creonte, Euridice's father, and Andrea Silvestrelli as Pluto. The chorus, so important in this work, is fresh and well disciplined.

Armida (complete).
*** Ph. (IMS) 432 438-2 (2). Norman, Ahnsjö, Norma Burrowes, Ramey, Leggate, Rolfe Johnson, Lausanne CO, Dorati.

More than most of Haydn's works in this form, *Armida* presents a psychological drama, with the myrtle tree the most obvious of symbols. On CD it makes a fair entertainment, with splendid singing from Jessye Norman, even if she scarcely sounds malevolent. Claes Ahnsjö as the indecisive Rinaldo does better than most tenors in coping with the enormous range. The whole team of soloists is one of the most consistent in Dorati's Haydn opera series, with Norma Burrowes particularly sweet as Zelmira. As well as some advanced passages, *Armida* also has the advantage that there is little *secco* recitative. The 1978 recording quality is outstanding.

La fedeltà premiata (complete).
*** Ph. (IMS) 432 430-2 (3). Valentini Terrani, Landy, von Stade, Titus, Cotrubas, Alva, Mazzieri, Lövaas, SRO Ch., Lausanne CO, Dorati.

La fedeltà premiata shows its composer on his finest form. It was the first of Dorati's series of Haydn opera recordings for Philips, launched with characteristic effervescence, helped by an excellent Haydn-sized orchestra and a first-rate cast. The proud Aramanta is superbly taken by Frederica von Stade, while Haydn's unconventional allocation of voices brings a fine baritone, Alan Titus, to match her as the extravagant Count Perrucchetto. But the sweetest and most tender singing comes from Ileana Cotrubas as the fickle nymph, Nerina. The recording is intimate but with plenty of atmosphere. It is well transferred to CD, but at times one feels the cueing could be more generous.

(i) *L'incontro improviso* (complete). Arias for: (ii) *Acide e Galatea*. (iii) SARTI: *I finti eredi*. (iv) TRAETTA: *Ifigenia in Tauride*. (ii–iv) Terzetto from: Pasticcio: *La Circe, ossia L'isola incantata*.
*** Ph. 432 416-2 (3) [id.]. (i; iv) Ahnsjö; (i) Zoghby, Trimarchi, Luxon, M. Marshall, Della Jones, Prescott; (ii) Devlin; (iii) Baldin; Lausanne CO, Dorati.

In eighteenth-century Vienna the abduction opera involving Moorish enslavement and torture became quite a cult. The greatest instance is Mozart's *Entführung*, but this example of the genre from Haydn is worthy of comparison, with its very similar story; the result is musically delightful. The most heavenly number of all is a trio for the three sopranos in Act I, *Mi sembra un sogno*, rather like *Soave sia il vento* in *Così fan tutte*. The tenor's trumpeting arias are beautifully crisp and the vigorous canzonettas for the two *buffo* basses include a nonsense song or two. Benjamin Luxon and Domenico Trimarchi are delectable in those roles. Claes Ahnsjö is at his finest, resorting understandably to falsetto for one impossible top E flat; the role of the heroine is superbly taken by Linda Zoghby, and she is well supported by Margaret Marshall and Della Jones. The layout places each of the three Acts on a single CD and makes room on the third for two arias which Haydn devised for operas by other composers, plus one for his own *Acide e Galatea*.

L'infedeltà delusa (complete).
*** Ph. (IMS) 432 413-2 (2). Mathis, Hendricks, Baldin, Ahnsjö, Devlin, Lausanne CO, Dorati.
(M) **(*) HM/BMG 05472 77316-2 (2) [id.]. Argenta, Lootens, Prégardien, M. Schäfer, Varcoe, La Petite Bande, Sigiswald Kuijken.

L'infedeltà delusa may not be dramatically the most imaginative of stage works, but by the standards of the time it is a compact piece, punctuated by some sharply noteworthy ideas. The opera brings many memorable numbers, such as a laughing song for Nencio (on Philips the admirable Claes Ahnsjö) and a song of ailments for the spirited and resourceful heroine, Vespina (Edith Mathis, lively and fresh). Dorati draws vigorous, resilient performances from everyone (not least from the delightful Barbara Hendricks). The Philips recording is splendidly full-blooded and neatly transferred on to a pair of CDs, with one Act complete on each.

The plot of the opera is unusual for the time in giving the role of the heavy father to the tenor (well taken on RCA by Christoph Prégardien), reflecting the fact that it was expressly designed for Karl Friberth, literary adviser to Prince Esterházy as well as a singer. This alternative version on period instruments nicely captures the flavour of a semi-domestic performance in the prince's country palace. Both the RCA sopranos, Nancy Argenta and Lena Lootens, are agile and precise, if a little edgy. Both tenors, Markus Schäfer as well as Prégardien, are stressed by the range demanded but, like the bass, Stephen Varcoe, they have clean voices, suitable for Haydn on a small scale. *L'infedeltà delusa* may be no *Così fan tutte* but this too is a most enjoyable set, worth considering at mid-price, even if the Dorati version is a clear first choice.

L'isola disabitata (complete).
*** Ph. (IMS) 432 427-2 (2). Lerer, Zoghby, Alva, Bruson, Lausanne CO, Dorati.

(i) *L'isola disabitata* (complete); (ii) Cantata: *Arianna a Naxos*.
(N) *** Arabesque Dig. Z 6717-2 (2) Susanne Mentzer; (i) with Ying Huang, John Aler, Christopher Schaldenbrand, Padova CO, David Golub; (ii) Golub (piano).

L'isola disabitata, one of the last operas that Haydn wrote for Esterhàza, is described as an 'azione teatrale', more compact than most with seven solo numbers linked by orchestral recitative, and rounded off with a substantial quartet. David Golub and his orchestra from Padua give a warm, relaxed reading, with speeds consistently slower than on the rival Dorati version. The soloists are all first-rate, with Susanne Mentzer warm and firm as Costanza, Ying Huang fresh and girlish as Silvia and John Aler clear-toned as Gernando. Christopher Schildenbrand jibs at singing trills but is stylish otherwise. Well-balanced sound. *Arianna a Naxos* has Mentzer accompanied by Golub at the piano (unidentified in the booklet) to make a very welcome fill-up, to give a substantial advantage over the Dorati set.

Vocally, it is the second soprano on the Dorati set, Linda Zoghby, who takes first honours, though the baritone, Renato Bruson, is splendid too. The piece ends with a fine quartet of reconciliation, only the eighth number in the whole piece. The direction of recitatives is unfortunately not Dorati's strong point – here, as elsewhere in the series, rather too heavy – but with excellent recording, very vividly transferred to CD, and with just the right degree of ambience, this makes a useful alternative to Golub's Arabesque version. The two acts are given a CD apiece.

(i) *Il mondo della luna* (complete). (ii) Arias for: Cantata: *Miseri noi, misera patria*; Petrarch's sonnet from *Il Canzoniere: Solo e pensoso*. BIANCHI: *Alessandro nell'Indie*. CIMAROSA: *I due supposti conti*. GAZZANIGA: *L'isola di Alcina*. GUGLIELMI: *La Quakera spiritosa*. PAISIELLO: *La Frascatana*. Pasticcio: *La Circe, ossia l'Isola incantata*.
*** Ph. (IMS) 432 420-2 (3). (i) (i) Trimarchi, Alva, Von Stade, Augér, Mathis, Valentini Terrani, Rolfe Johnson, Lausanne CO, Dorati ; (ii) Edith Mathis, Lausanne CO, Jordan.

Il mondo della luna ('The world on the moon') is better known (by name at least) than the other Haydn operas that the Philips series has disinterred. Written for an Esterházy marriage, it uses the plot of a naïve but engaging Goldoni comedy. Much of the most charming music comes in the brief instrumental interludes, and most of the arias are correspondingly short. That leaves much space on the discs devoted to *secco* recitative and, as on his other Haydn opera issues, Dorati proves a surprisingly sluggish harpsichord player. Nevertheless, with splendid contributions from the three principal women singers, this is another Haydn set which richly deserves investigation by anyone devoted to opera of the period. The 1977 recording is first class, as is the CD transfer; and the layout, with one Act allotted to each of the three CDs, leaves room for eight substitution arias (recorded three years later) on the last disc, stylishly sung by Edith Mathis.

Orlando paladino (complete).
*** Ph. (IMS) 432 434-2 (3). Augér, Ameling, Killebrew, Shirley, Ahnsjö, Luxon, Trimarchi, Mazzieri, Carelli, Lausanne CO, Dorati.

One might infer from this delightful send-up of a classical story in opera that Haydn in his pieces for Esterháza was producing sophisticated charades for a very closed society. Though long for its subject-matter, this is among the most delightful of all, turning the legend of Roland and his exploits as a medieval champion into something not very distant from farce. There are plenty of touches of parody in the music: the bass arias of the King of Barbary suggest mock Handel and Charon's aria (after Orlando is whisked down to the Underworld) brings a charming exaggeration of Gluck's manner. Above all the Leporello-like servant figure, Pasquale, is given a series of numbers which match Mozart, including a hilarious duet when, bowled over by love, he can only utter monosyllables – cue for marvellous *buffo* singing from Domenico Trimarchi. The overall team is strong, with Arleen Augér as the heroine outstandingly sweet and pure. George Shirley as Orlando snarls too much in recitative, but it is an aptly heroic performance; and Elly Ameling and Gwendoline Killebrew in subsidiary roles are both excellent. The recitatives here, though long, are rather less heavily done than in some other Dorati sets, and the 1976 recording is first rate and splendidly transferred to three CDs, one for each Act.

La vera costanza (complete).
*** Ph. (IMS) 432 424-2 (2). Norman, Donath, Ahnsjö, Ganzarolli, Trimarchi, Lövaas, Rolfe Johnson, Lausanne CO, Dorati.

Like Mozart's *Marriage of Figaro*, *La vera costanza* has serious undertones, if only because it is the proletarian characters who consistently inspire sympathy while the aristocrats come in for something not far short of ridicule. The individual numbers may be shorter-winded than in Mozart, but Haydn's sharpness of invention never lets one down, and the big finales to each of the first two Acts are fizzingly impressive, pointing clearly forward to *Figaro*. Overall, the opera is nicely compact. In every way bar one this is a delectable performance. The conducting of Dorati sparkles, Jessye Norman is superb as the virtuous fisher-girl, Rosina, while the others make up an excellent team, well cast in often difficult roles designed for the special talents of individual singers at Esterháza. The snag is the continuo playing of Dorati himself, heavy and clangorous, holding up the lively singing of the *secco* recitatives. Apart from some discrepancy of balance between the voices and a touch of dryness in the acoustic, the recorded sound is excellent.

Haydn, Michael (1737–1806)

(i) *2 Flute concertos: in D, MH 81 and MH 105; Symphony in F, MH 25.*

**(*) Nimbus Dig. NI 5392 [id.]. (i) István-Zsolt Nagy, Austro-Hungarian Haydn O, Adam Fischer (with Josef HAYDN: *Symphony No.* 22 **(*))

These two *galant* flute concertos are slight but most engaging. The perky, rhythmically pointed main theme of the first movement of MH 105 (which opens the concert) is immediately inviting, especially when played with such character and finesse as it is by István-Zsolt Nagy. The *F major Symphony* is a recently discovered early work, conventional but with a characteristically amiable 'walking' *Andante*. It is a pity another Michael Haydn symphony could not have been recorded to complete the programme, instead of Josef's *Philosopher*. The recording is warmly resonant throughout, with the flute balanced well forward.

Symphonies Nos. 1 in C, P.35; 2 in C, P.2; 3 (Divertimento) in G; 4 in B flat, P.51; 5 in A, P.3; 6 in C, P.4; 7 in E, P.5; 8 in D, P.38; 9 in D, P.36; 10 in F, P.45; 11 in B flat, P.9; 12 in G, P.7; 15 in D, P.41; 16 in A, P.6; 18 in C, P.10; 25 in G, P.16; 26 in E flat, P.17; 27 in B flat, P.18; 28 in C, P.19. Sinfonia (Divertimento) in G, P.8.

(N) **(*) CPO Dig. CPO 999 591-2 (6) [id.]. Slovak CO, Bohdan Warchal.

Josef Haydn's younger brother Michael worked first in Vienna, but gained security and a permanent post as Musical Director at the Salzburg court in 1763, where he remained until his death. His 41 symphonies were composed over three decades from 1760 until 1789. This is the first time they have been decently played on record and we owe a debt to CPO for allowing us to follow the composer's development from modest beginnings to considerable achievement in the later symphonies, the best of which ought to be much better known. The early works are comparatively straightforward and seldom adventurous, usually simply scored for oboes, horns and strings; sometimes flutes were added. The invention, too, though often quite endearing, is not particularly individual. Even so almost all the symphonies written in the 1760s have at least one memorable movement and sometimes two. No. 3 in G (subtitled Divertimento) has striking high horns in the outer movements and they trill spectacularly in the Minuet. The gracious *Andante* of No. 4 (*La Confidenza*) alternates with quicker sprightly episodes. No. 6 opens like a familiar Handel chorus and has a wistful *Andante*, with the strings muted throughout; the *Minuet* acts as finale. No. 8 (1764) stands out and is most winning throughout. It is again drawn from a Divertimento, and scored for trumpets as well as horns. After a vigorous but light-hearted outer movement the *Andante* features pastoral flutes and introduces an aria on the bassoons, who return jocularly in the *Trio* of the *Minuet*, while the engaging finale even introduces clarinets. The concise No. 9, more like an Italian overture, produces one of the composer's loveliest tunes as its centrepiece. No. 10 is also a rather appealing three-movement work, with a charming *grazioso* slow movemet, and No. 11 has another delicate *Andantino* full of charm. The *Allegro molto* of No. 12 *in G* brings a light-hearted secondary theme on the violins worthy of Josef, an *Andante* decorated with flutes, and a striking rondo finale. The horns are again used jovially in the dancing finale of No. 15.

With No. 18 we move into the 1770s and find the most ambitious work so far (36 minutes 34 seconds with repeats); its scoring includes a solo cor anglais. For a long time, No. 25 *in G* (1783) was attributed to Mozart, and with some justice – its slow movement is rather fine and the finale spirited and graceful. Nos 26 to 28 all date from 1783–4 and show the composer at full stretch. All are in three movements and each has an outstanding slow movement. It is difficult to decide whether the *Adagietto affettuoso* of No. 26 or the *Poco Adagio* of No. 28 is the finer. Finales too are infectious and very neatly scored. No. 27 has an extended slow introduction, but it is No. 28 which caps the series so far. It is not for nothing that it is in *C major*, for its impressive fugato closing movement has much in common with the finale of Mozart's *Jupiter Symphony*. The Slovak Chamber Orchestra is an excellent modern-instrument ensemble and performances throughout are lively in the traditional sense, warm and committed. Warchal phrases most musically, but generally observes repeats, which makes some slow movements seem rather long. Occasionally one might enjoy the brighter sound and brisker tempi of period-instrument manners, but overall this well-recorded set remains a fine achievement.

Symphonies: in A, P.6; in B flat, P.9; in G, P.16; in E flat, P.26; in F, P. 32.

*** Chandos Dig. CHAN 9352 [id.]. L Mozart Players, Matthias Bamert.

Here are more performances of the Michael Haydn Symphonies that really do them full justice. P.6 and P.9 are both four-movement works but the others are in three-part Italian overture form. The elegance of the gentle *Andante* of the *A major Symphony* sets the seal on the playing, warm, polished and cultivated, while the *Allegro molto* finale, with its bold horns, might almost be by Mozart. The charming *Andantino* of P.9 is no less engaging, while the closing Rondo of P.16 has plenty of high spirits. None of this is great music, but all of it is enjoyable and the composer's penultimate F major work (1789) brings a strong, impressively constructed opening movement and a tender *Adagio* with muted strings. The well-detailed recording is pleasingly full and resonant.

Symphonies Nos. 21 in D, P.42; 30 in D, P.21; 31 in F, P.22; 32 in D, P. 23.
(N) *** CPO Dig. CPO 999 179-2 [id.]. Deutsche CO, Neuss, Johannes Goritzki.

For the later symphonies Michael Haydn remains faithful to the three-movement format, jettisoning the minuet. Both Nos 21 and 30 have slow introductions. By now his orchestration has become much more sophisticated, using woodwind quite subtly for colouring and enriching the textures, and, in the *Andante* of No. 21 (a particularly impressive work), the horns too. His melodic material is more refined and musical arguments are developed with much greater assurance, as in the quite excellent opening *Allegro assai* of No. 31 (1785). The following *Andante cantabile* uses orchestral soloists, including cor anglais, almost as in a sinfonia concertante. No. 32 (1786) is the only two-movement work in the series and very delightful it is. The playing of the Deutsche Chamber Orchestra is first rate. Allegros have splendid zest and the ensemble is polished as well as sensitive so that the music has even greater vitality in Neuss am Rhein than in Slovakia. The recording too is of the highest quality.

Symphonies Nos. 34 in E flat, P.26; 35 in G, P.27; 36 in B flat, P.28; 37 in D, P. 29; 38 in F, P.30; 39 in C, P.31.
(N) *** CPO Dig. CPO 999 379-2 [id.]. Deutsche CO, Neuss, Johannes Goritzki.

Michael Haydn wrote these six symphonies in a continuing burst of inspiration in seven weeks, at the beginning of 1788. He again chose the three-movement format and his invention is fecund and concentrated: all but No. 39 are under ten minutes in overall length. But they bring a bubbling torrent of ideas; and how much more skilfully they are scored than the early symphonies!

The *Adagietto* of No. 34 introduces a dolorous bassoon solo and the closing fugato is skilfully and wittily contrived, with even surprise interjections from the solo horn. The outer movements of No. 35 sail along on a tide of rhythmic energy, yet with an underlying lyricism, and the unusual *Andante* brings a florid concertante oboe contribution. No. 36 also buzzes along, and the *Andante con espressione* is full of galant charm, while the *Andantino* of No. 37 is songful. No. 38 opens with a spirited, gavotte-like rhythm, but is far more than a dance movement, and is most felicitously scored, including a horn solo. The slow movement brings a delightful cello and violin duet, with oboe echoes. The Josef Haydnesque humour in the finale *Allegro scherzante*, with strong dynamic contrasts, is most winning (one really smiles at the crisp, neat playing here). From its opening, No. 39 is strong and forward-looking; the *Andante* uses the full orchestral palette, and in the final fugato there is mature use of counterpoint to knit the ideas convincingly together, with a brief, powerful coda. All these works are superbly played, conveying an exhilarating mixture of verve and elegance. Again first-class sound.

String quintets: in B flat, P.105; in C, P.108; in G, P.109.
**(*) Sony Dig. SK 53897 [id.]. L'Archibudelli.

It is good to have modern recordings of Michael Haydn's *String quintets*. P.108/9 date from 1773, and Mozart knew and admired them. The *C major* with its engaging *Andante cantabile* slow movement was very popular in its day. P.105 is more of a cassation or serenade and has seven movements, including an attractive fourth-movement set of variations and a *marcia* finale. All the works are inventive. Here they are played freshly, elegantly and authentically, without edginess, and the only drawback for some ears may be the modest squeezing of phrases in slow movements plus some rather strong accents in minuets. The recording is fresh, with firmly focused yet transparent textures.

Ave Regina.
(N) (B) *** Decca Double 458 376-2 (2) [id.]. St John's College, Cambridge, Ch., ASMF, George Guest – HAYDN: *Masses 1a, 8, 9, & 13.* ***

This lovely antiphon, scored for eight-part double choir, looks back to Palestrina, and the Venetian school of the Gabrielis and the young Monteverdi. It is beautifully sung and recorded.

Headington, Christopher (1931–96)

(i) *Piano concerto;* (ii) *The Healing Fountain;* (iii) *Serenade for cello and string orchestra.*
(N) *** ASV Dig. CDDCA 969 [id.]. The Britten Sinfonia, Nicholas Cleobury with (i) Gordon Fergus-Thompson; (ii) Andrew Carwood. (iii) Alexander Baillie.

Only a few days before his untimely death in a skiing accident, Christopher Headington attended these recording sessions and expressed delight at the results. *The Healing Fountain* was composed in 1978 'in memoriam Benjamin Britten' and is a 26-minute cycle for high voice and chamber orchestra comprising settings of Auden, Sassoon, Wilfred Owen, Thomas Moore and Shelley. It is expertly fashioned and often imaginative though it is perhaps a little too close for comfort to the Britten idiom – indeed it quotes from *Peter Grimes*, *Death in Venice* and the underrated *Nocturne*. The *Piano concerto* was begun the following year but was put aside until 1991. Although it is not as haunting or personal as the *Violin concerto,* Headington's masterpiece, it is a strong piece, well structured and rewarding. The composer was an excellent pianist and his writing for the instrument is exhilarating and adroit. Those who respond to, say, Prokofiev or Britten will find much to admire here. The *Serenade* is the most recent work, and was commissioned by Julian Lloyd Webber and premièred by him in 1995. Fine and committed performances and very good recording too.

Violin concerto.
❁ *** ASV CDDCA 780 [id.]. Xue Wei, LPO, Glover – R. STRAUSS: *Violin concerto.* ***

The Headington *Violin concerto* is a warmly lyrical, unashamedly tonal work in which a fiery central Scherzo is framed by two longer, more reflective movements. The finale is a spacious set of variations in which the last and longest acts as a movingly meditative summary. Xue Wei plays with a passionate commitment, with Jane Glover and the London Philharmonic providing warmly sympathetic accompaniments. Excellent sound. Those looking for twentieth-century music that is accessible and rewards familiarity need not hesitate.

Heath, Dave (born 1956)

The Frontier.
(M) *** Virgin/EMI CUV5 61121-2. LCO, Warren-Green – ADAMS: *Shaker loops* *** ❁; GLASS: *Company* etc. ***; REICH: *8 Lines.* ***

In *The Frontier* Heath's incisive rhythmic astringency is tempered by an attractive, winding lyrical theme which finally asserts itself just before the spiky close. The work was written for members of the LCO, and their performance, full of vitality and feeling, is admirably recorded.

Hebden, John (18th century)

6 Concertos for strings (ed. Wood).
**(*) Chandos Dig. CHAN 8339 [id.]. Cantilena, Shepherd.

These concertos are Hebden's only known works, apart from some flute sonatas. Although they are slightly uneven, at best the invention is impressive. The concertos usually feature two solo violins and are well constructed to offer plenty of contrast. The performances here are accomplished, without the last degree of polish but full of vitality.

Heinichen, Johann David
(1683–1729)

Dresden concerti: in C, S 211; in G, S 213; in G (Darmstadt), S 214; in G (Venezia), S 214; in G, S 215; in F, S 217; in F, S 226; in F, S 231; in F, S 232; in F, S 233; in F, S 234; in F, S 235. Concerto movement in C min., S 240; Serenata di Moritzburg in F, S 204; Sonata in A, S 208.
*** DG (IMS) Dig. 437 549-2 (2) [id.]. Col. Mus. Ant., Reinhard Goebel.

Dresden concerti: in F, S 231; 233/5; in G, S 213; Concerto movement in C min., S 240; Sonata in A, S 208.
*** DG (IMS) Dig. 437 849-2. Col. Mus. Ant., Reinhard Goebel.

Johann David Heinichen, a contemporary of Bach, was a Dresden court musician and the concertos here were intended for the (obviously excellent) Dresden court orchestra. It is the orchestral colour that makes these concertos so appealing rather than their invention, which is more predictable. Goebel's Cologne forces obviously relish the delicacy of Heinichen's wind scoring and his neat and busily vital allegros. The recording is freshly vivid, clean and realistic. One would be tempted to recommend the single-disc selection, but DG have cunningly not included therein the lollipop of the set. This is the *Pastorell* second movement of the *C major Concerto*, Seibel 211, with its piquant drone (track 5 of the second CD). It is immediately followed by a peaceful *Adagio* for flute and strings and a sparkling finale.

Alma mater redemptoris; Beatus vir; De profundis; Lamentations of Jeremiah; Nicht das Band, das dich bestricket (oratorio); *Nisi Dominus aedificaverit; Warum toben die Heiden; Pastorale in A.*
**(*) DG (IMS) Dig. 447 092-2 (2) [id.]. Mechthild Georg, Axel Köhler, Jörg Dürmüller, Scot Weir, Raimund Nolte, Col. Mus. Ant., Goebel.

Here is a representative selection of Heinichen's vocal music. But (unlike Biber) Heinichen is not revealed as a composer of inspired originality here, though he has some individual ideas about orchestration. The singers here are all impressive, but Goebel is less so. He too often favours rhythmic plodding, and one wonders whether in other hands this music would sound more inspiring. The *Pastorale*, a brief instrumental composition, ends the programme.

Helweg, Kim (born 1956)

American fantasy (A tribute to Leonard Bernstein).
** Chandos Dig. CHAN 9398 [id.]. Safri Duo & Slovak Piano Duo – BARTOK: *Sonata for 2 pianos and percussion;* LUTOSLAWSKI: *Paganini variations.* ***

The *American fantasy* is a four-movement sonata and at the same time a set of variations on Bernstein's song, *America*, from *West Side Story*. But although it is obviously the work of a resourceful and intelligent musician, it is of insufficient individuality to reward repeated listening. Fine playing, stunning recording. The audience goes wild at the end of the performance.

Hely-Hutchinson, Victor (1901–47)

Carol Symphony.
(M) ** EMI CDM7 64131-2. Guildford Cathedral Ch., Pro Arte O, Barry Rose – QUILTER: *Children's overture;* VAUGHAN WILLIAMS: *Fantasia on Christmas carols.* **

Hely-Hutchinson's *Carol Symphony* dates from the late 1920s. Hely-Hutchinson's first movement could do with a little judicious pruning, the Scherzo is quite effective and in the finale he gathers all the threads together and ends with a triumphal presentation of *O come, all ye faithful*. But it is the *Andante* which remains in the memory with its deliciously imaginative gossamer texture against which the solo harp embroiders *Nowell*. The performance here is lively and sensitive if not distinctive, but the close-miked recording is curiously dry and unexpansive, bearing in mind that the 1966 venue was Guildford Cathedral.

Heming, Michael (1920–42)

Threnody for a soldier killed in action.
(M) (***) EMI mono CDM5 66053-2. Hallé O, Barbirolli – BRITTEN: *Violin concerto* (**); RUBBRA: *Symphony No. 5* etc. (***)

Michael Heming was a kind of Second World War Butterworth and when he was killed at El Alamein, Anthony Collins concocted (to use Michael Kennedy's word) the *Threnody for a soldier killed in action* from sketches that the young man had made. Barbirolli and the Hallé Orchestra recorded it in 1945. A moving piece in the English pastoral tradition and a welcome fill-up to this interesting disc.

Henselt, Adolf von (1814–89)

Piano concerto in F min., Op. 16; Variations de concert on 'Quand je quittai la Normandie' from Meyerbeer's Robert le Diable, Op.11.
(N) *** Hyperion Dig. CDA 66717 [id.]. Marc-André Hamelin, BBC Scotish SO, Martyn Brabbins – ALKAN: *Concerti da camera.* ***

Henselt's *F minor concerto* is fiendishly difficult (Egon Petri thought it one of the hardest pieces he had ever played) but it seems to present few problems for Marc-André Hamelin, who is more than equal to its challenges. The idiom, as one might expect, is much indebted to Mendelssohn and Chopin, but there is much to give delight quite apart from the virtuosity of the playing. Stunning playing throughout from this remarkable Canadian pianist, and very good recorded sound.

Henze, Hans Werner (born 1926)

The DG Henze Collection
(M) *** DG stereo/mono 449 860-2 (14) [id.]. Various artists.

To mark the occasion of Hans Werner Henze's seventieth birthday, DG have issued a handsomely presented 14-CD set of the repertoire that the composer himself recorded in the heyday of his relationship with the company, plus a handful of other items. DG are wise to make the discs available separately as there are few who would necessarily want or could afford the whole package, even though it is very competitive at mid-price.

For most collectors the best starting-point, perhaps, would be the symphonies, which come on a two-CD set. For R.L. the *Third* and *Fourth* remain the most haunting of the set, with the latter casting a particularly powerful spell, and its expressionist anguish is punctuated by moments of an all-pervasive melancholy which must spring from a deep personal experience. The *First Symphony* is also a delight. The *First Violin concerto* (1947), recorded here with Schneiderhan as soloist, is one of the most rewarding of Henze's early scores, even if his debt to Hindemith is not fully discharged.

The other CDs which would make an excellent introduction to the set include the beautiful *Double Concerto for oboe and harp*, played by its dedicatees, Heinz and Ursula Holliger, coupled with one of his most haunting and affecting scores, the *Fantasia for strings*. Likewise the beautiful *Five Neapolitan songs* with the young Fischer-Dieskau or the *Cantata della fiaba estrema*, expertly sung by Edda Moser, are wonderful pieces. The CD transfers, generally speaking, have an admirable clarity, but this is achieved at a certain cost: compared with the LPs there is less depth and less space round the aural image.

(i) *2 Ballet variations;* (ii) *Piano concerto No. 2;* (iii) *Tristan* (preludes for piano, tapes and orchestra); (iv) *3 Tientos for guitar.*
(M) **(*) DG mono/stereo 449 866-2 (2). (i)

RIAS SO, Ferenc Fricsay; (ii) Christoph Eschenbach, LPO; (iii) Homero Francesch, Cologne RSO; (ii; iii) cond. composer; (iv) Siegfried Behrend.

The *Piano concerto* has great originality and poetry. Eschenbach, for whom the concerto was written in 1967, is the magnificent soloist. It is an interesting, often moving work, full of a sad eloquence that bursts into occasional bitter outcries of some violence. The beauty of the recording captures all the refinement and delicacy of Henze's textures. The brief *Ballet variations* were written as music for a ballet without a narrative while Henze was strongly under the influence of the Stravinsky of the *Danses concertantes*. The three *Tientos for guitar*, though brief, are very imaginatively conceived.

Tristan, the other extended work here, is an extraordinary montage with a kinship with Wagner's opera, yet is very much like a musical nightmare, originally deriving from an extraordinary mélange of extra-musical sounds, mixed together on tape in a studio in Putney, London. The resulting work is a six-part structure lasting just over 43 minutes, splicing in a quotation from the opening of Brahms's *First Symphony*, synthesized Chopin excerpts and more distorted Brahms. A bizarre sequence of what the composer calls 'Burlesque dance movements' comes next, ending with a scream of death, with the tape supposedly reproducing the scream of a famous Wagnerian soprano. The closing *Epilogue* leads to rather more distinct distillations of Wagner, a child's heartbeat, bells chiming and so on. It is difficult to take seriously, but it certainly represents a new experience.

(i) *Ode to the west wind* (for cello and orchestra); (ii) *Concerto for double-bass;* (iii) *Violin concerto No. 1.*

(M) *** DG 449 865-2 [id.]. (i) Siegfried Palm; (ii) Gary Karr; (iii) Wolfgang Schneiderhan; (i; iii) Bav. RSO; (ii) ECO; all cond. composer.

The *Violin concerto* shows the influence of Hindemith, while the *Ode to the west wind* was inspired by Shelley's poem. Both works contain pages of some beauty, though the later piece employs a more fragmented and complex style than the predominantly serial *Concerto*. The *Violin concerto* is the more immediately appealing work and has an eloquent slow movement, and the performances, apart from having the composer's authority to commend them, are expertly recorded. The *Double-bass concerto* is not among the composer's most impressive pieces, though it fascinates by its resourceful treatment of an unpromising solo instrument. The performance is exemplary.

(i) *Double concerto for oboe, harp and strings. Fantasia for strings; Sonata for strings.*

(M) *** DG 449 864-2. Zurich Coll. Mus., Paul Sacher, with (i) Heinz and Ursula Holliger.

The language of the *Fantasia*, based on incidental music for a film, is more disciplined and diatonic than is often Henze's wont. It is a moving score with a vein of melancholy that is direct in utterance. The *Double concerto* was inspired by the astonishing artistry and virtuosity of Heinz Holliger on the oboe, who performs it here with his wife, Ursula, on the harp. Highly inventive and resourceful, this performance is authoritative and is given an exemplary recording.

Symphonies Nos. (i) *1–5;* (ii) *6.*

(M) *** DG 449 861-2 (2). (i) BPO; (ii) LSO; cond. composer.

These works are the product of a highly sophisticated imagination with a most refined and sensitive awareness of atmosphere and feeling for sonority. There is much nourishment and stimulus to be found here. The *First*, with its cool, Stravinskian slow movement, is a remarkable achievement for a 21-year-old. There is a dance-like feel to the *Third*, written while Henze was attached to the Wiesbaden Ballet. The *Fourth* is meant to connote 'an evocation of the living, breathing forest and the passing of the seasons'. There is at times an overwhelming sense of melancholy and a strongly Mediterranean atmosphere to its invention. The *Fifth* embraces the most violent angularity, with passages of exquisite poignancy and tranquillity; the language is strongly post-expressionist. The *Sixth Symphony* was composed while Henze was living in Havana. The performances are brilliant and the vivid recordings do not sound their age, those of the first five symphonies being over 35 years old.

VOCAL MUSIC

(i) *Being beauteous;* (ii) *Five Neapolitan songs;* (iii) *Versuch über Schweine (Essay on pigs);* (iv) *Whispers from heavenly death.*

(M) *** DG mono/stereo 449 869-2. (i; iv) Edda Moser; (i) RIAS Ch., BPO soloists; (ii) Dietrich Fischer-Dieskau, BPO soloists, Richard Kraus; (iii) Roy Hart, Philip Jones Brass Ens., ECO; (iv) BPO soloists; (i; iii–iv) cond. composer.

The *Versuch über Schweine* ('Essay on pigs') contains a voice-part that traverses an amazing range and certainly encompasses an extraordinary variety of timbre. *Being beauteous* is exquisite and quite moving, and *Whispers from heavenly death* is one of the composer's most fascinating works. The singing of Edda Moser is quite phenomenal both in purity of tone and in accuracy of intonation. The performances of all this repertoire could hardly be bettered, and the recording reproduces a wide dynamic range with admirable truthfulness of balance and quality of tone.

(i) *Cantata della fiaba estrema (Cantata of the ultimate fable);* (ii) *Moralitäten (Moralities);* (iii) *Musen Siziliens (Muses of Sicily).*

(M) *** DG 449 870-2. (i) Edda Moser, RIAS Ch., Berlin Philh. CO; (ii) Cornelius Schwarz, Dieter Leffler, Andreas Scheibner, Friedemann Jäckel, Titus Paspirgilis, Frieder Lang, Dresden Ch., Leipzig GO; (iii) Dresden Ch., Joseph Rollino, Paul Sheftel, Dresden State O soloists; all cond. composer.

The *Cantata* is a setting of a Roman love-poem. With Edda Moser the soloist, it cannot fail to communicate vividly. *Moralities* (with narrator), is a setting of 'three scenic plays' which W. H. Auden devised from three of Aesop's fables. Its manner is not in the least intimidating and the result is potently ironic rather than lightly humorous in spirit. The *Muses of Sicily* opens with a *Pastorale* dialogue, and ends with the *Song of Silenus*, recounting the creation of the world from the elements of earth, air, sea and liquid. The work is entirely choral, with a vivid accompaniment for two pianos, wind instruments and timpani. Even if one does not take readily to all this music, Henze could never be less than stimulating. Superb singing and very good recording.

El Cimarrón (autobiography of the runaway slave Esteban Montejo) (recital for four musicians).

(M) *** DG 449 872-2. William Pearson, Karlheinz Zoeller, Leo Brouwer, Stomu Yamash'ta, cond. composer.

El Cimarrón uses the words of a former slave, born in Cuba over 100 years ago, a simple but moving story. The live performance was impressive for the antics of the Japanese percussionist, Stomu Yamash'ta; but on disc the impact of the work is even more intense, because the improvisatory passages have been considerably tightened up, and the story is after all best imagined in the mind's eye – the poetic passage where the runaway lives in the forest, the biting account of the Revolution, the scene of the swaggering Yankees where a four-letter word is inserted (in English) in an otherwise German text. The performance is as near definitive as one could expect, beautifully recorded.

Das Floss der Medusa (The Raft of the Medusa) (oratorio).

(M) *** DG 449 871-2. Edda Moser, Dietrich Fischer-Dieskau, Charles Regnier, RIAS Chamber Ch., Members of the St Nikolai Hamburg Youth Ch., N. German R. Ch. & O, cond. composer.

This is a vividly imaginative work and whatever the political bias, the message is both dramatic and moving as told in the tragic story of the crew of a shipwrecked frigate cast adrift and left to die by their officers. Henze has conceived the simple but effective idea of having the members of the crew as represented by the chorus move from one side of the stage to the other, one by one called from the land of the living over to the side of Death (soprano soloist). A vivid experience, superbly realized.

Der langwierige Weg in die Wohnung der Natascha Ungeheuer (The Tedious way to Natascha Ungeheuer's apartment).

(M) **(*) DG 449 873-2. William Pearson, Fires of London, Philip Jones Brass Quintet, Gunter Hampel Free Jazz Ens., Giuseppe Agostini, Stomu Yamash'ta, cond. composer.

It was unfortunate that the composer used the word 'tedious' in his title, for the writing here has the air of a political tract and comes from the period when the composer was rejecting opera. The work is an allegory: Natasha Ungeheuer is 'the siren of a false Utopia who constantly lures the leftist intellectual into the cosy situation of so many middle-class socialists, who preach revolution while meanwhile living more or less the same old comfortable life'.

OPERA

Elegie für junge Liebende (Elegy for young lovers) (scenes).

(M) *** DG 449 874-2. Fischer-Dieskau, Driscoll, Dubin, Mödl, Berlin RSO & German Op. O, Berlin (members), cond. composer.

Elegie für junge Liebende is set in a mountain inn, from which the hero and heroine eventually go to their deaths in a storm; but the underlying psychology of the characters, their destinies dominated by the poet, Mittenhoffer, is most complex. So is the construction of the music, both in the variety of forms for the set pieces, and in the way each character is given his or her own musical personality by the individual use of specific instrumentation and note-groupings (intervals, rather than leitmotives). The composer shows his brilliant feeling for orchestral colour and, with Fischer-Dieskau as Mittenhoffer, Martha Mödl as a strong-voiced Carolina (the poet's patron) and Liane Dubin an appealing Elisabeth, the vocal writing is fully characterized. An excellent and enterprising issue.

Der junge Lord.

(M) *** DG 449 875-2 (2). Mathis, Grobe, McDaniel, Johnson, Driscoll, German Op., Berlin, Ch. & O, Dohnányi.

This 'opera buffa' is Henze at his most amiable, and it results for much of the time in his Stravinskian side dominating, though he also allows himself a warmer vein of lyricism than usual. The plot in its comedy is consciously cynical, involving a snobbish community duped by a titled Englishman. He introduces an alleged English lord who finally turns out to be an ape. There is an underlying seriousness to the piece, and in this excellent performance, recorded with the composer's approval, the full range of moods and emotions is conveyed. Very good (1967) sound.

OTHER RECORDINGS

Symphony No. 7; Barcarola.
*** EMI Dig. CDC7 54762-2. CBSO, Rattle.

The *Seventh Symphony* is not only the longest Henze has written, it is also the weightiest and most traditionally symphonic, Beethoven-like in four substantial movements. Rather belying its title, the *Barcarola* presents a similarly weighty and massive structure, an elegiac piece of over 20 minutes, inspired by the myth of the ferryman, Charon, crossing the Styx. The dramatic bite of both performances, recorded live in Symphony Hall, Birmingham, makes them instantly compelling. Full, colourful recording to bring out the richness of Henze's orchestral writing.

Symphony No. 9.
(N) *** EMI CDC5 56513-2. Berlin R. Ch., BPO, Ingo Metzmacher.

Henze refers to his *Ninth Symphony* as a *summa summorum* of his musical output. At this time of war and ethnic cleansing it could not be more apposite. Commissioned by the Berlin Philharmonic, it is choral throughout, a setting of seven poems by Hans-Ulrich Treichel based on Anna Segher's *The Seventh Cross*. It tells of seven prisoners condemned to be crucified who escape from a concentration camp and are hunted down and recaptured. Only one succeeds in eluding his pursuers, and the poems and Henze's settings portray the most powerful and nightmarish emotions. In his autobiography, *Bohemian Fifths* (Faber, 1998), Henze recounts his own youthful experiences in Nazi Germany, and there is no doubt of the intensity and depth of feeling that lies behind this symphony. The recording derives from the première at the Philharmonie in 1997; it is a meticulously prepared performance and the singing of the Berlin Radio Choir is superb in every way. Powerful and impressive.

Undine (complete ballet).
(N) ❀ *** DG Dig. 453 467-2 (2) [id.]. L. Sinf, Oliver Knussen.

Here at last is a long overdue recording of Henze's wonderfully resourceful and strongly atmospheric ballet written for Covent Garden in 1958, choreographed by Ashton and starring the legendary Fonteyn. Given DG's dedication to Henze's cause in the 1960s and 70s, it is puzzling that they waited so long before recording what must arguably be his most approachable and attractive score. The scenario tells of the water-nymph Undine and her infatuation for a mortal, and Henze's score was described at the time as 'a concerto for Fonteyn'. Henze himself pictured her as 'the radiant centre of the whole ballet . . . this wonder floating, almost above the ground'. From the very opening note to the closing passacaglia, one is struck by the sheer profusion of invention, as well as the richness and subtlety of the orchestral palette. The evocation of the sea in Act II (CD1: track 22) is quite masterly. (Some of the audience felt distinctly queasy at the Covent Garden when the sea heaved and the horizon sank and rose above the boat as the lovers set sail.) The score may not always bother to disguise Stravinskian touches, but if there is a bit of Stravinsky in it, there is so much more that is pure Henze, and richly imaginative Henze at that. Oliver Knussen gets superlative playing from the London Sinfonietta and the DG recording is extraordinarily vivid and present, transparent and full of body. With a totally committed and persuasive performance and recording of demonstration standard, this makes an ideal entry-point for the collector into Henze's world.

CHAMBER MUSIC

Piano quintet.
(N) *** Ph. Dig. 446 710-2 [id.]. Peter Serkin, Guarneri Qt. – BRAHMS: *Piano quintet.* ***

Henze's *Piano quintet* was composed in 1990–91 for Peter Serkin and the Guarneri Quartet, and this recording emanates from 1995. It is a compact three-movement piece lasting some twenty minutes. In the composer's own words, 'each of the movements contrasts sharply from one another, and each evokes a world of its own [though] there is a distinct feeling of progression from the first movement to the last'. As always with Henze there is a highly imaginative creation of texture and a strong atmosphere. It shares some of its invention with the *Requiem* composed at roughly the same time. First-rate playing and recording.

INSTRUMENTAL MUSIC

Royal Winter Music: Guitar sonatas Nos. 1 & 2.
(N) *** MDG MDGL 3110 [id.]. Reinbert Evers.

These two sonatas, the *First* from 1975–6 and the *Second* from 1979, rank among Henze's most resourceful and imaginative scores. They are 'sonatas on Shakespearean characters', the first ranging from Romeo and Juliet, Ariel, Ophelia to the malice and majesty of Richard III; the second encompassing Sir Andrew Aguecheek, Bottom's Dream from *A Midsummer Night's Dream* and a particularly compelling and effective portrait of Lady Macbeth. Henze exploits all the resources of the instrument with astonishing assurance, subtlety and imagination. Reinbert Evers despatches its many challenges with great virtuosity and brilliance. The 1983 recording still sounds first-class.

Voices.
*** Berlin Classics 2180-2 BC (2) [id.]. Roswitha Trexler, Joachim Vogt, Leipzig RSO Chamber Ens., Horst Neumann.

This massive and wide-ranging song-cycle of 22 numbers, lasting over 90 minutes, is among Henze's most inspired and characterful works, even including ironic songs echoing Kurt Weill, several of them setting poems by Bertolt Brecht. The wonder is that, so far from seeming too disparate a sequence, *Voices* gathers in richness as it progresses, with instruments including ocarina, accordion, mouth-organ and electric guitar, as well as a large percussion section. Some of the episodes are violent, but the work is rounded off with the most beautiful and most extended piece, a duet, *Blumenfest* ('Carnival of flowers'), which seems to suggest a final ray of hope, with bitterness gone. This analogue recording, made in Germany in 1980, presents a sharply focused performance, strong and dramatic, with two excellent, clean-cut soloists.

OPERA

Die Bassariden (The Bassarids).
*** Koch Schwann 314 006-2 (2) [id.]. Tear, Schmidt, Armstrong, Riegel, Lindsley, Wenkel, Burt, Murray, Berlin RIAS Chamber Ch. & RSO, Albrecht.

Henze's *The Bassarids*, based on the *Bacchae* of Euripides, presents a contrast of rival philosophies between the Dionysiac and the Apollonian, the sensual and the intellectual, and this fine account from Berlin amply confirms the work's power. The cast is first rate, including Kenneth Riegel, Andreas Schmidt, Robert Tear and Karen Armstrong, and the choral writing adds greatly to the impact, splendidly realized here by the RIAS Choir.

Herbert, Victor (1859–1924)

Cello concerto No. 2 in E min., Op. 30.
*** Sony SK 67173 [id.]. Ma, NYPO, Masur – DVORAK: *Cello concerto.* ***
(M) ** Mercury (IMS) 434 355-2 [id.]. Miquelle, Eastman-Rochester O, Hanson - GROFE: *Grand Canyon suite; Mississippi suite.* **(*)

The Victor Herbert concerto which sparked Dvořák into writing his masterpiece within the year makes an apt and unusual coupling for that superb work. Yo-Yo Ma gives a compelling, high-powered performance. Ma's use of rubato is perfectly judged, with the slow movement made the more tender at a flowing speed. The finale is then given a quicksilver performance, both brilliant and urgent.

Georges Miquelle is a very musical soloist, but his tonal image is modest and he is dynamically upstaged by the orchestra everywhere but in the slow movement. He plays the work sympathetically, but Ma's newest version is much more persuasive.

Hérold, Ferdinand (1791–1833)

La Fille mal gardée (ballet, arr. Lanchbery): complete.
(M) *** Decca Dig. 430 849-2 (2). ROHCG O, Lanchbery – LECOCQ: *Mam'zelle Angot.* ***

La Fille mal gardée: extended excerpts.
❀ (M) *** Decca 430 196-2 [id.]. ROHCG O, Lanchbery.

Lanchbery himself concocted the score for this fizzingly comic and totally delightful ballet, drawing primarily on Hérold's music, but interpolating the famous comic *Clog dance* from Hertel's alternative score, which must be one of the most famous of all ballet numbers outside Tchaikovsky. There is much else of comparable delight. Here, with sound of spectacular Decca digital fidelity, Lanchbery conducts a highly seductive account of the complete ballet with an orchestra long familiar with playing it in the theatre.

The alternative extended selection on Decca has a vintage Kingsway Hall recording. One cannot believe that it dates from 1962, for the combination of ambient bloom and the most realistic detail still places it in the demonstration bracket.The performance is also wonderfully persuasive and brilliantly played, displaying both affection and sparkle in ample quantity.

Herrmann, Bernard (1911–75)

(i) *The Devil and Daniel Webster:* suite; (ii) *Obsession* (abridged score); (i) *Welles raises Kane:* suite.
(M) *** Unicorn UKCD 2065 [id.]. (i) LPO; (ii) Nat. SO; composer.

The Devil and Daniel Webster suite is not first-grade Herrmann; *Welles raises Kane* is another matter. Beecham himself gave one of its first performances in New York during the war. The music is drawn from both Orson Welles's *Citizen Kane* and *The Magnificent Ambersons*, snappily and evocatively extrovert, showing a brilliant flair for orchestral colour. It is superbly played. For the reissue Unicorn have added a brilliant Decca recording of an abridged version of the music Herrmann wrote for *Obsession* (some 39 minutes overall). It offers some of his most spectacular and evocative writing, including choral effects.

Symphony; (i) *The Fantasticks* (song-cycle).
(M) *** Unicorn UKCD 2063 [id.]. (London) National PO, composer; (i) with Michael Rippon, Meriel Dickinson, John Amis, Gillian Humphreys, Thames Chamber Ch.

Underlying everything in this eclectic but enjoyable symphony the argument reflects the approach of a dedicated Sibelian and it is good to hear Herrmann extending himself and giving what is in effect a musical self-portrait. Admirable performance and very good recording. The coupled song-cycle – virtually a cantata – set to words by the Elizabethan poet Nicolas Breton has more of the composer's own personality and is obviously deeply felt music. With its nicely spiced word-imagery, the music communicates readily, and it is a pity that Gillian Humphreys, who is very sympathetic, has such a close vibrato. Otherwise the soloists are excellent and the orchestral playing quite lovely. Most rewarding when the sound is so atmospheric.

(i) *Moby Dick* (cantata); (ii) *For the fallen*.
(M) *** Unicorn UKCD 2061 [id.]. (i) John Amis, Robert Bowman, Kelly, Rippon, Aeolian Singers, LPO; (ii) Nat. PO; composer.

Herrmann's *Moby Dick* is written in an immediately approachable idiom. The soloists are first rate, and the chorus and orchestra convey their enthusiasm and excitement in such effective and rewarding music. The recording is also outstanding. *For the fallen* is a short elegiac obituary for the dead of the Second World War. Its pastoral feeling and understatement are gently haunting. It is beautifully played and recorded.

Wuthering Heights (opera): complete.
(M) *** Unicorn UKCD 2050/52 [id.]. Bainbridge, Kelly, Bell, Beaton, Kitchiner, Rippon, Ward, Bowden, Elizabethan Singers, Pro Arte O, composer.

Bernard Herrmann spent many years working on his operatic adaption of Emily Brontë's novel, and the result is confident and professional. Though the writing is purely illustrative rather than musically original, this performance, strongly conducted by the composer, makes for a colourful telling of the story. The solo singing is consistently good and the recording beautifully clear.

Hertel, Johann (1727–89)

Trumpet concerto No. 1 in E flat.
(N) *** EMI Dig. CDC5 55231-2 [id.]. Maurice André, Franz Liszt O, Budapest, János Rolla – HAYDN; HUMMEL: *Trumpet concertos* *** (with MARCELLO: *Concerto in D min*. **(*)).

Hertel's *E flat concerto* (the first of three) has a rather fine central *Larghetto*. André clearly relishes the work's high tessitura and plays it with aplomb.

Trumpet concerto in D.
*** Ph. Dig. 420 203-2 [id.]. Hardenberger, ASMF, Marriner – HAYDN *** ✽; HUMMEL *** ✽; STAMITZ: *Concertos*. ***

Johann Hertel's *D major Trumpet concerto* is typical of many works of the same kind written in the Baroque era. Håkan Hardenberger clearly relishes every bar and plays with great flair.

Hildegard of Bingen (1098–1179)

'*900 Years*' (1098–1998) Collection.
(N) **(*) HM/BMG Analogue/Dig. 05472 77505-2 (8) [id.]. Sequentia, Barbara Thornton.

Born almost exactly nine centuries ago, Abbess Hildegard of Bingen has over the last decade or so emerged as one of the great creative figures of medieval times: not just an inspired composer, but a poet, dramatist and theologian, a correspondent with emperors and popes. Her output is astonishing. In terms of the quantity of the music and religious poetry she left us, she stands head and shoulders above any other name in the twelfth or thirteenth centuries, and the quality and individuality of her writing are in no doubt. As many listeners have found, her melismas insinuate themselves into the consciousness and stay there. Following on Gothic Voices' best-selling disc for Hyperion (see below), the fine German group Sequentia has, under Barbara Thornton, created an eight-CD collected edition of her works. The recordings are all available separately and are discussed individually below.

Canticles of ecstasy.
(N) ✽ *** HM/BMG Dig. 05472 77320-2 [id.]. Sequentia, Barbara Thornton.

This first instalment makes a splendid introduction, a collection of Marian antiphons, sequences and responsories, plus eulogies to the Holy Spirit, where the poetic imagery is often drawn from nature. At speeds more spacious than those of the Gothic Voices, with women's voices alone, the elaborate monodic lines soar heavenwards even more sensuously, matching the imagery of Hildegard's poetry. For a meditative mood this outdoes Gregorian chant.

Voice of the blood.
(N) **(*) HM/BMG Dig. 05472 77346-2 [id.]. Sequentia, Barbara Thornton.

The sequence of music here is related to St Ursula, who, in the company of a group of eleven virgin noblewomen, was reputedly slaughtered in Cologne on her return from a pilgrimage to Rome. (The telling of her story, in the course of time, increased the number of virgins to 11,000!) As leader of a spiritual community of women, Hildegard felt a strong identification with Ursula, and the opening lament of the cycle, *O rubor sanguinis*, immediately brings the imagery of flowing blood. It is sung unaccompanied, but the following responsory has a long instrumental pedal note over which the vocal melisma floats. The poetry draws on the natural world. *Favus distillans* pictures the saint as 'A honeycomb dripping honey' and later her purity is compared with apple-blossoms. After a reference to the Trinity, the fifth piece is an address to Ecclesia, a female personification of the heavenly community, and this symbolic (and vulnerable) figure is to return in the closing pieces, of which the antiphon *Nunc gaudeant* brings an extraordinary burst of spiritual energy. Two purely instrumental interludes (constructed by Elizabeth Gaver for fiddle and organ) add variety to a carefully planned collection which is, understandably, often rather sombre in its basic mood.

O Jerusalem.

(N) *** HM/BMG Dig. 05472 77353-2 [id.]. Sequentia, Sons of Thunder Men's Vocal Ens., Instrumental Ens., Benjamin Bagby & Barbara Thornton.

On 1st May 1152, Hildegard's very own newly built church in Rupertsberg was dedicated, with considerable ceremony, to serve her personal Benedictine order, and this collection is devised as a conjectural programme of celebratory music to fit such an occasion. The bells of Bamberg Cathedral toll through the opening title piece, which also has the simple instrumental backing, and there is more purely instrumental music here than in previous collections, joining flute, rebec, organ and vielle (hurdy-gurdy). There follows a lively *Magnificat* for St Rupert and two very touching (and typical) melismas extolling his virtues. The following music, beginning with *O tu illustrata,* soaringly evokes a radiantly mystical image of the Virgin Mary, to stand as symbol for the consecration of the women who were to renounce the physical world and join Hildegard's order; but for the hymn to the holy spirit a male group enters impressively, before the closing rapturous Marian testament from the women.

Symphoniae (Spiritual songs).

(N) *** HM/BMG GD 77020 [id.]. Sequentia, Barbara Thornton; with Margriet Tindemans, Benjamin Bagby.

This is a reissue of Sequentia's very first collection, made in 1979. The analogue recording is of the very highest quality and the choice of music, both vocal (accompanied and unaccompanied) and instrumental (fiddle, flute, 15-string harp, psaltery), is particularly appealing. The collection divides into two groups – the first celebrating female divinities such as Mary, Ursula and her accompanying virgins, and even Wisdom, considered a type of feminine deity and for which Hildegard wrote one of her most eloquent tributes. The second group is of laudatory pieces – for the Apostles (a responsory, introduced with a plaintive flute solo), for the Holy Confessors, for the Patriarchs and Prophets, and for the Martyrs. In this last, remarkable piece the upper vocal line moves over a sustained lower note. The freshness of the singing here and the considerable instrumental interest makes this one of the most imaginatively conceived of the series.

Ordo virtutum (The Play of the Virtues).

(N) *** HM/BMG Dig. 05472 77394-2 (2) [id.]. Sequentia Vox Feminae, Sons of Thunder Men's Vocal Ens., Instrumental Ens., Barbara Thornton & Benjamin Bagby.

Ordo virtutum is a mystery play, and this 92-minute piece includes strikingly dramatic passages, with the Devil himself intervening. This was the second recording made by Sequentia – even more imaginatively theatrical than the first – and is superbly atmosperic and compelling as recorded here.

Saints.

(N) **(*) HM/BMG Dig. 05472 77378-2 (2) [id.]. Sequentia Vox Feminae, Sons of Thunder Men's Vocal Ens., Instrumental Ens., Barbara Thornton & Benjamin Bagby.

Apart from *Ordo virtutum*, the mystery play mentioned above, this two-disc set is Sequentia's most ambitious project so far. It covers a wide range of music created to be sung by monks as well as nuns in honour of the early Saints: Disibod, Eucharius and Maximin, Mattias (who joined the Apostles to replace Judas) and Saint Boniface. Sequentia's vigorous male group alternates with the Vox Feminae, sometimes with instrumental support. This is eloquent singing of stirring music, usually extrovert, with strong lyrical lines, more like Gregorian monody, less sensuous than much of Hildegard's output, except for the two tributes to Saint Ursula. It is all impressively sung, but a survey to be recommended to the Hildegard enthusiast rather than the general collector.

Other Recordings

Hymns and sequences: *Ave generosa; Columba aspexit; O Ecclesia; O Euchari; O Jerusalem; O ignis spiritus; O presul vere civitatis; O viridissima virga.*

*** Hyperion CDA 66039 [id.]. Gothic Voices, Muskett, White, Page.

This Hyperion CD by the Gothic Voices was the disc which put Hildegard firmly on the map. It draws widely on the Abbess of Bingen's collection of music and poetry, the *Symphonia armonie celestium revelationum* – 'the symphony of the harmony of celestial revelations'. These hymns and sequences, most expertly performed and recorded, have excited much acclaim – and rightly so. A lovely CD.

'*Heavenly revelations*': Hymns, sequences, antiphons, responds.

(N) (BB) ** Naxos Dig. 8.550998 [id.]. Oxford Camerata, Summerly.

The Oxford Camerata offer a simple presentation,

alternating female and male voices in consecutive works. The opening female melisma, *O Euchari* ('Eucharius, you walked in the paths of happiness when you remained with the son of God'), has a striking, recurring melodic line and establishes the group's unpretentious flowing style. Then follow two eulogies to the Virgin Mary, the first a rather dark *Alleluia* from the men, followed by a soaring female tribute, *Ave generosa* ('Hail noble one, shimmering and unpolluted girl'). There is no doubt that this music suits the Oxford female voices best (the later male praise for the Trinity here lacks any sense of euphoria), and the closing final accolade to the Virgin from the women certainly has a serene beauty. The conductor's restraint is palpable; there is very little feeling of ecstasy here.

Laudes of Saint Ursula.
(N) *** HM Dig. HMC 901626 [id.]. Ens. Organum, Marcel Pérès.
(N) (B) *** HM Dig. Trio HMX 290891.93 (3) (as above) Ens.Organum, Pérès – MACHAUT: *Messe de Nostre Dame*; OCKEGHEM: *Requiem*. ***

The sound of the Ensemble Organum directed by Marcel Pérès cannot fail to be stimulating. They sing at a lower than usual pitch, in a robustly vibrant style, darker than a normal West European vocal group. Pérès is concerned to present Hildegard's music alongside the Gregorian monody from which it springs, so it is heard in the context of a reconstruction of the liturgy for the office of Lauds (a celebration of the arrival of the sun and the end of night). The result is a great deal more chant than Hildegard, but the combination is certainly compelling. This CD additionally comes in a slip case as part of a Harmonia Mundi Trio at budget price which is highly recommendable, for the recordings of Machaut and Ockgehem are equally arresting.

Vision (The music of Hildegard; arranged and recomposed by Richard Souther).
(N) *(**) EMI CDC5 55246-2. Emily Van Evera, Sister Germaine Fritz (with chorus, instrumental contributions & synthesized rhythm).

Richard Souther's way-out recomposed versions are precociously and recklessly unauthentic, even including instrumental numbers (*The living light* and *Only the Devil laughed* are typical titles). The sophisticated rock style amplifies the music's sensuous hypnotic melodic flow, adding all kinds of extra-instrumental vocal and synthesized nourishment, with echo-chamber effects plus exotic live percussion. But Souther is obviously deeply involved in this very personal enterprise, and he has the advantage of the illustrious singing of Emily Van Evera, who really understands this repertoire, having also recorded it under authentic circumstances. Her beautiful voice is close-miked, 'pop style', unabashedly flattered with an acoustic halo. The programme opens with *O virga ac diadema purpure regis*, included on the Naxos disc, but the effect is extravagantly different. Certainly the emotional power of the music and its innate melodiousness projects vividly. The CD's title number, '*Vision*' (*O Euchari*) (also included in Jeremy Summerly's programme on Naxos), is heard twice, ending the programme in a more elaborate extended version. This is a disc to either wallow in or hate. Full translations are included.

Hindemith, Paul (1895–1963)

Concert music for brass and strings, Op. 50; (i) *Viola concerto (Schwanendreher). Nobilissima visione.*
*** Decca (IMS) Dig. 433 809-2 [id.]. San Francisco SO, Herbert Blomstedt, (i) with Geraldine Walther.

The three substantial works on the disc include his most sensuously beautiful score, *Nobilissima visione*. The *Concert music* is characteristic of Hindemith's early music, with its chunky tonal contrasts and emphatic rhythms set against a brief lyrical interlude. *Schwanendreher* is a concerto for viola (Hindemith's own instrument), based on German folk-themes, ending with a jolly set of variations. Blomstedt and the orchestra bring out the warmth as well as the rugged power.

Cello concerto.
*** RCA Dig. 09026 68027-2 [id.]. Starker, Bamberg SO, Russell Davies – SCHUMANN: *Cello concerto*. ***

The *Cello concerto* is played by Starker with finesse and elegance, and Dennis Russell Davies gets good results from the Bamberg orchestra too. However, it is not to be preferred to the Wallfisch–Tortelier account on Chandos (see below), which has the more logical coupling.

Cello concerto; (i) *Clarinet concerto.*
*** Etcetera KTC 1006 [id.]. Tibor de Machula; (i) George Pieterson; Concg. O, Kondrashin.

The *Cello concerto* is exhilarating and inventive, and Tibor de Machula proves an excellent protagonist. The *Clarinet concerto* is lyrical and eventful. The recordings (made in the Concertgebouw, Amsterdam) are public performances and emanate from the Hilversum Radio archives.

(i) *Cello concerto;* (ii) *The Four Temperaments* (Theme and variations for piano and strings).
*** Chandos Dig. CHAN 9124 [id.]. (i) Raphael Wallfisch; (ii) Howard Shelley; BBC PO, Tortelier.

Both the *Cello concerto* and *The Four Temperaments* are vintage Hindemith and well worth adding to your collection. The four variations of the latter are ingenious and subtle and are splendidly realized by Howard Shelley and the BBC Philharmonic under Yan Pascal Tortelier. Raphael Wallfisch is the eloquent soloist in the *Cello concerto*. The Chandos recording is very good indeed. These recordings set new standards in both works.

Cello concertos Nos. 1 in E flat, Op. 3; 2 (1940); *Kammermusik No. 3, Op. 36/2.*
(N) *** CPO Dig. CPO 999 375-2 [id.]. David Geringas, Queensland SO, Werner Andreas Albert.

The *Cello concerto*, Op. 3, comes from 1915–16 when the composer was entering his twenties. It is naturally a derivative piece with a lot of Reger and Strauss and not too much of the Hindemith we know. The 1940 *Concerto* is a fine piece, though not the equal of the *Violin concerto* of the previous year, and the programme is completed by the little concerto from the *Kammermusik*. David Geringas is a generally impressive soloist and the orchestral response maintains the eminently respectable standard we have come to expect from this series.

Kammermusik Nos. 1 for 12 instruments, Op. 24/1; (i) *2 (Piano concerto), Op. 36/1;* (ii) *3 (Cello concerto), Op. 36/2;* (iii) *4 (Violin concerto), Op. 36/3;* (iv) *5 (Viola concerto), Op. 36/4;* (v) *6 (Viola d'amore concerto), Op. 46/1;* (vi) *7 (Organ concerto), Op. 46/2; Kleine Kammermusik for wind quintet, Op. 24/2.*
*** Decca Dig. 433 816-2 (2). (i) Brautigam; (ii) Harrell; (iii) Kulka; (iv) Kaskkashian; (v) Blume; (vi) van Doeselaar; Concg. O, Chailly.
*** RCA Dig. 09026 61730-2 (2) [id.] (without *Kleine Kammermusik*). (i) Wiget; (ii) Stirling; (iii) Rundel; (iv) Dickel; (v) Just; (vi) Lücker; Ens. Modern, Markus Stenz.
(N) (B) *** Teldec/Warner Ultima 3984 21773-2 (2) [id.]. (i) van Blerk; (ii) Bylsma; (iii) Schröder; (iv) Doktor; (v) Vermeulen; (vi) de Klerk; Concerto Amsterdam.

The seven pieces Hindemith called *Kammermusik* show the composer at his most fertile and inventive and are mandatory listening, all highly refreshing and imaginative. The set also includes the delightful little *Wind quintet* (*Kleine Kammermusik*). The playing of the distinguished soloists and the members of the Concertgebouw is beyond praise and so is the Decca recording.

The RCA set from the Ensemble Modern and Markus Stenz may not have as well-known a line-up of soloists as the Decca set, but the performances are no less zesty and exuberant. Artistically it is a matter of swings and roundabouts. There is a really idiomatic feel to these Stenz performances, which have plenty of character and atmosphere. Of course the *Wind quintet*, the *Kleine Kammermusik*, is not included whereas it is in the Decca, which makes a considerable plus factor.

The Teldec performances come from 1968 and are not only very expert but beautifully engineered. At their budget price, these may well be more tempting for the collector who wants an introduction to these engaging pieces than either of the admirable full price alternatives.

Kammermusik Nos. 1 (with finale) for twelve solo instruments, Op. 24/1; (i) *4 (Violin concerto);* (ii) *5 (Viola concerto), Op. 36/3–4.*
*** EMI (SIS) Dig. CDC5 56160-2 [id.]. BPO, Abbado, with (i) Kolja Blacher; (ii) Wolfram Christ.

It is amazing what refinement and point Abbado and the Berlin Philharmonic bring to the *Kammermusic*. The recording helps, with the chamber textures given transparency, where often – as in Chailly's complete set of all seven *Kammermusik* works on Decca – the sound in its forwardness simulates a full orchestra. The soloists are excellent, with Kolja Blacher finding mercurial lightness in fast movements and warm expressiveness in the lovely *Nachtstuck*. Wolfram Christ, the orchestra's viola principal for many years, is an outstanding artist, flawless in tone and freely expressive.

Kammermusik No. 5, Op. 36/4; Konzertmusik for viola and orchestra, Op. 48; Viola concerto (Der Schwanendreher).
*** ASV Dig. CDDCA 931 [id.]. Cortese, Philh. O, Brabbins.

Paul Cortese is the accomplished soloist in all three works, including the fifth of the *Kammermusik*. The Philharmonia respond with some enthusiasm to Martyn Brabbins's direction, and although there are finer recordings of *Der Schwanendreher* to be had (above all, Tabea Zimmermann on EMI) this disc gives undoubted pleasure. The recording is very good indeed, with great presence and body.

(i) *Clarinet concerto;* (ii) *Horn concerto;* (iii) *Concerto for trumpet, bassoon & strings;* (iv) *Concerto for woodwinds, harp & strings.*
**(*) CPO 999 142-2 [id.]. (i; iv) Mehlhart; (ii) Neunecker; (iii) Friedrich; (iii–iv) Wilkening; (iv) Büchsel, Varcol, Cassedanne; Frankfurt RSO, Werner Andreas Albert.

The *Clarinet concerto* was written for Benny Goodman; the *Horn concerto* is comparatively familiar. The *Concerto for winds and harp* is the more rewarding of the other two works and more varied in texture. The *Trumpet and bassoon concerto* finds Hindemith in more routine mode. The soloist is rather too forward in the *Clarinet concerto* and, though the recording quality is decent, it is possible to imagine more transparent orchestral textures. The performances throughout are eminently acceptable.

Horn concerto.

(***) EMI mono CDC7 47834-2. Dennis Brain, Philh. O, composer – R. STRAUSS: *Horn concertos Nos. 1–2.* (***) ✿

The Hindemith *Concerto* is altogether drier than the Strauss couplings, but has a hauntingly original, ruminative finale, in which the soloist declaims a short poem – written by the composer – in such a way that the note values match the syllables of the words. Brain's performance is incomparable and the first-class mono recording has been transferred expertly.

Piano concerto.

*** First Edition LCD 002 [id.]. Lee Luvisi, Louisville O, Leighton Smith (with LAWHEAD: *Aleost* *(*)) – ZWILICH: *Symphony No. 2.* **

The *Piano concerto* (1945) is a work of great lyrical feeling and fertile imagination, and those who associate Hindemith with manufactured Teutonic *Gebrauchmusik* will find this music open in texture, delicate in its colourings and inspired in its material. Lee Luvisi and the Louisville Orchestra give a very good account of themselves and are more than adequately recorded.

Viola concerto (Der Schwanendreher).

*** EMI Dig. CDC7 54101-2. Tabea Zimmermann, Bav. RSO, David Shallon – BARTOK: *Viola concerto.* ***

Everything about this performance is excellent – indeed it is arguably the best now before the public – and is certainly better recorded than the rather cool sound Decca get for Geraldine Walther and Blomstedt in San Francisco. If you are prepared to pay full price for such short measure, you will be well rewarded in terms of both artistic and technical quality.

(i) *Viola concerto (Der Schwanendreher);* (ii) *Violin concerto; Kammermusik No. 4 (Violin concerto), Op. 36/3.*

(BB) **(*) RCA Navigator 74321 24219-2. (i) Igor Boguslavsky; (ii) David Oistrakh; USSR RSO, Rozhdestvensky.

David Oistrakh made his Russian recording of the *Violin concerto* the same year as his Decca version with the composer (see below). It is hardly less dazzling, and even if the sound cannot match its London counterpart it is fully acceptable; it is good to have in addition his hardly less charismatic account of the concerto which Hindemith placed fourth in his *Kammermusik*. The violist, Igor Boguslavsky, also makes an impressive solo contribution to another fine performance, of *Der Schwanendreher*, the central movement wonderfully warm. This has somewhat more refined sound, since in the two works for violin the soloist is balanced very forwardly. Rozhdestvensky provides vivid accompaniments and, although the Russian brass coarsens tuttis, this disc is more than worth its modest cost, even though the documentation is totally inadequate.

Violin concerto.

(M) *** Sony Stern Edition II SMK 64507 [id.]. Stern, NYPO, Bernstein – PENDERECKI: *Violin concerto.* ***

(i) *Violin concerto;* (ii) *Mathis der Maler (Symphony);* (iii) *Symphonic metamorphoses on themes of Weber.*

✿ (M) *** Decca 433 081-2 [id.]. (i) David Oistrakh, LSO, composer; (ii) SRO, Kletzki; (iii) LSO, Abbado.

Oistrakh's performance of the Hindemith *Violin concerto* is oustanding. The composer provides an overwhelmingly passionate accompaniment and the 1962 recording still sounds extraordinarily vivid and spacious. The Rosette is for the concerto but the couplings are well chosen, both also offering vintage late 1960s Decca sound. Abbado's *Symphonic metamorphoses on themes of Weber* is second to none. Kletzki's account of *Mathis der Maler* is also impressive, very well prepared and with a similar attention to detail. He, too has the advantage of finely balanced and truthful recording, and the Suisse Romande Orchestra still plays very well for him.

If Oistrakh's performance under Hindemith has an authority that no competitor can match, this American account is very fine indeed: Stern plays with eloquence, and Bernstein's accompaniment is always sympathetic and at times has something special to offer. In places it scores over the composer's own (towards the end of the slow movement, for example) but the recording is less analytical than the Decca and detail is less in evidence. The new coupling is admirably chosen

Concerto for winds, harp and orchestra; Konzertmusik for brass and strings, Op. 50; Mathis der Maler: Symphony.

(N) *** Chandos Dig. CHAN 9475 [id.]. Czech PO, Jiří Bělohlávek.

The *Concerto for winds, harp and orchestra* is the least-often played of the three works on Jiří Bělohlávek's recording with the Czech Philharmonic and it has never been heard to better effect on record. The *Konzertmusik for brass and strings* is hardly less imposing. Bělohlávek takes a broad and spacious view that is most impressive. Competition is of course much keener in the *Mathis der Maler Symphony* and here Bělohlávek is a little more detached and wanting in intensity. The playing of the Czech Philharmonic is as expert and responsive as one might expect, and the Chandos engineers cope well with the reverberant acoustic.

Der Dämon; (i) *Hérodiade* (two versions).
*** CPO Dig. CPO 999 220-2 [id.]. (i) Annie Gicquel; Siegfried Mauser, Frankfurt RSO, Albert.

Der Dämon (*The Demon*) (1922) is an early ballet which has great resource in matters of colour and is full of imaginative, original textures. There is a prominent role for the piano, brilliantly and sensitively played by Siegfried Mauser. *Hérodiade* dates from 1944 and derives its inspiration from Mallarmé's poem. It is an excellent idea to let us have it first with the text, then again without it, and Annie Gicquel speaks it in exemplary fashion. *Hérodiade* is a beautiful score and Werner Andreas Albert gets excellent results from his Frankfurt forces. The Hessischer Rundfunk engineers produce recordings that are a model of good balance. Strongly recommended.

(i) *The Four Temperaments; Nobilissima visione.*
**(*) Delos Dig. D/CD 1006 [id.]. (i) Carole Rosenberger; RPO, James de Preist.

The Four Temperaments, a set of variations, is one of Hindemith's finest and most immediate works. Carole Rosenberger gives a formidable reading of this inventive and resourceful score. James de Preist also secures responsive playing from the RPO strings and gives a sober, well-shaped account of the *Nobilissima visione* suite, doing justice to its grave nobility.

Mathis der Maler (symphony).
(M) *** EMI (SIS) CMS5 66109-2 (2) [id.]. BPO, Karajan – BRAHMS: *Tragic Overture;* BRUCKNER: *Symphony No. 8.* ***

Mathis der Maler (symphony); *Concert music, Op. 50; Symphonic metamorphoses on themes by Carl Maria von Weber.*
*** DG Dig. 429 404-2. Israel PO, Bernstein.

Mathis der Maler (symphony); *Nobilissima visione; Symphonic metamorphoses on themes by Weber.*
*** EMI (SIS) Dig. CDC5 55230-2 [id.]. Phd. O, Sawallisch.

Mathis der Maler (symphony); *Symphonic metamorphoses on themes by Weber; Trauermusik.*
*** Decca (IMS) Dig. 421 523-2 [id.]. San Francisco SO, Blomstedt.

It is good to hear the great Philadelphia Orchestra sounding itself again. Sawallisch draws a warm, rich-textured sound from them, and he also gives a performance of the *Nobilissima visione* that does justice to its breadth and dignity. Sawallisch's account of the *Symphonic metamorphoses on themes by Carl Maria von Weber* is not quite as sharp or fleet of foot as the Bernstein set, but it is still very well characterized. The *Mathis* scores over the rival Blomstedt on Decca in depth of characterization and orchestral opulence and, all things considered, should probably be the preferred recommendation.

Blomstedt has a strong feeling for *Mathis der Maler* and presents a finely groomed and powerfully shaped performance, with lucid and transparent textures. The famous *Trauermusik* has an affecting quiet eloquence and dedication: the solo viola, Geraldine Walther, is exceptionally sensitive. Blomstedt's reading of the *Symphonic metamorphoses on themes of Carl Maria von Weber* is appropriately light in touch; and the recording is exemplary in the naturalness of its balance.

It is good to have Karajan's recording back in the catalogue. It dates from 1957, but it was made in the Berlin Jesus-Christus-Kirche and the sound is impressively spacious, the strings gloriously full. The warm, full-blooded performance is remarkably dramatic and convincing, the central movement very touching. Though Hindemith's markings may occasionally be ignored, Karajan is convincing in everything he does.

High-voltage Hindemith from Bernstein and the Israel Philharmonic; it was recorded live in the Robert Mann Auditorium in Tel Aviv, whose dry acoustic is a handicap. In both the *Concert music for brass and strings* and the *Weber metamorphoses* the playing is exhilarating, and the *Mathis der Maler* performance is thrilling.

Pittsburgh Symphony; Ragtime; Symphonic dances.
(N) *** Chandos Dig. CHAN 9530 [id.]. BBC Philh. O, Yan Pascal Tortelier.

The *Symphonic dances* is one of Hindemith's most inventive and enjoyable works and its present neglect in the concert hall and in the recording studio quite unaccountable. Dating from 1937 it is full of resource and imagination and deserves to be as popular as the *Symphonic metamorphoses on themes of Weber*. The *Pittsburgh Symphony* comes from 1958 and was the last he composed. It has not had a good press but then few of his works of that period did. It is, however, a rewarding piece – not as high-spirited or poetic as the *Symphonic dances* but hard-edged and full of good ideas. Yan Pascal Tortelier and the BBC Philharmonic give meticulously prepared and committed performances and the Chandos sound is above reproach. One of the most valuable Hindemith releases in the last three years. Strongly recommended.

Sinfonia serena; Symphony (Die Harmonie der Welt).
✽ *** Chandos Dig. CHAN 9217 [id.]. BBC PO, Yan Pascal Tortelier.

The *Sinfonia serena* (1946) is a brilliant and inventive score, full of humour and melody. The scoring is inventive and imaginative. There is plenty of wit in the Scherzo, which paraphrases a Beethoven march from 1809. The *Symphony*, *Die Har-*

monie der Welt (1951), is another powerful and consistently underrated score. These well-prepared and finely shaped performances are given state-of-the-art recording quality. An outstanding issue.

Symphonic metamorphoses on themes by Weber.
(M) *** Decca 448 579-2. LSO, Abbado – JANACEK: *Sinfonietta;* PROKOFIEV: *Symphony No. 3.* ***

Abbado is content to follow the composer's own dynamic markings and the Decca engineers balance this so musically that the effect is preserved. This is symptomatic of the subtlety of Abbado's approach in a performance that in every respect is of the highest quality, while the vintage (1968) recording is surely worthy to be included in Decca's 'Classic Sound' series. Readers will note that this performance is also available coupled with the *Violin concerto* – see above.

Symphony in E flat; Overture Neues vom Tage; Nobilissima visione.
*** Chandos Dig. CHAN 9060 [id.]. BBC PO, Tortelier.

The *Symphony in E flat* is an inventive and resourceful score and is well worth investigating. Yan Pascal Tortelier gets excellent results from the BBC Philharmonic. Good, musicianly performances of *Nobilissima visione* and the much earlier *Neues vom Tage* Overture complete an admirable addition to the Hindemith discography.

CHAMBER MUSIC

(i) *Alto saxophone sonata;* (ii) *Bass tuba sonata;* (iii) *Bassoon sonata;* (iv) *Morgenmusik;* (v) *Trio;* (vi) *Trombone sonata;* (vii) *Trumpet sonata.*
** BIS CD159 [id.]. (i) Savijoki, Siirala; (ii) Lind, Harlos; (iii) Sonstevold, Knardahl; (iv) Malmö Brass Ens.; (v) Pehrsson, Jonsson, Mjönes; (vi) Lindberg, Pöntinen; (vii) Tarr, Westenholz.

(i) *Alto horn sonata in E flat;* (ii) *Bass tuba sonata;* (i) *Horn sonata;* (iii) *Trombone sonata;* (iv) *Trumpet sonata.*
(M) ** Sony SM2K 52671 (2) [id.]. (i) Mason Jones; (ii) Abe Torchinsky; (iii) Henry Charles Smith; (iv) Gilbert Johnson; Glenn Gould.

The *Alto saxophone sonata* and the *Alto horn sonata* are one and the same work. The BIS recordings are rather closely balanced though not disturbingly so. The Sony recordings are all from 1976 but unfortunately do not offer the *Recorder trio*, expertly played on the BIS by Claes Pehrsson, Anders-Per Jonsson and Anders Mjönes, or the exhilarating *Morgenmusik* for brass – not to mention the inventive *Bassoon sonata*. On the other hand, Sony's mid-price two-CD set gives you the *Alto horn sonata* with Mason Jones. Glenn Gould has great feeling for Hindemith and plays with strong personality and commitment throughout, even though the tiresome vocalise is a strain.

Bassoon sonata; Harp sonata; Horn sonata; Sonata for 2 pianos; Sonata for piano 4 hands.
(N) *** MDG Dig. MDG 304 0694-2 [id.]. Ens. Villa Musica with Klaus Thunemann, Helga Storck, Radovan Vlatkovic, Piret & Kalle Randalu.

Hindemith had an unfailingly resourceful musical mind, even if inspiration at times takes second place to sheer facility. These are not only well fashioned but often very satisfying pieces. Klaus Thunemann is an expert and persuasive advocate of the *Bassoon sonata* and its companions here receive highly accomplished performances. Throughout the Ensemble Villa Musica's Hindemith series we have heard so far, the recording is very faithful and lifelike.

(i) *Double bass sonata.* (ii) *Trombone sonata.* (iii) *Tuba sonata.* (iv) *Cello sonata; Small sonata for violoncello; A frog he went a-courting.*
(N) *** MDG Dig. MDG 304 0697-2 [id.]. Kalle Randalu with (i) Wolfgang Güttler; (ii) Branimir Slokar; (iii) Walter Hilgers; (iv) Martin Ostertag.

This collection is both artistically rewarding and technically excellent. The sound is very vivid and present and the programme intelligently laid out. Hindemith was enormously prolific and often composed on automatic pilot but these pieces are fresh and inventive.

Octet.
**(*) Nimbus Dig. NI 5461 [id.]. BPO Octet – BEETHOVEN: *Septet.* **(*)

The *Octet* is well fashioned but a bit manufactured, and many of the ideas find the composer at his most routine. The exception is the central slow movement, which has considerable eloquence. The playing is expert, but the recording is closely balanced and upfront.

Septet.
*** Virgin/EMI Dig. VC5 45056-2. Deutsche Kammerphilharmonie Wind – TOCH: *5 pieces for wind and percussion;* WEILL: *Violin concerto.* ***

The present performance of Hindemith's *Septet* by the wind of the Deutsche Kammerphilharmonie is outstanding in every way. Hindemith's use of sonority is consistently imaginative and the invention fresher than in the later *Octet*. Exemplary recording. The Toch and Weill couplings are both excellent.

String quartets Nos. 1 in C, Op. 2; 2 in F min., Op. 10; 3 in C, Op. 16; 4, Op. 22; 5, Op. 32; 6 in E flat; 7 in E flat.

(N) *(*) CPO Dig. CPO 999 287-2 (3) [id.]. Danish Qt.

The Hindemith quartets are not generously represented in the catalogue, so this issue is on the face of it particularly welcome. It also includes an early quartet (Op. 2) composed in 1915 and not recognized in the published order of the scores. Accordingly, what we have always known as the *Sixth quartet in E flat* of 1945 becomes the *seventh*, and each of its predecessors adds one. Unfortunately the Danish Quartet will not win over the unconverted; nor will they give much comfort and joy to those who like this repertory. Their playing lacks authority and is wanting in tonal finesse and colour.

String quartet No. 3, Op. 22.
❀ (***) Testament mono SBT 1052 [id.]. Hollywood Qt – PROKOFIEV: *Quartet No. 2;* WALTON: *Quartet in A min.* (***) ❀

The Hollywood Quartet possessed an extraordinary virtuosity and perfection of ensemble, and it is difficult to imagine more persuasive advocacy. The transfer is excellent and, although the mono sound is less than ideal, the performance still sweeps the board.

Viola sonata in F, Op. 11/4.
(N) (***) Biddulph mono LAB 148 [id.]. William Primrose, Jesús María Sandromá – BAX: *Fantasy sonata for viola and piano*; BLOCH: *Suite.* (***)
(N) *(*) Olympia Dig. OCD 625 [id.]. Yuri Bashmet, Sviatoslav Richter – BRITTEN: *Lachrymae, Op. 48;* SHOSTAKOVICH: *Viola sonata, Op. 147.* *(*)

The classic 1938 Primrose recording of Hindemith's most lyrical sonata, with Jesús María Sandromá, probably remains unsurpassed in sheer style and refinement of tone. Given the date, the sound is very acceptable.

Distinguished playing as you would expect from Bashmet and Richter, who were recorded live in Germany in 1985. But the sound is distinctly unappealing, too close and hard.

(Unaccompanied) *Viola sonatas Nos. 1; 2, Op. 11/5; 3, Op. 25/1; 4, Op. 31/4.*
*** ASV Dig. CDDCA 947 [id.]. Paul Cortese.

(i) *Viola sonatas* (for viola and piano) *Op. 11/4; Op. 25/4;* (Unaccompanied) *Viola sonatas: Op. 11/5; Op. 25/1; Op. 31/4.*
*** ECM Dig. 833 309-2 (2) [id.]. Kim Kashkashian, (i) Robert Levin.

The solo *Sonatas* are played with superb panache and flair – and, even more importantly, with remarkable variety of colour – by Kim Kashkashian, who has an enormous dynamic range. The performances of the sonatas with piano are hardly less imaginative and the recording is good.

Paul Cortese is a player of considerable accomplishments and he is persuasive in this somewhat forbidding repertoire. He is not perhaps always as imaginative or poetic as Kim Kashkashian (ECM), but the disc is certainly recommendable.

Violin sonatas No 1 in E flat, Op. 11/1; 2 in D, Op. 11/2; 3 in E; 4 in C.
*** BIS Dig. CD 761 [id.]. Ulf Wallin, Roland Pöntinen.

As with most Hindemith, both the Op. 11 sonatas are well crafted and inventive. The finest of the four is the last in C major, which is both individual and finely wrought. Ulf Wallin and Roland Pöntinen play this repertoire with real dedication and conviction, and the BIS recording is very lifelike and present. They include a fragment of an alternative finale for the *E flat Sonata*, Op. 11/1, that Hindemith subsequently discarded.

PIANO MUSIC

Berceuse; In einer Nacht, Op. 15; Kleines Klavierstück; Lied; 1922 Suite, Op. 26; Tanzstücke, Op. 19.
**(*) Marco Polo Dig. 8.223335 [id.]. Hans Petermandl.

Exercise in three pieces, Op. 31/I; Klaviermusik, Op. 37; Series of little pieces, Op. 37/II; Sonata, Op. 17; Two little piano pieces.
** Marco Polo Dig. 8.223336 [id.]. Hans Petermandl.

Ludus Tonalis; Kleine Klaviermusik, Op. 45/4.
** Marco Polo Dig. 8.223338 [id.]. Hans Petermandl.

Piano sonatas Nos. 1–3.
(N) *** MDG Dig. MDG 304 0693-2 [id.]. Kalle Randalu.

Piano sonatas Nos. 1–3; Variations.
** Marco Polo Dig. 8.223337 [id.]. Hans Petermandl.

Hindemith's three piano sonatas, all written in quick succession in 1936 just before he fled from Hitler's Germany, are firmly in the grand German tradition. Long neglected but among the most satisfying piano sonatas of the century, they owe a direct debt not just to Beethoven but to Bach's *Well-Tempered Clavier*. Hindemith's crisply contrapuntal piano writing brings a strong consistency to the three contrasted works. No. 1 is the most challengingly ambitious, with the compact No. 2 more easily lyrical. Yet it is No. 3, directly echoing the first of Beethoven's late sonatas, Opus 101, which is the clearest masterpiece. Built on strikingly memorable themes, and ending with a formidable double fugue, it inspires the Estonian, Kalle Randalu, to a powerful performance, very well recorded.

Hans Petermandl is an expert guide in this repertoire and presents it with real sympathy for, and understanding of, the idiom; his performances are very persuasive. The textures in Hindemith's piano music are often unbeautiful and less than transparent and, although neither the piano nor the acoustic of the Concert Hall of Slovak Radio is outstanding, the sound is perfectly acceptable.

Ludus tonalis.
*** Decca (IMS) Dig. 444 803-2 [id.]. Olli Mustonen – PROKOFIEV: *Visions fugitives.* ***

Ludus tonalis; Suite (1922), Op. 26.
**(*) Hyperion Dig. CDA 66824 [id.]. John McCabe.

Hindemith's *Ludus tonalis* – comprising 25 sections – is, in total, not far short of an hour in length. It has been recorded before, but not with more concentration and authority than it is on Hyperion by John McCabe. As if not wishing to compromise himself, instead of coupling it with something a little less formidably intellectual, he offers also the *Suite 1922* which, if anything, is thornier still. So if you are a Hindemith addict, this is surely a disc you will want to explore.

For the general listener, however, Olli Mustonen, using every imaginative device at his disposal, tries to communicate the intricacies and inner detail of Hindemith's argument, as he wends his way through the 25 studies; as much as it is possible to unravel Hindemith's progression, he manages to do so. He is excellently recorded.

Organ sonatas Nos. 1–3.
*** Chandos Dig. CHAN 9097 [id.]. Piet Kee – REGER: *Four organ pieces.* ***

Piet Kee plays on the Müller organ of St Bavo in Haarlem, an instrument more suited to Hindemith than the somewhat spacious acoustic in which it is recorded. This small point apart, Kee plays with his customary distinction and character. All three sonatas are rewarding, and no one investing in this disc is likely to be disappointed on either artistic or technical grounds.

VOCAL MUSIC

When lilacs last in the dooryard bloom'd (Requiem).
*** Telarc Dig. CD 80132 [id.]. DeGaetani, Stone, Atlanta Ch. & SO, Robert Shaw.

This 'Requiem for those we loved' is one of the composer's most deeply felt works and one of his best. Shaw gives a performance of great intensity and variety of colour and nuance. Both his soloists are excellent, and there is both weight and subtlety in the orchestral contribution. Splendid recording.

Mathis der Maler (opera; complete).
(M) *** EMI CDS5 55237-2 (3) [CDCC 55237]. Fischer-Dieskau, Feldhof, J. King, M. Schmidt, Meven, Cochran, Malta, Grobe, Wagemann, Bav. R. Ch. & SO, Kubelik.

There is little doubt that the opera *Mathis der Maler* is Hindemith's masterpiece. Fischer-Dieskau proves the ideal interpreter of the central role, the painter Mathias Grünewald. The performance includes other fine contributions from James King as the Archbishop, Donald Grobe as the Cardinal, Alexander Malta as the army commandant and Manfred Schmidt as the Cardinal's adviser. The women principals are less happily chosen; Rose Wagemann as Ursula is rather squally. But with splendid playing and singing from Bavarian Radio forces under Kubelik, this is a highly enjoyable as well as an important set. Moreover the first-class (1977) analogue recording is just as kind to the voices as to the orchestra, with the balance between soloists, chorus and orchestra very natural, and the CD transfer is a model of its kind.

(i; ii) *Sancta Susanna* (opera; complete). *Das Nusch-Nuschi: Dances, Op. 20. Tuttifäntchen: suite.* (i) *3 Songs, Op. 9.*
(N) *** Chandos Dig. CHAN 9620 [id.]. (i) Susan Bullock; (ii) Della Jones, Ameral Gunson, & Soloists, Leeds Fest. Ch.; BBCPO, Yan Pascal Tortelier.

This collection of early works by Hindemith is a revelation. One can rarely detect signs of his mature style, except perhaps in ingenious counterpoint, but each of the four works, sharply contrasted with each other, is strong and positive. The most ambitious is the one-act opera, *Sancta Susanna*. Hindemith's musical language at this stage in his career is distinctly expressionist, lyrical and atmospheric though with traces of Gallic influence (and in particular Debussy), and Puccinian elements happily intermingled. It is a far cry from the austere, monochrome contrapuntist of the later symphonies. Written immediately after the end of the First World War, it scandalized its first audiences by its erotic-cum-blasphemous character. It is the last of three one-acters, the other two being *Das Nusch-Nuschi* (1920), based on a play for Burmese marionettes, and *Mörder, Hoffnung der Frauen* (1919).

Susanna is a young nun (Susan Bullock), inflamed by the legend she is told by Sister Clementia (Della Jones) about a girl who comes to the altar naked to embrace the figure of Christ on the cross. For this blasphemy she is buried alive. Undeterred by this fate, Susanna strips off at the altar and rips the covering from Christ's torso. She is petrified when a huge spider falls on to her head from the crucifix and in a frenzy of remorse begs the other nuns to wall her up! The opening is highly imaginative and full of atmosphere, closer indeed to Schreker or even Szymanowski than the Hindemith we know. It is a short piece, some 23 minutes in length, but enormously intense and concentrated in feeling. The performance is gripping, splendidly sung and expertly played by Yan Pascal Tortelier and his BBC Philharmonic Orchestra.

The oriental elements in the *Nusch-Nuschi dances* simply adorn a 1920s-style score, while the suite from the children's pantomime, *Tuttifäntchen*, of 1922 is delightful in its use of tunes from children's games, with ragtime introduced in the *Dance of the dolls*. (It includes, incidentally, a quotation from Debussy's *Golliwog's cake-walk*.) The Straussian *Drei Gesänge, Op. 3*, written earlier in 1917, represent the 22-year-old breaking loose from his classical background. Echoing Schoenberg's *Gurrelieder*, they are luxuriant and rich, and again unlike anything we know from the mature composer. Susan Bullock sings them with great conviction and flair. This is all music of outstanding interest, superbly performed, with Jan-Pascal Tortelier the most persuasive advocate, and beautifully recorded.

Hoddinott, Alun (born 1929)

(i; ii) *Concertino for viola and small orchestra, Op. 14;* (iii; iv) *Nocturnes and cadenzas for cello and orchestra, Op. 62;* (v; ii) *Dives and Lazarus* (cantata), *Op. 39;* (vi; iv) *Sinfonia Fidei* (for soprano, tenor, chorus & orchestra), *Op. 95.*

*** Lyrita Analogue/Dig. SRCD 332. (i) Erdélyi; (ii) New Philh. O, David Atherton; (iii) Welsh; (iv) Philh. O, Groves; (v) Palmer, Allen, Welsh Nat. Op. Ch.; (vi) Jill Gomez, Burrowes, Philh. Ch.

Csaba Erdélyi, the superb principal viola of the New Philharmonia in the mid-1970s, makes an admirable advocate in the imaginatively conceived *Viola concertino* of 1958, the point of the argument made sharper by the lightness of the string section against a normal woodwind group. By comparison the *Nocturnes and cadenzas* is less easy to come to grips with, presenting a more withdrawn face, not helped by being based on an idea which rather limits the quota of fast music. Nevertheless Moray Welsh excels himself as the cello soloist, making his soliloquy seemingly improvisational, and Sir Charles Groves draws excellent playing from the Philharmonia Orchestra. In the succinct and emotionally concentrated cantata, *Dives and Lazarus*, the choral writing is highly individual, especially in the dramatic closing section, *When Lazarus died*, with its exultant '*Allelujas*'. *Sinfonia Fidei* (1977) returns to a more conservative idiom and is one of the most impressive of Hoddinott's later works, purposeful and dramatic. Soloists, chorus and orchestra join to project all this music with the most ardent advocacy and the recordings, spaciously atmospheric, whether analogue or digital, are in every respect first rate.

Symphonies Nos. (i; ii) *2, Op. 29;* (i; iii) *3, Op. 61;* (iv) *5, Op. 81.*

*** Lyrita SRCD 331. (i) LSO; (ii) Del Mar; (iii) David Atherton; (iv) RPO, Andrew Davis.

The *Second Symphony* dates from 1962 and is clearly the work of a composer who, though a serialist, still retains an allegiance to tonal centres and who uses twelve-note technique as a spur rather than a crutch. Its arguments are not difficult to follow and there is a great outburst of passionate lyricism from the strings at the climax of the *molto adagio*. Del Mar directs the work confidently, and the LSO respond with eloquence. The *Third Symphony* is even more powerfully wrought, dark in colouring and deeply imaginative. It is well laid out for the orchestra and is perhaps the most completely effective of the three works offered here. Atherton's performance (again using the LSO) is wholly convincing. The *Fifth Symphony* is a more abrasive work than the *Third* and less immediately approachable. It is splendidly powerful, and it reinforces Hoddinott's representation in the catalogue when so impressively played. The vintage recordings of both the *Third* and *Fifth Symphonies* were made by a Decca engineering team in the early 1970s and are spectacularly vivid in their presence, range and definition.

(i) *Chorales, variants and fanfares* (for brass and organ); *Quodlibet on Welsh nursery tunes; Ritornello 2, Op. 100/2.*

*** Nimbus Dig. NI 5466 [id.]. Fine Arts Brass Ens.; (i) with Kevin Bowyer (organ) – MATHIAS: *Summer dances; Soundings.* ***

The most remarkable and original work here is the *Chorales, variants and fanfares*, written in 1992 for the Swansea Festival. Its interweaving organ and brass textures bring a highly imaginative interplay, the organ at times taking a concertante role, at others becoming part of the group. The sombrely evocative opening leads to the virtuoso *Fanfares*, with the organ dancing along in bravura discourse with the brass, but the closing section of the work is valedictory. The concert opens with Hoddinott's witty scoring of five attractive Welsh nursery tunes and ends with the second of his three *Ritornelli*, which are rather less rewarding than the other two works. Performances are first class and the recording in the demonstration bracket, with the balance between organ and brass expertly managed within the warm ambience of St Mary's Collegiate Church, Warwick.

Hoffmeister, Franz (1754–1812)

Flute concertos: in D; in G.

(BB) **(*) ASV Quicksilva CDQS 6012 [(M) id. import]. Dingfelder, ECO, Leonard – C. P. E. BACH: *Concerto.* **(*)

Franz Hoffmeister's two *Flute concertos* are elegantly inventive, if not distinctive. They are well recorded and make pleasant late-evening listening. The performances are sprightly and polished, and the accompaniments have plenty of spirit. The sound is brightly lit, but not excessively so.

Hofmann, Leopold (1738–93)

Sinfonias: in B flat; in C; in D; in F; in F.
(BB) *** Naxos Dig. 8.553866 [id.]. Northern CO, Ward.

Leopold Hofmann became Kapellmeister at St Stephen's Cathedral, Vienna, in 1773 and, to judge from the wide distribution of his manuscripts in Europe, he enjoyed considerable celebrity in his lifetime. He was one of the earliest composers who consistently wrote four-movement symphonies with both slow introductions and minuets. He preceded Haydn in this respect. Incidentally, for a brief period in 1791 Mozart acted as an assistant to him, doubtless in the hope of receiving preferment when Hofmann died. The five symphonies recorded here show him to be lively and fresh, though no one could pretend that his music plumbs great depths – or indeed is consistently interesting. The performances are very alert and sprightly but the recording, though distinguished by clarity and presence, is handicapped by a rather dry acoustic.

Holborne, Antony (c.1560–1602)

Pieces for bandora: *Almain: The Night watch; Fantazia; A Ground*; for cittern: *A French toy; A Horne pype; The Miller; Praeludium; Sicke sicke and very sicke*; (i) for cittern with a bass: *Galliard; Maister Earles Pavane; Queenes galliard*; for lute: Almains: *Almaine; The Choice. Fantasia.* Galliards: *As it fell on a holie yve; The Fairy-rownde; Holburns passion; Muy linda; Responce; The Teares of the muses.* Pavans: *Heres paternus; Pavan*, and *galliard to the same; Posthuma; Sedet sola. A Toy. Variations: Il Nodo di gordio.*
(N) ❁ ASV *** Dig. CDGAU 173 [id.]. Jacob Heringman, with (i) Susanna Pell.

An entirely delightful representation on CD of an Elizabethan lutenist, composer and poet, now totally overshadowed by Dowland. Yet he wrote a great number of works for the lute and its two sister instruments, generally in a serious and contemplative vein. Indeed the melancholy pavane *Posthuma* has as much 'dolens' as almost anything by Dowland. It is this meditative quality which Jacob Heringman catches to perfection and which makes this collection so appealing. He improvises his own divisions when needed, as was expected by the composer, and his playing is appealingly spontaneous. The thoughtful simplicity of a piece like *The Night watch* contrasts with the musing, improvisational extended *Fantazia*, both played on the more sonorous bandora, for which Holborne wrote more music than any of his contemporaries. But there is lively writing too, like *The Miller* and *A French toy*; and how well they sound on the cittern, a robust-timbred instrument mostly favoured by the lower classes, and which came to be much played in barber shops. The composer took especial care over the four duet pieces for cittern with bass viol: as he describes them 'with some reasonable good chords and bindinges after a more heedful nature of composition'. Jacob Heringman is beautifully recorded in a most suitable ambience, providing the ideal CD for a late evening reverie.

Lute pieces: *Cradle pavane; Countess of Ormond's galliard; The fairy round; Fantasia No. 3; Galliards Nos. 2 & 17; Heres Paternus; Muy Linda; The Night watch; Last will and testament Pavans Nos. 2 & 11; Wanton.*
(N) (BB) **(*) Naxos Dig. 8.553974 [id.]. Christopher Wilson (lute) – ROBINSON: *Lute pieces and duets.* ***

Christopher Wilson plays these pieces very well, notably the lively items like *The Fairy Round* and *Wanton*, with *Muy Linda* a highlight. But he does not penetrate the inner core of the ruminative pieces as touchingly as Jacob Heringman. However there is not too much duplication here and this inexpensive Naxos disc is well worth getting for the coupled repertoire (including duets) by Holborne's contemporary, Thomas Robinson.

Holbrooke, Joseph (1878–1958)

The Birds of Rhiannon, Op. 87; The Children of Don: Overture, Op. 56; Dylan: Prelude, Op. 53.
** Marco Polo Dig. 8.223721-2 [id.]. Ukraine Nat. SO, Andrew Penny.

In Holbrooke's opera, *The Children of Don* (the first of a trilogy), neither overture nor prelude offers particularly memorable or individual ideas and, generally speaking, inspiration is pretty thin. There are touches of Wagner in the former but the musical language is predominantly diatonic, particularly in the tone-poem *The Birds of Rhiannon*. The longest piece is the *Prelude* to *Dylan*, which is pretty undistinguished stuff. The performances sound a bit under-rehearsed but are adequate (some may find the horn vibrato a bit excessive), and the recording is decent.

(i) *Piano quartet in G min., Op. 21;* (ii) *String sextet in D, Op. 43;* (iii) *Symphonic quintet No. 1 in G min., Op. 44.*
** Marco Polo Dig. 8 223736 [id.]. (i; iii) Endre Hegedüs; (ii) Sándor Papp, János Devich; New Haydn Qt.

All three works come from the early years of the present century. Although the music never falls below a certain level of melodic fluency and is expertly crafted, little of it remains in the memory. Probably the most memorable idea comes in the *Lament* that serves as the centrepiece of the *Piano quartet*, though the outer movements rather outstay their welcome. The *String sextet* makes the most immediate and positive impact but, after the CD has come to an end, one realizes why Holbrooke has not stayed the course. The fine Hungarian ensemble play these pieces with appropriate conviction and ardour. Decent recording, much better than for the orchestral disc.

Holloway, Robin (born 1943)

Second Concerto for orchestra, Op. 40.
*** NMC Dig. D015M [id.]. BBC SO, Oliver Knussen.

Holloway's *Second Concerto* made a powerful impression when it was first performed in 1979. It is a richly imaginative score and shows a sensitivity of high quality, as well as a considerable mastery of instrumental resource. The *Concerto* is a work of substance that is well worth getting to know and is well served by the BBC Symphony Orchestra and Oliver Knussen. The engineers produce a better sound from the Maida Vale Studios than we have heard on any other occasion.

(i) *Romanza for violin and small orchestra, Op. 31;* (ii) *Sea-surface full of clouds, Op. 28.*
*** Chandos Dig. CHAN 9228 [id.]. (i) Gruenberg; (ii) Walmsley-Clark, Cable, Hill, Brett, Hickox Singers; City of L. Sinfonia, Richard Hickox.

Both works recorded here show Holloway's sensitivity to colour and marvellous feeling for the orchestra. The *Sea-surface full of clouds* begins luminously, rather like Szymanowski, and has an at times magical atmosphere. There is an affecting and consuming melancholy about the *Romanza* for violin and orchestra. A composer of a refined intelligence and real sensibility.

Holmboe, Vagn (born 1909)

(i) *Cello concerto, Op. 120;* (ii) *Brass quintet, Op. 79;* (iii) *Triade, Op. 123;* (iv) *Benedic Domino, Op. 59.*
*** BIS Analogue/Dig. CD-78 [id.]. (i) Bløndahl Bengtsson, Danish RSO, Ferencsik; (ii) Swedish Brass Quintet; (iii) Edward Tarr, Elisabeth Westenholz; (iv) Camerata Ch., Per Enevold.

Vagn Holmboe's magificent *Cello concerto* is given an excellent performance here, and the account of the choral piece, *Benedic Domino*, shows an austere beauty and elevation of feeling that are rare in contemporary music. The *Brass quintet* is effective and stirring; and the *Triade* for trombone and organ is hardly less striking. Only the *Quintet* is a digital recording but its companions here are also strikingly good as sound.

(i) *Chamber concertos Nos. 1 for piano, strings and tympani, Op. 17;* (ii) *2 for flute, violin, strings and percussion, Op. 20;* (iii) *3 for clarinet and chamber orchestra, Op. 21.*
(N) *** Marco Polo/Dacapo Dig. 8.224038 [id.]. (i) Anne Oland; (ii) Eva Ostergaard, Mikkel Futtrup; (iii) Niels Tomsen; Danish R. Concert O, Hannu Koivula.

Chamber concertos Nos. (i; ii; iv) *4 for piano trio and chamber orchestra, Op. 30;* (iii) *5 for viola and chamber orchestra, Op. 31;* (ii) *6 for violin and chamber orchestra, Op. 33.*
(N) *** Marco Polo/Da capo Dig. 8.224063 [id.]. (i) Anne Oland; (ii) Mikkel Futtrup; (iii) Tim Fredericksen; (iv) Niels Ullner; Danish R. Sinf., Hannu Koivula.

Chamber concertos (i) *Nos. 7, for oboe, Op. 37*; *8 (Sinfonia concertante), Op. 38*; (ii) *9 for violin and viola, Op. 39.*
(N) *** Marco Polo/Da Capo Dig. 8.224086 [id.]. (i) Max Artved; (ii) Mikkel Futtrup, Tim Frederiksen; Danish R. Sinf, Hannu Koivula.

Chamber concertos: No. 10 for wood-brass-gut and orchestra, Op. 40; (i) *No. 11 for trumpet and chamber orchestra, Op. 44;* (ii) *No. 12 for trombone and orchestra, Op. 52;* (iii) *No. 13 for oboe, viola and chamber orchestra, Op. 67.*
(N) *** Marco Polo/Dacapo Dig. 8.224087 [id.]. (i) Ole Edvard Antonsen; (ii) Mauger; (iii) Artved, Frederiksen; Danish R. Sinf., Hannu Koivula.

Vagn Holmboe began his series of *Chamber concertos* way back in 1939, completing them in the mid 1950s. Many of them were composed for Lavard Friisholm and the Collegium Musicum, and are predominantly neoclassical in outlook. They are fresh, clean-textured pieces, full of musical interest and a zest for life. A good point to start is the third disc (Nos. 7–9), which covers the period 1944–6. The most substantial of the three is No. 8, the *Sinfonia concertante* with its inventive set of variations, which (along with No. 11) is the only one that made any headway into the repertory outside Denmark in the 1950s. It is somewhat Hindemithian in its stance yet distinctive. Holmboe is always very much his own man. No. 11 has been the most widely recorded. Rewarding music, very well performed and decently recorded.

Chamber concertos Nos. (i) *11 for trumpet and orchestra, Op. 44;* (ii) *12 for trombone, Op. 52;* (iii) *Tuba concerto, Op. 152. Intermezzo concertante, Op. 171.*

*** BIS Dig. CD 802 [id.]. (i) Håkan Hardenberger; (ii) Christian Lindberg; (iii) Jens-Bjørn Larsen; Aalborg SO, Owain Arwel Hughes.

The noble neo-baroque *Concerto No. 11 for trumpet* (1948) is not new to the catalogue. It could hardly be better served than by Håkan Hardenberger's account with the Aalborg orchestra, and one is tempted to add that any newcomer will have to be pretty good to match Christian Lindberg's account of the *Twelfth Chamber concerto*. These are inspiriting and inspiring pieces. The one-movement *Tuba concerto* explores the virtuoso possibilities of this instrument as do few others, as does the companion *Intermezzo concertante*. These are dazzling performances and the orchestral support under Owain Arwel Hughes is first class. The recording is state of the art. Highly recommended.

Flute concertos Nos. 1, Op. 126; 2, Op. 147; (i) *Concerto for recorder, strings, celesta and vibraphone, Op. 122.*

(N) *** BIS Dig. BIS CD 911 [id.]. Manuela Wiesler; (i) Daniel Laurin; Aarhus SO, Owain Arwel Hughes.

The *First flute concerto* and the *Concerto for recorder, strings, celesta and vibraphone* come from the mid 1970s and the *Second, Op. 147* from 1981–2, the year after the *Eleventh symphony*. These are wonderfully inventive scores whose luminous, shining textures captivate the mind and reaffirm the conviction that Holmboe stands head and shoulders above his contemporaries in the North. Strong performances from all concerned and splendid recording too. Don't miss this.

Epilog, Op. 80; Epitaph (symphonic metamorphosis), Op. 68; Monolith, Op.76; Tempo variabile, Op. 108.

(N) ✿ *** BIS Dig. CD 852 [id.]. Aarhus SO, Owain Arwel Hughes.

The first of Vagn Holmboe's *Symphonic metamorphoses* was among a number of works commissioned in 1956 by the BBC to mark the tenth anniversary of the Third Programme. (Holmboe's title, *Epitaph, Op. 68*, was to be all too prophetic.) The musical ideas unfold, change shape, assume new identities without losing sight of their individuality, in much the same way as does, say, the *Seventh Symphony* of Sibelius. Make no mistake, this is the product of a profound and commanding musical mind. Three like-minded successors followed in the next few years, all of them works of great concentration, cogency and power. They have undergone grievous neglect since their premières in the 1960s but the present performance goes a long way in making amends, for the playing of the Aarhus Orchestra is excellent and Owain Arwel Hughes in total sympathy with these magnificent scores. Small wonder that in the 1970s Robert Simpson should hail Holmboe as his favourite living Nordic composer. The recording is state-of-the-art. It is not important but just for the record, the work was first performed in December 1956, not 1954 as stated in the otherwise excellent booklet.

Symphonies Nos. 1, Op. 4; 3 (Sinfonia rustica), Op. 25; 10, Op. 105.

*** BIS Dig. CD 605 [id.]. Aarhus SO, Arwel Hughes.

The general outlook of the *First Symphony* (*Sinfonia da camera*) is neo-classical and its proportions are modest, but one recognizes the vital current of the later Holmboe, the lucidity of thinking and the luminous textures. The last movement has an infectious delight in life; so, too, has the exhilarating finale of the *Third* (*Sinfonia rustica*), the first of his three war-time symphonies. The *Tenth* is dark, powerful and imaginative; altogether one of the Danish composer's most subtle and satisfying works. The performances and recordings are altogether first class.

Symphony No. 2, Op. 15; Sinfonia in memoriam, Op. 65.

✿ *** BIS Dig. CD 695 [id.]. Aarhus SO, Owain Arwel Hughes.

The *Second Symphony* with its imaginative middle movement and its vital companions is a splendid pieces. The *Sinfonia in memoriam* is a dark work of striking power and imaginative breadth and is masterly in every way. Owain Arwel Hughes and the Aarhus orchestra give a performance that is in every way worthy of it, and the recording is in the demonstration bracket.

Symphonies Nos. (i) *4 (Sinfonia sacra), Op. 29; 5, Op. 35.*

**(*) BIS Dig. CD 572 [id.]. (i) Jutland Op. Ch.; Aarhus SO, Owain Arwel Hughes.

The *Fifth Symphony* makes a good entry point into Holmboe's world. In outlook it is strongly tonal and neo-classical and a distinctive musical landscape is immediately established. The only word to describe its outer movements is exhilarating. The slow movement has a modal character, but an anguished outburst in the middle serves as a reminder that this is a wartime work, composed during the dark days of the Nazi occupation. The *Fourth* (*Sinfonia sacra*) is a six-movement choral piece dedicated to the memory of his brother, who perished in a Nazi concentration camp. It encompasses a bracing vigour and underlying optimism alongside moments of sustained grief. Very good performances, though the strings are a little under-strength and the acoustic is on the dry side. But don't let this put you off this inspiriting music.

Symphonies Nos. 6, Op. 43; 7, Op. 50.
**(*) BIS Dig. CD 573. Aarhus SO, Owain Arwel Hughes.

Holmboe's *Sixth Symphony* is a much darker piece than its predecessor. Its distinctively Nordic world is established by the brooding, slow-moving fourths of the long introduction; there is writing of great luminosity too. The one-movement *Seventh Symphony* is a highly concentrated score, individual in both form and content, which encompasses great variety of pace and mood. Owain Arwel Hughes acquits himself very well, and this is music that speaks with so strong and distinctive a voice that it is self-recommending. There are few if any Nordic symphonies post-Nielsen and -Sibelius of this quality.

Symphonies Nos 8, Op. 56 (1951); *9* (1968).
✿*** BIS Dig. CD 618 [id.]. Aarhus SO, Arwel Hughes.

This conductor has real feeling for the composer and not only penetrates the spirit of the score of the *Eighth* but is scrupulous in his observance of the letter. One is left with the impression that this symphony has never really had its due until now. The *Ninth Symphony* is wholly unfamiliar. This is its première recording in the composer's revised version. A dark, powerful work, it is among the finest Holmboe has given us: Taruskin compared it to 'academic discourse of a thrillingly high order: "If you have ever left a lecture hall haunted and altered, this may offer a comparable cognitive adventure." ' This is music which, one can feel with some certainty, future generations will want to hear. The Aarhus orchestra are equally persuasive in the *Ninth* as in the *Eighth*, and the recording is the best so far in the cycle.

Symphonies Nos. 11, Op. 141; 12, Op. 175; 13, Op. 192.
*** BIS Dig. CD 728 [id.]. Aarhus SO, Owain Arwel Hughes.

The *Thirteenth Symphony* is an astonishing achievement for a composer in his mid-eighties. It is a veritable powerhouse. The *Twelfth* is tautly structured and well argued, though less inspired than the *Eleventh Symphony*, which finds Holmboe at his most visionary. The arabesque that opens the first movement seems as if it is coming from another world. Every credit is due to Owain Arwel Hughes and the Aarhus Symphony Orchestra for their fervent advocacy of this music and to the splendid BIS engineers for the vivid and superbly natural sound.

String quartets Nos. 1, Op. 46; 3, Op. 48; 4, Op. 63.
*** Danacord Dig. CDDC 9203 [id.]. Kontra Qt.

String quartets Nos. 2, Op. 47; 5, Op. 66; 6, Op. 78.
*** Marco Polo/DaCapo Dig. 8.224026. Kontra Qt.

These quartets have a certain reserve: nothing is overstated, everything is quietly but cogently argued and, once one has broken through their reticence, the rewards are rich. This is easily the finest post-war quartet cycle in Scandinavia, and those who respond to the quartets of Shostakovich or Robert Simpson should lose no time in investigating them. The *Second Quartet* has a particularly engaging main theme and these artists play it with conviction. The *Fifth* and *Sixth* are both finely argued works. What a rewarding composer Holmboe is, and how well played and recorded these quartets are!

String quartets Nos. 10, Op. 102; 11, Op. 111 (Quartetto rustico); 12, Op. 116.
(N) **(*) Marco Polo/DaCapo Dig 8.224101 [id.]. Kontra Qt.

The three quartets on this disc come from the period 1969–73, the period of the *Ninth* and *Tenth Symphonies*. The *Tenth* in two movements is arguably the most concentrated in feeling and powerfully structured. Its successor, the only one of his quartets to bear a subtitle, *Quartetto rustico*, is the most relaxed and smiling. The *Twelfth* is a five-movement piece whose central slow movement has great eloquence. The performances are excellent and the Danish Radio recording acceptable in quality though tone tends to harden a little above the stave.

Holmès, Augusta (1847–1903)

Andromeda (symphonic poem); *Ireland* (symphonic poem); (i) *Ludus pro patria: Night and love. Overture for a comedy; Poland* (symphonic poem).
*** Marco Polo Dig. 8.223449 [id.]. Rheinland-Pfalz PO, Samuel Friedmann; (i) Patrick Davin.

Augusta Holmès was the inspiring force behind the César Franck *Piano quintet* which embodied much of that master's strong feeling for her. She was from an Anglo-Irish family that had settled in France. She was a person of remarkable gifts for, apart from her musical talents, she was an accomplished painter and wrote well. Although the *Overture for a comedy* (1876) is trite, *Andromeda* is quite striking. It is by far the best piece on the disc, and the best scored, though limitations in Augusta Holmès's technique (particularly her reliance on sequence, and the relatively limited development of ideas) are evident. But this is music of much interest – and its composer was obviously no mean talent. She has been well served by the Rheinland-Pfalz Philharmonic under Samuel Friedmann. The recordings too are eminently satisfactory.

Holst, Gustav (1874–1934)

'The essential Holst': (i) Egdon Heath, Op. 47; (ii) *A Moorside suite;* (iii) *The Perfect Fool, Op. 39;* (iv) *The Planets, Op. 32;* (v) *St Paul's suite, Op. 29/2;* (vi) *Ave Maria, Op. 9b; Choral hymns from the Rig Veda* (Group 3), *Op. 26/3; The Evening watch, Op. 43/1;* (vii) *The Hymn of Jesus, Op. 37;* (vi) *This have I done for my true love, Op. 34/1.*

(B) *** Decca Double Analogue/Dig. 444 549-2 (2) [id.]. (i; iii) LPO, Boult; (ii) Grimethorpe Colliery Band, Howarth; (iv) LPO, Solti; (v) St Paul CO, Hogwood; (vi) Purcell Singers, I. Holst; (vii) BBC Ch. & SO, Boult.

The brilliant Decca recording of Solti's LPO version of the *Planets* combined with Boult's vintage accounts of *Egdon Heath* and *The Perfect Fool* ballet music is discussed below in its single-disc format. Boult's distinguished performance of the *Hymn of Jesus* is also available on another Double Decca, joined with music by Delius and Elgar. But if the present compilation is suitable, it could make a splendid basis for a Holst collection. The jolly, folksy *St Paul's suite* for strings could hardly be done better. *A Moorside suite* sounds splendid in its original, brass-band form, and it is superbly played by the Grimethorpe Colliery Band under Elgar Howarth, with recording approaching demonstration standard. Aptly, the first of the *Rig-Veda Choral hymns* (taken from a Sanskrit source), the *Hymn to the dawn*, brings echoes of *Neptune* from *The Planets*, while the fast and rhythmically fascinating *Hymn to the waters* is even more attractive. The vocal music serves to balance the picture of Holst as a composer, to show the more mystical side of his musical character. Beautifully atmospheric recording to match intense and sensitive performances.

Beni Mora (oriental suite); Egdon Heath; Fugal overture; Hammersmith; (i) *Invocation for cello and orchestra. Somerset rhapsody.*

(BB) *** Naxos Dig. 8.553696 [id.]. RSNO, David Lloyd-Jones; (i) with Timothy Hugh.

This first disc in a Holst series from Naxos could not be more welcome. The six works are neatly balanced, three dating from before the climactic period of *The Planets*, and three after. So the generously lyrical *Somerset rhapsody*, *Beni Mora* and the long-neglected *Invocation for cello and orchestra* (with Timothy Hugh a moving soloist) lead on to the tauter and more astringent post-war works: the Hardy-inspired *Egdon Heath*, the darkly intense prelude and fugue, *Hammersmith* and the *Fugal overture*. Fresh and idiomatic performances, superbly recorded in full and brilliant sound.

(i) *Beni Mora (oriental suite), Op. 29/1; A Fugal overture, Op. 40/1; Hammersmith – A Prelude and scherzo for orchestra, Op. 52;* (ii) *Japanese suite;* (i) *Scherzo (1933/4); A Somerset rhapsody, Op. 21.*

*** Lyrita SRCD 222. (i) LPO; (ii) LSO; Boult.

Beni Mora (written after a holiday in Algeria) is an attractive, exotic piece that shows Holst's flair for orchestration vividly. Boult clearly revels in its sinuosity. *The Japanese suite* is not very Japanese, although it has much charm. The most ambitious work here is *Hammersmith*, far more than a conventional tone picture, intensely poetic. The *Scherzo*, from a projected symphony that was never completed, is strong, confident music. The *Somerset rhapsody* is unpretentious but very enjoyable, and the brief, spiky *Fugal overture* is given plenty of lift and bite to open the concert invigoratingly. As with other records in this Lyrita series the first-class analogue recording has been splendidly transferred to CD.

Brook Green suite for strings; Capriccio for orchestra; (i) *Double violin concerto, Op. 49;* (ii) *Fugal concerto for flute, oboe and strings, Op. 40/2. The Golden Goose* (ballet music, arr. Imogen Holst), *Op. 45/1;* (iii) *Lyric movement for viola and small orchestra. A Moorside suite: Nocturne* (arr. for strings); *2 Songs without words, Op. 22.*

**(*) Lyrita SRCD 223. ECO, Imogen Holst, with (i) Emanuel Hurwitz, Kenneth Sillito; (ii) William Bennett, Peter Graeme; (iii) Cecil Aronowitz.

The *Capriccio* proves an exuberant piece, with some passages not at all capriccio-like. *The Golden Goose* was written as a choral work for St Paul's Girls' School; these orchestral snippets were put together by Imogen Holst. The *Double concerto*, with its bi-tonality and cross-rhythms, is grittier and with much less obvious melodic appeal, but it remains an interesting example of the late Holst. The first two movements of the *Fugal concerto* are much more appealing with their cool interplay of wind colour, particularly when the soloists are so distinguished. The *Lyric movement for viola and small orchestra* is certainly persuasive in the hands of Cecil Aronowitz and is one of the most beautiful of Holst's later pieces. The concert is completed with the comparatively familiar *Brook Green suite* and two *Songs without words*, early works that are tuneful and colourful. All the performances are sympathetically authentic and the recording is well up to Lyrita's usual high standard.

Brook Green suite for string orchestra; (i) *A Fugal concerto, Op. 40/2;* (ii) *Lyric movement for viola and small orchestra; St Paul's suite for string orchestra, Op. 29/2. Arrangements of Morris dance tunes: Bean setting; Constant Billy; Country gardens; How d'ye do; Laudanum bunches; Rigs o'Marlow; Shepherd's hey.*

*** Koch Dig. 3-7058-2 [id.]. New Zealand CO, Nicholas Braithwaite; with (i) Alexa Still, Stephen Popperwell; (ii) Vyvyan Yendoll.

The Fugal concerto features concertante solos for flute and oboe and is a beautifully crafted triptych of miniatures; the rather more ambitious *Lyric movement* is hardly less appealing and is warmly played here by Vyvyan Yendoll, who has a fine, rich timbre. The New Zealand Chamber Orchestra respond sensitively and persuasively to Nicholas Braithwaite, who is thoroughly at home in this repertoire. The textures of the *Brook Green suite* are pleasingly light and airy and in the *St Paul's suite* the gutsy opening *Jig* makes a complete contrast with the pianissimo delicacy of the *Ostinati*. The set of country dances is agreeably spontaneous. The recording is in the demonstration bracket.

Brook Green suite for string orchestra; (i) *Fugal concerto for flute and oboe. The Perfect Fool* (ballet suite), *Op. 39; St Paul's suite for string orchestra, Op. 26/2; A Somerset rhapsody, Op. 21/2.*
(M) *** EMI CD-EMX 2227. ECO, Lord Menuhin.

There are a number of collections of Holst's shorter orchestral works currently available on CD, but none better played or recorded than this and none less expensive. It includes warmly characterized performances of both the works Holst wrote for St Paul's Girls' School, not just the *St Paul's suite* but also the *Brook Green suite*, both sounding fresh, while the rarer *Somerset rhapsody* is also very atmospherically presented. There is some delightful solo playing from Jonathan Snowden and David Theodore in the *Fugal concerto*, and many will welcome Menuhin's vivid account of *The Perfect Fool*, Holst's most familiar orchestral suite after *The Planets*. If the programme suits, you need look no further.

Brook Green suite; (i) *Double violin concerto, Op. 49;* (ii) *Fugal concerto for flute, oboe and strings, Op. 40/2;* (iii) *Lyric movement for viola and small orchestra; 2 Songs without words, Op. 22; St Paul's suite, Op. 29/2.*
*** Chandos Dig. CHAN 9270 [id.]. (i) Ward, Watkinson; (ii) Dobing, Hooker; (iii) Tees; City of L. Sinf., Hickox.

The most striking piece here, a fine example of Holst's later, sparer style, is the *Double concerto* for two violins and small orchestra, very taut and intense. The delicacy of the solo playing in the central *Lament* of this fine work is matched by the ethereal pianissimo from Stephen Tees at the opening of the *Lyric movement*. The woodwind playing is delightful here too, as is the gentle clarinet solo which opens the *Country song*, the first of Holst's two *Songs without words*; the second, appropriately, is more robust. The *Brook Green suite* is wonderfully fresh and there is a comparable lightness of touch at the opening of the delightful *Fugal concerto*. What matters throughout this programme is the surging warmth that Richard Hickox draws from his modest forces. The recording is superb – very real indeed.

Cotswolds Symphony in F, Op. 8; A Hampshire suite, Op. 28/2 (orch. Gordon Jacob); *The Perfect Fool* (ballet suite); *Scherzo for orchestra* (1933/4); *Walt Whitman overture.*
*** Classico Dig. CLASSCD 284 [id.]. Munich SO, Douglas Bostock.

We have had the *Cotswolds Symphony* before on Lyrita (see below), also the *Scherzo*, but it is good to hear fine, new, modern recordings of both. The work completely new to CD is the *Walt Whitman overture*, written as early as 1899. It is a vigorous but untypical piece, its scoring strong on trombones (Holst's own instrument), with a bold *pesante* tune to provide a climax. The rather jolly *Cotswolds Symphony*, which followed the overture (in 1899/1900), immediately shows the Holstian flair for colourful orchestration and has a folksy influence. The melancholy slow movement (*An Elegy for William Morris*) brings a few slight hints of the later Holst; its scherzo has an attractive lumbering dance rhythm, and the finale brings quite a striking tune in 6/4 time. *A Hampshire suite* is Gordon Jacob's orchestration of the *First Suite for military band*, and he skilfully ensures that wind and brass textures predominate. The independent *Scherzo* was the composer's final orchestral flourish. He was working on a symphony of which it was to be a part when he died, but he just managed to complete the orchestration. It distils many aspects of his later orchestral personality, with a distinct reminder of *The Planets*. But it is the familiar suite from *The Perfect Fool* in which we hear the composer at his most inspired and, like the rest of the programme, is most vividly played and recorded, with the slow movement especially persuasive. It is remarkable how well this fine Munich orchestra takes to English music, under the expert guidance of Douglas Bostock.

Cotswolds Symphony in F (Elegy: In memoriam William Morris), Op. 8; Indra (symphonic poem), Op. 13; (i) *Invocation* (for cello and orchestra), *Op. 19/2;* (iii) *The Lure* (ballet music); *The Morning of the year: Dances, Op. 45/2. Sita: Interlude from Act III, Op. 23;* (ii) *A Song of the night* (for violin and orchestra), *Op. 19/1; A Winter idyll.*
*** Lyrita Dig./Analogue SRCD 209 [id.]. (i) Alexander Baillie; (ii) Lorraine McAslan; LPO or (iii) LSO; David Atherton.

The earliest work here, *A Winter idyll*, was written when Holst was in his early twenties. Lewis

Foreman's informative note speaks of the influence of Stanford, but both in this work and in the *Elegy*, which is a slow movement originally forming part of a *Cotswolds Symphony*, one can detect comparatively little of the mature Holst. The familiar fingerprints do surface, however, in *Indra* (1903) and *A Song of the night* (1905), which is among the scores Colin Matthews has edited. *The Lure* (1921) was written at short notice for Chicago and is characteristic, but the inspiration is not of the quality of *The Perfect fool*.

Hammersmith: Prelude and scherzo, Op. 52; Marching song, Op.22; Military band suites Nos. 1 in E flat; 2 in F, Op. 28/1–2. Arr. of BACH (attrib.): *Fugue à la gigue*.

(N) *** Chandos Dig. CHAN 9697 [id.]. Royal Northern College of Music Wind O, Timothy Reynish – VAUGHAN WILLIAMS: *English folk song suite* etc. ***

Truly marvellous bravura playing from the Royal Northern College of Music's Wind Orchestra, who achieve the highest professional standards, especially in the naughtily rhythmic *Song of the blacksmith* from the *Second Military Band Suite*. Timothy Reynish catches the jaunty quality of this attractive music and is especially perceptive in the way he sneaks the *Greensleeves* melody into the *Fantasia on the Dargason*. The only slight disappointment is the climax of the great *Chaconne*, at the opening of the *First suite*. The pacing is ideal, but less tension is generated here than in the famous Fennell versions, and the bass drum is submerged – not nearly as telling as on the Telarc recording. As a compensation we are given an inspired account of *Hammersmith*, the finest performance on record. The rollicking central climax of the *Scherzo* (so reminiscent of *The Planets)* is exultantly powerful, and the work's haunting atmosphere is fully captured. It is good too, to have Holst's effective arrangement of the spirited *Fugue à la gigue*, even if it turns out that it is probably not by Bach. Apart from the matter of the bass drum, the vivid Chandos recording is demonstration-worthy, with splendid range, detail and a rich underlying sonority. Most enjoyable!

Military band suites Nos. 1 in E flat; 2 in F.

❁ *** Telarc Dig. CD 80038 [id.]. Cleveland Symphonic Winds, Fennell – HANDEL: *Royal Fireworks music*. ***

Holst's two *Military band suites* contain some magnificent music. Frederick Fennell's Telarc versions have more gravitas though no less *joie de vivre* than his old Mercury set. They are magnificent, and the recording is truly superb – digital technique used in a quite overwhelmingly exciting way. The *Chaconne* of the *First Suite* makes a quite marvellous effect here. The playing of the Cleveland wind group is of the highest quality.

Military band suites Nos. 1–2. Hammersmith: Prelude and scherzo, Op. 52.

(BB) *** ASV CDQS 6021. L. Wind O, Denis Wick – VAUGHAN WILLIAMS: *English folksong suite* etc. ***

The London performances have great spontaneity, even if they are essentially lightweight, especially when compared with the Fennell versions. The sound is first class.

The Planets (suite), *Op. 32*.

*** DG Dig. 445 860-2 [id.]. Monteverdi Ch. women's voices, Philh. O, Gardiner – GRAINGER: *The Warriors*. ***

(M) *** Penguin Classics Decca Dig. 460 606-2 [id.]. Montreal Ch. & SO, Dutoit.

(M) *** Decca 452 303-2 [id.]. VPO, Karajan (with ELGAR: *Enigma variations* ***).

(M) *** EMI CDM7 64748-2 [id.]. LPO, Boult (with G. Mitchell Ch.) – ELGAR: *Enigma variations*. ***

(B) *** DG Classikon 439 446-2. Boston SO, Steinberg – ELGAR: *Enigma variations* ***.

*** DG Gold Dig. 439 011-2 [id.]. Berlin Ch., BPO, Karajan.

(M) **(*) EMI Dig. CDM7 64740-2. Philh. O, Rattle – JANACEK: *Sinfonietta*. ***

(M) **(*) Chandos Dig. CHAN 7082 [id.]. SNO & Ch., Gibson.

(BB) **(*) Carlton LSO Double Dig. 30368 01107 (2) [(B) id.]. LSO & Ch., Hickox – ORFF: *Carmina burana*. ***

(M) **(*) Ph. Dig. 442 408-2 [id.]. Berlin R. Ch., BPO, Sir Colin Davis.

(i) *The Planets;* (ii) *Egdon Heath, Op. 47;* (iii) *The Perfect Fool* (suite), *Op. 39*.

(M) *** Decca 440 318-2. LPO, cond. (i) Solti, with LPO Ch.; (ii; iii) Boult.

(N) (M) **(*) EMI CDM5 66934-2 [id.]. (i) New Philh. O, with Ch., Boult; (ii; iii) LSO, Previn.

(i) *The Planets;* (ii) *The Perfect Fool* (suite).

(B) *** Decca 433 620-2. (i) LAPO, Mehta; (ii) LPO, Boult.

(N) (BB) **(*) Virgin Classics Dig. Double VBD5 61510-2 (2) [CDVB 61510]. RLPO with Ch., Mackerras – ORFF: *Carmina burana*. **(*)

(i) *The Planets* (suite); *St Paul's suite* (for strings), *Op. 29*.

(M) *** Carlton Dig. 30366 0432 [id.]. (i) Ladies of New Queen's Hall Ch.; New Queen's Hall O, Roy Goodman.

(B) *** Tring Dig. TRP 007 [(M) id. import]. RPO, Vernon Handley, (i) with Ladies of Ambrosian Ch.

John Eliot Gardiner's set of *The Planets* offers a performance of high voltage, with plenty of panache and an acute feeling for atmospheric colour. With speeds never exaggerated, he avoids vulgarity, yet with his rhythmic flair he gives the pieces a new buoyancy. Outstandingly enjoyable are the two most extrovert pieces: *Jupiter, the bringer of jollity* has rarely sounded so joyful, with a hint of wildness at the start, and the dancing rhythms of *Uranus* have a scherzando sparkle, with timpani and brass stunningly caught in the full, brilliant recording. The offstage women's chorus at the end of *Neptune* has seldom been more subtly balanced. Gardiner's *Planets* stands alongside the other current highly recommendable versions. On DG the unusual Grainger coupling, typically rumbustious, pays tribute to the conductor's great-uncle, the composer Balfour Gardiner, who promoted the first performances of both works.

Charles Dutoit's natural feeling for mood, rhythm and colour, so effectively used in his records of Ravel, here results in an outstandingly successful version, both rich and brilliant, and recorded with an opulence to outshine almost all rivals. It is remarkable that, whether in the relentless build-up of *Mars*, the lyricism of *Venus*, the rich exuberance of *Jupiter* or in much else, Dutoit and his Canadian players sound so idiomatic. The final account of *Saturn* is chillingly atmospheric. This is one of the finest of Penguin's mid-priced Classics, with a special note by Karen Armstrong in the UK, and in the USA by Ethan Canin.

With Karajan at his peak, plus the challenge to an orchestra discovering this music for the first time, this extraordinarily magnetic and powerful 1961 account of *The Planets* is uniquely individual, bringing a rare tension, an extra magnetism, the playing combining polish and freshness. The superb Decca recording – produced by John Culshaw in the Sofiensaal – is fully worthy of reissue in Decca's Classic Sound series. *Mars* is remorselessly paced and, with its whining Wagnerian tubas, is unforgettable, while the ravishingly gentle portrayal of *Venus* brings ardent associations with the goddess of love, rather than seeking a peaceful purity. The gossamer textures of *Mercury* and the bold geniality of *Jupiter* contrast with the solemn, deep melancholy expressed by the VPO strings at the opening of *Saturn*. *Uranus* brings marvellous playing from the Vienna brass, given splendid bite.

Under Roy Goodman, a conductor more often associated with baroque and classical repertory, the New Queen's Hall Orchestra crowns its achievement so far in a performance favouring instruments of the kind in general use in the first quarter of the twentieth century, the result subtly different from the effect using modern instruments. The immediate impact with *Mars* is in no doubt. If there is initially less menace than usual, Goodman is tremendously urgent in his pacing, developing great ferocity at the close. *Venus* with its delicate horn solo and translucent flutes is truly the bringer of peace, and the woodwind colouring and transparency of the strings tickle the ear in *Mercury*. The opening of *Jupiter* is light and clean, with crisp string articulation characteristic of the lighter sounds of instruments using gut strings. *Saturn* opens gently and poignantly, with the timpani coming through thrillingly at the climax and the deep bass pedal subtle in its underlining. At the beginning of *Uranus* the chortling bassoons readily recall Dukas's apprentice, the brass – and notably the tuba – making the sharpest, fullest impact. The delicate flutes establish a gentle, lonely mysticism as *Neptune* steals in, the chorus ethereal and perfectly placed in relation to the woodwind. The refreshingly athletic account of the *St Paul's suite* which acts as an encore is a good demonstration of the bright, clean quality of gut strings; John Boydon's Abbey Road recording does the orchestra full justice, and the back-up notes are well detailed.

After a sinister opening, Handley builds the climax of *Mars* impressively and the well-separated closing chords have malignant impact. The noble tune of *Jupiter* develops a similar build-up of intensity. *Saturn*, too, brings a well-graduated, melancholy climax, and the choral diminuendo to silence in *Neptune* is beautifully managed by the Ambrosians. *Venus* is warm and beautiful rather than sensuous or withdrawn, and the resonance provides a lustrous *Mercury*, undoubtedly chimerical if less sharply etched than in some versions. But the sound overall is attractively rich, giving glowing orchestral colour, the horns expansively opulent. What makes this bargain disc especially worth considering is the bracingly fresh account of the *St Paul's suite*, offered as a bonus. The recording of the string body is also very realistic.

The Decca recording for Solti's LPO version is extremely brilliant, with *Mars* given a vivid cutting edge at the fastest possible tempo. Solti's directness in *Jupiter* (with the trumpets coming through splendidly) is certainly riveting, the big tune red-blooded and with plenty of character. In *Saturn* the spareness of texture is finely sustained and the tempo is slow, the detail precise; while in *Neptune* the coolness is even more striking when the pianissimos are achieved with such a high degree of tension. The CD gives the orchestra great presence, and the addition of Boult's classic versions of *Egdon Heath* and *The Perfect Fool* ballet music makes this reissue very competitive.

Sir Adrian Boult gives a performance at once intense and beautifully played, spacious and dramatic, rapt and pointed. The great melody of *Jupiter* is calculatedly less resonant and more flowing than previously but is still affecting, and *Uranus* as well as *Jupiter* has its measure of jollity. The spacious slow movements are finely poised and the recording still stands up well, with added presence and definition.

Mehta's set of *Planets* set a new standard for sonic splendour when it was first issued in 1971. The CD transfer still provides outstanding sound, but there is a touch more edge on the strings and the quality has lost just a little of its richness and amplitude; though definition is sharper, the background hiss is fractionally more noticeable. Even so, this is a superb disc and a strong bargain recommendation. As on the Solti *Planets*, Boult's splendid account of the ballet suite from *The Perfect Fool* has now been added. This was recorded a decade earlier, but the vintage Decca sound remains spectacular, with the LPO brass hardly less resplendent than their colleagues in Los Angeles.

Steinberg's Boston set of *Planets* is another outstanding version from a vintage analogue period. It remains one of the most exciting and involving versions and now sounds brighter and sharper in outline, though with some loss of opulence. *Mars* in particular is intensely exciting. At his fast tempo, Steinberg may get to his fortissimos a little early, but rarely has the piece sounded so menacing on record. The testing point for most will no doubt be *Jupiter*, and here Steinberg the excellent Elgarian comes to the fore, giving a wonderful *nobilmente* swagger.

Karajan's early (1981) digital recording is spectacularly wide-ranging, while the marvellously sustained pianissimo playing of the Berlin Philharmonic – as in *Venus* and the closing pages of *Saturn* – is very telling indeed. *Mars* has great impact, and the sound, full and firm in the bass, gives the performance throughout a gripping immediacy and presence. *Jupiter*, at its climax, still seems a bit fierce: ideally it needs a riper body of tone, yet the big melody has a natural flow and nobility. *Venus* brings sensuous string-phrasing, *Mercury* and *Uranus* have beautiful springing in the triplet rhythms, and the climax of that last movement brings an amazing glissando on the organ. In short this is a thrilling performance and highly recommendable, but it remains at full price and without a coupling.

For Simon Rattle, EMI's digital recording provides wonderfully atmospheric sound, and the quality in *Venus* and *Mercury* is also beautiful, clear and translucent. Otherwise it is not as distinctive a version as one might have expected from this leading conductor; it is sensibly paced but neither so polished nor so bitingly committed as Karajan or Boult, and *Jupiter* is disappointing, lacking in thrust and warmth.

Gibson's reading is characteristically direct and certainly well played. Other versions have greater individuality and are more involving, but there is no doubt that the Chandos recording has fine bite and presence, although there are moments when one would have expected a greater degree of transparency. With sound this vivid, the impact of such a colourful score is enhanced, and at mid-price this is much more competitive, a fine traditional account with plenty of character.

Richard Hickox's *Mars* is given an unremittingly fast pace and is angrily aggressive, the climax topped by ferocious percussion. The emphasized dissonance makes *Venus*, with its translucent serenity, the more striking, the playing cool and withdrawn. *Mercury* is attractively fleet, with a proper element of fantasy, and *Saturn* has an elegiac gravity of mood. The disappointments are *Jupiter* and *Uranus*: the former lacking in real jubilation, with the central melody rather square – though there is no lack of energy – and *Uranus* has a forcefulness of accentuation which precludes any geniality. *Neptune*'s mystic chorus disappears into infinity very convincingly. The recording, with its wide dynamic range, is certainly spectacular; it has excellent transparency and detail but rather misses out on expansive warmth.

Sir Colin Davis's *Mars* is menacingly fast, with weighty Berlin brass and barbaric accents adding to the forcefulness. The resonant recording brings sumptuous textures to *Venus*, while even *Saturn* has a degree of opulence. *Mercury*, however, is infectiously spirited, and *Jupiter*, with a grand central tune, is bucolic in its amplitude. *Uranus* brings galumphing brass, and the closing *Neptune* is both ethereal and sensuous, an unusual combination, brought about partly by the warm reverberation. There are more subtle versions than this, but it is easy to enjoy. However, this reissue offers no coupling.

Mackerras's usual zestful approach communicates readily and the Liverpool orchestra bring a lively response, but the over-reverberant recording tends to cloud the otherwise pungently vigorous *Mars*, and both *Venus* and *Saturn* seem a little straightforward and marginally undercharacterized, while again in the powerful climax of *Uranus* there is some blurring from the resonance. *The Perfect Fool*, with its vivid colouring and irregular rhythms, has much in common with *The Planets* and makes a fine coupling, especially when played with such flair. This now comes on a bargain Virgin Double coupled with an excitingly vivid account of Orff's *Carmina burana*, rather let down by inadequate documentation.

Boult's New Philharmonia performance, recorded in Kingsway Hall in 1966, is brilliantly recorded but does not match his newer LPO version in imaginative detail. It has its moments, of course: the beginning of the big string tune in *Jupiter* is a splendid example of truly British orchestral tone. But otherwise the transfer is not entirely flattering in the upper range. Previn gives a darkly intense performance of *Egdon Heath*, illuminatingly different from Boult's cooler, more detached approach. The rip-roaring ballet music from *The Perfect Fool* presents a colourful contrast, but the extremely vivid transfer has a hint of coarseness.

Air and variations; 3 Pieces for oboe & string quartet, Op. 2.
*** Chandos Dig. CHAN 8392 [id.]. Francis, English Qt – BAX: *Quintet;* MOERAN: *Fantasy quartet;* JACOB: *Quartet.* ***

The three pieces here are engagingly folksy, consisting of a sprightly little *March*, a gentle *Minuet* with a good tune, and a *Scherzo*. Performances are first class, and so is the recording.

VOCAL MUSIC

(i) *Ave Maria, H.49;* (ii–iv; vii) *A Choral fantasia, Op. 51 (H.177);* (iii–iv; vii) *A Dirge for two veterans, H.121;* (v–vii) *The Cloud messenger, Op. 30 (H.111);* (i) *The Evening watch, H.159;* (vi–vii) *The Hymn of Jesus, Op. 37 (H.140);* (iv; vi; vii) *Ode to Death, Op. 38 (H.144);* (i) *4 Partsongs;* (ii–iv; vii) *7 Partsongs, H.162;* (i) *This have I done for my true love, H.128.*
(N) (B) *** Chandos 2-for-1 Dig. 241-6 (2) [id.]. (i) Finzi Singers, Spicer; (ii) Patricia Rozario; (iii) Joyful Company of Singers; (iv) City of L. Sinfonia; (v) Della Jones; (vi) LSO Ch.; (vii) Hickox.

Richard Hickox proves a passionate advocate of the shorter choral works of Holst, demonstrating that the two Whitman settings, *A Dirge for two veterans* and *Ode to Death*, are among his finest pieces for voices. Both were inspired by Holst's response to the First World War: the *Dirge* written just after war had started in 1914, a grim processional for male voices, brass and percussion, and the *Ode* in 1919 when it was over and his disillusion was even more intense. That second work is in very much the same vein of inspiration as his masterpiece, the *Hymn of Jesus*, and, with the larger forces of the London Symphony Chorus, brings the most powerful performance here. It easily outshines even Sir Adrian Boult's vintage version for Decca. Hickox secures tauter and crisper ensemble, as well as treating the sections based on plainchant with an aptly expressive freedom. Modern digital sound makes an enormous difference in a work where the choral sounds are terraced so tellingly.

The long-neglected choral piece, *The Cloud messenger*, may lack the concentration of the *Hymn of Jesus* but it brings similarly incandescent choral writing. Warmly and positively realized by Hickox and his powerful forces, with Della Jones a fine soloist, it makes a major discovery, whatever its incidental shortcomings. Rich and ample Chandos recording adds to the involvement. Both the later works, the *Seven Partsongs* of 1925 as well as the *Choral fantasia* of 1930, set poems by Robert Bridges, with the choral writing fluently beautiful. Though Patricia Rozario is not on her finest form, the Joyful Company of Singers sing superbly in intense and moving performances, helped by rich and full Chandos sound.

A Choral Fantasia, Op. 51; Choral Symphony, Op. 41.
**(*) Hyperion Dig. CDA 66660 [id.]. Lynne Dawson, Guildford Choral Society, RPO, Hilary Davan Wetton.

Though the ensemble of the Guildford Choral Society is not ideally crisp, and one really wants more weight of sound, the originality of Holst's choral writing and the purposeful nature of the argument are never in doubt in this surprisingly rare coupling, with Lynne Dawson the radiantly beautiful soprano soloist in both works. Holst is nothing if not daring in using well-known texts of Keats in the *Choral Symphony*, adding a new dimension even to the 'Ode on a Grecian urn'.

(i) *A Choral Fantasia, Op. 51;* (ii) *Psalm 86.*
(M) *** EMI CDM5 65588-2 [id.]. (i) Janet Baker; (ii) Ian Partridge, Purcell Singers, ECO, Imogen Holst – FINZI: *Dies natalis;* VAUGHAN WILLIAMS: *5 Mystical songs* etc. ***

In Holst's *Choral Fantasia* – a setting of words written by Robert Bridges in commemoration of Purcell – Dame Janet Baker once again shows her supreme quality as a recording artist. The recording, though not lacking ambient warmth, is admirably clear (indeed the organ pedals are only too clear). The sound could perhaps be more open, but there is no lack of projection and vividness. The setting of *Psalm 86*, with its expressive tenor part sung beautifully by Ian Partridge, is also included in this generous compilation. The recording here is outstanding, and the success of both these performances owes much to the inspired direction of the composer's daughter.

Choral hymns from the Rig Veda (Groups 1–4), *H. 97–100; 2 Eastern pictures for women's voices and harp, H. 112; Hymn to Dionysus, Op. 31/2.*
**(*) Unicorn Dig. DKPCD 9046 [id.]. Royal College of Music Chamber Ch., RPO, Willcocks; Ellis.

The *Choral hymns from the Rig Veda* show Holst writing with deep understanding for voices, devising textures, refined, very distinctively his, to match atmospherically exotic texts. Though performances are not always ideally polished, the warmth and thrust of the music are beautifully caught. The *Hymn to Dionysus*, setting words from the *Bacchae* of Euripides in Gilbert Murray's translation, a rarity anticipating Holst's *Choral symphony*, makes a welcome and substantial fill-up, along with the two little *Eastern pictures*. Beautifully clean and atmospheric recording.

Choral hymns from the Rig Veda (Group 3), *H. 99, Op. 26/3.*
*** Hyperion CDA 66175 [id.]. Holst Singers & O; Davan Wetton – BLISS: *Lie strewn the white flocks;* BRITTEN: *Gloriana: Choral dances.* ***

The third group of *Choral hymns from the Rig Veda*, like the whole series, reveals Holst in his Sanskritic period at his most distinctively inspired. In this responsive performance, it makes an excellent coupling for the attractive Bliss and Britten items, atmospherically recorded.

(i) *Choral Symphony, Op. 41;* (ii) *The Hymn of Jesus, Op. 37.*
(M) *** EMI CDM5 65128-2. (i) Felicity Palmer, LPO Ch., LPO, Boult; (ii) St Paul's Cathedral Ch., London Symphony Ch., LPO, Groves.

In the *Choral Symphony*, Boult and his performers readily demonstrate the beauty and imagination of the writing, and in his totally unsentimental performance, he manages to draw the whole work together. The 1974 recording remains richly atmospheric in its CD format, although the Scherzo could ideally be more sharply focused. The Groves recording of *The Hymn of Jesus* is on the whole finer than Boult's older, Decca account which has served collectors well over the years. Sir Charles Groves brings great sympathy and conviction to this beautiful and moving score, whose visionary quality has never paled, and the recording has transferred very well to CD to make a highly desirable Holst coupling.

The Evening watch, H.159; 6 Choruses, H.186; Nunc dimittis, H.127; 7 Partsongs, H.162; 2 Psalms, H.117.
*** Hyperion Dig. CDA 66329 [id.]. Holst Singers & O, Hilary Davan Wetton.

Hilary Davan Wetton's performance of the comparatively austere but no less inspired *Evening watch* creates a rapt, sustained pianissimo until the very closing bars, when the sudden expansion is quite thrilling. The *Six Choruses* for male voices show the composer at his most imaginative, while the comparable *Partsongs* for women often produce a ravishingly dreamy, mystical beauty. The final song, *Assemble all ye maidens*, is a narrative ballad about a lost love, and its closing section is infinitely touching. The performances are gloriously and sensitively sung and unerringly paced.

OPERA

(i) *At the Boar's Head, Op. 42* (complete); (ii) *The wandering scholar, Op. 50* (complete).
(M) *** EMI Dig./Analogue CDM5 65127-2. (i) Langridge, Palmer, Ross, Tomlinson, Wilson-Johnson, Hall, Suart, George, RLPO, Groves; (ii) Burrowes, Tear, Rippon, Langdon, E. Op. Group, ECO, Bedford.

Finding that Shakespeare's lines went naturally to dances and tunes from Playford's collection, for his Falstaff opera, *At the Boar's Head*, Holst used that material on a libretto drawn entirely from the relevant scenes of *Henry IV, Parts I* and *II.* The result is busy-sounding in its emphasis on chattering comedy, and dramatically it is questionable. But on record the charm, colour and originality of the piece come over well. *The wandering scholar*, by contrast, works delightfully on stage, but on record its galumphing humour is less than sparkling. But whatever one's response to the comedy, the musical inspiration has the sharp originality and economy one associates with Holst's last period, a fascinating score. The recording comes from the mid-1970s and the CD is something of a revelation in opening up the choral sound while still retaining the atmosphere and bloom of the analogue originals. An outstanding reissue in every way.

(i) *Savitri* (complete); (ii) *Dream city* (song cycle, orch. Matthews).
**(*) Hyperion Dig. CDA 66099 [id.]. (i) Langridge, Varcoe, Palmer, Hickox Singers; (ii) Kwella; City of L. Sinfonia, Hickox.

Felicity Palmer is more earthy, more vulnerable as Savitri than Janet Baker was in the earlier Argo recording, her grainy mezzo well caught. Philip Langridge and Stephen Varcoe both sing sensitively with fresh, clear tone, though their timbres are rather similar. Hickox is a thoughtful conductor both in the opera and in the orchestral song-cycle arranged by Colin Matthews from Holst's settings of Humbert Wolfe poems. Patrizia Kwella's soprano at times catches the microphone rather shrilly.

Holst, Imogen (1907–84)

String quartet No. 1.
*** Conifer Dig. 74321 15006-2. Brindisi Qt – BRIDGE: *3 Idylls;* BRITTEN: *String quartet No. 2.* ***

Imogen Holst's two-movement *Quartet* is a shortish work; although not strongly personal, it is full of interest. Both performance and recording are of high quality.

Holt, Simon (born 1958)

. . . era madrugada . . .; Shadow realm; Sparrow night; (i) *Canciones.*
*** NMC Dig. D008 [id.]. (i) Fiona Kimm; Nash Ens., Lionel Friend.

Regularly Simon Holt has found inspiration in Spanish sources, particularly Lorca, and two of these four pieces are fine examples: . . . *era madrugada* is a sinister evocation of a Lorca poem about a man found murdered in the hour just before dawn (*madrugada*). Like the other three pieces, it was written for the Nash Ensemble, who here under Lionel Friend respond superbly to Holt's virtuoso demands. Fiona Kimm is the formidable mezzo soloist in three Spanish settings, *Canciones*; but rather more approachable are the two highly atmospheric instrumental works, *Shadow realm* and *Sparrow night*, which round the disc off. These two also bring sinister nightmare overtones. The superb recording is engineered by Holt's fellow-composer, Colin Matthews.

Holten, Bo (born 1948)

(i) *Clarinet concerto* (1987); (ii) *Sinfonia concertante for cello and orchestra* (1985–6).
*** Chandos Dig. CHAN 9272 [id.] (i) Jens Schou; (ii) Morten Zeuten; Danish National RSO; (i) Jorma Panula; (ii) Hans Graf.

Bo Holten's *Clarinet concerto* is certainly appealing. The *Sinfonia concertante* comes from a broadcast of 1987 and is long on complexity (36 minutes 6 seconds) and short on substance, but there are sufficient moments of poetic vision to encourage one to return to it. It is played with great zest and conviction by Morten Zeuten (cellist of the Kontra Quartet), and the recording has exemplary presence and clarity.

Honegger, Arthur (1892–1955)

(i) *Le chant de Nigamon; Monopartita; Napoleon (film incidental music): Les hombres*. (ii) *Mouvement symphonique No. 3; Pastorale d'été*. (i) *Phaedre: Prélude; Prélude, fugue et postlude; The Tempest: Prélude*. (ii) *Le Roi David*.
(N) (B) *** Erato/Warner Dig./analogue 3984 24244-2 (2) [id.]. (i) Monte Carlo PO, Marius Constant; (ii) Bavarian RO; (iii) Christianne Ed-Pierre, Jeannine Collard, Eric Tappy, Jean Desailly (narr.), Philippe Caillard Ch., Instrumental Ens; (ii; iii) Dutoit.

This Erato Ultima is outstanding value and highly recommendable. Charles Dutoit's *Le Roi David* uses the original instrumental forces, not the full orchestra favoured by most of his rivals on record. The recording comes from 1970, not that anyone coming to it afresh would guess that. It is a compelling performance of strong dramatic contrasts. Dutoit also gives an atmospheric and sympathetic account of *Pastorale d'été* and the *Mouvement symphonique No. 3*. The rest of the programme, directed by Marius Constant, is also well worth having. A warm welcome must be given to the music for *Phaedre*, which is highly imaginative and atmospheric. The earliest work included here is *La chant de Nigamon* (1917), a tone-poem concerning the fate of a native American chief who is burnt at the stake; and it is both graphic and powerful. The *Monopartita* is Honegger's last orchestral piece, coming from the same period as the *Fifth Symphony*. Again the invention is of the highest quality. Decent performances and acceptable, though not first-class digital sound.

Concertino for piano and orchestra.
*** Decca Dig. 452 448-2 [id.]. Jean-Yves Thibaudet, Montreal SO, Dutoit (with RAVEL: *Concertos* **) – FRANCAIX: *Concertino*. ***

Honegger's *Concertino* has a gamin-like charm and its jazzy finale has delightful zest and character. This is probably the best recording to have appeared so far. Like the Françaix with which it is coupled, it is an unqualified delight. The main works, the two Ravel *Concertos*, are good but in no way do they challenge existing recommendations, so we hope Decca will one day recouple the two *Concertinos*.

Horace victorieux; Mermoz: La traversée des Andes; Le vol sur l'Atlantique; Pacific 231; Rugby; Pastorale d'été; La tempête: Prélude.
*** DG (IMS) Dig. 435 438-2 [id.]. Toulouse Capitole O, Plasson.

Horace victorieux is a noisy score but full of imaginative touches, as are the two scenes recorded here for the film *Mermoz*. We are also offered a beautifully languorous account of *Pastorale d'été*, among the best committed to disc, and Plasson's accounts of *Pacific 231* and *Rugby* are full of high spirits. His version of the *Prélude*, composed for a production of Shakespeare's *Tempest* in the late 1920s, is as fierce and violent as the composer's own pioneering Parlophone 78-r.p.m. disc. DG provide a realistic and natural sound-picture with plenty of detail. Strongly recommended.

Pacific 231.
(M) *** Decca (IMS) 448 576-2 [id.]. SRO, Ansermet – CHABRIER: *España* **(*); DEBUSSY: *La Mer* **(*); DUKAS: *L'apprenti sorcier* ***; RAVEL: *Boléro; La Valse*. ***

Ansermet conveys all the grinding power of Honegger's railway evocation, and its surging lyricism too, but some of the detail is clouded by the resonance at the climax. An impressive performance just the same.

Pacific 231; Pastorale d'été; Rugby; (i) *Christmas cantata (Cantata de Noël)*.
(M) **(*) EMI CDM7 63944-2. O Nat. de l'ORTF, Martinon; (i) with Camille Maurane & Ch. d'Oratorio Maîtrise de l'ORTF.

The Orchestre National de l'ORTF plays well for Jean Martinon, though we have heard more atmospheric accounts of *Pastorale d'été* (Martinon is not always responsive to pianissimo indications here). The *Cantata de Noël* is given a strong performance, though not even the expert French Radio choir manages the highly exacting demands of Honegger's difficult (and not always effective) choral writing. Generally these are good performances – although the programme offers short measure at 46 minutes.

Symphonies Nos. 1; 2 for strings with trumpet obbligato; 3 (Symphonie liturgique); 4 (Deliciae Basilienses); 5 (Di tre re); 3 Symphonic movements: Nos. 1, Pacific 231; 2, Rugby.
(B) *** Erato/Warner Ultima 3984 21340-2 (2). Bav. RSO, Charles Dutoit.

Symphonies Nos. 1; 2 for strings with trumpet obbligato; 3 (Symphonie liturgique); 4 (Deliciae Basilienses); 5 (Di tre re); 3 Symphonic movements: Nos. 1, Pacific 231; 3, The Tempest: Prélude.
(M) *** Sup. 11 1566-2 (2) [id.]. Czech PO, Baudo.

Honegger's symphonies are currently much underrated. The *First* is a highly stimulating and rewarding piece: its level of energy is characteristic of the later symphonies. The *Second* is a probing, intense wartime composition that reflects something of the anguish Honegger felt during the German occupation. The *Third* (*Liturgique*) dates from the end of the war, while the *Fourth*, composed for Paul Sacher, makes use of Swiss folk material. Beneath its smiling surface there is a gentle vein of nostalgia and melancholy, particularly in the slow movement. The finale is sparkling and full of high spirits, though even this ends on a bitter-sweet note. The *Fifth* is a powerful work, inventive, concentrated and vital. Although the performances are slightly uneven, Dutoit's Ultima Double is an appealingly economical way of acquiring excellent, modern, digital recordings (dating from the early 1980s). In Dutoit's hands the phrasing of the Bavarian orchestra in the beautiful slow movement of the *First* has both dignity and eloquence. He again produces very cultured string-playing in the dark, introspective *Symphony for strings*, but here it is just a shade deficient in vitality and drive. The *Deliciae Basiliensis* also has rather measured tempi; however, this beautifully recorded performance serves to rekindle enthusiam for a much-underrated work whose sunny countenance and keen nostalgia bring unfailing delight. Dutoit then gives thoroughly idiomatic accounts of both the *Symphonie liturgique* and the *Di tre re Symphony*. In the *Fifth* he does not galvanize his orchestra into playing of the same volcanic fire and vitality that Serge Baudo secures from the Czech Philharmonic on Supraphon, but the Erato recording is fresher and more detailed. Room has been found for only two of the *Three Symphonic movements*. Both *Pacific 231* and *Rugby* are well done; although the latter may be found a little genteel; the playing and recording are more than adequate compensation.

The Supraphon performances come from the 1960s, but they are more than merely serviceable. The sound comes up very well indeed and the playing of the Czech Philharmonic for Baudo is totally committed. The performance of the *Fifth Symphony* has never been surpassed (except possibly by the pioneering Munch recording) and has amazing presence and detail for its period.

Symphony No. 2 for strings and trumpet.
*** Delos Dig. DE 3121 [id.]. Seattle SO, Gerard Schwarz – R. STRAUSS: *Metamorphosen;* WEBERN, arr. SCHWARZ: *Langsamer satz.* ***

In terms of recording quality, Schwarz's account can hold its own alongside the very best, and the playing of the Seattle strings is splendidly responsive. He is just a bit too slow at the very beginning, and the same reservation could be made about the slow movement, but there is plenty of atmosphere. Although it does not displace the Jansons or Karajan accounts or other recommendations, this performance is very fine indeed and will give much pleasure.

Symphony No. 2 for strings and trumpet obbligato; Monopartita; Mouvements symphoniques Nos. 1, Pacific 231; 2, Rugby; 3, Pastorale d'été.
(N) *** Decca Dig. 455 352-2 [id.]. Zurich Tonhalle O, David Zinman.

The Zurich Tonhalle Orchestra is a far more sophisticated and impressive body than it was in the early days of LP. David Zinman gets sensitive and subtly nuanced playing from them in the *Symphony*. The Zurich Orchestra commissioned *Monopartita* in 1950, and first performed it under Hans Rosbaud, so the work belongs to the period of the *Fifth Symphony*. It was actually the composer's last orchestral piece – and a powerfully concentrated one. The better-known orchestral evocations come off very well, with a splendidly powerful and purposeful *Pacific 231* which sounds as if it is going to be in on time. Good performances, and though Karajan remains a first choice for the symphony, the very good Decca recording makes this disc thoroughly recommendable.

Symphonies Nos. 2 for strings with trumpet obbligato; 3 (Symphonie liturgique).
❁ (M) *** DG 447 435-2 [id.]. BPO, Karajan – STRAVINSKY: *Concerto in D.* ***

Symphonies Nos. 2 for strings and trumpet obbligato; 3 (Liturgique); Pacific 231.
*** EMI (SIS) Dig. CDC5 55122-2 [id.]. Oslo PO, Jansons.

Karajan's accounts of these magnificent symphonies come from 1973 and still remain in a class of their own. Not even Munch's pioneering recording of the *Symphony No. 2* or its successors comes near to it for sheer poetic intensity, and the *Symphonie liturgique* has likewise never been surpassed. It is luminous, incandescent and moving. The only rival is the Jansons version with the Oslo Philharmonic on EMI, but this is at full price. It certainly deserves its place as one of DG's 'Legendary Originals'.

Jansons's account of these two symphonies is arguably the Oslo orchestra's best record to date. The playing has a virtuosity and tonal sophistication that are almost the equal of the Berliners' sumptuous string-tone in the *Symphony for strings*, and superb concentration and control. The recording is magnificently rich and present, detail is splendidly focused. The *Symphonie liturgique* is thrilling in their hands, and there is an excellent account of *Pacific 231* as well.

Symphonies Nos. 2 for strings and trumpet obbligato; 4 (Deliciae Basiliensis).
(N) *(*) Cyprès Dig. CYP 1602 [id.]. Zurich SO, Daniel Schweizer.

Daniel Schweizer and his Zurich Orchestra give well-prepared, and perfectly acceptable accounts of both symphonies which would pass muster in the absence of any competition. But the performances are not as sumptuous as Karajan and Jansons in the *Second Symphony* or as elegant as Baudo or Munch in the delightful *Deliciae Basiliensis*. The recording is again perfectly decent, though perhaps a little studio bound.

Symphonies Nos. 3; 5; Pacific 231.
*** Chandos Dig. CHAN 9176 [id.]. Danish Nat. R. O, Järvi.

The *Symphonie liturgique* has stiff competition to meet in the classic Karajan account, but Neeme Järvi and the Danish orchestra serve it very well indeed, and the digital Chandos recording is even more detailed and present, and certainly fuller, than the DG version. Järvi's version of the *Fifth Symphony* is also masterly, even if it does not match the hell-for-leather abandon of Baudo's Supraphon set (see above). But that is now over 30 years old and, though it still sounds pretty amazing, this is undeniably superior.

Symphony No. 5 ('Di tre re').
(M) (**) DG Originals mono 449 748-2 [id.]. Lamoureux O, Igor Markevitch – MILHAUD: *Les Choéphores* (**); ROUSSEL: *Bacchus et Ariane: suite No. 2.* **

Markevitch's account of the *Fifth Symphony* with the Orchestre Lamoureux was recorded in the Salle Wagram in 1957 – in mono. The sound has plenty of depth and good perspective; it is a little set back, though there is no lack of impact in tuttis and there is plenty of space round the instruments elsewhere. Markevitch generates plenty of atmosphere; his approach, which is lyrical, is strongly characterized but not a first choice.

Jeanne d'Arc au bûcher.
✪ *** DG (IMS) Dig. 429 412-2 [id.]. Keller, Wilson, Escourrou, Lanzi, Pollet, Command, Stutzman, Aler, Courtis, R. France Ch., Fr. Nat. O, Seiji Ozawa.

Honegger's 1935 setting of the Claudel poem is one of his most powerful and imaginative works, full of variety of invention, colour and textures. It is admirably served by these forces, and in particular by the Joan of Marthe Keller. The singers, too, are all excellent and the Choir and the six soloists of the Maîtrise of Radio France are as top-drawer as the orchestra. The DG engineers cope excellently with the large forces and the acoustic of the Basilique de Saint-Denis.

Judith.
**(*) Van. 08 9054 71 [id.]. Devrath, Christiansen, Madeleine Milhaud (nar.), Salt Lake Symphonic Ch., Utah SO, Abravanel.

Judith is a dramatic vocal–orchestral concert work with interspersed narration; some passages are marvellously imaginative and atmospheric (the Choral invocation to protect Judith on her voyage through the valley of fear to cross into the Assyrian lines is quite chilling). The performance dates from 1964 and is totally committed; the only let-down is in some of the choral singing, which could be stronger. The work is short (just under 45 minutes) and it would have added to the competitiveness of the issue to provide a fill-up. But if it is short on quantity, it is long on musical and dramatic interest.

Le Roi David (complete).
(M) *** Van. 08.4038.71 [OVC 4038]. Davrath, Sorensen, Preston, Singher, Madeleine Milhaud, Utah University Ch., Utah SO, Abravanel.

The Vanguard version is remarkably vivid, well detailed and present, and the playing of the Utah Symphony under Maurice Abravanel is very fine. The recording also stands up well. Netania Davrath is excellent too, and so is Madeleine Milhaud, the composer's wife, as the Witch of Endor. Thoroughly recommendable.

Horneman, Christian Frederik Emil (1840–1906)

Aladdin overture; Ouverture héroïque: Helteliv; (i) *Gurre* (incidental music).
*** Chandos Dig. CHAN 9373 [id.]. (i) Guido Päevatalu, Danish R. Ch.; Danish RSO, Schønwandt.

Horneman is an altogether delightful composer, and the music recorded here deserves the widest dissemination. The incidental music to Holger Drachmann's play, *Gurre*, the major work on the disc, is light-textured and full of charming, gracious invention and is beautifully scored. It is quite enchanting, particularly in such persuasive hands, and the baritone, Guido Päevatalu, sings his simple strophic songs with great character. The other two pieces, *Helteliv* ('A Hero's Life') and the *Aladdin overture*, are the only purely orchestral works Horneman ever wrote: the *Aladdin overture* is his first; it shows a real flair for colour. This is a most enjoyable disc, beautifully played and recorded. Strongly recommended.

Hotteterre, Jacques (1674–1763)

Pièces pour la flûte, Oeuvre II: *Echoes for solo flute; Suite in B flat for recorder and continuo; Suite in E min. for transverse flute and continuo.* Oeuvre III: *Trio sonatas: in C for 2 oboes and continuo; in D min. for 2 recorders and continuo; Suite in D for transverse flute and continuo.* Oeuvre V: *Suite in E min. for recorder and continuo. Suite-Sonata in C for oboe and continuo.* Oeuvre VI: *Suite in G for 2 transverse flutes.* Oeuvre VII: *L'Art de Préluder: Préludes: for recorder; for transverse flute; for oboe; for treble viola da gamba. Airs et brunettes:* Arrangements of music by Mr Lambert, Lully, de Bousset etc.: *Fanfare et les Dieux for 3 transverse flutes.* (i) *Brunette: L'autre jour ma Cloris;* (i–ii) *Air de Mr Lambert: Goûtons un doux repos.* (iii) *Méthode pour La Musette;* Oeuvre X: *Bourrée d'Achille; Contredanses: La pharaonne; La petite janeton, Marche des dragons (Air); Musette de Mr Clerambault; Menuet: La Badaut; Prélude et la Régence; Tes beaux yeux ma Nicole; Rigaudons.*

(B) *** Seon/Sony SB2K 62942 (2) [S2K 62942]. Frans Brüggen, Walter van Hauwe, Barthold Kuijken, Oswald van Olmen, Bruce Haynes, Wieland Kuijken, Gustav Leonhardt, Shelley Gruskin; with (i) Marjanne Kweksilber; (ii) Toyohiko Satoh (lute); (iii) Shelley Gruskin (musette).

Jacques Hotteterre wrote some of the earliest music for the transverse flute and encouraged its use. He also perfected the musette, a kind of miniature bagpipe which looks a bit like a large embroidered sock with a mouthpiece. (Most of the instruments used are pictured in the accompanying booklet.) The present pair of discs gathers together Hotteterre's complete wind music (written between 1708 and 1738). An original oboe and a musette, both made by the composer, are featured in their performance. The programme includes well over two hours of music and it should be approached with some caution. Some of it, intended for the composer's pupils among the nobility, is not too demanding. However, Hotteterre's invention is often resourceful, and the series of short dance-movements which make up the trio sonatas are certainly characterful. In his slow movements he languishes plaintively and with some individuality. The dolorous *Sarabandes* of the two *Suites for transverse flute and continuo* are quite affecting. The *Trio sonatas* for a pair of oboes (with a bassoon featured in the continuo) and for two transverse flutes are texturally most diverting, and the latter also has some fine, expressive writing. The *Suite-Sonata* for oboe consists of five vignettes, none of which outlasts its welcome, and the similarly brief *Préludes* for various instruments have an attractive, improvisatory feeling. The closing surprise number for soprano (the sensitive Marjanne Kweksilber) and viola da gamba is quite haunting. Of the *Airs et Brunettes, L'autre jour ma Cloris* and the *Air de Mr Lambert* also feature the soprano voice, the latter with lute. They are both marked *Tendrement* and are genuinely touching. It is a pity the documentation does not include the words! The pieces for musette (which sounds like mini-bagpipes) are all piquant: they are offered as a series of interludes between the major works. The performances by a group of very distinguished soloists are of the highest calibre, and the recording is first class. It is very well, if rather closely, recorded.

Hovhaness, Alan (born 1911)

Symphony No. 2 (Mysterious mountain), Op. 32; And God created great whales; Alleluia and fugue; Celestial fantasy; Prayer of St Gregory; Prelude and quadruple fugue.

*** Delos Dig. DE 3157 [id.]. Seattle SO, Gerard Schwarz.

The *Symphony No. 2* begins with pastoral, modal writing, leading to a central fugal climax and returning to rich, expressive serenity. *The Prayer of St Gregory* is essentially a chorale and is rather appealing in its innocence. But the most sensational piece here is *And God created great whales*, which reaches a huge climax and interpolates tapes of the actual song of the humpbacked whale. The effect is really very grandiose indeed, and everybody here rises to the occasion, including both the whales and the recording engineers.

Symphonies Nos. 22 (City of light), Op. 236; 50 (Mount St Helens), Op. 360.

*** Delos Dig. DE 3137 [id.]. Seattle SO, composer.

If you enjoyed the spectacle of Symphony No. 2, you'll really respond to the extravagant *Mount St Helens Symphony* with its haunting *Spirit Lake* central movement and awe-inspiring *Volcano* eruption for a finale, where some of the orchestral effects are quite grotesquely shattering. *City of Light* is more conventional, but agreeable enough. Performances and recording are first class, but this is not a record for a flat with thin walls.

Howells, Herbert (1892–1983)

Concerto for string orchestra; Elegy for viola, string quartet and strings; Suite for string orchestra; Serenade for strings.

(N) ✿ *** Chandos Dig. CHAN 9161 [id.]. City of L. Sinf., Hickox.

These three splendid and inspired works are all in the great and ongoing tradition of English string-writing, and it is extraordinary that they are not better known, or more often heard. The *Concerto* (1938) opens with a great burst of energy, but the secondary theme is hauntingly nostalgic, and the elegiac character of the slow movement (with a string trio first ruminating on the tender main theme) establishes the music's character. That it owes a debt to Elgar is no accident, for the work is dedicated jointly to him and the composer's only son, whose loss is also remembered in the *Hymnus paradisi*. The life force returns exuberantly in the closing Minuet. The viola *Elegy*, written much earlier (1917), is clearly modelled on Vaughan Williams's *Tallis fantasia*, yet it is masterly in its own right and very moving. The delicate one-movement *Serenade*, which also features a solo quartet, dates from the same year. The *Allegro deciso* and *Rondo* which open and close the *Suite* (1938) are rhythmically extrovert in a Holstian 'St Paul's' manner, but then, after a gentle, rapturous *Siciliano*, the Minuet opens with a deeper voiced pizzicato. The performances here are exemplary, superbly played and conducted by Hickox with deep commitment and understanding. The recording is warm, sonorous and clearly detailed.

(i) *Concerto for string orchestra;* (ii) *Hymnus paradisi.*

(N) (M) **(*) EMI CDM5 67119-2. (i) LPO, Boult; (ii) Harper, Tear, Bach Ch., King's College Ch., New Philh. O, Willcocks.

Boult's understanding and vigorous performance of the *Concerto for strings* – a work dedicated to him – draws a parallel with that other virtuoso string work which stands at the heart of the English tradition – Bliss's *Music for strings* – with which it was originally coupled on LP. The new coupling here with the *Hymnus paradisi* is appropriate, for both were written in memory of the composer's son. It is a dignified and beautifully wrought piece but also, and more importantly, is both moving and powerful. Willcocks's performance is eloquent and warmly persuasive within the glowing Kingsway Hall acoustics, but even so it does not match Handley's later account on Hyperion (see below) in intensity of feeling.

(i) *3 Dances for violin and orchestra. Suite for orchestra, the five 'B's;* (ii) *In green ways* (song cycle).

(N) *** Chandos Dig. CHAN 9557 [id.]. (i) Lydia Mordkovitch; (ii) Yvonne Kenny; LSO, Richard Hickox.

This disc in Hickox's excellent Howells series for Chandos makes one appreciate how brilliant Howells's early career was as an orchestral composer – an admirable and greatly enjoyable collection which demonstrates his skills as an inventive melodist, master of the orchestral palette and splendid musical craftsman. The inspired *Suite, the 'B's* celebrates the composer's musician friends and colleagues at the Royal College of Music at the beginning of the 1914–18 war. As such it has something in common with Elgar's *Enigma variations*, although Howells clearly identified each dedicatee. Two of them succumbed: Ivor Gurney, who was badly gassed, and Francis 'Bunny' Warren, a viola player, who died at Mons. Gurney (nicknamed 'Bartholemew') is remembered with a movingly passionate *Lament*, and Bunny is personified in a delicate *Minuet/Mazurka*, at times disconsolate, but with a blithe pastoral counterpart. 'Blissy' (Arthur Bliss) inspires a dainty, chimerical *Scherzo* – with the piano an orchestral soloist – yet with a balancing touch of nostalgia reminiscent of Elgar. These shorter evocations are framed by an exuberant *Overture* with a nobilmente lyrical expansiveness representing the composer himself ('Bublum'), and the finale ('Benjee' – Arthur Benjamin), which begins lightheartedly but ends grandiloquently, recalls the composer's own themes from the overture. The whole makes an excellent entertainment and ought to be familiar in the concert hall. The *Three dances for violin and orchestra*, another wartime work (1915), are in the best English folk/pastoral tradition and the ravishing, bitter-sweet solo line of the central *Quasi lento* is magical on the sympathetic bow of Lydia Mordkovitch. The other two works – the *3 Dances*, with Lydia Mordkovitch as a brilliant violin soloist, and the song-cycle, *In green ways*, with Yvonne Kenny – also include poignant elegies. The English countryside is strikingly evoked in this group of five songs, using lyrics by Shakespeare and Goethe (the beautiful and touching *Wanderer's night song*, freely translated by Howells himself), although it is perhaps the evocative setting of James Stephens's *The Goat paths* that haunts the memory most of all. Yvonne Kenny sings the whole group most affectingly and Richard Hickox and the LSO are ardent and communicative advocates of all this fine music. A highly recommendable disc, very well recorded indeed.

(i) *Fantasia; Threnody* (both for cello and orchestra). *The King's herald; Paradise Rondel; Pastoral rhapsody; Procession.*

*** Chandos Dig. CHAN 9410 [id.]. (i) Moray Welsh; LSO, Hickox.

Herbert Howells was so shy about his orchestral music that only since his death have such pieces as these emerged. The most personal works here are the *Fantasia* and *Threnody*, both for cello and orchestra, together forming a sort of rhapsodic concerto. Howells was reflecting his anguish over the death of his ten-year-old son, with flashes of anger punctuating the elegiac lyricism. The *Threnody*, simpler in its lyricism, was probably planned as the slow movement of a three-movement *Cello concerto*. The other major piece is the *Pastoral rhapsody*, written in 1923. This is more conventionally English, except for a radiant climax, with anglicized echoes of *Daphnis et Chloé* and *Petrushka*. Similarly pastoral but predominantly vigorous, the *Paradise Rondel* of 1925 is full of sharp contrasts, with one passage offering clear echoes of the *Russian dance* from *Petrushka*. The collection opens with the boldly extrovert *King's herald*, bright with Waltonian fanfares. *Procession* brings more echoes of *Petrushka*, again reflecting Howells's response to the Diaghilev Ballets Russes' appearances in London. Helped by rich, atmospheric sound, Richard Hickox draws performances that are both brilliant and warmly persuasive from the LSO, with Moray Welsh a movingly expressive soloist in the concertante works.

Oboe sonata.

(N) (B) *** Hyperion Helios Dig. CDH 55008 [id.]. Sarah Francis, Peter Dickenson – BOUGHTON: *Pastoral;* HARTY: *3 Pieces;* RUBBRA: Sonata. ***

Howell's *Oboe sonata* was written in 1942 for Leon Goossens. It is a florid work, but Sarah Francis surmounts its complexities very musically, echoed by her pianist, Peter Dickenson. She provides a full, singing tone. The balance is forward, within a resonant acoustic, and it is important not to set the volume control too high.

PIANO MUSIC

The Chosen tune; Cobbler's hornpipe; Gadabout; Lambert's clavichord: Lambert's fireside (Hughes' ballet; De la Mare's pavanne; Sir Hugh's galliard); Musica sine nomine; 3 Pieces, Op. 14; Sarum sketches; Slow dance (Double the Cape); Snapshots, Op. 30; Sonatina.

*** Chandos Dig. CHAN 9273 [id.]. Margaret Fingerhut.

Howells's output for piano is not perhaps among his most important music but, as this survey shows, he has a good feeling for keyboard sonorities and the invention among these works is remarkably high. The high-spirited writing, as in *Gadabout* (1928) and *Jackanapes* (the third of the *Three Pieces*, Op. 14), has a Grainger-like rhythmic exuberance, while Howells can also be touchingly solemn, as in the dark processional which is the last item of Op. 14 or in the second of the *Sarum sketches*. The *Sonatina* is astonishingly fresh, one of his very best works, spikily high-spirited and with a thoughtfully tender slow movement marked *serioso ma teneramente*, with something of Ravel in its thinking. Throughout this highly stimulating and enjoyable programme this fine pianist readily catches the composer's moods, light or grave, and she is most realistically recorded.

VOCAL MUSIC

3 Children's songs (Eight o'clock, the postman's knock; The days are clear; Mother, shake the cherry-tree); 3 Folksongs (I will give my love an apple; The brisk young widow; Cendrillon); 4 French chansons, Op. 29; A Garland for de la Mare (group of 11 unpublished songs); *In green ways* (song-cycle), *Op. 43; Peacock Pie* (song-cycle), *Op. 33; 2 South African settings (Loneliness; Spirit of freedom); 4 Songs, Op. 22 (There was a maiden; Madrigal; The widow bird; Girl's song)*. Miscellaneous songs: *An old man's lullaby; Come sing and dance; Flood; Gavotte; Goddess of the Night; Here she lies; King David; The little boy lost; Lost love; Mally O!; The Mugger's song; O garlands, hanging by the doors; O my deir hert; Old Meg; Old skinflint; The restful branches.*

*** Chandos Dig. CHAN 9185/6 (2) [id.]. Lynne Dawson, Catherine Pierard, John Mark Ainsley, Benjamin Luxon; Julius Drake.

This two-disc collection covers virtually all of Howells's completed songs, most of them previously unrecorded and many still unpublished. One of the driving forces behind the project is the pianist Julius Drake, who plays the accompaniments with a consistent rhythmic spring and a sense of fantasy. Two of the finest songs are among the best known, *King David* and *Come sing and dance*, and such a group of miniatures as *Peacock Pie*, settings of Walter de la Mare written early in Howells's career, have a characteristic point and charm. Far more searching are the 11 much longer settings of de la Mare poems. Among the other fascinating examples are two South African settings to words by the Afrikaans poet, Jan Celliers,including one still very topical, *Spirit of freedom*. The sopranos, Catherine Pierard and Lynne Dawson, both have aptly fresh, English-sounding voices, with John Mark Ainsley as the thoughtful tenor and Benjamin Luxon the characterful baritone, a fine team, even though the recording brings out some unevenness in the vocal production of both Ainsley and Luxon.

Chichester service: Magnificat; Nunc dimittis. A Hymn for Saint Cecilia; Like as the hart desireth the waterbrooks; My eyes for beauty pine; O salutaris Hostia; Salve Regina.

**(*) ASV Dig. CDDCA 851 [id.]. David Went, Ch. of The Queen's College, Oxford, Matthew

Owens – LEIGHTON: *Crucifixus pro nobis* etc.
***

Howells is nearly always at his best in his choral work and the pieces gathered here are all worth having. Neither in terms of ensemble nor intonation is The Queen's College, Oxford, choir in the first league, but the performances are committed and give pleasure, and they are well recorded. The disc has the advantage of coupling rarely heard music of quality by Kenneth Leighton.

Collegium regale: canticles; Behold, O God our defender; Like as the hart; St Paul's service: Canticles. Take him, earth, for cherishing. (Organ): *Psalm prelude: De profundis; Master Tallis's testament.*
*** Hyperion Dig. CDA 66260 [id.]. St Paul's Cathedral Ch., Scott; Christopher Dearnley.

All the music here is of high quality and the recording gives it resonance, in both senses of the word, with the St Paul's acoustic well captured by the engineers. A fine representation of a composer who wrote in the mainstream of English church and cathedral music but who had a distinct voice of his own.

Collegium regale: Te Deum and jubilate; Office of Holy Communion; Magnificat and Nunc dimittis. Preces & Responses I & II; Psalms 121 & 122; Take him, earth, for cherishing. Rhapsody for organ, Op. 17/3.
❀ *** Decca Dig. 430 205-2. Williams, Moore, King's College, Cambridge, Ch., Cleobury.

Here is an unmatchable collection of the settings inspired by the greatest of our collegiate choirs, King's College, Cambridge, presented in performances of heartwarming intensity in that great choir's 1989 incarnation. The boy trebles in particular are among the brightest and fullest ever to have been recorded with this choir. The disc sensitively presents the sequence in what amounts to liturgical order, with the service settings aptly interspersed with responses, psalm-chants, anthems with organ introits and voluntaries all by Howells. Even those not normally attracted by Anglican church music should hear this.

Hymnus Paradisi; An English Mass.
*** Hyperion Dig. CDA 66488 [id.]. Kennard, Ainsley, RLPO Ch., RLPO, Handley.

Hymnus Paradisi is a heartfelt expression of grief over the death of the composer's son at the age of ten; Handley conveys a mystery, a tenderness rather missing from the previous recording, made by Sir David Willcocks for EMI, strong as that is. Handley's soloists bring a moving compassion, as in the haunting setting of the 23rd Psalm which makes up the third movement. The Hyperion digital recording is warm, full and atmospheric. *An English Mass* is simpler yet also hauntingly beautiful.

Missa Sabrinensis.
*** Chandos Dig. CHAN 9348 [id.]. Janice Watson, Della Jones, Martyn Hill, Donald Maxwell, London Symphony Ch., LSO, Rozhdestvensky.

Rozhdestvensky here conducts a passionate account of what in many ways is the most powerful of all the composer's major works. The result is one of the most full-blooded and sustained expressions of ecstasy to be found in any setting of the Mass. There is little of the restraint that is typical of much of Howells' choral writing. Rather he exploits the lushest, most passionate elements in his richly post-impressionist style, and he hardly lets up over the whole span. It would be hard to imagine a more inspired performance than Rozhdestvensky's. Over the incandescent singing of the choir, the four excellent soloists give radiant performances, with the golden-toned soprano, Janice Watson, regularly crowning the mood of ecstasy in her solos. Full, glowing, atmospheric sound to match.

(i) (Organ): *Master Tallis's testament; 6 Psalm-preludes, Set 1, Op. 32/1–3; Set 2 /1–3; 3 Rhapsodies, Op. 17/1–3;* (ii) Anthems: *Behold O God our defender; Like as the hart. Collegium regale: Jubilate and Te Deum.* Motet: *Take him, earth, for cherishing. St Paul's Services: Magnificat and Nunc dimittis.*
(N) (B) ** Hyperion Dig. Dyad CDD 22038 (2) [id.]. Christopher Dearnley (organ); (ii) with St Paul's Cathedral Choir, John Scott.

A good deal of the music here is for organ and there are only two items (about 12 minutes in all) from the *St Paul's Service* which draws the eye as the heading on the frontispiece of this Dyad Double. Although the organ pieces provide contrast between the choral items, the *Psalm-preludes* are mostly gentle pieces, improvisatory in feeling (Op. 32/3 with its repeated bass is the most striking), and although the *Rhapsodies* are more flamboyant, their focus is not helped by the wide reverberation. The piece inspired by Tallis is the most individual, and some listeners may feel, like us, that the programme is a little overweighted with organ repertoire. Among the choral highlights are the two fine canticles associated with the *Collegium regale* and the eloquent motet, *Take him, earth* which was dedicated to John F. Kennedy. The anthems are splendid too, and all the choral music is of high quality. The recording gives it resonance in both sense of the word, with the St Paul's acoustic well captured by the engineers.

(Organ) *Psalm prelude, Set 1/1; Paean; Prelude: Sine nomine.* (Vocal): *Behold, O God our defender; Here is the door; Missa Aedi Christi: Kyrie; Credo; Sanctus; Benedictus; Agnus Dei; Gloria. Sing lullaby; A spotless rose; Where wast thou?.*

M) *** CRD Dig. CRD 3455; *CRDC 4155* [id.]. New College, Oxford, Ch., Edward Higginbottom (organ).

A further collection, splendidly sung by Edward Higginbottom's fine choir, while he provides the organ interludes in addition. Among the shorter pieces, the carol-anthem, *Sing lullaby*, is especially delightful, and the programme ends with the motet, *Where wast thou?*, essentially affirmative, in spite of the question posed at the opening. Beautifully spacious sound makes this highly rewarding.

Requiem. Motets: *The House of the Mind; A Sequence for St Michael*.
*** Chandos Dig. CHAN 9019 [id.]. Finzi Singers, Spicer – VAUGHAN WILLIAMS: *Lord thou hast been our refuge* etc. ***

Requiem; Take him, earth, for cherishing.
*** United Recordings Dig. 88033 [id.]. Sally Barber, Julia Field, Mark Johnstone, Andrew Angus, Vasari, Jeremy Backhouse – MARTIN: *Mass*. ***

Howells' *Requiem* is the work which prepared the way for *Hymnus Paradisi*, providing some of the material for it. For unaccompanied chorus, it presents a gentler, compact view of what in the big cantata becomes powerfully expansive. The Finzi singers, 18-strong, give a fresh and atmospheric, beautifully moulded performance, well coupled with two substantial motets with organ by Howells as well as choral pieces by Vaughan Williams.

On United, the soloists and Vasari, a choir conducted by Jeremy Backhouse, are absolutely first class and give a well-nigh exemplary performance, possibly finer than its immediate rival. Doubtless couplings will resolve the matter of choice. The present disc offers the *Requiem* in harness with another Mass from the inter-war years by Frank Martin.

Stabat Mater.
*** Chandos Dig. CHAN 9314 [id.]. Neill Archer, London Symphony Ch., LSO, Rozhdestvensky.

The *Stabat Mater* was Howells' last major work. Though the ecstasy is not as consistently sustained as in the earlier *Missa Sabrinensis*, with many more passages of hushed devotion, one registers with new intensity the agony of St John the Divine at the foot of the Cross, the companion of the Virgin Mary. The saint is personified in the tenor solos, here sung superbly by Neill Archer with a clear, heady tone, starting with his first thrilling entry on *O quam tristis*. As in the *Missa*, Rozhdestvensky proves the most passionate advocate, magnetically leading one through the whole rich score. Though ensemble sometimes suffers, it is a small price to pay for such thrusting, spontaneous-sounding conviction. Glowing, rich sound.

Hume, Tobias (*c*. 1575–1645)

Captain Humes Poeticall Musick (1607) (music for viols, lute and voice).
(BB) *** Naxos Dig. 8.55416/7 (available separately) [id.]. Les Voix Humains.

Tobias Hume was a mercenary who served in both the Swedish and Russian armies. Relatively little is known about him. The dedications of his two collections, the *First Part of Ayres* (1605) and the *Poeticall Musick* (1607), were designed to court favour, the first from the Earl of Pembroke and the second from Queen Anne. He was a champion of the viol as opposed to the lute, and the pieces recorded here vindicate him. It is obvious that he was an accomplished composer and this excellently recorded Canadian ensemble prove persuasive advocates. A most enjoyable and welcome addition to the catalogue.

Humfrey, Pelham (1647–74)

Verse anthems: *By the waters of Babylon; Have mercy on me, O God; Hear, O Heav'ns; Hear my prayer, O God; Hear my crying, O God; Lift up your heads; Like as the hart; O give thanks unto the Lord; O Lord my God*.
*** HM Dig. HMU 907053 [id.]. Donna Deam, Drew Minter, Rogers Covey-Crump, John Potter, David Thomas, Clare College, Cambridge, Ch., Romanesca, Nicholas McGegan.

Pelham Humfrey (or Humphrey) began his career about 1660 as a chorister at the Chapel Royal and made such an impression that he was sent abroad at the expense of the royal purse of Charles II to study in France and Italy. He brought back from Italy (and from Lully in France) a thorough absorption of the operatic style, and his verse anthems are remarkably dramatic and powerfully expressive, using soloists almost like operatic characters. Nicholas McGegan's fine performances reflect this histrionic dimension, helped by his soloists, who at times approach stylistic boundaries in their performance of what is essentially devotional music, even if intensely felt. With a highly sensitive instrumental contribution from the excellent Romanesca, this collection (about half of Humfrey's surviving output) is very freshly recorded and is strongly recommended to the adventurous collector.

Hummel, Johann (1778–1837)

Bassoon concerto in F.
(N) *** Chandos Dig. CHAN 9656 [id.]. Valeri Popov, Russian State SO, Polyansky – MOZART; WEBER: *Bassoon concertos*. ***

Now that the Denon version has gone, a first-class modern recording of Hummel's genial *Bassoon concerto* was needed, and Valeri Popov fits the bill, twinklingly good-natured and elegant, especially in the swinging 6/8 finale. His woody timbre (a French instrument, perhaps) is most appealing, and Polyansky provides a warmly polished accompaniment, helped by the resonant, but not clouded, recording.

(i; ii) *Mandolin concerto in G*; (iii) *Trumpet concerto in G*; (iv; ii) *Gesellschafts Rondo in D for piano and orchestra, Op. 117*; (v; ii) *Introduction, theme and variations in F for oboe and orchestra, Op. 102*. (vi) *Flute sonatas Nos. 1–3; Grand rondo brillante in G, Op. 126*.

(N) (B) *** Erato/Warner Ultima Dig./Analogue 3984 25596-2 (2) [id.]. (i) André Saint-Clivier, (ii) Pailliard CO, Jean-François Paillard; (iii) Maurice André, O de Paris Ens., Wallez; (iv) Anne Queffélec; (v) Jacques Chambon; (vi) András Adoran, Noël Lee.

A useful anthology which summarizes Hummel's achievement in several fields. The *Mandolin concerto* is ingenuous but pleasing, dependent on a personable soloist and a felicitous recording balance, both of which are supplied here. The inestimable Maurice André has recorded the famous *Trumpet concerto E flat* many times; this account dates from 1981, when his timbre was particularly warm, flattered by the comparatively resonant digital recording. The *Gesellschafts Rondo* is quite a find, a most impressive piece, played with flair by Anne Queffélec; the variations for oboe are comparatively facile, but also presented with agreeable brilliance. The *Flute sonatas* are discussed below: the performances here are every bit as expert and pleasing as those on the separate Naxos anthology, and are well recorded (though the sound is analogue).

Piano concertos: in A min., Op. 85; B min., Op. 89.

*** Chandos Dig. CHAN 8505 [id.]. Stephen Hough, ECO, Bryden Thomson.

(B) *** Discover Dig. DICD 920117 [id.]. Dana Protopopescu, Slovak R. New PO, Rahbari.

The *A minor* is Hummel's most often-heard piano concerto, never better played, however, than by Stephen Hough on this prize-winning Chandos disc. The coda is quite stunning; it is not only his dazzling virtuosity that carries all before it but also the delicacy and refinement of colour he produces. The *B minor*, Op. 89, is more of a rarity, and is given with the same blend of virtuosity and poetic feeling which Hough brings to its companion. He is given expert support by Bryden Thomson and the ECO – and the recording is first class.

At bargain price Discover offers an outstanding alternative coupling. Well accompanied by the Slovak Radio New Philharmonic, Dana Protopopescu, always sounding fresh and spontaneous, plays with lightness, point and poetry. On her smaller scale, she even rivals Stephen Hough, though Hough is more impulsive.

Trumpet concerto in E.

✿ *** Ph. Dig. 420 203-2 [id.]. Hardenberger, ASMF, Marriner – HAYDN *** ✿; HERTEL ***; STAMITZ: *Concertos*. ***

Trumpet concerto in E flat.

*** Sony MK 37846 [id.]. Marsalis, Nat. PO, Leppard – HAYDN: *Concerto* *** (with L. MOZART: *Concerto* ***).

(N) *** EMI Dig. CDC5 55231-2 [id.]. Maurice André, Franz Liszt O, Budapest, János Rolla – HERTEL; HAYDN: *Trumpet concertos* *** (with MARCELLO: *Concerto in D min.* ***).

Hummel's *Trumpet concerto* is usually heard in the familiar brass key of E flat, but the brilliant Swedish trumpeter, Håkan Hardenberger, uses the key of E, which makes it sound brighter and bolder than usual. Neither he nor Marriner miss the genial lilt inherent in the dotted theme of the first movement, the slow-movement cantilena soars beautifully over its jogging pizzicato accompaniment, and the finale captivates the ear with its high spirits and easy bravura. This is the finest version of the piece in the catalogue, for Marriner's accompaniment is polished and sympathetic.

Maurice André's latest digital recording dates from 1994. His playing has lost none of its charisma; the tone is noticeably more open (more 'trumpety') here than in the earlier Erato version (above), the phrasing and articulation if anything more stylish. He is helped by a warm but nicely scaled accompaniment from Rolla and his excellent Budapest orchestra.

Marsalis gives a fine account of Hummel's *Concerto*, but does not quite catch its full *galant* charm. In matters of bravura, however, he cannot be faulted; he relishes the sparkling finale.

Clarinet quartet in E flat.

(M) *** O-L (IMS) 444 167-2 [id.]. Alan Hacker, The Music Party – WEBER: *Clarinet quintet*. ***

A delectable work, played as beautifully as the Weber coupling. Alan Hacker uses a Goulding clarinet *circa* 1880, and this would be the sound Hummel himself would have recognized. Hacker plays allegros with plenty of character and spirit and, at times, a winning bite on the timbre, yet there is plenty of warmth in the lyrical music. The Music Party also use original instruments and lovers of the authentic style will find this very stimulating.

Piano quintet in E flat, Op.87.

(B) **(*) Hyperion Dyad Dig. CDD 22008 (2) [id.]. Schubert Ens. of L. – SCHUBERT: *Trout quintet;* SCHUMANN: *Piano quintet; Piano quartet*. **(*)

A strong account of an impressive work from the Schubert Ensemble of London, who approach the piece as one in the classical mainstream rather than a *galant* entertainment. There is plenty of energy and commitment, and the brief *Largo* is made a touching interlude; only the finale (admittedly marked *Allegro agitato*) might seem too strongly driven and with not enough balancing elegance. The recording has fine immediacy.

Piano trios Nos. 1–7.
(N) *** MDG Dig. MDG 3307/8 (2) [id.]. Trio Parnassus.

Hummel's *Piano trios* span a period of two decades: the first was published in 1804, and the last in the early 1820s. All show the fluency, elegant craftsmanship and easy melodic flow for which he is admired in his better known concertos. Comparing the first with the last of the trios shows no marked development of style of the kind one expects with the very greatest composers, but all seven of these works are individually rewarding in their diverse ways, and the composer's fund of ideas never dries up for a moment. The Trio Parnassus play throughout with consistent zest and spontaneity and they obviously enjoy the simple lyrical melodies. They are admirably recorded and this box can carry a strong recommendation.

Piano trios Nos. 1 in E flat, Op. 12; 5 in E, Op. 83; 7 in E flat, Op. 96.
(N) *** Chandos Dig. CHAN 9529 [id.]. Borodin Trio.

Piano trios Nos. 1 in E flat, Op. 12; 2 in F, Op. 22; 3 in G, Op. 35; 7 in E flat, Op. 96.
(N) *** Mer. Dig. CDE 84350 [id.]. Triangulus.

Both these single-disc collections share the first and last of the Trios, each among the finest of the series, and both sets of performances are enjoyable in their different ways. Rostislav Dubinsky, leading the Borodin Trio, is a bolder, more temperamental player than Alison Kelly of Triangulus, and this is immediately shown in the opening of the *First*, Op. 12 *Trio* with its memorable flowing theme on the violin, taken up by the piano. The *Andante* is no less warmly melodic and the finale has great rhythmic energy. Generally the Triangulus performance is more relaxed than the Borodin's, and we are inclined to prefer the stronger pulse of the latter's first movement; but in the finale they tend almost to rush, and here Triangulus score a point or two. The opening movement of the Op. 96 immediately produces the dotted rhythms which are Hummel's special trademark, while the simplicity of the melody at the heart of the *Poco Larghetto* is very winning in both performances; in the closing *Rondo alla Russe*, the Borodin account is that bit stronger. The finale of Op. 83 (included only by Chandos) is also very catchy; however, Triangulus offer an extra work, and the closing Rondo of Op. 35 sparkles delightfully and shows the Meridian players at their most captivating. Both recordings are well balanced and pleasing. It is very much a case of swings and roundabouts.

Septet in D min., Op. 74.
(M) *** CRD CRD 3344; *CRDC 4044* [id.]. Nash Ens. – BERWALD: *Septet.* ***

Hummel's *Septet* is an enchanting and inventive work with a virtuoso piano part, expertly dispatched here by Clifford Benson. A fine performance and excellent recording make this a highly desirable issue, particularly in view of the enterprising coupling.

Flute sonatas Nos. 1 in G, Op. 2/2; 2 in D, Op. 50; 3 in A, Op. 64; (i) *Flute trio in A, Op. 78. Grand rondeau brillant for flute and piano in G, Op. 126.*
(N) (BB) *** Naxos Dig. 8.553473 [id.]. Lise Daoust, Carmen Picard with (i) Dolin.

Hummel's elegant, easygoing melodic style seems custom-made for the flute, and his three lightweight sonatas are lacking in neither diversity nor charm. The *D major* work, for instance, has a flowing pastoral finale, while the rondo which ends the *A major* is a vivacious *vivace*. The *Grand rondeau brillant* is entertainingly like a Weber display piece. The performances on Naxos are both sunny and technically felicitous, and are warmly recorded. The *Trio* is an ingenuous set of variations on a Russian folk tune, which lends itself to sparkling divisions. Here the resonance rather emphasizes the pianist's bold bravura (until then Carmen Picard has been a model of decorum), and there is plenty of bustle before the work ends peacefully.

Piano sonatas Nos. 1 in C, Op. 2/3; 2 in E flat, Op. 13; 3 in F min., Op. 20.
(N) (B) *(*) Discover Dig. DICD 920237 [id.]. Dana Protopopescu (piano)

Piano sonatas Nos. 2 in E flat, Op. 13;3 in F min., Op. 20; 5 in F sharp min., Op. 81.
(N) (BB) *** Naxos Dig. 8.553296 [id.]. Hae-won Chang (piano).

Hummel's piano sonatas at their best can match those of Haydn, and the *E flat major* work (1805) in Hae-won Chang's hands makes an attractive introduction to the genre. The opening *Allegro* marches off engagingly, and the *Andante*, with harp-like arpeggios, introduces a touchingly gentle melody, while the finale is a 'galant' set of variations. The more thoughtful first movement of the *F minor Sonata* (1807) is interrupted by a recurring brief *Adagio*; the central *Adagio maestoso* is more imposing, with the tension released in the bravura finale. The *F sharp minor Sonata* was written a decade later, and is altogether more ambitious, a splendid work, nearer to Beethoven than Haydn, its kernel a memorable *Largo con molto expessione*, to be followed by a vigorous bravura finale. This is the first of a Naxos series, and very welcome it is when this accomplished Korean pianist is right inside the music, which she plays very persuasively indeed. She is excellently recorded.

Dana Protopopescu gives us the earliest sonata of all, from 1792, and begins very boldly and cleanly. Her approach is uncompromisingly classical and she begins the *F minor* with very crisp articulation verging on staccato. Throughout she presents these works in sharp focus rather than trying to coax the music or charm the listener. Unfortunately the Discover recording does not help her: it is rather shallow and clattery.

String quartets: in C; in G; in E flat, Op. 30/1–3.
*** Hyperion Dig. CDA 66568 [id.]. Delmé Qt.

Hummel's three quartets are closer to Haydn than Beethoven, though the first of the set in C major, with its impressive opening *Adagio e mesto* in the minor key, and fine *Adagio*, obviously leans towards the influence of the later composer, while the audacious quotation of *Comfort ye* from Handel's *Messiah* in the preceding *Andante* brings yet another example of Hummelian sleight of hand. In short these are fascinating works, highly inventive, and crafted with the composer's usual fluent charm. They are splendidly played by the Delmé group, who provide plenty of vitality and warmth. The Hyperion recording is fresh and believable.

String quartet in G, Op. 30/2.
*(*) Testament mono SBT 1085 [id.]. Hollywood Qt – HAYDN: *Quartet No. 72;* MOZART: *Quartet No. 17.* **(*)

Hummel's charming *G major Quartet* comes with the first half of a 1957 Festival Hall concert. This performance was recorded two years earlier in a Hollywood studio and, though dazzlingly played, is a bit shrill.

Violin sonatas: in E flat, Op. 5/3; in D, Op. 50; Nocturne, Op. 99.
*** Amon Ra CD-SAR 12 [id.]. Ralph Holmes, Richard Burnett.

Ralph Holmes's violin timbre is bright and the Graf fortepiano under the fingers of Richard Burnett has plenty of colour and does not sound clattery. Burnett has a chance to catch the ear in the finale of the *D major Sonata* when he uses the quaintly rasping cembalo device (without letting it outstay its welcome). The *Nocturne* is an extended piece (nearly 16 minutes) in variation form. A thoroughly worthwhile issue, 'authentic' in the most convincing way, which shows this engaging composer at his most assured and inventive.

Mass in B flat, Op. 77; Tantum ergo (after Gluck).
*** Koch Dig. 3-7117-2 [id.]. Westminster Oratorio Ch., New Brunswick CO, John Floreen.

Hummel wrote his *Mass in B flat* while working for the Esterházys. It is an unpretentious work of great charm and a real discovery. The Westminster Choir (from the College of that name in Princeton, New Jersey) give exactly the right kind of modest performance, emphasizing the work's warm lyricism; the conductor, while not lacking vigour, is careful not to be too forceful at climaxes. The orchestral accompaniment is nicely in scale, and the recording, though not crystal clear, has the most agreeable ambience.

Humperdinck, Engelbert
(1854–1921)

Christmas Lieder: *Altdeutsches Weihnachtslied; Christkindleins Wiegenlied; Das Licht der Welt; Der Stern von Bethlehem; Weihnachten.*
❁ *** EMI (SIS) Dig. CDC5 56204-2. Bär, Deutsch (with Recital: '*Christmas Lieder*' *** ❁).

These Christmas settings have all the character and charm one would expect from the composer of *Hänsel und Gretel*, and Olaf Bär's warmly flowing line consistently captures their easy lyricism. The closing *Weihnachten* has a Schubertian spontaneity of feeling and a lovely tune. Bär's relaxed, affectionate (yet at times dramatic) performances are perfectly judged, and he is beautifully accompanied by Helmut Deutsch. The recording, too, is balanced most naturally.

The Bluebird: Prelude; Star dance. Hänsel und Gretel: Overture. Königskinder: Overture; Preludes to Acts II & III. The Sleeping Beauty: suite.
(M) **(*) Virgin/EMI Dig. CUV5 61128-2. Bamberg SO, Karl Anton Rickenbacher.

By far the most memorable piece here is the *Hänsel und Gretel Overture*, although the Introduction to Act III of *Königskinder* is also very touching, characteristically using horns to evoke the Minstrel's last song. The *Overture* to the same opera is significant in demonstrating Humperdinck's characteristic failing – a prolixity of ideas, none of which is quite memorable enough to emerge from the ongoing energy of the writing. Rickenbacher secures warm, cultured playing from his Bambergers, and the Virgin sound is full and pleasing if lacking just a little in sparkle. Worth trying at mid-price.

The Canteen Woman (Die Marketenderin): Prelude. The Merchant of Venice: Love scene. Moorish rhapsody: Tarifa (Elegy of summer); Tangier (A night in a Moorish coffee-house);

Tetuan (A night in the desert). The Sleeping Beauty: suite.
**(*) Marco Polo Dig. 8.223369 [id.]. Slovak RSO (Bratislava), Martin Fischer-Dieskau.

The Love scene from *The Merchant of Venice* ('On such a night') is beautiful but rather over-extended, and all three sections of the *Moorish rhapsody* are much too long (the composite piece lasts some 32 minutes). The opening of the *Summer elegy* begins with raptly ethereal writing for the violins, but the jolly Moorish coffee-house sequence sounds as if the restaurant has been leased from the owner of a Bavarian bierkeller. The Slovak performances under Martin Fischer-Dieskau (the famous Lieder singer's grandson) are not ideally polished but have freshness and vitality, while the Marco Polo recording is open and reasonably full.

Hänsel und Gretel (complete).
*** Teldec/Warner Dig.4509 94549-2 (2) [id.]. Larmore, Ziesak, Schwarz, Weikl, Behrens, Tölz Boys' Ch., Bav. RSO, Runnicles.
*** EMI Dig. CDS7 54022-2 (2) [Ang. CDCB 54022]. Von Otter, Bonney, Lipovšek, Schwarz, Schmidt, Hendricks, Lind, Tölz Boys' Ch, Bav. RSO, Tate.
(M) *** EMI CMS5 67061-2 (2) [CDMB 67145]. Schwarzkopf, Grümmer, Metternich, Ilsovay, Schürhoff, Felbermayer, Children's Ch., Philh. O, Karajan.
(M) **(*) RCA 74321 25281-2 (2). Moffo, Donath, Fischer-Dieskau, Berthold, Ludwig, Augér, Popp, Bav. R. Ch. & RSO, Eichhorn.
(M) **(*) Decca 455 063-2 (2). Brigitte Fassbaender, Lucia Popp, Julia Hamari, Walter Berry, Norma Burrowes, Edita Gruberová, Anny Schlemm, V. Boys' Ch., VPO, Solti.

The success of the Teldec version of *Hänsel und Gretel* is largely due to Donald Runnicles, who has a lighter touch than his direct rivals, regularly favouring faster speeds than the others, including Tate. In the casting the emphasis more than ever is on fresh, youthful voices. So it was too with Barbara Bonney and Anne Sofie von Otter in the Tate set, but here the distinction between boy and girl is if anything even more sharply drawn. Ruth Ziesak as Gretel and Jennifer Larmore as Hänsel are above all natural-sounding, with little or no feeling of mature opera-singers pretending to be children, yet with no sense of strain and none of the edginess. Fresh clarity marks the other voices too, even that of the Witch as taken by Hanna Schwarz. Though aptly she uses a croaking voice, it makes the witch sharply sinister without being too frightening. Hildegard Behrens is strong and characterful, with Bernd Weikl firm and dark as the Father, while Rosemary Joshua makes a welcome recording début in opera as a bright-toned Sandman and Christine Schäfer, fuller and firmer, is warmly contrasted as the Dew Fairy. On balance a first recommendation, the set brings incidentally a fascinating supplement in a brief orchestral coda, just over a minute long, which Humperdinck wrote in 1894 for a production of the opera in Dessau with Cosima Wagner as director. Ingeniously he has the Dessau national anthem set in counterpoint against various themes from the opera, with toy trumpets providing a commentary.

Tate brings a Brucknerian glow to the *Overture*, and then launches into a reading of exceptional warmth and sympathy at speeds generally faster than those in rival versions. The Witch of Marjana Lipovšek is firm and fierce, using the widest range of expression and tone. The chill that Lipovšek conveys down to a mere whisper makes one regret, more than usual, that the part is not longer. All the casting matches that in finesse, with no weak link. Barbara Bonney as Gretel and Anne Sofie von Otter as Hänsel are no less fine than the exceptionally strong duos on the rival sets. There is only a slight question mark over the use of the Tölz Boys' Choir for the gingerbread children at the end. Inevitably they sound what they are, a beautifully matched team of trebles, and curiously the heart-tug is not quite so intense as with the more childish-sounding voices in the rival choirs. That is a minimal reservation, however, when the breadth and warmth of the recording add to the compulsion of the performance.

Karajan's classic 1950s set of Humperdinck's children's opera, with Schwarzkopf and Grümmer peerless in the name-parts, is enchanting; this was an instance where everything in the recording went right. The original mono LP set was already extremely atmospheric. In most respects the sound has as much clarity and warmth as rival recordings made in the 1970s. There is much to delight here; the smaller parts are beautifully done and Else Schürhoff's Witch is memorable. The snag is that the digital remastering has brought a curious orchestral bass emphasis, noticeable in the overture and elsewhere, but notably in the *Witch's ride*. This is now reissued, as one of EMI's 'Great Recordings of the Century'.

There are some fine solo performances on the mid-priced 1971 RCA set, notably from Helen Donath as Gretel and Christa Ludwig as the Witch; and Kurt Eichhorn's direction is vigorous, with excellent orchestral playing and full, atmospheric recording. It is a pity that a more boyish-sounding singer than Anna Moffo could not have been chosen for the role of Hänsel but, all told, this is a colourful and enjoyable account of a unique, eternally fresh opera, well worth considering.

Solti with the Vienna Philharmonic directs a strong, spectacular version, emphasizing the Wagnerian associations of the score. Solti does the *Witch's ride* very excitingly, and the VPO are encouraged to play with consistent fervour throughout. The result, though rather lacking in charm, is well sung, with the two children both engagingly characterized. Edita Gruberová is an excellent Dew Fairy and Walter Berry is first rate as Peter. Anny Schlemm's Witch is memorable if vocally unsteady, and there are some imaginative touches of stereo production associated with *Hocus pocus* and her other moments of magic. The recording is even more vivid in its CD transfer.

Königskinder (complete).
(M) *** EMI (SIS) CMS5 66360-2 (3). Donath, Prey, Dallapozza, Schwarz, Unger, Ridderbusch, Bav. R. Ch., Tolz Boys' Ch., Munich R. O, Wallberg.
**(*) Calig Dig. CAL 50968/70 (3) [id.]. Moser, Schellenberger, Henschel, Schmiege, Kohn, Munich Boys' Ch., Bav. R. Ch. & O, Fabio Luisi.

The success of *Hänsel und Gretel* has completely overshadowed this second fairy-tale opera of Humperdinck, which contains much fine music. Humperdinck had expanded his incidental music for a play to make this opera, which was given its première in New York in 1910. In a recording as fine as this EMI one, very well cast, it is a piece well worth investigation. Both the conducting and the singing of the principals are most persuasive.

It is good to have a new recording of a rich score, generally well sung and warmly conducted by Fabio Luisi, who uses the same choir and orchestra as the earlier, EMI set, recorded in 1976, with sound rather more spacious but not so immediate. An incidental shortcoming in both sets is that the libretto comes in German only, with the Calig libretto omitting even the stage directions. The tenor of Thomas Moser, taking the central role of the Prince, is more heroic than that of his EMI rival, Adolf Dallapozza, with the voice often shaded down beautifully. Though Dagmar Schellenberger as the Goosegirl lacks sweetness, hers is a feeling, well-characterized performance, and she finds a delicate *mezza voce* for the prayer to her parents. Marilyn Schmiege with her warm, firm mezzo makes rather a young Witch. All told, this is a performance marked by good teamwork, with the chorus bringing energetic echoes of Smetana's *Bartered Bride* in their brief contributions.

Hurlstone, William (1876–1906)

The Magic mirror: suite; Variations on a Hungarian air; Variations on an original theme.
*** Lyrita Dig. SRCD 208 [id.]. LPO, Braithwaite.

As a glance at his dates shows, William Hurlstone only just reached thirty before the ill-health which dogged him during his life claimed him. The *Variations on an original theme* date from 1896, though the theme on which they are based comes from a *Trio*, written two years earlier. They show considerable inventive resource and although, like the *Variations on a Hungarian air*, there is also a certain debt to Brahms, they have a lightness of touch and a feeling for the orchestra which is marked. *The Magic mirror suite* of 1900 also offers reminders of the Elgar of *The Wand of youth*. But it is not long before one can sense something quietly individual beginning to surface. The LPO and Nicholas Braithwaite give lively, cultured performances of this eminently well-crafted, immaculately scored and civilized music, and they are beautifully recorded.

Hvoslef, Ketil (born 1937)

(i) *Antigone (1982);* (ii) *Violin concerto.*
*** Aurora Dig. ACD4969 [id.]. (ii) Trond Saeverud; Bergen PO, cond. (i) Eggen; (ii) Kitaienko.

Ketil Hvoslef is the son of Harald Saeverud and one of the brightest and most individual figures in the Norwegian musical firmament. He has the same craggy, salty quality as his father, the same rugged independence of personality and creative resource. This CD offers *Antigone*, which comes from the early 1980s, and the *Violin concerto*, composed almost ten years later, in which the soloist is his son, Trond.

Ibert, Jacques (1890–1962)

Bacchanale; Bostoniana; (i) *Flute concerto. Escales (Ports of call); Hommage à Mozart; Louisville concerto; Paris (suite).*
*** Decca (IMS) Dig. 440 332-2. (i) Timothy Hutchins; Montreal SO, Charles Dutoit.

Escales has all the required sensuous, Mediterranean feeling and colour for this music, and Timothy Hutchins is an estimable soloist in the *Flute concerto*. *Bostoniana* is in fact the only finished movement of the composer's second symphony, written for the Boston Symphony; the *Louisville concerto* was commissioned by yet another American ensemble and the Ibertian tribute to Mozart came in time for the bicentennial celebrations of Mozart's birth. Needless to say, the recording with rich, clear textures is yet another example of Decca expertise in St Eustache, Montreal.

La Ballade de la Geôle de Reading; Féerique; 3 Pièces de Ballet (Les Rencontres); (i) *Chant de Folie; Suite Elisabéthaine.*
**(*) Marco Polo Dig. 8.223508 [id.]. (i) Slovak Ph. Ch.; Slovak RSO (Bratislava), Adriano.

The *Suite Elisabéthaine* is a nine-movement suite taken from the incidental music Ibert composed for

Shakespeare's *A Midsummer Night's Dream*. It is largely pastiche and four of the movements draw on Blow, Purcell, Bull and Gibbons. More characteristic is *La Ballade de la Geôle de Reading*, an exercise in neo-impressionism and highly accomplished. The *Chant de Folie* is an effective four-minute choral and orchestral piece inspired by the composer's experiences in the First World War . Good performances and eminently serviceable recording.

Divertissement.

*** Chandos Dig. CHAN 9023 [id.]. Ulster O, Yan Pascal Tortelier – MILHAUD: *Le Bœuf; Création;* POULENC: *Les Biches*. ***

(M) *** RCA 09026 61429-2 [id.]. Boston Pops O, Arthur Fiedler – OFFENBACH: *Collection*. **

(M) *** Decca (IMS) 448 571-2 [id.]. Paris Conservatoire O, Martinon – BIZET: *Jeux d'enfants* ***; BERLIOZ: *Overtures* **(*); SAINT-SAENS: *Danse macabre* etc. ***

Yan Pascal Tortelier provides at last a splendid, modern, digital version of Ibert's *Divertissement*. There is much delicacy of detail, and the coupled suite from Poulenc's *Les Biches* is equally delectable. Marvellous, top-drawer Chandos sound.

Fiedler's racy account of Ibert's *Divertissement* is as sparkling as you could wish, with genuine Gallic insouciance. The *Valse*, *Parade* and exuberant *Finale* have tremendous élan. The recording too is splendidly lively and atmospheric. It is a pity that the Offenbach collection which acts as coupling is recorded less successfully.

Martinon's 1960 account has never been surpassed for its sheer fizzing energy and wit, and it is a pity that the *Introduction* sounds rather thin and shrill. But after that the sound fills out and the performance has marvellous aplomb, especially the galloping finale, complete with its uninhibited police-whistle.

Escales (Ports of call).

(M) *** RCA 09026 61500-2 [id.]. Boston SO, Munch – DEBUSSY: *La Mer* **(*); SAINT-SAENS: *Symphony No. 3*. *** ❁

(M) **(*) Mercury (IMS) 432 003-2 [id.]. Detroit SO, Paray – RAVEL: *Alborada* etc. ***

Munch's *Escales* brings some ravishing textures from the Boston violins, and the finale, *Valencia*, has sparkling dance rhythms. The 1956 recording, if balanced rather closely, has brilliance and transparency; although it does not sound ideally rich and sumptuous, the effect is slightly preferable to Paray's fine Mercury version.

Paray's recording catches the Mediterranean exoticism of *Escales* admirably, and the 1962 Mercury recording has plenty of atmosphere as well as glittering detail. The Ravel couplings are very impressive too.

3 Pièces brèves.

(M) *** Chandos CHAN 6543 [id.]. Athena Ens. – GOUNOD: *Petite symphonie in B flat;* POULENC: *Sextet*. ***

Ibert's *Trois Pièces brèves* could hardly be played with more polish, wit and affection than in this brilliantly realized performance by the Athena group, the effect enhanced when they are recorded so realistically.

d'India, Sigismondo (*c*. 1582–*c*. 1630)

Duets, Laments and Madrigals: *Amico, hai vinto; Ancidetemi pur, dogliosi affanti; Che nudrisce tua speme; Giunto a la tomba; Langue al vostro languir; Occhi della mia vita; O leggiadr' occhi; Quella vermiglia rosa; Son gli accenti che ascolto; Torna il sereno zefiro.*

(B) **(*) HM HMA 901011 [id.]. Concerto Vocale – CESTI: *Cantatas*. **(*)

Sigismondo d'India was among the vanguard of the new movement founded by Monteverdi at the beginning of the seventeenth century, and his laments show him to be a considerable master of expressive resource. The performances are authoritative, though there are moments of slightly self-conscious rubato that hold up the flow. The recording is fully acceptable and the coupling is also of considerable interest; this is worth exploring.

Amico, hai vinto; Diana (Questo dardo, quest' arco); Misera me (Lamento d'Olympia); Piangono al pianger mio; Sfere fermate; Torna il sereno zefiro.

*** Hyperion CDA 66106 [id.]. Emma Kirkby, Anthony Rooley (chitarone) – MONTEVERDI: *Lamento d'Olympia* etc. ***

Sigismondo d'India's setting of the *Lamento d'Olympia* makes a striking contrast to Monteverdi's and is hardly less fine. This is an affecting and beautiful piece and so are its companions, particularly when they are sung as superbly and accompanied as sensitively as they are here. A very worthwhile CD début.

Il primo Libro de Madrigali (1606): *Interdette speranz'e van desio. Ottavo Libro de Madrigali: Il pastor fido,* Act IV, Scene 9: *Se tu, Silvio crudel, mi saetti* (five madrigal cycle).

❁ (M) *** Virgin Veritas/EMI Dig. VER5 61165-2. Chiaroscuro, L. Baroque, Nigel Rogers – MONTEVERDI: *Madrigals*. *** ❁

It is in the cycle from his Eighth Book of Madrigals, *Se tu, Silvio crudel, mi saetti*, that one experiences not only the composer's lyrical originality to the full but also his affinity with the operatic writing of his greater contemporary, Monteverdi. The vocal dialogue, which alternates solo and ensemble singing, is touching and dramatic by turns, and requires effortless vocal virtuosity. The quality of the performances is superlative, refined without a hint of preciosity, and always alive, while the accompaniments on theorbo and harpsichord are delicately balanced. An outstanding collection in every way.

Il Terzo libro de Madrigali.
(B) **(*) DHM Dig. 05472 77437-2 [id.]. The Consort of Musicke, Anthony Rooley.

Rooley's Consort blend admirably and sing *a cappella* with remarkable freshness in the early works, if perhaps a little coolly. The later numbers, from No. 13 onwards, are supported by a discreet continuo, and the singing of these last eight settings seems freer and richer. No translations are included, but this remains an attractive disc.

d'Indy, Vincent (1851–1931)

Diptyque méditerranéan; Poème des rivages (symphonic suite).
(M) **(*) EMI (SIS) Dig. CDM7 63954-2. Monte Carlo PO, Prêtre.

Apart from the influence of Franck, the *Soleil matinal* of the *Diptyque* has a blend of the Wagner of *Parsifal* and that quality of conservative impressionism which d'Indy made so much his own after the turn of the century. There are considerable beauties in this piece and in the *Poème* and, though the recording is not top-drawer, the sound does not lack allure. This is well worth investigating for, despite some unevenness of inspiration, Prêtre holds the music together impressively.

(i) *Fantasy on French popular themes* (for oboe and orchestra), *Op. 31. Saugelfleurie* (Legend after a tale by Robert de Bonnières); *Tableaux de voyage, Op. 36; L'Etranger: Prelude to Act II. Fervaal: Prelude to Act I.*
** Marco Polo Dig. 8.223659 [id.]. (i) Philippe Cousu; Württemberg PO, Gilles Nopre, or (i) Jean-Marc Burfin.

The tone-poem, *Saugelfleurie,* based on a tale by Robert de Bonnières, the evocative *Tableaux de voyage*, and the lovely *Prelude to Act I* of *Fervaal*, all offer music of quality, and writing which also has the seeds of popularity. The *Fantaisie sur des thèmes populaires françaises* for oboe and orchestra has a fervent charm which is very winning. The performances of all these pieces are variable; they fall short of distinction but are more than routine. The recording, too, is eminently satisfactory and aficionados of French music need not hesitate.

Jour d'été à la montagne, Op. 61; (i) *Symphonie sur un chant montagnard français, Op. 25.*
**(*) Erato/Warner Dig. 2292 45821-2 [id.].(i) Catherine Collard; R. France PO, Janowski.

Jour d'été à la montagne is one of d'Indy's most inspired pieces. This version is artistically superior to the (deleted) rival under Pierre Dervaux on EMI, though the late lamented Catherine Collard's version of the *Symphonie sur un chant montagnard français* is handicapped by some unsympathetic accompanying from Janowski and a synthetic balance which does not allow the sound to expand.

Symphonie sur un chant montagnard français (Symphonie cévenole).
(M) **(*) RCA 09026 62582-2 [id.]. Henriot-Schweitzer, Boston SO, Charles Munch (with BERLIOZ: *Harold in Italy* *(*)).
(BB) **(*) Naxos 8.550754 [id.]. Thiollier, Nat. SO of Ireland, Antonio de Almeida – FAURE: *Ballade;* FRANCK: *Symphonic variations.* **(*)

Nicole Henriot-Schweitzer plays the piano part most sympathetically and Munch presents a fresh and crisp performance. The early (1958) stereo recording comes up well.

On Naxos the French-born but American-trained François-Joël Thiollier gives an intelligent performance, perfectly well accompanied and decently recorded, and with an interesting coupling. It is worth the money, but there are finer accounts to be had.

(i) *Symphonie sur un chant montagnard français;* (ii) *Symphony No. 2 in B flat, Op. 57.*
(M) *** EMI (SIS) CDM7 63952-2. (i) Ciccolini, O de Paris, Baudo; (ii) Toulouse Capitole O, Plasson.

Aldo Ciccolini gives a good account of himself in the demanding solo part of the *Symphonie*, and the Orchestre de Paris under Serge Baudo give sympathetic support. The recording is pleasing and with a convincing piano image. In the *Second Symphony* Michel Plasson proves a sympathetic and committed advocate, and his orchestra responds with enthusiasm and sensitivity to his direction. The recording too is spacious, full and well focused.

Symphony No. 2 in B flat, Op. 57; Souvenirs, Op. 52.
**(*) Koch Dig. 37280-2 [id.]. Monte Carlo PO, James DePreist.

The *Second Symphony* remains one of the neglected masterpieces of turn-of-the-century French music. The first stereo version did not appear on the scene until Michel Plasson and the Toulouse orchestra on EMI (see above). Choice between that and this newcomer is a matter of swings and roundabouts and should rest perhaps on the coupling. DePreist does not have as fine an orchestra as the Toulouse Capitole, though they play with plenty of commitment, but the recording is slightly more detailed and DePreist gives us the affecting *Souvenirs* which d'Indy composed on the death of his wife. Newcomers to this noble composer may prefer the EMI version, the initiate will opt for the present account. You can't go far wrong with either.

String quartets Nos. 1 in D, Op. 35; 2 in E, Op. 45.
**(*) Marco Polo Dig. 8.223140 [id.]. Kodály Qt.

The *First Quartet* is a large-scale piece and beautifully crafted. The *Second* (1897) is hardly less ambitious and shows something of the composer's admiration for late Beethoven; it must also be said that greater variety of texture would be welcome. The excellent Kodály Quartet are recorded in the Italian Institute in Budapest, where the rather close balance tends to iron out dynamic extremes.

Ippolitov-Ivanov, Mikhail
(1859–1935)

Caucasian sketches (suite), *Op. 10.*
*** Chandos Dig. CHAN 9321 [id.]. BBC PO, Fedor Glushchenko – KHACHATURIAN: *Symphony No. 3* etc. ***
*** ASV Dig. CDDCA 773. Armenian PO, Tjeknavorian – KHACHATURIAN: *Gayaneh* etc. **(*)

Once a popular repertory piece, the colourful *Caucasian sketches* have fallen out of favour; only the final *Procession of the Sardar* is generously represented on CD. The present version by the BBC Philharmonic under Fedor Glushchenko is generally superior to the alternative on ASV.

The *Procession of the Sardar* is played by the Armenians with great brio. The other items rely mainly on picaresque oriental atmosphere for their appeal, which Tjeknavorian also captures evocatively in this brightly lit recording.

Symphony No. 1 in E min. Op. 46; Armenian Rhapsody, Op. 48; Caucasian Sketches, Op. 10; (i) *Mtzyri, Op. 54. War march, Op. 42/4.*
(N) *** Conifer Dig. 75605 51317-2 [id.] Bamberg SO, Gary Brain; (i) Claudia Barainsky.

Few will have encountered his *Symphony* in the concert hall, and this is its first appearance on CD. It dates from 1908. Although announced as No. 1, it remains the composer's only contribution to the genre, and is as colourful as you would expect from a pupil of Rimsky-Korsakov. *Mtzyri* comes from 1929 and is a programmatic piece based on a Lermontov poem and has strong reminiscences of his master. The *Armenian Rhapsody* is even earlier. No one would claim that any of these pieces is more than an effective example of Russian-national Romanticism without any great claims of originality, but it is all well worth recording and is splendidly played by the Bamberg Orchestra under Gary Brain.

Liturgy of St John Chrysostom, Op. 37; Vespers, Op. 43.
(M) *** Sony Dig. SMK 64091 [id.]. Lege Artis Chamber Ch., Boris Analyan.

These are beautiful pieces, not as profound, powerful or soulful as either Tchaikovsky's or Rachmaninov's settings, but well worth having. A useful and pleasing addition to the catalogue. The Lege Artis Chamber Choir rise excellently to the not inconsiderable demands made on them, and the recording has an appropriately warm acoustic.

Ireland, John (1879–1962)

Concertino pastorale; A Downland suite (arr. composer and Geoffrey Bush); *Orchestral poem; 2 Symphonic studies* (arr. Geoffrey Bush).
*** Chandos Dig. CHAN 9376 [id.]. City of L. Sinfonia, Richard Hickox.

The valedictory *Threnody* of the *Concertino pastorale* and the lovely *Elegy* from the *Downland suite* show the composer at his most lyrically inspired, and the rapt playing here does them full justice. The early *Orchestral poem* (1904) is a surprisingly powerful work as presented here with great passion, with splendid brass writing at its climax. The two *Symphonic studies* come from film music Ireland wrote for *The Overlanders*, not incorporated into the concert suites: the brass chromatics in the first have a familiar ring, the second has a wild momentum, recalling the cattle stampede in the film, but both stand up well as independent concert pieces.

Concertino pastorale; A Downland suite: Minuet and Elegy. The Holy boy.
(N) (M) **(*) Carlton Classics Dig. 30366 00602 [id.]. E. Sinf., John Farrer – VAUGHAN WILLIAMS: *Five Variants of Dives and Lazarus; Greensleeves; Partita.* **(*)

Some of Ireland's finest lyrical inspirations are here, played warmly and sympathetically. While the Hickox Chandos performances are finer still, some collectors may prefer Farrer's coupling with Vaughan Williams, and the Carlton CD also costs less. It is very pleasingly recorded.

Piano concerto in E flat.
*** Conifer Dig. 74321 15007-2 [id.]. Kathryn Stott, RPO, Handley – BRIDGE: *Phantasm;* WALTON: *Sinfonia concertante.* ***
*** Unicorn Dig. DKPCD 9056 [id.]. Tozer, Melbourne SO, Measham (with RUBBRA: *Violin concerto.* ***)

Piano concerto in E flat; Legend for piano and orchestra; Mai-Dun (symphonic rhapsody).
*** Chandos Dig. CHAN 8461 [id.]. Parkin, LPO, Thomson.

(M) (***) Dutton Laboratories mono CDAX 8001 [id.]. Eileen Joyce, Hallé O, Leslie Heward – MOERAN: *Symphony*. *** ❁

Kathryn Stott gives the most sympathetic reading of Ireland's *Piano concerto* on record since the original interpreter on disc, Eileen Joyce. Spaciously expressive in the lyrical passages and crisply alert in the jazzy finale, Stott plays with a sense of spontaneity, using freely idiomatic rubato. Generously and aptly coupled with the much more neglected Walton and Bridge works, and very well recorded, this version makes an easy first choice for the work.

Eric Parkin gives a splendidly refreshing and sparkling performance too, and benefits from excellent support from Bryden Thomson and the LPO. They are no less impressive in *Mai-Dun* and the beautiful *Legend for piano and orchestra*.

Geoffrey Tozer conveys the poetic feel of the slow movement and, though he takes a rather measured tempo in the finale, the music loses none of its freshness. The recording is a little studio-bound, but too much should not be made of this. Doubtless the coupling will decide matters for most collectors.

However, Eileen Joyce's classic 1942 recording, transferred from 78s with great skill by Mike Dutton, still remains very special. It readily demonstrates the flamboyant romanticism for which she was famous and even a moment or two of fantasy, plus the freshness of discovery. Leslie Heward accompanies with flair. There is a touch of wow on the piano tone (especially noticeable in the *Lento*) but the orchestral sound is full and warm.

A Downland suite; Elegiac meditation; The Holy Boy.

*** Chandos Dig. CHAN 8390 [id.]. ECO, David Garforth – BRIDGE: *Suite for strings*. ***

A Downland suite was originally written for brass band. However, the present version was finished and put into shape by Geoffrey Bush, who also transcribed the *Elegiac meditation*. David Garforth and the ECO play with total conviction and seem wholly attuned to Ireland's sensibility. The recording is first class, clear and naturally balanced.

Epic march; The Overlanders (film incidental music): *suite* (arr. Mackerras).

(M) *** Unicorn UKCD 2062 [id.]. W. Australian SO, David Measham – VAUGHAN WILLIAMS: *On Wenlock Edge*. ***

The Overlanders is not the best of Ireland, but it contains some good ideas and it is persuasively presented here. The *Epic march* is jolly and rhythmically folksy, then presents an almost elegiac grand tune. This is all recommendable enough, for the CD transfers are first rate and the Vaughan Williams coupling is most appealing.

A London overture.

(M) *** EMI CDM5 65109-2. LSO, Barbirolli – VAUGHAN WILLIAMS: *London symphony*. **(*)

One of Ireland's most immediately attractive works, and Barbirolli's performance of it is a great success, as is the remastering of an outstanding recording. The main theme (rhythmically conjuring up the bus conductor's call of 'Piccadilly!') is made obstinately memorable, and the ripe romanticism of the middle section is warmly expansive in Barbirolli's hands.

A London overture; Epic march; The Holy Boy; (i–ii) *Greater love hath no man; These things shall be;* (i–iii) *Vexilla Regis.*

(M) *** Chandos Enchant Dig. CHAN 7074 [id.]. LSO, Richard Hickox, with (i) London Symphony Ch.; (ii) Bryn Terfel; (iii) Paula Bott, Teresa Shaw, James Oxley.

Richard Hickox is a sympathetic interpreter of Ireland's music and obtains sensitive results (and good singing) in *The Holy Boy* and *These things shall be* (surprisingly, the latter is not otherwise available on silver disc). The disc is of particular interest in that it brings a rarity, *Vexilla Regis*, for chorus, brass and organ, composed when Ireland was nineteen and still a student of Stanford. First-class recorded sound.

(i) *Cello sonata;* (ii) *Fantasy sonata for clarinet and piano;* (i) *The Holy boy* (for cello and piano); (iii) *Phantasie trio; Piano trios Nos. 2–3;* (iv) *Violin sonatas Nos. 1–2.*

*** Chandos Dig. CHAN 9377/8 [id.]. (i; iii) Karine Georgian; (i; iii–iv) Ian Brown; (ii) Gervase de Peyer, Gwenneth Pryor; (iii–iv) Lydia Mordkovitch.

Few British composers have written with quite such easy lyricism as John Ireland. The first two of the *Piano trios*, well contrasted, are warmly appealing, but the masterpiece is the four-movement *Piano trio No. 3* of 1938, passionately intense. The two *Violin sonatas* are both superb works too, masterfully played here by Lydia Mordkovitch with Ian Brown, who also accompanies Karine Georgian in the *Cello sonata*. Completing the set, the recording of the *Fantasy sonata* of 1943 for clarinet dates from earlier, with Gervase de Peyer and Gwenneth Pryor playing with equal commitment.

String quartets Nos. 1 in D min; 2 in C min; The holy boy.

(N) **(*) ASV Dig. CDDCA 1017 [id.]. Holywell Ens.

Both quartets come from 1897, when Ireland was eighteen, and were published posthumously. There is little sign of individuality but each work is beautifully crafted and gives much pleasure. The idiom is close to Dvořák and the ideas are fluent and pleasing. The Holywell Ensemble offer decent performances and are well recorded.

Violin sonatas Nos. 1 in D min.; 2 in A min.; Bagatelle; Berceuse; Cavatina; The holy boy.
(N) *** Hyperion Dig. CDA 66853 [id.]. Paul Barritt, Catherine Edwards.

Paul Barritt and Catherine Edwards make an effective partnership and give very persuasive accounts of both these fine sonatas. An excellent, well-balanced recording earns this a recommendation alongside Lydia Mordkovitch and Ian Brown's 2-CD set on Chandos coupled with the three *Piano trios* and the *Cello sonata*.

PIANO MUSIC

The Almond tree; Decorations; Merry Andrew; Preludes: (The undertone; Obsession; The Holy Boy; Fire of spring); Rhapsody; Sonata in E min.; Summer evening; The Towing-path.
*** Chandos Dig. CHAN 9056 [id.]. Eric Parkin.

Amberley Wild Woods; Ballad; The darkened valley; Equinox; For remembrance; Greenways; In those days; Leaves from a child's sketchbook; London pieces; 2 Pieces; Prelude in E flat; Sonatina.
*** Chandos Dig. CHAN 9140 [id.]. Eric Parkin.

Ballade of London nights; Columbine; Month's mind; On a birthday morning; 3 Pastels; 2 Pieces (February's child; Aubade); 2 Pieces (April; Bergomask); Sarnia; A Sea idyll; Soliloquy; Spring will not wait.
*** Chandos Dig. CHAN 9250 [id.]. Eric Parkin.

It goes without saying that Eric Parkin is completely inside Ireland's idiom and he brings both dedication and sympathy to this repertoire. Moreover the sound is clean, well-rounded and pleasing.

Ballade; Columbine; In those days; London pieces; Prelude in E flat; Sarnia.
(BB) *** Naxos Dig. 8.553700 [id.]. John Lenehan.

As a pianist himself, Ireland wrote piano music which seems to fit under the fingers, and John Lenehan proves the most persuasive advocate, warmly expressive, using rubato in a totally idiomatic way. The four *London pieces* are among his most colourful, not just *Ragamuffin*, played here with quicksilver lightness, but also the barcarolle-like *Chelsea Reach*, tenderly emotional. The most ambitious work is the three-movement suite, inspired by Guernsey, *Sarnia*, far more than a set of atmospheric colour pieces.This music shows Ireland's poetic imagination to particular advantage and its last movement has echoes of the *Piano concerto in E flat*. John Lenehan is not always as well recorded (the sound hardens a little in loud passages) as Eric Parkin on Chandos at full price. However, this Naxos programme is very good indeed and bargain-hunters wanting this repertoire need not hesitate.

Isaac, Heinrich (*c.* 1450–1517)

Missa de Apostolis. Motets: *Optime pastor; Tota pulchra es; Regina caeli laetare; Resurrexi et adhuc tecum sum; Virgo prudentissima.*
*** Gimell Ph. 454 923-2 [id.]. Tallis Scholars, Peter Phillips.

The German contemporary of Josquin des Pres, Heinrich Isaac has not until recently been widely appreciated. The Mass setting is glorious, culminating in an ethereal version of *Agnus Dei*, flawlessly sung by the Tallis Scholars. Among the many striking passages is the opening of the six-part setting of *Virgo prudentissima* for two upper voices only, with women's rather than boys' voices all the more appropriate with such a text. Ideally balanced recording.

Ives, Charles (1874–1954)

Calcium light night; Country band march; Largo cantabile: Hymn; 3 Places in New England; Postlude in F; 4 Ragtime dances; Set for theatre orchestra; Yale–Princeton football game.
*** Koch Dig. 37025-2 [id.]. O New England, Sinclair.

This selection of shorter Ives pieces makes an ideal introduction for anyone wanting just to sample the work of this wild, often maddening, but always intriguing composer. Excellent performances and recording.

(i) *Central Park in the dark;* (ii–iii) *Holidays Symphony;* (ii) *The unanswered question.*
(M) *** Sony SMK 60203 [id.]. NYPO, (i) Seiji Ozawa & Maurice Peress (under the supervision of Bernstein); (ii) Bernstein; (iii) with Seymour Lipkin (assistant conductor), Camerata Singers, Abraham Kaplan – CARTER: *Concerto for orchestra.* ***

Central Park in the dark, as the title implies, provides a brilliant collection of evening sounds, evocative yet bewildering. The first three sections of the the so-called *Holidays Symphony*, with their still-startling clashes of impressionistic imagery, are well enough known. The fourth – full title: *Thanksgiving and/or Forefathers Day* – is more of a rarity, bringing in a full chorus to sing a single verse of a hymn at the close. The performance is red-bloodedly convincing yet has remarkably clear detail. *The unanswered question* is probably the most purely beautiful music Ives ever wrote, with muted strings (curiously representing silence) set against a trumpet representing the problem of existence. No need to worry about Ives's philosophy when the results are so naturally moving. Superb playing (the trumpeter is William Vacchiano) and vivid recording, but the forward balance means the lack of a true pianissimo, especially noticeable in *The unanswered question*.

Central Park in the dark; New England Holidays symphony; The unanswered question (original and revised versions).
*** Sony Dig. MK 42381 [id.]. Chicago Symphony Ch. & O, Tilson Thomas.

The *New England Holidays symphony* comprises four fine Ives pieces normally heard separately. The performance from Michael Tilson Thomas and his Chicago forces is in every way superb, while the wide-ranging CBS recording provides admirable atmosphere. This is now among the most impressive Ives records in the catalogue.

(i) *Central Park in the dark;* (ii) *Three places in New England;* (iii) *Piano sonata No. 2 (Concord, Mass., 1840–1860).*
(B) *** DG Classikon 439 480-2. (i) Boston SO, Ozawa; or (ii) Tilson Thomas; (iii) Roberto Szidon (with Dieter Sonntag, flute).

An outstanding and highly recommendable bargain anthology. The Boston Symphony Orchestra plays quite magnificently in the two orchestral works, so full of evocative atmosphere, and the DG engineers produce a most musical balance. Most remarkable of all is Roberto Szidon's unsurpassed account of the *Concord Sonata*, where the concentration of the performance here gives the reading enormous authority. Szidon is admirably recorded. In the last movement a brief melody is given to the flute. When questioned about this, Ives replied nonchalantly that the flute was right for that particular moment in the music and, as no one was likely to play the sonata anyway, there would be no performance difficulties!

(i) *New England Holidays Symphony; 3 Places in New England;* (i) *They are there!*
(N) ✿ *** Argo Dig. 444 860-2 [id.]. Baltimore SO, David Zinman; (i) with Baltimore SO Ch.

Opening with the exuberantly spectacular Sousa-esque choral march, *They are there!* (a true lollipop if ever there was one), this is now the finest CD coupling of Ives's two key masterworks, the *New England Symphony* and the *Three Places in New England*. The orchestral playing is splendid: the quiet, gentle evocations raptly sustained by the strings and woodwind, the multitude of quotations wittily evoked, and the polyphonic and polytonal clashes are presented with great vigour and panache. The vivid Decca recording is truly in the demonstration class, handling the complicated sound pictures with remarkable clarity, yet within a spacious ambience. The brief entry of the Baltimore Symphony Chorus at the close of *Thanksgiving and Forefathers' Day* is a truly arresting moment.

Orchestral set No. 2.
(M) *** Decca Phase Four 448 956-2 [id.]. LSO Ch., LSO, Stokowski – GROFE: *Grand Canyon suite*. *(*)

The *Second Orchestral set* consists of three highly evocative pieces crammed with the sort of wild devices that make Ives's music so distinctive. In such atmospheric music Stokowski's wonderful sense of dramatic development is perfectly exploited. The multi-channel Phase Four recording, made in 1970, is well suited to the music, and the LSO obviously enjoys the experience, not least in the ragtime of the second piece, and the Kingsway Hall ambience ensures plenty of atmosphere, especially in the spectacular choral finale.

Symphony No. 1 in D min.
*** Chandos Dig. CHAN 9053 [id.]. Detroit SO, Järvi – BARBER: *Essays 1–3*. ***

There is a certain freshness about the melodic invention of the *First Symphony* that is appealing; the idiom is polite and generally conservative, with Dvořák as perhaps the strongest influence, but there are already glimpses of iconoclasm in the modulatory shifts. Neeme Järvi gives a very persuasive account of it and there is a fresh and unforced virtuosity from the Detroit orchestra. Excellent, very natural recorded sound, excellently balanced.

Symphonies Nos. 1; 4.
*** Sony Dig. SK 44939 [id.]. Chicago SO, Michael Tilson Thomas.

Tilson Thomas's strong and brilliant Chicago performances make a generous and apt coupling, the more valuable for providing first recordings of the revised editions of the composer's tangled scores, with bright, well-detailed sound and superb playing.

Symphony No. 1 in D min.; Orchestral set No. 2; Robert Browning overture; The unanswered question.
(BB) **(*) RCA Navigator 74321 29246-2. Chicago SO, Morton Gould.

This very first recording of the *First Symphony*, an immediately attractive work, was made in 1965; it has that special quality of freshness almost always found in recording premières, with the mercurial spirit of Ives emerging every so often, so that the result is very enjoyable indeed. The *Orchestral set No. 2* is similarly vivid in colour and detail. The *Robert Browning overture* (at 20 minutes) has some good ideas but rather outstays its welcome, while *The unanswered question* is one of the composer's most beautiful and imaginative pieces. Gould's performances are sympathetic and very well played, but they just lack the intensity that Bernstein and others brought to them, although they are still pretty magnetic. The mid-1960s recordings are basically warm and atmospheric, even if the violins are very brightly lit, and even fierce at times.

Symphony No. 2.
*** Chandos Dig. CHAN 9390-2. Detroit SO, Järvi – CRESTON: *Symphony No. 2.* ***

The Chandos CD offers a very good performance, and has the great advantage of also offering Neeme Järvi's account of Paul Creston's vital and invigorating *Second Symphony*.

Symphony No. 2; Central Park in the dark; The gong on the hook and ladder; Hallowe'en; Hymn for strings; Tone roads No. 1; The unanswered question.
*** DG Dig. 429 220-2 [id.]. NYPO, Bernstein.

Bernstein's DG disc brings one of the richest offerings of Ives yet put on record, offering the *Symphony No. 2* plus six shorter orchestral pieces. They include two of his very finest, *Central Park in the dark* and *The unanswered question*, both characteristically quirky but deeply poetic too. The extra tensions and expressiveness of live performance here heighten the impact of each of the works. The difficult acoustic of Avery Fisher Hall in New York has rarely sounded more sympathetic on record.

Symphony No. 2; Symphony No. 3 (The camp meeting).
(M) *** Sony SMK 60202 [id.]. NYPO, Bernsein (with talk: 'Leonard Bernstein discusses Charles Ives').
**(*) Sony Dig. SK 46440 [id.]. Concg. O, Michael Tilson Thomas.

Bernstein re-recorded this music more recently for DG, but these earlier CBS/Sony recordings (from 1958 and 1965 respectively) have characteristic conviction and freshness. The remastered sound is amazingly improved over the old LPs, full and atmospheric. The balance is too close, but the dynamics of the playing convey the fullest range of emotion. The readings are in a class of their own. This reissue includes Bernstein's illustrated lecture on Ives (recorded in 1966).

Tilson Thomas's performances may not have the fervour of a Bernstein in this music – perhaps reflecting the fact that this is not an American orchestra – but they are strong and direct, and in No. 3 the revised edition is used.

Symphony No. 3 (The camp meeting).
*** Argo 417 818-2 [id.]. ASMF, Marriner – BARBER: *Adagio;* COPLAND: *Quiet City;* COWELL: *Hymn;* CRESTON: *Rumor.* ***
*** Pro Arte Dig. CDD 140 [id.]. St Paul CO, Russell Davies – COPLAND: *Appalachian spring* etc. ***

Russell Davies does not use the new edition of Ives's score; nevertheless, he gives a fine account of this gentlest of Ives's symphonies, with its overtones of hymn singing and revivalist meetings, and the beauty of the piece still comes over strongly.

Marriner's account is first rate in every way. It does not have the advantage of a digital master, but the 1976 analogue recording has slightly sharper detail in this remastered format.

Symphony No. 3; 3 Places in New England.
(M) *** Mercury [432 755-2]. Eastman-Rochester O, Howard Hanson – SCHUMAN: *New England triptych* *** (with MENNIN: *Symphony No. 5* **(*)).

Symphony No. 3; 3 Places in New England; A Set of pieces; The unanswered question.
(N) (M) *** DG Dig. 457 911-2 [id.]. Orpheus CO.

The Orpheus Chamber Orchestra never cease to amaze and their playing here is of their usual stunning order of accomplishment and artistry. Their account of the *Third Symphony* is as good as any in the catalogue, and the same goes for their evocative and imaginative accounts of the companion pieces. With first-class modern digital recording this is excellent value.

As Hanson readily shows, Ives's quixotic genius is at its most individual and harmonically daring in *Three places in New England*. Both works here are most understandingly presented on Mercury, and Hanson proves equally at home in the folksy imagery of the *Third Symphony*. The acoustics of the Eastman theatre are less than ideally expansive, but the 1957 recording is remarkably full-bodied and vivid. This CD is available only in the USA.

String quartets Nos. 1–2.
*** DG (IMS) Dig. 435 864-2 [id.]. Emerson Qt – BARBER: *Quartet.* **(*)

The *First* of Ives' *String quartets* comes from the composer's early twenties and makes liberal use of hymn-tunes in the first movement fugue. The *Second* is made of sterner stuff with its high norm of dissonance. It is undeniably an extraordinary musical document and is well worth study. The Emerson Quartet give it a performance of stunning efficiency and brilliance. Full-blooded and very present DG recording.

Songs: *Autumn; Berceuse; The cage; Charlie Rutlage; Down East; Dreams; Evening; The greatest man; The Housatonic at Stockbridge; Immortality; Like a sick eagle; Maple leaves; Memories: 1, 2, 3; On the counter; Romanzo di Central Park; The see'r; Serenity; The side-show; Slow march; Slugging a vampire; Songs my mother taught me; Spring song; The things our fathers loved; Tom sails away; Two little flowers.*
*** Etcetera Dig. KTC 1020 [id.]. Roberta Alexander, Tan Crone.

Roberta Alexander presents her excellent and illuminating choice of Ives songs in chronological order, starting with one written when Ives was only fourteen, *Slow march*, already predicting developments ahead. Sweet, nostalgic songs predominate, but the singer punctuates them with leaner, sharper inspirations. Her manner is not always quite tough enough in those, but this is characterful singing from an exceptionally rich and attractive voice. Tan Crone is the understanding accompanist, and the recording is first rate.

Jacob, Gordon (1895–1987)

Mini-concerto for clarinet and string orchestra.
*** Hyperion CDA 66031 [id.]. Thea King, NW CO of Seattle, Alun Francis – COOKE; RAWSTHORNE: *Concertos.* ***

Gordon Jacob in his eighties wrote this miniature concerto for Thea King, totally charming in its compactness. She proves the most persuasive of dedicatees, splendidly accompanied by the orchestra from Seattle and treated to first-rate 1982 analogue sound, splendidly transferred.

Symphonies No. 1 in C; A Little Symphony; Festival overture.
*** Classico Dig. CLASSCD 204 [id.]. Munich SO, Douglas Bostock.

Gordon Jacob, professor of composition and orchestration at the Royal College of Music, is best known as an accomplished and witty craftsman of small-scale works, showing a distinct melodic gift. But the two symphonies offered here demonstrate that he could write distinctively over a larger canvas. The *Second Symphony* (1944/5) is spirited and outgoing. The first movement, after its deceptively gentle introduction, is boisterously scored and full of energy, with a swinging string-melody for second subject. It is followed by an intense, searching *Adagio* which opens plangently on high strings, but later assumes the character of a threnody, reflecting not only the composer's recent wartime experience but also the 1914–18 conflict in which he lost a much-loved brother. The mood lightens with an engaging Scherzo where gossamer strings and dainty woodwind are punctuated by more assertive brass. The final *Ground* is a passacaglia, which begins unostentatiously but reaches a boisterous, confident conclusion. The *'Little' Symphony* is perhaps an even finer work, more succinct and more introspective, but with a splendidly vigorous Scherzo whose rhythmic character is arresting, and with a jaunty light-hearted finale, full of good humour. The *Festival overture*, written for the Essex Youth Orchestra, combines Waltonesque rhythmic exuberance with a characteristic Jacobian lyrical strain. The performances here by the excellent Munich orchestra under Douglas Bostock are alive and thoroughly persuasive and in no way unidiomatic; the recording is vivid and quite spacious.

Divertimento for harmonica and string quartet.
*** Chandos Dig. CHAN 8802 [id.]. Tommy Reilly, Hindar Qt – MOODY: *Quintet; Suite.* ***

Gordon Jacob's set of eight sharply characterized miniatures shows the composer at his most engagingly imaginative and the performances are deliciously piquant in colour and feeling. The recording could hardly be more successful.

Oboe quartet.
*** Chandos Dig. CHAN 8392 [id.]. Francis, English Qt – BAX: *Quintet;* HOLST: *Air and variations* etc.; MOERAN: *Fantasy quartet.* ***

Gordon Jacob's *Oboe quartet* is well crafted and entertaining, particularly the vivacious final Rondo. The performance could hardly be bettered, and the recording is excellent too.

Jadin, Hyacinthe (1775–1800)

String quartets, Opp. 1/3; 2/1; 4/1.
*** ASV Gaudeamus Dig. CDGAU 151 [id.]. Rasumovsky Qt – VACHON: *Quartets.* ***

Jadin, of Belgian descent, obviously studied the quartets of Haydn and Mozart, for Op. 1/3 is dedicated to the former master. In F minor, it is the most strikingly individual work here. The chromatic flavour of the opening of Op. 2/1 has just a little in common with Mozart's *Dissonance Quartet*, and the amiable Op. 4/1 in two movements is attractively lightweight. The Rasumovsky Quartet have obviously lived with this music, and they play it with appealing simplicity and dedication. They are well recorded with plenty of presence and a nice ambient warmth.

Keyboard sonatas: in B flat & G min., Op. 3/1–2; in A & F, Op. 6/2–3.
(N) * Audivis Valois Dig. V 4777 [id.]. Patrick Cohen (fortepiano).

Hyacinthe Jadin, born in Versailles, had a very short life and career. He played bassoon in the Chapelle Royale orchestra, but was also a youthful prodigy as a fortepianist. These four galant works (all but one in two movements) are quite agreeable, well crafted with some personable ideas, and perhaps more could be made of them. But Patrick Cohen (who is such an impressive chamber-music player) does them a disservice by his uneven pulse and agogic distortions of the rhythmic line, which are barely acceptable.

Janáček, Leoš (1854–1928)

Adagio for orchestra; Ballad of Blaník; Cossack dance; (i) *Danube Symphony. The Fiddler's child* (ballad); *Idyll for strings; Jealousy overture; Lachian dances;* (ii) *The Pilgrimage of the soul*

(Violin concerto); (iii) *Schluck und Jau* (incidental music): excerpts: *Andante & Allegretto. Serbian Kolo. Sinfonietta; Suite, Op. 3; Suite for strings; Taras Bulba* (rhapsody).
*** Sup. Dig. 11 1834-2 (3) [id.]. Brno State PO, František Jílek, with (i) Karolína Dvořáková; (ii) Ivan Zenatý; (i; iii) Jiří Beneš.

(i) *Danube Symphony. Sinfonietta;* (ii) *The Pilgrimage of the soul (Violin concerto);* (iii) *Schluck und Jau.*
*** Sup. Dig. 11 1422-2 [id.]. Brno State PO, František Jílek, with (i) Karolina Dvořáková; (ii) Ivan Zenatý; (i; iii) Jiří Beneš.

Jílek's performance of the *Sinfonietta* can hold its own with the best in terms of atmosphere and authority, though the recording is admittedly not in the demonstration bracket. There is some invention of great imagination in the *Danube Symphony*, as, indeed, there is in the *Violin concerto* (*The Pilgrimage of the soul*). Ivan Zenatý is an aristocrat of the violin and his performance is poignantly affecting. The incidental music to *Schluck und Jau* is a two-movement piece about as long as the *Violin concerto* and likewise full of characteristic ideas. Of the other two discs, the first offering the *Lachian dances*, the early *Suite for strings* and its seven-movement companion, the *Idyll*, is well filled, and the other disc brings such valuable scores as *Blaník, The Fiddler's Child* and *Taras Bulba*. Good, idiomatic performances and very good, though not demonstration-quality recordings.

Capriccio for piano left-hand and wind; Concertino for piano and seven instruments.
*** RCA Dig. 09026 60781-2. Rudolf Firkušný, Czech PO, Václav Neumann – DVORAK: *Piano concerto in G min.* ***

Firkušný himself is now older than Janáček was when he wrote these remarkable pieces, but he conveys a youthful fire which seems to burn almost as brightly as the earlier recordings he made in the 1950s and 1970s. A thoroughly worthwhile coupling with Dvořák.

(i) *Capriccio for piano and wind; Concertino for piano and chamber ensemble;* (ii) *Lachian dances;* (iii) *Sinfonietta;* (iv) *Suite for string orchestra;* (iii) *Taras Bulba;* (v) *Mládí* (suite for wind).
(B) *** Decca Double Analogue/Dig. 448 255-2 (2) [id.]. (i) Paul Crossley, L. Sinf., David Atherton; (ii) LPO, Huybrechts; (iii) VPO, Mackerras; (iv) LAPO, Marriner; (v) Bell, Craxton, Pay, Harris, Gatt, Eastop.

On this Double Decca Paul Crossley is the impressive soloist in the *Capriccio* and the *Concertino*, performances that can be put alongside those of Firkušný – and no praise can be higher. This account of *Mládí* is among the finest available; the work's youthful sparkle comes across to excellent effect here. In Mackerras's VPO coupling of the *Sinfonietta* and *Taras Bulba* the massed brass of the *Sinfonietta* has tremendous bite and brilliance as well as characteristic Viennese ripeness. *Taras Bulba* is also given more weight and body than usual, the often savage dance-rhythms presented with great energy. The performance of the *Lachian dances*, under the Belgian conductor, François Huybrechts, is highly idiomatic and effective, and he is helped by fine playing from the LPO. The *Suite for string orchestra* was Marriner's first recording with the Los Angeles Chamber Orchestra, and the sound is characteristically ripe. The *Suite* is an early and not entirely mature piece but, when played as committedly as it is here, its attractions are readily perceived, and it certainly does not want character. Excellent sound throughout.

(i) *Concertino for piano and seven instruments;* (ii) *Sinfonietta; Taras Bulba.*
(B) *** DG 439 437-2. (i) Rudolf Firkušný (Bav. RSO (members)); (ii) Bav. RSO; Kubelik.

(i) *Capriccio for piano and 7 instruments; Concertino for piano and 6 instruments. (Piano) Sonata (1.X.1905); In the mist; On an overgrown path I and II; Reminiscences; Zdenka variations.*
(M) *** DG 449 764-2 (2) [id.]. Rudolf Firkušný; (i) Bav. RSO (members), Kubelik.

Kubelik has a special feeling for this repertoire and partners Rudolf Firkušný in his thoroughly idiomatic earlier account of the *Concertino. Taras Bulba* is powerfully evoked with virtuoso playing from the Bavarian orchestra throughout, and much excitement generated in the last two sections. The orchestra is hardly less impressive in the *Sinfonietta* (and particularly so in the central movements), while at the opening and close of the work the spacious acoustic of the Munich Herculessaal is especially suited to the massed brass effects. The vintage (1970) recording has been superbly remastered and sounds amazingly fresh.

Now reissued in DG's series of 'Originals', this alternative collection is eminently recommendable. It again offers Firkušný in discerningly sympathetic accounts of the *Concertino* and *Capriccio*, but here differently coupled (and at mid-price). Firkušný played to Janáček as a small boy and has long been regarded as the most authoritative exponent of the piano music. Firkušný recorded the piano pieces in the early 1970s and he produces seamless legato lines, hammerless tone and rapt atmosphere. Kubelik then partners him in the concertante works. The recordings are all of high quality.

Capriccio (for piano left hand & chamber ensemble); *Concertino* (for piano & chamber orchestra); *Mládí (Youth)* for wind sextet; *March of the Blue Boys* for piccolo and piano; (i)

Nursery rhymes (Ríkadla) for chamber choir & chamber ensemble.
*** Chandos Dig. CHAN 9399 [id.]. Berman, Netherlands Wind Ens., Thierry Fischer; (i) with Prague Music Ac. Ch.

Though Firkušný remains in a class of his own, Boris Berman is a good soloist in both the *Concertino* and *Capriccio*. The astonishing *Ríkadla* are given with great character by the Netherlands Wind Ensemble and the Prague Academy Choir. Thierry Fischer directs the proceedings impressively: the playing throughout is full of life and sensitivity. Vibrant recorded sound - every detail tells.

(i) *The Fiddler's child;* (ii) *Idyll for string orchestra;* (i) *Jealousy: overture; Sinfonietta;* (ii) *Suite for strings;* (i) *Taras Bulba.* (i) *The Cunning little vixen: suite.*
(N) (B) *** Chandos 2-for-1 Dig. CHAN 241-7 (2) [id.]. (i) Czech PO, Bělohlávek; (ii) Jupiter O, Gregory Rose.

The *Idyll* and the *Suite for strings* are both early works from the late 1870s, the one warmly lyrical and easily tuneful, the other just as accessible but in some ways more searching; both have Dvořákian influences, yet are already showing the composer's individuality. They are ravishingly played by the Jupiter Orchestra, under Gregory Rose, who shows himself completely at home in the lilting Czech idiom, and who achieves rapt concentration in the touching slow movements. The warmly spacious Chandos recording could hardly be bettered. This marvellous music, still comparatively little known, is alone worth the cost of this Chandos 2-for-1 Double. But the rest of the programme is also very stimulating. There are more dramatic and fiery accounts available of *Taras Bulba*. Bělohlávek is perhaps less at home in this melodramatic piece than in the nature mysticism of the orchestral suite from *Cunning little vixen* or the pathos of *The Fiddler's child*. But his splendidly vivid account of the *Sinfonietta* is unsurpassed, and throughout all these performances the beauty of the orchestral playing, and opulence and detail of the recordings, add to the attractions of a very well-chosen compilation.

Sinfonietta.
(M) *** EMI Dig. CDM5 66980-2 [CDM5 66995]. Philh. O, Rattle – *Glagolitic Mass.* ***
(M) *** EMI Dig. CDM7 64740-2. Philh. O, Rattle – HOLST: *Planets.* **(*)
(M) *** DG (IMS) Dig. 445 501-2 [id.]. BPO, Abbado – BARTOK: *The Miraculous Mandarin* etc. ***
(M) *** Decca 448 579-2. LSO, Abbado – HINDEMITH: *Symphonic metamorphoses;* PROKOFIEV: *Symphony No. 3.* ***
*** Chandos Dig. CHAN 8897 [id.]. Czech PO, Bělohlávek – MARTINU: *Symphony No. 6;* SUK: *Scherzo.* ***
*** Sony Dig. SK 47182 [id.]. LSO, Tilson Thomas – *Glagolitic Mass.* ***
(B) *** EMI forte CZS5 72664-2 (2). Chicago SO, Seiji Ozawa – BARTOK: *Concerto for orchestra;* LUTOSLAWSKI: *Concerto for orchestra;* STRAVINSKY: *Firebird ballet.* **(*)
(M) **(*) Telarc CD 82010 [id.]. LAPO, André Previn – BARTOK: *Concerto for orchestra.* **(*)

Sinfonietta; Lachian dances; Taras Bulba.
(BB) *** Naxos Dig. 8.550411 [id.]. Slovak RSO (Bratislava), Ondrej Lenárd.

(i) *Sinfonietta;* (ii) *Taras Bulba;* (iii) *The cunning little vixen:* suite.
(BB) **(*) RCA Navigator 74321 29251-2. (i) USSR RSO, Bolshoi Theatre Brass O; (ii) USSR MoC SO; (iii) Leningrad PO; Rozhdestvensky.
(B ** Sony SBK 62404; *SBT 62404* [id.]. (i) Cleveland O, Szell; (ii) Toronto SO, A. Davis – KODALY: *Dances of Galánta; Dances of Marosszék.* **(*)

Rattle gets an altogether first-class response from the orchestra and truthful recorded sound from the EMI engineers and his coupling with the *Glagolitic Mass* is very attractive indeed. It is also available at medium price with a less successful Holst coupling.

Abbado's later DG digital recording finds the Berlin Philharmonic Orchestra on splendid form. The Jesus-Christus Kirche provides a superbly spacious sonority for the brass. The opening brings a tautening of the pace, but the interpretation is not greatly changed and the subtleties of colour are not diminished by the more robust body of the newer version.

In his earlier, Decca recording Abbado gives a splendid account of the *Sinfonietta* and evokes a highly sympathetic response from the LSO. His acute sensitivity to dynamic nuances and his care for detail are felt in every bar. The recording balance, too, allows the subtlest of colours to register while still having plenty of impact.

Jiři Bělohlávek's exultant and imaginative account of the *Sinfonietta* is one of the best currently on offer and is coupled with an outstanding version of Martinů's *Sixth Symphony*; the recording, made in the Smetana Hall, Prague, is impressive.

A strong, bold and brassy performance from Tilson Thomas, with the LSO at their virtuoso best, helped by very full recorded sound, bright as well as weighty. However, fine though this is, it would not be preferable to Rattle or to Abbado.

On Naxos we have the normal LP coupling of the *Sinfonietta* and *Taras Bulba*, but with the *Lachian dances* thrown in for good measure, all played by musicians steeped in the Janáček tradition – and all at a very modest cost. These are excellent performances; the recording, made in a fairly resonant studio, is natural and free from any artificially spotlit balance.

Ozawa's account too is brilliantly played and very well recorded (in 1969). The CD transfer is also very successful, full-bodied if not opulent. A useful alternative to Abbado, if the three couplings are suitable.

The amiability of Janáček's colourful and brassy work is what dominates Previn's performance rather than any more dramatic qualities. The Los Angeles Philharmonic has never been recorded with a warmer and more realistic bloom than here by Telarc. However, those looking for more bite and brilliance in this work will probably be happier with either Mackerras or Rattle.

On RCA Navigator, in the *Sinfonietta* the Bolshoi brass (with Slavonic vibrato) are pungent, and especially arresting at the close. The inner movements are strongly characterized by Rozhdestvensky, and he is equally impressive in the vibrantly atmospheric account of *Taras Bulba*. The suite from *The cunning little vixen* consists of two 'interludes', each about nine minutes in length. They are beautifully played at another live concert, but the audience indicates its presence only at the beginning and end. Excellent value and vivid sound.

Szell's 1965 recording of the *Sinfonietta* has long been admired for its orchestral virtuosity and control. It is a very spirited and colourful account, and the new transfer brings out the ambient effect of the Severance Hall recording, even if the dynamic range remains less expansive than it should be. But the real snag here is that Andrew Davis's *Taras Bulba* has an altogether lower voltage. What a pity that was included instead of Ormandy's *Háry János suite*.

Suite for string orchestra.
(B) *** Discover Dig. DICD 920234 [id.].
Virtuosi di Praga, Vlček – SUK: *Serenade for strings* etc. **(*)

The expanded Virtuosi di Praga give an appropriately ardent and certainly a bravura account of Janáček's six-movement *Suite for string orchestra*, yet this group of seventeen players (including the leader/director, Oldřich Vlček) possess a vividly full sonority, and they do not miss the work's more subtle touches.

CHAMBER MUSIC

(i; iii) *Allegro; Dumka; Romance; Sonata* (for violin and piano); (ii; iii) *Pohádka (Fairy tale); Presto* (for cello and piano); (iii) (Piano) *In the mists; 3 Moravian dances; On an overgrown path, Series I–II; Paralipomena; Reminiscence; Piano sonata in E flat min. (I. X. 1905); Theme and variations (Zdenka's variations).*
**(*) BIS Dig. CD 663/664 [id.]. (i) Ulf Wallin; (ii) Mats Rondin; (iii) Roland Pöntinen.

This excellent collection ranges from the *Romance* for violin and piano from the late 1870s to the much later *Reminiscence* for piano. Pöntinen is an unfailingly intelligent player. Ulf Wallin proves a strong yet sensitive advocate of the *Violin Sonata*, and the cellist Mats Rondin is no less admirable in the *Pohádka* (*Fairy tale*) and the *Presto* for cello and piano. Readers wanting this whole collection may rest assured that both playing and recording are of a generally high standard.

Pohádka.
(BB) *** ASV Quicksilva Dig. CDQS 6218 [id.].
Bernard Gregor-Smith, Yolande Wrigley – PROKOFIEV; SHOSTAKOVICH: *Cello sonatas;* MARTINU: *Variations.* ***

The husband-and-wife team of Bernard Gregor-Smith and Yolande Wrigley gives a lively and sympathetic account of the three-movement *Pohádka*, which Janáček composed in 1910. It makes an admirable makeweight for the Prokofiev and Shostakovich sonatas.

String quartet No. 1 (Kreutzer sonata).
✿ *** Koch Dig. 3-6436-2 [id.]. Medici Qt – BRITTEN: *Quartet No.3;* RAVEL: *Quartet;* SHOSTAKOVICH: *Quartet No. 8;* SMETANA: *Quartet No. 1.* *** ✿
*** RCA Dig. 09026 61816-2 [id.]. Vogler Qt – DEBUSSY: *Quartet* (with SHOSTAKOVICH: *Quartet* ***).

The Medici players grab the listener's attention in the very opening bars, and they give an unsurpassed performance which combines deep feeling with great subtlety of colour. The opening of the third movement is disarming yet gripping in its combination of poignant simplicity and spontaneous, passionate outbursts. The recording could not be more real and tangible.

Taken on its own merits this performance by the Vogler Quartet it is very impressive: intelligent and alive, and well recorded too.

String quartet No. 1 (Kreutzer sonata).
*** Testament SBT 1074 [id.]. Smetana Qt – DVORAK: *Piano quintet* etc. ***

String quartet No. 2 (Intimate letters).
*** Testament SBT 1075 [id.]. Smetana Qt – DVORAK: *String quartet No. 14* etc. ***

The Smetana Quartet's account of the *First Quartet (Kreutzer sonata)* is one of the very best versions of the work ever committed to disc. There is a wonderful feeling that these players have lived with this music all their lives – and in fact live *for* it, so committed do they sound. Recommended with some urgency. Worth every penny of its full price.

Like its companion reviewed above, the Smetana account of the *Intimate Letters* appears in Britain for the first time. It deserves the same accolade. In terms of subtlety, tonal finish and technical polish, this is absolutely flawless – and the 1960s sound is superb, and not just for its period. Strongly recommended alongside its companion.

String quartets Nos. 1 (Kreutzer); 2 (Intimate letters).
*** ASV Dig. CDDCA 749 [id.]. Lindsay Qt (with DVORAK: *Cypresses* ***).
*** RCA Dig. 09026 68286-2 (3) [id.]. Tokyo Qt – BARTOK: *Quartets Nos. 1–6.* ***
(N) **(*) Ph. Dig. 456 574-2 [id.]. Guarneri Qt.
(M)**(*) HM Suite Dig. HMT 7901380 [id.]. Melos Qt.
(N) ** Sony Dig. SK 66840 [id.]. Juilliard Qt. – BERG: *Lyric Suite.* ***

(i) *String quartets Nos. 1–2;* (ii) *Mladí: suite for wind sextet.*
**(*) Koch/Panton 11203-2 [id.]. (i) Vlach Qt; (ii) Foerster Wind Quintet, Josef Horák.

(i) *String quartets Nos. 1–2;* (ii) *On an overgrown path: suite No. 1.*
*** Calliope Dig. CAL 9699 [id.]. (i) Talich Qt; (ii) Radoslav Kvapil.

Pride of place must go to the Talich Quartet on Calliope, not because their recording is the best, but because of their extraordinary qualities of insight. They play the *Intimate letters* as if its utterances came from a world so private that it must be approached with great care. The disc's value is much enhanced by a fill-up in the form of the *First suite, On an overgrown path.* Radoslav Kvapil is thoroughly inside this repertoire.

The Lindsays on ASV are also eminently competitive and have the right blend of sensitivity and intensity. Theirs must certainly rank very highly among current recommendations. They are played with the same concentration and sensitivity they bring to all they do, and recorded with great naturalness.

The Tokyo offer both quartets as an appetizer to their Bartók cycle, accommodating them on the first CD before the first Bartók *Quartet*. There is plenty of fire and passion, and they seem fully attuned to Janáček's sensibility. Choice in this repertoire must be dictated by preferred couplings.

The account of the Janáček quartets from the Guarneri on Philips is a strong one: both are well characterized and well played, and the recording is truthful and well balanced. It would receive a strong recommendation, were it not handicapped by short measure (full price for 41 minutes is too much to ask these days, however enjoyable those may be). Many of its rivals are as good artistically and offer another major work.

The Melos Quartet also offer nothing in addition to the two *Quartets*, but theirs are performances of considerable character and fire and, though the playing-time is ungenerous and the recording a bit fierce, they are worth consideration at mid price.

All the same, the Koch/Panton coupling with the Vlach Quartet, recorded in 1969, and a 1970 version of *Mladí* should not automatically be dismissed on grounds of age. The performances are very idiomatic and appealing, the recording far from inferior; and this record will give pleasure.

Very good playing from the Juilliard but they are not as wholly attuned to the Janáček as they are to the Alban Berg. They tend not to allow the music to speak for itself and overstatement is not called for here. Very good recorded sound.

(i) *String quartets Nos. 1–2;* (ii) *Pohádka for cello and piano;* (iii) *Violin sonata.*
(BB) *** Naxos Dig. 8.553895 [id.]. (i) Vlach Qt; (ii) Mikael Ericsson; (ii–iii) František Maly; (iii) Jana Vlachová.

There are one or two finer performances of the two *Quartets* listed above, but the Vlach Quartet give well played, impassioned accounts of both and are warmly recorded. Moreoever the account of the *Violin sonata* by Jana Vlachová and František Maly is very fine, and the *Pohádka for cello and piano* is given as touching and imaginative a performance by Mikael Ericsson as any in the catalogue. Good recordings and excellent value for money.

Violin sonata.
*** Virgin/EMI Dig. VC5 45122-2. Christian Tetzlaff, Leif Ove Andsnes – DEBUSSY: *Sonata;* NIELSEN: *Sonata No. 2;* RAVEL: *Sonata.* ***
(*) DG (IMS) Dig. 427 351-2. Gidon Kremer, Martha Argerich – BARTOK: *Sonata No. 1;* MESSIAEN: *Theme and variations.* *
(N) ** Ph. Dig. 446 091-2 [id.]. Viktoria Mullova, Piotr Anderszewski – DEBUSSY; PROKOFIEV: *Violin sonatas.* **

Christian Tetzlaff and Leif Ove Andsnes play with commitment and dedication. Theirs is an eloquent – indeed at times inspired – performance, and they are accorded excellent recording.

The *Sonata* is also played with great imaginative intensity and power by Gidon Kremer and Martha Argerich, though it is less selfless here than with Tetzlaff and Andsnes on Virgin: there is some expressive exaggeration. Excellent DG recording.

Mullova and Anderszewski give a generally satisfying, well projected and eminently well-recorded account of the *Sonata* which will give pleasure. Not a first choice all the same.

PIANO MUSIC

Along an overgrown path: Books 1 & 2; *In the mists; 3 Moravian dances; A recollection; Piano sonata (1.X.1905).*
*** EMI (SIS) Dig. CDC7 54094-2. Mikhail Rudy.

Along an overgrown path: Suite No. 1; In the mists; Piano sonata (I.X.1905).
*** Virgin/EMI Dig. VC7 59639-2. Leif Ove Andsnes.

Mikhail Rudy proves a perceptive and sympathetic guide in this music. His is a fine account of the *Sonata*, and he succeeds in penetrating the world of the *Overgrown path* miniatures to perfection. He conveys their acute sense of melancholy and their improvisatory character with distinction, and the recorded sound is very natural.

Leif Ove Andsnes gives us a very well-thought-out and imaginatively realized recital, including a highly sensitive account of *In the mists*, which is second to none in conveying the pervasive melancholy and evocative atmosphere of these pieces. This is every bit as telling as Mikhail Rudy's EMI account, and beautifully recorded, but it includes less music.

VOCAL MUSIC

Coz ta nase briza (Our birch tree); Elegie na smrt dcery Olgy (Elegy on the death of daughter Olga); Hradcanske písnicky (Song of Hradcany); Holubicka (The dove); Kacena divoká (The wild duck); Kantor Halfar (Schoolmaster Halfar); Potulny silenec (The wondering madman); Ríkadla (Nursery rhymes); Vlcí stopa (The wolf's trail).
*** Ph. Dig. 442 534-2 [id.]. Netherlands Chamber Ch., Schoenberg Ens., Reinbert De Leeuw.

Janáček's choral music covers a wide range from such straightforward partsongs as *Our birch tree* or *The Dove* to the ingenious, dazzling *Ríkadla* ('Nursery rhymes') of his last years. The affecting *Elegy on the death of daughter Olga* begins as if we are in the middle of *On an overgrown path* and is as every bit as subtle. The Netherlands Chamber Choir and members of the Schoenberg Ensemble under Reinbert De Leeuw produce cultured, well-blended results, and the Philips recording is impressive in its clarity and presence. It is possible to imagine wilder and more passionate performances, particularly from Moravian choirs, but in an area of the repertoire which is not generously served this deserves a strong recommendation.

Glagolitic Mass (original version, ed. Wingfield).
*** Chandos Dig. CHAN 9310[id.]. Kiberg, Stene, Svensson, Cold, Danish Nat. R. Ch. & SO, Mackerras – KODALY: *Psalmus hungaricus*. ***

The scholar, Paul Wingfield, has managed to reconstruct Janáček's original score and the added rhythmic complexities of this version, as interpreted idiomatically by Mackerras, encourage an apt wildness which brings an exuberant, carefree quality to writing which here, more than ever, seems like the inspiration of the moment. The wildness is also reinforced by having the *Intrada* at the very beginning, before the Introduction, as well as at the end. The chorus sings incisively with incandescent tone, and the tenor soloist, Peter Svensson, by far the most important of the four, has a trumpet-toned precision that makes light of the high tessitura and the stratospheric leaps that Janáček asks for. The soprano Tina Kiberg, also bright and clear rather than beautiful in tone, makes just as apt a choice. The mezzo, Randi Stene, is excellent, and only a certain unsteadiness in Ulrik Cold's relatively light bass tone prevents this from being an ideal quartet. Recorded sound of a weight and warmth that convey the full power of the music. Only the organ solo of the penultimate movement lacks a little in bite, thanks to a backward balance, even if it makes up in clarity.

Glagolitic Mass.
(M) *** EMI Dig. CDM5 66980-2 [CDM5 66995]. Palmer, Gunson, Mitchinson, King, CBSO & Ch., Rattle – *Sinfonietta*. ***
*** Sony Dig. SK 47182 [id.]. Beňačková, Palmer, Lakes, Kotcherga, Scott, London Symphony Ch., LSO, Tilson Thomas – *Sinfonietta*. ***.
(N) *** Decca Dig. 460 213-2 [id.]. Eva Urbanová, Marta Beňačková, Vladimir Bogachov, Richard Novák, Slovak Philharmonic Ch., VPO, Chailly – KORNGOLD: *Passover psalm*; ZEMLINSKY: *Psalm 83*. ***
(M) **(*) Sony SMK 47569 [id.]. Pilarczyk, Gedda, Gaynes, Westminster Ch., NYPO, Bernstein – POULENC: *Gloria*. ***

Rattle's performance of the standard published score, aptly paired with the *Sinfonietta*, is strong and vividly dramatic, with the Birmingham performers lending themselves to Slavonic passion. The recording is first class and now reissued as one of EMI's 'Great Recordings of the Century'.

Tilson Thomas directs a powerful, virtuoso performance of the normal published score, superbly played and sung, and helped by full, weighty recorded sound. The soprano solos are both idiomatic and beautiful as sung by Beňačková, unsurpassed by any rival; and Gary Lakes, though not quite idiomatic, uses his clean-cut, firm Heldentenor tone in the important tenor solos with no strain whatever. The London Symphony Chorus is magnificent, and the LSO plays brilliantly.

Chailly directs a strong and refined reading of the *Glagolitic mass*, with fine detail brought out in the glowing Decca recording, though not as immediate as some. If the work's earthiness is a degree underplayed, the emotional depth is fully brought out, with fine idiomatic singing and a virtuoso display from Thomas Trotter in the final organ solo. Warmly recommended for those who fancy the rare couplings.

Though Bernstein's reading of the *Glagolitic Mass* is not entirely idiomatic, it is a fine red-blooded performance and one which has the merit of distinguished soloists who add much to the performance. The vivid (1963) recording is one of the best of those Bernstein made in the Avery Fisher Hall.

Mass in E flat; (i) *Otčenáš (The Lord's Prayer).*
(M) *** EMI Dig. CDM5 65587-2. King's College, Cambridge, Ch., Cleobury; Stephen Lane; (i) with Arthur Davies, Osian Ellis – KODALY: *Missa brevis.* **(*)

The *Mass* comes from 1907–8 and was never completely finished. Janáček's pupil, Vilém Petrželka, discovered the *Kyrie* and *Agnus Dei* and a part of the *Credo*, which he completed. It is a beautiful piece. *Otčenáš* (*The Lord's Prayer*) is earlier (1901), written originally for tenor, chorus and harmonium (or piano); accompaniment was replaced in 1906 by organ and harp. The singing is generally good, though the sound is (not unnaturally) English rather than Slavonic. There is no alternative version of either work, and they are both valuable additions to the Janáček discography.

OPERA

The Cunning Little Vixen (complete); *Cunning little vixen* (suite, arr. Talich).
*** Decca Dig. 417 129-2 (2) [id.]. Popp, Randová, Jedlická, V. State Op. Ch., Bratislava Children's Ch., VPO, Mackerras.
*** Sup. SU 3071/2 612 (2) [id.]. Tattermuschová, Zikmundová, Kroupa, Hlavsa, Prague Nat. Ch. & O, Gregor.

Mackerras's thrusting, red-blooded reading is spectacularly supported by a digital recording of outstanding, demonstration quality. The inspired choice of Lucia Popp as the vixen provides charm in exactly the right measure: sparkling and coquettish, spiteful as well as passionate. The supporting cast is first rate, too. Talich's splendidly arranged orchestral suite is offered as a bonus in a fine new recording.

Janáček's opera is given on Supraphon with plenty of idiomatic Slavonic feeling by the composer's compatriots, with the part of the little vixen here charmingly sung by Helena Tattermuschová. The recording is evocatively warm and atmospheric. While the digitally recorded Decca Mackerras set (with Lucia Popp) remains a more obvious first choice, this earlier Czech version can hold its own. While not missing the red-blooded nature of the composer's inspiration, Gregor also captures the woodland ambience with appealing warmth and colour.

(i) *The Cunning Little Vixen* (sung in English); (ii) *Taras Bulba.*
*** EMI CDS7 54212-2 (2). (i) Watson, Tear, Allen, ROHCG Ch. & O; (ii) Philh. O; Simon Rattle.

For anyone who wants the work in English, Simon Rattle's recording provides an ideal answer, with his warmly expressive approach to the score giving strong support to the singers. The cast is outstanding, with Lillian Watson delightfully bright and fresh as the Vixen and Thomas Allen firm and full-toned as the Forester. If Mackerras's Janáček style is more angular and abrasive, bringing out the jagged, spiky rhythms and unexpected orchestral colours, Rattle's is more moulded, more immediately persuasive, if less obviously idiomatic.

The excursions of Mr Brouček (complete).
*** Sup. 11 2153-2 (2) [id.]. Přibyl, Svejda, Jonášová, Czech PO Ch. & O, Jílek.

This performance comes over with real charm, thanks to the understanding conducting of Jílek, but also to the characterization of the central character, the bumbling, accident-prone Mr Brouček (literally Mr Beetle). Vilém Přibyl portrays him as an amiable, much-put-upon figure as he makes his excursions. The big team of Czech singers (doubling up roles in the different parts, with Vladimir Krejčik remarkable in no fewer than seven of them) is outstanding, bringing out both the warmth and the sense of fun behind the writing. The result is a delight, as sharp and distinctive as any Janáček opera. The analogue recording, made in Prague in 1980, is full and atmospheric with a fine sense of presence on CD.

(i) *From the house of the dead;* (iii) *Mládí* (for wind sextet); (ii; iii) *Říkadla* (for Chamber Ch. & 10 instruments).
*** Decca Dig. 430 375-2 (2) [id.]. (i) Jedlička, Zahradníček, Zídek, Zítek, V. State Op. Ch., VPO, Mackerras; (ii) L. Sinf. Ch.; (iii) L. Sinf., Atherton.

With one exception, the Decca cast is superb, with a range of important Czech singers giving sharply characterized vignettes. The exception is the raw Slavonic singing of the one woman in the cast, Jaroslav Janska as the boy, Aljeja, but even that fails to undermine the intensity of the innocent relationship with the central figure, which provides an emotional anchor for the whole piece. The chamber-music items added for this reissue are both first rate.

Jenufa (complete).
❁ *** Decca Dig. 414 483-2 (2) [id.]. Söderström, Ochman, Dvorský, Randová, Popp, V. State Op. Ch., VPO, Mackerras.
(M) **(*) EMI (SIS) CMS5 64576-2 (2). Domanínská, Kniplová, Přibyl, Zídek, Prague Nat. Theatre Ch. & O, Bohumil Gregor.

This is the warmest and most lyrical of Janáček's operas, and it inspires a performance from Mackerras and his team which is deeply sympathetic, strongly dramatic and superbly recorded. Elisabeth Söderström creates a touching portrait of the girl caught in a family tragedy. The two rival tenors, Peter Dvorský and Wieslav Ochman as the half-brothers Steva and Laca, are both superb; but dominating the whole drama is the Kostelnitchka of Eva Randová. Some may resist the idea that she should be made so sympathetic but, particularly on record, the drama is made stronger and more involving.

The main strength of the 1969 Prague version lies in the fine characterization of the mother, the Kostelnička, the most complex and dominant figure in the action. Though none of the singers may be absolutely first class, and they are not free from Slav vibrato, the company has fine teamwork and Bohumil Gregor directs the performance with genuine imaginative vitality. However, the acoustic of this recording is rather reverberant and detail is inevitably smudged when compared with the later, Decca set. Even so, it remains vibrantly enjoyable and is well documented, with a clearly printed libretto.

Káta Kabanová (complete).
(N) ** Sup. Dig. SU 3291-2 632 (3) [id.]. Vele, Straka, Randová, Kopp, Beňačková, Kundlak, Pecková, Harvánek, Bauerová, Burešová, Prague Nat. Theatre Ch., Czech PO, Mackerras.

(i) *Káta Kabanová* (complete); (ii) *Capriccio for piano and 7 instruments; Concertino for piano and 6 instruments*.
*** Decca 421 852-2 (2) [id.]. (i) Söderström, Dvorský, Kniplová, Krejčik, Márová, V. State Op. Ch., VPO, Mackerras; (ii) Paul Crossley, L. Sinf., Atherton.

Elisabeth Söderström dominates the cast as the tragic heroine and gives a performance of great insight and sensitivity; she touches the listener deeply and is supported by Mackerras with imaginative grip and flair. The other soloists are all Czech and their characterizations are brilliantly authentic. But it is the superb orchestral playing and the inspired performance of Söderström that make this set so memorable. The recording is vividly transferred to CD, with a double bonus added in the shape of the two concertante keyboard works, in which Paul Crossley is the impressive soloist.

Though Mackerras's Supraphon set offers digital sound and has an excellent Czech cast, it cannot match his earlier Decca version in colour or bite. Though his speeds are a degree faster than before, the result is less violent and less involving, thanks partly to the low-level recording set in a reverberant acoustic. Beňačková, rich and vibrant, is an exceptionally characterful Káta, arguably more idiomatic than Söderström on Decca, and the other principals are first-rate too, but at every point this pales before its rival.

(i) *The Makropulos affair (Věc Makropulos)*: complete; (ii) *Lachian dances*.
*** Decca 430 372-2 (2) [id.]. (i) Söderström, Dvorský, Blachut, V. State Op. Ch., VPO, Mackerras; (ii) LPO, Huybrechts.

Mackerras and his superb team provide a thrilling new perspective on this opera, with its weird heroine preserved by magic elixir well past her 300th birthday. Elisabeth Söderström is not simply malevolent: irritable and impatient rather, no longer an obsessive monster. Framed by richly colourful singing and playing, Söderström amply justifies that view, and Peter Dvorský is superbly fresh and ardent as Gregor. The recording, like others in the series, is of the finest Decca analogue quality. The performance of the *Lachian dances* is highly idiomatic and makes a good bonus.

Osud (complete in English).
(N) (M) *** Chandos Dig. CHAN 3029 [id.]. Langridge, Field, Harries, Bronder, Kale, Welsh Nat. Op. Ch. & O, Mackerras.

This single-disc recording of Janáček's most unjustly-neglected opera – richly lyrical, more sustained and less fragmented than his later operas – is not just a valuable rarity but makes an ideal introduction to the composer. It is a piece that was for generations rejected as being unstageable, thanks to the oddities of the libretto; until, however, the English National Opera presented it at the Coliseum in London in an unforgettable production by David Pountney. Though this recording – one of the series sponsored by the Peter Moores Foundation – was made with Welsh National Opera forces, its success echoes the ENO production. Philip Langridge is again superb in the central role of the composer, Zivny, well supported by Helen Field as Mila, the married woman he loves, and by Kathryn Harries as her mother – a far finer cast than was presented on a short-lived Supraphon set. That was done in the original Czech, whereas this performance, following ENO, uses Rodney Blumer's excellent English translation, adding to the immediate impact. Sir Charles Mackerras matches his earlier achievement in the prizewinning series of Janáček opera recordings for Decca, capturing the full gutsiness, passion and impetus of the composer's inspiration, from the exhilarating opening waltz ensemble onwards, a passage that vividly sets the scene in a German spa at the turn of the century. The warmly atmospheric EMI recording, with a playing-time of nearly 80 minutes, was made in the Brangwyn Hall, Swansea, and brings out the unusual opulence of the Janáček sound in this work, written immediately after *Jenufa*, yet it allows words to come over with fine clarity.

Janiewicz, Feliks (1762–1848)

Divertimento for strings.
(B) *** EMI forte CZS5 69524-2 [CDFB 69524] (2). Polish CO, Maksymiuk – MENDELSSOHN: *String symphonies;* ROSSINI: *String sonatas;* JARZEBSKI: *Tamburetta; Chromatica.* ***

Feliks Janiewicz was an almost exact contemporary of Rossini, and this delightful work (one of six, written in London around 1805) might well have been another of Rossini's string sonatas, for the writing shares their brilliance and wit. The finale is a *tour de force* of bravura, relished here by this excellent Polish string band. A real find.

Järnefelt, Armas (1869–1958)

Berceuse; Korsholm; Ouverture lyrique; Praeludium; The Promised land (Det förlovade landet): suite; The Song of the Crimson Flower (Sången om den eldröda blomman).
(N) ** Sterling Dig. CDS-1021-2 [id.]. Gävle SO, Hannu Koivula.

Järnefelt is best remembered nowadays for two light classics, the *Berceuse* and *Praeludium*, which still delight music-lovers. He came from a highly gifted family: his brother Arvid was a novelist, his brother Eero a fine painter and his sister Aino married Sibelius. As a conductor he was a celebrated Sibelius interpreter and in later years gave little time to composing. He settled in Stockholm just before the First World War, where he was conductor at the Royal Swedish Opera. This well-recorded CD shows him to be a composer of natural talent though he does not possess a strongly individual personality. He was one of the first Nordic composers to write for the cinema: *The Song of the Crimson Flower* dates from 1919. All this music is direct in feeling and has a touch of nobility. It is national-romantic in character, not dissimilar from, say, Sibelius's *King Christian II* music. It is appropriate that it should be played by a Swedish orchestra as he adopted Swedish nationality in the 1920s. Hannu Koivula's conducting disappoints. There is not enough charm in these performances. Worth hearing all the same.

Jarzebski, Adam (*c.* 1590–*c.* 1649)

Tamburetta; Chromatica.
(B) *** EMI forte CZS5 69524-2 [CDFB 69524] (2). Polish CO, Maksymiuk – MENDELSSOHN: *String symphonies;* ROSSINI: *String sonatas;* JANIEWICZ: *Divertimento.* ***

These two delightful lollipops show Adam Jarzebski to be a composer of real personality, the *Tamburetta* bouncing along joyously, with staccato bowing from the Polish strings adding to the rhythmic life, the second changing its mood from dance-like vivacity to stately yet slightly doleful elegance. Marvellous bravura playing from the Polish strings and vividly bright recording add to the music's projection.

Joachim, Joseph (1831–1907)

(i) *Violin concerto in Hungarian style, Op. 11. Overtures: Hamlet, Op. 4; Henry IV, Op. 7.*
(B) *** Carlton Dig. 30367 02092 [id.(M)]. (i) Elmar Oliveira; LPO, Leon Botstein.

Joseph Joachim's fame rests as a legendary performer and the dedicatee of the Brahms *Violin concerto*, rather than as a composer. Nevertheless his concerto, conservative in outlook, and indebted to Mendelssohn and Beethoven, is a very considerable achievement – as, for that matter, is the playing of Elmar Oliveira in this well-balanced recording. The conductor Leon Botstein also gives committed accounts of the splendid *Henry IV* and *Hamlet Overtures*. An enterprising and rewarding release.

Johansen, David Monrad (1888–1974)

String quartet, Op. 36.
(BB) *** Naxos Dig. 8.550879 [id.]. Oslo String Qt – GRIEG: *String quartets.* ***

David Monrad Johansen's *String quartet*, composed in 1969 when in his early eighties, is persuasively played by the Oslo String Quartet and is impeccably recorded. It is a well-crafted piece but not as distinctively personal as *Pan* or the best of his mature works.

Johnson, Robert (*c.* 1582–1633)

Lute and Theatre music: *Almans I–III; Corant; Fantasia; Galliard; Pavan;* Ayres: *Adieu, fond love; Arm, arm!; As I walked forth; Away delights; Care-charming sleep; Charon, oh Charon; Come away, Hecate; Come away, thou lady gay; Come, heavy sleep; Come hither, you that love; Full fathom five; Hark! hark! the lark!; Have you seen the white lily grow?; O let us howl; Tell me dearest; 'Tis late and cold; Where the bee sucks; Woods, rocks and mountains.*
❁ *** Virgin/EMI (SIS) Dig. VC7 59321-2 [id.]. Emma Kirkby, David Thomas, Anthony Rooley.

In this most engaging recital, Emma Kirkby sings with characteristic freshness and charm in Shakespearean numbers like *Hark! hark! the lark!* and *Where the bee sucks*, and she is utterly ravishing in the poignant *Come, heavy sleep*, and the following, equally beautiful *Care-charming sleep*. David Thomas is hardly less expressive in Ariel's *Full fathom five* from *The Tempest* with its gently tolling bell and *Have you seen the white lily grow?* (Ben Jonson). Like Kirkby, his decoration is felicitous, often florid but never fussy. After the drama of the male solo songs, Thomas is joined by Emma Kirkby in the dialogue interchange of *Come away, Hecate* (from Middleton's *The Witch*) complete with vociferous growls which suggest that the angst is not to be taken too seriously. Anthony Rooley then calms the atmosphere with delicately played lute solos. Two more duets end the programme. The recording is absolutely natural, and the lute is never made to seem larger than life.

Jolivet, André (1905–74)

Chant de Linos.
*** Koch Dig. 3-7016 [id.]. Atlantic Sinf. – JONGEN: *Concert;* DEBUSSY: *Sonata.* ***

The *Chant de Linos* was originally composed for flute and piano, but Jolivet subsequently made this highly effective transcription for flute, violin, viola, cello and harp. It is played with exemplary taste and effortless virtuosity by Bradley Garner and his colleagues of the Atlantic Sinfonietta and is most beautifully recorded.

Jones, Daniel (1912–93)

Symphonies Nos. (i) *6*; (ii) *9*; (i; iii) *The Country beyond the stars.*
(N) *** Lyrita SRCD 326 [id.]. (i) RPO, Sir Charles Groves: (ii) BBC Welsh SO, Bryden Thomson; (iii) with Welsh Nat. Op. Ch.

Daniel Jones, a prolific and musically talented Welshman, is another composer whose music has fallen by the wayside, trampled underneath by the supremacy of the avant garde and the lack of interest in traditional musical values. Jones's facility in the use of the orchestra is striking and if his *Sixth Symphony* is eclectic in style, it is strong in personality, and the cogency of the argument (all six movements use the same basic material) is matched by an ability to communicate emotional experience. No. 9 too is finely crafted and has a particularly intense slow movement. Both works show genuine integrity and power: they are the work of a real symphonist who has a sense of movement and a feeling for growth. Both are very well played by orchestras who show their commitment, and under conductors who respond naturally to the idiom. *The Country beyond the stars* is a comparatively short cantata designed to suit the traditional qualities of Welsh Choirs, warm, relaxed writing, easy on the ear. The five choral movements are settings of the Breconshire poet, Henry Vaughan, and are divided by a purely orchestral third movement, *Joyful visitors.* Again fine performance and a good sound balance, courtesy of the Welsh Arts Council. The remastering of these recordings from the 1970s is more than acceptable.

String quartets Nos. 1–8.
(N) *** Chandos Dig. CHAN 9535 (2) [id.]. Delmé Qt.

Although Daniel Jones's symphonies were reasonably well served by the gramophone during the LP era, his chamber music was not. The *First Quartet* is a particularly impressive work, with a certain cosmopolitanism and a distinct French tinge to its atmosphere. But Jones is always his own man. No. 2 is exploratory and has a characteristically concentrated *Lento espressivo.* Nos. 3–5 were the first to be recorded, in 1981. All are distinguished by seriousness of purpose and fine craftsmanship. And for the most part this is more than just expertly fashioned music: it consistently places matter before manner and there are rarely any superfluous gestures. The music is unflamboyant but all three works are of substance. The last three quartets are even more succinct (each lasting about a quarter of an hour). No. 6 marked the 250th birthday of Haydn, and uses two of that master's themes. Its mood is strongly focused, moving from a solemn introduction (and back again) via the Haydnesque scherzo and a simple slow movement. No. 7 is masterly, intensely concentrated: its central movement is marked *Penseroso.* The last quartet, full of memorable ideas, was left unfinished; it was skilfully completed from the composer's sketches by Giles Easterbrook. Appropriately, it has a hauntingly elegiac close. It is played here with enormous dedication and, like No. 7, holds the listener in a powerful emotional spell. A fitting conclusion to a splendid series, given definitive readings from a quartet closely identified with the music, and first-class Chandos sound.

Jones, Sidney (1861–1946)

The Geisha (complete).
(N) *** Hyperion Dig. CDA 67006 [id.]. Watson, Maltman, Walker, Suart, New London Light Opera Ch. & O, Corp.

Given first in 1896, and very much of its period, *The Geisha* makes a delightful, innocent romp, helped by a sparkling performance under Ronald Corp. Prompted by the impresario George Edwardes, Jones and his librettist, Owen Hall, sought to follow up the success of Gilbert and Sullivan's *Mikado.* The formula worked so well that this Japanese musical play ran for two years. Granted that Jones cannot match Sullivan in finesse or tuneful memorability, this has a striking sequence of numbers with such off-beat titles as *The amorous goldfish* and *The interfering parrot.* The choruses too work splendidly. Though Lillian Watson's bright soprano grows edgy at the top, she is charming as the heroine Mimosa, and though Christopher Maltman's baritone grows gritty and uneven under pressure, he makes a dashing hero. Best of all is Sarah Walker, with her voice as rich and firm as ever, relishing the idiom, just as she does in cabaret songs. Richard Suart is ideal in the comic role of Wun-Hi.

Jongen, Joseph (1873–1953)

(i) *Allegro appassionato for viola and orchestra, Op. 79; Suite for viola and orchestra, Op. 48*. (ii) *Symphonie concertante for organ and orchestra, Op. 81*.
**(*) Koch Schwann Dig. CD 315 012 [id.) (i) Thérèse-Marie Gilissen, RTBF SO, Brian Priestman; (ii) Hubert Schoonbroodt, Liège SO, René Defossez.

Symphonie concertante for organ and orchestra, Op. 81.
*** Telarc Dig. CD 80096 [id.]. Michael Murray, San Francisco SO, De Waart – FRANCK: *Fantaisie* etc. ***

Anyone who likes the Saint-Saëns *Third Symphony* should enjoy the Jongen *Symphonie concertante*. Even if the music is on a lower level of inspiration, the passionate *Lento misterioso* and hugely spectacular closing *Toccata* make a favourable impression at first hearing and wear surprisingly well afterwards. Michael Murray has all the necessary technique to carry off Jongen's hyperbole with the required panache. He receives excellent support from Edo de Waart and the San Francisco Symphony Orchestra and Telarc's engineers capture all the spectacular effects with their usual aplomb. A demonstration disc indeed.

The Koch Schwann version comes from 1975 and has the advantage of being coupled with the *Suite for viola and orchestra*, Op. 48, whose first movement almost calls to mind the elegiac tone of Lekeu's *Adagio* for quartet and strings. Neither version is top-drawer, and the spectacular Telarc version by Michael Murray remains an easy first choice.

Concert à cinq.
*** Koch Dig. 3-7016-2 [id.]. Atlantic Sinf. – DEBUSSY: *Sonata;* JOLIVET: *Chant de Linos*. ***

The three-movement *Concert à cinq* for flute, harp and string trio is a civilized piece very much in the post-impressionist style. It remains more pleasing than memorable, though these players do their utmost for it.

Joplin, Scott (1868–1917)

Rags: *Bethena (concert waltz); Cascades rag; Country club (ragtime two-step); Elite syncopations; The Entertainer; Euphonic sounds (A syncopated novelty); Fig leaf rag; Gladiolus rag; Magnetic rag (syncopations classiques); Maple leaf rag; Paragon rag; Pine apple rag; Ragtime dance; Scott Joplin's new rag; Solace (Mexican serenade); Stoptime rag; Weeping willow (ragtime two-step)*.
(M) *** Nonesuch Elektra/Warner 7559 79449-2 [id.]. Joshua Rifkin.

Joshua Rifkin is the pianist whose name has been indelibly associated with the Scott Joplin revival, originally stimulated by the soundtrack music of the very successful film, *The Sting*. His relaxed, cool rhythmic style is at times remarkably subtle and, although the piano timbre is full, there is a touch of monochrome in the tone-colour. The current remastering gives the piano a natural presence.

Josquin Desprez (died 1521)

Motets: *Absolom, fili mi; Ave Maria, gratia plena; De profundis clamavi; In te Domine speravi per trovar pietà; Veni, Sanctus Spiritus*. Chansons: *La déploration de la mort de Johannes Ockeghem; El grillo; En l'ombre d'ung buissonet au matinet; Je me complains; Je ne me puis tenir d'aimer; Mille regretz; Petite camusette; Scaramella va alla guerra; Scaramella va la galla*.
(M) *** Virgin Veritas/EMI (SIS) Dig. VER5 61302-2 [CDM 61302]. Hilliard Ensemble.

Josquin spent much of his life in Italy, first as a singer in the choir of Milan Cathedral and subsequently in the service of the Sforza family. The chansons recorded here have both variety of colour and lightness of touch, while the motets are sung with dignity and feeling by the Hilliard Ensemble. Indeed, these performances will kindle the enthusiasm of the uninitiated as will few others. The 1983 recording, made in London's Temple Church, is expertly balanced and eminently truthful.

Motets: *Ave Maria, gratia plena; Ave, nobilissima creatura; Miserere mei, Deus; O bone et dulcissime Jesu; Salve regina; Stabat mater dolorosa; Usquequo, Domine, oblivisceris me*.
*** HM Dig. HMC 901243 [id.]. Chapelle Royale Ch., Herreweghe.

The Chapelle Royale comprises some nineteen singers, but they still produce a clean, well-focused sound and benefit from excellent recording. Their account of the expressive *Stabat mater* sounds thicker-textured than the New College forces under Edward Higginbottom, but there is a refreshing sense of commitment and strong feeling.

Antiphons, Motets and Sequences: *Inviolata; Praeter rerum serium; Salve regina; Stabat mater dolorosa; Veni, sancte spiritus; Virgo prudentissima; Virgo salutiferi.*
*** Mer. ECD 84093 [id.]. New College, Oxford, Ch., Higginbottom.

The Meridian anthology collects some of Josquin's most masterly and eloquent motets in performances of predictable excellence by Edward Higginbottom and the Choir of New College, Oxford. An admirable introduction to Josquin, and an essential acquisition for those who care about this master.

Chanson: *L'homme armé; Missa L'homme armé super voces musicales; Missa L'homme armé sexti toni.*
(N) *** Gimell/Ph. 454 919-2 [id.]. Tallis Scholars, Peter Phillips.

Josquin wrote two masses using *L'homme armé* as the cantus firmus, but in the later (though not much later) *Sexti toni* (sixth mode), the last note of the cantus is different – F, instead of G as favoured by most other composers including Dufay (see above). The character of the melody is thus given given a more positive character with the major key implied. The Tallis performances are in their usual impeccable flowing style, and the performance of the later work undoubtedly brings out its greater complexity, although the closing *Agnus Dei* has a hauntingly beautiful bare simplicity.

Missa L'homme armé sexti toni. Motets: *Absalom fili mi; Ave Maria.*
❁ (BB) *** Naxos Dig. 8.553428 [id.]. Oxford Camerata, Jeremy Summerly (with VINDERS: *Lament on the death of Josquin* ***).

Another interesting feature of the Josquin setting is his interpolation of a trope (*Laeta Dies*) following the *Credo* and before the *Sanctus* using a non-liturgical text. The effect is undoubtedly dramatic at the centre of a work where the flowing lines of the polyphony have such a rich harmonic implication. The long *Credo* breaks free, with the polyphony becoming more animated, and so becomes the central focus of the whole Mass – and what a beautiful Mass it is; very beautifully sung and recorded here. The *Ave Maria* is used to create a tranquil mood before the Mass itself begins, and the very touching motet, *Absalon, fili mi*, makes a poignant coda. This is followed by the radiant elegy of Josquin's contemporary, Jheronimus Vinders, with its soaring treble line, surely a fitting tribute. With full texts provided, this CD is one of the very finest of this distinguished Naxos series.

Missa Pange lingua; Missa La sol fa re mi.
*** Gimell Ph. Dig. 454 909-2 [id.]. Tallis Scholars, Peter Phillips.

The Gimell recording of the *Missa Pange lingua* has collected superlatives on all counts and was voted record of the year in the *Gramophone* magazine's 1987 awards. The tone the Tallis Scholars produce is perfectly blended, each line being firmly defined and yet beautifully integrated into the whole sound-picture. Their recording, made in the Chapel of Merton College, Oxford, is first class, the best of the *Missa Pange lingua* and the first of the ingenious *Missa La sol fa re mi*. Not to be missed.

Kabalevsky, Dmitri (1904–87)

Colas Breugnon: Overture and suite: The Comedians (suite); Romeo and Juliet (suite).
(BB) *** Naxos Dig. 8.553411 [id.]. Moscow SO, Vasily Jelvakov.

Three of Kabalevsky's best-known scores coupled together at super-bargain price in very acceptable performances and in decent sound. Kabalevsky speaks a patois akin to the language of Shostakovich and Prokofiev but without a scintilla of their depth and genius. The opera *Colas Breugnon* is based on Romain Rolland's novel *Le maître de Clamécy* and dates from 1938, though it was revised twice after the war. The suite from *The Comedians*, composed to accompany a play called *The Inventor and the Comedians*, written two years later, is cheap and cheerful, quite attractive and very well laid out for the orchestra – though, as in the score for *Romeo and Juliet* (which derives from 1956), some of its faster movements are tiresomely scatty. Still, there are others which are inventive and atmospheric.

The Comedians (suite), *Op. 26.*
(N) (M) *** RCA 09026 63302-2 [id.]. RCA Victor SO, Kiril Kondrashin – KHACHATURIAN: *Masquerade suite.* RIMSKY-KORSAKOV: *Capriccio espagnole*; TCHAIKOVSKY: *Capriccio italien.* *** ❁

On the RCA collection the *Comedians' galop* follows on almost immediately after the finale of Khachaturian's *Masquerade*, and the impetuous stylistic link is obvious. Kondrashin's performance is affectionate and colourful as well as lively and the warm resonance of the recording helps to prevent the music from sounding too brash. The Tchaikovsky and Rimsky-Korsakov couplings are marvellous.

Cello concerto No. 1 in G min.
*** Sony Dig. MK 37840 [id.]. Yo-Yo Ma, Phd. O, Ormandy – SHOSTAKOVICH: *Cello concerto No. 1.* ***

The excellence of Ma's performance is matched by a fine recording which adds considerably to the refinement and presence of the sound, and its vividness is such as to seem to add stature to the music itself.

(i) *Cello concertos Nos. 1 in G min., Op. 49; 2 in C min., Op. 77. Spring* (symphonic poem), *Op. 65*.
(BB) **(*) Naxos Dig. 8.553788 [id.]. (i) Alexander Rudin; Moscow SO, Igor Golovschin.

The enchanting *First Concerto in G minor* was written in 1949 for Knushevitzky and it wears well. Alexander Rudin is a first-rate soloist who yields nothing to the majority of his full-priced rivals. The orchestral playing is decent and acceptable but falls short of distinction. Good recording: this Naxos disc is generally worth the money. The short, slight and charming symphonic poem is not otherwise available.

Cello concerto No. 2, Op. 77.
*** Chandos Dig. CHAN 8579 [id.]. Wallfisch, LPO, Thomson – GLAZUNOV: *Chant du ménestrel;* KHACHATURIAN: *Concerto*. ***
(N) (BB) *** Virgin Classics Dig. VBD5 61490-2 [CDVB 61490]. Steven Isserlis, LPO, Litton – BLOCH: *Schelomo (Hebraic rhapsody)* for cello and orchestra; ELGAR: *Cello concerto*; R. STRAUSS: *Don Quixote;* TCHAIKOVSKY: *Rococo variations* etc. ***
**(*) BIS CD 719 [id.]. Lindström, Gothenburg SO, Ashkenazy – KHACHATURIAN: *Cello concerto*. **(*)

The *Second Cello concerto* is played eloquently – and with the greatest virtuosity – by Raphael Wallfisch, who is well supported by Bryden Thomson and the LPO. Excellent recording too.

Stephen Isserlis on Virgin gives as compelling and ardent an account of the concerto as does Wallfisch on Chandos and, since the LPO play as well for Andrew Litton as they did for Brydon Thomson, there is little to choose between them. As far as recorded sound is concerned, both are impressive; perhaps Virgin uses a slightly less resonant acoustic. The coupling will probably settle matters. Chandos offers two key Russian cello works; the Virgin bargain Double offers fine performances of concertante cello works by no fewer than five different composers!

Mats Lindström also proves an admirably sensitive soloist in Kabalevsky's *Second Concerto*. The recording is of high quality and well balanced but is a shade over-resonant, although the ear adjusts. Not a first choice, but an enjoyable performance, with no lack of spontaneity.

Violin concerto in C, Op. 48.
(N) *** DG Dig. 457 064-2 [id.]. Gil Shaham, Russian Nat. O, Pletnev – GLAZUNOV: *Concerto*; TCHAIKOVSKY: *Souvenir d'un lieu cher* etc. ***
*** Chandos Dig. CHAN 8918 [id.]. Lydia Mordkovitch, SNO, Järvi - KHACHATURIAN: *Violin concerto*. ***

Kabalevsky's *Violin concerto* has never enjoyed the same popularity among players as either of the cello concertos. However, its effortless invention and Prokofievian charm lend it a genuine appeal. (It is certainly more worthwhile than any of the piano concertos.) Gil Shaham's brilliant account of the piece with Mikhail Pletnev and the Russian National Orchestra should win it many friends.

The concerto is also most persuasively presented on the competing Chandos CD. Throughout Lydia Mordkovitch plays with great flair and aplomb and is given first-class recording. This is coupled with an equally fine version of the Khachaturian concerto, which collectors who already have the Glazunov might prefer.

Symphonies Nos. 1 in C sharp min., Op. 18; 2 in C min., Op. 19.
** Olympia Dig. OCD 268 [id.]. Szeged PO, Acél.

Kabalevsky's *First Symphony* unfolds naturally and the musical procedures have real dignity, even if some of the material of the finale is banal. The *Second Symphony* is both more individual and tautly argued. Good, though not first-class, performances from the Szeged Philharmonic Orchestra under Erwin Acél; however, the recording is handicapped by a rather cramped and constricted acoustic.

(i) *Symphony No. 4 in C min., Op. 54;* (ii) *Requiem, Op. 72.*
** Olympia OCD 290 (2) [id.]. (i) Leningrad PO; (ii) Valentina Levko, Vladimir Valaitis, Moscow Artistic Educational Institute Ch., Moscow SO; Kabalevsky.

The *Fourth Symphony* is a rather conventional work which goes through the correct motions of sonata form, but the ideas are only intermittently engaging; indeed, many border on the commonplace. The *Requiem* is a more rewarding piece, even if much of it is hard work. But the longueurs are offset by some moving passages and a genuine, unforced dignity that grips the listener. The sound in the *Requiem* is very good indeed for the period – and the place.

24 Preludes, Op. 38; Sonata No. 3, Op. 46; Sonatina in C, Op. 13/1.
**(*) Olympia Dig. OCD 266 [id.]. Murray McLachlan.

Murray McLachlan makes out a persuasive case for Kabalevsky's *24 Preludes*, Op. 38. Each of the preludes is based on a folk tune, mostly drawn from Rimsky-Korsakov's collection, and in *No. 13 in F sharp minor* we encounter the theme made famous by Stravinsky in the closing bars of *Firebird*. McLachlan does the set with great fluency and clarity of articulation. He also gives us two of Kabalevsky's best-known piano pieces, the *Sonatina* (1930) and the *Piano Sonata No. 3* (1946), with its Prokofievian middle movement. In the *Sonata*,

Pizarro (see below) is the more imaginative in his handling of tone-colour and dynamic range. The piano-sound is decent but could do with greater transparency and bloom.

Piano sonatas Nos. 1 in F, Op. 6; 2 in E flat, Op. 45; 3 in F, Op. 46; 4 Preludes, Op. 5; Recitative and Rondo, Op. 84.
*** Collins Dig. 1418-2 [id.]. Artur Pizarro.

On the present disc Artur Pizarro collects the three Kabalevsky *Sonatas*, together with the early *Four Preludes*, Op. 5, and a *Recitative and Rondo* dating from 1967, the fiftieth anniversary of the October Revolution. The *Sonata No. 1 in F*, Op. 6, was composed in 1927 while Kabalevsky was still a pupil of Miaskovsky, and its opening reflects not only the latter's influence but, even more so, that of Scriabin. Pizarro makes much more of the *Third Sonata* than McLachlan and gives a highly polished account of all the pieces recorded here and there is much to give pleasure, particularly when it is played with such elegance. The piano-sound is truthful and reasonably fresh, though there is perhaps more resonance than some will like. Recommended.

Piano sonata No. 3, Op. 46.
(M) (***) RCA mono GD 60377 [60377-2-RG]. Vladimir Horowitz – BARBER; PROKOFIEV: *Sonatas* etc. (***)

Horowitz cannot give Kabalevsky's music the calibre of the Barber or Prokofiev sonatas with which it is coupled, and the 1947 recording is a bit subfusc. But the power of the playing certainly comes through, especially in the brilliant finale.

Colas Breugnon (complete).
*** Olympia OCD 291 A/B (2) [id.]. Boldin, Isakova, Kayevchenko, Maksimenko, Duradev, Gutorovich, Mishchevsky, Stanislavsky & Nemirovich-Danchenko Moscow Music Theatre Ch. & O, Zhemchuzhin.

This complete recording, made in Russia in the 1970s, confirms that the effervescent overture is not just a flash in the pan but part of an exceptionally winning piece, rhythmically inventive and full of good tunes, many of them drawn from French folk-song. The snag is that between Acts I and II in the three-Act layout there is a story-gap of 40 years. Enough of the same characters are still around to maintain continuity, but youthful effervescence is less apt for the aged characters in Acts II and III. Nevertheless the Russian performance and recording, made by members of the Moscow Music Theatre, is most convincing, with a cast superbly led by the baritone, Leonid Boldin, in the title-role. The other male singers are first rate too, with splendidly alert singing from the chorus (which, in good proletarian fashion, plays a key part in the opera). The women soloists are raw-toned in a very Russian way, and the whole performance under Georgy Zhemchuzhin reflects the confidence of experience on stage. The 1973 recording, rather dry but with fine presence, catches the voices splendidly, though the orchestra is backwardly placed. But reservations may be put to one side; this is a thoroughly worthwhile set.

Kalinnikov, Vasily (1866–1901)

Intermezzos Nos. 1 in F sharp min.; 2 in G.
*** Chandos Dig. CHAN 8614 [id.]. RSNO, Järvi – RACHMANINOV: *Symphony No. 3.* ***

These two colourful *Intermezzos* with a flavour of Borodin are charming.

Overtures: The Cedar and the palm; Tsar Boris.
(M) *** Chandos Enchant Dig. CHAN 7093 [id.]. RSNO, Järvi – RIMSKY-KORSAKOV: *Scheherazade* etc. ***

Kalinnikov's *Cedar and the palm overture*, his final work for orchestra, is an atmospheric piece (based on a Heine poem). It has eminently nostalgic Slavonic invention and, like its companion, *Tsar Boris*, vividly colourful scoring. Kalinnikov's portrayal of the *Tsar*, however, has none of the sombre desolation of Mussorgsky's opera and ends joyously with a resplendent fanfare. Järvi's performances with his responsive Scottish players are very sympathetic and the Chandos recording is in the demonstration class.

Symphonies Nos. 1 in G min.; 2 in A.
(N) *** Chandos Dig. CHAN 9544 [id.]. RSNO, Neeme Järvi.

Kalinnikov's *First Symphony* contains something akin to the flow and natural lyricism of Borodin, and the *Second* is also rewarding in a similar way if not quite as appealing as No. 1. Neeme Järvi and the Royal Scottish National Orchestra recorded these delightful works in 1987 and 1989 respectively, These are spacious, well-performed performances and exemplary recordings.

Karamanov, Alemdar (born 1934)

Symphonies Nos. 20 (Blessed are the dead); 23 (I am Jesus).
** Olympia Dig. OCD 486 [id.]. USSR SO, Vladimir Fedoseyev.

Symphonies Nos. 22 (Let it be); 23.
*** Decca Dig. 452 850-2. German SO, Berlin, Vladimir Ashkenazy.

Alemdar Karamanov is another recent discovery among Russian composers. Born in Simferopol in the Crimea (his father was Turkish), he studied in Moscow with Khrennikov and Kabalevsky. He is of a strongly religious temperament and his music found no favour with the Soviet regime, though he did earn the allegiance of Shostakovich, who hailed him as 'one of the most original and unique composers of our time'. In the early 1960s he returned to the Crimea, where he has lived almost as a recluse.

The present symphonies come from a cycle of six (Nos. 18–23) on the theme of the Apocalypse, written between 1976 and 1980. Nos. 20 and 23 on the Olympia disc were recorded in Moscow in 1982, when their Christian programme was disguised. No. 23 or *I am Jesus* was re-titled *Risen from the ashes*. The music has a certain ecstatic voluptuousness that is reminiscent of Scriabin, but there are also touches of Shostakovich, Rachmaninov and Glière. Karamanov is very imaginative, though a streak of sentimentality comes to the surface – fairly often in the case of No. 20. The Decca performances and recording are vastly superior and make a distinct first choice. The USSR Symphony Orchestra produce rather crude tone at times and there are moments when the wind intonation is flawed. There is a certain pervading sameness about the hot-house atmosphere of this writing and the Szymanowski-like textures, and all three symphonies sound very similar. One wonders how well they will wear on repetition. There is, however, no question as to their interest, and Ashkenazy draws very convincing playing from his fine Berlin orchestra.

Kern, Jerome (1885–1945)

Overtures: (i) *The Cat and the fiddle; The Girl from Utah; Have a heart; Leave it to Jane; O, Lady! Lady!;* (ii) *Show Boat;* (i) *Sitting pretty; Sweet Adeline; Very warm for May;* (i, iii) Film music: *Swing Time* (suite).

(B) ** EMI forte Dig. CZS5 68589-2 [CDFB 68589] (2). (i) Nat. PO; (ii) L. Sinf.; (iii) Ambrosian Ch.; McGlinn – GERSHWIN: *Broadway and film music* **(*); PORTER: *Overtures.* ***

These Jerome Kern overtures, recorded from the original band-parts of musicals dating from between 1914 (*The Girl from Utah*) and 1939 (*Very warm for May*), are musically unimpressive. They are all played with an infectious sense of style, but really memorable tunes are thin on the ground. In *Sweet Adeline*, instead of his own material, Kern uses a pot-pourri of period songs from the 1890s, including *Daisy, Daisy* and *The Band played on*. By far the most attractive music comes in the film score from *Swing Time*, which includes *The way you look tonight*. For this reissue, the *Overture* from McGlinn's complete recording of *Showboat* has been added, but that is not much more than a pot-pourri.

Songs from musicals: *Centennial Summer: All through the day. Cover Girl: Long ago and far away. High, Wide and Handsome: The folks who live on the hill. Lady be Good: The last time I saw Paris. Music in the Air: The song is you. Roberta: Yesterdays; Smoke gets in your eyes. Sally: Look for the silver lining. Show Boat: Can't help lovin' dat man. Swing Time: The way you look tonight. Very warm for May: All the things you are. You were never Lovelier: I'm old fashioned.*

*** EMI (SIS) Dig. CDC7 54527-2 [id.]. Dame Kiri Te Kanawa, L. Sinf., Jonathan Tunick.

Kiri Te Kanawa proves completely at home in these luscious and life-enhancing Kern favourites. Her rich vocal line is matched by a nice feeling for the wittier lyrics. But it's the tunes that count, and she revels in them. So does Jonathan Tunick, who has scored the accompaniments; and the London Sinfonietta obviously enjoy themselves too, yet there is also a sense of sophistication and style. Excellent recording.

Showboat (complete recording of original score).

❁ *** EMI Dig. CDS7 49108-2 (3) [Ang. A23 49108]. Von Stade, Hadley, Hubbard, O'Hara, Garrison, Burns, Stratas, Amb. Ch., L. Sinf., John McGlinn.

In faithfully following the original score, this superb set at last does justice to a musical of the 1920s which is both a landmark in the history of Broadway and musically a work of strength and imagination hardly less significant than Gershwin's *Porgy and Bess* of a decade later. The original, extended versions of important scenes are included, as well as various numbers written for later productions. As the heroine, Magnolia, Frederica von Stade gives a meltingly beautiful performance, totally in style, bringing out the beauty and imagination of Kern's melodies, regularly heightened by wide intervals to make those of most of his Broadway rivals seem flat. The London Sinfonietta play with tremendous zest and feeling for the idiom; the Ambrosian Chorus sings with joyful brightness and some impeccable American accents. Opposite von Stade, Jerry Hadley makes a winning Ravenal, and Teresa Stratas is charming as Julie, giving a heartfelt performance of the haunting number, *Bill* (words by P. G. Wodehouse). Above all, the magnificent black bass, Bruce Hubbard, sings *Ol' man river* and its many reprises with a firm resonance to have you recalling the wonderful example of Paul Robeson, but for once without hankering after the past. Beautifully recorded to bring out the piece's dramatic as well as its musical qualities, this is a heart-warming issue.

Ketèlbey, Albert (1875–1959)

The Adventurers: overture; Bells across the meadow; Caprice pianistique; Chal Romano; The Clock and the Dresden figures; Cockney suite, excerpts: *Bank holiday; At the Palais de Danse.*

In a Monastery garden; In the moonlight; In a Persian market; The Phantom melody; Suite romantique; Wedgwood blue.
** Marco Polo Dig. 8.223442 [id.]. Slovak Philharmonic Male Ch., Slovak RSO (Bratislava), Adrian Leaper.

The Marco Polo collection has the advantage of modern digital recording and a warm concert-hall acoustic, and the effect is very flattering to *In a Monastery garden*. Adrian Leaper's performance is romantically spacious and includes the chorus. If elsewhere his characterization is not always as apt as Lanchbery's, this is still an agreeable programme. It offers several novelties and, though some of these items (for instance *The Adventurers overture*) are not vintage Ketèlbey, there is nothing wrong with the lively Slovak account of the closing *In a Persian market*, again featuring the chorus.

'Appy 'Ampstead; Bells across the meadows; In a Chinese temple garden; In a monastery garden; In a Persian market; In the mystic land of Egypt; The Phantom melody; Sanctuary of the heart; Wedgwood blue.
(M) *** Decca 444 786-2 [id.]. RPO & chorus, Eric Rogers – *Concert of gypsy violin encores:* Josef Sakonov, L. Festival O. ***

Eric Rogers and his orchestra present the more famous pieces with both warmth and a natural feeling for their flamboyant style, while *Wedgwood blue* is so much the epitome of a salon piece that it becomes a caricature of itself. But in its way it is fetching enough; and the tunes throughout come tumbling out, vulgar but irresistible when played so committedly. The birds twittering in the monastery garden make perfect 'camp' but the playing is straight and committed, and the larger-than-life Phase Four recording suits the music admirably. Moreover it was a happy idea to couple this programme with a collection of Hungarian gypsy fireworks and other favourite lollipops, played with great panache by Josef Sakonov – see Concerts section, below.

Bells across the meadow; Chal Romano (Gypsy lad); The Clock and the Dresden figures; In a Chinese temple garden; In a monastery garden; In a Persian market; In the moonlight; In the mystic land of Egypt; Sanctuary of the heart.
(B) *** CfP CD-CFP 4637; [id.]. Vernon Midgley, Jean Temperley, Leslie Pearson (piano), Amb. S., Philh. O, Lanchbery – LUIGINI: *Ballet Egyptien.* ***

A splendid collection in every way. John Lanchbery uses every possible resource to ensure that, when the composer demands spectacle, he gets it. *In the mystic land of Egypt*, for instance, uses soloist and chorus in canon in the principal tune (and very fetchingly too). In the *Monastery garden* the distant monks are realistically distant, in *Sanctuary of the heart* there is no mistaking that the heart is worn firmly on the sleeve. The orchestral playing throughout is not only polished but warm-hearted – the middle section of *Bells across the meadow*, which has a delightful melodic contour, is played most tenderly and loses any hint of vulgarity. Yet when vulgarity is called for, it is not shirked – only it's a stylish kind of vulgarity! The recording is excellent, full and brilliant.

Khachaturian, Aram (1903–78)

Cello concerto in E min.
*** Chandos Dig. CHAN 8579 [id.]. Wallfisch, LPO, Thomson – GLAZUNOV: *Chant du ménestrel;* KABALEVSKY: *Cello concerto No.2.* ***
(*) BIS CD 719 [id.]. Mats Lindström, Gothenburg SO, Ashkenazy (with RACHMANINOV: *Vocalise* *) – KABALEVSKY: *Cello concerto.* **(*)

Khachaturian's *Cello concerto* of 1946 has some sinuous Armenian local colour for its lyrical ideas, but none of the thematic memorability of the concertos for violin and piano and the *Gayaneh ballet* score, on which Khachaturian's reputation must continue to rest. Raphael Wallfisch plays with total commitment and has the benefit of excellent and sympathetic support. The recording is of the usual high standard we have come to expect from Chandos.

The combined concentration of Lindström and Ashkenazy prevents the writing from sounding too inflated. The recording is a bit over-resonant, but otherwise faithful and well balanced. As an encore we are given a fine if restrained account of Rachmaninov's *Vocalise*. An enjoyable if not, in the last resort, memorable coupling.

Cello concerto in E min.; Concerto-rhapsody for cello and orchestra in D min.
**(*) Olympia Dig. OCD 539 [id.]. Marina Tarasova, Russian SO, Veronica Dudarova.

The *Concerto-rhapsody for cello and orchestra in D minor* comes from 1963 and was first given by Rostropovich in London. Marina Tarasova plays both works with great eloquence and expressive vehemence; she has a big tone and impeccable technique. The orchestral playing is gutsy and sturdy without, perhaps, the finesse that might have toned down some of the garishness of the orchestral colours. The recording is bright and breezy – not worth a three-star grading and nor is the orchestral contribution, though Tarasova certainly is.

Flute concerto (arr. Rampal/Galway); *Gayaneh: Sabre dance. Masquerade: Waltz. Spartacus: Adagio of Spartacus and Phrygia.*

*** RCA Dig. 07863 57010-2. Galway, RPO, Myung-Whun Chung.

Khachaturian's *Flute concerto* is a transcription of the *Violin concerto*; Galway has prepared his own edition of the solo part. Needless to say, the solo playing is peerless; if in the finale even Galway cannot match the effect Oistrakh makes with his violin, the ready bravura is sparklingly infectious. As encores, he offers three of Khachaturian's most famous melodies.

Piano concerto in D flat.

❁ (M) (**(*)) RCA mono GD 60921. William Kapell, Boston SO, Koussevitzky – LISZT: *Mephisto waltz* (**(*)); PROKOFIEV: *Piano concerto No. 3.* (**(*)) ❁

(M) **(*) Hyperion Dig. CDA 66293 [id.]. Servadei, LPO, Giunta – BRITTEN: *Piano concerto.* **(*)

(i) *Piano concerto in D flat. Dance suite; Polka; Waltz* (both for wind band).

*** ASV Dig. CDDCA 964 [id.]. (i) Dora Serviarian-Kuhn; Armenian PO, Tjeknavorian.

(i) *Piano concerto in D flat; Gayaneh* (ballet) *suite; Masquerade: suite.*

**(*) Chandos Dig. CHAN 8542 [id.]. (i) Orbelian, SNO, Järvi.

The Armenian partnership of Dora Serviarian-Kuhn and Loris Tjeknavorian provides a clear first recommendation for Khachaturian's somewhat uneven *Piano concerto*, easily the finest account to have appeared on disc since the pioneering versions of William Kapell and Moura Lympany. The sinuous poetry of the lyrical Armenian folk-themes is well caught, particularly in the *Andante*, where the conductor judiciously balances the flexatone so that it adds a whistling edge to the texture without seeming too prominent. The Russian dance finale has plenty of dash, but what makes the performance individual is the sense of quixotic fantasy Serviarian-Kuhn brings to her cadential bravura. The bright piano-timbre and comparatively lean orchestral textures are not a disadvantage in a work that can too easily sound inflated. The other pieces on the ASV disc are very slight but lively enough; easily the most memorable item is the second *Uzbek dance* in the *Dance suite*, quite extended and touchingly atmospheric.

It is difficult to imagine a better-played account of the *Piano concerto* than that by William Kapell and the Boston Symphony under Koussevitzky (though not so hard to imagine better recorded sound). This incandescent performance, which Kapell recorded in his early twenties, should persuade even those who normally find the Khachaturian concerto irredeemably cheap and tawdry. Koussevitzky gets stunning results from the orchestra and Kapell's virtuosity and delicacy are remarkable. Even if the sound calls for lots of tolerance (the recording dates from 1946), the performance soon has a mesmeric effect.

The Chandos recording is splendid technically, well up to the standards of the house. Constantin Orbelian, an Armenian by birth, plays brilliantly and Järvi achieves much attractive lyrical detail. Overall it is a spacious account, and though the finale has plenty of gusto, the music-making seems just a shade too easygoing in the first movement. The couplings, sumptuously played, are both generous and appealing.

Annette Servadei makes up in clarity and point for a relative lack of weight in the outer movements, which she takes at speeds marginally slower than usual. The slow movement brings hushed and intense playing, sympathetically supported by the LPO under Joseph Giunta in a digital recording that is well balanced and unaggressive. However, ideally this work needs a stronger grip than these artists exert – the first movement in particular could do with greater thrust.

(i) *Piano concerto in D flat;* (ii) *Violin concerto in D min.;* (iii) *Masquerade suite;* (iv) *Symphony No. 2.*

(B) **(*) Decca Double 448 252-2 (2) [id.]. (i) De Larrocha, LPO, Frühbeck de Burgos; (ii) Ricci, LPO, Fistoulari; (iii) LSO, Stanley Black; (iv) VPO, composer.

The key performance here is the composer's own – of the *Second Symphony*. His advocacy is passionate and the recording is spectacular (although the CD remastering does not help its garish qualities). The slow movement of the *Piano concerto* as interpreted by a Spanish pianist and a Spanish conductor sounds evocatively like Falla, and the finale is also infectiously jaunty. Not so the first movement, which is disappointingly slack in rhythm at a dangerously slow tempo. Ricci is a good deal more consistent in the *Violin concerto*. He does not supply quite the demonic energy which the outer movements ideally call for, but his lyrical approach has its own attractions, and the closing pages of the slow movement are wonderfully atmospheric. The late-1950s recording does not have the projection we would expect today, but Ricci's fine playing is well focused. The *Masquerade suite* is consistently alive and colourful and is vividly if forwardly recorded.

Violin concerto in D min.

*** Chandos Dig. CHAN 8918 [id.]. Lydia Mordkovitch, SNO, Järvi - KABALEVSKY: *Violin concerto.* ***

(*) EMI Dig. CDC7 47087-2 [id.]. Perlman, Israel PO, Mehta (with TCHAIKOVSKY: *Méditation* *).

(i) *Violin concerto in D min.; Gayaneh* (extended suite); *Masquerade suite.*

(***) EMI mono CDC5 55035-2 [id.]. (i) David Oistrakh; Philh. O, composer.

David Oistrakh's EMI mono recording of the *Violin concerto* was made in the Kingsway Hall in 1954. It has the advantage of first-class recording, and such is the freshness and power of the performance that one adjusts almost immediately to the absence of stereo, for the sound is well balanced and spacious. The couplings on EMI are welcome, and again no apologies have to be made for the bright EMI recording with its attractive ambience. The *Masquerade suite* and the eight best numbers from *Gayaneh* bring a refreshing sense of newness and discovery: the lyrical music is full of atmosphere, finding delicacy as well as warmth, while the famous *Sabre dance* bursts at the seams with energy.

Among recent performances of this attractively inventive concerto, Lydia Mordkovitch is probably the most competitive. She plays with real abandon and fire, and Chandos balance her and the orchestra in a thoroughly realistic perspective. This new version has far superior sound to Oistrakh on Chant du Monde (see below).

Perlman's performance sparkles too – indeed it is superb in every way, lyrically persuasive in the *Andante* and displaying great fervour and rhythmic energy in the finale. He is well accompanied by Mehta (who nevertheless does not match the composer's feeling for detail). However, on CD one's ear is drawn to the very forward balance of the soloist, and the generally bright lighting becomes rather fierce at the opening tutti of the finale – the comparatively dry Israeli acoustic does not provide an ideal bloom on the music-making. The coupling is attractive but offers very short measure.

(i; ii) *Concert rhapsody for cello and orchestra*; (i; iii) *Concert rhapsody for violin and orchestra*; (i; iv) *Violin concerto in D min.*; (v) *Gayaneh* (ballet): excerpts. *Spartacus* (ballet): *Adagio. Symphony No. 1 in E min.*

(N) (B) **(*) BMG/Melodiya Twofer 74321 59056-2 (2) [id.]. (i) USSR RTV Large SO; with (ii) Karine Georgian; (ii) Nicolai Petrov; (iv) David Oistrakh; (v) USSR SO; all cond. composer.

This music is of uneven quality, but with all of it conducted by the composer, and vividly if sometimes coarsely recorded, this Melodiya 'Twofer' is worth considering. The highlight is of course, the inspired *Violin concerto* (1940) played by David Oistrakh, who gave the work its première and is its dedicatee. He is peerless in its performance, not only in projecting its very Russian bravura, but also in his melting phrasing and timbre in the sinuous secondary theme of the first movement (which returns in the exhilarating finale) and in the equally haunting melody of the *Andante*. Indeed this performance is unlikely ever to be surpassed and fortunately the recording, if not entirely refined, is full, warmly atmospheric and well balanced.

The garish *Concert rhapsody for piano and orchestra* was revised in 1968 for Nicolai Petrov, who gives a barnstorming performance, creating torrential energy at the opening and in the motoric, overextended finale. It is a very noisy piece, but no one could say this performance is without vitality. The *Concert rhapsody for cello* (1963) was written for Rostropovich, and lends itself to the kind of passionate playing it receives here from the forwardly balanced Karine Georgian, full-bodied in tone and a convincing substitute for its dedicatee. Again tuttis are at times dissonantly noisy, and the piece is overextended (nearly 25 minutes). The composer is a convincing advocate of his *First Symphony*, and brings out its full colouring, so that while the first movement is inflated, the work is not short of ideas. Here the recording is fully acceptable. The *Gayaneh* excerpts are also strongly characterized, and the famous *Spartacus Adagio* makes an ardently expansive encore.

Gayaneh (ballet): complete final score.

(N) (B) **(*) BMG/Melodiya Twofer 74321 63459-2 (2) [id.]. USSR R & TV Large SO, Djansug Kakhidze.

Khachaturian's original full score for *Gayaneh*, dating from 1942, is perhaps his finest extended work. Fortunately Tjeknavorian made a complete recording of it for RCA, and this is in urgent need of reissue. The composer later reworked and added to the music in order to fit a new scenario (because the earlier narrative, with its ingenuous wartime moral tone, had become embarrassing to the Soviets). The fresh inspiration of the original is expanded and often vulgarized in the later version about love and jealousy among shepherds dwelling in the mountains. But plenty of striking ideas remain. This Russian recording from 1976 has great verve and energy but does not disguise the shallower invention and the inflation of the louder passages. Nevertheless the recording is vivid and, although brash, is not unacceptably so; and these performers know just how to present the folk dances. As a 'Twofer' it is good value.

Gayaneh (ballet): extended suite.

(M) **(*) Mercury (IMS) 434 323-2 [id.]. LSO, Dorati – SHOSTAKOVICH: *Symphony No. 5.* **(*)

Dorati understands this music as well as anyone, and his *Sabre dance* has plenty of energy; and the other dances admirably celebrate Khachaturian's local colour. The 1960 Mercury recording is brilliant, with a tendency to fierceness in the strings, which suits the music well enough. There are eight items here; Dorati omits *Gayaneh's Adagio*.

Gayaneh (ballet): *suite; Masquerade: suite; Spartacus* (ballet): *suite.*

**(*) ASV Dig. CDDCA 773. Armenian PO,

Tjeknavorian – IPPOLITOV-IVANOV: *Caucasian sketches*. ***

Gayaneh: suite; Spartacus: suite.
(M) **(*) Decca 417 737-2. VPO, composer – PROKOFIEV: *Romeo and Juliet*. ***

The composer's own first selection on Decca was recorded in 1962 and offers five items from *Gayaneh* and four from *Spartacus*. Khachaturian achieves a brilliant response from the VPO and everything is most vivid, notably the famous *Adagio* from *Spartacus*, which is both expansive and passionate. It is a pity that the Decca remastering process has brought everything into such strong focus; the massed violins now have an added edge and boldness of attack, at the expense of their richness of timbre.

The Armenians clearly relish the explosive energy of this music. The *Masquerade suite* relies rather more on charm for its appeal, but Tjeknavorian and his players bring a determined gusto, even to the *Waltz* and certainly to the ebullient closing *Galop*. Then the vibrant Spartacus and his ardent lover Phrygia come on stage with a great flair of passion in a melody that is justly famous. One wishes the recording were more sumptuous here, but for the most part its burnished primary colours suit the dynamic orchestral style.

Gayaneh (ballet): highlights; *Spartacus* (ballet): highlights.
(B) *** CfP CD-CFP 4634. LSO, composer (with GLAZUNOV: *The Seasons: Autumn:* Philh. O, Svetlanov ***).

The composer's 1977 pairing for EMI of selections from his two famous ballets offers one more item from *Gayaneh* than on his earlier (1962) Decca coupling. The EMI sound, obviously more modern than the Decca, is a shade reverberant for the more vigorous numbers, but the present remastering presents a firmer focus than on LP. The effect is realistically spectacular with full, rich strings so that the famous *Adagio of Spartacus and Phrygia* expands opulently as well as ardently. The LSO play excitingly throughout. There is a gorgeous response from the violins in the extra item, called *Invention*, from *Gayaneh*. The inclusion of *Autumn*, the most memorable section of Glazunov's *Seasons* – its vigorously thrusting string theme stirringly conducted by Svetlanov – increases the appeal of this CD. At bargain price it is now a best buy for those wanting a suite from the two Khachaturian ballets.

Greeting overture; Festive poem; Lermontov suite; Ode in memory of Lenin; Russian fantasy.
** ASV Dig. CDDCA 946 [id.]. Armenian PO, Tjeknavorian.

Although it has plenty of characteristic Armenian colour, most of this music is routine Khachaturian, or worse: the *Festive poem* (at nearly 20 minutes) is far too inflated for its content, and the *Ode to Lenin* is an all too typical Soviet tribute. The sub-Rimskian finale of the *Lermontov suite* is by far the best movement. The *Russian fantasy* uses an agreeable folk-like melody, but we hear it repeated too often before the final quickening. Good performances, but the resonant recording is acceptable rather than sparkling.

Masquerade suite.
(N) (M) *** RCA 09026 63302-2 [id.]. RCA Victor SO, Kiril Kondrashin – KABALEVSKY: *The Comedians suite*; RIMSKY-KORSAKOV: *Capriccio espagnol*; TCHAIKOVSKY: *Capriccio italien*. *** ✿

Kondrashin certainly knows how to play this music, with warmth as well as sparkle, and even a touch of romantic elegance when Oscar Shumsky plays the violin solo in the *Nocturne*. Yet the final *Galop* is as roisterous as one could wish. The resonant recording gives the orchestra a pleasing ambience.

Spartacus (ballet): *suites Nos. 1–3.*
*** Chandos Dig. CHAN 8927 [id.]. RSNO, Neeme Järvi.

The ripe lushness of Khachaturian's scoring in *Spartacus* narrowly skirts vulgarity. Järvi and the RSNO clearly enjoy the music's tunefulness and primitive vigour, while the warmly resonant acoustics of Glasgow's Henry Wood Hall bring properly sumptuous orchestral textures, smoothing over the moments of crudeness without losing the Armenian colouristic vividness.

Symphonies Nos. 1 in E min.; 3 in C (Symphonic poem).
*** ASV Dig. CDDCA 858 [id.]. Armenian PO, Loris Tjeknavorian.

Symphony No. 1 in E min.; (i) *Masquerade suite.*
** Russian Disc RDCD11005 [id.]. Moscow R. SO, Alexander Gauk; (i) composer.

The *First Symphony* was Khachaturian's exercise on graduating from Miaskovsky's class in 1934. It is far from negligible and in some ways is superior to some of his later work – certainly to the bombastic *Third*. Now there are two recordings: a modern account from Armenia under Tjeknavorian which enjoys the advantage of good digital recording, and an older one from the redoubtable Alexander Gauk, made in the late 1950s, whose sonic limitations may deter some enthusiasts. It does, however, have the advantage of the composer's performance of the *Masquerade* suite, recorded in stereo. Gauk keeps a stronger grip on proceedings than Tjeknavorian, but the better technical quality will doubtless be more widely preferred. The Armenian orchestra play well for Tjeknavorian, and his is the safer recommendation.

Symphony No. 2 in E min. (The Bell); Battle of Stalingrad (suite).

**(*) ASV Dig. CDDCA 859 [id.]. Armenian PO, Loris Tjeknavorian.

Symphony No. 2 (original version); *Gayaneh: suite* (excerpts).

*** Chandos Dig. CHAN 8945 [id.]. RSNO, Järvi.

The *Second Symphony* comes from 1943 but the composer subsequently made a number of revisions, the last in 1969, which Tjeknavorian has recorded. It acquired its nickname, '*The Bell*', because of a motive heard on tubular bells, and in the slow movement makes fascinating use of the *Dies irae*. Neeme Järvi and his Scottish forces give a very fine account of themselves and they enjoy the benefit of a superb recording. It runs to some 51 minutes, while Tjeknavorian's account of the final revision prunes the score down to 42 minutes 45 seconds. The suite from *The Battle of Stalingrad* is taken from a score composed for a patriotic film and is empty and inflated.

(i) *Symphony No. 3 (Symphonic poem). Triumphal poem.*

*** Chandos Dig. CHAN 9321 [id.]. BBC PO, Fedor Glushchenko, (i) with Simon Lindley. IPPOLITOV-IVANOV: *Caucasian sketches.* ***

If the *Third Symphony* was as strong on musical substance as it is on decibels, it would be something to reckon with. But, alas, it is garish and empty; there are no fewer than eighteen trumpets in all! Analgesics and earplugs will be in brisk demand in its vicinity. The BBC Philharmonic, spurred on by their Russian conductor, play as if they believe in it, and the Chandos recording is in the demonstration category. The three stars are for the performance and the recording – not for the music!

The Valencian Widow (incidental music): *suite; Gayaneh* (ballet): *suite No. 2.*

*** ASV Dig. CDDCA 884 [id.]. Armenian PO, Loris Tjeknavorian (with TJEKNAVORIAN: *Danses fantastiques* **(*)).

Khachaturian's early suite from his incidental music to the Spanish comedy, *The Valencian Widow* (1940), is probably his first major score and, brimming over with striking tunes as it is, one is surprised that it has not been discovered by the gramophone before this. This is the Khachaturian of *Gayaneh*, so the coupling of seven lesser-known excerpts from that fine ballet score is very appropriate. Tjeknavorian and his orchestra play this music with great spirit and relish its Armenian flavours; they are equally at home in Tjeknavorian's own suite of *Danses fantastiques*, full of energy and colour if essentially sub-Khachaturian. Splendidly vivid, yet spacious sound.

Clarinet trio.

(B) *** HM Musique d'Abord Dig.HMA 1901419 [id.]. Walter Boeykens Ens. – PROKOFIEV: *Overture on Jewish themes* etc. ***

Khachaturian's *Clarinet trio* is a slight but pleasing work, full of sinuous Armenian melodic lines. With a *Moderato* finale (in some ways the most striking movement, with the central dance section rather soberly framed), it is without the hyperbole which often characterizes this composer's orchestral writing. It is very well played and recorded.

PIANO MUSIC

10 Children's pieces; 2 Pieces; Poem; Sonata; Sonatina; Toccata; Waltz (from *Masquerade*).

**(*) Olympia Dig. OCD 423 [id.]. Murray McLachlan.

Apart from the *Toccata* (1932), which is a frequent encore, Khachaturian's piano music rarely features in piano recitals. At 80 minutes, this CD offers all of it with the exception of the *Scenes from childhood* and the *Recitative and fugues*. The early pieces, *Poem* (1927) and the *Valse-Caprice* and *Dance* (1926), are much like the *Toccata*, pretty empty, but the later pieces, including the *Sonatina* (1959), the *Ten Children's pieces* (1964) and the *Sonata* (1961), are worth a hearing, even though they are limited in range and rely on a small vocabulary of musical devices. Murray McLachlan is a persuasive guide. His recording, made at All Saints' Church, Petersham, is eminently serviceable though there are times when the attentions of a tuner would not have come amiss (particularly in the garrulous first movement of the *Sonata*).

Klami, Uuno (1900–61)

Kalevala suite, Op. 23; Karelian rhapsody, Op. 15; Sea pictures.

**(*) Chandos Dig. CHAN 9268 [id.]. Iceland SO, Sakari.

The *Kalevala suite* is Klami's best-known work but, like the other two pieces on this disc, it is highly derivative. Ravel and Schmitt mingle with Falla, Sibelius and early Stravinsky; while there are some imaginative and inspired passages (such as the opening of the *Terheniemi* or Scherzo), there is some pretty empty stuff as well. The performances under Petri Sakari are very good indeed. Playback level needs to be high if the recording is to be heard to anywhere near best advantage; there is good perspective and a wide dynamic range.

Lemminkäinen's island adventures; (i) *Song of Lake Kuujärvi; Whirls: suites Nos. 1 & 2.*

*** BIS Dig. CD 656 [id.]. (i) Esa Ruuttunen; Lahti SO, Osmo Vänskä.

Klami was a master of orchestral colour, as one might expect from a composer who had the benefit of Ravel's criticism. *Lemminkäinen's island adventures* dates from 1934 and is more Sibelian than is usual with this composer, but its musical substance does not really sustain its length. There is quite a lot of Prokofiev and Shostakovich in the ballet, *Whirls*, and in *Song of Lake Kuujärvi*, and greater depth in the orchestral song. The performances are good and Esa Ruuttunen is an excellent baritone, and the recording offers wide dynamic range and natural perspective.

Symphony No. 2, Op. 35; Symphonie enfantine, Op. 17.
** Ondine Dig. ODE 858-2 [id.]. Tampere PO, Ollila.

Uuno Klami's musical sympathies were predominantly Gallic. Best known for his *Kalevala suite*, which Petri Sakari and the Iceland Orchestra have recorded for Chandos, Klami also composed two symphonies, the second of which he finished at the war's end in 1945. If its tone is predominantly post-romantic in character, its musical coherence is less than impressive. It is stronger on rhetoric than on substance. The *Symphonie enfantine* is a slighter piece from the 1920s, heavily indebted to Ravel, and rather delightful. Though he may be of peripheral importance, Klami's representation on CD is far from negligible, and Tuomas Ollila and the Tampere Philharmonic effectively broaden our picture of him. The Ondine engineers produce sound of exemplary clarity and naturalness.

Kodály, Zoltán (1882–1967)

Concerto for orchestra; Dances of Galánta; Dances of Marosszék; Háry János: suite; Symphony in C; Summer evening; Theatre overture; Variations on a Hungarian folksong (The Peacock).
(B) *** Double Decca 443 006-2 (2) [id.]. Philh. Hungarica, Antal Dorati.

This is all music which, though it is always beautifully written and often colourful, is not always as cogent as it might be. The more ambitious pieces like the *Concerto for orchestra* and the three-movement *Symphony in C* are certainly enjoyable, but they lack the sharpness of inspiration that pervades the music of Kodály's friend Bartók. The *Symphony* comes from the composer's last years and lacks real concentration and cohesion. Even so, in Dorati's hands the passionate *Andante* is strong in gypsy feeling and the jolly, folk-dance finale, if repetitive, is colourful and full of vitality. *Summer evening*, too, is warmly evocative, but in the *Theatre overture*, brightly and effectively scored, the invention is thin. The 1973 sound remains of vintage quality and the CD transfers are first rate.

Dances of Galánta; Dances of Marosszék.
(B) **(*) Sony SBK 62404 [id.]. Phd. O, Ormandy (with JANACEK: *Sinfonietta; Taras Bulba* **).

(i) *Dances of Galánta; Dances of Marosszék;* (ii) *Háry János: suite.*
(B) *** EMI CfP CD-CFP 6029. LPO, Walter Susskind.
(M) *** Mercury (IMS) 432 005-2 [id.]. (i) Philharmonia Hungarica; (ii) Minneapolis SO, Dorati – BARTOK: *Hungarian sketches* etc. ***

Dances from Galánta; Dances from Marosszék; Háry János suite; (i) *Psalmus Hungaricus, Op. 13.*
(N) (M) *** DG mono/stereo 457 745-2 [id.]. Berlin R.I.A.S., Fricsay, with (i) Ernst Haefliger, St Hedwig's Cathedral Ch.

Dances of Galánta; Dances of Marosszék; Háry János suite; Variations on a Hungarian folksong (The Peacock).
*** Decca (IMS) Dig. 444 322-2 [id.]. Montreal SO, Charles Dutoit.

Dances of Galánta; Háry János: suite.
*** Delos Dig. DE 3083 [id.]. Seattle SO, Gerard Schwarz – BARTOK: *Miraculous Mandarin.* **(*)

Dances of Galánta; Háry János suite; Variations on a Hungarian theme (The Peacock).
*** Telarc Dig. CD 80413. Atlanta SO, Yoel Levi.

Charles Dutoit, like Antal Dorati before him on Decca, offers the four most popular of Kodály's orchestral works in richly resonant, purposeful performances, with rhythms crisply sprung and with superb playing from the fine soloists of the Montreal orchestra. Though Dorati and his Hungarian players may at times sound more idiomatic, Dutoit and his Montreal players gain in brilliance, helped by recording of demonstration quality, outstanding even by Montreal standards. The *Peacock variations* benefit most of all from the opulence of the Montreal sound.

Susskind's triptych is one of the very best CDs in the Classics for Pleasure catalogue. It was recorded (with Brian Culverhouse the producer and Kenneth Williamson the engineer) in Kingsway Hall in 1977. A famous bargain LP in its day, it has only recently appeared in this modern format. The transfer is in every way first class, and Susskind's attractive performances of Kodály's three most popular orchestral works are treated to sound of superb demonstration quality. In depth of focus and fidelity this not only compares with the best recordings from the 1970s but can upstage many modern, digital discs. Susskind's direction could be more resilient, yet he evokes a true Hungarian flavour (the cimbalom is most effectively balanced) and the playing of the LPO is excellent.

From sneeze to finale, the Minneapolis orchestral playing in the *Háry János suite* is crisp and vigorous; given the excellent 1956 Mercury stereo, Dorati went on to record the other two sets of dances with the Philharmonia Hungarica in 1958. The playing of the woodwind soloists in the slow dances is intoxicatingly seductive, and the power and punch of the climaxes come over with real Mercury fidelity. An outstanding disc, since the Bartók couplings are equally successful.

The Seattle Symphony Orchestra play Kodály's music with great vividness and warmth. The *Háry János suite* is more spaciously romantic in feeling than some versions – helped by the rich acoustics of Seattle Opera House – and there is less surface glitter. But *The Battle and defeat of Napoleon* and the *Entrance of the Emperor and his Court* have all the necessary mock-drama and spectacle, and it is good to hear the cimbalom again balanced so effectively within the orchestra. The *Galánta dances* have splendid dash. The recording is outstandingly real.

Ormandy and the Philadelphia Orchestra play these well-known sets of dances brilliantly and with characteristic panache. The 1962 recording too has been immeasurably improved and it is pity that the reissue is let down by the omission of the *Háry János suite*, recorded around the same time. Moreover there is no internal cueing.

Robert Shaw in his Telarc recordings has repeatedly demonstrated what a fine orchestra the Atlanta Symphony is, and here Yoel Levi carries on the good work in a coupling of Kodály's three most popular orchestral works. The digital recording is full and well balanced, and the performances are brilliant and persuasive, with some fine, sensitive playing from the wind principals in particular. The snag is that this issue comes into direct competition with the Decca versions of Dutoit and Dorati, both of which offer a bonus in an extra work, the *Marosszék dances*.

Fricsay's performances are crisp and exciting, the orchestra superbly on its toes, a notable passage being the beautifully managed horn solo in the central trio of the intermezzo in *Háry János*. The mono recording was demonstration-worthy in its day and is still pretty remarkable. The coupled performance of the *Psalmus Hungaricus* has characteristic electricity, and with fine soloists is effortlessly idiomatic and thrillingly alive. This disc is well chosen for DG's 'Originals'.

(i–iii; vi) *Háry János* (play with music): complete recording of music, with narration by Peter Ustinov; (iv) *The Peacock* (folksong for unaccompanied chorus); (ii; v–vi) *Psalmus Hungaricus;* (vi) *Variations on a Hungarian folksong (The Peacock).*

(M) **(*) Decca Double (IMS) 443 488-2 (2). (i) Olga Szönyi, Márgit László, Erszébet Komlössy, György Melis, Zsolt Bende, Lásló Palócz; (ii) Wandsworth School Boys' Ch.; (iii) Edinburgh Festival Ch.; (iv) London Symphony Ch.; (v) Lajos Kozma, Brighton Festival Ch.; (vi) LSO; all cond. Kertész.

All of Kodály's music for *Háry János* is included here, and the links are provided by Peter Ustinov in many guises. Whether the comedy stands the test of repetition is another matter, but it is good to have Kodály's full score, including a number of pieces as attractive as those in the well-known suite, and vocal versions of some that we know already. Superb recording. This Double Decca reissue also includes a much-valued performance of the *Psalmus Hungaricus*, Kodály's most vital choral work. The light tenor tone of Lajos Kozma is not ideal for the solo part, but again the authentic Hungarian touch helps. The *Peacock variations* make a marvellous display piece, and it was a happy idea to include the folksong itself, stirringly sung by the London Symphony Chorus. The CD transfers are first class throughout.

Háry János suite.

(B) *** Sony SBK 48162 [id.]. Cleveland O, Szell – MUSSORGSKY: *Pictures at an exhibition*; PROKOFIEV: *Lieutenant Kijé: suite.* ***

(BB) *** Naxos Dig. 8.550142; *4550142* [id.]. Hungarian State O, Mátyás Antal (with Concert: *'Hungarian festival'* ***).

(M) *** Decca Phase Four 448 947-2 [id.]. Netherlands R. O, Dorati – DVORAK: *Symphony No. 9.* ***

(M) (***) RCA mono GD 60279 [60279-2-RG]. NBC SO, Toscanini – DVORAK: *Symphony No. 9* (***); SMETANA: *Má Vlast: Vltava.* (**)

Szell – Budapest born – was in his element in *Háry János*. Superb Cleveland polish matches the vitality of the playing, with a humorous sparkle in Kodály's first two movements and the mock pomposity of the Napoleon episode wittily dramatized. The 1969 recording was one of the very finest from this source, bold with a too-forward cimbalom, but the engineers certainly capture the exhilaration of the playing in this way. The couplings are equally fine, and this is one of the very best of all the Szell/ Cleveland reissues on the Sony Essential Classics logo.

The Hungarian performance of the *Háry János suite* is also wonderfully vivid, with the cimbalom – here perfectly balanced within the orchestra – particularly telling. The grotesque elements of *The Battle and defeat of Napoleon* are pungently and wittily characterized and the *Entrance of the Emperor and his Court* also has an ironical sense of spectacle. The brilliant digital sound adds to the vitality and projection of the music-making, yet the lyrical music is played most tenderly.

The Decca recording too is exceptionally vivid and Dorati's direct manner produces the strongest musical characterization. The Phase Four techniques are not exaggerated and they do no harm to Kodály's bright orchestral colours.

There is nothing relaxed about Toscanini's view of *Háry János*. He seems not to realize that a joke is involved; but the intensity of the performance gives the music a new and bigger scale, whether appropriate or not.

(i) *Hungarian rondo. Summer evening; Symphony.*
**(*) ASV Dig. CDDCA 924 [id.]. (i) Christopher Warren-Green; Philh. O, Yondani Butt.

Nowadays Bartók completely overshadows his distinguished countryman so that we are apt to forget how good so much of Kodály's music is. The *Summer evening* is a beautiful piece – eminently well served by Yondani Butt. It comes with a well-characterized account of the *Symphony*, not more impressive than Dorati's version but, of course, a more up-to-date recording. Very good indeed, albeit not quite three-star.

Variations on a Hungarian folksong (The Peacock).
*** Decca Dig. 452 853-2 [id.]. VPO, Solti – ELGAR: *Enigma variations;* BLACHER: *Paganini variations.* ***

It is surprising that Solti waited over 40 years after his 1954 version with the LPO (in mono) before recording Kodály's colourful variations again. Though his interpretation of a fellow-Hungarian composer has altered less between recordings than the Elgar on this same fiftieth-anniversary disc, this performance too has extra warmth and subtlety, with the rhythmic verve just as sharply infectious as before, conveying joy. Vivid sound, capturing the warm acoustic of the Musikverein.

Intermezzo for string trio.
(N) *** ASV Dig. CD DCA 985 [id.]. Lyric Quartet – DOHNÁNYI: *String quartets Nos. 2 & 3.* ***

The *Intermezzo for string trio* is an early piece, dating from 1905, pleasant if not particularly individual. It makes a perfectly acceptable and appropriate makeweight to the two Dohnányi quartets.

(Unaccompanied) *Cello sonata, Op. 8; Cello sonata* (for cello and piano), *Op. 4.*
(B) *** HM Dig. HMA 1901325 [id.]. Lluís Claret, (i) with Rose-Marie Cabestany.

(Unaccompanied) *Cello sonata, Op. 8;* (i) *Cello sonata* (for cello & piano), *Op. 4; 3 Chorale preludes* (arr. from Bach, BWV 743, 747 & 762).
(BB) *** Naxos Dig. 8.553160 [id.]. Maria Kliegel; (i) with Jenö Jandó.

On the evidence of this record, the Andorran cellist, Lluís Claret, has a larger-than-life musical personality, and one is sorely tempted to use the word 'vintage' to describe his inspired performance of Op. 8. A memorably compulsive account of a work which, until now, Starker has made his own. Moreover the recording is real and tangible within a suitably open acoustic. Rose-Marie Cabestany joins Claret persuasively for the less ambitious but still impressive two-movement *Sonata for cello and piano*, Op. 4, and proves an excellent partner, so that this piece is by no means an anticlimax after the major work.

Maria Kliegel in Kodaly's magnificent solo *Cello sonata* offers a warm and fanciful performance, not quite as incisive as Claret's or Schiefen's on Arte Nova (see below) but just as powerful and rather more flowing. So in the long central slow movement Kliegel is not so daringly expansive or darkly tragic, but she is more easily lyrical. Jenö Jandó is an outstandingly sympathetic partner in the two-movement Op. 4 *Sonata*, a performance deeply introspective in the slow first movement and full of fantasy in the *Allegro con spirito* of the finale. The three *Chorale preludes* are romantic arrangements – with the cello generally underlining the chorale melodies – of organ pieces attributed to Bach but now thought spurious.

(Unaccompanied) *Cello sonata, Op.8;* (i) *Duo for violin and cello, Op. 7.*
*** Delos D/CD 1015 [id.]. Janos Starker, (i) Josef Gingold.
(BB) *** Arte Nova Dig. 74321 51623-2 [id.]. Guido Schiefen, (i) with Axel Strauss.

When, not long before the composer's death, Kodály heard Starker playing this *Cello sonata*, he apparently said: 'If you correct the ritard in the third movement, it will be the Bible performance.' The recording is made in a smaller studio than is perhaps ideal; the *Duo*, impressively played by Starker and Josef Gingold, is made in a slightly more open acoustic. There is a small makeweight in the form of Starker's own arrangement of the Bottermund *Paganini variations*.

Guido Schiefen gives a powerful, intense performance, fearless in attacking the bravura writing, with double-stopping clean and precise and with his full cello-tone made the more dramatic by the close recorded sound. Powerful and passionate as the outer movements are, the central *Adagio* at an exceptionally broad speed is particularly impressive in its hushed concentration. The *Duo*, written the previous year, receives an equally compelling performance, making the ideal coupling.

It is astonishing what full and rich sounds Kodály draws from just two instruments. Another outstanding bargain.

String quartet No. 2, Op. 10.
*** DG (IMS) Dig. 419 601-2. Hagen Qt – DVORAK: *String quartet No. 12* etc. ***
*** Testament SBT 1072 [id.]. Hollywood Qt – DVORAK ***; SMETANA: *Quartets.* (***)

The Hagen give a marvellously committed and beautifully controlled performance of the *Second* – indeed as quartet playing it would be difficult to surpass. In range of dynamic response and sheer beauty of sound, this is thrilling playing and welcome advocacy of a neglected but masterly piece. The recording is well balanced and admirably present.

Although American readers will know the Hollywood Quartet's account of this piece, it will be new to collectors on this side of the Atlantic. It was recorded in 1958 and, unlike the Dvořák and Smetana with which it is coupled, is in stereo. Once a frequent item on concert and radio programmes, the Kodály has become something of a rarity. The present performance can only be described as masterly, enhancing the attractions of an already excellent issue.

Missa brevis.
(M) **(*) EMI Dig. CDM5 65587-2. King's College, Cambridge, Ch., Cleobury; Stephen Lane – JANACEK: *Mass* etc. ***

The *Missa brevis*, as its subtitle, *In tempore belli*, suggests, was composed at the height of the Second World War; it was first conceived as an organ Mass; but in 1945, when the Russians were laying siege to Budapest, Kodály transcribed it for voices and organ, subsequently orchestrating it. It is one of Kodály's strongest and most deeply felt works, every bit as powerful as the *Psalmus Hungaricus*. Ferencsik's recording was of the orchestral version, whereas Stephen Cleobury gives it in its earlier form, as did Laszlo Heltay in the 1970s. Some of the treble lines could be more secure, but for the most part this is a good performance, even if it lacks the bite and intensity that Hungarian singers would bring to it.

Psalmus Hungaricus, Op. 13.
*** Chandos Dig. CHAN 9310 [id.]. Svensson, Copenhagen Boys' Ch., Danish Nat. R. Ch. & SO, Mackerras – JANACEK: *Glagolitic Mass.* ***
(N) *** Decca Dig. 458 929-2 [id.]. Daróczy, Agache, Hungarian Radio and TV Ch. and Children's Ch., Schola Cantorum Budapestiensis, Budapest Festival O, Sir Georg Solti – BARTOK: *Cantata profana*; WEINER: *Serenade.* ***

As the unusual but refreshing coupling for the Janáček *Mass*, the *Psalmus Hungaricus* is here infected with an element of wildness that sweeps away any idea of Kodály as a bland composer. As in the Janáček, the tenor Peter Svensson is an excellent, clear-toned and incisive soloist, if here rather more backwardly balanced. The glory of the performance lies most of all in the superb choral singing, full, bright and superbly disciplined, with the hushed pianissimos as telling as the great fortissimo outbursts. It is a mark of Mackerras's understanding of the music that the many sudden changes of mood sound both dramatic and natural. Full, warm and atmospheric recording, with plenty of detail.

Solti, in his very last recording sessions in Budapest, June 1997, paid tribute to all three of his principal teachers, Bartók, Kodály and Weiner. In representing Kodály with the *Psalmus Hungaricus* he was returning to a work he had first recorded right at the beginning of his recording career, offering a performance even warmer and more idiomatic, with incandescent choral singing, marred only by the unsteadiness of the tenor soloist.

Koechlin, Charles (1867–1961)

Les heures persanes, Op. 65.
*** Marco Polo Dig. 8.223504 [id.]. Reinland-Pfalz PO, Segerstam.

Koechlin's powers as an orchestrator are evident in these 16 exotic mood-pictures which were originally composed for the piano in 1913. They evoke a journey recorded by Pierre Loti in 1900. 'He who wants to come with me to see at Isfahan the season of roses should travel slowly by my side, in stages, as in the Middle Ages,' and the cynic might be tempted to say that we do. The work is generally slow-moving, but this music has tremendous atmosphere and exotic colours and the very titles of the movements (*Les collines au coucher de soleil*, *A l'ombre près de la fontaine marbre*, for example) conjure up some idea of its character. In the hands of Leif Segerstam and the Reinland-Pfalz Orchestra this music casts a powerful spell. It is also beautifully recorded.

The Jungle Book (Le livre de la Jungle).
*** Marco Polo Dig. 8.223484 [id.]. Reinland-Pfalz PO, Segerstam.

Koechlin's lifelong fascination for Kipling's *Jungle Book* is reflected in this extraordinary four-movement tone-poem whose composition extended over several decades. *La course de printemps*, Op. 95, the longest of them, is extraordinarily imaginative and pregnant with atmosphere: you can feel the heat and humidity of the rainforest and sense the presence of strange and menacing creatures. *La loi de la jungle* is the most static and the least interesting. Leif Segerstam is excellent in this repertoire and with his refined ear for texture distils a heady atmosphere and is beautifully recorded. Anyone with a feeling for the exotic will respond to this original and fascinating music.

Cello sonata, Op. 66; Chansons bretonnes, Op. 115.
(N) *** Hyperion Dig. CDA 66979 [id.]. Mats Lidström, Bengt Forsberg – PIERNE: *Cello sonata.* ***

Both works on this enterprising issue were composed at roughly the same time as the Debussy sonata. Koechlin's sonata is pensive and introspective, ruminative in character, and Mats Lidström and Bengt Forsberg give a cultured, finely controlled performance of compelling subtlety. The sound is natural and lifelike. Don't let the self-indulgent liner notes put you off. In every other respect this is a disc of quality.

Horn sonata, Op. 70; Morceau de lecture (for horn); *15 Pieces, Op. 180; Sonneries.*
*** ASV Dig. CDDCA 716 [id.]. Barry Tuckwell, Daniel Blumenthal.

Barry Tuckwell has discovered another composer who has a real facility for horn writing, understanding its historical evolution from hand-horn to the modern rotary-valved instrument, yet realizing, as did Britten in his *Serenade*, that with this instrument simplest is best. The *Sonata* is a richly conceived three-movement work, linked by its evocative opening idea. The *Morceau de lecture* is freer, more rhapsodic, immediately stretching up ecstatically into the instrument's higher tessitura. The 15 *Pieces* are delightful vignettes, opening with a rapturous evocation, *Dans la forêt romantique*. While some of them are skittish (notably the muted Scherzo (No. 4) or jolly *Allegro vivo* (No. 11)), many explore that special solemn melancholy which the horn easily discovers in its middle to lower register, as in Nos. 10 and 12 (both marked *doux*). Two others are for hunting horns, and they robustly use the open harmonics which are naturally out of tune (an effect Britten tried more sparingly), while the 11 brief *Sonneries* are all written for cors de chasse with a similar plangent effect when the tonality is imperfect. Many of the *Sonneries* are in two, three or four parts, which Tuckwell plays by electronic means. This is a collection to be dipped into rather than taken all at once, but Tuckwell's artistry sustains the listener's interest and the fine pianist, Daniel Blumenthal, makes the most of his rewarding part in the *Sonata*. The recording is excellent.

Kokkonen, Joonas (1921-96)

(i) *Cello concerto; Symphonic sketches; Symphony No. 4.*
*** BIS Dig. CD 468 [id.]. (i) Torleif Thedéen, Lahti SO, Osmo Vänskä.

The *Fourth Symphony* is the strongest work here: its ideas are symphonic, its structure organic and its atmosphere powerful. The *Cello concerto* is a lyrical and accessible piece, just a shade mawkish. The Swedish cellist, Torleif Thedéen, gives a performance of great restraint, mastery and sensitivity. Good orchestral playing and recording.

(i) *Sinfonia da camera*; *Il paesaggio*; (ii) '*. . . durch einen Spiegel . . .*' (iii) *Wind quintet.*
*** BIS Dig. CD 528 [id.]. (i; ii) Lahti SO; (i) Vänskä; (iii) Söderblom; (ii) with Tiensuu; (iii) Lahti Sinf. Wind Quintet.

Those coming new to Kokkonen's musical idiom should try the pretentiously titled but resourceful and imaginative '*. . . durch einen Spiegel . . .*', subtitled *Metamorphosis*, for twelve strings and harpsichord. There are some rewardingly individual sonorities. *Il paesaggio* is an evocative landscape study, and the earlier *Wind quintet* is a lively piece. The early *Sinfonia da camera* is grey general-purpose modern music deriving from Bartókian–Hindemithian roots. Very good performances and splendid recording.

Symphony No. 1; Music for string orchestra; (i) *The Hades of the birds* (song-cycle).
*** BIS Dig. CD 485 [id.]. Lahti SO, Söderblom; (i) Monica Groop.

The *Music for string orchestra* is a rather powerful piece lasting almost half-an-hour, well wrought and its invention finely sustained if slightly anonymous. The colourings are dark. *The Hades of the birds* is a short song-cycle, which shows Monica Groop's talents to strong effect, but it is the *First Symphony* which is the strongest piece on the disc. It is serious in purpose and as far as the orchestra is concerned shows considerable mastery of colour.

Symphony No. 2; Inauguratio; Erekhtheion (cantata); *The Last temptations* (opera): *Interludes.*
**(*) BIS Dig. CD 498 [id.]. Vihavainen, Grönroos, Akateeminen Laulu Ch., Lahti SO, Vänskä.

The *Second Symphony* is a work of some eloquence and its invention has a certain freshness and quality, even if it remains ultimately unmemorable. The interludes from his opera, *The Last temptations*, make a strong impression. Not an essential purchase.

Symphony No. 3; (i) *Opus sonorum;* (ii) *Requiem.*
*** BIS Dig. CD 508 [id.]. Lahti SO, Söderblom; (i) with Ilkka Sivonen; (ii) Iskoski, Grönroos, Savonlinna Op. Festival Ch.

Söderblom's account of the *Third Symphony* has detail and atmosphere, and the same must be said of the *Requiem*. In the *Opus sonorum*, written in reaction to the sight of the vast battery of percussion so common in the 1960s, Kokkonen assigns all the percussion part to a piano, played with great delicacy here.

(i) *Piano quintet; String quartets Nos. 1–3.*
*** BIS Dig. CD 458 [id.]. (i) Valsta; Sibelius Ac. Qt.

The *Quintet* is a slight but not unpleasing work; the *First Quartet*, which sounds like any chamber work of the period, has more gravitas. Like its companions it is very well played, but even such eloquent advocacy cannot disguise a certain facelessness. But three stars for the performers and the engineers.

The Last Temptations (opera): complete.
**(*) Finlandia/Warner 1576 51104-2 (2) [id.]. Auvinen, Ruohonen, Lehtinen, Talvela, Savonlinna Op. Festival Ch. & O, Söderblom.

The Last Temptations tells of a revivalist leader, Paavo Ruotsalainen, from the Finnish province of Savo and of his inner struggle to discover Christ. The opera is dominated by the personality of Martti Talvela, and its invention for the most part has a dignity and power that are symphonic in scale. All four roles are well sung, and the performance under Ulf Söderblom is very well recorded indeed.

Kolessa, Mykola (born 1903)

Symphony No. 1.
** ASV Dig. CDDCA 963 [id.]. Odessa PO, Hobart Earle – SKORYK: *Carpathian concerto* etc. **

Mykola Kolessa, now in his late nineties, is the grand old man of Ukrainian music. He studied in Prague with Novák and was active as conductor of the Lvov (spelt as Lviv throughout the notes and in the French and German translations). Bartók and the French music of the first half of the century were formative influences on Mykola Kolessa. The *First* of his two symphonies was composed in 1950 in the immediate wake of the Zhdanov affair, when any sense of harmonic adventure was discouraged. This piece at times sounds like Glière or Arensky. It is expertly written and is easy to listen to, but it could just as well have been composed in the 1890s. Very well played and recorded. The pieces by Kolessa's pupil, Myroslav Skoryk, are more interesting.

Koppel, Herman D. (born 1908)

Cello concerto, Op. 56.
*** BIS CD 80 [id.]. Erling Blondal Bengtsson, Danish Nat. RSO, Schmidt – NORHOLM: *Violin concerto.* ***

Herman D. Koppel's idiom stems from Stravinsky and Bartók, but the opening of his *Cello concerto* has something of the luminous quality of Tippett's *Midsummer Marriage*. Very good recording of an inventive and original piece that deserves to enter the wider international repertoire. It is more satisfying than either the Kokkonen or Sallinen concertos.

Kopylov, Aleksandr (1854–1911)

Concert overture in D min., Op. 31; Scherzo in A, Op. 10; Symphony in C min., Op. 14.
(N) *** ASV Dig. CD DCA 1013 [id.]. Moscow SO, Antonio de Almeida.

Aleksandr Kopylov, pupil of Rimsky-Korsakov in St Petersburg, was more of a teacher than a composer, but all three of these works, the sum total of Kopylov's orchestral music, will delight devotees of the Russian Romantics. The *Concert overture* has the strongest Russian flavour, with colourful themes and snapping rhythms in the main Allegro. The *Scherzo* too is fresh and open with well-contrasted themes. The *Symphony* is more like Balakirev watered down, beautifully made with clean-cut structures. Persuasive performances under Antonio de Almeida, in one of the last recordings he made before his untimely death.

Korngold, Erich (1897–1957)

(i) *Cello concerto in C, Op. 37;* (ii) *Piano concerto in C sharp for the left hand, Op. 17. Symphonic serenade for strings, Op. 39; Military march in B flat.*
*** Chandos Dig. CHAN 9508 [id.]. (i) Peter Dixon; (ii) Howard Shelley; BBC PO, Matthias Bamert.

The more one hears of Korngold's lesser-known music the more impressive he seems: 'more gold than corn' rather than the reverse. The least interesting piece is the *Cello concerto*, an adaptation of a short piece he composed in 1946 for the film *Deception* starring Bette Davis and Claude Rains. The work's première, incidentally, was given by Eleanor Aller, later of Hollywood Quartet fame. The *Concerto in C sharp for piano left hand* (1924) is an altogether different matter. Composed, like Ravel's concerto, Prokofiev's *Fourth* and the Strauss *Parergon*, for the one-armed pianist, Paul Wittgenstein, who had lost his right arm during the First World War, it is an extraordinarily imaginative and resourceful work. Although it springs from a post-Straussian world (Gary Graffman called it 'a keyboard *Salome*'), it is full of individual touches. Howard Shelley gives it a radiant performance and is given splendid support. To complaints that the *Military march* (1917) was rather fast, Korngold is said to have replied that it was intended to be played for the retreat! The *Symphonic serenade for strings* was composed after the Second World War and was premièred in 1950 by the Vienna Philharmonic and Furtwängler. It is a very beautiful (as well as beautifully crafted) work with a highly inventive Scherzo and an eloquent, rather Mahlerian slow movement. First-rate playing and opulent, well-balanced recording. Well worth exploring.

Violin concerto in D, Op. 35.
*** EMI CDC7 47846-2 [id.]. Perlman, Pittsburgh SO, Previn – GOLDMARK: *Concerto.* ***
*** Decca 452 481-2 [id.]. Chantal Juillet, Berlin RSO, Mauceri – KRENEK: *Violin concerto* ***; WEILL: *Violin concerto.* **
(BB) *** Naxos Dig. 8.553579 [id.]. Vera Tsu, Razumovsky Sinfonia, Yu Long – GOLDMARK: *Violin concerto.* ***

(i) *Violin concerto;* (ii) *Much Ado About Nothing* (suite), *Op. 11.*
*** DG Dig. 439 886-2 [id.]. Gil Shaham; (i) LSO, Previn; (ii) Previn (piano) – BARBER: *Violin concerto.* ***

The Korngold was written within five years of the Barber *Concerto* and makes a desirable coupling for it. Indeed the conjunction of Barber and Korngold works splendidly, when in the Barber the ripe performance brings out moments that are not too distant from the world of Hollywood music, and the Korngold then emerges as a central work in that genre. The Israeli violinist, Gil Shaham, gives a performance of effortless virtuosity and strong profile. Shaham may not have quite the flair and panache of the dedicatee, Jascha Heifetz, in his incomparable reading, but he is warmer and more committed than Itzakh Perlman in his Pittsburgh recording for EMI, again with Previn conducting. There is greater freshness and conviction than in the Perlman. The recording helps, far clearer and more immediate than Perlman's EMI. It is true that in his cooler way Perlman finds an extra tenderness in such passages as the entry of the violin in the slow movement, but Shaham and Previn together consistently bring out the work's sensuous warmth without making the result soupy. The suite from Korngold's incidental music to *Much Ado About Nothing* provides a delightful and apt makeweight, with Previn as pianist just as understanding and imaginative an accompanist and Shaham yearningly warm without sentimentality, clean and precise in attack.

Chantal Juillet concentrates on the poetry of the work in a much gentler treatment, and the natural balance given to the soloist by the Decca engineers in vivid sound enhances that. It may not be as passionate as its rivals, but it is certainly a valid view, no less moving. An imaginative and generous coupling, having violin concertos by two other Central European composers who found refuge in America.

Vera Tsu, born in Shanghai and then discovered by Isaac Stern and trained in America, is an outstanding soloist in a coupling which directly challenges the EMI disc from Itzhak Perlman. In every way this ripely romantic version of the Korngold is a match for that and other full-price rivals, thanks to Tsu's rich, ample tone and her flawless intonation, as well as her fearless attack in bravura writing. In the quality of sound the recording outshines most other versions, rich and free, both immediate and atmospheric, with fine dynamic range and with the Chinese conductor, Yu Long, drawing beautiful, refined playing from the Bratislava orchestra.

Sinfonietta, Op. 5; Sursum corda, Op. 13.
*** Chandos Dig. CHAN 9317 [id.]. BBC PO, Bamert.

Korngold's *Sinfonietta* is a product of his precocious boyhood, a substantial four-movement work, a symphony in all but name, betraying a prodigious technical expertise both in the management and organization of musical ideas and in the handling of the orchestra; and not only that, the ideas themselves are of real quality and individuality. At 43 minutes, it is an extraordinary achievement for a fourteen-year-old and in its way is comparable (though not quite, perhaps, in quality of inspiration) only with Mendelssohn in the *Octet* and *Midsummer Night's Dream* music – an adolescent composer springing as it were fully equipped on to the musical scene. When in 1938 Korngold was working against time to write the score for the Hollywood epic with Errol Flynn, *The Adventures of Robin Hood*, he thought back to the brilliant symphonic overture he had composed 18 years earlier, *Sursum corda*. The original virtuoso showpiece lasting 20 minutes is finer than one might expect, an extraordinarily sumptuous piece that in its wide range of moods keeps suggesting that it will turn into the *Pines of Rome*. There are alternative versions of the *Sinfonietta*, but the present performance by the BBC Philharmonic Orchestra under Matthias Bamert is a clear front-runner and the Chandos recording is altogether superb in terms of definition and opulence. A ripely enjoyable disc of beautifully played performances, and a valuable addition to the catalogue, with the sumptuous sound-picture a little distant.

Symphony in F sharp, Op. 40; (i) *Abschiedslieder, Op. 14.*
*** Chandos Dig. CHAN 9171 [id.]. (i) Linda Finnie; BBC PO, Downes.

The *Symphony* is a work of real imaginative power. It is scored for large forces – a big percussion section including piano, celeste, marimba, etc. – and the orchestra is used with resource and flair. A big, 50-minute work, its opening almost calls to mind Prokofiev's textures, though there is also a fair amount of Mahler. The BBC Philharmonic play with enthusiasm and sensitivity for Edward Downes. The *Abschiedslieder* are much earlier and were completed in 1920; there is a great deal of Strauss, Mahler and Zemlinsky here. Linda Finnie is a persuasive soloist, and the balance is eminently well judged. The Chandos recording is wide-ranging and lifelike.

(i) *Piano quintet in E, Op. 15;* (ii) *Suite for two violins, cello and piano left hand, Op. 23.*
(N) *** ASV Dig. CDDCA 1047 [id.]. (i) Jan Schmolk; (ii) Clare McFarlane; Schubert Ens. of London.

The *Piano quintet* was composed in 1921 in the immediate wake of *Die tote Stadt* when the already experienced composer was 24. It is powerfully wrought and superbly laid out for the medium, and rightly enjoyed much exposure in the 1920s. It became *Entartete Musik* when the Nazis came to power, and again succumbed to neglect when serialism and post-serialist music dominated the post-war scene. Its resurrection in this fine new recording is more than welcome, for it reaffirms the fertility of Korngold's imagination and the quality of his invention. The *Suite, Op. 23*, one of six works written for Paul Wittgenstein, has some splendid ideas: the third movement, *Grotesquerie*, is particularly striking. This performance is less larger-than-life than the rival account from Sony.

String sextet, Op.10.
*** Hyperion Dig. CDA 66425 [id.]. Raphael Ens. – SCHOENBERG: *Verklaerte Nacht.* ***

The Korngold *Sextet* is an amazing achievement for a seventeen-year-old. Not only is it crafted with musicianly assurance and maturity, it is also inventive and characterful. The Raphael Ensemble play it with great commitment and the Hyperion recording is altogether first class.

Suite for two violins, cello and piano left hand, Op. 23.
(N) *** Sony Dig. SK 48253 [id.]. Joseph Silverstein, Jaime Laredo, Yo-Yo Ma, Leon Fleischer – SCHMIDT: *Quintet for two violins, viola, cello and piano left hand.* ***

Having lain neglected for so long, the Op. 23 *Suite*, for the unusual combination of two violins, cello and piano left hand, has been taken out of the deep freeze and given a virtuosic performance by these distinguished players. Their Schmidt coupling, another work written for Wittgenstein, enhances the attractions of this well-recorded issue.

PIANO MUSIC

Fairytale pictures (Marchenbilder), Op. 3; 4 Little caricatures for children, Op.19; Don Quixote (suite); Much Ado About Nothing (incidental music): excerpts, *Op. 11; Tales of Strauss, Op. 11; 4 Waltzes; Die tote Stade: Pierrot's dance song.*
(N) (M) **(*) Carlton Dig. 30366 01102 [id.]. Ingrid Jacobs.

Korngold's precocity never fails to astonish. Judging by the *Märchenbilder, Op. 3*, written when he was thirteen, he must have been taking composition lessons in the womb. These are all short or shortish pieces yet they encompass a much wider expressive range than you would imagine, and they are very persuasively played. The recording is less successful: there is too much ambient sound.

VOCAL MUSIC

3 Lieder, Op. 18. Lieder: *Alt-spanisch; Gefasster Abschied; Glückwunsch; Liebesbriefchen; Sonett für Wien; Sterbelied.*
*** DG Dig. 437 515-2. Anne Sofie von Otter, Bengt Forsberg – BERG: *7 Early songs;* STRAUSS: *Lieder.* ***

Anne Sofie von Otter and Bengt Forsberg follow up the success of their prize-winning disc of Grieg songs with inspired playing and singing, not just in Berg and Strauss, relatively well known, but in these rare and immediately attractive songs by Erich Korngold. Though a few date from his early, precocious years in Vienna, including some of the most sensuously beautiful, such a charming miniature as *Alt-spanisch* is taken from the film music he wrote in 1940 for the swashbuckling Hollywood film, *The Sea Hawk.* Singer and pianist draw out the intensity of emotion to the full without exaggeration or sentimentality. A fascinating programme.

5 Lieder Op. 38; Songs of the Clown, Op. 29.
*** Sony SK 68344 [id.]. Angelika Kirchschlager, Helmut Deutsch – MAHLER: *Lieder und Gesänge.* ***

These two song-groups, written after Korngold went to America – charming miniatures most of them – are tuneful in an innocent way, similar in kind but opposite in scale to Korngold's Hollywood music. Some of them might almost be by British composers of earlier in the century. Even *Come away Death* fails to draw from the composer a deep response (no doubt reflecting his title for the group), gravitating quickly to the major mode. With Op. 29 here receiving its first recording, they add a pointful element to the début recital of this talented, fresh-voiced singer; well worth exploring.

Passover psalm.
(N) *** Decca Dig. 460 213-2 [id.]. Eva Urbanová, Slovak Philharmonic Ch., VPO, Chailly – JANACEK: *Glagolitic mass.* ZEMLINSKY: *Psalm 83.* ***

The *Passover psalm*, commissioned by a rabbi in Hollywood in 1941, is Korngold's only religious work, a brief, warm-hearted piece that makes an unusual coupling for the Janáček. Very well recorded.

OPERA

Die Kathrin (complete).
(N) *** CPO Dig. CPO 999 602-2 (3) [id.]. Melanie Dienar, David Rendall, Robert Hayward, Lillian Watson, Della Jones, BBC Singers, BBC Concert O, Martyn Brabbins.

Erich Korngold composed *Die Kathrin*, his last opera, in summers spent back home in Austria, between Hollywood trips when he wrote his Oscar-winning film scores. Not so much grand opera as grand operetta, it is a far warmer and more relaxed piece than his other operas. The opulent scoring and ripe lyricism go with a novelettish story of Kathrin, a servant-girl, and her wandering minstrel of a sweetheart. With echoes of Strauss's *Arabella*, Puccini's *Suor Angelica* and even Humperdinck's *Hänsel und Gretel*, Martyn Brabbins draws aptly sumptuous sounds from the BBC Concert Orchestra, in a recording taken from a BBC radio production. A characterful cast, including Della Jones and Lillian Watson in small roles, is headed by the radiant young German soprano, Melanie Diener, but with David Rendall rather strained as the hero, François.

Die tote Stadt (complete).
(M) *** RCA GD 87767 (2) [7767-2-RG]. Neblett, Kollo, Luxon, Prey, Bav. R. Ch., Tölz Ch., Munich R. O, Leinsdorf.

At the age of twenty-three Korngold had his opera, *Die tote Stadt*, presented in simultaneous world premières in Hamburg and Cologne! The score includes many echoes of Puccini and Richard Strauss, but its youthful exuberance carries the day. Here René Kollo is powerful, if occasionally coarse of tone, Carol Neblett sings sweetly in the equivocal roles of the wife's apparition and the newcomer, and Hermann Prey, Benjamin Luxon and Rose Wagemann make up an impressive cast. Leinsdorf is at his finest.

Violanta (complete).
**(*) Sony CD 79229 [MK 35909]. Marton, Berry, Jerusalem, Stoklassa, Laubenthal, Hess, Bav. R. Ch., Munich R. O, Janowski.

Korngold wrote this opera at the age of seventeen. Though luscious of texture and immensely assured, the writing lets one down by an absence of really memorable melody but, with a fine, red-blooded performance and with Siegfried Jerusalem a youthfully fresh hero, it makes a fascinating addition to the recorded repertory. Eva Marton, not always beautiful of tone, combines power and accuracy in the key role of the heroine. The recording is quite full if not especially refined.

Das Wunder der Heliane (complete).
*** Decca (IMS) Dig. 436 636-2 (3) [id.]. Tomowa-Sintow, Welker, De Haan, Runkel, Pape, Gedda, Berlin R. Ch. & RSO, Mauceri.

Like the Decca set of Krenek's *Jonny spielt auf*, this Korngold opera, also first performed in Vienna in 1927, comes in a series devoted to works banned by the Nazis, '*Entartete Musik*', so-called decadent music. The narrative itself is full of overt eroticism. Though the plot, with its tyrannical ruler, his wife and a mysterious stranger, is unconvincing, Decca's magnificent recording amply confirms the view that this is Korngold's masterpiece, musically even richer than his better-known opera, *Die tote Stadt*. The opening prelude, with its exotic harmonies and heavenly choir, will seduce anyone with a sweet tooth, and though in three Acts of nearly an hour each it is overlong, Korngold sustains the story with a ravishing score. Puccini as well as Strauss is often very close, with one passage in the big Act I love-duet bringing languorous echoes of the end of *Fanciulla del West*. Korngold's lavish Hollywood scores of the 1930s are thin by comparison. John Mauceri draws glorious sounds from the Berlin Radio Symphony Orchestra, and the cast is headed by three outstanding singers, the soprano Anna Tomowa-Sintow at her richest, an impressive American Heldentenor, John David de Haan, as the Stranger and Hartmut Welker as the Ruler.

Kozeluch, Leopold (1747–1818)

Clarinet concerto No. 2 in E flat.
*** ASV Dig. CDDCA 763 [id.]. Emma Johnson, RPO, Herbig – CRUSELL; KROMMER: *Concertos*. ***

The Bohemian composer, Leopold Kozeluch, was the cousin of the slightly better-known Jan (Johann), and his concerto is a highly agreeable work, especially when performed so magnetically by Emma Johnson. There is plenty of Johnsonian magic here to light up even the most conventional passage-work and the 'naturally flowing melodies' (the soloist's own description), and she is well accompanied and admirably recorded, with the slow movement made to sound recessed and delicate.

Symphonies in D; F; G min.
(N) *** Chandos Dig. CHAN 9703 [id.]. L. Mozart Players, Matthias Bamert.

Kozeluch was born near Prague but established himself in Vienna in 1778, where he was appointed to the Imperial Court as official composer and director of the orchestra; he also established his own publishing house, from which these three works emerged in 1787. They are pleasingly crafted and the *G minor* is a deeper work than you might expect, but each is distinguished by a graceful and appealing slow movement and a vigorous, lighthearted finale. They are very well played here and the fairly resonant Chandos recording ensures their weight and substance.

Kramář, František – see Krommer, Franz

Krása, Hans (1899–1944)

String quartet.
*** Decca Dig. 440 853-2 [id.]. Hawthorne Qt – HAAS: *Quartets Nos. 2 & 3.* ***

Hans Krása and his compatriot, Pavel Haas, were born in the same year and sent to the gas chambers at the Terezin or Teresienstadt camp on the same day. Krása came from Prague and became a pupil of Zemlinsky, but he was influenced by French music as much as by the Viennese school. His *String quartet* is a remarkably mature piece for a twenty-two-year-old and, along with the occasional echoes of Janáček and the French, also burlesques a theme from Smetana's *Bartered Bride*. Although there are rapidly changing moods and colours, the composer holds everything together with a keen and intelligent logic. The Hawthorne Quartet play very persuasively and are excellently recorded. A rewarding issue.

Kraus, Joseph Martin (1756–92)

Symphonies in C; C min.; E flat; Olympie overture.
(BB) *** Naxos Dig. 8.553734 [id.]. Swedish CO, Petter Sundquist.

Born in the same year as Mozart, Kraus was similarly short-lived, dying in the year after him. That has led to his being dubbed the 'Swedish Mozart', but these lively symphonies, freshly performed by the Swedish Chamber Orchestra, suggest that his music has more in common with that of Haydn, above all the *Sturm und Drang* period. Haydn, who met Kraus in both Vienna and Esterházy, praised his music highly. Unlike Mozart, Kraus was drawn to minor keys, not just in the *C minor Symphony*, and the tough streak in the writing is emphasized by the sharpness of syncopated rhythms. The symphonies – three from the total of 12 that have survived – were written in the 1780s, but the overture, in three sections, slow–fast–slow following the French pattern, dates from the year of Kraus's death, written for a stage production of Voltaire's play of that name. Full, warm sound and excellent performances, involving a substantial string section with first-rate wind and brass playing, notably from the horns. Well worth exploring.

Kreisler, Fritz (1875–1962)

Violin concerto in the style of Vivaldi.
*** DG Dig. 439 933-2. Gil Shaham, Orpheus CO – VIVALDI: *The Four Seasons.* ***

An amiable pastiche, which sounds almost totally unlike Vivaldi as we experience his music performed today – indeed the name of Boccherini could well have been substituted in the title credit and, even then, could not disguise the early-twentieth-century provenance of the work. It is warmly played and clearly enjoyed by its performers, and the sumptuousness of the sound is the more striking coming, as it does, immediately after Vivaldi's wintry winds.

Allegretto in the style of Boccherini; Aucassin and Nicolette; Berceuse romantique; Caprice viennoise; La gitana; Liebesfreud; Liebesleid; Marche miniature viennoise; Menuett in the style of Porpora; Polichinelle; Praeludium and allegro in the style of Pugnani; La Précieuse in the style of Louis Couperin; Rondino on a theme of Beethoven; Schön Rosmarin; Sicilienne and Rigaudon in the style of Francoeur; Syncopation; Tambourin chinois; Tempo di minuetto in the style of Pugnani; Toy-soldiers' march.
*** Decca Dig. 444 409-2 [id.]. Joshua Bell, Paul Coker.

As readily shown by the opening *Praeludium and allegro*, Joshua Bell refuses to treat this music as trivial, and there is a total absence of schmalz. *Tambourin chinois*, impeccably played, lacks something in charm, but not the neatly articulated *La Précieuse*. And what lightness of touch in *Schön Rosmarin*, what elegance of style in the *Caprice viennoise*, what panache in the paired *Liebesfreud* and *Liebesleid*, and how seductive is the simple *Berceuse romantique*, one of the novelties here, like the winning *Toy-soldiers' march* and the unexpected, almost Joplinesque rag, *Syncopation*. The recording is completely realistic.

Allegretto in the style of Boccherini; Caprice viennoise; Chanson Louis XIII and Pavane; Liebesleid; Liebesfreud; Minuet; The old refrain; Praeludium and allegro; Recitativo and Scherzo; Rondino on a theme of Beethoven; Schön Rosmarin; Tambourin chinois; Tempo di minuetto.
(M) *** Mercury (IMS) 434 351-2 [id.]. Henryk Szeryng, Charles Reiner (with LECLAIR: *Violin sonata No. 3 in D;* GLUCK, arr. KREISLER: *Mélodie*; LOCATELLI: *The Labyrinth* **).

It is good to have a reminder of the artistry of Henryk Szeryng, who made many of his best concerto recordings in the earliest days of stereo. His playing of these occasional pieces of Kreisler – not all of them by any means trifles – is superb. The 1963 recording is firmly focused and truthful. The remaining items are played as virtuoso encores rather than showing any natural sympathy for the baroque style, although no one could fail to be impressed by the bravura of Locatelli's *Labyrinth*.

However, in these pieces the Mercury sound brings rather more edge to the violin timbre.

Allegretto in the style of Boccherini; Allegretto in the style of Porpora; Caprice viennoise; Cavatina; La Chasse in the style of Cartier; La Gitana; Grave in the style of W. F. Bach; Gypsy caprice; Liebesfreud; Liebesleid; Praeludium and allegro in the style of Pugnani; Recitative and scherzo; Schön Rosmarin; Shepherd's madrigal; Sicilienne et rigaudon in the style of Francoeur; Toy soldiers' march; Viennese rhapsodic fantasia; arr. of *Austrian National Hymn.*
(BB) **(*) ASV Quicksilva CDQS 6039. Oscar Shumsky, Milton Kaye.

Oscar Shumsky's combination of technical mastery and musical flair is ideal for this music; and it is a pity that the rather dry recording and forward balance – well in front of the piano – makes the violin sound almost too close.

Aucassin et Nicolette; Caprice viennois; La Gitana; Marche miniature viennoise; 3 Old Viennese dances (Liebesfreud; Liebesleid; Schön Rosmarin); Praeludium and allegro in the style of Pugnani; Preghiera in the style of Martini; Sicilienne et rigaudon in the style of Francoeur; Slavonic fantasie on themes by Dvořák; Tambourin chinois. Arrangements of: CHAMINADE: *Sérénade espagnole.* DVORAK: *Slavonic dance, Op. 72/2.* SCOTT: *Lotus land.* TCHAIKOVSKY: *Chant sans paroles, Op. 2/3.* MENDELSSOHN: *Songs without words: Andante espressivo in G, Op. 62/1.* RACHMANINOV: *Rhapsody on a theme of Paganini: Variation.* LEHAR: *Frasquita: Serenade.* ANON.: *Londonderry Air.* ALBENIZ: *España: Tango, Op. 165/2.* HEUBERGER: *Midnight bells.*
(M) *** Classic fM Dig. 75605 57020-2. Joji Hattori, Joseph Seiger.

Joji Hattori, winner of the Menuhin International Violin Competition in 1989, brings to these Kreisler trifles not only a brilliant technique and rich, firm violin-tone, but the rhythmic flair and naughty pointing of phrase which makes them sparkle. Here is an artist who plainly loves the instrument, as Kreisler himself did. The 22 encores include not only original pieces by Kreisler, but his inspired violin arrangements of favourite pieces by such composers as Dvořák, Tchaikovsky, Rachmaninov, Lehár and others. Also a sequence of the pieces he wrote, originally attributing them to then-neglected eighteenth-century composers like Pugnani, Francoeur and Martini. The gently lyrical *Preghiera* after Martini inspires Hattori to hushed, meditative playing just as intense as his bravura fireworks in such pieces as *Tambourin chinois*. Joseph Seiger is a comparably inspired accompanist, relishing the glissando display in such a piece as *La Gitana*. Warm, full recording. A best buy among mid-priced recordings of the repertoire.

Caprice viennoise; Chanson Louis XIII & Pavane in the style of Couperin; La Gitana; Liebesleid; Liebesfreud; Polichinelle; La Précieuse in the style of Couperin; Rondino on a theme by Beethoven; Scherzo alla Dittersdorf; Tambourin chinois; Schön Rosmarin. Arrangements: BACH: *Partita No. 3 in E, BWV 1006: Gavotte.* BRANDL: *The old refrain.* DVORAK: *Humoresque.* FALLA: *La vida breve: Danza española.* GLAZUNOV: *Sérénade espagnole.* HEUBERGER: *Midnight bells (Im chambre séparée).* POLDINI: *Poupée valsante.* RIMSKY-KORSAKOV: *Sadko: Chanson hindoue.* SCHUBERT: *Rosamunde: Ballet music No. 2.* SCOTT: *Lotus Land.* TCHAIKOVSKY: *Andante cantabile from Op. 11.* WEBER: *Violin sonata No. 1 in F, Op. 10: Larghetto.* TRAD.: *Londonderry air.*
(***) EMI mono CDH7 64701-2. Fritz Kreisler, Franz Rupp or Michael Rachelsein; or (in *Scherzo*) Kreisler String Qt.

Impeccable and characterful performances by Fritz Kreisler of his own lollipops, including those 'in the style of' pieces with which – until he owned up – he fooled his audiences into believing they were actually written by the composers in question. Most of the recordings were made with Franz Rupp in 1936 or 1938, and the transfers offer a convincingly realistic if studio-ish balance and are of excellent technical quality; a few (the *Polichinelle*, the pieces in the style of Couperin, the Schubert *Rosamunde ballet music*, the Glazunov and Weber arrangements, *The old refrain* (especially) and an indulgent performance of Heuberger's *Im chambre séparée*) date from 1930 and here the piano balance is poor, the piano badly defined. However, these were recorded before Kreisler's accident and the violin timbre is noticeably more opulent. A valuable document.

Caprice viennoise, Op. 2; La Gitana; Liebesfreud; Liebesleid; Polichinelle; La Précieuse; Recitativo and scherzo caprice, Op. 6; Rondo on a theme of Beethoven; Syncopation; Tambourin chinois; Zigeuner (Capriccio). Arrangements: ALBENIZ: *Tango, Op. 165/2.* WEBER: *Larghetto.* WIENIAWSKI: *Caprice in E flat.* DVORAK: *Slavonic dance No. 10 in E min.* GLAZUNOV: *Sérénade espagnole.* GRANADOS: *Danse espagnole.*
(M) *** DG 423 876-2 [id.]. Shlomo Mintz, Clifford Benson.

Shlomo Mintz plays with a disarmingly easy style and absolute technical command, to bring out the music's warmth as well as its sparkle. A very attractive programme, given first-class recording and splendid presence without added edge on CD.

Caprice viennoise; La Gitana; Grave; Liebesfreud; Liebesleid; Praeludium & allegro in the style of Pugnani; La Précieuse, in the style of Couperin; Rondino on a theme by Beethoven; Scherzo in the style of Dittersdorf; Schön Rosmarin; Sicilienne & rigaudon in the style of Francoeur. (Arr of: DVORAK: *Slavonic dances Nos. 1 in G min.; 2 in E min.* LECLAIR: *Tambourin.* GLUCK: *Mélodie (Orfeo ed Euridice).* WEBER: *Larghetto.* RAMEAU: *Tambourin.* TRADITIONAL: *Londonderry air* (all arr. for violin and orchestra by Peter Wolf)).
(N) **(*) Sony Dig. SK 62692 [id.]. Isaac Stern, with Franz Liszt CO.

These concertante arrangements serve to some extent to mask the fact that Stern's timbre is less sweet than it once was. If he can no longer match today's young lions in tonal sophistication, he still knows how to present this material with panache, and *Schön Rosmarin* shows him at his most dashing. Gluck's famous theme from *Orfeo* too is beautifully phrased. The recording is forward but truthful.

Krenek, Ernst (1900–1991)

Violin concerto No. 1, Op. 29.
*** Decca 452 481-2 [id.]. Chantal Juillet, Berlin RSO, Mauceri – KORNGOLD: *Violin concerto* ***; WEILL: *Violin concerto.* **

The Krenek *Violin concerto*, buried since its one and only performance in 1924, makes a welcome novelty, generously coupled with better-known concertos by fellow Europeans who also settled in America. Though this is a flawed work, not as tautly structured as it might be, it proves involvingly autobiographical, inspired by the composer's unhappy love-affair with a glamorous violinist, Alma Moodie. The late Berthold Goldschmidt in the liner-notes gives a detailed commentary, having attended the first performance with Alma Moodie (when Krenek ostentatiously kept away). Hearing the 1995 sessions for this recording, his memories came vividly back, so that he can explain how one key passage represents a night journey by train in a sleeping-car. Though the work fades out limply at the end, Chantal Juillet gives a warmly expressive performance, helped by vivid Decca sound, confirming this as a valuable addition to the 'Entartete Musik' series.

Symphonic elegy for string orchestra.
(M) (***) Sony mono MH2K 62759 (2) [id.]. NYPO, Dimitri Mitropoulos – BERG: *Wozzeck* (***); SCHOENBERG: *Erwartung.*(**(*))

Krenek wrote this powerful piece for strings as a direct response to hearing the news of the tragic death of his friend, Anton Webern. In homage he adopts full serial technique, but the result has little of the spareness of Webern; in its overtly emotional approach and lyrical warmth it comes nearer to Berg in style. Recorded in 1951, like *Wozzeck* and *Erwartung*, it makes an unexpected but valuable fill-up, very well played. (This set costs rather more than our usual upper-mid-price limitation.)

Jonny spielt auf (complete).
**(*) Decca (IMS) Dig. 436 631-2 (2). Kruse, Marc, St Hill, Kraus, Posselt, Leipzig Op. Ch., Leipzig GO, Zagrosek.

Ernst Krenek's opera, *Jonny spielt auf* ('Jonny plays on'), was acclaimed as the first jazz opera, even though the composer always resisted that description. Yet it proved a flash in the pan. Paris was unimpressed, and back in Germany it was quickly banned by the Nazi regime, which condemned it as '*Entartete Musik*', decadent music. Hearing the opera now in a fine recording, based on a 1990 Leipzig production – made just before the composer died at the age of ninety – it stands as more than a historical curiosity. Contradicting its reputation, it is a lyrical post-romantic piece. One's first disappointment is that it hardly matches the Kurt Weill operas. The idiom is far milder, with syncopations used more gently in the jazzy passages and with the instrumentation less abrasive. Though the Leipzig Gewandhaus Orchestra under Lothar Zagrosek does not always sound at home in the jazzy sequences, the recording provides the most convincing evidence yet that the piece deserves reappraisal. Heinz Kruse as Max sustains his long monologues impressively, and Krister St Hill as Jonny also sings well, even if the microphone catches an unevenness in their voices. It is Alessandra Marc as the heroine, Anita, who emerges as the main star, relishing lush Krenek melodies that yet never quite stick in the mind.

Kreutzer, Conradin (1780–1849)

Septet (for clarinet, horn, bassoon, violin, viola, cello & double-bass), *Op. 62;* (i) *Trio in E flat* (for piano, clarinet & bassoon), *Op. 43.*
❁ (BB) *** Arte Nova Dig. 74321 54462-2 [id.]. Mithras Octet (members), (i) with Paul Rivinius (piano).

In the early days of mono LP one of the plums of the Decca catalogue was a recording of a then unfamiliar *Septet*, by Conradin Kreutzer, winningly played by members of the Vienna Octet. Since then the work seems to have been neglected; but now comes yet another delightful performance to suggest that it is almost more infectiously enjoyable than the Beethoven *Septet* on which it was modelled (in 1824). The members of the Mithras Octet have the full measure of the music, playing with grace and elegance and an infectious charm, while the recording is excellent in every respect. The *Trio* is a similarly amiable and inventive work, if less distinctive. It has a doleful *Andante grazioso* and is capped by another memorably light-hearted finale. It is very well played here, but unfortunately the piano, recorded too resonantly, outbalances the pair of woodwind instruments, and this reduces the listener's enjoyment. The Rosette is for the *Septet*, which is not to be missed.

Kreutzer, Joseph (1778-1832)

Grand trio for flute, clarinet and guitar, Op. 16.
*** Mer. Dig. CDE 84199 [id.]. Conway, Silverthorne, Garcia – BEETHOVEN: *Serenade;* MOLINO: *Trio.* ***
(N) *** Koch Dig. 3-7404-2. Still, Alemany, Falletta – BEETHOVEN: *Serenade, Op. 8;* SCHUBERT: *Quartet for flute, guitar, viola and cello.* ***

Joseph Kreutzer, thought to be the brother of Rodolphe Kreutzer, dedicatee of Beethoven's *A major Violin sonata*, wrote many works for the guitar, of which this is a delightful example. The guitar, given at least equal prominence with the other instruments, brings an unusual tang to the textures of this charming piece, ending with a rousing *Alla Polacca*. A nicely pointed performance, very well recorded in warm, faithful sound.

Little is known of Joseph Kreutzer, except that he was an expert nineteenth-century Viennese guitarist. However this charmingly inconsequential work shows him also as a fair musical craftsman. Stylishly played and very well recorded, it makes an agreeable bonus for the more substantial pieces by Beethoven and Schubert.

Krommer, Franz (1759–1831)

Clarinet concerto in E flat, Op. 36.
*** ASV Dig. CDDCA 763 [id.]. Emma Johnson, RPO, Herbig – CRUSELL: *Concerto No. 1;* KOZELUCH: *Concerto No. 2.* ***

Emma Johnson is at her most winning in this attractive concerto, which is made to sound completely spontaneous in her hands, particularly the engaging finale, lolloping along with its skipping main theme. The *Adagio* is darker in feeling, its mood equally well caught. Excellent accompaniments and warm, refined recording make this a most engaging triptych.

Clarinet concerto in E flat, Op. 36; (i) *Double clarinet concertos in A flat, Opp. 35 & 91.*
(BB) ** Naxos Dig. 8.553178 [id.]. Kálmán Berkes; (i) Kaori Tsutsui; Nicolaus Esterházy Sinfonia.

Both the soloists here are good players and they blend very well together; but slow movements are rather deadpan and not all the music's sense of fun comes over. Neither clarinettists nor orchestra are helped by the reverberant recording, which means a forward balance for the soloists and tends to coarsen the tuttis by spreading the sound. Even so, the *Double concerto*, Op. 91, a winner if ever there was one, is very enjoyable, with the first movement swinging along merrily and the *Polacca* finale, with its jaunty duet theme introduced against orchestral pizzicatos, equally fluent.

Partitas: in F, Op. 57; E flat, Op. 71; B flat, Op. 78. Marches, Op. 31/3–5.
(BB) *** Naxos Dig. 8.553498 [id.]. Budapest Wind Ens.

The Budapest Wind, led by their exuberant clarinettist, Kálmán Berkes, are a first-rate ensemble, full of spirit and personality. They yield nothing in terms of artistic excellence or recording quality to any rivals.

Symphonies Nos. 2 in D, Op. 40; 4 in C min., Op. 102.
*** Chandos Dig. CHAN 9275 [id.]. LMP, Bamert.

A delightful addition to the representation of Krommer (born František Kramář) in the catalogue. Collectors who acquired the *Harmonien*, played by the Netherlands Wind Ensemble, will know how infectiously high-spirited this composer is; and they will not be disappointed by the two symphonies played here by the London Mozart Players under Matthias Bamert. They present a different picture of him: the *D major Symphony* (1803) opens in something of the manner of *Don Giovanni*, while much else conveys a distinctly Beethovenian visage. The *C minor*, Op. 102, composed towards the end of the second decade of the nineteenth century, already has a whiff of the changing sensibility that we find in Schubert and Weber. Very interesting and refreshing music, played with evident enthusiasm and well recorded.

Kuhlau, Friedrich (1786–1832)

(i) *Concertino for two horns, Op. 45;* (ii) *Piano concerto in C, Op. 7; Overture Elverhøj (The elves' hill), Op. 100.*
*** Unicorn Dig. DKPCD 9110 [id.]. (i) Ib Lansky-Otto, Frøydis Ree Wekre; (ii) Michael Ponti; Odense SO, Othmar Maga.

The overture *Elverhøj* or *The elves' hill* is probably Kuhlau's best-known work and is certainly the finest piece on this disc. The *Piano concerto in C*, Op. 7, is modelled on Beethoven's concerto in the same key. The *Concertino for two horns* (1821) is full of initially engaging, but eventually unmemorable, ideas. Very good performances from all concerned, and satisfactory recording.

Piano concerto in C, Op. 7.
(N) ** Chandos Dig. CHAN 9699 [id.]. Amalie Malling, Danish Nat. RSO, Michael Schønwandt – GRIEG: *Piano concerto.* *

Kuhlau's *C major concerto* was composed in 1810, half a century before the coupled Grieg concerto. This was the year when the young German fled to Denmark to avoid being conscripted into Napoleon'sarmy. The concerto was written before he settled in Copenhagen and is modelled on the Beethoven concerto in the same key. Unlike the latter, it is pretty nondescript in character and little of it resonates in the memory. Amalie Manning is more persuasive here than in the Grieg, of which she gives a routine account, and Michael Schønwandt gets alert and crisp playing from the Danish Radio Orchestra. Excellent sound.

Overtures: *Elisa; Elverhøj (The Elf's hill); Hugo and Adelheid; Lulu; The Magic harp; The Robber's castle; The Triplet brothers from Damask; William Shakespeare.*
(N) *** Chandos Dig. CHAN 9648 [id.]. Danish National RSO, Schonwandt.

Which composer other than Berg wrote an opera called *Lulu*, and one called *William Shakespeare*? The answer is Friedrich Kuhlau, a German who settled in Denmark, an exact contemporary of Weber and similarly short-lived. *Lulu* is a fairy-tale opera from the same source as *Zauberflöte*, while *William Shakespeare* is based on the bard's youthful exploit (alleged) of poaching deer. This delightful disc, brilliantly played and recorded, offers all seven of Kuhlau's opera overtures, plus his most famous work, the overture to the classic Danish play, *Elverhøj* (*Elf's Hill*).

Violin sonatas Nos. 1 in F min., Op. 33; 2 in E flat, Op. 64; 3 in F; 4 in F min.; 5 in C, Op. 79/1–3.
*** CPO Dig. CPO 999 363-2 [id.]. Dora Bratchkova, Andreas Meyer-Hermann.

Kuhlau is best known for his piano sonatinas – with which many novices at the piano are familiar – so this collection of his complete *Violin sonatas* is a delightful surprise. Written between 1820 and 1827, they have much in common with the violin sonatas of Beethoven, and it is surprising how often one is reminded of that master when listening to these attractive and in no way superficial works. The slow movement of the *F minor* and also the finale bring the most striking echoes, but the composer's own personality also emerges strongly, notably in the attractive variations on a Danish folksong which form the slow movement of the *E flat* work and in the *Rondo* finale. The three Opus 79 works are undoubtedly masterpieces, full of life and with invention of a consistently high order. Try the witty finale of Op. 79/1 or the engaging *Andantino* central movement of Op. 79/2, which has a delightful *Polacca* for its closing *Rondo*. The performances by the Bulgarian violinist, Dora Bratchkova, and Andreas Meyer-Hermann (who, like the composer, was born in lower Saxony and later studied in Hamburg) are in every way first rate, and they are most naturally balanced and realistically recorded. If you enjoy the Beethoven violin sonatas, you will certainly enjoy these.

Elverhøj (The elves' hill), Op. 100.
** DaCapo Dig. DCCD 8902 [id.]. Gobel, Plesner, Johansen, Danish R. Ch. & SO, John Frandsen.

Kuhlau's incidental music to J. L. Heiberg's play, *Elverhøj*, is endearingly fresh. Not so the recording however; this sounds really rather dryish, as if recorded in a fully packed concert hall. The music has great charm and the performance too under John Frandsen is very sympathetic.

Lulu (opera): complete.
*** Kontrapunkt/HM 32009/11 [id.]. Saarman, Frellesvig, Kiberg, Cold, Danish R. Ch. & SO, Schønwandt.

This *Lulu* comes from 1824 and is surely too long: the spoken passages are omitted here – but, even so, the music takes three hours. The opening of Act II has overtones of the Wolf's Glen scene in *Der Freischütz* and the dance of the black elves in the moonlight is pure Mendelssohn – and has much charm. The invention is generally fresh and engaging, though no one would claim that it has great depth. The largely Danish cast cope very capably with the not inconsiderable demands of Kuhlau's vocal writing, the Danish Radio recording is eminently truthful and vivid, and Michael Schönwandt draws excellent results from the Danish Radio Chorus and Orchestra.

Kuhnau, Johann (1660–1722)

Der Gerechte kommt um (motet).
(M) *** O-L 443 199-2. Christ Church Ch., AAM, Preston (with BACH: *Magnificat*) – VIVALDI: *Nisi dominus* etc. ***

Kuhnau was Bach's predecessor in Leipzig. He wrote this charming motet with a Latin text; it was later arranged in a German version, and there are signs of Bach's hand in it. The piece makes an excellent makeweight coupling for the original version of Bach's *Magnificat*.

Lachner, Franz Paul (1803–90)

Symphony No. 5 in C min. (Passionata), Op. 52 (Preis-Symphonie).
**(*) Marco Polo Dig. 8.223502 [id.]. Slovak State PO (Košice), Paul Robinson.

Franz Lachner's *Fifth Symphony* is an ambitious work, lasting an hour, lyrical and well crafted. Its ideas unfold naturally and with a certain fluency;

its scoring is effective and its idiom is close to the world of Schubert and Mendelssohn. It is a little conventional: phrase structures are rather four-square and predictable. All the same, one can see why the work enjoyed esteem in more conservative circles. It has more than mere curiosity value, and the Slovak orchestra under Paul Robinson play it with obvious enjoyment. Decent recording.

Septet in E Flat.
*** Marco Polo 8.223282 [id.]. Ens. Villa Musica – FUCHS: *Clarinet quintet.*

Lachner's *Septet* has an easygoing charm which is quite winning. Here it is elegantly played and well recorded.

Lajtha, László (1892–1963)

Hortobágy, Op. 21; Suite No. 3, Op. 56; Symphony No. 7, Op. 63 (Revolution Symphony).
**(*) Marco Polo Dig. 8.223667 [id.]. Pécs SO, Nicolás Pasquet.

László Lajtha was one of the leading Hungarian composers and scholars to emerge after the generation of Bartók and Kodály. The *Seventh Symphony* is a well-wrought and eclectic score that is worth hearing, even if it does not possess the concentration or profile one expects of a major symphonist. The suite from *Hortobágy*, a memorable film set in the plains of Hungary, and the *Two symphonic portraits* are effectively scored but their material is insufficiently distinctive. Good performances and recording.

Lalo, Edouard (1823–92)

Cello concerto No. 1 in D min., Op. 33.
*** RCA Dig. 09026 68420-2 [id.]. Ofra Harnoy, Bournemouth SO, Antonio de Almeida – OFFENBACH: *Concerto militaire.* ***
*** ASV Dig. CDDCA 867 [id.]. Sophie Rolland, BBC PO, Gilbert Varga – MASSENET: *Fantaisie;* SAINT-SAENS: *Cello concerto No. 1.* ***
*** EMI CDC5 55528-2 [id.]. Jacqueline du Pré, Cleveland O, Barenboim – R. STRAUSS: *Don Quixote.* ***
(B) *** Decca Eclipse Dig. 448 712-2. Lynn Harrell, Berlin RSO, Chailly – SAINT-SAENS; SCHUMANN: *Concertos.* ***
*** Finlandia/Warner Dig. 4509 95768-2 [id.]. Arto Noras, Finnish RSO, Saraste – ELGAR: *Cello concerto.* ***
*** DG (IMS) Dig. 427 323-2. Matt Haimovitz, Chicago SO, Levine – SAINT-SAENS: *Concerto No. 1;* BRUCH: *Kol Nidrei.* ***
(B) *** DG 431 166-2. Heinrich Schiff, New Philh. O, Mackerras – FAURE: *Elégie;* SAINT-SAENS: *Concerto No. 1.* ***
(M) **(*) Mercury (IMS) 432 010-2 [id.]. Janos Starker, LSO, Skrowaczewski – SAINT-SAENS; SCHUMANN: *Concertos.* ***
(B) **(*) Sony SBK 48278 [id.]. Leonard Rose, Phd. O, Ormandy – BLOCH: *Schelomo;* FAURE: *Elégie;* TCHAIKOVSKY: *Rococo variations.* ***

Ofra Harnoy is as thoroughly at home in Lalo as she is in the rare Offenbach coupling. As usual, the soloist's subtle use of the widest range of dynamic and her ever-poetic line give the performance a sense of ongoing spontaneity. Although the degree of reverberation may trouble some listeners, the balance between cello and orchestra is nicely managed.

Sophie Rolland's account reveals a formidable talent. She plays with effortless eloquence and is given responsive support from the BBC Philharmonic under Gilbert Varga, though he is a little brusque in the *Intermezzo*. An enjoyable and convincing performance. The excellence of the BBC/ASV recording makes for a strong recommendation.

Jacqueline du Pré's recording of the Lalo *Concerto* was taken live from a broadcast in Cleveland in January 1973, in one of her last remissions from multiple sclerosis. It is a masterly performance and is totally involving, even though the cello is balanced rather more backwardly than in du Pré's studio recordings. In spite of that, her fire at the opening grabs the attention, leading on to a performance that is both passionate and poetic.

Lynn Harrell's account is also highly recommendable. There is a yearning intensity in the *Intermezzo*, while the outer movements combine spontaneity and vigour. Chailly's accompaniment is attractively bold and the recording, made in the Berlin Jesus-Christus Kirche, has an attractively warm ambience.

Arto Noras is an aristocrat among cellists and he receives very responsive support from Saraste and excellent recording.

An outstandingly impressive début from young cellist Matt Haimovitz; the performance throughout combines vitality with expressive feeling in the most spontaneous manner. The recording is very well balanced indeed and highly realistic.

Schiff's 1977 account is youthfully fresh and enthusiastic and very well recorded for its period. A fine bargain.

Janos Starker's 1962 recording with the LSO under Stanislaw Skrowaczewski sounds remarkably good for its age. Though the tutti chords are brutal and clipped, Starker plays splendidly, and the famous Mercury recording technique lays out the orchestral texture quite beautifully and with remarkable transparency.

Leonard Rose gives a strong, spontaneous account of this sometimes intractable concerto, bringing out its melodic character as well as its vitality of invention. Ormandy's accompaniment is wonderfully supportive and it is a pity that the orchestral sound has a hint of edginess in the violins and is a bit two-dimensional.

Namouna (ballet): extended excerpts: *(suites Nos. 1–2 & Allegro vivace; Tambourin; La Gitane; Bacchanale).*
**(*) Audivis Valois Dig. V 4677 [id.]. Monte-Carlo PO, David Robertson.

Namouna (ballet): *suites Nos. 1–2; Valse de la cigarette.*
**(*) ASV Dig. CDDCA 878 [id.]. RPO, Yondani Butt (with GOUNOD: *Mors et Vita: Judex*).

There is no complete version available of Lalo's ballet, but David Robertson has added four more items to the content of Lalo's two suites, plus the charmingly Gallic *Valse de la cigarette* (which the composer extracted as a separate number). He has also re-established the music in ballet-order, whereas in the suites Lalo reassembled the items for concert performance. Robertson secures sensitive, polished playing from his Monte Carlo orchestra, who resound with warmth, and the recording, if not quite top-drawer, has plenty of colour and ambience.

Yondani Butt achieves performances of the suites and the *Valse de la cigarette* which have comparable colour and finesse, and the RPO play extremely well. Even so, they don't necessarily upstage their French competitors and they offer less music. Where they gain is in the *Prélude*, which is an unashamed crib from Wagner's *Das Rheingold*. The ASV disc offers a big *religieuse* Gounod tune as an encore, but more of *Namouna* would have been preferable.

Namouna: Suite No. 1. Overture: Le roi d'Ys.
(M) *** Mercury 434 389-2 [id.]. Detroit SO, Paul Paray – BARRAUD: *Offrande;* CHAUSSON: *Symphony.* **(*)

These 1958 recordings come up very well indeed, and the performances have sparkle and great lightness of touch. What delightful music it is, particularly in such authoritative hands.

Symphonie espagnole (for violin and orchestra), *Op. 21.*
*** EMI Dig. CDC5 55292-2 [id.]. Sarah Chang, Concg. O, Dutoit – VIEUXTEMPS: *Violin concerto No. 5.* ***
(B) *** EMI Eminence Dig. CD-EMX 2277. Tasmin Little, Royal SNO, Vernon Handley – BRUCH: *Scottish fantasy.* ***
(M) *** DG Dig. 445 549-2 [id.]. Perlman, O de Paris, Barenboim – SAINT-SAENS: *Concerto No. 3;* BERLIOZ: *Rêverie et caprice.* ***
(M) *** Decca Dig. 460 007-2. Kyung Wha Chung, Montreal SO, Dutoit – RAVEL: *Tzigane;* VIEUXTEMPS: *Violin concerto No. 5.* ***
(M) *** Sony Stern Edition II SM2K 64501 (2) [id.]. Stern, Phd. O, Ormandy (with Concert ***).
(*) RCA Dig. 74321 24213-2 [09026 60942-2]. Anne Akiko Meyers, RPO, López-Cobos – BRUCH: *Scottish fantasia.* *
(M) **(*) Sony SBK 48274 [id.]. Zukerman, LAPO, Mehta – VIEUXTEMPS: *Concerto No. 5.* **(*)
(B) **(*) [EMI Red Line Dig. CDR5 69861]. Mutter, O Nat. de France, Ozawa – BIZET: *Carmen: suites* etc.; SARASATE: *Zigeunerweisen.* **(*)
(**(*)) APR Signature mono APR 5506 [id.]. Huberman, VPO, Szell – BEETHOVEN: *Violin concerto.* (***)

Symphonie espagnole, Op. 21 (omitting *Intermezzo*).
(M) (**(*)) RCA Heifetz Collection mono 09026 61753-2 [id.]. Heifetz, RCA Victor SO, Steinberg – CHAUSSON: *Poème* **(*); SAINT-SAENS: *Havanaise* etc.; SARASATE: *Zigeunerweisen.* (***)

Sarah Chang's dazzling account of Lalo's five-movement feast of Spanish dance-rhythms goes readily to the top of the list. Dutoit provides a vigorous backing and the soloist's seductive lilt in the shimmering malaguena of the first movement is matched by the sparkling seguidilla rhythms of the Scherzo and the bouncing habanera of the Intermezzo, with the music's contrasting languor fully reflecting the Mediterranean sunshine. After a nostaglically songful *Andante* (where the Concertgebouw brass makes itself sonorously felt) the finale scintillates. The orchestra readily echoes Chang's sparkle and the expansively resonant recording (far preferable to the comparatively dry sound which DG provide for Perlman) is ideally balanced.

Tasmin Little too has the gift of sounding totally spontaneous on disc, with no feeling of strict studio manners, here giving a bold and characterful reading of the Lalo, warmly projected and well coupled with Bruch's comparable evocation of Scotland. She is greatly helped by the splendid, keenly polished playing of the Scottish orchestra under Vernon Handley, a most sympathetic partner. Handley is excellent in pointing the rhythms of the fast movements of the Lalo, matching his soloist, and the recording is superb, with brass in particular vividly caught.

The 1980 DG recording regularly pops in and out of the catalogue and, although the lively digital sound remains a trifle dry, Perlman's performance easily maintains its place near the top of the list. For the reissue in the Masters series, the Berlioz *Rêverie et caprice* makes an attractive if brief bonus.

Kyung Wha Chung has the advantage of a first-class Decca digital recording, with a highly effective, natural balance. Hers is an athletic, incisive account, at its most individual in the captivatingly light-weight finale, with an element almost of fantasy. Miss Chung does not have quite the panache of Perlman, but Charles Dutoit's accompaniment is first class and the orchestral characterization is strong throughout.

Stern's version from the late 1960s has all the rich, red-blooded qualities that have made this artist world-famous. Reservations concerning the close balance are inevitable (although Ormandy's fine accompaniment is not diminished), but the playing makes a huge impact on the listener and, although the actual sound-quality is far from refined, the charisma of this performance is unforgettable.

Anne Akiko Meyers' account offers a genuine alternative view. Her approach to the first movement's secondary theme has a beguilingly light touch, the seductive Spanish lilt pastel-shaded, and her sense of fantasy brings a similar airy lightness to the Scherzo. She introduces the lovely melody of the *Andante* with magically hushed intensity. The finale brings appealing sparkle and delicacy of articulation. López-Cobos does not quite match his young soloist in concentration. However, he has the advantage of really first-class recording, achieving a natural balance with the soloist.

Heifetz's 1951 account has superb panache and there are no complaints about the mono recording. Alas, he omitted the *Intermezzo* (a practice curiously common in his time), which is our loss, but the performance of the rest, like all the music on this CD, is dazzling.

Zukerman's performance is outstandingly successful. He plays with great dash and fire yet brings a balancing warmth. His couplings are more generous than Perlman's, but the effect of the DG recording is to give Perlman's account slightly more romantic finesse.

Anne-Sophie Mutter's account is second to none, with its dazzling display of bravura, the first movement immediately commanding. The Scherzo has an engaging element of fantasy; the finale is scintillating. However, there is a slight technical drawback: while the orchestral detail is good, the balance projects the violin well to the front and the slightly-too-close microphones add a touch of shrillness to the upper range. A degree of digital edge affects the orchestra, too; the orchestral violins sound thin above the stave. This disc is only available in the USA.

When Huberman recorded the *Symphonie espagnole* in 1930, it was common practice to omit the central *Intermezzo*, and so it is here, for that cut allowed the work to fit on to three 78-r.p.m. discs instead of four. Yet as a historic document this makes a welcome coupling for Huberman's classic reading of the Beethoven concerto with the same accompanists. Here more than in the Beethoven, Huberman indulges in surprising swoops of *portamento* – another sign of the times – though always with perfect control to match the sweetly expressive style.

Piano trios Nos. 1 in C min., Op. 7; 2 in B min.; 3 in A min, Op. 26.

*** ASV Dig. CDDCA 899 [id.]. Barbican Piano Trio.

As always with Lalo, this is the kind of unpretentious, inventive, well-crafted and delightful music which nineteenth-century civilization seemed able to foster and their composers to produce – and of which the late twentieth is conspicuously and lamentably bare. There is little to say about the music (always a good sign) and not much more about the performances, except to note their excellence and poise. A rewarding issue, and well recorded into the bargain.

Lambert, Constant (1905–51)

Aubade héroïque; (i) *The Rio Grande; Summer's last will and testament.*

*** Hyperion Dig. CDA 66565 [id.]. Sally Burgess, Jack Gibbons, William Shimell, Ch. of Opera North and Leeds Festival, (i) with Jack Gibbons; English N. Philh., Lloyd-Jones.

The Rio Grande, Lambert's jazz-based choral concerto setting a poem by Sacheverell Sitwell, is one of the most colourful and atmospheric works from the 1920s. The *Aubade héroïque* is an evocative tone-poem inspired by Lambert's memory of a beautiful morning in Holland in 1940 when, with the Nazi invasion, it was far from certain whether he and his colleagues would be able to get back to England. *Summer's last will and testament* is a big, 50-minute choral work setting lyrics by the Elizabethan, Thomas Nashe, on the unpromising subject of the threat of plague. Lloyd-Jones and his outstanding team, mainly from Opera North, bring out the vitality and colour of the writing, with each of the nine substantial sections based on Elizabethan dance-rhythms. The recording in all three works is full, vivid and atmospheric.

(i; ii) *Concerto for piano and nine players*; (i) *Piano sonata*; (iii; i) *8 Poems of Li-Po*; (iv; i) *Mr Bear Squash-you-all-flat.*

*** Hyperion Dig. CDA 66754 [id.]. (i) Ian Brown; (ii) Nash Ens., Lionel Friend; with (iii) Philip Langridge; (iv) Nigel Hawthorne.

Constant Lambert's remarkable qualities are in excellent evidence here in the Nash Ensemble's anthology which brings two of his most powerful works, the *Concerto for piano and nine players* and the *Piano sonata*, as well as one of his most delicately wrought, the *Eight Poems of Li-Po*, in a lovely performance from Philip Langridge. Ian Brown proves an equally exemplary advocate in the *Concerto* and the *Piano sonata*, which is not generously represented on disc. *Mr Bear Squash-you-all-flat* is Lambert's first composition, an entertainment written at roughly the same time as Walton's *Façade*, when Lambert was still in his teens, and based on a Russian fairy story. Imaginative and accomplished but, hardly surprisingly, not first-class Lambert. It is not certain whether Lambert meant the text to be spoken, but Sir Nigel Hawthorne speaks it excellently; he is somewhat reticently balanced (a fault on the right side).

The Rio Grande.
(M) **(*) Decca Dig. 452 324-2. Della Jones, Kathleen Stott, BBC Singers, BBC Concert O, Barry Wordsworth – ELGAR: *Sea pictures* etc. **(*)

With bright, forward recording, this account of *The Rio Grande* is rather aggressive. Wordsworth is also literal, less than idiomatic in the interpretations of jazzy syncopations. The performance is not warmly expressive, but the power and the colour of the writing come across with fine bite and clarity.

Horoscope (ballet): *suite.*
❁ *** Hyperion CDA 66436 [id.]. E. N. Philh. O, Lloyd-Jones (with BLISS: *Checkmate*) – WALTON: *Façade*. ***

The music for *Horoscope* is sheer delight, and it seems incredible that the only previous complete recording of the suite was made in the mid-1950s by Robert Irving for Decca. David Lloyd-Jones is equally sympathetic to its specifically English atmosphere. He wittily points the catchy rhythmic figure which comes both in the *Dance for the followers of Leo* and, later, in the *Bacchanale*, while the third-movement *Valse for the Gemini* has a delectable insouciant charm. Excellent playing and first-class sound, perhaps a shade resonant for the ballet pit, but bringing plenty of bloom.

Pomona (ballet); *Tiresias* (ballet).
(N) *** Hyperion Dig. CDA 67049 [id.]. E. Northern Philh. O, David Lloyd-Jones.

Première recordings of Lambert's first and last ballet scores make an ideal coupling, vigorously played and warmly recorded. Neither is quite as striking as Lambert's best-known ballet, *Horoscope*, but each offers colourful, atmospheric music vividly orchestrated. *Pomona*, written for Diaghilev in 1927, finds Lambert deftly echoing the neoclassical Stravinsky and Les Six, in his sequence of formal dances. *Tiresias*, completed not long before Lambert died, is more ambitious, the work of a composer steeped in the dramatic needs of ballet. The thematic material may not be so memorable as in Lambert's finest works, but with strong rhythmic invention and rich sounds – the piano often prominent – it is most attractive, only disappointing in the downbeat ending.

Lambert, Michel (*c.* 1610–96)

Airs de cour: *Admirons notre jeune et charmante Déesse; Ah! qui voudra desormais s'engager; C'en est fait, belle Iris; D'un feu secret je me sens consumer; Il faut mourir plutost que le changer; Iris n'est plus, mon Iris m'est ravie; Je suis aymé de celle que j'adore; Ma bergère est tendre et fidelle; Ombre de mon amant; Par mes chants tristes et touchants; Pour vos beaux yeux, Iris; Le repos, l'ombre, le silence; Tout l'univers obéit à l'amour; Trouver sur l'herbette.*
(B) *** HM Musique d'Abord HMA 1901123 [id.]. Les Arts Florissants, William Christie.

Grove speaks of Michel Lambert's airs as models of elegance and grace, in which careful attention was paid to direct declamation. The 300 or so that survive show his artistry in characterization and dialogue to have been of the highest order. They are beautifully performed and expertly recorded by members of Les Arts Florissants and William Christie and are altogether delightful. Unlike some bargain issues, there is excellent documentation with the original texts and translation.

Lampe, John Frederick (1702/3–51)

(i) *Pyramus and Thisbe* (A mock opera); (ii) *Flute concerto in G (The Cuckoo).*
*** Hyperion Dig. CDA 66759 [id.]. (i) Padmore, Bisatt, Opera Restor'd, Peter Holman; (ii) Rachel Brown.

Pyramus and Thisbe, written in 1745, is a reworking of the entertainment given by the rude mechanicals in Shakespeare's *Midsummer Night's Dream*, with the role of the heroine, Thisbe, taken not by a man but by a soprano. The Opera Restor'd company, with Jack Edwards as stage director, here present it complete with spoken Prologue for several attendant characters. Following the overture come 16 brief numbers, with the score edited and completed by the conductor, Peter Holman. Mark Padmore is outstanding as Pyramus, with Susan Bisatt a fresh-toned Thisbe. The warm, immediate recording brings out the distinctive timbre of the period instruments, notably the braying horns. As an agreeable makeweight, the disc also offers Lampe's only surviving independent orchestral work, the *G major Flute concerto*, with its three crisp movements lasting little more than 5 minutes.

Lanchbery, John (born 1923)

Tales of Beatrix Potter (ballet arranged from popular tunes of the Victorian era).
(B) **(*) CfP CD-CFP 6074. ROHCG O, John Lanchbery.

Here is a companion score to John Lanchbery's

arrangement of *La Fille mal gardée*. The music is not as distinguished melodically as the compilation of Hérold tunes, but the colourful and witty orchestration is a source of delight. This was top-drawer analogue Abbey Road sound from the beginning of the 1970s, although the resonance has brought some loss of focus in the CD transfer, as the opening bars readily show. But there is a fine ambient glow on wind and strings alike, and this still makes an attractive aural entertainment. The composer-arranger used Victorian tunes (including some by Sullivan) of the period of the Beatrix Potter stories, and they are linked so skilfully that one would think the score had been composed as original music. The ballet itself has a strong visual appeal for children but can prove boring for adults, though the music itself is very listenable.

Landowski, Marcel (born 1915)

(i) *Concerto for ondes martenot, strings and percussion;* (ii) *Piano concerto No. 2;* (iii) *Concerto for trumpet, strings and electro-acoustic instruments.*

*** Erato/Warner 4509 96972-2. (i) Jeanne Loriod, O de Chambre de Musique Contemporain, Jacques Rondon; (ii) Annie d'Arco, ORTF, Jean Martinon; (iii) Maurice André, Strasbourg PO, Alain Lombard.

Marcel Landowski is little more than a name outside France, where he is much respected – and rightly so, if his symphonies are anything to go by: his handling of complex orchestral textures and orchestral colours is highly imaginative. In the *Piano concerto* of 1963, the balance places the soloist too prominently and the instrument itself sounds tubby. The musical invention can be compared to certain kinds of conversation, civilized and intelligent, which holds you while it goes on but which remains ultimately unmemorable. The *Concerto for ondes martenot* of 1954 is stronger in atmosphere and invention; its idiom is a cross between Honegger and Shostakovich. Add Bartókian *Night music* to that mix, and you have the opening of the *Trumpet concerto* (1976). Scored for small forces (no oboes, two horns and one trombone), it also makes discreet use of magnetic tape. It is even finer than the *Concerto for ondes martenot* and its seriousness of purpose and powerful atmosphere make a strong impression. The 1978 Strasbourg recording is excellent and Maurice André plays it with total commitment.

Symphonies Nos. (i) *1 (Jean de la peur);* (ii) *2;* (i) *3 (Des espaces); 4.*

*** Erato/Warner Dig. 4509 96973-2 (2) [2292 45018-2]. (i) French Nat. O; Georges Prêtre; (ii) ORTF, Jean Martinon.

The *First*, *Third* and *Fourth* of Landowski's symphonies were recorded in 1988 and have been available before. To them Erato have now added an analogue recording from 1970 of the *Second Symphony*, conducted by Jean Martinon (economically packaged in one single jewel-case). Like its companions the musical language and thought processes have their roots in Honegger; the musical argument is well sustained and has a certain dignity. Even if he does not possess a strongly distinctive profile, Landowski has a powerful and fertile imagination, a resourceful sense of orchestration, and a commanding symphonic grip. He holds the listener from the first bar to the last. If you have the opportunity of sampling this set, try the opening minute or so of the *Fourth Symphony*, and if you respond to its world you will enjoy all these pieces. Generally excellent recorded sound.

Langgaard, Rued (1893–1953)

Symphony No. 1 (Klippepastoraler); Fra Dybet.

*** Chandos Dig. CHAN 9249 [id.]. Danish Nat. RSO & Ch., Segerstam.

Rued Langgaard began this symphony when he was fourteen; he was only eighteen when he finished revising it. Langgaard was a figure of undoubted but flawed talent, but as this banal, five-movement overblown sprawl slowly unwinds its 67 minutes, one realizes that the composer subjected this particular piece to no real critical scrutiny. Not to put too fine a point upon it, he was essentially a windbag. There are some imaginative moments in the finale. *Fra Dybet* ('From the Deep') comes from the other end of his career and was completed not long before his death: it opens rather bombastically but soon lapses into sentimentality at the entrance of the choir. Good recording.

Symphonies Nos. 4 (Løfvald: The falling of the leaf); 5 (Steppelands); 6 (Himmelrivende: The storming of the heavens).

*** Chandos Dig. CHAN 9064 [id.]. Danish Nat. RSO, Neeme Järvi.

Rued Langgaard's *Fourth Symphony*, subtitled *The falling of the leaf* or, rather less romantically, *Defoliation*, has retained little more than a foothold on the repertoire. The *Sixth* (*Himmelrivende* – variously translated as *The storming of the heavens* or, on this CD, as *Heavens asunder*) is another work which hovers on the periphery of the catalogue. In fact this Chandos collaboration with Danish Radio makes a useful introduction to this far from uninteresting composer, for these works have passages that almost persuade one as to the justice of the claims made by his admirers; what is lacking in Langgaard is any real sense of organic growth and ultimately, it must be said, a distinctive and original personality. However, Neeme Järvi makes out a strong case for this music and the Danish Radio Orchestra play with conviction and sympathy. They are given excellent recorded sound.

Symphonies Nos. 4 (Løvfald); 6 (Den Himmelrivande); (i) *Sfærernas Musik.*
**(*) Danacord DACOCD 340/341 [id.]. (i) Edith Guillaume, Danish R. Ch.; Danish RSO, John Frandsen.

Sfærernas musik (*The Music of the spheres*), written in 1918 in between the two symphonies recorded here, is an extraordinary piece of undoubted vision and originality. It has a wild-eyed intensity and a quasi-mystical quality that is unusual in the Nordic music of its time. One has the feeling that it could equally stop earlier or go on longer, but formal coherence is not Langgaard's strong suit. The performances are good and the recording eminently satisfactory without being quite in the Chandos league.

Symphonies Nos. 10 (Yon Dwelling of Thunder); 11 (Ixion); 12 (Helsingeborg); Sfinx (tone-poem).
** Danacord Dig. DACOCD 408 [id.]. Artur Rubinstein PO, Ilya Stupel.

The *Eleventh* and *Twelfth Symphonies* are shorter than they seem; in fact the *Eleventh* lasts less than six minutes but its main theme is of awesome vapidity. It is openly neo-romantic, which would not in itself matter were the musical invention tinged with a flicker of real distinction. The Artur Rubinstein Philharmonic Orchestra turns in serviceable performances and are decently enough recorded, but do not dispel the impression that this is music of shadows rather than substance.

Symphonies Nos. 13 (Faithlessness); 16 (The Deluge of Sun); Anti-Christ (opera): *Prelude.*
** Danacord Dig. DACOCD 410. Artur Rubinstein PO, Ilya Stupel.

The *Sixteenth Symphony* opens rather like Strauss, then comes to an abrupt stop, before launching into a short, Schumannesque Scherzo of about 1 minute in the same key, and thence into a *Dance of chastisement*. The *Elegy* which follows also has touches of Schumann and there is a short and unconvincing finale. In the *Thirteenth* (*Undertro*, 'Faithlessness') the composer returns to material he had first used in his *Seventh Symphony*, which he had in turn borrowed from his countryman, Axel Gade. What it lacks in substance it makes up for in bombast. Probably the best thing here is the *Prelude* to the opera, *Anti-Christ*, a much earlier piece dating from the 1920s. The performances and recordings are respectable rather than distinguished.

Langlais, Jean (born 1907)

(i) *Messe solennelle;* (i; ii; iii) *Missa Salve regina;* (Organ): (i) *Paraphrases grégoriennes, Op. 5: Te Deum. Poèmes évangéliques, Op. 2: La Nativité. Triptyque grégorien: Rosa mystica.*
*** Hyperion Dig. CDA 66270 [id.]. Westminster Cathedral Ch., David Hill, (i) with J. O'Donnell; (ii) A. Lumsden; (iii) ECO Brass Ens.

Jean Langlais' organ music owes much to Dupré's example, and the two Masses are archaic in feeling, strongly influenced by plainchant and organum, yet with a plangent individuality that clearly places the music in the twentieth century. The style is wholly accessible and the music enjoys fervent advocacy from these artists, who are accorded sound-quality of the high standard one expects from this label.

Larsson, Lars-Erik (1908–86)

Symphonies Nos. 1 in D, Op. 2; 2, Op. 17.
**(*) BIS Dig. CD 426 [id.]. Helsingborg SO, Hans-Peter Frank.

The *First Symphony* is derivative but a work of obvious promise, fluent and well put together. There are obvious echoes of the Russian post-nationalists as well as Nielsen and Sibelius. Much the same could be said of the more mature *Second Symphony* (1936–7), which is genial and unpretentious. Good performances and recording, but the music itself is not Larsson at his strongest.

Symphony No. 3 in C min., Op. 34; (i) *Förklädd Gud (A God in disguise), Op. 24.*
** BIS CD 96 [id.]. (i) Nordin, Hagegård, Jonsson, Helsingborg Concert Ch.; Helsingborg SO, Frykberg.

A God in disguise was a production for Swedish Radio. The choral suite for two soloists and narrator that Larsson fashioned from it has great freshness and charm. This 1978 performance has some fine singing from Håkan Hagegård, and the Helsingborg chorus and orchestra give a serviceable account of the score. The symphony is as diatonic as *A God in disguise* and, though not completely successful, is strong enough to deserve rescue.

Croquiser, Op. 38; 7 Little fugues with preludes in the old style, Op. 58; Sonatinas Nos. 1, Op. 16; 2, Op. 39; 3, Op. 41.
*** BIS Dig. CD 758 [id.]. Hans Pålsson.

Larsson is better represented in the catalogue than in the concert hall. The eloquent *Violin concerto* of 1953 ought to be a repertory piece, and the *Music for orchestra* (1950) is equally deserving. The piano music is slight but far from insignificant. It is beautifully fashioned, always intelligent and often witty. Hans Pålsson serves it with exemplary taste and expertise. It is well recorded, and those who like Larsson's music need not hesitate.

Lassus, Orlandus (*c.* 1532–94)

Chansons and Moresche: *Allala, pia Calia; Canta Giorgia Cathalina; Chi chilichi?; Elle s'en va; En un chasteau; Fuyons tous d'amour le jeu; Hai Lucia; Je l'ayme bien; Las! me faut-il; Lucescit jam o socii; Lucia, celu; O foible esprit; O Lucia; Mais qui pourroit estre celuy; La nuict froid et sombre; Quand mon mary vient de dehors; Si du malheur; Une puce j'ay dedans l'oreille; Un triste coeur; Un jeune moine est sorti du couvent; Vignon, vignon, vignette.* Lute solos: *J'ay un mary; Quand mon mary; Le tems peult bien.*

(B) *** HM Dig. HMC 90856.58 (3) [(M) id. import]. Ens. Clément Jannequin, Dominique Visse – BANCHIERI: *Barca di Venetia per Padova* ***; MARENZIO: *Madrigals* **(*); VECCHI: *Madrigal comedies.* ***

One tends to think of the madrigals of Lassus as of a predominantly dolorous nature, and indeed the opening number here, *Las! me faut il* ('Alas must I needs bear so much woe'), and other settings like *Si du malheur* and *La nuict froide et sombre*, carry their full weight of expressive melancholy. They are sung simply and beautifully here. But this excellently varied collection shows another side to this remarkable composer: his sense of fun and the grotesque, and a ready response to the most ribald goings-on. The singers here enter fully into the boisterous spirit of this lively music and, led by their counter-tenor director, Dominique Visse, project the Rabelaisian texts with a characterful aplomb, remarkable precision and, at times, a slightly nasal tonal edge which is very fitting. Excellent recording, with fine presence. The disc comes as part of a Harmonia Mundi CD Trio of *'Comédies madrigalesques'*, which is well worth exploring if you have a taste for such repertoire. Good documentation.

Chansons: *Bon jour mon cœur* (ensemble and solo versions); *Fleur de quinz ans; J'ayme la pierre précieuse; Margot labourez les vignes; La nuict froide et sombre; Pour courir en poste a la ville; Susanne ung jour* (with ANON.: Intablature for lute from the Wickhambrook Lute Manuscript); Motets: *Cum natus esset Jesus; In monte Oliveti; Stabat Mater.*

(M) *** Virgin Veritas/EMI Dig. VER5 61166-2. Hilliard Ens., Paul Hillier.

One half is devoted to motets, the other to chansons; both are sung one voice to a part. The tonal blend is as perfect as is usual with this ensemble, intonation is extraordinarily accurate, and there is no vibrato. The sacred pieces, and in particular the setting of the *Stabat Mater* which opens the first half, are most impressive. In some of the chansons there is a discreet lute accompaniment to lend variety. Of the chansons, *La nuict froide et sombre* is quite magical and given with great feeling and colour. One of the other songs tells of an unscrupulous friar, in which all suggestions of virtuous behaviour bring the refrain: 'Brother Lubin can't do it'; others include a simple expression of delight in a loved one, a tale of attempted seduction based on the story of Susanna and the Elders, and a hopeful offer to a fifteen-year-old girl to '*vous faire apprendre*' (teach you how it is done!). For all these racier poems, Lassus provides the most refined setting. A useful addition to the Lassus discography and beautifully recorded.

De profundis clamavi; Exaltabo te, Domine; Missa octavi toni; Missa qual donna.

*** Nimbus Dig. NI 5150 [id.]. Christ Church Cathedral Ch., Oxford, Stephen Darlington.

The *Missa qual donna* is a late work, expressive and mellifluous, and very well sung by the choir of Christ Church Cathedral, Oxford. As a pendant, the disc also includes Cipriano de Rore's Petrarch setting, *Qual donna a gloriosa fama*, which the Mass takes as its inspiration. The motet, *De profundis clamavi*, one of the great penitential Psalms, is almost the most eloquent and expressive of the pieces here. At times one could wish for more ardent tone from the trebles; but unquestionably these are fine performances, and the recording is very good indeed.

Le Lagrime di San Pietro a 7.

(BB) *** Naxos Dig. 8.553311 [id.]. Ars Nova, Bo Holten.

*** HM Dig. HMC 901483 [id.]. Kiehr, Koslowsky, Berridge, Türk, Lamy, Koay, Peacock, Ens. Voc. Européen, Herreweghe.

Le Lagrime de San Pietro ('The Tears of St Peter') is a setting of 20 verses of the poet Luigi Transillo (1510–68), a Neapolitan best known for his lyrical love-sonnets. Like much Renaissance music, it can be performed by a vocal consort or a choir, with or without instruments. The music is rich in variety of expressive means: Howard Mayer Brown calls it a work of 'almost Baroque religious fervour'. The Naxos performance by a first-class Danish choir (6 sopranos, 2 altos, 2 counter-tenors, 4 tenors and 3 basses) is comparatively robust yet offers singing of great sensitivity and a wide dynamic range. The recording, made at the Copenhagen Grundtvigskirken, has a properly spacious ambience, yet is admirably clear.

The *Lagrime di San Pietro* is full of symbolism – seven being the number associated with suffering; the writing is in seven parts, and there are 21 pieces in all (a multiple of seven), the last of which is a Latin motet on the theme of suffering. It is a work of great expressive purity and is performed by Herreweghe's forces with dedication and perfection in the matter of intonation. Excellent recording.

9 Lamentationes Hieremiae.
*** HM Dig. HMC 901299 [id.]. Paris Chapelle Royale Ens., Herreweghe.

(i) *9 Lamentationes Hieremiae.* (ii) *Missa pro defunctis (Requiem)* for 4 voices. (i) *Aurora lucis rutilat* (hymn for Lauds); *Magnificat on Aurora lucis rutilat*. Motets: *Christus resurgens; Regina coeli laetare; Surgens Jesus.*
(B) *** Hyperion Dyad Dig. CDD 22012 (2) [id.]. Pro Cantione Antiqua, (i) Bruno Turner; (ii) Mark Brown.

The competing Harmonia Mundi set of the *Lamentations* is available on a single, premium-priced disc, whereas for approximately the same cost this Hyperion Dyad offers much more music. Within this set, Bruno Turner's 1981 digital recording of the *Lamentations* is also now accommodated on a single CD, while the second includes a selection of music for Easter Sunday, including the glorious *Aurora lucis rutilat* for two five-part choirs and the *Magnificat* based on the motet, plus Mark Brown's fine performance of the four-part *Requiem*. The performances under Bruno Turner are expressive and vital. The recording too is spacious and warm. So for that matter is the Harmonia Mundi recording for the Chapelle Royale and Philippe Herreweghe, whose performances of the *Lamentations* are hardly less admirable.

Missa Ad imitationem Vinum bonum; Motet: *Vinum bonum; Missa super Quand'io pens'al martire* (with ARCADELT: Madrigal: *Quand'io pens'al martire*). *Missa super triste départ* (with GOMBERT: Chanson: *Triste départ*).
*** Decca (IMS) Dig. 444 335-2. King's College, Cambridge, Ch., Stephen Cleobury.

It is good to welcome the King's College Choir back on Decca with a generous 70-minute programme, superbly sung, offering three of Lassus's finest Masses, together with their secular source-material. The parody Mass in praise of wine was first published in Paris in 1577 and is quite surprisingly extrovert, as is the motet on which it is based, singing the praises of good wine but also referring to the miracle at Cana. The *Missa super Quand'io pens'al martire* is a particularly appealing and beautiful work, and again this is not surprising when Arcadelt's four-part madrigal is such a fine piece. An outstanding addition to the growing Lassus discography.

Missa Bell'Amfitrit'alterna.
(BB) *** Naxos Dig. 8.550836 [id.]. Oxford Schola Cantorum, Jeremy Summerly – PALESTRINA: *Missa Hodie Christus natus est* etc. ***
(M) **(*) EMI Dig. CD-EMX 2180 [(M) id. import]. St John's College, Cambridge, Ch., Guest – ALLEGRI: *Miserere* **(*); PALESTRINA: *Veni sponsa Christi.* ***

This magnificent Mass of Palestrina's great Flemish contemporary, Lassus, makes a superb coupling for the outstanding performances of Palestrina masterpieces on the Naxos disc. This is the full Schola Cantorum of Oxford, not just the smaller Camerata group, and arguably it is too large for the dedicated, intimate polyphony of Lassus; but the singing is superb and the recording is warm and atmospheric. Yet another outstanding Naxos issue of early music.

Amphitrite was not only the mythological goddess of the sea but also a nickname for Venice, and this Mass is almost certainly connected with the city rather than with Poseidon's wife. It is a complex and varied piece of remarkable textural diversity, and it is also finely sung by the St John's Choir under Guest, although perhaps a little more Latin fervour would have been in order. The digital recording is first class.

Missa Osculetur me; Motets: *Alma Redemptoris Mater; Ave regina caelorum; Hodie completi sunt; Osculetur me; Regina caeli; Salve Regina; Timor et tremor.*
*** Gimell/Ph. Dig. 454 918-2 [id.]. Tallis Scholars, Peter Phillips.

Lassus learned the technique of double-choir antiphonal music in Italy. The Mass is preceded by the motet, *Osculetur me* (*Let him kiss me with the kisses of his lips*), which provides much of its motivic substance and is glorious in its sonorities and expressive eloquence. The singing of the Tallis Scholars under Peter Phillips is as impressive as it was on their earlier records, and the recording is beautifully present.

Prophetiae Sibyllarum. Settings of Petrarch, Ronsard and du Bellay: Chansons: *Amour donne-moy pays; Bon jour mon coeur; Comme un qui prend; J'ay de vou voir; J'espère et crains; La nuict froide et sombre; O foible esprit; Ronds-moi mon cœur; La terre les eaux va Beuvant; La vita fugge.* Madrigals: *Crudele acerba; I vo piangendo; Mia benigna fortun'e; Soleasi nel mio cor; Standomi un giorno.*
*** HM/BMG Dig. 05472 77304-2 [id.]. Cantus Cölln, Konrad Junghänel.

The *Prophetiae Sibyllarum* ('Sibylline Prophecies') sets a cycle of humanistic Latin verse based on Neapolitan legends that tell how the caves at Cumae were the home of the Sibyls who foretold the coming of God. Jerome Roche in his 1982 monograph writes of the work as 'mysterious, brooding music, but never unsettling emotionally in the manner of Gesualdo'. In addition, we have the madrigal-cycle, *Standomi un giorno*, and five other Petrarch settings, as well as settings by two of *La Pléiade*, Pierre de Ronsard and Joachim du Bellay. It is difficult to imagine these better performed than they are here by the Cantus Cölln and Konrad Junghänel, and they are excellently recorded too.

St Matthew Passion; Exsultet; Visitatio.
**(*) HM Dig. HMU 907076 [id.]. Paul Elliot, Theatre of Voices, Paul Hillier.

This is Lassus at his most austere and devotional, with more chant than polyphony; it is not the best entry-point into his music for those unfamiliar with its opulence. The *Visitatio* (*Easter Dialogue*), which uses the edition by John Stevens, and the *Exsultet* from the Paschal Vigil, are purely chant. In the *Passion* Paul Elliot sings the part of the Evangelist, Paul Hillier that of Christ. The recording, made in California, is exemplary.

Lawes, Henry (1596–1662)

Songs: *Amintor's welladay; The angler's song; Come sad turtle; Fairwell despairing hopes; Hark, shepherd swains; I laid me down; I prithee send me back my heart; The Lark; My soul the great God's praises sings; O King of heaven and hell; Sing, fair Clorinda; Sitting by the streams; Slide soft you silver floods; Sweet stay awhile; Tavola; Thee and thy wondrous deeds; This mossy bank.*
*** Hyperion CDA 66315 [id.]. Emma Kirkby, Consort of Musicke, Anthony Rooley.

The Lawes songs were enormously popular in their time. Today their direct, declamatory style seems comparatively unsubtle alongside Purcell. The melancholy is tangible, but not overtly expressive. The brief but effective *Tavola* is like an arietta from an Italian opera. The Hyperion collection is fairly wide in its range: the title-number (*Sitting by the streams*) is a verse anthem. There are plenty of secular songs too, notably the engaging *Angler's song*, and admirers of Emma Kirkby – here in radiant voice – and Rooley's immaculately stylish Consort of Musicke will find much to enjoy.

Lawes, William (1602–45)

Fantasia suites for 2 violins, bass viol and organ Nos. 1–8.
*** Chandos Dig. CHAN 0552 [id.]. Purcell Qt.

Lawes studied with Coperario when the latter was organizing a performing group for Prince Charles which he called 'Coperarios Musique', in which Orlando Gibbons played the organ. Lawes's own *Fantasia suites* are based on those of his mentor and are simpler, usually more extrovert works than the *Consort suites*. They are in three movements, in each case a *Fantazy* followed by two *Aires*, in essence dance movements, alman and galliard, later corant or saraband. The organ does not just play a continuo role but is important in its own right. The music itself is lively in invention and by no means predictable, with surprise moments of passing dissonance, and the composer's individuality comes out in his special brand of lyricism. The performances here have plenty of life, and the recording balance is very successful: the result is enjoyably fresh.

Royal consorts Nos. 1–10.
*** Chandos Dig. CHAN 0584/5 [id.]. Purcell Consort.

Royal consorts Nos. 1 in D min.; 3 in D min.; 6 in D; 7 in A min.; 9 in F.
*** ASV Gaudeamus Dig. CDGAU 146 [id.]. Greate Consort, Monica Huggett.

Royal consorts Nos. 2 in D min.; 4 in D; 5 in D; 8 in C; 10 in B flat.
*** ASV Gaudeamus Dig. CDGAU 147 [id.]. Greate Consort, Monica Huggett.

The ten *Royal Consorts*, even though they are in four rather than five or six parts like the *Setts*, in many ways represent Lawes's most ambitious undertaking. There is evidence that he conceived the works as simple quartets (two violins and two viols) around 1620, but a decade later theorbos (archlutes) were added to provide a basic continuo and increase the range of textural colour. Each suite is in six or seven movements, the first of which is the most extended, sometimes taking as long as the remaining charming *Aires* and increasingly lively *Almans*, *Corants* and *Sarabands* all put together. Indeed these opening expressive *Fantazys* or *Pavanes* offer the kernel of the arguments and contain the most adventurous music, combining nobility of feeling with ear-catching contrapuntal lines.

Each *Consort* has its own distinct character, but we are offered here two markedly different styles of performance. The playing of the Purcell Consort is notably sprightly, the recording fresh and vividly clear, but within an open acoustic of some depth. The brightness and transparency of the sound, without loss of sonority, means that the individual instruments are cleanly delineated, although blending well together, never better demonstrated than in the splendidly managed *Echo* movement that ends the first work of the series.

Monica Huggett and her Greate Consort are very slightly recessed; their sound is warmer and the expressive music is given a fuller texture by the resonance. Some will feel that, presented in this way, this music is afforded more atmosphere. They also play at a slightly lower pitch, which means that the effect is inevitably mellower when compared directly with the brighter Chandos sound, although on ASV detail is by no means unclear. Both sets of performances are very rewarding, and if we are inclined, marginally, to favour the bright projection and added transparency of Chandos, many collectors will surely respond differently.

Collections

Consort sets a 5: in A min. & C ; Divisions on a Pavan in G min. for 2 bass viols & organ; Royal consorts Nos. 1 in D min.; 6 in D; Set a 4 in G min. (with 2 theorbos); *Lute duets: Alman; 2 Corants.*

(BB) **(*) Naxos Dig. 8.550601 [id.]. Rose Consort of viols; Jacob Herigan, David Miller (lutes), Timothy Roberts (organ).

Naxos provide an attractive cross-section of Lawes's instrumental music, using an all-viol texture for the string parts in the *Consorts* (with organ where appropriate).The group also include a fascinatingly bravura set of *Divisions for viols and organ* on the same *Pavane* which opens the four-part *Set in G minor*. The pieces for two lutes could have been given more lively projection, although they are well enough played. The excellent balance helps to make this inexpensive sampler recommendable, which readers might well try.

Leclair, Jean-Marie (1697–1764)

6 Concertos, Op. 7; 6 Concertos, Op. 10.

(M) *** Erato/Warner 0630 11225-2 (3). Jarry, Lardé, Paillard CO, Paillard.

Flute concerto in C, Op. 7/3; Violin concertos: in F; in A, Op. 7/4 & 6; in A, Op. 10/2.

*** Chandos Dig. CHAN 0564 [id.]. Rachel Brown; Simon Standage, Coll. Mus. 90.

Violin concertos: in D min., Op. 7/1; in D; F; G min, Op. 10/3–4 & 6.

*** Chandos Dig. CHAN 0589 [id.]. Simon Standage, Coll. Mus. 90.

Violin concertos: Op. 7/2 in D; 7/5 in A min.; Op. 10/1 in B flat; 10/5 in E min.

*** Chandos Dig. CHAN 0551 [id.]. Simon Standage, Coll. Mus. 90.

The twelve concertos of Opp. 7 and 10 make up Leclair's complete orchestral output. Op. 7 was composed in 1737 and Op. 10 in 1743–4; generally speaking, they are underrated and their merits are considerable. Although one cannot include among these a strongly individual lyrical power, the *Aria gracioso* of No. 1 is quite ear-catching, while both the *Adagio* of Op. 7/4 and the *Largo* of Op. 7/5 are distinctly appealing. The *Andante* of Op. 10/3 could well have been written by Vivaldi. Finales too are sprightly in their invention. Op. 7/3 is optionally for flute or oboe, and Rachel Brown makes a pleasing case for the use of a baroque flute, especially in the rather winning slow movement. Simon Standage is a stylish soloist of impeccable technique and Collegium Musicum 90 (4.4.2.2.1) provide authentic, spirited accompaniments. The recordings were made either in St Jude's in north-west London or in All Saints', East Finchley, and textures are transparent and have good sonority.

The performances by the violinist Gérard Jarry and flautist Christian Lardé are of exemplary style and virtuosity. Those who must have the music played with the benefit of period sonorities can turn to the alternative Chandos/Simon Standage ongoing series or to Jaap Schröder's selection (see below); but there is nothing in this Erato set that is wanting in stylistic sense or musical verve, and the recording is first class and most naturally transferred to CD. There are excellent and extensive notes by Harry Halbreich.

Violin concertos: in C & A min., Op. 7/3 & 5; in G min., Op. 10/6.

(M) *** Teldec/Warner 4509 92180-2 [id.]. Jaap Schröder, Concerto Amsterdam (with NAUDOT: *Recorder concerto in G, Op. 17/5:* Brüggen, VCM, Harnoncourt **).

Distinguished playing from Jaap Schröder and his colleagues, who make outstanding advocates of these concertos. Leclair is a stronger composer than he is often given credit for. The *G minor Concerto*, Op. 10/6, is a work of real sensibility and imagination, and one only has to sample the slow movements of both the other concertos to discover that Leclair's melodic lines are individual and pleasing. The performances are on period instruments or copies and can be recommended to *aficionados*, as the 1978 analogue sound is both flattering and vivid. The *Recorder concerto* by Jacques-Christophe Naudot (*c.* 1690–1762) which is provided as a bonus is less individual but very well played. However, here the sound of the supporting group is thin and less well focused.

Sonatas for 2 violins without basso continuo, Op. 3/1–6; Op. 12/1–6.

(N) (B) *** Erato Ultima 3984 24245-2 (2). Chiara Banchini, John Holloway.

Although this set is probably aimed at the specialist collector with an interest in the violin's musical history, these works are by no means dull or repetitive and the music itself is often surprisingly attractive. Leclair uses all the special devices of which the instrument's technique was capable in the early years of the eighteenth century, with sustained multiple-stopped chords (very effective in the opening of Op.3/3), and even simulating a drone effect on one instrument while its companion ruminates melodically above (the *Adagio* of the same work). The first set dates from 1730, and although the second set was not published until 1746, these sonatas were probably composed around the same time. The sonatas of Op. 3 are written in a three-movement structure; four of the six sonatas of Op.12 extend to four movements, yet the invention in the first set is if anything fresher than in the second. Leclair is always light-hearted, never austere, and his slow movements are often touchingly expressive. The performances here are first-class in every way: clearly these two players are enjoying themselves, and the recording is beautifully balanced, the violin timbres natural and never edgy or scratchy.

Trio sonatas, Book 3, Op. 5/3, 4, 6 (Le Tombeau) 10 & 11.
(N) * Hyperion Dig. CDA 67033 [id.]. Convivium.

It is difficult to welcome these period-instrument performances – the first of a new series – when the string sound (Elizabeth Wallfisch and Richard Tunnicliffe, with Paul Nicholson, harspichord) is so edgy and buzzy. The very opening *Grave* of the *C minor Sonata (Le Tombeau)* is singularly uningratiating. The performers bring plenty of vitality to allegros, but the ear quickly wearies of these disagreeable textures.

Trio sonatas: in D (première récréation de musique d'une exécution facile), Op. 6; in A, Op. 14; Double violin sonata in D, Op. 3/6.
**(*) Chandos Dig. CHAN 0582 [id.]. Coll. Mus. 90 (Simon Standage, Micaela Comberti, Jane Coe, Nicholas Parle).

The pair of *Trio sonatas* prove to be elegant and tuneful French suites and, although the composer advertised the *D major* as making few technical demands on the players, it is by no means simplistic and the extensive decorated *Chaconne* with which it ends (splendidly played here) is hardly music for beginners! The *Double violin sonata* opens with a tenderly melancholy *Andante* but proves a lively and engaging work with a dancing finale, even though the central *Largo* is again rather doleful. In short this is all highly attractive music with a consistently high standard of invention, and it is played on period instruments with fine style and much vitality. The recording cannot be faulted. The sole reservation, and it is not unimportant, is that Simon Standage's timbre has a characteristic cutting edge which some ears may find wearing after a time.

Lecocq, Alexandre (1832–1918)

Mam'zelle Angot (ballet, arr. Gordon Jacob).
(M) *** Decca 430 849-2 (2) [id.]. Nat. PO, Bonynge – HEROLD: *La Fille mal gardée*. ***

Mam'zelle Angot is a gay, vivacious score with plenty of engaging tunes, prettily orchestrated in the modern French style. Bonynge offers the first recording of the complete score, and its 39 minutes are consistently entertaining when the orchestral playing has such polish and wit. The Kingsway Hall recording is closely observed: the CD brings sharp detail and tangibility, especially at lower dynamic levels.

Lecuona, Ernesto (1895–1963)

Danzas Afro-Cubanas; Gardenia; Noche de Estrellas; Porcelana China (Danza de Muñecos); Polka de los Enanos; (i) *Rapsodia Cubana; Valses Fantásticos; Vals del Nilo; Yo te Quiero Siempre.*
** BIS Dig. CD 794 [id.]. Thomas Tirino, (i) with Polish Nat. RSO, Michael Bartas.

Ernesto Lecuona hails from Cuba and made a career for himself outside Latin and Central America. His reputation extended to Spain and France as well as North America, and he numbered Ravel and Gershwin among his admirers. A pupil of Joaquín Nin, he founded the Havana Symphony Orchestra and the Lecuona Cuban Boys Band and also served as an honorary cultural attaché in Washington (as at one time had the pianist, Jorge Bolet). He was active in both the Columbia and RCA recording studios until the 1930s, when he concentrated on composing. He obviously enjoyed a strong technique, particularly for the left hand, for which he writes with both virtuosity and ingenuity. With the exception of the *Rapsodia Cubana*, which is conspicuously slight in invention, this is light music in the Latin-American style but distinguished by an inventive and resourceful use of rhythm. Thomas Tirino is equal to its demands, although this recording – which emanates from New York and Katowice, not BIS's usual venues – is not three-star. Nor is the music; however, although it is all very limited, there are rewarding moments of sophistication.

Piano music: *Ante El Escorial; La cardenese. Pièces caractéristicas: La Habanera; Mazurka glissando. Preludio en la noche. Diary of a child: Canción de luna. Danzas Afro-Cubanas; La comparsa; La Conga de media noch; Danza de los ñañigos; Danza lucumí; Danza negra; . . . Y ma negra bailaba!. Ella y yo. Miniature No. 1: Bell-Flower. San Francisco El Grande. Valses fantásticos: Valse apasionato; Valse arabesque; Valse brilliante; Valse maracilloso; Valse patéco; Valse poetico; Valse romantico. Yo te quiero siempre.*
(N) *** EMI Dig. CDC5 56803-2 [id.]. Kathryn Stott.

Popular Cuban music has been the melting-pot for many ethnic influences, but the most famous rhythms – bolero, conga, habanera, guarache and rumba – have a shared Black and Spanish origin. Lecuona, best known for his songs, was also a virtuoso pianist, and for his piano pieces he fused these elements into a popular art form of considerable sophistication. His miniatures are not only tuneful, but well crafted. Evocations like *Ante El Escorial* and *Saint Franciso El Grande* are quite ambitious, while the romantic numbers like the sultry *Ella y yo* ('She and I') and *Yo te quiero siempe* ('I will always love you') in the sensitive hands of Kathryn Stott are gently seductive. The suite of *Valses fantásticos* shows her at her most stylish and sparkling. The *Valse arabesque* has an ongoing moto perpetuo flow which is played with the crispest delicacy; *Valse patéco* and *Valse poetico* bring a pleasingly subtle rhythmic feeling, and the others all have an engaging syncopated lilt. Though not to be taken all at once, this music has character and enjoyable individuality. Excellent recording, bright but not hard.

Le Flem, Paul (1881–1984)

Symphony No. 4; (i) *Le grand jardinier de France* (film music). *7 Pièces enfantines; Pour les morts (Tryptique symphonique No. 1).*
** Marco Polo Dig. 8.223655 [id.]. Rhenish PO, James Lockhart, (i) with Gilles Nopre.

Paul Le Flem is another of the French composers who is emerging from the shadows into which he has been so prematurely cast. The *Fourth Symphony* bears witness to an amazing creative vitality, when one thinks that its composer was just ninety years young at the time (1971–2). (As his dates will show at a glance, he lived to be 103.) The *Sept Pièces enfantines* is an orchestral transcription of a set of children's pieces for piano, and *Le grand jardinier de France* is a film score. Both have a certain charm and would have more, had the orchestra been allowed more rehearsal. Wind intonation is not always flawless. Le Flem is not, perhaps, a major personality, but the *Fourth Symphony* is in its way quite remarkable, and had the performance greater finesse, the disc would have rated a three-star recommendation.

Lehár, Franz (1870–1948)

The Czarevitch (sung in English).
*** Telarc Dig. CD 80395 [id.]. Nancy Gustafson, Jerry Hadley, Naomi Itami, Lynton Atkinson, Jeffrey Carl, ECO, Bonynge.

Though it lacks the really memorable melodies which make the finest Lehár operettas so winning, *The Czarevitch* is a delightful piece which, with Richard Bonynge as a most understanding conductor, is full of charm and sparkle, with Russian colour from balalaikas nicely touched in. Anyone wanting this in English translation will not be disappointed, with the second couple of principals readily matching up to Jerry Hadley and Nancy Gustafson.

Friederike (complete).
(M) *** EMI CMS5 65369-2 (2). Donath, Dallapozza, Fuchs, Finke, Grabenhorst, Bav. R. Ch., Munich R. O, Wallberg.

The idea of Richard Tauber inspiring Lehár to write an operetta with the poet Goethe as the main character may sound far-fetched, but that is just what *Friederike* is, more ambitious than a genuine operetta and bringing the obvious snag for non-German speakers that there is a great deal of spoken dialogue, the more disruptive because there is no libretto, let alone an English translation. However, there is a track-by-track synopsis of each number, and in every other respect this is a delightful reissue, with Helen Donath charming and sensitive in the name-part. Dallapozza has a light, heady tenor, at times stressed by the weight of the part of Goethe but rising above all to the great Tauber number, *O Mädchen, mein Mädchen!*, based (like other numbers) on a Goethe poem, *Mailied*. Heinz Wallberg is a lively and persuasive director, and the 1980 recording has the bloom one associates with German EMI productions.

(i) *Giuditta* (complete). (ii) *Der Zarewitsch*: highlights.
(N) (B) **(*) Decca Double 458 552-2 (2). (i; ii) Hilde Gueden, Waldemar Kmentt; (i) Emmy Loose, Murray Dickie, Oskar Czerwenka, Walter Berry; (i) Vienna State Op., Ch. & O, Moralt; (ii) Vienna Volksoper Ch. & O, Max Schönherr.

The classic Decca recording of *Giuditta* dates from 1958 and it is good to have this late and comparatively ambitious opera reissued complete, even if musically it is more uneven than Lehár's two most famous operettas. The performance is affectionately idiomatic in a Viennese way, very well sung and vividly presented. Hilde Gueden is in fresh, sparkling form, and Waldemar Kmentt makes an excellent Octavio: their duet, *Schön wie die blau Sommernacht*, makes another attractive hit to put alongside Gueden's delightful *Mein Lippen, sie küssen so heiss*. The score also has some more routine Lehár, but the infectious singing and bright, slightly garish sound injects it with plenty of life.

The highlights from *Der Zarewitsch* and *Der Graf von Luxemburg* (coupled with the *The Merry Widow* – see below) were recorded a decade later in the Sofiensaal. Although the offerings are not especially generous, with approximately half an hour from each operetta, the recording itself (produced by Christopher Raeburn) is splendid, as demonstrated by the atmospheric opening scenes, with lively support from the chorus and orchestra. The two principals are on top form so that the *Wolgalied* in *Der Zarewitsch* and the charming *Kosende Wellen* are matched by the delightful waltz-duet of *Der Graf von Luxemburg*. There are no librettos but good plot summaries detail individual numbers.

Das Land des Lächelns (The Land of smiles) (complete).

(M) **(*) EMI CMS5 65372-2 (2). Rothenberger, Gedda, Holm, Friedauer, Moeller, Bav. R. Ch., Graunke SO, Willy Mattes.

This 1967 recording has on the whole transferred well to CD. Don't be put off by the sound of the overture, which seems thin because of the relatively small orchestra for the opening scene, but then has plenty of theatrical presence. The recording is atmospheric and real, not only in conveying the songs but also in the spoken dialogue, which is well produced. The cast is strong. Gedda is in excellent form and, besides Anneliese Rothenberger, Renate Holm makes a charming contribution as Mi. The famous tunes, including '*You are my heart's delight*', are splendidly done. Yet again there is no libretto, especially desirable in the operetta; but we are offered a track-by-track synopsis of each number.

The Land of smiles (sung in English).

*** Telarc Dig. CD 80419 [id.]. Nancy Gustafson, Jerry Hadley, Naomi Itami, Lynton Atkinson, ECO, Bonynge.

Richard Bonynge proves as warmly understanding of the Lehár idiom as he is in Bellini, while Jerry Hadley winningly takes the Tauber role of Prince Sou-Chong. He also provides a new translation, with the hit-number, 'You are my heart's delight', becoming *My heart belongs to you*, with diction commendably clear. Nancy Gustafson makes a bright heroine and Lynton Atkinson sings with winning lightness in the second tenor-role. Recommended.

The Merry Widow (Die lustige Witwe; complete, in German).

*** DG Dig.439 911-2 [id.]. Studer, Skovhus, Bonney, Trost, Terfel, Monteverdi Ch., VPO, Gardiner.

✿ *** EMI (SIS) CDS7 47178-8 (2) [Ang. CDCB 47177]. Schwarzkopf, Gedda, Waechter, Steffek, Knapp, Equiluz, Philh. Ch. and O, Matačić.

(***) EMI (SIS) mono CDH7 69520-2 [id.]. Schwarzkopf, Gedda, Kunz, Loose, Kraus, Philh. Ch. & O, Ackermann.

A single-disc version of *The Merry Widow*, with full text and ample dialogue, neatly packaged with libretto, makes an attractive recommendation ahead of any rival. John Eliot Gardiner has the bonus of the Vienna Philharmonic very much on home ground, playing not only with a natural feeling for the idiom but with unrivalled finesse and polish. The characteristic spring which Gardiner brings to the rhythms goes with idiomatic rubato, often daringly extreme. As Hanna Glawari, the widow of the title, Cheryl Studer gives her most endearing performance yet. She may not have quite the vivacity of Elisabeth Schwarzkopf, but Studer's very first entry establishes her authority and charm, and the gentle half-tone on which she opens the soaring melody of the *Viljalied* is ravishing. Consistently she sings with sweet, firm tone and the Danish baritone, Boje Skovhus, as Danilo makes an animated, raffish hero. The second couple, Valencienne and Camille, are delectably taken by Barbara Bonney and Rainer Trost, clear and youthful-sounding, outshining all rivals. The rest make an outstanding team, with Bryn Terfel, ripely resonant, turning Baron Mirko into more than a *buffo* character, while the choristers of Gardiner's Monteverdi Choir, obviously enjoying their Viennese outing, bring to Lehár the point and precision they have long devoted to the baroque repertory.

Elisabeth Schwarzkopf was surely born to take the role of Hanna and Matačić provides a magical set, guaranteed to send shivers of delight through any listener with its vivid sense of atmosphere and superb musicianship. It is one of Walter Legge's masterpieces as a recording manager, creating a sense of theatre that is almost without rival in gramophone literature. The CD opens up the sound yet retains the full bloom, and the theatrical presence and atmosphere are something to marvel at.

It was the mono set, of the early 1950s, which established a new pattern in recording operetta. Ten years later in stereo Schwarzkopf was to record the role again, if anything with even greater point and perception, but here she has extra youthful vivacity, and the *Viljalied* – ecstatically drawn out – is unique. Some may be troubled that Kunz as Danilo sounds older than the Baron, but it is still a superbly characterful cast, and the transfer to a single CD is bright and clear.

(i) *Die lustige Witwe (The Merry Widow)* complete. (ii) *Der Graf von Luxemburg*: highlights.

(N) (M) *** Decca Double 458 549-2 (2). (i; ii) Hilde Gueden, Waldemar Kmentt, (ii) Per Grunden, Emmy Loose, Karl Dönch, Kurt Equiluz, Peter Klein, Marjan Rus; (i) Vienna State Op. O, Robert Stolz; (ii) V. Volksoper Ch. & O, Max Schönherr.

As with *Giuditta*, the classic Decca *Merry Widow* dates from 1958, and was recorded in Vienna with characteristic engineering flair. After Robert Stolz's inflated but enjoyable overture, we are taken straight into the Pontevedrian Embassy with its multitude of guests, laughter and talk, clinking cocktail glasses and rustling dresses. This extraordinary ambient effect swirls into the room in the most spectacular manner and the *Polonaise* at the beginning of Act II and the entrance of the grisettes in Act III have similar startling presence. The recording itself has splendid atmosphere and sparkle throughout (one really feels oneself in the front stalls). Hilde Gueden gives a melting performance as the Widow and she sings the *Viljalied* most seductively (helped at the close with an aura of resonance). Per Grunden makes Danilo a heady tenor role (it is usually sung by a baritone); Waldemar Kmentt is an appealing Camille de Rosillon and the other parts are well up to standard. Robert Stolz conducts an entirely authentic performance, missing not a whit of sparkle or allure, with the Vienna State Opera Orchestra adding a characteristic lilt to the music; indeed in its idiomatic Viennese inflection, this set in every way challenges the famous Schwarzkopf versions on EMI.

The coupled highlights from *Der Graf von Luxemburg* come first on disc 1, and immediately create a proper carnival atmosphere. The selection concentrates on four key excerpts, two from each act, and the singing of the two principals is hardly less enjoyable. *Bist du's, lachendes Glück* is a hit, if ever there was one!. Brief plot summaries place each number in narrative perspective.

Leighton, Kenneth (1929–88)

(i) *Cello concerto;* (ii) *Symphony No. 3 (Laudes Musicae).*

*** Chandos Dig. CHAN 8741 [id.]. (i) Wallfisch; (ii) Mackie; SNO, Bryden Thomson.

The symphony is in part a song-cycle, and its glowing, radiant colours and refined textures are immediately winning. Raphael Wallfisch plays the *Concerto* as if his life depended on it, and the *Symphony* draws every bit as much dedication from its performers. The recording is very immediate, and has stunning clarity and definition.

Veris gratia (for cello, oboe and strings), *Op. 9.*

*** Chandos Dig. CHAN 8471 [id.]. Wallfisch, Caird, RLPO, Handley – FINZI: *Cello concerto.* ***

Finzi is the dedicatee of Kenneth Leighton's *Veris gratia*, and so it makes an appropriate coupling for his *Cello concerto*, more particularly as its English pastoral style nods in his direction. The performance is highly sympathetic, George Caird the excellent oboist, and the naturally balanced recording is first class.

Conflicts, Op. 51; Fantasia contrappuntistica, Op. 24; Household pets, Op. 86; Sonatina No. 1; 5 Studies, Op. 22.

**(*) Abacus Dig. ABA 402-2 [id.]. Eric Parkin.

Kenneth Leighton was one of the most musical of pianists and wrote beautifully for the instrument. The *Household pets* is a sensitive piece, refined in craftsmanship, and the *Fantasia contrappuntistica* is comparably powerful. Eric Parkin plays it with total sympathy, and the recording is eminently serviceable.

Crucifixus pro nobis; Give me the wings of faith; O sacrum convivium; The second service: Magnificat; Nunc dimittis. Solus ad victimam.

*** ASV Dig. CDDCA 851 [id.]. David Went, Ch. of The Queen's College, Oxford, Matthew Owens – HOWELLS: *Chichester service* etc. **(*)

As a chorister in his youth, Kenneth Leighton wrote with an inborn sympathy for the voice and a natural feeling for line. These are beautiful pieces with an occasional reminder of Britten, and they are well sung, too, by the Choir of The Queen's College, Oxford, where Leighton was a student.

Lekeu, Guillaume (1870–94)

Adagio for quartet and orchestra (Les fleurs pâles de souvenir . . .) arr. for quartet with piano by Gérard Inglésia; *Molto Adagio for string quartet (Commentaire sur les paroles du Christ)*; (i) *Larghetto for cello and instrumental septet; Piano quartet* (completed D'INDY). (ii) *3 Poèmes: (Sur une tombe; Ronde; Nocturne).*

(N) *** HM Dig. HMC 901455 [id.]. Ens. Musique Oblique; (i) with Isabelle Veyrier; (ii) Rachel Yakar, Alice Adler.

The Belgian composer Guillaume Lekeu died at the age of twenty-four, leaving only a small number of works, all of which, although influenced by Franck (especially the passionate first movement of the unfinished *Piano quartet*), have a haunting post-Wagnerian *fin de siècle* atmosphere, seemingly looking forward with a sense of foreboding. Indeed the slow movement of his unfinished *Piano quartet*, the beautiful *Larghetto* for solo cello and instrumental septet with its voluptuous tenderness, and the (arranged) *Adagio* for string quartet and piano all resonate in the memory. In many ways the early extended *Molto adagio for quartet and strings*, with its strange 5/4 rhythmic pulse, inspired by Christ's lament in the Garden of Gethsemane, is most remarkable of all, not only in itself, but in having a germinal influence on the later works. The playing here by the Ensemble Musique Oblique catches the music's passionate feeling, and at times almost despairing intensity, although perhaps the account of the *Molto adagio* could be tauter. The recording, though closely observed, has plenty of ambience. The collection ends with three delightful contrasting *Poèmes* for soprano (the sensitive Rachel Yakar) and piano, where the sombre mood melts away in the central *Ronde*, but is felt again in the closing *Nocturne*. Let the reader not think this is depressing music; on the contrary it is spiritually uplifting, and is full of striking sound patterns, not least the bold horn solos in the *Larghetto*.

(i) *Piano quartet* (2nd movt ed. D'INDY); (ii) *Cello sonata in F*.
*** Koch Schwann Dig. 310 185 [id.] (i–ii) Blumenthal, (i) Adamopoulos, Desjardins, (i–ii) Zanlonghi.

Lekeu's *Cello sonata* was written when he was a mere eighteen and is a powerful, big-boned piece whose first movement alone takes well over 20 minutes (the whole work lasts just under 50). The *Piano quartet*, composed at the instigation of Ysaÿe, was left incomplete when Lekeu succumbed to typhus; it was finished by d'Indy, who was a supportive figure after the death of Franck. The style is heavily indebted to these masters, but there is a dignity and melancholy at the heart of Lekeu's music which is moving. Excellent performances and vividly present recording.

Piano trio in C min.
**(*) Koch Schwann Dig. 310 060 [id.] Blumenthal, Adamopoulos, Zanlonghi.

The *Piano trio* has a secure grasp of form and is full of expressive intensity. The main influence, apart from that of his master, is Wagner, whose music Lekeu had encountered the previous year. Lekeu is a thoughtful composer and, though the slow movement perhaps outstays its welcome, there are relatively few *longueurs*. The performance is dedicated, and the only reservation is the quality of the piano-tone, which is thick at the bottom end of the register; the acoustic is a bit over-reverberant.

Lemba, Artur (1885–1960)

Symphony in C sharp min.
*** Chandos Dig. CHAN 8656 [id.]. SNO, Järvi (with Concert: *'Music from Estonia'*: Vol. 2***).

Lemba's *Symphony in C sharp minor* was the first symphony ever to be written by an Estonian. It sounds as if he studied in St Petersburg: at times one is reminded fleetingly of Glazunov, at others of Dvořák (the scherzo) – and even of Bruckner (at the opening of the finale) and of Elgar. This is by far the most important item in an enterprising collection of Estonian music.

Leoncavallo, Ruggiero (1858–1919)

I Pagliacci (complete).
(M) *** DG 449 727-2 [id.]. Carlyle, Bergonzi, Taddei, Panerai, La Scala, Milan, Ch. & O, Karajan.
*** DG 419 257-2 (3) cast as above, La Scala, Milan, Ch. & O, Karajan – MASCAGNI: *Cavalleria rusticana*. ***
(M) *** EMI CMS7 63967-2 [CDMB 63967] (2). Amara, Corelli, Gobbi, La Scala, Milan, Ch. & O, Von Matačić – MASCAGNI: *Cavalleria rusticana*. **(*)
(M) *** RCA 74321 50168-2 (2) [09026 60865-2]. Caballé, Domingo, Milnes, John Alldis Ch., LSO, Santi – PUCCINI: *Il Tabarro*. **(*)
(***) EMI mono CDS5 56287-2 [CDFB 56287] (2). Callas, Di Stefano, Gobbi, La Scala, Milan, Ch. & O, Serafin – MASCAGNI: *Cavalleria rusticana*. (***)
(M) **(*) EMI CMS7 63650-2 (2). Scotto, Carreras, Nurmela, Amb. Op. Ch., Philh. O, Muti – MASCAGNI: *Cavalleria rusticana*. **(*)
(B) **(*) Naxos Dig. 8.660021 [id.]. Gauci, Martinucci, Tumagian, Dvorsky, Skovhus, Slovak Philh. Ch., Czech RSO, Rahbari.
(M) (**(*)) Nimbus mono NI 7843/4 [id.]. Gigli, Pacetti, Basiola, Nessi, Paci, La Scala Ch. & O, Ghione – MASCAGNI: *Cavalleria rusticana*. (**)

Karajan's *Pagliacci* has dominated the catalogue for three decades alongside its natural operatic partner, *Cavalleria rusticana*, so it is apt that DG have chosen it for separate reissue in their series of 'Originals', freshly remastered. Karajan does nothing less than refine Leoncavallo's melodrama, with long-breathed, expansive tempi and the minimum of exaggeration. Karajan's choice of soloists was clearly aimed to help that – but the passions are still there; and rarely if ever on record has the La Scala Orchestra played with such beautiful feeling for tone-colour. Bergonzi is among the most sensitive of Italian tenors of heroic quality, and it is good to have Joan Carlyle as Nedda, touching if often rather cool. Taddei is magnificently strong, and Benelli and Panerai could hardly be bettered in the roles of Beppe and Silvio. The combined set remains available (and unsurpassed) but on three records at premium price – although, as well as *Cav.*, DG provide a splendid set of performances of operatic intermezzi as a filler. However, the separate *Pagliacci* is something of a bargain.

The EMI (originally Columbia) recording under Von Matačić dates from the early 1960s and is especially notable for the contribution of the tenor, Franco Corelli, as Canio, which calls for some superlatives. He is not nearly as imaginative as some of the great tenors of the past, yet he shows a natural feeling for the phrases. It is not just a question of making a big, glorious noise – though of course he does that too – but of interpreting the music; and a performance like this puts several others, by more obviously starry names, in the shade. The coupled *Cav.* is dramatically not quite so striking, but this still makes a clear first choice in the mid-priced range for those who want the pairing with Mascagni.

For those who do not want that obvious coupling, the alternative RCA set is a first-rate recommendation, with fine singing from all three principals, vivid playing and recording, and one or two extra passages not normally included – as in the Nedda–Silvio duet. Milnes is superb in the Prologue.

It is thrilling to hear *Pagliacci* starting with the Prologue sung so vividly by Tito Gobbi. Di Stefano, too, is at his finest, but the earlier EMI performance inevitably centres on Callas and there are many points at which she finds extra intensity, extra meaning. Serafin's direction is strong and direct. The mono recording is greatly improved in the new transfer, with voices well forward, but this set is overpriced.

Under Muti's urgent direction both *Cav.* and *Pag.* represent the music of violence. In both he has sought to use the original text, which in *Pag.* is often surprisingly different, with many top notes eliminated and Tonio instead of Canio delivering (singing, not speaking) the final *La commedia è finita*. Muti's approach represents the antithesis of smoothness, and the coarse rendering of the *Prologue* in *Pag.* by the rich-toned Kari Nurmela is disappointing. Scotto's Nedda goes raw above the stave, but the edge is in keeping with Muti's approach, with its generally brisk speeds. Carreras seems happier here than in *Cav.*, but it is the conductor and the fresh look he brings which will prompt a choice here. The sound is extremely vivid.

Alexander Rahbari conducts his Slovak forces in a vigorous, red-blooded reading which with first-rate solo singing makes an excellent bargain recommendation, very well recorded, if with the chorus a little distant. Miriam Gauci is a warmly vibrant Nedda, with plenty of temperament, and Eduard Tumagian is an outstanding Tonio, not only firm and dark of tone but phrasing imaginatively. As Canio, Nicola Martinucci has an agreeable tenor that he uses with more finesse and a better line than many more celebrated rivals, even though his histrionics at the beginning and end of *Vesti la giubba* are unconvincing.

The Nimbus transfer of the classic 1934 recording with Gigli focuses the voices effectively enough, giving them a mellow bloom – though the orchestra, often rather recessed, is relatively muffled. Gigli is very much the centre of attention, with Iva Pacetti as Nedda clear and powerful rather than characterful.

I Pagliacci (in English; complete).
(N) (M) *** Chandos Dig. CHAN 3003 [id.]. Tonio (Alan Opie), Nedda (Rosa Mannion), Canio (Dennis O'Neil), Beppe (Peter Bronder), Geoffrey Mitchell Ch., Peter Kay Children's Ch., LPO, David Parry.

David Parry conducts a powerful performance in the Peter Moores Foundation's 'Opera in English' series, building the drama persuasively. The cast is one of the finest in the series yet, with Rosa Mannion a touching Nedda, and Alan Opie and William Dazeley both outstanding and well contrasted in the baritone roles. Dennis O'Neill sings very well too as Canio, but faces greater problems with translating the tragic clown into an English-speaking hero. No longer *On with the motley* but 'Put on your costume'. Warm, atmospheric sound with voices beautifully focused.

I Pagliacci: highlights.
(M) **(*) EMI (SIS) CDM5 66048-2. Scotto, Carreras, Nurmela, Allen, Amb. Op. Ch., Philh. O, Muti – MASCAGNI: *Cavalleria rusticana:* highlights. **(*)

Muti uses the original text, which is often surprisingly different, with Tonio instead of Canio delivering (singing not speaking) the final *La commedia è finita*. It is an urgent performance and very involving, but the rendering of the Prologue by Kari Nurmela brings a coarse start to the proceedings.

Leoni, Franco (1884–1949)

L'Oracolo (opera): complete.
*** Decca 444 396-2. Sutherland, Gobbi, Van Allan, Tourangeau, Davies, John Alldis Ch., Finchley Children's Music Group, Nat. PO, Bonynge.

L'Oracolo, heard first at Covent Garden in 1905, the work of a contemporary of Puccini who settled in London, tells the lurid story of the wicked Cim-Fen, who finally gets strangled, to the delight of everyone, with his own pigtail. In the meantime the heroine goes mad after the murder of her beloved, and the whole drama is set against sound-effects which are superbly caught in this brilliant first recording, made in the Kingsway Hall in 1975. The very opening – three bangs on the bass drum, two crowings of a cockerel and a great jabber in Chinese from the chorus – might almost be a hi-fi demonstration.

The piece gives marvellous opportunities not only to the veteran Tito Gobbi (relishing the character's wickedness) but also to Joan Sutherland, specialist in mad scenes, and to Richard Van Allan as the doctor who finally dispatches Cim-Fen. If Leoni's actual idiom is rather too bland for so dark a story, and his melodies, although often lusciously attractive, never quite come up to Puccini standard, the piece makes a fine compact entertainment in such a performance as this, directed with passionate conviction by Richard Bonynge, with superb playing from the National Philharmonic. This enterprising set is well worth having: it grows more compelling on repeated hearings.

Leonin (c. 1163–90)

Organa: *Alleluya, Epulemur Azamis; Gaude Maria; Propter veritatem; Viderunt omnes.*
*** Lyrichord LEMS 8002 [id.]. Russell Oberlin, Charles Bressler, Donald Perry – PEROTINUS: *Organa.* ***

Over eight centuries have passed since the construction of the Cathedral of Notre Dame began and Leonin, the cathedral's composer, was writing this music. It is in two parts, with the top voice moving in unison or octaves, or over a sustained or only occasionally moving second part. Sometimes both voices sing in unison. The present performances are extraordinarily convincing and take us back in time to the very beginning of written music. Excellent recording.

Le Roux, Gaspard (d. c. 1705)

Pièces de clavecin: Suites Nos. 1–7.
*** O-L (IMS) Dig. 443 329-2. Christophe Rousset (harpsichord).

Christophe Rousset, playing a Hemsch harpsichord reputed to have been used by Le Roux himself, here adds to his laurels and our knowledge of French keyboard literature with this vivid and surprisingly individual music of an almost unknown composer. If you enjoy Rameau and have already investigated Rousset's companion collection of the music of Pancrace Royer, this is the composer to try next.

Liadov, Anatol (1855–1914)

Baba-Yaga, Op. 56; The Enchanted lake, Op. 62; Kikimora, Op. 63.
*** DG Dig. 447 084-2 [id.]. Russian Nat. O, Pletnev – RIMSKY-KORSAKOV: *Le Coq d'or;* TCHEREPNIN: *La Princesse lointaine* etc. ***

(i) *Baba Yaga, Op. 56; The Enchanted lake, Op. 62; Kikimora, Op. 63;* (ii) *8 Russian folksongs.*
(BB) **(*) Naxos Dig. 8.550328 [id.]. Slovak PO, (i) Gunzenhauser; (ii) Kenneth Jean – Concert: *'Russian Fireworks'.*

Anatol Liadov is almost as well known for what he did not write as for what he actually accomplished. It was he whom Diaghilev commissioned to write *The Firebird* and it was his dilatory response that prompted the impresario to turn to Stravinsky. These are exquisite miniatures, full of atmosphere and colour, which owe much to Rimsky but are at the same time distinguished by an individual fantasy and a remarkable feeling for orchestral colour. Mikhail Pletnev and his Russian National Orchestra give evocative performances of them: indeed their account of *The Enchanted lake* is the best since Koussevitzky's magical 78-r.p.m., and there can be no finer tribute. Excellent sound.

It is good to have inexpensive recordings of these key Liadov works, particularly the *Russian folksongs*, eight orchestral vignettes of great charm, displaying a winning sense of orchestral colour. The performances are persuasive, and the digital recording is vivid and well balanced.

Ligeti, György (born 1923)

(i) *Cello concerto; Chamber concerto;* (ii) *Piano concerto.*
*** Sony Dig. SK 58945 [id.]. (i) Miklós Perényi; (ii) Ueli Wiget; Modern Ens., Peter Eötvös.

These three concertos span two decades of Ligeti's output. The *Cello concerto* and the *Chamber concerto*, for 13 instruments, are vivid in colour, complex in detail and undoubtedly full of energy. To some ears their content may not match their undoubted prolixity of surface comment. The *Piano concerto* has five movements. The most striking movement is the second; perhaps the others, exuberant as they are, outlast their welcome. Dedicated Ligetians (are there many, we wonder) will welcome these obviously skilled and committed performances, well recorded, with Wiget a striking advocate of the demanding solo role in the concertante work for piano.

(i) *Cello concerto;* (ii) *Piano concerto;* (iii) *Violin concerto.*
*** DG Dig. 439 808-2 [id.]. (i) Queras; (ii) Aimard; (iii) Gawriloff; Ens. InterContemporain, Boulez.

Those interested in sampling the music of this famous exponent of the avant garde could not do better than try this concertante triptych which won the *Gramophone* magazine's Contemporary Music Award in 1996. The composer's imaginative inventiveness is never in doubt, but his musical purpose is not always easy to fathom. All the performers believe that this music has an underlying profundity; all three performances are musically and technically impressive and communicate strongly.

Chamber concerto.
(B) *** DG Classikon Dig. 439 452-3. Ens. InterContemporain, Boulez – LUTOSLAWSKI: *Chain 3* etc.; SCHNITTKE: *Concerto grosso No. 1.* ***

This bargain DG CD presents a performance of the *Chamber concerto* that is a useful supplement to that offered above, and admirers of this composer's cloudy sound-textures can safely investigate. In this work the specific notes matter less than the washes of colour. Excellent performance and recording.

Bagatelles.
*** Crystal CD 750 [id.]. Westwood Wind Quintet – CARLSSON: *Nightwings;* MATHIAS: *Quintet;* BARBER: *Summer music.* ***

Ligeti's folk-inspired *Bagatelles* are highly inventive and very attractive; and they are played with dazzling flair and unanimity of ensemble by this American group.

Le grand macabre (complete opera).
(N) *** Sony S2K 62312 (2) [id.]. Sibylle Ehlert, Graham Clark, Willard White, Van Nes, Lee Ragin, Cole, Suart, L. Sinf. Voices, Philh. O, Salonen.

Le grand macabre, one of the most successful modern operas on stage, was first heard in 1977, but revised twenty years later, when the composer tautened the piece, replacing much of the spoken dialogue with musical settings of the text, making judicious cuts and slimming down the orchestration. It is that revised version which is recorded here under supervision from the composer, using an English text. Set in Breughelland, this apocalyptic vision lightens its macabre theme – of the ending of the world – with humour, viciously satirical and anarchic, setting out from a witty prelude for tuned motor-horns, with tongue-in-cheek echoes of a baroque toccata. Salonen is a brilliant advocate, drawing colourful playing from the Philharmonia. Sibylle Ehlert is dazzling in the coloratura role of Gepopo, Graham Clark a characterful Piet the Pot, and Willard White aptly baleful as Le Grand Macabre himself, the sinister Nekrotzar. This may be an off-beat piece, but as audiences have found, it has a sparkle which has one simultaneously laughing and thinking. Atmospheric sound, recorded live at the Theatre du Châtelet.

Lilburn, Douglas (born 1915)

Symphonies Nos. 1 (1949); *2* (1951); *3 in one movement* (1961).
*** Continuum Dig. 1069 [id.]. New Zealand SO, John Hopkins.

Douglas Lilburn is the doyen of New Zealand composers. The three symphonies collected here on this well-filled disc show an impressive musical mind at work. There is a strong affinity with Scandinavian music, induced perhaps by the similarities of latitude and landscape, and an imposing formal coherence. The opening of the *Third Symphony in one movement* almost suggests an antipodean Holmboe. The musical invention shows a consistently high level of imagination, and the performances are thoroughly committed. Excellent, well-balanced recorded sound enhances the claims of this disc. Strongly recommended.

Lindberg, Magnus (born 1958)

'Meet the composer': (i) *Action – Situation; Signification;* (ii–iii) *Kinetics;* (i–ii; iv) *Kraft;* (v; iii) *Rittrato;* (vi–vii; iii) *Zona;* (Instrumental) (viii–ix) *Ablauf;* (x)*. . . De Tartuffe, je crois* (for piano quintet); (viii; xi) *Linea d'ombra;* (vi) *Stroke;* (Piano) (xii) *Twine.*
(B) *** Finlandia/Warner Dig. Double 0630 19756-2 (2). (i) Toimili Ens.; (ii) Finnish RSO; (iii) Salonen; (iv) Swedish RSO; (v) Avanti! CO; (vi) Anssi Karttunen; (vii) L. Sinf.; (viii) Krikku; (ix) Aaltonen, Ohenoja; (x) Endymion Ens., John Witfield; (xi) Ferchen, Pohjola, Virtanen; (xii) Tuija Hakkila.

Magnus Lindberg belongs to the younger generation of Finnish composers now moving into their middle years. He studied with Paavo Heininen in Helsinki and with Bryan Ferneyhough at the Darmstadt summer courses in the early 1980s. He also studied with Franco Donati in Siena and with Vinko Globokar in Paris. His breakthrough as a composer came with *Kraft* (the second item on the first CD), which had its première in 1984 and brought him to international attention. This Finlandia '*Meet the Composer*' set of two CDs gives a good cross-section of his work during the 1980s, when he was still in his late twenties and early thirties. If you do not respond to avant-garde music, you may still find something to reward you here, for Lindberg is a composer of imagination and intelligence.

Linkola, Jukka (born 1955)

'Meet the composer': (i) *Boogie Woogie waltz;* (ii–iii) *Crossings;* (iv) *Trumpet concerto;* (i) *Malaria*; (v; iii) *Ronia, the Robber's daughter (5 movements);* (vi; iii) *The Snow Queen* (film incidental music); (vii) *Evoe!*
(B) *** Finlandia/Warner Dig. Double 0630 19808-2 (2). (i) Jukka Linkola Octet; (ii) Juhani Aaltonen, Helsinki PO; (iii) cond. composer; (iv) Jouko Harjanne, Finnish RSO, Segerstam; (v) Finnish Nat. Op. O; (vi) O; (vii) Helsinki University Ch., Matti Hyökki, with Kristian & Laura Attila.

Jukka Linkola began life as a jazz musician, and it was an encounter with the music of Lutoslawski which turned him in the direction of serious contemporary music. Although his is not a voice of great individuality, he is obviously a composer of both sophistication and imagination. *Crossings* for tenor saxophone and orchestra from 1983 reveals traces of Messiaen and French music, as well as his past in the world of jazz. Kimmo Korhonen's note speaks of it as 'an exceptionally seamless and functional synthesis of the worlds of jazz and serious music'. The excerpts from the ballet, *Ronia, the*

Robber's daughter, have more than the occasional reminder of Stravinsky and Prokofiev and the average Hollywood score. Even so, Linkola has the capability of taking the listener by surprise. Though not a major figure, he is far from negligible, and he is resourceful, rarely less than an entertaining aural companion and always intelligent.

Liszt, Franz (1811–86)

Piano concertos Nos. 1–2; Fantasia on Hungarian folksongs; Fantasia on themes from Beethoven's 'Ruins of Athens'; Grande fantaisie symphonique on themes from Berlioz's 'Lélio'; Malédiction; Polonaise brillante on Weber's Polonaise brillante in E (L'Hilarité); Totentanz (paraphrase on the *Dies Irae*); SCHUBERT/LISZT: *Wanderer fantasia.*
(B) *** EMI Rouge et Noir (SIS) CZS5 69662-2 (2) [CDZB 69662]. Michel Béroff, Leipzig GO, Kurt Masur.

Béroff's 1977 account of the two concertos can hold its own with the best of the competition: here there is nothing routine or slapdash, but instead excitement, warmth and spontaneity, along with his remarkable technical prowess. The piano timbre has plenty of body and colour, as well as sparkle. This is an exhilarating and rewarding set which can be given a strong recommendation on all counts.

(i) *Piano concertos 1–2; Totentanz* (paraphrase on the '*Dies irae*'). *Années de pèlerinage: Book 1: 1st year: Switzerland; Book 2: 2nd year (Italy); Book 3: 3rd Year (Italy) excerpts: Aux cyprès de la Villa d'Este; Sunt lachrimae rerum; Sursum corda* (only). *Sonata in B min.; Concert paraphrase of 'Isolde's Liebestod' from Wagner's 'Tristan'. Csárdás macabre; En rêve (Nocturne); Harmonies poétiques et religieuses (Invocations; Bénédiction de Dieu dans la solitude; Pensée des morts); Funérailles. Klavierstück in F sharp; Légendes Nos. 1–2; La lugubre gondola Nos. 1–2; Mosonyis Grabgeleit; Nuages gris; Prelude and fugue on the name 'BACH'; RW (Venezia); Schlaflos! Frage und Antwort; Unstern (Sinistre); Valse oubliée No. 1; Vexilla regis Prodeunt; Weinachtsbaum (Christmas tree) suite (excerpts); Variations on 'Weinen, Klagen, Sorgen Zagen'.*
(M) *** Ph. Brendel Edition Analogue/Dig. 446 924-2 (5). Alfred Brendel, (i) LPO, Haitink.

Brendel's 1972 recordings of the *Concertos* and *Totentanz* have long been among the key versions of these volatile works and Haitink is a persuasive accompanist. Brendel's set of the *Second year* of the *Années de pèlerinage* was recorded that same year and proved no less outstanding. The performances are of superlative quality, the playing highly poetic and brilliant, while the analogue recording offers Philips's most realistic quality. The *First year* (*Switzerland*) came 14 years later and was recorded digitally. It has many impressive moments but also some ugly fortissimi that are not wholly the responsibility of the engineers. Brendel plays the pieces *segue*, without pauses, and, although there is some atmospheric playing in the set, the moments of magic are relatively few. The four excerpts from the *Third year* were recorded as part of an outstanding (1979) analogue recital, which included the extraordinary late pieces, many of whose names are unfamiliar. The music is often surprisingly stark and bitter and Brendel's presentation of them is distinguished by a concentration and subtlety of nuance that are wholly convincing, helped by extremely lifelike recording. The *Prelude and fugue on the name 'BACH'* and the *Variations* on *'Weinen, Klagen, Sorgen, Zagen'* are better known as organ pieces but sound no less impressive on the piano when played so masterfully, and the *Harmonies poétiques et religieuses* are hardly less distinguished. However, the *Sonata* is something of a disappointment. Brendel has recorded this work three times and Philips have chosen the most recent version, made in 1991. It was a great pity that his second recording (also digital) was not chosen. The newest account brings a similarly wide range of colour, yet there is not the same spontaneity nor a comparable firmness of grip. There is much brilliant pianism, but the overall purpose of the reading seems much less clear and even the recording, though bright and clean, is less impressive than either the 1983 version or even the analogue record, made in the 1960s. But overall this box shows Brendel as a superb Lisztian.

(i) *Piano concertos Nos. 1 in E flat; 2 in A; Totentanz for piano and orchestra;* (ii) *Piano sonata in B min.; Années de pèlerinage, 2nd Year: Après une lecture du Dante (Dante sonata); Sonetti de Petrarca Nos. 104 & 123.*
(B) *** Teldec/Warner Ultima 3984 21092-2 (2). (i) Boris Berezovsky, Philh. O, Hugh Wolff; (ii) Elisabeth Leonskaya.

Too often when a Double features different performers on each of the two paired CDs, one or another lets the side down. Not in this case, however. Berezovsky's thrillingly extrovert yet highly musical accounts of the two concertos and the rumbustious *Totentanz* are ideally balanced by Elisabeth Leonskaya's imaginative recital of solo piano music. Berezovsky plays throughout with enormous panache and bravura, yet with melting poetic feeling too. Hugh Wolff proves a splendid partner, and the Philharmonia Orchestra play with great gusto. The full-blooded, resonantly spacious recording was made at Aldeburgh in 1994.

Leonskaya then takes over for the *Sonata*, and she gives a very impressive reading indeed. She has a firm grip on this wayward piece, especially in the more reflective writing, where she displays much poetic feeling. The central *Allegro energico* is played superbly. The two *Petrarch sonnets* are played very freely, with flexible rubato which suits No. 123 particularly well. Even if you already have some of the music on record, this set is well worth investigating.

(i) *Piano concertos Nos. 1–2;* (ii) *Hungarian rhapsody No. 2.*
(M) *** [RCA Basic 100 09026 62679-2]. (i) Barry Douglas, LSO, Hirokami; (ii) Boston Pops, Fiedler.

(i) *Piano concertos Nos. 1–2;* (ii) *Hungarian rhapsody No. 2; Liebesträum; Les Préludes.*
(BB) **(*) RCA Navigator 74321 29244-2. (i) Leonard Pennario, RPO, Leibowitz; (ii) Boston Pops O, Arthur Fiedler.

Piano concertos Nos. 1–2; Totentanz.
✿ *** DG Dig. 423 571-2 [id.]. Zimerman, Boston SO, Ozawa.
(M) *** Ph. 426 637-2. Alfred Brendel, LPO, Haitink.

Piano concertos Nos. (i) *1 in E flat;* (ii) *2 in A. Années de pèlerinage: Sonetto 104 del Petrarca. Hungarian rhapsody No. 6; Valse oubliée.*
(M) *** Mercury (IMS) 432 002-2 [id.]. Byron Janis, (i) Moscow PO, Kondrashin; (ii) Moscow RSO, Rozhdestvensky (also with SCHUMANN: *Romance in F sharp; Novellette in F.* FALLA: *Miller's dance.* GUION: *The harmonica player* ***).

Piano concertos Nos. (i) *1 in E flat;* (ii) *2 in A. Piano sonata in B min.*
(M) *** Ph. 446 200-2 [id.]. Sviatoslav Richter, (i–ii) with LSO, Kirill Kondrashin.

Krystian Zimerman's record of the two *Concertos* and the *Totentanz* is altogether thrilling, and he has the advantage of excellent support from the Boston orchestra under Ozawa. It has poise and classicism and, as one listens, one feels this music could not be played in any other way – surely the mark of a great performance! This record is outstanding in every way, and still remains a first choice for this repertoire.

Sviatoslav Richter's 1961 performances on Philips are very distinguished indeed, and the recent remastering by Wilma Cozart Fine makes the very most of the recording, originally engineered by the Mercury team. Richter's playing is unforgettable and so is his rapport with Kondrashin and the LSO, whose playing throughout is of the very highest order. For the current reissue, Richter's electrifying and highly poetic new recording of the *Sonata* has been added; Philips are, however, reluctant to suggest a recording date. The sound is vivid and present but the acoustic is rather dry for full comfort. However, given playing of this calibre, one soon adjusts.

Around the time they were recording Richter's Liszt *Concertos* for Philips in London (1962), the Mercury engineers paid a visit to Moscow to record Byron Janis in the same repertoire, and his is a comparably distinguished coupling. Janis's glittering articulation is matched by his sense of poetry and drama, and there is plenty of dash in these very compelling performances, which are afforded characteristically brilliant Mercury sound, although the piano is too close. The encores which follow the two *Concertos* are also very enjoyable.

Brendel's Philips recordings from the early 1970s hold their place at or near the top of the list and are discussed under the Brendel Liszt edition. The recording is one of Philips's best.

Barry Douglas commands a wide variety of keyboard colour and keeps the flamboyant showmanship in hand, while displaying a good deal of poetic feeling. Moreover his readings are well thought out and never unimaginative. He gets highly musical support from Hirokami, and the recording is excellent. Fiedler provides the encore, a vivid account of the most famous of Liszt's orchestral rhapsodies. This is one of the very best of RCA's Basic 100 series.

Pennario's performances are assured and brilliant, yet the slow movement of No. 1 is touchingly wistful. Leibowitz provides excellent support and the opening of the *A major Concerto* is enticingly atmospheric. The recording, though forward, is full and vivid, and the result is sensitive, sparkling and spontaneous, with a thrilling lack of inhibition at the close of the *Second Concerto*. There is nothing much wrong with Fiedler's exciting Boston Pops accounts of the two orchestral works, which are also vividly recorded. It was a pity that the famous *Liebesträum* could not have been provided in its original piano format, though the orchestral version is undoubtedly luscious. This bargain-basement collection is first-class value.

Piano concerto No. 1 in E flat.
*** Chesky CD 93 [id.]. Earl Wild, RPO, Sargent – CHOPIN: *Concerto No. 1* **(*); FAURE: *Ballade for piano and orchestra.* ***
(M) *** DG 449 719-2 [id.]. Argerich, LSO, Abbado – CHOPIN: *Piano concerto No. 1.* ***
(BB) **(*) Naxos Dig. 8.550292 [id.]. Joseph Banowetz, Czech RSO, Bratislava, Oliver Dohnányi – CHOPIN: *Concerto No. 1.* **(*)

(i; ii) *Piano concerto No. 1 in E flat;* (i) *Piano sonata in B min.; Hungarian rhapsody No. 6;* (iii) *Années de pèlerinage: Vallée d'Obermann; Les jeux d'eau à la Villa D'Este.*
(B) **(*) DG Classikon 439 409-2. (i) Martha Argerich; (ii) LSO, Abbado; (iii) Lazar Berman.

(i) *Piano concerto No. 1 in E flat; Fantasia in E min. on Hungarian folksongs; Hungarian rhapsodies Nos. 8–11, 13.*
(***) Sony mono MHK 62338. Claudio Arrau, (i) with Phd. O, Ormandy.

Earl Wild is in his element and gives a glittering and powerful account of Liszt's famous warhorse, yet one that does not lack either delicacy or warmth. The famous triangle Scherzo is crystalline in its clarity and the full-blooded recording matches the extravagance of Liszt's exciting finale.

For some reason Martha Argerich (in 1968) recorded only Liszt's *First Concerto* and not the *Second*. However, in the *E flat Concerto* there is an excellent partnership between the pianist and Abbado, and this is a performance of flair and high voltage which does not ever become vulgar. It is very well recorded and, in this reissue coupled with Chopin for DG's 'Legendary Recordings' series of 'Originals', it sounds better than ever. The performance is also available on DG's bargain Classikon label, coupled with the *Sonata*, which Argerich recorded three years later.

The Arrau recordings come from 1952 and have not been in circulation here for many years. The *E flat Concerto* was done in one take and prompted Ormandy to say after the playback, 'Well, what is there to say? We're done. It can't be better than this!' The rest of the programme has just as much electricity. Arrau had an aristocratic poise and a refined musicianship which were unique in this repertoire. The sound is amazingly good. This disc costs rather more than upper-mid-price.

A splendid, energetic account of the *First Concerto* from Banowetz, well coupled with Chopin, has the full measure of the work's flamboyance and its poetry. The wide-ranging sound is excellent though the triangle solo in the Scherzo is only just audible.

Piano concerto No. 2 in A.

*** Virgin/EMI Dig. VC7 59613-2 [id.]. Leif Ove Andsnes, Bergen PO, Dmitri Kitaenko – GRIEG: *Piano concerto* etc. ***

Leif Ove Andsnes is a real musician who plays with great tenderness and poetic feeling as well as bravura. Marvellous sound, too, with a piano in perfect condition (not always the case on records) and an excellent balance.

Dante Symphony.

(N) *** DG Dig. 457 614-2 [id.]. Dresden State Op. Ch., and State O, Sinopoli (with BUSONI: *Doktor Faust: Saraband und Cortège* ***).

(i) *Dante Symphony;* (ii) *Années de pèlerinage, Book 2: Après un lecture du Dante (Fantasia quasi sonata).*

*** Teldec/Warner Dig. 9031 77340 [id.]. (i) Women's voices of Berlin R. Ch., BPO, Daniel Barenboim; (ii) Barenboim (piano).

Liszt's *Dante Symphony* divides naturally into two very expansive, equally balanced halves – *Inferno* and *Purgatorio* – each lasting about 21 minutes, with a relatively short choral *Magnificat* as a finale. The work opens diabolically, with the rasping trombones evoking the gates of Hell, followed by a sustained frenzy of writing for strings and brass; later in a romantic interlude we meet Francesca da Rimini in all her grief. Interestingly, she is introduced by a bass clarinet in a not dissimilar way to her entrance on the clarinet in Tchaikovsky's symphonic poem. A blinding flash of harps introduces the malignant Scherzo, and the movement reaches a tremendous climax. The second movement is calming – some might say becalmed in its spacious paragraphs. Finally the heavenly chorus enters and lusciously proclaims salvation.

Sinopoli, on one of his very finest records, gives a grippingly inspired account, unashamedly using accelerandos to increase the tension and not shirking the flamboyant melodrama of the brilliantly descriptive opening *Inferno* sequence. He draws a clear parallel, not only with Tchaikovsky's *Francesca da Rimini*, but also with the *Manfred Symphony*. The refined and beautiful playing of the Dresden Orchestra easily sustains the long central *Purgatorio*, and the luminous and superbly sung choral entry in the finale creates a magical apotheosis. The DG recording is in the demonstration bracket, wonderfully spacious and clear. For an imaginative coupling we are offered the two pieces Busoni composed in 1918/19 as 'a reduced-size model' while working on his opera, *Doktor Faust*. Their orchestral treatment is more subtle than Liszt's, but they are still brilliantly scored and well worth having when played so impressively.

Barenboim too really has the measure of this overextended but remarkable work and controls its rhapsodic structure admirably, holding the tension throughout the first movement and creating enormous visceral excitement at the close. He is helped by marvellous playing from the BPO, who really sound as if they believe in it all, and the radiant choral effects are superbly brought off. The resonant acoustic of Berlin's Schauspielhaus lets everything expand with Wagnerian amplitude and the result is very impressive indeed. As an encore, Barenboim leaves the rostrum for the piano and offers the *Dante Sonata*, which has the same literary basis but offers a quite different musical treatment. The performance is flamboyantly arresting, but the piano recording is curiously shallow.

Fantasia on Hungarian folk tunes for piano and orchestra.

(M) *** Decca Dig. 430 726-2. Bolet, LSO, Ivan Fischer – ADDINSELL: *Warsaw concerto* ***; GERSHWIN: *Rhapsody* **(*); GOTTSCHALK: *Grand fantasia* ***; LITOLFF: *Scherzo*. ***

Bolet is a masterful soloist and he plays here with characteristic bravura. Like the pianist, the Hungarian conductor is an understanding Lisztian, and the accompaniment from the LSO is first rate, with a recording balance of demonstration quality.

(i) *Fantasia on Hungarian folk tunes. Hungarian rhapsodies Nos. 2, 4–5; Mazeppa; Mephisto waltz No. 2; Les Préludes; Tasso, lamento e trionfo.*
(B) *** DG Double 453 130-2 (2) [id.]. BPO, Karajan; (i) with Cherkassky.

This DG Double generally shows Karajan at his finest. Shura Cherkassky's glittering 1961 recording of the *Hungarian fantasia* is an affectionate performance with some engaging touches from the orchestra, though the pianist is dominant and his playing is superbly assured. The rest of the programme is comparably charismatic. Here as elsewhere the remastering for CD has brought out the range and body of the sound impressively, with firm detail throughout the orchestra. The cellos and basses sound marvellous in the *Fifth rhapsody* and *Tasso*, and even the brashness of *Les Préludes* is a little tempered. *Mazeppa* is a great performance, superbly thrilling and atmospheric, with a riveting coda – worthy of a Rosette. A set showing Karajan and his Berlin orchestra at their finest.

A Faust symphony.
(N) *** Ph. Dig. 454 460-2 [id.]. Peter Blochwitz, Hung. Radio Ch., Budapest Fest. O, Iván Fischer.
(N) *** Teldec/Warner Dig. 3984 22948-2 [id.]. Placido Domingo, Ch. of German Op., BPO, Barenboim.
(M) *** DG 447 449-2 [id.]. Kenneth Riegel, Tanglewood Festival Ch., Boston SO, Bernstein.
*** EMI Dig. CDC5 55220-2 [id.]. Peter Seiffert, Ernst-Senff Ch. Male voices, Prague Philharmonic Ch., BPO, Rattle.

Iván Fischer's recording of *A Faust symphony*, with the Budapest Festival Orchestra and Peter Blochwitz as the tenor soloist in the finale, is quite simply the best since Beecham. Obviously it has the advantage of exceptionally rich and present recording with great range and body. An additional point of interest is the ending: we are offered a choice between Liszt's original ending, which is purely orchestral (preferred by Wagner), and the familiar more extended choral ending. An outstanding issue.

Barenboim's flamboyant account is at one with his fine companion version of the *Dante Symphony*. It has great gusto, especially in the choral finale, and his freely moulded spontaneous style suits the opening movement when the tension is so well sustained – as it is in the gentle portrayal of Gretel in the *Andante*, where there is most beautiful playing from the Berlin Orchestra. Another plus point is the ardent and memorable solo contribution from Placido Domingo in the last movement. Fine spacious recording makes this an enjoyable alternative to Fischer on Philips, which remains first choice.

Bernstein on DG seems to possess the ideal temperament for holding together grippingly the melodrama of the first movement, while the lovely *Gretchen* centrepiece is played most beautifully. Kenneth Riegel is an impressive tenor soloist in the finale, there is an excellent, well-balanced choral contribution, and the Boston Symphony Orchestra produce playing which is both exciting and atmospheric. While Fischer's version remains first choice, the Bernstein account (reissued as one of DG's 'Originals') makes a fine, mid-priced alternative.

Rattle's début recording with the Berlin Philharmonic brings an exceptionally warm and persuasive reading. That it was recorded live is particularly helpful in this expansively episodic work. Rattle's spontaneity of expression, whether in pointing the main melodies or in moulding the all-important transitions, carries the ear on magnetically. He is helped by ravishing playing from the Berlin players, not least the strings, with the central movement, *Gretchen*, emerging as the high point of the performance. That the recording, made in the Philharmonie, sets the orchestra at a slight distance, notably the brass, prevents tuttis from biting as hard and as dramatically as they can. The impact of Bernstein's masterly (mid-priced) analogue version from Boston is more powerful, but Rattle is closer to Beecham's pioneering stereo set, and on its own terms one quickly adjusts to the balances of the Berlin sound, relishing its beauty. The performance culminates in a rapt account of the choral apotheosis, with the men's chorus clearly focused and with Peter Seiffert singing radiantly, headily beautiful through the range.

Hungarian rhapsodies Nos. 1–6.
(M) **(*) Mercury 432 015-2 [id.]. LSO, Dorati – ENESCU: *Roumanian rhapsody No. 1.* ***

Hungarian rhapsodies Nos. 1–6; Hungarian battle march; Rákóczy march.
(M) **(*) EMI CDM7 64627-2. Philh. Hungarica or LPO, Boskovsky.

Dorati's is undoubtedly the finest set of orchestral *Hungarian rhapsodies*. He brings out the gypsy flavour and, with lively playing from the LSO, there is both polish and sparkle. The Mercury recording is characteristically vivid.

Boskovsky does not fully catch the mercurial element, the sudden changes of mood which is the gypsy heritage of these pieces, but the Philharmonia Hungarica (who play in Nos. 1, 4 and 6 – *Carnival in Pest*) are obviously at home; and the LPO clearly enjoy the famous No. 2. The freshly remastered recordings (from 1977/8) sound well and, though Dorati on Mercury takes pride of place in this repertoire, this EMI disc certainly gives pleasure.

Hungarian rhapsodies Nos. 1 in F min.; 4 in D min.; Les Préludes.
(M) **(*) Sony SMK 47572 [id.]. NYPO, Bernstein – ENESCU: *Roumanian Rhapsody No. 1* (with BRAHMS: *Hungarian dances Nos. 5–6* **(*)).

Notable for the vivid coupled performance of the Enescu *Rhapsody*, this collection shows characteristic Bernstein brilliance, with first-rate orchestral playing throughout.

Hungarian rhapsodies Nos. 2, 6, 9, 12, 14 & 15 (arr. Peter Wolf).
(B) *** HM Musique d'Abord Dig. HMA 1903046 [id.]. Franz Liszt CO, János Rolla.

These transcriptions for strings are most enjoyable, giving the rhapsodies a chimerical lightness of texture. They are very well played indeed by this excellent orchestra, and Rolla's performances have nicely calculated rubato and plenty of spirit. Excellent, fresh recording. Not an alternative to the usual full-orchestra versions but a worthwhile bargain supplement.

Hungarian rhapsody No. 2 in C sharp min.
(N) *** Decca Dig. 452 482-2 [id.]. Montreal SO, Charles Dutoit. – ALFVEN, DVORAK, ENESCU, GLAZUNOV: *Rhapsodies etc.* ***

Very vivid recording and an eminently enjoyable account of the *Hungarian Rhapsody No. 2* from Montreal and Dutoit, distinguished by a recording of great clarity and presence.

Mephisto waltz.
(M) *** RCA 09026 61246-2 [id.]. Chicago SO, Reiner – TCHAIKOVSKY: *Symphony No. 6* etc. **(*)

Reiner's account of the *Mephisto waltz* is the star item on this CD, unsurpassed on disc. The Chicago playing is superb.

SYMPHONIC POEMS

Symphonic poems: *Ce qu'on entend sur la montagne (Bergsinfonie); Festklänge; Hunnenschlacht; Die Ideale; Von der Wiege bis zum Grabe;* (i) *Dante symphony.*
(B) *** EMI forte (SIS) CZS5 68598-2 [CDFB 68598] (2). Leipzig GO, Masur; with (i) Arndt, Leipzig Thomaskirche Ch.

On the whole Masur's survey of Liszt's symphonic poems is the finest we have had so far. The performances have a dramatic vitality that eludes Haitink, and the Leipzig orchestra's playing is even finer than that of the LPO on Philips. Some of the earlier pieces, such as *Ce qu'on entend sur la montagne* and *Festklänge*, suffer not only from formal weakness but also from a lack of interesting melodic invention. However, these performances – and, whatever one may think of it, this music – cast a strong spell, and with rare exceptions Masur proves a most persuasive advocate. It is the rich sonority of the lower strings, the dark, perfectly blended woodwind-tone and the fine internal balance of the Leipzig Gewandhaus Orchestra that hold the listener throughout.

Ce qu'on entend sur la montagne; Festklänge; Mazeppa; Orpheus; Les Préludes; Prometheus; Tasso, lamento e trionfo.
(B) **(*) Ph. Duo 438 751-2 (2). LPO, Bernard Haitink.

Hamlet; Héroïde funèbre; Hungaria; Hunnenschlacht; Die Ideale; Mephisto waltz No. 1; Von der Wiege bis zum Grabe.
(B) **(*) Ph. Duo 438 754-2 (2). LPO, Bernard Haitink.

Haitink's set includes all the tone poems in two double-CD sets as opposed to the five pieces plus *Dante Symphony* on offer from Masur. They are fine performances and recorded in exemplary sound even if they perhaps lack the histrionic dimension and vulgarity that is part of Liszt's make-up. The recordings have never sounded better – far more vivid than on the original LPs. Liszt invented the symphonic poem; here is an inexpensive and, for the most part, rewarding way to sample his achievement overall. There is good documentation.

Symphonic poems: *From the cradle to the grave (Von der Wiege bis zum Grabe); Hamlet; Die Ideale; Orpheus.*
(N) (BB) *(**) Naxos Dig. 8.553355 [id.]. New Zealand SO, Halász.

Michael Halász gets a vital and sensitive response from his fine New Zealand Orchestra in these tone poems, with some beautiful string playing at the opening of *From the cradle to the grave* – an elusive, extended work that he holds together very well – and the opening of *Orpheus* is most evocative. He does not shirk the melodrama in *Die Ideale*, and *Hamlet* too is powerfully done. Artistically this is very impressive, but the recorded sound brings problems that will worry some listeners more than others. There is no lack of vividness but the balance is too close, and while all is well in *piano* and *pianissimo* passages, tuttis are less comfortable, with a degree of glare and congestion and a lack of space round the climaxes. Impressive just the same, and good value.

Hamlet; Mazeppa; Orpheus; Les Préludes.
(N) * Sony Dig. SK 66834 [id.]. BPO, Zubin Mehta.

Four celebrated symphonic poems with the Berlin Philharmonic conducted by Zubin Mehta do not send the pulse racing. Mehta gets what might be called general-purpose performances. There is no special identification with what are well-prepared, well-held-together accounts with little poetic feeling. The disc is remarkable in one respect: Mehta manages to get the Berlin Philharmonic sounding just like any other orchestra, rather than the incomparable body they are.

Mazeppa; Les Préludes; Prometheus; Tasso, lamento e trionfo (symphonic poems).
(BB) *** Naxos Dig. 8.550487 [id.]. Polish Nat. RSO (Katowice), Michael Halász.

Michael Halász has the full measure of this repertoire and this is one of the most successful collections of Liszt's symphonic poems to have emerged in recent years. He draws some remarkably fine playing from the Katowice Radio Orchestra. The brass playing is very impressive throughout, especially the trombones and tuba, who have the epic main theme of *Mazeppa*, but its grandiloquence is no less powerful in *Les Préludes*, weighty and never brash. The recording is spacious, with full natural string textures, but it is the resounding brass one remembers most.

Les Préludes
(N) *(**) Decca 452 305-2 [id.]. Paris Conservatoire O, Ataulfo Argenta – BERLIOZ: *Symphonie fantastique*. **

Though the sound is not so weighty or cleanly defined as in the Berlioz, Argenta's account of the most famous Liszt symphonic poem also brings an exceptionally powerful, purposeful performance.

Tasso, lamento e trionfo.
(N) **(*) Testament mono SBT 1129 [id.]. Philh. O., Constantin Silvestri – TCHAIKOVSKY: *Manfred Symphony*. *(*)

Silvestri's version of *Tasso* was one of his best recordings (second only perhaps to his account of Elgar's *In the South*). It comes up well in this new transfer but the Tchaikovsky coupling does not show the Romanian maestro at his best.

CHAMBER MUSIC

Elégies Nos. 1–2; La lugubre gondola; Romance oubliée; Die Zelle in Nonnenwerth.
*** RCA Dig. 09026 68290-2 [id.]. Steven Isserlis, Stephen Hough – GRIEG: *Cello sonata;* RUBINSTEIN: *Cello sonata No. 1*. ***

The five cello pieces of Liszt, all of them brief and all of them adapted from earlier works, are used to frame two high-romantic cello sonatas by Grieg and Rubinstein, with the latter in danger of neglect. Isserlis and Hough give inspired performances, bringing out the distinctive lyricism of Liszt's writing for cello. The *Romance oubliée* ('Forgotten romance'), adapted from an early song, was originally written for viola, with an added arpeggio passage at the end reflecting Berlioz's *Harold in Italy*, which Liszt had arranged for viola and piano. In the two *Elégies* Isserlis is most persuasive in the improvisation-like passages, while the disc is rounded off by two Liszt pieces that are slightly more substantial than the others: *Die Zelle in Nonnenwerth* is a late adaptation of an early song, spare in texture; and Liszt's tribute to Wagner after his death, *La lugubre gondola*, is only one of Liszt's many different adaptations. Warm, well-balanced sound.

PIANO MUSIC

Complete piano music, Vol. 1: *Albumblatt in waltz form; Bagatelle without tonality; Caprice-valses Nos. 1 & 2; Ländler in A flat; Mephisto waltzes Nos. 1–3; Valse impromptu; 4 Valses oubliées.*
*** Hyperion Dig. CDA 66201 [id.]. Leslie Howard.

Complete piano music, Vol. 2: *Ballades Nos. 1–2; Berceuse; Impromptu (Nocturne); Klavierstück in A flat; 2 Légendes; 2 Polonaises.*
**(*) Hyperion Dig. CDA 66301. Leslie Howard.

Complete piano music, Vol. 3: *Fantasia and fugue on B-A-C-H; 3 Funeral odes: Les morts; La notte; Le triomphe funèbre du Tasse; Grosses Konzertsolo; Prelude on Weinen, Klagen, Sorgen, Sagen; Variations on a theme of Bach.*
** Hyperion Dig. CDA 66302 [id.]. Leslie Howard.

Complete piano music, Vol. 4: *Adagio in C; Etudes d'éxécution transcendante; Elégie sur des motifs de Prince Louis Ferdinand de Prusse; Mariotte.*
** Hyperion Dig. CDA 66357 [id.]. Leslie Howard.

Complete piano music, Vol. 5: Concert paraphrases: BERLIOZ: *L'Idée fixe; Overtures: Les Francs-Juges; Le Roi Lear; Marche des pèlerins; Valse des Sylphes.* CHOPIN: *6 Chants polonais.* SAINT-SAENS: *Danse macabre.*
*** Hyperion Dig. CDA 66346 [id.]. Leslie Howard.

Complete piano music, Vol. 6: Concert paraphrases: AUBER: *3 Pieces on themes from La muette de Portici.* BELLINI: *Réminiscences de Norma.* BERLIOZ: *Benvenuto Cellini: Bénédiction et serment.* DONIZETTI: *Réminiscences de Lucia di Lammermoor; Marche funèbre et Cavatina (Lucia).* ERNST (Duke of Saxe-Coburg-Gotha): *Tony: Hunting chorus.* GLINKA: *Ruslan and Ludmilla: Tscherkessenmarsch.* GOUNOD: *Waltz from Faust.* HANDEL: *Almira: Sarabande and Chaconne.* MEYERBEER: *Illustrations de L'Africaine.* MOZART: *Réminiscences de Don Juan.* VERDI: *Aida: Danza sacra & Duetto finale.* TCHAIKOVSKY: *Eugene Onegin: Polonaise.* WAGNER: *Tristan: Isoldes Liebestod.* WEBER: *Der Freischütz: Overture.*

*** Hyperion Dig. CDA 66371/2 [id.]. Leslie Howard.

Complete piano music, Vol. 7: Chorales: *Crux ave benedicta; Jesu Christe; Meine Seele; Nun danket alle Gott; Nun ruhen all Wälder; O haupt; O Lamm Gottes; O Traurigkeit; Vexilla Regis; Was Gott tut; Wer nur den Lieben; Via Crucis; Weihnachtsbaum; Weihnachtslied.*
** Hyperion Dig. CDA 66388 [id.]. Leslie Howard.

Complete piano music, Vol. 8: *Alleluia and Ave Maria; Ave Marias 1–4; Ave Maria de Arcadelt; Ave Maris stella; Harmonies poétiques et religieuses* (complete); *Hungarian Coronation Mass; Hymnes; Hymne du Pape; In festo transfigurations; Invocation; O Roma nobilis; Sancta Dorothea; Slavimo slavno slaveni!; Stabat mater; Urbi et orbi; Vexilla regis prodeunt; Zum Haus des Herrn.*
** Hyperion Dig. CDA 66421/2 [id.]. Leslie Howard.

Complete piano music, Vol. 9: *6 Consolations; 2 Elégies; Gretchen* (from *Faust Symphony*); *Sonata in B min.; Totentanz.*
** Hyperion Dig. CDA 66429 [id.]. Leslie Howard (piano).

Complete piano music, Vol. 10: Concert paraphrases: BELLINI: *Hexaméron (Grand bravura variations* on the *March* from *I Puritani).* BERLIOZ: *Symphonie fantastique. Un portrait en musique de la Marquise de Blocqueville.*
**(*) Hyperion Dig. CDA 66433 [id.]. Leslie Howard.

Complete piano music, Vol. 11: *Abschied (Russisches Volkslied); Am Grabe Richard Wagners; Carrousel de Madame P-N; Dem Andenken Petöfis; Epithalium; Klavierstück in F sharp; En Rêve; 5 Klavierstücke; Mosonyis Grabgeleit; Recueillement; Resignazione; Romance oubliée; RW (Venezia); Schlaflos! Frage und Antwort; Sospiri; Toccata; Slyepoi (Der blinde Sänger); Die Trauergondel (La lugubre gondola); Trauervorspiel und Trauermarsch; Trübe Wolken (Nuages gris); Ungarns Gott; Ungarisches Königslied; Unstern: Sinistre; Wiegenlied (Chant de berceau).*
**(*) Hyperion Dig. CDA 66445 [id.]. Leslie Howard.

Complete piano music, Vol. 12: *Années de pèlerinage, 3rd Year (Italy); 5 Hungarian folksongs; Historical Hungarian portraits.*
** Hyperion Dig. CDA 66448 [id.]. Leslie Howard.

Complete piano music, Vol. 13: Concert paraphrases: ALLEGRI/MOZART: *A La Chapelle Sistine: Miserere d'Allegri et Ave verum corpus de Mozart.* BACH: *Fantasia and fugue in G min.; 6 Preludes and fugues for organ.*
** Hyperion Dig. CDA 66438 [id.]. Leslie Howard.

Complete piano music, Vol. 14: *Christus; Polonaises de St Stanislas; Salve Polonia; St Elizabeth.*
**(*) Hyperion Dig. CDA 66466 [id.]. Leslie Howard.

Complete piano music, Vol. 15: Concert paraphrases of Lieder: BEETHOVEN: *Adelaïde; An die ferne Geliebte; 6 Gellert Lieder; 6 Lieder von Goethe; An die ferne Geliebte.* DESSAUER: *3 Lieder.* FRANZ: *Er est gekommenin Sturm und Regen; 12 Lieder.* MENDELSSOHN: *7 Lieder* including *Auf Flügeln des Gesanges.* CLARA & ROBERT SCHUMANN: *10 Lieder* including *Frühlingsnacht; Widmung.*
**(*) Hyperion Dig. CDA 66481/2 [id.]. Leslie Howard.

Complete solo piano music, Vol. 16: Piano transcriptions: DAVID: *Bunte Reihe* (24 character pieces for violin and piano), *Op. 30.*
*** Hyperion Dig. CDA 66506 [id.]. Leslie Howard.

Complete piano music, Vol. 17: Concert paraphrases: DONIZETTI: *Spirito gentil* from *La Favorita; Marche funèbre* from *Don Sebastien.* GOUNOD: *Les Sabéennes (Berceuse)* from *La Reine de Saba.* GRETRY: *Die Rose (Romance)* from *Zémire et Azor.* MEYERBEER: *3 Illustrations du Prophète; Fantasia and fugue* on *Ad nos, ad salutarem undam* on a theme from *Le Prophète.* MOSONYI: *Fantasy on Szép Ilonka.* WAGNER: *Spinning song and Ballade* from *Der fliegende Holländer; Pilgrims' chorus and O du, mein holder Abendstern* from *Tannhäuser; Valhalla* from *The Ring; Feierlicher Marsch zum heiligen Grail* from *Parsifal.*
**(*) Hyperion Dig. CDA 66571/2 [id.]. Leslie Howard.

Complete piano music, Vol. 18: Concert paraphrases: BEETHOVEN: *Capriccio alla turca; Fantasy* from *Ruins of Athens.* LASSEN: *Symphonisches Zwischenspiel zu Calderons Schauspiel über allen Zauber Liebe.* MENDELSSOHN: *Wedding march and dance of the elves* from *A Midsummer night's dream.* WEBER: *Einsam bin ich, nicht alleine* from *La Preciosa.* HEBBEL: *Nibelungen.*
**(*) Hyperion Dig. CDA 66575 [id.]. Leslie Howard.

Leslie Howard's ambitious project to record the complete music of Liszt proceeds apace and at least two of these issues have already collected a Grand Prix du Disque in Budapest (Volumes 5 and 6). The performances are very capable and musicianly, and there are moments of poetic feeling, but for the most part his playing rarely touches distinction. The kind of concentration one finds in great Liszt pianists such as Arrau, Kempff and Richter (and there are many younger artists whose names also spring to mind) rarely surfaces. Howard's technical equipment is formidable but poetic imagination and the ability to grip the listener are here less developed: his rushed account of the *Sonata* does not really stand up against the current competition. One of the most interesting issues is Volume 16, the *Bunte Reihe* of Ferdinand David (1810–70), a contemporary of Mendelssohn. These are transcriptions of music for violin and piano in which the violin seems hardly to be missed at all. Leslie Howard plays them beautifully. Certainly the coverage so far is remarkable and, if this playing rarely takes the breath away either by its virtuosity or its poetic insights, it is unfailingly intelligent and the recordings are first class.

Complete piano music, Vol. 19: *Die Lorelei; 3 Liebesträume; Songs for solo piano, Books 1–2.*
*** Hyperion Dig. CDA 66593 [id.]. Leslie Howard.

Complete piano music, Vol. 20: *Album d'un voyageur: Années de pèlerinage*, 1st, 2nd & 3rd years (first versions); *Chanson du Béarn; Fantaisie romantique sur deux mélodies suisses; Faribolo pastour.*
*** Hyperion Dig. CDA 66601/2 [id.]. Leslie Howard.

Complete piano music, Vol. 21: ROSSINI: *Soirées musicales; Grande fantaisie on motifs from Soirées musicales; 2nd Fantaisie on motifs from Soirées musicales.* DONIZETTI: *Nuits d'été à Pausilippe.* MERCADANTE: *Soirées italiennes. 3 Sonetti di Petrarca* (1st version); *Venezia e Napoli* (1st set).
*** Hyperion Dig. CDA 66661/2 [id.]. Leslie Howard.

Complete piano music, Vol. 22: Concert paraphrases of Beethoven Symphonies: *Symphonies Nos. 1–9.*
** Hyperion Dig. CDA 66671/5 [id.]. Leslie Howard.

Complete piano music, Vol. 23: BERLIOZ: (i) *Harold in Italy.* LISZT: (i) *Romance oubliée.* GOUNOD: *Hymne à Sainte Cécile.* MEYERBEER: *Le moine; Festmarsch.*
**(*) Hyperion Dig. CDA 66683 [id.]. Leslie Howard, (i) with Paul Coletti.

Complete piano music, Vol. 24: Concert paraphrases: BEETHOVEN: *Septet, Op. 20.* MOZART: *Requiem mass, K.626: Confutatis; Lacrimosa. Ave verum corpus, K.618.* VERDI: *Requiem mass: Agnus dei.* ROSSINI: *Cujus animam: Air du Stabat Mater; 3 Chœurs religieux: La Charité.* GOLDSCHMIDT: *7 Tödsunden: Liebesszene und Fortunas Kugel.* MENDELSSOHN: *Wasserfahrt und der Jäger Abschied.* WEBER: *Schlummerlied mit Arabesken; Leyer und Schwert-Heroïde.* HUMMEL: *Septet No. 1 in D min.*
** Hyperion Dig. CDA 66761/2 [id.]. Leslie Howard.

Complete piano music, Vol. 25: *San Francesco: Prelude: The canticle of the sun; Canticle of the sun of St Francis of Assisi. Ave maris stella; Gebet; Ich liebe dich; Il m'aimait tant; O pourquoi donc; Ora pro nobis; O sacrum convivium* (2 versions); *Rezignazione – Ergebung; Salve regina; Von der Wiege bis zum Grabe; Die Zelle in Nonnenwerth.*
**(*) Hyperion Dig. CDA 66694 [id.]. Leslie Howard.

Complete piano music, Vol. 26: *Allegro di bravura; Apparitions; Berceuse; 12 Etudes; Feuilles d'album; Galop de bal; Hungarian recruiting dances; Impromptu brillant on themes of Rossini and Spontini; Klavierstücke (aus der Bonn Beethoven-Kantatej); 2 Klavierstücke; Marche hongroise; Notturno No. 2; Rondo di bravura; Scherzo in G min.; Variation on a waltz of Diabelli; Variations on a theme of Rossini; 5 Variations on a theme from Méhul's Joseph; Waltz in A; Waltz in E flat.*
**(*) Hyperion Dig. CDA 66771/2 [id.]. Leslie Howard.

Complete piano music, Vol. 27: *Canzone napolitana* (2 versions); *La cloche sonne; Gleanings from Woronince; God save the Queen; Hungarian national folk tunes (Ungarische Nationalmelodien); Hussite song; La Marseillaise; Rákóczi march; Szózat and Hungarian hymn; Vive Henri IV.*
*** Hyperion Dig. CDA 66787 [id.]. Leslie Howard.

Complete piano music, Vol. 28: *Bulow-Marsch; Heroischer Marsch im Ungarischer Geschwindmarsch; Csárdás; Csárdás macabre; Csárdás obstiné; Festmarsch zur Goethejubiläumsfeier; Festpolonaise; Festvorspiel; Galop in A min.; Grand galop chromatique; Huldigungsmarsch; Kunstierfestzug zur Schillerfeier; Marche héroïque; Mazurka brillante; Mephisto polka; Petite valse; Rákóczy Marsch; Vorn Fels zurn Meer; La favorite; Scherzo and march; Siegesmarsch; Ungarischer Marsch zur Krönungsfeier in Ofen-Pest; Ungarischer Stürmmarsch; Zweite Festmarsch.*
**(*) Hyperion Dig. CDA 66811/2 [id.]. Leslie Howard.

The two Liszt *Songbooks* offer 12 early Lieder in engagingly simple transcriptions. Leslie Howard plays them beautifully, as he does the three *Liebesträume*, of which only the third is really familiar. Volume 20 centres on what Leslie Howard prefers to call *Album d'un Voyager*, the early edition of what we know as the *Années de pèlerinage* (which the composer tried, unsuccessfully, to suppress). Book I includes a flamboyant extra item, *Lyon*, inspired by a workers' uprising, and only two of the pieces in Book II, *Fleurs mélodiques des Alpes*, were retained in the final set of *Années de pèlerinage*. Apart from the *Paraphrases* in Book III, this collection also includes an unknown major improvisatory work of the same period and inspiration, the 18-minute-long *Fantaisie romantique sur deux mélodies suisses*, with plenty of opportunities for bravura in the latter part. A fascinating collection, very well played indeed. Volume 21 is lightweight, opening with the Rossini *Soirées musicales*, which we know from the much later Britten orchestrations, and *Soirées italiennes*, based on rather less interesting music by Mercadante. For the second disc Howard returns to the initial versions of the *Années de pèlerinage*, including the *Petrarch Sonnets* and *Venezia e Napoli*. The second CD ends with a pair of *Grand fantasias* on themes from the *Soirées* which began the recital.

Volume 22 brings us to Liszt's paraphrases of the nine Beethoven symphonies. Leslie Howard's 'interpretations' are sound throughout; he makes more of some movements than others (the first movement of the *Eroica* could be more compelling) and the resonance of the recording is not ideal for revealing detail. The *Ninth* works impressively, if not as earth-shaking as Katsaris's version on Teldec. Overall, this is surprisingly enjoyable to listen to; without the orchestral colour, one notices the more what is happening in the internal arguments of these inexhaustible works.

Volume 23 is an effective transcription of Berlioz's *Harold in Italy* for viola and piano, and Howard takes the opportunity to include Liszt's own *Romance oubliée* for the same combination. Here Paul Coletti joins the pianist, and the performances are well played and spontaneous, if not earth-shaking. The transcriptions of the Beethoven and Hummel *Septets*, however, do not really work at all. This music either needs the instrumental colour or a much more witty approach (and the resonant recording is not helpful). However, there are some other paraphrases here that are much more effective, notably the excerpts from Goldschmidt's *Die sieben Todsünden* and two transcribed Mendelssohn choruses.

The *Cantico del Sol di San Francesco d'Assisi* is pleasantly based on *In dulci jubilo*. Then comes the chrysalis of the symphonic poem, *From the cradle to the grave*, which was greatly expanded in its orchestral form. Volume 26 is almost entirely devoted to works written when Liszt was a teenager, and the *Variations* show his mettle. Volume 27 offers patriotic songs and airs in a much more interesting and varied programme than it looks at first glance. *God save the Queen* was written for a British tour in 1840/41 and the tune is immediately interestingly varied in the opening bars. *La Marseillaise* starts off straightforwardly and the variants come later, but the tune reasserts itself strongly. The *Ungarische Nationalmelodien* is in effect a sketch for the *Sixth Hungarian rhapsody*. But there are plenty of enticing ideas here, notably the three-part suite, *Glanes de Woronince*, and the delightful French folksong arrangements, *Vive Henry IV* and *La cloche sonne*. Howard is at his most imaginative. Volume 28 is essentially a collection of marches and lively extrovert pieces, but they are very well presented.

Complete piano music, Vol. 29: *Hungarian themes and rhapsodies, Nos. 1–22*.
** Hyperion Dig. CDA 66851/2 [id.]. Leslie Howard.

Here is the source material for Liszt's *Hungarian rhapsodies* and the *Hungarian fantasia* in earlier, more earthy form, before the dances became sophisticated concert repertoire. There is even an early version (subsequently discarded) of the *Consolation No. 3*. Of course not all the music here is equally interesting, but Leslie Howard brings it to life fluently. His playing has convincing rubato but lacks something in flair and adrenalin.

Complete piano music, Vol. 30: Operatic fantasies, concert paraphrases and transcriptions: DONIZETTI: *Valse de concert on 2 motifs of Lucia de Lammermoor and Parisina*. GOUNOD: *Les Adieux (Rêverie on a theme from Roméo et Juliette)*. ERKEL: *Schwanengesang and march to Hunyadi László*. MEYERBEER: *Réminscences de Robert le diable: Cavatine; Valse infernale*. MOZART: *Fantasy on themes from Nozze di Figaro and Don Giovanni*. VERDI: *Ernani; Rigoletto; Il Trovatore: Miserere* (concert paraphrases); *Réminiscences de Simon Boccanegra*. WAGNER: *Lohengrin: Elsa's bridal procession; Wedding march; Elsa's dream; Lohengrin's reproof. Fantasy on themes from Rienzi*. WEBER: overture: *Oberon*.
** Hyperion Dig. CDA 66861/2 [id.]. Leslie Howard.

It is difficult for present-day music-lovers to appreciate that in Liszt's time even a piece as familiar as Weber's *Oberon overture* was relatively inaccessible outside the opera house, though it must be said that Howard does not make a great deal of it – the allegros sound unpianistic. But of course Liszt's operatic paraphrases were designed both to entertain and to remind listeners not only of the tunes that made up the best-known operas of Mozart, Verdi and Wagner but those of lesser composers too. Some of this music ideally needs a Horowitz, but for the most part Leslie Howard is up to the display and pyrotechnics which Liszt's embellishments require. However, Mozart's *Là ci darem* is heavily romanticized and the Verdi paraphrases also need more impetus. The Wagner transcriptions are more successful.

Complete piano music, Vol. 31: 'The Schubert transcriptions' (Vol. 1): *Ave Maria; Der Gondelfahrer; Erlkönig; Märche für das Pianoforte übertragen: Trauermarsch (Grande marche funèbre); Grande marche; Grande marche characteristique. Marche militaire* (concert paraphrase); *Mélodies hongroises; Die Rose; La Sérénade; Soirées de Vienne; 2 Transcriptions for Sophie Menter.*
** Hyperion Dig. CDA 66951/3 [id.]. Leslie Howard.

Complete piano music, Vol. 32: 'The Schubert transcriptions' (Vol. 2): *Die Forelle; Frühlingsglaube; Marche hongroise* (2 versions); *Meeresstille; 6 Mélodies favorites de la belle meunière; 6 Mélodies of Franz Schubert; 4 Sacred songs; Schuberts Ungarische Melodien; Schwanengesang; 12 Songs from Winterreise; Ständchen (Leise flehen).*
** Hyperion Dig. CDA 66954/6 [id.]. Leslie Howard.

Complete piano music, Vol. 33: 'The Schubert transcriptions' (Vol. 3): *Die Forelle; Die Gestirne; 2 Lieder; 12 Lieder* (2 versions); *Marche hongroise; Meerestille* (2 versions); *Müllerlieder; Die Nebensonnen; Schwanengesang; Soirées de Vienne: Valse caprice No. 6; 12 songs from Winterreise.*
** Hyperion Dig. CDA 66957/9 [id.]. Leslie Howard.

Liszt obviously admired Schubert enormously and wanted to champion him as well as play his music. The songs were obvious candidates because of their sheer tunefulness, but he was also attracted to Schubert's lighter dance music. The *Soirées de Vienne* really suit Howard and are played with a pleasantly Schubertian feeling and nicely judged rubato, while the *Valse caprice* is quite charming. And what of the songs? The four *Geistliche Lieder* (*Sacred songs*) which open the collection are made to seem unremittingly sombre, and Howard has a tendency to over-characterize the darker songs elsewhere. *Die Forelle* and some of the other most famous songs are not very imaginatively done, although *Erlkönig* comes off well. But not everyone will want two complete *Schwanengesangs* without a singer. Of course the transcriptions are free – sometimes (but not often) very free – and there is more Liszt than Schubert. Leslie Howard plays them (as Liszt surely would have done) with comparable freedom in matters of phrasing and rubato, and for the most part he is convincing, if at times his tempi seem a little too indulgent.

Complete piano music, Vol. 34: *12 Grandes études; Morceau de salon.*
*** Hyperion Dig. CDA 66973 [id.]. Leslie Howard.

These *Grandes études* were the pilot version of the *Etudes d'exécution transcendente*, which appeared a quarter of a century later, in 1851. This (as with so much of this invaluable series) is their first recording, as the composer expressly forbade their performance. This music demands great bravura, and Leslie Howard surpasses himself in rising to the challenge with remarkable confidence. There is much to tickle the ear here, and all this music is Liszt's own and is not borrowed from others!

Complete piano music, Vol. 35: *Arabesques (2 mélodies russes):* (ALABIEV: *Le rossignol.* P. BULAKHOV: *Chanson bohémienne*). Russian transcriptions: AN AMATEUR FROM ST PETERSBURG: *Mazurka.* (Liszt's) *Prelude à la Polka de Borodin.* BORODIN: (i) *Polka.* K. BULAKHOV: *Galop russe.* CUI; DARGOMIZHSKY: *Tarentelles.* WIELHORSKY: *Autrefois.* Hungarian transcriptions: *Rákóczi-march.* ABRANYI: *Flower song.* FESTETICS: *Spanish Ständchen.* SZECHENYI: *Introduction and Hungarian march.* SZABADI/MASSENET: *Revive Szegedin!* VEGH: *Valse de concert.* ZICHY: *Valse d'Adèle.*
*** Hyperion Dig. CDA 66984 [id.]. Leslie Howard, (i) with Philip Moore.

Liszt was especially enthusiastic about new Russian music and, as can by seen from the piece based on the *Mazurka* of 'An Amateur from St Petersburg', he didn't restrict his interest to famous names, although they are all here. He composed his own piano solo introduction to Borodin's engaging four-handed *Polka*, which is included here with the help of Philip Moore. Most of the Hungarian names are unfamiliar but the music itself, if slight, is often delightful. The two opening *Arabesques* are enticing; but everything tickles the ear, especially Abranyi's *Flower song*, and no one can say that Leslie Howard does not relish its glittering colours. As usual, good recording. This is a most enjoyable collection.

Complete piano music, Vol. 36: *Consolations Nos. 1–6; Elégie: Entwurf der Ramann; Excelsior! (Prelude to The bells of Strasburg Cathedral); Fanfare for the unveiling of the Carl August memorial; Geharnischte Lieder; National hymn (Kaiser Wilhelm!); Rosario Schlummerlied im Grabe; Die Zelle in Nonnenwerth* (2 versions); *Weimars Volkslieder Nos. 1–2.*
**(*) Hyperion Dig. CDA 66995 [id.]. Leslie Howard.

The first version of the six *Consolations* misses out the most famous *Third in D flat* and substitutes a less memorable piece in *C sharp minor*, but in all other respects these earlier pieces are valid in their own right and are well worth having on disc, although the performances do tend to languish a bit. The rest of the programme consists of novelties, including cathedral bells (celebrated here by the two versions of *Die Zelle in Nonnenwerth* as well as by *Excelsior!*), all unknown, many of them occasional pieces and of no great interest except for *Rosario*, three gentle settings of *Ave Maria* which are persuasively atmospheric.

Complete piano music, Vol. 37: BULOW: *Tanto gentile e tanto onesta*. CONRADI: *Zigeuner polka*. ERNST: *Die Gräberinsel der Fürsten zu Gotha*. HERBECK: *Tanzmomente Nos. 1–8; No. 4* (alternative). LASSEN: *Ich weil' in teifer Einsamkeit; Löse, Himmel meine Seele* (2 versions). LESSMAN: *3 Lieder from Julius Wolff's Tannhäuser*. LISZT/LOUIS FERDINAND: *Elégie sur des motifs du Prince Louis Ferdinand de Prusse*.
** Hyperion Dig. CDA 67004 [id.]. Leslie Howard.

Liszt's interest in Johann Ritter von Herbeck reflects the latter's importance in Viennese musical life of the time. He was choirmaster as well as composer, and his *Tanzmomente* consists of eight dances, many of them waltzes of some charm. Liszt's transcriptions flatter them agreeably and he expands the finale considerably and to good effect. Otto Lessen was a journalist and theatre manager, and his songs also make agreeable transcriptions, as does Hans von Bülow's *Tanto gentile*. The closing *Zigeuner-Polka* of August Conradi was a pop hit in its day, and Liszt's arrangement adds a bit of spice to the melodic sequence. All this music is exceedingly rare, but its musical interest is frankly limited. The Lassen and Bülow pieces are the highlights.

Complete piano music, Vol. 38: *Concert études and Episodes from Lenau's Faust: Les préludes; 3 Etudes de concert; 2 Concert studies; 2 Episodes from Lenau's Faust*.
*** Hyperion Dig. CDA 67015 [id.]. Leslie Howard.

Volume 38 is a good deal more substantial than its predecessor, starting off with the popular *Les Préludes*, which anticipates the orchestral version fairly closely, with a few minor differences near the end. The transcription is made in pianistic terms and works well. The three *Etudes de concert* continue in familiar territory, especially the third, a Lisztian romantic blossoming better known as '*Un Sospiro*' (which Howard presents boldly). *Waldesrauschen* and *Gnomenreigen* (beautifully done) are equally welcome, as is the opportunity of hearing the two *Faust* pieces together in their piano versions, of which the *Mephisto waltz* is easily the more famous. A rewarding collection, very well played and recorded.

Complete piano music, Vol. 39: *Années de pèlerinage, 1st year (Switzerland); 3 Morceaux suisses*.
** Hyperion Dig. CDA 67026 [id.]. Leslie Howard.

With Volume 39 of his continuing Liszt survey Leslie Howard moves on to the first year of the *Années de pèlerinage*, for the most part playing the second versions. But this is music we know well in the hands of artists like Wilhelm Kempff. Howard provides thoroughly musical performances, but without finding the degree of poetry and magic that these evocative pieces deserve. The three *Morceaux suisses* come off brightly and quite spontaneously. Liszt's descriptive powers are more literally used here, with a storm graphically depicted in the second, *Un soir dans la montagne*.

Complete piano music, Vol. 40: *Ballade No. 2* (first version); *Festmarsch zur Säkularfeier von Goethes Geburtstag; Seconde Marche hongroise; Nocturne (Impromptu);* Concert paraphrases and transcriptions: *Galop russe* (Bulhakov); *Gaudeamus igitur* (2 versions: *Paraphrase; Humoreske*); *Lyubila ya* (Wielhorsky); *La Marche pour le Sultan Abdul Médjid-Khan* (Donizetti); *Seconda Mazurka di Tirindelli; Le Rossignol-Air russe* (Alyabiev); *Una stella amica-Valzer* (Pezzini).
** Hyperion Dig. CDA 67034 [id.]. Leslie Howard.

This collection is described as *Pièces d'occasion*, and much of the music here is desperately trivial. Liszt's paraphrase on *Gaudeamus igitur* at nine minutes outlasts its welcome, while the second version, called *Humoreske*, is even less entertaining. Howard takes everything fairly seriously and, though his playing is secure technically, he seldom dazzles the ear, which is surely what the composer would have done.

Complete piano music, Vol. 41: Recitations with piano: (i) *A holt költo szerelme (The Dead poet's love);* (ii) *Helge's Treue (Helge's loyalty); Lenore; Der traurige Mönch (The Sad monk);* (iii) *Slyepoi (The Blind man)*.
*(**) Hyperion Dig. CDA 67045 [id.]. Leslie Howard, with (i) Sandor Eles; (ii) Wolf Kahler; (iii) Yuri Stepanov.

A real curiosity, but essentially a specialist compilation. While one is willing to follow an opera libretto alongside a recording, to have to listen to a spoken poetic narrative in German, Hungarian or Russian alongside its musical illustration while following the translation is a different matter. Certainly the ballades here are not lacking in melodrama. *Lenore*, whose lover fails to come back from the wars, cries out blasphemously against God. Night falls, and she hears the sound of hooves clip-clopping: there he is on his horse to take her to the bridal bed. They travel 'a hundred miles' through the night, later followed by demons, and at the end of the journey her lover is no more than a brittle skeleton. All the lurid tales here obviously excited Liszt's imagination, and Howard rises to the occasion. But one wonders how often one would want to return to a CD of this kind.

Complete piano music, Vol. 42: Concert paraphrases: AUBER: *Tyrolean melody* from *La Fiancée; Tarantelle di bravura* from *Masaniello.* BELLINI: *Réminiscences des Puritains; Introduction et Polonaise* from *I Puritani; Grosse Concert-fantaisie* on *La Sonnambula.* DONIZETTI: *Réminiscences de Lucrezia Borgia: Grandes fantaisies I & II.* MEYERBEER: *Réminiscences des Huguenots.* (i) MOZART: *Song of the two armed men* from *Die Zauberflöte* (piano duet). RAFF: *Andante finale* and *Marsch* from *König Alfred.* VERDI: *Coro di festa e marcia funebre* from *Don Carlos; Salve Maria de l'opéra de Jérusalem* from *I lombardi* (two versions). WAGNER: *Pilgrims' chorus* from *Tannhäuser; Am stillen Herd – Lied* from *Die Meistersinger.*
** Hyperion Dig. CDA 67101/2 [id.]. Leslie Howard, with (i) Philip Moore.

Liszt wrote his concert paraphrases in order to present his audiences with music they would hear but rarely in the opera house. To come off, they need to be played with dazzling virtuosity and – above all – real charisma. Leslie Howard is reliably equal to most of their technical demands but he does not titillate the ear, and much of this music tends to lose the listener's attention. These records have been praised elsewhere, but for us they did not prove very stimulating listening. For instance, Howard takes the *Pilgrims' chorus* from *Tannhäuser* unbelievably slowly; he is at his best in the Bellini items. As a sound document to demonstrate the range of Liszt's operatic interest this is valuable, but the playing is seldom very exciting in itself.

Complete piano music, Vol. 43: *Années de pèlerinage, 1st Year, Switzerland: Au bord d'une source* (with coda for Sgambati). *Années de pèlerinage, 2nd Year, Italy; Supplement: Venezia e Napoli.*
**(*) Hyperion Dig. CDA 67107 [id.]. Leslie Howard.

This is one of Howard's more spontaneous recitals. *Au bord d'une source* comes off delightfully, and the brief nine-bar additional coda which Liszt wrote for his friend, the young composer/pianist Giovanni Sgambati, makes a charming (if superfluous) postlude. Howard is also at his best in the *Venezia e Napoli Supplement*, in which the closing *Tarantella* sparkles iridescently. The earlier pieces of the *Second Year* come off well enough, but the *Dante Sonata* needs more grip and fire than Howard finds for it. Excellent recording.

Complete piano music, Vol. 44: Concert paraphrases: BEETHOVEN: *Symphonies Nos. 3 (Marche funèbre); 5–7* (complete) (first versions); *No. 6 (fifth movement)* (second version); *No. 7* (fragment); *Adelaïde* (two versions); *Fantasy* from *Ruins of Athens* (first version). BERLIOZ: *Marche au supplice* from *Symphonie fantastique* (second version). LISZT: *Cadenza for 1st movement of Beethoven's Piano concerto No. 3.*
** Hyperion Dig. CDA 67111/3 [id.]. Leslie Howard.

Once again these recordings are valuable as documentation in showing how brilliantly Liszt transcribed Beethoven's orchestral works, preserving all the important detail. But Leslie Howard seems concerned to lay the music out before us with care for every bit of that detail, without seeking to create enough thrust to take the music onwards. The account of the *Fifth Symphony*, which opens the first disc, has almost no adrenalin whatsoever and proceeds onward as a very routine affair, while the *Marche funèbre* from the *Eroica* is similarly very literal in feeling. The *Pastoral Symphony* might be thought to work well with a simple, straightforward approach, especially when Howard's playing of the Scherzo and the storm sequence generates proper bravura. But then the *Shepherd's hymn of thanksgiving* is presented with little warmth of feeling. The opening of the *Seventh* has a false start, for we are first given only a fragment. When Howard begins again, the *Introduction* seems to go on for a long time but the allegro has momentum, and the other movements have more life than the other symphonies – especially the Scherzo, which really sparkles – although the articulation in the finale could be cleaner. The programme ends with excerpts from Berlioz's *Symphonie fantastique*, with first the *idée fixe* languorously turned into a 'nocturne' (which does not work especially well), followed by a bold, lively *Marche au supplice* which at least ends the programme vigorously. As with the rest of this series, the recording is excellent.

Complete piano music, Vol. 45: *Feuille morte – Elégie d'après Soriano; Grand concert fantasia on Spanish themes; Rapsodie espagnole; La romanesca* (first and second versions); *Rondeau fantastique* on *El contrabandista.*
(N) **(*) Hyperion Dig. CDA 67145 [id.]. Leslie Howard.

Collecting virtually all of Liszt's Spanish-inspired solo piano music, this is one of Howard's more impressive discs. There is not quite all the necessary dash in the *Grand concert fantasia*, but there is some glittering fingerwork in the more familiar *Rapsodie espagnole*. He does not find a great deal of inspiration in the alternative versions of *La romanesca*, but plays the *Feuille morte* beautifully, with just the right touch of romantic feeling. This comes as an interlude before the closing *Rondeau fantastique*, which produces arresting digital dexterity, but where one feels he could have let his hair down just a little bit more. He is excellently recorded.

Complete piano music, Vol. 46: 'Meditations': *Responsories and antiphons*.
(N) ** Hyperion Dig. CDA 67161/2 [id.]. Leslie Howard.

This set is in essence a series of simple chorales: settings of the matutinal plainchant responsories from the Offices for Christmas (12) and Holy Week – Maundy Thursday (22), Good Friday (19), Holy Saturday (19) – and for the Office for the Dead (24), with ('for completeness' sake') eleven alternative harmonizations. The chants are accompanied for the most part in four and occasionally three parts. Liszt's harmony is innocently simple, reflecting the Lutheran hymn tradition, without frills. Howard plays them simply too, but dedicatedly and never didactically. However, with the average timing of each item around a minute, these are not collections to listen to in bulk, for monotony inevitably sets in after just a few of these essentially ingenuous arrangements.

Complete piano music, Vol. 47: Music intended for a first cycle of *Harmonies poétiques et religieuses* (1847): *Litanies de Marie* (first and second versions); *Miserere* (first version); *Pater noster d'après la Psalmodie de l'Eglise* (first version); *Hymne de l'enfant à son réveil* (second version); *Prose des morts – De profundis* (second version); *La lampe du temple* (first version); *Hymne; Bénédiction* (second version). Earlier related pieces: *Prière d'un enfant à son réveil; Prélude* (first version).
(N) *** Hyperion Dig. CDA 67187 [id.]. Leslie Howard.

This is surely one of the most valuable of Leslie Howard's pioneering series, and all Lisztians should have it. Almost all the music recorded here is unpublished, and none of it has been previously recorded. The *Harmonies poétiques et religieuses* is one of the composer's key works and its gestation in these earlier pieces is both fascinating and musically rewarding. Howard has never played better, and his account of the remarkable *Prose des morts/ De profundis* is arresting, as are both versions of *Litanies de Marie*, sombre and commanding. He shows the composer at his most flamboyantly garrulous in the *Hymne*, with its cascades of notes. But his playing in the gentler pieces is even more memorable, notably the *Hymne* et *Prière de l'enfant* and *La lampe du temple* while the *Bénédiction* is quite magical. Excellent recording.

Complete piano music, Vol. 48: *Etudes d'exécution transcendante d'après Paganini* (complete); with *No. 1* (second version); *No. 5* (alternative); *Grandes études de Paganini* (complete); *Mazeppa* (intermediate version); *Technische Studien No. 62: Sprünge mit der Tremolo-Begleitung*.
(N) **(*) Hyperion Dig. CDA 67193 [id.]. Leslie Howard.

It would be a pity if Leslie Howard's glittering accounts of Liszt's *Grandes études de Paganini* escaped the attention of the general collector because they are 'hidden away' in this ongoing complete survey. He is clearly enjoying himself and his delectable digital dexterity is consistently ear-tickling, with the familiar numbers like *La Campanella* sounding crisply minted. Rhythms are lifted spontaneously, even wittily, and these sparkling performances leap out of the speakers. He plays the more difficult *Etudes d'exécution transcendante d'après Paganini* with flair also, but here there are some technical smudges, although not enough to impair enjoyment; the alternative version of No. 1, incorporating a study by Schumann (Op. 10/2), is well worth having on disc. The 'intermediate' version of *Mazeppa* is structurally unconvincing yet demands enormous virtuosity; here it sounds flurried and overstressed, obviously reaching the outer limit of Leslie Howard's technique.

Complete piano music, Vol. 49: '*Schubert and Weber transcriptions*': SCHUBERT: *Impromptus in E flat; in G flat, D.899; Die Rose* (intermediate version); *Wanderer fantasy in C*. WEBER: *Jubel overture; Konzertstück; Polonaise brillante*.
(N) **(*) Hyperion Dig. CDA 67203 [id.]. Leslie Howard.

Liszt reorganized the pianistic layout of the Schubert *Wanderer fantasy* with the excuse of taking advantage of the greater compass of the keyboard in the mid nineteenth century and making the score more 'pianistic'. His own version involved considerable changes in the finale, which now sounds weightily orchestral, without using an orchestra. Leslie Howard gives a commanding and convincing account of the Liszt score, yet playing with real Schubertian feeling in the serenely lyrical *Adagio*. But the biggest surprise here comes in Liszt's shortened version of Schubert's famous *Impromptu in G flat*, where at the reprise of the main theme the melody is taken up an octave, with a much more elaborate accompaniment. The result is (enjoyably) highly romantic, but not at all Schubertian. Liszt's brilliant transcriptions of Weber's *Konzertstück* and *Jubel overture* adhere fairly closely to the original texts, but demand great virtuosity, especially so in the concertante work, where the orchestral and piano parts are combined, to be played by two very busy hands. The *Polonaise brillante* (also originally for piano and orcestra) is more freely transcribed, with Weber's ideas further extended, notably in the introduction. Howard plays all this music with vigour and enthusiasm, and if at times bravura detail is lost in the pianistic stampedes, this is still impressive; the Lisztian flamboyance is well projected.

Complete piano music, Vol. 50: 'Liszt at the opera V': Concert paraphrases: AUBER: *Souvenir de La Fiancée* (third version); *Tarantelle di bravura* from *Masaniello* (first version). BELLINI: *Fantaisie sur des motifs favoris* from *La sonnambula* (second version). DONIZETTI: *Fantaisie sur des motifs* from *Lucrezia Borgia*. HALEVY: *Réminiscences de La juive*. MEYERBEER: *Réminiscences des Huguenots* (first version). PACINI: *Grande fantaisie sur des thèmes* from *Niobe*. ROSSINI: *William Tell overture*. WAGNER: *Festspiel und Brautlied* from *Lohengrin; Einzug der Gäste auf der Wartburg* from *Tannhäuser*.

(N) **(* Hyperion Dig. CDA 67231/2 [id.]. Leslie Howard.

Complete piano music, Vol. 51: '*Paralipomènes*': *Après une lecture du Dante: Dante sonata* (first, second and third versions); *A la chapelle Sistine – Miserere d'Allegri et Ave verum de Mozart* (first version); *Elégie (Die Zelle in Nonnenwerth)* (first version); *Grand solo de concert* (first version); *Prelude and fugue on B-A-C-H* (first version); *Ungarische National-Melodien Nos. 1–3 & Rákóczi marsch; Romance oubliée* (draft); *Sposalizio* (first version); *Weihnachtsbaum (Christmas tree suite)*.

(N) *** Hyperion Dig. CDA 67233/4 [id.]. Leslie Howard.

To have three different early versions of the *Dante sonata* (altogether about an hour of music) might be thought by the average collector as being too much of a good thing, but Howard plays them all with prodigious virtuosity. This famous highlight of the second year of the *Années de pèlerinage* started life under the title *Paralipomènes à la Divina Commedia*, and originally had two distinct sections, the first of which comes to a full close. It has one thematic idea, which the composer later deleted. The second revised single-movement version bears the familar title, *Après une lecture du Dante – Fantasia quasi sonata*, and this resembles the final (fourth version) fairly closely. But the third version has more additions, including a hair-raising bravura section in the final peroration, which Liszt prudently later excised. Leslie Howard plays it with thrilling abandon, and in many ways this is the most exciting of the three accounts. But each interpretation is different in structural control and variations of dynamics, so that although there is much music common to all three scores, Howard achieves a feeling of fresh spontaneity with each – a remarkable achievement. The first version of *Sposalizio* and the solo *Elégie* bring calmer waters, even if the *Grand solo de concert* again shows the composer at his most rhetorically flamboyant. The second disc opens with the piano transcription of the *B-A-C-H Prelude and fugue* for organ (technically hair-raising but less effective than the original), and includes both the ingenuous *Christmas tree suite*, with its series of innocent chorales, and the ear-tickling conflation of Allegri and Mozart, in which Liszt characteristically misses the simple atmospheric beauty of the originals. The Hungarian pieces make a lively and colourful interlude. A formidable achievement, splendidly recorded.

Complete piano music, Vol. 52: *Hungarian romanzero Nos. 1–18* (complete); *2 Marches dans le genre hongrois*.

(N) ** Hyperion Dig. CDA 67235 [id.]. Leslie Howard.

Volume 52 has greater documentary than musical interest. The '*Hungarian romances*' exist only in an unpublished manuscript dating from the early 1850s, held in the Wagner Museum in Bayreuth – a volume of Hungarian dance themes arranged for piano, sometimes simply, sometimes more elaborately. They are all quite short and appear to be a kind of detailed musical notebook for future use. (Liszt had already completed and published his set of *Hungarian rhapsodies*.) Leslie Howard makes the most of relatively unpromising material, tickling the ear whenever he can. The two unfinished *Hungarian marches* date from ten years earlier, and have been edited and completed by Howard himself.

Complete piano music, Vol. 53a: Music for piano and orchestra (Vol. 1): *Piano concerto No. 1; Piano concerto in E flat, op. posth.; Concert paraphrase on Weber's Polonaise brillante; Fantasy on motives from Beethoven's Ruins of Athens; Grand solo de concert; Hexaméron; Lélio fantasy; Malédiction (Concerto in E min. for piano and strings); Totentanz* (2nd version).

(N) *** Hyperion Dig. CDA 67401/2 [id.]. Leslie Howard, Budapest SO, Karl Rickenbacher.

Complete piano music, Vol. 53b: Music for piano and orchestra. (Vol.2): *Piano concerto No. 2; Concerto pathétique* (orch. Reuss); *De profundis; Hungarian fantasia; Totentanz* (1st version). SCHUBERT, arr. LISZT: *Wanderer fantasy*. WEBER arr. LISZT: *Konzertstück*.

(N) *** Hyperion CDA 67403/5 [id.]. Leslie Howard, Budapest SO, Rickenbacher – MENTER: *Concerto in the Hungarian style*. ***

Crowning his monumental project to record every note of piano music that Liszt ever wrote, Leslie Howard here tackles the concertante works: not just the handful of popular pieces but no fewer than fifteen works, sixteen if you count the two very different versions of *Totentanz*. Each of the two volumes centres round one of the numbered concertos, and then branches out to rarities. So after a bright and sparkling account of the *First concerto*, Volume 1 offers a sequence of eight mid-length pieces. They include not just the final version of *Totentanz*, with its grim variations on the *Dies Irae*, but *Malédiction*, a concerto for piano and strings, and the *Fantasy on motives from Beethoven's Ruins of Athens*. Rarer still, and even more interesting, are the works which Howard himself has helped to edit, usually from manuscript sources. Outstanding among these is the *Concerto in E flat*, written in the late 1830s, and reconstructed only recently after much detective work by the scholar Jay Rosenblatt, a taut sequence of five sections introduced by unaccompanied timpani. The longest work is the *Grande fantaisie symphonique on themes from Berlioz's Lélio*, which Berlioz himself conducted in 1834 with Liszt at the piano. It may be over-long for the material, but it is full of incident and, like much of this music, gives a clear idea of Liszt's style of improvisation.

Volume 2 follows up the *Second Concerto* (which Howard prefers to No. 1) with an extraordinary 36-minute piece, *De Profundis*, using a plainchant theme in a vastly expanded sonata-form. The *Concerto pathétique* is fascinating too, as not long before he died, Liszt added linking passages between sections in his late, spare style. Add to that the popular *Hungarian fantasy* and Liszt's own distinctive versions of Schubert's *Wanderer Fantasy* and Weber's *Konzertstück*. On a third bonus disc (at no extra cost) comes the oddest item of all, a colourful concert piece based on Hungarian gypsy themes by Sophie Menter, which almost certainly Liszt helped to write. Howard's dedication is clear in all his playing here, with clear, crisp articulation vividly caught in finely balanced sound.

Complete piano music, Vol. 54: 'Liszt at the opera VI': Concert paraphrases: AUBER: *Grande fantaisie on Tyrolean melodies* from *La Fiancée* (first version). BELLINI: *Réminiscences des Puritains* (second version); *Fantaisie sur des motifs favoris* from *La sonnambula* (first version). DONIZETTI: *Valse à capriccio sur deux motifs de Lucia et Parisina* (first version). GLINKA: *Marche des Tcherkesses* from *Ruslan and Ludmila* (first version). MERCADANTE: *Réminiscences de La Scala*. MEYERBEER: *Réminiscences des Huguenots* (second version). VERDI: *Ernani: Prière paraphrase de concert*. WAGNER: *Tannhäuser overture*. WEBER: *Fantasie über Themen* from *Der Freischütz*.
(N) *** Hyperion Dig. CDA 67406/7 [id.]. Leslie Howard.

Both these two-disc selections of operatic paraphrases are entertaining, and in many cases they re-serve their original purpose – to disseminate operatic melodies to a public unlikely to hear them in the opera-house. Many of the operas here, by Auber, Donizetti, Mercadante, Halévy, Pacini and even Meyerbeer, are either forgotten or seldom performed, and Liszt's selections are often as extended as they are elaborately set out and embroidered. The more familiar Bellini pot-pourris are very characterful, and Leslie Howard clearly enjoys playing them. However, he has problems with the raging torrent of notes surrounding the Pilgrim's chorale in the closing section of the *Tannhäuser overture*: surely this is only feasible in a four-handed version. The *William Tell overture* on the other hand is a great success, as are the sparkling Auber *Tarantella* from *Masaniello*, and Glinka's March from *Ruslan and Ludmila*. Howard's vitality, commitment and strong characterization here make up for any imprecisions in the thundering scalic passages. This is not music to hear all at once, but it tells us a great deal about popular operatic taste in the mid nineteenth century.

Complete piano music, Vol.55: *Années de pèlerinage: Angelus! Prière aux anges gardiens* (4 drafts); *Den Cypressen der Villa d'Este – Thrénodie II; Le lac de Wallenstadt* (early drafts). *Grand galop chromatique; Grande fantaisie di bravura* and *Grande fantaisie sur des thèmes de Paganini; Historische ungarische Bildnisse; Huldigungsmarsch; Hungaria; Legend: St Francis of Paola walking on the water* (simplified version); *Mélodie polonaise; Mephisto waltz No. 4; Petite valse favorite; Rákóczi march; St Elizabeth* (excerpts); *Sunt lacrymae rerum; Valse-impromptu; Valse mélancolique* (2 versions); *Valse oubliée No. 3; Variations sur Le Carnaval de Venise (Paganini)*.
(N) **(*) Hyperion Dig. CDA 67408/9/10 [id.]. Leslie Howard.

Leslie Howard describes the contents of this three-disc set as 'first thoughts and second drafts' and indeed there is much here of interest which the composer discarded in later versions. And although the first draft of the *Mephisto waltz* is surprisingly brief, there are many delights here, especially among the Valses, and notably among early drafts of pieces from the *Années de pèlerinage*. Howard plays the intermediate version of *Le lac de Wallenstadt* beautifully, as he does the much less familiar transcription of *The Miracle of the Roses* from *St Elizabeth*. The *Historal Hungarian portraits* – the composer's last cycle of piano pieces, almost unknown in the recital room – is remarkable for the austerity of texture and feeling, while the rhetorical symphonic poem *Hungaria* seems hopelessly inflated, for all Howard's powerful advocacy. Yet the *Huldigungsmarsch* is quite a find. The three extended *Paganini Fantasias*, using *La Campanella*, the *Carnival of Venice* or both, are rather overextended, but Howard treats them thoughtfully and poetically, rather than as vehicles for mere display, and his performances have many felicities. Excellent recording as always in this series.

Other piano music

Années de pèlerinage (complete): *Book 1, 1st Year: Switzerland; Book 2, 2nd Year: Italy;*

Supplément: Venezia e Napoli; Book 3, 3rd Year: Italy.
(B) *** DG 437 206-2 (3). Lazar Berman.

The *Années de pèlerinage* contain some of Liszt's very finest inspiration, and Lazar Berman's 1977 recording is enormously authoritative, free of empty display and virtuoso flamboyance, even though its brilliance is never in question. Berman brings searching qualities to this music: he is thoughtful and inward-looking in pieces like *Angelus* and *Sunt lachrymae rerum*. The imaginative colour and flair he displays in *Les cloches de Genève* and the simple freshness of *Eglogue* are matched by the felicity of the watery evocations, *Au lac de Wallenstadt* and *Les jeux d'eaux à la Villa d'Este*, while the power of the *Dante sonata* is equalled by the coruscating glitter of his articulation of the *Tarantella* from the *Supplément*, *Venezia e Napoli*. The recording, made in the Munich Alter Herkulessaal, is excellent. It is firmly and faithfully transferred to CD and does full justice to Berman's range of colour and dynamics. Moreover, this box is remarkably inexpensive.

(i) *Années de pèlerinage: Book 1, lst Year: Switzerland; Book 2, 2nd Year: Italy;* (ii) *Book 3, 3rd Year: Italy.*
(N) (B) ** Ph. Duo Dig. 462 312-2 (2). (i) Alfred Brendel; (ii) Zoltán Kocsis.

Brendel made some of his finest conquests in the recording studio in this repertoire and his 1959 analogue survey of the first book of the *Années de pèlerinage* was among the best. This later digital set of both the first and second years has many impressive moments, but also some ugly *fortissimi* that are not wholly the responsibility of the engineers. Brendel plays the *First Book* segue, without pauses, and although there is some atmospheric playing in the set, the moments of magic are relatively few. Brendel is always to be heard with respect, but this playing is out of scale and over-projected. For *Book 3*, Kocsis takes over and he gives the most compelling account of these sober and imaginative pieces; apart from beautiful pianism, he also manages to convey their character without exaggeration. He has impeccable technical control and can convey the dark power of the music without recourse to percussive tone. He is splendidly recorded and it is a pity that Philips decided to reissue his parformances in harness with those of Brendel. Readers will note that the set omits the *Book 2* supplement (*Venezia e Napoli*).

Années de pèlerinage: 1st Year (Switzerland); 2nd (with supplement) & 3rd Years (Italy): complete. *Hungarian rhapsodies Nos. 1–19* (complete).
(M) **(*) EMI CMS7 64882-2 (4) [id.]. Georges Cziffra.

Cziffra's accounts of the complete *Années de pèlerinage* show the same prodigious virtuosity and keyboard command that make his set of *Hungarian rhapsodies* unforgettable. His account of the *Dante sonata* is enormously dramatic and produces the same fabulous digital dexterity that makes the *Tarantella* from the Italian Supplement, *Venezia e Napoli*, so breathtaking. In the more poetic pieces from Book 1, *Au lac de Wallenstadt* and *Au bord d'une source*, he finds more restrained romantic feeling, and in the Third Year *Les jeux d'eau à la Villa d'Este* brings some most delicate articulation. He is not helped by a degree of hardness on piano timbre that is already somewhat dry. Remarkable pianism just the same. As can be seen below, the *Hungarian rhapsodies* (in which he is in his element) are available separately.

Années de pèlerinage, 1st Year (Switzerland).
*** Decca (IMS) Dig. 410 160-2. Jorge Bolet.
(BB) *** Naxos Dig. 8.550548 [id.]. Jenö Jandó.

This recording of the Swiss pieces from the *Années de pèlerinage* represents Bolet at his very peak, with playing of magical delicacy as well as formidable power. The piano sound is outstandingly fine.

Even remembering his excellent Beethoven and Haydn recordings, Jandó's performances of the Liszt *Années de pèlerinage* are an impressive achievement. The solemn opening of *La chapelle de Guillaume Tell* immediately shows the atmospheric feeling he can generate in this remarkable music, and its later, more grandiose rhetoric is handled with powerful conviction. First class recording, and the feeling throughout is very much of the spontaneity of live music-making.

Années de pèlerinage, 2nd Year (Italy) (complete).
*** Decca Dig. 410 161-2 [id.]. Jorge Bolet.

Années de pèlerinage, 2nd year (Italy); Supplement: Venezia e Napoli.
(BB) *** Naxos Dig. 8.550549 [id.]. Jenö Jandó.

Jandó offers Lisztian playing of the highest order, confirming the *Années de pèlerinage* as being among the supreme masterpieces of the piano. *Sposalizio* is superbly evoked, and the three contrasted *Petrarch Sonnets* bring the most imaginatively varied characterization, with No. 123 especially chimerical. But clearly Jandó sees the *Dante sonata* as the climactic point of the whole series. His performance has tremendous dynamism and power. One has the sense of Liszt himself hovering over the keyboard. Again first-class recording and the feeling of a continuous live recital. This is the disc to try first, and we have awarded it a token Rosette.

The pianistic colourings in this second fine instalment in Bolet's Liszt series are magically caught here, whether in the brilliant sunlight of *Sposalizio* or the visionary gloom of *Il penseroso*. The *Dante sonata* brings a darkly intense performance, fresh and original and deeply satisfying.

Années de pèlerinage, 3rd Year (Italy) (complete).
(BB) *** Naxos Dig. 8.550550 [id.]. Jenö Jandó.

The opening *Angelus* shows Jandó at his most imaginatively expansive and commanding, while *Les jeux d'eau à la Villa d'Este* sparkles and glitters: this is playing of great appeal. The secret of Jandó's success is that he is deeply involved in every note of Liszt's music.

Années de pèlerinage, Book 2; Supplement: Venezia e Napoli (Gondoliera; Canzone; Tarantella); 3rd Year: Les jeux d'eau à la Villa d'Este; Ballade No. 2 in B min.; Harmonies poétiques et religieuses: Bénédiction de Dieu dans la solitude.
*** Decca (IMS) Dig. 411 803-2. Jorge Bolet.

A dazzling pendant to Liszt's Italian *Années de pèlerinage*, and the recital includes two of Liszt's weightiest conceptions, the *Bénédiction* and the *Ballade*, both spaciously conceived and far too little known. Vivid and full piano recording.

Années de pèlerinage, 1st Year: Au bord d'une source. 2nd Year: Sonetto del Petrarca No. 104. 2 Concert studies: Waldesrauschen; Gnomenreigen. Mephisto waltz No. 1; Rhapsodie espagnole.
*** Sony Dig. SK 47180 [id.]. Murray Perahia – FRANCK: *Prélude, choral et fugue.* ***

Murray Perahia's Liszt shows all the keyboard distinction and poetic insight we associate with him. This is memorable and very distinguished Liszt playing, and the Sony engineers do full justice to him.

Années de pèlerinage, 2nd year: 3 Sonetti di Petrarca (Nos. 47, 104 & 123). Concert paraphrase on the *Quartet* from Verdi's *Rigoletto; Consolations Nos. 1–5; Liebesträume Nos. 1–3.*
(M) *** DG 435 591-2. Daniel Barenboim.

Daniel Barenboim proves an ideal advocate for the *Consolations* and *Liebesträume*, and he is highly poetic in the *Petrarch sonnets*. His playing has an unaffected simplicity that is impressive and throughout there is a welcome understatement and naturalness, until he arrives at the *Rigoletto paraphrase*, which is played with plenty of flair and glitter. The quality of the recorded sound is excellent.

Années de pèlerinage, 2nd Year (Italy): Sposalizio; Il penseroso; Canzonetta del Salvator Rosa; Sonetto del Petrarca Nos. 47, 104 & 123; Supplement: Venezia e Napoli: Gondoliera. 2 Legends: St Francis of Assisi preaching to the birds; St Francis of Paola walking on the water.
(M) *** DG 449 093-2 [id.]. Wilhelm Kempff.

In the early days of mono LP, Kempff made a famous record of Liszt piano music for Decca. He plays much of the same programme here, adding *Sposalizio*, and he had lost none of his magic and sense of poetry in the intervening years. Few listeners will fail to respond to these evocative and masterly performances, and one wonders why DG chose not to reissue this outstanding recital as a 'Legendary Recording' rather than putting it on their mid-priced Galleria label. The recording is excellent.

Recital I: *Années de pèlerinage, 3rd Year: Tarantella. Harmonies poétiques et religieuses: Pensées des morts; Bénédiction de Dieu dans la solitude; Legend: St Francis of Assisi preaching to the birds. Mephisto waltz No. 1; Rhapsodie espagnole.* Recital II: *Années de pèlerinage, 2nd Year: Aux cyprès de la Villa d'Este; Après une lecture du Dante (Dante Sonata). 3rd Year: Aux cyprès de la Villa d'Este; Les jeux d'eau à la Villa d'Este. Ave Maria; Ave Maria (Die Glöcken von Rom); La lugbre gondola* (2 versions); *Recueillement.*
(BB) *** Virgin Classics Dig. Double VBD5 61439-2 [CDVB 61439]. Stephen Hough.

Few pianists of the younger generation have quite such a magic touch as Stephen Hough, and this budget-priced Virgin Double rescues two of his finest recitals. The first, from 1987, has been reissued before, but the second, published four years later, appeared and disappeared very quickly. The performances are all magnetic. On the first disc, he brings sparkle and wit to the fireworks of the *Mephisto waltz* and the *Tarantella* from the third year of the *Années de pèlerinage* with phenomenal articulation, and he plays the extended slow movement of the *Bénédiction* with velvety warmth. The second collection is mainly of rarer music and is imaginatively chosen to include two different versions of both *Aux cyprès de la Villa d'Este* and the darkly original *La lugubre gondola*, in each case with the second version longer and more elaborate than the first. The cascades of *Les jeux d'eau à la Villa d'Este* make a glittering centrepiece. The recording is excellent, but the documentation is abysmal, and even the frontispiece (a detail from Giordano's *L'archange Michel écrasant les anges rebelles*) seems far less appropriate than the pictures of the actual fountains and cypresses at the Villa d'Este which illustrated the second recital when it first appeared at full price. Nevertheless the concentration of the playing here is unforgettable.

Ave Marias in D flat; G; E; d'Arcadelt; 6 Consolations; Harmonies poétiques et religieuses, Nos. 7–10; Ungarns Gott (left-hand).
(BB) *** Naxos Dig. 8.553516 [id.]. Philip Thomson.

Harmonies poétiques et religieuses, Nos. 1–6; Les morts; Resignazione; Ungarns Gott (two-hand).

(BB) *** Naxos Dig. 8.553073 [id.]. Philip Thomson.

Philip Thomson is a Canadian pianist who has specialized in Liszt. He exhibits considerable artistry in the two discs listed above and commands not only the virtuosity which this repertoire calls for in abundance but also great poetic feeling. (He seems to be a remarkable all-rounder, having occupied teaching posts in both China and the United States, being an accomplished violinist, champion table-tennis player, and even parachute jumper.) He commands a wide range of keyboard colour and refinement of pianissimo tone and has the benefit of very good recorded sound as well. Both his Liszt recitals are touched by distinction and are a real bargain.

Concert paraphrases: BEETHOVEN: *Symphony No. 5 in C min.; Symphony No. 6 (Pastoral):* 1st movt.
(M) *(*) Sony SMK 52636 [id.]. Glenn Gould.

It is not easy to comment on Glenn Gould's Liszt–Beethoven transcriptions – or, for that matter, on anything by this artist. For his admirers he can do nothing wrong, while his detractors find him perverse. However, no one can deny his remarkable keyboard prowess and mastery – and even the most sceptical are impressed by his insights. These performances come from the 1960s and are handicapped by shallow recorded sound. Nor – even at mid-price – are they particularly generous on playing-time.

Concert paraphrase: BEETHOVEN: *Symphony No. 6 (Pastoral)*.
(M) * Sony SMK 52637 [id.]. Glenn Gould.

Gould certainly holds your attention – but this is distinctly short measure. The sound is shallow and coarse.

Concert paraphrases: BELLINI: *Réminiscences de 'Norma'*. VERDI: *Rigoletto; Miserere du Trovatore*. WAGNER: *Tannhäuser overture; Am stillen Herd* from *Die Meistersinger; Liebestod* from *Tristan und Isolde. Années de pèlerinage, 2nd Year: Sonetti del Petrarca Nos. 123 & 124; Consolation No. 3; Hungarian rhapsody No. 12 in C sharp min.*
(BB) **(*) CfP Silver Double CDCFPSD 4745 (2) [id.]. Craig Sheppard – *Sonata* etc. ***

Craig Sheppard was the second prizewinner in the Leeds Piano Competition of 1972, a formidable challenger to the eventual winner, Murray Perahia. Though he lacks Perahia's individuality, Sheppard's playing of Liszt on this record is a fine tribute to his musicianship and technique, especially in the *Concert paraphrases*. He does not manage to disguise the awkwardness of the *Pilgrim's chorus* section of *Tannhäuser*, where the pianist is expected to play the big tune and the swirling (string) accompaniment simultaneously with only two hands. But the *Trovatore* scene has fine, red-blooded melodrama, and the passion of the *Liebestod* is excitingly projected. The *Réminiscences de 'Norma'*, too, are stylishly done. The other items come from his début recital in 1973 and are almost equally compelling. The piano tone is bold and clear. It was a happy idea on this Silver Double reissue to couple these performances with a memorable account of the *Sonata* by another celebrated prizewinner, Bernard d'Ascoli – see below.

Concert paraphrases: Faust waltzes; Réminiscences de 'Don Juan' (Mozart); Réminiscences de 'Robert le Diable': Valse infernale (Meyerbeer); Concert study: Gnomenreigen; Mephisto polka; Mephisto waltz No. 1.
(M) **(*) Van. 08.4035.71 [OVC 4035]. Earl Wild.

The title of this recital is '*The demonic Liszt*', and as a display of brilliant piano playing it could hardly be bettered. Earl Wild's technique is prodigious. The articulation in *Gnomenreigen* has a fairy lightness and the *Mephisto polka* has a similar blithe delicacy of touch. The more sinister waltz which follows is played with formidable energy and power. There is glittering upper tessitura in the *Don Juan fantasy*. But one ideally needs a programme designed to give more contrast, and the 1968 piano recording is on the dry side.

Concert paraphrases of Rossini: *Soirées musicales; Overture William Tell.*
(BB) *** Naxos Dig. 8.553961 [id.]. Kemal Gekić.

Liszt made his Rossini transcriptions in 1836, and they are rarely heard in the recital room or on record. The only rival is Leslie Howard's set on Hyperion, and this performance by the Yugoslav-born Kemal Gekić at super-bargain price has infinitely more wit, lightness of touch and subtlety of articulation. Were the price-tags reversed, this would still be the preferred recommendation. In fact this is dazzling playing that sparkles when required and has an effortless brilliance that is quite captivating. Gekić has real flair and is very well recorded too, with natural, life-like quality. One looks forward to returning to this disc.

Concert paraphrase of sacred music: *Alleluja; Ave maris stella; 11 Chorales; Hungarian Coronation Mass: Benedictus; Offertorium. L'Hymne du pape; In festo transfigurationis; O Roma nobilis; Sancta Dorothea; Stabat Mater; Urbi et orbi; Weihnachtslied; Zum Haus des Herrn ziehen wir.*
(BB) *** Naxos Dig. 8.553659 [id.]. Philip Thomson.

This Canadian-born pianist made a strong impression earlier in this Liszt survey, and he does so again now. These transcriptions from the 1860s and '70s are rarely heard in recital and, apart from Leslie Howard's survey, are seldom encountered on disc. Philip Thomson brings a wide dynamic range and a fund of keyboard colour to this repertoire. As in the earlier discs, the recording is eminently acceptable without being outstanding.

Concert paraphrases of Schubert Lieder: *Auf den Wasser zu singen; Aufenthalt; Erlkönig; Die Forelle; Horch, horch die Lerch; Lebe wohl!; Der Lindenbaum; Lob der Tränen; Der Müller und der Bach; Die Post; Das Wandern; Wohin.*
*** Decca (IMS) Dig. 414 575-2. Jorge Bolet.

Superb virtuosity from Bolet. He is not just a wizard but a feeling musician, though here he sometimes misses a feeling of fun. First-rate recording.

Concert paraphrases of Schubert Lieder: *Auf dem Wasser zu singen; Gretchen am Spinnrade; Der Müller und der Bach; Ständchen. Hungarian rhapsody No. 12.*
(M) *** DG Dig. 445 562-2 [id.]. Yevgeny Kissin – BRAHMS: *Fantasias;* SCHUBERT: *Wanderer fantasia.* **(*)

There is – as always – much to admire in Kissin's playing, and he is in good form in these Liszt–Schubert transcriptions. Both *Der Müller und der Bach* and *Ständchen* are beautifully done. The Brahms and the *Wanderer fantasia* find him in good rather than outstanding form.

Concert paraphrase of Verdi's *Rigoletto; Etudes d'exécution transcendante d'après Paganini: La Campanella. Harmonies poétiques et religieuses: Funérailles. Hungarian rhapsody No. 12; Liebestraum No. 3. Mephisto waltz No. 1.*
*** Decca Dig. 410 257-2 [id.]. Jorge Bolet.

Bolet's playing is magnetic, not just because of virtuosity thrown off with ease, but because of an element of joy conveyed, even in the demonic vigour of the *Mephisto waltz No. 1*. The relentless thrust of *Funérailles* is beautifully contrasted against the honeyed warmth of the famous *Liebestraum No. 3* and the sparkle of *La Campanella*. First-rate recording.

3 Concert studies; 2 Concert studies; 6 Consolations; Réminiscences de Don Juan (Mozart).
*** Decca (IMS) 417 523-2. Jorge Bolet.

In the *Concert studies* the combination of virtuoso precision and seeming spontaneity is most compelling in the splendid account of the *Don Juan* paraphrase. The *Consolations* show Bolet at his most romantically imaginative: he plays them beautifully.

Etudes d'exécution transcendante (complete).
*** Teldec/Warner 4509 98415-2 [id.]. Boris Berezovsky.

Boris Berezovsky shows astonishing flair and technical assurance. His charisma in the bravura writing is totally commanding yet in *Feux follets* he plays with the utmost delicacy, and the ruminative poetry of *Ricordanza* is melting. The piano is recorded boldly and brilliantly, not as full and sonorous as with Arrau, but there is no lack of pianistic colour in the gentler lyrical writing. The colour portrait of Liszt on the back of the accompanying booklet demonstrates why so many women succumbed to his physical charms!

(i) *12 Etudes d'exécution transcendante, G. 139;* (ii) *6 Etudes d'exécution transcendante d'après Paganini, G. 140;* (i) *3 Etudes de concert (Il lamento; La leggierezza; Un sospiro), G. 144; 2 Etudes de concert (Waldesrauschen; Gnomenreigen), G. 145.*
(B) **(*) Ph. Duo 456 339-2 (2). (i) Claudio Arrau; (ii) Nikita Magaloff.

Arrau made his recording of the twelve *Etudes d'exécution transcendante* in 1974, a formidable achievement for an artist in his seventies. Arrau always played with great panache and musical insight, which more than compensates for the occasional smudginess in the recorded sound. He always produced a wonderfully distinctive tone, and his enormous range of keyboard colour was splendidly captured by the Philips engineers of the day. Younger players, Cziffra for one, have brought more obvious virtuosity to these pieces, but Arrau's playing is most masterly and poetic, and the recording, if too reverberant, is admirably truthful and rich in timbre. The three *Etudes de concert*, too, are strongly characterized; indeed some might find Arrau's richly textured romanticism in *Un sospiro* a little overwhelming. However, his bravura in *Gnomenreigen* is riveting. So too is Nikita Magaloff's virtuosity in the *Paganini studies*, and here the bright, less sumptuous piano-tone projects his digital dexterity with fine glitter. He gives scintillating accounts of *La campanella* and *Arpeggio* and tickles the ear with a delectably sparkling *La chasse*. The set, of course, ends with variations on the famous theme used also by Brahms and Rachmaninov, also played with fine dash. Overall this is most impressive and can be recommended enthusiastically.

Etudes d'exécution transcendante d'après Paganini: Nos. 3 (La Campanella); 5 (La Chasse). Etudes d'exécution transcendante: Feux follets; Polonaise No. 2 in E.
(M) *** Nimbus Dig. NI 8810 [id.]. Ferruccio Busoni (piano) – BACH: *Chaconne;* CHOPIN: *Preludes.* **

Very convincingly reproduced from a 1915 Duo-Art piano-roll, in first-class digital sound, this gives a stunning impression of Busoni's transcendental technique in music which calls for the kind of scintillating virtuosity this remarkable artist could so readily provide. Occasionally in *Feux follets* he seems somewhat wilful, but the bravura is prodigious, and the two *Paganini studies* are superb, while there is some glittering upper tessitura in the central section of the characterful *Polonaise*. Fascinating.

12 Etudes d'exécution transcendante; 2 Legends.
(N) *(*) EMI Dig. CDC5 56684-2. François-René Duchable.

Duchable's performances display no lack of virtuosity, but the far too reverberant recording blurs the bravura, makes the playing sound unfocused.

Grandes Etudes de Paganini Nos. 1–8.
(BB) *** Koch Discover Dig. DICD 920423 [id.]. Evelyne Brancart – BRAHMS: *Paganini variations*. ***

Evelyne Brancart displays a glittering technique, fine musicianship and a Lisztian sensibility. The recording is rather bright and forward but this is not ineffective in such repertoire. An enjoyable disc – though, even at super-bargain price, it is rather short measure at under 48 minutes.

Hungarian rhapsodies Nos. 1–19; Rhapsodie espagnole.
(B) *** DG Double 453 034-2 (2) [id.]. Roberto Szidon.

Hungarian rhapsodies Nos. 1–15; Rhapsodie espagnole.
(B) *** EMI (SIS) Rouge et Noir CZS5 69003-2 (2). György Cziffra.

Cziffra's performances are dazzling. They are full of those exciting spurts of energy and languorous rubato that immediately evoke the unreasonably fierce passions of gypsy music. Yet the control is absolute (try the delectably free opening of *No. 12 in C sharp minor*, or the *D minor* (No. 7)). There is plenty of power in reserve, and poetry too. The high degree of temperament in the playing, with hardly two consecutive phrases at an even tempo, makes even Szidon (who has the full measure of the music) seem almost staid. Cziffra, with coruscating brilliance, sets every bar of the music on fire. Some might find him too impulsive for comfort (and they should turn to the DG alternative), but this is surely the way Liszt would have played them: the *Rákóczy march* (No. 15) is a *tour de force*. The recording, made in the Salle Wagram, Paris, in 1957/8 (or, in the case of Nos. 2, 6, 12 and 15, in the Hungaraton Budapest Studio a year earlier), is a little dry and close but otherwise truthful, and it does not lack sonority. The *Rouge et Noir* reissue offers two discs for the price of one.

Roberto Szidon offers Liszt playing of the highest order. He has flair and panache, genuine keyboard command and, when required, great delicacy of tone. He is well recorded too, and this DG Double is not only inexpensive but also provides (as does Cziffra on EMI) an excellent version of the *Rhapsodie espagnole*. Cziffra's performances are from an artist of an even more volatile personality, but Szidon is by no means upstaged: his style is equally valid and his approach is always imaginatively illuminating.

Hungarian rhapsodies Nos. 2–3, 8, 13, 15 (Rákóczy march); 17; Csárdás obstinée.
(M) *** Van. 08.4024.71 [OVC 4024]. Alfred Brendel.

Although the Vanguard recording is not a recent one, it sounds very good in this excellent CD transfer, and the playing is very distinguished indeed. There are few more charismatic or spontaneous accounts of the *Hungarian rhapsodies* available, and there is no doubt about the brilliance of the playing nor the quality of musical thinking that informs it.

Mephisto waltz.
(M) (**(*)) RCA mono GD 60921. William Kapell – KHACHATURIAN: *Piano concerto;* PROKOFIEV: *Piano concerto No. 3*. (**(*))

William Kapell's *Mephisto waltz*, recorded in 1945, must be one of the most dazzling ever, and it ranks alongside the likes of Horowitz, Cziffra, Richter and Pletnev. Moreover, it comes with incandescent accounts of the Khachaturian *Piano concerto* (with Koussevitzky, no less), and the Prokofiev *Third Piano concerto*.

Piano sonata in B min.
(M) *** RCA 09026 61614-2 [id.]. Emil Gilels – SCHUBERT: *Sonata No. 17*.
(B) *** EMI forte CZS5 69527-2 (2) [CDFB 69527]. Anievas – CHOPIN: *Sonata No. 3* **; RACHMANINOV: *Preludes Nos. 1–24* etc. **(*)
(M) **(*) RCA 09026 62590-2 [id.]. Artur Rubinstein – BACH: *Chaconne;* FRANCK: *Prelude, chorale and fugue*. ***

Piano sonata in B min.; Années de pèlerinage, 2nd year: Après une lecture du Dante (Fantasia quasi Sonata); Concert study: Gnomenreigen; Harmonies poètiques et religieuses: Funérailles.
(N) *** DG Dig. 457 629-2 [id.]. Mikhail Pletnev.

Piano sonata in B min.; Berceuse; Concert study: Gnomenreigen. Liebestraum No. 3 in A flat; Valse oubliée No. 1.
(M) *** Decca 452 306-2 [id.]. Clifford Curzon (with SCHUBERT: *Impromptu in A flat, D.935/2*).

Piano sonata; 3 Concert studies.
*** Chandos Dig. CHAN 8548 [id.]. Louis Lortie.

Piano sonata; Concert study No. 2 (La Leggierezza).
(BB) *** CfP Silver Double Dig. CDCFPSD 4745

(2). Bernard d'Ascoli – *Concert paraphrases* etc. **(*)

Piano sonata; Grand galop chromatique; Liebesträume Nos. 1–3; Valse impromptu.
*** Decca (IMS) Dig. 410 115-2. Jorge Bolet.

Piano sonata; 2 Legends; Scherzo and March.
*** Hyperion Dig. CDA 66616 [id.]. Nikolai Demidenko.

This is one of Pletnev's most remarkable discs. His earlier account of the *B minor Sonata*, made when he was in his twenties (briefly available on Olympia) had dazzling virtuosity and brilliance. This newcomer has even greater tonal finesse, articulation and control of keyboard colour; there is no ostentation about its virtuosity, but a tremendous grip, depth and majesty. All his keyboard brilliance is totally at the service of the music, and the breadth of the *Sonata* is deeply impressive. A performance of stature among the very best that this great pianist has yet given us. The remainder of the programme is hardly less gripping. It is difficult to imagine many pianists surviving the close scrutiny that DG's engineers give him, but the reservations concerning balance do not obscure the artistry and distinction of this recital.

Gilels's version of the Liszt *Sonata* is masterly. It is as penetrating in its way as Horowitz's famous pre-war record was virtuosic, and the playing here is equally astonishing technically. The 1964 recording leaves little cause for complaint on CD. It is vividly transferred and is not without body.

Nikolai Demidenko's account of the *Sonata* has won golden opinions, and rightly so. His is a keenly dramatic and powerfully projected account that has the listener on the edge of his or her seat. It must be numbered among the finest performances he has given us and is free from the slight mannerisms and the disruptive rubati that sometimes mar his recitals. The excitement and virtuosity are second to none and almost call to mind Horowitz: his playing can be measured against that of Brendel and Pletnev. He has the advantage of exceptionally vivid recorded sound, and the remainder of the recital goes equally well.

Curzon shows an innate understanding of the *Sonata*'s cyclic form, so that the significance of the principal theme is brought out subtly in relation to the music's structural development. There are only a few performances to compare with this and none superior, and Decca's recording matches the playing in its excellence. The shorter pieces too are imaginatively played. The excellent recording was made in the Sofiensaal in 1963, but the fairly close microphones create something of a studio effect. For the reissue in Decca's Classic Sound series, Curzon's warm and beautiful account of Schubert's *A flat Impromptu* has been added. This was recorded at The Maltings, and the sound is noticeably richer and fuller.

Louis Lortie gives almost as commanding a performance of the Liszt *Sonata* as any in the catalogue; its virtuosity can be taken for granted and, though he does not have the extraordinary intensity and feeling for drama of Pletnev, he has a keen awareness of its structure and a Chopinesque finesse that win one over. The Chandos recording, though a shade too reverberant, is altogether natural.

Bernard d'Ascoli displays classical qualities in his refreshing and intense reading of this most romantic of sonatas. It is the sort of interpretation that one might have expected Wilhelm Kempff to have given, with articulation of pearly clarity, wonderful singing legato in the big melodies and an emphasis on control and concentration rather than thrusting urgency. Yet there is no lack of power, and the result is most satisfying. The delicate account of *La Leggierezza* makes a fine encore. The early (1982) digital recording is dry but faithful, and the coupled recital from Craig Sheppard, another prizewinner, makes this a very recommendable Silver Double.

The power, imagination and concentration of Bolet are excellently brought out in his fine account of the *Sonata*. With the famous *Liebestraum* (as well as its two companions) also most beautifully done, not to mention the amazing *Grand galop*, this is one of the most widely appealing of Bolet's outstanding Liszt series. However, the *Sonata* is also available in a Double Decca set – see below.

Anievas gives a fine and memorable performance, notable for its thoughtfulness and its subtlety in the control of tension. The lyrical impulse is finely balanced to bring out the music's poetry as well as its fire and strength. There may be more flamboyant interpretations available which more readily project the music's bravura, but few other recorded performances are as satisfying or are more successful in revealing the work's stature. The recording too is generally very good and, although the reverberation prevents absolute clarity in the bass in florid passages, the effect is firmer in the excellent CD transfer.

Rubinstein's performance of the *Sonata* was recorded in 1965, and there is some hardness of timbre in fortissimos. But at *piano* and *mezzo forte* levels (and there is a wider range of dynamic here than on some Rubinstein records) the tone is subtly coloured, and Rubinstein's mercurial approach to the music is wonderfully spontaneous, bringing an astonishing fire and brilliance for a pianist of his age, and considerable poetry to the more thoughtful moments.

Miscellaneous Recitals

Piano sonata; Années de pèlerinage, 1st Year: Au bord d'une source; 2nd Year: Sonetto 104 del Petrarca; 3rd Year: Les jeux d'eau à la Ville d'Este; Concert paraphrases: Die Forelle;

Erlkönig (Schubert); *Réminiscences de Don Juan* (Mozart); *Rigoletto* (Verdi). *Consolation No. 3; Etudes d'exécution transcendante d'après Paganini: La campanella. Etudes de concert: Gnomenreigen; Un sospiro. Harmonies poétiques et religieuses: Funérailles. Hungarian rhapsody No. 12 in C sharp min.; Liebesträume No. 3 in A flat; Mephisto waltz No. 1.*

(B) *** Decca Double Dig. 444 851-2 (2). Jorge Bolet.

The full range of the late Jorge Bolet's achievement for Decca in the music of Liszt is admirably surveyed here, ending with his commanding account of the *Sonata*. He can be romantic without sentimentality, as in the *Consolation*, *Un sospiro* or the most famous of the *Liebesträume*, yet can dazzle the ear with bravura or beguile the listener with his delicacy of colouring, as in the *Années de pèlerinage*. All the recordings here save the Mozart *Concert paraphrase* are digital and are as clear and present as one could wish.

ORGAN MUSIC

Fantasia and fugue on 'Ad nos, ad salutarem undam'; Prelude and fugue on B-A-C-H; Variations on 'Weinen, Klagen, Sorgen, Zagen'.

(BB) *** ASV CDQS 6127 [id.]. Jennifer Bate (Royal Albert Hall organ) – SCHUMANN: *4 Sketches*. ***

Jennifer Bate gives superb performances of the three major Liszt warhorses. The clarity and incisiveness of her playing go with a fine sense of line and structure, and there is plenty of exuberance in the *'Ad nos' Fantasia and fugue*. Even making no allowance for the Royal Albert Hall's acoustic problems, the analogue recording captures an admirable combination of definition and atmosphere, well conveyed on CD. This makes a fine super-bargain alternative to the competing digital versions, which are only marginally more sharply defined.

VOCAL MUSIC

Lieder: *Blume und Duft; Der du von dem Himmel bist; Du bist wie eine Blume; Die drei Zigeuner; Einst; Es war ein König in Thule; Freudvoll und leidvoll; Hohe Liebe; Ich möchte hingehn; Ihr Auge; Im Rhein, im schönen Strome; Mignons Lied (Kennst du das Land); O lieb' so lang du dieben kannst; Uber allen Gipfeln ist Ruh; Und wir dachten der Toten; Was Liebe sei; Wieder möcht' ich dir begegnen.*

*** Decca (IMS) Dig. 430 512-2. Brigitte Fassbaender, Jean-Yves Thibaudet.

The sensitive poetry of Thibaudet's playing goes with powerful singing from Fassbaender in superb, characterful voice, with each highly individual artist challenging the other in imagination. There are few collections of Liszt songs to match this generous one in either range or intensity. Outstanding in every way, with excellent, helpful sound.

Lieder: *Blume und Duft; Die drei Zigeuner; Der du von dem Himmel bist* (2 settings); *Ein Fichtenbaum steht einsam; Es muss ein Wunderbares sein; Es rauschen die Winde; Der Hirt; Ihr Auge; Ihr Glocken von Marling; Freudvoll und leidvoll; Die Loreley; O komm im Traum; Des Tages laute Stimmen schweigen; Uber allen Gipfeln ist Ruh; Vergiftet sind meine Lieder.*

*** Capriccio Dig. 10 294 [id.]. Mitsuko Shirai, Hartmut Höll.

There are only one or two collections of Liszt songs as searchingly persuasive as this, and none more beautiful. Provocatively, the record starts with Shirai at her most vehement in *Vergiftet sind meine Lieder*, written when Liszt's long relationship with the Countess d'Agoult was breaking up. Regrettably, no English translations are provided with the text, only a commentary.

Lieder: *Comment, disaient-ils; Es muss ein Wunderbares sein; Es rauschen die Winde; Go not happy day; Ihr Auge; Im Rhein, im schönen Strome; Oh, quand je dors; La tombe et la rose; Die Vätergruft; Vergiftet sind meiner Lieder; Wanderers Nachtlied.*

*** EMI (SIS) Dig. CDC5 55047-2. Thomas Hampson, Geoffrey Parsons – BERLIOZ; WAGNER: *Lieder*. ***

On his disc of romantic songs, Thomas Hampson ranges wide in his selection of 11 by Liszt, ending magically with one of the best known, his setting of Victor Hugo, *Oh, quand je dors*. Characteristic, in that he finds a wider range of expressiveness and dynamic than almost any of his rivals, building from the drawing-room charm of the opening to a tremendous climax. He is helped by Geoffrey Parsons's accompaniment and the fine, warm recording. Other fascinating songs include Liszt's setting of Tennyson in English, *Go not happy day*, with the words oddly stressed. There is also a still, hushed and intense setting of Goethe's *Wanderers Nachtlied*, best known from Schubert. Magnetic, rich-voiced performances.

Litolff, Henri (1818–91)

Concerti symphoniques Nos. 2 in B min., Op. 22; 4 in D min., Op. 102.

*** Hyperion Dig. CDA 66889 [id.]. Peter Donohoe, Bournemouth SO, Litton.

The *Fourth Concerto symphonique* is the source of the famous Litolff *Scherzo*, so often heard in the days of 78s. The complete work has been recorded before, by Gerald Robbins with the Monte Carlo Opera Orchestra under Eduard van Remoortel; it was issued on a Genesis LP, when we dismissed the first movement as rhetorical, the slow movement as uninspired, and the finale as empty. But what a difference a really fine performance makes! Indeed we have to revise our view of the piece. The first movement is certainly rhetorical but opens with endearing flamboyance under the baton of Andrew Litton, while the passage-work scintillates in the hands of Peter Donohoe. The secondary material has both delicacy and charm. The famous *Scherzo* which follows is taken a fraction too fast and loses some of its poise, the articulation not always absolutely clean; but one adjusts to the breathless virtuosity, and it remains the work's finest inspiration. The *Adagio religioso* opens with some lovely horn-playing, its solemn mood nicely offset later by the pianistic decoration. The finale, marked *Allegro impetuoso*, is certainly all of that, with more twinkling bravura from Donohoe.

The *Second Concerto* is also well worth while. True, its opening *Maestoso* is hopelessly inflated, but in the Chopinesque secondary material Donohoe finds an engaging charm as well as brilliance. The second movement is another scintillating Scherzo, and if not quite as memorable as its more famous companion, it has a tripping centrepiece worthy of Saint-Saëns, especially as presented here. With a warm, naturally balanced recording, this entertaining Hyperion CD is very much worth having.

Concerto symphonique No. 4: Scherzo.
(M) *** Decca Legends 466 376-2 [id.]. Clifford Curzon, LPO, Sir Adrian Boult – BRAHMS: *Piano concerto;* FRANCK: *Symphonic variations*. ***
(B) *** Ph. Dig. 411 123-2 [id.]. Misha Dichter, Philh. O, Marriner (with Concert of concertante music ***).
(M) *** Decca Dig. 430 726-2. Ortiz, RPO, Atzmon – ADDINSELL: *Warsaw concerto* ***; GERSHWIN: *Rhapsody* **(*); GOTTSCHALK: *Grand fantasia* ***; LISZT: *Hungarian fantasia*. ***

Curzon provides all the sparkle Litolff's infectious *Scherzo* requires, and the 1958 Walthamstow Town Hall recording makes a delightful encore for the Brahms *Concerto* and the Franck *Symphonic variations* in this reissue in Decca's Classic Sound series. The fine qualities of the original sound, freshness and clarity, remain impressive.

Misha Dichter gives a scintillating account of Litolff's delicious *Scherzo*, played at a sparklingly brisk tempo. Marriner accompanies sympathetically and the recording is excellent.

Cristina Ortiz's version may lack extrovert brilliance but it has an agreeable elegance. The intimacy of this version is emphasized by the balance, which places the piano within the orchestral group, making the gentle central section especially effective. The Decca couplings are all appealing and the CD is impressively natural.

Lloyd, George (1913–98)

Piano concerto No. 3.
**(*) Albany Dig. TROY 019-2 [id.]. Kathryn Stott, BBC PO, composer.

The *Third Piano concerto* is very eclectic in style, with flavours of Prokofiev (with diluted abrasiveness) and even of Khachaturian – minus vulgarity – in outer movements which have a toccata-like brilliance and momentum. Kathryn Stott plays with a pleasing, mercurial lightness and makes the most of the music's lyrical feeling. But the slow movement is too long and its climax does not show Lloyd at his best. On the other hand, the wistful tune at the centre of the finale is rather appealing. The composer achieves a fine partnership with his soloist and the performance has undoubted spontaneity.

(i) *Piano concerto No. 4; The lily-leaf and the grasshopper; The transformation of that Naked Ape.*
*** Albany AR 004 [id.]. Kathryn Stott; (i) LSO, composer.

The *Fourth Piano concerto* is a romantic, light-hearted piece with a memorable 'long singing tune' (the composer's words), somewhat Rachmaninovian in its spacious lyricism, contrasting with a 'jerky' rhythmic idea. The performance by Kathryn Stott and the LSO under the composer is ardently spontaneous from the first bar to the last. The solo pieces are eclectic but still somehow Lloydian. The recording is first rate.

Symphonies Nos. 1 in A; 12.
*** Albany Dig. TROY 032-2 [id.]. Albany SO, composer.

The pairing of George Lloyd's first and last symphonies is particularly appropriate, as they share a theme-and-variations format. The *First*, written in 1932 but recently revised, is relatively lightweight. The mature *Twelfth* uses the same basic layout but ends calmly with a ravishingly sustained pianissimo, semi-Mahlerian in intensity, that is among the composer's most beautiful inspirations. At the beginning of the work, the listener is soon aware of the noble lyrical theme which is the very heart of the *Symphony*. The Albany Symphony Orchestra gave the work its première and they play it with enormous conviction and eloquence. The concentration of the music-making throughout is that of a live performance, helped by the superb acoustics of the Troy Savings Bank Music Hall, which produces sound of demonstration quality. This record therefore makes an admirable starting point for anyone wishing to begin an exploration of the music of a composer who communicates readily.

Symphonies Nos. 2 and 9.
*** Albany Dig. TROY 055 [id.]. BBC PO, composer.

Lloyd's *Second Symphony* is a lightweight, extrovert piece, conventional in form and construction, though in the finale the composer flirts briefly with polytonality, an experiment he did not repeat. The *Ninth* (1969) is similarly easygoing; the *Largo* is rather fine, but its expressive weight is in scale, and the finale, 'a merry-go-round that keeps going round and round', has an appropriately energetic brilliance. Throughout both works the invention is attractive, and in these definitive performances, extremely well recorded, the composer's advocacy is very persuasive.

Symphony No. 3 in F; Charade (suite).
*** Albany Dig. TROY 90 [id.]. BBC PO, composer.

The *Third Symphony* dates from the composer's nineteenth year, and after some consideration he decided to leave it unrevised. On the whole it works well, its idiom undemanding but agreeable. Although it is described as a one-movement piece, it clearly subdivides into three sections and it is the central *Lento* which has *the* tune, a winding, nostalgic theme that persists in the memory. It is atmospherically prepared and eventually blossoms sumptuously. *Charade* dates from the 1960s and attempts to portray the London scene of the time, from aggressive *Student power* and *LSD* to *Flying saucers* and *Pop song*. The ironic final movement, *Party politics*, is amiable rather than wittily abrasive. The composer is good at bringing his music vividly to life, and he is very well recorded indeed.

Symphony No. 4.
*** Albany AR 002 [id.]. Albany SO, composer.

George Lloyd's *Fourth Symphony* was composed during his convalescence after being badly shell-shocked while serving in the Arctic convoys of 1941/2. The first movement is directly related to this period of his life, and the listener may be surprised at the relative absence of sharp dissonance. After a brilliant scherzo, the infectious finale is amiable, offering a series of quick, 'march-like tunes', which the composer explains by suggesting that 'when the funeral is over the band plays quick cheerful tunes to go home'. Under Lloyd's direction, the Albany Symphony Orchestra play with great commitment and a natural, spontaneous feeling. The recording is superb.

Symphony No. 5 in B flat.
*** Albany Dig. TROY 022-2 [id.]. BBC PO, composer.

The *Fifth Symphony* is a large canvas, with five strong and contrasted movements, adding up to nearly an hour of music. It was written during a happy period spent living simply on the shore of Lac Neuchâtel, during the very hot summer of 1947. In the finale the composer tells us: 'everything is brought in to make as exhilarating a sound as possible – strong rhythms, vigorous counterpoints, energetic brass and percussion'. The symphony is played with much commitment by the BBC Philharmonic under the composer, who creates a feeling of spontaneously live music-making throughout. The recording is first class.

(i) *Symphonies Nos. 6;* (ii) *10 (November journeys);* (i) *Overture: John Socman.*
**(*) Albany Dig. TROY 15-2 [id.]. (i) BBC PO; (ii) BBC PO Brass, composer.

The bitter-sweet lyricism of the first movement of *November journeys* is most attractive, but the linear writing is more complex than usual in a work for brass. In the finale a glowing *cantando* melody warms the spirit, to contrast with the basic *Energico*. The *Calma* slow movement is quite haunting, no doubt reflecting the composer's series of visits to English cathedrals, the reason for the subtitle. The *Sixth Symphony* is amiable and lightweight; it is more like a suite than a symphony. Lloyd's performances are attractively spontaneous and well played, and the equally agreeable *John Socman overture* also comes off well, although it is rather inconsequential.

Symphony No. 7.
*** Albany Dig. TROY 057 [id.]. BBC PO, composer.

The *Seventh Symphony* is a programme symphony, using the ancient Greek legend of Proserpine. The slow movement is particularly fine, an extended soliloquy of considerable expressive power. The last and longest movement is concerned with 'the desperate side of our lives – ''Dead dreams that the snows have shaken, Wild leaves that the winds have taken'' ' – yet, as is characteristic with Lloyd, the darkness is muted; nevertheless the resolution at the end is curiously satisfying. Again he proves an admirable exponent of his own music. The recording is splendid.

Symphony No. 8.
*** Troy Dig. TROY 230 [id.]. Philh. O, composer.

After his severe depression and nervous breakdown, Lloyd gave up composing entirely for many years, earning his living instead as a mushroom farmer, only gradually turning back to composition. The *Eighth Symphony*, written in 1961 – the first to be heard in public – is a product of that long recuperative period, and in the openness of inspiration (passionately English) it both belies earlier depression and testifies to the success of composition as therapy. Linked by a six-note leitmotif, the work holds well together. Even if the scherzando finale is arguably a little too long for its material, the elliptical first movement (opening and closing atmospherically and with a richly memorable secondary theme) and the eloquently sustained *Largo* both show the composer at his finest. Sir Edward Downes, who gave the first broadcast performance in 1977, subsequently made a fine LP of the work for Lyrita, but that has long been out of the catalogue and is now inevitably superseded by the composer's own highly spontaneous and very well-played Philharmonia account. The recording, made in the spacious acoustics of Watford Town Hall, is first class.

Symphony No. 11.
*** Albany Dig. TROY 060 [id.]. Albany SO, composer.

The urgently dynamic first movement of the *Eleventh* is described by the composer as being 'all fire and violence', but any anger in the music quickly evaporates, and it conveys rather a mood of exuberance, with very full orchestral forces unleashed. With the orchestra for which the work was commissioned, Lloyd conducts a powerful performance, very well played. The recording, made in the Music Hall of Troy Savings Bank near Albany, is spectacularly sumptuous and wide-ranging.

PIANO MUSIC

An African shrine; The aggressive fishes; Intercom baby; The road through Samarkand; St Anthony and the bogside beggar.
**(*) Albany Dig. AR 003 [id.]. Martin Roscoe.

The most ambitious piece here is *An African shrine*, in which the composer's scenario is linked (not very dissonantly) to African violence and revolution. *The road through Samarkand* (1972) has travellers from the younger generation leaving for the East; while *The aggressive fishes* are tropical and violently moody, changing from serenity to anger at the flick of a fin. The two most striking pieces are the picaresque tale of the *Bogside beggar* and the charming lullaby written for a baby whose mother is in another room listening with the aid of modern technology. Martin Roscoe's performances are thoroughly committed and spontaneous, and the recording is first class.

Aubade (fantasy suite); *Eventide; The Road through Samarkand.*
(N) *** Albany Dig. Troy 248 [id.]. Anthony Goldstone & Caroline Clemmow (piano duet).

Aubade, written in 1971, is a substantial suite of some 38 minutes' length. The composer describes it as a dream-like fantasy, with pictures flitting through his mind at dawn. Its evocations are impressionistic, its flavour distinctly Gallic. Included are *Charcoal burners*, ghostly but robust *Tin soldiers*, who gambol uninhibitedly after Waterloo, a Satie-esque *Love duet* and a quirkily ungainly *Waltz* (the imaginary participants are Lady Hamilton and the Duke of Wellington). There are tinkling *Bells, Monks and Lutherans,* a pair of *Moths*, who flit through a sparkling moto perpetuo, and a strong finale in which the bells return, now more dominant. It is all brilliantly imagined and its colourful imagery is vividly realized in a bravura performance by Anthony Goldstone and Caroline Clemmow. *Eventide* is a touching re-presentation and elaboration of a carol from the composer's youth – a simple melody which is charmingly ingenuous and not sentimentalized. *The Road to Samarkand* is a virtuoso toccata dominated by a simple motto theme. It recalls a trek to the East by the youth of the 1960s ('with burning hearts they danced their way from Calais to Calcutta, but what did they find?'). It is full of rhythmic interest, often syncopated, and the players clearly relish the virtuosity it demands. In short these are first-rate performances of highly communicative music which shows the composer at his most successfuly spontaneous. The recording is vivid but somewhat over-reverberant.

VOCAL MUSIC

A Litany.
**(*) Troy Dig. 200 [id.]. Janice Watson, Jeremy White, Guildford Choral Soc., Philh. O, composer.

A Litany, a setting of 12 verses from the John Donne poem, was Lloyd's penultimate work. Completed in 1995, it was first performed in London in 1996 and was recorded soon afterwards. If anything, the recording is more successful than that first performance, with the choir enthusiastically at home in music which communicates readily, even if the soloists are less than ideal, both having rather wide vibratos. *A Litany* is not as inspired as the *Symphonic Mass*. It is unfortunate that the very opening brings a curious reminder of *The Phantom of the Opera* and *Belshazzar's Feast*, with a whiff of Ketèlbey for good measure. But the music soon settles down and there is much fine choral writing in the first two sections, even if it is the third, unaccompanied, section, 'a song of thanks to the Virgin', that is the heart of the piece. The finale is quixotic in its mood changes but ends very positively. The spacious recording is well up to Albany's usual high standard.

A Symphonic Mass.
*** Albany Dig. TROY 100 [id.]. Brighton Festival Ch., Bournemouth SO, composer.

George Lloyd's *Symphonic Mass* is his masterpiece. Written for chorus and orchestra (but no soloists) on the largest scale, the work is linked by a recurring main theme, a real tune which soon lodges insistently in the listener's memory, even though it is modified at each reappearance. It first appears as a quiet setting of the words *Christe eleison*, nearly four minutes into the *Kyrie*. The climax of the whole work is the combined *Sanctus* and *Benedictus*, with the latter framed centrally. To the words *Dominus Deus* the great melody finds its apotheosis in a passage marked *largamente con fevore*. Then the *Sanctus* reasserts itself dramatically and, after a cry of despair from the violins, the movement reaches its overwhelmingly powerful and dissonant dénouement. Peace is then restored in the *Agnus Dei*, where the composer tells us the words *Dona nobis pacem* became almost unbearably poignant for him.

The performance is magnificent and the recording is fully worthy, spaciously balanced within the generous acoustic of the Guildhall, Southampton, and overwhelmingly realistic, even in the huge climax of the *Sanctus* with its shattering percussion.

The Vigil of Venus (Pervigilium Veneris).
*** Albany Dig. TROY 170 [id.]. Carolyn James, Thomas Booth, Welsh Nat. Op. Ch. & O, composer.

Following up the success of his recordings of his symphonies, George Lloyd here directs Welsh National Opera forces in this ambitious oratorio. Here, as in the symphonies, he thumbs his nose at fashion in a score which both pulses with energy and cocoons the ear in opulent sounds. Delian ecstasy is contrasted against the occasional echo of Carl Orff, an attractive mixture, even if – for all the incidental beauties – there is dangerously little variety of mood in the nine substantial sections. The composer was not entirely happy with what he was able to achieve in that first recording; even so, his performance certainly does not lack intensity and the recording (made by Argo engineers) is excellent, given the inherent problems of the recording venue in Swansea.

Iernin (opera; complete).
*** Albany Dig. TROY 121/3 (3) [id.]. Hill Smith, Pogson, Herford, Rivers, Powell, BBC Singers & Concert O, composer.

George Lloyd was only 21 when in the early 1930s he wrote this ambitious opera, and there is an open innocence in the warmly atmospheric, lyrical score. The piece was inspired by an ancient Cornish legend about ten maidens turned into a circle of stones, one of whom, Iernin (pronounced Ee-er-nin), returns in human form. Though this is ostensibly an old-fashioned opera, it deserves revival, and on the recording – taken from a BBC Radio 3 presentation in 1988 – the composer conducts a red-blooded, warmly expressive reading. Though some of the ensemble writing is less distinguished, the offstage choruses of faery folk are most effective. As to the soloists, Marilyn Hill Smith sings brightly in the title-role with all the agility needed, and the tenor, Geoffrey Pogson, copes well with the hero's role, if with rather coarse tone. The most distinguished singing comes from the rich-toned contralto, Claire Powell, as Cunaide. The third disc includes a half-hour interview with the composer, which makes up in part for the absence of background notes in the booklet with the libretto. Excellent, well-balanced BBC sound.

Lloyd Webber, William (1914–82)

(i) *Aurora (tone poem); Invocation; Lento; Serenade for strings; 3 Spring miniatures.* (ii) *Benedictus* (for violin and organ) (iii) *Nocturne* (for cello and harp); (iv) *Jesus, dear Jesus*; (i;v) *Love divine, all loves excelling; Mass (Princeps pacis).*
(N) *** Chandos Dig. CHAN 9595 [id.]. (i) City of L. Sinf., Richard Hickox; (ii) Tasmin Little, Ian Watson; (iii) Julian Lloyd Webber, Skaila Kanga; (iv) Hollie Cook, Arts Educational School, London, Gareth Jones; John Antrobus (organ); (v) Westminster Singers.

William Lloyd Webber demonstrates in ten short works that he wrote tunes every bit as fluently as his son, Andrew. Lloyd Webber senior, church organist and teacher, was yet an arch-romantic at heart, whose style sets English pastoral alongside Rachmaninov-like surges of passion. The most ambitious piece is the symphonic poem, *Aurora*, which starts like Bartók as smoothed over by Vaughan Williams, then develops in a colourfully orchestrated sequence of ideas. A forthright setting of the *Mass* written for Westminster Cathedral happily reconciles Roman and Anglican manners, yet every one of these unpretentious miniatures, beautifully performed and recorded, offers music of winning openness.

(i) *Air and variations; Fantasy trio; Frensham pond (Aquarelle); The gardens at Eastwell (A late summer impression); Mulberry cottage; Sonatina; A song for the morning; 3 Spring miniatures.* (ii) Songs: *The call of the morning; The forest of wild thyme; How do I love thee; I looked out into the morning; Love, like a drop of dew; Over the bridge; Sun-Gold; To the Wicklow hills.*
(N) *** Hyperion Dig. CDA 67008 [id.]. (i) Nash Ens.; (ii) John Mark Ainsley, Ian Brown.

Lloyd Webber's chamber and piano pieces span a far wider period than the songs, starting with the *Fantasy trio* of 1936, written when the composer was 22. The pieces inspired by particular places, like his very last known work, *The Gardens at Eastwell* for flute, are as freely lyrical as the songs. Very English in idiom, this music echoes not just early Bridge but occasionally Ireland too, as in the brisk, chattering piano piece, *Tree tops*. The Nash Ensemble soloists are all outstanding, with the pianist, Ian Brown, an inspired linchpin in every item. Again, the gift of melody revealed in the eight songs included here is a rare one. In idiom rather like early Frank Bridge they have tunes ready to latch in the mind, largely predictable but with unexpected twists. This is music written primarily for the delight of the composer, a sudden outpouring in the early 1950s. John Mark Ainsley is a most sensitive interpreter and again Ian Brown makes a fine contribution.

Aria; Chorale, cantilena and finale; Choral march; Elegy; Festal march; 3 Interludes on Christmas carols; Intermezzo; Meditation on Stracathro; Prelude; Prelude on Winchester New; 3 Recital pieces: (Prelude; Barcarolle; Nuptial march); Slumber song; Solemn procession; Song without words; Trumpet minuet; Vesper hymn.
(N) *** Priory Dig. PRCD 616 [id.]. Jane Watts (Willis organ of Salisbury Cathedral).

Like other discs of William Lloyd Webber's music, the Priory issue of organ pieces consistently reveals his fluent tunefulness, even if this is much more a specialist issue, the first recording made on the refurbished Willis organ at Salisbury Cathedral. Roughly half the 22 pieces here are typical examples of hushed and meditative organ music designed to fill in discreetly between items in a service, with five more designed as bright and energetic voluntaries for speeding congregations out of church. There are Franckian echoes in the chromaticism of the *Chorale, cantilena and finale*, but generally the style is very similar to that of the orchestral pieces. Sympathetic performances, very well recorded.

(i) *Missa Sanctae Mariae Magdalenae;* (ii) Arias: *The Divine compassion: Thou art the King. The Saviour: The King of Love. 5 Songs.* (iii; iv) *In the half light (soliloquy); Air varié* (after Franck); (iv) *6 Piano pieces.*
*** ASV Dig. CDDCA 584 [id.]. (i) Richard Hickox Singers, Hickox; I. Watson (organ); (ii) J. Graham Hall; P. Ledger; (iii) Julian Lloyd Webber; (iv) John Lill.

In this varied collection, the *Missa Sanctae Mariae Magdalenae* is both the last and the most ambitious of these works, strong and characterful. John Lill is a persuasive advocate of the *Six Piano pieces*, varied in mood and sometimes quirky, and accompanies Julian Lloyd Webber in the two cello pieces, written – as though with foresight of his son's career – just as his second son was born. Graham Hall, accompanied by Philip Ledger, completes the recital with beautiful performances of a group of songs and arias. Recording, made in a north London church, is warm and undistracting.

Lôbo, Duarte (*c.* 1565–1646)

Missa pro defunctis.
(BB) *** Naxos Dig. 8.550682 [id.]. Oxford Schola Cantorum, Jeremy Summerly – CARDOSO: *Missa pro defunctis.* ***

Here is another new name from the great age of Renaissance polyphony to conjure with – the Portuguese composer, Duarte Lôbo, Mestre de Capela at Lisbon Cathedral. He was an almost exact contemporary of Manuel Cardoso, whose music we have already discovered and who provides an eloquent coupling for this splendid Naxos CD. As performed here, Lôbo's *Missa pro defunctis* for double choir is a work of beautiful flowing lines (following directly on from Palestrina), bold dramatic contrasts and ardent depth of feeling. The *Agnus Dei* is particularly beautiful. A solo treble briefly introduces each section except the *Kyrie*, which adds to the effect of the presentation. This is another triumph from Jeremy Summerly and his excellent Oxford group (38 singers), who catch both the Latin fervour and the underlying serenity of a work which has a memorably individual voice.

Motets: *Audivi vocem de caelo; Pater peccavi.*
(BB) *** Naxos Dig. 8.553310 [id.]. Ars Nova, Bo Holten (with Concert of Portuguese polyphony ***) – CARDOSO: *Motets;* MAGALHAES: *Missa O Soberana luz* etc. ***

Lôbo's two beautiful motets, *Audivi vocem de caelo* ('I heard a voice from heaven') and *Pater peccavi* ('Father, I have sinned'), confirm the individuality of his writing. They are part of an outstandingly sung collection which is among the most desirable records of its kind in the catalogue.

Locatelli, Pietro (1695–1764)

L'Art del violino (12 violin concertos), *Op. 3.*
*** Hyperion Dig. CDA 66721/3 [id.]. Elizabeth Wallfisch, Raglan Bar. Players, Nicholas Kraemer.

Pietro Locatelli was a younger contemporary of Handel and Vivaldi. It was in 1733 that he wrote the present set of concertos, each of which in its outer movements includes an extended *Capriccio* of enormous technical difficulty with fast, complicated, sometimes stratospheric upper tessitura. Elizabeth Wallfisch not only throws off the fireworks with ease but also produces an appealingly gleaming lyrical line. Although Locatelli has not as strong a melodic personality as his famous contemporaries, the invention here has rhythmic vitality (which at times mirrors Vivaldi) and, in the Largo slow movements, a series of flowing ideas that have an inherent Handelian grace. With excellent, vital and stylish support from Kraemer and his Raglan Baroque Players, this may be counted a stimulating authentic re-creation of a set of concertos which had a profound influence on the violin technique of the time. The very well-balanced recording (the soloist real and vivid) is admirably clear yet has plenty of ambience.

Concerti grossi, Op. 1/1–12.
(BB) *** Naxos Dig. 8.553445/6 [id.]. Capella Istropolitana, Jaroslav Krec̆ek.
**(*) Hyperion Dig. CDA 66981/2 [id.]. Raglan Bar. Players, Elizabeth Wallfisch, Nicholas Kraemer.

Locatelli's Op. 1 first appeared in 1721 but was revised in 1729 when its composer settled in Amsterdam. Though indebted to Corelli (with the eighth of the set ending with a Christmas *Pastorale*), they have a style and personality of their own. Their invention is vigorous, their expressive range appealing. The Capella Istropolitana play with crisp attack, plenty of sparkle and resilient rhythms; the style of the slow movements reveals a keen identity with the lessons of period performances, even though modern instruments are used and phrasing is unexaggerated by bulges. The recording is admirable, with textures clear and with attractive, light sonorities. Most enjoyable and highly recommended.

The performances on Hyperion are lively enough, but there is at times an element of routine, a feeling of jogging along, as if the players recognize that this is not a very distinctive Opus. Elizabeth Wallfisch leads the concertino and is fully up to the bravura demands placed on her, though in the lyrical music her 'authentic' style of phrasing seems slightly more intrusive than usual. The recording is bright and vivid, the ambience spacious.

Concerti grossi, Op. 1/2, 5 & 12; Il Pianto d'Arianna, Op. 7/6; Sinfonia in F min. (composta per le esequie della sua Donna che si celebrarono in Roma).
*** Opus 111 OPS 30-104 [id.]. Europa Galante, Fabio Biondi.

The composer himself set great store by his Opus 1 and they are remarkable works, full of individuality. The Sonata subtitled *Il Pianto d'Arianna*, from Opus 7, is even more ambitious, with ten brief movements, an occasional whiff of Vivaldi, and plenty of drama. Perhaps most striking of all here is the *Sinfonia 'for the funeral of his lady which took place in Rome'*, which opens with an accented *Lamento* of rare intensity, in which the composer could be suggesting a heartbeat. It has to be said that this is not certainly by Locatelli but, heard in context, it sounds like it. The performances here are full of cleanly articulated, bouncing rhythmic vitality and are also persuasively expressive. Fabio Biondi, who really knows his way about this repertoire, uses a triple rather than a double layout, with the concertino, a further tutti group still made up of soloists, plus the real tutti or ripieno. The organ continuo adds subtle extra colour. The recording is most vividly clear yet not too close, with plenty of natural ambience. Highly recommended.

12 Flute concertos, Op. 2.
(M) ** Van. Dig. 99099 (2) [id.]. Jed Wentz, Musica ad Rhenum.

The Vanguard set is fluent and highly musical, and the continuo group (including organ in Nos. 2, 4, 6, 9 and 11) is very effective; but Jed Wentz's period flute sounds a little pale. Even so, this is offered at mid-price and is very well recorded. Readers will note that the cueing goes wrong for the final double sonata (in which, presumably, Wentz plays a duet with himself), which starts at track 19 (not 18), since the previous sonata has four sub-divisions, not the indicated three.

6 Introduttioni teatrali, Op. 4/1–6; 6 Concerti grossi, Op. 4/7–12.
*** Hyperion Dig. CDA 67041/2 [id.]. Raglan Bar. Players, Elizabeth Wallfisch.

(i) *6 Introduttioni teatrali, Op. 4: Nos. 1 in D; 2 in F; 3 in B flat; 4 in G; 5 in D; 6 in C.* (ii) *Trio sonatas: in E min., Op. 5/2; in D & A, Op. 8/2 & 10.*
*** DHM Dig. 0542 77207-2. (i) Freiburg Bar. O, Thomas Hengelbrock; (ii) Gottfried von Goltz, Guido Larisch, Torsten Johann.

There is simply no better introduction to the music of Locatelli than this superbly invigorating collection of his six *Theatrical introductions*. They are essentially (highly inventive) small-scale concerti grossi, with a concertino of four players, written in the fast–slow–fast manner of an Italian overture. Indeed the finale of No. 5 reminds one of the fifth concerto grosso of Handel's Op. 6. The fast movements erupt with vitality and bravura in these sparkling accounts from the excellent Freiburg Baroque Orchestra (4;3;2;2;1 plus harpsichord), who use period instruments brightly and freshly, and entirely without edgy acerbity, while the accented chords which are an integral part of Locatelli's allegros are played with gutsy incisiveness. These young players are not intimidated by the expressive writing and, although vibrato is minimal, there is no lack of sunshine. To add diversity, the *Introduttioni* are presented in pairs, and in between the concertino step forward to offer three *Trio sonatas* which are mellower but hardly less inventive. The recording, in an ideal acoustic, is first class. A most rewarding disc.

Whereas the Freiburg players provide interludes in their survey by playing three *Trio sonatas*, the Raglan Baroque Players instead offer the other six *Concerti grossi* which make up the rest of Locatelli's Op. 4. They too show him on his finest form, particularly the *Concerto No. 8 in F à immitazione de Corni da caccia*, where the opening *Grave* is quite profound, and then in later movements the solo violin of the concertino uses double-stopping ingeniously to depict a pair of horns. The remaining works are not as novel as this, but No. 10 (*Da Camera*) is a reworking of the *Sixth Sonata* of Locatelli's Op. 8 (see below) and includes the remarkable *Minuetto* with extended bravura variations, which are superbly played here by Elizabeth Wallfisch. No. 11 opens with another remarkably sombre *Grave* and then produces a jewelled sequence of brief movements (five in all). The final concerto of the set features four solo violins and was surely influenced by Vivaldi's famous work in this format which he included in *L'Estro armonico*. It deserves to be better known. The playing of the Raglan Baroque Ensemble, directed from the violin by the estimable Elizabeth Wallfisch, is supremely vital and expressively alive. The aural brightness is rather more sharply etched than in the DHM set, but the basic sonorities are full and the ambience is appealing.

CHAMBER MUSIC

6 Trio sonatas, Op. 5.
(M) **(*) Van. Dig. 99087 [id.]. Musica ad Rhenum.

Locatelli's Op. 5 *Trio sonatas* are full of agreeable, singing melody and have plenty of lively invention too. It is optional to use a pair of flutes or two violins in their performance, and it might have been a good idea to vary the instrumentation, as two flutes used continually can prove too much of a good thing. However, Jed Wentz and Marion Moonen play with style and they blend nicely together; the continuo group includes a bassoon for added colour. Good performances, without any of the acerbities one associates with period performance, nicely recorded.

Violin sonatas (for 1 or 2 violins) *and continuo, Op. 8/1–10.*
*** Hyperion Dig. CDA 67021/2 [id.]. Locatelli Trio.

Locatelli's Op. 8 consists of six works for solo violin, of which the last is the most impressive with its closing *Aria di minuetto* with eight variations, demanding considerable bravura from the soloist. All the sonatas start with a slow, expressive introduction, with faster movements following. The remaining works are *Trio sonatas*; with their format of (usually) four (or sometimes five) movements, they offer the composer even greater opportunities for variety and he is obviously intending to please his cultivated listeners. The very agreeable (penultimate) *Cantabile* of No. 7, for instance, is followed by an unusual *Allegro* alternating more sustained passages with bursts of activity. But the invention in these later works is deft in imaginative touches, and the contrapuntal writing is genially spirited. Provided you don't respond adversely to Elizabeth Wallfisch's tendency in playing to bulge very slightly on expressive phrasing, the performances are admirable, crisply detailed and refreshingly alive. The Hyperion recording is well up to standard.

Locke, Matthew (*c.* 1621–77)

Consort of Fower Parts: suites Nos. 1 in D min.; 2 in D min./maj.; 3 & 4 in F; 5 in G min.; 6 in G.
*** Astrée Audivis Dig. E 8519 [id.]. Hespèrion XX.

Consort of Fower Parts: suites Nos. 1–6. Duos for 2 bass viols Nos. 1 in C; 2 in D.
**(*) Virgin Veritas/EMI (SIS) Dig. VC5 45142-2. Fretwork, with Nigel North & Paul Nicholson.

Matthew Locke, born in Devon, was a choirboy at Exeter Cathedral but later moved to work as a musician in London; here in 1660, when Charles II was restored to the throne of England, Locke became Master of the King's Music at the royal court. At that time he had 24 violins at his disposal, but he probably wrote the *Consort of Fower Parts* earlier, in the 1650s. If they are less ambitious in instrumentation, they are much more so in musical achievement. Indeed the remarkably ethereal *Fantazie* opening the *Fifth suite in G minor*, which is magnetically presented in the Hespèrion performance, can be measured against comparable music by Purcell. Each suite opens with a *Fantazie* and then follows a standard sequence of *Courante*, *Ayre* and *Saraband*. Locke's suites were regarded at the time as being composed 'after the old style', but the music itself is forward-looking and by no means predictable. It seems likely that they would have been performed with continuo, a practice followed sparingly in both the Fretwork and Hespèrion performances, the former using archlute and organ, the later preferring a double harp to the lute.

Both sets of performances are highly musical, scholarly and well recorded, but there is a clear first choice. In the dance movements there is an extra rhythmic vigour and buoyancy with Hespèrion, and in the *Ayres* of the *First* and *Second suites*, for instance, there is an extra expressive warmth, compared with a faster tempo and relative austerity of feeling with Fretwork. The latter's playing brings somewhat more refined textures, and the Virgin Veritas programme includes two extra works: a pair of *Duos* (each in six movements) for two bass viols. Of these, it is the second that is obviously the more appealing and it has a subtle organ continuo (although the booklet suggests the reverse – that the organ is involved in the *C major Duo*). But in spite of this bonus, it is the Hespèrion playing which is the more penetrating in this fine music.

Psyche.
*** O-L (IMS) Dig. 444 336-2. Catherine Bott,

Christopher Robson, Andrew King, Paul Agnew, Michael George, Simon Grant, Julia Gooding, Helen Parker, Julian Podger, Ch. & New L. Cons., Pickett.

Psyche dates from 1675, a year after Locke's success with *The Tempest*. But he worked on *Psyche* (broadly based on the Lully equivalent) in partnership with Giovanni Draghi, who provided the instrumental parts of the score, which are now lost. So they have been inspirationally reconstituted by Philip Pickett and Peter Holman by making arrangements from Draghi's keyboard music, and the result is very vivid and colourful. The vocal music is very engaging too, from the *Chorus of Nymphs* to the Forge scene, complete with anvil noises. The soloists all rise to the occasion, especially Catherine Bott who is perfectly cast as Venus. Michael George is also splendid, and there is no weak link here, while the New London Chorus obviously enjoy themselves and make a lively contribution. This is not on the level of Purcell, but it still makes a most enjoyable entertainment.

Loewe, Carl (1796–1869)

Ballads and Lieder: *Archibald Douglas; Canzonette; Die drei Lieder; Edward; Elvershöh; Erlkönig; Freibeuter; Frühzeitiger Frühling; Der getreue Eckart; Gottes ist der Orient!; Die Gruft der Liebenden; Gutmann und Gutweib; Der heilige Franziskus; Heinrich der Vogler; Herr Oluf; Hinkende Jamben; Hochzeitlied; Ich denke dein; Im Vorübergehen; Kleiner Haushalt; Lynkeus, der Türmer, auf Fausts Sternwarte singend; Meeresleuchten; Der Mohrenfürst auf der Messe; Der Nöck; Odins Meeresritt; Prinz Eugen; Der Schatzgräber; Süsses Begräbnis; Tom der Reimer; Der Totentanz; Trommelständchen; Turmwächter Lynkeus zu den Füssen der Helena; Die Uhr; Die wandelnde Glocke; Wandrers Nachtlied; Wenn der Blüten Frühlingsregen; Der Zauberlehrling.*

(M) *** DG 449 516-2 (2). Fischer-Dieskau, Demus.

For the most part this set was recorded in 1968–9, with a second group of songs added a decade later. With the great German baritone consistently in fine voice, it makes an ideal selection of some of Loewe's most memorable songs and ballads. Fischer-Dieskau, admirably accompanied by Jörg Demus, gives performances which have the commitment and intensity of spontaneous expression while remaining flawlessly controlled and strongly thought through. This alternative setting of the *Erlkönig*, preferred by many in the nineteenth century, is in its way as dramatic as Schubert's, if musically less subtle. The following *Edward* is also extraordinarily dramatic, while the magnificent *Die Uhr* ('The timepiece') opens lightly but develops an unexpected depth of feeling. The story-telling in other songs is also so graphic that it might be thought that even a non-German speaker would have little need to refer to the translations. However, it is an excellent feature of the set that these are provided in full. Splendidly vivid recording: if you enjoy Schubert, you can hardly fail to relish the best of Loewe.

Frauenliebe (song-cycle) *Op. 60*. Goethe, Heine and Rückert Lieder: *Der du von dem Himmel heist; Erste Liebe; Hinkende Jamben; Ich hab in Traume geweinet; Im Traume sah ich die Geliebte; Irrlichter; Die Lotusblume; Mädchenwünsche; Meine Ruh ist hin; O süsse Mutter; Die Pfarrjüngferchen; Sehnsucht; Süsses Begräbnis; Szene aus Faust; Uber allen Gipfeln ist Ruh.*

(M) *** DG (IMS) Dig. 445 575-2. Brigitte Fassbaender, Cord Garben.

Frauenliebe, Loewe's cycle to poems of Chamisso, inevitably invites comparison with Schumann's *Frauenliebe und Leben*, but if it has less depth than the latter, Loewe's sequence remains infinitely touching; Brigitte Fassbaender sings it tenderly and with much charm. There are nine songs in all, although the composer published only seven of them as his Op. 60. Loewe's heroine is impulsive and soon falls deeply in love, and we follow her progress to a Schubertian dream of happiness, the wedding ring and revelling in marital bliss, her lover's sudden death and the poignant epilogue addressed to her daughter who, by the nature of things, will follow in her mother's footsteps. The final words of blessing are not sung but gently spoken. Not all the other songs here suit Fassbaender so well; she is best in the gentler settings. Goethe's *Scene with Faust* is lovely, as is *Uber allen Gipfeln ist Ruh*, while Rückert's *Irrlichter* ('Will-o'-the-wisps'), sung precociously fast, is captivating. But it is a pity that the recital opens with Goethe's *Meine Ruh ist hin*, which brings some repeated ugly upward scoops. Nevertheless this rare CD is not to be missed.

Lombardini, Maddelena Laura

(1735–99) – see under **Sirmen, Maddelena**

Lortzing, Albert (1801–51)

Die Opernprobe.

(M) *** CPO/EMI CPO 999 557-2. Marheineke, Gedda, Hirte, Litz, Lövaas, Berry, Bav. State Op. Ch. & O, Suitner.

Best known for his opera, *Der Wildschütz*, still popular in Germany today, Lortzing wrote this light-hearted satire in 1851, his very last piece, given its first performance on the day before he died. As a singer and actor himself, writing his own librettos, he had the gift of composing operas which, helped by his easy tunefulness, work well. *Die Opernprobe* ('The opera rehearsal') involves disguises and confusions of identity in the household of a music-loving Count who encourages his servants to perform. In a sparkling overture and ten numbers, mostly brief, it tells a simple story of true love triumphant, ending with a substantial finale in Mozartian style. Otmar Suitner directs a lively performance, very well sung and well produced in its dialogue, with first-rate (1974) EMI sound.

Lotti, Antonio (*c.* 1667–1740)

Crucifixus.

(B) *** Decca Double 443 868-2 (2) [id.]. St John's College, Cambridge, Ch., Philomusica, Guest – BONONCINI: *Stabat Mater* ***; PERGOLESI: *Magnificat in C; Stabat Mater* **(*); D. SCARLATTI: *Stabat Mater;* A. SCARLATTI: *Domine, refugium factus es nobis; O magnum mysterium;* CALDARA: *Crucifixus.* ***

(B) *** Decca Double 455 017-2. St John's College, Cambridge, Ch., L. Philomusica, Guest – CALDARA: *Crucifixus* ***; PERGOLESI: *Magnificat* etc. **(*)

This short *Crucifixus*, which takes less than four minutes, may well have inspired the noble Caldara setting with which it frames Bononcini's beautiful *Stabat Mater* in this highly desirable collection of choral music. The Lotti setting is less elaborate in texture than Caldara's but it is hardly less noble or affecting. Performance and recording are excellent. Alongside the Caldara setting, this fine piece also comes as a filler for Decca's alternative compilation which centres on Pergolesi.

Lovenskiold, Herman (1815–70)

La Sylphide (ballet) complete.

(M) *** Chandos Dig. CHAN 6546 [id.]. Royal Danish O, David Garforth.

La Sylphide (1834) predates Adam's *Giselle* by seven years. It is less distinctive than Adam's score, but it is full of grace and the invention has genuine romantic vitality – indeed the horn writing in the finale anticipates Delibes. The wholly sympathetic playing is warm, elegant, lively and felicitous in its detailed delicacy, yet robust when necessary and always spontaneous. A most enjoyable disc, superbly recorded.

Ludford, Nicholas (1485–1557)

Masses; Magnificat benedicta & Motets (as listed below).

✿ (M) *** ASV/Gaudeamus CDGAX 426 (4) [id.]. The Cardinall's Musick, Andrew Carwood.

Nicholas Ludford is one of the least familiar of the Tudor masters; he never enjoyed the fame of his older contemporary, Fayrfax, or the much younger Tallis. According to Dr John Bergsagel's *Grove* article, Ludford composed 11 complete Masses and three incomplete, thus making him 'the most prolific of English composers of masses'. This four-CD box gathers together the four splendid discs of Ludford's music performed by Andrew Carwood and his excellent group of singers, who are individually as impressive as in the blended whole. This is music of remarkably passionate feeling, and it brings to life a composer who spent much of his working life in St Stephen's Chapel at St Margaret's, Westminster. He was an ardent Catholic and was very happily married – he paid for his wife to have her own pew and gave her an elaborate ceremonial burial. He then married again, and his second wife was instructed to prepare something more modest for his interment alongside his beloved first spouse. His music is little short of extraordinary, and we hope our Rosette will tempt collectors to explore it, either through this comprehensive box, or by trying one of the individual issues.

Missa Benedicta et venerabilis; Magnificat benedicta.

*** ASV/Gaudeamus Dig. CDGAU 132 [id.]. The Cardinall's Musick, Andrew Carwood.

Ludford uses the same plainchant for both works, but the voicing has a distinct emphasis at the lower end of the range, not only adding to the weight but also bringing a certain darkness to the sonority. The performance has the same spontaneous feeling that distinguishes this magnificent series throughout, and it confirms Ludford as one of the most emotionally communicative and original musicians of his age. The plainsong proper relates the music to the Feast of the Assumption. Excellent, full recording.

Missa Christi Virgo dilectissima; Motet: Domine Ihesu Christie.

*** ASV/Gaudeamus Dig. CDGAU 133 [id.]. The Cardinall's Musick, Andrew Carwood.

This is music of great beauty, whose expressive eloquence and floating lines quite carry the listener away. Andrew Carwood proves an excellent advocate and the sound is also spacious and well balanced.

Missa Lapidaverunt Stephanum; Ave Maria ancilla trinitatis.

*** ASV/Gaudeamus Dig. CDGAU 140 [id.]. Cardinall's Musick, Andrew Carwood.

This Mass, celebrating St Stephen the Martyr, is thought to have been written soon after he was appointed verger and organist there in 1527. In five-part polyphony the scale is formidable, culminating in a magnificent *Agnus Dei*. The performances, fresh and stylish, are punctuated by apt plainsong.

Missa Videte miraculum; Motet: Ave cuius conceptio.
*** ASV/Gaudeamus Dig. CDGAU 131 [id.]. The Cardinall's Musick, Andrew Carwood.

The six-part *Missa Videte miraculum* brings a remarkable double treble line running together, often in thirds. Overall this work is as fine as the others in the series, and it is gloriously sung.

Luigini, Alexandre (1850–1906)

Ballet Egyptien, Op. 12 (suite).
(B) *** CfP CD-CFP 4637 [id.]. RPO, Fistoulari – KETELBEY: *Collection.* ***

Because of its bandstand popularity, Luigini's amiable and tuneful *Ballet Egyptien* has never been taken very seriously. However, the four-movement suite is highly engaging (both the two central sections have good tunes), especially when played as affectionately and stylishly as here under that master conductor of ballet, Anatole Fistoulari. The 1958 recording has come up remarkably freshly, and this makes an excellent bonus for an outstanding Ketèlbey concert.

Lully, Jean-Baptiste (1632–87)

Petits motets: *Anima Christe; Ave coeli; Dixit Dominus; Dominum salvum fac Regem; Exaudi Deus; Laudate pueri; O dulcissime; Omnes gentes; O Sapientia; Regina coeli; Salve Regina.*
(N) *** HM Dig. HMC 901274 [id.]. Les Arts Florissants, William Christie.

Lully's Italianate *Petits Motets* range in length from two to nine minutes. Recent scholarship has rejected several attributed works, but has confirmed the present group as authentic. They are written for three voices, usually sopranos – since the music was intended for a Paris Convent Choir – and the sopranos here are appealingly fresh-voiced. The continuo (with Christie himself at the organ) is tellingly and discreetly managed, and the performances have a pleasing sweetness of timbre and lightness of touch.

Dies irae; (i) *Te Deum.*
(M) **(*) Erato/Warner 0630 11226-2. Jennifer Smith, Devos; (i) Bessac, Vandersteene, Huttenlocher; Valence Vocal Ens., Paillard CO, Paillard.

The *Dies irae* is a noble piece encapsulating a mood of dark melancholy, and it makes a strong impression here, with a notably dedicated contribution from the two soloists. The effect has a striking, elegiac beauty. The sudden choral interjections at a faster pace are convincingly managed. Here the choral focus in the CD transfer could be cleaner, but the sound has plenty of body and a most attractive ambience. The better-known *Te Deum* dates from 1677. It opens regally with brilliant high trumpets and is a work of contrasting splendour and breadth rather than the general-purpose pomp often favoured by Lully and his followers. Paillard and his forces give a thoroughly committed and eloquent account of the piece, and the recording is richly expansive, with the choral sound cleaner. Incidentally, it was while conducting this work that Lully vigorously brought down the heavy stick that served to mark the beat on to his right foot; gangrene eventually set in, and a couple of months later he died!

Les Comédies ballets: excerpts from: (i) *Les Amants magnifiques; L'Amour médecin; Le Bourgeois Gentilhomme; George Dandin (Le Grand Divertissement royal de Versailles); Monsieur de Pourceaugnac (Le Divertisement de Chambourd); Pastoral comique; Les Plaisirs de l'île enchantée.*(ii) *Phaëton* (tragédie en musique; complete).
(N) (B) *** Erato/Warner Dig. Ultima 3984 26998-2 (2) [id.]. (i) Poulenard, Mellon, Ragon, Laplénie, Verschaeve, Delétré, Cantor; (ii) Crook, Yakar, J. Smith, Gens, Thereul, Sagittarius Vocal Ens.; Musiciens du Louvre, Minkowski.

This immensely rewarding Ultima Double combines a selection of highlights from the *comédies ballets* which Lully wrote in collaboration with Molière, with his '*tragédie en musique*', *Phaëton*. One despairs at the absence of texts and translations – how can a major record company be so parsimonious in this way? – and the documentation provided instead is totally inadequate. (Otherwise this would have received a ✿). But the music is so delightful, and the performances so alive and spirited that this Ultima Double must be strongly recommended, even to those who are totally unfamiliar with this repertoire. The series of *comédies-ballets* represented here were written between 1663 and 1670, and their tuneful and often outrageous burlesque represents an unparalleled comic partership between composer and playwright – French insouciance combined with wittily *bucolique* music which obviously reflects the influence of Italian comic opera, yet never loses its Gallic character, especially in the charming and often beautiful pastoral airs. The ensemble of ironic salutation to men of medicine (Lully despised doctors) in *L'Amour médecin* is matched by the robust *bouffe* male interchanges wallowing in the hedonistic pleasures of *L'île enchantée*, and there are similar comically boisterous ensembles in the divertissement, *George Dandin*, although they are perhaps capped by the extraordinary excerpt from *Monsieur de Pourceaugnac* which makes fun of polygamy. The two longest selections come from *Le Bourgeois Gentilhomme*, infectiously spirited, which includes one syncopated number which anticipates '*America*' in Bernstein's *West Side Story*, and finally, the masterly third *intermède* of *Les Amants magnifiques*, which combines a gentler humour with graceful lyricism. The team of soloists clearly relishes every ridiculous situation, and the presentation has consistent sparkle and spontaneity, while the lyrical music is most persuasively phrased by singers and orchestra alike.

Phaëton tells of the attempt of the son of the Sun God to drive across the heavens in his father's chariot. The horses bolt and this threatens to set fire to the earth, whereupon Jupiter strikes him dead, to the apparent rejoicing of everyone. When Libye can then be partnered by her beloved Epaphus, it is hardly a tragedy at all, with their love celebrated earlier in two brief, but intensely beautiful duets, punctuating the many solo airs. The cast is strong – Véronique Gens is most affecting as Libye, with Rachael Yakar and Jennifer Smith impressive too, and Howard Crook clean-focused and stylish in the name part. Throughout the two discs Marc Minkowski's direction is compellingly fresh and resilient. Both recordings are co-productions between Erato and Radio France and are strikingly vivid and immediate. Again one laments the appalling presentation, or lack of it, but this is still a set not to be missed.

Le Bourgeois Gentilhomme (comédie-ballet; complete).
(M) *** HM/BMG GD 77059 (2) [77059-2-RG]. Nimsgern, Jungmann, Schortemeier, René Jacobs, Tölz Ch., La Petite Bande, Leonhardt – CAMPRA: *L'Europe galante*. ***

The performance here puts Lully's music into the correct stage perspective and, with such sprightly and spirited performers as well as good 1973 recording, this can hardly fail to give pleasure. The orchestral contribution under the direction of Gustav Leonhardt is distinguished by a splendid sense of the French style.

Atys (opera): complete.
*** HM Dig. HMC 901257/9 (3). Guy de Mey, Mellon, Laurens, Gardeil, Semellaz, Rime, Les Arts Florissants Ch. & O, Christie.

Christie and his excellent team give life and dramatic speed consistently to the performance of *Atys*, and there are many memorable numbers, not least those in the sleep interlude of Act III. Outstanding in the cast are the high tenor, Guy de Mey, in the name-part and Agnès Mellon as the nymph, Sangaride, with whom he falls in love.

Atys: highlights.
(B) *** HM Dig. HMT 7901249 [HMC 901249] (from complete recording, with Guy de Mey, Agnès Mellon, Les Arts Florissants, cond. Christie).
(B) *** HM Dig. HMX 290844/46 (3) [id.] (from complete recording, cond. Christie) – CAMPRA: *Idomenée:* highlights; RAMEAU: *Castor et Pollux:* highlights. ***

Atys remains one of Christie's greatest successes on record; it is full of good things, and many of them are also included on the single-disc highlights selection (notably the delightful Sleep scene of Act III). With consistently fine singing and superb recording, this disc contains about a third of the opera (68 minutes).

This CD is also offered as part of one of Harmonia Mundi's enterprising 'Trios', in this case offering three discs of operatic highlights together in a slip-case at bargain price. But unlike its companions, *Idomenée* and *Castor et Pollux*, no translation is included for *Atys*. Christie's performance is highly recommended by us (see above), with Guy de Mey memorable in the principal role, and this 68-minute selection includes the remarkable 'Sleep fantasy' in Act III. Taken as a package with its two companions, this collection of highlights costs only a fraction of the price of the three-disc complete set.

Lumbye, Hans Christian (1810–74)

Amager polka; Amelie waltz; Champagne galop; Columbine polka mazurka; Copenhagen Steam Railway galop; Dream pictures fantasia; The Guard of Amager (ballet): *Final galop. Helga polka mazurka; Hesperus waltz; Lily polka (dedicated to the ladies); Queen Louise's waltz; Napoli* (ballet): *Final galop. Salute to August Bournonville; Salute to our friends; Sandman galop fantastique.*
*** Unicorn Dig. DKPCD 9089 [id.]. Odense SO, Peter Guth.

This superb Unicorn collection offers 75 minutes of the composer's best music, with wonderfully spontaneous performances demonstrating above all its elegance and gentle grace. It opens with a vigorous *Salute to August Bournonville* and closes with a *Champagne galop* to rival Johann junior's polka. In between comes much to enchant, not least the delightful *Amelie waltz* and the haunting *Dream pictures fantasia* with its diaphanous opening textures and lilting main theme. But Lumbye's masterpiece is the unforgettable *Copenhagen Steam Railway galop*. This whimsical yet vivid portrait of a local Puffing Billy begins with the gathering of passengers at the station – obviously dressed for the occasion in a more elegant age than ours. The little engine then wheezingly starts up and proceeds on its journey, finally drawing to a dignified halt against interpolated cries from the station staff. Because of the style and refinement of its imagery, it is much the most endearing of musical railway evocations, and the high-spirited lyricism of the little train racing through the countryside, its whistle peeping, is enchanting. This is a superbly entertaining disc, showing the Odense Symphony Orchestra and its conductor, Peter Guth, as naturally suited to this repertoire as are the VPO under Boskovsky in the music of the Strauss family. The recording has a warm and sympathetic ambience and gives a lovely bloom to the whole programme.

Amelie waltz; Britta polka; Champagne galop; Columbine polka mazurka; Concert polka (for 2 violins and orchestra); *Copenhagen Steam Railway galop; Dream pictures* (fantasy); *The Lady of St Petersburg* (polka); *The Guards of Amager: Final galop. My salute to St Petersburg* (march); *Napoli* (ballet): *Final galop. Polonaise with cornet solo; Queen Louise's waltz; Salute to August Bournonville; St Petersburg champagne galop.*
*** Chandos Dig. CHAN 9209 [id.]. Danish Nat. RSO, Rozhdestvensky.

This new Chandos disc opens with an arresting fanfare and sets off into the *Champagne galop* with much brio. Throughout his programme, Rozhdestvensky's approach is altogether more extrovert than Guth's on Unicorn, and the Royal Danish Orchestra, without loss of finesse, play almost everything here with great gusto. The Copenhagen Steam Railway engine becomes a mainline express and reaches an exhilarating momentum before slamming on its brakes, to be vociferously welcomed by the Danish porters as it arrives at its destination. One cannot but respond to the energy and vivacity of the playing here, while the lovely *Dream pictures* creates a total contrast and is most poetically done. The recording is spectacularly resonant and adds to the impact.

Britta polka; Canon galop; Cecilie waltz; Dancing tune from Kroll Waltz; Indian war dance; King Christian IX March of honour; King George I March of honour; Manoeuvre galop; Memories from Vienna waltz; Nordic brotherhood; Pegasus galop; Summernight at Møns Cliff galop; Sophie waltz; Velocipedes galop; Victoria quadrille; Welcome mazurka; Les Zouaves galop.
*** Unicorn Dig. DKPCD 9143. Odense SO, Peter Guth.

A further, essentially energetic selection of sparkling Lumbye repertoire, splendidly played with much spirit by the excellent Odense orchestra under Guth. The *Velocipedes galop* makes an engaging and vivacious opener, and the *Canon galop* which closes the concert has properly spectacular effects, plus a final bang to make the listener jump. The *Memories from Vienna waltz* has a particularly winning lilt, but there is nothing here that quite matches the *Copenhagen Steam Railway galop*.

Lutoslawski, Witold (1916–94)

(i) *Chain II. Chain III; Novelette;* (i; ii) *Partita.*
(M) *** DG Dig. 445 576-2 [id.]. (i) Mutter, (ii) Philip Moll; (i; ii) BBC SO, composer.

Chain III; Novelette.
(B) *** DG Dig. 439 452-3 [(M) 431 664-2]. BBC SO, composer – LIGETI: *Chamber concerto;* SCHNITTKE: *Concerto grosso No. 1.* ***

Chain II, a 'dialogue for violin and orchestra', follows up the technique of *Chain I* (of which at present there is no really satisfactory recording), contrasting fully written sections with *ad libitum* movements, where chance plays its part within fixed parameters. *Chain III* then makes a sustained contrast with its ear-catching orchestral colours. The *Partita* is a development of a piece for violin and piano which Lutoslawski originally wrote for Pinchas Zukerman, with the first, third and fifth movements now scored for violin and orchestra. With Mutter and the composer the most persuasive advocates, both concertante pieces establish themselves as among the finest examples of Lutoslawski's late work. *Novelette*, an attractive, scherzo-like piece, full of incandescent energy, is common to both the main, mid-priced programme and the Classikon reissue, coupled with other stimulating works by Ligeti and Schnittke. DG here are obviously treading water to see if they can sell this kind of *avant-garde* music in a wider marketplace at budget price.

Cello concerto.
*** EMI (SIS) CDC7 49304-2. Rostropovich, O de Paris, composer – DUTILLEUX: *Cello concerto.* ***

The *Cello concerto* was written in response to a commission by Rostropovich, whose 1975 recording is now reissued at full price, retaining the original catalogue number and still sounding extremely vivid. As in some other Lutoslawski pieces, there are aleatory elements in the score, though these are carefully controlled. The sonorities are fascinating and heard to good advantage on the EMI CD. The soloist is rather forward, but in every other respect the recording is extremely realistic. Rostropovich is in his element and gives a superb account of the solo role, and the composer's direction of the accompaniment is grippingly authoritative.

Concerto for orchestra.
(B) **(*) EMI forte CZS5 72664-2 (2) [CDFB 72664]. Chicago SO, Seiji Ozawa – BARTOK: *Concerto for orchestra* **(*); JANACEK: *Sinfonietta* ***; STRAVINSKY: *Firebird ballet.* **(*)

The Swiss orchestra on Decca – see below – play impressively for Kletzki and are very well recorded. But they are no match for Ozawa's virtuoso players, and this EMI forte set is similarly priced and offers attractive couplings. The acoustics of Chicago's Medinah Temple posed problems for the engineers and the overall sound is somewhat two-dimensional and dryish.

Concerto for orchestra; Mi-parti; Overture for strings; Three poems by Henri Michaux.
(N) (BB) *** Naxos Dig. 8.553779 [id.]. Camerata Silesia, Anna Szostak; Polish Nat. RSO, Antoni Wit.

This fifth volume of Naxos's excellent Lutoslawski series brings together two of the early works which helped to make his name, alongside later, more radical inspirations. The disc provides an excellent cross-section for anyone wanting to sample this inspired composer's work. The *Concerto for orchestra* of 1954 remains among his most popular works, and like the *Overture* of five years earlier reflects the influence of Bartók and of neo-classicism. The settings of the surrealist poet, Henri Michaux, dating from the early 1960s are highly original in their use of choral textures, and *Mi-parti* in a single span, slow then fast, points forward in the brilliance and originality of its interplay of instruments to the later symphonies. Strong and purposeful performances vividly recorded in full, immediate sound.

(i) *Concerto for orchestra;* (ii) *Paganini variations* (for piano and orchestra); (iii) *Musique funèbre;* (iv) *Paroles tissées*.
(B) **(*) Decca Double Analogue/Dig. 448 258-2 (2) [id.]. (i) SRO, Kletzki; (ii) Jablonski, RPO, Ashkenazy; (iii) Cleveland O, Dohnányi; (iv) Peter Pears, LSO, composer – SZYMANOWSKI: *Violin concerto No. 2; Symphonies Nos. 2–3.* **(*)

Kletzki directs a brilliant account of the *Concerto for orchestra*, and the Swiss orchestra play very well for him; moreover they are given vintage Decca sound from 1968. Kletzki makes a small cut in the second movement, albeit with the composer's permission. However, this is an exciting performance. *Musique funèbre* (not perhaps one of the composer's most inspired pieces) is very well played and recorded, but it does not generate the last degree of tension. The *Paganini variations* for two pianos is very successful indeed, however: it is one of Lutoslawski's earliest and most readily appealing works. Peter Jablonski plays it in the much later transcription for piano and orchestra, and his pleasure and delight will surely be shared by the listener. The digital recording is first class. The *Paroles tissées* were written for Peter Pears, who sings the cycle here, and Lutoslawski's writing shows extraordinary understanding of that singer's special qualities and the colour of his voice. The texts are from poems of Jean-François Chabrun, with haunting imagery recurring in a manner mirrored exactly by the composer's finely textured, sharply conceived writing. Performances and recording are ideal.

Piano concerto.
*** Koch Dig. 3-6414-2 [id.]. Ewa Kupiec, Bamberg SO, Judd – SZYMANOWSKI: *Symphony No. 4.* **

(i) *Piano concerto. Chain 3; Novelette.*
*** DG (IMS) Dig. 431 664-2 [id.]. (i) Krystian Zimerman; BBC SO, composer.

(i) *Piano concerto. Little suite; Symphonic variations; Symphony No. 2.*
(BB) *** Naxos 8.553169 [id.]. (i) Paleczny; Polish Nat. RSO, Wit.

Ewa Kupiec gives a compelling performance of this difficult concerto, with its fragmentary writing in slow movements and chattering passage-work in the second-movement Scherzo. Even more than the dedicatee, Krystian Zimerman, or Piotr Paleczny in the previous recordings, she finds fun in the Scherzo and, warmly supported by Judd and the Bamberg orchestra, gives point and purpose to the seemingly improvisatory writing of the other movements. Excellent sound. The Szymanowski symphony with its important piano part makes an interesting but ungenerous coupling.

The *Piano concerto* is also marvellously played by Zimerman and the BBC Symphony Orchestra under the composer. It is beautiful to listen to, but for all its diversity of aural incident and activity here one is left wondering whether there is much of enduring substance. The two remaining works are also very convincingly presented. Absolutely first-rate recording.

The early, tonal *Symphonic variations* make an attractive introduction to the second of Naxos's discs in what aims to cover his complete orchestral music. The *Little suite* is an approachable work too, before the much tougher and more substantial symphony and concerto which make up the great part of the disc. In two massive movements, *Hesitant* and *Direct*, the *Symphony No. 2* is an uncompromising piece, and here is helped by a purposeful, very well-rehearsed performance. The *Piano concerto* is even more elusive, often fragmentary, but again the performance is magnetic: Piotr Paleczny plays with a clarity and brilliance that sound totally idiomatic. Excellent sound, with good presence.

Dance preludes (for clarinet and orchestra).
*** Hyperion Dig. CDA 66215 [id.]. Thea King, ECO, Litton – BLAKE: *Clarinet concerto;* SEIBER: *Concertino.* ***
*** Chandos Dig. CHAN 8618 [id.]. Janet Hilton, SNO, Bamert – COPLAND; NIELSEN: *Concertos.* ***

Lutoslawski's five folk-based vignettes are a delight in the hands of Thea King and Andrew Litton, who give sharply characterized performances, thrown into bold relief by the bright, clear recording. Janet Hilton also emphasizes their contrasts with her expressive lyricism and crisp articulation in the lively numbers. Excellent recording.

(i) *Postlude No. 1;* (ii) *Preludes and fugues for 13 solo strings;* (iii) *Paroles tissées;* (iv) *3 Poèmes d'Henri Michaux.*

(M) *** EMI CDM5 65865-2. (i) Polish Nat. RSO; (ii) Polish CO; (iii) Louis Devos; (iv) Krakow R. Ch.; all cond. composer.

The searching *Preludes and fugues for thirteen solo strings* (1970–72) shows the mature Lutoslawski; the choral *Poèmes* were written a decade earlier. With their variety of effects, including whispering and syllabic monotones, the writing readily contrasts with the atmospheric *Paroles tissées* ('woven words') with its mystical feeling and remarkable word-imagery. Together with the elliptical *Postlude* this programmes offers a well-planned demonstration of the composer's breadth of achievement. Performances and recordings are of a high standard, as is the recording from the late 1970s.

Symphonies Nos. 1–2; Symphonic variations.

(M) *** EMI CDM5 65076-2. Polish R. Nat. SO, composer.

The wholly beguiling *Symphonic variations*, with its Szymanowskian palette and luminosity, is an early work (1938); the symphonies date from 1947 and 1966/8, respectively. The latter consolidates the new language the composer formed after his change of style in the mid-1950s; the *First* is written against a musical background influenced by Hindemith, Bartók and Prokofiev and perhaps by Stravinsky too. But the work has its own individuality and is well worth hearing. The composer is an eloquent advocate, and the 1976/7 recordings are spacious and full-bodied with bright detail.

Symphonies Nos. 3–4; (i) *Les espaces du sommeil.*

*** Sony Dig. SK 66280 [id.]. LAPO, Esa-Pekka Salonen; (i) with John Shirley-Quirk.

The format of the *Fourth*, Lutoslawski's culminating symphony, is elliptical, its broodingly atmospheric opening building to an almost Waltonian lyrical cantilena and a darkly passionate climax. This slowly disintegrates until a brief, emphatically rhythmic coda produces a sudden resolution. It is a remarkable piece, aurally fascinating as well as gripping. Salonen gives deeply committed, passionate accounts of both this and the dramatic *Third Symphony*, also built in one continuous span. Here he challenges the composer's own interpretation, and in *Les espaces du sommeil* Salonen provides a different slant from the composer himself, making it – with the help of John Shirley-Quirk as an understanding soloist – much more evocative and sensuous in full and well-balanced sound.

Symphony No. 3; (i) *Variations on a theme of Paganini;* (ii) *Les espaces du sommeil;* (iii) *Paroles tissées.*

(BB) *** Naxos Dig. 8.553423 [id.]. (i) Bernd Glemser; (ii) Adam Kruszewski; (iii) Piotr Kusiewicz; Polish Nat. RSO (Katowice), Antoni Wit.

The earliest piece here, the *Paganini variations* for two pianos, comes from 1941; during this period Lutoslawski played as a duo with a fellow composer, Andrzej Panufnik, in occupied Warsaw. But in 1978 the composer rearranged the piece for piano and orchestra. This and the *Third Symphony* from 1982 – arguably one of his finest works – are well played and recorded. Less persuasive, perhaps, is *Les espaces du sommeil* (the soloist is a bit forward, though he sings well). In the *Paroles tissées* the singer is less at ease both with the musical idiom and with the French language. All the same, this well-filled CD is recommendable in every other respect.

Symphony No. 4;(i) *Chain II; Interlude; Partita. Musique funèbre.*

(BB) *** Naxos Dig. 8.553202 [id.]. (i) Bakowski; Polish Nat. RSO, Wit.

This is the most approachable of the first issues in Naxos's adventurous Lutoslawski series. The *Symphony No. 4* is his culminating masterpiece which, in its concentration over two linked movements, seems to echo Sibelius's *Seventh.* The darkly intense *Funeral music* in memory of Bartók is another beautiful and concentrated work, while the two violin concertante works, *Chain II* and *Partita*, here come with the separating *Interlude*, similarly thoughtful, which Lutoslawski wrote as a link. In almost every way, not least in the playing of the violinist, Krzysztow Bakowski, these Polish performances match and even outshine earlier recordings conducted by the composer, helped by full, brilliant sound.

Paganini variations (arr. Ptasazynska).

*** Chandos Dig. CHAN 9398 [id.]. Safri Duo & Slovak Piano Duo – BARTOK: *Sonata for 2 pianos and percussion* ***; HELWEG: *American fantasy.* **

A slight piece from Lutoslawski's youth, dressed up by Marta Ptasazynska for the same forces as the Bartók *Sonata*. It is brilliantly played and no less remarkably recorded at a Danish Radio concert. There is enthusiastic applause, which is understandable, and whistling, which is unfortunate.

Lyatoshynsky, Boris (1895–1968)

Symphony No. 1 in A min., Op. 2; Overture on 4 Ukrainian themes, Op. 20; Poem of reunification, Op. 40.
*** Russian Disc Dig. RDCD 11055 [id.]. Ukrainian State SO, Vladimir Gnedash.

Symphonies Nos. 2, Op. 26; 3 in B min., Op. 50.
*** Marco Polo Dig. 8.223540 [id.]. Ukrainian State SO, Theodore Kuchar.

Symphonies Nos. 4 in B flat min., Op. 63; 5 in C ('Slavonic'), Op. 67.
*** Marco Polo Dig. 8.223541 [id.]. Ukrainian State SO, Theodore Kuchar.

Symphony No. 4 in B flat min., Op. 63; (i) *On the banks of the Vistula, Op. 59;* (ii) *Lyric poem.*
** Russian Disc Dig. RDCD 11062 [id.]. Ukrainian State SO, Igor Blazhkov; (i) Viktor Sirenko; (ii) Fedor Glushchenko.

Lyatoshynsky began writing his *First Symphony* immediately after the First World War, while he was still studying with Glière in Kiev, and it is a well-crafted, confident score that inhabits the world of Russian post-nationalism, Strauss and Scriabin. It abounds in contrapuntal elaboration and abundant orchestral rhetoric. The *Second Symphony* followed in 1936, but its air of pessimism did not sit well in post-*Lady Macbeth* Russia and it was not premièred until 1964, when it was still out of tune with the prevailing Soviet ideological climate. The *Third* is a decade or more later (1951), some three years after the Zhdanov affair had plunged Soviet composers into temporary paralysis. Lyatoshynsky was still denounced during this period for his 'formalism, decadence, aggression, sadism and cacophony' – not bad going. Although the *Third Symphony* tries hard to be a good Soviet symphony, it does not wholly ring true. (Incidentally, Mravinsky's recording of it, coupled with the Shostakovich *Festival overture*, Liadov's *Enchanted lake* and *Baba-Yaga*, is available on Russian Disc RD CD10900.)

The *Fourth Symphony* (1963) reflects something of the cultural thaw in the Soviet Union and is more directly Shostakovichian than its predecessors. Its middle movement depicts what must be a mysterious, chimerical city to a Ukrainian (just as it is a source of wonder to everyone else), namely, Bruges. There is striking use of bells and celesta, and at times a suggestion of Messiaen. The *Fifth (Slavonic)* certainly pays tribute to his master in using the Rus theme, *Il'ya Mourametz*, as well as a wide variety of Russian, Bulgarian and Serbian liturgical melodies. It aspires to explore the common roots of the Slavonic peoples; hence its title. There are many touches of colour and some token modernity, but basically this looks back to earlier masters – Glière, Rimsky-Korsakov and the Russian post-nationalists.

Those with exploratory tastes will find much to interest them in these symphonies, provided they are not expecting masterpieces. As far as performances are concerned, the Ukraine orchestra obviously is inside this music, and none of the playing is second rate. The Marco Polo recordings are more than marginally superior to the Russian Disc, and the performances sound much better rehearsed than is usually the case with this label, while the odd fillers on the Russian Discs are not of sufficient interest to tip the scales in their favour.

McCabe, John (born 1939)

(i) *Symphony No. 2;* (ii) *The Chagall windows;* (i; iii) *Notturni ed alba.*
(N) (M) *** EMI CDM5 67120-2 [id.]. (i) CBSO, Frémaux; (ii) Hallé O, Loughran; (iii) Jill Gomez.

John McCabe is a composer who refuses to worry too much about fashion. These are warm, approachable and atmospheric works, which should communicate immediately to most music-lovers, if only because McCabe in his chosen idiom is often intent on charming the listener's ear, even when his argument is far from simple. The *Symphony*, in contrasted sections, fast and slow, within a single-movement framework, has an underlying bitterness to it, an expression of tension not entirely resolved. *Notturni ed alba*, with its lovely writing for the soprano, is a setting of Latin words, which yet inspire often passionate music, exciting sounds, a joy in sonorities. Fine committed performances of these two works, richly recorded. The commissioning of *The Chagall windows* by the Hallé, his inspiration and composition, not to mention a visit to Jerusalem, and the stained-glass windows designed by Chagall to symbolize the twelve tribes of Israel, were vividly depicted in a TV programme, and this colourful recording first appeared soon after. McCabe used the visual stimulus as his starting point, but the result, readily approachable, is satisfying on its own musical terms. Loughran's vigorous direction adds to the attractiveness of the piece.

String quartets Nos. 3, 4 & 5.
*** Hyperion Dig. CDA 67078 [id.]. Vanbrugh Qt.

Few twentieth-century string quartets have such a haunting opening as John McCabe's masterly *Third*, written in 1979; this indelibly simple phrase resonates throughout the *Variants* of the first movement, which alternate between intense slow sections and quixotic and sometimes aggressive faster passages. Two chimerical Scherzi frame the central *Romanza*, passionate and restless, and the work ends with a Passacaglia which 'derives its overall shape and flow from the concept of a lakeland stream', tumbling down in irregular patterns until the return of that memorable opening motive leads to a wonderful sense of calm. The single-movement *Fourth Quartet* (1982) is hardly less compelling. It again uses variation form and opens with pianissimo evocation as the main theme rises and falls chromatically. Its treatment is at times serene, at others very vigorous indeed. Once again the close is comparatively peaceful, with an expressive cello soliloquy. The *Fifth Quartet* (1989) is programmatic and, as the very beginning makes plain, was inspired by a series of Graham Sutherland's aquatints called *The Bees*. We follow these small but energetic creatures through larval and hatching stages, the first flight, the partnership of bee and flower, a wild nest, the expulsion and killing of an enemy intruder, and finally a domestic fight between workers and drones, which ends brusquely and positively. The aural results are most intriguing and require much virtuosity from the players, which is readily forthcoming. Indeed, these three remarkable works could hardly be presented with greater concentration or more commitment, and the recording is first class.

5 Bagatelles; Haydn variations; Studies Nos. 3 (Gaudi);4 (Aubade); 6 (Mosaic); Variations, Op. 22.

(N) *** British Music Society Dig. BMS 424DC [id.]. Composer.

John McCabe was born at Huyton near Liverpool, and the Royal Liverpool Philharmonic Orchestra celebrated his 60th birthday with performances of two of his large-scale works, including the spectacular *Concerto for orchestra*. It is good to have the reissues of his orchestral music. However, the British Music Society have now published a major survey of his piano music, from the early *Variations* (1963) to the much more complex *Haydn variations* of 1983, while the pianistically exploratory *Studies* span the decade between 1970 and 1980. The early *Variations* use a theme encompassing a tri-tone (and thus provide a link with the structure of the *First Symphony*, written two years later). The development is not difficult to follow, but the later *Haydn variations* are much more complex and individual, and made less approachable for the listener in that the Haydn theme (from the *Piano sonata in G minor*, Hob XVI:44) does not appear until more than halfway into the work. The *Bagatelles*, five brief vignettes, in the words of the composer 'were written to a request for not-too-difficult 12-note pieces', but the third and sixth *Studies* are extended works, architecturally inspired. McCabe is a formidable pianist and is obviously an ideal exponent of his own music, which is highly atmospheric in pianistic terms, but intellectually stimulating rather than lyrical in the melodic sense. This is not for the faint-hearted, but repeated listening undoubtedly brings its own rewards. Excellent recording.

MacCunn, Hamish (1868–1916)

Concert overture: *The Land of the Mountain and the Flood.*

(B) *** CfP CD-CFP 4635. RSNO, Gibson – GERMAN: *Welsh rhapsody;* HARTY: *With the wild geese;* SMYTH: *Wreckers overture.* ***

Concert overture: *The Land of the Mountain and the Flood; The Dowie Dens o'Yarrow; The Ship o' the Fiend. Cantata:* (i) *The Lay of the Last Minstrel: Breathes there the man; O Caledonia! Jeannie Deans* (opera): excerpts.

(N) *** Hyperion Dig. CDA 66815 [id.]. BBC Scottish SO, Martyn Brabbins; (i) with Watson, Milne, MacDougal, Sidholm, Gadd, Danby, Scottish Opera Ch.

Hamish MacCunn was the son of a Greenock shipowner and proved something of a musical prodigy, composing an oratorio (uncompleted) at the age of twelve. For many years his name has been kept alive by Sir Alexander Gibson's dramatically sympathetic account of his colourful and melodramatic concert overture, *The Land of the Mountain and the Flood*, written when he was only eighteen. It is a very well-constructed piece, with a memorable tune which became a signature tune for a Scottish TV series. Martyn Brabbins and the BBC Scottish Orchestra, in a brilliant new performance, give it fresh life, and the Chandos recording has more range and sparkle than the (fully acceptable) CfP version.

The Dowie Dens o' Yarrow is a very similar piece, with comparable rhythmic impetus and another attractive secondary theme, given to the oboe. The even more atmospheric *Ship o' the Fiend* uses both solo horn and oboe most evocatively at the opening, then introduces another endearing lyrical cello theme reminiscent of *The Land of the Mountain and the Flood*. Thus the three works are in many ways linked, and are all worth hearing in performances as committed and convincing as these.

MacCunn's opera, *Jeannie Deans* was premièred in 1894 by the touring Carl Rosa Opera, and stayed in that company's repertoire until the 1920s; it since has been twice revived by others. The libretto is ingenuous, but it is a tuneful and colourful piece with plenty of musical vitality. One thinks at times of a Scottish Edward German, but sometimes of Boughton too. Effie's aria, *Oh that I again could see* (she is imprisoned in the Tolbooth), and the following *Lullaby* are touchingly sung here by Janice Watson, and the choral contribution is very spirited. Some of the singing is vibrato-afflicted, but the performance is thoroughly alive and freshly enjoyable. The excerpt from the cantata, *The Lay of the Last Minstrel*, brings a suitably vigorous closing chorus, *O Caledonia!*

MacDowell, Edward (1861–1908)

Piano concertos Nos. 1 in A min., Op. 15; 2 in D min., Op. 23.
❀ *** Olympia Dig. OCD 353 [id.]. Donna Amato, LPO, Paul Freeman.

Of MacDowell's two *Piano concertos* the *First* is marginally the lesser of the two: the melodic content, though very pleasing, is slightly less memorable than in the *Second*. This is a delightful piece, fresh and tuneful, redolent of Mendelssohn and Saint-Saëns. Donna Amato's scintillating performance is entirely winning, and she is equally persuasive in the *A minor*. This music needs polish and elegance as well as fire, and Paul Freeman's accompaniments supply all three. The recording, made in All Saints', Tooting, has an agreeable ambient warmth. A highly rewarding coupling in all respects.

Piano concerto No. 2 in D min., Op. 23.
*** Chesky CD 76 [id.]. Earl Wild, RCA Victor SO, Freccia – RACHMANINOV: *Piano concerto No. 3*. ***
(M) **(*) RCA 09026 64820-2 [id.]. Van Cliburn, Chicago SO, Walter Hendl – BRAHMS: *Piano concerto No. 2*. **(*)

(i) *Piano concerto No. 2 in D min., Op. 23. Woodland sketches: To a wild rose, Op. 51/1.*
(M) **(*) [RCA 60420-2-RG]. Van Cliburn, (i) Chicago SO, Hendl – SCHUMANN: *Concerto*. ***

Earl Wild never played more brilliantly or more appealingly on record than in these coupled recordings of MacDowell and Rachmaninov, engineered by Decca in the mid-1960s. The performance of the MacDowell concerto is technically dazzling, and so assured and sympathetic is Wild's style that the concerto is almost made to sound a masterpiece. Massimo Freccia provides excellent support, and Wild is much better balanced and recorded than Van Cliburn on RCA.

Van Cliburn is not helped by a recording balance which consistently makes him sound rather too loud; but the performance otherwise has the advantage of warm Chicago acoustics, and Walter Hendl's vigorous and sympathetic support, with its fire and spontaneity, triumphs over the technical problems. The Scherzo is superb. The newer coupling with Brahms is certainly worth considering, especially by admirers of this fine pianist.

On the alternative coupling MacDowell's most famous solo piano piece makes a pleasing encore, though the performance is a trifle cool. (This record is currently available in the USA only.)

PIANO MUSIC

Fireside tales, Op. 61; New England idylls, Op. 62; Sea pieces, Op. 55; Woodland sketches, Op. 51.
**(*) Marco Polo Dig. 8.223631 [id.]. James Baragallo.

MacDowell's most famous piano piece opens this recital: *To a wild rose* (named by his wife) is the first of the ten *Woodland sketches*. They are all pleasant if not distinctive vignettes, most lasting a little over a minute. The other three suites are very similar. Not a CD to listen to all at once but to be dipped into; one can appreciate that James Baragallo is a thoroughly sympathetic exponent, and he is well recorded.

McEwen, John Blackwood (1868–1948)

Three Border ballads: *Coronach; The Demon lover; Grey Galloway*.
(N) *** Chandos Dig. CHAN 9241 [id.]. LPO, Alasdair Mitchell.

McEwen was a much more flamboyantly romantic composer than MacCunn. His orchestral tapestries are at once sumptuous and translucent in texture, and show a remarkably individual feeling for colour. These three *Border ballads*, written between 1906 and 1908, are symphonic poems, well-stocked with distinctive ideas, and with a strong Lisztian inheritance. *The Demon lover*, the most ambitious in scale (some might feel too ambitious), has a kind of luscious melodramatic post-Wagnerian chromaticism that isn't too far from the world of Scriabin. Even the first to be written, *Coronach*, has a sensuous feeling that one associates with more southern climes, yet the nobility of its main theme also suggests links with Parry and Elgar. The performances here are warmly sympathetic and very well played and recorded, and almost convince one that these works are masterpieces.

A Solway Symphony; (i) *Hills o'heather; Where the wild thyme blows.*
*** Chandos Dig. CHAN 9345 [id.]. (i) Moray Welsh; LPO, Mitchell.

Sir John McEwen wrote his highly evocative *Solway Symphony* in 1911, a triptych of seascapes marked by magically transparent orchestration and crisply controlled argument. McEwen was influenced by the folksong movement – notably here in *Hills o'heather* with its hints of reels – but the flavour is quite individual, with occasional echoes of Sibelius in the sparer moments. Above all, this is warm-hearted music. The first of the three movements of the symphony, *Spring tide*, is built on a striking motif, argued with clean-cut directness. The second movement, *Moonlight*, is developed, Sibelius-like, over a gently nagging ostinato, while the finale, *The sou'west wind*, opens with brassy exuberance in galloping compound time, and only later develops a stormy side, before ending darkly in F sharp minor. *Hills o'heather* is a charming movement for cello and orchestra, while *Where the wild thyme blows* uses slow pedal points to sustain harmonically adventurous arguments. The performances, conducted by Alasdair Mitchell, who edited the scores, are outstanding, a well-deserved tribute to a neglected composer who was far more than an academic. The recording is sumptuously atmospheric.

Machaut, Guillaume de

(*c*. 1300–1377)

Ballades, motets, rondeaux & virelais: *Amours me fait desirer; Dame se vous m'estés lointeinne; De Bon Espoir – Puis que la douce rousee; De toutes flours; Douce dame jolie; Hareu! hareu! le feu; Ma fin est mon commencement; Mes esperis se combat; Phyton le mervilleus serpent; Quant j'ay l'espart; Quant je suis mis au retour; Quant Theseus – Ne quier veoir; Se ma dame m'a guerpy; Se je souspir; Trop plus est belle – Biauté paree – Je ne sui mie certeins.*

(M) *** Virgin Veritas/EMI VED5 61284-2 (2). Early Music Cons. of L., David Munrow (within Recital: '*The art of courtly love*' ***).

This collection is within 'Guillaume Machaut and his age', which is itself part of David Munrow's wide-ranging collection, 'The art of courtly love'. Treasures here include cantatas with James Bowman and Charles Brett beautifully matched as soloists. Everything reveals both the remarkable individuality of Guillaume de Machaut as a highly influential composer who spanned the first three-quarters of the fourteenth century, and the life and energy which Munrow consistently brought to early music. Excellent transfers.

Messe de Nostre Dame (with Plainsong for the Proper of the Mass of Purification for the Blessed Virgin (Candlemas)).

**(*) HM Dig. HMC 901590 [id.]. Soloists, Ens. Organum, Marcel Pérès.

(N) (B) *** HM Dig. Trio HMX 290891.93 (3) (as above) Ens.Organum, Pérès – OCKEGHEM: *Requiem;* HILDEGARD: *Laudes of Saint Ursula.* ***

Messe de Nostre Dame; Le Lai de la Fonteinne (The Lay of the Fountain); Rondeau: *Ma fin est mon commencement (My end is my beginning).*

**(*) Hyperion Dig. CDA 66358 [id.]. James, Stafford, Covey-Crump, Potter, Padmore, Nixon, Hillier, George, Hilliard Ens., Paul Hillier.

Messe de Nostre Dame. Le Livre dou Voir dit (excerpts): *Plourez dames; Nes qu'on porroit* (ballades); *Sans cuer dolens* (rondeau); *Le lay de bonne esperance; Puis qu'en oubli* (rondeau); *Dix et sept cinq* (rondeau).

(BB) ***(*) Naxos Dig. 8.553833 [id.]. Oxford Camerata, Jeremy Summerly.

With his *Messe de Nostre Dame* (dedicated to the Virgin Mary), Guillaume de Machaut wrote the first known complete setting of the Ordinary of the Mass: *Kyrie*, *Gloria*, *Credo*, *Sanctus* and *Agnus Dei*. He chose to finish with his own simple interpolation: *Ite missa est*, which very briefly tells us, 'The mass is ended; thanks be to God.' Machaut's writing is full of extraordinary, dissonant clashes and sudden harmonic twists which are immediately resolved, so the music is both serene and plangently stimulating: here is an epoch-making work of great originality. Both the Hilliard Ensemble and the Oxford Camerata present the Mass as it stands (and therefore they have room for extra items), whereas Marcel Pérès has inserted the plainsong for the Proper of the Mass, taken from the Candlemas liturgy for the Purification of the Virgin, which is presented in the same florid style as is Machaut's setting of the Ordinary.

Of the three performances here, Jeremy Summerly's account is undoubtedly the most eloquently serene; it is beautifully controlled and modulated, rather after the fashion of the famous Willcocks/King's College accounts of the Byrd Masses. The harmonic pungencies are cleanly presented but unexaggerated and – compared with Hillier and (especially) Pérès – the musical lines, although by no means bland, flow in relative tranquillity. The singers apparently experimented freely with plicas – notational signs indicating some kind of ornament – the meaning of which is uncertain but which appear frequently; but there is none of the audacious decoration which is so striking on the Harmonia Mundi version.

Hillier's approach certainly does not lack repose or linear beauty, but he presses the music onwards with a much greater sense of drama than obtains in Oxford. His *Kyrie* is three minutes shorter than Summerly's, and the *Gloria* brings freely passionate accelerandos, which are highly involving but may or may not be authentic. The Hilliard group is superbly recorded with a strong presence, and there is no doubt that the music's unexpected dissonances are more dramatically brought out here than on Naxos.

However, the boldness of effect produced by the Ensemble Organum under Marcel Pérès in every way dramatically upstages its two competitors. In his (confident and very interesting) notes, Pérès laments that 'The art of ornamentation is little practised by performers today, which is much to be regretted. Ornamentation is essential, for it creates the active force of the work.' And in this performance it certainly does – to an extraordinary degree.

The Ensemble Organum bring a distinctly Arab flavour with the dark pungency of male timbre and twirling embellishments to the ornamentation. The singing itself is powerfully resonant and the dissonances ring out boldly. After this the other performances sound a bit pale. Certainly this is a record to hear and be thrilled by, if hardly a 'library' addition for a collection. The recording is splendid. This CD additionally comes in a slip case as part of a Harmonia Mundi Trio at budget price which is highly recommendable, for the recordings of Hildegard and Ockeghem are equally arresting.

On Naxos the chansons were recorded, equally effectively, at the BBC's Maida Vale studio; they celebrate Machaut as poet/lover as well as composer and, at its modest price, the disc is worth having for these alone. Indeed *Le Livre dou voir dit* is one of the most remarkable cycles of poems of the Middle Ages. Its 9,094 lines of verse, arranged in octosyllabic rhyming couplets, were inspired by the passionate love between the elderly composer (Machaut was in his sixties when he wrote all the music here) and his adolescent student admirer, Péronne d'Armetières. It draws on their correspondence, which frequently shared poems, some set to music by Machaut and intended for his beloved to sing. The music itself is lighter in lyrical feeling than the Mass and its melodic and harmonic style, while recognizably similar, is far less plangent. This is one of Naxos's real bargains.

The solo singing in the extra items on the Hyperion disc is very impressive indeed, as might be expected from the cast-list. *Le Lai de la Fonteinne* is another elaborate poem of 12 stanzas in praise of the Virgin, six polyphonic, six monodic, beautifully sung by Mark Padmore, Rogers Covey-Crump and John Potter, while the shorter rondeau, an expressive piece if restlessly so, is ingeniously constructed, and is a 'crab' canon by inversion, in that the imitating part, instead of being presented straightforwardly, is written backwards and upside down – appropriately so, to fit the text: 'My end is my beginning.'

Mackenzie, Alexander (1847–1935)

Benedictus, Op. 37/3; Burns – 2nd Scottish rhapsody, Op. 24; Coriolanus (incidental music): *suite, Op. 61; The cricket on the hearth: Overture, Op. 62; Twelfth Night* (incidental music): *Overture/suite, Op. 40.*

*** Hyperion Dig. CDA 66764 [id.]. BBC Scottish SO, Martyn Brabbins.

Sir Alexander Mackenzie wrote in the Stanford/Elgar/Parry tradition rather than showing any strong Scottish traits. However, in the *Burns rhapsody* he uses three Scottish folk tunes quite felicitously, notably '*Scots! wha hae*', which is very emphatic. The second movement has charm, and indeed Mackenzie's own lyrical gift is quite striking in the jolly, at times Sullivanesque *Cricket on the hearth overture* (which also shows his deft orchestral skill), and of course the *Benedictus* with a melody typical of its time. The incidental music for *Twelfth Night* is in the form of an overture, subdivided into six sections, with a Shakespeare quotation for each to identify its mood. These vignettes are attractively scored and have considerable character. The whole programme is presented with commitment and polish by the BBC Scottish Symphony Orchestra and makes a very agreeable hour and a quarter of not too demanding listening. The recording is excellent.

Scottish concerto, Op. 55.

(N) *** Hyperion Dig. CDA 67023. Steven Osborne, BBC Scottish SO, Brabbins – TOVEY: *Piano concerto in A.* ***

Hyperion's imaginative series of Romantic piano concertos here offers two works by composers associated with Scotland. Unlike Tovey, Sir Alexander Mackenzie was Scottish by birth – Sir Donald Tovey (best-known for his analytical essays) by adoption. Built on Scottish themes, Mackenzie's *Concerto*, premiered by Paderewski, centres round its lyrical slow movement, framed by a rhapsodic first movement and a dance finale based on *Green grow the rushes O.* The young Scottish pianist, Steven Osborne, is a brilliant advocate, Brabbins a natural partner.

MacMillan, James (born 1959)

(i). . . *as others see us; 3 Dawn rituals; Untold;* (ii) *Veni, veni, Emmanuel (concerto for percussion and orchestra);* (iii) *After the Tryst (miniature fantasy for violin and piano).*

✽ *** RCA Catalyst Dig. 09026 61916-2 [id.]. (i) Scottish CO (members), composer; (ii) Evelyn Glennie, SCO, Saraste; (iii) Ruth Crouch, composer.

Veni, veni, Emmanuel, written for Evelyn Glennie, instantly reveals the composer's rare gift of communicating with electric intensity to a wide audience, rare in new music today. His dedication, strongly motivated by his devout Catholicism and his equally passionate left-wing stance, invariably colours what he writes, making us share not his precise beliefs but the spiritual intensity that goes with them. In *Veni, veni, Emmanuel* MacMillan has written a concerto for percussion that in its energy as well as its colour consistently reflects both the virtuosity and the charismatic personality of Evelyn Glennie. Taking the Advent plainsong of the title as his basis, he reflects in his continuous 26-minute sequence the theological implications behind the period between Advent and Easter. The five contrasted sections are in a sort of arch form, with the longest and slowest section in the middle. The very close of the work brings a crescendo of chimes intended to reflect the joy of Easter in the Catholic service and the celebration of the Resurrection. In this superb recording the orchestra as well as Evelyn Glennie play with both brilliance and total commitment, if not with quite the extra thrill that at the end is experienced in live performances. In the fill-up works – brief pieces marked by the same dramatic intensity – MacMillan himself as conductor inspires strong, positive performances from various groups of SCO players. With first-rate, atmospheric sound – *Veni, veni, Emmanuel* recorded in Usher Hall, Edinburgh, the rest in City Hall, Glasgow – this is an outstanding first issue on BMG's Catalyst label.

(i) *The Berserking* (a concerto for piano and orchestra); (ii) *Britannia; Sinfonietta; Sowetan spring*.
*** RCA Dig. 09026 68328-2 [id.]. Royal SNO; (i) with Peter Donohoe, Stenz; (ii) composer.

James MacMillan is a composer with a demon when it comes to vivid communication. In their widely contrasted ways, all four of the works here have an agenda, political and social, yet the high-voltage electricity which results is very different from propaganda music, whether of the right or left, when so colourfully each work reflects the composer's intensely personal responses. So *The Berserking* – a term drawn from frenzied Viking warriors – was written in response to MacMillan's frustration as an ardent Scot to his compatriots' 'seeming facility for shooting themselves in the foot'. The manically energetic first movement of this 33-minute piano concerto – brilliantly played by Peter Donohoe – may represent 'swaggering futility', but it is exciting music in its own right, and it resolves on two slower, more contemplative movements which finally bring peace in a modal mood not all that distant from Vaughan Williams. Similarly *Britannia*, with its ironic references to English music from *Knees up Mother Brown* to *God save the Queen* and *Cockaigne*, proves to be a thoroughly enjoyable Ivesian fantasy. Implanted in the meditations of the one-movement *Sinfonietta* is a violent, ironic reference to an Ulster marching song, which serves to intensify the beauty of the rest. Only the very serious agenda of *Sowetan spring* results in an obsessive piece with too much reliance on minimalism, though that too is memorable. With superb performances, brilliantly recorded, this is a disc to attract more than the devotee of new music.

The Confession of Isobel Gowdie; Tryst
*** Koch/Schwann Dig. 3-1050-2 [id.]. BBC Scottish SO, Maksymiuk.

Inspired by the horrific execution in 1662 of Isobel Gowdie, tortured into confessing herself a witch, MacMillan has used the story as a metaphor for twentieth-century witch-hunting, including what he sees as resurgent fascism today. The result is rather like Vaughan Williams's *Tallis fantasia* updated and then invaded by Stravinsky's *Rite of spring*. The other piece on the disc, *Tryst* – marginally longer at 28 minutes – has similar qualities. In juxtaposition it emerges as the obverse of *Isobel Gowdie*, similarly a massive single movement in arch form. This time the music works from violence at the beginning and end to a long slow meditation in the middle, again with echoes of ecclesiastical chant a basic element. Maksymiuk proves a dedicated interpreter.

Triduum, an Easter triptych, Part 1: (i) *The world's ransoming* (for cor anglais and orchestra); Part 2: (ii) *Cello concerto*.
(N) *** BIS Dig. CD 989 [id.].(i) Christine Pendrill; (ii) Raphael Wallfisch; BBC Scottish SO, Osmo Vänskä.

The world's ransoming and the *Cello concerto*, each self-contained, are the first two in a sequence of three related works representing MacMillan's response to Christ's Passion and the Easter story. *The world's ransoming*, with its poignant writing for cor anglais set against violent interruptions, provides the emotional prelude and is intensely involving music, often wild in its expressionism. In its energy it mixes styles and idiom with abandon. This is religious inspiration at the farthest remove from that of John Tavener or Arvo Pärt, but just as likely to strike a chord with listeners of whatever faith, or none. Christine Pendrill is the superb soloist, and though Raphael Wallfisch is just as expressive as the soloist in the *Cello concerto*, conveying Christ's agony, sadly the balance sets him at a distance. This three-movement work, a response to Good Friday and the Crucifixion, is even more violent – using thunder-sheet amid heavy brass and percussion, the embodiment of earthquake and storm, both physical and spiritual. Brilliant performances, spaciously recorded.

Triduum, an Easter triptych, Part 3: *Symphony (Vigil)*.
(N) *** BIS Dig. CD 900 [id.]. Fine Arts Brass Ens., BBC Scottish SO, Osmo Vänskä.

The *Symphony (Vigil)* in three movements – *Light*, *Tuba insonet salutaris* and *Water* – forms the climax of the *Triduum* triptych, longer than either of the preceding works. Predictably it moves from darkness to light, with violence at the start of the first movement echoing the music of the *Cello concerto*. The second movement brings fanfares spread spaciously, the last trump graphically portrayed, while the resolution of the final movement, longer than the other two put together, brings no easy salvation. Even the meditative close still implies the memory of pain, ever more pauseful, fading into nothing. Here too as in the companion disc Vänskä draws brilliant, warmly committed playing from the

BBC Scottish Symphony orchestra, vividly recorded.

Veni, veni Emmanuel; Tryst.
(N) (BB) *** Naxos Dig. 8.554167 [id.]. Colin Currie, Ulster O, Takuo Yuasa.

With Colin Currie, the young prizewinning percussionist, matching his compatriot predecessor, Evelyn Glennie, in flair and panache, the Naxos version of the brilliant and dramatic percussion concerto, *Veni veni, Emmanuel*, cannot be recommended too highly. Takuo Yuasa is a strong and persuasive conductor, not just in *Veni, veni Emmanuel*, but in the earlier work, *Tryst*, an extended and colourful fantasy in five sections built on a setting of a Scottish song. Recorded in the helpful acoustic of the Ulster Hall, Belfast, the sound is exceptionally full and vivid, matching the excellent playing of the orchestra.

(i) *Seven last words from the Cross* (for choir and string orchestra); (ii) *Cantos sagrados* (for choir and organ).
*** RCA Catalyst Dig. 09026 68125-2 [id.]. Polyphony, with (i) LCO, composer; (ii) Christopher Bowers-Broadbent.

Seven last words from the Cross is a modern choral counterpart of Haydn's masterpiece. On one level it is just another of the slow-moving, easily mellifluous expressions of religious devotion that have had such spectacular success on CD. Each of these seven movements for chorus and strings intensifies each message from the Cross in dramatic contrasts and illustration. In four of them the title-words are amplified by liturgical texts in Latin or English, with the layering of musical ideas matching that of the words. Consistently they bring out the meaning so as to make one share Christ's suffering. *Cantos sagrados* illustrates the layering device again. In each of the three movements MacMillan juxtaposes poems by Spanish-American authors (in translation) alongside traditional Latin texts, setting the violence and tragedy of political persecution against the consolations of faith. So the last and most poignant of the three, about a firing-squad, resolves on the words, ever gentler, of one of the executioners, 'Forgive me, *compañero*.' The idiom is clear and approachable, but hardly conventional. The performances, vividly recorded, are electrifying, with the players of the London Chamber Orchestra and the organist Christopher Bowers-Broadbent (in *Cantos sagrados*), as well as the fine singers of Stephen Layton's group, Polyphony, consistently inspired by the music and its composer-conductor. Characteristically, MacMillan's notes are terse, clear and helpful.

Maconchy, Elizabeth (born 1907)

Concertinos Nos. 1 (1945); 2 (1984).
*** Hyperion Dig. CDA 66634 [id.]. Thea King, ECO, Wordsworth – ARNOLD: *Clarinet concertos* etc.; BRITTEN: *Clarinet concerto movement.* ***

The two Maconchy *Concertinos*, each in three movements and under ten minutes long, have a characteristic terseness, sharp and intense, that runs no risk whatever of seeming short-winded. Not only Thea King but the ECO under Barry Wordsworth bring out the warmth as well as the rhythmic drive, as in the other attractive works on the disc.

String quartets Nos. 1–4.
*** Unicorn Dig. DKPCD 9080 [id.]. Hanson Qt.
String quartets Nos. 5–8.
*** Unicorn Dig. DKPCD 9081 [id.]. Bingham Qt.
String quartets Nos. 9–13.
*** Unicorn Dig. DKPCD 9082 [id.]. Mistry Qt.

All these works testify to the quality of Maconchy's mind and her inventive powers. She speaks of the quartet as 'an impassioned argument', and there is no lack of either in these finely wrought and compelling pieces. Even if there is not the distinctive personality of a Bartók or a Britten, her music is always rewarding. Though the playing may occasionally be wanting in tonal finesse, all three groups play with total commitment and are well recorded.

Madetoja, Leevi (1887–1947)

Symphonies Nos. 1 in F, Op. 29; 2 in E flat, Op. 35; 3 in A, Op. 55; Comedy overture, Op. 53; Okon Fuoko, Op. 58; Pohjolaisia suite, Op. 52.
(N) (M) *** Chandos Dig. CHAN 7097(2) [id.]. Iceland SO, Petri Sakari.

Symphonies Nos. 1 in F, Op. 29; (i) *2 in E flat, Op. 35*; (ii) *3 in A, Op. 55;* (iii) *Comedy overture, Op. 53*; (iv) *Okon Fuoko, Op. 58; Pohjalaisa Suite, Op. 52.*(i) *Kullervo, Op. 15.*
(N) (B) **(*) Finlandia/Warner Double 4509 99967-2 (2). Finnish Radio SO, Segerstam, (ii) Saraste, (i) Tampere PO, Rautio; (iii) Helsinki PO, Panula; (iv) Finnish Radio SO, Segerstam, Okko Kamu.

Apart from Sibelius himself, with whom Madetoja briefly studied, there are many influences to be discerned in the *First Symphony* (1915–26) – figures like Strauss, the Russian post-nationalists, Reger and above all the French, for whom Madetoja had a lifelong admiration. The *Second Symphony* (1917–18), composed at about the same time as Sibelius was working on the definitive version of his *Fifth*, is expertly fashioned and despite the obvious debts there is some individuality too. The *Third* was written in the mid 1920s while Madetoja was living in Houilles, just outside Paris. Gallic elements surface most strongly in this piece (he had hoped to study with Vincent d'Indy and as a conductor championed both d'Indy and Debussy, as well as such contemporaries as Szymanowski and Janáček). The French critic Henri-Claude Fantapié mentioned Madetoja's affinities with that 'little known but important branch of French music which evolved in the shadow of impressionism' and which was represented by Roussel, Magnard or Paul Le Flem. The *Comedy overture* (1923) is an absolute delight, and both the suite from the opera *Pohjalaisa (The Ostrobothnians)* and the ballet–pantomime *Okon Fuoko* show an exemplary feeling for colour and atmosphere. Now that the excellent Chandos set under Petri Sakari has been transferred to the Double format at mid-price, it deserves to carry our first recommendation. Both the performances and the spacious natural recordings are exemplary and Sakari gets imaginative and sensitive playing from his Reykjavik forces.

No real grumbles about the Finlandia performances, which are well worth the money and will give pleasure, but the Icelandic is the more distinguished of the two and worth the extra cost.

'Meet the composer': Complete songs for male voice choir (52 songs).
(B) *** Finlandia/Warner Double Dig. 0630 19807-2 (2) [(M) id. import]. Helsinki University Ch., Matti Hyökki.

The present Finlandia Double assembles the contents of three previous issues, recorded in 1990–91, devoted to Madetoja's output for male voice choir, and offers no fewer than 52 part-songs, many of them of signal quality. The male voice choir is a popular medium in both Finland and Sweden, and both countries have produced a rich repertory of songs and expert groups to sing them. The Helsinki University Choir is among the very finest, and they certainly sing these pieces with wonderful ensemble and fervour. The notes (by the conductor, Matti Hyökki) provide exemplary background information as well as the texts themselves. Many of the songs have something of the modal quality of Sibelius's output in this genre; and the later songs, which Madetoja composed in the 1940s when ill-health inhibited him from finishing a fourth symphony and a violin concerto, are striking. A rewarding set.

The Ostrobothnians (Pohjalaisa) (complete); *Suite from the opera, Op. 52a.*
(N) (M) *** Finlandia/Warner Dig. 3984 21440-2 (2) [id.]. Jorma Hynninen, Raimio Sirkiä, Monica Groop, Ritva-Liisa Auvinen, Finnish R. Ch; Finnish R. SO, Jukka-Pekka Saraste.

Madetoja's opera dates from the early 1920s and is set in the western Finnish plains of Ostrobothnia which Madetoja knew well, and its central theme is the Bothnian farmer's love of personal liberty and his abhorrence of authoritarian restraints. The nationalist tone of the original play was prompted by the growing Russification of Finland in the period leading up to and including the First World War. In the nineteenth century, the peasantry had been prepared to co-operate with a centrally appointed governor or sheriff, but the brutal authority into which these had turned inspired strong hostility. Against this background of tension, there is a simple love story. Antti, one of the farmers, is imprisoned after a stabbing incident; the first Act centres on his relationship with Maija, and the increased tension between her brother Jussi and the sheriff. In the second, Antti escapes during an attack by the sheriff's thugs, whose leader is soundly beaten by Jussi. In the last Act a chance remark leads the sheriff mistakenly to believe that Jussi was implicated in the escape and the opera ends with Jussi's death at the sheriff's hands. The opera is also interspersed with humorous elements that lighten the mood and lend the work variety. Unlike Merikanto's *Juha*, composed at much the same time, Madetoja's language is not ahead of its time: it springs from much the same soil as most Scandinavian post-nationalists. However, the score makes often imaginative use of folk material and Madetoja's sense of theatre and lyrical gift are in good evidence. *Pohjalaisa* is effective theatre and this new recording completely supersedes the 1975 set under Jorma Panula – also with Hynninen as the hero – both artistically and technically. Like its predecessor it offers excellent teamwork from the soloists, and keen and responsive playing from the Finnish Radio forces under Saraste. The work lasts barely two hours, and the fill-up derives from a 1993 recording.

Magalhães, Filipe de (1571–1652)

Missa O Soberana luz; Motets: *Commissa mea pavesco; Vidi aquam.*
(BB) *** Naxos Dig. 8.553310 [id.]. Ars Nova, Bo Holten – CARDOSO; LOBO *Motets.* ***

Filipe de Magalhães was the youngest of the three great Portuguese composers who all became pupils of Manuel Mendes (*c.* 1547–1605) at Evora in eastern Portugal. The others, Cardoso and Lobo, are also represented in this outstanding concert, but Magalhães was reputedly the favourite pupil. One can see why, listening to his highly individual writing in both the Mass *O Soberana luz* and the two hardly less memorable motets, *Vidi aquam* ('I beheld the water') and *Commissa mea pavesco* ('I tremble at my sins') with its instantly poignant opening. The flowing perfection of the linear writing and the imaginative contrasts of tempo between sections of the Mass are striking enough, but the ravishing beauty of the chorale-like, 'harmonized' passages is even more remarkable. In the Mass the *Sanctus* soars radiantly and the lovely *Benedictus* is equally affecting, only to be capped by the *Agnus Dei*. The Danish performances are wonderfully eloquent and the recording, made at Kasterskirken, Copenhagen, has an ideal ambience and is beautifully clear.

Magnard, Albéric (1865–1914)

Symphonies Nos. 1 in C min., Op. 4; 2 in E, Op. 6.

(N) *** Hyperion Dig. CDA 67030 [id.]. BBC Scottish SO, Ossonce.

Symphonies Nos. 3 in B flat min., Op. 11; 4 in C sharp min., Op. 21.

(N) *** Hyperion Dig. CDA 67040 [id.]. BBC Scottish SO, Ossonce.

Albéric Magnard, the neurotic, self-doubting son of a rich father, is generally remembered as the composer who in 1914, quixotically firing on German invaders, was burnt alive in his chateau, along with many of his manuscripts. This superb set of his four symphonies, neatly fitted on two separately available CDs, easily outshines earlier rivals, with warm, cleanly focused sound. The works, crowned by his *Fourth* and last symphony of 1913, amply confirm him as one of the finest of French symphonists, translating Wagnerian influences in keenly original ways. Excellent notes by Francis Pott.

Mahler, Gustav (1860–1911)

Symphonies Nos. 1–9.

(B) *** Decca Dig./Analogue 430 804-2 (10). Buchanan, Zakai, Chicago Ch. (in No. 2); Dernesch, Ellyn Children's Ch., Chicago Ch. (in No. 3); Te Kanawa (in No. 4); Harper, Popp, Augér, Minton, Watts, Kollo, Shirley-Quirk, Talvela, V. Boys' Ch., V. State Op. Ch. & Singverein (in No. 8); Chicago SO, Solti.

Symphonies Nos. 1–9; 10 (Adagio).

(B) **(*) Ph. 442 050-2 (10). Concg. O, Haitink (with Ameling, Heynis & Netherlands R. Ch. in No. 2; Forrester, Netherlands R. Ch. & St Willibrord Boys' Ch. in No. 3; Ameling in No. 4; Cotrubas, Harper, Van Bork, Finnila, Dieleman, Cochran, Prey, Sotin, Amsterdam Choirs in No. 8).

(N) (BB) *** EMI Digital/Analogue CZS5 72941-2 (11) [id.]. LPO, Tennstedt (with Mathis, Soffel (in No. 2); Wenkel & Southend Boys' Ch. (in No. 3); Lucia Popp (in No. 4); Connell, Wiens, Lott, Schmidt, Denize, Versalle, Hynninen, Sotin, Tiffin School Boys' Ch. (in No. 8); LPO Ch. (in Nos. 2, 3 & 8)).

Symphonies Nos. 1–10.

(B) **(*) DG 435 162-2 (13). Hendricks, Ludwig, Wittek, M. Price, Blegen, Zeumer, Baltsa, Schmidt, Reigel, Prey, Van Dam, Brooklyn Boys' Ch., Westminster Ch., NY Choral Artists, V. Boys' Ch., V. Singverein, V. State Op. Ch., Concg. O, NYPO, or VPO, Bernstein.

Solti's achievement in Mahler has been consistent and impressive, and this reissue is a formidable bargain that will be hard to beat. Nos. 1–4 and 9 are digital recordings, Nos. 5–8 are digitally remastered analogue. Solti draws stunning playing from the Chicago Symphony Orchestra, often pressed to great virtuosity, which adds to the electricity of the music-making; if his rather extrovert approach to Mahler means that deeper emotions are sometimes understated, there is no lack of involvement; and his fiery energy and commitment often carry shock-waves in their trail. All in all, an impressive achievement.

It is a measure of Bernstein's greatness as a Mahler interpreter and the electricity he consistently conveys in these edited live recordings that, despite obvious shortcomings, they so readily add up to more than the sum of their parts. The wilfulness of some of the readings, the heaviness of underlining, the exaggeratedly slow speeds, notably in Nos. 3 and 9, even seem to enrich the total experience. This is a personal statement by one great musician on another, and represents a monumental achievement.

Haitink's set of Mahler *Symphonies* comes at bargain price and offers characteristically refined and well-balanced Philips recording. The performances bring consistently fine playing from the Concertgebouw Orchestra, but Haitink is not by nature an extrovert Mahlerian. While he is always sensitive and thoughtful – and this works well enough in Nos. 1 (his earlier recording is included) and 4 (with Elly Ameling a freshly appealing soloist) and they have an attractive simplicity of approach – Nos. 2 and 8 lack the necessary sense of occasion, and No. 8 also needs greater overall grip and a more expansive recording. No. 5 is fresh and direct (the *Adagietto* a little cool) but No. 6 has more refinement than fire. The finest of the set are the deeply satisfying accounts of No. 3 (with fine contributions from both Maureen Forrester and the choristers) and the finely wrought and intensely convincing performance of No. 7. However, the series is capped by an outstanding performance of No. 9. Here Haitink is at his most inspirational and the last movement has a unique concentration, with its slow tempo maintained to create the greatest intensity of feeling. As usual from Philips, the original recordings are consistently enhanced by the CD transfers, and only No. 8 is technically disappointing.

Tennstedt's complete Mahler cycle is now most temptingly offered in a handsome super-bargain box, with the conductor's photograph on each of the eleven cardboard inners. Tennstedt's interpretations should find many admirers, for they find a convincing middle course between the intensity of Solti's view of Mahler with its voluptuous Chicago sound, or the passionate wilfulness of Bernstein, and the more refined, more introvert manner of Haitink. No. 1 – the first to be recorded in Abbey Road, in 1977 – sets the style of Tennstedt's approach, with textures fresh, the opening evocation of spring comparatively gentle. The precision and directness, however, do not preclude coaxing use of rubato and the finale is spaciously passionate. The *Resurrection*, if less tinglingly dramatic than some, is consistently dedicated. No. 3 is one of the most eloquent of the cycle and No. 4 is hardly less successful, with impressive solo contributions in both. Like Barbirolli, Tennstedt takes a ripe, measured view of the *Fifth*, while the *Sixth* and the two *Nachtmusik* movements of No. 7 are notable for their extra warmth of expressiveness. If the *Eighth* does not have the searing intensity that marks Solti's overwhelming Decca version, Tennstedt's broader, grander view makes at least as powerful an impact, and its great glory is the splendid choral contribution. The *Ninth* brings another performance of warmth and distinction, characteristically underlining nobility rather than any neurotic tensions. The playing is excellent both here and in the *Adagio* of the *Tenth*, and throughout the set the recordings, whether analogue or digital, are impressively full and well balanced. A splendid bargain in every way.

Symphonies Nos. 1 (including *Blumine*); *2–9* (complete); *10 (Adagio)*.

(N) ** Chandos Dig. CHAN 9972 (12) [id.]. Copenhagen Boys' Ch., Danish Nat. Ch. & RSO, Leif Segerstam; (with Tina Kilberg, Kirsten Dolberg in Nos. 2 & 8; Anne Gjevang in Nos. 3 & 8; Eva Johansson in No. 4; Inga Nielsen, Majken, Henrietta Bonde-Hansen, Raimo Sirkiä, Jorma Hynninen, Carsten Stabell, BPO Ch. in No. 8).

The main advantages of the Chandos set are fine playing by a clearly committed and dedicated orchestra and superbly rich and expansive recording. Inner detail is not sharp, but it is not blurred either and the concert-hall feeling means that Mahler's most expansive sounds are superbly contained, notably the brass and chorus in the powerful finale of the *Resurrection Symphony*, although the vocal balance in No. 8, as so often, is less than ideal. Segerstam's is a very relaxed view of Mahler, and he takes us through the Mahlerian pastoral scenery as in an affectionate guided tour. Immediately in the *First Symphony* one notices a lack of grip in the opening evocation and throughout the series the relaxed tempi and Segerstam's lack of firmness mean that although the playing itself is committed and always sensitive there is a loss of sustained intensity. Inner movements are often delightfully coloured, and the famous *Adagio* of the *Fifth Symphony* is warmly atmospheric but very laid back. Similarly Segerstam opens the *Fourth* in the most coaxing manner, but remains very relaxed and the explosive *fortissimo* of the slow movement could be more biting. In the great *Adagio* of the *Ninth* there is the widest range of dynamic and some beautiful *pianissimo* playing, but the final pull of tension from the conductor which makes for a compellingly great performance is missing. The layout too is less than ideal, with the first five symphonies not coming in numerical order, so initially finding one's way about the twelve CDs takes some care.

Symphony No. 1 in D (Titan).

(N) (B) *** CfP Dig. 573 5102. RLPO, Mackerras.

(N) *** Decca Dig. 448 813-2 [id.]. Concg. O, Chailly (with BERG: *Sonata, Op. 1*, orch. VERBEY ***).

*** DG Dig. 431 769-2 [id.]. BPO, Claudio Abbado.

(M) *** Unicorn UKCD 2012. LSO, Horenstein.

(N) ** Koch Dig. 3-7405-2 [id.]. Houston SO, Christoph Eschenbach.

(N) (**) Sony mono MHK 63328 [id.]. NYPO, Walter – BRAHMS: *Variations on a theme of Haydn*. (**)

(N) (*) Sony mono MHK 62348 [id.]. Minneapolis SO, Dmitri Mitropoulos – RACHMANINOV: *Isle of the Dead*. (**)

Mackerras's version, now reissued on CfP, is not only one of the best-recorded of all, but it offers a performance which, with crisply sprung rhythms, brings out the youthful freshness of Mahler's inspiration. The natural warmth and spontaneity of the reading have one concentrating on Mahler's arguments rather than on points of interpretation. Speeds are consistently well chosen and though the finale is not quite so biting as the rest, the joy of the inspiration comes over winningly, so that the whole performance hangs magnetically together, making this an outstanding choice, irrespective of price.

Helped by immaculate playing from the Concertgebouw, meticulous on detail and with sound of demonstration quality, Chailly's direct, positive reading is magnetic in its control of the long line. More subjective interpretations may characterize more strongly, but this is consistently satisfying, and comes with an unusual coupling in an orchestration of the early Berg *Sonata* by the Dutch composer, Theo Verbey.

Abbado's Berlin reading, like others in his Mahler series, was recorded live and, though one or two coughs intrude, the sound is fresh and full, bringing out the beauty and clarity of the Berlin strings. Though Abbado occasionally exaggerates the pointing of rhythms and speed-changes (as in the Ländler), the high voltage of the whole performance makes it most compelling, if not an obvious first choice.

Horenstein's version has a freshness and concentration which put it in a special category among the many rival accounts. Fine recording from the end of the 1960s, though the timpani is balanced rather too close.

Eschenbach's live recording, made in Vienna, brings a fresh, objective reading, very well played, though marred by audience noises and with sound that is not ideally clear in heavy tuttis.

Bruno Walter's mono account of the *First Symphony* comes from 1954 and was recorded at Carnegie Hall. Sonically it is naturally not as fresh or open as his later stereo version but despite a certain congestion and coarseness in climaxes, it has the spontaneity and refinement that characterize this great conductor. As with the other recordings in this Heritage series, the set is beautifully presented, but this also means (like the Mitropoulos version below) it is rather expensive.

Mitropoulos's account comes from 1940, the era of 78s, and was originally issued in the UK in 1953, when it was not well received because of the recording quality, which is dry and coarse. It has a fervour that almost lifts it beyond its sonic confines but a good deal of tolerance is called for. Great care has been taken over the transfer, and the presentation – as with most issues in this series – is both handsome and induces much nostalgia.

Symphony No. 1 in D min.; (i) *Lieder eines fahrenden Gesellen.*
(M) **(*) DG 449 735-2 [id.]. Bav. RSO, Kubelik, (i) with Dietrich Fischer-Dieskau.

Kubelik gives an intensely poetic reading. He is here at his finest in Mahler and though, as in later symphonies, he is sometimes tempted to choose a tempo on the fast side, the result could hardly be more glowing. The rubato in the slow funeral march is most subtly handled. In its CD reissue the quality is a little dry in the bass and the violins have lost some of their warmth, but there is no lack of body. In the *Lieder eines fahrenden Gesellen* the sound is fuller, with more atmospheric bloom. No one quite rivals Fischer-Dieskau in these songs, and this is a very considerable bonus at 'Originals' price.

Symphony No. 1 in D (Titan) (with *Blumine*).
**(*) HM Dig. HMU 907118-2 [id.]. Florida PO, Judd.
(B) **(*) [EMI Red Line Dig. CDR5 69816]. Israel PO, Mehta.
** EMI Dig. CDC7 54647-2. CBSO, Rattle.

James Judd demonstrates the virtuoso qualities of the Florida Philharmonic in a warm, well-pointed, spontaneous-sounding performance, slightly marred by a slow and rather heavy reading of the second-movement Ländler, which yet includes a most delicate account of the central Trio. The atmospheric recording sets the orchestra at a slight distance, which may take away some of the bite but enhances the beauty of the string-tone, not least in a dedicated performance of *Blumine*, which comes as a supplement after the symphony.

Mehta's version with the Israel Philharmonic brings a hybrid – the regular four-movement version in its revised instrumentation, into which is inserted the lyrical *Blumine* movement from the original version, which Mahler later excised. Mehta's reading of the whole work, though not the most individual or illuminating, is satisfyingly warm and direct, helped by very full, forward recording, among the best in the difficult acoustic of the Mann Auditorium. A worthwhile reissue (available only in the USA).

Recorded live in Symphony Hall, Birmingham, Rattle's account with the CBSO is rather lacking in the spontaneity one expects. Speed-changes in the first movement sound self-conscious, as do the exaggerations of dotted rhythms in the Ländler movement. It remains an acceptable reading, well recorded, but hardly matches Rattle's achievement in other Mahler recordings. As a preface to the main work, the *Blumine* movement, which Mahler excised from the original version of the symphony, is given with a freshness and spontaneity that rather shows up the rest.

Symphonies Nos. (i) *1;* (ii) *2 (Resurrection).*
(B) *** Decca Double 448 921-2 (2) [id.]. (ii) Harper, Watts, London Symphony Ch.; LSO, Solti.
(M) ** Sony SM2K 47573 (2) [id.]. (i) NYPO; (ii) J. Baker, S. Armstrong, Edinburgh Festival Ch., LSO; Bernstein.

Solti's 1964 LSO account of No. 2 remains a demonstration of the outstanding results Decca were securing with analogue techniques at that time, although on CD the brilliance of the *fortissimos* may not suit all ears. Helen Watts is wonderfully expressive, while the chorus has a rapt intensity that is the more telling when the recording perspectives are so clearly delineated. Coupled with his outstanding version of No. 1, it makes a genuine bargain at Double Decca price.

Bernstein's earlier (1966) account of the *First Symphony* is an excellent, red-blooded version but, when competition is so intense in this work, it falls below a top recommendation because of the close-up (originally CBS) sound. Similarly the *Resurrection Symphony*, recorded in Ely Cathedral in September 1973 and concluded in George Watson's College, Edinburgh, a few months later, is far too badly balanced for the discs to have a general recommendation. The performance is idiosyncratic but deeply felt and has superb contributions from the two soloists, not to mention the chorus and the orchestra.

Symphonies Nos. (i) *1 (Titan);* (ii) *2 (Resurrection);* (iii) *Lieder eines fahrenden Gesellen.*

(M) *** Sony SMK 64447 (2) [id.]. (i) Columbia SO; (ii) Emilia Cundari, Maureen Forrester, Westminster Ch., NYPO; (iii) Mildred Miller, Columbia SO; Bruno Walter.

As part of the initial volume of Sony's Bruno Walter Edition, his stereo recordings of the *First* and *Second Symphonies* are now economically coupled on a pair of discs together with the *Lieder eines fahrenden Gesellen*. The *First Symphony* was recorded in Hollywood in 1961 with a specially assembled orchestra of first-class musicians; in its newly remastered form the recording sounds better than ever, richer and fuller at the bottom end of the spectrum, and the dynamic range seemingly extended. Even more than the *First Symphony*, the 1958 set of the *Resurrection Symphony* is among the gramophone's indispensable classics. In the first movement there is a restraint and in the second a gracefulness which provide a strong contrast with a conductor like Solti. The recording was one of the last Walter made in New York – in Carnegie Hall – before his series with the Columbia Symphony Orchestra; it was remarkably good for its period and the dynamic range is surprisingly wide. In the newest remastering, detail registers more clearly; while the sound is not sumptuous, in the finale the balance with the voices still gives the music an ethereal resonance, with the closing section thrillingly expansive. In the 1960 recording of the *Lieder eines fahrenden Gesellen* the superb orchestral detail glows as never before. Mildred Miller is perhaps not an inspirational soloist, but she sings well enough, and Walter ensures that the performance is dramatically alive. The tangibility of both voice and orchestra is striking and the balance is first class.

Symphonies Nos. 1 in D; 9 in D min.; (i) *Lieder eines fahrenden Gesellen.*

(B) **(*) Teldec/Warner Ultima Dig. 3984 21339-2 (2). NYPO, Kurt Masur; (i) with Håkan Hagegård.

In a two-disc package Masur's live Mahler recordings with the NYPO from the early 1990s are certainly worth considering. On the first disc the *Symphony No. 1* and the related *Wayfaring Lad* song-cycle are given attractively fresh, unsentimental readings, even if ironic undertones are muted, with Hagegård a clear, firm baritone soloist. The *Symphony No. 9*, complete on the second disc, is more variable. If the first movement establishes the directness of Masur's approach, powerful but lacking in mystery, and the second and third movements follow a similar pattern, clean and precise, the long, slow finale crowns the performance in a reading strong and purposeful rather than tenderly elegiac. The recording, made in Avery Fisher Hall (like that of the companion disc), has less air round it.

Symphonies Nos. 1 in D min. (Titan); 10 (Adagio).

(N) (M) ** Sony SMK 60732 [id.]. NYPO, Bernstein.

Bernstein's is an excellent red-blooded version of the *First*, and the voltage is high, but when competition is so intense in this work it falls below a top recommendation if only because of the close-up mid 1960s sound, although the occasional self-indulgence in the interpretation (as in the trio of the Ländler) will not please the dedicated Mahlerian. In the *Tenth*, recorded a decade later in 1975, Bernstein uses the old fallible edition, but the passionate commitment of his performances is hard to resist, with contrasts underlined between the sharpness of the *Andante* passages and the free expressiveness of the main *Adagio*.

Symphonies Nos. (i) *1 in D (Titan);* (ii) *10: Adagio* (arr. Krenet, ed. Jokl).

(B) **(*) Sony Dig./Analogue SBK 53259 [id.]. (i) NYPO, Mehta; (ii) Cleveland O, Szell.

Mehta's Sony/CBS digital version of the *First Symphony*, successfully recorded in the Avery Fisher Hall in 1980, is far preferable to his later, Israeli, Decca CD. It has no less urgency and drama, but here Mehta's Viennese training comes out in the lilt of the Ländler second movement while his freely expressive rubato in the third, after the dark opening, is very appealing. While the strings lack a genuine pianissimo in the slow introduction, detail is attractively colourful and the reading overall has undoubted spontaneity. Many will also welcome the reissue of Szell's 1958 recording of the *Adagio* from the *Tenth Symphony* in Jokl's edition. Although today we are used to hearing the whole work in Deryck Cooke's performing version of the sketch, the Cleveland orchestral playing is stylish as well as eloquent. The sound, too, is very good.

Symphony No. 2 in C min. (Resurrection).

❁ *** EMI CDS7 47962-8 (2) [Ang. CDCB 47962]. Augér, J. Baker, CBSO Ch., CBSO, Rattle.

*** Ph. Dig 438 935-2 (2) [id.]. McNair, Van Nes, Ernst Senff Ch., BPO, Haitink.

(M) *** Chandos CHAN 6595/6 [id.]. Lott, Hamari, Latvian State Ac. Ch., Oslo Philharmonic Ch., Oslo PO, Jansons.

(B) *** Double Decca 440 615-2 (2) [id.]. Ileana Cotrubas, Christa Ludwig, V. State Op. Ch., Mehta – SCHMIDT: *Symphony No. 4.* ***

*** DG 439 953-2 (2) [id.]. Studer, Meyer, Arnold Schoenberg Ch., VPO, Abbado.

(N) *** Conifer Dig. 76505 51337-2 [id.]. Benita

Valente, Maureen Forrester, Ardwyn Singers, BBC Welsh Ch., Cardiff Philharmonic Ch., Dyfed Ch., LSO Ch., LSO, Gilbert Kaplan.

(i) *Symphony No. 2 in C min. (Resurrection)*; (ii) *Lieder eines fahrenden Gesellen;* (iii) *Lieder und Gesang aus der Jugendzeit:* excerpts.
(M) *** DG (IMS) Dig. 445 587-2 (2). (i) Fassbaender, Plowright, Philh. Ch.; (ii) Fassbaender; (iii) Weikl; Philh. O, Sinopoli.

Simon Rattle's reading of Mahler's *Second* is among the very finest records he has yet made, superlative in the breadth and vividness of its sound and with a spacious reading which in its natural intensity unerringly sustains generally slow, steady speeds to underline the epic grandeur of Mahler's vision. The playing of the CBSO is inspired. The choral singing, beautifully balanced, is incandescent, while the heart-felt singing of Arleen Augér and Dame Janet Baker is equally distinguished and characterful.

Bernard Haitink's 1993 version with the Berlin Philharmonic also brings one of his very finest Mahler recordings, weighty and bitingly powerful. The sound of the Berlin Philharmonic in the Philharmonie is caught with a vividness and sense of presence rarely matched. Above all Haitink conveys the tensions of a live occasion, even though this was a studio performance, leading up to a glorious apotheosis in the Judgement Day finale. The soloists are outstanding, and the chorus immaculately expands from rapt, hushed singing to incandescent splendour. Outstanding in every way, this can be placed alongside Rattle's superb CBSO set.

Sinopoli's version of the *Resurrection* has the advantage of including the *Lieder eines fahrenden Gesellen*, beautifully sung by Brigitte Fassbaender, and the *Songs of Youth* ('*aus der Jugendzeit*'), skilfully orchestrated by Harold Byrns and well sung by Bernd Weikl, bringing extra anticipations of the mature *Des Knaben Wunderhorn* songs. In the symphony Sinopoli has meticulous concern for detail, yet he still conveys consistently the irresistible purposefulness of Mahler's writing, fierce at high dramatic moments and intense too, rarely relaxed, in moments of meditation, with *Urlicht* beautifully sung with warmth and purity by Fassbaender. The recorded sound, though not quite as full and vivid as that for Rattle, is among the most brilliant of any in this work. Rosalind Plowright is a pure and fresh soprano soloist, contrasting well with the equally firm, earthier-toned mezzo of Fassbaender.

The crisp attack at the start of the opening funeral march sets the pattern for an exceptionally refined and alert reading of the *Resurrection Symphony* from Jansons and his Oslo orchestra. During the first four movements, this may seem a lightweight reading, but the extra resilience of rhythm brings out the dance element in Mahler's *Knaben Wunderhorn* inspirations rather than ruggedness or rusticity, while at the finale the whole performance erupts in an overwhelming outburst for the vision of Resurrection. That transformation is intensified by the breathtakingly rapt and intense account of the song, *Urlicht*, which precedes it. In the finale, power goes with precision and meticulous observance of markings, when even Mahler's surprising diminuendo on the final choral cadence is observed. With the Oslo Choir joined by singers from Jansons's native Latvia, the choral singing is heartfelt, to crown a version which finds a special place even among the many distinguished readings on a long list.

Zubin Mehta sounds a different conductor, not at all like his NYPO self, when he is drawing as sympathetic a Mahler performance as this from the Vienna Philharmonic. The refinement of the playing, recorded with vivid clarity and warmth, puts this among the finest versions of the symphony. The second movement has *grazioso* delicacy and, though the third movement begins with the sharpest possible timpani strokes, there is no hint of brutality, and the *Wunderhorn* rhythms have a delightful lilt. *Urlicht* finds Christa Ludwig in superb form. The enormous span of the finale brings clarity as well as magnificence, with fine placing of soloists and chorus and glorious atmosphere in such moments as the evocation of birdsong over distant horns, as heavenly a moment as Mahler ever conceived. The CD transfer has brightened the analogue sound somewhat, but there is still plenty of ambient warmth.

Abbado's recording with the Vienna Philharmonic was made live in 1992 in the Musikverein, offering a predictably fine, beautifully paced performance, but one that rather suffers, compared both with his Berlin version of the *Fifth*, recorded live six months later, and with Haitink's Berlin account of the *Second*. The Vienna Philharmonic's ensemble is less refined than that of the Berliners, even in the strings, and the sound is less immediate and involving. Tensions are not helped when the audience is so noisy. Yet with powerful soloists and a superb choir, it is still a strong reading.

This Kaplan reissue now replaces the more elaborate (and much more expensive) Conifer set which included a CD-ROM package of photographs and paintings of Mahler, and the reminiscences of musicians who knew the composer, plus the *Adagietto* of the *Fifth Symphony*. Kaplan's performance of the *Resurrection Symphony* is not only thoroughly idiomatic and full of enthusiasm but totally compelling. He gets keenly dramatic and highly responsive playing from the LSO, and the recording is of demonstration quality, indeed second to none. The performance runs to just over 83 minutes so has been issued in a Double format to compete with other full-priced versions on a single CD.

Symphony No. 3 in D min.
*** Ph. Dig. 432 162-2 (2) [id.]. Jard van Nes, Tölz Boys' Ch., Ernst-Senff Ch., BPO, Haitink.
*** DG Dig. 410 715-2 (2) [id.]. J. Norman, V. State Op. Ch., V. Boys' Ch., VPO, Abbado.
(M) *** Unicorn UKCD 2006/7 [id.]. Procter, Wandsworth School Boys' Ch., Amb. S., LSO, Horenstein.
(N) **(*) BBC Legends BBCL 4004-7 [id.]. Kerstin Meyer, Ladies of the Hallé Ch., Boys of Manchester Grammar School, Hallé O, Sir John Barbirolli.
(N) *(*) Sony Dig. S2K 60250 (2) [id.]. Anna Larsson, Los Angeles Master Chorale (Women), Paulist Boy Choristers of California, LAPO, Esa-Pekka Salonen.
(N) *(*) Telarc Dig. 2CD 80481 (2) [id.]. Michelle DeYoung, May Festival Ch., Cincinnati College, Children's Ch, Cincinnati SO, López-Cobos.

(i) *Symphony No. 3. Kindertotenlieder.*
**(*) Chandos Dig. CHAN 9117/18 [id.]. Finnie, RSNO, Järvi; (i) with R. Scottish Ch. & Junior Ch.

(i) *Symphony No. 3;* (ii) *Kindertotenlieder; Des Knaben Wunderhorn: Das irdische Leben. 3 Rückert Lieder: Ich atmet' einen linden Duft; Ich bin der Welt abhanden gekommen; Um Mitternacht.*
(M) *** Sony SM2K 47576 (2) [id.]. (i) Martha Lipton, Schola Cantorum Ch., Boys' Ch. of Church of Transfiguration; (ii) Jennie Tourel; NYPO, Bernstein.

(i) *Symphony No. 3 in D min; (ii) Des Knaben Wunderhorn: 8 Lieder.*
(N) *** EMI Dig. CDS5 56657-2 (2) [CDCC 56657]. (i) Birgit Remmert, CBSO Women's Ch.; (ii) Simon Keenlyside; CBSO, Rattle.

Symphony No. 3; 5 Rückert Lieder.
(M) *** Sony M2K 44553 (2) [id.]. Janet Baker, London Symphony Ch., LSO, Tilson Thomas.

Rattle conducts an outstanding version of No. 3, magnetic from the very start, rich, bold and opulent and very well recorded with an exceptionally full bass. The subtlety of Rattle's phrasing and rubato not only brings out the work's deeper qualities, with the visionary intensity of the long finale superbly caught, but far more than most the joy and humour of the lighter movements. Simon Keenlyside's beautiful, finely detailed readings of the *Knaben Wunderhorn* songs make a very welcome bonus, with an extra song, *Ablösung im Sommer* (which is quoted in the third movement of the *Symphony*), aptly included in an arrangement by Berio.

Michael Tilson Thomas inspires the orchestra to play with bite and panache in the bold, dramatic passages and to bring out the sparkle and freshness of the *Knaben Wunderhorn* ideas; but what crowns the performance is the raptness of his reading of the noble, hymn-like finale, hushed and intense, beautifully sustained. There is a formidable bonus in Dame Janet Baker's searching performances of the five *Rückert Lieder*. Excellent CBS sound, both warm and brilliant.

With the Berlin Philharmonic producing glorious sounds, recorded with richness and immediacy, Haitink conducts a powerful, spacious reading. It culminates in a glowing, concentrated account of the slow finale, which gives the whole work a visionary strength often lacking. The mystery of *Urlicht* is then beautifully caught by the mezzo soloist Jard van Nes.

With sound of spectacular range, Abbado's performance is sharply defined and deeply dedicated. The range of expression, the often wild mixture of elements in this work, are conveyed with extraordinary intensity, not least in the fine contributions of Jessye Norman and the two choirs. The recording has great presence and detail on CD.

Horenstein is at his most intensely committed. The manner is still very consistent in its simple dedication to the authority of the score and its rejection of romantic indulgence; but with an extra intensity the result has the sort of frisson-creating quality one knew from live Horenstein performances and the recording quality is both full and brilliant. Fine vocal contributions from Norma Procter, the Ambrosian Singers and the Wandsworth School Boys' Choir.

Bernstein's 1961 account of Mahler's *Third Symphony*, strong and passionate, has few of the stylistic exaggerations that sometimes overlaid his interpretations. Here his style in the slow movement is more heavily expressive than Horenstein's, but many will respond to his extrovert involvement. The remastered recording, made in New York's Manhattan Center, the venue of so many of the best of his early records, has added spaciousness and body in this very successful remastering for CD; it is rather less refined than the Unicorn sound but is better balanced. The vocal contributions from Martha Lipton and the two choirs contribute to the success of this venture and the generous Lieder coupling is well worth having, and Jennie Tourel is in excellent voice.

Barbirolli's BBC *Third Symphony* was recorded at a concert at the Free Trade Hall, Manchester, in May 1969, the same year as Sir John's celebrated *Fifth* with the New Philharmonia. There is much of the fervour and warmth that characterized all he did, which compensates for various shortcomings. The recording is generally very good, though the cellos and double-basses are wanting in weight. Kerstin Meyer displays artistry, but has an unwelcome and obtrusive vibrato. For some reason the engineers cut off the applause and the resulting edit on the last D major chord is ugly. The disc also includes an interesting conversation between Sir John and the critic, C. B. Rees.

Järvi conducts a warmly expressive, spontaneous-sounding reading which brings out the joy behind Mahler's inspiration rather than any tragedy. This makes light of the epic qualities in this massive work. Though the ensemble of the Royal Scottish National Orchestra is not as immaculate as that of some distinguished rivals, the bite of communication is always intense, helped by full, atmospheric Chandos recording. Järvi brings out the folk-like elements in the second and third movements, and Linda Finnie is a dedicated soloist and gives a felt, expressive reading of the *Kindertotenlieder*.

Salonen conducts his Los Angeles forces in a bold, strong reading, forwardly recorded in full open sound, which in its insistence on power lacks subtler Mahlerian qualities, with no mystery even in the visionary last movement.

López-Cobos and the Cincinnati Orchestra give a crisp, well-pointed reading, rather undercharacterized, with first-rate recording which yet conveys a thinness in string-tone. Choral singing is good, though the unsteady singing of Michelle DeYoung is a blot.

Symphonies Nos. 3 in D min.; 6 in A min.; Symphony No. 10: Adagio.

(N) (**) Conifer mono 75605 51279-2 (3). VSO, Charles Adler.

Charles Adler sponsored these historic, pioneering recordings of Mahler in 1950–51, and though the playing is not always polished, his natural feeling for the apt speed and his unerring concentration make them well worth hearing. This was the first-ever commercial recording of No. 6, and it still stands the test of time. Limited sound.

Symphony No. 4 in G.

(N) *** EMI Dig. CDC5 56563-2 [id.]. Amanda Roocroft, CBSO, Sir Simon Rattle.

(N) (BB) *** CfP Dig. 573 4372. Felicity Lott, LPO, Welser-Möst.

(M) *** DG 419 863-2 [id.]. Edith Mathis, BPO, Karajan.

(N) *** BBC Legends BBCL 4014-2 [id.]. Heather Harper, BBC SO, Sir John Barbirolli (with BERLIOZ: *Overture: Le Corsaire, Op. 21*).

(BB) *** Naxos Dig. 8.550527 [id.]. Lynda Russell, Polish Nat. RSO, Antoni Wit.

(BB) *** Arte Nova/BMG Dig. 74321 46506-2 [id.]. Hellen Kwan, Gran Canaria PO, Adrian Leaper.

(BB) **(*) RCA Navigator 74321 21286-2. Lisa Della Casa, Chicago SO, Reiner – R. STRAUSS: *Burleske*. **(*)

(M) **(*) Van. 08 6164 71 [OVC 4007]. Netania Davrath, Utah SO, Abravanel.

(N) (M) ** Sony SMK 60733 [id.]. Reri Grist, NYPO, Bernstein.

Symphonies Nos. 4 in G; 5 (Adagietto).

(B) *** [EMI Red Line Dig. CDR5 69817]. Popp, LPO, Tennstedt.

(i) *Symphony No. 4 in G;* (ii) *Des Knaben Wunderhorn: Das irdische Leben; Wo die schönen Trompeten blasen. Rückert Lieder: Ich atmet' einen linden Duft; Ich bin der Welt abhanden gekommen; Um Mitternacht.*

(N) (M) **(*) EMI CDM5 67035-2. [CDM 69667]. (i) Elizabeth Schwarzkopf; (ii) Christa Ludwig; Philh. O, Klemperer.

(i) *Symphony No. 4 in G;* (ii) *Lieder eines fahrenden Gesellen.*

❁ (B) *** Sony SBK 46535 [id.]. (i) Judith Raskin, Cleveland O, Szell; (ii) Frederica von Stade, LPO, Andrew Davis.

(i) *Symphony No. 4 in G;* (ii) *Lieder und Gesang aus der Jugendzeit.*

(M) (***) Sony mono SMK 64450 [id.]. Desi Halban; (i) NYPO, Bruno Walter; (ii) Walter (piano).

George Szell's 1966 record of Mahler's *Fourth* represented his partnership with the Cleveland Orchestra at its highest peak and the digital remastering for CD brings out the very best of the original recording. The performance remains uniquely satisfying: the music blossoms, partly because of the marvellous attention to detail (and the immaculate ensemble), but more positively because of the committed and radiantly luminous orchestral response to the music itself. In the finale Szell found the ideal soprano to match his conception. An outstanding choice, generously coupled. In contrast with most other recorded performances, Frederica von Stade insinuates a hint of youthful ardour into her highly enjoyable account of the *Wayfaring Lad* cycle.

Rattle's performance begins with an idiosyncratic but valid reading of the opening bars, at first very slow then brisk for the main *Allegro*. It demonstrates the thoughtfulness on detail of his approach to Mahler, reflected in an unusually refreshing account, youthfully urgent, which rises to a spacious, songful reading of the long slow movement. Amanda Roocroft sings with warm, creamy tone in the finale. Refined recording to match. This stands high among modern recordings of this beautiful symphony.

Welser-Möst's outer movements are fresh and beautifully shaped, with Felicity Lott a youthful-sounding soloist, and the Ländler second movement clean-cut and crisp. It is the third movement *Adagio* that crowns the performance, hushed and intense from the start, with the emotional outbursts strongly controlled. At bargain-price with excellent modern digital sound, spacious like the performance, it makes an outstanding recommendation, a fine alternative to Szell.

Karajan's refined and poised, yet undoubtedly affectionate account remains among the finest versions of this lovely symphony, and Edith Mathis's sensitively composed contribution to the finale matches the conductor's meditative feeling. With glowing sound, this makes another outstanding mid-priced recommendation alongside Szell's renowned Cleveland CD.

Barbirolli's live BBC recording, made in Prague, comes from a series of performances he conducted while on tour. With the orchestra very well drilled, responding warmly to the fluctuations of Barbirolli's expressive Mahler style, this is an account to set alongside Barbirolli's classic studio recording of the *Fifth* in its passionate generosity. As in the *Fifth*, he tends to prefer broad speeds, but controls them masterfully with all the familiar warmth and conviction one expects from this conductor. The result may be weightier than usual, but this is a symphony that welcomes alternative views, and rhythms are so crisply pointed that slow speeds never drag. The glowing, seamless reading of the slow movement leads on to a spacious account of the finale, with Heather Harper a radiant soloist. Full, warm, well-balanced sound to match. The Berlioz overture, dashingly done, and brilliantly played by this fine orchestra, is a welcome makeweight.

Tennstedt's reading of the *Fourth Symphony* conveys spaciousness and strength, yet his agreeably light touch in the outer movements brings an innocence entirely in keeping with this most endearing of the Mahler symphonies. He makes the argument seamless in his easy transitions of speed, yet here he never deliberately adopts a coaxing, overtly charming manner; and in that he is followed most beautifully by Lucia Popp, the pure-toned soloist in the finale. The peak of the work as Tennstedt presents it lies in the long slow movement, here taken very slowly and intensely. The 1982 digital recording, made in the Kingsway Hall, is among EMI's finest, full and well balanced. Tennstedt's account of the *Adagietto* lacks the full tenderness of Barbirolli's (starting with a slightly intrusive balance for the harp) but still makes a worthwhile bonus.

Antoni Wit conducts a fresh, spontaneous-sounding reading, beautifully played and recorded, that can be warmly recommended at Naxos's bargain price. Lynda Russell is a pure-toned soprano soloist in the finale, both fresh and warm, with Wit giving a good lilt to the rhythm. Excellent sound, which gives a good bite and focus to the woodwind, so important in Mahler.

Spaciously recorded, the Arte Nova version offers a fresh, crisply paced reading from Adrian Leaper, demonstrating what polished ensemble the Gran Canaria Philharmonic can achieve. Woodwind soloists are most imaginative, and most striking of all is the refinement of the strings. with the opening of the slow movement bringing the gentlest pianissimo, ravishingly sustained. The finale is then beautifully sprung, with the Korean soprano, Hellen Kwan, a golden-toned soloist, aptly young-sounding. Without being in the same class as the famous Szell version, this is thoroughly recommendable in the budget range.

Klemperer is slow in the first movement and, strangely, fractionally too fast in the slow movement. Yet the Philharmonia make some ravishing sounds, and one can easily fall under Klemperer's spell. The two highlights of the reading are the marvellously beautiful Ländler, which forms the central section of the second movement, and the simplicity of Elisabeth Schwarzkopf's singing in the finale. This is a record to enjoy, but perhaps not the one to buy as a single representation of Mahler's *Fourth* in a collection. In the Lieder other performers may find a deeper response to the words but the freshness of the singing, when Christa Ludwig's voice was in its early prime and at its richest, here gives much pleasure.

The *Fourth Symphony*, relatively lightweight, suits the Utah orchestra better than the weightier Mahler symphonies, and Abravanel directs a characteristically fresh and crisp reading, marked by some fine solo playing. The strings in the slow movement may not be quite as refined as in the finest rival versions, but the hushed intensity is most convincing, and the finale, with Netania Davrath a firm, boyish soloist, is light and urgent, bringing out the joy of the inspiration. Fair sound, fuller than in others in the Vanguard series. As with the other issues, no recording date is given.

Walter's glowingly radiant reading suffers from the fairly limited mono sound (especially at the climax of the slow movement). But the remastering of the 1945 recording has worked wonders, and orchestral textures are clear and yet warm. Desi Halban's contribution is refreshingly individual, dramatic as well as touching, and she is comparably impressive in the songs, which Walter accompanies discreetly at the piano. Her account of *Ich ging mit Lust durch einen grünen Wald* is enchanting.

Reiner's version was made in 1958. The recording has been digitally remastered, with great improvement to the sound, which remains brightly lit but has attractively vivid detail, naturally glowing within the acoustic bloom of the hall. The performance is wayward, but lovingly so; and everything Reiner does sounds spontaneous. The slow movement has striking intensity, with its rapt closing pages leading on gently to the finale, in which Lisa della Casa, in ravishing voice, matches Reiner's mood.

Bernstein's version, dating from 1960, brings a rather erratic reading, less controlled than his finest Mahler performances, and although well transferred, not really competitive in quality of sound. His later DG digital version with the Royal Concertgebouw Orchestra makes this earlier performance sound heavy-handed by comparison, although not everyone will respond to his use of a boy-treble in the finale. In that respect Reri Grist's contribution is less controversial.

(i) *Symphony No. 4*; (ii; iii) *Lieder eines fahrenden Gesellen*; (iii; iv) *Des Knaben Wunderhorn: Das irdische Leben; Wer hat dies Liedlein erdacht?*
(N) (***) BBC Legends mono/stereo BBCB 8004-2 [id.]. (i) Joan Carlyle, LSO; (ii) Anna Reynolds; (iii) ECO; (iv) with Elly Ameling, Benjamin Britten.

The *Fourth* was a special Britten favourite and his mono account with the LSO, recorded at Orford Church, Suffolk during the 1961 Aldeburgh Festival, makes a striking contrast with the Barbirolli version listed above. It brings a most distinctive reading, with the spareness of Mahler's textures matched by the bright, clear playing of the LSO strings. Britten is brisker, more classical in approach, yet his feeling for this music always shines through. Though the very opening threatens chaos, when Britten launches the main *Allegro* at a very fast tempo, evidently taking the players by surprise, it is still a revelatory account, in some ways neo-classical in its freshness, edgy and abrasive in the *Scherzo*, tender in the slow movement and light and jaunty in the child-heaven finale, with Joan Carlyle the boyish soloist. Though the sound is not as full as most in this series, the impact of the performance is unimpaired. The fill-ups, both in stereo, come from two other Aldeburgh Festival concerts of a decade later, with Anna Reynolds rich and firm in the *Wayfaring lad* cycle and Elly Ameling sweet and true, though not helped by the washy sound. The two songs from *Des Knaben Wunderhorn*, with Elly Ameling in radiant form, were recorded in 1969 and the *Lieder eines fahrenden Gesellen* with Anna Reynolds three years later at Snape Maltings. No one with an interest in Britten as interpreter should neglect this issue.

(i) *Symphonies Nos. 4 in G;* (ii) *5 in C sharp min.*
(N) (B) ** Decca Double 458 383-2 (2) [id.]. (i) Sylvia Stahlman, Concg. O; (ii) Chicago SO; Solti.

Solti's earlier performance of the *Fourth symphony* is disappointing. It is extremely well-balanced as a recording but the conductor is not altogether happy in the first movement and, besides a wilfulness of style, there are dull patches which he is unable to sustain with any richness of emotional expression. He does the finale best, and here Sylvia Stahlman sings charmingly. The opening *Funeral march* sets the tone of his reading of the *Fifth*. At a tempo faster than usual, it is wistful rather than deeply tragic, even though the dynamic contrasts are superbly pointed, and the string tone could hardly be more resonant. In the pivotal *Adagietto* too, Solti secures intensely beautiful playing, but the result lacks the 'inner' quality one finds so abundantly in Barbirolli's interpretation. Full-bodied if slightly over-reverberant recording.

Symphony No. 5 in C sharp min.
(N) *** Decca Dig. 458 860-2 [id.]. Concg. O, Chailly.
*** DG Dig. 437 789-2 [id.]. BPO, Abbado.
(N) ❁ (M) *** EMI CDM5 66910-2 [CDM 66962]. New Philh. O, Barbirolli.
(N) *** Conifer Dig. 75605 51318-2 [id.]. RPO, Daniele Gatti.
(M) *** EMI Dig. CD-EMX 2164; *TC-EMX 2164*. RLPO, Mackerras.
(M) *** DG 447 450-2 [id.]. BPO, Karajan.
(N) (M) *** Decca Penguin Classics Dig. 460 625-2 [id.]. Cleveland O, Dohnányi.
(BB) **(*) RCA Navigator 74321 29249-2 [Basic 100 09026 68365-2]. Boston SO, Erich Leinsdorf.
(B) (**(*)) Millennium mono MCD 80081 [id.] V. State Op. O, Hermann Scherchen.

Chailly excels himself in his strong, clear-sighted, but deeply felt reading of No. 5, with his concentration reflected in superlative playing from the Concertgebouw, caught with exceptional clarity in the full and brilliant Decca recording. The beauty of Mahler's orchestration has rarely been conveyed so vividly, with the hushed intensity of the *Adagietto* the more moving for its reticence, and with the joyful finale dazzling in its crisp detail. Other, more personal readings may be more distinctive, but none is more widely recommendable.

Abbado's is another outstanding new version, recorded live in the Philharmonie, Berlin, with the dramatic tensions of a concert performance vividly captured. Abbado's view is clean-cut and taut, bringing out the high contrasts between movements, pointing rhythms not just precisely but with often-Viennese seductiveness. The great *Adagietto* is raptly done, wistful rather than openly romantic at a flowing tempo, and the *Wunderhorn* finale is at once refined and exuberant. With excellent sound, there are few versions to match this, presenting Abbado at his peak.

Barbirolli's famous analogue 1969 recording (made in Watford Town Hall) has now been splendidly remastered for EMI's 'Great recordings of the century' series and sounds fuller, clearer, more atmospheric than ever. On any count this is one of the greatest, most warmly affecting accounts ever committed to disc, expansive, yet concentrated in feeling: the *Adagietto* is very moving indeed. A classic version which many will prefer even to Abbado's newer digital account.

Daniele Gatti draws a colourful, impulsive

reading of No. 5 from his RPO players, not as highly polished as some, and not so weightily recorded, but this is still an engagingly warm and relaxed performance to be recommended strongly.

Mackerras in his well-paced reading sees the work as a whole, building each movement with total concentration. There is a thrilling culmination on the great brass chorale at the end, with polish allied to purposefulness. Barbirolli in his classic reading may find more of a tear-laden quality in the great *Adagietto*; but Mackerras, with fewer controversial points of interpretation and superb modern sound, makes an excellent alternative choice at mid-price.

Dohnányi conducts the Cleveland Orchestra in an exceptionally high-powered reading, superbly played and recorded, which can still relax totally in expressive warmth. The toughness of the first two movements – with superb discipline bringing immaculate articulation in the second – gives way to an equally polished but nicely lilting Ländler in the third, finely shaded. Though the hushed *Adagietto* keeps a degree of reserve, the songful freshness and purity are very sympathetic, before the thrustful and dramatic finale. The brilliance of the Cleveland playing is matched by the vivid recorded sound. The descriptive essay is written by Hilary Spurling.

Karajan's 1973 recording (previously available on DG's bargain label) now reverts to mid-price as a 'Legendary Performance' in DG's series of 'Originals'. Karajan's characteristic emphasis on polish and refinement goes with sharpness of focus. His is at once one of the most beautiful and one of the most intense versions available, starting with an account of the first movement which brings more biting funeral-march rhythms than any rival. Radiant playing from the Berlin Philharmonic and full, atmospheric recording, made in the Berlin Jesus-Christus Kirche. However, the CD transfer is very brightly lit and some softening of the brilliance on top is needed for complete comfort.

Leinsdorf is predictably less gentle than some in the famous *Adagietto* – indeed he brings out its underlying neurosis – but elsewhere his directness makes for an unexpectedly strong and convincing result. The recording from 1963 has first-class playing from the great Boston orchestra and is the least expensive recommendable version of the Mahler *Fifth* in the catalogue, though it is by no means a first choice.

Dating from 1953, Scherchen's version with the Vienna State Opera Orchestra offers a powerful, rugged performance with mono sound astonishingly full and vivid for the period. The opening *Funeral march* has ample power and thrust, and the second movement is fast and furious, while the celebrated *Adagietto* is tender, sweet and flowing rather than elegiac. The finale brings a ripely joyful conclusion, attractively wild in the coda.

(i) *Symphony No. 5*; (ii; iii) *Lieder eines fahrenden Gesellen*; (ii; iv) *Des Knaben Wunderhorn*.

(N) (BB) ** Virgin Classsics Double Dig. VBD5 61507-2 (2) [CDVB 61507]. (i) Finnish RSO, Saraste; (ii) Ann Murray; (iii) RPO, Andrew Litton; (iv) Thomas Allen, LPO, Mackerras.

Saraste and the Finnish Radio Orchestra offer a refined and well-paced reading of the *Fifth*, which gives a relatively lightweight view of the symphony, Mahlerian neurosis is largely missing, which might be justified in a work that ends in joy. Rhythms are beautifully sprung, and the *Adagietto* is the more tenderly moving for being a degree reticent and understated. The recording is refined to match, warm and naturally balanced. On the second disc Ann Murray gives a warmly responsive account of *Lieder eines fahrenden Gesellen*, and is particularly touching in the two outer songs. She is joined by Thomas Allen in *Des Knaben Wunderhorn*, directed with imagination and character by Mackerras. Some of the songs are reallotted between the singers, and comparison with Schwarzkopf and Fischer-Dieskau on the famous old Szell recording cannot always be useful, although two of the highlights are Allen's noble *Rheinlegendchen*, and Murray's ravishing performance of the closing song, *Wo die schönen Trompeten blasen*, here a solo rather than a duo. The recording is warmly resonant and spacious, which by widely spreading the orchestral tapestry puts the effect of the performance at some remove from the intimacy of a Lieder cycle.

Symphony No. 6 in A min.

*** Ph. Dig. 426 257-2 [id.]. BPO, Haitink – *Lieder eines fahrenden Gesellen*. ***

*** DG Dig. 445 835-2 [id.]. VPO, Boulez.

(B) *** Sony SBK 47654 [id.]. Cleveland O, Szell.

(N) (M) *** Carlton Dig. 30366 01007 (2) [id.]. Boston PO, Benjamin Zander.

(M) **(*) Sony SMK 60208 [id.]. NYPO, Bernstein.

(BB) *** Naxos Dig. 8.550529 (2) [id.]. Polish Nat. RSO (Katowice), Antoni Wit.

(B) *** Decca (IMS) Double 444 871-2 (2). Concg. O, Chailly – ZEMLINSKY: *Maeterlinck Lieder*. ***

(M) *** Unicorn UKCD 2024/5. Stockholm PO, Jascha Horenstein.

(M) **(*) Decca 425 040-2 [id.]. Chicago SO, Solti.

(B) **(*) EMI forte CZS5 69349-2 [CDFB 69349]. New Philh. O, Barbirolli – R. STRAUSS: *Ein Heldenleben*. ***

(B) **(*) EMI CZS7 67816-2 (2). New Philh. O, Barbirolli – R. STRAUSS: *Metamorphosen*. **(*)

**(*) EMI Dig. CDS5 56925-2. CBSO, Simon Rattle.

(N) **(*) Telarc Dig. CD 80444 [id.]. Atlanta SO, Yoel Levi.

Symphony No. 6 in A min.; (i) *Kindertotenlieder; 5 Rückert Lieder.*

(N) (M) *** DG 457 716-2 (2) [id.]. BPO, Karajan; (i) with Christa Ludwig.

With superlative playing from the Berlin Philharmonic, Karajan's reading of the *Sixth* is a revelation, above all in the slow movement, which emerges as one of the greatest of Mahler's slow movements, and the whole balance of the symphony is altered. Though the outer movements firmly stamp this as one of the darkest of the Mahler symphonies, in Karajan's reading their sharp focus makes them both compelling and refreshing. The fine mid 1970s DG recording, with its wide dynamic, adds enormously to the impact. This is well worthy of reissue as one of DG's Originals, especially as Christa Ludwig's moving account of the *Kindertotenlieder* has been added to the previously coupled *Rückert Lieder*; fine, positive performances with comparable distinction and refinement in the orchestral playing.

Haitink conducts a noble reading of this difficult symphony, underplaying the neurosis behind the inspiration, but, in his clean-cut concentration and avoidance of exaggeration, making the result the more moving in its degree of reticence, yet intensely committed. Jessye Norman's rich-toned account of *Lieder eines fahrenden Gesellen* makes a powerful bonus. Excellent sound, both full-blooded and refined.

Boulez conducts a performance of the most enigmatic symphony which in its power and sharpness of focus transcends almost any rival. Rarely if ever has the Vienna Philharmonic been recorded with such fullness and immediacy in the Musikvereinsaal as here. Boulez's control of speeds is masterful, never rushed, even though this is a performance squeezed on to a single disc, and the slow movement brings hushed, ravishingly beautiful playing of a refinement it would be hard to match. The finale is rugged and weighty, with crisp pointing of rhythms, making this an outstanding recommendation alongside Karajan, who, on two discs, also includes Christa Ludwig's five *Rückert Lieder* and *Kindertotenlieder*. Though RL found this a performance observed rather than felt at white heat, EG was totally involved.

Szell's powerful outer movements are masterfully shaped and unerringly paced, with the second-movement scherzo beautifully sprung to bring out the grotesquerie. The *Andante moderato* then brings a uniquely delicate and moving account, hauntingly wistful, tender without a hint of sentimentality. The CD transfer gives a fuller, more atmospheric impression of what the orchestra sounded like in Severance Hall, Cleveland, than most of the studio recordings of the time. At budget price, squeezed on to a single disc, this is buried treasure and a fine counterpart to Szell's classic reading of Mahler's *Fourth*.

Recorded live, Zander's reading may lack the full weight of some – mainly a question of recording – but, with fine rhythmic control married to keen concentration, his is a consistently compelling version, which rises to an eloquent account of the long finale, so spacious that a second disc is needed.

It is good that Sony have now separated Bernstein's enormously gripping NYPO account of the *Sixth* from the *Eighth* (see below). Now on a single, mid-priced disc it is highly competitive. The remastering has further improved the sound; although the close balance remains a drawback, the actual sounds are impressive, and the performance itself is very compelling indeed.

The excellent quality of the Katowice Orchestra of Polish Radio is impressively demonstrated in all four movements of this difficult symphony. The ensemble can hardly be faulted, and the full, atmospheric recording enhances that quality with string-sound that is fresh and radiant. Wit conducts a spacious performance, clean and well sprung, with the varying moods sharply contrasted. On two full discs it becomes less of a super-bargain than some Naxos issues, but it stands comparison with any rival.

Chailly's version with the Concertgebouw offers brilliant playing and spectacular sound in a reading remarkable for the broad, rugged approach in the outer movements. There is relentlessness in the slow speed for the first movement, with expressive warmth giving way to a square purposefulness, tense and effective. The third movement brings a comparably simple, direct approach at a genuine flowing *Andante*. In its open songfulness it rouses *Wunderhorn* echoes. Anyone fancying the unexpected but attractive Zemlinsky coupling need not hesitate.

In the first movement, Horenstein finds extra weight by taking a more measured tempo than most conductors. It is a sober reading that holds together with wonderful concentration, yet the slow movement brings the most persuasive rubato. The finale brings another broad, noble reading. Yet some will feel that 33 minutes is short measure for the second CD.

Solti draws stunning playing from the Chicago orchestra. The sessions were in March and April 1970, and this was the first recording he made with them after he took up his post as principal conductor; as he himself said, it represented a love-affair at first sight. The electric excitement of the playing confirms this, with brilliant, immediate but atmospheric sound. Solti's rather extrovert approach is here at its most impressive. His fast tempi may mean that he misses some of the deeper emotions, and the added brightness of the CD transfer perhaps emphasizes this, but it is still a very convincing and involving performance.

Barbirolli gives a characteristically expansive account of Mahler's *Sixth Symphony*, and there are many of the same fine qualities as in his version of the *Fifth*, recorded with the same orchestra a year later. But, particularly in the first movement, the slow tempo is allowed to drag a little, so that tension falls. Such wavering of concentration will not trouble everyone, but the 1967 Kingsway Hall recording has now lost some of its bloom. Moreover there is nothing like the same illusion of a live Barbirolli performance as there is with the *Fifth*. There is a choice of couplings, and the pairing with *Ein Heldenleben* is to be preferred as it has a superior CD transfer. The alternative brings one of the most beautiful performances of Strauss's *Metamorphosen* ever recorded; but again the sound is less full than on the original LPs.

At spacious speeds Rattle directs a thoughtful, finely detailed reading of what has become a favourite symphony for him. The performance yet lacks the electric tension which usually marks his work with this orchestra, with ensemble less crisp. One admires without being involved in the way Mahler demands, even in Rattle's tender and hushed account of the slow movement, which he places second in the scheme instead of third, following Mahler's last thoughts on the work rather than what is published. The sound is full and warm, but in its diffuseness it undermines tension further compared with the finest versions.

By dint of omitting the exposition repeat in the first movement Yoel Levi's version is squeezed on to a single disc, despite an exceptionally spacious reading of the finale. His is generally an extrovert approach to Mahler, leading occasionally to heaviness, though with finely disciplined playing from the Atlanta Orchestra, vividly recorded.

Symphony No. 6 (arr.for piano duet by Zemlinsky).
(N) ** MDG Dig. MDGL 300 [id.]. Silvia Kenker, Evelinde Trenker.

Zemlinsky's piano duet arrangement of No. 6 makes a fascinating curiosity, beautifully played with keen concentration by the German duo, and presented in very vivid sound.

Symphony No. 7 in E min.
*** DG (IMS) Dig. 419 211-2 (2) [id.]. NYPO, Bernstein.
(M) *** Decca 425 041-2 [id.]. Chicago SO, Solti.
(M) *** DG Dig. 445 513-2 [id.]. Chicago SO, Abbado.
(N) (M) *** Sony SMK 60564 [id.]. NYPO, Bernstein.
**(*) EMI Dig. CDC7 54344-2 [id.]. CBSO, Rattle.
(BB) **(*) Naxos Dig. 8.550531 [id.]. Polish Nat. RSO, Michael Halász.

Leonard Bernstein's *Seventh* for DG was recorded from live performances. It is a riveting performance from first to last, ending with a searingly exciting account of the finale which triumphantly flouts the idea of this as a weak conclusion. It is a performance to send you off cheering – a splendid example of Bernstein's flair in Mahler. The recording is a little harsh at times, next to the finest modern digital sound.

In interpretation, Solti's version is as successful as his fine account of the *Sixth Symphony*, extrovert in display but full of dark implications. The tempi tend to be challengingly fast – at the very opening, for example, and in the scherzo (where Solti is mercurial) and in the finale (where his energy carries shock-waves in its trail). The second *Nachtmusik* is enchantingly seductive, and throughout the orchestra plays superlatively. This is one of Solti's finest Mahler records and the recording is brilliant and full – the CD transfer increases the brightness.

Abbado's command of Mahlerian characterization has never been more tellingly displayed than in this most problematic of the symphonies; even in the loosely bound finale Abbado unerringly draws the threads together. The precision and polish of the Chicago orchestra go with total commitment, and the recording is one of the finest DG has made with this orchestra.

In 1965, Bernstein drew an earlier performance of the *Seventh* of characteristic intensity and beauty from the New York Philharmonic; his love of the music is evident in every bar. The playing is fabulous, yet there are also reservations. His warmth of phrasing in the second subject makes Bernstein's pointing sound self-conscious and tense, and in the Night music of the second and fourth movements, where the New York orchestra produces playing of heavenly refinement, the same feeling is present. Even in the finale, where Bernstein's thrusting dynamism holds the disparate structure together, there is the feeling that he is unable to relax into simplicity. The recording, made in the Avery Fisher Hall, is vivid and forward, not as full-bodied or refined as the later, DG version, which is worth the considerable extra outlay.

Rattle, as ever, proves a sensitive and persuasive Mahlerian, in this most equivocal Mahler symphony. He made this recording live in The Maltings at Snape, disappointed with an earlier, studio version, which he did not want to have issued. Sadly, live or not, this performance does not have the biting tension and thrust that makes Rattle's recording of the *Second Symphony* so compelling, and the sound is not as full. The first movement suffers most, and the finale is the most successful. But as a single-disc version of the symphony – when most other versions take two CDs – this is still well worth considering.

Very well played and treated to refined and well-balanced digital recording, the Naxos version offers excellent value on a single disc at super-bargain price. With well-chosen speeds, often brisk but unhurried, with crisp ensemble and good rhythmic point, the only snag is that, by the standards of the finest versions, it is undercharacterized, lacking both flamboyance and tragic weight. Even there one has an advantage in the haunting melody of the second *Nachtmusik*, which is the more moving for being treated in a restrained way.

Symphony No. 8 (Symphony of 1000).
(M) *** Decca Legends 460 972-2 [id.]. Harper, Popp, Augér, Minton, Watts, Kollo, Shirley-Quirk, Talvela, V. Boys' Ch., V. State Op. Ch. & Singverein, Chicago SO, Solti.
(B) *** Sony SBK 48281 [id.]. Robinson, Marshall, Heichele, Wenkel, Laurich, Walker, Stilwell, Estes, Frankfurt Kantorei, Singakademie, Limburger Boys' Ch., Op. & Museum O, Gielen.
(N) **(*) BBC Legends BBCL 4002-7 [id.]. Barker, Hatt, Giebel, Meyer, Watts, Neate, Orda, van Mill, BBC Ch. and Choral Soc., Goldsmith's Ch. Union, Hampstead Ch. Soc., Emanuel School Boys' Ch., Orpington Jun. Singers, LSO, Jascha Horenstein.
**(*) DG Dig. 445 843-2 (2) [id.]. Studer, McNair, Rost, Von Otter, Lang, Seiffert, Terfel, Rootering, Tölz Boys' Ch., Berlin R. & Prague Philharmonic Ch., BPO, Abbado.
(N) ** RCA Dig. 09026 68348-2(2) [id.]. Marc, Sweet, Norberg-Schulz, Kasarova, Liang, Heppner, Leiferkus, Pape, Bayerischen Rundfunks Ch., Berlin Rundfunkchor, Stuttgart Südfunk Ch., Tölzer Knabenchor, Bayerischen Rundfunks SO, Sir Colin Davis.

(i) *Symphony No. 8 (Symphony of 1000). Symphony No. 10: Adagio.*
(N) (B) *** DG Double Dig. 459 406-2 (2). (i) Studer, Blasi, Jo, Lewis, Meier, Nagai, Allen, Sotin, Southend Boys' Ch.; Philh. O, Sinopoli.
**(*) DG (IMS) 435 102-2 (2). VPO, Bernstein, (i) with Price, Blegen, Zeumer, Schmidt, Baltsa, Riegel, Prey, Van Dam, V. Op. Ch., V. Boys' Ch.

Giuseppe Sinopoli gives a ripely passionate account of this most extravagant symphony, recorded with a richness and body that outshine any digital rival. In vividness of atmosphere it is matched only by Solti's magnificent analogue version, recorded in Vienna, which has the added advantage of now being available on a single CD – now reissued in Decca's Legends series – which makes a strong alternative choice. Sinopoli, flexible in his approach to speed, here conveys a warmth of expression that brings joyful exuberance to the great outburst of the opening *Veni creator spiritus*. It builds into one of the most thrilling accounts ever, helped by a superb team of soloists and incandescent choral singing, recorded with fine weight and body. In the long second movement and its setting of the closing scene of *Faust*, Sinopoli's approach is almost operatic in its dramatic flair, magnetically leading from one section to another, with each of the soloists characterizing strongly. As in the first movement, the chorus sings with fine control and incandescent tone, from the hypnotic first entry through to a thrilling final crescendo on '*Alles vergangliche*'. The *Adagio* from the *Tenth Symphony* makes a useful fill-up, but Sinopoli's very slow reading, with detail very heavily underlined, takes away the dark purposefulness of the argument.

Bernstein's DG version of the *Eighth*, also coupled with the *Adagio* from the *Tenth*, is certainly compelling – and better recorded (in 1975) than his earlier CBS/Sony version. But at full price it is hardly a primary recommendation, even though the sound is quite full and atmospheric.

Recorded live at the opening of the Alte Oper in Frankfurt in August 1981, Gielen's version offers a direct, fresh reading, full of atmosphere, in which brisk speeds allow ample weight. The analogue recording is less full than some, but it is naturally balanced with plenty of presence, if with brass a little distant. The chorus sings with heartfelt intensity, and the soloists make a distinguished team, except that the ringing Heldentenor, Mallory Walker, develops a beat in the voice under stress as Dr Marianus. On a single disc at budget price in Sony's Essential Classics series, it makes an outstanding bargain.

When the BBC mounted Horenstein's monumental performance of the *Eighth Symphony* at the Royal Albert Hall in March 1959, there was only one commercial recording in existence (the Rotterdam Philharmonic under Eduard Flipse on Philips) – and that was in mono, and the work had not been heard in public in the U.K. since Sir Adrian Boult directed it in 1948. Bernard Keeffe describes how the performance came into being. The Third Programme was in danger of underspending its allowance and rather than having it trimmed in the following year, decided at relatively short notice to mount one of the most expensive works in the repertoire. Horenstein's reading conveys a thrilling sense of occasion, and though it does not challenge some of the later commercial recordings, it is the feeling that they were engaged in something special that makes this so memorable. Though audience noises are intrusive at times, the atmosphere is vividly caught, with the conductor's unforced, firmly paced reading magnetic from beginning to end, always natural, never exaggerated. Other readings may have a higher voltage or present a more distinctive view, but this has a special place in the Mahler archive. The sound the BBC engineers get from the Festival Hall holds up very well. The second disc includes a conversation between Horenstein and the critic, Alan Blyth.

Claudio Abbado's 1994 recording, keenly analytical and precisely balanced, fails to capture the very quality one would expect in a live account: a sense of atmosphere. Except in the final chorus, '*Alles vergangliche*', where the tension and slow momentum are irresistible, making a magnificent climax, this is too often a detached-sounding reading, clear and transparent rather than intense, relating the music more than usual to Mahler's *Knaben Wunderhorn* inspirations.

Sir Colin Davis has the benefit of the wonderful Bavarian Orchestra, who play with great eloquence and commitment, and excellent engineering from his RCA team. There is some very fine choral singing and the sweep and grandeur of Mahler's vision comes over clearly. But the performance is flawed by some of the female singers. The soloists are too close to the microphone and are uneven, in what is otherwise a well-balanced sound picture. Alessandra Marc's vibrato is intrusive and neither Sharon Sweet nor Ning Liang gives much pleasure.

Symphony No. 9 in D min.
*** DG Gold Dig. 439 024-2 (2) [id.]. BPO, Karajan.
(N) *** EMI Dig. CDS5 56580-2 (2) [id.]. VPO, Sir Simon Rattle – R. STRAUSS: *Metamorphosen for 23 solo strings.* ***
*** DG (IMS) 435 378-2 [id.]. BPO, Leonard Bernstein.
(N) (M) *** Sony SMK 60597 [id.]. NYPO, Bernstein.
(M) *** EMI CDM7 63115-2 [id.]. BPO, Barbirolli.
(N) (M) *** EMI CMS5 67036-2 (2). New Philh. O, Klemperer – R. STRAUSS: *Metamorphosen;* WAGNER: *Siegfried idyll.* ***
(B) (***) Dutton Lab. mono CDEA 5005 [id.]. VPO, Bruno Walter.
(N) ** DG Dig. 457 581-2 [id.]. Chicago SO, Pierre Boulez.

Symphony No. 9 (with rehearsal & conversation between Bruno Walter and Arnold Michaelis).
(M) *** Sony SMK 64452 (2) [id.]. Columbia SO, Bruno Walter.

Symphony No. 9 in D (with separate talk by the conductor on performing and listening to the symphony).
(N) (M) **(*) Telarc Dig. 3CD 80527 (3 for cost of 1) [id.]. Philh. O, Benjamin Zander.

Symphony No. 9; Symphony No. 10: Adagio.
*** Nuova Era Dig. 6906/7 (2). Mahler-Jugend O, or European Community Youth O, James Judd.

Symphony No. 9; (i) *Kindertotenlieder; 5 Rückert Lieder.*
(B) *** DG Double 453 040-2 (2). BPO, Karajan; (i) with Christa Ludwig.

Symphony No. 9; (i) *Das Lied von der Erde.*
(N) (B) *** Ph. Duo 462 299-2 (2) [id.]. Concg. O, Haitink; (i) with Dame Janet Baker, James King.

Fine as Karajan's other Mahler recordings have been, his two accounts of the *Ninth* transcend them. In the earlier analogue version it is the combination of richness and concentration in the outer movements that makes for a reading of the deepest intensity, while in the middle two movements there is point and humour as well as refinement and polish. Helped by full, spacious recording, the sudden pianissimos which mark both movements have an ear-pricking realism such as one rarely experiences on record, and the unusually broad tempi are superbly controlled. In the finale Karajan is not just noble and stoic; he finds the bite of passion as well, sharply set against stillness and repose.

Yet within two years Karajan went on to record the work even more compulsively at live performances in Berlin. The major difference in that later recording is that there is a new, glowing optimism in the finale, rejecting any Mahlerian death-wish and making it a supreme achievement. The 'original-image' bit-processing has added to the projection, but the strings have plenty of body.

The earlier (1980) analogue performance makes a remarkable bargain alternative, reissued as a DG Double and costing half as much as the later, digital recording. Moreover the performances of the *Kindertotenlieder* and *Rückert Lieder* have a distinction and refinement of playing which stand out above all.

Haitink is at his very finest in Mahler's *Ninth*, and the last movement, with its slow expanses of melody, reveals a unique concentration. Unlike most other conductors he maintains his intensely slow tempo from beginning to end. This is a great performance, beautifully recorded at the end of the 1960s, and with the earlier movements superbly performed – the first movement a little restrained, the second pointed at exactly the right speed, and the third gloriously extrovert and brilliant – this will be for many Mahlerians a primary recommendation, particularly as it now comes generously recoupled in Duo format with Haitink's famous set of *Das Lied von der Erde* with Baker and King. This is also available separately, and on an alternative Duo coupled with other Mahler song cycles – see below.

Rattle's reading, recorded live in the Musikverein in Vienna, consistently brings out the deeper qualities in No. 9, the hushed, tender intensity of the outer movements erupting in monumental climaxes with dynamic contrast matched by emotional power. Equally the central movements are just as sharply characterized, with the fun and wit behind the writing conveyed with winning lightness, aptly Viennese. The sound is not as full or immediate as in some versions, but the beauty and subtlety of the Vienna Philharmonic's playing comes over vividly. Strauss's *Metamorphosen* makes an excellent fill-up.

Bernstein's version of Mahler's *Ninth*, made live in 1979, was the solitary occasion when he was permitted to conduct Karajan's own orchestra, and the response is electric, with playing not only radiant and refined but also deeply expressive in direct response to the conductor. Highly spontaneous, with measured speeds superbly sustained in a tautly concentrated reading. Bernstein conveys a comparably hushed inner quality.

Barbirolli greatly impressed the Berliners with his Mahler performances live, and this recording reflects the players' warmth of response. He opted to record the slow and intense finale before the rest, and the beauty of the playing makes it a fitting culmination. The other movements are strong and alert too, and the sound remains full and atmospheric, though now more clearly defined. An unquestionable bargain.

Bernstein's New York *Ninth* – a lucky symphony on record – is undoubtedly a great performance. Here Bernstein's sense of urgency has its maximum impact, though in the finale he does not quite achieve the visionary intensity of his later recording, for DG with the Berlin Philharmonic. The recording, made in the Avery Fisher Hall at the same time as his equally successful *Seventh*, is forwardly balanced but has plenty of body.

Zander is a natural Mahlerian, and his is a powerful, red-bloodedly passionate, yet at times relatively intimate view of this visionary symphony. The concentration of the performance is immensely compelling throughout, with the hushed intensity of the final *Adagio* superbly caught, enhanced by an exceptionally spacious tempo, very well sustained. That said, while the orchestra is given great presence, the sound lacks full body as recorded in the difficult acoustic of the Barbican Hall. This detracts from the weight of impact, in spite of the electricity of live performance. Nevertheless this is a very gripping account indeed. Zander is a major new international personality on the rostrum, and (like Bernstein before him) he is a great communicator. His illuminating and thoughtful extended talk on the third disc is a distinct bonus. The three discs come for the cost of one, and apart from the normal documentation, there is a folded facsimile of the first page of Mahler's score, with the conductor's markings. Even if you have another recording of this symphony, Zander's version is worth considering for there is no doubt of his special insights.

Walter's Sony (originally CBS) performance was recorded in late January and early February 1961, and the producer, John McClure, took the opportunity to record a working portrait of the occasion. That is supplemented here by a 16-minute conversation between the conductor and Arnold Michaelis, dating from five years earlier. Walter's performance lacks mystery at the very start, but through the long first movement he unerringly builds up a consistent structure, controlling tempo more closely than most rivals, preferring a steady approach. The middle two movements similarly are sharply focused rather than genial, and the finale, lacking hushed pianissimos, is tough and stoically strong. A fine performance, quite different from his famous 1938 VPO account which (courtesy of Mike Dutton) is now available in a really first-class transfer.

Klemperer's performance was recorded in 1967 after a serious illness. His refusal to languish pays tribute to his spiritual defiance, and the physical power is underlined when the sound is full-bodied and firmly focused. The sublimity of the finale comes out the more intensely, with overt expressiveness held in check and deep emotion implied rather than made explicit. Now recoupled both with the Strauss *Metamorphosen* and Wagner's *Siegfried idyll*, this is one of the more important reissues in EMI's 'Klemperer Legacy'.

Judd conducts the brilliant young players of the Mahler-Jugend Orchestra in a deeply moving account of the *Ninth*, recorded live in Bratislava in April 1990. With recording of spectacular range and vividness, this makes one of the most appealing of all versions. The searing emotional commitment of the players comes out consistently, and no allowance whatever need be made on technical grounds for their youth. The performance of the *Adagio* from *No. 10* is not quite so distinguished, though warmly satisfying; it was recorded in August 1987 by the rival band from EEC countries, the European Community Youth Orchestra.

Bruno Walter's 1938 version with the Vienna Philharmonic was the first recording of this symphony ever issued. The opening is not promising, with coughing very obtrusive; but then, with the atmosphere of the Musikvereinsaal caught more vividly than in most modern recordings, the magnetism of Walter becomes irresistible in music which he was the first ever to perform. Ensemble is often scrappy in the first movement, but intensity is unaffected; even at its flowing speed, the finale brings warmth and repose with no feeling of haste. The new Dutton transfer (transferred direct from 78-r.p.m. shellac discs) can do little about the audience noises, but the sound-balance is further enhanced over the EMI transfer (CDH7 63029-2), and the last movement in particular offers amazingly natural and believable string-sound.

Boulez's grasp of the work's architecture is impressive and he charts this territory with unfailing clarity and intelligence without fully revealing its spiritual landscape. He seems determined to give us the facts without the slightest trace of hysteria, and his objectivity makes for a thought-provoking reading. He draws from the Chicago Orchestra the most powerful playing – strong, resonant and seamless – with DG's immediate recording adding to the impact. This is Mahler seen in broad daylight. There is no hint of sentimentality in the long *Adagio* finale, which is the more moving for its hint of restraint at a slow speed.

Symphony No. 10 in F sharp (Unfinished) (revised performing edition by Deryck Cooke).
*** EMI Dig. CDC7 54406-2 [id.]. Bournemouth SO, Rattle.
(B) **(*) Decca Double Dig. 444 872-2 (2) [id.]. Berlin RSO, Chailly (with SCHOENBERG: *Verklärte Nacht* **).

With digital recording of outstanding quality, Simon Rattle's vivid and compelling reading of the Cooke performing edition has one convinced more than ever that a remarkable revelation of Mahler's intentions was achieved in this painstaking reconstruction. The Bournemouth orchestra plays with dedication, marred only by the occasional lack of fullness in the strings.

Reissued at bargain price on this Double Decca, Chailly's Decca version is superbly recorded and his grasp of the musical structure is keen. The Berlin Radio Orchestra is highly responsive, although the internal tension of the music-making is not as high as in Rattle's version.

LIEDER AND SONG-CYCLES

7 frühe Lieder (with piano); *11 frühe Lieder* (arr. Berio); *Lieder eines fahrenden Gesellen*.
*** Teldec/Warner Dig. 9031 74002-2. Thomas Hampson, David Lutz or Philh. O, Berio.

Thomas Hampson is in magnificent voice for his unusual collection of Mahler songs. He does the first seven of the early songs and the *Wayfaring Lad* songs with piano accompaniment by David Lutz. He then turns to the remaining early songs in the distinctive orchestral arrangements made by Luciano Berio. Though Berio follows Mahlerian practice in many of his orchestral colourings, his instrumentation overall is far thicker and weightier. Though these arrangements are less 'authentic', they have their fascination when sung as warmly and sensitively as by Thomas Hampson. First-rate sound.

7 early Lieder: *Ablosung im Sommer; Fruhlingsmorgen; Hans und Grete; Nicht Wiedersehen!; Selbstgefühl; Starke Einbildungskraft; Zu Strassburg Auf der Schanz'* (orch. D. and C. Matthews).
*** Unicorn Dig. DKPCD 9120 [id.]. Jill Gomez, Bournemouth Sinf., Carewe (with MATTHEWS: *Cantiga, Introit; September music* ***).

Some years before they took on the task of helping Deryck Cooke with the performing edition of Mahler's *Tenth Symphony*, David and Colin Matthews made this orchestration of Mahler's so-called 'Youth' songs. As is shown in this sensitive performance from Jill Gomez and the Bournemouth Sinfonietta under John Carewe, their feeling for the Mahler sound is unerring, making these a most rewarding addition to the tally of regular Mahler song-cycles with orchestra. It proves a very apt coupling for the warmly sympathetic works of David Matthews on the disc, notably the dramatic scena, *Cantiga*, powerful and immediately attractive.

Kindertotenlieder.
(M) (**) Decca (IMS) mono 425 995-2. Kathleen Ferrier, Concg. O, Klemperer – BRAHMS: *Liebeslieder Waltzes*. (***)

Kindertotenlieder; Des Knaben Wunderhorn: 3 songs; *Lieder eines fahrenden Gesellen; 4 Rückert Lieder*.
**(*) Decca (IMS) Dig. 425 790-2. Brigitte Fassbaender, Deutsches SO, Berlin, Chailly.

(i) *Kindertotenlieder; Lieder eines fahrenden Gesellen;* (ii) *5 Rückert Lieder*.
✿ (M) *** EMI CDM5 66981-2 [CDM 566996]. Dame Janet Baker, Hallé or New Philh. O, Barbirolli.
(BB) *** Naxos Dig. 8.554156 [id.]. Bernadette Greevy, Nat. SO of Ireland, (i) James Fürst; (ii) Franz-Paul Decker.

Dame Janet Baker's collaboration with Barbirolli represents the affectionate approach to Mahler at its warmest, intensely beautiful, full of breathtaking moments. The spontaneous feeling of soloist and conductor for this music comes over as in a live performance and brings out the tenderness to a unique degree. An indispensable CD.

Bernadette Greevy uses her opulent mezzo, firm and even, to bring out the lyrical beauty of Mahler's writing in all three of these orchestral song-cycles. She may lack a degree of vitality in such a song as the second of the *Wayfaring Lad* cycle, the song that gave Mahler his first theme in his *First Symphony*, but her poise in such a great song as the Rückert setting, *Ich bin der Welt abhanden gekommen*, is most satisfying, readily compensating for any lack of emotional weight compared with the finest interpretations. On the disc that song is placed third in the series of five and not – as is more usual – at the end. The Irish National Symphony Orchestra play with rich, velvety tone in every section, not least the strings, matching the soloist, helped by the warmly atmospheric recording, made in the National Concert Hall in Dublin.

Fassbaender gives fearless, vividly characterized performances of Mahler's three shorter orchestral song-cycles, adding for good measure three songs from *Des Knaben Wunderhorn*, including *Urlicht*, usually heard as part of the *Symphony No. 2*. In that last, her voice is not quite as even as usual, and the orchestra in *Kindertotenlieder* is slacker than elsewhere; but otherwise this is an issue to recommend to anyone who fancies these songs with a woman's voice.

The Ferrier version with Klemperer is a live recording taken from a broadcast in July 1951, some two years after her EMI recording with Bruno Walter. Though the voice is caught vividly and the richness of her interpretation has, if anything, intensified, the surface-hiss is daunting. Unusually coupled with the Brahms, in which Ferrier's role is only incidental.

(i) *Kindertotenlieder;* (ii) *Lieder eines fahrenden Gesellen;* (i) *4 Rückert Lieder (Um Mitternacht; Ich atmet' einen linden Duft; Blicke mir nicht in die Lieder; Ich bin der Welt).*

*** DG (IMS) 415 191-2 [id.]. Dietrich Fischer-Dieskau, (i) BPO, Boehm; (ii) Bav. RSO, Kubelik.

Only four of the *Rückert Lieder* are included (*Liebst du um Schönheit* being essentially a woman's song), but otherwise this conveniently gathers Mahler's shorter and most popular orchestral cycles in performances that bring out the fullest range of expression in Fischer-Dieskau at a period when his voice was at its peak.

Kindertotenlieder; 3 Rückert Lieder (Ich atmet einen linden Duft; Ich bin der Welt abhanden gekommen; Um Mitternacht).

(B) *** Sony SBK 63039 [id.]. Jennie Tourel, NYPO, Bernstein – WALTON: *Belshazzar's Feast.* ***

Jennie Tourel was in excellent voice when she recorded these Mahler songs at the beginning of the 1960s. The three *Rückert* songs are particularly beautiful and, with Bernstein providing warmly affectionate accompaniments, this is one of her finest recordings. It is a pity that the new coupling is inappropriate, although it is most enjoyable.

Kindertotenlieder; 5 Rückert Lieder; Das Lied von der Erde: Der Einsame im Herbst.

(N) **(*) EMI Dig. CDC5 56443-2 [id.]. Thomas Hampson, Wolfram Rieger.

With piano accompaniment instead of orchestra, much of the colouring is missing in these songs, but it concentrates attention all the more on the voice, bringing greater intimacy. Hampson here sings with evenly beautiful tone and fine feeling for detail. With a male voice the *Rückert Lieder* work better than *Kindertotenlieder*, with half-tones exquisitely shaded. The baritone version of the second song from *Das Lied von der Erde* makes a welcome bonus. Warm, well-balanced recording.

Das klagende Lied: complete *(Part 1, Waldmärchen; Part 2: Der Spielmann; Part 3, Hochzeitsstücke).*

(N) *** EMI Dig. CDC5 66406-2 [DC 47089]. Helena Döse, Alfreda Hodgson, Robert Tear, Sean Rea, CBSO Ch., CBSO, Rattle.

*** Decca (IMS) Dig. 425 719-2. Susan Dunn, Markus Baur, Fassbaender, Hollweg, Schmidt, Düsseldorf State Musikverein, Berlin RSO, Chailly.

(M) **(*) Sony SMK 45841 [id.]. Hoffman, Söderström, Haefliger, Nienstedt, Lear, Burrows, LSO, Boulez.

(N) *(*) Erato/Warner Dig. 3984 21664-2. Eva Urbanová, Jadwiga Rappé, Hans Peter Blochwitz, Håkan Hagegård, Hallé Ch. & O, Kent Nagano.

Rattle brings out the astonishing originality of Mahler's cycle, but adds urgency, colour and warmth, not to mention deeper, more meditative qualities. So the final section, *Wedding Piece*, after starting with superb swagger in the celebration music, is gripping in the minstrel's sinister narration and ends in the darkest concentration on a mezzo-soprano solo, beautifully sung by Alfreda Hodgson. The ensemble of the CBSO has a little roughness, but the bite and commitment could not be more convincing. Dating from 1983–4, this is one of Rattle's earliest Mahler recordings, but it sounds excellent in what appears to be a new transfer.

The strength of the Chailly version lies with the splendid singing of the Düsseldorf Choir and the demonstration-worthy Decca recording, full of presence. While not quite upstaging Simon Rattle in revealing the music's marvellously imaginative detail, Chailly pulls one special trick out of the hat in *Waldmärchen* by using a boy alto (Markus Baur) to represent the voice from the grave, a tellingly sepulchral effect.

Boulez is a distinctive Mahlerian. His clear ear concentrates on precision of texture, but the atmospheric ambience adds warmth despite the forward balance. Certainly the chill at the heart of this gruesome story of the days of chivalry and knights in armour is sharply conveyed. *Waldmärchen* is less effective than the rest. Good singing from the chorus, less good from the soloists.

Boldly claiming to be the 'world première recording of the Original version', the Nagano version offers not just the introductory movement, *Waldmärchen*, which Mahler set aside, but the unrevised texts of the other two movements. Snags outweigh any advantages, and the performance cannot match the finest rivals, with choral sound often unclear.

Des Knaben Wunderhorn.
*** EMI CDC7 47277-2. Schwarzkopf, Fischer-Dieskau, LSO, Szell.

Szell's warmth and tenderness, coupled with the most refined control of pianissimo in the orchestra, match the tonal subtleties of his two incomparable soloists. Wit and dramatic point as well as delicacy mark these widely contrasted songs, and the device of using two voices in some of them is apt and effective.

(i) *Des Knaben Wunderhorn;* (ii) *Lieder eines fahrenden Gesellen.*
(B) **(*) Carlton IMP PCD 2020 [id.]. (i) Dame Janet Baker, Sir Geraint Evans, LPO; (ii) Roland Hermann, Symphonica of L.; (i; ii) Wyn Morris.

Dame Janet and Sir Geraint recorded Mahler's cycle in 1966 for Delysé, long before they both received the royal accolade. This was also Wyn Morris's first major essay in the recording studio; though he secures crisp playing from the LPO, the orchestral phrasing could ideally show more affection and be less metrical in charming songs that need some coaxing. Dame Janet in particular turns her phrases with characteristic imagination, and her flexibility is not always matched by the orchestra. Baker could hardly be more ideally cast, but Sir Geraint is more variable. However, it is good to have this recording available again at bargain price. Roland Hermann's performance of the *Lieder eines fahrenden Gesellen* is fresh, committed and intelligent, though his baritone is not always flattered by the otherwise atmospheric stereo.

Des Knaben Wunderhorn (excerpts): *Verlor'ne Müh; Rheinlegendchen; Wo die schönen Trompeten blasen; Lob des hohen Verstandes; Aus! Aus!. Lieder: Erinnerung; Frühlingsmorgen; Ich ging mit Lust durch einen grünen Wald; Phantasie aus Don Juan; Serenade aus Don Juan.*
*** DG (IMS) Dig. 423 666-2. Anne Sofie von Otter, Rolf Gothoni – WOLF: *Lieder.* ***

The Mahler half of Anne Sofie von Otter's brilliant recital is just as assured and strongly characterized as the formidable group of Wolf songs. Rolf Gothoni's sparkling and pointed playing makes this a genuinely imaginative partnership, bringing out the gravity as well as the humour of the writing. Excellent, well-balanced recording.

Lieder eines fahrenden Gesellen.
*** Ph. Dig. 426 257-2 [id.]. Jessye Norman, BPO, Haitink – Symphony No. 6. ***

Jessye Norman is a joy to the ear, with Haitink, in his accompaniment for the jaunty second song, providing the necessary lightness. The stormy darkness of the third song fits the soloist more naturally, always a magnetic singer. It makes a valuable extra for Haitink's deeply satisfying version of the *Sixth Symphony.*

Lieder eines fahrenden Gesellen; Lieder und Gesänge (aus der Jugendzeit); Im Lenz; Winterlied.
❁ *** Hyperion CDA 66100 [id.]. Dame Janet Baker, Geoffrey Parsons.

Dame Janet presents a superb collection of Mahler's early songs with piano, including two written in 1880 and never recorded before, *Im Lenz* and *Winterlied*; also the piano version of the *Wayfaring Lad* songs in a text prepared by Colin Matthews from Mahler's final thoughts, as contained in the orchestral version. The performances are radiant and deeply understanding from both singer and pianist, well caught in atmospheric recording. A heart-warming record.

Lieder und Gesänge.
*** Sony Dig. SK 68344 [id.]. Angelika Kirchschlager, Helmut Deutsch (with Alma MAHLER: *5 Lieder*) – KORNGOLD: *5 Lieder, Op. 38; Songs of the Clown.* ***

Angelika Kirchschlager from Salzburg is one of the most talented Lieder singers of her generation, fresh, bright and girlish of tone and with keen insight into word meaning. In Mahler's youth songs she may not have the subtlety of Dame Janet Baker in the same repertory, with tonal contrasts far more limited, but the girlishness and direct approach are arguably more apt for these early songs with their folk flavours, often settings of *Des Knaben Wunderhorn.* The five additional songs by Alma Mahler were written in the early years of her marriage to Gustav: charming inspirations, tuneful and direct but full of subtle modulations, and quite unlike her husband's work. They make an attractive extra item in this impressive début recording.

Das Lied von der Erde.
(M) *** Ph. 432 279-2 [id.]. Dame Janet Baker, James King, Concg. O, Haitink.
(M) *** DG 419 058-2 [id.]. Ludwig, Kollo, BPO, Karajan.
(N) *** EMI Dig. CDC5 56200-2 [id.]. Peter Seiffert, Thomas Hampson, CBSO, Sir Simon Rattle.
*** DG (IMS) Dig. 413 459-2 [id.]. Fassbaender, Araiza, BPO, Giulini.
(N) (M) *** EMI CDM5 66892-2 [CDM 66944]. Christa Ludwig, Fritz Wunderlich, Philh. & New Philh. O, Klemperer.
(M) **(*) Sony SMK 64455 [id.]. Mildred Miller, Ernst Haefliger, NYPO, Bruno Walter.
(B) **(*) DG 439 471-2 [id.]. Nan Merriman, Ernst Haefliger, Concg. O, Jochum.
(**) Decca mono 414 194-2. Ferrier, Patzak, VPO, Walter.
(N) (B) (*(**)) Naxos mono 8.110029 [id.].

Kathleen Ferrier, Set Svanholm, NYPO, Bruno Walter.

(N) *(*) DG Dig. 453 437-2GH. Iris Vermillion, Keith Lewis, Staatskapelle, Dresden, Giuseppe Sinopoli.

(N) *(*) DG Dig. 439 948-2. Jessye Norman, Siegfried Jerusalem, Berlin PO, Levine.

(i) *Das Lied von der Erde;* (ii) *Des Knaben Wunderhorn;* (iii) *Kindertotenlieder; Lieder eines fahrenden Gesellen.*

(B) *** Ph. Duo 454 014-2 (2) [id.]. (i) J. Baker, King; (ii) J. Norman, Shirley-Quirk; (iii) Hermann Prey; Concg. O, Haitink.

The combination of this most deeply committed of Mahler singers with Haitink, the most thoughtfully dedicated of Mahler conductors, produces radiantly beautiful and moving results, helped by refined and atmospheric recording. James King cannot match his solo partner, but his singing is intelligent and sympathetic. However, this version – vividly re-transferred – is now additionally offered on a Philips Duo set, coupled with Mahler's three other key song-cycles, and as such is very tempting. In *Des Knaben Wunderhorn* the singing of both Jessye Norman and John Shirley-Quirk brings out the purely musical imagination of Mahler at his finest, while Haitink's accompaniments are refined and satisfying, especially when the 1976 analogue sound is vividly atmospheric. Hermann Prey's performances of *Kindertotenlieder* and the *Lieder eines fahrenden Gesellen* are fresh and intelligent, and the colour of the baritone voice brings a darkness of timbre which is especially poignant, as in the third song of the *Wayfaring lad* cycle. Haitink's accompaniments are again understanding, yet they create urgency through the briskness of the chosen tempi. If in the last instance Prey cannot quite match Fischer-Dieskau in intensity of expression, these performances are still estimable, and the Philips recording (from 1970) is of very high quality – the effect is most beautiful.

Karajan presents *Das Lied* as the most seductive sequence of atmospheric songs, combining characteristic refinement and polish with a deep sense of melancholy. He is helped enormously by the soloists, both of whom have recorded this work several times, but never more richly than here. The sound on CD is admirably vivid and does not lack a basic warmth.

Sir Simon Rattle in a thoughtful, refined reading brings out the poetry of *Das Lied von der Erde*. Peter Seiffert makes an outstanding choice of tenor soloist, bringing together lyric and heroic qualities, singing with purity and refinement, with fine feeling for word meaning. What will decide choice more than anything is Rattle's preference for a baritone soloist instead of a mezzo. Thomas Hampson sings with both weight and refinement, using a wider dynamic range than most mezzos, not least in the final *Abschied*, where Rattle's concentration and depth of expression is matched by Hampson's singing.

Giulini conducts a characteristically restrained reading. With Araiza a heady-toned tenor rather than a powerful one, the line *Dunkel ist das Leben* in the first song becomes unusually tender and gentle, with rapture and wistfulness keynote emotions. In the second song, Fassbaender gives lightness and poignancy rather than dark tragedy to the line *Mein Herz ist müde*; and even the final *Abschied* is rapt rather than tragic, following the text of the poem; and the playing of the Berlin Philharmonic could hardly be more beautiful.

Klemperer's way with Mahler is at its most individual in *Das Lied von der Erde* – and that will enthral some, as it must infuriate others. True, there is less case for Klempereran nobility in so evocative and orient-inspired a piece as *Das Lied* than there is in the symphonies; if the ear is open, however, Klemperer's preference for slow tempi and his refusal to languish reveal qualities far removed from the heaviness his detractors deplore. With slower speeds, the three tenor songs seem initially to lose some of their sparkle and humour; however, thanks to superb expressive singing by the late Fritz Wunderlich – one of the most memorable examples of his artistry on record – and thanks also to pointing of rhythm by Klemperer himself, subtle but always clear, the comparative slowness will hardly worry anyone intent on hearing the music afresh, as Klemperer intends. As for the mezzo songs, Christa Ludwig sings them with a remarkable depth of expressiveness; in particular, the final *Abschied* has the intensity of a great occasion. Excellent digitally remastered recording (1967 vintage), apart from a forward woodwind balance. This is now reissued in EMI's 'Great recordings of the century' series.

Though Bruno Walter's 1960 New York version does not have the tear-laden quality in the final *Abschied* that made his earlier Vienna account (in mono) with Kathleen Ferrier unique, that is the only serious shortcoming. Haefliger sparkles with imagination and Miller is a warm and appealing mezzo soloist, lacking only the last depth of feeling you find in a Ferrier or Janet Baker; and the maestro himself has rarely sounded so happy on record, even in Mahler. The remastered recording has been freshly remastered for the Bruno Walter Edition and now has even more vivid detail.

Generally Jochum avoided conducting Mahler – as a Brucknerian, underlining the point that these massive masters of symphony are totally contrasted. His reading of *Das Lied*, beautiful and compelling as it is, helps to explain why, for it speaks of the radiant calm of the Bruckner temperament rather than of Mahlerian tensions. Excellent solo singing and fine, clean recording, vivid and kind to the voices: worth considering at bargain price.

It is a joy to have the voice of Kathleen Ferrier

so vividly caught on CD – not to mention that of the characterful Patzak – in Bruno Walter's classic Vienna recording for Decca. The sad thing is that the violin tone in high loud passages has acquired a very unattractive edge, not at all like the Vienna violins, and this makes for uncomfortable listening.

The historic recording from Naxos, taken from an NBC broadcast in January 1948, gives a valuable slant on Kathleen Ferrier's unique interpretation. She is even more deeply expressive than in her Decca studio recording of four years later, also with Walter conducting. Svanholm gives a powerful yet finely detailed reading of the tenor songs, yet many will find the scrubby orchestral sound a serious stumbling block to enjoyment, when the surface noise is often very intrusive. Even so, few will fail to note the desolation and poignancy of Ferrier in the final *Abschied*. An important historical document.

From Iris Vermillion and Keith Lewis a far from negligible performance. The recording quality has both presence and transparency even though the soloists are a bit too upfront and Sinopoli, who can so often prove intrusive, is restrained and supportive. It is the kind of performance one would applaud in the concert hall, but be disinclined to return to.

Levine in what is claimed as a live recording conducts a heavyhanded account of *Das Lied*, weighty and often contrived, lacking flow. Neither soloist is helped by the very close balance. Jessye Norman sounds self-conscious in her detailing, missing the mystery of the final song, and Jerusalem is less subtle than he can be.

(i) *Das Lied von der Erde;* (ii) *5 Rückert Lieder.*
(B) **(*) Sony SBK 53518 [id.]. (i) Lilli Chookasian, Richard Lewis, Philadelphia O, Ormandy; (ii) Fredericka von Stade, LPO, Andrew Davis.

A coupling for *Das Lied* is rare enough, but so generous a one as the *Rückert Lieder* on a bargain-label issue is worth investigating. Ormandy conducts a purposeful, superbly played reading, dating from 1966, that may lack something in Mahlerian magic but which, with fine solo singing, carries you magnetically through to the final climax. Richard Lewis is by his standards sometimes a little rough in tone, but his perception is unfailing, and Lilli Chookasian's warm, weighty mezzo, with vibrato well controlled, brings poise and gravity to her songs, not least the final *Abschied*. Fredericka von Stade makes a characterful soloist in the *Rückert Lieder*, sometimes colouring the voice too heavily; but, with fine bloom on the 1976 sound, she brings out ravishing tonal contrasts, helped by Andrew Davis's sympathetic accompaniment.

(i) *Das Lied von der Erde. 2 Rückert Lieder:* (ii) *Ich atmet' einen linden Duft;* (iii) *Ich bin der Welt abhanden gekommen.* (iv) *Symphony No. 5: Adagietto.*
(B) (***) Dutton Lab. mono CDEA 5014 [(M) id.]. (i; iii) Thorborg; (i–ii) Kullman; (i; iii–iv) VPO, Walter; (ii) O, Sargent.

This is the first of the two great pioneering recordings of Mahler, made in the mid-1930s by Bruno Walter with the Vienna Philharmonic. As with the *Ninth Symphony* two years later, it was a live recording, made in the Musikverein. Here, as in the symphony, the intensity and concentration of the performance are heightened, making this one of the supreme accounts of this now much-recorded score. It is arguably even finer than Walter's later recording for Decca with Kathleen Ferrier, though ensemble is not always crisp, and audience noises intrude. The soloists here are excellent, both with clear, firm voices that convey full expressiveness without strain. The recording is drier than the later one of the *Ninth Symphony*, but voices are very well caught, and the Dutton transfer does wonders in improving the orchestral sound. The generous fill-ups are also welcome. *Ich bin der Welt abhanden gekommen* with Thorborg was recorded from the same concert as the main work, while the other *Rückert* setting – using an English translation – was recorded by Kullman in 1938 with Sargent conducting for the twentieth-century volume of the Columbia History of Music. Walter's 1938 studio recording of the *Adagietto* from the *Fifth Symphony* is fascinating for being so much faster than latter-day readings, while still conveying total repose.

Malipiero, Gianfrancesco
(1882–1973)

String quartets Nos. 1–8.
*** ASV Dig. CDDCD 457 (2) [id.]. Orpheus Qt.

Malipiero's eight *String quartets* are all modest in length: the longest being the *First* (*Rispetti e strambotti*) (1920), which runs to twenty minutes, while the *Eighth* (1963–4), written when the composer was in his early eighties, takes only twelve. None falls below a certain level of distinction, all are beautifully crafted and there is much freshness and fertility of invention. They are all played with expertise and conviction by the Orpheus Quartet, and very well recorded indeed.

Marais, Marin (1656–1728)

L'Arabesque; Le Badinage; Le Labyrinthe; Prélude in G; La Rêveuse; Sonnerie de Sainte Geneviève du Mont de Paris; Suite in G; Tombeau pour Monsieur de Sainte-Colombe.
(BB) *** Naxos Dig. 8.550750 [id.]. Spectre de la Rose – SAINTE-COLOMBE: *Le Retour* etc. ***

Naxos have stepped in enterprisingly and chosen a programme that is not only most attractive in its own right, but which also includes the key items used in the fascinating conjectural film about the relationship between Marin Marais and his reclusive mentor, Sainte-Columbe (*Tous les matins du monde*). Spectre de la Rose consists of a first-rate group of young players, led by Alison Crum, who plays in a dignified but austere style which at first seems cool but which is very effective in this repertoire. *Le Badinage* is perhaps a little stiff and unsmiling, but the key item, Marais's eloquent lament for his teacher, *Tombeau pour Monsieur de Sainte-Colombe*, is restrained and touching. Good, bright, forward recording, vividly declaiming the plangent viola da gamba timbre. But be careful not to play this record at too high a volume setting.

La Gamme en forme de petit opéra; Sonata à la marésienne.
(B) *** HM Musique d'Abord HMA 1901105 [id.]. L. Baroque.

La Gamme is a string of short character-pieces for violin, viola de gamba and harpsichord that takes its inspiration from the ascending and descending figures of the scale. Although it is *en forme de petit opéra*, its layout is totally instrumental and the varied pieces and dramatic shifts of character doubtless inspire the title. The *Sonata à la marésienne* also has variety and character. The London Baroque is an excellent group, and they are well recorded too.

Pièces en trio: Les Contrefaiseurs (for descant recorder, violin, viola da gamba & continuo). *6 Suites* – edited into *10 Suites: in B flat* (for oboe, viola da gamba & continuo); *in B flat* (for treble recorder, oboe, viola da gamba & continuo); *in C* (for treble recorder, violin, oboe, viola da gamba & continuo); *in C* (for treble recorder, oboe, viola da gamba & continuo); *in C min.* (for treble recorder, violin, viola da gamba & continuo); *in D* (for voice flute, descant recorder, violin, oboe, viola da gamba & continuo); *in D min.* (for oboe, viola da gamba & continuo); *in E min.* (for voice flute, violin, oboe, viola da gamba & continuo); *in G min.* (for recorder, violin, oboe, viola da gamba & continuo); *in G min.* (for treble recorder, violin, viola da gamba and continuo).
(M) **(*) Virgin/EMI Veritas Dig. VMD5 61365-2 (2) [ZDMB 61365]. Musica Pacifica.

These ten suites are arranged by the performers here from the composer's collection of six *Pièces en trio pour le flute, violon et dessus de viole avec b. c.* (basso continuo) which were published in Paris in 1692. For instance, some of the movements in the *E minor Suite* have been transposed down to make a *D minor Suite* and suit the chosen instrumentation. In addition, extra movements have been added elsewhere, taken from a manuscript collection of chamber trios by Lully and Marais (*Trios pour le coucher du Roy*), which almost certainly belong to Marais. The music is often doleful in its expressive feeling, but it needs all the advocacy it can get: it would be idle to pretend that it always commands attention. Unlike some of Marais's gamba writing, these suites are of limited musical interest and belong among that repertoire which it is more rewarding to play than to hear. Some might feel that to stretch out the available music to fill a pair of CDs (136 minutes) was too much of a good thing! Aficionados can be assured of the refinement and expertise of both playing and recording.

Suites for viols: in D min.; in G; Tombeau de Mr Meliton.
*** HM/BMG Dig. RD 77146 [77146-2-RC]. Kenneth Slowik, Jaap ter Linden, Konrad Junghänel.

The viol music of Marin Marais is, like certain white wines, an acquired taste; however, once acquired, it is quite addictive. Kenneth Slowik and Jaap ter Linden alternate between bass viol and gamba in the two suites, with Konrad Junghänel on theorbo, and they give vibrant, spirited performances that are most persuasive. The recording needs to be played at a lower than usual level-setting if a realistic result is required.

Marcello, Alessandro (1669–1747)

6 Oboe concertos (La Cetra).
(M) *** DG (IMS) 427 137-2. Heinz Holliger, Louise Pellerin, Camerata Bern, Füri.

The six concertos of *La Cetra* reveal a pleasing mixture of originality and convention; often one is surprised by a genuinely alive and refreshing individuality. These performances are vital and keen, full of style and character, and the recording is faithful and well projected.

Oboe concerto in D min.
(BB) **(*) Naxos Dig. 8.550556 [id.]. József Kiss, Ferenc Erkel CO – C. P. E. BACH: *Concertos.* **(*)

This enjoyable concerto, once attributed (in a different key) to Benedetto Marcello, is given a good performance here by József Kiss and is very well recorded. One might have preferred more dynamic contrast from the soloist, but his timbre is right for baroque music and he plays with plenty of spirit. This disc is well worth its modest cost for the C. P. E. Bach couplings.

Marek, Czeslaw (1891–1985)

Meditations, Op. 14; Sinfonia, Op. 28; Suite for orchestra, Op. 25.
*** Koch Dig. 36429-2. Philh. O, Gary Brain.

Czeslaw Marek was a Polish-born Swiss composer who, when he died in 1985 at the age of 94, left a handful of finely crafted, warmly post-Romantic works which virtually no one had heard. Modest to a fault, and happily rich enough not to care, he gave up composing in 1940 and refused even to promote any performances of his music, let alone recordings. This first of seven discs covering his complete works offers ripely convincing performances in spectacular sound of three richly orchestrated works. Earliest is the four-movement suite, *Meditations*, written in 1913, with very skilful orchestral writing for a 22-year-old. The *Suite*, Op. 25, dates from 1926, consisting of five colourful and atmospheric movements, with a hint of neo-classicism in the romantic mixture. Most rewarding of all is the inspired one-movement *Sinfonia* of 1929, over half an hour long, echoing Sibelius's *Seventh* in its formal control and concentration. This was one of the works which in 1928 vied with Atterburg's *Symphony No. 6* and Havergal Brian's *Gothic Symphony* for the first prize in the Schubert centenary competition.

Marenzio, Luca (1553–99)

Madrigals: Book VI: *Se quel dolor* (madrigal-cycle in 6 voices); Book VII: *Care mie selve; Cruda Amarilli; Questa vaghi concenti.*

(B) **(*) HM Dig. HMC 90856.58 [(M) id. import]. Ens. Clément Jannequin, Dominique Visse – BANCHIERI: *Barca di Venetia per Padova;* LASSUS; VECCHI: *Madrigal comedies.* ***

It is appropriate that Banchieri's comic dramatized account of a trip on *A boat from Venice to Padua* should be coupled with a group of these much more serious madrigals by Marenzio, for an affectionate pastiche of a work by his older contemporary is featured by Banchieri as an elegant centrepiece of the journey. Marenzio's *Cruda Amarilli* is justly celebrated, but the other settings here also carry the aristocratic lines and eloquent pathos which are the hallmark of Marenzio's writing. The singing here is given added colour and warmth by a judicious instrumental accompaniment, but more subtlety in the matter of light and shade within the continually flowing lines would have been welcome. Good documentation with full translations.

Madrigals: *Come inanti de l'alba; Crudele, acerba; Del cibo onde il signor; Giunto a la tomba; Rimanti inpace; Sola angioletta* (sestina); *Strider faceva; Tirsi morir volea; Venuta era; Vezzosi augelli.*

(B) *** HM Musique d'Abord HMA 1901065 [id.]. Concerto Vocale, René Jacobs.

Luca Marenzio enjoyed an enormous reputation during his lifetime, particularly in England, and this record gives an altogether admirable picture of his breadth and range. There are poignant and expressive pieces such as *Crudele, acerba*, from the last year of his life, which is harmonically daring, and lighter pastoral madrigals such as *Strider faceva* and the more ambitious sestina, *Sola angioletta*, which this excellent group of singers, occasionally supported by theorbo and lute, project to striking effect. Fine singing and recording and a modest price serve to make this a most desirable issue.

Markevitch, Igor (1912–83)

(i) *The Flight of Icarus;* (ii) *Galop;* (iii) *Noces;* (iv) *Serenade.*

*** Largo Dig. 5127 [id.]. (i) Lyndon-Gee, Lang, Gagelmann, Haeger; (ii) Markevitch Ens., Köln; (i; iii; iv) Lessing; (iv) Meyer, Jensen.

Born in Kiev, the son of the pianist, Boris Markevitch, the young Igor moved with his family to Switzerland and, after the war, became a pupil of Cortot at the Paris Conservatoire. *Noces*, for piano, was composed in 1925 when Markevitch was only thirteen, and it was on the strength of this and a *Sinfonietta* that Diaghilev was prompted to take him up. Indeed it was with a *Piano concerto* commissioned by Diaghilev that he made his London début in 1929. The young composer-conductor was only twenty when he composed *L'Envol d'Icare*, which Lifar commissioned but subsequently never produced. It is heard here not in its orchestral form but in the transcription for two pianos and percussion. *Noces*, neatly played by Kolja Lessing, is close to the world of Poulenc and Satie, and it is obvious that Markevitch knew his Ravel. The *Serenade* is akin to the Milhaud of the *Petites symphonies*, and there is tremendous energy and a lot of Stravinsky in *L'Envol d'Icare*. This disc does not reveal Markevitch to be a great composer, but it gives an insight into his talent and musicianship which will be of interest to all those who care about the Diaghilev years and Paris between the wars.

Marsh, John (1752–1828)

Symphonies Nos. 1 in B flat (ed. Robins); *3 in D; 4 in F; 6 in D; A Conversation Symphony for 2 Orchestras* (all ed. Graham-Jones).

** Olympia Dig. OCD 400 [id.]. Chichester Concert, Ian Graham-Jones.

John Marsh was essentially a musical amateur (in the best sense). In his way he was innovative: because of the continuing influence of Handel the symphony format was not fashionable in England at that time. For the most part they each consist of three short movements and, while the tunes sometimes have a whiff of Handel, there is a strong element of the English village green. The *Conversation Symphony* does not divide into two separate ensembles but makes contrasts between higher and lower instrumental groupings. Five of his works are presented here with enthusiasm by an aptly sized authentic

Baroque group; they play well and are quite effectively recorded.

Martin, Frank (1890–1974)

Ballades for: (i) *cello & small orchestra;* (ii) *flute, strings & piano;* (iii) *piano & orchestra;* (iv) *saxophone & small orchestra;* (v) *viola, wind, harpsichord, timpani & percussion;* (vi) *trombone & piano.*

*** Chandos Dig. CHAN 9380 [id.]. (i) Peter Dixon; (ii) Celia Chambers; (ii–iii; v–vi) Roderick Elms; (iv) Martin Robertson; (v) Philip Dukes, Rachel Masters; (vi) Ian Bousfield; LPO, Matthias Bamert.

The *Ballades* are among Martin's most personal utterances. Only three are otherwise currently available; there are no alternative versions of the *Saxophone ballade* or the *Ballade for cello*, except in the version with piano. The only other recording of the *Ballade for viola and wind* was by Menuhin and has long been out of circulation. So the present issue is a most valuable addition to the Martin discography, particularly in view of the excellence and commitment of the performances. Subtle, state-of-the-art recording with no false 'hi-fi' brightness, but a natural and unobtrusive presence. An indispensable disc for admirers of this subtle and rewarding master.

(i) *Ballade for piano and orchestra;* (ii) *Ballade for trombone and orchestra;* (iii) *Concerto for harpsichord and small orchestra.*

**(*) Jecklin-Disco JD 529-2. (i) Sebastian Benda; (ii) Armin Rosin; (iii) Christiane Jaccottet; Lausanne CO, composer.

The *Harpsichord concerto* is a highly imaginative and inventive piece, arguably the most successful example of the genre since the Falla *Concerto*. The orchestral texture has a pale, transparent delicacy that is quite haunting, and the atmosphere is powerful – as, indeed, it is in the fine *Ballade*. Christiane Jaccottet is a committed advocate and her performance has the authority of the composer's direction.

(i) *Piano concerto No. 2;* (ii) *Violin concerto.*

** Jecklin-Disco JD 632-2 [id.]. (i) Badura-Skoda; (ii) Schneiderhan; Luxembourg RSO, composer.

The *Violin concerto* is a score of great subtlety and beauty. Don't be put off by the less than lustrous sound, for this is a masterpiece and has the benefit of having Martin himself at the helm. The *Second Piano concerto* is not as lyrical as the *Violin concerto* but is still worth investigation for its thoughtful slow movement.

(i; ii) *Violin concerto;* (ii) *Concerto for 7 wind instruments, timpani, percussion & strings; Etudes for strings;* (iii) *Passacaglia for strings;* (ii; iv) *Petite symphonie concertante for harp, harpsichord, piano & double string orchestra;* (ii; v) *In terra pax* (oratorio).

(B) (***) Decca Double mono/stereo 448 264-2 (2) [(M) id. import]. (i) Schneiderhan; (ii) SRO, Ansermet; (iii) Stuttgart CO, Münchinger; (iv) Jamet, Vaucher-Clerc, Rossiaud; (v) Buckel, Höffgen, Haefliger, Mollet, Stämpfli, Union Ch. & Lausanne Women's Ch.

This set contains not only the pioneering record of the *Petite symphonie concertante* but also Schneiderhan's superb (1955) performance of the *Violin concerto*, often ethereal in its beauty. Both performances have a concentration and atmosphere that have rarely been matched since. The 1951 recording of the *Petite symphonie concertante* brings a thin edge to the upper string timbre, which seems to be emphasized by the CD transfer; the *Violin concerto*, however, sounds much better, with Schneiderhan's gloriously pure timbre captured very naturally. The other orchestral recordings are vivid enough, and Münchinger's shaping of the powerful, 12-minute *Passacaglia* shows him at his most concentrated and the Stuttgart strings in excellent form. *In terra pax* is a 1963 stereo recording. The oratorio was commissioned by the Swiss Radio in preparation for the end of the 1939–45 war and it was first performed by Ansermet. Martin's music has an appropriate eloquence and spirituality, and he is admirably served by his fine soloists. The score falls into four short sections, all with biblical texts, and its sincerity and sense of compassion leave a strong impression. No complaints about the sound here.

Concerto for 7 wind instruments, percussion and strings; (i) *Erasmi monumentum* (for organ and orchestra); *Etudes for strings.*

*** Chandos Dig. CHAN 9283 [id.]. (i) Leslie Pearson; LPO, Matthias Bamert.

Erasmi monumentum is a substantial piece of some 25 minutes. The first movement, *Homo pro se* ('The independent man'), alludes to the name given to Erasmus by his contemporaries; the second is *Stulticiae Laus* ('In praise of folly'), and the third is *Querela Pacis* ('A plea for peace'). The outer movements are pensive and atmospheric; the middle movement is less convincing. Matthias Bamert's account of the *Concerto for seven wind instruments* is very assured, relaxed and animated; although thoroughly persuasive he makes rather heavy weather of the *Etudes*.

The Four elements; (i) *In terra Pax.*

*** Chandos Dig. CHAN 9465 [id.]. (i) Judith Howarth, Della Jones, Martyn Hill, Roderick Williams, Stephen Roberts, Brighton Festival Ch.; LPO, Bamert.

Les quatre éléments, written for Ansermet's eightieth birthday in 1967, is a highly imaginative work which exhibits to striking effect Martin's feeling for the orchestra and his subtle mastery of texture. This is its first recording since Haitink's in the late 1960s, coupled with the roughly contemporaneous *Cello concerto*, and this supersedes it. *In terra Pax* is a noble work, and this makes a distinguished addition to the growing Martin discography. The singers are not perhaps quite as impressive as in the Ansermet set, but in every other respect the new recording is superior.

Symphonie concertante (arr. of *Petite symphonie concertante* for full orchestra); *Symphony; Passacaglia.*
❁ *** Chandos Dig. CHAN 9312 [id.]. LPO, Matthias Bamert.

The *Symphony* is new to the gramophone and is a haunting and at times quite magical piece. It has all the subtlety of colouring of the mature Martin and is a piece of great imaginative resource. The slow movement in particular has an other-worldly quality, suggesting some verdant, moonlit landscape, strongly related in its muted colouring to the world of Debussy's *Pelléas et Mélisande*. The two pianos are effectively used and though, as in the *Petite symphonie concertante*, lip service is paid to the twelve-note system, the overall effect is far from serial. Its main companion here is the transcription Martin made for full orchestra of the *Petite symphonie concertante* the year after its first performance, without the harp, harpsichord and piano soloists and with an ample complement of wind, brass and other instruments. Harp and piano are in fact used for colouristic effects but completely relinquish any hint of soloist ambitions. The *Passacaglia* is the only modern digital recording of Martin's 1962 transcription for full orchestra of his much (and rightly) admired (1944) organ piece. Sensitive playing from the LPO under Matthias Bamert and exemplary Chandos recording.

(i) *Ballade for cello and piano*; (ii) *Ballade for flute and piano. Piano quintet*; (iii) *Violin sonata*; (iv) *4 Sonnets à Cassandre.*
(N) *** ASV Dig. CDDCA1010 [id.]. Ian Burnside, Pears–Britten Ens.; (i) Paul Watkins; (i–iv) Ian Burnside; (ii) Karen Jones; (iii) Laurence Jackson; (iv) Barbara Rearick.

This rewarding issue brings us the rarely heard *Piano quintet* of 1919 in which Martin's debts to Ravel (particularly in the trio section of the second movement) and Fauré are clearly evident. The *Violin sonata* comes from 1932 and is a three-movement piece much indebted to the Debussy *G minor sonata* written fifteen years earlier, which would have been new music then. All these pieces, save for the *Ballades* for flute and cello, pre-date the period in which Martin found his true idiom – in such works as *Le vin herbé* and *Der Cornet*. The performances are as alert and sensitive as one could wish and the recordings are very good too.

Piano quintet; String quintet (Pavane couleur de temps); String trio; Trio sur des mélodies populaires irlandaises.
*** Jecklin-Disco JD 646-2 [id.]. Zurich Ch. Ens.

The *Piano quintet* has an eloquence and an elegiac dignity that are impressive; the short string quintet, subtitled *Pavane couleur de temps* (the title is taken from a fairy story in which a young girl wishes for 'a dress the colour of time'), is a beautiful piece. The *Piano trio on Irish popular themes* is full of imagination and rhythmic life. The *String trio* is a tougher nut to crack; its harmonies are more astringent and its form more concentrated. To summarize: altogether a most satisfying disc, offering very good performances and recordings.

VOCAL MUSIC

Cantate pour le 1er août; Chansons: *Sonnet; Le coucou; Ode; Le petit village; Janeton; Petite église; Ste Charlotte avait voulu. Mass for double choir;* (i) *Ode à la musique. Songs of Ariel.*
*** Collins Dig. 1467-2 [id.]. (i) Simon Birchall; The Sixteen, Harry Christophers.

The most substantial work here is the *Mass for double choir*. It is a beautiful work and well represented in the catalogue. Harry Christophers and The Sixteen give us a performance that can rank alongside any of them, and which has the additional attraction of couplings that are not otherwise available. The *Fünf Gesänge des Ariel*, written in 1950 for Felix de Nobel's celebrated Nederlands Kamerkoor, served as a kind of sketch for episodes in *The Tempest*, but it is marvellous in its own right. All of the vocal writing is resourceful and much of it inspired. Both the *Trois Chansons* of 1931, to texts by Ronsard and the 1944 *Chansons* are pleasing, though not perhaps as inventive as the *Ode à la musique*, a setting of some verses by the composer Machaut. Splendid singing from all concerned, including the baritone Simon Birchall in the *Ode à la musique*. This, incidentally, is a later piece, written just before *Les quatre éléments*. The *Cantate pour le 1er août* was written during the war years and comes between *Le vin herbé* and *Der Cornet*, though it does not match their level of inspiration. In every respect, however, this is a rewarding and beautiful record that will give all who value this great composer much satisfaction.

Der Cornet.
*** Orfeo Dig. S 164881A [id.]. Marjana Lipovšek, Austrian RSO, Zagrosek.
*** Ph. Dig. 442 535-2. Jard van Nes, Amsterdam Nieuw Sinf., Reinbert de Leeuw.

Der Cornet or, to give it its full title, *Die Weise von Liebe und Tod des Cornets Christoph Rilke* ('The Lay song of the love and death of Cornet Christoph Rilke'), is one of Martin's most profound and searching works. It sets all but four of the 27 stanzas of Rainer Maria Rilke's poem, which tells of a youthful ensign who dies in 1660 'under the sabres of the Turks into an ocean of flowers'. Each of the prose-poems gives a different aspect of the narrative, from the ensign's homesick adolescence and enforced maturity to his discovery of youthful love and early death. Though Rilke's poem sold only 300 copies when it first appeared in 1899, it became a best-seller once the 1914–18 war broke out. Martin's setting for contralto and small chamber orchestra was written at the height of the war and in the immediate wake of *Le vin herbé*, his oratorio on the Tristan legend. The shadowy, half-real atmosphere often reminds one of the world of *Pelléas*; and Martin's responsiveness to the rhythm and music of the words is as idiomatic as Debussy's, even though German was not his native tongue. All his fingerprints are there, and the restrained, pale colourings provide an effective backcloth to the vivid and poignant outbursts which mark some of the settings. It would feature more often in concert performances were singers able to sustain it. It is demanding for the soloist and emotionally exhausting for the listener. The performance by Jard van Nes is no less remarkable than that of Marjana Lipovšek on Orfeo – and honours are equally divided. Sensitive orchestral playing under Reinbert de Leeuw and faithfully balanced, well-recorded sound. This music casts a powerful spell and is strongly atmospheric. Whether you get this or the Orfeo rival does not matter, so long as you do not miss this wonderful work.

(i) *Golgotha* (oratorio).(ii) *Mass for double choir*.
(N) (B)*** Erato Ultima Analogue/Dig. Double 3984 24237-2 (2) [id.]. (i) Wally Stampfli, Marie-Lise de Montmollin, Eric Tappy, Pierre Mollet, Philip Huttenlocher, Faller Ch., Lausanne University Ch., SO, Robert Faller; (ii) Midi Chamber Ch., Denis Martin.

Martin's post-war oratorio *Golgotha* is a work of power and substance whose neglect, like that of *Le vin herbé*, is puzzling. It has all the qualities that his finest work exhibits, nobility and elevation of feeling, and its inspiration runs at a high level. This recording appeared on LP in the late 1960s and briefly on CD, but its reissue at this price level makes it even more recommendable. Some have argued that it is possibly the greatest Passion since Bach but, in contradistinction to Bach, the narrative passes freely between the various soloists and the body of the choir. This is the only recording so far of *Golgotha* and it comes with a recommendable digital account of the *Mass for double choir*, not the equal of the Westminster version, but nonetheless eminently worthwhile.

Mass for double choir.
*** United Recordings 88033 [id.]. Vasari, Jeremy Backhouse – HOWELLS: *Requiem* etc. ***
(*) Nimbus Dig. NI 5197 [id.]. Christ Church Cathedral Ch., Oxford, Stephen Darlington – POULENC: *Mass in G* etc. *

(i) *Mass for double choir;* (ii) *Passacaille for organ*.
(N) ❀*** Hyperion Dig. CDA 67017 [id.]. Westminster Cathedral Ch., James O'Donnell – PIZZETTI: *Messa di requiem; De profundis*. *** ❀

The *Mass for double choir* is one of Martin's purest and most sublime utterances. It was written in 1922 for his own satisfaction without the thought of performance. Martin added the *Agnus Dei* in 1926 but kept the whole work in a drawer until the 1960s. In recent years it has at last come into its own on record. The latest version from the Westminster Cathedral Choir under James O'Donnell (Hyperion) is the most outstanding. The boys produce marvellously focused tone of great purity and expressive power, and the tonal blend that James O'Donnell achieves throughout is little short of miraculous. This is a reading whose fervour and eloquence haunts the listener. It won *Gramophone* magazine's 'Record of the Year' Award in 1998, and deservedly so. As a fill-up James O'Donnell offers the *Passacaille* for organ, together with two magnificent Pizzetti works.

Irrespective of the above competition, the United Recordings version is also quite masterly in every respect and Vasari, a choir conducted by Jeremy Backhouse, get remarkably fine results. A very convincing performance and an exemplary recording.

The Choir of Christ Church Cathedral, Oxford, under Stephen Darlington also give a good account of themselves: their tone is clean and beautifully balanced. The boys' voices are moving in a different way from that of the Frankfurt choir, but the English performance does not add up to quite as impressive or richly imaginative a musical experience. The Nimbus disc is eminently well recorded.

(i) *6 Monologues from Everyman;* (ii) *Maria triptychon;* (i) *The Tempest:* 3 excerpts.
*** Chandos Dig. CHAN 9411 [id.]. (i) David Wilson-Johnson (ii) Linda Russell; LPO, Bamert.

Only three excerpts from Frank Martin's opera, *The Tempest* (1953–5), have so far been recorded (on both occasions by Fischer-Dieskau, once with the composer himself and on another occasion under Ansermet), and such is their quality that the appetite is whetted for the whole work. As with the present Chandos CD, Fischer-Dieskau's DG recording coupled them with the *Everyman monologues*, one of the most powerful song-cycles of the twentieth century; it is a measure of David Wilson-Johnson's artistry here that in both instances one forgets the exalted comparison that the appearance of this new record invites. He sings with intense – but not excessive – dramatic feeling and total commitment and conviction. The extra rarity on this disc is the *Maria triptychon*, which Martin wrote in response to a commission from Wolfgang Schneiderhan for a work that he could perform together with his wife, the soprano Irmgard Seefried. The central movement, *Magnificat*, originally stood on its own and was first given in 1968 under Haitink, but Martin subsequently added the two outer movements, *Ave Maria* and *Stabat Mater*. The former is one of his most inspired pieces, and Linda Russell and the violinist Duncan Riddell give a totally dedicated account of it. This is a most beautiful work, and Bamert and the LPO give a thoroughly sympathetic account of it. They generate a keen sense of atmosphere, and the Chandos recording is every bit as good as the other issues in this splendid series.

Requiem.
*** Jecklin-Disco JD 631-2 [id.]. Speiser, Bollen, Tappy, Lagger, Lausanne Women's Ch., Union Ch., SRO, composer.

This is arguably the most beautiful *Requiem* to have been written since Fauré's and, were the public to have ready access to it, would be as popular. The recording, made at a public performance that the (then 83-year-old) composer conducted in Lausanne Cathedral, is very special. The analogue recording is not in the demonstration class, but this music and performance must have three stars.

Le vin herbé (oratorio).
*(**) Jecklin-Disco JD 581/2-2 [id.]. Retchitzka, Tuscher, Comte, Morath, De Montmollin, Diakoff, De Nyzankowskyi, Tappy, Jonelli, Rehfuss, Vessières, Olsen, composer, Winterthur O (members), Desarzens.

Martin's oratorio on the Tristan legend is laid out for a madrigal choir of twelve singers, who also assume solo roles, and a handful of instrumentalists, including the piano, played here by the septuagenarian composer himself. It is powerful and hypnotic, and there is some fine singing here from Tuscher, Tappy and Rehfuss. The instrumental playing, though not impeccable, is dedicated (and the same must be said for the choral singing). The 1960s sound is much improved in the CD format.

Martini, Johannes (*c.* 1440–97/8)

Ave Maris stella; Magnificat terti toni; O beate Sebastiane; Salve regina.
(N) *** ASV Dig. CDGAU 171 [id.]. Clerks' Group, Edward Wickham – OBRECHT: *Laudes Christo; Missa Malheur me bat.* ***

Though Martini cannot compare with Obrecht in imagination, the motets recorded here have a simple beauty made the more compelling by the dedicated performances of the Clerks' Group; atmospherically recorded.

Martinů, Bohuslav (1890–1959)

La Bagarre; Half-time; Intermezzo; The Rock; Thunderbolt.
*** Sup. SUP 001669 [id.]. Brno State O, Vronsky.

La Bagarre and *Half-time* are early evocations, the latter a Honeggerian depiction of a roisterous half-time at a football match that musically doesn't amount to a great deal. The three later works are much more interesting – *Intermezzo* is linked to the *Fourth Symphony* – and the collection as a whole will be of great interest to Martinů addicts, if perhaps not essential for other collectors. All the performances are alive and full of character, and the recording is vividly immediate.

(i) *Concertino in C min. for cello, wind instruments and piano;* (ii) *Harpsichord concerto;* (iii) *Oboe concerto.*
*** Sup. Dig. 11 0107-2 031 [id.]. (i) Alexandr Večtomov, Vladimir Topinka, members of Czech PO; (ii) Zuzana Růžičková, Václav Rehák; (iii) Jiří Krejči; (ii; iii) Czech Philharmonic Chamber O; (i, iii) Petr Skvor; (ii) Václav Neumann.

Zuzana Růžičková has made a number of recordings of the *Harpsichord concerto* but this is her most successful. The sound is agreeably spacious, though the balance is synthetic and the piano has equal prominence with the solo harpsichord. However, the playing is spirited and sympathetic; and the *Oboe concerto* is heard to excellent advantage too, with very good playing and a well-laid-out sound-picture. The early *Concertino for cello* with piano, wind and percussion is more than acceptably played and recorded.

Cello concertos Nos. 1–2.
**(*) Sup. 1110 3901-2 [id.]. Angelica May, Czech PO, Václav Neumann.

Cello concertos Nos. 1–2; Concertino in C min. for cello, wind instruments, piano & percussion.
*** Chandos Dig. CHAN 9015 [id.]. Raphael Wallfisch, Czech PO, Bělohlávek.
(N) *(*) Kontrapunkt Dig. 33256 [id.] Michaela Fukacová; Odense SO, Peter Csaba.

The *Cello concerto No. 1* was composed in 1930 but has been revised twice, in 1939 and 1955. It is in this third form that both artists have recorded it. The *Cello concerto No. 2*, written in New York at the turn of the year 1944–5, is the bigger of the two, some 36 minutes in all, and had to wait until Saša Večtomov performed it in 1965, six years after Martinů's death. It opens with a very characteristic and infectiously memorable B flat tune, and there is much of the luminous orchestral writing one associates with the *Fourth* and *Fifth Symphonies*. It is a warm-hearted, lyrical score with a Dvořák-like radiance.

Angelica May, a Casals pupil, gives a good account of both scores and, in the absence of the Wallfisch, this is perfectly recommendable. But as both performance and recording, her version is outclassed by the Chandos, which has much greater definition and presence and also has the advantage of offering the *Concertino for cello, wind, piano and percussion* (1924).

Michaela Fukacová is an eloquent player and no one investigating her performances will have great grounds for disappointment. But the orchestral playing of the Odense Orchestra is not first-class, nor is Peter Csaba's direction, and while it would be wrong to call the recording congested, the sound is not as transparent as the Chandos and does not have quite enough space in which to expand.

(i; ii) *Concerto for double string orchestra, piano and timpani;* (iii) *Concerto for string quartet and orchestra. 3 Frescoes of Piero della Francesca;* (i; iv) *3 Ricercari* (for chamber orchestra with 2 pianos). (i) *Sinfonietta La Jolla; Toccata e due canzoni.*

(N) (B) ** Erato/Warner Dig. Ultima Double 3984 24238-2 (2) [id.]. (i) Jean-François Heisser; (ii) Jean Camosi; (iii) Brandis Qt. (iv) Alain Planès; O National de France, James Conlon.

On both these Erato discs joined together as a Double, the balance is close and unnatural. One soon becomes aware that the microphones are too near to the violins. There is plenty of impact and some vigorous, spirited playing from the strings of the Orchestre National, but overall this is not a match for the Czech Philharmonic and Jiří Bělohlávek on Chandos. The *Concerto for quartet and orchestra* is again very forwardly balanced and the perspective quite unnatural, though the performance by the Brandis Quartet with the orchestra under James Conlon certainly sounds convincing. Conlon also gets some very good playing from the Orchestre National in the *Frescoes*. In the *Toccata e due canzoni*, written at the same time as the *Fifth Symphony* in 1946, the piano is very prominent and the effect, with close lower strings and percussion, is bottom-heavy. The mix is again synthetic; the overall effect is over-lit. The acoustic of Studio No. 104 in the Maison de la Radio in Paris is dryish and there is not enough space round the instruments. In the *Frescoes* the balance is more successful but there is still the aural equivalent of glare. These are marvellously evocative and tuneful scores, but the cramped acoustic diminishes the pleasure these performances would otherwise have given.

Concerto for double string orchestra, piano and timpani; (i) *Sinfonietta giocosa for piano and orchestra;* (ii) *Rhapsody-concerto for viola and orchestra.*

**(*) Conifer Dig. 76505 51210-2. Brno State PO, Mackerras; (i) Dennis Hennig, Australian CO, Mackerras; (ii) Rivka Golani, Berne SO, Peter Maag.

Rivka Golani's unaffected account of the *Rhapsody-concerto*, all the more eloquent for being understated, is here added to the *Double concerto* reviewed below, and the delightful *Sinfonietta giocosa*, both previously coupled with music by different composers. The wartime but apparently carefree *Sinfonietta giocosa* gets a delightfully fresh performance and an acceptable recording, though the balance is a bit synthetic, with little back-to-front depth.

Concerto for double string orchestra, piano and tympani; Spalíček – ballet suites.

*** Conifer Dig. 74321 17919-2 [id.]. Brno State PO, Mackerras.

The ballet *Spalíček* is an engaging score, based on traditional Czech fairytale tunes and nursery rhymes. The music is delightful and some of the numbers, particularly the *Dance of the Ladies of Honour*, captivating. If you enjoy the Dvořák of the *Slavonic dances*, you will respond to this fresh and open-hearted music. Mackerras also includes the powerful *Concerto for double string orchestra, piano and tympani*, again well played and recorded, though the pianist produces some less-than-elegant tone at climaxes. Eminently recommendable, though in the *Double concerto* Bělohlávek perhaps gives the more concentrated reading.

Concerto for double string orchestra, piano and tympani; Symphony No. 1.

*** Chandos Dig. CHAN 8950 [id.]. Czech PO, Jiří Bělohlávek.

Jiří Bělohlávek's dedicated and imaginative account of the *First Symphony* is very good indeed. Bělohlávek is totally inside this music, and the recording, made in the agreeably resonant Spanish Hall of Prague Castle, is very natural. The *Double concerto* is one of the most powerful works of the present century, and its intensity is well conveyed in this vital, deeply felt performance. Strongly recommended for both works.

Oboe concerto.

*** Nimbus Dig. NI 5330 [id.]. John Anderson, Philh. O, Simon Wright – FRANCAIX: *L'horloge de flore;* R. STRAUSS: *Concerto.* ***

The newest Nimbus account, by John Anderson, principal of the Philharmonia, is outstanding in every way, with the *Andante* quite ravishing when the soloist's timbre is so rich. The recording is first class and the couplings particularly attractive.

Piano concertos Nos. 2; 3; 4 ('Incantation').
❁*** RCA Dig. 09026 61934 [id.]. Rudolf Firkušný, Czech PO, Libor Pešek.

The present set by Rudolf Firkušný, who premièred all three concertos and was the dedicatee of No. 3, was well worth waiting for. The finest of them is *Incantation* (*Piano concerto No. 4*), which here receives a performance that is unlikely ever to be surpassed. Its exotic colourings and luminous, other-worldly landscape with its bird-like cries and extraordinary textures have never been heard to better advantage. It is a work of strong atmosphere and mystery, and Firkušný is its ideal advocate. In the *Fourth Concerto* nothing is hurried and every phrase is allowed to breathe – and the same goes for its two companions. The recording is very good indeed.

Violin concertos Nos. 1–2; Rhapsody concerto for viola and orchestra.
(M) **(*) Sup. 11 1969-2 [id.] Josef Suk, Czech PO, Václav Neumann.

The *Second Violin concerto* was written for Mischa Elman, who had heard and liked the *First Symphony* and immediately commissioned a concerto. It is an appealing and inventive score and of greater substance than its predecessor from the 1930s. This came to light only in the early 1970s and finds Martinů very much in concerto-grosso mode. It is resourceful nevertheless, and Josef Suk is the only violinist so far to record it. By far the most poignant and eloquent of these three works is the *Rhapsody-concerto* for viola and orchestra, in which Suk is also the soloist and which dates from the period of the *Fantaisies symphoniques*. Suk is a masterly player, of course, and the Czech Philharmonic play with obvious pleasure. The recordings are analogue and inner detail is not quite as sharply focused as in the very best discs from the 1970s; at mid-price, however, this is quite competitive.

Spalíček (ballet; complete); *Dandelion* (Romance); *5 Duets on Moravian folksongs.*
*** Sup. Dig. 11 0752-2 (2). Soloists, Kantilena Children's Ch., Kühn Mixed Ch., Brno State PO, František Jílek.

The original of Martinů's engaging ballet, *Spalíček*, dates from 1931–2 and must in some sense have been a reaction against the sophistication of life in Paris. This is the first recording of the complete score and it makes an even more positive impression than the more conventionally scored suites (see above). The dances familiar from the suites are interspersed with vocal episodes, both solo and choral, and there is inevitably far greater variety of texture and pace than is evident from the suites. Its three Acts last some 97 minutes and, although there are some longueurs, they are very few. For the most part this music is quite captivating, particularly given the charm of this performance. Two shorter works complete the set: *Dandelion Romance* for mixed chorus and soprano, and *Five Duets on Moravian folksong texts* for female voices, violin and piano, both of which come from his last years. All in all, a delightful addition to the Martinů discography.

Symphonies Nos. 1–6 (Fantaisies symphoniques).
(M) *** Sup. 11 0382-2 (3) [id.]. Czech PO, Václav Neumann.

Symphonies Nos. 1–4.
*** BIS Dig. CD 362-3 [id.]. Bamberg SO, Järvi.

Martinů always draws a highly individual sound from his orchestra and secures great clarity, even when the score abounds in octave doublings. He often thickens his textures in this way, yet, when played with the delicacy these artists produce, they sound beautifully transparent. On hearing the *First*, Virgil Thomson wrote, 'the shining sounds of it sing as well as shine', and there is no doubt this music is luminous and life-loving. The BIS recording is in the demonstration class yet sounds completely natural, and the performances under Neeme Järvi are totally persuasive and have a spontaneous feel for the music's pulse.

Neumann's set was recorded in the Dvořák Hall of the House of Artists, Prague, between January 1976 (No. 6) and 1978 (No. 5). The transfers to CD are excellently done: the sound is full, spacious and bright; it has greater presence and better definition than the original LPs.

Symphonies Nos. 1; 3; 5.
*** Multisonic 31 0023-2 (2). Czech PO, Ančerl.

This is the real thing. Whether or not you have modern versions of these Martinů symphonies, you should obtain these powerful, luminous performances; they come from Czech Radio recordings made in 1963, 1966 and 1962 respectively. They are such superb and convincing readings that readers should not hesitate. The music glows in Ančerl's hands and acquires a radiance that quite belies its date.

Symphonies Nos. 3–4.
(M) **(*) Sup. 11 1967-2 011 [id.]. Czech PO, Václav Neumann.

The Supraphon recordings were made in the 1970s and are analogue. No harm in that, of course, though the sound is a little diffuse and wanting in detail. The performances are good though they are neither better nor more imaginative than those by Neeme Järvi (BIS 363: same coupling) or, in the case of the *Fourth Symphony* alone, Bělohlávek (Chandos). Both of those are full price and the present issue retails at mid-price. Those not wanting to pay more will find these (as one would expect) thoroughly idiomatic accounts. However, if sound is not a primary concern, Ančerl's account of No. 3 has stronger artistic claims.

Symphony No. 4; Memorial to Lidice; (i) *Field Mass.*
*** Chandos Dig. CHAN 9138 [id.]. (i) Ivan Kusjner, Czech Ph. Ch.; Czech PO, Jiří Bělohlávek.

Despite its wartime provenance the *Fourth Symphony* is one of the composer's sunniest works; the infectious high spirits of the Scherzo and the luminous, glowing textures of the slow movement and its harmonic resource are irresistible. There is a radiance about this work that is quite special, and Bělohlávek's account of it is quite the best that has appeared in recent years. The *Memorial to Lidice*, composed in response to a Nazi massacre, is a powerful and haunting piece, and so is the *Field Mass*, which receives its best performance until now – by far. An indispensable item in any Martinů discography.

Symphony No. 5; Les Fresques de Piero della Francesca; Memorial to Lidice; The Parables.
**(*) Supraphon mono/stereo 11 1931–2 [id.]. Czech PO, Ančerl.

Most of these are pioneering recordings. The *Fifth Symphony* comes from 1955 and the *Memorial to Lidice* from 1957 and, although the sound is naturally constricted in range, it never detracts for one moment from the stature of these performances. They have great radiance and give enormous pleasure. The *Three Frescoes* and *The Parables* are in stereo and were made in 1959 and 1961 respectively. The *Three Frescoes* are given a marvellously glowing performance and, though it has still not been possible to remove the slight glassiness and shrillness in the string-tone above the stave, there is rather more detail and body than in the LP. *The Parables*, never released in stereo on LP in the UK, sound better, and the performances have tremendous authority, conveying that luminous quality that make the Martinů sound-world so special. An indispensable element in any Martinů collection.

Symphonies Nos. 5; 6 (Fantaisies symphoniques).
*** BIS Dig. CD 402 [id.]. Bamberg SO, Järvi.

The *Fifth* is a glorious piece and Järvi brings to it that mixture of disciplined enthusiasm and zest for life that distinguishes all his work. Wonderfully transparent, yet full-bodied sound, in the best BIS manner.

Symphony No. 6 (Fantaisies symphoniques).
*** Chandos Dig. CHAN 8897 [id.]. Czech PO, Bělohlávek – JANACEK: *Sinfonietta;* SUK: *Scherzo.* ***

This Chandos version has the inestimable benefit of the Czech Philharmonic. Moreover the interpretation has great dramatic strength and is fully characterized; undoubtedly these players believe in every note. It is an outstanding performance that does full justice to the composer's extraordinarily imaginative vision and is very well recorded.

CHAMBER MUSIC

Cello sonatas Nos. 1 (1939); *2* (1942); *3* (1952).
*** Hyperion Dig. CDA 66296 [id.]. Steven Isserlis, Peter Evans.

Steven Isserlis and Peter Evans offer very good playing and very acceptable recording, and this can be strongly recommended.

(i) *Madrigal sonata for flute, violin and piano;* (ii) *Five madrigal stanzas for violin and piano;* (i) *Promenades for flute, violin and harpsichord;* (iii) *Scherzo for flute and piano; Sonata for flute and piano*; (i) *Sonata for flute, violin and piano.*
(N) *** Fleurs de Lys Dig. FL 2 3031 [id.]. (i) Angèle Dubeau, Marc-André Hamelin, Alain Marion; (ii) Angèle Dubeau, Marc-André Hamelin; (iii) Alain Marion, Marc-André Hamelin.

The performances are as fresh and exhilarating as the music itself. The *Sonata for flute, violin and piano* and the *Promenades* come from the late 1930s when Martinů was living in Paris. The *Flute Sonata* comes from 1945 and both the *Madrigal Stanzas* and the *Madrigal Sonata* were composed in 1942–3 at about the time of the *First Symphony*. They are delightfully inventive and vital, and give little clue as to their troubled provenance. All three artists play with imagination and virtuosity, and the recording has exemplary clarity and presence. The jazz-like *Scherzo* from the late 1920s comes off particularly well.

4 Madrigals for oboe, clarinet and bassoon; 3 Madrigals for violin and viola; Madrigal sonata for piano, flute and violin; 5 Madrigal stanzas for violin and piano.
*** Hyperion Dig. CDA 66133 [id.]. Dartington Ens.

These delightful pieces exhibit all the intelligence and fertility of invention we associate with Martinů's music. The playing of the Dartington Ensemble is accomplished and expert, and the recording, though resonant, is faithful.

Nonet; Trio in F for flute, cello and piano; La Revue de cuisine.
*** Hyperion CDA 66084 [id.]. Dartington Ens.

A delightful record. Only one of these pieces is otherwise available on CD and all of them receive first-class performances and superb recording. The sound has space, warmth, perspective and definition. An indispensable issue for lovers of Martinů's music.

Oboe quartet (for oboe, violin, cello & piano); *Piano quartet; String quintet; Viola sonata*.
(BB) *** Naxos 8.553916 [id.]. Artists of 1994 Australian Festival of Chamber Music.

The best thing here is the captivating *Oboe quartet*, which is quite a discovery. Like the fine *Viola sonata* and the early *String quintet*, whose slow movement is crossed by the shadow of Martinů's master, Roussel, it is not otherwise represented. Its appearance at budget price is doublý welcome in that the performances are lively and spirited and the recording eminently natural.

Piano quintet No. 2.
*** ASV Dig. CDDCA 889 [id.]. Peter Frankl, Lindsay Qt – DVORAK: *Piano quintet*. ***

Martinů's *Second Piano quintet* is a remarkably successful piece, characteristically original in its content and rhythmic style. The Lindsays with Peter Frankl have its full measure. The recording is lively and present, with the piano well integrated, although there is just a touch of thinness on the strings. An outstanding coupling.

(i) *Piano trio No. 1 (Cinq pièces brèves);2 in D min.; 3 in C*. (ii) *Duo No. 2 for violin and cello*.
(N) (BB) *** ASV Quicksilva Dig. CDQS 6230 [id.]. (i) Angell Trio; (ii) Jan Peter Dvhmolvk, Richard May.

Excellent performances of these engaging pieces recorded in very good sound. Anyone wanting the Martinů piano trios need really look no further.

Sonata for 2 violins and piano.
(*) Hyperion Dig. CDA 66473 [id.]. Osostowicz, Kovacic, Tomes – MILHAUD: *Violin duo* etc. **(*); PROKOFIEV: *Violin sonata*. *

Martinů's *Sonata for two violins and piano* finds him full of invention and vitality. Krsyia Osostowicz, Ernst Kovacic and Susan Tomes play it with all the finesse and sensitivity you could want and are excellently recorded. The disc would be even more recommendable if it had a longer playing time than 46 minutes.

String quartets Nos. 1–7.
**(*) Sup. 110 994-2 (3) [id.]. Panocha Qt.

The Panocha Quartet's recordings of the Martinů cycle were made at various times between 1979 and 1982. The *First* of the quartets is both the longest and the most derivative; it is heavily indebted to the world of Debussy and Ravel. The *Third* is by far the shortest (it takes barely 12 minutes) and has the nervous energy and rhythmic vitality characteristic of the mature composer. The *Fourth* and *Fifth* are close to the *Double Concerto for two string orchestras, piano and timpani*. The *Fifth* is the darkest of the quartets and in its emotional intensity is close in spirit to Janáček's *Intimate Letters*. The *Sixth* – and in particular its first movement – is a powerful and disturbing piece, and there is a sense of scale and a vision that raise it above its immediate successor, which is fluent, well crafted and nicely fashioned but wanting in the freshness and spontaneity that distinguishes, say, the *Sinfonietta giocosa*. To be frank, the quartets do not show Martinů at his most consistently inspired but are still worth investigating. The Panocha set is eminently recommendable, even though it is a bit steep to ask full price for it, and the recordings are a bit two-dimensional.

Violin sonatas Nos. 2–3; 5 Madrigal sonatas.
** Sup. Dig. 11 0099-2 [id.]. Josef Suk, Josef Hála.

The *Second Violin sonata* is a short and attractive work, while the bigger-boned *Third* speaks much the same language as the symphonies. Josef Suk and Josef Hála give excellent acounts of all three pieces, though the 1987 recording is less than appealingly balanced. The sound is rather synthetic and too close.

Variations on a Slovak folksong.
(BB) *** ASV Quicksilva Dig. CDQS 6218 [id.]. Bernard Gregor-Smith, Yolande Wrigley – PROKOFIEV; SHOSTAKOVICH: *Cello sonatas;* JANACEK: *Pohádka*. ***

The *Variations on a Slovak folksong* are not top-drawer Martinů, considering that they come from his last year, in many ways a vintage period. The husband-and-wife team of Bernard Gregor-Smith and Yolande Wrigley gives a lively and persuasive account of it and, even if the piano is slightly too prominent, the recording is lively and fresh.

VOCAL MUSIC

The Butterfly that stamped (ballet): 5 scenes (arr. Rybár).
** Sup. Dig. 11 0380-2 [id.] Women's voices of Kühn Ch., Prague SO, Bělohlávek.

Martinů's choral ballet, *The Butterfly that stamped*, is an early work from his Paris years, based on one of Kipling's *Just-So* stories. Unfortunately Kipling's publisher demanded payment for the copyright, and Martinů, who was eking out a penurious existence, had to abandon the project. The five scenes have been put into a performing edition by Jaroslav Rybár. The score has a great deal of Gallic charm and does not follow the avant-garde line of *La Bagarre*. A pity that Supraphon market this slight but charming score (lasting only 41 minutes 47 seconds) at full price – without the addition of a fill-up. (One of his other works of the period could easily have been accommodated on it.)

Recommended to collectors with a penchant for Martinů all the same.

The Epic of Gilgamesh (oratorio).
*** Marco Polo Dig. 8.223316 [id.]. Depoltová, Margita, Kusnjer, Vele, Karpílšek, Slovak Ph. Ch. & O, Zdeněk Košler.
*** Sup. 11 1824 [id.]. Machotková, Zahradníček, Zítek, Proůša, Brousek, Czech Philh. Ch., Prague SO, Bělohlávek.

The Epic of Gilgamesh comes from Martinů's last years and is arguably his masterpiece. It evokes a remote and distant world, full of colour and mystery. Gilgamesh is the oldest poem known to mankind: it predates the Homeric epics by 1,500 years, which places it at 7000 BC or earlier. The work abounds with invention of the highest quality and of consistently sustained inspiration. The Marco Polo performance is committed and sympathetic and the recording very natural in its balance.

Bělohlávek's version can hold its own artistically with the excellent Marco Polo account. The latter was intended to underline the inspired quality of the music itself as much as the quality of performance and recording. This does not displace the Marco Polo but it can certainly be recommended alongside it.

OPERA

Ariane.
** Sup. Dig. 10 4395-2. Lindsley, Phillips, Doležal, Novák, Czech PO, Václav Neumann.

Ariane is a slight work to which Martinů turned as a relaxation from *The Greek Passion*. It is based on the play, *Le voyage de Thésée*, by Georges Neveux. Apparently the demanding role of Ariane was inspired by Callas; it is all quite engaging and high-spirited without being Martinů at his very best. Written in the course of a month, it is a short piece, no longer than 43 minutes, though it is housed in a two-CD format so as to accommodate a multilingual booklet and libretto. The singers (and in particular Celina Lindsley) are very good indeed: only Richard Novák's wide vibrato is problematic. Decent rather than outstanding recording quality.

The Greek Passion (sung in English).
*** Sup. Dig. 10 3611/2 [id.]. Mitchinson, Field, Tomlinson, Joll, Moses, Davies, Cullis, Savory, Kuhn Children's Ch., Czech PO Ch., Brno State PO, Mackerras.

Written with much mental pain in the years just before Martinů died in 1959, this opera was the work he regarded as his musical testament. It tells in an innocent, direct way of a village where a Passion play is to be presented; the individuals – tragically, as it proves – take on qualities of the New Testament figures they represent. Mackerras makes an ideal advocate, and the recording is both brilliant and atmospheric. With the words so clear, the absence of an English libretto is not a serious omission, but the lack of any separate cues within the four Acts is a great annoyance. Extraordinarily vivid recording.

Julietta (complete).
*** Sup. 10 8176-2 (3) [id.]. Tauberová, Zídek, Zlesák, Otava, Bednář, Mixová, Jedenáctík, Procházková, Hanzalíková, Soukupová, Jindrák, Veverka, Svehla, Zlesák, Lemariová, Berman, Prague Nat. Theatre Ch. & O, Jaroslav Krombholc.

Described by the composer as a Dreambook, *Julietta* was given first in Prague in March 1938. This vintage Supraphon recording, made in 1964, captures that surreal quality vividly. You would never guess the date of the recording, for the ear is mesmerized from the very start, when the howling of a high bassoon introduces the astonishingly original prelude. The voices as well as the orchestra are then presented with a bright immediacy which reinforces the power and incisiveness of Krombholc's performance. The sharpness of focus adds to the atmospheric intensity, as when in the first Act The Man in the Window plays his accordion. Ivo Zídek gives a vivid portrait of the central character, Michel, perplexed by his dream-like search, and there is no weak link in the rest of the cast. Informative notes and libretto come with multiple translations.

Martucci, Giuseppe (1856–1909)

(i) *Piano concerto No. 1 in D min.;* (ii) *Le canzone dei ricordi.*
** ASV Dig. CDDCA 690 [id.]. (i) Caramiello; (ii) Yakar; Philh. O, D'Avalos.

The *First Piano concerto* (with Francesco Caramiello a capable soloist) is inevitably derivative, and it is the song-cycle that is the chief attraction here: Rachel Yakar sings beautifully and is particularly affecting in the Duparc-like *Cantavál ruscello la gaia canzone*. The recording is generally faithful.

(i) *Piano concerto No. 2 in B flat, Op. 66;* (ii) *Le canzone dei ricordi.*
*** Sony Dig. SK 64582 [id.]. (i) Carlo Bruno; (ii) Mirella Freni; La Scala, Milan, PO, Riccardo Muti.

The *Second Piano concerto in B flat* is a massively powerful work whose first movement alone runs to 23 minutes. It is Brahmsian in both its scope and scale; however, although it is indebted to him, there is far more to it than that: this is Brahms distilled through very individual filters, and there is no question of the mastery with which the composer unfolds his argument. No doubts either about the virtuosity and sensibility which the impressive soloist brings to bear. Carlo Bruno's name is at present unfamiliar to us but he is a commanding artist whom we would like to hear on more familiar terrain. The performance exhibits infinitely greater authority and finesse than Francesco Caramiello and d'Avalos on ASV, and it is recorded with far greater subtlety and naturalness. It emerges as a far more interesting piece (CD DCA 691). Mirella Freni brings to *Le canzone dei ricordi* all the warmth and delicacy of feeling this lovely score calls for. Muti conducts with evident conviction and gets very fine results from the Milan orchestra. Strongly recommended.

Giga, Op. 61/3; Notturno, Op. 70/1; Novelletta, Op. 82.
*** Sony Dig. SK 53280 [id.]. La Scala PO, Muti – BUSONI: *Turandot suite;* CASELLA: *Paganiniana.* ***

The three Martucci pieces are played with infinitely greater sensitivity and finesse than in the ASV survey of Martucci's symphonies and concertos by d'Avalos. They were all composed at about the turn of the century and have the gentleness and elegiac quality of Fauré and Elgar with a touch of Wagner (Martucci conducted the Italian première of *Tristan*). This is altogether a most valuable issue and can be strongly recommended.

Symphony No. 1 in D min., Op. 75; Notturno, Op. 70/1; Novelletta, Op. 82; Tarantella, Op. 44.
** ASV Dig. CDDCA 675 [id.]. Philh. O, d'Avalos.

The *First Symphony* is greatly indebted to Brahms, but elsewhere there is a vein of lyricism that is more distinctive. The performances by the Philharmonia under Francesco d'Avalos are serviceable rather than distinguished, but the recording is very truthful and well balanced.

Symphony No. 2 in F, Op. 81; Andante in B flat, Op. 69; Colore orientale Op. 44/3.
** ASV Dig. CDDCA 689 [id.]. Philh. O, d'Avalos.

The *Second Symphony* is a relatively late work. Though the performance falls short of distinction, it leaves the listener in no doubt as to Martucci's quality as a composer and the nobility of much of his invention. The *Colore orientale* is an arrangement of a piano piece; the beautiful *Andante*, a work of depth, has a Fauréan dignity. The recording is a bit too closely balanced.

Le canzone dei ricordi; Notturno, Op. 70/1.
*** Hyperion Dig. CDA 66290 [id.]. Carol Madalin, ECO, Bonavera – RESPIGHI: *Il tramonto.* ***

Le canzone dei ricordi is a most beautiful song-cycle, and its gentle atmosphere and warm lyricism are most seductive. At times Carol Madalin has a rather rapid vibrato, but she sings the work most sympathetically and with great eloquence. The *Notturno* is beautifully played. Recommended with all possible enthusiasm.

Mascagni, Pietro (1863–1945)

L'amico Fritz (complete).
(N) *** EMI CDS7 47905-8 [CDCB 47905] (2). Pavarotti, Freni, Sardinero, ROHCG Ch. & O, Gavazzeni.

The haunting *Cherry duet* from this opera whets the appetite for more, and it is good to hear so rare and delightful a piece, one that is unlikely to enter the repertory of our British opera houses. The performance could not be more refined, and Freni and Pavarotti were both at their freshest in 1969 when it was recorded. While the dramatic conception is at the opposite end of the scale from *Cavalleria rusticana*, one is easily beguiled by the music's charm. The Covent Garden Orchestra responds loyally; the recording is clear and atmospheric and has transferred most successfully to CD.

Cavalleria rusticana (complete).
(M) *** RCA 74321 39500-2. Scotto, Domingo, Elvira, Amb. Op. Ch., Nat. PO, Levine.
*** DG 419 257-2 (3). Cossotto, Bergonzi, Guelfi, Ch. & O of La Scala, Milan, Karajan – LEONCAVALLO: *I Pagliacci* *** (also with collection of Operatic intermezzi ***).
(***) EMI mono CDS5 56287-2 (2) [CDCB 56287]. Callas, Di Stefano, Panerai, Ch. & O of La Scala, Milan, Serafin – LEONCAVALLO: *I Pagliacci.* (***)
(M) **(*) Decca 458 224-2 [425 985-2]. Tebaldi, Björling, Bastianini, Maggio Musicale Fiorentino Ch. & O, Erede.
(M) **(*) EMI CMS7 63967-2 (2) [CDMB 69367]. De los Angeles, Corelli, Sereni, Rome Op. Ch. & O, Santini – LEONCAVALLO: *Pagliacci.* ***
(M) **(*) EMI CMS7 63650-2 (2). Caballé, Carreras, Hamari, Manuguerra, Varnay, Amb. Op. Ch., Southend Boys' Ch., Philh. O, Muti – LEONCAVALLO: *I Pagliacci.* **(*)
**(*) Decca 444 391-2 [414 590-2]. Varady, Pavarotti, Bormida, Cappuccilli, Gonzales, Nat. PO, Gavazzeni.
(M) (***) RCA mono GD 86510 [RCA 6510-2-RG]. Milanov, Björling, Merrill, Robert Shaw Chorale, RCA O, Cellini.
(B) **(*) Naxos Dig. 8.660022 [id.]. Evstatieva, Aragall, Tumagian, Di Mauro, Michalková, Slovak Philh. Ch., Czech RSO, Rahbari – LEONCAVALLO: *I Pagliacci.* **(*)
(M) (**) Nimbus mono NI 7843/4 [id.]. Gigli, Bruna Rasa, Marcucci, Bechi, Simionato, La Scala Ch. & O, composer – LEONCAVALLO: *I Pagliacci.* (**(*))

Now reissued at mid-price (pleasingly presented in

a slip-case with libretto) in RCA's Opera Treasury series, this now stands as a clear first recommendation for Mascagni's red-blooded opera, with Domingo giving a heroic account of the role of Turiddù, full of defiance. Scotto is strongly characterful too, and James Levine directs with a splendid sense of pacing, by no means faster than his rivals (except the leisurely Karajan) and drawing red-blooded playing from the National Philharmonic. The recording is vivid and strikingly present in its CD transfer.

Karajan pays Mascagni the tribute of taking his markings literally, so that well-worn melodies come out with new purity and freshness, and the singers have been chosen to match that. Cossotto quite as much as Bergonzi keeps a pure, firm line that is all too rare in this much-abused music. Not that there is any lack of dramatic bite. The CD transfer cannot rectify the balance, but voices are generally more sharply defined, while the spacious opulence is retained.

Dating from the mid-1950s, Callas's performance as Santuzza reveals the diva in her finest form, with edginess and unevenness of production at a minimum and with vocal colouring at its most characterful. The singing of the other principals is hardly less dramatic and Panerai is in firm, well-projected voice.

The early (1957) Decca recording with Tebaldi offers a forthright, lusty account of Mascagni's piece of blood and thunder and has the distinction of three excellent soloists. Tebaldi is most moving in *Voi lo sapete*, and the firm richness of Bastianini's baritone is beautifully caught. As always, Björling shows himself the most intelligent of tenors, and it is only the chorus that gives serious cause for disappointment; they are very undisciplined. The CD sound is strikingly bright and lively.

Though not as vibrant as Von Matačić's *Pagliacci* coupling, this beautifully sung, essentially lyrical Santini performance could give considerable satisfaction, provided the bitterness of Mascagni's drama is not a first consideration. Like the coupling, it shows Corelli in good form; both he and de los Angeles are given scope by Santini to produce soaring, Italianate singing of Mascagni's richly memorable melodies. The recording is suitably atmospheric.

There are fewer unexpected textual points in Muti's EMI *Cav.* than in *Pag.*, but the conductor's approach is comparably biting and violent, brushing away the idea that this is a sentimental score, though running the risk of making it sound vulgar. The result is certainly refreshing, with Caballé – pushed faster than usual, even in her big moments – collaborating warmly. So *Voi lo sapete* is geared from the start to the final cry of *Io son dannata*, and she manages a fine snarl on *A te la mala Pasqua*. Carreras does not sound quite so much at home, though the rest of the cast is memorable, including the resonant Manuguerra as Alfio and the veteran Astrid Varnay as Mamma Lucia, wobble as she does. The recording is forward and vivid.

With Pavarotti loud and unsubtle as Turiddù – though the tone is often most beautiful – it is left to Julia Varady as Santuzza to give the 1976 Decca recording under Gavazzeni its distinction. Though her tone is not heavyweight, the impression of youth is most affecting; the sharpness of pain in *Voi lo sapete* is beautifully conveyed, and the whole performance is warm and authentic. Cappuccilli's Alfio is too noble to be convincing, and the main claim to attention lies in the brilliant forward recording. This set is now issued separately, but remains at full price.

Admirers of Milanov will not want to miss her beautiful singing of *Voi lo sapete*, and in the duet Merrill's dark, firm timbre is thrilling. Björling brings a good measure of musical and tonal subtlety to the role of Turiddù, normally belted out, while Cellini's conducting minimizes the vulgarity of the piece.

As in his parallel recording of *Pag.*, Alexander Rahbari conducts a red-blooded reading of *Cav.*, making it a first-rate super-bargain choice. Stefka Evstatieva is a warmly vibrant Santuzza, well controlled, no Slavonic wobbler, and Giacomo Aragall as Turiddù, not quite as fresh-sounding as he once was, yet gives a strong, characterful performance, with Eduard Tumagian excellent as Alfio, firm and dark. Well-focused digital recording.

EMI's vintage (1940) version of *Cav.*, conducted by the composer with Gigli as Turiddù, came out on CD in an ungenerous two-disc package from EMI, and we await its reissue. It is good to have it again available from Nimbus, along with the curious little speech of introduction that Mascagni himself recorded. Yet the composer's sluggish speeds mean that this opera has to start awkwardly at the end of the *Pag.* disc. Nimbus's transfer captures the voices well, giving them a mellow bloom, though the focus is not nearly as sharp as on the old EMI transfer.

Cavalleria rusticana: highlights.
(M) **(*) EMI CDM5 66048-2. Caballé, Carreras, Varnay, Manuguerra, Hamari, Amb. Op. Ch., Philh. O, Muti – LEONCAVALLO: *I Pagliacci:* highlights. **(*)

Caballé is in good form here and receives good support from the rest of the cast. With Muti conducting strongly, this a recommendable sampler of a highly dramatic performance, vividly recorded.

Cavalleria rusticana (complete; in English).
(M) **(*) Chandos Dig. CHAN 3004 (2) [id.]. Miricioiu, O'Neill, Joll, Montague, Bainbridge, Geoffrey Mitchell Ch., LPO, David Parry.

As in other recordings sponsored by Peter Moores, notably those for Opera Rara, David Parry proves a deeply sympathetic conductor of Italian opera, with a natural feeling for expressive rubato. This is a warmly atmospheric reading of the Mascagni score which, as well as bringing out its atmospheric beauty, helped by opulent Chandos recording with fine bloom on the LPO strings, brings home the high drama, as in the big duet between Turiddù and Santuzza and at the very end. Nelly Miricioiu is an inspired choice to take the role of the heroine, her rich, vibrant voice firmly under control, with fine legato and passionately declaimed climaxes. Dennis O'Neill with his clear Italianate tone is also excellent as Turiddù, passionate and intense whether in the big emotional outbursts or in the playful *brindisi* at the end. It is good to hear the fruity and characterful Elizabeth Bainbridge as Mamma Lucia, and Diana Montague sings with creamy beauty in Lola's Song. The serious blot comes with the Alfio of Phillip Joll, most damagingly in the Carter's song, in which the voice is pitched so vaguely it is half-way to talking, with notes spreading under pressure. A pity, when the rest is so convincing.

Iris (complete).

*** Sony Dig. M2K 45526 (2) [id.]. Domingo, Tokody, Pons, Giaiotti, Bav. R. Ch., Munich R. O, Patanè.

Musically, *Iris* brings a mixture of typical Mascagnian sweetness and a vein of nobility often echoing Wagner. With a strong line-up of soloists including Domingo, and with Giuseppe Patanè a persuasive conductor, this recording makes as good a case for a flawed piece as one is ever likely to get. Domingo's warm, intelligent singing helps to conceal the cardboard thinness of a hero who expresses himself in generalized ardour. The Hungarian soprano, Ilona Tokody, brings out the tenderness of the heroine, singing beautifully except when under pressure. Juan Pons, sounding almost like a baritone Domingo, is firm and well projected as Kyoto, owner of a geisha-house, and Bonaldo Giaiotti brings an authentically dark Italian bass to the role of Iris's father. Full, atmospheric recording.

Mason, Benedict (born 1954)

Lighthouses of England and Wales.

**(*) Collins Dig. Single 2004-2 [id.]. BBC SO, Zagrosek.

Mason's piece is based on the distinctively rhythmic light signals of dozens of specific lighthouses (plus a fog-signal or two). It then develops into an evocative seascape, in its way a descendant of Debussy's *La mer*. Lothar Zagrosek directs a finely concentrated performance, and the recorded sound is outstanding.

Massenet, Jules (1842–1912)

Le Carillon (ballet): complete.

(B) *** Decca Double Dig. 444 836-2 (2) [id.]. SRO, Richard Bonynge – DELIBES: *Coppélia.* ***

Le Carillon was written in the same year as *Werther*. The villains of the story who try to destroy the bells of the title are punished by being miraculously transformed into bronze jaquemarts, fated to continue striking them for ever! The music of this one-act ballet makes a delightful offering – not always as lightweight as one would expect. With his keen rhythmic sense and feeling for colour, Bonynge is outstanding in this repertory, and the 1984 Decca recording is brilliant and colourful. A fine bonus (37 minutes) for a desirable version of Delibes' *Coppélia*, at the cheapest possible price.

Le Cid: ballet suite.

(B) *** Decca Double 448 095-2 (2) [425 475-2]. New Philh. O, Richard Bonynge – DELIBES: *Sylvia* (complete). ***

(M) *** Decca 444 110-2. Nat. PO, Bonynge – MEYERBEER: *Les Patineurs* (with DELIBES: *Naïla*, LSO, Bonynge; THOMAS: *Hamlet: ballet music* ***).

Over the years, Decca have made a house speciality of recording the ballet music from *Le Cid* and coupling it with Constant Lambert's arrangement of Meyerbeer (*Les Patineurs*). Bonynge's version is the finest yet, with the most seductive orchestral playing, superbly recorded, with the remastering for CD adding to the glitter and colour of Massenet's often witty scoring, and made the more attractive at Double Decca price. For the single-disc reissue in Decca's Ballet Gala series, Delibes's charming *Naïla Intermezzo* (a dainty little valse) and the lively, easily melodic – if less distinctive – ballet from Act IV of Thomas's *Hamlet* have been added, played with characteristic flair.

Piano concerto in E flat.

*** Hyperion Dig. CDA 66897 [id.]. Stephen Coombs, BBC Scottish SO, Ossonce – HAHN: *Piano concerto in E.* ***

Massenet, much the most successful French opera composer of his day, unexpectedly completed this substantial concerto at the age of sixty, and received little appreciation. Based on sketches written many years earlier, before his operatic career took off, it regularly reveals Massenet's love of the keyboard, and in a performance like Stephen Coombs's the result is a delight. One might argue that the light manner and lack of weight in the argument do not match the impressive scale of the work – which may have disconcerted early critics – but the writing is full of attractive ideas. That is so, even when in the Slovak dance of the finale the main theme barely skirts banality, providing an extra challenge for Coombs to magick it with sparkling articulation. As in the Hahn concerto – an apt coupling, when it occupies a similar place in that composer's career – Jean-Yves Ossonce is a most sympathetic accompanist, drawing idiomatic playing from the BBC Scottish Symphony, helped by warm, well-balanced sound.

Don Quichotte: 2 Interludes; Scènes alsaciennes; Scènes de féerie; Scènes dramatiques; Scènes pittoresques; La Vierge: The last sleep of the Virgin.
(N) (B) **(*)Erato/Warner Ultima Double 3484 26999-2 (2) [id.]. Monte Carlo Op. O, Gardiner.

These recordings were made in 1978 and this Ultima Double gathers together four of Massenet's seven orchestral suites, plus a few encores, including one of Sir Thomas Beecham's favourites, *The last sleep of the Virgin*. In fact this is all music which would respond to the Beecham touch. John Eliot Gardiner secures quite impressively characterized performances. The *Scènes pittoresques* are bright and fresh, the horns tolling in the *Angelus* with resonant impact. The *Scènes alsaciennes* also come off colourfully. The Monte Carlo Orchestra play well enough and the full recording has rather more presence than we remember from its last appearance; it is natural enough, although some ears will seek more sparkle. However, the slight excess of resonance disguises any deficiencies, for the wind solos are well taken, and the orchestral response is generally persuasive. But the two discs only play for 45 and 41 minutes respectively and the Naxos alternative below fits the four suites comfortably onto one.

Fantaisie (for cello and orchestra).
*** ASV Dig. CDDCA 867 [id.]. Sophie Rolland, BBC PO, Gilbert Varga – LALO: *Cello concerto;* SAINT-SAENS: *Cello concerto No. 1.* ***

Massenet composed his three-movement *Fantaisie for cello and orchestra* in 1897 while on holiday in Aix-les-Bains. Music for the sweet-toothed (and none the worse for that), though its ideas are not anywhere near as memorable as those of its two companions on this disc. The Canadian cellist, Sophie Rolland, and the BBC forces under Gilbert Varga play it with total commitment and fervour as if they believe every note. Excellent recording.

Hérodiade (ballet) *suite; Orchestral suites Nos. 1; 2 (Scènes hongroises); 3 (Scènes dramatiques).*
(BB) ** Naxos Dig. 8.553124 [id.]. New Zealand SO, Jean-Yves Ossonce.

The ballet suite from *Hérodiade* comes in the final scene of the opera and the five movements are nicely scored, including flutes and harp, delicate dancing strings, a luscious tune in the middle strings, decorated by chirpy woodwind, and a vigorous dance finale. The other orchestral suites are also well worth hearing, offering a further series of sharply memorable vignettes, demonstrating Massenet's ready store of tunes and his charmingly French orchestral palette. In the *Scènes hongroises* the charming *leggiero* second movement is followed by characteristic *risoluto* brass writing. The more histrionic *Scènes dramatiques* (with a Shakespearean inspiration) brings a touching and very balletic central *Mélodrame*, originally entitled *Le sommeil de Desdémone*. The playing of the New Zealand orchestra is first class, polished and vivid, though it is a pity that the microphones are somewhat close. The wind have plenty of colour, but the string tuttis are made to sound a bit tight and fierce.

Orchestral suite No. 1, Op. 13; Cendrillon (opera): *suite. Esclarmonde* (opera): *suite.*
** Marco Polo Dig. 8.223354 [id.]. Hong Kong PO, Kenneth Jean.

The delicate atmosphere of *L'île magique* and *Hymenée* from *Esclarmonde*, and the charming *Nocturne* from the *Suite*, Op. 13, is matched by the vigour of the finales from both, the *Marche et Strette* of Op. 13 and *La Chasse*, with its hunting horns, in the operatic suite. The charming *Cendrillon* vignettes also have plenty of sparkle. The playing does not find the degree of Beechamesque finesse that makes for totally memorable results in such repertoire, but this remains an enjoyable collection.

Orchestral suites: *Scènes alsaciennes; Scènes de féerie; Scènes napolitaines; Scènes pittoresques.*
(BB) *** Naxos Dig. 8.553125 [id.]. New Zealand Symphony O, Jean-Yves Ossonce.

Massenet's orchestral suites are in essence picture-postcard music, but they include plenty of tunes (perhaps not always first-rate ones) and the scoring has characteristic Gallic charm and colour. Best known are the somewhat ingenuous *Scènes pittoresques* and the *Scènes alsaciennes.* The most touching movement is the beautiful *Sous les tilleuls* ('Under the lime trees'), with its wilting dialogue between cello and clarinet, played here with an affectionate finesse worthy of a Beecham. With full, sparkling, yet warmly atmospheric recording, this is a first-class disc in every way. Why pay more?

Eve (mysterium in 3 parts).
(N) (BB) ** Arte Nova Dig. 74321 58964-2 [id.]. Geb, Kolczyk, Simos, Steidler, Three Nation Ch., Euregio SO, Jeanpierre Faber.

Eve, described as a mysterium, is a compact oratorio lasting just under an hour. Written in 1875, it tells the story of the Fall of Man, bringing echoes of Mendelssohn and Gounod, as well as cross-references to Massenet's operas. The orchestration is often exotic, regularly including the harp, and with the impact of the Fall intensified on fortissimo timpani. The choruses in particular are most attractive, whether lyrical or dramatic. They are very well performed here under the energetic direction of Faber, by a chorus drawn from three nations – Germany, Austria and the Czech Republic. Sadly, the three soloists are all disappointing, singing with unsteady tone. Warmly atmospheric recording. The French text is given but no translation.

OPERA

Cendrillon (complete).
**(*) Sony CD 79323 (2) [M2K 35194]. Von Stade, Gedda, Berbié, Welting, Bastin, Amb. Op. Ch., Philh. O, Rudel.

Julius Rudel directs a winning performance of Massenet's Cinderella opera. The Fairy Godmother is the bright-toned Ruth Welting and Cendrillon a soprano. Von Stade gives a characteristically strong and imaginative performance, untroubled by what for her is high tessitura. The pity is that the role of the prince, originally also written for soprano, is here taken by a tenor, Gedda, whose voice is no longer fresh-toned. Jules Bastin sings most stylishly as Pandolfe, and the others make a well-chosen team. The recording is vivid, but spacious too. Worth exploring, even at full price.

Chérubin (complete)
❀ *** RCA/BMG Dig. 09026 60593-2 (2) [60593-2]. Von Stade, Ramey, Anderson, Upshaw, Bav. State Op. Ch., Munich RSO, Steinberg.

What Massenet did in this delightful *comédie chantée* of 1903 (he was sixty at the time) was to follow up what happened to Cherubino after the *Marriage of Figaro*. There is none of the social comment of Beaumarchais, or of da Ponte or Mozart, just a frothy entertainment, one brimming with ear-tickling ideas, from the dazzlingly witty overture onwards. In this superb RCA recording the cast is both starry and ideal, with June Anderson powerful and flamboyant as the dancer with whom Cherubino has a fling, Dawn Upshaw sweet and pure as Nina, his faithful sweetheart, and Samuel Ramey warm and firm as the Philosopher. Yet finest of all is Frederica von Stade in the title-role. Cherubino is a perky figure, much more self-confident and pushy than in Mozart, master of his own household, though still full of youthful high spirits. What seals this as an exhilarating experience is the conducting of Pinchas Steinberg with the Munich Radio Symphony Orchestra, strong and thrustful yet responsive to the dramatic subtleties, plainly a conductor who should be used more often in recordings. The sound is fresh and atmospheric, bringing out the sparkle and fantasy of the piece.

Le Cid (complete).
** Sony CD 79300 (2) [M2K 34211]. Bumbry, Domingo, Bergquist, Plishka, Gardner, Camp Chorale, NY Op. O, Queler.

The CBS recording is taken from a live performance in New York and suffers from boxy recording quality. Only with the entrance of Domingo in the second scene does the occasion really get going, and the French accents are often comically bad. Domingo, not always as stylish as he might be, is in heroic voice and Grace Bumbry as the proud heroine responds splendidly. The popular ballet music is given a sparkling performance. But this should have been reissued at mid-price.

Cléopâtre (complete).
**(*) Koch/Schwann Dig. 3 1032-2 (2) Harries, Streiff, Olmeda, Henry, Maurette, Hacquard, Festival Ch., Nouvel O de Saint-Étienne, Fournillier.

Cléopâtre was the very last of Massenet's operas, written in 1912, the year he died. With exotic choruses, fanfares, dances and marches, it makes one regret that Massenet – unlike Erich Korngold – did not live to become a Hollywood composer: *Cléopâtre* has much of the easy opulence of a film spectacular. This première recording was taken from a live performance at the Massenet Festival in Saint-Etienne in 1990, with Patrick Fournillier conducting. The cast has no serious weakness, and the two principal roles are splendidly taken, with Didier Henry firm and responsive as Mark Antony and with Kathryn Harries demonstrating what a rich role for a singing actress this Cléopâtre is. Miss Harries with her rich mezzo should be used more on record, when her expressive intensity here in her big solos is magnetic. That is particularly so in the concluding scenes. Antony's death-throes bring first an extended love-duet leading to what becomes a Massenet equivalent of Isolde's *Liebestod.* The Koch live recording is not helped by the dryness of the orchestral sound, though only the brass is seriously affected, and the voices are vividly caught.

Don Quichotte (complete).
*** EMI (SIS) Dig. CDS7 54767-2 (2). Van Dam, Fondary, Berganza, Toulouse Capitole Ch. & O, Plasson.

(i) *Don Quixote* (complete); (ii) *Scènes alsaciennes*.
(M) *** Decca 430 636-2 (2) [id.]. (i) Ghiaurov, Bacquier, Crespin, SRO Ch. & O, Kord; (ii) Nat. PO, Bonynge.

Massenet's operatic adaptation of Cervantes' classic novel gave him his last big success. There is genuine nobility as well as comedy in the portrait of the knight, and that is well caught here by Ghiaurov, who refuses to exaggerate the characterization. Bacquier makes a delightful Sancho Panza, but it is Régine Crespin as a comically mature Dulcinée who provides the most characterful singing, flawed vocally but commandingly positive. Kazimierz Kord directs the Suisse Romande Orchestra in a performance that is zestful and electrifying, and the recording is outstandingly clear and atmospheric.

Michel Plasson conducts a sumptuous account of Massenet's charming Cervantes-based opera, with José van Dam singing gloriously as the Don, producing consistently firm and velvety tone. Alain Fondary as Sancho Panza is equally strong and firm vocally, shadowing and matching his master instead of contrasting, never indulging in exaggeratedly comic effects. Teresa Berganza as Dulcinée adds to the sensuousness of the performance, with the Toulouse acoustic bringing out the richness and beauty of Massenet's orchestral writing. No one will be disappointed, but the 1977 Decca set still has clear advantages. The Decca analogue sound is more clearly focused than the EMI digital, with the chorus full and immediate and with stage effects creating a vivid atmosphere. At mid-price the Decca set also comes with an attractive fill-up, the *Scènes alsaciennes*, brightly and colourfully presented by Bonynge and the National Philharmonic Orchestra.

Esclarmonde (complete).

(M) *** Decca 425 651-2 (3). Sutherland, Aragall, Tourangeau, Davies, Grant, Alldis Ch., Nat. PO, Bonynge.

**(*) Koch Schwann Dig. 3-1269-2 (3) [id.]. Gavazzeni-Daviola, Sempere, Parraguin, Tréguier, Courtis, Gabelle, Massenet Festival Ch., Budapest Liszt SO, Fournillier.

Joan Sutherland is the obvious diva to encompass the demands of great range, great power and brilliant coloratura of the central role of *Esclarmonde*, and her performance is in its way as powerful as it is in Puccini's last opera. Aragall proves an excellent tenor, sweet of tone and intelligent, and the other parts are well taken too. Richard Bonynge draws passionate singing and playing from chorus and orchestra, and the recording has both atmosphere and spectacle to match the story, based on a medieval romance involving song-contests and necromancy.

Recorded live at concert performances in October/November 1992, the Koch set is among the most successful sets to have come from the Massenet Festival in Saint-Etienne. The digital recording is full and clear, coping very well with the massed forces, giving plenty of detail, and Patrick Fournillier as a specialist interpreter of this composer persuades singers and players alike to perform with sympathy for the Massenet idiom. The Italian soprano, Denia Gavazzeni-Daviola, with a voice bright and clear at the top but which has fair weight down below, tackles here the weightiest of the Massenet roles and, though she cannot match Sutherland in the warmth and weight of her singing in this music, the element of vulnerability in the princess with magic powers is more readily conveyed than with Sutherland. The Spaniard, José Sempere, sings freshly and clearly as the hero, Roland, if less ringingly and with less warmth than Giacomo Aragall, the tenor who sings opposite Sutherland on her Decca recording. Reissued on CD at mid-price, that remains the first recommendation.

Grisélidis (complete).

*** Koch Schwann Dig. 3-1270-2 (2) [id.]. Command, Viala, Larcher, Desnoues, Courtis, Henry, Treguier, Sieyès, Lyon Ch., Franz Liszt SO of Budapest, Fournillier.

Grisélidis is a curious opera, one which, against his usual practice, took Massenet several years to complete. One reason may be that the subject – a medieval morality found in Plutarch, Boccaccio and Perrault – fits awkwardly with a broadly realistic style representing high Romanticism. To suggest the medieval atmosphere and the purity of the heroine, Grisélidis, Massenet exceptionally dallies with modal writing, if not very consistently, and the introduction of the Devil as a comic figure, henpecked by his wife, gets in the way of one taking the threat to Grisélidis and her virtue seriously. Michèle Command sings warmly as the heroine and Jean-Luc Viala sings splendidly in the incidental tenor role of the shepherd, Alain, in love with Grisélidis, but pushed aside by the Marquis, who sweeps her off her feet, only to prove an overpossessive husband. As the Marquis, Didier Henry is in rather gritty voice, and it is a pity that Jean-Philippe Courtis does not bring out the comedy of the Devil's role more positively, though he sings well enough. Clear, generally well-balanced 1992 'live' recording.

Hérodiade (complete).

*** EMI Dig. CDC5 55378-2 (3) [CDCC 55378]. Studer, Denize, Heppner, Hampson, Van Dam, Capitole Toulouse Ch. & O, Plasson.

Massenet's opera about Salome and John the Baptist, completed in 1880, has little in common with either the Bible story or the violent Strauss opera based on Oscar Wilde's play. The title itself is misleading, for Hérodiade, mother of Salome and wife of Herod, is in no way the central figure. To illustrate the idiosyncratic approach, one merely notes that the final scene, so far from involving Salome in asking for John's head, has an ecstatic duet for them both, 'hymning the chaste flame of their immortal love' – as the EMI synopsis graphically puts it. When John is executed, Salome then kills herself. What matters is that the opera offers five fat parts for well-contrasted voices, and it is good to have two fine new recordings, each offering leading singers.

Michel Plasson's studio recording offers well-balanced sound, opulent and firmly focused, with none of the snags inevitable in a live recording made during a stage performance. His text is complete too, using the final and fullest version of a work which Massenet revised several times. Add to that a consistent cast, in which you have outstanding singers not only in the roles of Salome and John (Jean) but also in the three other main roles. As Hérodiade herself, Nadine Denize sings with gloriously rich, firm tone, and Thomas Hampson's portrait of Hérode could hardly be richer either vocally or dramatically, with words brought out vividly. It would be hard to imagine a finer Phanuel than José van Dam, with his well-contrasted bass-baritone incisive in attack. As for Cheryl Studer as Salome, she has rarely sung with such expressive range and beauty of tone, with words crystal-clear. Sam Heppner as Jean confirms in his clear, firmly focused delivery earlier impressions of his development as a genuine heroic tenor with few rivals today. There are first-rate singers too in the small roles, and the Toulouse orchestra plays with glowing warmth and intensity, helped by the acoustic of the Halle aux Grains, far less washy than the Capitole, where EMI recordings used to be made. A warmly enjoyable set from first to last, admirably filling a major gap in the catalogue.

Manon (complete).
**(*) EMI Dig. CDC7 49610-2. Cotrubas, Kraus, Quilico, Van Dam, Toulouse Capitole Ch. & O., Plasson.
(N) (B) (**) Naxos 8.110003/5 (3). Bidu Sayao, Sydney Rayner, Richard Bonelli, Metropolitan Ch. & O, Abravanel.

We are currently promised a new recording of *Manon*; meanwhile the Plasson Toulouse set is a more than adequate stop-gap. It is a stylish performance, well characterized and well sung. Ileana Cotrubas is a charming Manon, more tender and vulnerable than De los Angeles was on an earlier mono set, but not so golden-toned, and with a more limited development of character from the girlish chatterbox to the dying victim. Alfredo Kraus betrays some signs of age, but his is a finely detailed and subtle reading, with none of the blemishes that marred his *Werther* performance, also for EMI. Louis Quilico has a delightfully light touch as Lescaut, and José Van Dam is a superb Comte Des Grieux. The warm reverberation of the Toulouse studio is well controlled to give bloom to the voices and, though Plasson is rougher with the score than Monteux was on an older mono version, his feeling for French idiom is very good.

Taken from an NBC broadcast in 1937, the Naxos historic issue offers limited and variable sound, but clearly demonstrates the merits, vocal and technical, of the pre-war company at the Met in New York. This marked the début of the Brazilian, Bidu Sayao, whose light, bright soprano with a hint of rapid flutter in the tone exactly matches the role, perfectly conveying the provocative as well as the tender side of the heroine, totally at home in the French idiom. The American tenor, Sydney Rayner, makes a virile hero, using his rather baritonal voice stylishly if with occasional heaviness. Bonelli makes an excellent Lescaut too, but it is Maurice Abravanel, then in charge of the French repertory at the Met, who provides the impetus, drawing brilliant playing from the orchestra, recessed as it is behind the clearly focused voices.

Manon: highlights.
(N) (M) (***) Dutton Lab. mono CDLX 7023 [id.]. Maggie Teyte, Heddle Nash, Dennis Noble, Norman Walker, Roy Henderson, BBC Theatre O, Stanford Robinson.

This collection, almost 80 minutes of fragments from a radio broadcast of 1939 – starting with a prim BBC announcer – is a period piece. It celebrates the meeting of the French tradition – represented by Maggie Teyte, who first won fame there – with the more staid English tradition. It says much for Teyte's characterful dominance that, with Stanford Robinson bringing out the warmth of the score, Massenet and France triumphantly win out, even in face of a stilted English translation. Heddle Nash, the finest British operatic tenor of the period, like Teyte sings with a ravishing range of tone, his diction equally perfect, and the others represent the best of British singing of the time. Excellent transfers of flawed sound, with the voices well caught but the orchestra rather thin.

La Navarraise (complete).
(M) *** RCA 74321 50167-2. Horne, Domingo, Milnes, Zaccaria, Bacquier, Ryland Davies, Amb. Op. Ch., LSO, Henry Lewis.

La Navarraise, a compact 'lyric episode' lasting barely 50 minutes, finds Massenet challenging the *verismo* school and succeeding convincingly. The flavour is a cross between *Carmen* and *Cavalleria rusticana*, with a touch of *Il tabarro*. To earn her dowry before marrying her beloved, the intrepid heroine penetrates the enemy lines in the Carlist wars and for money assassinates the royalist general's direct adversary. Following a misunderstanding, the hero follows her and is mortally wounded. In despair she promptly goes mad – a great deal of story for so short a piece. It says much for Massenet's dramatic powers that he makes the result as convincing as he does, and the score is full of splendid, atmospheric effects. It was produced in the same year as *Thaïs* (1894), with a première at Covent Garden. Massenet originally had a heavyweight, 'Carmen' voice in mind, and Marilyn Horne seems an apter choice for the role of heroine than her competitor on the CBS/Sony set (which is currently out of the catalogue). Even if her upper register is not as firm as it was, it remains an appealing performance, and Domingo is characteristically rich-toned. Henry Lewis conducts with a sense of the work's atmosphere and grandeur, and this is an opera ideally suited to the gramophone.

The recording, made at Walthamstow in 1975, is appropriately spacious, if not always absolutely refined. The documentation for this reissue in the RCA Opera Treasury series is excellent, with a full libretto. This is not currently available in the USA.

Le Roi de Lahore (complete).
❁ (M) *** Decca Dig. 433 851-2 (2) [id.]. Sutherland, Lima, Milnes, Ghiaurov, Morris, Tourangeau, L. Voices, Nat. PO, Bonynge.

Le Roi de Lahore was Massenet's first opera for the big stage of L'Opéra in Paris and marked a turning point in his career, even introducing the supernatural, with one Act set in the Paradise of Indra. The characters may be stock figures out of a mystic fairytale, but in the vigour of his treatment Massenet makes the result red-blooded in an Italianate way. This vivid performance under Bonynge includes passages added for Italy, notably a superb set-piece aria which challenges Sutherland to some of her finest singing. Sutherland may not be a natural for the role of the innocent young priestess, but she makes it a magnificent vehicle with its lyric, dramatic and coloratura demands. Luis Lima as the King is somewhat strained by the high tessitura, but his is a ringing tenor, clean of attack. Sherrill Milnes as the heroine's wicked uncle sounds even more Italianate, rolling his 'r's ferociously; but high melodrama is apt, and with digital recording of demonstration splendour and fine perspective this shameless example of operatic hokum could not be presented more persuasively on CD.

Thaïs (complete).
(M) ** EMI CMS5 65479-2 (2) [CDMB 65479]. Sills, Milnes, Gedda, Van Allan, John Alldis Ch., New Philh. O, Maazel.

Thaïs is an exotic period-piece, set in Egypt in the early Christian era, the story of a monk who seeks to save a beautiful courtesan and is himself destroyed. Sentimental as the plot is, it inspired Massenet to some of his characteristically mellifluous writing, with atmospheric choruses and sumptuous orchestration. Maazel's conducting is crisply dramatic (and he plays the violin solo himself most tastefully in the famous *Meditation*). The casting is good, except for the heroine. Beverly Sills has a bright, almost brittle voice, and here it sounds neither seductive nor idiomatic, for the unevenness of the production, already noticeable in earlier recordings, has grown more obtrusive. She is at her best as the reformed *Thaïs* in the later scenes. Sherrill Milnes is a powerful but conventional Athanaël and, though Nicolai Gedda as Nicias sings with his usual intelligence, it is not a young enough voice for the role. A good, warm recording, well transferred on to CD, and with a complete text and translation.

Thérèse (complete).
*** Decca 448 173-2. Huguette Tourangeau, Ryland Davies, Louis Quilico, Linden Singers, New Philh. O, Bonynge.

This story of the French Revolution, depicting a conflict of love and loyalty, has so many parallels with Puccini's *Tosca* and Giordano's *Andrea Chénier* of the previous decade that it is surprising Massenet chose it. He was then (1905) at the end of his career and was freshly inspired by the charms of a young mezzo-soprano, Lucy Arbell, who by all accounts was (vocally at least) unworthy of his attentions. The result was this passionate score, compressed and intense, lacking only the last degree of memorability in the melodies that make Massenet's finest operas so gripping. Bonynge is a splendid advocate, amply proving how taut and atmospheric the writing is. There is some first-rate singing from the three principals. The vivid vintage recording, produced by James Walker in the Kingsway Hall in 1973, is excellent, and the reissue now includes a libretto with a new translation.

Werther (complete).
*** Ph. 416 654-2 (2) [id.]. Carreras, Von Stade, Allen, Buchanan, Lloyd, Children's Ch., ROHCG O, C. Davis.
(N) (M) *** Orfeo C494982I (2) [id.]. Plácido Domingo, Brigitte Fassbaender, Marianne Seibel, Hans Günter Nöcker, Bav. State Op. Ch., Bav. State O, Jésus López-Cobos.
(N) *** Warner/Erato Dig. 0630 17790-2 (2) [id.]. Jerry Hadley, Anne Sofie von Otter, Dawn Upshaw, Gérard Théruel, Lyon Opera Ch. & O, Kent Nagano.
(M) **(*) EMI CMS7 63973-2 (2) [Ang. CDMB 63973]. Gedda, De los Angeles, Mesplé, Soyer, Voix d'Enfants de la Maîtrise de l'ORTF, O de Paris, Prêtre.

Sir Colin Davis has rarely directed a more sensitive or more warmly expressive performance on record than his account of *Werther*, based on a stage production at Covent Garden. Frederica von Stade makes an enchanting Charlotte, outshining all current rivals on record. Carreras uses a naturally beautiful voice freshly and sensitively. Thomas Allen as Charlotte's husband Albert and Isobel Buchanan as Sophie, her sister, are excellent, too. The CD transfer on to a pair of discs has been highly successful, with a single serious reservation: the break between the two CDs is badly placed in the middle of a key scene between Werther and Charlotte, just before *Ah! qu'il est loin, ce jour!*

At mid-price the Bavarian Radio recording on Orfeo makes an excellent alternative choice, with Plácido Domingo an ardent hero, even more warmly expressive than he was on the (now deleted) DG version conducted by Barenboim. Opposite him as Charlotte, far preferable to the seriously flawed Obraztsova on DG, is Brigitte Fassbaender in peak form, rich and firm as well as passionately expressive. Marianne Seibel and Hans Günter Nöcker are first-rate too, as Sophie and Albert. López-Cobos is an ardently red-blooded interpreter of Massenet, and though in this live recording, stage noises are obtrusive at times and balances are not always perfect, they hardly detract from the impact of the whole.

With an excellent cast, Kent Nagano conducts his Lyon Opera team in a warm, well-paced reading. With the orchestra backwardly placed, this is a relatively intimate performance, with the two principals, Jerry Hadley and Anne Sofie von Otter, sounding youthful and characterizing well, with neurotic tensions implied. Dawn Upshaw is excellent too as a characterful Sophie. Though this cannot quite match the excellent Colin Davis version with Carreras and von Stade, it makes a good digitally recorded alternative.

Victoria de los Angeles's golden tones, which convey pathos so beautifully, are ideally suited to Massenet's gentle melodies and, though she is recorded too closely (closer than the other soloists), she makes an intensely appealing heroine. Gedda makes an intelligent romantic hero, though Prêtre's direction could be subtler.

Mathias, William (1934–92)

(i) *Oboe concerto. Helios, Op. 76; Requiescat, Op. 79; Symphony No. 3.*
(N) *** Nimbus Dig. NI 5343 [id.]. (i) David Cowley; BBC Welsh SO, Grant Llewellyn.

One could hardly better this splendidly played and superbly recorded Nimbus disc as a way of getting to know the orchestral music of a highly individual Welsh composer, whose muse is both powerful and accessible. His command of the orchestral palette is very impressive in the evocation of *Helios*, where, in the words of the composer, 'the transparency and translucence of the Greek landscapes and seascapes had an effect on the scoring', with 'Greek dance rhythms sometimes evoked'. The *Oboe concerto* (with a first-rate soloist) brings a complex opening movement, with barely a pause for breath, balanced by the pensive *Adagio espressivo* and the jocular, off-beat rondo finale, which in its chromaticism has a curiously oriental tinge. *Requiescat* is a plangently affecting threnody for an admired colleague, Sir Ben Owen Thomas, prime founder of the North Wales Music Festival. The *Third Symphony* again shows the composer's great resource and imagination in the command of orchestral colour and sonority. The first movement is driven by a wildly motoric toccata which provides the material for the rest of the work; the elegiac *Lento* brings a haunting cor anglais melody (which is not too distantly related to the slow movement of the *Oboe concerto*) and the energetic finale, with its 'brazen, ritualistic brass fanfares', acts as a kind of metamorphosis of what has gone before.

(i) *Clarinet concerto;* (ii) *Harp concerto;* (iii) *Piano concerto No. 3.*
*** Lyrita SRCD 325 [id.]. (i) Gervase de Peyer; (ii) Osian Ellis; (iii) Peter Katin; LSO or New Philh. O, Atherton.

Helped by vividly immediate recording, the *Clarinet concerto* with its clean-cut, memorable themes sparks off an inspired performance from Gervase de Peyer, not just in the lively outer movements, but in the poignant *Lento espressivo* in the middle. The *Harp concerto* (1970) is less outward-going, but it prompts Mathias to create evocative, shimmering textures, very characteristic of him. The harp, superbly played by the dedicatee, Osian Ellis, is set alongside exotic percussion, with the finale a snappy jig that delightfully keeps tripping over its feet. In the *Piano concerto No. 3* of 1968 the outer movements bring jazzily syncopated writing, like Walton with a difference, here incisively played by Peter Katin. They frame an atmospheric central *Adagio* with echoes of Bartókian 'night music', like Bartók with a difference.

(i; ii) *Dance overture, Op. 16;* (iii; ii) *Divertimento for string orchestra, Op. 7;* (i; ii) *Invocation and dance, Op. 17;* (iv; ii) *'Landscapes of the mind': Laudi, Op. 62; Vistas, Op. 69.* (iii; ii) *Prelude, Aria and Finale for string orchestra, Op. 25;* (v) *Sinfonietta, Op. 34.*
*** Lyrita SRCD 328 [id.]. (i) LSO; (ii) David Atherton; (iii) ECO; (iv) New Philh. O; (v) Nat. Youth O of Wales, Arthur Davison.

As this collection readily bears out, William Mathias was a composer of genuine talent, versatile as well as inventive. The joyful *Dance overture* is vividly scored, rather after the manner of Malcolm Arnold, and the *Invocation and dance* has genuine spontaneity. Undoubtedly the two most remarkable works here are the two pieces described by their composer as 'Landscapes of the mind'. *Laudi*, written in 1973, a 'landscape of the spirit', opens with temple bells and then contrasts bold cross-rhythms with gently voluptuous string sonorities, closing with a serene yet sensuous benediction, somewhat after the manner of Messiaen. The evocative *Vistas* was inspired by the composer's visit to the USA in 1975. Here an Ivesian influence is unmistakable. Performances throughout are of the highest calibre with Atherton at his most perceptive, and the recordings (engineered by Decca for the most part) are outstanding.

Summer dances; Soundings.
*** Nimbus Dig. NI 5466 [id.]. Fine Arts Brass Ens. – HODDINOTT: *Chorales, variants and fanfares* etc. ***

Mathias's seven *Summer dances* (1990) bring witty

rhythmic quirkiness but, if the writing is consistently skilful, the invention is at times rather conventional. His *Soundings* (commissioned by the Philip Jones Brass and first performed in 1988) is much more entertaining with its kinky *March* (its humour agreeably lugubrious), a darkly nostalgic *Elegy* and a catchy but unpredictable final *Capriccio*. Fine playing and splendid recording in an ideal acoustic that brings plenty of sonority but provides firmly focused detail.

String quartets Nos. 1–3.
*** Metier Dig. MSVCD 92005 [id.]. Medea Qt.

Spanning the years 1967–86, Mathias's three string quartets make a fine sequence, illuminating his whole achievement. The *First Quartet*, in a single 20-minute movement, pithily argued, has a Stravinskian directness. The idiom brings momentary echoes of Britten, but might best be described as music by a composer who has thoroughly digested the Bartók quartets. The *Second Quartet* dates from 1980–81, and in each of its four compact movements Mathias echoes medieval music in different ways. The result is stylistically as individual as the *First Quartet*, never sounding merely derivative. The *Third Quartet*, dating from 1986, brings together elements of both the earlier works, with the first of its three movements developing from a deceptively light opening into a taut, large-scale structure comparable with the *Quartet No. 1*. All three quartets, very well recorded, are outstandingly well performed by the young Medea Quartet, formed as recently as 1991 at the Royal Academy of Music.

Wind quintet.
*** Crystal CD 750 [id.]. Westwood Wind Quintet – CARLSSON: *Nightwings;* LIGETI: *Bagatelles;* BARBER: *Summer music.* ***

Of the five movements of this spirited *Quintet* the Scherzo is particularly felicitous and there is a rather beautiful *Elegy*. The playing of the Westwood Wind Quintet is highly expert and committed, and the recording is very good indeed.

Lux aeterna, Op. 88.
*** Chandos Dig. CHAN 8695 [id.]. Felicity Lott, Cable, Penelope Walker, Bach Ch., St George's Chapel Ch., Windsor, LSO, Willcocks; J. Scott (organ).

Just as Britten in the *War Requiem* contrasted different planes of expression with Latin liturgy set against Wilfred Owen poems, so Mathias contrasts the full choir singing Latin against the boys' choir singing carol-like Marian anthems, and in turn against the three soloists, who sing three arias and a trio to the mystical poems of St John of the Cross. Overall, the confidence of the writing makes the work far more than derivative, an attractively approachable and colourful piece, full of memorable ideas, especially in this excellent performance, beautifully sung and played and atmospherically balanced.

Missa brevis; Rex gloriae; Anthems: Ad majorem Dei gloriam; Angelus; Alleluia; Doctrine of Wisdom; Except the Lord build the house; Hodie Christus natus est; The Lord is my Shepherd; Veni sancte spiritus.
(N) ✪ *** Paraclete Press Dig. GDCD 026 [id.]. Gloriæ Dei Cantores, Elizabeth Patterson.

As a Welshman, it is not surprising that it is Mathias's choral music which has gained him world-wide recognition, and special acclaim in the United States. Like his English colleague, John Rutter, his name is kept alive by choral societies who know a good thing when they hear it. His writing is traditional in the best sense, and the flowing melodic lines, with the harmony bringing characteristic stabs of dissonance, means that anyone who enjoys the music of John Tavener will surely respond to the collection here, which consistently reflects Mathias's view that 'Music is an immense celebration'.

That feeling certainly comes over from the very opening of this splendidly sung programme from Gloriæ Dei Cantores, a 44-voice choir from Cape Cod, Massachusetts, directed by Elizabeth Patterson. They have the advantage of the superb acoustics of the Methuan Music Hall and the use of its famous organ, which Mathias uses very orchestrally – and often in the *Missa brevis* to provide 'instrumental' obbligatos. The thrilling opening of *Sanctus* establishes this as the emotional kernel of the work, with the organ then creating darker woodwind colours to introduce the very touching *Agnus Dei*. The highlight of the *Rex gloriae* is the gloriously rich *Victimae paschali*, with its suspended choral lines seemingly floating in space, as a backgound for a soaring treble solo.

The anthems are hardly less individual and inspired. Trumpets and percussion annnounce the exultant setting of *Except the Lord build the house* while the celestial *Angelus* brings a surprisingly effective use of the piano. *The Lord is my shepherd* is very Welsh in feeling, a passionate declaration of faith; *The Doctrine of Wisdom* again uses the organ very atmospherically, and its melodic simplicity is telling. The device of dissonant suspensions is used again in *Veni sancte spiritus* (the most ambitious setting) with sustained trumpets blending with the choir, followed by organ undulations which recall Messiaen. Then the trumpets return in fanfare to share the exultant *Alleluja*. With singing of such commitment and intensity, yet exploiting the widest range of dynamics, every piece here is memorable. Mathias could hardly have hoped for more persuasive advocacy, nor finer recording. If you have difficulty in getting this disc the Choir's website address is:

www.paraclete-press.com

Matthews, Colin (born 1946)

Hidden variables; Memorial; Quatrain; Machines and dreams.
*** Collins Dig. 1470-2 [id.]. LSO, Michael Tilson Thomas.

Like Knussen's excellent disc for DG, this grouping of orchestral pieces by Matthews, each lasting between 10 and 16 minutes, demonstrates his impressive range of expression. Regularly his writing reveals his joy in sound, his love of mixing unexpected colours, whether inventively dallying with minimalism in *Hidden variables* or searching more deeply in *Memorial* (written in memory of Britten, to whom he was musical amanuensis over the last years) and *Quatrain*. In many ways most striking of all is *Machines and dreams*, a toy symphony written for the Festival of Children at the Barbican in London in 1991. The disc contains the live recording made then, with a virtuoso children's ensemble playing the toy instruments alongside the full London Symphony Orchestra. If the humour may initially seem naïve, it grows on you with repetition, such is the wit and sense of fun behind Matthews's use of bird noises (with affectionate nods in the direction of Messiaen), toy pianos, sirens, football rattles, metronomes, and so on. The wonder is that poetry emerges too. An intriguing disc, very well performed and brilliantly recorded.

(i) *Cello concerto;* (ii) *Sonata No. 5 (Landscape), Op. 17.*
(M) *** Unicorn Dig. UKCD 2058 [id.]. (i) Alexander Baillie, L. Sinf.; (ii) Berlin RSO, John Carewe.

Colin Matthews' *Sonata No. 5*, subtitled *Landscape*, is one of the most powerful and ambitious orchestral works to have been written by a British composer of the younger generation, in effect a large-scale symphony in a single movement, richly and evocatively scored. This is a formidable achievement and a splendid celebration of a fast-growing talent. The *Cello concerto* too is an impressive piece, again confidently argued on a broad scale. It is a pity that, with this of all instruments, Matthews does not allow himself a warmer lyricism; but with Alexander Baillie brilliantly bringing out the power of the declamatory writing and intensifying the underlying darkness of the piece, this too emerges as a fine, ambitious work, warm in its emotions. On this CD it is as well recorded as it is dedicatedly played.

Broken symmetry; 4th Sonata for orchestra; Sun dances.
*** DG Dig. 447 067-2 [id.]. London Sinf., Oliver Knussen.

These three fine works, given superb performances by Oliver Knussen and the London Sinfonietta, present a strong portrait of an outstanding and imaginative composer, each taken from a different period of his career. The *Fourth Sonata*, from the mid-1970s, presents Matthews's response to minimalism in its repetitive rhythms but with ideas kept continually alert in a well-planned structure. *Sun dances*, from the mid-1980s, is a ballet for ten instruments which brilliantly transcends that limitation of forces. *Broken symmetry*, from the early 1990s, is a scherzo movement for large orchestra, leading to a dramatic conclusion. The excellent recording brings both bloom and sharp focus.

Matthews, David (born 1942)

Symphony No. 4, Op. 52.
**(*) Collins Single Dig. 2008-2 [id.]. East of England O, Malcolm Nabarro.

David Matthews is a gifted and imaginative composer with a good musical mind, whose work deserves wider exposure. There is a lot of Britten, Stravinsky and Tippett in his musical thinking, but all the same he is his own man. His *Fourth Symphony* takes 27 minutes and is well worth hearing. The orchestral playing is spirited, though the strings are not world class; but the recording is very vivid and well detailed.

Maunder, John (1858–1920)

Olivet to Calvary (cantata).
(B) **(*) CfP CD-CFP 4619 [id.]. John Mitchinson, Frederick Harvey, Guildford Cathedral Ch., Barry Rose; P. Morse (organ).

It is easy to be patronizing about music like this but, provided one accepts the conventions of style in which it is composed, the music is effective and often moving. The performance has an attractive simplicity and genuine eloquence. Frederick Harvey is particularly moving at the actual moment of Christ's death; in a passage that, insensitively handled, could be positively embarrassing, he creates a magical, hushed intensity. The choir sing beautifully, and in the gentler, lyrical writing (the semi-chorus *O Thou whose sweet compassion*, for example) sentimentality is skilfully avoided. The 1964 recording is first class in every way, and it has been admirably transferred to CD.

Maw, Nicholas (born 1935)

Flute quartet; Night thoughts for solo flute; (i) *Roman canticle for mezzo-soprano, flute, viola and harp.*
(N) *** Koch Dig. 37355-2H1 [id.]. Auréole Trio (i) Mary Nessinger – R. R. BENNETT: *Sonata after Syrinx etc.* ***

All these Maw pieces come from the 1980s and have been recorded before. The *Roman canticle* for flute, viola and harp is sung here by a mezzo-soprano rather than a baritone . She is well balanced here and not too forward in the aural picture. In the inventive *Flute quartet* there should ideally be a little more space round the players; the flautist is a bit upfront. However this should not put off collectors interested in this fine composer.

(i) *Flute quartet;* (ii) *Piano trio.*
*** ASV Dig. CDDCA 920 [id.]. Monticello Trio; with (i) Judith Pearce; (ii) Paul Coletti.

Commissioned by the Koussevitzky Foundation, the *Piano trio* is among Maw's most impressive and ambitious chamber works. It was written in 1991 for the Monticello Trio, who here record it in a warmly expressive performance, fiery where necessary. The *Flute quartet* of 1981 was written for Judith Pearce of the Nash Ensemble, who plays it most beautifully here; it is another fine example of Maw's broad romanticism, powerful and lyrical, often sensuous, approachable yet clearly contemporary. Though the central slow movement opens as a fugue, it develops emotionally to become an atmospheric nocturne, leading to a scurrying finale. Excellent performances and sound.

Maxwell Davies, Peter (born 1934)

Ave maris stella; Image, reflection, shadow; (i) *Runes from a holy island.*
(M) *** Unicorn UKCD 2038. Fires of London, (i) cond. composer.

This is a CD compilation of key Maxwell Davies works. *Ave maris stella*, essentially elegiac, finds the composer at his most severe and demanding. The second piece, *Image, reflection, shadow*, is a kind of sequel. *Runes*, conducted by the composer, is much shorter yet just as intense in its rapt slowness. Ideal performances, well recorded, from the group for which all this music was written.

The Boyfriend; The Devils (film-scores): suites. (i) *Seven in nomine.*
*** Collins Dig. 1095-2 [id.]. (i) Mary Thomas; Aquarius, Nicholas Cleobury.

In 1971 Maxwell Davies did the sharply imagined scores for two Ken Russell films. Maxwell Davies's distorting lens works surprisingly well in both. Nicholas Cleobury draws alert playing from Aquarius, though in *The Boyfriend* the distant recording takes away some of the necessary bite. From the same crisply economical period *Seven in nomine* is a series of rather severe reworkings of the *In nomine* theme of John Taverner, which somewhat obsessed Maxwell Davies while writing his opera on that Tudor composer.

Caroline Mathilde – concert suite
*** Collins Dig. Single 2002-2. BBC PO, composer.

The composer conducts the BBC Philharmonic in these vivid performances, brilliantly recorded. A valuable addition to Collins's 20th-Century Plus series of CD singles.

(i) *Carolisima; The MacDonald dances*; (ii) *Mavis in Las Vegas; Ojai festival overture*; (iii) *An Orkney wedding with sunrise*; (i) *Serenade for chamber orchestra*; (i) *A Spell for green corn.*
(N) (B) *** Collins Dig. 1524-2 [id.]. (i) SCO, (ii) BBC PO, (iii) RPO with George McIlwham (bagpipes).

This attractive collection represents Maxwell Davies at his most relaxed, generally using a very approachable tonal idiom, often with references to popular material. That very much applies to the jolly piece which gives the disc its name, *Mavis in Las Vegas*, inspired by a misunderstanding in a hotel over the composer's name. The *Festival overture* and *Orkney wedding*, with its role for the bagpipes, are equally uninhibited, with the more extended *Carolisima* and *Spell for green corn* striking a more serious note. Excellent sound and performances.

(i) *Piano concerto*; (ii) *Piccolo concerto. Maxwell's reel, with Northern Lights.*
(N) *** Collins Dig. 1520-2 [id.]. (i) Kathryn Stott; (ii) Stewart McIlwham; RPO, composer.

The large-scale *Piano concerto*, written for Kathryn Stott, is one of Maxwell Davies's grittier works, with angular, often abrasive writing for the solo instrument, modified in the dark, central slow movement. The *Piccolo concerto* is much lighter and more approachable, with the solo instrument given a role not just decorative but lyrical over three compact movements. *Maxwell's reel* with its medley of Scottish dances makes an attractive fill-up. Very well-balanced sound and fine performances.

(i) *Trumpet concerto;* (ii) *Symphony No. 4.*
*** Collins Dig. 1181-2 [id.]. (i) John Wallace, RSNO; (ii) SCO; composer.

Inspired by the dazzling and poetic playing of the Philharmonia principal, John Wallace, the soloist on the record, the *Trumpet concerto*, written in 1988, is one of the most rewarding of Maxwell Davies's later works. Another source of inspiration has been St Francis, and the slow movement links with the saint's sermon to the birds, deeply meditative; the final coda in its Messiaenic jangling represents sublime glorification when St Francis receives the stigmata. The *Fourth Symphony* of 1984 brings similarly striking landmarks. Though it uses chamber forces, this four-movement work is texturally the thorniest of the composer's symphonies, not an easy piece but one with a powerful physical impact. The playing both of the RSNO in the concerto and of the SCO in the symphony is strongly committed, with excellent recorded sound.

Violin concerto.
(M) *** Sony Stern Edition II Dig. SMK 64506 [id.]. Stern, RPO, Previn – BARBER: *Violin concerto.* ***

Maxwell Davies wrote this massive *Violin concerto* (over half an hour long) specifically with Isaac Stern in mind, to a commission from the RPO to celebrate its fortieth anniversary. There are parallels here with the Walton *Violin concerto* of over 40 years earlier. The composer was inspired to draw on a more warmly lyrical side that he has displayed rarely. Davies claims to have been influenced by his favourite violin concerto, Mendelssohn's, but there is little of Mendelssohnian lightness and fantasy here; for all its beauties, this is a work which has a tendency to middle-aged spread, not nearly as taut in expression as the Walton. Stern, understandably, seems less completely involved here than in the inspired Barber coupling.

Renaissance and Baroque realisations: PURCELL: *Fantasia & 2 pavans; Fantasia upon one note.* BACH: *Well-tempered Clavier: Preludes & fugues in C sharp major and min.* (i) GESUALDO: *Tenebrae super Gesualdo.* DUNSTABLE: *Veni sancte – Veni creator spiritus.* KINLOCH: *His fantaisie. 3 Early Scottish motets.*
(M) *** Unicorn UKCD 2044 [id.]. Fires of London, (i) with Mary Thomas; composer.

These pieces mainly represent the composer in the 1960s abrasively distorting into foxtrot and other dance rhythms pieces by Purcell, Bach, Dunstable and others. It is like painting a moustache on the Mona Lisa, only more fun.

Sinfonia; Sinfonia concertante.
(M) *** Unicorn Dig. UKCD 2026 [id.]. SCO, composer.

In his *Sinfonia* of 1962 Peter Maxwell Davies took as his inspiration Monteverdi's *Vespers* of 1610, and the dedication in this music, beautifully played by the Scottish Chamber Orchestra under the composer, is plain from first to last. The *Sinfonia concertante* is a much more extrovert piece for strings plus solo wind quintet and timpani. In idiom this is hardly at all neo-classical and, more than usual, the composer evokes romantic images, as in the lovely close of the first movement. Virtuoso playing from the Scottish principals, not least the horn. Well-balanced recording.

Sinfonia accademica; (i) *Into the labyrinth.*
(M) *** Unicorn UKCD 2022. (i) Neil Mackie; SCO, composer.

Into the labyrinth, in five movements, might be regarded more as a song-symphony than as a cantata, a prose-poem inspired by the physical impact of Orkney. The fine Scottish tenor, Neil Mackie, gives a superb performance, confirming this as one of Maxwell Davies's most beautiful and moving inspirations. The *Sinfonia accademica* provides a strong and attractive contrast, and again evokes the atmosphere of Orkney. Strong, intense performances under the composer, helped by first-rate recording.

Symphony No. 2.
*** Collins Dig. 1403-2 [id.]. BBC PO, composer.

Written for the centenary of the Boston Symphony Orchestra, the *Second* represents the composer's search for a latter-day equivalent, personal to him, of the traditional conflicts of symphonic form. Like Sibelius, he has also taken inspiration directly from nature, the seascape near his Orkney home which has been an important force in many of his later works. The outer, most obviously symphonic, movements are the ones that benefit most from repetition on disc, but the whole work, with its reposeful slow movement and shadowy Scherzo, makes an immediate impact, though under the composer the playing of the BBC Philharmonic is not as taut as it might be. Excellent sound.

(i) *Symphony No. 5;* (ii) *Chat Moss; Cross Lane Fair;* (i) *5 Klee pictures.*
*** Collins Dig. 1460-2 [id.]. (i) Philh. O; (ii) BBC PO; composer.

Maxwell Davies's *Fifth Symphony* is in a single movement lasting only 25 minutes, half the length of his previous symphonies. The 34 sections, some lasting several minutes and others only a few seconds, convey the tautness of a passacaglia, with groups of sections linked to produce a structure which, like Sibelius's *Seventh*, echoes the contrasted movements of a conventional symphony. Davies has sharpened his idiom too, making it more approachable and lyrical, with an underlying reliance on two plainchants from the *Liber Usualis*. Just as strikingly, his instrumental writing has a new beauty, not least in the rapt slow passages, and in the concertante passages for flute, trumpet, timpani and other instruments. A bold climax leads finally to a deeply reflective coda, confirming this as the most memorable yet of Davies's symphonies. The other works here, much lighter, all reflect in different ways the composer's preoccupation with childhood and youth. The composer draws intense performances from both the Philharmonia (in the *Symphony*) and the BBC Philharmonic.

(i) *Vesalii Icones; The Bairns of Brugh; Runes from a Holy Island.*
(M) *** Unicorn-Kanchana Analogue/Dig. UKCD 2068 [id.]. (i) Jennifer Ward Clarke, Fires of London, composer.

Maxwell Davies has the great quality of presenting

strikingly memorable visions, and *Vesalii Icones* is certainly one, an extraordinary cello solo with comment from a chamber group. It was originally written to accompany a solo dancer in a fourteen-fold sequence, each dance based on one of the horrifying anatomical drawings of Vesalius (1543) and each representing one of the Stations of the Cross. Characteristically, the composer has moments not only of biting pain and tender compassion but also of deliberate shock tactics – notably when the risen Christ turns out to be Antichrist and is represented by a jaunty fox-trot. This is difficult music, but the emotional landmarks are plain from the start, and that is a good sign of enduring quality. Jennifer Ward Clarke plays superbly, and so do the Fires of London, conducted by the composer. The 1970 recording is excellent. The two shorter pieces, digitally recorded more than a decade later, make a valuable fill-up, *The Bairns of Brugh* a tender lament (viola over marimba) and *Runes* a group of brief epigrams.

Resurrection.
** Collins Dig. 7034-2 (2) [id.]. Della Jones, Robson, Martyn Hill, Jenkins, Herford, Finley, J. Best, Blaze, BBC PO, composer.

Resurrection is an oddity, a musical autobiography in stylized operatic form offering a ragbag of situations and experiences. The Hero is a stuffed dummy who, through the Prologue and long single Act, is consistently humiliated to make him conform with the prejudices of today. The composer's aim of satirizing society should have sparked off a whole series of the kind of parodistic pieces which he conceived so brilliantly in the 1960s. Yet the edge here is blunted, and the deliberate banality of TV jingles and the like falls into its own trap. The introduction of a Rock Band (Blaze) and an Electronic Vocal Quartet merely adds to the impression of the composer flailing about, unselfcritically throwing in every idea that occurs to him. What makes the discs exciting to hear is the quality of the performance, featuring an excellent team of soloists, with the composer drawing fine, incisive playing from the BBC Philharmonic, helped by superb sound. Della Jones in particular is outstanding both as the Elder Sister and at the end as the Antichrist.

OPERA

The Doctor of Myddfai.
(N) *** Collins Dig. 7046-2 (2) [id.]. Paul Whelan, Lisa Tyrrell, Gwynne Howell, Welsh Nat Op. Ch. & O, Richard Armstrong.

Recorded live in a performance in Cardiff when the WNO production was new, this gives a welcome airing to a dark and elusive opera which deserved to be studied more closely than is possible in a one-off performance. Following Celtic legend, the Doctor of Myddfai is a mythical figure with powers of healing. The conflict between him and the ruler of an unnamed state would be more involving if the story was less stylized and more specific, and the music might have been more animated. But with his librettist, David Pountney, Davies is tackling a serious theme, often with deep feeling, and he is very well served by Armstrong and the WNO company in a performance very well sung and played, with Paul Whelan and Gwynne Howell outstanding in the two central roles. Good clear sound.

The Lighthouse (chamber opera; complete).
*** Collins Dig. 1415-2 [id.]. Mackie, Keyte, Comboy, BBC PO, composer.

The Lighthouse, one of the most successful of recent chamber operas, tells the story of three lighthouse keepers who mysteriously disappeared without explanation from a solitary lighthouse off the coast of the Outer Hebrides in 1900. The first half consists of a long Prologue involving the Court of Inquiry, where three officials are questioned wordlessly by the solo horn. The second, main section, *The Cry of the Beast*, goes back to the lighthouse itself, presenting the three keepers, taken by the same singers, who are introduced in characteristic songs, a vulgar music-hall song for Blaze, a sentimental love-ballad for Sandy, and – most significantly – a vehement revivalist song about God's revenge on the Children of Israel for Arthur, a rabble-rousing Evangelical. It is Arthur's obsession that infects all three, insisting that the Beast is coming, and the climax comes in a storm when they are all convinced that the Antichrist has arrived. The coda presents the arrival of three more keepers, the same figures transformed. It is a powerful story, simply and directly told, and though in a recording one misses the atmospheric help of a stage set, this fine performance, conducted by the composer – with the tenor, Neil Mackie, outstanding among the three soloists, undaunted by the high tessitura – brings the story home powerfully, with all its overtones, aided by the printed text.

The Martyrdom of St Magnus.
*** Unicorn Dig. DKPCD 9100 [id.]. Dives, Gillett, Thomson, Morris, Kelvin Thomas, Scottish Chamber Op. Ens., Michael Rafferty.

With Gregorian chant providing an underlying basis of argument, Davies has here simplified his regular idiom. The musical argument of each of the nine compact scenes is summarized in the interludes which follow. The story is baldly but movingly presented, with St Magnus translated to the present century as a concentration camp victim, finally killed by his captors. Outstanding among the soloists is the tenor, Christopher Gillett, taking among other roles that of the Prisoner (or saint).

Mayerl, Billy (1902–59)

All-of-a-twist; Autumn crocus; Bats in the belfry; The harp of the winds; Insect oddities: Praying mantis; Wedding of an ant. Jazzaristrix; The Jazz master; Jill all alone; Look lively; Loose elbows; Marigold; Railroad rhythm; Shallow waters; Sweet William. Arrangements: *Body and soul; Limehouse blues; Peg o' my heart; Phil the Fluter's ball; Smoke gets in your eyes.*
(M) *** Virgin/EMI Ultraviolet Dig. CUV5 61323-2. Susan Tomes.

Billy Mayerl believed he had achieved a specially English style of jazz. During the 1920s and 1930s his name was a household word, and 20,000 students enrolled in his mail-order School of Music to learn syncopated piano. He left an indelible legacy of light pieces of high quality, with writing that is often much more complex and sophisticated than the rags of Joplin and his contemporaries. His most famous lyrical numbers, such as *Marigold* and *Autumn crocus*, (to quote Susan Tomes) combine 'a blend of elegance, wistfulness, nonchalance and high spirits – qualities which stamped his whole output'. The best of his pieces sound surprisingly undated, and in the hands of this stunning pianist they emerge with a refreshing spontaneity. The recording is splendidly real.

Aquarium suite; Autumn crocus; Bats in the belfry; Four Aces suite: Ace of Clubs; Ace of Spades. 3 Dances in syncopation, Op. 73; Green tulips; Hollyhock; Hop-o'-my-thumb; Jill all alone; Mistletoe; Parade of the sandwich-board men; Sweet William; White heather.
**(*) Chandos Dig. CHAN 8848 [id.]. Eric Parkin.

Eric Parkin obviously enjoys this repertoire and plays the music with much sympathy and vivacious rhythmic freedom, even if his shoulders are not quite as loose as those of Susan Tomes. His programme is well chosen to suit his own approach to Mayerl's repertoire, and this Chandos record is certainly very enjoyable, as he is very well treated by the recording engineers.

Mazzocchi, Domenico (*c*.1592–1665)

Sacrae concertationes: *Concilio de' farisei*; (i–v) *Dialogo della cantica. Dialogo della Maddalena; Dialogo dell'apocalisse; Dialogo di Lazaro*; (i; iv; v) *Gaudebunt labia mea; Jesu, dulcis memoria. Lamento di David.* (i; iii) *Miseris omnium, Domine*; (i; ii; v) *Peccantem me quotidie. Vide, Domine, afflictionem nostram.*
(N) (M) *** Harmonia Mundi Suite HMT 7901357 [id.]. (i) Maria Cristina Kiehr; (ii) Barbara Borden; (iii) Andras Scholl; (iv) Gerd Türk; (v) Ulrich Messthaler. Netherlands Chamber Ch., Jacobs, with Rousset, Swarts, Schröder.

Domenico Mazzocchi was in a sense a musical amateur. First a Priest and Doctor of both Theology and Law, he later became a prosperous 'Gentleman of the Chamber' to the influential Aldobrandi family in Rome (one of whom had been elected as the Pope in the year of Mazzocchi's birth). They secured him a good church benefice and paid him a salary. There is nothing in the least unprofessional about Mazzocchi's writing for voices. He almost certainly studied music in Rome and the present *Sacred concertantes* form part of his last work to be published in 1664, though probably dating from much earlier. Whether writing for soloists, solo groups, chorus or a combination of them all, his part-writing is blended and interwoven with skill, and his invention is of high quality. He was almost exactly contemporary with Barbara Strozzi, whose taste for telling harmonic chromaticisms he shared (though with less overt sensuality). His music includes deeply expressive solo melismas – as in the lovely *Peccantem me quotidie* ('Since daily I sin') – or chordal writing (*Jesu, dulcis memoria*), or both (the deeply touching *Dialogo della Maddalena*) alternated with bursts of Italianate exuberance. The *Lamento di David* has a remarkable closing section which includes all these features. Performances here are wonderfully sympathetic. The soloists include outstanding contributions from Maria Cristina Kiehr (who can also be heard in Strozzi's music – see below) and the bass, Ulrich Messthaler, who has some splendidly resonant low notes to sing, while we should not underpraise the other members of the solo team here, or the excellent choir, admirably accompanied by a continuo led by Christophe Rousset, and directed very persuasively indeed by René Jacobs. The recording too is first-class.

Medtner, Nikolai (1880–1951)

(i) *Piano concertos Nos. 1 in C min., Op. 33; 2 in C min., Op. 50; 3 in E min. (Ballade), Op. 60.* (Piano) *Sonata-Ballade in F sharp, Op. 27.*
*** Chandos Dig. CHAN 9040 (2) [id.]. Geoffrey Tozer; (i) LPO, Järvi.

(i) *Piano concerto No. 1 in C min., Op. 33; Sonata-Ballade in F sharp, Op. 27.*
*** Chandos Dig. CHAN 9038 [id.]. Tozer, (i) LPO, Järvi.

(i) *Piano concerto No. 1 in C min., Op. 33;* (ii) *Piano quintet in C, Op. posth.*
**(*) Hyperion Dig. CDA 66744 [id.]. Dmitri Alexeev, with (i) BBC SO, Lazarev; (ii) New Budapest Qt.

Piano concertos Nos. 2 in C min., Op. 50; 3 in E min., Op. 60.
*** Hyperion Dig. CDA 66580 [id.]. Nikolai

Demidenko, BBC Scottish SO, Jerzy Maksymiuk.
*** Chandos Dig. CHAN 9039 [id.]. Tozer, LPO, Järvi.

After some years of neglect, the recording industry is taking more interest in Medtner, this Russian aristocrat of the piano who spent his last years in London. Chandos offer the three concertos together as a package or separately. Their soloist is the Australian Geoffrey Tozer, who also plays the *Sonata-Ballade*, Op. 27, for good measure. In the *Second* and *Third Concertos* they come into direct competition with Hyperion with Nikolai Demidenko as soloist. Tozer has obvious feeling for this composer and his playing has no lack of warmth and virtuosity. He has the advantage over his rival of a richer, more transparent recording and a more sympathetic and responsive accompanist in Järvi and the London Philharmonic. Demidenko, on the other hand, has the greater fire and dramatic flair, and his performance with the BBC Scottish Orchestra under Jerzy Maksymiuk has one very much on the edge of one's chair. He is by no means as well recorded as Tozer: the sound of the piano is shallow and the orchestra lacks real transparency and is a bit two-dimensional in terms of front-to-back perspective. All the same, many will feel that this is a small price for playing of such thrilling quality.

Dmitri Alexeev plays the *First Piano concerto* with virtuosity, flair and sympathy, and the BBC Symphony Orchestra under Alexander Lazarev give excellent support. The recording is very good and generally well balanced, and overall gives better results than the coupling, the late *Piano quintet in C major*. Alexeev plays it with dedication, but the New Budapest Quartet are conscientious rather than committed or inspired partners. The two-dimensional and rather congested recording does not help.

Piano concertos Nos. 2 in C min., Op. 50; 3 in E min. (Ballade), Op. 60; Arabesque in A min., Op. 7/2; Tale in F min., Op. 26/3.
(***) Testament mono SBT 1027 [id.]. Composer, Philh. O, Dobrowen.

At last we have two of the celebrated set of Medtner concerto recordings which the Maharajah of Mysore funded in the late 1940s. Medtner was then in his sixties but his playing is still pretty magisterial. These two concertos and the early miniatures that make up the disc still possess an aristocratic allure and a musical finesse that it is difficult to resist. The performances were never reissued in the UK in the days of LP, and their reappearance at long last is as welcome as it is overdue. Good transfers.

(i) *Piano concerto No. 2 in C min., Op. 50;* (ii) *Piano quintet in C.*
(BB) *** Naxos Dig. 8.553390 [id.]. Konstantin Scherbakov, with (i) Moscow SO, Golovschin; (ii) Danel, Tedla, Bourová, Pudhoransk.

On Naxos a very good performance of the Medtner *Second Piano concerto* from Konstantin Scherbakov, who generates plenty of excitement. Perhaps there is a higher voltage in Demidenko's full-price, prize-winning (but not ideally recorded) Hyperion version, coupled with the *Third Piano concerto*, but Scherbakov is highly sympathetic and offers very musical playing, less narcissistic than his full-price rival. The Moscow Symphony Orchestra play well for Igor Golovschin, though they sound as if they could do with more rehearsal. There is plenty of space round the sound. Scherbakov communicates a more sympathetic musical personality than Demidenko and many will prefer him. There is an appealing makeweight in the form of the finely wrought *Piano quintet* of 1946.

(i) *Piano quintet in C, Op. posth.;* (ii) *Violin sonata No. 2 in G, Op. 44.*
** Russian Disc RDCD 11019 [id.]. Svetlanov, with (i) Borodin Qt; (ii) Labko.

The *Piano quintet*, on which Medtner laboured for so long, is played with much greater variety of tone and dynamics by Svetlanov and the Borodin Quartet than in the more recent Hyperion issue (see above). The 1968 recording calls for tolerance, but it is worth extending for the sake of some fine music-making. Alexander Labko plays the *Second Violin sonata* with conviction and eloquence. He is well partnered by Yevgeni Svetlanov, who proves a sensitive pianist. Unfortunately the 1968 recording is not good, even for its age, and is wanting in frequency range.

(i) *Piano quintet in C. Sonata triad, Op. 11;* (ii) *Two pieces for 2 pianos, Op. 58/1–2.*
(M) *** Carlton Classics Dig. 30366 00582 [id.]. Veniamin Korobov, with (i) State Prokofiev Qt; (ii) Lyudmila Kuznetsova.

The *Sonata triad* is made up of three relatively short sonata movements: *No. 1 in A*, a *Sonata elegy in D minor* and a third in *C major*; they come from the first decade of the century and feature Medtner's personal blend of Brahms, Schumann and Rachmaninov. The two Op. 58 pieces, the *Khovorod* and *Knight Errant*, with Lyudmila Kuznetsova playing the first piano part, come off well and are better than the full-price alternative on Hyperion. There is nothing to choose between the present account of the *Piano quintet* and its Naxos rival. Korobov is a fine pianist, and though at the end of the *A major sonata* and in the *Second* there is very occasionally some less-than-refined fortissimo tone, the recording may contribute to that effect. In any event this is well worth the money.

Violin sonatas Nos. 1 in B min., Op. 21; 2 in G, Op. 44; 3 in E min., Op. 57 (Epica); Canzonas and Dances, Op. 43; 3 Nocturnes, Op. 16.
**(*) Russian Disc MK Dig. 417109 (2) [id.]. Alexander Shirinsky, Dmitri Galynin.

Violin sonatas Nos. 1–2.
*** Chandos Dig. CHAN 9293 [id.]. Lydia Mordkovitch, Geoffrey Tozer.

The two Russian CDs comprise Medtner's complete output for violin and piano – indeed his entire chamber music save for the *Piano quintet*. The *Second* and *Third Sonatas* are both big-boned works, lasting almost 50 minutes apiece, and despite their apparent air of rhapsody are held together closely. They are not easy listening and call for keen concentration; more approachable is the much shorter *First Sonata*, which has genuine charm. The *Nocturnes* and their lyrical companions on this disc should be repertoire pieces. The performances are good and the recording acceptable but not top-drawer.

The first two of Medtner's three *Violin sonatas* also come on a well-recorded Chandos release. Lydia Mordkovitch proves a most imaginative and thoughtful advocate of the sonata. As far as the *G major Sonata* is concerned, the Chandos issue must remain the preferred recommendation among those now available; Lydia Mordkovitch betrays an effortless expressive freedom, and both she and her partner are well recorded too.

Violin sonata No. 3 (Sonata epica), Op. 57.
*** Erato/Warner Dig. 0630 15110-2 [id.]. Repin, Berezovsky – RAVEL: *Violin sonata*. ***

Vadim Repin and Boris Berezovsky make a formidable partnership, and they give what is arguably the most sensitive and certainly the most persuasive account of the *Sonata epica* since David Oistrakh and Alexander Goldweiser's celebrated Melodiya LP. Composed in the years preceding the Second World War, Medtner's third and last *Violin sonata* runs for three-quarters of an hour, but in the hands of these artists it does not outstay its welcome. They bring to it a wide range of colour and dynamics and infuse every phrase with life. Repin uses the Guarneri which belonged to Isaac Stern for almost half a century, and it sounds magnificently responsive in his hands. Very natural recording-balance adds to the pleasure this CD gives.

PIANO MUSIC

Canzona matinata, Op. 39/4; Canzona serenata, Op. 38/6; Dithyrambe, Op. 10/2; Fairy tale, Op. 20/1; Sonata elegia in D min., Op. 11/2; Sonata reminiscenza in A min., Op. 38/1; Sonata tragica in C min., Op. 39/5; Theme and variations in C sharp min., Op. 55.
** Hyperion Dig. CDA 66636 [id.]. Nikolai Demidenko.

No one who has heard Medtner's own playing, which is simple, direct and totally free of any affectation, or who recalls Gilels's account of the *Sonata reminiscenza* will find Demidenko's perfumed account entirely acceptable. By their side Demidenko sounds posturing and self-regarding. As a guide to Medtner, the less glamorous Hamish Milne (CRD) remains the truer interpreter. The quality of the Hyperion recording has also been overpraised. It is good without being distinguished and there is a lack of transparency, particularly in the middle range.

Dancing fairy tale, Op. 48/1; Fairy tale (1915); Fairy tales in D min., Op. 51/1; in E min., Op. 34/2; in F min., Op. 26/3; in G sharp min., Op. 31/3. Funeral march, Op. 31/2; The Organ grinder, Op. 54/3; Russian fairy tale, Op. 42/1; Sonata in G min., Op. 22; Sonata reminiscenza in A min., Op. 38/1.
*** Chandos Dig. CHAN 9050 [id.]. Geoffrey Tozer.

Tozer takes much less time over the *Sonata reminiscenza* than Demidenko but creates the illusion of unhurried calm. He allows the music to speak for itself without recourse to ostentation or flamboyance. The lifelike recording enhances the claims of this issue and bodes well for the enterprise (a complete survey of the keyboard music) as a whole.

Fairy tales, Op. 51; Forgotten melodies, Op. 38; Sonata triad, Op. 11.
(N) **(*) Chandos Dig. CHAN Dig. 9153 [id.]. Geoffrey Tozer.

Forgotten melodies, Opp. 39–40; Sonata in A min., Op. 30.
(N) **(*) Chandos Dig. CHAN 9692 [id.]. Geoffrey Tozer.

Sonatas in B flat min. (Sonata romantica), Op. 53/1; in F min., Op. 5; in F min. (Sonata minacciosa), Op. 53/2.
(N) **(*) Chandos Dig. CHAN 9691 [id.]. Geoffrey Tozer.

Complete piano music (as above).
(N) *** Chandos Dig. CHAN 9723 (4) [id.]. Geoffrey Tozer.

Geoffrey Tozer has long championed Medtner, and his excellently recorded series for Chandos has put collectors in his debt. His playing is unfailingly reliable and scrupulously conscientious and often persuasive. Where, in the *Sonatas*, for instance, he duplicates repertoire recorded by Marc-André Hamelin, his imaginative and poetic limitations can be discerned. All the same he has good fingers and a keen musical intelligence. The Chandos discs are all available separately, as well as in a box at a slightly reduced price.

Dithyramb, Op. 10/2; Elegy, Op. 59/2; Skazki (Fairy tales): No. 1 (1915); in E min., Op. 14/2;

in G, Op. 9/3; in D min. (Ophelia's song); in C sharp min., Op. 35/4. Forgotten melodies, 2nd Cycle, No. 1: Meditation. Primavera, Op. 39/3; 3 Hymns in praise of toil, Op. 49; Piano sonata in E min. (The Night Wind), Op. 25/2; Sonata Triad, Op. 11/1–3.
(M) *** CRD CRD 3338/9 [id.]. Hamish Milne.

Improvisation No. 2 (in variation form), Op. 47; Piano sonata in F min., Op. 5.
(M) *** CRD Dig. CRD 3461 [id.]. Hamish Milne.

3 Novelles, Op. 17; Romantic sketches for the young, Op. 54; Piano sonatas in G min., Op. 22; A min., Op. 30; 2 Skazki, Op. 8.
(M) *** CRD Dig. CRD 3460 [id.]. Hamish Milne.

Medtner's art is subtle and elusive. He shows an aristocratic disdain for the obvious, a feeling for balance and proportion, and a quiet harmonic refinement that offer consistent rewards. There is hardly a weak piece here, and Milne is a poetic advocate whose technical prowess is matched by first-rate artistry. The recording too is very truthful and vivid, and at mid-price this series is very competitive indeed.

Forgotten melodies, Opp. 38–39; 3 Marches, Op. 8; Sonata ballada in F sharp, Op. 27; Sonata idylle in G, Op. 56; Sonata skazka in C min., Op. 25/1; Sonata triad, Op. 11; Sonatas in A min., Op. 30; in B flat min. (Sonata romantica), Op. 53/1; in E min. (Night wind), Op. 25/2; in F min., Op. 5; in F min. (Sonata minacciosa), Op. 53/2; in G min., Op. 22.
(N) *** Hyperion Dig. CDA 67221-4 (4) [id.]. Marc-André Hamelin.

Medtner's music calls for the most persuasive and committed advocacy. Every note must come as a surprise and a discovery, for Medtner's is often the art of understatement and any hint of routine phrasing or lack of sensitivity to dynamic nuance or keyboard colour can be ruinous. No such problems here, for Marc-André Hamelin's artistry is to be found at its most consummate in this four-CD set of the sonatas and miscellaneous piano music. If you find Medtner just a little bland or predictable, then try this set, for in Hamelin's hands it is neither. Playing touched by distinction.

Russian round dance; Knight errant, Op. 58/1–2.
*** Hyperion Dig. CDA 66654 [id.]. Nikolai Demidenko, Dmitri Alexeev – RACHMANINOV: *Suite* etc. ***

The Russian round-dance or *khorovod* was written in 1946 and Medtner and Moiseiwitsch recorded it the same year for EMI. Here it is given with great lightness of touch, though this partnership loses beauty of tone-production above fortissimo.

Méhul, Etienne-Nicolas (1763–1817)

Symphonies Nos. 1–4; Overtures: La chasse de jeune Henri; Le trésor supposé.
*** Nimbus Dig. NI 5184/5 [id.]. Gulbenkian Foundation O, Swierczewski.

Méhul was a contemporary of Cherubini and flourished during the years of Napoleon. He was enormously prolific and wrote no fewer than 25 operas in the period 1790–1810. The four symphonies recorded here come from 1808–10 (Nos. 3 & 4 have been discovered only in recent years by David Charlton, who has edited them) and are well worth investigating. The invention is felicitous and engaging, and in *No. 4 in E major* Méhul brings back a motif of the *Adagio* in the finale, a unifying gesture well ahead of its time. The performances are eminently satisfactory even if the strings sound a shade undernourished.

Melartin, Erkki (1875–1937)

(i) *Violin concerto, Op. 60. Sleeping Beauty (suite), Op. 22; Suite lyrique No. 3 (Impressions de Belgique).*
(N) ** Ondine ODE 923-2 [id.]. (i) John Storgårds; Tampere PO, Leif Segerstam.

Ten years younger than Sibelius, Erkki Melartin is an interesting figure: he was a gifted painter, exhibiting on at least two occasions, and possessed a formidable knowledge of literature and languages. His music shows a considerable lyrical talent and expertise in writing for the orchestra. The *Violin concerto* (1910–13) has a lot going for it and John Storgårds takes its formidable difficulties in his stride. At one point its slow movement even brings Delius to mind. However, the folksy finale rather lets it down. The atmospheric *Suite lyrique* is a set of six impressionistic sketches inspired by a visit the composer made to Bruges in 1914, and the incidental music to Topelius's play, *The Sleeping Beauty*, dates from 1910. Decent recording, but the Tampere Orchestra is a bit too raw-toned and ill-tuned to do this music full justice. Worth hearing all the same.

Mendelssohn, Fanny (1805–47)

Piano trio in D, Op. 11.
*** Hyperion Dig. CDA 66331 [id.]. Dartington Piano Trio – Clara SCHUMANN: *Trio in G min.* ***

Like Clara Schumann's *G minor Trio* with which it is coupled, the *Piano trio* has impeccable craftsmanship and great facility. Its ideas are pleasing, though not strongly individual. The Dartington Piano Trio play most persuasively and give much pleasure. Excellent recording.

3 Pieces for piano, 4 hands.
*** Sony Dig. SK 48494 [id.]. Tal & Groethuysen – Felix MENDELSSOHN: *Andante and allegro* etc. ***

Yaara Tal and Andreas Groethuysen are a wonderful duo and have the capacity to transform dust into gold – not that Fanny Mendelssohn's *Pieces* are inferior. They have charm, and seem even more charming than they are in this duo's hands.

Mendelssohn, Felix (1809–47)

Capriccio brillant for piano and orchestra, Op. 22.
(B) ** Sony SBK 48166 [id.]. Rudolf Serkin, Phd. O, Ormandy – BRAHMS: *Concerto No. 1;* SCHUMANN: *Intro. and allegro appassionato.* **(*)

Serkin is on good form here. This is a brilliant performance, not without panache, if not especially strong on charm. The recording is a little shallow, but otherwise good.

(i; ii) *Capriccio brillant in B min. for piano and orchestra, Op. 22;* (iii) *Piano concerto in A min.* (for piano and strings); (i; iv) *Piano concertos Nos. 1 in G min., Op. 25; 2 in D min., Op. 40;* (iii; v) *Double piano concerto in E* (for two pianos and strings); (i; ii) *Rondo brillant in E flat for piano and orchestra, Op. 29;* (vi) *Rondo capriccioso in E, Op. 14.*
(B) *** Decca Double 452 410-2 (2). (i) Peter Katin; (ii) LPO, Martinon; (iii) John Ogdon, ASMF, Marriner; (iv) LSO, Anthony Collins; (v) with Brenda Lucas; (vi) Jorge Bolet.

This well-filled Double Decca conveniently gathers together all Mendelssohn's major concertante works for the piano except the *Double concerto in A flat*. However, the present compilation is tempting in its own right, as Katin's classic 1956 performances of the two best-known solo concertos have come up very freshly on CD. The two concertante pieces were recorded earlier (1954) and find Katin in sparkling form. Here a mono master is used; but this is an amazing example of the way Arthur Haddy's Decca recording team could use the Kingsway Hall ambience to give an impression of stereo. The ambitious and successful *A minor Concerto* was written when the composer was thirteen and the *Double concerto* comes from approximately two years later. These delightful concertante rarities both have engaging ideas and are played with great verve and spirit by John Ogdon and his wife. The orchestral playing is equally lively and fresh throughout, and the vivid (originally Argo) 1969 Kingsway Hall recording has hardly dated. Jorge Bolet (recorded digitally in 1985) offers the solo *Rondo capriccioso* as a closing encore with the lightest of touch.

(i) *Capriccio brillant, Op. 22*; (i; ii) *Double concerto for violin and piano.* (i) *Rondo brillant, Op. 29*; *Serenade and Allegro giocoso, Op. 43* (BIS CD 713); *Piano concertos Nos. 1 in G min., Op. 25; 2 in D min., Op. 40; Piano concerto in A min.* (BIS CD 718); (iii) *Double piano concertos: in A flat; E* (BIS CD 688); (ii) *Violin concerto in D min.; Violin concerto in E min., Op. 64 (1844 version). Octet, Op. 20: Scherzo* (orchestral version) (BIS CD 935).
(N) (M) *** BIS Dig. CD 966/69 [id.]. (i) Ronald Brautigam; (ii) Isabelle van Keulen; (iii) Love Derwinger, Roland Pöntinen, Amsterdam New Sinf., Lev Markiz.

These are exemplary recordings of exemplary performances. Indeed it is difficult to flaw them. They are available separately (the individual catalogue numbers are listed within the titles above), but there is a price advantage in purchasing them altogether. The interesting account of the *E minor Violin concerto* in its original form (beautifully played by Isabelle van Keulen) is of particular interest. Mendelssohn spent seven years working over what is perhaps his most successful concertante work (1838–45) and this is its earlier draft. Its gestation is discussed in greater detail in the accompanying notes for the individual disc, but the notes here are still pretty copious.

Piano concertos Nos. 1 in G min., Op. 25; 2 in D min., Op. 40; Capriccio brillant in B min., Op. 22.
*** Chandos Dig. CHAN 9215 [id.]. Howard Shelley, LMP.

Piano concertos Nos. 1–2; Capriccio brillant, Op. 22; Rondo brillant in E flat, Op. 29.
(BB) *** Naxos Dig. 8.550681-2 [id.]. Benjamin Frith, Slovak State PO (Košice), Robert Stanovsky.

Howard Shelley offers marvellous playing in every respect: fresh, sparkling and dashing in the fast movements, poetic and touching in the slower ones. The London Mozart Players are a group of exactly the right size for these works and they point rhythms nicely and provide the necessary lift. Shelley is particularly good in the finales and certainly conveys the scherzando quality in the closing *Presto* of No. 2. He despatches the *Capriccio brillant* with similar aplomb, and the recording-balance is admirably judged, with rich, truthful recorded sound.

Benjamin Frith on Naxos is a hardly less personable and nimble soloist: he is sensitively touching in the slow movements and makes much of the fine *Adagio* of No. 2. The Slovak orchestra accompany with vigour and enthusiasm, and if the effect is at times less sharply rhythmic this is partly the effect of a somewhat more reverberant acoustic. The piano balance here is bolder, more forward, although the orchestra certainly makes a strong impression. What makes the Naxos disc very competitive, is the inclusion of the *Rondo brillant*, which Frith dispatches with admirable vigour and sparkle. This disc is very good value indeed.

Piano concertos Nos. 1 and 2; Capriccio brillant, Op. 22; Rondo brillant, Op. 29; Serenade and Allegro giocoso, in B min., Op.43.
(N) *** Hyperion Dig. CDA 66969. Stephen Hough, CBSO, Foster.

It says much for Stephen Hough, a natural recording artist, that he readily matches such outstanding rivals in the Mendelssohn piano concertos as Murray Perahia, Howard Shelley and Benjamin Frith. Like them he treats these compact minor-key works with a biting intensity. Yet with freer expressiveness and bigger contrasts he also brings out extra poetry, and in the finales a sparkling wit. He also has the advantage of the most generous and very apt couplings, three other, rare concertante piano works by Mendelssohn. The point and delicacy of Hough's passage-work is a constant delight.

(i) *Piano concertos Nos. 1–2. Prelude and fugue, Op. 35/1; Rondo capriccioso, Op. 14; Variations sérieuses, Op. 54.*
(M) *** Sony SMK 42401 [id.]. Murray Perahia; (i) ASMF, Marriner.

Perahia's playing catches the Mendelssohnian spirit with admirable perception. There is sensibility and sparkle, the slow movements are shaped most beautifully and the partnership with Marriner is very successful, for the Academy give a most sensitive backing. The recording could be more transparent but it does not lack body, and the piano timbre is fully acceptable. At mid-price, a very recommendable issue.

(i) *Piano concertos Nos. 1 in G min., Op. 25; 2 in D min., Op. 40. Songs without words, Op. 19/1, 2, & 6 (Venetian gondola song); Op. 30/4 & 6 (Venetian gondola song); Op. 38/6; Op. 53/1; Op. 62/ 1 & 6 (Spring song); Op. 67/4 (Spinning song) & 6; Op. 85/6; Op. 102/5.*
(N) (M) *** Decca Dig. 466 425-2 [id.]. András Schiff, with (i) Bav. RSO, Dutoit.

András Schiff plays both concertos marvellously, with poetry, great delicacy and fluency, while his virtuosity is effortless. He is given excellent acccompaniments by Dutoit and the Bavarian players, and the Decca recording is first-class. His simplicity of style suits the *Songs without words*, although some might find his approach a little cool. Yet the famous *Spring song* shows him at his best. The recording is again most natural and realistic.

Double piano concertos: in A flat; in E.
*** Hyperion Dig. CDA 66567 [id.]. Coombs, Munro, BBC Scottish SO, Maksymiuk.
(BB) *** Naxos Dig. 8.553416 [id.]. Benjamin Frith, Hugh Tinney, Dublin RTE Sinf., O Duinn.

Mendelssohn's *Double concerto in A flat* is the most ambitious of all his concertante works, and the work in E brings an expansive first movement too; they provide formidable evidence of the teenage composer's fluency and technical finesse. Stephen Coombs and Ian Munro prove ideal advocates, playing with delectable point and imagination, finding a wit and poetry in the writing that might easily lie hidden, with even the incidental passagework magnetizing the ear. The recording of the pianos is on the shallow side, and the string-tone is thin too, but that is not inappropriate for the music.

This Naxos disc challenges comparison with the outstanding Hyperion issue coupling these same two charming double concertos. Mendelssohn wrote them in his early teens for his sister Fanny and himself to play. If the Irish players are not quite as persuasive as their Scottish counterparts on Hyperion, their playing is just as refined, and Frith and Tinney are a fair match for Coombs and Munro, less powerful but just as magnetic and even more poetic. The transparent recording helps, very appropriate for such youthful music.

Double piano concerto in E.
**(*) Ph. Dig. 432 095-2. Katia and Marielle Labèque, Philh. O, Bychkov – BRUCH: *Double concerto.* **(*)

The Labèques play Mendelssohn's ambitious *E major Double concerto* with enthusiasm and flair, and Bychkov accompanies manfully. But, partly because of the resonant acoustic, the effect is rather inflated and the ear looks for more transparency and lightness of texture in such an amiable piece.

2 Concert pieces for clarinet and basset horn: in F min., Op. 113; in D min., Op. 114.
(B) *** Hyperion Dyad Dig. CDD 22017 (2) [id.]. Thea King, Georgina Dobrée, LSO, Francis (with Concert – see below ***).

These Mendelssohn duets for clarinet and basset horn are most diverting, with their jocular finales; and they are played with a nice blend of expressive spontaneity and high spirits. Georgina Dobrée proves a nimble partner for the ever-sensitive Thea King. This is part of an excellent two-disc set, including other attractive concertante works by Max Bruch, Crusell, Spohr and other less familar names.

Piano concerto in A min. (i) *Concerto for violin and piano.*
(N) **(*) Teldec/Warner Dig. 0630 13152-2. Andreas Staier, Concerto Köln; (i) with Rainer Kussmaul.

These two boyhood concertos of Mendelssohn, dating from his early teens, make an excellent coupling. As these works were first heard in the Sunday salons of the composer's banker father, it is logical that they should be recorded here not just on period instruments but with a small band of strings – in places one instrument per part. What is less welcome is that the strings of Concerto Köln are too acid sounding even by period standards. By contrast, the solo violinist, Rainer Kussmaul, plays with rare freshness and purity, allowing himself just a measure of vibrato, and if Staier takes second place, that is not just a question of balance between the violin and an 1825 fortepiano, but of the young composer's piano writing, regularly built on passage-work – often in arpeggios – rather than straight melodic statements. That also applies to the piano writing in the solo concerto too, and it is striking that though each work is astonishing from a composer so young, a clear progression is revealed between 1822, the date of the solo concerto, and March 1823, when the double concerto was completed in time for his 14th birthday.

Violin concertos: in D min. (for violin & strings); in E min., Op. 64.

*** RCA Dig. 09026 62512-2 [id.]. Kyoko Takezawa, Bamberg SO, Claus Peter Flor.

*** Ph. Dig. 432 077-2 [id.]. Viktoria Mullova, ASMF, Marriner.

(N) (BB) **(*) Virgin Classics Dig. Double VBD5 61504-2 [CDVB 61504] (2). Mayumi Seiler, City of L. Sinf., Hickox – BEETHOVEN: *Concerto.* **(*)

Kyoko Takezawa gives winning accounts of both the great Mendelssohn *Violin concerto in E minor* and the youthful D minor work, resurrected over 40 years ago by Yehudi Menuhin. These are performances which consistently reflect the joy of the performers in the music. Takezawa's reading of the *D minor* is full of fantasy, with each movement sharply characterized to make the piece seem more mature than it is.

Purity is the keynote of Mullova's fresh and enjoyable readings of both concertos, the early *D minor* as well as the great *E minor* which is tenderly expressive rather than flamboyant in the expression of emotion, yet with concentration keenly maintained. So the central *Andante* is sweet and songful and the finale, light and fanciful, conveys pure fun in its fireworks. The early work follows a similar pattern, with youthful emotions given full rein and with the finale turned into a headily brilliant Csardas. The Philips recording is admirably natural and beautifully balanced, but Takezawa is now a first choice for this coupling.

It is good to have a recommendable bargain pairing of Mendelssohn's youthful and mature concertos. Mayumi Seiler is fresh and appealing in the one, and then gives a sparkling account of the famous *E minor* work with the slow movement serene in its simplicity, as with the coupled Beethoven concerto. Hickox is in good form and the recording is pleasingly balanced; although the timbre of the soloist is small, it is perfectly focused.

Violin concerto in E min., Op. 64.

(M) *** Sony Dig. SMK 64250 [id.]. Cho-Liang Lin, Philh. O, Tilson Thomas – BRUCH: *Concerto;* VIEUXTEMPS: *Concerto No. 5.* ***

(N) (M) *** Decca Legends 460 976-2 Kyung Wha Chung, Montreal SO, Dutoit – BRUCH: *Violin concerto No. 1*; *Scottish fantasy.* ***

(M) *** Decca Dig. 460 015-2. Kyung Wha Chung, Montreal SO, Charles Dutoit (as above) – ELGAR: *Violin concerto.* ***

(N) *** EMI Dig. CDC5 56418-2 [id.]. Sarah Chang, BPO, Mariss Jansons – SIBELIUS: *Violin concerto.* ***

(N) *** Teldec/Warner 0630-15870-2 [id.]. Perlman, Chicago SO/Barenboim – BRAHMS: *Double concerto.* ***

(BB) *** Naxos Dig. 8.550153 [id.]. Nishizaki, Slovak PO, Jean – TCHAIKOVSKY: *Concerto.* ***

(M) *** DG Dig. 445 515-2 [id.]. Anne-Sophie Mutter, BPO, Karajan – BRAHMS: *Violin concerto.* ***

*** EMI Dig. CDC5 66220-2 [id.]. Nigel Kennedy, ECO, Tate – BRUCH: *Concerto No. 1;* SCHUBERT: *Rondo.* ***

*** ASV CDDCA 748 [id.]. Xue-Wei, LPO, Ivor Bolton – BRAHMS: *Violin concerto.* ***

(M) *** Carlton IMP Dig. PCD 2005 [id.]. Jaime Laredo, SCO – BRUCH: *Concerto No. 1.* ***

(M) *** EMI CDM5 66906-2 [CDM 66958]. Menuhin, Philh. O, Kurtz – BRUCH: *Concerto No. 1.* ***

(BB) *** Belart 461 355-2. Campoli, LPO, Boult – BEETHOVEN: *Violin concerto.* ***

(B) *** [EMI Red Line CDR5 69863]. Itzhak Perlman, LSO, Previn – BRUCH: *Violin concerto.* ***

(N) (M) *** Penguin Classics 460 619-2 [id.]. Nathan Milstein, VPO, Abbado – TCHAIKOVSKY: *Concerto.* ***

(B) *** DG Double 453 142-2 (2). Nathan Milstein, VPO, Abbado – BEETHOVEN: *Concerto* ***; BRAHMS: *Concerto* **(*); TCHAIKOVSKY: *Concerto.* ***

**(*) RCA 09026 61743-2 [RCA 61743-2-RC]. Heifetz, Boston SO, Munch – TCHAIKOVSKY: *Concerto* etc. **(*)

(***) Testament mono SBT 1037 [id.]. Martzy, Philh. O, Kletzki – BRAHMS: *Concerto.* (***)

(M) (***) EMI mono CDM5 66975-2 [CDM 66990]. Yehudi Menuhin, BPO, Furtwängler – BEETHOVEN: *Concerto.* (***)

(***) Beulah mono 1PD 10. Alfredo Campoli, LPO, Boult – ELGAR: *Violin concerto.* (***)

(M) **(*) Sony Stern Edition I SMK 66827 [id.]. Stern, Phd. O, Ormandy (with DVORAK: *Violin concerto; Romance.* **)

(B) **(*) Discover Dig. DICD 920122 [id.]. Evgeny Bushkov, Slovak New PO, Rahbari (with TCHAIKOVSKY: *Concerto*. **)

(M) **(*) Sup. SU 1939-2 011 [id.]. Josef Suk, Czech PO, Karel Ančerl – BERG: *Concerto* ***; (with BRUCH: *Concerto*. **)

(M) (**(*)) EMI mono CDH5 65191-2. Heifetz, RPO, Beecham – MOZART: *Concerto No. 5;* VIEUXTEMPS: *Concerto No. 5*. (***)

Cho-Liang Lin's vibrantly lyrical account now reappears with the Bruch *G minor* plus the Vieuxtemps No. 5, to make an unbeatable mid-priced triptych. They are all three immensely rewarding and poetic performances, given excellent, modern, digital sound, and Michael Tilson Thomas proves a highly sympathetic partner in the Mendelssohn *Concerto*.

Chung favours speeds faster than usual in all three movements, and the result is sparkling and happy, with the lovely slow movement fresh and songful, not at all sentimental. With warmly sympathetic accompaniment from Dutoit and the Montreal orchestra, amply recorded, the result is one of Chung's happiest records. The Elgar coupling works well, but the alternative of Bruch's *G minor concerto* and *Scottish fantasy* in Decca's Legends series is more attractive still.

Unlike the Sibelius with which it is coupled, Chang's account of the Mendelssohn was recorded under studio conditions in the Philharmonie, Berlin. Here too she offers an astonishingly mature reading, more restrained than some, but still magnetic in its thoughtfulness and spontaneous poetry. Warm, atmospheric sound.

Perlman's 1993 Chicago version, strong and volatile, was recorded live and originally issued in coupling with the second Prokofiev. It makes an excellent, more generous coupling in the new format with the powerful Perlman/Ma version of the Brahms *Double concerto*.

Takako Nishizaki gives an inspired reading of the *Concerto*, warm, spontaneous and full of temperament. The central *Andante* is on the slow side, but well shaped, not sentimental, while the outer movements are exhilarating, with excellent playing from the Slovak Philharmonic. Though the forwardly placed violin sounds over-bright, the recording is full and warm. A splendid coupling at super-bargain price.

In the Mendelssohn *E minor*, even more than in her Brahms coupling, the freshness of Anne-Sophie Mutter's approach communicates vividly to the listener, creating the feeling of hearing the work anew. Her gentleness and radiant simplicity in the *Andante* are very appealing, and the light, sparkling finale is a delight. Mutter is given a small-scale image, projected forward from the orchestral backcloth; the sound is both full and refined.

Kennedy establishes a positive, masculine view of the work from the very start, but fantasy here goes with firm control. The slow movement brings a simple, songful view of the haunting melody, and the finale sparkles winningly, with no feeling of rush. With a bonus in the rare Schubert *Rondo* and clear, warm recording, it makes an excellent recommendation.

Xue-Wei's version, clean and fresh if a little reticent emotionally, makes a generous and attractive coupling for his equally recommendable version of the Brahms. There are more strongly characterized readings than this but, with its pastel-shaded lyricism, this is undoubtedly satisfying, helped by first-rate recording.

Laredo's version on a mid-price CD brings an attractively direct reading, fresh and alert, marked by consistently sweet and true tone from the soloist. The orchestral ensemble is amazingly good when you remember that the soloist himself is directing. The recording is vivid and clean.

The restrained nobility of Menuhin's phrasing of the famous principal melody of the slow movement has long been a hallmark of his reading with Efrem Kurtz, who provides polished and sympathetic support. The sound of the CD transfer is bright, with the soloist dominating but the orchestral texture well detailed.

It is good to have Campoli's delightful performance back in the catalogue. His perfectly formed tone and polished, secure playing are just right for the Mendelssohn *Concerto*. A delightful performance, notable for its charm and disarming simplicity. The 1958 (originally Decca) recording is brightly lit in the CD transfer, and the vividness is marred by a degree of roughness in the orchestral focus; but no matter, this very inexpensive record gives much pleasure and is a fine reminder of a superb violinist. This is also available in an alternative coupling with the Elgar concerto.

Perlman gives a performance of the Mendelssohn that is full of flair, superbly matched by the LSO under Previn, always an illuminating interpreter of this composer. Ripe recording quality.

Milstein's DG version comes from the early 1970s. His is a highly distinguished performance, very well accompanied. His account of the slow movement is more patrician than Menuhin's and his slight reserve is projected by DG sound which is bright, clean and clear in its CD remastering. This now comes either as a Penguin Classic (with an author's sleeve note by Jan Morris) in its original coupling with Tchaikovsky, or on a DG Double which also includes the Beethoven and Brahms concertos.

As one might expect, Heifetz gives a fabulous performance. His speeds are consistently fast, yet in the slow movement his flexible phrasing sounds so inevitable and easy that it is hard not to be convinced. The finale is a tour de force, light and sparkling, with every note in place. The recording has been digitally remastered with success and the sound is smoother than before.

It is not just the perfect sweetness and purity of Martzy's tone that is so impressive, coupled with flawless intonation, but also her natural imagination in phrasing. Her freely flexible rubato always sounds spontaneous, and the hushed tenderness of her pianissimo playing is breathtaking, as in the link into the second subject of the first movement and in the central *Andante*. The performance is also remarkable for the quicksilver energy of the finale and, with the soloist well forward, the mono sound is full and clear.

Menuhin's unique gift for lyrical sweetness has never been presented on record more seductively than in his classic, earlier version of the Mendelssohn *Concerto* with Furtwängler. The digital transfer is not ideally clear, yet one hardly registers that this is a mono recording from the early 1950s.

Another totally memorable performance by Stern from the late 1950s. It has great bravura, culminating in a marvellously surging account of the finale. The slow movement too is played with great eloquence and feeling but, when pianissimos are non-existent – partly, but not entirely, the fault of the close recording-balance – the poetic element is diminished, even though there is a full flood of romanticism. However, Stern is much less at home in the Dvořák *Concerto*.

The latest bargain digital recording from Discover introduces a brilliant young Russian soloist, Evgeny Bushkov, a pupil of Leonid Kogan. His small, sweet, silvery timbre suits the Mendelssohn *Concerto* admirably, and he prepares and plays the secondary theme of the opening movement with appealing tenderness. The *Andante*, too, has a matching simplicity and the finale no lack of bravura and fire. He is well accompanied, and the recording, made in the Concert Hall of Slovak Radio, Bratislava, is full and well balanced. Not a first choice, however, for the coupled Tchaikovsky *Concerto* sounds less spontaneous.

Suk's small, sweet timbre is particularly suited to the Mendelssohn *Concerto* and his intonation is immaculate. This is a highly congenial performance, not as individual as some, with a straightforwardly lyrical slow movement and a finale which gains from not being rushed off its feet. An excellent CD transfer, firm and full. However, Suk's style is less suited to the Bruch *Concerto*.

Anything that Heifetz does is pretty well without compare, and his dazzling virtuosity is well in evidence in this 1948 performance of the Mendelssohn with the RPO and Beecham. However, there would seem to be less warmth and rapport between Heifetz and Sir Thomas than there was between the violinist and Barbirolli in the coupled Mozart *Concerto*.

(i) *Violin concerto in E min., Op. 64;* (ii) *Symphonies Nos. 3 (Scottish); 4 (Italian);* (iii) *A Midsummer Night's Dream: Overture and incidental music: Scherzo; Intermezzo; Nocturne; Wedding march.*

(B) *** Teldec/Erato/Warner Analogue/Dig. Ultima 0630 18954-2 (2). (i) Olivier Charlier, Monte Carlo Op. O, Lawrence Foster; (ii) Leizig GO, Kurt Masur; (iii) LPO, Raymond Leppard.

For this Ultima reissue Warner Classics have drawn on both the Erato and Teldec back-catalogues to make another very attractive compilation. At its centre is Masur's highly recommendable coupling of Mendelssohn's two best-loved symphonies. He observes exposition repeats in both, and his choice of speeds brings out the freshness of inspiration judiciously, avoiding any suspicion of sentimentality in slow movements, which are taken at flowing tempi. However the reverberant Leipzig recording tends to obscure detail in tuttis; the Scherzo of the *Scottish*, for example, becomes a blur, losing some of its point and charm. Otherwise, the sound of the orchestra has all the characteristic Leipzig bloom and beauty. Indeed the orchestral sound is glorious and the cultured playing always a joy to listen to, while at the climax of the first movement, by bringing out the timpani strongly, Masur finds a storm sequence almost to match *Fingal's Cave*. Olivier Charlier's account of the *Violin concerto* is warm, lyrically fresh, and nicely paced. Lawrence Foster accompanies persuasively and this is enjoyably spontaneous. Leppard's suite from *A Midsummer Night's Dream* is also very sensitively played and well recorded.

(i) *Violin concerto in E min.*; (ii) *Symphony No. 4 (Italian); Overtures: The Hebrides (Fingal's Cave); A Midsummer Night's Dream; Ruy Blas.*

(BB) *** EMI Seraphim CES5 68524-2 (2) [CEDB 68524]. LSO, with (i) Sir Yehudi Menuhin, cond. Rafael Frühbeck de Burgos; (ii) Previn – BRUCH: *Violin concerto No. 1.* ***

Menuhin's second stereo recording, with Rafael Frühbeck de Burgos, has its moments of roughness, but it has magic too: at the appearance of the first movement's second subject and in the slow movement, even if the timbre itself is a little spare. The recording sounds fuller than the earlier account with Kurtz, and this makes a good bargain on EMI's new Seraphim label, coupled with the Bruch *Concerto* and Previn's 1979 version of the *Italian Symphony*, plus the three most popular overtures. Previn, always an inspired Mendelssohnian, gives exuberant performances. In the symphony the outer movements are urgent, without sounding at all breathless, and are finely sprung; the essential first-movement exposition repeat is included. Recording balance has the strings a little less forward than usual, but the overall effect is agreeably full.

Overtures: Athalia; Calm sea and prosperous voyage; Fingal's Cave (The Hebrides); Ruy Blas. Symphonies Nos. 3 (Scottish); 4 (Italian); (i) *A Midsummer Night's Dream: Overture and incidental music* (complete).
(B) *** RCA Twofer Dig. 74321 34177-2 (2). Bamberg SO, Claus Peter Flor; (i) with Lucia Popp, Marjana Lipovšek, Bamberg SO Ch.

Claus Peter Flor has a wonderfully warm affinity with Mendelssohn's music, and this RCA Twofer cannot be too highly recommended, even if some duplication is involved. His collection of overtures (which received a Rosette from us in its original format, when it also included *The Marriage of Camacho*) remains the most desirable the catalogue has ever offered. The magically evocative opening of *Calm sea and prosperous voyage*, followed by an allegro of great vitality, is a demonstrable example of the spontaneous imagination of these performances, and there is no finer or more atmospheric version of *Fingal's Cave*, with its lyrical secondary theme phrased with memorable delicacy of feeling. The bold *Ruy Blas* and the nobly contoured *Athalia* are also greatly enjoyable, especially when played with such freshness and polish. The recording, made in the Dominikanerbau, Bamberg, has splendid bloom, for the hall ambience is just right for this repertoire.

The *Midsummer Night's Dream* incidental music is recorded equally beautifully, glowing and radiant. The little melodramas are omitted, but the performance is otherwise complete. Flor's stylish yet relaxed control brings the kind of intimacy one expects from a chamber group. Again the Bamberg acoustic adds to the character of these performances, unforced and beaming.

Symphonies for strings Nos. 1–12; 13 in C min. (single movement).
*** RCA Dig. 09026 68069-2 (3) [id.]. Hanover Band, Roy Goodman.
(N) *** BIS Dig. CD 938/940 [id.]. Amsterdam New Sinf., Lev Markiz.

Mendelssohn's early symphonies for strings, lost for 150 years, were rediscovered in 1950. The first ten were student works and the last two, together with the virtually unknown *Symphony movement in C minor* (No. 13), had all been completed before their young composer reached the age of fourteen. The special novelty on the RCA set is the fully scored version (for woodwind, brass and timpani) of No. 8, one of the more ambitious of the series, with a performance time of 30 minutes. Mendelssohn rewrote the Trio of the very jolly Minuet and uses the woodwind and horns most effectively throughout: this is a splendid movement which could readily fit into one of the later, mature symphonies. Otherwise the composer left the music very much as it had been in its original string version. The first six symphonies are in three-movement, Italian overture form; then, from No. 7 onwards, Mendelssohn moves into the four-movement format of the Haydn and Mozart symphonies, often with a slow introduction. No. 11, the most ambitious (40 minutes 32 seconds), has five, with a second-movement Scherzo and fourth-movement Minuet which frame the beautiful, serene central *Adagio* (in layout recalling Haydn's early Divertimenti/Quartets). The arresting *Symphoniesatz*, too, is remarkably imaginative in its construction and towards the close even anticipates a style of writing which its young composer would use later in his teenage years.

Bustling energy and drive are the keynote of Goodman's period-instrument performances. Allegros sparkle and the comparatively brief *Andantes* of the earliest works are sensitively presented, even if one feels here that the music could occasionally smile more. But the later symphonies, which have brought maturity from experience, are superbly characterized. The playing is as alert and vigorous as ever, yet Goodman's readings balance energy with gravitas and weight, and their persuasive, expressive feeling shows the players as totally involved in this remarkable, precocious writing.

We welcomed the first of the BIS Mendelssohn *String symphonies* to appear (comprising Nos. 2, 3, 9, 10) in earlier volumes; the remaining instalments by this fine Amsterdam ensemble fully live up to the expectations it aroused. The playing of the Amsterdam New Sinfonietta is vibrant and alive, and the recording has a warmth and clarity that give the set the edge over its current rivals. This music is full of charm, and the quality of Mendelssohn's youthful invention is little short of astonishing.

Symphonies for strings Nos. 1–12.
(N) *** Teldec/Warner Dig. 0630 17433-2 (3) [id.]. Concerto Köln.

The early Mendelssohn symphonies are here accommodated on a three-CD set made by the conductorless Concerto Köln. Although the usual original-instrument sonority is not to all tastes, those whose preference is for period instruments should also consider these. The performances are very musical and the recorded sound is excellent.

Symphonies for string orchestra Nos. 1 in C; 2 in D; 3 in E min.; 4 in C min.; 5 in B flat; 6 in E flat.
(BB) *** Naxos Dig. 8.553161 [id.]. N. CO, Nicholas Ward.

Symphonies for string orchestra Nos. 7 in D min.; 8 in D; 9 in C.
(BB) *** Naxos Dig. 8.553162 [id.]. N. CO, Nicholas Ward.

Symphonies for string orchestra Nos. 10 in B min.; 11 in F; 12 in G min.; 13 in C min. (Sinfoniesatz).

(BB) *** Naxos Dig. 8.553163 [id.]. N. CO, Nicholas Ward.

Nicholas Ward and the Northern Chamber Orchestra follow up the success of their Haydn recordings for Naxos with an outstanding series of the boy Mendelssohn's string symphonies, matching and even outshining rivals at whatever price. The freshness and incisiveness of the performances are enhanced by bright, clean recording, made in the Concert Hall of Broadcasting House in Manchester. Not only does Ward bring out the exhilarating sparkle and vigour of the fast movements – with Mendelssohn, even at the age of eleven, giving clear anticipations of his mature style – but he also gives apt emotional weight to such beautiful lyrical movements as the *Andante* of No. 2 or the darkly slow introduction to the one-movement *No. 10 in B minor*. All three discs can be warmly recommended to everyone.

Symphonies for string orchestra Nos. 2 in D; 3 in E min.; 5 in B flat; 6 in E flat.

(B) *** EMI forte Dig. CZS5 69524-2 (2) [CDFB 69524]. Polish CO, Maksymiuk – JANIEWICZ: *Divertimento;* JARZEBSKI: *Chromatica; Tamburetta;* ROSSINI: *String sonatas.* ***

This collection of the boy Mendelssohn's early *String symphonies* (written when he was only twelve) is most invigorating. These earlier symphonies from the series of 12 may look to various models from Bach to Beethoven, but the young composer keeps showing his individuality and, however imitative the style, the vitality of the invention still bursts through. The slow movement of *Symphony No. 2*, for example, is a Bachian meditation that in its simple beauty matches later Mendelssohn. The Polish strings are set in a lively acoustic, giving exceptionally rich sound, but the playing also has plenty of dash.

Symphonies Nos. 1–5.

(M) *** DG 429 664-2 (3). Mathis, Rebman, Hollweg, German Op. Ch., BPO, Karajan.

(B) **(*) RCA 74321 20286-2 (3) [Eurodisc 69237-2 RV]. Casapietra, Stolte, Schreier, Leipzig R. Ch. (in *No. 2*); Leipzig GO, Masur.

Symphonies Nos. 1 in C min., Op. 11; (i) *2 in B flat (Hymn of praise), Op. 52;* (ii) *Die erste Walpurgisnacht, Op. 60.*

(N) (B) *** Decca Double 460 236-2 (2) [id.]. VPO, Dohnányi with (i) Ghazarian, Gruberová, Krenn, V. State Op. Ch.; (ii) Lilowa, Laubenthal, Krause, Sramek, V. Singverein.

Symphonies Nos. 3 in A min. (Scottish), Op. 56; 4 in A (Italian), Op. 90; 5 in D min. (Reformation), Op. 107; Athalie, Op. 74: Overture and War march of the priests; Overtures: Calm sea and prosperous voyage, Op. 27; The Hebrides (Fingal's Cave), Op. 26.

(N) (B)*** Decca Double Analogue/Dig. 460 239-2 [id.]. VPO, Dohnányi.

Symphonies Nos. 1–5; Overture: The Hebrides (Fingal's Cave).

(M) *** Chandos Enchant Dig. CHAN 7090 (3) [id.]. Philh. O, Walter Weller (with Cynthia Haymon, Alison Hagley, Peter Straka, Philh. Ch. in *Symphony No. 2*).

Symphonies Nos. 1–5; Overtures: Fair Melusina, Op. 32; The Hebrides (Fingal's Cave), Op. 26; A Midsummer Night's Dream, Op. 21; Octet, Op. 20: Scherzo.

*** DG Dig. 415 353-2 (4). LSO, Abbado (with Connell, Mattila, Blochwitz and London Symphony Ch. in Symphony No. 2).

Abbado's is a set to brush cobwebs off an attractive symphonic corner; in the lesser-known symphonies it is his gift to have you forgetting any weaknesses of structure or thematic invention in the brightness and directness of his manner. The toughness of the piece makes one marvel that Mendelssohn ever substituted the scherzo from the *Octet* for the third movement (as he did in London), but helpfully Abbado includes that extra scherzo, so that on CD, with a programming device, you can readily make the substitution yourself. Good, bright recording, though not ideally transparent. However, this set remains at full price.

Weller's set of the Mendelssohn symphonies comes up against considerable competition but can stand comparison with the finest alternatives, including Karajan and Abbado. Certainly it is the most beautifully recorded, the Chandos sound richly full-bodied, though not sharply defined. He plays the *First Symphony* as if it were a mature work, not the inspiration of a fifteen-year-old, making the strongest contrast between fast outer movements and a spaciously moulded Andante. The *Scottish* and *Italian Symphonies* convey the sense of live performances caught on the wing here and throughout the series, compensating for the occasional lack of crispness in ensemble. These are warm, affectionate readings which include exposition repeats and build excitingly to climaxes. In the *Reformation Symphony* and in *Fingal's Cave*, which follows, there is an emotional thrust that is very involving, leading to a joyfully exultant conclusion in the finale. Again in the *Hymn of Praise* (No. 2) from the opening trombone solo onwards it is the warmth and weight of the recorded sound that tells, with a large chorus set against full-bodied, satisfyingly string-based orchestral sound. Though again speeds are often dangerously slow, as in the lovely duet for the two sopranos, *Ich harrete des Herrn*, the sense of spontaneity in the performance makes it compelling throughout. And how sympathetically Weller sustains the lilting second-movement

Allegretto. In the finale, Cynthia Haymon and Alison Hagley are warm-toned soloists, with Peter Straka an expressive if slightly fluttery tenor, but with a timbre which suits Mendelssohn. A considerable achievement.

Dohnányi's pair of Decca Doubles (which includes two key overtures, lesser-known *Athalie* items and a half-hour cantata, as well as the symphonies) brings performances which are fresh and direct, often relying on faster and more flowing speeds than in Abbado's full-price set, more clearly rebutting any idea that this music might be sentimental. The most striking contrast comes in the *Hymn of Praise*, where Dohnányi's speeds are often so much faster than Abbado's that the whole character of the music is changed, as in the second-movement Scherzo, sharp in one, gently persuasive in the other. Many will prefer Dohnányi in that, particularly when the choral sound is brighter and more immediate too. The *Reformation Symphony* comes off particularly well. The vintage recordings were made in the Sofiensaal between 1976 and 1978, and the two overtures and the *Italian Symphony* are digital, the Decca engineers producing sound which was among the finest of its period. The snag of the set is that Dohnányi, unlike Abbado, omits exposition repeats, which in the *Italian Symphony* means the loss of the substantial lead-back passage in the first movement.

Die erste Walpurgisnacht, with its unexpected anti-Christian stance (reflecting Goethe's sardonic tone of voice in his dramatic poem), is an oddity but one full of interest for the modern listener. Witches and druids are angrily pursued by Christians on the Brocken, and some of the more dramatic moments suggest that had he been given the right libretto, Mendelssohn might have made an opera composer. It makes an excellent contribution to the first of the two Doubles.

Karajan's distinguished set of the Mendelssohn *Symphonies* was recorded in 1971/2 in the Berlin Jesus-Christus Kirche. The early C minor work sounds particularly fresh, and the *Hymn of Praise* brings the fullest sound of all; the very fine choral singing is vividly caught. The soloists make a good team, rather than showing any memorable individuality; but overall Karajan's performance is most satisfying. The *Scottish Symphony* is a particularly remarkable account and the *Italian* shows the Berlin Philharmonic in sparkling form: the only drawback is Karajan's characteristic omission of both first-movement exposition repeats. There are few reservations to be made about the *Reformation Symphony*, and the sound has been effectively clarified without too much loss of weight.

Recorded by Eurodisc in 1971/2, the earlier of Masur's two Mendelssohn *Symphony* cycles, reissued in RCA's Symphony Edition, makes an excellent bargain-priced alternative to the strongly characterized later set for Teldec (see below). The recording is warmer and more immediate, and Masur's preference for flowing speeds in slow movements is not so marked, often with more affectionate moulding of phrase. The performances are often more vivid and more spontaneous-sounding, notably that of No. 2, the *Hymn of Praise*, where the forward focus of the voices adds to the impact of a most refreshing reading. Sadly, the two most popular symphonies, the *Scottish* and *Italian*, are the least successful, with generally slow speeds and slacker ensemble than in the rest. Masur here observes the exposition repeat in the *Italian* but not in the *Scottish*, but this is a case where Masur's mid-priced Teldec alternative coupling of these two key works is clearly preferable. The symphonies in the RCA set have also been issued separately at mid-price: *Symphonies Nos. 1* and *3* (74321 20287-2); *Symphony No. 2* (74321 20288-2); *Symphonies Nos. 4* and *5* (74321 20289-2).

(i) *Symphonies Nos. 1 in C min., Op. 11;* (ii) *2 in B flat (Hymn of Praise), Op. 52;* (i) *3 in A min. (Scottish), Op. 56; Overture The Hebrides (Fingal's Cave), Op. 26.*

(B) *** Ph. Duo 456 071-2 (2) [id.]. LPO; (i) Haitink; (ii) M. Price, Burgess, Jerusalem, LPO Ch., Chailly.

(i) *Symphonies Nos. 4 in A (Italian), Op. 90; 5 in D min. (Reformation), Op. 107; Calm sea and prosperous voyage overture, Op. 27;* (ii–iii) *Violin concerto in E min.;* (iii–iv) *A Midsummer Night's Dream: Overture, Op. 21; Incidental music, Op. 61.*

(B) *** Ph. Duo 456 074-2 (2) [id.]. (i) LPO; (ii) Grumiaux; (iii) Concg. O; (iv) with Woodland, Watts, Women of Netherlands R. Ch.; all cond. Haitink.

When Bernard Haitink in 1980 was prevented from rounding off his planned Mendelssohn symphony cycle with the Symphony No. 2 (*Lobgesang – Hymn of Praise*), Riccardo Chailly stepped in to record it in his place. This compilation brings together what, despite the change of conductor, is an outstanding cycle, fresh and energetic, with a geniality that regularly puts a smile on Mendelssohn's face. If one compares this with rival cycles at mid-price, this one is more warmly expressive, more lightly pointed than either Sawallisch's (the previous Philips cycle) or Dohnányi's on Decca, both of which seem plainer, even at times fierce, next to this. Only in the first movement of the *Italian Symphony* does Haitink press too hard, and even then he has time to spring rhythms. Broadly, Chailly follows a similar pattern in *Lobgesang*, another excellent performance with an outstanding trio of soloists, helped by full and vivid sound, though the fine chorus is backwardly balanced. The fourth disc contains Haitink's brilliant Concertgebouw version of the *Midsummer Night's Dream* incidental music

– ten movements, including a dazzling account of the Overture – as well as the excellent Grumiaux version of the *Violin concerto*, also with Haitink and the Concertgebouw, with 1960s sound still fresh and clear.

Symphonies Nos. 1 in C min., Op. 11; (i) *2 in B flat (Hymn of Praise), Op. 52. 5 in D (Reformation), Op. 107.*

(B) **(*) Teldec/Warner Ultima Dig. 3984 21341-2 (2) [(M) id. import]. Leipzig GO, Kurt Masur; (i) with Barbara Bonney, Michael Schönheit, Leipzig R. Ch.

Masur's mastery in Mendelssohn in his later, Teldec set is due in good measure to his ability to adopt relatively fast speeds and make them sound easy and relaxed, not hurried and breathless. Mendelssohn himself, conductor of this same Leipzig orchestra, was renowned for adopting fast speeds, and in all three symphonies here Masur is faster than his principal rivals on disc, not just in allegros but in slower movements too. In Nos. 1 and 5 that works very well indeed, bringing an alert freshness with no hint of sentimentality; but the fast speeds in the big choral symphony will for many be too extreme. Where Abbado on DG, no sentimentalist, takes 29 minutes over the three instrumental movements which open the work, Masur takes only 21 minutes, an astonishing discrepancy. Nevertheless, as ever, Masur avoids breathlessness, and with excellent soloists and choir, freshly recorded with plenty of detail, the two-disc package is still competitive in bringing together Mendelssohn's three less popular symphonies.

Symphonies Nos. 1 in C min., Op. 11; 5 in D (Reformation), Op. 107; Octet, Op. 20: Scherzo.

(M) *** DG Dig. 445 596-2 [id.]. LSO, Abbado.

The *First* and *Fifth* are Mendelssohn's least-played and least-recorded symphonies, so Abbado's coupling is very welcome. His version includes a sparkling version of the Scherzo from the Octet which Mendelssohn substituted for the original when he presented it in London, so that you can readily programme the substitution yourself. His direct manner suits the *Reformation Symphony* equally well. Brightly lit, early-digital recording (1984), but with the warm ambience of St John's, Smith Square, adding overall bloom.

Symphony No. 2 in B flat (Hymn of praise), Op. 52.

*** DG (IMS) Dig. 423 143-2 [id.]. Connell, Mattila, Blochwitz, London Symphony Ch., LSO, Abbado.

(M) *** DG 431 471-2. Mathis, Rebmann, Hollweg, German Op. Ch., BPO, Karajan.

*** Opus 111 OPS 30-98. Soile Isokoski, Mechthild Bach, Frieder Lang, Chorus Musicus Köln, Das neue Orchester, Christoph Spering.

We have already praised the 1972 Karajan recording of the *Hymn of Praise* within the context of his complete set of Mendelssohn symphonies above. In some ways Abbado's full-price digital version is even finer, if not more clearly recorded, brushing aside all sentimentality, both fresh and sympathetic and, though the recording is not ideally clear on inner detail, the brightness reinforces the conductor's view. The chorus, well focused, is particularly impressive, and the sweet-toned tenor, Hans-Peter Blochwitz, is outstanding among the soloists.

It is timely that Spering, following up the success of Herreweghe's Harmonia Mundi version of *Elijah*, here presents a performance of the *Hymn of Praise* in period style. Spering is relaxed in his choice of tempos, but in no way does he let the music drag or become sentimental. With clean, crisp textures this is a most refreshing performance, full of incidental beauties. For example, the once-celebrated duet for the two soprano soloists, *Ich harrete des Herrn* ('I waited for the Lord'), is intensely beautiful in its simplicity, with Soile Isokoski (also in Herreweghe's *Elijah*) and Mechthild Bach both angelically sweet yet nicely contrasted. The tenor soloist, Frieder Lang, is also exceptionally sweet-toned, though his projection is keen enough to make the *Huter, ist die Nacht bald hin?* ('Watchman, what of the night?') episode very intense and dramatic. Though not always clear in inner definition, the freshness of the choral singing matches that of the whole performance.

Symphony No. 3 in A min. (Scottish), Op. 56.

(N) ((**)) Orfeo C 488 981 B [id.]. BPO, Mitropoulos – DEBUSSY: *La Mer*; SCHOENBERG: *Variations*. (**)

Mitropoulos's account of the *Scottish Symphony* comes from the 1960 Salzburg Festival. It is an extraordinary performance in every way. The slow movement has enormous eloquence and both the scherzo and the finale are taken as fast as the Berlin Philharmonic can play them. Spellbinding though this is, the Austrian Radio recording is execrable. Its frequency range is narrow and the sound of the strings above the stave is shrill and strident. Artistically this rates three stars but as a recording this strains tolerance to the limit.

Symphony No. 3 in A min. (Scottish), Op. 56; A Midsummer Night's Dream: Overture, Op. 21 and excerpts, Op 61; Overture: The Hebrides (Fingal's Cave).

(M) **(*) Decca 443 578-2 [id.]. LSO, Peter Maag.

Under Maag, the *Scottish Symphony* is played most beautifully, and its pastoral character, occasioned by Mendelssohn's considerable use of strings throughout, is amplified by a Kingsway Hall recording of great warmth. The response of the LSO has quite remarkable freshness in this highly spontaneous performance. The opening string cantilena is poised and very gracious and thus sets the mood for what is to follow. The first-movement exposition repeat is not observed. Maag is too ponderous in the final *Maestoso*, but there is a compensating breadth and the effect is almost Klempererian. The remastered sound is first class, with a natural balance and glowing woodwind detail. Only a degree of thinness of timbre in the violins when playing above the stave betrays the age of the original. *Fingal's Cave* is no less successful. Maag's *Overture* and excerpts from a *A Midsummer Night's Dream* derive from a more extended LP selection, dating from the earliest days of stereo (1957). The recording is clean and well projected; in the remastering, the luminous quality one remembers in the original has been retained. These vintage recordings play for 76 minutes.

Symphony No. 3 in A min. (Scottish), Op. 56; Overtures; Calm sea and a prosperous voyage; The Hebrides (Fingal's cave); Ruy Blas.
(BB) **(*) Naxos Dig. 8.550222; *4.550222* [id.]. Slovak PO, Oliver Dohnányi.

Oliver Dohnányi conducts a joyful account of the *Scottish Symphony* on Naxos, given the more impact by forward recording. Mendelssohn's lilting rhythms in all the fast movements are delightfully bouncy, and though the slow movement brings few hushed pianissimos, its full warmth is brought out without sentimentality. The three overtures, also very well done, not least the under-appreciated *Ruy Blas*, make an excellent coupling.

Symphonies Nos. 3 in A min. (Scottish); 4 in A (Italian), Op. 90.
*** Decca (IMS) Dig. 433 811-2 [id.]. San Francisco SO, Herbert Blomstedt.
*** Mer. Dig. CDE 84261 [id.]. Apollo CO, Chernaik.
(M) *** DG Dig. 427 810-2 [id.]. LSO, Abbado.
(BB) *** ASV CDQS 6004. O of St John's, Lubbock.
*** Ph. (IMS) Dig. 442 130-2. ASMF, Sir Neville Marriner.
*** Teldec/Warner Dig. 9031 72308-2 [id.]. COE, Harnoncourt.
(M) **(*) DG (IMS) 439 980-2. Israel PO, Bernstein.

(i) *Symphonies Nos. 3 in A min. (Scottish), Op. 56;* (ii) *4 in A (Italian), Op. 90;* (i) *Hebrides overture (Fingal's cave), Op. 26.*
(M) *** DG Originals 449 743-2 [id.]. BPO, Karajan.
(M) *** Classic fM Dig. 75605 57013-2. Ulster O, Sitkovetsky.

Of all the many discs coupling Mendelssohn's two most popular symphonies, the *Scottish* and the *Italian*, there is none finer than Blomstedt's. Not only does he choose ideal speeds – not too brisk in the exhilarating first movement of the *Italian* or sentimentally drawn out in slow movements – he conveys a feeling of spontaneity throughout, springing rhythms infectiously. The sound is outstandingly fine, outshining any direct rival.

Karajan's 1971 account of the *Scottish* is justly included among DG's 'Originals', as it is one of his finest recordings. The coupling was originally the *Fingal's Cave*, a characterful and evocative account, but now the *Italian Symphony* has been added, recorded two years later. This is also played very beautifully and brilliantly but, good though the performance is, it does not quite match that of the *Scottish* and it is just a shade wanting in spontaneity and sparkle.

Dmitry Sitkovetsky, forsaking his violin, has since 1996 been principal conductor of the Ulster Orchestra, in succession to another violinist-conductor, Yan-Pascal Tortelier. Here he draws superb performances from the orchestra of both symphonies as well as the overture, helped by outstandingly full and rich recording, made in the Ulster Hall. Consistently Sitkovetsky conveys the feeling of live performances caught on the wing. With speeds beautifully chosen and with rhythms crisp and well sprung, his readings are full of light and shade, warmly dramatic, demonstrating an expressive freedom – notably in pressing ahead – which always sounds natural, never self-conscious. With refined playing from every section, at once tense and polished, textures are exceptionally clear and transparent, so that inner details are brought out that are often obscured. The strings in particular produce some magical pianissimos, reflecting Sitkovetsky's own mastery as an instrumentalist. A very generous and apt coupling, with the exposition repeat observed in the *Italian Symphony* but not in the *Scottish*.

The dynamic young American conductor, David Chernaik, gives performances of these two symphonies which in their vitality and freshness are most exhilarating. Although the recording is live, the audience is notably quiet and shows its presence only by clapping perfunctorily at the end of each work, a distraction which could and should have been edited out. The London-based Apollo Chamber Orchestra, on its toes throughout, is exactly the right size for these two symphonies, and the recording (in St John's, Smith Square) has been beautifully balanced so that detail is transparently clear, yet a warm ambience remains. Wind and string playing alike are consistently fresh. The *Scottish* is particularly fine, with a vigorous opening movement, a vivaciously buoyant Scherzo, a songful *Adagio* (ideally paced) and a particularly satisfying final coda, exuberant but not rushed. Chernaik includes the essential exposition repeats in both symphonies, and in the *Italian* the light, sparkling string articulation in the outer movements bounces infectiously, the *Saltarello* finale particularly joyful with its chortling woodwind vying with scintillating bravura from the violins, particularly neat in their pianissimos.

Abbado's fine digital recordings of the *Scottish* and *Italian Symphonies*, coupled together from his complete set, make a splendid mid-price bargain. The recording is admirably fresh and bright – atmospheric, too – and the ambience, if not absolutely sharply defined, is very attractive. Both first-movement exposition repeats are included.

Lubbock's coupling of the *Scottish* and *Italian Symphonies* makes an outstanding super-bargain issue, offering performances of delightful lightness and point, warmly and cleanly recorded. The string section may be of chamber size but, amplified by a warm acoustic, the result sparkles, with rhythms exhilaratingly lifted. The slow movements are both on the slow side but flow easily with no suspicion of sentimentality, while the *Saltarello* finale of No. 4, with the flute part delectably pointed, comes close to Mendelssohnian fairy music.

Marriner in his 1994 Philips version offers direct and sensitive readings of both symphonies, generally a fraction faster than those he recorded earlier for Decca. This time too he observes the exposition repeats in both symphonies. In the slow movements, the more flowing speeds bring a clear advantage, particularly when the Academy violins are even sweeter and purer than before, helped by recording that is a degree more refined. All in all, an enjoyable disc, but not a first choice for this coupling.

As in Beethoven and Schubert, Nikolaus Harnoncourt's happy relationship with the Chamber Orchestra of Europe brings performances which on modern instruments might be counted 'historically aware', with shortened phrasing, limited string vibrato, rasping horns and clean-cut timpani. The cleanness of texture is enhanced by Harnoncourt's generally relaxed speeds, which allow Mendelssohnian rhythms to have an infectious spring. Natural, well-balanced sound.

Bernstein and the Israel orchestra, recorded live in Munich in 1979, give a loving performance of the *Scottish Symphony* but their expansive tempi run the risk of overloading Mendelssohn's fresh inspiration, with heavy expressiveness making the slow introduction and slow movement sound almost Mahlerian. The rhythmic lift of the Scherzo and finale makes amends; but it is a performance to bring out for an interesting change, rather than a version to recommend for repeated listening. The recording is well balanced and full. The sparkling account of the *Italian* was made a year earlier in the Mann Auditorium, Tel Aviv, but remains convincingly atmospheric if not ideally clear. It is also available at bargain price, coupled with the *Midsummer Night's Dream* incidental music – see below.

Symphonies Nos. 3 in A min., Op. 56 (Scottish); 4 in A, Op. 90 (Italian); 5 in D min., Op. 107 (Reformation); Overtures: Calm Sea and a prosperous voyage; The Hebrides (Fingal's Cave).

(N) *** Ph. Dig. 456 267-2. O of the 18th Century, Frans Brüggen.

Even if you do not respond to period-instrument performances, this is worth investigating. The orchestral playing is splendidly uninhibited and at times virtuosic. The finale of the *Italian* is quite staggering. Textures are beautifully transparent and the only cause for reservation is the string tone, which though pure lacks the weight of sonority and the singing quality of modern instruments. Those who warm to period instruments will know what to expect, and will welcome these highly musical performances with enthusiasm. First-rate recording.

Symphony No. 4 in A (Italian), Op. 90.

(M) *** DG Dig. 445 514-2 [id.]. Philh. O, Sinopoli – SCHUBERT: *Symphony No. 8.* *** ✿

**(*) Decca (IMS) Dig. 440 476-2 [id.]. VPO, Sir Georg Solti – SHOSTAKOVICH: *Symphony No. 5.* **(*)

Sinopoli's great gift is to illuminate almost every phrase afresh. His speeds tend to be extreme – fast in the first movement but with diamond-bright detail, and on the slow side in the remaining three. Only in the heavily inflected account of the third movement is the result at all mannered but, with superb playing from the Philharmonia and excellent Kingsway Hall recording, this rapt performance is most compelling. For refinement of detail, especially at lower dynamic levels, the CD is among the most impressive digital recordings to have come from DG.

In the *Italian Symphony* you would never recognize this live performance with the Vienna Philharmonic as the work of the same conductor as Solti's earlier, Chicago recording. Though in the first movement the speed is even faster than before, if only fractionally, the lightness and resilience of the Viennese players make it seem far less tense and far more buoyant. In the finale too, the Vienna performance is lighter and more resilient, and in the middle two movements the contrasts are even more extreme, with speeds kept flowing, so avoiding the heaviness of the Chicago performance. The recording is acceptable, though it could be fuller-bodied.

Symphonies Nos. 4 (Italian), Op. 90; 5 Reformation, Op. 105.

(N) (M) (**(*)) RCA mono 74321 59480-2 (2) [id.]. NBC SO, Toscanini – SCHUBERT:

Symphonies Nos. 5; 8(Unfinished); 9 in C (Great). (**(*))

Though there is still an edge on high violins, this new RCA transfer of Toscanini's NBC performances offers fuller sound with plenty of body. The playing in this surprisingly rare coupling is characteristically brilliant, but not entirely without charm, and the *Reformation Symphony* is certainly arresting. With the three Schubert symphonies, this makes an attractive coupling.

Symphonies Nos. 4 (Italian); 5 (Reformation); A Midsummer Night's Dream: Scherzo. Octet, Op. 20: Scherzo.

(N) (M) (**) BMG/RCA mono GD 60284 NBC SO, Toscanini.

Though the dry NBC recording allows for too little dynamic contrast, and the tautness of Toscanini's direction is at times uncomfortable, the electricity behind Mendelssohn's inspiration is never in doubt, with the *Reformation Symphony* given new strength. The two *Scherzos* make a brilliant supplement.

Symphonies Nos. 4 (Italian; original and revised versions), Op. 90; 5 (Reformation), Op. 105.

(N) *** DG Dig. 459 156-2. VPO, John Eliot Gardiner.

John Eliot Gardiner draws incandescent playing from the Vienna Philharmonic in both works, helped by the warm Musikverein acoustic. In both versions of the *Italian* and in the live recording of the *Reformation* – with all Victorian cobwebs blown away – he brings out both the transparency and the urgency of Mendelssohn's inspiration, generally preferring fast but never breathless speeds. The *coup* is that the revised version of the last three movements of the *Italian* have never been recorded before. The composer made the revisions in the year following the London première. Surprisingly for so discriminating a composer, he undermined the exuberant inspiration of the original – smoothing over melodic lines (as in the *Pilgrim's march*) and extending linking passages. Even so, a fascinating insight into the creative process and the danger of second thoughts on what was originally white-hot inspiration.

(i) *Symphony No. 4 in A (Italian), Op. 90; Overture The Hebrides (Fingal's Cave);* (ii) *A Midsummer Night's Dream: Overture, Op. 21; Scherzo; Nocturne; Wedding march, Op. 61.*

(B) *** DG 439 411-2. (i) Israel PO, Bernstein; (ii) Bav. RSO, Kubelik.

(M) **(*) Virgin/EMI CUV5 61131-2. LSO, Barry Wordsworth.

(i) *Symphony No. 4 in A (Italian); Overtures: The Hebrides (Fingal's Cave);* (ii) *Ruy Blas; A Midsummer Night's Dream: Overture; Scherzo; Intermezzo; Nocturne; Wedding march.*

(B) **(*) Decca Dig. 448 237-2 [(M) 430 722-2]. (i) VPO, Dohnányi; (ii) Montreal SO, Dutoit.

Bernstein's performance of the *Italian Symphony* (exposition repeat included) is sparkling and persuasive. The 1978 recording was made at a public concert and, though speeds are often challengingly fast in outer movements, they never fail to convey the exhilaration of the occasion. *Fingal's Cave* is also a live recording, made a year later, and while it has plenty of romantic warmth and Bernstein is slightly more indulgent, it too sounds spontaneously alive. In the items from *A Midsummer Night's Dream* the Bavarian orchestra are on top form, especially in the *Overture* which is beautifully played. The recording, made in the Herkules-Saal, Munich, still sounds excellent, and this bargain Classikon CD would grace any collection.

Wordsworth combines a sparkling version of the *Italian Symphony* (with attractively light articulation in the bracing outer movements and the essential first-movement exposition repeat included), with the four most important items from *A Midsummer Night's Dream* and a very lively performance of *Fingal's Cave*. If the programme is suitable, this is certainly enjoyable and the recording is first class.

Dohnányi's is a refreshing account of the *Italian*, never pushed too hard, and with the *Saltarello* taken exhilaratingly fast. It is a pity that the first-movement exposition repeat is omitted. However, the CD is generously full for, besides Dohnányi's slow and romantic account of the *Hebrides overture*, there is Dutoit's splendidly vital *Ruy Blas* with its commanding brass opening ringing out superbly and the scurrying violins very vivid and tangible. Indeed both this and the 32-minute selection from the *Midsummer Night's Dream* incidental music are marvellously recorded. The acoustics of Saint-Eustache in Montreal are ideal, giving a wonderful bloom to the dancing strings and a very convincing, concert-hall illusion to the whole programme. However, the playing in the incidental music is altogether more routine: the very brisk *Scherzo* conveys little charm, although the *Wedding march* is grand without being pompous.

Symphony No. 4 in A (Italian), Op. 90; A Midsummer Night's Dream: Overture, Op. 21; (i) *Incidental music, Op. 61* (complete).

(N) (M) *** EMI CDM5 67038-2. [id.]. Philh. O, Klemperer; (i) with Heather Harper, Dame Janet Baker, Philh. Ch.

Klemperer takes the first movement of the *Italian Symphony* substantially slower than we are used to, but this is no heavily monumental and humourless reading. The Philharmonia playing sparkles and has an incandescence which outshines many other versions with more surface sparkle. There is again a slowish speed for the second movement, but the way Klemperer moulds and floats the main theme over the moving bass defeats all preconceptions in its sustained beauty. A fast tempo in the minuet, but still with wonderful phrasing: and it is the beautiful shaping of a phrase that makes the finale so fresh and memorable. There is no lack of exultation, yet none of that feeling of being rushed off one's feet, that some conductors give. In the Overture and incidental music from *A Midsummer Night's Dream* the orchestral playing is again superb, the wind solos so nimble that even the *Scherzo*, taken more slowly than usual, has a light touch. The contribution of the celebrated soloists and the Philharmonia Chorus is first class and the quality of the remastered 1960 recording is full and fresh. This is another of the more notable reissues in the 'Klemperer Legacy'.

(i) *Symphony No. 4 (Italian);* (ii) *A Midsummer Night's Dream: Overture, Op. 21; Incidental music, Op. 61: Scherzo; Intermezzo; Nocturne; Wedding march; Fanfare & funeral march; Dance of the rustics.*
(BB) *** LaserLight Dig. 15 526 [id.]. (i) Philh. O, János Sándor; (ii) Budapest PO, Kovacs.

A first-class coupling in the super-bargain range from LaserLight. Sándor gives a fresh and exhilarating account of the *Italian Symphony*, with particularly elegant Philharmonia playing, and the digital sound is excellent. The performance of a generous selection from the *Midsummer Night's Dream* incidental music also shows the Budapest orchestra on top form: this is most beguiling and is recorded in a pleasingly warm acoustic which does not cloud detail.

Symphony No. 4 (Italian); Overtures: Fair Melusina, Op. 32; The Hebrides (Fingal's Cave), Op. 26; Son and stranger (Die Heimkehr aus der Fremde), Op. 89.
(M) *** Carlton IMP Dig. PCD 2003 [id.]. Berne SO, Peter Maag.

Peter Maag, making a welcome return to the recording studio with his Berne orchestra, here offers a winningly relaxed performance of the *Italian Symphony* (including exposition repeat), plus an attractive group of overtures, which once more confirms him as a supreme Mendelssohnian. *The Hebrides* receives a spacious reading and the two rarer overtures are a delight too, particularly *Son and stranger*, which in Maag's hands conveys radiant happiness. At bargain price, with full and brilliant recording, it is first rate.

Symphony No. 5 in D min. (Reformation), Op. 107.
(M) *** DG 449 720-2 [id.]. BPO, Maazel – FRANCK: *Symphony in D min.* ***

The *Reformation Symphony* springs grippingly to life in Maazel's hands. The Berlin Philharmonic brass make an immediate impact in the commanding introduction and the orchestral playing throughout continues on this level of high tension. The finale is splendidly vigorous, the chorale, *Ein' feste Burg is unser Gott*, ringing out resplendently. If ever one were choosing a 'best buy' for this individual symphony, Maazel's interpretation would rank very high on the list. It was aptly chosen for reissue in DG's series of 'Legendary Recordings', and the Franck coupling is hardly less impressive. The recording is spacious and has been vividly enhanced by the DG CD transfer.

CHAMBER AND INSTRUMENTAL MUSIC

Cello sonatas Nos. 1 in B flat, Op. 45; 2 in D, Op. 58; Assai tranquillo; Song without words, Op. 109; Variations concertantes, Op. 17.
*** Hyperion Dig. CDA 66478 [id.]. Richard Lester, Susan Tomes.

Cello sonatas Nos. 1 in B flat, Op. 45; 2 in D, Op. 58; Songs without words, Op. 19/1; Op. 109; Variations concertantes, Op. 17.
*** RCA Dig. 09026 62553-2 [id.]. Steven Isserlis, Melvyn Tan (fortepiano).

There are few cello sonatas so exhilarating as the second of the two written by Mendelssohn. Susan Tomes, the inspired pianist of the group, Domus, and her cellist colleague, Richard Lester, give a performance full of flair on this ideally compiled disc of Mendelssohn's collected works for cello and piano, brimming with charming ideas. As well as the works with opus number they include a delightful fragment, *Assai tranquillo*, never previously recorded.

Steven Isserlis and Melvyn Tan convey a freshness, delight and authenticity in music-making that rekindles enthusiasm for this delightful repertoire. They pace both sonatas expertly and are faithfully served by the RCA engineers. Like their colleagues, Richard Lester and Susan Tomes on Hyperion, they command poetry as well as virtuosity.

Cello sonata No. 2 in D, Op. 58.
(M) *** Mercury 434 377-2 [id.]. Starker, Sebök – BRAHMS: *Cello sonatas.* ***

Starker and Sebök give an outstanding account of Mendelssohn's finest *Cello sonata*, spontaneously full of ardour, yet with plenty of light and shade in the central movements, and topped by a sparkling finale, which yet retains the lyrical feeling. The 1962 recording is truthful and admirably balanced within a warm acoustic with a clear focus.

Octet in E flat, Op. 20.
*** Hyperion Dig. CDA 66356 [id.]. Divertimenti – BARGIEL: *Octet.* ***

Divertimenti give a very natural and unforced account of the celebrated *Octet* which, though it may not be the most distinguished in the catalogue, still gives great pleasure. Excellent recorded sound.

Octet in E flat, Op. 20; String quintet No. 2 in B flat, Op. 87.
(B) *** Ph. Virtuoso 420 400-2 [id.]. ASMF Chamber Ens.

This Philips account comes from just over a decade after the Academy's earlier record of Mendelssohn's *Octet* and the playing has greater sparkle and polish. The recorded sound is also superior and sounds extremely well in its CD format. The *Second Quintet* is an underrated piece and it too receives an elegant and poetic performance. A fine bargain.

Piano quartets Nos. 1 in C min.; 2 in F min.; 3 in B min., Opp. 1–3.
(M) *** Virgin/EMI (SIS) Dig. CUV5 61203-2. Domus.

Piano quartet No. 1 in C min., Op. 1; Piano sextet in D, Op. 110.
(BB) **(*) Naxos Dig. 8.550966 [id.]. Bartholdy Piano Qt (augmented).

Piano quartets Nos. 2 in F min., Op. 2; 3 in B min., Op. 3.
(BB) **(*) Naxos Dig. 8.550967 [id.]. Bartholdy Piano Qt.

The *Piano quartet No. 1 in C minor* was the composer's first published composition and was succeeded the following year by another, equally fluent and accomplished. However, none of the ideas of this *F minor* work is as remarkable as those of its successor in *B minor* of 1825. All three pieces have charm, vitality and musicianship, particularly in the hands of Domus, who play with the taste and discernment we have come to expect from them. Excellent recording.

The Bartholdy Quartet have an excellent pianist in Pier Narciso Masi, and his mercurial style is just right for these early works. The string players are always fluent and show a light-hearted vivacity in Mendelelssohn's scherzos (especially in the very winning *Allegro molto* of No. 3) and finales, and they play the simple slow movements gracefully. The *Piano sextet* also comes from the composer's youth and, like the other works, it has an engaging immediacy. The recording was made in the fairly resonant Clara Wieck Auditorium in Heidelberg, which means that the microphones are fairly close to the strings and the balance is slightly contrived. Nevertheless the sound is good and the piano well caught. While Domus remain a clear first choice, this Naxos set is worth considering.

Piano quartet No. 1 in C min., Op. 1.
(N) (BB) *** ASV Quicksilva Dig. CDQS 6199 [id.]. Schubert Ens. of London – BRAHMS: *Piano quartet No. 2.* ***

Musicianly and well-recorded performances that will give satisfaction at this (or any other) price level. Sensible tempi and very well-articulated phrasing.

Piano quartet No. 3 in B min., Op. 3.
(BB) *** ASV Dig. Quicksilva CDQS 6198 [(M) id.]. Schubert Ens. of London – BRAHMS: *Piano quartet No. 3.* ***

Mendelssohn's *Piano quartet No. 3 in B minor* comes from 1824–5, at roughly the same time as the *C minor Symphony*, when the composer was about fifteen or sixteen. In his *Master Musicians* survey, Philip Radcliffe speaks of 'the breadth of the material and the Weberian exuberance of the piano writing . . . the slow movement recalls Spohr in its luxuriant chromaticism'. This B minor work (which Mendelssohn dedicated to Goethe) has undoubted charm and, even if there are garrulous moments, they evince an astonishing precociousness. William Howard plays with great expertise and the instrumentalists are well balanced. If the coupling is suitable, this is worth its modest outlay.

Piano trios Nos. 1 in D min., Op. 49; 2 in C min., Op. 66.
(M) *** HM Suite Dig. HMT 7901335 [id.]. Trio de Barcelona.
**(*) Sony Dig. SK 66351 [id.]. Wanderer Trio.
**(*) Chandos Dig. CHAN 8404 [id.]. Borodin Trio.

Lovely music, and lovely performances of both works from the excellent Trio de Barcelona, as warm-hearted as they are fresh. Each *Andante* is beautifully played – and how sprightly they are in the two Scherzos. The pianist, Albert Attenelle, clearly holds the performances together, but the balance is admirable and he never dwarfs his fine string colleagues, Gérard and Lluis Claret. The one drawback is the acoustic, which is a bit too reverberant. It does not cloud detail, however; the players are given a realistic presence, and the ear soon adjusts when the music-making is so spontaneously enjoyable.

The Sony recordings follow the style of their competitors by being much too resonant. But these are strong and ardent readings, with notably fine playing in both slow movements and with the cellist, Raphael Pidoux, standing out, although the pianist, Vincent Coq, also makes a very considerable contribution. Marginally a first choice on performance grounds.

The Borodin Trio are also recorded in a very resonant acoustic and are rather forwardly balanced. They give superbly committed but somewhat overpointed readings. All the same, there is much musical pleasure to be found here.

Piano trio No. 2 in C min., Op. 66.
*** Ph. (IMS) Dig. 432 125-2. Beaux Arts Trio – SMETANA: *Piano trio in G min.* ***

Although most collectors will probably want the

Mendelssohn *Piano trios* together (and there is a fair choice of such a coupling), those happy to take the *C minor Trio* alone, coupled with Smetana, will find the Beaux Arts distinguished in all respects and very well recorded.

String quartets: in E flat; Nos. 1 in E flat, Op. 12; 2 in A min., Op. 13; 3–5, Op. 44/1–3; 6 in F min., Op. 80; 4 Pieces, Op. 81.
*** Hyperion Dig. CDS 44051/3 [id.]. Coull Qt.

String quartets Nos. 1–6.
*** EMI (SIS) CDS7 54514-2 (3). Cherubini Qt.

The young Mendelssohn in Berlin in his teens was able to study the scores of late Beethoven quartets even before he had a chance to hear the music performed. His own youthful quartets reflect that influence from what at the time was the most avant-garde music imaginable. For those wanting a complete set, the Coull survey is eminently satisfactory, the playing alive and spontaneous, well paced and musically penetrating. Moreover they bring the advantage of both freshness and completeness (including the early (1823) *Quartet*, written a year before the *C minor First Symphony*). The quietly intense playing in the slow movements of the later works – and indeed in Op. 13 – and the charming, graceful *Intermezzo* of this same quartet show the group's affinity with this repertoire, while the *Canzonetta* of Op. 12 introduces Mendelssohn's fairies, tripping in gracefully. The Scherzo of Op. 44/3 is another highlight, and the opening of Op. 44/2 is particularly warm and well paced. The recording is realistic and well balanced.

A new set of the six regular Mendelssohn *Quartets* is most welcome from the young members of the Cherubini Quartet who consistently play with warmth as well as intensity. Here with a light touch they bring out the mercurial charm of Mendelssohn as well as his vigour and high spirits. Unlike the Coull set, the Cherubini do not include two works from opposite ends of Mendelssohn's career that provide an extra insight into his development: the early *E flat Quartet* (without opus number), written when he was only fourteen, and the collection of four movements, Op. 81, that in shape and sequence group themselves satisfyingly together. One only wishes that the Cherubinis, consistently imaginative, had been persuaded to do the extra items as well.

String quartets: in E flat; Nos. 1 in E flat, Op. 13; 2 in A min., Op. 13.
(N) *** H M Dig. HMU 907245 [id.]. Eroica Qt.
(N) *** Audivis Astrée Dig. E 8622 [id.]. Mosaïques Qt.

The Eroica Quartet was formed in 1993 by four London period-instrument players who are committed to performing the nineteenth-century repertoire in nineteenth-century style. In addition to the first two numbered quartets, written when Mendelssohn was in his late teens, they include the *E flat quartet*, written when he was fourteen, but not published until after his death. The performances are distinguished by good ensemble, clean articulation and well-focused textures. Good recorded sound too.

The Mosaïques Quartet apply their delicacy of style and subtle grading of texture with winning results to the *A minor Quartet*, particularly in the delectable *Intermezzo*, which is as light as thistledown. They open the *B flat major* with great concentration, and the *Canzonetta* has an airy fragilty. Some ears might prefer the fuller, suaver quality of modern instruments in the *Andante espressivo* and finale, but certainly these performances have a character of their own, which aficionados will relish, and they are very well recorded.

String quartets Nos. 1 in E flat, Op. 12; 2 in A min., Op. 13; 2 Pieces, Op. 81.
*** Hyperion Dig. CDA 66397 [id.]. Coull Qt.

For those wanting the first two *Quartets* only, the Coull Quartet give fresh and unaffected accounts of both and have the benefit of very good recorded sound. Tempi are well judged and everything flows naturally. The Coull offer the additional inducement of two of the *Four pieces*, Op. 81, which were published after Mendelssohn's death.

String quartet No. 2 in A min., Op. 13.
(M) *** Cal. CAL 6698 [id.]. Talich Qt – BOCCHERINI: *Quartet, Op. 58/2;* HAYDN: *Quartet No. 74;* MICA: *Quartet No. 6.* ***

Mendelssohn's *Quartet in A minor*, Op. 13, has a serene and remarkably searching slow movement, before its charmingly memorable 'Intermezzo' which is linked to the lively but lyrical *Presto* finale, which has something of the character of a Mendelssohn Scherzo. A most enjoyable work, played with spirit, warmth and cultivated elegance by this superb group, who are most naturally recorded. The couplings are all equally recommendable.

String quartets Nos. 2 in A, Op. 13; 4 in E min., Op. 44/2; 2 Pieces, Op. 81/1–2.
(N) *(*) Chandos Dig. CHAN955 [id.] Sorrel Qt.

The Sorrel Quartet do not produce a really beautiful sound or enough polish to be convincing candidates in these pieces. Excellent recording.

String quintets Nos. 1 in A, Op. 18; 2 in B flat, Op. 87.
(M) *** Sony/CBS MPK 45883. Laredo, Kavafian, Ohyama, Kashkashian, Robinson.

Laredo and his ensemble achieve good matching of timbre, and they give lively accounts of both these neglected works, lacking neither warmth nor finesse. The 1978 recording has responded well to remastering, and has body and presence.

PIANO MUSIC

Andante and allegro brilliant in A, Op. 92; Andante and variations in B flat, Op. 83a; Piano trio No. 2 in C min., Op. 66.
*** Sony Dig. SK 48494 [id.]. Tal & Groethuysen – Fanny MENDELSSOHN: *3 Pieces for piano, 4 hands.* ***

Playing of exceptional quality from this remarkable duo. Everything, including the transcription of the *C minor Piano trio*, sparkles, and the recording does them full justice.

Andante and rondo capriccioso in E min., Op. 14; Prelude and fugue in E minor/major, Op. 35/1; Sonata in E, Op. 6; Variations sérieuses in D min., Op. 53.
*** Sony Dig. MK 37838 [id.]. Murray Perahia.

Perahia is perfectly attuned to Mendelssohn's sensibility and it would be difficult to imagine these performances being surpassed. The quality of the CBS recording is very good indeed.

Capriccio in F sharp min., Op. 5; 7 Characteristic pieces, Op. 7; Fantasia (Sonata écossaise) in F sharp Min., Op. 28; Prelude and fugue in E min; Sonata movement in B flat.
(N) (BB) *** Naxos Dig. 8. 553541 [id.]. Benjamin Frith.

This collection gives a very different idea of Mendelssohn's piano-writing from that in the *Songs without words*. The *Characteristic pieces* present fascinating evidence of the influence of Bach on the young composer, with some impressive contrapuntal writing in fugues both brilliant and thoughtful. Also some echoes of Scarlatti. The three-movement *Fantasia* and the *Capriccio* as well, inspire Frith to sparkling playing, vividly recorded.

Etude in F min.; Preludes & 3 Etudes, Op. 104; 6 Preludes & fugues, Op. 35; Prelude & fugue in E min.
**(*) Nimbus NI 5071 [id.]. Martin Jones.

Fantasy in F sharp min., Op. 28; 3 Fantaisies et caprices, Op. 16; Fantasy on 'The last rose of summer', Op. 15; Variations: in E flat, Op. 82; in B flat, Op. 83; Variations sérieuses in D min., Op. 53.
**(*) Nimbus NI 5072 [id.]. Martin Jones.

Sonatas: in E, Op. 6; in G min., Op. 105; in B flat, Op. 106; Kinderstücke, Op. 72.
**(*) Nimbus NI 5070 [id.]. Martin Jones.

In his collection of Mendelssohn piano music, Martin Jones provides a fascinating slant on the composer, particularly his youthful inspirations. In many ways the disc of sonatas is the most interesting of all, reflecting Mendelssohn's devotion to Beethoven and his sonatas. The *Preludes and fugues* inevitably reflect his even deeper devotion to Bach, then still under-appreciated. The sets of variations on the third disc were mostly written later in his career, examples of his high skill and love of the keyboard, rather than works of genius. Martin Jones is an excellent advocate, playing dedicatedly and persuasively, not always immaculately but without mannerism. The recordings, made in the 1970s, come up very well in the CD transfers, with the atmosphere of a small hall realistically conveyed.

Preludes and fugues Nos. 1–6, Op. 35; 3 Caprices, Op. 33; Perpetuum mobile in C, Op. 33.
(BB) *** Naxos Dig. 8.550939 [id.]. Benjamin Frith.

In the first of what is obviously going to be a distinguished series, Benjamin Frith offers a highly imaginative set of the Op. 35 *Preludes and fugues*, full of diversity, from the flamboyant opening *Prelude in E minor* to the expansive *Prelude No. 6 in B flat*. The three *Caprices* are equally varied in mood and colour and are most sensitively presented, with the last one opening solemnly and then providing characteristically light-hearted Mendelssohnian dash. The *Perpetuum mobile* makes a scintillating encore. Acceptably full if not remarkable piano sound, recorded in St Martin's Church, East Woodhay. But the playing promises well for what is to follow.

Scherzo from A Midsummer Night's Dream, Op. 61 (trans. Rachmaninov).
*** Hyperion CDA 66009 [id.]. Howard Shelley – RACHMANINOV: *Variations* etc. ***

Howard Shelley, with fabulously clear articulation and delectably sprung rhythms, gives a performance of which Rachmaninov himself would not have been ashamed.

Piano sonata in B flat, Op. 106; Albumblatt, Op. 117; Andante cantabile e presto agitato in B; 3 Fantaisies et caprices, Op. 16; Rondo capriccioso in E, Op. 14; Variations in E flat, Op. 82.
(BB) *** Naxos Dig. 8.553186 [id.]. Benjamin Frith.

Benjamin Frith's inexpensive survey is timely. The *B flat Sonata*, Op. 106, comes from 1827 when Mendelssohn was eighteen and much in awe of the Beethoven *Hammerklavier*. (Ironically, when the piece was published posthumously it was allotted the same opus number, Op. 106.) The sonata has been called 'a comfortable and domestic' version of the Beethoven and 'disappointingly pedestrian'. However, Benjamin Frith is so persuasive that he almost dispels this impression. His playing is nothing less than a delight, and in the celebrated *Rondo capriccioso* and the more conventional *Variations in E flat* of 1841 he is as light of touch as one could possibly wish.

Piano sonata in G min., Op. 105; Capriccio in E, Op. 118; Etude in F min.; Fantasia on 'The last

rose of summer', Op. 15; 2 Pieces: Andante cantabile; presto agitato. Scherzo a capriccio in F sharp min.; Variations in B flat, Op. 83.
(BB) *** Naxos Dig. 8.553358 [id.]. Benjamin Frith.

The *G minor sonata*, Op. 105, is the earliest of Mendelssohn's published works and was completed in 1821 when the twelve-year-old youngster was already an accomplished and assured composer. It is distinctly Haydnesque, and there is perhaps more charm than individuality. Although the *Fantasia on 'The last rose of summer'* is pretty thin stuff, in such imaginative fingers, however, it sounds delightful and marvellously fresh. Naxos provide quite excellent recording and the series so far is touched with distinction.

Songs without words, Books 1–8 (complete); *No. 49 in G min., Op. posth.*
(B) **(*) Hyperion Dyad Dig. CDD 22020 (2) [id.]. Lívia Rév.

Songs without words, Books 1–8 (complete); *Albumblatt, Op. 117; Gondellied; Kinderstücke, Op. 72; 2 Klavierstücke.*
(B) *** DG Double 453 061-2 (2) [id.]. Daniel Barenboim.

Songs without words (complete); *Andante and variations in E flat, Op. 82; Andante cantabile e presto agitato in B; Variations in B flat, Op. 83.*
(B) *** Ph. Duo 438 709-2 (2) [id.]. Ilse von Alpenheim.

This 1974 set of Mendelssohn's complete *Songs without words*, which Barenboim plays with such affectionate finesse, has dominated the catalogue for nearly two decades. For this reissue the six *Kinderstücke* (sometimes known as 'Christmas pieces') have been added, plus other music. The sound is first class. At DG Double price this sweeps the board in this repertoire.

Ilse von Alpenheim's set of *Songs without words* may not have quite the distinctive character of Barenboim, but she plays this music with an appealing spontaneous simplicity. The (1980) recording of the piano is first class, well up to Philips's usual high standard. Not a first choice, perhaps, but an undoubted bargain.

Lívia Rév is a thoughtful, sensitive and aristocratic artist. Her survey of the *Songs without words* has charm and warmth, and she includes a hitherto unpublished piece. The set is handsomely presented and the recording is warm and pleasing; it is, however, somewhat bottom-heavy. Yet the slightly diffuse effect suits the style of the playing. This might well now be seriously considered at its new price, especially by those who enjoy intimate music-making and want digital sound with its silent background.

Songs without words, Opp. 19/1, 6; 30/6; 38/4, 6; 53/2–4; 62/1, 5–6; 67/3–4; 85/4, 6; 102/3, 5.
(N) (M) *(**) EMI mono CHS5 66775-2 (2) [CDHB 66775]. Walter Gieseking – GRIEG: *Lyric pieces*. *(**)

Gieseking's Mendelssohn was much admired in its day but these recordings made towards the end of his life do not find him at his most inspired. Of course some are touched by his special poetry but others sound – dare one say it – a little 'casual'. (They were, incidentally, produced by Alec Robertson and William Mann.) The recorded sound is a little studio bound.

ORGAN MUSIC

Organ sonatas Nos. 1–6, Op. 65/1–6; Preludes and fugues Nos. 1–3, Op. 37/1–3; Andantes in D & F; Allegro in B flat; Allegro, chorale and fugue in D; Allegro maestoso in C; Fugues: (Allegro) in E min.; (Lento) in F min.
(B) *(*) Hyperion Dyad Dig. CDD 22029 (2) [id.]. John Scott (organ of St Paul's Cathedral).

John Scott's survey of Mendelssohn's organ music is pretty comprehensive, but the choice of the St Paul's Cathedral organ was a mistake. The ample sounds and blurring resonance prevent any kind of bite – particularly striking in the *Allegro con brio* which opens the *Fourth Sonata*. He is undoubtedly a master of this repertoire technically speaking (witness the closing *Allegro, choral and fugue in D*, which pays direct homage to Bach) but alongside Peter Hurford his style seems embedded in Victorian tradition.

VOCAL MUSIC

Lieder: *Allnächtlich im Traume; Altdeutsches Liede; And'res Maienlied; An die Entfernte; Auf der Wanderschaft; Auf Flügeln des Gesanges ('On wings of song'); Bei deder Wiege; Der Blumenkranz; Da lieg' ich unter den Bäumen; Entelied; Erster Verlust; Das erste Veilchen; Es lauschte das Lamb; Frühlingslied* (3 versions: Lenau, Lichtenstein and Klingemann settings); *Grüss; Hirtenlied; Jagdlied; Minnelied* (Deutsches Volkslied); *Minnelied* (Tieck); *Der Mond; Morgengruss; Nachtlied; Neue Liebe; O Jugend; Pagenlied; Reiselied* (2 versions: Heine and Ebert); *Scheindend; Schiflied; Schlafloser Augen Leuchte; Tröstung; Venetianisches Gondellied; Volkslied (Feuchtersleben); Das Waldschloss; Wanderlied; Warnung vor dem Rhein; Wenn sich zwei Herzen scheiden; Winterlied.*
(M) **(*) EMI (SIS) CMS7 64827-2 (2). Fischer-Dieskau, Sawallisch.

Though Mendelssohn generally reserved his finest song-like inspirations for the *Songs without words*, the lyrical directness of these settings of Heine, Eichendorff, Lenau and others assures him of a niche of his own among Lieder composers. Fischer-Dieskau conveys the joy of fresh discovery but in some of the well-known songs – *Grüss* or *On wings of song* – he tends to overlay his singing with heavy expressiveness. Lightness should be the keynote, and that happily is wonderfully represented in the superb accompaniments of Sawallisch. Excellent, natural recording.

Elijah (oratorio), *Op. 70*.
*** Chandos Dig. CHAN 8774/5 [id.]. White, Plowright, Finnie, A. Davies, London Symphony Ch., LSO, Hickox.
(B) *** EMI forte CZS5 68601-2 [CDFB 68601] (2). Gwyneth Jones, Janet Baker, Gedda, Fischer-Dieskau, Woolf, Wandsworth School Boys' Ch., New Philh. Ch. & O, Frühbeck de Burgos.
**(*) Decca Dig. 455 688-2 (2) [id.]. Bryn Terfel, Renée Fleming, Patricia Bardon, John Mark Ainsley, Edinburgh Festival Ch., OAE, Paul Daniel.
**(*) Teldec/Warner Dig. 9031 73131-2 (2). Alastair Miles, Helen Donath, Jard van Nes, Donald George, Leipzig MDR Ch., Israel PO, Masur.
**(*) Ph. Dig. 432 984-2 (2) [id.]. Kenny, Dawson, Von Otter, Rigby, Rolfe Johnson, Begley, Allen, Connell, Hopkins, ASMF Ch., ASMF, Marriner.
**(*) HM Dig. HMC 901463/4. Petteri Salomaa, Soile Isokoski, Monica Groop, John Mark Ainsley, Delphine Collot, La Chapelle Royale, Coll. Voc., O des Champs-Elysées, Herreweghe.

Richard Hickox with his London Symphony Chorus and the LSO secures a performance that both pays tribute to the English choral tradition in this work and presents it dramatically as a kind of religious opera. Willard White may not be ideally steady in his delivery, sometimes attacking notes from below, but he sings consistently with fervour. Rosalind Plowright and Arthur Davies combine purity of tone with operatic expressiveness, and Linda Finnie, while not matching the example of Dame Janet Baker in the classic EMI recording, sings with comparable dedication and directness in the solo, *O rest in the Lord*. The chorus fearlessly underlines the high contrasts of dynamic demanded in the score. The Chandos recording, full and immediate yet atmospheric too, enhances the drama.

Frühbeck de Burgos proves an excellent Mendelssohnian. The choice of Fischer-Dieskau as the prophet is more controversial. His pointing of English words is not always idiomatic, but his sense of drama is infallible and goes well with this Mendelssohnian new look. Gwyneth Jones and Nicolai Gedda similarly provide mixed enjoyment, but the splendid work of the chorus and, above all, the gorgeous singing of Dame Janet Baker, make this a memorable and enjoyable set, very well recorded (in the late 1960s) and spaciously and realistically transferred to CD. Offered in EMI's forte double series it makes a remarkable bargain.

The glory of Paul Daniel's Decca set is the fiercely dramatic portrayal of the central character by Bryn Terfel, spanning the wide range of expression and tone. This Elijah is the very personification of an Old Testament prophet, with Terfel rightly responding to the operatic element in Mendelssohn's score. It adds to the operatic feeling that, unlike most rival sets, this one lavishly offers alternative singers in minor roles, not just the quartet of principal soloists strictly required. Renée Fleming sings most beautifully as the principal soprano, strong rather than reflective in *Hear ye, Israel*. There are no weak links among the others, even if there are no stars either, with Patricia Bardon's *O rest in the Lord*, with tempo pressed ahead, sounding rather matter-of-fact. Many will find it refreshing that with a period orchestra Paul Daniel takes a crisp, direct view of the work, helped by fresh, cleanly focused singing from the Edinburgh Festival Chorus. Yet not only is there a lack of orchestral weight, Daniel is at times too metrical to conceal the squareness of some of the work's weaker passages. A warmly idiomatic reading such as Hickox's on Chandos is both more persuasive and kinder to Mendelssohn. Clean, well-separated sound.

Masur as a Mendelssohnian consistently eliminates any hint of sentimentality, but in *Elijah* his determination to use a new broom involves many fast speeds that fail to let this dramatic music blossom, not least in the exuberant final chorus. Yet anyone wanting a fine, modern, digital recording using the German text, crisply and urgently done, should not be too disappointed, particularly when Alastair Miles sings so freshly and intelligently in the title-role.

Marriner in his line-up of soloists may look unmatchable, and there is much fine singing; but with the mellifluous Elijah of Thomas Allen balanced rather backwardly in the live recording, less dominant than he should be, the result is refined rather than dramatically powerful. Marriner and his splendid forces are in danger of sounding too well-mannered. He gives the quartets and double-quartets to the soloists, whereas Hickox, following the English tradition, has the chorus singing them.

Herreweghe's reading, using period forces, recorded live in Metz in February 1993, is predictably clean, fresh and light-textured. With a German text, this is as far removed from the English choral tradition as could be. Yet in its way it is quite compelling, thanks to the bright, clear choral singing. Petteri Salomaa is a lightweight Elijah, occasionally fluttery in timbre, and Soile Isokoski is less sweet-toned than in the Opus 111 recording of the *Hymn of Praise*, but John Mark Ainsley and Monica Groop are both excellent. Clear, atmospheric recording.

Infelice; Psalm 47 (As pants the hart), Op. 42.
(BB) *** Virgin Classics Dig. Double VBD5 61469-2 (2) [CDVB 61469]. Dame Janet Baker, City of L. Sinf., Hickox – BERLIOZ: *Les Nuits d'été* etc.; BRAHMS: *Alto rhapsody* etc.; RESPIGHI: *La Sensitiva*. ***

The scena, *Infelice* – a piece which harks back to an earlier tradition – and the Psalm-setting both have the solos prescribed for soprano, but they suit Dame Janet well, here making a welcome foray out of official retirement for a recording. The voice is in superb condition, with the weight of expressiveness as compelling as ever. The Psalm sounds very like an extra item from *Elijah*.

A Midsummer Night's Dream: Overture, Op. 21 (incidental music): suite
(M) *** Sony SBK 48264 [id.]. Cleveland O, Szell – BIZET: *Symphony;* SMETANA: *Vitava*. ***

Seldom can Mendelssohn's score have been played so brilliantly on record as under Szell. The orchestral ensemble is superb, the fairies dance with gossamer lightness in the violins, yet the tension is high so that the listener is gripped from the first bar to the last of the *Overture*. The *Scherzo* is infectious and in the *Nocturne* the solo horn is cool but very sensitive. This may not be everyone's idea of Mendelssohn but of its kind it is first class, and the 1967 recording sounds smoother and fuller than on the old LP.

A Midsummer Night's Dream: Overture, Op. 21; Incidental music, Op. 61 (complete; with melodramas and text).
*** DG Dig. 439 897-2 [id.]. Kathleen Battle, Frederica von Stade, Tanglewood Festival Ch., Boston SO, Ozawa (with excerpts from play spoken by Dame Judi Dench).

(i) *A Midsummer Night's Dream: Overture, Op. 21; Incidental music, Op. 61* (including spoken passages with the melodramas); *Symphony No. 4 (Italian)*.
*** Sony SK 62826. (i) Sylvia McNair, Angelika Kirchschlager, Kenneth Branagh (speaker), Ch.; BPO Abbado.

Like the Sony version below, Ozawa's virtually complete performance presents Mendelssohn's enchanting incidental music – which is most beautifully played throughout by the Boston Symphony Orchestra – complete with the Shakespearean text, which is spoken over the melodramas by Judi Dench. With two excellent soloists and a fine choral contribution, the only omission here is the brief excerpt which is No. 6 in the score; but the fragmentary reprise of the *Wedding march*, and the two little comic snippets, the Bergomask (*Dance of the clowns*) and ironic little *Funeral march*, intended for the Rude Mechanicals' 'Pyramus and Thisbe' playlet, are included, whereas they are missing in the competing Sony version with Kenneth Branagh. Judi Dench speaks the Shakespeare text in the simplest way, without any of Branagh's occasional exuberance of style, and in her performance Shakespeare's words seem to glow as magically as Mendelssohn's music. This means that Mendelssohn's little melodramas become so much more than orchestral snippets. The recording is first class, one of the finest made in Symphony Hall in recent years, and the balance, with Dench's narration quite intimate but with every word clear, is very well judged indeed. This DG alternative has no coupling and plays for only 56 minutes, but every one of them is delightful.

It certainly makes an attractive package having Mendelssohn's *Midsummer Night's Dream* music dramatically presented (with Kenneth Branagh taking every role from Titania to Puck), and then very generously coupled with Mendelssohn's most popular symphony. Sony have managed to squeeze in 50 minutes of the incidental music, which means that the only omissions are the fragmentary reprise of the *Wedding march* and the two little comic pieces, *Bergomask* and *Funeral march*. Some may resist Branagh's style – burring his 'r's for a Mummerset Puck, coming near to an Olivier imitation in Oberon's final speech – but in his versatility he is very persuasive. Having speech over music in melodrama certainly makes sense of the more fragmentary passages of the score which most other discs omit. Abbado's performances are a delight, fresh and transparent in the fairy music, with generally fast speeds made exhilarating, never breathless. The chorus is balanced atmospherically, with the two excellent soloists, Sylvia McNair and Angelika Kirchschlager, set more forwardly. The recording, made live in the Philharmonie in Berlin, is rather more vivid, a degree less recessed than in the symphony, where the orchestra is placed at a slight distance. Abbado's reading has changed little since his LSO recording of 1985, a fresh, beautifully sprung reading. By any reckoning he remains one of the most persuasive interpreters of this delectable work.

(i) *A Midsummer Night's Dream: Overture, Op. 21; Incidental music, Op. 61;* (ii) *Die erste Walpurgisnacht, Op. 60*.
*** Teldec/Warner Dig. 9031 74882-2 [id.]. (i) Coburn, Van Magnus, Bantzer (speaker); (ii) Remmert, Heilmann, Hampson, Pape; Arnold Schoenberg Ch., COE, Harnoncourt.

Harnoncourt gets the best of both worlds, simultaneously visiting both Mendelssohn's fairy kingdom and his not-too-serious evocation of satanic revelry and the traditional religious response.

Soloists, chorus and a narrator for the Shakespearean text (translated into German) all participate in this vivid, condensed version of the *Midsummer Night's Dream* incidental music which manages to include the *Overture*, *Scherzo*, *Nocturne*, *Intermezzo* and *Wedding march*, plus the vocal numbers, including the finale. Harnoncourt is nothing if not dramatic in the *Overture*, with the feather-light violins opening *pianopianissimo* and the tuttis strong and rhythmic. The playing of the COE is of a virtuoso order and the *Scherzo* is wonderfully light and crisp in articulation. After the serene close, the atmosphere changes abruptly for Mendelssohn's Ballade, *Die erste Walpurgisnacht*, which has never before been performed so dramatically on record. He has an excellent team of soloists, with Thomas Hampson standing out, while the singing of the Arnold Schoenberg Choir is unforgettably vivid, helped by an exceptionally lively and spacious recording. This is one of Harnoncourt's very finest records.

A Midsummer Night's Dream: Overture, Op. 21; Incidental music, Op. 61 (complete).

*** EMI CDC7 47163-2 [id.]. Watson, Wallis, Finchley Children's Music Group, LSO, Previn.

(B) *** CfP Dig. CD-CFP 4593. Wiens, Walker, LPO Ch. & O, Litton.

(M) (***) RCA mono GD 60314. Eustis, Kirk, University of Pennsylvania Women's Glee Club, Phd. O., Toscanini – BERLIOZ: *Romeo and Juliet: Queen Mab scherzo*. (**)

On EMI, Previn offers a wonderfully refreshing account of the complete score; the veiled pianissimo of the violins at the beginning of the *Overture* and the delicious woodwind detail in the *Scherzo* certainly bring Mendelssohn's fairies to life. Even the little melodramas which come between the main items sound spontaneous here, and the contribution of the soloists and chorus is first class. The *Nocturne* (taken slowly) is serenely romantic and the *Wedding march* resplendent. The recording is naturally balanced and has much refinement of detail.

Andrew Litton also includes the melodramas and, like Previn, he uses them most effectively as links, making them seem an essential part of the structure. He too has very good soloists; in the *Overture* and *Scherzo* he displays an engagingly light touch, securing very fine wind and string playing from the LPO. The wide dynamic range of the recording brings an element of drama to offset the fairy music. Both the *Nocturne*, with a fine horn solo, and the temperamental *Intermezzo* are good examples of the spontaneity of feeling that permeates this performance throughout and makes this disc a bargain.

Toscanini's Philadelphia recording offers the seven most popular numbers from the *Midsummer Night's Dream* music, including the song with chorus, *You spotted snakes*, and the final melodrama. In sparkling performances it offers a fine example of his more relaxed manner in his one Philadelphia season.

(i) *A Midsummer Night's Dream: Overture, Op. 21; Incidental music, Op. 61* (complete); (ii) *Overtures: The Hebrides (Fingal's Cave); Ruy Blas*.

(BB) **(*) Belart 461 354-2. (i) Hannecke van Bork, Alfreda Hodgson, Amb. S., New Philh. O, Frühbeck de Burgos; (ii) SRO, Ansermet.

Frühbeck de Burgos's 1969 recording of just the music is complete. The orchestral playing is very fine throughout – and notably so in the *Nocturne* and *Scherzo*. The performance of the *Overture* is not quite as magical as Flor's account, and the Decca recording, though full-bodied and with plenty of bloom, is not as clear-cut and transparent. But this remains very good value at super-bargain price, for Ansermet's accounts of the two overtures are full of vitality and drama, while the romantic element in *Fingal's Cave* is not missed. The mid-1960s sound is excellent.

3 Psalms, Op. 78.

**(*) Nimbus Dig. NI 5171 [id.]. Oslo Cathedral Ch., Terje Kvam – GRIEG: *4 Psalms*. **(*)

All three *Psalms* have considerable beauty and dignity, especially the first, a setting of Psalm 11 with its ingenious four-part canon. Good performances by the Oslo Cathedral Choir, and eminently serviceable recording. However, at under 45 minutes, the CD offers short measure.

St Paul, Op. 36.

(N) (BB) *** Arte Nova Dig. 74321 59219-2 (2) [id.]. Kwon, Ardam, Blochwitz, Lika, Bach-Ens. of Europa ChorAkademie, SWWR SO, Joshard Daus.

**(*) Ph. (IMS) 420 212-2 (2). Janowitz, Lang, Blochwitz, Stier, Polster, Adam, Leipzig R. Ch. & GO, Masur.

On the Arte Nova label Joshard Daus's version makes an excellent bargain. It is a fresh, sensitive reading with some lively choral singing and first-rate soloists, including the outstanding Helen Kwon and Hans Peter Blochwitz. Kwon is appealingly girlish in the big aria, *Jerusalem*. The chorus is rather backwardly placed, lessening its impact, but adding to the impression of a performance rather more intimate than most. The beauty of the orchestral writing is also the more apparent. The German text is provided but no translation. Though in memorable ideas this earlier oratorio cannot match *Elijah*, it has a devotional intensity in a performance like this which is most compelling, with its echoes of Bach and Handel.

Masur, always a persuasive interpreter of Mendelssohn, here directs a performance which, without inflating the piece, conveys its natural gravity. Theo Adam is not always steady, but otherwise the team of soloists is exceptionally strong, and the chorus adds to the incandescence, although placed rather backwardly. The Leipzig recording is warm and atmospheric.

OPERA

Die beiden Pädagogen (complete).
(M) *** CPO/EMI CPO 999 550-2. Fuchs, Laki, Dallapozza, Fischer-Dieskau, Wewel, Hirte, Bav, Op. Ch. & O, Wallberg.

Mendelssohn wrote this jolly piece, *Die beiden Pädagogen* ('The two pedagogues'), when he was only twelve, attacking the pedantry of schoolmasters, and with a side-swipe at ambitious fathers. It is a charming work that lay dormant from 1821 until 1960, when by chance the dialogue for this little *Singspiel* was discovered in Oxford. Starting with a brilliant overture, remarkable for deft woodwind writing, the musical ideas are charming, the manner light and sparkling in a way astonishing from a boy, even one as talented as Mendelssohn. In a piece lasting under an hour there are 11 vocal numbers, mainly brief duets and trios, culminating in a quartet with chorus much longer and more complex than the rest. In this denouement, solos are often superimposed on the choral writing with almost Mozartian skill. Under Heinz Wallberg, this CPO disc, very well recorded, offers a reissue of an EMI/Electrola recording made in 1978 with a first-rate cast. Fischer-Dieskau with great zest and style takes the *buffo* role of the schoolmaster, Kinderschreck (unnecessarily translated even in the cast-list as 'Bogy'), with Adolf Dallapozza clear and fresh in the principal tenor role of Carl, and with Krisztina Laki and Gabriele Fuchs well contrasted in the two soprano roles. A charming rarity. There is no libretto, only a detailed note and synopsis.

Die Heimkehr aus der Fremde (complete).
(M) *** CPO/EMI CPO 999 555-2. Donath, Schreier, Schwarz, Fischer-Dieskau, Kusche, Bav. Op. Ch. & O, Wallberg.

It was at the time of his first visit to England in 1829 at the age of twenty that Mendelssohn wrote this lighthearted little one-act *Singspiel*, *Die Heimkehr aus der Fremde* ('The return from abroad'). The plot recounts the return to his home village of Hermann, who for six years has served in the Foreign Legion. Matters are complicated by the involvement of an impostor, but everything works out well in the end. Lasting just over an hour, the 14 numbers plus overture skilfully and briskly take one through the plot. After the opening *Romanza* for the mother, a mezzo role, and a duet, the heroine Lisbeth is given a hauntingly beautiful aria in G minor, very sweetly sung here by Helen Donath. Hermann, the returning hero, also has a tender aria, more extended than the rest, with the young Peter Schreier perfectly cast. By that time the impostor, Kauz, has already made his mark in a jolly *buffo* aria referring to the *Dudelsack* (bagpipes), brilliantly sung by Fischer-Dieskau. The plot leads to a confrontation between the rivals which brings an echo of Beethoven's *Fidelio*. A resolution is crisply achieved, leading to a mellifluous final ensemble very characteristic of the composer. Like *Die beiden Pädagogen*, this is a rarity well worth investigating in this vividly recorded, first-rate performance.

Menotti, Gian-Carlo (born 1911)

Piano concerto in F.
(M) **(*) Van. 08.4029.71 [OVC 4071]. Earl Wild, Symphony of the Air, Jorge Mester – COPLAND: *Concerto.* ***

Menotti's *Piano concerto*, like most of his music, is easy and fluent, never hard on the ear. Its eclectic style brings a pungent whiff of Shostakovich at the opening, and there are hints of Khachaturian elsewhere. Even if it is unlikely to bear repeated listening, the charisma and bravura of Earl Wild's playing make the music sound more substantial than it is.

Amahl and the Night Visitors (opera): complete.
*** That's Entertainment CDTER 1124. Lorna Haywood, John Dobson, Curtis Watson, Christopher Painter, James Rainbird, ROHCG Ch. & O, David Syrus.

Recorded under the supervision of the composer himself, this is a fresh and highly dramatic performance, very well sung and marked by atmospheric digital sound of striking realism. Central to the success of the performance is the astonishingly assured and sensitively musical singing of the boy treble, James Rainbird, as Amahl, while Lorna Haywood sings warmly and strongly as the Mother, with a strong trio of Kings.

Amahl and the night visitors: Introduction; March; Shepherd's dance. Sebastian (ballet): suite.
*** Koch Dig. 3-7005-2 [id.]. New Zealand SO, Schenck – BARBER: *Souvenirs.* ***

This seven-movement suite from *Sebastian* is beautifully crafted and expertly scored music whose attractions are strong, as are the three movements from *Amahl and the night visitors*. The players under the late Andrew Schenck, sound as if they are enjoying themselves, and are well recorded.

The Consul (complete).
(N) *** Chandos Dig. CHAN 9706 (2) [id.]. Susan Bullock, Louis Otley, Jacalyn Kreitzer, Victoria Livengood, Graeme Broadbent, 1998 Spoleto Festival O, Richard Hickox.

It is astonishing that so powerfully involving a work

as *The Consul* should have been neglected on disc for so long. This ripely red-blooded performance, recorded live at the Spoleto Festival in 1998, finds Richard Hickox a passionate interpreter of this early response to the cold war and the human tragedies involved. Though initially in the 1950s the piece was immensely popular with a wide public, Menotti's achievement has tended to be disparaged by critics. In context today, it now emerges as a positive strength that Menotti unashamedly echoes Puccini in his emotional assault on the listener, whether in dramatic coups such as the very opening, which echoes the opening of *Tosca*, or in sweeping tunes that immediately catch in the memory. With a simple and direct story, and clear motivation, Menotti also has room to heighten tension in cunningly placed ensembles, as in the brilliant quintet in Act I, based on a haunting tune, for those hopelessly waiting at the Consulate. With the scenes beautifully balanced and contrasted, two per act, Hickox builds the structure masterfully, firmly controlling tension. He is helped by an excellent orchestra and a good cast, led by Susan Bullock in the central role of Magda. Her big outburst against bureaucracy at the end of Act II brings the emotional highpoint of the whole opera, an overwhelming moment worthy of Puccini. None of the others quite matches Bullock vocally, with some voices rather unsteady. Jacalyn Kreitzer is warmly affecting as the Mother, and Charles Austin sings strongly as the Secret Agent, giving a rounded portrait. Full-toned vivid recording, with ample detail.

(i) *Martin's Lie* (complete); (ii) *Canti della lontananza: Impossible lovers; The Letter; Pegasus asleep; Resignation; The Seventh glass of wine; Snowy morning; The Spectre;* (iii) 5 songs: *The Eternal prisoner; My ghost; The Idle gift; The Longest wait; The Swing.*

(N) *** Chandos Dig. CHAN 9605 [id.]. (i) Tees Valley Boys' Ch., Northern Sinfonia, Richard Hickox; (ii) Robin Leggate, Malcolm Martineau; (iii) Judith Howarth, Malcolm Martineau.

As Gian Carlo Menotti is one of the rare opera composers today who has a genuinely popular touch, updating Puccini, it is astonishing how neglected he has been by the record companies. Richard Hickox, the new music director of Menotti's Spoleto Festival, here sets out on a welcome Menotti series for Chandos. *Martin's Lie* was written as a follow-up to the children's piece for TV, *Amahl and the Night Visitors*, a sinister medieval story with a moral, fluently told in 45 minutes; warmly involving singing and playing. Judith Howarth and Robin Leggate are the singers in the two brief song-cycles, with Menotti's writing all the richer in the Italian settings.

Merbecke, John (*c.* 1505–*c.* 1585)

Missa per Arma Iustitie; Antiphona per arma iustitie (plainsong); Ave Dei patris filia; Domine Ihesu Christe; A virgin and mother.

*** ASV/Gaudeamus Dig. CDGAU 148 [id.]. Cardinall's Musick, Andrew Carwood.

The Tudor composer John Merbecke was a polyphonic master to bracket with his exact contemporary, Thomas Tallis, but his Latin church music has largely disappeared, perhaps destroyed by him after he became a devout Calvinist. This disc brings together all the major items that survive, a magnificent extended setting of the Mass and two splendid anthems, one early and direct in its polyphony, the other dauntingly complex. In the hands of Andrew Carwood and his fine choral group, Cardinall's Musick, the disc proves as revelatory and as beautiful as their previous, highly acclaimed issues of earlier Tudor masters, Nicholas Ludford and John Fayrfax.

Mercadante, Saverio (1795–1870)

Flute concertos: in D; E; E min.

*** RCA Dig. 09026 61447-2 [id.]. James Galway, Sol. Ven., Scimone.

These three *Flute concertos* show Mercadante to be an excellent craftsman with a nice turn for lyrical melody in the slow movements with their simple, song-like cantilenas. Both the *Andante alla siciliana* of the *D major Concerto* and the *Largo* of the *E minor* are appealing, especially with Galway as soloist, while the *Rondo Russo* or *Polacca* finales are inventively spirited. Scimone makes the most of the often exuberantly florid tuttis of the opening movements, and elsewhere he accompanies Galway's silvery melodic line, sparkling and delicate by turns, with style and polish. The sound is excellent.

Merikanto, Aarre (1893–1958)

'Meet the composer': (i) *Violin concertos Nos. 2 & 4;* (ii) *Fantasy for orchestra;* (iii) *Konzertstück for cello and orchestra;* (ii) *Largo misterioso;* (iv) *Notturno;* (ii) *Pan;* (iv) *10 Pieces for Orchestra;* (ii) *Symphonic study;* (v) *Genesis* (for soprano, chorus & orchestra).

(B) *** Finlandia/Warner Double 4509-99970-2 (2). (i) Kaija Saarikettu, Helsinki PO, James DePreist; (ii) Finnish RSO, Segerstam; (iii) Anssi Karttunen, London Sinf., Esa-Pekka Salonen; (iv) Avanti CO, Ari Angervo; (iv) Finnish RSO, Jukka-Pekka Saraste; (v) Karita Mattila, Savonlinna Op. Ch., Lahti SO, Söderblom.

As with previous issues in their '*Meet the composer*'

series, Finlandia have assembled the bulk of previous LP and CD issues to give a good cross-section of Merikanto's output. He is the most rewarding of the Finnish composers after Sibelius, and this is undoubtedly a set of exceptional musical interest. After studying with Reger in the years before the First World War, Merikanto went on to Moscow, where he came into contact with the music of Scriabin among others, thus laying the foundations of the radical style he developed in the inter-war years. Works like the *Fantasy for orchestra* (1923) and *Pan* (1924) are searching in idiom and set great store by refinement of colour. The *Ten Pieces* date from 1930, the orchestra the composer had in mind being the newly founded 23-man Helsinki Radio Orchestra. The first, *Largo misterioso*, also included in a fuller orchestration, is a haunting example of expressionism, highly original and powerful in its atmosphere. There are many reminders of Szymanowski in the *Second Violin concerto*, never played during the composer's lifetime, for the received wisdom was that after the Second World War Merikanto's inspiration declined in quality. To quote Seppo Heikinheimo's note in a previous issue of the concertos, 'In 1945 . . . Merikanto managed to break his morphine addiction, but his music never fully returned to what it once had been'. The collector can here judge for him or herself. The *Fourth Violin concerto* (1954) is more 'conventional in outlay': it opens with a Prokofiev-like ostinato figure and there is some lush and imaginative writing in the slow movement which again comes close to Szymanowski. Kaija Saarikettu is a commanding and brilliant soloist, and she is well accompanied by the Helsinki Philharmonic and James DePreist. *Genesis* (1956), too, is powerful and inspired music of high quality that enhances the claims of this composer on a wider public. Very strongly recommended.

Andante religioso; 4 Compositions for orchestra; Lemminkäinen, Op. 10; Pan, Op. 28; Scherzo.

(N) ** Ondine Dig. ODE 905-2 [id.]. Tampere PO, Tuomas Ollila.

Lemminkäinen comes from 1916, when Merikanto was finishing his studies in Moscow and is derivative (Russian post-nationalism, Sibelius and a dash of Scriabin). *Pan* is more radical and is highly imaginative with an evocative and powerful atmosphere. The *Four Compositions for orchestra* come from the 1930s as does the *Scherzo*. Good performances and decent recording, though the Tampere studio is a bit on the dry side.

(i) *Piano concerto Nos. 2 & 3; 2 Studies for small orchestra; 2 Pieces for orchestra.*

(N) ** Ondine Dig. ODE 915-2 [id.]. (i) Matti Raekallio; Tampere PO, Tuomas Ollila.

Although neither of the piano concertos is the equal of the *Second Violin concerto*, they are both inventive and rewarding. The *Second piano concerto* comes from the mid-1930s and the *Third* from 1955. Its middle movement with its strong evocation of nature is one of Merikanto's most haunting inspirations. The orchestral pieces are less interesting. Matti Raekallio is a very capable player and the Tampere Orchestra, though obviously a provincial band, copes well under Tuomas Ollila. The sound is synthetic with little front-to-back perspective. Worth investigating all the same.

Messiaen, Olivier (1908–92)

Des canyons aux étoiles; Couleurs de la cité céleste; Oiseaux exotiques.

*** Sony Dig. MK 44762 [id.]. Paul Crossley, L. Sinf., Salonen.

The power of the writing in Messiaen's vast symphonic cycle, *Des canyons aux étoiles*, comes out vividly in Esa-Pekka Salonen's CBS version, with Paul Crossley as soloist both incisive and deeply sympathetic. Salonen's performance is not obviously devotional in the first five movements; but then, after Michael Thompson's virtuoso horn solo, in the sixth movement Salonen and his players increasingly find a sharper focus, with the playing of the London Sinfonietta ever more confident and idiomatic. *Oiseaux exotiques* find Crossley in inspired form as soloist, and with *Couleurs de la cité céleste* made tough rather than evocative. The recording is sharply focused, but has good presence and atmosphere.

(i) *Couleurs de la cité céleste;* (ii) *Et exspecto resurrectionem mortuorum.*

(M) ** Sony SMK 68332 [id.]. Groupe Instrumental à percussion de Strasbourg, with (i) Yvonne Loriod; (ii) O du Domaine Musical; Boulez (with STRAVINSKY: *Symphonies of wind instruments;* with NYPO **).

In Messiaen's own words, his *Couleurs de la cité céleste* 'turns on itself like a rose-window', bringing together, with astonishing assurance, elements from plainsong, Greek and Hindu music, not to mention the persistent birdsong which runs through so much of this composer's writing. Boulez's account, helped by close microphones, centres on sharpness of detail rather than atmosphere; the result seems literal and fails to be seductive. Similarly, in the larger scale of *Et exspecto resurrectionem* the concentration of a series of clearly differentiated sounds and sonorities brings a negative effect. One cannot help feeling here that the musical content is spread rather thin, with too meandering a tempo predominating – pregnant pauses repeated overmuch lose their pregnancy. The Stravinsky encore makes a rather more positive impression, but this is essentially a reissue for Boulez aficionados rather than for the general collector.

Eclairs sur l'Au-Delà (Illuminations of the Beyond).

(N) *** DG Dig. 439 929-2 [id.]. Paris Bastille Opéra O, Myung-Whun Chung.

Collectors will be forgiven if they register a double take on observing Messaien's title, for what is an intensely mystical symphonic work; it has nothing in common with patisserie, but reveals an undoubted connection with the visionary *Turangalîla Symphony*. Especially so in the longest movement, a haunting *adagio* for strings, *Demeurer dans l'Amour*. This magical sequence returns to close the work in translucent radiance, portraying *Le Christ, lumière du Paradis*. Of course, the music features the composer's beloved bird-song (six different species on six flutes and in the third movement, an exotically vivid portrayal of the Australian Lyre-bird). There are also evocations of constellations in the night sky 'in all their glory', and of 'seven angels with seven trumpets'. Myung-Whun Chung is at his most persuasive in holding this evocative score together, and this superbly played performance is even finer than his reading of *Turangalîla*; the DG sound is spaciously atmospheric yet beautifully clear.

Turangalîla Symphony.

(B) *** EMI forte CZS5 69752-2 (2) [CDFB 69752]. Michel Béroff, Jeanne Loriod, LSO, Previn – POULENC: *Concert champêtre; Organ concerto.* ***

*** Decca Dig. 436 626-2 [id.]. Jean-Yves Thibaudet, Takashi Harada, Concg. O, Chailly.

*** DG Dig. 431 781-2 [id.]. Yvonne & Jeanne Loriod, Bastille O, Chung.

(N) **(*) Chandos Dig. CHAN 9678 [id.]. Howard Shelley, Valérie Hartmann-Claverie, BBC PO, Yan Pascal Tortelier.

(i) *Turangalîla symphony;* (ii) *Quartet for the end of time.*

*** EMI Dig. CDS7 47463-8 (2). (i) Donohoe, Murail, CBSO, Rattle; (ii) Gawriloff, Deinzer, Palm, Kontarsky.

Messiaen's *Turangalîla Symphony* was written at a time (1946–8) when – Shostakovich notwithstanding – the symphonic tradition seemed at its lowest ebb. Messiaen's conception is on an epic scale, seeking to embrace almost the totality of human experience. This is immediately implied in the Sanskrit title, a complex word suggesting the interplay of life forces, creation and dissolution, but which is also divisible: *Turanga* is Time and also implies rhythmic movement; *Lîla* is love, and with a strong inspiration from the Tristan and Isolde legend Messiaen's love-music dominates his conception of human existence. The actual love-sequences feature the ondes martenot with its 'velvety glissandi'. The piano obbligato is also a strong feature of the score. Previn's vividly direct approach, helped by spectacular recording, has much electricity. He is at his best in the work's more robust moments, for instance the jazzy fifth movement, and he catches the wit at the beginning of the *Chant d'amour 2*. The idyllic *Garden of the sleep of love* is both serene and poetically sensuous, and the apotheosis of the love theme in the closing pages is jubilant and life-enhancing. Chailly's full-priced Decca account may have the advantage of even finer, digital recording, and it costs about the same; being (just) fitted on to a single CD, however, it is without Previn's considerable bonus: outstanding versions of two of Poulenc's finest concertos.

Among the new generation of one-disc versions of *Turangalîla*, Chailly's powerful, dramatic reading with the Concertgebouw makes an outstanding first choice. The richness of the sound goes with beautiful balance, fine clarity and a keen sense of presence, heightening the impact of Chailly's clean-cut, brilliant interpretation. Chailly's sharpness at a fast tempo in the catchy fifth movement, *Joie du sang des étoiles*, conveys its joy with a jazzy lilt, and the following *Jardin du sommeil d'amour* conveys sensuousness rather than spiritual intensity, taken at a flowing tempo. In the seventh movement, *Turangalîla II*, the wit and point of Thibaudet's playing heighten the sharpness of focus and, though some will prefer a warmer reading, no one will fail to appreciate the concentration and intensity of Chailly's performance. The Decca recording is in the demonstration class.

Chung's reading with the Bastille Orchestra was recorded in 1990 in the composer's presence, not long before he died. Messiaen's endorsement is confirmed when the soloists are his wife and his sister-in-law, at times less precise than rivals, but bringing a unique, expressive intensity. Their contributions, particularly the pointed piano-playing of Yvonne Loriod, heighten the natural warmth of Chung's reading, less high-powered and at times less precise than Chailly's rival one-disc version, and less cleanly recorded, but very persuasive.

Simon Rattle conducts a winning performance of *Turangalîla*, not only brilliant and dramatic but atmospheric and convincing. The recording is warm and richly co-ordinated while losing nothing in detail. Peter Donohoe and Tristan Murail play with comparable warmth and flair. Led by Aloys Kontarsky, the performance of the *Quartet for the end of time* provides a contrasting approach to Messiaen from Rattle's, where atmospheric warmth is only an incidental.

In many ways the Yan Pascal Tortelier Chandos version falls between that of Chailly and Chung. It opens excitingly, has undoubted grip, and the recording is exceptionally vividly detailed, with Howard Shelley's piano contribution always crystal clear. But the very positive characterization seems to give the work a more episodic nature. In the freely rhythmic *Joie du sang des étoiles* the jazzy element is unemphasized, and the *Jardin du sommeil d'amour* is delicately refined in its erotic feeling, less overtly sensuous than Chailly. The reading overall is not as warmly expressive as Chung's, partly the effect of the sound balance, and this is especially striking in the brilliant finale.

Quatuor pour la fin du temps.

(N) *** Decca Dig. 452 899-2 [id.]. Olli Mustonen, Joshua Bell, Steven Isserlis, Michael Collins – SHOSTAKOVICH: *Piano trio No. 2.* ***

*** Delos Dig. D/CD 3043 [id.]. Chamber Music Northwest – BARTOK: *Contrasts.* ***

(N) *** Collins Dig. 1393-2 [id.]. Joanna MacGregor, Madeleine Mitchell, Christopher van Kampen, David Campbell (with Zygmunt KRAUZE: Quatuor pour la Naissance ***).

(i) *Quatuor pour la fin du temps (Quartet for the end of time);* (ii) *Le merle noir.*

(M) *** EMI CDM7 63947-2. (i) Gruenberg, De Peyer, Pleeth, Béroff; (ii) Zöller, Kontarsky.

Messiaen's visionary and often inspired piece was composed during his days in a Silesian prison camp. Among his fellow-prisoners were a violinist, a clarinettist and a cellist who, with the composer at the piano, made its creation possible. The 1968 EMI account is in the very highest class, the players meeting every demand the composer makes upon them, and the fine, clear Abbey Road recording gives the group striking presence while affording proper background ambience. The bonus, *Le merle noir*, exploits the composer's love of birdsong even more overtly and is splendidly played and recorded here.

Undoubtedly the new Decca version is the finest among recent digital recordings. All four artists distinguish thmselves, and Messiaen's other-worldly piece is beautifully played and has great concentration and atmosphere. The one snag is the wide dynamic range of the recording (which also affects the superb Shostakovich coupling), although the clarinettist, Michael Collins, makes the very most of it with his *pianissimos*. It is difficult (but not impossible) to find a volume setting in which the gentler passages register, yet *fortissimos* do not become just a shade fierce, and the ear is conscious that the microphones are fairly close. Nevertheless this is very fine, and as on the earlier EMI version, the Abbey Road ambience is well judged.

We already know the calibre of David Shifrin's playing from his recording of Copland's *Clarinet concerto*. Here, like his colleagues, he fully captures the work's sensuous mysticism, while the solos of Warren Lash (cello) and Williams Doppmann have a wistful, improvisatory quality: both *Louange à l'éternité de Jésus* and the closing *Louange à l'immortalité de Jésus* are played very beautifully. The Delos recording is naturally balanced and very realistic, while the ambience is suitably evocative.

The performance on Collins is also highly involving, with both Joanna MacGregor and David Campbell making memorable contributions, while the players create a haunting *pianissimo* in the two sections of the work named after Jésus. The one slight drawback is the reverberant acoustic which detracts a little from the intimacy. What makes this CD particularly interesting is the inclusion of the *Quatuor* by Zygmunt Krauze, obviously modelled on Messiaen's work and having much of the same compelling atmosphere.

(i) *Quatuor pour la fin du temps;* (ii) *Cinq rechants* (for 12 voices).

(M) *** Erato/Warner 4509 91708 [id.]. Fernandez, Deplus, Neilz, Petit; (ii) Solistes des Chœurs de l'ORTF, Marcel Couraud.

The French Ensemble on Erato give a strong, powerfully integrated performance, well held together by the pianist, Marie-Madeleine Petit. The recording is very good, clear and well balanced. The coupling, *Cinq rechants*, is written for a choir of twelve soloists. The composer's inspiration of human passion brings both lyrical intensity and extraordinary irregular rhythmic effects (some of which have an Indian source) and the various bursts and cascades of vocal tone give the work a stimulatingly original vitality. The performance is remarkably assured and full of ardent spontaneity, and the group are vividly recorded. Excellent notes are provided by the composer.

(i) *Quatuor pour la fin du temps;* (ii) *Theme and variations for violin and piano.*

(N) (B) **(*) DG Classikon. (i) Yordanoff, Tetard, Desurmont, Barenboim; (ii) Kremer, Argerich.

Barenboim and his colleagues recorded the *Quatuor pour la fin du temps* in the presence of the composer. Barenboim is a strong personality who carries much of this vibrant and atmospheric performance in his own hands and inspired his colleagues with his own commitment to the music. There are fine contributions from the cellist Albert Tetard and the clarinettist Claude Desurmont. The 1979 recording was originally a very good one and retains its ambience. But the CD transfer has added a degree of edginess to Luben Yordanoff's violin timbre, making this less attractive than the original LP from which the recording derives. The *Theme and variations* (a digital recording from 1990), is something of a rarity on disc, but is in every way successful. It is also available differently coupled (see below).

Theme and variations.
*** DG (IMS) Dig. 427 351-2. Gidon Kremer, Martha Argerich – BARTOK: *Sonata No. 1* ***; JANACEK: *Sonata.* **(*)

Messiaen's *Theme and variations* is an early work and the music's fervour is well captured here.

PIANO MUSIC

Catalogue d'oiseaux (complete); *Petites esquisses d'oiseaux.*
(BB) *** Naxos Dig. 8.553532/4 (3) [id.]. Håkan Austbø.

The Norwegian pianist, Håkan Austbø, has already distinguished himself in composers such as Scriabin and Messiaen. His earlier Naxos account of the *Vingt regards sur l'enfant Jésus* (see below) can hold its own with any full-price version in the catalogue. The same goes for these dedicated readings. The seven books of the *Catalogue d'oiseaux* occupied Messiaen between 1956 and 1958, and they include 13 ornithological portraits. (It was this work which prompted one French critic to write that if the birds really sing like this, '*la chasse doit devenir un devoir social*'.) The *Petites esquisses d'oiseaux* are much later. Whatever one's reactions to Messiaen's music, he creates a world entirely his own. Håkan Austbø is completely attuned to this sensibility, and the recording is exemplary. Aficionados of Messiaen need not hesitate.

Catalogue d'oiseaux, Books 1–3.
*** Unicorn Dig. DKPCD 9062 [id.]. Peter Hill.

Catalogue d'oiseaux, Books 4–6: L'alouette calandrelle; La bouscarle; La merle de roche; La rousserolle effarvatte.
*** Unicorn Dig. DKPCD 9075 [id.]. Peter Hill.

Peter Hill prepared this music in Paris with the composer himself and thus has his imprimatur. He evokes the wildlife pictured in this extraordinary music to splendid effect, and is recorded with the utmost clarity and definition.

Catalogue d'oiseaux, Book 7; Supplement: La fauvette des jardins.
*** Unicorn Dig. DKPCD 9090 [id.]. Peter Hill.

In addition to the last book of the *Catalogue d'oiseaux* we have here *La fauvette des jardins*, which the sleeve annotator describes as the perfect parergon to the cycle. The composer himself has spoken with great warmth of this artist and, given what we hear on this disc, has every reason to.

4 Etudes de rythme; Petites esquisses d'oiseaux; 8 Préludes; Vingt regards sur l'enfant Jésus.
(M) *** Erato/Warner 4509 96222-2 (3) [id.]. Yvonne Loriod.

The 1973 recording by Yvonne Loriod – the composer's second wife – of *Vingt regards* has long been considered very special in its understanding and feeling for the composer's musical soundworld. The piano recording is full but is otherwise acceptable rather than outstanding – yet the magnetism of the playing overcomes the lack of the sharpest focus. This now returns to the catalogue at mid-price, coupled with other key repertoire played with equal distinction.

8 Préludes pour piano; Vingt regards sur l'enfant Jésus.
(B) **(*) EMI (SIS) Rouge et Noir CZS5 69668-2. Michel Béroff.

The *Préludes* are early works but, like *Vingt regards*, they show Béroff at his most inspired, generating the illusion of spontaneous creation. Clean, well-focused sound – but a little wanting in richness and sonority.

Vingt regards sur l'enfant Jésus.
*** Collins Dig. 7033-2 [id.]. Joanna MacGregor.
(BB) *** Naxos Dig. 8.550829/30 [id.]. Håkon Austbø.

Joanna MacGregor's powerful and highly atmospheric set of *Vingt regards* now takes its place as a primary recommendation for Messiaen's remarkable, visionary and often uncompromising work. She does not shirk the percussive Bartókian pianism of a movement like *La parole toute-puissante* ('The all-powerful word') and is equally impressive in evoking the 'fiery flames' of *Regard des Anges*. Yet in the *Regard du silence* the quiet evocation is compelling and the contemplative *Je dors, mais mon cœur veille* ('I sleep, but my heart is awake') has comparable concentration. The closing section, *Regard de l'Eglise d'Amour*, brings a superb sense of apotheosis. The recording is very fine indeed, with just the right degree of ambient warmth.

Håkon Austbø as one-time prize-winner of the Olivier Messiaen Competition for Contemporary Music in Royan has excellent credentials in this repertoire. His is an individual view, with a wider range of tempi and dynamic than Loriod. His account of the opening *Regard du Père* and the later *Regard du Fils sur le Fils* is paced much more slowly, but his playing has great concentration and evocative feeling so that he readily carries the slower tempo, and in *Par lui tout a été fait* articulation is bolder, giving the music a stronger profile, helped by the clearer, Naxos digital focus. This is undoubtedly a performance that grips the listener and can be strongly recommended as an alternative view.

Visions de l'Amen.
*** EMI (SIS) CDC7 54050-2. Alexandre Rabinovitch, Martha Argerich.
*** New Albion Dig. NA 045 CD [id.]. Double Edge (Edmund Niemann & Nurit Tilles).

Messiaen's *Visions de l'Amen* for two pianos is a long, eloquent work in seven sections with a powerful sense of mystery, and is played with uncommon conviction by the Russian pianist-composer, Alexandre Rabinovitch, with Martha Argerich at the second piano.

The performance from Edmund Niemann and Nurit Tilles is hardly less spontaneous. They capture the work's colour and atmosphere powerfully and evocatively – it is Messiaen at his most compelling – and some may prefer the sound of the New Albion recording. The two pianists are set back in a fairly reverberant but not over-reverberant acoustic.

ORGAN MUSIC

Organ music: *Apparition de l'Eglise éternelle; L'Ascension (4 Méditations); Le banquet céleste; Le corps glorieux (7 Visions de la vie des ressuscités); Diptyque (Essai sur la vie terrestre et l'éternité religieuse); Livre d'Orgue (Reprises par interversion; Première pièce en trio; Les mains de l'abîme; Chants oiseaux; Deuxième pièce en trio; Les yeux dans les roues; Soixante-quatre durées). Messe de la Pentecôte; La Nativité du Seigneur (9 Méditations).*

(M) *** EMI (SIS) mono CZS7 67400-2 (4) [id.]. Composer (Cavaillé-Coll organ de L'Eglise de la Sainte-Trinité, Paris).

In an intensive series of sessions which began at the end of May and continued through June and July 1956, Olivier Messiaen returned to the organ in Sainte-Trinité, with which all his music is associated, and recorded everything he had written and published before that date. These performances not only carry the imprint of the composer's authority, but also the inspiration of the occasion. The large-scale works have a concentration and compelling atmosphere that are unforgettable. No apologies at all need be made for the range, breadth and faithfulness of the recording, although some must be made for the organ itself, which is not always perfectly tuned. There is minor background hiss, which is not troublesome, and technically the CD transfers are a remarkable achievement.

Livre du Saint Sacrement.

*** Unicorn Dig. DKPCD 9067/8 [id.]. Jennifer Bate (organ of Sainte-Trinité, Paris).

What a sound! This is a quite spectacular recording and carries the composer's imprimatur. Jennifer Bate makes an impressive and compelling case for these hypnotic pieces, and the recording is in the demonstration bracket.

La Nativité du Seigneur (9 meditations); Le banquet céleste.

❁ *** Unicorn Dig. DKPCD 9005 [id.]. Jennifer Bate (organ of Beauvais Cathedral).

'*C'est vraiment parfait!*' said Messiaen after hearing Jennifer Bate's Unicorn recording of *La Nativité du Seigneur*, one of his most extended, most moving and beautiful works. For the CD issue, *Le banquet céleste* also provides an intense comment on the religious experience which has inspired all of the composer's organ music. The recording of the Beauvais Cathedral organ is of demonstration quality.

Meyerbeer, Giacomo (1791–1864)

Les Patineurs (ballet suite, arr. & orch. Lambert).

(B) *** Decca Dig. 444 110-2 [id.]. Nat. PO, Richard Bonynge – MASSENET: *Le Cid* etc. ***

Les Patineurs was arranged by Constant Lambert using excerpts from two of Meyerbeer's operas, *Le Prophète* and *L'Etoile du Nord*. Bonynge's approach is warm and comparatively easy-going and, with such polished orchestral playing, this version is extremely beguiling. The sound too is first rate.

Il Crociato in Egitto (complete).

*** Opera Rara OR 10 (4). Kenny, Montague, Della Jones, Ford, Kitchen, Benelli, Platt, Geoffrey Mitchell Ch., RPO, David Parry.

This was the sixth and last opera which Meyerbeer wrote for Italy. The musical invention may not often be very distinctive, but the writing is consistently lively, notably in the ensembles. With one exception – Ian Platt, ill-focused in the role of the Sultan – the cast is a strong one, with Dianna Montague outstanding in the castrato role of the Crusader-Knight, Armando. Della Jones, too, in the mezzo role of Felicia, whom Armando has abandoned in favour of Palmide, the Sultan's daughter, sings superbly with agile coloratura and a rich chest register. Yvonne Kenny is brilliant as Palmide. Bruce Ford, with his firm, heroic tone, and Ugo Benelli are very well contrasted in the two tenor roles. Though the chorus is small, the recording is clear and fresh.

Les Huguenots (complete).

(M) *** Decca (IMS) 430 549-2 (4) [id.]. Sutherland, Vrenios, Bacquier, Arroyo, Tourangeau, Ghiuselev, New Philh. O, Bonynge.

Sutherland is predictably impressive, though once or twice there are signs of a 'beat' in the voice, previously unheard on Sutherland records. The rest of the cast is uneven, and in an unusually episodic opera, with passages that are musically less than inspired, that brings disappointments. Gabriel Bacquier and Nicola Ghiuselev are fine in their roles and, though Martina Arroyo is below her best as Valentine, the star quality is unmistakable. The tenor, Anastasios Vrenios, copes with the extraordinarily high tessitura and florid diversions. Vrenios sings the notes, which is more than almost any rival could. Fine recording to match this ambitious project, well worth investigating by lovers of

French opera. The work sounds newly minted on CD.

Le Prophète (complete).
**(*) Sony M3K 79400 (3) [id.]. Horne, Scotto, McCracken, Hines, Dupony, Bastin, Boys' Ch. of Haberdasher's Aske's School, Amb. Op. Ch., RPO, Henry Lewis.

This recording anticipated the 1977 production at the New York Met. with the same conductor and principal soloists. None of the soloists is quite at peak form, though they all sing more than competently. Nevertheless, with vigorous direction by Henry Lewis – rather brutal in the Coronation scene – there is much to enjoy. The recording is vividly transferred to CD but would have benefited from a more atmospheric acoustic.

Miaskovsky, Nikolay (1881–1950)

Cello concerto in C min., Op. 66.
❁ (M) *** EMI CDM5 65419-2. Rostropovich, Philh. O, Sargent – TANEYEV: *Suite de concert.* ***
(N) *** Virgin/EMI Dig. VC5 45310-2 [id.]. Truls Mørk, CBSO, Paavo Järvi – PROKOFIEV: *Sinfonia concertante.* ***
*** DG Dig. 449 821-2 [id.]. Mischa Maisky, Russian National O, Mikhail Pletnev – PROKOFIEV: *Sinfonia concertante.* ***

(i) *Cello concerto;* (ii) *Cello sonatas Nos. 1 in D, Op. 12; 2 in A min., Op. 81.*
*** Olympia Dig. OCD 530 [id.]. Marina Tarasova, with (i) Moscow New Op. O, Yevgeny Samoilov; (ii) Alexander Polezhaev.

The Miaskovsky *Cello concerto* has an overwhelming sense of nostalgia and an elegiac atmosphere that is quite individual. Its very directness of utterance and diatonic simplicity can easily mask its depths. Although it does not encompass as wide a range as does the Elgar, it has a similarly powerful expressive impact. Marina Tarasova earns praise for coupling it so logically with the two *Cello sonatas*. The *Sonata in D major*, Op. 12 (1911, revised 1930), does not differ in idiom from its much later companion, *No. 2 in A minor*, Op. 81. Tarasova has a strong musical personality and produces a magnificent tone; she receives sympathetic support from her accompanists, and decent recording.

The Norwegian cellist Truls Mørk, with Paavo Järvi and the City of Birmingham Symphony Orchestra, couple the concerto with the Prokofiev *Sinfonia concertante*. They enjoy superb and very balanced recorded sound. Truls Mørk does not wear his heart anywhere near his sleeve and his restrained reading deserves a prime position among modern recordings.

Mischa Maisky shows admirable finesse and some restraint in Miaskovsky's elegiac concerto. Those who find him sometimes too gushing, too ready to lay bare his breast, will be relieved. Like the Prokofiev coupling, this is a strongly characterized performance. Pletnev keeps a firm grip on proceedings, and the Russian National Orchestra play with impeccable taste and aristocratic feeling. This will now probably be a first choice for many collectors. It is well recorded and, though the soloist is forwardly balanced, it is not at the expense of orchestral detail.

However, Rostropovich's pioneering account with Sir Malcolm Sargent is still in a class of its own. It could not be played with greater eloquence and restraint, and the (1956) Abbey Road recording is amazingly full and fresh – one would never guess its age.

(i) *Lyric concertino for flute, clarinet, horn, bassoon, harp and string orchestra, Op. 32/3; Salutation overture in C, Op. 48; Serenade for chamber orchestra in E flat, Op. 32/1; Sinfonietta for string orchestra in B min., Op. 32/2.*
*** Olympia Dig. OCD 528 [id.]. Moscow New Op. O, Samoilov.

The *Serenade* has great charm and strong lyrical appeal; the *Lyric concertino*, and particularly its slow movement, has considerable harmonic subtlety. The performance under Yevgeny Samoilov is much finer than the earlier account by Vladimir Verbitzky (see below), and he gives a sensitive reading of the *Sinfonietta for strings*. These are endearing pieces; not so the *Salutation overture*, written for Stalin's 60th birthday, which is worth giving a miss. Very good recording.

Sinfonietta for strings in B min., Op. 32/2; Theme and variations; 2 Pieces, Op. 46/1; Napeve.
*** ASV Dig. CDDCA 928 [id.]. St Petersburg CO, Roland Melia.

The *Sinfonietta for strings* will appeal to anyone of a nostalgic disposition. The players give an affectionate, well-prepared account of it and convey the wistful, endearing nature of the slow movement to perfection. The *Theme and variations* (on a theme of Grieg) also has the same streak of melancholy. The first of the *Two Pieces*, Op. 46, No. 1, is a transcription and reworking for strings of the inner movements, reversing their order, of Miaskovsky's *Symphony No. 19 for military band*, composed in 1939. The St Petersburg Chamber Orchestra is an expert and responsive ensemble, and the ASV recording does them proud.

Symphonies Nos. (i) *1 in C min., Op. 3;* (ii) *19 in E flat for wind band, Op. 46.*
**(*) Russian Disc RDCD 11 007 [id.]. (i) USSR Ministry of Culture SO, Gennady Rozhdestvensky; (ii) Russian State Brass O, Nikolai Sergeyev.

Miaskovsky's *First Symphony* is a student work, very much in the received tradition. It is obvious from the very start that Miaskovsky was a composer who could think on a big scale. The *Nineteenth Symphony in B flat* for military band was written in 1939 for the 21st anniversary of the Red Army and is a slighter piece, worth hearing for its inner movements, a wistful *Moderato* and a well-written *Andante*. The *First Symphony* is well played by the Ministry of Culture Orchestra under Gennady Rozhdestvensky, though the brass sound a bit raw, as indeed do the upper strings. The *Nineteenth* is played with great brio and genuine affection. The less-than-three-star recording-quality should not deter collectors from investigating this work.

Symphonies Nos. 5 in D, Op. 18; 9 in E min., Op. 28.
*** Marco Polo Dig. 8.223499 [id.]. BBC PO, Downes.

The *Fifth Symphony* is a sunny, pastoral score dating from 1918, very much in the tradition of Glazunov and Glière. Downes's recording with the BBC Philharmonic, recorded in an admittedly over-resonant venue in Derby, is to be preferred both artistically and sonically to its earlier rival by the USSR Symphony Orchestra under Ivanov on Olympia. The *Ninth Symphony* is somewhat better served than No. 5 so far as the sound is concerned. It is vintage Miaskovsky, more cogently argued and more interesting in thematic substance than the *Eighth*. Very good performances and good enough recording – just – to make three stars.

Symphony No. 6 in E flat min. (Revolutionary), Op. 23.
(**(*)) Russian Disc mono RDCD 15008 [id.]. Yurlov Russian Ch., USSR SO, Kirill Kondrashin.

Here, at long last on CD, is the pioneering set of the mammoth *Sixth Symphony* with choral finale, which alerted many collectors to Miaskovsky's real stature. There are echoes of Miaskovsky's master, Glière, and also of Scriabin but, in the trio of the Scherzo, Miaskovsky strikes that note of nostalgia and lost innocence he was to make so much his own in the *Cello concerto* - and the *Violin concerto* too. It is a highly individual and often masterly score, although let down a little by its (somewhat inflated) choral finale, which employs folk and revolutionary songs, including the *Carmagnole*, which earned the symphony its nickname, *The Revolutionary*. Though the present recording dates from 1959, it is the one to have.

Symphony No. 8 in A, Op. 26.
** Marco Polo Dig. 8.223297 [id.]. Slovak RSO (Bratislava), Robert Stankovsky.

Although the *Eighth* is not one of Miaskovsky's finest symphonies, it is still worth investigating. There are some characteristic ideas, and initially unfavourable impressions are soon dispelled as one comes closer to it. Neither the performance nor the recording is distinguished, but both are thoroughly acceptable; there is a lack of subtlety here, but not of vitality and commitment.

Symphony No. 12 in G min., Op. 35; Silence (symphonic poem after Poe), *Op. 9.*
**(*) Marco Polo Dig. 8.223302 [id.]. Slovak RSO (Bratislava), Robert Stankovsky.

The *Twelfth Symphony* is endearingly old-fashioned and has strong appeal. Although some of the big rhetorical gestures of the *Sixth Symphony* are to be found in the second movement, there are also some pre-echoes of things to come in the later symphonies. It is highly enjoyable, particularly when it is as well played as it is here by the Bratislava Radio Orchestra under their gifted young conductor, Robert Stankovsky. The tone-poem *Silence* draws for its inspiration on Edgar Allan Poe's *The Raven* and has a strongly atmospheric quality with a distinctly *fin-de-siècle* air: if you enjoy Rachmaninov's *Isle of the dead*, you should investigate it. The orchestra play with enthusiasm and they are decently recorded.

CHAMBER MUSIC

Cello sonata No. 1 in D, Op. 12.
*** Virgin/EMI Dig. VC5 45119-2. Truls Mørk, Jean-Yves Thibaudet – RACHMANINOV: *Cello sonata* etc. ***

The Norwegian cellist, Truls Mørk, plays this lovely piece with both feeling and restraint. No doubt the most logical choice in this work is Marina Tarasova on Olympia, for she also offers its later companion in *A minor*, Op. 81, and the elegiac *Cello concerto*. For those wanting the present coupling, however, these artists give a very fine account both of the *Sonata* and of the Rachmaninov coupling. Well-balanced recording.

String quartets Nos. 1 in A min., Op. 33/1; 4 in F min., Op. 33/4.
** Russian Disc RDCD 11013 [id.]. Taneyev Qt.

The Taneyev Quartet of Leningrad recorded all the Miaskovsky *Quartets* on LP during the course of the 1980s, and their release on CD is warmly to be welcomed. Miaskovsky composed half as many quartets as symphonies (thirteen as opposed to twenty-seven), but they are hardly less important, always finely crafted and possessing moments of restrained depth. Like so much of Miaskovsky's music, they are conservative in idiom but their ideas are often memorable. The *First Quartet* finds him more among the avant-garde of Russian composers than the conservative figure he became, and it has a far higher norm of dissonance than we are used to. It is a surprisingly fascinating and powerful score. The *Fourth*, in F minor, is less challenging and more overtly lyrical and traditional in outlook.

These imaginative and thought-provoking works are eminently well played, but the recording lets things down. The players are forwardly balanced, the sound is hard and vinegary and needs to be tamed above the stave. All the same, such is the interest of this disc that it must have a strong recommendation.

PIANO MUSIC

Piano sonatas Nos. 1 in D min., Op. 6; 2 in F sharp min., Op. 13; 3 in C min., Op. 19; 6 in A flat, Op. 64/2.
**(*) Olympia Dig. OCD 214 [id.]. Murray McLachlan.

In its way, the *First Sonata* is an oddity; its opening, like that of the Balakirev *B flat minor Sonata* written two years earlier, is fugal, but much of the second movement is more akin to the early Scriabin sonatas. So, too, is the *Second*, though Taneyev, Glazunov and Medtner also spring to mind. Murray McLachlan possesses a very considerable talent. An enterprising issue in every way, and well recorded.

Piano sonatas Nos. 4 in C min., Op. 27; 5 in B, Op. 64/1; Sonatine in E min., Op. 57; Prelude, Op. 58.
*** Olympia Dig. OCD 217 [id.]. Murray McLachlan.

The middle movement of the *Sonatine*, marked *Narrante e lugubre*, is dark and pessimistic, and quite haunting. McLachlan speaks of the 'enormous tactile pleasure' it gives to the performer, and his playing is both authoritative and persuasive. Perhaps this is the record to try first, since both *Sonatas*, not just the more 'radical' *Fourth*, are of interest and substance. Good recording.

Piano sonatas Nos. 6 in A flat, Op. 62/2; 7 in C, Op. 82; 8 in D min., Op. 83; 9 in F, Op. 84.
**(*) Marco Polo Dig. 8.223178 [id.]. Endre Hegedüs.

Piano sonatas Nos. 7 in C, Op. 82; 8 in D min., Op. 83; 9 in F, Op. 84; Reminiscences, Op. 29; Rondo-Sonata in B flat min., Op. 58; String quartet No. 5: Scherzo (trans. Aliawdina): *Yellowed Leaves, Op. 31.*
**(*) Olympia Dig. OCD 252 [id.]. Murray McLachlan.

The sonatas on the Olympia disc are all from 1949. The music is of the utmost simplicity but has an endearing warmth. As in the earlier discs, McLachlan provides scholarly and intelligent notes. The recording is good though the acoustic ambience is perhaps not absolutely ideal.

The Marco Polo disc brings the last four sonatas. The young Hungarian pianist, Endre Hegedüs, is often the more imaginative interpreter: he colours the second theme of the *Barcarolle* section of the *Eighth Sonata* with greater tenderness and subtlety than Murray McLachlan on Olympia, though the latter has great freshness. The sound is a little wanting in bloom. On balance, then, honours are fairly even between these two artists.

Míča, Jan František Adam

(1746–1811)

String quartet No. 6 in C.
(M) *** Cal. CAL 6698 [id.]. Talich Qt – BOCCHERINI: *Quartet, Op. 58/2;* HAYDN: *Quartet No. 74;* MENDELSSOHN: *Quartet No. 2.* ***

The Bohemian composer Jan Míča writes elegantly in the *galant* style, and this *C major Quartet* (his sixth) brings an enticing opening theme, then continues in a cultivated and courtly style. Yet the *Rondo* finale produces a quite touching central interlude and one is reminded of Boccherini. Throughout, the warmth and finesse of the Talich playing ensure our enjoyment of what is a slight but well-crafted little work.

Milán, Luis de (*c.* 1500–*c.* 1561)

El Maestro: Fantasias Nos. 7, 8, 9 & 16; Pavanas Nos. 1, 4, 5 & 6; Tento No. 1.
(M) *** RCA 09026 61606-2. Julian Bream (lute) (with MUDARRA: *Fantasia*) – NARVAEZ: *Collection.* ***

This music was originally written for the vihuela. It was Milán who produced the first published book of this music in 1535, calling it *El Maestro* and including also instruction. Julian Bream seeks and achieves nobility of feeling in this repertoire and often chooses slow, dignified tempi. It all sounds splendid here on a proper lute, especially when so beautifully recorded.

Milano, Francesco Canova da

(1497–1543)

(i) Lute duets: *Canon; Fantasia quarta; Fantasia quinta; Fantasia sexta; Ricercar prima; Ricercar seconda; Ricercar terza; La spagna.* Pieces for solo lute: *Fantasias Nos. 30; 55–6; 63–7; 81–3; Ricercars Nos. 2; 10; 13; 69–70; 73; 76 & 79.*
(BB) *** Naxos Dig. 8.550774 [id.]. Christopher Wilson, (i) with Shirley Rumsey.

During his lifetime Francesco Canova da Milano was known as 'Il Divino' and was, by all accounts, 'a miraculous lute player'. By the time he was twenty-two he was already in the employ of the Pope. He served the Gonzaga Court at Mantua and Cardinal Ippolito de' Medici, though he spent most of his years in the papal court. In 1538 he accompanied Paul III to Nice for his meeting with

Charles V and François I, and possibly visited Paris, since two of his compositions are attributed to 'Francesco da Parigi'. He published four collections of works in Venice, Milan and Naples during his lifetime, but his music is widely encountered – in no fewer than 40 printed tablatures. He was the most prolific lute composer of his day, even more so than his close contemporary, the Spanish vihuelist and composer, Luis de Milán.

Christopher Wilson plays this collection of pieces, including duets with Shirley Rumsey, with a natural and unforced authority. Cultured playing of highly civilized music – recorded with admirable clarity, though it is advisable to reduce the level setting to get the most lifelike and natural result.

Milhaud, Darius (1892–1974)

L'Apothéose de Molière, Op. 286; Le bœuf sur le toit, Op. 58; (i) *Le carnaval d'Aix, Op. 83b. Le carnaval de Londres, Op. 172.*

*** Hyperion Dig. CDA 66594 [id.]. (i) Jack Gibbons; New L. O, Ronald Corp.

Le carnaval d'Aix is a carefree work full of high spirits and is bathed in Mediterranean sun with the occasional poignant moment of nostalgia – a delight from start to finish, and very expertly played by Jack Gibbons and the New London Orchestra under Ronald Corp. They also convey the Satie-like circus-music character of *Le bœuf sur le toit* to excellent effect. What delightful music this is, and so expertly fashioned by this lovable composer. The Molière pastiche and the arrangement of melodies from *The Beggar's Opera* are not top-drawer Milhaud, but they are still worth having. Very good recording from the Hyperion team.

(i) *Ballade, Op. 61; Le carnaval d'Aix, Op. 83b* (both for piano and orchestra); *Piano concertos Nos. 1, Op. 127; 4, Op. 295; 5 Etudes for piano and orchestra, Op. 61;* (ii) *Le bœuf sur le toit, Op. 58;* (ii–iii) *Harp concerto, Op. 323;* (ii) *La création du monde, Op. 81.*

(B) *** Erato/Warner Ultima Double Dig. 3984 21347-2 (2) [(M) id. import]. (i) Claude Helffer, O. Nat. de France, David Robertson; (ii) Lyon Op. O, Nagano; (iii) with Frédérick Cambreling.

This admirable Erato Ultima Double combines two highly recommendable collections from the early 1990s and includes a great deal of Milhaud's most attractive music, very well recorded. Claude Helffer's account of Milhaud's delightful *Le carnaval d'Aix* with the Orchestre National must rank high in terms of easy-going charm and Mediterranean atmosphere. All the pieces on this disc, incidentally, are for piano and orchestra. The *Ballade* was composed for Roussel, and Milhaud made his piano début at its première in New York: its languorous opening seems to hark back to his days in Brazil. The first of the *Cinq Etudes* shows Milhaud in window-breaking, polytonal mode, as does the third. The *First Piano concerto* is a relaxed, charming work not dissimilar to, though more complex in texture than, Jean Françaix's well-known *Concertino*. The *Fourth Piano concerto*, Op. 295 (1949), is an inventive piece of some substance with a particularly imaginative, dream-like slow movement.

Kent Nagano and the Orchestra of the Opéra de Lyon give a splendid account of themselves in both the ballets. In *La création* the playing is full of character (the jazz fugue comes off marvellously). The 1953 *Harp concerto* was written in America for Nicanor Zabaleta. It is not top-drawer Milhaud; there is more activity than substance for much of the time, but the slow movement has many beautiful things and Cambreling makes out a very good case for the high-spirited finale.

Le bœuf sur le toit.

(M) *** Mercury (IMS) 434 335-2 [id.]. LSO, Dorati – AURIC: *Overture;* FETLER: *Contrasts;* FRANCAIX: *Piano concertino;* SATIE: *Parade.* ***

Dorati's reading, effervescent and light-hearted, catches the idiom splendidly and the music's lilt is infectiously conveyed. The LSO are obviously enjoying themselves and their playing, subtle as well as vivid, catches the audacious mood of a piece which is a trifle long for its content but which still entertains. The (1965) Mercury recording is perfectly judged, giving the music both transparency, vibrant colour and its proper edge.

Le bœuf sur le toit, Op. 58; La création du monde, Op. 81.

*** Chandos Dig. CHAN 9023 [id.]. Ulster O, Yan Pascal Tortelier – IBERT: *Divertissement;* POULENC: *Les Biches.* ***

A most engaging account of *Le bœuf sur le toit* from Tortelier and his Ulster players, full of colourful detail, admirably flexible, and infectiously rhythmic. Perhaps *La création du monde* is without the degree of plangent jazzy emphasis of a French performance, but its gentle, desperate melancholy is well caught, and the playing has plenty of colour and does not lack rhythmic subtlety. The Chandos recording, although resonant, is splendid in every other respect, and so are the couplings.

(i) *Le bœuf sur le toit;* (ii) *La création du monde;* (iii) *Saudades do Brasil; Suite provençale;* (iv) *Scaramouche* (for 2 pianos).

(***) EMI (SIS) mono/stereo CDC7 54604-2. (i) Champs-Elysées Theatre O; (ii) Ens. of 19 soloists; (iii) Concert Arts O, composer; (iv) Marcel Meyer, composer.

Milhaud's own account of *La création du monde*

has a certain want of abandon but is otherwise well played, and this *Scaramouche* has an altogether special charm. Older collectors will recall the Capitol mono LP coupling of the captivating *Suite provençale* and the carefree and catchy *Saudades do Brasil*, which now appears for the first time in stereo sounding very sprightly indeed. The Hollywood players who comprised the 'Concert Arts' orchestra respond to the composer with evident delight, and they make this a most desirable issue. In addition there is *Le bœuf sur le toit* that Milhaud made with a Champs-Elysées orchestra in 1958 which will be new to most collectors and which makes a welcome makeweight to an altogether delightful (and, for lovers of this composer, indispensable) issue. However, it was curmudgeonly of EMI to put the disc in the full-price range.

La création du monde.
(M) *** EMI (SIS) CDM7 63945-2. Paris Conservatoire O, Prêtre – DUTILLEUX: *Le Loup;* POULENC: *Les Biches.* ***
(M) *** Virgin/EMI Dig. CUV5 61206-2. Lausanne CO, Zedda – DEBUSSY: *Danse; Sarabande;* PROKOFIEV: *Sinfonietta.* ***

Prêtre's recording of *La création du monde* is unsurpassed in catching both the bitter-sweet sensuousness of the creation scene and the jazzy pastiche of the mating dance – the rhythmic touch is very much in the authentic spirit of 1920s French jazz. The 1961 sound has been transformed in the CD remastering: it is fresh and vivid, yet admirably atmospheric. The couplings are no less attractive.

La création comes off well in Alberto Zedda's highly spontaneous account and the vivid recording makes a bold dynamic contrast between the work's tender and abrasive moments.

Suite française.
(M) *** CDWHL 2067. L. Wind O, Wick – GRAINGER: *Irish tune from County Derry* etc.; POULENC: *Suite française.*

Milhaud's *Suite française* for wind is an enchanting piece, full of Mediterranean colour and vitality. It would be difficult to imagine a more idiomatic or spirited performance than this one, which has excellent blend and balance. Vivid recording.

Symphonies for chamber orchestra Nos. 1 (Le Printemps); 2 (Pastoral); 3 (Serenade); 5 (Dixtour d'instruments).
**(*) Koch Dig. 3-7067-2 [id.]. Sinfonia O of Chicago, Barry Faldner (with DEBUSSY: *Symphony in B min.;* GOUNOD: *Petite symphonie for winds* **).

Barry Faldner and his Chicago Sinfonia, drawn from principals and other winds of the Chicago Symphony, give expert accounts of four of the little symphonies Milhaud composed in the 1920s. It would have made better sense (as well as rendering them more competitive) to have recorded all six rather than offering Faldner's orchestral transcription of Debussy's 10-minute symphony. The performances of the Milhaud are very alert, characterful and polished – and very well recorded indeed. They give much pleasure.

Symphonies Nos. 1 (1939); *2* (1944); *Suite provençale.*
❁ *** DG (IMS) Dig. 435 437-2. Toulouse Capitole O, Michel Plasson.

The *Second Symphony* is richly imaginative, melodically inventive and rewarding. Sample the fourth movement, *Avec sérénité*, and you will see just how sunny, relaxed and easy-going this music is; try also the slow movement of the *First* for its powerful, nocturnal atmosphere. The Orchestre du Capitole de Toulouse and Michel Plasson play these melodious scores with total commitment and convey their pleasure in rediscovering this music. The recording is very natural with a refined tone and well-balanced perspective. The delightful *Suite provençale* is as good as a holiday in the south of France – and cheaper!

Symphonies Nos. 2, Op. 247; (i) *3 (Te Deum), Op. 271.*
(N) *** CPO Dig. CPO 999 540-2 [id.]. (i) Basel Theatre Ch.; Basel Radio SO, Alun Francis.

Milhaud's first two symphonies come from his wartime exile in the United States. The *First* was written for Chicago, and the *Second* (1944) in response to a commission from another great American orchestra, the Boston Symphony and Koussevitzky. The central slow movement conveys some of the grief of the war years but elsewhere (particularly in the captivating fourth movement), the carefree atmosphere that distinguishes Milhaud's music and its Mediterranean light are much in evidence. The *Third* (1946) was composed on his return to France in 1946 and commissioned by the French Radio (whose director-general was the composer Henry Barraud) to celebrate victory over the Nazis. Particularly effective is the atmospheric slow movement with its wordless chorus. Good performances and a natural and well-balanced recording that holds its own with rival versions.

Symphonies Nos. 7, Op. 344; 8 (Rhôdanienne), Op. 362; 9, Op. 380.
*** CPO Dig. CPO 999 166-2 [id.]. Basel RSO, Alun Francis.

The *Seventh* and *Ninth* are both three-movement. Alun Francis actually makes more sense of the slow movement of the *Seventh* than does Plasson, holding it together at an altogether more realistic tempo. It is a powerful and often searching movement, even if there is a fair amount of note-spinning in its companions. For that matter, so there is in the *Ninth*, though it begins splendidly with a short and lively

Modérément animé. If the *Eighth Symphony* is full of colour, the scoring is also open to the charge of being a bit too dense. The acoustic is drier than that of the Halle aux Grains in Toulouse, which is why the tempi are more taut and detail better defined. The Basel Radio Orchestra is a far from second-rate ensemble and in the *Seventh Symphony* hold up well against their French colleagues.

(i) *Symphony No. 8 (Rhôdanienne), Op. 362;* (i; ii) *Scaramouche for saxophone, Op. 165c;* (iii) *La Cheminée du Roi René, Op. 205;* (iv) *Organ preludes, Op. 231b/3, 7–8;* (v) *Cantique du Rhône, Op. 155.*
** Praga PR 250 013 [id.]. (i) Czech PO, Neumann, (ii) with Neidenbach-Rahbari; (iii) Mihule, Vaček, Hůlka, Uher, Svárovsky; (iv) Tvrzský; (v) Czech R. Mixed Ch., Kühn.

The 1966 performance of the *Eighth Symphony* (*Rhôdanienne*) is not superior to the composer's own on Erato, but the disc is well worth acquiring even if it involves duplication. The *Cantique du Rhône* for a cappella choir, a setting of words by Claudel in praise of the Rhône, composed in Aix in 1936, is a beautiful piece, well sung here by the Pavel Kühn Choir and, like *Scaramouche*, recorded in 1987. The saxophone version of *Scaramouche* is played with plenty of character and a certain artful charm by Sohre Neidenbach-Rahbari and the Czech Philharmonic and was recorded at a live performance. *La Cheminée du Roi René* for wind quintet has an abundant charm, much of which is conveyed in this 1979 studio performance.

(i; ii) *Symphony No. 10, Op. 382;* (i; iii) *Concertino d'hiver for trombone and strings, Op. 327;* (iv) *Music for Prague, Op. 415;* (i; v) *Hommage à Comenius, Op. 421.*
** Praga PR 250 012 [id.]. (i) Prague R.O; (ii) Košler; (iii) Pulec, cond. Krombholc; (iv) Czech PO, composer; (v) Zikmundová, Jindrák, Hrnčíř.

The *Concertino d'hiver* comes from the set of 'Four Seasons' that Milhaud composed over a period of two decades and subsequently linked together. Not as inventive as the pre-war *Concertino de printemps*, it is given a very good performance by Zdenek Pulec and the Prague Radio Orchestra under Jaroslav Krombholc (1976). The quality in the 1970 performance of the *Tenth Symphony* with Zdenek Košler conducting is sonically superior to Milhaud's own account on Koch. *Musique pour Prague* was commissioned for the Prague Spring Festival in 1966, and this performance under Milhaud's own baton sounds a little better than the Koch rival. The textures are occasionally thick and hyperactive, but on the whole it is more rewarding than the symphony itself. Also associated with Prague is the cantata for soprano and baritone Milhaud composed in honour of the Czech philosopher and bishop Comenius (1592–1670), a pioneer of universal education, which is new to the catalogue. This, like the symphony, is a studio performance from 1970, though the soprano, Eva Zikmundová, has a characteristic Slavonic vibrato.

CHAMBER MUSIC

Caprice, Op. 335a; Duo concertant, Op. 351; Petit concert, Op. 192; Le printemps, Op. 18; Violin sonata No. 2, Op. 40; Sonatine, Op. 100; Le voyageur sans bagage (suite) *Op. 157b.*
** Schwann Dig. 3-1310-2 [id.]. Trio Bellerive.

Very bright, up-front recording in the suite from the music to *Le voyageur sans bagage* (1936) for clarinet, violin and piano, though it is very well played. The sound is better in the *Violin sonata No. 2* and *Le printemps*, though the balance rather favours Robert Hairgrove's piano than Sandra Goldberg's violin. The pieces for clarinet and piano, the *Petit concert*, the *Sonatine*, Op. 100, and the two pieces from the mid-1950s (the *Caprice*, Op. 335a, and the *Duo concertant*, Op. 351) are played with spirit, but the close, unrelieved recording is a handicap.

Duo for 2 violins, Op. 243; (i) *Sonata for 2 violins and piano, Op. 15.*
(*) Hyperion Dig. CDA 66473 [id.]. Osostowicz, Kovacic, (i) Tomes – MARTINU: *Violin sonata* **(*); PROKOFIEV: *Violin sonata.* *

The *Sonata for two violins and piano* of 1914 is beautifully crafted and has a charming slow movement but is very slight. Not as slight, though, as the *Duo*, the first two movements of which were composed at a dinner party; the finale was written the following morning. Musically it is all rather like having *canapés* and *petits fours* and missing out the meal! Elegant performances from Krysia Osostowicz and Ernst Kovacic – and in the *Sonata* Susan Tomes.

Music for wind: *La Cheminée du Roi René, Op. 105; Divertissement en trois parties, Op. 399b; Pastorale, Op. 47; 2 Sketches, Op. 227b; Suite d'après Corrette, Op. 161b.*
(M) **(*) Chandos CHAN 6536 [id.]. Athena Ens., McNichol.

Though none of this is first-class Milhaud, it is still full of pleasing and attractive ideas, and the general air of easy-going, life-loving enjoyment is well conveyed by the alert playing of the Athena Ensemble. One's only quarrel is the somewhat close balance.

(i) *Oboe sonatina, Op. 337;* (ii) *Suite d'après Corette, Op. 161b;* (iii) *Violin sonata No. 1, Op. 240;* (iv) *4 Visages, Op. 238;* (v) *Organ pastorale, Op. 229;* (vi) *3 Chansons de Négresse,*

Op. 148b; (vii) *2 Poems by Blaise Cendrars, Op. 113.*
*** Praga PR 250 008 [id.].(i) Adamus, Bogunia; (ii) Hedba, Nechvatal, Zedník; (iii) Spelina, Friesl; (iv) Christ, Klánský; (v) Grubich; (vi) Fassbaender, Gage; (vii) Smíšený, Kühn Mixed Ch., Kühn.

All are live performances, made in Prague between 1981 and 1990, and are of decent to excellent quality. The two choral settings of poems by Blaise Cendrars are of striking quality and are very well sung by Pavel Kühn's choir. The *Trois Chansons de Négresse* hark back to Milhaud's years in Rio, and are sung with great character and charm by Brigitte Fassbaender. Wolfram Christ is the excellent soloist in the *Sonata No. 1*, based on eighteenth-century French tunes, and the *Quatre Visages* for viola and piano: this is a portrait of four ladies from California, Wisconsin, Brussels and Paris. Like Jean Françaix's *Cinq Portraits de jeunes filles* for piano, it has character and a winning charm. A valuable addition to the Milhaud discography.

String quartets Nos. 1, Op. 5; 2, Op. 16.
(B) *** Discover Dig. DICD 920290 [id.]. Arriaga Qt.

The *First Quartet* comes from 1912 and is dedicated to the memory of Milhaud's fellow-Provençal, Cézanne. It is among the most diatonic of all his works, and is unusual in having two slow movements, both of which find him at his most serene. There are occasional hints of the Debussy *Quartet* and even a faint shadow of Franck in the *Grave* movement. The *Second* was composed during the first of the war years (1914–15) at about the time Milhaud was embarking on that key work in his development, *Les Choéophores*, and there are signs of an emergent fascination with polytonality. The Arriaga Quartet are very persuasive and communicate their feeling for the music.

String quartets Nos. 1, Op. 5; 7 in B flat, Op. 87; 10, Op. 218; 16, Op. 303.
*** Cybella Dig. CY 804 [id.]. Aquitaine National Qt.

The *Seventh Quartet* speaks Milhaud's familiar, distinctive language; its four short movements are delightful, full of melody and colour. The *Tenth*, too, is attractive; the *Sixteenth* was a wedding anniversary present for his wife: its first movement has great tenderness and warmth. The Aquitaine Quartet has excellent ensemble, intonation is good and their playing is polished. The recording has a wide dynamic range and a spacious tonal spectrum.

String quartets Nos. 5, Op. 64; 8, Op. 121; 11, Op. 232; 13, Op. 268.
*** Cybella Dig. CY 805 [id.]. Aquitaine National Qt.

The *Fifth Quartet* is not one of Milhaud's most inspired; the *Eighth*, on the other hand, has much to commend it, including a poignant slow movement. No. 11 has a splendid pastoral third movement and a lively jazzy finale; No. 13 has overtones of Mexico in its finale and a beguiling and charming *Barcarolle*. Both performance and recording are very good.

PIANO MUSIC

Music for 2 pianos: *Le bal Martiniquais, Op. 249; Le bœuf sur le toit, Op. 58a; Carnaval à la Nouvelle-Orléans, Op. 275; Kentuckiana, Op. 287; La libertadora, Op. 236; Scaramouche, Op. 165b; Songes, Op. 237.*
(N) *** Hyperion Dig. CDA 67014 [id.]. Stephen Coombs, Artur Pizarro.

Hyperion assemble the bulk of Milhaud's music for two pianos from the popular and irresistible *Scaramouche* through to the duet arrangement of *Le bœuf sur le toit*. An entertaining and delightful issue which brings some high-spirited pianism from these fine players and very good recorded sound.

Piano sonata No. 1; L'automne; Printemps, Books 1 & 2; 4 Sketches (Esquisses); Sonatine.
(B) ** Discover Dig. DICD 920 167 [id.]. Billi Eidi.

Milhaud was a capable pianist. Here is a good cross-section of his output covering four decades from the *Première Sonate* to the *Sonatine*. Some of the music, such as the first book of *Printemps* or the *Quatre Esquisses*, is charming; none of it makes great demands on either the pianist or the listener, and some of it is pretty inconsequential. All the same, there is much that gives pleasure – and would give more if the recording were not quite so bottom-heavy or wanting in transparency. Billi Eidi's playing is fluent, sensitive and totally committed.

VOCAL MUSIC

Les Choéphores, Op. 24.
*** Sony MHK 62352 [id.]. Vera Zorina (narr.), McHenry Boatwright, Irene Jordan, Virginia Babikian, NY Schola Cantorum, NYPO, Bernstein (with HONEGGER: *Rugby, Pacific 231* **) – ROUSSEL: *Symphony No. 3.* **(*)
(M) (**) DG Originals mono 449 748-2 [id.]. Geneviève Moizan, Hélène Bouvier, Heinz Rehfuss, Claude Nollier, Chorale de L'Université, Lamoureux O, Igor Markevitch – HONEGGER: *Symphony No. 5* (**); ROUSSEL: *Bacchus et Ariane: Suite No. 2.* **

Les Choéphores is the second part of Milhaud's setting of Paul Claudel's translation of the *Oresteia* of Aeschylus. It was composed in 1915 at the height of the First World War and comprises seven scenes which cover the same events as are depicted in Strauss's *Elektra*. Milhaud scores the work for large forces, including a spoken role – effectively declaimed on Sony by Vera Zorina – plus soloists, chorus and orchestra. It marked a bold and radical departure in Milhaud's style, making use of polytonality, choral speech and arresting dramatic effects. Bernstein's 1961 performance never appeared on this side of the Atlantic on LP, though the Honegger and Roussel items did. The performance is thrilling and the recording sounds excellent for the period. This is an important issue, much enhanced by the interest of the Roussel coupling and the excellence of the presentation.

Markevitch's 1957 recording has a lot going for it. The performance is strongly characterized, though less virtuosic than Leonard Bernstein's vivid stereo account, made in New York four years later. The mono recording is well balanced with plenty of front-to-back depth and good perspective, though it has the inevitable tonal frailty one might expect after 40 years. The soloists are generally good, but Bernstein scores with the superiority of the orchestral playing and the choral singing.

Minkus, Léon (1826–1917)

La Bayadère (complete; arr. Lanchbery).
*** Decca Dig. 436 917-2 (2). ECO, Richard Bonynge.

Lanchbery has provided the present score, and though officially he is responsible for the orchestration, who knows, perhaps he had a hand in its content, as in his vintage arrangement of Hérold's *La fille mal gardée*. Whatever the case, the result is highly engaging. Unlike Adam's rather disappointing *Le Corsaire* (also recorded by the same forces), this work is full of attractive melody and sparkling orchestral effects. If you like late-nineteenth-century ballet music, then here is nearly two hours of it, played with much vivacity, elegance and drama, and given Decca's top-quality sound.

Moeran, Ernest J. (1894–1950)

(i) *Cello concerto;* (ii–iii) *Violin concerto;* (iii) *2 Pieces for small orchestra: Lonely waters; Whythorne's shadow.*
(M) *** Chandos Enchant Dig. CHAN 7078 [id.]. (i) Raphael Wallfisch, Bournemouth Sinf., Del Mar; (ii) Lydia Mordkovitch; (iii) Ulster O, Handley.

The *Cello concerto* (1945) is a pastoral work with elegiac overtones, save in its rather folksy finale. Raphael Wallfisch brings an eloquence of tone and a masterly technical address to this neglected piece, and he receives very responsive orchestral support from Norman Del Mar and the Bournemouth players. The *Violin concerto* is also strongly lyrical in feeling. The first movement is thoughtful and rhapsodic, its inspiration drawn from Moeran's love of the west coast of Ireland; the middle movement makes use of folk music; while the finale, a ruminative elegy of great beauty, is the most haunting of the three. Lydia Mordkovitch plays with great natural feeling for this music and, quite apart from his sensitive support in the *Concerto*, Vernon Handley gives an outstanding account of *Lonely waters*. Superb recording. This is one of the most attractive and generous (78 minutes) reissues on Chandos's new mid-priced label, Enchant, with the sobriquet here entirely appropriate.

Serenade in G (complete original score); (i) *Nocturne*.
*** Chandos Dig. CHAN 8808 [id.]. Ulster O, Vernon Handley, (i) with Mackey, Renaissance Singers – WARLOCK: *Capriol suite* etc. ***

The *Serenade in G* is a welcome addition to the catalogue, a work which has a good deal in common with Warlock's *Capriol suite* in its orchestral dress. Both use dance forms from a previous age and transform them with new colours and harmonic touches. Handley and the Ulster Orchestra present it with striking freshness and warmth in its original version. The *Nocturne*, a setting of a poem by Robert Nichols for baritone and eight-part chorus, much admired by Britten receives a wholly sympathetic performance and recording here, and the resonant acoustics of the Ulster Hall, Belfast, provide a warmly atmospheric ambient glow.

Symphony in G min.
✿ (M) *** Dutton Laboratories mono CDAX 8001 [id. full price]. Hallé O, Leslie Heward – IRELAND: *Piano concerto*. (***)

There is always something special about first recordings, but this is remarkable in more than one respect. First, it is a wonderful performance of a great British symphony. Secondly, it celebrates a great British conductor, working at white-hot intensity, who died just over a year after the original 78s appeared. Walter Legge produced the sessions in Manchester's Houldsworth Hall, and his mono sound-balance was completely natural, using the slightly dry hall acoustics to maximum advantage. Finally, no praise can be too great for Michael Dutton's CD transfer, made direct from the 78-r.p.m. shellac pressings, using the Cedar system to suppress the surface noise, yet providing sound for which no apologies whatsoever need be made, with no edginess to ruin the strings: the violins sound particularly fresh. The composer was present at the sessions and gave his imprimatur. This CD is fully worthy of it. The Ireland coupling is hardly less indispensable.

Symphony in G min.; (i) *Rhapsody for piano and orchestra in F sharp*.
(N) *** Chandos Dig. CHAN 7106 [id.]. (i) Fingerhut; Ulster O, Handley.

Moeran's superb *Symphony in G minor* is in the best English tradition of symphonic writing and worthy to rank with the symphonies of Vaughan Williams and Walton. But for all the echoes of these composers (and Holst and Butterworth, too) it has a strong individual voice. Vernon Handley gives a bitingly powerful performance, helped by superb playing from the Ulster Orchestra, totally committed from first to last. The *Rhapsody* (written for Harriet Cohen and first heard at a 1943 Promenade concert) is obviously more lightweight than the symphony, but is by no means insubstantial. Using three themes, the piece is melodically attractive (with a folksy touch) and well integrated. It is splendidly played here (Margaret Fingerhut a brilliantly spontaneous soloist) and throughout the disc the Chandos recording is superb.

Fantasy quartet for oboe and strings.
*** Chandos Dig. CHAN 8392 [id.]. Francis, English Qt – BAX: *Quintet;* HOLST: *Air and variations* etc.; JACOB: *Quartet*. ***

Moeran's folk-influenced *Fantasy quartet*, an attractively rhapsodic single-movement work, is played admirably here, and the recording is excellent, well balanced too.

String quartets Nos. 1 in E flat; 2 in A min.; String trio.
(BB) *** Naxos 8.554079 [id.]. Maggini Qt.

Moeran's chamber music has been seriously neglected on disc, and this delightful issue could not be more welcome. The *String quartet in A minor* (1921) has a certain pastoral quality, with Irish echoes in the dance rhythms and ending on a flamboyant Rondo. The *String trio* of 1931, beautifully written with no feeling of thinness, is even subtler, with the pastoral idiom more equivocal in its tonal shiftings. The CD also offers something of a discovery in the form of an earlier *Quartet in E flat* that the cellist Peer Coetmore (Moeran's widow) found among the composer's papers after his death. Moeran apparently lost faith in the piece and suppressed it. Although it is not a masterpiece, there are some quite inspired things in it and the Maggini play throughout with great dedication and commitment. The recording is very lifelike and present. A first-class bargain.

(i) *String quartet in A min.;* (ii) *Violin sonata in E min*.
*** Chandos Dig. CHAN 8465 [id.]. (i) Melbourne Qt; (ii) Donald Scotts, John Talbot.

There is a strong folksong element in the *Quartet*, and some French influence too; these pieces are stronger than they have been given credit for. Good performances and recording.

Molino, Francesco (1775–1847)

Trio, Op. 45.
*** Mer. Dig. CDE 84199 [id.]. Conway, Silverthorne, Garcia – BEETHOVEN: *Serenade;* JOSEPH KREUTZER: *Grand Trio*. ***

Italian-born, Molino first settled in Spain, before going on to London and Paris, where he built a reputation as a violinist and guitarist. Undemanding music to complete a charming disc for a rare combination. First-rate playing and recording.

Mompou, Federico (1893–1987)

Escenas infantiles (orch. Tansman); *Suburbis* (orch. Rosenthal); (i) *Combat del Sueño;* (ii) *Los Improperios*.
*** HM Dig. HMC 901482 [id.]. O of Cambra Theatre, Lliure, Josep Pons, with (i; ii) Virginia Parramon; (ii) Jerzy Artysz, Valencia Ch.

The two orchestral works were scored by other hands, but the writing itself has much charm and the pastel-shaded colouring is inherent in the music itself. Not surprisingly, the flavour and impressionistic influences are both Spanish and French, with whiffs of Ravel and the Debussy of *Ibéria*. The oratorio, *Los Improperios*, is much more ambitious and – although there are reminders of Poulenc and even of Delius – the music has an individual voice, both orchestrally and in its serene, gleaming choral writing. *Combat del Sueño* is a triptych of ardent yet poignant love songs – somewhat like Ravel's *Shéhérazade* – combining memorable melodic lines with spare and delicate orchestration. They are seductively sung here by Virginia Parramon. Jerzy Artysz joins her in the oratorio, and the excellent choral and orchestral contributions under the persuasive Josep Pons, plus warm yet vividly atmospheric recording, ensure a strong recommendation for this very rewarding collection. Mompou may be eclectic, but he is also very personable.

Suite compostellana (for guitar).
(M) *** RCA Dig. 09026 61596-2 [id.]. Julian Bream (with RECITAL: *'Twentieth-century guitar'* ***).

Mompou's *Suite compostellana* is his only work for guitar – and very fine it is, beautifully written for the instrument and with a prevailing mood of wistful melancholy. Bream's performance is wonderfully sympathetic and spontaneous and the digital recording is first class.

Cancións y danzas Nos. 1, 3, 5, 7, 8–9; Cants magics; Charmes; Dialogues Nos. I–II; Paisajes;

Preludios Nos. 1, 5 (Palmier d'étoiles), 6 (for the left hand), 7, 9–10; 3 Variations.

(N) ❁ *** Hyperion Dig. CDA 66963 [id.]. Stephen Hough.

This exceptionally generous (77 minute) and wide-ranging *Gramophone*-Award-winning recital makes an obvious first choice for those wanting to explore, on a single CD, the fullest possible range of Mompou's piano music. Stephen Hough, who provides the illuminating notes, imaginatively describes this as 'the music of evaporation . . . There is no development of material, little counterpoint, no drama or climaxes to speak of; and this simplicity of expression – elusive, evasive and shy – is strangely disarming.' Hough frames and integrates his collection with six of the *Preludios* and six of the *Cancións y danzas* (which together span the years between 1921 and 1979), and includes also the *Cants magics*, Mompou's first published work, then follows with the *Charmes* (1920/1), *Variations* (1921), *Dialogues* (1923) and the visionary *Paisajes* (Landscapes), written between 1942 and 1960. He is completely inside Mompou's fastidious, Satie-esque sound world and understands the absorbed influences which make this music as much French as Spanish. The recording too is excellent if a little reverberant.

Not even Mompou himself equalled, let alone surpassed Hough in this repertoire. Of course he conveyed their rhapsodic character, tranquillity and inwardness with distinction, but Hough possesses a technique and imagination which enables him to realize their withdrawn yet intense world to perfection. Here is a pianist whose concentration of mood and mastery of the subtleties of keyboard colour and dynamic nuance is second to none.

Cancións y danzas Nos. 1–12, 14; Charmes; Scènes d'enfants.

(N) (BB) *** Naxos Dig. 8.554332 [id.]. Jordi Masó.

In many ways Jordi Masó's excellent Naxos collection is not upstaged by the competition. Moreover this is to be the first of a continuing series. He gives us the complete *Cancións y danzas* (except for No. 13 which is for guitar), plus the engagingly diverse, but at times almost mystical *Charmes*, and his playing is imbued with gentle poetic feeling. Masó's pianistic sensibility is never self-aware, always at the service of the composer, and the music's soft-hued colours are perceptively graduated. The unostentatious innocence of the *Scènes d'enfants* is beautifully caught. Excellent recording makes this a disc to recommend even if it cost far more than it does.

Cancións y danzas Nos. 1–12. 14; Impresiones intimas.

(N) ** Collins Dig. 1515-2 [id.]. Artur Pizarro.

Artur Pizzaro's recital for Collins differs in detail from the Hyperion collection. He offers very good playing but he is far less inward and imaginative than Hough. His command of the dynamic nuances between *pianopianissimo* and *pppp,* not to mention keyboard colour, does not really match the Hyperion disc.

7 Cancións y danzas; Impresiones intimas; Música callada; Preludio a Alicia de Larrocha.

(N) (B) *** Decca Double Analogue/Dig. 433 929-2 (2) [id.]. Alicia de Larrocha – '*Música española*' (Recital). ***

This is for the most part gentle, reflective music and its quiet ruminative quality finds an eloquent exponent in Alicia de Larrocha, to whom Mompou dedicated one of his preludes. The *Impresiones intimas* date from 1911–14 and is the composer's first work of note. Like Falla and Turina, Mompou was drawn to Paris, and these pieces have absorbed some of the delicacy of Debussy in their poetic feeling, fine detail and well-calculated proportions. Alicia de Larrocha plays these poetic miniatures *con amore*, and the Decca recording is superbly real. This is reissued economically as part of a Decca Double linked to a generous and stimulating recital of music by Mompou's Spanish contemporaries.

14 Cançons i dansas; Preludes Nos. 5; 6 (for the left hand); 7 (Fireworks).

*** RCA Dig. 09026 62554-2 [id.]. Alicia de Larrocha.

Alicia de Larrocha has previously recorded a group of the *Cançons i dansas* for Decca as part of a recital of '*Musica española*' (see below). Now she offers the whole set and is given first-class, modern, digital recording. The sense of repose in No. 5, the delicate loveliness of No. 7 and the wistful charm of No. 11 are characteristic of the intimacy of feeling of this playing. The performances have much warmth and grace. The present recital also includes four *Preludes*, of which No. 11 is aptly dedicated to the pianist.

8 Cancións y danzas; Escenas de niños; Fiestas lejanas; Paisajes; Pessebres; Suburbis.

(M) *** EMI (SIS) CDM7 64470-2. Gonzalo Soriano or Carmen Bravo.

Gonzalo Soriano plays these reflective miniatures simply and with the right degree of restrained eloquence. Carmen Bravo also finds poetry in the rest of the programme and is charmingly perceptive in his portrayal – in *Suburbis* – of *L'home de l'aristo* (the *aristo* was a cross between a hand-held miniature barrel-organ and a hurdy-gurdy). A rewarding and generous recital, given remarkably good recording, even though it dates from the early days of stereo.

Jeunes filles au jardin; El carrer, el guitarrista i el vell cavall; Cancións y danzas Nos. 5, 6 & 8; La fuente y la compaña.

(M) (***) EMI mono CDC7 54836-2 [id.]. (i) Composer – FALLA: *Harpsichord concerto* etc.; GRANADOS: *Danzas españolas* etc.; NIN: *Cantos populares españolas*. (***)

One of the most valuable of the marvellously documented and beautifully restored 'Composers in Person' CDs that EMI have recently published. Federico Mompou was the most long-lived of the Spanish composers recorded on this disc. He remains the most intimate and the most intensely private of Spanish composers. He recorded these six pieces while in London in 1950, though unaccountably they were never published until 1983. They are slight but beautiful and enhance what is a highly interesting disc.

Mondonville, Jean-Joseph Cassanéa de (1711–72)

6 Sonates en Symphonies, Op. 3.
*** DG Dig. 457 600-2 [id.]. Les Musiciens du Louvre, Minkowski.

This entirely captivating set of *Symphonies* confirms Mondonville as a great deal more than a historical figure. They originated as sonatas for violin and obbligato harpsichord in 1734, but the composer later skilfully orchestrated them. Each is in three movements, with an expressively tuneful centrepiece framed by sprightly allegros. Their invention is consistently fresh, and they are played here with great élan and spontaneity, and are beautifully recorded. Highly recommended.

Pièces de clavecin avec voix ou violon, Op. 5/1-8.
(B) *** HM Musique d'abord HMA 1901045 [id.]. Judith Nelson, Stanley Ritchie, William Christie.

Mondonville is credited with developing the harpsichord sonata with obbligato violin, which he called *Pièces de clavecin en sonates* (Op. 3). But Mondonville experimented too with the voice as a chamber-music instrument alongside a stringed instrument. In his *Pièces de clavecin avec voix ou violon* the music was composed independently of any text. The composer then fitted religious Latin texts to the musical line. What is striking is how naturally vocal the music sounds. The fine balance and expert playing of Stanley Ritchie and William Christie's sensitive harpsichord contribution add much to this presentation. But the greater part of the credit must go to the lovely singing of Judith Nelson, whose many shakes and turns are a pleasure in themselves. The sequential lines of Mondonville's writing are followed most sensitively. Altogether an outstanding disc, and very well recorded.

Titon et L'Aurore (complete).
*** Erato/Warner Dig. 2292 45715-2 (2). Fouchécourt, Napoli, Huttenlocher, Smith, Monoyios, Les Musiciens du Louvre, Minkowski.

Described as a 'heroic-pastoral', *Titon et L'Aurore* tells of the mortal Titon who has the temerity to fall in love with Aurora, goddess of the dawn. Some of the instrumental effects are most vivid and the work is full of charming ideas, presented with freshness and vigour. Marc Minkowski proves an ideal interpreter, directing a performance of the highest voltage, which yet allows the singers a full range of expressiveness. Jean-Paul Fouchécourt proves an outstanding example of the French *haute-contre*, sustaining stratospheric lines with elegance and no strain. Catherine Napoli is bright and clear, if shallow at times as Aurore, while Anne Monoyios sings with ideal sweetness as L'Amour.

Montemezzi, Italo (1875–1952)

L'amore dei tre re (complete).
(M) **(*) RCA 74321 50166-2 (2). Moffo, Domingo, Elvira, Siepi, Ryland Davies, Amb. Op. Ch., LSO, Nello Santi.

In 1913 at La Scala, Milan, Italo Montemezzi, one of Puccini's young successors, delivered this lurid melodrama based on a play by Sem Benelli. Set in a medieval palace ruled over by a blind king, Archibaldo, the obvious dramatic echoes of *Tristan* and *Pelleas*, combined with a red-blooded, lyrical score, brought it success not just in Italy, but more significantly in the United States, where Toscanini conducted the opera at the Met. in 1914. What it lacks, compared to Puccini – let alone to Wagner or Debussy – are memorable ideas. The melodic fragments rarely adding up to a genuine tune, and with no sustained set numbers to punctuate the free-flowing progress of the music. Nevertheless, with colourful scoring and an economical structure it makes easy listening. Even by operatic standards the plot is absurd: the heroine, Fiora, on refusing to disclose the name of her lover to the blind king, is promptly strangled by him. After that, in the final Act Archibaldo smears Fiora's lips with deadly poison, catching in turn not only the returning lover, Avito, but his own son, the heroine's husband, Manfredo, who consciously sacrifices himself by pressing his lips to those of the corpse.

This 1977 recording with Nello Santi a thrustful conductor makes as good a case for the piece as one is likely to get. Anna Moffo is an old-sounding if dramatic Fiora, but Plácido Domingo is in glowing form as Avito, and Cesare Siepi vividly heightens the melodrama as Archibaldo. As Manfredo, the baritone, Pablo Elvira, sings with firm, clean attack, as does Ryland Davies in the role of the castle guard, Flaminio. Full, warm, well-balanced sound. Synopsis and libretto with translation are provided but no background information on the work or the composer.

Monteverdi, Claudio (1567–1643)

Madrigals, Book I (complete); *Book 7: Tempro la cetra; Tirsi e Clori.*
(M) *** Virgin Veritas/EMI (SIS) VC5 45143-2. Consort of Musick, Anthony Rooley.

At the time of this first collection of madrigals Monteverdi was just nineteen years of age and already beginning to explore a world which he was to make very much his own. Two-thirds of his chosen texts here are concerned with love's disappointments, the words full of torments and aching hearts, which gives him plenty of opportunity for expressive colour. Though these early madrigals are usually brief and without the sharp poignancy of later examples (it was not until the Third Book that his originality began to make itself felt to the full) there is much here that is imaginative and there is consistent lyrical beauty. The simple presentation, with good tuning and fine blending, seems just right for this repertoire. Rooley ends his programme with two rather more ambitious pieces from Book VII, with instrumental accompaniment – the engaging introductory sonnet, where the poet tunes his lyre and finds it will respond only to themes of love, and the charming pastoral ballet, *Tirsi e Clori*, written for the Mantua Court, about the joy of requited love and faithfulness. With good soloists, the performances readily capture the music's happiness. The recording is first class.

Madrigals, Book 2 (complete).
*** Opus 111 Dig. OPS 30-111 [id.]. Concerto Italiano, Rinaldo Alessandro.
(M) *** Virgin Veritas/EMI (SIS) Dig. VC7 59282-2. Cons. of Musicke, Rooley.

Rinaldo Alessandro and his superb Concerto Italiano are singing their sunny Italianate way through Monteverdi's complete madrigal sequence. Apart from being of Italian birth, all the performers here have studied early Italian and therefore bring a special idiomatic feeling to the words. The Second Book, about half of whose five-part settings are from Tasso, demands and receives a simpler style of presentation than the later works, and there is radiant freshness about the singing here which is particularly appealing. The recording has the most pleasing acoustic.

It is good that Rooley too is turning to the earlier Books of the Monteverdi madrigals, including the very effective Tasso settings. Much of this music is simpler in its appeal and imagery than the later writing, but it all comes to life with great freshness here. Immaculate recording.

Madrigals, Book 3 (complete).
(M) *** Virgin Veritas/EMI (SIS) Dig. VC7 59283-2. Cons. of Musicke, Rooley.

This is a livelier, more vibrant collection than Book 2, and Rooley and his group respond accordingly. A most stimulating concert.

Madrigals, Books 3 & 4 (for 5 voices); *Book 7; Book 8 (Madrigali guerrieri et amorosi;* includes: *Il ballo delle ingrate; Il combattimento di Tancredi e Clorinda*); *Book 9 (Scherzi musicali).*
(N) (B) **(*)Ph. 462 243-2 (8). Armstrong, Burrowes, Harper, Howells, Watson, Hodgson, Kern, Collins, Watts, Alva, Ryland Davies, Oliver, Tear, Wakefield, Partridge, Luxon, Dean, Lloyd, John Alldis Ch., Glyndebourne Op. Ch. & Ambrosian S. (members), ECO, Leppard.

Beginning in 1969 (and continuing through the early 1970s) Philips inaugurated a project, directed by Raymond Leppard, to make the first complete recording of Monteverdi's enormous total output of madrigals, but the enterprise foundered, bypassed by recording history as more authentic styles of performance arrived. *Book 8* was the first to be recorded and it got the venture off to a splendid start. With his star-studded cast, Leppard ensured that there was nothing earnest or pedestrian about the results. The warmth and richness, not only of the opening Sinfonia, but also of the pair of magnificent six-part choruses which open each set (both *guerrieri* and *amorosi*) may seem a little opulent to today's ears but here, as elsewhere, Leppard is demonstrating the enormous variety of expression of the composer's three described musical styles, *concitato, temperato*, and *molle*, and the string accompaniments on modern instruments sound very much in place. *Book 8* also includes the longer stage works – almost concise operas – *Il ballo delle ingrate* and *Il combattimento di Tancredi e Clorinda* both vividly sung.

Books 3 and *4* followed. These earlier madrigals (*Book 3* was published in 1592, *Book 4* in 1603) show the transition from Monteverdi's early mastery in the accepted genre to the full flowering of his individual originality in *Book 4*, where he chooses to set poems much more overtly emotional. However, with choral madrigals limited here to a handful in *Book 4*, there is not the same variety as in *Books 8–10* and this proved a stumbling block for Leppard and his forces. Though the style and direction are as captivating as ever, at least one of the soloists is fallible in ensembles of five voices which need meticulous tuning. The rest of the present set is given over to the *Scherzi musicali* in *Book 9*. Overall there is a great deal of fine music-making here and some stylish singing and playing. Raymond Leppard indulges his taste for excessive continuo ornamentation, and the sumptuous string tone in *Il ballo delle ingrate* jars a bit. But there is more to enjoy in this well-recorded series than there are grounds to cavil. The music is most rewarding and the performances are full of life and style.

Madrigals, Book 4 (complete).
*** Opus 111 Dig. OPS 30-81 [id.]. Concerto Italiano, Rinaldo Alessandro.

The Fourth Book, published in 1603 and again for five voices, marks an added richness of expressive feeling over Monteverdi's earlier settings, well recognized by Rinaldo Alessandro and his superbly blended vocal group. This series goes from strength to strength and can be strongly recommended. The recording continues to match the singing in excellence.

Madrigals, Books 4–5 (complete). *Book 7: Con che soavità, labbra odorate; Tempro la cetra. Book 8: (Madrigali guerrieri et amorosi): Mentre vaga; Ogni amante è guerrier.*
(B) *** O-L Dig. Double 455 718-2 (2) [id.]. Consort of Musicke, Anthony Rooley.

This Oiseau-Lyre Double offers exceptional value in including the whole of the contents of Book 4 (dating from 1603) and Book 5 (1605), plus four substantial accompanied madrigals which come from the composer's later, Venetian years. Under Anthony Rooley, the well-integrated singers of the Consort of Musicke, led by Emma Kirkby, give masterly performances of the fourth book, which suits their vocal style especially well. One has only to sample the moving and beautifully sung opening piece, *Ah dolente partita!*, to note the tonal beauty, flexibility and control of dramatic contrast. Book 5 marked a turning-point in Monteverdi's madrigal output, for the last six works bring an obligatory continuo and are much freer in style than their predecessors, even semi-operatic in their use of freely individual vocal solos. It might be said that the change of style in the singing here is less marked than in the competing (full-priced) collection of these works by the Concerto Italiano directed by Rinaldo Alessandro, whose singing is distinctly Italianate and more extrovert. Nevertheless the comparatively restrained approach of Rooley's group brings its own rewards, and their refinement is reflected in the delicate lute continuo in the later numbers. The later madrigals are even more successful, their quixotic mood-changes superbly caught. All four are among Monteverdi's most imaginative dialogue settings, displaying much operatic feeling. *Tempro la cetra* ('I tune the lute') has a noble introductory instrumental ritornello, but the most ambitious, *Ogni amante è guerrier*, crowns the programme at the end of the second CD. The recording is excellent throughout and full translations are provided.

Madrigals, Book 5 (complete).
✿ *** Opus 111 Dig. OPS 30-166 [id.]. Concerto Italiano, Rinaldo Alessandro.

As we have noted Book 5 marks a turning-point in Monteverdi's madrigal output, for the last six works introduce continuo support and are very much freer in style, even semi-operatic in their use of freely individual vocal solos. The performances by this superb Italian vocal group, at one moment blending richly together, at another asserting solo individuality, cannot be too highly praised, and again they are beautifully recorded.

Madrigals, Book 6 (complete).
(M) *** Virgin Veritas/EMI Dig. VC7 59605-2. Consort of Musicke, Anthony Rooley.

Il sesto libro de madrigali (1614) includes the five-part transcription of the *Lamento d'Arianna* and *Zefiro torno*, and also pieces from Monteverdi's years at Mantua. The Consort of Musicke maintain the high standards of taste and artistry with which we associate them. Excellent recording.

Madrigals from Books 7 and 8: *Amor che deggio far; Altri canti di Marte; Chiome d'oro; Gira il nemico insidioso; Hor ch'el ciel e la terra; Non havea Febo ancora – Lamento della Ninfa; Perchè t'en fuggi o Fillide; Tirsi e Clori (ballo concertato for 5 voices and instruments).*
(B) *** HM HMA 1901068 [id.]. Les Arts Florissants, Christie.

The singing of this famous group is full of colour and feeling and, even if intonation is not absolutely flawless throughout, it is mostly excellent. Much to be preferred to the bloodless white tone favoured by some early-music groups. Good recording. A bargain.

Madrigals, Book 8: *Madrigali guerrieri et amorosi (Madrigals of war and love).*
(BB) **(*) Virgin Classics Dig. Double VBD5 61570-2 (2). Soloists, Consort of Muicke, Anthony Rooley.

Monteverdi published his Eighth Book after a long gap in his madrigal output. It is in two parts and one of the very greatest of his songs in the *Madrigali amorosi* is *Lamento della ninfa* in what Monteverdi called the *stile rappresentativo* or theatre style, and that is affectingly done here. The *Madrigali guerrieri* are also very theatrical and include *Il ballo delle ingrate* and *Il combattimento di Tancredi e Clorinda*, which are also available separately in other individual versions. The performances here are distinctive, and anyone collecting Rooley's series, should find this inexpensive Double well worth its modest cost. The cast list is strong, including Emma Kirkby and Evelyn Tubb, but Andrew King is the narrator in *Il combattimento* and his approach is less than robustly full-blooded, while in both works the performances under Pickett and Christie are more dramatically arresting (see below).

Madrigal collections

Madrigals and motets (collection)

Disc 1: Madrigals: *Addio Florida bella; Ahi com'a un vago sol; E così a poco a poco torno farfalla; Era l'anima mia; Luci serene e chiare; Mentre vaga Angioletta ogn'anima; Ninfa che scalza il piede; O mio bene, a mia vita; O Mirtillo, Mirtill'anima mia; Se pur destina; Taci, Armelin deh taci; T'amo mia vita; Troppo ben può questo tiranno amore.*

Disc 2: Madrigals: *Bel pastor dal cui bel guardo; Lamento d'Arianna; Non è gentil cor; O come sei gentile; Ohimé, dov'é il mio ben; Zefiro torna* (with Benedetto FERRARI: *Queste pungenti spine* (cantata); (attributed FERRARI): Final duet for MONTEVERDI: *L'Incoronazione di Poppea: Pur ti miro, pur ti godo*).

Disc 3: Motets for 1, 2 & 3 voices: *Confitebor tibi, Domine* (solo); *Duo seraphim* (a 3); *Ego flos campi* (solo); *Fugge, anima mea* (a 2); *Jubilet; Laudate Dominum; Nigra sum* (all three solos); *O beata viae* (a 2); *O quam pulchra es* (solo); *Pulchra es, amica mea* (a 2); *Salve, O Regina* (solo).

(B) **(*) HM Analogue Dig. HMX 290841/3 [id.]. Concerto Vocale, René Jacobs.

One of Harmonia Mundi's bargain 'trios', this Monteverdi programme is presented by the Concerto Vocale directed by René Jacobs, whose vocal artistry and virtuosity dominate many of the performances. It offers an admirable, inexpensive survey of Monteverdi's music, both his madrigals and his church music. The disc called *'Un concert spirituel'* is the highlight of the set and might have received a Rosette as an independent issue. It opens with the remarkable and beautiful *Duo seraphim* which juxtaposes overlapping long notes and rapid virtuoso diminutions, suggesting angels' wings as well as a celestial chorale. Both the solo *Confitebor tibi, Domine* and the duet *Fugge, anima mea* are in essence miniature cantatas, with complex duets followed by solos which additionally bring a violin obbligato. This was originally played by the soloist, who was expected to be an instrumentalist as well as a singer. *Pulchra es* is the first of Monteverdi's chamber duets, with the second voice entering unexpectedly to fill out the texture richly. The dramatically expressive *Nigra sum* soon becomes lyrically quite sensuous, especially at the decorated closing section, and *O quam pulchra es* is very like one of the composer's operatic laments, and very touching. Both are set to words from the Song of Songs. Their dolorous feeling is well caught by Jacobs, whose decoration is very convincing. The *Laudate Dominum* and *Jubilet* are sung delightfully by Judith Nelson. An outstanding concert, with imaginatively varied continuo accompaniments (including organ as well as harpsichord). They are recorded in an atmospheric acoustic, adding bloom to voices and instruments alike, without clouding detail.

The first madrigal collection is also available separately on a bargain Musique d'Abord CD (HMA 190184). It is a highly attractive collection of generally neglected items, briskly and stylishly performed, and, with continuo accompaniment, the contrasting of vocal timbres is achieved superbly. Again excellent recording.

The third programme offers more familiar repertoire including the famous *Lamento d'Arianna*. Jacobs allots the lead vocal role to Helga Müller-Molinari, whose general approach is too redolent of grand opera, while her opulent voice does not blend readily with the instrumental support. The interest of this disc is also increased by the inclusion of music by Benedetto Ferrari, a Venetian composer of the generation following Monteverdi, and also a playwright and theorbo player. He is best remembered for a handful of operas and his three books of *Musiche varie*. His *Queste pungenti spine* is a spiritual cantata which comes from the 1637 book and is accompanied on the CD by the final duet from *L'Incoronazione di Poppea*, which has been attributed to him by some scholars. Listening to the one, it is very difficult to believe he really did compose the other, for the Monteverdi madrigals are on a much higher level of inspiration. This collection is now also available separately in Harmonia Mundi's mid-price Suite series (HMT 7901129).

Madrigals: *Ab aeterno ordinata sum; Confitebor tibi, Domine* (3 settings); *Deus tuorum militum sors et corona; Iste confessor Domini sacratus; Laudate Dominum, O omnes gentes; La Maddalena: Prologue: Su le penne de venti. Nisi Dominus aedificaverit domum.*

✿ *** Hyperion Dig. CDA 66021 [id.]. Kirkby, Partridge, Thomas, Parley of Instruments.

There are few records of Monteverdi's solo vocal music as persuasive as this. The three totally contrasted settings of *Confitebor tibi* (Psalm 110) reveal an extraordinary range of expression, each one drawing out different aspects of word-meaning. Even the brief trio, *Deus tuorum militum*, has a haunting memorability – it could become to Monteverdi what *Jesu, joy of man's desiring* is to Bach – and the performances are outstanding, with the edge on Emma Kirkby's voice attractively presented in an aptly reverberant acoustic. The accompaniment makes a persuasive case for authentic performance on original instruments. The CD sounds superb.

Madrigals: *Alcun non mi consigli; Ardo e scoprir; Bel pastor; Eccomi pronta ai baci; Eri già tutta mia; Lamento d'Arianna; Lamento della Ninfa; Ohimè, ch'io cado; Tu dormi; Una donna fra l'altre.*

(N) (B) **(*) Sony Seon SBK 60707 [id.]. Marjanne Kweksilber, René Jacobs, Marius van Altena, Michiel ten Houte de Lange, Floris Rommerts, Gustav Leonhardt.

This is an exceptionally attractive selection of ten of Monteverdi's very finest madrigals, including the famous five-voiced setting of the operatic *Lamento d'Arianna* and the companion four-part *Lamento della Ninfa*, with its remarkable opening dissonances darkly blended, and Marjanne Kweksilber singing exquisitely in '*Amor*', the lament itself. She also joins delightfully with Marius van Altena in the engaging dialogue of *Bel pastor*. What is continually stimulating is the way all these distinguished soloists, each with an individual vocal personality, can match their timbres, when singing together (as with the two tenors, van Altena and Michiel ten Houte de Lange in *Ardo e scopir*), or in a group. René Jacobs is individually impressive in his two solos, *Ohimè ch'io cado*, and *Eri già tutta mia*. The balance with Gustav Leonhardt's harpsichord accompaniment is excellent, the recording is natural, and the only snag with an otherwise outstanding disc is the absence of translations, or any kind of guide to what the individual madrigals are about. The playing time is also short at 45 minutes, but the musical quality is very high.

Madrigals: *'Batto', qui pianse Ergasto; Gira, il nemico insidioso amore; Hor che'l ciel e la terra; O come sei gentile; Ogni amante è guerrir; Zefiro torna.*

❁ (M) *** Virgin Veritas/EMI (SIS) Dig. VER5 61165-2. Chiaroscuro, L. Baroque, Nigel Rogers – D'INDIA: *Madrigals*. *** ❁

A hand-picked half-dozen of Monteverdi's finest madrigals, superlatively sung, consistently bringing out the expressive originality and the extraordinary variety of the settings, to say nothing of their inherent vocal bravura. *Zefiro torna* is justly famous, but *'Batto', qui pianse Ergasto* is hardly less remarkable, and the two *Madrigali guerrieri et amorosi* are very telling indeed. The engagingly lyrical *O come sei gentile* follows immediately after the d'India dramatized cycle from *Il pastor Fido* and makes a fascinating comparison. Accompaniments are nicely balanced and the recording has an exceptionally real and vivid presence.

Madrigali erotici: Chiome d'oro; Come dolci hoggi l'auretta; Con che saovita; Mentre vaga Angioletta; Ogni amante e guerrier; Ohimè, dov'è il mio ben?; Parlo misero, o taccio; S'el vostro cor, Madonna; Tempro la cetra; Vorrei baciarti o Filli.

*** O-L (IMS) Dig. 421 480-2. Emma Kirkby, Nelson, Holden, Elliot, King, Thomas, Cons. of Musicke, Rooley.

Most of the madrigals on this CD come from the Seventh Book of 1619, very much a watershed in Monteverdi's output. In many instances they are for virtuoso singers and make a break with the past in that they call for instrumental accompaniment. The recording is excellently balanced. Strongly recommended.

Madrigals (Duets and solos): *Chiome d'oro, bel thesoro; Il son pur vezzosetta pastorella; Non è di gentil core; O come sei gentile, caro augellino; Ohimè dov'è il mio ben?; Se pur destina e vole il cielo, partenza amorosa.* Sacred music: *Cantate Domino; Exulta, filia Sion; Iste confessoe II; Laudate Dominum in sanctis eius; O bone Jesu, o piissime Jesu; Sancta Maria, succurre miseris; Venite, siccientes ad aquas Domini.* (Opera) *Il Ritorno d'Ulisse in patria: Di misera regina (Penelope's lament).*

(M) *** Carlton Dig. 30366 00442 [id.]. Emma Kirkby, Evelyn Tubb, Consort of Musicke, Rooley.

Admirers of Emma Kirkby will surely revel in this collection, mostly of duets in which she is joined by Evelyn Tubb. The two voices are admirably matched and both artists ornament their lines attractively and judiciously. Evelyn Tubb is given a solo opportunity in Penelope's lament from *Il ritorno d'Ulisse*, which she sings dramatically and touchingly. Anthony Rooley's simple accompaniments with members of the Consort of Musicke are also imaginatively stylish. We are pleased to report that the current reissue has been properly documented with notes and full translations.

Lamento d'Olympia; Maladetto sia l'aspetto; Ohimè ch'io cado; Quel sdengosetto; Voglio di vita uscia.

*** Hyperion CDA 66106 [id.]. Emma Kirkby, Anthony Rooley (chitarone) – D'INDIA: *Lamento d'Olympia* etc. ***

A well-planned recital from Hyperion contrasts the two settings of *Lamento d'Olympia* by Monteverdi and his younger contemporary, Sigismondo d'India. The performances by Emma Kirkby, sensitively supported by Anthony Rooley, could hardly be surpassed; this ranks among her best records.

Church Music

Motets: *Ego flos campi; Ego sum pastor bonus; Exulta, filia Sion; Fuge, fuge anima mea, mundum; Iusti tulerunt spolia; Lapidabant Stephanum; Lauda, Jerusalem; Laudate Dominum; Nigra sum; O bone Jesu, illumina oculos meos; O bone Jesu, O piissime Jesu; O quam pulchra es; Pulchra es; Salve Regina; Spuntava al dì; Sugens Jesus, Dominus noster; Surge propera, amica mea; Veni in hortum meum* (with PICCININI: *Toccata X*).

*** Virgin/EMI Dig. VC7 59602-2. Brigitte

Lesne, Gérard Lesne, Josep Benet, Josep Cabré, Il Seminario Musicale, Tragicomedia.

The music on this disc encompasses all periods of Monteverdi's career; the earliest comes from his first published collection, the *Sacrae Canticulicae* (1582) composed when he was only fifteen. Other pieces, such as the *Salve Regina*, come from the *Selva Morale* (1640), while *Pulchra es* and *Nigra sum* are performed on instruments alone. The solo motet *O quam pulchra es* is preceded by a *Toccata* by Alessandro Piccinini about which the excellent notes are silent. The performances here are expert and totally committed. Excellent recording.

Missa de cappella a 4; Missa de cappella a 6 (In illo tempore); Motets: *Cantate domino a 6; Domine ne in furore a 6.*

*** Hyperion Dig. CDA 66214 [id]. The Sixteen, Christophers; M. Phillips.

Harry Christophers draws superb singing from his brilliant choir, highly polished in ensemble but dramatic and deeply expressive too, suitably adapted for the different character of each Mass-setting, when the four-part Mass involves stricter, more consistent contrapuntal writing and the six-part, in what was then an advanced way, uses homophonic writing to underline key passages. Vivid, atmospheric recording.

Selva morale e spirituale: excerpts: *Adoramus; Beatus vir a 6 voci; Chi vol che m'innamori; Confitebor terzo alla francese; Confitebor tibi Domine; E questa vita un lampo; Gloria a 7 voci; Laudate Dominum; O ciechi ciechi.*

(N) *** HM Dig. HMC 901250 [id.]. Les Arts Florissants, William Christie.

Monteverdi's *Selva morale e spirituale* (1640) is a huge collection of nearly 40 separate works, written over three decades. Christie's programme here gives an idea of its range, from *Beatus vir*, the vivid large scale psalm-setting for six voices and violins, and the splendid seven-voiced *Gloria*, with its burst of vocal virtuosity at the opening, to the succinct *Adoramus te*, and the more modest *Laudate dominum* for bass voice with continuo. All the performances here are imbued with a flowing vitality, and combine breadth and devotional feeling with vocal and instrumental refinement. As usual from this source the recording is admirably clear and spacious.

Vespro della Beata Vergine (Vespers).

✿ *** DG Dig. 429 565-2 (2) [id.]. Monoyios, Pennicchi, Chance, Tucker, Robson, Naglia, Terfel, Miles, H. M. Sackbutts & Cornetts, Monteverdi Ch., London Oratory Ch., E. Bar. Soloists, Gardiner.

(M) *** Virgin Veritas/EMI Dig. VMD5 61347-2 (2). Kirkby, Nigel Rogers, Davis Thomas, Taverner Ch., Cons. & Players, Parrott.

(BB) *** Hyperion Dyad Dig. CDD 22028 (2) [id.]. The Sixteen, Harry Christophers.

(B) **(*) Teldec/Warner Ultima Dig. 0630 18955-2 (2) [2292 42671-2]. Margaret Marshall, Felicity Palmer, Philip Langridge, Kurt Equiluz, Thomas Hampson, Arthur Korn, Tölz Boys' Ch., Soloists from V. Hofbur Ch., Arnold Schœnberg Ch., VCM, Harnoncourt.

(M) **(*) Teldec/Warner 4509 92175-2 (2). Hansmann, Jacobeit, Rogers, Van t'Hoff, Van Egmond, Villisech, V. Boys' Ch. soloists, Hamburg Monteverdi Ch., Plainsong Schola of Munich Capella Antiqua, VCM, Jürgen Jürgens.

Gardiner's second recording of the *Vespers* vividly captures the spatial effects that a performance in the Basilica of St Mark's, Venice, made possible. Gardiner made his earlier recording for Decca in 1974 using modern instruments (see below). Here, with the English Baroque Soloists and a team of soloists less starry but more aptly scaled, all of them firm and clear, he directs a performance even more compellingly dramatic. It would be hard to better such young soloists as the counter-tenor Michael Chance, the tenor Mark Tucker and the bass Bryn Terfel. Without inflating the instrumental accompaniment – using six string-players only, plus elaborate continuo and six brass from His Majesties Sackbutts and Cornetts – he combines clarity and urgency with grandeur. Gardiner's version more than any other conveys the physical thrill which above all has established this long-neglected work as music for today, bringing it into the central repertory alongside the choral masterpieces of later centuries. Gardiner (as before) does not include plainchant antiphons, and so has room on the two discs for the superb alternative setting of the *Magnificat*, in six voices instead of seven, in another dedicated performance.

Though Andrew Parrott uses minimal forces, with generally one instrument and one voice per part, so putting the work on a chamber scale in a small church setting, its grandeur comes out superbly through its very intensity. Brilliant singing here by the virtuoso soloists, above all by Nigel Rogers, whose distinctive timbre may not suit every ear but who has an airy precision and flexibility to give expressive meaning to even the most taxing passages. Fine contributions too from Parrott's chosen groups of players and singers, and warm, atmospheric recording. At mid-price this is very competitive.

The Sixteen's version of Monteverdi's 1610 *Vespers* on Hyperion, beautifully scaled, presents a liturgical performance of what Graham Dixon suggests as Monteverdi's original conception. Dixon noted that this was one of the texts used in the Gonzaga family's traditional celebrations for their patron saint, St Barbara. He infers from this that Monteverdi's first idea was to be a work in her honour. In practice the occasional changes of text are minimal; the booklet accompanying the set even includes an order of tracks if anyone wishes to hear the *Vespers* in traditional form. As it is, with a liturgical approach, the performance includes not only relevant Gregorian chant but antiphon substitutes, including a magnificent motet of Palestrina, obviously relevant, *Gaude Barbara*. The scale of the performance is very satisfying, with The Sixteen augmented to 22 singers (7.4.6.5) and with members of the group taking the eight solo roles. Christophers provides a mean between John Eliot Gardiner's unashamedly grand view, with modern instruments and pitch, and Andrew Parrott's vital, scholarly re-creation of an intimate, princely devotion. This makes a clear first choice in the lower-priced category for those wanting a modern, digital recording, although Schneidt's fine DG Archiv set should certainly be considered (see below).

Harnoncourt's admirers may well be attracted to his 1986 recording, particularly as it is now available as an Ultima bargain Double. It was recorded live and gives a keen sense of occasion, with the grandeur of the piece linked to a consciously authentic approach. There is an entirely apt ruggedness in the interpretation, which is lightened by the characterful refinement of the solo singing from an exceptionally strong team of soloists, not to mention the fine singing from all three choirs. Ample, atmospheric recording.

Recorded in Vienna in 1966/67 the Jürgens set is scholarly yet not without warmth. The liturgical sequence is respectful, and authentic instruments are used. The continuo tends to be somewhat lightweight, but there is a sure sense of style. The opening chorus is vivid with the colour of renaissance trumpets and recorders, but the CD transfer cannot disguise a lack of sharpness of focus here and in the more complex analogue choral textures. At mid-price this is fair value, for the soloists are all fine artists and the choral singing is committed and polished. Documentation is excellent.

Vespro della Beata Vergine (with *Magnificat II*); *Missa in illo tempore*.

(B) *** DG 447 719-2 (2). Paul Esswood, Kevin Smith, Ian Partridge, John Elwes, David Thomas, Christopher Keyte, Instrumental soloists, Regensburg Cathedral Ch., Schneidt.

When Schneidt's DG Archiv set was issued on LP in 1975, we gave it a Rosette as the most dedicated and beautiful performance of Monteverdi's choral masterpiece then on record, finer than Gardiner's first Decca set, which was also a landmark in its day. In its excellent transfer to CD it comes up as freshly as ever. With male voices alone – soloists as well as choir – and a small, authentic band of instrumentalists (the cornetti squeaking delightfully), its intimacy is set against a gloriously free church acoustic which yet allows clarity. The Regensburg Choir uses young voices, and the tenor and bass singing is not always as incisive as it might be, but the rest is sensitive, not just the bright-sounding trebles but also the superb team of soloists, all of them from Britain. In live performance it may not be possible for two male altos to take the solo parts in *Pulchra es*, but here Paul Esswood and Kevin Smith sing radiantly, while Ian Partridge in *Nigra sum* excels even his standards of expressiveness and beautiful tone-colour. Not the least attraction of this inexpensive reissued set is that, besides including the alternative and scarcely less elaborate setting of the *Magnificat*, Schneidt adds the superb *Missa in illo tempore*.

(i) *Vespro della Beata Vergine (Vespers)*; (ii) Motet: *Exultent caeli*.

(B) *** Decca Double 443 482-2 (2) [id.]. (i) Gomez, Palmer, Bowman, Tear, Langridge, Shirley-Quirk, Rippon, Monteverdi Ch. & O, Salisbury Cathedral Boys' Ch., Philip Jones Brass Ens., Munrow Recorder Consort; (ii) Monteverdi Ch., Philip Jones Brass & Wind Ens.; Gardiner (with (ii) Christmas motets: G. GABRIELI: *Angelus ad pastores; Audite principes; O magnum mysterium; Quem vidistis pastores?; Salvator noster*. BASSANO: *Hodie Christus natus est* ***).

Gardiner's earlier Decca recording was made before he had been won over entirely to the claims of the authentic school. Modern instruments are used and women's voices, but Gardiner's rhythms are so resilient that the result is exhilarating as well as grand. Singing and playing are exemplary, and the recording is one of Decca's most vividly atmospheric, with relatively large forces presented and placed against a helpful, reverberant acoustic. Now issued as a Double Decca (two CDs for the price of one), this set is well worth considering, with the addition to the *Vespers* of a collection of Christmas motets, mostly by Giovanni Gabrieli, first issued in 1972. The rich, sonorous dignity of Gabrieli's *Sonata pian'e forte* sounds resplendent, and in the choral numbers the vocal and instrumental blend is expert. The most impressive work here is Gabrieli's glorious *Quem vidistis pastores?* Monteverdi's *Exultent caeli* is shorter, but one is again amazed by the range of expressive contrast. Then there is Gabrieli's fine *Salvator noster*, a motet for three five-part choirs, jubilantly rejoicing at the birth of Christ. The CD transfer is admirable.

OPERA AND OPERA-BALLET

Il ballo dell'Ingrate; Il combattimento di Tancredi e Clorinda; Tirsi e Clori (opera-ballets).

❁*** O-L Dig. 440 637-2 [id.]. Bott, King, Ainsley, Bonner, George, New London Consort, Pickett.

The star of this outstanding Monteverdi disc is Catherine Bott. It collects all three of these inspired opera-ballets, a generous triptych. Pickett presents them with a sharp clarity and concern for dramatic impact, to match and outshine any of the various rivals in each work. The voices are especially well chosen for contrast as well as for clarity. The narration in *Tancredi* is taken by John Mark Ainsley with his clean-cut tenor that is yet darker and weightier than that of Andrew King, who sings Tancredi. Yet it is Catherine Bott who more than anyone brings the narrative to life, with delectably pointed and finely shaded singing, using a wider tonal range than is common in Monteverdi. Similarly as Venus in the *Ballo dell'Ingrate* she is well contrasted with Tessa Bonner as Amore and Michael George as a sepulchral Plutone. The third work is much shorter but presents the simple dialogue of the lovers in similarly dramatic terms, with Bott partnered by Andrew King as Tirsi, joined at the end by the chorus of other soloists. First-rate, well-balanced sound.

Alfred Deller Edition: (i) *Il ballo delle ingrate;* (ii) *Lamento d'Arianna.*
(M) **(*) Van. 08.5063.71 [id.]. (i) Alfred Deller, McLoughlin, Ward, Cantelo, Amb. S., L. Chamber Players, Denis Stevens; (ii) Shepard, Le Sage, Worthley, Todd, Deller, Bevan, Deller Consort, Deller.

Denis Stevens's pioneering stereo version of Monteverdi's *Il ballo delle ingrate* dates from 1956 and has an impressive cast, well backed up by the Ambrosian Singers and London Chamber Players. Although the orchestral sound seems rather ample to ears used to original instruments, this account rings true and there is much that is authentic, not least the decoration of the vocal line, by Deller himself who is most moving as Venus. Eileen McLoughlin makes a delightful Amor, and David Ward is suitably stentorian as Pluto. It is all emotively communicated here and the recording is vivid, if rather close. In addition Deller directs a performance of the famous *Lamento d'Arianna*, sung by a vocal sextet comprising Honor Sheppard, Sally le Sage, Max Worthley, Philip Todd, Maurice Bevan and Deller himself. Here the individual voices, while having plenty of character, do not always match ideally in consort. Nevertheless a thoroughly worthwhile reissue in the Alfred Deller Edition.

Il ballo delle ingrate; Sestina: Lagrime d'amante al sepolcro dell'amata.
(M) *** HM Dig. HMT 1901108. Mellon, Laurens, Reinhardt, Feldman, Les Arts Florissants, Christie.

William Christie directs refreshingly dramatic accounts of both *Il ballo delle ingrate* and the complex but very beautiful *Sestina*. Some may find the lovely final lament of *Il ballo* too plaintive, but it is certainly touching and in keeping with the rest of the performance. In the glorious *Sestina* the richness of Christie's interpretation makes for compelling listening, and both performances are beautifully and vividly recorded. With full translations included, this is a fine bargain.

Il combattimento di Tancredi e Clorinda.
(BB) *** HM Solo Dig. HM 926015 [id.]. Françoise Semeliaz, Adrian Brand, Nicolas Rovenq, Les Arts Florissants, Christie.

Like his companion CD of *Il ballo delle ingrate*, Christie's account of *Il combattimento* is very dramatic, with the storytelling vividly projected and with Françoise Semeliaz a touching Clorinda in the tragic closing scene. The recording is admirably vivid too. The libretto is in Italian and French only, but the narrative is easy enough to follow.

(i) *Il combattimento di Tancredi e Clorinda. Lamento della Ninfa; Mentre vaga Angioletta; Ogni amante e guerrier.*
(M) *** Teldec/Warner Dig. 4509 92181-2 [id.]. (i) Equiluz, Schmidt, Hollweg, Murray, Langridge, Hartman, Perry, Palmer, Mühle, Franzden; VCM, Harnoncourt.

Harnoncourt directs sharply characterized readings of substantial items from Monteverdi's eighth Book of Madrigals plus two *Canti amorosi*. The substantial scena telling of the conflict of Tancredi and Clorinda is made sharply dramatic in a bald way. *Ogni amante e guerrier*, almost as extended, is treated with similar abrasiveness, made attractively fresh but lacking subtlety. The two *Canti amorosi* are treated quite differently, in a much warmer style, with the four sopranos of *Mentre vaga Angioletta* producing sensuous sounds. *Lamento della Ninfa*, perhaps the most celebrated of all Monteverdi's madrigals, brings a luscious performance with the solo voice (Ann Murray) set evocatively at a slight distance behind the two tenors and a bass. On CD the recording is extremely vivid, with voices and instruments firmly and realistically placed. The documentation is first class in every way, with full translations and the composer's own fascinatingly detailed instructions as to how *Il Combattimento* should be staged.

L'Incoronazione di Poppea.
*** DG Dig. 447 088-2 (3) [id.]. McNair, Von Otter, Hanchard, Chance, D'Artegna, E. Bar. Soloists, Gardiner.
(M) **(*) Teldec/Warner 2292 42547-2 (4) [id.]. Donath, Söderström, Berberian, Esswood, VCM, Harnoncourt.

With an exceptionally strong and consistent cast in which even minor roles are taken by star singers, Gardiner presents a purposeful, strongly characterized performance. He is helped by the full and immediate sound of the live recording, made in concert at the Queen Elizabeth Hall, London. Sylvia McNair is a seductive Poppea and Anne Sofie von Otter a deeply moving Ottavia, both singing ravishingly. Francesco d'Artegna, a robustly Italian-sounding bass, makes a stylish Seneca, and there are clear advantages in having a counter-tenor as Nero instead of a mezzo-soprano, particularly one with a slightly sinister timbre like Dana Hanchard. So in the sensuous duet which closes the opera, the clashing intervals of the voices are given a degree of abrasiveness, suggesting that, though this is a happy and beautiful ending, the characters still have their sinister side. The text has been modified with newly written ritornellos by Peter Holman, using the original, authentic bass line, and aiming to be 'closer to what Monteverdi would have expected' than the usual flawed text.

Nikolaus Harnoncourt's well-paced and dramatic version makes a welcome reappearance at mid-price in Teldec's Harnoncourt series. First issued in 1974, it offers a starry cast, with Elisabeth Söderström as Nero (imaginative but not always ideally steady), Helen Donath pure-toned as Poppea and Cathy Berberian as the most characterful and moving Ottavia on disc. Others include Paul Esswood and Philip Langridge, and Harnoncourt's bold and brassy instrumentation adds to the bite. The snag is that, unnecessarily, the set stretches to four discs instead of three, which cancels out the price advantage over the excellent rival set from Richard Hickox.

Orfeo (opera): complete.

*** O-L Dig. 433 545-2 (2) [id.]. Ainsley, Gooding, Bott, Bonner, George, Grant, New L. Cons., Pickett.

*** DG Dig. 419 250-2 (2) [id.]. Rolfe Johnson, Baird, Lynne Dawson, Von Otter, Argenta, Robson, Monteverdi Ch., E. Bar. Soloists, Gardiner.

(M) *** EMI Dig. CMS7 64947-2 (2) [CDMB 64947]. Rogers, Kwella, Kirkby, J. Smith, Chiaroscuro, L. Bar. Ens., L. Cornett & Sackbutt Ens., Charles Medlam.

(M) ** Teldec/Warner 2292 42494-2 (2). Kozma, Hansmann, Berberian, Katanosaka, Villisech, Van Egmond, Munich Cappella Antiqua, VCM, Harnoncourt.

(BB) ** Naxos Dig. 8.554094-2 (2) [id.]. Carmignani, Pennichi, Frisani, Pantasuglia, Cappella Musicale di San Petronio di Bologna, Vartolo.

Pickett has not tried to treat *Orfeo* with kid gloves but has aimed above all to bring out its freshness. Compared with John Eliot Gardiner, whose DG Archiv recording combines precision and alertness in presenting the drama, Pickett is rougher, not caring quite so much about pinpoint ensemble, preferring less extreme speeds and relying more on dramatic contrasts in instrumentation. So, in the dark *Sinfonia* with its weird chromatic writing which at the opening of Act III represents Orfeo's arrival in the underworld, Pickett cuts out strings and uses brass instruments alone. As Orfeo, John Mark Ainsley may have a less velvety tenor than Anthony Rolfe Johnson on the Gardiner set, but his voice is more flexible in the elaborate decorations of *Possente spirto*, Orfeo's plea to Charon. Outstanding among the others is Catherine Bott. In *Orfeo* she not only sings the elaborate role given to La Musica in the Prologue, sensuously beautiful and seductive in her coloration, but also the part of Proserpina and the key role of the Messenger, who graphically describes the death of Euridice.

John Eliot Gardiner very effectively balances the often-conflicting demands of authentic performance – when this pioneering opera was originally presented intimately – and the obvious grandeur of the concept. So the 21-strong Monteverdi Choir conveys, on the one hand, high tragedy to the full, yet sings the lighter commentary from nymphs and shepherds with astonishing crispness, often at top speed. However, Gardiner is strong on pacing. This is a set to take you through the story with new involvement. Though editing is not always immaculate, the recording on CD is vivid and full of presence.

In the EMI version Nigel Rogers – who recorded the role of Orfeo ten years earlier for DG Archiv – has the double function of singing the main part and acting as co-director. Rogers has modified his extraordinarily elaborate ornamentation in the hero's brilliant pleading aria before Charon and makes the result all the freer and more wide-ranging in expression, with his distinctive fluttering timbre adding character. The concentration of the whole performance is all the greater, telling the story simply and graphically; and Euridice's plaint, beautifully sung by Patrizia Kwella, is the more affecting for being accompanied very simply on the lute. The other soloists make a good team, though Jennifer Smith as Proserpina, recorded close, is made to sound breathy. The brightness of the cornetti is a special delight, when otherwise the instrumentation used – largely left optional in the score – is modest. Excellent, immediate recording, making for a fine mid-priced alternative to Gardiner.

In Harnoncourt's version, the ritornello of the Prologue might almost be by Stravinsky, so sharply do the sounds cut. He is altogether more severe than John Eliot Gardiner. In compensation, the simple and straightforward dedication of this performance is most affecting, and the solo singing, if not generally very characterful, is clean and stylish. One exception is Cathy Berberian as the Messenger. She is strikingly successful and, though slightly differing in style from the others, she sings as part of the team. Excellent recording. The extra clarity and sharpness of focus – even in large-scale ensembles – add to the abrasiveness from the opening *Toccata* onwards, and the 1968 recording sounds immediate and realistic.

With some first-rate solo singing and a restrained, scholarly approach, there is much to enjoy in the Naxos version. However Sergio Vartolo's speeds are consistently slow. Alessandro Carmignani is a fine, clear Orfeo, coping splendidly with all the technical problems, and his singing in the big solos has a dedicated intensity, but at such slow speeds there is a sleepwalking quality in the results, however beautiful. More seriously, the exchanges between characters never have the dramatic intensity needed. In the instrumental numbers the strings are often uncomfortably edgy. It is as well that full text and translation are provided, when the CD tracks on the disc are radically different from those indicated in the booklet. For once the discs provide too many separate tracks, with even ritornelli of five or six seconds separately indexed. Clear, well-balanced sound, recorded in the Theatre of Puy-en-Velay in France.

Il ritorno d'Ulisse in patria (complete).
*** HM Dig. HMC 90 1427/9 [id.]. Prégardien, Fink, Högeman, Hunt, Visse, Tucker, D. Thomas, Concerto Vocale, René Jacobs.
(M) **(*) Teldec/Warner 2292 42496-2 (3) [id.]. Eliasson, Lerer, Hansen, Baker-Genovesi, Hansmann, Equiluz, Esswood, Wyatt, Walters, Van Egmond, Mühle, Junge Kantorei, VCM, Harnoncourt.

René Jacobs offers a scholarly performance that is not afraid of being expressive. As a singer himself, he is most understanding of the need to give his soloists free rein, and they make a first-rate team, with Christoph Prégardien splendid as Ulisse, firm and heroic but light enough to cope with the elaborate ornamentation. Bernarda Fink with her rich, firm mezzo gives full weight to Penelope's agony, and it is encouraging to find such excellent British singers as Martyn Hill, Mark Tucker and David Thomas taking character roles. Dominique Visse is also excellent, both as Human Frailty in the Prologue and as one of Penelope's suitors, with Guy de Mey in the comic role of the glutton, Iro. Jacobs explains that with the surviving manuscripts raising dozens of textual questions, he decided to return to the original five-Act division of the text which, as he suggests, is better-balanced. He also inserts music by Rossi and Caccini for the choruses included in the text but missing from the score.

Harnoncourt's 1971 recording of *Il ritorno d'Ulisse* brings a sympathetic performance, generally not quite as brisk as Jacobs in his recording from the Montpellier Festival, and rather more square in rhythm, but bringing a keener sense of repose, important in Monteverdi. The solo singing is not as characterful as that on the Jacobs set, nor as Harnoncourt's *Poppea*, though Norma Lerer makes a touching Penelope, with Sven Olaf Eliasson a stylish Ulisse, not ideally pure of timbre.

Moody, James (born 1907)

(i) *Quintet for harmonica and string quartet;* (ii) *Suite dans le style français.*
*** Chandos Dig. CHAN 8802 [id.]. Tommy Reilly; (i) Hindar Qt; (ii) Skaila Kanga – JACOB: *Divertimento.* ***

James Moody's *Suite in the French style* may be pastiche but its impressionism is highly beguiling. The *Quintet* is more ambitious, less charming perhaps, but likely to prove even more rewarding on investigation, especially the very diverse theme and variations of the finale, the longest movement. The performance and recording are hardly likely to be bettered.

Moreno Torroba, Federico
(1891–1982)

Sonatina for guitar and orchestra; Interludes I & II.
(N) *** Analekta Fleur de Lys Dig. Fl 2 3049 [id.]. Rémi Boucher, Amati Ens., Raymond Dessaints – ABRIL: *Concierto Mudéjar.* ***

Moreno Torroba's *Sonatina* was written in the early years of the twentieth century for Segovia. It belongs more readily to the nineteenth, but is none the worse for that; the composer made the concertante arrangement of the solo work not long before he died. The outer movements with their Castilian atmosphere are gay and engaging, and the Romance which forms the central *Andante* is quite captivating, especially when the performance has such a simple spontaneity and is not too overladen with expressive feeling. The two *Interludes* are also both highly evocative. The first is not without moments of Andalusian temperament, while the second is essentially ruminative; both were composed for wind quintet, and later arranged by the composer's son. They are most winning in their present format. Rémi Boucher is a splendid soloist and Dessaints gives him affectionate support. The warmth of the truthful and very well-balanced recording adds to the listener's pleasure.

Luisa Fernanda (complete).
(N) *** Valois Audivis Dig. V 4759 [id.]. Plácido Domingo, Veronica Villaroel, Juan Pons, Ana Rodrigo, Madrid Univ. Ch., Madrid SO, Antoni Ros Marba.

This is an ideal recommendation for anyone wanting to investigate the zarazuela, the Spanish genre of operetta. Moreno Torroba, best known for his guitar music, here offers in three compact acts a sequence of catchily tuneful numbers, brightly orchestrated.

Led by Domingo in glowing form as the hero, Javier, an army colonel, the cast is as near ideal as possible, with Veronica Villaroel in the title role, and Juan Pons as Javier's rich rival. Bright, immediate sound.

Morley, Thomas (1557–1603)

Ayres and madrigals: *Absence, hear thou my protestation; Arise, awake; Besides a fountain; Deep lamenting; Fire and lightning; Hard by a crystal fountain; Hark! Alleluia; In every place; Mistress mine; No, no Nigelia; O grief ev'n on the bud; Phyllis I fain would die now; Singing alone; Sleep slumbr'ing eyes; Stay heart, run not so fast; With my love.*

(N) (B) *** Decca Double 458 093-2 (2). Consort of Musicke, Anthony Rooley – GIBBONS; WILBYE: *Madrigals.* ***

Morley is generally thought of as a lesser figure than his contemporaries, even though he was the pioneering English madrigalist. This collection should do something to modify the picture of him, for although the lighter canzonetti and balletti based on Italian models (and in particular Gastoldi) are in evidence, there are more searching and thoughtful pieces. *Deep lamenting* and *O grief ev'n on the bud* are very touching, while Rooley himself provides lute accompaniments for Emma Kirkby's lovely *Sleep slumb'ring eyes* and the ambitious *Absence, hear thou my protestation*, the longest song in the whole programme, sensitively sung by Andrew King. *Mistress mine* is unexpectedly precocious, and there are others that make one feel that the range of Morley's musical personality has not been adequately reflected before. This is a rewarding recital and has the benefit of well-projected performances and very good recording. Full texts are provided.

The First Booke of Ayres: A painted tale; Thyrsis and Milla; She straight the light greensilken coats; With my love; I saw my lady weeping; It was a lover; Who is it that this dark night?; Mistress mine; Can I forget; Love winged my hopes; What is my mistress; Come, sorrow, stay; Fair in a morn; Absence, hear thou; Will you buy a fine dog?; Sleep slumb'ring eyes.

(M) ** Teldec/Warner 3984 21334-2. Nigel Rogers, Nikolaus Harnoncourt, Eugen Dombois.

This integral recording of Morley's *First Booke of Songs* first appeared at the beginning of the 1970s and remains unique in a catalogue not notably generous to Morley's music. The settings show the scope of the composer's imagination in his sensitivity to the words themselves, in the variety of style and metre, and in the diversity of manner of the accompaniments. The performances are fresh and direct and scholarly in the use of decoration.

Mosonyi, Mihály (1815–70)

(i) *Piano concerto in E min.;* (ii) *Symphony No. 1 in D.*

** Marco Polo Dig. 8.223539 [id.]. (i) Körmendi, Slovak State Philh. O (Košice); (ii) Slovak RSO (Bratislava); Stankovsky.

Mihály Mosonyi is hardly a household name in this country and his representation on disc is meagre. Originally Michael Brand and born in Bradford, he adopted Hungarian nationality and changed his name in 1859, some years after settling in Pest. Despite his origins, Mosonyi is thought of as one of the most representative nineteenth-century Hungarian composers – apart, of course, from the more obvious major figures, Liszt and Erkel. The *Symphony No. 1 in D* is an early work, composed in his late twenties and modelled on the Viennese classics in general and Beethoven in particular. The *Piano concerto in E minor*, which comes from about the same time, shows the influence of Chopin and Weber. If, like the symphony, it is not strong on individuality, it is at least well-crafted, well-bred music and well worth an occasional airing. Klára Körmendi is the fluent soloist and receives decent orchestral support from Robert Stankovsky and his Slovak forces.

Moszkowski, Moritz (1854–1925)

Piano concerto in E, Op. 59.

*** Hyperion Dig. CDA 66452 [id.]. Piers Lane, BBC Scottish SO, Maksymiuk – PADEREWSKI: *Piano concerto.* ***

(i) *Piano concerto in E, Op. 59. From foreign lands, Op. 23.*

(N) (BB) *** Naxos Dig. 8.553989 [id.]. (i) Markus Pawlik; Polish Nat. RSO (Katowice), Wit.

Moszkowski is most often remembered for his dazzling piano miniatures, but he is just as fluent in this big four-movement *concerto*, written for the Polish virtuoso, Josef Hofmann. An extended first movement leads to a lyrical slow movement, a sparkling tarantella Scherzo and a finale rather like an Offenbach galop. The young German, Markus Pawlik, proves a magnetic soloist, playing with the crispest articulation, readily matching the fine version from Piers Lane in Hyperion's parallel Romantic piano concerto series. The fill-up, a suite of colourful orchestral pieces, is delightful.

It was Piers Lane's performance of this concerto, in partnership with the volatile Jerzy Maksymiuk, which inaugurated Hyperion's highly successful series, and anyone fancying a coupling with Paderewski will not be disappointed by this brilliant alternative version, certainly full of vitality and both expressively sympathetic and subtle in detail. Excellent recording too.

Air de ballet, Op. 36/5; Albumblatt, Op. 2; Au Crépuscule, Op. 68/3; Barcarolle from *Offenbach's Tales of Hoffmann; Chanson bohème* from *Bizet's Carmen; Danse Russe; En Automne, Op. 36/4; Expansion, Op. 36/3; La Jongleuse, Op. 52/4; Minuetto, Op. 68/2; Nocturne, Op. 68/1; Poème de Mai; Près de berceau; Rêverie, Op. 36/2; Serenata, Op. 15/1; Tarantella, Op. 27/2; Valse Mignonne.*
**(*) Collins Dig. 1412-2. Seta Tanyel.

Famous in their day, Moszkowski's *Spanish dances* are all but forgotten now, and his piano music seems faded too. Seta Tanyel characterizes the music well enough, but she is hard put to sustain interest through a 69-minute recital of genre pieces that are heard most effectively as encores at the end of a more substantial programme. Good recording.

3 Etudes de concert, Op. 24; Fantaisie impromptu; Grand valse de concert, Op. 88; 3 Morceaux, Op. 42; 3 Morceaux, Op. 73; Transcription of Wagner's Isolde's death.
(N) *** Collins Dig. 1473-2 [id.]. Seta Tanyel.

Seta Tanyel is completely at home in Moszkowski's musical world. She brings all these pieces to life and finds both glitter and an ingenuous charm in the *Etudes*, the *Grande valse de concert* and *Fantaisie impromptu*. If the composer's inspiration cannot match Chopin's similarly named works, he writes for the piano with striking facility. The unambitious *Morceaux* are pleasingly coloured miniatures, given here with the lightest touch. Indeed Tanyel's second collection is generally more appealing than the first, and this lightweight but well-crafted music could hardly be more persuasively presented, or better recorded.

Mourant, Walter (born 1910)

The Pied Piper.
*** ASV Dig. CDDCA 568 [id.]. MacDonald, N. Sinfonia, Bedford – COPLAND; FINZI: *Concertos.* ***

Walter Mourant's *Pied Piper* is a catchy, unpretentious little piece for clarinet, strings and celeste, which in a gently syncopated style effectively contrasts 3/4 and 6/8 rhythms. It makes an attractive filler after the Copland *Concerto*.

Mozart, Leopold (1719–87)

Cassation in G: Toy symphony (attrib. Haydn). (i) *Trumpet concerto in D.*
*** Erato/Warner Dig. 2292 45199-2. (i) Touvron; Paillard CO, Paillard – W. A. MOZART: *Musical Joke.* ***

One could hardly imagine this *Cassation* being done with more commitment from the effects department directed by Paillard, while the music itself is elegantly played. After this, the more restrained approach to the excellent two-movement *Trumpet concerto* seems exactly right. The recording has plenty of presence and realism.

Mozart, Wolfgang Amadeus
(1756–91)

Adagio and fugue in C minor: see also below, in VOCAL MUSIC, under Complete Mozart Edition, Volume 22.

Cassations, Divertimenti and Serenades

Cassations Nos. 1 in G, K. 63; 2 in B flat K.99; Divertimenti for strings Nos. 1–3, K.136/8; Divertimenti Nos. 1 in E flat, K. 113; 2 in D, K.131; 7 in D, K. 205; 10 in F, K.247; 11 in D K. 251; 15 in B flat, K.287; 17 in D, K.334. A Musical joke, K. 522. Serenades Nos. 1 in D, K.100; 3 in D, K.185; 4 in D (Colloredo), K. 203; 5 in D, K. 204; 6 in D (Serenata notturna), K.239; 7 in D (Haffner), K. 250; 8 in D, for four orchestras, K.286; 9 in D (Posthorn), K. 320; 13 in G (Eine kleine Nachtmusik), K.525.
(N) (B) *** Decca 458 310-2 (8) [id.]. V. Mozart Ens., Willi Boskovsky.

Recorded in the Vienna Sofiensaal between 1967 and 1978, this splendid series was one of Willi Boskovsky's finest achievements for Decca, every bit as impressive as his survey of the dance music of the Strauss family. This set covers all Mozart's major divertimenti and serenades, except those for wind instruments alone. Even the earliest works bring delight. The very first *Cassation*, K. 63 has two enchanting slow movements. The first is a delicate *Andante* (nicely atmospheric here); the second introduces a cantilena for solo violin. No. 2 (K.99) is almost equally attractive. Boskovsky's performances immediately set the manner for the whole series. The playing is marvellously alive and stylish, investing comparatively lightweight works with unexpected stature. The recording balance is flawless. The three *String divertimenti* sparkle, as does the *Serenata notturna*, while *Eine kleine Nachtmusik* is one of the freshest accounts on disc. And if the larger-scale *Divertimenti* (K. 247, K. 287 and K.334 for instance) which Mozart intended for solo instruments, are to be heard in orchestral dress, none could be more elegant than this. The *Serenade for four orchestras*, K. 286, without gimickry, gains much from Decca's stereo set-up and Boskovsky even succeeds with a piece like the *Musical joke*, making it appear an almost unqualified masterpiece. The large-scale *Haffner* and *Posthorn Serenades* combine vitality with charm and elegance and Boskovsky's own solo violin contributions to the former are wholly admirable. The recordings have been remastered and the bloom of the Sofiensaal ambience now adds to one's aural pleasure.

Complete Mozart Edition, Volume 3: *Cassations Nos. 1 in G, K.63; 2 in B flat, K.99; Divertimento No. 2 in D, K.131; Galimathias musicum, K.32; Serenades Nos. 1 in D, K.100* (with *March in D, K.62); 3 in D, K.185* (with *March in D, K.189); 4 in D (Colloredo), K.203* (with *March in D, K.237); 5 in D, K.204* (with *March in D, K.215); 6 in D (Serenata notturna), K.239; 7 in D (Haffner), K.250* (with *March in D, K.249); 8 in D (Notturno for 4 orchestras), K.286; 9 in D (Posthorn), K.320* (with *Marches in D, K.335/1–2); 13 in G (Eine kleine Nachtmusik), K.525.*
(M) *** Ph. Dig. 422 503-2 (7) [id.]. ASMF, Sir Neville Marriner.

Marriner and his Academy are at their very finest here and make a very persuasive case for giving these works on modern instruments. The playing has much finesse, yet its cultivated polish never brings a hint of blandness or lethargy; it is smiling, yet full of energy and sparkle. In the concertante violin roles Iona Brown is an ideal soloist, her playing full of grace. Throughout this set the digital recording brings an almost ideal combination of bloom and vividness.

Cassations Nos. 1 in G, K.63; 2 in B flat, K.99; Adagio and fugue in C min., K.546.
*** Capriccio Dig. 10 192 [id.]. Salzburg Camerata, Végh.

Cassations Nos. 1 in G, K.63; 2 in B flat, K.100; 3 (Serenade No. 1) in D, K.100.
(BB) *** Naxos Dig. 8.550609 [id.]. Salzburg CO, Harald Nerat.

The super-budget Naxos label issues a great many recorded performances that are inexpensive but are otherwise of only moderate appeal; every now and then, however, a winner appears – and this is one of them. For all their charms, these early *Cassations* (otherwise miniature serenades or divertimenti) are not likely to be a top priority for many collectors but, played with style and excellently recorded, they are very attractive at Naxos price, and they would still be so if they cost more. All three are given lively, nicely turned performances, very well – if resonantly – recorded. This admirable disc is certainly worth its modest cost and nicely fills a gap in the catalogue.

Sándor Végh and the Salzburg Camerata too give excellent performances of the early *Cassations*. Their playing combines vitality with finesse and they find plenty of drama in the *Adagio and fugue*. Very good recording.

CONCERTOS

Complete Mozart Edition, Volume 9: (i) *Bassoon concerto;* (ii) *Clarinet concerto;* (iii) *Flute concertos Nos. 1–2; Andante in C for flute & orchestra;* (iii; iv) *Flute and harp concerto;* (v) *Horn concertos Nos. 1–4; Concert rondo in E flat for horn and orchestra;* (vi) *Oboe concerto. Sinfonia concertante in E flat, K.297b; Sinfonia concertante in E flat, K.297b* (reconstructed R. Levin).
(M) **(*) Ph. Dig. 422 509-2 (5) [id.]. (i) Thunemann; (ii) Leister; (iii) Grafenauer; (iv) Graf; (v) Damm; (vi) Holliger; ASMF, Marriner (except (vi) Holliger).

The principal wind concertos here are recent digital versions. They are all well played and recorded. However, there is a slightly impersonal air about the accounts of the *Bassoon* and *Clarinet concertos*, well played though they are; and there are more individual sets of the works for horn. The *Sinfonia concertante* is offered both in the version we usually hear (recorded in 1972, with the performance attractively songful and elegant) and in a more modern recording of a conjectural reconstruction by Robert Levin, based on the material in the four wind parts.

Bassoon concerto in B flat, K.191.
(N) *** Chandos Dig. CHAN 9656 [id.]. Valeri Popov, Russian State SO, Polyansky – HUMMEL; WEBER: *Bassoon concertos.* ***
*** Caprice Dig. CAP 21411. Knut Sönstevold, Swedish RSO, Comissiona – PETTERSSON: *Symphony No. 7.* ***

Though not as individual as Gwydion Brooke with Beecham, Valeri Popov's playing has character and warmth. He is at his most personable in the Minuet Rondo finale. Polyansky's accompaniment is warmly supportive, and the Chandos recording is well up to standard.

Knut Sönstevold's performance of Mozart's concerto is good enough to compete in an already crowded market, but Mozartians are likely to turn elsewhere in search of a more logical coupling. A good, big-band performance, which gives pleasure, and is very well recorded.

(i) *Bassoon concerto in B flat, K.191;* (ii) *Clarinet concerto in A, K.622;* (iii) *Flute concerto No.1 in G, K.313; Andante in C, K.315;* (iii; iv) *Flute and harp concerto in C, K.299;* (v) *Horn concertos Nos. 1–4;* (vi) *Oboe concerto in C, K.314; Sinfonia concertante in E flat, K.197b.*
(M) *** DG (IMS) Dig. 431 665-2 (3). (i) Morelli; (ii) Neidlich; (iii) Palma; (iv) Allen; (v) Jolley or Purvis; (vi) Wolfgang; Orpheus CO.

Randall Wolfgang's plaintive, slightly reedy timbre is especially telling in the *Oboe concerto* and he plays with the lightest possible touch, as does Susan Palma in the *Flute concerto*. The *Sinfonia concertante* for wind is pleasingly fresh. All the works are given excellent modern recordings and this is a very persuasive collection, probably a 'best buy' for those wanting all the music in a digital format.

(i) *Bassoon concerto;* (ii) *Clarinet concerto;* (iii) *Oboe concerto, K.314.*

*** Decca Dig. 443 176-2 (i) David McGill; (ii) Franklin Cohen; (iii) John Mack; Cleveland Orchestra, Dohnányi.

(BB) **(*) Naxos Dig. 8.550345 [id.]. (i) Turnovský; (ii) Ottensamer; (iii) Gabriel; V. Mozart Academy, Wildner.

In this favourite trio of Mozart concertos for reed instruments, Christoph von Dohnányi and the Cleveland Orchestra successfully follow up their record of the *Flute and harp concerto* and *Sinfonia concertante for violin, viola and orchestra* (see below) with an impressive showcase disc using three more soloists from the orchestra. It is beautifully recorded and attractively balanced. Franklin Cohen steals the limelight with his mastery and polish in the *Clarinet concerto*. The oboist, John Mack, has an appealingly sweet (but not too sweet) timbre; he plays most stylishly and his sprightly closing rondo is a delight. Then David McGill, in the third work instantly establishes keen individuality, matching the high polish of his colleagues but readily assumes the central role ahead of the conductor. He does not overdo the humour in the finale. Very enjoyable music-making by musicians who are clearly at one with Mozart.

In the *Oboe concerto* the soloist on Naxos, Martin Gabriel, is excellent. The clarinettist, Ernst Ottensamer, is also a sensitive player, his slow movement is full of feeling; and there is an accomplished performance of the *Bassoon concerto* from Stepan Turnovský, who has the measure of the work's character and wit. Recommendable.

(i) *Bassoon concerto in B flat, K.191;* (ii) *Clarinet concerto in A, K.622;* (iii) *Violin concerto No. 3 in G, K.216.*

(M) *** EMI stereo/mono CDM7 63408-2. (i) Brooke; (ii) Brymer; (iii) De Vito; RPO, Beecham.

Beecham's romantically expansive reading of the Mozart *Clarinet concerto* with Jack Brymer is a 1958 classic recording, totally individual in every phrase, with conductor and soloist inspiring each other. The account of the *Bassoon concerto* has equal magic, thanks to the comparable partnership between Beecham and Gwydion Brooke. But the surprise here is the equally inspired and highly personal 1949 mono account of the *G major Violin concerto*, with Gioconda de Vito as soloist. She too conveys magic comparable to Beecham's own, with the slow movement again luxuriantly expansive.

(i) *Bassoon concerto in B flat, K.191;* (ii) *Flute and harp concerto in C, K.299. Sinfonia concertante in E flat, K.297b.*

(M) *** Classic fM Dig. 76505 57038-2. (i) Julie Andrews; (ii) Kate Hill, Lucy Wakeford; soloists, Britten Sinfonia, Nicholas Cleobury.

Like the companion Classic fM disc offering concertos for clarinet, flute, and oboe (see below), all the soloists here play with charm, spontaneity and style in the best tradition of British orchestral wind-playing. Julie Andrews gives Mozart's droll *Bassoon concerto* a genial lift-off, while the flautist, Kate Hill, and the harpist, Lucy Wakeford, create winningly delicate tracery in the *Concerto for flute and harp*. Both slow movements are beautifully phrased, and the team of soloists is no less persuasive in the *Sinfonia concertante*, not least in the light-hearted finale. The recording and balance are altogether first class.

(i) *Bassoon concerto in B flat, K.191. Divertimento No. 15 in B flat, K.287; Symphony No. 35 in D (Haffner), K.385; Overture: Le nozze di Figaro.*

(M) (**) BMG/RCA mono 09026 60286-2 [id.]. (i) Leonard Sharrow; NBC SO, Toscanini.

Leonard Sharrow, principal bassoon of Toscanini's NBC orchestra, gives a brilliant account of the solo part in the *Bassoon concerto*, undaunted by any rigidity in the conducting, bringing out the youthful exuberance of the writing. The *Haffner Symphony* is less extreme, if a degree less sparkling, than the classic 1929 version that Toscanini recorded with the New York Philharmonic, with the middle movements flowing more easily, while the *Divertimento* makes an attractive filler, despite the omission of the second Minuet, with the first violins together taking the solo violin role. Dry, limited sound.

(i) *Clarinet concerto in A, K.622;* (ii–iii) *Andante, K.315;* (ii; iv) *Flute and harp concerto in C, K.299.*

(M) *** [RCA Basic 100 09026 68024-2; *68024-4*]. (i) Stolzman, ECO, Schneider; (ii) James Galway; (iii) Lucerne Festival O, Baumgartner; (iv) Marisa Robles, LSO, Mata.

Richard Stolzman's distinguished account of the *Clarinet concerto* makes a thoroughly recommendable coupling, in RCA's Basic 100 series, for the two works with James Galway (see below).

(i) *Clarinet concerto in A, K.622;* (ii) *Flute concerto No. 1 in G, K.313;* (iii) *Oboe concerto in C, K.314.*

(M) *** Classic fM Dig. 75605 57001-2. (i) Joy Farrall; (ii) Kate Hill; (iii) Nicholas Daniel; Britten Sinfonia, Nicholas Cleobury.

No composer ever bettered Mozart's natural facility in writing for wind. His music seems to go right to the heart of the instrument for which he is writing and reveals, in glowing fashion, every facet of its personality. All three soloists on the Classic fM disc are distinguished British orchestral players, and each plays with much individuality of character. In the *Clarinet concerto* Joy Farrall's solo style lies somewhere between the freely spontaneous manner of Emma Johnson and the flexible, classical directness of Thea King. Nicholas Daniel is equally appealing in the stylishly infectious account of the *Oboe concerto*. Kate Hill's *Flute concerto* is hardly less delectable, especially the touching *Adagio*. The neatly pointed minuet finale is delightful. Excellent balancing and fine recording make this mid-priced triptych from Classic fM hard to beat.

(i) *Clarinet concerto;* (ii) *Flute and harp concerto in C, K.299.*
*** ASV Dig. CDDCA 532 [id.]. (i) Emma Johnson; (ii) Bennett, Ellis; ECO, Leppard.
(B) *** Carlton IMP Dig. PCD 2011 [id.]. (i) Campbell; (ii) Davies, Masters; City of L. Sinfonia, Hickox.

Emma Johnson's account of the *Clarinet concerto* has a sense of spontaneity and natural magnetism. There may be some rawness of tone in places, but that only adds to the range of expression, which breathes the air of a live performance. Leppard and the ECO are in bouncing form, as they are too for the *Flute and harp concerto*, though here the two excellent soloists are somewhat on their best behaviour, until the last part of the finale sends Mozart bubbling up to heaven. First-rate recording.

David Campbell's agile and pointed performance of the clarinet work brings fastish speeds and a fresh, unmannered style in all three movements. His tonal shading is very beautiful. The earlier flute and harp work is just as freshly and sympathetically done, with a direct, unmannered style sounding entirely spontaneous.

(i) *Clarinet concerto in A, K.622;* (ii) *Flute and harp concerto in C, K.299;* (iii) *Serenade No. 13 in G (Eine kleine Nachtmusik), K.525.*
(B) **(*) Belart 450 035-2. (i) Harold Wright, Boston SO, Ozawa; (ii) Karl-Heinz Zöller, Nicanor Zabaleta, BPO, Märzendorfer; (iii) VPO, Karl Boehm.

Harold Wright's Boston performance of the *Clarinet concerto* is thoroughly musical and well recorded. The warm tone of the clarinet is especially appealing and the soloist enterprisingly plays his own cadenza in the slow movement. However, Ozawa's accompaniments, though well fashioned and neatly laid out, are rather matter-of-fact, and the overall orchestral effect is accomplished rather than inspired. There are no strictures about the Zöller/Zabaleta account of the *Flute and harp concerto*. The flautist is a most sensitive player and his phrasing a constant source of pleasure, while Zabaleta's sense of line knits the overall texture of this solo-duet most convincingly. The early-1960s recording is clear and clean, if not as rich as we would expect today. Of the many excellent versions of Mozart's famous *Night music* in the catalogue, Karl Boehm's 1976 performance is among the finest: polished and spacious, with a graceful *Andante* and a neat, lightly pointed finale. Excellent value.

(i) *Clarinet concerto in A;* (ii) *Oboe concerto in C, K.314;* (i; ii; iii) *Sinfonia concertante, K.297b.*
*** ASV Dig. CDCDA 814 [id.]. (i) Richard Hosford; (ii) Douglas Boyd; (iii) O'Neill, Williams; COE, Schneider.

It would be hard to imagine a performance of the *Oboe concerto* that conveys more fun in the outer movements, infectiously pointed and phrased, both by Douglas Boyd and his colleagues. The wind soloists in this live recording of the *Sinfonia concertante* are four COE artists who each know when to take centre stage and when to hold back in turn. The variations of the finale are pure delight. Richard Hosford in his reading of the *Clarinet concerto* uses a basset clarinet with its extended lower range, allowing Mozart's original intentions to be realized. At slowish speeds he leans towards the lyrical rather than the dramatic, even in the first movement, and ends with a delightfully bouncy account of the finale. Full, atmospheric recording.

(i) *Clarinet concerto;* (ii) *Clarinet quintet in A, K.581.*
*** Hyperion Dig. CDA 66199 [id.]. Thea King, (i) ECO, Tate; (ii) Gabrieli Qt.
(M) **(*) Ph. 442 390-2. Jack Brymer, with (i) LSO, Sir Colin Davis; (ii) Allegri Qt.

Thea King's coupling brings together winning performances of Mozart's two great clarinet masterpieces. She steers an ideal course between classical stylishness and expressive warmth, with the slow movement becoming the emotional heart of the piece. The Gabrieli Quartet is equally responsive in its finely tuned playing. For the *Clarinet concerto* Thea King uses an authentically reconstructed basset clarinet. With Jeffrey Tate an inspired Mozartian, the performance – like that of the *Quintet* – is both stylish and expressive, with the finale given a captivating bucolic lilt. Excellent recording.

Jack Brymer's (1964) Philips account of the *Clarinet concerto* with Sir Colin Davis has an eloquent autumnal serenity and the reading a soft lyricism that is very appealing. However, the leisurely (1970) interpretation of the *Quintet* is more controversial. Generally the very slow tempi throughout are well sustained, although in the finale the forward flow of the music is reduced to a near-crawl. Good transfers.

(i) *Clarinet concerto; Serenades Nos.10 for 13 wind in B flat, K.375; 13 in G (Eine kleine Nachtmusik).*

(N) *** RCA 09026 62531-2 [id.].
(i) Karl-Heinz Steffens; Bavarian RSO, Sir Colin Davis.

This is a delightful disc, bringing together three outstanding performances. The two serenades – the first of the two great wind octet serenades and *Eine kleine Nachtmusik* – both gain from being recorded live; fresh and urgent with rhythms well-sprung and phrases persuasively moulded but without mannerism, even if *Eine kleine Nachtmusik* brings a relatively large-scale performance. In K.375 – with the Bavarian wind section joined by a double bass – the ripeness of horn tone and the reediness of the oboes is a delight. Karl-Heinz Steffens, soloist in the *Clarinet concerto*, recorded in the Herkulessaal, plays with comparable individuality, pointing rhythms, shaping phrases and using the subtlest dynamic contrasts, as in echo phrases. Not just the soloist but the orchestra too sound just as spontaneous as in the two live performances.

(i) *Clarinet concerto in A, K.622;* (ii) *Serenade No. 10 for 13 wind instruments, K.361: Adagio* (only).

*** EMI Dig. CDC5 55155-2 [id.]. Sabine Meyer; (i) Dresden State O., Hans Vonk; (ii) with Wind Ens – STAMITZ: *Clarinet concerto No. 10*; WEBER: *Clarinet concerto No. 1.* ***

(i) *Clarinet concerto in A, K.622*; (ii) *Sinfonia concertante for oboe, clarinet, horn, bassoon and orchestra in E flat, K. 297b.*

(N) (M) *** EMI Dig. CDM5 66897-2 [CDM 66949]. (i) Sabine Meyer, Dresden State O; (ii) cond. Hans Vonk.

Using the original basset clarinet, Sabine Meyer gives a highly seductive performance of Mozart's beautiful concerto and at the same time accompanies herself by directing a rich-textured modern instrument backing from the excellent Dresden orchestra, resonantly recorded. The solo playing has much warmth and great finesse, bringing the most sophisticated use of colour and light and shade. Indeed some listeners may feel that this music-making has an element of self-consciousness, especially at the gentle muted reprise of the *Adagio*. But the finale trips along gracefully and her beauty of tone and line is enticing, and it is good to have a performance of such individuality.

She participates also in a sonorously solemn account of the *Adagio* from the so-called *Grand Partita*, in which she joins the principal oboe (Diethelm Jonas) to lead the plaintive melodic flow. The couplings, too, are very impressive.

Meyer's performance has also been reissued paired with Vonk's persuasively stylish account of the *Sinfonia concertante*, with Meyer joining the team of soloists. The *Adagio*, in which she pairs with the principal oboe (Diethelm Jonas) to lead the plaintive melodic flow, again has a characterful solemnity, yet the finale is jocular in the most attractive manner. The sound is excellent, but this coupling is a less than apt candidate for EMI's 'Great recordings of the century' series.

(i) *Flute concertos Nos. 1–2; Andante in C, K.315;* (ii) *Flute and harp concerto, K.299;* (iii) *Sinfonia concertante for flute, oboe, horn & bassoon, K.297b* (reconstructed R. Levin); (iv) *4 Flute quartets, K.285, K.285a, K.285b; K.298.*

(B) **(*) Ph. Duo 442 299-2. (i) Aurèle Nicolet, Cong. O, Zinman; (ii) Hubert Barwahser, Osian Ellis, LSO, C. Davis; (iii) Nicolet, Holliger, Baumann, Thunemann, ASMF, Marriner; (iv) William Bennett, Grumiaux Trio.

Aurèle Nicolet's performances of the *Flute concertos* and *Andante for flute and orchestra* are very positive, and the solo playing throughout is expert and elegantly phrased. Barwahser and Ellis give a sparkling account of the *Flute and harp concerto* and Sir Colin accompanies them with the greatest sprightliness and sympathy. If these are not a top choice in this repertoire, the William Bennett accounts of the four *Flute quartets* with the Grumiaux Trio certainly are. They are, to put it in a nutshell, exquisitely played and very well recorded. The wind *Sinfonia concertante* in which the oboe and clarinet parts are replaced by flute and oboe respectively, is an interesting conjectural experiment rather than an essential part of a Mozart collection. The recordings throughout are smoothly remastered and sound fine.

Flute concertos Nos. (i) *1 in G, K.313;* (ii) *2 in D, K.314.*

(B) *** Carlton IMP PCD 2036 [id.]. Judith Hall, Philh. O, Peter Thomas.

Flute concertos Nos. 1 in G, K.313; 2 in D, K.314; Andante in C, K.315.

(BB) **(*) Naxos Dig. 8.550074; *4550074* [id.]. Herbert Weissberg, Capella Istropolitana, Sieghart.

Judith Hall produces a radiantly full timbre. Moreover she is a first-class Mozartian, as she demonstrates in her cadenzas as well as in the line of the slow movements, phrased with a simple eloquence that is disarming. There is plenty of vitality in the allegros, and Peter Thomas provides polished, infectious accompaniments to match the solo playing. The balance is good and the 1987 sound is bright and clear. However, at 45 minutes playing time this is not particularly generous.

The Naxos record by Herbert Weissberg and the Capella Istropolitana under Martin Sieghart can hold its head quite high alongside the competition. Weissberg does not have the outsize personality of some of his rivals but he is a cultured player, and the quality of the recording is excellent. In short, good value for money and very pleasant sound.

(i) *Flute concerto No. 1 in G, K.313; Andante in C, K.315;* (ii) *Flute and harp concerto in C, K.299.*

(M) *** RCA GD 86723 [6723-2-RG]. James Galway; (i) Lucerne Festival O, Baumgartner; (ii) with Marisa Robles, LSO, Mata.

(M) *** Erato/Warner 2292 45832-2 [id.]. Rampal, (i) VSO, Guschlbauer; (ii) Lily Laskine, Paillard CO, Paillard.

James Galway's silvery timbre seems as unlike an original instrument as could possibly be imagined. Galway is well supported by the Lucerne orchestra, rather reverberantly recorded, with the solo flute placed well forward. The *Flute and harp concerto* has seldom sounded more lively than it does here, with an engaging element of fantasy in the music-making, a radiant slow movement and a very spirited finale. Marisa Robles makes a characterful match for Galway and they are well accompanied.

Rampal and Lily Laskine also create a genuine symbiosis in the *Flute and harp concerto*: their interplay has great charm and delicacy, and the slow movement is a delight. The solo concerto and *Andante* find Rampal in equally good form and he is well accompanied in both instances. With well-transferred recordings from the mid-1960s, this CD is well worth its mid-price.

(i) *Flute concertos Nos. 1–2, K.313/4;* (ii) *Flute and harp concerto in C, K.299.*

(N) *** RCA Dig. 09026 68256-2 [id.]. James Galway; (i) Marisa Robles, ASMF, Marriner.

(M) *** Decca 440 080-2. (i) William Bennett, ECO, Malcolm; (ii) Werner Tripp, Hubert Jellinek, VPO, Münchinger.

(N) **(*) EMI Dig. CDC5 56356-2 [id.]. Emmanuel Pahud; (i) Marie-Pierre Langlamet, BPO, Abbado.

Galway and his favourite harpist partner, Marisa Robles – always characterful – take an expansive, warmly expressive view of the slow movement of the *Flute and harp concerto*. As in previous recordings with Galway she also matches him in a delightfully bouncy account of the finale, sharper in focus than the Berlin one. In the solo concertos too Galway takes an expansive, expressive view of the slow movements, and a winningly relaxed one of the allegros.

William Bennett gives a beautiful account of the concertos, among the finest in the catalogue. Every phrase is shaped with both taste and affection, and the playing of the ECO under George Malcolm is fresh and vital. The earlier Vienna recording of the *Flute and harp concerto* has also stood the test of time, and again the recording is smooth, full, nicely reverberant and with good detail. Refinement and beauty of tone and phrase are a hallmark throughout, and Münchinger provides most sensitive accompaniments. A first-rate (75 minutes) compilation.

The fast speeds in the Berlin performance have a light, taut touch, with the ever-imaginative Pahud set against a modest-sized Berlin Philharmonic. Next to Pahud, the harp soloist, Marie-Pierre Langlamet is rather reticent in the *Flute and harp concerto*, though always sensitive.

(i) *Flute concerto No. 1 in G, K.313;* (ii) *Flute and harp concerto in C, K.299;* (iii) *Oboe concerto in C, K.314;* (iv) *Sinfonia concertante in E flat, K.297b.*

(BB) **(*) CfP Silver Double Dig. CDCFPSD 4808 (2). (i; ii) Snowden; (ii) Thomas; (iii) Hunt; (iv) Theodore, Hill, Price, Busch; LPO, (i; iv) Mackerras; (ii–iii) Litton.

Jonathan Snowden's account of the *Flute concerto* is attractive, sprightly, stylish and polished (though some might not take to his comparatively elaborate cadenzas). The performance of the *Flute and harp concerto* is even more winning. Where Gordon Hunt in the *Oboe concerto* seems a less natural concerto soloist, Snowden, in collaboration with Caryl Thomas on the harp, is both sparkling and sensitive, regularly imaginative in his individual phrasing. In the first movement of the *Sinfonia concertante* for wind, Mackerras is characteristically brisk, and his performance has plenty of life throughout, and charm too, in the closing variations. The solo playing here (by a different group) is of high quality; the *Adagio* is persuasive, if with no striking individuality. With excellent digital recording, this makes an enjoyable if not a distinctive collection.

(i) *Flute and harp concerto in C, K.299;* (ii) *Oboe concerto in C, K.271.*

*** Chandos Dig. CHAN 9051 [id.]. (i) Susan Milan, Skaila Kanga; (ii) David Theodore; City of L. Sinf., Hickox – SALIERI: *Double concerto.* ***

A warmly elegant modern-instrument account of this beguiling concerto, with the delicate interweaving of flute and harp given a delightful bloom by the resonant recording. The *Oboe concerto* is equally sensitive, again with the line of the *Adagio* delectably sustained by David Theodore, whose creamy tone is so enticing. Both soloists play their own cadenzas. Again the ear notices the very resonant orchestral sound, but in all other respects this is highly recommendable and it has a charming surprise for its coupling.

(i) *Flute & harp concerto, K.299. Serenade in G (Eine kleine Nachtmusik), K.525;* (ii) *Sinfonia concertante in E flat for violin, viola & orchestra, K.364.*
*** Decca (IMS) Dig. 443 175-2 [id.]. Cleveland O, Christoph von Dohnányi, with (i) Joshua Smith, Lisa Wellbaum; (ii) Daniel Majeske, Robert Vernon.

Here are two more eminently acceptable performances. The *Sinfonia concertante* is very well paced and completely free from any interpretative egocentricity. A musicianly, rather aristocratic performance, free from any playing to the gallery. The recording reproduces very faithfully and freshly. The *Concerto for flute, harp and orchestra* comes off nicely and has an appropriate *joie de vivre.* Not necessarily a first choice in either work, but worth considering alongside the best, and eminently recommendable if you want this particular coupling.

(i) *Flute and harp concerto in C, K.299; Sinfonia concertante in E flat, K.297b.*
(BB) *** Naxos Dig. 8.550159; *4550159* [id.]. (i) Jiri Válek, Hana Müllerová; Capella Istropolitana, Richard Edlinger.

Richard Edlinger's account of the *Flute and harp concerto* is thoroughly fresh and stylish, and the two soloists are excellent. Although the *Sinfonia concertante in E flat*, K.297b, is not quite so successful, it is still very impressive, and it gives much pleasure. Both performances are very decently recorded; in the lowest price-range they are a real bargain.

Horn concertos Nos. 1 in D, K.412; 2–4 in E flat, K.417, 447 & 495.
(N) *** Crystal Dig. CD 515 [id.]. John Cerminaro, Seattle SO, Schwarz.
(N) (B) *** CfP Dig. 573 4392. Claire Briggs, RLPO, Kovacevich – HAYDN: *Trumpet concerto.* ***
(B) *** DG Classikon 449 856-2 [(M) id. import]. Gerd Seifert, BPO, Karajan.
(M) **(*) Teldec 0630 17429-2 [id.]. Hermann Baumann, VCM, Harnoncourt.
(M) **(*) Carlton Dig. 30366 00972 [id.]. William Ver Meulen, Houston SO, Eschenbach

Horn concertos Nos. 1 in D, K.412 (with *Rondo*, reconstructed J. Humphries); *2–4 in E flat, K. 417, K.447 & K.495; Concert rondo in E flat, K.371* (reconstructed J. Humphries); *Rondo in D, K.514* (completed Süssmayr).
❁ *** O-L Dig. 443 216-2 [id.]. Anthony Halstead, AAM, Hogwood.

Horn concertos Nos. 1 in D, K.412 (with alternative versions of Rondo); *2–4 in E flat, K.417, K.447 & K.495; Allegro, K.370b & Concert rondo in E flat* (ed. Tuckwell); *Fragment in E, K.494a.*
*** Collins Dig. 1153-2 [id.]. Barry Tuckwell, Philh. O.

Horn concertos Nos. 1–4; Concert rondo in E flat, K.371 (ed. Civil or E. Smith).
*** Sony Dig. SK 53369 [id.]. Ab Koster, Tafelmusik, Bruno Weil.
*** Chandos Dig. CHAN 9150 [id.]. Frank Lloyd, N. Sinfonia, Richard Hickox.
(M) *** Ph. 442 397-2. Alan Civil, ASMF, Marriner.
(BB) *** Naxos Dig. 8.550148; *4.550148* [id.]. Miloš Stevove, Capella Istropolitana, Josef Kopelman.
(B) **(*) Carlton IMP Dig. PCD 2013. Richard Watkins, City of L. Sinfonia, Hickox.

Horn concertos Nos. 1–4; Concert rondo in E flat, K.371 (arr. Tuckwell).
(M) *** EMI (SIS) Dig. CDM7 64851-2. Radovan Vlatkovic, ECO, Tate – R. STRAUSS: *Horn concerto No. 1.* ***

Horn concertos Nos. 1–4; Concert rondo, K.371 (ed. Tuckwell); *Fragment, K.494a.*
(N) (BB) *** Virgin Classics Dig. Double VBD5 61573-2 (2) [id.]. Timothy Brown (hand-horn), O of Age of Enlightenment, Kuijken – Concert arias. ***
(M) *** EMI CDM7 69569-2. Barry Tuckwell, ASMF, Marriner.

Horn concertos Nos. 1–4; Concert rondos: in E flat, K.371 (completed John Humphries); *in D, K.514* (completed Süssmayr); *Fragment for horn and orchestra in E flat, K.370b* (reconstructed Humphries).
(BB) *** Naxos Dig. 8.553592 [id.]. Michael Thompson, Bournemouth Sinf.

As well as offering superb performances of the four regular concertos using revised texts prepared by John Humphries, this outstanding Naxos issue includes reconstructions of two movements designed for a horn concerto dating from soon after Mozart arrived in Vienna. The *Rondo* completed by Süssmayr is the version generally used as the second movement of K.412, which, according to the latest scholarship, was the last of the concertos to be written, not the first. The *Rondo* played here as the second movement of K.412 is Humphries's reconstruction from sources recently discovered, much more imaginative than the Süssmayr version. It is fascinating too to have extra passages in No. 4, again adding Mozartian inventiveness. Thompson plays with delectable lightness and point, bringing out the wit in finales, as well as the tenderness in slow movements. He also draws sparkling and refined playing from the Bournemouth Sinfonietta, very well recorded in clear, atmospheric sound.

Like Michael Thompson, Halstead plays the

music as modified by John Humphries. By using two different hand-horns, Halstead shows us the full range of tonal possibilities of the eighteenth-century instrument. For the earlier works, K.371, K.417 and K.447, he favours a modern copy of a Bohemian hand-horn of Mozart's own time; for K.495 and the *D major Concerto*, another copy of a more sophisticated and slightly smaller-bore Raoux instrument of 1795, to which most virtuosi of the time, including the famous Giovanni Punto, turned in the latter part of the century. As for the playing itself, it cannot be praised too highly for its imaginative musical phrasing, technical fluency and spontaneity. So pleasing is the orchestral sound that, apart from the transparent detail, one would hardly believe one was listening to period instruments.

Barry Tuckwell's Collins CD, his fourth recording of the Mozart *Horn concertos*, remains a splendid alternative choice for those wanting a modern-instrument performance with first-class, digital sound. They are fresh, without a suspicion of routine, and are played with rounded tone and consistently imaginative phrasing. Moreover the Collins collection is unusually complete. Besides the *Fragment*, K.494a, Tuckwell includes both the familiar *Concert Rondo*, K.371, plus an *Allegro* first movement which Mozart wrote to go with it. Tuckwell also includes his own alternative *Rondo* finale of the *Concerto in D*, K.412, based directly on Mozart's autograph, placing the two alternative finales side by side.

EMI have also effectively remastered Tuckwell's second set of the *Horn concertos* with Marriner, and the 1972 recording sounds quite full and fresh. This mid-priced CD also includes the *Concert rondo* and the *Fragment in E*.

We must also give the most cordial welcome to a splendid authentic set from Tafelmusik, which makes a very tempting alternative. Ab Koster is a very personable soloist and he plays on an Austrian hand-horn, built by Ignaz Lorenz of Linz. His plump timbre is very different from Tuckwell's – obviously very like the sound Mozart would have recognized, with stopped notes neatly incorporated into the melodic line. Melodic lines are allowed to breathe in the most attractive way while allegros are as spirited as one would wish, and the fresh, transparent textures of the accompanying Tafelmusik group (a sizeable band: 9.8.4.3.2, plus wind) are equally refreshing. Splendid recording, but this CD includes only the four *Concertos* plus the *Rondo*, K.371.

The other performance on original instruments is hardly less enjoyable. Timothy Brown also uses an open hand-horn without valves. He uses stopped notes with especially smart effect in the Rondos, and more sparingly and more subtly in the lyrical music. His control of the upper range of the instrument is remarkably free and even, yet the ear is often subtly aware that certain notes are being contrived. Far from being a drawback, this tends to increase the range of colour. Brown's lyrical line is very persuasive. In short these performances sound delightfully fresh, and give constant pleasure. Timothy Brown includes the additional *Rondo* and also the *Fragment*, which he leaves in mid-air, at the point at which the composer abandoned his manuscript. Kuijken's accompaniments, while light, bright and transparent, are also pleasingly smooth and cultivated. But it seems a strange idea to couple this repertoire (even as a super-bargain Virgin Double) with concert arias.

Among the other more recent versions is a fine set by Frank Lloyd, an outstanding soloist of the new generation. He plays these works with great character and poetic warmth; his phrasing is supple and his tone full, though never suave. Like Tuckwell, he uses a modern German double horn with great skill and sensitivity. Hickox provides admirable accompaniments, and the Chandos recording is well up to the high standards of the house.

Claire Briggs also gives brilliant performances of all four *Concertos*, with the celebrated finale of No. 4 taken exceptionally fast. Even that is superbly articulated without any feeling of breathlessness, though it lacks some of the fun that others have brought.

Miloš Stevove is principal horn with the Slovak Philharmonic Orchestra, and with his Bohemian background he is naturally at home in this genial music. He uses the slightest trace of vibrato but it is never obtrusive, and one has only to listen to the *Larghetto* of K.447 or the *Andante cantabile* of K.495 to discover his naturally warm feeling for a Mozartian phrase. Allegros are lively and the Rondos have agreeable lift. In short, with excellent, stylish accompaniments from the Capella Istropolitana this is enjoyably spontaneous. The recording is very good too; though not quite as beautiful as the Chandos, it has a compensating freshness.

John Cerminaro, at present principal with the Seattle Orchestra, is a splendid soloist. His tone is rich and glowing (a little plump as recorded), and the hints of vibrato add to the individuality of his supple phrasing, for he shows a warmly elegant feeling for the Mozartian line. There are plenty of imaginative touches, and in slow movements subtle dynamic touches bring out the expressive depth. Rondos bounce along genially. One of the highlights is the outstanding account of the *First Concerto*, into which he interpolates a soaring account of the slow movement of the *Horn quintet*. He is warmly and persuasively accompanied by Schwarz – himself a brass player of distinction. But at full price, and without the *Concert rondo*, this can hardly be a top recommendation.

Gerd Seifert has been principal horn of the Berlin Philharmonic since 1964, and his velvety, warm tone is familiar on many records. His articulation is light and neat here, and his nimbleness brings an effective lightness to the gay Rondos. Karajan almost matches his earlier accompaniments for Dennis Brain, and the orchestral playing is strong in character, although he never overwhelms his soloist. The 1969 recording now brings just a hint of over-brightness on the *forte* violins, but this adds to the sense of vitality without spoiling the elegance. This is now offered on DG's bargain Classikon label but, unlike some of its competitors, there are no added items.

Hermann Baumann also successfully uses the original hand-horn, without valves, for which the concertos were written, and the result is not achieved at the expense of musical literacy or expressive content. Baumann lets the listener hear the stopped effect only when he decides that the tonal change can be put to good artistic effect. In his cadenzas he also uses horn chords (where several notes are produced simultaneously by resonating the instrument's harmonics), but as a complement to the music rather than as a gimmick. Unfortunately the remastering has not been entirely successful: the original recording was mellow and reverberant; now it is noticeably drier. The solo horn is given a bold – indeed, rather too tangible – presence, yet its outline is not absolutely sharp, while there is also some roughness of focus in the strings.

Alan Civil's Philips set was made in 1973. The recording is obviously modern and the performances are highly enjoyable, with Sir Neville Marriner's polished and lively accompaniments giving pleasure in themselves. The balance has the effect of making the horn sound slightly larger than life.

Radovan Vlatkovic's tone is very full, with the lower harmonics telling more resonantly than is characteristic of a British soloist; there is also at times the slightest hint of vibrato, but it is applied with great discretion and used mostly in the cadenzas. His performances are full of imaginative touches and he has the perfect partner in Jeffrey Tate, who produces sparkling accompaniments. All in all, another outstanding set, most winningly different from the playing of the British generation. Moreover Vlatkovic includes both the *Concert rondo*, K.371, and, very appropriately, a quite outstanding account of the *First Horn concerto* of Richard Strauss which has so much in common with the spirit of the Mozart concertos.

Richard Watkins has the advantage of first-class modern digital recording on a bargain-priced label. He is an expert player and shows a genuine Mozartian sensibility. But this easy lyrical flow does mean that slow movements are very limpid and relaxed, and even the Rondos, articulated lightly, take wing more gently than usual. Hickox's accompaniments, on the other hand, are efficient and positive. But generally there is a somewhat self-effacing quality to the solo performances which detracts from the music's projection, and Barry Tuckwell's Collins set has an altogether stronger profile.

William Ver Meulen, principal horn of the Houston Symphony, is a fine expondent of what European horn-players tend to describe as the super-charged American style of playing. His performances are both strong and sensitive, with a wide expressive and tonal range. Eschenbach is a sympathetic accompanist and the recording is full and immediate. But at mid-price and with no coupling it is hardly competitive with such outstanding issues as the Naxos disc.

(i) *Horn concertos Nos. 1–4;* (ii) *Piano and wind quintet in E flat, K.452.*

(M) (***) EMI mono CDM5 66898-2 [CDM 566950]. Dennis Brain; (i) Philh. O, Karajan; (ii) Colin Horsley & members of Dennis Brain Wind Ens.

EMI have reissued Dennis Brain's famous (1954) mono record of the concertos with Karajan, and the disc now rightly appears in EMI's 'Great recordings of the century' series. Brain's horn timbre was unique. As for the playing, Brain's glorious tone and phrasing – every note is alive – is life-enhancing in its warmth; the *espressivo* of the slow movements is matched by the joy of the Rondos, spirited, buoyant, infectious and smiling. Karajan's accompaniments, too, are a model of Mozartian good manners and the Philharmonia at their peak play wittily and elegantly. Brain's distinguished earlier recording of the *Piano and wind quintet* has been added, with Colin Horsley making a fine contribution on the piano.

Oboe concerto in C, K.314.

*** ASV Dig. CDCOE 808 [id.]. Douglas Boyd, COE, Berglund – R. STRAUSS: *Oboe concerto.* ***

Douglas Boyd is never afraid to point the phrasing individually, spontaneously and without mannerism. Others may be purer in their classicism, but this is a very apt reading next to Strauss. Recorded in Henry Wood Hall, the sound is full and vivid.

Piano concertos

Complete Mozart Edition, Volume 7: (i) *Piano concertos, K.107/1–3;* (ii) *Nos. 1–4;* (iii) *5, 6, 8, 9, 11–27; Concert rondos 1–2;* (iii; iv) *Double piano concertos, K.242 & K.365;* (v) *Triple concerto in F, K.242.*

(M) **(*) Ph. Analogue/Dig. 422 507-2 (12) [id.]. (i) Ton Koopman, Amsterdam Bar. O; (ii) Haebler, Vienna Capella Academica, Melkus; (iii) Brendel, ASMF, Marriner; (iv) Imogen Cooper; (v) Katia and Marielle Labèque, Bychkov, BPO, Bychkov.

Piano concertos Nos. 1–6; 8–9; 11–27; Rondo in D, K.382.
(B) *** EMI CES5 72930-2 [CDZ5 62825] (10). Daniel Barenboim, ECO.

Piano concertos Nos. 1–6; 8–9; 11–27; Rondos Nos. 1–2, K.382 & 386.
❁ (M) *** Sony Analogue/Dig. SX12K 46441 (12). Murray Perahia, ECO.

(i) *Piano concertos Nos. 1–6; 8, 9, 11–27; Concert rondos Nos. 1 in D, K.382;* (ii) *2 in A, K.386;* (iii) *Double piano concerto in E flat, K.365;* (iii; iv) *Triple piano concerto in F, K.242.*
(B) *** Decca Analogue/Dig. 443 727-2 (10) [id.]. Ashkenazy, (i) with Philh. O; (ii) LSO, Kertész; (iii) Barenboim, ECO; (iv) Fou Ts'ong.

Piano concertos Nos. (i) *1–4;* (ii) *5;* (iii) *6;* (ii) *8–9;* (iv) *11;* (iii) *12;* (iv) *13–16;* (iii) *17;* (iv) *18;* (iii) *19;* (ii) *20;* (iii) *21;* (iv) *22;* (iii) *23;* (iv) *24;* (ii) *25;* (iii) *26;* (ii) *27; Concert rondos for piano and orchestra: in D, K.382; in A, K.386;* (ii; v) *Double piano concerto in E flat, K.365;* (ii; v; vi) *Triple concerto in F (Lodron), K.242.*
(B) **(*) Ph. 454 352-2 (10). Ingrid Haebler ((i) fortepiano or (ii–iv) piano), with (i) V. Capella Academica, Edward Melkus; (ii–vi) LSO; (ii) Galliera; (iii) Rowicki; (iv) Sir Colin Davis; (v) Ludwig Hofmann; (vi) Sas Bunge.

Piano concertos No. 20 in D min., K.466; 21 in C, K.467.
(BB) **(*) Belart 450 055-2 (from above). Ingrid Haebler, LSO; (i) Galliera; (ii) Rowicki.

By omitting the four early concertos after J. C. Bach, Sony have been able to reissue the Perahia set on twelve mid-priced CDs. The cycle is a remarkable achievement; in terms of poetic insight and musical spontaneity, the performances are in a class of their own. There is a wonderful singing line and at the same time a sensuousness that is always tempered by spirituality. About half the recordings are digital and of excellent quality and, we are glad to report, the earlier, analogue recordings have been skilfully remastered with first-class results, both in this complete set and in the separate issues below. The strings now sound smooth and full (the previously noticed edginess has disappeared) and the balance gives no cause for complaint. This is an indispensable set in every respect.

Those wanting a modern digital set of the Mozart concertos and for whom the flatteringly resonant sound of the Schiff/Végh series offers problems (see below) can readily turn to Ashkenazy, where the Decca recording is more crisply focused, with bright, athletic strings against a warm backgound ambience. Ashkenazy's set with the Philharmonia appeared over more than a decade: the early *Concertos* are the most recent (1987), while the *G major*, K.453, and the *C major*, K.467, come from 1977. The account of the *E flat Concerto*, K.365, with Barenboim and the ECO and the *Triple concerto* with Fou Ts'ong to complete the trio, is earlier still (1972). These performances have won golden opinions over the years, and the clarity of both the performances and the recordings is refreshing: indeed the fine Decca sound is one of their strongest features.

The sense of spontaneity in Barenboim's performances of the Mozart concertos, his message that this is music hot off the inspiration line, is hard to resist, even though it occasionally leads to over-exuberance and idiosyncrasies. These are as nearly live performances as one could hope for on record, and the playing of the English Chamber Orchestra is splendidly geared to the approach of an artist with whom the players have worked regularly. They are recorded with fullness, and the sound is generally freshened very successfully in the remastering. The set has been reissued in a handsomely produced super-bargain box, alongside his equally recommendable survey of the Beethoven piano sonatas, and EMI have appropriately chosen a different photograph of Barenboim to adorn the ten cardboard inner sleeves. The recordings were made at Abbey Road between 1967 and 1974.

The Philips Mozart Edition *Piano concertos* box is based on Brendel's set with the ASMF under Marriner. Throughout, his thoughts are never less than penetrating. The transfers are consistently of the very highest quality, as is the playing of the Academy of St Martin-in-the-Fields under Sir Neville Marriner. To make the set complete, Ingrid Haebler gives eminently stylish accounts of the first four *Concertos* on the fortepiano, accompanied by Melkus and his excellent Vienna Capella Academica; the sound is admirably fresh. However, on disc two the ear gets rather a shock when Ton Koopman presents the three works after J. C. Bach. Convincing though these performances are, it seems a strange idea to offer an authentic approach to these three concertos alone, particularly as at the end of the disc we return to a delightfully cultured performance on modern instruments of the alternative version for three pianos of the so-called *Lodron Concerto*, K.242, provided by the Labèque duo.

Ingrid Haebler recorded the Mozart concertos with the LSO for Philips between 1965 and 1968, alternating among three different conductors, then completing the set in 1973 with eminently stylish accounts of the first four concertos played appropriately on the fortepiano, accompanied by Melkus and his excellent Vienna Capella Academica. Her readings of the remainder are distinguished by a singular poise, meticulous finger-control and great delicacy of touch. She is less concerned with dramatic intensity; but with her carefully delineated boundaries she undoubtedly gives considerable pleasure by her restrained sensibility and musicianship. She is helped throughout by finely judged recordings, warm and spacious yet crystal clear, and the orchestral response is most sympathetic, particularly in the concertos conducted by Witold Rowicki and Colin Davis. She is at her most characteristic in the early masterpiece, No. *9 in E flat*, K.371, with a clean, classical approach; her account of K.413 (No. 11) is also beautifully alert and the slow movement immediately impresses with its poetry; but eventually the lack of forward movement becomes more obvious. It would be difficult to imagine a more poised account of No. *17 in G major*; the playing may lack the ultimate in forward drive, but Haebler plays lovingly and with great poetry, even if one regrets a certain want of temperament. Both the *B flat Concerto* (No. 18) and the great *E flat Concerto* (No. 22) show her at her finest: she is unfailingly musical and, though she is meticulous in her attention to detail, this does not detract from the scale of the music; the fine accompaniments from Davis contribute to the success of these performances. Summing up: as a complete survey this cannot measure up to Perahia, even if Sony's recordings do not consistently match the Philips sound-quality. But Haebler has her own insights to offer, she is a highly individual Mozartian and there is much here to give pleasure when the recorded sound is so good.

For those wanting a characteristic sample of the series, Belart have made available a super-bargain coupling of the two top favourite concertos, *Nos. 20 in D minor* and *21 in C major*, the latter with its 'Elvira Madigan' associations – although Haebler's exquisitely dispassionate view of the famous *Andante* would hardly have been suitable for the soundtrack. The recordings are beautifully transferred.

Piano concertos Nos. 5–6, 8–9, 11–27.
(M) *** Decca Dig. 448 140-2 (9). András Schiff, Salzburg Mozarteum Camerata Academica, Végh.

András Schiff's cycle with the Salzburg Mozarteum Camerata Academica under Sándor Végh proves to be one of the most satisfying of recent years and – along with the new Shelley series on Chandos – arguably the finest since Murray Perahia's cycle of the late 1970s. Schiff plays a Bösendorfer piano and its relatively gentle, cleanly focused timbre has something of the precision of a fortepiano without any loss of the colour which comes with a more modern instrument. The recording is consistently more beautiful than in Perahia's Sony set, with sweet strings and glowing woodwind and the piano usually balanced naturally and integrated with the orchestra. For some listeners in certain works the warm resonance may offer a problem. The recordings were made in a variety of venues between 1984 and 1990, although the balance and warm ambience seem fairly consistent. This is agreeably relaxed music-making, though not in the least lacking in intensity or weight. Just occasionally Schiff dots his 'i's and crosses his 't's a little too precisely, but for the most part he is so musicianly and perceptive that this seems unimportant. In short, these are lovely performances, enhanced by the quality of the accompaniment under Végh, who is unfailingly supportive. For the most part Schiff plays his own cadenzas, but in the first movement of K.466 he uses a cadenza by Beethoven, and the finale of K.488 brings one by George Malcolm. There is an accompanying booklet which includes two essays: 'A performer's approach' by Schiff himself, and a general survey by Jeremy Siepmann called 'Mozart's Utopian visions'. All these records are also available separately in their original couplings.

Piano concertos Nos. 5–6; 8–9; 11–27; Rondo in D, K.382.
**(*) Ph. Dig. 438 207-2 (9) [id.]. Mitsuko Uchida, ECO, Jeffrey Tate.

Mitsuko Uchida, following up her stylish and sensitive accounts of the *Piano sonatas*, began a cycle of the concertos in 1985 with Nos. 20 and 21, which set the style for the series (recorded over a period of nearly five years) with playing of considerable beauty and performances guaranteed never to offend and most likely to delight. There is some lovely playing, although her cultured approach at times offers more than a glimpse of Dresden china. She is unfailingly elegant but a little over-civilized; some will find a faint hint of preciosity here and there. Uchida is eminently alive and imaginative, although at times one would welcome a greater robustness of spirit, a lively inner current, and this applies particularly to the last two concertos, K.537 and K.595. Throughout, Jeffrey Tate draws splendid playing from the ECO, and these artists have the benefit of exceptionally good recorded sound; although the perspective favours the piano, the timbre of the solo instrument is beautifully captured.

Piano concertos Nos. 5–6, 8–9, 11–27; (i) *Double piano concerto, K.365;* (i; ii) *Triple piano concerto, K.242. Concert Rondos 1–2.*
(M) *** DG Dig. 431 211-2 (9) [id.]. Malcolm Bilson (fortepiano), E. Bar. Soloists, Gardiner, (i) with Robert Levin; (ii) Melvyn Tan.

Malcolm Bilson's complete set of the Mozart *Piano concertos* appears on nine mid-price CDs. Bilson is an artist of excellent musical judgement and good taste, and his survey is the only one at present available on the fortepiano. For the most part, there is little to quarrel with here and much to enjoy.

Piano concertos Nos. 5 in D, K.175; 25 in C, K.503.
*** Sony Dig. SK 37267 [id.]. Perahia, ECO.

Murray Perahia has the measure of the strength and scale of the *C major*, K.503, as well as displaying tenderness and poetry; while the early *D major*, K.175, has an innocence and freshness that are completely persuasive. The recording is good, but the upper strings are a little fierce and not too cleanly focused.

Piano concerto No. 6 in B flat, K.238.
(M) **(*) Decca 448 598-2 [id.]. Vladimir Ashkenazy, LSO, Schmidt-Isserstedt – BACH: *Clavier concerto No. 1* **(*); CHOPIN: *Piano concerto No. 2.* ***

This is an eloquent performance of a charming work, beautifully accompanied. The 1968 recording is excellent for its period, though perhaps an unexpected choice for reissue in Decca's Classic Sound series. The coupled Chopin concerto is the highlight of this reissue.

Piano concertos Nos. 6 in B flat, K.238; 8 in C, K.246; 19 in F, K.459.
(BB) *** Naxos Dig. 8.550208; *4550208* [id.]. Jenö Jandó, Concentus Hungaricus, Mátyás Antal.

No. 19 in F is a delightful concerto and it receives a most attractive performance, aptly paced, with fine woodwind playing, the finale crisply sparkling. No. 6 is hardly less successful; if No. 8 seems plainer, it is still admirably fresh. With excellently balanced recording this is a genuine bargain.

Piano concertos Nos. 6 in B flat, K.238; 13 in C, K.415.
*** Sony SK 39223 [id.]. Murray Perahia, ECO.

Perahia brings a marvellous freshness and delicacy to the *B flat Concerto*, K.238, but it is in the *C major*, with its sense of character and subtle artistry, that he is at his most sparkling and genial. Even if the acoustic ambience is less than ideally spacious, the CBS sound is still good.

Piano concertos Nos. 6 in B flat, K.238; 17 in G, K.453; 21 in C, K.467.
(M) *** DG 447 436-2 [id.]. Géza Anda, Salzburg Mozarteum Camerata Academica.

It is proper that Géza Anda's Mozart concerto series from the 1960s should find a place in DG's 'Originals' series. His poetic account of the *C major Concerto*, K.467, is one of the most impressive from his cycle, notably for a beautifully poised account of the slow movement. In the *G major*, K.453, Anda, who directs from the keyboard, there is both strength and poetry, while the DG recording is excellent in both balance and clarity. The *B flat Concerto*, K.238, is played simply and eloquently. The recording is not quite so cleanly transferred in the early work. It comes last on the CD and is by no means of lesser appeal, and this remains a most enjoyable triptych.

Piano concertos Nos. 8 in C (Lützow), K.246; 9 in E flat (Jeunehomme), K.271; Concert rondo No. 2 in A, K.386.
✿ (M) *** Decca 443 576-2 [id.]. Ashkenazy, LSO, Kertész.
(BB) *** Discover DICD 920517 [id.]. Susan Kagan, Suk CO, Petr Macecek.

Ashkenazy's earlier, 1966 coupling with Kertész, which includes also the *A major Concert rondo*, has now been appropriately reissued in Decca's Classic Sound series and the recorded quality remains beautifully fresh and realistic. The magnificent performances originally earned the LP a Rosette and we see no reason not to carry it forward. Ashkenazy has the requisite sparkle, humanity and command of keyboard tone, and his readings can only be called inspired. He is very well supported by the LSO under Kertész, and they make an excellent case for a partnership with a sympathetic conductor, rather than having the soloist direct the proceedings from the keyboard.

These performances by the American performer and scholar, Susan Kagan are notable for an appealingly direct simplicity of approach. These are not self-conscious interpretations, but Mozart played freshly and spontaneously. The recording, in an intimate, slightly dry acoustic, is real and immediate. Though without the experienced insights of a Perahia, of its kind this is first class.

Piano concertos Nos. 8 in C, K. 246; 13 in C, K. 415; 25 in C, K. 503.
(B) **(*) HMA 1903022 [id.]. Kocsis, Franz Liszt CO, János Rolla.

Robust and thoroughly lively and musical accounts of Mozart's three C major concertos. The slow movement of K.503 comes off especially well and the finale is infectious. Fine, modern, digital recording and a good balance ensure the appeal and value of the disc; even if the sound is a shade resonant, everything is clearly focused.

(i) *Piano concertos Nos. 9 in E flat, K.271; 14 in E flat, K.449.*
(M) *** Van. 8.4015.71 [OVC 4015]. Alfred Brendel; (i) I Solisti di Zagreb, Janigro.

Brendel's 1968 performance of No. 9 is quite outstanding, elegant and beautifully precise. The classical-sized orchestra is just right and the neat, stylish string-playing matches the soloist. The performance of K.449 is also first rate, with a memorably vivacious finale. Altogether this is an outstanding reissue with natural sound which hardly shows its age in the clean remastering.

Piano concertos Nos. 9 in E flat, K.271; 15 in B flat, K.450; 22 in E flat, K.482; 25 in C, K.503; 27 in B flat, K.595.
(B) *** Ph. Duo 442 571-2 (2) [id.]. Alfred Brendel, ASMF, Marriner.

A first-class follow-up to Brendel's first Duo collection of Mozart piano concertos (see below). The account of the opening *Jeunehomme* is finely proportioned and cleanly articulated, with a ravishing account of the slow movement. The finale has great sparkle and finesse and the recording has exemplary clarity. Brendel is hardly less fine in K.450, and the *E flat Concerto* has both vitality and depth. Brendel's first movement has breadth and grandeur as well as sensitivity, while the *Andante* has great poetry. No. 25 (there is well-deserved applause at the close) was recorded at a live performance and has life and concentration, and a real sense of scale. Here as elsewhere the playing of the ASMF under Marriner is alert and supportive. K.595 is also among Brendel's best Mozart performances, with a beautifully poised *Larghetto* and a graceful, spirited finale. The recordings were made between 1974 and 1981 (No. 15 is digital) and offer characteristically fresh and natural sound. Highly recommended.

Piano concertos Nos. 9 in E flat, K.271; 17 in G, K.453.

(M) *** Chandos Dig. CHAN 9068 [id.]. Howard Shelley, LMP.

Piano concertos Nos. 9 in E flat (Jeunehomme), K.271; 17 in G, K.453; Rondo in D, K.382.

(M) *** DG (IMS) Dig. 447 291-2 [id.]. Malcolm Bilson (fortepiano), E. Bar. Soloists, Gardiner.

Howard Shelley is the latest to embrace the challenge of directing Mozart concertos from the keyboard. Shelley's playing is a delight and is possessed of a refreshing naturalness which should win many friends. There is spontaneity and elegance, a strong vein of poetic feeling and extrovert high spirits. His *G major concerto* belongs in the most exalted company and can withstand comparison with almost any rival. But both performances are touched by distinction, and they are beautifully recorded too.

Malcolm Bilson shows himself a lively and imaginative artist, well matched by Gardiner. The CD catches the lightness and clarity of the textures, with the fortepiano sound not too twangy and with wind balances often revelatory. The darkness of the C minor slow movement of K.271 is eerily caught; K.453, as ever, is a delight, with Bilson allowing himself a natural degree of expressiveness, within the limits of classical taste. The lightness of the keyboard action encourages the choice of fast allegros, but never at the expense of Mozart.

(i) *Piano concertos Nos. 9 in E flat (Jeunehomme), K.271; 17 in G, K.453; 20 in D min., K.466. Adagio and fugue in C min., K.546.*

(N) **(*) ECM Dig. ECM 1624/25 [id.]. (i) Keith Jarrett; Stuttgart CO, Dennis Russell Davies.

Admirers of Keith Jarrett should be well satisfied with his newest Mozartian venture, apart from the short measure. For the *Adagio and fugue*, well played as it is, only lasts for just over seven minutes! Dennis Russell and the excellent Stuttgart Orchestra set the scene in each of the three concertos very impressively: the opening *ritornello* of K.271 is remarkably mature-sounding and the dramatic outer movements of the *D minor Concerto* are equally forward-looking. Jarrett plays fluently and responsively throughout: only in the central *Romance* of the latter work does he seem not ideally relaxed. But the movement's roving central section is impressively done, and the *Andante* of K. 453, taken slowly and reflectively, shows him at his most thoughtful, while the finale is delightfully light-hearted. Excellent recording, well balanced, full bodied and clear.

Piano concertos Nos. 9 in E flat (Jeunehomme), K.271; 20 in D min., K.466; 21 in C, K.467; 23 in A, K.488; 27 in B flat, K.595.

(B) **(*) EMI Rouge et Noir CZS5 69991-2 (2). Daniel Barenboim, ECO.

The youthful *Jeunehomme concerto*, K.271, sets the style of these highly enjoyable performances, full of spirit and demonstrating masterly pianism, with an alert and musical direction of the orchestra. It also demonstrates Barenboim's willingness at times to display too great an awareness of refinements of tone and dynamics that are, strictly speaking, anachronistic. In K.271 the most serious reservation concerns the minuet at the centre of the final rondo which is far too measured. Barenboim's performances of *No. 20 in D minor* and No. 23, K.488, have all the sparkle and sensitivity one could ask for. The orchestral accompaniment is admirably alive, and one's only serious reservation concerns the somewhat fast tempo he adopts in the finale of K.466. The account of No. 23 is enchanting. There are moments when his delicacy of fingerwork comes close to preciosity, but it never quite goes over the edge. (It is a pity that this concerto is split between the two CDs.) There need be no reservations about the performance of No. 21 either; it is accomplished in every way. His version of K.595 is, however, more controversial. He again indulges in great refinement of touch and his reading of the slow movement is overtly romantic. The recordings (from the late 1960s) are fresh and naturally balanced; they are admirably transferred to CD.

Piano concertos Nos. 9 in E flat, K.271; 21 in C, K.467.

*** Sony SK 34562 [id.]. Murray Perahia, ECO.

(N) (B) ** CfP Dig. 573 4402. Stephen Hough, Hallé O, Bryden Thomson.

Perahia's reading of K.271 is wonderfully refreshing and delicate, with diamond-bright articulation, urgently youthful in its resilience. The famous *C major Concerto* is given a more variable, though still highly imaginative performance. Faithful, well-balanced recording.

As in his prizewinning Chandos record of the two Hummel concertos, Stephen Hough plays with fine freshness, point and clarity; but where in the Hummel he gave the works a bigger stature than you might expect, here he tends to prettify two of Mozart's strongest concertos, minimizing their greatness. This delicate, Dresden-china treatment would have been more acceptable half-a-century ago, but now leaves out too much that is essential.

Piano concertos Nos. 11 in F, K.413; 12 in A, K.414; 13 in C, K.415.
(B) *** EMI Debut CDZ5 72525-2 [id.]. Patrick Dechorgnat, Henschel Qt.

There is a special kind of intimate pleasure in hearing these three simple but masterly concertos of 1782 with just a string quartet accompaniment. The interplay between the stylish Patrick Dechorgnat and the polished and sympathetic Henschel Quartet is heard at its most appealing in the *Larghetto* of the *F major Concerto*, K.413, yet the touching *Andante* of K.414 is hardly less winning, and the recording throughout is so expertly balanced that all three works are a great success. A first-rate début for soloist and string quartet alike.

Piano concertos Nos. 11 in F, K.413; 12 in A, K.414; 14 in E flat, K.449.
*** Sony SK 42243 [id.]. Murray Perahia, ECO.

These performances remain in a class of their own. When it first appeared, we thought the *F major*, K.413, the most impressive of Perahia's Mozart concerto records so far, its slow movement wonderfully inward; and the *E flat Concerto*, K.449, is comparably distinguished. The current remastering is very successful.

Piano concertos Nos. 12 in A, K.414; 14 in E flat, K.449; 21 in C, K.467.
(BB) *** Naxos Dig. 8.550202; *4550202* [id.]. Jenö Jandó, Concentus Hungaricus, András Ligeti.

In Jandó's hands the first movement of K.449 sounds properly forward-looking; the brightly vivacious K.414 also sounds very fresh here, and its *Andante* is beautifully shaped. The excellent orchestral response distinguishes the first movement of K.467: both grace and weight are here, and some fine wind playing. An added interest in this work is provided by Jandó's use of cadenzas provided by Robert Casadesus. Jandó is at his most spontaneous throughout these performances and this is altogether an excellent disc, well recorded.

Piano concertos Nos. 12 in A, K.414; 19 in F, K.459.
(M) *** Chandos Dig. CHAN 9256 [id.]. Howard Shelley, LMP.

Another fine disc in Howard Shelley's musically rewarding and beautifully recorded series. Admirers of this artist need not hesitate in investing here, with the music's expressive range fully encompassed without mannerism, slow movements eloquently shaped and outer movements aptly paced and alive with vitality.

Piano concertos Nos. 12 in A, K.414; 20 in D min., K.466; Rondo in D, K.382.
*** RCA Dig. 09026 60400 [id.]. Kissin, Moscow Virtuosi, Spivakov.

The *D major Rondo*, K.382, has an elegance and delicacy worthy of the greatest Mozart players of the day. The *A major Concerto* shows the same immaculate technical finesse and musical judgement (save, perhaps, in the slow movement, which some could find a little oversweet). There are perhaps greater depths in the *D minor Concerto* than Kissin finds but, even so, the playing is musical through and through and gives unfailing pleasure. The recorded sound is very good and the disc as a whole deserves the attention of any Mozartian.

Piano concertos Nos. 12 in A, K.414; 21 in C, K.467.
(M) (***) Dutton Lab mono CDCLP 4000. Moura Lympany, Philh. O, Menges – TURINA: *Rapsodia sinfonica.* (***)

These performances originally appeared on a plum-label HMV LP in 1955. (Even Moura Lympany's dazzling account of the Prokofiev and Rachmaninov *Concertos* was assigned to this less prestigious label.) Not that Dame Moura's playing is in any way lacking in distinction – indeed, these are readings of the highest finesse and subtlety. Herbert Menges gets very good playing from the Philharmonia and the sound, beautifully refurbished by Michael Dutton, sounds very fresh. Strongly recommended.

Piano concertos Nos. 13 in A, K.415; 20 in D min., K.466.
(BB) **(*) Naxos Dig. 8.550201 [id.]. Jenö Jandó, Concentus Hungaricus, András Ligeti.

These performances set a high standard in their communicative immediacy, and if they have not quite the individuality of Perahia or Ashkenazy, they are worth a place in any collection and are very modestly priced. Jandó uses Beethoven's cadenzas with impressive authority. The balance and recording are most believable and there is good documentation throughout this series.

Piano concertos Nos. 13 in C, K.415; 24 in C min., K.491.
(M) *** Chandos Dig. CHAN 9326 [id.]. Howard Shelley, LMP.

Like Perahia before him, Howard Shelley directs from the keyboard and this, the fifth in his ongoing series, is as distinguished as its predecessors. He has immaculate keyboard manners and his strong, natural musicianship is always in evidence. An instinctive yet thoughtful Mozartian whose consummate artistry places his cycle among the very finest now on the market.

Piano concertos Nos. 14 in E flat, K.449; 15 in B flat, K.450; 16 in D, K.451.

(N) **(*) Teldec/Warner 0630 16827-2. Berlin PO/Barenboim.

The Teldec disc of the same three related concertos completed Daniel Barenboim's second survey of all the solo works from K.271 in *E flat* (*No. 9*) to the final K.595, which has been a mixed success. With two of the three works here recorded live, there is the same concentration, freshness and sense of spontaneity as in his EMI recordings of 30 years earlier, now recoupled together. But overall these latest performances are a shade heavier and more muscular, with fewer pianissimos. Interpretatively, the big difference is that slow movements flow more easily, in a lighter, less romantically expressive style; in principle, a positive gain, though with less magic in the results. Thanks to the recording, the modest-sized orchestra, playing immaculately, sounds rather beefy in tuttis. The EMI disc remains the one to go for.

(i) *Piano concertos Nos. 14 in E flat, K.449; 15 in B flat K.450; 19 in F, K.459; 21 in C, K.467; 26 in D (Coronation), K.537; 27 in B flat, K.595;* (i; ii) *Double piano concerto in E flat, K.365. Adagio in B min., K.540; Piano sonatas Nos. 8 in A min., K.310; 11 in A, K.331; 13 in B flat, K.333; 14 in C min., K.457; Fantasia in C min., K.475; Rondo in A min., K.511.*

(M) **(*) Ph. Brendel Edition Analogue/Dig. 446 921-2 (5). Alfred Brendel, with (i) ASMF, Marriner; (ii) Imogen Cooper – HAYDN: *Andante & variations in F min.; Piano sonatas.* ***

Among Brendel's many fine recordings of the Mozart concertos, the *E flat major*, K.449, ranks highly, distinguished by beautifully clean and alive passage-work, while there is superb control and poise. The main ideas are well shaped without being overcharacterized. Tempi are wisely chosen and perfectly related. He is hardly less impressive in K.450. In K.467 each detail of a phrase is meticulously articulated, every staccato and slur carefully observed in an almost didactic fashion. But there is so much to delight in these performances. In the *Coronation concerto*, as always, Brendel's articulation and intelligence excite admiration. Only in the slow movement does one feel a trace of didacticism. There are no such reservations about No. 27, which is in every way distinguished and is beautifully recorded. Similarly the *Double concerto* (with Imogen Cooper) is elegant and poised, combining vigour with tonal refinement, and here as elsewhere Marriner's accompaniments are comparably polished. The *Sonatas*, however, bring a few reservations. The pianism is masterly, as one would expect from this great artist, but the performances of Nos. 8 and 14 strike one as the product of excessive ratiocination. There is no want of inner life, the texture is wonderfully clean and finely balanced, but the listener is all too aware of the mental preparation that has gone into the interpretations. The staccato markings in the slow movement of K.310 are exaggerated and the movement as a whole is unsmiling and strangely wanting in repose. Self-conscious playing, immaculately recorded. Both Nos. 11 and 13, however, are a joy, and beautifully recorded too.

Piano concertos Nos. 14 in E flat, K.449; 23 in A, K. 488; 24 in C min., K.491.

(M) *** DG Dig. 447 295-2. Malcolm Bilson (fortepiano), E. Bar. Soloists, Gardiner.

Here are three key Mozart concertos in a generous triptych, with the tough *E flat Concerto* coming last. The much-loved *A Major*, K.488, is as fresh as you could wish for, with plenty of zing in outer movements – the horns ringing through the texture – the *Adagio* very poised. Here the ear notices the comparative lack of the darker sonority of a modern instrument, but this is still most sensitive playing, not over-elaborated. Gardiner and the English Baroque Soloists provide vigorous, large-scale orchestral tuttis, matching Bilson's expressiveness on the one hand, while on the other relishing the fast speeds he prefers in the finales and bringing wit to the last movement of K.488. The *Larghetto* of the *C minor* brings no reservations and this is a performance which combines drama with poetry; here the tempo of the finale is a moderate *Allegretto*, allowing the detail to register admirably. Excellent recording, fresh and full-bodied, yet clear.

Piano concertos Nos. 14 in E flat, K.449; 27 in B flat, K.595.

(M) *** Chandos Dig. CHAN 9137 [id.]. Howard Shelley, LMP.

Admirable performances, stylish and with a fine Mozartian sensibility. This is altogether most refreshing, and the recording is very good indeed.

(i) *Piano concerto No. 15 in B flat, K.450; Symphony No. 36 in C (Linz), K.425.*

(M) **(*) Decca (IMS) 448 570-2 [id.]. (i) Leonard Bernstein (piano); VPO, Bernstein.

An enjoyably light-hearted Mozartian coupling. In the performance of the *Linz Symphony* one relishes the carefree quality in the playing. The *Concerto*, even more than the *Symphony*, conveys the feeling of a conductor enjoying himself on holiday. Bernstein's piano playing may not be poised in every detail, but every note communicates vividly.

Piano concertos Nos. 15 in B flat, K.450; 16 in D, K.451.

*** Sony Dig. SK 37824 [id.]. Perahia, ECO.

Perahia's are superbly imaginative readings, full of seemingly spontaneous touches and turns of phrase very personal to him, which yet never sound mannered. His version of the *B flat Concerto* has sparkle, grace and intelligence; both these performances are very special indeed. The recording is absolutely first rate, intimate yet realistic and not dry, with the players continuously grouped round the pianist.

Piano concertos Nos. 16 in D, K.451; 25 in C, K.503; Rondo in A, K.386.
(BB) *** Naxos Dig. 8.550207; *4550207* [id.]. Jenö Jandó, Concentus Hungaricus, Mátyás Antal.

Jenö Jandó gives a very spirited and intelligent account of the relatively neglected *D major Concerto*, K.451, in which he receives sensitive and attentive support from the excellent Concentus Hungaricus under Mátyás Antal. The performance has warmth. The players sound as if they are enjoying themselves and, although there are greater performances of the *C major Concerto*, K.503, on record, few are at this extraordinarily competitive price.

Piano concertos Nos. 17 in G, K.453; 18 in B flat, K.456.
*** Sony Dig. SK 36686 [id.]. Perahia, ECO.
(BB) *** Naxos Dig. 8.550205; *4550205* [id.]. Jenö Jandó, Concentus Hungaricus, Mátyás Antal.

The *G major Concerto* is one of the most magical of the Perahia cycle and is on no account to be missed. The *B flat*, too, has the sparkle, grace and finesse that one expects from him. Even if you have other versions, you should still add this to your collection, for its insights are quite special.

This is also one of the finest in Jandó's excellent super-bargain series. Tempi are admirably judged and both slow movements are most sensitively played. The variations which form the *Andante* of K.456 are particularly appealing in their perceptive use of light and shade, while the very lively *Allegro vivace* finale of the same work is infectiously spirited. Jandó uses Mozart's original cadenzas for the first two movements of K.453 and the composer's alternative cadenzas for K.546. Excellent sound.

Piano concertos Nos. 17 in G, K.453; 21 in C, K.467.
*** DG Dig. 439 941-2 [id.]. Maria João Pires, COE, Abbado.

We admired Maria João Pires's Mozart concertos, recorded with the Lisbon orchestra way back in the 1970s, and are pleased to welcome this newcomer. Her playing, both in the mercurial *G major Concerto* and in its more ceremonial *C major* companion, is elegant, searching and intelligent. She has taste and fine musicianship, and the Chamber Orchestra of Europe under Abbado give excellent support. In the *C major* we would not necesarily recommend her in preference to Perahia, Shelley or Brendel, but there is none of the preciosity that marred Uchida's cycle with Jeffrey Tate. Good recording.

Piano concertos Nos. 18 in B flat, K.456; 19 in F, K.459.
*** HM Dig. HMU 907138 [id.]. Melvyn Tan, Philh. Bar. O, McGegan.

No one is more convincing on the fortepiano than Melvyn Tan. The pointedly rhythmic main theme of the *F major Concerto* suits the fortepiano particularly well – which is not to say that the *Allegretto* isn't equally winning, with some delightful wind playing from these characterful period instrumentalists. The *B flat Concerto* is hardly less successful: the gentle melancholy of its G minor slow movement has an engaging fragility, and the superb finale – one of Mozart's most ambitious – is given its full character. McGegan and his players are clearly completely at one with their soloist. The recording is more intimate, slightly drier than in Malcolm Bilson's DG series, and the result is most persuasive.

Piano concertos Nos. 19, K.459; 20, K.466; 21, K.467; 23, K.488; 24, K.491; Concert rondos Nos. 1–2, K.382 & 386.
❁ (B) *** Ph. Duo 442 269-2 [id.]. Alfred Brendel, ASMF, Marriner.

This must be the Mozartian bargain of all time, five piano concertos and two concert rondos – all for the cost of one premium-price CD. A Rosette then for generosity, to say nothing of the distinction of the performances. Indeed the playing exhibits a sensibility that is at one with the composer's world and throughout the set the Philips sound-balance is impeccable.

Piano concertos Nos. 19 in F, K.459; 22 in E flat, K.482.
(B) *** Decca Eclipse Dig. 448 992-2. Alicia de Larrocha, VSO, Uri Segal – HANDEL: *Keyboard suite No. 5.* ***

Alicia de Larrocha can hold her own against most of her rivals in terms of both scale and sensitivity, though her K.482 is perhaps not as completely integrated or as touching as the Perahia, which has particularly eloquent playing from the ECO wind. She is also on good form in the *F major*; the Decca recording is beautifully transparent and clear, as well as being warmly resonant, which increases the tinge of romantic feeling in these performances.

Piano concertos Nos. 19 in F, K.459; 23 in A, K.488.
❁ *** Sony Dig. SK 39064 [id.]. Murray Perahia, ECO.

Murray Perahia gives highly characterful accounts of both *Concertos* and a gently witty yet vital reading of the *F Major*, K.459. As always with this artist, there is a splendidly classical feeling allied to a keenly poetic sensibility. His account of K.488 has enormous delicacy and inner vitality, yet a serenity that puts it in a class of its own.

Piano concertos Nos. 19 in F, K.459; 25 in C, K.503.

(N) **(*) Erato Dig. 3984-23299-2. Till Fellner, Camerata Ac. Salzburg, Janiczek.

With the young, prizewinning Viennese pianist, Till Fellner, as a crisp and sparkling soloist, this imaginatively brings together two concertos with military manners. His fine musicianship, clean articulation and classical poise are heard to admirable effect in both works, and these performances are best described as fresh and light. Though Fellner is a former pupil of Brendel, his Mozart style is quite different, with articulation of diamond-like precision, enhanced by the excellent Erato recording, cleanly separated. In slow movements he is at once poetic and unmannered. There is a good rapport between him and the Camerata Academica Salzburg led by Alexander Janiczek, who draws clean, fresh playing from the fine Salzburg orchestra, yet on the cool side. Some may find both the first and last movements a shade too brisk, but generally speaking it is difficult to fault these performances. Taken in their own right they give considerable pleasure.

Piano concerto No. 20 in D min., K.466.

(N) (B) **(*) EMI double fforte Dig. CZS5 73329-2 (2). Egorov, Philh. O, Sawallisch – BEETHOVEN: *Symphony No. 9; Piano concerto No. 5.* **(*)

It seems a curious idea to couple this (albeit inexpensively) with part of Sawallisch's Beethoven symphony cycle. But Egorov is stylish enough and Sawallisch finds plenty of drama in the outer movements, and the slow movement, too, is elegantly shaped. Good, bright 1985 recording, made at Abbey Road.

Piano concertos Nos. 20 in D min., K.466; 21 in C, K.467.

✽ *** DG Dig. 419 609-2 [id.]. Malcolm Bilson (fortepiano), E. Bar. Soloists, Gardiner.

(M) *** RCA GD 87967 [7967-2-RG]. Rubinstein, RCA Victor SO, Wallenstein (with HAYDN: *Andante & variations in F min.* ***).

(i) *Piano concertos Nos. 20 in D min., K.466; 21 in C, K.467.* (ii) *Serenade No. 13 in G (Eine kleine Nachtmusik), K.525.*

(BB) *** RCA Navigator 74321 17888-2. (i) Géza Anda, VSO; (ii) Bamberg SO, Jochum.

These are vital, electric performances by Bilson and the English Baroque Soloists, expressive within their own lights, neither rigid nor too taut in the way of some period Mozart, nor inappropriately romantic. This is a disc to recommend even to those who would not normally consider period performances of Mozart concertos, fully and vividly recorded with excellent balance between soloist and orchestra – better than you would readily get in the concert hall.

Rubinstein has seldom been caught so sympathetically by the microphones, and the remastered 1961 recording has the orchestral sound admirably freshened. In each concerto the slow movement is the kernel of the interpretation. Rubinstein's playing is melting. Wallenstein is an excellent accompanist, for finales have plenty of sparkle. The Haydn *Andante and variations*, a substantial bonus recorded a year earlier, again demonstrates Rubinstein's aristocratic feeling for a classical melodic line: it is played most beautifully.

Both performances by Anda have an attractive simplicity and are admirably spontaneous, with slow movements sensitive and graciously phrased. The delicacy of the solo playing entirely avoids any suggestions of Dresden china, while the orchestral introduction to the *D minor* has plenty of atmosphere. Excellent value.

(i) *Piano concertos Nos. 20 in D min., K.466; 21 in C, K.467;* (ii) *22 in E flat, K.482; 23 in A, K.488.*

(BB) *** EMI Seraphim CES5 68529-2 (2). Annie Fischer, Philh. O; (i) Sawallisch; (ii) Boult.

This is one of the real bargains on EMI's Seraphim (two-for-the-price-of-one medium-price-CD) label and well worth having, even if duplication is involved. Annie Fischer's coupling of Nos. 21–22 was very highly regarded when it first appeared in 1959 on mono only. Fischer's gentle, limpid touch, with its frequent use of half-tones, gives a great deal of pleasure. In the *C major Concerto* she uses cadenzas by Busoni and in the *E flat Concerto* the first-movement cadenza is by Hummel, which adds another point of interest to this coupling. In the *D minor Concerto* Boult's tempi are sensible and the orchestral playing is again felicitous, particularly from the wind. The reading perhaps misses the ultimate in breadth and dramatic fire, but it is a very good performance all the same. In K.488, Fischer plays with liveliness of feeling and refinement of touch. Beethoven's cadenzas are used in the *D minor Concerto*.

(i) *Piano concertos Nos. 20 in D min., K.466; 21 in C, K.467; 23 in A, K.488; 24 in C min., K.491; 25 in C, K.503.*

(B) *** Decca Double Dig./Analogue 452 958-2 (2) [id.]. Ashkenazy, Philh. O.

This Double Decca set, reissued for Ashkenazy's sixtieth birthday, now includes both the D minor and C minor masterpieces, but not K.595 (No. 27), which, however, remains available on a slightly different permutation at a similar cost – see below. K.491 and K.503 are among the finest in his series, so the present grouping is particularly attractive. The Kingsway Hall recordings cannot be faulted.

They were made between 1977 and 1983; Nos. 20, 23 and 25 are digital.

(i) *Piano concertos Nos. 20 in D min., K.466; 21 in C, K.467; 23 in A, K.488; 27 in B flat, K.595. Piano sonata No. 17 in D, K.576; Rondo in A min., K.511.*
(B) *** Decca Double Analogue/Dig. 436 383-2 (2). Vladimir Ashkenazy, Philh. O.

This alternative set, with slightly different contents, is also highly recommendable on all counts, with the three favourite Mozart piano concertos included, plus a splendid *Sonata* and a charming *Rondo*. Ashkenazy's performance of the *B flat Concerto* is as finely characterized as one would expect. The *Sonata* and *Rondo* were recorded earlier (in 1967); the playing is equally fine.

Piano concertos Nos. 20 in D min., K.466; 21 in C, K.467; 25 in C, K.503; 27 in B flat, K.595.
(B) **(*) DG Double 453 079-2 (2). Friedrich Gulda, VPO, Abbado.

Abbado had much greater luck in his Mozartian partnership with Gulda than he was to experience with Serkin a decade or so later. Even so it was a pity that these two discs (from the mid-1970s) had to be reissued in tandem, for the first is much more successful than the second. Gulda uses a Bösendorfer and in Nos. 20 and 21 his tone is crisp and clear with just a hint of a fortepiano about it, admirably suited to these readings, which have an element of classical restraint. In Nos. 25 and 27, however, Gulda is strangely cool, though he disciplines his responses impressively and there is no basic want of feeling or finesse, as for instance in the second group of the first movement of K.503. But overall there is a lack of charm. There are felicitous moments elsewhere, but the account of K.595 does not compare with the finest available, despite very good playing from the Vienna Philharmonic. The digital transfer is bright and clear, but there is also a certain shallowness of sonority.

Piano concertos Nos. 20 in D min., K.466; 23 in A, K.488.
(M) *** Chandos Dig. CHAN 8992 [id.]. Howard Shelley, LMP.
(N) **(*) Hänsler Dig. CD 98.142 [id.]. Ivan Moravec, ASMF, Marriner.
(B) *** Ph. Virtuoso 422 466-2. Kovacevich, LSO, Davis.

Those wanting this coupling with modern instruments will find Howard Shelley's performances immensely rewarding. Characterization is strong, yet the slow movement of K.488 is very beautiful and touching. Splendid Chandos recording.

Ivan Moravec, born in Prague in 1930, has not been appreciated on disc as much as he deserves. These are fresh, thoughtful readings which never get in the way of Mozart, and Marriner and the Academy match him with playing of similar refinement. The *Romance* of the *D minor Concerto* and the *Adagio* of the *A major* are both on the slow side, next to the outstanding performances of the same concertos with Howard Shelley as soloist–director, on Chandos. That also has a price advantage.

If the coupling of the *D minor* and the *A major* from Kovacevich and Davis lacks some of the magic of their earlier pairing of the two *C major Concertos*, it is largely that the playing of the LSO is less polished. Nevertheless the minor-key seriousness of the outer movements of K.466 and the F sharp minor *Adagio* of K.488 come out superbly. It is a token of the pianist's command that, without any expressive exaggeration, the K.488 slow movement conveys such depth and intensity. The recording is full and clear in its new format, and in the bargain range this is very tempting.

Piano concertos Nos. 20 in D min., K.466; 23 in A, K.488; Rondo in A min., K.511.
(M) *** [RCA Basic 100 09026 68337-2; *68337-4*]. Rubinstein, RCA Victor SO, Wallenstein.

These works are also available differently coupled – the present pairing is equally recommendable.

Piano concertos Nos. 20 in D min., K.466; 27 in B flat, K.595.
✿ (M) *** Decca (IMS) 417 288-2. Clifford Curzon, ECO, Britten.
*** Sony SK 42241 [id.]. Murray Perahia, ECO.

In September 1970 Clifford Curzon went to The Maltings at Snape, and there with Benjamin Britten and the ECO he recorded these two concertos. K.595, the last concerto of all, was always the Mozart work with which he was specially associated and, not surprisingly – when he was the most painfully self-critical and mistrusting of recording artists – he wanted to do it again. Just before he died, in September 1982, sessions had been organized to make such a recording (as they had on several previous occasions). But it was not to be, and anyone hearing this magical record, full of the glow and natural expressiveness which always went with Britten's conducting of Mozart, will recognize both performances as uniquely individual and illuminating, with Curzon at his very finest. The record was kept from issue on LP until after Sir Clifford's death, when it received its Rosette from us. It now arrives on CD still sounding full and beautiful.

Perahia produces wonderfully soft colourings and a luminous texture in the *B flat Concerto*, yet at the same time he avoids underlining too strongly the valedictory sense that inevitably haunts this magical score. In the *D minor Concerto* none of the darker, disturbing undercurrents go uncharted, but at the same time we remain within the sensibility of the period. An indispensable issue, well recorded and excellently transferred.

Piano concertos Nos. 21 in C, K.467; 22 in E flat, K.482.
*** Chandos Dig. CHAN 9404 [id.]. LMP, Howard Shelley.

Howard Shelley's cycle continues to delight, and his survey of the Mozart canon survives the most exalted comparisons. The *C major* has dignity, intelligence and poetic feeling. The *E flat* has poise and breadth, and the winds of the London Mozart Players are heard to good advantage. These performances can be confidently recommended alongside the very finest rivals, such as Perahia (Sony) and András Schiff/Sándor Végh (Decca).

Piano concertos Nos. 21 in C, K. 467; 22 in E flat, K. 482; 24 in C min., K.491; 27 in B flat, K. 595.
(N) (B) **(*) Carlton Dig. Double 30366 01167 (2) [id.]. Fou Ts'ong, Sinfonia Varsovia.

Fou Ts'ong and the Sinfonia Varsovia give us very musical playing and have the advantage of exemplary recording, well balanced and in a warm, beautifully spacious acoustic. There is much to admire, the playing lacking neither in style nor vividness. However the occasional mannerism must be noted (and the pianist-conductor's humming is occasionally audible), and there are times in all four works when one feels that the vital sense of flow is not vital enough. On the whole, K.482 is the most memorable account of the four with expressive and bracing playing in good balance, but there are more deeply searching readings of the *C minor*. But now these two discs have been reissued as a Double, they are far more competitive.

Piano concertos Nos. 21 in C, K.467; 23 in A, K.488.
(M) *** Virgin/EMI Dig. CUV5 61123-2. Jean-Bernard Pommier, Sinfonia Varsovia.
(N) (M) *** Penguin Classics Ph. 460 621-2. Alfred Brendel, ASMF, Marriner.

A surprisingly rare coupling of what are now arguably the two favourite Mozart piano concertos here works very well indeed. Both performances have plenty of sparkle in outer movements – the first movement of K.467 is particularly arresting – and both slow movements are played simply and beautifully. Jean-Bernard Pommier's *Adagio* in K.488 compares favourably with Brendel's, and the string playing at the famous opening of the *Andante* of K.467 is ravishing in its transparent delicacy and gentle warmth. The finale of the same work is brisk but never sounds rushed. The sound is first class.

Brendel's coupling has been issued as a Penguin Classic in the UK but, curiously, not in the USA. They are characteristically discerning performances, with No. 23 especially beautiful. Playing and recording are both immaculate. The Penguin disc comes with the usual author's essay, in this case by Tom Sharpe, who is a great admirer of Brendel as well as of Mozart.

Piano concertos Nos. 21 in C, K.467; 24 in C min., K.491.
(M) *** Carlton IMP Dig. PCD 2007 [id.]. Howard Shelley, City of L. Sinfonia.

Howard Shelley gives delightfully fresh and characterful readings of both the popular *C major* and the great *C minor* concertos, bringing out their strength and purposefulness as well as their poetry, never overblown or sentimental. His Carlton (formerly Pickwick) disc makes an outstanding digital bargain, with accompaniment very well played and recorded.

Piano concertos Nos. 21 in C, K.467; 25 in C, K.503.
(B) *** Ph. 426 077-2. Kovacevich, LSO, C. Davis.

The partnership of Kovacevich and Colin Davis almost invariably produces inspired music-making. Their balancing of strength and charm, drama and tenderness, make for performances which retain their sense of spontaneity but which plainly result from deep thought, and the weight of both these great C major works is formidably conveyed. The 1972 recording is well balanced and refined.

(i) *Piano concertos Nos. 21 in C, K.467; 26 in D (Coronation), K.537;* (ii) *12 Variations on 'Ah, vous dirai-je, Maman', K.265.*
❀ (B) *** Sony SBK 67178 [id.]. (i) Robert Casadesus, Columbia SO or Cleveland O, Szell; (ii) André Previn (piano).

The ravishing slow movement of K.467 has never sounded more magical than here, and Casadesus then takes the finale at a tremendous speed; but, for the most part, this is exquisite Mozart playing, beautifully paced and articulated. Casadesus's Mozart may at first seem understated, but the imagination behind his readings is apparent in every phrase.

Piano concertos Nos. 21 in C, K.467; 27 in B flat, K.595.
*** Sony Dig. SK 46485 [id.]. Murray Perahia, COE.

Murray Perahia gives performances of characteristic understanding and finesse with the Chamber Orchestra of Europe. There are new and different insights into both works though neither reading necessarily displaces his earlier accounts with the ECO, which may have a slight edge on the newcomer in terms of freshness and spontaneity.

Piano concertos Nos. 22 in E flat, K.482; 23 in A, K.488.
*** Ph. Dig. 420 187-2 [id.]. Mitsuko Uchida, ECO, Tate.

In balance, fidelity and sense of presence, few recordings of Mozart piano concertos can match Uchida's fine coupling of the late *E flat*, K.482, with its immediate successor, the beautiful *A major*, and Uchida's thoughtful manner, at times a little understated, is ideally set against outstanding playing from the ECO with its excellent wind soloists.

Piano concertos Nos. 22 in E flat, K.482; 24 in C min., K.491.
*** Sony SK 42242 [id.]. Perahia, ECO.

Not only is Perahia's contribution inspired in the great *E flat Concerto*, but the wind players of the ECO are at their most eloquent in the slow movement. Moreover the *C minor Concerto* emerges here as a truly Mozartian tragedy, rather than as foreshadowing Beethoven, which some artists give us. Both recordings are improved in focus and definition in the CD transfer.

Piano concertos Nos. 22 in E flat, K.482; 26 in D (Coronation), K.537.
(M) *** DG (IMS) Dig. 447 283-2 [id.]. Malcolm Bilson (fortepiano), E. Bar. Soloists, Gardiner.

The *Coronation concerto* is presented strongly as well as elegantly, with the authentic timpani cutting dramatically through the textures in the first movement. Full and spacious recording in a helpful acoustic. The earlier concerto is hardly less vibrant and lyrically convincing, with the contrasts of the finale particularly effective.

Piano concertos Nos. 23 in A, K.488; 24 in C min., K.491.
(M) *** DG 423 885-2. Kempff, Bamberg SO, Leitner.
*** Virgin/EMI (SIS) Dig. VC7 59280-2. Mikhail Pletnev, Deutsche Kammerphilharmonie.
(M) **(*) Decca 452 888-2 [id.]. Clifford Curzon, LSO, Kertész.

(i) *Piano concertos Nos. 23 in A, K.488;* (ii) *24 in C min., K.491; Rondo in A, K.511.*
(M) *** RCA GD 87968 [7968-2-RG]. Rubinstein, RCA Victor SO, (i) Alfred Wallenstein; (ii) Josef Krips.

Kempff's outstanding performances of these concertos are uniquely poetic and inspired, and Leitner's accompaniments are comparably distinguished. The 1960 recording still sounds well, and this is strongly recommended at mid-price.

Rubinstein brings characteristic finesse and beauty of phrasing to his coupling; K.488 is especially beautiful. In K.491 the crystal-clear articulation is allied to the aristocratic feeling characteristic of vintage Rubinstein: the slow movement is memorable in its poise. Krips's accompaniment acts as a foil to the tragic tone of this great and wonderfully balanced work. The recordings, from 1958 and 1961 respectively, sound fresh, and the *Rondo*, recorded in 1959, is equally distinguished.

Pletnev and the Deutsche Kammerphilharmonie have obviously established a close rapport and there is great personality here – whether you like everything about it or not. In Pletnev's hands the slow movement of the *A major Concerto* is among the most beautiful on record, the finale the most rushed. In the *C minor Concerto* he is intensely dramatic, Beethovenian in feeling and powerful in conception: his own first-movement cadenza looks even more forward into the nineteenth century. There is nothing bland here: commanding playing from all concerned.

Curzon's vintage Kingsway Hall recording from 1968 was produced by Ray Minshull and engineered by Gordon Parry. It still sounds first class, full, warm and naturally balanced. It is certainly worthy of Decca's Classic Sound series. Curzon's account of these two concertos is immaculate and no connoisseur of the piano will fail to derive pleasure from them. Curzon has the advantage of sensitive support from Kertész and the LSO, and only an absence of the last ounce of sparkle and spontaneity prevents this from being strongly recommended.

Piano concertos Nos. 23 in A, K.488; 27 in B flat, K.595.
(M) *** Ph. 442 391-2. Alfred Brendel, ASMF, Marriner.

On Philips, two of the best of Brendel's Mozart concertos. However, these performances are included in Brendel's two Duo sets of Mozart concertos (one in each) and these represent marvellous value; the present disc remains of interest for those preferring uninterrupted performances as *Piano concerto* No. 23 is split across the two discs in its Duo format.

(i) *Piano concerto No. 27 in B flat, K.595.*
(M) **(*) Decca 448 600-2 [id.]. Backhaus, VPO, Boehm – BRAHMS: *Piano concerto No. 2.* ***

Backhaus is magisterial and, if he is rhythmically rather uneven and the performance of the concerto does not always flow smoothly, the performance, very well accompanied by Boehm, has great character. The manner is a little unsmiling in its directness, but the classicism is appealing in its total lack of romantic overlay. There is something very compelling about this music-making, for Backhaus's personality projects strongly in every bar. The early (1955) stereo is remarkably truthful – worthy of Decca's Classic Sound series.

Piano concerto No. 27 in B flat, K.595; (i) *Double piano concerto in E flat, K.365.*
✿ (M) *** DG 419 059-2. Emil Gilels, VPO, Boehm, (i) with Elena Gilels.

Gilels's is supremely lyrical playing that evinces all the classical virtues. No detail is allowed to detract from the picture as a whole; the pace is totally unhurried and superbly controlled. All the points are made by means of articulation and tone, and each phrase is marvellously alive, while Boehm and the Vienna Philharmonic provide excellent support. The performance of the marvellous *Double concerto* is no less enjoyable. Its mood is comparatively serious, but this is not to suggest that the music's sunny qualities are not brought out. The quality on CD is first class, refining detail yet not losing ambient warmth.

Piano concerto No. 27 in B flat, K.595; Symphony No. 35 (Haffner); Ov. Marriage of Figaro.
(N) (B) (**) Naxos 8.110809 [id.]. Mieczyslaw Horszowski, NBCSO, Toscanini.

Toscanini's Mozart performances rarely have any charm. This concert, recorded in 1943, brings taut and refreshing, but somewhat unyielding accounts of the *Symphony* and the *Overture*, but Toscanini responds much more illuminatingly to the classical poise and point of Horszowski's playing in Mozart's last piano concerto, allowing him surprising freedom. Typically dry, rough sound.

(i; ii) *Piano concerto No. 27 in B flat, K.595*; (iii) *Piano quartet in G min., K.478*; (iv; ii) *Exsultate, jubilate, K.165.*
(N) *** BBC Music Legends BBCB 8005-2 (i) Sviatoslav Richter; (ii) ECO/Britten; (iii) Britten, Kenneth Sillito, Cecil Aronowitz, Kenneth Heath; (iv) Elly Ameling.

This compilation of BBC radio recordings winningly captures the magic of Britten as performer of Mozart at the Aldeburgh Festival. Elly Ameling has never sounded more sweetly radiant on disc than in this account of *Exsultate, jubilate*, technically immaculate. Britten as conductor in Richter's reading of K.595 is warmer in his Mozart style than his soloist, just as persuasive as he is in his recording with Clifford Curzon. Best of all is the *Piano quartet*, where Britten's expressiveness even in the simplest scale passage has one magnetized, a great performance. The power of the first movement is heightened, when both halves are repeated. Though the string sound in the *Concerto* is a little thin, the other two recordings are excellent.

(i) *Double piano concerto in E flat, K.365;* (ii) *Sinfonia concertante for violin, viola and orchestra in E flat, K.364.*
(N) *** Chandos Dig. CHAN 9695 [id.]. (i) Håvard Gimse, Vebjørn Anvik; (ii) Iona Brown, Lars Tomter; Norwegian CO, Brown.

It is surprising that these two greatest of Mozart's '*double concertos*' are not regularly coupled, occupying adjacent Köchel numbers, both dating from 1779. Over the years since 1981, when she took over as music director, Iona Brown has built the Norwegian Chamber Orchestra into a superb body. It is good to welcome two brilliant young Norwegian pianists in K.365, light and agile, each articulating with refreshing clarity, relishing the antiphonal effects. In the elegant, spontaneously expressive account of *Sinfonia concertante* the contrast between the soloists is far more extreme, when Iona Brown's clear, bright violin tone is set against the nut-brown warmth of Tomter's viola. Full, clear Chandos sound. Highly recommended.

Violin concertos

Complete Mozart Edition, Volume 8: (i) *Violin concertos Nos. 1–5; 7 in D, K.271; Adagio in E, K.261; Rondo in B flat, K.269; Rondo in C, K.373.* (i; ii) *Concertone, K.190;* (iii; iv) *Double Concerto in D for violin, piano and orchestra, K.315f;* (iii; v; vi) *Sinfonia concertante in A, for violin, viola, cello and orchestra, K.320e;* (iii; v) *Sinfonia concertante in E flat, K.364.*
(M) **(*) Ph. Analogue/Dig. 422 508-2 (4). (i) Szeryng, (ii) with Poulet, Morgan, Jones; New Philh. O, Gibson; (iii) Iona Brown, with (iv) Shelley; (v) Imai; (vi) Orton; ASMF, Marriner.

Philip Wilby has here not only completed the first movement of an early *Sinfonia concertante for violin, viola and cello* (Mozart's only music with concertante cello) but also, through shrewd detective work, has reconstructed a full three-movement *Double concerto* from what Mozart left as 'a magnificent torso', to use Alfred Einstein's description; it is for violin, piano and orchestra. The result here is a delight, a full-scale 25-minute work which ends with an effervescent double-variation finale, alternately in duple and compound time. That is superbly done with Iona Brown and Howard Shelley as soloists; and the other ASMF items are very good too, with Iona Brown joined by Nobuko Imai most characterfully on the viola in the great *Sinfonia concertante*, K.364. What is a shade disappointing is to have Henryk Szeryng's readings of the main violin concertos from the 1960s instead of the Grumiaux set. Szeryng is sympathetic but a trifle reserved and not as refreshing as Grumiaux.

Violin concertos Nos. 1–5; Adagio in E, K.261; Rondo in C, K.373; Rondo concertante in B flat, K.269.
(B) *** O-L Double Dig. 455 721-2 (2) [id.]. Simon Standage, AAM, Hogwood.
(M) *** Virgin/EMI VCD5 45214-2 (2) [ZDCB 45214]. Christian Tetzlaff, Deutsche Kammerphilharmonie.

(B) **(*) EMI forte Dig. CZS5 69355-2 (2) [CDFB 69355]. Zimmermann, Württemberg CO, Faerber.

(M) **(*) DG Dig. 445 535-2 (2). Itzhak Perlman, VPO, Levine.

(BB) **(*) RCA Navigator 74321 21277-2 (*Nos. 1–3 & Rondo, K.373*); 74321 21278-2 (*Nos. 4–5; Adagio, K.261 & Rondo K.269*) [(M) id. import]. Josef Suk, Prague CO, Libor Hlaváček.

Violin concertos Nos. 1–5; Adagio in E, K.261; Rondo in C, K.373.

(B) **(*) Sony SBK 46539/40 [id.]. Zukerman, St Paul CO.

(B) **(*) RCA Twofer 74321 34170-2 (2). Josef Suk, Prague CO, Libor Hlaváček.

(i) *Violin concertos Nos. 1–5;* (ii) *Adagio in E, K.261; Rondo in C, K.373;* (i; iii) *Sinfonia concertante in E flat, K.364.*

(B) *** Ph. Duo 438 323-2 (2) [id.]. Arthur Grumiaux, (i) LSO, C. Davis; (ii) New Philh. O, Leppard; (iii) with Arrigo Pellicia.

Violin concertos Nos. 1–5; Adagio in E, K.261; Rondo concertante in B flat, K.269.

(N) (BB) *** Virgin Veritas Dig. Double VBD5 61576-2 (2) [id.]. Monica Huggett, OAE.

Violin concertos Nos. 1–5; (i) *Sinfonia concertante in E flat for violin, viola and orchestra, K.364.*

(BB) **(*) EMI Seraphim (SIS) CES5 68530-2 (2). Lord Menuhin, Bath Festival O; (i) with Rudolph Barshai.

Anyone seeking period-instrument performances of Mozart's concertante music for violin and orchestra need look no further than this superb Oiseau-Lyre set, which, for stylishness and spontaneity, can be ranked alongside the finest versions on modern instruments. The first two concertos are particularly felicitous. Hogwood's accompaniments are beautifully sprung, with no lack of warmth, the orchestral violins articulating neatly and gracefully to match the soloist, and the transparent textures revealing every detail of the orchestral scoring. Standage's beautifully focused, silvery tone is a constant joy. The shorter pieces are also given fine performances and are never just treated as encores: the *E major Adagio* has a touchingly wistful air and the *C major Rondo* closes the programme amiably. The 1990 Abbey Road recording is first rate throughout, beautifully balanced and with not a trace of edginess anywhere.

Monica Huggett provides an admirable alternative. She directs from the bow and she is a superb soloist: spontaneous, vital, warm and elegant. She plays her own cadenzas, and very good they are too. Orchestral textures are fresh and transparent, ensemble is excellent, and the solo playing is without even a drop of vinegar; indeed the violin timbre, if not opulent, is firm, well focused and sparkling. The Virgin Double omits the *Rondo in C*, but costs somewhat less than its Oiseau-Lyre competitor.

Grumiaux's accounts of the Mozart *Violin concertos* come from the early 1960s and are among the most beautifully played in the catalogue at any price. The orchestral accompaniments have sparkle and vitality, and Grumiaux's contribution has splendid poise and purity of tone. For this generous reissue on their bargain Duo label, Philips have added the *Adagio*, K.261, and *Rondo*, K.373, recorded later in 1967, and also a fine performance of the great *Sinfonia concertante*, K.364, with Arrigo Pellicia proving a sensitive partner for Grumiaux, especially in the *Andante*. The new CD transfers are brightly lit but still faithful.

Christian Tetzlaff is a first-class player and an equally first-class Mozartian. He plays all five concertos with great freshness and he simultaneously directs the Deutsche Kammerphilharmonie in polished and sympathetic accompaniments. His pacing of allegros is brisk, but exhilaratingly so, and his expressive phrasing in slow movements matches the clean, positive style of his contribution to faster movements. However, for a somewhat lower cost on a Philips Duo one can get Grumiaux, who is unsurpassed; and that set includes also the *Sinfonia concertante in E flat*. We also have a very soft spot for the Double Decca, similarly priced, in which the excellent Mayumi Fujikawa offers all the repertoire above and she is given a vintage Decca analogue sound of striking warmth and naturalness.

Zukerman's set has the advantage of excellent digital recording and a good balance, the violin forward but not distractingly so. The playing of outer movements is agreeably simple and fresh, and in slow movements Zukerman's sweetness of tone will appeal to many, although his tendency to languish a little in his expressiveness, particularly in the *G major*, K.216, rather less so in the *A major*, K.219, may be counted a less attractive feature, and he is not always subtle in his expression of feeling. Nevertheless this is still enjoyably spontaneous and his admirers will certainly not be disappointed with K.219.

Frank Peter Zimmermann is also most impressive. His interpretations do not quite match those of Grumiaux (with whom, at the price, he comes into direct competition), Stern, Perlman or Fujikawa; but they are distinguished by fine musicianship and an effortless technical command. Zimmermann uses cadenzas by Zukerman and Oistrakh in No. 2 and Joachim in No. 4. The digital recordings have agreeable warmth and freshness and are very well balanced. Jörg Faerber is an excellent partner and gets extremely alive playing from the Württemberg orchestra. Not a first recommendation then, but certainly worth considering.

Perlman gives characteristically assured, virtuoso readings of these concertos of Mozart's youth, which, with Levine as a fresh and undistracting Mozartian, bring exceptionally satisfying co-ordination of forces. The virtuoso approach sometimes involves a tendency to hurry, and the power is emphasized by the weight and immediacy of the recording. Warmth is here rather than charm; but Perlman's individual magic makes for magnetic results all through, not least in the intimate intensity of slow movements. Those of the first two concertos are particularly graceful, but at times (and notably in the two most popular concertos, Nos. 3 and 5) he treats the works rather more as bravura showpieces than is common. However, Perlman's virtuosity is effortless and charismatic, and the orchestral playing is first class. The DG recording is well balanced, with the soloist close but not too excessively so, and the perspective is on the whole well judged.

However, the alternative set (available as a 'Twofer' or separately) on RCA's super-bargain Navigator label is by no means upstaged. Josef Suk's recordings date from 1972. The solo playing has character, warmth and humanity, and its unaffected manner is especially suited to the first two concertos. The last three concertos have an agreeable simplicity and a freedom from histrionic gestures that is most welcome, and the recording, though not as vividly detailed as the DG, is agreeably smooth and natural. Hlaváček does not always make enough of the dynamic contrasts and, throughout, this music-making is dominated by Suk. This is partly a matter of the recording balance. But with any reservations noted, these are delightful performances and very good value.

Menuhin's recordings date from the early 1960s, a fruitful period for this fine artist, when he was closely associated with the Bath Festival. Most violinists use cadenzas by Joachim, but in all but No. 3 (where he chooses those by Franco) Menuhin uses cadenzas of his own, and many may feel that they are not Mozartian. Otherwise the style is sensibly exploited, and these performances give an engaging sense of musicians making intimate music together for the joy of it. One is always conscious that this is the phrasing of a master musician who can also provide the lightest touch in finales, which are alert and extrovert. In the *Sinfonia concertante* Menuhin and Barshai comprise a splendid team with happily similar views. Throughout, the stereo has a bright sheen and, with the remastering, the orchestral violins are made to sound glassy above the stave, but the ear adjusts when the music-making is so distinctive and the acoustic is basically warm.

Violin concertos Nos. (i) *1 in B flat, K.207;* (ii) *2 in D, K.211;* (iii) *3 in G, K.216;* (ii) *4 in D, K.218;* (i) *5 in A (Turkish), K.219;* (ii) *Adagio in E, K.261; Rondo in C, K.373;* (iv) *Concertone for 2 violins and orchestra in C, K.190; Sinfonia concertante in E flat for violin, viola and orchestra, K.364.*

(M) **(*) Sony Stern Edition I SM3K 66475 (3) [id.]. Isaac Stern, with (i) Columbia SO, Szell; (ii) ECO, Schneider; (iii) Cleveland O, Szell; (iv) Zukerman, ECO, Barenboim.

It goes without saying that Stern's solo playing is always splendid; but he is not always as sensitive to detail as his rivals, and this especially applies to No. 1 and rather less so to No. 5 where the accompaniment is provided by the Columbia Symphony Orchestra under Szell. The great *Sinfonia concertante* stands among the finest available and is certainly the jewel in this set, presenting as it does two soloists of equally strong musical personality, and listening to the solo concertos again, so impressively remastered, is to relish the sheer beauty of Stern's tone and phrasing. The *Concertone* is attractive enough, if not one of Mozart's most inspired pieces, and here the dryness of the acoustic rather detracts from the charm of a work which on any count goes on too long for its material. Stern, Zukerman and Barenboim pay the central *Andantino grazioso* the compliment of a really slow tempo, and though this makes a very long movement the concentration is superb. Whatever the shortcomings of the recording, the artistry of the soloists shines out through every bar.

Violin concertos Nos. 1 in B flat, K.207; 2 in D, K.211; Rondo in B flat, K.269; Andante in F (arr. Saint-Saëns from *Piano concerto No. 21, K.467*).

(BB) **(*) Naxos Dig. 8.550414 [id.]. Takako Nishizaki, Capella Istropolitana, Johannes Wildner.

This was the last disc to be recorded (in 1990) of Takako Nishizaki's fine survey of the violin concertos. The opening movement of K.207 is brisk and fresh, although this is the least individual of Nishizaki's readings. The *Second Concerto*, K.211, has rather more flair, the *Andante* touchingly phrased, and the finale has a winning lightness of touch. The *Rondo* is also an attractively spontaneous performance, and as an encore we are offered Saint-Saëns's arrangement of the famous *'Elvira Madigan'* theme from the *C major Concerto*, K.467.

(i) *Violin concertos Nos. 2 in D, K.211; 4 in D, K.218;* (ii) *Divertimento for strings No. 1, K.136.*

(B) *** [EMI Red Line Dig. CDR5 69865]. (i) Anne-Sophie Mutter, Philh. O; (ii) BPO; Muti.

Anne-Sophie Mutter made her Mozartian début with Karajan on DG with a famous youthful coupling of the *G major*, K.216, and *A major*, K.219. She went on to record the two *D major Concertos* for EMI with a different orchestra and conductor. The results are hardly less successful. She is given very sensitive support from the Philharmonia under Muti. Her playing combines purity and classical feeling, delicacy and incisiveness, and is admirably expressive. Its freshness is also most appealing. The early digital recording is very good, the images sharply defined, but the balance satisfactory. The finest of Mozart's three string divertimenti makes a good bonus.

Violin concerto No. 3 in G, K.216.
(B) *** EMI forte CZS5 69331-2 (2) [CDFB 69331]. David Oistrakh, Philh. O – BEETHOVEN: *Triple concerto;* BRAHMS: *Double concerto;* PROKOFIEV: *Violin concerto No. 2.* ***
*** EMI Dig. CDC5 55426-2 [id.]. Frank Peter Zimmermann, BPO, Sawallisch – BRAHMS: *Violin concerto.* **(*)

David Oistrakh was at his finest in this beautiful 1958 performance of Mozart's *G major Concerto.* His supple, richly toned yet essentially classical style suits the melodic line of this youthful work and gives it the stature of maturity. The orchestral contribution is directed by the soloist himself and is eminently polished. EMI provide admirably smooth yet vivid sound, and this is just one of four marvellous performances which make up this forte compilation, one of the finest concertante bargains in the catalogue.

With the the string complement of the Berlin Philharmonic aptly reduced, and with Sawallisch at his most sparkling, Zimmermann's studio recording of Mozart's *G major Concerto* is a delight, with a quicksilver lightness in the outer movements, very different from the traditional big bow-wow approach, and a compelling repose and concentration in the central *Adagio.* In its own right this is superb music-making.

(i) *Violin concertos Nos. 3 in G, K.216; 4 in D, K.218;* (ii) *Duo for violin and viola in G, K.423.*
(M) **(*) DG (IMS) Dig. 439 525-2. Gidon Kremer; (i) VPO, Harnoncourt; (ii) Kim Kashkashian.

Kremer and Harnoncourt make a characterful partnership in the Mozart violin concertos, although Harnoncourt is nothing if not eccentric. In the *G major*, K.216, the first movement flows at just the right pace, and then in the *Andante* a comma is placed to romanticize the climbing opening phrase of the main theme slightly. But with Kremer playing sweetly throughout, such individual touches may be found very acceptable (including a long cadenza in the first movement of No. 3) when there is plenty of vitality and Harnoncourt's tuttis are always strong. The *Duo* (quite substantial at 17 minutes) makes an interesting bonus, with skilful playing and a good balance between Kremer and Kashkashian. But there is more to this music than these players find.

(i) *Violin concertos Nos. 3 in G, K.216; 4 in D, K.218. Serenade: Eine kleine Nachtmusik, K.525.*
(M) **(*) Sony stereo/mono SMK 64468 [id.]. (i) Zino Francescatti; Columbia SO, Walter.

Francescatti's coupling of the *Third* and *Fourth* Mozart *Concertos* is probably his best record, and in their remastered CD format these fine performances from 1958, recorded in California, are given a new lease of life. The playing is at times a little wayward, but Bruno Walter accompanies throughout with his usual warmth and insight and falls into line sympathetically with his soloist. Both slow movements are beautifully played, albeit with an intensity that barely stops short of romanticism. In some ways the *D major* suits Francescatti's opulent style of playing best. The whole atmosphere of this music-making represents the pre-authentic approach to Mozart at its most rewarding. The 1954 New York recording of the *Night music* is no great bonus: the sound is harsh and ill-focused.

Violin concertos Nos. 3 in G, K.216; 4 in D, K.218; 5 in A, K.219.
(B) **(*) DG Classikon 449 850-2. Wolfgang Schneiderhan, BPO.

This reissue is drawn from Schneiderhan's complete set of the violin concertos, made in the late 1960s. He plays with effortless mastery and a strong sense of classical proportion. The Berlin orchestra plays well for him, although there is a slightly unsmiling quality at times. The *A major Concerto* was perhaps the finest of the set and makes a suitable coupling for his famous record of the Beethoven, made six years earlier (see below). The sound is realistically balanced.

Violin concertos Nos. 3 in G, K.216; 5 in A (Turkish), K.219.
(N) (M) DG 457 746-2 [id.]. Anne-Sophie Mutter, BPO, Karajan.
(BB) *** Naxos Dig. 8.550063 [id.]. Takako Nishizaki, Capella Istropolitana, Stephen Gunzenhauser.

Violin concertos Nos. 3 in G, K.216; 5 in A (Turkish), K.219; Adagio in E, K.261.
(B) **(*) Tring Dig. TRP 060 [(M) id. import]. Jonathan Carney, RPO.

Extraordinarily mature and accomplished playing from Anne-Sophie Mutter, who was a mere fourteen years old when her recording was made. The instinctive mastery means that there is no hint of immaturity: the playing has polish, but fine artistry too and remarkable freshness. Karajan is at his most sympathetic and scales down the accompaniment to act as a perfect setting for his young soloist. The recording has been brilliantly transferred to CD, though some might feel that the orchestral strings are a shade too brightly lit. A fine candidate for DG's 'Originals'.

This is the finest of Nishizaki's three discs of the Mozart violin concertos on Naxos. The readings are individual and possess the most engaging lyrical feeling and the natural response of the soloist to Mozartian line and phrase. A good balance, the soloist forward, but convincingly so, and the orchestral backcloth in natural perspective. A real bargain.

Jonathan Carney successfully directs the RPO from the bow, but he favours brisk tempi in outer movements, and the finale of K.216 is dangerously fast. Even so, these lively and expressive performances are very enjoyable, and well recorded too. But even though Carney offers a bonus, Takako Nishizaki takes precedence in this coupling.

Violin concerto No. 4 in D, K.218.

(M) (***) DG mono 457 720-2 [id.]. Wolfgang Schneiderhan, BPO, Rosbaud – HAYDN: *Symphonies Nos. 92 & 104.* (***)

We share DG's enthusiasm for the eminently stylish classical playing of Wolfgang Schneiderhan in Mozart's *D major Violin concerto*. He plays it very beautifully indeed, and there may be more points of detail in the orchestra which Rosbaud presents to the listener rather more clearly than in Schneiderhan's later, stereo version, where he directed the Berlin Philharmonic himself. Nevetherless the (well-balanced) 1956 mono recording is marginally less flattering to his timbre than the stereo, and for most collectors that later version will probably be the preferred choice, unless the present Haydn coupling is thought essential, and it is certainly impressive.

Violin concerto No. 4 in D, K.218; (i) *Sinfonia concertante in E flat, for violin, viola and orchestra, K.364.*

(BB) **(*) Naxos Dig. 8.550332 [id.]. Takako Nishizaki, (i) Ladislav Kyselak; Capella Istropolitana, Stephen Gunzenhauser.

A fine account of No. 4, with Takako Nishizaki's solo playing well up to the high standard of this series and with Stephen Gunzenhauser's perceptive pacing adding to our pleasure. The *Sinfonia concertante* is very enjoyable too, if perhaps slightly less distinctive. The finale is infectious in its liveliness, its rhythms buoyantly pointed. Again, a good balance and excellent sound.

Violin concertos Nos. 4, K.218; 5 (Turkish), K.219.

*** Nimbus Dig. NI 5009. Oscar Shumsky, SCO, Yan Pascal Tortelier.

Oscar Shumsky's performances with the Scottish Chamber Orchestra have the advantage of being totally unaffected, natural and full of character. Yan Pascal Tortelier secures a very alive and thoroughly musical response from the orchestra. The recording is nicely balanced.

Violin concertos Nos. 4 in D, K.218; 5 in A (Turkish), K.219; Adagio in E, K.261; Rondos Nos. 1 in B flat, K.269; 2 in C, K.373.

(M) **(*) EMI (SIS) CDM7 64868-2. David Oistrakh, BPO.

David Oistrakh's performances come from his complete set, recorded in 1970/71. The slow movement of K.219 is particularly fine, and so too is the finale. The three shorter concertante works also show the soloist at his finest; though the accompaniment for the *Adagio*, K.261, remains richly upholstered, this is played very beautifully. With 77 minutes of music this is excellent value, for the soloist is truthfully caught and the balance is convincing.

Violin concerto No. 5 in A (Turkish), K.219.

(M) *** RCA 09026 61757-2 [61757-2-RG]. Heifetz with CO – *String quintet, K.516* etc. ***

(M) *** DG 447 403-2 [id.]. Wolfgang Schneiderhan, BPO, Jochum – BEETHOVEN: *Violin concerto.* *** ✪

(***) EMI mono CDH5 65191-2. Heifetz, LPO, Barbirolli – MENDELSSOHN: *Concerto* (**(*)); VIEUXTEMPS: *Concerto No. 5.* (***)

Marvellously exhilarating Mozart from Heifetz; his actual entry in the first movement is quite ethereal. He directs the accompanying group himself, the only time he did so on record. The early (1954) stereo is fully acceptable and the performance memorable, with the crystalline clarity of articulation matched by warmth of timbre and aristocratic phrasing.

This was perhaps the finest of the complete set of Mozart's violin concertos which Schneiderhan recorded with the Berlin Philharmonic in the late 1960s. The recording is realistically balanced, and this makes a generous coupling for his famous record of the Beethoven, made six years earlier.

Heifetz's EMI recording first appeared in 1934 and it is evident that there was a good rapport between him and the young John Barbirolli, whom Fred Gaisberg had chosen as partner. The playing has a commendable warmth and spontaneity which is less striking in the Mendelssohn coupling, where Beecham is at the helm.

(i) *Concertone in C, K.190;* (ii) *Sinfonia concertante in E flat, for violin, viola and orchestra, K.364.*

✪ *** DG 415 486-2 [id.]. Perlman, Zukerman, Israel PO, Mehta.

*** Sony Dig. SK 47693 [id.]. Cho-Liang Lin, Jaime Laredo, ECO, Leppard.

The DG version of the *Sinfonia concertante* was recorded in Tel Aviv at the Huberman Festival in December 1982. It is balanced with the soloists a fraction too near the microphones. The performance is in a special class and is an example of 'live' recording at its most magnetic, with the inspiration of the occasion caught on the wing. Zubin Mehta is drawn into the music-making and accompanies most sensitively. The *Concertone* is also splendidly done; the ear notices the improvement in the sound-balance of the studio recording of this work. But the *Sinfonia concertante*, with the audience incredibly quiet, conveys an electricity rarely caught on record.

Cho-Liang Lin's outstanding performance of the *Sinfonia concertante* is also mandatory listening. The playing has great finesse and style, and Lin makes a natural partnership with Laredo. Neil Black (oboe) and Charles Tunnell (cello) add to the distinction of the *Concertone*. The recording is reverberant, which brings a large-scale orchestral image, but it is fuller and smoother than the DG alternative.

(i; ii) *Concertone in C, K. 190; Sinfonia concertante for violin, viola and orchestra in E flat, K.364*; (i) *Rondo in C, K.373.*
(N) *** Virgin Veritas/EMI Dig. VC 545290-2 [id.]. (i) Monica Huggett, (ii) Pavlo Beznosiuk, Portland Bar. O, Huggett.

Recordings of the great *Sinfonia concertante*, K.364, using period instruments, are surprisingly rare, and this warmly expressive one is welcome for being ideally coupled with the early *Concertone* as well as the *C major Rondo*. The Portland Baroque Orchestra, founded in 1984 in Portland, Oregon, offers sympathetic support for two soloists well known in Europe. Playing with period purity which avoids astringency, the style of both Monica Huggett (also the director) and of Pavlo Beznosiuk (on both viola and violin) is free rather than strictly controlled, with ensemble less crisp than in the earlier period performance on Cala. The outer movements of the *Concertone*, less complex, work extremely well – fresh and alert – and so does the *Rondo in C*. A welcome issue, when direct rivalry is limited.

Dances and Marches

Contredanses: La Bataille, K.535; Das Donerwetter, K.534; Les filles malicieuses, K.610; Der Sieg vom Helden Koburg, K.587; Il trionfo delle donne, K.607. Gallimathias musicum (quodlibet), K.32; 6 German dances, K.567; 3 German dances, K.605; German dance: Die Leyerer, K.611. March in D, K.335/1. A Musical joke, K.522.
*** DG (IMS) Dig. 429 783-2. Orpheus CO.

A splendid sampler of the wit and finesse, to say nothing of the high quality of entertainment, provided by Mozart's dance music, which kept people on their feet till dawn at masked balls in the 1780s and early 1790s. The playing of the Orpheus group is winningly polished, flexible and smiling, and they bring off the *Musical joke* with considerable flair, both in the gentle fun of the *Adagio cantabile*, which is exquisitely played, and in the outrageous grinding dissonance of the 'wrong notes' at the end. First-class sound, fresh, transparent and vividly immediate.

Complete Mozart Edition, Volume 6: *La Chasse, KA.103/K.299d; Contredanses, K.101; K.123; K.267; K.269b; K.462; (Das Donnerwetter) K.534; (La Bataille) K.535; 535a; (Der Sieg vom Helden Koburg) K.587; K.603; (Il trionfo delle donne) K.607; (Non più andrai) K.609; K.610; Gavotte, K.300; German dances, K.509; K.536; K.567; K.571; K.586; K.600; K.602; K.605; Ländler, K.606; Marches, K.214; K.363; K.408; K.461; Minuets, K.61b; K.61g/2; K.61h; K.94, 103, 104, 105; K.122; K.164; K.176; K.315g; K.568; K.585; K.599; K.601; K.604; Minuets with Contredanses, K.463; Overture & 3 Contredanses, K.106.*
❁ (M) *** Ph. 422 506-2 (6). V. Mozart Ens., Willi Boskovsky.

Much of the credit for this remarkable undertaking should go to its expert producer, Erik Smith, who, besides providing highly stylish orchestrations for numbers without Mozart's own scoring, illuminates the music with some of the most informative and economically written notes that ever graced a record. The CD transfers preserve the excellence of the mid-1960s sound. The collector might feel that he or she is faced here with an *embarras de richesses* with more than 120 *Minuets*, nearly 50 *German dances* and some three dozen *Contredanses*, but Mozart's invention is seemingly inexhaustible, and the instrumentation is full of imaginative touches.

German dances, K.509/1–6; K.536/1–6; K.567/1–6; K.571/1–6; 12 German dances, K. 586.
*** Sony Dig. SK 46696 [id.]. Tafelmusik, Bruno Weil.

Of period-instrument ensembles, Tafelmusik must be numbered among the most persuasive. They bring the advantages of authentic instruments (clarity of texture and lightness of articulation) without the attendant aural discomfort. Bruno Weil directs light and refreshing accounts of all these pieces and is very truthfully and cleanly recorded. Readers will find most of them enjoyable and some altogether captivating.

12 German dances, K.586; 6 German dances, K.600; 4 German dances, K.602; 3 German dances, K.605.
(BB) *** Naxos Dig. 8.550412 [id.]. Capella Istropolitana, Johannes Wildner.

Fresh, bright, unmannered performances of some of the dance music Mozart wrote right at the end of his life. The playing is excellent and the recording is bright and full. An excellent super-bargain alternative to the Boskovsky Decca CD.

Complete Mozart Edition, Volume 45: *'Rarities and curiosities': Contredanses in B flat & D* (completed Smith); *The London Sketchbook:* (i) *3 Contredanses in F; 2 Contredanses in G; 6 Divertimenti*. (ii) *Wind divertimenti* arr. from

operas: *Don Giovanni* (arr. Triebensee); *Die Entführung aus dem Serail* (arr. Wendt) & (i) *March, K 384*. (i; iii) *Rondo in E flat for horn and orchestra, K 371* (completed Smith); (iv) *Larghetto for piano and wind quintet, K 452a;* (v) *Modulating prelude in F/E min*. (vi) *Tantum ergo in B flat, K 142; in D, K 197;* (vii) *Idomeneo: Scene & rondo*. (viii) *Musical dice game, K.516*.
(M) *** Ph. 422 545-2 (3) [id.]. (i) ASMF, Marriner; (ii) Netherlands Wind Ens.; (iii) Timothy Brown; cond. Sillito; (iv) Uchida, Black, King, Farrell, O'Neil; (v) Erik Smith (harpsichord); (vi) Frimmer, Leipzig R. Ch. & SO, Schreier; (vii) Mentzler, Hendricks, Bav. RSO, C. Davis; (viii) Marriner & Smith.

The first CD includes the innocent little piano pieces from the child Mozart's 'London Notebook'. Erik Smith has orchestrated them and, if the results may not be important, they charm the ear at least as much as Mozart's early symphonies, with many unexpected touches. Marriner and the Academy are ideal performers and the 1971 recording is warm and refined. Then come the arrangements for wind of selections from two key operas, elegantly played by the Netherlands Wind Ensemble. Finally come the rarities and curiosities, the *Rondo for horn and orchestra* with the missing 60 bars (discovered only in 1989) now added, and the other music made good by Erik Smith. There is a curious finale in which Erik Smith and Sir Neville Marriner participate (with spoken comments) in a *Musical dice game* to decide the order of interchangeable phrases in a very simple musical composition. The result, alas, is something of a damp squib.

Divertimenti and Serenades

Complete Mozart Edition, Volume 4: *Divertimenti for strings Nos. 1–3, K.136/8; Divertimenti for small orchestra Nos. 1 in E flat, K.113; 7 in D, K.205* (with *March in D, K.290); 10 in F, K.247* (with *March in F, K.248); 11 in D, K.251; 15 in B flat, K.287; 17 in D, K.334* (with *March in D, K.445); A Musical joke, K.622; Serenade (Eine kleine Nachtmusik), K.525*.
(M) *** Ph. Dig. 422 504-2 (5) [id.]. ASMF CO.

This is one of the most attractive of all the boxes in the Philips Mozart Edition. The music itself is a delight, the performances are stylish, elegant and polished, while the digital recording has admirable warmth and realistic presence and definition.

Divertimenti for strings Nos. 1–3, K.136–8; Serenades Nos. 6 in D (Serenata notturna), K.239; 13 in G (Eine kleine Nachtmusik), K.525.
(M) **(*) Classic fM Dig. 75605 57024-2. City of L. Sinfonia, Andrew Watkinson.

Divertimenti for strings Nos. 1–3, K.136–8; Serenade No. 13 (Eine kleine Nachtmusik), K.525.
*** Collins Dig. 1378-2 [id.]. Consort of L., Robert Haydon Clark.

Robert Haydon Clark's accounts of the three string *Divertimenti* (or so-called 'Salzburg symphonies') remind us of Marriner's early analogue set with the ASMF. They are hardly less polished and are stylish and very crisply played indeed. There is no need for original instruments when a modern string group can sound as fresh as this. *Eine kleine Nachtmusik* is equally persuasive. Moreover the conductor has here interpolated the 'missing' Minuet and Trio. In fact, as the accompanying notes readily admit, it is most unlikely to be the correct replacement, but it works rather well in context. Excellent, vividly real recording.

These are delightful performances from the City of London Sinfonia: fresh, warm and polished. *Eine kleine Nachtmusik* is elegant, graceful and nicely paced, and the same can be said of the three engaging *String divertimenti*. The *Serenata notturna* features the leaders of each section (two violins, viola and double-bass) as a solo concertino group, and with the timpani not over-dominant. The resonance of the recording is rather excessive but if you don't mind that, this Classic fM programme is very recommendable.

Divertimenti for strings Nos. 1–3, K.136–8.
(N) *(*) Finlandia/Warner Dig. 0630 17674-2 [id.]. Ostrobothnian CO, Juha Kangas – SCHUBERT: *5 German dances with 7 trios and coda; 5 Minuets and 6 Trios, D.89*. *(*)

Kangas draws crisp and polished playing with high contrasts from his Ostrobothnian players, but with fast, frantic speeds and rhythms totally unsprung, the charm is totally missing. That is until an element of wit and point enters in K.138.

Divertimenti Nos. 2 in D, K.131; 15 in B flat, K.287.
(BB) *** Naxos Dig. 8.550996 [id.]. Capella Istropolitana, Harald Nerat.

The playing of the Capella Istropolitana under Harald Nerat is beautifully turned and polished. They phrase elegantly; the sound is full and transparent, bringing the sweetest modern violin timbre, yet the effect is as refreshing as any period performance. The *D major Divertimento* is charmingly scored for flute, oboe, bassoon, four horns and strings, with woodwind adding frequent touches of colour, but it has a gracious second-movement *Adagio* cantilena of disarming simplicity for strings alone. The *B flat Divertimento* was written five years later, in Salzburg, and is scored more simply for two horns and strings. The lovely E flat major *Adagio* has that touch of gentle pathos that is Mozart's very own, and the finale brings a recitativo from the principal violin before its lighthearted conclusion, with a feather-light response from the violins.

Divertimenti Nos. 10 in F, K.247; 11 in D, K.331.
**(*) Capriccio 10 203 [id.]. Salzburg Mozarteum Camerata Academica, Végh.

The playing, as in Végh's previous issues, has striking freshness and vitality; these are chamber orchestral performances on modern instruments, but the scale is admirable and the resonance adds a feeling of breadth. Although slow movements tend to be on the slow side, while not lacking grace, allegros sparkle and have dash without ever seeming hurried, even if ensemble isn't always absolutely immaculate.

Divertimento No. 11 in D, K.251; Serenade No. 9 in D (Posthorn), K.320; 2 Marches in D, K.335/1–2.
**(*) Sony Dig. SK 53277 [id.]. BPO, Claudio Abbado.

Abbado uses a modest chamber group from the orchestra for the *Divertimento* and larger forces for the *Posthorn Serenade*. The playing is lively and cultivated, with plenty of rhythmic character and much finesse from the strings and a charming delicacy from the woodwind in the *concertante* movement of the *Serenade*. In the first Trio of the second Minuet of the latter work, Andrea Blau plays what sounds very like a treble recorder, a curious but effective change of colour. This is an enjoyable concert, very well recorded (the serenade at a live performance), but a smaller scale can be even more effective in this repertoire.

Wind divertimenti and Serenades

Adagios: in F, K,410; in B flat, K.411; Divertimenti for wind Nos. 3 in E flat, K.166; 4 in B flat, K.186; 8 in F, K.213; 9 in B flat, K.240; 12 in E flat, K.252; 13 in F, K.253; 14 in B flat, K.270; 16 in E flat, K.289; in E flat, K.Anh. 226; in B flat, K.Anh. 227. Serenades Nos. 10 in B flat, for 13 wind instruments, K.361; 11 in E flat, K.375; 12 in C min., K.488.
(B) **(*) Decca 455 794-2 (3). L. Wind Soloists, Jack Brymer.

The coverage is remarkably comprehensive and the playing here of the highest order, and the only drawback is the too-close balance for the large-scale *B flat major Serenade*. All the recordings were made in Decca's West Hampstead studio and in this work the effect is rather dry; the digital remastering has taken much of the ambient bloom from the sound. However, Brymer's group gives a strong, stylish performance with plenty of imagination in matters of phrasing. Elsewhere there is presence and bloom in equal measure. There are countless felicities: all the finales have a wonderfully light touch, but one remembers especially the engaging three-movement *Divertimento in F*, K.253, with its charming first-movement theme and variations and its slow Minuet with its playful Trio.

Complete Mozart Edition, Volume 5: *Divertimentos for wind Nos. 3 in E flat, K.166; 4 in B flat, K.186; 6 in C, K.188; 8 in F, K.213; 9 in B flat K.240; 12 in E flat, K.252; 13 in F, K.253; 14 in B flat, K.270; 16 in E flat, K.289; in E flat, K.Anh. 226; in B flat, K.Anh. 227; Divertimentos for 3 basset horns, K.439b/1–5; Duos for 2 horns, K.487/1–12; Serenades for wind No. 10 in B flat, K.361; 11 in E flat, K.375; 12 in C min., K.388; Adagios: in F; B flat, K.410–11.*
(M) *** Ph. Analogue/Dig. 422 505-2 (6) [id.]. Holliger Wind Ens. (or members of); Netherlands Wind Ens., De Waart (or members of); ASMF, Marriner or Laird.

Mozart's wind music, whether in the ambitious *Serenades* or the simpler *Divertimenti*, brings a naturally felicitous blending of timbre and colour unmatched by any other composer. It seems that even when writing for the simplest combination of wind instruments, Mozart is incapable of being dull. The playing of the more ambitious works is admirably polished and fresh, and it is interesting to note that Holliger's group provides a stylishly light touch and texture with the principal oboe dominating, while the blending of the Netherlanders is somewhat more homogeneous, though the effect is still very pleasing.

Divertimenti for wind Nos. 3 in E flat, K.166; 4 in B flat, K.186; 8 in F, K.213; 9 in B flat, K.240; 12 in E flat, K.252; 13 in F, K.253; 14 in B flat, K.270; Serenades Nos. 10 in B flat, for 13 wind instruments, K.361; 11 in E flat, K.375; 12 in C min., K.488.
(M) *** Audivis Astrée Dig. E 8627 [id.]. Zefiro Ens.

Audivis Astrée offer a new digital set at mid-price (three records for the cost of two), offering the same three major *Serenades* as Jack Brymer, plus seven of the *Divertimenti*, played on period instruments by a highly sensitive Italian group called Ensemble Zefiro – they take their name very appropriately from the Greek mythological God of the Western Wind. There would have been room here for the other *Divertimenti*, but those offered are the major masterpieces and the performances are very recommendable on all counts. The sounds of the period instruments are delightfully fresh and the blending of timbres most felicitous. Moreover the ambient effect of the recording has just the right degree of resonance, affording an agreeable overall bloom, without any kind of clouding. The playing itself brings a characteristic Italianate sunny quality to Mozart yet is remarkably subtle in detail. The *Gran Partita* is particularly seductive, with only one tiny flaw. At the opening of its eloquent *Adagio* the initial oboe entry begins a little below the note: some ears might find this disturbing on repetition.

Otherwise intonation is impeccable and the brilliant playing on natural horns by Raul Diaz and Dileno Baldin is most infectious. In the *C minor Serenade* with its darker sonorities, the Italians miss the sombre touch which the English players manage so adroitly, but overall the Zefiro group play with such glowing finesse and spontaneity that this Audivis set must marginally take pride of place.

Complete Mozart Edition, Volume 25: (i) *Idomeneo* (ballet music), *K.367;* (ii) *Les petits riens* (ballet), *K.299b; Music for a pantomime (Pantalon und Colombine), K.446* (completed and orch. Beyer); *Sketches for a ballet intermezzo, K.299c* (completed and orch. Erik Smith); (iii) *Thamos, King of Egypt* (incidental music), *K.345*.
(M) *** Ph. 422 525-2 (2) [id.]. (i) Netherlands CO, David Zinman; (ii) ASMF, Marriner; (iii) Eickstädt, Pohl, Büchner, Polster, Adam, Berlin R. Ch. & State O, Klee.

This volume collects together Mozart's theatre music and makes a particularly enticing package. Zinman and his Netherlanders give a neatly turned account of the ballet from *Idomeneo*, musical and spirited. Marriner takes over with modern digital sound for *Les petits riens* and the two novelties, and the ASMF playing has characteristic elegance and finesse. The *Sketches for a ballet intermezzo* survive only in a single-line autograph, but Erik Smith's completion and scoring provide a series of eight charming vignettes, most with descriptive titles, ending with a piquant *Tambourin*. The music for *Pantalon und Columbine* (more mime than ballet) survives in the form of a first violin part, and Franz Beyer has skilfully orchestrated it for wind and strings, using the first movement of the *Symphony*, K.84, as the overture and the last movement of *Symphony*, K.120, as the finale. Beautifully played as it is here, full of grace and colour, this is a real find and the digital recording is first rate. *Thamos, King of Egypt* is marvellous music which it is good to have on record, particularly in such persuasive hands as these. The choral singing is impressive and the orchestral playing is excellent.

Masonic funeral music: see below, in VOCAL MUSIC, under Complete Mozart Edition, Volume 22

A Musical joke, K.522.
*** Erato/Warner Dig. 2292 45199-2. Paillard CO, Paillard – L. MOZART: *Cassation* etc. ***

Happily paired with a high-spirited version of Leopold Mozart's *Toy symphony*, Paillard's account of Mozart's fun piece makes the most of its outrageous jokes, with the horns in the opening movement boldly going wrong and the final discordant clash sounding positively cataclysmic; yet it takes into account the musical values, too.

Overtures: *Apollo et Hyacinthus; Bastien und Bastienne; La clemenza di Tito; Così fan tutte; Don Giovanni; Die Entführung aus dem Serail; La finta giardiniera; Idomeneo; Lucio Silla; Mitridate, rè di Ponto; Le nozze di Figaro; Il rè pastore; Der Schauspieldirektor; Die Zauberflöte.*
(BB) *** Naxos Dig. 8.550185; *4550185* [id.]. Capella Istropolitana, Barry Wordsworth.

Wordsworth follows up his excellent series of Mozart symphonies for Naxos with this generous collection of overtures, no fewer than 14 of them, arranged in chronological order and given vigorous, stylish performances. In Italian overture form, *Mitridate* and *Lucio Silla*, like miniature symphonies, have separate tracks for each of their three contrasted sections. Very well recorded, the disc is highly recommendable at super-bargain price.

Overtures: *Bastien and Bastienne; La clemenza di Tito; Così fan tutte; Don Giovanni; Die Entführung aus dem Serail; La finta giardiniera; Idomeneo; Lucio Silla; Mitridate; Le nozze di Figaro; Il rè pastore; Der Schauspieldirektor; Die Zauberflöte.*
(N) [M] *** Classic fm Dig. 75605 57032-2. Sinfonia Varsovia, Lord Menuhin.

This delightful disc offers fresh and alert performances of all the overtures to Mozart's operas, not just the later works but the boyhood pieces too. Menuhin has long had a special relationship with this superb Polish orchestra (formerly the Polish Chamber Orchestra) and here, as in his recordings of late Mozart symphonies for Virgin, the performances are electric, with speeds generally brisk but never rushed. Though the overture to *Bastien und Bastienne* may be little more than a flourish, its opening strikingly anticipates the first theme of the *Eroica*. Those to two other early operas, *Lucio Silla* and *Mitridate* are like miniature symphonies. The recording is full and clear with ample bloom.

Overtures: *La clemenza di Tito; Così fan tutte; Don Giovanni; Die Entführung aus dem Serail; Idomeneo; Le nozze di Figaro; Der Schauspieldirektor; Die Zauberflöte. Serenade No. 13 (Eine kleine Nachtmusik).*
*** Sony Dig. SK 46695 [id.]. Tafelmusik, Bruno Weil.

Sparkling and vital performances by this Canadian period-instrument group under Bruno Weil. Mozart overtures do not come much fresher than this, and the players convey pleasure and delight in what they are doing. Very clean recording quality from the Sony team of engineers.

Serenades Nos. 1 in D, K.100; 7 in D (Haffner), K.250; 9 in D (Posthorn), K.320; 13 in G (Eine kleine Nachtmusik), K.525; Serenata notturna, K.239.

(B) **(*) Decca Double 443 458-2 (2) [id.].
Vienna Mozart Ens., Willi Boskovsky.

Boskovsky and the Vienna Mozart Ensemble play with elegance and sparkle, and these performances still sound outstandingly bracing and vivid. The recordings were made in the Sofiensaal over a decade between 1968 and 1978. The account of *Eine kleine Nachtmusik*, one of the freshest and most attractive on disc and dating from 1968, here has a somewhat astringent treble, while Boskovsky's 1973 *Posthorn Serenade*, which has a natural musicality and is very well balanced, seems rather dry in the matter of string-timbre, though the bloom remains on the wind and the posthorn is tangible in its presence. Like the *Haffner serenade*, it is marvellously alive, full of the sparkle and elegance we associate with this group, with admirable phrasing and feeling for detail, yet the *Haffner* (dating from 1972) has a distinctly warmer ambience. The very engaging earliest *Serenade in D*, K.100, has the greatest glow of all, although it was recorded in 1970. Nevertheless many will count this excellent value for money in Decca's two-for-the-price-of-one series, offering 159 minutes of music on the pair of CDs.

Serenades Nos. 3 in D, K.185; 4 in D (Colloredo), K.203.
(BB) *** Naxos Dig. 8.550413; *4550413* [id.].
Salzburg CO, Harald Nerat.

Well-played, nicely phrased and musical accounts on Naxos, recorded in a warm, reverberant acoustic, but one in which detail clearly registers. The Salzburg Chamber Orchestra has real vitality, and most readers will find these accounts musically satisfying and very enjoyable.

Serenades Nos. 6 in D (Serenata notturna), K.239; 7 in D (Haffner), K.250.
(M) **(*) Erato/Warner Dig. 0630 13737-2. Pavlo Beznosiuk, Amsterdam Bar. O, Koopman.

Koopman's account is bold and his accents robust, especially in Minuets; indeed the energetic timpani are little short of explosive. But he has an excellent violin soloist in Pavlo Beznosiuk, and he ensures that the delectable *moto perpetuo* sparkles daintily. The extra transparency means that detail registers throughout. The timpani come through strongly and cleanly in the *Serenata notturna* and tend to dominate aurally, but the string playing remains elegantly turned.

Serenades Nos. (i) *6 (Serenata notturna), K.239; 7 in D (Haffner), K.250; 9 in D, K.320.*
*** Telarc Dig. CD 80161 [id.]. Prague CO, Mackerras.

In Mackerras's coupling the playing is lively and brilliant, helped by warm recorded sound, vivid in its sense of presence, except that the reverberant acoustic clouds the tuttis a little. The violin soloist, Oldrich Viček, is very much one of the team under the conductor rather than a virtuoso establishing his individual line. By omitting repeats in the *Haffner*, Mackerras leaves room for the other delightful *Serenade*, just as haunting, with the terracing between the solo string quartet (in close focus) and the full string band aptly underlined.

Serenades Nos. (i) *6 (Serenata notturna), K.239; 7 in D (Haffner), K.250; 9 in D (Posthorn), K.320;* (ii) *13 in G, K.525.*
(B) ** DG Double 453 076-2 (2). (i) BPO; (ii) VPO; Karl Boehm.

These are characteristic Boehm performances from the early 1970s. A large orchestra is used and, as it is the Berlin Philharmonic, one can take it for granted that they will play with polish and refinement. The effect is warm and civilized (including the posthorn solos). There is a degree of suavity, although there is spirit in the allegros. The *Posthorn Serenade* also brings a certain dourness on the part of Boehm. He doesn't find much fun and sparkle in the music, although this is somewhat offset by Thomas Brandis's stylish solo violin contribution. The real snag is the sheer weight of sound, and on the first disc the string focus is not absolutely clean, not even in the opening *Eine kleine Nachtmusik*, which lacks textural refinement, even though Boehm's reading is polished and spacious, with a neat, lightly pointed finale.

Serenades Nos. 6 in D (Serenata notturna), K.239; 13 in G (Eine kleine Nachtmusik), K.525.
(B) *** Carlton IMP 30367 02242 [(M) id.].
Serenata of London, Barry Wilde – ELGAR: *Serenade for strings;* GRIEG: *Holberg suite.* ***

These performances by the Serenata of London under Barry Wilde are first class in every way and, with truthful, modern recording, they are very recommendable indeed. In the *Serenata notturna* the timpani are not too resonantly dominant, yet they add much character to the opening *Marcia-maestoso*. Wilde's pacing of the *Night music* is admirable and the playing is consistently fresh and stylish.

Serenades Nos. 6 in D (Serenata notturna), K.239; 13 (Eine kleine Nachtmusik), K.525; Serenade for wind No. 12 in C min., K.388.
(M) **(*) DG Dig. 439 524-2. Orpheus CO.

The *Serenata notturna*, which can easily sound bland, has a fine sparkle here. The famous *Night music*, however, is rather lacking in charm with a very brisk opening movement, alert enough and very polished, but somewhat unbending. The *Wind serenade* restores the balance of excellence, alert and sympathetic and full of character. The digital recording is first class throughout.

Serenade No. 7 in D (Haffner), K.250; March in D, K.249.
*** Sony Dig. SK 66270 [id.]. Isaac Stern, Franz Liszt CO, Rampal.
(BB) **(*) Naxos Dig. 8.550333 [id.]. Takako Nishizaki, Capella Istropolitana, Johannes Wildner.

Easily the finest of recent accounts of the delightful *Haffner Serenade* is the new Sony version from the Franz Liszt Chamber Orchestra. Here Isaac Stern teams up with Jean-Pierre Rampal, who directs a performance which combines vigour and energy with elegance and grace. Stern's solo contribution is a bit thin in timbre but his phrasing is sure, and what makes this performance so enjoyable is the warmth and elegance of the playing of the Liszt Chamber Orchestra in the three movements which follow the miniature violin concerto: indeed the first Minuet is truly *galant*, as Mozart indicated. The finale fizzes with energy and geniality, with nice trills from bassoons and flutes adding to the sense of high spirits.

The K.249 *March* is given twice on Naxos, as both prelude and postlude to the main *Serenade* in the authentic manner. Wildner brings out the vigour rather than the charm of the fast movements, with the Minuets on the heavy side, but with the big final allegro superbly articulated and erupting in rustic jollity. The important violin solos in earlier movements are played superbly by Takako Nishizaki. Bright, full recording. Even with the above reservations, this is an excellent bargain.

Serenade No. 7 (Haffner), K.250; Symphony No. 35 in D (Haffner), K.385.
(N) *** Hänssler Dig. CD 98.173 [id.]. ASMF, Iona Brown.

The coupling of the *Haffner Symphony* and *Haffner Serenade*, specially apt, is surprisingly rare. In the *Symphony* Brown, unlike Marriner, follows the autograph in omitting an exposition repeat. Iona Brown herself is the virtuoso soloist in the *Serenade*, as she was in the Marriner version on Philips, lighter than ever in the moto perpetuo scurryings of the fourth movement *Rondo*. Hänssler describe this issue and the companion disc of the *Posthorn Serenade* as part of their Academy series, and such refreshing discs, vividly recorded, could not be more promising.

Serenades Nos. 9 in D (Posthorn); 13 (Eine kleine Nachtmusik), K.525.
**(*) Telarc CD 10108 [id.]. Prague CO, Mackerras.

(i) *Serenades Nos. 9 in D (Posthorn), K.320; 13 in G (Eine kleine Nachtmusik), K.525;* (ii) *6 German dances, K.509; Minuet in C, K.409.*
(B) **(*) Sony SBK 48266 [id.]. (i) Cleveland O, George Szell; (ii) LSO, Leinsdorf.

Serenade No. 9 in D (Posthorn), K.320; (i) *Bassoon concerto in B flat, K.191.*
**(*) RCA Dig. 09026 61927-2 [id.]. (i) Eberhard Marschall; Bav. R. O, Sir Colin Davis.

Serenade No. 9 in D (Posthorn); Idomeneo (ballet music), K.367; 2 Marches in D, K.335/1–2.
**(*) O-L Dig. 452 604-2. AAM, Hogwood.

The Prague strings have great warmth and Mackerras gets vital results from his Czech forces. Rhythms are lightly sprung and the phrasing is natural in every way. The Telarc acoustic is warm and spacious with a wide dynamic range (some might feel it is too wide for this music), though most ears will find the effect agreeable.

Marvellously vivacious playing from the Clevelanders in the *Posthorn Serenade*, especially in the exhilarating presto finale, yet there is no lack of tenderness in the *concertante* third movement. *Eine kleine Nachtmusik* is similarly polished and vital, and in both works the Severance Hall acoustic provides a full ambience, but it is a pity that the close balance means a reduced dynamic range. Even so, this is music-making of great character. Leinsdorf's *German dances* make a lively bonus, if not as distinctive as the Szell performances.

Sir Colin Davis's account of the *Posthorn Serenade* cannot be faulted. The recording was made 'live' and it is admirably paced and elegantly played, and the *Concertante* section which features a group of wind players (instead of the solo violin which Mozart had interpolated in previous serenades) is pleasingly colourful. The ample resonance of the Dresden acoustic (the more remarkable as there is an audience present) serves to inflate the textures in a way we do not expect today. The *Bassoon concerto* is similarly affected and the first tutti sounds overblown. But the bassoonist, Eberhard Marschall, is such a personable and characterful player that one cannot help but revel in his solo contribution, while Davis shapes the central *Andante* with appealing breadth. The Minuet finale rounds the work off with much flair from all concerned.

If you are a follower of Hogwood's Mozart, this will not disappoint. The playing has style and finesse; it is also strong in character. Indeed the *Serenade* (with its pair of bold Marches which act as introduction and postlude) is unusually symphonic in feeling; although the graceful secondary material is well appreciated, some listeners might feel that the music could smile more. However, when it finally appears, the posthorn makes a vibrant impression. The recording is excellent.

Serenade No.9 (Posthorn), K 320; Symphony No. 33 in B flat, K 319.
(N) *** Hänssler Dig.CD 98.129 [id.]. ASMF, Iona Brown.

Challenging earlier recordings by the Academy

under Sir Neville Marriner, Iona Brown neatly offers another popular Serenade alongside a symphony contemporary with it. The sound is outstandingly good, with plenty of bloom but no excessive reverberation. These are attractively fresh Mozart performances, using modern instruments, which have concern for the crisper manners encouraged by period performance. Speeds are consistently brisker than those of the Marriner versions which we have used for comparison. The finale of *Symphony No. 33* for example, brings a hectic speed which does not sound at all breathless, with feather-light triplets, and similarly in the finale of the *Posthorn Serenade* with which it is coupled.

Serenade No. 10 in B flat for 13 wind instruments, K.361.

*** ASV Dig. CDCOE 804 [id.]. COE Wind Soloists, Schneider.

*** Ph. (IMS) Dig. 412 726-2 [id.]. ASMF, Marriner.

**(*) Accent ACC 68642D [id.]. Octophorus, Kuijken.

Serenade No. 10 in B flat for 13 wind instruments, K.361; Divertimento in F (for 2 oboes, 2 horns & 2 bassoons), K.213.

(M) **(*) Chandos Dig. CHAN 6575. SNO Wind Ens., Paavo Järvi.

The brilliant young soloists of the Chamber Orchestra of Europe, inspired by the conducting of Alexander Schneider, give an unusually positive, characterful reading. Right at the start, the flourishes from the first clarinet are far more effective when played as here, not literally, but with Schneider leading them on to the first forte chord from the full ensemble. From then on the individual artistry of the players is most winning. The sound is exceptionally vivid and faithful.

The Marriner version fits very stylishly in the Academy's series of Mozart wind works, characteristically refined in its ensemble, with matching of timbres and contrasts beautifully judged, both lively and graceful with rhythms well sprung and speeds well chosen, yet with nothing mannered about the result. Full, warm recording that yet allows good detail.

On period instruments Barthold Kuijken directs his talented team in an authentic performance where the distinctive character of eighteenth-century instruments brings a sparer, lighter texture, as it should. Speeds tend to be on the cautious side but the liveliness of the playing makes up for that. The recording adds to the clarity.

The SNO Wind Ensemble's version under Paavo Järvi is enjoyably spontaneous-sounding, though ensemble is not quite as polished as in the finest versions. Speeds are well chosen, and the recording is warm, though the detail is sometimes masked by the lively acoustic. The little *Divertimento* makes an attractive bonus. Not a first choice but, at mid-price and with digital recording, worth considering.

Serenades Nos. 10 in B flat for 13 wind instruments, K.361; 11 in E flat, K.375; 12 in C min., K.388; Wind divertimenti: in B flat, K. 240; in E flat, K.252; in F, K.253; in B flat, K.270.

(N) (B) *** Decca Double 458 096-2 (2) [id.]. Amadeus Winds, Christopher Hogwood.

Anyone wanting period performances of Mozart's three supreme *Serenades for wind* can safely have these Amadeus Winds versions recommended to them. Moreover this collection offers a fascinating aural comparison. K.375 and K.388 were recorded first in 1985 in New York, and the effect is undoubtedly more plangent than in the later performances recorded in Boston in 1987 (K.361) and 1989 (the four *Divertimenti*). In the *C minor Serenade* the extra darkness of colour adds to the character of the music, although the blending is well matched and characterful. Both here and K.375 (similarly bold), where one might expect speeds faster than usual, these are on the leisurely side, except in the finales, though well lifted both rhythmically and in phrasing. The speeds are perhaps a recognition of the players' technical problems, coping with intonation and less sophisticated mechanisms, a point brought home in the clear, full digital recording, with much clicking of keys. By the time they came to record the *Grand Partita* two years later, the group's integration is much smoother and the effect is much more sophisticated. Indeed this is an outstandingly characterful account, preferable to the Brymer version on modern instruments (see above), not lacking finesse, and making the strongest possible case for authenticity. Both the *Adagio* and *Romance* are lyrically mellow, and the *Theme and variations* is almost Schubertian in its innocent charm. The jocular Finale goes like the wind, pressed home with a virtuosity, surmounting almost all difficulties. The four *Divertimenti* are also very successful, with the vivid colouring preventing any possible feeling of blandness.

Serenades Nos. 10 in B flat; 12 in C min., K.388.

(B) *** HM Dig. HMA 1903051 [id.]. Budapest Wind Ens., Zoltán Kocsis.

The Budapest wind players blend beautifully in slow movements and phrase with pleasingly simple, expressive warmth; allegros are infectiously buoyant, especially the Rondo finale of the so-called *Grand Partita in B flat*, which also has a satisfyingly full sonority. Both works contain a notable set of variations: in K.361 it is the penultimate movement, in K.388 the finale, and the colour and diversity of the playing make a high point in each work. Kocsis himself composes a brief oboe cadenza for the latter and a clarinet cadenza for the lovely *Romance* in K.361.

Serenades for wind Nos. 11 in E flat, K.375; 12 in C min., K.388.

*** ASV Dig. CDCOE 802 [id.]. COE, Schneider.

With Schneider as a wise and experienced guide, the COE Wind give performances which combine brilliance and warmth with a feeling of spontaneity. K.375 in particular is a delight, as genial as it is characterful, conveying the joy of the inspiration. K.388 might have been more menacing at the C minor opening, but the result is most persuasive, with excellent digital sound set against a warm but not confusing acoustic.

Serenades Nos. 11 in E flat, K.375; 12 in C min., K.388; Overtures: Le nozze di Figaro (arr. Vent); *Don Giovanni* (arr. Triebensee); *Die Zauberflöte* (arr. Heidenreich).

*** Hyperion Dig. CDA 66887 [id.]. E. Concert Winds.

One of the most enjoyable records of Mozart's wind music to appear for a long time. Fresh, spirited playing; firmly focused and well-blended sound both from the players and from the engineers. A delight!

Serenade No. 13 in G (Eine kleine Nachtmusik), K.525.

*** Ph. Dig. 410 606-2 [id.]. I Musici (with concert of Baroque music***).

I Musici play the music with rare freshness, giving the listener the impression of hearing the work for the first time. The playing is consistently alert and sparkling, with the *Romanze* particularly engaging. The recording is beautifully balanced.

(i) *Serenade No. 13 in G (Eine kleine Nachtmusik), K.525;* (ii) *Allegro in D, K.121; 3 German dances, K.605; Marches in D, K.249, 335; Minuet in C, K.409.*

(N) (M) ** Mercury 434 398-2 [id.]. (i) LSO, (i; ii) Festival CO; Dorati – HANDEL: *Fireworks music; Water music.* **(*)

The LSO sparkle in Mozart's most famous *Serenade* and a similar spick-and-span rhythmic point gives a characteristic Dorati brightness to the other genre pieces, as played by the Festival Chamber Orchestra, whoever they may be! The Watford Town Hall recording is pleasingly warm but the Telefunken microphones give a somewhat glassy upper range to the violins.

Sinfonia concertante for violin, viola and orchestra in E flat, K.364.

(M) ** EMI CDM7 64632-2. David & Igor Oistrakh, BPO, D. Oistrakh – BRAHMS: *Violin concerto.* **(*)

Although the solo playing is rich-timbred and beautifully matched, the orchestral accompaniment polished and the recording full and pleasing, there is a curiously literal approach to the music-making here, and the imaginative spark which can bring this glorious work fully to life is missing.

(i) *Sinfonia concertante in E flat for violin, viola and orchestra, K.364;* (ii) *Sinfonia concertante in E flat for oboe, clarinet, horn, bassoon and orchestra, K.297b.*

(B) *** Virgin/EMI Dig. CUV5 61205-2. (i) Warren-Green, Chase; (ii) Hunt, Collins, Thompson, Alexander; LCO, Warren-Green.

*** DG (IMS) Dig. 429 784-2 [id.]. (i) Todd Phillips, Maureen Gallagher; (ii) Stephen Taylor, David Singer, William Purvis, Orpheus CO.

(BB) **(*) ASV Quicksilva Dig. CDQS 6139 [id.]. (i) McAslan, Inque; (ii) Anderson, Hacker, Gambold, Taylor; L. Festival O, Ross Pople.

In the ideal coupling of Mozart's paired *Sinfonias concertantes*, Christopher Warren-Green is joined by Roger Chase to provide a characteristically vital account of Mozart's inspired work for violin and viola. The *Andante* is slow and warmly expressive, yet without a trace of sentimentality. This is very satisfying, with its full-timbred sound from soloists and orchestra alike. The coupling, K.297b, is even more delectable and it would be hard to imagine a more persuasive team of wind players than those here. The full-bodied recording has plenty of space and atmosphere and the soloists in both works remain real and tangible.

The performances from members of the Orpheus Chamber Orchestra have an appealing warmth and intimacy. The dialogue between the violin and viola soloists in K.364 is both lively and very sensitive, with a warm expansiveness for the lovely secondary group, while the slow movement brings a comparably felt espressivo, and the finale is buoyant. This is most satisfying, and the comparable work with wind soloists gives a similar feeling of a chamber performance, with the soloists not lacking individuality but blending exceptionally well as a team. Here the first movement is briskly paced, the *Adagio* is warm and leisurely, and the finale light and graceful. The recording is very truthful and the warm acoustic gives pleasing inner definition.

The outer movements of K.364 have a fine rhythmic spring on ASV, and the *Andante* is touchingly expressive in a pleasingly restrained manner. Lorraine McAslan is rather near the microphone, which is not entirely flattering to her upper range in the first movement, but the viola is not too backward, and the recording projects vividly. The account of K.297b brings a lively, alert performance with speeds relaxed enough to allow a winning lift to rhythms. Only in the finale is the result a little heavy, but the 6/8 coda becomes all the more playful. Alan Hacker's distinctive reedy clarinet provides an extra tang, and the way the soloists appear in turn as protagonists in the variations finale is delightfully done. The sound is bright, firm and realistic. Good value.

Sinfonia concertante in E flat for oboe, clarinet, horn, bassoon and orchestra, K.297b.

(N) (***) Cala mono CACD 0523 [id.]. Marcel Tabuteau, Bernard Portnoy, Sol Schoenbach, Mason Jones, Phd. O, Stokowski – BEETHOVEN: *Symphony No. 6 (Pastoral).* (***)

Stokowski recorded the *Sinfonia concertante* in December 1940, ready for issue the following year to mark the 250th anniversary of the composer's death. Surprisingly, it was his first and only Mozart recording made in his quarter-century directing the Philadelphia Orchestra. The result is sheer joy. His graceful string phrasing may have romantic elements, but the warmth is ever persuasive, especially in the lovely slow movement, and notably its coda. His expert group of orchestral soloists (balanced forwardly and clearly) blend well together – with the single proviso that the bassoonist at times produces a rather close vibrato. Yet they retain their individuality and the opening of the finale is delightful. The transfer is excellent and the sound, though a bit subfusc is always fully acceptable, with a wider dynamic range than on the coupled Beethoven. A disc to treasure for all Stokowskians.

(i) *Sinfonia concertante in E flat, K.297b;* (ii) *Piano and wind quintet in E flat, K.452.*

❁ (***) Testament mono SBT 1091 [id.]. (i) Dennis Brain, Cecil James, Sidney Sutcliffe, Bernard Walton, Philh. O, Karajan; (ii) Gieseking, Philh. Wind Ens. – BEETHOVEN: *Piano and wind quintet.* (***) ❁

The Mozart *Quintet* is one of the classic chamber-music recordings of all time. Gieseking and members of the Philharmonia Wind (Dennis Brain, Sidney Sutcliffe, Bernard Walton and Cecil James) recorded it over 40 years ago, and in terms of tonal blend and perfection of balance and ensemble it has few rivals, although among modern versions Perahia's account with members of the ECO remains very highly recommendable at mid-price, also coupled with Beethoven (see below).

To the original quintet coupling Testament have added the *Sinfonia concertante* for wind, which these distinguished players recorded with Karajan in 1953, a performance of comparable stature. Not to be missed. The mono sound comes up wonderfully fresh in this Testament transfer. This is a full-price reissue and is worth every penny of the asking price.

Complete Mozart Edition, Volume 21: (i) *Sonatas for organ and orchestra (Epistle sonatas) Nos. 1–17* (complete). *Adagio & allegro in F min., K.594; Andante in F, K.616; Fantasia in F min., K.608.*

(M) **(*) Ph. 422 521-2 (2). Daniel Chorzempa (organs at Stift Wilhering, Linz, Austria; Schlosspfarrkirche, Obermarchtal, Germany – K.594; K.608); (i) German Bach Soloists, Helmut Winschermann.

The *Epistle sonatas* derive their name from the fact that they were intended to be heard between the Epistle and Gospel in the Mass. Admittedly they are not great music or even first-class Mozart; however, played with relish they make a strong impression. The final *Sonata*, K.263, becomes a fully fledged concerto. The set is completed with the other works by Mozart which are usually heard on the organ, and here Chorzempa's registration is particularly appealing.

Sonatas Nos. 1–17 (Epistle sonatas) for organ and chamber orchestra.

(BB) **(*) Naxos Dig. 8.550512 [id.]. János Sebestyén, Budapest Ferenc Erkel CO.

While it is understood that, apart from No. 16 in C, K.329, which has a specific solo part, the organ is not intended as a solo instrument in these *Chiesa sonatas*, it seems perverse to balance the instrument so that it blends in completely with the orchestral texture, as the Naxos engineers have done. Otherwise these alert, polished and nicely scaled performances could hardly be improved on and, apart from the controversial matter of the relationship of the organ to the orchestra, the recording is first class.

SYMPHONIES

Symphonies Nos. 1–47 (including alternative versions); in C, K.35; in D, K.38; in F, K.42a; in B flat, K.45b; in D, K.46a (K.51); in D, K.62a (K.100); in B flat, K.74g (K.216); in F, K.75; in G, K.75b (K.110); in D, K.111a; in D, K.203, 204 & 196 (121); in G, K.425a (K.444); in A min. (Odense); in G (New Lambacher).

(B) *** O-L Analogue/Dig. 452 496-2 (19) [id.]. AAM, Schröder, Hogwood.

The monumental complete recording of the Mozart symphonies, using authentic instruments, made between 1978 and 1985, now returns as a complete set on 19 bargain-priced CDs. With Jaap Schröder leading the admirably proportioned string group (9,8,4,3,2) and Christopher Hogwood at the keyboard, this was a remarkably successful joint enterprise. The playing has great style, warmth and polish and, if intonation is not always absolutely refined, that is only to be expected with old instruments. The survey is complete enough to include No. 37 – in fact the work of Michael Haydn but with a slow introduction by Mozart. The *Lambacher* and *Odense Symphonies* are also here, plus alternative versions, with different scoring, of No. 40; while the *Paris Symphony* is given two complete performances with alternative slow movements. Although Pinnock's more recent recording remains first choice (see below), it is much less comprehensive, and Hogwood's overall achievement is remarkable. The recording is well balanced and has plenty of ambience, the CD transfers are very successful, and the accompanying documentation is very good.

Symphonies Nos. (i) *1 in E flat, K.16; 4 in D, K.19; in F, K.19a; 5 in B flat, K.22; 6 in F, K.43; 7 in D, K.45; in G (Neue Lambacher); in G (Alte Lambacher), K.45a; in B flat, K.45b; 8 in D, K.48; 9 in C, K.73; 10 in G, K.74; in F, K.75; in F, K.76; in D, K.81; 11 in D, K.84; in D, K.95; in C, K.96; in D, K.97; 12 in G, K.110; 13 in F, K.112; 14 in A, K.114; 15 in G, K.124; 16 in C, K.128; 17 in G, K.129; 18 in F, K.130; 19 in E flat, K.132* (with alternative slow movement); *20 in D, K.133; in D, K.161 & 163; in D, K.111 & 120; in D, K.196 & 121; in C, K.208 & 102. Minuet in A, K.61g/1;* (ii) *21 in A, K.134; 22 in C, K.162; 23 in D, K.181; 24 in B flat, K.182; 25 in G min., K.183; 26 in E flat, K.184; 27 in G, K.199; 28 in C, K.200; 29 in A, K.201; 30 in D, K.202; 31 in D (Paris), K.297* (with alternative slow movement); *32 in G, K.318; 33 in B flat, K.319; 34 in C, K.338; 35 in D (Haffner), K.385; 36 in C (Linz), K.425; 38 in D (Prague), K.504; 39 in E flat, K.543; 40 in G min., K.550; 41 in C (Jupiter), K.551.*

(B) **(*) Ph. 454 085-2 (12) [id.]. (i) ASMF, Marriner; (ii) Concg. O, Krips.

Complete Mozart Edition, Volume 1: *Symphonies Nos. 1 in E flat, K.16; 4 in D, K.19; in F, K.19a; 5 in B flat, K.22; 6 in F, K.43; 7 in D, K.45; in G (Neue Lambacher), G.16; in G (Alte Lambacher), K.45a; in B flat, K.45b; 8 in D, K.48; 9 in C, K.73; 10 in G, K.74; in F, K.75; in F, K.76; in D, K.81; 11 in D, K.84; in D, K.95; in C, K.96; in D, K.97; 12 in G, K.110; 13 in F, K.112; 14 in A, K.114; 15 in G, K.124; 16 in C, K.128; 17 in G, K.129; 18 in F, K.130; 19 in E flat, K.132* (with alternative slow movement); *20 in D, K.133; in D, K.161 & 163; in D, K.111 & 120; in D, K.196 & 121; in C, K.208 & 102. Minuet in A, K.61g/1.*

(M) *** Ph. 422 501-2 (6) [id.]. ASMF, Marriner.

The first half of this 12-CD box (also available separately in a 6-CD set) is a reissue of Volume 1 of the Philips Complete Mozart Edition. Marriner's recordings confirm the Mozartian vitality of the performances and their sense of style and spontaneity. The Philips engineers respond with alive and vivid recording. Except perhaps for those who insist on original instruments, the finesse and warmth of the playing here is a constant joy. The Dutch players for Krips also bring warmth, as well as proving characteristically stylish in phrasing and execution. Quick movements can be bracingly vigorous. Both the previously underrated *No. 28 in C* and the first great masterpiece in A major, both aptly paced, are very persuasively done, with an almost ethereal delicacy from the strings in the beautiful *Andante* of No. 29 and the horns thrusting exuberantly in the coda of the finale. Although Krips's Mozartian sensibility never deserts him, the readings of some of the later symphonies are somewhat wanting in character, however, and do not do full honour to the fine Mozartian that Krips was. No. 39 goes well enough and the first movement of the *G minor* is not pressed too hard, but in the *Jupiter* Krips holds the tension much more slackly. The ample Concertgebouw sound, with its resonant bass, emphasizes the breadth of scale of the music-making, yet the digital remastering gives an attractive freshness to the violins, although the Minuets sound well upholstered. Throughout, the orchestral playing is a pleasure in itself, especially nimble in finales, which are never raced.

Symphonies Nos. 1–41.

(B) **(*) DG 453 231-2 (10). BPO, Karl Boehm.

Boehm's Mozart symphony recordings with the Berlin Philharmonic, made between 1959 and 1968, were in fact just as much a pioneering project, setting the pattern for Antal Dorati's Haydn series for Decca, completed five years later. All the earlier symphonies were recorded in intensive sessions in March and November 1968, a real voyage of discovery, with performances warm and genial, with bold contrasts of dynamic and well-sprung rhythms. This latest CD reissue, on ten discs instead of twelve, also brings the advantage of fuller and more forward transfers, with good body and presence. The new bargain box, unlike the previous one, has essays on Boehm as Mozartian by Peter Cosse and Mozart as symphonist by Heinz Becker. An excellent bargain, and not just for the historical specialist, but for all Mozartians.

Symphonies Nos. 1 in E flat, K.16; 4 in D, K.19; in F, K.19a; 5 in B flat, K.22; in G, K.45a; 6–36; 38–41.

(M) **(*) DG (IMS) 435 360-2 (11) [id.]. VPO, Levine.

James Levine was the players' own surprising choice of conductor when the Vienna Philharmonic agreed to record the complete Mozart symphonies for the bicentenary year, and though the performances may sometimes be heavy-handed and may lack charm, there is no lack of energy, and no risk of Mozart being sentimentalized. The string forces used are modest, even though slow movements such as that of the *Jupiter* have a Viennese smoothness. The recording is full-bodied but in places bright to the point of edginess, particularly on string-tone in allegros. Mackerras on Telarc may offer a complete Mozart cycle with more finesse and exhilaration, but all these Levine performances are enjoyable and never boring. The set comes out somewhere between mid- and bargain-price.

Symphonies Nos. 1 in E flat, K.16; 4 in D, K.19; in F, K.19a; 5 in K.22; in G, K.45a; 6–36; 38–41.

(M) *** Telarc Dig. CD 80300 (10) [id.]. Prague CO, Mackerras.

Mackerras's is an outstanding series, with electrifying performances of the early as well as the later symphonies. There is not a suspicion of routine, with the playing full of dramatic contrasts in rhythm, texture or dynamic. Mackerras has a keen feeling for Mozart style, not least in the slow movements and minuets, which he regularly takes faster than usual. His flowing andantes are consistently stylish too, with performances on modern instruments regularly related to period practice. An outstanding instance comes in the G minor *Andante* of *No. 5 in B flat*, K.22, where Mackerras, fastish and light, makes others seem heavy-handed in this anticipation of romanticism, underlining the harmonic surprises clearly and elegantly. Consistently Mackerras finds light and shade in Mozart's inspirations, both early and late, though some may feel that, with warm reverberation characteristic of this Prague orchestra's recording venue, the scale is too large, particularly in the early symphonies. Harpsichord continuo, where used, is usually well balanced.

Symphonies Nos. 14 in A, K.114; 15 in G, K.124; 16 in C, K.128; 17 in G, K.129; 18 in F, K.130.

*** Telarc Dig. CD 80242 [id.]. Prague CO, Mackerras.

No. 14 in A is a particularly fine work (as indeed are all Mozart's A major symphonies) and, like the others here, it receives an invigorating account with brisk Allegros and a strong, one-in-a-bar tempo for the Minuet (this suits the Minuet of *No. 18 in F* even better as it is very folksy). Slow movements, however, are very direct and are pressed onwards, slightly unbending; here some might find Mackerras's approach too austere. The bright recording is resonant, which prevents absolute clarity, but the clean lines of the playing ensure plenty of stimulating impact.

Symphonies Nos. 15 in G, K.124; 16 in C, K.128; 17 in G, K.129; 18 in F, K.129.

(BB) **(*) Naxos Dig. 8.550874 [id.]. Northern CO, Nicholas Ward.

Symphonies Nos. 19 in E flat, K.132; 20 in D, K.133; 37 in G Introduction only (with remainder of the symphony by Michael Haydn).

(BB) *** Naxos Dig. 8.550875 [id.]. Northern CO, Nicholas Ward.

Nicholas Ward continues his stylish Mozart series, with his fourth and fifth Naxos discs offering six symphonies written in 1772. The orchestral string-phasing is particularly elegant in slow movements (notably the wistful *Andante* of *No. 15 in G* and the charming melody which forms the centre-piece of No. 17), while the lively first movement of *No. 18 in F* effervesces neatly. Elsewhere allegros are alert and strong. Excellent, full and well-balanced recording, though not ideally sharply detailed.

No. 19 is scored for four horns, two in E flat *alt*, and they give added weight and character to the orchestral texture in outer movements but are sensibly reduced to just a pair in the *Andante*. No. 20 is given extra brightness by a pair of trumpets. But it is the delectable *Andante* that catches the ear with its charming flute solo over muted violins. Mozart contributed just the rather grand opening *Adagio maestoso* to the symphony once mistakenly regarded as his No. 37. It is played most persuasively: this disc is well worth having on all counts.

Symphonies Nos. 16 in C, K.128; 17 in G, K.129; 18 in F, K.130; 19 in E flat, K.132; 20 in D, K.133; 21 in A, K.134; 22 in C, K.162; 23 in D, K.181; 24 in B flat, K.182; 25 in G min., K.183; 26 in E flat, K.184; 27 in G, K.199; 28 in C, K.200; 29 in A, K.201.

*** DG Dig. 439 915-2 (4). E. Concert, Trevor Pinnock.

This invigorating DG box of the Salzburg Symphonies is a splendid follow-up to Pinnock's collection of the earlier juvenile works. The playing has polish and sophistication, fine intonation and spontaneity and great vitality, balanced by warm, lyrical feeling in slow movements. Indeed the account of *No. 29 in A major* is among the finest available (on either modern or original instruments) and the earlier A major work (No. 21) is very impressive too, as is the G minor, K.183, and the very 'operatic' *No. 23 in D major*. Another clear first choice, and not only for authenticists.

Symphonies No. 19 in E flat, K.132; 20 in D, K.133; 21 in A, K.134; 22 in C, K.162; 23 in D, K.162b.

*** Telarc Dig. CD 80217 [id.]. Prague CO, Mackerras.

Mackerras is equally lively in these early works from Mozart's Salzburg period. The surprising thing is how fast his speeds tend to be. In one instance the contrast is astonishing, when at a very brisk *Andantino grazioso* Mackerras turns the slow middle movement of No. 23 into a lilting Ländler, quite different from other performances. The recording is reverberant, as in the later symphonies, giving relatively weighty textures; with such light scoring, however, there is ample clarity, with braying horns riding beautifully over the rest.

Complete Mozart Edition, Volume 2: *Symphonies Nos. 21–36; 37: Adagio maestoso in G, K.44* (Introduction to a symphony by M. Haydn); *38–41; Minuet for a Symphony in C, K.409.*

(M) **(*) Ph. 422 502-2 (6) [id.]. ASMF, Marriner.

As with the early works, the later symphonies in the Marriner performances, as reissued in the Philips Mozart Edition, are conveniently laid out on six mid-priced CDs, offered in numerical sequence, without a single symphony having to be divided between discs. However, the over-resonant bass remains in the recording of No. 40 and the *Haffner* (both of which date from 1970, nearly a decade before the rest of the cycle was recorded). Otherwise the transfers are of Philips's best quality, and the performances generally give every satisfaction, even if their style does not show an awareness of the discoveries made – in terms of texture and balance – by the authentic school.

Symphonies Nos. 24 in B flat, K.173; 26 in E flat, K.161a; 27 in G, K.161b; 30 in D, K.202.
*** Telarc Dig. CD 80186 [id.]. Prague CO, Mackerras.

Where in later symphonies Mackerras chooses more relaxed speeds, here he tends to be more urgent, as in the finale of No. 26 or the *Andantino grazioso* slow movement of No. 27, where he avoids the questionable use of muted strings. The reverberation of the recording gives the impression of a fairly substantial orchestra, without loss of detail, and anyone fancying this particular group of early Mozart symphonies need not hesitate.

Symphonies Nos. 24 in B flat, K.182; 25 in G min., K.183; 26 in E flat, K.184; 27 in G, K.199; 32 in G, K.318.
(B) *** [EMI Red Line Dig. CDR5 69818]. ASMF, Marriner.

Symphonies Nos. 31 in D (Paris), K.297; 33 in B flat, K.319; 34 in C, K.338.
(B) *** [EMI Red Line Dig. CDR5 69819]. ASMF, Marriner.

Symphonies Nos. 40 in G min., K.550; 41 in C (Jupiter), K.551.
(B) **(*) [EMI Red Line Dig. CDR5 69820]. ASMF, Marriner.

Marriner's third set of Mozart symphony recordings, made for EMI, is the most beautifully recorded of all. The playing, too, is graceful and elegant. With bracing rhythms and brisker pacing than in his earlier, Philips set, these readings are positive yet unidiosyncratic. Phrasing is supple and the Mozartian spirit is always alive here. There is a degree of disappointment in the *Jupiter Symphony*, which is slightly undercharacterized. For the most part, however, this music-making will give a great deal of pleasure.

Symphonies Nos. 24–36; 38–41.
(M) *** EMI Dig. [CDMF 638562] (4). ASMF, Marriner.

Symphonies Nos. 28 in C, K.200; 29 in A, K.201; 30 in D, K.202; 40 in G min., K.550; 41 in C (Jupiter), K.551.
(B) **(*) EMI Dig. CZS7 67564-2 (2). ASMF, Marriner.

In his continuing series for EMI, Marriner secures warm and gracious playing from the Academy in the three early symphonies but, with articulation that brings neat rather than sharp rhythmic incisiveness. Slow movements are very persuasive, in both their delicacy of touch and elegant contours. In No. 29 Marriner observes more repeats than before and the performance has an affectionate breadth, with plenty of energy reserved for the last movement. Marriner is at his very best in No. 40, a work he always did very sympathetically. In the last two movements he is strikingly dramatic, with crisper articulation and faster speeds than in his earlier recording for Philips, and this time in the slow movement he observes the first-half repeat. The *Jupiter* is also very well done, but the effect is less charismatic – though, as in the others in this digital series, the recording is first rate.

Symphonies Nos. 25 in G min., K.183; 29 in A, K.201; 31 in D (Paris), K.297.
(M) **(*) DG (IMS) 449 552-2. BPO, Karl Boehm.

These three symphonies come from the complete box (see above) that Boehm recorded in the 1960s. The playing of the Berlin Philharmonic is quite superlative, but here enjoyment is occasionally marred by the want of spontaneity that sometimes distinguished Boehm's direction. Marriner, for instance, is far more spirited in No. 25, though the orchestral playing is less cultured. The easy-going tempi are acceptable until the finale, which is very slow. The finales of Nos. 29 and 31 are more lively, but the weighty opening of the *Paris* will not appeal to everyone, although the violins articulate gracefully, and the Berlin wind phrase exquisitely throughout the disc. The mid-1960s recording is full-bodied (perhaps too much so for today's ears) and does not sound too dated.

Symphonies Nos. 25 in G min., K.183; 32 in G, K.318; 41 in C (Jupiter), K.551.
(BB) *** Naxos Dig. 8.550113 [id.]. Capella Istropolitana, Barry Wordsworth.

Symphonies Nos. 27 in G, K.199/161b; 33 in B flat, K.319; 36 in C (Linz), K.425.
(BB) *** Naxos Dig. 8.550264 [id.]. Capella Istropolitana, Barry Wordsworth.

Symphonies Nos. 28 in C, K.200; 31 in D (Paris), K.297; 40 in G min., K.550.
(BB) *** Naxos Dig. 8.550164 [id.]. Capella Istropolitana, Barry Wordsworth.

Symphonies Nos. 29 in A, K.201; 30 in D, K.202; 38 in D (Prague), K.504.
(BB) *** Naxos Dig. 8.550119 [id.]. Capella Istropolitana, Barry Wordsworth.

Symphonies Nos. 34 in C, K.338; 35 in D (Haffner), K.385; 39 in E flat, K.543.
(BB) *** Naxos Dig. 8.550186 [id.]. Capella Istropolitana, Barry Wordsworth.

Symphonies Nos. 40 in G min., K.550; 41 in C (Jupiter), K.551.
(BB) *** Naxos Dig. 8.550299 [id.]. Capella Istropolitana, Barry Wordsworth.

Barry Wordsworth's series of 15 symphonies on the Naxos super-bargain-priced label brings consistently refreshing and enjoyable performances. The Capella Istropolitana consists of leading members of the Slovak Philharmonic Orchestra of Bratislava; though their string-tone is thinnish, it is very much in scale with the clarity of a period performance but tonally far sweeter. The recording is outstandingly good, with a far keener sense of presence than in most rival versions and with less reverberation to obscure detail in tuttis. Wordsworth observes exposition repeats in first movements, but in the finales only in such symphonies as Nos. 38 and 41, where the movement particularly needs extra scale. In slow movements, as is usual, he omits repeats. He often adopts speeds that are marginally slower than we expect nowadays in chamber-scale performances; but, with exceptionally clean articulation and infectiously sprung rhythms, the results never drag, even if No. 29 is made to sound more sober than usual. In every way these are worthy rivals to the best full-priced versions, and they can be recommended with few if any reservations. Anyone wanting to sample might try the coupling of Nos. 34, 35 and 39 – with the hard-stick timpani sound at the start of No. 39 very dramatic. The *Linz* too is outstanding. For some, the option of having the last two symphonies coupled together will be useful.

Symphonies Nos. 25 in G min., K.183; 28 in C, K.200; 29 in A, K.201.
*** Telarc Dig. CD 80165 [id.]. Prague CO, Mackerras.

If you want performances on modern instruments, these are as fine as any, fresh and light, with transparent textures set against a warm acoustic and with rhythms consistently resilient. Mackerras's speeds are always carefully judged to allow elegant pointing but without mannerism, and the only snag is that second-half repeats are omitted in slow movements, and in the finale too of No. 29.

Bruno Walter Edition

(i) *Symphonies Nos. 25 in G min., K.183; 28 in C, K.200; 29 in A, K.201;* (ii) *35 in D (Haffner), K.385.*
(M) (***) Sony mono SMK 64473 [id.]. (i) Columbia SO; (ii) NYPO, Bruno Walter.

'The birth of a performance' (recorded rehearsals of *Symphony No. 36*); (i) *Symphonies Nos. 36 in C (Linz) K.425;* (ii) *38 in D (Prague), K.504.*
(M) (***) Sony mono SM2K 64474 (2) [id.]. (i) Columbia SO; (ii) NYPO, Bruno Walter.

Symphonies Nos. 39 in E flat, K.543; 40 in G min., K.550; 41 in C (Jupiter), K.551.
(M) (**) Sony mono SMK 64477 [id.]. NYPO, Bruno Walter.

Walter's recordings were made in the 1950s and have been impressively transferred. The early symphonies on the first CD show his touch at its lightest (especially in K.201) and there is some lovely playing, both graceful and delicate, from the New York violins in slow movements. The *Haffner* sparkles with vitality; this and the *Linz* (offered together with its justly famous rehearsal sequence) and the *Prague* all show Walter at his finest – stylish and vital yet always making the music sing. *No. 39 in E flat* is a strong performance, but the *G minor*, K.550, is curiously heavy and unspontaneous, while the *Jupiter*, more appropriately weighty, lacks incandescence.

Symphonies Nos. 25 in G min., K.183; 31 in D (Paris), K.297; Symphony in D (The Posthorn), after K.320; Masonic funeral music (Maurerische Trauermusik), K.477.
*** Sony Dig. SK 48385-2 [id.]. BPO, Abbado.

Claudio Abbado and the Berlin Philharmonic defy the fashion for period performance in exhilarating accounts of Mozart using modern instruments. Like his other Mozart recordings made for Sony in Berlin, this is warmly recommended to those who want to hear Mozart playing which marries sweetness and purity to crisp rhythms and dramatic bite. Although the string band is substantial, the purity and clarity of the playing aerates textures. Woodwind doubling is always clearly audible. The recording also captures very tellingly the lugubrious timbres of the *Masonic funeral music*, made dark with extra weight of wind set against a string section without cellos.

Symphonies Nos. 25 in G min., K.183; 39 in E flat, K.543.
(N) **(*) Ph. Dig. 454 443-2 [id.]. VPO, Muti.

The very opening of the slow introduction to No. 39 makes it very clear that Muti has no thought of being influenced by latterday ideas of period performance. The result is big, bold and weighty, with a full and warm Philips recording which yet reveals good inner detail. In No. 25, the little *G minor*, Muti is fast and fierce in the first movement, with no sense that this is an early work, and in the second movement *Andante* he keeps the violins unmuted, bringing out more sharply the tonal contrasts with the woodwind in alternate phrases.

Symphonies Nos. 26 in E flat, K.184; 27 in G, K.199; 28 in C, K.200; 30 in D, K.202; 32 in G, K.318.
*** ASV Dig. CDDCA 762 [id.]. LMP, Jane Glover.

Glover's generous coupling of five early symphonies brings typically fresh and direct readings, marked by sharp attack and resilient rhythms, at speeds on the fast side. With tuttis a little weightier than with most rivals, these are brightly enjoyable performances.

Symphonies Nos. 28 in C, K.200; 29 in A, K.201; 35 in D (Haffner).
*** Sony Dig. SK 48063 [id.]. BPO, Claudio Abbado.

Though Abbado's Berlin sound is weighty, the results are not just big-scaled but elegant too, with horns whooping out brightly. Abbado is never mannered and his phrasing and pointing of rhythm are delicately affectionate, conveying an element of fun and with speeds never allowed to drag. Slow movements are kept flowing, and finales are hectically fast, but played with such verve and diamond-bright articulation that there is no feeling of breathlessness. The Sony engineers have coped splendidly with the acoustic problems of the Philharmonie to give a full and forward sound, with good presence.

Symphonies Nos. 29 in A, K.201; 31 in D (Paris), K.297; 32 in G, K.318; 33 in B flat, K.319; 34 in C, K. 338; 35 in D (Haffner), K.385; 36 in C (Linz), K.425; 38 in D (Prague), K.504; 39 in E flat, K.543; 40 in G min., K.550; 41 in C (Jupiter), K.551.
**(*) Ph. Dig. 442 604-2 (5). E. Bar. Soloists, Gardiner.

Recorded between 1984 and 1989, these performances originally appeared on five separate discs, offering period performances which lean towards the nineteenth rather than eighteenth century, with dark-toned, weighty tuttis set in high contrast to transparent treatment of lightly scored passages. Had Gardiner made the recordings a year or so later, he would probably have used fewer agogic hesitations and underlinings for, by his standards, they sometimes lack a little in spontaneity. But anyone fancying late Mozart symphonies with a Beethovenian tinge and with extreme dynamic contrasts need not hesitate, for the playing avoids the abrasiveness of earlier period performances, and the recordings are generally full and weighty.

Symphonies Nos. 29 in A, K.201; 31 in D (Paris), K.297; 34 in C, K.338.
(B) (***) Dutton Lab. mono CDEA 5008 [id.]. LPO, Sir Thomas Beecham.

In Dutton's budget-priced Essential Classics series it is good to welcome these incomparable performances, which date from between 1937 and 1940. Although Beecham re-recorded many Mozart symphonies with the RPO after the war, he never returned to Nos. 29 or 34. Beecham's are elegant and cultivated accounts which in many ways are unique, though No. 29 brings one of his most controversial readings. One can readily accept the absence of exposition repeats and can adjust to Beecham's expansiveness and affectionate manner in all the slow movements, but in No. 29 the pace of the opening movement is eccentrically slow, even if Beecham is very persuasive in his pointing. In his note Lyndon Jenkins points out that Beecham had conducted No. 29 four times in the month before he recorded it, which must mean that the speeds were well calculated. In the finales by contrast Beecham prefers really fast speeds, exhilarating in all three here. The superb new transfers are fuller and have much finer presence, transparency and, above all, body than the earlier, EMI versions that appeared some years ago.

Symphonies Nos. 29 in A, K.201; 32 in G, K.318; 33 in B flat, K.319; 35 (Haffner); 36 (Linz); 38 (Prague); 39 in E flat, K.543; 40 in G min., K.550; 41 (Jupiter).
(M) *** DG 429 668-2 (3) [id.]. BPO, Karajan.

With Nos. 29, 32 and 33 added to the original LP box (see below), these are beautifully played and vitally alert readings; and the recordings, made between 1966 and 1979, are well balanced and given full, lively transfers to CD.

Symphonies Nos. 29 in A, K. 201; 33 in B flat, K.319; 40 in G min., K.550.
(N) *** DG Dig. 453 425-2. Orpheus CO.

With the three works presented in reverse chronological order, the great *G minor* comes in a strong and positive reading, which defies the idea that a corporate interpretation necessarily lacks individuality, with outer movements fast but not breathless, and the slow movement full of dramatic contrasts. Equally recommendable is the Orpheus reading of No. 33, again with exhilaratingly fast speeds for the outer movements, and with the slow movement smoother than the rest. Though the very opening of No. 29 brings playing a little less taut, the same qualities quickly emerge in a reading at once fresh and highly polished. Immediate, full-bodied sound adds to the impact, with braying horns vividly caught. A very successful triptych.

Symphonies Nos. 29 in A, K.201; 41 in C (Jupiter); Serenade No. 13 in G (Eine kleine Nachtmusik), K.525.
(***) Testament mono/stereo SBT 1093 [id.]. Philh. O, Klemperer.

Klemperer's 1954 Mozart symphony recordings of Nos. 29 and 41, unavailable for many decades, marked the turning-point in his accident-prone career. They were the very first recordings which he made with the Philharmonia Orchestra – from then on providing the focus of his work, belatedly establishing him as a central interpreter of the great German classics. Only the first movement of No. 29

bears out the later image of Klemperer as slow and rugged. After that, all is exhilaration, with superlative playing from the Philharmonia, with rhythms beautifully sprung and phrases elegantly turned. The *Jupiter* in particular is electrifying, one of the very finest versions on disc, both powerful and polished, while *Eine kleine Nachtmusik* (in stereo) for once is made to sound like late Mozart, both strong and elegant. Outstanding transfers.

Symphonies Nos. 31 in D (Paris), K.297; 32 in G, K.318; 33 in B flat, K.319; 34 in C, K.338; 35 in D (Haffner), K.385; 36 in C (Linz), K.425; 38 in D (Prague), K.504; 39 in E flat, K.543; 40 in G min., K.550; 41 in C (Jupiter), K.551.
*** DG Dig. 447 043-2 (4). English Concert, Pinnock.

Among period performances of Mozart symphonies Pinnock's stand out above all others, and this four-disc collection covering the masterpieces from the *Paris* to the *Jupiter* can be warmly recommended not just to period enthusiasts but also to non-specialist collectors. It is the joy and exhilaration in Mozart's inspiration that consistently bubble out from these performances, even from the dark *G minor* or the weighty *Jupiter*. The rhythmic lift which Pinnock consistently finds is infectious throughout, magnetizing the ear from the start of every movement, and few period performances are as naturally and easily expressive as these. Allegros are regularly on the fast side but never hectically so, and it is a measure of Pinnock's mastery that when in a slow movement such as that of the *Prague* he chooses an unusually slow speed, there is no feeling of dragging. Where Gardiner in these same works exaggerates the dynamic contrasts, Pinnock keeps them firmly in the eighteenth-century tradition, with textural contrasts more clearly integrated. The performances are all billed as being 'directed from the harpsichord', but that continuo instrument is never obtrusive, and one can only register surprise that such subtlety and exuberance have been achieved without a regular conductor. Clear, well-balanced sound, with the orchestra in some symphonies set more distantly than in others.

Symphonies Nos. 31 in D (Paris), K.297; 33 in B flat, K.319; 34 in C, K.338.
**(*) Telarc Dig. CD 80190 [id.]. Prague CO, Mackerras.

Mackerras and the Prague Chamber Orchestra give characteristically stylish and refined performances, clean of attack and generally marked by brisk speeds. As in their accounts of the later symphonies, all repeats are observed – even those in the *da capos* of minuets. However the reverberant Prague acoustic, more than in others of the Telarc series, clouds tuttis: the Presto finale of the *Paris* brings phenomenal articulation of quavers at the start, which then in tuttis disappear in a mush.

(i) *Symphonies Nos. 31 in D (Paris), K.297; 36 in C (Linz), K.425;* (ii) *Overture: Le nozze di Figaro.*
(BB) *** ASV Quicksilva CDQS 6033. (i) LSO; (ii) RPO, Bátiz.

After a sprightly account of the *Figaro overture* from the RPO, the LSO under Bátiz provide two spirited and polished accounts of favourite named symphonies. Tempi in outer movements are brisk, but the *Presto* finale of the *Linz* (for instance) produces some sparkling playing from the strings; and in both slow movements the phrasing is warm and gracious. With excellent digital recording, this makes an enjoyable super-bargain pairing.

Symphonies Nos. 31 in D (Paris), K.297; 36 in C (Linz), K.425; 38 in D (Prague), K.504.
*** ASV Dig. CDDCA 647 [id.]. LMP, Jane Glover.

Jane Glover and the London Mozart Players offer a particularly attractive and generous coupling in the three Mozart symphonies associated with cities. Happily, exposition repeats are observed in the outer movements. The performances are all fresh and vital in traditional chamber style, with little influence from period performance. Tuttis are not always ideally clear on inner detail; but the result is nicely in scale, not too weighty, with the delicacy beautifully light and airy.

Symphonies Nos. 32 in G, K.318; 33 in B flat, K.319; 34 in C, K.338.
(M) **(*) Teldec/Warner Dig. 4509 97487-2. Concg. O, Harnoncourt.

Symphonies Nos. 35 in D (Haffner), K.385; 36 in C (Linz), K.425.
(M) **(*) Teldec/Warner Dig. 4509 97488-2. Concg. O, Harnoncourt.

Symphonies Nos. 38 in D (Prague), K.504; 39 in E flat, K.543.
(M) **(*) Teldec/Warner Dig. 4509 97489-2 [9031 77596]. Concg. O, Harnoncourt.

Nikolaus Harnoncourt's Mozart, for all its merits, is nothing if not wilful, turning from conducting an ensemble of original instruments to the glories of the Concertgebouw Orchestra and establishing his personality immediately, with strong, even gruff accents, yet at times with an approach which (notably in slow movements, with speeds rather slower than usual) is relatively romantic in its expressiveness. He constantly secured fine playing, and the Teldec engineers rewarded him with bright, clear, yet resonant recording, very different from the sound the Philips engineers get from this orchestra. Overall the results are of mixed appeal. Both the *Paris Symphony* and *No. 33 in B flat* are among Harnoncourt's most successful performances, with beautiful, cleanly articulated playing. In No. 33 Harnoncourt overdoes his slowness in the *Andante* but adds to the breadth of the finale by giving the repeats of both halves. The performances of No. 34 and the *Haffner* are refreshingly direct, certainly dramatic, marked by relatively unforced tempi; but charm is somewhat missing. *No. 32 in G* again shows Harnoncourt at his best, although it is made to sound weightier than usual. In the *Linz* he observes even more repeats than are marked in the regular scores, making it, like K.318, a more expansive work than usual. The *Prague* is generally very successful, superbly played, and Harnoncourt is again very generous with repeats (it runs for 38 minutes). Tempi are again erratic in No. 39 (the Minuet is rushed), although the first movement of this symphony is well judged.

Symphonies Nos. 32 in G, K.318; 35 in D (Haffner), K.385; 36 in C (Linz), K.425; 39 in E flat, K.543; 41 in C (Jupiter), K.551.
(BB) *** Virgin Classics Double Dig. VBD5 61451-2 (2) [CDVB 61451]. SCO, Jukka-Pekka Saraste.

This Virgin Classics Double brings together an exceptionally successful grouping of performances. More than most other versions on modern instruments, Saraste's vividly alive accounts of the three earlier symphonies reflect the new lessons of period performance. These are more detached, less sostenuto than many modern-instrument chamber-orchestra versions and, with all repeats observed, are highly stimulating in their resilience. The recording, helpfully reverberant, yet gives lightness and transparency to textures, conveying an apt chamber scale. Saraste then offers two of the finest accounts of the two late symphonies available on any disc: fresh, again light and resilient in allegros, elegant in slow movements and with clean, transparent recording. Wordsworth and the Capella Istropolitana may have more weight in these works, but Saraste has extra polish and refinement, with generally brisker speeds, notably in slow movements and Minuets. These two CDs, offered for the cost of one mid-priced disc, make a remarkably inexpensive way of collecting four of Mozart's greatest symphonies, plus a vivacious account of the *G major Italian overture*.

Symphonies Nos. 32 in G, K.318; 35 in D (Haffner), K.385; 38 in D (Prague), K.504.
(B) **(*) Tring Dig. TRP 059 [(M) id. import]. RPO, Howard Shelley.

With the RPO strings reduced (11.9.7.6.4), Howard Shelley conducts relaxed and amiable readings of three symphonies, very well recorded. In the *Haffner* and *Prague* some may want a higher-powered, more dramatic view, notably in the latter, where Shelley does not bring out the *Don Giovanni* overtones, but these are consistently refreshing performances, clear and transparent and very well played. No. 32, in Italian overture form, is a delight, with Jeffrey Bryant leading the RPO horn section in glorious playing.

Symphonies Nos. 32 in G, K.318; 33 in B flat, K.319; 35 in D (Haffner), K.385; 36 in C (Linz), K.425.
(M) *** DG (IMS) 435 070-2. BPO, Karajan.

Symphonies Nos. 35 in D (Haffner), K.385; 36 in C (Linz), K.425; 38 in D (Prague), K.504; 39 in E flat, K.543; 40 in G min., K.550; 41 in C (Jupiter), K.551.
(B) *** DG Double 453 046-2 (2) [id.]. BPO, Karajan.
(M) **(*) DG 447 416-2 (2) [id.]. BPO, Boehm.

Here on DG is Karajan's big-band Mozart at its finest. Although there may be slight reservations about the Minuet and Trio of the *Linz*, which is rather slow (and the other minuets are also somewhat stately), overall there is plenty of life here, and slow movements show the BPO at their most graciously expressive. The opening of the *G minor* may not be quite dark enough for some tastes. The *Jupiter*, although short on repeats, has power as well as surface elegance. The remastered sound is clear and lively, full but not over-weighted. The separate issue makes a good sampler.

Karl Boehm's way with Mozart in the early 1960s was broader and heavier in texture than we are used to nowadays, and the exposition repeats are the exception rather than the rule; but these Berlin Philharmonic performances are warm and magnetic, with refined and strongly rhythmic playing, and there is an attractive honesty and strength about them. The *Linz*, for instance, is an example of Boehm at his finest, with an agreeable, fresh vitality; but overall there is a comfortable quality of inevitability here, perpetuating a long Mozart tradition. The recordings sound full, vivid and well balanced in the new transfers.

Symphonies Nos. 32 in G, K.318; 35 in D (Haffner), K.385; 39 in E flat, K.543.
*** Telarc Dig. CD 80203 [id.]. Prague CO, Mackerras.
(BB) *** ASV Quicksilva Dig. CDQS 6071. ECO, Mackerras.

On Telarc, Mackerras is fresh rather than elegant, yet with rhythms so crisply sprung that there is no sense of rush. His whirling one-in-a-bar treatment of Minuets may disconcert traditionalists, but brings exhilarating results. The third movements of both the *Haffner* and No. 39 become scherzos, not just faster but fiercer than regular minuets, and generally his account of No. 39 is as commanding as his outstanding versions of the last two symphonies. The clanging attack of harpsichord continuo is sometimes disconcerting, but this music-making is very refreshing.

Mackerras's ASV version was recorded digitally, in 1985, before he moved on to make his integral set for Telarc. Mackerras here anticipates the urgent style of the later recordings, especially in the Minuets and, with generally brisk speeds, the ASV readings are attractively fresh and full of momentum. Mackerras rarely seeks to charm, but unfussily presents each movement with undistractingly direct manners. The strong character of the music-making is in no doubt, and the sound is appealingly bright and vivid; at super-bargain price this undoubtedly remains competitive.

Symphonies Nos. 34 in C, K.338; 35 in D (Haffner), K.385; 39 in E flat, K.543.
*** ASV Dig. CDDCA 615 [id.]. LMP, Jane Glover.

Tackling three major works, Jane Glover provides freshly imaginative performances that can compete with any in the catalogue, given the most vividly realistic recorded sound; Nos. 34 and 39 are especially striking. This collection can be recommended with enthusiasm.

Symphonies Nos. (i) *34 in C, K.338*; (ii) *39 in E flat, K.543; 41 in C (Jupiter).*
(N) **(*) Testament mono/stereo SBT 1092 [id.]. (i) LPO, (ii) RPO, Kempe.

The Testament disc of Kempe in Mozart, very well transferred, offers 1956 stereo recordings of Nos. 39 and 41 previously unissued, as well as a 1955 mono account of No. 34. Though the results initially may seem smooth and soft-grained, the conductor's warmth and understanding magnetize the ear. No. 34 has an exhilarating account of the 6/8 finale. The only reservation is over the slowness of the *Minuets* in Nos. 39 and 41.

(i) *Symphonies Nos. 35 in D (Haffner), K.385; 36 in C (Linz), K.425;* (ii) *Divertimento No. 1 for strings, K.136; Serenade No. 6 (Serenata notturna).*
(M) *** Virgin/EMI Dig. CUV5 61204-2. (i) Sinfonia Varsovia; (ii) Lausanne CO, Lord Menuhin.

As in Menuhin's winning versions of the last four Mozart symphonies, Mozart is again presented with a smile on his face. Though modern instruments are used, the scale is intimate, with textures beautifully clear. There is elegance and charm as well as energy in outer movements, and in the slow movements Menuhin moulds the phrasing with Beechamesque magic, yet never adopts excessively slow speeds or over-romantic manners. The *Serenata notturna* and the *Divertimento* make a generous coupling. Performances are similarly fresh and elegant, though, as recorded, the strings of the Lausanne Chamber Orchestra are a degree less sweet, and the acoustic is bigger and more reverberant.

Symphonies Nos. 35 in D (Haffner), K.385; 36 in C (Linz); 38 in D (Prague).
(B) (***) Dutton Lab. mono CDEA 5001 [(M) id.]. LPO, Sir Thomas Beecham.
(BB) *** RCA Navigator 74321 24198-2 [Basic 100 09026 68364-2; *68364-4*]. ECO, Jean-François Paillard.

It was Beecham's advocacy in the early years of the century which led to the late Mozart symphonies finally achieving their rightful position among the greatest masterpieces of the symphonic repertoire. These recordings, which were to dominate the catalogue until the arrival of LP, were made in 1939–40, either at Abbey Road or Kingsway Hall. The *Haffner* used both venues, and the ear can detect the change of acoustic 4½ minutes into the first movement. Beecham's dictum was to present Mozart with 'the maximum of virility coupled with the maximum of delicacy', coupled also with loving care with phrasing and subtle attention to dynamic nuance. The first movement of the *Linz* is endearingly characteristic of his boldness of style, steadily paced, without any loss of vitality. Beecham's way with Minuets, however, was to present them with genial stateliness to contrast with the brilliant articulation of the dancing finales. (He even includes the exposition repeat in the finale of No. 36, as there was room for it on the 78 side.) These Dutton transfers come into direct competition with those of EMI. The contrasts are not quite consistent. In the *Haffner* and *Prague*, the Dutton sound is marginally warmer and more rounded, with the boxiness gone, where the EMI sound is brighter and more immediate, with a hint of harshness. In the slow movement of the *Haffner* it is astonishing how different the woodwind solos sound, with the balance somehow altered. Curiously, in the *Linz* the contrasts between Dutton and EMI are rather the other way about. As to the subtly pointed magic of Beecham in Mozart, that hardly needs commendation, readily defying this purist age. Highly recommended at bargain price.

Stylish, excellently paced performances from Paillard and the ECO, with warmly expressive slow movements – that for the *Linz* is particularly fine – and sparkling finales. Those enjoying these works in lively, traditional performances will find there is both polish and warmth here, and plenty of vitality. The recording is resonant but not so much as to obscure detail. An excellent bargain-basement triptych.

Symphonies Nos. 35 in D (Haffner), K.385; 38 in D (Prague), K.504.
(N) ** Ph. Dig. 462 587-2 [id.]. VPO, Muti.

Immaculate playing from the VPO and opulent sound. But this is not one of the most recommendable of Muti's Mozart series with the Vienna Philharmonic, fierce in the outer movements at speeds that come to sound breathless.

Symphonies Nos. 35 in D (Haffner), K.385; 40 in G min., K.550; 41 in C (Jupiter), K.551.
(B) *** Sony SBK 46333 [id.]. Cleveland O, Szell.

As in his companion triptych of late Haydn symphonies, Szell and his Clevelanders are shown at their finest here. The sparkling account of the *Haffner* is exhilarating, and the performances of the last two symphonies are equally polished and strong. Yet there is a tranquil feeling to both *Andantes* that shows Szell as a Mozartian of striking sensibility and finesse. He is at his finest in the *Jupiter*, which has great vigour in the outer movements and a proper weight to balance the rhythmic incisiveness; in spite of the lack of repeats, the work's scale is not diminished. Here the sound is remarkable considering the early date (late 1950s), and the remastering throughout is impressively full-bodied and clean.

Symphonies Nos. 35 in D (Haffner), K. 385; 41 in C (Jupiter), K. 550.
(N) (M) *** Penguin Classics Dig. 460 615-2 [id.]. VPO, Bernstein.

The *Jupiter* brings one of the very finest of Bernstein's Mozart recordings, edited together from live performances. Bernstein observes the repeats in both halves of the finale, and his powerful concentration sustains the length. The *Haffner* brings a similarly satisfying reading until the finale, when Bernstein in the heat of the moment breaks loose with a speed so fast that even the Vienna violins find it hard to articulate exactly. It remains very exciting, and with recording on CD only slightly cloudy in louder tuttis it makes an excellent recommendation, not so heavy in texture as most using regular symphony orchestras. The accompanying author's note, obligatory with this Penguin series, comes from Jane Smiley.

Symphonies Nos. 36 in C (Linz); 38 in D (Prague); 39 in E flat, K.543; 40 in G min., K.550; 41 in C (Jupiter).
(B) *** Ph. Duo 438 332-2 (2). ASMF, Marriner.

This is an inexpensive way of acquiring first-class performances of Mozart's last five symphonies. The recordings are of high quality, all being made in 1978 or 1980, except for No. 40, which dates from a decade earlier (1970). Here the bass is a shade over-resonant, but the present transfer has made it seem firmer than previously. In terms of finesse and elegance of phrasing, the orchestral playing is of very high quality and Marriner's readings are satisfyingly paced, full of vitality and warmth. There is not a whiff of original-instrument style here, but those who enjoy the sound of Mozart in a modern orchestra of a reasonable size should be well satisfied.

Symphonies Nos. 37 in G, K.444: Introduction (completed by M. Haydn); *40 in G min., K.550; 41 in C (Jupiter), K.551.*
*** ASV Dig. CDDCA 761 [id.]. LMP, Jane Glover.

This is an excellent example of Jane Glover's work with the LMP. Anyone who fancies this generous coupling need hardly hesitate, particularly when in the two last Mozart symphonies Glover does not skimp on repeats, as she might have done. She omits them – as most versions do – in the slow movements, but includes exposition repeats in the finales as well as in first movements, particularly important in the *Jupiter*, with its grandly sublime counterpoint. There Glover's speed is exceptionally fast, with ensemble not quite so refined or crisp as in some rival versions, but still making for a strong and enjoyable reading.

Symphony No. 38 in D (Prague), K.504.
(M) (**) Mercury mono 434 387-2 [id.]. Chicago SO, Kubelik – DVORAK: *Symphony No. 9 (New World)*. (***)

Kubelik's 1953 account of the *Prague* is splendid: the outer movements are alert and sparkling, the *Andante* is ideally paced, gracefully phrased and beautifully played. The effect is undoubtedly refreshing; the ambience of Chicago's Orchestral Hall adds warmth, and the only snag is the consistent edge imparted by the single Telefunken microphone to the violin timbre.

Symphonies Nos. 38 in D (Prague) K.504; No. 39 in E flat, K.543; Serenata notturna.
(N) (**(*)) Testament mono SBT 1094 [id.]. Philh. O, Klemperer.

This mono version of the *Prague Symphony* brings one of Klemperer's very finest Mozart performances, strong and rugged, but finely sprung and phrased, with the *Don Giovanni* relationship firmly established. This mono version of No. 39 too is fresher than the stereo remake, while the *Serenata notturna* brings a typical Klemperer contrast, with the orchestra providing rugged, four-square support for the soloists, who by contrast are allowed their measure of charm and elegance.

Symphonies Nos. 39 in E flat, K.543; 40 in G min., K.550; 41 in C (Jupiter), K.551.
(B) (***) Dutton Lab. mono CDEA 5012 [(M) id.]. LPO, Beecham.
(M) (**) BMG/RCA mono GD 60285 [id.]. NBC SO, Toscanini.

It is good to have the continuing Dutton series of reissues of Beecham's pre-war Mozart with the LPO rounded off with this generous coupling of the last three symphonies – a coupling made possible when exposition repeats are omitted in Nos. 39 and 41. As ever, the rhythmic point of the playing, not least from the LPO woodwind, is delectable so that, with brisk allegros set against expressive slow movements, these readings seem as fresh as ever, whatever changes in performance practice we have come to accept in Mozart. These always were among the best EMI recordings of the 1930s, and the Dutton transfers are excellent. Curiously, the fullest-bodied of the three recordings is the earliest recorded, that of the *Jupiter*, dating from 1934. At bargain price in the Essential Classics series, this is an exceptionally attractive issue that no Beecham admirer should miss.

There is an astonishing discrepancy between the three Mozart performances from Toscanini. Where in No. 39 the great Italian conductor's thrustful approach seems very brutal, with rhythms and phrasing so unyielding and speeds so fast that all charm is eliminated, even in the Minuet, the great *G minor Symphony* – recorded in conjunction with Toscanini's very first concert with the NBC orchestra in 1938 – is treated more sympathetically, even if the middle movements again are plain and charmless. The *Jupiter*, bigger and more challenging, inspires Toscanini to quite a different degree. The performance is searingly powerful in the outer movements, even exuberant in the finale, and the slow movement and Minuet given a rhythmic lift missing in the earlier symphonies. Limited sound with fizzy strings in No. 39.

Symphony No. 40 in G min., K.550.
*** RCA Dig. 09026 68032-2 [id.]. N. German RSO, Wand – TCHAIKOVSKY: *Symphony No. 5.* ***
(B) **(*) Carlton Dig. 30367 02372 [(M) id.]. O of St John's, Smith Square, Lubbock – HAYDN: *Symphony No. 44.* ***
(M) (**) RCA mono GD 60271 [60271-2-RG]. NBC SO, Toscanini – BEETHOVEN: *Symphony No. 3.* (***)

Unexpected as this pairing of Mozart and Tchaikovsky may be, Wand in live recordings brings them together with a radiant consistency. Though in Mozart Wand follows many of the performing manners of an earlier generation, notably with a very slow, lovingly moulded account of the second-movement *Andante*, the remarkable point is how transparent he makes the textures. Also remarkable in Wand's performance is the lightness and speed of the Minuet, a whirling one-in-a-bar to match any authenticist. The refinement of approach means that, even in the first-movement development, he seems reluctant to find menace in the music; rather he concentrates on beauty, and that without any lack of intensity. A fascinating coupling for a unique account of the Tchaikovsky, vividly recorded.

Lubbock's is a pleasingly relaxed account of Mozart's *G minor Symphony*, well played – the Minuet particularly deft – and nicely proportioned. The last ounce of character is missing from the slow movement, but the orchestra is responsive throughout, and the recording is in the demonstration class.

Dating from March 1950, Toscanini's version was recorded in the notoriously dry Studio 8-H in Radio City, New York; though the sound is uncomfortable, the high voltage of the interpretation makes considerable amends, with expressive warmth tempering the conductor's characteristic urgency. The slow movement is elegantly done, and even though the finale brings a measure of fierceness, Toscanini eases lovingly into the second subject.

Symphonies Nos. 40 in G min., K.550; 41 in C (Jupiter), K.551.
✿ (M) *** DG Dig. 445 548-2 [431 040-2]. VPO, Bernstein.
(M) *** Virgin/EMI (SIS) Dig. CUV5 61133-2. Sinfonia Varsovia, Sir Yehudi Menuhin.
*** Ph. (IMS) Dig. 426 315-2 [id.]. E. Bar. Soloists, Gardiner.
*** Telarc Dig. CD 80139 [id.]. Prague CO, Mackerras.

(i) *Symphonies Nos. 40–41;* (ii) *Serenade: Eine kleine Nachtmusik, K.525.*
(B) **(*) DG 439 472-2. (i) BPO; (ii) VPO; Boehm.

Symphonies Nos. 40–41; Overture: The Marriage of Figaro.
(B) *** RPO TRP 004 [id.]. RPO, Glover.

Bernstein's electrifying account of No. 40 is keenly dramatic, individual and stylish, with the finale delightfully airy and fresh. If anything, the *Jupiter* is even finer: it is exhilarating in its tensions and observes the repeats in both halves of the finale, making it almost as long as the massive first movement. Bernstein's electricity sustains that length, and one welcomes it for establishing the supreme power of the argument, the true crown in the whole of Mozart's symphonic output. Pacing cannot be faulted in any of the four movements and, considering the problems of making live recordings, the 1984 sound is first rate, lacking only the last degree of transparency in tuttis. This mid-price reissue on DG's Masters label now takes its place again at the top of the list of recommendations for this coupling.

Recorded in exceptionally vivid, immediate sound, Menuhin's versions of both symphonies with the Sinfonia Varsovia find a distinctive place in an overcrowded field, with playing of precision, clarity and bite which is consistently refreshing, giving a feeling of live music-making. Menuhin reveals himself again as very much a classicist, preferring speeds on the fast side, rarely indulging in romantic tricks. He is generous with repeats – observing exposition repeats in both first movement and finale of the *Jupiter*, for example. With such vivid sound, this is the best current recommendation for this favourite pairing.

Gardiner's coupling is also very impressive indeed and, for those wanting period instruments, this is a clear first choice. These are both large-scale conceptions with the strings fuller and with less edge than usual, and there are no eccentric tempi. Allegros are strongly motivated and slow movements spacious, that of the *Jupiter* strikingly so, and played with great eloquence. The finale has great vitality and purpose yet certainly does not lack weight. The second repeat is not taken here, which is a pity; but these remain powerful and stimulating readings, very well played and recorded.

On Telarc, with generally fast speeds, so brisk that he is able to observe every single repeat, Mackerras takes a fresh, direct view which, with superb playing from the Prague Chamber Orchestra, is also characterful. The speeds that might initially seem excessively fast are those for the Minuets, which – with fair scholarly authority – become crisp country dances, almost Scherzos. On the question of repeats, the doubling in length of the slow movement of No. 40 makes it almost twice as long as the first movement, a dangerous proportion – though it is pure gain having both halves repeated in the magnificent finale of the *Jupiter*.

At super-bargain price in the Royal Philharmonic Collection, Jane Glover conducts fresh, urgent performances, stylishly moulded, which include exposition repeats that generally outshine her own earlier, smaller-scale readings with the London Mozart Players on ASV. With rhythms crisply sprung in fast movements and with slow movements warmly lyrical and relaxed without becoming over-romantic, these performances, brightly recorded, stand comparison with almost any version, and the *Figaro overture* provides a welcome makeweight, though on ASV the *Symphony No. 37* (mainly by Michael Haydn) was even more generous.

By its side Boehm sounds mellow and cultivated but still magnetic and strong. He, of course, is much less generous in the matter of repeats, but the Berlin Philharmonic play very beautifully and the recording is agreeably warm and full, the reissue inexpensive. *Eine kleine Nachtmusik* was recorded a decade and a half later, and the VPO playing is polished and fresh, with a neat, lightly pointed finale.

CHAMBER MUSIC

(i) *Adagio and fugue in C min., K.546;* (ii) *Adagio and rondo in C for glass harmonica, flute, oboe, viola & cello;* (iii) *Clarinet quintet in A, K.581;* (iv) *String quintets Nos. 4 in G min., K.516; 5 in D, K.593; 6 in E flat, K.614.*

(B) **(*) Ph. Duo 456 058-2 [id.]. (i) Italian Qt; (ii) Hoffmann, Nicolet, Holliger, Schouten, Decroos; (iii) Jack Brymer, Allegri Qt; (iv) Grumiaux Trio, Gérecz, Lesueur.

(i) *Horn quintet in E flat, K.407;* (ii) *Piano and wind quintet in E flat, K. 452;* (iii) *String quintets Nos. 1 in B flat, K.174; 2 in C min., K.406; 3 in C, K.515; Adagio in B flat for 2 clarinets & 3 basset horns.*

(B) **(*) Ph. Duo 456 055-2 (2). (i) Timothy Brown, ASMF Chamber Ens.; (ii) Ingrid Haebler, Bamberg Wind Qt (members); (iii) Grumiaux Trio, Gérecz, Lesueur; (iv) Netherlands Wind Ens.

Of the additional music above, the *Adagio and fugue* is splendidly played by the Quartetto Italiano. The *Adagio and rondo* for glass harmonica with Bruno Hoffmann playing that rare instrument, and the *Adagio in B flat* for clarinets and basset horns are delectable in these performances. Of the other major works, Brymer's reading of the *Clarinet quintet* is warm and relaxed and very agreeable, if not distinctive. Timothy Brown is a personable soloist and the *Horn quintet* is given a well-projected and lively account. However, in spite of Ingrid Haebler's characteristically stylish contribution to the *Piano and wind quintet*, the Bamberg performance does not take flight, a straightforward rather than an imaginative account. Throughout all four CDs the recordings are admirably balanced and given high-quality analogue sound.

Complete Mozart Edition, Volume 14: (i) *Adagio in C for glass harmonica, K.356;* (i; ii) *Adagio in C min. & Rondo in C for glass harmonica, flute, oboe, viola & cello;* (iii) *Clarinet trio in E flat (Kegelstatt), K.498;* (iv; v) *Piano quartets Nos. 1–2;* (iv) *Piano trios Nos. 1–6; Piano trio in D min., K.442;* (vi) *Piano and wind quintet in E flat, K.452.*

(M) *** Ph. Dig./Analogue 422 514-2 (5) [id.]. (i) Bruno Hoffmann; (ii) with Nicolet, Holliger, Schouten, Decroos; (iii) Brymer, Kovacevich, Ireland; (iv) Beaux Arts Trio, (v) with Giuranna; (vi) Brendel, Holliger, Brunner, Baumann, Thunemann.

This compilation of Mozart's chamber music with piano has no weak link. The last three discs contain the complete *Piano trios* recorded by the Beaux Arts Trio in 1987, a first-rate cycle which includes not only the six completed trios but also the composite work, put together by Mozart's friend, the priest Maximilian Stadler, and listed by Köchel as K.442. The Beaux Arts' teamwork – with the pianist Menahem Pressler leading the way – brings consistently fresh and winning performances, as it also does in the two great *Piano quartets* where, in recordings made in 1983, they are joined by the viola-player, Bruno Giuranna. The *Piano and wind quintet*, K.452, recorded in 1986, subtly contrasts the artistry of Alfred Brendel at the piano with that of the oboist, Heinz Holliger, leading a distinguished team of wind-players. The only non-digital recordings are those of the *Kegelstatt trio*, characterfully done by Stephen Kovacevich with Jack Brymer and Patrick Ireland, and of the two shorter works involving glass harmonica.

Adagio and rondo for flute, oboe, viola, cello and piano, K.617; (i) *Clarinet trio in E flat (Kegelstatt), K.498;* (ii) *Flute quartets Nos. 1–4, K.285, K.285a, K.285b & K.298;* (iii) *Horn quintet in E flat, K.407;* (iv) *Oboe quartet in F, K.370.*

(BB) *** Virgin Classics Dig. Double VBD5 61448-2 (2) [CVBD 61448]. Nash Ens., with (i) Michael Collins; (ii) Philippa Davies; (iii) Frank Lloyd; (iv) Gareth Hulse.

This inexpensive Virgin Double offers two CDs which pair naturally together. In the *Adagio and rondo*, originally written for glass harmonica, the wind instruments blend together most felicitously. Michael Collins proves a winningly personable soloist in the *Clarinet trio*, a work much rarer on record than the *Quintet*. Gareth Hulse plays exquisitely in the *Oboe quartet* and the Nash Ensemble blend in most sensitively, and give excellent support to Frank Lloyd's warmly lyrical account of the *Horn quartet*. The second disc contains the four *Flute quartets*, with Philippa Davies both a nimble and a highly musical flautist who has a natural feeling for Mozartian line. She is very well balanced with her Nash colleagues and these are pleasingly warm, intimate performances, nicely turned, if perhaps not distinctive. But the two discs together add up to a very pleasing concert.

Canons for strings; Canons for woodwind: see below, under VOCAL MUSIC: Complete Mozart Edition, Volume 23.

Complete Mozart Edition, Volume 10: (i; vi) *Clarinet quintet;* (ii) *Flute quartets Nos. 1–4;* (iii; vi) *Horn quintet;* (iv; vi) *Oboe quartet;* (v) *Sonata for bassoon and cello, K.292;* (vi) Fragments: *Allegro in F, K.App. 90/580b for clarinet, basset horn, & string trio; Allegro in B flat. K.App. 91/K.516c for a clarinet quintet; Allegro in F, K.288 for a divertimento for 2 horns & strings; String quartet movements: Allegro in B flat, K.App. 72/464a; Allegro in B flat, K.App. 80/514a; Minuet in B flat, K.68/589a; Minuet in F, K.168a; Movement in A, K.App. 72/464a. String quintet No. 1 in B flat, K.174:2 Original movements: Trio & Finale. Allegro in A min., K.App. 79 for a string quintet. Allegro in G, K.App. 66/562e for a string trio* (completed, where necessary, by Erik Smith).

(M) *** Ph. Analogue/Dig. 422 510-2 (3) [id.]. (i) Pay; (ii) Bennett, Grumiaux Trio; (iii) Brown; (iv) Black; (v) Thunemann, Orton; (vi) ASMF Chamber Ens.

These are highly praised performances of the major chamber works featuring modern wind instruments (Antony Pay uses a normal clarinet). The rest of the items are by no means inconsequential offcuts but provide music of high quality, notably the *String quartet movement*, K.514a. The *Minuet in B flat*, K.589a, in the rhythm of a polonaise and possibly the first draft for the finale of the *Hunt quartet*, is a real charmer which, had it received more exposure, might well have become a Mozartian lollipop like the famous and not dissimilar Minuet in the *D major Divertimento*, K.334. The two pieces with solo clarinet are also very winning. The performances here are all polished and spontaneous and beautifully recorded.

Clarinet quintet in A, K.581.

(N) *** Ph. Dig. 442 149-2 [id.]. Harold Wright, Boston SO Chamber Players – BRAHMS: *Clarinet quintet.* ***

(N) (B) *** HM Dig. HMN 911 691 [id.]. Alessandro Carbonare, Luc Hery, Florence Binder, Nicolas Bone, Muriel Pouzenc. – BRAHMS: *Clarinet quintet.* ***

(B) *** Decca Eclipse Dig. 448 232-2. Peter Schmidl, Vienna Octet (members) – BEETHOVEN: *Septet in E flat, Op. 20.* ***

(BB) **(*) Belart 450 056-2 [(M) id. import]. Jack Brymer, Allegri Qt – SCHUBERT: *Trout quintet.* ***

A truly lovely performance from Harold Wright and the Boston Chamber Players, beautifully recorded, goes to the top of the list of modern versions of this very fresh masterwork, especially if you want the Brahms coupling. The very opening creates a beguiling mood of warmth and delicacy of atmosphere. The slow movement has an appealing simplicity of line and the finale the lightest rhythmic touch, with much subtle light and shade in the variations. The sound balance is right out of Philips's top drawer.

With talented young performers in Harmonia Mundi's bargain series, Les Nouveaux Interprètes, this apt and rare coupling is most welcome. Alessandro Carbonare, principal clarinet of the Orchestre Nationale of France, produces exceptionally beautiful, liquid tone-colours over the widest dynamic range. Clear and fresh as the outer movements are, the high point is the *Larghetto*, magically gentle and with the main melody tastefully elaborated on its reprise. The four string-players, also members of the Orchestre Nationale, are not quite so distinctive yet provide most sympathetic support. One slight irritation is that the recording from time to time picks up the clicking of Carbonare's keys.

Peter Schmidl, using a basset clarinet, is sometimes just a little cool, but his intimate approach has its own appeal. He phrases with imagination and much delicacy in matters of light and shade. Of course these Viennese players use modern instruments, and the sound they make is consistently full and smooth. The 1989 Decca recording is state of the art, and while this would not necessarily be a clear first choice for the *Quintet*, it is very distinguished, and the splendid Beethoven coupling makes this Eclipse reissue an outstanding bargain.

Brymer's interpretation of the *Clarinet quintet* is warm and leisurely, and he chooses slow tempi throughout. With his tone so succulent, and with velvety support from the Allegri Quartet, he is almost entirely successful in sustaining them although, as the finale proceeds, the forward flow of the music is reduced to a near crawl before the quickening at the coda. The recorded sound is warm and flattering, and this is still very beguiling.

Clarinet quintet in A, K.581; Clarinet quintet fragment in B flat, K.516c; (i) *Quintet fragment in F for clarinet in C, basset-horn and string trio, K.580b* (both completed by Duncan Druce).
*** Amon Ra/Saydisc CD-SAR 17 [id.]. Alan Hacker, Salomon Qt, (i) with Lesley Schatzberger.

Leading the CD versions of the *Clarinet quintet* (alongside Thea King's outstanding coupling with the *Clarinet concerto* on Hyperion – see above) is a superb recording by Alan Hacker with the Salomon Quartet, using original instruments. Hacker's gentle sound on his period instrument is displayed at its most ravishing in the *Larghetto*. Tempi are wonderfully apt and the rhythms of the finale are infectious, the music's sense of joy fully projected. The recording balance is near perfect. Hacker includes a fragment from an earlier projected *Quintet* and a similar sketch for a work featuring C clarinet and basset-horn with string trio. Both are skilfully completed by Duncan Druce.

(i; ii) *Clarinet quintet in A, K.581;* (i; iii) *Clarinet trio (Kegelstatt) for clarinet, viola and piano, K.498;* (i; ii) *Allegro assai in B flat, K.516c* (completed Robert Levin).
(N) [M] ** Carlton Classics Dig. 30366 01192 [id.]. (i) John Denman; (ii) Flesch Qt; (iii) Mark Denman, Paula Fan Denman.

This mid-price issue usefully brings together Mozart's two principal chamber works for clarinet, plus a clarinet quintet movement left as a fragment. The sound is warm and immediate, bringing out the full-toned beauty of the playing, with the roundness of John Denman's clarinet tone matched by that of the string players. The matching and intonation are flawless, but the performances are too well mannered to make their full impact, with speeds too often sluggish.

(i) *Clarinet quintet in A, K.581;* (ii) *Flute quartet No. 1 in D, K.285;* (iii) *Oboe quartet in F, K.370.*
(B) **(*) EMI Dig. CDZ5 69702-2 [id.]. (i) Nicholas Carpenter; (ii) Jaime Martin; (iii) Jonathan Kelly; Brindisi Qt (members).

The three soloists introduced here in EMI's Debut series are all principals with various British orchestras. Each is a first-rate artist and all three performances here are fresh and enjoyable, with the *Flute quartet* the most successful of the three, perhaps because its charming, serenade-like *Adagio*, with the soloist poised over a pizzicato accompaniment, cannot fail to beguile the listener. In both the other works the slow movements, although played persuasively, are just a little plain; to make up for it, all three finales are sprightly, with that of the *Clarinet quintet* being particularly successful. The members of the Brindisi Quartet provide admirable support, and the recording is excellent, vivid and transparent.

(i) *Clarinet quintet in A, K.581;* (ii) *Horn quintet in E flat, K.407;* (iii) *Oboe quartet in F, K.370.*
(B) *** Ph. 422 833-2. (i) Antony Pay; (ii) Timothy Brown; (iii) Neil Black; ASMF Chamber Ens.

It is a delightful idea to have the *Clarinet quintet, Oboe quartet* and *Horn quintet* on a single CD. Here, Antony Pay's earlier account of the *Clarinet quintet*, played on a modern instrument, with the Academy of St Martin-in-the-Fields players must be numbered among the strongest now on the market for those not insisting on an authentic basset clarinet. Neil Black's playing in the *Oboe quartet* is distinguished, and again the whole performance radiates pleasure, while the *Horn quintet* comes in a well-projected and lively account with Timothy Brown. The recording, originally issued in 1981, is of Philips's best.

(i) *Clarinet quintet;* (ii) *Oboe quartet in F, K.370.*
(B) *** CfP CD-CFP 4377. (i) Andrew Marriner; (ii) Gordon Hunt, Chilingirian Qt.
(B) *** Carlton Dig. 30367 02332 [(M) id. import]. (i) Keith Puddy; (ii) Douglas Boyd; Gabrieli Qt.

On the bargain-priced CfP version, recorded in 1981, the young Andrew Marriner's persuasive account occupies the front rank, quite irrespective of price. Marriner's playing in the *Quintet* is wonderfully flexible; it reaches its apex in the radiantly beautiful reading of the slow movement, although the finale is also engagingly characterized. The *Oboe quartet* is delectable too, with Gordon Hunt a highly musical and technically accomplished soloist. The CfP issue was recorded in the Wigmore Hall and the sound-balance is most believable.

The alternative bargain-priced Carlton CD brings a reading of the *Clarinet quintet* which is clean and well paced and, if lacking the last degree of delicacy in the slow movement, is never less than stylish. Douglas Boyd gives an outstanding performance in the shorter, less demanding work, with the lilting finale delectably full of fun. The digital recording is vividly immediate and full of presence, with even the keys of the wind instruments often audible.

(i) *Clarinet quintet in A, K.581; String quartet No. 18 in A, K.464.*

(N) **(*) ASV Dig. CDDCA 1042 [id.]. (i) Janet Hilton; Lindsay Qt.

Janet Hilton gives a disarmingly simple, unaffected account of the *Clarinet quintet* and gets excellent support from the Lindsays. The performance of the *A major Quartet* is characteristically perceptive and vital, with the *Andante* on the whole beautifully played, although some may find dynamics a little overstressed. The balance is forward and vivid.

(i) *Clarinet quintet in A, K.581; String quartet No. 20 in D (Hoffmeister), K.499.*

(M) **(*) Whitehall Associates Dig. MQCD 6001 [id.]. (i) Jack Brymer; Medici Qt.

The Medici String Quartet have set up their own label. Jack Brymer joins them for their first Mozart CD and has a benign influence in a fine, mellifluous performance of the *Clarinet quintet*. He plays the *Adagio* as a sustained half-tone and conjures from the strings comparably soft playing. Perhaps a little more dynamic variety would have been an advantage, but the concentration is sustained right through. The finale is delightful; there is an attractive improvisational feeling in the lyrical variation before the main theme makes its joyful return. The recording is truthful, but the close balance is more noticeable in the coupled *Hoffmeister quartet*, which is a lively, well-integrated performance, if without the individuality of the *Quintet*. However, at mid-price this coupling is certainly worth considering.

(i) *Clarinet quintet in A, K.581;* (ii) *Violin sonatas in F, K.376; E flat, K.481.*

(M) *** Cal. Approche CAL 6628 [id.]. (i) Bohuslav Zahradnik, Talich Qt; (ii) Peter Messiereur, Stanislav Bogunia.

The *Clarinet quintet* is exquisitely done. Bohuslav Zahradnik's contribution has much delicacy of feeling and colour; he is highly seductive in the slow movement, and even in the finale the effect is gentle in the most appealing way without any loss of vitality. The recording balance is exemplary. The two *Violin sonatas* are also beautifully played in a simple, direct style that is wholly persuasive. The recording is clearly detailed and well balanced, if slightly more shallow.

Clarinet trio in E flat (Kegelstatt), K.498.

** Sony Dig SK 57499 [id.]. Stoltzman, Ax, Ma – BEETHOVEN; BRAHMS: *Clarinet trios.* ***

The Brahms and Beethoven trios come off better than the Mozart *Kegelstatt Trio*. Yo-Yo Ma plays the viola part on the cello, which presents no problems. However, the performance is not without tiny little mannerisms, which diminish pleasure.

Complete Mozart Edition, Volume 13: (i) *Divertimento in E flat for string trio, K.563;* (ii) *Duos for violin and viola Nos. 1–2, K.423/4;* (i) *6 Preludes and fugues for string trio, K.404a;* (iii) *Sonata (String trio) in B flat, K.266.*

(M) *** Ph. 422 513-2 (2) [id.]. (i) Grumiaux, Janzer, Szabo; (ii) Grumiaux, Pelliccia; (iii) ASMF Chamber Ens.

(B) *** Ph. Duo 454 023-2 (2). As above.

Grumiaux's 1967 recorded performance of the *Divertimento in E flat* remains unsurpassed; he is here joined by two players with a similarly refined and classical style. In the *Duos*, which are ravishingly played, the balance is excellent, and Arrigo Pelliccia proves a natural partner in these inspired and rewarding works. The *Sonata for string trio* is well played by the ASMF Chamber Ensemble and it has a modern, digital recording. Of the six *Preludes and fugues*, the first three derive from Bach's *Well-tempered clavier*, the fourth combines an *Adagio* from the *Organ sonata*, BWV 527, with *Contrapunctus 8* from the *Art of fugue*, the fifth is a transcription of two movements from the *Organ sonata*, BWV 526, and the sixth uses music of W. F. Bach. The performances here are sympathetic and direct, the recorded sound bold, clear and bright.

Divertimento in E flat for string trio, K.563.

*** Sony Dig. MK 39561 [id.]. Kremer, Kashkashian, Ma.

Gidon Kremer, Kim Kashkashian and Yo-Yo Ma turn in an elegant and sweet-toned account on Sony/CBS and are excellently recorded. Indeed, the sound is fresh and beautifully realistic. There are many perceptive insights, particularly in the *Adagio* movement which is beautifully done.

Flute quartets Nos. 1 in D, K.285; 2 in G, K.285a; 3 in C, K.285b; 4 in A, K.298.

*** Sony Dig. SK 66240 [id.]. Irena Grafenauer, Gidon Kremer, Veronika Hagen, Clemens Hagen.

(M) *** Van. 08.4001.71 [OVC 4001]. Paula Robinson, Tokyo Qt (members).

*** Accent ACC 48225D. Bernhard and Sigiswald Kuijken, Van Dael, Wieland Kuijken.

*** Sony Dig. MK 42320 [id.]. Rampal, Stern, Accardo, Rostropovich.

Mozart professed an aversion for the flute (partly because at the time its intonation was suspect and its timbre could be watery), yet he wrote some delightful music for it, none more so than these delicious, lightweight quartets. This newest Sony CD is second to none. Irene Grafenauer's playing is in every way memorable, with the most elegant phrasing and an appealing timbre and the accompanying group, led by Kremer, are highly supportive. Of course the flute dominates throughout, and this is reflected in the recording balance, which is very natural in all respects.

The Vanguard recording of the *Flute quartets* (presumably from the 1960s – no date is given) is most winning. Paula Robinson displays a captivating lightness of touch and her silvery timbre seems eminently suited to Mozart. Needless to say, the Tokyo Quartet provide polished accompaniments which combine warmth with much finesse, and the recording is most naturally balanced.

Readers normally unresponsive to period instruments should hear these performances by Bernhard Kuijken, for they have both charm and vitality; they radiate pleasure and bring one close to this music. This record is rather special and cannot be recommended too strongly. The playing is exquisite and the engineering superb.

It would be hard to dream up a more starry quartet of players than that assembled on the alternative Sony disc. But the recording was made in a relatively dry studio, and the acoustic emphasizes the dominance of Rampal's flute in the ensemble, with the three superstar string-players given little chance to shine distinctively except in the finale of K.285. A delectable record none the less.

(i) *Flute quartets Nos. 1 in D, K.285; 2 in G, K.285a; 3 in C, K.285b; 4 in A, K.298*; (ii) *Andante for flute and orchestra in C, K.315.*
(B) *** DHM 05472 77442-2 [id.]. Barthold Kuijken; (i) Members of Coll. Aur.; (ii) La Petite Band.

The Collegium Aureum set is the only bargain version using period instruments. Kuijken plays a beguilingly soft instrument from Dresden, made by August Grenser in 1789, and the effect has great charm, even to ears not much enamoured of period instruments. The playing of the three string instruments is also very smooth and accomplished, and the ensemble is beautifully recorded in a warm acoustic. The pitch is lower by a semitone, but few listeners will mind this. The *Andante for flute and orchestra* makes an engaging encore.

(i) *Flute quartets Nos. 1–4;* (ii) *Oboe quartet in F, K.370.*
(M) *** DG (IMS) 453 287-2 [id.]. (i) Andreas Blau; (ii) Lothar Koch; Amadeus Qt (members).

Andreas Blau is a fine artist and the Amadeus accompany him with subtlety and distinction. These performances are matched by the refinement of Koch in the *Oboe quartet*. With creamy tone, nice embellishments (especially in the finale) and very stylish phrasing, he is splendid. The Amadeus accompany with sensibility and the balance is flawless. The excellent analogue recordings date from the late 1970s. Other recommended versions of the flute works have no extra work, so this superior, mid-priced DG disc is very competitive indeed.

Flute quartets Nos. 1–4; Oboe quartet (arr. for flute, Galway), *K.370.*
**(*) RCA Dig. 09026 60442-2 [id.]. James Galway, Tokyo Qt.

James Galway is an impeccable soloist and the Tokyo Quartet provide admirable support. The recording too is fresh and well balanced and, if Galway dominates, that is partly the result of Mozart's writing and the use of a modern instrument. Some may feel that in slow movements his sweet, silvery timbre and individual vibrato are too much of a good thing. The transcription of the *Oboe quartet* is more questionable, although it must be admitted that here the *Adagio* sounds refreshingly different on the flute, and the performance cannot be faulted.

Horn quintet in E flat, K. 407; Horn duos in E flat, K.487/496a.
(N) (B) *** EMI Debut Dig. CDZ5 72822-2 [id.]. Andrew Clark, (waldhorn); (i) Ensemble Galant; (ii) Roger Montgomery – BEETHOVEN: *Horn sonata; Sextet, Op. 81b*; BRAHMS: *Horn trio.****

On EMI's bargain Debut label, Andrew Clark uses a waldhorn and displays considerable panache. As in the Brahms *Trio*, his virtuosity is well matched by his partners, also using period instruments. The two rare Mozart *Duos* are guaranteed to win the listener. Strongly recommended.

(ii) *Horn quintet in E flat, K.407;* (ii) *Oboe quartet in F, K.370; A Musical Joke, K.522.*
(BB) **(*) Naxos Dig. 8.550437 [id.]. (i) József Kiss; (ii) Jenö Keveházi; Kodály Qt.

Highly musical if not especially individual performances of the *Horn quintet* and *Oboe quartet*; in the latter the oboe is balanced forwardly and seems a bit larger than life; but no matter, the recordings have a pleasingly resonant bloom. The *Musical Joke* really comes off well: the horn players have a great time with their wrong notes.

Piano quartets Nos. 1 in G min., K.478; 2 in E flat, K.493 (see also above, under Complete Mozart Edition, Volume 14).
(N) *** Sony Dig. SK 66841 [id.]. Emanuel Ax, Isaac Stern, Jaime Laredo, Yo-Yo Ma.
*** Ph. (IMS) Dig. 410 391-2 [id.]. Beaux Arts Trio with Giuranna.
*** Decca Dig. 444 115-2 [id.]. András Schiff, Shiokawa, Höbarth, Perényi.

The grouping of star names by Sony offers performances of keen imagination and insight, with the line-up of three string soloists bringing extra individuality compared with members of a string quartet. Speeds are beautifully chosen and in both works the performances consistently convey a sense of happy spontaneity. It is striking that Emanuel

Ax, in the many passages in which the piano is set against the strings, establishes the sort of primacy required, pointing rhythms and moulding phrases persuasively. The recording, made in the Manhattan Center, New York, in 1994, is a degree drier than in many previous versions, suggesting a small rather than a reverberant hall.

The Beaux Arts group provide splendidly alive and vitally sensitive accounts that exhilarate the listener, just as does the Curzon–Amadeus set (see below), and they have the advantage of first-class digital recording. The Beaux Arts play them not only *con amore* but with the freshness of a new discovery, and the sound (particularly that of the piano) is exceptionally lifelike.

Not only does András Schiff play Mozart's fortepiano, an Anton Walter of about 1780, but Yuuko Shiokawa plays his violin, a mid-eighteenth-century instrument from Mittenwald in Bavaria (as is Miklós Perényi's 1770 cello), while Erich Höbarth uses a viola made by Carlo Antonio Testore of Milan, also believed to have belonged to Mozart. The stringed instruments produce real warmth in the acoustic of the Wienersaal of the Salzburg Mozarteum, though the fortepiano sounds somewhat papery and wanting in timbre. Generally, these are articulate and affectionate performances which will give pleasure, though this should not be an only recommendation in this repertoire. The Beaux Arts, using modern instruments, are rather special.

(i) *Piano quartets Nos. 1–2;* (i) *Horn quintet in E flat, K.407.*

✽ (M) *** Decca mono 425 960-2. (i) Clifford Curzon, Amadeus Qt; (ii) Dennis Brain, Griller Qt.

All versions of the Mozart *Piano quartets* rest in the shadow of the recordings by Clifford Curzon and members of the Amadeus Quartet. No apologies need be made for the 1952 mono recorded sound. The performances have a unique sparkle, slow movements are elysian. One's only criticism is that the *Andante* of K.478 opens at a much lower dynamic level than the first movement, and some adjustment of the controls needs to be made. The *Horn quintet* coupling was recorded in 1944 and the transfer to CD is even more miraculous. The slight surface rustle of the 78-r.p.m. source is in no way distracting and Dennis Brain's performance combines warmth and elegance with a spirited spontaneity, and the subtleties of the horn contribution are a continuous delight. A wonderful disc that should be in every Mozartian's library.

Piano quartet No. 1 in G min., K.478.

*** Ph. Dig. 446 001-2 [id.]. Alfred Brendel, Thomas Zehetmair, Tabea Zimmermann, Richard Duven – SCHUBERT: *Trout quintet.* ***

Brendel's performance of the *G minor Piano quartet* has vigour and sensitivity and, not surprisingly, an admirable sense of style. It very well recorded too and, although most collectors will prefer a disc containing both piano quartets, this is a sizeable bonus for an outstanding account of Schubert's *Trout quintet*.

Piano trios Nos. 1–6 (see also above, under Complete Mozart Edition, Volume 14).

Piano trios Nos. 1 in B flat, K.254; 2 in G, K.496; 3 in B flat, K.502; 4 in E, K.542; 5 in C, K.548; 6 in G, K.564.

(M) *** Teldec/Warner Dig. 0630 12336-2 (2) [2292 46439-2]. Trio Fontenay.

*** Chandos Dig. CHAN 8536/7 (2). Borodin Trio.

(N) (B) **(*) EMI double fforte CZS5 73350-2 (2). Vienna Schubert Trio.

Piano trios Nos. 1–6; Piano trio in D min., K.442.

*** Ph. Dig. 422 079-2 (3). Beaux Arts Trio.

(i) *Piano trios Nos. 1 in B flat, K.254; 2 in G, K.496; 3 in B flat, K.502; 4 in E, K.542; 5 in C, K. 548; 6 in G, K.564;* (ii) *Clarinet trio (Kegelstatt) in E flat, K. 498.*

(B) *(**) Ph. (IMS) Duo 446 154-2 (2) [id.]. (i) Beaux Arts Trio; (ii) Brymer, Kovacevich, Ireland.

The Trio Fontenay have already given us excellent accounts of the Brahms and Dvořák *Piano trios* and they are equally happy in the music of Mozart. As before, the splendid pianist, Wolf Harden, dominates the music-making by strength of personality, although the others are well in the picture, and the playing of the cellist, Niklas Schmidt, is notable. The playing of this group is consistently fresh and spontaneous. Indeed these musicians are completely at one with Mozart and the recording is truthful and well balanced. Although the earlier Beaux Arts set remains very tempting on a Philips Duo (which throws in the *Clarinet trio* for good measure), this Teldec set has the advantage of modern digital recording and carries the strongest recommendation at mid-price. The only snag is the absence of accompanying musical notes.

Apart from including the *D minor trio* completed by Stadler, the Beaux Arts are more generous with repeats, which accounts for the extra disc in their digital version. Their performances are eminently fresh and are no less delightful and winning. There is a somewhat lighter touch here compared with the Chandos alternative, thanks in no small degree to the subtle musicianship of Menahem Pressler. The Philips recording is strikingly realistic and present.

The Borodin Trio are slightly weightier in their approach and their tempi are generally more measured than the Beaux Arts, very strikingly so in the *Allegretto* of the *G major*. All the same, there is, as usual with this group, much sensitive playing and every evidence of distinguished musicianship. The balance in the Philips set tends to favour the piano a little; the Chandos, recorded at The Maltings, Snape, perhaps produces the more integrated sound.

Claus-Christian Schuster, the pianist on the EMI Vienna set, is a stylishly elegant player. He very much dominates his colleagues, but the recording itself is smooth and natural. These performances are lightweight, but they certainly give pleasure.

The Beaux Arts Trio's earlier performances, made in the late 1960s, still sound vivid and fresh. As music-making, this has almost equal artistic claims on the listener and, though the timbre of Daniel Guilet's violin is a bit thin and pinched, it is well focused. Different ears and different reproducers will react to this with varying degrees of dissatisfaction; but Menahem Pressler's piano playing is most naturally caught. In the *Clarinet trio* the balance is such that Jack Brymer's clarinet dominates and Stephen Kovacevich's piano is slightly recessed, but the overall effect is beautiful, warmer than in the *Piano trios*. But the later, digital set of the *Piano trios* is well worth the extra cost.

Piano and wind quintet in E flat, K.452.
(M) *** Sony Dig. SMK 42099 [id.]. Perahia, members of ECO – BEETHOVEN: *Quintet.* ***

An outstanding account (now at mid-price) of Mozart's delectable *Piano and wind quintet* on CBS, with Perahia's playing wonderfully refreshing in the *Andante* and a superb response from the four wind soloists, and in particular Neil Black's oboe. Clearly all the players are enjoying this rewarding music, and they are well balanced, with the piano against the warm but never blurring acoustics of The Maltings at Snape.

String quartets

Complete Mozart Edition, Volume 12: *String quartets Nos. 1–23.*
(M) *** Ph. 422 512-2 (8) [id.]. Italian Qt.

The earliest recordings by the Italians now begin to show their age (notably the six *Haydn Quartets*, which date from 1966): the violin timbre is thinner than we would expect in more modern versions. But the quality is generally very satisfactory, for the Philips sound-balance is admirably judged. As a set, the performances have seen off all challengers for two decades or more; one is unlikely to assemble a more consistently satisfying overview of these works, or one so beautifully played. They hold a very special place in the Mozartian discography.

String quartet No. 1 in G, K.80.
(B) *** Discover Dig. DICD 920171 [id.]. Sharon Qt – BEETHOVEN: *Harp quartet;* RAVEL: *Quartet in F.* **(*)

The Sharon Quartet give an excellent account of Mozart's *First* divertimento-like *Quartet*, which he wrote in Italy at the age of fifteen. The playing has life and finesse and, although the recording (made in a Cologne church) is reverberant, detail is clear; indeed the acoustic rather suits the music.

String quartets Nos. 8 in F, K.168; 9 in A, K.169; 10 in C, K.170; 11 in E flat, K.171; 12 in B flat, K.172.
*** Cal. Dig. CAL 9247 [id.]. Talich Qt.

The Talich are the soul of finesse and play with great expressive simplicity, while bringing vitality to allegros and conveying a consistent feeling of spontaneous vitality throughout. They are naturally if forwardly balanced, and beautifully recorded. There are few records of Mozart's earlier quartets to match this collection.

String quartets Nos. 14 in G, K.387; 15 in D min., K.421; 16 in E flat, K.428; 17 in B flat (Hunt), K.458; 18 in A, K.464; 19 in C (Dissonance), K.465 (Haydn Quartets); 20 in D (Hoffmeister), K. 499; 21 in D, K.575; 22 in B flat, K.589; 23 in F, K.590 (Prussian Quartets Nos. 1–3).
(M) *** Teldec/Warner 4509 95495-2 (4) [9031 72480-2]. Alban Berg Qt.

The Teldec recordings were made by the Alban Berg in the latter half of the 1970s; the performances have not since been surpassed, and now they make one of the most distinguished sets of Mozart's late quartets currently available, with the additional advantage of economy. The playing is thoroughly stylish and deeply musical; it is entirely free from surface gloss and there are none of the expressive exaggerations of dynamics and phrasing that marred this group's later records for EMI. The *Haydn Quartets* are consistently successful; the *Hunt* (1979) is still possibly the finest on the market and the *Dissonance* too is first class, with a wonderfully expressive account of the slow movement.

String quartets Nos. 14–19 (Haydn Quartets); 20 in D (Hoffmeister), K.499; 21–23 (Prussian Nos. 1–3).
(B) *** Nimbus Dig. NI 1778 (5) [id.]. Franz Schubert Qt of Vienna.

Among modern recordings this is an outstanding set in every way, and for those wanting Mozart's last ten and – by general consent – greatest quartets, this Nimbus bargain box rather sweeps the board. The Franz Schubert Quartet play with a refreshing lack of affectation, natural warmth, and great sweetness of tone. There is nothing narcissistic about their playing, and the listener is held from start to finish. In the six *Haydn Quartets* comparison with the Talich and (at full price) the Chilingirians, is in no way disadvantageous to the Viennese group, who have the benefit of first-class, modern, digital recording (made between 1992 and 1994), most naturally balanced in a pleasing acoustic.

String quartets Nos. 14 in G, K.387; 15 in D min., K.421; 16 in E flat, K.428; 17 in B flat (Hunt), K.458; 18 in A, K.464; 19 in C (Dissonance), K.465 (Haydn Quartets).

❁ (M) *** Audivis Astrée Dig. E 8596 (3) [id.] (*K.387 & K.421:* E 8746; *K.428 & K.458:* E 8747; *K.464 & K.465:* E 8748). Mosaïques Qt.

(M) *** CRD CRD 3362; *CRDC 4062* (*Nos. 14–15*); 3363; *4063* (*Nos. 16–17*); 3364; *4064* (*Nos. 18–19*) [id.]. Chilingirian Qt.

*** Hyperion Dig. CDS 44001/3 [id.]. Salomon Qt.

(i) *String quartets Nos. 14–19 (Haydn Quartets)*; also *String quartet No. 3 in G, K.156;* (ii) *Violin sonata No. 18 in G, K.301.*

(M) *** Cal. CAL 3241/3 [id.]. (i) Talich Qt; (ii) Peter Messiereur, Stanislav Bogunia (with HAYDN: *String quartet No. 74 in G min., Op. 74/3* **(*)).

String quartets Nos. 14 in G, K.387; 15 in D min., K.421.

(M) **(*) Whitehall Associates Dig. MQCD 6004 [id.]. Medici Qt.

String quartets Nos. 16 in E flat, K.428; 19 in C (Dissonance), K.465.

(M) **(*) Whitehall Associates Dig. MQCD 6002 [id.]. Medici Qt.

String quartets Nos. 17 in B flat (Hunt), K.458; 18 in A, K.464.

(M) **(*) Whitehall Associates Dig. MQCD 6003 [id.]. Medici Qt.

Although we have long had a special liking for the full-price Chilingirian performances on CRD, this new set by the Mosaïques Quartet on period instruments must take pride of place, the more particularly as it is offered at mid-price. As with their previous award-winning performances of Haydn, this is playing of great distinction which offers new insights in every one of the six quartets. Phrasing is wonderfully musical, textures are elegantly blended, there is great transparency yet a full sonority, and this music-making unfolds freshly and naturally with absolutely none of the disadvantages one usually associates with period performances. Slow movements have great concentration and often rapt intensity, yet allegros are alert and vital and finales are a joy. The recording is first class, real and present, while allowing the widest range of dynamic. The three CDs are separately packaged but come in a slip-case so we assume that later they will be available separately.

For those wanting performances on modern instruments, the Chilingirian Quartet plays with unforced freshness and vitality, avoiding expressive mannerism but always conveying the impression of spontaneity, helped by the warm and vivid recording. Unlike most quartets, they never sound superficial in the elegant but profound slow movements. The three CDs are packaged separately and offer demonstration quality.

The playing of the Salomon Quartet is highly accomplished and has a real sense of style; they do not eschew vibrato, though their use of it is not liberal, and there is admirable clarity of texture and vitality of articulation. There is no want of subtlety and imagination in the slow movements. The recordings are admirably truthful and lifelike, and those who seek 'authenticity' in Mozart's chamber music will not be disappointed.

The performances by the Talich Quartet are immaculate in ensemble and the performances have a special kind of shared intimacy which is yet immediately communicative. There is complete understanding of what Mozart is trying to say and a warmth and elegance of phrasing which is totally appealing. The analogue recordings are beautiful, very smooth on top, the balance slightly middle- and bass-orientated. The set has now been issued complete on three mid-priced discs with a pair of bonuses. The *Violin sonata* comes after the *Dissonance Quartet*; the *Haydn Quartet*, Op. 74/3, after the *Hunt*, K.458, at a disconcertingly higher level. This too is a fine performance – but be prepared! Perhaps the *Dissonance* could have a stronger profile but it, too, is beautifully played and recorded.

The Medici provide a polished, well-integrated set of *Haydn Quartets*, fresh and alert, if without always the touch of extra individuality that appears in their account of the *Clarinet quintet*. The studio recordings are rather closely balanced (although they are not airless) and the leader is obviously near the microphone. These records are competitively priced and certainly give pleasure.

String quartet No. 14 in G, K.387; (i) *String quintet No. 4 in G min., K.516.*

*** ASV Dig. CDDCA 923 [id.]. Lindsay Qt, (i) with Patrick Ireland.

This is what chamber-music playing is about. The Lindsays radiate a delight in their music and judge the character of each piece of music exactly. There is none of the chromium-plated perfection of the Emersons, and one has only to sample the finale of K.387, played with enormous vitality and sparkle (even with an element of risk in the virtuosity), with that of the Quatuor Ysaÿe on Decca to sense immediately that the music-making is a world apart. The slow movement of the *G minor String quintet* is very touching in its gentle intensity. These are among the finest modern recordings of either work. They were made in All Saints', Petersham, and the fairly close microphones are in no way intrusive, capturing the players against a very attractive ambience. The disc must be recommended with enthusiasm.

String quartets Nos. 15 in D min, K.421; 16 in E flat, K.428; 18 in A, K.464.

(N) (***) Testament mono/stereo SBT 1117 [id.]. Smetana Qt.

Older readers who possessed the Columbia mono LP coupling made by the Smetana Quartet in the mid-1950s of the *D minor*, K.421 and *E flat*, K.428 *quartets*, will need no reminders of their excellence. These are performances of a singular distinction, supremely classical in every way. At no point do the Smetanas invite admiration for their perfect ensemble or tonal finesse, both are at the service of Mozart. The slow movement of K.428 has rarely sounded more affecting (only the pre-war Pro Arte surpass it). This quartet appears in stereo for the first time. The *A major*, K.464, has not been issued before, and gives equal satisfaction. A very special record.

String quartets Nos. 15 in D min., K.421; 21 in D, K.575.
*** DG (IMS) Dig. 449 136-2. Hagen Qt.

The Hagen Quartet here reinforce their Mozartian credentials. In both the quartets recorded here, they are highly sensitive to dynamic markings without ever exaggerating them. They are pensive and inward-looking (at times as if they are viewing Mozart through Schubertian eyes) and they make the listener think anew about this great music. Exemplary recorded sound.

String quartet No. 15 in D min., K.421; String quintet No. 5 in D, K.593.
(N) **(*) ASV Dig. CDDCA 1018 [id.]. Lindsay Qt.

These are perceptive, highly musical and essentially dramatic accounts, very well played. But as with the other issues in this series, accents are strong, and in the *Andante* of the *D minor Quartet*, and the *Adagio* of the *Quintet* there are dynamic surges, which not all listeners will find quite comfortable. Alternative versions of the Finale of the *Quintet* demonstrate how the main theme can either be presented as a descending chromatic scale, or a simplified 'zig-zag' rhythmic pattern. With CD cueing you can take your choice. Vividly forward sound.

String quartets Nos. 16 in E flat, K.428; 17 in B flat (Hunt), K.458.
(N) (B) **(*) Philips Virtuoso 422 832-2. Italian Qt.

The Italian players give a fine, unaffected account of the *Hunt quartet*, although some may feel that it is a shade undercharacterized in places. K.428 however gives little cause for complaint, the playing unfailingly perceptive and most musical. In the present transfer, the ambient effect of the 1977 recording remains pleasing but the upper range is thinner, noticeably less smooth than the CRD recording of the Chilingirians.

String quartet No. 17 (Hunt), K.458.
(M) *** DG (IMS) 449 092-2 [id.]. Amadeus Qt – HAYDN: *String quartets Nos. 77–78.* ***
**(*) Testament mono SBT 1085 [id.]. Hollywood Qt – HUMMEL: *Quartet in G* *(*); HAYDN: *Quartet No. 76.* **(*)

The Amadeus, recorded in 1963, give a strikingly fine account of the *Hunt*, famous in its day. The reading is well characterized and, though there are some touches that will not have universal appeal (in the slow movement, for example, these artists do not always allow the music to speak for itself), this is, generally speaking, a most satisfying version, notable for a finely blended and naturally balanced recording, which has been transferred beautifully to CD.

The Hollywood Quartet's performance was recorded at a memorable concert in London's Royal Festival Hall in September 1957, and also included the Haydn coupling. The performance is as impeccable as one would expect from these artists and the sound astonishingly good for the period.

String quartets Nos. 17 in B flat (Hunt), K.458; 19 in C (Dissonance), K.465.
(B) *** EMI CfP CD-CFP 6034. Lindsay Qt.
(BB) **(*) Naxos Dig. 8.550105 [id.]. Moyzes Qt.

A highly competitive issue at CfP price. There is also a justly famous Amadeus version of the *Hunt* on DG (see above) and the Lindsay Quartet can well withstand the comparison. They play most beautifully, with unforced expressiveness and an alert and vital sensitivity. In the slow movement some readers may even prefer them to their rivals, for they are without the slightest affectation. Their recording too is more modern (1975) and wider in range. In the *Dissonance Quartet*, so called because of its bold opening, there is again much sensitivity. Recommended on all counts.

The Moyzes Quartet come from Bratislava and are an accomplished ensemble, distinguished by a generally sweet and light tone and decently recorded in the clean acoustic of the Concert Hall of Slovak Radio. The performances are very well prepared and neatly played, phrasing is musical and often sensitive. Greater diversity of colour would be welcome, and the players do not command quite a wide enough range of dynamics, so that the overall effect is just a little bland. But the performances still have a lot going for them and can be recommended.

String quartets Nos. 20 in D (Hoffmeister), K.499; 21 in D, K.575; 22 in B flat, K.589; 23 in F, K.590 (Prussian Quartets Nos. 1–3).
(M) *** CRD CRD 3427/8; *CRDC 4127/8* [id.]. Chilingirian Qt.

The Chilingirian Quartet give very natural, unforced, well-played and sweet-toned accounts of the last four *Quartets*. They are very well recorded too, with cleanly focused lines and a warm, pleasing ambience; indeed in this respect these two discs are second to none.

(i) *String quartets Nos. 20 in D, K.499; 21 in D, K.575;* (ii) *Violin sonata No. 17 in C, K.296.*
*** Calliope CAL 9244. (i) Talich Qt; (ii) Peter Messiereur, Stanislav Bogunia.

The Talich coupling of K.499 and K.575 is digital and the recording brighter and more present than in the *Haydn Quartets*. The playing has comparable sensibility and plenty of vitality.

String quartets Nos. 20 in D (Hoffmeister), K.499; 23 in F, K. 590.
(N) **(*) Arcana Dig. A 8. Festetics Qt.

These are fine, characterful performances, with splendid vigour and ensemble showing the Festetics Quartet in more relaxed form than in their coupling of K.575 and K.590. However slow movements could still loosen up a bit more, they still sound very considered. Excellent recording.

String quartets Nos. 21 in D, K.575; 22 in B flat, K.589.
*** Nimbus Dig. NI 5351 [id.]. Franz Schubert Qt.

The Franz Schubert Quartet play with refreshing lack of affectation and great sweetness of tone; but at the same time it must be said that there is nothing narcissistic about the playing, and the listener is held from start to finish. They are very well recorded too.

String quartets Nos. 21 in D, K.575; 23 in D, K.590 (Prussian).
(N) *** Audivis Astrée Dig. E 8659 [id.]. Mosäiques Qt.
**(*) Arcana Dig. A 9 [id.]. Festetics Qt.

The Mosaïques Quartet make an easy first choice in this coupling, and even those collectors who do not normally respond to period instrument performances should be swayed by the warmth and finesse of their playing, and for their lightness of touch in the finale of K.590. The closing *Allegretto* of K.575 is revealing in quite a different way, and both slow movements have a searching intensity; yet there is an underlying lyrical feeling, which often brings the sun out from behind the clouds. The thoughtful subtlety of this playing is matched by a spontaneous response to Mozart at his most penetrating. The recording is extremely lifelike.

The Hungarian Quatuor Festetics, who also play '*sur instruments d'époque*', as the French so engagingly put it, approach Mozart with a degree of severity that not all will take to. The opening of K.575 is superbly poised, and the *Andante* is most eloquent. But never a suspicion of a smile until the arrival of the Minuet, and even this is very purposeful. Strong accents abound, and there is something a bit spare about the finale too, vital though it is. A record to be greatly admired, but not one to fall in love with. The recording is made in an unlikely venue, the Zögernitz Casino in Vienna, and is vividly faithful, if a bit close.

String quartets Nos. 22 in B flat, K.589; 23 in F, K. 590.
(N) *** Delos Dig. DE 3192 [id.]. Shanghai Qt.

The New York based Shanghai Quartet, who play modern instruments, have won glowing opinions from the American press and elsewhere, and no wonder. Their accounts of Mozart's last two quartets are second to none. They create a beautifully blended sound, warm and refined. Slow movements have a natural expressive flow, and there is all the delicacy of articulation needed for the dancing finales. They are most naturally recorded in a pleasingly spacious ambience.

String quartets Nos. 21 in D, K.575; 22 in B flat, K.589; 23 in F, K.590.
(B) *** MDG Double Dig. MDG 307 0936-2 (2). Leipzig Qt.

Although they use modern instruments – and with great finesse – the splendid Leipzig Quartet play with all the transparency of texture associated with period style, and in that they are helped by a recording which has clear separation and striking presence and realism. Their performances of Mozart's last three quartets are second to none, and have all the spontaneity of live music-making. They rather upstage the Shanghai Quartet on Delos by including an extra work for the same cost, and fill up the rest of the space on the second CD by ingeniously creating a 'sampler' composite quartet. This combines the opening Allegro of Schubert's D.353 with the glorious *Lento assai* of Beethoven's Op. 135, followed by the Scherzo from Brahms's Op. 51/2 and the finale from Beethoven's Op. 59/3. In principle one would resist such an idea, but all four movements are superbly played, and the amalgam works astonishingly well.

String quintets

Complete Mozart Edition, Volume 11: *String quintets Nos. 1–6.*
(M) *** Ph. 422 511-2 (3). Grumiaux Trio, with Gerecz, Lesueur.

The Grumiaux ensemble's survey of the *String quintets* offers immensely civilized and admirably conceived readings. Throughout the set the vitality and sensitivity of this team are striking, and in general this eclipses all other recent accounts. The remastering of the 1973 recordings for CD is very successful indeed.

Complete quintets: String quintets Nos. 1 in B flat, K.174; 2 in C min., K.406; 3 in C, K.515; 4 in G min., K.516; 5 in D, K.593; 6 in E flat, K.614 (i) *Clarinet quintet in A, K.581.*

❀ *** Calliope CAL9231/3 [id.]. Talich Qt. with Rehák (i) Zahradnik.

The six Mozart *String quintets* played by the Talich Quartet and Karel Rehák are available in a mid-priced box, together with a radiant account of the *Clarinet quintet* (with Bohuslav Zahradnik the sensitive soloist), on three Calliope discs which cost approximately the same as the pair of Duos above. The Calliope set will in the long run prove a far better investment. However bargain hunters preferring the Grumiaux ensemble's immensely civilized 1973 survey of just the *String quintets* will find them also available on three mid-priced discs, as Volume 11 of the Philips Mozart Edition (422 511-2).

String quintets (Nos. 1) in B flat, K.174 (with original version of *Trio of the Minuet and Finale*); *(2) in C, K.515.*
(BB) **(*) Naxos Dig. 8.553103 [id.]. Eder Qt, with János Fehérvári.

String quintets (Nos. 4) in C min., K.406; (3) in G min., K.516.
(BB) *(*) Naxos Dig. 8.553104 [id.]. Eder Qt, with János Fehérvári.

String quintets Nos. (5) in D, K.593; (6) in E flat, K.614.
(BB) *** Naxos Dig. 8.553105 [id.]. Eder Qt, János Fehérvári.

The augmented Eder Quartet move on to offer a complete set of the *String quintets*, and the first disc again displays their unexaggerated Mozartian style, a fine blend of tone and musicianship. The *Andante* of the *C major Quintet* is particularly eloquent, the finale as lively as it is graceful. The recording (again using the Budapest Unitarian Church) is full and natural, with the resonance adding ambient bloom without too much inflation. While not a match for the Talich, these performances are eminently recommendable to those with limited budgets. But after the success of the first disc, the second is disappointing. The playing is still thoughtful and ensemble is clean, but there is an element of routine, and neither performance really takes off. It is not until the opening *Adagio* of the finale of the *G minor Quartet* that the Eder account achieves real concentration. The last two quartets come off very well indeed. The opening *Larghetto* of the *D major* is warmly intense, and the allegro immediately lifts off. The *Adagio* is beautifully played, the finale delightfully light-hearted. The *E flat major Quintet* is similarly well judged, with a poised *Andante* and another infectious closing movement. The recording is close but very realistic.

*String quintets (Nos. 2) in C, K.515; (3) in G min., K.516; 5 in D, K.593; 5 in E flat, K.614*1
(M) *** Virgin Veritas/EMI Dig. VCD 45169-2 (2). Hausmusik.

Those seeking period performances of the four finest of the Mozart *Quintets* should be more than satisfied with the playing of Hausmusik. These recordings were made in 1991/2, and for some reason the set was not completed. But as the very opening of the *C major* readily demonstrates, this playing brings a wonderfully light rhythmic touch and is remarkably airy in texture. The first movement of the *G minor* is managed no less beautifully, while the allegros of both the *D major* and *E flat major Quintets* burst with energy. Slow movements have a movingly restrained espressivo, withdrawn but without a feeling of austerity, and the *Adagio* of the *G minor* is hauntingly dark in its gentle melancholy. Finales bounce along joyfully and, although quite different in character, these performances are every bit as rewarding as those on modern instruments by the Talich. The EMI recording is very distinguished in its fine balance and naturalness.

String quintets (Nos. 2) in C, K.515; (3) in G min., K.516.
**(*) Sony Dig. SK 66259 [id.]. L'Archibudelli.
(M) **(*) HM Suite Dig. HMT 7901512 [id.]. Ensemble 415.

String quintets (Nos. 2) in C, K.515; (3) in G min., K.516; 5 in D, K.593; 6 in E flat, K.614.
(B) **(*) Hyperion Dyad Dig. CDD 22005 [id.]. Salomon Qt, Simon Whistler.

The Salomon Quartet use period instruments, and this Dyad reissue comes into direct competition with the full-price Virgin Veritas collection of the same four quintets by Hausmusik (which is currently awaiting reissue). The Salomon group, understandably, are at their very best in the *G minor Quintet*, with the beauty of the *Adagio* sensitively caught. The final work is also splendidly played, but the *C major* and *D major Quintets* are cooler. The Hyperion recording is excellent, and this Dyad costs the same as a single premium-priced CD; but on almost all counts Hausmusik, who are also most realistically recorded, find greater depth in this music and in particular bring out a hauntingly dark yet gentle melancholy in slow movements, while finales bounce along joyfully.

With L'Archibudelli, allegros (including Minuets) have a pleasing lilt and rhythmic lift, and the fresh, transparent textures avoid edginess. Some might find the accents in the slow movement of the *C major* a shade too forceful; but in the beautiful *Adagio* of the *G minor*, where a minimum of vibrato creates a somewhat austere beauty, the concentration is in no doubt The tension is carried over to the sustained opening of the finale, which then takes off infectiously when the allegro arrives. Excellent vivid recording within an open acoustic. But there is less grace and charm here than with Hausmusik.

Ensemble 415 (leader Chiara Banchini) couple the two favourite Mozart *String quintets* and play them with warmth and the delicacy of texture possible from period instruments. Although one has to adjust to some linear swelling, this music-making is certainly enjoyable. Opening movements have plenty of rhythmic lift and slow movements are refined in feeling, although without quite the degree of rapt concentration found by Hausmusik. However, the finale of the *G minor* (which opens with a hushed *Adagio* and then finds its release in the following allegro) is very succesful. The recording is excellent.

Violin sonatas

Complete Mozart Edition, Volume 15: *Violin sonatas Nos. 1–34; Sonatinas in C & F, K.46d & 46e; Sonatina in F (for beginners), K.547; Sonata in C, K.403* (completed Stadler); *Adagio in C min., K.396; Allegro in B flat, K.372; Andante & allegretto in C, K.404; Andante in A & Fugue in A min., K.402* (completed Stadler); *12 Variations on 'La bergère Célimène', K.359; 6 Variations on 'Hélas, j'ai perdu mon amant', K.360.*
(M) **(*) Ph. Analogue/Dig. 422 515-2 (7). Gérard Poulet, Blandine Verlet; Arthur Grumiaux, Walter Klien; Isabelle van Keulen, Ronald Brautigam.

The early sonatas, from K.6 through to K.31, were recorded in the mid-1970s by Gérard Poulet with Blandine Verlet on harpsichord. The various fragments, sonatinas, sonatas (K.46d, K.46e, K.403 and K.547) and variations by Isabelle van Keulen and Ronald Brautigam come from 1990. For the remaining four CDs, Philips have turned to the set by Arthur Grumiaux and Walter Klien, recorded digitally in the early 1980s. There is a great deal of sparkle and some refined musicianship in these performances, and pleasure remains undisturbed by the balance which, in the 1981 recordings, favours the violin. The later recordings, from 1982 and 1983, are much better in this respect.

Violin sonatas Nos. 1–16, K.6–15 & 26–31.
(B) *** Ph. Duo (IMS) 438 803-2 (2) [id.]. Gérard Poulet, Blandine Verlet.

This set derives from Volume 15 of Philips's Complete Mozart Edition (see above) and is well worth having as a separate issue. There is much to delight and fascinate the ear, although these are records to dip into rather than to play all through!

Violin sonatas Nos. 17 in C, K.296; 18 in G, K.301; 19 in E flat, K.302; 20 in C, K.303.
(N) (BB) **(*) Naxos Dig. 8.553111 [id.]. Takako Nishizaki, Jenö Jandó.

Violin sonatas Nos. 21 in E min., K.304; 22 in A, K. 305; 23 in D, K. 306; 25 in F, K. 377.
(N) (BB) **(*) Naxos Dig. 8.553110 [id.]. Takako Nishizaki, Jenö Jandó.

Violin sonatas Nos. 26 in B flat, K.378; 27 in G, K.379; 28 in E flat, K.380.
(N) (BB) **(*) Naxos Dig. 8.553112 [id.]. Takako Nishizaki, Jenö Jandó.

Violin sonatas Nos. 32 in B flat, K.454; 33 in E flat, K.481.
(N) (BB) **(*) Naxos Dig. 8.553590 [id.]. Takako Nishizaki, Jenö Jandó.

In the earlier of the more mature sonatas, which date from 1778, the violin often takes a subsidiary role and here, the balance and Jandó's strong personality emphasize the effect. This is slightly less striking in K.379–80 (on the third disc) which are later (1781) and in which the part writing is more equal – witness the lively Rondo finale of K.378 or the delightful *Theme and variations*, which forms the second movement of K. 379, which are very attractively shared here. However the sonatas on the second disc are pleasingly spontaneous. On the fourth CD of the series we move on to K. 454 and K.481, which date from 1785 and 1786, respectively. The two instruments now form a much more equal partnership, and in the *B flat* work (written for the Italian violinist, Regina Strinasacchi) the violin takes an accompanied solo role in the *Andante* and leads the way into the finale. In the *E flat* work the piano sometimes returns to dominance, but the partnership is assured, and in the *Andante* the violin leads; then the two instruments engagingly share the theme and variatons of the finale. Takako Nishizaki's tone is small, and at times a little thin and uncovered (rather like a period instrument), but seems perfectly scaled for Mozart; her playing is highly musical and these artists strike a Mozartian symbiosis that is appealing in its fresh simplicity of approach.

Violin sonatas Nos. 17 in C, K.296; 18 in G, K.301; 19 in E flat, K.302; 20 in C, K.303; 21 in E min., K.304; 22 in A, K.305; 23 in D, K.306; 24 in F, K.376; 25 in F, K.377; 12 Variations in G on 'La bergère Célimène', K.359.
(B) *** Ph. Duo 462 185-2 (2) [id.]. Henryk Szeryng, Ingrid Haebler.

Ingrid Haebler brings an admirable vitality and robustness to her part. Her playing has sparkle and great spontaneity. Szeryng's contribution is altogether masterly, and all these performances find both partners in complete rapport. The analogue recordings from the mid-1970s provide striking realism and truthfulness, and they have been transferred immaculately to CD. The *Variations* included in the set are managed with charm. The intimate atmosphere of these performances is particularly appealing.

Violin sonatas Nos. 17 in C, K.296; 18 in G, K.301; 19 in E flat, K.302; 20 in C, K.303; 21 in E min., K.304; 22 in A, K.305; 23 in D, K.306; 24 in F, K.376; 25 in F, K.377; 26 in B flat,

K.378; 27 in G, K.379; 28 in E flat, K.380; 32 in B flat, K.454; 33 in E flat, K.481; 34 in A, K.526; Violin sonatina in F, K.547.
(B) *** Decca 448 526-2 (4). Szymon Goldberg, Radu Lupu.

This was one of Radu Lupu's first recordings for Decca and he plays with uncommon freshness and insight, while Szymon Goldberg brings a wisdom, born of long experience, to these sonatas which is almost unfailingly revealing. Lupu gives instinctive musical support to his partner and both artists bring humanity and imagination to their performances. In short, very distinguished playing from both artists. The recordings were made in the Kingsway Hall in 1974 and were expertly balanced by Christopher Raeburn. They have been most naturally transferred to CD, and this Decca bargain box can be given the strongest recommendation.

PIANO MUSIC

Complete works for piano

Piano duet: (i–ii) *Andante and variations, K.501; Sonatas, K.19d; K.381; K.357–8; K.497; K.521.* 2 Pianos: *Fugue, K.426; Sonata, K.448;* (iii) *Larghetto & Allegro in E flat* (reconstruction). Solo piano music: (i) *Sonatas Nos. 1–18;* (iv) *8 Variations in G, K.24; 7 Variations in D, K.25; 12 Variations in C, K.179; 6 Variations in G, K.180; 9 Variations in C, K.264; 12 Variations in C, K.265; 8 Variations in F, K.352; 12 Variations in E flat, K.353; 12 Variations in E flat, K.354; 6 Variations in F, K.398; 10 Variations in G, K.455; 12 Variations in B flat, K.500; 9 Variations in D, K.573; 8 Variations in F, K.613; Adagio in B min., K.540; Eine kleine Gigue in G, K.574; Fantasia in D min., K.397; Minuet in D, K.355; Rondos: in D, K.485; in A min., K.511; 21 Pieces for keyboard, K.1, K.1a–1d;1f; K.2–5; K.5a; K.33b; K.94; K.312; K.394–5; K.399–401; K.408/1; K.453a; K.460.*
(B) **(*) Ph. 456 132-2 (10) [(M) id. import]. (i) Ingrid Haebler; (ii) Ludwig Hoffmann; (iii) Jörg Demus and Paul Badura-Skoda; (iv) Ingrid Haebler (piano) or Ton Koopman (harpsichord).

Ingrid Háebler with the help of several other artists gives us a complete ten-disc survey of Mozart's keyboard music for two and four hands. She has the solo sonatas to herself and, above all, she gets the scale right. In this repertoire it is quite wrong, on the one hand, to inflate or romanticize; on the other, it is equally unfair to miniaturize them. Haebler's classical approach avoids both these pitfalls. There is sparkle and lightness in the allegros, but also real thoughtfulness – without rhythmic exaggerations in slow movements. The early sonatas are very successful. The intensity with which, for instance, she plays the opening *Adagio* of *No. 4 in E flat*, K.282, varying the tension with the mood of the material, is magical. The well-known later works show a similar feeling for colour and atmosphere. Ton Koopman's despatches various juvenilia with spme brusqueness but he is not helped by the close balance of his harpsichord. The quality of the piano-sound, however, is very good indeed, beautiful and true in Philips's best analogue manner. The piano duet music is also available separately on a Philips Duo and is discussed below.

Piano duet

(i) *Andante with 5 variations, K.501; Fugue in C min., K.426; Sonatas for piano duet: in C, K.19d; D, K.381; G, K.357; B flat, K.358; F, K.497; C, K.521; Sonata in D for two pianos, K.448;* (ii) *Larghetto and Allegro in E flat* (reconstructed Badura-Skoda).
(M) ** Ph. 422 516-2 (2). (i) Haebler, Hoffmann; (ii) Demus, Badura-Skoda.
(B) **(*) Ph. Duo 454 026-2 (2). (i) Haebler, Hoffmann; (ii) Demus, Badura-Skoda.

This two-CD set includes all the music Mozart composed for piano duet or two pianos, in elegant (if at times a little too dainty) performances by Ingrid Haebler and Ludwig Hoffmann in recordings dating from the mid-1970s. Also included is a Mozart fragment, the *Larghetto and Allegro in E flat*, probably written in 1782–3 and completed by Paul Badura-Skoda, who recorded it in 1971 for the Amadeo label with Jörg Demus. Despite the occasional distant clink of Dresden china, all these performances give pleasure and are very decently recorded.

Andante with 5 variations, K.501; Sonata in D for 2 pianos, K.448.
*** Chandos Dig. CHAN 9162 [id.]. Louis Lortie, Hélène Mercier – SCHUBERT: *Fantasia in F min.* ***

The Louis Lortie–Hélène Mercier partnership give one of the most sensitive accounts of the *D major Sonata*, K.448, currently available on disc, and their account of the *Andante and variations* is equally fine. The Schubert coupling is also recommendable. Very good recording.

Sonata in D, K.448.
*** Sony SK 39511 [id.]. Murray Perahia, Radu Lupu – SCHUBERT: *Fantasia in F min.* ***

With Perahia taking the primo part, his brightness and individual way of illuminating even the simplest passage-work dominate the performance, producing magical results and challenging the more inward Lupu into comparably inspired playing. Pleasantly ambient recording made at The Maltings, Snape, and beautifully caught on CD.

Sonatas: in F, K.497; in C, K.521; Pieces for mechanical organ: *Adagio and allegro in F min., K.594; Adagio and allegro in F min., K.608.*
✿ *** Ottavio Dig. OTR C129242. Imogen Cooper and Anne Queffélec.

Above all, these performances convey a sense of joy in the music. The *Sonatas* – both highly inspired – are framed by the two works for mechanical clock, which here sound both thoughtful and unusually commanding: the opening *Adagio* of K.594 is wonderfully serene. The first movement of the *C major Sonata* sets off with great spirit, yet detail is always imaginatively observed; the *Andante* which follows is delightfully poised, and the finale has the lightest touch. The slow movement of K.497 reminds the listener immediately of the horn concertos, a lovely, flowing melody, so persuasively presented, while the finale has a most engaging lilt. Altogether this is playing of great distinction. Everything is marvellously fresh and there is never the least suspicion of Dresden china. Very strongly recommended.

Solo piano music

Piano sonatas Nos. 1–18 (complete).
(M) *** EMI CZS7 67294-2 (5). Daniel Barenboim.

Piano sonatas Nos. 1–18; Fantasia in C min., K.475.
✿ (M) *** Ph. Dig. 422 517-2 (5). Mitsuko Uchida.
(B) *** Decca 443 717-2 (5) [id.]. András Schiff (piano).
(M) ** Nimbus NI 1775 (6) [id.]. Marta Deyanova.

Piano sonatas Nos. 1–18; Sonatas in C, K.46d; in F, K.46e.
(B) *** DG 419 445-2 (5). Christoph Eschenbach.

On Philips, Mitsuko Uchida's collection, with beautiful and naturally balanced digital recording made in the Henry Wood Hall, London, has now been reissued on 5 mid-priced CDs by omitting the shorter pieces, except for the *C minor Fantasia*. Miss Uchida's set of the Mozart *Sonatas* brings playing of consistently fine sense and sound musicianship. There is every indication that this will come to be regarded as a classic series to set alongside those of Gieseking and Walter Klien. Every phrase is beautifully placed, every detail registers, and the early *Sonatas* are as revealing as the late ones. The piano recording is completely realistic, slightly distanced in a believable ambience. This series is available in the USA on separate CDs.

Barenboim's distinguished set of the Mozart *Piano sonatas* is reissued not only at mid-price but now on five CDs instead of the original six. Barenboim, while keeping his playing well within scale in its crisp articulation, refuses to adopt the Dresden china approach to Mozart's *Sonatas*. Even the little *C major*, K.545, designed for a young player, has its element of toughness, minimizing its 'eighteenth-century drawing-room' associations. Though – with the exception of the two minor-key sonatas – these are relatively unambitious works, Barenboim's voyage of discovery brings out their consistent freshness, with the orchestral implications of some of the allegros strongly established. The recording, with a pleasant ambience round the piano sound, confirms the apt scale.

András Schiff's earlier, Decca recordings now also reappear, in a bargain box. Schiff, without exceeding the essential Mozartian sensibility, takes a somewhat more romantic and forward-looking view of the music. His fingerwork is precise yet mellow, and his sense of colour consistently excites admiration. He is slightly prone to self-indulgence in the handling of some phrases, but such is the inherent freshness and spontaneity of his playing that one accepts the idiosyncrasies as a natural product of live performance. The piano is set just a little further back than in the Philips/Uchida recordings, and the acoustic is marginally more open, which suits his slightly more expansive manner.

Christoph Eschenbach gives consistently well-turned, cool and elegant performances without affectation or mannerism. Those looking for an unidiosyncratic, direct approach to Mozart should find this poised, immaculate pianism to their taste. The famous *Andante grazioso* variations which form the first movement of the *Sonata in A*, K.331, are entirely characteristic, played very simply and directly. Other pianists are gentler, more romantic, but Eschenbach's taste cannot be faulted.

Marta Deyanova is an excellent Mozartian and she has her own distinct insights to offer in these sonatas: her style is crisp and clean, without artifice. There is an attractive sense of poise, as at the opening of the *F major*, K.289, while the *Adagio* of the same work is a fine demonstration of her thoughtful lyricism in slow movements, full of imaginative touches of light and shade, yet never precocious or out of style. But while we enjoyed these performances a great deal, the characteristically resonant recording which Nimbus sometimes favour for their piano records slightly blurs the outlines of the playing, and the empty hall effect will not be to all tastes.

Piano sonatas Nos. 1–18; Fantasias: in D min., K.397; C min., K.475.
*** DG (IMS) Dig. 431 760-2 (6). Maria João Pires.

Piano sonatas Nos. 1 in C, K.279; 2 in F, K.280; 9 in D, K.311; 18 in D, K.576.
*** DG (IMS) Dig. 435 882-2 [id.]. Maria João Pires.

Piano sonatas Nos. 3 in B flat, K.281; 4 in E flat, K.282; 15 in F: Andante and allegro, K.533; Rondo, K.494.
*** DG (IMS) Dig. 437 546-2 [id.]. Maria João Pires.

Piano sonatas Nos. 5 in G, K.283; 6 in D, K.284; 10 in C, K.330.
*** DG (IMS) Dig. 437 791-2 [id.]. Maria João Pires.

Piano sonatas Nos. 7 in C, K.309; 12 in F, K.332; 17 in B flat, K.570.
*** DG (IMS) Dig. 439 769-2 [id.]. Maria João Pires.

Piano sonatas Nos. 8 in A min., K.310; 13 in B flat, K.333; 16 in C, K.545.
*** DG (IMS) Dig. 427 768-2 [id.]. Maria João Pires.

Piano sonatas Nos. 11 in A, K.331; 14 in C min., K.457; Fantasias: in C min., K.475; in D min., K.397.
*** DG (IMS) Dig. 429 739-2 [id.]. Maria João Pires.

Maria João Pires is a stylist and a fine Mozartian, as those who have heard any of her cycle on Denon will know. But this splendid new DG set marks a step forward over her earlier interpretations. Pires is always refined yet never wanting in classical feeling, and she has a vital imagination. In these new readings there is even more life: she strikes an ideal balance between poise and expressive sensibility, conveying a sense of spontaneity in everything she does. Moreover, the DG recording is fuller, with greater depth than the Denon set, and the slight dryness to the timbre suits the interpretations, which are expressively fluid and calm without a trace of self-consciousness. With allegros always alert and vital yet never too predictable in their expressive contrasts, this is playing to stimulate the listener consistently – even the hackneyed *C major Sonata*, K.545, sounds freshly minted. While Uchida's much-praised versions are full of personal intimacy, Pires's more direct style with its tranquil eloquence is no less satisfying.

Piano sonatas Nos. 1 in C, K.279; 2 in F, K.280; 3 in B flat, K.281.
(N) *** BIS Dig. CD 835 [id.]. Ronald Brautigam (fortepiano).

Piano sonatas Nos. 4 in E flat, KV.282; 5 in G, KV.283; 6 in D, K.284.
(N) *** BIS Dig. CD 836 [id.]. Ronald Brautigam (fortepiano).

Piano sonatas Nos. 7 in C, KV.309; 8 in D, KV.311; 9 in A min., KV.310.
(N) *** BIS Dig. CD 837 [id.]. Ronald Brautigam (fortepiano).

Piano sonatas Nos. 10 in C, KV.330; 11 in A, KV.331; 12 in F, KV.332.
(N) *** BIS Dig. CD 838 [id.]. Ronald Brautigam (fortepiano).

Piano sonatas Nos. 13 in B flat K.333/315c; 14 in C min., KV.457; Fantasia in C min., KV.475.
(N) *** BIS Dig. CD 839 [id.]. Ronald Brautigam (fortepiano).

Piano sonatas Nos. 15 in F, KV.533 and KV.494; 16 in C, KV.545; 17 in B flat, KV.570; 18 in D, KV.576.
(N) *** BIS Dig. CD 840 [id.]. Ronald Brautigam (fortepiano).

Adagio in B min., K.540; Eine kleine Gigue in G, K.574; Prelude in C, K.284a; Prelude & Fugue in C, K.394; 12 Variations in E flat, K.354; 8 Variations in F, K.613.
(N) *** BIS Dig. CD 896 [id.]. Ronald Brautigam (fortepiano).

Fantasy-fragment in D Min., K. 397; Klavierstück in F, K. 33b; Kleiner Trauermarsch in C min., K. 453a; 8 Variations in F on Grétry's 'Dieu d'amour', K. 352; 10 Variations in G on 'Unser dummer Pöbel meint', K. 455; 12 Variations in C on a Minuet by J. C. Fischer, K. 179.
(N) *** BIS Dig. CD 895 [id.]. Ronald Brautigam (fortepiano).

Modulation Prelude in F/E minor; Rondo in A min., K. 511; 6 Variations in F on 'Salve tu, Domine' from Paisiello's I filosofi immaginarii; 8 Variations in G on a Dutch song by C. E. Graaf, K. 24; 12 Variations in C on 'Ah vous dirai-je maman', K. 265; 12 Variations in B flat, on an Allegretto, K.500; 12 Variations in E flat on a French song, 'La belle Français'. K. 353.
(N) *** BIS Dig. CD 894 [id.]. Ronald Brautigam (fortepiano).

Rondo in D, K.485; Theme and 5 variations in F, K. 547; 2 Variations in A on the aria Come un' agnello by Sarti; 6 Variations in G on Salieri's Mio caro Adone, K.180; 7 Variations in D on the Dutch song, Willem van Nassau; 9 Variations in C on an ariette, Lison dormait, by Dezéde, K. 264; 9 Variations in D on a Minuet by Jean Pierre Dupont, K.573.
(N) *** BIS Dig. CD 897 [id.]. Ronald Brautigam (fortepiano).

Ronald Brautigam's set is extraordinarily refreshing. It is bursting with life and intelligence. He uses a 1992 copy (made in his native Amsterdam) of a fortepiano by Anton Gabriel Walter from about 1795. It is a very good instrument and he is a very good player. Dip in anywhere in this set and you will be rewarded with playing of great imagination and sensitivity – not to mention sureness and agility of mind and fingers. At every turn he commands both delicacy and vitality, and he is completely inside the Mozartian sensibility of the period. Even if you prefer Mozart's keyboard music on the piano, you should investigate this set without delay. It brings Mozart to life in a way that almost no other period-instrument predecessor has done. It starts off very well from the early *C major Sonata*, K.279, with playing that sparkles and delights – and continues as it has begun. This series has given great pleasure as it has appeared over the last couple of years and it is beautifully recorded too.

Piano sonatas Nos. 1–18; Fantasia, K.475; Fantasia, K.396; Variations, K. 353; Variations, K.398; Variations, K.460; Allegro, K.312; Minuet, K.355; Rondo, K.511; Adagio, K.540; Gigue, K.574.

(N) (M) *** Music & Arts CD-1001 (5) [id.]. Lili Kraus.

Lili Kraus, born in Budapest in 1905, recorded this cycle of the Mozart sonatas, as well as shorter pieces, in New York for the Haydn Society in 1954. Compared with her later recording, issued by Sony, the closeness of the sound allows one to appreciate more the diamond clarity of Kraus's playing with its high dynamic contrasts, even if pianissimos are not as hushed as they might be. The important point is that with Kraus one is never in danger – as so many commentators have been – of underprizing these sonatas. These earlier performances are not only more dramatic but more spontaneous sounding too, with firmer technical control. The mono sound is well transferred to make it firm and vivid. In both recordings Kraus omits the composite *Sonata in F*, K.533/494, which Mozart created by adding to two late movements an earlier *Rondo* in less complex style.

Adagio in B min., K.540; Andantino in E flat, K.236; Fantasia in C min., K.475; Gigue in G, K.574; Minuet in D, K.355; Rondo in A min., K.511; Piano sonatas Nos. 14 in C min., K.457; 15 in F, K.533.

(N) (M) **(*) Carlton Classics Dig. 30366 01112 [id.]. Fou Ts'ong.

This is not inconsiderable playing. The *F major Sonata* is particularly fine. But in the *Fantasia in C minor* Fou Ts'ong seems to be looking towards Beethoven and this large-scale performance moves to the very edge of Mozartian sensibility. But there is much to admire here and the recording is lifelike and immediate. Incidentally the *Gigue*, K.174 was chosen by Tchaikovsky for his Mozartiana suite.

Piano sonatas Nos. 3 in B flat, K.281; 10 in C, K.330; 13 in B flat, K.333; Adagio in B min., K.540; Rondo in D, K.485.

(M) *** DG Dig. 445 517-2 [431 274-2]. Vladimir Horowitz.

Playing of such strong personality from so great an artist is self-recommending. With Horowitz there were astonishingly few reminders of the passage of time and the artistry and magnetism remain undiminished. The recordings were made in the pianist's last vintage period, between 1985 and 1989, in either a New York studio, the pianist's home, or an Italian studio in Milan (K.333). As usual, the piano is tightly tuned and the sound is slightly shallow, though very suitable for Mozart. Remarkable playing, not always completely free from affectation; but for variety of articulation just sample the *Allegretto grazioso* finale of K.333 and, for simply expressed depth of feeling, the *Adagio*, K. 540.

Piano sonatas Nos. 8 in A min., K.310; 11 in A, K.331; 13 in B flat, K.333; 14 in C min., K.457; Adagio in B min., K.540; Fantasia in C min., K.475; Rondo in A min., K.511; 9 Variations in D on a minuet by Dupont, K.573.

(B) **(*) Ph. Duo Analogue/Dig. 454 244-2 (2). Alfred Brendel.

The recordings of the *A major Sonata*, K.331, and the *B flat*, K.333, come from 1971 and 1975 respectively and they show Brendel at his very finest, while (not to be forgotten) the *B minor Adagio* is also memorable. So thoughtful and illuminating are Brendel's insights in these works that, even if you possess other versions of them, this will uncover new areas of feeling. K.331, with its engaging opening theme and variations and justly famous *Alla turca* finale, is a joy. The analogue recording, too, is most realistic. However, the *A minor*, K.310, and the *C minor*, recorded digitally in the following decade, are more controversial. The pianism is masterly, as one would expect from this great artist, but both performances strike one as the product of excessive ratiocination. There is no want of inner life, the texture is wonderfully clean and finely balanced, but the listener is too aware of the mental preparation that has gone into it. The first movement of the *A minor* has immaculate control but is more than a little schoolmasterly, particularly in the development. The staccato markings in the slow movement are exaggerated and the movement as a whole is unsmiling and strangely wanting in repose. Brendel seems unwilling to seduce us by beauty of sound, and the result is self-conscious playing, immaculately recorded. Fortunately he is back on form in the *Fantasia in C minor*, the *Rondo* and the *Variations*.

Piano sonatas No. 8 in A min., K.310; 11 in A, K.331; 15 in F, K.533.

✽ *** Sony Dig. SK 48233 [id.]. Murray Perahia.

Murray Perahia celebrated his return to the recording studios after a sabbatical with this recital, which is the finest Mozart sonata record for some years. Such is his artistry that one is never consciously aware of it. Again we have the old story of the search for truth producing beauty almost as a by-product. Nothing is beautified, nor does he shrink from conveying that hint of pain that fleetingly disturbs the symmetry of the slow movements. The Sony engineers provide excellent sound. Here is one of the records that will be reissued in 2010 or thereabouts as a 'Great Recording of the Last Century'.

Piano sonatas Nos. 12 in F, K.332; 13 in B flat, K.333; 14 in C min., K.457; Fantasy in C min.
*** Sony Dig. SK 46748 [id.]. Andreas Haefliger.

The Swiss-born, Juilliard-trained Andreas Haefliger is still in his twenties and shows himself to be an impressive Mozartian. These are finely poised and well-integrated performances with plenty of sensitivity. The Sony recording is very clean and firm. Eminently recommendable.

Piano sonata No. 17 in B flat, K.570.
(***) Testament mono SBT 1089 [id.]. Emil Gilels – CHOPIN: *Sonata No. 2;* SHOSTAKOVICH: *Preludes and fugues Nos. 1, 5 & 24.* (***)

The *B flat Sonata* was recorded in Paris at the Théâtre des Champs-Elysées in March 1954. The sound is a little dry and close, but the playing has a simplicity and poetry that completely transcend sonic limitations.

Complete Mozart Edition, Volume 18: *8 Variations in G, K.24; 7 Variations in D, K.25; 12 Variations in C, K.179; 6 Variations in G, K.180; 9 Variations in C, K.264; 12 Variations in C, K.265; 8 Variations in F, K.352; 12 Variations in E flat, K.353; 12 Variations in E flat, K.354; 6 Variations in F, K.398; 10 Variations in G, K.455; 12 Variations in B flat, K.500; 9 Variations in D, K.573; 8 Variations in F, K.613; Adagio in B min., K.540; Eine kleine Gigue in G, K.574; Fantasia in D min., K.397; Minuet in D, K.355; Rondos: in D, K.485; in A min., K.511; 21 Pieces for keyboard, K.1, K.1a–1d; 1f; K.2–5; K.5a; K.33b; K.94; K.312; K.394–5; K.399–401; K.408/1; K.453a; K.460.*
(M) ** Ph. Analogue/Dig. 422 518-2 (5) [id.]. Ingrid Haebler or Mitsuko Uchida (both piano), Ton Koopman (harpsichord).

Ingrid Haebler is an intelligent and perceptive artist who characterizes these variations with some subtlety. The quality of the sound is very good indeed: there is both warmth and presence. Mitsuko Uchida gives us various short pieces, such as the *A minor Rondo*, K.511, and the *B minor Adagio*, K.540, which she plays beautifully – though at less than 40 minutes her disc offers rather short measure. However, Haebler and Koopman make up for that, the latter offering 21 short pieces, including some juvenilia, which are very brightly recorded.

ORGAN MUSIC

Andante in F, K.616; Fantasia in F min. (Adagio and allegro), K.594; Fantasia in F min. (Allegro and Andante), K.608 (all for musical clock; ed. Trotter). *Adagio in C, K.356* (originally for glass harmonica). Organ pieces: *Adagio in B min., K.40; Andantino in E flat, K.236; Fugue in C min., K.401; Gigue in G, K.574; Prelude (Fantasia) and fugue in C, K.394; Suite, K.399: Overture. Molto allegro in G, K.72a; 4 Pieces from London Notebook, K.15.*
*** Decca (IMS) Dig. 443 451-2. Thomas Trotter (organ of Nederlands Hervormde Kerk, Farsum).

Mozart is never really thought of as a composer for the organ, but he loved its challenge and, whenever he travelled, always made the point of seeking out a local instrument. The problem for us was that he liked best of all to improvise and seldom wrote anything down. Until now, the only 'organ works' we have had on record have been the three pieces he wrote for Count Deym's mechanical organ attached to a clock. Mozart had no opinion of the mechanism for which his music was commissioned and is known to have wished the pieces were intended for a large instrument. These two major *Fantasias* sound quite splendid on the Dutch organ here and Thomas Trotter plays them with great flair, while he finds an entirely suitable registration for the ocarina-like *Andante*, K.616, with its charming decorative effects. The *Adagio for glass harmonica* is also sweetly evoked. Of the other pieces, four are engagingly simple miniatures from the Notebook of Mozart's first juvenile visit to London in 1764. The other, much later, works include a splendid *Fugue in G minor*, K.401, which he finished, all but the eight-bar coda, later added by Stadler; and there is also a lollipop *Gigue in G major*, K.574, written for the Court organist in Dresden, probably in 1789. But the most remarkable remaining piece here is the masterly *Prelude and fugue in C*, K.394, whose dazzling passage-work reminds one just a little of Bach's most famous *D minor Toccata*, although the joyous bravura style is all Mozart's own. It is an extraordinary piece, and Thomas Trotter's account of it is a *tour de force*. The recording is wonderfully vivid, sonorous and clear.

VOCAL MUSIC

Complete Mozart Edition, Volume 22: (i) *Adagio and fugue in C min., K.546; Maurerische Trauermusik, K.477;* (ii) *La Betulia liberata* (oratorio), *K.118;* (iii) *Davidde penitente* (cantata), *K.469;* (iv) *Grabmusik (Funeral music), K.42;* (v; i) Masonic music: *Dir, Seele des Weltalls, K.429; Ihr unsre neuen Leiter, K.484; Die ihr unermesslichen Weltalls Schöpfer, ehrt, K.619; Lasst uns mit geschlung'gnen Händen, K.623; Laut verkünde unsre Freude, K.623; Lied zur Gesellenreise, K.468; Lobgesang auf die feierliche Johannisloge, K.148; Die Maurerfreude, K.471; Zerfliesset heut, geliebte*

Brüder, K.483; (vi) *Passionslied: Kommet her, ihr frechen Sünder, K.146;* (vii) *Die Schuldigkeit des ersten Gebots* (Singspiel), K.35.

(M) **(*) Ph. Analogue/Dig. 422 522-2 (6) [id.]. (i) Dresden State O, Schreier; (ii) Schreier, Cotrubas, Berry, Fuchs, Zimmermann, Salzburg Chamber Ch. & Mozarteum O, Hager; (iii) M. Marshall, Vermillion, Blochwitz; (iv) Murray, Varcoe; (v) Schreier, Blochwitz, Schmidt, Leipzig R. Ch.; (vi) Murray; (vii) M. Marshall, Murray, Nielsen, Blochwitz, Baldin; (iii; iv; vi; vii) Stuttgart RSO, Marriner.

The two big oratorios are both early works, *La Betulia liberata* and (even earlier, dating from his twelfth year) *Die Schuldigkeit des ersten Gebots* ('The Duty of the First Commandment'). *Davidde penitente* is the cantata largely derived from the torso of the *C minor Mass*, while the sixth disc, in many ways the most inspired of all, contains the Masonic music, vividly done in Dresden under the direction of Peter Schreier. For convenience that disc also includes the purely instrumental Masonic music, the *Maurerische Trauermusik* and the *Adagio and fugue in C minor*. Directed by Leopold Hager, *La Betulia liberata* is a plain, well-sung performance that does not quite disguise the piece's excessive length. Sir Neville Marriner is the conductor both of *Die Schuldigkeit* and of *Davidde penitente*, giving sparkle to the early oratorio and vigour to the cantata, a fine piece. Full texts are given, and informative notes on individual works.

Complete Mozart Edition, Volume 20: (i) *Alma Dei creatoris, K.277;* (ii) *Ave verum corpus, K.618;* (i) *Benedictus sit Deus Pater, K.117; Cibavit eos ex adipe frumenti, K.44;* (iii) *Dixit et Magnificat, K.193;* (i) *Ergo interest, an quis, K.143;* (ii) *Exsultate jubilate, K.165;* (i) *God is our refuge* (motet), *K.20; Inter natos Mulierum, K.72;* (iii) *Litaniae de BMV (Lauretanae), K.109 & K.195;* (i) *Kyries, K.33; K.90–91; K.322–3;* (ii) *Kyrie, K.341;* (iii) *Litaniae de venerabili altaris sacramento, K.125 & K.243;* (i) *Miserere mei, Deus, K.85; Misercordias Domini, K.222; Quaerite primum regnum Dei, K.86; Regina coeli, laetare, K.108; K.127; K.276; Sancta Maria, mater Dei, K.273; Scande coeli limina, K.34; Sub tuum praesidium, K.198; Te Deum laudamus, K.141; Veni, Sancte Spiritus, K.47; Venite, populi, venite, K.260;* (ii) *Vesperae solennes de confessore, K.339;* (iii) *Vesperae solennes de Domenica, K.321.*

(M) *** Ph. 422 520-2 (5) [id.]. (i) Nawe, Reinhardt-Kiss, Schellenberger-Ernst, Selbig, Burmeister, Lang, Büchner, Eschrig, Ribbe, Pape, Polster; (ii) Te Kanawa, Bainbridge, Ryland Davies, Howell, London Symphony Ch. & LSO, Sir Colin Davis; (iii) Frank-Reinecke, Shirai, Burmeister, Riess, Büchner, Polster; (i; iii) Leipzig R. Ch. & SO, Kegel.

It is fascinating to find that the boy Mozart's very first religious piece is an unaccompanied motet, written in London to an English text, *God is our refuge*. Herbert Kegel with the Dresden Staatskapelle and his Leipzig Radio Choir are responsible for the great majority of the pieces here, fresh and alert if on occasion rhythmically too rigid. The big exception is the great setting of the *Solemn vespers*, K.339, for which Sir Colin Davis's 1971 version has understandably been preferred, when the young Kiri Te Kanawa sings the heavenly soprano setting of *Laudate Dominum* so ravishingly. She is also the soloist in the early cantata *Exsultate jubilate* with its brilliant *Alleluia*. Those 1971 recordings, made in London, are bass-heavy, but the rest brings very fresh and clean recording, with the choir generally more forwardly placed than in the recordings of Mozart's Masses, made by the same forces.

Complete Mozart Edition, Volume 23: (i) *2 Canons for strings; 14 Canons for woodwind; 10 Interval canons for woodwind;* (ii) *6 Canons for female voices; 3 Canons for mixed voices; 13 Canons for male voices; 4 puzzle canons for mixed voices;* (iii) *53 Concert arias. Aria* (with ornamentation by Mozart) for: J. C. BACH: *Adriano in Siria;* (iv) *8 Vocal Duets, Trios and Quartets;* (v) Alternative arias and duets for: *Così fan tutte; Don Giovanni; Die Entführung aus dem Serail; La finta semplice; Idomeneo; Lucio Silla; Mitridate; Le nozze di Figaro.*

(M) *** Ph. 422 523-2 (8) [id.]. (i) Bav. RSO (members); (ii) Ch. Viennensis, Mancusi or Harrer; (iii) Moser, Schwarz, Popp, Mathis, Gruberová, Sukis, Araiza, Ahnsjö, Lloyd, Berry, Kaufmann, Blochwitz, Lind, Burrows, Eda-Pierre; (iv) Blochwitz, Schariner, Pape, Kaufmann, Lind, Jansen, Schreier; (v) Blochwitz, Szmytka, Wiens, Gudbjörnson, Vermillion, Schreier, Mathis, Burrows, Tear, Terfel, Kaufmann, Lind, Scharinger.

This Philips set offers not just a collection of a dozen or so ensembles and a whole disc of 35 canons (some of them instrumental) but also some fascinating alternative versions and substitute arias for different Mozart operas, from *La finta semplice* and *Mitridate* through to the three Da Ponte masterpieces. It is fascinating to have Bryn Terfel, for example, as Figaro in a varied recitative and slightly extended version of the Act I aria, *Non piu' andrai*. Eva Lind is vocally a less happy choice for the items involving Susanna and Zerlina, and generally the sopranos chosen for this collection, stylish Mozartians as they are, have less sumptuous voices than those on the Decca set.

Complete Mozart Edition, Volume 24: (i) Lieder: *Abendempfindung; Als Luise die Briefe ihres ungetreuen Liebhabers; Die Alte; An Chloe; An die Freude; An die Freundschaft; Die betrogene Welt; Dans un bois solitaire; Geheime Liebe; Der Frühling; Gessellenreise; Die grossmütige Gelassenheit; Ich würd' auf meinem Pfad; Das Kinderspiel; 2 Kirchenlieder (O Gottes Lamm; Als aus Agypten); Des kleinen Friedrichs Geburtstag; Die kleine Spinnerin; Komm, liebe Zither, komm; Lied der Freiheit; Das Lied der Trennung; Un moto di gioia; Oiseaux, si tous les ans; Ridente la calma; Sehnsucht nach dem Frühling; Sei du mein Trost; Das Traumbild; Das Veilchen; Verdankt sei es dem Glanz der Grossen; Die Verschweigung; Warnung; Wie unglücklich bin ich nit; Der Zauberer; Die Zufriedenheit (2): (Was frag' ich viel nach Geld und Gut; Wie sanft, wie ruhig fühl' ich hier); Die Zufriedenheit im niedrigen Stande;* (ii) *6 Notturni for voices and woodwind, K.346; K.436/9 & K.549.*

(M) *** Ph. 422 524-2 (2) [id.]. Elly Ameling, (i) with Dalton Baldwin (piano or organ) or Benny Ludemann (mandolin); (ii) with Elisabeth Cooymans, Peter van der Bilt, Netherlands Wind Ens. (members).

Elly Ameling is the ideal soprano for such fresh and generally innocent inspirations, with her voice at its purest and sweetest when she made the recordings in 1977. In the 1973 recordings of the *Notturni* (setting Italian texts by Metastasio) she is well matched by her soprano and baritone partners, though these are mostly plainer, less distinctive miniatures. Included are two hymns with organ and two tiny songs with mandolin, while aptly the very last of the series, K.598, is one of the lightest of all, *Children's games*, sparklingly done. The recordings come up with fine freshness and presence.

Songs: *Abendempfindung; Als Luise die Briefe; An Chloe; Die betrogene Welt; Dans un bois solitaire; Komm, liebe Zither; Oiseaux, si tous les ans; Sehnsucht nach dem Frühling; Der Zauberer.*

*** DG Dig. 447 106-2. Anne Sofie von Otter, Melvyn Tan (fortepiano) – HAYDN: Songs. ***

A delightful recital in all respects. There is a winning charm in the opening *Komm, liebe Zither*, and *Oiseaux, si tous les ans* is hardly less appealing. Melvyn Tan accompanies most sensitively and – as so often with this artist – makes one feel that nothing other than a fortepiano could have been used to give these songs the right lift. The balance seems just about ideal, and the Haydn couplings are equally pleasing.

51 Concert arias.

(B) *** Decca 455 241-2 (5) [id.]. Kiri Te Kanawa, Edita Gruberová, Teresa Berganza, Krisztina Laki, Elfrieda Hobarth, Gösta Winbergh; VCO, György Fischer; or LSO, John Pritchard; Dietrich Fischer-Dieskau, V. Haydn O, Reinhard Peters; Fernando Corena, ROHCG, Argeo Quadri.

This very comprehensive coverage is based on a five-LP Decca set of the complete concert arias for female voice, published in 1981, to which those for male voice have subsequently been added. The use of the Kingsway Hall or Vienna Sofiensaal has ensured full, spacious recording. Originally each of five female artists was given a record apiece, which means that the order of items is arbitrary. Berganza's collection includes the most demanding soprano aria of all, *Ch'io me scordi di te*, recorded (with Pritchard and the LSO) a decade earlier than the rest. Te Kanawa opens the programme, and her items range from one of the very earliest arias, *Oh temerario Arbace!*, already memorably lyrical, to the late *Vado, ma dove?* Gruberová's contribution is hardly less brilliant and charming, her singing full of sparkle and character, and superbly articulated. The others, Elfrieda Hobarth and Krisztina Laki, are less individual personalities but do not disappoint vocally. Laki immediately displays a delightfully fresh voice with a true, clear upper range and impressive coloratura in her opening aria, the little-known *Fra cento affanni*, K.88, and she is equally impressive in the lyrical flow of *Non curo l'affetto*, which again demands comparable bravura. Elfrieda Hobarth's style is more operatic and she becomes a veritable Queen of the Night in tackling the fearsome upper tessitura of *Ma che vi fece, o stelle*, K.368, and *Mia speranza adorata!*, K.416, both of which are accomplished with confident bravado. If she displays less in the way of seductive charm, this is still remarkably well-focused singing.

The digital recordings by Gösta Winbergh, an exceptionally stylish Mozart tenor, were added later; he rises splendidly to the challenges of such splendid arias as *Per pietà non ricercate*, K.420, and *Aura che intorno spiri*, K.431, using his clean, heady tenor very effectively if without the final degree of personal charisma. Throughout the series György Fischer's conducting is lively and responsive but is sometimes lacking in detail. Fischer-Dieskau's contribution was a separate undertaking, recorded in 1969, and it includes a beautiful aria from 1787, *Mentre ti lascio*, which reveals Mozart's inspiration at its keenest. The other items too bring their delights. Fischer-Dieskau sings most intelligently and Fernando Corena's three contributions were among the first of any Mozart arias to be recorded in stereo, in 1960. In *Alcandro, lo confesso . . . Non so d'onde viene*, K.512, and *Per questa bella mano*, K.612 (which includes a virtuoso double bass solo in the orchestra), he is less than ideally stylish and in the latter not always absolutely secure in intonation. Admittedly, some of the florid passages are fiendishly difficult for a bass to cope with but, when strained, Corena has a tendency to slide between the notes to ungainly effect. Yet he is at his very finest in the *buffo* aria, *Rivolcete a lui lo sguardo*, K.584, originally written for *Così fan tutte* and later cut because of its length. It is a superb piece which Alfred Einstein called 'the most remarkable *buffo* aria ever written', and it suits Corena's voice well, so that the full power is brought out magnificently. The CD transfers throughout are of high quality, and full translations are included, but the accompanying essay by Kenneth Chalmers documents the music only sketchily, because of limited space.

Concert arias: *Ah! lo previdi . . . Ah, t'invola, K.272; Alma grande e nobil core, K.578; A questo seno . . . Or che il cielo, K.374; Bella mia fiamma . . . Resta, o cara, K.528; Betracht dies Herz und frage mich, K.42; Misera, dove son! . . . Ah! non son io che parlo, K.369; Vado, ma dove? o Dei!, K.583.*

(M) *** DG 449 723-2 [id.]. Gundula Janowitz, VSO, Wilfried Boettcher.

In 1966 when this recording was made (in the Grosser Saal of the Vienna Musikverein) Gundula Janowitz's voice combined a glorious tonal beauty with a surprising degree of flexibility so that Mozart's cruelly difficult divisions – usually written deliberately to tax the original ladies involved – present no apparent difficulty. Janowitz is helped by a flattering, reverberant acoustic, but there is no mistaking the singer's ability to shade and refine the tone at will. An excellent collection of delightful concert arias that are too often neglected nowadays, thanks to the vagaries of modern concert-planning.

Concert arias: *Ah! lo previdi . . . Ah t'invola, K.272; Bella mia fiamma . . . Resta oh cara, K.528; Chi sa, K.582; Nehmt meinen Dank, ihr holden Gönner, K.383; Non più, tutto ascolta . . . Non temer, amato bene, K.490; Oh temerario Arbace! . . . Per quel paterno amplesso, K.79/ K.73d; Vado, ma dove?, K.583.* Opera arias: (ii) *Le nozze di Figaro: Porgi amor; E Susanna non vien! . . . Dove sono;* (iii) *Der Schauspieldirektor: Bester Jüngling!*

(M) *** Decca 440 401-2 [id.]. Kiri Te Kanawa: (i) V. CO, György Fischer; (ii) LPO, Solti; (iii) VPO, Pritchard.

Kiri Te Kanawa's Decca set of Mozart's concert arias for soprano, recorded in 1982, makes a beautiful and often brilliant recital. Items range from one of the very earliest arias, *Oh temerario Arbace!*, already memorably lyrical, to the late *Vado, ma dove*, here sung for its beauty rather than for its drama. Atmospheric, wide-ranging recording, which has transferred well to CD. The arias from *Figaro* and *Schauspieldirektor* come from the complete Decca sets and show the singer at her finest.

Concert arias: *Alcandro, io confeso, K.512; Così dunque tradici, K.432; Mentre ti lascio, K.513; Per questa bella mano, K.612; Rivolgete a lui, K.584.* Opera arias from: *Don Giovanni; Le nozze di Figaro; Die Zauberflöte.*

(N) *** RCA Dig. 09026 61428-2 [id.]. Thomas Quasthoff, Württemberg CO, Faerber.

Thomas Quasthoff's bass-baritone is among the most beautiful ever, rich, firm and heroic, far more lyrical and cleanly projected than one expects of a voice in such a dark register. It is fascinating here to have him interpreting concert arias with operatic point and light of eye, as well as portraying a range of the Mozart characters we know – Figaro's Act IV aria biting yet still beautiful, Don Giovanni and Leporello delightfully contrasted, not just Papageno but Sarastro too. The tragedy is that Quasthoff's disability as a thalidomide victim must prevent him from taking these roles on stage, but recording is different, and one hopes for many more revelations to come.

Concert arias: *Alma grande e nobil core, K.578; Ch'io mi scordi di te?, K.505; Nehmt meinen Dank, K.383; Vado, ma dove?, K.583.* Lieder: *Abendempfindung; Als Luise die Briefe; Die Alte; An Chloë; Dans un bois solitaire; Im Frühlingsanfang; Das Kinderspiel; Die kleine Spinnerin; Das Lied der Trennung; Oiseaux, si tous les ans; Ridente la calma; Sehnsucht nach dem Frühling; Das Trumbild; Das Veilchen; Der Zauberer; Die Zuhfriedenheit.*

(M) *** EMI mono/stereo CDH7 63702-2 [id.]. Schwarzkopf, Gieseking; Brendel; LSO, Szell.

Schwarzkopf's classic series of the Mozart songs with Gieseking makes a splendid reissue at mid-price; it includes the most famous one, *Das Veilchen*. As a generous coupling, the disc also includes Schwarzkopf's much later recordings, with Szell conducting four concert arias – including the most taxing of all, *Ch'io mi scordi di te?*, with Brendel playing the piano obbligato. Though the voice is not quite so fresh in the concert arias, the artistry and imagination are supreme, and stereo recording helps to add bloom.

Concert arias: *A questo seno deh vieni...Or che il cielo, K.374; Ah, lo previdi! . . . Ah, t'invola agl'occhi miei . . . Deh, non vacar, K.272; Bella mia fiamma . . . Resta oh, cara, K.528; Clarice cara, K.256; Miserero! O sogno . . . Aura che intorni spiri, K.431; Se ai labbro mio non credi, K.295; Si mostra la sorte, K.209; Va dai furor portata, K.211 Voi avete un cor fedele, K.217.*

(N) (BB) *** Virgin Veritas Dig. Double VBD5 61573-2 (2). Lena Lootens, Christoph Prégardien, La Petite Bande, Kuijken – MOZART: *Horn concertos.* ***

This is a highly authentic collection of concert arias, several comparatively rare, divided between two fine artists, who not only have appealing voices, but understand about period style, and ornamentation.

Lena Lootens produces nimble coloratura (as in the engaging *Voi avete un cor fedele*) and can be dramatic or provide a lovely legato line, and in both respects Christophe Prégardien is consistently her equal. The accompaniments are fresh, the recording is vivid; but it was a curious idea to couple this programme with the *Horn concertos*, even though they are also first-rate period performances.

Arias: *Artaserse: Per pietà, bell'idol mio. Il barbiere di Siviglia: Schon lacht der holde Frühling* (arr. BEYER). *Demofoonte: Se tutti i mali miei. Didone abbandonata: Basta, vincesti . . . Ah, non lasciarmi. I due baroni di Rocca Azzura: Alma grande e nobil core. A questo seno deh vieni . . . Or che il cielo a me ti rende. Ezio: Misera, dove son? . . . Ah! non son io che parlo. Le nozze di Dorina: Voi avete un cor fedele. Le nozze di Figaro: Un moto di gioia.* Arias from: *Der Schauspieldirektor; Die Entführung aus dem Serail.*
(M) *** Decca Analogue/Dig. 448 249-2 [id.]. Edita Gruberová, VCO, Fischer.

This collection comes from the above Decca box, covering all the Mozart arias and concert arias for soprano, which first appeared at the beginning of the 1980s (see above). It brings brilliant and charming performances from Gruberová. Among the other rare items it includes an alternative aria for Susanna in *Figaro*, *Un moto di gioia*. The excerpts from *Der Schauspieldirektor* and *Die Entführung* come from much later but are also impressively sung.

Concert arias: *Bella mia fiamma . . . Resta, o cara!, K.528; Ch'io mi scordi di te?, K.505.* Arias: *Don Giovanni: Or sai chi l'onore; Crudele! Ah, no, mio bene; Non mi dir. Idomeneo: Se il padre perdei; O smania! . . . D'Oreste e d'Ajace. Le nozze di Figaro: Porgi, amor; Deh vieni non tardar; E Susanna non vien! . . . Dove sono. Il re pastore: L'amerò, sarò costante. Die Zauberflöte: Ach, ich fühl's.*
(M) *** RCA 09026 61357-2 [id.]. Leontyne Price, New Philh. O, Adler or Santi; RCA Italiana Op. O, Molinari-Pradelli; LSO, Downes.

This record is an adjunct to Leontyne Price's four-disc miscellaneous 'Prima donna' collection and the items here make an equally outstanding representation of her art. One does not think of her primarily as a Mozartian, yet the very opening concert aria, *Ch'io mi scordi*, shows the extra dimension of drama in her vocal personality. She is thrilling as Electra and *Or sai chi l'onore* (*Don Giovanni*) is scarcely less vehement. The glorious legato line is heard at its most ravishing in the major *Figaro* arias, whether as Susanna (*Deh vieni*) or the Countess (*Dove sono*), and the excerpt from *Il rè pastore, L'amerò, sarò costante*, with its weaving violin obbligato, is radiant. Nearly all these recordings were made in the late 1960s, when the voice was at its freshest. Accompaniments are highly sympathetic and the vocal quality is most natural and vivid, and with lovely orchestral sound.

Ave verum corpus, K.618; Exsultate, jubilate, K.165; Kyrie in D minor, K.341; Vesperae solennes de confessore in C, K.339.
**(*) Ph. 412 873-2 [id.]. Te Kanawa, Bainbridge, Ryland Davies, Howell, London Symphony Ch., LSO, C. Davis.

This disc could hardly present a more delightful collection of Mozart choral music, ranging from the early soprano cantata, *Exsultate, jubilate*, with its famous setting of *Alleluia*, to the equally popular *Ave verum*. Kiri Te Kanawa is the brilliant soloist in the cantata, and her radiant account of the lovely *Laudate Dominum* is one of the highspots of the *Solemn vespers*, here given a fine, responsive performance. The 1971 recording has been remastered effectively, although the choral sound is not ideally focused.

(i–ii) *Ave verum corpus, K.618;* (iii–iv) *Exsultate, jubilate, K.165; Masses Nos.* (i–iii; v) *10 in C (Missa brevis): Spatzenmesse, K.220;* (ii–iii; vi) *16 in C (Coronation), K.317.*
(M) *** DG 419 060-2. (i) Regensburg Cathedral Ch.; (ii) Bav. RSO, Kubelik; (iii) Edith Mathis; (iv) Dresden State O, Klee; (v) Troyanos, Laubenthal, Engen; (vi) Procter, Grobe, Shirley-Quirk, Bav. R. Ch.

Kubelik draws a fine, vivid performance of the *Coronation Mass* from his Bavarian forces and is no less impressive in the earlier *Missa brevis*, with excellent soloists in both works. Then Edith Mathis gives a first-class account of the *Exsultate, jubilate* as an encore. The concert ends with Bernard Klee directing a serenely gentle account of the *Ave verum corpus* (recorded in 1979).

Concert arias: (i) *Ch'io mi scordi di te? Nehmt meinen Dank, ihr holden Gönner!, K. 383; Vo, avete un cor fedele, K.21; Il re pastore: Aer tranquillo e di sereni;* (ii) *L'amerò, sarò costante* (with Christopher Hirons, violin). *Zaïde: Ruhe sanft, mein holdes Leben; Trostios schluchzet Philomele.*
(N) (B) *** Decca Double 458 084-2 (2) [id.]. Emma Kirkby, AAM, Hogwood; (i) with Stephen Lubin (fortepiano); (ii) Christopher Hirons – RECITAL ***

This delightful recital, recorded in 1988–9, is admirably suited to Emma Kirkby's sweetly confident line and dazzling coloratura. She is ideally cast as Amita (originally a castrato role) in *Il re pastore* and as the heroine of *Zaïde*. Indeed her rapturous line in *L'amerò, sarò costante* is fully worthy of Mozart's imaginative accompaniment (including violin obbligato). She is a compellingly passionate

Andromeda in projecting the pain and rage of *Ah, lo previdi*, and very touching in the equally ambitious, but more expressive *Ch'io mi scordi di te?* Here Stephen Lubin contributes the fortepiano accompaniment, which Mozart himself played at its first performance in Vienna by Nancy Storace (who created the role of Susanna in *Le nozze di Figaro*). Hogwood's accompaniments are both stylish and warmly, dramatically supportive, and the Walthamstow recording has a fine, spacious bloom. This is part of a desirable Decca Double, including music by Arne, Handel, Haydn and Lampe (see Vocal Recitals below).

Exsultate, jubilate, K.165 (Salzburg version); Motets: *Ergo interest, K.143; Regina coeli* (2 settings), *K.108, K.127.*
*** O-L Dig. 411 832-2 [id.]. Emma Kirkby, Westminster Cathedral Boys' Ch., AAM Ch. and O, Hogwood.

The boyish, bell-like tones of Emma Kirkby are perfectly suited to the most famous of Mozart's early cantatas, *Exsultate, jubilate*, culminating in a dazzling account of *Alleluia*. With accompaniment on period instruments, that is aptly coupled with far rarer but equally fascinating examples of Mozart's early genius, superbly recorded.

(i) *Exsultate jubilate, K.165;* (ii) *Litaniae Lauretanae in D, K.195; Mass No. 16 (Coronation), K.317;* (iii) *Requiem mass (No. 19) in D min., K.626.*
(B) **(*) Double Decca 443 009-2 (2) [id.]. (i) Erna Spoorenberg; (ii; iii) Cotrubas, Watts, Tear, Shirley-Quirk; (ii) Oxford Schola Cantorum; (iii) ASMF Ch; (i–iii), ASMF, Marriner.

It is good to have Marriner's 1971 (Argo) recordings of two of Mozart's most appealing early choral works, the *Litaniae Lauretanae* and the *Coronation Mass*, back in the catalogue on this Double Decca set. The solo work is particularly good (notably Ileana Cotrubas in the two lovely *Agnus Dei* versions) and the Academy Choir is on its best form. Erna Spoorenberg's impressive *Exsultate jubilate* was recorded earlier (1966). However, Marriner generates less electricity than usual in the coupled (1977) *Requiem Mass*. It is interesting to have a version which uses the Beyer Edition and a text which aims at removing the faults of Süssmeyr's completion. Solo singing is good, and some of the choruses (the *Dies irae*, for instance) are vibrant, but at other times they are less alert and the tension slackens. The sound is excellent, well balanced and vivid.

(i) *Litaniae Lauretanae in D, K.195;* (ii; iii) *Litaniae de venerabili altaris sacramento, K.243;* (iii; iv) *Mass No. 12 in C (Spaur), K.259;* (iii; iv) *Vesperae solennes de confessore, K.339;* (ii; iii) *Vesperae solennes de Domenica, K.321.*
(N) (B) *** Decca Double 458 379-2 (2) [id.]. (i) Cotrubas, Watts, Tear, Shirley-Quirk, Oxford Schola Cantorum, ASMF, Marriner; (ii) Marshall, Cable, Evans, Roberts; (iii) St John's College, Cambridge, Ch., Wren O, Guest; (iv) Palmer, Cable, Langridge, Roberts.

Readers will note that Marriner's performance of the *Litaniae Lauretanae in D,* K.195, is also available on another Decca Double (see above). However, many collectors may prefer the present programme. Mozart made four settings of the Litany of which the *Litaniae de venerabili altaris sacramento* is the last, written in 1776. It is ambitiously scored for an orchestra of double wind, two horns and three trombones – used to add sonorous gravity to many of the choral passages and to bring point and drama to the choral fugue, *Pignus futurae gloriae*; in the beautiful *Dulcissimum convivium* the solo soprano is accompanied with flutes, added to the orchestra in the place of the oboes. It is Mozart at his most imaginative and vital; the artists here rise to the occasion and give a highly responsive performance, with Margaret Marshall outstanding among the soloists. The *Spaur Mass* is not among Mozart's most inspired, but its directness is appealing and the *Benedictus* offers a fine Mozartian interplay of chorus and soloists. In Guest's vigorous performance it is very enjoyable. The vibrant *Vesperae solennes de Domenica* opens with a series of brilliant choral settings (with contrasting solo quartet), accompanied by trumpet and strings. Margaret Marshall is appropriately agile in the lively soprano solo of the *Laudate Dominum*, and the work closes with an ambitious *Magnificat*, in which all the participants are joined satisfyingly together. The collection is completed with the masterly *Vesperae solennes de confessore*, and although Guest's account does not always match Sir Colin Davis's Philips version (see above under *Ave verum corpus*) – with Felicity Palmer a less poised soloist than Kiri Te Kanawa – the Decca has the advantage of authenticity in the use of boys in the chorus. Moreover the CD transfer of these (originally Argo) recordings offers a brighter, sharper focus than the less well-defined Philips sound.

Masonic music (see also above, in Complete Mozart Edition, Volume 22)

Masonic music: *Masonic funeral music (Maurerische Trauermusik), K.477; Die ihr des unermesslichen Weltals Schöpfer ehrt* (cantata), *K.619; Die ihr einen neuen Grade, K.468; Dir, Seele des Weltalls* (cantata), *K.429; Ihr unsre neuen Leiter* (song), *K.484; Lasst uns mit geschlungnen Händen, K.623a; Laut verkünde unsre Freude, K.623; O heiliges Band* (song),

K.148; Sehen, wie dem starren Forscherange, K.471; Zerfliesset heut', geliebte Brüder, K.483.

(M) *** Decca (IMS) 425 722-2. Werner Krenn, Tom Krause, Edinburgh Festival Ch., LSO, Kertész.

This Decca reissue contains the more important of Mozart's masonic music in first-class performances, admirably recorded. Most striking of all is Kertész's strongly dramatic account of the *Masonic funeral music*; the two lively songs for chorus, *Zerfliesset heut'* and *Ihr unsre neuen Leiter*, are sung with warm humanity and are also memorable. Indeed the choral contribution is most distinguished throughout, and Werner Krenn's light tenor is most appealing in the other items which he usually dominates.

Complete Mozart Edition, Volume 19: *Masses Nos. 1 in G (Missa brevis), K.49; 2 in D min. (Missa brevis), K.65; 3 in C ('Dominicus'), K.66; 4 in C min. (Weisenhaus), K.139; 5 in G (Pastoral), K.140; 6 in F (Missa brevis), K.192; 7 in C (Missa in honorem Ssmae Trinitatis), K.167; 9 in D (Missa brevis), K.194; 10 in C (Spatzenmesse; 'Sparrow Mass'), K.220; 11 in C ('Credo'), K.257; 12 in C (Spaur-Messe), K.258; 13 in C ('Organ solo'), K.259; 14 in C (Missa longa), K.262; 15 in B flat (Missa brevis), K.275; 16 in C ('Coronation'), K.317; 17 in C (Missa solemnis), K.337; 18 in C min. (Great), K.427; 19 in D min. (Requiem), K.626.*

(M) **(*) Ph. Analogue/Dig. 422 519-2 (9) [id.]. Mathis, Donath, M. Price, McNair, Montague, Shirai, Casapietra, Trudeliese Schmidt, Lang, Schiml, Markert, Burmeister, Knight, Schreier, Araiza, Heilmann, Baldin, Ryland Davies, Rolfe Johnson, Ude, Jelosits, Adam, Polster, Andreas Schmidt, Hauptmann, Rootering, Grant, Eder; Leipzig R. Ch.; Monteverdi Ch.; V. Boys' Ch.; John Alldis Ch.; Ch. Viennensis; Leipzig RSO; E. Bar. Soloists; Dresden State O; LSO; VSO; Dresden PO; Kegel; C. Davis; Gardiner; Schreier; Harrer.

Only the *C minor Mass* has period performers. John Eliot Gardiner's inspired reading, with superb soloists as well as his Monteverdi Choir and English Baroque Soloists, has rightly been chosen, and the *Requiem* comes in another outstanding modern version, with the Dresden Staatskapelle and Leipzig Radio Choir conducted by Peter Schreier, as imaginative a conductor as he is a tenor. That same choir and orchestra under the choir's regular conductor, Herbert Kegel, is responsible for the great bulk of the rest of the Masses. With the chorus tending to be placed a little backwardly, it does not always sound its freshest, but performances – with consistently clean-toned soloists, including latterly Mitsuko Shirai – are bright and well sprung. Sir Colin Davis and the LSO in the earliest recording here, dating from 1971, take a weightier view than any in the *Credo Mass*, K.257, with sound bass-heavy, but again his vigour and freshness are very compelling. Two favourite Masses, the *Coronation Mass* and the *Spatzenmesse* (Sparrow Mass), come in performances conducted by Uwe Christian Harrer with the Vienna Symphony Orchestra and the Vienna Boys' Choir; boys also distinctively take the soprano and alto solos. Though Harrer's speeds tend to be slow, the rhythmic buoyancy is most compelling, with choral sound full and forward.

Mass No. 3 in C (Dominicus), K.66; Vesperae de Domenica, K.321.

(M) *** Teldec/Warner Dig. 2292 46469-2. Margiono, Bonney, Von Magnus, Heilmann, Cachemaille, Arnold Schoenberg Ch., V. Hofburgkapelle Choral Scholars, VCM, Harnoncourt.

Harnoncourt is at his finest in this splendidly lively Mass which the thirteen-year-old Mozart wrote for a personal friend ten years his senior when he took holy orders. It has sixteen brief jewels of movements, and the direct Harnoncourt style with its strong accents and positive characterization brings every one of them vividly to life. The bright tempi too are apt and the soloists equally strong. The more ambitious *Vesperae de Domenica*, written a decade later, with its plainsong introduction to each of six sections, forms a neat and joyful *Missa brevis*, here refreshingly alive and brimful of variety of invention. Again the singing of chorus and soloists alike is highly stimulating, and Harnoncourt's affection brings a committed and vivacious approach which is entirely successful. The recording is first rate.

Mass No. 4 in C min. (Weisenhausmesse), K.139.

(M) *** DG (IMS) 427 255-2. Janowitz, Von Stade, Moll, Ochman, V. State Op. Ch., VPO, Abbado.

(i; ii) *Mass No. 4 in C min. (Weisenhaus), K.139;* (i) *Exsultate jubilate, K.165.*

(M) **(*) Teldec/Warner Dig. 2292 44180-2 [id.]. (i) Barbara Bonney; (ii) Rappé, Protschka, Hagegård, Arnold Schoenberg Ch., VCM, Harnoncourt.

By any standards this is a remarkably sustained example of the thirteen-year-old composer's powers, with bustling allegros in the *Kyrie*, *Gloria* and *Credo*, as well as at the end of the *Agnus Dei*, while the *Gloria* and *Credo* end with full-scale fugues. This far from negligible piece sounds at its very best in Abbado's persuasive hands.

This lively early work responds to strong characterization and, with excellent soloists and vibrant choral singing, is another refreshing example of Harnoncourt's view of authenticity. Barbara Bonney's *Exsultate jubilate* is enjoyably bracing, though it is sung a semitone lower than in modern instrument performances. The sound is satisfactory. However, for those not insisting on original instruments Abbado's DG recording remains a more obvious first choice.

Masses Nos: (i–ii) *4 in C min. (Weisenhaus), K.139;* (iii) *7 in C (Missa in honorem Ssmae Trinitas), K.167;* (i–ii) *11 in C (Credo), K.257; 257;* (ii; iv) *16 in C (Coronation), K.317; 17 in C (Missa solemnis), K.337.*

(B) **(*) Decca Double 455 032-2 (2). (i) Susanne Mentzer, Bernadette Manca di Nissa, Neil Mackie, Stephen Roberts; (ii) King's College, Cambridge, Ch., ECO, Cleobury; (iii) V. State Op. Ch., VPO, Münchinger; (iv) with Margaret Marshall, Ann Murray, Rogers Covey-Crump, David Wilson-Johnson.

Mozart's early *C minor Mass* was composed for the dedication of a new orphanage church, the Waisenhausekirche am Rennweg, in 1768, and it is notable both for its rich choral writing and for the fine *Benedictus*, a dialogue between soprano and chorus. The tenor's *Agnus Dei* is then sonorously introduced by a trombone chorale, and all the soloists then join the chorus, with the trumpets entering resplendently for the *Amen*. It is presented here most effectively by Cleobury and his team. The *Missa Trinitas*, written in Salzburg five years later, is even more ambitious, using a big orchestra with copious brass (four trumpets and three trombones) as well as oboe, strings and organ. Münchinger offers a strong, direct account, but the disappointment of this 1974 recording, made in the Sofiensaal, is how little is made of the trumpets which, even in the *Credo*, are backwardly balanced. However, one does not want to make too much of this, for the choral singing is admirably fresh and beautifully recorded, and the overall balance with the orchestra is well judged. The other recordings are digital and were made a decade later. Stephen Cleobury, inheritor of the King's choral tradition in the 1980s, is perhaps at his finest in the *Credo Mass* and, with the help of his excellent soloists, gives a vividly exuberant performance of a work that shows its composer at his most sunnily high-spirited throughout. The *Missa solemnis in C major*, K.337, was the very last of the 15 settings that Mozart wrote for Salzburg, another work that is just as inspired as the better-known *Coronation Mass* (they were written for the Easter celebrations of 1779 and 1780), and with a similar anticipation of the Countess's music for *Figaro* in the *Agnes Dei* (reminding us of *Dove sono* in K.317, of *Porgi amor* in K.337). Though Cleobury's direction here could be rhythmically more lively, both performances are of high quality, with excellent soloists and fresh choral singing.

Masses Nos. (i) *10 in C (Missa brevis) K.220: Spatzenmesse*; (ii) *18 in C min. (Great) K.427*; (iii) *19 (Requiem) Mass in D min., K.626.*

(N) (B) **(*) DG Double Analogue/Dig. 459 409-2. (i) Mathis, Troyanos, Laubenthal, Engen, Regensburg Cathedral Ch., Bav. RSO, Kubelik; (ii) Battle, Cuberli, Seiffert, Moll, V. State Op. Konzertvereinigung, VPO, Levine; (iii) Tomowa-Sintow, Baltsa, Krenn, Van Dam, V. Singverein, VPO, Karajan.

Kubelik's direct but lively account of the *Missa brevis* does not disappoint: his soloists, led by Edith Mathis make a good team and the recording from the early 1970s is fresh and clear. (This is also available coupled with the *Ave verum corpus* and *Coronation mass* – see above.) Karajan's 1975 analogue recording of the *Requiem* is outstandingly fine, deeply committed. The toughness of his approach is established from the start with incisive playing and clean-focused singing from the chorus, not too large and set a little behind. The fine quartet of soloists too is beautifully blended, and through everything – whatever the creative source, Süssmayr or Mozart – the conductor superbly establishes a sense of unity. The reading has its moments of romantic expressiveness, but nothing is smoothed over and with splendidly vivid recording, such a passage as the *Dies irae* has exceptional freshness and intensity. Levine's recording of the *C minor Mass* is digital and dates from 1987, although for some reason it was not originally pubished until 1991. Perhaps DG had doubts about the tremulous soprano line in the chorus, which otherwise sings powerfully: *Gratias agimus tibi* is arresting, and the *Qui tollis peccata mundi* is monolithic in its remorseless progress. The soloists are individually impressive (Kathleen Battle shines in the *Laudamus te*), but the ensemble of the *Quoniam* is less than ideally polished, and the performance overall is a little rough round the edges. Yet the VPO adds an element of finesse and the music's emotional power is never in doubt, for Levine's reading has a compelling, spontaneous vigour. The recording too, is very live and vivid.

Mass No. 16 in C (Coronation), K.317.

(M) **(*) DG (IMS) Dig. 445 543-2 (2). Battle, Schmidt, Winbergh, Furlanetto, V. Singverein, VPO, Karajan – BEETHOVEN: *Missa solemnis.***(*)

(B) **(*) DG Double 453 016-2 (2) [423 913-2]. Tomowa-Sintow, Baltsa, Krenn, Van Dam, V. Singverein, BPO, Karajan – BEETHOVEN: *Missa solemnis.* ***

(N) (M) *** DG 457 744-2 [id.]. Stader, Dominguez, Haefliger, Roux, Brasseur Ch., LOP, Markevitch – CHERUBINI: *Requiem No. 2 in D min.* ***

(i) *Mass No. 16 in C (Coronation), K.317; Vesperae solennes de confessore, K.339;* (ii) *Epistle sonata in C, K.278/271e.*

*** O-L Dig. 436 585-2 [id.]. AAM, Hogwood, with (i) Kirkby, Robbin, Ainsley, George,

Winchester College Quiristers and Cathedral Ch.; (ii) Alastair Ross.

Oiseau-Lyre offers easily the finest CD, a coupling of the *Coronation Mass* and the *Vespers*, and indeed it is one of Hogwood's most succesful records. In using boy trebles he quite upstages Harnoncourt, and the choral singing has both vitality and a sense of joy. The soloists are an excellent team overall, but it is Emma Kirkby's glorious contributions one remembers especially, not least her radiant *Laudate Dominum* in the *Solemn vespers*. The organ sonata is an attractive if not essential bonus, and the recording is spacious and naturally balanced as well as vivid.

Karajan's 1985 recording of Mozart's *Coronation Mass* is certainly vibrant, with fine choral singing and good soloists. Kathleen Battle sings beautifully in the *Agnus Dei*, and the recording is bright, if not ideally expansive.

Karajan's 1976 recording of the *Coronation Mass* is a dramatic reading, lacking something in rhythmic resilience perhaps; but, with excellent solo singing as well as an incisive contribution from the chorus, there is no lack of strength and the score's lyrical elements are sensitively managed. The current remastering has further improved the sound.

Markevitch's performance, though not always completely refined, is incisively brilliant and its sheer vigour is infectious. That is not to say that its lyrical moments are not equally successful. He has an impressive team of soloists and they are well matched in ensemble as well as providing very good individual contributions. The *Agnus Dei* is especially fine. The brightly remastered recording has plenty of life and detail, but it is the coupled Cherubini that makes this disc especially attractive.

Masses Nos. 16 in C (Coronation), K.317; 17 in C (Missa solemnis), K.337; (i) *Epistle sonatas Nos. 16, K.329; 17, K.336.*

**(*) Virgin Veritas/EMI Dig. VER5 61244-2 [id.]. Patrizia Kwella, Ulla Groenwold, Christoph Prégardien, Franz-Josef Selig, Cologne Chamber Ch., Coll. Cartusianum, Peter Neumann.

Peter Neumann directs a most enjoyably spirited account of the *Coronation Mass* and couples it with the much rarer *Missa solemnis*, K.336, which is on a similar scale and which is also very well sung. The singers, a well-blended team, are balanced somewhat backwardly within an ecclesiastical acoustic, which takes off a little of the bite from the chorus too, but the effect remains vivid. Hogwood's version of the *Coronation Mass* (paired with the *Vespers*) is even finer, and he has Emma Kirkby as a radiant soprano soloist (see above). But that is at full price, and Patrizia Kwella makes fine solo contributions to both the Virgin performances.

Masses Nos. (i; ii) *16 in C (Coronation), K.317;* (i; iii) *18 in C min. (Great), K.427;* (i; iv) *Requiem Mass, K.626.*

(B) **(*) Ph. Duo 438 800-2 (2) [id.]. (i) Helen Donath, Ryland Davies; (ii) Gillian Knight, Stafford Dean; John Alldis Ch., LSO; (iii) Heather Harper, Stafford Dean, L. Symphony Ch., LSO; (iv) Yvonne Minton, Gerd Nienstedt, Alldis Ch., BBC SO; Sir Colin Davis.

These very successful CD transfers demonstrate the best features of the original recordings, which date from between 1967 and 1971. Sir Colin Davis's vital account of the *Coronation Mass* is given with a fine team of soloists; and in the so-called *'Great' Mass in C minor* the use of the Robbins Landon edition – which rejects the accretions formerly used to turn this incomplete torso of a work into a full setting of the liturgy – prompts him to a strong and intense performance which brings out the darkness behind Mozart's use of the C minor key. Again he is helped by fine soprano singing from Helen Donath, and from Heather Harper too. The *Requiem*, with a smaller choir, is more intimate and the soloists are more variable, yet with his natural sense of style Davis finds much beauty of detail. While the scale is authentic and the BBC orchestra is in good form, this reading, enjoyable as it is, does not provide the sort of bite with which a performance on this scale should compensate for sheer massiveness of tone.

Mass No. 18 in C min. (Great), K.427.

*** DG Gold Dig. 439 012-2 [id.]. Hendricks, Perry, Schreier, Luxon, V. Singverein, BPO, Karajan.

*** Ph. Dig. 420 210-2 [id.]. McNair, Montague, Rolfe Johnson, Hauptmann, Monteverdi Ch., E. Bar. Soloists, Gardiner.

*** Decca Dig. 425 528-2. Augér, Dawson, Ainsley, D. Thomas, Winchester Cathedral Ch. & Winchester College Quiristers, AAM, Hogwood.

Mass No. 18 in C min., K.427; Kyrie in D min., K.341.

(M) **(*) Virgin Veritas/EMI Dig. VER5 61167-2. Barbara Schlick, Monika Frimmer, Christoph Prégardien, Klaus Mertens, Cologne Chamber Ch., Collegium Cartusianum, Neumann.

(i) *Mass No. 18 in C min., K.427; Meistermusik* (1785 original choral version of *Masonic funeral music*), *K.477.*

(N) **(*) HM HMC 941393 [id.]. (i) Christiane Oelze, Jennifer Larmore, Scot Weir, Peter Kooy, Collegium Vocale, Chapelle Royale O of Champs Elysées, Herreweghe.

In his (1982) digital recording of the *C minor Mass* Karajan gives Handelian splendour to this greatest of Mozart's choral works and, though the scale is large, the beauty and intensity are hard to resist. Solo singing is first rate, particularly that of Barbara Hendricks, the dreamy beauty of her voice ravishingly caught. Woodwind is rather backward, yet the sound is both rich and vivid – though, as the opening shows, the internal balance is not always completely consistent. Nevertheless this digitally remastered CD in the Karajan Gold series sounds more vivid than ever, and the chorus is tangibly present.

John Eliot Gardiner, using period instruments, gives an outstandingly fresh performance of high dramatic contrasts, marked by excellent solo singing – both the sopranos pure and bright-toned and Anthony Rolfe Johnson in sweet voice. With the recording giving an ample scale without inflation, this too can be warmly recommended.

Hogwood's version can be considered alongside the fine Gardiner account, even though his control of rhythm is less resilient and often squarer. The soloists if anything are even finer, and many Mozartians will prefer having boy trebles in the chorus and German pronunciation of Latin. Hogwood also opts for an edition by Richard Maunder which, among other things, adds appropriate instruments to the incomplete orchestrations of the *Credo* and *Et incarnatus est*. This is particularly impressive in the *Credo*, where trumpets and timpani bring an aptly festive flavour, adding to the panache of the opening. The sound has a vivid sense of presence, with treble tone cutting through very freshly.

Herreweghe also directs a satisfying and very well-recorded period performance of Mozart's *C minor Mass*, K.427, if not as vital as those of Gardiner and Hogwood. He opens somewhat squarely, but the performance soon opens out. The choral singing is always vivid, and both soprano soloists are outstanding: Christiane Oelze sweetly nimble in the *Et incarnatus est* and Jennifer Larmore giving a brilliant and moving account of the *Laudamus te*. The fill-up is the original choral version of the *Masonic funeral music* and here Herreweghe achieves just the right feeling of sombre ceremonial.

Peter Neumann's account of the *C minor Mass* has a great deal going for it: fine soloists – with Barbara Schlick always fresh and captivating in the *Laudamus te* – spacious choral singing, gloriously if somewhat backwardly recorded, and excellent playing from an authentic-sized orchestra on original instruments. The *Sanctus* is properly expansive and the overall conception warmly persuasive in its relaxed way. But in the last resort the chorus lacks the bite to make the performance really gripping. The rather solemn *Kyrie* has plenty of character with the performance darkly lyrical rather than dramatic.

Requiem Mass (No. 19) in D min., K.626.

*** DG Dig. Gold 439 023-2 [id.]. Tomowa-Sintow, Müller Molinari, Cole, Burchuladze, V. Singverein, VPO, Karajan.

*** Ph. Dig. 411 420-2. Margaret Price, Schmidt, Araiza, Adam, Leipzig R. Ch., Dresden State O, Schreier.

(BB) *** RCA Navigator 74321 29238-2. Equiluz, Eder, Vienna Boys' Ch., V. State Op. Ch. & O, Gillesberger – HAYDN: *Te Deum.* ***

(N) (M) **(*) Chan. Dig. CHAN 7059 [id.]. Yvonne Kenny, Sarah Walker, William Kendall, David Wilson-Johnson, St John's College, Cambridge, ECO, Guest.

(B) **(*) [EMI Red Line CDR5 69867]. Donath, Ludwig, Tear, Lloyd, Philh. Ch. & O, Giulini.

(B) **(*) Ph. Virtuoso 420 353-2 [id.]. Donath, Minton, Ryland Davies, Nienstedt, John Alldis Ch., BBC SO, Sir Colin Davis.

(N) (M) **(*) Penguin Classics 460 607-2 [id.]. (Soloists as above with Alldis Ch., BBC SO, Sir Colin Davis.)

Requiem Mass (No. 19) in D min., K.626; Kyrie, K.341.

*** HM Dig. HMC 901620 [id.]. Sibylla Rubens, Annette Markert, Ian Bostridge, Hanno Müller-Brachmann, La Chapelle Royale Coll. Vocale, O des Champs Elysées, Herreweghe.

*** Ph. Dig. 420 197-2 [id.]. Bonney, Von Otter, Blochwitz, White, Monteverdi Ch., E. Bar. Soloists, Gardiner.

(i) *Requiem Mass (No. 19) in D min.; Maurerisches Trauermusik, K.477.*

(N) (BB) *** Virgin Classics Dig. Double VBD5 61501-2 (2) [CDVB 61501]. Kenny, Hodgson, Davies, Howell, L. Sinf. Ch., N. Sinf. Ch. & O., Hickox – BRUCKNER: *Missa solemnis; Psalms.* ***

(N) (B) *** Audivis Dig. ES 9915 [id.]. Soloists, La Capella Reial de Catalunya; Concert des Nations, Savall.

Herreweghe is arresting from the very dramatic opening bars, and in the work's central Sequenz (*Dies irae*; *Tuba mirum*; *Rex Tremendae*; *Recordare*; *Confutatis* and the moving *Lacrimosa*) he achieves a remarkable emotional thrust. The orchestra gives weighty support, and one is hardly aware that this is a period-instrument performance, with the horns and trumpets capping climaxes forcefully. The soloists make an excellent team, singing with individuality (especially Ian Bostridge) but also blending together. The sound is spacious, but there is no feeling that the choral impact is blunted. After Süssmayr's completion, it seems entirely appropriate to end the record with the simple and very touching *Kyrie*, K.341, which is from Mozart's own hand.

Richard Hickox's excellent version of the *Requiem Mass* on the Virgin Ultraviolet label matches any in the catalogue. With generally brisk speeds and light, resilient rhythms, it combines gravity with authentically clean, transparent textures in which the dark colourings of the orchestration, as with the basset horns, come out vividly. All four soloists are outstandingly fine, and the choral singing is fresh and incisive, with crisp attack. The voices, solo and choral, are placed rather backwardly; otherwise the recording is excellent. This now comes as part of a super-bargain Virgin Double, aptly coupled with the rare Bruckner *Missa solemnis*, which is also very well sung, the only drawback being sparse documentation and an absence of texts.

John Eliot Gardiner with characteristic panache gives one of the most powerful performances on record, for while the lighter sound of the period orchestra makes for greater transparency, the weight and bite are formidable. The soloists are an outstanding quartet, well matched but characterfully contrasted too, and the choral singing is as bright and luminous as one expects of Gardiner's Monteverdi Choir. The superb *Kyrie in D minor* makes a very welcome and generous fill-up, to seal a firm recommendation.

Savall's Audivis bargain reissue of Mozart's *Requiem Mass* is controversially individual, but the result is stimulatingly different. The dark intensity of the opening is powerfully compelling, yet the soprano solos from Monserrat Figueras bring a blissfully serene contrast, and later the solo ensemble singing is equally radiant. The performance by La Capella Reial de Catalunya and Les Concert des Nations directed by Jordi Savall is both gutsy and expressive; at times tempi have great urgency – witness the thrilling *Dies irae* and the strong accents of the opening of the *Confutatis*, then contrasted by the angelic soprano line. The solo trombonist (Guy Van Waas) is a particularly fine player; indeed the trombones make a remarkable contribution throughout, and especially in the *Benedictus* and *Agnus Dei*. The recording is absolutely first-class and certainly no other version of the *Requiem* makes more impact on the listener. It is aptly introduced by the plangent timbres of the *Maurerische Trauermusik*. At the time of going to press, the disc comes in a slip case with a full Audivis/Fontalis catalogue.

Karajan's 1987 digital version of the *Requiem* is a large-scale reading, but one that is white-hot with intensity and energy. The power and bite of the rhythm are consistently exciting. The solo quartet is first rate, though Helga Müller Molinari is on the fruity side for Mozart. Vinson Cole, stretched at times, yet sings very beautifully, and so does Paata Burchuladze with his tangily distinctive, Slavonic bass tone. The close balance adds to the excitement. As with all these reprocessed Karajan Gold CDs, the sound is made marginally firmer by the remastering, but readers will note that this CD in consequence now reverts from mid- to full price.

Peter Schreier's is a forthright reading of Mozart's valedictory choral work, bringing strong dramatic contrasts and marked by superb choral singing and a consistently elegant and finely balanced accompaniment. The singing of Margaret Price in the soprano part is almost finer than any other yet heard on record, and the others make a first-rate team, if individually more variable. Only in the *Kyrie* and the final *Cum sanctis tuis* does the German habit of using the intrusive aitch annoy. Altogether this is most satisfying.

The surprise version is Gillesberger's. Using treble and alto soloists from the Vienna Boys' Choir, who sing with confidence and no little eloquence, this performance also has the advantage of a dedicated contribution from Kurt Equiluz. Gillesberger's pacing is well judged and the effect is as fresh as it is strong and direct. The 1982 recording is excellent, vivid yet full, and the result is powerful but not too heavy. This is very well sung indeed, as is the rare Haydn coupling. This is a real bargain.

Guest has the advantage of first-class singing from his St John's choristers, strong and eloquent, and an outstanding Chandos recording, full, vivid and clear. The performance is vigorous and positive, and well held together. The soloists, however, though making an excellent team and never letting the performance down, are not individually memorable, and altogether this cannot quite match Karajan or Hickox.

Giulini directs a large-scale performance which brings out both Mozartian lyricism and Mozartian drama, and anyone who fancies what by today's standards is an inauthentic approach may consider this version. The choir is in excellent, incisive form, and the soloists are a first-rate quartet. As one would expect, what Giulini's insight conveys is the rapt quality of such passages as the end of the *Tuba mirum* and the *Benedictus*. The recording is warm rather than brilliant.

Davis gives a comparatively small-scale performance which in principle should have given the sort of 'new look' to the Mozart *Requiem* that was such a striking success in Handel's *Messiah*. But somehow that does not happen, for the choral sound itself is weighty and thick, and, while this account is enjoyable, in the last resort it is not memorable. Readers will note that this performance is also available on a Philips Duo, above, combined with the *Coronation* and *Great C minor Masses*, and overall that seems to be a rather more enticing proposition. As can be seen above, the Davis version is also available as one of the mid-priced Penguin Classics (with a note by D. M. Thomas). However the Philips Virtuoso CD is the more economical proposition.

Requiem mass (No. 19) in D min. (ed. Maunder).
**(*) O-L Dig. 411 712-2. Emma Kirkby, Watkinson, Rolfe Johnson, David Thomas, Westminster Cathedral Boys' Ch., AAM Ch. and O, Hogwood.

Hogwood's version cannot be compared with any

other, using as it does the edition of Richard Maunder, which aims to eliminate Süssmayr's contribution to the version of Mozart's unfinished masterpiece that has held sway for two centuries. So the *Lacrimosa* is completely different, after the opening eight bars, and concludes with an elaborate *Amen*, for which Mozart's own sketches were recently discovered. This textual clean-out goes with authentic performance of Hogwood's customary abrasiveness, very fresh and lively to underline the impact of novelty.

(i; ii) *Requiem Mass (No. 19) in D min.* (edited and revised Duncan Druce); (ii) *Ave verum corpus. Maurerisches Trauermusik, K.477.*
(N) (M) **(*) Virgin Veritas/EMI VM5 61520-2 [CDC 54525]. (i) Nancy Argenta, Catherine Robbin, John Mark Ainsley, Alastair Miles; (ii) L. Schütz Ch.; L. Classical Players, Norrington.

Norrington goes even further than Hogwood in aiming to restore the *Requiem* so that it may come (conjecturally) nearer to the composer's original intentions. He uses an entirely new score by Duncan Druce, rejecting Süssmayr and other additional editorial material. Duncan Druce's revisions are considerable, even presenting recomposed music, with alterations as early as the *Recordare* and *Sanctus*. The result is fascinating, and in its way is undoubtedly successful, once one adjusts to the changes. Norrington certainly believes in it, and his account is both vibrant and compelling, with unpredictable tempi at times, but never eccentric. The soloists too are very impressive and so is the recording. As bonuses Norrington offers a tranquil (though not dallying) *Ave verum corpus* and a strongly characterized version of the *Mauerische Trauermusik*, moved forward with more drive than usual. This acts as as a rather effective prelude to the main work.

Ridente la calma, K.152.
*** Decca Dig. 440 297-2 [id.]. Cecilia Bartoli, András Schiff – BEETHOVEN: *Che fa il mio bene?* etc.; HAYDN: *Arianna a Naxos;* SCHUBERT: *Da quel sembiante appresi* etc. ***

Ridente la calma is invested with much innocent charm by Cecilia Bartoli within an interesting collection of Italian songs by German composers.

OPERA

Complete Mozart Edition, Volume 26: *Apollo et Hyacinthus* (complete).
(M) *** Ph. 422 526-2 (2) [id.]. Augér, Mathis, Wulkopf, Schwarz, Rolfe Johnson, Salzburg Chamber Ch. & Mozarteum O, Hager.

The opera was written when Mozart was eleven, with all but two of the parts taken by schoolchildren. The style of the writing and vocalization is rather simpler than in other dramatic works of the boy Mozart, but the inspiration is still remarkable, astonishingly mature. The orchestration is assured and full of imaginative touches. The performance here is stylish and very well sung. Excellent, clear and well-balanced recording, admirably transferred to CD.

Complete Mozart Edition, Volume 30: *Ascanio in Alba* (complete).
(M) **(*) Ph. 422 530-2 (3) [id.]. Sukis, Baltsa, Mathis, Augér, Schreier, Salzburg Chamber Ch., Salzburg Mozarteum O, Hager.

Ascanio in Alba (complete).
(B) *** Naxos Dig. 8.660040-2 (2). Windsor, Chance, Feldman, Milner, Mannion, Paris Sorbonne University Ch., Budapest Concerto Armonico, Jacques Grimbert.

Mozart at the age of fifteen wrote this charming, ever-inventive 'festa teatrale' for the coronation of the Archduke Ferdinand to an Italian princess in Milan in 1771. A court entertainment rather than an opera proper, it designedly identifies characters in a classical story, with the bride and bridegroom taking part in a delightful and original closing trio. The Naxos version, squeezing the dozens of arias and choruses on to two 79-minute discs, easily outshines previous recordings with a lightly sprung, stylishly conducted performance featuring an outstanding cast. The counter-tenor, Michael Chance, sings flawlessly in the castrato role of Ascanio, son of Venus, even-toned and brilliantly flexible. The others are fresh-toned too. Lorna Windsor, bright and clear as Venus, is nicely contrasted with the girlish-sounding Silvia of Jill Feldman, who sings with fine assurance in one of the two extended arias. The other, even more extended and demanding, is given to Fauno, with Rosa Mannion arguably the most accomplished soloist of all. The excellent tenor taking the role of Aceste is Howard Milner. Well recorded with transparent textures, if with chorus backwardly balanced, this makes an outstanding bargain in every way, rare Mozart that for most will be a delightful discovery.

Hager makes an excellent start with an exceptionally lively account of the delightful overture, but then the choruses seem relatively square, thanks to the pedestrian, if generally efficient singing of the Salzburg choir. Hager's speeds are sometimes on the slow side, but the singing is excellent, with no weak link in the characterful cast, though not everyone will like the distinctive vibrato of Lilian Sukis as Venus. The 1976 analogue recording is full and vivid. But this set is now completely upstaged by the new Naxos version.

Bastien und Bastienne (complete). Concert arias: *Mentre ti lascio, o figlia, K.513; Misero! o sogno . . . Aura, che intorno spiri, K.431. Le nozze di*

Figaro: Giunse alfin il momento . . . Deh vieni; Un moto di gioia.
*** Sony Dig. SK 45855 [id.]. Gruberová, Cole, Polgar, Liszt CO, Leppard.

Complete Mozart Edition, Volume 27: *Bastien und Bastienne* (complete); Lieder: *Komm, liebe Zither, komm; Die Zufriedenheit.*
(M) *** Ph. Dig. 422 527-2 [id.]. Dominik Orieschnig, Georg Nigl, David Busch, V. Boys' Ch., VSO, Harrer.

Leppard conducts a near-ideal performance of the eleven-year-old Mozart's charming little one-Acter, very well recorded. Edita Gruberová is delectably fresh and vivacious as the heroine, Vinson Cole is a sensitive and clean-voiced Bastien and Laszlo Polgar is full of fun in the buffo role of Colas. The Liszt Chamber Orchestra of Budapest plays with dazzling precision. As a generous fill-up, the three soloists sing Mozart arias, including the big scena for tenor, *Misero! o sogno*, and a replacement aria for Susanna, especially written for the 1789 production of *Le nozze di Figaro*: *Un moto di gioia.*

On Philips, the opera is performed by boy trebles instead of the soprano, tenor and bass originally intended. Members of the Vienna Boys' Choir give a refreshingly direct performance under Uwe Christian Harrer, missing little of the piece's charm. The two songs with mandolin accompaniment, also sung by one of the trebles, make an attractive fill-up. First-rate 1986 digital sound.

Complete Mozart Edition, Volume 44: *La clemenza di Tito* (complete).
(M) *** Ph. 422 544-2 (2) [id.]. Dame Janet Baker, Minton, Burrows, Von Stade, Popp, Lloyd, ROHCG Ch. & O, Sir Colin Davis.

La clemenza di Tito (complete).
*** EMI (SIS) Dig. CDS5 55489-2 (2). Winbergh, Vaness, Ziegler, Senn, Barbaux, V. State Op. Ch., VPO, Muti.
*** DG Dig. 431 806-2 (2). Rolfe Johnson, Von Otter, McNair, Varady, Robbin, Hauptmann, Monteverdi Ch., E. Bar. Soloists, Gardiner.
*** Teldec/Warner Dig. 4509 90857-2 (2) [id.]. Langridge, Popp, Ziesack, Murray, Ziegler, Polgár, Zurich Op. Ch. & O, Harnoncourt.
**(*) O-L Dig. 444 131-2 (2) [id.]. Heilmann, Bartoli, Della Jones, Montague, Bonney, Ch. & AAM, Christopher Hogwood.

Sir Colin Davis's superb set is among the finest of his many Mozart recordings. Not only is the singing of Dame Janet Baker in the key role of Vitellia formidably brilliant; she actually makes one believe in the emotional development of an impossible character, one who progresses from villainy to virtue with the scantiest preparation. The two other mezzo-sopranos, Minton as Sesto and Von Stade in the small role of Annio, are superb too, while Stuart Burrows has rarely if ever sung so stylishly on a recording as here. Davis's swaggering manner transforms what used to be dismissed as a dry *opera seria*. Excellent recording.

Recorded live on stage at the 1988 Salzburg Festival, Muti's version is vividly dramatic, full of expressiveness of a kind underplayed in period performance, with the Vienna Philharmonic producing traditional, consistently beautiful, orchestral sound. The tension of the live performance is powerfully conveyed, underlining the emotional thrust behind a piece long dismissed as uninvolving. The cast is a strong one, with Carol Vaness as Vitellia and Delores Ziegler as Sesto intense and characterful, two singers who built their Mozartian reputations at Glyndebourne, although Vaness comes under strain by the end of this live event. Gösta Winbergh makes a noble Tito, heroic of tone and never strained, and the others are good if not always ideally sweet of tone. A good alternative to the Colin Davis version, if you want a recording on modern instruments, though in this Muti set live performance involves interruption from stage noises and audience applause. Atmospheric sound, despite oddities of balance for voices.

Again, with his vitality and bite, Gardiner turns the piece into a genuinely involving drama. Though the team of soloists is not quite as consistent as on Sir Colin Davis's 1977 recording, Anthony Rolfe Johnson is outstanding in the title-role, matching the vivid characterization of both Anne Sofie von Otter as Sesto and Julia Varady as Vitellia. Sylvia McNair is an enchanting, pure-toned Servilia and Catherine Robbin a well-matched Annio, though the microphone catches an unevenness in the voice, as it does with Cornelius Hauptmann in the incidental role of Publio. More seriously, DG's vivid, immediate recording picks up a distracting amount of banging and bumping on stage in the Süssmayr recitatives.

Nikolaus Harnoncourt is expansively romantic. In keeping with this approach, he uses modern, not period instruments. Even so, he has not forgotten his early devotion to period performance, making this a very viable account for anyone wanting a half-way approach. Though recorded in association with Zurich Opera, this is a studio, not a live, recording like Gardiner's. It gains from not having stage noises in recitative. Ann Murray is at her finest as Sesto, if not quite as firm or dominant as von Otter for Gardiner. Philip Langridge is a splendid Tito, and it is good to have Lucia Popp so affecting in her very last recording. Ruth Ziesak and Delores Ziegler complete a strong team which will not disappoint anyone, even if it cannot quite compare with Gardiner's, singer for singer.

With clean, crisp manners Hogwood draws transparent textures from the players in the Academy, pointing rhythms and phrases more lightly and almost as imaginatively as Gardiner. Sesto as portrayed by the characterful Cecilia Bartoli is clearly established as the central figure in the drama, with Della Jones as Vitellia comparably positive, though neither of them produces quite such beautiful and even, cleanly focused tone as their opposite numbers for Gardiner, the magnificent Anne Sofie von Otter and Julia Varady. Diana Montague as Annio and Barbara Bonney as Servilia both weigh in favour of Hogwood, but Uwe Heilmann with his slightly fluttery tenor conveys nothing like the heroic strength of Anthony Rolfe Johnson in the title-role for Gardiner. Clean, well-balanced studio sound.

La clemenza di Tito: highlights.
(N) (M) *** Teldec/Warner Dig. 0630 15800-9 [id.]. (from above complete recording with Langridge, Popp, Ziesack, Murray; cond. Harnoncourt).

The highlights from the Harnoncourt set are eminently recommendable at medium price, well selected (72 minutes) and with full translation included.

Complete Mozart Edition, Volume 42: *Così fan tutte* (complete).
(M) *** Ph. 422 542-2 (3) [id.]. Caballé, Dame Janet Baker, Cotrubas, Gedda, Ganzarolli, Van Allan, ROHCG Ch. & O, Sir Colin Davis.

Così fan tutte (complete).
*** Decca Dig. 444 174-2 (3). Renée Fleming, Anne Sofie von Otter, Frank Lopardo, Olaf Bär, Adelina Scarabelli, Michele Pertusi, COE, Solti.
❀ (M) *** EMI CMS7 69330-2 (3) [Ang. CDMC 69330]. Schwarzkopf, Ludwig, Steffek, Kraus, Taddei, Berry, Philh. Ch. & O, Boehm.
*** Ph. Dig. 422 381-2 (3). Mattila, Von Otter, Szmytka, Araiza, Allen, Van Dam, Amb. Op. Ch., ASMF, Marriner.
❀ (M) (***) EMI mono CMS5 67064-2 (3) [CMS5 67138]. Schwarzkopf, Otto, Merriman, Simoneau, Panerai, Bruscantini, Philh. Ch. & O, Karajan.
(N) (B) **(*) Decca Double 455 476-2 (2) [417 185-2]. Lisa della Casa, Christa Ludwig, Emmy Loose, Anton Dermota, Erich Kunz, Paul Schöffler, V. St. Op. Ch., VPO, Boehm.
(N) *** HM Dig. HMC 951663/5 [id.]. Véronique Gens, Bernarda Fink, Marcel Boone, Werner Güra, Graciela Oddone, Pietro Oddone, Cologne Chamber Ch. & O, René Jacobs.
*** DG Dig. 437 829-2 (3) [id.]. Roocroft, Mannion, Gilfry, Trost, James, Feller, E. Bar. Soloists, Gardiner.
*** EMI (SIS) Dig. CDS7 47727-8 (3) [Ang. CDCC 47727]. Vaness, Ziegler, Watson, Aler, Duesing, Desderi, Glyndebourne Ch., LPO, Haitink.
(M) *** Erato/Warner 4509 98494-2 (3) [id.]. Te Kanawa, Stratas, Von Stade, Rendall, Huttenlocher, Bastin, Rhine Op. Ch., Strasbourg PO, Lombard.
**(*) EMI Dig. CDS5 56170-2 (3) [CDCC 56170]. Hillevi Martinpelto, Hagley, Murray, Streit, Finley, Allen, OAE, Rattle.
(N) (M) **(*) DG 449 580-2 (3). Irmgard Seefried, Nan Merriman, Herman Prey, Ernst Haefliger, Erika Köth, Dietrich Fischer-Dieskau, Berlin RIAS Chamber Ch., BPO, Jochum.

In contrast to his prickly and straight-faced recording of the early 1970s, Solti's digital *Così*, recorded live at the Royal Festival Hall in 1994, is as sparkling and full of humour as you could want. With the youthful and starry cast acting the story out on stage so as to sharpen the dramatic point, Solti takes a fast and light approach which yet has none of his old fierceness. The speeds may challenge the singers, notably in the many ensembles, but Solti gives his performers every consideration in moulding the arch of phrases or in allowing time for elaborate decorations. Though such meditative passages as the lovely little trio, *O soave sia il vento*, and the opening of Fiordiligi's aria, *Per pietà*, are taken at flowing speeds, faster than usual, they have a poise that holds one rapt. Much is owed to the superb playing of the Chamber Orchestra of Europe and, though the Festival Hall acoustic means that violin-tone has an edge on it, the Decca engineers have managed to overcome the snags of that notoriously difficult venue brilliantly. Renée Fleming as Fiordiligi, brought in as substitute at the last minute, yet proves a central focus among the soloists. She excels even over her performances in the role at Glyndebourne, singing with a firm, full voice that is yet brilliant and flexible, ranging down to a satisfyingly strong chest register. Dazzling as her *Come scoglio* is in Act I, *Per pietà* in Act II brings even greater emotional depth, poised and commanding, intensified by contrasts of dynamic more daringly extreme than in rival versions. Frank Lopardo too, as Ferrando, most sensitively uses his distinctive tenor over an unusually wide dynamic range, so that in the lovely aria, *Un aura amorosa*, he sings the reprise in a gentler, more beautiful half-tone than anyone else on disc. Anne Sofie von Otter predictably makes a characterful Dorabella, well contrasted with Fleming, and Olaf Bär a keenly intelligent Guglielmo, while two Italian singers, less well known but well chosen, Adelina Scarabelli and Michele Pertusi, complete the team in the manipulative roles of Despina and Alfonso. Altogether Solti's finest Mozart recording yet, outshining even his *Figaro*.

Boehm's classic set has been handsomely repackaged and remains a clear alternative choice, despite the attractions of the new Gardiner version.

Its glorious solo singing is headed by the incomparable Fiordiligi of Schwarzkopf and the equally moving Dorabella of Christa Ludwig; it remains a superb memento of Walter Legge's recording genius and still bears comparison with any other recordings made before or since.

Marriner directs a fresh and resilient performance, beautifully paced, often with speeds on the fast side, and with the crystalline recorded sound adding to the sparkle. Though the women principals make a strong team, the men are even finer: Francisco Araiza as Ferrando, Thomas Allen as Guglielmo and José van Dam as Alfonso all outstanding so that, though the reading is lighter in weight than those of Boehm, Karajan, Haitink or Davis, it has more fun in it, bringing out the laughter in the score.

Boehm's 1955 Decca stereo set is not as polished a performance as his later one for EMI, and the cutting of brief passages from the ends of arias may worry those who know the opera very well. But it remains a captivatingly spontaneous account of the frothiest of Mozart's comedies and has a vocal cast without flaw. Lisa della Casa is strong and sweet-toned, Christa Ludwig is admirably fresh-voiced, and the rest are sparklingly good, especially Emmy Loose's deliciously knowing portrayal of Despina. Paul Schöffler was nearing the end of his career when the recording was made, but in the role of Don Alfonso his singing is most appealing. This was one of Decca's early stereo experiments and there is little attempt at stage production, but the result is still surprisingly vivid and immediate. The sense of the singers acting out the comedy just beyond the speakers is uncannily realistic. This set is a great favourite of I. M.'s. At Decca Double price it is easily worth its modest cost even as a second version. Decca's new-style synopsis – with the narrative first given briefly 'in a nutshell' followed by suggested highlights, and listener-friendly cueing of the action – is a distinct asset.

Commanding as Schwarzkopf is as Fiordiligi in the 1962 Boehm set, the extra ease and freshness of her singing in the earlier (1954) mono version under Karajan makes it even more compelling. Nan Merriman is a distinctive and characterful Dorabella, and the role of Ferrando has never been sung more mellifluously on record than by Leopold Simoneau. The young Rolando Panerai is an ideal Guglielmo, and Lisa Otto a pert Despina; while Sesto Bruscantini in his prime brings to the role of Don Alfonso the wisdom and artistry which made him so compelling at Glyndebourne. Karajan has never sparkled more naturally in Mozart than here, for the high polish has nothing self-conscious about it. The recording has been impressively remastered for reissue as one of EMI's 'Great Recordings of the Century'.

René Jacobs with the Concerto Köln directs an intimate period performance of *Così fan tutte*, often light and brisk, but occasionally marked by surprisingly slow speeds, extremely so in the Act I farewell quintet, *Di scrivermi*. Véronique Gens, golden-toned, makes a delightful Fiordiligi, scaling down *Come scoglio* to match the rest, with Bernarda Fink also singing with creamy beauty. Werner Güra is a charming, expressive Ferrando, but Marcel Boone is far less focused as Guglielmo. A thoroughly enjoyable set, well co-ordinated, though not a first choice.

John Eliot Gardiner chooses voices that are both fresh and well focused, with the roles of all four of the lovers taken by young singers – Amanda Roocroft, Rosa Mannion, Rainer Trost and Rodney Gilfry. For this comedy, Gardiner, more controversially, opted to get the engineers to record a live performance not in concert but on stage. Stage noises are often intrusive, with laughter and applause punctuating the performance, not always helpfully. Whatever the snags, the full flavour of *Così*, its effervescence as well as its deeper qualities, comes over the more intensely as a result and Gardiner secures ensemble as crisp as you would expect in a studio recording. Though Roocroft and Mannion do not sound quite as sweet and even as they can, few tenors on disc can rival the German, Rainer Trost, in the heady beauty of his voice, above all in Ferrando's aria, *Una aura amorosa*. The poise and technical assurance of all the singers, not least Rodney Gilfry as Guglielmo, put this among the very finest versions of *Così*, outshining many with far starrier (and older) casts. DG offers the alternative of a video version (072 436-31), also made on stage, but at the Théâtre du Châtelet in Paris instead of Ferrara, and with Claudio Nicolai instead of Carlos Feller as Alfonso. The unscripted noises are here explained in the detail of Gardiner's own (sometimes excessive) staging, but with delectably pretty scenery. The crowning achievement on both CD and video is that the dénouement in the long Act II finale has a tenderness and depth rarely matched.

With speeds often more measured than usual, Haitink's EMI version still conveys the sparkle of live performances at Glyndebourne. The excellent teamwork, consistently conveying humour, makes up for a cast-list rather less starry than that on some rival versions. This is above all a sunny performance, sailing happily over any serious shoals beneath Da Ponte's comedy. Claudio Desderi as Alfonso helps to establish that Glyndebourne atmosphere, with recitatives superbly timed and coloured. If Carol Vaness and Delores Ziegler are rather too alike in timbre to be distinguished easily, the relationship becomes all the more sisterly when, quite apart from the similarity, they respond so beautifully to each other. John Aler makes a headily unstrained Ferrando, beautifully free in the upper register; and Lilian Watson and Dale Duesing make up a strong team. The digital recording gives fine bloom and an impressive dynamic range to voices and orchestra alike.

The energy and sparkle of Sir Colin Davis are set against inspired and characterful singing from the three women soloists, with Montserrat Caballé and Janet Baker proving a winning partnership, each challenging and abetting the other all the time. Cotrubas equally is a vivid Despina, never merely arch. Though Gedda has moments of rough tone and Ganzarolli falls short in one of his prominent arias, they are both spirited, while Richard van Allan sings with flair and imagination. Sparkling recitative, and recording which has you riveted by the play of the action.

On Erato, Kiri Te Kanawa's voice sounds radiant, rich and creamy of tone; she is commanding in *Come scoglio*, and tenderly affecting in *Per pietà*. Lombard is a sympathetic accompanist, if not always the most perceptive of Mozartians; some of his tempi are on the slow side, but his sextet of young singers make up a team that rivals almost any other, giving firm, appealing performances. With warm recording of high quality, this is most enjoyable and could be a first choice for any who follow the singers in question.

Following the impressive versions of John Eliot Gardiner and Sir Georg Solti, Sir Simon Rattle offers this sizzling account of *Così*, also recorded live, with the period instruments of the Orchestra of the Age of Enlightenment. In its often hectic speeds from the overture onwards, it may miss some of the sparkle of the piece, but Rattle knows how to bring out the emotional high points, so that the superb Fiordiligi, Hillevi Martinpelto, at a measured speed sings with aching beauty in *Per pietà*. With less pointed playing, the set may not replace Gardiner, Boehm or Solti, but the cast is the most consistent of the three, including Thomas Allen as a masterly Alfonso, Kurt Streit a clear-toned Ferrando and Gerald Finley a youthfully ardent Guglielmo. It is refreshing too to have a soprano Dorabella, particularly when the lovely timbre of Alison Hagley's voice is clearly contrasted with the brighter tones of Martinpelto. As ever, Ann Murray is a characterful Despina. The acoustic of Symphony Hall, Birmingham, adds brightness to the sound, though this is not focused quite as well as Birmingham recordings made without an audience.

Few conductors match Jochum in his pacing of this score or his feeling for detail, making his a delightful set, and though the team of soloists is flawed (Erika Köth an edgy Despina), they work superbly together, all of them characterizing strongly. And though Seefried is past her very finest as Fiordiligi, her charm is irresistible. Warm, full 1962 sound.

Così fan tutte (excerpts).
(***) Testament mono SBT 1040 [id.]. Jurinac, Thebom, Lewis, Kunz, Borriello, Glyndebourne Festival O, Fritz Busch; Alda Noni, Philh. O, Susskind.

The superb Testament transfer of excerpts from *Così fan tutte* in the 1950 Glyndebourne production gives a vivid idea of the way that even in the first year when the re-established Glyndebourne Festival was recovering its pre-war format, standards were never higher. Fritz Busch in his penultimate season was as incisive as before the war, directing performances at once superbly disciplined yet easy and amiable. Sena Jurinac as Fiordiligi, clear and vibrant, provides the central glory, with both her two big arias included, as well as six of her ensemble numbers, and three substantial rehearsal 'takes'. Blanche Thebom too, as Dorabella, sings with clarity and freshness, and the others make a splendid team. Alda Noni, the Despina, was not recorded at the Glyndebourne sessions but later, at Abbey Road, with Susskind and the Philharmonia. The recording brings out a flutter in her voice, less steady than the others. As in pre-war days, a piano is used instead of harpsichord for recitatives.

Così fan tutte (English version by Ruth & Thomas Martin).
(N) (***) Sony mono MH2K 60652 (2) [id.]. Eleanor Steber, Blanche Thebom, Roberta Peters, Richard Tucker, Frank Guarrera, Lorenzo Alvary, Met. Op. Association Ch. & O, Fritz Stiedry.

In the Masterworks Heritage series it is fascinating to hear this English-language version of *Così fan tutte*, recorded in 1951 with a front-line team of soloists from the Met in New York. In close-up sound, with every word clearly audible, it makes a lively offering at generally brisk speeds. Eleanor Steber, a superb soprano too little appreciated outside America, makes an outstanding Fiordiligi, whose account of *Come scoglio* ('Strongly founded') is breathtaking, one of the very finest on disc. Her positive characterization is well matched by Blanche Thebom and Roberta Peters, with Richard Tucker nicely scaling down his Italianate tenor, and Frank Guarrera (Toscanini's choice of Ford for Falstaff) stylish too. Ferrando, Guglielmo and Despina each lose an aria in Act II, convertional cuts at the time.

Così fan tutte: highlights.
(B) (***) EMI Eminence mono CD-EMX 2211 (from above complete recording, with Schwarzkopf, Merriman, Otto, Panerai, Simoneau, Bruscantini; cond. Karajan).
(BB) **(*) Belart 450 114-2 (from complete recording, with Janowitz, Fassbaender, Prey, Schreier, Grist, VPO, cond. Boehm).
(M) **(*) Teldec/Warner Dig. 0630 15801-9 [9031 76455-2] (from complete recording, with Margiono, Delores Ziegler, Anna Steiger, Van der Walt, Cachemaille, Hampson, Netherlands Op. Ch., Concg. O, Harnoncourt).

For those without the complete set (given a Rosette

– see above), the highlights CD from the 1954 Karajan mono set, with Schwarzkopf at her very finest, is surely indispensable, even if the documentation is inadequate and there is no proper cued synopsis.

These Belart highlights come from Karl Boehm's third (DG) recording of the opera and, with 72 minutes of music included, it makes an attractive memento. It was recorded live during the Salzburg Festival performance on the conductor's eightieth birthday. It has a splendid cast, and the zest and sparkle of the occasion come over delightfully. Even if at times ensemble leaves a good deal to be desired, at super-budget price it makes a genuine bargain.

Harnoncourt, the period-instrument specialist, as in his other Mozart opera recordings here favours an orchestra of modern instruments while adopting speeds of period style. He gives a quirkily magnetic reading and many will be glad of a fairly comprehensive sampler (74 minutes), especially when – as usual with the Warner Classics Opera Collection series – it is documented with a full translation and linking narrative. Though *O soave sia il vento* is raced along, Fiordiligi's great Act II aria, *Per pietà*, is taken very slowly indeed. Even so, Charlotte Margiono sustains the line immaculately, and she is similarly accommodating over another of Harnoncourt's eccentricities, making the emphatic opening of Fiordiligi's other big aria, *Come scoglio*, into a hushed meditation. There is no real weak link in the cast, but Harnoncourt's perverse tempi prevent a full recommendation for the complete set.

(i) *Così fan tutte;* (ii) *Don Giovanni;* (iii) *Le nozze di Figaro*.

(B) *** Ph. 456 375-2 (9). (i–iii) Ganzarolli; (i) Caballé, J. Baker, Cotrubas, Gedda; (i–ii) Van Allan, ROCG Ch. & O; (ii) Arroyo, Te Kanawa, Burrows, Roni; (ii–iii) Wixell, Freni; (iii) Norman, Minton, Casula, Grant, Tear, BBC Ch., BBC SO; all cond. Sir Colin Davis.

Philips wisely decided to omit Sir Colin Davis's recording of *Die Zauberflöte* from this very tempting bargain box; it was the least successful of his Mozart opera series and in any case is available separately and inexpensively on a Duo (see below). The other three performances are sheer delight. The sparkling *Così fan tutte* brings a superb female trio in Caballé, Janet Baker and Cotrubas, and the men fall only slightly short of this very high standard. In *Don Giovanni* the very consistency of the whole cast is its major asset, led by Kiri Te Kanawa as Donna Elvira and Mirella Freni's engaging Zerlina, while Ingvar Wixell and Wladimiro Ganzarolli strike sparks off each other as the Don and Leporello; and the same comment applies to *Nozze di Figaro*, where those same two male singers are equally successful in the comparable master and servant roles. Throughout all three operas Davis's lively pacing brings a flowing spontaneity as at live performances. The Philips sound, from clean CD transfers of recordings made between 1971 and 1974, is always fresh and immediate.

Complete Mozart Edition, Volume 41: *Don Giovanni* (complete).

(M) *** Ph. 422 541-2; *422 541-4* (3/2) [id.]. Wixell, Arroyo, Te Kanawa, Freni, Burrows, Ganzarolli, ROHCG Ch. & O, Sir Colin Davis.

Don Giovanni (complete).

*** EMI CDS5 56232-2 (3) [CDCC 56232]. Waechter, Schwarzkopf, Sutherland, Alva, Frick, Sciutti, Taddei, Philh. Ch. & O, Giulini.

*** DG Dig. 445 870-2 (3). Gilfry, Orgonasova, Margiono, James, d'Arcangelo, Prégardien, Clarkson, Silvestrelli, Monteverdi Ch., E. Bar. Soloists, Gardiner.

(M) *** Decca 411 626-2 (3) [id.]. Siepi, Danco, Della Casa, Corena, Dermota, V. State Op. Ch., VPO, Krips.

*** DG Dig. 419 179-2 (3) [id.]. Ramey, Tomowa-Sintow, Baltsa, Battle, Winbergh, Furlanetto, Malta, Burchuladze, German Op. Ch., Berlin, BPO, Karajan.

*** EMI Dig. CDS7 47037-2 (3) [Ang. CDCC 47036]. Allen, Vaness, Ewing, Gale, Lewis, Van Allan, Rawnsley, Kavrakos, Glyndebourne Ch., LPO, Haitink.

(M) *** EMI (SIS) CMS7 63841-2 (3) [Ang. CDMC 63841]. Ghiaurov, Claire Watson, Ludwig, Freni, Gedda, Berry, Montarsolo, Crass, New Philh. Ch. & O, Klemperer.

(M) (***) EMI mono CHS5 66657-2 (3). Gobbi, Schwarzkopf, Welitsch, Seefried, Kunz, Dermota, Poell, Greindl, V. State Op. Ch., VPO, Furtwängler.

(M) (***) EMI mono CHS7 63860-2 (3) [Ang. CDHB 63860]. Siepi, Schwarzkopf, Berger, Grümmer, Dermota, Edelmann, Berry, Ernster, V. State Op. Ch., VPO, Furtwängler.

(M) **(*) Decca 448 973-2 (3). Bacquier, Sutherland, Lorengar, Horne, Krenn, Gramm, Monreale, Grant, Amb. S., ECO, Bonynge.

**(*) O-L Dig. 425 943-2 (3). Hagegård, Cachemaille, Augér, Della Jones, Van der Meel, Bonney, Terfel, Sigmundsson, Drottningholm Court Theatre Ch. & O, Ostman.

(M) **(*) DG (IMS) 437 341-2 (3). Fischer-Dieskau, Jurinac, Stader, Seefried, Haefliger, Kohn, Sardi, Kreppel, Berlin RIAS Chamber Ch. & R.O, Fricsay.

(M) (**(*)) Naxos mono 8.110013/14 [id.]. Pinza, Novotna, Bampton. Sayão, Kullman, Kipnis, Harell, Cordon, NY Met. Op. Ch. & O, Walter.

(N) (M) ** RCA 74321 57737-2 (3) [id.]. George London, Lisa della Casa, Sena Jurinac, Erich Kunz, Anton Dermota, Irmgard Seefried,

Walter Berry, Ludwig Weber, V. St. Op.Ch. & O, Karl Boehm.

(N) ** Decca Dig. 455 500-2 (3) [id.]. Bryn Terfel, Renée Fleming, Ann Murray, Michele Pertusi, Herbert Lippert, Monica Groop, Roberto Scalriti, Mario Luperi, L. Voices, LPO, Solti.

(N) (M) ** Virgin Veritas/EMI Dig. VMT5 61601-2 (3). Andreas Schmidt, Gregory Yurisich, Amanda Halgrimson, Lynne Dawson, John Mark Ainsley, Nancy Argenta, Gerald Finley, Alistair Miles, Schütz Ch. of L., LCP, Norrington.

The classic Giulini EMI set, lovingly remastered to bring out even more vividly the excellence of Walter Legge's original sound-balance, sets the standard by which all other recordings have come to be judged. Elisabeth Schwarzkopf, as Elvira, emerges as a dominant figure to give a distinctive but totally apt slant to this endlessly invigorating drama. The young Sutherland may be relatively reticent as Anna but, with such technical ease and consistent beauty of tone, she makes a superb foil. Taddei is a delightful Leporello, and each member of the cast – including the young Cappuccilli as Masetto – combines fine singing with keen dramatic sense.

John Eliot Gardiner's set was recorded mainly live but with tidying sessions afterwards. As in his *Figaro*, the result is vividly dramatic, beautifully paced and deeply expressive, with little or none of the haste associated with period practice. The performance culminates in one of the most thrilling accounts ever recorded of the final scene, when Giovanni is dragged down to hell, presented in sound of spine-tingling immediacy. Stage noises are minimally intrusive, and much is gained from having the music paced in relation to live performances. Gardiner opts for a text that is neither that of the original Prague version nor the usual amalgam of Prague and Vienna. Dramatically the result is tauter, and the numbers omitted are here included in an appendix. Sometimes lightness goes too far, as when Charlotte Margiono as Donna Elvira sings '*Ah fuggi il traditor*' in a half-tone, but increasingly Gardiner encourages his soloists, particularly Anna and Elvira, to sing expansively, bringing out the full weight of such arias as '*Mi tradi*' and Anna's '*Non mi dir*'. Fine as Margiono is, Luba Orgonasova is even more assured and characterful as Anna, and the agility of both is exemplary. Rodney Gilfry excels himself, on one side tough and purposeful, on the other a smooth seducer, with the clean-toned voice finely shaded. Ildebrando d'Arcangelo is suitably darker-toned as Leporello, lithe and young-sounding, hardly a *buffo*. Julian Clarkson makes a crotchety Masetto, and Eirian James a warmer, tougher Zerlina than usual, aptly so for her extra scene. The Commendatore of Andrea Silvestrelli, though recessed on the recording, is magnificently dark and firm, not least in the final confrontation. A recording that sets new standards for period performance, and vies with the finest of traditional versions.

Sir Colin Davis has the advantage of a singing cast that has fewer shortcomings than almost any other on disc and much positive strength. Martina Arroyo controls her massive dramatic voice more completely than one would think possible, and she is strongly and imaginatively contrasted with the sweetly expressive Elvira of Kiri Te Kanawa and the sparkling Zerlina of Mirella Freni. As in the Davis *Figaro*, Ingvar Wixell and Wladimiro Ganzarolli make a formidable master/servant team with excellent vocal acting, while Stuart Burrows sings gloriously as Don Ottavio, and Richard Van Allan is a characterful Masetto. Davis draws a fresh and immediate performance from his team, riveting from beginning to end, and the recording is now better defined and more vivid than before.

Krips's recording of this most challenging opera has kept its place as a mid-priced version that is consistently satisfying, with a cast of all-round quality headed by the dark-toned Don of Cesare Siepi. The women are not ideal, but they form an excellent team, never overfaced by the music, generally characterful, and with timbres well contrasted. To balance Siepi's darkness, the Leporello of Corena is even more saturnine, and their dramatic teamwork is brought to a superb climax in the final scene – quite the finest and most spine-tingling performance of that scene ever recorded. The 1955 recording – genuine stereo – still sounds remarkably well.

Even if ensemble is less than perfect at times in the Karajan set and the final scene of Giovanni's descent to hell goes off the boil a little, the end result has fitting intensity and power. Though Karajan was plainly thinking of a big auditorium in his pacing of recitatives, having Jeffrey Tate as continuo player helps to keep them moving and to bring out word-meaning. The starry line-up of soloists is a distinctive one. Samuel Ramey is a noble rather than a menacing Giovanni, consistently clear and firm.

Haitink's set superbly captures the flavour of Sir Peter Hall's memorable production at Glyndebourne, not least in the inspired teamwork. The only major change from the production on stage is that Maria Ewing comes in as Elvira, vibrant and characterful, not ideally pure-toned but contrasting characterfully with the powerful Donna Anna of Carol Vaness and the innocent-sounding Zerlina of Elizabeth Gale. Keith Lewis is a sweet-toned Ottavio, but it is Thomas Allen as Giovanni who – apart from Haitink – dominates the set, a swaggering Don full of charm and with a touch of nobility when, defiant to the end, he is dragged down to hell – a spine-chilling moment as recorded here. Rarely has the *Champagne* aria been so beautifully sung, with each note articulated – and that also reflects Haitink's flawless control of pacing, not always conventional but always thoughtful and convincing. Excellent playing from the LPO – well practised in the Glyndebourne pit – and warm, full recording, far more agreeable than the dry sound in the old auditorium at Glyndebourne.

The lumbering tempo of Leporello's opening music will alert the listener to the predictable Klemperer approach and at that point some may dismiss his performance as 'too heavy' – but the issue is far more complex than that. Most of the slow tempi which Klemperer regularly adopts, far from flagging, add a welcome breadth to the music, for they must be set against the unusually brisk and dramatic interpretation of the recitatives between numbers. Added to that, Ghiaurov as the Don and Berry as Leporello make a marvellously characterful pair. In this version the male members of the cast are dominant and, with Klemperer's help, they make the dramatic experience a strongly masculine one. Nor is the ironic humour forgotten with Berry and Ghiaurov about, and the Klemperer spaciousness allows them extra time for pointing. Among the women, Ludwig is a strong and convincing Elvira, Freni a sweet-toned but rather unsmiling Zerlina; only Claire Watson seriously disappoints, with obvious nervousness marring the big climax of *Non mi dir*. It is a serious blemish but, with the usual reservations, for those not allergic to the Klemperer approach, this stands as a good recommendation – at the very least a commanding experience. The set now reappears at mid-price, its catalogue number unchanged, but the presentation more stylish.

The 1950 EMI set with Tito Gobbi in the title-role should not be confused with the later Furtwängler recording, also made at the Salzburg Festival and issued by EMI, with Schwarzkopf as Elvira. The speeds, spacious by most standards, are here a degree faster than they became four years later. Gobbi, not usually a Mozartian, yet gives a commanding, keenly characterful portrayal of the Don, very much the centre of the drama, swaggering and snarling, a menacingly dangerous seducer. Schwarzkopf as ever is a comparably commanding and characterful Elvira, no wilting flower, and Ljuba Welitsch in 1950 was at her peak, a radiant Anna, with Irmgard Seefried a magical Zerlina and Anton Dermota a honeyed Ottavio. Erich Kunz is the vintage Leporello, and if neither Alfred Poell as Masetto nor Josef Greindl as the Commendatore can match the others vocally, the team could otherwise hardly be stronger. The sound is rough on the orchestra but improves after the overture, while voices are very well caught, though stage balances vary.

The alternative Furtwängler performance was recorded live by Austrian Radio at the 1954 Salzburg Festival, barely three months before the conductor's death. Though speeds are often slow by today's standards, his springing of rhythm never lets them sag. Even the very slow speed for Leporello's catalogue aria is made to seem charmingly individual. With the exception of a wobbly Commendatore, this is a classic Salzburg cast, with Cesare Siepi a fine, incisive Don, dark in tone, Elisabeth Schwarzkopf a dominant Elvira, Elisabeth Grümmer a vulnerable Anna, Anton Dermota a heady-toned Ottavio and Otto Edelmann a clear and direct Leporello. Stage noises often suggest herds of stampeding animals, but both voices and orchestra are satisfyingly full-bodied in the CD transfer, and the sense of presence is astonishing.

Richard Bonynge's reading of *Don Giovanni*, recorded in 1968 and originally dismissed as too lightweight, was in many ways ahead of its time, using a chamber orchestra, with plentiful appoggiaturas in the vocal lines, even if some *Andantes* are on the slow side. The Kingsway Hall recording vividly captures an ideal scale. Though the overture is rather underpowered, tension never lapses after that, and the cast is exceptionally strong, finer than in most modern versions. Sutherland is commanding as Donna Anna, even finer than for Giulini on EMI. Gabriel Bacquier, at his peak as the Don, makes a vigorous hero, with Donald Gramm a firm if sober-sided Leporello and Werner Krenn an outstanding, heady-toned Ottavio, while Clifford Grant sings with thrillingly black tone as the Commendatore. Pilar Lorengar, with a hint of flutter in the voice, is a vulnerable rather than a biting Elvira, while the choice of Marilyn Horne as a full mezzo Zerlina, strange by latterday standards, follows historic precedent, with the singer scaling her powerful voice down. A mid-priced set for more than Sutherland devotees.

Ostman follows up his earlier recordings of *Così fan tutte* and *Le nozze di Figaro* with this period performance of *Don Giovanni*. This time, with a far darker score, he has modified his stance. Though speeds are still often fast, this time they rarely seem breathless. Håkan Hagegård as Giovanni could be sweeter-toned, but his lightness and spontaneity, particularly in exchanges with the vividly alive Leporello of Gilles Cachemaille, are most winning, with recitative often barely vocalized. Arleen Augér is a radiant Donna Anna, while Della Jones is a full-toned Elvira and Bryn Terfel a resonant Masetto. Understandably, the original Prague text is used. Such essential additions as Ottavio's *Dalla sua pace* (beautifully sung by Nico van der Meel) and Elvira's *Mi tradi* are given in an appendix on the third disc.

As he has shown in his recording of *Die Zauberflöte*, Fricsay is a forceful, dramatic Mozart conductor, but here the absence of charm is serious. This is mainly felt in some ridiculously fast speeds. Zerlina, Masetto and their rustic friends are hustled unmercifully along in 6/8, and poor Zerlina has an even worse time when it comes to her aria, *Batti*

batti. Seefried being the superb artist she is, her charm comes through. The cast is generally strong, but unfortunately there is a serious blot in the Donna Elvira of Maria Stader; she is made to sound shrill and some of her attempts to get round the trickier florid passages leave a good deal to be desired. Yet most of the singing is very stylish. Haefliger shows himself as one of the finest Mozart tenors of the time, Karl Kohn is a fine, incisive Leporello, Ivan Sardi an exceptionally rich-voiced Masetto, and Seefried a truly enchanting Zerlina. As so often on records, Sena Jurinac is not quite as thrilling here as one remembers her in the flesh. Fischer-Dieskau is a particularly interesting choice of Don; his characterization proves powerful and forwardly projected. Yet with all these plus points, the set does not quite add up to the sum of its parts, even though there is much to enjoy. The 1958 recording was made in the Berlin Jesus-Christus Kirche, so the stereo is remarkably atmospheric.

The vintage Bruno Walter recording, made live at the Met. in New York in March 1942, is one of the most desirable of the Naxos historic issues. To get such a performance, so starrily cast, at bargain price on only two discs makes it an obvious recommendation. Bruno Walter's brisk speeds may not allow the sort of detailed expressiveness one finds in either of the Furtwängler versions, but the bite of the drama is irresistible. Ezio Pinza is an engagingly characterful Don, even if he is not the most natural Mozartian, and he takes the *Champagne aria* at an impossibly fast speed. Even so, his is a commanding performance vocally, matched by the rest of the cast. Few Annas equal Rose Bampton for her combination of purity and power, with every note cleanly in place; though Jarmila Novotna as Elvira is less polished, it is a strong performance, and Bidu Sayão makes a charming Zerlina. Charles Kullman – earlier Walter's tenor soloist in his 1936 *Das Lied von der Erde* – is a clear-toned Ottavio, and though Alexander Kipnis as Leporello is not at his best in Act I, the biting clarity of his performance is magnetic. The 1942 sound, one of the better recordings from this source, has voices forwardly balanced. Whether to fit the opera on to two discs, or simply following the original Prague score, Elvira's aria, *Mi tradi*, is omitted.

The Boehm RCA version, recorded live by Austrian Radio and given in German, is a historic curiosity – a performance that in 1955 marked the reopening of the Vienna State Opera. Vocally, it is worth hearing for the contributions of the three women principals, with Lisa della Casa creamy-toned as Donna Anna, Sena Jurinac at her magical peak as Donna Elvira and Irmgard Seefried the most charming of Zerlinas. George London is a strong but sour-toned Giovanni. The others are not at their finest either, not helped by the dry acoustic and odd balances.

Recorded live at the Royal Festival Hall in London in October 1996, Solti's version is disappointing despite the promising cast list. It lacks the keen electricity that marks his live recording of *Così fan tutte*, and not one of the singers is on top form. Even Renée Fleming's beautiful voice sounds clouded, and Ann Murray as Elvira is seriously strained. Monica Groop as Zerlina, sweet enough in her arias, is edgy elsewhere, while Roberto Scaltriti is a gritty Masetto and Michele Pertusi often rough as Leporello. Bryn Terfel, so inspired a Leporello, proves an unpersuasive lover, with the tone tending to become unfocused. Dryish sound.

Sir Roger Norrington's version not only provides a period performance which on the orchestral side outshines the Ostman Drottningholm set on Oiseau-Lyre, but also ingeniously offers the alternative of playing the original Prague version or Mozart's revision for Vienna. This it does by having long sections on separate tracks, instead of tracking each individual number. The snag is that if you want to find a particular aria, it is far less convenient, and many numbers are duplicated when there are alternative sections for Prague or Vienna. Sadly, the singing cast cannot match that in the Ostman set. Though Lynne Dawson as Elvira, John Mark Ainsley as Ottavio, Gregory Yurisich as Leporello and Alastair Miles as the Commendatore all sing impressively, they hardly outshine their Drottningholm opposite numbers, and most of the others fall seriously short, including Andreas Schmidt as an ill-focused Don and Amanda Halgrimson as a shrill Donna Anna. Good, well-balanced sound.

Don Giovanni: highlights.

(M) *** EMI CDM5 65567-2 [ZDM 63078] (from recording, with Sutherland, Schwarzkopf, Waechter, Philh. Ch. & O, cond. Giulini).

*** DG Dig. 449 139-2 (from above recording, with Gilfry, Orgonasova; cond. Gardiner).

(B) **(*) [EMI Red Line Dig. CDR5 69824] (from complete recording, with Shimell, Ramey, Studer, VPO, Muti).

(N) *(*) Telarc Dig. CD 80442 [id.]. (from complete set with Boje Skovhus, Alessandro Corbelli, Christine Brewer, Felicity Lott, Jerry Hadley, Nuccia Focile, Umberto Chiummo; cond. Mackerras).

(N) ** Decca Dig. 466 065-2 [id.]. (from above complete recording with Bryn Terfel, Renée Fleming, Ann Murray; cond. Solti).

Not surprisingly, the Giulini EMI selection concentrates on Sutherland as Donna Anna and Schwarzkopf as Donna Elvira, so that the Don and Leporello get rather short measure, but Sciutti's charming Zerlina is also given fair due. The selection from the Gardiner set is at full price but runs to 73 minutes.

Muti's *Don Giovanni* is on a big scale but is nevertheless refreshingly alert (using a fortepiano continuo). It is perhaps a set to sample rather than to have complete. Shimell makes a rather gruff Don, not as insinuatingly persuasive as he might be; like the others, he is not helped by the distancing of the voices. With Samuel Ramey convincingly translated here to the role of Leporello and Cheryl Studer an outstanding Donna Anna, the rest of the casting is strong and satisfying. The selection of highlights is not particularly generous but does include most of the key numbers.

Mackerras's 1995 recording of *Don Giovanni* is vividly dramatic and perfectly paced, with modern instruments echoing period practice. The teamwork is excellent, but individually the casting is flawed, so the performance is better approached through a highlights disc. This one is generous enough (77 minutes), although the booklet offers only historical notes on the opera and a synopsis which is uncued, which is surely unacceptable for a full-priced CD. In any case Bo Skovhus as the Don may be seductive in expression but his vocal focus too often grows woolly under pressure. Felicity Lott, as recorded, is in disappointing voice as Elvira, not nearly so sweet as usual and there is too much acid in the soprano tones of Christine Brewer as Donna Anna, though Nuccia Focile makes a characterful Zerlina. The sound has a pleasing ambience but does not provide much sparkle.

Solti's live recording is a disappointment in almost all respects, and this full-priced set of highlights (74 minutes), will be mainly of interest to collectors seeking a sampler of Bryn Terfel's assumption of the title-role, which is generously represented here. Full texts and translations are included.

Die Entführung aus dem Serail (complete).

*** DG Dig. 435 857-2 (2) [id.]. Orgonasova, Sieden, Olsen, Peper, Hauptmann, Mineti, Monteverdi Ch., E. Bar. Soloists, Gardiner.

(M) *** DG 429 868-2 (2). Augér, Grist, Schreier, Neukirch, Moll, Leipzig R. Ch., Dresden State O, Boehm.

(BB) *** Arte Nova/BMG Dig. 74321 49701-2 (2) [id.]. Habermann, Ellen, Bezcala, Kalchmair, Ringelhahn, Linz Landestheater Ch., Linz Bruckner O, Sieghart.

(N) *** Erato/Warner Dig. 3984 25490-2 (2). Christine Schäfer, Patricia Petibon, Ian Bostridge, Iain Paton, Alan Ewing, Les Arts Florissants, William Christie.

(N) (M) *** EMI CMS7 63263-2 (2). Anneliese Rothenberger, Lucia Popp, Nicolai Gedda, Gerhard Unger, Gottlob Frick, V. St. Op. Ch., VPO, Josef Krips.

(M) *** Teldec/Warner Dig. 2292 44184-2 (2) [id.]. Kenny, Watson, Schreier, Gamlich, Salminen, Zurich Op. Ch. & Mozart O, Harnoncourt.

(N) ** DG mono 457 730-2 (2) [id.]. (i) Maria Stader, Rita Streich, Ernst Haefliger, Josef Greindl, Martin Vantin, Berlin RIAS Chamber Ch. & SO, Fricsay (with (i) *Exsultate jubilate, K. 165*. ***)

Unlike Gardiner's *Idomeneo* and *La clemenza di Tito*, *Entführung* was not recorded live but in the studio immediately after a concert performance. With a comedy like this, studded with spoken dialogue, that was a wise decision. The overture immediately establishes the extra zest of the performance, with wider dynamic contrasts, more body in the sound, and with more spring in the rhythm and a keener sense of fun. So Konstanze's great heroic aria, *Martern aller Arten*, has tremendous swagger; thanks also to glorious singing from Luba Orgonasova, at once rich, pure and agile, the close is triumphant. Curiously, Gardiner exaggerates the *ad lib.* markings in the first half of that climactic aria. Orgonasova sounds far richer than Lynne Dawson, the outstanding Konstanze for Hogwood; and in the other great aria, *Traurigkeit*, she is warmer too, less withdrawn. As Belmonte, Stanford Olsen for Gardiner is firmer and more agile than the fluttery Uwe Heilmann for Hogwood, and though Cornelius Hauptmann, Gardiner's Osmin, lacks a really dark bass, he too is firmer and more characterful than the unsteady Günther von Kannen for Hogwood. Add to that a recording which gives a clearer idea of staging, and you have a version of *Entführung* to be recommended as first choice even for those who would not normally go for a period performance.

Boehm's is also a delectable account, superbly cast and warmly recorded. Arleen Augér proves the most accomplished singer on record in the role of Constanze, girlish and fresh, yet rich, tender and dramatic by turns, with brilliant, almost flawless coloratura. The others are also outstandingly good, notably Kurt Moll whose powerful, finely focused bass makes him a superb Osmin, one who relishes the comedy too. The warm recording is beautifully transferred, to make this after Gardiner easily the most sympathetic version of the opera on CD, with the added attraction of being at mid-price.

With an excellent cast of young singers, the Arte Nova set offers an outstanding version of *Entführung* to rival almost any in the catalogue. With Martin Sieghart a crisp and urgent conductor, stylistically impeccable, drawing fine playing from the Linz Bruckner Orchestra, the performance gains from having been recorded in conjunction with live performances on stage, a point consistently reflected in the interplay between the soloists. Ingrid Habermann is a formidable Konstanze, fresh and clear, bright in coloratura yet creamy of tone in lower registers, undaunted by the demands of *Martern aller Arten*. The American, Donna Ellen, is a lively Blonde with a clear, unstrained top register. The Polish tenor, Piotr Bezcala, is a stylish, honey-toned Belmonte, with power as well as lyric beauty, only occasionally lachrymose in attack, while Oliver Ringelhahn is a well-contrasted Pedrillo, though pushed to the limit in his big Act II aria, *Frisch zum Kampfe*. Best of all is the Osmin of Franz Kalchmair, whose firm, dark bass copes masterfully with every demand of the role, cleanly focused from top to bottom. Still youthful-sounding, he yet conveys a compelling portrait of this prickly character. Good sound, though the spoken dialogue (well edited) is not consistent. At super-bargain price, the set comes with full libretto, including English translation.

William Christie with an excellent cast conducts a typically crisp and light account of *Entführung*. His speeds are consistently on the fast side, even imperilling articulation in the overture, and allowing less spring to rhythms than in the finest rival period performances. Christine Schäfer makes a ravishing Konstanze, powerful in *Martern aller Arten* and touchingly tender in *Traurigkeit*, though Christie's flowing speed prevents it from having the poignancy which more spacious treatment allows. Ian Bostridge, in the context of a light performance, is ideal as Belmonte, finely detailed both in words and musical treatment, always individual. Patricia Petibon is a light, bright, minxish Blonde, Iain Paton a clear Pedrillo. Most controversial is the choice of the velvet-toned Alan Ewing as Osmin, singing beautifully, but generally avoiding buffo characterization. The chorus is fresh and incisive, though at high speed the Janissaries at their entry are very rushed.

Recorded in 1966, the Krips EMI version brings an amiable and highly enjoyable performance with a formidable line-up of soloists. The team of Popp, Gedda, Unger and Frick could hardly be bettered at the time, each of them singing beautifully and with vivid characterization. Anneliese Rothenberger, potentially the weak link as Konstanze, not only sounds amply powerful as recorded, but sings with a purity and sweetness rarely caught on her discs. This is arguably her finest recording ever. The stereo sound is warm and well balanced, with spoken dialogue well presented. Act I comes on the first disc, with Acts II and III fitted complete on the second.

Harnoncourt's version establishes its uniqueness at the very start of the overture, tougher and more abrasive than any previous recording, with more primitive percussion effects than we are used to in his Turkish music. It is not a comfortable sound, compounded by Harnoncourt's often fast allegros racing singers and players off their feet. Slow passages are often warmly expressive, but the stylishness of the soloists prevents them from seeming excessively romantic. The men are excellent: Peter Schreier singing charmingly, Wilfried Gamlich both bright and sweet of tone, Matti Salminen outstandingly characterful as an Osmin who, as well as singing with firm dark tone, points the words with fine menace. Yvonne Kenny as Konstanze and Lilian Watson as Blonde sound on the shrill side, partly a question of microphones. Readers will note that this has now been reissued on two (instead of three) CDs and at mid-price. There is also a highlights disc (75 minutes) on Teldec 0630 13811-9.

Though lacking in body, the mono sound for Fricsay's recording brings splendid detail, with voices well caught. Fricsay characteristically opts for fast, generally refreshing speeds and crisp attack, though Konstanze's great aria of lamentation, *Traurigkeit*, lacks tenderness. Maria Stader is appealing in that role, even though the sweet voice grows less secure on top. Haefliger as Belmonte brings weight but little lyrical beauty. Greindl is a strong but often gritty Osmin and Martin Vantin a boyish Pedrillo, while the finest singing comes from Rita Streich as Blonde. The dialogue is mainly spoken by actors. *Exsultate jubilate*, with Stader, makes a welcome fill-up.

Complete Mozart Edition, Volume 33: *La finta giardiniera* (complete).
(M) *** Ph. 422 533-2 (3) [id.]. Conwell, Sukis, Di Cesare, Thomas Moser, Fassbaender, Ihloff, McDaniel, Salzburg Mozarteum O, Hager.

Leopold Hager has a strong vocal team, with three little-known soloists taking the women's roles – Jutta-Renate Ihloff, Julia Conwell (in the central role of Sandrina, the marquise who disguises herself as a garden-girl) and Lilian Sukis (the arrogant niece). Brigitte Fassbaender sings the castrato role of Ramiro, and the others are comparably stylish. It is a charming – if lengthy – comedy, which here, with crisply performed recitatives, is presented with vigour, charm and persuasiveness. The recording, made with the help of Austrian Radio, is excellent.

Complete Mozart Edition, Volume 28: *La finta semplice* (complete).
(M) *** Ph. Dig. 422 528-2 (2) [id.]. Hendricks, Lorenz, Johnson, Murray, Lind, Blochwitz, Schmidt, C. P. E. Bach CO, Schreier.

Schreier's version replaces the earlier, Orfeo full-priced set from Leopold Hager, particularly when it comes at mid-price on two discs instead of three. The digital recording is wonderfully clear, with a fine sense of presence, capturing the fun of the comedy. Ann Murray has never sung more seductively in Mozart than here as Giacinta, and the characterful Barbara Hendricks is a delight in the central role of Rosina.

Idomeneo (complete).
✿ *** DG Dig. 431 674-2 (3) [id.]. Rolfe Johnson, Von Otter, McNair, Martinpelto,

Robson, Hauptmann, Monteverdi Choir, E. Bar. Soloists, Gardiner.
*** DG Dig. 447 737-2 (3) [id.]. Bartoli, Domingo, Vaness, Grant Murphy, Hampson, Lopardo, Terfel, Met. Op. Ch. & O, Levine.
(M) *** DG 429 864-2 (3). Ochman, Mathis, Schreier, Varady, Winkler, Leipzig R. Ch., Dresden State O, Boehm.
*** Decca (IMS) Dig. 411 805-2 (3) [id.]. Pavarotti, Baltsa, Popp, Gruberová, Nucci, V. State Op. Ch., VPO, Pritchard.

With its exhilarating vigour and fine singing, Gardiner's aim has been to include all the material Mozart wrote for the original 1781 production, and he recommends the use of the CD programming device for listeners to select the version they prefer. Gardiner's Mozartian style is well sprung and subtly moulded rather than severe. The principals sing beautifully, notably Anne Sofie von Otter as Idamante and Sylvia McNair as Ilia, while Anthony Rolfe Johnson as Idomeneo is well suited here, with words finely projected. The electrifying singing of the Monteverdi Choir adds to the dramatic bite.

From the very opening of the overture it is clear what tense dramatic control James Levine has over this masterpiece of an *opera seria*, reflecting in the recording his experience in the opera house. It stands as his finest Mozart opera performance on disc. The superb sound helps, fuller and more vivid than in any previous recording, with the Met. Orchestra both stylish and incisive, and with woodwind principals outstanding. The text is roughly that of the Munich first performance, with Elettra given her culminating aria and Arbace both of his, and with recitatives given nearly complete – as satisfying and practical a solution to the textual problem as could be devised.

The cast is not just starry but stylish, with Plácido Domingo a commanding Idomeneo, giving a noble, finely controlled performance, which makes it a pity that the shorter version of his big aria, *Fuor del mar*, is preferred. Carol Vaness is a powerful, dramatic Elettra, well focused, and Cecilia Bartoli characterizes well as Idamante, wonderfully pure-toned in the Trio, while Heidi Grant Murphy is a charmingly girlish Ilia with a light, bright soprano. Completing this unrivalled team, you have Thomas Hampson as a superb Arbace and Bryn Terfel commanding in the brief solo given to the Oracle. The Met. chorus, like the orchestra, is incisively dramatic. John Eliot Gardiner's splendid DG Archiv set includes almost every textual alternative, but for those who prefer modern rather than period instruments and who fancy an exceptionally powerful line-up of soloists this is a clear choice.

Boehm's conducting is a delight, often spacious but never heavy in the wrong way, with lightened textures and sprung rhythms which have one relishing Mozartian felicities as never before. As Idomeneo, Wieslaw Ochman, with tenor tone often too tight, is a comparatively dull dog, but the other principals are generally excellent. Peter Schreier as Idamante also might have sounded more consistently sweet, but the imagination is irresistible. Edith Mathis is at her most beguiling as Ilia, but it is Julia Varady as Elettra who gives the most compelling performance of all, sharply incisive in her dramatic outbursts, but at the same time precise and pure-toned, a Mozartian stylist through and through.

In the Decca version, spaciously conducted by Sir John Pritchard, Pavarotti is the only tenor among the principal soloists. Not only is the role of Idamante given to a mezzo instead of a tenor – preferable, with what was originally a castrato role – but that of the High Priest, Arbace, with his two arias is taken by a baritone, Leo Nucci. The wonder is that though Pavarotti reveals imagination in every phrase, using a wide range of tone colours, the result remains well within the parameters of Mozartian style. Casting Baltsa as Idamante makes for characterful results, tougher and less fruity than her direct rivals. Lucia Popp as Ilia tends to underline expression too much, but it is a charming, girlish portrait. Gruberová makes a thrilling Elettra, totally in command of the divisions, as few sopranos are; owing to bright Decca sound, the projection of her voice is a little edgy at times.

Lucio Silla (slightly abridged).
*** Teldec/Warner Dig. 2292 44928-2 (2). Schreier, Gruberová, Bartoli, Kenny, Upshaw, Schoenberg Ch., VCM, Harnoncourt.

The sixteen-year-old Mozart wrote his fifth opera, on the subject of the Roman dictator Sulla (Silla), in double quick time. There are many pre-echoes of later Mozart operas, not just of the great *opera seria*, *Idomeneo*, but of *Entführung* and even of *Don Giovanni*. On Philips the castrato roles are splendidly taken by Julia Varady and Edith Mathis, and the whole team could hardly be bettered. The direction of Hager is fresh and lively, and the only snag is the length of the *secco* recitatives. However, with CD one can use these judiciously.

What Harnoncourt has done is to record a text which fits on to two generously filled CDs, not just trimming down the recitatives but omitting no fewer than four arias, all of them valuable. Yet his sparkling direction of an outstanding, characterful team of soloists brings an exhilarating demonstration of the boy Mozart's genius, with such marvels as the extended finale to Act I left intact. As in the earlier set, Schreier is masterly in the title-role, still fresh in tone, while Dawn Upshaw is warm and sweet as Celia, and Cecilia Bartoli is full and rich as Cecilio. The singing of Edita Gruberová as Giunia and Yvonne Kenny as Cinna is not quite so immaculate, but still confident and stylish. The Concentus Musicus of Vienna has rarely given so bright and lightly sprung a performance on record. Excellent digital sound.

Complete Mozart Edition, Volume 29: *Mitridate, rè di Ponto* (complete).
(M) **(*) Ph. 422 529-2 (3) [id.]. Augér, Hollweg, Gruberová, Baltsa, Cotrubas, Salzburg Mozarteum O, Hager.

Mitridate, rè di Ponto (complete).
(N) *** Decca Dig. 460 772-2 (3) [id.]. Cecilia Bartoli, Natalie Dessay, Giuseppe Sabbatini, Brian Asawa, Les Talens Lyriques, Christophe Rousset.

Mozart was only fourteen when he composed this, his first full *opera seria*, and though it has its longueurs, it has many beauties too. This is only the second recording to be issued, but it completely outshines the first (part of the Philips Mozart Edition). One big advantage is that Christophe Rousset conducts his period forces with a panache that disguises the weaknesses, pointing rhythms infectiously. Though the cast in the earlier set is an excellent one, the new line-up is even more characterful, with Cecilia Bartoli outstanding as the hero, Sifare, in love with Aspasia. In that prima donna role, Natalie Dessay is both rich of tone and brilliantly agile in coloratura, a match even for Arleen Augér on the earlier set.The counter-tenor, Brian Asawa, is firm and characterful as the predatory Farnace, and though in the title role Giuseppe Sabbatini is overstrenuous at times, his is a heroic performance, clean in attack. The softer-grained Sandrine Piau as Ismene is well contrasted with the others. Vivid, well-balanced sound. An excellent set, unlikely to be easily supplanted.

Hager's fresh and generally lively performance (the rather heavy recitatives excepted) also brings illumination to the long-hidden area of the boy Mozart's achievement. Two of the most striking arias (including an urgent G minor piece for the heroine, Aspasia, with Arleen Augér the ravishing soprano) exploit minor keys most effectively. Ileana Cotrubas is outstanding as Ismene, and the soloists of the Salzburg orchestra cope well with the often important obbligato parts. The CD transfer is vivid and forward and a little lacking in atmosphere.

Complete Mozart Edition, Volume 40: *Le nozze di Figaro* (complete).
(M) *** Ph. 422 540-2 (3) [id.]. Freni, Norman, Minton, Ganzarolli, Wixell, Grant, Tear, BBC Ch. & SO, Sir Colin Davis.

Le nozze di Figaro (complete).
*** Decca Dig. 410 150-2 (3). Te Kanawa, Popp, Von Stade, Ramey, Allen, Moll, LPO & Ch., Solti.
(M) *** EMI CMS7 63266-2 (2) [Ang. CDMB 63266]. Schwarzkopf, Moffo, Cossotto, Taddei, Waechter, Vinco, Philh. Ch. & O, Giulini.
❁ (B) *** CfP CD-CFPD 4724 (2) [id.]. Sciutti, Jurinac, Stevens, Bruscantini, Calabrese, Cuénod, Wallace, Sinclair, Glyndebourne Ch. & Festival O, Gui.
*** DG Dig. 439 871-2 (3) [id.]. Terfel, Hagley, Martinpelto, Gilfry, Stephen, McCulloch, Feller, Egerton, Backes, Monterverdi Ch., E. Bar. Soloists, Gardiner.
(M) **(*) Decca Legends 466 369-2 (3) [id.]. Gueden, Danco, Della Casa, Dickie, Poell, Corena, Siepi, V. State Op. Ch., VPO, Erich Kleiber.
*** Teldec/Warner Dig. 4509 90861-2 (3) [id.]. Scharinger, Bonney, Margiono, Hampson, Lang, Moll, Langridge, Netherlands Op. Ch., Concg. O, Harnoncourt.
(M) *** DG 449 728-2 (3) [id.]. Janowitz, Mathis, Troyanos, Fischer-Dieskau, Prey, Lagger, German Op. Ch. & O, Boehm.
(M) **(*) EMI (SIS) CMS7 63849-2 (3). Grist, Söderström, Berganza, Evans, Bacquier, Hollweg, Alldis Ch., New Philh. O, Klemperer.
**(*) DG Dig. 445 903-2 (3) [id.]. McNair, Gallo, Studer, Skovhus, Bartoli, V. State Op. Ch., VPO, Abbado.
**(*) Telarc CD-80388 (3) [id.]. Miles, Focile, Vaness, Corbelli, Mentzer, Murphy, Ryland Davies, Rebecca Evans, SCO and Ch., Mackerras.
(M) (**(*)) EMI mono CMS5 67068-2 (2) [CMS5 67142]. Schwarzkopf, Seefried, Jurinac, Kunz, Majkut, London, V. State Op. Ch., VPO, Karajan.
(M) (**(*)) EMI (SIS) mono CHS5 66080-2 (3) [CDHC 66080]. Kunz, Seefried, Schwarzkopf, Schöffler, Gueden, V. State Op. Ch., VPO, Furtwängler.

Solti opts for a fair proportion of extreme speeds, slow as well as fast, but they rarely if ever intrude on the quintessential happiness of the entertainment. Samuel Ramey, a firm-toned baritone, makes a virile Figaro, superbly matched to the most enchanting of Susannas on record, Lucia Popp, who gives a sparkling and radiant performance. Thomas Allen's Count is magnificent too, tough in tone and characterization but always beautiful on the ear. Kurt Moll as Dr Bartolo sings an unforgettable *La vendetta* with triplets very fast and agile 'on the breath', while Robert Tear far outshines his own achievement as the Basilio of Sir Colin Davis's amiable recording. Frederica von Stade is a most attractive Cherubino, even if *Voi che sapete* is too slow; but crowning all is the Countess of Kiri Te Kanawa, challenged by Solti's spacious tempi in the two big arias, but producing ravishing tone, flawless phrasing and elegant ornamentation throughout. With superb, vivid recording this now makes a clear first choice for a much-recorded opera.

However, in view of the strong competition, Decca should find a way of reducing its price.

Like others in EMI's series of Mozart operas, Giulini's set has been pleasingly repackaged and has a cleanly printed, easy-to-read libretto, giving an advantage over the competing CfP set. It remains a classic, with a cast assembled by Walter Legge that has rarely been matched, let alone surpassed. Taddei with his dark bass-baritone makes a provocative Figaro; opposite him, Anna Moffo is at her freshest and sweetest as Susanna. Schwarzkopf as ever is the noblest of Countesses, and it is good to hear the young Fiorenza Cossotto as a full-toned Cherubino. Eberhard Waechter is a strong and stylish Count. On only two mid-priced discs it makes a superb bargain, though – as in the other EMI two-disc version, the Gui on CfP – Marcellina's and Basilio's arias are omitted from Act IV.

The effervescent 1955 stereo Glyndebourne recording makes a bargain without equal on only two CDs from CfP. The transfer on CD brings sound warmer, more naturally vivid and with more body than on many modern recordings. Just as Sesto Bruscantini is the archetypal Glyndebourne Figaro, Sena Jurinac is the perfect Countess, with Graziella Sciutti a delectable Susanna and Risë Stevens a well-contrasted Cherubino, vivacious in their scenes together. Franco Calabrese as the Count is firm and virile, if occasionally stressed on top; and the three character roles have never been cast more vividly, with Ian Wallace as Bartolo, Monica Sinclair as Marcellina and the incomparable Hugues Cuénod as Basilio. The only regret is that Cuénod's brilliant performance of Basilio's aria in Act IV has had to be omitted (as it so often is on stage) to keep the two discs each within the 80-minute limit. There is no libretto; instead a detailed synopsis is provided, with cueing points conveniently indicated. But this set costs little more than a third of the price of the Decca/Solti version.

Gardiner's version was recorded live in concert performances at the Queen Elizabeth Hall in London in 1993, and this brings disadvantages in occasional intrusive stage noises, but it also offers a vividly dramatic and involving experience. In one instance the effect of the moment goes too far, when Cherubino (Pamela Helen Stephen) sings '*Voi che sapete*' for the Countess in a funny, nervous voice. That is very much the exception, for Gardiner's approach is lively and often brisk, with period manners made more genial and elegant than on the rival period recording from Drottningholm on Oiseau-Lyre. One of the most consistent and characterful of modern casts is led superbly by Bryn Terfel as Figaro, already a master in this role, with the enchanting, bright-eyed Alison Hagley as Susanna. Rodney Gilfry and Hillevi Martinpelto are fresh and firm as the Count and Countess, aptly younger-sounding than usual. Carlos Feller is a characterful *buffo* Bartolo, and Francis Egerton a wickedly funny Basilio. In Act III Gardiner adopts the revised order, suggested by Robert Moberly and Christopher Raeburn, with the Countess's aria placed earlier. More controversially, in Act IV he divides the recitative for Figaro's aria so that part of it comes logically before Susanna's '*Deh vieni*'.

Kleiber's famous set was one of Decca's Mozart bicentenary recordings of the mid-1950s. It remains a memorably strong performance with much fine singing. Few sets since have matched its constant stylishness. Gueden's Susanna might be criticized but her golden tones are certainly characterful and her voice blends with Della Casa's enchantingly. Danco and Della Casa are both at their finest. A dark-toned Figaro in Siepi brings added contrast and, if the pace of the recitatives is rather slow, this is not inconsistent within the context of Kleiber's overall approach. The closing scene of Act II is marvellously done. This set is a top favourite with I. M. who welcomes the new carefully remastered recording in Decca's Legend series.

The pacing of Sir Colin Davis has a sparkle in recitative that directly reflects experience in the opera house, and his tempi generally are beautifully chosen to make their dramatic points. Vocally the cast is exceptionally consistent. Mirella Freni (Susanna) is perhaps the least satisfying, yet there is no lack of character and charm. It is good to have so ravishingly beautiful a voice as Jessye Norman's for the Countess. The Figaro of Wladimiro Ganzarolli and the Count of Ingvar Wixell project with exceptional clarity and vigour, and there is fine singing too from Yvonne Minton as Cherubino, Clifford Grant as Bartolo and Robert Tear as Basilio. The 1971 recording has more reverberation than usual, but the effect is commendably atmospheric and on CD the voices have plenty of presence.

Harnoncourt on Teldec makes the Royal Concertgebouw Orchestra produce fresh, light and transparent sounds close to period style. Speeds are relaxed, bringing out the fun and sparkle of the piece. The excellent cast has Thomas Hampson as a dominant Count, Charlotte Margiono as a tenderly sweet Countess, with Barbara Bonney a charmingly provocative Susanna and Anton Scharinger a winning Figaro, both tough and comic. Recitative at flexible speeds conveys the dramatic confrontations and complications vividly. A version that gets the best of both interpretative worlds, new and old.

Boehm's version of *Figaro*, reissued by DG as a 'Legendary Recording', is also among the most consistently assured performances available. The women all sing most beautifully, with Janowitz's Countess, Mathis's Susanna and Troyanos's Cherubino all ravishing the ear in contrasted ways. Prey is an intelligent if not very jolly-sounding Figaro, and Fischer-Dieskau gives his dark, sharply defined reading of the Count's role. All told, a great success, with fine playing and recording, here impressively remastered.

Klemperer may seem to have been the most solemn of conductors but he had a great sense of humour. Here he shows very clearly how his humour fits in with the sterling characteristics we all recognize. Though the tempi are often slow, the pointing and shading are most delicate and the result, though hardly sparkling, is full of high spirits. A clue to the Klemperer approach comes near the beginning with Figaro's aria *Se vuol ballare*, which is not merely a servant's complaint about an individual master but a revolutionary call, with horns and pizzicato strings strongly defined, to apply to the whole world: 'I'll play the tune, sir!' Sir Geraint Evans is masterly in matching Klemperer; though his normal interpretation of the role of Figaro is more effervescent than this, he is superb here, singing and acting with great power. Reri Grist makes a charming Susanna and Teresa Berganza is a rich-toned Cherubino. Gabriel Bacquier's Count is darker-toned and more formidable than usual, while Elisabeth Söderström's Countess, though it has its moments of strain, gives ample evidence of this artist's thoughtful intensity. Though this is not a version one would regularly laugh over, it represents a unique experience. The recording has transferred very well to CD.

Drawing beautiful sounds from the Vienna Philharmonic, Claudio Abbado with a cast of mainly young singers turns the opera into an immaculate recital. At generally brisk speeds and with recitatives trippingly delivered, the plot moves speedily but with little sparkle or sense of fun. The basic reason is that Abbado adopts a surprisingly metrical, unyielding approach, failing to bend rhythms and phrases to suit the needs of words or plot or the natural expressiveness of singers. Sylvia McNair as Susanna, Cheryl Studer as the Countess and Cecilia Bartoli as Cherubini are all characterful and musically imaginative enough to overcome much of the dulling effect of this, but the character-roles of Dr Bartolo, Marcellina and Basilio are all displayed colourlessly, with young voices unable to present the characters convincingly. Lucio Gallo is a dark-voiced Figaro who finds it hard to point comedy, similar in tone to the Count of Boje Skovhus, who however has a less pleasing, grittier voice. Most disappointing of all are the big ensembles, the Act III sextet as well as the finales to Acts II and IV, where with unexpectedly slow speeds and metrical rhythms the comedy evaporates. Happily, the final resolution on '*Contessa perdono*' is done ravishingly, with Cheryl Studer crowning a totally radiant performance. McNair also sings enchantingly and Bartoli is ideally cast. It is worth hearing the set for these three alone. The recording, faithful to voices, is slightly cavernous.

The big advantage of the Telarc version is that Sir Charles Mackerras with the Scottish Chamber Orchestra provides some 34 minutes of alternative items and variants. It is fascinating, for example, to have two alternative versions of the Count's Act III aria, with the difficult triplets largely removed, and there is also a heavily ornamented version of Cherubino's '*Voi che sapete*'. Mackerras also encourages his singers to provide ornamentation in their arias and, more than his rivals, he inserts appoggiature, avoiding 'blunt endings'. Like Harnoncourt, Mackerras aims to get the best of both interpretative worlds, but with the balance more towards period performance, using modern instruments but in a small orchestra and with speeds generally brisker and bowing lighter. Orchestrally, this is an exceptionally characterful reading, more so than for the singing of the arias and ensembles. Alastair Miles as Figaro sings superbly with clean focus but, next to his main rivals, he is straight-faced, and similarly the Susanna of Nuccia Focile is a little lacking in charm and humour, while Carol Vaness as the Countess is perhaps stressed by Mackerras's slow speeds (an exception) for her two big arias. The Count of Alessandro Corbelli is rather rough in tone, and Alfonso Antoniozzi is too light and unsteady as Bartolo, but Ryland Davies is a superb Basilio and Susanne Mentzer a strong Marcellina, both given their arias in Act IV, which comes complete on disc 3, along with the appendices. Any reservations are made relative to only the finest rivals; with warm sound, the set can be strongly recommended.

Recorded in 1950, Karajan's first recording of *Figaro* offers one of the most distinguished casts ever assembled; but, curiously at that period, they decided to record the opera without the *secco* recitatives. That is a most regrettable omission when all these singers are not just vocally immaculate but vividly characterful – as for example Sena Jurinac, later the greatest of Glyndebourne Countesses, here a vivacious Cherubino. The firmness of focus in Erich Kunz's singing of Figaro goes with a delightful twinkle in the word-pointing, and Irmgard Seefried makes a bewitching Susanna. Schwarzkopf's noble portrait of the Countess – not always helped by a slight backward balance in the placing of the microphone for her – culminates in the most poignant account of her second aria, *Dove sono*. The sound, though obviously limited, presents the voices very vividly. However, this seems a curious choice as a 'Great Recording of the Century'.

Furtwängler's vintage recording of *Figaro* from the Salzburg Festival was made by Austrian Radio in 1953, the only year when he conducted it there. Fascinatingly, at the conductor's insistence the performance is in German, reverting to the pre-war custom in Salzburg. It is a revelation to compare his reading of *Figaro* with Karajan's in the EMI studio recording made only a year earlier with the same orchestra, the Vienna Philharmonic, and with three of the same principals: Elisabeth Schwarzkopf as the Countess, Irmgard Seefried as Susanna and Erich Kunz as Figaro. Next to Furtwängler, Karajan

– who recorded the opera without the *secco* recitatives – sounds stiff and plain, surprisingly lacking in humour. By contrast, many of Furtwängler's speeds are very broad though, even at their most extreme, there is always a lift to the rhythm to give Mozartian sparkle. The result is an exceptionally warm and relaxed reading, in which all the principals joyfully bring out the comedy, Kunz and Seefried above all. Schwarzkopf is in superb voice, rich and full, more creamy-toned than with Karajan, though her later performance on Giulini's 1959 recording is finest of all. Hilde Gueden as Cherubino and Paul Schöffler as the Count are also most characterful, even if Schöffler no longer sounds young. The snag is that, even with Basilio's and Marcellina's arias cut in the last act – as habitually they were in those days – the performance stretches to three CDs. Also, as with other EMI historic issues, no libretto is provided, just a detailed synopsis.

Le nozze di Figaro: highlights.
(M) *** EMI CDM5 66049-2 [id.] (from complete recording, with Schwarzkopf, Moffo, Cossotto, Taddei, Waechter, Philh. Ch. & O, cond. Giulini).
(N) (M) **(*) Decca 458 225-2 [id.] (from complete recording with Tomowa-Sintow, Cotrubas, Von Stade, Van Dam, Krause; cond. Karajan).
(M) *** Teldec/Warner Dig. 4509 97958-2 [id.] (from complete recording, with Scharinger, Bonney, Margiono, Hampson, Lang, Moll, Langridge, Netherlands Op. Ch., Concg. O, Harnoncourt).
(B) *** DG Classikon 439 449-2 [429 822-2] (from above set, with Janowitz, Mathis, Prey, Fischer-Dieskau; cond. Boehm).
(M) **(*) Decca 452 732-2 [id.] (from above recording, with Siepi, Gueden, della Casa, Danco, Poell; cond. Erich Kleiber).
**(*) Telarc Dig. CD 80449 [id.] (from above set with Milnes, Focile, Vaness, Corbelli, Mentzner; cond. Mackerras).

The Giulini CD makes a clear first choice for a highlights CD from *Nozze di Figaro*. The selection may play for only 62 minutes but every item is treasurable, not least *Non più andrai*, the Countess's two arias, and the long excerpt from the Act II finale. The new transfer is extremely vivid, and the synopsis relates the excerpts to the narrative.

The Karajan set of highlights is exceptionally generous (73 minutes), and very well documented, with full translation. The complete set would not be a first choice – Karajan's approach is rather too smooth and polished – but the singing, especially from the ladies, is often very fine and this gives an impressive overall survey of Mozart's inspired score, and is very well recorded.

Harnoncourt's *Nozze di Figaro* is relaxed and sparkling – one of his very best Mozart opera sets, with Barbara Bonney a charmingly provocative Susanna and Anton Scharinger a winning Figaro. Thomas Hampson proves a dominant Count and Charlotte Margiono a tenderly sweet Countess. The 76-minute selection of highlights (like the others in the Teldec series) comes with a full translation and can be recommended in its own right.

Boehm's selection includes many of the key numbers, but with a little over an hour of music it is less than generous and inadequately documented; but the singing is first class and the sound vivid.

It is good to have a reminder of Erich Kleiber's classic 1956 set. It is a pity that the selection, though not really ungenerous (66 minutes), did not find room for an extended excerpt at the close of Act II (where Kleiber's overall control was revelatory); but the disc ends with the final ten minutes of Act IV, which is some compensation and, of course, includes the key arias. Gueden's enchanting Susanna both blends and contrasts beautifully with Della Casa's Countess (their Letter duet in Act III is delightful); and Danco, too, is at her finest as Cherubino. The new transfer is vivid, smoother than before, and the cued synopsis is well managed. An essential purchase for all lovers of this wonderful opera who do not already have the complete set.

A well-selected 77 minutes from the Mackerras Scottish set, with most of the key items, will be useful as this is not likely to be a first choice for the complete opera, except for those with a special interest in the singers or the additional items which Mackerras includes (but which are not offered here). There is a good synopsis, but it is not cued.

Complete Mozart Edition, Volume 39: *L'Oca del Cairo* (complete).
(M) *** Ph. Dig. 422 539-2 [id.]. Nielsen, Wiens, Coburn, Schreier, Johnson, Fischer-Dieskau, Scharinger, Berlin R. Ch. (members), C. P. E. Bach CO, Schreier – *Lo sposo deluso*. ***

We owe it to the Mozart scholar and Philips recording producer, Erik Smith, that these two sets of Mozartian fragments, *L'Oca del Cairo* and *Lo sposo deluso*, have been prepared for performance and recorded. *L'Oca del Cairo* ('The Cairo goose'), containing roughly twice as much music as *Lo sposo deluso*, involves six substantial numbers, most of them ensembles, including an amazing finale to the projected Act I, with contrasted sections following briskly one after the other. It is very well conducted by Peter Schreier, who also takes part as one of the soloists. Dietrich Fischer-Dieskau takes the *buffo* old-man role of Don Pippo, and Anton Scharinger is brilliant in the patter aria in tarantella rhythm for the major-domo, Chichibio, bringing a foretaste of Donizetti. Fresh, bright digital recording.

Complete Mozart Edition, Volume 35: *Il rè pastore* (complete).
(M) **(*) Ph. Dig. 422 535-2 (2) [id.]. Blasi,

McNair, Vermillion, Hadley, Ahnsjö, ASMF, Marriner.

Il rè pastore (complete).
(M) **(*) RCA 74321 50165-2 (2). Grist, Popp, Saunders, Alva, Monti, O of Naples, Vaughan.

'There is nothing for Mozart to do but write beautiful music,' says Alfred Einstein of this early piece, written in 1775 for a state occasion in Salzburg. It is a pastoral story of shepherds and shepherdesses, and not a single character is anything but utterly, boringly good. Not exactly a music drama, then, but still a splendid example of Mozart's youthful genius at work, the more enchanting for being performed here with real style and verve. Denis Vaughan – once a Beecham protégé – is a lively advocate and, when first issued in 1967, this recording reinforced his then blossoming reputation. Among the singers, Lucia Popp is wonderfully sweet-toned and her high legato phrases never concede even a momentary blemish. Reri Grist's voice is harder, less smooth, but in a way that is fitting enough in the castrato role of Aminta, and her singing of the most famous number, *L'amerò*, is expressively beautiful. Arlene Saunders is a graceful Tamiri, and Nicola Monti and Luiga Alva make a quite stylish pair of tenors, even if their florid singing is not always quite immaculate. Not the least important quality of Denis Vaughan's direction is his editing, very scholarly for the late 1960s, with a plentiful sprinkling of appoggiature smoothing the blunt phrase-endings. He also plays the continuo in the recitatives most effectively. The one slight snag is the CD transfer, which has brightened what was a pleasingly full and lively analogue sound: the voices now have a degree of added edge and the orchestral tuttis bring some rough moments. However, this remains a vivid musical experience, and a full libretto is provided.

The alternative version by Marriner and the Academy, with a first-rate cast and with plenty of light and shade, and superbly played, does not efface memories of the 1979 DG version conducted by Leopold Hager, which offered even purer singing. Here Angela Maria Blasi, despite a beautiful voice, attacks notes from below, even in *L'amerò*. Excellent sound.

Complete Mozart Edition, Volume 36: *Der Schauspieldirektor* (complete).
(M) **(*) Ph. 422 536-2 (2) [id.]. Welting, Cotrubas, Grant, Rolfe Johnson, LSO, Sir Colin Davis – *Zaïde*. ***

(i–v; viii) *Der Schauspieldirektor*. Concert arias: (ii; vii; ix) *Misera, dove son!, K.369; Un moto di gioia, K.579; Schon lacht der holde Frühling, K.580*. (i; vii; ix) *Vado, ma dove? oh Dei!, K.583; Bella mia fiamma, addio, K.529; Nehmt meinen Dank, ihr holden Gonner!* (iv; vi; x) *Die Entführung: Ha! Wie will ich triumpheren*. (v; viii) *Le nozze di Figaro: Overture*.
(M) *** Decca (IMS) Dig. 452 624-2. (i) Te Kanawa, (ii) Gruberová, (iii) Heilmann, (iv) Jungwirth; (v) VPO; (vi) V. Haydn O; (vii) VCO; (viii) Pritchard; (ix) Fischer; (x) Kertész.

This Decca recording of the four musical numbers from *Der Schauspieldirektor* (presented 'dry' with no German dialogue) was made only six months before Sir John Pritchard died, an apt last offering from him, a great Mozartian. Having two such well-contrasted star sopranos adds point to the contest, and the performances are a delight, though the recorded sound is not as well focused as usual from this source. The *Figaro overture*, also conducted by Pritchard, is another completely new item. The rest is reissue material, with three concert arias each from Gruberová and Dame Kiri, taken from Decca's 1981 boxed set of the collected arias. Manfred Jungwirth's bitingly dark account of Osmin's aria from *Entführung* dates from ten years before that, a welcome extra. The single mid-priced disc comes with full translations and note and the reissue is something of a bargain.

There is no contest whatsoever between the two rival prima donnas presented in the Philips recording. *Ich bin die erste Sängerin* ('I am the leading prima donna'), they yell at each other; but here Ileana Cotrubas is in a world apart from the thin-sounding and shallow Ruth Welting. Davis directs with fire and electricity a performance which is otherwise (despite the lack of spoken dialogue) most refreshing and beautifully recorded (in 1975) in a sympathetic acoustic.

Complete Mozart Edition, Volume 31: *Il sogno di Scipione* (complete).
(M) *** Ph. 422 531-2 (2) [id.]. Popp, Gruberová, Mathis, Schreier, Ahnsjö, Thomas Moser, Salzburg Chamber Ch. & Mozarteum O, Hager.

Il sogno di Scipione presents an allegorical plot with Scipio set to choose between Fortune and Constancy. Given the choice of present-day singers, this cast could hardly be finer, with Edita Gruberová, Lucia Popp and Edith Mathis superbly contrasted in the women's roles (the latter taking part in the epilogue merely), and Peter Schreier is joined by two of his most accomplished younger colleagues. Hager sometimes does not press the music on as he might, but his direction is always alive. With fine recording, vividly and atmospherically transferred to CD, the set is not likely to be surpassed in the immediate future.

Complete Mozart Edition, Volume 39: *Lo sposo deluso*.
(M) *** Ph. 422 539-2 [id.]. Palmer, Cotrubas,

Rolfe Johnson, Tear, Grant, LSO, Sir Colin Davis – *L'Oca del Cairo*. ***

The music presented here from *Lo sposo deluso* is the surviving music from an unfinished opera written in the years before *Figaro*, and it contains much that is memorable. The *Overture*, with its trumpet calls, its lovely slow middle section and recapitulation with voices, is a charmer, while the two arias, reconstructed by the recording producer and scholar, Erik Smith, are also delightful: the one a trial run for Fiordiligi's *Come scoglio* in *Così*, the other (sung by Robert Tear) giving a foretaste of Papageno's music in *The Magic Flute*.

Complete Mozart Edition, Volume 36: *Zaïde*.
(M) *** Ph. 422 536-2 (2) [id.]. Mathis, Schreier, Wixell, Hollweg, Süss, Berlin State O, Klee – *Der Schauspieldirektor*. **(*)

Zaïde, written between 1779 and 1780 and never quite completed, was a trial run for *Entführung*. Much of the music is superb, and melodramas at the beginning of each Act are strikingly effective and original, with the speaking voice of the tenor in the first heard over darkly dramatic writing in D minor. Zaïde's arias in both Acts are magnificent: the radiantly lyrical *Ruhe sanft* is hauntingly memorable, and the dramatic *Tiger* aria is like Constanze's *Martern aller Arten* but briefer and more passionate. Bernhard Klee directs a crisp and lively performance, with excellent contributions from singers and orchestra alike – a first-rate team, as consistently stylish as one could want.

Die Zauberflöte (complete).
*** Ph. Dig. 426 276-2 (2) [id.]. Te Kanawa, Studer, Lind, Araiza, Bär, Ramey, Van Dam, Amb. Op. Ch., ASMF, Marriner.
*** DG Dig. 449 166-2 (2); Video VHS 072 447-3. Oelze, Schade, Sieden, Peeters, Finley, Backes, Monteverdi Ch., E. Bar. Soloists, Gardiner.
*** Erato/Warner Dig. 0630 12705-2 (2). Mannion, Blochwitz, Dessay, Hagen, Scharinger, Les Arts Florissants, William Christie.
✿ (M) (***) DG mono 435 742-2 (2). Stader, Streich, Fischer-Dieskau, Greindl, Haefliger, Berlin RIAS Ch. & SO, Fricsay.
*** EMI CDS5 67071-2 (2) [CMS5 67165]. Janowitz, Putz, Popp, Gedda, Berry, Frick, Schwarzkopf, Ludwig, Hoffgen (3 Ladies), Philh. Ch. & O, Klemperer.
(M) *** EMI (SIS) mono CHS7 69631-2 (2) [Ang. CDHB 69631]. Seefried, Lipp, Loose, Dermota, Kunz, Weber, V. State Op. Ch., VPO, Karajan.
*** EMI Dig. CDS7 47951-8 (3) [Ang. CDCC 47951]. Popp, Gruberová, Lindner, Jerusalem, Brendel, Bracht, Zednik, Bav. R. Ch. & SO, Haitink.
*** Telarc Dig. CD-80302 (2). Hadley, Hendricks, Allen, Anderson, Lloyd, SCO & Ch., Mackerras.
(B) *** Naxos Dig. 8 660030/31 (2) [id.]. Norberg-Schulz, Kwon, Lippert, Leitner, Tichy, Rydl, Hungarian Festival Ch., Failoni O, Budapest, Halász.
(M) **(*) DG Originals 449 749-2 (2) [id.]. Lear, Peters, Wunderlich, Fischer-Dieskau, Crass, Hotter, BPO, Boehm.
(B) (***) Dutton mono 2CDEA 5011 (2) [id.]. Lemnitz, Roswaenge, Hüsch, Berger, Strienz, BPO, Beecham.
**(*) O-L Dig. 440 085-2 (2) [id.]. Bonney, Sumi Jo, Streit, Cachemaille, Sigmundsson, Drottningholm Court Theatre Ch. & O, Ostman.
(M) **(*) RCA 74321 32240-2. Donath, Geszty, Schreier, Adam, Hoff, Leib, Vogel, Leipzig R. Ch., Dresden State O, Suitner.
*** Telarc Dig. CD-80302 (2). Hadley, Hendricks, Allen, Anderson, Lloyd, SCO & Ch., Mackerras.
(N) (B) ** Decca Double 448 734-2 (2) [id.]. Gueden, Lipp, Simoneau, Berry, Böhme, Schöffler, V. St. Op. Ch., VPO, Boehm.

Marriner directs a pointed and elegant reading of *Zauberflöte*, bringing out the fun of the piece. It lacks weight only in the overture and finale, and the cast is the finest in any modern recording. Dame Kiri lightens her voice delightfully, while Olaf Bär, vividly characterful, brings the Lieder-singer's art to the role of Papageno. Araiza's voice has coarsened since he recorded the role of Tamino for Karajan, but this performance is subtler and conveys more feeling. Cheryl Studer's performance as Queen of the Night is easily the finest among modern recordings; and Samuel Ramey gives a generous and wise portrait of Sarastro. This is now the finest digital version, superbly recorded, with the added advantage that it comes on only two discs instead of the three used for most other recent recordings.

John Eliot Gardiner rounds off his outstanding series for DG Archiv of Mozart's seven great mature operas with an electrifying account of *Zauberflöte*. In almost every way it surpasses even the finest period-performance rivals, even though the generally inspired casting is marred by the underpowered and uneven Sarastro of Harry Peeters. The recording was made in studio conditions over the same period as staged performances at the Ludwigsburg Festival, getting the best of both worlds. William Christie in his Erato version, based similarly on live festival performances, is more relaxed in his approach, bringing out more fun in the piece, but Gardiner, at once more daring in his choice of speeds, both fast and slow, finds more depth, drawing more polished and incisive playing from his English Baroque Soloists. One can appreciate far more clearly in this bigger-scale view the other essential elements in Mozart and Schikaneder's complex entertainment, not just an allegory involving masonic ritual, but above all an intensely human quest, with the plight of the heroine, Pamina, involving us if anything even more than that of the hero, Tamino.

In this Gardiner is helped enormously by his choice of singer as Pamina, a young German soprano with a ravishingly pure and sweet voice, flawlessly controlled, Christiane Oelze. In the agonized Act II aria, *Ach, ich fühl's*, she conveys a depth of emotion rarely matched. Also superb is the American soprano who takes the role of Queen of the Night. With a voice as full and silvery as it is flexible, Cyndia Sieden has none of the tinkly shallowness of many coloraturas, while the Tamino of Michael Schade has youthful freshness combined with keen imagination; though there are more characterful Papagenos than Gerald Finley, few sing as freshly and cleanly as he. With recording clear and well balanced, the set offers an incidental practical advantage in putting the spoken dialogue on separate tracks, so that it can readily be programmed out. Recommended strongly alongside Marriner's modern-instrument version.

Based on a production at the Aix-en-Provence Festival, and recorded in 1995 in collaboration with Radio France, William Christie's Erato set otherwise sweeps the board for recordings using period instruments. Arnold Ostman's Drottningholm set similarly re-creates the sparkle and exuberance of a live performance, but that is a small-scale reading, and the very opening of the overture under Christie instantly demonstrates that this is a performance which, along with lighter qualities, can where necessary convey the full weight of Mozart's masonic inspiration, with the instruments of Les Arts Florissants firm and full. More than his rivals, Christie wears his period manners easily and amiably, with fast speeds crisp and light, and with some numbers – such as Papageno's first aria – relaxedly expansive. There is no weak link in the cast, with Rosa Mannion a warm, touching Pamina, able to bring out deeper feelings as in *Ach, ich fühl's*, and Blochwitz is an imaginative, sweetly expressive Tamino, while Natalie Dessay as Queen of the Night is unusually warm-toned for the role, not so much a frigid figure as a fully rounded character, with the coloratura display dazzlingly clear. Scharinger is a genial, rich-toned Papageno, and Hagen a Sarastro satisfyingly clean of focus. Above all, the joyful vigour of Mozart's inspiration captures one from first to last, making this a strong contender, even if you would normally choose a modern-instrument version.

From the early LP era Fricsay's is an outstandingly fresh and alert *Die Zauberflöte*, marked by generally clear, pure singing and well-sprung orchestral playing at generally rather fast speeds. In some ways Fricsay anticipates the Mozart tastes of a later generation, even if his approach to ornamentation is hardly in authentic-period style. Maria Stader and Dietrich Fischer-Dieskau phrase most beautifully, but the most spectacular singing comes from Rita Streich as a dazzling Queen of the Night – the finest on record – and the relatively close balance of the voice gives it the necessary power such as Streich generally failed to convey in the opera house. It is this unique contribution which nudges us towards a Rosette; but Ernst Haefliger, too, is at his most honeyed in tone as Tamino, and only the rather gritty Sarastro of Josef Greindl falls short – and even he sings with a satisfyingly dark resonance. This was the first version to spice the musical numbers with brief sprinklings of dialogue, just enough to prevent the work from sounding like an oratorio. Even including that, DG has managed to put each of the Acts complete on a single disc. The transfer of the original 1954 mono recording (made in the Berlin Jesus-Christus Kirche) is remarkably full-bodied, with a pleasant ambience and sense of presence.

Klemperer's conducting of *The Magic Flute* is one of his finest achievements on record; indeed he is inspired, making the dramatic music sound more like Beethoven in its breadth and strength. But he does not miss the humour and point of the Papageno passages, and he gets the best of both worlds to a surprising degree. The cast is outstanding – look at the distinction of the Three Ladies alone – but curiously it is that generally most reliable of all the singers, Gottlob Frick as Sarastro, who comes nearest to letting the side down. Lucia Popp is in excellent form, and Gundula Janowitz sings Pamina's part with a creamy beauty that is just breathtaking. Nicolai Gedda too is a firm-voiced Tamino. The transfer to a pair of CDs, made possible by the absence of dialogue, is managed expertly. However, like Klemperer's set of Beethoven's *Fidelio*, this recording has reverted to full price and, even though it has been repackaged, such an increase in cost seems in no way justifiable.

Apart from the Fricsay set with Rita Streich which includes some spoken dialogue, there has never been a more seductive recording of *Zauberflöte* than Karajan's mono version of 1950. The Vienna State Opera cast here has not since been matched on record: Irmgard Seefried and Anton Dermota both sing with radiant beauty and great character, Wilma Lipp is a dazzling Queen of the Night, Erich Kunz as Papageno sings with an infectious smile in the voice, and Ludwig Weber is a commanding Sarastro. There is no spoken dialogue; but on two mid-priced CDs instead of three LPs, it is a Mozart treat not to be missed, with mono sound still amazingly vivid and full of presence.

Haitink directs a rich and spacious account of *Zauberflöte*, superbly recorded in spectacularly wide-ranging digital sound. The dialogue – not too much of it, nicely produced and with sound effects adding to the vividness – frames a presentation that has been carefully thought through. Popp makes the most tenderly affecting of Paminas and Gruberová has never sounded more spontaneous in her brilliance than here as Queen of the Night: she is both agile and powerful. Jerusalem makes an outstanding Tamino, both heroic and sweetly Mozartian; and though neither Wolfgang Brendel as Papageno nor Bracht as Sarastro is as characterful as their finest rivals, their personalities project strongly and the youthful freshness of their singing is most attractive. The Bavarian chorus too is splendid.

Though the recording puts a halo of reverberation round the sound, Mackerras and the Scottish Chamber Orchestra find an ideal scale for the work. His speeds are often faster than usual, not least in Pamina's great aria of lament, *Ach, ich fühl's*, but they always flow persuasively. This is the version among recent ones which best conveys the fun of the piece, as well as its power. Jerry Hadley makes a delightfully boyish Tamino, with Thomas Allen the most characterful Papageno, singing beautifully. Robert Lloyd is a noble Sarastro, and though June Anderson is a rather strenuous Queen of the Night, it is thrilling to have a big, dramatic voice so dazzlingly agile. Barbara Hendricks is a questionable choice as Pamina, not clean enough of attack, but the tonal quality is golden. Among modern recordings this is a set to put beside Haitink's very enjoyable EMI version, despite the reverberant sound.

Though Kurt Rydl is the only established recording artist among the soloists, the Naxos set offers a very satisfying performance, well conducted and well recorded, with some very stylish solo singing. At budget price with a fair measure of German dialogue included (but on separate tracks to allow it to be programmed out if preferred), this makes a first-rate recommendation, competitive with some of the classic sets. As Tamino, Herbert Lippert is a good, clean-cut Germanic tenor, hardly ever strained, with fine legato in *Dies Bildnis*. The young Norwegian, Elisabeth Norberg-Schulz, is a bright, girlish Pamina, who sustains a slow speed for *Ach, ich fühl's* very effectively, tenderly making it an emotional high point. Rydl is a powerful Sarastro, if not always perfectly steady, and Tichy is a delightful Papageno, defying Halász's uncharacteristically stodgy tempo for his first aria, and from there consistently conveying characterful humour without vocal exaggeration. Perhaps the most exciting newcomer is Hellen Kwon, an outstanding Queen of the Night, using full, firm tone with bright attack in her two big arias. The recording is clear and well balanced, with the Queen's thunder vividly caught.

One of the glories of Boehm's DG set is the singing of Fritz Wunderlich as Tamino, a wonderful memorial to a singer much missed. Fischer-Dieskau, with characteristic word-pointing, makes a sparkling Papageno on record and Franz Crass is a satisfyingly straightforward Sarastro. The team of women is well below this standard – Lear taxed cruelly in *Ach, ich fühl's*, Peters shrill in the upper register (although the effect is exciting), and the Three Ladies do not blend well – but Boehm's direction is superb, light and lyrical, but weighty where necessary to make a glowing, compelling experience. Fine recording, enhanced in this new transfer for reissue as one of DG's 'Originals'. It is now divested of its previous coupling of *Der Schauspieldirektor* and fitted on to two instead of three CDs.

Beecham's magical pre-war set of *Zauberflöte* has had three earlier CD transfers, all of them seriously flawed, which makes it specially welcome that Mike Dutton comes up with a transfer which at last does justice to the original sound, full and vivid; and the two discs are offered at bargain price. There is glorious singing from Tiana Lemnitz as Pamina, brilliant coloratura from Erna Berger as Queen of the Night, and sharp characterization from Gerhard Hüsch as Papageno. Helge Roswaenge is a Germanic Tamino and Wilhelm Strienz a firm but lugubrious Sarastro. No spoken dialogue, but much warmth and sparkle.

In contrast with his earlier Drottningholm recordings of Mozart operas, often rushed and brittle, Ostman in his Oiseau-Lyre series offers a far more sympathetic set of *Zauberflöte*. It may lack weight but it rarely sounds rushed, for consistently Ostman gives a spring to the rhythms. That was something which disappointingly is missing from Roger Norrington on EMI, a rival recording using period forces. Ostman's cast too is markedly preferable to Norrington's, with no weak link. Barbara Bonney is a charming Pamina, with Kurt Streit a free-toned Tamino and with Gilles Cachemaille as Papageno both finely focused and full of fun. Sumi Jo is a bright, clear Queen of the Night and, though the Sarastro of Kristian Sigmundsson is lightweight, that matches the overall approach.

The RCA (originally Eurodisc) set is well cast, directed with breadth and spirit, and vividly recorded. Indeed, considering that the recording was made at the beginning of the 1970s, it sounds remarkably well, although with a forward balance there is not the subtlety of perspective one finds in more modern sets. There are no real flaws here. The finest performances come from Peter Schreier, an outstanding Tamino, ardent and stylish; Sylvia Geszty's Queen of the Night is fierce to the point of shrillness, but it is a forceful projection and balances with Donath's somewhat ingenuous portrayal of Pamina, prettily sung. Theo Adam is a commanding Sarastro and Renata Hoff and Günther Leib make an attractive team as Papagena and Papageno; while the orchestral playing is first rate, the contribution of the Leipzig Radio Choir is less impressive. There is a minimum of dialogue and it is separately cued. Not a top choice, but enjoyable just the same. The accompanying libretto is in German with no translation.

The principal attraction of this Decca Double reissue from the earliest days of stereo, apart from its modest cost, is the conducting of Karl Boehm. With surprisingly good recording quality (vintage 1955) – vivid, warm and full in the bass – that might well be counted recommendation enough in spite of the absence of dialogue, particularly when the Tamino of Léopold Simoneau and the Papageno of Walter Berry are strongly and sensitively sung, and Wilma Lipp proves an impressive Queen of the Night. But the rest of the singing is variable, with Hilde Gueden a pert, characterful Pamina, unhappy in the florid divisions, and Kurt Böhme a gritty and ungracious Sarastro. The new cued synopsis is a great improvement on the previous reissue and includes new documentation intended to offer a helpful guide for the newcomer to the opera.

Die Zauberflöte: highlights.
*** Ph. Dig. 438 495-2 [id.] (from above recording, with Te Kanawa, Studer, Araiza, Bär, Ramey; cond. Marriner).
(M) *** EMI CDM5 65568-2 (from complete recording, with Janowitz, Putz, Popp, Gedda, Berry, Frick, Schwarzkopf, Ludwig, Hoffgen (3 ladies), Philh. Ch. & O, Klemperer).
(B) *** [EMI Red Line Dig. CDR5 72098] (from complete recording, with Popp, Gruberová, Lindner, Jerusalem, Brendel, Bav. RSO & Ch., Haitink).
(M) (***) EMI mono CD-EMX 2220 [id.] (from above recording with Seefried, Lipp; cond. Karajan).
(B) **(*) DG Classikon 449 845-2 [429 825-2] (from above recording, with Lear, Peters, Wunderlich, Fischer-Dieskau, Crass; cond. Boehm).
(M) **(*) Decca 458 213-2 [421 302-2] (from complete recording, with Lorengar, Deutekom, Burrows, Talvela, Prey, Stoltze, V. State Op. Ch., VPO, Solti).
(N) *** DG Dig. 453 443-2 [id.]. (from above complete set with Oelze, Schade, Sieden, Peeters, Finley, Backes, Monteverdi Ch., cond. Gardiner).

First choice goes to Marriner with his outstanding cast and first-class, modern, digital recording. The selection includes the *Overture* and plays for 69 minutes. Otherwise, those looking for a first-rate set of highlights from *Die Zauberflöte* will find the mid-priced Klemperer disc hard to beat. It makes a good sampler of a performance which, while ambitious in scale, manages to find sparkle and humour too. A synopsis details each individual excerpt, and in this case the inclusion of the *Overture* is especially welcome. The remastered sound has plenty of presence, but atmosphere and warmth too.

This selection from the full-priced Haitink set is well made to include many favourites, with the Papageno/Papagena music well represented to make a contrast with the lyrical arias and the drama of the Queen of the Night. Gruberová has never sounded more spontaneous in her brilliance than here; in that role she is both agile and powerful. Popp makes the most tenderly affecting of Paminas. The gravitas of Haitink's approach does not miss the work's elements of drama and charm, though nothing is trivialized. Superb recording in spectacularly wide-ranging, digital sound.

The Karajan Vienna State Opera selection on Eminence will be a good way for many to sample a highly enticing mono set with a superb cast, all on the top of their form. The selection lasts 68 minutes, but seven of these are taken up by the Overture, a less than sensible idea, even if it is superbly played. It is disgraceful, though, that the front of this CD – aimed at a popular market – does not make it absolutely clear that the sound is mono.

The hour of excerpts from Boehm's recording is not obviously directed towards bringing out its special qualities, although there would have been room on the CD (which includes the *Overture*) for at least another quarter of an hour of music, to measure up with the companion selection from *Don Giovanni*. One would have liked more of Wunderlich's Tamino, one of the great glories of the set. However, the key arias are all included and the sound is fresh and full. This is now on DG's bargain Classikon label, which means that the synopsis is not cued.

Solti's highlights, which come from his earlier (1970) analogue set, are certainly worth sampling. On the male side the cast is very strong indeed, with Stuart Burrows a stylish, rich-toned Tamino. Martti Talvela is a bold Sarastro and Hermann Prey rounds out the character of Papageno with intelligent pointing of words. Pilar Lorengar's Pamina is sweetly attractive as long as your ear is not worried by her intrusive vibrato, while Cristina Deutekom's Queen of the Night is technically impressive, though the coloratura has a curious colouristic flaw. Solti's reading is tough and brilliant, but it is aguable that in highlights this is less worrying than in a complete set, even if the almost total absence of charm is disconcerting. The selection is generous (73 minutes) and the disc is handsomely packaged in Decca's Opera Gala series, with a full translation included.

The full-priced DG Archiv selection from the Gardiner set is comprehensive (72 minutes) but only a cued synopsis is included.

Recitals

'*The Mozart experience*': Arias from *Ascanio in Alba; Così fan tutte; Die Entführung aus dem Serail; Le nozze di Figaro; Die Zauberflöte; Zaïde.*

(N) **(*) Conifer Classics Dig. 75605 55031-2 [id.]. Lynne Dawson; Inger Dam-Jensen; Della Jones; Anthony Rolfe Johnson; François Le Roux; ROHO/Nicholas McGegan.

This is a mixed bag of a Mozart compilation, starting with the Overture to *La clemenza di Tito*, and then presenting a variable collection of arias early and late. Inger Dam-Jensen is disappointingly edgy in her two items from *Zaïde*, but the other soprano, Lynne Dawson, sings ravishingly both in *Ascanio in Alba* and as the Countess in *Figaro*. Della Jones is strong and characterful in a range of items, and Anthony Rolfe Johnson too sings with immaculate point and style in the great tenor arias from *Entführung*, *Così* and *Zauberflöte*. François Le Roux is disappointingly variable, until the Papageno items at the end find him at his most winningly characterful. Clear, well-balanced sound.

Arias from: *La clemenza di Tito; Così fan tutte; Don Giovanni; Die Entführung aus dem Serail; Idomeneo; Le nozze di Figaro; Die Zauberflöte.*
(M) *** Ph. (IMS) Dig. 442 410-2. Cheryl Studer, ASMF, Marriner.

This is a very impressive recital indeed. Only the aria from *Idomeneo* could be considered a little under-characterized – and that is a marginal criticism; the Queen of the Night's arias from *Die Zauberflöte* are superbly done, as is the opening *Martern aller Arten* (from *Die Entführung*) and the excerpts from *Così* and *Don Giovanni* are hardly less memorable in a quite different way. Excellent accompaniments and recording, but the measure is fairly short (55 minutes).

Arias: *La clemenza di Tito: S'altro che lagrime. Così fan tutte: Ei parte . . . Sen . . . Per pietà. La finta giardiniera: Crudeli fermate . . . Ah dal pianto. Idomeneo: Se il padre perdei. Lucio Silla: Pupille amate. Il rè pastore: L'amerò, sarò costante. Zaïde: Ruhe sanft, mein holdes Leben. Die Zauberflöte: Ach, ich fühl's es ist verschwunden.*
*** Ph. (IMS) Dig. 411 148-2 [id.]. Kiri Te Kanawa, LSO, C. Davis.

Kiri Te Kanawa's is one of the loveliest collections of Mozart arias on record, with the voice at its most ravishing and pure. One might object that Dame Kiri concentrates on soulful arias, ignoring more vigorous ones; but with stylish accompaniment and clear, atmospheric recording, beauty dominates all.

Arias from: *Così fan tutte; Don Giovanni; Clemenza di Tito; Idomeneo; Lucio Silla; Mitridate; Le nozze di Figaro;*
(N) *** RCA Dig. 09026 68661-2 [id.]. Vesselina Kasarova, Dresden State O, Sir Colin Davis.

The young Bulgarian, Vesselina Kasarova, with her tangy, sharply projected mezzo, is both characterful and magnetic. Here in a formidable collection of Mozart arias, much enhanced by Colin Davis's accompaniment, she demonstrates not only her stylishness and technical prowess – with not a single intrusive aitch allowed – but her musical flair. At the very start, she launches into the recitative before Dorabella's aria in *Così fan tutte* with a vehemence that takes the breath away, and vehemence is a quality that draws many of these portrayals together, whether as Donna Elvira in *Don Giovanni* (giving way to tenderness when required), Vitellia in *Clemenza* or a whole range of trouser roles, including those in the early *Mitridate* and *Lucio Silla*.

Arias from: *Don Giovanni; Die Entführung aus dem Serail; La finta giardiniera; Il rè pastore; Le nozze di Figaro; Il sogno di Scipione; Die Zauberflöte. Concert aria: Nehmt meinen Dank.*
*** Decca Dig. 452 602-2 [id.]. Renée Fleming, O of St Luke's, Mackerras.

Renée Fleming has rarely sounded quite so beautiful on disc as in this wide-ranging collection of Mozart arias, one of the finest available. If it is disappointing not to have her singing the role of the Countess in *Figaro*, the two Susanna items are both welcome – *Deh vieni* bringing out her most golden tone and the big alternative aria, *Al desio*, challenging her to her most brilliant singing. Her account of La Fortuna's aria from *Il sogno di Scipione* is commanding too, and her ornamentation is phenomenally crisp and brilliant throughout, not least in *Ach ich liebte* from *Entführung*. The only reservations come with the brisk treatment, period-style, of Pamina's *Ach, ich fühl's* and the lovely aria from *Zaïde*, both of which could be much more tenderly expressive. Excellent, stylish accompaniment and first-rate recording.

Arias: *Don Giovanni; Die Entführung aus dem Serail; Idomeneo; Le nozze di Figaro; Die Zauberflöte.*
(M) (***) EMI mono CDH7 63708-2 [id.]. Elisabeth Schwarzkopf (with various orchestras & conductors, including John Pritchard).

Just how fine a Mozartian Schwarzkopf already was early in her career comes out in these 12 items, recorded between 1946 and 1952. The earliest are Konstanze's two arias from *Entführung*, and one of the curiosities is a lovely account of Pamina's *Ach, ich fühl's*, recorded in English in 1948. The majority, including those from *Figaro* – Susanna's and Cherubino's arias as well as the Countess's – are taken from a long-unavailable recital disc conducted by John Pritchard. Excellent transfers.

ANTHOLOGIES

'Fifty Years of Mozart singing on record': (i) *Concert arias;* Excerpts from: (ii) *Mass in C min., K.427;* (iii) *La clemenza di Tito;* (iv) *Così fan*

tutte; (v) *Don Giovanni;* (vi) *Die Entführung aus dem Serail;* (vii) *La finta giardiniera;* (viii) *Idomeneo;* (ix) *Le nozze di Figaro;* (x) *Il rè pastore;* (xi) *Zaïde;* (xii) *Die Zauberflöte.*

(M) (***) EMI mono CMS7 63750-2 (4) [id.]. (i) Rethberg, Ginster, Francillo-Kaufmann; (ii) Berger; (iii) Kirkby-Lunn; (iv) V. Schwarz, Noni, Grümmer, Hahn, Kiurina, Hüsch, Souez, H. Nash; (v) Vanni-Marcoux, Scotti, Farrar, Battistini, Corsi, Leider, Roswaenge, D'Andrade, Pinza, Patti, Maurel, Renaud, Pernet, McCormack, Gadski, Kemp, Callas; (vi) Slezak, L. Weber, Tauber, Lehmann, Nemeth, Perras, Ivogün, Von Pataky, Hesch; (vii) Dux; (viii) Jurinac, Jadlowker; (ix) Stabile, Helletsgruber, Santley, Gobbi, Lemnitz, Feraldy, Schumann, Seinemeyer, Vallin, Rautawaara, Mildmay, Jokl, Ritter-Ciampi; (x) Gerhart; (xi) Seefried; (xii) Fugère; Wittrisch; Schiøtz, Gedda, Kurz, Erb, Kipnis, Galvany, Hempel, Sibiriakov, Frick, Destinn, Norena, Schöne, Kunz.

This is an astonishing treasury of singing, recorded over the first half of the twentieth century. It begins with Mariano Stabile's resonant 1928 account of Figaro's *Se vuol ballare*, snail-like by today's standards, while Sir Charles Santley in *Non piu andrai* a few tracks later is both old-sounding and slow. The stylistic balance is then corrected in Tito Gobbi's magnificently characterful 1950 recording of that same aria. Astonishment lies less in early stylistic enormities than in the wonderful and consistent purity of vocal production, with wobbles – so prevalent today – virtually non-existent. That is partly the result of the shrewd and obviously loving choice of items, which includes not only celebrated marvels like John McCormack's 1916 account of Don Ottavio's *Il mio tesoro* (breaking all records for breath control, and stylistically surprising for including an appoggiatura), but many rarities. The short-lived Meta Seinemeyer, glorious in the Countess's first aria, Germaine Feraldy, virtually unknown, a charming Cherubino, Johanna Gadski formidably incisive in Donna Anna's *Mi tradi*, Frieda Hempel incomparable in the Queen of the Night's second aria – all these and many dozens of others make for compulsive listening, with transfers generally excellent. There are far more women singers represented than men, and a high proportion of early recordings are done in languages other than the original; but no lover of fine singing should miss this feast. The arias are gathered together under each opera, with items from non-operatic sources grouped at the end of each disc. Helpfully, duplicate versions of the same aria are put together irrespective of date of recording, and highly informative notes are provided on all the singers.

Muffat, Georg (1653–1704)

Armonico tributo cioè sonata da camera: Nos. 2 in G min.; 5 in G.

**(*) HM/BMG Dig. 05472 77303-2 [id.]. Freiburg Bar. Cons. – BIBER: *Sonatae tam Aris.* **(*)

Muffat's sonatas (1682) are almost exactly contemporary with the Biber sonatas with which they are coupled but they are much more conventional works. Yet they attractively provide a touch of gravitas between the chimerical Biber pieces. They are played authentically and with spirit, and are well recorded. But with a playing time of 59 minutes there would have been room here for yet another work by each composer.

Muldowney, Dominic (born 1952)

(i) *Piano concerto;* (ii) *Saxophone concerto.*

(M) *** EMI CDM5 66528-2. (i) Peter Donohoe, BBC SO, Mark Elder; (ii) John Harle, L. Sinf., Diego Masson.

Dominic Muldowney, now in his late forties, has been music director at the National Theatre since 1976. These two colourful and dramatic concertos are excellent examples of his more recent style, far more approachable than his earlier work. His *Piano concerto* is a formidable work in a continuous half-hour span of many different sections. It uses Bachian forms, along with tough Bachian piano figuration, to move kaleidoscopically in a kind of musical collage of references to different genres, including jazz and the popular waltz. With Peter Donohoe giving one of his finest performances on record, and with colourful playing from the BBC Symphony Orchestra under Mark Elder, the piece emerges powerfully, with occasional gruff echoes of Hindemith. The *Saxophone concerto* (written for the outstanding virtuoso of the instrument, John Harle, who plays it on the record) is a more compact, strongly characterized work in three movements, each throwing up a grateful number of warm, easy tunes without any sense of compromise or incongruity. Warm, well-balanced recording.

Mundy, William (*c.* 1529–*c.* 1591)

Vox Patris caelestis.

*** Gimell Ph. 454 939-2 [id.]. Tallis Scholars, Phillips – ALLEGRI: *Miserere;* PALESTRINA: *Missa Papae Marcelli.* ***

Mundy's *Vox Patris caelestis* was written during the short reign of Queen Mary (1553–8). The work is structured in nine sections in groups of three, the last of each group being climactic and featuring the whole choir, with solo embroidery. Yet the music flows continuously, like a great river, and the complex vocal writing creates the most spectacular effects, with the trebles soaring up and shining out over the underlying cantilena. The Tallis Scholars give an account which balances linear clarity with considerable power. The recording is first class and the digital remastering for CD improves the focus further.

Mussorgsky, Modest (1839–81)

The Capture of Kars (Triumphal march); St John's night on the bare mountain (original score); *Scherzo in B flat. Khovanshchina: Prelude to Act I;* (i) *Introduction to Act IV. The Destruction of Sennacherib.* (i; ii) *Joshua.* (i) *Oedipus in Athens: Temple chorus. Salammbô: Priestesses' chorus* (operatic excerpts all orch. Rimsky-Korsakov).

❁ (M) *** RCA 09026 61354-2 [id.]. (i) London Symphony Ch.; (ii) Zehava Gal; LSO, Abbado.

To commemorate the centenary of Mussorgsky's death, in 1981 Abbado and the LSO came up with this very attractive and revealing anthology of shorter pieces. It is particularly good to have so vital and pungent an account of the original version of *Night on the bare mountain*, different in all but its basic material from the Rimsky-Korsakov arrangement. Rimsky was right to prune it: at 12 minutes, without the slow end-piece, it is a shade over-long, but Mussorgsky's scoring is so original and imaginative that the ear is readily held. Best of all are the four choral pieces; even when they are early and untypical (*Oedipus in Athens*, for example), they are immediately attractive and very Russian in feeling, and they include such evocative pieces as the *Chorus of Priestesses* (intoning over a pedal bass) from a projected opera on Flaubert's novel. The recording is first rate and the CD transfer enhances the original considerably, giving the chorus greater presence without loss of atmosphere or perspective. This is one of the most attractive Mussorgsky records in the catalogue and is not to be missed: the performers are on their toes throughout.

Night on the bare mountain (orch. Rimsky-Korsakov).

(M) *** EMI (SIS) CDM5 65715-2 [id.]. O de Paris, Rostropovich – RIMSKY-KORSAKOV: *Scheherazade; Capriccio espagnol.* **(*)

(M) *** Mercury (IMS) 432 004-2 [id.]. LSO, Dorati – PROKOFIEV: *Romeo and Juliet suites.* ***

A bold, exciting account from Rostropovich, emphasizing the richness of Rimsky-Korsakov's orchestration rather than the starkness of Mussorgsky's original conception – but not necessarily the worse for that, when the recording is full-blooded to match.

Dorati's fine 1960 account of *Night on the bare mountain* comes as an encore for Skrowaczewski's outstanding Prokofiev, and it is interesting at the end of *Romeo and Juliet* to note the subtle shift of acoustic from the Minneapolis auditorium to Wembley Town Hall.

(i) *Night on the bare mountain* (arr. Rimsky-Korsakov); (ii) *Pictures at an exhibition* (orch. Ravel).

*** DG (IMS) Dig. 429 785-2 [id.]. NYPO, Sinopoli – RAVEL: *Valses nobles et sentimentales.* **(*)

*** Telarc Dig. CD 80042 [id.]. Cleveland O, Maazel.

(M) *** RCA [id.]. 09026 61958-2 [id.]. Chicago SO, Reiner – *Concert of Russian showpieces.* ***

(B) **(*) Decca Eclipse Dig. 448 233-2 [id.]. Montreal SO, Dutoit – RIMSKY-KORSAKOV: *Capriccio espagnol* etc. **(*)

Sinopoli's electrifying New York recording of Mussorgsky's *Pictures at an exhibition* not only heads the list of modern digital versions but also it again displays the New York Philharmonic as one of the world's great orchestras, performing with an epic virtuosity and panache that recall the Bernstein era of the 1960s. The playing of violins and woodwind alike is full of sophisticated touches, so well demonstrated by their colourful, brilliant articulation in *Tuileries Gardens* and *Limoges*, the wittily piquant portrayal of the *Unhatched chicks*, and the firm, resonant line of the lower strings in *Samuel Goldenberg and Schmuyle*. But it is the brass that one rememembers most, from the richly sonorous opening *Promenade*, through the ferocious bite and subtle grotesquerie of *Gnomus*, the bleating trumpet of *Schmuyle*, the stabbing sforzandos at the opening of *Catacombs*, to the malignantly forceful rhythms of *The hut on fowl's legs*, with the playing of the trombones and tuba often assuming an unusual yet obviously calculated dominance of the texture. The finale combines power with dignified splendour, and the bells toll out from their tower to emphasize the Byzantine character of Hartmann's picture of the *Kiev Gate*. *A Night on the bare mountain* is comparably vibrant, with the Rimskian fanfares particularly vivid and the closing pages full of Russian nostalgia. The splendid digital recording, made in New York's Manhattan Center, has breadth and weight, and its fullness comes with a believable overall perspective and excellent internal definition.

The quality of the Telarc Cleveland recording is apparent at the very opening of *Night on the bare mountain* in the richly sonorous presentation of the deep brass and the sparkling yet unexaggerated percussion. With the Cleveland Orchestra on top form, the *Pictures* are strongly characterized; this may not be the subtlest reading available, but each of Mussorgsky's cameos comes vividly to life. After a vibrantly rhythmic *Baba-Yaga*, strong in fantastic menace, the closing *Great Gate of Kiev* is overwhelmingly spacious in conception and quite riveting as sheer sound, with the richness and amplitude of the brass which make the work's final climax unforgettable. Unfortunately the *Pictures* are not cued separately.

Reiner's RCA *Pictures* (recorded in 1957) is another demonstration of vintage stereo using simple microphone techniques to achieve a natural concert-hall balance.The sound-balance is full and atmospheric and Reiner's approach is evocative to match – the sombre picture of *The old castle*, the lumbering *Ox-wagon*, the unctuous picture of *Samuel Goldenberg* (powerfully drawn in the strings) and the superb brass playing in the *Catacombs* sequence are all memorable. The final climax of *The Great Gate of Kiev* is massively effective, if not quite matching the Cleveland Telarc version in sheer spectacle. The Chicago brass is again very telling in *Night on a bare mountain*, made two years later, a performance just as strongly characterized. The current CD transfers are very impressive indeed.

Dutoit's *A Night on the bare mountain* is strong and biting, but again the adrenalin does not flow as grippingly as in, say, Solti's version. Dutoit's *Pictures* have each movement strongly characterized and there is a sense of fun in the scherzando movements. But overall this is less involving than with Reiner, and the brilliant recording is not as sumptuous as some other versions, although it has the bloom characteristic of the Montreal sound.

A night on the bare mountain; Pictures at an exhibition; Khovanshchina, Act IV: Entr'acte. Boris Godunov: symphonic synthesis (all arr. and orch. Stokowski).
*** Chandos Dig. CHAN 9445 [id.]. BBC PO, Matthias Bamert.

These highly characteristic transcriptions all come from the peak period of Stokowski's association with the great orchestra he helped to create in Philadelphia. The skilfully tailored 24-minute *Boris Godunov* synthesis dates from November 1936, the *Pictures from an exhibition* from 1939, and *Night on bald mountain* (the correct title, and nearer the original Russian meaning) was scored for Disney in 1940. Anyone who has seen *Fantasia* will find the music indelibly associated with the imagery of the film, and the spectacularly plangent orchestration (especially the highly individual use of the percussion) is in many respects nearer to Mussorgsky's *St John's night on the bare mountain* than the Rimsky version, with Rimsky's interpolated brass fanfares omitted. Thus Mussorgsky's satanic conception makes a spectacularly sinister impact, with the coda by contrast sumptuously romantic. (One wonders why Matthias Bamert chose not to tack on Schubert's *Ave Maria*, as Stokowski did for the film.) The sombre power of the operatic synthesis from *Boris Godunov*, with its Kremlin bells and chanting monks, and the haunted portrait of Boris himself, are also gripping, while the *Entr'acte* from *Khovanshchina* is even finer, one of Stokowski's most telling transcriptions, rich in its sonorities and played very tellingly under Bamert. We like the vividness of Stokowski's *Pictures* too, particularly the way in which the the unison horns swell out vocally near the climax of *Bydlo*, while to choose a cor anglais for the main theme in *The old castle* is every bit as telling as Ravel's saxophone, perhaps more so. Not surprisingly, Stokowski scores for the violins rather more readily than Ravel, as instanced by the opening *Promenade*. The one moment when Ravel's orchestration is truly inspired is the interchange between *Goldenberg and Schmuyle*; Stokowski has the solo trumpet echoed by the woodwind and the effect is mockingly bizarre, but less bleatingly obsequious than Ravel's version. However, the *Catacombs* sequence makes a sumptuously weighty impact, and *Baba-Yaga* is grotesquely pointed with imaginative orchestral comments. Two numbers are omitted: *Tuileries* and *Limoges*; according to Edward Johnson's authoritative notes, Stokowski considered them 'too French' and 'not Mussorgskian'. *The Great Gate of Kiev*, massively scored, including tolling bells and organ, makes a huge final apotheosis. In all, this record is a great success, for the Chandos sound is fully worthy and would surely have delighted the old orchestral magician with its richness of amplitude – the effect far preferable to the somewhat bloated Phase 4 quality of Stokowski's own earlier recordings for Decca.

(i) *Night on the bare mountain* (arr. Rimsky-Korsakov); *Pictures at an exhibition* (arr. Funtek); (ii) *Songs and dances of death* (arr. Aho).
*** BIS Dig. CD 325 [id.]. (i) Finnish RSO, (i) Leif Segerstam; (ii) Järvi, with Talvela.

This fascinating CD offers an orchestration by Leo Funtek, made in the same year as Ravel's (1922); it is especially fascinating for the way the different uses of colour change the character of some of Victor Hartman's paintings: the use of a cor anglais in *The old castle*, for instance, or the soft-grained wind scoring which makes the portrait of *Samuel Goldenberg and Schmuyle* more sympathetic, if also blander. The performances by the Finnish Radio Orchestra under Leif Segerstam both of this and of the familiar Rimsky *Night on the bare mountain* are spontaneously presented and very well recorded. The extra item is no less valuable: an intense, darkly Russian account of the *Songs and dances of death* from Martti Talvela with the orchestral accompaniment plangently scored by Kalevi Aho.

Night on the bare mountain (trans. Tchernov).
❁ *** Teldec/Warner Dig. 4509 96516-2 [id.]. Boris Berezovsky – BALAKIREV: *Islamey*. *** ❁

This remarkable transcription by Konstantin Tchernov sounds hardly less dazzling in Berezovksy's hands than the outstanding *Islamey* with which it is coupled. The engineers capture very good piano sound.

(i) *Night on the bare mountain* (arr. and orch. Stokowski); (ii) *Boris Godunov: symphonic synthesis* (arr. Stokowski).

(M) ** Decca Phase 4 443 896-2 [id.]. (i) LSO; (ii) SRO; Stokowski – BORODIN: *Polovtsian dances* ***; (with TCHAIKOVSKY: *1812 overture*; *Marche slave*. **(*))

Pictures at an exhibition. (arr. and orch. Stokowski).

(M) ** Decca Phase 4 443 898-2 [id.]. New Phil. O, Stokowski – SCRIABIN: *Poème de l'extase;* STRAVINSKY: *Firebird suite* etc. **(*)

Stokowski's *Night on the bare mountain* opens with a grotesque balance at the opening, with the heavy brass to the fore. This is Stokowski's own orchestration, so gauche emphasis is fair enough. Few records have more noise on them at climaxes, but the bizarre orchestral effects are telling in a crude way, and the gentle coda is beautifully done in Stokowski's romantically drenched, ecstatic manner. The complete *1812* and *Marche slave* are similarly eccentric. The former includes an overwhelming carillon and chorus at the climax.

The extended symphonic synthesis from *Boris Godunov* has a technicolor flavour; yet, for all the hyperbole of the presentation, Stokowski's magnetism ensures that the music's power communicates, even if the stark austerity of Mussorgsky's original is missing.

Similarly Stokowski's arrangement of *Pictures at an exhibition* is not notable for its subtlety. The pictures are blown up with Phase Four immediacy, so that the orchestra sounds right on top of the listener. With a restricted dynamic range, the sound is very coarse and the inner tension is stretched to breaking point. The closing climax is harsh. Even so, the sheer personality of this music-making makes its impact.

Pictures at an exhibition (orch. Cailliet).

(N) (***) Biddulph mono WHL 046 Phd. O, Ormandy – TCHAIKOVSKY: *Symphony No. 6*. (***)

This 1937 recording, one of the first Ormandy made in Philadelphia, offers the only version yet of Lucien Cailliet's orchestration of *Pictures*, specially commissioned by Ormandy from the orchestra's 'house arranger' and principal bass clarinet. Surprisingly for a wind player, Cailliet uses full strings markedly more than Ravel in his orchestration, so that the result is less transparent, often warmer, and some would say more conventional. One bonus is that Cailliet includes the long *Promenade*, after *Goldenberg* and before *Limoges*, which Ravel omits. The transfer is clear and fresh, with remarkably little feeling of limitation. With the Tchaikovsky coupling, a timely tribute to a conductor too often underestimated.

Pictures at an exhibition (orch. Ravel).

(M) *** DG 447 426-2 [id.]. BPO, Karajan – DEBUSSY: *La Mer;* RAVEL: *Boléro*. ***

❀ (M) *** RCA 09026 61401-2 [id.]. Chicago SO, Fritz Reiner – RESPIGHI: *The Fountains of Rome; The Pines of Rome*. *** ❀

*** DG Gold (IMS) Dig. 439 013-2. BPO, Karajan – RAVEL: *Boléro* etc. ***

(M) *** DG Penguin Classics Dig. 460 633-2 [id.]. LSO, Abbado – RAVEL: *Boléro*. ***

(M) *** DG (IMS) 415 844-2. Chicago SO, Giulini – RAVEL: *Ma mère l'Oye; Rapsodie espagnole*. ***

(M) *** EMI (SIS) Dig. CDM7 64516-2. Phd. O, Muti – STRAVINSKY: *Rite of spring*. ***

(B) *** Sony SBK 48162 [id.]. Cleveland O, Szell – KODALY: *Háry János suite;* PROKOFIEV: *Lieutenant Kijé suite*. ***

(M) *** Decca Dig. 417 754-2 [id.]. Chicago SO, Solti – BARTOK: *Concerto for orchestra*. ***

(M) (***) Mercury mono 434 378-2 [id.]. Chicago SO, Rafael Kubelik – BARTOK: *Music for strings, percussion and celesta*. (***)

(BB) **(*) EMI Seraphim Dig. CES5 68539-2 (2). Philh. O, Maazel – DEBUSSY: *La Mer; Nocturnes* *** (with RAVEL: *Alborada* etc. **(*)).

(M) (**) RCA mono GD 60287 [60287-2-RG]. NBC SO, Toscanini – ELGAR: *Enigma variations*. (***)

Among the many fine versions of Mussorgsky's *Pictures* on CD, Karajan's 1966 record stands out. It is undoubtedly a great performance, tingling with electricity from the opening Promenade to the spaciously conceived finale, *The Great Gate of Kiev*, which has real splendour. The remastered analogue recording still sounds marvellous, and this reissue, in DG's 'Originals' series of legendary recordings, includes a uniquely evocative performance of Debussy's *La Mer* as well as a very exciting account of Ravel's *Boléro*.

Reiner's 1957 Chicago performance was orginally issued in the UK in October 1958 (as RCA SB 2001), around the same time as Karajan's Philharmonia account. With the advantage of the rich acoustics of Symphony Hall, the RCA sound-balance is more atmospheric than the EMI recording, if less sharply focused. The finale climax of *The Great Gate of Kiev* shows the concentration of the playing. The remastering is fully worthy, and there is excellent documentation.

Karajan's 1986 recording is one of the most impressive of DG's digital recordings remastered by their Original-image-bit processing. The tangibility of the sound is remarkable, with the opening brass *Promenade* and the massed strings in *Samuel Goldenberg and Schmuyle* notable in their naturalness of sonority. The power of *Bydlo* is as impressive as the tension in the pianissimo tremolando strings in *Cum mortuis in lingua mortua*. With superb Berlin Philharmonic playing and the weight of the climaxes contrasting with the wit of *Tuileries* and the exhilaration of *The market at Limoges*, this is certainly now among the top recommendations. Even the spacious finale, where Karajan fails to detach the massive chords – if not quite as electrifying as his earlier, analogue version – is given greater impact by the added weight and makes a fittingly grandiose culmination.

Abbado takes a straighter, more direct view of Mussorgsky's fanciful series of pictures than usual. He is helped by the translucent and naturally balanced digital recording; indeed, the sound is first class, making great impact at climaxes yet also extremely refined, as in the delicate portrayal of the unhatched chicks. Abbado's speeds tend to be extreme, with both this and *Tuileries* taken very fast and light, while *Bydlo* and *The Great Gate of Kiev* are slow and weighty. This now reappears on Penguin Classics at mid-price, coupled with Ravel. The author's essay is by Richard Ford.

Giulini's 1976 Chicago recording has always been among the front runners. He is generally more relaxed and often more wayward than Karajan, but this is still a splendid performance and the finale generates more tension than Karajan's most recent, digital version, though it is not as overpowering as the earlier, analogue recording.

Muti's reading, given the excellence of its recorded sound, more than holds its own, although the balance is forward and perhaps not all listeners will respond to the brass timbres at the opening. The lower strings in *Samuel Goldenberg and Schmuyle* have extraordinary body and presence, and *Baba-Yaga* has an unsurpassed virtuosity and attack, as well as being of a high standard as a recording. The coupling is no less thrilling. This can be recommended even to those readers who have not always responded to later records from this conductor.

Szell's 1963 Cleveland performance also remains among the greatest of all recordings of Ravel's vividly inspired orchestration and is recommendable alongside Karajan. Even if the recording has a somewhat less expansive dynamic-range, the character of each portrait is firmly drawn with vivid strokes of orchestral colour, helped by the feeling that the orchestral players are enjoying their own effortless virtuosity. The portrayal of *Goldenberg and Schmuyle* brings superbly full articulation from the lower strings and *Baba-Yaga* makes the most incisive impact. Indeed it is the precision with which Ravel's instrumentation is conveyed that makes each thumbnail sketch so indelible. Whether in the cheeping and chattering of the unhatched chicks, the bravura swirl of the *Limoges Market*, or the dignified grandiloquence of that final great gateway of Kiev, the controlled brilliance of the recording projects everything with extraordinary vividness.

Solti's performance is fiercely brilliant rather than atmospheric or evocative. He treats Ravel's orchestration as a virtuoso challenge, and with larger-than-life digital recording it undoubtedly has demonstration qualities, and the transparency of texture, given the forward balance, provides quite startling clarity.

Kubelik's famous (1951) mono version of Ravel's masterly scoring was the Mercury recording which coined the term (and subsequent trademark) 'Living presence', taken from Howard Taubman's review in *The New York Times*. The realism of the recording (in spite of some thinness in the top range of the strings) still has the power to astonish. It is most naturally balanced and, although without the additional illumination of stereo, still conveys much of the splendid acoustic of Chicago's Orchestral Hall. The success of the record is not just technical, but musical too. The performance has great freshness with not a hint of routine anywhere; there are many subtleties, particularly as one picture or promenade is dovetailed into another.

Maazel has the advantage of first-class playing from the 1962 Philharmonia Orchestra, and all these pictures spring to life colourfully, even if the characterization is not as sharp as with Karajan. After a comparatively subtle portrait of *Baba-Yaga*, Maazel draws out the final climax of *The Great Gate of Kiev* very spaciously indeed.

Toscanini's regimented view of the exotic Mussorgsky–Ravel score is at its least sympathetic in the opening statement of the opening *Promenade*, not just rigidly metrical but made the coarser by the cornet-like trumpet tone. Many of the individual movements are done with greater understanding – but too often Toscanini's lack of sympathy undermines the character of this rich score. Clean, bright transfer.

(i) *Pictures at an exhibition* (orch. Ravel); (ii) *Boris Godunov* (original version): highlights (including *Death scene*).

(M) *** Sony Theta Dig. SMK 60008 [id.]. (i) BPO, Giulini; (ii) Nicolai Ghiaurov, Nicola Ghiuselev, Dimiter Petrov, Josef Frank, Sofia Nat. Op. Ch., Bodra Smyana Children's Ch., Sofia Festival O, Tchakarov.

It was a splendid idea to reissue Giulini's newest (1989) Sony account of Mussorgsky's *Pictures* (discussed above) with highlights from Tchakarov's Sofia *Boris Godunov*. Ghiaurov gives a magnificent performance as Boris and Tchakarov brings out the reflective side of the score well. But the complete set is flawed. It is partly a question of backward balance, partly a lack of bite in the performance. But the opening chorus of wandering minstrels from the *Prologue* makes a fine impact and the intensity of Boris's monologue, *I have achieved power*, and above all the death scene (both included here), with Ghiaurov singing beautifully, rarely snarling in sing-speech, make this set of excerpts particularly valuable. Nicola Ghiuselev is magnificent as Pimen in his Act I aria, *Just one last story*, and if Dimiter Petrov is at times an unsteady Varlaam, he is not ineffective in his contribution to the second scene of Act I, and this is the only drawback in a thoroughly worthwhile and unusual coupling.

(i) *Pictures at an exhibition* (orch. Ravel); (ii) *Pictures at an exhibition* (original piano version).
(M) **(*) Ph Dig. 442 650-2. (i) VPO, Previn; (ii) Brendel.

Previn's Philips version was recorded during live performances in Vienna. Obviously the Philips engineers had problems with the acoustics of the Musikvereinsaal, as the bass is noticeably resonant and inner definition is far from sharp. Otherwise the balance is truthful; but the performance, though not lacking spontaneity, is not distinctive, and there is a lack of the kind of grip which makes Karajan's version so unforgettable.

Brendel's performance of the original piano score has its own imaginative touches and some fine moments. Brendel keeps the music moving but effectively varies the style of the Promenades. The closing pages, however, need to sound more unbuttoned: Brendel is weighty, but fails to enthral the listener. The recording is faithful.

Pictures at an exhibition; St John's night on the bare mountain (original version); (i) *The destruction of Sennacherib;* (ii) *Joshua; Oedipus in Athens: Chorus of people in the temple. Salambô: Chorus of priestesses.*
*** DG Dig. 445 238-2. BPO, Abbado; with (i) Prague Philharmonic Ch.; (ii) and Elena Zaremba.

Abbado included the four choral items on an outstanding mid-priced RCA record (see above). This was coupled with other short orchestral pieces besides *St John's night on the bare mountain* and is splendidly played and sung. This new CD offers an equally vivid account of *St John's night on the bare mountain*. The choral pieces are richly sung and the short cantata, *Joshua*, is particularly successful with its central solo, *The Amorite women weep*, movingly sung by Elena Zaremba. There is also much to praise in the spacious performance of the *Pictures* with its individually observed detail. It is not as electrifying as Karajan's analogue version or Sinopoli's highly recommendable digital account, but it is notable for the refinement of its colouring and evocation, often more gently evocative than usual.

Pictures at an exhibition (original piano version).
✿ *** Virgin/EMI Dig. VC7 59611-2. Mikhail Pletnev – TCHAIKOVSKY: *Sleeping Beauty*: excerpts. *** ✿

Pictures at an exhibition (piano version, ed. Horowitz).
(M) (***) RCA mono GD 60321. Vladimir Horowitz – TCHAIKOVSKY: *Piano concerto No. 1*. (***) ✿

Pictures at an exhibition (piano version, ed. Horowitz); *Sunless: On the river* (arr. Horowitz).
(M) (***) RCA mono GD 60449 [60449-2-RG]. Horowitz – TCHAIKOVSKY: *Piano concerto No. 1*. (***)
(N) * Hyperion Dig. CDA 67018 [id.]. Nikolai Demidenko – PROKOFIEV: Romeo & Juliet: 10 pieces; Toccata, Op. 11. **

There are remarkable effects of colour and of pedalling in Pletnev's performance – easily the most commanding to have appeared since Richter and, one is tempted to say, a re-creation rather than a performance. Pletnev does not hesitate to modify the odd letter of the score in order to come closer to its spirit. *The Ballet of the unhatched chicks* has great wit and the *Great Gate of Kiev* is extraordinarily rich in colour. An altogether outstanding issue.

Horowitz's famous 1951 recording, made at a live performance at Carnegie Hall, is as thrilling as it is perceptive. Mussorgsky's darker colours are admirably caught and the lighter, scherzando evocations are dazzlingly articulated. This has now been reissued as Volume 44 in the Toscanini Edition, admirably paired with his equally devastating account of Tchaikovsky's *First Piano concerto*, recorded at a live concert in 1943. This is an indispensable coupling and no admirer of great pianism should be without this record. RCA have also reissued this version of the *Pictures*, plus Horowitz's arrangement of *On the river* from Mussorgsky's song-cycle, *Sunless*, coupled with the 1941 *studio* recording of the Tchaikovsky concerto, a performance which we find less satisfying.

No doubts about Demidenko's virtuosity and keyboard command here, or the excellence of the Hyperion sound. There are doubts however about many of the highly idiosyncratic touches that are so pervasive so that he attracts more attention to himself than Mussorgsky!

(i) *Pictures at an exhibition* (arr. Leonard for piano and orchestra). *3 Pictures from the Crimea* (orch. Goehr); *Night on the bare mountain* (arr. & orch. Rimsky-Korsakov); *Scherzo in B flat* (orch. Rimsky-Korsakov); *From my tears* (orch. Kindler); *Khovanshchina: Prelude* (orch. Rimsky-Korsakov); *Golitsyn's journey* (orch. Stokowski); *Sorochinsky Fair: Gopak* (orch. Liadov).

*** Cala Dig. CACD 1012; *CAMC 1012*. (i) Tamás Ungár; Philh. O, Geoffrey Simon.

Lawrence Leonard's arrangement of Mussorgsky's *Pictures* for piano and orchestra is remarkably effective and very entertaining. The concertante format works admirably, especially powerful in *Gnomus* and *The hut on fowl's legs*, charmingly depicting the *Unhatched chicks* (a piquant mixture of keyboard and woodwind, spiced with xylophone). There are many added touches of colour. The other pieces are all well worth having, notably Rimsky's chimerical scoring (following the composer's orchestral sketch) of the *Scherzo in B flat*. The three *Pictures from the Crimea* are darkly nostalgic, and the lively *Gopak*, like the *Khovanshchina* excerpts (Stokowski's arrangement of *Golitsyn's journey* is sombrely characterful), are very welcome. All Geoffrey Simon's performances have plenty of life, and Tamás Ungár makes an exciting contribution and is fully equal to all the technical demands of the revised piano-part. The recording is warm, full and expansive, but not always sharply defined.

SONGS

The Complete Songs.

✿ (M) (***) EMI (SIS) mono CHS7 63025-2 (3) [Ang. CHS 63025]. Boris Christoff, Alexandre Labinsky, Gerald Moore, French R. & TV O, Georges Tzipine.

Boris Christoff originally recorded these songs in 1958; they then appeared in a four-LP mono set with a handsome book, generously illustrated with plates and music examples, giving the texts in Russian, French, Italian and English, and with copious notes on each of the 63 songs. Naturally the documentation cannot be so extensive in the CD format – but, on the other hand, one has the infinitely greater ease of access that the new technology offers. The Mussorgsky songs constitute a complete world in themselves, and they cast a strong spell: their range is enormous and their insight into the human condition deep. Christoff was at the height of his vocal powers when he made the set with Alexandre Labinsky, his accompanist in most of the songs; and its return to circulation cannot be too warmly welcomed. This was the first complete survey, and it still remains the only really recommendable set.

Song-cycles: The nursery; Songs and dances of death. Songs: Darling Savishna; Forgotten; The He-Goat; The Puppet-show; Mephistopheles' Song of the flea.

✿ *** Conifer Dig. 7605 51229-2 [id.]. Sergei Leiferkus, Semion Skigin.

These are impressive performances; not only does Sergei Leiferkus make a beautiful sound, but his singing has immense character and power. He can be passionate, earthy and yet aristocratic, touching and then magisterial by turn. He seems to command an unlimited range of colour and to be able to draw forth all the drama and variety of vocal timbre these songs demand. In Semion Skigin he has a pianist of commanding dramatic talent and, at the same time, exemplary restraint. This is the only Mussorgsky song-recital of recent times that can rank alongside the classic pre-war records of Kipnis or the majestic 1950s Christoff set. The Conifer recording is first class, too.

Song-cycles: *The Nursery; Sunless; Songs and dances of Death*. Songs: *Gopak; Hebrew song; Song of the flea*.

*** Sony Dig. SK 66858 [id.]. Marjana Lipovšek, Graham Johnson.

Marjana Lipovšek always imparts intensity and meaning to the music she sings. Her mezzo has a sumptuous yet subtle quality, and the rapport between her and partner, Graham Johnson, is close. His playing is of the highest imaginative order. Although *The Nursery* has been recorded by a number of female singers (Galina Vishnevskaya, Margaret Price and others), the bulk of the songs on this disc fall within the preserve of the male singer. Yet even if you are collecting Sergei Leiferkus's magisterial survey of the complete songs on Conifer, this recital is still well worth your attention. Lipovšek brings special musical and poetic insights to all this repertoire; her range of colour and sonority is impressively wide, and she and Johnson remain admirably free of the constraints of the bar line. In a word, their interpretations aspire to the quality of a pitched poetic speech. The recording has plenty of bloom, and the balance between singer and pianist is very natural. A lovely recital.

Songs and dances of death (orch. Shostakovich).

*** EMI Dig. CDC7 55232-2 [id.]. Lloyd, Phd. O, Jansons – SHOSTAKOVICH: *Symphony No. 10*. ***

Robert Lloyd gives a commanding and sonorous account of the Shostakovich transcription of Mussorgsky's gripping *Songs and dances of death* as a fill-up to Jansons' intense and powerful reading of the Shostakovich *Tenth Symphony*.

OPERA

Boris Godunov ((i) 1869 & (ii) 1872 versions).

(N) (M) *** Ph. Dig. 462 230-2 (5) [id.]. (i) Boris (Nikolai Putilin), Grigory (Viktor Lutsuk); (ii) Boris (Vladimir Vaneev), Grigor (Vladimir Galusin); (i; ii) Pimen (Nikolai Ohotnikov), Varlaam (Fyodor Kuznetsov), Xenia (Olga Trifonova), Feodor (Zlata Bulycheva), Shuisky (Konstantin Pluzhnikov), Simpleton (Evgeny Akimov), Kirov Opera Ch. & O, Gergiev.

It makes a fascinating contrast in Gergiev's St Petersburg set – five discs for the price of three – to have the original 1869 version of seven scenes set against the 1872 revision with its amplification in the extra Polish act and elsewhere. Gergiev's incisive, keenly dramatic readings bring out the differences very effectively, and the casting of Boris in each heightens that. In 1869 the character is more direct, more of a villain, less of a victim – reflected in Nikolai Putilin's virile and firm singing – where in the expanded 1872 portrait the character is more equivocal, more self-searching, clearly verging on madness, and there you have Vladimir Vaneev bringing out the element of thoughtfulness and mystery over a wider expressive range. The role of Grigory, the Pretender, brings alternative casting too, but it is only in the 1872 version that the character plays a full part, very well taken by the ringing and clear, very Russian-sounding tenor, Vladimir Galusin. The others make a first-rate team, individually strong and idiomatic, and all enhancing the drama, obviously experienced on stage. Outstanding are Olga Borodina as Marina and Konstantin Pluzhnikov as a sinister Shuisky. The sound is fresh and forward, with voices set in front of the orchestra, more powerful in wind and brass than in the strings. The Abbado set on Sony (see below) offers a starrier cast and a more spacious reading, often more warmly expressive, but the practical advantages of the Gergiev set make it even more recommendable.

Boris Godunov (original version; complete).
*** Sony Dig. S3K 58977 (3) [id.]. Kotcherga, Leiferkus, Lipovšek, Ramey, Nikolsky, Langridge, Slovak Philharmonic Ch., Bratislava, Tölz Boys' Ch., Berlin RSO, Abbado.
**(*) EMI CDS7 54377-2 (3) [id.]. Talvela, Gedda, Mróz, Kinasz, Haugland, Krakow Polish R. Ch., Polish Nat. SO, Semkow.

Claudio Abbado recorded *Boris Godunov* in its original version in conjunction both with live concert performances in Berlin and with the subsequent stage production at the Salzburg Festival. The result may initially seem to dilute the essential ruggedness of this work but, with speeds which regularly press ahead, the urgency of the composer's inspiration is conveyed as never before on disc, without reducing the epic scale of the work or its ominously dark colouring. Abbado inserts the beautiful scene in front of St Basil's at the start of Act IV, but then omits from the final Kromy Forest scene the episode about the Simpleton losing his kopek, which would otherwise come in twice – as it does in the Semkow (EMI) set. Vocally, the performance centres on the glorious singing of Anatoly Kotcherga as Boris. Rarely has this music been sung with such firmness and beauty as here and, so far from losing out dramatically compared with rivals who resort to *parlando* effects for emphasis, the performance gains in intensity. Kotcherga may not have as weighty a voice as Talvela on EMI, but with Abbado encouraging high contrasts, the darkly meditative depth of the performance is enhanced without loss of power. The other principal basses, Samuel Ramey as the monk, Pimen, and Gleb Nikolsky as Varlaam, are well contrasted, even if Ramey's voice sounds un-Slavonic. The tenor, Sergei Larin, sings with beauty and clarity up to the highest register as the Pretender, not least in the Polish act, while Marjana Lipovšek is a formidably characterful Marina, if not quite as well focused as usual. Having Philip Langridge as Shuisky and Sergei Leiferkus as Rangoni reinforces the starry strength of the team. The sound is spacious, more atmospheric than usual in recordings made in the Philharmonie in Berlin, and allowing high dynamic contrasts, with the choral ensembles – so vital in this work – full and glowing.

Though the EMI version offers (at full price) only an analogue recording of 1977, its warmth and richness go with a forward balance and a high transfer level that many will prefer to digital rivals. The voices have an extra bite, not least the firm, weighty bass of Martti Talvela as Boris or of Aage Haugland, magnificent as Varlaam. Nicolai Gedda is excellent as the Pretender, if not as free on top as Larin in the Abbado set. The other soloists, as well as the chorus, make up a formidable Polish team, with hardly a weak link. Bozena Kinasz as Marina is particularly impressive. Jerzy Semkow may not convey such bite and beauty as Abbado, but in his rugged, measured way he conveys more intensity at moments of high drama than the other Sony rival, Tchakarov, helped by the firm, full sound. If this were reissued at mid-price it would be a strong contender.

Boris Godunov (arr. Rimsky-Korsakov).
*** Decca (IMS) 411 862-2 (3) [id.]. Ghiaurov, Vishnevskaya, Spiess, Maslennikov, Talvela, V. Boys' Ch., Sofia R. Ch., V. State Op. Ch., VPO, Karajan.

With Ghiaurov in the title-role, Karajan's superbly controlled Decca version, technically outstanding, comes far nearer than previous recordings to conveying the rugged greatness of Mussorgsky's masterpiece. Only the Coronation scene lacks something of the weight and momentum one ideally wants. Vishnevskaya is far less appealing than the impressive Slavonic Marina of Bozena Kinasz on EMI, but overall this Decca set has much more to offer. However, Decca need to reissue the Karajan at mid-price, when it would still be competitive.

Boris Godunov (original, 1869 version): excerpts: *Coronation Scene; Varlaam's song; Apartment scene; St Basil scene; Death scene* (sung in English).
✿ (M) *** Chandos CHAN 3007. Tomlinson,

Kale, Bayley, Rodgers, Best, Opera North Ch., E. N. Philh. O, Paul Daniel.

This generous, 75-minute selection of excerpts from *Boris Godunov* is an important addition to the excellent series of operatic recordings in English, sponsored by Peter Moores, and is highly recommendable even when compared with current Russian versions of Mussorgsky's masterpiece. John Tomlinson has never been in finer voice on disc than here, with his dark bass-baritone perfectly focused. This is an exceptionally lyrical view of the self-tortured tsar, both dramatically powerful and warmly expressive, letting one appreciate the beauty of Mussorgsky's melodies. Tomlinson is helped by Paul Daniel's inspired direction and opulent recorded sound, with excellent support from singers in the vintage Opera North production, including Stuart Kale as Prince Shuisky, Clive Bayley as Varlaam, Joan Rodgers as Xenia and Matthew Best as Pimen. Anyone who supports the ideas of opera sung in English should not miss this highly compelling disc.

Khovanshchina (complete).

*** DG (IMS) Dig. 429 758-2 (3) [id.]. Lipovšek, Burchuladze, Atlantov, Haugland, Borowska, Kotscherga, Popov, V. State Op. Ch. & O, Abbado.

**(*) Ph. (IMS) Dig. 432 147-2 (3) [id.]. Minjelkiev, Galusin, Steblianko, Ohotnikov, Borodina, Kirov Theatre Ch. & O, Gergiev.

Abbado's live recording brings the most vivid account of this epic Russian opera yet on disc. He uses the Shostakovich orchestration (with some cuts), darker and harmonically far more faithful than the old Rimsky-Korsakov version. Yet Abbado rejects the triumphant ending of the Shostakovich edition and follows instead the orchestration that Stravinsky did for Diaghilev in 1913 of the original subdued ending as Mussorgsky himself conceived it. When the tragic fate of the Old Believers, immolating themselves for their faith, brings the deepest and most affecting emotions of the whole opera, that close, touching in its tenderness, is far more apt. Lipovšek's glorious singing as Marfa, the Old Believer with whom one most closely identifies, sets the seal on the whole performance. Aage Haugland is a rock-like Ivan Khovansky and, though Burchuladze is no longer as steady of tone as he was, he makes a noble Dosifei. Stage noises sometimes intrude and voices are sometimes set back, but this remains a magnificent achievement.

Gergiev does not disguise the squareness of much of the writing and his performance lacks the flair and brilliance of Abbado. He stays faithful to the Shostakovich version of the score to the very end. There he simply adds a loud version of the *Old Believers' chorale* on unison brass – hardly a subtle solution! The Kirov soloists make a fine team, but on almost all counts Abbado is more persuasive.

Mysliveček, Josef (1737–81)

Violin concerto in C.

(B) *** Discover Dig. DICD 920265 [id.]. Ivan Zenaty, Virtuosi di Praga, Oldrich Vlček (with DVORAK: *Romance; Mazurka* ***) – VANHAL: *Violin concerto.* ***

Born in Bohemia almost a generation before Mozart, Mysliveček wrote fresh, vigorous music, of which this violin concerto is a fine example, its central slow movement a brief, gentle interlude. The Vanhal coupling is a comparable work, equally attractive. On this well-recorded bargain issue Ivan Zenaty with his clean, full tone proves an outstanding advocate, with the Virtuosi di Praga providing lively support on modern instruments. In the two shorter concertante works of a century later, Zenaty and the orchestra readily adapt their style to the romanticism of Dvořák, tender in the *Romance*, flamboyant in the *Mazurka*.

Octets Nos. 1 in E flat; 2 in E flat; 3 in B flat.

**(*) EMI Dig. CDC5 55512-2 [id.]. Sabine Meyer Wind Ens. – DVORAK: *Serenade in D min.* **(*)

The Sabine Meyer Wind Ensemble offer three charming *Octets* by Mysliveček as their fill-up to an eminently satisfying if laid-back account of the Dvořák *Wind serenade*. Too many claims should not be made for this music, which is of no great substance but is nevertheless genuinely charming, particularly in the slow movements. The excellent, well-balanced EMI recording makes for pleasurable listening.

Nancarrow, Conlen (born 1912)

3 Canons for Ursula; Studies for player-piano Nos. 3c, 6 & 11.

(N) *** Collins Dig. 7043-2 (2) [id.]. Joanna MacGregor (piano) – BACH: Art of fugue. ***

It was an inspired idea to combine a selection from Conlen Nancarrow's formidably complex twentieth-century excursions into intricate polyphony with Bach's *Art of fugue*. Because of the extremely irregular linear-metrical relationships between the parts, many of Nancarrow's pieces were considered virtually unplayable by human hands, so he chose to use a player-piano which could juxtapose the parts (individually running at different tempi) with absolute precision. But Joanna MacGregor – with the aid of multi-tracking – manages the impossible and reveals these miniatures as both witty and jazzy as well as physically and intellectually dazzling.

Narváez, Luys de (1500–c. 1555)

El Delphin de Musica, Book 1: *Fantasia No. 5.* Book 2: *Fantasias Nos. 5–6.* Book 3: *La canción del Emperor.* Book 4: *O gloriosa domina (Seys differencias).* Book 5: *Arde coracón, arde; Ye se asiente el Rey Raminor.* Book 6: *Conde claros; Guárdame las vacas; Tre diferencias por otra parte; Baxa de contrapunto.*

(M) *** RCA 09026 61606-2. Julian Bream (lute) – MILAN: *Collection.* ***

The collection Bream plays here is more diverse than the coupled Milán pieces and he includes some arrangements of the popular songs of the time and some of the earliest-known *differencias* (variations). Bream is in his element in this repertoirė and each piece is eloquently felt and strongly characterized; the music's nobility is readily conveyed. The recording is first class.

Nepomuneco, Alberto (1864–1920)

Galhofeira, Op. 13/4; Improviso, Op. 27/2; Nocturnes: Nos. 1 in C; 2 in G (for the left hand); 5 Pequenas peças (for the left hand); Nocturne, Op. 33; Sonata in F min., Op. 9; Suite antiga, Op. 11.

(N) ** Marco Polo Dig. 8.223548 [id.]. Maria Inês Guimarães.

Alberto Nepomuneco has every right to be called the father of Brazilian music. He studied in Berlin, Rome and Paris where he became a pupil of Guilmant, knew Brahms and was a friend of Grieg, who much admired his *Suite antiga*. Later, Nepomuneco was active as a teacher and for a time director of the National Institute of Music in Rio da Janeiro, helping the youthful Villa Lobos. Although he composed in most genres, little of his output has been recorded, so this disc of his piano music is welcome. Much of it is derivative – Brahmsian or Schumannesque – but it shows him to be far from negligible. Morever there is a trace of the kind of popular Brazilian music that fascinated Milhaud in his *Saudades do Brasil*. The *Cinco Pequenas peças* and the *Nocturnes* of 1919 were both written for Nepomuneco's daughter who was born without a right arm. Maria Inês Guimarães is not the most imaginative of pianists and is somewhat wanting in finesse, but those with a taste for off-beat repertoire may find this worth investigating.

Nevin, Arthur (1871–1943)

From Edgeworth Hills.

*** Altarus Dig. AIR-CD 9024 [id.]. Donna Amato – Ethelbert NEVIN: *A Day in Venice* etc. ***

Arthur Nevin was without his older brother's melodic individuality, but he wrote spontaneously and crafted his pieces nicely. The most striking number of *From Edgeworth Hills* is the tripping *Sylphs*, very characteristic of its time, while *As the moon rose* has an agreeably sentimental tune, and the picaresque *Firefly* sparkles nicely here. *Toccatella* is rhythmically a bit awkward but is quite a showpiece, and Donna Amato plays it with real dash. Excellent recording.

Nevin, Ethelbert (1862–1901)

A Day in Venice (suite), *Op. 25; Etude in the form of a Romance; Etude in the form of a scherzo, Op. 18/1–2; May in Tuscany* (suite), *Op. 21; Napoli (En passant), Op. 30/3; Mighty lak' a rose* (after the transcription by Charles Spross); *O'er hill and dale* (suite); *The Rosary* (arr. Whelpley); *Water scenes, Op. 13.*

*** Altarus Dig. AIR-CD 9024 [id.]. Donna Amato – Arthur NEVIN: *From Edgeworth Hills.* ***

Ethelbert Nevin was born in Edgeworth, Pennsylvania, scored his first great success when *Narcissus* became a world-wide hit, and *The Rosary* was Nevin's other hit, with the sheet music selling over a million copies in the decade following its publication in 1898. Donna Amato grew up in the area where he was born, and she takes care not to sentimentalize these genre pieces, which can be just a little trite but also quite engaging. *Mighty lak' a rose*, another favourite, retains all its charm. The recording is clear and natural in a pleasing acoustic.

Nicolai, Carl Otto (1810–49)

The merry wives of Windsor (Die lustigen Weiber von Windsor): complete.

(N) (B) *** Decca Double 460 197-2 (2) [id.]. Karl Ridderbusch, Wolfgang Brendel, Alexander Malta, Helen Donath, Trudeliese Schmidt, Bav. R. Ch. & SO, Kubelik.

(M) **(*) EMI (SIS) CMS7 69348-2 (2). Frick, Gutstein, Engel, Wunderlich, Lenz, Hoppe, Putz, Litz, Mathis, Ch. & O of Bav. State Op., Heger.

Kubelik's performance may be slightly lacking in dramatic ebullience, but its extra subtlety has perceptive results – as in the entry of Falstaff in Act I, where Kubelik conveys the tongue-in-cheek quality of Nicolai's *pomposo* writing. Ridderbusch portrays a straight and noble Falstaff. Although as an opera this may not have the brilliant insight of Verdi or all the atmosphere of Vaughan Williams, it has its own brand of effervescence which is equally endearing and is well caught here. The dialogue is crisply edited, and the recording, while fairly reverberant, is vividly atmospheric. *Faute de mieux*, it should receive a strong recommendation. This is particularly welcome as a Decca Double, although the documentation includes only a cued synopsis.

As Falstaff, Gottlob Frick in magnificent voice, even if he sounds baleful rather than comic. It is good too to have the young Fritz Wunderlich as Fenton opposite the Anna Reich of Edith Mathis. Though the others hardly match this standard – Ruth-Margret Putz is rather shrill as Frau Fluth – they all give enjoyable performances. The effectiveness of the comic timing is owed in great measure to the conducting of the veteran, Robert Heger. From the CD transfer one could hardly tell the age of the recording, with the voices particularly well caught.

Nielsen, Carl (1865–1931)

Aladdin (suite); *A fantasy-journey to the Færoes* (rhapsodic overture); *Helios Overture; Maskarade: Overture; Prelude to Act II, Dance of the cockerels. Pan and Syrinx; Saga-drøm.*
*** DG Dig. 447 757-2. Gothenburg SO, Järvi.

Of the anthologies of Nielsen's orchestral music other than the symphonies, this is now the best on offer. The performances are vital and affectionate, with the orchestra playing with their usual finesse and enthusiasm. Both *Pan and Syrinx* and *Saga-drøm* are atmospheric. Two minor reservations: the *Helios Overture* is too swiftly paced (the sun rises over the Aegean in fast-forward mode). The recording is very fine indeed.

At the bier of a young artist; Little suite for strings, Op. 1.
*** Virgin/EMI Dig. VC5 45224-2 [CDC 45224]. Norwegian CO, Iona Brown – GRIEG: *At the cradle* etc. ***

The Norwegian Chamber Orchestra are an excellent group and their account of Nielsen's first opus, the *Little suite for strings*, is about the best in the catalogue. His moving elegy, the *Andante lamentoso* (*At the bier of a young artist*) is equally eloquent in their hands. The recording, made in the glorious acoustic of Eidsvoll Church in Norway, is very real and tangible. Very strongly recommended.

Clarinet concerto, Op. 57.
*** Chandos Dig. CHAN 8618 [id.]. Janet Hilton, SNO, Bamert – COPLAND: *Concerto;* LUTOSLAWSKI: *Dance preludes.* ***

Janet Hilton gives a highly sympathetic account of the Nielsen *Concerto*, but it is characteristically soft-centred and mellower in its response to the work's more disturbing emotional undercurrents than Olle Schill's splendid account on BIS – see below. The Chandos recording is first class.

(i) *Clarinet concerto, Op. 57;* (ii) *Flute concerto;* (iii) *Violin concerto, Op. 33.*
*** Chandos Dig. CHAN 8894 [id.]. (i) Thomsen; (ii) Christiansen; (iii) Sjøgren; Danish RSO, Schønwandt.

Niels Thomsen's powerfully intense account of the late *Clarinet concerto* is completely gripping. Michael Schønwandt gives sensitive and imaginative support, both here and in the two companion works. Toke Lund Christiansen is hardly less successful in the *Flute concerto*. Kim Sjøgren and Schønwandt give a penetrating and thoughtful account of the *Violin concerto*; there is real depth here, thanks in no small measure to Schønwandt. The recording is first class.

(i) *Clarinet concerto, Op. 57;* (ii) *Flute concerto;* (iii) *Violin concerto, Op. 33, An imaginary journey to the Faroe Islands (Rhapsodic overture); Helios overture, Op. 17; Pan and Syrinx, Op. 49; Saga-drøm, Op. 39; Symphonic rhapsody.*
(B) *** EMI forte CZS5 69758-2 (2) [CDFB 69758]. (i) Stevennson; (ii) Lemmser; (iii) Tellefsen; Danish RSO, Blomstedt.

Arve Tellefsen is a first-class soloist in the *Violin concerto* and his recording stands up well alongside more recent, full-priced versions. Kjell-Inge Stevennson is pretty stunning in the remarkable and other-worldly *Clarinet concerto*. The charm and subtleties of the *Flute concerto* are hardly less well realized by Frantz Lemmser's nimble and sensitive account. Moreover, since the orchestra is Danish, the other works (such as the marvellous *Pan and Syrinx* and the atmospheric *Helios overture*) are played with authentic accents. The collection also includes a novelty in the *Symphonic rhapsody* (1889), composed before the *First Symphony*. Throughout the EMI engineers secure a natural sound-balance. In its economical new format this is a most attractive proposition, and the recordings still sound very warm and fresh.

(i) *Clarinet concerto;* (ii) *Flute concerto. An Imaginary journey to the Faeroe Islands; Saul and David: Prelude;* (iii) *Springtime in Fünen, Op. 42.*
**(*) Sony Dig. SK 53276 [id.]. Swedish RSO, Salonen, with (i) Håkan Rosengren; (ii) Per Flemström; (iii) Asa Bäverstam, Kjell Sandve, Per Høyer, Linnéa Ekdale, Andréas Thors, Swedish R. Ch. & Boys' Ch.

Håkan Rosengren has the measure of the *Clarinet concerto*, which he plays with considerable flair, and he receives excellent support from Salonen. The *Flute concerto* fares equally well. The *Prelude* to *Saul and David* comes off pesuasively, but the earthy (yet seraphic) innocence and simplicity of *Springtime in Fünen* elude Salonen altogether. The concertos, though not first recommendations, deserve three stars but the cantata falls well short of that. Good recording, as one would expect from this source.

(i) *Clarinet concerto, Op. 57. Overture: Amor og digteren (Love & the poet), Op. 54; Little suite for strings, Op. 1; Pan and Syrinx, Op. 49.*
(M) *** HM Suite Dig. HMT 7901489 [id.]. (i) Walter Boeykens; Beethoven Academie, Jan Caeyers.

Walter Boeykens gives a remarkably perceptive account of the *Clarinet concerto*, one which gets to the heart of this often elusive and other-worldly score. This artist blends taste and grace on the one hand with the vociferous and awkward outbursts which Nielsen perceived in the personality of its dedicatee, Aage Oxenvad. There is always an undercurrent of tenderness and poetic feeling. The makeweights include a rarity in the late overture, *Amor og digteren* (1930). Jan Caeyers has as genuine a feeling for Nielsen as has Boeykens in the concerto, and *Pan and Syrinx* comes off very well indeed.

(i) *Clarinet concerto, Op. 57;* (ii) *Symphony No. 3 (Sinfonia espansiva). Maskarade overture.*
*** BIS Dig. CD 321 [id.]. (i) Olle Schill; (ii) Pia Raanoja, Knut Skram; Gothenburg SO, Myung-Whun Chung.

Olle Schill brings brilliance and insight to what is one of the most disturbing and masterly of all modern concertos. The young Korean conductor secures playing of great fire and enthusiasm from the Gothenburgers in the *Third Symphony* and he has vision and breadth – and at the same time no want of momentum. Two soloists singing a wordless vocalise are called for in the pastoral slow movement, and their contribution is admirable. Myung-Whun Chung also gives a high-spirited and sparkling account of the *Overture* to Nielsen's comic opera, *Maskarade*. The BIS recording is marvellous, even by the high standards of this small company.

(i) *Clarinet concerto, Op. 57;* (ii) *Serenata in Vano;* (iii) *Wind quintet, Op. 43.*
(***) Clarinet Classics mono CC 002 [id.]. (i) Cahuzac, Copenhagen Op. O, Frandsen; (ii) Oxenvad, Larsson, Sorensen, Jensen, Hegner; (iii) Royal Chapel Wind Quintet.

These are pioneering recordings. The *Clarinet concerto* was to have been recorded by its dedicatee, Aage Oxenvad, who is heard in both the *Quintet* and the *Serenata in Vano*, but death intervened and the eminent French clarinettist Louis Cahuzac filled the breach. This lovely performance of the *Quintet* is so full of character that in some ways it remains unsurpassed. These transfers are a great improvement on the earlier ones on Danacord LPs, a bit dry but eminently clean and well detailed in the case of the *Concerto*, which Cahuzac plays with great feeling.

(i) *Flute concerto; Symphony No. 1; Rhapsody overture: An imaginary journey to the Faeroe Islands.*
*** BIS Dig. CD 454 [id.]. (i) Patrick Gallois; Gothenburg SO, Myung-Whun Chung.

The *Flute concerto* is given a marvellous performance by Patrick Gallois, and Myung-Whun Chung and the Gothenburg orchestra have an instinctive feeling for Nielsen. They play with commendable enthusiasm and warmth, and Chung shapes the *Symphony* with great sensitivity to detail and a convincing sense of the whole. The *Rhapsody overture: An imaginary journey to the Faeroe Islands* is not the composer at his strongest, but it has a highly imaginative opening.

Violin concerto, Op. 33.
✽ *** Sony Dig. SK 44548 [id.]. Cho-Liang Lin, Swedish RSO, Salonen – SIBELIUS: *Violin concerto.* *** ✽

(i) *Violin concerto, Op. 33.* (ii) *Symphony No. 1 in G min., Op. 7.*
(N) **(*) Finlandia/Warner Dig. 3984-22836-2 [id.]. (i) Henrik Hannisdal; Norwegian RO, Ari Rasilainen or (ii) Terje Mikkelsen.

(i) *Violin concerto, Op. 33. Symphony No. 5, Op. 50.*
*** BIS Dig. CD 370. (i) Dong-Suk Kang, Gothenburg SO, Myung-Whun Chung.

Cho-Liang Lin brings as much authority to Nielsen's *Concerto* as he does to the Sibelius and he handles the numerous technical hurdles with breathtaking assurance. His perfect intonation and tonal purity excite admiration, but so should his command of the architecture of this piece; there is a strong sense of line from beginning to end. Salonen is supportive here and gets good playing from the Swedish Radio Symphony Orchestra.

Dong-Suk Kang is more than equal to the technical demands of this concerto and is fully attuned to the Nordic sensibility. He brings tenderness and refinement of feeling to the searching slow movement and great panache and virtuosity to the rest. The *Fifth Symphony* is hardly less successful and is certainly the best-recorded version now available. Myung-Whun Chung has a natural feeling for Nielsen's language and the first movement has real breadth.

The Norwegian Radio Orchestra is very good indeed, even if their strings do not match the excellence of the Oslo Philharmonic. Nor for that matter do the wind and brass. Under their Finnish conductor they turn in a very natural and unaffected account of the *First symphony* and a hardly less appealing version of the *Violin concerto*. Henrik Hannisdal was once the leader or concertmaster and his playing gives consistent pleasure, particularly when the recorded sound is so well balanced. If you want the pairing this is worth considering, but neither performances displace first recommendations with other couplings.

En aften paa Giske: Prelude (1889); Bøhmiske-dansk folketone; Helios, Overture, Op. 17; Paraphrase on 'Nearer my God, to thee', for wind band; Rhapsodic overture: An imaginary journey to the Faeroe Islands; Saga-drøm, Op. 39; Symphonic rhapsody (1888).

**(*) Chandos Dig. CHAN 9287 [id.]. Danish Nat. RSO, Rohzdestvensky.

The *Paraphrase on the Psalm, 'Nearer, my God, to thee', for wind band* is both noble and individual. Rozhdestvensky gives musicianly, well-prepared and often poetic accounts of the more familiar pieces, though his *Helios, Overture* must be the slowest ever – over 14 minutes! His account of *Saga-drøm* ('The Dream of Gunnar') is also spacious. Very good recording, but in the last analysis these performances are a little deficient in zest.

Symphonies Nos. (i) *1 in G min. Op. 7; 2 in B min., Op. 16;* (i & ii) *3 (Espansiva), Op. 27;* (iii) *4 (Inextinguishable), Op. 29;* (i) *5, Op. 50;* (iii) *6 (Sinfonia semplice);* (i; iv) *Clarinet concerto, Op. 57;* (i; v) *Flute concerto;* (i; vi) *Violin concerto, Op. 33.*

(M) *** BIS Dig. CD 614/6 (4) [id.]. Gothenburg SO, (i) Myung-Whun Chung; (ii) with Raanoja, Skram; (iii) Neeme Järvi; (iv) with Olle Schill; (v) Patrick Gallois; (vi) Dong-Suk Kang.

Symphonies Nos. 1 in G min., Op. 7; 2 (Four Temperaments), Op. 16; (i) *3 (Sinfonia espansiva), Op. 27;* (ii) *Aladdin (suite). Maskarade overture.*

*** Decca Dig. Double 460 985-2 (2) [id.]. San Francisco SO, Blomstedt (i) with Nancy Wait Kromm, Kevin McMillan ; (ii) San Francisco SO Ch.

(i)*Symphonies Nos. 4 (Inextinguishable), Op. 29; 5, Op. 50; 6 (Sinfonia semplice).* (ii) *Little suite, Op. 1;* (ii;iii) *Hymnus amoris, Op. 12.*

*** Decca Dig. Double 460 988-2 (2) [id.]. (i) San Francisco SO, Blomstedt; (ii) Danish Nat. RSO, Ulf Schirmer; (iii) with Bonney, Pedersen, Mark Ainsley, M. & B. Hansen, Danish Nat. R Ch., Copenhagen Boys' Ch.

Symphonies Nos. (i) *1 in G min., Op. 7;* (ii) *2 (Four Temperaments), Op. 16;* (iii) *3 (Sinfonia espansiva), Op. 27;4 (Inextinguishable), Op. 29;* (i) *5, Op. 50;* (iii) *6 (Sinfonia semplice).*

*** Chandos Dig. CHAN 9163/5 [id.]. Royal Scottish O, Bryden Thomson.

(B) *** RCA Dig. 74321 20290-2 (3). Royal Danish O, Paavo Berglund (with soloists in *No. 3*).

(**(*)) Danacord mono DACOCD 351/3. Danish RSO; (i) Erik Tuxen; (ii) Launy Grøndahl; (iii) Thomas Jensen.

Symphonies Nos. 1 in G min. Op. 7; 2 in B min., Op. 16.

**(*) DG Dig. 439 775-2. Gothenburg SO, Neeme Järvi.

Symphonies Nos. (i) *3 (Espansiva), Op. 27; 4 (Inextinguishable), Op. 29.*

**(*) DG Dig. 439 776-2. Gothenburg SO, Neeme Järvi, (i) with Hynninen.

Symphonies Nos. 5, Op. 50; 6 (Sinfonia semplice).

**(*) DG Dig. 439 777-2. Gothenburg SO, Neeme Järvi.

Blomstedt's complete Decca set of the symphonies now reappears on a pair of Decca Doubles, and is pretty well self-recommending. All six performances are among the finest available: the *First Symphony* has vitality and freshness, and there is a good feel for Nielsen's natural lyricism. Nos. 2 and 3 are possibly the finest of the cycle: Blomstedt finds just the right tempo for each movement and nowhere is this more crucial than in the finale of the *Espansiva*. The two soloists are good and the orchestra play with all the freshness and enthusiasm one could ask for. The opening of Blomstedt's *Fourth* has splendid fire: this must sound as if galaxies are forming. The finale is exhilarating, yet held on a firm rein. The *Fifth Symphony*, too, is impressive: it starts perfectly and is almost as icy in atmosphere as those pioneering recordings of the 1950s. In the *Sixth Symphony* there is no want of intensity, though a broader tempo would have helped generate greater atmosphere in the first movement. However, the performance is undeniably impressive and like the rest of the series enjoys the advantage of first-class recording.

The fill-ups are also very recommendable. Blomstedt is an eminently reliable guide to the *Aladdin suite*, though both Myung-Whun Chung (BIS) and Rozhdestvensky (Chandos) are more atmospheric. Ulf Schirmer too, shows a natural affinity for Nielsen and on the second of the two Doubles, he gives us Nielsen's early cantata, *Hymnus amoris*, one of his warmest and most openhearted scores. It gets a good performance and recording, with excellent and responsive singing from the distinguished soloists, and there is also a persuasive account of Nielsen's first published opus, the endearing *Little suite for strings*. To put it briefly, this remains the best all-round modern set of the symphonies and can be purchased with confidence; the reservation concerning No. 6, where a broader tempo would have helped generate greater evocation in the opening movement, is relatively insignificant against the overall success of this series.

Though individual symphonies in the BIS set score very highly, the performances are generally speaking not the equal of the Blomstedt, and the pair of Decca Doubles hold their own.

Myung-Whun Chung's accounts of the *First* and *Second Symphonies* can also hold their own against the best, and his version of the *Sinfonia espansiva* is one of the *very* best – and can be recommended alongside Blomstedt (Decca). It has the inestimable advantage of the Gothenburg Hall acoustic and warm, splendidly present recording. The concertos are all excellent – some may even prefer them to the rival collection on Chandos. Dong-Suk Kang's reading of the *Violin concerto* is eloquent in every respect and a worthy alternative to Cho-Liang Lin on Sony; and both Patrick Gallois and Olle Schill are magnificent soloists. The package as a whole with four records for the price of three is eminently competitive.

Generally speaking Bryden Thomson's Nielsen symphonies are eminently sound and straightforward, without the extra ounce of finish that we find with the Blomstedt set. If they are not as beautifully recorded as Järvi on DG, they still sound impressive and as performances have the merit of being totally unmannered and unfussy, with generally well-chosen tempi. Thomson's version of the *Sixth* is arguably the best now on the market, and his *Fourth* has great fire. The set can hold its own with most of the first recommendations without displacing any of them – except in the two cases mentioned.

Berglund's set with the Royal Danish Orchestra, in which Nielsen once served, was recorded between 1987 and 1989. The ever-fresh *First Symphony* is given a thoroughly straightforward account and the *Sinfonia espansiva* (No. 3) is perhaps the finest of his cycle. His two soloists, though unnamed, are very good and the general architecture of the work is well conveyed. The *Fourth* (*Inextinguishable*) is more problematic. In his desire to convey the sense of drama and urgency, Berglund tends to be impatient to move things on, particularly in the closing paragraphs. The *Fifth* opens with a strong sense of atmosphere and the second movement's complex structure is well controlled and satisfyingly resolved. In the *Sinfonia semplice* (No. 6) Berglund again proves a perceptive guide. His performance matches Blomstedt's in integrity and insight. Here as elsewhere, the playing of the Royal Danish Orchestra is beautifully prepared and full of vitality and the RCA engineers produce a recording of splendid body and presence. In the event, Berglund's set can be strongly recommended alongside (though not in preference to) Blomstedt, and it also has a distinct price advantage.

Neeme Järvi's DG Nielsen cycle as a whole has much going for it – absolutely first-class recording with a completely natural balance. The Gothenburg orchestra play with great enthusiasm and responsiveness. At the same time, not all the performances can be wholeheartedly recommended. Järvi does not allow the atmosphere and mystery of the *Fifth Symphony*'s first movement to register fully, and in the *First Symphony* he is a shade too brisk in the outer movements though not unacceptably so, while the inner movements are played with real eloquence. The inner movements of the *Second Symphony* have plenty of character, though Järvi does make a little too much of the *allargando* markings in the third, which becomes a little overblown. Again the finale is rather rushed off its feet, particularly at the very end. The *Sinfonia espansiva* is well paced, and the slow movement features some particularly sensitive singing from Hynninen. The finale is let down by some uncharacteristic moments of bombast.

The Danacord set of three CDs tells us more about Nielsen than almost any later performances. Only one commercial disc is included: Jensen's masterly account of the *Sixth Symphony*. Launy Grøndahl's version of the *Second Symphony* (*The Four Temperaments*) has tremendous fire, and Jensen's accounts of the *Third* (*Sinfonia espansiva*) and *Fourth* (*Inextinguishable*) are pretty electrifying. Although allowances must be made for the poor quality of sound in some instances, these performances radiate an authenticity of atmosphere and love of the scores that is quite infectious.

Symphonies Nos. 1 in G min., Op. 7; 2 in B min., Op. 16 (The 4 Temperaments).
*** Chandos Dig. CHAN 8880 [id.]. Royal Scottish O, Bryden Thomson.

Strong, vigorous accounts of both symphonies from the Royal Scottish Orchestra under Bryden Thomson, with a particularly well-characterized reading of *The Four Temperaments*. The second movement is perhaps a shade too brisk, but in most respects these performances are difficult to fault.

(i) *Symphonies Nos. 1 in G min., Op. 7; 5, Op. 50;* (ii) *Helios overture, Op. 17.*
❁ (M) *** Dutton Lab. mono CDLXT 2502 [id.]. Danish State RSO; (i) Thomas Jensen; (ii) Erik Tuxen.

These are exemplary transfers of the première recording of the *First Symphony* and the first LP recordings of the *Fifth* (the very first was on 78s under Tuxen) and the *Helios Overture*. Jensen and Tuxen both played under Nielsen, and their performances have a special authenticity. The quality of these Decca recordings is captured with absolute fidelity in these stunning transfers; the engineers of the day, working in the pleasingly warm yet crisp acoustic of the Danish Radio concert hall produced remarkably truthful results. An indispensable issue that belongs in every Nielsen collection.

Symphonies Nos. 1 in G min., Op. 7; 6 (Sinfonia semplice).
(BB) **(*) Naxos Dig. 8.550826 [id.] Nat. SO of Ireland, Leaper.

Very good performances indeed of Nielsen's first and last symphonies from Adrian Leaper and the National Symphony Orchestra of Ireland. The sound is exceptionally well balanced, with exemplary detail and good perspective. The playing is well prepared, full of vitality, and phrasing is always intelligent. Blomstedt on Decca and Berglund with the Danish Orchestra on RCA are finer still (these players have the music in their blood), but the Naxos disc remains very good value for money.

Symphony No. 2 (The Four Temperaments), Op. 16; Aladdin suite, Op. 34.
*** BIS CD 247 [id.]. Gothenburg SO, Myung-Whun Chung.

Symphonies Nos. 2 (The Four Temperaments); (i) *3 (Espansiva), Op. 27.*
(BB) *** Naxos Dig. 8.550825. Nat. SO of Ireland, Adrian Leaper.

Myung-Whun Chung has a real feeling for this repertoire and his account of the *Second Symphony* is among the best, while the *Aladdin suite* is particularly successful. The Gothenburg Symphony Orchestra proves an enthusiastic and responsive body of players. The recording is impressive, too, and can be recommended with enthusiasm.

Adrian Leaper gets vibrant and involving playing from the Dublin orchestra in *The Four Temperaments, which* is as good as any in the catalogue (save for the Jensen), and the *Espansiva* is well paced, with tempi well judged throughout. The orchestra sounds better rehearsed and more accustomed to the Nielsen idiom than they did in their earlier disc, and they are certainly well enough recorded. Not necessarily a first choice but highly competitive.

(i) *Symphonies Nos. 3 (Sinfonia espansiva), Op. 27;* (ii) *5, Op. 50.*
*** Chandos Dig. CHAN 9067 [id.]. (i) Bott, Roberts; Royal Scottish O, Bryden Thomson.
(M) **(*) Sony SMK 47598-2. (i) Ruth Guldbaeck, Niels Moller, Royal Danish O; (ii) NYPO, Bernstein.

Bryden Thomson's chosen tempi in the *Sinfonia espansiva* are just right, particularly in the finale. In the slow movement Catherine Bott and Stephen Roberts are excellent, and the performance has a refreshing directness that is most likeable. The *Fifth Symphony* is equally committed and satisfying. The recordings are very good indeed, though one feels the need for heavily scored passages to open out a little more. Recommended, albeit not in preference to Blomstedt, who is differently coupled.

Bernstein's genial *Espansiva* with the Royal Danish Orchestra has a lot going for it. And yet, for all the excellence of the orchestral playing, this performance misses something of the music's innocence. Bernstein is at his finest in the *Fifth*, giving an immensely powerful reading, and the passion of the string cantilena and the following movement through into the finale are indicative of the spontaneous feeling which pervades the whole symphony. The well-detailed, resonant recording adds to the impact of the performance.

Symphony No. 4 (Inextinguishable), Op. 29.
(M) *** DG (IMS) Dig. 445 518-2 [id.]. BPO, Karajan – SIBELIUS: *Tapiola.* ***

Symphony No. 4 (Inextinguishable); Pan and Syrinx.
(M) *** EMI CDM7 64737-2. CBSO, Rattle – SIBELIUS: *Symphony No. 5.* ***

One of the very finest performances of Nielsen's *Fourth* comes from Karajan. The orchestral playing is altogether incomparable; there is both vision and majesty in the reading and a thrilling sense of commitment throughout. The wind playing sounds a little over-civilized – but what exquisitely blended, subtle playing this is. It is also excellently recorded, although there is an editing error in the finale.

Simon Rattle's version of the *Inextinguishable* dates from the late 1970s and is also very fine indeed: it deserves a strong recommendation, particularly given the fact that it is at mid-price and comes with an altogether outstanding account of *Pan and Syrinx* (the best ever on record) and his classic account of Sibelius's *Fifth Symphony*. Excellent sound.

Symphonies Nos. 4 (Inextinguishible), Op. 29; 5, Op. 50.
(N) *** Finlandia Dig. 3984-21439-2. Finnish RSO, Jukka-Pekka Saraste.

Saraste's coupling of the *Fourth* and *Fifth symphonies* is the best to have appeared in recent years, and it makes a worthy alternative to Blomstedt's San Francisco pairing. Saraste and the Finnish Radio Orchestra capture the explosive character of the opening of No. 4 to perfection and although there are moments when one feels that the current could flow with a higher charge, for the most part this performance is splendidly shaped and impressively executed. The *Fifth* is hardly less successful; the conception is spacious yet there is no want of movement. The recorded sound has plenty of clarity though the acoustic is a shade dry. This new CD deserves to be recommended alongside the Decca.

Symphonies Nos. 4 (Inextinguishable); 6 (Sinfonia semplice).
❀ *** Chandos Dig. CHAN 9047 [id.]. Royal Scottish O, Bryden Thomson.

The late Bryden Thomson's coupling of the *Fourth* and *Sixth Symphonies* is by far the most successful of his Nielsen cycle and possibly the finest recording of his career. The *Fourth Symphony* has great sweep and excitement and this account of the *Sixth Symphony* is quite simply the finest version now before the public, and arguably the most penetrating since Thomas Jensen's first recording. Indeed no one brings us closer to the spirit of this music than Thomson, and the recording is very good too. Recommended with enthusiasm.

CHAMBER MUSIC

Canto serioso; Fantasias for oboe and piano, Op. 2; The Mother (incidental music), Op. 41; Serenata in vano; Wind quintet, Op. 43.
**(*) Chandos CHAN 8680 [id.]. Athena Ens.

This reissue gathers together Nielsen's output for wind instruments in chamber form, with everything played expertly and sympathetically. The recording is balanced very close; nevertheless much of this repertoire is not otherwise available, and this is a valuable disc.

String quartets Nos. 1 in G min., Op. 13; 2 in F min., Op. 5; 3 in E flat, Op. 14; 4 in F, Op. 44. (i) *String quintet in G* (1888); (ii) *Andante lamentoso (At the bier of a young artist)* (1910).
*** BIS Dig. CD 503/4 [id.]. Kontra Qt, (i) Philipp Naegele; (ii) Jan Johansson.

String quartets Nos. 1 in G min., Op. 13; 2 in F min., Op. 5; 3 in E flat, Op. 14; 4 in F, Op. 44. 5 quartet movements, FS2.
*** Kontrapunkt Dig. 32150-1 [id.]. Danish Qt.

The new set from the Danish Quartet is the best since the Copenhagen Quartet's LPs: these players are sensitive to the shape of the phrase, they produce a wide dynamic range, including really soft pianissimo tone when required. They are not always the last word in polish, but everything they do is musical and leaves one marvelling at the freshness of invention Nielsen commanded, which makes one forgive the occasional rough edge and the somewhat dry quality and rather close balance of the recording. This shortcoming should not be overstressed but deserves mention. The set also includes five short movements that Nielsen wrote in his late teens and early twenties, emphatically not great music but of undoubted interest for students of the composer. Recommended.

There is an ardour and temperament to the playing by the Kontra Quartet, which most listeners will find very persuasive. In addition we are given by far the finest account yet recorded of the *G major String quintet*, where they are joined by the American violist Philipp Naegele, and the only current account of the *Andante lamentoso* (*At the bier of a young artist*) in its chamber form. The BIS recordings, made in the Malmö Concert Hall, have plenty of presence and clarity, and are rather forwardly (but not unpleasingly) balanced. Recommended, alongside the Danish Quartet.

String quartets Nos. 1 in G min, Op. 13; 4 in F, Op. 44; Little suite for strings, Op. 1 (arr. Zapolski).
(N) * Chan. Dig. CHAN9635 [id.]. Zapolski Qt.

The Zapolski Quartet is so concerned with projecting Nielsen's ideas that the music is never allowed to speak for itself. Those who know these delightful works will view both performances with some impatience, though the playing as such is accomplished and the recording more than acceptable.

String quartets Nos. 3 in E flat, Op. 14; 4 in F, Op. 44.
(N) (BB) *** 8.553907 [id.]. Oslo Qt.

The performances by the Oslo Quartet are spirited, sensitive and very alive. There is a touch of fierceness in the recording quality (they are rather closely balanced) but artistically they are a first recommendation. They also enjoy a hefty price advantage over their Danish rivals.

String quintet in G (1888), FS5.
*** Chandos Dig. CHAN 9258 [id.]. ASMF Ens. – SVENDSEN: Octet. ***

The *String quintet in G major* is very well fashioned and owes more to Svendsen, under whose baton the composer was to play, than to his teacher, Gade. It makes both an agreeable and an appropriate companion for Svendsen's early and delightful *Octet*. It receives a three-star performance and recording.

Violin sonata No. 2 in G min., Op. 35.
*** Virgin/EMI (SIS) Dig. VC5 45122-2. Christian Tetzlaff, Leif Ove Andsnes – DEBUSSY; JANACEK; RAVEL: *Sonatas*. ***

Nielsen's *G minor Sonata* is a transitional work in which Nielsen emerges from the geniality of the *Sinfonia espansiva* into the darker and more anguished world of the *Fourth Symphony*. It has much of the questing character of the latter and much of its muscularity. Christian Tetzlaff and Leif Ove Andsnes give a very distinguished – at times inspired – performance, and are accorded excellent recording.

PIANO MUSIC

Chaconne, Op. 32; Dream of Merry Christmas ; Festival Prelude; Humoresque-Bagatelles, Op. 11; Piano pieces for young and old, Op. 53; 3 Pieces, Op. 59; 5 Pieces, Op. 3; Suite, Op. 45; Symphonic suite, Op. 8; Theme and variations, Op. 40.
(N) (B) ** DanaCord Dig. DACOCD 498/499 [id.]. Mina Miller.

Mina Miller is an American academic who edited the texts of the piano music for the Wilhelm Hansen

Edition in 1981 and subsequently recorded them for Hyperion in 1986, of which this is a Double reissue. She really understands what this music is about but does not command the keyboard authority or range of sonority of an Andsnes. His one-CD disc on Virgin gives the quintessential Nielsen piano music and is the one to have (see below).

Chaconne, Op. 32; Humoresque bagatelles, Op. 11; The Luciferian (suite), Op. 45; Piano music for young and old, Books I–II, Op. 53; 5 Pieces, Op. 3; 3 Pieces, Op. 59; Symphonic suite, Op. 8; Theme and variations, Op. 40.
(N) *(*) Marco Polo dacapo Dig. 8.224095/6 (2) [id.]. Herman Koppel.

Apart from his distinction as a composer, Herman D. Koppel was a fine pianist. His interpretations of Nielsen provide a link with the composer, for as a young man of 21, he played for him. He recorded the *Chaconne* and the *Theme and variations* in 1940, and again in 1952, in the early days of LP, when he also committed the *Suite*, the *3 Piano pieces*, Op. 59 and other important works to disc. The present set was recorded in 1982–3, when he was in his mid-seventies and beyond his prime. There is insufficient subtlety in tonal colour and dynamic shading.

Chaconne, Op. 32; Humoresque-bagatelles, Op. 11; 5 Pieces, Op. 3; 3 Pieces, Op. 59; Suite luciferique, Op. 45.
❁ *** Virgin/EMI Dig. VC5 45129-2 [CDC 45129]. Leif Ove Andsnes.

Nielsen's piano music is unmissable! The early pieces have great charm and the later *Suite* and the *Three Pieces*, Op. 59, great substance. Although their finest exponent up to now, the Danish pianist Arne Skjold Rasmussen, committed them to disc, he never enjoyed the international exposure to which his gifts entitled him. But now at last they have found a princely interpreter in the Norwegian, Leif Ove Andsnes, who has a natural feeling for and understanding of this music. Indeed these are performances of eloquence and nobility that are unlikely to be surpassed for some years to come, and the recorded sound is vivid and life-like.

VOCAL MUSIC

Amor and the Poet; An evening at Giske; Cosmus; Sir Oluf he rides; Tove; Willemoes (incidental music).
**(*) BIS Dig. CD 641 [id.] Henriette Bonde-Hansen, Susanne Persson; Jan Lund; Jesper Vigant, Danish Nat. Op. Ch.; Aalborg SO, Tamas Vetö.

The music to *Herr Oluf han rider* (*Sir Oluf he rides*) occupies almost half the CD. It was written at high speed (in one number Nielsen even presses one of his early piano pieces, Op. 3, into service). The overture is very imaginative and deserves to enter the repertoire, but for the most part the music is slight. *An evening at Giske* (*En aften paa Giske*), the earliest piece on the disc, is well held together. The Overture, *Love and the Poet* (*Amor og Digtaren*) is not dissimilar in style or quality to *An imaginary journey to the Fœroe Islands*. More engaging than the Kontrapunkt collection with *Hagbarth og Signe*, but of specialist rather than general interest.

(i) *Hymnus amoris, Op. 12;* (ii) *3 Motets, Op. 55; The sleep, Op. 18;* (iii) *Springtime in Fünen, Op. 43.*
*** Chandos Dig. CHAN 8853 [id.]. Soloists; (i) Copenhagen Boys' Ch.; (ii–iii) Danish Nat. R. Ch.; (iii) Skt. Annai Gymnasium Children's Ch., Danish Nat. RSO; (i; iii) Segerstam; (ii) Parkman.

Hymnus amoris is full of glorious music whose polyphony has a naturalness and freshness that it is difficult to resist, and which is generally well sung. The harsh dissonances of the middle *Nightmare* section of *Søvnen* ('The Sleep') still generate a powerful effect. Segerstam gets very good results both here and in the enchanting *Springtime in Fünen*, and the solo singing is good. The three motets actually contain a Palestrina quotation. Generally excellent performances and fine recorded sound.

6 Songs, Op. 10.
(N) *** Virgin/EMI Dig. VC5 45273-2 [id.]. Solveig Kringelborn, Malcolm Martineau – GRIEG, RANGSTROM, SIBELIUS: *Songs.* ***

Solveig Kringelborn's anthology includes a half-dozen songs by four composers from each of the Nordic countries. The most neglected are Nielsen's, perhaps because of their uniformly strophic folk-like character. The Op. 10 set is among the most delightful and she sings them with great purity and does them full justice. Only in *Lake of memory* does she falter. (She is a little under the note.) But this apart, this is a lovely group and we are not well endowed with alternative readings. Malcolm Martineau is superb throughout. Excellent recorded sound too.

(i) *Springtime in Fünen. Aladdin suite, Op. 34.*
*** Unicorn Dig. DKPCD 9054 [id.]. (i) Ingo Nielsen, Von Binzer, Klint, Lille Muko University Ch., St Klemens Children's Ch.; Odense SO, Veto.

Springtime in Fünen is one of those enchanting pieces to which everyone responds when they hear it, yet which is hardly ever performed outside Denmark. The engaging *Aladdin* orchestral suite is well played by the Odense orchestra. This disc is a little short on playing time – but no matter, it is well worth its cost and will give many hours of delight.

STAGE WORKS

Aladdin (complete incidental music), *Op. 34.*
*** Chandos Dig. CHAN 9135 [id.]. Ejsing, Paevatalu, Danish R. Chamber Ch. & SO, Rozhdestvensky.

Until now the *Aladdin* music has been known only from the 20-minute, seven-movement suite, but the complete score runs to four times its length. Some numbers are choral, and there are songs and a short piece for solo flute. Thirteen of the movements are designed to accompany spoken dialogue and, although not all of it is of equal musical interest and substance, most of it is characteristically Nielsenesque, and much of it is delightful. The two soloists, Mette Ejsing and Guido Paevatalu, are very good and the Danish Radio forces respond keenly to Rozhdestvensky's baton. This is not top-drawer Nielsen but, given such a persuasive performance and excellent recording, one is almost lulled into the belief that it is.

OPERA

Maskarade (complete).
(N) *** Decca Dig. 460 227-2 (2) [id.]. Aage Haugland, Susanne Resmark, Gert Henning Jensen, Bo Skovhus, Michael Kristensen, Kurt Ravn, Henriette Bonde-Hansen, Marianne Rørholm, Danish Nat. R. Ch. & SO, Ulf Schirmer.
**(*) Unicorn DKPCD 9073/4 [id.]. Hansen, Plesner, Landy, Johansen, Serensen, Bastian, Brodersen, Haugland, Danish R. Ch. & SO, Frandsen.

It is sad that so brilliant and delightful an opera as *Maskarade* has so far failed to get a foothold in the international repertory, but this superb recording should help to change that, an ideal work for enjoying on disc. The original play by Ludwig Holberg is one of the classics of Danish theatre, adapted here by Nielsen himself and the poet, Vilhelm Andersen. The plot is the classic one of young lovers being coerced into arranged marriages by heavy-handed fathers, with the masquerade as the symbol of freedom. The result in the opera is a charming mixture, with echoes of Verdi's *Falstaff* as well as of Johann Strauss's *Fledermaus*. Going one better than Strauss, Nielsen reserves his party scene, the masquerade, for his climactic last act, a brilliant conclusion. With eighteenth-century flavours invading the idiom, Nielsen has also learnt from Mozart's da Ponte operas.

Central to the success of the recording is the weighty performance of the bass, Aage Haugland, as the heavy father, Jeronimus. Though the tenor, Gert Henning Jensen, is lightweight as the son, he characterizes well, as do the rest of the cast, including Susanne Resmark as the wife, Henriette Bonde-Hansen as the heroine, Leonora (who appears only in the second half of the opera) and above all, Bo Skovhus as the servant, Henrik, a key commentator. Ulf Schirmer draws sparkling and idiomatic playing from the Danish Radio Orchestra, recorded in warm, opulent sound.

Maskarade is a buoyant, high-spirited score, full of strophic songs and choruses, making considerable use of dance and dance-rhythms, and having the unmistakable lightness of the *buffo* opera. It is excellently proportioned. The performance on Unicorn is delightful, distinguished by generally good singing and alert orchestral support. The disappointment is the CD transfer which, in trying to clarify textures, has in fact made the focus less clean.

Saul and David (complete).
❀ *** Chandos Dig. CHAN 8911/12 [id.]. Haugland, Lindroos, Kiberg, Westi, Ch. & Danish Nat. RSO, Järvi.

Nielsen's first opera is here sung in the original language, which is as important with Nielsen as it is with Janáček, and it has the merit of an outstanding Saul in Aage Haugland. The remainder of the cast is very strong and the powerful choral writing is well served by the Danish Radio Chorus. The opera abounds in wonderful and noble music, the ideas are fresh and full of originality. It convinces here in a way that it rarely has before, and the action is borne along on an almost symphonic current that disarms criticism. A marvellous set.

Nielsen, Ludolf (1876–1939)

Symphony No. 1 in B min. Op. 3; Fra Bjœrgene (From the mountains: symphonic suite), Op. 8.
(N) ** Maro Polo dacapo 8.224093 [id.]. Danish PO, Frank Cramer.

Ludolf Nielsen was eleven years younger than his famous namesake, and like his exact contemporary, Hakan Børresen, a pupil of Svendsen. Like Carl Nielsen, his background was rural and in his student days he formed a string quartet. His *First Symphony* (1903) has real symphonic feeling and a natural grasp of form. The ideas have a touch of Bruckner and of Carl Nielsen too, and it is obvious that Ludolf possessed an original mind. The advent of the First World War shattered his faith in humanity and although his creative fires did not wholly burn out, he was occupied during the late 1920s and early 1930s, in building up the music department of the Danish Radio. The Danish Philharmonic is the South Jutland Orchestra, based at Odense, and the playing under the German conductor, Frank Cramer, is perfectly acceptable though the recording is not top-drawer. Both the symphony and the suite, Op. 8, are well worth investigating.

Nin, Joaquín (1879–1949)

Cantos populares españoles Nos. 3, 4, 6, 7, 19 & 20.

(M) (***) EMI (SIS) mono CDC7 54836-2. Ninon Vallin, composer – FALLA: *Harpsichord concerto* etc.; GRANADOS: *Danzas españolas* etc.; MOMPOU: *Piano pieces*. (***)

Joaquín Nin's *Cantos populares españoles* are rather similiar in character to the celebrated Falla set. The incomparable Ninon Vallin sings six of them with great simplicity and Nin proves himself a charming accompanist. The recordings, made in Paris in 1929, when Vallin was at the height of her powers, sound remarkably good.

Norby, Erik (born 1936)

The Rainbow snake.

*** BIS CD 79 [id.]. Danish Nat. RO, Frandsen – BENTZON: *Feature on René Descartes;* JORGENSON: *To love music.* **

The Rainbow snake is an American Indian fable which tells how drought had produced infertility in the land. The snake heard of this and let itself be thrown, coiled up, into the sky where it uncoiled until it touched the earth at both ends. It then arched its back and scraped down the blue ice which had given rise to the drought, thus restoring life to the earth. Every time the sun and rain meet, the snake stretches its luminous body across the heavens. The scoring is highly colourful, the harmonic language impressionist. All highly atmospheric, with kaleidoscopic changes of harmony against an almost static rhythmic background. It is very well played and recorded.

Nørgård, Per (born 1932)

Symphony No. 1 (Sinfonia austera); Symphony No. 2.

(N) *** Chan Dig. CHAN 9450 [id.]. Danish Nat. RSO, Leif Segerstam.

Per Nørgård is the leading Danish composer of his generation, a pupil of Vagn Holmboe and Hilding Rosenberg, and an influential mentor of younger figures such as Ruders. He is highly prolific and an enormously talented figure, as such early works as *Konstellationer* (1958) – his first work to appear on LP in the UK – and the *Sinfonia austera* show. The *Sinfonia austera*, Nørgård's *First Symphony*, comes from 1955 and has a strong atmosphere with something of Holmboe's sense of power and forward movement; impressive and compelling. The *Second* (1970) is different in kind, static in feeling and hypnotic in effect. The 'infinite series' which shaped his *Voyage into the golden screen* dominates the whole piece. There are some striking and imaginative effects here. Very good performances too from Leif Segerstam and the Danish National Radio Symphony Orchestra. A good launching pad to start exploring this composer who is now well represented on CD.

Nørholm, Ib (born 1931)

Violin concerto, Op. 60.

*** BIS CD 80 [id.]. Leo Hansen, Danish Nat. RSO, Herbert Blomstedt – KOPPEL: *Cello concerto*. ***

Ib Nørholm's *Violin concerto* not only evinces considerable imaginative powers but contains some music of real beauty and is expertly laid out for the orchestra. The Danish Radio recording, while not state of the art, is more than acceptable, and it comes with a rewarding coupling.

(i) *Symphonies Nos. 4 (Décreation), Op. 76. 5 (The 4 Elements), Op. 80.*

** Kontrapunkt Dig. CD 32212 [id.]. (i) Pavlovski, Dahlberg, Høyer, Ib Nørholm, Danish Nat. R. Ch.; Danish Nat. RSO, Serov.

The *Fourth Symphony* (*Décreation*) is highly self-conscious – the sub-title itself, *Moralities* or *There may be many miles to the nearest spider*, puts you in the picture, although there are many imaginative touches during its course. Sadly, inspiration is intermittent and the work as a whole is deficient in thematic vitality. There is a lot going on but very little actually happens. The *Fifth Symphony* (*The Four Elements*) is better, though again its neo-expressionism outstays its welcome. The performances under Eduard Serov are obviously committed, and in the *Fourth* the composer himself is the narrator. Decent recording.

Novák, Vitězslav (1870–1949)

(i) Symphonic poems: *About the Eternal longing, Op. 33; In the Tatras, Op. 26;* (ii) *Moravian-Slovak suite, Op. 32.*

(M) **(*) Sup. 11 0682-2 [id.]. (i) Czech PO; (ii) Brno State PO, Karel Sejna.

In the Tatras (1902), an opulent Straussian tone-poem, and *About the Eternal longing* (1903/4) were inspired by unrequited love for a beautiful young pupil, Růžena. The *Slovak suite* is a heavenly score. *Two in love*, its third movement, could well become as widely popular as any piece of music you care to think of. *In the church*, the opening movement, has something in common with Mozart's *Ave verum corpus*, though more obviously romantic, and the closing *At night* is beguilingly atmospheric. All three works here are persuasively played. The recording of the two symphonic poems is atmospheric and clear but a bit pale in the more expansive tuttis; the suite has slightly more body and colour.

Eternal longing, Op. 33; In the Tatra mountains, Op. 26; Slovak suite, Op. 32.
*** Virgin/EMI Dig. VC5 45251 [CDC 45251]. RLPO, Libor Pešek.

Novák's two best-known tone-poems date from the first years of the century – as, for that matter, does the enchanting *Slovak suite*. *In the Tatra mountains* (1902) might be thought of as a kind of Bohemian *Alpine Symphony* and is no less striking, while *Eternal longing* (1903–4) blends expressionism and impressionism in a wholly individual fashion. The *Slovak suite* has a refreshing spontaneity and fertility of invention, second only to his master, Dvořák. Libor Pešek and the Liverpool orchestra put us firmly in their debt with this issue. Both performance and recording are first rate.

De profundis, Op. 67; Overture, Lady Godiva, Op 41; South Bohemian suite, Op. 64.
(***) Sup. mono 11 1873-2 011 [id.]. Brno State PO, Jaroslav Vogel.

These classic performances all come from 1960, except for the *De profundis*, which Jaroslav Vogel recorded two years later. The recordings still sound very good for their period and the performances are unlikely to be surpassed. What attractive music it is, too. Recommended.

Pan (symphonic poem), *Op. 43.*
*** Marco Polo Dig. 8.223325 [id.]. Slovak PO, Zdeněk Bílek.

Novák's five-movement symphonic poem, *Pan*, has some lovely music in it, and there is a pantheistic sensibility here. The scoring has great delicacy and imaginative resource, and there is a distinctly Gallic feeling to much of it. Lyrical, often inspired (occasionally a bit overlong – particularly the last movement) and rewarding, this score is beautifully played by the Slovak Philharmonic under Zdeněk Bílek, and no less beautifully recorded.

The Storm, Op. 42.
(M) *** Sup. SU 3088-2 211 [id.]. Soloists, Czech PO Ch. & O, Košler.

The Storm is a work of great beauty and imagination, scored with consummate mastery and showing a lyrical gift of a high order. It has warmth and genuine individuality; the idiom owes something to Richard Strauss as well as to the Czech tradition, and there is an impressive command of both melody and structure. The performance is fully worthy and has splendid dramatic feeling, helped by good soloists and a fine chorus. The recording, too, is admirably balanced, and there is depth, and plenty of weight, even if the soloists are rather too forward. This is one of the best Supraphon reissues for some time.

Nyman, Michael (born 1948)

(i) *Piano concerto;* (ii) *On the Fiddle; Prospero's Books.*
(B) *** Tring Dig. TRP 097 [id.]. (i) Peter Lawson; (ii) Jonathan Carney; RPO, Carney.

(i) *Piano concerto;* (ii) *MGV.*
*** Argo Dig. 443 382-2 [id.]. (i) Kathryn Stott, Royal Liverpool PO; (ii) Michael Nyman Band, O; composer.

Michael Nyman's brand of minimalism has been most effective in illustrating a whole sequence of films, including the Oscar-winning *The Piano*, in which this concerto was evocatively used. This Tring version of that work, with Peter Lawson a fine, muscular soloist, costs only a third as much as the Argo issue with the composer conducting and is just as powerful as that original, helped by fuller and more immediate sound. (However, for R. L. the sound-picture is too forward and over-resonant: he feels minimalist music needs the widest range of dynamic to make its fullest effect.)

On the fiddle is drawn from Nyman's music for three films directed by Peter Greenaway; its third section, *Miserere paraphrase*, derives from *The Cook, The Thief, His Wife and Her Lover*. Here, with the solo violin taking a central role, Nyman reverts to warmly melodic writing, and the RPO leader, Jonathan Carney, is a most persuasive advocate, both as soloist and as conductor. The music for the Shakespeare-based film with John Gielgud, *Prospero's Books*, is more conventionally minimalist, with nagging repetitions at generally fast speeds. This too is magnetic in its way, using a smaller ensemble. With any reservations, this is an excellent bargain for anyone who has responded to Nyman's film music.

Kathleen Stott's account of the concerto is as fine as one would expect, and the coupling on the Argo CD, *Musique à grande vitesse* was commissioned for the inauguration of the high-speed TGV train from Paris to Lille. Not surprisingly, it relies on train rhythms, with all their unexpected syncopations. The Michael Nyman Band, heavily amplified, is set as a ripieno group alongside the orchestra, giving the piece what the composer thinks of as concerto grosso associations. Powerful, forward recording.

The convertibility of lute strings; For John Cage; Self-laudatory hymn of Inanna and her omnipotence; Time will pronounce.
*** Argo Dig. 440 282-2 [id.]. James Bowman, Fretwork, Trio of London, Virginia Black, London Brass.

Inspired by the first onslaught of the war in Bosnia, *Time will pronounce* uses a piano trio alternately to evoke the pain of war and the violence, but with more slow music than is usual with this highly charged, self-indulgent composer. At the end the music fades inconclusively to nothing. The *Self-laudatory hymn* is a weird but magnetic piece for the odd combination of counter-tenor and consort of viols, setting an ancient Near Eastern text with biblical overtones. It should not work, but with such performers as James Bowman and Fretwork, for whom it was written, it does. The least appealing piece is *The convertibility of lute strings*, in which Nyman exploits his aggressive vein in heavy, jangling writing for solo harpsichord. The only piece with jollity in it is *For John Cage*, using the ten instruments of London Brass with wit as well as colour, ending with a slow, chorale-like section with a crescendo at the end, leaving one hanging in mid-air. Whatever reservations have to be made about such minimalist inspirations, the individuality is undeniable, and performances and recording are vividly colourful.

Noise, sounds and sweet airs.
*** Argo (IMS) Dig. 440 842-2 [id.]. Bott, Summers, Bostridge, Ensemble Instrumental de Basse-Normandie, Dominique Debart.

The musical material here is drawn from his opera-ballet, *La princesse de Milan*, with new vocal lines superimposed over the top, setting a text drawn from Shakespeare's *The Tempest*, 'very heavily and idiosyncratically edited', as Nyman says himself. The oddest idiosyncrasy is that the three different voices keep switching roles, so that the words of Prospero, Miranda and other characters are divided among all three singers. The performance and recording are superb, as vivid as any Nyman on disc, giving the result a hypnotic fascination. The three soloists in particular sing magnificently, each with clear, firm, richly focused voice. Catherine Bott, always compelling, is well matched by the alto, Hilary Summers and the clear-toned young tenor, Ian Bostridge.

Nystroem, Gösta (1890–1966)

(i) *Viola concerto (Hommage à la France). Ishavet (Arctic Sea);* (ii) *Sinfonia concertante for cello and orchestra.*
*** BIS Dig. CD 682 [id.]. (i) Nobuko Imai; (ii) Niels Ullner; Malmö SO, Paavo Järvi.

Niels Ullner is a fine cellist with an opulent tone and eloquent phrasing and his is a thoughtful, well-integrated performance of the *Sinfonia concertante*, and the music has both quality and depth. The *Viola concerto* has a neo-classical and eminently Gallic *joie de vivre*, as well as poignancy. Nobuko Imai plays it superbly and, throughout the whole programme, the Malmö orchestra are in excellent form under Neeme Järvi's son, Paavo. The recording is transparent and has excellent presence and definition.

Sinfonia espressiva; Sinfonia seria.
(N) *** BIS Dig. CD 782 [id.]. Malmö SO, Paavo Järvi.

As good an introduction to the music of this Swedish composer as any. Along with the *Sinfonia concertante* for cello and orchestra, the *Sinfonia espressiva* is probably Nystroem's finest work; finely crafted and purposeful. The fires of inspiration burn less brightly in the *Sinfonia seria* of 1963, though its opening, which recalls Honegger a little, has a certain promise. Paavo Järvi and the Malmö Orchestra give committed accounts of both pieces and the BIS engineers produce excellent results.

Obradors, Fernando Jaumandreu (1897–1945)

Symphonic suite: El Poema de la jungla.
(N) *** ASV Dig. CDDCA 1043 [id.]. Gran Canaria PO, Leaper – RODO: *Symphony No. 2.* ***

Fernando Obradors is best known for his collection of classical Spanish songs, *Canciones clásicas española*. The rest of his output languishes in obscurity including his opera, *La maja de los lunares*. *El Poema de la jungla* was begun at the outset of the Spanish civil war and shows his remarkable skill as an orchestrator. It is less imaginative and resourceful than Koechlin's *Le livre de la jungle*, but colourful and atmospheric all the same. The disc is particularly useful in bringing to light the *Second Symphony* of another Catalan, Gabriel Rodó, who also served as conductor of the Gran Canaria Filarmónica. Good performances and excellent recorded sound too.

Obrecht, Jacob (1457–1505)

Laudes Christo; Missa Malheur me bat.
(N) *** ASV Dig. CDGAU 171 [id.]. Clerks' Group, Edward Wickham – MARTINI: *Motets & Magnificat.* ***

The Dutch composer, Jacob Obrecht, was one of the pioneers in developing a new, more closely organized polyphonic style, notably in his use of segmentation. This is well illustrated in this fine *Mass*, with the theme on which the work is based successively fragmented. There is a sublime summation at the end when the theme is restored to its original form. The music is radiantly performed by the Clerks' Group, and given warmly atmospheric sound. The coupling is apt – Obrecht ended up as maestro di capella at the court of Ferrara, where Martini had spent his career.

Missa Caput; Salve Regina: in 4 parts; in 6 parts. Venit ad Petrum.
(BB) *** Naxos Dig. 8.553210 [id.]. Oxford Camerata, Jeremy Summerly.

The *Missa Caput* survives in a manuscript at the court of Ferrara but could possibly have been compiled in Bruges. Both of the *Salve Regina* settings are based on plainchant melody and are *alternatim* settings, the music alternating between a polyphonic treatment of the chant and the unadorned chant itself. Jeremy Summerly and his Oxford Camerata, recorded in the Chapel of Hertford College, Oxford, give expert and committed accounts of this music and they are accorded first-class sound. To adapt the comment of the author of the accompanying notes, listening to this music persuades one of the fifteenth-century view that 'music was capable of lifting one's soul to a contemplation of heavenly things'.

Ockeghem, Johannes (*c.* 1410–97)

Alma Redemptoris Mater; Ave Maria; Missa L'homme armé.
❁ (BB) *** Naxos Dig. 8.554297 [id.]. Oxford Camerata, Jeremy Summerly (with Josquin DESPREZ: *Memor esto veri tui* ***).

The soaring opening *Ave Maria*, gloriously sung, immediately sets the seal on the inspirational power of Ockeghem's music. It is followed by the plainchant, *Alma Redemptoris Mater*, and then its polyphonic setting, simple and flowing and harmonically rich. The robust ballad, *L'homme armé*, follows ('The armed man must be feared'), sounding vigorously jolly, like a carol. It must have been hugely popular in its day since so many composers used it as a basis for a Mass. While the polyphony in the *Gloria* and *Credo* moves onward inventively, the work's dramatic and emotional peak is readily found in the extended *Sanctus* (by far the longest section) and resolved in the sublime melancholy of the *Agnus Dei*. In short, this is a work of striking individuality and beauty, and it is sung superbly here, and marvellously paced. Josquin's setting of sixteen verses from Psalm 119, *Memor esto verbi tui*, with its expressively fertile imitative devices, makes an eloquent postlude, and the recording, made in the Chapel of Hertford College, Oxford, could hardly be bettered. It dates from February 1997, thus aptly celebrating the 500th anniversary of Ockeghem's death.

Alma redemptoris mater; Missa Mi-Mi; Salve Regina.
*** ASV Dig. CD GAU 139 [id.]. The Clerks' Group, Edward Wickham (with motets by BUSNOIS, ISAAC and OBRECHT).

Ockeghem's *Salve Regina*, the motet *Alma redemptoris mater* and the *Missa Mi-Mi* are contrasted here with motets by three of his contemporaries. The *Missa Mi-Mi* is so named because of the recurring descending fifth, both named 'mi' in the natural and soft hexachords. These performances have a refreshing enthusiasm and the approach to rhythm is remarkably free. The Clerks' Group and Edward Wickham specialize in the music of the late Middle Ages and early Renaissance, and readers can invest in the series with confidence.

Missa caput; Ma Maistresse; Missa Ma Maistresse: Kyrie & Gloria.
(N) *** ASV Gaudeamus Dig. CDGAU 186 [id.]. Clerks' Group, Edward Wickham (with ANON: Hymn: *O solis ortus cardine;* Motets: *O sidus Hispanie; Gaude Marie*. SARUM CHANT: Antiphon: *Venit ad Petrum*).

Only two movements survive of the *Missa Ma Maitresse*, but very fine they are, bright and extrovert in feeling, making ingenious use of the song material. The song itself is solo-led, ravishingly sung: Ockeghem's lovely setting is fully worthy of the words: '*My mistress and my greatest love, perfect in attributes as ever woman was*'. The cantus firmus of the *Missa Caput* is dervived from the long melisma on the word 'caput' which we have already heard at the end of the Sarum Antiphon, *Venit ad Petrum*. It is perhaps an awkward basis for a mass, but Ockeghem's polyphony rises to the challenge, and the work is both texturally and aurally intriguing, yet moves forward on a seemingly inevitable course, in spite of Ockeghem's frequent use of cadences. The three anonymous motets can be found in the same manuscript which is the earliest source of this mass and it is possible that *O sidus Hispanie*, an eulogy for St Anthony of Padua, was written by Du Fay, who greatly admired this Saint. All the performances here are of the highest order and the recording is first-class too.

Missa De plus en plus; Missa Fors seulement.
(N) *** Lyrichord Dig. LEMS 8029 [id.]. Schola Discantus, Kevin Moll.

This Lyrichord disc joins the beautiful middle-period four-part *Missa De plus en plus* with a later five-part work, *Missa Fors seulement*, based on one of the composer's own chansons, which is unfortunately not included here as it is on Edward Wickam's ASV disc (see below). However the performances are finely sung and blended here and have an appealing simplicity. Kevin Moll's varied pacing is convincing. The *Missa Fors seulement* (which only consists of a *Kyrie, Gloria* and *Credo*) is especially striking for its use of two basses, which darkens the texture very strikingly, although Moll takes care not to provide an exaggerated balance.

Missa prolationum.
(N) (BB) *** ASV Gaudeamus Dig. CDGAU 143 [id.]. Clerks' Group, Edward Wickham (with

BUSNOIS: *Gaude coelestis Domina; In hydraulis*. JOSQUIN DESPREZ: *Illibata Dei Virgo nutric*. OBRECHT (attrib.): *Humilium decus*. PULLOIS: *Flos de spina* ***).

Missa prolationum; Requiem; Intemerata Dei mater.
(N) (BB) **(*) Naxos Dig. 8.554260 [id.]. Musica Ficta, Bo Holten.

Ockeghem was a mathematician as well as a composer, and his *Missa prolationum* is famous for its intellectually complex polyphony based on double canons, while the rhythmic discipline is also carefully calculated. To all but the most analytical listener this will not matter too much, for the resulting music has a seemingly effortless flow, although the eight-voiced Clerks' Group, without losing melismatic sonority, certainly don't miss the special rhythmic relationships. They support the mass with five diverse motets by Ockeghem's contemporaries (nearly all set to Marian texts), to make a stimulating introduction to other Franco-Netherlands composers of this period. Excellent recording.

The performances by this first-class Danish Choir under Bo Holten on Naxos, use a larger group (fourteen in all) and one in which the rich-voiced women singers refine their tone to sound very like boy-trebles when required. The account of the *Missa prolationum* is particularly rich-textured, and beautifully balanced: the *Sanctus* and *Benedictus* strikingly so. The *Requiem* is also superbly sung, if with the rough edges smoothed off. The result is remarkably homogeneous, with the different sections of the work given a more convincing unity than in some performances. The *Intemerata Dei Mater*, opens the programme. It is sung with considerable feeling and immediately shows the splendid inner blend commanded by this group. Holten moves the polyphony forward with just the right degree of momentum. The choir is very beautifully recorded, but the disc (unusually for Naxos) is let down a little by the absence of English translations.

Masses for 3 voices: *Missa sine nomine; Missa quinti toni*.
*** Lyrichord Dig. LEMS 8010 [id.]. Schola Discantus, Kevin Moll.

Here is a natural follow-up to the superb Lyrichord CD of organa by Leonin and Perotinus. The very austerity of Ockeghem's part-writing, with its serenely flowing polyphony, adds to the potency of his music for modern ears. It is very beautifully sung by a vocal quartet of high quality whose tonal matching and fine tuning are ideal. The recording, too, is clear yet has a perfectly judged ambience.

Requiem (Missa pro defunctis).
(N) *** HM Dig. HM 901441 [id.]. Ensemble Organum, Pages de la Chapelle, Marcel Pérès.
(N) (B) *** HM Dig. Trio HMX 290891.93 (3) (as above) Ens. Organum, Pérès – MACHAUT: *Messe de Nostre Dame*; HILDEGARD: *Laudes of Saint Ursula*. ***

Requiem; Motet and *Missa Fors seulement*.
*** ASV Gaudeamus CDGAU 168 [id.]. Clerks' Group, Edward Wickham.

Requiem (Missa pro defunctis); Missa Mi-Mi (Missa quarti toni).
(M) *** Virgin Veritas/EMI Dig. VER5 61219-2 [id.]. Hilliard Ens., Hillier.

Ockeghem's *Requiem* remains one of the riddles of medieval liturgical music. Its various surviving movements are very different in style, notation and part-writing, and (rather like the Du Fay *St Anthony Mass* see above) it was long thought that the manuscript might be a collection of fragments from a number of different works. Even so the *Requiem* holds together with a convincing unity. Of all the available recordings, that by Marcel Pérès and the Ensemble Organum carries the darkest medieval feeling. The conductor's reconstruction is a quite arbitrary one. He even sings the solo plainchants himself, lugubriously but resonantly. At the opening the ear is struck by the dark sonorities of Pérès's uniquely low pitching of the male voices, an extraordinary sound. Later he adds the (missing) *Sanctus* and *Communion* from a Mass by Antonius Divitis, emphasizing the change by the inclusion of trebles (Les Pages de la Chapelle). Inevitably this must be a controversial account, but it is both gripping and aurally stimulating. This CD additionally comes in a slipcase as part of a Harmonia Mundi Trio at budget price which is highly recommendable, for the recordings of Hildegard and Machaut are no less stimulating.

Certainly every bar of the music is memorable in such a dedicated performance as we have from the Clerks' Group under Edward Wickham, who offer fine blending and tuning, clearly detailed inner parts and a richly flowing line which is seemingly ideally paced. In addition we are offered the *Kyrie*, *Gloria* and *Credo* of the *Missa Fors seulement*, plus the rondeau on which it is based, and further arrangements of the latter by Pierre de la Rue and Antoine Brumel, which offer more splendid music to intrigue the inquisitive ear.

The *Missa Mi-Mi* is his most widely performed Mass and survives in three different sources in the Vatican Library; in one it is called *Missa Quarti Toni* and in another *My-My*. These performances, reissued on Virgin Veritas, have the expertise, secure intonation, blend and ensemble that one expects from these singers, and the music itself has an austere and affecting simplicity. Although alongside the account of the *Requiem* by the Clerks' Group it has a certain blandness, it would be curmudgeonly not to welcome such generally persuasive accounts of both works. At mid-price these make an eminently serviceable introduction to the sacred music of this composer and they are very well recorded, too.

Offenbach, Jacques (1819–80)

Andante for cello and orchestra; Concerto militaire in G for cello and orchestra (completed Jean-Max Clément).
*** RCA Dig. 09026 68420-2 [id.]. Ofra Harnoy, Bournemouth SO, Antonio de Almeida – LALO: *Concerto.* ***

The *Concerto militaire* dates from 1847. The published score, as recorded here, is revised by the French cellist, Jean-Max Clément, who orchestrated the last two movements and also reconstructed the solo part (notably in the finale, where he provides the cadenza), which appears never to have been written out in full by its composer: it bristles with bravura, sometimes in registers more in keeping with a violin than a cello! The composer himself richly revised the scoring of the second-movement *Andante* as an independent piece, and it is presented here separately, after the complete performance of the concerto. It has a glorious main theme, and in Harnoy's ravishing performance it is the highlight of this CD. The concerto is robbed a little of its sparkle here by a somewhat over-resonant recording. Harnoy has the full measure of the work: she essays the technical hurdles of the solo part with aplomb, yet her lyrical lines, the true stuff of operetta, soar ardently; her playing imaginatively uses the widest range of dynamic to add to the sense of spontaneity. The jaunty finale is full of high spirits. Almeida accompanies sympathetically and persuasively, and cello and orchestra are naturally balanced, but it is a pity about the high degree of resonance.

Gaîté parisienne (ballet, arr. Rosenthal): complete.
❁ (M) *** RCA 09026 61847-2 [id.]. Boston Pops O, Arthur Fiedler – ROSSINI/RESPIGHI: *Boutique fantasque.* ***
(M) ** EMI CDM7 63136-2. Monte Carlo Op. O, Rosenthal – WALDTEUFEL: *Waltzes.* ***

Fiedler's *Gaîté parisienne* is irresistible – one of his very finest records. The orchestra are kept exhilaratingly on their toes throughout and are obviously enjoying themselves, not least in the elegantly tuneful waltzes and in the closing *Barcarolle*, which Fiedler prepares beautifully and to which the generous acoustic of Symphony Hall affords a pleasing warmth without in any way blunting or coarsening the brilliance. The percussion, including bass drum in the exuberant *Can-Can*, adds an appropriate condiment and John Pfeiffer's superb new transfer makes the recording sound remarkably fresh and full. Unbelievably it dates from 1954, one of the very first of RCA's 'Living Stereo' records and still one of the finest.

Maurice Rosenthal's absolutely complete version from the mid-1970s has now been restored to the catalogue. The performance, though often idiomatically persuasive, has not the verve and glamour of that by Fiedler and Karajan. The sound, however, has been greatly improved, with the original excess resonance considerably tempered.

(i) *Gaîté parisienne* (ballet, arr. Rosenthal; complete); (ii) *Overtures and suites* from: *Orpheus in the Underworld* (1874 version, with *Pastoral ballet*); *Le voyage dans la lune* (with *Snowflakes ballet*).
(M) *** Ph. 442 403-2 [id.]. (i) Pittsburgh SO, Previn; (ii) Philh. O, Almeida.

An outstanding coupling. In *Gaîté parisienne* Previn realizes that tempi can remain relaxed and the music's natural high spirits will still bubble to the surface. The orchestral playing is both spirited and elegant, with Previn obviously relishing the score's delightful detail. Perhaps the tuba thumping away in the bass is a shade too present, but it increases one's desire to smile through this engagingly happy music. The *Snowflakes ballet* from *Le voyage dans la lune* is a charmer, and the ballet from *Orpheus in the Underworld* is hardly less delectable. The other surprise is the *Orpheus overture*, not the one we know but a more extended work in pot-pourri style, with some good tunes. Almeida is no less high-spirited than Previn, and the Philharmonia's response is both polished and elegant. Excellent recording too.

Gaîté parisienne (ballet, arr. Rosenthal): extended excerpts.
(B) *** DG 429 163-2 [id.]. BPO, Karajan – CHOPIN: *Les Sylphides* *** ❁; DELIBES: *Coppélia:* suite. ***

Karajan's selection is generous. On the DG disc, only Nos. 35, 7 and 19–21 are omitted. The remastering of the 1972 recording is highly successful; textures have been lightened to advantage, and the effect is to increase the raciness of the music-making, while its polish and sparkle are even more striking.

Musette (Air de ballet). Overtures: *La Belle Hélène; La Grande-Duchesse de Gérolstein; Orpheus in the Underworld. Les belles Américaines: Waltz* (orch. Robert Russell Bennett). *Contes d'Hoffmann: Intermezzo; Introduction; Minuet; Barcarolle. Geneviève de Brabant: Galop. La Périchole:* Pot-pourri.
(M) ** RCA 09026 61429-2 [id.]. Boston Pops O, Arthur Fiedler – IBERT: *Divertissement.* ***

For once the CD transfer of this RCA 'Living Stereo' recording from 1956 is disappointing. The Boston resonance intrudes on the music-making and tends to blunt the effect of the playing, so that one has the impression that Fiedler is fielding a second team. But the selection is interesting and generous, and Samuel Mayes is a sympathetic cello soloist in the *'Air de ballet from the 17th Century'*. Curiously, the Ibert *Divertissement* which acts as coupling and which was recorded a month later, is as racy as you could wish, and the recorded sound is comparably lively.

Overtures: *La Belle Hélène; Bluebeard; La Grande-Duchesse de Gérolstein; Orpheus in the Underworld; Vert-vert. Barcarolle from Contes d'Hoffmann.*
**(*) DG (IMS) Dig. 400 044-2 [id.]. BPO, Karajan.

Other hands besides Offenbach's helped to shape his overtures. Most are on a pot-pourri basis, but the tunes and scoring are so engagingly witty as to confound criticism. Karajan's performances racily evoke the theatre pit. The Berlin playing is very polished and, with so much to entice the ear, this cannot fail to be entertaining; however, the compact disc emphasizes the dryness of the orchestral sound; the effect is rather clinical, with the strings lacking bloom.

Le Papillon (ballet; complete).
(B) *** Decca Double 444 821-2 (2) [id.]. Nat. PO, Bonynge – TCHAIKOVSKY: *Nutcracker*. ***

Le Papillon is Offenbach's only full-length ballet and it dates from 1860. The quality of invention is high and the music sparkles from beginning to end. In such a sympathetic performance, vividly recorded (in 1972 in the Kingsway Hall), it cannot fail to give pleasure.

Cello duos, Op. 54: Suites Nos. 12.
(B) *** HM Musique d'Abord 1901043. Roland Pidoux and Etienne Péclard.

Offenbach was himself a very accomplished cellist, and these two works are tuneful and imaginatively laid out to exploit the tonal possibilities of such a duo. Offenbach's natural wit is especially apparent in the *First Suite in E major*. The performances are excellent and so is the recording.

OPERA

La Belle Hélène (complete).
(N) *** EMI (SIS) CDS7 47157-8 (2). Jessye Norman, Alliot-Lugaz, Aler, Burles, Bacquier, Lafont, Capitole Toulouse O, Plasson.

The casting of Jessye Norman in the name-part of *La Belle Hélène* may seem too heavyweight, but the way that great soprano can lighten her magisterial voice with all the flexibility and sparkle the music calls for is a constant delight, and her magnetism is irresistible. John Aler, another American opera-singer who readily translates to the style of French operetta, makes a heady-toned Paris, coping superbly with the high tessitura in the famous Judgement couplets and elsewhere. The rest of the cast is strong too, not forgetting Colette Alliot-Lugaz as Oreste, who had such a dazzling success in the central role of Chabrier's *L'étoile* in John Eliot Gardiner's brilliant recording. Michael Plasson here produces similarly fizzing results, with excellent ensemble from the chorus and orchestra of the Capitole. Excellent, lively recording, less reverberant than some other CDs from this source, although it is very important not to set the volume level too high or the spoken dialogue will seem unrealistically close.

Les brigands (complete).
**(*) EMI Dig. CDS7 49830-2 (2). Raphanel, Alliot-Lugaz, Raffalli, Trempont, Le Roux, Lyon Opera Ch. & O, Gardiner.

Les brigands has a Gilbertian plot about brigands and their unlikely association with the court of Mantua, with the carabinieri behaving very like the police in *The Pirates of Penzance*. The tone of the principal soprano, Ghislaine Raphanel, is rather edgily French, but the rest of the team is splendid. Outstanding as ever is the characterful mezzo, Colette Alliot-Lugaz, in another of her breeches roles. Warm, well-balanced recording. (This recording has been deleted as we go to press.)

Les Contes d'Hoffmann (The Tales of Hoffmann): complete.
✿ *** Decca 417 363-2 (2) [id.]. Sutherland, Domingo, Tourangeau, Bacquier, R. Suisse Romande and Lausanne Pro Arte Ch., SRO, Bonynge.
**(*) Ph. 422 374-2 (3) [id.]. Francisco Araiza, Eva Lind, Cheryl Studer, Jessye Norman, Anne Sofie von Otter, Samuel Ramey, Dresden Ch. & State O, Tate.

On Decca Joan Sutherland gives a virtuoso performance in four heroine roles, not only as Olympia, Giulietta and Antonia but also as Stella in the *Epilogue*. Bonynge opts for spoken dialogue, and puts the Antonia scene last, as being the more substantial. His direction is unfailingly sympathetic, while Sutherland is impressive in each role, notably as the doll Olympia and in the pathos of the Antonia scene. As Giulietta she hardly sounds like a *femme fatale*, but still produces beautiful singing. Domingo gives one of his finest performances on record, and so does Gabriel Bacquier. It is a memorable set, in every way, much more than the sum of its parts.

Jeffrey Tate in this textually troubled work uses a new expanded edition prepared by Michael Kaye. One big difference here from the complete Oeser edition is that dialogue replaces all the recitatives written by Ernest Guiraud. The Prologue is more extended, showing the transformation of the Muse into Nicklausse, with extra material in the Olympia and Antonia Acts too, such as the striking trio for Hoffmann, Nicklausse and Coppélius. It is a pity that a single singer was not chosen for all the heroines, as in the Bonynge/Sutherland set. As it is, Jessye Norman, the Antonia of the new set, cunningly lightens her voice, making it sound as girlish as she can, and she urges the music on at a brisker speed than usual in the charming duet, *C'est une chanson d'amour*, but it is still hard to imagine her as the fragile young girl destined to die. Tate's determination to adopt an authentic text leads him to reject the wonderful septet, based on the *Barcarolle* theme, not even including it in an appendix. Nor is Dapertutto's *Scintille, diamant* included, drawn originally from another Offenbach work, when the authentic *Tourne, tourne miroir*, is restored at that point. The new set uses the sour alternative ending to the Venice Act, with Giulietta accidentally taking poison. Samuel Ramey sings very well in all four villainous roles, with satisfyingly firm, dark tone, even if he finds it hard to sound really sinister, but principal vocal honours go to Anne Sofie von Otter as a superb Muse and Nicklausse, making one relish all the extra music given the character in this version. Eva Lind is bright and clear, if a little edgy and shallow, as Olympia, perfectly doll-like in fact; and Cheryl Studer is technically very strong and confident, even if she does not quite sound in character. Francisco Araiza makes an agreeable Hoffmann, but he lacks the flair of his finest rivals, and the voice tends to lose its focus under pressure. Even with reservations, there is a very strong textual case for this set, and admirers of the opera will surely want to have it alongside the first choice with Sutherland, Domingo and Bacquier.

Les Contes d'Hoffmann: highlights.
(M) *** Decca 458 234-2 (from above set, cond. Bonynge).

The newly compiled Decca highlights disc is one of the finest set of excerpts of its kind from any opera. With about 70 minutes of music, it offers a superbly managed distillation of nearly all the finest items and is edited most skilfully, including both the vocal and orchestral versions of the famous *Barcarolle*.

Orphée aux enfers (Orpheus in the Underworld; 1874 version).
(N) *** EMI (SIS) CDS7 49647-2 (2). Sénéchal, Mesplé, Rhodes, Burles, Berbié, Petits Chanteurs à la Croix Potencée, Toulouse Capitole O, Plasson.

Plasson recorded his fizzing performance – the first complete set in French for 30 years – using the far fuller four-act text of 1874 instead of the two-act version of 1858, so adding such delectable rarities as the sparkling *Rondo* of Mercury and the Policemens' chorus. Mady Mesplé as usual has her shrill moments, but the rest of the cast is excellent, and Plasson's pacing of the score is exemplary. The recording is brightly atmospheric and the leavening of music with spoken dialogue just enough. The newer recording by Minkowski of the alternative version is a disappointment (in spite of an impressive cast), over-driven and without the effervescence of the Plasson set.

Orpheus in the Underworld: highlights of English National Opera production (in English).
**(*) That's Entertainment Dig. CDTER 1134. Kale, Watson, Angas, Squires, Bottone, Pope, Belcourt, Styx, Burgess, E. Nat. Op. Ch. & O, Mark Elder.

The sparkling English National Opera production depends a lot for its fun on the racy new adaptation and translation by Snoo Wilson and the ENO producer, David Pountney. Offenbach devotees should be warned: there is little of Parisian elegance in this version and plenty of good knockabout British fun, brilliantly conveyed by the whole company, including Bonaventura Bottone's hilariously camp portrait of a prancing Mercury. Bright, vivid recording to match the performance.

La Périchole (complete).
(M) *** Erato/Warner 2292 45686-2 (2) [id.]. Crespin, Vanzo, Bastin, Lombard, Friedmann, Trigeau, Rhine Op. Ch., Strasbourg PO, Lombard.
(N) **(*) EMI (SIS) Dig. CDS7 47362-8 (2). Berganza, Carreras, Bacquier, Sénéchal, Trempont, Delange, Toulouse Capitole Ch. & O, Plasson.

Though both Régine Crespin in the title-role and Alain Vanzo as her partner, Piquillo, were past their peak at that time, their vocal control is a model in this music, with character strongly portrayed but without any hint of vulgar underlining. Crespin is fresh and Vanzo produces heady tone in his varied arias, some of them brilliant. Jules Bastin is characterful too in the subsidiary role of Don Andres, Viceroy of Peru. Lombard secures excellent precision of ensemble from his Strasbourg forces, only occasionally pressing too hard. The recorded sound is vivid and immediate, and the libretto provides a detailed synopsis of the action between the texts and translations of numbers.

A good modern recording of this delightful piece was badly needed, and in many ways this EMI set fits the bill for, though the sound (in Toulouse) is over-reverberant, the CD remastering has sharpened the impact, and ensemble work is excellent, with diction surprisingly clear against the full orchestral sound. The incidental roles are superbly taken, but it is odd that Spaniards were chosen for the two principal roles. José Carreras uses his lovely tenor line to fine effect but is often unidiomatic, while Teresa Berganza – who should have made the central character into a vibrant figure, as Régine Crespin used to – is surprisingly heavy and unsparkling. The CD disc-break is well placed between the Acts, but cueing might have been more generous.

Robinson Crusoe (sung in English).
*** Opera Rara ORC 7 (3) [id.]. Brecknock, Kenny, Kennedy, Hartle, Hill Smith, Oliver, Browne, Geoffrey Mitchell Ch., RPO, Alun Francis.

More ambitious than Offenbach's operettas, *Robinson Crusoe* offers a sequence of fresh and tuneful numbers with many striking ensembles. The plot is derived less from Daniel Defoe than from the British pantomime tradition. Characterization is strong and amusing, with a secondary couple shadowing Crusoe and his beloved Edwige. The casting is also from strength, with John Brecknock and Yvonne Kenny outstanding as Crusoe and Edwige, while Man Friday, as in the original Paris production, is sung by a mezzo, Sandra Browne. On the three discs are three hours of music, covering numbers which the composer cut even from the original production. The witty English translation, very freely adapted from the French text, with some changes of plot, is by Don White, and words are admirably clear.

La vie parisienne (complete).
(N) *** EMI (SIS) CDS7 47154-8 (2). Crespin, Mesplé, Masson, Sénéchal, Trempont, Benoit, Chateau, Lublin, Toulouse Capitole Ch. & O, Plasson.

Hardly less effervescent than the parallel version of *Orpheus in the Underworld*, also conducted by Michel Plasson for EMI, *La vie parisienne* is a scintillating example of Offenbach's work, an inconsequential farce around the heady days of the International Exhibition in Paris. Though the EMI recording is not quite as consistent as the one of *Orphée aux enfers*, the performance and presentation sparkle every bit as brilliantly, with the spoken dialogue for once a special attraction. Régine Crespin, in a smaller role, is most commanding and, though the cast lacks the excellent Vanzo and Massard, the style is captivatingly authentic. The CD transfer is vivid, without loss of ambient atmosphere.

'The world of Offenbach': Overtures: (iii) *La Belle Hélène;* (iii–iv) *La Fille du tambour-major;* (iii) *Orpheus in the Underworld;* (iii–iv) *Le Papillon: Pas de deux* (excerpt); *Valse des rayons. Les Contes d'Hoffmann:* (v; i; iv) *Ballad of Kleinzach; O Dieu! De quelle ivresse* (vi; i; iv) *Doll song* (vi–vii; i; iv) *Barcarolle* (2 versions). *La Grande Duchess de Gérolstein:* (vii–ix) *Portez armes . . . J'aime les militaires. La Périchole:* (viii; i; x) *O mon cher amant (Air de lettre); Ah! quel dîner.* (vi; i; iv) *Robinson Crusoé: Conduisez-moi vers celui que j'adore (Waltz song).* (xi; iv) *Valse tyrolienne.*
✽ (M) *** Decca Analogue/Dig. 452 942-2. (i) SRO; (ii) Ansermet; (iii) LSO; (iv) Bonynge; (v) Domingo; (vi) Sutherland; (vii) Tourangeau; (viii) Crespin; (ix) V. Volksopernorchester; (x) Lombard; (xi) Sumi Jo, ECO.

This 'lucky-bag' of Offenbachian goodies which Decca have expanded for CD from the original LP selection is bursting with lollipops to make a marvellously entertaining 74 minutes. The programme now opens and closes with the *Barcarolle*. Ansermet and Bonynge offer much character in the overtures; even if the former takes the famous can-can which closes the *Orpheus* overture more slowly than usual, he invests it with much rhythmic vigour. Bonynge has another scintillating can-can to offer in *La Fille du tambour-major*, which opens with an arresting side-drum, and he now also includes two items from Offenbach's only ballet, *Le Papillon*. The various excerpts from Bonynge's complete *Contes d'Hoffmann* are matched by Régine Crespin's delightful contribution as *La Périchole*, and Sutherland returns to sing the *Waltz song* from *Robinson Crusoé*. The other additional item is Sumi Jo's sparkling *Valse tyrolienne*. With splendidly vivid recording this is an unmissable sampler, to match and even surpass 'The world of Borodin'.

Onslow, Georges (1784–1853)

String quintets: in C min. (The Bullet), Op. 38; in E, Op. 39; in B min., Op. 40.
**(*) Sony Dig. SK 64308 [id.]. L'Archibudelli & Smithsonian Chamber Players.

Georges Onslow produced 34 string quintets, of which his fifteenth is nicknamed *The Bullet*. It is associated with a very serious hunting accident, in which he was struck in the head by a bullet intended for a wild boar. He was severely injured but survived to finish the work with its highly descriptive, indeed spectacular, Minuet describing his suffering and subsequent fever and delirium. The group here go over the top in this movement, with their anguished sforzandos and glissandos; but they play the peaceful *Andante sostenuto* (subtitled *Convalescena*) very beautifully. The energetic and optimistic finale describes his recovery, and it is presented here with appropriate spirited vitality. The other two *Quintets* are not quite so striking, though the *E major* has an expressive *Adagio grandioso* and the *B minor Quintet* has a strong opening movement and its *Adagio*, like the *E major*, has something of the dignity of Haydn. In short these quintets are well worth getting to know; if the 'authentic' sounds here are on the astringent side, this is still first-class quartet playing.

Orff, Carl (1895–1982)

Carmina Burana.

*** EMI (SIS) Dig. CDC5 55392-2 [id.]. Natalie Dessay, Thomas Hampson, Gérard Lesne, Chœur d'enfants de Midi-Pyrénées, Orféon Donostiarra, Toulouse Capitole O, Plasson.

*** Decca Dig. 430 509-2 [id.]. Dawson, Daniecki, McMillan, San Francisco Boys' & Girls' Choruses, San Francisco Symphony Ch. & SO, Blomstedt.

(M) *** Ph. Dig. 462 063-2 [id.]. Gruberoval, Aler, Hampson, Shinyukai Ch., Knaben des Staats & Berlin Cathedral Ch., BPO, Ozawa.

❀ (M) *** Sony SBK 47668 [id.]. Harsanyi, Petrak, Presnell, Rutgers University Ch., Phd. O, Ormandy.

*** EMI CDM5 66899-2 [CDM5 66951]. Armstrong, English, Allen, St Clement Danes Grammar School Boys' Ch., London Symphony Ch., LSO, Previn.

(N) *** DG Dig. 435 587-2 [id.]. Christiane Oelze, David Kuebler, Simon Keenlyside, German Opera Ch. & O, Berlin, Thielemann.

(M) *** DG 447 437 [id.]. Janowitz, Stolze, Fischer-Dieskau, Schöneberger Boys' Ch., Berlin German Op. Ch. & O, Jochum.

(BB) *** Carlton LSO Double Dig. 30368 01107 (2) [(B) id.]. Walmsley-Clark, Graham-Hall, Maxwell, Southend Boys' Ch., London Symphony Ch., LSO, Hickox – HOLST: *The Planets*. **(*)

(BB) *** RCA Navigator Dig. 74321 17908-2 [Basic 100 09026 68085-2]. Hendricks, Aler, Hagegård, St Paul's Cathedral Boys' Ch., L. Symphony Ch., LSO, Mata.

*** RCA Dig. 09026 61673-2 [id.]. McNair, Aler, Hagegård, St Louis Ch. & SO, Slatkin.

(N) (BB) **(*) Virgin Classics Dig. Double VBD5 61510-2 [CDVB 61510] (2). Janice Watson, James Boman, Donald Maxwell, Highcliffe Junior Ch., Waynflete Singers, Bournemouth Symphony Ch. & SO, David Hill – HOLST: *The Planets*; *Perfect Fool* (suite). **(*)

**(*) Teldec/Warner Dig. 9031 74886-2 [id.]. Sumi Jo, Jochen Kowalski, Boje Skovhus, LPO Ch., Southend Boys' Ch., LPO, Mehta.

(B) **(*) [EMI Red Line CDR5 69868]. Augér, van Kesteren, Summers, Southend Boys' Ch., Philh. Ch. & O, Muti.

Carmina Burana is very well served on CD, but Michel Plasson's new EMI performance, recorded in Toulouse, is rather special. It is sumptuously packaged, as CDs seldom are, and the design is suitably hedonistic, with a golden, slimly statuesque female form to represent the *Cours d'amours*. Moreover, not only is the choral singing extraordinarily vivid, it is as seductively warm in pianissimos as it is incisively vibrant in fortissimos. The three soloists are the finest on record. Thomas Hampson's tender first entry, *Omnia sol temperat* ('The sun rules over all'), is matched by his great vigour in the *Tavern scene*, *Estuan interius* ('Burning inside'). The orchestral introduction for the *Song of the roast swan* is bizarrely piquant and Gérard Lesne's alto timbre is uniquely suited to its wailing upper tessitura, while the orchestra adds sinister little snarls. The trebles open *Amor volat undique* with knowing Gallic delicacy, helped by the daintiness of the flutes, and Lesne and Hampson combine to make the sequence *Si puer cum puella* ('If a boy with a girl') quite delectable, topped by Natalie Dessay's tenderly ravishing *Stetit puella*, which is to be followed later by her moment of tender submission (*Dulcissime*) with its thrilling upward leap. The choral *Tempus est iocundum* brings the fullest expression of sexual rapture into which the trebles from the Midi-Pyrénées enter with enthusiasm, if without quite the knowing exuberance which English boy-trebles bring to it. But Plasson's closing *Ave formosissima O Fortuna* has splendid grandeur, and this outstandingly recorded new version must go straight to the top of the list.

Blomstedt's is also among the finest modern versions of Orff's exhilaratingly hedonistic cantata. Throughout the choral singing, men, boys, and girls, all enjoy themselves hugely as they should, with such stimulating words to sing. They generate great passion and energy and all three soloists are equally outstanding. John Daniecki's use of vocal colouring is entertainingly diverse, while Kevin McMillan is a splendidly unctuous Abbot, and Lynne Dawson portrays the girl in the red tunic with sensuous innocence. Blomstedt's reading is full of imaginative touches of light and shade, yet the flow of passionate energy is paramount. He is helped by the remarkable range and sonority of the Decca recording, very much in the demonstration bracket.

Ozawa's digital recording of Orff's justly popular cantata carries all the freshness and spontaneity of his earlier successful Boston version. The *Cours d'amours* sequence is the highlight of his reading, with the soprano, Edita Gruberová, highly seductive; Thomas Hampson's contribution is also impressive. Ozawa's infectious rubato in *Oh, oh, oh, I am bursting out all over*, interchanged between male and treble chorus towards the end of the work, is wonderfully bright and zestful, with the contrast of the big *Ave formosissima* climax which follows made to sound spaciously grand. Taken overall, this Philips version holds its position near the top of the list alongside Ormandy, and it has the additional advantage of spectacular, demonstration-worthy, digital recording. It comes handsomely repackaged as part of the Philips 'Choral Edition', but it is a pity that a translation could not have been included.

Ormandy and his Philadelphians have just the right panache to bring off this wildly exuberant picture of the Middle Ages by the anonymous poets of former days, and there is no more enjoyable analogue version. It has tremendous vigour, warmth and colour and a genial, spontaneous enthusiasm from the Rutgers University choristers, men and boys alike, that is irresistible. The soloists are excellent, but it is the chorus and orchestra who steal the show; the richness and eloquence of the choral tone is a joy in itself. This is quite splendid, one of Ormandy's most inspired recordings and, even if you already have the work in your collection, this exhilarating version will bring additional delights.

Previn's 1975 analogue version, vividly recorded, is even more sharply detailed than Ozawa's. It is strong on humour and rhythmic point. The chorus sings vigorously, the men often using an aptly rough tone; and the resilience of Previn's rhythms, finely sprung, brings out a strain not just of geniality but of real wit. This is a performance which swaggers along and makes you smile. Among the soloists, Thomas Allen's contribution is one of the glories of the music-making, and in their lesser roles the soprano and tenor are equally stylish. The digital remastering is wholly successful: the choral bite is enhanced, yet the recording retains its full amplitude.

Using a chorus and orchestra from the Opera in Berlin, the brilliant young German conductor Christian Thielmann offers a boldly dramatic reading of Orff's naggingly memorable score, helped by full, atmospheric recording. It is a performance of extremes, with the fast, insistent sections brisk and incisive and the lyrical passages warmly expansive. Though the chorus is backwardly balanced, the terracing of textures is clearly defined. The soloists are among the finest on record, with the soprano Christiane Oelze ravishingly pure in her high-flown solos, the tenor, David Kuebler, unstrained even by the *Roast Swan* passage, and Simon Keenlyside superb as the baritone Master of Ceremonies. All in all, a competitive and enjoyable version, but not a first choice.

Jochum's 1968 recording of *Carmina Burana* has never sounded better than it does in this reissue in DG's 'Originals' series. The choral pianissimos lack the very last degree of immediacy, but the underlying tension of the quiet singing is very apparent. Fischer-Dieskau's singing is refined but not too much so, and his first solo, *Omnia Sol temperat*, and later *Dies, nox et omnia* are both very beautiful, with the kind of tonal shading that a great Lieder singer can bring; he is suitably gruff in the Abbot's song so much so that for the moment the voice is unrecognizable. Gerhard Stolze too is very stylish in his falsetto *Song of the roasted swan*. The soprano, Gundula Janowitz, finds a quiet dignity, rather than an overt sensuality for her contribution and this is finely done. The closing scene is moulded by Jochum with wonderful control, most compelling in its restrained power.

Richard Hickox, on his brilliantly recorded Carlton CD, uses the combined London Symphony forces, but adds the Southend Boys' Choir, who make sure we know they understand all about sexual abandon – their *Oh, oh, oh, I am bursting out all over* is a joy. Penelope Walmsley-Clark, too, makes a rapturous contribution: her account of the girl in the red dress is equally delectable. The other soloists are good but less individual, and the chorus rises marvellously to climaxes, while the sharp articulation of consonants when the singers hiss out the words of *O Fortuna* in the closing section is a highlight. The documentation provides a vernacular narrative for each band but no translation. Coupled with Hickox's brilliant account of Holst's *Planets*, this is one of the most successful of Carlton's LSO Doubles.

Mata's splendid 1980 digital recording now comes at super-bargain price and is highly recommendable on all counts. It is a joyously alive and volatile reading, not as metrical in its rhythms as most; this means that at times the London Symphony Chorus is not as clean in ensemble as it is for Previn. The choristers of St Paul's Cathedral sing with purity and enthusiasm but are perhaps not boyish enough, though the soloists are first rate (with John Aler coping splendidly, in high, refined tones, with the Roast Swan episode). There is fine warmth of atmosphere and no lack in the lower range; indeed in almost every respect the sound is superb. This is unbeatable value for those wanting a bargain-priced version.

Slatkin's new RCA recording was made in St Louis in 1992 and is notable for another fine trio of soloists, two of whom are featured on Mata's earlier recording. But one especially remembers Sylvia McNair's ravishing portrayal of the girl in the red tunic, whose final submission is so seductively sweet. The choral singing is enjoyably rhythmic and vigorously crisp. Slatkin's reading is spacious and certainly brings out the grandeur of the opening and closing sections, but in the Court of Love his trebles are very chaste; their racily knowing '*Oh, Oh, Ohs*' are without the pubescent sexual abandon of the British performances variously under Previn, Hickox and Mata. But this remains overall a very convincing performance, if not a first choice. The acoustic of St Louis Powell Symphony Hall is suitably rich and expansive but the chorus is not very sharply defined when singing softly.

David Hill's Bournemouth recording has a choral bite and an exhilarating rhythmic zest that carries the music thrustfully forward. Among the soloists Donald Maxwell makes a strenuously boisterous Abbot, his solo punctuated with spectacular percussion; but one wonders whether a counter-tenor was a good choice for the song about the roasting swan. Here a falsetto can have a more piquant edge. Janice Watson sings with enticing femininity: her red shift is obviously just a temporary covering. The boys' chorus are as pubescently eager as you could wish. This is excitingly vivid, and it is a pity that this reissue is so poorly documented. There are no texts or translations included, indeed virtually no information whatsoever to inform the listener of the meaning of the Latin titles of the work's twenty-five cued sections.

Mehta's newest Teldec version is often enjoyably vigorous, it has good soloists and an excellent choral response, with the Southend boys throatily enjoying their pubescent spree. Sumi Jo is a seductive and rather knowing Girl in the Red Shift who submits willingly, rising nimbly up her ascending scale to a spectacularly floated pianissimo. But Boje Skovhus makes a strongly vibrant rather than a subtle contribution. The recording, made at The Maltings, Snape, is resonantly spectacular, especially in the matter of the orchestral percussion, but the quieter choral passages are a little recessive. In the last resort this is not a first choice, for Mehta's direction is not as imaginative or as spontaneously exuberant as that of his finest competitors.

Muti's is a reading which underlines the dramatic contrasts, both of dynamic and of tempo, so the nagging ostinatos as a rule are pressed on at breakneck speed; the result, if at times a little breathless, is always exhilarating. The soloists are first rate; the Philharmonia Chorus is not quite at its most polished, but the Southend Boys are outstandingly fine. However, the digital remastering of the 1980 analogue recording is disappointing. The chorus and soloists seem to have lost a degree of immediacy.

Catulli Carmina.

(M) *** DG (IMS) 449 097-2 [id.]. Arleen Augér, Wieslaw Ochman, Berlin Op. Ch., 4 pianos & percussion, Jochum EGK: *The Temptation of St Anthony.* ***

Catulli Carmina; Trionfo di Afrodite.

❀ *** EMI (SIS) Dig. CDC5 55517-2 [id.]. Dagmar Schellenberger, Lothar Odinius, Linz Mozart Ch., Munich R. O, Franz Welser-Möst.

Orff's sequel to *Carmina Burana* (using much the same formula, but with the accompaniment scored for four pianos and percussion) cannot match its predecessor in memorability, but for anyone hypnotized by the composer's vital rhythmic ostinatos this is the work to recommend next, and certainly so in Franz Welser-Möst's vibrant performance, complete with enthusiastic crowd noises and superlative choral singing that in its sharpness and precision lifts the music clear of banality. The soloists, too, are excellent, the soprano, Dagmar Schellenberger, revelling in the sensuous upper tessitura which is so like the music for the Girl in the Red Tunic in *Carmina Burana.*

Trionfo di Afrodite, the third work in Orff's sequence, is a wedding cantata, and here the composer is in fresh imaginative form, exploring the marriage rites of Ancient Greece by combining two dramatic choral odes by Catullus in Greek style with poems by Sappho and a chorus from Euripides's *Hippolytus.* It is scored for large orchestra, including three pianos and plentiful percussion; with more nagging rhythmic repetitions it pays its hedonistic tribute to the pleasures of love in a similarly exhilarating manner. Although it opens in the familiar Orff style with alternating choruses of eager young men and willing virgins, there is an added dimension in the tender writing, when young men and maidens alike consider the implications of the forthcoming nuptials, ending with an extraordinary closing choral glissando. The vibrant *Invocation to Hymenaeus* brings a curious reminder of *Petrushka* but stirringly returns us to Orff's world of ostinatos until the arrival of the bride at the wedding chamber brings a series of spoken exhortations by the leader of the guests with vehement choral interruptions. There follows a chorus, first touching then ardent, celebrating marital bliss. The bridegroom then joins his bride admiringly in the wedding chamber, to which she responds with wordless coloratura. The work ends dramatically with a vision of Aphrodite, which brings an immensely bold closing chorus and a final explosion of enthusiasm from the assembled guests. It is an extraordinary dramatization, and it is brought thrillingly to life by Welser-Möst and his combined soloists, singers and orchestra, working splendidly as a team and superbly recorded.

Until the arrival of the Welser-Möst version, Jochum's performance of *Catulli Carmina* was never surpassed. His chorus sings with sharp, rhythmic point and, if imagination is called for in such music, Jochum matches flexibility with a spark of humour in his control of mechanistic rhythms. His soloists are individual and sweet-toned. The recording is very fine, although even on CD evocative pianissimos sound a little recessed.

(i) *Die Kluge;* (ii) *Der Mond.*

(M) *** EMI CMS7 63712-2 (2). (i) Cordes, Frick, Schwarzkopf, Wieter, Christ, Kusche; (ii) Christ, Schmitt-Walker, Graml, Kuen, Lagger, Hotter; Philh. Ch. & O, Sawallisch.

Sawallisch's pioneering Orff recordings of the mid-1950s are vivid and immediate on CD, with such effects as the thunderbolt in *Der Mond* impressive still. Elisabeth Schwarzkopf is characterful and dominant as the clever young woman of the title in *Die Kluge.* It is good too to hear such vintage singers as Gottlob Frick and Hans Hotter in unexpected roles. Musically, these may not be at all searching works, but both short operas provide easy, colourful entertainment, with Sawallisch drawing superb playing from the Philharmonia. No texts are provided, but the discs are very generously banded. (This set has currently been withdrawn.)

Pacius, Fredrik (1809–91)

Kung Karls Jakt (King Charles's Hunt) (opera): complete.
(M) *** Finlandia/Warner Dig. [1576 51107-2]. Törnqvist, Lindroos, Krause, Grönroos, Jubilate Ch., Finnish Nat. Op. O, Söderblom.

Fredrik Pacius became known as 'the father of Finnish music', for he brought the Finnish capital, then a provincial backwater, into contact with the mainstream of European music. His opera *King Charles's Hunt* brings pretty simple musical ideas. Some are pleasant but there is little evidence of much individuality. There is some fine singing from Pirkko Törnqvist as the fisherman's daughter, Leonora, Peter Lindroos as her fiancé, and from Walton Grönroos as the coup leader, Gustaf Gyllenstjerna. The young King is a speaking role. Much care has been lavished on the production and Ulf Söderblom holds things together admirably. No masterpiece is uncovered but it will be of interest to collectors with a specialist interest in the beginnings of opera in the northern countries.

Paderewski, Ignaz (1860–1941)

Piano concerto in A min., Op. 17.
(N) *** Hyperion Dig. CDA 66452 [id.]. Piers Lane, BBC Scottish SO, Jerzy Maksymiuk – MOSZKOWSKI: *Piano concerto.* ***

Paderewski's *Piano concerto* opens with strong thematic promise, and the secondary lyrical material is attractive too. The central *Romanza* brings another very winning theme, and throughout the invention has genuine vitality. Even if some of the passagework is relatively conventional, the work is well worth having back in the catalogue, especially when Piers Lane gives a performance that is poetic and subtly coloured, as well as vivacious. In that he has an accompaniment from the BBC Scottish Orchestra under Maksymiuk that is as alert as it is spirited. The recording is naturally balanced; indeed, at times one might feel the piano image could be more forward.

Symphony in B min. (Polonia), Op. 28.
(N) **(*) Hyperion Dig. CDA 67056 [id.]. BBC Scottish SO, Jerzy Maksymiuk.

Paderewski's *Symphony in B minor* is a mammoth affair. Its first movement alone takes half-an-hour, and the finale is almost as long. It occupied him for five years (1903–8) and runs to 74 minutes. It would have been longer had he added a scherzo as he had originally planned. Although some of the ideas are unmemorable and the symphony is undoubtedly overblown, it is far from negligible. There are reminders of Liszt, Tchaikovsky, Richard Strauss, Elgar, and in the opening paragraphs even Sibelius. Moreover it has a certain sweep and is very well laid out for the orchestra. If, for example, you enjoy the Glière symphonies, you should try it. The BBC Scottish Symphony Orchestra play well for Jerzy Maksymiuk and the only minor reservation which inhibits a strong three-star recommendation is the recording quality which is a bit opaque.

Paganini, Niccolò (1782–1840)

Andante amaroso; Balletto campestre (Variations on a comic theme; orch. Tamponi); *Larghetto con passione; Moto perpetuo in C, Op. 11; Polacca with variations in A; Sonata for grand viola; Sonata Maria Luisa in E; Sonata Varsavia; Variations on The Carnival of Venice; Variations on a theme from Rossini's Mosè.*
(B) *** EMI (SIS) CZS7 67567-2 (2). Salvatore Accardo, COE, Tamponi.

Salvatore Accardo here explores the by-ways of Paganini's concertante music for violin and orchestra (with one piece for viola), and much of the virtuosity is stunning – sample the *Moto perpetuo*. As can be seen from the listing, Paganini's favourite device was a set of variations on a simple, often ingenuous theme, alternating *galant* lyricism with fiendish bravura. Accardo is equally at home in both. The orchestral accompaniments are of minimal interest but they are warmly supportive; the flattering ambience of the recording and the good balance ensure that the sounds reaching the listener are pleasingly believable: the CD transfers are admirably faithful. The two discs are offered for the price of one. There are, however, no notes about the music.

Violin concertos Nos. 1–6.
(M) *** DG 437 210-2 (3). Accardo, LPO, Dutoit.

Violin concertos Nos. 1 in D, Op. 6; 2 in B min. (La Campanella), Op. 7.
*** DG (IMS) 415 378-2 [id.]. Accardo, LPO, Dutoit.

Violin concertos Nos. 3 in E; 4 in D min.
*** DG (IMS) 423 370-2 [id.]. Accardo, LPO, Dutoit.

Violin concerto No. 5 in A min.; Maestosa sonata sentimentale; La primavera in A.
*** DG (IMS) 423 578-2. Accardo, LPO, Dutoit.

Violin concerto No. 6 in E min., Op. posth.; Sonata with variations on a theme by Joseph Weigl; Le streghe (Variations on a theme of Süssmayr), Op. 8; Variations of Non più mesta from Rossini's La Cenerentola.
*** DG 423 717-2. Accardo, LPO, Dutoit.

Paganini's concertos can too often seem trivial and long-winded; it is a tribute to the virtuosity and artistry of Salvatore Accardo that they reveal so much musical interest in his hands. But – as we have observed before – Accardo's technique is formidable and his intonation marvellously true; these qualities, blended with good taste, make this series of performances distinctive. Apart from No. 5 (which, like No. 6, was orchestrated by Federico Mompellio), these are all genre works written to a formula in which the composer produced a series of contrasting lyrical operatic melodies to offset the fireworks of the outer movements. Having said this, Paganini's invention holds up well throughout these works. Tuttis are stereotyped but have plenty of impulse, the lyrical tunes are all very engaging, and the violinistic display is consistently ear-tickling when presented with such panache. Accardo is beautifully accompanied by Dutoit who always keeps even the most conventional passage-work alive. The recordings were made in Barking Town Hall in 1974/5 and the remastering preserves the hall ambience, yet has a cleaner orchestral bass than the LPs.

Violin concerto No. 1 in D, Op. 6.
❀ *** EMI CDC7 47101-2 [id.]. Itzhak Perlman, RPO, Foster – SARASATE: *Carmen fantasy*.*** ❀
*** DG Dig. 429 786-2 [id.]. Gil Shaham, NYPO, Sinopoli – SAINT-SAENS: *Concerto No. 3*. ***
**(*) EMI Dig. CDC5 55026-2 [id.]. Sarah Chang, Phd. O, Sawallisch – SAINT-SAENS: *Havanaise; Intro & Rondo capriccioso*. **(*)

(i) *Violin concerto No. 1 in D, Op. 6. Caprices for solo violin Nos. 1, 3–4, 9–11, 14, 16–17, 24.*
(B) *** DG 439 473-2. Salvatore Accardo; (i) LPO, Charles Dutoit.

Violin concerto No. 1 in D, Op. 6; I Palpiti; Perpetuela; Sonata napoleone.
(M) *** DG 439 981-2 [id.]. Accardo, LPO, Dutoit.

Itzhak Perlman demonstrates a fabulously clean and assured technique and, with the help of the EMI engineers, he produces a gleamingly rich tone, free from all scratchiness. Lawrence Foster matches the soloist's warmth with an alive and buoyant orchestral accompaniment. Provided one does not feel strongly about Perlman's traditional cuts, there has been no better record of the *D major Concerto*.

Although Perlman's EMI version of Paganini's *First Concerto* is special, Accardo's account is second to none in its sense of lyrical style, finesse and easy bravura. The selection of solo *Caprices*, too, is well made, including the most famous of all, which so many other composers have used for variations of their own. Accardo presents his selection with an eloquence far beyond mere display. Excellent recording.

Accardo's account is also available, recoupled at mid-price with attractive, shorter concertante pieces, of which the *Perpetuela* is quite dazzling and *I Palpiti* is like an operatic air with variations.

Gil Shaham's technical ease in the histrionics of Paganini's stratospheric tessitura, harmonics and all, is breathtaking, and he can phrase an Italianate lyrical melody – and there are some good ones in this *Concerto* – with disarming charm and ravishing timbre. His dancing spiccato in the finale is a joy and, however high he ascends, there is never a hint of scratchiness. Sinopoli's finely graduated and often dramatic accompaniment could hardly be more sympathetic.

Sarah Chang made her début with this famous bravura concerto in the Avery Fisher Hall at the age of eight and at the relatively mature age of twelve (!), she recorded it in Philadelphia. The slow movement is fresh and direct rather than romantic, but she knows how to charm the ear gently. The finale is dazzling. While Perlman remains supreme in this work, Chang can bounce her bow with aplomb and never fails to entice the ear. Sawallisch gives her admirable support, but the recording is flattering neither to soloist (balanced close) nor to orchestra, which lacks sumptuousness.

Violin concertos Nos. 1 in D, Op. 6; 2 in B min. (La Campanella), Op. 7.
(BB) *** Naxos Dig. 8.550649 [id.]. Ilya Kaler, Polish Nat. RSO, Gunzenhauser.
(B) *** DG 429 524-2 [id.]. Shmuel Ashkenasi, VSO, Esser.

The young Russian virtuoso, Ilya Kaler, was a pupil of Leonid Kogan and is fully equal to Paganini's once devilish technical demands and the phrasing of warm Italianate melody. His bouncing staccato in the sparkling spiccato finales of both concertos is managed adeptly and in every respect his technique is commandingly secure. Stephen Gunzenhauser is a sympathetic accompanist throughout, and the Polish Radio Orchestra play with suppleness and bring a sense of elegance and style to this music. There is no lack of dazzle in the fireworks, and no damp squibs here. With very good notes, this is an excellent example of a Naxos super-bargain at its best.

At bargain price on CD, Ashkenasi's coupling of the two favourite Paganini *Concertos* is also very good value. He surmounts all the many technical difficulties in an easy, confident style and, especially in the infectious *La Campanella* finale of No. 2, shows how completely he is in control. The microphone is close, but his timbre is sweet and the high tessitura and harmonics are always cleanly focused.

Allegro di concert (Moto perpetuo) in C, Op. 11; Cantabile in D, Op. 17; Centone si sonate: in D; in A, Op. 64/2 & 4; Guitar and violin sonatas: in A; A min.; E min., Op. 3/1, 4 & 6; Grand sonata for violin & guitar in A, Op. posth.; Sonata concertata in A, Op. 61; Sonata a preghiera (arr. Hannibal).

*** DG (IMS) Dig. 437 837-2 [id.]. Gil Shaham, Göran Söllscher.

The atmosphere of much of this repertoire is comparatively intimate, something these artists readily appreciate, and their playing is immaculate and amiably easy-going. Perhaps at times here the style of performance could with advantage have been more extrovert, but the present hour-long recital will make attractive late-evening entertainment (not taken all at once, of course). The recording has a realistic balance and fine presence.

Cantabile for violin and guitar; 5 Centone di sonate, Lerrera A; 12 Sonatas for violin and guitar, Op. 2/1–6; Op. 3/1–6; Sonata concertata in A; Grand sonata in A; Fantasia on a theme from Rossini's Mosè in Egitto; Tarantella in A min. (all for violin and guitar).
(B) *** Teldec/Warner Double 4509 97974-2 (2). György Terebesi, Sonja Prunnbauer.

This valuable collection contains works that came to light only in 1910. When Paganini's effects were auctioned, a substantial number of pieces for violin and guitar were discovered, all highly accomplished. If they are lightweight and undemanding they are also tuneful and entertaining. In the sets of sonatas the violin is very much predominant and the guitar part is designed so that almost any reasonably proficient accompanist would have no trouble at all in giving support to the violin line. The aptly named *Sonata concertata* and the *Grand sonata* are much more demanding, the former giving the guitar a fair share of the limelight and the latter bristling with bravura for that instrument. György Terebesi is a most appealing player, with a sweet timbre, and he is well supported by Sonja Prunnbauer. The recording is excellent and the set is in no way inferior to the DG selection above; it costs very little more and offers more than twice as much music. No back-up notes are included, but this is music intended for light-hearted enjoyment – to be dipped into and not played all at once.

Violin and guitar: *Cantabile; Centone di sonate No. 1 in A; Sonata in E min., Op. 3/6; Sonata concertata in A.*
*** Sony MK 34508 [id.]. Itzhak Perlman, John Williams – GIULIANI: *Sonata.* ***

Superb playing from Perlman and John Williams, and a good balance; the music-making here gives much pleasure, and this is a generally distinguished disc.

Cantabile and valse; 6 Sonatas for violin and guitar, Op. 2; Sonata for gran viola and guitar; Variations di bravura on Caprice No. 24.
(BB) **(*) Naxos Dig. 8.550759 [id.]. Scott St John, Simon Wynberg.

Cantabile in D; 6 Sonatas for violin and guitar, Op. 3; Sonata concertata in A; Variations on Barucabà, Op. 14.
(BB) **(*) Naxos Dig. 8.550690 [id.]. Scott St John, Simon Wynberg.

As can be seen, Naxos are planning a complete edition of Paganini's music for violin and guitar. Scott St John plays with flair and considerable virtuosity: his approach has more extrovert dazzle and rather less charm than the performances on Teldec, and he dominates the performances strongly. The recording venue is resonant, which means close microphones, but the violin timbre is bright without being edgy.

Centone di sonate for violin and guitar, Nos. 1–12.
(BB) **(*) Naxos Dig. 8.553141 (Nos. 1–6); 8.553142 (Nos. 7–12) (available separately). Moshe Hammer, Norbert Kraft.

Moshe Hammer plays with plenty of character and an agreeable cantabile line: his style lies somewhere between those of Scott St John and Terebesi on Teldec. He is truthfully recorded in a resonant ecclesiastical acoustic, and the effect is slightly smoother in Volume II (*Sonatas Nos. 7–12*), made three months after Volume I. But both records reproduce realistically and offer enjoyable music-making.

24 Caprices, Op. 1.
(M) *** DG 429 714-2; *429 714-4* [id.]. Salvatore Accardo.
*** EMI CDC7 47171-2 [id.]. Itzhak Perlman.
(BB) *** Naxos Dig. 8.550717 [id.]. Ilya Kaler.
(M) *** Decca (IMS) 440 034-2. Ruggiero Ricci.
*** Telarc Dig. CD 80398 [id.]. James Ehnes.
(M) **(*) Teldec/Warner Dig. 9031 76259-2 [id.]. Thomas Zehetmair.

Accardo succeeds in making Paganini's most routine phrases sound like the noblest of utterances and he invests these *Caprices* with an eloquence far beyond the sheer display they offer. There are no technical obstacles and, both in breadth of tone and in grandeur of conception, he is peerless. He observes all the repeats and has an excellent CD transfer.

Perlman's playing is also flawless, wonderfully assured and polished, yet not lacking imaginative feeling. The transfer to CD of the 1972 recording is extremely natural. But this is at full price.

Those looking for a bargain will surely not be disappointed with the Russian fiddler, Ilya Kaler, on Naxos. A pupil of Leonid Kogan, his playing is technically very assured, the lyrical bowing vibrant in a Slavic way, and, like Ricci, he projects a strong profile. The 1992 Naxos recording is truthful and real: how attractively this colours the opening of the famous *No. 9 in E major*, which has superb variety of bowing!

Ricci's Decca recording dates from 1959 but it

is remarkably vivid and present. Ricci's playing often offers a breathtaking display of bravura and, oddly enough, his very occasional imperfections (usually minor slips of intonation) come at points where they are least expected – in the easier rather than the more difficult parts. The playing has great personality and the quicksilver articulation is often dazzlingly precise, conveying enormous dash, for instance in *No. 5 in A minor*. However, Perlman and Accardo are even more polished.

James Ehnes is Juilliard-trained and has technique to burn. He tosses off these pieces with great bravura and aplomb. His playing has real personality, even if others have managed to find greater subtlety and delicacy. Accardo plays them as if they are more than bravura pieces and invests them with an eloquence far beyond the sheer display they offer. All the same, there is much to relish in his youthful ardour and the splendid sound the Telarc engineers give us.

Thomas Zehetmair has a somewhat more reticent personality and seems to want to avoid virtuosity for its own sake. His style of articulation in the faster passages at times has an almost throwaway quality, but he soars most agreeably in the lyrical writing and his timbre above the stave is richly caught by the recording. There is much to appreciate and enjoy in these performances, but in the last resort Zehetmair projects less charisma than his competitors.

24 Caprices, Op. 1 (arr. for violin and piano by Schumann).
(N) *** DG Dig. 453 489-2 [id.]. David Garrett, Bruno Canino.

When he recorded Paganini's famous display pieces in 1997, David Garrett was only sixteen and to put it mildly, he is pretty amazing. Schumann added a discreet piano accompaniment by way of tribute to the Genovese wizard towards the end of his life. He was not the only one, for nineteenth-century musicians were a little uneasy about an unaccompanied violin. Ferdinand David, for whom Mendelssohn wrote his *violin concerto*, Kreisler, Adolf Busch and, surprisingly, Szymanowski all had a go at providing keyboard back-ups. David Garrett plays with dazzling virtuosity and an effortless fluency that almost makes one fear for him. Where can he go from here? Bruno Canino makes a supportive partner, and DG offer admirably vivid recorded sound.

Caprice No. 24, Op. 1/24; Grand sonata in A.
(B) *** Sony SBK 62425 [id.]. John Williams (guitar) – GIULIANI: *Variations on a theme by Handel;* D. SCARLATTI: *Sonatas;* VILLA-LOBOS: *5 Preludes.* ***

Grand sonata in A.
(B) **(*) Decca Eclipse 448 709-2. Eduardo Fernández – GIULIANI; VIVALDI: *Concertos.* **(*)

John Williams is in excellent form in the *Grande sonata*, with its charming central *Romanza* and ingenuous closing *Andantino variato* (originally a duo for guitar and violin), and the famous *Caprice*, for violin solo, both arranged by Williams. The recording is only marginally balanced too forwardly and is otherwise truthful. Most enjoyable.

Fernández's playing is rightly much admired by fellow guitarists. His technique is immaculate and his somewhat self-effacing approach always puts the composer first. He is beautifully recorded and the effect is engagingly intimate to suit the gentle, improvisatory nature of his playing, especially the pensive central *Romanza*. Some might feel that the finale needs more extrovert feeling, but there is certainly no lack of dash or bravura.

Paine, John Knowles (1839–1906)

Symphony No. 1 in C min., Op. 23; Overture, As you like it.
*** New World Dig. NW 374-2 [id.]. NYPO, Mehta.

Paine's symphonies were milestones in the history of American music, and it is good that at last Mehta's fine recordings of both of them will allow them to be appreciated more widely. Paine consciously inspires echoes of Beethoven, with little feeling of dilution – though, after his dramatic C minor opening, he tends to relax into sweeter, more Mendelssohnian manners for his second subject and the three other movements. What is striking is the bold assurance, and the overture is also full of charming ideas. Mehta is a persuasive advocate, helped by committed playing and full, well-balanced recording.

Symphony No. 2 in A, Op. 34.
*** New World Dig. NW 350-2 [id.]. NYPO, Mehta.

Written four years after the *First Symphony*, this magnificent work is both more ambitious and more memorable than its predecessor and, far more remarkably, anticipates Mahler. The idiom is notably more chromatic than that of the *First*, and the other movements – introduced by an extended slow introduction – bring an element of fantasy, as in the fragmented rhythms and textures of the Scherzo. Mehta draws a strongly committed performance from the New York Philharmonic, and the sound is first rate.

Paisiello, Giovanni (1740–1816)

Piano concertos Nos. 1–8.
**(*) ASV Dig. CDDCS 229 (2) [id.]. Monetti, ECO, Gonley.

Piano concertos Nos. 1 in C; 5 in D; 7 in A; 8 in C.
*** ASV Dig. CDDCA 873 [id.]. Monetti, ECO, Gonley.

Piano concertos Nos. 2 in F; 3 in A; 4 in G min.; 6 in B flat.
**(*) ASV Dig. CDDCA 872 [id.]. Monetti, ECO, Gonley.

Mariaclara Monetti reveals herself to be an artist who can produce a silk purse out of more humble material, for her playing here is both sparkling and elegant. Paisiello obviously was primarily an opera composer, and these concertos, though not wanting grace or fluency, are often very conventional in most other respects. But with a ready facility Paisiello could certainly spin an expressive cantilena. No complaints about the recording, and on the whole the first of the two discs is the one to go for. As can be seen, the eight concertos are also available as a boxed set, though with no saving in cost.

Palestrina, Giovanni Pierluigi da (1525–94)

Ave Regina Caelorum; Lamentations of Jeremiah I–III; Gloriosi principes terrae; Missa in duplicibus minoribus II.
*** HM/BMG Dig. 05472 77317-2 [id.]. Maîtrise de Garçons de Colmar, Ens. Gilles Binchois, Cantus Figuratus, Dominique Vellard.

This ensemble produce singing of exceptional purity and quality. The Marian antiphon, *Ave Regina Caelorum*, is for two choruses, one high and one low, and was printed in 1575. The *Missa in duplicibus minoribus*, which belongs to the Mantuan repertory, was discovered in Milan as late as 1950 and is not otherwise available. All this material is sung with impressive control, a wonderfully integrated balance and great beauty of tone. Those who find Palestrina too bland should investigate this eloquent and beautifully recorded disc.

Canticum canticorum Salomonis (Fourth Book of Motets for 5 voices from the *Song of Songs*).
*** Hyperion Dig. CDA 66733 [id.]. Pro Cantione Antiqua, Bruno Turner.

The *Canticum canticorum Salomonis* is one of Palestrina's most sublime and expressive works, possibly wider in its range than anything else he composed, and certainly as deeply felt. His disclaimer in the dedication to Pope Gregory XIII, which Bruno Turner quotes at the beginning of his notes ('There are far too many poems with no other subject than love of a kind quite alien to the Christian faith'), cannot disguise the fervour which he poured into these 29 motets. The ten members of the Pro Cantione Antiqua under Bruno Turner bring an appropriate eloquence and ardour, tempered by restraint. They are accorded an excellently balanced and natural-sounding recording. This music is not generously represented on disc, but no one acquiring this is likely to be disappointed.

Canticum canticorum; Madrigals for 5 voices, Book I: 8 Madrigali spirituali.
(M) *** Virgin Veritas/EMI (SIS) Dig. VED5 61168-2 (2) [ZDMB 61168]. Hilliard Ens., Paul Hilliard.

The Hilliard Ensemble provide beautifully shaped performances, with refined tonal blend and perfect intonation, but they are more remote and ultimately rather cool in emotional temperature. The second CD includes eight Petrarch settings from the First Book of Madrigals. Excellent recording.

Lamentations of Jeremiah the Prophet I–III (Fourth Book for 4 & 5 voices).
(M) *** Carlton Dig. 30366 00762 [(M) id.]. Pro Cantione Antiqua, Bruno Turner.

Many composers have set the Lamentation Lessons for the Tenebrae services on Maundy Thursday, Good Friday and Holy Saturday but, remarkably, Palestrina did so on five different occasions. The present (fourth) setting was discovered only at the beginning of the nineteenth century, and it is recorded here complete for the first time. The music has a serene but poignant simplicity, which Bruno Turner captures admirably with spacious tempi. The concentration is obvious and the quality of the singing from a group of eight (including several famous names) is of a high order. So is the recording, which is very well balanced in the warm acoustic of St Alban's Church, Brook Street, London.

Masses

'The Palestrina 400 collection': Missa Assumpta est Maria (with Plainchant: *Assumpta est Maria*); Motet: *Assumpta est Maria. Missa Benedicta es* (with Plainchant: *Benedicta es.* JOSQUIN: *Benedicta es*). *Missa brevis; Missa Nasce la gioja mia* (with PRIMAVERA: *Madrigal: Nasce la gioja mia*). *Missa Nigra sum* (with Plainchant: *Nigra sum.* LHERITIER: *Nigra sum*). *Missa Papae Marcelli. Missa Sicut lilium inter spinas;* Motet: *Sicut lilium inter spinas I.*
(M) *** Gimell/Ph. Analogue/Dig. 454 890-2 (4). Tallis Scholars, Peter Phillips.

This highly recommendable and well-documented box gathers together four CDs recorded by the Tallis Scholars between 1981 and 1989. As is their practice, this group records the Masses together with the motets on which they are based, even if they are by other composers. Their account of the most famous of Palestrina's works, the *Missa Papae Marcelli*, brings a characteristically eloquent performance.

Missa Aeterna Christi munera (with *Hymn*); *Missa l'homme armé*.
(M) **(*) Carlton Dig. 30366 00772 [(M) id.]. Pro Cantione Antiqua, Mark Brown.

This 1992 Carlton coupling of two fine Palestrina masses from the Pro Cantione Antiqua under Mark Brown could hardly be bettered in terms of ensemble and accomplishment. This is an all-male ensemble (there are 12 singers in all, counter-tenors, tenors and basses) and the forces are modest – one to a part for much of the time – with resultant textural clarity, though the vocal colour is inevitably dark and there is no lack of weight. This suits *L'homme armé* particularly well, and this is the more memorable of the two performances. The balance could with advantage have been more distant, as it is in the chants with which the Mass movements are interspersed; more air round the voices would have given greater aural variety and relief, though a somewhat lower-than-usual level setting helps matters. The singing itself is superb. The group includes such distinguished singers as Michael Chance, Ian Partridge and Stephen Roberts, and the impact of the performances is enhanced by the closeness of the sound, set in the warm but intimate acoustic of St Jude's, Hampstead. Many will also appreciate the inclusion of apt plainsong passages between the sections of the liturgy.

Missa Aeterna Christi munera; Missa Papae Marcelli.
(BB) **(*) Naxos Dig. 8.550573 [id.]. Oxford Camerata, Jeremy Summerly.

Summerly's are bold, flowing performances, lacking something in mysticism and ethereal dynamics, but sung very confidently, with textures clear and the performances alive and compelling. The Oxford Camerata consists of twelve singers, of whom a third are female, and the blend is impressive. The account of the lesser-known *Missa Aeterna Christi munera* is particularly compelling. The recording was made in Dorchester Abbey, so the ambience is flattering, although the balance is fairly close.

Mass & Motet: *Assumpta est Maria*. Motets: *Ave Maria; Beata es, Virgo Maria; Hodie gloriosa semper Virgo Maria; Regina coeli; Magnificat septimi toni.*
(B) **(*) EMI Dig. CDZ5 69703-2 [CDZ 69703]. Clare College, Cambridge, Ch., Timothy Brown.

This is an exceptionally well-chosen collection, mainly of shorter works, but also including the splendid *Missa Assumpta est Maria*. The programme ends with an equally fine *Magnificat* setting. We are familiar with the excellent Clare College Choir and their rich sound, partly achieved by using women's voices, from earlier recordings under their previous director, John Rutter. This EMI Debut CD introduces their new conductor, Timothy Brown, and the choir responds expressively to his melismatic direction, immediately arresting in the beautiful opening motet with which the Mass is associated. The choir is beautifully recorded, and the only minor criticism is the relatively restricted dynamic range, which may partly be caused by the microphone placing, but which certainly reduces the dramatic contrast of the singing. But this remains a thoroughly worthwhile bargain disc, although it is a pity that the documentation has so little to say about the music.

Missa: Assumpta est Maria; Missa: Sicut lilium.
*** Gimell Ph. Dig. 454 920-2 [id.]. Tallis Scholars, Peter Phillips.

After the *Missa Papae Marcelli*, the *Missa: Assumpta est Maria* is one of Palestrina's most sublime works. Its companion on this CD is based on the motet, *Sicut lilium inter spinas* ('Like a lily among thorns'). As is their practice, the Tallis Scholars record the Masses together with the motets on which they are based, and sing with their customary beauty of sound and well-blended tone. They are superbly recorded in the Church of St Peter and St Paul in Salle, Norfolk.

Antiphon: Assumpta est Maria; Missa: Assumpta est Maria. Antiphon, Motet and Missa: Veni sponsa Christi. Magnificat VI toni.
(M) *** Decca 433 678-2 [id.]. St John's College, Cambridge, Ch., Guest.

The older St John's record of *Assumpta est Maria* sounds splendid on CD, if perhaps not so refined in texture as its digital competitor, and the St John's performance is thoroughly persuasive. The Decca couplings are even more generous (70 minutes) than on the Gimell CD and equally attractive. Some may find the presentation a little lacking in Latin fervour: the trebles sound distinctly Anglican. But this is fine singing by any standards, and has great purity of tone and beauty of phrasing.

Missa: Benedicta es (with *Plainchant*).
*** Gimell Ph. 454 901-2 [id.]. Tallis Scholars, Peter Phillips (with JOSQUIN: *Motet: Benedicta es*).

Palestrina's Mass is coupled with the Josquin motet, *Benedicta es*, on which it is based, together with the plainchant sequence on which both drew. It would seem that this Mass was the immediate predecessor of the *Missa Papae Marcelli* and was composed while the music of *Benedictus es* was still at the forefront of the composer's mind. The Tallis Scholars and Peter Phillips sing with impressive conviction and produce an expressive, excellently blended sound.

Masses: Ecce ego Joannes; Sine nomine.
(BB) *** Belart 461 018-2. Mary Thomas, Jean Allister, Edgar Fleet, Christopher Keyte, Carmelite Priory Ch., London, John McCarthy – VICTORIA: Mass & Motet: *O quam gloriosum*. ***

The reissue of these distinguished (originally Oiseau-Lyre) recordings by the London Carmelite Priory Choir under John McCarthy, made in the early 1960s, is very welcome indeed on Polygram's super-budget label, Belart. The two works offered here make a good foil for each other, for they are contrasted in style and texture. The Mass 'without name' is a small-scale work, whereas *Ecce ego Johannes* is more ambitious and dramatic. Both are beautifully sung and very well recorded. With the availablity of this record so inexpensively and with extra works by Victoria (not on the original LP) included for good measure, one hopes that more music-lovers will be tempted to sample this wonderfully expressive and rewarding music.

Missa Hodie Christus natus est; Motet: Hodie Christus natus est; Stabat Mater.
(BB) *** Naxos Dig. 8.550836 [id.]. Oxford Schola Cantorum, Jeremy Summerly – LASSUS: *Missa Bell'Amfitrit'alterna*. ***

Where in their account of Palestrina's *Missa aeterna Christi munera*, Summerly's group are restrained in their devotional manner, this celebrated Mass for Christmas has them joyful and exuberant. The choir, over 30 strong, brings out both the beauty and the drama of the writing, and equally so in the brief motet setting the Christmas words. The magnificent *Stabat Mater* is wisely given to a smaller group of 16 singers, two to a part, with added clarity in the complex polyphony. Well coupled with one of Lassus's best-loved Masses, representing the work of Palestrina's close contemporary from Flanders, the two supreme polyphonic masters who died in the same year.

Missa brevis; Missa: Nasce la gioia mia (with PRIMAVERA: *Madrigal: Nasce la gioia mia*).
*** Gimell Ph. Dig. 454 908-2 [id.]. Tallis Scholars, Phillips.

The *Missa: Nasce la gioia mia* is a parody Mass, modelled on the madrigal, *Nasce la gioia mia* by Giovan Leonardo Primavera. The Tallis Scholars and Peter Phillips give expressive, finely shaped accounts of both the *Missa brevis* and the *Mass*, which they preface by the madrigal itself. A most rewarding disc: no grumbles about the recording.

Missa: Nigra sum (with motets on *Nigra sum* by LHERITIER; VICTORIA; DE SILVA).
*** Gimell Ph. Dig. 454 903-2 [id.]. Tallis Scholars, Phillips.

Palestrina's *Missa: Nigra sum* is another parody Mass, based on a motet by Jean Lheritier, and follows its model quite closely; its text comes from the Song of Solomon. On this record, the plainchant and the Lheritier motet precede Palestrina's *Mass*, plus motets by Victoria and Andreas de Silva, a relatively little-known Flemish singer and composer who served in the Papal chapel and later in Mantua. The music is inspiring and the performances exemplary. This is a most beautiful record and the acoustic of Merton College, Oxford, is ideal.

Missa Papae Marcelli.
*** Gimell Ph. 454 939-2 [id.]. Tallis Scholars, Phillips – ALLEGRI: *Miserere;* MUNDY: *Vox Patris caelestis*. ***

Missa Papae Marcelli; Missa brevis.
*** Hyperion Dig. CDA 66266 [id.]. Westminster Cathedral Choir, David Hill.

Missa Papae Marcelli; Tu es Petrus (motet).
*** DG (IMS) 415 517-2 [id.]. Westminster Abbey Ch., Preston (with ANERIO: *Venite ad me omnes;* NANINO: *Haec dies;* GIOVANNELLI: *Jubilate Deo* ***; ALLEGRI: *Miserere* **(*)).

David Hill and the Westminster Cathedral Choir give an imposing and eloquent *Missa Papae Marcelli* that many collectors may prefer to the finely sung Gimell issue from the Tallis Scholars. They, too, have the advantage of a spacious acoustic and excellent recording.

The account by the Westminster Abbey choristers is a performance of great fervour, married to fine discipline, rich in timbre, eloquent both at climaxes and at moments of serenity. The singing is equally fine in the hardly less distinctive motet, *Tu es Petrus*. Felice Anerio, Giovanni Bernardino Nanino and Ruggiero Giovannelli represent the following generation of composers. Their contributions to this collection are well worth having, particularly Giovannelli's *Jubilate Deo* which makes a splendid closing item. The digital recording is first class.

The Gimell alternative is an analogue recording from 1980. The singing has eloquence, purity of tone, and a simplicity of line which is consistently well controlled.

Missa Papae Marcelli; Alma redemptoris Mater; Magnificat 1 toni; Nunc dimittis. Stabat Mater; Surge illuminare.
*** Gimell Ph. Dig. 454 994-2 [id.]. Tallis Scholars (with ALLEGRI: *Miserere* ***).

The Tallis Scholars are here recorded in the Basilica of Maria Maggiore in Rome, where Palestrina was a choirboy and, later, master of the choristers. The most celebrated of Palestrina's masses, *Missa Papae Marcelli*, receives as eloquent a performance as any in the catalogue. The Tallis Scholars have wonderful fluidity and the sense of movement never flags in this finely tuned, well-paced reading. Much the same goes for the remaining motets here and, of course, for the Allegri *Miserere*, which had a unique association with the Sistine Chapel until Mozart heard it and wrote it down from memory for performance elsewhere. As the recording was made before an audience, there is applause, which is quite inappropriate and very tiresome. In every other respect this is a first-class issue and can be warmly recommended.

Missa Papae Marcelli; Alma Redemptoris Mater (antiphon); *Peccantem me quotidie* (motet); *Stabat Mater*.
(BB) **(*) ASV CDQS 6086. L. Pro Cantione Antiqua, Bruno Turner.

Bruno Turner uses small forces throughout his well-conceived programme, and these are most beautiful performances of all four pieces, offering both intelligence and sensitivity in the handling of each line. Partly because of the recording balance, which is rather forward, one can hear the inner parts with uncommon clarity and, although this is not achieved at the expense of the overall sonority, some might feel that the clear and precise acoustic robs the music of some of its mystic atmosphere. This is not the only way of performing and recording Palestrina, but it is none the less impressive, and it makes one listen to the linear detail with fresh ears.

Missa Papae Marcelli; Stabat Mater.
(M) *** Carlton Dig. 30366 0070-2 [(M) id.]. Pro Cantione Antiqua, Mark Brown.

Mark Brown and the Pro Cantione Antiqua give an account of these celebrated pieces that aspires to total authenticity in that the forces used are those Palestrina himself would have known: no boys' voices, no women and just one-to-a-part, with the Mass sections interspersed with plainchant. The Pro Cantione Antiqua sing with eloquence and power against the background of a resonant acoustic. The 1986 recording is splendidly balanced. Whatever other versions you may have of either work, this has special claims, and its outward severity does not preclude depth of feeling – rather the reverse.

Veni sponsa Christi.
(M) *** EMI Dig. CD-EMX 2180. St John's College, Cambridge, Ch., Guest (with ALLEGRI: *Miserere*); LASSUS: *Missa super bella*. **(*)

Veni sponsa Christi is a parody Mass – which means that it uses pre-existing music, here an earlier Palestrina motet based on Gregorian chant. Every section of the Mass is introduced by the same idea with much subtle variation, and this impressive work ends with two *Agnus Dei* settings, the second with an additional tenor part. It receives an eloquent, imaginatively detailed and finely shaped performance here, and the relative restraint of the Anglican choral tradition suits Palestrina's flowing counterpoint better than it does the Lassus Venetian coupling.

COLLECTIONS

Hodie Beata Virgo; Litaniae de Beata Virgine Maria in 8 parts; Magnificat in 8 parts (Primi Toni); Senex puerum portabat; Stabat Mater.
(M) *** Decca Legends 466 373-2 [id.]. King's College Ch., Willcocks – ALLEGRI: *Miserere*. ***

The flowing melodic lines and serene beauty which are the unique features of Palestrina's music are apparent throughout this programme, and there is no question about the dedication and accomplishment of the performance. The recording is no less successful, sounding radiantly fresh and clear as remastered for Decca's Legend series.

Palmgren, Selim (1878–1951)

'Meet the composer': Piano concertos Nos. (i–ii) *1, Op. 13;* (iii; ii) *2 (The River), Op. 33;* (iv; ii) *3 (Metamorphoses), Op. 41;* (iii; ii) *4 (April), Op. 85;* (v; ii) *5, Op. 99;* (ii) *Pictures from Finland, Op. 24;* (vi) *Piano sonata in D min., Op. 11;* Piano pieces: *Raindrops, Op. 54/1; Preludes Nos. 12 (The Sea); 24 (The War), Op. 17/12 & 24; Spring: Dragonfly; May night, Op. 27/3–4; Dusk, Op. 47/1*.
(B) *** Finlandia/Warner Double Dig. 0630 19810-2 (2) [(M) id. import]. (i) Eero Heinonen; (ii) Turku PO, Jacques Mercier; (iii) Juhani Lagerspetz; (iv) Matti Raekallio; (v) Raija Kerppo; (vi) Izumi Tateno.

Palmgren was a fine pianist and accompanied his wife, the singer Maikki Järnefelt, who by her first marriage had been Sibelius's sister-in-law and a noted interpreter of his songs. Palmgren taught briefly in America at the Eastman School of Music when Howard Hanson had become its first director. This valuable Double in Finlandia's '*Meet the Composer*' series collects the five *Piano concertos*, which range in the composer's career from 1903 to 1941, and some of his piano miniatures, as well as the early *Sonata in D minor*, Op. 11, of 1900. All the soloists are persuasive in the concertos and are well supported by the Turku orchestra under Jacques Mercier. The orchestra gives an eminently acceptable account of the *Pictures from Finland*, Op. 24, from 1908. In the *Sonata* and the solo miniatures the pianist is the Japanese-born Izumi Tateno. He plays these pieces with great sympathy and is very well recorded. A useful survey of Palmgren's music, recorded in very decent sound.

Barcarolle, Op. 14; Finnish rhythms, Op. 31; Illusion, Op. 1/2; Intermezzo Op. 3/4; 3 Piano pieces, Op. 54; Snowflakes, Op. 57/2; Sonette,

Op. 4/3; Spring, Op. 27; Spring, Op. 47: 2 Pieces; Youth, Op. 28.
*** Finlandia Dig. 4509-98991-2 [id.]. Izumi Tateno.

Palmgren will be remembered here by the older generation of piano students brought up on pieces like *May night* and *Moonlight*. He was spoken of as the 'Chopin of the north' for he wrote more idiomatically for the piano than Sibelius; but his music is limited both in its emotional range and in its repertory of pianistic devices. The present disc collects some of his early and middle-period music, from *Illusion* (which comes from his first published collection of 1899) through to the *Three Piano pieces*, Op. 54, of 1918. There is a certain poetic feeling, tinged at times by a hint of gentility. Palmgren was influenced by impressionism, though his melancholic sensibility is undoubtedly Nordic. Izumi Tateno is Japanese-born but has lived in Finland since his student days. He plays these pieces with great sympathy and is very well recorded.

24 Preludes, Op. 17; Piano sonata in D min., Op. 11.
(N) *** Finlandia/Warner Dig. 4509 95868-2 (2) [id.]. Izumi Tateno.

These are early works. The *Sonata* is modestly imposing, at its best in the rhapsodical finale. Tateno makes the most of it, without inflation. The *24 Preludes* are a homage to Chopin, although the piano technique they exploit is much narrower, and they also have a French influence at times. The opening two pieces are characteristic, appealing in their simplicity, and many of them have charm, such as the chattering *Bird song* (No. 19). They are played very pleasingly and are truthfully recorded.

Pandolfi Mealli, Giovanni Antonio (*fl.* 1660–69)

Violin sonatas: La cesta; La castella; La Clemente; La Sabbatina, Op. 3/2, 4, 5 & 6; La Bernabea; La Biancuccia; La vinciolina, Op. 4/1, 4 & 6; (i) Anon.: *Harpsichord suites in A, C & D.*
*** Channel Dig. CCS 5894 [id.]. Andrew Manze, (i) Richard Egarr, Fred Jacobs.

Giovanni Antonio Pandolfi Mealli's reputation rests on a single surviving copy of two sets of violin sonatas, six sonatas in each. Seven are recorded here, interspersed with three anonymous, French-influenced harpsichord suites, very different in style. The notes suggest the possibility that the composer was Christian Flor (1626–97). These are all rewarding and interesting scores, marvellously played by all concerned, and very well recorded too.

Panufnik, Andrzej (1914–91)

(i) *Arbor Cosmica;* (ii) *Symphony No. 3 (Sinfonia sacra).*
*** Elektra Nonesuch/Warner Dig. 7559 79228-2 [id.]. (i) NY Chamber Symphony; (ii) Concg. O; composer.

The *Sinfonia sacra* is one of Panufnik's most warmly and immediately communicative works, and here receives a magnificent performance from the Concertgebouw under the composer. As the title implies, *Arbor Cosmica* directly reflects a visual concept, this time the branches of a tree. The 12 'evocations' are all generated from a single three-note chord, each with the structure mapped out like a tree. The composer draws dedicated performances both from the Concertgebouw and the New York Chamber Symphony, with the former inevitably sounding richer and fuller.

(i) *Autumn music; Heroic overture;* (i, ii) *Nocturne;* (iii) *Sinfonia rustica;* (i) *Tragic overture.*
(M) *** Unicorn UKCD 2016. (i) LSO, Horenstein; (ii) with Anthony Peebles; (iii) Monte Carlo Op. O, composer.

The *Autumn music* and *Nocturne* may strike some listeners as musically uneventful, but the opening of the *Nocturne* is really very beautiful indeed and there is a refined feeling for texture and a sensitive imagination at work here. The *Sinfonia rustica* is the most individual of the works recorded here and has plenty of character. The performance under the composer is thoroughly committed. The LSO under Horenstein play with conviction and they are very well recorded.

(i) *Bassoon concerto;* (ii) *Violin concerto;* (iii) *Hommage à Chopin.*
*** Conifer Dig. 74321 16188-2 [id.]. (i) Thompson; (ii) Smietana; (iii) K. Jones; L. Musici, Stephenson.

The *Hommage à Chopin* owes its origin to a commission from Unesco. Panufnik composed five vocalises for voice and piano that make use of folk music from Masovia, in 1966 transcribing them for flute and orchestra; they could not have more persuasive advocacy than they do from Karen Jones and the London Musici. The *Bassoon concerto* (1985) is a darker piece, dedicated to the memory of the Polish priest, Jerzy Popieluszko, who was murdered that year; Robert Thompson plays it with great sensitivity. The London Musici under Mark Stephenson play with dedication throughout and, as the recording was made in the presence of the composer, it can be assumed to be authoritative. The *Violin concerto*, which was championed by Menuhin (see below) is a strongly atmospheric piece and is well worth a place in the repertory; it is beautifully played here by Krzysztof Smietana. The Conifer sound, very well balanced at The Maltings, Snape, is first class.

Cello concerto.
*** NMC Dig. Single D 0105 [id.]. Rostropovich, LSO, Hugh Wolff.

The *Cello concerto* of Sir Andrzej Panufnik, his very last work, completed only days before his death in September 1991, is here presented by Rostropovich. The recording is even more successful at conveying the purposefulness of the writing than the first performance, bringing out the tautness of the palindromic structure, with the two movements, each in arch form, a mirror-image of the other, slow then fast. The result is not a drily schematic work, as one might expect, but a piece that in its warmth reflects the player who inspired it, strong and eventful with a more open lyricism than in many previous Panufnik compositions.

(i) *Piano concerto. Symphony No. 9 (Sinfonia della speranza).*
*** Conifer Dig. 74321 16189-2 [id.]. (i) Ewa Poblocka; LSO, composer.

In a massive single movement of 41 minutes Panufnik's *Ninth Symphony* brings a formidable example of the composer's fascination with translating geometric concepts into notes. The visual analogy here is with light travelling through a prism, and the accompanying booklet provides a diagram illustrating how the formula works, using a three-note cell refracted in various ways. The result has similarities with a gigantic passacaglia and there is no denying the symphony's strength. Panufnik's *Piano concerto* is not so extended, but carries comparable weight. The opening *Entrata* has a neoclassical flavour in its ostinatos for the solo instrument, leading to a bald, spare central slow movement. The mood is rather like that of some of Bartók's night music. By contrast, the finale is violently rhythmic with jazzy syncopations. Though the piano writing gives the soloist relatively little chance for conventional keyboard display, her playing adds to the power of the composer's purposeful interpretation. The piano tone is a degree too clangy, but otherwise the recording is spacious and full.

(i) *Concerto festivo;* (ii) *Concerto for timpani, percussion and strings; Katyn epitaph; Landscape;* (iii) *Sinfonia sacra (Symphony No. 3).*
(M) *** Unicorn UKCD 2020. (i) LSO, (ii) with Goedicke & Frye; (ii) Monte Carlo Op. O, composer.

This splendidly recorded collection might be a good place for collectors to begin exploring Panufnik's output. The *Concertos* are both readily communicative and the *Katyn epitaph* is powerfully eloquent. The best of this music is deeply felt. The *Sinfonia sacra* serves to demonstrate the spectacular quality of the vividly remastered recording, with its compelling introductory 'colloquy' for four trumpets, followed by a withdrawn section for strings alone. In the finale of the second part of the work, Hymn, the trumpets close the piece resplendently.

(i) *Concerto for timpani, percussion and strings. Harmony* (a poem for chamber orchestra); (ii) *Sinfonia concertante for flute, harp and strings.*
*** Conifer Dig. 75605 51217-2 [id.]. L. Musici, Mark Stephenson, with (i) Richard Benjafield, Graham Cole; (ii) Karen Jones, Rachel Masters.

The *Concertino* is a highly effective work based on a four-note motif, F-G-B-C; Panufnik creates an imaginative sound-world using both tuned and untuned percussion. The *Sinfonia concertante* is highly atmospheric, often hauntingly so, but somewhat more static. Karen Jones and Rachel Masters make a highly persuasive solo partnership. By far the most impressive work here is *Harmony*, written for the composer's wife in celebration of their 25th wedding anniversary. Opening with a poignantly ethereal pianissimo on the violins, this distinctive 16-minute piece alternates passages for strings and wooodwind; then they finally join together and move to a passionately piercing climax. The performance here has great intensity and, given greater exposure, this piece could become really popular, after the manner of Barber's *Adagio*, though thematically it is more diffuse. Performance and recording throughout are first class.

Symphony No. 8 (Sinfonia votiva).
*** Hyperion Dig. CDA 66050 [id.]. Boston SO, Ozawa – SESSIONS: *Concerto for orchestra.* ***

The *Sinfonia votiva* has a strongly formalistic structure, but its message is primarily emotional. Though Panufnik's melodic writing may as a rule reflect the formalism of his thought rather than tapping a vein of natural lyricism, the result is most impressive, particularly in a performance of such sharp clarity and definition as Ozawa's, very well recorded.

Paray, Paul (1886–1979)

Mass for the 500th anniversary of the death of Joan of Arc.
(M) **(*) Mercury (IMS) 432 719-2 [id.]. Yeend, Bible, Lloyd, Yi-Kwei-Sze, Rackham Ch., Detroit SO, Paul Paray – SAINT-SAENS: *Symphony No. 3.* ***

Paray's *Mass*, much admired by the composer, Florent Schmitt, could hardly have a more eloquent performance. The soloists are good and the choir are inspired to real fervour by their conductor, who at the close (in a brief recorded speech) expresses his special satisfaction with the singing of the closing, very romantic *Agnus Dei*. Excellent (1957) Mercury stereo, using the Ford Auditorium in Detroit.

Parry, Hubert (1848–1918)

(i) The Birds: Bridal march; (ii) English suite; Lady Radnor's suite (both for strings); *Overture to an unwritten tragedy; Symphonic variations.*
*** Lyrita SRCD 220 [id.]. (i) LPO; (ii) LSO; Boult.

The *Bridal march* comes from Parry's equivalent to Vaughan Williams's *Wasps*, a suite of incidental music for *The Birds*, also by Aristophanes. Here the rich, *nobilmente* string melody asserts itself strongly over any minor contributions from the woodwind aviary. The two *Suites* of dances for strings have some charming genre music and the *Overture* is very strongly constructed. But best of all is the *Symphonic variations*, with its echoes of Brahms's *St Anthony* set and its foretastes of *Enigma*. Boult's advocacy is irresistible. and the CD transfer demonstrates the intrinsic excellence of the analogue recordings, with gloriously full string sound.

Piano concerto in F sharp min.
*** Hyperion Dig. CDA 66820 [id.]. Piers Lane, BBC Scottish SO, Martyn Brabbins – STANFORD: *Piano concerto.* ***

The *Piano concerto in F sharp minor* may at first seem rather naïve in the way it embraces a grand manner but, written in 1880, it is a relatively early work which appeals openly with its directness and lyricism. The Brahmsian echoes are supplemented in the finale by clear if momentary echoes of Bizet's *Carmen*, then a very new work. Piers Lane plays with feeling and brilliance, helped by beautiful sound.

An English suite; Lady Radnor's suite.
(M) *** EMI Dig. CDM5 66541-2. City of L. Sinfonia, Hickox – ELGAR: *Elegy for strings* etc. ***

On EMI, Parry's two elegant and beautifully crafted suites make an unusual and very apt coupling for the Elgar string music. The combination of straightforward, warm expression with hints of melancholy below the surface is very Elgarian. Both suites were written later than the Elgar *Serenade*, with *An English suite* published only after the composer's death. The Bach tributes in *Lady Radnor's suite* are surface-deep; the slow minuet for muted strings is particularly beautiful. Refined playing and first-rate recording.

Lady Radnor's suite.
*** Nimbus Dig. NI 5068 [id.]. E. String O, Boughton – BRIDGE: *Suite;* BUTTERWORTH: *Banks of green willow* etc. ***

Parry's charming set of pastiche dances, now given an extra period charm through their Victorian flavour, makes an attractive item in an excellent and generous English collection, one of Nimbus's best-sellers. Warm, atmospheric recording, with refined playing set against an ample acoustic.

Symphonies Nos. 1–5; Symphonic variations in E min.
*** Chandos Dig. CHAN 9120-22 [id.]. LPO, Matthias Bamert.

The rehabilitation of Parry has been long overdue; Chandos have now done this remarkable British nineteenth-century 'English Renaissance' musician full justice by recording the complete set of the symphonies. Bamert takes us convincingly through the symphonic terrain of a highly influential composer about whom Elgar declared, 'He is our leader – no cloud of formality can dim the healthy sympathy and broad influence he exerts upon us. Amidst all the outpourings of modern English music the work of Parry remains supreme.' Bamert's set, discussed in detail below, is offered here complete on three CDs and includes also Parry's best-known orchestral work, the *Symphonic variations.*

Symphony No. 1 in G; Concertstück in G min.
*** Chandos Dig. CHAN 9062 [id.]. LPO, Bamert.

Parry began work on his *First Symphony* in December 1880. Only a few weeks previously he had made his acquaintance with Brahms's *First*, and it had an obvious influence on him, not least in the grand main theme of his own finale. Bamert immediately demonstrates his response to the composer's muse in the way the opening *Con fuoco* sails off with a powerful thrust in the first movement. His control of the overall structure with its interrelated thematic material is most convincing, through the eloquent *Andante* and the Scherzo with its double trio, until he brings the finale to an impressively up-beat conclusion. He also offers the earlier *Concertstück for orchestra*, though here the Wagnerian influences remain incompletely absorbed. The spacious Chandos recording seems exactly right for this pre-Elgarian opulence of symphonic thought.

Symphony No. 2 in F (Cambridge); Symphonic variations.
*** Chandos Dig. CHAN 8961 [id.]. LPO, Matthias Bamert.

The *Second Symphony* opens confidently (with distinct Mendelssohnian associations) and Brahms's influence reappears in the main lyrical idea of the finale. In between there are reminders of Dvořák and Schumann but for all its eclecticism and occasional longwindedness, notably in the finale, Parry finds his own voice and the music has a genuinely vital flow. Bamert's advocacy certainly holds the listener's attention and the orchestra responds with obvious relish. The *Symphonic variations* makes an admirable makeweight. Excellent, full-bodied sound of the best Chandos vintage.

Symphony No. 2 in F min. (Cambridge); Overture to an unwritten tragedy; Symphonic variations.
(BB) **(*) Naxos Dig. 8.553469 [id.]. Royal SNO, Andrew Penny.

Challenging the outstanding Parry series from Chandos conducted by Matthias Bamert, Naxos here offers a very acceptable alternative to the *Symphony No. 2*, similarly coupled with the *Symphonic variations* and with an extra item in the *Overture*. The playing of the Royal Scottish National Orchestra is just as polished as that of the LPO on Chandos, but Penny's manner is less warmly expressive at speeds generally a little faster, and the recorded sound is rather less opulent.

Symphonies Nos. 3 in C (English); 4 in E min.
*** Chandos Dig. CHAN 8896 [id.]. LPO, Matthias Bamert.

No. 3 is the most immediately approachable of the symphonies, with its bold melodies, often like sea-shanties, and its forthright structure. Yet it is No. 4 which proves the more rewarding, a larger-scale, ambitious work which, amazingly, was never performed at all between the first performance of the revised version in 1910 and the present recording. The bold opening, in its dark E minor, echoes that of Brahms's *First Piano concerto*, leading to an ambitious movement lightened by thematic transformation that can take you in an instant into infectious waltz-time. The elegiac slow movement and jolly and spiky scherzo lead to a broad, noble finale in the major key. Bamert again proves a masterly interpreter, bringing out the warmth and thrust of the writing, akin to that of Elgar but quite distinct. The sound is rich and full to match the outstanding playing.

Symphony No. 5 in B min.; Symphonic variations; Elegy to Johannes Brahms; (i) *Blest pair of Sirens.*
(M) *** EMI CDM5 65107-2. LPO, Boult, (i) with LPO Ch.

Symphony No. 5 in B min.; Elegy for Brahms; From death to life.
*** Chandos Dig. CHAN 8955 [id.]. LPO, Bamert.

The *Fifth* and last of Parry's symphonies is in four linked movements, terser in argument than the previous two, and often tougher, though still with Brahmsian echoes. After the minor-key rigours of the first movement, *Stress*, the other three movements are comparably subtitled *Love*, *Play* and *Now*, with the Scherzo bringing echoes of Berlioz and the optimistic finale opening with a Wagnerian horn-call. The *Elegy for Brahms* conveys grief, but its vigour rises above passive mourning into an expression of what might almost be anger. *From death to life* consists of two connected movements, exuberantly melodic, with a theme in the second which echoes Sibelius's *Karelia*. It would be hard to imagine finer, more committed performances than those on Chandos, or richer sound.

This was the last record made by Sir Adrian Boult, whose recording of the slow movement is particularly beautiful here. Equally impressive is the *Elegy*, not merely an occasional piece but a full-scale symphonic movement which builds to a powerful climax. The *Symphonic variations* fills out the Parry portrait. Recording and performances are exemplary, a fitting coda to Sir Adrian's recording career. To make the CD even more representative, it is good to welcome so enjoyably professional a motet as Parry's *Blest pair of Sirens*. The performance by the London Philharmonic Choir should be more incisive, but it still conveys much of the right atmosphere. Throughout, the digital remastering has been wholly beneficial.

Nonet in B flat.
*** Hyperion Dig. CDA 66291 [id.]. Capricorn – STANFORD: *Serenade (Nonet)*. ***

Parry's *Nonet* is for flute, oboe, cor anglais and two each of clarinets, bassoons and horns. Although the finale is perhaps a little lightweight, it is a delight from beginning to end. If one did not know what it was, one would think of early Strauss, for it is music of enormous accomplishment and culture as well as freshness. An excellent performance and recording.

(i) *Piano quartet in A flat; Piano trio No. 1 in E min.*
**(*) Mer. Dig. CDE 84248 [id.]. Deakin Piano Trio, (i) with Yuko Inoue.

After the success of the Chandos series of the Parry symphonies, it is good to have his chamber music appearing in a comparable Meridian series. In his actual idiom, Brahms and Schumann were still the more important influences, with diatonic melody providing clear-cut thematic material, well argued. The *E minor Piano trio* is both shorter and more direct than the *Piano quartet*, which is more ambitious, with a darkly meditative slow introduction echoing late Beethoven. Though the performance on the disc is not as polished as one would like, Parry's melodic writing is more than distinctive enough to rebut the charge of mere imitation, with such a movement as the dashing tarantella-like Scherzo of the *Piano quartet* very effective indeed. The recording balances the piano rather behind the rest, which is a pity when Catherine Dubois so often takes the lead.

Piano trios Nos. 2 in B min.; 3 in G.
*** Mer. Dig. CDE 84255 [id.]. Deakin Piano Trio.

In the two *Piano trios* the English element in Parry's invention is more clearly identifiable, with some themes bringing anticipations of Elgar. Equally, the healthy outdoor feel of the triple-time main themes of the finales of both trios has a hint of English folk-music, while the folky element in the third-movement Scherzo of No. 2 is like a cross between Dvořák and Stanford, with Czech and Irish elements attractively intermingled. Both works are richly enjoyable, with the warm, open lyricism of the slow movement of No. 2 particularly attractive. The players of the Deakin Piano Trio seem more happily adjusted to the rigours of recording than in the first volume, with rather better matching and intonation.

Violin sonata in D, Op. 103; Fantasie-sonata in B, Op. 75; 12 short pieces.
*** Hyperion CDA 66157 [id.]. Erich Gruenberg, Roger Vignoles.

The *Fantasie-sonata* provides a fascinating example of cyclic sonata form, earlier than most but also echoing Schumann. The three-movement *Sonata in D* is another compact, meaty piece, the strongest work on the disc. The *Twelve short pieces*, less demanding technically, are delightful miniatures. Gruenberg and Vignoles prove persuasive advocates, and the recording is first rate.

PIANO MUSIC

Hands across the centuries (suite); *10 Shulbrede tunes; Theme and 19 variations in D min.*
*** Priory Dig. PRCD 451 [id.]. Peter Jacobs.

On the evidence of this very enjoyable recital, Parry is a much more rewarding piano composer than his contemporary, Stanford. Shulbrede Priory was the remains of a substantial twelfth-century Augustinian settlement, turned into a country house, where the composer's married daughter lived with her family. Parry was captivated by its charm and atmosphere when he first paid a visit there in 1902 and he returned frequently. In 1914 he published a set of ten delightful miniatures which showed this affection and the strong spell the house wielded over him. The style of the ten Shulbrede tunes may be eclectic, but how colourful and warmly melodic they are. The mock-baroque *Hands across the centuries suite* is hardly less diverting, and its invention equally varied. The more ambitious *Theme and variations* is rather prolix but is very well organized. Peter Jacobs, obviously enjoying himself, plays all this music with flair and the nimblest fingers (very necessary at times) and there is never a dull bar here. Excellent natural recording, too. A real find – you should try it, if you admire Parry.

VOCAL MUSIC

English lyrics: *And yet I love her till I die; Blow, blow, thou winter wind; Bright star; From a city window; Looking backward; Love is a bable; Marian; No longer mourn for me; O mistress mine; On a time the amorous Silvy; Take, O take those lips away; There; There be none of beauty's daughters; Thine eyes still shine for me; Welsh lullaby; When comes my Gwen; When lovers meet again; Weep you no more; When icicles hang by the wall; When we two parted.*
(BB) **(*) Belart 461 493-2. Robert Tear, Philip Ledger – VAUGHAN WILLIAMS: *Songs of travel; Linden Lea.* ***

Between the 1880s and 1920 Parry published a dozen sets of what he called 'English lyrics', 74 in all. He was perhaps not among the greatest of English song composers but his melodic line is always fresh, and these songs are all appealing in their easy lyricism. Robert Tear sings them with conviction and the right lightness of touch; his voice here has developed a beat since he recorded the Vaughan Williams songs, seven years earlier in 1972, but this is still an enjoyable recital, not least because of Ledger's sympathetic and stylish accompaniments.

Blest pair of sirens; I was glad (anthems).
*** Chandos Dig. CHAN 8641/2 [id.]. London Symphony Ch. & LSO, Hickox – ELGAR: *Dream of Gerontius.* ***

Parry's two finest and most popular anthems make an attractive coupling for Hickox's fine, sympathetic reading of Elgar's *Dream of Gerontius*. The chorus for Parry is rather thinner than in the main work but is very well recorded.

Evening Service in D (Great): Magnificat; Nunc dimittis. Hear my words, ye people; I was glad when they said unto me; Jerusalem; Songs of farewell.
*** Hyperion CDA 66273 [id.]. St George's Chapel, Windsor, Ch., Christopher Robinson, Roger Judd (organ).

Everyone knows *Jerusalem*, which highlights this collection resplendently. In the *Songs of farewell* trebles are used and the effect is less robust than in Marlow's version, but undoubtedly very affecting. Perhaps the stirring coronation anthem, *I was glad*, needs the greater weight of an adult choir, but it is still telling here. The excerpts from the *Great Service in D* are well worth having on record, as is the anthem, *Hear my words, ye people*. Excellent recording, the chapel ambience colouring the music without blunting the words.

Job (oratorio).
(N) **(*) Hyperion Dig. CDA 67025 [id.]. Peter Coleman-Wright, Toby Spence, Neal Davies, Jaime Morgan Hitchcock, Guildford Choral Soc., RPO, Hilary Davan Wetton.

Though Parry, as a Victorian, sidesteps the problem of conveying the pain and bitterness in the story of Job, this is a warm, beautifully written oratorio which is most welcome on disc, very English and optimistic. It would be even better, had Hilary Davan Wetton drawn a more biting response from the chorus and had Peter Coleman-Wright in the title role, clear and direct as he is, sounded less respectful. The other soloists are first rate, notably Toby Spence in the tenor part of Satan, and the recording is warm and atmospheric, though with the chorus rather backwardly placed. For all its limitations a highly enjoyable curiosity.

Songs of farewell.
*** Conifer Dig. 75605 51155-2 [id.]. Trinity College, Cambridge, Ch., Richard Marlow – STANFORD: *Magnificat* etc. ***

Parry's *Songs of farewell* represent his art at its deepest. Finest and most searching of the set is the Donne setting, *At the round earth's imagined corners*, with its rich harmonies poignantly intense and beautiful. Richard Marlow with his splendid Trinity Choir, using fresh women's voices for the upper lines instead of trebles, directs thoughtful, committed performances, very well recorded, which capture both the beauty and the emotion.

The Soul's ransom (sinfonia sacra); The Lotos eaters.
*** Chandos Dig. CHAN 8990 [id.]. Jones, Wilson-Johnson, LPO and Ch., Bamert.

Using a biblical text *The Soul's ransom*, with its sequence of solos and choruses, forms a broadly symphonic four-movement structure with references back not only to Brahms and the nineteenth century but to much earlier choral composers, notably Schütz. This 45-minute piece is generously coupled with *The Lotos eaters*, a setting for soprano, chorus and orchestra of eight stanzas from Tennyson's choric song of that name, with Della Jones again the characterful soloist. Full and atmospheric recording to match the incandescent performances.

Pärt, Arvo (born 1935)

(i) *Arbos* (two performances); (ii) *Pari Intervallo;* (iii) *An den Wassern zu Babel; De Profundis;* (iv; v) *Es sang vor langen Jahren;* (iii) *Summa;* (iii; v; vi) *Stabat Mater.*
*** ECM Dig. 831 959-2 [id.]. (i) Brass Ens., Stuttgart State O, Davies; (ii) Bowers-Broadbent; (iii) Hilliard Ens., Hillier; (iv) Bickley; (v) Kremer, Mendelssohn; (vi) Demenga.

All the music recorded here gives a good picture of Pärt's musical make-up with all its strengths and limitations. *Arbos*, which is heard in two different versions, 'seeks to create the image of a tree or family tree'. It does not modulate and has no development, though pitch and tempi are in proportional relationships. The *Stabat Mater* (1985) for soprano, counter-tenor, tenor and string trio is distinguished by extreme simplicity of utterance and is almost totally static. This music relies for its effect on minimal means and invites one to succumb to a kind of mystical, hypnotic repetition rather than a musical argument. The artists performing here do so with total commitment and are excellently recorded.

(i) *Cantus in memory of Benjamin Britten; Festina lente; Summa;* (i; ii) *Tabula rasa;* (ii) *Fratres; Spiegel im Spiegel.*
(M) *** EMI Dig. CD-EMX 2221. (i) Bournemouth Sinf., Richard Studt; (ii) Tasmin Little, Martin Roscoe.

An admirable and enterprising compilation from EMI Eminence to tempt those who have not yet sampled this composer's highly individual sound-world with its tintinnabulation. *Summa* is another version of the vocal *Creed* and is certainly effective, if not superior in its new costume. In the two chamber works Tasmin Little holds the listener's attention by the intensity of her commitment and the powerful projection of her playing. But most striking of all is the ambitious *Tabula rasa* with strong contrasts between the erupting energy of the opening *Ludus* and the aptly named second-movement *Silentium* which, of course, isn't silent but spins a compulsive atmospheric web. Fine performances and evocative sound, spread within an ecclesiastical acoustic, and first-rate recording combine to give this programme persuasive advocacy.

Collage on B-A-C-H; Cantus in memory of Benjamin Britten.
*** RCA Dig. 09026 68061-2 [id.]. Moscow Virtuosi, Vladimir Spivakov – SHOSTAKOVICH: *Chamber symphony No. 2;* DENISOV: *Variations;* SHCHEDRIN: *Stalin cocktail.* ***

These intense and very well-played performances show Pärt at his most imaginatively approachable. The three brief, neo-baroque movements (a spiccato *Toccata*, lyrical *Sarabande* – with engaging oboe solo, interrupted by saturated chords for strings and piano – and the dissonantly contrapuntal *Ricercar finale*) are like Bach seen through a distorting prism. The result is both inventive and colourful, while the Britten work uses descending scales against a tolling bell yet creates both brilliant textures and an intense climax. First-class recording and stimulating couplings.

Fratres (6 versions); *Cantus in memory of Benjamin Britten; Festina lente.*
*** Telarc Dig. CD 80387 [id.]. Jane Manning, France Springuel, Mireille Gleizes, I Fiamminghi, Rudolph Werthen.

For all the repetitions involved in Pärt's minimalist progressions there are no more hypnotic examples of his curiously compelling, ritualistic writing than this sequence of six settings of a very simple monastic chorale which he calls *Fratres*. We hear it first slowly swelling up from a *piano-pianissimo* on strings, with unobtrusive decorative percussion, then sinking away again. Then follow variants featuring first a solo violin, then for a carefully blended wind octet, for eight cellos used in their higher register, then returning to a string group and quickening to achieve the flavour of an elegant baroque dance, further adapted to the more economical texture of a string quartet, and finally rustling on the cello with the piano tolling a bell-like accompaniment until a closing climax builds and abates. The Britten tribute and *Festina lente for strings and harp ad libitum* are used as interludes. The playing here has great atmosphere and concentration, while Telarc's glowing sound adds to the sensuous physical beauty.

Fratres; Summa (string quartet versions).
*** Virgin/EMI Dig. VC5 45023-2 [id.]. Chilingirian Qt – TAVENER: *Last Sleep of the Virgin* etc. ***

Like the Tavener works with which they are generously coupled on this 74-minute CD, these are both atmospheric works with a liturgical basis, using sparse basic material, which try to convey a sense of eternity. The performances here, obviously felt, make an interesting comparison with the alternative versions discussed above. But it must be admitted that, as music, they are less potent than the Tavener pieces.

And one of the Pharisees; (i) *The Beatitudes; Cantate Domino (Psalm 95);* (ii) *De Profundis (Psalm 129); Magnificat; 7 Magnificat Antiphons;* (i) *Missa Sillabica. Solfeggio; Summa (Credo).*
*** HM Dig. HMU 907182 [id.]. Theatre of Voices, Paul Hillier; (i) with Christopher Bowers-Broadbent (organ); Dan Kennedy (percussion).

The cover of this CD indicates that it includes just *De Profundis*, whereas this 76-minute collection covers a very wide range of Pärt's choral output, from the short *Solfeggio* of 1964, which seems to float in space, to *The Beatitudes* (1990) of which this is the recording première. This work opens in stillness and calm but, as so often with this composer, leads on to a great climax, here over an organ pedal; then, after an exultant 'Amen', the organ has a brief but prolix postlude. *De Profundis* (1980) brings a similarly elliptical structure, based on a simple climbing phrase in the bass; it again uses an organ pedal to underpin the climax. The *Missa Sillabica* (1977), heard here in a slightly revised version, is a fine example of Pärt's use of the simplest means to communicate his expression of the liturgical text, the repetitions within the 'Credo' a characteristic example. *And one of the Pharisees* is a setting for three voices of a text from chapter 7 of St Luke's Gospel and its powerful medieval atmosphere, including solo chants, reminds us of the link which Pärt's liturgical music has with the distant past. The performances here could hardly be more powerful or atmospheric, yet they are firmly controlled. They are magnificently recorded.

Passio Domini Nostrum Jesu Christi secundum Joannem.
*** ECM Dig. 837 109-2 [id.]. Michael George, John Potter, Hilliard Ens., Western Wind Chamber Ch. (Instrumental group), Paul Hillier.

Pärt's *Passion of our Lord Jesus Christ according to St John* was composed in a bleak narrative style that reminds one of a mixture of Stravinsky and Schütz. It repeats the same scraps of ideas over and over again; it takes 70 minutes and never seems to leave the Aeolian mode, and it ought to be intolerable; yet in its way it is a strangely impressive experience, albeit not a wholly musical one. Impeccable recording and a dedicated performance.

Patterson, Paul (born 1947)

Concerto for orchestra, Op. 45; Europhony, Op. 55; (i) *Missa brevis, Op. 54.*
(M) *** EMI Dig. CDM5 66529-2. LPO, Owain Arwel Hughes; (i) with LPO Ch.

This disc offers representative examples of Patterson's recent work, much more approachable in idiom than his earlier music. The gem of the collection is the *Missa brevis*, using a seemingly simple style boldly and freshly. It must be as grateful for the singers as it is for the listener, with moments of pure poetry as in the *Benedictus*. The two orchestral pieces, though less individual, are colourful and immediately attractive. Their openness of idiom conceals the ingenuity of their construction, with *Europhony* clearly developing on variation form. Vigorous performances and wide-ranging recording.

Penderecki, Kryszstof (born 1933)

(i) *Anaklasis;* (ii; iii) *Capriccio for violin and orchestra;* (iii) *De natura sonoris I & II; The dream of Jacob; Fonogrammi; Threnody for the victims of Hiroshima;* (iv) *Canticum canticorum Salomonis.*
(M) *** EMI CDM5 65077-2 [id.]. (i) LSO; (ii) Wanda Wilkomirska; (iii) Polish Nat. RSO; (iv) Krakow Philharmonic Ch.; composer.

A splendid anthology and an admirable introduction to Penderecki's music. The longest work is the setting of a text from the *Song of Solomon* for large orchestra and sixteen solo voices. The other, shorter pieces will probably have a more lasting impact. The beautiful and touching *Threnody* for 53 strings (1959–61) is the best-known piece and originally made the composer's name internationally; it is here given a magnificent performance. So is the ambitious *Capriccio* in which Wilkomirska proves a superb soloist. *Anaklasis*, an inventive piece for strings and percussion, and *De natura sonoris* are more obviously brilliant in their use of contrasts, while *The dream of Jacob* of 1974 is as inventive as the rest but sparer and more cogent. Performances are definitive and the recordings, a co-production between EMI and Polish Radio, are of a very high standard.

(i; iii) *Cello concerto;* (iii) *Emanationen for 2 string orchestras;* (ii–iii) *Partita for harpsichord and orchestra;* (iv) *Symphony*.

(M) *** EMI CDM5 65416-2. (i) Siegfried Palm; (ii) Felicja Blumenthal; (iii) Polish RSO; (iv) LSO; composer.

For those who admire such athematic music, these 1972–3 recordings of Penderecki's works in authentic performances under the composer's own direction will have much to commend them. Penderecki's music relies for its appeal on its resourceful use of sonorities, and his sound-world is undoubtedly imaginative, albeit limited. The *Symphony*, the composer's most ambitious orchestral work so far, was commissioned by a British engineering firm and first heard in Peterborough Cathedral. That setting has influenced the range of sumptuous orchestral colours devised by the composer. You may regard this as merely a sequence of brilliant effects rather than a logically argued symphony, but in this committed performance it is certainly striking and memorable. Fine recording enhances the value of this disc, and the CD transfers combine fullness with admirable presence.

Violin concerto.

(M) *** Sony Stern Edition II SMK 64507 [id.]. Stern, Minnesota O, Skrowaczewski – HINDEMITH: *Violin concerto*. ***

This concerto, written for Isaac Stern in 1977, marked Penderecki's return to a more conservative idiom. Even so, his fingerprints are clearly identifiable and the compression of thematic material, combined with spare, clean textures, makes for memorable results. The single movement, which lasts nearly 40 minutes, contains within it the traces of a funeral march, a Scherzo and a meditative adagio. The performance here is passionately committed, with Stern at his most inspired, and the recording is splendidly detailed. With its hardly less valuable Hindemith coupling, this is a key reissue in the second Box of Sony's Stern Edition.

Penella, Manuel (1880–1939)

El gato montes (The wild mountain cat).

(N) (B) *** DG Double Dig. 459 427-2 (2) [id.]. Plácido Domingo, Veronica Villarroel, Juan Pons, Teresa Berganza, National Lyrical Theatre Zarzuela Ch., Madrid SO, Miguel Roa.

This is a red-blooded performance of a melodramatic piece half-way between opera and zarzuela, which Plácido Domingo has a special affection for. He sings the role of the bullfighter, Rafael, in love with the heroine Soleá, who still keeps her affection for the bandit, Juanillo, *El gato montes*, 'The wildcat'. The highly coloured plot ends with the death of all three, Rafael gored to death in the ring, Soleá dying of a broken heart and *El gato montes* cornered by the police. The writing is fluent and lyrical, with scenes punctuated by attractive orchestral pieces, notably the most celebrated, a paso doble. The musical invention may not be distinguished, but in such beefy performances, with Juan Pons in the title-role a genuine rival for Domingo, it is certainly attractive. The casting of the women principals is strong too, with Veronica Villarroel fresh and bright as the heroine and Teresa Berganza as characterful as ever as the Gypsy. Full, forward sound.

Pergolesi, Giovanni (1710–36)

(i) *Magnificat in C;* (ii) *Miserere II in C min.;* (iii) *Salve Regina in C min.;* (iv) *Stabat Mater* (revision and organ part by M. Zanon).

(B) **(*) Decca Double 455 017-2 (2). (i) Vaughan, J. Baker, Partridge, Keyte, King's College Ch., ASMF, Marriner; (ii) Wolff, James, Covey-Crump, Suart, Magdalen Coll., Oxford, Ch., Wren O, Bernard Rose; (iii) Kirkby, AAM, Hogwood; (iv) Raskin, Lehane, O. Rossini di Napoli, Caracciolo – CALDARA: *Crucifixus*. LOTTI: *Crucifixus*. ***

This more ambitious if slightly uneven collection of Pergolesi's choral music (although only the *Salve Regina* and the *Stabat Mater* are almost certainly authentic) makes a useful alternative to the Double Decca set below, with the Willcocks performance of the *C major Magnificat* common to both. The *Stabat Mater* is modest in its demands, requiring originally two castrati plus strings and continuo. The orchestral accompaniment is spirited and the warm acoustic of the Naples Conservatorio adds richness to a fairly small body of strings. The *Miserere*, whether authentic or not, is undoubtedly moving. The singers here are all of quality, particularly Richard Suart; Bernard Rose secures expressive and persuasive results from the Magdalen College choir and the Wren Orchestra. The (originally Argo) recording sounds magnificently real and vivid. Last but not least comes Emma Kirkby's radiantly expressive and spirited *Salve Regina*, the finest solo contibution to this collection. Here period instruments enter the sound-picture, and the accompaniment from Hogwood's Academy matches Kirkby's depth of feeling, particularly in the touching closing '*O clemens*'.

(i) *Magnificat in C;* (ii) *Stabat Mater.*
(B) **(*) Decca Double 443 868-2 (2) [id.]. (i) Vaughan, J. Baker, Partridge, Keyte, King's College Ch., ASMF, Willcocks; (ii) Palmer, Hodgson, St John's College, Cambridge, Ch., Argo CO, Guest – BONONCINI: *Stabat Mater;* D. SCARLATTI: *Stabat Mater;* A. SCARLATTI: *Domine, refugium factus es nobis; O magnum mysterium;* CALDARA: *Crucifixus;* LOTTI: *Crucifixus.* ***

This well-planned Double Decca collection centres on three different settings of the *Stabat Mater dolorosa*. Pergolesi's version dates from 1735 and, subsequently, settings were made by many other composers, including Vivaldi and Haydn. Pergolesi conceived a work which has secular and even theatrical overtones, and its devotional nature is unexaggerated. George Guest directs a sensible, unaffected performance, simple and expressive, with relaxed tempi, not overladen with romantic sentiment. The *Magnificat* – doubtfully attributed, like so much that goes under this composer's name – is a comparatively lightweight piece, notable for its rhythmic vitality. The King's College Choir under Willcocks gives a sensitive and vital performance, and the recording matches it in intensity of atmosphere.

Stabat Mater.
(N) ❁ *** Opus 111 Dig OPS 30-160 [id.]. Gemma Bertagnolli, Sara Mingardo, Concerto Italiano, Rinaldo Alessandrini – A. SCARLATTI: *Stabat Mater.* ***
*** DG 415 103-2 [id.]. Margaret Marshall, Valentini Terrani, LSO, Abbado.
(N) (B) (**) Dutton 2CDAX 2005 (3) [id.]. Joan Taylor, Kathleen Ferrier, Oriana Ch., Roy Henderson – BACH: *St Matthew Passion.* (**(*))

(i; ii) *Stabat Mater;* (ii) *In coelestibus regnis;* (i) *Salve Regina in A.*
*** Hyperion Dig. CDA 66294 [id.]. (i) Gillian Fisher; (ii) Michael Chance; King's Consort, Robert King.

Both the soprano, Gemma Bertagnolli, and the contralto, Sara Mingardo (with her remarkably resonant lower register) have extraordinarily colourful voices, which blend beautifully at the work's sustained opening, but which only display their full richness in their solos, notably *Cujus animam gementem* and *Fac ut portem Christ mortem*. This is a totally Italianate performance of both high drama and moving pathos. The closing *Quando corpus morietur*, in which both singers join in sustained legato is very moving indeed, followed by a passionately final affirmation of faith. Alessandrini's instrumental support could not be more telling and the recording is made in an ideal acoustic.

Abbado's account brings greater intensity and ardour to this piece than any rival, and he secures marvellously alive playing from the LSO – this without diminishing religious sentiment. The DG recording has warmth and good presence and the perspective is thoroughly acceptable. But there is no coupling.

The Hyperion recording makes a very good case for authenticity in this work. The combination of soprano and male alto blends well together yet offers considerable variety of colour. Gillian Fisher's *Salve Regina* is quite a considerable piece in four sections, whereas Michael Chance's motet is brief but makes an engaging postlude. Excellent sound.

The 1946 Decca recording of the *Stabat Mater* makes a welcome fill-up to the Bach *St Matthew Passion*, thanks to the contribution of Kathleen Ferrier. The rest is less distinguished, with Joan Taylor a fluttery soprano soloist.

Stabat Mater (revised Alberto Soresina).
(M) **(*) Ph. 462 054-2. Lear, Ludwig, RIAS Ch., Berlin RSO, Maazel – VIVALDI: *Stabat Mater.* **(*)

This is an unashamedly romantic performance of Pergolesi's most famous choral work. Evelyn Lear and Christa Ludwig could hardly be bettered when it comes to expressive musicianship and beauty of tone, but those who have concern for authenticity of style may be disturbed by the weight of emotion the performers find in what is fundamentally simple music. In this Maazel must take most of the blame. It is music that can so easily sound sentimental, something he narrowly skirts. But the singing itself is glorious, and it is easy to be swayed by the rich opulence of the sounds here, with the chorus joining in vigorously at the close. The reissue comes as part of the Philips Choral Collection, which means handsome packaging, but a limited 'sleeve-note' and no texts.

Perotinus Magister (*c.* 1160–1225)

Organa: *Alleluya, Nativitas; Sederunt principes.*
*** Lyrichord LEMS 8002 [id.]. Russell Oberlin, Charles Bressler, Donald Perry, Seymour Barab – LEONIN: *Organa.* ***

Perotinus extended the simple polyphony of Leonin from two to three and four parts, and the ear is very aware of the intervals which characterize the organum: unison, octave, fourths and fifths. This music is more florid, freer than the coupled works written several decades before. The performances here are totally compelling and the recording excellent.

Peterson-Berger, Wilhelm

(1867–1942)

Symphony No. 1 in B flat (The Banner); Last summer (suite).
(N) *** CPO Dig. CPO 999 561-2 [id.]. Saarbrücken RSO, Jurowski.

The Swedish composer, Wilhelm Peterson-Berger enjoyed some notoriety in his lifetime as a critic. Some of his countrymen have compared his writing to Bernard Shaw's but his wit does not have the light touch, or the memorable turn of phrase of the latter, and there is a certain pomposity too. As a composer he is essentially a miniaturist, a water-colourist, whose ideas are not ideally suited to the symphonic canvas. His *First Symphony* (*Banéret* or *The Banner*) was composed when he was in his early twenties but revised later on in life. It is heavily indebted to Grieg and Wagner, and has some appealing moments. As a symphony it is pretty flimsy in structure and by the side of Stenhammar or Alfvén conveys little sense of real mastery. In the quieter, pastoral moments the scoring is fresh but elsewhere it is far from expert. The suite, *Last summer* is the better piece. Both receive sympathetic and persuasive performances, and excellent recording.

Flowers from Frösö: Book I, Op. 16; Book II; Book III (Humoresques and idylls for piano).
(N) *** BIS Dig. CD 925 [id.]. Norika Ogawa.
(N) (BB) *** Naxos Dig. 8.554343 [id.]. Niklas Sivelöv.

The author of the notes of the BIS CD compares Peterson-Berger with César Cui – neither could come to terms with not being a great composer and as critics they took it out on their betters. *Fröslomster* is variously described on these discs as *Frösöflowers* and *Flowers from Fröso Island* but they are the same pieces. Peterson-Berger's talent was far better suited to the miniature than the large-scale orchestral canvas, and these miniatures, though not earth-shattering in any way, have a pallor and charm that is all their own. Norika Ogawa plays them with grace and much sensitivity – and the BIS recording is exemplary.

Niklas Sivelöv is hardly less successful in conveying the fineness of these pieces. There is a Grieg-like salon quality about them redeemed by a certain freshness, and Sivelöv plays with style and elegance, He is recorded in St George's, Brandon Hill, Bristol and the sound is excellent. Price apart, there is nothing to choose between his set and Norika Ogawa on sonic or artistic grounds.

Pettersson, Allan (1911–80)

(i) *Viola concerto. Symphony No. 5.*
*** BIS Dig. CD 480 [id.]. (i) Nobuko Imai; Malmö SO, Moshe Atzmon.

Allan Pettersson's *Fifth* is a one-movement work and begins well. However, invention flags and the brooding, expectant atmosphere and powerful ostinatos arouse more promise of development than fulfilment. The *Viola concerto* comes from the last year of Pettersson's life and is pretty amorphous. Both pieces lack the concentration and quality of Tubin or Holmboe. The three stars are for the performers and the recording team.

Symphony No. 7.
*** Caprice Dig. CAP 21411. Swedish RSO, Comissiona – MOZART: *Bassoon concerto.* ***

The *Seventh Symphony* is a long, dark work which wears an anguished visage and packs a considerable emotional punch. Its musical substance is less weighty than appears to be the case on first acquaintance, and the ideas seem static and thinly spread; but it has a strong emotional appeal for many music-lovers and its atmosphere is quite powerful. Those who dismiss its composer impatiently as a self-pitying windbag should hear this work, which has an undoubted eloquence. Sergiu Comissiona gives a dedicated and sensitive account of the score that is every bit as fine as Dorati's première recording. The rather bizarre coupling is unlikely to sway the collector one way or the other.

Symphonies Nos. 7; 11.
*** BIS Dig. CD 580 [id.]. Norrköping SO, Leif Segerstam.

The music of Allan Pettersson inspires partisan feeling. There seems to be no middle course, and if you are among his admirers the present CD, which shows him at his best, can be recommended. Segerstam and his fine Norrköping players bring great feeling to the *Seventh* and give the somewhat shorter *Eleventh Symphony* the most sympathetic advocacy. If you want to explore further, you could try the *Fifth Symphony* (BIS CD 480), but the present disc seems the best possible place to start.

Symphonies Nos. 8; 10.
(N) *** BIS Dig. CD 880 [id.]. Norrköping SO, Leif Segerstam.

The *Eighth Symphony* is long, often static, at times powerful and at others totally wanting in any kind of symphonic coherence. The *Tenth* is shorter but good though this performance is, it does not dispel the impression made by an earlier LP account that it is still essentially empty: the music of gesture not substance, and deficient in thematic vitality. Those who are on Pettersson's wavelength (and he has a following in both Germany and Sweden) need not have any hesitations about either the performances or recordings on this BIS CD.

Symphony No. 9.
*** CPO Dig. CPO 999 231-2. Berlin RSO, Alun Francis.

Pettersson's *Ninth Symphony* (1970) was composed in the valley of the shadow of death and has had a powerful effect on many of his admirers. Life being short and sweet, one can only say that the 70 minutes which it takes to unfold seems an eternity. Not surprisingly, given the sudden beatification he received with the *Seventh Symphony* and the enthusiasm with which his supporters hailed him, fame went to Pettersson's head and he began to assume that any utterance from his pen, irrespective of quality, had to be committed to paper, and that his every quaver was significant. The three stars are for the performance and recording, so that admirers of the composer can proceed accordingly.

Barfota sånger (Barefoot songs); 6 songs.
(N) ** CPO Dig. CPO 999499-2 [id.]. Monica Groop, Cord Garben.

These songs come from the war years when Pettersson was working as an orchestral player. The *Barefoot songs* precede any of his seventeen symphonies and are of the utmost simplicity. They are all strophic, and few last more than a couple of minutes. They are superbly sung by Monica Groop but not even she and her expert pianist can disguise their naïvety and in some cases emptiness. Admirers of the composer may not find their charms so eminently resistable or the melodic invention so unmemorable.

Pfitzner, Hans (1869–1949)

Das Herz: Liebesmelodie (Love theme); *Das Kaethchen von Heilbronn: Overture. Palestrina: Preludes to Acts I, II & III.*
(*) DG Dig. 449 571-2 [id.]. German Opera, Berlin, O, Thielemann – R. STRAUSS: *Capriccio* etc. *

Thielemann believes passionately in Pfitzner, and here he confirms the impression he created in his 1997 Covent Garden performance of *Palestrina*. In the three *Preludes*, the playing is passionate yet at the same time restrained. The *Love theme* from Pfitzner's last opera, and the extended prelude to his early opera, *Das Kaethchen von Heilbronn*, if overlong, are more sparkling than the rest. Both add to a fairly persuasive portrait, though the Strauss items prove much more memorable, and one has the feeling that this is not music to which one would return very often. The Orchestra of the Berlin Deutsches Oper does not possess the opulent string-tone found at the *Philharmonie* but they play with conviction. The DG recording is very good without being state of the art.

String quartets: in D, Op. 13; in C min., Op. 50.
*** CPO Dig. CPO 999 072-2 [id.]. Franz Schubert Qt.

We think of Pfitzner primarily as a composer of opera and Lieder, but this first-class CPO string quartet coupling serves to show him as a composer of fine chamber music in the mainstream of the German romantic tradition. The two works are aptly paired to span his career; the *D major*, from 1903, was dedicated to Alma Mahler. The opening is gentle and elegiac, and the mood nostalgic. The *C minor Quartet*, written 40 years later, carries a mood of resignation which hauntingly dominates the first and third movements, but the *Andantino*, which comes second, jauntily restores the composer's good humour. Altogether these are two thoroughly rewarding works, finely crafted, with a ready flow of appealing variations and subtly individual harmonic progressions. They are splendidly played by the richly blended Schubert Quartet, whose chording is immaculate and who respond to the bittersweet, *fin de siècle* flavour of the writing. Excellent, realistic recording.

Palestrina (opera) complete.
(M) *** DG 427 417-2 (3). Gedda, Fischer-Dieskau, Weikl, Ridderbusch, Donath, Fassbaender, Prey, Tölz Boys' Ch., Bav. R. Ch. & SO, Kubelik.

Though Pfitzner's melodic invention hardly matches that of his contemporary, Richard Strauss, his control of structure and drawing of character through music make an unforgettable impact. It is the central Act, a massive and colourful tableau representing the Council of Trent, which lets one witness the crucial discussion on the role of music in the church. The outer Acts – more personal and more immediately compelling – show the dilemma of Palestrina himself and the inspiration which led him to write the *Missa Papae Marcelli*, so resolving the crisis, both personal and public. At every point Pfitzner's response to this situation is illuminating, and this glorious performance with a near-ideal cast, consistent all through, could hardly be bettered in conveying the intensity of an admittedly offbeat inspiration. This CD reissue captures the glow of the Munich recording superbly and, though this is a mid-price set, DG has not skimped on the accompanying booklet.

Philips, Peter (c. 1561–1640)

Motets: *Ave verum corpus; Ave Maria gratia plena; Ecce vicit Leo; Factum est silentium; Gaudent in coelis; Hodie nobis de coelo; O bone Jesu; O crux ave spes unica; O quam suavis.*
**(*) EMI Dig. CDM5 66788-2 [id.]. King's

College, Cambridge, Ch., Cleobury – DERING: *Motets.* **(*)

Both Peter Philips and his younger contemporary, Richard Dering, were Catholics and spent much of their lives on the Continent. This CD contrasts and compares the two composers' beautiful and expressive settings of the same texts. The performances are faithful, but the actual sound is not always perfect in either focus or blend, partly but not solely due to the recording.

Pierné, Gabriel (1863–1937)

Cello sonata in F sharp min., Op. 46.

(N) *** Hyperion Dig. CDA 66979 [id.]. Mats Lidström, Bengt Forsberg – KOECHLIN: *Cello sonata* etc. ***

Both works on this enterprising issue were composed at roughly the same time as the Debussy sonata. Best known in his lifetime as a conductor, Pierné was an interesting and cultured composer. His sonata is finely wrought with touches of real individuality, and well worth getting to know. Mats Lidström and Bengt Forsberg play with great intelligence and refinement and are well served by the engineers.

(i; iii) *Piano quintet in E min., Op. 41;* (i; ii) *Violin sonata, Op. 36;* (iv) *Les enfants à Bethléhem* (mystère for narrator, soloists, and children's chorus).

(N) (B) **(*) Erato/Warner Ultima Double 3984 24239-2 (2) [id.]. (i) Jean Hubeau; (ii) Olivier Charlier; (iii) Viotti Qt; (iv) Deiber (narr.), Chamonin, Schaer, Orliac, Frémeau, French R. Maîtrise & PO, Michel Lasserre de Rozel.

It is good that the catalogue is at long last paying some attention to Pierné. The *Piano quintet* is quite a powerful piece, Franckian in influence, but with its own voice. Its scherzo seductively borrows the rhythms of a Basque dance. The *Violin sonata* is impressive too, with a most engaging central *Andante tranquillo*. Both are well played; the digital sound is a bit reverberant, but acceptable. *Les enfants à Bethléhem* is a work of great charm, for narrator (who sets the scene and closes the work, but does not outstay his welcome), adult and child soloists, and children's chorus. It sees the Nativity through the eyes of a child and could hardly be better presented: the performance has an engaging enthusiam and innocence. The recording too is admirably atmospheric. Alas, the documentation is poor and there is no text for the cantata.

Pijper, Willem (1894–1947)

String quartets Nos. 1–5.

*** Olympia Dig. OCD 457 [id.]. Schönberg Qt.

Willem Pijper was a dominant force in Dutch music between the wars. This CD collects all five of his *String quartets*. The post-war *Fifth Quartet* (1946) was left unfinished at his death, though two movements were completed. Pijper's music is concentrated and thoughtful, eminently civilized and predominantly gentle in outlook, even if it falls short of having that unmistakable and distinctive voice betokening a great composer. The Schönberg Quartet is one of the finest Dutch ensembles, and they are beautifully recorded. A rewarding disc, well worth investigating.

Pinto, George Frederick (1785–1806)

Piano sonatas Op. 3/1–2; Fantasia and sonata in C min.; Grand sonata in C min. (To his friend, John Field).

** Olympia OCD 494 [id.]. Riko Fukuda (fortepiano).

Pinto was a musical prodigy in London at the turn of the eighteenth century and these works date from between 1801 and 1808. They show Pinto to be a conventional composer, although undoubtedly he anticipates the style of early Beethoven. He has a few good ideas (as at the very opening of the *Sonata*, Op. 3/1, or the *Adagio* of Op. 3/2), but his allegros seldom mine any deep level of argument. Riko Fukuda's performances are robust but sympathetic. Truthful recording.

Piston, Walter (1894–1976)

(i; ii) *Capriccio for harp and strings;* (ii) *3 New England sketches;* (iii) *Serenata;* (ii) *Symphony No. 4.*

✿ *** Delos Dig. DE 3106 [id.]. (i) Wunrow; (ii) Seattle SO; (iii) NY CO; Gerard Schwarz.

Piston's *Fourth* is arguably the finest American symphony, as powerful in its forward sweep as the Harris *Third* and better held together than either Barber's *First* or Copland's *Third*. The remaining pieces, not only the *New England sketches* but also the inventive *Capriccio for harp and strings*, are well worth seeking out. The fine recording and Gerard Schwarz's natural and unforced direction make this a most desirable CD. The slow movement of the *Serenata*, equally well played by New York forces, is quite inspired.

Violin concertos Nos. 1–2; Fantasia for violin and orchestra.

(N) ✿(BB *** Naxos Dig. 8.559003 [id.]. James Boswell, Ukraine Nat. SO, Theodor Kucher.

It is quite extraordinary that a work as inspired as Piston's *First Violin concerto* (1939) is not already in the standard repertory alongside the Barber, with which it has much in common, including a comparable profusion of individual, lyrical melody. The second subject of the first movement persists in the memory until, most engagingly, it is rhythmically transformed to become the secondary theme of the riotous Rondo finale, the kind of movement that would bring down the house at a Promenade Concert. In between comes a pensive *Andantino molto tranquillo* with just a hint of Gershwin in its bluesy opening. The *Second Concerto* was written two decades later. Its atmosphere is more elusive, but its opening is no less haunting. The first movement is a two-part structure, developing two ideas, one sinously 'expressible' (which is to reach a passionate climax), the other pungently rhythmic and angular. The extended *Adagio* introduces a calm and very beautiful theme which is later to form a canonic duet with the flute. The finale is another sparkling, jaunty Rondo, less immediately appealing perhaps, but certainly not less vigorous and spirited than that which closes its predecessor. The *Fantasia* is a late work, first performed in 1973. Ruminative and searching, its language is more dissonant; it is in five intricately related sections, with hectic bravura allegros framed by adagio passages in which the soloist also thoughtfully participates, which have been described as 'painfully aware and transcendentally serene'. The work's closing section is profoundly gentle. It may seem remarkable that these works should be given their CD début by a Russian orchestra, but they play the music with security, splendid commitment and feeling. Their conductor, Theodor Kucher, moved to the Ukraine from Cleveland, Ohio, and he is also currently Music Director of the Boulder Philharmonic and the newly formed Sinfonia of Colorado. James Boswell, who studied at Juilliard (and who made his solo début with the NYPO at the age of seven), is a superbly accomplished, dedicated and spontaneous soloist, and the recording is first class, often approaching demonstration standard.

The Incredible flutist (ballet; complete); *New England sketches; Symphony No. 6* (1955).
*** RCA Dig. RD 60798 [60798-2-RC]. St Louis SO, Leonard Slatkin.

Walter Piston's ballet, *The Incredible flutist*, is one of the most refreshing and imaginative of all American scores. The most powerful work on Slatkin's disc is the *Sixth Symphony*, about which Piston wrote rather disarmingly, 'It seemed as though the melodies were being written by the instruments themselves as I just followed along,' and there is an inexorable sense of logic and inevitability. Piston is a cultivated, refined symphonist who does not wear his heart on his sleeve. The playing of the St Louis orchestra under Leonard Slatkin both here and in the *New England sketches* is sensitive and brilliant, and the RCA engineers give them excellent quality.

(i) *Sinfonietta;* (ii) *Symphonies Nos. 2; 6.*
(N) *** Delos Dig. DE 3074 [id.]. (i) NY CO; (ii) Seattle SO, Gerard Schwarz.

Gerhard Schwarz's coupling of the *Second* and *Sixth Symphonies* is a welcome addition to the Piston discography. The sound has amplitude and warmth, and the playing of the Seattle Orchestra has plenty of enthusiasm and vitality. This makes an admirable alternative to Slatkin's RCA version of the *Sixth*. One wonders why RCA have not transferred the pioneering version by the dedicatees, Charles Münch and the Boston Symphony. The *Sinfonietta* of 1942 is neoclassical in outlook – fresh and inventive with a touch of Hindemith about it.

Symphonies Nos. 5; (i) *7 and 8.*
** Albany AR 011 [id.]. Louisville O, Whitney, (i) Mester.

The *Fifth Symphony* has a sureness of purpose and feeling for organic growth that are the hallmark of the true symphonist. The *Seventh* and *Eighth Symphonies*, though not quite the equal of the finest Piston, are powerful and rewarding works which will speak to those who are more concerned with substance than with surface appeal. The Louisville performances are thoroughly committed and good, without being outstanding. The recordings sound better than they did on LP.

(i) *Piano quintet. Passacaglia; Piano sonata; Toccata.*
**(*) Northeastern/Koch Int. Dig. NR 232-CD [id.]. Leonard Hokanson; (i) Portland Qt.

The *Piano quintet* must be numbered among the finest post-Second World War piano quintets; it is a work of great vitality and integrity. These artists give a more than respectable account of it, and Leonard Hokanson proves no less convincing and responsive in the early *Piano sonata*. The recording is fully acceptable.

String quartets Nos. 1–3.
** Northeastern/Koch Dig. NR 9001-CD [id.]. Portland Qt.

Piston's five *String quartets* are finely crafted pieces, sinewy and Hindemithian at times (the first movement of No. 1), thoughtful and inward-looking at others (the Lento opening of No. 2 and the slow movement of No. 3). His music never wears its heart on its sleeve, but if its emotional gestures are restrained there is no real lack of warmth. The Portland Quartet play well and the recordings are clear, although the acoustic is a little on the small side.

Pizzetti, Ildebrando (1880–1968)

Messa di requiem. De profundis.
(N) ✿ *** Hyperion Dig. CDA67017 [id.]. Westminster Cathedral Ch., James O'Donnell - MARTIN: *Mass for double choir* etc. *** ✿

Pizzetti's 'serene and lyrical Requiem' (as his biographer, Guido Gatti puts it) comes from the same year as the Martin *Mass for double choir* with which it is coupled. It is a work of surpassing beauty which will be a revelation to those who have not encountered it before, particularly in this fervent and inspired performance. It comes with the *De profundis* he composed in 1937 to mark the healing of his breach with Malipiero. Fine though the performance by the Danish Radio Chamber Choir under Stefan Parkman was (Chandos CHAN8964), coupled with other Pizzetti choral pieces, this Westminster Cathedral version completely supplants it.

Messa di Requiem. Due composizioni corali: Il giardino dia rossette here. Afrodite; Piena sorgeva la luna. Tre composizioni corali: Cade la sera; Ululate; Recordare, Domine.
**(*) Chandos Dig. CHAN 8964 [id.]. Danish Nat. R. Chamber Ch., Stefan Parkman.

The Chandos issue has the merit of offering two other Pizzetti rarities in performances of high quality by the Danish Radio Chamber Choir, and there is no doubt that this is a most rewarding issue.

Murder in the Cathedral (Mord in der Kathedral) (complete).
(M) (**(*)) DG mono 457 671-2 (2). Hotter, Equiluz, Dermota, Stolze, Schöffler, Berry, Ludwig, V. State Op. Ch. & O, Karajan.

In 1960, during his controversial reign as music director of the Vienna State Opera, Karajan conducted Pizzetti's thoughtful adaptation of T. S. Eliot's play about Thomas à Becket, *Murder in the Cathedral*. This important première on disc offers an Austrian Radio recording in mono of a live performance using the German translation. The sound is limited, with the orchestra sounding rather thin, but the result is convincingly atmospheric, with the formalistic structure which Pizzetti took from Eliot compellingly conveyed. In an economically planned adaptation of the play, nicely tailored, the idiom is easily lyrical without using memorable melodic material, giving the impression of a pageant rather than an opera. The all-star cast helps to intensify Karajan's powerful, concentrated reading, with such fine singers as Christa Ludwig, Anton Dermota and Walter Berry in incidental roles, and with Hans Hotter outstanding in the title-role, strong and characterful, more smoothly lyrical than in Wagner.

Platti, Giovanni Benedetto (1697–1763)

Solo for oboe and continuo in C min.; Sonata for oboe, cello and continuo in G min.; Sonata in D for violin, oboe and continuo; Sonata a tre in G for violin or oboe, cello and continuo; Trio for flute, violin or oboe and continuo in G; Trio for oboe, bassoon obbligato and continuo in D min.
(N) *** Tactus Dig. TC 691601 [id.]. J. M. Anciuti Ens.

Giovanni Benedetto Platti was born in or near Padua, but in 1722 he left Italy for Germany and spent the rest of his life and career at the Court in Würzburg. He was prolific, and besides his vocal music he established a reputation with twelve harpsichord sonatas, published in Nuremberg between 1742 and 1746. This attractive collection of chamber sonatas reveals him as a musician of resource, skill and imagination. Where there is a choice in instrumentation, the excellent baroque oboeist Paollo Palastri, takes the lead, and a period bassoon (Alberto Santi) is used as the continuo in the *C minor* Solo as well as in the *Trio in D minor*. With the flute leading in the *Trio in G major*, there is plenty of colour, and as Platti's invention is always appealing – particularly the plaintive slow movements – this collection gives much pleasure. The recording is intimate and naturally balanced.

Pleyel, Ignaz (1757–1831)

(i) *Sinfonia concertante for violin, cello and strings in D. Symphony in A; Flute quartet in B.*
(B) ** Discover Dig. DICD 920130 [id.]. (i) Bushkov, Kozodov; Moscow Concertino (members), Evgueni Bushkov.

The name of Ignaz Pleyel is famous as a French manufacturer of pianos but, around the time that Haydn was visiting London for the Salomon concerts, Pleyel was far better known as a composer and his easily tuneful, facile music was enormously popular. His writing is a bit like Boccherini without the pathos. Here the *Flute quartet* (for flute, violin, viola and cello) has surface charm and the *Symphony* is fluent, if rather too long. The *Sinfonia concertante* – easily the best work here, and half as long as the *Symphony* – is full of neat invention and has an engaging finale. The whole programme is given persuasive advocacy by this excellent Russian group who are thoroughly within the style of the music and play with expert precision and much vitality. They are forwardly balanced and rather dryly recorded, and the dynamic contrast of their playing is reduced by the close microphones. Even so, this inexpensive disc gives a fascinating glimpse of an interesting and distinctly talented musician.

Ponce, Manuel (1882–1948)

Folia de España (Theme and variations with fugue).
(B) *** Sony SBK 47669 [id.]. John Williams (guitar) – BARRIOS: *Collection.* ***

Ponce's *Variations on 'Folia de España'* are subtle and haunting, and their surface charm often conceals a vein of richer, darker feeling. The performance is first rate and the sound admirably clean and finely detailed, yet at the same time warm.

Ponchielli, Amilcare (1834–86)

La Gioconda (complete).
*** Decca (IMS) Dig. 414 349-2 (3) [id.]. Caballé, Baltsa, Pavarotti, Milnes, Hodgson, L. Op. Ch., Nat. PO, Bartoletti.
*** EMI CDS5 56291-2 [CDCB 56291]. Callas, Cossotto, Ferraro, Vinco, Cappuccilli, Companeez, La Scala, Milan, Ch. & O, Votto.

The colourfully atmospheric melodrama of this opera gives the Decca engineers the chance to produce one of their most vivid opera recordings. Caballé is just a little overstressed in the title-role but produces glorious sounds. Pavarotti has impressive control and heroic tone. Commanding performances too from Milnes as Barnaba, Ghiaurov as Alvise and Baltsa as Laura, firm and intense all three. Bartoletti proves a vigorous and understanding conductor, presenting the blood and thunder with total commitment but finding the right charm in the most famous passage, the *Dance of the hours*.

Maria Callas gave one of her most vibrant, most compelling, most totally inspired performances on record in the title-role of *La Gioconda*, with flaws very much subdued. The challenge she presented to those around her is reflected in the soloists – Cossotto and Cappuccilli both at the very beginning of distinguished careers – as well as the distinctive tenor Ferraro and the conductor Votto, who has never done anything finer on record. The recording still sounds well, though it dates from 1959.

Popov, Gavril (1904–1972)

(i) *Symphonies Nos. 1, Op. 7;* (ii) *2 (Motherland), Op. 39.*
**(*) Olympia Dig./Analogue OCD 576 [id.]. (i) Moscow State SO; (ii) USSR R. & TV SO; Gennady Provatorov.

Along with Shostakovich, Prokofiev and Miaskovsky, Gavril Popov was singled out for condemnation at the Soviet composers' conference, presided over by Zhdanov in 1948. An accomplished all-round musician and a pupil of Vladimir Shcherbachov in Leningrad, Popov appeared as a pianist with Shostakovich in the Mozart *E flat Concerto*, K.365, and was a prolific composer for the cinema, providing music for 38 films, including some by Eisenstein. He gave us six symphonies in all, plus a good deal of chamber music as well as an opera on *Alexander Nevsky*. His *First Symphony* occupied him during 1928–34 and not long before the *Lady Macbeth* affair was denounced as formalistic and 'ideologically alien to Soviet order'. He had established himself sufficiently in early 1930s Germany with his *Septet* for Malko, Klemperer, Scherchen and Erich Kleiber to compete with one another for the first performance of the *First Symphony*. The first movement is over 20 minutes long, inventive and powerful, though indebted to Shostakovich, his junior by two years. The wartime *Second Symphony* (1943) opens with a long and expansive slow movement, not without overtones of the cinema, while the lively *Presto* sounds as if it has strayed out of *Petrushka*. Perhaps the most eloquent movement is the third, a soulful and powerfully sustained threnody. Small wonder Shostakovich admired his music, which is finely paced, expertly constructed and brilliantly scored. The performances under Gennady Provatorov are totally committed, though the recordings are not wholly satisfactory. The *First* was made in 1989 and is digital; the *Second* dates from 1961 and is perhaps a little shallow but perfectly acceptable. This should not, however, deter readers from investigating this interesting music which is every bit as rewarding as Vainberg, Kancheli and Schnittke – probably more so.

Porter, Cole (1891–1964)

Overtures: *Anything goes; Can-Can; Gay divorce; Kiss me, Kate. Night and day* (from *Gay divorce*).
(B) *** EMI forte Dig. CZS5 68589-2 [CDFB 68589] (2). L. Sinf., McGlinn – GERSHWIN: *Broadway and film music* **(*); KERN: *Overtures.* **

These overtures were not put together or scored by the composer but by the professionals of the day. As *Gay divorce* does not include the most famous number from the show, a separate arrangement of *Night and day* has been included, richly scored. The performances here are definitive and the bright recording fits the music like a glove.

Song arrangements for orchestra: *Anything goes; Begin the beguine; Blow, Gabriel blow; In the still of the night; It's de-lovely; I've got you under my skin; My heart belongs to Daddy; Night and day; It's all right with me; Ridin' high; So in love; You'd be so nice to come home too* (all orch. Ray Wright).
(M) **(*) Mercury (IMS) 434 327-2 [id.]. O,

Frederick Fennell – GERSHWIN: *Song arrangements*. **(*)

The lyrics are missed more than most with orchestral arrangements of Cole Porter songs and, though Ray Wright's scoring is imaginative and admirably sophisticated, this is essentially a CD to use as a pleasing background for a dinner party, rather than for concentrated listening. Unusually for this label, the recording is multi-miked, so the stereo effects are unashamedly directional. But the sound is silky-smooth as well as being clearly defined and, of its kind, this is very good indeed.

Kiss me Kate (musical).
*** EMI (SIS) Dig. CDS7 54033-2 (2). Barstow, Hampson, Criswell, Dvorsky, Burns, Evans, Amb. Ch., L. Sinf., John McGlinn.

Having two opera-singers, Josephine Barstow and Thomas Hampson, in the principal roles of the ever-argumentative husband-and-wife team who play Kate and Petruchio in *The Taming of the Shrew* works excellently, both strong and characterful. Kim Criswell is delectable as Lois Lane, brassy but not strident in *Always true to you, darling, in my fashion*. Strong characterization too from George Dvorsky, Damon Evans and Karla Burns, with the London Sinfonietta playing their hearts out. The recording is full and vivid with enough atmosphere to intensify the sense of presence.

Songs: *Begin the Beguine; Bring me back my butterfly; Bull Dog; Don't fence me in; Drink; Easy to love; A fool there was; How's your romance?; I concentrate on you; In the still of the night; It was written in the stars; I've got you under my skin; My cozy little corner in the Ritz; Night and day; Two little babes in the wood; When I had a uniform on; When my baby goes to town; Who said Gay Paree?*.
*** EMI Dig. CDC7 54203-2 [id.]. Thomas Hampson, Ambrosian Ch., LSO, McGlinn.

Thomas Hampson proves an ideal baritone for this repertory, totally inside the idiom, yet bringing to it a gloriously firm, finely controlled voice. The selection is a delightful one, including not just popular 'standards' but unexpected rarities. Excellent sound.

Let's do it; Miss Otis regrets; My heart belongs to Daddy; The physician; Night and day.
(*) Unicorn Dig. DKPCD 9138 [id.]. Jill Gomez, Martin Jones, Instrumental Ens. – BRITTEN: *Songs*. *

Though the accompanist, Martin Jones, is too stiff and deadpan in these five classic Cole Porter songs, Jill Gomez is so warmly expressive a singer that the dry backing serves to add to the poignancy of songs like 'Miss Otis Regrets'. Despite the reservations, a good coupling for the Britten items.

Poulenc, Francis (1899–1963)

EMI Centenary Edition Volume 1: Concertos, orchestral and sacred music: (i–iii) *Aubade (Concerto choréographique);* (ii; iii) *Les animaux modèles;* (iv; v; iii) *Les Biches* (ballet; complete); (iv; iii) *Bucolique;* (vi; ii; vii) *Concert champêtre (for harpsichord and orchestra);* (viii; ii; iii) *Concerto in G min. for organ, strings and timpani;* (i–iii) *Piano concerto in C sharp min.*; (ix; ii; vii) *Double piano concerto in D min.*; (x) *Gnossienne No. 3* (Satie, orch. Poulenc); (xi; iii) *2 Marches et un intermède (for chamber orchestra); Les mariés de la Tour Eiffel;* (iv; iii) *Matelote provençale*; *Pastourelle;* (xi; iii) *Suite française; Sinfonietta.* (Vocal): (xii) *Ave verum corpus; Exultate Deo;* (xiii; xiv; iii) *Gloria;* (xv) *Laudes de Saint Antoine de Padoue;* (xvi) *Litanies à la Vierge Noire;* (xvii) *Mass in G; 4 Motets pour le temps de Noël;* (xiv; xviii) *4 Motets pour un temps de pénitence;* (xix) *4 petites prières de Saint François d'Assise;* (xx; iii) *7 Répons des ténèbres*; (xii) *Salve Regina;* (xxi; ii; iii) *Stabat Mater*.
(N) (M) **(*) EMI stereo/mono Analogue/Dig. CMS5 66837-2 (5) [ZDME 66837-2]. (i) Tacchino; (ii) Paris Conservatoire O; (iii) Prêtre; (iv) Philh. O; (v) Ambrosian Singers; (vi) Van der Wiele; (vii) Dervaux; (viii) Duruflé; (ix) Février, composer; (x) Toulouse Capitole O, Plasson; (xi) O de Paris; (xii) Groupe Vocal de France, Alldis; (xiii) Cateri; (xiv) French R & TV Ch. & O; (xv) The Sixteen, Christophers; (xvi) French R. Children's Ch., Joineau; Roget; (xvii) Winchester Cathedral Ch., Neary; (xviii) Resnel; (xix) The King's Singers; (xx) Carpentier, Various Choirs, New PO of R France; (xxi) Crespin, René Duclos Ch.

Like most of the recordings in this EMI Centenary Edition, those of the orchestral and choral music are vintage versions, with Georges Prêtre the leading interpreter. The composer's own recording of the *Double piano concerto* with Jacques Fevrier goes back to 1957, a high-spirited account, at times unpolished; and so does the *Concert champêtre* with Aimée van der Wiele, made all the more effective thanks to a clangorous Pleyel harpsichord of the kind intended by the composer. The *Organ concerto*, with the original soloist, Maurice Duruflé, brings some suspect intonation, but the performance is lively and dramatic. *Les biches*, comes in the full ballet version with chorus, not the usual suite. Readers will note that this, and much of the other orchestral and concertante music are also available separately on the two-disc set below. In the religious music, the choral singing is variable, with the British choirs and groups generally setting a higher standard than the French, although the Groupe Vocal de

France under John Alldis is the exception. For all the unevenness and occasional roughness of sound, a valuable and enjoyable collection. As in the rest of the series, the five CDs come in stout cardboard inners within a stylish box. There are excellent notes, with original texts provided (in French or Latin), but no translations. At present the discs are not available separately.

EMI Centenary Edition, Volume 2: Chamber and piano music: (i; ii) *Bagatelle for violin and piano;* (ii; iii) *Cello sonata;* (ii; iv) *Clarinet sonata;* (iv; v) *Sonata for 2 clarinets*; (iv; vi) *Sonata for clarinet and bassoon;* (ii; vii) *Elégie for horn and piano;* (ii; viii) *Flute sonata;* (vii; ix) *Sonata for horn, trumpet & trombone;* (x) *3 Mouvements perpétuels for chamber ensemble;* (xi) *Sarabande for guitar;* (ii; xii) *Oboe sonata;* (ii; xiii) *Sextet for piano, flute, oboe, clarinet, bassoon & horn;* (xiv) *Suite française for cello and piano;* (ii; xv) *Trio for piano, oboe & bassoon;* (xvi) *Villanelle for flute and piano* (xvii) *Violin sonata*. Piano duet: (xviii; ii) *Capriccio; Elégie; L'embarquement pour Cythère; Sonata for piano, 4 hands; Sonata for 2 pianos*. Solo piano: (xviii) *Badinage; Bourrée au Pavillon d'Auvergne; 3 Feuillets d'album; Française; Humoresque; 5 Impromptus; 15 Improvisations; 3 Intermezzi; Mélancolle; Pastourelle;* 3 Mouvements perpétuels; (ii) *Napoli;* (xviii) *8 Nocturnes; 3 Novelettes; 3 Pièces; Pièce brêve; Presto in B flat; Promenades;* (ii) *Les soirées de Nazelles;* (xviii) *Suite française; Suite in C;* (ii) *Thème varié;* (xviii) *Valse in C; Valse improvisation; Villageoises.*

(N) (M) ** EMI Analogue/Dig. CMS5 66831-2 (5) [ZDME 66831]. (i) Grimal; (ii) Février; (iii) Fournier; (iv) Portal; (v) Gaal; (vi) Wallez; (vii) Civil; (viii) Debost; (ix) Wilbraham, Iveseon; (x) Members of O de la Garde Républicaine, F. Boulanger; (xi) Ghiglia; (xii) Bourgue; (xiii) Wind Ens.; (xiv) Phillips, Strosser; (xv) Casier, Faisandier; (xvi) Pottier, Strosser; (xvii) Zimmermann, Lonquich; (xviii) Tacchino.

This is a pretty comprehensive collection of Poulenc's chamber music, but not all the performances are equally distinguished. It is good to have Fournier's elegant account of the *Cello sonata* and Zimmermann's more recent one of the *Violin sonata*; Bourgue's performance of the *Oboe sonata* is also very enjoyable, and the other wind sonatas are effective enough, if less individual. Both the *Trio for piano, oboe and bassoon* and the *Sextet* are rather dryly recorded; however, although the playing could have more elegance, there is a high-spirited, knockabout quality here that is eminently likeable. The brass trio is one of the highlights, very entertainingly played and given good sound. Most of the recordings date from the 1970s but one or two are more modern. Jacques Février's pianism, both in the sonatas and the two-piano works, does not always have the finish such repertoire ideally demands. Tacchino's playing of the solo piano music is often technically brilliant and strongly characterized (perhaps at times a shade too strongly), but it does not have the degree of charm or the gamin quality which are ideally required. The recording too, closely balanced, is a bit hard and lacking bloom.

EMI Centenary Edition Volume 3: Mélodies and chansons: *Airs chantés; A se guitare; Banalités; Le Bestiare ou Cortège d'Orphée* (with unpublished supplement: *La Colombe; Le serpent; La Puce*). *Calligrammes* (cycle); *Bleuet; Ce doux petit visage; Chanson à boire; 3 Chansons de Federico Garcia Lorca; Chansons Gailliardes; 7 Chansons for mixed choir, a capella; 8 Chansons françaises; 8 Chansons polonaises;4 Chansons pour enfants; Un chanson de porcelaine; Chansons villageoises; Les Chemins de l'amour; Cocardes; Colloque; La Courte Paille* (cycle); *Dernier poème; Le disparu; Epitaphe; Fancy; Fiançailles pour rire; La Fraicheur et le feu* (cycle); *Le Grenouillière; Hymne; Main dominée par le coeur; Mazurka; 2 Mélodies: (Le souris; Nuage); 2 Mélodies de Guillaume Apollinaire; Métamorphoses; Miroirs brûlants; Nos souvenirs qui chantent; Paul et Virginie; Petites voix* (cycle); *Pierrot; 2 Poèmes de Guillaume Apollinaire* (2 sets); *4 Poèmes de Guillaume Apollinaire; 3 Poèmes de Louise Lalanne; 3 Poèmes de Louis de Vilmorin; 4 Poèmes de Max Jacob; 5 Poèmes de Max Jacob; 2 Poèmes de Louis Aragon; 5 Poèmes de Paul Eluard; 5 Poèmes de Pierre de Ronsard; Le portrait; Priez pour la paix; Rapsodie nègre; Rosamonde; Tel jour telle nuit* (cycle); *Toréador; La Travail du peintre* (cycle); *Vive Nadia; Vocalise.*

(N) (M) *** EMI stereo/mono Analogue/Dig. CMS5 66849-2 (5) [ZDME 66849]. Benoit, Rivenq, Fouchécourt, La Roux, Van Dam, Streich, Souzay, Ameling, Gedda, Mesplé, Bernac, Berton, Sénéchal, Parker, Bacquier, Norman, Develiereau, French Radio Children's Ch., Besson, The Sixteen, Christophers, Stockholm Chamber Ch., Erikson. Accompanists include Collard, Baldwin, Parsons, Tacchino, Francis Poulenc, Février.

A fine gallery of singers is presented here, in vintage performances covering the full span of Poulenc's work as a song composer, with his cabaret style happily set alongside deeper songs. There is an immense variety here and though there have been more refined performances on rival discs, there are none more idiomatic than these, with each singer characterizing vividly. Rita Streich, Jessye Norman and Elly Ameling are very well represented alongside native French singers ranging back to the composer's friend and associate, Pierre Bernac. The close-up sound, transferred with fine immediacy, hardly shows its age. Entirely new are the a cappella choral recordings, very well performed by the Sixteen and the Stockholm Chamber Choir. An indispensable collection.

EMI Centenary Edition, Volume 4: Vocal works ('*Oeuvres lyriques*'): (i) *Le Bal masqué;* (ii) *Les Chemins de l'amour;* (iii) *La Dame de Monte-Carlo;* (iv) *Dialogues des Carmélites;* (v) *Esquisse pour une fanfare;* (vi) *Figure humaine* (vii) *Le Gendarme incompris;* (viii) *L'Histoire de Babar le petit éléphant;* (ix) *L'Invitation au château;* (x) *Les Mamelles de Tiresias;* (xi) Sécheresses; (vi) *Un soir de neige;* (xii) *La voix humaine*.

(N) (M) (***) EMI mono/stereo Analogue/Dig. CMS5 66843-2 (5) [ZDME 66843]. (i) Benoit, Charpentier, Paris Conservatoire O (Soloists), Prêtre; (ii) Yvonne Printemps, O, Cariven; (iii) Mesplé, Monte-Carlo PO, Prêtre; (iv) Duval, Crespin, Scharley, Berton, Gorr, Depraz, Finel, Paris Op. O, Dervaux; (v) Toulouse O (members), Cardon; (vi) The Sixteen, Christophers; (vii) Rivenq, Fouchécourt, Benoit, Garde Républican Soloists' O, F. Boulanger; (viii) Peter Ustinov, Paris Conservatoire O, Prêtre; (ix) Strosse, Grimal, Guyot; (x) Duval, Giraudeau, Opéra-Comique Ch. & O, Cluytens; (xi) New O of R. France, Prêtre; (xii) Duval, Opéra-Comique, O, Prêtre.

Although not everything here has been satisfactorily re-recorded, and the vintage performances in this collection of Poulenc's stage works may not measure up to more recent rivals in opulence of recording, yet the immediacy, intensity and feeling for idiom have never been surpassed, and the singers are all well chosen, firm and true even in face of the close-up sound favoured by the French EMI engineers. So the *Dialogues des Carmelites*, much the longest work, lacks atmospheric beauty, but makes its dramatic point with overwhelming force, and Poulenc's favourite soprano, Denise Duval, could not be more characterful, both there and in *Les Mamelles de Tirésias* and *La voix humaine*. Peter Ustinov narrates the story of *Babar the elephant* charmingly in French. Totally new and beautifully done by the Sixteen under Harry Christopher, are the secular cantatas at the end, *Figure humaine* and *Un soir de neige*. Texts in French are provided but no translations.

ORCHESTRAL MUSIC

(i) *Les animaux modèles: suite;* (iii) *Aubade. La baigneuse de Trouville; Les Biches (ballet): suite. Les mariés de la Tour Eiffel: Discours du général. Matelote provençale* (from *La Guiriande de Campra). Pastourelle* (from *L'Eventail de Jeanne); 2 Préludes posthumes et une Gnossienne* (SATIE, orch. POULENC); *Valse;* (from Album des six) (452 937).

(i) *Bucolique; Fanfare; 2 Marches et un intermède; Pièce brève sur le nom d'Albert Roussel; Sinfonietta; Suite française;* (iii) *Concert champêtre* (for harpsichord and orchestra) ✽ (452 665).

(ii; iv) *Concerto in G min. for organ, strings and timpani;* (ii; iii) *Piano concerto;* (ii; iii; v) *Double piano concerto in D min.* (436 546).

Complete Orchestral music and concertos (as above).

(N) (M) *** Decca Dig. 460 597-2 (3) [id.]. (CDs available separately). (i) O Nat. de France, or (ii) Phil.O; Dutoit; with (iii) Pascal Rogé (piano or harpsichord); (iv) Peter Hurford; (v) Sylvianne Deferne.

This Decca set makes a clear first choice for those wanting a complete survey of Poulenc's concertante and orchestral works. The box comes at mid-price, but the discs are available separately (at premium price) for those wanting to fill in gaps in a collection. The first disc is new and well up to the standard of the others, with the *Aubade* particularly delightful, and the richly coloured orchestral arrangement of Satie's *Gnossiennes* ending the disc magnetically. The only slight proviso concerns the suite from *Les Biches*. It is a pity the complete ballet was not chosen (as on the EMI Rouge et Noir set below). Dutoit readily catches the music's languid warmth and veiled eroticism, notably in the beautiful *Adagietto*, but the opening *Rondeau*, with its pert, jazzy trumpet solo, might have had more bite, partly the fault of the warm resonance of the recording.

The major works on the second disc (to which we awarded a ✽ on its first issue) are the *Sinfonietta*, which comes off marvellously and the *Concert champêtre*, where Pascal Rogé proves as fine a clavecinist as pianist and his account, equally strong on charm and elegance, ranks very highly indeed. The smaller pieces greatly enhance the already strong attractions of this disc. The excellence of the performances is matched by first-rate and meticulously balanced Decca sound.

Rogé's playing in the third collection, (the first to be issued, in 1993), is hardly less captivating, so it will be no surprise that his accounts of the *Piano concerto* (with its moments of tenderness and gamin-like *joie de vivre*) and the delightful D minor *Concerto for two pianos* (partnered by Silvia Deferne) are completely attuned to the sensibility and spirit of this still underrated master. One of Poulenc's most extraordinary qualities is his ability to effect an abrupt change of mood from the highest of spirits to a sudden glimpse of melancholy and desolation, which is mirrored here. Hurford is hardly less successful in the *Organ concerto* and the Philharmonia Orchestra produces a cultivated sound for Dutoit, marginally less characterful and idiomatic perhaps than the French Orchestra on the companion discs, but warmly elegant. The recording is excellent.

(i) *Les animaux modèles;* (ii; iii) *Les Biches* (complete ballet); (ii) *Bucolique;* (i; iv) *Concert champêtre (for harpsichord & orchestra);* (i; v) *Double piano concerto in D min.;* (vi) *2 Marches et un intermède (for chamber orchestra); Les mariés de la Tour Eiffel (La baigneuse de Trouville; Discourse du Général);* (ii) *Matelote provençale; Pastourelle;* (vi) *Sinfonietta; Suite française.*

(B) *** EMI Rouge et Noir Analogue/Dig. CZS5 69446-2 (2). (i) Paris Conservatoire O; or (ii) Philh. O; (iii) with Amb. S.; (iv) with Van de Wiele, or (v) composer and Février; (vi) O de Paris; all cond. Prêtre.

Les Biches comes here in its complete form, with the choral additions that Poulenc made optional when he came to rework the score. The music is a delight, and so too is the group of captivating short pieces, digitally recorded at the same time (1980): *Bucolique*, *Pastourelle* and *Matelote provençale*. High-spirited, fresh, elegant playing and sumptuous recorded sound enhance the claims of all this music. The *Suite française* is another highlight. It is well played and recorded in a pleasing, open acoustic. Poulenc himself was a pianist of limited accomplishment, but his interpretation with Jacques Février of his own skittish *Double concerto* is infectiously jolly. In the imitation pastoral concerto for harpsichord, Aimée van de Wiele is a nimble soloist, but here Prêtre's inflexibility as a conductor comes out the more, even though the finale has plenty of high spirits. The *Sinfonietta*, too, could have a lighter touch. *Les animaux modèles* is based on the fables of La Fontaine, with a prelude and a postlude, but here the recording is rather lacking in bloom, and the *Deux Marches* are also a trifle overbright. With nearly 156 minutes' playing time, these CDs are well worth exploring.

(i) *Aubade (Concerto choréographique);* (ii) *Concert champêtre for harpsichord and orchestra;* (iii) *Organ concerto in G min.;* (i) *Piano concerto in C sharp min.;* (i; iv) *Double piano concerto in D min.*

(B) *** Erato/Warner Ultima 3984 21342-2 (2). Rotterdam PO, James Conlon; with (i) Duchable; (ii) Koopman; (iii) Alain; (iv) Collard.

The Erato Ultima Double is one of the most attractive of all Poulenc issues. The *Aubade* is an exhilarating work of great charm. It dates from the late 1920s and is a send-up of Mozart, Stravinsky etc. The *Piano concerto* has a most beguiling opening theme and evokes the faded charms of Paris in the 1930s. The performances of two of the solo works by François-René Duchable and the Rotterdam orchestra have a certain panache and flair that are most winning. The *Double concerto* too captures all the wit and charm of the Poulenc score, and the 'mock Mozart' slow movement is particularly elegant. Perhaps in these two solo works Duchable is a shade too prominent, but not sufficiently so to disturb a strong recommendation, for the sound is otherwise full and pleasing. The *Organ concerto*, too, has never come off better on record than in Marie-Claire Alain's performance using the excellent Flenthrop organ in Rotterdam's concert hall, the Doelen. The *Concert champêtre* always offers problems of balance as it is scored for a full orchestra, but the exaggerated contrast was clearly intended by the composer. The performance is most perceptive, with a particularly elegant and sparkling finale. James Conlon provides admirable accompaniments throughout a highly recommendable pair of discs.

(i) *Aubade;* (ii) *Double piano concerto in D min.; Sinfonietta.*

*** Virgin/EMI VCS5 45028-2. (i–ii) Jean-Bernard Pommier, with (ii) Anne Queffélec; City of London Sinf., Richard Hickox.

Jean-Bernard Pommier gives a thoroughly idiomatic and incisive account of the *Aubade*, and both he and Anne Queffélec play the *Concerto for two pianos* to the manner born. They have the measure of the pastiche Mozart slow movement and the quasi-Gamelan first. Good though the Duchable–Collard performance is, this has the better recording. Hickox gives an affectionate and charming account of the *Sinfonietta* that matches – almost – the splendid account from the Orchestre National under Dutoit. Very recommendable.

Aubade; Sinfonietta.

*** Hyperion Dig. CDA 66347 [id.]. New London O, Corp – HAHN: *Le bal de Béatrice d'Este.* ***

The *Sinfonietta* is a fluent and effortless piece, full of resource and imagination, and Ronald Corp and the New London Orchestra do it proud. Julian Evans is an alert soloist in the *Aubade*: his is a performance of real character and, though less well balanced than the *Sinfonietta*, his account can hold its own artistically with the competition. The Hahn rarity with which it is coupled enhances the interest and value of this release.

Les Biches (ballet suite).

*** Chandos Dig. CHAN 9023 [id.]. Ulster O, Yan Pascal Tortelier – IBERT: *Divertissement*; MILHAUD: *Le bœuf; La création.* ***

(M) *** EMI (SIS) CDM7 63945-2. Paris Conservatoire O, Prêtre – DUTILLEUX: *Le Loup;* MILHAUD: *Création du Monde.* ***

Yan Pascal Tortelier and the Ulster Orchestra give an entirely winning account of Poulenc's ballet suite. Here the opening has delightfully keen rhythmic wit, and the playing is equally polished and crisply articulated in the gay *Rag-Mazurka* and infectious *Final*. The lovely *Adagietto* is introduced with tender delicacy, yet reaches a suitably plangent climax. Top-drawer Chandos sound and splendid couplings ensure the overall success of this admirable compilation.

Prêtre has re-recorded *Les Biches* digitally in its complete format (see above). This 1961 recording of the suite, omitting the chorus, is well worth having in its own right: the racy style of the orchestral playing is instantly infectious in the opening *Rondeau* with its catchy trumpet solo. The remastered sound-picture is much better focused than in its old LP format; and this is one example where the bright vividness of CD is entirely advantageous, for there is just the right degree of ambient atmosphere. With excellent couplings this is a most desirable triptych.

Concert champêtre (for harpsichord); *Concerto in G min. for organ, strings and timpani.*

(B) *** EMI forte CZS5 69752-2 (2) [CDFB 69752]. Simon Preston, LSO, Previn – MESSIAEN: *Turangalîla Symphony.* ***

On EMI forte each of the recordings is realistically balanced, and Simon Preston, who plays the solo parts in both concertos produces readings of great fluency and authority, to say nothing of wit in the work for harpsichord. Previn too has a genuine feeling for the music: the orchestral playing is always musical, often sparkling, and the recording is first class. It set new standards in its day (1977).

Concerto in G min. for organ, strings and timpani.

(*) Chandos Dig. CHAN 9271 [id.]. Ian Tracey (organ of Liverpool Cathedral), BBC PO, Yan Pascal Tortelier – GUILMANT: *Symphony No. 1;* WIDOR: *Symphony No. 5.* *

The wide reverberation period of Liverpool Cathedral produces gloriously plushy textures (the orchestra strings are radiantly rich in colour) but little plangent bite, and some may feel that the effect is too overwhelmingly sumptuous for Poulenc's *Concerto*. Yet it is easy to wallow in the gloriously full sounds, and the performance itself, spacious to allow for the resonance, is certainly enjoyable.

Double piano concerto in D min.

(M) *** Teldec/Warner Dig. 4509 97445-2 [id.]. Güher and Süher Pekinel, French R. PO, Janowski – SAINT-SAENS: *Carnival of the animals.* ***

The Pekinel Duo come from mixed Spanish/Turkish parentage and their account of Poulenc's *Double concerto* is given with great dash and sparkle. Janowski provides a lively and thoroughly supportive accompaniment, and the recording balance is excellent. But even at mid-price 38 minutes is short measure even if the Saint-Saëns zoological fantasy is equally enticing and attractive disc.

The story of Babar the elephant (orch. Jean Françaix).

✿ (BB) *** Naxos Dig. 8.554170 [id.]. Barry Humphries, Melbourne SO, John Lanchbery – BRITTEN: *Young person's guide to the orchestra*; PROKOFIEV: *Peter and the wolf.* ***

Barry Humphries adopts an engagingly cultivated male persona to tell *The story of Babar* with an elegance and a sense of innocence which make the narrative seem completely believable, within a children's world where elephants can assume human vanities and aspirations. He is genial, gently touching and animated by turns, but always stylish; and so is Lanchbery's matching orchestral accompaniment, which catches the moments of nostalgia and joy with equal sensitivity and flair. The dance after the wedding (in Jean Françaix's uninhibited scoring) momentarily recalls *Les Biches*. The effect here is infinitely more involving than the composer's rather bald, original piano version. Jean de Brunhoff's tale has never been presented more effectively on record, or better recorded. A delight and very highly recommended, as the couplings are first rate too.

Suite française.

(M) *** ASV CDWHL 2067. L. Wind O, Wick – GRAINGER: *Irish tune from County Derry* etc.; MILHAUD: *Suite française.* ***

This engaging suite is based on themes by the sixteenth-century composer, Claude Gervaise. Poulenc scored them for a small ensemble of wind instruments and they come up very freshly in these artists' hands. Excellent recording and couplings. Thoroughly recommended.

CHAMBER MUSIC

(i) *Elégie for horn and piano;* (ii) *Violin sonata;* Music for 2 pianos: *Le Bal masqué (Capriccio); Elégie; L'Embarquement pour Cythère; Sonata; Sonata for piano* (4 hands).

*** Decca Dig. 443 968-2. (i) Cazalet; (ii) Juillet; Rogé, Collard.

Poulenc has the capacity to charm and enchant. His lightness of touch and elegance often mask a vein of deeper feeling into which he can briefly move to striking and original effect. No one is more closely attuned to Poulenc's world than Pascal Rogé, and his presence ensures the authenticity of feeling that distinguished his earlier Poulenc. His masterly compatriot, Jean-Philippe Collard, is no less superb. In the *Elégie* for horn, written in memory of Dennis Brain, André Cazalet is an eloquent player and so, too, is Chantal Juillet in the *Violin sonata*. An outstanding issue.

(i) *L'invitation au château (for clarinet, violin & piano);* (ii) *Mouvements perpétuels for flute, oboe, clarinet, bassoon, horn, violin, viola, cello & bass;* (iii) *Rapsodie nègre for flute, clarinet, string quartet, baritone & piano;* (iv) *Sextet for flute, oboe, clarinet, bassoon, horn & piano;* (v) *Sonata for clarinet; Sonata for clarinet & bassoon;* (vi) *Sonata for 2 clarinets;* (vii) *Sonata for flute and piano;* (viii) *Oboe sonata;* (ix) *Trio for oboe, bassoon & piano;* (x) *Villanelle for piccolo & piano.*

(B) *** Cala Dig. CACD 1018 (2) [id.]. (i–vi) James Campbell; (i–ii) Peter Carter; (i) John York; (ii–iv; vii; x) William Bennett; (ii; iv; viii; ix) Nicholas Daniel; (ii; iv–v; ix) Rachel Gough; (ii; iv) Richard Watkins; (ii) Roger Tapping, Bruno Schrecker, Chris West; (iii) Allegri Qt (Peter Carter, David Roth, Roger Tapping, Bruno Schrecker), Peter Sidhom; (iii; viii–ix) Julius Drake; (iv; vii; x) Clifford Benson; (vi) David Campbell – RAVEL: *Introduction and allegro* etc. ***

These Cala discs are a terrific bargain. The Poulenc accounts for the bulk of the two CDs (two hours' music in fact), all of it full of sparkle and freshness of invention. The discs comprise the complete chamber music for woodwind by Ravel and Poulenc, with the exception of works written primarily for the voice. The performances have great elegance and finesse. There are rarities, such as the *Rapsodie nègre* and *L'invitation au château* for clarinet, violin and piano which Cala claim as a first recording. Poulenc has this rare gift of being able to move from the most flippant high spirits to the deepest poignancy, as in the *Oboe sonata*, expressively played by Nicholas Daniel. His pianist, Julius Drake, is highly sensitive, though the piano is not always ideally focused in the excessively resonant acoustic. Elsewhere, in the captivating incidental music to a play by Jean Cocteau and Raymond Radiguet, *L'invitation au château*, the playing is expert, tasteful and stylish. The *Mouvements perpétuels*, the *Sextet* and the various wind sonatas are beautifully played with great relish and spirit. This is a most attractive set, which deserves the widest dissemination. Had the piano been as well balanced as it is played, this would have earned a Rosette.

Sextet (for piano and wind).

(M) *** Chandos CHAN 6543 [id.]. Ian Brown, Athena Ens. – GOUNOD: *Petite symphonie in B flat;* IBERT: *3 Pièces brèves*. ***

From Ian Brown and the Athena Ensemble a bravura and responsive performance of Poulenc's many-faceted *Sextet*, catching its high spirits as well as its wit, and the gentle melancholy which intervenes at the close of the boisterous finale. The recording is excellent, slightly dry, yet with a nice ambience. Even though the programme is short measure, every minute is enjoyable.

Sextet for piano & wind; Trio for piano, oboe & bassoon; (i) *Le Bal masqué; Le Bestiaire.*

*** CRD Dig. CRD 3437; *CRDC 4137* [id.]. (i) Thomas Allen; Nash Ens., Lionel Friend.

Thomas Allen is in excellent voice and gives a splendid account of both *Le Bal masqué* and *Le Bestiaire*. The Nash play both the *Trio* and the *Sextet* with superb zest and character. The wit of this playing and the enormous resource, good humour and charm of Poulenc's music are well served by a recording of exemplary quality and definition. Not to be missed.

(i) *3 Mouvements perpétuels;* (ii) *Le Bal masqué;* (iii) *Le Bestiare; Cocarde;* (iv) *Le Gendarme incompris;* (iii) *4 Poèmes de Max Jacob;* (ii) *Rapsodie nègre (1919).*

*** Decca Dig. 452 666-2 [id.]. (i–ii) Pascal Rogé; Fr. Nat. O (members); (ii–iv) François Le Roux; (iv) Dominique Visse, Lambert Wilson; Charles Dutoit.

An engaging and charming addition to the growing representation of Poulenc in the Decca catalogue. Most of these pieces are early (1917–21) settings of Apollinaire, Cocteau and Max Jacob and are offered together with the later, better-known and always captivating *Le Bal masqué*. Such was the popularity of the *Trois Mouvements perpétuels* that Poulenc orchestrated them in 1925 and made a second arrangement for nine instruments, as offered here. *Le Bestiare* is recorded in its original form for baritone and a small instrumental ensemble without piano. This is one of the few pieces on this CD in which Pascal Rogé does not participate. *Le Gendarme incompris* ('The misunderstood policeman') is a spoken entertainment, a *comédie-bouffe*, lasting about 20 minutes, a curtain-raiser interspersed with some songs for boarding schools to words by Cocteau and Raymond Radiguet (1903–23). As always with Poulenc there is a lot of charm, but an undercurrent of deeper feeling too. Elegant and polished performances, expertly balanced by the Decca engineers.

Violin sonata.

(B) *** EMI Eminence CD-EMX 2244 [(M) id. import]. Tasmin Little, Piers Lane – DEBUSSY: *Violin sonata*; RAVEL: *Violin sonata; Tzigane.* ***

*** Sony Dig. SK 66839 [id.]. Cho-Liang Lin, Paul Crossley – DEBUSSY: *Violin sonata;* RAVEL: *Violin sonatas & Tzigane.* ***

In this well-designed collection of violin-and-piano music, Tasmin Little and Piers Lane give outstanding performances, very well recorded, aptly and subtly changing style for each composer, as here in Poulenc's *Sonata*, longer but generally lighter in tone than the other works included. In the slow movement Little produces her sweetest, warmest tone, and she relishes the virtuoso demands of the *Moto perpetuo* finale.

Cho-Liang Lin and Paul Crossley give a vibrant, well-argued account of Poulenc's characterful and pungent *Sonata*, to which Sony accord excellent recording. Apart from Tasmin Little, the main rivals are Chantal Juillet and Pascal Rogé (see above), and there is a spirited bargain challenge from Dong-Suk Kang and Pascal Devoyon on Naxos (8.550276 – see Instrumental Recitals, below). However, this present issue has much going for it: apart from the quality of the playing and the exemplary recorded sound, there is the generous programme on offer.

PIANO MUSIC

Piano duet

Capriccio; Elégie; L'embarquement pour Cythère; Sonata for piano, four hands; Sonata for two pianos.
*** Chandos Dig. CHAN 8519 [id.]. Seta Tanyel, Jeremy Brown.

These two artists have a very close rapport and dispatch this repertoire with both character and sensitivity. The Chandos recording is excellent, very vivid and present.

Solo piano music

Complete piano music (as listed on the three CDs below).
(N) ✽ (M) *** Decca Dig.460 598-2 (3) [id.]. Pascal Rogé.

Pascal Rogé's survey is of the highest calibre and is surely unsurpassable, for the Decca recording is fully worthy of the playing. The three CDs listed below remain available separately but are offered in a medium-priced box, to which we have transferred the ✽ originally awarded to the first disc.

Badinage; Bourrée, au Pavillon d'Auverge; Feuillets d'album; Française d'après Claude Gervaise; 5 Impromptus; Mélancolie; Napoli; 3 Pastorales; Pièce brève sur le nom d'Albert Roussel; Promenades; Suite française d'après Claude Gervaise; Valse-improvisation sur le nom de Bach.
(N) *** Decca Dig. 460 329-2 [id.]. Pascal Rogé.

This CD (72 minutes) completes Rogé's distinguished coverage of Poulenc's piano music, and it is just as delightful and wide-ranging in mood as its two companions. Who but Poulenc would have written a frivolous *Valse-improvisation* to celebrate the name of B-A-C-H, and his light-hearted manner is equally felicitous in the delicious *Third Impromptu* or the gentle melancholy of *Badinage*. But he is perhaps at his most touching in his suite of pieces paying a tribute to Claude Gervaise, which is thoroughly imbued with personal nostagia. As before, Rogé is beautifully recorded.

Humoresque; Improvisations Nos. 4, 5, 9–11 & 14; 2 Intermezzi; Intermezzo in A flat; Nocturnes; Presto in B flat; Suite; Thème varié; Villageoises.
*** Decca (IMS) Dig. 425 862-2 [id.]. Pascal Rogé.

Pascal Rogé's second Poulenc recital is every bit as captivating as his earlier disc (see below). The acoustic is somewhat reverberant but not excessively so. Elegant playing, responsive to all the rapidly changing shifts of tone in Poulenc's music, and strongly recommended.

Improvisations Nos. 1–3; 6–8; 12–13; 15; Mouvements perpétuels; 3 Novelettes; Pastourelle; 3 Pièces; Les soirées de Nazelles; Valse.
*** Decca Dig. 417 438-2 [id.]. Pascal Rogé.

This music is absolutely enchanting, full of delight and wisdom; it has many unexpected touches and is teeming with character. Rogé is a far more persuasive exponent of it than any previous pianist on record; his playing is imaginative and inspiriting, and the recording is superb.

Badinage; Les Biches: Adagietto; Intermezzo No. 3 in A flat; 3 Mouvements perpétuels; Napoli; 3 Pièces; Les soirées de Nazelles; Suite in C; Valse-improvisation sur le nom de Bach.
*** Chandos Dig. CHAN 8637 [id.]. Eric Parkin.

Humoresque; 15 Improvisations; Intermezzi Nos. 1 in C; 2 in D flat; Mélancolie; 3 Novelettes; Presto in B flat; Suite française d'après Claude Gervaise; Thème varié; Villageoises (Petites pièces enfantines).
*** Chandos Dig. CHAN 8847 [id.]. Eric Parkin.

Eric Parkin is an artist of instinctive taste and a refined musical intelligence who is completely inside this idiom: he has plenty of spirit and character and abundant sensitivity. Perhaps Rogé has the greater pianistic finesse plus a gamin-like charm, but Parkin too has charm and, in many of the pieces where they overlap, there is often little to choose between them. The Chandos recording is rather more resonant, though not unacceptably so.

CHORAL MUSIC

Ave verum corpus; Exsultate Deo; Laudes de Saint-Antoine de Padoue; (i) *Litanies à la Vierge Noire; 4 Motets pour le temps de Noël; 4 Motets pour le temps de pénitence; Salve Regina.*

(M) *** EMI CDM5 65156-2. Groupe Vocale de France, John Alldis; (i) with Marie-Claire Alain.

An outstanding collection. This is music that ideally needs French voices, and John Alldis has trained his French group splendidly so that they combine precision and fervour with a natural feeling for the words. The soaring *Ave verum* is matched by the exhilaration of the *Exsultate Deo* and the originality of the *Litanies* with its stabbing bursts of organ tone. The *Salve Regina* is very fine too, and the four *Christmas motets* have the right extrovert joyfulness and sense of wonder. The recording is made within an ecclesiastical ambience, yet definition is admirable.

(i) *Figure humaine*; (ii) *Laudes de Saint Antoine de Padoue*; (i) *Mass in G*; (ii) *4 Motets pour un temps de Pénitence*; (i) *Petites prières de Saint Françoise d'Assise*; (iii) *La Voix humaine*.

(N) (B) *** Erato/Warner Ultima Analogue/ Dig. 3984 25598-2 (2) [id.]. (i) Marianne Mellnäs, Thomas Sunnegärdh, Uppsala Academic Chaber Ch., Kfum Chamber Ch., Olo Stenlund; (ii) Jocelyn Chamonin, Stéphane Caillat, Vocal Ens., Caillat; (iii) Julia Migenes, O. Nat de France, Prêtre.

Figure humaine is a wartime work, written during the occupation to words of Paul Eluard. It is perhaps Poulenc's most substantial and deeply felt work in this medium and these Swedish forces convey its eloquence to good effect. The pre-war *Mass in G major* is less intense but contains a moving soprano solo, which is beautifully done here. The four male-voiced *Prières* are post-war and are effectively projected by these fine Uppsala singers. For this reissue the more familiar *Laudes* and *Motets* have been added in ardent and idiomatic accounts from the Stéphane Caillat Ensemble. Good atmospheric analogue sound throughout.

The second CD contains Julia Migenes's rivetingly dramatic and very moving performance of Poulenc's theatrical telephone monologue, *La voix humaine*, a setting of Cocteau. She conveys the utter despair of a woman brought to the verge of suicide by the desertion of her lover, at first pathetically hoping he will call her back, and the final hopeless resignation. The lyrical writing is both Puccinian but Ravelian too in its moments of tenderness. Prêtre holds the piece together admirably, but then he conducted the work's première. The digital sound could not be more vivid. This is the finest modern version on record so this Ultima Double is surely one of the most important bargain reissues made for the centenary.

Figure humaine; Laudes de Saint Antoine de Padoue; 4 Motets pour le temps de Noël; 4 Motets pour un temps de pénitence; 4 Petites prières de Saint François d'Assise.

*** Virgin/EMI (SIS) Dig. VC7 59192-2. The Sixteen, Harry Christophers.

A lovely record which assembles the cantata for double choir, *Figure humaine*, with some of the composer's most celebrated *a cappella* motets. These performances can be recommended strongly, both on artistic grounds and for the excellence of the sound.

Gloria.

(B) *** Decca Eclipse 448 711-2. Greenberg, SRO Ch., Lausanne Pro Arte Ch., SRO, López-Cobos – DURUFLE: *Requiem;* FAURE: Pavane. ***

(M) *** Sony SMK 47569 [id.]. Judith Blegen, Westminster Ch., NYPO, Bernstein – JANACEK: *Glagolitic Mass.* ***

The *Gloria* is one of Poulenc's last compositions and is among his most successful. López-Cobos gives a fine account, expansive yet underlining the Stravinskian elements in the score. The recording is first class, full-bodied and with clean definition.

Bernstein produces a vividly etched and clean-textured account which makes excellent sense in every way and is free from excessive sentiment. Judith Blegen is an appealing soloist, and the 1976 recording, made in New York's Manhattan Center, though not the last word in refinement, is clear, well detailed and spacious. With its vibrant Janáček coupling, this is one of the most attractive reissues in the Bernstein Edition.

(i; ii) *Gloria; Ave verum corpus; Exsultate Deo;* (ii) *Litanies à la Vierge Noire; 4 Motets pour le temps de Noël; 4 Motets pour un temps de pénitence; Salve regina.*

*** Coll. COLCD 108. (i) Donna Deam, Cambridge Singers; (ii) City of L. Sinfonia, John Rutter.

A generous selection of Poulenc's choral music, much of it of great beauty and simplicity, in very fresh-sounding performances and well-focused sound.

Mass in G; 4 petites prières de Saint François d'Assise; Salve Regina.

*** Nimbus Dig. NI 5197 [id.]. Christ Church Cathedral Ch., Oxford, Stephen Darlington – MARTIN: *Mass for double choir*. **(*)

The *Mass in G* is a work of strong appeal and greater dramatic fire than the *Salve Regina* or the more intimate *Quatre petites prières de Saint François d'Assise* for men's voices. The choir of Christ Church Cathedral, Oxford, under Stephen Darlington sing with clean tone and excellent balance, and the Nimbus recording is very good indeed.

(i) *Mass in G. Exsultate Deo;* (ii) *Litanies à la Vierge Noire. Salve Regina.*

(B) *** Double Decca 436 486-2 (2) [id.].

St John's College, Cambridge, Ch., Guest; (i) with Jonathon Bond; (ii) Stephen Cleobury – FAURE; DURUFLE: *Requiems*. ***

As an extraordinarily generous bonus for the two great *Requiems* of Fauré and Duruflé, this Double Decca set offers the Poulenc *Mass in G* together with two motets, *Exsultate Deo* and *Salve Regina*, finely wrought pieces in performances of great finish. Then, together with Stephen Cleobury, they give us the cool, gently dissonant *Litanies à la Vierge Noire*, a dialogue between voices and organ in which the voices eventually take dominance. It is beautifully done and the St John's College forces cope with the delicacy and sweetness of Poulenc's chromatic harmony throughout. The (originally Argo) recording is eminently realistic and truthful.

Stabat Mater; Litanies à la Vierge Noire; Salve Regina.
*** HM Dig. HMC 905149 [id.]. Lagrange, Lyon Nat. Ch. and O, Baudo.

In the *Stabat Mater* Serge Baudo certainly makes the most of expressive and dynamic nuances; he shapes the work with fine feeling and gets good singing from the Lyon Chorus. Michèle Lagrange has a good voice and is an eminently expressive soloist. The coupling offers the short *Salve Regina* and the *Litanies à la Vierge Noire*, an earlier and somewhat more severe work.

SONGS

Mélodies: *Airs chantés; Bleuet; La Courte Paille; Fancy; La grenouillère; Montparnasse; Monsieur Sans-Souci, il fait tout lui-même; Nous voulons une petite soeur; Le petit garçon trop bien portant; 2 Poèmes de Louis Aragon; 3 Poèmes de Louise Lalanne; 5 Poèmes de Max Jacob; Le portrait; Priez pour paix; Toréador; La tragique histoire du petit René.*
(N) *** Decca Dig. 458 859-2 [id.]. Felicity Lott, Pascal Rogé.

Felicity Lott is a stylist par excellence and her sympathy for and affinity with the songs of Poulenc is long standing. This recital with Pascal Rogé whose understanding of this repertoire is *sans pareil* centres on the theme of childhood, and range from *La courte paille* – written for Denise Duval, Poulenc's favourite soprano, to sing for her young son – and the *Cinq poèmes de Max Jacob* which evoke childhood memories of Brittany. Dame Felicity is in excellent form throughout and brings the right blend of feeling and style to everything here. *Hier*, the third of the *Trois poèmes de Louise Lalanne*, is marvellously characterized and quite haunting. Excellent recording.

Mélodies: *Allons plus vite; Banalités; Le Bestiaire; Ce doux petit visage; Chansons gaillardes; Les Chemins de l'amour; Colloque; Fiançailles pour rire; Hyde Park; Main dominée par le cœur; Métamorphoses; 3 Poèmes de Louise de Vilmorin; La Souris; Tu vois le feu du soir.*
(N) **(*) Decca Dig. 436 991-2 [id.]. Catherine Dubosc, Gilles Cachemaille, Pascal Rogé.

Catherine Dubosc was a memorable Blanche in the *Dialogues des Carmélites* and is thoroughly at home in the Poulenc idiom. She is perhaps less successful in varying the character of each song (her approach tends to very different moods tends to be a little uniform). Like her fellow artist, the baritone Gilles Cachemaille, she is rather forwardly balanced. Pascal Rogé is his impeccable self in this repertoire. Recommended, if with less enthusiasm than its companion listed above. Both are included in the four-disc set of Poulenc's songs on Decca 460 599-2 (below).

Mélodies: Disc 1: *A sa guitare; Le bestiaire (unpublished): La colombe; La puce; Le serpent. Calligrammes; Une chanson de porcelaine; Cocardes; 2 Poèmes de Guillaume Apollinaire; Poèmes de Ronsard; Tel jour telle nuit; Le travail du peintre; Vive Nadia* (460 327). Disc 2: *3 Chansons de F. Garcia-Lorca; Epitaphe; Mazurka; Paul et Virginie; Pierrot; 5 Poèmes de Paul Eluard; Chansons villageoises; Dernier poème; Le disparu; Le fraîcheur et le feu; Hymne; ... mais mourir; Nuage; Parisiana; 2 Poèmes de Guillaume Apollinaire; 4 Poèmes de Guillaume Apollinaire; Rosemonde;* (v) *8 Chansons polonaises* (460 328). *Melodies.*
(N) **(*) Decca 460 326-2 (2) [id.]. François Le Roux, Gilles Cachemaille, Urszula Kryger, Pascal Rogé.

This two-disc collection, most sensitively sung by fine French singers of today, concentrates on cycles and sequences of Poulenc songs, mainly from the later years of his life. Francois le Roux, a high baritone who can cope with the demanding tessitura of the songs written for the composer's friend, Pierre Bernac, takes on the major share, including all the songs on the first disc – notably the fine cycle, *Tel jour, telle nuit*. He also sings superbly the three extra songs for *Le bestiaire*, only recently published. On the second disc, Gilles Cachemaille, a warmer but less versatile baritone and Urszula Kryger provide contrast in an equally varied selection. Throughout the series Pascal Rogé is the intensely poetic accompanist.

Complete Mélodies (as above)
(N) (M) *** Decca Dig. 460 599-2 (4) [id.]. (CDs available separately as above). Lott, Dubosc, Kryger, Le Roux, Cachemaille, Rogé.

At mid-price, this collection repackages Decca's four discs of Poulenc songs accompanied by the ever-sensitive Pascal Rogé. For those who insist on fine modern recording, this provides consistently refined and idiomatic performances, making it an ideal alternative to the EMI collection of vintage recordings also issued to celebrate the Poulenc centenary (see above). If the EMI set offers even more characterful performances, the results here with only five specialist singers are more consistent.

Mélodies: *Banalités: Hôtel; Voyage à Paris. Bleuet. C; Calligrammes: Voyage. 4 Chansons pour enfants: Nous voulons une petite soeur. Les chemins de l'amour. Colloque; Hyde Park; Métamorphoses; Miroirs brûlants: Tu vois le feu du soir. Montparnasse; 2 Poèmes de Louis Aragon; 3 Poèmes de Louise Lalanne; Priez pour paix; Tel jour, telle nuit; Toréador.*
*** Hyperion Dig. CDA 66147 [id.]. Songmakers' Almanac: Lott, Rolfe Johnson, Murray, Johnson.

Felicity Lott sings the great majority of the songs here, joyful and tender, comic and tragic by turns. The other soloists have one song apiece, done with comparable magnetism, and Richard Jackson joins Felicity Lott (one stanza each) in Poulenc's solitary 'song for two voices', *Colloque*. First-rate recording, though Lott's soprano is not always as sweetly caught as it can be.

Dialogue des Carmélites (complete).
*** Virgin/EMI Dig. VCD7 59227-2 (2) [CDCB 59227]. Dubosc, Gorr, Yakar, Fournier, Van Dam, Viala, Dupuy, Lyon Opéra O, Kent Nagano.

The opening of Poulenc's *Dialogue des Carmélites* with its very Stravinskian ostinatos for a moment suggests a minimalist opera, written before its time. Much is owed to the dynamic Nagano, who gives an extra momentum and sense of contrast to a work that with its measured speeds and easily lyrical manner can fall into sameness. That the male casting is so strong, with the principal roles taken by José van Dam and the tenor, Jean-Luc Viala, compensates for any lack of variety in having women's voices predominating in an opera about nuns. Catherine Dubosc in the central role of the fear-obsessed, self-doubting Blanche is fresh and appealing, with Brigitte Fournier charming as the frivolous nun, Constance, and the veteran Rita Gorr as the old Prioress and Rachel Yakar as the new Prioress both splendid. The vivid recording, helped by a stage production in Lyon, culminates in a spine-chilling rendering of the final execution scene, with the sound of the guillotine ever more menacing.

(i) *Les mamelles de Tiresias* (opéra-bouffé); (ii) *La bal masque* (cantata).
(N) ** Ph. Dig 456 504-3 [id.]. (i–ii) Wolfgang Holzmair; (i) Barbara Bonney, Jean-Paul Fouchécourt, Jean-Philippe Lafont, Mark Oswald, Graham Clark, Gordon Gietz, Anthony Griffey, Akemi Sakamoto, Tokyo Opera Singers; Saito Kinen O, Ozawa.

With the help of a fine team of soloists from the West, Seiji Ozawa conducts his Japanese forces in refined, polished performances of both works, with rhythms crisply sprung. With refined recording to match, this gives a muted idea of the witty Poulenc. In *Le bal masque*, a 'cantata profana', Wolfgang Holzmair sings beautifully, but the necessary sharpness in this 1920s piece for voice and chamber group is largely missing. *Les mamelles de Tiresias* dates from much later, 1944, but the same satirical spirit is still there in this romp. There too the impact is muted, in a performance not quite idiomatic.

La voix humaine (complete).
(N) (M) ** HM Suite Dig. HMT 7901474 [id.]. Françoise Pollet, Lille Nat. O, Jean-Claude Casadesus.

Françoise Pollet sings with poignant warmth in this telephone monodrama for soprano, sustaining the length well, bringing out the heart-break of the woman whose lover is leaving her. She may not have the intensity of the original interpreter, Denise Duval, or Julia Migenes's very dramatic Erato version (see above) – and the spacious acoustic, coupled with speeds on the broad side, makes this less intimate than it might be – but the warm expressiveness of the writing is persuasively caught.

Power, Leonel (d. 1445)

Missa Alma redemptoris mater. Motets: *Agnus Dei; Ave Regina; Beata viscera; Credo; Gloria; Ibo michi ad montem; Quam pulchra es; Salve Regina; Sanctus.*
(M) *** Virgin Veritas/EMI Dig. VER5 61345-2. Hilliard Ens., Hillier.

Power was a contemporary of Dunstable and was born probably in the mid-1370s. One of the leading composers represented in the Old Hall MS. (some 20 pieces are attributed to him), Power spent the last years of his life at Canterbury, but the music on this disc is earlier, coming from the period before 1413. The *Missa Alma redemptoris mater* is probably the earliest, in which all the Mass sections are linked by a common cantus firmus and there is also a complex mathematical design. The music is of an austere beauty that is quite striking, as indeed is the remarkable singing of the Hilliard Ensemble. The digitally remastered recording comes from the early 1980s and is vivid and present. Strongly recommended.

Praetorius, Michael (1571–1621)

Christmas motets and chorale concertos: *In dulci jubilo; Joseph, lieber Joseph mein; Der Morgenstern ist aufgedrungen; Nun komm der Heiden Heiland; Omnis mundus jocundetur; Psalitte; Puer natus: Ein Kind geborn zu*

Bethlehem; Singet und klinget; Vom Himmel hoch; Wachet auf, ruft uns die Stimme; Wie schön leuchtet der Morgenstern. Missa gantz Teudsch: Kyrie eleison.

**(*) MDG Dig. MDG 614 0660-2 [id.]. Hassler Consort, Franz Rami.

The skill of Praetorius as a polyphonist is readily demonstrated in the more ambitious works here, with the settings varying within the chorale concertos between three and fifteen parts. Indeed the busy contrapuntal textures of the opening *Wachet auf* stretch up to nineteen different lines. They are full of interest, and *Nun komm der Heiden Heiland* is similarly lively and inventive. *Puer natus est* (à 3, 7 and 11) alternates slow and jolly, energetic sections very appealingly, while the two movements from the *Mass* show the composer at his most unconventionally individual: both are unexpectedly vigorous, with echoes in the solo vocal parts of the *Kyrie* and the *Gloria* more rhythmically forceful with alternating declamatory passages. But it is the simpler and more lyrical settings that one remembers most affectionately. *In dulci jubilo* for double choir with solo lines simply embellished is quite delightful, and the solo interweaving at the opening of *Joseph, lieber Joseph mein* is equally lovely. The brief *Psallitte*, lightly sprung in its rhythms, is also memorable. *Der Morgenstern* is first heard in a simple evocative presentation then, in the chorale variations which follow, it is expanded, but not too flamboyantly. Of the two closing items *Omnis mundus jocundetur* is appealingly carol-like, pastoral in feeling, in spite of its complexity of texture. *Singet und klinget* reintroduces the melody, so associated with this composer, which we have heard before as the basis for *Joseph, lieber Joseph mein.* The performances here are on a chamber scale, with solo voices well matched and blended, if lacking something in individuality. But the freshness of the music-making is never in doubt and, although the balance is immediate, the recording is very good, integrating the various textural strands within a pleasing acoustic, even if the sound tends to congeal a little rather than separating out naturally.

Dances from Terpsichore (extended suite).

*** Decca Dig. 414 633-2. New L. Cons., Philip Pickett.

Terpsichore is a huge collection of some 300 dance tunes used by the French-court dance bands of Henri IV. They were enthusiastically assembled by the German composer, Michael Praetorius, who also harmonized them and arranged them in four to six parts; however, any selection is conjectural in the matter of orchestration. Philip Pickett's instrumentation is sometimes less exuberant than that of David Munrow before him; but many will like the refinement of his approach, with small instrumental groups, lute pieces and even what seems like an early xylophone! There are also some attractively robust brass scorings (sackbuts and trumpets). The use of original instruments is entirely beneficial in this repertoire; the recording is splendid.

Dances from Terpsichore (Suite de ballets; Suite de voltes). (i) Motets: *Eulogodia Sionia: Resonet in laudibus; Musae Sionae: Allein Gott in der Höh sei Ehr; Aus tiefer Not schrei ich zu dir; Christus der uns selig macht; Gott der Vater wohn uns bei; Polyhymnia Caduceatrix: Erhalt uns, Herr, bei deinem Wort.*

**(*) Virgin Veritas/EMI VER5 61289-2 [CDM 61289]. Early Music Cons. of L., Munrow; (i) with boys of the Cathedral and Abbey Church of St Alban.

David Munrow's main purpose was to bring the music fully to life and, at the same time, imaginatively to stimulate the ear of the listener. This record, made in 1973, is one of his most successful achievements. Munrow's instrumentation is imaginatively done: the third item, a *Bourrée* played by four racketts (a cross between a shawm and comb-and-paper in sound), is fascinating. The collection is a delightful one. After this stimulating aural feast, Munrow offers six of the composer's eloquent motets, the finest of which is *Erhalt uns, Herr, bei deinem Wort* for four choirs, each with its own accompanying instrumental group, although the shorter *Gott der Vater wohn uns bei* for double choir is hardly less resplendent, and the joyful *Allein Gott in der Höh sei Ehr* (for counter-tenor and triple choir) is also most stimulating, with crumhorns added to the third accompanying group. The only snag is the lack of a really clean focus in the CD transfer, especially in the exultant closing *Christus der uns selig macht*. The Abbey Road acoustic is reverberant, creating a wide amplitude, and the remastering has not altogether been a success in trying to sharpen up the focus. But the result remains rich in amplitude, and this inspired music, which often reminds the listener of Giovanni Gabrieli, is sung superbly by the choir.

Christmas music: *Polyhymnia caduceatrix et panegyrica Nos. 9–10, 12 & 17. Puericinium Nos. 2, 4 & 5. Musae Sionae VI, No. 53: Es ist ein Ros' entsprungen. Terpsichore: Dances Nos. 1; 283–5; 310.*

*** Hyperion Dig. CDA 66200 [id.]. Westminster Cathedral Ch., Parley of Instruments, David Hill.

Praetorius was much influenced by the polychoral style of the Gabrielis; these pieces reflect this interest. The music is simple in style and readily accessible, and its performance on this atmospheric Hyperion record is both spirited and sensitive.

Christmas music: *Polyhymnia caduceatrix et panegyrica Nos. 10, Wie schön leuchtet der*

Morgenstern; 12, Puer natus in Bethlehem; 21, Wachet auf, ruft uns die Stimme; 34, In dulci jubilo.
(M) *** Virgin Veritas/EMI VM5 61353-2. Taverner Cons. Ch. & Players, Parrott – SCHUTZ: *Christmas oratorio.* ***

This is the finest collection of Praetorius's vocal music in the current catalogue. The closing setting of *In dulci jubilo*, richly scored for five choirs and with the brass providing thrilling contrast and support for the voices, has great splendour. Before that comes the lovely, if less ambitious *Wie schön leuchtet der Morgenstern*. Both *Wachet auf* and *Puer natus in Bethlehem* are on a comparatively large scale, their combination of block sonorities and florid decorative effects the very essence of Renaissance style. The recording is splendidly balanced, with voices and brass blending and intertwining within an ample acoustic, and all the more welcome in this mid-priced Veritas reissue.

Previn, André (born 1929)

(i) *Peaches for flute and piano; Trio for piano, oboe and bassoon*; (ii) *Triolet for brass;* (i) *Wedding waltz for 2 oboes and piano;* (iii) (Piano) *Variations on a theme by Haydn.*
(N) *** Arabesque Dig. Z 6701 [id.]. (i) André Previn (piano) with Elizabeth Mann, Stephen Taylor, Dennis Godburn, Melanie Field; (ii) Brass Ens; (iii) Wo Han.

These works bring out the fluency of Previn's writing in a lighter vein. The *Trio for piano, oboe and bassoon* begins and ends as fun music, with a deeply emotional slow movement between. The *Triolet* is a display piece written for the Philip Jones Brass ensemble, and the piano *Variations*, using the slow movement theme from Haydn's *Symphony No. 82 (The Bear)*, set grittily purposeful writing against two warmly expressive slow variations. The two little occasional pieces, *Peaches* and the *Wedding waltz* also bring out Previn's lyrical side. A charming collection, very well performed and recorded.

Violin sonata (Vineyard).
(N) *** DG Dig. 453 470-2 [id.]. Gil Shaham, André Previn – BARBER: *Canzone*; COPLAND: *Violin sonata; Nocturne;* GERSHWIN: *3 Preludes.* ***

The inspired collaboration between Previn and Gil Shaham is crowned in their formidable performance of Previn's own *Violin sonata*, one of the most ambitious of his chamber works. If there are echoes of Walton's writing in the mixture of rhythmic energy and warm lyricism, the idiom is distinctively Previn's own, over the broad span of three substantial movements. Part of a fine, attractive survey of twentieth-century American violin music.

A Streetcar named Desire (complete).
(N) *** DG Dig. 459 366-2 (3) [id.]. Fleming, Futral, Gilfry, Griffey, San Francisco Op. Ch. & O, Previn.

André Previn's first opera, *A Streetcar named Desire*, based on Tennessee Williams' play, was first presented in San Francisco in September, 1998. This live recording, conducted by Previn himself, confirms this as by far his most powerful score yet, not just colourful and atmospheric but agonizingly intense in its portrait of the central character, Blanche. That role was specifically created for the soprano, Renée Fleming, and in the recording she responds magnificently. The inbred tensions created by Blanche's arrival in the home of her sister and the coarse Stanley Kowalski, build up relentlessly over the first two acts. They erupt in Act III in a sequence of solos for Blanche as she loses her mind, that have an overwhelming impact, at once sensuous and sinister. The final solo, as beautiful as it is moving, leads on to the chill of the final scene of Blanche's departure for the asylum. The whole is a great operatic concept, brilliantly achieved. Its impact may owe something to Previn's early experience in Hollywood, but this rises far above heightened film music, distinctive in its lyricism and subtle in its orchestration. Fleming gives a heart-rending performance, well supported by Elizabeth Futral as Blanche's sister (if rather too close in timbre to Fleming), Rodney Gilfry as Stanley and Anthony Dean Griffey as the wimpish Mitch. Warm, atmospheric recording, with voices well caught and good detail in the orchestral sound.

Prokofiev, Serge (1891–1953)

Andante for strings, Op. 50 bis; Autumn (symphonic sketch), *Op. 8; Lieutenant Kijé: suite, Op. 60; The Stone flower: suite, Op. 118; Wedding suite, Op. 126.*
*** Chandos Dig. CHAN 8806 [id.]. RSNO, Järvi.

The *Andante* is a transcription for full strings of the slow movement of the *First String quartet*, and its eloquence is more telling in this more expansive format. *Autumn*, on the other hand, is an early piece, much influenced by Rachmaninov and full of imaginative touches. Järvi takes it at a fairly brisk tempo but it remains appropriately atmospheric. The *Wedding suite* is drawn from *The Stone flower* and complements the Op. 118 suite from Prokofiev's last full-length ballet. The performances and recording are in the best traditions of the house.

Boris Godunov, Op. 70 bis: Fountain scene; Polonaise. Dreams, Op. 6. Eugene Onegin, Op. 71: Minuet, Polka, Mazurka. 2 Pushkin waltzes, Op. 120. Romeo and Juliet (ballet): *suite No. 2, Op. 64.*

*** Chandos Dig. CHAN 8472 [id.]. RSNO, Järvi.

Järvi's second suite from *Romeo and Juliet* has sensitivity, abundant atmosphere, a sense of the theatre, and is refreshingly unmannered. A fuller selection of the music Prokofiev wrote for a production of *Eugene Onegin* is available – see below – but what is offered here, plus the *Two Pushkin waltzes*, are rather engaging lighter pieces. The performances are predictably expert, the balance finely judged and detail is in exactly the right perspective.

Chout (ballet): *suite, Op. 21a; Love for 3 Oranges: suite, Op. 33a; Le pas d'acier: suite, Op. 41a.*
*** Chandos Dig. CHAN 8729 [id.]. RSNO, Järvi.

Järvi has a natural affinity for this repertoire and gets splendid results from the RSNO; and the recording is pretty spectacular.

Cinderella (ballet; complete), *Op. 87.*
(N) (B) *** Decca Double Dig. 455 349-2 (2) [id.]. Cleveland O, Ashkenazy – GLAZUNOV: *The Seasons*. ***

Cinderella (ballet; complete), *Op. 87; Summer night: suite, Op. 123.*
✪ *** DG Dig. 445 830-2 (2). Russian Nat. O, Mikhail Pletnev.

Cinderella (ballet; complete), *Op. 87; Symphony No. 1 in D (Classical), Op. 25.*
(B) *** EMI Dig./analogue. forte CZS5 68604-2 (2) [CDFB 68604]. LSO, Previn.

Pletnev produces playing of terrific life, lightness of touch, poetic feeling and character. Quite simply the best-played, most atmospheric and affecting *Cinderella* we have ever had on disc. We found its effect tremendously exhilarating, and have had difficulty in stopping playing it! Don't hesitate – on every count this is one of the best recordings, not only of the year but the 1990s.

Otherwise artistic honours are very evenly divided between the Ashkenazy and Previn recordings of Prokofiev's *Cinderella*. Some dances come off better in Previn's EMI version and there is an element of swings and roundabouts in comparing them. Detail is more closely scrutinized by the Decca engineers; Ashkenazy gets excellent results from the Cleveland Orchestra. On CD, the recording's fine definition is enhanced, yet not at the expense of atmosphere, and the bright, vivid image is given striking projection. The appeal of the Decca digital set (now reissued as a Double) is greatly increased by the inclusion of Ashkenazy's splendid account of Glazunov's finest ballet score, *The Seasons*. However, the EMI engineers have a more spacious acoustic within which to work and yet lose no detail. Moreover this now comes on EMI's similarly economical two-for-the-price-of-one forte series, and the CD reissue adds a splendid account of the *Classical Symphony*, sunlit and vivacious and hardly less well recorded five years previously.

Cinderella: suite No. 1, Op. 107; Lieutenant Kijé (suite); The Love for 3 Oranges: March; Scherzo; The Prince and Princess. Romeo and Juliet: Madrigal; Dance of the girls with lilies.
(BB) *** Naxos Dig. 8.550381 [id.]. Slovak State PO, (Košice), Andrew Mogrelia.

The calibre of this excellent Slovak orchestra is well demonstrated here, and its perceptive conductor, Andrew Mogrelia, is at his finest in his gently humorous portrait of *Lieutenant Kijé*, the three 'best bits' from *The Love for Three Oranges* and the charming items from *Romeo and Juliet*. Excellent recording.

Cinderella: ballet suite; 2 Pushkin waltzes, Op. 120; The Stone flower (ballet), Op. 118: 2 Waltzes; Waltz suite, Op. 110.
(M) *** Chandos Enchant Dig. CHAN 7076 [id.]. RSNO, Järvi.

The Chandos full-price catalogue is rich in Prokofieviana, always giving stimulation and pleasure in the hands of Neeme Järvi. This mid-priced collection, entitled '*Waltz suite*', is lightweight but very winning. From the full score of *Cinderella* Prokofiev chose three suites, and the selection here draws on the First and Third, opening with the ballet's yearning Introduction, moving on to the *Quarrel* between the Ugly Sisters and including the Courtiers' elegant *Pavane* and the *Adagio* danced by Cinderella and the Prince. The *Waltz suite*, Op. 110, is drawn from various works, including *Cinderella* and the opera, *War and Peace*, while the final *Mephisto waltz* comes from incidental music for the film, *Lermontov*. The pair of excerpts from *The Stone flower* come from the fourth scene and include the *Waltz of the Diamonds*, and the two equally engaging *Pushkin waltzes*, one passionate, the other more delicate, are part of the music Prokofiev wrote for a production of *Eugene Onegin*. The variety of the composer's invention and his often piquant scoring negate any suggestion that a succession of pieces in triple time could be too much of a good thing. The orchestral playing throughout is very persuasive, with the sensuousness of much of the writing brought out, especially in *Cinderella*, the highlight of the programme. The recording is first class.

(i) *Concertino in G min. for cello and orchestra, Op. 132* (completed and orch. Kabalevsky & Rostropovich); *Sinfonia concertante in E min. for cello and orchestra, Op. 125;* (ii) *Cello sonata in C, Op. 119.*
(N) (M) (**) Revelation mono RV10102 [id.].

Rostropovich,(i) USSR SO, Rozhdestvensky; (ii) Sviatoslav Richter.

Concertino in G min. for cello and orchestra, Op. 132; Symphony-concerto in E min. for cello and orchestra, Op. 125; 2 Pushkin waltzes, Op. 120.
(BB) *** Naxos Dig. 8.553624 [id.]. Rudin, Ukraine Nat. SO, Kuchar.

Rostropovich's performances of this coupling with the USSR Symphony Orchestra under Rozhdestvensky previously appeared on Russian Disc (mono RDCD 11103). They were made at public concerts in 1964 and 1960 respectively (the performance is a composite one). Some allowance must be made for the sound here and in the 1951 recording of the *Cello sonata*, once briefly available on the Monitor label, but what a performance!

The Russian cellist, Alexander Rudin, proves a powerful interpreter of these two concertante works, consistently incisive in attack and with clean intonation, not just breasting the technical problems but playing with natural warmth. Rudin can match and even outshine most other rivals, not least in the beauty of his half-tones, as in the slow movements of both works. He and the conductor, Theodore Kuchar, inspire the Ukraine orchestra to play with similar incisiveness, helped by vivid, immediate sound. Here more than usual, the *Concertino* – completed after Prokofiev's death by Kabalevsky and Rostropovich – with its warm lyricism emerges as fully representative of the composer. The two charming Pushkin-based *Waltzes* make an attractive fill-up, winningly pointed.

(i) *Flute concerto* (orch. Palmer); (ii) *Humoresque scherzo, Op. 12 bis; Overture on Hebrew themes, Op. 34 bis; Sonata for unaccompanied violins, Op. 115; Symphony No. 1 in D (Classical), Op. 25.*
**(*) Conifer Dig. 74321 15910-2 [id.]. (i) Jonathan Snowden; (ii) Alexander, Gatt, Mackie, Orford; L. Musici, Mark Stephenson.

The *Flute concerto* is an arrangement of the *Sonata in D major*, expertly scored by Christopher Palmer but is in no sense a concerto, the orchestra's role being confined to that of accompaniment. The *Humoresque scherzo* is in Prokofiev's own transcription for four bassoons, and the *Sonata*, Op. 115, was originally intended to be heard played by violins in unison, and sounds effective in this form. The *Overture on Hebrew themes* is well played and recorded, and so is the *Classical Symphony*, though it is rather on the slow side. Jonathan Snowden gives an excellent account of the arrangement of the *D major Sonata* and the recordings are well balanced, natural and realistic.

Piano concertos Nos. 1–5.
(B) *** Decca Double 452 588-2 (2) [id.]. Ashkenazy, LSO, Previn.
(N) *** Ph. Dig. 462 048-2 (2) [id.]. Alexander Toradze, Kirov O, Very Gergiev.
*** Chandos Dig. CHAN 8938 (2) [id.]. Boris Berman (in Nos. 1, 4 & 5); Horacio Gutiérrez (in Nos. 2 & 3), Concg. O, Järvi.
(B) **(*) Teldec/Warner Ultima Dig. 3984 21038-2 (2). Vladimir Krainev, Frankfurt RSO, Dmitri Kitaenko.

Piano concertos Nos. 1 in D flat, Op. 10; 3 in C, Op. 26; 4 in B flat, Op. 53.
(BB) *** Naxos Dig. 8.550566 [id.]. Kun Woo Paik, Polish Nat. RSO (Katowice), Antoni Wit.

Piano concertos Nos. 2 in G min., Op. 16; 5 in G, Op. 55.
(BB) *** Naxos Dig. 8.550565 [id.]. Kun Woo Paik, Polish Nat. RSO (Katowice), Antoni Wit.

(i) *Piano concertos Nos. 1–5;* (ii) *Autumnal, Op. 8;* (iii) *Overture on Hebrew themes, Op. 34.*
(M) *** Decca 448 126-2 (*Nos. 1, 2 & 4*); 448 127-2 (*Nos. 3 & 5; Autumnal; Overture*) [id.]. (i) Ashkenazy, LSO, Previn; (ii) LSO, Ashkenazy; (iii) Puddy, Ashkenazy & Gabrieli Qt.

(i) *Piano concertos Nos. 1–5;* (ii) *Overture on Hebrew themes. Visions fugitives, Op. 22.*
(B) **(*) EMI Rouge et Noir CZS5 69452-2 (2) [CDZB 62542]. Michel Béroff; (i) with Leipzig GO, Masur; (ii) with Portal, Parrenin Qt.

Ashkenazy is a commanding soloist in both the *First* and *Second Concertos*, and his virtuosity in the *First* is quite dazzling. If he is curiously wayward in the opening of the *Second*, there is no question that this too is a masterly performance. The *Third Concerto* is keen-edged and crisply articulated, and the only reservation here concerns the slow movement which at times is uncharacteristically mannered. Ashkenazy is authoritative in No. 4 and gives an admirable account of No. 5: every detail of phrasing and articulation is well thought out, and yet there is no want of spontaneity or any hint of calculation. Throughout, Previn and the LSO accompany sympathetically, and the recently remastered recording makes the most of the vintage mid-1970s Kingsway Hall sound. The early *In Autumn* is eminently worth having, as is the chamber performance of the *Overture on Hebrew themes*. As can be seen, the five concertos are also available, slightly differently laid out even more economically on a Double Decca set, without the additional items. The transfers appear to be identical.

The merits of the Berman single discs are discussed below. As a package, their claims are strong, both artistically and in terms of recording quality.

Kun Woo Paik's playing throughout these five concertos has exhilarating bravura. Tempi are dangerously fast at times and occasionally he has the orchestra almost scampering to keep up with him, but they do, and the result is often electrifying. The famous theme and variations central movement of the *Third concerto* is played with great diversity of mood and style and the darkly expressive *Larghetto* of No. 5 is very finely done. The *First concerto*, which comes last on the first CD has great freshness and compares well with almost any version on disc. In short, with vivid recording in the Concert Hall of Polish Radio, which has plenty of ambience, this set is enormously stimulating and a remarkable bargain. It has far better sound than the remastered Decca recording for Ashkenazy.

Alexander Toradze is a powerful pianist in whose musical armoury virtuosity is not in short supply. Superb recorded sound of impressive clarity and presence enhances the appeal of these performances, which were made in Jyväskylä in Finland. The actual instrument is better conditioned than in some rival recordings, and the performances are spirited, big-boned and powerful. As in the Scriabin *Prometheus* (coupled with Stravinsky's *Firebird*), this is a formidable partnership.

Vladimir Krainev and the Frankfurt Radio Orchestra under Dmitri Kitaenko are also formidable contenders in their Ultima Double format. The recordings were made in 1992 and offer sound of considerable warmth and naturalness. Krainev is a virtuoso of the first order and, apart from the *Third*, which has greater brilliance than poetic feeling, his accounts of these concertos have much to recommend them. Though not quite the equal of Ashkenazy, these are eminently worthwhile accounts that will give pleasure.

A satisfying Rouge et Noir set from Michel Béroff, who plays masterfully and is a pianist of genuine insight where Prokofiev is concerned; Masur gives him excellent support. Béroff is free from some of the agogic mannerisms that distinguish Ashkenazy in the slow movement of the *Third*, and he has great poetry. The balance is good; although the overall sound-picture is not wholly natural, it is certainly vivid, and the timbre of the piano is captured sympathetically. However, in the transfer to CD, a degree of hardness and opaqueness has crept in.

(i) *Piano concerto No. 1 in D flat. Suggestion diabolique, Op. 4/4.*

(M) *** EMI (SIS) CDM7 64329-2 [id.]. Gavrilov, (i) LSO, Rattle – BALAKIREV: *Islamey;* TCHAIKOVSKY: *Piano concerto No. 1.* ***

A dazzling account of the *First Piano concerto* from Andrei Gavrilov. This version is second to none for virtuosity and sensitivity. Apart from its brilliance, this performance scores on other fronts too; Simon Rattle provides excellent orchestral support and the EMI engineers offer most vivid recording, while the *Suggestion diabolique* makes a hardly less dazzling encore after the concerto.

Piano concertos Nos. 1 in D flat, Op. 10; 3 in C, Op. 26.

*** DG Dig. 439 898-2 [id.]. Kissin, BPO, Abbado.

(N) **(*) EMI CDC5 56654-2 [id.]. Martha Argerich, Montreal SO, Charles Dutoit – BARTOK: *Piano concerto No. 3.* **(*)

(i) *Piano concertos Nos. 1 in D flat, Op. 10; 3 in C, Op. 26. Piano sonata No. 7 in B flat, Op. 83.*

*** ASV Dig. CDDCA 786 [id.]. Mari Kodama, (i) with Philh. O, Kent Nagano.

Yevgeni Kissin gives a virtuosic, dashing account of both concertos and is given highly sensitive and responsive support from the Berlin Philharmonic under Abbado. It is unfailingly brilliant, aristocratic in feeling and wonderfully controlled pianism. After the big theme in the *First Piano concerto*, Kissin does not dash away in quite the same way as did Richter (in his mono recording from the late 1950s on Supraphon, which sounds pretty marvellous even as sound), and in the *Third* there is none of the wild abandon of William Kapell (see below). But this is playing of artistry and distinction; and the recording is very good. It is a pity that DG did not offer a fill-up, for example one of the sonatas from Kissin, as this CD offers only 42 minutes 27 seconds of playing time. All the same, it is very highly recommendable.

ASV's coupling should win great favour since it brings performances of real panache and style, together with a highly competitive account of the *Seventh Sonata*. Mari Kodama is a vital and imaginative player and the performances are wonderfully alert and fresh-eyed; there is splendid rapport between soloist and conductor (not surprisingly since they are husband and wife) and they benefit from first-class recording. A strong recommendation not only for newcomers to Prokofiev but for the experienced collector.

Argerich is pretty dazzling in the *First Concerto*, though there is perhaps more grace than fire. Indeed some will find it just a shade underpowered. The *Third*, too, has many felicitous touches and great refinement though it does not supersede the earlier version she made in Berlin for DG with Abbado. She still commands a wide range of tone colour and a technical finesse of formidable quality.

Piano concertos Nos. 1 in D flat, Op. 10; 3 in C, Op. 26; 5 in G, Op. 55.

*** Sony SK 52483 [id.]. Yefim Bronfman, Israel PO, Zubin Mehta.

Yefim Bronfman's Sony recording offers the *Fifth Piano concerto* instead of the *Sonata* (as on ASV), which makes a more logical and competitive choice – and the recording is similarly excellent in quality. Bronfman is hardly less remarkable or sensitive than Mari Kodama; indeed he is a player of subtlety and possesses a formidable technique and a cultured restraint. The Israel orchestra under Mehta gives good, well-phrased and athletic support. Existing recommendations are not displaced, but for those wanting this particular coupling this deserves a three-star recommendation.

Piano concertos Nos. 1 in D flat, Op. 10; 4 in B flat for the left hand, Op. 53; 5 in G, Op. 55.
*** Chandos Dig. CHAN 8791 [id.]. Boris Berman, Concg. O, Järvi.
(N) *(*) Hyperion Dig. CDA 67029 [id.]. Nikolai Demidenko, LPO, Alexander Lazarev.

On Chandos, very fine performances of all three *Concertos* and very distinguished orchestral playing. Boris Berman has established an enviable reputation in this repertoire, and he plays with great panache and dazzling virtuosity. He holds the music on a taut rein and has the nervous energy and ebullience this music needs. The superb recording quality will sway many collectors in his favour.

Nikolai Demidenko possesses formidable technical address but his musical personality is too intrusive for this to be the kind of recommendation his virtuosity should ensure. We do not care for these performances any more than we did for Nos. 2 and 3 (CDA 66838). Tone above *forte* is not always beautiful, *pianissimo* markings are not always observed, and though there is much to admire, it is the pianist rather than the composer to whom one's attention is too often drawn. On the whole there is good support from the LPO under Alexander Lazarev and good recording quality.

Piano concerto No. 3 in C, Op. 26.
(M) *** DG 447 438-2 [id.]. Martha Argerich, BPO, Abbado – RAVEL: *Piano concerto in G* etc. ***
(M) *** Mercury (IMS) 434 333-2 [id.]. Byron Janis, Moscow PO, Kondrashin (with PROKOFIEV: *Toccata;* SCHUMANN: *Sonata No. 3;* MENDELSSOHN: *Songs without words, Op. 61/1;* PINTO: *3 Scenes from childhood* ***) – RACHMANINOV: *Piano concerto No. 1.* ***
(M) **(*) RCA 09026 62691-2 [id.]. Van Cliburn, Chicago SO, Reiner – SCHUMANN: *Piano concerto.* ***
(BB) **(*) Belart 450 081-2. Israela Margalit, New Philh. O, Maazel (with MUSSORGSKY: *Pictures* **(*)).
❁ (M) (**(*)) RCA mono GD 60921 [id.]. William Kapell, Dallas SO, Dorati – KHACHATURIAN: *Piano concerto* (**(*)) ❁; LISZT: *Mephisto waltz.* (**(*))

Another ideal choice for reissue in DG's 'Originals' series of 'Legendary Recordings'. Martha Argerich made her outstanding record of the Prokofiev *Third Concerto* in 1968, while still in her twenties. There is nothing ladylike about the playing, but it displays countless indications of feminine perception and subtlety. The *C major Concerto* was once regarded as tough music but here receives a sensuous performance, and Abbado's direction underlines that from the very first, with a warmly romantic account of the ethereal opening phrases on the high violins. When it comes to the second subject, the lightness of Argerich's pointing has a delightfully infectious quality, and surprisingly a likeness emerges with the Ravel *G major Concerto*, which was written more than a decade later. This is a much more individual performance of the Prokofiev than almost any other available and brings its own special insights. The 1967 recording, made in the Berlin Jesus-Christus Kirche, always excellent, sounds even more present in this new transfer.

Byron Janis's record with Kondrashin has a certain historical éclat in containing the first recordings made in the Soviet Union (in 1962) by non-Russian recording engineers. The result was a triumphant success, artistically and technically. Janis's account of the Prokofiev *Third Concerto* is outstanding in every way, soloist and orchestra plainly challenging each other in a performance full of wit (particularly in the delightfully managed slow-movement variations), drama and warmth. Even though it was made three decades ago, the Mercury recording sounds amazingly clean and faithful. The recital (recorded in Russia the following year – except for the Schumann, which was made in the USA) is comparatively low-key, except perhaps for the captivating *Scenes from childhood* of Octavio Pinto, which combine charm with glittering yet unostentatious bravura.

Van Cliburn plays with both sympathy and astonishing digital brilliance. However, the 1960 recording is closely balanced, as if the producer, Richard Mohr, decided to counteract the richness of the Chicago ambience with his microphone placing. With a very forward (indeed at times too forward) piano-image and a relatively sharp focus for the violins, he has certainly made his point, and there is no doubting the strong projection of the music-making.

The performance by Israela Margalit and Maazel is not the most poised available but it has a splendid feeling of spontaneity and enjoyment, and there is no lack of wit in the central theme and variations. The recording balance is somewhat contrived, the resonance of the acoustic competing with the microphone spotlighting, but the end-result is unfailingly vivid and the piano image is tangible. It is not unlikely that those who buy this disc for the Mussorgsky may find themselves turning just as readily to the concerto, for the personality and colour of the score emerge strongly here.

William Kapell's account of the *Third Piano concerto* is dazzlingly brilliant, and the Dallas orchestra under Antal Dorati rise to the occasion too. Indeed this is arguably the most incandescent and vital performance of this concerto ever committed to disc. It comes with an equally remarkable performance of the Khachaturian with the Boston Symphony under Koussevitzky, a powerhouse of vitality. Playing like this silences any criticism one might voice about the recorded sound, which admittedly is pretty grim.

(i) *Piano concerto No. 3 in C, Op. 26;* (ii; iii) *Violin concerto No. 1 in D, Op. 19;* (iii) *Lieutenant Kijé (suite), Op. 60.*
(B) *** DG Classikon Analogue/Dig. 439 413-2. (i) Martha Argerich, BPO; (ii) Shlomo Mintz; (iii) Chicago SO; all cond. Abbado.

Martha Argerich's highly individual performance of Prokofiev's *C major Concerto* (see above) is here coupled with the *First Violin concerto*, which also has a magical opening, and once again Abbado's accompaniment is peerless, while Mintz phrases with imagination and individuality. *Lieutenant Kijé* is hardly less successful and also sounds splendid; Abbado gets both warm and wonderfully clean playing from the Chicago orchestra. This compilation is one of the very finest reissues on DG's bargain Classikon label.

Piano concerto No. 4 in B flat for the left hand, Op. 53.
*** Sony Dig. SK 47188 [id.]. Fleisher, Boston SO, Ozawa – BRITTEN: *Diversions;* RAVEL: *Left-hand concerto.* ***

The *Fourth Piano concerto* was commissioned, like the Ravel, for Paul Wittgenstein who lost his right hand during the First World War. He did not like it, however, and the piece remained long neglected (its first UK performance was by Malcolm Binns in 1960). It is a powerful and resourceful piece which Fleisher performs with great sympathy and skill. Although his does not necessarily eclipse earlier versions by Michel Béroff and Ashkenazy, it is an interpretation of strong character and comparable stature, and is well accompanied by Ozawa and the Boston orchestra, and is splendidly recorded.

(i) *Piano concerto No. 5 in G, Op. 55. Piano sonata No. 8 in B flat, Op. 84; Visions fugitives, Op. 22/3, 6 & 9.*
(M) *** DG Originals 449 744-2 [id.]. Richter, (i) with Warsaw PO, Rowicki.

Richter's account of the *Fifth Piano concerto* is a classic. It was recorded in 1959, yet the sound of this excellent CD transfer belies the age of the original in its clarity, detail and vividness of colour. In any event it cannot be recommended too strongly to all admirers of Richter, Prokofiev and great piano-playing. Richter then plays the *Eighth Sonata* and the excerpts from the *Visions fugitives* with comparable mastery, the latter deriving from a live recital. In both cases the recording is surprisingly good.

Violin concertos Nos. (i) *1;* (ii) *2. Solo Violin sonata in D, Op. 115; Sonata for 2 Violins in C, Op. 56;* (iii) *Violin sonatas Nos. 1–2; 5 Melodies, Op. 35b; Love for 3 Oranges: March* (arr. Heifetz).
(M) **(*) EMI Dig. CMS5 66605-2. Frank Peter Zimmermann; (i) BPO, Maazel; (ii) Philh. O, Janssons; (iii) Alexander Longquich.

EMI on two mid-priced discs have here compiled a complete collection of Prokofiev's violin works in thoughtful, refined readings from Frank Peter Zimmermann. If he does not quite compete with the finest rivals in the two concertos, it is useful to have them together, when they originally appeared with different couplings. The solo and duo sonatas were recorded at different times in Holland, with Zimmermann taking both parts in the curious *Two-violin Sonata*. These are outstanding performances. Otherwise Zimmermann offers finely crafted performances, marked by poetry in the lyrical movements and quicksilver lightness in such a movement as the central *Scherzo* of the *First Concerto*, which is taken exceptionally fast. Zimmermann's is a relatively relaxed style, with a degree of restraint and consistently sweet, pure tone. Though that means there is a lack of bite and spikiness in the concertos and the violin-and-piano sonatas, it works very well in the *Cinq mélodies*, transcribed from the *Songs without words*, written in 1920 as vocalises for the soprano, Nina Koshetz. In the *Sonatas* Zimmermann is not helped by the slightly distant recording-balance, and the pianist is sometimes rhythmically a little square, not as responsive as his partner. Nevertheless the set is well worth considering.

Violin concerto No. 1 in D, Op. 19.
*** Teldec/Warner Dig. 4509 92256-2 [id.]. Maxim Vengerov, LSO, Rostropovich – SHOSTAKOVICH: *Violin concerto No. 1.* ***
*** Sony SK 66567 [id.]. Julian Rachlin, Moscow RSO, Vladimir Fedoseyev – TCHAIKOVSKY: *Violin concerto.* ***
(N) *** Erato/Warner Dig. 0630 17722-2 [id.]. Anne-Sophie Mutter, Nat. SO, Rostropovich – GLAZUNOV: *Violin concerto, Op. 82;* SHCHEDRIN: *Stihira.****

Maxim Vengerov's coupling not only won the *Gramophone*'s Concerto Award in 1995, but was also voted 'Record of the Year'. Vengerov's magnetism in both concertos is in no doubt; his playing is full of life and spontaneous feeling, helped by Rostropovich's highly supportive accompaniments. In the Prokofiev, Julian Rachlin displays rather more poetic subtlety but his pairing is with Tchaikovsky, and many will feel that Vengerov's Shostakovich coupling is even more appropriate, while his performance has its own special character and insights. The recording is excellent too.

The yearning, hushed beauty of Rachlin's treatment of the great opening melody recalls Philip Hope-Wallace's description of Galli-Curci's singing: 'like a nightingale half asleep'. This is not only a movingly poetic performance, with the lyrical outer movements both lighter and faster-flowing than usual, but one which consistently brings out the wit and fun in the writing. It may not be everyone's first choice, but there is no more distinctive reading on disc than this, and anyone who wants this unusual coupling need not hesitate, with the Tchaikovsky also more meditative than usual.

As in the Glazunov, Mutter gives a warmly sympathetic account of the *First* Prokofiev concerto, responding to the inspirational direction of Rostropovich. The great melodies of the outer movements are tenderly expressive and the central *Scherzo* delightfully witty. The Washington recording, airy and spacious, has the soloist forwardly balanced.

Violin concertos Nos. 1 in D, Op. 19; 2 in G Min., Op. 63.

❁*** Sony Dig. SK 53969 [id.]. Cho-Liang Lin, LAPO, Salonen – STRAVINSKY: *Concerto*. ***

(N) (BB) *** Virgin Classics 2-for-1 Dig. VBD5 61633-2 [CDBV 61630] (2). Dmitri Sitkovetsky, LSO, Sir Colin Davis – SHOSTAKOVICH: *Concertos*. ***

(M) *** Decca 425 003–2 [id.]. Kyung-Wha Chung, LSO, Previn – STRAVINSKY: *Concerto*. ***

*** Chandos Dig. CHAN 8709 [id.]. Mordkovitch, RSNO, Järvi.

**(*) EMI Dig. (SIS) CDC7 47025-2 [id.]. Perlman, BBC SO, Roshdestvensky.

(M) **(*) Sony Stern Edition II Dig. SMK 64503 [id.]. Isaac Stern, NYPO, Mehta – BARTOK: *Rhapsodies*. **

The two Prokofiev concertos are among the composer's most richly lyrical works, and Lin brings out their romantic warmth as well as their dramatic bite. Salonen's understanding support – helped by sound more refined than this orchestra usually gets, if with weighty bass – culminates in ravishing accounts of the outer movements of No. 1 and the central slow movement of No. 2. The Stravinsky coupling is another powerful and warmly expressive reading, although here Chung is in some ways even more stimulating.

The Virgin two-for-one Double makes an amazing bargain in offering first-class versions of both the paired concertos of Prokofiev and Shostakovich, and all for the cost of a single mid-priced CD! Dmitri Sitkovetsky conveys the demonic side of the *First Concerto* more effectively than any other player, without losing sight of its lyricism or sense of line. His version of the Scherzo touches an ironic, almost malignant nerve, while he has the measure of the ice-maiden fairy-tale element at the opening. He has a sympathetic collaborator in Sir Colin Davis and the *Second Concerto* is hardly less powerful. The soloist is rather more forward than is ideal, but orchestral detail is never masked and the internal orchestral balance is very natural.

Chung on mid-price Decca offers hardly less compelling Prokofievian readings in excellent analogue sound, more overtly emotional if not quite so commanding. Her performances emphasize the lyrical quality of these concertos with playing that is both warm and strong, tender and full of fantasy. Previn's accompaniments are deeply understanding, while the Decca sound has lost only a little of its fullness in the digital remastering, and the soloist is now made very present. The Stravinsky coupling is equally stimulating.

Perlman's coupling is still at full price. His performances bring virtuosity of such strength and command that one is reminded of the supremacy of Heifetz. Though the EMI sound has warmth and plenty of bloom, the balance of the soloist is unnaturally close, which has the effect of obscuring important melodic ideas in the orchestra behind mere passage work from the soloist. Nevertheless one is left in no doubt that both works are among the finest violin concertos written this century. Apart from the balance the recording is a fine one.

Lydia Mordkovitch enters a hotly contested field and gives readings of strong personality and character. She is well supported by the RSNO and Järvi, and more than holds her own with rival versions. There are some splendidly malignant sounds in the Scherzo of No. 1, and much intensity and panache throughout both works. She does not displace Lin or Sitkovetsky, both of them rather special, nor Chung in lyrical warmth, but both performances make a very satisfying alternative and have first-class sound.

In his digital recordings, made in the Avery Fisher Hall in 1982, Stern's are warm and boldly extrovert readings, a degree freer in expression and more spontaneous-sounding than his 1965 versions, recorded in Philadelphia, even if Ormandy offered riper accompaniments than Mehta does here. Stern may here lack the depth of poetry of Chung, and the fearless brilliance of Perlman, but his accounts are full of character and not without distinction in their own right.

(i) *Violin concertos Nos. 1 in D, Op. 19; 2 in G min., Op. 63;* (ii) *5 Mélodies, Op. 35b.*

(N) ** RCA Dig. 09026 68353-2 [id.]. Anne Akiko Meyers, with (i) Frankfurt RSO, Dmitri Kitaenko; (ii) Li Jian.

In both *concertos* Meyers offers warm and confident performances which yet lack a degree of refinement, missing the mystery which many others convey. Meyers attacks such an outward-going movement as the finale of the *Second Concerto* with splendid panache, but this remains a disc to be recommended simply to those who want this all-Prokofiev coupling, with the *Cinq mélodies* also rather heavy-handed. Balance favours the soloist.

(i) *Violin concerto No. 1 in D, Op. 19. Symphony No. 1 in D (Classical), Op. 25; Visions fugitives, Op. 22* (orch. Barshai).
(N) * Chandos Dig. CHAN9615 [id.]. (i) Ilya Grubert; Moscow CO, Constantine Orbelian.

All these pieces date from 1917, but the *Classical Symphony* apart, they receive pretty lacklustre performances. Ilya Grubert undergoes too close a scrutiny from the recording engineers and in the *Visions fugitives*, their American conductor sets somewhat slow tempi. Subfusc recording.

Violin concerto No. 2 in G min., Op. 63.
(M) *** RCA 09026 61744-2 [61744-2-RG]. Heifetz, Boston SO, Munch – GLAZUNOV; SIBELIUS: *Concertos*. ***
(B) *** EMI forte CZS5 69331-2 (2) [CDFB 69331]. David Oistrakh, Philh. O, Galliera – BEETHOVEN: *Triple concerto;* BRAHMS: *Double concerto;* MOZART: *Violin concerto No. 3*. ***
(N) *** Teldec/Warner Dig. 4509 98255-2 [id.]. Itzhak Perlman, Chicago SO, Barenboim – STRAVINSKY: *Violin concerto*. ***

In the *arioso*-like slow movement, Heifetz chooses a faster speed than is usual, but there is nothing unresponsive about his playing, for his expressive rubato has an unfailing inevitability. In the spiky finale he is superb, and indeed his playing is glorious throughout. The recording is serviceable merely, though it has been made firmer in the current re-mastering. But no one is going to be prevented from enjoying this ethereal performance because the technical quality is dated.

David Oistrakh's account of Prokofiev's *G minor Concerto*, made in 1958, occupies a place of honour in the catalogue. In some respects it has never been surpassed, though Heifetz's recordings with Koussevitzky and Munch fall into a special category. Oistrakh's is a beautifully balanced reading which lays stress on the lyricism of the concerto, and the orchestral support he receives could hardly be improved upon. The 1958 recording is admirably spacious and atmospheric, with finely focused detail and great warmth. The CD transfer is immaculate. An altogether marvellous performance, and this forte compilation of four very distinguished recordings is extraordinary value for money.

Though Perlman's coupling of Prokofiev's *Second concerto* and the Stravinsky is most ungenerous, this performance, recorded live, is more compelling than his earlier studio recording, with Barenboim adding to the urgency and energy.

Divertimento, Op. 43; The Prodigal Son, Op. 46; Symphonic song, Op. 57; Andante (Piano Sonata No. 4).
*** Chandos Dig. CHAN 8728 [id.]. RSNO, Järvi.

The *Divertimento* is a lovely piece: its first movement has an irresistible and haunting second theme. Its long neglect is puzzling since it is highly attractive and ought to be popular. So, for that matter, should *The Prodigal Son*, some of whose material Prokofiev reused the following year in the *Fourth Symphony*. Another rarity is the *Symphonic song*, a strange, darkly scored piece. The recording is first class – as, indeed, are the performances. An indispensable item in any Prokofiev collection.

The Gambler: 4 Portraits, Op. 49; Semyon Kotko: Symphonic suite, Op. 81 bis.
*** Chandos Dig. CHAN 8803 [id.]. RSNO, Järvi.

Prokofiev's *Four Portraits* enshrine the best of the opera and are exhilarating and inventive. *Semyon Kotko*, though not top-drawer Prokofiev, is still thoroughly enjoyable. Järvi gives a thoroughly sympathetic reading in vivid and present sound.

Lieutenant Kijé (incidental music): *suite, Op. 60*.
(B) *** Sony SBK 48162 [id.]. Cleveland O, Szell – KODALY: *Háry János suite*; MUSSORGSKY: *Pictures at an exhibition*. ***

Szell, even more than in the *Háry János* coupling, is on his highest form. Seldom on record has the *Lieutenant Kijé* music been projected with such drama and substance, and Szell is wonderfully warm in the *Romance* without a suggestion of sentimentality. The recording, like the couplings, is balanced too closely, but the orchestral playing is so stunning one hardly minds, for the opening and closing trumpet-calls are properly distanced.

The Love for 3 Oranges: suite.
(B) ** Sony SBK 53621 [id.]. Phd. O, Ormandy – SHOSTAKOVICH: *Symphony No. 5* etc. **(*)

(i) *Love for 3 Oranges* (suite); (ii) *La pas d'acier:* suite, *Op. 41 bis;* (i) *Scythian suite, Op. 20.*
(B) (**) EMI Rouge et Noir mono CZS5 69674-2 (2). (i) French Nat. R. O; (ii) Philh. O, Markevitch – STRAVINSKY: *Le baiser de la fée* etc. (***)

(i) *Love for 3 Oranges* (suite), *Op. 33a; Scythian suite, Op. 20;* (ii) *Symphony No. 5, Op. 100.*
(M) **(*) (IMS) Mercury 432 753-2 [id.]. (i) LSO; (ii) Minneapolis SO, Antal Dorati.

Dorati's account of Prokofiev's powerful and atmospheric *Scythian suite* was recorded at Watford Town Hall in 1957; the remastering confirms the excellence of the original engineering. The suite from the *Love for Three Oranges* is similarly striking in its characterization and vivid primary colours, with the resonance not blunting the rhythms. The CD is worth considering for these two performances; but the *Fifth Symphony*, recorded in Minneapolis two years later, is less successful. Dorati's reading is similarly forceful but the effect is hard and often unsympathetic.

Superb orchestral playing of course, but Ormandy's view of the score is larger than life, spectacle seemingly more important than subtlety, which the close recording tends to emphasize. The excitement is undeniable, but the famous *March* seems rather inflated and heavy.

Sharply characterized performances from Markevitch, brilliantly played. No apologies need be made for the mono sound, which is both brilliant and atmospheric and is transferred to CD without added edge or thinness. However, it is the Stravinsky coupling which makes this reissue distinctive. The pair of CDs are now offered in EMI's French 'two for the price of one' series.

Peter and the wolf, Op. 67.

❁ (M) *** Virgin/EMI Dig. CU5 61137-2 [id.]. Gielgud, Ac. of L., Richard Stamp – SAINT-SAENS: *Carnival.* ***

(BB) *** Naxos Dig. 8.554170 [id.]. Dame Edna Everage, Melbourne SO, John Lanchbery – BRITTEN: *Young person's guide to the orchestra* ***; POULENC: *The story of Babar.* *** ❁

(BB) *** ASV Quicksilva CDQS 6017 [(M) id. import]. Angela Rippon, RPO, Hughes – SAINT-SAENS: *Carnival.* ***

(B) **(*) Tring Dig. TRP 046 [(M) id.]. Sir John Gielgud, RPO, Andrea Licata – BIZET: *Jeux d'enfants;* ** SAINT-SAENS: *Carnival.* **(*)

(i) *Peter and the wolf;* (ii) *Lieutenant Kijé* (suite).

(M) **(*) Decca Phase Four 444 104-2 [id.]. (i) Sean Connery (nar.), RPO; (ii) Netherlands R. PO; Dorati – BRITTEN: *Young person's guide.* **(*)

(i; ii) *Peter and the wolf;* (iii) *Lieutenant Kijé: suite;* (iv) *Love for 3 Oranges: suite;* (ii) *Symphony No. 1 in D (Classical).*

❁ (B) *** Decca 433 612-2. (i) Sir Ralph Richardson, (ii) LSO, Sargent; (iii) Paris Conservatoire O, Boult; (iv) LPO, Weller.

Sir John Gielgud's highly individual presentation of Prokofiev's masterly narrative with orchestra brings a worthy successor to our previous favourite version, by Sir Ralph Richardson for Decca; moreover Richard Stamp and the Academy of London have the advantage of a superb, modern, digital recording, warmly atmospheric but with a strikingly wide dynamic range. At the end, Sir John, who has presided over these events with a wonderfully benign involvement, becomes Grandfather himself with his restrained moral questioning of Peter's youthful bravado. Throughout, his obvious relish for the colour as well as the narrative flow of the text has been splendidly matched by the detail and impetus of Richard Stamp's accompaniment.

Sir Ralph Richardson brings a great actor's feeling for words to the narrative; he dwells lovingly on their sound as well as their meaning, and this genial preoccupation with the manner in which the story is told matches Sargent's feeling exactly. Sir Malcolm Sargent's direction of the accompaniment shows his professionalism at its very best. The original coupling, Sargent's amiable, polished account of the *Classical Symphony*, has now been restored. All the tempi, except the finale, are slow but Sir Malcolm's assured elegance carries its own spontaneity. The sound is vivid. Boult's Paris recording of *Lieutenant Kijé* offers more gusto than finesse, but the result is exhilaratingly robust and the very early (1955) stereo comes up remarkably well. Weller's *Love for three oranges* is a first-class performance, given top-drawer 1977 recording. But our Rosette is for *Peter and the wolf.*

If you react adversely to Dame Edna Everage's exuberantly eccentric persona, the Naxos version cannot be recommended. But for those willing to be included among her possums it is a highly entertaining and very dramatic narrative, with the orchestral accompaniment splendidly paced to match the gripping onward flow of the story. The wolf-horns positively snarl, the flute-bird chirps merrily and the cat-clarinet has a certain elegant insouciance, while the hunter's guns are like thunder. There are twee moments, but children will readily respond to Dame Edna's very positive involvement with her characters, and so will most parents. At the close she throws away the humour of Grandfather's grumble but not the childish delight on discovering that the duck is still alive after all, inside the wolf. The couplings are equally splendid.

Angela Rippon narrates with charm yet is never in the least coy; indeed she is thoroughly involved in the tale and thus also involves the listener. The accompaniment is equally spirited, with excellent orchestral playing, and the recording is splendidly clear, yet not lacking atmosphere. This makes an excellent super-bargain recommendation.

Sean Connery uses a modern script by Gabrielle Hilton which brings a certain colloquial friendliness to the narrative and invites a relaxed style, to which the actor readily responds. If you can accept such extensions as 'dumb duck' and a pussy cat who is 'smooth, but greedy and vain', you will not be disappointed with Connery's participation in the climax of the tale, where Dorati supports him admirably. Both *Peter and the wolf* and *The Young person's guide to the orchestra* start with the orchestra tuning up, to create an anticipatory atmosphere, and the introductory matter is entirely fresh and informal. In *Lieutenant Kijé* Dorati is characteristically direct, with everything boldly characterized, and he secures excellent playing from the Netherlands orchestra. As with *Peter and the wolf,* the extremely vivid Decca Phase Four recording (not unnaturally balanced but ensuring every detail is clear) gives the performance a strong projection.

Sir John Gielgud made his second recording of *Peter and the wolf* six years after the first, which is orchestrally superior. In this new version the narrative may be more mature but the manner is just as friendly and avuncular; Gielgud becomes increasingly caught up in the story as it progresses, and so do we. The moment when the wolf catches its prey is vividly exciting (and the oboe soloist here responds poignantly) and at the end of the story Gielgud's pleasure in discovering that the duck is still alive bubbles over with merriment. The Italian conductor directs competently and there is some good solo playing from the RPO, but it is the enthusiastic participation of Gielgud and his wonderfully varied vocal inflexions that make this performance so enjoyable. Voice and orchestra are recorded in different acoustics but are quite well edited together.

Romeo and Juliet (ballet), *Op. 64* (complete).
(M) *** Decca Double 452 970-2 (2) [id.]. Cleveland O, Lorin Maazel.
(B) *** EMI forte CZS5 68607-2 (2) [CDFB 68607]. LSO, Previn.

Almost simultaneously in 1973 two outstanding versions of Prokofiev's complete *Romeo and Juliet* ballet appeared, strongly contrasted to provide a clear choice on grounds of interpretation and recording. Previn and the LSO made their recording in conjunction with live performances at the Royal Festival Hall, and the result reflects the humour and warmth which went with those live occasions. Previn's pointing of rhythm is consciously seductive, whether in fast, jaunty numbers or in the soaring lyricism of the love music. The Kingsway Hall recording quality is full and immediate, yet atmospheric too.

Maazel by contrast will please those who believe that this score should above all be bitingly incisive. The rhythms are more consciously metrical, the tempi generally faster, and the precision of ensemble of the Cleveland Orchestra is little short of miraculous. The recording is one of Decca's most spectacular, searingly detailed, but atmospheric too. With the reissue of the Maazel set as a Double Decca, honours are even between both sets: if you want the finest sound and a gripping sense of drama, choose Maazel; if you prefer a more genial manner, Previn is your man.

Romeo and Juliet (ballet), *Op. 64:* highlights.
*** Sony Dig. SK 42662 [id.]. BPO, Salonen.
*** Virgin/EMI Dig. VC7 59278-2 [id.]. RLPO, Libor Pešek.

With magnificent playing from the Berlin Philharmonic Orchestra, Esa-Pekka Salonen's set of excerpts seems marginally a first choice for those wanting a full-priced disc of highlights from Prokofiev's masterly score. The Berlin Philharmonic playing has an enormous intensity and a refined felicity in the score's more delicate evocations. One is touched and deeply moved by this music-making, while the selection admirably parallels the ballet's narrative. The recording, made in the Philharmonie, matches sumptuousness with a potent clarity of projection, and the dynamic range is dramatically wide.

Pešek's selection follows the narrative line, and one feels that the conductor and his players are highly involved in the course of events; in the closing numbers Pešek tightens the screws so that the *Death of Juliet* is devastating. The Royal Liverpool Philharmonic Orchestra play very well indeed and achieve great freshness and spontaneity; they are given a satisfying concert-hall balance. This Virgin CD offers 71 minutes from Prokofiev's inspired score, and every minute is stimulating and enjoyable.

Romeo and Juliet (ballet): *suites Nos. 1 & 2, Op. 64.*
(M) *** Mercury (IMS) 432 004-2 [id.]. Minneapolis SO, Skrowaczewski – MUSSORGSKY: *Night.* ***
(B) **(*) Decca Double 440 630-2 (2) [id.]. SRO, Ansermet – TCHAIKOVSKY: *Swan Lake.* **(*)

Skrowaczewski's recording of the two ballet suites was made in 1962. The playing of the Minneapolis orchestra is on a virtuoso level. The crystal-clear acoustic of the hall in Edison High School, with its backing ambience, seems ideally suited to the angular melodic lines and pungent lyricism of this powerful score, to underline the sense of tragedy without losing the music's romantic sweep. The fidelity and spectacle of the Mercury engineering reach a zenith in the powerful closing sequence of *Romeo at Juliet's tomb.* At mid-price this is highly recommendable.

Ansermet's performances have both atmosphere and passion (notably *Romeo with Juliet before his departure*). After the ominous introduction, the playing is rhythmically a bit sluggish. But *Juliet as a young girl* and the *Madrigal* are charming, and the love scene of *Romeo and Juliet* is genuinely touching; the *Death of Tybalt* bursts with energy, and *Masks* is nicely pointed. If the Suisse Romande Orchestra in 1961 was not one of the world's greatest ensembles, Ansermet was very persuasive and he brings everything vividly to life. The dramatically vibrant recording is well up to Decca's vintage standard of the early 1960s.

Romeo and Juliet: suites Nos. 1 & 2: excerpts.
*** Telarc Dig. CD 80089 [id.]. Cleveland O, Yoel Levi.

Levi seems to have a special affinity with Prokofiev's score, for pacing is unerringly apt and characterization is strong. There are some wonderfully serene moments, as in the ethereal introduction of the flute melody in the first piece (*Montagues and Capulets*). The quicker movements have an engaging feeling of the dance and the light, graceful articulation in *The child Juliet* is a delight; but the highlights of the performance are the *Romeo and Juliet love scene* and *Romeo at Juliet's before parting*, bringing playing of great intensity, with a ravishing response from the Cleveland strings. The rich Telarc recording is in the demonstration class, but this offers less music than several of its competitors.

Romeo and Juliet (ballet): excerpts (including *suites 1–3*).
(N) ** DG Dig. 453 439-2 [id.]. BPO, Abbado.

Abbado's new selection from *Romeo* has some exemplary playing from the Berlin Philharmonic and the DG engineers offer us very well-balanced recorded sound. This 70-minute anthology is assembled from the three published concert suites, as well as the ballet itself. Everything is well shaped and finely characterized, but Myung-Whun Chung's version with the Concertgebouw Orchestra on the same label has greater atmosphere and dramatic flair. The problem is that it offers much less music!

Romeo and Juliet (ballet): *suites Nos. 1 & 3*.
*** DG Dig. 439 870-2 [id.]. Concg. O, Myung-Whun Chung.

Myung-Whun Chung gets playing of great atmosphere, virtuosity and dramatic fire from the Royal Concertgebouw Orchestra, and DG provide a recording of great range and presence, comparable with the very best now in currency. A pity that they did not include the second suite, for which there would have been time, a self-inflicted wound which handicaps a record that should enjoy and certainly deserves the widest exposure. Those who invest in it will not be disappointed.

Romeo and Juliet (ballet): excerpts (including *suite No. 2*).
(N) (M) *** Classic fM Dig. 75605 57047. RPO, Daniele Gatti – TCHAIKOVSKY: *Romeo and Juliet (fantasy overture)*. ***

After a bitingly pungent opening (*Montagues and Capulets*), Daniele Gatti's 50-minute selection effectively encapsulates the ballet's dramatic narrative in nine key numbers. The RPO characterizes very strongly indeed and, with generally brisk tempi, the strongest contrast is made between the bold, pungent rhythms of the more vigorous dances and the exquisite delicacy of the gentler, romantic evocation with its wonderfully transluscent orchestral colouring. The portrait of *Friar Laurence* is touchingly gentle, but the ballet's passionate climax could not be more heart-rendingly plangent. The recording is superb, very much in the demonstration bracket, and the coupling with Tchaikovsky's fantasy overture is made the more apt by Gatti's highly romantic approach to that quite different response to Shakespeare's tragedy.

Romeo and Juliet (ballet): *suite*.
(M) *** Decca 417 737-2 [id.]. Cleveland O, Maazel – KHACHATURIAN: *Gayaneh; Spartacus*. **(*)

An intelligently chosen selection of six pieces (including *Juliet as a young girl*, the *Balcony scene* and *The last farewell*) makes a generous coupling for Decca's Khachaturian ballet scores.

Russian overture, Op. 72; Summer night: suite from *The Duenna, Op. 123; War and Peace* (suite, arr. Christopher Palmer).
*** Chandos Dig. CHAN 9096 [id.]. Philh. O, Järvi.

The *Russian overture* is determinedly popular in appeal, and it teems with ideas, both lyrical and grotesque, and has plenty of vitality. It is played here in a slightly reduced scoring. The *Summer night suite* is notable for its delicate *Serenade* and a charmingly romantic movement called *Dreams*. But the finest music here is Christopher Palmer's suite of interludes from *War and Peace*, full of splendid ideas. It ends triumphantly with the magnificent patriotic tune associated with Marshal Kutuzov, the architect of the Russian victory. Järvi and the Philharmonia Orchestra are thoroughly at home in these scores, and the Chandos recording is characteristically spectacular. This is well worth exploring.

Sinfonia concertante for cello and orchestra, Op. 125. (see also above under *Concertino*).
(N) *** Virgin/EMI Dig. VC5 45310-2 [id.]. Truls Mørk, CBSO, Paavo Järvi – MIASKOVSKY: *Cello concerto, Op. 66*. ***
*** DG Dig. 449 821-2 [id.]. Mischa Maisky, Russian Nat. O, Pletnev – MIASKOVSKY: *Cello concerto*. ***

Virgin bring the Norwegian Truls Mørk and the Birmingham Orchestra under Paavo Järvi in an exhilarating and masterly performance that, as far as the solo playing is concerned, certainly matches if not surpasses its DG rival. So, too, does the Virgin recording, which is both richer and more present. It is unique in offering the alternative version of the finale on a second CD.

Mischa Maisky is often over-emotional, but in Prokofiev's masterpiece his intensity is not misplaced. This is a highly characterful account that can withstand the most exalted comparisons. Pletnev and the Russian National Orchestra give a superb account of themselves and produce a real Prokofievian sonority, full of the mordant flavour the composer commands and with a splendid rhythmic spring. Judging from this, Pletnev would do a superlative Prokofiev symphony cycle, and one can only hope that DG will let him start with the *Sixth* and *Seventh*, written at roughly the same period. The Miaskovsky coupling enhances the attractiveness of this CD which, for the *Sinfonia concertante*, will now be a first choice for many collectors.

Sinfonietta in A, Op. 48 (see also below, under *Symphony No. 7*)
(M) *** Virgin/EMI Dig. CUV5 61206-2 [id.]. Lausanne CO, Zedda – DEBUSSY: *Danse* etc.; MILHAUD: *Création du monde*. ***

Prokofiev could not understand why the early *Sinfonietta* failed to make an impression on the wider musical public, and neither can we. Alongside the *Classical Symphony* the *giocoso* outer movements have a more fragile geniality but they are highly delectable, as are the somewhat angular *Andante*, the brief *Intermezzo* and the witty Scherzo. The use of the orchestral palette is as subtle as it is engaging and, with Alberto Zedda's affectionately light touch and fine Lausanne playing, the piece emerges here with all colours flying. The fairly resonant sound, with the orchestra slightly recessed, adds to the feeling of warmth without blunting the orchestral articulation.

The Stone Flower (ballet): complete.
(N) (M) *** CPO Dig. CPO 999385-2 (3) [id.]. Hanover Radio PO, Michail Jurowski.
(N) (B) *** BMG/Melodiya Twofer 74321 63458-2 (2) [id.]. Bolshoi Theatre O, Rozhdestvensky.

The Stone Flower is grievously (if understandably) neglected in favour of its two full-length companions, *Romeo and Juliet* and *Cinderella*. It is not as distinguished, characterful or inventive as they, but Prokofiev at second-best is still worth more than a lot of composers firing on all cylinders. There is much that is imaginative in this score, even if it is not the equal of its two companions in terms of consistency and inspiration. The new version from Hanover under Michail Jurowski has a lot going for it. The orchestral playing is polished and characterful, and the CPO recording is fresh and well detailed. Indeed, it must now be a first recommendation, though it is much the more expensive on three mid-price discs, when the Russian recording has been reissued as a 'Twofer'. Incidentally, the 1991 Kirov video production (Teldec 9031-76401-3) is not to be missed: a joy to the eye, very well danced and well worth buying; but the score is not complete.

Rozhdestvensky's Bolshoi performance dates from 1968 and still sounds pretty good on CD.

SYMPHONIES

Symphonies Nos. 1–7.
*** Chandos Dig. CHAN 8931/4 [id.]. RSNO, Järvi.

Symphonies Nos. 1–7; Overture russe, Op. 72; Scythian suite, Op. 20.
(B) **(*) Decca 430 782-2 (4). LSO or LPO, Walter Weller.

These Chandos recordings from the mid-1980s are of the highest quality. They have been shorn of their couplings in this box, the only important loss being the delightful *Sinfonietta*. Both versions of the *Fourth Symphony* are included: the 1947 revision appears with the *Classical* on the first disc, while the 1930 original is coupled with the *Third*. Nos. 2 and 6 are on the third disc, and 5 and 7 on the last, so that no side-breaks are involved. As performances, these are the equal of the best.

Weller began his 1970s Kingsway Hall recordings with the LSO (Nos. 1, 5 and 7) then turned to the LPO. The performances are polished and very well played, though at times they are emotionally a little earthbound. Transfers are well managed, though there is some loss of naturalness in the upper range. The finest of the set is No. 2. Elsewhere, the bitter tang of Prokofiev's language is again toned down and the hard-etched lines smoothed over. The *Seventh* suits Weller's approach readily and he catches the atmosphere of its somewhat balletic second movement particularly well. The *Russian overture* has plenty of energy but the *Scythian suite*, too, needs more abrasiveness. However, those who normally find Prokofiev's orchestral writing too pungent could well be won over by these performances.

Symphony No. 1 in D (Classical), Op. 25.
*** DG Dig. 423 624-2 [id.]. Orpheus CO – BIZET: *Symphony;* BRITTEN: *Simple symphony*. ***

The Orpheus performance has freshness and wit – the droll bassoon solo in the first movement against sparkling string figurations is delightful. In the cantilena of the *Larghetto*, some ears might crave a greater body of violin tone; but the playing has a fine poise, and the minuet and finale have equal flair. Excellent, truthful recording to make this a highly desirable triptych.

Symphonies Nos. 1 in D (Classical); 4 in C, Op. 112 (revised 1947 version).
*** Chandos Dig. CHAN 8400 [id.]. RSNO, Järvi.

Järvi succeeds in making out a more eloquent case for the revision of the *Fourth Symphony* than many of his predecessors. He also gives an exhilarating account of the *Classical Symphony*, one of the best on record. The slow movement has real douceur and the finale is wonderfully high-spirited. On CD, the recording has fine range and immediacy, but in the *Fourth Symphony* the upper range is a little fierce in some of the more forceful climaxes.

Symphonies Nos. 1 in D (Classical), Op. 25; 5 in B flat, Op. 100; Romeo and Juliet: excerpts; Chout: final dance.
✿ (M) (***) RCA mono 09026 61657-2 [id.]. Boston SO, Koussevitzky.

Koussevitzky's *Fifth Symphony* and the four movements from *Romeo and Juliet* are quite simply breathtaking and have never been equalled, except perhaps by Karajan's 1969 record with the Berlin Philharmonic. Yet this has even more fire, zest and virtuosity, and the recordings, made in 1945–6, are remarkably good. The *Classical Symphony* is not to be confused with Koussevitzky's sparkling account on 78-r.p.m. records. Both the *Classical Symphony* and the *Danse finale* from *Chout* come from 1947 and were recorded when the orchestra were on a visit to Carnegie Hall, New York. Likewise these are thrilling performances on which it would be very difficult to improve and, again, few allowances have to be made for the sound-quality. An outstanding issue in every way.

Symphonies Nos. 1 (Classical); 7, Op. 131; Love for 3 oranges (opera): *suite.*
(B) *** CfP CD-CFP 4523. Philh. O, Malko.

All the performances here are quite excellent, and the *Seventh Symphony*, of which Malko conducted the UK première, is freshly conceived and finely shaped. What is so striking is the range and refinement of the 1955 stereo recording: the excellence of the balance and the body of the sound are remarkable.

(i) *Symphony No. 1 in D (Classical);* (ii) *Romeo and Juliet* (ballet): highlights.
(B) *** DG Classikon Dig. 439 492-2. (i) Orpheus CO; (ii) Boston SO, Ozawa.

An outstanding coupling. The Orpheus performance of the *Classical Symphony* is first class in every way while *Romeo and Juliet* was one of Ozawa's finest recordings. The playing has elegance and an attractive rhythmic lightness and point. There is no lack of drama or feeling, but it is the stylishness and beauty of the playing one remembers, together with the conductor's obvious affection for the score. The sound throughout is of DG's best, warm yet transparent and with a most attractive ambience.

Symphonies Nos. 1 in D (Classical), Op. 25; 5 in B flat, Op. 100.
(M) *** DG 437 253-2 [id.]. BPO, Karajan.
(M) *** Ph. (IMS) Dig. 442 399-2. LAPO, André Previn.
(M) *** [RCA Dig. 09026 61350-2]. LPO or St Louis SO, Slatkin.
(M) **(*) Sony SBK 53260 [id.]. Phd. O, Ormandy.
(BB) **(*) Naxos Dig. 8.550237 [id.]. Slovak PO, Stephen Gunzenhauser.

Karajan's 1969 recording of the *Fifth* is in a class of its own. The playing has wonderful tonal sophistication and Karajan judges tempi to perfection so that proportions seem quite ideal. The recording has an excellent perspective and allows all the subtleties of orchestral detail to register; however, the digital remastering has overtly brightened the upper range, while the bass response is drier. Nevertheless this remains among the most distinguished *Fifths* ever recorded, and it is coupled with Karajan's 1982 digital recording of the *Classical Symphony*, in which his performance is predictably brilliant and the playing beautifully polished, with grace and eloquence distinguishing the slow movement.

In the first movement of the *Fifth*, Previn's pacing seems exactly right: everything flows so naturally and speaks effectively. The Scherzo is not as high-voltage as some rivals, but Previn still brings it off well; and in the slow movement he gets playing of genuine eloquence from the Los Angeles orchestra. He also gives an excellent account of the perennially fresh *Classical Symphony*. The recording is beautifully natural, with impressive detail, range and body. Although Karajan reigns supreme in this coupling, his analogue recording does not match this Philips competitor, and those wanting modern, digital sound will find Previn an ideal mid-priced alternative.

Ultimately the same holds for Slatkin's St Louis performance on RCA at mid-price. It is eminently well shaped, spacious and characterful, and there is no want of virtuosity or lyricism. Thoroughly recommendable, without being a first choice.

The Philadelphia Orchestra play superbly and with much wit in the *Classical Symphony*. Ormandy's expansive warmth in the *Adagio* and the easy brilliance of the orchestral articulation in the second and fourth movements make for splendid results in the *Fifth*. Although the early stereo recording could be more opulent and less brightly lit, it still conveys impressively the ample body of tone this great orchestra was creating in the late 1950s.

The Naxos recording coupling the most popular of the Prokofiev symphonies, Nos. 1 and 5, on the face of it is very good value indeed. The recording is altogether first class: there is splendid detail and definition, and the balance is extremely well judged. Moreover the American conductor, Stephen Gunzenhauser, gets very good playing from the excellent Slovak Philharmonic and the performances have the merit of being straightforward and unaffected. All the same, tempi are generally well judged in No. 5. The first movement of the *'Classical' Symphony* is a bit sedate and wanting in sparkle; the finale comes off best.

Symphony No. 2 in D min., Op. 40; Romeo and Juliet (ballet): *suite No. 1, Op. 64.*
**(*) Chandos Dig. CHAN 8368 [id.]. RSNO, Järvi.

The *Second Symphony* reflects the iconoclastic temper of the early 1920s; the violence and dissonance of its first movement betray Prokofiev's avowed intention of writing a work 'made of iron and steel'. Neeme Järvi produces altogether excellent results from the Royal Scottish National Orchestra and the Chandos recording is impressively detailed and vivid. The *Romeo and Juliet* suite comes off well; the RSNO play with real character.

Symphony No. 3 in C min., Op. 44.
(M) *** Decca 448 579-2. LSO, Abbado – HINDEMITH: *Symphonic metamorphoses on themes of Weber.* JANACEK: *Sinfonietta.* ***

In the *Third Symphony* Abbado penetrates the atmosphere and mystery of the highly imaginative inner movements most successfully. These movements exert quite a powerful spell, and their impact is all the greater for Abbado's total lack of exaggeration. The outer movements are slightly less successful, needing a shade more bite and momentum. But the Decca recording has fine body and presence, and if the couplings are suitable this is still very recommendable.

Symphonies Nos. 3; 4 in C, Op. 47 (original, 1930 version).
*** Chandos Dig. CHAN 8401 [id.]. RSNO, Järvi.

Neeme Järvi's account of the *Third* is extremely successful. In many ways the original of the *Fourth Symphony* seems more like a ballet suite than a symphony: its insufficient tonal contrast tells – yet the Scherzo, drawn from the music for the Temptress in *The Prodigal Son* ballet, is particularly felicitous.

Symphony No. 4 in C (revised 1947 version), *Op. 112; The Prodigal son* (ballet; complete), *Op.46.*
(N) (BB) *** Naxos Dig. 8,553055 [id.]. Ukraine NSO, Theodore Kuchar.

It makes an ideal coupling having the *Symphony No. 4* alongside the ballet score from which Prokofiev drew most of the material. He originally wrote the symphony in 1929–30 for the 50th anniversary of the Boston Symphony Orchestra, using the ballet score written only months before for Diaghilev. The 1947 revision of the symphony, now generally preferred, is richer in both structure and instrumentation. Kuchar's readings are both powerful and idiomatic, with crisply disciplined playing from the Ukraine orchestra bringing home the weight and violence of much of the writing. These are performances to match and even outshine current rivals at whatever price; the Naxos recording is satisfyingly full-bodied, not least in vivid brass and percussion sounds, with the piano both clear and well integrated in the symphony.

Symphony No. 5 in B flat, Op. 100.
*** Chandos Dig. CHAN 8576 [id.]. Leningrad PO, Jansons.

Symphony No. 5 in B flat, Op. 100; Romeo and Juliet: excerpts.
(N) ** Teldec/Warner Dig. 4509 96301-2 [id.]. NYPO, Kurt Masur.

Symphony No. 5 in B flat, Op. 100; Scythian suite, Op. 20.
*** EMI Dig. CDC7 54577-2 [id.]. CBSO, Simon Rattle.

Symphony No. 5 in B flat, Op. 100; Waltz suite, Op. 110.
*** Chandos Dig. CHAN 8450 [id.]. RSNO, Järvi.

Rattle's brilliantly recorded account of the *Fifth Symphony* with the CBSO is very fine indeed, full of fire and vitality; given the quality of the sound, it must rank along with the best now available. The slow movement comes off particularly well – though perhaps it is invidious to single out one particular movement, for these are really stimulating performances with many imaginative touches. Thoroughly recommendable.

Mariss Jansons's reading with the Leningrad Philharmonic was recorded at a live concert in Dublin. Needless to say, the playing is pretty high voltage, with firm, rich string-tone, particularly from the lower strings, and distinctive wind timbre. Jansons goes for brisk tempi – and in the slow movement he really is too fast. The Scherzo is dazzling and so, too, is the finale, which is again fast and overdriven. An exhilarating and exciting performance, eminently well recorded, recommended to those willing to accept the ungenerous measure.

Järvi's credentials in this repertoire are well established and his direction unhurried, fluent and authoritative. His feeling for the music is unfailingly natural. The three *Waltzes* which derive from various sources are all elegantly played. The Chandos recording is set just a shade further back than some of its companions in the series, yet at the same time every detail is clear.

Kurt Masur's account of the *Fifth Symphony* with the New York Philharmonic Orchestra derives from concert performances at Avery Fisher Hall. The playing is eminently cultured and the performance would be enjoyable in the concert hall were it not for the abrupt hiatus at the *l'istesso tempo* section (fig. 48) of the Scherzo which will rule it out of court for many collectors. The recording is very full-bodied and well detailed. The six movements from *Romeo and Juliet* are studio recordings and paradoxically enough, sound more spontaneous but even so there is nothing here to disturb existing recommendations.

Symphony No. 6 in E flat min., Op. 111; Romeo and Juliet (ballet): excerpts.
(N) **(*) Decca Dig. 458 190-2 [id.]. NHK SO, Charles Dutoit.

Dutoit gives warmth to one of Prokofiev's most

elusive works, missing some of the darker qualities. Warm, full recording made in a regular Decca venue, the Vienna Konzerthaus. The excerpts from the *Romeo and Juliet ballet* were recorded in Tokyo, again with warmth in both the sound and performance, making the focus less sharp than it might be.

Symphony No. 6 in E flat min., Op. 111. Waltz suite, Op. 110, Nos. 1, 5 and 6.
*** Chandos Dig. CHAN 8359 [id.]. RSNO, Järvi.

Though it lags far behind the *Fifth* in popularity, the *Sixth Symphony* goes much deeper than any of its companions; indeed it is perhaps the greatest of the Prokofiev cycle. Neeme Järvi has an instinctive grasp and deep understanding of this symphony; he shapes its detail as skilfully as he does its architecture as a whole. These artists have the measure of the music's tragic poignancy more than almost any of their predecessors on record. The fill-up, as its title implies, is a set of waltzes, drawn and adapted from various stage works.

Symphony No. 7 in C sharp min., Op. 131; Sinfonietta in A, Op. 5/48.
*** Chandos Dig. CHAN 8442 [id.]. SNO, Järvi.

Neeme Järvi's account of the *Seventh Symphony* is hardly less successful than the other issues in this cycle. He draws very good playing from the SNO and has the full measure of this repertoire. The early *Sinfonietta* is a highly attractive coupling (what a sunny and charming piece it is!). The digital recording has great range and is excellently balanced.

CHAMBER AND INSTRUMENTAL MUSIC

Cello sonata in C, Op. 119.
(N) *** Virgin/EMI Dig. VC5 45274-2 [id.]. Truls Mørk, Lars Vogt – SHOSTAKOVICH: *Cello sonata.* STRAVINSKY: *Suite italienne.* ***
*** Chandos Dig. CHAN 8340 [id.]. Yuli Turovsky, Luba Edlina – SHOSTAKOVICH: *Sonata.* ***
(BB) *** ASV Quicksilva Dig. CDQS 6218 [(M) id. import]. Bernard Gregor-Smith, Yolande Wrigley – MARTINU: *Variations;* JANACEK: *Pohádka;* SHOSTAKOVICH: *Cello sonata.* ***
(BB) **(*) Arte Nova Dig. 74321 27805-2 [id.]. Emil Klein, Cristian Beldi – SHOSTAKOVICH: *Cello sonata.* **(*)

Truls Mørk and Lars Vogt give a perceptive and thoughtful account of the *Sonata* and are expertly recorded in the Eidsvoll Church, Norway. This is probably the best of recent versions and in addition to the Shostakovich has the advantage of an additional item, the Stravinsky *Suite italienne.*

Yuli Turovsky and Luba Edlina are eloquent advocates of this *Sonata*. A finely wrought and rewarding score, it deserves greater popularity, and this excellent performance and recording should make it new friends. The balance is particularly lifelike on CD.

Both these ASV and Arte Nova performances are very serviceable and are unlikely to disappoint. Bernard Gregor-Smith and Yolande Wrigley have the benefit of the better recording: there is greater bloom and a more lively acoustic, though the piano is sometimes more dominant in the aural picture than is ideal. They are more relaxed and thoughtful in approach than the Romanian partnership.

However, Emil Klein and Cristian Beldi give a very well-characterized account of the *Sonata*, tautly held together and vital in feeling, though the sound is a bit drier than the ASV listed above. The balance between cello and piano is better-judged, even if the timbre of the latter is less realistic. Artistically there is not a great deal to choose between these performances, though, if choose one must, the ASV would be the one to have on account of the fresher sound and the additional Martinů and Janáček items.

Flute sonata in D, Op. 94.
(M) *** RCA 09026 61615-2 [id.]. James Galway, Martha Argerich – FRANCK; REINECKE: *Sonatas.* ***

Prokofiev's *Flute sonata* (1943) is one of his sunniest and most serene wartime compositions. It is difficult to imagine a more delightful performance than this one, with its combination of effortless virtuosity and spontaneity of feeling; every detail falls naturally into place. The recording is most sympathetic.

Overture on Hebrew themes (for clarinet, piano & string quartet), *Op. 34; Quintet* (for oboe, clarinet, violin, viola & cello), *Op. 39.*
(B) *** HM Musique d'Abord Dig. HMA 1901419 [id.]. Walter Boeykens Ens. (with KOKAI: *Clarinet quartettino* ***) – KHACHATURIAN: *Clarinet trio.* ***

Prokofiev composed his *Overture on Jewish themes* in 1919 at the request of a Jewish commission from a small ensemble of musical refugees in New York (hence the instrumentation). He warmed to a pair of melodies taken from a collection provided by the commission, and the result is a delightful work, at first nostalgic, then energetic and jocular. The *Quintet* was written to accompany a ballet commissioned by a Russian dancer whom the composer had met while working with Diaghilev. It has a wide range of moods: gentle, sardonic, burlesque; while highly characteristic of its composer, it also brings clear rhythmic influences from Stravinsky. Both works are performed here with vigour, affection and wit; indeed they are beautifully played and recorded.

The *Quartetettino* (for clarinet and string trio) by Rezsö Kókai (1906–62) provided as a bonus is deliciously flimsy in texture (suggesting Françaix with Hungarian inflexions) but with a touching folk-tune-like *Canzonetta* for its slow movement.

String quartets Nos. 1 in B min., Op. 50; 2 in F, Op. 92.
*** Olympia Dig. OCD 340 [id.]. American Qt.

(i) *String quartets Nos. 1 in B min., Op. 50; 2 in F, Op. 92;* (ii) *Cello sonata, Op. 119.*
(BB) *** Naxos Dig. 8.553136 [id.]. (i) Aurora Qt; (ii) Grebanier, Guggenheim.

The American Quartet play the *First Quartet* far more persuasively than any earlier version and reveal it to be a work of some appeal as well as substance. The *Second* incorporates folk ideas from Kabarda in the Caucasus, to highly characteristic ends. Although the performance does not have quite the bite and zest of the Hollywood Quartet, it does not fall far short of it, and the recording is absolutely first class. A rewarding issue.

The members of the Aurora Quartet all come from the San Francisco Symphony and give thoroughly straightforward, unaffected accounts of both *Quartets*. They are recorded in a warm, resonant acoustic. The performance of the *Second Quartet* may not have the character of the pioneering Hollywood set (reissued on Testament; see below) but then what other account has! The *Cello sonata* makes a substantial bonus. Michael Grebanier is a principal cellist of the San Francisco Symphony and Janet Goodman Guggenheim is a pupil of Rosina Lhevinne, who teaches at the University of California at Berkeley. Theirs is a thoroughly musical account, not perhaps as strongly characterized as some, but eminently satisfying, and well recorded. A more than acceptable makeweight to the two *Quartets*, and this CD is well worth the money.

String quartet No. 2 in F, Op. 92.
✪ (***) Testament mono SBT 1052 [id.]. Hollywood Qt – HINDEMITH: *Quartet No. 3;* WALTON: *Quartet in A min.* *** ✪

There have been innumerable recordings of Prokofiev's *Second Quartet* since the pioneering Hollywood Quartet version first appeared on these shores in 1952. Not one has matched let alone surpassed this stunning performance, which has an extraordinary precision and intensity (as well as repose when this is required). The transfer sounds excellent and, although the mono sound does not represent the state of the art these days, the performance surely does.

Violin sonata (for solo violin), *Op. 115; Sonata for two violins.*
*** Chandos Dig. CHAN 8988 [id.]. Mordkovitch, Young – SCHNITTKE: *Prelude;* SHOSTAKOVICH: *Violin sonata.* ***

Sonata for 2 violins, Op. 56.
*** Hyperion Dig. CDA 66473 [id.]. Osostowicz, Kovacic – MARTINU: *Violin sonata;* MILHAUD: *Violin duo* etc. **(*)

The solo *Violin sonata in D*, Op. 115, is a crisply characteristic piece in three short movements. The *Sonata in C for two violins*, written much earlier, is just as effective, played – as here – by solo violins. The warmth of Lydia Mordkovitch is well matched by her partner, Emma Young.

The *Sonata for two violins* gives the impression of being vintage Prokofiev, as performed by Krysia Osostowicz and Ernst Kovacic. The slow movement is played with exceptional imagination and poetry.

Violin sonatas Nos. 1 in F min., Op. 80; 2 in D, Op. 94a.
(M) *** DG Dig. 445 557-2. Shlomo Mintz, Yefim Bronfman – RAVEL: *Violin sonata in G.* ***

(i) *Violin sonatas Nos. 1–2;* (ii) *Violin concerto No. 2 in G min., Op. 63.*
(M) *** RCA 09026 61454-2 [id.]. Itzhak Perlman; (i) Vladimir Ashkenazy; (ii) Boston SO, Leinsdorf.

Both the *Violin sonatas* date from the years immediately after Prokofiev returned to the Soviet Union. The *F minor Sonata* is one of his very finest works, and the *D major*, originally written for the flute, has a winning charm and melodiousness. Both works are masterly and rewarding.

Shlomo Mintz made a great impression with his coupling of the two *Concertos*, and his recording of the *Sonatas* is hardly less successful. Mintz has a wonderful purity of line and immaculate intonation, and his partner, Yefim Bronfman, is both vital and sensitive. These are commanding performances, imaginative in phrasing and refined in approach. The DG recording is excellent. This is a clear first choice.

Perlman and Ashkenzy also play both works superbly, and the 1969 recording is well balanced, slightly dry in timbre but otherwise truthful. Their coupling is the *Second Violin concerto*, recorded three years earlier. It is an enjoyably fresh and spontaneous account and, even if Leinsdorf provides an accomplished rather than a highly individual accompaniment, the finale comes off particularly vividly. Good recording, with the soloist balanced well forward.

Violin sonata No. 1 in F min., Op. 80.
(N) *** Orfeo C489981B [id.]. David Oistrakh, Sviatoslav Richter – BRAHMS: *Sonata No. 2.* ***

(N) ** Ph. Dig. 446 091-2 [id.]. Viktoria Mullova, Piotr Anderszewski – DEBUSSY: JANACEK: *Violin sonatas.* **

This Orfeo disc records the Oistrakh–Richter

partnership in a live concert at the 1972 Salzburg Festival at the very top of their form. The playing, as one might expect, silences criticism and the recording from ORF (Austrian Radio) is perfectly serviceable.

Viktoria Mullova and Piotr Anderszewski give a well-projected account of the *Sonata* and are recorded with tremendous clarity and realism. For all the excellence of the sound though, as a musical experience it does not equal Oistrakh and Richter listed above.

PIANO MUSIC

10 Pieces from Romeo and Juliet, Op. 75; Toccata in D min., Op. 11.
(N) ** Hyperion Dig. CDA 67018 [id.]. Nikolai Demidenko. – MUSSORGSKY: *Pictures.* *

No doubts about Demidenko's virtuosity and keyboard command, particularly in the *Toccata*, or the excellence of the Hyperion sound. His playing in the *Romeo and Juliet* often delights, but there are exasperating mannerisms that attract attention to the pianist rather than Prokofiev.

10 Pieces from Romeo and Juliet, Op. 75; War and peace: Waltz, Op. 96/1. The Love of three oranges, Op. 33b: Scherzo; March. 6 Pieces from Cinderella, Op. 102.
*** Decca Dig. 452 062-2 [id.]. Vladimir Ashkenazy.

Ashkenazy's recital concentrates on Prokofiev's music for the stage in the composer's own adroit transcriptions for the keyboard. Excerpts from two operas, including the beguiling *Waltz* from *War and peace*, the ten pieces from *Romeo and Juliet* and six from *Cinderella*, make an attractive and appealing hour's listening, particularly when they are as well characterized and vividly recorded as they are here. If this programme appeals, there is no need to hesitate.

Piano sonatas 1–9 (complete); *Lieutenant Kijé* (suite, transcribed Chiu).
**(*) HM Dig. HMU 907086/8 (3) [id.]. Frederic Chiu.

Frederic Chiu is a brilliant Chinese-American pianist now in his early thirties. This is exciting playing. His tempi can be a little extreme, and there are greater extremes of dynamics and colours. The *Seventh* is brilliant and can be ranked along with the best, and the *Sixth*, though not superior to either of the Kissin accounts, is pretty dazzling. Throughout the cycle he impresses with his marvellous fingers, abundant energy and good musical taste. Unfortunately the recording lets him down: the tone is shallow and the balance a bit too close. Otherwise this would have been a strong three-star recommendation.

Piano sonata No. 1 in F min., Op. 1; 4 Pieces, Op. 4; Prelude and Fugue in D min. (Buxtehude, arr. Prokofiev); *2 Sonatinas, Op. 54; Gavotte (Hamlet, Op. 77 bis); 3 Pieces, Op. 96.*
*** Chandos Dig. CHAN 9017 [id.]. Boris Berman.

Piano sonata No. 2 in D min., Op. 14; Cinderella: 3 Pieces, Op. 102; Dumka; 3 Pieces, Op. 69; Waltzes (Schubert, arr. Prokofiev).
*** Chandos Dig. CHAN 9119 [id.]. Boris Berman.

Piano sonata No. 3 in A min., Op. 28; Cinderella: 6 pieces, Op. 95; 10 Pieces, Op. 12; Thoughts, Op. 62.
*** Chandos Dig. CHAN 9069 [id.]. Boris Berman.

Piano sonata No. 4, Op. 29; Music for children, Op. 65; 6 Pieces, Op. 52.
*** Chandos Dig. CHAN 8926 [id.]. Boris Berman.

Piano sonata No. 5 in C, Op. 38/135; 4 Pieces, Op. 32; Love for three oranges: Scherzo and March; Romeo and Juliet: 10 Pieces, Op. 75.
*** Chandos Dig. CHAN 8851 [id.]. Boris Berman.

Piano sonatas Nos. 5 in C, Op. 38; 6 in A, Op. 82; 10 in E min., Op. 137 (fragment); *Gavotte (Classical Symphony, Op. 25); Juvenilia; Toccata, Op. 11.*
*** Chandos Dig. CHAN 9361 [id.]. Boris Berman.

Piano sonata No. 7; Sarcasms, Op. 17; Tales of an old grandmother, Op. 31; Visions fugitives, Op. 22.
*** Chandos Dig. CHAN 8881 [id.]. Boris Berman.

Piano sonata No. 8; Cinderella: 10 Pieces, Op. 97; 4 Pieces, Op. 3.
*** Chandos Dig. CHAN 8976 [id.]. Boris Berman.

Piano sonata No. 9; Choses en soi, Op. 45; Divertissement, Op. 43 bis; 4 Etudes, Op. 2.
*** Chandos Dig. CHAN 9211 [id.]. Boris Berman.

Boris Berman's survey of the complete Prokofiev piano music has proved the most satisfactory all-round set of the sonatas so far. Berman always plays with tremendous concentration and control. He commands a finely articulated and vital rhythmic sense as well as a wide range of keyboard colour. The first CD brings some transcriptions. He does not play these with quite the same elegance and distinction that mark the *Sonatinas*, which are beautifully characterized and splendidly recorded. In the *Second Sonata in D minor* Berman is quite magnificent and full of panache. The *Third* is coupled with the inventive but unaccountably neglected *Ten Pieces*, Op. 12. This also has the *Pensées*, Op. 62, and remains one of the most desirable of the set.

The *Fourth Sonata*, like its predecessor, takes its inspiration from Prokofiev's earlier notebooks. The Op. 52 *Pieces* are transcriptions of movements from other works: the ballet *The Prodigal Son*, the *Andante* from the *First Quartet*, the Scherzo from the *Sinfonietta* and one of the *Songs without words*, Op. 35. Berman plays them incisively, with marvellous articulation and wit. On CHAN 8851 he plays the post-war revision of the *Fifth Sonata*, and its crisp, brittle inner movement is heard to splendid advantage. The other works are presented with equal perception. State-of-the-art recording from Chandos, made at The Maltings, Snape. Of course with the *Sixth Sonata* Berman is traversing hotly contested ground. Yet his cooler and more collected reading remains eminently recommendable. He then gives us the original (1923) version of the *Fifth Sonata* (generally to be preferred to the revision) but also the minute or so that survives of a *Tenth Sonata*. Berman is completely inside the astringent idiom and subtle character of the *Seventh Sonata*, and his playing in the *Sarcasms* could scarcely be bettered. He gives altogether outstanding performances of all four works, and the superbly vivid recording greatly enhances the sheer musical satisfaction this disc gives.

In the expansive *Eighth Sonata*, there is more pianistic refinement in Berman's account than in the Lill reviewed below, though it is in the ten numbers from *Cinderella* and the Op. 3 *Pieces* that Berman's command of atmosphere and character tells most. The quality of the recorded sound is excellent.

Berman plays the *Ninth Sonata* with tremendous concentration and control. His finely articulated and vital rhythms are matched by a good command of keyboard colour; aided by the clean, well-balanced (though rather forward) recording, he presents this sonata in the most persuasive light. The *Choses en soi* ('Things in themselves') come from the period of the *Third Symphony*, though there is a momentary hint of *The Prodigal Son*. The *Divertissement* is a delightful piece in Prokofiev's most acerbic manner which derived from the ballet, *Trapeze*. Berman couples them with the brilliant Op. 2 *Etudes* of 1909 with which Prokofiev made his Moscow début. A very satisfying recital.

Piano sonatas Nos. 2 in D min., Op. 14; 3 in A min., Op. 28; 5 in C, Op. 38; 9 in C, Op. 103.
*** Sony Dig. SK53273 [id.]. Yefim Bronfman.

Bronfman is highly articulate and meticulously attentive to details of dynamics and phrasing. The brittle rhythms and the energy of the writing are always effectively conveyed. He plays the earlier version of the inventive *Fifth Sonata*. The recorded sound is excellent, and readers wanting this particular coupling need not hesitate. A good three-star recommendation, and the equal of any of the modern versions now on the market.

Piano sonatas Nos. 2 in D min., Op. 14; 7 in B flat, Op. 83; 8 in B flat, Op. 84.
(N) *** DG Dig. 457 588-2 [id.]. Mikhail Pletnev.

Pletnev's 1997 account of the *Seventh Sonata* seems broader and deeper than his early version made soon after he won the Tchaikovsky competition in 1978. Yet in duration they differ only in a matter of seconds, and it is the mastery of pacing and characterization that gives this impression. The variety of keyboard colour and the control of voicing is stunning both here and in the *Eighth Sonata*. The latter can be named in the same breath as the Gilels and Richter versions – and so, for that matter, can the *Second*. Stunning playing and good recording.

Piano sonata No. 6 in A, Op. 82.
❁ *** DG Dig. 413 363-2 [id.]. Pogorelich – RAVEL: *Gaspard de la nuit*. ***

Pogorelich's performance of the *Sixth Sonata* is quite simply dazzling; indeed, it is by far the best version of it ever put on record. It remains Pogorelich's most brilliant record so far and can be recommended with the utmost enthusiasm in its CD format.

Piano sonata No. 7 in B flat, Op. 83.
(M) *** DG 447 431-2 [id.]. Maurizio Pollini – *Recital*. ***

This is a great performance by Pollini, well in the Horowitz or Richter category. It is part of a generous CD of twentieth-century music.

Piano sonata No. 7; Toccata in C, Op. 11.
(M) (***) RCA mono GD 60377 [id.]. Vladimir Horowitz – BARBER; KABALEVSKY: *Sonatas* etc. (***)

Horowitz's account of the *Seventh Sonata* is justly legendary. When he had recorded it in 1945 he sent a copy of the disc to the composer, who returned an autographed score to express his admiration. The better-known *Toccata* is hardly less electrifying, and the somewhat confined mono sound is never distracting with playing of this degree of magnetism.

Piano sonatas Nos. 7 in B flat, Op. 83; 8 in B flat, Op. 84.
*** Sony Dig. MK 44680 [id.]. Yefim Bronfman.

Yefim Bronfman has a formidable technique and his clarity of articulation and tonal finesse are unfailingly impressive. The opening of No. 8 has a good sense of forward movement. Highly accomplished playing throughout, though it is distinctly short measure these days. All the same, it is very recommendable.

Piano sonatas Nos. 7 in B flat, Op. 83; 8 in B flat, Op. 84; 9 in C, Op. 103.
*** ASV Dig. CDDCA 755 [id.]. John Lill.

This disc, coupling the last three *Sonatas*, offers exceptionally good value, and the excellent ASV recording was made in Henry Wood Hall. All three performances are of high quality, and John Lill is never less than a thoughtful and intelligent guide in this repertoire.

Visions fugitives, Op. 22.
*** Decca Dig. 444 803-2 [id.]. Olli Mustonen – HINDEMITH: *Ludus tonalis*. ***

You are not likely to buy Mustonen's CD for this Prokofiev coupling, but rather to enjoy this attractive suite as an antidote to Hindemith's much more intractable *Ludus tonalis*. If you venture so bravely into Hindemith's world you will find Mustonen's account of the *Visions fugitives* perceptive, strongly characterized and vividly coloured. It is also very well recorded.

VOCAL MUSIC

(i) *Alexander Nevsky* (cantata), *Op. 78;* (ii) *Ivan the Terrible, Op. 116* (film music, arr. Lankester).
*** Sony Dig. S2K 48387 (2) [id.]. (i) Dolora Zajic; (ii) Christopher Plummer (nar.), Sinyavskaya, Leiferkus; L. Symphony Ch., LSO, Rostropovich.

Rostropovich's set offers not the usual cantata version of Prokofiev's music for the Eisenstein film but one, more comprehensive, prepared by Michael Lankester, which tells the story of the Tsar by way of an elaborate narration, dotted with biblical quotations. Having snatches of music joined by spoken narration suits this subject well, though having so much speech means that the piece spreads to a second disc. Particularly moving is the humming chorus which starts the second of the two discs, a hushed and meditative version of the great surging melody which later became a central theme in Prokofiev's epic opera, *War and Peace*, representing General Kutuzov's patriotic defiance. Christopher Plummer is the oratorical narrator, with Sergei Leiferkus and the fruity-toned Tamara Sinyavskaya the excellent soloists, and the London Symphony Chorus both powerful and refined. As a fill-up on the second disc comes the *Alexander Nevsky* cantata. Dolora Zajic is the moving mezzo soloist in the great *Lament for the dead* after the *Battle on the ice*, with Rostropovich again drawing an inspired performance from the LSO and Chorus.

(i) *Alexander Nevsky* (cantata), *Op. 78;* (ii) *Ivan the Terrible, Op. 116* (film music, arr. in oratorio form by Stasevich).
(N) (B) *** EMI double fforte CZS5 73353-2 (2) [CDFB 73353]. (i) Anna Reynolds, LSO & Ch., Previn; (ii) Arkhipova, Mokrenko, Morgunov (narrator), Amb. Ch., Philh. O, Muti – RACHMANINOV: *The Bells*.

All the weight, bite and colour of the *Alexander Nevsky* score are captured by Previn and though the timbre of the singers' voices may not suggest Russians, they cope very confidently with the Russian text; Previn's direct and dynamic manner ensures that the great *Battle on the ice* scene is powerfully effective. Anna Reynolds sings the lovely *Lament for the dead* most affectingly. The sound is sharply defined, with plenty of bite; a little of the old analogue ambient fullness has gone. Like Rostropovich, Muti uses the version of *Ivan the Terrible* with spoken narration (in Russian), and this could well prove irritating on repetition when no texts are provided. Nevertheless, with fine playing and choral singing, there is much here to relish, not least those broad, folk-like melodies. The Kingsway Hall recording is admirably spacious and though the histrionic style of the narrator, Boris Morgunov, is unappealing, the two other soloists are excellent in their limited roles. The remastering has been successful and the effect is often thrillingly vivid, with the chorus especially telling.

(i) *Alexander Nevsky, Op. 78. Lieutenant Kijé (suite), Op. 60.*
(M) *** RCA GD 60176 [60176-2-RG]. (i) Rosalind Elias, Chicago SO Ch.; Chicago SO, Reiner – GLINKA: *Ruslan Overture*. ***

(i) *Alexander Nevsky, Op. 78;* (ii) *Lieutenant Kijé, Op. 60; Scythian suite, Op. 20.*
(M) *** DG 447 419-2 [id.]. (i) Elena Obraztsova; London Symphony Ch., LSO; (ii) Chicago SO; Claudio Abbado.

(i) *Alexander Nevsky, Op. 78. Scythian suite, Op. 20.*
*** Chandos Dig. CHAN 8584 [id.]. (i) Linda Finnie, RSNO Ch.; RSNO, Järvi.

Abbado's performance of *Alexander Nevsky* culminates in a deeply moving account of the tragic lament after the battle (here very beautifully sung by Obraztsova), made the more telling when the battle itself is so fine an example of orchestral virtuosity. The chorus is as incisive as the orchestra. The digital remastering of the 1980 recording has been all gain, and the sound is very impressive indeed. A fine account of *Lieutenant Kijé* and what is probably the best version of the *Scythian suite* to appear in many years make this a desirable reissue in DG's 'Legendary Recordings' series.

The bitter chill of the Russian winter can be felt in the orchestra at the very opening of Järvi's reading and the melancholy of the choral entry has real Slavic feeling. His climactic point is the enormously spectacular *Battle on the ice*, with the recording giving great pungency to the bizarre orchestral effects and the choral shouts riveting in their force and fervour. Linda Finnie sings the final lament eloquently and Järvi's apotheosis is very affecting. As coupling, Järvi also chooses the *Scythian suite*.

Reiner's version, recorded in 1959, was another of the astonishingly vivid early achievements of the RCA stereo catalogue. The performance is gripping from the first bar to the last, with choral singing of great fervour and a movingly eloquent contribution from Rosalind Elias in the great *Lament*. The *Lieutenant Kijé suite*, recorded two years earlier, is another colourful example of the Chicago orchestra at their peak, the sound again full and atmospheric.

Cantata for the 20th anniversary of the October Revolution, Op. 74.
*** Chandos Dig. CHAN 9095 [id.]. Rozhdestvensky (speaker), Philh. Ch. & O, Järvi – *Stone Flower suite*. ***

Even Prokofiev rarely wrote so wild and totally original a piece as this cantata, designed to celebrate the twentieth anniversary of the 1917 Revolution. The key movement, centrally placed and the longest, uses such exotic percussion as rattles and sirens, with shouting from the chorus, in a graphic description of the revolution in St Petersburg. Järvi, here with his fellow-conductor Gennadi Rozhdestvensky as narrator, has made a first complete recording with the Philharmonia Chorus and Orchestra. A performance by a Russian chorus might have been even more bitingly uninhibited, but it is good to have so sharply original and refreshingly dramatic a piece complete on disc at last, an occasional work that rises far above its first inspiration. As a valuable fill-up comes a suite of excerpts from the folk-tale ballet of 1948, *The Stone Flower*.

Eugene Onegin (incidental music), *Op. 71; Hamlet* (incidental music), *Op. 77; Lieutenant Kijé* (suite), *Op. 60.*
*** Chant du Monde Dig. LDC 288 027/8 (2) [id.]. Koroleva, Stetsenko, Blagovest Ch., Maly Moscow SO, Vladimir Ponkin.

Prokofiev's incidental music for *Eugene Onegin* proves to be a major find, with an inspiration comparable to *Romeo and Juliet* in lyric fervour and melodic sweep. *Hamlet* is less ambitious, offering ten vignettes, but including three engaging songs for Ophelia charmingly sung here by Ludmila Koroleva. The orchestral playing in both scores is fresh and ardent, and the Russian wind and brass playing is suitably vibrant. The performance of *Lieutenant Kijé* brings out the music's laconic melancholy in a specially Russian way. Excellent, modern, digital recording throughout. This is an indispensable set for any true Prokofievian.

On guard for peace, Op. 124.
(N) *** RCA Dig. 09026 68877-2 [id.]. Marton, Rjavkin (nar.), Bulitcheva, Rjavkin, Glinka College Boys' Ch., St Petersburg Ch. & PO, Temirkanov – SHOSTAKOVICH: *Song of the forests*. ***

Like Shostakovich, Prokofiev was required by the Soviet authorities to write his quota of propaganda pieces, and this cantata is a good example, though it cannot compare in imagination with the *Revolution cantata* of 1937. The writing is inventive, even if it lacks distinctive Prokofiev melody, while the use of a reciter (in Russian) is questionably effective. Nonetheless in coupling with the fine Shostakovich work, strongly and persuasively performed and recorded, it is very welcome.

5 Poems of Anna Akhmatova, Op. 27; 2 Poems, Op. 9; 5 Poems of Konstantin Balmont, Op. 36; 3 Romances, Op. 73.
**(*) Chandos Dig. CHAN 8509 [id.]. Carole Farley, Arkady Aronov.

Rare and valuable repertoire. The songs are powerful and full of resourceful and imaginative touches. The Akhmatova settings are quite beautiful. The *Three Romances*, Op. 73, to words of Pushkin, are full of the wry harmonic sleights of hand that are so characteristic of his musical speech. The American soprano, Carole Farley, responds to the different moods and character of the poems and encompasses a rather wide range of colour and tone, although at times her voice is rather edgy and uneven in timbre. The accompaniments of Arkady Aronov are highly sensitive and perceptive. The recording is completely truthful.

OPERA

L'amour des trois oranges (The Love for 3 oranges): complete.
**(*) Virgin/EMI (SIS) Dig. VCD7 59566-2 (2). Bacquier, Bastin, Dubosc, Gautier, Viala, Lyon Opera Ch. & O, Kent Nagano.

French was the language used when the opera was given its first, lavish production in Chicago in December 1921. It inevitably brings a degree of softening in vocal texture, but the brilliant young conductor, Kent Nagano, and his Lyon Opera House team make up for any loss in knife-edged precision of ensemble. Gabriel Bacquier as the King and Jules Bastin as the monstrous Cook, guardian of the three oranges, are well matched by the others, including Jean-Luc Viala as an aptly petulant Prince and Catherine Dubosc as a sweetly girlish Princess Ninette. The recorded sound is not ideally focussed so that the commenting chorus – very much a part of the action in *commedia dell'arte* style – is not always clear. Happily, the solo voices are better served. However, it is irritating that there are so few cueing points on the CDs (just one for each scene), even if this is very much an ensemble opera, with few set solos.

Betrothal in a monastery.

(N) *** Ph. Dig. 462 107-2(3) [id.]. Nikolai Gassie, Anna Netrebko, Alexander Gergalov, Larissa Diadkova, Evgeny Akimov, Marianna Tarassova, Sergei Alexashkin, Kirov Opera Ch. & O, Gergiev.

(N) [M] **(*) BMG/Melodiya Dig. 74321 60318-2 (2) [id.]. Alexei Maslennikov, Lyudmilla Sergienko, Vladimir Redkin, Galina Borisova, Arkady Mishenkin, Marina Shutova, Mikhail Krutikov, Vladislav Verestnikov, Bolshoi Theatre, Moscow Ch. & O, Alexander Lazarev.

The cumbersome title, *Betrothal in a monastery*, conceals a charmer among Prokofiev's operas. Completed in 1940, it is based on Sheridan's play, *The Duenna*, using all the conventional trappings of *opera buffa* – secret lovers, comic old father pressuring the heroine, rich suitor thwarted and so on. This is a gentler piece than Prokofiev would have written earlier, wittily pointed in its comic writing, but regularly giving foretastes of the ripe lyricism that was to blossom in his last, most masterly opera, *War and Peace*. The beauty of such numbers as Antonio's love-song for Louisa is regularly heightened by sensuous orchestration.

The Philips set from the Kirov, St Petersburg, follows up the success of Gergiev's earlier opera sets, with stage performances recorded live and edited together. Stage noises and odd balances are only occasionally distracting, and the dry, intimate acoustic suits the scale of the comedy, even if voices are not helped, with the orchestra a little cloudy. Outstanding in the cast – outshining her fruity opposite number in the rival Bolshoi set – is the sweet and youthful-sounding Anna Netrebko as the heroine, Louisa. The male soloists are relatively light-toned, with a sharp contrast between the two principal tenors, the buffo Don Jerome and the light-weight Don Antonio. The big advantage is that Philips's three-disc set offers a full libretto, translation and excellent background notes.

The Bolshoi version, recorded for Melodiya in 1990, presented on two mid-priced discs has the merit of a strong cast headed by the characterful Maslennikov, with a first-rate Duenna and a powerful team of male soloists. With a reverberant studio recording, there is plenty of bloom on the voices, with the beauty of the orchestral writing evocatively brought out. Lazarev's well-chosen speeds, generally a little broader than those of Gergiev on the Kirov set, allow an extra infectious spring to Prokofiev's repetitive rhythms. The snag is that at mid-price no libretto is offered, only a detailed synopsis.

The Fiery Angel (complete).

❁ *** Ph. Dig. 446 078-2 (2) (Video 070 198-3; LD 070 198-1). Gorchakova, Leiferkus, Pluzhnikov, Ognovanko, soloists; Kirov Op. Ch. & O, Gergiev.

Impressive as Neeme Järvi's 1990 recording for DG of this elusive but powerful opera was Gergiev's with Kirov forces is even finer. Based on a novel by Valery Bryusov, *The Fiery Angel* is set in and around Cologne in the 1520s. The opera centres on Renata's obsession with the vision of Madiel, a fiery angel who consumed her thoughts in childhood but who left her when, on reaching puberty, she asked him to consummate their relationship. His image possesses her, and she marries the Count Heinrich, believing that in him Madiel has returned to earth. From the very outset the style is declamatory in a way that recalls Mussorgsky. The vocal line is largely heightened speech, but Prokofiev does provide a series of leitmotivs which are identified with characters or situations in the opera. Indeed, in terms of fantasy and sheer imaginative vision, *The Fiery Angel* reaches heights which Prokofiev never surpassed, and its atmosphere resonates for a long time.

This is the finest of the Philips Kirov series yet, a live recording which, with full, forward sound, avoids most of the snags of a recorded stage-performance. Above all, it offers in the singing and acting of Elena Gorchakova in the central role of Renata, the hysterical woman obsessed by demons, one of the most compelling operatic performances in years. It was she who, when this production was given at Covent Garden, magnetized the audience; here, with experience, the intensity is if anything even greater, with the timbre of the voice often sensuously beautiful, even when stretched to the limit. Sergei Leiferkus as Ruprecht with his clear, firm baritone is also ideally cast; the remainder of the cast, from the Landlady of Evgenia Perlasova to the resonant Inquisitor of Vladimir Ognovanko, are absolutely first class, while the Kirov team provides outstanding, always idiomatic and individual performances in smaller roles. Gergiev proves an inspired conductor who secures orchestral playing of great dramatic eloquence: the players sound as though they have the music in their blood, bringing out the full power of this weird score. There are the inevitable stage noises and not all the voices in big ensembles are properly balanced, but any snag is quickly forgotten.

The presence of vision in the finely directed video tape and laserdisc serves to underline an implicit ambiguity in the opera – whether Madiel and the spirits conjured up in Act II are real or are just Renata's paranoid delusions. Here the use of mimed figures, unseen by the protagonists but perceived by the audience, was a brilliant solution. The frenetic, highly charged atmosphere of the final Convent scene, in which Renata confronts the Inquisitor, and the mass possession to which the nuns succumb, benefits by vision particularly in this splendid production. The sound in the laserdisc version has marvellous presence and detail.

War and peace (complete).

✪ (M) *** Erato/Warner 2292 45331-2 (4). Vishnevskaya, Miller, Ciesinski, Tumagian, Ochman, Ghiuselev, Smith, Paunova, Petkov, Toczyska, Zakai, Gedda, Fr. R. Ch. & Nat. O, Rostropovich.

*** Ph. Dig. 434 097-2 (3) [id.]. Gergalov, Prokina, Gregoriam, Borodina, Gerelo, Bogachova, Okhotnikov, Morozov, Kirov Theatre Ch. & O, Gergiev.

War and Peace is not just epic in scale but warmly approachable, with a fund of melody rarely matched this century. Moreover a really complete rendering of Prokofiev's text – never heard by the composer in its finished form – shows triumphantly how the components cohere into an opera of epic achievement. Rostropovich's complete account on record, flawed in some of the casting, nevertheless confirms equally that this is one of the great operatic masterpieces of the century. However, no one should be deceived by the ease of listening into thinking that the writing lacks strength or intensity; rather, Prokofiev, in his game with the Soviet authorities, was submitting to the impossible restrictions of writing a 'people's opera' and succeeding masterfully, knowing that only he could have done it.

In Rostropovich's powerful reading one revels – thanks also to the lively Erato recording – in the vividness of the atmosphere, both in the evocative love scenes and ball scenes of the first half (Peace) and in the high tensions of the battle scenes in the second (War). The opera culminates in a great patriotic chorus, using the most haunting tune of all, earlier sung by General Kutuzov after the Council of Fili, and the emotional thrust is overwhelming. The French Radio Choir sings that chorus with real Russian fervour – though anyone remembering the ENO production will be disconcerted to find the opera starting, not with the shattering choral epigraph which hit so hard at the Coliseum, but with a pot-pourri overture airing some of the main themes. Prokofiev wrote it as an option, and what Rostropovich has done, with fair logic, is to reserve the choral epigraph – telling of the invasion of Russia – for the beginning of the second half and the scenes of war. It was natural that Rostropovich's wife, Galina Vishnevskaya, should sing the central role of Natasha, as she did in the earlier, much-cut, Bolshoi recording. It is extraordinary how convincingly this mature soprano in her early sixties characterizes a young girl; there may be raw moments, but she is completely inside the role. The Hungarian baritone, Lajos Miller, not flawless either, is a clear-voiced Andrei, and Wieslaw Ochman is a first-rate Pierre, with the veteran, Nicolai Gedda, brought in as Kuragin. Katherine Ciesinski is a warm-toned Sonya, but Dimiter Petkov is disappointingly unsteady as Natasha's father, Count Rostov. The small role of Napoleon is strongly taken by Eduard Tumagian, while Nicola Ghiuselev is a noble Kutuzov, in some ways the most impressive of all. The libretto contains French and English translations, but no Russian transliteration, only the Cyrillic text in a separate section.

The Kirov performance under Valery Gergiev, at rather more urgent speeds than Rostropovich's, may be less warmly expressive and atmospheric, but it brings the advantage of having in the principal roles younger voices. Many will prefer the Kirov Natasha, Yelena Prokina, to the controversially cast Vishnevskaya on the Rostropovich set. The voice is fresher as well as younger-sounding, though the tone becomes hard under pressure, losing any sweetness. Alexandr Gergalov, Prince Andrei in the Kirov performance, is attractively young-sounding too, lighter and more lyrical than Rostropovich's principal, also good, the Hungarian baritone, Lajos Miller. Otherwise the Kirov principals, including Nikolai Okhotnikov as Kutuzov, are almost all as characterful and assured as their generally starrier rivals on Erato, and the sense of purpose from a very large company, well drilled in the music, counterbalances in part, though not entirely, the unhelpful dryness of the sound. The economical layout on three CDs may seem to favour Philips, but there is no price-advantage, when Rostropovich's Erato comes at mid-price in the Libretto series. The three-disc format on Philips is made possible by Gergiev's faster speeds and a briefer text for the final patriotic chorus, though the breaks between discs come awkwardly in the middle of scenes.

Puccini, Giacomo (1858–1924)

Capriccio sinfonico; Crisantemi; Minuets Nos. 1–3; Preludio sinfonico; Edgar: Preludes, Acts I & III. Manon Lescaut: Intermezzo, Act III. Le Villi: Prelude; La Tregenda (Act II).

(M) *** Decca Dig. 444 154-2. Berlin RSO, Ricardo Chailly.

In a highly attractive collection of Puccinian juvenilia and rarities, Chailly draws opulent and atmospheric playing from the Berlin Radio Symphony Orchestra, helped by outstandingly rich and full recording. The CD is of demonstration quality. The *Capriccio sinfonico* of 1876 brings the first characteristically Puccinian idea in what later became the opening Bohemian motif of *La Bohème*. There are other identifiable fingerprints here, even if the big melodies suggest Mascagni rather than full-blown Puccini. *Crisantemi* (with the original string quartet scoring expanded for full string orchestra) provided material for *Manon Lescaut*, as did the three little *Minuets*, pastiche eighteenth-century music.

Crisantemi for string quartet.
*** CRD CRD 3366 [id.]. Alberni Qt – DONIZETTI: *Quartet No. 13;* VERDI: *Quartet.* ***

Puccini's brief essay in writing for string quartet dates from the late 1880s. The piece is given a warm, finely controlled performance by the Alberni Quartet and makes a valuable makeweight for the two full-scale quartets by fellow opera-composers. The sound is excellent.

Crisantemi; Fugues 1–3; Minuets 1–3; Scherzo in A min.; String Quartet in D.
(N) *** ASV Dig. CDDCA 909 [id.]. Puccini Qt. – CATALANI: *String quartet in A; A sera; Serenatella.* ***

Puccini's three *Fugues* and the *Quartet movement in D* (with the jolliest, most trivial of main themes) are mere student exercises, technically adept and charming but with no stylistic personality. The *Minuets*, more developed, are hardly identifiable as by Puccini, though they provided material for *Manon Lescaut*, with the second, much-adapted, supplying the bustling opening theme of Act I. Then suddenly, the full Puccini emerges in the beautiful *Crisantemi* of 1890, which provided key material for the final death scene in *Manon Lescaut*. It is strange that though Puccini's musical personality began to emerge early in his choral and orchestral works, this sparer genre found him more anonymous, even in his melodies. Nonetheless, a delightful disc, warmly played and atmospherically recored, with Catalani's quartet music providing an ideal coupling.

(i) *Crisantemi; Minuets Nos. 1–3; Quartet in A min.: Allegro moderato; Scherzo in A min.;* (ii) *Foglio d'album; Piccolo tango;* (iii; ii) *Avanti Urania; E l'uccellino; Inno a Diana; Menti all'avviso; Morire?; Salve regina; Sole e amore; Storiella d'amore; Terra e mare.*
*** Etcetera KTC 1050. (i) Raphael Qt; (ii) Tan Crone; (iii) Roberta Alexander.

It is fascinating to find among early, rather untypical songs like *Storiella d'amore* and *Menti all'avviso* a charming little song, *Sole e amore*, written jokingly for a journal, 'Paganini', in 1888, which provided, bar for bar, the main idea of the Act III quartet in *La Bohème* of eight years later. The two piano pieces are simple album-leaves; among the six quartet pieces, *Crisantemi* is already well known; the rest are student pieces, including a delightful fragment of a Scherzo. Performances are good, though Roberta Alexander's soprano is not ideally Italianate. The recorded sound is vivid and immediate against a lively hall ambience.

Messa di gloria.
(M) *** Erato/Warner Dig. 4509 96367-2 [id.]. Carreras, Prey, Amb. S., Philh. O, Scimone.
(M) *** Ph. 434 170-2. Lövaas, Hollweg, McDaniel, West German R. Ch., Frankfurt RSO, Inbal (with MOZART: *Vesperae solennes, K.339: Laudate Dominum:* Te Kanawa, LSO, C. Davis ***).

Puccini's *Messa di gloria*, completed when he was twenty, rebuts any idea that this composer was a late developer. Very much under the influence of Verdi (hearing *Aida* was a profound formative experience), Puccini still showed his positive character as a composer, writing bold melodies with just a hint here and there of individual fingerprints and using the orchestra with astonishing maturity. The various parts were written at different times and even for different purposes; but with the exception of an over-sweet setting of *Agnus Dei* (later used in *Manon Lescaut*) the work stands well together. Best of all is the ambitious and strong setting of the *Gloria*, the longest section and the earliest written. It has a cheeky recurring march theme which may be doubtfully apt for church but which is richly enjoyable. The section ends with a formidable fugue, echoing Beethoven's *Missa solemnis*, no less.

The return of Scimone's second (1983) digital recording of the Puccini *Messa di gloria* at mid-price makes this version much more competitive, even though it has no fill-up. He and a fine team are brisker and lighter than their predecessors on record, yet effectively bring out the red-bloodedness of the writing. José Carreras turns the big solo in the *Gratias* into the first genuine Puccini aria. His sweetness and imagination are not quite matched by the baritone, Hermann Prey, who is given less to do than usual, when the choral baritones take on the yearning melody of *Crucifixus*. Excellent, atmospheric sound.

This 1975 Philips version, available as a limited edition, is excellent value at mid-price. It has stylish soloists, a fine choral contribution and clean, well-balanced recording. Kiri Te Kanawa's ravishing account of the *Laudate Dominum* from Mozart's *Solemn Vespers* is thrown in as an enticing encore.

OPERA

La Bohème (complete).
❀ *** EMI Dig. CDC5 56120-2 [Ang. CDCB 56120]. Vaduva, Alagna, Swenson, Hampson, Keenlyside, Ramey, L. Voices, boys from L. Oratory School, Philh. O, Pappano.
(***) EMI mono CDS5 56236-2 [CDCB 56236]. De los Angeles, Björling, Merrill, Reardon, Tozzi, Amara, RCA Victor Ch. & O, Beecham.
*** Decca 421 049-2 (2) [id.]. Freni, Pavarotti, Harwood, Panerai, Ghiaurov, German Op. Ch., Berlin, BPO, Karajan.
(B) *** Decca Double 448 725-2 (2) [id.]. Tebaldi, Bergonzi, Bastianini, Siepi, Corena, D'Angelo, St Cecilia Ac. Ch. & O, Serafin.

(B) (***) Decca Double mono 440 233-2 (2) [id.]. Tebaldi, Prandelli, Gueden, Inghilleri, Corena, Arié, Luise, Santa Cecilia Ac., Rome, Ch. & O, Erede.

(***) EMI mono CDS5 56295-2 (2) (CDCB 56295]. Callas, Di Stefano, Moffo, Panerai, La Scala, Milan, Ch. & O, Votto.

(M) **(*) EMI (SIS) CMS7 69657-2 (2). Freni, Gedda, Adani, Sereni, Mazzoli, La Scala, Milan, Ch. & O, Schippers.

(M) **(*) RCA 74321 39496-2 (2) [09026 61725-2]. Caballé, Domingo, Milnes, Raimondi, Alldis Ch., Wandsworth School Boys' Ch., LPO, Solti.

(N) (M) ** RCA 09026 63179-2 (2) [id.]. Anna Moffo, Richard Tucker, Mary Costa, Robert Merrill, Giorgio Tozzi, Rome Opera Ch. & O, Leinsdorf.

(B) ** Naxos Dig. 8.660003/4 [id.]. Orgonasova, Welch, Gonzales, Previati, Senator, Slovak Philharmonic Ch., Slovak RSO (Bratislava), Will Humburg.

(M) ** Nimbus mono NI 7862/3 [id.]. Albanese, Gigli, Oili, Menotti, Baracchi, Baronti, La Scala, Milan, Ch. & O, Berrettoni.

Pappano's recording of *Bohème* is the finest in over 20 years or even longer – sumptuously played and recorded, and characterfully sung by a starry cast. Above all, it is conducted with ever-fresh imagination by Antonio Pappano, who brings out not just subtle emotions alongside high passion, but also the fun of the piece in lightly sprung rhythms. This is a performance in which nothing is routine and where, over and over again, you hear Puccini afresh. It is Pappano's gift – and one registers it from the start – that extremes are made to sound totally natural, not forced or self-conscious, whether of extreme speeds, both fast and slow, of extreme dynamics, superbly caught by the engineers, or of extreme flexibility in rubato. So the exchanges when Mimì arrives have the most moving intimacy at the gentlest pianissimo, with the singers given full expressive freedom within a purposeful frame. The great set-piece numbers at the end of Act I, *Che gelida manina*, *Mi chiamano Mimì* and *O soave fanciulla*, then have the freshness of genuine emotion – of Rodolfo tenderly concerned, of Mimì vulnerable, of their realization of love swelling in a radiant, towering crescendo. Alagna's tenor may not be velvety, but it has a fine tonal range with a heroic ring, and Vaduva is similarly characterful rather than just sweet. The others make a superb team, virtually incomparable today – Ruth Swenson using her dramatic timbres most delicately even in the outburst of the waltz song, Thomas Hampson a swaggering Marcello, with Samuel Ramey and Simon Keenlyside characterfully contrasted as the other two Bohemians, all relishing the fun. With the Philharmonia inspired to playing of consistent flair, notably the woodwind soloists, this is a version to stand alongside the classics of the past.

Beecham's is a uniquely magical performance with two favourite singers, Victoria de los Angeles and Jussi Björling, challenged to their utmost in loving, expansive singing. The voices are treated far better by the CD remastering than the orchestra, which is rather thinner-sounding than it was on LP, though as ever the benefits of silent background are very welcome in so warmly atmospheric a reading. With such a performance one hardly notices the recording, but those who want fine modern stereo can turn readily to Karajan.

Karajan too takes a characteristically spacious view of *Bohème*, but there is an electric intensity which holds the whole score together as in a live performance. Pavarotti is an inspired Rodolfo, with comic flair and expressive passion, while Freni is just as seductive as Mimì. Elizabeth Harwood is a charming Musetta. Fine singing throughout the set. The reverberant Berlin acoustic is glowing and brilliant in superb Decca recording, with the clean placing of voices enhancing the performance's dramatic warmth.

Tebaldi's Decca set with Bergonzi dominated the catalogue in the early days of stereo; technically it was an outstanding recording in its day, and it still sounds astonishingly vivid, with a very convincing theatrical atmosphere. At Double Decca price, it is one of the great operatic bargains in the current catalogue. Vocally the performance achieves a consistently high standard, with Tebaldi as Mimì the most affecting. Carlo Bergonzi is a fine Rodolfo; Bastianini and Siepi are both superb as Marcello and Colline, and even the small parts of Benoit and Alcindoro (as usual taken by a single artist) have the benefit of Corena's magnificent voice. The veteran Serafin was more vital here than on some of his records. The recording, not far off 40 years old, has its vividness and sense of stage perspective enhanced on CD. The set comes with a perfectly adequate cued synopsis, for *La Bohème* is an exceptionally easy opera to follow.

The very early Decca set, one of the very first complete operas to appear on LP. Recorded in 1951, it immediately won glowing praise, above all for Tebaldi's radiant and rich-voiced portrayal of Mimì. The effect is still extraordinarily atmospheric in its sense of stage perspective, with sound effects mostly adding to the realism and not overdone. Like the companion early Decca *Die Fledermaus*, the one drawback was the whistly sound of the violins (something to do with the microphones in use at Decca at that time). The CD transfer has improved the violin focus, but the effect is still emaciated above the stave. Yet one soon adjusts to this, for the acoustic is basically warm and evocative. It is still a lovely performance, and there are no appreciable weaknesses in the cast: Gueden (if not always completely Italianate in style) an exceptionally characterful Musetta (a part that fitted her like a glove), Pradelli a most likeable Rodolfo, engagingly light-voiced yet stirring at climaxes, Inghilleri rather old-sounding but still interesting as Marcello. Erede keeps the music flowing: he is not a great conductor but he controls the great love duet of Act I spaciously. The atmospheric opening of Act III at the Paris toll-gate is remarkably evocative, with the kind of production values that were to lead on to the vintage Decca opera recordings of the stereo era already apparent. Indeed, at times here one could almost think stereo had already arrived.

Callas, flashing-eyed and formidable, may seem even less suited to the role of Mimì than to that of Butterfly, but characteristically her insights make for a vibrantly involving performance. Though Giuseppe di Stefano is not the subtlest of Rodolfos, he is in excellent voice here, and Moffo and Panerai make a strong partnership as the second pair of lovers. Votto occasionally coarsens Puccini's score but he directs with energy. The comparatively restricted dynamic range means that the singers appear to be 'front stage', but there is no lack of light and shade in Act II, and the sound of the new transfer is greatly improved.

The engineers placed Freni rather close to the microphone, which makes it hard for her to sound tentative in her first scene, but the beauty of the voice is what one remembers, and from there to the end her performance is conceived as a whole, leading to a supremely moving account of the Death scene. Nicolai Gedda's Rodolfo is not rounded in the traditional Italian way, but there is never any doubt about his ability to project a really grand manner of his own. Thomas Schippers' conducting starts as though this is going to be a hard-driven, unrelenting performance, but after the horseplay he quickly shows his genuinely Italianate sense of pause, giving the singers plenty of time to breathe and allowing the music to expand. The resonant, 1964 recording has transferred vividly to CD and the set has been attractively repackaged with an excellently printed libretto.

The glory of Solti's set of *Bohème* is the singing of Montserrat Caballé as Mimì, an intensely characterful and imaginative reading which makes you listen with new intensity to every phrase, the voice at its most radiant. Domingo is unfortunately not at his most inspired. *Che gelida manina* is relatively coarse, though here as elsewhere he produces glorious heroic tone, and he never falls into vulgarity. The rest of the team is strong, but Solti's tense interpretation of a work he had never conducted in the opera house does not quite let either the full flexibility of the music or the full warmth of romanticism have their place. The recording, however, is both vivid and atmospheric, and this recording is welcome back to the catalogue, pleasingly packaged in RCA's mid-priced Opera Treasury series. At the moment it remains at full price in the USA.

On the Leinsdorf set Anna Moffo is an affecting Mimì, Mary Costa a characterful Musetta, while Merrill and Tozzi provide strong support. Tucker gives a positive characterization as Rodolfo, though he has lachrymose moments. Sadly, Leinsdorf's rigid direction, with speed fluctuations observed by instruction and never with natural expression, sets the singers against a deadpan, unsparkling accompaniment. Dated recording, impressively remastered.

Well played and atmospherically recorded, the Naxos version of *La Bohème* offers an outstanding performance by Luba Orgonosova as Mimì. The creamy quality of the voice, coupled with her warm expressiveness and her vocal poise, brings out the tenderness of the character to the full; and it is a pity that none of the others matches her. Jonathan Welch as Rodolfo and Fabio Previati as Marcello are both strained and unsteady at times, while Carmen Gonzales tries too hard as Musetta. Yet with Will Humburg pacing the opera effectively, and with the well-disciplined Slovak Philharmonic Chorus adding to the atmospheric beauty, this is a fair bargain.

It is good to have the classic recording with Gigli restored to the catalogue in Nimbus's Prima Voce series, when EMI's own CD transfer, drier and less atmospheric, has been deleted. The Nimbus transfer process (recording an acoustic-horn gramophone in a large room) works well here, with plenty of body in the sound, without too much masking of reverberation, and with a bloom on the voices. The glory of the set is Gigli's Rodolfo, with a chuckle in the voice bringing out the fun, while Gigli uses his pouting manner charmingly, with the occasional sob adding to the charm. He adds little touches, as when he murmurs '*Prego*' when ushering Mimì out, before she discovers she has lost her key. He dwarfs the others, with even Albanese a little shrill as Mimì.

La Bohème (complete; sung in English).
(N) *** Chandos Dig. CHAN 3008 (2) [id.].
Mimì (Cynthia Hayman), Rodolfo (Dennis O'Neill), Musetta (Marie McLaughlin), Colline (Alistair Miles), Schaunard (William Dazeley), Geoffrey Mitchell Ch., Peter Kay Children's Ch., Philh. O, David Parry.

This is one of the most enjoyable issues yet in the Peter Moores Foundation's 'Opera in English' series. The magic mixture of humour and pathos in this unsinkable masterpiece is brought all the closer for having it in translation, even if the occasional line may ring false. Dennis O'Neill reinforces his high reputation as the regular tenor in the series, despite some intrusive vibrato under pressure, and Cynthia Haymon as a touching Mimì has never sounded more beautiful on disc, with the widest range of expression and tone. Marie McLaughlin is a warm-toned Musetta, temperamental rather than just flighty, and the other three Bohemians are ideally cast. Voices are vividly caught in the atmospheric recording, with the crowd scenes of Act II beautifully clarified. Highest praise too for David Parry who knows how to relax in tenderness, as well as when to press home hard. Warm, refined playing from the Philharmonia. Highly recommended to all who enjoy opera in English.

La Bohème: highlights.

(N) (M) ** Penguin Classics Decca 460 617-2 [id.] (from above recording with Tebaldi, Bergonzi; cond. Serafin).

(N) (M) (**) EMI mono CDM5 66670-2 [id.] (from above recording with Callas, di Stefano; cond. Votto).

The sets of excerpts from the Tebaldi and Callas recordings are little more than samplers. Although both include the Love duet from Act I, and the closing scene, the overall playing time is only 54 minutes for the EMI disc, and a minute or so more for the Decca. There is a cued synopsis for Callas, but the Decca selection offers merely a very brief cued narrative summary. However, the one compensation here is the usual Penguin Classics author's note and it is most engagingly written by Rabbi Lionel Blue.

Edgar (complete).

(N) (M) ** Sony M2K 79213 (2) [id.]. Scotto, Bergonzi, Sardinero, Killibrew, NY Schola Cantorum and Op. O, Queler.

'What is wanted is a subject which palpitates with life and is believable', wrote Puccini after one performance of *Edgar*, his second opera; a work which, as we know now, took him in the wrong direction, away from realism towards medieval fantasy in which the knightly hero has to choose between the loves of the symbolically named Fidelia and Tigrana (a Carmen figure without the sparkle). The motivation was made even less convincing by the cutting which Puccini carried out in later editions; but, as this recording makes plain, there is much to enjoy. The melodies are not quite vintage Puccini, but Scotto as Fidelia, Killibrew as Tigrana, and Bergonzi as Edgar give them compelling warmth. Eve Queler proves a variably convincing conductor, with Act III in need of more rehearsal. But this set, edited from live performances at Carnegie Hall, and commendably well recorded, makes a welcome stop-gap.

La Fanciulla del West (The Girl of the Golden West) complete.

❁ (M) *** Decca (IMS) 421 595-2 (2) [id.]. Tebaldi, Del Monaco, MacNeil, Tozzi, St Cecilia Ac., Rome, Ch. & O, Capuana.

**(*) DG 419 640-2 (2) [id.]. Neblett, Domingo, Milnes, Howell, ROHCG Ch. and O, Mehta.

The Decca set of *La Fanciulla del West* has been remastered for CD with spectacular success. Tebaldi gives one of her most warm-hearted and understanding performances on record, and Mario del Monaco displays the wonderfully heroic quality of his voice to great – if sometimes tiring – effect. Cornell MacNeil as the villain, Sheriff Rance, sings with great precision and attack, but unfortunately has not a villainous-sounding voice to convey the character fully. Jake Wallace's entry and the song *Che faranno i viecchi miei* is one of the high spots of the recording, with Tozzi singing beautifully. Capuana's expansive reading is matched by the imagination of the production, with the closing scene wonderfully effective.

On DG, Mehta's manner – as he makes clear at the very start – is on the brisk side, not just in the cakewalk rhythms but even in refusing to let the first great melody, the nostalgic *Che faranno i viecchi miei*, linger into sentimentality. Sherrill Milnes as Jack Rance makes that villain into far more than a small-town Scarpia, giving nobility and understanding to the first-Act arioso. Domingo, as in the theatre, sings heroically, disappointing only in his reluctance to produce soft tone in the great aria *Ch'ella mi creda*. The rest of the team is excellent, not least Gwynne Howell as the minstrel who sings *Che faranno i viecchi miei*; but the crowning glory of a masterly set is the singing of Carol Neblett as the Girl of the Golden West herself, gloriously rich and true and with formidable attack on the exposed high notes. Full, atmospheric recording to match, essential in an opera full of evocative offstage effects, but the slight drying-out process of the digital sound adds some stridency in tuttis, readily acceptable with so strong a performance.

Gianni Schicchi (complete).

(M) *** RCA Dig. 74321 25285-2. Panerai, Donath, Seiffert, Bavarian R. Ch., Munich R. O, Patanè.

The RCA (formerly Eurodisc) recording of *Gianni Schicchi* brings a co-production with Bavarian Radio, and the recording is vivid and well balanced. Central to the performance's success is the vintage Schicchi of Rolando Panerai, still rich and firm. He confidently characterizes the Florentine trickster in every phrase, building a superb portrait, finely timed. Peter Seiffert as Rinuccio gives a dashing performance, consistently clean and firm of tone, making light of the high tessitura and rising splendidly to the challenge of the big central aria. Helen Donath would have sounded even sweeter a few years earlier, but she gives a tender, appealing portrait of Lauretta, pretty and demure in *O mio babbino caro*. Though Italian voices are in the minority, it is a confident team. In its reissued form, access to the disc has been greatly improved and there are now seven cues.

Madama Butterfly (complete).

*** Decca 417 577-2 (3) [id.]. Freni, Ludwig, Pavarotti, Kerns, V. State Op. Ch., VPO, Karajan.

*** DG Dig. 423 567-2 (3) [id.]. Freni, Carreras, Berganza, Pons, Amb. Op. Ch., Philh. O, Sinopoli.

(B) *** Decca Double 452 594-2 (2) [id.]. Tebaldi, Bergonzi, Cossotto, Sordello, St Cecilia, Rome, Ac. Ch. & O, Serafin.

(M) *** RCA GD 84145 (2) [4145-2-RG]. Moffo, Elias, Valletti, Cesari, Catalani, Rome Op. Ch. & O, Leinsdorf.

(M) *** EMI CMS7 69654-2 (2) [Ang. CDMB 69654]. Scotto, Bergonzi, Di Stasio, Panerai, De Palma, Rome Op. Ch. & O, Barbirolli.

(N) (***) Testament mono SBT 2168 (2) [id.]. Victoria de los Angeles, Giuseppe di Stefano, Tito Gobbi, Rome Opera Ch. & O, Gavazzeni.

(M) **(*) EMI CMS7 63634-2 (2) [Ang. CDMB 63634]. De los Angeles, Bjoerling, Pirazzini, Sereni, Rome Op. Ch. & O, Santini.

(***) EMI mono CDS5 56298-2 (2). Callas, Gedda, Borriello, Danieli, La Scala, Milan, Ch. & O, Karajan.

(B) (**(*)) Decca Double mono 440 230-2 (2) [id.]. Tebaldi, Campora, Inghilleri, Rankin, Santa Cecilia Academy, Rome, Ch. & O, Alberto Erede.

Karajan's set is extravagantly laid out on three discs instead of two as for most of the rival sets – slow speeds partly responsible. However, he inspires singers and orchestra to a radiant performance which brings out all the beauty and intensity of Puccini's score, sweet but not sentimental, powerfully dramatic but not vulgar. Freni is an enchanting Butterfly, consistently growing in stature from the young girl to the victim of tragedy, sweeter of voice than any rival on record. Pavarotti is an intensely imaginative Pinkerton, actually inspiring understanding for this thoughtless character, while Christa Ludwig is a splendid Suzuki. The recording is one of Decca's most resplendent, with the Vienna strings producing glowing tone.

However expansive his speeds, Sinopoli is never sentimental or self-indulgent. Puccini's honeyed moments are given, not sloppily, but with rapt intensity. They are then set the more movingly against the biting moments, from the opening fugato of Act I, sharply incisive, through to the final aria, tough and intense. As she was for Karajan in his classic Decca set, Freni is a model Butterfly; though the voice is no longer so girlish, she projects the tragedy even more weightily than before. José Carreras is similarly presented as a large-scale Pinkerton. Juan Pons is a virile Sharpless and Teresa Berganza an equally positive, unfruity Suzuki. This is a set which in its spacious but intensely concentrated way brings a unique and unforgettable experience. But like the Karajan set it is on three CDs.

Serafin's sensitive and beautifully paced reading finds Tebaldi at her most radiant. Though she was never the most deft of Butterflies dramatically (she never actually sang the role on stage before recording it), her singing is consistently rich and beautiful, breathtakingly so in passages such as the one in Act I when she tells Pinkerton she has changed her religion. The excellence of the Decca engineering in 1958 is amply proved in the CD transfer, the current remastering now providing full, atmospheric sound from the very beginning, opening out further as the orchestration grows fuller, with voices very precisely and realistically placed. At Double Decca price this is a pretty formidable bargain.

Anna Moffo's Butterfly proves delightful, fresh and young-sounding, and the *Flower duet* with Rosalind Elias is enchanting. Valletti's Pinkerton has a clear-voiced, almost Gigli-like charm – preferable to most rivals – and with Corena as the Bonze the only blot on the set vocally is the unimaginative Sharpless of Renato Cesari. Leinsdorf is efficient and undistracting and, with vivid recording (balanced in favour of the voices), this makes a first-class mid-priced recommendation, costing less than half the price of the Decca Karajan set with Freni, Ludwig and Pavarotti.

Under Sir John Barbirolli, players and singers perform consistently with a dedication and intensity rare in opera recordings made in Italy, and the whole score glows more freshly than ever. There is hardly a weak link in the cast. Bergonzi's Pinkerton and Panerai's Sharpless are both sensitively and beautifully sung; Anna di Stasio's Suzuki is more than adequate, and Renata Scotto's Butterfly has a subtlety and perceptiveness in its characterization that more than make up for any shortcoming in the basic beauty of tone-colour.

The *Butterfly* set with Victoria de los Angeles on Testament, is her mono recording, made in 1954, when the voice was at its fullest and most golden, even fresher and warmer than her stereo remake. It is a magical performance, with de los Angeles meltingly beautiful, bringing out the tender vulnerability of Puccini's heroine. Giuseppe di Stefano is also at his very finest as Pinkerton, with Tito Gobbi giving unexpected depth to the role of Sharpless, and Gavazzeni's timing heightening the pathos. The superb transfer is clearer and more forward than EMI's earlier CD version.

Victoria de los Angeles' 1960 recording displays her art at its most endearing, her range of golden tone-colour lovingly exploited. Opposite her, Jussi Bjoerling produces a flow of rich tone to compare with that of the heroine. Mario Sereni is a full-voiced Sharpless, but Miriam Pirazzini is a disappointingly wobbly Suzuki; Santini is a reliable, generally rather square and unimaginative conductor who rarely gets in the way. With recording quality freshened, this fine set is most welcome either on a pair of mid-priced CDs or in its CfP cassette format.

Callas's view, aided by superbly imaginative and spacious conducting from Karajan, gives extra dimension to the Puccinian little woman, and with some keenly intelligent singing too from Gedda as Pinkerton this is a set which has a special compulsion. The performance projects the more vividly on CD, even though the lack of stereo in so atmospheric an opera is a serious disadvantage, and the new transfer is full and fairly spacious.

Astonishingly, this Decca mono set was made (in 1951) before Tebaldi ever sang the part in the opera house. In the last resort she lacks temperament but there is much magnificent singing. Campora is a fine Pinkerton and the fresh young voices of the two lovers are particularly convincing in Act I. Erede's conducting is strong and dramatic, and there is much to relish, not least the amazingly atmospheric Decca recording, which is very kind to the voices. The orchestra sounds thinner, but the violins have more body here than on those old Ace of Clubs LP pressings. The two CDs come in a single jewel-case with an independent plot summary unrelated to the 40 cues.

Madama Butterfly: highlights.

(N) (M) *** Decca 458 223-2 [421 873-2]. (from above complete set with Tebaldi, Bergonzi; cond. Serafin).

(M) *** EMI CDM5 65580-2 [ZDM 64311] (from above complete set, with Scotto, Bergonzi, Di Stasio; cond. Barbirolli).

If you want just a set of highlights from *Butterfly* the excerpts from the 1957 Decca stereo Tebaldi set fit the bill. The selection is quite generous (68 minutes), and singing and recording are splendid; moreover the documentation includes a full translation. But with only a little more outlay one can get this version of the complete opera on a Double Decca, which seems a far more sensible investment.

The EMI selection (54 minutes) does include the essential *Humming chorus*. For those owning another complete set, it offers a fine sampler of Barbirolli's deeply felt performance with its admirably consistent cast. Scotto's Butterfly was one of her finest recorded performances. The transfer does reveal the age of the 1966 recording in the orchestral sound, but the voices are full and vividly projected.

Madame Butterfly: highlights (sung in English).

(B) **(*) CfP CD-CFP 4600. Collier, Craig, Robson, Griffiths, Sadler's Wells O, Brian Balkwill.

This 1960 recording was the first of a series of Sadler's Wells highlights discs of opera in English. There are few better examples, for the clear recording lets the listener hear almost every word, and this is achieved without balancing things excessively in favour of the voices. Marie Collier got inside the part very well; she has a big, full voice and she sings most movingly. Charles Craig is a splendid Pinkerton: his singing achieves international standards and he was in particularly fresh voice when this record was made. As to the choice of extracts, the one omission which is at all serious is the entry of Butterfly. As it is, the duet of Pinkerton and Sharpless cuts off just as she is about to come in. The recording wears its years lightly; just occasionally the bright CD transfer brings a touch of peakiness in the vocal climaxes, but the performance remains very involving.

Manon Lescaut (complete).

*** Decca Dig. 440 200-2 (2) [id.]. Freni, Pavarotti, Croft, Taddei, Vargas, Bartoli, NY Met. Op. Ch. & O, Levine.

*** DG Dig. 413 893-2 (2) [id.]. Freni, Domingo, Bruson, ROHCG Ch., Philh. O, Sinopoli.

(N) (B) *** Decca Double Dig. 460 750-2 (2) [id.]. Kiri Te Kanawa, Carreras, Paolo Coni, Tajo, Matteuzzi, Ch. & O of Teatro Cumunale di Bologna, Chailly.

(B) *** Naxos Dig. 8.660019/20 (2) [id.]. Gauci, Sardinero, Kaludov, BRT Philh. Ch. & O, Rahbari.

(M) (***) RCA mono GD 60573 (2) [60573-2-RG]. Albanese, Bjoerling, Merrill, Rome Op. Ch. & O, Perlea.

(***) EMI mono CDS5 56301-2 (2). Callas, Di Stefano, Fioravanti, La Scala, Milan, Ch. and O, Serafin.

(M) **(*) EMI CMS7 64852-2 (2) [Ang. CDMB 64852]. Caballé, Domingo, Amb. Op. Ch., New Philh. O, Bartoletti.

With Luciano Pavarotti as a powerful Des Grieux, James Levine conducts a comparably big-boned performance of *Manon Lescaut*, bringing out the red-blooded drama of Puccini's first big success, while not ignoring its warmth and tender poetry. The impact is enhanced by exceptionally full, vivid sound, with the voices balanced close, well in front of the orchestra in a way one associates with opera recordings of the 1950s. It represents an opposite view to that taken by the DG engineers when in one of the last Kingsway Hall sessions they recorded the Sinopoli version. There too the title-role was taken by Mirella Freni and, though the closeness of balance on the newer set exposes some inevitable blemishes of age in the voice, its fullness and warmth are more faithfully captured in a performance even warmer and more relaxed. It culminates in an account of the big Act IV aria, *Sola, perduta, abbandonata*, more involving and passionate than any in recent years, with the voice showing no signs of wear. Consistently, Levine conveys the tensions and atmosphere of a stage performance in a way that plainly owes much to his experience at the Met., avoiding the feeling of a studio performance.

Pavarotti's contribution as Des Grieux is more

controversial. He tackles his little opening aria challenging the girls to make him fall in love, *Tra voi belle*, with a beefy bravado that misses the subtlety and point of Domingo, for example. But then he characteristically points word-meaning with a bright-eyed intensity that compels attention. The closeness of balance means that in volume his singing rarely drops below mezzo-forte, and as a vocal demonstration Domingo's performance is consistently more refined, but there is little harm in having so passionate a portrait of Des Grieux as Pavarotti's. The rest of the cast is strong too, with Dwayne Croft a magnificent Lescaut who brings out the character's wry humour. The veteran Giuseppe Taddei is superbly cast as Geronte, very characterful and still full-throated, while Cecilia Bartoli makes the unnamed singer in the Act II entertainment into far more than a cipher. One incidental advantage over most rivals is that the break between discs comes after Act II, avoiding any break within an Act.

Plácido Domingo's portrait of Des Grieux on DG is far subtler and more detailed, with finer contrasts of tone and dynamic, than in his earlier, EMI recording opposite Caballé. Freni proves an outstanding choice: her girlish tones in Act I rebut any idea that she might be too mature. Of the others, a first-rate team, Renato Bruson nicely brings out the ironic side of Lescaut's character, and having Brigitte Fassbaender just to sing the *Madrigal* adds to the feeling of luxury, as does John Tomlinson's darkly intense moment of drama as the ship's captain. The voices are more recessed than is common, but they are recorded with fine bloom, and the brilliance of the orchestral sound comes out impressively.

The digital Chailly set dates from as recently as 1988 and makes a splendid bargain as a Decca Double. It comes with Decca's new reissue documentation including a 'listening guide' which offers good documentation and a simple cued synopsis. Dame Kiri gives an affecting characterization of Manon, at times rather heavily underlined but passionately convincing in the development from innocent girl to fallen woman. The playing from Chailly's Bologna orchestra cannot quite match that of the Philharmonia for Sinopoli, yet Chailly is a degree more idiomatic in his pacing. Carreras is in good form, but sounds a little strained at times. The Decca sound, with the voices well forward is characteristically vivid.

On the bargain Naxos issue, Miriam Gauci gives one of the most sensitive performances of this role on any set. Her Act II aria, *In quelle trine morbide*, is beautifully poised and her monologue in the death scene, *Sola, perduta, abbandonata*, is the more moving for being restrained at the start, building from there in intensity without sacrificing musical values. The young Bulgarian, Kaludi Kaludov, is a clean-cut, virile Des Grieux, opening up impressively in his big moments. Vincente Sardinero makes a powerful Lescaut, and Rahbari, as in his Bratislava recordings of *Cav.* and *Pag.*, is a red-blooded interpreter of Italian opera, generally pacing well, even if at the very start he is disconcertingly hectic. Though the Brussels orchestra plays with refinement – the strings in particular – the sound is thinner than in the Slovakian recordings, with the orchestra set slightly back. This is the least expensive *Manon Lescaut* in the catalogue but, even if it cost more, it would still be very recommendable.

In Perlea's 1954 recording, the mono sound may be limited, but no Puccinian should miss it, when Jussi Bjoerling gives the finest ever interpretation on record of the role of Des Grieux. Robert Merrill too is superb as Manon's brother, giving delightful irony to the closing scene of Act I, which has rarely sounded so effervescent. The Manon of Licia Albanese is sensitively sung, but the voice is not at all girlish.

It is typical of Callas that she turns the final scene into the most compelling part of the opera. Serafin, who could be a lethargic recording conductor, is here electrifying, and Di Stefano too is inspired to one of his finest complete opera recordings. The cast-list even includes the young Fiorenza Cossotto, impressive as the singer in the Act II *Madrigal*. The recording – still in mono, not a stereo transcription – minimizes the original boxiness and gives good detail.

The EMI version, conducted by Bartoletti, is chiefly valuable for the performance of Montserrat Caballé as the heroine, one of her most affecting, with the voice alluringly beautiful. Otherwise the set is disappointing, with Plácido Domingo unflattered by the close acoustic, not nearly as perceptive as in his much later, DG performance under Sinopoli. Bartoletti's conducting is also relatively coarse, with the very opening forced and breathless. The new transfer to CD, however, has improved the sound, which is now much more vivid and atmospheric; and the presentation, with a clearly printed libretto, is also attractive.

Manon Lescaut: highlights.
(M) *** DG Dig. 445 466-2 (from above recording, with Freni, Domingo; cond. Sinopoli).

Most of the key items are included in this well-chosen mid-price selection of highlights from the brilliant Sinopoli set which is a strong alternative recommendation for this opera. An adequate synopsis with track cues is provided in lieu of a libretto. The playing time is 66 minutes.

'*The Puccini Album*': *Manon Lescaut: Intermezzo*; Act IV (complete). *Tosca: Recondita armonia*. Act I: *Love duet; Vissi d'arte*; Act III (complete).
(N) **(*) Ph. 456 586-2. Galina Gorchakova,

Neil Shicoff, Maggio Musicale Fiorentino O, Ozawa.

The title is misleading when this offers simply substantial extracts from only two operas, concentrating on scenes rather than arias. The idea is reasonable, but it feels rather like having off-cuts from complete recordings that failed to get finished, with incidental voice-parts all included. Both Gorchakova and Shicoff sing powerfully, but the overall impression is rather generalized. Gorchakova, in splendid voice, rises superbly to the challenge of Manon's big monologue, *Sola perduta, abbandonata*, the climax of the whole disc.

La Rondine (complete).
*** Sony Dig. M2K 37852 [id.]. Te Kanawa, Domingo, Nicolesco, Rendall, Nucci, Watson, Knight, Amb. Op. Ch., LSO, Maazel.

(i) *La Rondine* (complete). (ii) *Le Villi: Prelude, L'Abbandono; La Tregenda; Ecco la casa . . . Torna al felice;* (iii) Song: *Morire!*.
*** EMI Dig. CDS5 56338-2 (2) [id.]. (i–iii) Roberto Alagna; (i) Gheorghiu, Mula-Tchako, Matteuzzi, Rinaldi; (i–ii) London Voices, LSO, Pappano; (iii) Pappano (piano).

Puccini's ill-timed attempt to outshine Lehár in an operetta-like subject has long been counted a failure. The two previous recordings have each modified that idea, but Pappano on this EMI issue transforms the work, revealing it to be another masterpiece. He is aided by the partnership of Angela Gheorghiu, most moving in the Violetta-like role of the heroine, Magda, and of Alagna as the ardent young student she falls in love with. Puccini cunningly interweaves elements not just of *La Traviata* but of *The Merry Widow* and *Fledermaus*, not to mention earlier Puccini operas, with a melodic style for the most part simpler than before, with one striking theme following another in profusion, each subtly interwoven.

Pappano consistently brings out the poetry, drawing on emotions far deeper than are suggested by this operetta-like subject, thanks also to Gheorghiu's superb performance, translating her mastery as Violetta to this comparable character, tenderly expressive, as in Magda's first big solo, *Che il bel sogno di Doretta*. Consistently she makes you share the courtesan's wild dream of finding her young student. Most striking of all is the way she convinces you of her heartbreak, when in Act III she finally gives up Ruggero, not through any opposition from his family, but out of love for him, knowing the liaison would ruin him.

As Ruggero, the hero, Alagna winningly characterizes the ardent young student, singing in his freshest voice. What will specially delight Puccinians in this set is that he is given an extra aria about Paris, *Parigi e un citta*, which transforms his otherwise minimal contribution to Act I. Adapting it from a song, Puccini included it in the 1920 Viennese version of the score but never incorporated it in the original, Italian version, as it certainly deserves. The role of the poet, Prunier, is also transformed thanks to the casting of the clear-toned William Matteuzzi in what is normally a comprimario role. Not only is his relationship with Magda beautifully drawn, his improbable affair with the skittish maid, Lisette (clone of Adèle in *Fledermaus*), is made totally convincing too, mirroring Magda's affair. Inva Mula-Tchako is equally well cast in that soubrette role, bright, clear and vivacious, with Alberto Rinaldi making the sugar-daddy, Rambaldo, the dull dog intended. The excerpts from *Le Villi*, warm and dramatic, include two orchestral showpieces. Alagna also gives a ringing account of Roberto's aria, as he does of the song, *Morire!* – with Pappano at the piano – the source of the extra aria for Ruggero included in the main opera.

Maazel's is a strong, positive reading, crowned by a superb and radiant Magda in Dame Kiri Te Kanawa, mature yet glamorous. Domingo, by age too mature for the role of young hero, yet scales his voice down most effectively in the first two Acts, expanding in heroic warmth only in the final scene of dénouement. Sadly, the second pair are far less convincing, when the voices of both Mariana Nicolesco and David Rendall take ill to the microphone.

Suor Angelica (complete).
(M) **(*) RCA 74321 40575-2. Popp, Lipovšek, Schiml, Jennings, Bav. R. Ch., Munich R. O, Patanè.

Suor Angelica (complete); *Tosca: Vissi d'arte*.
(M) *** Decca 458 218-2 [id.]. Sutherland, Ludwig, Collings, London Op. Ch., Finchley Children's Music Group, Nat. PO, Bonynge.

Puccini's atmospheric picture of a convent is superbly captured in the Decca version, with sound of spectacular depth. Bonynge's direction is most persuasive, and Sutherland rises superbly to the big dramatic demands of the final scenes. With Sutherland, Angelica is in no sense a 'little woman' or even an inexperienced girl, but a formidable match for the implacable Zia Principessa, here superbly taken by Christa Ludwig, detailed and unexaggerated in her characterization. The supporting cast is outstanding, and the pity is that Sutherland did not record the piece rather earlier, before the beat developed in her voice. The first offstage entry and opening scene catch it rather distractingly. The recording is attractively repackaged in Decca's Opera Gala series, with full translation included, plus an encore, *Vissi d'arte* from *Tosca*, recorded six years earlier in 1972.

Patanè's performance is idiomatic and consistently well placed. Neither Lucia Popp as Angelica nor Marjana Lipovšek as the vindictive Zia

Principessa is ideally cast – the one overstressed, the other sounding too young – but these are both fine artists who sing with consistent imagination, and the recording is pleasingly atmospheric. There is a libretto/translation provided, and the only snag is the lack of cueing: only two tracks are indicated, one 28 minutes into the opera and the second 12 minutes later.

Il Tabarro (complete).

(M) *** RCA 74321 45081-2. Nimsgern, Tokody, Lamberti, Pane, Bav. R. Ch., Munich R. O, Patanè.

(M) **(*) RCA 74321 50168-2 (2) [09026 60865-2]. Leontyne Price, Domingo, Milnes, John Alldis Ch., New Philh. O, Leinsdorf – LEONCAVALLO: *I Pagliacci*. ***

Patanè in his larger-than-life direction may at times run the risk of exaggerating the melodrama, but the result is richly enjoyable. Ilona Tokody, already well known from Hungaroton opera sets, makes a powerful, strongly projected Giorgetta, somewhat showing up the relative weakness of the tenor, Giorgio Lamberti, as her lover, Luigi. His over-emphatic underlining mars his legato, but the main love-duet comes over with gutsy strength. Siegmund Nimsgern makes a powerful Michele, a shade too explosive in the climactic final aria, but generally firm and clean in his projection, making the character more sinister. The full and brilliant recording has voices set convincingly on a believable stage, well balanced against the orchestra, the effect appealingly atmospheric. There is a libretto/translation and the reissue is much more generously cued than before, providing ten tracks in all.

Leontyne Price may not be ideally cast as the bargemaster's wife, but she is fully in character. Sherrill Milnes is rather young-sounding for the bargemaster, but he sings memorably in the climactic aria. Plácido Domingo makes a fresh-voiced and well-characterized young bargee, while Leinsdorf is at his most sympathetic. This RCA set is handsomely repackaged with libretto in the Opera Treasury series.

Tosca (complete).

✽ *** EMI mono CDM5 66444-2 (2) [CDM 66444]. Callas, Di Stefano, Gobbi, Calabrese, La Scala, Milan, Ch. and O, De Sabata.

(B) *** Decca Double 452 620-2 (2) [id.]. Leontyne Price, Di Stefano, Taddei, V. State Op. Ch., VPO, Karajan.

(N) (M) *** Decca Legends 466 384-2 (2) Price, Di Stefano, Taddei, V. State Op. Ch. , VPO Karajan (as above).

*** DG Dig. 431 775-2 (2). Freni, Domingo, Ramey, Terfel, ROHCG Ch., Philh. O, Sinopoli.

(M) *** RCA 74321 39503-2 (2) [RCD-2-0105]. Leontyne Price, Domingo, Milnes, Plishka, Alldis Ch., Wandsworth School Boys' Ch., New Philh. O, Mehta.

*** DG 413 815-2 (2) [id.]. Ricciarelli, Carreras, Raimondi, Corena, German Op. Ch., BPO, Karajan.

(B) (***) Decca Double (IMS) mono 440 236-2 (2) [id.]. Tebaldi, Campora, Mascherini, Santa Cecilia Academy, Rome, Ch. & O, Alberto Erede.

**(*) Decca (IMS) Dig. 414 597-2 (2) [id.]. Te Kanawa, Aragall, Nucci, Welsh Nat. Opera Ch., Nat. PO, Solti.

(M) **(*) EMI Dig. CMS5 66504-2 (2) [CDMB 66504]. Scotto, Domingo, Bruson, Amb. Op. Ch., St Clement Danes School Boys' Ch., Philh. O, Levine.

There has never been a finer recorded performance of *Tosca* than Callas's first, with Victor de Sabata conducting and Tito Gobbi as Scarpia. Gobbi makes the unbelievably villainous police chief into a genuinely three-dimensional character, and Di Stefano as the hero, Cavaradossi, was at his finest. The conducting of De Sabata is spaciously lyrical as well as sharply dramatic, and the mono recording is superbly balanced in Walter Legge's fine production. Though there is inevitably less spaciousness than in a stereo recording, the voices are caught gloriously.

Now reissued on a Double Decca, Karajan's Vienna set is unbeatable value. Karajan deserves equal credit with the principal singers for the vital, imaginative performance, recorded in Vienna. Taddei himself has a marvellously wide range of tone-colour, and though he cannot quite match the Gobbi snarl he has almost every other weapon in his armoury. Leontyne Price is at the peak of her form and Di Stefano sings most sensitively. The sound of the Vienna orchestra is enthralling – both more refined and richer than usual in a Puccini opera – and it sounds quite marvellous in its digitally remastered format, combining presence with atmosphere and making a superb bargain. It is also currently due for reissue on Decca's Legends label at mid-price, including a full libretto.

Even more than the Puccini operas he had previously recorded – always with spacious, finely moulded treatment – *Tosca* seems to match Sinopoli's musical personality, helped by DG recording of spectacular weight and range. Ramey's is not a conventional portrait of the evil police-chief, but the role has rarely been sung with more sheer beauty, with such a climax as the *Te Deum* at the end of Act I sounding thrilling in its firmness and power. Domingo's heroic power is formidable too, and unlike many of his opera recordings for DG this one presents him in close-up, not distanced. Freni's is not naturally a Tosca voice, but it is still a powerful, heartfelt performance.

Price made her second complete recording of

Tosca (for RCA) ten years after the first under Karajan, and the interpretation remained remarkably consistent, a shade tougher in the chest register – the great entry in Act III a magnificent moment – and a little more clipped of phrase. That last modification may reflect the relative manners of the two conductors – Karajan more individual in his refined expansiveness, Mehta more thrustful. On balance, taking Price alone, the preference is for the earlier set, but Mehta's version also boasts a fine cast, with the team of Domingo and Milnes at its most impressive. The recording, too, is admirable, even if it yields to the Decca in atmosphere and richness. The current reissue in RCA's Opera Treasury series (at the moment for the UK only) is very agreeably packaged. The set remains at premium price in the USA.

On Karajan's DG version the police chief, Scarpia, seems to be the central character, and his unexpected choice of singer, a full bass, Raimondi, helps to show why, for this is no small-time villain but a man who in full confidence has a vein of nobility in him. Katia Ricciarelli is not the most individual of Toscas, but the beauty of singing is consistent. Carreras gives a powerful, stylish performance. The recording is rich and full, with the stage picture clearly established and the glorious orchestral textures beautifully caught.

Tosca was one of Tebaldi's finest parts, and her earlier Decca mono set showed her at her most moving. In addition, Campora and Ezo Mascherini gave far more satisfying support as Cavaradossi and Scarpia respectively than did del Monaco and George London in the later Decca stereo set. The 1951 recording too stands the test of time remarkably well, the orchestra a little distant but the whole effect satisfyingly atmospheric. The choral climax with Scarpia in the *Te Deum* at the end of Act I is remarkably effective, even without the advantage of stereo. Erede's conducting is fittingly full-blooded, and Tebaldi admirers should not hesitate at the very reasonable price, even if there is no libretto/translation, only a synopsis.

Rarely has Solti phrased Italian melody so consistently *con amore*, his fiercer side subdued but with plenty of power when required. Even so, the timing is not always quite spontaneous-sounding, with transitions occasionally rushed. But the principal *raison d'être* of the set must be the casting of Dame Kiri as the jealous opera-singer. Her admirers will relish the glorious sounds, but the jealous side of Tosca's character is rather muted.

With extreme speeds, both fast and slow, and with fine playing from the Philharmonia Orchestra, Levine directs a red-blooded performance which underlines the melodrama. Domingo here reinforces his claim to be the finest Cavaradossi today, while the clean-cut, incisive singing of Renato Bruson presents a powerful if rather young-sounding Scarpia. Renata Scotto's voice is in many ways ideally suited to the role of Tosca, certainly in its timbre and colouring; as caught on record, however, the upper register is often squally. The digital recording is full and forward.

Tosca: highlights.

(B) *** DG Classikon 439 461-2 (from complete recording, with Ricciarelli, Carreras, Raimondi, Corena, German Op. Ch., BPO, Karajan).

(N) (M) ** EMI CDM5 66666-2 [id.]. (from above recording with Callas, Bergonzi, Gobbi; cond. Prêtre).

The new bargain Classikon 70-minute selection from Karajan's powerful, closely recorded Berlin version is welcome. The breadth of Karajan's direction is well represented in the longer excerpts; there is also Tosca's *Vissi d'arte* and Carreras's two famous arias from the outer Acts. Now Scarpia's music in Act II is much better represented, essential when Raimondi is such a distinctive Scarpia with his dark, bass timbre.

Even to Callas admirers her stereo remake of Tosca must be a disappointment when it fails so obviously to match the dramatic tension of the first version under Sabata. This is another sampler-length selection with only 56 minutes of music.

Tosca (complete; sung in English).

*** Chandos Dig. CHAN 3000 (2) [id.]. Eaglen, O'Neill, Yurisich, Geoffrey Mitchell Ch., Peter Kay Children's Ch., Philh. O, Parry.

With opera in English becoming at last a less neglected cause, the Peter Moores Foundation here sponsors the most persuasive example yet on CD of opera in translation. Above all, it offers the first recording to demonstrate the powers of Jane Eaglen at full stretch in one of the most formidable, vocally satisfying portrayals of the role of Tosca in years. The thrilling security with which she attacks one top note after another is a delight, vehement in presenting Tosca's jealousy. She is well matched by Dennis O'Neill as Cavaradossi, aptly Italianate in every register, with only occasional unevenness. Gregory Yurisich makes a powerful Scarpia, younger-sounding than most, and a plausible lover, with David Parry proving an outstanding Puccinian, pacing the score masterfully to heighten tensions, helped by opulent recording.

Il Trittico: (i) *Il Tabarro;* (ii) *Suor Angelica;* (iii) *Gianni Schicchi.*

(N) ❁ *** EMI Dig. CDS5 56567-2 [CDCC 54587] (3). (i; iii) Angela Gheorghiu, Roberto Alagna; (i) Carlo Guelfi, Maria Guleghina, Neil Schicoff; (ii) Cristina Gallardo-Domas, Bernadette Manca di Nissa; (ii–iii) Felicity Palmer; (iii) José van Dam, Luigi Roni; (i–ii) London Voices; (ii) Tiffin Boys' Ch., LSO or Philh. O, Pappano.

(M) *** EMI mono/stereo CMS7 64165-2 (3). (i; iii) Gobbi; (i) Pradelli, Mas; (ii–iii) De los Angeles; (ii) Barbieri; (iii) Canali, Del Monte, Montarsolo; Rome Op. Ch. & O; (i) Bellezza; (ii) Serafin; (iii) Santini.

**(*) Sony CD 79312 (3) [M3K 35912]. (i; ii) Scotto; (i; iii) Domingo; (i) Wixell, Sénéchal; (ii) Horne; (ii; iii) Cotrubas; (iii) Gobbi, Amb. Op. Ch.; (ii) Desborough School Ch.; (i; ii) Nat. PO; (iii) LSO, Maazel.

Antonio Pappano here anticipates his superb *La Bohème* and brilliantly follows up his outstanding set of *La Rondine*. No previous recordings of the three one-acters in Puccini's triptych bring quite such warmth or beauty or so powerful a drawing of the contrasts between each – in turn Grand Guignol melodrama, pure sentiment and high comedy. Pacing each opera masterfully, he heightens emotions fearlessly to produce at key moments the authentic gulp-in-throat, whether for the cuckolded bargemaster, Michele, for sister Angelica in her agonized suicide and heavenly absolution, or for the resolution of young love at the end of *Gianni Schicchi*.

Angela Gheorghiu and Roberto Alagna do not, as in *La Rondine*, take centre-stage, but as well as making a tiny cameo appearance in *Il Tabarro* as the off-stage departing lovers, they sing radiantly as Lauretta and Rinuccio in *Gianni Schicchi*, with the happy ending most tenderly done. Having different sopranos in each opera sharpens the contrasts between them. Maria Guleghina, well known for her fine Tosca, makes a warm, vibrant Giorgetta, and the touch of acid at the top of the voice adds character. Even more remarkable is the singing of the young Chilean soprano, Cristina Gallardo-Domas as Sister Angelica. This is a younger, more tender, more vulnerable Angelica than usual. Her vocal subtlety and commanding technique go with a fully mature portrayal of the nun's agony. As with Gheorghiu the dynamic shading brings pianissimos of breathtaking delicacy, not least in floated top-notes. The casting in the middle opera is as near flawless as could be. The Zia Principessa is sung with chilling power by Bernadette Manca di Nissa, her tone firm and even throughout. Felicity Palmer with her tangy mezzo tone is well contrasted as the Abbess, and she is just as characterful as the crabby Zita in *Gianni Schicchi*. Among the men, Carlo Guelfi makes a superb Michele in *Il Tabarro*, incisive, dark and virile. In range of tone he cannot match Tito Gobbi on the early EMI set, but he tellingly brings out both anger and poignancy in the bargemaster. Neil Shicoff makes a fine Luigi, his nervy tenor tone adding character. As Gianni Schicchi, José van Dam is in fine voice, with his clean focus bringing out the sardonic side of Schicchi, and his top Gs wonderfully strong and steady still. The recording is comfortingly sumptuous and atmospheric, very wide in its dynamic range, with magical off-stage effects.

The classic EMI set of *Il Trittico* has dominated the catalogue since the earliest days of LP, with Tito Gobbi giving two of his ripest characterizations. The central role of the cuckolded bargemaster, Michele, in *Il Tabarro* inspires him to one of his very finest performances on record. Though this version of Puccini's *grand guignol* opera, set on a barge on the Seine in Paris, is a mono recording, not stereo, it conveys the sense of horror far more keenly than any, with Gobbi's voice vividly caught on CD. The central leaf of the triptych, *Suor Angelica*, brings a glowing performance from Victoria de los Angeles, giving a most affecting portrayal of Angelica, the nun ill-treated by her noble family, with Fedora Barbieri formidable as her unfeeling aunt, the Zia Principessa. De los Angeles reappears, charmingly girlish as Lauretta, in *Gianni Schicchi*, where the high comedy has never fizzed so deliciously outside the opera house. She and Gobbi come together just as characterfully in this final opera. Though Gobbi's incomparable baritone is not by nature comic-sounding, he is unequalled as Schicchi, sardonically manipulating the mourning relatives of Buoso Donati, as he frames a new will for them. Puccini, the master of tragedy, here emerges a supreme master of comic timing too. Only *Gianni Schicchi*, recorded last in 1958, is in genuine and excellent stereo; *Il Tabarro* (1955) and *Suor Angelica* (1957) are mono, but all the transfers are expert, clear and convincingly balanced.

Il Tabarro may most seriously lack atmosphere in Maazel's version, but his directness is certainly refreshing, and in the other two operas it results in powerful readings; the opening of *Gianni Schicchi*, for example, has a sharp, almost Stravinskian bite. In the first two operas, Scotto's performances have a commanding dominance, presenting her at her finest. In *Gianni Schicchi* the veteran Tito Gobbi gives an amazing performance, in almost every way as fine as his EMI recording of twenty years earlier – and in some ways this is even more compelling. The only snag is the lack of cueing; CBS provide only one track for the whole of *Il Tabarro* and only two each for *Gianni Schicchi* and *Suor Angelica*, the second in each case being used to indicate the main soprano aria.

Turandot (complete).

*** Decca 414 274-2 (2) [id.]. Sutherland, Pavarotti, Caballé, Pears, Ghiaurov, Alldis Ch., Wandsworth School Boys' Ch., LPO, Mehta.

(M) *** EMI CMS7 69327-2 (2) [Ang. CDMB 69327]. Nilsson, Corelli, Scotto, Mercuriali, Giaiotti, Rome Op. Ch. & O, Molinari-Pradelli.

*** DG Dig. 423 855-2; *423 855-4* (2) [id.]. Ricciarelli, Domingo, Hendricks, Raimondi,

V. State Op. Ch., V. Boys' Ch., VPO, Karajan.
(***) EMI mono CDS5 56307-2 (2) [id.]. Callas, Fernandi, Schwarzkopf, Zaccaria, La Scala, Milan, Ch. & O, Serafin.
(M) **(*) EMI CMS5 65293-2 (2) [Ang. CDMB 65293]. Caballé, Carreras, Freni, Plishka, Sénéchal, Maîtrise de la Cathédrale, Ch. of L'Opéra du Rhin, Strasbourg PO, Lombard.
(N) *(*) RCA Dig. 74321 60617-2 (2) [id.]. Giovanna Casolla, Sergei Larin, Barbara Frittoli, Maggio Musicale Fiorentino Ch. & O, Mehta.

Joan Sutherland gives an intensely revealing and appealing interpretation, making the icy princess far more human and sympathetic than ever before, while Pavarotti gives a performance equally imaginative, beautiful in sound, strong on detail. To set Caballé against Sutherland was a daring idea, and it works superbly well; Pears as the Emperor is another imaginative choice. Mehta directs a gloriously rich and dramatic performance, superlatively recorded, still the best-sounding *Turandot* on CD, while the reading also remains supreme.

The EMI set brings Nilsson's second assumption on record of the role of Puccini's formidable princess. As an interpretation it is very similar to the earlier, RCA performance, but its impact is far more immediate, thanks to the conducting of Molinari-Pradelli. Corelli may not be the most sensitive prince in the world, but the voice is in glorious condition. Scotto's Liù is very beautiful and characterful too. With vividly remastered sound, this makes an excellent mid-priced recommendation, though the documentation, as yet, does not include an English translation.

In Karajan's set, Hendricks is almost a sex-kitten with her seductively golden tone, and one wonders how Calaf could ever have overlooked her. This is very different from the usual picture of a chaste slave-girl. Ricciarelli is a far more vulnerable figure than one expects of the icy princess, and the very fact that the part strains her beyond reasonable vocal limits adds to the dramatic point, even if it subtracts from the musical joys. By contrast, Plácido Domingo is vocally superb, a commanding prince; and the rest of the cast present star names even in small roles.

With Callas, the character seems so much more believably complex than with others, and this 1957 recording is one of her most thrillingly magnetic performances on disc. Schwarzkopf provides a comparably characterful and distinctive portrait as Liù, far more than a Puccinian 'little woman', sweet and wilting. Eugenio Fernandi sounds relatively uncharacterful as Calaf, but his timbre is pleasing enough. By contrast, Serafin's masterly conducting exactly matches the characterfulness of Callas and Schwarzkopf, with colour, atmosphere and dramatic point all commandingly presented. With such a vivid performance, the 1957 mono sound hardly seems to matter, and the sound is much more expansive in the new transfer

Having earlier sung Liù opposite Joan Sutherland for Decca, Caballé went on to assume the more taxing role of Turandot. With Mirella Freni as Liù there is again a powerful confrontation, not between black and white but between subtler, less fixed characters. So from the very start Caballé conveys an element of mystery while Freni underlines the dramatic rather than the lyrical side of Liù's role. The pity is that the recording is unflattering to the voices – allowing Caballé less warmth and body of tone than usual, while setting Freni so close that a flutter keeps intruding. Lombard, so alert and imaginative in French music, proves a stiff and unsympathetic Puccinian so that the tenor, José Carreras, for example is prevented from expanding as he should in the big arias. Nor is the Strasbourg Philharmonic a match for the LPO on Decca. A good CD transfer and excellent back-up documentation.

It was a bold venture to go to Peking, where Turandot is set, and there present a spectacular production in an authentic building from the Ming dynasty, now called the People's Cultural Palace. The recording which resulted offers a strong performance under Zubin Mehta (conductor of the outstanding Decca recording with Sutherland and Pavarotti) in beefy, if at times abrasive, sound, with ample space round the voices. The musicians from the Maggio Musicale Fiorentino generally perform well, if with some rough moments, while the casting of the principals is seriously flawed. Sergei Larin is outstanding among Russian tenors, and he sings with fine dramatic thrust, though his voice grows strained towards the end. Giovanna Casola has a big voice with a pronounced flutter, so that the tone grows sour, and at the top pitching becomes vague under stress, so that *In questa reggia* ends with a squeal. Barbara Frittoli is even less well cast as Liù, with her heavy vibrato and reluctance to sing softly.

Turandot: highlights.
(M) *** Decca 458 202-2 [id.] (from complete recording, with Sutherland, Pavarotti, Caballé, Ghiaurov, John Alldis Ch., Wandsworth School Boys' Ch., LPO; cond. Mehta).

A generous and shrewdly chosen 70-minute collection of excerpts from the glorious full-priced Decca set of *Turandot*. *Nessun dorma*, with Pavarotti at his finest, is here given a closing cadence for neatness. The vintage Decca sound is outstandingly full and vivid. The reissue in Decca's Opera Gala series is neatly packaged in a slipcase and includes a full translation.

Le Villi: complete.

*** Sony MK 76890 [MK 36669]. Scotto, Domingo, Nucci, Gobbi, Amb. Op. Ch., Nat. PO, Maazel.

Maazel directs a performance so commanding, with singing of outstanding quality, that one can at last assess Puccini's first opera on quite a new level. Scotto's voice tends to spread a little at the top of the stave but, like Domingo, she gives a powerful performance, and Leo Nucci avoids false histrionics. A delightful bonus is Tito Gobbi's contribution reciting the verses which link the scenes; he is as characterful a reciter as he is a singer. The recording is one of CBS's best.

COLLECTIONS

'Gala': La Bohème: (i) *Che gelida manina; Si, mi chiamano Mimi*; (ii) *Quando m'en vo*; (iii) *Donde lieta usci*; (iv) *La Fanciulla del West: Ch'ella mi creda*; (v) *Gianni Schicchi: O mio babbino caro*; (i) *Madama Butterfly: Un bel dì; Addio fioriti asil*; (iii) *Manon Lescaut: In quelle trine morbide*; (vi) *Donna non vidi mai*; (v) *La Rondine: Sogno di Doretta*; (iii) *Suor Angelica: Senza mamma*; (vii) *Tosca: Recordita armonia; Vissi d'arte; E lucevan le stelle*; (viii) *Turandot: Signore ascolta!; Non piangere Liù!; Ah! Per l'ultima volta!; In questa reggia; Tu che di gel sei cinta; Nessun dorma!*

(N) (M) *** Decca 458 212-2 [id.]. (i) Freni, Pavarotti; (ii) Elizabeth Harwood; (iii) Maria Chiara; (iv) Sherrill Milnes; (v) Tebaldi; (vi) José Carreras; (vii) Corelli, Nilsson; Sutherland, Caballé, Pavarotti, Ghiaurov.

This generous (71-minute) 'Gala' collection, with 22 items, opens predictably with Freni and Pavarotti in the Act I love scene from Karajan's 1972 *Bohème*, and they sing again in Karajan's 1974 *Butterfly*. The programme closes ambitiously, with six major excerpts from Mehta's *Turandot* with Sutherland, Caballé, and Pavarotti. Tebaldi is at her most ravishing in arias from *La rondine* and *Gianni Schicchi*, and imaginatively, the 1966 Nilsson/Corelli/Maazel recording is chosen for the three items from *Tosca*. Decca are skilled at this kind of anthology, and particularly welcome is the inclusion of three arias from Maria Chiara's magical 1971 début recital, including lyrically very beautiful accounts of 'In quelle trine morbide' (*Manon Lescaut*) and 'Senza mamma' (*Suor Angelica*), recorded when her voice sounded wonderfully young and fresh. The documentation is excellent and full translations are included.

'Sole e amore': Arias and Duets: *La Bohème: Donde lieta usci; Si,mi chiamano Mimi.* (i) *Canto d'anime. Gianni Schicchi: O mio babbino caro. Madama Butterfly: Intermezzo Atto II, Parte seconda; Un bel di vedremo. Manon Lescaut: In quelle trine morbide; Intermezzo Act III; Sola perduta, abandonnata;* (i) *Morire. La Rondine: Ch'il bel sogno di Doretta;* (i) *Sole e amore. Suor Angelica: Senza Mamma, o bimbo. Tosca: Vissi d'arte. Turandot: Signore ascolta; Tu che di gel sei cinta. Le Villi: Se come voi.*

(N) *** Erato/Warner Dig. 0630 17071-2 [id.]. Kiri Te Kanawa, (i) Roger Vignoles with Nat. Op. O de Lyon, Kent Nagano.

This is a Puccini recital disc with a difference. The title, '*Sole e amore*' (Sunshine and love), is taken not from an aria but from one of the three Puccini songs included, the one written as a magazine contribution in 1888, which he later raided for the Act III Quartet from *La Bohème*. Rightly, Dame Kiri sings it not as an opera excerpt *manqué* but – encouraged by Roger Vignoles's imaginative accompaniment – as the trivial album-leaf intended. Those three songs with piano provide a welcome variety in a Puccini collection which, avoiding Minnie and Turandot, might have lacked contrast. Tosca's *Vissi d'arte* comes as an introduction, but then the ordering is chronological. The orchestral interludes from *Manon Lescaut* and *Butterfly* are beautifully done, but more songs with piano would have been preferable. With a recording lacking in bloom on top, the voice is not quite as creamy as it once was, if still very beautiful.

'The Essential Puccini': Preludio sinfonico; Famous arias, duets and choruses from: *La Bohème; La Fanciulla del West; Gianni Schicchi; Madama Butterfly; Manon Leseaut; La Rondine; Suor Angelica; Tosca; Turandot.*

(B) **(*) Decca Double Analogue/Dig. 444 555-2 (2) [id.]. Caballé, Chiara, Freni, Te Kanawa, Sutherland, Tebaldi, Bergonzi, Bjoerling, Carreras, Pavarotti, Corena, Ghiaurov, Krause, Milnes, Siepi (with various orchestras & conductors).

Many collectors will welcome a sampler of the vintage set of *La Bohème* with Tebaldi and Bergonzi at the height of their powers. Five items are included here, including the love scene from Act I. Tebaldi is also at her most seductive in *Madama Butterfly*, which is generously represented with well over half an hour of excerpts, including the whole of the Act I Love duet. She also provides the key arias from *Gianni Schicchi* and *La Rondine*, while Suor Angelica's ravishing *Senza mamma, o bimbo, tu sei morto* comes from Maria Chiara's glorious 1971 début recital, which Decca should urgently restore to the catalogue. Dame Kiri gives a movingly passionate if comparatively unsubtle characterization of *Manon Lescaut*; with three numbers included, her partner, Carreras, recorded just before his illness, sounds a little strained. It was a pity that Rescigno's recording was chosen for the 30 minutes or so of *Tosca* excerpts, especially as a highlights disc from that set is already available. Freni as Tosca is below her best form and, though Sherrill Milnes does not disappoint as Scarpia, Pavarotti's *E lucevan le stelle* is the high point. Joan Sutherland's assumption of the role of the formidable *Turandot* is justly esteemed, as is Caballé's melting Liù, while Pavarotti delivers a splendid *Nessun dorma*. With Bjoerling on hand to provide a superb *Ch'ella mi creda* from *Fanciulla del West*, this is something of a (143-minute) Puccini feast, with the ripely expansive Decca sound fairly consistent throughout (although the early Tebaldi recordings give some indication of their age in the violin tone). The snag is that the documentation is totally inadequate.

'Puccini heroines'; La Bohème: Sì, mi chiamano Mimì; Donde lieta uscì; Musetta's waltz song. Edgar: Addio, mio dolce amor. La Fanciulla del West: Laggiù nel Soledad. Gianni Schicchi: O mio babbino caro. Madama Butterfly: Bimba, bimba non piangere (*Love duet,* with Plácido Domingo); *Un bel dì. Manon Lescaut: In quelle trine morbide; Sola, perduta, abbandonata. La Rondine: Ore dolci a divine. Tosca: Vissi d'arte. Turandot: In questa reggia. Le Villi: Se come voi piccina.*
*** RCA RD 85999 [RCA 5999-2-RC]. Leontyne Price, New Philh. O or LSO, Downes; Santi.

This collection is a formidable demonstration of the art of Leontyne Price at the very peak of her career, still marvellously subtle in control (the end of Tosca's *Vissi d'arte* for example), powerfully dramatic, yet able to point the *Rondine* aria with delicacy and charm. The *Love duet* from *Butterfly* in which she is joined by Domingo is particularly thrilling, and there is much else here to give pleasure. The remastering is extremely vivid and the voice is given fine bloom and presence. A Puccinian feast!

Arias: *La Bohème: Quando m'en vo' soletta. Gianni Schicchi: O mio babbino caro. Madama Butterfly: Un bel dì. Manon Lescaut: In quelle trine morbide. La Rondine: Chi il bel sogno di Doretta. Tosca: Vissi d'arte. Le Villi: Se come voi piccina.*
*** Sony Dig. MK 37298 [id.]. Kiri Te Kanawa, LPO, Pritchard – VERDI: *Arias.* ***

The creamy beauty of Kiri Te Kanawa's voice is ideally suited to these seven lyrical arias, including such rarities as the little waltz-like song from *Le Villi*, well recorded and sounding especially believable on CD.

Arias: *La Bohème; Sì, mi chiamano Mimì; Donde lieta uscì. Gianni Schicchi: O mio babbino caro. Madama Butterfly: Un bel dì; Tu, tu piccolo Iddio. Manon Lescaut: In quelle trine morbide; Sola, perduta, abbandonata. La Rondine: Chi il bel sogno di Doretta. Tosca: Vissi d'arte. Turandot: Signore, ascolta!; Tu che di gel sei cinta. Le Villi: Se come voi piccina.*
*** EMI CDC7 47841-2 [id.]. Montserrat Caballé, LSO, Mackerras.

Montserrat Caballé uses her rich, beautiful voice to glide over these great Puccinian melodies. The effect is ravishing, with lovely recorded sound to match the approach. This is one of the loveliest of all operatic recital discs and the comparative lack of sparkle is compensated for by the sheer beauty of the voice. The CD transfer is extremely successful, vivid yet retaining the full vocal bloom.

Arias: *La Bohème: Si, mi chiamano Mimì; Donde lieta uscì. Gianni Schicchi: O mio babino caro. Madama Butterfly: Un bel dì; Con onor muore. Manon Lescaut: In quelle trine morbide; Sola, perduta. Suor Angelica: Senza mamma. Turandot: Signore acolta!; In questa reggia; Tu che di gel sei cinta.*
(M) (***) EMI mono CDM5 66463-2 [id.]. Maria Callas, Philh. O, Serafin.

This collection of Puccini arias was Callas's first EMI recital, recorded in mono in Watford Town Hall in September 1954. Now reissued as part of EMI's Callas Edition, it brings a classic example of her art. She was vocally at her peak. Even when her concept of a Puccinian 'little woman' has eyes controversially flashing and fierce, the results are unforgettable, never for a moment relaxing on the easy course, always finding new revelation, whether as Turandot or Liù, as Manon, Mimì or Butterfly. Well-balanced recording, with the voice vividly projected by the transfer and with plenty of depth and detail in the orchestra.

Arias and duets from: *La Bohème; Madama Butterfly; Manon Lescaut; Tosca; Turandot.*
(N) (BB) *(*) Arts Music 47518-2. Peter Dvorský, Hungarian State Op. O, András Mihaly or Berlin RSO, Roberto Paternostro.

The Czech tenor, Peter Dvorský, is generally associated on disc with the Slavonic repertory, but he has had a formidable international career singing in a far wider range of works and here ably tackles Puccini, modifying his Slavonic tone towards roundness. The items recorded in Budapest, notably Des Grieux's Act III aria from *Manon Lescaut*, are more impressive than those from Berlin. Much the longest item, the Love duet from *Butterfly*, is not helped by the rather raw singing of Fiamma Izzo in the title-role. The booklet has texts but no translation. A fair recommendation at super-bargain price for admirers of this singer, even if the recording is not ideally clear.

Arias: *Madama Butterfly: Un bel dì; Tu? tu? piccolo Iddio!* (Death of Butterfly). *La Rondine: Che il bel sogno di Doretta. Tosca: Vissi d'arte. Turandot: Signore ascolta; Tu che di gel sei cinta.*

(M) **(*) RCA 09026 68883-2 [id.]. Leontyne Price, Rome Opera O, Oliviero de Fabritiis or Artur Basile – VERDI: *Arias.* ***

There is some glorious singing in this recital from the beginning of the 1960s. Perhaps Leontyne Price does not always get right inside each heroine at this stage in her career, but *Un bel dì* is thrilling, with a sharp contrast of tone between the incisiveness of the opening and the delicacy of *Chi sarà, Chi sarà*. In *Vissi d'arte* she forces a little too hard so that her vibrato becomes a wobble, but the two *Turandot* arias are very beautiful. Most welcome of all is Magda's aria from *La Rondine*, sweet, charming and lyrical. The recording was always very good indeed, and it sounds even more vivid in this CD transfer, without any loss of bloom.

Purcell, Henry (1659–95)

Gardiner Purcell Collection

'Gardiner Purcell Collection'.

(M) *** Erato/Warner 4509 96371-2 (8) [id.]. Soloists, Monteverdi Ch. & O, Equale Brass Ens., E. Bar. Soloists, Gardiner.

To commemorate the tercentenary of Purcell's death, the following reissued Erato recordings, all directed with distinction by John Eliot Gardiner, are also available together in a slip-case (at a slightly reduced price); they would make a splendid basis for any Purcell collection. All these discs are also available separately.

Come, ye sons of art away; Funeral music for Queen Mary (1695).

(M) *** Erato/Warner 4509 96553-2 [id.]. Lott, Brett, Williams, Allen, Monteverdi Ch. & O, Equale Brass Ens., Gardiner.

Come, ye Sons of art, the most celebrated of Purcell's birthday odes for Queen Mary, is splendidly coupled here with the unforgettable funeral music he wrote on the death of the same monarch. With the Monteverdi Choir at its most incisive and understanding the performances are exemplary, and the recording, though balanced in favour of the instruments, is clear and refined. Among the soloists Thomas Allen is outstanding, while the two counter-tenors give a charming performance of the duet, *Sound the trumpet*. The *Funeral music* includes the well-known *Solemn march* for trumpets and drums, a *Canzona* and simple anthem given at the funeral, and two of Purcell's most magnificent anthems setting the *Funeral sentences*. Recording made in 1976 in Rosslyn Hill Chapel, London.

Ode on St Cecilia's day (Hail! bright Cecilia).

(M) *** Erato/Warner Dig. 4509 96554-2 [id.]. Jennifer Smith, Stafford, Gordon, Elliott, Varcoe, David Thomas, Monteverdi Ch., E. Bar. Soloists, Gardiner.

Gardiner's characteristic vigour and alertness in Purcell come out superbly in this delightful record of the 1692 *St Cecilia Ode* – not as well known as some of the other odes he wrote, but a masterpiece. Soloists and chorus are outstanding even by Gardiner's high standards, and the recording excellent. Recording made in 1982 in the Barbican Concert Hall, London.

Dioclesian; Timon of Athens.

(M) *** Erato/Warner Dig. 4509 96556-2 (2) [id.]. Dawson, Fisher, Covey-Crump, Elliott, George, Varcoe, Monteverdi Ch., E. Bar. Soloists, Gardiner.

The martial music, shining with trumpets, is what stands out in *Dioclesian*, adapted from a Jacobean play first given in 1622. Gardiner is such a lively conductor, regularly drawing out the effervescence in Purcell's inspiration, that the result is delightfully refreshing, helped by an outstanding team of soloists. The incidental music for *Timon of Athens* offers more buried treasure, including such enchanting inventions as *Hark! how the songsters of the grove*, with its 'Symphony of pipes imitating the chirping of birds', and a fine *Masque for Cupid and Bacchus*, beautifully sung by Lynne Dawson, Gillian Fisher and Stephen Varcoe. Excellent Erato sound. Recordings made in Rosslyn Hill Chapel, London, in 1987.

The Indian Queen (incidental music; complete).

(M) *** Erato/Warner 4509 96551-2 [id.]. Hardy, Fisher, Harris, Smith, Stafford, Hill, Elwes, Varcoe, Thomas, Monteverdi Ch., E. Bar. Soloists, Gardiner.

The reissued Erato version is fully cast and uses an authentic accompanying baroque instrumental group. The choral singing is especially fine, with the close of the work movingly expressive. John Eliot Gardiner's choice of tempi is apt and the soloists are all good, although the men are more strongly characterful than the ladies; nevertheless the lyrical music comes off well. The recording is spacious and well balanced. Recording made in 1979 in Henry Wood Hall, London.

King Arthur (complete).

(M) *** Erato/Warner Dig. 4509 96552-2 (2) [id.]. Jennifer Smith, Gillian Fischer, Priday, Ross, Stafford, Elliot, Varcoe, Monteverdi Ch., E. Bar. Soloists, Gardiner.

Gardiner's solutions to the textual problems carry complete conviction, as for example his placing of the superb *Chaconne in F* at the end instead of the start. Solo singing for the most part is excellent, with Stephen Varcoe outstanding among the men.

Fairest isle is treated very gently, with Gill Ross, boyish of tone, reserved just for that number. Throughout, the chorus is characteristically fresh and vigorous, and the instrumentalists beautifully marry authentic technique to pure, unabrasive sounds. Digital recording, made in 1983 in St Giles, Cripplegate, London.

The Tempest (incidental music).
(M) *** Erato/Warner 4509 96555-2 [id.]. Jennifer Smith, Hardy, Hall, Elwes, Varcoe, David Thomas, Earle, Monteverdi Ch. & O, Gardiner.

Whether or not Purcell himself wrote this music for Shakespeare's last play (the scholarly arguments are still unresolved), Gardiner demonstrates how delightful it is, a masterly collection, in performances both polished and stylish and with excellent solo and choral singing. At least the overture is clearly Purcell's, and that sets a pattern for a very varied collection of numbers, including three *da capo* arias and a full-length masque celebrating Neptune for Act V. The 1979 recording, made in London's Henry Wood Hall, is full and atmospheric; the words are beautifully clear, and the transfer to CD is admirably natural.

INSTRUMENTAL MUSIC

3 Fantasias for 5 viols; 9 Fantasias for 4 viols; Fantasia on one note for 5 viols; In nomine for 6 viols; In nomine for 7 viols.
*** Virgin Veritas/EMI (SIS) Dig. VC5 45062-2 [CDC 45062]. Fretwork.

Purcell wrote these *Fantasias* in 1680 at the time of his twenty-first birthday, consciously adopting what was then considered an archaic style, but displaying not only an astonishing contrapuntal skill but also a harmonic and structural adventurousness which leaps the centuries, sounding to us amazingly modern still in its daring chromaticisms. The players of Fretwork use viols with a concern for matching, tuning and balance which is quite exceptional, and their natural expressiveness matches the deeper implications of these masterpieces in microcosm. This makes a superb modern successor to the earlier recordings by Wenzinger and his Schola Cantorum Basiliensis and by Harnoncourt, both included in DG's Archiv Purcell Collection, above.

(i) *3 Fantasias for 3 Viols; 9 Fantasias for 4 Viols; Fantasia on one note for 5 viols; In nomine for 6 viols; In nomine for 7 viols;* (ii) *Chacony in G min.*
(M) **(*) DG 447 153-2. (i) VCM, Alice Harnoncourt; (ii) E. Concert, Pinnock.

The Purcell *Fantasias* and *In nomines* are among the most searching and profound works in all music, and the 1963 Vienna Concentus, led by Alice Harnoncourt (with Nikolaus at the time playing 'second fiddle'), provide a set of performances of these wonderful pieces, darkly sombre in colour, using original instruments with a minimum of vibrato. Then at track 16 there is a splash of cold water in the face as Trevor Pinnock and his English Concert (recorded two decades later) demonstrate modern ideas of authenticity of style and pitch with a brightly astringent and strikingly vital account of the famous *Chacony in G minor*. This transition is not entirely comfortable, and it is better to listen to this piece as a separate item.

Sonatas in 3 parts: Nos. 1–12 (complete).
(M) *** HM Suite Dig. HMT 7901439 [id.]. London Baroque.

Purcell's set of 12 *Sonatas in 3 Parts* was published in 1683. The Italian influence is undeniable but they remain very much Purcell's own in their contrapuntal interest, their deeply expressive harmonic richness and their English seriousness of purpose. The period performances from London Baroque are full of vitality and warmth; indeed the rich blending of the violons of Ingried Seifert and Richard Gwilt in partnership with the viola da gamba of Charles Medlam gives the music plenty of warmth. The full resonance of the recording is helpful, but that in itself brings the one drawback: the effective dynamic range is reduced, although there is no lack of light and shade in the playing itself; and the continuo, featuring both harpsichord and organ (as was the practice at the time), comes through as it should, beautifully. So this fine set must receive the strongest advocacy, for the music itself is very rewarding indeed.

Sonatas of 3 Parts Nos. 1–12, Z.790/801; Sonatas of 4 Parts Nos. 1–10, Z.802/810; Chacony in G min., Z.730; Pavans, Z.438/52; Three parts upon a ground in D, Z.731.
*** Chandos Dig. CHAN 0572/3 [id.]. Purcell Qt.

Sonatas of 3 parts Nos. 1–7, Z.790–6; Pavans: in A min.; B flat; G min., Z.749, Z.750, Z.752.
*** Chandos Dig. CHAN 8591 [id.]. Purcell Qt.

Sonatas of 3 Parts Nos. 8–12, Z.797–801; Sonatas in 4 Parts Nos. 1–2, Z.802–3; Chacony in G min., Z.751; Fantasia on a Ground in D & F; Pavans in A, Z.748; G min., Z.751.
*** Chandos Dig. CHAN 8663 [id.]. Purcell Qt.

Sonatas of 4 Parts Nos. 3–10, Z.804–811; Prelude for solo violin in G min., Z.773; Organ voluntaries Nos. 2 in D min.; 4 in G, Z.718 & 710.
*** Chandos Dig. CHAN 8763 [id.]. Purcell Qt.

In these *Sonatas* Purcell turned to the new, concerted style which had been developed in Italy. Interspersed among the *Sonatas* are three earlier and highly chromatic *Pavans*, composed before Purcell embraced the sonata discipline. If anything, the second volume is more attractive than the first, for it includes the indelible *Chacony in G minor*. The third leaves room for a solo violin *Prelude* and two organ *Voluntaries*, both admirably presented and, like the *Sonatas*, offering very realistic sound. The Purcell Quartet give a first-class account of themselves: their playing is authoritative and idiomatic, and the artists are firmly focused in a warm but not excessively reverberant acoustic. Strongly recommended. These authoritative and thoroughly enjoyable accounts of Purcell's *Sonatas* have now been gathered together on two CDs without the miscellaneous items which filled out a third. Whichever is chosen, this set can be thoroughly recommended.

KEYBOARD MUSIC

Harpsichord suites Nos. 1–8, Z.660/663; 666–9; Ground in G min., Z.221; A new Ground in E min., Z.682; Hornpipe, Z.685.
**(*) HM Dig. HMC 901496 [id.]. Kenneth Gilbert (harpsichord).

Not surprisingly, Kenneth Gilbert gives authoritative, stylish and completely spontaneous accounts of these fine suites. He plays a Couchet-Taskin of 1671 but the reverberant recording spreads the harpsichord sound so that it tends to become aurally tiring.

'The Purcell Manuscript': *Suites: in A min. & C; Prelude; 3 Minuets; 3 Airs; Thus happy and free; Trumpet minuet; Minuet; 3 Hornpipes.*
*** Virgin/EMI Dig. VC5 45166-2 [id.]. Davitt Moroney (virginals or harpsichord) (with Giovanni DRAGHI: *Suites: in A; C min.; G; G min.;* GIBBONS: *Prelude in G* ***).

This charming disc presents the complete contents of a keyboard lesson-book, discovered in London towards the end of 1993, one of only 15 or 16 Purcell manuscripts to have survived. In his own hand he copied out pieces evidently for a pupil to play. Of the 20 Purcell pieces here, mostly miscellaneous but including *Suites in A minor* and *C major*, five were previously unknown, and six more are arrangements of theatre-pieces unique to this book. Tiny as they are, between them they significantly amplify the picture we have of Purcell's keyboard music. The manuscript also includes a favourite keyboard piece of Orlando Gibbons, the *Prelude in G*, and four suites by Purcell's contemporary, Giovanni Batista Draghi (*c*. 1640–1708), a rival teacher who may well have taken over the pupil's lessons after Purcell's early death. Crisp and bright, Davitt Moroney uses a virginals for the Purcell and two different harpsichords for the more elaborate Draghi pieces.

VOCAL MUSIC

Anthems & Services, Vol. 1: *It is a good thing to give thanks; Let mine eyes run down with tears; My beloved spake; O give thanks unto the Lord; O praise God in his holiness; O sing unto the Lord; Praise the Lord, O Jerusalem.*
*** Hyperion Dig. CDA 66585 [id.]. Witcomb, Finnis, Hallchurch, Bowman, Daniels, George, Evans, King's Cons., Robert King.

Anthems & Services, Vol. 2: *Behold now praise the Lord; Blessed are they that fear the Lord; I will give thanks unto Thee, O Lord; My song shall be alway; Te Deum and Jubilate.*
*** Hyperion Dig. CDA 66609 [id.]. Bowman, Covey-Crump, George, New College, Oxford, Ch., King's Cons., Robert King.

Anthems & Services, Vol. 3: *Begin the song, and strike the living lyre; Blessed Virgin's expostulation: Tell me, some pitying angel. Blow up the trumpet in Zion; Hear my prayer, O Lord; Hosanna to the highest; Lord, I can suffer thy rebukes; The Lord is King, be the people never so impatient; O God, Thou has cast us out; O Lord, our governor; Remember not Lord our offences; Thy word is a lantern unto my feet.*
*** Hyperion Dig. CDA 66623 [id.]. Dawson, Bowman, Daniels, George, Evans, King's Cons. Ch., King's Cons., Robert King.

Anthems & Services, Vol. 4: *Awake ye dead; Behold I bring you glad tidings; Early, O Lord, my fainting soul; The earth trembled; Lord, not to us but to thy name; Lord, what is man?; My heart is inditing of a good matter; O all ye people, clap your hands; Since God so tender a regard; Sing unto God; Sleep, Adam and take thy rest; The way of God is an undefiled way.*
*** Hyperion Dig. CDA 66644 [id.]. Witcomb, Finnis, Hallchurch, Kennedy, O'Dwyer, Gritton, Bowman, Covey-Crump, Daniels, George, Varcoe, R. Evans, New College, Oxford, Ch., King's Cons., Robert King.

Anthems & services, Vol. 5: *Awake, and with attention hear; How long, great God; Let the night perish (Job's Curse); O God, the king of glory; O God, Thou art my God; O, I'm sick of life; O Lord, rebuke me not; Praise the Lord, O my soul, and all that is within me; Rejoice in the Lord alway; We sing to him, whose wisdom form'd the ear; When on my sick bed I languish; With sick and famish'd eyes.*
*** Hyperion Dig. CDA 66656 [id.]. Witcomb, Finnis, Hallchurch, Kennedy, Gritton, Bowman, Covey-Crump, Daniels, George, Evans, King's Cons. Ch., King's Cons., Robert King.

Anthems & Services, Vol. 6: *Great God and just; Hear me, O Lord, the great support; I will love Thee, O Lord; Lord, who can tell how oft he offendeth?; My heart is fixed, O God; O Lord, grant the King a long life; O praise the Lord, all ye heathen; Plung'd in the confines of despair; Thou wakeful shepherd that dost Israel keep; Who hath believed our report?; Why do the heathen so furiously rage together?*

*** Hyperion Dig. CDA 66663 [id.]. Witcomb, Kennedy, O'Dwyer, Bowman, Covey-Crump, Daniels, Agnew, George, New College, Oxford, Ch., King's Cons., Robert King.

Anthems & Services, Vol. 7: *Beati omnes qui timent; In the black dismal dungeon of despair; I was glad* (2 settings: coronation anthem & verse anthem); *Jubilate in B flat; O consider my adversity; Music for the funeral of Queen Mary; Save me O God; Te Deum in B flat; Thy way O God is holy.*

✿ *** Hyperion Dig. CDA 66677 [id.]. Kennedy, O'Dwyer, Goodman, Gritton, Bowman, Short, Covey-Crump, Daniels, Milhofer, George, R. Evans, King's Cons. Ch., King's Cons., Robert King.

Anthems & Services, Vol. 8: *Be merciful unto me; Benedicte in B flat; Blessed is the man that feareth the Lord; Bow down thine ear, O Lord; Full of wrath, his threatening breath; In Thee, O Lord, do I put my trust; Jehova, quam multi sunt hostes mei; Magnificat and Nunc Dimittis in G min.; They that go down to the sea in ships.*

*** Hyperion Dig. CDA 66686 [id.]. O'Dwyer, Kennedy, Bowman, Covey-Crump, Daniels, Padmore, Milhofer, George, King's Cons. Ch., King's Cons., Robert King.

Robert King follows up the success of his collection of Purcell's Odes and Welcome songs (see below) with an equally illuminating collection of the church music. The different categories of work, Services, Verse Anthems, Motets (or Full Anthems) and devotional songs, cover the widest range of style and expression, with King's own helpful and scholarly notes setting each one in context. Generally the most adventurous in style are the Full Anthems, with elaborate counterpoint often bringing amazingly advanced harmonic progressions. Yet the Verse Anthems too include some which similarly demonstrate Purcell's extraordinary imagination in contrapuntal writing. So though Volume 6 is confined to Verse Anthems and devotional songs, they too offer passages of chromatic writing which defy the idea of these categories as plain and straightforward. As the title suggests, the devotional song, *Plung'd in the confines of despair*, is a particularly fine example. Although all the earlier volumes are full of good things, Volume 7 (to which we award a token Rosette for the extraordinary achievement of this series) is the one to recommend first to anyone simply wanting to sample Purcell's church music. Not only does it contain the *Music for the Funeral of Queen Mary* in 1695, with drum processionals, the solemn *March* and *Canzona for brass* and *Funeral sentences*, it has the *B flat Morning service*, two settings of the Coronation anthem, *I was glad*, (one of them previously unrecorded), a magnificent Full Anthem, three Verse Anthems and two splendid devotional songs. Robert King's meticulous notes include a detailed account of Queen Mary's funeral, providing evidence for his view that the *March* was not played with drums accompanying, but on its own. Volume 8, too, is full of fine music. The opening Verse Anthem, *In Thee, O Lord, do I put my trust*, opens with a very striking, slightly melancholy *Sinfonia*, with a six-note figure rising up from a ground bass, which sets the expressive mood. The closing anthem, so appropriate from an island composer, *They that go down to the sea in ships*, is characteristically diverse, with Purcell helping the Lord 'maketh the storm to cease' and at the end providing a joyful chorus of praise. It is astonishing how many of the pieces have never appeared on record before, and that includes some of the finest. King's notes and documentation closely identify each item, adding to one's illumination. An outstanding series, full of treasures, with King varying the scale of forces he uses for each item. Often he uses one voice per part, but he regularly expands the ensemble with the King's Consort Choir or turns to the full New College Choir, which includes trebles.

Odes and Welcome songs Vols. 1–8 (complete).

*** Hyperion Dig. CDS 44031/8 [id.]. Soloists, New College, Oxford, Ch., King's Cons., Robert King.

Odes & Welcome songs, Vol. 1: *Arise my muse (1690); Now does the glorious day appear (1689) (Odes for Queen Mary's birthday); Ode for St Cecilia's Day: Welcome to all pleasures (1683).*

*** Hyperion Dig. CDA 66314 [id.]. Fisher, Bonner, Bowman, Chance, Daniels, Ainsley, George, Potts, King's Cons., Robert King.

Odes & Welcome songs, Vol. 2: *Ode on St Cecilia's Day (Hail! bright Cecilia!)* (1692). *Ode for the birthday of the Duke of Gloucester: Who can from joy refrain* (1695).

*** Hyperion Dig. CDA 66349 [id.]. Fisher, Bonner, Bowman, Covey-Crump, Ainsley, George, Keenlyside, New College, Oxford, Ch., King's Cons., King.

Odes & Welcome songs, Vol. 3: *Ode for Queen Mary's birthday: Celebrate this festival* (1693). *Welcome song for Charles II (1683): Fly, bold rebellion* (1683). *Welcome song for James II: Sound the trumpet, beat the drum* (1687).

*** Hyperion Dig. CDA 66412 [id.]. Fisher, Bonner, Bowman, Kenny, Covey-Crump, Müller, George, Pott, King's Cons., King.

Odes & Welcome songs, Vol. 4: *Ode for Mr*

Maidwell's School: Celestial music did the gods inspire (1689). *Ode for the wedding of Prince George of Denmark and Princess Anne: From hardy climes and dangerous toils of war* (1683). *Welcome song for James II: Ye tuneful muses* (1686).

*** Hyperion Dig. CDA 66456 [id.]. Fisher, Bonner, Bowman, Kenny, Covey-Crump, Daniels, George, Pott, King's Cons., Robert King.

Odes & welcome songs, Vol. 5: *Ode for the birthday of Queen Mary: Welcome, welcome, glorious morn* (1691). *Ode for the Centenary of Trinity College, Dublin: Great parent, hail to thee* (1694). *Welcome song for King Charles II: The Summer's absence unconcerned we bear* (1682).

*** Hyperion CDA 66476 [id.]. Fisher, Tubb, Bowman, Short, Covey-Crump, Ainsley, George, Pott, King's Cons., Robert King.

Odes & Welcome songs, Vol. 6: *Ode for Queen Mary's birthday: Love's goddess sure was blind* (1692). *Ode for St Cecilia's Day: Laudate Ceciliam* (1683). *Ode for St Cecilia's Day: Raise, raise the voice* (*c*. 1685). *Welcome song for Charles II: From those serene and rapturous joys* (1684).

*** Hyperion Dig. CDA 66494 [id.]. Fisher, Seers, Bowman, Short, Padmore, Tusa, George, Evans, King's Cons., King.

Odes & Welcome songs, Vol. 7: *Welcome song for Charles II: Swifter Isis, swifter flow* (1681). *Welcome song for the Duke of York: What shall be done in behalf of the man?* (1682). *Yorkshire feast song: Of old, when heroes thought it base* (1690).

*** Hyperion Dig. CDA 66587 [id.]. Fisher, Hamilton,, Bowman, Short, Covey-Crump, Daniels, George, Evans, King's Cons., King.

Odes & welcome songs, Vol. 8: *Ode for the birthday of Queen Mary: Come ye sons of Art, away* (1694). *Welcome song for Charles II: Welcome, viceregent of the mighty king* (1680). *Welcome song for King James: Why, why are all the Muses mute?*

*** Hyperion Dig. CDA 66598 [id.]. Fisher, Bonner, Bowman, Chance, Padmore, Ainsley, George, Evans, Ch. of New College, Oxford, King's Cons., King.

Just what a wealth of inspiration Purcell brought to the occasional music he wrote for his royal and noble masters comes out again and again in Robert King's splendid collection of the Odes and Welcome songs. It is sad that for three centuries this fine music has been largely buried, with just a few of the Odes achieving popularity. In those, King's performances do not always outshine the finest of previous versions, but with an outstanding team of soloists as well as his King's Consort the performances achieve a consistently high standard, with nothing falling seriously short. Being able to hear previously unrecorded rarities alongside the well-known works sets Purcell's achievement vividly in context, helped by informative notes in each volume, written by King himself. Volume 1 includes the shorter of the two *St Cecilia odes* and immediately – among the fine team of soloists – it is a delight to hear such superb artists as the countertenors James Bowman and Michael Chance in duet. Volume 3 with the 1693 *Birthday ode* and Volume 7 with the fascinating *Yorkshire feast song* are two more CDs that would make good samplers. Those who want to dive in at the deep end should invest in the complete set, where all eight CDs are offered in a slip-case. First-rate sound throughout.

(i) *Odes for Queen Mary's birthday: Come ye sons of art; Love's Goddess sure.* (ii) *Funeral music for Queen Mary (March; Canzone;* Funeral sentences: *Man that is born of woman; In the midst of life; Thou knowest, Lord; March;* Anthems: *Hear my prayer, O Lord; Remember not, Lord, our offences).* Anthems: *Blessed are they that fear the Lord; My beloved spake; Rejoice in the Lord alway.* (iii) (Organ) *The Queen's doleur; Trumpet minuet in C* (including *March* from *The Married Beau); Trumpet tunes in C & D; Voluntary in A.*

(B) *** EMI Rouge et Noir (SIS) CZS5 69270-2 (2). (i) Burrowes, Bowman, Lloyd, Brett; Ch.; York Skinner, Hill, Shaw, Lloyd; L. Early Music Cons., Munrow; (ii) Cockerhan, King, Hayes, Chilcott, Morell, Castle, Byram-Wigfield, Robarts, Grier, King's College Ch., ASMF, Philip Jones Brass Ens., Ledger; (iii) Jean-Patrice Brosse (organ of Cathedral of Sainte Marie de Saint Bertrand de Comminges).

Purcell wrote a series of ceremonial odes for the birthdays of Queen Mary, and rarely has a courtier writing occasional pieces been so deeply and genuinely inspired. *Come ye sons of art* is the richest of the sequence, with its magnificent overture or symphony (no doubt intended to outdo those French at Versailles), and such memorable pieces as the duet, *Sound the trumpet. Love's goddess sure,* though not quite so grand, brings more Purcellian delights. David Munrow inspires fine playing and singing from his excellent forces and gives sensitive, intelligent performances of both works, which deliberately opt for an intimate scale, using old instruments and an authentic style of string playing; the results are entirely congenial to the ear. The intimacy clearly detracts from the sense of grandeur and panoply which are apt for this music but, with refined yet full sound to match, this alternative approach is equally satisfying. The coupling, made around the same time (1976/7), at King's is hardly less stimulating. As can be seen from the listing above, *Queen Mary's funeral music* consists of far more than the unforgettable *March* for lugubrious trombones (sackbuts) with punctuating timpani (later repeated without timpani), which still sounds so modern to our ears. Philip Ledger has the advantage of spacious sound (the original LP was issued in quadraphony) and his account of the *March* is darkly memorable. The anthems are well sung too, if slightly less alertly. The organ pieces, very well played, are particularly characterful heard on a comparatively pungent French organ. They are used as a postlude for the two birthday odes, while the voluntary (on disc 2) becomes an overture to introduce the three great verse anthems. The trumpet ayres are jolly, with a hurdy-gurdy effect in the Minuet framing a march from *The Married Beau*; the *Voluntary in C* is dark in timbre to match the dolorous piece specifically dedicated to the Queen.

Alfred Deller Edition: (i) *Come ye sons of art (Ode on the birthday of Queen Mary, 1694);* Anthems: (ii) *My beloved spake;* (iii) *Rejoice in the Lord alway (Bell anthem);* (iv) *Welcome to all the pleasures (Ode on St Cecilia's Day, 1683).*
(M) **(*) Van. 08.5060 71 [id.]. Alfred Deller, Deller Consort; (i) Mark Deller, Mary Thomas, Bevan, Oriana Concert Ch. & O; (ii) Cantelo, English, Bevan; (iii; iv) Kalmar O; (iii) Thomas, Sheppard, Tear, Worthley; Oriana Concert O; (iv) Cantelo, McLoughlin, English, Grundy, Bevan.

An enjoyable anthology, now reissued as part of the Alfred Deller Edition, showing Deller at his finest. The other soloists are good too, especially the tenor, Gerald English. The two anthems make a fine centrepiece, responding to the demand of Charles II for composers 'not to be too solemn' and to 'add symphonies, etc., with instruments' to their sacred vocal music. The warm, expressively played accompaniments are rather different from the effect one would achieve today with original instruments. The recording is closely balanced; although made at either Walthamstow or Cricklewood Church, the effect is not quite as spacious as one would expect, though pleasingly full.

Come, ye sons of art away (Ode on the birthday of Queen Mary, 1694); Funeral music for Queen Mary (1695); Funeral sentences; Odes for St Cecilia's day: Hail! bright Cecilia; Welcome to all the pleasures.
(N) (BB) *** Virgin Veritas/EMI Dig. VBD5 61582-2 (2) [id.]. Kirkby, Chance, Kevin Smith, Covey-Crump, Elliott, Grant, George, Thomas, Taverner Ch. & Players, Parrott.

A most inexpensive collection of key Purcell works with many individual touches in Andrew Parrott's performances. His speeds are generally slower and rhythms less alert than those of Trevor Pinnock (see below), but these are still very fine performances, sounding more intimate as recorded. Parrott takes the view that Purcell would have used a high tenor and not a second counter-tenor in *Sound the trumpet*, and it works well, with John Mark Ainsley joining the counter-tenor, Timothy Wilson. In his pursuit of authenticity Parrott has eliminated the timpani part from the well-known solemn march for slide trumpets (performed here on sackbutts) in the *Queen Mary Funeral music* – a pity when it becomes far less effective. The central anthem is beautifully done, and it is good also to have the three *Funeral sentence anthems*, written a few years earlier. *Hail! bright Cecilia* is also relatively reticent, but brings another performance full of incidental delights, particularly vocal ones from a brilliant array of no fewer than twelve solo singers, notably five excellent tenors. With pitch lower than usual, some numbers that normally require counter-tenors can be sung by tenors. Interestingly, Parrott includes the *Voluntary in D minor* for organ before the wonderful aria celebrating that instrument and St Cecilia's sponsorship of it, *O wondrous machine*. And, if you feel it holds up the music's flow, it can easily be omitted.

Come, ye sons of art, away (Ode on the birthday of Queen Mary); Ode for St Cecilia's Day: Welcome to all the pleasures. Of old when heroes thought it base (The Yorkshire Feast song).
(B) *** DG Classikon Dig. 449 853-2. Jennifer Smith, Michael Chance, Timothy Wilson, Stephen Richardson, John Mark Ainsley, Michael George, E. Concert Ch., E. Concert, Pinnock.

Pinnock directs exuberant performances of all three works. The weight and brightness of the choral sound go with infectiously lifted rhythms, making the music dance, as in the first chorus of *Welcome to all pleasures*, the best-known of the Queen Mary *Odes*, the one for 1694. There the line, 'to celebrate this triumphant day', could not come over more catchingly. The soloists are all outstanding, with the counter-tenor duetting of Michael Chance and Timothy Wilson for *Sound the trumpet* delectably pointed. The neglected *Yorkshire Feast song* (composed in 1690 for 'an otherwise obscure gathering of York nobility') is full of wonderful inspirations, like the tenor and counter-tenor duet, *And now when the renown'd Nassau* – a reference to the new king, William III.

Funeral music for Queen Mary: March, Anthem and Canzona; 3 Funeral sentences; 2 Elegies; 2 Coronation anthems; Anthem for Queen Mary's birthday, 1688: Now does the glorious day appear.
*** Sony Dig. SK 66243 [id.]. Kirkby, Tubb, Chance, Bostridge, Richardson, Birchall, Westminster Abbey Ch., New London

Consort, Martin Neary (with music by TOLLETT; PAISIBLE; MORLEY; BLOW).

Funeral music for Queen Mary: March, Anthem and Canzona; 3 Funeral sentences; 2 Elegies; Anthem for Queen Mary's birthday, 1692: Love's goddess sure was blind.
*** Collins Dig. 1425-2 [id.]. The Sixteen, Harry Christophers (with MORLEY: *Funeral sentences;* TOLLETT; PAISIBLE: *Marches*).

Funeral music for Queen Mary: March & canzona in C min.; Funeral sentences; Anthems: Give sentence with me, O Lord; Hear my prayer, O Lord; Jehova, quam multi sunt hostes mei; My beloved spake; O God, Thou art my God; O, I'm sick of life; Rejoice in the Lord alway (Bell anthem); Remember not, Lord, our offences; Organ voluntaries: in C; in G.
**(*) Argo Dig. 436 833-2 [id.]. Winchester Cathedral Ch., David Dunnett (organ), L. Bar. Brass, Brandenburg Cons., Hill.

With the help of the scholar, Bruce Wood, Harry Christophers was the first on disc to restore the original sequence of musical numbers given at the funeral of Queen Mary in 1695. The well-known *March* and *Canzona*, as well as the beautiful anthem, *Thou know'st, Lord, the secrets of our hearts*, are presented along with the settings of the remaining funeral sentences by Thomas Morley, equally inspired, as well as marches by James Paisible and Thomas Tollett. Authentic military drums are used on their own, so that the marches are less atmospheric than usual, but, with superb, crisply precise singing from the Sixteen in the choral numbers, the whole programme is electric in its intensity. Not least of the delights is the performance of the 1692 Birthday ode, *Love's goddess sure was blind*, given in Bruce Wood's edition with tenor replacing soprano, as well as two magnificent elegiac anthems to Latin words. Excellent sound, both atmospheric and clear.

In the ample acoustic of Westminster Abbey, where the music was first performed in 1695, Martin Neary, until recently Purcell's latterday successor as master of music there, gives the same sequence of funeral music as Harry Christophers on his excellent Collins disc, plus an even more generous collection of other works inspired by Queen Mary. The result is less polished, less clear, with the sound of traffic murmuring in from outside, but undeniably more atmospheric, conveying a weightier devotional intensity. One has a genuine sense of a great ceremonial, not just in the funeral music but in the other works too, including the glorious 1688 Birthday ode, *Now does the glorious day appear*, the first that Purcell composed for the new Queen. Preference between this and the Collins disc might be left to a choice between fresh soprano voices, as used in The Sixteen's disc, and the boy trebles of the Abbey Choir, more authentic and beautifully tuned but not quite so precise. The soloists are outstanding, notably the counter-tenor, Michael Chance, and the tenor, Ian Bostridge.

David Hill and the Winchester Choir plus instrumentalists provide an interesting alternative to Robert King (see below) in the *Queen Mary funeral music*, opting – like most previous interpreters, but unlike King – to have the drum recessionals simultaneously with the *March*. Though the boy-trebles are attractively fresh-toned, the Winchester ensemble is markedly less polished than King's. The choice of other items includes a number of Purcell's most celebrated anthems, as well as the *Organ Voluntary in C*. Good, atmospheric sound.

Funeral music for Queen Mary (with (i) *Queen's epicedium*); *March and canzona on the death of Queen Mary*. Funeral sentences: *Man that is born of a woman; In the midst of life are we in death; Thou knowest, Lord, the secrets of our hearts.* Anthems: *Hear my prayer; Jehova quam multi sunt.* (ii) *3 (Organ) Voluntaries: in D min.; in G; in C.*
(BB) *** Naxos Dig. 8.553129 [id.]. Oxford Camerata, Summerly; with (i) Carys-Ann Lane; (ii) Laurence Cummings.

The glorious, darkly intense funeral music which Purcell wrote on the death of Queen Mary is here given an outstandingly fresh and clear rendering, vividly recorded, matching even the finest rival versions. The sharpness of focus in the sound means that Purcell's adventurous harmonies with their clashing intervals are given extra dramatic bite in these dedicated performances, marked by fresh, clear soprano tone in place of boy trebles. The choice of extra items – full anthems with their inspired counterpoint rather than verse anthems – is first rate, including as it does the magnificent *Jehova, quam multi sunt* and the wonderfully compressed *Hear my prayer*, both beautifully done. Aptly, the extended solo song for soprano (with simple organ accompaniment), *The Queen's epicedium*, is also included with the funeral music, sung with boyish tone by Carys-Ann Lane.

Anthems: *Man that is born of woman; O God, thou has cast us out; Lord, how long wilt thou be angry?; O God, thou art my God; O Lord God of hosts; Remember not, Lord, our offences; Thou knowest, Lord, the secrets of our hearts.* Verse anthems: *My beloved spake; My heart is inditing; O sing unto the Lord; Praise the Lord, O Jerusalem; They that go down to the sea in ships. Morning Service in B flat: Benedicte omnia opera; Cantate Domino; Deus miscreatur; Magnificat; Nunc dimittis. Evening service in G min.: Magnificat; Nunc dimittis. Latin Psalm: Jehovah, quam multi sunt hostes mei. Te Deum and Jubilate in D.*

(M) *** DG (IMS) 447 150-2 (2). David Thomas, Christ Church Cathedral, Oxford, Ch., E. Concert, Simon Preston.

The admirable Christ Church two-disc collection of anthems, verse-anthems and excerpts from service settings was recorded in the London Henry Wood Hall in 1980. With some of the music not otherwise available, it is self-recommending. Apart from David Thomas's fine contribution (in the verse-anthems) the soloists come from the choir – and very good they are too, especially the trebles. The performances are full of character, vigorous yet with the widest range of colour and feeling, well projected in a recording which simulates a cathedral ambience yet is naturally focused and well detailed – analogue sound at its best.

In guilty night (Saul and the Witch of Endor); Man that is born of woman (Funeral sentences); Te Deum and Jubilate Deo in D.

(B) **(*) HM Musique d'Abord HMA 190207 [id.]. Deller Cons., Stour Music Festival Ch. & O, Deller.

In guilty night is a remarkable dramatic scene depicting Saul's meeting with the Witch of Endor. The florid writing is admirably and often excitingly sung by Alfred Deller himself as the King and Honor Sheppard as the Witch. The *Te Deum and Jubilate* are among Purcell's last and most ambitious choral works; the *Funeral sentences* from early in his career are in some ways even finer in their polyphonic richness. The chorus here is not the most refined on record but, with sensitive direction, this attractive collection is well worth hearing. The recording is good.

Jubilate Deo in D; The noise of foreign wars; Ode for St Cecilia's Day; Raise, raise the voice; Te Deum; (i) *Trumpet sonata.*

(BB) *** Naxos Dig. 8.553444 [id.]. Bern, Bisatt, Robson, Purefoy, Honeyman, Guthrie, The Golden Age Ch. & O, Robert Glenton; (i) with David Staff.

These superb examples of Purcell's choral music, both church music and secular cantatas, as well as a brief, joyful trumpet sonata, make an attractive collection, well recorded. The singing is excellent from a group which includes such distinguished singers as the counter-tenor, Christopher Robson, though the instrumental group is lacking in bite in the string section, hardly matching the wind. But this is not enough to detract from the pleasure of the music-making overall. David Staff on the trumpet is outstanding, in both the sonata and the choral works too. Specially fascinating is the première recording of the *Noise of foreign wars*, a substantial fragment of a cantata only recently identified as being by Purcell.

SONGS

Songs: *Ah! How sweet it is to love; The earth trembled; An evening hymn; If music be the food of love; I'll sail upon the dog star; I see she flies me ev'rywhere; Let the night perish; Lord, what is man; Morning hymn; A new ground.* Arias: *Birthday ode for Queen Mary: Crown the altar. Bonduca: Oh! Lead me to some peaceful gloom. History of Dioclesian: Since from my dear Astrea's sight. The Indian Queen: I attempt from love's sickness to fly. The Mock marriage: Man that is for woman made. Oedipus: Music for a while. Pausanias: Sweeter than roses. The Rival sisters: Take not a woman's anger ill.*

(BB) *** ASV Quicksilva CDQS 6172 [id.]. Ian Partridge, Jennifer Partridge – BRITTEN: *Winter words.* ***

Appropriately entitled 'Sweeter than Roses', this is a warmly sympathetic collection of favourite Purcell songs from a tenor whose honeyed tones are ideally suited to recording. The style smoother than we have come to expect latterly – this is a reissue of an earlier Enigma issue – but with ever-sensitive accompaniment from George Malcolm, who also contributes one brief solo, this is an excellent recommendation for those who resist the pursuit of authenticity. Atmospheric recording, with the voice well forward. The CD transfer is very faithful, with the voice caught in its presence and natural bloom and the harpsichord image believable and nicely focused.

Songs: *Come, let us drink; A health to the nut brown lass; If ever I more riches; I gave her cakes and I gave her ale; Laudate Ceciliam; The miller's daughter; Of all the instruments; Once, twice, thrice I Julia tried; Prithee ben't so sad and serious; Since time so kind to us does prove; Sir Walter enjoying his damsel; 'Tis women makes us love; Under this stone; Young John the gard'ner.*

*** HM HMC 90242 [id.]. Deller Cons., Deller.

One section of this charming and stylish collection has a selection of Purcell's catches, some of them as lewd as rugby-club songs of today, others as refined as *Under this stone* – all of which the Deller Consort take in their stride. The final two pieces are extended items; *If ever I more riches*, a setting of Cowley, has some striking passages. The re-mastering for CD has greatly improved the sound, with voices fresh and first-rate recording of the instruments.

Songs: *Cupid, the slyest rogue alive; Dear pretty youth; From silent shades; The fatal hour comes on apace; If music be the food of love; Incassum Lesbia; Not all my torments; Now that the sun hath veil'd his light; O solitude* (2 versions); *Stripp'd of their green; Tell me, some pitying*

angel. Theatre songs: *Dioclesian: Let us dance; Don Quixote: From rosy bow'rs. The Indian Queen: I attempt from love's sickness to fly. King Arthur: Fairest isle. The Massacre of Paris: Beneath a poplar's shadow. Pausanias: Sweeter than roses. Tyrannic Love: Ah! how sweet it is to love.*
*** Virgin/EMI (SIS) Dig. VC7 59324-2. Nancy Argenta, Nigel North, Richard Boothby, Paul Nicholson.

All but two of these songs were published in Henry Playford's celebratory Purcell collection, *Orpheus Britannicus*, and every one is inspired, offering a remarkable variety of mood and expression. Nancy Argenta's voice seems exactly suited to the repertoire, her tone consistently beautiful but never bland, her feeling for the words matched by her skill at not-too-elaborate ornamentation. The accompaniments are most beautifully managed, judiciously using archlute, viola da gamba and harpsichord and, in *Now that the sun hath veil'd his light*, a chamber organ. The recording is most natural and realistic.

Songs: *An Evening hymn; Not all my torments; O solitude*. Arias: *Bonduca: O lead me to some peaceful gloom. Don Quixote: From rosy bow'rs. The Fairy Queen: The Plaint; Thrice happy lovers. History of Dioclesian: Since from my dear Astrea's sight. The Indian Queen: I attempt from love's sickness to fly. King Arthur: Fairest isle. Gentleman's Journal of June: If music be the food of love. Oedipus: Music for a while. Pausanias: Sweeter than roses. The History of the Sicilian usurper: Retired from any mortal's sight.*
(N) **(*) HM HMC 190249 [id.]. Alfred Deller, with continuo led by William Christie.

During the LP era, the English counter-tenor, Alfred Deller had a great influence on extending the Purcell discography, and helping to popularize songs like these (to say nothing of introducing the wider musical public to the then unfamilar counter-tenor timbre). He opens here with a touching account of *The Plaint* and is heard at his best in *I attempt from love's sickness to fly*, *Fairest isle*, and especially the ravishing *Music for a while*, which he made his own. Although in the late 1970s, his voice was no longer quite as smooth on top as on his earlier Vanguard discs, his artistry is if anything even more penetrating, and the stylish accompanying continuo group with Christie at the harpsichord is a great asset.

Songs: *The fatal hour comes on apace; Lord, what is man?; Love's power in my heart; More love or more disdain I crave; Now that the sun hath veiled his light; The Queen's epicedium; Sleep, Adam, sleep; Thou wakeful shepherd; Who can behold Florella's charms*. Arias: *History of Dioclesian: Since from my dear Astrea's sight. Indian Queen: I attempt from love's sickness to fly. King Arthur: Fairest isle. Oedipus: Music for a while. Pausanias: Sweeter than roses. The Rival Sisters: Take not a woman's anger ill. Rule a wife and have a wife: There's not a swain.*
*** Etcetera Dig. KTC 1013 [id.]. Andrew Dalton; Uittenbosch; Borstlap.

Andrew Dalton has an exceptionally beautiful counter-tenor voice, creamy even in its upper register to make the extended 'Hallelujahs' of *Lord, what is man?* and *Now that the sun* even more heavenly than usual. A delightful disc, well recorded.

Duets and solos for counter-tenor: *Bonduca: Sing, sing ye Druids. Come, ye sons of art: Sound the trumpet. Elegy on the death of Queen Mary: O dive custos Auriacae domus. The Maid's last prayer: No, resistance is but vain. Ode on St Cecilia's Day: In vain the am'rous flute. O solitude, my sweetest choice. The Queen's epicedium: Incassum, Lesbia rogas. Timon of Athens: Hark how the songsters.*
*** Hyperion Dig. CDA 66253 [id.]. James Bowman, Michael Chance, King's Cons., King – BLOW: *Ode* etc. ***

A sparkling collection of solos and duets which show both the composer and these fine artists in inspirational form. The performances are joyous, witty and ravishing in their Purcellian melancholy, with often subtle response to word meanings, and King's accompaniments have plenty of character in their own right. Excellent recording.

Songs and dialogues: *Go tell Amynta; Hence fond deceiver; In all our Cinthia's shining sphere; In some kind dream; Lost is my quiet; Stript of their green; What a sad fate is mine; What can we poor females do; Why my poor Daphne, why complaining*. Theatre music: *Amphitryon: Fair Iris and her swain. Dioclesian: Tell me why. King Arthur: You say 'tis love; For love every creature is formed by his nature. The Old Bachelor: As Amoret and Thyrsis lay.*
*** Hyperion CDA 66056 [id.]. Kirkby, Thomas, Rooley.

This nicely planned Hyperion collection has one solo apiece for each of the singers, but otherwise consists of duets, five of them from dramatic works. These near-ideal performances, beautifully sung and sensitively accompanied on the lute, make a delightful record, helped by excellent sound.

Other Collections

Pavans 1–4; Beati omnes qui timent Dominum; In guilty night (Saul and the Witch of Endor); Jehova, quam multi sunt hostes mei; My beloved spake; Te Deum & Jubilate (for St Cecilia's Day, 1694); Te Deum; When on my sick bed I languish.

*** Virgin/EMI Dig. VC5 45061-2. Taverner Ch., Consort & Players, Andrew Parrott.

Starting with an exceptionally brisk and compelling account of the *Te Deum and Jubilate*, Parrott and his team provide a refreshing and illuminating survey of Purcell's vocal music, punctuated by four of the adventurous, intense *Pavans* which Purcell wrote in his youth, at about the same time as the great sequence of string *Fantasias*. In the relatively brief span of 70 minutes Parrott ranges wide, with the elaborately contrapuntal Latin anthem, *Jehova, quam multi sunt*, one of Purcell's finest, made the more moving, if less grand, with one voice per part, and with the scena about the Witch of Endor, *In guilty night*, thrillingly dramatic. Well-matched singing and playing, atmospherically recorded.

(i) *Abdelazar: suite;* (i; ii) *Cibell for trumpet and strings;* (i) *Dioclesian: Dances from the Masque; Overtures: in D min.; G min.;* (i; ii) *Sonata for trumpet and strings;* (i) *Staircase overture; Suite in G, Z.770; Timon of Athens: Curtain tune;* (Keyboard): (iii) *New Irish tune; New Scotch tune; Sefauchi's farewell; Suite No. 6 in D;* Songs: (iv; i) *Hark how all things; If Love's sweet passion;* (iv; iii) *If music be the food of love; Lord what is man (Divine hymn);* (iv; i) *See even night is here; Thus the ever grateful Spring.*

*** Chandos CHAN 0571 [id.]. (i) Purcell Qt; (ii) Mark Bennett; (iii) Robert Woolley; (iv) Catherine Bott.

Catherine Bott opens this 72-minute concert with a glorious account of one of Purcell's most famous Shakespearean settings, most artfully decorated: *If music be the food of love*; if anything, the later song, *See, even Night herself is here*, is even more ravishing, given an ethereal introduction by the string group. The instrumental items are most rewarding, notably the attractive unpublished suite of dances in G, while the three Overtures are full of plangent character. Robert Woolley's harpsichord contribution is most infectious (the *New Irish tune*, incidentally, is 'Lilliburlero') and he is beautifully recorded, the harpsichord set back in an intimate acoustic and perfectly in scale. There are few better Purcell anthologies than this, and overall the CD gives an ideal introduction to the music of one of the very greatest English composers. The Chandos recording is first class, well up to the standards of the house.

'Music for England, my England': Sonata for trumpet and strings in D; Abdelazar: Rondeau. The Married beau: Overture. Come ye sons of art (Birthday Ode, 1694): Sound the trumpet. Music for Funeral of Queen Mary: March; Canzona; 3 Funeral sentences. Saul and the Witch of Endor. Dido and Aeneas: Dido's lament. The Indian Queen: Adagio. King Arthur: Fairest Isle; Upon a quiet conscience; Act III (complete).

*** Erato/Warner 0630 10700-9 [id.]. Chance, Bowman, Dawson, Graham, Argenta, Varcoe, Monteverdi Ch., E. Bar. Soloists, Gardiner.

Tony Palmer's film on Purcell to a provocative script by the late John Osborne prompted John Eliot Gardiner to make these fine recordings of music for the sound-track. This generous selection provides an excellent sampler of the composer's work.

'Pocket Purcell': *Fantasia VIII; Three parts upon a ground;* Anthem: *Rejoice in the Lord, alway.* Funeral sentences: *Man that is born of woman; In the midst of life; Thou knowest Lord.* (Keyboard) *Ground in Gamut; Organ voluntary in D min.* Songs: *Close thine eyes; If music be the food of love;* Duets: *Close thine eyes; Of all the instruments. Suite of theatre music.*

**(*) Virgin/EMI VC5 45116-2. Taverner Consort Ch. & Players, Andrew Parrott.

This attempt at an authentic 'Pocket Purcell' nearly comes off. If perhaps it tries to do too many different things in the space of one 66-minute CD, it certainly shows the composer's breadth and variety of achievement. Opening with a four-movement *Suite of theatre music* brightly played (and including the inevitable *Rondeau* from *Abdelazar* which Britten borrowed for his *Young person's guide*). There is also a touching *Fantasia for viols*, a delightful set of keyboard divisions on a *Ground in Gamut*, admirably played by John Toll, and an equally engaging joke-duet for two tenors, *Of all the instruments that are*. Fine, vivid recording; but this would be far more attractive at mid-price.

Ayres, Theatre music and Sacred songs: *Awake awake, ye dead (Hymn for the Day of Judgement); Birthday ode for Queen Mary: Strike the viol. Dioclesian: O how happy's he; Chaconne. The earth trembled (A hymn on our Saviour's Passion). The Fairy Queen: One charming night. How plaisant is this flow'ry plain and grove* (ode). *The Indian Queen: Ye twice ten hundred deities; Wake Quivera. Ode for St Cecilia: Raise, raise the voice; Oedipus: Hear, ye sullen pow'rs below; Come away, do not stay. The Old Bachelor: Thus to a ripe consenting maid. Olinda: There ne'er was so wretched a lover as I* (duet). *Timon of Athens: Hark how the songsters. Pavane and Trio.*

(B) **(*) HM Musique d'Abord HMA 190214 [id.]. Deller Cons. & Ens., Deller.

Deller has put together what one might regard as a sampler of Purcell's vocal music, a varied collection which includes some of his finest inspirations. Always fresh and often lovely performances, given good if not outstanding recording.

Benedicite: O all ye works of the Lord. Coronation music for King James II: I was glad. Funeral music for Queen Mary: Man that is born of woman; In the midst of life; Thou knowest, Lord, the secrets of our hearts. Anthems: Blow up the trumpet in Sion; Hear my prayer, O Lord; I will sing unto the Lord; Jubilate; Lord, how long wilt Thou be angry; O God, Thou art my God; O God, Thou hast cast us out; O Lord God of Hosts; Remember not, Lord, our offences; Save me, O God.

*** Conifer Dig. 74321 16849-2 [id.]. Trinity College Ch., Cambridge, Marlow; Matthews; G. Jackson (organ).

Richard Marlow gets good results from his singers; such expressive anthems as *Remember not, Lord, our offences* and *Hear my prayer, O Lord* are eloquently done and beautifully recorded. Excellent performances from all concerned – not least the Conifer recording team.

Songs of welcome and farewell: *O dive custos Auriacae domus (Elegy on the death of Queen Mary); Incassum, Lesbia rogas (The Queen's Epicedium); Raise, raise the voice (Ode for St Cecilia's day); Welcome, vicegerent of the mighty king (Welcome song for Charles II); Why, why are all the Muses mute? (Elegy on the death of Thomas Farmer); Young Thirsis' fate, ye hills and groves, deplore (Elegy on the death of Thomas Farmer); The Fairy Queen: O let me ever, ever weep.*

*** Teldec/Warner Dig. 4509 95068-2 [id.]. Suzie le Blanc, Barbara Borden, Steve Dugardin, Douglas Nasrawi, Harry van der Kamp, Simon Grant, Tragicomedia, Stephen Stubbs & Erin Headley.

Tragicomedia here involves eight talented singers from America and Europe who, with clean, firm voices, sharp attack and precise ensemble, give refreshing performances of a well-varied selection of seven of Purcell's occasional pieces. Those who resist the idea of following Robert King's outstanding series for Hyperion (see above) might opt for this disc, very well recorded. As well as well-known items like the two magnificent *Elegies* for Queen Mary's Funeral, it includes several rarities to cherish. Clean, forward sound to match.

STAGE WORKS AND THEATRE MUSIC

Instrumental suites from: *Dioclesian; The Fairy Queen; The Indian Queen; King Arthur*.

**(*) Sony Dig. SK 66169 [id.]. Tafelmusik, Jean Lamon.

Although Purcell's standard of invention is high and these period performances are vital and alive, if not always strong on expressive charm, it seems perverse to offer 71 minutes of mostly instrumental snippets from essentially vocal works. When the trumpets enter, there is an element of grandeur, certainly, but this is not a disc to play all at once. The bright recording has great immediacy.

Dido and Aeneas (complete).

❁ (M) *** Decca Legends 466 387-2. Dame Janet Baker, Herincx, Clark, Sinclair, St Anthony Singers, ECO, Anthony Lewis.

*** Erato/Warner Dig. 4509-98477-2 [id.]. Gens, Berg, Marin-Degor, Brua, Fouchécourt, Les Arts Florissants, William Christie.

*** Teldec/Warner Dig. 4509 91191-2. Della Jones, Harvey, Donna Dean, Bickley, Murgatroyd, St James's Singers & Baroque Players, Ivor Bolton.

*** Chandos Dig. CHAN 0586 [id.]. Ewing, Daymond, MacDougall, R. Evans, Burgess, Bowman, Coll. Mus. 90, Hickox.

*** Ph. Dig. 416 299-2 [id.]. Jessye Norman, McLaughlin, Kern, Allen, Power, ECO and Ch., Leppard.

*** Chandos Dig. CHAN 0521 [id.]. Kirkby, Thomas, Nelson, Noorman, Rees, Taverner Ch. & Players, Parrott.

(***) EMI mono CDH7 61006-2. Flagstad, Schwarzkopf, Hemsley, Mermaid Theatre Singers & O, Geraint Jones.

(BB) **(*) Naxos Dig. 8.553108 [id.]. Scholars Bar. Ens.

Janet Baker's 1962 recording of *Dido* is a truly great performance. The radiant beauty of the voice is obvious enough, but the emotion is implied, as it should be in this music, not injected in great uncontrolled gusts. Listen to the contrast between the opening phrase of *When I am laid in earth* and its repeat a few bars later: it is a model of graduated mezza voce. Then with the words *Remember me!*, delivered in a monotone, she subdues the natural vibrato to produce a white tone of hushed, aching intensity. Anthony Lewis and the ECO (Thurston Dart a model continuo player) produce the crispest and lightest of playing, which never sounds rushed. The other soloists and chorus give very good support. Herincx is a rather gruff Aeneas, but the only serious blemish is Monica Sinclair's Sorceress. She overcharacterizes in a way that is quite out of keeping with the rest of the production. Like most vintage Oiseau-Lyre recordings, this was beautifully engineered, and it is due for reissue on the Decca Legends label during the lifetime of this book.

On Erato the scale is intimate, with one instrument per part, and one voice per part in choruses, yet the emotions conveyed are the opposite of miniature. Christie cunningly varies the pace to intensify the drama. Though speeds are generally fast, with tripping rhythms and light textures, bringing out the joy of so many numbers, Christie points an extreme contrast in Dido's two big arias, giving them full expressiveness at measured speeds. In the final exchanges between Dido and Aeneas the hastening speed of the recitative directly reflects the mounting tensions. What then sets this above other period performances is the tragic depth conveyed by Véronique Gens in Dido's great *Lament*, taken very slowly, with the voice drained and agonized in a way that Janet Baker supremely achieved. Though not all the other French singers match Gens in her fine English pronunciation, this is an exceptionally strong and well-contrasted team of singers with cleanly focused voices. The young Canadian baritone, Nathan Berg, dark and heroic of tone, is outstanding as Aeneas, making this thinly drawn character for once more than a wimp. Textually this version is interesting for supplying two very brief extra numbers to fill in the music missing from the end of Act II, as indicated in the suriviving libretto, a *Chorus of triumph* for the witches – a capable pastiche of Purcell to fit Nahum Tate's text – plus a *Grove's dance*, taken from the *Magicians' dance* written for the play, *Circe*. Together they last less than 90 seconds.

Ivor Bolton and the St James's Singers and Players present a period performance, intimately scaled, which avoids the snags of earlier versions, with Della Jones as Dido giving her finest recorded performance yet. She has a weightier mezzo than her rivals in other period performances, yet her flexibility over ornamentation is greater, and *Dido's Lament* is the more moving when, unlike Von Otter on DG Archiv, she is restrained over expressive gestures, keeping a tender simplicity. She shades her voice tonally very much as Dame Janet Baker did in her classic recording with Sir Anthony Lewis and the ECO, made in 1961, long before period manners were adopted. Ivor Bolton's team, recorded with bright immediacy, has no weak link, with Peter Harvey as Aeneas, Susan Bickley as a clear-toned Sorceress, Donna Dean as a characterful Belinda, and Andrew Murgatroyd as the Sailor, a tenor who plays no stylistic tricks. Setting the seal on the performance's success, the choir is among the freshest and liveliest, and the use of a guitar continuo as well as brief guitar interludes (suggested by the original libretto) enhances the happy intimacy of the presentation.

Richard Hickox's version was linked to a striking television presentation marking the Purcell tercentenary in 1995. That revolved round the magnetically characterful portrayal of the central role by Maria Ewing, not a singer one normally associates with baroque music. In the event her performance, as recorded, is both distinctive and stylish. Combined with Hickox's lively direction, unmarred by intrusive re-allocation of voices, it makes an impressive version, with Karl Daymond making Aeneas a more complex character than usual, with Rebecca Evans a radiant Belinda, matching Ewing in emotional intensity, and with Sally Burgess a characterful, unexaggerated Sorceress. Add the excellent contributions of James Bowman and Jamie MacDougall, and it makes a strong contender, certainly for admirers of Maria Ewing.

Authenticists should keep away, but the security and dark intensity of Jessye Norman's singing make for a memorable performance, heightened in the recitatives by the equally commanding singing of Thomas Allen as Aeneas. The range of expression is very wide – with Norman producing an agonized whisper in the recitative just before *Dido's Lament*. Marie McLaughlin is a pure-toned Belinda, Patrick Power a heady-toned Sailor, singing his song in a West Country accent, while Patricia Kern's performance as the Sorceress uses conventionally sinister expression. Leppard's direction is relatively plain and direct, with some slow speeds for choruses. Excellent recording.

Andrew Parrott's concept of a performance on original instruments has one immediately thinking back to the atmosphere of Josias Priest's school for young ladies where Purcell's masterpiece was first given. The voices enhance that impression, not least Emma Kirkby's fresh, bright soprano, here recorded without too much edge but still very young-sounding. It is more questionable to have a soprano singing the tenor role of the Sailor in Act III; but anyone who fancies the idea of an authentic performance need not hesitate. The CD is exceptionally refined, the sound well focused, with analogue atmosphere yet with detail enhanced.

Though Flagstad's magnificent voice may in principle be too weighty for this music, she scales it down superbly in her noble reading, which brings beautiful shading and masterly control of breath and tone. Schwarzkopf is brightly characterful as Belinda, and though Thomas Hemsley is not ideally sweet-toned as Aeneas, he sings very intelligently; even in this age of period performance, this traditional account under the late Geraint Jones sounds fresh and lively still, not at all heavy. The mono sound, obviously limited, yet captures the voices vividly, and this above all is Flagstad's set.

Using minimum forces, with one-to-a-part strings, the Scholars Baroque Ensemble offer an intimate view of Purcell's compressed epic, taking their cue from the first documented performance in Josias Priest's girls' school in Chelsea. Though the instrumental sections are rather rough in ensemble, the performance is vigorous and compelling, with choral ensemble excellent. Speeds are well chosen, often on the brisk side, yet with Dido's two great ground-bass arias – not just *Dido's lament* at the end but *Ah Belinda!* at the beginning – both given necessary emotional weight. Kym Amps is a warmly expressive heroine, singing with moving restraint in the *Lament*, while Anna Crookes as Belinda sings with fresh, clear tone, and Sarah Connolly with her rich mezzo makes an impressive Sorceress. Though David van Asch, leader of the group, is a dry-toned Aeneas, he compensates by his expressiveness. Two improvised guitar dances and an interlude for two violins are added to the surviving musical text where the libretto suggests. Clear, immediate recording.

Well worth having at its modest cost, though Dame Janet reigns supreme in this opera.

(i) *Dido and Aeneas* (ed. Britten; complete). (ii) Evening hymn: *When night her purple veil had softly spread*.

(N) (**(*)) BBC Legends mono/stereo BBCB 8003-2 [id.]. Claire Watson, Peter Pears, Jeannette Sinclair, Arda Mandikian, Patricia Clark, Jean Allister, Rosemary Phillips, John Hahessy, Michael Ronayne, Purcell Singers, EOG O, Britten; (ii) Dietrich Fischer-Dieskau; Howard Davies; Peter Pople; Benjamin Britten.

Britten's own performance of *Dido and Aeneas*, using the edition he and Imogen Holst prepared for the English Opera Group, was recorded in mono in the Maida Vale studio in 1959. The distinctive point about the text is that three brief Purcell items are added at the end of Act II, setting the passage in the libretto missing from the score. Britten's direction is alert, with rhythms crisply articulated and speeds on the slow side only in choruses. Though the EOG's strings are relatively sumptuous, he is ahead of his time in use of ornamentation. What is disappointing is the casting. Claire Watson – Britten's choice for Ellen Orford in his *Peter Grimes* recording – is a reliable soprano, but hardly a characterful one, even though she puts great feeling into the *Lament*. As in his Decca recording of almost 20 years later, Peter Pears is an expressive Aeneas, treating recitative in a Lieder-like way, though in a low-lying role his tone is sometimes gritty. Arda Mandikian repeats the performance she gave earlier as the Witch in the Flagstad recording, characterful but at times ungainly, and Jeannette Sinclair, a fresh, bright Belinda, has moments of shrillness. Following the Britten edition, boy-trebles are used for the roles of Spirit and the Sailor, with often disconcerting results. Britten's edition of Purcell's extended *Evening hymn* makes a valuable bonus, triumphing over current stylistic fashion when it inspires Fischer-Dieskau to give such a moving and intense performance, one of the items he gave in his recital in Jubilee Hall, Aldeburgh, when in June 1965 he gave the première of Britten's Blake song-cycle.

Dido and Aeneas: Dido's lament (arr. Stokowski).

(M) *** EMI CDM5 66760-2 [id.]. RPO, Stokowski – DVORAK: *String serenade;* VAUGHAN WILLIAMS: *Fantasia on a theme by Thomas Tallis*. ***

Stokowski's indulgent arrangement of Purcell's famous *Lament* is certainly not for purists. But Stokowski feels this music deeply: it is beautifully played and recorded, and the lovely melody is genuinely touching.

Dioclesian; Timon of Athens: Masques only.

*** Chandos Dig. CHAN 0568 [id.]. Pierard, Bowman, Ainsley, Padmore, George, Coll. Mus. 90, Hickox.

Dioclesian; Timon of Athens (Masque).

*** Chandos Dig. CHAN 0569/70 [id.]. Pierard, Bowman, Ainsley, George, Coll. Mus. 90, Hickox.

Following John Eliot Gardiner on Erato, Richard Hickox on Chandos offers the same apt coupling of *Dioclesian* and *Timon of Athens*, both sets of theatre music involving masques. Both versions can be warmly recommended, and choice might well be left to a preference over soloists in each. Gardiner (who has a considerable price advantage) in his 1988 recording is rather more abrasive than his more recent rivals, but that helps to sharpen the focus, with his rhythmic thrust second to none. Hickox takes a lighter view, at times more detached, often adopting faster speeds and using on balance the most consistent team of soloists, including in smaller roles such outstanding younger singers as Ian Bostridge and Nathan Berg. On the other hand, he does not include the overture to *Timon* which Gardiner does offer. The single Chandos CD contains the masque music only.

The Fairy Queen (complete).

*** DG Dig. 419 221-2 (2) [id.]. Harrhy, Jennifer Smith, Nelson, Priday, Penrose, Stafford, Evans, Hill, Varcoe, Thomas, Monteverdi Ch., E. Bar. Soloists, Gardiner.

*** HM Dig. HMC 901308/9; *HMC 401308/9* [id.]. Argenta, Dawson, Daniels, Loonen, Correas, Les Arts Florissants, William Christie.

(B) *** Naxos Dig. 8.550660-1 (2) [id.]. Diane Atherton, Kym Amps, Angus Davidson & Soloists, The Scholars Bar. Ens., led by David van Asch.

(N) (B) **(*) HM Musique d'abord HMA 190257/8 [id.]. Sheppard, Knibbs, Bevan, Platt, Alfred Deller, Jenkins, Mark Deller, Buttrey, Clarke, Stour Music Ch. & O, A. Deller.

**(*) Erato/Warner Dig. 4509 98507-2 (2) [id.]. Bott, Thomas, Schopper, Amsterdam Bar. Ch. & O, Koopman.

Purcell's setting of Shakespeare's *Midsummer Night's Dream*, written in 1692, followed in the wake of the great success of *Dido and Aeneas*. The music takes the form of five masques, each symbolizing one aspect of the play. Gardiner's performance is a delight from beginning to end, for, though authenticity and completeness reign, scholarship is worn lightly and the result is consistently exhilarating, with no longueurs whatever. The fresh-toned soloists are first rate, while Gardiner's regular choir and orchestra excel themselves, with

Purcell's sense of fantasy brought out in each succeeding number. Beautifully clear and well-balanced recording.

William Christie uses a far bigger team of both singers and instrumentalists than John Eliot Gardiner on the rival, DG Archiv set, allowing a wider range of colours. The bite of the performance is increased by the relative dryness of the recorded sound. Among Christie's soloists, Nancy Argenta and Lynne Dawson are outstanding, and the whole team is a strong one. The number of singers in solo roles allows them to be used together as chorus too – an authentic seventeenth-century practice. This makes a vigorous and refreshing alternative to the fine Gardiner set; but the Harmonia Mundi booklet is inadequate.

For Naxos at bargain price the Scholars Baroque Ensemble offer an outstanding version of Purcell's semi-opera, not always quite as beautifully sung as the finest rivals, but stylishly presented with a refreshing vigour in its scholarly approach. The recording too is exceptionally bright and immediate, regularly giving the illusion of a dramatic entertainment on stage. Logically this version, unlike previous ones, presents the purely instrumental numbers designed as interludes for *A Midsummer Night's Dream* as an appendix, rather than including them during the course of the musical entertainment of five separate masques. So the performance starts with the very brief Overture instead of the First Musick Prelude, and the variety of expression throughout is well caught and contrasted. The humour of the Scene of the Drunken Poet is touched in delightfully without exaggeration, thanks to David van Asch, as is the Dialogue between Corydon and Mopsa, though the counter-tenor, Angus Davidson, has a flutter in the voice that the recording exaggerates. One or two of the others are not always quite steady either. Outstanding among the sopranos are Diane Atherton, singing most beautifully in the Night solo of Act II, and Kym Amps, not only bright and agile in *Hark! The ech'ing air* but making the plaint, *O ever let me weep*, of Act V into the emotional high-point of the whole performance. In the edition specially prepared for the Ensemble it is made the more affecting with lamenting oboe obbligato. Instrumental playing on period instruments is first rate, and the chorus sings consistently with bright, incisive attack.

Deller's set was recorded – very well too – at the Stour Music Festival in 1972 and, although the balance is rather forward, the acoustic is pleasingly warm and the voices and orchestra combine effectively. All the solo singing is of a high standard, with Honor Sheppard particularly memorable as Night in Act II, well matched by Jean Knibbs's Mystery in some of Purcell's most evocative writing. Norman Platt is a suitably bucolic Drunken Poet in Act I and becomes one of a pair of West Country haymakers (Alfred Deller obviously enjoying himself as his companion, Mopsa) in Act III. The many ensembles are eloquently sung and, although this has not quite the sophistication of Gardiner's set, its robust warmth and Deller's considerable concern for detail make for an enjoyable entertainment, well worth its modest price when so smoothly and vividly transferred to CD.

Ton Koopman's version is generally rather mellower than its period-performance rivals, starting with a very spacious account of the opening of the overture. Koopman's approach to each successive number is strongly characterized, at times idiosyncratic, but always convincing, and he offers some fine solo singing from the three billed soloists, notably from Catherine Bott whose accounts of *Ye gentle spirits*, taken very slowly, and of *Hark! The ech'ing air* have an unsurpassed richness and intensity. The soloists billed in small print are less consistent, but Koopman's understanding of this enigmatic Purcell masterpiece is never in doubt, including its humour, as in his bluff account of the dialogue of Corydon and Mopsa. He is helped by excellent singing and playing from the Amsterdam Choir and Orchestra.

The Indian Queen (complete).
*** O-L Dig. 444 339-2 [id.]. Kirkby, Bott, Ainsley, D. Thomas, Finley, Williams, AAM Ch. & O, Hogwood.

The Indian Queen (incidental music; complete).
*** HM HMC 90243 [id.]. Knibbs, Sheppard, Mark and Alfred Deller, Elliot, Bevan, Deller Singers, King's Musick, Deller.

Hogwood's recording of Purcell's fourth and last semi-opera, left incomplete at his death, is the first to include the Wedding cantata which the composer's brother, Daniel, wrote to round off the entertainment. It makes an attractive if inconsistent addition to a score which, despite the oddity of the play that inspired the music, contains vintage Purcell inspirations, notably the solo with chorus, *All dismal sounds*, which was the last part of the work completed by Purcell himself. The elaborate chromatics in that confirm the continuing vigour of Purcell's genius to the end. With John Mark Ainsley, Emma Kirkby and Catherine Bott all making outstanding solo contributions, and with clean-cut period playing from the orchestra, this performance on a relatively grand scale is consistently convincing, by turns lively and moving. The rival Gardiner version at mid-price on Erato (made in 1979, soon after he turned to period instruments) lacks the final masque and is more abrasive in sound, though the bass, David Thomas, is firmer than in the later set.

Deller's group is at its liveliest and most characterful in *The Indian Queen*. *Ye twice ten hundred deities* is sung splendidly by Maurice Bevan; and the duet for male alto and tenor, *How happy are we* (with Deller himself joined by Paul

Elliot), as well as the best-known item, the soprano's *I attempt from love's sickness to fly* (Honor Sheppard), are equally enjoyable.

The Indian Queen (complete; with Daniel PURCELL (*c.* 1661–1717): *The Masque of Hymen*).
(BB) **(*) Naxos Dig. 8.553752 [id.]. Soloists, Ch., Scholars Baroque Ens.

The music which Purcell wrote in 1694, the year before he died, to turn the play *The Indian Queen* (Dryden one of the two authors) into a semi-opera with a sequence of masques works well on disc. In this Naxos version it comes with the added bonus of the concluding *Masque of Hymen*, which Daniel Purcell added after his brother's death, making a celebratory instead of a tragic conclusion. Though Daniel Purcell hardly matches his brother in originality, that generous supplement is welcome, though arguably the finest music of all comes at the very end of the main work in the tragic slow fugal sinfonia and chorus – all dismal sounds.

The work overall suits the lively style of the Scholars Baroque Ensemble admirably, on a scale rather more intimate than you find on most rival versions, with one instrument per part. Bright, clear recording to match, with dances and trumpet-tunes well sprung. The choral work is first rate; but when the singers come to their solos, the voices (mostly unidentified as to who sings what) are uneven, often with delivery rather unsteady. The fresh-toned soprano, Anna Crookes, makes an honourable exception. Yet solos are usually short, and what matters is the overall freshness, vigour and intensity.

King Arthur (complete).
❀ *** Erato/Warner Dig. 4509 98535-2 (2). Gens, McFadden, Padmore, Best, Salomaa, Les Arts Florissants, William Christie.
*** DG (IMS) Dig. 435 490-2 (2). Argenta, Gooding, Perillo, MacDougal, Tucker, Bannatyne-Scott, Finley, Ch. & E. Concert, Pinnock.

Recorded at sessions immediately after Christie's spectacular production of *King Arthur* in Paris in February 1995 – complete with the Dryden play – this Erato recording of the musical numbers consistently reflects stage experience. Some may not like the crowd noises in the more rollicking numbers but, more than his rivals, Christie brings out the jollity behind much of the piece. Even the pomposo manner of some of the Act Tunes (or interludes) has fun in it, with the panoply of the ceremonial music swaggering along genially. Few will resist the jollity of *Your hay it is mow'd* when the chorus even includes 'gentlemen of the orchestra' in the last verse. Unlike the earlier, Gardiner version (also Erato), this one does not in that character number have the bass soloist (Petteri Salomaa) singing in a broad Mummerset dialect, but it is still earthy enough. Christie's soloists are generally warmer and weightier than Gardiner's, notably Véronique Gens as Venus, sustaining Christie's exceptionally slow speed for *Fairest isle*. Otherwise speeds are generally on the fast side, with *Shepherd, shepherd, cease decoying* deliciously light and brisk. The vigour of Purcell's inspiration in this semi-opera has never been more winningly conveyed in a period performance on disc, with full-bodied instrumental sound set against a helpful but relatively dry acoustic, giving immediacy to the drama.

Pinnock opens with the *Chaconne*, which is placed before the *Overture*. His performance is consistently refreshing and can be recommended alongside, though not in preference to Gardiner's. Linda Perillo makes a charming Philidel. Brian Bannatyne-Scott is superb in Aeolus's *Ye blust'ring brethren*, and in his *Frost aria* he achieves an unusual if controversial effect by beginning his series of shakes from slightly under the note. Not surprisingly, Nancy Argenta sings beautifully in the double roles of Cupid and Venus and her *Fairest isle* will not disappoint; both chorus and orchestra sing and play throughout with consistent vitality. The DG recording is first class, but why no coupling? The second CD plays for only 39 minutes.

Theatre music (collection).

Disc 1: *Abdelazar: Overture and suite. Distressed Innocence: Overture and suite. The Gordian Knot Untied: Overture and suite; The Married Beau: Overture and suite. Sir Anthony Love: Overture and suite.*

Disc 2: *Bonduca: Overture and suite. Circe: suite. The Old Bachelor: Overture and suite. The Virtuous Wife: Overture and suite.*

Disc 3: *Amphitrion: Overture and suite; Overture in G min.; Don Quixote: suite.*

Disc 4: *Overture in G min. The Double Dealer: Overture and suite. Henry II, King of England: In vain, 'gainst love, in vain I strove. The Richmond Heiress: Behold the man. The Rival Sisters: Overture; 3 songs. Tyrannic Love: Hark my Damilcar!* (duet); *Ah! how sweet it is to love. Theodosius:* excerpts. *The Wives' Excuse:* excerpts.

Disc 5: *Overture in D min.; Cleomenes, the Spartan Hero: No, no, poor suff'ring heart. A Dialogue between Thirsis and Daphne: Why, my Daphne, why complaining? The English Lawyer: My wife has a tongue:* excerpts. *A Fool's Preferment:* excerpts. *The History of King Richard II: Retir'd from any mortal's sight. The Indian Emperor: I look'd and saw within. The Knight of Malta: At the close of the ev'ning. The Libertine:* excerpts. *The Marriage-hater Match'd: As soon as the chaos . . . How vile are the sordid intregues. The Massacre of Paris: The genius lo* (2 settings). *Oedipus:* excerpts. *Regulus: Ah me!*

to many deaths. Sir Barnaby Whigg: Blow, blow, Boreas, blow. Sophonisba: Beneath the poplar's shadow. The Wives' Excuse: excerpts.

Disc 6: *Chacony; Pavans Nos. 1–5; Trio sonata for violin, viola de gamba & organ. Aureng-Zebe: I see, she flies me. The Canterbury Guests: Good neighbours why? Epsom Wells: Leave these useless arts. The Fatal Marriage: 2 songs. The Female Virtuosos: Love, thou art best. Love Triumphant: How happy's the husband. The Maid's Last Prayer:* excerpts. *The Mock Marriage: Oh! how you protest; Man is for the woman made. Oroonoko: Celemene, pray tell me. Pausanius: Song (Sweeter than roses) and duet. Rule a Wife and Have a Wife: There's not a swain. The Spanish Friar: Whilst I with grief.*

(M) *** O-L (IMS) 425 893-2 (6). Kirkby, Nelson, Lane, Roberts, Lloyd, Bowman, Hill, Covey-Crump, Elliott, Byers, Bamber, Pike, David Thomas, Keyte, Shaw, George, Taverner Ch., AAM, Hogwood.

Most of the music Purcell wrote for the theatre is relatively little heard and much of the music comes up with striking freshness in these performances using authentic instruments. As well as the charming dances and more ambitious overtures, as the series proceeds we are offered more extended scenas with soloists and chorus, of which the nine excerpts from *Theodosius*, an early score (1680), are a particularly entertaining example. Before that, on Disc 3 we have already had the highly inventive *Overture and incidental music* for *Don Quixote*, with much enchanting singing from both the soprano soloists, Emma Kirkby and Judith Nelson. Disc 4 also includes a delightful duet from *The Richmond Heiress*, representing a flirtation in music. There are other attractive duets elsewhere, for instance the nautical *Blow, blow, Boreas, blow* from *Sir Barnaby Whigg*, which could fit admirably into *HMS Pinafore* (Rogers Covey-Crump and David Thomas) and the jovial *As soon as the chaos* from *The Marriage-hater Match'd*. In *Ah me! to many deaths* from *Regulus*, Judith Nelson is at her most eloquent while, earlier on Disc 5, she sings charmingly the familiar *Nymphs and shepherds*, which comes from *The Libertine*, a particularly fine score with imaginative use of the brass. The equally famous *Music for a while*, beautifully sung by James Bowman, derives from *Oedipus*. The last disc also includes a splendidly boisterous *Quartet* from *The Canterbury Guests*. The collection is appropriately rounded off by members of the Academy giving first-class performances of some of Purcell's instrumental music, ending with the famous *Chacony*. The discs are comprehensively documented and with full texts included.

Quantz, Joseph Joachim
(1697–1773)

Flute concertos: in C; in D (For Potsdam); G; G min.

*** RCA Dig. RD 60247 [60247-2-RC]. James Galway, Württemberg CO, Heilbron, Faerber.

Quantz was a skilled musician and all four concertos here are pleasing, while their slow movements show a genuine flair for melody. The *Arioso mesto* of the *G major* is particularly charming but the *Amoroso* of the *C major* is appealing too. Quantz also wrote well-organized allegros, and the opening *Allegro assai* of the *G major* shows him at his most vigorous, even if perhaps the *Potsdam concerto* is overall the best of the four works here. The thoroughly musical James Galway is most winning in the lyrical cantilenas, and the Württemberg group accompany with polish and much vitality. Excellent sound.

Quilter, Roger (1877–1953)

A Children's overture.

(M) ** EMI CDM7 64131-2. Light Music Society O, Sir Vivian Dunn (with TOMLINSON: *Suite of English folk dances*) – HELY-HUTCHINSON: *Carol Symphony;* VAUGHAN WILLIAMS: *Fantasia on Christmas carols.* **

This charming overture, skilfully constructed from familiar nursery rhymes, hitherto has not been available on CD except for a full-priced Marco Polo version (see below). Its neglect is inexplicable. Sir Vivian Dunn gives a good if not remarkable performance and the recording too is pleasing rather than outstanding. But the music itself is a delight. Ernest Tomlinson's suite of six folk-tunes, simply presented and tastefully scored, makes an attractive bonus. Again the sound is acceptable but could be richer.

A Children's overture; Country pieces; 3 English dances; As you like it: suite; The Rake: suite; Where the Rainbow ends: suite.

**(*) Marco Polo Dig. 8.223444. Slovak RSO (Bratislava), Adrian Leaper.

Adrian Leaper plays the enchanting *Children's overture* with the lightest touch, and the transparency of the recording ensures that all the woodwind detail comes through nicely, even if his performance could ideally have had a shade more momentum. One might also have wished for a bigger band with a more opulent string sheen, but the texture here well suits the suites of incidental music, an agreeable mixture of the styles of Edward German (especially the *Country dance* from *As you like it*), Eric Coates and sub-Elgar of the *Nursery suites*. All this nicely scored and amiably tuneful music is freshly and spontaneously presented and the recording is nicely resonant.

Rabaud, Henri (1873–1949)

Divertissement sur des chansons russes, Op. 2; Eglogue, Op. 7; Mârouf, savetier du Caire: dances; Symphonic poem after Lenau's Faust (Procession nocturne), Op. 6; Suites anglaises Nos. 2–3.
** Marco Polo Dig. 8.223503 [id.]. Rheinland-Pfalz PO, Segerstam.

Henri Rabaud is best known for his opera, *Mârouf, savetier du Caire*, though it has not been available since the days of LP. His music has enjoyed little exposure on records. Leif Segerstam's recording with the Baden-Baden or Rheinland-Pfalz Philharmonic has the field more or less to itself. Rabaud was not prolific, for the bulk of his time was consumed by conducting and by his administrative duties at the Paris Conservatoire, of which he was director during the inter-war years. (He had a short spell with the Boston Symphony just before Monteux took it over in the early 1920s.) The *Eglogue* was Rabaud's first orchestral piece, written in Italy during his period as a Prix de Rome scholar, and derives its inspiration from the first *Eclogue* of Virgil. The dances from *Mârouf, savetier du Caire* have an appropriately oriental flavour since the opera itself is based on an episode from the *Arabian Nights*. The *Procession nocturne* is a tone-poem based on the same Lenau poem which inspired Liszt's *Nächtlige Zug* and is the most atmospheric of the pieces on this disc. The *Suites anglaises* are arrangements of Byrd, Farnaby and other Elizabethan composers that Rabaud made for a 1917 production of *The Merchant of Venice*. Like Roger-Ducasse, Rabaud's music is not strongly personal, but it is distinctly Gallic and well worth investigating. As with their Koechlin (*Le livre de la jungle* and *Les heures persanes*) and Florent Schmitt's *La tragédie de Salomé*, Segerstam and his orchestra show a real sympathy with this turn-of-the-century French repertoire, and they are decently recorded too.

Rachmaninov, Sergei (1873–1943)

Piano concertos Nos. (i) *1;* (ii) *2* (2 versions); (i) *3–4;* (ii) *Rhapsody on a theme of Paganini;* (iii) *The Isle of the Dead; Symphony No. 3; Vocalise.* (piano, 4 hands): (iv) *Polka italienne.* (Solo piano): *Barcarolle, Op. 10/3; Daisies* (song transcription); *Etudes-tableaux, Op. 33/2 & 7 & Op. 39/6; Humoresque, Op. 10/5; Lilacs* (song transcription; 2 versions); *Mélodie, Op. 3/3; Moment musical, Op. 16/2; Oriental sketch; Polichinelle, Op. 3/4; Polka de W. R.* (3 versions). *Preludes: in C sharp min., Op. 3/2* (3 versions); *in G min.; in G flat, Op. 23/5 & 10; in E, G, F min., F, G sharp, Op. 32/3, 5–7, 12; Serenade, Op. 3/5* (2 versions); (v) BEETHOVEN: *Violin sonata No. 8 in G, Op. 30/3.* SCHUBERT: *Violin sonata in A, D.574.* GRIEG: *Violin sonata in C min., Op. 45.* BACH: *Partita No. 4, BWV 828: Sarabande.* HANDEL: *Suite No. 5: Air and variations (The Harmonious blacksmith).* MOZART: *Piano sonata in A, K.331: Theme and variations; Rondo alla Turca.* BEETHOVEN: *32 Variations in C min. WoO 80.* LISZT: *Concert paraphrase of Chopin: Polish songs (Return home; The maiden's wish). Concert paraphrases of Schubert: Das Wandern; Serenade. Polonaise No. 2; Concert study: Gnomenreigen; Hungarian rhapsody No. 2.* MENDELSSOHN: *Song without words: Spinning song, Op. 67* (2 versions). *Etudes, Op. 104b/2–3.* SCHUBERT: *Impromptu in A flat, Op. 90/4.* GLUCK: *Orfeo ed Euridice: Mélodie.* SCHUMANN: *Der Kontrabandiste* (arr. Tausig); *Carnaval, Op. 9.* PADEREWSKI: *Minuet, Op. 14/1.* CHOPIN: *Sonata No. 2 (Funeral march); Nocturnes, Op. 9/2; Op. 15/2; Waltzes: Op. 18 (Grand valse brillante), Op. 34/3; Op. 42; Op. 64/1* (2 versions); *Op. 64/2; Op. 64/3* (2 versions); *Op. 69/2; Op. 70/1; in E min., Op. posth.; Ballade No. 3; Mazurkas, Op. 63/3, Op. 68/2; Scherzo No. 3.* BORODIN: *Scherzo in A flat.* TCHAIKOVSKY: *The Seasons: November (Troika;* 2 versions). *Humoresque, Op. 10/2; Waltz, Op. 40/8.* SCRIABIN: *Prelude, Op. 11/8.* Johann STRAUSS Jnr: *Man lebt nur einmal (One lives but once;* arr. Tausig). DAQUIN: *Le coucou.* SAINT-SAENS: *Le Cygne* (arr. Siloti). GRIEG: *Lyric pieces: Waltz; Elfin dance.* DOHNANYI: *Etude, Op. 28/6.* HELSELT: *Etude, Op. 2/6 (Si oiseau j'étais).* MOSZKOWSKI: *Etude, Op. 52/4 (La jongleuse).* DEBUSSY: *Children's corner: Dr Gradus ad Parnassum; Golliwog's cakewalk.* Domenico SCARLATTI: *Pastorale* (arr. Tausig). Transcriptions: KREISLER: *Liebesfreud* (3 versions). BACH: (Unaccompanied) *Violin Partita No. 3, BWV 1003: Preludio; Gavotte & Gigue.* MENDELSSOHN: *A Midsummer Night's Dream: Scherzo.* SCHUBERT: *Wohin?.* MUSSORGSKY: *Gopak.* TCHAIKOVSKY: *Lullaby, Op. 16/1.* RIMSKY-KORSAKOV: *Flight of the bumble bee.* BEETHOVEN: *Ruins of Athens: Turkish march.* BIZET: *L'Arlésienne: Minuet.* TRAD.: (vi) *Powder and Paint.*
(M) (***) RCA mono 09026 61265-2 (10) [id.]. Sergei Rachmaninov (piano); with Phd. O, (i) Ormandy; (ii) Stokowski; (iii) cond. composer; (iv) with Natalie Rachmaninov; (v) Fritz Kreisler; (vi) Nadejda Plevitskaya.

(i) *Piano concerto No. 2; Rhapsody on a theme of Paganini;* (ii) *Vocalise.*
(M) (***) Carlton mono GLRS 104 [id.]. Rachmaninov, Phd. O, Stokowski; (ii) composer, Phd. O.

Spurred by the 50th anniversary of Rachmaninov's death, RCA has issued a ten-disc box at mid-price collecting all the recordings the composer made from 1919, the time he arrived in America, until 1942, the year before his death. These include all four of his *Piano concertos* (No. 3 with the cuts Rachmaninov himself made) as well as the *Paganini rhapsody*, the *Third Symphony* and the tone-poem, *The Isle of the Dead*. Among Rachmaninov's many solo piano recordings it is fascinating to compare his different readings of the most celebrated piece of all, the *Prelude in C sharp minor*. The stiff performance of 1919 (made for Edison) leads to a much freer and subtler reading in 1921, while the 1928 version, using the new electrical process, remains free and subtle but is emotionally less charged. The acoustic recordings, made between 1920 and 1925, are on balance the most cherishable of all, with the sound astonishingly full and the readings sparkling and spontaneous. That is true even of his 1924 recording of the *Piano Concerto No. 2*, now for the very first time issued complete. As in his classic electrical recording of five years later, he is partnered by Stokowski and the Philadelphia Orchestra, but the earlier one has a more volatile quality, with the fingerwork even clearer. Interpreting Chopin, Rachmaninov was also at his freshest and most imaginative in the early recordings, yet dozens of items here bear witness to the claim often made that he was the greatest golden-age pianist of all, bar none. The delicacy of his playing in Daquin's little piece, *Le coucou*, shows how he was able to scale down his block-busting virtuosity and, though in Beethoven's *32 Variations in C minor* he omitted half-a-dozen variations so as to fit the piece on two 78 sides, it is full of flair. There is magic too in his collaborations with Fritz Kreisler, not just in Beethoven but also in the Grieg and Schubert sonatas, and in the private recordings, when he accompanies a gypsy singer in a traditional Russian song or plays a piano duet, the *Polka italienne*, with his wife, Natalie. Transfers are commendably clean but with high background hiss. The ten discs come in a box at mid-price.

For those who want just the two electrical concertante recordings made with Stokowski, the Pickwick CD serves admirably. The transfers are slightly less sharp in detail but agreeably full. Both here and in the RCA version of the second recording of the *C minor Concerto* the woodwind triplets which accompany the reprise of the main theme of the slow movement come out vividly as in no other recording. Even in a live performance these very effective decorations tend to become buried.

Piano concertos Nos. 1–4.

(B) *** Decca Double 444 839-2 (2) [id.]. Vladimir Ashkenazy, LSO, Previn.

(B) *** EMI CZS7 67419-2 (2). Collard, Capitole Toulouse O, Plasson.

(M) *** Chandos CHAN 7114 (2) [id.]. Earl Wild, RPO, Horenstein.

(i) *Piano concertos Nos 1–4;* (ii) *Rhapsody on a theme of Paganini.*

(B) *** BMG/Melodiya Twofer Dig. 74321 40068-2 (2). Victor Eresko; (i) USSR SO, Gennady Provotorov; (ii) Leningrad PO, Vladimir Ponkin.

Piano concertos Nos. (i) *1 in F sharp min;* (ii) *2 in C min;* (iii) *3 in D min.;* (i) *4 in G min.;* (ii) *Rhapsody on a theme of Paganini, Op. 43.*

(B) **(*) EMI forte (SIS) CZS5 68619-2 (2) [CDFB 68619]. Anievas, New Philh. O; (i) Frühbeck de Burgos; (ii) Atzmon; (iii) Ceccato.

The new Double Decca set of the four Rachmaninov concertos now tends to sweep the board. The current transfers (unlike the previous, mid-priced incarnation) are admirable, fully capturing the Kingsway Hall ambient warmth yet not lacking brilliance and clarity, and with the *Third Concerto* better focused than when it first appeared on LP. The vintage 1972 performances, with their understanding partnership between Ashkenazy and Previn, have achieved classic status. The *Second Concerto*'s slow movement is particularly beautiful; it is almost matched by the close of the first movement of the *Third* and the restrained passion of the opening of the following *Adagio*. The individuality and imagination of the solo playing throughout, combined with the poetic feeling of Previn's accompaniments and the ever-persuasive response of the LSO, provide special rewards. An outstanding bargain in every way.

Issued as a 'Twofer', two discs for the price of one, the Melodiya digital versions of the four Rachmaninov *Piano Concertos* (1984) plus the *Paganini rhapsody* (1983) make an excellent bargain in performances full of flair. The notes give no information about the pianist, Victor Eresko, but he proves a formidable virtuoso who in No. 3 opts for the weightier and more difficult of Rachmaninov's two cadenzas. In his articulation Eresko plays with the crispest definition, not just in bravura passage-work, but magically in the light, quicksilver skeins of notes so characteristic of Rachmaninov, and in such movements as the finales of Nos. 3 and 4 he points rhythms with a sparkle of wit, making most others seem a little plain. He also brings off the virtuoso codas to each of these works with splendid panache, to set this up as a most attractive set, well recorded and a first-rate bargain.

Jean-Philippe Collard's recordings of the four Rachmaninov concertos date from the late 1970s. Collard is completely at home in this repertoire; his account of the *First* has splendid fire and can hold its own with all comers (even Pletnev and Ashkenazy, though the former is incomparable in the slow movement); and much the same goes for its companions. Perhaps the *Third Piano Concerto* is the least incandescent in his hands, but readers wanting an alternative, inexpensive set (all four concertos for the price of one CD) should consider this, for this is playing of real quality, and the recording, though not outstanding, is fully acceptable.

The Earl Wild set with Horenstein originally derived from RCA. It was produced by the late Charles Gerhardt and was recorded at the Kingsway Hall in 1965. They worked marvellously together, with Horenstein producing an unexpected degree of romantic ardour from the orchestra and both artists finding the natural feeling for the ebb and flow of phrases. Earl Wild's technique is prodigious and sometimes (as in the first movement of the *Fourth Concerto*) he almost lets it run away with him. What is surprising is how closely the interpretations here seem to be modelled on the composer's own versions – not slavishly, but in broad conception. This applies strikingly to the *First Concerto* and the *Rhapsody*. The first movement of the *C minor Concerto* is faster than usual, but the expressive fervour is in no doubt; the *Adagio*, too, blossoms readily. In terms of bravura, the *Third Concerto* is in the Horowitz class. The digital remastering is a great success, the overall balance is truthful and the hall ambience brings a rich orchestral image and plenty of brilliance. However, he makes the three cuts Rachmaninov sanctioned in the *Third Concerto*, one in the second movement and two in the third, a total of 55 bars. Horenstein does not quite match Stokowski's flair, although his rather straighter approach is still idiomatically sensitive and is helped by the rich body given to the strings by the Kingsway ambience. All in all, this is a first-class and very rewarding set, and the sumptuousness of the sound belies the age of the recording.

Anievas cannot match Ashkenazy as a searching and individual interpreter of Rachmaninov, but his youthful freshness makes all these concerto performances highly enjoyable. With three Mediterranean conductors to help him, and with bright, vivid EMI recording, not as atmospheric as the quality Decca provide for Ashkenazy, the result brings a combination of brilliance and romanticism which never lets go, even if it rarely produces the moments of magical illumination that mark the most inspired interpretations. Like Ashkenazy, Anievas gives the *Third Concerto* absolutely uncut and uses the longer, more difficult version of the first-movement cadenza. It is a strong, direct interpretation, though at the very end of the finale the presentation of the big melody nearly goes over the top.

(i) *Piano concertos Nos. 1–4; Rhapsody on a theme of Paganini, Op. 43.* (ii) (2 Pianos): *Suites Nos. 1–2, Opp. 5 & 17; Russian rhapsody; Symphonic dances, Op. 45.* (Piano) *Etudes-tableaux, Opp. 33 & 39; 24 Preludes* (complete); *Piano sonata No. 2 in B flat min., Op. 36; Variations on a theme by Corelli, Op. 42.*

(B) ❀ *** Decca 455 234-2 (6) [id.]. Ashkenazy; (i) LSO, Previn; (ii) with André Previn (piano).

This bargain box was perhaps the finest of Decca's special reissues made to celebrate Ashkenazy's 60th birthday. All these performances are very distinguished indeed. The vintage Decca recordings (made over a decade and a half between 1971 and 1986, mostly in the Kingsway Hall, but also at Walthamstow and All Saints', Petersham) are fully worthy of the quality of the music-making. Ashkenazy's readings, with Previn an admirable partner (whether conducting or at the keyboard), are unsurpassed on CD, except by the composer's own historic versions; while they are also available on a series of Double Deccas, any collector not involved in too much duplication will find this bargain box will make an ideal linchpin for a Rachmaninov collection.

Piano concerto No. 1 in F sharp min., Op. 1.

(M) *** Mercury (IMS) 434 333-2 [id.]. Byron Janis, Moscow PO, Kondrashin – PROKOFIEV: *Piano concerto No. 3.* ***

As in the Prokofiev coupling, on the occasion of the first Western-engineered recordings made in the USSR, soloist and orchestra plainly challenged each other to the limit, and the American technical team brilliantly captured the warmly romantic and charismatic interpretation which resulted. The solo playing stands alongside that of Horowitz in this repertoire, scintillating in the finale, yet never offering virtuosity simply for its own sake. Even now the recording is impressive for its clarity of texture and subtle detail within a warm acoustic. The CD is one of Wilma Cozart Fine's most successful transfers.

(i) *Piano concerto No. 1 in F sharp min., Op. 1;* (ii) *Rhapsody on a theme of Paganini, Op. 43.*

*** Virgin/EMI Dig. VC7 59506-2. Pletnev, Philh. O, Pešek.

Mikhail Pletnev's accounts of the *F sharp minor Concerto* and the *Rhapsody on a theme of Paganini* with the Philharmonia Orchestra under Libor Pešek are very fine indeed. The *Paganini rhapsody* is distinguished not only by quite stunning virtuosity and unobtrusive refinement but also by great feeling. This is playing of classic status, strong in personality and musicianship, and with especially vivid sound.

Piano concertos Nos. (i) *1 in F sharp min., Op. 1;* (ii) *3 in D min., Op. 30.*

(M) *** RCA 09026 68762-2 [id.]. Byron Janis; (i) Chicago SO, Fritz Reiner; (ii) Boston SO, Munch.

Byron Janis in his late twenties (in March 1957) gives a dashing account of the *F sharp minor Concerto*, freshly charismatic. With Reiner at the helm the performance cannot help but be commanding:

how beguilingly warm and relaxed is the phrasing of the lyrical string-melody in the finale! Then in December of the same year Janis went to Boston to record the greater *D minor* work, with Munch an equally perceptive partner; here it is the acoustics of Boston's Symphony Hall which cast a glow over the proceedings and the piano balance is very well judged. Janis's reading is basically lyrical, not unlike Ashkenazy's, but more impetuous and with a particularly exciting finale. Janis's tempo for the main theme of the first movement is brisk (he tells us the reason for his choice in the accompanying notes); but the contrast with the second subject is nicely made and Munch's orchestral backcloth reveals much subtlety of colour-shading. He is an excellent partner and contributes a strong surge of romanticism to the *Adagio*. Janis was to go on to re-record both works for Mercury, but the present coupling has a youthful spontaneity which is hard to resist.

Piano concertos Nos. 1 in F sharp min.; 4 in G min.; Rhapsody on a theme of Paganini, Op. 43.
(BB) *** Naxos Dig. 8.550809 [id.]. Bernd Glemser, Polish Nat. RSO, Wit.

This exceptionally generous Naxos disc is worth anyone's money. Bernd Glemser has a boldly impetuous way with Rachmaninov and, with excellent support from the Polish National Radio Orchestra under Antoni Wit, he generates plenty of excitement and expressive fervour in all three works here. If Janis and Reiner are that bit more characterful in the *F sharp minor Concerto*, and Rubinstein is even more charismatic in the *Rhapsody*, Glemser is by no means unimaginative or wanting in poetic feeling, and he gives a very enjoyable account of the more elusive *Fourth Concerto*.

Piano concerto No. 2 in C min., Op. 18.
*** Hänssler Dig. CD 98.932 [id.]. Garrick Ohlsson, ASMF, Marriner – TCHAIKOVSKY: *Piano concerto No. 1.* ***
(M) *** RCA 09026 61961-2 [id.]. Van Cliburn, Chicago SO, Reiner (with BEETHOVEN: *Concerto No. 5.* ***)
(M) *** DG 447 420-2 [id.]. Sviatoslav Richter, Warsaw PO, Stanislaw Wislocki – TCHAIKOVSKY: *Piano concerto No. 1.* (**)
(B) *** Decca Eclipse Dig. 448 221-2. Cristina Ortiz, RPO, Moshe Atzmon (with TCHAIKOVSKY: *Piano concerto No. 1.* *(*))

Ohlsson and Marriner combine to give a satisfyingly romantic account of this favourite concerto, and they are able to relax in the outer movements without loss of grip or tension. The climax of the first movement is broad and very powerful, and the finale, while not lacking brilliance, makes the very most of Rachmaninov's great secondary melody with a gorgeously expansive final presentation; the coda is then satisfyingly positive, rather than being rushed off its feet. The *Adagio* is equally persuasive, creating a simple lyrical flow, with the reprise tenderly beautiful, rapt in its gentle concentration. The recording is full-bodied and natural and is admirably balanced. If you want a modern, digital recording of this coupling, this Hänssler CD is hard to beat.

With Reiner making a splendid partner, Van Cliburn's 1958 account of the Rachmaninov *C minor Concerto* is second to none. The pacing of the first movement is comparatively measured, but the climax is unerringly placed, remaining relaxed yet enormously telling. The finale too does not seek to demonstrate runaway bravura but has sparkle and excitement, with the lyrical element heart-warming to match the very beautiful account of the central *Adagio*, full of poetry and romantic feeling. The recording is wonderfully rich, with the Chicago acoustic adding a glorious ambient glow, while the piano, though forwardly placed, has an unexpected body and fullness of timbre. The coupling with Beethoven's *Emperor* is unusual but stimulating, with Reiner again participating impressively.

With Richter the long opening melody of the first movement is taken abnormally slowly, and it is only the sense of mastery that he conveys in every note which prevents one from complaining. The slow movement too is spacious – with complete justification this time – and the opening of the finale lets the floodgates open the other way, for Richter chooses a hair-raisingly fast *allegro*. He does not, however, let himself be rushed in the great secondary melody, so this is a reading of vivid contrasts. The sound is very good. It's a great pity that the performance chosen as the new coupling for DG's series of Legendary Recording performances should be Tchaikovsky's *First Concerto*, with Karajan and the Berlin Philharmonic. The Rachmaninov readily fits this description, but the Tchaikovsky certainly does not, except as an example of a performance where two great artists pull simultaneously in different directions.

Cristina Ortiz's account has the advantage of rich Decca digital sound. The performance is warmly romantic, the first-movement climax satisfyingly expansive and the *Adagio* glowingly poetic, while the finale brings sparklingly nimble articulation from Ortiz and a fine expressive breadth from the strings in the famous lyrical melody. However, the Postnikova version of the Tchaikovsky *B flat minor Concerto* which acts as coupling is too eccentric to be recommendable.

Piano concertos Nos. 2 in C min., Op. 18; 3 in D min., Op. 30.
(M) **(*) Decca Legends 466 375-2 [id.]. Ashkenazy, (i) Moscow PO, Kondrashin; (ii) LSO, Fistoulari.
(N) (M) **(*) Erato/Teldec Dig. 0630 18411-2 [id.]. (i) François-René Duchable, Strasbourg

Philh. O., Theodor Guschlbauer; (ii) Boris Berezovsky, Philh. O, Eliahu Inbal.

(N) ** BIS Dig. CD 900 [id.]. Norika Ogawa, Malmö SO, Owain Arwel Hughes.

Piano concertos Nos. (i) *2 in C min, Op. 18;* (ii) *3 in D min., Op. 30. Preludes: in C sharp min., Op. 3/2; in E flat, Op. 23/6.*

(M) *** Mercury 432 759-2 [id.]. Byron Janis; (i) Minneapolis SO; (ii) LSO, Antal Dorati.

Byron Janis has the full measure of this music: his shapely lyrical phrasing and natural response to the ebb and flow of the melodic lines is a constant source of pleasure. In the finale there is all the sparkling bravura one could ask for, but the great lyrical tune is made beguilingly poetic. Although the 1960 recording has plenty of ambience, the Minneapolis violins lack the richness of the LSO strings, recorded at Watford in 1961. The simple opening of the *Third Concerto* benefits from the extra warmth, and Janis lets the theme unwind with appealing spontaneity, and in the great closing climax of the finale the passion is built up – not too hurriedly – to the greatest possible tension. Janis makes two cuts (following the composer's own practice), one of about ten bars in the second movement and a rather longer one in the finale. Two favourite *Preludes*, with the *E flat* coming first, most persuasively played, make some compensation.

Ashkenazy's first (1963) recording of the *C minor Concerto* is more successful than his much later, digital account with Haitink, but less compelling than his version with Previn, which remains uniquely beautiful. But the performance with Kondrashin offers superb Walthamstow sound and, though Kondrashin does not hold the first movement at a consistent level of tension and its climax is almost over-stated in its accented emphasis, the close of the *Andante* is ravishing and no one should be disappointed with the passionate climax of the finale. The *Third Concerto* is another matter. Anatole Fistoulari proved a splendid partner, and this reading is the freshest and most spontaneous of Ashkenazy's four recordings. Both CD transfers are outstandingly successful and the vintage (again Walthamstow) sound-balance is very satisfying, present, full-bodied and vivid.

Duchable's 1985 performance of the *Second Concerto* with Theodor Guschlbauer and the Strasbourg Orchestra is well paced and involving, though for all his keyboard mastery, this would not be a first choice. Boris Berezovsky's aristocratic performance of the *Third* with the Philharmonia Orchestra under Eliahu Inbal is an admirable example of his elegant pianism and artistic finesse. There is playing of great delicacy though he does at times seem a little reluctant to let himself go. In the finale he cuts from two bars after fig 52 through to 54 (an excision which Rachmaninov himself made but which is unusual nowadays). Very good recording balance.

Norika Ogawa is a cultured and musical artist but she does not have quite the tempestuous, barnstorming brilliance that any pianist aspiring to the *Third Piano Concerto* must command if he or she is to convince. She gives us the bigger cadenza, which seems to have replaced the more exhilarating one that Rachmaninov and Horowitz recorded. This is all rather low voltage though the Malmö Orchestra under Owain Arwel Hughes are very supportive and the BIS recording is first-class.

Piano concertos Nos. (i) *2 in C min., Op. 18;* (ii) *3 in D min., Op. 30* (transfers use alternative takes).

(N) (***) Biddulph mono LHW 036 [id.]. (i) Sergei Rachmaninov, Phd. O, Stokowski; (ii) Vladimir Horowitz, LSO, Albert Coates.

Two classics of the Rachmaninov discography: the 1929 account of the *C minor Concerto* the composer recorded with the Philadelphia Orchestra, coupled with the first (and in some ways most exciting) of Horowitz's recordings of the *Third,* made in London the following year with Albert Coates conducting. An electrifying performance. The Biddulph transfers made by Mark Obert Thorn are first-rate and in the *C minor*, use is made of alternative takes made at the original sessions. An invaluable supplement to RCA's Complete Rachmaninov Edition and a mandatory purchase for collectors of this repertoire.

(i) *Piano concerto No. 2;* (ii) *Rhapsody on a theme of Paganini.*

✿ (M) *** Decca Penguin Classics 460 632-2 [id.]. Ashkenazy, LSO, Previn.

(BB) *** Naxos Dig. 8.550117; *4550117* [id.]. Jandó, Budapest SO, Lehel.

(B) *** CfP Dig. CD-CFP 9017. Tirimo, Philh. O, Levi.

(M) *** Decca 448 604-2 [417 880-2]. Julius Katchen; (i) LSO, Solti; (ii) LPO, Boult – DOHNANYI: *Variations on a nursery tune.* ***

For those not investing in the Double Decca, which includes all four concertos played by the same artists, Decca's recoupling of Ashkenazy's earlier recordings with Previn is a very desirable CD indeed. At mid-price on Penguin Classics it makes a first choice. In the *Concerto*, the gentle, introspective mood of the *Adagio* is among the most beautiful on record. The finale is broad and spacious yet very exciting, and the scintillating, unforced bravura provides all the sparkle necessary. The *Rhapsody* too is outstandingly successful. The Kingsway Hall sound is rich and full-bodied in the best analogue sense. The commentary is by Reynolds Price.

Katchen re-recorded the *C minor Concerto* with Solti in stereo in 1958, seven years after his mono recording with Fistoulari, and the *Paganini vari-*

ations with Boult the following year. Even today the Kingsway Hall stereo is impressively rich and full, especially in the famous *Eighteenth Variation*. If there remains something very special about Katchen's earlier mono versions, most listeners will revel in the vintage sound of this remake, fully worthy of reissue in Decca's Classic Sound series. Katchen's performances of both works offer drama and excitement in plenty – the outer movements of the *Concerto* reach the highest peak of excitement, with bravura very much to the fore. Solti makes a splendid partner here; Boult sees that the *Rhapsody* is superbly shaped and has diversity and wit as well as romantic flair. With three works offered, this reissue can be recommended very highly.

Jenö Jandó's performances of both works are strongly recommendable. Jandó has the full measure of the ebb and flow of Rachmaninov's musical thinking, and the slow movement is romantically expansive and the finale has plenty of dash and ripe, lyrical feeling. The *Rhapsody* is as good as any around. The digital recording is satisfyingly balanced, with a bold piano image and a full, resonant orchestral tapestry.

Concentrated and thoughtful, deeply expressive yet never self-indulgent, Tirimo is outstanding in both the *Concerto* and the *Rhapsody*, making this another of the most desirable versions irrespective of price. Speeds for the outer movements of the *Concerto* are on the fast side, yet Tirimo's feeling for natural rubato makes them sound natural, never breathless, while the sweetness and repose of the middle movement are exemplary. The digital recording is full, clear and well balanced.

Piano concerto No. 2 in C min., Op. 18; Rhapsody on a theme of Paganini, Op. 43; Preludes in C sharp min., Op. 3/2; G sharp min., Op. 32/12.

(N) (M) * Classic fM Dig. 75605 57005-2. Evelyn Chen, Philh. O, Leonard Slatkin.

Very capable but low-voltage performances from Evelyn Chen, well recorded, but no challenge to the three-star recommendations above.

(i, iii) *Piano concerto No. 2 in C min., Op. 18;* (ii, iii) *Rhapsody on a theme of Paganini, Op. 43;* (iv) *Suite No. 2 in C, Op. 17.*

(N) (***) Dutton Lab. mono CDCLP 4004 [id.]. Cyril Smith, with (i) Liverpool PO; (ii) Philh. O; (iii) Sargent; (iv) Phylis Sellick.

Cyril Smith's version of the *C minor Concerto*, made with the Liverpool Philharmonic in the Abbey Road Studios in 1947, has been underrated. It was passed over by the authors of *The Record Guide* in the early 1950s in favour of Rachmaninov (understandably so, perhaps) and Moiseiwitsch (another splendid performance, which I. M. at the time preferred to the composer's own version). However it has the real Rachmaninov sound and a great deal of feeling (Sir Malcolm Sargent too is an exemplary and supportive accompanist). Well worth investigating – as are the *Paganini Rhapsody*, again with Sargent and the Op. 17 *Suite* which Cyril Smith recorded with his wife the following year. The sound is remarkably good for its day and the transfer in the best traditions of the house.

(i) *Piano concerto No. 2 in C min.; Rhapsody on a theme of Paganini, Op. 43;* (ii) *Vocalise.*

(M) *** [RCA Basic 100 09026 61851-2; *09026 61851-4*]. (i) Rubinstein, Chicago SO, Reiner; (ii) Anna Moffo, American SO, Stokowski.

Rubinstein was in his seventies when he recorded both works and he could still show the muscular virtuosi a thing or two. Unlike Katchen, he refuses to take the first and last movements of the concerto any faster than he wants. He shows that a more measured speed can be just as exciting and in the long run gives a warmer, more sympathetic result. Rubinstein has the uncanny knack in almost any recording of creating the tension of a live performance, and here the result is most compelling in both works. The Chicago acoustics add much to the attractions of this disc, which has a highly seductive encore, the *Vocalise*, sung as a wordless melisma by Anna Moffo, warmly accompanied by Stokowski.

(i) *Piano concertos Nos. 2–3; Rhapsody on a theme of Paganini. Preludes: in C sharp min., Op. 3/2; in B flat & G min., Op. 23/2 & 5; in B min. & D flat, Op. 32/10 & 13; Etudes-tableaux, Op. 39/1, 2 & 5.*

(B) *** Double Decca 436 386-2 (2). Ashkenazy, (i) LSO, Previn.

This pair of Decca CDs includes outstanding performances of Rachmaninov's three greatest concertante works for piano and orchestra, plus five favourite *Preludes* and three of the Op. 39 *Etudes-tableaux*. The digital remastering offers first-class transfers, full and well balanced, with the Kingsway Hall ambience casting a pleasing glow over the proceedings. This is very highly recommendable, including as it does Ashkenazy's outstanding version of the *C minor Piano concerto*, where the slow movement is memorably beautiful.

(i) *Piano concerto No. 2 in C min., Op. 18; Etudes-tableaux, Op. 39/1–2, 4–6 & 9.*

*** RCA Dig. 07863 57982 [7982-2-RC]. Evgeny Kissin, (i) LSO, Valentin Gergiev.

Evgeny Kissin phrases intelligently and resists the temptation to play to the gallery in any way. He produces a beautiful sound throughout and it is a compliment to him that any comparisons that spring to mind are with great pianists. The LSO under Valentin Gergiev give him every support. The six *Etudes tableaux* are imaginatively played and impressively characterized. The recording is well balanced and truthful.

Piano concerto No. 3 in D min., Op. 30.
*** Ph. 446 673-2 [id.]. Martha Argerich, Berlin RSO, Chailly – TCHAIKOVSKY: *Piano concerto No. 1.* ***
*** Chesky CD 76. Earl Wild, RPO, Horenstein – MACDOWELL: *Piano concerto No. 2.* ***
(***) Testament mono SBT 1029 [id.]. Gilels, Paris Conservatoire O, Cluytens (with SHOSTAKOVICH: *Prelude and fugue in D*) – SAINT-SAENS: *Piano concerto No. 2.* (***)
*(**) RCA 09026 61564 [id.]. Horowitz, NYPO, Ormandy.
(*(**)) VAI mono VAIA IPA 1027 [id.]. William Kapell, Toronto SO, Sir Ernest MacMillan – KHACHATURIAN: *Piano concerto.* (**)

(i) *Piano concerto No. 3 in D min., Op. 30. Barcarolle in G min., Op. 23/5; Mélodie in E, Op. 3/3; Preludes: in C sharp min., Op. 3/2; in G min., Op. 23/5; in G sharp min., Op. 32/12.*
*** Decca (IMS) Dig. 448 401-2. Shura Cherkassky, (i) with RPO, Temirkanov.

(i) *Piano concerto No. 3. Prelude in B flat, Op. 23/2; Vocalise, Op. 34/14.*
** RCA Dig. 09026 61548-2 [id.]. Kissin; (i) Boston SO, Ozawa.

(i) *Piano concerto No. 3. Sonata No. 2 in B flat min., Op. 36; Moment musical in E flat min., Op. 16/2; Polka; Prelude in C, Op. 32/5.*
(M) (***) RCA (mono) GD 87754 [7754-2-RC-]. Vladimir Horowitz; (i) with RCA SO, Reiner.

There are few finer examples of live recording than Martha Argerich's electrifying performance of Rachmaninov's *Third concerto*, recorded in Berlin in 1982. Her volatility and dash are entirely at one with the romantic spirit of this music, and her interpretation is so commanding that individual eccentricities seem a natural part of the musical flow. Moreover she plays with great tenderness (well supported by Chailly) in the *Adagio* and the lyrical theme of the finale. Throughout the concerto her bursts of scintillating bravura are quite hair-raising (comparison with Horowitz is not to her disadvantage), yet at the end of the last movement there is a touching pause before she dashes into the final straight with coruscating brilliance. The rush of romantic adrenalin at the close (well supported by the orchestra) is thrilling and brings forth a well-deserved response from the audience in which the listener is tempted to join. The recording is very good; the strings might have been better flattered in the studio but the overall sound-picture satisfyingly demonstrates the skill of the Philips engineering team.

Shura Cherkassky's playing could always be relied on for both individuality and finesse. It is something of a *tour de force* for an octogenarian and, although there are others with greater fire and zest, this has a poetic grace which in its way is rather special. Nothing Cherkassky did was without its special musical insights, and readers who respond to Cherkassky's pianism should snap up this last opportunity of hearing him, for he made no more records after this.

Earl Wild's *Third Concerto* is also among the very finest versions of this work on record. Wild favours the less elaborate version of the first-movement cadenza and plays it with compelling bravura. Horenstein proves a most understanding partner. This alternative coupling on Chesky of the *Third Concerto* with the MacDowell *Second Concerto* is very attractive, but it is a full-priced CD, whereas the Chandos Rachmaninov pairing of the *Second* and *Third Concertos* (see above) is at mid-price.

Horowitz's RCA account with Reiner dates from 1951. As a performance it is full of poetry, yet electrifying in its excitement. In spite of its dated sound and a less than ideal balance, its magic comes over and it is to be preferred to his later performance with Ormandy. The *Sonata* comes from live concerts in 1980 and is also pretty electrifying. He plays the conflation he made (and which Rachmaninov approved) of the 1913 original and the 1931 revision plus a few further retouchings he subsequently added. An indispensable part of any Rachmaninov collection which, in its digitally remastered form, sounds better than it has before.

In January 1978 Horowitz was persuaded to re-record the work in stereo, this time at a live concert, with Ormandy drawing a committed and romantically expansive accompaniment from the New York Philharmonic Orchestra. Perhaps just a little of the old magic is missing in the solo playing, but it remains prodigious and Horowitz's insights are countless. The snag is the recording, which was originally very dry and clinical, the piano timbre lacking bloom. For CD, the remastering has altered the sound-picture radically, considerably softening the focus to bring a more romantic aura to the music-making. The result is that at lower dynamic levels the image appears to recede. The effect is disconcerting – but one can adjust to it, and certainly the effect is more agreeable than the 'bare bones' of the original LP sound-quality.

Gilels's classic account of the *Concerto* with André Cluytens and the Paris Conservatoire Orchestra comes from 1955 and belongs among the 'greats'. The piano-sound is a bit shallow and at times the balance favours the soloist unduly – but what lovely playing. Rachmaninov's own account cannot be displaced, nor, for that matter, the Horowitz/Reiner version, but this should still be in the collections of all who have an interest in Rachmaninov and piano playing.

During his short life William Kapell was closely

identified with this concerto, and this performance was recorded in Toronto at a public concert in 1948 when he would have been in his mid-twenties. It is obvious that he knew Rachmaninov's own recording, and equally obvious that he is also very much his own man. He is one of the very few pianists who can be compared to Horowitz and Rachmaninov himself. He plays the same cadenza as they did. The sound is very poor indeed, but the playing is absolutely electrifying. If only some of the more recent performances the companies have been offering had a tenth its level of energy, sheer abandon and poetic ardour.

Piano concertos Nos. 3 in D min, Op. 30; 4 in G min., Op. 40.

(N) (M) *** Penguin Classics Decca 460 608-2 [id.]. Ashkenazy, LSO, Previn.

(M) **(*) Van. Classics Dig. 99091 [id.]. Nikolai Lugansky, Russian State Ac. SO, Ivan Shpiller.

Ashkenazy's performances with Previn are thoroughly recommendable on all counts. But for only a little more outlay one can get a Decca Double including all four concertos. The author's note here is provided by William Boyd.

Nikolai Lugansky is a young Russian pianist of quality, born in 1972 (which makes him a year or so younger than Evgeni Kissin and Leif Ove Andsnes). These performances do not have the slightest trace of ostentation. He produces a wonderful sound, allows phrases to breathe naturally and the music to unfold freely. In short he is content to serve Rachmaninov rather than his own ego. He plays the cadenza that Rachmaninov himself recorded rather than the overblown alternative favoured by the majority of pianists these days, and in the *Fourth Concerto* his playing is wonderfully fluid. There is ample virtuosity, but it takes second place to poetic fantasy. To put it in a nutshell, Lugansky is a real artist whose thoughts about the music carry more weight for this listener than many barnstorming virtuosi. There are drawbacks, however, for the orchestral playing is not of comparable distinction. The strings of the Russian Academic Symphony Orchestra do not produce as sumptuous or opulent a tone as they did in the days of Svetlanov, and the horn vibrato may worry some collectors; moreover the recording is not in the very first flight, though it is far from inadequate. Both these shortcomings should produce a two-star rating, but the artistic merits of Lugansky's unfailingly musical and aristocratic playing just carry it across into a three-star bracket.

It is odd to look back at the 5th edition of *Grove's Dictionary of Music and Musicians* to see in what low esteem Rachmaninov was held in the 1950s. Eric Blom, no less, wrote of his 'artificial and gushing tunes' and more or less wrote off the *Fourth Concerto* altogether, 'as a failure from the start'.

Piano concerto No. 4 in G min., Op. 40 (see also below, under *Monna Vanna*).

❁ *** EMI CDC7 49326-2. Michelangeli, Philh. O, Gracis – RAVEL: *Piano concerto in G.* ***

This is one of the most brilliant piano records ever made. It puts the composer's own recorded performance quite in the shade, and the Ravel coupling is equally illuminating. The recording does not quite match the superlative quality of the playing but still sounds pretty good.

(i) *Piano concerto No. 4; Rhapsody on a theme of Paganini, Op. 43. Variations on a theme of Corelli, Op. 42.*

(N) *(*) Nimbus Dig. NI 5478 [id.]. John Lill; (i) BBC Nat O of Wales, Otaka.

From John Lill a reliable rather than an inspired performance of all three pieces. The piano tone is inclined to be a tad shallow and the soloist, whom we have often admired, comes close to being pedestrian.

(i) *Piano concerto No. 4 in G min., Op. 40; Variations on a theme of Corelli, Op. 42; Piano sonata No. 2 in B flat min., Op. 36; Prelude in C sharp min., Op. 3/2.*

(N) ** Decca Dig 458 930-2 [id.]. Jean-Yves Thibaudet; (i) Cleveland O, Vladimir Ashkenazy.

Jean-Yves Thibaudet's account of the *Fourth Piano concerto* is brilliant and fluent without achieving the panache and flair of Michelangeli, or poetic feeling of such players as Ashkenazy (also Decca) or Nikolai Lugansky (Vanguard). Likewise in his dashing account of the *Variations on a theme of Corelli*, something of the soul of this music eludes him. Thibaudet plays the 1931 revision of the *B flat minor Sonata*.

The Isle of the dead, Op. 29.

(M) *** RCA 09026 61250-2. Chicago SO, Reiner – Concert: '*The Reiner sound*'. ***

(M) *** DG (IMS) Dig. 445 558-2. BPO, Maazel – RIMSKY-KORSAKOV: *Scheherazade.* **

(N) (**) Sony mono MHK 62348 [id.]. Minneapolis SO, Mitropoulos – MAHLER: *Symphony No. 1.* (**)

Reiner builds the arch-like span of the music to an impassioned climax and manages the return to the sombre opening mood with equal distinction. The recording, made in 1957, is eminently spacious and shows Reiner at his finest.

At a fast speed Maazel's powerful reading of *The Isle of the dead* is less sombre and brooding than usual; but the climaxes have real fervour, and the result is intensely compelling. The 1981 recording is strikingly vivid and full, and it is a pity that the Rimsky-Korsakov coupling is far less recommendable.

Mitropoulos's account of *The Isle of the dead* comes from the 78 era, and was recorded in 1945.

It has the intensity that marked so much of what he did, though its murky sound is no match for later recordings. Great care has been taken over the transfer, and the presentation – as with most issues in this series – is both handsome and induces much nostalgia. But this is not inexpensive.

The isle of the dead, Op. 29; The rock, Op. 7; Symphonic dances, Op. 45.
(N) *(*) Finlandia/Warner Dig. 0630 19091-2 [id.]. R. Stockholm PO, Andrew Davis.

Andrew Davis gets good playing from the Stockholm Philharmonic throughout and the Finlandia engineers reward them with first-rate sound. All the same, one does not feel that heady rush of passion which great Rachmaninov music-making must communicate. The orchestral sound is cultured, the overall sonority well blended and refined. The recording is impressively detailed but ultimately these are not particularly memorable performances.

The Isle of the dead, Op. 29; Symphonic dances, Op. 45.
(M) *** Decca Dig. 430 733-2. Concg. O, Ashkenazy.
(BB) **(*) Naxos Dig. 8.550583 [id.]. RPO, Enrique Bátiz.

Ashkenazy's is a superb coupling, rich and powerful in playing and interpretation, *The Isle of the dead* relentless in its ominous build-up, while the *Symphonic dances* have extra darkness and intensity too. The splendid digital recording highlights both the passion and the fine precision of the playing.

Bátiz gives the *Symphonic dances* an attractively spontaneous performance, full of lyrical intensity, with some splendid playing from the RPO strings. The vivid recording helps give the feeling that Bátiz almost goes over the top in his extremely passionate climax for *The Isle of the dead*. The performance certainly does not lack darker feelings, and at super-bargain price this remains well worth considering.

Rhapsody on a theme of Paganini, Op. 43.
(M) *** RCA 09026 68886-2 [id.]. Rubinstein, Chicago SO, Reiner – CHOPIN: *Andante spianato & Grande Polonaise;* FALLA: *Nights in the gardens of Spain.* ***

Rubinstein's early stereo (1956) account of Rachmaninov's romantic showpiece is new to the British catalogue. There is no finer version. Rubinstein's playing is dazzling and it continually delights with its poetic sensibility and flair. Reiner is with him in every bar, orchestral detail persuasively delineated, and the warm Chicago acoustic ensures a glorious blossoming of string-tone at the *Eighteenth*. Both pianist and conductor relish the *Dies irae* each time it appears, and the closing pages reach a high pitch of excitement. The recording, with the piano forward but not unattractively so, sounds little short of ideal in Richard Mohr's splendid new remastering.

(i) *Rhapsody on a theme of Paganini, Op. 43. Etudes-tableaux, Opp. 33 & 39; Piano sonata No. 2, Op. 36; Moment musical, Op. 16/3; Preludes: Op. 3/2; Op. 23/1, 2 & 4; Op. 32/12; Variations on a theme of Corelli, Op. 42.*
(B) *** EMI Rouge et Noir CZS5 69677-2 (2) [CDZB 69677]. Jean-Philippe Collard; (i) Capitole Toulouse O, Plasson.

These are impressive and competitive performances, recorded in the 1970s when this artist was beginning to make a name for himself. In the *Rhapsody on a theme of Paganini* he can hold his own with the finest, though he is not as well recorded as Ashkenazy. His account of the *Variations on a theme of Corelli* is exemplary and the *Second Sonata* is no less powerful. Collard plays the 1913 version but, like Horowitz, incorporates elements of the revision. Playing of real distinction and very competitively priced.

Symphonic dances, Op. 45; (i) *The Bells, Op. 35.*
(M) **(*) BMG/Melodiya 74321 32046-2 [id.]. (i) Shumskaya, Dovenman, Bolshakov, Russian State Chamber Ch. Moscow PO, Kyrill Kondrashin.

Kondrashin's classic 1969 performance with the Moscow Philharmonic returns in a less than distinguished transfer. One wonders whether the impression, that our LPs sounded better, is deceptive – until you hear them side by side. All the same, this is an electrifying performance and, like *The Bells*, which comes from 1966, shines through all sonic limitations.

SYMPHONIES

Symphonies Nos. 1–3; The Isle of the dead, Op. 29; Symphonic dances; (i) *The Bells, Op. 35.*
(B) *** Decca 455 798-2 (3) [id.]. Concg. O, Ashkenazy; (i) with Natalia Troitskaya, Ryszard Karczykowski & Concg. Ch.

Symphonies Nos. 1–3.
(B) *** Decca Double Dig. 448 116-2 (2) [id.]. Concg. O, Ashkenazy.

Symphonies Nos. 1–3; The Isle of the dead, Op. 29; Symphonic dances, Op. 45; Vocalise, Op. 34/14; Aleko: Intermezzo & Women's dance.
(M) *** EMI CMS7 64530-2 (3) [EMIC 64350]. LSO, André Previn.

Symphonies Nos. 1–3; The Rock, Op. 7.
(M) **(*) DG (IMS) Dig. 445 590-2 (2). BPO, Maazel.

Symphonies Nos 1–3; Vocalise, Op. 34/14.
✿ (B) *** Sony SB2K 63257 (2) [id.]. Phd. O, Ormandy.

Ormandy pioneered the recording of the three Rachmaninov symphonies in stereo, and in many ways his performances remain unsurpassed. Certainly they have never sounded as good as they do in these splendid new transfers. The *Second Symphony* came first in 1959 and has perhaps the most naturally balanced sound. The performance has great intensity of feeling and passion. The *First Symphony* had to wait until 1966 and yet was still the work's first stereo version; an exceptionally strong performance it is too. Ormandy's thrustful view of the outer movements is supported by superbly committed Philadelphia playing, with the orchestra on top form. The conductor's own commitment is obvious in every bar. The balance has woodwind solos spotlighted, but the spacious acoustic of Philadelphia Town Hall provides the necessary ambient warmth. In some ways the *Third Symphony* is even more distinguished and now that the artificial brilliance of the old LP has been tamed one can at last appreciate the body of tone this great orchestra commanded in its heyday. The playing itself is marvellous, and this warmth of feeling carries over into the touchingly shaped *Vocalise* which acts as a final encore. A bargain set not to be missed, even if you have more modern versions of these splendid works.

The Ashkenazy digital set of the three symphonies, made between 1980 and 1982, now comes either as a Double Decca or in a bargain box of three discs, one symphony to each CD and coupled respectively with *The Isle of the dead*, *Symphonic dances* and the dramatic cantata, *The Bells*, outstanding in every way. The performances of the symphonies, passionate and volatile, are intensely Russian; the only possible reservation concerns the slow movement of the *Second*, where the clarinet solo is less ripe than in some versions. Elsewhere there is drama, energy and drive, balanced by much delicacy of feeling, while the Concertgebouw strings produce great ardour for Rachmaninov's long-breathed melodies. The vivid Decca sound within the glowing Concertgebouw ambience is ideal for the music.

While Ashkenazy's digital Double Decca set of the three Rachmaninov symphonies with the Concertgebouw Orchestra will probably remain first choice for many collectors, Previn's LSO set at mid-price offers some alternative couplings. His 1973 account of the *Second Symphony* – a passionately committed performance, with a glorious response from the LSO strings – has been remastered for CD a second time, with improvement in the body of the string timbre. No. 1 is a forthright, clean-cut performance, beautifully played and very well recorded. It may lack some of the vitality that one recognizes in Russian performances (Ashkenazy is more volatile and remains first choice in this work) but is still very enjoyable. Previn's account of the *Third*, however, is outstanding and the LSO's playing again has enormous bravura and ardour. This, like *The Isle of the dead* and *Symphonic dances*, has been remastered very successfully and the performances of the two shorter works have plenty of atmosphere and grip. With the *Aleko* excerpts and the *Vocalise* also included, this EMI box remains very competitive.

Maazel's set offers superb playing from the Berlin Philharmonic. However, the DG engineers secured a less sumptuous sound in the Berlin Philharmonic than their Decca colleagues in Amsterdam. The climaxes of the *Second Symphony* in particular would have been enhanced by a warmer middle and lower range. Maazel's readings are not to be dismissed: the *First Symphony* is particularly fine, with Rachmaninov's often thick orchestration beautifully transparent. The *Third* too is distinctive, unusually fierce and intense. The result is sharper and tougher than one expects, less obviously romantic, and the finale for all its brilliance lacks joyful exuberance. Moreover (although it also includes *The Rock*) this is at mid-price, while the Ashkenazy recordings are on a Double Decca – two discs for the cost of one premium-priced CD.

Symphony No. 1 in D min.; Etudes-tableaux, Op. 39/2, 6, 7 & 9 (orch. Respighi).
*** Nimbus Dig. NI 5311 [id.]. BBC Welsh SO, Tadaaki Otaka.

Symphony No. 1 in D min., Op. 13; The isle of the dead, Op. 27.
(N) *** EMI Dig. CDC5 56754-2 [id.]. St. Petersburg PO, Mariss Jansons.

Symphony No. 1 in D min.; The Rock (fantasy), *Op. 7; Vocalise, Op. 34/14; Aleko: Intermezzo.*
(B) *** DG Classikon Dig. 449 854-2. BPO, Maazel.

Mariss Jansons and his St Petersburg musicians do not wear their hearts on their sleeves but give a totally committed and finely shaped performance of the *First Symphony*. Jansons maintains a firm hold over the architecture of the piece and produces playing of great poetic feeling. *The isle of the dead* is highly atmospheric, a convincing and indeed haunting performance. The recording is beautifully natural, with transparent string sound and plenty of space round the instruments, and no want of presence. A very satisfying issue and now first choice among separate recordings of the symphony.

Tadaaki Otaka's is a characterful and excellently shaped reading of the *First Symphony*. The recording, too, is very acceptable, though detail is not as well defined or as cleanly laid out as in some other three-star versions, thanks no doubt to the resonance of the acoustic. Respighi's masterly transcriptions of the four *Etudes-tableaux* comprise an appealing makeweight and may sway many collectors. This Nimbus disc is not a first choice but still merits three stars.

Maazel's is a superb performance, beautifully transparent and consistently clarifying detail. He lacks something in Slavonic passion but, with generous fill-ups, the positive strength of the reading stands up well. The 1984 recording is drier than Ashkenazy's Decca.

Symphony No. 2 in E min., Op. 27.
✿ (M) (***) DG mono 449 767-2 [id.]. Leningrad PO, Kurt Sanderling.
(BB) *** ASV Quicksilva CDQS 6107 [id.]. Philh. O, Ling Tung.
(M) **(*) Chandos Dig. CHAN 6606 [id.]. SNO, Sir Alexander Gibson.
**(*) Ph. Dig. 438 864-2 [id.]. Kirov O, Gergiev.

Symphony No. 2 in E min., Op. 27; The Rock, Op. 7.
**(*) DG Dig. 439 888-2 [id.]. Russian Nat. O, Pletnev.

Symphony No. 2 in E min., Op. 27; (i) *3 Russian Songs, Op. 41.*
(N) *(*) Chan. Dig. CHAN 9665 [id.]. Russian State SO, Valéry Polyansky; (i) with Russian State Sym. Capella.

Symphony No. 2 in E min., Op. 27; Scherzo in D min.; Vocalise, Op. 34/14.
*** EMI (SIS) Dig. CDC5 55140-2 [id.]. St Petersburg PO, Jansons.

Symphony No. 2; (i) *Vocalise, Op. 34/14.*
**(*) Telarc Dig. CD 80312 [id.]. (i) Sylvia McNair; Baltimore SO, David Zinman.

Sanderling's famous mono recording dates from 1956, but one would never guess, so voluptuously full is the sound of this current DG re-transfer and so remarkably refined the detail. Here is a great Russian orchestra at their very peak, obviously inspired by their conductor, Kurt Sanderling, and carried away on a tide of passion, underpinned by the very Russian melancholy of the slow movement, and especially at its close. (There is a haunting clarinet solo and some lovely oboe playing too.) The string playing throughout is glorious, reaching its apotheosis in the great climaxes of the finale, where Rachmaninov bares his very soul in a flood of yearning romantic feeling. From the first note to the last this is the kind of live performance one would only dream of experiencing – yet amazingly it was made in the studio. Of other recorded versions only Ormandy's (see above) reaches this intensity of feeling, and even he cannot quite match the Russian fervour of the Leningrad violins as they are caught up in that tremendous final climax. A great performance and, astonishingly, the mono sound is fully worthy of it.

Jansons's newest St Petersburg account offers a strong, warm reading in which climaxes are thrust home powerfully, with full dramatic impact. Phrasing is warmly idiomatic, even if occasionally over-moulded, and the recording gives fine body and immediacy to the sound, outshining most latter-day rivals. In Russian fashion the clarinet in the slow movement sounds like an organ stop. A warm, exciting reading which stands among the best modern versions. The coupling is generous, when in addition to *Vocalise*, beautifully done, it offers the early orchestral *Scherzo* of 1887.

Ling Tung's reading is refined but he knows just how to mould the sweeping lines necessary to bring out the rapture inherent in this lovely symphony, notably at the climax of the slow movement and at the very satisfying close. This is a case where the CD transfer brings a striking improvement in the vividness of a 1978 recording which is backwardly balanced. One needs to play back at a fairly high level, then the Philharmonia strings emerge with a warmly natural, radiant sheen of tone. At super-bargain price this is well worth considering.

Gibson and the Scottish National Orchestra have the advantage of an excellent digital recording, made in the Henry Wood Hall in Glasgow. The brass sounds are thrilling, but the slightly recessed balance of the strings is a drawback and there is not the body of tone demonstrated by the best version recommended above. But this is a freshly spontaneous performance and overall the sound is admirably natural, even if it includes some strangely unrhythmic thuds at climaxes (apparently the conductor in his excitement stamping on the podium).

Pletnev brings a fresh mind to this symphony, with his approach very much controlled, giving a strong sense of onward current and producing none of the heart-on-sleeve emotion that can often afflict the slow movement, which seems to be conceived in one long paragraph. The clarity and lightness of articulation that distinguish his piano playing seem to be in ample evidence and, throughout the work, feeling is held in perfect control. It is a performance of quality, though the recording, while good, could be cleaner-detailed in the lower end of the range. Ensemble is endangered by some frenetically fast speeds – as in the finale. *The Rock*, inspired by Lermontov, makes a generous coupling.

As in his opera recordings, Gergiev gives a strong and well-paced reading, if lacking a little in individuality. Although he takes what one might think of as a more traditional approach, he brings an appropriate warmth and also possesses considerable command of the architecture. His first movement (with repeat) is very spacious (22 1/2 minutes).

After a slack start Zinman builds the symphony persuasively, if with less character than some, helped by first-rate playing from the Baltimore orchestra. Good, clean sound. The coupling is an attraction when, unlike most rivals, Zinman has *Vocalise* with soprano soloist, the radiant Sylvia McNair. Even with that extra, Zinman manages to observe the exposition repeat in the first movement of the symphony.

Valéry Polyansky's account of the *Second Symphony* with the Russian State Orchestra is far from negligible but it is equally far from distinguished. The most attractive feature of the disc is the Op. 41 set of *Three Russian songs*, a glorious triptych, full of character, which are given decent, full blooded performances.

Symphony No. 3 in A min., Op. 44.
*** Chandos Dig. CHAN 8614 [id.]. LSO, Järvi – KALLINIKOV: *Intermezzos*. ***

Symphony No. 3 in A min.; Isle of the dead, Op. 29.
*** Nimbus Dig. NI 5344 [id.]. BBC Welsh SO, Tadaaki Otaka.

Symphony No. 3 in A min., Op. 43. Symphonic dances.
(N) (M) *** EMI CDM5 73475-2. LSO, Previn.
(N) *** DG Dig. 457 598-2 [id.]. Russian Nat. O, Mikhail Pletnev.

Symphony No. 3 in A min., Op. 44; Vocalise, Op. 34/14.
(M) *** EMI CDM5 66759-2 [id.]. Nat. PO, Stokowski.

It was Stokowski who in 1936 in Philadelphia conducted the first performances of Rachmaninov's last symphony. Nearly 40 years later he re-recorded it with Sydney Sax's fine group of selected orchestral players, and the result is rewarding and exciting. There are idiosyncrasies aplenty, not least a tempo for the finale that whirls one along in exhilarating danger; but this is a splendid example of Stokowski's energy in old age, his ability to inspire players to a totally individual and riveting performance, full of romantic warmth and fervour, not directly comparable with others. The recording, made at West Ham Central Mission, has a wide dynamic range and good definition and it produces the richest patina of string-tone.

Previn's EMI CD brings an outstanding performance; the digital remastering brings plenty of body alongside the sharpened detail. Previn conveys the purposefulness of the writing at every point, revelling in the richness, but clarifying textures. The LSO has rarely displayed its virtuosity more brilliantly in the recording studio, and, with its new *Symphonic Dances* coupling, after Stokowski this is a first choice for this symphony.

Tadaaki Otaka's performance of the *Third Symphony* unfolds with complete naturalness and unfailing musical instinct that reflect great credit on their gifted Japanese conductor. Apart from excellent orchestral playing, the technical side of the recording is also handled expertly. A natural concert-hall perspective with plenty of warmth from the acoustic but no lack of detail. The *Isle of the dead* is no less well served and this can be recommended along with the very best on the market.

The Russian National Orchestra and Mikhail Pletnev also couple the symphony with the late *Symphonic Dances*. If you have acquired Pletnev's CD of the *Second Symphony* you will know that he has a special feeling for this composer and is completely steeped in his spiritual climate. So completely indeed is he attuned to the Rachmaninov sensibility that he can persuade you that his interpretative idiosyncrasies – the very slow tempo he adopts for the interlude in the finale, just about seven minutes in, or his phrasing of the second subject of the first movement – are absolutely right. The opulent sound world of this wonderful score is beautifully served by his players (and in particular the strings). However this is not a first choice.

Järvi in his weighty, purposeful way misses some of the subtleties of this symphony, but with superb playing from the LSO – linking back to André Previn's unsurpassed reading with them – the intensity is magnetic, with even a very slow *Adagio* for the outer sections of the middle movement made to sound convincing, and with the finale thrusting on at an equivalently extreme tempo.

Symphony No. 3 in A min., Op. 44; Isle of the dead, Op. 29; Vocalise, Op. 34/14.
❁ (M) (***) RCA mono 09026 62532-2 [id.]. Phd. O, Sergei Rachmaninov.

RCA deserve congratulations for making these wonderful recordings available on a separate CD, an immense boon for those who cannot afford the ten-CD Complete Rachmaninov Edition. Rachmaninov's own recording of the *Third Symphony*, *Isle of the dead* and *Vocalise*, made in 1939 and 1929 respectively, are an indispensable part of any serious collector's library. They also sound magnificent – and not simply for their age.

CHAMBER AND INSTRUMENTAL MUSIC

Cello sonata in G min., Op. 19; Danse orientale in A, Op. 2/2; Lied (Romance) in F min.; Mélodie in D; Prelude in F, Op. 2/1; Romance in F, Op. 4/3; Vocalise in E min., Op. 34/14.
(N) (BB) *** Naxos Dig. 8.550987 [id.]. Michael Grebanier, Janet Guggenheim.

Rachmaninov's *Cello sonata*, written at the same period as such masterpieces as the *Second Symphony* and the *Second Piano concerto*, is one of the greatest in the repertory. Michael Grebanier, principal cellist of the San Francisco Symphony Orchestra for over 20 years, gives it a powerful, richly expressive reading, with Janet Guggenheim an incisive partner, very clearly focused if not always as warm. The slow movement is most moving, the headlong finale thrilling in its clarity. The shorter pieces make up an excellent bargain disc to match rivals at premium price.

Cello sonata in G min., Op. 19; 2 Pieces, Op. 2; Vocalise, Op. 34/14.
*** Virgin/EMI Dig. VC5 45119-2 [VCL 45119]. Truls Mørk, Jean-Yves Thibaudet – MIASKOVSKY: *Cello sonata No. 1*. ***

The gifted Norwegian cellist Truls Mørk plays with

a restrained eloquence that is totally compelling. The demanding (and commanding) piano part is given with authority and conviction by Thibaudet, and they handle the companion pieces excellently. The value of this well-recorded and well-balanced issue is enhanced by the attractive Miaskovsky coupling.

Trios élégiaques Nos. 1 in G min., Op. 8; 2 in D min., Op. 9.
*** Chandos Dig. CHAN 8431 [id.]. Borodin Trio.

The *Trios* are both imbued with lyrical fervour and draw from the rich vein of melancholy so characteristic of Rachmaninov. The performances by the Borodin Trio are eloquent and masterly, and the recording is admirably balanced.

PIANO MUSIC

Piano duet

Music for 2 pianos: (i) *Suites Nos. 1–2, Opp. 5 & 17; Symphonic dances, Op. 45; Russian rhapsody;* (Solo piano) *Etudes-tableaux, Op. 33; Variations on a theme by Corelli, Op. 42.*
(B) *** Decca Double 444 845-2 (2) [id.]. Vladimir Ashkenazy, (i) with André Previn.

The colour and flair of Rachmaninov's writing in the two *Suites* (as inspired and tuneful as his concertos) are captured with wonderful imagination. The two-piano version of the *Symphonic dances* is masterly and dazzling, and they are hardly less persuasive in the early *Russian rhapsody*. Ashkenazy's superb solo performances of the *Etudes-tableaux* and the *Corelli variations* (a rarity and a very fine work) cap the appeal of this bargain Double. The recording throughout is superb, with a natural presence and a most attractive ambience.

Suites Nos. 1–2, Opp. 5 & 17; Symphonic dances, Op. 45.
*** Hyperion Dig. CDA 66375 [id.]. Howard Shelley, Hilary Macnamara.

Howard Shelley and Hilary Macnamara give strong performances of both the *Suites* and the *Symphonic dances*. In the *Suites* their responses are not quite as imaginative as those of Ashkenazy and Previn, but there is plenty of dramatic fire in the *Symphonic dances* in this generously filled disc.

Suite No. 2, Op. 17; Russian rhapsody, Op. posth.; Symphonic dances, Op. 45.
**(*) Hyperion Dig. CDA 66654 [id.]. Nikolai Demidenko, Dmitri Alexeev – MEDTNER: *Russian round dance* etc. **(*)

There are some beautiful things on the Alexeev–Demidenko disc. They shape the second group of the first of the *Symphonic dances* with exquisite sensitivity and colour, and there are many other felicities elsewhere. However, even allowing for the hazards of two pianos, there is some ugly fortissimo tone, which one never finds in a Kissin or a Pletnev recording. All the same there is much to delight the listener, even though Previn and Ashkenazy are to be preferred in this repertoire.

Solo piano music

Barcarolle in G min., Op. 10/3; Etudes-tableaux, Op. 39/4 & 6; Humoresque in G, Op. 10/5; Lilacs, Op. 21/5; 5 Morceaux de fantaisie, Op. 3: (Elégie in E flat min.; Prelude in C sharp min.; Mélodie in E; Polichinelle in F sharp min.; Sérénade in B flat min.); Polka de W. R.; Prelude in G min., Op. 23/5. Transcriptions: MUSSORGSKY: *Hopak.* SCHUBERT: *Wohin?.* RIMSKY-KORSAKOV: *Flight of the bumblebee.* KREISLER: *Liebeslied; Liebesfreud. The Star-spangled banner.*
(M) *** Decca 425 964-2 [id.]. Sergei Rachmaninov (Ampico Roll recordings, 1919–29).

The Decca disc offers the composer's Ampico piano-roll recordings, made between 1919 and 1929, when Rachmaninov was at his technical peak. The Ampico recordings were reproduced on a specially adapted Estonia concert grand in the Kingsway Hall and recorded in stereo in 1978/9. On CD the sound is outstandingly real and the impression on the listener is quite uncanny when the recital opens with the *Elégie in E flat minor*, which was put on roll in October 1928 yet has all the spontaneity and presence of live music-making. The Ampico system at that time could accurately reflect what was played, including note duration and pedalling, but the *strength* at which the notes were struck had to be edited on to the roll afterwards by a skilled musician/technician. It can only be said that listening to these Ampico recordings never brings a feeling of any mechanical tone graduation, and in pieces like the *Humoresque in G major* or the *Polka de W. R.* not only does Rachmaninov's scintillating bravura sound absolutely natural, but also his chimerical use of rubato is more convincing on the earlier recordings. *The Flight of the bumblebee* is a *tour de force* of exuberant articulation.

Etudes-tableaux, Opp. 33 & 39; Fragments; Fughetta in F; Mélodie in E; Moments musicaux; Morceaux de fantaisie; Morceaux de salon; 3 Nocturnes; Oriental sketch; 4 Pieces; Piece in D min.; 25 Preludes (complete); *Sonatas 1–3* (including original & revised versions of *No. 2*); *Song without words; Transcriptions* (complete); *Variations: on a theme of Chopin ; on a theme of Corelli.*
(M) *** Hyperion Dig. CDS 44041/8 (8). Howard Shelley.

Hyperion have collected Howard Shelley's exemplary survey of Rachmaninov into a mid-price, eight-CD set, and very good it is, too. Shelley can hold his own against most rivals not only in terms of poetic feeling (as you would expect from a distant descendant of the great poet) but in keyboard authority and virtuosity. The recordings are variable in quality but are mostly excellent.

Elégie, Op. 3/1; Etudes-tableaux, Op. 39/3 & 5; Moments musicaux, Op. 16/3–6; Preludes, Op. 23/1, 2, 5 & 6; Op. 32/12.
(B) *** EMI CD-EMX 2237 [EMI Red Line CDR5 69869 (with RAVEL: *Gaspard de la nuit*)]. Andrei Gavrilov – SCRIABIN: *Preludes.* ***

There is some pretty remarkable playing here, especially in the stormy *B flat major Prelude*, while the *G sharp minor* from Op. 32 has a proper sense of fantasy. More prodigious bravura provides real excitement in the *F sharp minor Etude-tableau*, Op. 39/3, and in the *E minor Moment musical*, while Gavrilov relaxes winningly in the *Andante cantabile* of Op. 16/3 and the *Elégie*. Sometimes his impetuosity almost carries him away, and the piano is placed rather near the listener so that we are nearly taken with him, but there is no doubt about the quality of this recital.

Etudes-tableaux, Opp. 33 & 39.
*** Hyperion CDA 66091 [id.]. Howard Shelley.

The conviction and thoughtfulness of Shelley's playing, coupled with excellent modern sound, make this convenient coupling a formidable rival to Ashkenazy's classic versions, which in any case are not coupled together on CD.

Moments musicaux, Op. 16; Morceaux de salon, Op. 10.
*** Hyperion Dig. CDA 66184 [id.]. Howard Shelley.

Howard Shelley has a highly developed feeling for Rachmaninov and distinguishes himself here both by masterly pianism and by a refined awareness of Rachmaninov's sound-world. The recording is eminently realistic and natural.

24 Preludes; Preludes in D min. and F; Morceaux de fantaisie, Op. 3.
*** Hyperion CDA 66081/2 (available separately) [id.]. Howard Shelley.

24 Preludes (complete); Piano sonata No. 2 in B flat min., Op. 36.
(BB) *** Decca Double 443 841-2 (2) [id.]. Vladimir Ashkenazy.

(i) *24 Preludes* (complete); (ii) *Suite No. 2 for 2 pianos, Op. 17.*
(N) (B) **(*) Erato/Warner Dig. Analogue Ultima 3984 25599-2 (2) [id.]. (i) Dame Moura Lympany; (ii) Katia and Marielle Labèque.

There is superb flair and panache about Ashkenazy's playing. Perhaps the stormy *B flat major Prelude*, Op. 23/2, is even more hair-raising in Sviatoslav Richter's hands but, as the *G minor Prelude* demonstrates, Ashkenazy's poetic feeling is second to none. At Double Decca price this sweeps the board. As a bonus, the compact discs offer the *Second Piano sonata*, with Ashkenazy generally following the 1913 original score but with some variants. He plays with great virtuosity and feeling, and the result is a *tour de force*.

Moura Lympany's Erato recording of the Rachmaninov *Préludes* repeats an early success. While the pieces that need bravura seem to offer her no real problems, she is at her finest in the lyrical preludes, which truly blossom in her hands. The whole set moves forward spontaneously and the piano recording is full and vivid. This now costs half as much as its original premium-priced issue and can be recommended, though not in preference to Ashkenazy. The snag is that the Labèques' performance of the Opus 17 *Suite for 2 pianos*, offered as a bonus, is much less appealing, partly because the analogue recording (from 1974) is somewhat shallow.

Shelley is a compellingly individual interpreter of Rachmaninov. Each one of the *Preludes* strikes an original chord in him. These are very different readings from those of Ashkenazy but their intensity is well caught in full if reverberant recording.

Preludes: Op. 3/2; Op. 23/1–2, 4–6; Mélodie, Op. 3/3; Polichinelle, Op. 3/4; Variations on a theme of Corelli, Op. 42.
*** Conifer Dig. 75605 51159-2 [id.]. Kathryn Stott.

Kathryn Stott has a good feeling for Rachmaninov and gives well-considered accounts of all the pieces on this generously filled CD; there is a strong rhythmic grip and her phrasing is keenly articulate.

Piano sonatas Nos. 1 in D min., Op. 28; 2 in B flat min., Op. 36 (revised 1931).
*** Hyperion CDA 66047 [id.]. Howard Shelley.

Howard Shelley offers here the 1931 version of the *B flat Sonata*. He has plenty of sweep and grandeur and an appealing freshness, ardour and, when required, tenderness. He is accorded an excellent balance by the engineers.

Piano sonata No. 2 in B flat min., Op. 36 (original version); *Etudes-tableaux, Op. 33/1, 39/4 & 7; Morceaux de fantaisie, Op. 3/3 & 5; Preludes, Op. 23/1 & 7; 32/2, 6, 9 & 10.*
❁ *** Ph. Dig. 446 220-2. Zoltán Kocsis.

One of the finest Rachmaninov recitals of recent years. Be it in the smaller, reflective pieces or in the bigger-boned *B flat minor Sonata*, Zoltán Kocsis's piano speaks with totally idiomatic accents, effortless virtuosity and keen poetic feeling. A most distinguished offering and is recommended with enthusiasm. Excellent recording.

Piano sonata No. 2 in B flat min., Op. 36 (original version); *Fragments in A flat; Fughetta in F; Gavotte in D; Mélodie in E; Morceau de fantaisie in G min.; Nocturnes Nos. 1–3; Oriental sketch in B flat; Piece in D min.; 4 Pieces; Prelude in E flat min.; Romance in F sharp min.; Song without words in D min.*
*** Hyperion CDA 66198 [id.]. Howard Shelley.

Howard Shelley now gives us the original version of Op. 36 and his performances here show unfailing sensitivity, intelligence and good taste. They have the merit of excellent recorded sound. A valuable issue.

Transcriptions: *Daisies; Lilacs; Polka de W. R.; Vocalise.* BACH: *Prelude; Gavotte; Gigue.* BIZET: *Minuet from L'Arlésienne.* KREISLER: *Liebesleid; Liebesfreud.* MENDELSSOHN: *Midsummer Night's Dream: Scherzo.* MUSSORGSKY: *Sorochinsky Fair: Gopak.* RIMSKY-KORSAKOV: *Flight of the bumble-bee.* SCHUBERT: *Wohin?.* TCHAIKOVSKY: *Lullaby.*
*** Hyperion Dig. CDA 66486 [id.]. Howard Shelley.

Shelley plays with an authority and sensitivity that is wholly persuasive and dispatches the virtuoso transcriptions to the manner born. The transcription of the *Vocalise* is by Zoltán Kocsis, but otherwise all are Rachmaninov's own.

Variations on a theme of Chopin, Op. 22; Variations on a theme of Corelli, Op. 42; Mélodie in E, Op. 3/3.
*** Hyperion CDA 66009 [id.]. Howard Shelley – MENDELSSOHN: *Scherzo.* ***

Howard Shelley gives dazzling, consistently compelling performances, full of virtuoso flair. First-rate piano sound.

VOCAL MUSIC

Songs: *All passes; All was taken from me; At my window; Before the icon; By a fresh grave; Christ is risen; Fate; The fountain; Night; Fragments from A. Musset; How pained I am; How peaceful; I am again alone; I am not a prophet; I beg for mercy; Lilacs; Let us leave, my sweet; Melody; Night is sorrowful; On the death of a siskin; The ring; There are many sounds; They replied; To my children; Twilight; Two farewells; We shall rest; Yesterday we met.*
(N) *** Chan. Dig. CHAN 9451 [id.]. Joan Rodgers, Maria Popescu, Alexandre Naoumenko, Sergei Leiferkus, Howard Shelley.

Fluent in Russian, Joan Rodgers with her richly expressive voice makes a perfect interpreter of Rachmaninov songs, ideally partnered by the pianist, Howard Shelley, a specialist in this composer's music. Taken from Chandos's complete edition of the songs, this generous selection of those for soprano ranges through the whole of the composer's songwriting career up to his exile from Russia in 1917, when in rejection of his roots he stopped completely. Loveliest of the songs is the extended wordless *Vocalise*, here set against its neighbour in Op. 34, the dramatic song, *Dissonance*. Most distinctive are the six forward-looking songs, Op. 38, to words by symbolist poets.

The Bells, Op. 35.
(N) (B) *** EMI double fforte CZS5 73353-2 [CDFB 73353] (2). Sheila Armstrong, Robert Tear, John Shirley-Quirk, LSO & Ch., Previn – PROKOFIEV: *Alexander Nevsky; Ivan the Terrible.* ***
*** Telarc Dig. CD 80363 [id.]. Renée Fleming, Karl Dent, Victor Ledbetter, Atlanta Ch. & SO, Robert Shaw – ADAMS: *Harmonium.* ***

The Bells, Op. 35; 3 Russian songs, Op. 41; Spring, Op. 20.
*** Decca (IMS) Dig. 440 355-2. Alexandrina Pendachanska, Kaludi Kaludov, Sergei Leiferkus, Choral Arts Society, Phd. O, Dutoit.

In *The Bells*, the London Symphony chorus sings convincingly in the original language, as they do in *Alexander Nevsky*. Previn's concentration on purely musical values as much as on evocation of atmosphere produces powerful results, even when the recording has lost just a little of its original ambient warmth in favour of added presence and choral brilliance. The soloists are excellent.

Charles Dutoit's disc with the Philadelphia Orchestra conveniently couples all three of Rachmaninov's choral works with orchestra. The performances have subtle dynamic shadings and half-tones rather than dramatic intensity. *Spring*, the rarest work here, is not as striking in its musical material as *The Bells* but it builds up in Dutoit's fine performance to a magnificent climax. The Russian soloists sing idiomatically and, though the chorus is backwardly placed, the dynamic range is impressive. Well worth having, alongside its competitors, if only to hear this great orchestra, so well recorded by the Decca team.

The late Robert Shaw conducts a colourfully expansive performance of Rachmaninov's cantata. The special melancholy of the finale is touchingly conveyed, with a fine orchestral response as well as an ardent contribution from the choir. All three soloists are impressive and if Renée Fleming, who sings beautifully, is not especially Slavonic, in the closing *Lento lugubre* the baritone, Victor Ledbetter, catches the darkly expressive mood admirably. While this is not superior to Dutoit, he has a quite different coupling, and anyone wanting the spectacular Adams work should be well satisfied with Shaw's Rachmaninov.

Liturgy of St John Chrysostom, Op. 31.
✿ (B) *** EMI forte CZS5 68664-2 (2). Maximova, Zorova, Vidov, Stoytsov, Petrov, Bulgarian R. Ch., Milkov.
*** Hyperion Dig. CDA 66703 [id.]. Corydon Singers, Matthew Best.

Rachmaninov's *Liturgy of St John Chrysostom*, written in 1910, is an even fuller setting than Tchaikovsky's of 1878, and it had no more success than its predecessor in convincing the church dignitaries that its powerful emotional feeling was not too secular for use within the context of a religious service. Yet listening to this glorious performance by the Chorus of Bulgarian Radio, recorded in the spacious acoustics of the Alexander Nevsky Memorial Cathedral in Sofia, one can be in no doubt that the work's powerful expressive feeling has an underlying deep spirituality, while the performance itself conveys great religious fervour. Apart from the continuing dialogue between cantor (Ivan Petrov) and chorus (in which the soloists also participate), there are moments of overwhelming simple beauty, as in the sublime, sustained *Cheroubikon* ('Cherubic hymn'). It would be difficult to imagine this superbly recorded performance being bettered and, although the spacious tempi (which are sustained with continuing concentration) mean that the work runs to 97 minutes, the set is offered in EMI's forte series so that the two discs are offered for the price of one. It is a pity that a full text with translation is not included, but the presentation is otherwise fully acceptable.

The fine Hyperion alternative is a sharper, more cleanly enunciated account – the choral sound is without that misty focus which is so much part of the character of Slavic *a capella* singing. It is immensely stimulating, and very well recorded and documented. However, the Corydons curiously omit the prayer dialogue which is the centrepiece of the *Cherubic hymn* and which in Sofia brings such a strikingly exhilarating response from the chorus. There are various other versions in the catalogue, including a superbly sung and deeply moving account from the St Petersburg Chamber Choir under Nikolai Korniev (Philips 442 776-2). But this has been cut to fit on to a single CD. If you have already succumbed to the *Vespers*, you won't be disappointed with *St John Chrysostom's Liturgy*.

6 Songs, Op. 4; 6 Songs, Op. 8; 12 Songs, Op. 14; 12 Songs, Op. 21; 15 Songs, Op. 26 (including (i) *Two partings*); *14 Songs, Op. 34; 6 Songs, Op. 38; Again you leapt, my heart; April! A festive spring day; By the gates of the holy dwelling; Did you hiccup?; Do you remember that evening?; A flower fell; From St John's Gospel; I shall tell you nothing; Letter to Konstantin Stanislavsky; Night; Powdered paint* (folksong); *Song of disappointment; Twilight has fallen*. (Piano solo): *Daisies; Lilacs*.
(M) *** Decca 436 920-2 (3). Elisabeth Söderstrom, Vladimir Ashkenazy, (i) with John Shirley-Quirk.

Recorded between 1974 and 1979, Elisabeth Söderström's set of the major Rachmaninov songs is a glittering jewel in the Decca catalogue. She is a fluent and radiant soloist, often inspired by her accompanist to performances of pure poetry, ranging over the wide span of Rachmaninov's career as well as his whole emotional range, so that you find, for instance, the highly characteristic *Brooding*, or the richly intense *O do not grieve*, alongside a comic skit on a drinking song, *Did you hiccup, Natasha?*. Sonia's final speech in Chekhov's *Uncle Vanya* becomes a song which nicely skirts sentimentality, and there is also a letter in music sent to Stanislavsky on the tenth anniversary of the Moscow Arts Theatre. John Shirley-Quirk joins the team for the wry dialogue, *Two partings*, and Ashkenazy allows himself two solo items in the composer's transcriptions of *Daisies* and *Lilacs*. The recording is vivid in its immediacy and presence. Full translations are provided.

Vespers, Op. 37.
✿ *** HM Chant du Monde Russian Season Dig. LDC 288050 [T88050]. St Petersburg Capella, Chernuchenko.
(N) *** Virgin/EMI Dig. VC5 45124-2 [id.]. Malena Emman, Per Björsund, Nils Höglund, Swedish R Ch., Tönu Kaljuste.
*** Hyperion Dig. CDA 66460 [id.]. Corydon Singers, Matthew Best.
(N) *** EMI Dig. CDC5 56752-2 [EMIC 56439]. King's College Ch., Stephen Cleobury.

Rachmaninov's *Vespers* – more correctly the 'All-night vigil' – rank not only among his most soulful and intensely powerful music but are also the finest of all Russian choral works. The St Petersburg Capella is in fact the Mikhail Glinka Choir and their lineage goes back to the fifteenth century. Their earlier recording of the piece was pretty impressive. Even so, this newcomer surpasses it and offers singing of an extraordinarily rapt intensity. The dynamic range is enormous, the perfection of ensemble and blend and the sheer beauty of tone such as to exhaust superlatives. Vladislav Chernuchenko gets performances of complete conviction from them, and it is hard to imagine that their singing can be surpassed. The recording does them justice and is made in a suitably atmospheric acoustic.

Under Eric Ericsson the Swedish Radio Choir became one of the most admired in Europe, and their 1994 account of the *Vespers* under Tönu Kaljuste shows that they have lost nothing of their sensitivity or command of sonority. They can produce a wonderful range of colour from the darkest to the most luminous. Their Russian sounds totally authentic too. This is undoubtedly one of the finest versions available, with its own special character.

Though Matthew Best's British choir, the Corydon Singers, lacks the dark timbres associated with Russian choruses and though the result could be weightier and more biting, theirs is still a most beautiful performance; very well sung and recorded in an atmospheric, reverberant setting.

It also makes a moving experience having the Anglican tradition, as ideally represented by the choir of King's College, Cambridge, meeting the Russian Orthodox tradition, represented by Rachmaninov's supremely beautiful setting of the *All-night Vigil*. Against the warm acoustic of King's College Chapel, beauty and refinement are the keynotes. The precision of ensemble and subtlety of dynamic shading – remarkable from a choir of young singers – are given extra freshness with the high dramatic contrasts. However, of the English versions, Matthew Best has the more authentic ring, and the St Petersburg Capella (as the Leningrad Glinka Choir became) under Vladislav Chernushenko remains specially authoritative.

Vocalise, Op. 34/14 (arr. Dubensky).
(M) *** RCA 09026 62600-2. Anna Moffo, American SO, Stokowski – CANTELOUBE: *Songs of the Auvergne;* VILLA-LOBOS: *Bachianas Brasileiras No. 5*. ***

Rachmaninov's *Vocalise* was a favourite showpiece of Stokowski, usually in a purely orchestral arrangement; but here with Moffo at her warmest it is good to have the vocal version so persuasively matching the accompaniment.

OPERA

(i) *Monna Vanna* (incomplete opera: Act I, orch. Buketoff); (ii) *Piano concerto No. 4* (original version).
**(*) Chandos Dig. CHAN 8987 [id.]. (i) Milnes, McCoy, Walker, Karoustos, Thorsteinsson, Blythe; (ii) William Black; Iceland SO, Buketoff.

Monna Vanna is the fragment of an opera based on Maeterlinck which Rachmaninov wrote around the inspired period of his *Second Symphony*. He thought so well of the fragment that it was the one score he brought away from Russia after the Revolution. Igor Buketoff, who knew the composer, has rescued this Act I score and orchestrated it very sensitively to make an interesting curiosity. In its ripely romantic manner the writing has lyrical warmth and flows freely, thrusting home climactic moments with the same sureness as Rachmaninov's symphonies. Buketoff's performance with the Iceland Symphony is warmly convincing, but the singing is flawed, with Sherrill Milnes, as Monna Vanna's jealous husband, standing out from an indifferent team, otherwise thin-toned and often wobbly. Buketoff's resurrection of the original score of the *Fourth Piano concerto* is rather more expansive than the text we know. William Black is the powerful soloist, though the piano sound, unlike that of the orchestra, lacks weight.

Raff, Joachim (1822–82)

Symphony No. 1 in D (An das Vaterland), Op. 96.
** Marco Polo Dig. 8.223165 [id.]. Rhenish PO, Friedman.

Symphony No. 2 in C, Op. 140; Overtures: Macbeth; Romeo and Juliet.
** Marco Polo Dig. 8.223630 [id.]. Slovak State PO (Košice), Urs Schneider.

Symphonies Nos. 3 in F (Im Walde), Op. 153; 10 in F min. (Zur Herbstzeit), Op. 213.
** Marco Polo Dig. 8.223321 [id.]. Slovak State PO (Košice), Urs Schneider.

Symphonies Nos. 3 in F; 4 in G min., Op. 167.
(N) (B) **(*) Hyperion Helios Dig. CDH 55017 [id.]. Milton Keynes City O, Hilary Davan Wetton.

Symphonies Nos. 4 in G min.; 11 in A min. (Der Winter), Op. 214.
*(*) Marco Polo Dig. 8.223529 [id.]. Slovak State PO (Košice), Urs Schneider.

Symphony No. 5 in E (Lenore), Op. 177.
(M) *** Unicorn UKCD 2031. LPO, Bernard Herrmann.

Symphony No. 5 in E; Overture, Ein feste Burg ist unser Gott, Op. 127.
*(*) Marco Polo Dig. 8.223455 [id.]. Slovak State PO (Košice), Urs Schneider.

Raff was Liszt's assistant at Weimar during the early 1850s and helped prepare his orchestral scores. He enjoyed enormous standing during his lifetime though nowadays he is best remembered for a handful of salon pieces. However, he composed no fewer than eleven symphonies between 1864 and 1883, some of which have excited extravagant praise. (The composer-conductor Bernard Herrmann called No. 5, which he recorded for Unicorn, 'one of the finest examples of the Romantic Programme school – it deserves a place alongside the *Symphonie fantastique* of Berlioz, the *Faust Symphony* of Liszt and the *Manfred Symphony* of Tchaikovsky'.) Yet generally speaking Raff's music is pretty bland, though far from unambitious. The *First Symphony* (*An das Vaterland*), takes itself very seriously and runs to over 70 minutes. To be frank, it places some strain on the listener's concentration, and many will not stay the course. Although the well-played and -recorded *Symphony No. 2 in C* has a certain charm, it is predominantly Mendelssohnian and, although outwardly attractive, it remains pretty insubstantial. Sampling the performances listed above, one is left in no doubt that they are conscientious in approach but are recommendable to the initiate rather than to the unconverted.

Of the eleven symphonies it is the *Fifth* (*Lenore*) which has captured the imagination of many. No doubt this may be accounted for by the somewhat macabre programme that inspired its finale. Although the symphony itself is more inspired than some of its companions (it has a particularly eloquent slow movement), it does need rather better advocacy than it receives from the Slovak Philharmonic under Urs Schneider. The Unicorn-Kanchana version by the LPO under Bernard Herrmann, made over a quarter of a century ago, has greater polish and allure, and the recording holds up well against this digital newcomer. The Overture, *Ein feste Burg ist unser Gott*, is hardly sufficient to tip the scales in its favour.

The *Eleventh Symphony in A minor* was left incomplete on Raff's death in 1882 and is not otherwise available; the *Fourth* of 1871, available on the Hyperion version under Hilary Davan Wetton, is insufficiently persuasive. This music has moments of charm but is essentially second-rate and must have the most expert advocacy and opulent recorded sound if it is to be persuasive; neither of these two versions is really first class. One needs a Beecham to work his magic on these scores. In these performances they are merely amiable but insignificant.

Raid, Kaljo (born 1922)

Symphony No. 1 in C min.
*** Chandos Dig. CHAN 8525 [id.]. SNO, Järvi – ELLER: *Dawn; Elegia* etc. ***

Raid's *First Symphony* shows a genuine feel for form and a fine sense of proportion, even though the personality is not fully formed. Well worth hearing. Neeme Järvi gets very committed playing from the Scottish National Orchestra and the recording is warm and well detailed.

Rameau, Jean Philippe (1683–1764)

Overtures: *Acante et Céphise, ou La Sympathie; Castor et Pollux; Dardanus; Les fêtes de l'Hymen et de l'amour, ou Les Dieux d'Egypte; Les fêtes de Polymnie; Hippolyte et Aricie; Les Paladins; Naïs; Pigmalion; Platée; Les surprises de l'amour: Prologue (le retour d'Astrée); Act I (L'enlèvement d'Adonis); Les Talens lyriques (Les fêtes d'Hébé); Le temple de la Gloire; Zaïs; Zoroastre.*
(N) *** O-L Dig. 455 293-2 [id.]. Les Talens Lyriques, Christophe Rousset.

This collection of overtures is well nigh comprehensive. It covers three decades from 1733 (*Hippolyte et Aricie*) through to *Les Paladins* of 1761. The familiar, such as *Platée*, *Dardanus*, *Les indes galantes* and so on, is leavened by the unfamiliar, *Acante et Céphise*. Rameau's mastery of instrumental colour is little short of amazing and completely original. Try *Platée* or *Zaïs* or the *Feu d'artifice* section of *Acante* with its cannon fire. Christophe Rousset and his accomplished musicians play with flair and imagination and are superbly recorded. One of the best discs of its kind for the last three years.

Les Boréades: orchestral suite; Dardanus: orchestral suite.
*** Ph. (IMS) Dig. 420 240-2. O of 18th Century, Brüggen.

The orchestral suite from *Les Boréades* occupies the larger part of the disc. The invention is full of resource and imagination, and the playing here of both this and *Dardanus* is spirited and sensitive and will provide delight even to those normally unresponsive to authentic instruments.

6 Concerts en sextuor (for strings).
(M) ** Cal. CAL 6838 [id.]. Caen CO, Dautel – BOISMORTIER: *Première suite de clavecin.* **

The anonymous arrangement of Rameau's five suites of *Pièces de clavecin en concert* for string sextet is a novelty and a pleasing one. The arranger used Rameau's instrumental version for harpsichord and two violins: the two violin parts are retained, the upper voice of the harpsichord is given to the third violin, its middle voice to the viola, and the cello follows the bass line. However, these two instruments are not always divided, and the music becomes a true sextet only when the bass has a separate part. The additional *Sixth Suite* is a further transcription of four pieces taken from the third book for the harpsichord, published in 1728, and is very effective, including the famous *La Poule* (clucking realistically on violins to anticipate Saint-Saëns). The music is played spiritedly on modern instruments by the Caen Chamber Orchestra under Jean-Pierre Dautel; if, as recorded, the violins seem a shade pallid, this approaches the sound (if not always the degree of polish) we expect from a period group.

Dardanus: suite; *Les Indes galantes:* suite.
(BB) *** DHM Baroque Esprit 05472 77420-2 [id.]. Coll. Aur.

This early example of authentic performance dates from the 1960s. Any abrasiveness deriving from the use of original instruments is countered by the generous acoustics of the Cedernsaal in the Schloss Kirchheim. But the playing has both life and elegance and the sound, though warm and full, is by no means bland: the flutes and oboes (and trumpets in *Les Indes galantes*) bring plenty of added colour. The selection from *Les Indes galantes* is shorter than that provided by Herreweghe, but many will welcome the coupling with *Dardanus*. At super-bargain price this is very recommendable.

Hippolyte et Aricie: orchestral suite.
(M) *** DHM/BMG GD 77009 [77009-2-RG]. La Petite Bande, Kuijken.

This record collects virtually all the orchestral music from *Hippolyte et Aricie*; the melodic invention is fresh and its orchestral presentation ingenious. Sigiswald Kuijken gets delightful results from his ensemble. In every way an outstanding release – and not least in the quality of the sound.

Les Indes galantes: suites for orchestra.
(B) *** HM HMA 1901130 [id.]. Chappelle Royale O, Philippe Herreweghe.

Besides the harpsichord arrangements listed below, Rameau also arranged his four 'concerts' of music from *Les Indes galantes* for orchestra. The result makes nearly three-quarters of an hour of agreeable listening, especially when played so elegantly – and painlessly – on original instruments, and very well recorded (in 1984) by Harmonia Mundi.

Naïs: orchestral suite. Le Temple de la Gloire: orchestral suite.
*** HM Dig. HMU 907121 [id.]. Philharmonia Bar. O, Nicholas McGegan.

There is much delightful music here and the playing by the Philharmonia Baroque Orchestra has ravishing finesse, showing original instruments at their most persuasively delicate, textures always transparent; the ear is continually beguiled by this warm and polished playing, beautifully recorded. A quite lovely disc.

Les Paladins (comédie-ballet): *orchestral suite.*
*** Ph. (IMS) Dig. 432 968-2. O of Age of Enlightenment, Leonhardt.

Gustav Leonhardt's recording of the ballet numbers with the Orchestra of the Age of Enlightenment is little short of a triumph. There is a liveliness, freshness and delight in the colours and rhythms of this inventive score that will captivate the listener and lay to rest any fears of scholarly caution. There is more than an hour's music here, all of it of quality and all played with a panache and style that will win many friends for this composer. The recording, made at St Giles's, Cripplegate, is equally crisp and well detailed. Strongly recommended.

Pièces de clavecin en concert Nos. 1–5.
(B) *** HM Dig. HMX 2901418 [HMC 901418]. Christophe Rousset, Ryo Terakado, Kaori Uemura.

The instrumental *Pièces de clavecin* usually include a flute, but they are equally valid in this format with baroque violin and viola da gamba. The Harmonia Mundi team are attractively spirited and rhythmically buoyant; the effect with period instruments brings a slightly abrasive edge at times, but not disagreeably so. The star here is Christophe Rousset, whose very imaginative contribution lights up this music-making. The recording is realistic, the balance excellent. At bargain price this is well worth considering.

KEYBOARD MUSIC

Les Indes galantes: excerpts (harpsichord transcriptions).
*** HM HMC 1901028. Kenneth Gilbert.

These transcriptions are Rameau's own, including not only dance numbers and orchestral pieces but arias as well. Kenneth Gilbert, playing a fine instrument in contemporary tuning, reveals these miniatures as the subtle and refined studies they are. He could not be better served by the recording engineers.

Music for harpsichord: *Book 1* (1706); *Pièces de clavecin* (1724); *Nouvelles suites de pièces de clavecin* (*c.* 1728); *5 Pièces* (1741); *La Dauphine* (1747).
*** O-L (IMS) Dig. 425 886-2 (2). Christophe Rousset (harpsichord).

Rousset's playing is marvellously persuasive and vital, authoritative and scholarly, yet fresh and completely free from the straitjacket of academic rectitude. He plays a Hemsch in a perfect state of preservation and a 1988 copy of a 1636 Ruckers harpsichord, modified by Hemsch. The sound is excellent.

Pièces de clavecin: Suite (No. 1) in A min.; L'Agaçante; La Dauphine; L'Indiscrète; La Livri; La Pantomime: La Timide.
(M) *** CRD CRD 3320; *CRDC 4020* [id.]. Trevor Pinnock.

Trevor Pinnock chose a mellow instrument here, making his stylish, crisply rhythmic performances even more attractive. The selection includes *La Dauphine*, the last keyboard piece which Rameau wrote, brilliantly performed. Excellent recording.

Harpsichord suites: in A min. (1728); *in E min.* (1724).
(M) *** CRD CRD 3310; *CRDC 4010* [id.]. Trevor Pinnock.

Harpsichord suites: in D min./maj. (1724); *in G maj./min.* (1728).
(M) *** CRD CRD 3330; *CRDC 4030* [id.]. Trevor Pinnock.

Trevor Pinnock is restrained in the matter of ornamentation, but his direct manner is both eloquent and stylish. The harpsichord is of the French type and is well recorded.

Suite de clavecin in E min. (1724).
(BB) *** HM Solo HMS 926018 [id.]. William Christie (harpsichord).

Rameau's *E minor Suite* is one of his most inventive, from the bursting birdsong of *Le Rappel des oiseaux* to the charming portrait of *La villageoise*, while the penultimate movement, a tender *Musette en rondeau*, is splendidly contrasted with the rumbustious closing *Tambourin*. William Christie plays the whole suite with infectious spontaneity and in fine style, and his Goujon-Swanen harpsichord is vividly recorded. This makes a splendid and inexpensive sampler for those unwilling to venture into a full-length programme of this attractive keyboard repertoire.

Grand motets: *In convertendo; Quam dilecta. Laboravi.*
(B) *** HM Musique d'abord HMA 1901078 [HMC 901078]. Gari, Monnaliu, Ledroit, De Mey, Varcoe, Chapelle Royale Ch., Ghent Coll. Voc., Herreweghe.

These two motets are among Rameau's finest works. The Ghent Collegium Vocale is stiffened by forces from La Chapelle Royale in Paris. They produce excellent results, and the soloists are also very fine indeed. The instrumental ensemble includes several members of La Petite Bande, so its excellence can almost be taken for granted. The brief *Laboravi* makes an appealing little encore. This CD is even more attractive at bargain price.

OPERA-BALLET AND OPERA

(i) *Anacréon* (opéra-ballet; complete); (ii) *Le berger fidèle* (cantata).
*** DG Dig. 449 211-2. (i–ii) Véronique Gens; (ii) Thierry Félix, Annick Massis, Rodrigo del Pozo, Ch.; Les Musiciens du Louvre, Marc Minkowski.

Rameau composed two works on the theme of the ancient Greek poet, Anacreon, famed for his devotion to Cupid and Bacchus. This is the second, originally designed as an *acte de ballet* to a libretto by P.-J. Bernard and composed in 1757. The music has both vivacity and charm, and they are fully revealed in this splendidly alive, DG Archiv performance from Minkowski and his excellent Chœur and Musiciens du Louvre, who are given first-class recording. The plot asks the question: can love and wine coexist? There is real drama at the opening of Scene 2 when Anacreon's unremitting wining and dining is interrupted by the angry arrival of Bacchus's Priestess (the excellent Véronique Gens) to destroy a statue of Cupid and abduct Anacreon's neglected lover, Lycoris. Scene 3 opens with an atmospheric evocation reminiscent of Vivaldi: *Sommeil-Pluie* (delicate pizzicati) *-Orage*; here as elsewhere the ear is caught by the contributions from the petites flûtes (transverse baroque piccolos), which so enhance the orchestral colour, chattering away in their obbligatos for the arias and returning piquantly to add brightness to the closing *Contredanse* after the problem has been resolved with the very happy compromise: wine should be one of the joys of lovers, not an alternative diversion! As an encore, Véronique Gens sings very affectingly an equally inspired 15-minute solo cantata which juxtaposes happiness and sacrifice with all the drama of the operatic stage. Once again the power of love wins out and tragedy is averted. This fine coupling now replaces Christie's earlier, Harmonia Mundi version of *Anacréon* with Les Arts Florissants (HMC 90190).

Les Boréades (complete).
(M) *** Erato/Warner 2292 45572-2 (3). Jennifer Smith, Rodde, Langridge, Aler, Lafont, Monteverdi Ch., E. Bar. Soloists, Gardiner.

It was John Eliot Gardiner who in April 1975 conducted the first-ever public performance of this last opera of Rameau, written after he had reached his eighties. The composer died during the rehearsal at the Paris Opéra, and the piece was not staged until 1982, when Gardiner presented it at the Aix-en-Provence Festival with the present cast. Though the story – involving the followers of Boreas, the storm god – is highly artificial, the music, involving many crisp and brief dances and arias, is as vital and alive as anything Rameau ever wrote, completely contradicting any idea of classical opera as static or boring. Gardiner here directs an electrifying performance with generally first-rate singing, except that Jennifer Smith's upper register, in the central role of Alphise, Queen of Baltria, is not sweet. Chorus and orchestra are outstanding and the recording excellent. Bizarre copyright problems prevented a libretto from being included, which makes it hard to follow the plot because the synopsis is not cued. However, the set is very welcome on CD as part of the Gardiner 'French Baroque Edition'.

Castor et Pollux (complete).
*** HM Dig. HMC 901435/7 [id.]. Crook, Corréas, Mellon, Gens, Schirrer, Brua, Piau, Les Arts Florissants Ch. & O, William Christie.
(M) **(*) Erato/Warner Dig. 4509 95311-2 (2) [id.]. Jeffes, Huttenlocher, Jennifer Smith, Buchan, Wallington, Parsons, Rees, E. Bach Festival Singers & Bar. O, Charles Farncombe.

Recorded in 1992, following stage performances at Aix-en-Provence the preceeding year, Christie's performance of Rameau's second *tragédie en musique* uses the original 1733 text, quite different from the 1754 text recorded by Charles Farncombe. Christie's performance consistently benefits from the dramatic timing, not least in the fluently alert and idiomatic exchanges in recitative, as well as in the broad, expressive treatment of set numbers like

Telaire's lament, *Tristes apprets*, beautifully sung by Agnès Mellon. With such fine sopranos as Véronique Gens and Sandrine Piau in relatively small roles, the cast has no weakness. Howard Crook has the clear tenor needed for the role of Castor (who appears very late in the drama), with Jérôme Corréas a stylish Pollux. The sound is a little drier and less warm than is usual with Christie, but it is fresh and immediate and has plenty of body, with military percussion beautifully caught. This is now a clear first choice.

Farncombe uses the revised edition of 1754 and though, after a brisk and refreshing account of the Overture, he fails to spring rhythms brightly enough, this is an admirable mid-priced set, marked by an agreeably authentic orchestral contribution and some stylish singing, notably from Huttenlocher as Pollux, who was not in the stage performances. Excellently clear, 1982 digital recording with a most attractive ambience, made at All Saints', Tooting. The documentation, too, is admirable.

Castor et Pollux: highlights.
(B) *** HM Dig. HMX 290844/46 (3) [id.] (from above set; cond. Christie) – CAMPRA: *Idomenée:* highlights; LULLY: *Atys:* highlights. ***
(N) (B) *** HM Musique d'abord Dig. HMA 1901501 (as above).

This is one of Harmonia Mundi's enterprising 'Trios', compiling three discs of operatic highlights at bargain price, in this case with full documentation, including translation. *Castor et Pollux* is a masterpiece, vividly recorded, and this 70-minute selection, if taken with its two companions, costs but a fraction of the price of the three-disc complete set. As can be seen this is now also available as a separate Musique d'abord disc, also including full texts and translations.

Dardanus (complete).
(M) **(*) Erato/Warner 4509 95312-2 (2) [id.]. Gautier, Eda-Pierre, Von Stade, Devlin, Teucer, Soyer, Van Dam, Paris Op. Ch. & O, Raymond Leppard.

Though the French chorus and orchestra (using modern instruments) here fail to perform with quite the rhythmic resilience that Leppard usually achieves on record, the results are refreshing and illuminating, helped by generally fine solo singing and naturally balanced (if not brilliant) 1980 analogue recording, smoothly transferred to CD, with the choral sound quite vivid. José van Dam as Ismenor copes superbly with the high tessitura, and Christiane Eda-Pierre is a radiant Venus. The story may be improbable (as usual), but Rameau was here inspired to some of his most compelling and imaginative writing. Well documented and well worth exploring.

(i) *Dardanus*: extended orchestral suite; (ii) Les Fêtes d'Hébé: 3rd Entreé: *La Danse* (Acte de ballet).
(N) (B) *** Erato/Warner Dig./Analogue Ultima 3984 27002-2 (2) [id.]. (i) E. Bar. Soloists; (ii) Gomez, Rode, Orliac, Monteverdi Ch. & O, Gardiner.

Gardiner offers a substantial selection (58 minutes) from the orchestral music of both versions of *Dardanus* (the 1739 score and the score for the 1744 revival, which involved radical rewriting of the last two Acts). There is plenty of variety here, from lightly orchestrated dance music to the powerful closing *Chaconne*. Very good, if perhaps not outstanding digital recording, a little lacking in depth. The coupling, *Les Fêtes d'Hébé*, was first staged in Paris in 1739. Its third Act (which is given here) is a pastoral interspersed with dances in which Mercury courts the shepherdess, Eglé. The music is inventive and delightful. As in *Dardanus*, Gardiner's performance is distinguished by his great feeling for this composer and an alive sensitivity: he secures excellent singing and playing from his first-rate team. Here the analogue recording is smoothly transferred, with lovely textures, choral and orchestral, both warm and transparent, with the soloists most naturally balanced. All in all this makes an ideal and inexpensive introduction to the music of Rameau.

Dardanus (orchestral suite); *Platée* (orchestral suite).
(N) *** Conifer Dig. 75605 51313-2 [id.]. Philh. Bar. O, Nicholas McGegan.

McGegan offers rather less music from *Dardanus* than Gardiner (about half-an-hour), but includes a charmingly Beechamesque *Air gracieux pour les Plaisirs*, omitted in the Erato suite. This makes room for the more extended suite from *Platée*, a 'ballet bouffon' dating from 1745 written as an entertainment at a royal wedding between the king's son and a princess noted for her plain appearance! Platée herself is an unlovely nymph who rules over a swamp full of frogs and insects (we hear them croaking in the *Passepieds* and *Tambourins*). However she fancies herself as a catch for the roving eye of the amorous Jupiter. He is in trouble with Juno for his unfaithful dalliances, so pretends to woo her, sure that his wife could never take the affair seriously when she sees Platée face to face. The mock nuptials are finally interrupted by Folie and Momus (the God of Ridicule). McGegan and his period-instrument orchestra are if anything more crisply resilient than Gardiner and not a whit less graceful. Moreover the Conifer recording is first-class and the suite from *Dardanus* is given a warmer ambience, notable in the lovely *Le sommeil*. The music for *Platée* has plenty of character and charm and like *Dardanus* ends with a memorable

Chaconne, for which – as it is interrupted in the ballet – McGegan provides a concert ending.

Hippolyte et Aricie (complete).
*** Erato/Warner Dig. 0630 15517-2 (3). Padmore, Panzarella, Hunt, Naouri, James, Les Arts Florissants, William Christie.
*** DG Dig. 445 853-2 (3). Gens, Fouchécourt, Fink, Feighan, Massis, Naouri, Smythe, Sagittarius Vocal Ens., Les Musiciens du Louvre, Minkowski.

It was through *Hippolyte et Aricie* that, in Anthony Lewis's 1965 Oiseau-Lyre recording, Christie first discovered Rameau while still a student at Harvard. His love for the piece brims out from his superb recording, which has the benefit of using the text specially prepared for the complete Rameau Edition by Sylvie Bouissou. In this, as she explains in a note, she aims to restore fully the original (1733) edition, long buried, which was later altered and modified, not for artistic reasons, but under pressure from a conservative public. Marc Minkowski in his fine, crisply alert DG Archiv recording uses a text substantially similar, and both of them – unlike Lewis – include the Prologue. The contrasts with Minkowski are striking, for Christie, using rather larger forces to produce warmer textures and timbres, consistently brings out the sensuous beauty of much of the writing as well as its dramatic point. At speeds fractionally broader, he bounces rhythms more infectiously and allows himself more flexible phrasing, regularly more relaxed in his manner, without undermining the classical purity of style. Though Anne-Maria Panzarella as Aricie is not as golden in tone as Véronique Gens for Minkowski, she is fresh and bright, responding immediately to Christie's timing which more consistently seems geared to stage presentation, with a conversational quality given to passages of recitative. Mark Padmore is a more ardent Hippolyte than his opposite number and Lorraine Hunt a weightier, more deeply tragic Phèdre, with Eirian James a warm Diana and Laurent Naouri as Thésée weightier than Russell Smythe. The Erato sound too is warmer and more immediate than the DG Archiv.

Mark Minkowski conducts an outstanding account of the first of Rameau's great tragédies-lyriques, a performance that firmly holds together the many jewelled fragments which make up the allegorical Prologue and five extended Acts. He is helped by an excellent cast, with the two young lovers of the title ideally taken by the sweet, silver-toned Véronique Gens, enchantingly girlish, and the light, very French-sounding tenor, Jean-Paul Fouchécourt, similarly conveying depth of feeling in formal melodic lines. Also central to the set's success is the powerful performance of Bernarda Fink as Phèdre, firm and rich, well contrasted with Gens, as memorable in its way as Dame Janet Baker's on the original Argo set conducted by Anthony Lewis, which yet omitted the Prologue. Though in the other major role of Thesée Russell Smythe's baritone is not always sweet, he sings with clear focus and expression, with Luc Coadou aptly sinister as Tisifone and Laurent Naouri sepulchral as Pluton. In the formal scheme the longest, most sustained aria which comes at the very end, celebrating the nightingale, is given to an incidental character, a shepherdess, and is sung here sweetly and charmingly by Annick Massis. Minkowski also draws crisp, alert performances from his chorus and well-tuned orchestra. In an opera for which the composer provided many alternatives, he chooses the original, 1733 text with the first cuts restored, but with minor amendments for which he provides detailed reasons.

Les Indes galantes (complete).
(M) *** Erato/Warner 4509 95310-2 (3) [id.]. Jennifer Smith, Hartman, Elwes, Devos, Huttenlocher, Ens. Vocale à Cœur Joie de Valence, Paillard O, Valence, Paillard.

The plot of *Les Indes galantes* is complicated but brings opportunities for a splendid tempest and sailors' chorus in Act I, which is set in Turkey. Act II moves to Peru, with a Sun Festival and a volcano erupting (admittedly not as spectacular as the tempest), and Act III with its floral festival is appropriately pastoral and picturesque. Finally we are taken to an Amazonian forest, where the two principal European characters are courting an Indian girl, Zima. She chooses one of her own tribe instead, but a pipe of peace ensures a final reconciliation; there are spectacular trumpets and a triumphant aria from the heroine before the closing ballet. The work is full of lyrical inspiration, and Jennifer Smith sings ravishingly in the roles of Phani, Fatime and Zima, while John Elwes as Tacmas and Adario brings a headily beautiful light-tenor response. Gerda Hartman as Hébé, Emilie and Zaire is charmingly lightweight, if not always quite as secure as Smith, and Philippe Huttenlocher sings all his roles with distinction. The duets and ensembles are often inspired, and the quartet, *Tendre amour*, in Scene 7, which comes before the ballet divertissement of Act III, is fully worthy of Mozart. Paillard directs the proceedings with much flair and warmth, and the 1974 recording is vividly atmospheric. With first-class documentation and a full translation, this is a set to cherish.

Naïs (complete).
(M) *** Erato/Warner 4509 98532-2 (2). Russell, Caley, Caddy, Tomlinson, Jackson, Parsons, Ransome, E. Bach Festival Ch. and Bar. O, McGegan.

Rameau's opera *Naïs* tells of Neptune's courtship of the water-nymph Naïs and is full of bold invention. The overture has some astonishing dissonances and syncopations, and the opening battle scenes in which the Heavens are stormed by the Titans and Giants are quite striking. The performance, based on the 1980 English Bach Festival production, is full of spirit and uses authentic period instruments to good effect. The work is not long, and the rewards of the music are such as to counterbalance any reservations one might have as to imperfections in ensemble or the like. Admirers of Rameau will need no prompting to acquire this attractive reissue. The unconverted should sample the opening, which will surely delight and surprise. The sound of this 1980 recording is strikingly well balanced, vivid and present. Highly recommended.

Platée (complete).
** Erato/Warner Dig. 2292 45028-2 (2) [id.]. Ragon, Jennifer Smith, Guy de Mey, Le Texier, Gens, Ens. Vocale Françoise Herr, Musiciens du Louvre, Minkowski.

Platée, written in 1745 and described as a '*ballet bouffon*', is in fact a comic opera, based on a classical theme. With such a send-up of classical tradition, the performers here understandably adopt comic expressions and voices, which in a recording, as opposed to a stage performance, become rather wearing on the listener. Also almost all the soloists aspirate heavily in florid passages. Within that convention this is a lively, brisk performance, very well conducted by Marc Minkowski, but marred by the dryness of the recording. As a work, *Platée* certainly provides a fascinating side-glance at Rameau's mastery.

La Princesse de Navarre (complete).
(M) *** Erato/Warner 0630 12986-2 (3) [id.]. Hill-Smith, Harrhy, Chambers, Rees, Goldthorpe, Caddy, Wigmore, Savidge, E. Bach Festival Singers and Bar. O, McGegan.

La Princesse de Navarre is a collection of dance movements which Rameau used in other works, as well as interludes for the Voltaire comédie. The finest is a chaconne of some magnificence, in which dancers and singers participate. This edition is the first to incorporate all the music Rameau composed for the work. He made substantial revisions, probably more than once and possibly as late as 1763 when Voltaire added a new Prologue for a performance at Bordeaux. There is some altogether delightful music here and those older readers who saw the Covent Garden staging in 1976 will not need reminding as to its quality. Of course, listening to 55 minutes of dances (even though some of them are choral) in close proximity is not the ideal way of enjoying Rameau, but a cued CD recording gives one the opportunity to pick and choose. Very good performances, and excellent recording too.

(i) *Pygmalion* (Acte de ballet); (ii) *Nélée et Myrthis* (Acte de ballet).
(N) ❁ (M) *** HM Dig. HMT 7901381 [id.]. (i) Howard Crook, Sandrine Piau; (i; ii) Agnès Mellon, Michel-Dansac Donatienne; (ii) Jérôme Corréas, Françoise Semellaz; (ii) Caroline Pelon; Ch. & O, Les Arts Florissants, Christie.

Pygmalion (Acte de ballet). *Le Temple de la gloire* (excerpts): *Air gay; Ces oiseaux par leur doux ramage.*
(N) (M) **(*) Virgin Veritas VM5 61539-2. Jean-Paul Fouchécourt, Greta de Reyghere, Nicole Fournié, Sandrine Piau.

Unlike the extended opera-ballets, Rameau's *Actes de ballet* are comparatively concise, although it seems likely that *Nélée and Myrthis* was originally part of a longer work. Its frivolous – but in Rameau's setting, very touching – story is of the heroine, Myrthis being put to the test by her lover, who encourages her to think his attentions are roving elsewhere. This is balanced by the famous legend of *Pygmalion*, who falls in love with a female statue he has sculpted. The statue is then (by the courtesy of Venus) brought to life by that very love – a moment of sheer orchestral magic in Rameau's delightful score. Both works have happy endings. The performances under Christie are comparatively intimate, giving the effect of chamber-operas, and are ideally cast. Howard Crook is a most sympathetic Pygmalion, and Agnes Mellon charming as Céphise, who cannot accept that Pygmalion should spurn her for a marble alternative. But then Donatienne Michel-Dansac is a soaringly sweet-voiced statue, who finds it even more remarkable that she is taking human form because of her creator's deep feelings for her. The celebrated scene where the Statue learns to dance (in various different tempi) brings delightfully elegant and sprightly playing from the orchestra, where the piccolos are very telling. In the hardly less appealing companion piece, Mellon is equally well cast as a touching Myrthis, as is Françoise Semellaz as her apparent rival, Corinne. Beautifully balanced recording and a fully translated libretto earns this coupling the highest recommendation. The only slight snag is the comparatively meagre allotment of cues.

The alternative Virgin Veritas version is more robustly operatic, immediately obvious in the Overture, with its boldly repeated notes, superbly articulated which may (or may not) have been intended by Rameau to simulate the sculptor's chisel. Jean-Paule Fouchécourt gives a strong characterization of Pygmalion, but most listeners will find Howard Crook more sympathetic, and apart from Sandrine Piau as the Statue, her two female colleagues are more histrionic but less sweet voiced than their rivals on Harmonia Mundi. Moreover, the excerpts from *Le Temple de la gloire* are quite brief (about 8 minutes), and while the Virgin Veritas reissue includes good notes and a libretto in French, there is no English translation.

Zoroastre (complete).
(M) **(*) DHM/BMG GD 77144 (3). Elwes, De Reyghere, Van der Sluis, Nellon, Reinhart, Bona, Ghent Coll. Vocale, La Petite Bande, Kuijken.

Though Kuijken's characteristically gentle style with his excellent authentic group, La Petite Bande, fails to give the piece all the bite and urgency it needs, this is nevertheless a fine presentation of a long-neglected masterpiece, with crisp and stylish singing from the soloists, notably John Elwes in the name-part and Gregory Reinhart as Abramane. The Ghent Collegium Vocale, placed rather close, sing with vigour in the choruses, but the individual voices fail to blend. The excellent documentation (144 pages, including translations) puts the mid-priced issues of many of the large international companies to shame.

Rangström, Ture (1884–1947)

Symphony No. 1 in C sharp min. (August Strindberg in memoriam); Dithyramb; Spring hymn.
**(*) CPO Dig. CPO999 367-2 [id.]. Norrköping SO, Michail Jurowski.

Symphonies Nos. 1 in C sharp min. (August Strindberg in memoriam); (i) *3 in D sharp (Song under the stars).*
** Sterling CDS 1014-2 [id.]. Swedish RSO, Leif Segerstam; (i) Helsingborg SO, Janos Fürst.

Rangström's *First Symphony* dates from 1914, two years after the death of Strindberg, to whose memory it is dedicated, as indeed is the *Vårhymn* (*Spring hymn*) of 1942 on the CPO disc. This also includes his very first orchestral work, the *Dithyramb* of 1909. To be frank, it is not in the same league, either in terms of musical substance or craftmanship, as the symphonies of Alfvén and Atterberg. Rangström studied briefly with Pfitzner, though he was basically self-taught, and the prime influences are Franck and early Sibelius. There are some individual things in the slow movement but elsewhere, and particularly in the finale, the rhetoric is overblown and the ideas second rate. For sheer banality the second group of the finale has to be heard to be believed. It is strange that a composer who could write with such artlessness and inspiration in his songs or in the *Divertimento elegiaco* should exhibit such lapses of taste.

Of the two performances, Michail Jurowski is the more persuasive and he gets very good playing from the Norrköping orchestra. Not that Leif Segerstam's 1979 account with the Swedish Radio Orchestra is in any way negligible; indeed he draws an accomplished performance from his players and is decently recorded in good analogue sound. It is difficult to work up much enthusiasm for the Sterling coupling, the *Third Symphony* (*Sång under stjärnorna* – 'Song under the stars'), which is also rather corny. No grumbles about the playing of the Helsingborg Symphony Orchestra under Janos Fürst.

Symphonies Nos. 3 in D flat (Song under the Stars); (i) *4 in E flat (Invocatio).*
** CPO Dig. CPO 999 369-2 [id.]. (i) Mark Fahlsjö; Norrköping SO, Michail Jurowski.

The *Third Symphony* (1929) takes one of his songs, *Bön till natten* ('Prayer to the night') as its starting point, but the result is terribly inflated. The *Fourth Symphony* (1933–6) is best described as a suite for orchestra and organ. Its invention is very uneven, though there is a charming *Intermezzo*, which forms the central movement. Good performances and recordings, but neither work is remotely convincing symphonically.

The Girl under the new moon (Flickan under nymånen); Melody; The only moment; Pan; Prayer to the Night (Bön till natten); Villemo.
(N) *** Virgin/EMI Dig. VC5 45273-2. Solveig Kringelborn, Malcolm Martineau – GRIEG, NIELSEN, SIBELIUS: *Songs.* ***

Rangström is Sweden's leading *romans* composer and the simplicity and eloquence of his best songs – and the present half dozen are among his very finest – are affecting. Although Solveig Kringelborn does not eradicate memories of Söderström or von Otter, she does these lovely songs justice and her pianist Malcolm Martineau is superb throughout. Excellent recorded sound too.

Rautavaara, Einojuhani (born 1928)

Anadyomene (Adoration of Aphrodite); (i) *Flute concerto, Op. 63*; (ii) *On the last frontier.*
(N) *** Ondine Dig. ODE 921-2 [id.]. Helsinki PO, Leif Segerstam; with (i) Patrick Gallois; (ii) Finnish Philharmonic Ch.

Anadyomene or the *Adoration of Aphrodite* comes from 1969, and is highly atmospheric and compelling. Its original inspiration was Joyce's *Finnegans Wake*. The *Flute concerto*, subtitled *Dances with the winds*, was written five years later for the Swedish flautist, Gunilla von Bahr, and employs bass flute, alto flute and piccolo. It is one of Rautavaara's most imaginative and resourceful scores, and its many hurdles are effortlessly despatched by the distinguished French soloist. *On the last frontier*, a fantasy for chorus and orchestra, is one of Rautavaara's most recent works (1997), inspired by Edgar Allan Poe's description of Antartica, at the end of *The Narrative of Arthur Gordon Pym*. Vaughan Williams occasionally comes to mind in its pages. All three pieces are expertly performed by these Helsinki forces under Leif Segerstam and superbly recorded.

(i) *Angel of Dusk (Concerto for double bass and orchestra);* (ii) *Cantos I–III for string orchestra;* (iii) *Cantus Articus (Concerto for birds and orchestra);* (iv) *Epitaph for Béla Bartók; Hommage à Ferenc Liszt; Hommage à Zoltán Kodály;* (v) *A Requiem in our time for brass ensemble;* (vi) *Clarinet sonata;* (vii) *String quartet No. 2.*

(N) (B) *** Finlandia/Warner Dig./Analogue Ultima 3984 27003-2 (2) [id.]. (i) Kosonen, Finish RSO, Segerstam; (ii) Tapiola Sinfonietta, Lamminmäki; (iii) Klementi Institute SO, Pekkanen; (iv) Helsinki Strings, Csaba & Géza Szilvay; (v) Helsinki PO, Panula; (vi) Kojo, Lagerspetz; (vii) Sibelius Qt.

Even more than the Naxos disc below, this generously full Finlandia Ultima Double seems an ideal way of entering Rautavaara's highly individual sound world. The *Angel of Dusk* is a hauntingly unconventional way of writing a darkly atmospheric yet bravura concertante work for double bass and orchestra, with the Angel's 'closing appearance', a plaintive blending of toccata and threnody, finally fading into silence. In the *Cantus Articus* the taped Arctic birds are full throated and equally balanced with the warmly sinuous orchestral melismas. The kernel of the searchingly restless *String quartet* is the concentrated and deeply felt Adagio; the yearning finale is ambivalent, but curiously satisfying. The performance by the Jean Sibelius Quartet is deeply felt and well recorded.

Angels and visitations; (i) *Violin concerto. Isle of bliss.*

✿ *** Ondine Dig. ODE 881-2 [id.]. (i) Elmar Oliveira; Helsinki PO, Leif Segerstam.

Rautavaara's wholly original *Violin concerto* is truly memorable and must surely be ranked alongside other outstanding modern works in this form by Samuel Barber and Christopher Headington. Like their music, it is hauntingly accessible and wholly grips the listener. It moves from an ethereal opening cantilena, through a series of colourful events and experiences until, after a final burst of incandescent energy, it makes a sudden but positive homecoming. The lively opening of the *Isle of bliss* is deceptive, for the music centres on a dreamy, sensual romanticism and creates a rich orchestral tapestry with a sense of yearning ecstasy, yet overall it has a surprisingly coherent orchestral structure. *Angels and visitations* is close to the visions of William Blake and (as the composer tells us) brings a sense of 'holy dread'. The extraordinary opening evokes a rustling of angels' wings, which is then malignantly transformed, becoming a ferocious multitude of bumblebees. It is a passage of real imaginative power, in some ways comparable to the storm sequence in Sibelius's *Tapiola*. The work is in a kind of variation form and moves from the ethereal nature of angels to demons quite readily, while later taking on board forceful rhythmic influences from Stravinsky's *Rite of spring* and *Petrushka*. Its orchestration and impact are spectacular, hardly music for a small flat! Elmar Oliveira is the inspired soloist in the *Violin concerto*, floating his line magically and serenely in the opening *Tranquillo* and readily encompassing the work's adventurous shifts of colour and substance. Segerstam provides a shimmering backing and directs a committed and persuasively spontaneous orchestral response throughout all three works. The recording is superbly balanced, spacious and vivid in detail.

Cantus Arcticus (Concerto for birds and orchestra), Op. 61; (i) *Piano concerto, Op. 45; Symphony No. 3, Op. 20.*

(N) (BB) *** Naxos Dig. 8.554147 [id.]. (i) Laura Mikkola; R Scotttish Nat. O, Hannu Lintu.

The *Cantus Arcticus* (1972) which uses taped Arctic bird-cries against an evocative orchestral background has gained much popularity in recent years. The *Third Symphony* (1959–60) has genuine breadth and space: indeed there is an allusion to Bruckner at the very opening. Rautavaara speaks of it as being 'freely constructed and emphatically tonal'. It has a strong feeling for nature. The later *Piano concerto No. 1* (1969) has a certain neo-romantic feel to it, with its harmonic language deriving from Bartók, Ravel and Prokofiev. Laura Mikkola is a fervent exponent of it, and the Royal Scottish National Orchestra under Hannu Lintu play with real commitment and are well recorded. An inexpensive introduction to a composer in whom interest has consistently grown in the past decade.

Symphonies 1–3.

*** Ondine Dig. ODE 740-2 [id.]. Leipzig RSO, Max Pommer.

Einojuhani Rautavaara has been overshadowed outside Finland by Joonas Kokkonen and Aulis Sallinen, but the present disc shows him to be a symphonist to reckon with. Ideas never outstay their welcome and there is a sense of inevitability about their development. Those with a taste for Shostakovich or Simpson should find these pieces congenial. Good performances by the Leipzig Radio Orchestra under Max Pommer and very decent recorded sound too.

Symphony No. 6 (Vincentiana); (i) *Cello concerto, Op. 41.*

*** Ondine Dig. ODE 819-2 [id.]. (i) Marko Ylönen; Helsinki PO, Max Pommer.

The *Sixth Symphony* comes from 1992 and is a large-scale work of over 42 minutes, which draws on material from the opera, *Vincent* (1985–7), based on the life of van Gogh. There is, appropriately enough, no lack of colour, though the score tends to be both eclectic and amorphous. The orchestral scoring itself is quite sumptuous and there is no lack of incident. However, the invention is hardly symphonic and the canvas does not fully sustain interest. It comes with a much earlier and more cogently argued piece, the *Cello concerto* of 1968, which is expertly played by Marko Ylönen. The recording is very impressive, well detailed and present, and is in the demonstration bracket.

Symphony No. 7 (Angel of Light); (i) *Annunciations.*
*** Ondine Dig. ODE 869-2 [id.]. (i) Kari Jussila; Helsinki PO, Leif Segerstam.

The *Seventh Symphony* is the more substantial piece and is both powerful and atmospheric. There is a good deal of Sibelius in its first movement and there is a pervasive sense of nature. Rautavaara betrays some affinities with the minimalists but offers greater musical substance. *Annunciations* for organ, brass quintet, winds and percussion, written in 1976–7, strikes a more dissonant note but it is brilliant and well thought out. Kari Jussila is the virtuoso soloist, and the Helsinki orchestra under Segerstam are eminently well served by the Ondine engineers.

Ravel, Maurice (1875–1937)

(i) *Alborada del gracioso; Une barque sur l'océan; Boléro;* (ii) *Daphnis et Chloé* (ballet) *suite No. 2;* (i) *L'Eventail de Jeunne: Fanfare. Menuet antique; Pavane pour une infante défunte; Rapsodie espagnole; Shéhérazade: Ouverture de féerie. Le tombeau de Couperin; La valse; Valses nobles et sentimentales.*
(N) (B) *** DG Double Dig./Analogue 459 439-2 (2). (i) LSO; (ii) Boston SO with New England Conservatory Ch., Claudio Abbado.

Abbado's DG Double Ravel anthology is highly appealing, even if its content is not entirely predictable. Only the *Second Suite* is included from *Daphnis et Chloé*, using his early 1970 Boston account. His feeling for the music's atmosphere is matched by his care for detail, and the glowing analogue recording was one of the best made in Symphony Hall in the analogue era: it is warmly resonant, but there is no resulting inflation of tone and texture brought about by too-close microphones. *Ma Mère l'Oye* is omitted, yet the early overture to *Shéhérazade* (which is completely unrelated to the song cycle), is included alongside the two transcriptions from *Miroirs*, the *Alborada* and *Un barque sur l'océan*. Abbado gets delicious sounds in all three, as he does in the *Valses nobles et sentimentales*. The sultry atmosphere of *Rapsodie espagnole* is very evocative and the *Pavane* has a grave, withdrawn melancholy. All these LSO recordings are digital (made between 1981 and 1987) and the characteristically polished and refined playing is matched by sound with a wide dynamic range, a fine focus, and yet plenty of ambience and warmth. *Boléro* and the exquisitely played *Le tombeau de Couperin* are also included on another single disc anthology below.

(i) *Alborada del gracioso;* (ii) *Une barque sur l'océan; Boléro;* (i; iii) *Piano concerto for the left hand;* (ii; iv) *Daphnis et Chloé* (complete ballet); (ii) *Fanfare pour L'Eventail de Jeanne; Menuet antique; Ma Mère l'Oye* (complete ballet); (i) *Pavane pour une infante défunte; Rapsodie espagnole;* (ii) *Shéhérazade: Ouverture de féerie. Le tombeau de Couperin; La valse; Valses nobles et sentimentales.*
(M) **(*) Sony SM3K 45842 (3) [S3K 45842]. (i) Cleveland O; (ii) NYPO; Boulez; (iii) with Entremont; (iv) Camerata Singers.

Boulez's distinguished Sony set offers a glitteringly iridescent account of the *Ouverture de féerie*, which is omitted by Dutoit. Entremont's account of the *Left-hand concerto* is strong and characterful and not lacking in colour; but the rather fierce CBS sound does not flatter the piano timbre. On the whole, however, the remastering makes the most of recordings which were originally among the best of their period (1972–5). Boulez allows all the music ample time to breathe; gentler textures have the translucence for which this conductor is admired. There is no doubt that this music-making with its cleanly etched sound is immensely strong in character, and many listeners will respond to it very positively.

Alborada del gracioso; Une Barque sur l'océan; Boléro; Daphnis et Chloé: suite No. 2. L'Eventail de Jeanne: Fanfare. Menuet antique; Ma Mère l'Oye (complete); Pavane pour une enfante défunte; Rapsodie espagnole; Le tombeau de Couperin; La valse; Valses nobles et sentimentales.
(N) ❁ *** Decca Dig. Double 460 214-2 (2) [id.]. Montreal SO, Dutoit.

Anyone beginning a Ravel collection, or coming fresh to most of this repertoire and willing to duplicate, will find this Decca Double unbeatable value, including as it does all the key orchestral works, though not the piano concertos (by no means a disadvantage, when there is plenty of choice available). The orchestral playing is wonderfully sympathetic and the recording ideally combines atmospheric evocation with vividness. The balance is most musically judged and very realistic; indeeed the sound remains in the demonstration class.

Alborada del gracioso; Une barque sur l'océan; Boléro; Ma Mère l'Oye (complete); *Menuet antique; Ouverture de féerie; Pavane pour une Infante défunte; Rapsodie espagnole; Le tombeau de Couperin; La valse; Valses nobles et sentimentales.*

(B) *** EMI forte CZS5 68610-2 (2) [CDFB 68610]. O de Paris, Martinon.

Like his version of *Daphnis et Chloé*, Martinon's *Ma Mère l'Oye* is exquisite, among the finest ever put on record. Although the *Valses nobles et sentimentales* and *La valse* do not eclipse the 1961 Cluytens versions (see below) and the present *La valse* has a rather harsh climax, there is much ravishing delicacy of orchestral playing, notably in *Le tombeau de Couperin* and the rare *Ouverture de féerie* (*Shéhérazade*). The sound is warm and luminously coloured and the refined virtuosity of the Orchestre de Paris is a constant source of delight. Excellent value.

Alborada del gracioso; Une barque sur l'océan; Boléro; Ma Mère l'Oye (complete ballet); *Menuet antique; Pavane pour une infante défunte; Rapsodie espagnole; Le tombeau de Couperin; La valse; Valses nobles et sentimentales.*

(M) *** EMI (SIS) CZS7 67897-2 (2) [id.]. Paris Conservatoire O, Cluytens.

These 1961 performances, made in the Salle Wagram, Paris, are as good as any in the catalogue. They have a strongly idiomatic and atmospheric feel; the *Rapsodie espagnole*, *La valse* and the *Valses nobles* are exceptionally good, and so too is the complete *Ma Mère l'Oye*. The only snag is the wide vibrato of the horn in *Pavane pour une infante défunte*. The recordings still sound remarkably realistic, and not just for the period: they are very good by present-day standards. The two-disc set makes a genuine bargain.

Alborada del gracioso; Boléro; Daphnis et Chloé (ballet): *Suite No. 2; Menuet antique; Ma Mère l'Oye* (complete ballet); *Pavane pour une infante défunte; Rapsodie espagnole; Le tombeau de Couperin; La valse; Valses nobles et sentimentales.*

(B) **(*) Ph. (IMS) Duo 438 745-2 (2) [id.]. Concg. O, Bernard Haitink.

Although Haitink's Ravel collection, recorded in the early 1970s, is not as magical as the superb companion Debussy set on Philips Duo, these are still good performances. The playing of the Amsterdam orchestra is eminently polished and civilized, even if the heady, intoxicating qualities of Ravel are missed. Yet the orchestral playing seduces the ear with its refinement and finish, and the engineers produce a sound to match: the perspective is truthful and the overall effect on CD most pleasing, with the remastered recordings improved in firmness of outline without loss of atmosphere or bloom.

(i) *Alborada del gracioso;* (ii) *Boléro;* (i) *Pavane pour une infante défunte; Rapsodie espagnole;* (ii) *Le tombeau de Couperin; La valse.*

(N) (M) *** Sony Theta SMK 60303 [id.]. (i) Cleveland O; (ii) NYPO; Boulez.

These recordings come from the three-disc Boulez anthology above, showing him at his very finest, securing top-class performances from both orchestras. Atmosphere is not sacrificed to detail, and the concentration of the playing is remarkable. This is all distinguished music-making, full of character, and the recordings from the early 1970s have all been impressively remastered.

(i) *Alborada del gracioso;* (ii) *Boléro; Pavane pour une infante défunte; Rapsodie espagnole;* (iii) *Tzigane;* (ii) *La valse.*

(M) **(*) [RCA Basic 100 09026 61712-2; *61712-4*]. (i) Chicago SO, Reiner; (ii) Boston SO, Munch; (iii) Perlman, LSO, Previn.

We have a special affection for these Munch performances as they were originally discussed (in 1960) in our very first hardback *Stereo Record Guide*. In spite of effective remastering, neither *Boléro* nor *La valse* is in the first class now – in the former the dynamic range is relatively restricted and the opening side-drum, though clear enough, is too loud in relation to the final climax. In those heady early days of stereo we were taken by the Boston sound, which we found full-blooded yet well separated. *La valse* is exciting, but with the closing pages hard-driven and rather frenetic. Reiner's *Alborada* comes from the same period, and his reading misses nothing in colour or atmosphere, with the Chicago acoustic adding to the vividness and sense of space. Perlman's earliest stereo recording of the *Tzigane* is brilliantly involving, and Previn accompanies imaginatively; but, as too often with this artist, the violin is given an exaggeratedly close balance.

(i) *Alborada del gracioso; Boléro; Pavane pour une infante défunte; La valse;* (ii) *Valses nobles et sentimentales.*

(BB) **(*) EMI Seraphim Analogue/Dig. CES5 68539-2 (2) [CDEB 68539]. (i) New Philh. O, Maazel; (ii) RPO, Previn – DEBUSSY: *La Mer; Nocturnes* ***; MUSSORGSKY: *Pictures at an exhibition.* **(*)

Previn gives here a provocatively languorous account of the *Valses nobles et sentimentales*, lazy of tempo and affectionately indulgent, and afforded glowing (1985) digital sound. Maazel directs the rest of this Ravel collection which offers more first-class orchestral playing. His are brilliant, extrovert performances, with plenty of glitter in the *Alborada* and the *Pavane* played gently and beautifully. The climaxes of both *Boléro* and *La valse* are rhythmically mannered, but there is no lack of adrenalin; the sound, from the early 1970s, is spectacular, if a bit brash.

Alborada del graciso; Boléro; Rapsodie espagnole; (i) *Daphnis et Chloé* (complete ballet). *Le tombeau de Couperin; La valse; Valses nobles et sentimentales.*

(B) *** RCA Twofer Dig. 74321 34171-2 (2). Dallas SO; (i) with Ch.; Eduardo Mata.

In the late 1970s Eduardo Mata helped to build the Dallas orchestra into a splendid band, and here he directs a warmly atmospheric and magnetic reading of *Daphnis et Chloé* for which RCA (in 1979) produced one of the finest of their early digital recordings. Two decades later it remains near the demonstration bracket for its clarity and allure (helped by the splendid acoustics of the Dallas auditorium). The closing pages with chorus are particularly impressive.

Mata's *Le tombeau de Couperin* has elegance and finesse, while the expansive climaxes of *Boléro* and *La valse* are very compelling. The recording has the most spectacular dynamic range, while the Dallas hall provides plenty of atmosphere. The *Alborada* flashes, the *Rapsodie* shimmers and there is a balmy underlying patina of sensuous colour. At bargain price this is highly recommendable. The climax of the *Valses nobles et sentimentales* again impresses for its dynamic range and fine orchestral playing, and altogether this makes an outstanding compilation.

(i) *Alborado del gracioso; Boléro; Rapsodie espagnole; Le tombeau de Couperin;* (ii) *Valses nobles et sentimentales.*
(B) **(*) Sony SBK 48163 [id.]. Phd. O, (i) Ormandy; (ii) Munch.

Ormandy was a first-class Ravel conductor, as those who can recall his wartime *Daphnis et Chloé* (and, for that matter, its successors) can testify. These performances are eminently well worth the money at bargain price, even if the recording is not three-star by 1990s standards.

Alborada del gracioso; Fanfare for L'Eventail de Jeanne; Ma Mère l'Oye (complete ballet); *Miroirs: La vallée des cloches* (arr. Percy Grainger); *La valse;* (i) *Shéhérazade* (song-cycle).
*** EMI Dig. CDC7 54204-2. (i) Maria Ewing; CBSO, Simon Rattle.

The recording of the CBSO, made in the Arts Centre of Warwick University, is spectacular, with a state-of-the-art sound-balance of the widest range and amplitude. The orchestral playing is superb. Rattle captures the lambent allure of Percy Grainger's orchestration of the last of the *Miroirs* and gives an equally glowing account of *Ma Mère l'Oye*. At the beginning of the programme, Maria Ewing's *Shéhérazade* is matched in voluptuous intensity by Rattle and his players; in the aching yearning of *La flûte enchantée* the atmosphere becomes more impressionistic. But it is essentially a dramatic performance, and the shimmering *Alborada* is well placed to follow on afterwards.

Alborada del gracioso; Pavane pour une infante défunte; Rapsodie espagnole; Le tombeau de Couperin; La valse.
(M) *** Mercury (IMS) 432 003-2 [id.]. Detroit SO, Paray – IBERT: *Escales.* **(*)

Paray's Ravel performances enjoyed a high reputation in the 1960s. His *Rapsodie espagnole* can be spoken of in the same breath as the Reiner/RCA and Karajan/EMI versions, with its languorous, shimmering textures and sparkling *Feria*. His *Alborada* glitters and the *Pavane* is glowingly elegiac. *La valse*, too, is impressively shaped and subtly controlled. *Le tombeau de Couperin* has great refinement and elegance: the solo oboist plays beautifully. All have been excellently remastered.

Alborada del gracioso; Pavane pour une infante défunte; Rapsodie espagnole; Valses nobles et sentimentales.
❁ (M) *** RCA GD 60179 [60179-2-RG]. Chicago SO, Reiner – DEBUSSY: *Ibéria.* ***

These performances are in an altogether special class. In the *Rapsodie espagnole*, the *Prélude à la nuit* is heavy with fragrance and atmosphere; never have the colours in the *Feria* glowed more luminously, while the *Malagueña* glitters with iridescence. In the three and a half decades since it first appeared, this is the recording we have turned to whenever we wanted to hear this work for pleasure. No one captures its sensuous atmosphere so completely as did Reiner, and the recorded sound with its natural concert-hall balance is greatly improved in terms of clarity and definition.

Alborada del gracioso; Rapsodie espagnole.
*** Chandos Dig. CHAN 8850 [id.]. Ulster O, Yan Pascal Tortelier – DEBUSSY: *Images.* ***

Yan Pascal Tortelier gives very good performances of both works and has the advantage of excellent Chandos sound. His *Rapsodie espagnole* is not quite as gripping as some celebrated accounts (Reiner, Karajan, Giulini and others) but it is highly atmospheric all the same, and some collectors may be swayed by the claims of the outstanding digital recording.

Boléro.
(M) *** DG 447 426-2 [id.]. BPO, Karajan – DEBUSSY: *La Mer;* MUSSORGSKY: *Pictures.* ***

Boléro; Daphnis et Chloé: suite No. 2.
(M) *** DG 427 250-2. BPO, Karajan – DEBUSSY: *La mer; Prélude.* ***

Karajan's 1964 *Boléro* is a marvellously controlled, hypnotically gripping performance, with the Berlin Philharmonic at the top of its form. It is available either with a superb suite from *Daphnis et Chloé*, or among DG's Legendary Recordings series of 'Originals'; the couplings on both discs show Karajan at his very finest.

Boléro; Rapsodie espagnole; La valse.
(M) *** DG Dig. Penguin Classics 460 633-2

[id.]. LSO, Abbado – MUSSORGSKY: *Pictures at an exhibition*. ***

Abbado has impeccable taste in this repertoire, and it goes without saying that the LSO plays superbly throughout, although near the climax of *Boléro* Abbado makes a perceptible gear-change, pressing the tempo forward. No complaints about the 1986 digital recording either. The author's essay is by Richard Forde.

Boléro; (i) *Daphnis et Chloé: suite No. 2; Ma Mère l'Oye (suite); Valses nobles et sentimentales.*

(BB) *** Naxos Dig. 8.550173; *4550173* [id.]. (i) Slovak Philharmonic Ch.; Slovak RSO (Bratislava), Kenneth Jean.

The Slovak Radio Orchestra, which is a fine body and is superbly recorded, respond warmly to Kenneth Jean. At the price, this is very good value indeed; the *Ma Mère l'Oye* can hold its own alongside all but the most distinguished competition: indeed *Les entretiens de la belle et de la bête* is as keenly characterized as Dutoit at mid-price, and *Le jardin féerique* is enchanting. For those wanting these pieces this is a real bargain.

Boléro; Jeux d'eau (orch. Viacava); *Ma Mère l'Oye: suite;* (i) *Tzigane. La vallée des cloches* (orch. Grainger); *La valse;* (ii) *5 Mélodies populaires grecques.*

**(*) Cala Dig. CACD 1004 [id.]. (i) Stephanie Chase; (ii) Sally Burgess; Philh. O, Geoffrey Simon.

A record of unusual interest in that it offers orchestral transcriptions of two Ravel piano pieces that are new to the catalogue: Viacava's orchestration of *Jeux d'eau*, made in 1951, and Percy Grainger's exotic and imaginative scoring of *La vallée des cloches* from 1944. The test of good orchestration is to convey the illusion that the music could have existed in no other form, as do Ravel's own transcriptions of *Alborada del gracioso* and *Ma Mère l'Oye*, and it is a tribute to Viacava's cunning and expertise that he succeeds as well as he does (albeit not completely) to disguise the keyboard origins of *Jeux d'eau*. Percy Grainger's *La vallée des cloches* is quite remarkable, calling as it does on an exotic array of glockenspiel, vibraphone, marimba, celeste and dulcitone plus the strings of a piano struck by a mallet. It is not perhaps wholly Ravel in sensibility, but it is highly effective in its own right. Geoffrey Simon directs good performances from the Philharmonia, though his *Ma Mère l'Oye* doesn't banish memories of Giulini, Cluytens or Dutoit. Simon's two soloists in the *Cinq mélodies populaires grecques* and *Tzigane* are excellent, and the recording is very good indeed. The liner-notes by Grant Cathro are full of insights into Ravel's music and are very perceptive.

Boléro; Rapsodie espagnole.

*** DG (IMS) Gold Dig. 439 013-2. BPO, Karajan – MUSSORGSKY: *Pictures*. ***

Karajan's later versions of *Boléro* and *Rapsodie espagnole* find the Berlin Philharmonic in characteristically brilliant form, recorded in very wide-ranging digital sound; the thrust of *Boléro* and the sensuousness of the *Rapsodie* are conveyed with unerring power and magnetism, and the close of the *Feria* of the *Rapsodie espagnole* is spectacular indeed!

Boléro; La valse.

(M) *** Decca (IMS) 448 576-2 [id.]. SRO, Ansermet – CHABRIER: *España* **(*); DUKAS: *L'apprenti sorcier* ***; DEBUSSY: *La Mer* **(*); HONEGGER: *Pacific 231*. ***

Outstanding 1963 performances from Ansermet, very well recorded. Nearly all the music included here shows the Swiss conductor at his best.

Piano concerto in G.

✿ *** EMI CDC7 49326-2. Michelangeli, Philh. O, Gracis – RACHMANINOV: *Concerto No. 4*. ***

(N) (M) *** Carlton Classics 30366 01002 [id.]. Stephen Drury, Boston PO, Zander – STRAVINSKY: *Petrushka*. ***

Piano concerto in G; Piano concerto in D for the left hand.

(*) Chandos Dig. CHAN 8773 [id.]. Louis Lortie, LSO, Frühbeck de Burgos – FAURE: *Ballade*. *

(N) (M) *(*) EMI CDM5 66905-2 [CDM 66957]. Samson François, Paris Conservatoire O, Cluytens.

(i) *Piano concerto in G; Piano concerto for the left hand. Une barque sur l'océan; L'Eventail de Jeanne: Fanfare; Menuet antique.*

**(*) Decca Dig. 410 230-2. (i) Rogé; Montreal SO, Dutoit.

(i–ii) *Piano concerto in G; Piano concerto for the left hand;* (ii) *La valse;* (i) (Piano) *Valses nobles et sentimentales.*

(B) *** CfP CD-CFP 4667 [id.]. (i) Philip Fowke; (ii) LPO, Baudo.

(i; ii) *Piano concerto in G;* (i; iii) *Piano concerto for the left hand*; (ii) *Valses nobles et sentimentales.*

(N) ✿ *** DG Dig. 449 213-2 [id.]. (i) Kryztian Zimerman, (i; ii) Cleveland O or (iii) LSO, Pierre Boulez.

(i) *Piano concerto in G; Gaspard de la nuit.*

(M) *** DG 447 438-2 [id.]. Martha Argerich, (i) BPO, Abbado – PROKOFIEV: *Piano concerto No. 3*. ***

Zimerman's *G major Concerto* and the *Valses nobles et sentimentales* were recorded with the

Cleveland Orchestra in 1994 and the *Left-hand concerto* in Watford in 1996. They were not released until the spring of 1999 and have perhaps been treated like a good wine and allowed to mature. Not to beat about the bush, they are well nigh perfect in every respect. Boulez's account of the *Valses nobles* are quite wonderfully atmospheric, indeed magical, and in the concertos the delicacy and finesse of Krystian Zimerman's pianism is dazzling, his refinement of nuance and clarity of articulation a source of wonder – or rather would be, were it not for the fact that these are selfless performances that put the composer first and the interpreter second. Beautifully balanced and finely detailed recording.

Michelangeli plays the *G major Concerto* with superlative brilliance which yet has great sympathy for the tender moments. The exquisite playing in the slow movement makes up for any deficiencies of dimensional balance. The recording has been remastered very successfully and is of high quality: clear, with bold piano timbre and excellent orchestral detail.

Argerich's half-tones and clear fingerwork give the *G major Concerto* unusual delicacy, but its urgent virility – with jazz an important element – comes over the more forcefully by contrast. Other performances may have caught the uninhibited brilliance in the finale more fearlessly, but in the first movement few other versions can match Argerich's playing. The compromise between coolness and expressiveness in the slow minuet of the middle movement is tantalizingly sensual. Her *Gaspard de la nuit* abounds in character and colour. The remastered recordings (the concerto comes from 1967, *Gaspard* from 1975) sound first class. The reissue is rightly part of DG's 'Originals' series of 'Legendary Recordings'.

The performances of both *Concertos* by Philip Fowke with Baudo and the LPO are particularly attractive in the way they bring out the jazzy side of Ravel's inspiration, treating the misplaced accents and syncopations less strictly than some, but with winning results. In the slow movement of the *G major Concerto* the Spanish overtones also come out strongly, and Fowke's solo playing in the *Valses nobles et sentimentales* is clean, bright and rhythmic in a muscular way, without ever becoming brutal or unfeeling; nor does he lack poetry. Baudo and the orchestra also give a strongly characterized reading of *La valse*, brisker than some, with waltz rhythms powerfully inflected. Excellent 1988 recording, made in St Augustine's, Kilburn, vivid and attractively atmospheric; this disc and tape are irresistible at bargain price.

Pascal Rogé brings both delicacy and sparkle to the *G major Concerto*, which he gives with his characteristic musical grace and fluency. He brings great poetry and tenderness to the slow movement; but in the *Left-hand concerto* he is a good deal less dynamic, even though there is much to admire in the way of pianistic finesse – and charm. The Decca recording offers excellent performances of three short orchestral pieces as a makeweight.

With persuasively alive and perceptively detailed support from Zander and his excellent Boston Orchestra, and a warm, naturally balanced recording, Stephen Drury gives an appealingly intimate account of the *G major Concerto*, one in which vividness and delicacy of feeling are nicely balanced. The slow movement is tender and gentle, to contrast with the dazzling finale – uninhibited, yet carefully controlled so that there is poise as well as exhilaration. The 'live' recording is naturally balanced within a most appealing ambience. No wonder there is enthusiastic applause at the close.

Louis Lortie's account of the two *Concertos* on Chandos has the advantage of altogether outstanding recording. In the *G major* he is often highly personal without becoming unduly idiosyncratic, with a fastidious sense of colour at his command. In the *Left-hand concerto* he really takes his time over the cadenzas and his agogic hesitations are sometimes over-indulgent. Immaculate playing as such, and superb recording.

Samson François has good analogue sound in his favour (his two recordings were made in the Salle Wagram in 1959 and 1967, respectively), and good playing from the Paris Conservatoire Orchestra under Cluytens. But the choice of this pairing for EMI's 'Great recordings of the century' series is surely misguided, however much affection the French may feel for the soloist. Especially so when Michelangeli's incandescent account of the *G major concerto* was readily available to fill this role. François was not always a particularly sensitive player and there is little to recommend in his efficient but prosaic performance of one of Ravel's most magical works. Fortunately his spirited account of the *Left-hand Concerto* is much more competitive, although it would have been more so at Classics-for-Pleasure price, which was the format for the LP. The piano is forwardly balanced, but not at the expense of orchestral detail.

(i) *Piano concerto in G; Piano concerto for the left hand in D. A la manière de Borodine; A la manière de Chabrier; Gaspard de la nuit; Jeux d'eau; Menuet antique; Menuet sur le nom de Haydn; Miroirs; Pavane pour une infante défunte; Prélude; Sonatine; Le tombeau de Couperin; Valses nobles et sentimentales.*
(B) **(*) Ph. Duo 438 353-2 (2) [id.]. Werner Haas; (i) Monte-Carlo Opéra O, Galliera.

This well-recorded pair of CDs offers virtually all Ravel's piano music at a bargain price. Werner Haas has a genuine Ravel sensibility and he plays with delicacy and a fine feeling for the music's colour and its moments of gentle rapture. The performances of the two *Concertos* match the rest, refined and satisfying. Perhaps the playing here is a little strait-laced (elsewhere Haas is often pleasingly flexible) but Galliera's fine accompaniments add to the authority of these performances, and the 1968 recording is well balanced. These are performances one could live with.

Piano concerto for the left hand in D.
(BB) *** ASV Quicksilva Dig. CDQS 6092. Osorio, RPO, Bátiz – FRANCK: *Symphonic variations* **(*); SAINT-SAENS: *Wedding-cake* ***; SCHUMANN: *Concerto.* ***
*** Sony Dig. SK 47188 [id.]. Fleisher, Boston SO, Ozawa – BRITTEN: *Diversions;* PROKOFIEV: *Concerto No. 4.* ***

Jorge Federico Osorio's account of the *Left-hand concerto* can hold its own with the best and it is very well recorded. With its tempting couplings, about which there are only minor reservations, this disc is a genuine bargain. He also gives a crisp and colourful performance of the *Alborada* in an alternative, full-price coupling with Prokofiev.

Leon Fleisher's account of the Ravel *Concerto for the left hand* is strongly characterized and full of life and colour. Apart from its general artistic excellence, the strength of his CD also lies in the interest of the coupling. All three works share a common origin in that they were commissioned by the one-armed Austrian pianist, Paul Wittgenstein. Fleisher's account of the Ravel deserves to rank high among current recommendations, and choice will inevitably depend upon couplings. Both the orchestral support and the Sony recording are very good indeed.

(i) *Piano concerto for the left hand.* (ii) *Berceuse sur le nom de Gabriel Fauré, A la manière de Chabrier; A la manière de Chabrier; Gaspard de la nuit*; (ii) *Habanera. Jeux d'eau; Menuet antique; Menuet sur le nom de Haydn*; (ii) *Ma Mère l'Oye. Miroirs; Pavane pour un infante défunte; Prélude in A min.; Sonatine; Le tombeau de Couperin; Valses nobles et sentimentales.*
(N) (**) Sony mono MH2K 63316 (2) [id.]. Robert Casadesus; with (i) Phd. O, Ormandy; (ii) Gaby Casadesus.

In his day Robert Casadesus was a great exponent of this repertoire and these mono recordings were eagerly sought after by collectors, despite their rather two-dimensional sound. They come mostly from 1951 (although the concerto dates from 1947 and the *Berceuse* a year earlier) and have been cleanly remastered. Returning to the set proved something of a disappointment. The performances are as authoritative and sure-fingured, of course, and in *Miroirs* one admires the crystalline clarity of the *Noctuelles* and *Une barque sur l'ocean*, but the special qualities with which the memory invested them are curiously elusive. The *Left hand concerto* remains impressive, in spite of indifferent recording, partly because of Ormandy, but unlike the best of the Casadesus Mozart concertos, which hold up very well in their CD incarnation, these solo Ravel performances strike one as less remarkable than they had once seemed. There are some fine moments, of course, notably in the *Valses nobles et sentimentales*, while the *Toccata* from *Le tombeau de Couperin* is special. Other pieces are less sensitive: *Jeux d'eau* and even *Gaspard de la nuit* find him less responsive to dynamic nuance, a shade routine, and the *Sonatine* is quite offhand. The pianism is sometimes less than subtle, and the unexpansive, colourless studio and relatively compressed range of dynamics do not do Casadesus full justice. The set is attractively presented and well documented, but this has the drawback of taking it outside the mid-price range.

Daphnis et Chloé (ballet; complete).
✽ (M) *** RCA 09026 61846-2 [id.]. New England Conservatory & Alumni Ch., Boston SO, Munch.
*** Decca (IMS) Dig. 443 934-2 [id.]. Het Groot Ch., Conc. O, Chailly – DEBUSSY: *Khamma.* ***
(N) *** Testament SBT 1128 [id.]. Choeurs René Duclos, Paris Conservatoire O, André Cluytens – FRANCK: *Psyché.* (***)
(N) (BB) ** Arte Nova Dig. 74321 63641-2 [id.]. Europa Akademie Ch., SWR SO, Michael Gielen.

(i) *Daphnis et Chloé* (ballet; complete); *Alborada del gracioso; Boléro.*
(M) **(*) DG Dig. 445 519-2 [id.]. LSO, Abbado; (i) with L. Symphony Ch.

Daphnis et Chloé (complete); *Boléro.*
(B) *** [EMI Red Line Dig. CDR5 69830]. CBSO & Ch., Rattle.

Daphnis et Chloé (complete); *Pavane pour une infante défunte; Rapsodie espagnole.*
(M) *** Decca 448 603-2 [id.]. ROHCG Ch., LSO, Pierre Monteux.

Daphnis et Chloé (complete); *Pavane pour une défunte; La valse.*
(M) *** Decca Legends Dig. 458 605-2. Montreal SO & Cho., Dutoit.

(i) *Daphnis et Chloé* (ballet; complete); (ii) *Shéhérazade.*
(M) **(*) Sony SMK 47604 (i) Schola Cant., NYPO; (ii) Horne, Fr. Nat. R. O; Bernstein.

Speaking of his ballet score, *Daphnis and Chloé*, Ravel once described it as 'a vast musical fresco, loyal to my visionary Greece, which is fairly close to the Greece imagined and depicted by French painters at the end of the eighteenth century'. Ravel also told Pierre Leroi that he would like to die lulled in the tender and voluptuous embrace of Debussy's *Prélude à l'après-midi d'un faune*, this 'unique miracle in all of music'. One can only say that *Daphnis* is hardly less miraculous and hope that the strains of *Lever du jour* greeted his entry into the next world – for its inspiration is nothing if not heavenly.

Charles Munch's Boston account is one of the great glories of the 1950s. The playing in all departments of the Boston orchestra is simply electrifying. The sound here may not be as sumptuous as the Dutoit on Decca, but the richness of colour lies in the playing, and there is a heady sense of intoxication that at times sweeps you off your feet, and the integration of the chorus is impressively managed. Try the *Danse de supplication de Chloé* (track 15) and the ensuing scene in which the pirates are put to flight, and you will get a good idea of how dazzling this is, with the ballet ending in tumultous orchestral virtuosity.

Dutoit adopts an idiomatic and flexible style, observing the minute indications of tempo change but making every slight variation sound totally spontaneous. The final *Danse générale* finds him adopting a dangerously fast tempo, but the Montreal players – combining French responsiveness with transatlantic polish – rise superbly to the challenge, with the choral punctuations at the end adding to the sense of frenzy. The digital recording is wonderfully luminous, with the chorus ideally balanced at an evocative half-distance, fully worthy of Decca's Legends series. The CD is now generously cued.

Monteux conducted the first performance of *Daphnis et Chloé* in 1912; Decca's 1959 recording, a demonstration disc in its day, captured his poetic and subtly shaded reading in vivid colours in the most agreeably warm ambience. The performance was one of the finest things Monteux did for the gramophone. Decca have added his 1962 recording of the *Pavane*, wonderfully poised and played most beautifully, and the highly spontaneous *Rapsodie espagnole*. A worthy addition to the Classic Sound series.

Riccardo Chailly conducts a remarkably fine *Daphnis*. Perhaps the last ounce of magic is missing, but there is plenty of colour and no lack of atmosphere. The excellence of the orchestral playing can be taken for granted, and the same goes for the luminous Decca recording, perhaps the finest the work has received. Not necessarily a first recommendation, but a choice that is unlikely to disappoint.

With André Cluytens's 1962 version with the Paris Conservatoire Orchestra you are confronted with the orchestral tradition that Ravel himself would have known (including the saxophone-like horns, and the sweet-sour, almost scented woodwind), and although the orchestral virtuosity in Paris is no match for, say, the 1955 Boston Symphony Orchestra under Charles Münch or the 1958 Monteux and the LSO, they have a voluptuousness all their own. The *Danse de Pan* is wonderfully atmospheric (and marvellously played) and the stereo recording beautifully open and natural. This was before the days when naturalness became a casualty in the engineers desire to astonish us with *their* own brilliance.

Simon Rattle conducts the CBSO in a most warmly expressive reading of Ravel's great ballet score. The moulding of phrase and subtle flexibility of rubato bear tribute not only to his feeling for Ravel but to the responsiveness of the Birmingham orchestra as well as its fine chorus, trained by Simon Halsey. The sensuous beauty of the slow sequences is enhanced by the mistily evocative recording, though the dynamic range is extreme. Such showpiece numbers as the *Danse guerrière* and the final *Danse générale* have a winning resilience and energy. *Boléro* is relatively slow and easily expressive, not as hard-edged as it can be.

Bernstein's *Daphnis et Chloé* comes with an altogether seductive *Shéhérazade* with Marilyn Horne, one of the most sensuous accounts committed to disc. Bernstein is at his very best here and each movement is characterized to perfection. The sound, too, is very good. Horne's *Shéhérazade* weaves the most erotic tales, and while one is under its spell the claims of the incomparable Suzanne Danco and Régine Crespin are almost (though not quite) forgotten. By comparison, Bernstein's 1961 *Daphnis* is less successful; there are good things, of course – most notably the last part, which comprises the second suite. The sound is a vast improvement on the CBS original – but then it needed to be. In spite of the *Daphnis*, this record is a must.

The brilliant playing of the LSO under Abbado is helped by an exceptionally analytical DG recording which has the widest possible dynamic range – so much so that the *pianissimo* at the very opening is barely audible for almost thirty seconds. For all its refinement and virtuosity, this is a performance to admire rather than love, lacking the atmospheric warmth that marks, say, the Dutoit version.

Gielen, as a twentieth-century specialist, conducts a cleanly disciplined, finely detailed reading, with polished playing from the radio orchestra vividly recorded. Though such numbers as the *Danse guerrière* are brilliantly done, the performance is unidiomatic in such key passages as *Daybreak*, where Gielen's slow, steady pace undermines the thrust of the music. There are no index points, only a single CD track of 58 minutes.

(i; ii) *Daphnis et Chloé* (ballet): *suites Nos. 1–2*; (iii) *Ma Mère l'Oye (Mother Goose) suite;* (i; iv) *La valse;* (i; iv; v) *Shéhérazade* (song-cycle).
❀ (M) *** Dutton Lab. CDK 1201 [id.]. (i) Paris Conservatoire O; (ii) Munch; (iii) Nat. SO, Sidney Beer; (iv) Ansermet; (v) with Suzanne Danco.

Despite an apology about the opening – 'Noise at start of Track 1 as original master' – the detail and depth of focus of the early *ffrr* 78 recording for *Daphnis* are remarkable, with *Daybreak* matching later Munch readings in warmth – indeed its sense of ecstasy has never been surpassed on disc – and with the final *Danse générale* given tremendous thrust. The recording was made at Walthamstow in October 1946, and *La valse* under Ansermet at Kingsway Hall followed a year later. The sound is fuller in bass with even greater clarity, but under Ansermet the ensemble is rougher in a work that cries out for virtuoso treatment. Ansermet is far stronger in *Shéhérazade*, recorded with the same orchestra in Paris in May 1948. With the bright-toned, very French-sounding Danco enunciating the text to bring out every word, it is a taut and purposeful rather than an atmospheric reading, but it still has a flavour all its own. The conductor in *Ma Mere l'Oye* is Sidney Beer, with the orchestra he himself assembled from among London's leading players of the time, many still in the armed forces. Though he sounds rather matter-of-fact at the start after Munch or Ansermet, there is plenty of charm later, with excellent solo work and with the final *Le jardin féerique* rapt in concentration. This Kingsway Hall recording is so luminous that one can hardly believe it is mono, or that the uncannily present and vivid transfers are made direct from 78 shellac discs dating from 1945. The Rosette, however, is for Munch's *Daphnis et Chloé*.

Daphnis et Chloé: suite No. 2.

(M) *** Decca Phase Four 455 152-2 [id.]. L. Symphony Ch., LSO, Stokowski – DEBUSSY: *La Mer* etc. ***

Stokowski's Phase Four version comes from 1969 and was recorded in the Kingsway Hall to impressive effect. He secures a glowing performance with sumptuous playing, and the multi-channel technique is used to produce exactly the right disembodied, ethereal effect for the off-stage chorus. It is true that the close balance highlights some of the woodwind bird-noises excessively, but with the chorus the pervading presence is richly satisfying. Stokowski takes the choral parts from the complete ballet rather than the usual *Suite No. 2*. He adds a fortissimo chord at the very end, but after such an involving performance few will begrudge him that.

Daphnis et Chloé: suite No. 2; Pavane pour une infante défunte.

(***) Testament mono SBT1017 [id.]. Philh. O, Cantelli – CASELLA: *Paganiniana;* DUKAS: *L'apprenti sorcier;* FALLA: *Three-cornered hat.* (***)

Cantelli's account of *Daphnis* was among his last – and finest – records. It sounds remarkably good in this splendid transfer. Along with Koussevitzky, Ormandy and Karajan, this has classic status.

(i) *Introduction and allegro for harp, flute, clarinet and strings* (orchestral version); (ii) *Ma Mère l'Oye* (ballet suite); (iii) *Pavane pour une infante défunte;* (iv) *La valse.*

(B) *** Sony SBK 63056 [id.]. (i) Cleveland O, Louis Lane; (ii) Philh. O, Tilson Thomas; (iii) Cleveland O, Szell; (iv) Phd. O, Ormandy – DEBUSSY: *Petite suite;* SATIE: *Gymnopédies Nos. 1 & 3.* ***

This is a first-class anthology which gives great satisfaction. The orchestral version of Ravel's haunting *Introduction and allegro* is less delicately textured than the chamber version, but as played by the splendid Cleveland Orchestra under Louis Lane it does not lose its magic or its refinement of feeling. The 1969 recording is not too forwardly balanced. Michael Tilson Thomas is wholly attuned to the sensibility of Ravel's ravishing *Ma Mère l'Oye*. This is a highly seductive performance, glowingly played and lustrously recorded (digitally in 1988). Szell takes over the Cleveland podium for the *Pavane*, which brings more first-class playing, particularly from the orchestra's principal horn. Finally Ormandy and the Philadelphia Orchestra give a sensuous, exciting, bravura account of *La valse*, with the 1963 sound suitably spacious and with plenty of atmosphere.

Ma Mère l'Oye (complete ballet).

(N) (M)*** Philips Virtuoso 462 938-2. Pittsburgh SO, Previn – SAINT-SAENS: *Carnival of the animals*; DUKAS: *L'apprenti sorcier*; Rotterdam PO, Zinman. ***

Ma Mère l'Oye - suite.

(M) *** Mercury (IMS) 434 343-2 [id.]. Detroit SO, Paray – DEBUSSY: *Ibéria* etc. ***

(B) *** CfP CD-CFP 4086. SNO, Gibson – BIZET: *Jeux d'enfants;* SAINT-SAENS; *Carnival.* ***

Ma Mère l'Oye - suite; *Rapsodie espagnole.*

(M) *** DG (IMS) 415 844-2. LAPO, Giulini – MUSSORGSKY: *Pictures.* ***

In Previn's version, played and recorded with consummate refinement, the quality of innocence shines out. The recording is superb, with the Philips engineers presenting a texture of luminous clarity. Now at bargain price this is very competitive indeed, particularly as Philips have added Zinman's attractive version of Dukas's narrative masterpiece.

Paray's gently evocative *Ma Mère l'Oye* is most beautifully played and recorded. The score's calm innocence with its undercurrent of quiet ecstasy is caught perfectly. So lustrous is the sound that it is almost impossible to believe the early recording date: 1957.

The Giulini Los Angeles performance conveys much of the sultry atmosphere of the *Rapsodie espagnole*. Indeed some details, such as the sensuous string responses to the cor anglais tune in the *Feria*, have not been so tenderly caressed since the intoxicating Reiner version. The *Ma Mère l'Oye* suite is also sensitively done; though it is cooler, it is still beautiful.

Gibson is highly persuasive, shaping the music with obvious affection and a feeling for both the innocent spirit and the radiant textures of Ravel's beautiful score. The orchestral playing is excellent and, with excellent couplings, this is very recommendable.

Ma Mère l'Oye (ballet): *suite* (with narration).
(N) (BB) *** Naxos Dig. 8.554463 [id.]. Johnny Morris (nar.), Slovak RSO, Kenneth Jean – DUKAS: *L'apprenti sorcier*; SAINT-SAENS: *Carnival of the animals* **(*).

Ma Mère l'Oye is exquisite music and it is most beautifully played by the Slovak orchestra under Kenneth Jean. Johnny Morris provides a friendly spoken introduction for each fairy-tale number which has been admirably and concisely written by Keith and Anthony Anderson. To link them with Ravel's music is surely a marvellous way of familiarizing younger children with the music.

Tzigane (for violin and orchestra).
(M) *** EMI (SIS) CDM5 66058-2. Itzhak Perlman, O de Paris, Barenboim – SAINT-SAENS: *Havanaise;* VIEUXTEMPS: *Violin concertos Nos. 4 & 5.* ***
*** EMI (SIS) Dig. CDC7 47725-2 [id.]. Perlman, O de Paris, Martinon – CHAUSSON: *Poème;* SAINT-SAENS: *Havanaise* etc. ***
(M) *** DG Dig. 447 445-2 [id.]. Itzhak Perlman, NYPO, Mehta – BERG; STRAVINSKY: *Concertos.* ***
(M) *** Decca Dig. 460 007-2. Kyung Wha Chung, RPO, Dutoit – LALO: *Symphonie espagnole;* VIEUXTEMPS: *Violin concerto No. 5.* ***
(N) (B) **(*) Ph. 420 887-2. Szeryng, Monte Carlo Op. O, Remoortel – SAINT-SAENS: *Violin concerto No. 3* etc. **(*)

Perlman's classic (1974) account of Ravel's *Tzigane* for EMI is marvellously played; the added projection of the CD puts the soloist believably at the end of the living room. The opulence of his tone is undiminished by the remastering process and the orchestral sound retains its atmosphere, while gaining in clarity. As can be seen this is offered on alternative couplings.

Perlman's later digital version is very fine and the recording is obviously modern. But the earlier, EMI performance has just that bit more charisma.

With its seemingly improvisatory solo introduction, *Tzigane* is a work which demands an inspirational artist, and Kyung Wha Chung is ideally cast, catching the atmosphere of this elusive piece with natural affinity.

Szeryng was at the height of his powers when he recorded this splendidly strong and committed account of Ravel's *Tzigane*, flexible and responsive as well as brilliant in execution. The recording spotlights him so that the rather less distinguished orchestral contribution, well enough held together by Eduard van Remoortel, emerges less strongly. However, the current remastering does somewhat improve the orchestral profile.

Valses nobles et sentimentales.
(*) DG (IMS) Dig. 429 785-2 [id.]. NYPO, Sinopoli – MUSSORGSKY: *Night* etc. *

With Sinopoli Ravel's *Valses nobles et sentimentales* is perhaps a shade too idiosyncratic, even though it is played superbly by the New York Philharmonic.

CHAMBER MUSIC

Berceuse; Pièce en forme de habañera; Tzigane.
*** DG Dig. 445 880-2. Dumay, Pires – DEBUSSY; FRANCK: *Violin sonatas.* ***

Polished and elegant performances of these Ravel pieces. There would, of course, have been room on this disc for the 1922 *Sonata*, which at premium price would have made better sense as well as value for money. However, no complaints about these performances or the recording quality.

Introduction and allegro for harp, flute, clarinet and string quartet.
✿ (M) *** Decca 452 891-2. Osian Ellis, Melos Ens. – DEBUSSY: *Sonata*; ROUSSEL: *Sérénade*; ROPARTZ: *Prélude, marini et chansons.* *** ✿
(***) Testament mono SBT 1053 [id.]. Gleghorn, Lurie, Stockton, Hollywood Qt – CRESTON: *Quartet;* DEBUSSY: *Danse sacrée* etc. TURINA: *La Oración del torero;* VILLA-LOBOS: *Quartet No. 6.* (***)

The beauty and subtlety of Ravel's sublime septet are marvellously realized by this 1962 Melos account. The interpretation has great delicacy of feeling, and the recording hardly shows its age at all. A superb disc in every way.

The Hollywood Quartet's version of the *Introduction and allegro* gives us an example of the exquisite flute playing of Arthur Gleghorn as well as the artistry of Mitchell Lurie and Ann Mason Stockton. A fine performance, sounding remarkably fresh for a 1951 recording.

(i) *Introduction and allegro;* (ii) *Pièce en forme de habañera.*
(B) *** Cala Dig. CACD 1018 (2) [id.]. James Campbell; (i) William Bennett, Ieuan Jones, Allegri Qt; (ii) John York – POULENC: *L'invitation au château* etc. ***

These Cala performances are recommendable in their own right, but they come in a particularly valuable two-CD set for the price of one, which includes over two hours of music for wind instruments by Poulenc. It is sheer delight from start to finish and cannot be too strongly recommended.

Piano trio in A min.

*** Ph. (IMS) Dig. 411 141-2. Beaux Arts Trio – CHAUSSON: *Piano trio.* ***

*** Chandos Dig. CHAN 8458 [id.]. Borodin Trio – DEBUSSY: *Violin and Cello sonatas.* ***

(BB) **(*) Naxos Dig. 8.550934 [id.]. Joachim Trio – DEBUSSY: *Piano trio in G;* SCHMITT: *Piano trio: Très lent.* **(*)

The most recent Beaux Arts account of the Ravel *Trio* is little short of inspired and is even finer than their earlier record of the late 1960s. The recording, too, is of high quality, even if the piano is rather forward.

The Borodin Trio are excellently recorded and their playing has great warmth and is full of colour. Some may find them too hot-blooded by the side of the Beaux Arts.

The Naxos version by the Joachim Trio who comprise Rebecca Hirsch, Caroline Dearnley and the pianist John Lenehan is worth any collector's notice. They play with sensitive musicianship and finesse. Their performance is imaginative and beautifully recorded, and it is far from uncompetitive.

Piano trio in A min.; Sonata for violin and cello; (i) *Chansons madécasses; 3 Poèmes de Stéphane Mallarmé* (song-cycle).

(BB) **(*) Virgin Classics Double Dig. VBD5 61427-2 (2) [CDVB 61427]. Nash Ens. (members), (i) with Sarah Walker – DEBUSSY: *Chamber music.* **

The Virgin anthology offers a very good introduction to the less familiar Ravel, if you exclude the *Piano trio*. The *Sonata for violin and cello* is expertly played by Marcia Crayford and Christopher van Kampen – as good an account as any – and in the *Piano trio* Ian Brown joins them in a performance of real stature and eloquence. In the *Chansons madécasses* and the exquisite *Trois poèmes de Stéphane Mallarmé* Sarah Walker is *primus inter pares* rather than a soloist, though she is not balanced as reticently by Andrew Keener's team as is Delphine Seyrig in the Debussy *Chansons de Bilitis*. This is a pity, but it is not an insuperable obstacle to an apt and inexpensive Ravel coupling.

(i) *Piano trio in A min.;* (ii) *String quartet in F;* (iii) *Violin sonata in G.*

(M) **(*) Ph. 454 134-2. (i) Beaux Arts Trio; (ii) Italian Qt; (iii) Grumiaux, Hajdu.

Ravel's *String quartet* usually comes in harness with the Debussy *Quartet*; here it is offered as part of a triptych of Ravel's key chamber-works. The performance by the Quartetto Italiano has long been praised by us. The Beaux Arts give a predictably fine account of the *Trio*, though the violinist, Daniel Guilet is a shade wanting in charm. In the *Violin sonata* Grumiaux's playing has great finesse and beauty of sound. The recordings date from 1966 and are very naturally balanced, but the CD transfer demonstrates their age by a degree of shrillness of the fortissimo string-timbre.

String quartet in F.

✿ *** Koch Dig. 3-6436-2 [id.]. Medici Qt – BRITTEN: *Quartet No. 3;* JANACEK: *Quartet No. 1;* SHOSTAKOVICH: *Quartet No. 8;* SMETANA: *Quartet No. 1.* ***

*** DG (IMS) Dig. 437 836-2 [id.]. Hagen Qt – DEBUSSY; WEBERN: *Quartets.* ***

*** Sony Dig. SK 52554 [id.]. Juilliard Qt – DEBUSSY; DUTILLEUX: *Quartets.* ***

(B) *** Ph. 420 894-2. Italian Qt – DEBUSSY: *Quartet.* ***

(B) *** CfP Dig. CD-CFP 4652. Chilingirian Qt – DEBUSSY: *Quartet.* ***

(*) ASV Dig. CDDCA 930 [id.]. Lindsay Qt – DEBUSSY: *String quartet* **(*); STRAVINSKY: *3 Pieces.* *

(B) **(*) Discover Dig. DICD 920171 [id.]. Sharon Qt – BEETHOVEN: *Harp quartet* **(*); MOZART: *Quartet No. 1.* ***

(B) **(*) Sony SBK 62413 [id.]. Tokyo Qt – DEBUSSY: *Quartet* **(*); FAURE: *Piano trio.* (*)

String quartet in F; (i) *Introduction & allegro for harp, flute, clarinet and string quartet.*

(BB) *** Naxos Dig. 8.550249 [id.]. Kodály Qt, (i) with Maros, Gyöngyössy, Kovács – DEBUSSY: *Quartet.* **(*)

**(*) RCA Dig. 09026 62552-2 [id.]. Tokyo Qt, (i) with Galway, Stolzman, Lehwalder – DEBUSSY: *Quartet.* **(*)

In the hands of the Medici players the opening of the Ravel *Quartet* is utterly magical, its subtlety of atmosphere and gentle radiance caught with a perfection rare in the concert hall, let alone on record. This is a great performance of a masterly work, for the *Assez vif – très rhythmé* brings comparable finesse and concentration, while the stillness at the opening of the *Très lent* make one hold one's breath at the music's *tendresse*. The recording is completely tangible: it is as if these players were at the end of one's room.

The equally impressive Hagen Quartet, by adding the Webern, are perhaps even more competitive They give a performance of great finesse and tonal refinement, and are beautifully recorded to boot, very well served by an excellent balance from one of DG's best engineers, Wolfgang Mitelehner.

The Juilliard are very impressive too, not quite so youthful, elegant and fresh in their approach but eminently polished and sensitive. This Sony disc is to be recommended primarily to those attracted to the fine Dutilleux bonus. However, the earlier (and less expensive) versions remain very competitive.

For many years the Italian Quartet held pride of place in this coupling. Their playing is perfect in ensemble, attack and beauty of tone, and their performance remains highly recommendable, one of the most satisfying chamber-music records in the catalogue.

The Chilingirian recording has plenty of body and presence, and also has the benefit of a warm acoustic. The players give a thoroughly committed account, with well-judged tempi and very musical phrasing. The Scherzo is vital and spirited, and there is no want of poetry in the slow movement. At mid-price this is fully competitive and the sound is preferable to that of the Italian Quartet on Philips.

The Naxos version can more than hold its own. Artistically and technically this is a satisfying performance which has the feel of real live music-making. The *Introduction and allegro* is not as magical or as atmospheric as that of the Melos Ensemble from the 1960s, nor is it as well balanced (the players, save for the harp, are a bit forward), but it is still thoroughly enjoyable.

The Tokyo Quartet are equally impressive on RCA, and although their performance is not entirely free from some self-regarding touches its tonal finesse is a joy in itself. In the *Introduction and allegro*, the balance tends to favour Galway, to put it mildly, and there is at times a danger of it becoming a flute concerto!

A highly accomplished and finely etched performance from the Lindsays, who play with their usual aplomb and panache. There are splendid things here, notably the youthful fire of the opening movement and the vivid finale. They do not always match the poetic feeling and the *douceur* which some rivals find, but this is not a neglible account, and it is well recorded.

The Sharon Quartet are completely at home in this music and play with ardour and sensitivity. The resonant acoustic (a Cologne church) suits the work better than the Beethoven coupling. It certainly does not cloud the Scherzo or the energetic account of the finale (which also has much delicacy of feeling) and adds warmth and atmosphere to the *très lent*. Very good playing: if the couplings are suitable, this is a bargain.

The Tokyo Quartet on Sony play with great finesse and tonal beauty, especially in the warm yet refined account of the *très lent*. They certainly observe the marking of the finale, *vif et agité* and perhaps elsewhere there could be a touch more poise. But their music-making is thoroughly alive. The sound is very good.

Violin sonata in G.
*** Virgin/EMI Dig. VC5 45122-2. Tetzlaff, Andsnes – DEBUSSY: *Sonata;* JANACEK: *Sonata;* NIELSEN: *Sonata No. 2*. ***
(M) *** DG (IMS) Dig. 445 557-2. Shlomo Mintz, Yefim Bronfman – PROKOFIEV: *Violin sonatas*. ***
*** Erato/Warner Dig. 0630 15110-2. Vadim Repin, Boris Berezovsky – MEDTNER: *Sonata No. 3 (Sonata epica)*. ***

Violin sonata; Tzigane.
(B) *** EMI Eminence Dig. CD-EMX 2244. Tasmin Little, Piers Lane – DEBUSSY; POULENC: *Violin sonatas*. ***

(i; ii) *Violin sonata (1897); Violin sonata in G;* (i; iii) *Sonata for violin and cello;* (i; ii) *Berceuse sur le nom de Gabriel Fauré; Kaddish; Pièce en forme de habanera; Tzigane.*
*** Decca Dig. 448 612-2. (i) Chantal Juillet; (ii) Pascal Rogé; (iii) Truls Mørk.

Violin sonata (1897); Violin sonata in G; Tzigane; Berceuse sur le nom de Gabriel Fauré.
*** Sony Dig. SK 66839 [id.]. Cho-Liang Lin, Paul Crossley – DEBUSSY; POULENC: *Violin sonatas*. ***

The Ravel *Violin sonata* has come into its own in recent years. The performance from Christian Tetzlaff and Leif Ove Andsnes proves as characterful and imaginative as any available, and an additional attraction is the interest of the couplings, in particular the Nielsen *Second Sonata*. Excellent recording too.

Shlomo Mintz and Yefim Bronfman's account offers highly polished playing, even if it is not so completely inside Ravel's world in the slow movement. The glorious sounds both artists produce are a source of unfailing delight and they are beautifully recorded too. At mid-price, coupled with outstanding versions of the two Prokofiev *Sonatas*, this is very recommendable.

But the Sony issue is if anything even more competitively coupled, for it offers very good value in terms of playing time and, more importantly, artistic satisfaction. Cho-Liang Lin plays with his usual effortless virtuosity and impeccable taste, and he is well supported by Paul Crossley. The early (1897) *Sonata* has rarely sounded more captivating. Sony provide these artists with exemplary recorded sound.

The Decca is an all-Ravel record and, in addition to the two *Sonatas*, gives us the *Tzigane*, a handful of other shorter pieces and the *Sonata for violin and cello*. Chantal Juillet and Pascal Rogé present a *Tzigane* with a difference in that Rogé uses a piano luthenal (an instrument modified to sound like a cimbalom, which was used in the first performance in 1922) and Juillet sounds more zigeuner-like than most of her rivals. Their accounts of the two *Sonatas* are predictably cultured and (equally unsurprisingly) beautifully recorded. Pascal Rogé scores over Cho-Liang Lin's partner in terms of sheer responsiveness, and Chantal Juillet and Truls Mørk are first rate in the *Duo sonata*. Strongly recommended, if this programme is suitable.

In their well-designed collection of violin-and-piano music, Tasmin Little and Piers Lane give outstanding performances, very well recorded, aptly and subtly changing style for each composer, equally bringing out the contrast of tone in the two

Ravel works here, the *Sonata* fleeting and elusive, the *Tzigane* more rhetorical and extrovert. Pointing of rhythm could hardly be more persuasive, with Little relishing the colour-changes in the central Blues movement of the *Sonata*. Excellent sound.

Vadim Repin and Boris Berezovsky on Erato offer an unusual coupling though it is difficult to see what Ravel and Medtner have in common. These two artists command a wide range of colour and dynamics, infuse every phrase with life, and have the full measure of the 'Blues' movement. Repin plays the Guarneri with which Isaac Stern delighted us for almost half a century and it sounds magnificently responsive in his hands. Very good and completely natural recording.

PIANO MUSIC

Piano duet

Boléro; Introduction and allegro; Ma Mère l'Oye; Rapsodie espagnole; La valse.
❀ *** Chandos Dig. CHAN 8905 [id.]. Louis Lortie and Hélène Mercier.

Lortie's recital for piano (four hands and two pianos) with his Canadian partner, Hélène Mercier, is quite magical; these artists command an exceptionally wide range of colour and dynamic nuance. The acoustic is that of The Maltings, Snape, and the result is quite outstanding sonically: you feel that you have only to stretch out and you can touch the instruments. Ravel's transcriptions are stunningly effective in their hands, even, surprisingly, *Boléro*.

Ma Mère l'Oye.
*** Ph. (IMS) Dig. 420 159-2. Katia and Marielle Labèque – FAURE: *Dolly;* BIZET: *Jeux d'enfants.* ***

The Labèque sisters give an altogether delightful performance of Ravel's magical score, which he later orchestrated and expanded. The recording could not be more realistic and present.

Solo piano music

Complete solo piano works: *A la manière de Borodine; A la manière de Chabrier; Gaspard de la nuit; Jeux d'eau; Menuet antique; Menuet sur le nom de Haydn; Miroirs; Pavane pour une enfante défunte; Prélude; Sérénade grotesque; Sonatine; Le tombeau de Couperin; La valse; Valses nobles et sentimentales.* (i) *Sites auriculaires; Ma mère l'Oye* (i–ii) *Frontispièce.*
(B) *** EMI CES5 72376-2 (3). Jean-Philippe Collard, with (i) Michel Béroff; (ii) Katia Labèque – DEBUSSY: *En blanc et noir* etc. ***

Jean-Philippe Collard is arguably the greatest French pianist of his generation and his Ravel playing never falls below distinction. The recordings were made between 1977 and 1980. What a beautiful sense of line he achieves in *Ondine*, the first of the *Gaspard de la nuit*, though it must be admitted that the right-hand ostinato is far from the *pianopianissimo* which Ravel marks. The recording, made in the Salle Wagram, is not wholly sympathetic; there is a glassy, shallow quality, particularly in the upper part of the spectrum.

A la manière de Borodine; A la manière de Chabrier; Gaspard de la nuit; Jeux d'eau; Menuet antique; Menuet sur le nom de Haydn; Miroirs; Pavane pour une infante défunte; Prélude; Sérénade grotesque; Sonatine; Le tombeau de Couperin; Valses nobles et sentimentales.
*** Decca Dig. 433 515-2 (2). Jean-Yves Thibaudet.
*** CRD Dig. CRD 3383/4; *CRDC 4083/5* [id.]. Paul Crossley.
(M) *** Chandos Dig. CHAN 7004/5 [id.]. Louis Lortie.
(N) (BB) **(*) Virgin Classics Double Dig. VBD5 61489-2 (2) [CDVB 61489]. Anne Queffélec.

Jean-Yves Thibaudet's collected Ravel has won golden opinions everywhere, for this is quite outstanding playing on all counts; Thibaudet exhibits flawless technique, perfect control, refinement of touch and exemplary taste. He distils just the right atmosphere in *Oiseaux tristes* and *Une barque sur l'océan* – but then, one might as well choose any other piece from *Miroirs*, and his *Gaspard* can hold its own with any in the catalogue. The recording is of real distinction too.

Paul Crossley's accounts of all these works are beautifully fashioned. He is aristocratic, with an admirable feeling for tone-colour and line, and rarely mannered (the end of *Jeux d'eau* is an exception). His version of *Le tombeau de Couperin* has a classical refinement and delicacy that are refreshing. The CRD recording is very good indeed.

Chandos have now put Louis Lortie's two Ravel discs together. The first, including *Le tombeau de Couperin*, *Jeux d'eau*, *La valse* and the *Valses nobles et sentimentales*, was warmly welcomed in our 1992 edition and we found his *Gaspard de la nuit* with its chilling and atmospheric account of *Le gibet* particularly impressive. Now that these are repackaged at mid-price, let us hope that they will gain the wider dissemination to which their merits entitle them. The Chandos sound, which emanates from The Maltings, Snape, is very realistic and truthful.

No quarrels with Anne Queffélec's playing, which is alert, intelligent and vital, as one would expect from so excellent a stylist. There are some masterly and enjoyable interpretations here, but it is all far too closely observed, as if one were in the front row of the concert hall; as a result not all the atmosphere registers to full effect, once the dynamics rise above *mf*. However this has been very inexpensively reissued on a Virgin Double (two discs for the cost of one medium-priced CD) and is now the least expensive way of collecting a complete survey of the solo piano music in really distinguished performances.

A la manière de Borodine; A la manière de Chabrier; Menuet antique; Menuet sur le nom de Haydn; Miroirs; Pavane pour une infante défunte; Prélude; Sérénade grotesque; Sonatine.
**(*) ASV Dig. CDDCA 809 [id.]. Gordon Fergus-Thompson.

Gaspard de la nuit; Jeux d'eau; Le tombeau de Couperin; Valses nobles at sentimentales.
**(*) ASV Dig. CDDCA 805 [id.]. Gordon Fergus-Thompson.

Turning to Gordon Fergus-Thompson's Ravel immediately after Thibaudet is to enter a different imaginative world. There is not quite the same concentration that distinguishes Thibaudet's set, nor quite the same keyboard control. However, there is an ample and rich colour-palette, and he exhibits considerable personality and imagination. Not to be preferred to the Decca set, but readers considering it can be assured that it is very well recorded.

A la manière de Borodine; A la manière de Chabrier; Menuet antique; Prélude; Le tombeau de Couperin; Valses nobles et sentimentales.
**(*) Nimbus NI 5011 [id.]. Vlado Perlemuter.

Gaspard de la nuit; Jeux d'eau; Miroirs; Pavane.
**(*) Nimbus NI 5005 [id.]. Vlado Perlemuter.

Though Perlemuter's technical command is not as complete as it had been, he gives delightful, deeply sympathetic readings; the sense of spontaneity is a joy. There may be Ravel recordings which bring more dazzling virtuoso displays, but none more persuasive. Nimbus's ample room acoustic makes the result naturally atmospheric on CD.

Gaspard de la nuit.
*** DG Dig. 413 363-2 [id.]. Pogorelich – PROKOFIEV: *Sonata No. 6.* ***

Pogorelich's *Gaspard* is out of the ordinary. In *Le gibet*, we are made conscious of the pianist's refinement of tone and colour first, and Ravel's poetic vision afterwards. But for all that, this is piano playing of astonishing quality. The control of colour and nuance in *Scarbo* is dazzling and its eruptive cascades of energy and dramatic fire have one sitting on the edge of one's seat.

VOCAL MUSIC

Mélodies: *Ballade de la Reine; Morte d'Aimer; Canzone italiana; Chanson du rouet; Chanson espagnole; Chanson française; Chanson hébraïque; Chansons madécasses; 5 mélodies populaires grecques; 2 Epigrammes de Clément Marot; 2 Mélodies hébraïques; Don Quichotte à Dulcinée; Un grand sommeil nuit; Les grands vents venus d'outremer; Histoires naturelles; Manteau de fleurs; Noël des jouets; Rêves; Ronsard à son âme; Sainte; Scottish song; Shéhérazade* (complete); *Si morne!; Sur l'herbe; Tripatos; 3 Poèmes de Stéphane Mallarmé; Vocalise en forme de Habanera.*
(B) *** EMI (SIS) Dig. CZS5 69299-2 (2). Norman, Mesplé, Lott, Berganza, Van Dam, Bacquier, Capitole Toulouse O or Paris CO, Plasson; Dalton Baldwin (piano).

With a composer whose expressive range in song-form (or mélodie) might have seemed limited, it is an excellent idea in the EMI set to have six strongly contrasted singers, each given an apt area to cover. So Teresa Berganza as well as singing *Shéhérazade* has two songs inspired by Spain, the *Vocalise in the form of an Habanera* and the *Chanson espagnole* from the set of five *Chants populaires*, each of which is allotted to a different singer. Felicity Lott's *Chanson écossaise* is a rarity, *Ye banks and braes* sung in a convincing Scots accent. For all the shallowness of Mady Mesplé's voice, it works well in the *Mélodies populaires grecques*, while Jessye Norman, rich-toned if not quite as characterful as usual, has the *Chansons madécasses* as well as lesser-known songs. It is the contribution of the two men that provides the sharpest illumination: José van Dam magnificently dark-toned in the *Don Quichotte* songs and the *Mélodies hébraïques* (making *Kaddish* thrillingly powerful in its agony of mourning), while Gabriel Bacquier twinkles in Figaro tones in the point songs. Excellent sound, and the pair of CDs particularly generous (136 minutes) in offering the contents of three LPs and now being offered as an inexpensive Rouge et Noir reissue.

3 Chansons.
*** Ph. Dig. 438 149-2 [id.]. Monteverdi Ch., O Révolutionnaire et Romantique, Gardiner – FAURE: *Requiem;* DEBUSSY; SAINT-SAENS: *Choral songs.* ***

With his superb choir, Gardiner lightly and crisply touches in the wit and humour behind the two outer songs with their sixteenth-century overtones, and he draws out the lyrical beauty of the central one. A welcome addition to the fascinating group of works chosen by Gardiner as coupling for his expressive reading of the Fauré *Requiem*.

(i) *Chansons madécasses;* (ii) *Don Quichotte à Dulcinée; 5 mélodies populaires grêcques;* (iii) *3 poèmes de Stéphane Mallarmé.*
(M) *** Sony SMK 64107 [id.]. (i) Norman, Ens. InterContemporain; (ii) José van Dam; (iii) Jill Gomez; BBC SO, – ROUSSEL: *Symphony No. 3.* **(*)

With three characterful and strongly contrasted soloist's, this collection of Ravel songs with orchestra (including arrangements) makes a delightful mid-priced collection and is especially valuable as the *Don Quichotte* and the *Greek popular songs* are rarely heard in this orchestral form. Van Dam may not be as relaxed here as he was with piano accompaniment but the dark, firm voice is just as impressive. Excellent sound, full and atmospheric, with translations provided; the addition of Boulez's 1975 version of Roussel's *Third Symphony* makes this reissue all the more desirable.

'*Chant d'amour': 4 Chansons populaires; 2 Mélodies hébraïques; Tripatos; Vocalise-étude en forme de Habanera.*
*** Decca Dig. 452 667-2 [id.]. Cecilia Bartoli, Myung-Whun Chung – BIZET; BERLIOZ; DELIBES: *Mélodies*. ***

Cecilia Bartoli is just as much at home in the music of Ravel as she is with the songs of the other composers represented in this outstanding recital of French songs. Myung Whun-Chung, too, proves himself a natural accompanist.

Shéhérazade (song-cycle).
*** Decca 417 813-2. Régine Crespin, SRO, Ansermet (with *Recital of French songs* ***).
(M) **(*) Sony Theta Dig. SMK 60031. Frederica von Stade, Boston SO, Ozawa – BERLIOZ: *Nuits d'été*; DEBUSSY: *La Damoiselle élue*. *(*)

Crespin is right inside these songs and Ravel's magically sensuous music emerges with striking spontaneity. She is superbly supported by Ansermet who, aided by the Decca engineers, weaves a fine tonal web round the voice. Her style has distinct echoes of the opera house; but the richness of the singer's tone does not detract from the delicate languor of *The enchanted flute*, in which the slave-girl listens to the distant sound of her lover's flute playing while her master sleeps.

Ozawa is an experienced and sympathetic advocate of Ravel, and he and the Boston orchestra provide a seductive web of sound for von Stade's beguiling account of this most sensuous of French song-cycles. The centrepiece, *La flûte enchantée*, is particularly ravishing; as the recording is warm and atmospheric, it is a pity that the Berlioz and Debussy couplings are so much less successful.

OPERA

L'enfant et les sortilèges (complete).
✿ (***) Testament mono SBT 1044 [id.]. Nadine Sautereau, André Vessières, Solange Michel, Denise Scharley, Yvon Le Marc'Hadour, Joseph Peyron, Martha Angelici, French Nat. R. Ch. and O, Ernest Bour.

Testament here offer a superlative transfer of the unsurpassed first recording of Ravel's charming one-Acter under Ernest Bour. There is a magic about this performance that completely captivates the listener. Each part, from Nadine Sautereau's Child, Yvon Le Marc'Hadour's Tom-Cat and Clock and Solange Michel's touching Squirrel, to Denise Scharley as the Dragonfly and the Mother, could not be improved upon in character, subtlety and style. The singing and playing of the French Radio forces are vital and imaginative. Ravel's exquisite score is heard to best advantage in this extraordinary transfer, in which every detail in the recording comes across to perfection. Though the 1947 mono sound is short on mystery, the sharpness of focus, with voices firm and immediate, heightens the authentic Frenchness of the reading, both jewelled and purposeful. With no stars but with no weak link, the singers make an outstanding team, helped by sound which, with background hiss eliminated, has astonishing presence. No other version casts quite such a strong spell.

Previn's dramatic and highly spontaneous reading of *L'Enfant* certainly brings out the refreshing charm of this still neglected masterpiece. Helped by a strong and stylish team of soloists, this makes superb entertainment. On CD, the precision and sense of presence of the digital recordings come out the more vividly, with subtle textures clarified and voices – including the odd shout – precisely placed. That precision goes well with Previn's performance, crisply rhythmic rather than atmospherically poetic. Those wanting a modern, digital recording should be well satisfied with this at mid-price, for a full libretto with translation is included.

L'heure espagnole (complete).
(M) (***) EMI (SIS) mono CDM5 65269-2. Duval, Giraudeau, Vieuille, Herent, Clavensy, O. du Théâtre Nat. de l'Opéra-Comique, André Cluytens.

This recording, with Denise Duval as Concepcion and Jean Giraudeau as Gonzalve, was recorded at the Théâtre des Champs-Elysées in 1952 and makes its first appearance in Britain. Denise Duval is altogether superb, as is the rest of the cast for that matter. Apart from the quality of the singing, the artists of this period understood the importance of diction and acting. The sound comes up very well indeed, and the set should give much pleasure.

(i) *L'heure espagnole;* (ii) *L'enfant et les sortilèges* (both complete).
(M) *** DG 449 769-2 (2) [id.]. (i) Berbié, Sénéchal, Giraudeau, Bacquier, Van Dam, Paris Opera O; (ii) Ogéas, Collard, Berbié, Sénéchal, Gilma, Herzog, Rehfuss, Maurane, RTF Ch. & Boys' Ch., RTF Nat. O; Maazel – RIMSKY-KORSAKOV: *Capriccio espagnol;* STRAVINSKY: *Le chant du rossignol*. ***

Maazel's recordings of Ravel's two one-Act operas were made in the early 1960s and, though the solo voices in *L'enfant* are balanced rather closely, the remastered sound in both operas is wonderfully vivid and atmospheric and each performance is splendidly stylish. The singing is delightful: neo-classical crispness of articulation goes with refined textures that convey the ripe humour of one piece, the tender poetry of the other. The inclusion of Maazel's superb early stereo accounts of Rimsky's *Capriccio* (with the Berlin Philharmonic), and *Le chant du rossignol* glitteringly played by the Berlin Radio Orchestra, two classics of the gramophone, ensures this set a place at the top of the list of DG's illustrious 'Originals'.

Rawsthorne, Alan (1905–71)

Clarinet concerto.

*** Hyperion CDA 66031 [id.]. Thea King, NW CO of Seattle, Alun Francis – COOKE: *Concerto;* JACOB: *Mini-concerto.* ***

Though the *Clarinet concerto* is an early work of Rawsthorne's it already establishes the authentic flavour of his writing with a certain gritty and angular quality masking the obvious depth of feeling behind. That constraint makes for musical strength, the more obviously so in a performance as persuasive as this from soloist and orchestra alike. Excellent 1982 analogue recording, expertly transferred.

(i) *Concertante pastorale for flute, horn and strings; Concerto for string orchestra; Divertimento for chamber orchestra; Elegiac rhapsody for string orchestra; Light music for strings (based on Catalan tunes);* (ii) *Suite for recorder and string orchestra* (orch. McCabe).

(N) (BB) *** Naxos Dig. 8.553567 [id.]. Norther CO, David Lloyd-Jones; (with (i) Conrad Marshall, Rebecca Goldberg; (ii) John Turner.

This collection of Rawsthorne's shorter pieces for string orchestra brings out his most attractive side. Though the melodic writing is rarely as memorable as that of, say, Walton, all the works here are beautifully crafted, not least the *Concerto for string orchestra*, with two dark movements followed by lightness and open intervals. The *Concertante* is most evocative with beautiful solos for flute and horn. The *Light music* represents Rawsthorne's pre-war left-wing propagandist period, and the neo-classical *Recorder suite* has been deftly arranged by John McCabe from an original with piano. Finest of all is the *Elegiac rhapsody*, written in memory of Rawsthorne's friend, the poet Louis MacNeice, touching a deeper vein, erupting from lamentation into anger. Outstanding performances, brilliant and intense, vividly recorded.

Piano concertos Nos. 1–2; (i) *Double piano concerto.*

*** Chandos Dig. CHAN 9125 [id.]. Tozer, (i) with Cislowski; LPO, Bamert.

The *First Piano concerto* was a wartime work and the *Second* (1951) was composed for the Festival of Britain and is also rewarding, though the finale with its cheap opening idea is a bit of a let-down. The *Concerto for two pianos* is likewise stimulating. Tozer gives a good account of the concertos, not perhaps as compelling or understanding as the (now deleted) Malcolm Binns version on Lyrita or Moura Lympany's pioneering disc. The opening of No. 1 is a bit rushed; Tamara-Anna Cislowski is an excellent partner in the 1968 concerto. Matthias Bamert and the LPO are very supportive and the recording is in the best traditions of the house.

Piano concertos Nos.(i) *1*; (ii, iii) *2.* (iv) *Practical cats.* (ii) (Piano) *Bagatelles.*

(N) (M) *** EMI stereo/mono CDM5 66935-2. (i) Dame Moura Lympany, Philh. O, Menges; (ii) Denis Matthews; (iii) BBC SO, Sargent; (iv) Robert Donat, Philh. O, composer.

Moura Lympany's account of the *First Piano concerto* (1939) with the Philharmonia Orchestra under Herbert Menges, uses the revision for larger orchestra of 1943 and – like Denis Matthews's recording with Sir Malcolm Sargent of the *Second*, composed for the 1951 Festival of Britain – has the benefit of stereo. Sargent had also conducted the first recording with Clifford Curzon on a Decca 10-inch LP. (The *Bagatelles*, recorded in 1943, originally appeared on the last side of the Moeran *Symphony*: Denis Matthews had to learn them in three days.) Of particular interest is *Practical cats*, which has long been out of circulation and has the advantage of Donat's impeccable reading and the composer's own direction. Great care has been taken over the transfers.

(i) *Violin concertos No. 1–2. Fantasy overture: Cortèges.*

(BB) *** Naxos Dig. 8.554240 [id.]. (i) Rebecca Hirsch; BBC Scottish SO, Lionel Friend.

The Naxos recording brings the accomplished Rebecca Hirsch as soloist, with excellent orchestral support from the BBC Scottish Symphony under Lionel Friend. Apart from her championship of Poul Ruders's music (his *Second Concerto* is dedicated to her), she has established herself also as a fine chamber musician and is a member of the Joachim Trio. Her performances hold their own with distinguished rivals, and the value of the disc is enhanced by another première recording of Rawsthorne's *Cortèges*, commissioned by the BBC and first performed at the 1945 Prom season. It is an imaginative and at times haunting piece, very well played and recorded here.

Symphonies Nos. (i) *1;* (ii) *2 (Pastoral);* (iii) *3.*

*** Lyrita Analogue/Dig. SRCS 291 [id.]. (i) LPO, Pritchard, or (ii) Nicholas Braithwaite; with Tracey Chadwell, (iii) BBC SO, Norman Del Mar.

The symphonies are distinguished by impeccable craftsmanship and first-rate invention, as is readily demonstrated by the *First*, played with such evident enjoyment by the LPO under Sir John Pritchard. But, of the three, the *Second (Pastoral) Symphony* is the most readily approachable, since its thematic material catches the ear, especially in the expressive ideas of the *Poco lento* and the gay country-dance Scherzo. Rawsthorne uses a soprano soloist in the finale, with a succinct text by Henry Howard, Earl of Surrey (1516–47), giving brief impressions of three of the four seasons: spring, summer and winter. The music has a powerful atmosphere, and Tracey Chadwell copes successfully with the rather angular vocal-line to catch the essential melancholy of the poem. All three works receive superb performances and the recording is outstanding with the sense of space and splendid detail we expect from Lyrita.

Clarinet quartet.
*** Redcliffe Dig. RR 010 [id.]. Nicholas Cox, Redcliffe Ens. – BLISS; ROUTH: *Clarinet quintets.* ***

Rawsthorne's *Clarinet quartet* is more ambivalent in feeling than the Bliss *Quintet*, but its quirky opening movement is appealing and the darker *Poco lento* hardly less striking. In the finale, a purposeful *Allegro risoluto* leads to a slower section before the movement's tensions are resolved by the effective return of the main theme of the opening movement. With Nicholas Cox a most winning soloist, the performance here could hardly be improved upon, and the recording is first class.

4 Bagatelles; Ballade; 4 Romantic pieces; Sonatina; Theme and four studies.
(N) **(*) Paradisum Dig. PDS-CD2 [id.]. John Clegg – LENNOX BERKELEY: *Six Preludes, Op. 23.* **(*)

In the 1960s and 1970s, John Clegg was frequently heard in broadcasts of rare repertoire before his duties as a professor of mathematics took its toll on his time. On this CD he presents the whole of Rawsthorne's output for the piano (apart from the two concertos). Inventive and civilized music, every bar bearing his personal stamp, and persuasively played. The only snag is the rather claustrophobic acoustic in which it is recorded.

Rebel, Jean-Féry (1661–1747)

Les caractères de la Danse; Les Elémens; Le tombeau de M. de Lully.
*** Erato/Warner Dig. 2292 45974-2. Les Musiciens du Louvre, Marc Minkowski.

The eloquent trio sonata, *Le tombeau de M. de Lully*, was written on the death of the great French composer whose pupil Rebel had become as a boy of eight, and *Les Elémens* is one of the most original works of the period. With its representation of chaos in which all the notes of the harmonic scale are heard simultaneously, it is certainly quite astonishing in effect. The performance and recording are of the highest quality, and this is to be preferred to the rival accounts from Christopher Hogwood and the Academy of Ancient Music, and Reinhard Goebel and the Musica Antiqua Köln.

Rebelo, João Lourenço (1610–61)

Lamentations for Maundy Thursday; Vesper Psalms.
*** Sony Dig. SK 53115 [id.]. Huelgas Ens., Paul van Nevel.

João Lourenço Rebelo was court composer to John (João) IV of Portugal. His leaning was towards the polychoral Venetian style of Giovanni Gabrieli rather than the polyphony of Palestrina, and he was one of the first to compose specific parts for instruments in his polyphonic works. The *Vesper Psalms* and the *Lamentations* recorded here are of striking expressive power and are both played and recorded marvellously with vivid realism. Those who admire Gabrieli and Schütz will find this a congenial yet distinctive voice.

Reger, Max (1873–1916)

Ballet suite, Op. 130; 4 Böcklin tone-pictures, Op. 128; Variations and fugue on a theme by Beethoven, Op. 86.
(N) *** BIS Dig. CD 601 [id.]. Norrköping SO, Leif Segerstam.

Segerstam gets a very good response from the Norrköping Orchestra and gives a more atmospheric account of the *Vier Böcklin Tondichtungen, Op. 128* than most of his rivals. He obviously cares for this music and makes the most of it without succumbing to the expressive exaggeration which spoils some of his other work. Both the *Ballet suite* and the *Beethoven variations* are very well served, and while others have the benefit of world-class orchestras, none is as well recorded and with as wide a range as this BIS CD.

(i) *Concerto in olden style, Op. 123;* (ii) *Sinfonietta, Op. 90.*
**(*) Koch Dig. 31354-2 [id.]. (i) Harald Orlovsky; (i; ii) Peter Rosenberg; Bamberg SO, Horst Stein.

The *Concerto in olden style* is Reger's tribute to the great Baroque masters, though his Op. 123 is scored for somewhat larger forces! The *Sinfonietta in A major* is an ambitious work, full of luxuriant invention, and richly and at times thickly scored; at others, it is a model of delicacy. The *Largo* is absolutely inspired. Horst Stein gets very good playing from the Bamberg orchestra and the recording is very warm and sonorous, perhaps not transparent enough at the top end of the spectrum.

Piano concerto in F min., Op. 114.
(N) *** RCA Dig 09026 68028-2 [id.]. Barry Douglas, French R. PO, Janowski – Richard STRAUSS: *Burleske.* ***

Reger's *Piano concerto* is a remarkable and powerful composition. The slow movement is a contemplative, rapt piece that touches genuine depths.

Barry Douglas receives exemplary recording from the RCA/Radio France engineers, and gives a very persuasive account of this uncompromising and at times intractable score. This is probably its best recording and certainly Barry Douglas's best disc so far.

(i) *Symphonic prologue to a tragedy, Op. 108;* (ii) *2 Romances for violin and orchestra, Op. 50.*
**(*) Schwann CD311 076. (i) Berlin RSO, Albrecht; (ii) with Maile; cond. Lajovic.

The tragedy in question is Sophocles' *Oedipus Rex*, and Reger's *Symphonic prologue* is one of his very finest and most powerful works. Inspiration runs consistently high. The violin *Romances* are beautiful pieces and are very well played by Hans Maile and the Berlin Radio Orchestra. Strongly recommended, even if the 1982 recording is serviceable rather than distinguished.

Symphonic prologue to a tragedy, Op. 108; Variations and fugue on a theme of Mozart, Op. 132.
(N) *** BIS Dig. CD 771 [id.]. Norrköping SO, Segerstam.

The Norrköping Orchestra may not be the equal of the Concertgebouw or the Bavarian Radio Orchestras but given Segerstam's obvious dedication to the spirit and the letter of these scores, it rises to their challenge admirably. The BIS recording is of demonstration standard.

4 Tone poems after Böcklin, Op. 128; Variations on a theme by Hiller, Op. 100.
*** Chandos Dig. CHAN 8794 [id.]. Concg. O, Järvi.

Of the four *Tone poems* here, textures in *Der geigende Eremit* ('Hermit playing the violin') are unexpectedly transparent, and *Im spiel der Wellen* has something of the sparkle of the *Jeu de vagues* movement of *La Mer* photographed in sepia; while the *Isle of the dead* is a lovely and often very touching piece. The *Hiller variations* are gloriously inventive. These works are beautifully recorded and Neeme Järvi's performances have the combination of sensitivity and virtuosity that this composer needs.

ORGAN WORKS

Aus tiefer Not schrei ich zu dir, Op. 67/3; Intermezzo in F min., Op. 129/7; Introduction and Passacaglia in D min., Op. posth.; Prelude in D min., Op. 65/7.
*** Chandos Dig. CHAN 9097 [id.]. Piet Kee – HINDEMITH: *Organ sonatas.* ***

The Müller organ of St Bavo in Haarlem seems ideally suited to this repertoire, as is the slightly reverberant acoustic which rather softens the textures and contours of the Hindemith. Piet Kee plays with his customary authority and distinction. A rewarding and satisfying issue.

Chorale fantasia on Straf' mich nicht in deinem Zorn, Op. 40/2; Chorale preludes, Op. 67/4, 13, 28, 40, 48; Introduction, passacaglia and fugue in E min., Op. 127.
*** Hyperion Dig. CDA 66223 [id.]. Graham Barber (Klais organ of Limburg Cathedral).

The *Introduction, passacaglia and fugue* is bold in conception and vision and is played superbly on this excellently engineered Hyperion disc by Graham Barber. The five *Chorale preludes* give him an admirable opportunity to show the variety and richness of tone-colours of this instrument.

PIANO MUSIC

5 Humoresques, Op. 20; Variations and fugue on a theme of Johann Sebastian Bach, Op. 81; Variations and fugue on a theme of Georg Philipp Telemann, Op. 134.
(N) ❁ *** Hyperion Dig. CDA66996 [id.]. Marc-André Hamelin.

Like Brahms, Reger was one of the greatest masters of the variation form. The Bach and Telemann sets are generally acknowledged to be among his finest keyboard works and it is difficult to think of more persuasive performances of either than those by the Canadian pianist, Marc-André Hamelin. His playing has enormous eloquence and imagination as well as a wide range of both dynamics and tonal colour. This has an elegance and refinement that never calls attention to itself. The finest accounts of either work that we have heard on or off record. Superbly natural recorded sound too.

Variations and fugue on a theme of Bach, Op. 81.
(BB) **(*) Naxos Dig. 8.550469 [id.]. Wolf Harden – SCHUMANN: *Humoreske.* **(*)

Wolf Harden's account of the Reger *Variations and fugue on a theme of Bach*, Op. 81, is very fine. The piano sounds much drier here than in the Schumann coupling. Yet the compelling quality of his playing is in no doubt.

VOCAL MUSIC

Christmas Lieder: *Christkindleins Wiegenlied; Ehre sei Gott in der Höhe! Maria am Rosenstrauch; Morgengesang; Uns ist geboren ein Kindelein.*

❀ *** EMI Dig. CDC5 56204-2 [id.]. Bär, Deutsch (with Recital: '*Christmas Lieder*' *** ❀).

Max Reger's Christmas Lieder sustain the most serious mood of any of the songs in Olaf Bär's superb recital, especially the closing *Ehre sei Gott in der Höhe!* But the imagination of Bär's word-colouring and his wide range of dynamic prevent any feeling of heaviness. The opening *Morgengesang*, describing the 'morning star', brings a delightfully fresh spontaneity, and *Mary in the Rosebower* has a gentle, rocking lyricism, beautifully realized in Helmut Deutsch's flowing accompaniment.

Reich, Steve (born 1936)

8 Lines.

(M) *** Virgin/EMI Dig. CUV5 61121-2. LCO, Warren-Green – ADAMS: *Shaker loops* *** ❀; GLASS: *Company* etc. ***; HEATH: *Frontier.* ***

Steve Reich's *8 Lines* is minimalism in its most basic form, and, although the writing is full of good-humoured vitality, the listener without a score could be forgiven for sometimes thinking that the music was on an endless loop. The performance is expert.

Music for 18 musicians.

(N) *** RCA Dig. 09026 68672-2 [id.]. Ens. Modern.

Dating from 1974–6, *Music for 18 Musicians* until recently only existed as a set of parts in what the composer describes as 'musical shorthand'. Recently – by using a computer plus musical notation software – a full score and complete parts were created by Marc Mellits, a graduate student at Cornell University, and it was possible for the present performance – which has the imprimatur of the composer – to be recorded. The work derives from and returns to a pulsing 11-chord cyclic 'theme', framing 12 connected sections, which have comparatively simple additional material superimposed upon them, as the music proceeds. As the recording is cued into 14 separate tracks, the listener can readily isolate the changes within the basic structure. In his accompanying notes, Frank Oteri draws a parallel between Reich's sonic architecture and Beethoven's *Eroica Symphony*. This is going a bit far, but there is no doubt that this is a hypnotic performance of a key work in Reich's continuing odyssey in musical minimalism.

(i) *Six Pianos;* (ii) *Music for mallet instruments;* (iii) *Variations for winds, strings and keyboards.*

(B) *** DG Analogue/Dig. 439 431-2. (i–ii) Chambers, Preiss, Hartenberger, Becker, Velez, composer; (ii) Ferchen, Harms, Jarrett, LaBarbara, Clayton; (iii) San Francisco SO, De Waart.

This collection also admirably charts the progress of Reich's minimalism. Both the first two pieces exploit the composer's technique of endlessly repeating a very brief fragment which gradually becomes transformed, almost imperceptibly, by different emphases being given to it. The *Variations* mark a new departure, using a large orchestra. The recording throughout is of high quality.

Tehillim.

** ECM 827 411-2 [id.]. Steve Reich & musicians, George Manahan.

Steve Reich is listed among the percussion players in *Tehillim*, with Manahan conducting. The central focus, in this Hebrew setting of Psalms 19 and 18 (in that order), is on the vocal ensemble of four voices. The result – with clapping and drumming punctuating the singing – has an element of charm rare in minimalist music. With jazzy syncopations and Cuban rhythms, the first of the two movements sounds like Bernstein's *Chichester Psalms* caught in a groove. The second starts slowly but speeds up for the verses of praise to the Lord and the final *Hallelujahs*. Clear, forward, analogue recording.

Variations for winds, strings & keyboard.

(N) (B) *** Ph. Virtuoso 412 214-2 [id.]. San Francisco SO, De Waart – ADAMS: *Shaker loops.* ***

Reich's *Variations*, written for the San Francisco orchestra in 1980, marked a new departure in the writing of this leading minimalist, using a large orchestral rather than a small chamber scale. The repetitions and ostinatos, which gradually get out of phase, are most skilfully used to produce a hypnotic kind of poetry, soothing rather than compelling. This disc now comes at bargain price.

Reicha, Antonín (1770–1836)

(i) *Sinfonia concertante in G for flute, violin and orchestra. Symphony in E flat, Op. 41; Overture in D.*

*** MDG Dig. MDG 335 0661-2 [id.]. (i) Ida Bieler, Jean-Claude Gérard; Wuppertal SO, Peter Gülke.

The first movement of Reicha's *Sinfonia concertante* brings engaging textures but is otherwise relatively conventional.The galant *Andante* however, brings a charming little violin melody over a tick-tock flute accompaniment; later the two instruments change roles. The *Overture in D minor* is, remarkably, in 5/8 time and its nagging ostinato main theme is at first quite catching. The snag is that, despite its variety of colour, it is a shade over-long. The *Symphony* is a different matter. Its main *allegro* is very confidently constructed in a style very like the later symphonies of Haydn and Mozart. The *Andante un poco adagio* doesn't disappoint, while in the lively finale the composer keeps a card or two up his sleeve until the very end. A real discovery, which invites repeated hearings. The orchestra is a fine ensemble and, with two first-class soloists here, offers a rewarding collection, well recorded.

Flute quartets Nos. 1 in E min., Op. 98; 2 in A; 3 in D, Op. 98/1–3.
*** MDG Dig. MDG 311 0630-2 [id.]. Konrad Hünteler, Rainer and Jürgen Küssmaul, Roel Dietiens.

In the opening *Quartet*, a particularly fine piece, one thinks often of Mozart, and Reicha's invention is seldom inferior. The piquant opening of the *Second Quartet* has a charming insouciance, and in the *Third Quartet* the quaint little tune, marching along slowly and elegantly is again Bohemian in spirit, and its appeal is almost matched by the following *Allegro*. The finale, marked *Folie harmonique*, begins with little shudders, perhaps at the thought of the witty fugal writing that is subsequently to appear in the string parts. Throughout all three works the solo flute part demands, and receives, the utmost virtuosity from its performer, here Konrad Hünteler, who either dominates or blends with his colleagues, all excellent players. The vivid recording completes the listener's pleasure.

Oboe quintet in F, Op. 107.
(B) *** Hyperion CDH 55015 [id.]. Sarah Francis, Allegri Qt – CRUSELL: *Divertimento* (with R. KREUTZER: *Grand quintet*. ***)

Antonín Reicha's *F major Quintet* is unmemorable but always amiable. The present performance is of high quality and very well recorded.

Wind quintets: in F (1811); in E flat; in B flat, Op. 88/2 & 5; in D; in A, Op. 91/3 & 5.
(B) *** Hyperion Dyad Dig. CDD 22006 (2) [id.]. Academia Wind Quintet of Prague.

Czech wind-playing in Czech wind music has a deservedly high entertainment rating, and the present performances are no exception. The music itself has great charm and geniality; it is ingenuous yet cultivated, with some delightful, smiling writing for the bassoon. The players are clearly enjoying themselves, yet they play and blend expertly. The sound too is admirable.

Reinecke, Carl (1824–1910)

Fantasiestücke, Op. 43.
*** EMI Dig. CDC5 55166-2. Caussé, Duchable – BEETHOVEN: *Notturno* ***; SCHUBERT: *Arpeggione sonata*. **(*)

Reinecke's musical language is Schumannesque and the *Fantasiestücke*, Op. 43, owe an obvious debt to Schumann's *Märchenbilder*. They are very slight, but Caussé and Duchable make out the best possible case for them.

Flute sonata (Undine), Op. 167.
(M) *** RCA 09026 61615-2 [id.]. James Galway, Martha Argerich – FRANCK; PROKOFIEV: *Sonatas*. ***

Some of Reinecke's invention here is quite striking (as in the sonata's first movement). His writing, which has sudden florid bursts, makes an engaging vehicle for an artist of Galway's calibre, and this makes a fine bonus for the coupling of two masterly works by Prokofiev and Franck.

String trio in C min., Op. 249.
(N) *** MDG Dig. MDG 634 0841-2 [id.]. Belcanto Strings – FUCHS: *Trio in A, Op. 94*. ***

Like his companion composer (Robert Fuchs) on this CD, Carl Reinecke was a much admired teacher: he numbered Grieg and Svendsen among his pupils. He was enormously prolific and a composer of some quality. This *C minor Trio* comes from around 1898 and is conservative in style, finely crafted and cultured music, superbly played and recorded.

Respighi, Ottorino (1879–1936)

(i) *Adagio con variazioni* (for cello and orchestra); *The Birds; 3 Botticelli pictures;* (ii) *Il tramonto*.
*** Chandos Dig. CHAN 8913 [id.]. (i) Wallfisch; (ii) Linda Finnie; Bournemouth Sinf., Vásáry.

Raphael Wallfisch is very persuasive in Respighi's *Adagio*. *The Birds* brings lovely playing and the luminous recording gives much pleasure. The lambent Italianate evocation of the *Three Botticelli pictures* is also aurally bewitching. But what caps the success of this Chandos Respighi anthology is Linda Finnie's ravishing account of *Il tramonto*, even finer than Carol Madalin's on Hyperion – see below. Her vocal timbre is fresh yet has an element of gentle voluptuousness just right for this ecstatic setting of Shelley. Again very responsive orchestral playing and the recording is in the demonstration class throughout this CD.

(i) *Ancient airs and dances: suites Nos. 1–3;* (ii) *Belfagor:* overture; (iii) *The Birds* (suite); (ii) *The Fountains of Rome; The Pines of Rome;* (iii) *3 Botticelli pictures (Trittico Botticelliano).*
(B) **(*) EMI forte Dig. CZS5 69358-2 (2) [CDFB 69358]. (i) LACO, or (iii) ASMF; Marriner; (ii) LSO, Gardelli.

Sir Neville Marriner's account of the suites of dances is attractively light and gracious, offering an almost French elegance, with pleasingly transparent textures. *The Birds* and *Trittico Botticelliano* are no less delightful, and they are beautifully recorded. So far so good; but Lamberto Gardelli's performances of *The Pines* and *Fountains of Rome*, though warmly sympathetic and finely played, bring less of a feeling of drama, and generate neither the atmospheric magic nor electricity experienced in the competing versions from Reiner or Karajan. The *Belfagor overture* is an acceptable bonus, a dramatic and lively piece, strongly characterized and vivid.

Ancient airs and dances: suites Nos. 1–3; The Birds (suite).
*** Van./Omega Dig. 08.1007.71. Australian CO, Gee.

Ancient airs and dances: suites Nos. 1–3; 3 Botticelli pictures (Trittico Botticelliano).
*** Telarc Dig. CD 80309 [id.]. Lausanne CO, Jesús López-Cobos.

Christopher Gee's performance of *The Birds* is a complete delight, opening and closing vigorously, yet providing the most refined portraits of the dove, nightingale and cuckoo, with particularly lovely oboe playing in *The dove*. The opening of the *First suite* of *Ancient airs and dances* has a comparable grace and delicacy of feeling throughout. The recording, made at the ABC Studio at Chatsworth, Sydney, is in the demonstration class.

Opening brightly and comparatively robustly, the Lausanne performance yet has both warmth and finesse. The rhythmic pulse is lively without being heavy, and there is much engaging woodwind detail; at the graceful beginning of the *Third suite* textures are agreeably light and transparent. The Telarc recording is first rate and even more impressive in the *Botticelli pictures*, with *La primavera* burgeoning with the extravagantly exotic spring blossoming, and *The birth of Venus* rapt in its radiantly expansive ecstasy.

(i) *Ancient airs and dances: suites Nos. 1–3; The Birds (Gli uccelli); 3 Botticelli pictures (Trittico botticelliano);* (ii) *Feste romane; the Fountains of Rome; The Pines of Rome.*
(B) *** Teldec/Warner Ultima Dig. 0630 18970-2 (2) [(M) id. import]. (i) St Paul CO, Hugo Wolff; (ii) LPO, Carlo Rizzi.

The playing of the St Paul Chamber Orchestra in the first group of works on this Ultima Double is excellent: they are responsive equally to dynamic contrasts and to changes of colour. Hugo Wolff gets a sympathetic and spirited response throughout and the *Ancient airs and dances* are beautifully played; the recording is bright but spacious. Carlo Rizzi's vivid acount of the Roman triptych is hardly less impressive. The recording is immensely spectacular and its moments of hyperbole are thrilling in a very physical way, as at the huge, overwhelming climax of *The Pines of the via Appia* and, in *Feste romane*, the crude spectacle of *Circuses* with its distant brass effects. The *Fountains* too are brilliantly pictorial, while Respighi's gently luminous evocation of *The Pines of the Janiculum* and the heady, sensuous nostalgia of *Villa Medici at sunset* are drawn with subtle colours. The LPO respond with superb virtuosity and dash, balanced by warm sensitivity.

Ancient airs and dances: suite No. 3 for strings; The Fountains of Rome; The Pines of Rome.
(M) *** DG 449 724-2 [id.]. BPO, Karajan (with BOCCHERINI: *Quintettino;* ALBINONI: *Adagio in G min.* (arr. Giazotto) ***).

In the symphonic poems Karajan is in his element, and the playing of the Berlin Philharmonic is wonderfully refined as well as exciting. The opening of the *Ancient airs* brings ravishing tone from the strings, and they sound even more lavish in Giazotto's famous arrangement of Albinoni's *Adagio*, while Boccherini's *Quintettino* makes an engaging additional lollipop.

Le astuzie di Colombina; La pentola magica; Sèvres de la vieille France.
*** Marco Polo Dig. 8.223346 [id.]. Slovak RSO (Bratislava), Adriano.

Sèvres de la vieille France is based on seventeenth- and eighteenth-century airs, scored with great elegance and charm; *La pentola magica* makes use of Russian models. *Le astuzie di Colombina*, described as a 'Scherzo Veneziano', uses popular Venetian melodies among other things. The scores contain some winning and delightful numbers. Decent performances and good recording.

Ballata delle Gnomidi; (i) *Concerto gregoriano; Poema autunnale.*
*** Chandos Dig. CHAN 9232 [id.]. (i) Lydia Mordkovitch; BBC PO, Downes.

The *Concerto gregoriano* is a meditative, lyrical outpouring making free use of Gregorian modes. Apart from some moments of brilliant display, the slightly later *Poema autunnale* for violin and orchestra is also predominantly lyrical and has moments of a Delius-like mysticism. Again Lydia Mordkovitch gives most affecting accounts of both piece and is very well supported by Downes and the BBC Philharmonic. The *Ballata delle Gnomidi* (1920) finds Respighi in his most exotic *Roman trilogy* mode: it is a dazzling exercise in colour and orchestration. This issue is one of the high points in the current Chandos survey of the composer.

Belfagor overture; 3 Corali; (i) *Fantasia slava for piano and orchestra; Toccata for piano and orchestra.*
*** Chandos Dig. CHAN 9311 [id.]. (i) Geoffrey Tozer; BBC PO, Downes.

The best thing here is the *Toccata for piano and orchestra*. It is better argued and structured, more inventive and novel, as well as more musically rewarding, than either of the piano concertos, and Tozer plays it with considerable bravura and panache and the BBC Philharmonic under Sir Edward Downes are admirably supportive. The *Fantasia slava* is shorter and less interesting, and the same goes for the three chorale arrangements. The *Belfagor* is a re-composition based on themes from his opera, and not the curtain-raiser heard in the theatre. Excellent in every way, and with recording of first-class quality.

Belkis, Queen of Sheba: suite. Metamorphoseon modi XII.

*** Chandos Dig. CHAN 8405 [id.]. Philh. O, Simon.

The ballet-suite *Belkis, Queen of Sheba*, is a score that set the pattern for later Hollywood biblical film music; but *Metamorphoseon* is a taut and sympathetic set of variations. It has been ingeniously based on a medieval theme, and though a group of cadenza variations relaxes the tension of argument in the middle, the brilliance and variety of the writing have much in common with Elgar's *Enigma*. Superb playing from the Philharmonia, treated to one of the finest recordings that even Chandos has produced, outstanding in every way.

(i) *The Birds* (suite); *Brazilian impressions;* (ii) *The Fountains of Rome; The Pines of Rome.*

(M) **(*) Mercury 432 007-2 [id.]. (i) LSO; (ii) Minneapolis SO, Antal Dorati.

In Dorati's hands the opening and closing evocations of the *Fountains of Rome* have a unique, shimmering brightness which certainly suggests a sun-drenched landscape, although in Minneapolis the turning-on of the Triton fountain brings a shrill burst of sound that almost assaults the ears. The tingling detail in the companion *Pines of Rome* is again matched by Dorati's powerful sense of atmosphere, while the finale has an overwhelming juggernaut forcefulness. The coupling of *The Birds* and *Brazilian impressions* was made in the smoother, warmer acoustics of Watford Town Hall in 1957, and here the vividness of detail particularly suits Dorati's spirited account of *The Birds*, bringing pictorial piquancy of great charm and strongly projected dance-rhythms. *Brazilian impressions* certainly glitters in Dorati's hands even if overall this work does not represent Respighi at his finest.

The Birds (Gli uccelli); Church windows (Vetrate di chiesa).

(B) **(*) Sony SBK 60311 [id.]. Phd., Ormandy – SCARLATTI: *The Good-humoured ladies.* **(*)

In *Church windows* the picture of the baby Jesus in *The flight into Egypt* has a Latin intensity of feeling which suits Ormandy and the rich-textured Philadelphia sound, while the following evocation of St Michael, sword in hand, is spectacularly painted with broad strokes of the orchestral brush. The finale, a papal blessing scene, is on the largest scale. Ormandy rises to the occasion and the spectacular recording is a match for the Philadelphia big guns – although subtlety is not the keynote here and the listener is all but overwhelmed. *The Birds* is slighter, but the playing is full of charm, especially the delicate tracery of the final cuckoo evocation.

3 Botticelli pictures; (i) *Aretusa;* (ii) *Lauda per la Nativita del Signore;* (i) *Il tramonto.*

✿ *** Collins Dig. 1349-2 [id.]. (i) Dame Janet Baker; (ii) Patricia Rosario, Louise Winter, Lynton Atkinson, Hickox Singers; City of L. Sinfonia, Hickox.

Aretusa was the first work in which Respighi established his mature style, with lightly surging fountain music that anticipates the *Fountains* and *Pines of Rome*. *Il tramonto* ('The sunset') evokes a mood remarkably similar to *Beim Schlafengehen* from Strauss's *Four Last Songs* and, with Dame Janet Baker as soloist, is just as beautiful. *Lauda* is a nativity cantata which touchingly presents the story as a simple pastoral sequence, with the tenderly expressive woodwind accompaniment suggesting rustic pipe music. The *Trittico Botticelliano* establishes its seductiveness in the shimmering sounds at the very opening of the first movement, *Primavera*. Refined playing and recording.

Brazilian Impressions.

(N) ** Decca Dig. 455 983-2 [id.]. Montreal SO, Charles Dutoit – ROSSINI: *La Boutique fantasque* (arr. RESPIGHI). **(*)

Respighi's *Brazilian Impressions* have not been well served on CD, but Dutoit conveys their heady atmosphere very successfully, and the Decca recording is well up to the expected Montreal standard.

Brazilian impressions; Church windows (Vetrate di chiesa).

**(*) Chandos Dig. CHAN 8317 [id.]. Philh. O, Simon.

Geoffrey Simon is sympathetic if not distinctive and he secures very fine playing from the Philharmonia. On CD, the wide dynamic range and a striking depth of perspective create the most spectacular effects.

Burlesca; Overture Carnevalesca; Prelude, chorale & fugue; Suite in E; Symphonic variations.

**(*) Marco Polo Dig. 8.223348 [id.]. Slovak RSO (Bratislava), Adriano.

The *Symphonic variations*, an early work, is very well crafted, with a lot of Brahms and Franck – though the scoring already betrays Respighi's future expertise. In the *Suite in E major* the influences are mainly Slavonic; primarily Dvořák and Rimsky-

Korsakov, but in the *Burlesca* of 1906 with its whole-tone scale one can discern a whiff of Debussy. The release discovers no masterpieces but does afford a valuable insight into Respighi's creative development. Good performances from Adriano and the Slovak Radio Orchestra and decent recording.

Piano concerto in A min.; Concerto in modo misolidio.
**(*) Chandos Dig. CHAN 9285 [id.]. Geoffrey Tozer, BBC PO, Downes.

Respighi wrote his *Piano concerto in A minor* in 1902, just after graduating, with the result that the influences of Rachmaninov and Grieg are strong. It is aptly coupled with a much later and more ambitious concertante work with piano, the *Concerto in modo misolidio* ('in the mixolydian mode'), which reflects Respighi's fascination with early Church music and is rather too diffuse a work, too extended for its material. The impact of Geoffrey Tozer's playing in both works is undermined by the backward balance of the piano, with only the A minor work taking fire.

Piano concerto in A min.; Fantasia slava for piano and orchestra; Toccata for piano and orchestra.
(BB) *** Naxos Dig. 8.553207 [id.]. Konstantin Scherbakov, Slovak RSO (Bratislava), Howard Griffiths.

An enterprising Naxos CD offers three concertante piano works of Respighi, missing out the *Concerto in modo misolidio* and including instead the much finer if rather extended *Toccata*, written in 1928, three years after the former piece. The concise and rather engaging *Fantasia slava* suddenly surprises the listener by quoting a tune familiar from a Dvorák *Slavonic dance*. The Russian pianist, Konstantin Scherbakov, is a persuasive and at times dazzlingly brilliant soloist and he is accompanied persuasively by the Slovak Radio Symphony Orchestra (Bratislava) under Howard Griffiths. The recording is excellent and this disc is well worth its modest cost.

Concerto in modo misolidio; (i) *Concerto a cinque.*
(N) (BB) *** Naxos Dig. 8.553366 [id.]. Konstantin Scherbakov, Slovak RSO, Howard Griffiths; (i) Capella Istropolitana, Ewald Danel.

Konstantin Scherbakov is an extremely fine player, highly imaginative in his use of colour and dynamics, fully alive to every shading and nuance of this music. His account of the *Concerto in modo misolidio* is superior in every way (except recorded quality) to Tozer's on Chandos – and a third of the price. The *Concerto a cinque* makes a delightful and inventive makeweight.

The Fountains of Rome.
(N) (***) Testament mono SBT 1108 [id.]. St Cecilia, Ac., Rome O, Victor de Sabata – DEBUSSY: *La mer; Jeux; Nuages; Fêtes.* (***)

Victor de Sabata's 1947 account of *The Fountains of Rome* was the earliest post-war set and superseded Albert Coates's early 1930s version with the LSO also on HMV. It is a magical performance with many touches that, though different from Reiner, Toscanini and Karajan, are of comparable subtlety and atmosphere.

Feste romane; The Fountains of Rome; The Pines of Rome (symphonic poems).
*** EMI Dig. CDC5 55600-2 [id.]. Oslo PO, Mariss Jansons.
*** Conifer Dig. 75605 51292 [id.]. Santa Cecilia Ac. O, Gatti.
(BB) *** Naxos Dig. 8.550539 [id.]. RPO, Bátiz.
(M) *** Decca Dig. 430 729-2. Montreal SO, Dutoit.
*** EMI Dig. CDC7 47316-2 [id.]. Phd. O, Muti.
(B) **(*) Sony SBK 48267 [id.]. Phd. O, Ormandy.
(BB) **(*) RCA Navigator 74321 24208-2 [09026 61401-2]. Phd. O, Eugene Ormandy.
(M) (**(*)) RCA mono GD 60262; *GK 60262* [60262-2-RG; *60262-4-RG*]. NBC SO, Toscanini.

The Fountains of Rome; The Pines of Rome.
✿ (M) *** RCA 09026 61401-2 [id.]. Chicago SO, Fritz Reiner – MUSSORGSKY: *Pictures at an exhibition.* *** ✿
✿ (M) *** RCA 09026 68079-2 [id.]. Chicago SO, Fritz Reiner – DEBUSSY: *La Mer.* ***

Jansons's splendidly vivid account of the *Feste romane* is here recoupled with *The Pines* and *The Fountains*, which are equally magnificent: Jansons has their full measure. There is more to this music than just colour, Mediterranean atmosphere and virtuoso orchestration. One expects the latter from a pupil of Rimsky-Korsakov, but there is a rather special quality of bitter-sweetness and a sense of longing and nostalgia that are beautifully realized here. The orchestral playing is of the first order, marvellous wind and brass throughout; and the Oslo recording scores over its immediate rival in having the deeper and more sumptuous acoustic ambience.

Daniele Gatti also brings something special to all three works: a rapt intensity, an extraordinary feeling for atmosphere and a total dedication to these glowing, richly coloured scores that is completely involving. The Santa Cecilia Orchestra plays wonderfully for him, and the Conifer recording, while not quite as spacious and open as the Oslo, is very well detailed. The wide dynamic range needs some help in some of the *pianopianissimo* sections, at the end of the *Fountains*, for example, where you will need to adjust the volume control. However, except for this, these Gatti performances can be recommended alongside the EMI CD.

Reiner's legendary recordings of *The Pines* and *Fountains of Rome* were made in Symphony Hall, Chicago, on 24 October 1959, and the extraordinarily atmospheric performances have never been surpassed since for their sultry Italian warmth. Yet the turning on of the Triton fountain brings an unforced cascade of orchestral brilliance. The marvellous orchestral playing is matched by the skill of RCA's new generation of transfer engineers, who have put it all on CD with complete fidelity. Reiner's performances are available with alternative couplings, Debussy's *La Mer* and his equally riveting (1957) recording of the Mussorgsky/Ravel *Pictures at an exhibition*.

The Naxos recording, engineered by Brian Culverhouse in St Barnabas, Mitcham, is also in the demonstration bracket. The climax of *The Fountain of Trevi at mid-day*, when Neptune parades across the heavens, is enormously spectacular, and here a computer organ was used to provide the underlying sustained pedal. The *Pines* and *Fountains* bring extremely fine playing with much warmth and finesse from the RPO. The sharp focus of the Naxos recording brings an extra degree of brazen splendour to the tumultuous popular crowd sequences in the *Circus* and *Jubilee* scenes of the *Feste romane*, while at the close of the *October festival* the mandolin serenade emerges more tangibly.

Dutoit, as in other brilliant and colourful pieces, draws committed playing from his fine Montreal orchestra. Where many interpreters concentrate entirely on brilliance, Dutoit finds a vein of expressiveness too, which – for example in the opening sequence of *The Pines of Rome* – conveys the fun of children playing at the Villa Borghese. The recorded sound is superlative on CD, where the organ pedal sound is stunning. At mid-price, this is now very competitive, especially for those who enjoy the Montreal ambience.

Muti gives warmly red-blooded performances of Respighi's Roman trilogy, captivatingly Italianate in their inflexions. With brilliant playing from the Philadelphia Orchestra and warmly atmospheric recording, these are exceptional for their strength of characterization.

Ormandy's Sony/CBS *Feste romane* dates from the early days of stereo. The performance has great electricity and enormous surface excitement, and it is a pity that the sound-quality is fiercely brilliant. In the other two works the effect is more opulent, and the Philadelphia playing is fabulous, while the recording has come up astonishingly well. It is a pity that such electrifying performances need some technical indulgence because of the microphone balance, but this is still a very exciting example of the Ormandy/Philadelphia regime at its most spectacularly compelling.

On Navigator, Ormandy again plays all three works with enormous gusto and panache, and the orchestral virtuosity is thrilling, with the robust vulgarity of *Feste romane* breathtaking in its unbuttoned zest. The cascade at the turning on of the Triton fountain is like a dam bursting, and all the pictorial effects spring vividly to life. But again the (1973–4) recording, though atmospheric, is brightly lit to the point of garishness, and not all ears will respond to the tingling brilliance. But the performances make an unforgettable impact.

Toscanini's recordings of the Roman trilogy are in a class of their own; they (and Reiner in the *Pines* and the *Fountains*) are the yardstick by which all others are measured. This is electrifying playing, which comes over well in this transfer – though, to be fair, the old LPs had a rounder, fuller (less acidulated) tone on the strings above the stave.

The Pines of Rome.

(N) *** BBC Legends BBCL 1007-2 [id.]. Bournemouth SO, Constantin Silvestri – TCHAIKOVSKY: *Manfred Symphony*. **(*)

Silvestri's account of the *Pines* comes from the Colston Hall, Bristol and 1967. It sounds remarkably good technically and the performance is very fine indeed. Atmospheric and evocative, and well worth considering. Not as subtle nor as masterly as Reiner but far from negligible. Unfortunately the *Manfred Symphony* is not so competitive, given the outstanding versions now available.

Sinfonia drammatica.

*** Chandos Dig. CHAN 9213 [id.]. BBC PO, Downes.

Respighi's *Sinfonia drammatica* (1914) is a work of ambitious proportions: epic in scale, it lasts just over an hour, the first movement alone taking 25 minutes. Yet it proves rich in incident and lavish in its orchestral colours and virtuosity; even if it is not organic in conception or symphonic in the classical sense, it is an immensely worthwhile addition to the catalogue. If you enjoy the *Alpine Symphony*, you should try this. An excellent performance and outstanding recording.

Violin sonata in B min.

(M) *** DG Dig. 457 907-2 [id.]. Kyung Wha Chung, Krystian Zimerman – R. STRAUSS: *Sonata*. ***

A splendid disc. Kyung Wha Chung is at her best and Krystian Zimerman brings an enormous range of colour and dynamics to the piano part – the clarity of his articulation in the *Passacaglia* is exceptional. This is undoubtedly the finest performance to appear on record since the Heifetz version. The close of the first movement and the rapturous opening of the *Andante* are particularly beautiful. This coupling originally won a *Gramophone* Award and no wonder!

PIANO MUSIC

Ancient airs and dances; 6 Pieces; 3 Preludi sopra melodie gregoriane; Sonata in F min.
(BB) *** Naxos Dig. 8.553704 [id.]. Konstantin Scherbakov.

Respighi followed his famous orchestral set of *Antiche Danze ed Arie* (transcriptions from lute tablature), with some for the piano. He also transcribed others: the first by the Genovese, Simone Molinaro, *Balletto detto Il Conte Orlando* bears a strong resemblance to the first movement of *The Birds*, as does the *Gagliarda* by Vincenzo Galileo (father of the famous scientist). Of the other pieces, the *Notturno* from the *Six Pieces* has a distinctly Rachmaninovian feel. The *F minor Sonata* (1897–8) is a rarity, and it is difficult to imagine a performance that is more persuasive than this – at any price level. Konstantin Scherbakov is a pianist of quality, combining the highest musicianship with sensitivity and refinement. He is excellently recorded too.

VOCAL MUSIC

(i) *Deità silvane;* (i; ii) *Lauda per la Nativitá del Signore. 3 Botticelli pictures (Trittico botticelliano).*
(B) *** Decca Double 444 842-2 (2) [id.]. (i) Robert Tear; (ii) Jill Gomez, Meriel Dickinson; L. Chamber Ch.; Argo CO, Heltay (with ROSSINI: *Petite messe solennelle.* **)

The two rarities here are most appealing. The *Lauda per la Nativitá del Signore* is a setting of words attributed to Jacapone da Todi, a Franciscan of the thirteenth century, and is ingeniously scored for two flutes, piccolo, oboe, cor anglais, two bassoons, piano (four hands) and triangle, while the voices are wonderfully handled. The *Deità silvane* is scored for single wind, horn, percussion, harp and strings – to great effect. All this music, including the much better-known *Botticelli pictures*, shows great skill in the handling of pastel colourings, and the performances reflect credit on all concerned, including the recording team. It is a pity that the Rossini coupling is much less readily recommendable.

La Primavera; (i) *4 Liriche su poesie popolari armene (1921)* (arr. Adriano).
**(*) Marco Polo Dig. 8.223595 [id.]. Henrietta Lednárová, Jana Valásková, Beata Geriová, Miroslav Dvorsky, Richard Haan, Vladimir Kubovčic, Slovak Ph. Ch., Slovak RSO (Bratilava); (i) Denisa Slepkovská, Ens., Adriano.

La Primavera is an ambitious cantata for six soloists, chorus and orchestra. It takes 45 minutes and is not vintage Respighi. But, although it has moments of bombast and periodically finds his muse on automatic pilot, it has some music of real quality and in particular the sixth of the seven movements; there are evocative and opulently scored orchestral interludes. The *Quattro liriche su poesie popolari armene* are simple and affecting. They are given here in Adriano's arrangement for flute, oboe, clarinet, bass clarinet, bassoon, trombone and harp. The performances throughout are more than adequate and are acceptably recorded.

La Sensitiva.
(BB) *** Virgin Classics Dig. Double VBD5 61469-2 (2) [CDVB 61469]. Dame Janet Baker, City of L. Sinf., Hickox – BERLIOZ: *Les Nuits d'été* etc.; BRAHMS: *Alto rhapsody* etc.; MENDELSSOHN: *Infelice* etc. ***

Tautly structured over its span of more than half an hour, Respighi's setting of Shelley's poem, *The sensitive plant* (in Italian translation), is a most beautiful piece which Dame Janet and Richard Hickox treat to a glowing first recording. The vocal line, mainly declamatory, is sweetly sympathetic and the orchestration is both rich and subtle. Altogether this makes a quite outstanding anthology.

Il tramonto.
*** Hyperion Dig. CDA 66290 [id.]. Carol Madalin, ECO, Bonavera – MARTUCCI: *Le canzone dei ricordi; Notturno.* ***

Respighi's *Il tramonto* (*The sunset*) is a glorious work which at times calls to mind the world of late Strauss. A most lovely record. Recommended with all possible enthusiasm.

Rezniček, Emil von (1860–1945)

Symphonies Nos. 3 in D; 4 in F min.
(N) **(*) Koch Schwann Dig. 3 1203-2 [id.]. Philh. Hungarica, Gordon Wright.

The Baron Emil Nikolaus von Rezniček is known only by his enchanting, irresistible *Donna Diana* Overture but he was a prolific composer with 12 operas, four symphonies, a violin conerto and four string quartets to his credit. He was torn between law and music, and alongside composition he pursued a career as conductor in Mannheim, Prague, the Warsaw Opera and the Komische Oper, Berlin. Those expecting anything approaching the inventiveness of the overture will be disappointed here. The symphonies date from 1918 and 1919, not long before he joined the staff of the *Hochschüle für Musik* in Berlin where he lived until his death in 1945. Well crafted and expertly fashioned even if originality is not their strong suit. All the same there are some delightful ideas, the minuet of the *D major Symphony* would be quite a teaser in a quiz. It begins like Haydn or Schubert and there are overtones of Mahler, and some of the humour of *Donna Diana*. Elsewhere in the *F minor Symphony* there are echoes of Mahler, Bruckner, Wagner and Dvořák. Well worth trying, decently performed, and the recordings made in the mid-1980s are very acceptable without being distinguished.

Rheinberger, Joseph (1839–1901)

Organ concerto No. 1 in F, Op. 137.
*** Telarc Dig. CD 80136 [id.]. Michael Murray, RPO, Ling – DUPRE: *Symphony*. ***

Rheinberger's *Concerto* is well made, its invention is attractive and it has suitable moments of spectacle that render it admirable for a coupling with the Dupré *Symphony*, with its use of the massive Albert Hall organ. The performance here is first rate. A fine demonstration disc.

Richafort, Jean (*c*.1480–*c*.1547)

Requiem Mass.
(N) ❀ *** Signum Dig. SIGCD 005 [id.]. Chapelle du Roi, Alistair Dixon (with GUERRERO: *Gradual & Tract*. GOMBERT: *Dicite in magni*. INFANTAS: *Domine ostende*. JOSQUIN DESPRES: *Nimphes nappés*. LOBO: *Versa est in luctum; Libera me*).

This superbly recorded collection is entitled '*Music for Philip [II] of Spain*', and it gathers together music that might have been sung at the spectacular Royal Exequies which was celebrated at San Jerónimo, Madrid on 18 October 1598, five weeks after the King had died. A great catafalque was built, housing a symbolic coffin, surrounded by a great many unbleached wax candles (2,500 were used during the various services, which went on through the night). It is not certain which music accompanied the celebrations, but scholarly detective work suggests that the *Missa pro defunctis* for six voices, composed by Jean Richefort around 1532, might have been chosen, supplemented here by Guerrero's *Gradual* and *Tract*. As a prelude, Alistair Dixon presents Gombert's motet written to celebrate Philip's birth in 1527, and he has also interpolated Josquin's great song of mourning, *Nimphes nappés*. Richafort's setting of the *Missa pro defunctis* is in a darkly solemn, chordal polyphonic style which has a grave beauty. So when, after the *Sanctus*, we hear Alonso Lobo's radiant motet *Versa est in luctum* (for the elevation of the Host) it is like a light shining down from heaven, and it is Lobo's equally beautiful Respond, *Libera me*, which concludes this remarkable vocal memento of the death of a long-dead monarch. Whether or not these actual settings were used in 1598, this enterprise achieves a satisfying linking together of some remarkable music, all sung with devotion and with the beautiful tonal blending for which the Chapelle du Roi are renowned.

Rihm, Wolfgang (born 1952)

Gesungene Zeit (Time chant).
*** DG Dig. 437 093-2 [id.]. Mutter, Chicago SO, Levine – BERG: *Violin concerto*. ***

Under the title *Gesungene Zeit* ('Time Chant'), Rihm has written what in effect is an extended lyrical meditation for the soloist, heightened and illustrated by the orchestra in the most discreet way. As in the Berg, Mutter is inspired, playing with an inner hush that used only rarely to mark her recordings.

Riisager, Knudåge (1897–1974)

Erasmus Montanus overture, Op. 1; Etudes (ballet; complete); *Qarrtsiluni, Op. 36.*
*** Chandos Dig. CHAN 9432 [id.]. Danish Nat. RSO, Rozhdestvensky.

Both the *Etudes* and *Qarrtsiluni* are classics of the Danish ballet. Knudåge Riisager, born in Estonia, pursued his musical studies in Paris with Roussel and Paul Le Flem, and his admiration for *Les six* is evident in the elegance and wit that distinguish the *Etudes* (1948), a pastiche based on Czerny, and *Qarrtsiluni* (1938). There is a zest and sparkle about his music, though it neither aims for nor has any great depth. The attractive *Erasmus Montanus overture* is a highly accomplished first opus, neatly performed and superbly recorded.

Riley, Terry (born 1935)

The Heavenly ladder, Book 7; The Walrus in memoriam.
(N) *** Telarc Dig. CD 80513 [id.]. Gloria Cheng-Cochran – ADAMS: *China gates; Phrygian gates*. ***

The five pieces which make up *The Heavenly ladder* were written in 1994 and represent the composer's move away from an aleatory improvisational style into written 'paper music'. The jazz element remains and is never more effectively interpolated than in the third piece, the polyponic *Ragtempus fugatum*. *Venus in '94* is a bizarre waltz-scherzo and the *Fandango on the heavenly ladder* (the most extended movement) intriguingly combines melancholy with energy. Its three themes are then gently re-explored in the closing *Simone's lullaby*, a set of variations marked *pianissimo* throughout, and dedicated to the composer's newly arrived granddaughter. *The Walrus in memoriam* is a witty ragtime encore piece ending more reflectively, as it is intended as a memorial to John Lennon. The performances here are persuasive: Gloria Cheng-Cochran is very sensitive to the composer's eclectic but very personal pianistic excursions, and with the stimulating Adams couplings (dating from the late

1970s) this is an important issue for those interested in the way mimimalism is developing.

Rimsky-Korsakov, Nikolay
(1844–1908)

Capriccio espagnol, Op. 34.

(N) (M) *** RCA 09026 63302-2 [id.]. RCA Victor SO, Kiril Kondrashin – KABALEVSKY: *The Comedians suite*; KHACHATURIAN: *Masquerade suite*; TCHAIKOVSKY: *Capriccio italien.* *** ❁

(M) *** DG 449 769-2 (2) [id.]. BPO, Lorin Maazel – RAVEL: *L'heure espagnole; L'enfant et les sortiléges* ***; STRAVINSKY: *Le chant du rossignol.* *** ❁

Kondrashin's 1958 performance is among the finest ever recorded, ranking alongside Maazel's famous Berlin Philharmonic account, but with the advantage of slightly more sumptuous string textures. Like the coupled Tchaikovsky *Capriccio* it has great flair and excitement, with glittering colour and detail in the variations and the *Scena e canto gitana*. The orchestral zest is exhilarating, yet there is warmth too and the resonant recording still sounds very good indeed. Choice between this and Maazel must rest with preferred couplings.

Maazel's 1960 recording of the *Capriccio espagnol* is also memorable in every way, and remains one of his finest recorded performances. With gorgeous string and horn playing and a debonair, relaxed virtuosity in the *Scene e canto gitano*, leading to remarkable bravura in the closing sequence, every note in place, this is unforgettable. The remastering has restored the recording's analogue allure and, although the fortissimo violins are a little thin above the stave, the ear readily adjusts when the playing is so exciting. A true candidate for DG's 'Originals'.

(i) *Capriccio espagnol;* (ii) *Le coq d'or: suite; Dubinushka;* (iii) *May night overture;* (iv) *Russian Easter festival overture; Scheherazade;* (ii) *Snow Maiden: suite;* (v) *Tsar Sultan:suite;* (i) *Flight of the bumblebee.*

(B) **(*) EMI Rouge et Noir CZS5 69680-2 (2). Philh. O, with (i) André Cluytens; (ii) Efrem Kurtz; (iii) Constantin Silvestri; (iv) Lovro von Matačić; (v) Paul Kletzki.

These recordings were made at Abbey Road between 1956 and 1963, and although some of the allure in the treble has been lost with the CD remastering, the bright colouring remains, and the Philharmonia are on top form, as they immediately demonstrate in an exciting *Scheherazade*. Matačić's direction has plenty of drive in the opening movement, and the silky strings in the slow movement are matched by the lustre of the woodwind solos. The finale is really exciting. The *Russian Easter festival overture* wrings every ounce of colour from the music, and the famous trombone solo is played with great dignity. Efrem Kurtz is thoroughly at home in *Le coq d'or* and *The Snow Maiden*, and Kletzki is vibrant in *Tsar Sultan*. Cluytens closes the first disc and opens the second with virtuoso accounts of the *Capricio espagnol* and *Flight of the bumblebee* respectively; in the former the sound is brilliant but lacking in voluptuousness.

Capriccio espagnol, Op. 34; Le coq d'or: suite; Russian Easter festival overture, Op. 36.

(M) *** Mercury (IMS) 434 308-2 [id.]. LSO, Antal Dorati – BORODIN: *Prince Igor: Polovstian dances.* **(*)

Dorati's 1959 *Capriccio espagnol* brings glittering bravura and excitement from the LSO players, and the *Russian Easter festival overture*, recorded at Walthamstow at the same sessions, is equally dynamic and colourful. Even more remarkably, the rich-hued and vibrant *Le coq d'or* dates from as early as 1956, yet hardly sounds dated. The playing has plenty of allure in its evocation of Queen Shemakha, yet has drama and well defined detail.

Capriccio espagnol; Russian Easter festival overture.

(B) **(*) Decca Eclipse Dig. 448 233-2 [id.]. Montreal SO, Dutoit – MUSSORGSKY: *Night on the bare mountain* etc. **(*)

Dutoit's *Capriccio espagnol* is comparatively genial and relaxed; the *Russian Easter festival overture* is strong, with a fine climax . In both works the Montreal recording is full, with iridescent detail.

Christmas eve (suite); Le Coq d'or: suite; Legend of the invisible city of Kitezh: suite; *May night:* overture; *Mlada:* suite; *The Snow Maiden:* suite; *The Tale of the Tsar Saltan:* suite.

*** Chandos Dig. CHAN 8327/9 (3) [id.]. RSNO, Järvi.

Apart from the feast of good tunes here, the composer's skilful and subtle deployment of the orchestral palette continually titillates the ear. Neeme Järvi draws the most seductive response from the SNO; he consistently creates orchestral textures which are diaphanously sinuous. Yet the robust moments, when the brass blazes or the horns ring out sumptuously, are caught just as strikingly and the listener is assured that here is music which survives repetition uncommonly well. However, this set now seems rather expensive.

Christmas eve: suite; Le coq d'or: suite; The Tale of Tsar Saltan: suite; Flight of the bumblebee.

*** ASV Dig. CDDCA 772 [id.]. Armenian PO, Tjeknavorian.

Tjeknavorian and his fine Armenian orchestra are completely at home in Rimsky's sinuous orientalism, with its glittering, iridescent windcolouring. The racy vigour and sparkle of the playing brings a jet-setting bumble bee and the carolling horns and bold brass add to the vividness. The Tchaikovskian *Polonaise* music from *Christmas eve* exudes similar sparkling vitality within a glowing palette. In short this is one of the most desirable and generous Rimsky-Korsakov collections in the current catalogue, and only a degree of thinness in the violin timbre above the stave prevents the use of the adjective, sumptuous. In all other respects this is in the demonstration bracket.

Christmas Eve (suite); Dubinushka, Op. 62; May night overture; Russian Easter Festival overture, Op. 36; Sadko (musical picture), Op. 5; (i) *Scheherazade, Op. 35; The Snow Maiden (suite). Tsar Saltan (suite), Op. 57; Tsar Saltan* (opera): *The Flight of the bumblebee.*

(B) **(*) Decca Double 443 464-2 (2) [id.]. SRO, Ansermet, (i) with Geneva Motet Ch.

This is all repertoire for which Ansermet was famous in the early stereo era, and *Scheherazade* must be counted a historic recording. It dates from 1960, and the sound still offers quality regarded as of demonstration standard in its day and not very far short of it now. Ansermet's skill as a ballet conductor comes out persuasively. The outer movements with their undoubted sparkle are the finest: the first is dramatic and the last is built steadily to a climax of considerable impact. The music's sinuous qualities are not missed and every bar of the score is alive. *May Night* was recorded a year earlier and the strings have far less lustre; but the *Tsar Saltan suite*, also made in 1959, shows Ansermet and the Decca engineers in glittering form, especially in the recording of brass and woodwind. The *Flight of the bumblebee* is rather leisurely, but Ansermet is at his finest in the *Christmas Eve suite*, played with much affection, plus that mixture of spontaneity and a remarkably graphic orchestral palette which made Ansermet's performances special. *Dubinushka* has some typical brass fanfare writing and Ansermet is (again in 1958) well served here by the engineers, as he is in *Sadko*, an exotic fairy-tale handled with characteristic aplomb. The earliest recording offered here is *The Snow Maiden suite* (1957) and once again the sound is remarkably warm and richly coloured. This set can certainly be recommended at Double Decca price, especially to Ansermet aficionados.

Concert phantasy on Russian themes for violin and orchestra in B min., Op. 33.

(N) **(*) Globe Dig. GLO 5174 [id.]. Lubotsky, Estonian Nat. SO, Volmer – ARENSKY; TCHAIKOVSKY: *Violin concertos.* **(*)

The *Concert fantasy in B minor on two Russian themes* comes from 1886–7 (not 1866–7 as quoted on the back of the sleeve, where it is also quoted inaccurately as being a world première recording). It is a slight but colourful piece, and is persuasively performed here. It makes an admirable fill-up to Arensky's endearing *Violin concerto* and the Tchaikovksy which inspired it. Good orchestral playing under Arvo Volmer and naturally balanced sound.

Piano concerto in C sharp min., Op. 30.

*** Hyperion Dig. CDA 66640 [id.]. Malcolm Binns, E. N. Philh. O, Lloyd-Jones – BALAKIREV: *Concertos Nos. 1–2.* ***

Malcolm Binns proves a sensitive and intelligent exponent in the Rimsky-Korsakov concerto, which comes aptly coupled with Balakirev's two essays in the form. The Northern Philharmonia under David Lloyd-Jones give excellent support and the Hyperion recording is first class.

Le Coq d'or (suite).

*** DG Dig. 447 084-2 [id.]. Russian Nat. O, Pletnev – TCHEREPNIN: *La Princesse lointaine* etc; LIADOV: *Baba-Yaga*, etc. ***

Mikhail Pletnev and the Russian National Orchestra, which he founded in 1990, give this exotic suite a performance of exemplary atmosphere and colour, and theirs is likely to remain special for a long time. The coupling is of particular interest in that it brings music by two Rimsky pupils, Liadov and Nikolai Tcherepnin, the latter otherwise currently unrepresented in the catalogue. An outstanding issue.

Le Coq d'or; The Maid of Pskov; Pan Voyevoda: suites.

✿ *** Impetus Kontrapunct Dig. 32247 [id.]. Odense SO, Edward Serov.

Serov is a complete master of the repertoire, and the playing of the Odense orchestra is glorious, the glowing woodwind palette matched by the most seductive and transparent string textures. Serov's performance of *Le coq d'Or* is every bit as fine as Pletnev's on DG, and the recording here is even more luxuriant. Indeed it is very much in the demonstration bracket. In *The Maid of Pskov* suite, *The Tsar hunting in the wood and Tempest* has much of the imaginative pictorial evocation and imagery of Berlioz's *Royal hunt and storm*. Again it is superbly presented, as is the hardly less attractive *Pan Voyevoda* which opens with a pastoral evocation rather like Wagner's *Forest murmurs*, and includes three brilliantly scored *Russian dances*. Very highly recommended: marvellous music, its magic fully realized, and sound which could hardly be bettered.

Scheherazade (symphonic suite), *Op. 35.*

(M) *** EMI CDM5 66998-2. RPO, Beecham – BORODIN: *Polovtsian dances.* ***

*** DG Dig. 437 818-2 [id.]. O de l'Opéra Bastille, Chung – STRAVINSKY: *Firebird suite.* ***

(M) *** RCA GD 60875 [60875-2-RG]. Chicago SO, Fritz Reiner – DEBUSSY: *La Mer.* ***

(M) *** RCA 09026 68168-2 [id.]. Chicago SO, Fritz Reiner – STRAVINSKY: *Chant du rossignol.* ***

(M) *** Penguin Classics DG 460 618-2 [id.]. BPO, Karajan – BORODIN: *Polovtsian dances*. ***

**(*) Decca (IMS) Dig. 443 703-2. Concg. O, Chailly (with STRAVINSKY: *Scherzo fantastique*).

(N) (M) **(*) Mercury 462 953-2 [id.]. Minneapolis SO, Dorati (with LSO: LISZT: *Les Préludes;* SIBELIUS: *Valse triste;* SMETANA: Vltava. **).

(B) ** EMI forte CZS5 69361-2 (2) [CDFB 69361]. LSO, Svetlanov – ARENSKY: *Variations on a theme by Tchaikovsky;* GLAZUNOV: *The Seasons; Concert waltzes*. ***

(N) (**) Testament mono SBT 1139 [id.]. Philh. O, Stokowski – STRAVINSKY: *Petrushka*. (***)

Scheherazade; Capriccio espagnol, Op. 34.

✿ *** Telarc Dig. CD 80208 [id.]. LSO, Sir Charles Mackerras.

(N) (M) *** Classic fm Dig. 74605 57055-2. LPO, Alexander Lazarev.

**(*) EMI Dig. CDC7 55227-2 [id.]. LPO, Jansons.

(B) **(*) DG Analogue/Dig. 439 443-2. (i) Boston SO, Ozawa; (ii) Gothenburg SO, Neeme Järvi.

(BB) **(*) Tring Dig. TRP 003 [id.]. RPO, Barry Wordsworth.

(M) **(*) EMI CDM5 65715-2. O de Paris, Rostropovich – MUSSORGSKY: *Night on the bare mountain*. ***

(i–ii) *Scheherazade;* (iii–iv) *Capriccio espagnol;* (i; iv) *Russian Easter festival overture, Op. 36.*

(M) *** Ph. 442 643-2. (i) Concg. O; (ii) Kondrashin; (iii) LSO; (iv) Markevitch.

Scheherazade (symphonic suite), *Op. 35; Dubinushka, Op. 62; Tale of Tsar Saltan: Flight of the bumble-bee.*

(M) *** Chandos Enchant Dig. CHAN 7093 [id.]. RSNO, Järvi – KALINNIKOV: *Overtures*. ***

Scheherazade; Fairy tale (Skazka), Op. 29; Sadko, Op. 5; Song of India, from Sadko (arr. Tjeknavorian).

*** ASV Dig. CDDCA 771 [id.]. Armenian PO, Tjeknavorian.

Scheherazade; Russian Easter festival overture; The Maid of Pskov: Hunt and storm.

(M) (***) Biddulph mono WHL 010 [id.]. Phd. O, Stokowski.

(i–ii) *Scheherazade;* (i; iii) *Russian Easter festival overture, Op. 36;* (iv) *Tsar Saltan* (opera): *Flight of the bumblebee; March.*

(M) *** [RCA Basic 100 09026 68335-2; *68335-4*]. (i) Chicago SO; (ii) Reiner; (iii) Stokowski; (iv) LSO, Previn.

Scheherazade; Tsar Saltan: orchestral suite.

(BB) *** Naxos Dig. 8.550726. Philh. O, Bátiz.

Mackerras's reading combines gripping drama with romantic ardour, subtlety of colour with voluptuousness; he is helped by a wonderfully beguiling portrait of Scheherazade herself, provided by his orchestral leader, in this case Kees Hulsmann. The charming closing reverie, with the Sultan lying peacefully satiated in the arms of his young wife, their themes blissfully intermingled, is unforgettable. After an appropriate pause, Mackerras then delivers a thrilling bravura account of *Capriccio espagnol*, lushly opulent in the variations, glittering in the exotic *Scena e canta gitano*, and carrying all before it in the impetus of the closing *Fandango asturiano*. Telarc's digital recording is very much in the demonstration class.

Kondrashin's version of *Scheherazade* with the Concertgebouw Orchestra has the advantage of splendidly glowing (1980) analogue recorded sound. Hermann Krebbers's exquisitely seductive portrayal of Scheherazade is cleverly used by Kondrashin to provide a foil for the expansively vibrant contribution of the orchestra as a whole, and he creates an irresistible forward impulse, leading to a huge climax at the moment of the shipwreck. Markevitch gives an excellent account of the *Russian Easter festival overture* with the same orchestra; the *Capriccio espagnol*, too, is brilliantly played by the LSO, and in both the sound also has considerable allure, with the present CD transfer much more vivid than the original LP.

Beecham's 1957 *Scheherazade* is a performance of extraordinary drama and charisma. Alongside the violin contribution of Stephen Staryk, all the solo playing has great distinction; in the second movement Beecham gives the woodwind complete metrical freedom. The sumptuousness and glamour of the slow movement are very apparent and the finale has an explosive excitement, rising to an electrifying climax. Now finally reissued at mid-price, as one of EMI's 'Great recordings of the Century' this could well be first choice for some collectors, although the *fortissimo* massed strings in the first movement are on the thin side and show the age of the recording (1957).

The newest digital coupling of Rimsky-Korsakov's two most popular orchestral works from Alexander Lazarev on Classic fM is very successful indeed. The recording, made at Watford Colosseum, combines brilliance and lustre with body and warmth. The LSO are consistently on top form, with seductive horn and string playing in the *Variazioni* of the *Capriccio*, sparkling detail in the *Scena e canto gitano* and a highly zestful closing *Fandango asturiano*. Lazarev opens *Scheherazade* very boldly, but the heroine's entry (Jaokim Svenheden, the violin soloist) is sharply contrasted, delicately alluring. The first movement is spacious, but the tension is built up steadily to a powerful climax. Lazarev's idyllic languour in the slow movement then brings the most glowingly seductive response from the LPO, strings and woodwind alike, to contrast with a thrillingly uninhibited finale. After its climactic peak, the closing reverie is the more beguiling for its gentle hint of resigned melancholy.

On ASV a refreshing and totally gripping new-look recording of *Scheherazade* from Eastern Russia. Yuri Boghosian immediately presents a seductively slight and sinuous image for the heroine-narrator and throughout the central movements one is made aware of the lustrous oriental character of Rimsky's melodies. The finale, with its spectacular storm and shipwreck, has exhilarating animation and bite. Tjeknavorian shows great imaginative flair in the two shorter folk tales and also offers his own gently luscious arrangement of the *Chant hindu*, which caresses the ear beguilingly. The brilliant recording has great vividness and projection, but relatively little sumptuousness. But it suits the performances admirably.

There is a certain freshness about the newest Paris account under Myung-Whun Chung; nothing is routine and the playing has a certain enthusiasm. Very fast and effective tempo in the finale. The sound has warmth and perspective, thanks to Wolfgang Mitlehner, one of DG's best *Tonmeister*, though the timpani resonate perhaps a bit too much. All the same, a very enjoyable newcomer.

Reiner's first movement opens richly and dramatically and has a strong forward impulse. The unnamed orchestral leader, naturally balanced, plays most seductively. Reiner's affectionate individual touches have much in common with Beecham's (full-price) version and sound comparably spontaneous and the finale, brilliant and very exciting, has a climax of resounding power and amplitude. The Chicago Hall ambience makes up in body and spaciousness for any lack of internal clarity.

Reiner's recording also comes, differently coupled, in RCA's Basic 100 collection (available only in the USA). Most notable is Stokowski's *Russian Easter festival overture* (also recorded in Chicago), but the two colourful excerpts from *Tsar Saltan* show Previn and the LSO in top form, and they too are vividly recorded.

Järvi's version of *Scheherazade* with the RSNO is given one of Chandos's most sumptuous and spectacular digital recordings and, as with Kondrashin, Järvi's reading generates a vivid narrative feeling. The playing is no less fine, and this is well worth considering, and it offers a similarly brilliant account of the colourful *Dubinushka*, plus a buzzing, convincingly scaled *Bumblebee*. The coupled overtures by Kalinnikov are also well worth having.

Bátiz's reputation for spontaneity in the recording studio is demonstrated at its most telling. His performance is impulsive, full of momentum and seductively volatile. David Nolan's picture of Scheherazade is rhapsodically evanescent and in the key second movement the lilting Philharmonia wind solos are a constant pleasure. The slow movement combines refinement with its sensuous patina, and the finale has fine zest and excitement. The colourful *Tsar Saltan suite* is comparably dramatic and vivid. In short, with first-class recording, both clear in detail and full-bodied, at super-bargain price this is hard to beat.

Jansons gives us a very well-played and warmly distinctive version of Rimsky-Korsakov's *Scheherazade* with much to recommend it. What comes out in all four movements is the way he points rhythms, lilting, bouncy and affectionate, to distinguish this from most other versions, bringing a satisfying resolution at the great climax towards the end of the finale, with Joakim Svenheden a warmly expressive soloist. The *Capriccio espagnol* brings a similar combination of expressive warmth and exuberance. But the recorded sound has less bloom and transparency than others made in Abbey Road Studio No. 1 and is a bit lacking in front-to-back depth.

Karajan's 1967 recording, now reissued as one of the Penguin Classics, brings much ardour from the glorious Berlin strings in the *Andante*. The outer movements have great vitality and thrust, and the bright percussion transients add to the feeling of zest. Yet Michel Schwalbé's sinuously luxuriant violin solos are still allowed to participate in the narrative. The fill-up is a sizzling account of the Borodin *Polovtsian dances*, with no chorus, but managing perfectly well without. The author's note is by David Lodge.

Chailly's newest Decca *Scheherazade* has sound out of Decca's top drawer, with all the glowing lustre one expects from the Concertgebouw acoustics, but Jaap van Zweden's assumption of the role of voluptuous storyteller, though sweetly sinuous, does not have a strong enough profile to dominate the narrative, especially at the opening and close of the work. It is in the sensuous grace of the two central movements, with their translucent detail, that the performance is at its most appealing. The brief Stravinsky encore is beautifully played and has never been recorded more richly.

Mercury *aficianados* will be glad to have this very well remastered CD transfer of Dorati's fine 1958 performance, which sounds much better than the old LP. The Minneapolis orchestra play very well for him and, if the first movement is not especially arresting, the finale is very brilliant indeed. It has to be said that in terms of panache, this account is no real match for Beecham's, made at about the same time, but the remastered sound is somewhat fuller in the upper range than the EMI transfer, in spite of the basically dry Minneapolis acoustic. The encores were recorded two years later in the more flattering ambience of Wembley Town Hall, though the massed violins still reveal the recording date.

Liszt's *Les Préludes* is outstandingly successful, with dignity and warm romantic feeling as well as excitement. *Valse triste* is sombrely characterful, and only Smetana's *Vltava* brings a measure of disappointment when the flowing opening string tune fails to lift off as much as it can.

Ozawa's earlier (1977) Boston *Scheherazade* is an attractive performance, richly recorded; if the last degree of vitality is missing from the central movements, the orchestral playing is warmly vivid. The reading as a whole has plenty of colour and atmosphere, however, and is certainly enjoyable. Moreover Järvi's digital *Capriccio espagnol* is a distinctive and worthwhile bonus, brilliantly recorded.

Barry Wordsworth's RPO version is offered in the lowest price-range and is certainly recommendable. While the solo violin (Jonathan Carney) is rather forwardly balanced, it means that *Scheherazade* immediately takes a dominating role. The first movement has a fine, spacious sweep and, if the wind solos in the second movement are made to seem rather less spontaneous, the slow movement has an agreeable allure at the opening, and the finale brings plenty of orchestral bravura and excitement. What makes this disc particularly attractive is the outstanding coupling, a brilliant and colourful *Capriccio espagnol* with a vibrant close. The Tring recording produces a vivid orchestral presence.

Rostropovich's performance of the first movement, spacious and opulent, is very convincing, but in the second the conductor's flexibility in the matter of rubato is not entirely matched by precision in the orchestral playing. This is perhaps a small matter when there is so much lambent allure in the central movements and in the performance as a whole; there is much infectious rhythmic pointing, while the finale is splendidly exciting. The *Capriccio espagnol*, recorded four years later, is similarly sumptuous and appealing.

This collection of Leopold Stokowski's recordings of Rimsky-Korsakov centres on the first of his five versions of *Scheherazade*. Made in 1927, it is wilder and more passionate than later ones; fascinatingly, an alternative version of the first movement, never issued before, is included as a supplement. At a slightly broader speed, spreading to an extra 78-r.p.m. side, it is even more persuasive. Equally impressive is Stokowski's intense, volatile account of the *Russian Easter festival overture*, dating from 1929, while the *Hunt and storm* sequence from the *The Maid of Pskov* comes from ten years later, with the sound drier and marginally less full. The Biddulph transfers are excellent, with plenty of body.

Svetlanov's 1978 version with the LSO is disappointing, despite John Georgiadis's subtly seductive image of Scheherazade herself. The broad, powerful opening movement, taken very spaciously indeed, is balanced by a finale which is almost aggressively brilliant. The inner movements are extremely volatile and less contrasted than usual. The LSO wind solo playing is impressive, but the strings sometimes have an almost febrile timbre which is less than glamorous. Svetlanov's conception undoubtedly brings out the Russianness of the score; but in such a competitive field this could hardly be a strong contender, which is a pity when the Arensky and Glazunov couplings are so seductive.

Stokowski's 1950s Philharmonia recording of the *Scheherazade* offers some superb playing – what performances under his baton did not! – but it is actually less likeable than his pre-war Philadelphia set. His rubati are intrusive in the slow movement and he pulls phrases out of shape elsewhere. Good sound and an excellent transfer.

Symphonies Nos. 1 in E min., Op. 1; 2 in F sharp min., Op. 9 (Antar).
*** RCA Dig. 09026 62558-2 [id.]. State SO of Russia, Yevgeni Svetlanov.

Symphonies Nos. 1 in E min., Op. 1; 2 (Antar), Op. 9; 3 in C, Op. 32; Capriccio espagnol, Op. 35; Russian Easter festival overture, Op. 36.
*** DG (IMS) Dig. 423 604-2 (2). Gothenburg SO, Järvi.

Symphonies Nos. 1 in E min., Op. 1; 2 (Antar), Op. 9; 3 in C, Op. 32; Capriccio espagnol, Op. 36; (i) *Piano concerto in C sharp min., Op. 30. Russian Easter festival overture, Op. 36; Sadko, Op. 5.*
(M) **(*) Chandos Dig. CHAN 7029 (3) [id.]. (i) Geoffrey Tozer; Bergen PO, Kitaienko.

Whatever Rimsky-Korsakov's symphonies may lack in symphonic coherence they make up for in colour and charm. Some of the material is a little thin but there is some highly attractive invention as well. *Antar* is not quite as strong as some of its protagonists would have us believe, but it should surely have a stronger presence in the concert and recorded repertoire than it has. The performances under Neeme Järvi have considerable merit and the Gothenburg orchestra is excellently recorded; moreover the addition of the *Capriccio espagnol* and the *Russian Easter festival overture* makes the set a very attractive proposition.

However, Yevgeni Svetlanov's later digital accounts of the first two symphonies may well be a preferred choice for some collectors. The Russians respond well to Svetlanov's impulsive and full-blooded approach. The recording, made while the orchestra was on tour in France, is very good indeed, and despite one or two interpretative exaggerations this rates a three-star recommendation.

Kitaienko draws very good playing from the Bergen Philharmonic throughout and the first two symphonies are generally successful. In the *Third Symphony* the lustrous colours of the secondary material glow appealingly, but the Scherzo lacks sparkle. He gets very lively results in the *Capriccio espagnol*, but *Sadko* takes a while to warm up, although it has a spectacular close. With Tozer at the keyboard he shares a warmly lyrical view of the *Piano concerto* but, partly because of the resonant sound, the finale lacks something in sparkle, and Malcolm Binns on Hyperion (see above) is preferable.

Symphony No. 2 (Antar), Op. 9.
(M) *** DG (IMS) Dig. 445 568-2 [id.]. Gothenburg SO, Järvi – BORODIN: *Symphony No. 2*, etc. ***

As with the Borodin coupling, Järvi's account is essentially spacious. Glorious playing from the Gothenburg strings and warm, lustrous DG recording combine to make the most of Rimsky's languor, and the central movements are by no means lacking in vitality.

Symphony No. 3 in C, Op. 32; Sadko (Tableau musical), Op. 5; Mlada: Procession of the Nobles. The Maid of Pskov: Overture. The Tsar's Bride: Overture. The Tale of Tsar Saltan: Three Miracles.
*** RCA Dig.09026 62684-2 [id.]. State SO of Russia, Svetlanov.

Yevgeni Svetlanov is ideally at home in this repertoire and this will for most people supersede the rival versions. Choice resides between the new, excellently recorded Svetlanov and Neeme Järvi on DG.

Tsar Saltan: suite
(N) *** Belair BAM 9724. New Russian Orchestra, Oleg Poltevsky – BORODIN: *Symphony No. 2 in B min.* *(*)

The young Russian, Oleg Poltevsky, conducts this hand-picked Russian orchestra in an electrifying account of the colourful *Tsar Saltan* music, well recorded. An excellent, if ungenerous coupling for a rather ponderous reading of the Borodin.

Piano and wind quintet in B flat.
*** Hyperion CDA 66163 [id.]. Capricorn – GLINKA: *Grand Sextet.* ***
(M) *** CRD CRD 3409; *CRDC 4109* [id.]. Ian Brown, Nash Ens. – ARENSKY: *Piano trio No. 1.* ***

Rimsky-Korsakov's youthful *Quintet for piano, flute, clarinet, horn and bassoon* is a thoroughly diverting piece. It is like a garrulous but endearing friend whose loquacity is readily borne for the sake of his charm and good nature. The main theme of the finale is pretty brainless but singularly engaging, and the work as a whole leaves a festive impression. Capricorn's account has great vivacity and is very well recorded.

The Nash Ensemble also give a spirited and delightful account of it on CRD that can be warmly recommended for its dash and sparkle and full, naturally balanced sound; though those used to digital records might like sharper inner definition, the effect is very pleasing with no lack of presence.

OPERA

The Maid of Pskov.
(N) *** Dig. 446 678-2 (2) [id.]. Galina Gorchakova, Vladimir Ognovienko, Vladimir Galusin, Ludmilla Filatova, Kirov Op. Ch. & O, Gergiev.

Diaghilev introduced the first of Rimsky-Korsakov's operas, *The Maid of Pskov*, to Western audiences in 1909 under the title *Ivan le Terrible* as a vehicle for the artistry of Chaliapin. Although it was his first opera, he subsequently revised it twice, and the Kirov offer the third and last version. Much has been made by commentators of the parallels between *The Maid of Pskov* and Mussorgsky's *Boris*, particularly in light of the fact that the two composers shared a room at one stage while writing them; they were even written at the same table and worked out on the same piano! Both tackle serious historic themes and concerned tormented monarchs; both have sumptuous crowd scenes and splendid bell-ringing (the *Coronation scene* in *Boris* is matched by the council summons in Act II of *The Maid of Pskov*); both aspire to naturalistic declamation and to a kind of 'formlessness' in the name of realization, though both operas have set-pieces. The characterization of Rimsky's Tsar Ivan may not equal Mussorgsky's Tsar in *Boris* either in depth or psychological understanding, but there is no lack of effective characterization elsewhere. Olga, marvellously sung by Gorchakova, is in fact an illegitimate daughter of Ivan, whom his vice-regent Prince Tokmakov has brought up. It is the Tsar's recognition of her that tips the scales in favour of the city of Pskov to which he was preparing to lay siege. Her abduction and subsequent death enable him to show the more human side of his personality in much the same way as did Boris in Mussorgsky's opera. The well-known orchestral interlude from the third Act, the *Hunt and storm*, was written under the influence of Berlioz's *Royal hunt and storm* from *Les Troyens*. The cast is strong and Gerigev gets very good singing from the chorus and orchestra. There is a lot of striking music here and the Philips team do it proud.

Sadko (complete).
*** Ph. Dig. 442 138-2 (3) [id.]. Galusin, Tsidipova, Tarassova, Minjelkiev, Gergalov, Grigorian, Alexashin, Diadkova, Boitsov, Bezzubenkov, Ognovenko, Gassiev, Putilin, Kirov Op. Ch. & O, Gergiev.

Whatever its dramatic weaknesses, *Sadko* is full of glorious musical invention, sumptuously orchestrated, which puts the listener completely under its spell. Vladimir Galusin's assumption of the name role is very good, though his handling of dynamic nuance is not always subtle. The vibrato to which one is long accustomed in Russian sopranos is not worrying in Valentina Tsidipova's portrayal of the Sea Princess, Volkhova. Indeed most of the roles are well sung, with the possible exception of Gegam Grigorian's rather tight-throated Hindu merchant. Valery Gergiev brings great warmth and feeling for colour to the opera. The recording is very good, though there are some stage noises, inevitable in stage performances. There is an excellent video (070 439-1 for the laserdisc; 070 439-3 for the VHS cassette), well directed for the cameras by Brian Large; both sound and vision are particularly impressive on Laserdisc. Thoroughly recommended.

Robinson, Thomas (*fl.*1589–1609)

Lute pieces: *Bonny sweet boy; A Galliard; A Gigue; Go from my window; A Toy*. Lute duets: (i) *A Fantasy for 2 lutes; Pazzamezzo galliard; A Plaine song for 2 lutes; the Queen's goodnight; A Toy for 2 lutes; Twenty ways upon the bells*.

(N) (BB) *** Naxos Dig. 8.553974 [id.]. Christopher Wilson (lute); (i) with Shirley Rumsey – HOLBORNE: *Lute pieces*. **(*)

Thomas Robinson, an almost exact Elizabethan contemporary of Holborne, was above all a teacher, rather than a virtuoso lutenist. He taught the future Queen Anne in Denmark before she married King James. He liked to write and play duets with his pupils and the '*Goodnight*' here is obviously addressed to her. It is engaging but rhythmically complicated, so she must have been an accomplished pupil. All the duets here are delightful, particularly *Twenty ways upon the bells* with its two players ingeniously ringing the changes. The solo pieces, too, are full of character, notably the melancholy solo *Toy*, worthy of Dowland. But Robinson has a personality in his own right and it is good to have his music rediscovered. Christopher Robinson and his pupil Shirley Rumsey play everything intimately and spontaneously, readily conveying their pleasure in the music. They are truthfully recorded (not too close) in a pleasant acoustic.

Rodgers, Richard (born 1902)

'*Rodgers and Hammerstein songs*' from: *Allegro; Carousel; The King and I; Me and Juliet; Oklahoma!; The Sound of Music; South Pacific; State Fair*.

*** DG Dig. 449 163-2 [id.]. Bryn Terfel, Opera North Ch., E. N. Philh., Paul Daniel.

Bryn Terfel masterfully embraces the Broadway idiom, projecting his magnetic personality in the widest range of songs, using a remarkable range of tone, from a whispered head voice (as he does magically at the end of *Some enchanted evening*) to a tough, almost gravelly *fortissimo* at climaxes, from the biting toughness of *Nothing like a dame* or Billy Bigelow's big soliloquy in *Carousel* (using a very convincing American accent) to the warmth of *If I loved you* and *You'll never walk alone* (with chorus). It is a comment on the quality of performance that in that final item you get the authentic gulp in the throat without any hint of sentimentality. Specially welcome are the rarities, including one number from *Me and Juliet* and four from the stylized and underprized *Allegro*, including the powerfully emotional *Come home*. With excellent sound and fine playing from Opera North forces under Paul Daniel, this is a wide-ranging survey of Rodgers and Hammerstein (supplemented by first-rate notes) to have one valuing their achievement more than ever. It deserves the widest circulation.

Slaughter on 10th Avenue (ballet from the musical, *On Your Toes*).

(M) *** RCA 09026 68550-2 [id.]. Boston Pops O, Arthur Fiedler – Concert. **(*)

Rodger's brief (nine-minute) ballet score, written for the musical *On Your Toes* and choreographed by Balanchine, has three splendid tunes, two of them quite unforgettable, the one gloriously lyrical, the other bouncingly rooty-tooty. Fiedler makes the very most of them and integrates the score splendidly in a frisson-creating performance that has never been surpassed. The orchestra plays superbly, and the early stereo recording also has an amplitude and bite which fit the music exactly. This comes as part of one of the earliest Boston Pops 'Living Stereo' reissues – the RCA equivalent of Decca's 'Classic Sound'.

Rodó, Gabriel (1904–63)

Symphony No. 2.

(N) *** ASV Dig. CDDCA 1043 [id.]. Gran Canaria PO, Adrian Leaper – OBRADORS: *El Poema de la jungla*. ***

Gabriel Rodó was a cellist and conductor who studied composition in Paris with Alexandre Tansman. He spent his last years (1951–62) as conductor of the Gran Canaria Filarmónica and subsequently as first cellist in Bogotá where he died. His *Second Symphony* was composed in 1957 following the death of Sibelius, whom he admired. It is a powerful and well-argued piece and though not highly individual, it is well worth investigating, particularly in such a good performance and recording.

Rodrigo, Joaquín (1902–99)

A la busca del más allá; (i) *Concierto Andaluz* (for 4 guitars); (ii) *Concierto de Aranjuez* (for guitar); (iii) *Concierto de estío* (for violin); (iv) *Concierto en modo galante* (for cello); (v) *Concierto heroico* (for piano); (vi) *Concierto madrigal* (for 2 guitars); (vii) *Concierto pastoral* (for flute); (viii) *Concierto serenata* (for harp). (ii) *Fantasia para un gentilhombre. Música para un jardín; Per la flor del Iliri blau; 5 Piezas infantiles; Soleriana; Zarabanda lejana y villancico.*

(M) *** EMI Dig. CDZ7 67435-2 (4) [id.]. (i) Moreno, Garibay, López, Ruiz; (ii) Alfonso Moreno; (iii) Augustín Léo Ara; (iv) Robert Cohen; (v) Jorge Osorio; (vi) Moreno, Mariotti; (vii) Lisa Hansen; (viii) Nancy Allen; LSO; Mexico State PO; RPO, Enrique Bátiz.

The only missing concertos here are the second *Guitar concerto* (*Concierto para una Fiesta*) and the later *Cello concerto* (*Concierto como un divertimento*) commissioned by Julian Lloyd Webber. The present EMI recordings were made between 1980 and 1985, many of them in Watford Town Hall, and are of excellent quality, although the early digital technique often brings an overlit sound to the treble, perhaps appropriate for music drenched in Spanish sunshine. The *Summer concerto* for violin ('conceived in the manner of Vivaldi') is the composer's own favourite, and Augustin Léo Ara catches its neo-classical vitality admirably. The *Cello concerto* is given a masterly performance by Robert Cohen; the *Concierto serenata* for harp has both piquancy and charm. Nancy Allen consistently beguiles the ear with her gentleness. The opening of *Concierto pastoral* is far from pastoral in feeling, but Rodrigo's fragmented melodies soon insinuate themselves into the consciousness. Rodrigo's *Piano concerto* has a programmatic content, with the four movements written 'under the sign of the Sword, the Spur, the Cross and the Laurel'. The performers give a strong, extrovert account of the piece. The *Concierto Andaluz* has its weaknesses but remains engaging if a trifle inflated. A similar comment might be made about the effect of the duo *Concierto madrigal*, but the four guitar soloists here do not achieve the strongest profile, and this is also one reason why Alfonso Moreno's account of the famous *Concierto de Aranjuez*, though bright and sympathetic, is in no way outstanding.

The symphonic poem, *A la busca del más allá*, is evocative and powerfully scored; *Música para un jardín* is a quartet of cradle songs, originally conceived for the piano and scored with all the piquancy at the composer's command. The *Five Children's pieces* are delightful, while the two neo-classical evocations of eighteenth-century Spain (*Soleriana*) are also unostentatiously appealing. *Per la flor del Iliri blau* is based on a Valencian legend, and Rodrigo is more impressive in moments of gently atmospheric detail than in the melodrama. The *Zarabanda lejana* was Rodrigo's first work for guitar. He later orchestrated it and added the *Villancico* to make a binary structure, the first part nobly elegiac, the second a gay dance movement.

(i) *Concierto Andaluz* (for 4 guitars); (ii) *Concierto de Aranjuez;* (ii; iii) *Concierto madrigal* (for 2 guitars); (ii) *Concierto para una fiesta; Fantasia para un gentilhombre.* Solo guitar pieces: *Bajando de la Meseta; En los trigales; Fandango; Junto al Generalife; 3 Little Pieces; Romance de Durandarte; Sonata a la española; Tiento antiquo.*

(M) *** Ph. 432 581-2 (3) [id.]. (i) Los Romeros; (ii) Pepe Romero; (iii) Angel Romero; ASMF, Marriner.

This distinguished set gathers together all Rodrigo's major concertante guitar works in first-class performances and adds a rewarding recital of solo works as a postlude, all played with natural spontaneity and complete authority by an artist who feels this music from his innermost being. The *Sonata* is no less strongly Spanish in character and the genre pieces are comparably picturesque in evoking Mediterranean atmosphere and local dance-rhythms. Throughout, Marriner and the Academy provide accompaniments which are thoroughly polished and have much warmth, and the Philips sound is most natural and beautifully balanced.

(i) *Concierto Andaluz* (for 4 guitars); (ii) *Concerto de Aranjuez* (for guitar); (ii; iii) *Concierto madrigal* (for 2 guitars); (ii) *Concierto para una fiesta; Fantasia para un gentilhombre*; *Sones en la Giralda*; (iv) *Concierto serenata* (for harp).

(N) (B) *** Ph. Duo 462 296-2 (2) [id.]. (i) Los Romeros; (ii) Pepe Romero; (iii) Angel Romero; (i–iii) ASMF, Marriner; (iv) Catherin Michel, Monte Carlo Op. O, Almeida.

This Duo includes all Rodrigo's splendid concertante guitar works, most of which are included in the above three-disc set, the exception being the *Sones en la Giralda*. The omission of the solo pieces makes room for the *Concierto serenata* for harp and orchestra, a delectable and unaccountably neglected work in which Catherine Michel is a seductive soloist, neatly accompanied by Almeida. La Giralda is the ancient tower of Seville Cathedral. Its character and associations obviously stimulated Rodrigo's imagination so that the first of its two sections is eerily atmospheric; then the clouds clear away and the finale sparkles with the flamenco dance rhythms of the *Sevillanas*. The work was conceived for harp and orchestra, and it is a pity it was not allotted to Michel; but Pepe Romero and Marriner show an immediate response to its evocation and spirit, and the result is memorable, helped by the first-class recording which pertains throughout these two generously filled CDs.

Concierto de Aranjuez (for guitar and orchestra).
❁ (M) *** Decca Dig. 430 703-2 [id.]. Carlos Bonell, Montreal SO, Dutoit – FALLA: *El amor brujo*, etc. *** ❁
(M) *** Sony SMK 60022 [id.]. John Williams, ECO, Barenboim – CASTELNUOVO-TEDESCO; VILLA-LOBOS: *Guitar concerto*. ***
(BB) *** Naxos Dig. 8.550729 [id.]. Norbert Kraft, N. CO, Nicholas Ward – CASTELNUOVO-TEDESCO: *Concerto* ***; VILLA-LOBOS: *Concerto*. **(*)

Concierto de Aranjuez; (i) *Concierto madrigal* (for 2 guitars); *Fantasia para un gentilhombre*.
(M) *** Ph. 432 828-2 [id.]. Pepe Romero; (i) Angel Romero; ASMF, Marriner.

(i) *Concierto de Aranjuez;* (ii) *Fantasia para un gentilhombre*.
(B) *** Decca Eclipse Dig. 448 243-2. Carlos Bonell, Montreal SO, Dutoit – ALBENIZ: *Rapsodia española*; TURINA: *Rapsodica sinfónica*. ***
(M) *** Decca Dig. 417 748-2. Carlos Bonell, Montreal SO, Dutoit (with FALLA: *Three-cornered hat* ***).

The Bonell/Dutoit *Concierto* was originally paired with the *Fantasia para un gentilhombre*. Decca made this issue even more attractive by adding a bonus of three dances from Falla's *Three-cornered hat* (taken from Dutoit's complete set). In the *Fantasia*, the balance between warmly gracious lyricism and sprightly rhythmic resilience is no less engaging. There is now a third, even more generous coupling on Decca's Eclipse bargain label which is well worth considering, as the Albéniz and Turina concertante works for piano are given dazzling, sultry performances by De Larrocha and Frühbeck de Burgos.

John Williams's 1974 recording of the *Concierto de Aranjuez* with Barenboim is superior to his earlier version with Ormandy (see below). The playing has marvellous point and spontaneity, and the famous *Adagio* has rarely been played with this degree of poetic spontaneity. This performance can challenge the best of its competitors. The balance is characteristically forward, but the result is extremely vivid and clearly focused.

Pepe Romero's performance of the *Concierto de Aranjuez* has plenty of Spanish colour, the musing poetry of the slow movement beautifully caught. The account of the *Fantasia* is warm and gracious, with the Academy contributing quite as much as the soloist to the appeal of the performance. Angel joins Pepe for the Renaissance-inspired duet, *Concierto madrigal*, which is very attractive indeed, making this a very viable alternative to the Decca couplings.

Norbert Kraft is a soloist of personality and he receives spirited, sensitive accompaniments from the Northern Chamber Orchestra under Nicholas Ward. Indeed the work sounds remarkably fresh using a smaller-sized orchestral group, which can bring a degree of intimacy yet produce sufficient body of violin-tone for the rapturous tutti near the end of the *Adagio*. This Naxos CD deserves a place near the very top of the list. The recording is very well balanced, with the guitar given a most convincing relationship with the orchestra and the sound itself vividly realistic.

The balance is near ideal, with the guitar nicely placed in relation to the orchestra in a pleasingly atmospheric ambience. Williams was to record the *Concierto* again with greater charisma, but this early, more intimate account remains appealing, and the couplings are good, too.

The Julian Bream Edition
Concierto de Aranjuez.
(M) *** RCA 09026 61598-2. Julian Bream, Melos Ens., Colin Davis – ARNOLD: *Concerto;* BENNETT: *Concerto* ***.
(M) *** RCA Dig. 09026 61605-2 [id.]. Julian Bream, COE, Gardiner – BERKELEY; BROUWER: *Concertos*. ***
*** EMI Dig. CDC7 54661-2 [id.]. Julian Bream, CBSO, Rattle – ARNOLD: *Concerto;* TAKEMITSU: *To the edge of dream*. ***

(i) *Concierto de Aranjuez;* (ii) *Fantasia para un gentilhombre. Invocation and dance (Hommage à Manuel de Falla); 3 Piezas españolas*.
(M) *** RCA Dig. 09026 61611-2. Julian Bream, (i) COE, Gardiner; (ii) RCA Victor CO, Leo Brouwer.

The differences between Bream's two earlier RCA readings of the *Concierto*, the first (analogue) with Colin Davis in 1963, the second (digital) with Gardiner in 1982, are almost too subtle to analyse and perhaps depend as much on the personalities of the two conductors as on that of the soloist. Certainly neither account is upstaged by the most recent version with Rattle. Colin Davis's direction is at its best in the opening movement, as crisply rhythmic as you could like, and in the slow movement Bream is raptly inspirational. Maybe the Gardiner version has a little extra dash and, for those who prefer an all-Rodrigo programme, this could be a good choice and the famous *Adagio* is played in a very free, improvisatory way, with some highly atmospheric wind solos in the orchestra. In the *Fantasia para un gentilhombre* Leo Brouwer, himself a guitarist, brings plenty of orchestral vitality to the later sections of the score. The *Tres Piezas españolas* add to the value of the disc, and both this and the

Homage to Falla show Bream at his most inspirationally spontaneous. The alternative coupling is with concertos by Berkeley and Brouwer.

The later, EMI recording of the *Concierto* with Rattle is also very enjoyable in a slightly more relaxed way. This is not to suggest a lack of point and alertness but, with warmer, somewhat more modern digital sound, the effect is more opulent, although Bream maintains his ruminative, improvisatory style convincingly. The finale is engagingly spirited and lighthearted. In the end choice will depend on couplings.

Concierto de Aranjuez (arr. for harp).
(N) (B) *** Decca Double 433 938-2 (2) [id.]. – Marisa Robles, Philh. O, Dutoit – Recital: *Música española for harp*; SARASATE: *Music for violin and piano*. ***

The glowing acoustic of St Barnabas Church, London creates an attractively romantic aura for Marisa Robles's magnetic and highly atmospheric account of the composer's own arrangement for harp of his famous concerto. Miss Robles is so convincing an advocate that for the moment the guitar original is almost forgotten, particularly when, with inspirational freedom, she makes the beautiful slow movement sound like a rhapsodic improvisation. It is a haunting performance, and coupled not only with a hardly less magical solo recital of Spanish music, but also with some comparatively rare Sarasate, played with panache by Campoli and Ricci.

(i) *Concierto pastoral* (for flute and orchestra); *Fantasia para un gentilhombre* (arr. Galway for flute and orchestra); (ii) *Concierto de Aranjuez* (for guitar and orchestra).
(M) *** RCA Analogue/Dig. 09026 68428-2 [id.]. (i) James Galway, Philh. O, Mata; (ii) Kazuhito Yamashita, Paillard CO, Paillard.

The *Concierto pastoral* was composed for James Galway in 1978. At first hearing, the material seems thinner than usual, but the slow movement is especially effective, with a witty *scherzando* centrepiece framed by the *Adagio* outer sections. Galway's performance is truly superlative, showing the utmost bravura and matching refinement. The arrangement of the *Fantasia* is a very free one, necessitating re-orchestration, exchanging clarinet and horn instrumentation for the original scoring for trumpet and piccolo. The result is, to be honest, not an improvement on the original. But Galway is very persuasive, even if there is a persistent feeling of inflation. The brilliant Japanese guitar player, Kazuhito Yamashita, is not mentioned at all on the front of the CD, yet he contributes a memorable solo contribution to the famous *Concierto de Aranjuez*, especially in the slow movement, where he adds a cadenza. Paillard and his orchestra support him well enough, although the orchestral playing at times lacks refinement. But this digitally recorded performance may be regarded as a bonus.

SOLO GUITAR MUSIC

Tres Piezas españolas.
❁ (BB) *** RCA Navigator Dig. 74321 17903-2. Julian Bream (guitar) – ALBENIZ: *Collection;* GRANADOS: *Collection*. *** ❁

Rodrigo's *Three Spanish pieces* are characteristically inventive, the central *Passacaglia* quite masterly and the closing *Zapateado* attractively chimerical in Julian Bream's nimble figers. This 1983 recording has been added to what was already one of the finest of all recorded guitar recitals of Spanish music. An outstanding bargain in every way.

PIANO MUSIC

Music for 2 pianos: (i) *5 Piezas infantiles* (piano, 4 hands): *Atardecer; Gran marcha de los subsecretarios; Sonatina para dos Muñecas;* (solo piano): *Air de ballet sur le nom d'une jeune fille; Album de Cecilia; A l'ombre de Torre Bermeja; Bagatela; Berceuse d'automne; Berceuse de printemps; Danza de la Amapola; 3 Danzas de españa; 4 Estampas andaluzas; 3 Evocaciones; Pastorale; 4 Piezas (Caleseras: Homenaje a Chueca; Fandango del Ventorrillo; Plegaria de la Infanta de Castilla; Danza Valenciana); Preludio de Añoranza; Preludio al Gallo mañanero; Serenata española; Sonada de adiós (Hommage à Paul Dukas); 5 Sonatas de Castilla, con Toccata a modo de Pregón: Nos. 1–2 in F sharp min.; 3 in D; 4 in B min. (como un tiento); 5 in A. Suite: Zarabanda lejana.*
❁ *** Bridge BCD 9027 A/B [id.]. Gregory Allen (i) with Anton Nel.

Rodrigo's keyboard music is all but unknown and, as this first-class and comprehensive survey shows, for all its eclecticism it is well worth exploring. In his earliest piano work, the *Suite* of 1923, with its sprightly *Prelude*, cool *Sicilienne* and Satie-ish minuet, the link with the French idiom is obvious, while the glittering brilliance of the *Preludio al Gallo mañanero* is unmistakably Debussian. The *Cinq Sonatas de Castilla* look back further in time and draw continually on the keyboard writing of Scarlatti. But they are spiced with piquant dissonances which the Italian composer would have disowned. The *Serenata española* marks Rodrigo's positive adoption of an overtly Andalusian style, while the *Cuatro Piezas* and the *Cuatro estampas andaluzas* are as sharply Spanish in character as any of the similarly picaresque miniatures of Granados or Albéniz. Rodrigo's children's pieces have especial charm. The darker side of Rodrigo's nature, sometimes brooding, sometimes nostalgic, is at its most expressive in the nocturne, *Atardecer*, an ambitious piece for two players; but it also colours some of the miniatures, not least the austere yet deeply felt *Plegaria de la Infanta de Castilla* from the *Cuatro Piezas*. The recording is uncommonly real and has great presence. In the duo works Allen is admirably partnered by Anton Nel.

A l'ombre de Torre Bermeja; 2 Berceuses; 4 Estampas Andaluzas; 3 Evocaciones (Homenaje a Joaquin Turina); 4 Piezas; 5 Piezas del Siglo XVI (Diferencias sobre Antonio de Cabezón's Canto del Caballero; 2 Pavans of Muis de Milan; Pavan of Enríquez de Valderrábano; Fantasia que contrahace la harpa de Ludovico of Alonso Mudarra).
*** Collins Dig. 1434-2 [id.]. Artur Pizarro.

It is good to have a highly recommendable single-CD representation of Rodrigo's evocative and sharply characterized piano music, opening with five pieces in which the composer draws on earlier Spanish musicians of the sixteenth century – after the fashion of Ravel's *Le tombeau de Couperin*. Of the two gentle *Berceuses*, the *Berceuse d'Automne*, with its sombre, tolling-bell-like figure, is particularly haunting, while the *Turina Evocations* and the even more overtly Spanish *Estampas Andaluzas* glitteringly demonstrate a wide palette of pianistic colour. Artur Pizarro is thoroughly at home in this repertoire and plays with panache, demonstrating a striking Spanish sensibility and feeling for dynamic nuance. His account of the last piece on this disc, *A l'ombre de Torre Bermeja*, is a *tour de force* of spontaneous pianistic flair. He is splendidly recorded.

Roger-Ducasse, Jean-Jules
(1873–1954)

Au jardin de Marguérite: Interlude; Epithalame; Prélude d'un ballet; Suite française.
*** Marco Polo Dig. 8.223641 [id.]. Rheinland-Pfalz Philh. O, Segerstam.

Le joli jeu de furet: Scherzo; Marche française; Nocturne de printemps; Orphée: 3 fragments symphoniques; Petite suite.
*** Marco Polo Dig. 8.223501 [id.]. Rheinland-Pfalz Philh. O, Segerstam.

The music of Roger-Ducasse has both elegance and atmosphere. The *Nocturne de printemps* and the fragmentary but imaginative *Prélude d'un ballet* show a post-impressionist, Debussy-like figure with a refined feeling for the orchestra; elsewhere, in *Orphée* for example, the influence of d'Indy can be discerned. There are touches of Ravel and in the *Epithalame* something of the high spirits of Les Six. Segerstam has a good feeling for this repertoire and gets atmospheric and sensitive performances from his Baden-Baden forces and good, serviceable recordings from the Marco Polo and radio engineers.

Roman, Johan Helmich (1694–1758)

(i) *Violin concertos: in D min.; E flat; F min.; Sinfonias: in A; D and F.*
*** BIS Dig. CD 284 [id.]. (i) Nils-Erik Sparf; Orpheus Chamber Ens.

Of the five *Violin concertos*, the three recorded here are certainly attractive pieces, particularly in such persuasive hands as those of Nils-Erik Sparf and the Orpheus Chamber Ensemble, drawn from the Stockholm Philharmonic. None of the *Sinfonias* have appeared on disc before. Very stylish and accomplished performances that are scholarly in approach.

Drottningholm music; Little Drottningholm music.
(BB) *** Naxos Dig. 8.553733 [id.]. Uppsala CO, Halstead.

In 1744 Johan Helmich Roman wrote 24 pieces for the very grand four-day ceremonies celebrating the marriage of the future King of Sweden to a daughter of Frederick the Great of Prussia. From first to last they are full of delightful invention, starting with a swaggering *Allegro* which, like other movements, owes something to the example of Handel's *Water music*, and ending with a bouncy *vivace Jig*. Halstead also includes eight extra pieces, written to be used in reserve at the wedding, under the title *Little Drottningholm music*. Unlike the recording on Musica Sueciae (see below), Halstead's Naxos version – just as exhilarating, often at brisker speeds – uses period instruments to bring out the great variety of instrumental colour. Fresh, lively performances and excellent sound.

Little Drottningholm Music; Sjukmans Music; (i) *Piante amiche.*
*** Musica Sveciae Dig. MSCD 417 [id.]. (i) Pia-Maria Nilsson; Stockholm Nat. Museum CO, Claude Génetay.

Génetay offers all 17 dances of the *Little Drottningholm Music* plus the somewhat earlier *Sjukmansmusiquen* which has no less appeal. The performances by the Stockholm National Museum Orchestra convey real pleasure in the music-making. The disc includes a short cantata probably (but not certainly) by Roman, *Piante amiche*, which is attractive whatever its authenticity, and nicely sung too by Pia-Maria Nilsson. The recorded sound is well balanced and truthful.

(i) *Assaggi for violin in A, in C min. and in G min., BeRI 301, 310 & 320;* (i; ii) *Violin and harpsichord sonata No. 12 in D, BeRI 212;* (ii) *Harpsichord sonata No. 9 in D min., BeRI 233.*
*** Cap. CAP 21344 [id.]. (i) Jaap Schröder; (ii) Johann Sönnleitner.

The *Assaggi* (essays) recorded here often take one by surprise, particularly when played with such imagination as they are by Jaap Schröder. The harpsichord sonata is also more inward-looking than many others of Roman's pieces, and the only work that one could possibly describe as fairly predictable is the opening *Sonata for violin and continuo*. Excellent performances and recording, as well as exemplary presentation.

Ropartz, Joseph Guy (1864–1955)

Symphony No. 3 (for soloists, chorus and orchestra).

(M) *** EMI (SIS) Dig. CDM7 64689-2. Pollet, Stutzman, Dran, Vassar, Orféon Donostiarra Ch., Toulouse Capitole O, Plasson.

Like the Magnard symphonies, the *Third Symphony* of Ropartz has much nobility and there is a sense of scale and grandeur. There is much in the pantheistic vision of its opening pages that one cannot fail to respond to, and some felicitous harmonic invention. There is a personality here, and all lovers of French music will find it rewarding. Even if the recording (and some of the solo singing) is not of the very highest order, the orchestral playing under Michel Plasson is thoroughly committed.

Prélude, marine et chansons for flute, violin, viola, cello and harp.

❁ (M) *** Decca 452 891-2 [id.]. Osian Ellis, Melos Ens. – DEBUSSY: *Sonata for flute, viola and harp;* RAVEL: *Introduction and allegro;* ROUSSEL: *Sérénade for flute, violin, viola, cello and harp.* *** ❁

Ropartz's *Prélude, marine et chansons* has a comparable intimacy of feeling with the works by his more famous contemporaries. It abounds in Gallic delights to charm the listener's ear, especially the wistful central movement, which is exquisitely played, as is the charmingly perky finale. The recording could hardly be more enticing in its delicacy of atmosphere.

Rore, Cipriano da (*c.* 1515–65)

Missa Praeter rerum seriem. Motets: *Ave regina; Descendit in hortum meum; Infelix ego; Parce mihi.*

*** Gimell/Ph. Dig. 454 920-2 [id.]. Tallis Scholars, Peter Phillips (with JOSQUIN DES PRES: Motet: *Praeter rerum seriem* ***).

Cipriano da Rore was Josquin's successor at the Italian Court d'Este at Ferrara. His *Missa Praeter rerum seriem* is appropriately preceded by the richly textured six-part Josquin motet based on the same melodic sequence. Rore's piece was intended as a tribute to his illustrious predecessor and is a worthy accolade, lyrically powerful, contrapuntally fascinating, spiritually serene and beautifully sung by these highly experienced singers, whose director knows just how to pace and inflect its linear detail and shape its overall structure. The four motets are hardly less impressive, and Gimell's recording, as ever, is virtually flawless.

Rosenberg, Hilding (1892–1985)

Concertos for strings Nos. 1, 4; Suite on Swedish folk tunes for strings, Op. 36.

(N) *** CPO Dig. CPO 999 573-2 [id.]. Deutsche Kammerakadmie Neuss, Goritzki.

Older collectors may recall Carl Garaguly's 78 r.p.m. recording with the Stockholm Concert Association Orchestra (as the Philharmonic was then called) of the *First concerto* for strings of 1946, one of Rosenberg's most inventive and engaging scores. This completely supersedes it as a performance and, understandably enough, as a recording. Johannes Goritzki and his superb Deutsche Kammerakademie Neuss couple it with the early and often charming *Suite on Swedish folk songs* from 1927 and the much later *Fourth concerto* also for strings from 1966. The latter is not quite as inventive or fresh as its companion but it is persuasively played here by these artists and the balance is eminently truthful. Those who are on Rosenberg's wavelength need not hesitate.

Orfeus i sta'n (Orpheus in town): ballet suite; (i) *Sinfonia concertante for violin, viola, oboe, bassoon and orchestra;* (ii) *Violin concerto No. 1. Symphony Nos. 3 (The Four Ages of Man;* 1939 version); (iii) *4 (Johannes Uppenbarelse: The Revelation of St John the Divine):* excerpts; (iv) *5 (Ortagårdsmästaren);* (v) *Den heliga natten (The Holy Night);* (vi) *Suite in D: Pastorale.*

(***) Caprice mono CAP 21510 (3) [id.]. Swedish RO or Stockholm PO, composer; with (i) Barter, Berglund, Lännerholm, Lavér; (ii) Charles Barkel; (iii) Anders de Wahl, Swedish R. Ch.; (iv) Lorri Lail, Swedish R. Ch.; (v) Björker, Lail, Lindberg-Torlind, Nilsson, Ohlson, Saedén, Widgren, Chamber Ch.; (vi) Lotte Andriesson.

The majority of these Archive recordings were made between 1940 and 1947. The suite from the ballet, *Orpheus in Town*, shows the sophisticated man-about-town side of the composer and is inventive and witty, while his inspiration in the oratorio, *The Holy Night*, is spread rather thin – despite some memorable singing from the baritone, Erik Saedén. There is nothing thin about the *Third Symphony*, based on Romain Rolland's *The Four Ages of Man* and interspersed with narration before each of the four movements, read by the composer. His pacing, particularly in the first movement, is expansive and, above all, convincing, and the same measured style emerges in the excerpts from the *Fourth Symphony* (*The Revelation of St John the Divine*), recorded in 1940 with narrator rather than baritone. The *Fifth Symphony*, for soprano, chorus and orchestra, has a serenity, eloquence and strength which are very striking. For the most part it finds Rosenberg at his most deeply characteristic best. The *Sinfonia concertante* is a good piece in neo-classical idiom (sounding like a Swedish Martinů) but the *Violin concerto No. 1* is of lesser interest and finds the composer in manufactured mode. It is good to hear him as pianist, accompanying Lotte Andriesson in 1935 in the *Pastorale* movement from his *Suite in D* for violin and piano. The documentation could not be more comprehensive or researched more scrupulously. A valuable issue of great interest.

(i) *Symphonies Nos. 3;* (ii) *6 (Sinfonia semplice).*
(N) *** Phono Suecia PSCD 100 [id.]. Stockholm PO, Herbert Blomstedt; (ii) Stockholm SO, Stig Westerberg.

Both recordings come from the 1960s and are analogue. Apart from Tubin, who was Estonian-born and naturalized Swedish, Hilding Rosenberg is undoubtedly the finest Swedish symphonist after Stenhammar. But although the *Second (Sinfonia breve)* and his *Fourth Symphony (The Revelation of St John the Divine)* have appeared on CD, neither Nos. 3 nor 6 have been re-recorded since these versions first came out. The *Third* originally bore the subtitle *The Four Ages of Man* and was inspired by Romain Rolland's novel, *Jean Christophe*. Originally there was narration between each of the four movements, and a Swedish Radio recording, made in 1948 with the composer conducting, exists on the Caprice label. In it he can also be heard reading the links, the latter recorded in the 1970s.

After this Rosenberg had second thoughts about the symphony, withdrawing the literary programme and excising a fugal section in the scherzo. It is strong, purposeful music and its slow movement, with its delicately wrought textures, muted colours and transparent scoring, shows the composer at his best. Blomstedt and the Stockholm Philharmonic are persuasive advocates and the 1966 recording sounds well. The *Sinfonia semplice* radiates the poetic feeling and sense of melancholy that pervade the Swedish summer nights. There is a keen awareness of nature throughout. The 1960 recording made by the augmented Swedish Radio Orchestra, here called the Stockholm Symphony, under Sixten Ehrling is very good and the performance excellent. Rosenberg possesses a richly stocked imagination and his music has a distinctively individual stamp. Robert Simpson spoke of him as an Old Testament figure and there is indeed a nobility and dignity about his music that yields rich rewards. It would be more competitive at mid rather than full price but nevertheless this CD is strongly recommended.

Symphony No. 4 (Johannes Uppenbarelse: The Revelation of St John the Divine).
*** Caprice Dig. CAP 21429. Håkan Hagegård, Swedish R. Ch., Pro Musica Ch., Rilke Ens., Gothenburg SO, Ehrling.

Rosenberg's remarkable 80-minute symphony-oratorio to texts from the Bible and by the Swedish poet, Hjalmar Gullberg, is for large forces and is a powerful work of real vision. Its opening fourths recall the world of Walton's *Belshazzar's feast* or of Hindemith, and one's thoughts occasionally turn to Honegger's *King David*. The biblical text inspires the most vividly expressive music, while the Gullberg poems are in an archaic and often serene style. Despite occasional longueurs, the overall impact of this score is very powerful. A splendid performance, very well recorded, though it needs to be played at a slightly higher-level setting than usual.

Rosetti, Antonio (*c.* 1750–92)

Horn concerto in D min., Kaul III:43.
(M) **(*) Teldec/Warner 0630 12324-2 [id.]. Hermann Baumann, Concerto Amsterdam, Jaap Schröder – DANZI: *Horn concerto in E;* HAYDN: *Horn concerto in D.* **(*)

The Bohemian composer, born Franz Anton Rössler, who adopted an Italian name, wrote prolifically and attractively for the horn: the present concerto is characteristic of the taxing melodic line he provides for the soloist. He was especially good at *rondo* finales, and the present example shows him at his melodically most exuberant. Baumann's recording could do with more warmth in the orchestra: the string-tone is close-miked and rather dry, while the horn-timbre by contrast resonates openly; but this makes an attractive collection, despite the less than ideal orchestral sound.

Rossini, Gioachino (1792–1868)

Ballet music from: *Mosè; Otello; Le siège de Corinthe; William Tell.*
(B) **(*) Ph. (IMS) Duo 442 553-2 (2) [id.]. Monte Carlo Op. O, Antonio de Almeida – DONIZETTI: *Ballet music.* ***

Not all these items are lightweight, and Almeida draws positive and vigorous performances from the Monte Carlo orchestra. The strings often play with finesse, notably in the famous *William Tell ballet*, but the orchestra cannot quite provide the colour and degree of zestful brilliance which makes the Philharmonia Donizetti coupling so attractive. The sound in Monte Carlo, although agreeable, is less vivid than in London. Even so, this is very enjoyable.

La boutique fantasque (ballet, arr. Respighi) complete.
(B) **(*) Decca Eclipse Dig. 448 984-2. Nat. PO, Bonynge – CHOPIN: *Les Sylphides*. **(*)
(N) **(*) Decca Dig. 455 983-2 [id.]. Montreal SO, Charles Dutoit – RESPIGHI: *Brazilian impressions*. **

Decca have long made a speciality of recording this delightful, sparkling ballet score – from Ansermet's early mono LP with the LSO – onwards. This modern recording by Dutoit and the Montreal Orchestra is well up to house standards. The Decca sound is particularly well detailed and spacious. But the performance itself, though very well played, is just a little bland, especially alongside Bonynge.

Bonynge goes for sparkle and momentum above all in Respighi's brilliant and sumptuous rescoring of Rossini, a magical ballet if ever there was one. The Decca compact disc has great brilliance and the orchestral colours glitter and glow within the attractive resonance of Kingsway Hall, although there is a degree of digital edge on the treble. Bonynge's exuberance is certainly exhilarating when the sound is so spectacular.

La boutique fantasque: extended suite.
(M) *** RCA 09026 61847-2 [id.]. Boston Pops O, Arthur Fiedler – OFFENBACH: *Gaîté parisienne*. *** ✿

Fiedler offers nearly half an hour of the ballet, not missing out much of importance. The performance sparkles, the playing has warmth and finesse and the Boston acoustics add the necessary atmosphere at the magically evocative opening. John Pfeiffer's remastering of this 1956 recording leaves little to be desired and the coupling is indispensable.

La boutique fantasque (ballet, arr. Respighi): *suite*.
(M) **(*) Chandos CHAN 6503 [id.]. SNO, Gibson – DUKAS: *L'apprenti sorcier;* SAINT-SAENS: *Danse macabre*. **(*)
(M) **(*) Sony SBK 46340 [id.]. Phd. O, Ormandy (with TCHAIKOVSKY: *Sleeping Beauty:* highlights. **)

Gibson's version of the suite is strikingly atmospheric. Helped by the glowing acoustics of Glasgow's City Hall, the opening has much evocation. The orchestra is on its toes and plays with warmth and zest, and the 1973 recording has transferred vividly to CD.

Ormandy presents Respighi's glittering orchestration with much brilliance and dash, and the Philadelphia Orchestra has all the sumptuousness one could ask for. This is more extrovert music-making than Gibson's and it is undoubtedly exhilarating, and matched by the sumptuously glossy and generous Tchaikovsky coupling.

Introduction, theme and variations in C min. for clarinet and orchestra.
*** ASV Dig. CDDCA 559 [id.]. Emma Johnson, ECO, Groves – CRUSELL: *Concerto No. 2* *** ✿; BAERMANN: *Adagio* ***; WEBER: *Concertino*. ***

As in all her recordings, Emma Johnson's lilting timbre and sensitive control of dynamic bring imaginative light and shade to the melodic line. Brilliance for its own sake is not the keynote, but her relaxed pacing is made to sound exactly right. Vivid recording.

String sonatas Nos. 1–6 (complete).
(BB) *** Decca Double 443 838-2 (2) [id.]. ASMF, Marriner (with CHERUBINI: *Etude No. 2 for French horn and strings* (with Barry Tuckwell); BELLINI: *Oboe concerto in E flat* (with Roger Lord) ***) – DONIZETTI: *String quartet*. ***
*** ASV CDDCA 767 [id.]. Serenata of London (members).
*** Hyperion Dig. CDA 66595 [id.]. O of Age of Enlightenment (members).
(B) *** EMI forte (SIS) Analogue/Dig. CZS5 69524-2 (2) [CDFB 69524]. Polish CO, Maksymiuk – MENDELSSOHN: *String symphonies;* JANIEWICZ: *Divertimento;* JARZEBSKI: *Chromatica; Tamburetta*. ***

We have a very soft spot for the sparkle, elegance and wit of these ASMF performances of the Rossini *String sonatas*, amazingly accomplished products for a 12-year-old. Marriner offers them on full orchestral strings but with such finesse and precision of ensemble that the result is all gain. The 1966 recording still sounds remarkably full and natural, and the current CD transfer adds to the feeling of presence. The overall playing time of just over 80 minutes means that the six sonatas will not comfortably fit on a single CD, so the new Double Decca two-for-the-price-of-one format is ideal, with other music added. Apart from the Donizetti *Quartet*, which has an appropriately Rossinian flavour, the two minor concertante works are well worth having, with both Barry Tuckwell (in what is in essence a three-movement horn concertino) and Roger Lord in excellent form.

The Serenata of London, working as a string quartet, and a comparably sized group from the Orchestra of the Age of Enlightenment, playing period instruments, each manage to include all six of the *String sonatas* on one CD. As might be expected, the Serenata, playing modern instruments and led by the easily brilliant Barry Wilde, give the warmer, more sunny bouquet to Rossini's string textures; their competitors, led by the dazzling Elizabeth Wallfisch, offer a slightly drier vintage, though their approach is by no means unsmiling. Indeed their bass player, ChiChi Nwanoku, brings added sharpness of attack to his moments of bravura, where Michael Brittain, with comparable virtuosity, at times sounds rather deadpan. On both discs the recording is truthful and naturally balanced.

Jerzy Maksymiuk with the Polish Chamber Orchestra consistently chooses challengingly fast speeds, and the playing is bracingly brilliant. Though some of the fun is lost, the wit remains, and these virtuoso performances are still most enjoyable for their exhilarating dash. Nos. 2, 3, 4 and 5 were recorded in analogue sound, earlier than the rest, but the difference is minimal and no one will complain at the quality, which is excellent. A fine alternative to the Marriner versions, and made the more attractive by the couplings, notably the Janiewicz *Divertimento*, so like Rossini in style, and also the two Jarzebski lollipops which stand out for their strength of personality.

(i) *Sonatas for strings Nos. 1–6*; (ii) *Overtures: Il barbiere di Siviglia; (iii) L'Italiana in Algeri; Otello; Maometto II; Semiramide; Le siège de Corinthe.*

(N) (B) **(*) Erato/Warner Ultima Double 3984 24242-2 (2). (i) I Solisti Veneti; (ii) Lausanne CO, (iii) Philh. O; (i;iii) Scimone; (ii) López-Coboz.

String sonatas Nos. 1–3; (i) *Andante and theme with variations in E flat for clarinet and orchestra;* (ii) *Une Larme for double bass.*

(N) (BB) ** Naxos Dig. 8.554418 [id.]. Hungarian Virtuosi, Tamás Benedek with (i) János Szepesi; (ii) Vilmos Buza.

String sonatas Nos. 4–6; (i) *Variations in C for violin and small orchestra.*

(N) (BB) ** Naxos Dig. 8.554419 [id.]. Hungarian Virtuosi, Tamás Benedek with (i) Miklós Szenthelyi.

Scimone gives affectionate and nicely turned performances of the *String sonatas* – their geniality not missed – and his lively tempi (without rushing) ensure that all six fit on a single CD. The overtures are also played with enthusiasm and polish in London and more resonantly recorded (*Il barbiere* in Lausanne is rather more intimate). Although Marriner's set of the sonatas remains in a class of its own, if the programme appeals this Ultima Double is certainly worth considering.

The Naxos performances are very well played, warm and elegant enough, but surprisingly, with a Hungarian virtuoso group, have neither fizz not wit. Of the extra items the *Variations* for clarinet has an attractively jocular finale. No complaints about the recording.

VOCAL MUSIC

Cantata: *Giovanna d'Arco*. Songs: *L'âme délaissée; Ariette à l'ancienne; Beltà crudele; Canzonetta spagnuola (En medio a mis colores); La grande coquette (Ariette pompadour); La légende de Marguerite; Mi lagnerò tacendo* (5 settings including *Sorzico* and *Stabat Mater*); *Nizza; L'Orpheline du Tyrol (Ballade élégie); La pastorella; La regata veneziana* (3 songs in Venetian dialect); *Il risentimento; Il trovatore.*

*** Decca Dig. 430 518-2 [id.]. Cecilia Bartoli, Charles Spencer.

The songs of Rossini's old age were not all trivial, and this brilliantly characterized selection – with the pianist as imaginative as the singer – gives a delightful cross-section. Bartoli's artistry readily encompasses such a challenge, a singer who, even at this early stage of her career, is totally in command both technically and artistically. The recording, too, has splendid presence.

(i) *Cantata in onore del Sommo Pontefice Pio Nono*; (ii) *La morte di Didone.*

(N) **(*) Decca Dig. 458 843-2 [id.]. (i;ii) Mariella Devia; (i) Paul Austin Kelly, Michele Pertusi, Francesco Piccoli, La Scala Philharmonic Ch. & O, Chailly.

The two cantatas here are separated by over 30 years: *La morte di Didone* comes from 1811, not long after Rossini had abandoned his studies in Bologna, while the *Cantata in onore del Sommo Pontefice Pio Nono* was written for the accession of Pope Pius IX in 1847 – of whom liberal opinion at first had high hopes, soon dashed after the turbulence of 1848. The latter is significantly longer, and was more of a compilation, since Rossini recycled material from *Ermione*, *Armide* and *Ricciardo e Zoraide*, operas that had by this time fallen into obscurity. The autograph of *La morte di Didone* does not survive and the editor has collated the five manuscript copies and fragments to produce a convincing reconstruction. Neither work is top-drawer Rossini by any manner of means but Chailly gives lightly articulated and well-sprung accounts of both and draws excellent singing from his splendid team. Mariella Devia, the soloist in the early cantata, brings a splendid ardour to her part. The Decca recording is very good without being in the first flight.

Petite messe solennelle.

(M) **(*) Decca Dig. 444 134-2 (2) [id.]. Dessì, Scalchi, Sabbatini, Pertusi, Bologna Teatro Comunale Ch. & O, Chailly.

(i) *Petite messe solennelle;* (ii) *Stabat Mater.*

(B) **(*) EMI forte Dig. CZS5 68658-2 (2) [CDFB 68658]. (i) Popp, Fassbaender, Gedda, Kavrakos, King's College Ch., Katia & Marielle Labèque, Briggs, Cleobury; (ii) Malfitano, Baltsa, Gambill, Howell, Maggio Musicale Fiorentino Ch. & O, Muti.

Rossini's *Petite messe solennelle* must be the most genial contribution to the church liturgy in the history of music. Sawallisch's recording of Rossini's original score of this work – originally Ariola, later Eurodisc – remains the finest on record, but perversely it remains out of the catalogue. However, the EMI/King's version provides a different and contrasting view from Sawallisch's, very enjoyable in its own right. The use of the refined trebles of King's College Choir brings a timbre very different from what Rossini would have expected from boys' voices – but, arguably, close to what he would have wanted. That sound is hard to resist when the singing itself is so movingly eloquent. The work's underlying geniality is not obscured, but here there is an added dimension of devotional intensity from the chorus which, combined with outstanding singing from a fine quartet of soloists and beautifully matched playing from the Labèque sisters, makes for very satisfying results. The recording, too, attractively combines warmth with clarity. Rossini loses nothing of his natural jauntiness in his setting of the coupled *Stabat Mater*, but Muti's view is a dramatic one, and it is sad that he did not record it with the Philharmonia or the Vienna Philharmonic, with whom he gave a memorable reading at the 1983 Salzburg Festival. As it is, the Florence Festival forces are sometimes rough – notably the orchestra – and the singing at times unpolished, though the solo quartet is a fine one. Warm but rather unrefined recording.

Chailly chooses Rossini's orchestral version (made in 1867), although Rossini himself preferred his original, as do we. Nevertheless, with a fine solo team, Daniella Dessì and Gloria Scalchi both singing beautifully (and ravishing in their *Qui tollis* duet), and with the bass rising to the occasion in the *Quoniam tu solus sanctus*, this is a very considerable account. The Bologna Chorus are not helped by a somewhat backward balance which, within the warmly resonant acoustic, does not provide an ideal sharpness of focus. But they sing with much ardour, especially in the *Gloria* and *Credo*, and Chailly ensures that the *Et resurrexit* caps the performance ebulliently. Apart from the choral balance (and that is not a real problem when the performers are so committed), the recording is glowing and vivid.

Soirées musicales (excerpts): *La partenza; La pesca; La promessa; La regata veneziana.*

(N) *** BBC Legends BBCB 8001-2 [id.]. Heather Harper, Dame Janet Baker, Benjamin Britten – BRAHMS: *Liebeslieder waltzes, Op. 52.* TCHAIKOVSKY: *4 Duets.* ***

Both the tongue-in-cheek humour and the outright fun (as in the gondolier race of *La regata veneziana*) are vividly caught in this BBC recording from the 1971 Aldeburgh Festival. Heather Harper and Janet Baker match beautifully, while remaining characterfully distinct, yet Britten at the piano remains master of ceremonies in family music-making idealized.

Stabat Mater.

✿ *** Chandos Dig. CHAN 8780 [id.]. Field, Della Jones, A. Davies, Earle, London Symphony Ch., City of L. Sinfonia, Hickox.

(B) (***) DG Double mono 439 684-2 (2) [id.]. Stader, Radev, Haefliger, Borg, Berlin RIAS Chamber Ch., St Edwige's Cathedral Ch., Berlin RIAS SO, Fricsay – VERDI: *Requiem.* (***)

Richard Hickox rightly presents Rossini's *Stabat Mater* warmly and with gutsy strength. This is a most winning account which has one marvelling that a work written piecemeal should have such consistently memorable invention, much of it anticipating – or reflecting – early Verdi. All four soloists here are first rate, not Italianate of tone but full and warm, and the London Symphony Chorus sings with fine attack as well as producing the most refined *pianissimos* in the unaccompanied quartet, here as usual given to the full chorus rather than to the soloists. Full-bodied and atmospheric sound.

It is the vitality and drama that come over most strongly in Fricsay's strong and spontaneous account of a work that can easily sound lightweight. Even the tenor's *Cujus animam*, jaunty as the rhythm may be, has a warm, lyrical resilience, and the fervour of the choral singing is matched by the soloists. The effect is very much of compellingly live music-making; and this makes a worthy coupling for Fricsay's electrifying account of the Verdi *Requiem*. The mono recording from the mid-1950s has astonishing vividness and the conveyed atmosphere means that no apologies whatever need be made for the sound.

OVERTURES

Overtures: *Armida; Il barbiere di Siviglia; Bianca e Faliero; La cambiale di matrimonio; La Cenerentola; Demetrio e Poblibio; Edipo a Colono; Edoardo e Cristina;* (i) *Ermione. La gazza ladra; L'inganno felice; L'Italiana in Algeri; Maometto II; Otello.* (i) *Ricciardo e Zoraide. La scala di seta; Semiramide; Le siège de Corinthe; Il Signor Bruschino; Tancredi; Il Turco in Italia; Torvaldo e Dorliska; Il viaggio a Reims; William Tell. Sinfonia al Conventello; Sinfonia di Bologna.*

(M) *** Ph. 434 016-2 (3). ASMF, Marriner; (i) with Amb. S.

Marriner's three discs span all Rossini's overtures, but one must remember that the early Neapolitan operas, with the exception of *Ricciardo e Zoraide* and *Ermione*, make do with a simple Prelude, leading into the opening chorus. *Ricciardo e Zoraide*, however, is an extended piece (12 minutes 25 seconds), with the choral entry indicating that the introduction is at an end. *Maometto II* is on a comparable scale, while the more succinct *Armida* is an example of Rossini's picturesque evocation, almost like a miniature tone-poem. Twenty-four overtures plus two sinfonias make a delightful package in such sparkling performances, which eruditely use original orchestrations. Full, bright and atmospheric recording, spaciously reverberant, admirably transferred to CD, with no artificial brilliance.

Overtures: *Il barbiere di Siviglia; La cambiale di matrimonio; La Cenerentola; La gazza ladra; L'Italiana in Algeri; La scala di seta; Semiramide; Il Turco in Italia; William Tell.*
(M) *** Classic fM Dig. 75605 57031-2. Sinfonia Varsovia, Sir Yehudi Menuhin.

Mehuhin and his Polish group, the Sinfonia Varsovia present a stylishly enjoyable collection of nine favourite Rossini overtures. There is a nice balance between wit and finesse, geniality and grace. Tempi are often brisk, but when there is a surge of vivacity there is no loss of poise. The wind solos are elegantly done and the string phrasing combines neatness with graceful warmth. Above all there is spontaneity here, and even at times a Beechamesque twinkle. The recording, made in the No. 1 Studio of Polish Radio in Warsaw, is full and resonant but not excessively so.

Overtures: *Il barbiere di Siviglia; La cambiale di matrimonio; La gazza ladra; L'Italiana in Algeri; Otello; La scala di seta; Semiramide; Le siège de Corinthe; Il signor Bruschino; Tancredi; Torvaldo e Dorliska; Il Turco in Italia; Il viaggio a Reims; William Tell.*
(B) *** Decca Double 443 850-2 (2). Nat. PO, Riccardo Chailly.

In 1981 Chailly and the National Philharmonic made the first compact disc of Rossini overtures (in the Kingsway Hall) and these performances are now combined with their further compilation, recorded at Walthamstow Assembly Hall in 1984, to make a desirable bargain double. At times on the first disc there is a degree of digital edge on tuttis, but the bustle from the cellos is particularly engaging. The solo playing is fully worthy of such clear presentation, demonstrating that this is an orchestra of London's finest musicians. Under Chailly the spirit of the music-making conveys spontaneous enjoyment too, especially in *The thieving magpie* and the nicely paced account of *William Tell*. Incidentally, *Il viaggio a Reims* had no overture at its first performance, but one was cobbled together later, drawing on the ballet music from *Le siège de Corinthe*. The other novelties, *Otello* – played with great dash – and *Torvaldo e Dorliska*, with its witty interchanges between woodwind and strings, are among the highlights, and overall the performances are undoubtedly as infectious as they are stylish.

Overtures: *Il barbiere di Siviglia; La Cenerentola; La gazza ladra; L'Italiana in Algeri; La scala di seta; Semiramide; Il Signor Bruschino; Il Turco in Italia; William Tell.*
(M) *** Ph. 446 196-2. ASMF, Sir Neville Marriner.

This 76-minute collection of nine overtures is drawn from two separate LPs, originally published in 1974 and 1976. All the performances are vivacious and, for the earlier record (*Il Barbiere*, *L'Italiana in Algeri*, *La scala di seta*, *Il Signor Bruschino* and *Il Turco in Italia*), Marriner resurrected the original and lighter orchestrations (*sans* heavy brass and bass-drum). They emerge the more sparkling, and *Il Signor Bruschino* brings the tapping of a triangle stick, not the usual bows . However, no one need fear that *William Tell* is minus trombones or lacks an enthusiastic closing *galop*. There is no shortage of recommendable anthologies of Rossini overtures at mid- and bargain-price, but this is certainly among them.

Overtures: *Il barbiere di Siviglia; La Cenerentola; La gazza ladra; L'Italiana in Algeri; Le siège de Corinthe; Il Signor Bruschino.*
(M) *** DG (IMS) 419 869-2 [431 653-2]. LSO, Abbado.

Brilliant playing, with splendid discipline, vibrant rhythms and finely articulated phrasing – altogether invigorating and bracing. There is perhaps an absence of outright geniality here, but these are superb performances and this remains one of the very finest collections of Rossini overtures ever, for the wit is spiced with a touch of acerbity, and the flavour is of a vintage dry champagne which retains its bloom, yet has a subtlety all its own.

Overtures: *Il barbiere di Siviglia; La Cenerentola; La gazza ladra; La scala di seta; Il Signor Bruschino; William Tell.*
❀ (M) *** RCA GD 60387 [60387-2-RG]. Chicago SO, Fritz Reiner.

As with the others in RCA's remastered Reiner/Chicago series, the 1958 sound-quality has been improved phenomenally; they are preferable to most digital collections. The blaze of brass tone, supported by a rich orchestral backcloth and resonant bass drum, at the galop in the *William Tell overture*, is all-engulfing, a thrilling moment indeed; at the same time the scurrying violins display the utmost virtuosity. But it is the sparkle and vivacity of these performances that one remembers above all – and, in *La Cenerentola*, the wit, as well as fizzing orchestral bravura. One would have liked the opening flourish of *La scala di seta* to be neater – it is presented too lavishly here – but this is the solitary reservation over a magnificent achievement.

Overtures: *Il barbiere di Siviglia; La cambiale di matrimonio; L'inganno felice; L'Italiana in Algeri; La scala di seta; Il Signor Bruschino; Tancredi; Il Turco in Italia*. (i) *Introduction, theme and variations for clarinet and orchestra in E flat*.

✿ (M) *** DG Dig. 445 569-2 [id.]. Orpheus CO; (i) with Charles Neidlich.

This crackingly good CD by the conductorless Orpheus Chamber Orchestra has always been one of the most enjoyable collections of Rossini overtures ever put on disc; at mid-price and with Charles Neidlich's scintillating account of the concertante clarinet work also included, it is irresistible. The wit of the latter is caught with such sparkle and humour that one cannot help but smile with pleasure. In the overtures the orchestra displays astonishing unanimity of style and ensemble. Not only is the crispness of string phrasing a joy, but the many stylish wind solos have an attractive degree of freedom. The DG recording is marvellously real, with the perspective perfectly judged.

Overtures: *Il barbiere di Siviglia; La gazza ladra; L'Italiana in Algeri; La scala di seta; Semiramide; Le siège de Corinth; William Tell*.

*** RCA Dig. 09026 68139-2 [id.]. Hanover Band, Goodman.

This is a delight; it has an exuberance and pace which are quite captivating. If you want period-instrument performances, it will be difficult to beat these.

Overtures: *Il barbiere di Siviglia; La gazza ladra; L'Italiana in Algeri; La scala di seta; Semiramide; William Tell*.

(B) **(*) DG Classikon 439 415-2. BPO, Karajan.

Karajan's virtuoso performances are polished like fine silver. The main allegro of *La scala di seta* abandons all decorum when played as fast as this, and elsewhere bravura often takes precedence over poise. However, with the Berlin Philharmonic on sparkling form, there is wit as well as excitement. The 1971 recording was made (like so many other vintage Karajan recordings) in the Berlin Jesus-Christus Kirche, but the remastering casts very bright lighting on the upper range, which makes sonic brilliance approach aggressiveness in some climaxes.

Overtures: *Elisabetta, Regina d'Inghilterra; La scala di seta; Semiramide; Tancredi; Il Turco in Italia; William Tell*.

(M) *** [RCA Basic 100 09026 61554-2; *61554-4*]. LSO, Abbado (with VERDI: *Overtures: La forza del destino; I vespri siciliani* ***).

Zestful performances from Abbado, with exhilaratingly fast tempi, the LSO players kept constantly on their toes and obviously revelling in their own virtuosity. The exuberance comes to the fore especially in *Tancredi* – there is even a brief clarinet glissando – in a revised version by Philip Gosset. But some might feel that *La scala di seta* would be more effective if a fraction more relaxed and poised, something Beecham understood perfectly, and his account has never been surpassed. *Elisabetta, Regina* is our old friend, *The barber of Seville*. It is listed as such on the CD; but there is a subtle change here which surely implies the use of the proper title – a triplet in the first theme of the *allegro* which is consistently repeated each time the tune appears. This overture too is brilliantly played but does not lose its essential stylishness. The two Verdi overtures which act as a bonus are well suited by Abbado's spiritedly dramatic readings. The remastered recording is vividly bright, but it matches Abbado's approach. A pity that this enjoyable collection is not available in the UK.

Overtures: *La gazza ladra; L'Italiana in Algeri; Semiramide; Il Signor Bruschino; William Tell*.

(B) **(*) EMI forte CZS5 69364-2 (2) [CDFB 69364]. RPO, Sir Colin Davis – BEETHOVEN: *Symphony No. 7* *** ✿; SCHUBERT: *Symphony No. 9*. ***

Sir Colin Davis's 1962 collection, recorded at Abbey Road, brings playing that is admirably stylish with an excellent sense of nuance. *Semiramide* is superb, reminding one of Beecham, as does the spunky opening of *The Thieving Magpie*. *William Tell* is pretty good too, the opening beautifully played. In *Il Signor Bruschino* it seems as if the bow-tapping device is done by the leader alone, which is rather effective. The CD transfer is vivid, but very brightly lit, with some loss of the body of the original; but the orchestral balance is natural.

Semiramide: Overture.

(***) Testament mono SBT 1015 [id.]. BBC SO, Toscanini – BRAHMS: *Symphony No. 2* (***); (with MENDELSSOHN: *Midsummer Night's Dream* excerpt. (**)).

Toscanini's famous concerts with the BBC Symphony Orchestra were obviously very special. This overture from a 1935 concert has one on the edge of one's seat. Quite electrifying. The sound calls for tolerance – but what playing!

OPERA

Armida (complete).

*** Koch Europa Dig. 350211 [id.]. Gasdia, Merritt, Matteuzzi, Ford, Furlanetto, Workman, Amb. Op. Ch., I Sol. Ven., Scimone.

**(*) Sony Dig. S3K 58968 (3) [id.]. Fleming, Kunde, Francis, Kaasch, Bosi, Zennaro, Fowler, D'Arcangelo, Zadvorny, Teatro di Bologna Ch. & O, Gatti.

Armida brings some marvellous fire-eating moments of display, particularly in the last act, when the knight, Rinaldo, finally manages to resist the heroine's magic and escape. Her realization of defeat, dramatically conveyed on a repeated monotone, is intensely human. As Armida, Cecilia Gasdia may not be strikingly characterful (Maria Callas knew the role) but her singing is both powerful and agile, firm and bold in Rossini's brilliant coloratura. As for the problem of finding three high *bel canto* tenors capable of tackling elaborate ornamentation, William Matteuzzi and Bruce Ford more than match Chris Merritt as Rinaldo. Though the principal, he is the least gainly of the three, but still impressive, notably in the love duets with Armida. Ferruccio Furlanetto is excellent in two bass roles, and a fourth tenor, Charles Workman, might well have stood in for any of the others. The booklet includes an introduction in English, but no translation of the Italian libretto.

Under Daniele Gatti the Sony performance, recorded live in Bologna in upfront sound with a noisy audience, is lusty rather than subtle, but Renée Fleming sings commandingly in the title-role, with the voice both golden and flexible, extending down to a ripe chest-register. The four tenors, with three of them singing a splendid trio in Act III, make a generally stylish team, strongly led by Gregory Kunde as Rinaldo. However, first choice for this opera rests with the Koch Europa set, conducted by Scimone.

L'assedio di Corinto (*The siege of Corinth;* complete).

(M) **(*) EMI (SIS) CMS7 64335-2 (3) [CDMC 64335]. Sills, Verrett, Diaz, Theyard, Howell, Lloyd, Amb. Op. Ch., LSO, Schippers.

Thomas Schippers here encourages the coloratura prowess of the prima donna, Beverly Sills, at the expense of the composer's final thoughts, with display material from Rossini's earlier version. Some of the most striking passages are the patriotic choruses, recognizably Rossinian but not at all in the usual vein. Sills, as so often on record, is variable, brilliant in coloratura but rarely sweet of tone, and she is completely upstaged by Shirley Verrett, singing magnificently as Neocle. Some strong singing too among the others, though not all the men are very deft with ornamentation. The recording, made at All Saints', Tooting, has plenty of atmosphere and has achieved a very satisfactory CD transfer.

Il barbiere di Siviglia (complete).

*** Decca Dig. 425 520-2 (3) [id.]. Bartoli, Nucci, Matteuzzi, Fissore, Burchuladze, Ch. & O of Teatro Comunale di Bologna, Patanè.

*** Ph. Dig. 446 448-2 (2). Baltsa, Allen, Araiza, Trimarchi, Lloyd, Amb. Op. Ch., ASMF, Marriner.

*** Teldec/Warner Dig. 9031 74885-2 (2) [id.]. Larmore, Hagegård, Giménez, Corbelli, Ramey, Lausanne CO, López-Cobos.

*** EMI CDS5 56310-2 (2) [CDCB 56310]. Callas, Gobbi, Alva, Ollendorff, Philh. Ch. & O, Galliera.

(M) *** EMI CMS7 64162-2 (2) [CDMB 641622]. De los Angeles, Alva, Cava, Wallace, Bruscantini, Glyndebourne Festival Ch., RPO, Gui.

(N) (***) Testament mono SBT 2166 (2) [id.]. Victoria de los Angeles, Nicola Monti, Gino Bechi, Nicola Rossi-Lemeni, Milan Ch. & SO, Serafin.

(B) *** Naxos Dig. 8.660027/29 [id.]. Ganassi, Serville, Vargas, Romero, De Grandis, Hungaria R. Ch., Failoni CO, Budapest, Will Humburg.

(M) *** RCA 09026 68552-2 (3) [id.]. Merrill, Peters, Valletti, Tozzi, Corena, Met. Op. Ch. & O, Leinsdorf.

**(*) DG Dig. 435 763-2 (3) [id.]. Battle, Domingo, Lopardo, Raimondi, Ch. & COE, Abbado.

(N) (B) **(*) Decca Double 452 591-2 (2). Berganza, Ausensi, Benelli, Corena, Ghiaurov, Rossini Ch. & O of Naples, Varviso.

(M) ** DG 457 733-2 (2) [id.]. Teresa Berganza, Hermann Prey, Luigi Alva, Enzo Dara, Paolo Montarsolo, Amb. Ch., LSO, Abbado.

Cecilia Bartoli made this recording when she was still in her early twenties, and her rich, vibrant voice not only copes brilliantly with the technical demands but she also gives a winningly provocative characterization. In her big Act I aria, *Una voce poco fa*, she even outshines the memorable Agnes Baltsa on the excellent Marriner set. Like the conductor, Bartoli is wonderful at bringing out the fun. So is Leo Nucci, and he gives a beautifully rounded portrait of the wily barber. Burchuladze, unidiomatic next to the others, still gives a monumentally lugubrious portrait of Basilio, and the Bartolo of Enrico Fissore is outstanding, with the patter song wonderfully articulated at Patanè's sensible speed. The snag is that this Decca set is on three CDs; other recommended vresions manage with two.

Il Barbiere was Sir Neville's first opera recording and he finds a rare sense of fun in Rossini's witty score. His characteristic polish and refinement – beautifully caught in the clear, finely balanced recording – never get in the way of urgent spontaneity, the sparkle of the moment. Thomas Allen as Figaro – far more than a *buffo* figure – and Agnes Baltsa as Rosina – tough and biting too – manage to characterize strongly, even when coping with florid divisions, and though Araiza allows himself too many intrusive aitches he easily outshines latterday rivals, sounding heroic, not at all the small-scale tenorino, but never coarse either. Fine singing too from Robert Lloyd as Basilio.

López-Cobos conducts a scintillating performance, helped by brilliant ensembles, generally taken at high speed, with rhythms sprung delectably. Though Håkan Hagegård is a dry-toned Figaro, the recording sets him in a helpful ambience, which equally helps to enhance the comic atmosphere, with the interplay of characters well managed. There are few more stylish Rossini tenors today than Raúl Giménez and, though his voice is not as youthful as some, his musical imagination goes with fine flexibility and point. As for Jennifer Larmore, she is an enchanting Rosina, both firm and rich of tone and wonderfully agile. Crisply consistent, it makes a strong contender among modern digital versions, even next to the delectable Decca version featuring Cecilia Bartoli, particularly when it comes (like Marriner's Philips version) on two discs instead of three.

Gobbi and Callas were here at their most inspired and, with the recording quality nicely refurbished, the EMI is an outstanding set, not absolutely complete in its text, but so crisp and sparkling it can be confidently recommended. Callas remains supreme as a minx-like Rosina, summing up the character superbly in *Una voce poco fa*. The early stereo sound comes up very acceptably in this fine new transfer, clarified, fuller and more atmospheric, presenting a uniquely characterful performance with new freshness and immediacy.

Victoria de los Angeles is as charming a Rosina as you will ever find: no viper this one, as she claims in *Una voce poco fa*, and that matches the gently rib-nudging humour of what is otherwise a 1962 recording of the Glyndebourne production. It does not fizz as much as other Glyndebourne Rossini on record but, with a characterful line-up of soloists, it is an endearing performance which in its line is unmatched. The recording still sounds well. The CDs have been handsomely re-packaged and the documentation is freshly printed.

The Testament issue, superbly transferred, brings out of EMI's archive the long-buried set which Victoria de los Angeles recorded with Serafin in mono in 1952, when her voice was at its fullest and most golden. Though the orchestral playing is often rough, and Serafin is relaxed rather than sparkling, the performance of de los Angeles could not be more seductive. Not as light as her later account with Gui in stereo, this is even sunnier and more glowing. Gino Bechi is a strong if gruff Figaro, Nicola Monti a heady-toned Almaviva and Nicola Rossi-Lemeni a characterful Basilio.

Though the cast is not as starry as with most full-price rivals, the Naxos set makes a first-rate bargain. The singing is hardly less stylish, with Sonia Ganassi a rich-toned Rosina, controlling vibrato well, and with Ramon Vargas an agile and attractively youthful-sounding Almaviva. Roberto Serville as Figaro conveys the fun of the role brilliantly. The *buffo* characters are strongly cast too, with Basilio's *La calunnia* (Franco de Grandis) delightfully enlivened by comments from Bartolo (Angelo Romero), both very much involved in their roles. Will Humburg's often brisk speeds, with crisp recitative matched by dazzling ensembles, never prevent the music (and the singers) from breathing.

Roberta Peters sparkles as Rosina, her voice always sweet and her coloratura (not always avoiding intrusive aitches) exquisitely agile and pointed. Robert Merrill could be a more genuinely comic Figaro, but his vocal acting is certainly impressive and his voice is beautifully focused. Valletti, Corena and Tozzi are all splendid. Leinsdorf manages to provide genuine lightness and so convey the proper sparkling style. Within the fairly wide reverberation the sound remains clear, and the CD transfer has not lost its original bloom. While our first choice for this opera remains with Bartoli and Nucci on Decca, this RCA reissue is well worth having in its own right.

Domingo heads a cast that would be hard to beat today, including Kathleen Battle, Frank Lopardo and Ruggero Raimondi, with Claudio Abbado conducting the Chamber Orchestra of Europe. Domingo is the set's biggest success. Abbado is free and spontaneous-sounding, but his touch, as conveyed in dry, close-up sound, is much heavier-handed, missing much of the sparkle of his earlier DG set, with ensemble-work surprisingly rough. Even Raimondi as Basilio in his big aria, *La calunnia*, is relatively undisciplined, if spontaneous-sounding, and the big bangs at the climax are completely miscalculated. Kathleen Battle makes a minx of a Rosina, coy but full of flair, and Frank Lopardo is a stylish Almaviva, though not well contrasted with Domingo.

Vocally, the Decca Double set with Teresa Berganza an agile Rosina, is very reliable, and Silvio Varviso secures electrifying effects in many of Rossini's high-spirited ensembles. Manuel Ausensi as Figaro himself is rather gruff but Ugo Benelli is charming as the Count, a free-voiced 'tenorino', though he sounds nervous in his first aria. Corena's fine Dr Bartolo is justly famous, and Ghiaurov sings with characteristic richness as Basilio. The Decca 1964 sound is well up to standard and the reissued set comes with a good cued synopsis and is listener-friendly in its documentation. Good value.

Abbado's earlier recording of *Il barbiere* was a curious choice for inclusion among DG's 'Legendary Originals'. It is a clean, satisfying performance, but one which lacks the last degree of sparkle. Berganza's interpretation of the role of Rosina remains very consistent with her earlier performance on Decca, but the Figaro here, Hermann Prey, is more reliable, and the playing and recording have an extra degree of polish. The text is not absolutely complete, but the omissions are of minimal importance. With fresh recorded sound and plenty of immediacy, this remains competitive, but hardly a primary recommendation.

Il barbiere di Siviglia: highlights.
(M) *** EMI CDM5 66671-2 (from above recording, with Gobbi, Callas; cond. Galliera).
**(*) DG (IMS) Dig. 437 841-2 [id.] (from above recording, with Domingo, Battle; cond. Abbado).

The EMI highlights disc offers most of the key solo numbers from Act I, while in Act II it concentrates on Rossini's witty ensembles, including the extended Second Act *Quintet*. The *Overture* is included and, while it is stylishly played, it would have been better to have offered more of the vocal music. The overall playing time is only 57' 26".

Abbado's DG selection is more generous (73 minutes) and will be valuable for those wanting to sample Domingo's highly successful assumption of the title-role. But it is at full price.

The Barber of Seville (sung in English).
**(*) Chandos Dig. CHAN 7023/4 [id.]. Della Jones, Ford, Opie, Rose, ENO Ch. & O, Bellini.

Boldly, with help from the Peter Moores Foundation, long devoted to this cause, Chandos here offers at mid-price this *Barber* in English, using the bright translation of Amanda and Anthony Holden. Strongly cast, it is a genial performance, very well played and recorded. The only reservation is over the relaxed conducting of Gabriele Bellini which lacks dramatic bite. Compensating for that, the principal singers not only characterize vividly but together form a lively ensemble. Alan Opie is a strong, positive Figaro, while Della Jones as Rosina both exploits her rich mezzo tones and brings sparkle to the coloratura. It is good too to have so accomplished a Rossini tenor as Bruce Ford singing Almaviva. Peter Rose as Basilio and Andrew Shore as Dr Bartolo, both young-sounding for these roles, are fresh and firm too.

La cambiale di matrimonio (complete).
* Claves Dig. CD 50-9101 [id.]. Praticò, Rossi, Comencini, De Simone, Facini, Baiano, ECO, Viotti.

This was the first of the Claves series to be recorded in London, and while the voices have fair bloom on them, the recessed orchestra sounds washy, a significant flaw in such intimately jolly music, with ensembles suffering in particular. Viotti is a relaxedly stylish Rossinian, drawing pointed playing from the ECO, but the singing is poor. The tenor Maurizio Comencini sounds unsteady and strained, while Alessandra Rossi as the heroine, agile enough, is too shrill for comfort. The best singing comes from the buffo baritone, Bruno Praticò, as the heroine's father.

La Cenerentola (complete).
*** Decca Dig. 436 902-2 (2) [id.]. Bartoli, Matteuzzi, Corbelli, Dara, Costa, Banditelli, Pertusi, Teatro Comunale (Bologna) Ch. & O, Chailly.
*** Teldec/Warner Dig. 4509 94553-2 (2). Larmore, Giménez, Quilico, Corbelli, Scarabelli, ROHOCG Ch. & O, Rizzi.
(M) (***) EMI (SIS) mono CMS7 64183-2 (2). Gabarain, Oncina, Bruscantini, Noni, Glyndebourne Festival Ch. & O, Gui.
(N) (B) ** DG Double 459 448-2 (2). Berganza, Alva, Montarsolo, Capecchi, Scottish Op. Ch., Abbado.

Cecilia Bartoli makes an inspired Cenerentola. Her tone-colours are not just more sensuous than those of her rivals: her imagination and feeling for detail add enormously to her vivid characterization, culminating in a stunning account of the final rondo, *Non più mesta*. The rest of the cast has been just as carefully chosen, with William Matteuzzi as an engaging prince, sweeter of tone and more stylish than his direct rivals, while the contrasting of the bass and baritone roles is ideal between Alessandro Corbelli as Dandini, Michele Pertusi as the tutor, Alidoro (substitute for the fairy godmother in the Cinderella story), and Enzo Dara as Don Magnifico. Few Rossini opera-sets have such fizz as this, and the recording is one of Decca's most vivid. The video was recorded more recently at the Houston Grand Opera with Bartolli, Corbelli, Dara and Pertusi continuing in the principal roles and Bruno Campanella conducting with fine spirit. Visually the production is a delight. Subtitled in English, this is very highly recommended (Decca 071 444-3).

On Carlo Rizzi's Teldec version with Covent Garden forces, Jennifer Larmore makes an enchanting heroine, with her creamily beautiful mezzo both tenderly expressive in cantilena and flawlessly controlled through the most elaborate coloratura passages. She may not be the fire-eating Cenerentola the vibrant Cecilia Bartoli is on Chailly's outstanding Decca version, but this is a more smiling character, not least in the final exuberant rondo, *Non più mesta*, which sparkles deliciously, more relaxed than with Bartoli. As Ramiro, Raúl Giménez sings with a commanding sense of style, less youthful but more assured than his rival, while Alessandro Corbelli is far more aptly cast here as Don Magnifico than as Dandini in the Decca set. Here the Dandini of Gino Quilico is youthful and debonair, and Alastair Miles is a magnificent Alidoro. Though the Covent Garden forces cannot quite match the close-knit Bologna team in underlining the comedy as in a live performance, as directed by Carlo Rizzi they are consistently more refined, with more light and shade, bringing out the musical sparkle all the more. Excellent, well-balanced sound.

Gui's 1953 recording of *Cenerentola* has mono sound of amazing clarity and immediacy. Sadly the text is seriously cut, but the effervescence of Gui's live performances at Glyndebourne has been infectiously caught. Juan Oncina produces the most sweet-toned singing as the Prince, with the vintage baritone, Sesto Bruscantini, a vividly characterful Dandini, almost another Figaro. The title-role is sung by the Spanish mezzo, Marina de Gabarain, a strikingly positive singer with a sensuous flicker in the voice, very much in the style of the legendary Conchita Supervia.

Abbado's 1971 DG set now reappears inexpensively on a Double. Although enjoyable, it lacks the extrovert bravura and sparkle of an ideal performance. The atmosphere in places is almost of a concert performance, with excellent balance between the participants, helped by fine analogue recording. Berganza, agile in the coloratura, seems too mature, even matronly, for the fairy-tale role of Cinderella. Alva sings well enough but is somewhat self-conscious in the florid writing. Abbado, although hardly witty in his direction, inspires delicate playing throughout. The CD transfer is admirably fresh.

La Cenerentola: highlights.
(M) *** Teldec/Warner Dig. 4509 98819-2 (from complete recording, with Larmore, Giménez, Quilico, Corbelli, Scarabelli, ROHCG Ch. & O, Rizzi).

With vivid recording and nearly 75 minutes of music included, this makes a splendid choice for a disc of highlights, especially for collectors who have the competing Decca set with Cecilia Bartoli. As usual with the Warner Opera Collection series, a full translation is included.

Le Comte Ory (complete).
❁ (M) (***) EMI mono CMS7 64180-2 (2) [Ang. CDMB 64180]. Oncina, Roux, Jeannette and Monica Sinclair, Glyndebourne Festival Ch. & O, Gui.
❁ *** Ph. Dig. 422 406-2 (2). Sumi Jo, Aler, Montague, Cachemaille, Quilico, Pierotti, Lyon Op. Ch. & O, Gardiner.

Gui's classic recording of *Le Comte d'Ory*, with the same Glyndebourne forces who gave this sparkling opera on stage, brings pure delight. In limited but clearly focused mono sound, Gui conveys an extra sparkle and resilience, even over Gardiner's brilliant Philips version. There is a natural sense of timing here that regularly has you laughing with joy, as in the dazzling finale of Act I, one of the most infectiously witty of all recordings of a Rossini ensemble. Juan Oncina in his prime as the Count, the Hungarian Sari Barabas as the Countess Adèle and Michel Roux as the Count's friend are superbly matched by Monica Sinclair as the Countess's housekeeper and Ian Wallace as the Count's tutor. Some 10 minutes of text have been cut, but that allows the complete opera to be fitted on two CDs, each containing a complete act.

On Philips, Gardiner tends to be rather more tense than Gui was, with speeds on the fast side, and he allows too short a dramatic pause for the interruption to the Nuns' drinking choruses. But the precision and point are a delight. Though John Aler hardly sounds predatory enough as the Count, the lightness of his tenor is ideal, and Sumi Jo as Adèle and Diana Montague as the page, Isolier, are both stylish and characterful. So is the clear-toned Gino Quilico as the tutor, Raimbaud. With the cuts of the old Glyndebourne set opened out and with good and warm, if not ideally crystal-clear, recording, this set takes its place as a jewel of a Rossini issue.

La Donna del Lago (complete).
*** Sony Dig. M2K 39311 (2) [id.]. Ricciarelli, Valentini Terrani, Gonzalez, Raffanti, Ramey, Prague Philharmonic Ch., COE, Pollini.

Maurizio Pollini, forsaking the keyboard for the baton, draws a fizzing performance from the Chamber Orchestra of Europe. Katia Ricciarelli in the title-role of Elena, Lady of the Lake, has rarely sung so stylishly on record, the voice creamy and very agile in coloratura. Lucia Valentini Terrani is no less impressive in the travesti role of Elena's beloved, Malcolm; while Samuel Ramey as Elena's father, Douglas, with his darkly incisive singing makes you wish the role was far longer. Of the two principal tenors, Dalmacio Gonzalez, attractively light-toned, is the more stylish; but Dano Raffanti as Rodrigo Dhu copes with equal assurance with the often impossibly high tessitura. The recording is clear and generally well balanced and given added immediacy in the new format.

Elisabetta Regina d'Inghilterra (complete).
(M) *** Ph. 432 453-2 (2). Caballé, Carreras, Masterson, Creffield, Benelli, Jenkins, Amb. S., New Philh. O, Masini.

The overture, which turns out to be the one which we know as belonging to *Il barbiere di Siviglia*, is one of a whole sequence of self-borrowings which add zest to a generally delightful score. In a well-sprung performance like this, with beautiful playing from the LSO and some very fine singing, it is a set for any Rossinian to investigate. Of the two tenors, José Carreras proves much the more stylish as Leicester, with Ugo Benelli, in the more unusual role of a tenor-villain, singing less elegantly than he once did. Caballé produces some ravishing sounds, though she is not always electrifying. Lively conducting and splendid recording.

Ermione (complete).
(M) *** Erato/Warner Dig. 2292 45790-2 (2) [id.]. Gasdia, Zimmermann, Palacio, Merritt, Matteuzzi, Alaimo, Prague Philharmonic Ch., Monte Carlo PO, Scimone.

Ermione begins very strikingly with an off-stage chorus, introduced in the slow section of the overture, singing a lament on the fall of Troy. The use of dramatic declamation, notably in the final scene of Act II, also gives due weight to the tragedy; however, not surprisingly, Rossini's natural amiability keeps bursting through, often a little incongruously. Though the three tenors in this Monte Carlo set from Erato are good by modern standards – Ernesto Palacio (Pirro), Chris Merritt (Oreste) and William Matteuzzi (Pilade) – they are uncomfortably strained by the high tessitura and the occasional stratospheric top notes. Cecilia Gasdia makes a powerful Ermione, not always even enough in her production but strong and agile; while Margarita Zimmermann makes a firm, rich Andromaca. Scimone, not always imaginative, yet directs a strong, well-paced performance. The recording is rather dry on the voices, but the hint of boxiness is generally undistracting and this set is a must for true Rossinians.

Guglielmo Tell (*William Tell:* complete, in Italian).
*** Decca (IMS) 417 154-2 (4) [id.]. Pavarotti, Freni, Milnes, Ghiaurov, Amb. Op. Ch., Nat. PO, Chailly.

Rossini wrote his massive opera about William Tell in French, but Chailly and his team here put forward a strong case for preferring Italian, with its open vowels, in music which glows with Italianate lyricism. Chailly's is a forceful reading, particularly strong in the many ensembles, and superbly recorded. Milnes makes a heroic Tell, always firm, and though Pavarotti has his moments of coarseness he sings the role of Arnoldo with glowing tone. Ghiaurov too is in splendid voice, while subsidiary characters are almost all well taken, with such a fine singer as John Tomlinson, for example, ripely resonant as Melchthal. The women singers too are impressive, with Mirella Freni as the heroine Matilde providing dramatic strength as well as sweetness. The recording, made in 1978 and 1979, comes out spectacularly on CD. The *Pas de six* is here banded into its proper place in Act I.

Guillaume Tell (William Tell) (sung in French).
(M) *** EMI (SIS) CMS7 69951-2 (4) [CDMD 69951]. Bacquier, Caballé, Gedda, Mesplé, Amb. Op. Ch., RPO, Gardelli.

The interest of the 1973 EMI set is that it is sung in the original French. Gardelli proves an imaginative Rossini interpreter, allying his formidable team to vigorous and sensitive performances. Bacquier makes an impressive Tell, developing the character as the story progresses; Gedda is a model of taste, and Montserrat Caballé copes ravishingly with the coloratura problems of Mathilde's role. While Chailly's full-price Decca set puts forward a strong case for using Italian with its open vowels, this remains a fully worthwhile alternative, with excellent CD sound. Indeed the current remastering is first class in every way and the choral passages, incisively sung, are among the most impressive; moreover the set now comes with full translation.

L'inganno felice (complete).
*(*) Claves Dig. CD 50-9211 [id.]. De Carolis, Felle, Zennaro, Previato, Serraiocco, ECO, Viotti.

L'inganno felice is stylishly and energetically conducted by Viotti with sprung rhythms and polished playing, but with a flawed cast. As the heroine, Amelia Felle is agile but too often raw-toned, even if on occasion she can crown an ensemble with well-phrased cantilena. As the hero, Bertrando, Iorio Zennaro has an agreeable natural timbre, but his tenor is not steady enough and strains easily. The buffo, Fabio Previato, is the soloist who comes closest to meeting the full challenge. The recorded sound has a pleasant bloom on it, but the orchestra is too recessed, and though the recitatives are briskly done, with crisp exchanges between the characters, the degree of reverberation is a serious drawback.

L'Italiana in Algeri (complete).
✿ *** DG 427 331-2 (2) [id.]. Baltsa, Raimondi, Dara, Lopardo, V. State Op. Konzertvereinigung, VPO, Abbado.
*** Sony Dig. M2K 39048 (2) [id.]. Valentini Terrani, Ganzarolli, Araiza, Cologne R. Ch., Capella Coloniensis, Ferro.
(M) *** Erato/Warner 2292 45404-2 (2) [id.]. Horne, Palacio, Ramey, Trimarchi, Battle, Zaccaria, Prague Ch., Sol. Ven., Scimone.

Abbado's brilliant version was recorded in conjunction with a new staging by the Vienna State Opera, with timing and pointing all geared for wit on stage to make this the most captivating of all recordings of the opera. Agnes Baltsa is a real fire-eater in the title-role, and Ruggero Raimondi with his massively sepulchral bass gives weight to his part without undermining the comedy. The American tenor, Frank Lopardo, proves the most stylish Rossinian, singing with heady clarity in superbly articulated divisions, while both buffo baritones are excellent too. Like the CBS set, this uses the authentic score, published by the Fondazione Rossini in Pesaro.

The fine Sony version not only uses the critical edition of the score, it goes further towards authenticity in using period instruments, including a fortepiano instead of harpsichord for the recitatives (well played by Georg Fischer). Lucia Valentini Terrani here gives her finest performance on record to date, with her seductively rich, firm voice superbly agile in coloratura. Francisco Araiza as Lindoro peppers the rapid passage-work with intrusive aitches – but not too distractingly – and the strength of the voice makes the performance heroic with no suspicion of the twittering of a tenorino. Ganzarolli treats the role of the Bey, Mustafa, as a conventional buffo role, with a voice not ideally steady but full of character; the rest of the cast is strong, too.

Scimone's highly enjoyable version is beautifully played and recorded with as stylish a team of soloists as one can expect nowadays. The text is complete and alternative versions of certain arias are given as an appendix. Marilyn Horne makes a dazzling, positive Isabella, and Samuel Ramey is splendidly firm as Mustafa. Domenico Trimarchi is a delightful Taddeo and Ernesto Palacio an agile Lindoro, not coarse, though the recording does not always catch his tenor timbre well. Nevertheless the sound is generally very good indeed.

L'Italiana in Algeri: highlights.
(M) *** Sony SMK 53504 [id.] (from above recording, with Terrani, Araiza; cond. Ferro).

On Sony a set of highlights (72 minutes) from a first-rate version, with Lucia Valentini Terrani seductively leading a consistently strong cast.

Maometto II (complete).
*** Ph. (IMS) Dig. 412 148-2 (3). Anderson, Zimmermann, Palacio, Ramey, Dale, Amb. Op. Ch., Philh. O, Scimone.

Claudio Scimone's account of *Maometto II* has Samuel Ramey magnificently focusing the whole story in his portrait of the Muslim invader in love with the heroine. The other singing is less sharply characterized but is generally stylish, with Margarita Zimmermann in the travesti role of Calbo and June Anderson singing sweetly as Anna. Laurence Dale is excellent in two smaller roles, while Ernesto Palacio mars some fresh-toned singing with his intrusive aitches. Excellent recording.

Mosè in Egitto (complete).
(M) *** Ph. 420 109-2 (2). Raimondi, Anderson, Nimsgern, Palacio, Gal, Fisichella, Amb. Op. Ch., Philh. O, Scimone.

Scimone here justifies his claim that the 1819 version is dramatically more effective than both the earlier Italian one and the later Paris one. Rossini's score brings much fine music and, among the soloists, Raimondi relishes not only the solemn moments like the great invocation in Act I and the soaring prayer of Act III, but also the rage aria in Act II, almost like Handel updated if with disconcerting foretastes of Dr Malatesta in Donizetti's *Don Pasquale*. The writing for the soprano and tenor lovers (the latter the son of Pharaoh and in effect the villain of the piece) is relatively conventional, though the military flavour of their Act I cabaletta is refreshingly different. Ernesto Palacio and June Anderson make a strong pair, and the mezzo, Zehava Gal, is another welcome newcomer as Pharaoh's wife. Siegmund Nimsgern makes a fine Pharaoh, Salvatore Fisichella an adequate Arone (Aaron). The well-balanced recording emerges most vividly on CD.

L'occasione fa il ladro (complete).
(M) ** Claves Dig. CD 50-9208/9 [id.]. Bayo, De Carolis, Zennaro, Provvisionato, Previati, Massa, ECO, Viotti.

On two discs, this is one of the longer one-Acters in the Claves series, bringing one of the more recommendable performances, with Viotti at his most relaxed. Maria Bayo as the heroine sings warmly and sweetly, with no intrusive aspirates in the coloratura. The soubrette role of Ernestina is also charmingly done, and the buffo characters sing effectively, though the tenor, Iorio Zennaro, is hardly steady enough for Rossinian cantilena. The two discs come in a single hinged jewel-box at upper-mid-price.

Otello (complete).
(M) *** Ph. 432 456-2 (2). Carreras, Von Stade, Condò, Pastine, Fisichella, Ramey, Amb. S., Philh. O, López-Cobos.

The libretto of Rossini's *Otello* bears remarkably little resemblance to Shakespeare – virtually none at all until the last Act. It is some tribute to this performance, superbly recorded, and brightly and stylishly conducted by López-Cobos, that the line-up of tenors is turned into an asset, with three nicely contrasted soloists. Carreras is here at his finest – most affecting in his recitative before the murder, while Fisichella copes splendidly with the high tessitura of Rodrigo's role, and Pastine has a distinct timbre to identify him as the villain. Frederica von Stade pours forth a glorious flow of beautiful tone, well-matched by Nucci Condò as Emilia. Samuel Ramey is excellent too in the bass role of Elmiro.

La pietra del paragone (complete).
(M) **(*) Van. 08 9031 73 (3) [id.]. Carreras, Wolff, Bonazzi, Elgar, Reardon, Foldi, Diaz, Murcell, Clarion Concerts Ch. & O, Jenkins.

This recording of the *opera buffa*, *La pietra del paragone*, made by Vanguard in New York in 1972, presents the young José Carreras in an incidental role, just one in an attractively fresh-voiced cast of soloists. It is given a vigorous, if occasionally hard-pressed performance under Newell Jenkins with what is called the Clarion Concerts Orchestra and Chorus. The plot of disguises and deceit is a throwback to artificial eighteenth-century conventions, involving a house-party with a couple of poets and a venal critic brought in. For modern performance the problem is the length, though on disc that evaporates when Rossini's invention is at its peak in number after number.

La scala di seta (complete).
*** Claves Dig. 50-9219/20 [id.]. Corbelli, Ringholz, Vargas, De Carolis, Provvisionato, Massa, ECO, Viotti.

The overture is among the best known of all that Rossini wrote, and here Viotti establishes his individuality with an unusually expansive slow introduction leading to a brisk and well-sprung allegro, scintillatingly played by the ECO. The cast here is stronger vocally than those in the rest of the Claves series, with Teresa Ringholz delightful as the heroine, Giulia, warm and agile, shading her voice seductively. She and the buffo, sung by Alessandro Corbelli, have the biggest share of the solo work, and he is also first rate. The tenor Ramon Vargas sings without strain – rare in this series – and the mezzo, Francesca Provvisionato, sings vivaciously as the heroine's cousin, with a little aria in military rhythm a special delight. Warm sound with good bloom on the voices.

Semiramide (complete).
*** DG (IMS) Dig. 437 797-2 (3). Studer, Larmore, Ramey, Lopardo, Amb. Op. Ch., LSO, Ion Marin.

Semiramide (complete, but with traditional cuts).
(M) *** Decca (IMS) 425 481-2 (3). Sutherland, Horne, Rouleau, Malas, Serge, Amb. Op. Ch., LSO, Bonynge.

Rossini concentrates on the love of Queen Semiramide for Prince Arsace (a mezzo-soprano), and musically the result is a series of fine duets, superbly performed here by Sutherland and Horne (in the mid-1960s when they were both at the top of their form). In Sutherland's interpretation, Semiramide is not so much a Lady Macbeth as a passionate, sympathetic woman and, with dramatic music predominating over languorous cantilena, one has her best, bright manner. Horne is well contrasted, direct and masculine in style, and Spiro Malas makes a firm, clear contribution in a minor role. Rouleau and Serge are variable but more than adequate, and Bonynge keeps the whole opera together with his alert, rhythmic control of tension and pacing. The vintage Decca recording has transferred brilliantly to CD.

On this DG version, Marin opens out many traditional cuts, notably in the role of the tenor, Idreno. Lopardo sings Idreno's splendid Act I aria magnificently, a scene omitted on Decca; and the newer performance, even at speeds generally faster, altogether lasts almost 40 minutes longer, though most of the extra material – recitative, repeats, introductions – is not of major importance. Though Cheryl Studer cannot match Sutherland in command or panache as the Babylonian queen, hers is still a strong, aptly agile performance. Jennifer Larmore sings superbly in the breeches role of Arsace, less powerful than Marilyn Horne but even more convincing in character, with the voice more youthfully fresh. What above all prevents Semiramide and Arsace's great duet, *Serbami ognor*, from sounding so seductively idiomatic is the conducting of Ion Marin, strong and purposeful but often too mechanical, generally missing the helpful rubatos that mark the Bonynge reading. The role of Assur is strongly sung by Samuel Ramey, but he gives little idea of the character's villainous side. The mid-'60s sound of the Decca, transferred to CD at mid-price, is still very vivid, but the digital DG recording provides extra brilliance and range.

Il Signor Bruschino (complete).
*** DG (IMS) Dig. 435 865-2 [id.]. Battle, Ramey, Lopardo, Desderi, Larmore, ECO, Ion Marin.

You could hardly devise a starrier cast for this 'comic farce in one act' than that assembled by DG, with even the tiny role of the maid, Marianna, taken by Jennifer Larmore. Ion Marin springs rhythms very persuasively, with the first Cavatina of Gaudenzio, the tutor, so delectably pointed in the introduction that one registers the character even before Samuel Ramey enters. Kathleen Battle makes a provocative heroine and the tenor, Frank Lopardo, sings sweetly and freshly as Sofia's lover, Florville. He is delightfully agile in his patter duet with Filiberto, the innkeeper, taken by Michele Pertusi. Excellent, well-balanced sound. The single disc (76 minutes) comes complete with libretto, translation and notes in a double-disc jewel-case.

Tancredi (complete).
(B) *** Naxos Dig. 8.660037/8 [id.]. Podles, Jo, Olsen, Spagnoli, Di Micco, Lendi, Capella Brugensis, Brugense Coll. Instrumentale, Alberto Zedda.

The enterprise of Naxos in recording one of the rarer operas of Rossini is triumphantly rewarded, for this set completely displaces the previous versions from Sony and RCA, and the eminent Rossini scholar and conductor, Alberto Zedda, proves a far more resilient, generally brisker and lighter Rossini interpreter than his predecessors. Sumi Jo is superb as the heroine, Amenaide, in dazzlingly clear coloratura, as well as imaginative pointing of phrase, rhythm and words. The mezzo, Ewa Podles, is less characterful, yet the voice is firm and rich as well as flexible; but it is the tenor, Stanford Olsen, previously heard as Belmonte on John Eliot Gardiner's recording of *Entführung*, who offers some of the freshest, most stylish and sweetly tuned singing from a Rossini tenor in recent years. The recording is a little lacking in body, but that partly reflects the use of a small orchestra, and the voices come over well. Having a studio recording means that ensembles are crisper and better focused. An Italian libretto is provided but no translation. Instead, a helpful synopsis is geared to the different tracks on the discs; had there been a libretto, this could well have received a Rosette.

Il Turco in Italia (complete).

*** Ph. (IMS) Dig. 434 128-2 (2). Sumi Jo, Alaimo, Fissore, Giménez, Mentzer, Corbelli, Bronder, Amb. Op. Ch., ASMF, Marriner.

(N) **(*) Decca Dig. 458 924-2 (2) [id.]. Cecilia Bartoli, Alessandro Corbelli, Michele Pertusi, Raymón Vargas, La Scala Milan Ch. & O, Chailly.

(***) EMI mono CDS5 56313-2 (2) [CDCB 56313]. Rossi-Lemeni, Callas, Gedda, Stabile, Ch. & O of La Scala, Milan, Gavazzeni.

On Philips, Sumi Jo as Fiorilla, the sharp-tongued heroine, unhappily married to old Don Geronio, is no fire-eater, as Callas was in her vintage recording, but she sparkles delightfully, a most believable young wife. What seals the success of the Philips version is the playing of the St Martin's Academy under Sir Neville Marriner, consistently crisp and light, wittily bringing out the light and shade in Rossini's score and offering a full text. As for the rest of the Philips cast, Simone Alaimo as the visiting Turkish prince, Selim, may lack sardonic weight, but it is a fine voice, and the buffo role of Geronio finds Enrico Fissore agile and characterful in his patter numbers. Raúl Giménez is the stylish tenor in the relatively small role of Narciso, which happily acquires an extra aria. Altogether a most welcome follow-up to Marriner's excellent set of the *Barber*.

Winner of the *Gramophone* Opera Award in 1998, Chailly's Decca version – his earlier recording with Caballé was for Sony – centres round the brilliantly characterful singing of Cecilia Bartoli as a fire-eating Fiorilla, following up the success of her earlier Rossini performances for Decca. The tessitura is high for a mezzo, but she copes with sparkling confidence. Chailly, as before, paces the many ensembles most effectively, with a first-rate team of soloists to back up Bartoli. Even so, the Marriner's version on Philips with Sumi Jo as Fiorilla remains preferable, when the sound is so much clearer and more immediate than in this rather mushy Milan recording. Marriner also draws far crisper, better sprung playing from the St Martin's Academy than Chailly gets from his Italian players, whose violins are thinner and edgier. Though Sumi Jo has a lighter voice than Bartoli, she is no less positive and just as agile and sparkling.

Callas was at her peak when she recorded this rare Rossini opera in the mid-1950s. As ever, there are lumpy moments vocally, but she gives a sharply characterful performance as the capricious Fiorilla, married to an elderly, jealous husband and bored with it. Nicola Rossi-Lemeni as the Turk of the title is characterful too, but the voice is ill-focused, and it is left to Nicolai Gedda as the young lover and Franco Calabrese as the jealous husband to match Callas in stylishness. It is good too to have the veteran Mariano Stabile singing the role of the Poet in search of a plot. Walter Legge's production has plainly added to the sparkle. On CD the original mono recording has been freshened and given added bloom, despite the closeness of the voices. It is a vintage Callas issue, her first uniquely cherishable essay in operatic comedy.

Il Turco in Italia: highlights.

(N) *** Decca Dig. 466 063-2 [id.]. (from above complete set with Bartoli, Corbelli, Pertusi, Vargas; cond. Chailly).

(M) **(*) Sony Dig. SMK 53505 [id.]. Ramey, Caballé, Dara, Palacio, Berbié, Amb. Op. Ch., Nat. PO, Chailly.

The Bartoli Decca set is not a first choice, partly on grounds of recording, so many collectors will be glad to have this 72-minute selection in which the heroine is well enough represented. Full texts and translations are included.

Chailly's earlier Sony recording is very well conducted, with a good feeling for theatrical timing. His cast is strong. Montserrat Caballé as Fiorilla is less girlish than she might be, and Samuel Ramey is a rather strait-laced Selim, but his singing is splendid; and this makes an enjoyable selection, brightly recorded.

Il viaggio a Reims (complete).

❁ *** DG Dig. 415 498-2 (2) [id.]. Ricciarelli, Valentini Terrani, Cuberli, Gasdia, Araiza, Giménez, Nucci, Raimondi, Ramey, Dara, Prague Philharmonic Ch., COE, Abbado.

**(*) Sony Dig. S2K 53336 (2) [id.]. McNair, Valentini Terrani, Serra, Studer, Giménez, Matteuzzi, Ramey, Raimondi, Berlin R. Ch., BPO, Abbado.

This DG set is one of the most sparkling and totally successful live opera recordings available, with Claudio Abbado in particular freer and more spontaneous-sounding than he generally is on disc, relishing the sparkle of the comedy, and the line-up of soloists here could hardly be more impressive, with no weak link. Apart from the established stars the set introduced two formidable newcomers in principal roles, Cecilia Gasdia as a self-important poetess and, even finer, Lella Cuberli as a young fashion-crazed widow. Abbado's brilliance and sympathy draw the musical threads compellingly together with the help of superb, totally committed playing from the young members of the Chamber Orchestra of Europe.

It seems strange that Sony should so soon make a new recording of so rare – if delightful – an opera as this in competition with DG's prize-winning version, particularly when Claudio Abbado is again the conductor and the cast features many of the same singers. Again it is a live recording but, with more distanced sound and voices less clear, it sparkles less. The Berlin Philharmonic is less attuned to Rossini than the Chamber Orchestra of Europe. Though the Sony cast is strong, no individual singer significantly outshines any predecessor, and most are less impressive.

Zelmira (complete).
*** Erato/Warner Dig. 2292 45419-2 (2). Gasdia, Fink, Matteuzzi, Merritt, Amb. S., Sol. Ven., Scimone.

Scimone takes a generally brisk view of both the arias and the ensembles of this underrated opera, but never seems to race his singers. In this performance the choice of singers underlines the contrast between the two principal tenor-roles. Chris Merritt combines necessary agility with an almost baritonal quality as the scheming Antenore, straining only occasionally, and William Matteuzzi sings with heady beauty and fine flexibility in florid writing as Ilo. Star of the performance is Cecilia Gasdia in the name-part, projecting words and emotions very intensely in warmly expressive singing. She is well matched by the mezzo, Barbara Fink, as her friend, Emma, and only the wobbly bass of José Garcia as the deposed Polidoro mars the cast.

COLLECTIONS

Arias and duets & choruses from: (i) *Armida. Bianca e Falliero* (with chorus); (i) *La Cenerentola. La Donna del Lago* (with chorus); *L'Italiana in Algeri* (with chorus); (i) *Otello. Semiramide*.
(N) **(*) RCA Dig. 74321 7131-2 [id.]. Vesselina Kasarova, (i) Juan Diego Florez, Bavarian R Ch., Munich RO, Artur Fagen.

Vesselina Kasarova is impressive in the original mezzo versions of Rossini arias and duets, though it is a pity that her least attractive singing comes right at the start in the rare aria from *Bianca e Falliero*, where under stress the pitching is vague. That said, she is at her most impressive in the more dramatic numbers in the items from *Semiramide, Armida* and, not least, the title-role in *Otello* transposed up for mezzo. The lighter items from *Italiana in Algeri* and *La Cenerentola* lack a little in sparkle, partly the fault of the conductor, though the voice is as tangily attractive as ever, and the coloratura brilliant and secure. The tenor, Juan Diego Florez, makes a good foil.

Arias from *L'assedio di Corinto; Bianca e Faliero; Elisabetta, Regina d'Inghilterra; Guglielmo Tell; Otello; Semiramide; Tancredi*.
(M) **(*) Virgin/EMI CUV5 61139-2. Katia Ricciarelli, Lyon Op. Ch. & O, Ferro.

Admirers of this artist will surely want this recital, even if Ricciarelli was past her peak when it was recorded in 1989. There is rare material here, sung with much character and at times (as the opening excerpt from *L'assedio di Corinto* and the *Romanza* from *William Tell* readily show) her line is beautifully spun. But elsewhere, when under stress, she sounds less comfortable, although her vigorous sense of dramatic style often carries the day. Ferro conducts sympathetically and the Lyon Opera Chorus gives good support. The recording is vivid, too.

Arias: *L'assedio di Corinto: L'ora fatal s'appressa . . . Giusto ciel! Avanziam . . . Non temer, d'un basso affetto . . . I destini tradir ogni speme! . . . Signor che, tutto puoi . . . Sei tu che stendi, o Dio! La Cenerentola: Nacqui all'affanno . . . Non più mesta. La donna del lago: Mura felici; Tanti affetti. L'Italiana in Algeri: Cruda sorte! Semiramide: Bel raggio lusinghier. Tancredi: Di tanti palpiti.*
✿ (M) *** Decca 458 219-2 [id.]. Marilyn Horne, SRO or ROHCG O, Henry Lewis.

For this reissue in Decca's Opera Gala series, Marilyn Horne's now famous Rossini recital disc is more generously filled than ever, making one of the most cherishable of all Rossini aria records ever issued. Moreover full translations are included, which is especially valuable in the long 25-minute scene from *L'assedio di Corinto* which (with the excerpts from *La donna del lago*) dates from 1972. The rest of the selection derives from two recitals the great mezzo also recorded with her then husband, Henry Lewis, in 1964–6 when she was at the zenith of her powers. The voice is in glorious condition, rich and firm throughout its spectacular range, and is consistently used with artistry and imagination, as well as brilliant virtuosity in coloratura. By any reckoning this is thrilling singing, the more valuable for the inclusion of the rarities – which, with Horne, make you wonder at their neglect. The sound is full and brilliant, hardly showing its age at all.

Arias from: *Il barbiere di Siviglia; La Cenerentola; La donna del lago; L'Italiana in Algeri; Maometto II; Semiramide; Tancredi*.
(BB) *** Naxos Dig. 8.553543 [id.]. Ewa Podles, Hungarian State Op. Ch. & O, Morandi.

The Hungarian mezzo, Ewa Podles, earlier the star singer in the complete set of Rossini's *Tancredi* on Naxos, is here even more impressive in one of the finest Rossini recitals in years. Hers is a rich and even voice which is not only weighty throughout its range but is also extraordinarily agile, dazzling in the elaborate divisions in all these coloratura numbers. She may find it hard to convey the fun and sparkle in Rossini, but the bright-eyed intensity provides fair compensation even with Cinderella or Rosina, and the cabaletta of Cinderella's final aria is breathtaking in its bravura at a formidably fast tempo. By contrast, this great voice is an ideal vehicle for the *opera seria* arias here, with the male characters very well characterized. First-rate accompaniment too.

Arias: *La Cenerentola: Nacqui all'affano. Guglielmo Tell: S'allontano alfin!; Selva opaca. Semiramide: Bel raggio lusinghier.*
(M) **(*) EMI CDM5 66464-2 [id.]. Callas, Paris Conservatoire O, Rescigno – DONIZETTI: *Arias.* **

These recordings from 1963–4 have been admirably remastered so that the orchestra always provides a vivid and atmospheric backing for the voice. If the performances show a degree of cautiousness that rarely marked Callas's earlier work, this only goes to show how conscious she was of all the criticisms and how she did her utmost to avoid any real blots. In general she succeeds, often producing golden tone. The Rossini excerpts rightly come first on the CD, for they offer much for aficionados to enjoy. Yet there is something less positive about the end result than in her earlier recordings of this repertory, and, more seriously, the performances do not have that refinement of detail which at her peak lit up so many phrases and made them unforgettable. Good documentation and full translations are provided.

Arias: *La Cenerentola: Non piu mesta. La Donna del Lago: Mura felici . . . Elena! O tu, che chiamo. L'Italiana in Algeri: Cruda sorte! Amor tiranno! Pronti abbiamo . . . Pensa all patria. Otello: Deh! calma, o ciel. La Pietra del Paragone: Se l'Italie contrade . . . Se per voi lo care io torno. Tancredi: Di tanti palpiti. Stabat Mater: Fac ut portem.*
*** Decca Dig. 425 430-2 [id.]. Cecilia Bartoli, A. Schoenberg Ch., V. Volksoper O, Patanè.

Cecilia Bartoli's first recital of Rossini showpieces brings a formidable demonstration not only of Bartoli's remarkable voice but of her personality and artistry, bringing natural warmth and imagination to each item without ever quite making you smile with delight. Yet there are not many Rossini recitals of any vintage to match this. Vocally, the one controversial point to note is the way that Bartoli articulates her coloratura with a half-aspirate, closer to the Supervia 'rattle' than anything else, but rather obtrusive. Accompaniments are exemplary, and Decca provided the luxury of a chorus in some of the items, with hints of staging. Full, vivid recording. Recommended.

'Rossini heroines': Arias from: *La donna del lago; Elisabetta, Regina d'Inghilterra; Maometto II; Le nozze di Teti e Peleo; Semiramide; Zelmira.*
*** Decca Dig. 436 075-2 [id.]. Cecilia Bartoli, Ch. & O of Teatro la Fenice, Marin.

Cecilia Bartoli follows up the success of her earlier Rossini recital-disc with this second brilliant collection of arias, mostly rarities. The tangy, distinctive timbre of her mezzo goes with a magnetic projection of personality to bring to life even formal passage-work, with all the elaborate coloratura bright and sparkling. The rarest item of all is an aria for the goddess Ceres from the classically based entertainment, *Le nozze di Teti e Peleo*, making a splendid showpiece. The collection is crowned by a formidably high-powered reading of *Bel raggio* from *Semiramide*, with Bartoli excitingly braving every danger.

Rott, Hans (1858–84)

Symphony in E.
*** Hyperion Dig. CDA 66366 [id.]. Cincinnati Philh. O, Gerhard Samuel.

It is astonishing to encounter in Hans Rott's *Symphony* ideas that took root in Mahler's *First* and *Fifth Symphonies*. Structurally the work is original, each movement getting progressively longer, the finale occupying nearly 25 minutes. But the music is full of good ideas and, anticipations of Mahler apart, has a profile of its own. The Cincinnati Philharmonia are a student orchestra who produce extraordinarily good results under Gerhard Samuel. The recording is good. Readers should investigate this issue without delay.

Rousseau, Jean-Jacques (1712–78)

Le devin du village (complete).
(M) *** CPO/EMI CPO 999 559-2 [id.]. Micheau, Gedda, Roux, Ch. Raymond St-Paul, Louis de Froment CO, Froment.

The one-act Intermezzo, *Le devin du village* ('The village soothsayer'), is Rousseau's most celebrated work, written in 1752, an unpretentious piece in what he conceived as the Italian style of the day, which he vigorously supported against the French, even though he here uses a French text. Starting with an overture in the Italian style, fast–slow–fast, it is charming in a plain and straightforward style, hardly original, and the baldness of the writing is rather underlined in this performance with continuo in bare chords. The 25 sections, mostly very short indeed, last well under an hour, offering a simple story of the soothsayer reconciling the estranged lovers, for a price. All three soloists are first rate, with Micheau at her most seductive, and the young Gedda heady-toned.

Roussel, Albert (1869–1937)

(i; ii) *Aeneas* (ballet), *Op. 54;* (iii) *Bacchus et Ariane* (complete ballet); (i) *Le festin de l'araignée* (complete); (i) *Petite suite, Op. 39*; (i) *Pour une fête de printemps, Op. 22*; (iv) *Sinfonietta, Op. 52*; (iii) *Suite in F, Op. 33.*
(N) (B) *** Erato/Warner Ultima Analogue/Dig. 3984 24240-2 (2) [id.]. (i) O. Nat de l'ORTF, Martinon (ii) Ch. de l'ORTF (iii) O. de Paris, Dutoit (iv) Paillard CO, Paillard.

The quintessential Roussel is all assembled on this two-CD set. Performances are at best excellent, and always good. Martinon's beautifully played account of the complete *Le festin de l'arraignée* is particularly welcome, and there is currently no alternative version of his later ballet, *Aeneas* with chorus (not identified in the documentation but that of the French Radio). This is a rarity dating from 1935. Neither recording is digital but none the worse for that – indeed most of these come from the late 1960s early 1970s – save for the *Suite en fa* and *Bacchus* which are from 1986 and digital. Abundant testimony to the musical resource and richly endowed imagination Roussel possessed, and very much worth getting.

Bacchus et Ariane (complete ballet), *Op. 43*; *Le festin de l'araignée (The spider's feast), Op. 17.*
*** Chandos Dig. CHAN 9494 [id.]. BBC PO, Yan Pascal Tortelier.

Bacchus et Ariane (complete ballet), *Op. 43; Le festin de l'araignée (The spider's feast): symphonic fragments.*
(M) *** EMI (SIS) Dig. CDM7 64690-2 [id.]. O Nat. de France, Prêtre.

Tortelier offers the best *Bacchus et Ariane* yet – and what a marvellously inventive and resourceful score it is. The BBC Philharmonic play with tremendous zest and give a sensitive and atmospheric account of *Le festin de l'araignée*. They offer us the complete banquet, not just the chosen dishes on the set menu! Splendid recording and performances of rewarding and colourful music that deserves to be more widely heard.

The EMI recording, made in the generous acoustic of the Salle Wagram, is a shade too reverberant at times, but no essential detail is masked. Georges Prêtre obtains an excellent response from the Orchestre National de France in both scores. The CD freshens detail a little, although the resonance means that the improvement is relatively limited. However, the background silence is certainly an asset in *The spider's feast*.

Bacchus et Ariane: Suite No. 2.
(M) ** DG Originals 449 748-2 [id.]. Lamoureux O, Igor Markevitch – HONEGGER: *Symphony No. 5*; MILHAUD: *Les Choéphores*. (**)

Markevitch's spirited and atmospheric account of the second suite from *Bacchus et Ariane* comes from 1960 and, unlike its companions (Honegger's *Fifth Symphony* and Milhaud's *Les Choéphores*), is in stereo. It is very well played and recorded with plenty of space round the aural image, but the sound naturally lacks the body and focus of a modern recording, although it is fully acceptable.

Suite in F, Op. 33.
(M) **(*) Mercury 434 303-2 [id.]. Detroit SO, Paul Paray – CHABRIER: *Bourrée fantasque*, etc. ***

The outer movements of Roussel's *Suite in F* have a compulsive drive which also infects the harmonically complex, bitter-sweet central *Sarabande*. The scoring is rich (some might say thick), and the resonance of the Detroit Ford Auditorium makes it congeal a little. It is well played and alive, with Paray at his best in the closing *Gigue*.

Symphonies Nos. 1 in D min. (Le poème de la forêt), Op. 7; 2 in B flat, Op. 23; 3 in G min., Op. 42; 4 in A, Op. 53.
*** RCA Dig. 09026 61511-2 (2) [id.]. R. France PO, Janowski.
(B) **(*) Erato/Warner Ultima Dig. 3984 21090-2 (2). Fr. Nat. O, Charles Dutoit.

The Roussel symphonies have not been ideally served on disc, and the present RCA set is a source of celebration and is well worth having. On this showing Marek Janowski has a natural feel for the Roussel idiom. His version of the *First* (*Le poème de la forêt*) is the best to appear so far, and his *Second* is very good indeed and far more idiomatic than the Dutoit. The *Third* is impressive too, though the Scherzo is a shade too fast, and the *Fourth* receives a very fine performance. The set is neatly packaged (two discs in the space of one) and the recording, made in the Salle Olivier Messiaen of Radio France, has plenty of body, presence and detail. This is now the standard recommendation for these rewarding and resourceful scores.

Dutoit does not quite match the Janowski set. Not that his readings are wanting in character. He gets first-class playing from the Orchestre National, who are in excellent form, while the CD transfers do particular justice to the richness of Roussel's scoring and are most imposing in the definition at the bottom end of the register. So, with any minor reservations, this is certainly a recommendable alternative and splendid value for money.

Symphony No. 3 in G min., Op. 42.
(M) **(*) Sony Heritage MHK 62352 [id.]. NYPO, Leonard Bernstein (with HONEGGER: *Rugby; Pacific 231* **) – MILHAUD: *Les Choéphores*. ***
(M) **(*) DG (IMS) Dig. 445 512-2 [id.]. O Nat. de France, Bernstein – FRANCK: *Symphony*. **(*)
(M) **(*) Sony SMK 64107 [id.]. NYPO, Boulez – RAVEL: *Chansons*. ***

On Sony Heritage, a vividly characterized and enormously vital account of Roussel's magnificent *Third Symphony*. It was Bernstein's mentor, Koussevitzky, who commissioned the work for the 50th anniversary of the Boston Symphony Orchestra, and Bernstein's reading is as highly charged as one could wish for. The Sony performance comes from 1961 and in the original LP format was shrill and reverberant. The present transfer has tamed some though not all of its ferocity and cleaned up some of the detail. Though the recording is not perfect, this is still the best performance of the symphony in the current catalogue, and it comes with a Milhaud rarity new to these shores.

In his later DG version, Bernstein again compulsively brings out all its energy and pungent dissonance, and yet he lightens the mood attractively for the high-spirited finale. The 'live' recording is extremely vivid if a shade harsh. But his Sony account is even finer,

Boulez's first movement is surprisingly slow (it is still pungent but has less electricity and brilliance than Bernstein's CBS disc). The slow movement, however, has great warmth and humanity. Unfortunately, the recording, made in the Manhattan Center in 1975, is not as first rate as the performance: the acoustic is reverberant and there is plenty of body, but the upper strings are rather shrill. Nevertheless, with the splendid Ravel couplings, this makes an alternative mid-priced recommendation.

Symphonies Nos. 3; 4 in A, Op. 53; Bacchus et Ariane, suite No. 2; Sinfonietta for string orchestra, Op. 52.
**(*) Chandos Dig. CHAN 7007 [id.]. Detroit SO, Neeme Järvi.

Neeme Järvi's account of the *Third Symphony* has an engaging vitality and character, and the playing of the Detroit orchestra is highly responsive. In the slow movement he indulges in a rather steep *accelerando* after the fugal section. Likewise his finale feels too fast. But it is a committed performance. Some may find the acoustic a shade too resonant, given the complexity of Roussel's textures, but the overall balance is very natural and pleasing. Not absolutely ideal performances, perhaps, but certainly very recommendable, given the superior sound and Järvi's obvious enthusiasm for this repertoire.

Symphony No. 4 in A, Op. 53.
❁ (M) *** EMI mono CDM5 66595-2. Philh. O, Karajan – BALAKIREV: *Symphony No. 1.* (***) ❁

Karajan's pioneering version of Roussel's marvellous *Fourth Symphony* was recorded in November 1949, yet it still sounds exceptionally fresh. Having treasured this in its 78-r.p.m. form and on LP and in its brief CD incarnation, it is good to have it back again. What a performance! It is vastly superior to most of its successors. Like the Balakirev with which it is coupled, it is a performance of real stature.

CHAMBER MUSIC

Andante and Scherzo for flute and piano, Op. 51; Andante from an unfinished Wind trio for oboe, clarinet and bassoon; Aria No.2 for oboe and piano; Divertissement for wind quintet and piano, Op. 6; Duo for bassooon and double bass; Impromptu for harp solo, op. 21; Joueurs de flûte for flute and piano, Op. 27; Music from Elpénor (poème radiophonique) for flute and string quartet, Op. 59; Piano trio in E flat, Op. 2; Pipe for piccolo and piano; 2 Poèmes de Ronsard for flute and soprano, Op. 25; Segovia for guitar, Op. 29; Sérénade for flute, string trio and harp, Op. 30; String quartet, Op. 45; String trio, Op. 58; Trio, Op. 40 for flute, viola and cello; Violin sonatas Nos. 1 in D min., Op. 11; 2, Op. 28.
(M) *** Olympia Dig. OCD 706 ABC (3). Paul Verhey (flute or piccolo); Jet Röling (piano); Hans Roerade (oboe); (iv) Frank van den Brink (clarinet); Jos de Lange (bassoon); Herman Jeurissen (horn); Quirijn van Altena (double bass); Erika Waarsenburg (harp), Schoenberg Qt. (members); Jean-Jacques Kantorow (violin); Herre-Jan Stegenga (cello); Ireene Maessen (soprano); Jan Goodswaard (guitar).

Roussel's chamber music is not so well represented on CD that we can afford to be too unwelcoming to the present set. Indeed there is no need to be. These are good performances, well presented here by these fine Dutch artists. This is eminently civilized music and, without going into too much detail, artistically these would carry a three-star rating. The recordings are eminently serviceable. The *Sérénade* for flute, string trio and harp, a lovely piece – and very well played indeed – is not as finely focused as on the old Melos recording (Decca), and the piano in the *Joueurs de flûte* seems to be in a slightly more resonant acoustic than the flute. All the same this is as economical a way as any of exploring this interesting repertoire. Although the ideas are not always as memorable as are the symphonies, the writing is always intelligent and expert. The three discs are not now available separately, but if you respond to Roussel, this set is well worth considering, especially at mid-price.

(i) *Evocations, Op. 15;* (ii) *Résurrection (Prélude symphonique d'après Tolstoi), Op. 4.*
(M) *** EMI (SIS) Dig. CDM5 65564-2. (i) Gedda, Stutzmann, Van Dam, Orféon Donostiarra, Anton Ayestaran; (ii) Toulouse Capitole O, Plasson.

Évocations dates from 1910–11 and reflects something of the impression that Roussel's travels in the Far East and, more particularly, India made on him. It is full of exotic colours and atmosphere, which come splendidly to life in this eminently satisfactory (1986) recording. Plasson directs an excellent performance and adds *Résurrection*, the very first orchestral piece Roussel composed while still under the tutelage of Vincent d'Indy.

Sérénade for flute, violin, viola, cello and harp, Op. 30.

✪ (M) *** Decca 452 891-2 [id.]. Osian Ellis, Melos Ens. – DEBUSSY: *Sonata for flute, viola & harp;* RAVEL: *Introduction and allegro;* ROPARTZ: *Prélude, marine et chansons.* *** ✪

Roussel's charming *Sérénade* fits naturally into this collection of greater and lesser masterpieces of twentieth-century French chamber music. Osian Ellis's musicianship is very much in evidence, his fine technique and musicality matching the degree of sensitivity of the other members of the group. This Melos version has held its place in the catalogue for more than three decades. It is an inspired account and is beautifully engineered, well worthy of inclusion in Decca's Classic Sound series.

Songs: *Jazz dans la nuit, Op. 38; Light, Op. 19/12; 2 Mélodies, Op. 20; 2 Poèmes chinois, Op. 35.*

(M) **(*) Unicorn-Kanchana Dig. UKCD 2078 [id.]. Sarah Walker, Roger Vignoles – DEBUSSY: *Mélodies;* ENESCU: *Chansons.* ***

Sarah Walker may not plumb the full emotions of some of the deceptively deep songs in her Roussel group – *Light*, for example – but the point and charm of *Jazz dans la nuit* are superbly caught, and the group makes an attractive and generous coupling for the Debussy and Enescu songs, all superbly recorded, with Vignoles a most sensitive accompanist.

Routh, Francis (born 1927)

Clarinet quintet.

*** Redcliffe Dig. RR 010 [id.]. Redcliffe Ens. – BLISS: *Clarinet quintet;* RAWSTHORNE: *Clarinet quartet.* ***

Routh's *Quintet* was written for Nicholas Cox, who plays it with great skill and understanding. Its variety of mood makes up for the melodic fragmentation, and its invention is lively throughout. Excellent recording.

Royer, Pancrace (1705–55)

Pièces de clavecin (1746): *La majestueuse; La Zaïde; Les matelots; Tambourins 1–2; L'incertaine; L'aimable; La bagatelle; Suite de la bagatelle; La remouleuse; Les tendres sentiments; Le vertigo; Allemande; La sensible; La marche des Scythes. La chasse de Zaïde.*

✪ *** O-L (IMS) Dig. 436 127-2. Christophe Rousset (harpsichord).

Pièces de clavecin (1746).

(B) *** HM Musique d'Abord Dig. HMA 901037 [id.]. William Christie (harpsichord).

Royer's *Pièces de clavecin*, his only collection to appear in print, had their origins in his stage works but, unlike Rameau, who transcribed instrumental dances for the keyboard, Royer drew on arias and choral pieces as well. Similarly, *La chasse de Zaïde* comes from his *ballet-héroïque*, *Zaïde* (1739). All these pieces show flashes of real imagination and a refined and developed sensibility. Rousset plays a harpsichord from 1751 by Henri Hemsch which once belonged to Rameau's patron *fermier general*, La Poupelinière, and was in all probability played by Rameau himself. Rousset plays with great flair and poetic imagination and he is impeccably recorded; he also provides the useful and scholarly notes.

William Christie's Harmonia Mundi recording, made in the 1980s, is hardly less fine and at bargain price deserves an enthusiastic recommendation alongside the Rousset.

Rózsa, Miklós (1907–94)

Symphony in 3 movements, Op. 6a (ed. Palmer); *The Vintner's daughter, Op. 23a.*

*** Koch Dig. 37244-2 [id.]. New Zealand SO, James Sedares.

Rózsa's early attempt in 1930 to write a large-scale symphony proved abortive, and the present structure, minus a Scherzo and heavily edited by Christopher Palmer, relies on an incomplete manuscript. However, as we know from his film scores, Rózsa had no difficulty finding memorable musical ideas and in the first movement uses them cogently and with intensity. The second-movement *Andante* is highly evocative and the finale does not lack fire and energy, even if structurally it remains the least convincing part of the work. *The Vintner's daughter*, a picturesque set of variations, again shows the composer's melodic appeal, and again he uses the orchestral palette as seductively as in his film music. James Sedares and his New Zealand players are obviously caught up in the music and present it persuasively, with the conductor showing a notably firm grip on the first movement of the symphony. The recording has plenty of body and colour.

Rubbra, Edmund (1901–86)

(i) *Viola concerto, Op. 75;* (ii) *Violin concerto, Op. 103.*

*** Conifer Dig. 75605 51225-2 [id.]. (i) Rivka Golani; (ii) Tasmin Little; RPO, Vernon Handley.

The *Viola concerto* is a work of euphony and depth, and Rivka Golani's account is a first recording. Tasmin Little's version of the *Violin concerto* has an effortless and masterly virtuosity; she is well recorded and the RPO under Vernon Handley give excellent support.

Sinfonietta (for strings), Op. 163; 4 Medieval Latin lyrics, Op. 32; 5 Spenser sonnets, Op. 42; Amoretti: 5 Spenser sonnets, 2nd series, *Op. 43.*
(N) (M) *** EMI Dig. CDM5 66936-3 [id.]. Martyn Hill, Wilson-Johnson, Endellion Qt, City of L. Sinfonia, Schönzeler.

The *Sinfonietta for strings* is Rubbra's last work and alone is worth the price of the record. It is short but concentrated and is eloquently played by the City of London Sinfonia under Hans-Hubert Schönzeler. The songs are all much earlier and are rewarding pieces, the settings are strikingly melodic and full of atmosphere with each collection very distinct in character, and a certain pastiche period flavour imbuing the music of each group.

Symphony No. 1, Op. 44; (i) *Sinfonia concertante for piano and orchestra, Op. 38; A Tribute, Op. 56.*
(N) *** Chandos Dig. CHAN 9538 [id.] BBC Nat. O. of Wales, Richard Hickox;(i) with Howard Shelley.

At long last Rubbra's music of the 1930s is receiving attention. When the *First Symphony* received its first performance under Sir Adrian Boult in 1937, it caused quite a stir and prompted comparisons with the Walton *Symphony* and Vaughan Williams's *Fourth*. The *Sinfonia concertante* for piano and orchestra which preceded it, though it was revised in 1942, also made a strong impression, and these performances show why. Less easy to understand is the neglect into which they have been cast ever since. Both have been broadcast once or twice, but this is their first appearance on CD, LP or 78. The first movement of the symphony is fiercely turbulent, reflecting the spirit of the times; a French dance tune, a *Périgourdine*, forms the basis of the middle movement, but the pensive, inward-looking finale, which is as long as the first two movements put together, is the most powerful and haunting of the three. The *Sinfonia concertante* is no less symphonic in character and substance. The opening *Fantasia* begins with a reflective lento passage which anticipates the tranquillity of the *G major Piano concerto*, though it is the final *Prelude and fugue*, composed in memory of his teacher, Gustav Holst which lingers longest in the memory. Howard Shelley is an inspired soloist and the sometimes thick textures of the symphony sound remarkably lucid in Richard Hickox's hands. The BBC National Orchestra of Wales play splendidly and the Chandos sound is in the best traditions of the house.

Symphonies Nos. 2 in D, Op. 45; 6, Op. 80.
*** Chandos Dig. CHAN 9481 [id.]. BBC Nat. O of Wales, Richard Hickox.

Richard Hickox and his fine players do make the score of the *Second Symphony* more lucid than Handley's Lyrita recording from the 1970s. The performance is meticulously prepared and yet flows effortlessly, and the slow movement speaks with great eloquence. The heart of the *Sixth Symphony* is the serene *Canto* movement which is not dissimilar in character to the *Missa in honorem Sancti Dominici*. It is arguably the finest of the cycle after No. 9, and Hickox and his fine players do it proud. So, too, do the Chandos engineers.

Symphonies Nos. (i) *2 in D, Op. 45;* (ii) *7 in C, Op. 88;* (i) *Festival overture, Op. 62.*
*** Lyrita SRCD 235 [id.]. (i) New Philh. O., Handley; (ii) LPO, Boult.

The *Seventh Symphony* is a very considerable piece. The longest and most ambitious of its three movements – perhaps the most enigmatic, too – is the finale, an extended passacaglia and fugue displaying the composer's naturally contrapuntal mode of thought at its most typical. The first movement brings a cogent argument based on a simple four-note motif, and the second a rhythmic Scherzo that leads to a more lyrical, noble climax. Boult's performance is outstandingly successful. A good performance too from Handley of both the *Second Symphony* and the overture which bears an adjacent opus number to the *Fifth*. Both recordings, from the 1970s, are up to the high standards of realism one expects from this label. A thoroughly worthwhile and generous coupling (78 minutes).

Symphonies Nos. 3, Op. 49; 4, Op. 53; Resurgam overture, Op. 149; A Tribute, Op. 56.
*** Lyrita Dig. SRCD 202 [id.]. Philh O, Norman Del Mar.

The opening of the *Fourth Symphony* is of quite exceptional beauty and has a serenity and quietude that silence criticism; there is a consistent elevation of feeling and continuity of musical thought. Rubbra's music is steeped in English polyphony and it could not come from any time other than our own. Unquestionably both symphonies have a nobility and spirituality that is rare in any age. The fine *Resurgam overture* is a late work.

Symphonies Nos. 3, Op. 49; 7 in C, Op. 88.
(N) ❀ *** Chandos Dig. CHAN 9634 [id.]. BBC Nat. O. of Wales, Richard Hickox.

The *Third Symphony* (1939) once enjoyed repertory status – at least in BBC programmes – but completely fell out of establishment favour from the 1960s through to the late 1980s. It has a pastoral character and a certain Sibelian feel to it (woodwind in thirds), though Rubbra is always himself. In the final movement there is even a hint of Elgar in the fourth variation. This is a more eloquent and ultimately more convincing account than the fine Philharmonia version under Norman Del Mar on Lyrita. The *Seventh Symphony* (1956) receives a performance of real power from Hickox and his Welsh Orchestra. This is music that speaks of deep and serious things and its opening paragraphs are among the most inspired that Rubbra ever penned. Noble performances and excellent recorded sound.

Symphonies Nos. 4, Op. 53; 10 (Sinfonia da camera), Op. 145; 11, Op. 153.
*** Chandos Dig. CHAN 9401 [id.]. BBC Nat. O of Wales, Hickox.

Richard Hickox offers a particularly imaginative account of the *Eleventh Symphony* in one movement (1979), which is new to the catalogue. Like so much of Rubbra's music, it has an organic continuity and inner logic that are immediately striking. And in common with the *Tenth Symphony*, also in one movement, its textures are spare and limpid. The *Fourth Symphony* (1940–42), a wartime work, has great serenity and tranquillity. Its opening is among the most beautiful in all English music of our time. Hickox's account is totally convincing. The Chandos recording is excellent in every respect, with plenty of warmth and transparency of detail.

Symphony No. 5 in B flat, Op. 63.
(M) *** Chandos CHAN 6576 [id.]. Melbourne SO, Schönzeler – BLISS: *Checkmate* ***; TIPPETT: *Little music.* **(*)

Rubbra's *Fifth Symphony* is a noble work which grows naturally from the symphonic soil of Elgar and Sibelius. Although the Melbourne orchestra is not in the very top division, they play this music for all they are worth, and the strings have a genuine intensity and lyrical fervour that compensate for the opaque effect of the octave doublings. Altogether, though, this is an imposing performance which reflects credit on all concerned. The recording is well balanced and lifelike; but the ear perceives that the upper range is rather restricted.

Symphonies Nos. 5 in B flat, Op. 63; 8 (Hommage à Teilhard de Chardin), Op. 132; (i) *Ode to the Queen, Op. 83.*
(N) *** Chandos Dig. CHAN 9714 [id.]. BBC Nat. O. of Wales, Richard Hickox;(i) with Susan Bickley.

Richard Hickox's recording of the *Fifth Symphony* is only the third to have been made in the 50 years since its composition. (At one time it was the most frequently performed of all the Rubbra symphonies, but after the 1960s it virtually disappeared from the repertoire.) Hickox's reading is easily the finest and most penetrating; the slow movement has depth and, thanks to a magnificent recording, a greater clarity than either of its predecessors. Tempi are unerringly judged and he brings great breadth and gravitas to the very opening of the work. He gives, too, a more intense account of the *Eighth (Hommage à Teilhard de Chardin)* than we have had before. Teilhard de Chardin was the French Jesuit priest, philosopher and paleontologist with whose ideas Rubbra had great sympathy. *Ode to the Queen*, commissioned by the BBC for the Coronation in 1953, is a newcomer to the catalogue and particularly welcome. It is a setting of three poems, variously by Richard Crashaw, Sir William d'Avenant and Thomas Campion, for mezzo-soprano and full orchestra and is strong in inspiration. Excellent performances and outstanding recorded sound from the Chandos/BBC team.

Symphony No. 5 in B flat, Op. 63; Loth to depart (Improvisations on virginal pieces by Giles Farnaby), Op. 50/4.
(M) (***) EMI mono CDM5 66053-2. Hallé O, Barbirolli – BRITTEN: *Violin concerto* (**); HEMING: *Threnody for a soldier killed in action.* (***)

This was the very first recording of any Rubbra symphony. Made in 1950, it originally appeared on seven 78-r.p.m. discs with the haunting *Loth to depart* as a fill-up. Although it has reappeared on LP both in the early 1950s and in HMV's British Music series in the late 1960s, it has never sounded as fresh and 'present' as it does in Andrew Walter's exemplary transfer. Sir Adrian Boult gave its première in 1949 but Barbirolli was quick to take it up, and his spacious and affectionate reading stands up well nearly half a century after its composition.

(i) *Symphonies Nos. 6, Op. 80; 8 (Hommage à Teilhard de Chardin), Op. 132;* (ii) *Soliloquy for cello and orchestra, Op. 57.*
*** Lyrita SRCD 234 [id.]. (i) Philh. O, Norman Del Mar; (ii) Rohan de Saram, LSO, Handley.

The *Sixth* is one of the most admired of Rubbra's symphonies and its slow movement is arguably the most beautiful single movement in all of Rubbra's output. The *Eighth* has something of the mystical intensity that finds its most visionary outlet in the *Ninth Symphony*. In Norman Del Mar's hands Rubbra's music speaks here with directness and without artifice; the Philharmonia play marvellously and the composer's sound-world is very well served by the recording balance. The *Soliloquy* has a grave beauty which exerts a strong appeal. Rohan de Saram plays with a restrained eloquence that is impressive and he has excellent support from the LSO under Vernon Handley.

(i) *Symphony No. 9 (Sinfonia sacra), Op. 140. The Morning Watch for chorus and orchestra, Op. 55.*
✽ *** Chandos Dig. CHAN 9441 [id.]. (i) Lynne Dawson, Della Jones, Stephen Roberts; BBC Nat. Ch. of Wales, BBC Nat. O of Wales, Hickox.

The *Ninth Symphony*, arguably Rubbra's greatest work, is an unqualified masterpiece whose eloquence is of the order of Elgar's *Dream of Gerontius*, Britten's *War Requiem* and Tippett's *A Child of our time*. Subtitled *The Resurrection*, it was inspired by a painting of Donato Bramante and has something of the character of the Passion, which the three soloists relate in moving fashion. Apart from a BBC performance in the 1980s, this wonderful score has remained unperformed and unrecorded since its first performance in 1973! *The Morning Watch*, a setting of Henry Vaughan for chorus and orchestra, which was originally to have formed part of a choral fifth symphony, is another score of great nobility, which has taken even longer (half a century) to be recorded. Both works are superbly served here by all these fine musicians, and the Chandos recording is no less magnificent.

Symphony No. 10 (Sinfonia da camera), Op. 145; Improvisations on virginal pieces by Giles Farnaby, Op. 50; A tribute to Vaughan Williams on his 70th birthday (Introduction and danza alla fuga), Op. 56.
(M) *** Chandos CHAN 6599. Bournemouth Sinf., Schönzeler.

Rubbra's *Tenth Symphony* is a short, one-movement work, whose opening has a Sibelian seriousness and a strong atmosphere that grip one immediately. Schönzeler is scrupulously attentive to dynamic nuance and internal balance, while keeping a firm grip on the architecture as a whole. The 1977 recording has been impressively remastered. It has a warm acoustic and reproduces natural, well-placed orchestral tone. The upper range is crisply defined. The *Farnaby variations* is a pre-war work whose charm Schönzeler uncovers effectively, revealing its textures to best advantage. *Loth to depart*, the best-known movement, has gentleness and vision in this performance. Strongly recommended. Even though this CD plays for only 40 minutes, it remains indispensable.

Oboe sonata in C, Op. 100.
(N) (B) *** Hyperion Helios Dig. CDH 55008 [id.]. Sarah Francis, Peter Dickenson – BOUGHTON: *Pastoral;* HARTY: *3 Pieces*; HOWELLS: *Sonata*. ***

Rubbra's *Oboe sonata* has a songful, rhapsodic opening movement, which leads naturally into the soulful central *Elegie*; the fluent finale is rondo with a semi-oriental melodic line. The performance here is of quality, but these artists are not helped by the forward balance and the background resonance. It is important not to have the volume level set too high.

String quartets Nos. 1 in F min., Op. 35; 2 in E flat, Op. 51; 3, Op. 112; 4, Op. 150.
(M) ** Conifer Dig. 75605 51260-2 (2) [id.]. Sterling Qt.

These are impressive quartets and have been hailed as masterpieces; they deserve the most dedicated, subtle and persuasive advocacy. The Sterling Quartet have the dedication, but the sound they produce is wanting in bloom and is at times raw and unpleasant. No doubt the close balance is partly to blame. Nor, in the *First Quartet*, do they produce as wide a dynamic range as the music demands. This music is important, so the set must perforce be recommended *faute de mieux*.

Songs: (i & ii) *A hymn to the virgin; The jade mountain; Jesukin; Mystery; Orpheus with his lute; Rosa mundi*. Instrumental pieces: (ii & iii) *Discourse, Op. 127*; (iii) *Fukugawa; Improvisation, Op. 124*. (ii) Harp pieces: *Pezzo ostinato, Op. 102*; *Transformations, Op. 141*.
(N) *** ASV Dig. CDDCA 1036 [id.]. (i) Tracey Chadwell, (ii) Danielle Perrett, (iii) Timothy Gill. (with Lennox BERKELEY: *Nocturne for harp*; HOWELLS: *Prelude*. ***)

Many of these pieces are first recordings and enrich our picture of this fine composer. The CD reflects his lifelong interest in the Orient from the early *Fukagawa* (1929), an arrangement of a Japanese melody, to *The Jade Mountain* songs (1962). The two pieces for harp, the *Pezzo ostinato* and the *Transformations*, both reflect the fascination that Indian music exercised. They are both impressive – indeed, exalted is the word that springs to mind. Some of the very early pieces reflect the spell cast by Holst and Cyril Scott but the bulk of the music here finds him at his most individual. Tracy Chadwell sings ethereally though there is perhaps a little too much echo round her voice, but the harp pieces are both exquisitely played and could hardly be more authoritative. A most rewarding and recommendable issue.

(i) *Magnificat and Nunc dimittis in A flat, Op. 65. Missa in honorem Sancti Dominici, Op. 66; 3 Hymn tunes, Op. 114; 3 Motets, Op. 78.*
*** ASV Dig. CDDCA 881 [id.]. Gonville & Caius College, Cambridge, Ch., Geoffrey Webber; (i) Phillips (organ) – HADLEY: *Lenten cantata*, etc. ***

The most important work here is the *Missa in honorem Sancti Dominici* (1948), written at about the time of the *Fifth Symphony* and one of the most beautiful of twentieth-century *a cappella* choral pieces written in this or any other country. None of the other works on the disc is its equal. The performance by the Choir of Gonville & Caius College, Cambridge, under Geoffrey Webber, is dedicated and sensitive, though it does not altogether banish memories of Richard Hickox's RCA version from the 1970s. Excellent balance, though the organ is obtrusive, particularly so in the first of the Op. 78 *Motets*.

Rubinstein, Anton (1829–94)

Piano concertos Nos. 1 in E, Op. 25; 2 in F, Op. 35.

** Marco Polo Dig. 8.223456 [id.]. Joseph Banowetz, Czech State PO, Alfred Walter.

Piano concertos Nos. 3 in G, Op. 45; 4 in D min., Op. 70.

** Marco Polo Dig. 8.223382 [id.]. Banowetz, Slovak State PO (Košice), Stankovsky.

Piano concerto No. 5 in E flat, Op. 94; Caprice russe, Op. 102.

**(*) Marco Polo Dig. 8.223489 [id.]. Joseph Banowetz, Slovak RSO (Bratislava), Stankovsky.

Rubinstein was the first composer of concertos in Russia and was enormously prolific. His *First Piano concerto in E major*, dating from 1850, is greatly indebted to Mendelssohn though it is more prolix. As David Brown puts it, Rubinstein's 'enormous facility was unhindered by originality, and he was unashamedly eclectic and conservative'. The *Third Piano concerto in G* (1853–4) is more concentrated, and there is a recording of the *Fourth in D minor* (1864) by his pupil, Josef Hofmann; no later pianist has equalled that. By the mid 1860s Rubinstein's perspective had broadened (rather than deepened), and the *Fifth Piano concerto in E flat* (1874) is an ambitious piece, longer than the *Emperor* and almost as long as the Brahms *D minor*. No less a pianist than Joseph Lhévinne championed it during the early years of the century and no doubt its prodigious technical demands (it was not dedicated to Alkan for nothing) have stood in the way of its wider dissemination. It has all the fluent lyricism one expects of Rubinstein, though most of its ideas, attractive enough in themselves, overstay their welcome.

Joseph Banowetz has now recorded all the concertos for Marco Polo and, although the orchestral support and the recording do not rise much above routine, there is nothing ordinary about Banowetz's pianism. The *Fifth*, at least, is worth investigating (for the *Fourth*, one should turn to Cherkassky). The *Caprice russe* was written four years after the concerto, but the fires were obviously blazing less fiercely. All the same, this is an issue of some interest, and the solo playing has conviction.

Piano concerto No. 4 in D min., Op. 70; Melody in F.

*** Decca (IMS) Dig. 448 063-2. Cherkassky, RPO, Ashkenazy (with encores by TCHAIKOVSKY; GLAZUNOV; MOSZKOWSKI; GODOWSKY).

Cherkassky was 85 when he recorded the *Fourth* and, by common consent, best of the *Piano concertos*. It is a performance of distinction and, though not quite as dazzling as the famous 1937 Josef Hofmann performance, is stamped with much the same ring of authenticity. The encores are all taken from an analogue 1974 recital, previously issued on a Oiseau-Lyre LP. Some remarkable pianism there, too, particularly in the Godowsky pieces.

Cello sonata No. 1 in D, Op. 18.

*** RCA Dig. 09026 68290-2 [id.]. Steven Isserlis, Stephen Hough – GRIEG: *Cello sonata;* LISZT: *Elégies*, etc. ***

In these exhilarating performances Isserlis and Hough challenge each other in spontaneously imaginative interplay to bring out all the high-romantic qualities of the music while keeping firmly disciplined control. After a strongly characterized first movement, Isserlis and Hough adopt a genuine flowing *allegretto* for the siciliana rhythms of the central movement, made charmingly fresh; and the exuberant finale finds Hough at his most brilliant in the shimmering piano-writing. Warm, full sound.

Piano sonatas Nos. 1 in E min., Op. 12; 2 in C min., Op. 20; 3 in F, Op. 41; 4 in A min., Op. 100.

(B) *** Hyperion Dyad Dig. CCD 22007 (2) [id.]. Leslie Howard.

Leslie Howard proves highly persuasive in all four works. The 1981 recordings sound excellent, and this set is more enticing as a Dyad, with two discs offered for the price of one. Returning to these works, one is surprised to find how enjoyable the music is, with some good lyrical ideas, phrased romantically, to balance the arrestingly flamboyant rhetoric which Leslie Howard obviously relishes.

Ruders, Poul (born 1949)

(i) *Concerto for clarinet and twin orchestra;* (ii) *Violin concerto No. 1;* (iii) *Drama trilogy No. 3 for cello and orchestra 'Polydrama'*.

*** Unicorn Dig. DKPCD 9114 [id.]. (i) Thomsen; (ii) Hirsch; (iii) Zeuten; Odense SO, Tamás Vetö.

This *Violin concerto* is a tribute to the sunny atmosphere of Italian baroque music in general and Vivaldi's *Four Seasons* in particular. Apart from its neo-classicism there is a whiff of minimalism about much of it. The *Clarinet concerto* is strong stuff; to quote Ruders himself, the soloist is a 'Pierrot-like *vox humana* caught in a vice of orchestral onslaught', and the effect is often disturbing and almost surrealistic. He is an imaginative composer with a vein of lyrical feeling and melancholy that surfaces in the *Cello concerto*. A rewarding and interesting figure.

Rutter, John (born 1943)

(i; ii) *The Falcon;* (ii) *2 Festival anthems: O praise the Lord in heaven; Behold, the tabernacle of God;* (ii; iii) *Magnificat.*

*** Coll. Dig. COLCD 114; *COLC 114* [id.]. (i) St Paul's Cathedral Choristers; (ii) Cambridge Singers, City of L. Sinfonia; (iii) with Patricia Forbes; all cond. composer.

The Falcon was Rutter's first large-scale choral work. Its inspiration was a medieval poem, which is linked to the Crucifixion story, but the core of the piece is the mystical central *Lento*. The *Magnificat* has the usual Rutter stylistic touches, with a syncopated treatment of the opening *Magnificat anima mea*, and a joyous closing *Gloria Patri*. The two anthems are characteristically expansive and resplendent with brass. Fine performances and recording in the best Collegium tradition.

(i) *Gloria;* (ii) Anthems: *All things bright and beautiful; For the beauty of the earth; A Gaelic blessing; God be in my head; The Lord bless you and keep you; The Lord is my Shepherd; O clap your hands; Open thou my eyes; Praise ye the Lord; A prayer of St Patrick.*

*** Coll. Dig. COLCD 100; *COLC 100* [id.]. Cambridge Singers, (i) Philip Jones Brass Ens.; (ii) City of L. Sinfonia, composer.

Rutter has a genuine gift of melody and his use of tonal harmony is individual and never bland. The resplendent *Gloria* is a three-part piece, and Rutter uses his brass to splendid and often spectacular effect. The anthems are diverse in style and feeling and, like the *Gloria*, have strong melodic appeal – the setting of *All things bright and beautiful* is delightfully spontaneous. It is difficult to imagine the music receiving more persuasive advocacy than under the composer, and the recording is first class in every respect.

3 Musical fables: (i) *Brother Heinrich's Christmas;* (ii) *The Reluctant Dragon; The Wind in the Willows.*

**(*) Coll. COLCD 115; *COLC 115* [id.]. City of L. Sinf.; with (i) Brian Kay, Cambridge Singers, composer; (ii) Richard Baker, King's Singers, Hickox.

Brother Heinrich's Christmas is a musical narrative with choir, telling the story of how one of the most famous of all carols was introduced late at night by the angels to Brother Heinrich, just in time for it to be included in the monks' Christmas Day service. It is all highly ingenuous but engagingly presented, and should appeal to young listeners who have enjoyed Howard Blake's *The Snowman*. The settings of the two famous Kenneth Grahame stories are no less tunefully communicative and include simulations of pop music of the 1940s (among other derivations), notably a Rodgers-style ballad which sentimentalizes the end of *The Wind in the Willows* episode, after Toad's escape from prison. All the music is expertly sung and played and blends well with the warmly involving narrative, splendidly done by Richard Baker.

(i) *Requiem;* (ii) *Magnificat.*

(N) ❁ (M) *** CSCD 504 [id.]. (i) Caroline Ashton, Donna Dean; (ii) Patricia Forbes; Cambridge Singers, City of L. Sinf., composer.

John Rutter's melodic gift, so well illustrated in his carols, is here used in the simplest and most direct way to create a small-scale *Requiem* that is as beautiful and satisfying in its English way as the works of Fauré and Duruflé. The penultimate movement, a ripe setting of *The Lord is my Shepherd* with a lovely oboe obbligato, sounds almost like an anglicized Song of the Auvergne; while Caroline Ashton's performance of the delightful *Pie Jesu* is wonderfully warm and spontaneous, most beautifully recorded on CD, with the equally glorious *Magnificat* setting (see above) making a superb bonus on this mid-priced reissue.

(i) *Requiem. Cantata Domino;* (ii) *Cantus. Hymn to the Creator of light; Veni sancte spiritis; What sweeter music;* (ii) *Te Deum.*

(N) *** EMI Dig. CDC5 56605-2 [id.]. King's College, Cambridge Ch., Stephen Cleobury; with (i) Edward Saklatvala, Thomas Harries, City of L. Sinfonia; (ii) the Wallace Collection.

(i; ii) *Requiem. Cantata Domino; Choral fanfare; Draw on sweet night;* (ii) *Gaelic blessing. God be in my head; Hymn to the Creator of light; My true love hath my heart;* (ii) *The Lord bless you and keep you. Open thou mine eyes; A prayer for Saint Patrick.*

(N) *** Hyperion Dig. CDA 66947 [id.]. Polyphony, Stephen Layton; with (i) Rosa Manion; (ii) Bournemouth Sinf.

These two new recordings are of high quality and both bring first-class digital sound. There is something special about hearing this music within the King's acoustic, and using boy trebles in the choir as well as for the two solos. At times there is an ethereal resonance here, although climaxes emerge strongly.

Polyphony uses women's voices (as does Rutter himself) in a choir of 25 voices. The balance is slightly more forward, and the result brings a radiant richness of sound which is hardly less enjoyable. Both choirs complete their programmes with some of Rutter's shorter choral works. Three of them – the memorable *Veni sanctus spiritus*, *What sweeter music* and the *Cantus*, with its resonant brass accompaniment – were written for King's, but both choirs give us the refreshingly lively *Cantate Domino* and the remarkable *Hymn to the Creator of Light* for double chorus, which was written in memory of Herbert Howells but reminds one also of Tavener. The King's programme ends with the exultant *Te Deum*; Polyphony include the lovely *Gaelic blessing* and *Draw on sweet light*, plus Rutter's beautiful setting of the *Benediction*, which introduces one of his friendliest tunes.

Ryba, Jakob Jan (1765–1815)

Czech Christmas mass; Missa pastoralis.

(N) (BB) *** Naxos Dig. 8.554428 [id.]. Soloists, Czech Madrigalists Ch. & O, Frantisek Xaver Thuri.

The Czech composer, Jakob Jan Ryba, contemporary with Mozart, wrote these *Christmas masses* – one long, one short – as seasonal cantatas. With only token references to the liturgy, obvious enough in the *Gloria*, they relate the story of the shepherds visiting the baby Jesus to the various sections of the Mass. Understandably, with their simple folk-like tunes and harmonies, they have long been part of traditional Czech celebrations at Christmas, and here receive winningly fresh and direct performances, atmospherically recorded.

Sæverud, Harald (1897–1992)

Peer Gynt Suites Nos. 1 & 2, Op. 48.

(N) *** Finlandia/Warner Dig. 0630 17675-2 [id.]. Anne-Margarethe Eikaas, Norwegian Radio O, Ari Rasilainen. – GRIEG: *Peer Gynt suites.* ***

This disc contrasts the two scores for Ibsen's *Peer Gynt*: Grieg's romantic setting of 1874 on which he later based his two orchestral suites, and Harald Sæverud's anti-Romantic, altogether rougher, incidental music of 1947. The Norwegian Radio Orchestra under their Finnish conductor, Ari Rasilainen, give a stimulating account of the piece, every bit as enjoyable and full of character as the Stavanger account on BIS listed below. Excellent recording.

Symphony No. 6 (Sinfonia dolorosa), Op. 19; Galdreslåtten, Op. 20; Kjæmpevise-slåtten, Op. 22; Peer Gynt Suites Nos. 1 & 2, Op. 28.

*** BIS Dig. CD 762 [id.]. Stavanger SO, Alexander Dmitriev.

The *Sixth Symphony* (*Sinfonia dolorosa*) is a short but intense piece from the war years, dedicated to a close friend who perished in the resistance, and the *Kjæmpevise-slåtten* ('Ballad of Revolt') comes from the same years. It is an inspiriting work, an outraged, combative reaction to the sight of the Nazi occupation barracks near his Bergen home. The *Peer Gynt* music, written for a post-war production of Ibsen's play, could not be further removed from Grieg's celebrated score. It is earthy and rambunctious and it makes Grieg sound positively genteel. So, too, does the delightful, inventive and wholly original *Galdreslåtten*. Eminently satisfactory performances from the Stavanger orchestra under Alexander Dmitriev, brought vividly to life by the BIS recording team.

Symphony No. 7 (Salme), Op. 27; (i) *Bassoon concerto, Op. 44. Lucretia (suite), Op. 10.*

(N) *** BIS Dig. CD 822 [id.] (i) Robert Rønnes; Stavanger SO, Alexander Dmitirev.

The one-movement *Seventh* (1945) is the last of Sæverud's wartime symphonies, *Salme-symfoni*, a deeply felt work, a hymn of thanksgiving for peace. It has never sounded better than it does in this recording. Both the *Lucretia suite* and the *Bassoon concerto* are first recordings. The suite derives from the incidental music Sæverud wrote in 1936 for André Obey's play on which Benjamin Britten based his opera, *The Rape of Lucretia*. Much of it is highly imaginative (the evocation of night in the fourth movement, for example) and the charming middle movement, Lucretia sleeping. There are some Nielsenesque touches in the second movement which portrays Lucretia spinning. The *Bassoon concerto* (1965) was revised towards the end of Sæverud's long life in collaboration with Robert Rønnes, the soloist here. Absolutely first-class performances and recordings.

Symphony No. 9, Op. 45; (i) *Piano concerto, Op. 31. Fanfare and Hymne, Op. 48.*

(N) ✿ *** BIS Dig. CD 962 [id.]. Stavanger SO, Dmitriev with (i) Noriko Ogawa.

Alexander Dmitriev and the Stavanger orchestra are very persuasive in the *Ninth Symphony*, which is currently unrepresented on CD now that Per Dreier's RPO recording has gone. There is a strong sense of the Norwegian landscape here and the BIS recording conveys it all with striking clarity and presence. The *Piano concerto* of 1950 is a delightful piece, full of quirky, robust humour. It opens in somewhat neo-classical mode with a Stravinskian flourish but Sæverud's original dialect soon surfaces. It is a work that haunts and fascinates, and the farmyard noises of the finale together with the strongly atmospheric slow movement linger in the memory. Norika Ogawa is an alert, sensitive player who has the measure of this piece, and Alexander Dmitriev and the Stavanger orchestra are eminently supportive. The short *Fanfare and Hymn* was commissioned by the City of Bergen to celebrate its 900th anniversary. The sound is in the demonstration bracket.

Sainte-Colombe (died *c.* 1700)

Concerts à deux violes: Bourrasque; La dubois; La raporté; Le retour; Tombeau les regrets.

*** Astrée Audivis Dig. E 7729 [id.]. Jordi Savall, Wieland Kuijken.

Concerts à deux violes: La conférence; Dalain; Le figuré; La rougeville; Le tendre.
*** Astrée Audivis Dig. E 8743 [id.]. Jordi Savall, Wieland Kuijken.

Le Retour; Tombeau les Regrets.
(BB) *** Naxos Dig. 8.550750 [id.]. Spectre de la Rose – MARAIS: *Tombeau pour M. de Sainte-Colombe*, etc. ***

The success of the film (*Tous les matins du monde*) about this reclusive composer and his relationship with his pupil, Marin Marais, has led to the soundtrack becoming a bestseller. However, this enterprising and inexpensive Naxos recital includes the 'hits' from the film. The two Sainte-Colombe works included are austerely but certainly touchingly played by a fresh-sounding 'authentic' group led by Alison Crum (viola da gamba) and Marie Knight (baroque violin). The Naxos recording is vivid, but its forward balance means that for a realistic effect a modest setting of the volume control should be chosen.

Those who are then tempted to explore the music of Sainte-Colombe further might invest in the pair of excellent Audivis CDs featuring Jordi Savall, who was associated with the film. They are performed by artists who have this music in their bones, and the playing is more subtle than it is on Naxos and has even greater emotional depth. The two CDs are excellently recorded and are available separately; the second duplicates nothing on the Naxos CD.

Saint-Saëns, Camille (1835–1921)

(i) *Africa fantasy for piano and orchestra, Op. 89. Ascanio: Valse-finale; Parysatis: Airs de ballet. Sarabande et Rigaudon, Op. 93; Suite algérienne, Op. 60: Marche militaire française.* (ii) *Tarantelle for flute, clarinet and orchestra, Op. 6;* (iii) *Messe de Requiem, Op. 54.*
**(*) Cala Dig. CACD 1015; *CAMC 1015* [id.]. LPO, Geoffrey Simon, with (i) Gwendolyn Mok; (ii) Susan Milan, James Campbell; (iii) Olafimihan, Wyn-Rogers, Roden, Kirkbride, Hertfordshire Ch., Harlow Ch., East London Ch.

La jota aragonesa, Op. 64; (i) *La muse et le poète. La princesse jaune: Overture;* (ii) *Symphony No. 3 in C min.;* (iii) *Danse macabre* (original vocal version). *Grande fantaisie on themes from Samson et Dalila* (arr. Luigini).
** Cala Dig. CACD 1016; *CAMC 1016* [id.]. LPO, Geoffrey Simon, with (i) Stephanie Chase, Robert Truman; (ii) James O'Donnell; (iii) Anthony Roden.

Geoffrey Simon is an amiably persuasive advocate of these Saint-Saëns novelties and his affectionate approach emphasizes the music's surface elegance. The resonant acoustics of All Hallows Church, Gospel Oak, cast a warm glow over the proceedings, and detail could be sharper. However, the nicely scored *Airs de Ballet*, which come from the incidental music for *Parysatis*, are certainly enticing. The gracious *Sarabande* and genial *Rigaudon* certainly tickle the ear, as does the tuneful *Valse-finale* from *Ascanio*. But it is the lively and charming *Tarantelle* for flute, clarinet and orchestra which is the vivacious highlight of the first CD. It is winningly played by Susan Milan and James Campbell. The rich sonority of the sound suits the melodically catchy *Marche militaire française*, with its resplendent brass, but the exotically oriental *Africa fantasy for piano and orchestra* loses some of its point and glitter when the acoustic is so resonant. Even so, the performance is full of charm, and Gwendolyn Mok plays with flair. The *Messe de Requiem* is a real find, even if here the focus of the choral sound needs to be sharper. In its unpretentious, expressive style it is a kind of French equivalent of Rossini's *Petite messe solennelle*. Pretty good choral singing, a well-matched team of soloists, and the recording gives the work a fine, sonorous impact, even if more bite is needed.

The undoubted highlight of the second disc is the fascinating original vocal version of *Danse macabre*, very much shorter than the familiar tone-poem. It takes less than three minutes and almost seems to be cut off. The effect is semi-operatic, interrupted by the cock-crow. *La muse et le poète* is an extended duo for violin and cello with orchestra. It opens dreamily, but as it becomes more passionate it also becomes technically demanding. Stephanie Chase and, especially, the cellist Robert Truman are good if not distinctive soloists. The *Jota aragonesa* is very like the Glinka fantasy and needs a recording with more glitter. The *Grande fantaisie on Samson et Dalila* arranged by Luigini is rather inflated but is not helped by Geoffrey Simon's very leisurely tempo for *Softly awakes my heart*, even though there is some lovely warm Philharmonia string-playing. The *Overture La princesse jaune* is presented with real charm but Geoffrey Simon then chooses to end his second CD with the *Organ Symphony* – an agreeable account, but no more than that.

(i) *Caprice andalou, Op. 122; Morceau de concert, Op. 62: Romance, Op. 36* (all for violin and orchestra); *Morceaux de concert:* (ii) *for harp and orchestra, Op. 64;* (iii) *for horn and orchestra, Op. 94; Romance for horn and orchestra, Op. 48. Spartacus: overture.*
*** EMI (SIS) Dig. CDC5 55587-2. (i) Olivier Charlier; (ii) M. Nordmann; (iii) R. Vlatkovič; O de Paris Ens., Kantorow.

This is an appealing collection of concertante miniatures. Saint-Saëns ready melodic flow and natural craftsmanship are always endearing; The *Morceau de concert* for violin and orchestra may lack the memorability of the *Introduction and rondo capriccioso* but there is much to delight the ear. The two works for horn and orchestra are more robust. Both Olivier Charlier and Radovan Vlatkovič are persuasive soloists. The overture *Spartacus* brings no anticipations of Khachaturian. Indeed its style veers nearer to that of Lalo. It also brings a melodic whiff of Verdi in its secondary string tune. If perhaps a shade overlong, it is presented persuasively by Kantorow and his players. The recording, made in the Salle Wagram, is very satisfactory.

Carnival of the animals.

(M) *** Teldec/Warner Dig. 4509 97445-2 [id.]. Güher and Süher Pekinel, French R. PO, Janowski – POULENC: *Double piano concerto.* ***

(M) *** Virgin/EMI Dig. CUV7 61137-2 [id.]. Anton Nel, Keith Snell, Ac. of L., Richard Stamp – PROKOFIEV: *Peter.* *** ✪

(N) (B)*** Ph. Virtuoso 462 938-2 [id.]. Villa, Jennings, Pittsburgh SO, Previn – RAVEL: *Ma Mère l'Oye* (complete) (with DUKAS: *L'apprenti sorcier;* Rotterdam PO, Zinman ***).

(B) *** CfP CD-CFP 4086. Katin, Fowke, SNO, Gibson – BIZET: *Jeux d'enfants;* RAVEL: *Ma Mère l'Oye.* ***

(BB) *** ASV Quicksilva CDQS 6017. Goldstone, Brown, RPO, Hughes – PROKOFIEV: *Peter.* ***

(BB) **(*) Tring Dig. TRP 046 [id.]. RPO, Andrea Licata (with BIZET: *Jeux d'enfants;* **) – PROKOFIEV: *Peter.* **(*)

Güher and Süher Pekinel – of mixed Turkish/Spanish parentage – make a sparklingly spontaneous contribution to Saint-Saëns's zoological fantasy, readily dominating the performance with their scintillating pianism. Janowski and the French Radio Orchestra provide admirable support, and Saint-Saëns's portrait gallery comes vividly and wittily to life. The gentle dignity of Eric Levionnais's *Le Cygne* makes a touching highlight, leading on to an exhilarating finale. The performance is beautifully recorded and naturally balanced within an attractively warm ambience; although the playing time is short, this mid-priced CD remains highly recommendable.

Richard Stamp directs an outstanding version, full of affectionate humour. Throughout, one responds to the polished overall presentation and sense of fun; although some may feel that the recording is rather resonant, it adds a genial warmth to the vitality of the proceedings.

Previn's version makes a ready alternative. The music is played with infectious rhythmic spring and great refinement. It is a mark of the finesse of this performance – which has plenty of bite and vigour, as well as polish – that the great cello solo of *Le Cygne* is so naturally presented. Fine contributions too from the two pianists, although their image is rather bass-orientated, within a warmly atmospheric recording. At bargain price this is very attractive, particularly as Philips have now added a very enjoyable account of Dukas's *Sorcerer's apprentice.*

On CfP the solo pianists, Peter Katin and Philip Fowke, enter fully into the spirit of the occasion, with Gibson directing his Scottish players with affectionate, unforced geniality. The couplings are attractive and the CD transfer confirms the vivid colourfulness and presence of the mid-1970s recording.

The two pianists on ASV also play with point and style, and the accompaniment has both spirit and spontaneity. *The Swan* is perhaps a trifle self-effacing, but otherwise this is very enjoyable, the humour appreciated without being underlined. The recording is excellent, and this makes a good super-bargain CD recommendation.

With a pair of unnamed pianists who play brilliantly and enjoy their wrong notes in the self-portrait, this is a vivid performance on Tring, with the solo orchestral instruments closely miked, with the effect of changing the balance in each portrait. The double-bass sounds lugubriously larger-than-life, but the cello plays his famous portrayal of *The swan* in a very melancholy fashion.

Carnival of the animals (with narration).

(N) (BB) **(*) Naxos Dig. 8.554463 [id.]. Johnny Morris (nar.), Slovak RSO, Lenárd – DUKAS: *L'apprenti sorcier;* RAVEL: *Ma Mère l'Oye.* ***

This Naxos collection is clearly aimed at younger children, and many adults could find Johnny Morris's very personal (and often eccentric) descriptions and rhymes, which adorn this performance, too much to take. But the playing of the Slovak orchestra, with a persuasively spontaneous contribution from the two anonymous pianists, is most attractive. If Morris's friendly delivery and lazy timing of his own text bring children to the music, all to the good, especially if they remember the musical association past childhood. They will surely not mind Morris's singing along in a quavery fashion with the Tortoise, and in the Aquarium, even though he drowns the music! His opening poem gives an idea of what to expect:

'The whole world is a sort of zoo,
Where people look like animals,
And animals look like you.
The man who lives in that large villa,
reminds one of a big gorilla.
The only difference being that,
He goes to work in a bowler hat.'

The orchestral playing is most sensitive, and the recording balance warmly intimate: the pianists sound real.

'The essential Saint-Saëns': (i) Carnival of the animals; (ii) Piano concerto No. 2 in G min., Op. 22; (iii) Violin concerto No. 3 in B min., Op. 61; (iv) Danse macabre, Op. 40; (v) Havanaise, Op. 83; Introduction and rondo capriccioso, Op. 28; (vi) Symphony No. 3 in C min. (Organ), Op. 78; Samson et Dalila: (vii) Air et danse bacchanale; (viii) Mon cœur s'ouvre à ta voix.

(B) **(*) Decca Double 444 552-2 (2) [id.]. (i) Ortiz; (i; ii) Rogé; (iii) Bell; (v) Kyung Wha Chung; (vi) Priest; (viii) Horne; (i) L. Sinf.; (ii; v) RPO; (iii; vii) Montreal SO; (iv) Philh. O; (i–v; vii) cond. Dutoit; (vi) LAPO, Mehta.

Mehta's Los Angeles account of the *Third Symphony* is among the more recommendable versions of this much-recorded work, for he draws a well-disciplined and exuberant response from all departments of the orchestra. Joshua Bell's performance of the *Violin concerto* is very attractive indeed: the *pianissimo* opening is full of atmosphere and the *Andantino* has a pleasingly lyrical simplicity. The disappointment is Dutoit's *Carnival of the animals* – in a crisp, clean, digital recording with very bright sound – which is lacking charactization and charm. *The Swan* is played in a very matter-of-fact way. Dutoit shows himself in a better light in his deft account of the *Danse macabre*, while Kyung Wha Chung is on top form, playing with flair in both the famous violin showpieces. Marilyn Horne's ripe characterization of Saint-Saëns's most famous aria, 'Softly awakes my heart', will not disappoint, and nor will the excerpts from *Samson et Dalila*. Pascal Rogé's account of the favourite Saint-Saëns *Second Piano concerto* is second to none.

(i) *Carnival of the animals;* (ii) *Le Cygne; Piano concertos Nos.* (iii) *2 in G min., Op. 22;* (iv) *4 in C min., Op. 44;* (v) *Violin concerto No. 3 in B min., Op. 61;* (vi) *Danse macabre, Op. 40;* (v) *Introduction and Rondo capriccioso, Op. 28;* (vii) *Symphony No. 3 in C min. (Organ), Op. 78.*

(B) **(*) Ph. Duo 442 608-2 (2) [id.]. (i) Villa, Jennings, Pittsburgh SO, Previn; (ii) Gendron, Gallion; (iii) Davidovich, Concg. O, Järvi; (iv) Campanella, Monte Carlo Op. O, Ceccato; (v) Szeryng, Monte Carlo Op. O, Remoortel; (vi) Concg. O, Haitink; (vii) Chorzempa, Rotterdam PO, Edo de Waart.

This inexpensive Duo collection is described as 'The Best of Saint-Saëns' and indeed it does include good and sometimes fine performances of many of the composer's most attractive orchestral and concertante works. Notable here is Previn's 1980 *Carnival of the animals*, as fine as almost any available (see above). (Philips have also included a second performance of *Le Cygne* by the inestimable Maurice Gendron.) Bella Davidovich gives a most sympathetic account of the *G minor Piano concerto* and draws pleasing tone-quality from the instrument, even if she lacks the last degree of brilliance and flair. She has the advantage of excellent orchestral support from the Concertgebouw Orchestra, who also give a lively account of the *Danse macabre* under Haitink. In the *C minor Concerto* (which is analogue) the effect is harder, partly because Michele Campanella is a more boldly extrovert soloist; but this account has undoubted vitality and no lack of *espressivo*. Henryk Szeryng gives clean, immaculate performances of the *B minor Violin concerto* and the *Introduction and Rondo capriccioso*. His approach is aristocratic rather than seductive. The contribution of the Monte Carlo orchestra is adequate. De Waart's 1976 recording of the *Organ Symphony* is not among the most exciting versions available but, with polished orchestral playing and refined Philips sound, it is certainly enjoyable.

(i) *Carnival of the animals;* (ii) *Danse macabre, Op. 40; Suite algérienne, Op. 60: Marche militaire française. Samson et Dalila: Bacchanale.* (ii; iii) *Symphony No. 3 in C min., Op. 78.*

(B) *** Sony SBK 47655 [id.]. (i) Entremont, Gaby Casadesus, Régis Pasquier, Yan Pascal Tortelier, Caussé, Yo-Yo Ma, Lauridon, Marion, Arrignon, Cals, Cerutti; (ii) Phd. O, Ormandy; (iii) with E. Power Biggs.

(i) *Carnival of the animals;* (ii) *Danse macabre;* (iii) *Symphony No. 3;* (iv) *Wedding-cake* (caprice-valse for piano and orchestra), *Op. 76.*

**(*) ASV Dig CDDCA 665 [id.]. (i) Guillermo Salvador Snr & Jnr, Mexico City PO; (ii) Mexicana State SO; (iii) Noel Rawsthorne, LPO; (iv) Osorio, RPO; Bátiz.

It would be churlish to bracket the third star for the generous Sony collection because the opening of the *Carnival of the animals*, performed in its original chamber version, is a bit lacklustre. The ear adjusts to the rather dry effect. It is a starry cast: Yo-Yo Ma personifies *The Swan* gently and gracefully. Ormandy and his splendid orchestra play the other orchestral lollipops with fine panache. No complaint about the 1962 sound in the *Symphony*. The performance is fresh and vigorous, with Ormandy at his most involved.

The *Carnival of the animals* and *Danse macabre* have plenty of genial vitality on ASV but are less strong on finesse, and the forwardly balanced recording adds to the robust feeling. Jorge Federico Osorio, however, dispatches the charming *Wedding-cake caprice-valse* with a winning sparkle. Bátiz's version of the spectacular *Organ symphony* was the first digital success for this work. The orchestral playing is exhilarating in its energy, while the *Poco Adagio* balances a noble, elegiac feeling with romantic warmth. The organ entry is an impressive moment and the sense of spectacle persists in the closing pages.

Cello concertos Nos. 1 in A min., Op. 33; 2 in D min., Op. 119; Allegro appassionato in B min.,

Op. 43; Suite in D min., Op. 16; Carnival of the animals: The Swan (orch. Vidal).
(BB) **(*) Naxos Dig. 8.553039 [id.]. Kliegel, Bournemouth Sinf., Monnard.

The Naxos issue brings together Saint-Saëns's cello music in sensitive, warmly expressive performances, marred by the rather thin string sonority. Maria Kliegel proves a most sympathetic soloist, technically immaculate, undeterred even by the relatively ungrateful writing for the cello in the *Second Concerto*, so much less striking a work than No. 1. It is good to have the early *Suite*, a colourful collection of genre pieces, and the dashing *Allegro appassionato*, both originally with piano accompaniment and here arranged by the composer himself. Saint-Saëns's most celebrated cello piece, *The Swan*, makes an attractive supplement, played in an orchestral arrangement by Paul Vidal, which adds strings to the usual harp accompaniment.

Cello concerto No. 1 in A min., Op. 33.
*** EMI Dig. CDC5 56126-2 [id.]. Han-Na Chang, LSO, Rostropovich – BRUCH: *Kol Nidrei* ***; FAURE: *Elégie* ***; TCHAIKOVSKY *Rococo variations*. *** ❁
*** ASV Dig. CDDCA 867 [id.]. Sophie Rolland, BBC PO, Gilbert Varga – LALO: *Cello concerto in D min.;* MASSENET: *Fantaisie*. ***
(B) *** Decca Dig. Eclipse 448 712-2; *448 712-4* [(M) id. import]. Lynn Harrell, Cleveland O, Marriner – LALO; SCHUMANN: *Concertos*. ***
(B) *** DG 431 166-2. Heinrich Schiff, New Philh. O, Mackerras – FAURE: *Elégie;* LALO: *Cello concerto*. ***
❁ (M) (***) Sony Heritage mono MHK 62876 [id.]. Gregor Piatigorsky, Chicago SO, Stock – BRUCH: *Kol Nidrei;* DVORAK: *Cello concerto*. (***)
(M) *** Mercury (IMS) 432 010-2 [id.]. Janos Starker, LSO, Dorati – LALO: *Concerto* **(*); SCHUMANN: *Concerto*. ***

Han-Na Chang's account of the Saint-Saëns *Concerto* is second to none, full of ardour, yet light-hearted in its bravura. Chang's delicacy of feeling, natural sense of line and wide range of dynamic show an instinctive musicianship and a mastery of her instrument that recalls the young Menuhin, while the sophistication of the performance is extraordinarily mature, helped in no small part by Rostropovich's always supportive accompaniment and the superb playing of the LSO. The EMI Abbey Road recording is first class in every way and beautifully balanced.

Sophie Rolland's performance of the *A minor Cello concerto* demonstrates a formidable talent. She takes its technical hurdles in her effortless stride and is very well supported by the BBC Philharmonic under Gilbert Varga. Perhaps their opening is marginally too fast for an *Allegro non troppo*, but the performance is in every respect a highly enjoyable one. The excellence of the BBC/ASV recording makes for a strong recommendation.

Harrell's reading of the Saint-Saëns, altogether more extrovert than Yo-Yo Ma's (see below), makes light of any idea that this composer always works on a small scale. The opening is positively epic, and the rest of the performance is just as compelling, with the minuet-like *Allegretto* crisply neo-classical. The addition of the Lalo *Concerto* makes this reissue very competitive.

Schiff gives as eloquent an account of this concerto as any on record. He sparks off an enthusiastic response from Mackerras, and the recorded sound and balance are excellent. At bargain price, this deserves the strongest recommendation.

Piatigorsky's account of the Saint-Saëns *A minor Concerto* must rank among the very best ever made. While you are listening to it, you think it cannot have been surpassed since. The orchestral accompaniment under Frederick Stock shows the Chicago orchestra to have been every bit as fine when this was made as they were in their heyday under Reiner. Stock brings delicacy and virtuosity to this score, and not the least astonishing is the quality of the recorded sound, which dates from March 1940! It is superior to the post-war Philadelphia recordings with which it is coupled. The presentation, as always with this series, is distinguished and reproduces the handsome original covers of the 78-r.p.m. sets. This disc costs rather more than an ordinary mid-priced issue but is well worth it.

Starker plays the Saint-Saëns *A minor* with charm and grace, and Dorati provides first-class support. The 1964 recording comes up amazingly well and is excellently (and naturally) balanced.

(i) *Cello concerto No. 1, Op. 33;* (ii) *The swan;* (iii) *Allegro appassionato, Op. 43; Cello sonata No. 1, Op. 32; Chant saphique, Op. 91; Gavotte, Op. posth.; Romances Nos. 1 in F, Op. 36; 2 in D, Op. 51;* (iv) *Prière* (for cello & organ).
*** RCA Dig. 09026 61678-2 [id.]. Steven Isserlis; (i) LSO, Tilson Thomas; (ii) Tilson Thomas, Dudley Moore; (iii) Pascal Devoyon; (iv) Stephen Grier.

Steven Isserlis's account of the *Cello concerto in A minor* is among the best on record. Of particular interest is the *Cello sonata No. 1 in C minor*, composed in the same year, in which he is accompanied with elegance and finesse by Pascal Devoyon. Isserlis himself plays with the musicianship and virtuosity one has come to expect from him. Most of the remaining pieces are both worthwhile and entertaining, particularly the *Allegro appassionato*. The *Prière*, Op. 159, for cello and organ, was written as late as 1919, and is a small but affecting addition to the Saint-Saëns discography. The recorded sound is very good indeed.

(i) *Cello concerto No. 1 in A min., Op. 33;* (ii) *Piano concerto No. 2 in G min., Op. 22;* (iii) *Violin concerto No. 3, Op. 61.*

✪ (M) *** Sony Dig. SMK 66935 [id.]. (i) Yo-Yo Ma, O Nat. de France, Maazel; (ii) Cécile Licad, LPO, Previn; (iii) Cho-Liang Lin, Philh. O, Tilson Thomas.

Three outstanding performances from the early 1980s are admirably linked together in this highly desirable CBS mid-price reissue. Yo-Yo Ma's performance of the *Cello concerto* is distinguished by fine sensitivity and beautiful tone, while Cécile Licad and the LPO under Previn turn in an eminently satisfactory reading of the *G minor Piano concerto* that has the requisite delicacy in the Scherzo and seriousness elsewhere. Cho-Liang Lin's account of the *B minor Violin concerto* with the Philharmonia Orchestra and Michael Tilson Thomas is exhilarating and thrilling; indeed, this is the kind of performance that prompts one to burst into applause; his version is arguably the finest to have appeared for years.

(i) *Cello concerto No. 1 in A min, Op. 33; Suite, Op. 16;* (ii) *Allegro appassionato, Op. 43; Carnaval of the animals: The Swan Romance in F, Op. 36; Cello sonata No. 1 in E min., Op. 32.*

(N) ** DG Dig. 457 599-2 [id.]. Mischa Maisky, (i) Orpheus CO; (ii) Daria Hovora.

Mischa Maisky plays with great virtuosity and brings splendid vitality as well as brilliance to the quicker movements of the *A minor concerto*. But for all his virtuosity and beauty of tone, expressive exaggeration is not alien to his nature and he is prone to emote heavily at the slightest pretext. Of course he makes a glorious sound and the Orpheus Chamber Orchestra play with splendid attack. One longs for the finesse and understatement of a Fournier.

Piano concertos Nos. 1 in D, Op. 17; 2 in G min., Op. 22; 3 in E flat, Op. 29; 4 in C min., Op. 44; 5 in F (Egyptian), Op. 103.

(B) *** Decca Double 443 865-2 (2) [id.]. Pascal Rogé, Philh. O, RPO or LPO, Dutoit.

(B) *** EMI (SIS) Rouge et Noir CZS5 69258-2 (2) [ZDMB 694432]. Aldo Ciccolini, O de Paris, Serge Baudo.

Piano concertos Nos. 1–5; Africa fantaisie, Op. 89; Wedding-cake caprice-valse, Op. 76 (both for piano and orchestra).

(N) (B) *** EMI double fforte Dig. CZS5 73356-2 (2) [CDFB 73356]. Jean-Philippe Collard, RPO, Previn.

(i) *Piano concertos Nos. 1 in D, Op. 17; 2 in G min., Op. 22; 3 in E flat, Op. 29; 4 in C min., Op. 44; 5 in F ('Egyptian'), Op. 103;* (ii) *Septet in E flat, Op. 65.*

(B) (***) EMI Rouge et Noir mono CZS5 69470-2 (2). Jeanne-Marie Darré, with (i) French Nat. RO, Louis Fourestier; (ii) Delmotte, Logerot, Pascal Qt.

As always with Collard there is splendid character and a dazzling technique. He brings panache and virtuosity to these concertos, as well as impressive poetic feeling. Apart from the beauty of sound, he commands a wide dynamic range and a subtle tonal palette. At one point in the *Fifth (Egyptian) concerto* Collard exploits Saint-Saëns's genius in manipulating the piano to suggest Eastern sonorities, and makes his instrument sound exactly like an Arab *qunan* or zither. Throughout, Previn and the Royal Philharmonic Orchestra are sensitive accompanists, and this set tends to trump the opposition by including not only the celebrated (and scatty) *Wedding-cake caprice-valse*, but also a sparkling account of the exuberant, pseudo-exotic *Africa-Fantaisie*. Although in many respects allegiance to Pascal Rogé on Decca remains strong, Collard with his greater dynamic range and authority often makes even more of this music. The digital sound is very good too, at times slightly more transparent than the Decca, but there is a distinct touch or hardness on top.

Played as they are on Decca, these concertos can exert a strong appeal: Pascal Rogé brings delicacy, virtuosity and sparkle to the piano part and he receives expert support from the various London orchestras under Dutoit. Altogether delicious playing and excellent piano-sound from Decca, who secure a most realistic balance.

The performances from Ciccolini and Baudo on EMI are also admirably spirited and emerge freshly on CD. The vibrant, at times slightly brash, 1970 sound gives the music-making strong character and projection. This is another very welcome reissue in EMI's French 'two for the price of one' series.

Jeanne-Marie Darré is little known outside her native France, where her recordings of the Saint-Saëns *Piano concertos* enjoy classic status. The performances come from the 1950s and are wonderfully high-spirited and vivacious. She is said to have played all five concertos in the course of one concert in celebration of her 21st birthday! Both in the concertos and in the delightful *Septet*, in which Roger Delmotte is the trumpeter, she sparkles and glitters. Well worth considering even if you have a good modern set, for the sound is very good.

Piano concerto No. 2 in G min., Op. 22.

(M) *** RCA 09026 61863-2 [id.]. Rubinstein, Phd. O, Ormandy – FALLA: *Nights in the gardens of Spain*, etc. **(*); FRANCK: *Symphonic variations for piano and orchestra*. ***

(***) Testament mono SBT 1029 [id.]. Gilels, Paris Conservatoire O, Cluytens (with SHOSTAKOVICH: *Prelude and fugue in D, Op. 87/5*) – RACHMANINOV: *Piano concerto No. 3*. (***)

(M) **(*) BMG/Melodiya 74321 40721-2 [id.]. Grigori Sokolov, USSR SO, Neeme Järvi – TCHAIKOVSKY: *Piano concerto No. 1*.**(*)

Rubinstein's version was made in 1969, and he is

partnered by that most understanding of accompanists, Eugene Ormandy. Rubinstein's secret is that, though he appears sometimes to be attacking the music, his phrasing is full of little fluctuations so that his playing never sounds stilted. The recording of the piano is rather dry, even hard at times, but the glitter seems just right for the centrepiece.

Gilels's celebrated account of the Saint-Saëns *G minor concerto* comes from 1954 and is masterly in every respect. Its delicacy and refinement still come across in spite of the limitations of the recording, and Gilels gets marvellous support from the Paris orchestra under André Cluytens. Excellent transfers.

Grigory Sokolov was a mere 16 when he gave his dazzling account of the Saint-Saëns *G minor Concerto*, with which he won the Tchaikovsky Piano Competition in 1966. The publicity material quotes Harold Schonberg in the New York *Times* calling it 'a startling performance' and hailing the 'truly refined lightness of the finale'. The Tchaikovsky concerto from the following year is no less remarkable, not just for virtuosic display but also for poetic depth. A remarkable response from both the young soloist and from the USSR Symphony Orchestra and Neeme Järvi. The recording may be pretty rough-and-ready but what playing!

Piano concertos Nos. 2 in G min., Op. 22; 4 in C min., Op. 44.

(BB) **(*) Naxos Dig. 8.550334 [id.]. Idil Biret, Philh. O, James Loughran.

At least on this occasion Idil Biret has the benefit of decent sound, for the recording was made at St Barnabas, London. She makes rather heavy weather of the opening of the *G minor Concerto* and her performance sounds just a little portentous and wanting in charm, though the scherzo is played with delicacy and character. The accompaniment by the Philharmonia Orchestra under James Loughran is very good and the recording is very good indeed. There are performances of greater subtlety to be had – albeit not at this price.

Violin concertos Nos. 1 in A, Op. 20; 2 in C, Op. 58; 3 in B min., Op. 61; Caprice andalou, Op. 122; Le Déluge, Op. 45: Prélude. Havanaise, Op. 83; Introduction and Rondo capriccioso, Op. 28; Morceau de concert, Op. 62; Romances: in D, Op. 37; in C, Op. 48; (i) *La Muse et le Poète, Op. 132.* (Also includes: YSAYE: *Caprice d'après l'Etude en forme de valse, Op. 52/6.*)

(BB) **(*) EMI Rouge et Noir (SIS) CZS5 72001-2 (2). Ulf Hoelscher, New Philh. O, Pierre Dervaux; (i) with Ralph Kirshbaum.

This two-CD box collects all Saint-Saëns's music for violin and orchestra (with a short bonus from Ysaÿe) in performances of excellent quality. Ulf Hoelscher is an extremely accomplished soloist who plays with artistry as well as virtuosity. The *Second concerto* has a most attractive *Andante* and a catchy *Allegro scherzando* finale, while the first of the two *Romances* deserves to be much better known. The *Morceau de concert* is most engaging and the relatively ambitious extended duo concertante piece, *La Muse et le Poète*, in which Hoelscher is admirably partnered by Ralph Kirschbaum, seems much more substantial here than usual. In this EMI set Pierre Dervaux directs excellent accompaniments, and the recording (made at Abbey Road in 1977) is basically of excellent quality even though the forward balance of the soloist does not enhance Hoelscher's timbre in the upper range.

Violin concertos Nos. (i) *1 in A, Op. 20;* (ii) *3 in B min., Op. 61*; (iii) *Havanaise, Op. 83; Introduction and Rondo capriccioso.*

(M) *** Decca 460 008-2. Kyung Wha Chung, (i) Montreal SO, Charles Dutoit; (ii) LSO, Lawrence Foster; (iii) RPO, Dutoit.

Saint-Saëns's *First Violin concerto* is a miniature – in three sections, but playing altogether for only just over 11 minutes. Kyung Wha Chung presents it delightfully and receives admirable support from Dutoit. She gives a passionate account of the *B minor Concerto*, so intense that even a sceptical listener will find it hard not to be convinced that this is a great work. Such music needs this kind of advocacy, and Miss Chung is splendidly backed up by the LSO under Lawrence Foster. The 1975 analogue recording is slightly less flattering than the 1980 digital sound in Montreal, but it remains full and clear.

Violin concerto No. 3 in B min., Op. 61.

(M) *** DG Dig. 445 549-2 [id.]. Perlman, O de Paris, Barenboim – LALO: *Symphonie espagnole;* BERLIOZ: *Rêverie et caprice.* ***

*** DG (IMS) Dig. 429 786-2 [id.]. Gil Shaham, NYPO, Sinopoli – PAGANINI: *Concerto No. 1.* ***

*** ASV Dig. CDDCA 680 [id.]. Xue Wei, Philh. O, Bakels – BRUCH: *Concerto No. 1.* ***

Violin concerto No. 3 in B min., Op.61; Havanaise; Introduction and Rondo capriccioso (for violin and orchestra).

(N) (B) **(*) Ph. 420 887-2. Szeryng, Monte Carlo Op. O, Remoortel – RAVEL: *Tzigane.* **(*)

(i) *Violin concerto No. 3 in B min., Op. 61;* (ii) *Introduction and rondo capriccioso, Op. 28.*

(M) *** Sony Stern Edition II SM2K 64501 (2) [id.]. Isaac Stern, with (i) O de Paris, Barenboim; (ii) Philadelphia O, Ormandy (with Concert ***).

On DG, Perlman achieves a fine partnership with Barenboim, in a performance that is both tender and strong, while Perlman's verve and dash in the finale are dazzling. The forward balance is understandable in this work, but orchestral detail could at times be sharper. The Berlioz *Rêverie et caprice* has been added for this reissue.

One only has to sample the delectable way Gil Shaham presents the enchanting *Barcarolle*, which forms the principal theme of Saint-Saëns's *Andante*, to discover the distinction of his performance, which balances elegant *espressivo* with great dash and fire: neither the soloist nor the conductor lets even the slightest suspicion of routine into a reading which dazzles and charms in equal measure. The recording is first class.

Stern's violin is for once balanced naturally against the orchestra, and paradoxically it gives his splendid performance of the Saint-Saëns more strength than close-up sound does. Though this is not as persuasively affectionate as with Gil Shaham, it remains among the finest versions, and the *Introduction and rondo capriccioso* is dazzling.

Xue Wei's account is full of flair from the very first entry onwards. The orchestral accompaniment is strongly characterized as well, while the soloist creates an ideal mixture of ruminative lyricism and dash, especially in the slow movement. The sound is vivid, even if the balance, within a church acoustic, seems artificially contrived.

Clean and immaculate performances from Szeryng, whose approach is aristocratic rather than indulgent. The orchestral contribution, adequate rather than distinguished, is not helped by the balance of the recording, which spotlights the violin and does not add a great deal of lustre to the accompaniment. However, the present remastering has improved the orchestral presence while the ambience remains pleasing.

Danse macabre, Op. 40; (i) *Havanaise, Op. 83; Introduction and Rondo capriccioso, Op. 28. Le jeunesse d'Hercule, Op. 50; Marche héroïque, Op. 34; Phaéton, Op. 39; Le rouet d'Omphale, Op. 31.*

(M) *** Decca 425 021-2 [id.]. (i) Kyung Wha Chung, RPO; Philh. O; Charles Dutoit.

A splendidly conceived anthology. The symphonic poems are beautifully played, and the 1979 Kingsway Hall recording lends the appropriate atmosphere. Charles Dutoit shows himself an admirably sensitive exponent, revelling in the composer's craftsmanship and revealing much delightful orchestral detail in the manner of a Beecham. Decca have now added Kyung Wha Chung's equally charismatic and individual 1977 accounts of what are perhaps the two most inspired short display-pieces for violin and orchestra in the repertoire.

Danse macabre; Le rouet d'Omphale.

(M) *** Decca 448 571-2 [id.]. Paris Conservatoire O, Martinon (with BIZET: *Jeux d'enfants* ***) – BERLIOZ: *Overtures* **(*); IBERT: *Divertissement.* ***

Martinon's are delightful, Beechamesque performances, offering excellent orchestral playing and a characteristic sense of delicacy and style. The 1960 recording is excellent, and this collection of French music, reissued in Decca's 'Classic Sound' series, is well worth exploring.

Havanaise, Op. 83.

(M) *** EMI CDM5 66058-2. Itzhak Perlman, O de Paris, Barenboim – RAVEL: *Tzigane;* VIEUXTEMPS: *Violin concertos Nos. 4 & 5.* ***

Havanaise, Op. 83; Introduction and Rondo capriccioso, Op. 28.

*** EMI (SIS) Dig. CDC7 47725-2 [id.]. Perlman, O de Paris, Martinon – CHAUSSON: *Poème;* RAVEL: *Tzigane.* ***

(M) (***) RCA Heifetz Collection mono 09026 61753-2 [id.]. Heifetz, RCA Victor SO, Steinberg – CHAUSSON: *Poème* **(*); LALO: *Symphonie espagnole* (**(*)); SARASATE: *Zigeunerweisen.* (***)

**(*) EMI Dig. CDC5 55026-2 [id.]. Sarah Chang, Phd. O, Sawallisch – PAGANINI: *Violin concerto No. 1.* **(*)

Perlman plays these Saint-Saëns warhorses with splendid panache and virtuosity on EMI; his tone and control of colour in the *Havanaise* are ravishing. The digital remastering brings Perlman's gorgeous fiddling right into the room, at the expense of a touch of aggressiveness when the orchestra lets rip; but the concert-hall ambience prevents this from being a problem.

The Heifetz performances also have quite extraordinary panache: his bowing in the coda of the *Havanaise* is utterly captivating. Indeed this dazzling playing is unsurpassed on record and the 1951 mono recording, if closely balanced, is very faithful. Even if you have these works in more modern versions, this marvellous disc should not be passed by.

Although she misses some of the sultry seductiveness in the *Havanaise*, the 12-year-old Sarah Chang still captures the gleaming Spanish sunshine. She is well supported by Sawallisch but is not flattered by the close recording-balance.

Henry VIII: ballet music.

(BB) *** Naxos Dig. 8.553338/9 [id.]. Razumovsky Sinfonia, Mogrelia – DELIBES: *Sylvia.* ***

This ballet-divertissement, described as a '*fête populaire*', comes in Act II of the opera, and in the outer movements Saint-Saëns wittily introduces first a Scottish reel then an Irish jig with Gallic insouciance. But all six numbers, which are enjoyably tuneful, unashamedly incorporate a great many airs from both countries, and Mogrelia presents them affectionately and vividly. With excellent recording, this is a genuine bonus to a pleasing account of Delibes's *Sylvia*.

Introduction & Rondo capriccioso.
(M) *** DG Dig. 457 896-2. Mintz, Israel PO, Mehta – LALO: *Symphonie espagnole;* VIEUXTEMPS: *Violin concerto No. 5.* ***
(N) (M) (***) Dutton Lab. mono CDK 1204 [id.]. Ida Haendel, Nat.SO, Basil Cameron – DVORAK: *Violin concerto* (***); TCHAIKOVSKY: *Violin concerto in D, Op. 35.* (***) ✪

Mintz dazzles the ear with Saint-Saëns's fireworks, while always playing with elegance and finesse. If the couplings are suitable, this is highly recommendable.

Ida Haendel recorded the Saint-Saëns display piece at the same time as her superb account of the Tchaikovsky concerto and it has a comparable freshness and sparkle. The recording is amazingly lifelike and the transfer most natural.

Symphonies: in A; in F (Urbs Roma); Symphonies Nos. 1–3.
(B) *** EMI (SIS) Rouge et Noir CZS5 69683-2 (2) [CDMB 62643]. French Nat. R. O, Martinon (with Bernard Gavoty, organ de l'église Saint-Louis des Invalides in *No. 3*).

The *A* and *F major* works were totally unknown and unpublished at the time of their recording and have never been dignified with numbers. Yet the *A major*, written when the composer was only 15, is a delight and may reasonably be compared with Bizet's youthful work in the same genre. More obviously mature, the *Urbs Roma Symphony* is perhaps a shade more self-conscious, and more ambitious too, showing striking imagination in such movements as the darkly vigorous Scherzo and the variation movement at the end.

The first of the numbered symphonies is a well-fashioned and genial piece, again much indebted to Mendelssohn and Schumann, but with much delightfully fresh invention. The *Second* is full of excellent ideas. Martinon directs splendid performances of the whole set, well prepared and lively. The account of the *Third* ranks with the best: freshly spontaneous in the opening movement, and the threads knitted powerfully together at the end of the finale. Here the recording could do with rather more sumptuousness. Elsewhere the quality is bright and fresh, with no lack of body.

Symphony in F (Urbs Roma); Symphony No. 2 in A min., Op. 55; (i) *Africa for piano and orchestra, Op. 89*
(N) *** BIS Dig. CD 790 [id.]. (i) Laura Mikkola; Tapiola Sinfonietta, Jean-Jacques Kantorow.

The *F major 'Urbs Roma' symphony* and the delightful *Second Symphony in A minor* are played with great spirit and zest by the Tapiola Sinfonietta and Jean-Jacques Kantorow. *Africa*, a fantasy for piano and orchestra, is a later piece, written after Saint-Saëns had returned from a trip to Ceylon (as Sri Lanka was then known) and Egypt. Laura Mikkola is the excellent pianist. If the coupling is suitable, these intelligent and well-recorded performances can be recommended.

(i) *Symphonies Nos. 1 in E flat, Op. 2; 2 in A min., Op. 55*; (ii) *Piano concerto No. 4 in C min., Op. 44*; (i) *La jeunesse d'Hercule, Op. 50*; (iii) *Le rouet d'Omphale, Op. 31.*
(N) (B) ** Erato Ultima Analogue/Dig. 3984 24236-2 [id.]. (i) VSO, Prêtre; (ii) Duchable, Strasbourg PO, Lombard; (iii) O. Nat. de l'O.R.T.F., Martinon.

This Ultima double is attractive in assembling very serviceable performances of the composer's two lesser-known published symphonies (useful for those who already have No. 3), plus one of the most attractive of the piano concertos, and the seldom-heard *La jeunesse d'Hercule*. Prêtre does not quite match Martinon's flair in the symphonies, but he gets some refined playing fom the VPO in the central movements (the two scherzi are highlights), and finds a pleasing energetic lightness for the first-movement fugato and the tarantella-finale of the *Second*. Duchable then opens the *C minor Concerto* pleasingly (what a seductive work it is!) and the solo playing is never thoughtless or slipshod. Yet his bold assertiveness later in the work brings a hint of agressiveness to music which should above all captivate the listener with its charm. *La jeunesse d'Hercule* is quite strongly characterized if a bit melodramatic; then Martinon's extremely vivid *Le rouet d'Omphale, Op. 31* arrives to show us what the earlier performances lacked in natural spontaneity and panache.

Symphony No. 2 in A min., Op. 55; Phaéton, Op. 39; Suite algérienne, Op. 60.
*** ASV Dig. CDDCA 599 [id.]. LSO, Butt.

Symphonies Nos. 2 in A min.; (i) *3 in C min., Op. 78.*
*** Chandos Dig. CHAN 8822 [id.]. Ulster O, Yan Pascal Tortelier; (i) with Gillian Weir.

If you want the *Second Symphony*, it is particularly well played by the LSO under Butt, with the freshness of a major orchestra discovering something unfamiliar and enjoying themselves. The companion pieces are also thoroughly enjoyable and are just as attractively presented. The recording is warmly atmospheric.

Yan Pascal Tortelier's performance of the *Second* is also very attractive and very well recorded; but Yondani Butt's account of this work has greater freshness, and the slightly less reverberant ASV recording contributes to this. If, however, your main interest lies with the *Third Symphony*, this extra resonance proves no disadvantage. Some years ago, E. G. made a side-by-side comparison of all the then available recordings of the *Organ Symphony* and came out in favour of the Tortelier version as a 'best buy', both for the appeal of the performance overall and for the state-of-the-art Chandos recording.

Symphony No. 3 in C min., Op. 78.
✽ (M) *** RCA 09026 61500-2. Berj Zamkochian, Boston SO, Munch – DEBUSSY: *La Mer* **(*); IBERT: *Escales*. ***
*** DG Dig. 419 617-2 [id.]. Simon Preston, BPO, Levine – DUKAS: *L'apprenti sorcier*. ***
(B) **(*) DG Classikon 439 494-2. Gaston Litaize, Chicago SO, Barenboim – FRANCK: *Symphony*. *(*)
**(*) Teldec/Warner Dig. 4509 98416-2. BPO, Mehta – FRANCK: *Symphony in D min*. **(*)
(B) *** Carlton Dig. PCD 2010 [id.]. Chorzempa, Berne SO, Maag.
(M) *** Mercury (IMS) 432 719-2 [id.]. Marcel Dupré, Detroit SO, Paray – PARAY: *Mass*. **(*)

(i; ii) *Symphony No. 3;* (ii) *Danse macabre, Op. 40; Samson et Dalila: Bacchanale;* (i) *3 Rhapsodies sur des cantiques bretons, Op. 7.*
*** BIS Dig. CD 555 [id.]. (i) Hans Fagius; (ii) Royal Stockholm PO, James DePreist.

(i) *Symphony No. 3 in C min.; Cyprès et Lauriers, Op. 156. La Foi, 3 tableaux symphoniques, Op. 130.*
(M) *** EMI (SIS) Dig. CDC5 55584-2 (2). Toulouse Capitole O, Plasson; (i) with Matthias Eisenberg.

(i) *Symphony No. 3 in C min. Danse macabre, Op. 40; Phaéton, Op. 39; Samson et Dalila: Danse bacchanale.*
*** Sony SK 53979 [id.]. (i) Newman; Pittsburgh SO, Maazel.

Symphony No. 3 in C min., Op. 78; Phaéton, Op. 39; Le rouet d'Omphale, Op. 31.
(B) *** [EMI Red Line Dig. CDR5 69833]. O de France, Ozawa.

(i) *Symphony No. 3;* (ii) *Danse macabre; Le Déluge: Prélude, Op. 45; Samson et Dalila: Bacchanale.*
(M) *** DG 415 847-2 [id.]. (i) Litaize, Chicago SO, Barenboim; (ii) O de Paris, Barenboim.

Munch's Boston recording dates from 1960, yet in its currently remastered form it still sounds spectacular. The performance is stunning, full of lyrical ardour and moving forward in a single sweep of great intensity. The couplings, showing Munch and his Bostonians at their peak, are equally valuable, if not quite so outstandingly recorded.

Maazel's newest Sony recording must also go to the top of the list for audacious spectacle in the finale. The recording, rich and spacious, was made in the Heinz Hall in Pittsburgh, employing similar microphone techniques to those used by the RCA engineers in the late 1960s for Reiner's Symphony Hall recordings in Chicago. The organ part, admirably played by Anthony Newman, was recorded in the Church of St Ignatus Loyola in New York City, and laminated on afterwards. It makes a superb impact. Maazel presses the music onwards thrillingly to its close, the trombones very much to the fore, as in the climax of the first movement, and the tuba also very tangible. The close is overwhelming, cymbals ringing out, and the downward descent of the organ pedals underlining the whole edifice, while Maazel's accelerando in the coda tautens the excitement even further. *Phaéton* and *Danse macabre* come off splendidly and there is real abandon at the close of the *Bacchanale* from *Samson and Dalila*.

With the Berlin Philharmonic in cracking form, Levine's is a grippingly dramatic reading, full of imaginative detail. The great thrust of the performance does not stem from fast pacing: rather it is the result of incisive articulation, while the clarity of the digital recording allows the pianistic detail to register crisply. The thunderous organ entry in the finale makes a magnificent effect, and the tension is held at white heat throughout the movement. The Dukas coupling is equally memorable, and this remains among the first choices for modern, digital versions of the symphony.

From Stockholm comes another outstanding performance of the *Third Symphony* that is competitive even in a well-stocked market. DePreist is straight and unmannered, completely at the service of the music, and proves very persuasive in this repertoire. Hans Fagius plays the Stockholm Concert Hall organ so that, unlike some performances in which the organist is tacked on afterwards, this is a genuine performance. He plays the *Trois Rhapsodies sur des cantiques bretons* on the splendid Marcussen instrument of St Jakobs Kyrka in Stockholm to striking effect. The recording of all these items is full-blooded and has plenty of impact yet it is beautifully and naturally balanced.

Michel Plasson and the Orchestre du Capitole de Toulouse offer a particularly interesting package. Their account of the *Symphony No. 3*, made in the Basilique Notre-Dame La Daurade, Toulouse, with Matthias Eisenberg, is first rate and the recording first class, although brightly lit. The plangent, reedy sound of the Puget organ, very French and somewhat harsh, will not appeal to all ears and will probably reproduce differently on different equipment. But its spectacular impact cannot be denied. The symphony comes in a two-for-the-price-of-one format with two rarities, *Cyprès et Lauriers*, whose high opus number indicates its lateness in Saint-Saëns's output, and *La Foi*, three symphonic tableaux drawn from incidental music for Eugène Brieux's play, *False Gods*. With *Cyprès et Lauriers*, Saint-Saëns returned to the medium of organ and orchestra for the first time since the *Third Symphony*. It was completed to celebrate the ending of the 1914–18 war and is extravagantly scored: its first movement (*Cyprès*) is for organ solo, and here the organ sounds just right. The second (*Lauriers*) brings trumpet fanfares and a general sense of spectacle: clearly Saint-Saëns is greatly enjoying his bursts of rhetoric, and so do we. Indeed the work's rumbustious close is thoroughly endearing. *La Foi*, which runs for just over 30 minutes, comes on the second CD and has some of the fey, oriental charm that characterizes the *Egyptian piano concerto* (No. 5). Thoroughly convincing performances, and *La Foi* is well worth hearing. This is certainly excellent value.

Barenboim's inspirational 1976 version has long dominated the catalogue. The performance of the *Symphony* glows with warmth from beginning to end. The digital remastering is not wholly advantageous: while detail is sharper, the massed violins sound thinner and the bass is drier. In the finale, some of the bloom has gone, and the organ entry has a touch of hardness. It is now also available in a bargain Classikon disc, but here the Franck coupling is not an asset.

Ozawa's version is coupled with attractive performances of two of Saint-Saëns's most colourful symphonic poems in which the conductor is in his element. The *Symphony* too is very enjoyable, and this performance certainly wears well. Ozawa's finale makes a splendidly opulent effect. The sound is in the demonstration class.

Maag's extremely well-recorded Berne performance has a Mendelssohnian freshness and the sprightly playing in the Scherzo draws an obvious affinity with that composer. The closing pages have a convincing feeling of apotheosis and, although this is not the weightiest reading available, it is an uncommonly enjoyable one in which the sound is bright, full and suitably resonant.

The fine Paray/Mercury recording dates, astonishingly, from 1957. The early date brings just a hint of shrillness to the violins in the first movement; otherwise the sound remains bold, full and remarkably well detailed. Marcel Dupré's weighty organ entry introduces a finale which is powerfully co-ordinated, building to an impressive climax. However, not everyone may want the coupling, enjoyable as it is.

Under Mehta, the first-movement *Allegro* of the symphony immediately takes wing and very soon expands to become weighty too – the horns sing out vociferously at the climax, with the trumpets following. The *Poco adagio* makes a serene, cantabile contrast, its climactic ardour affecting. The bustling energy of the Scherzo is well caught, with the detail of the piano figurations sparkling, and Daniel Chorzempa's powerful organ entry certainly makes one sit up. The tension is well held, and the BPO produces a characteristically full body of sound. Sonically this is spectacular too, though not quite as impressive as Maazel's recent Pittsburgh recording for Sony, which also has the edge as a performance. But then that does not offer the Franck symphony as well.

Wedding-cake (Caprice-valse), Op. 76.
(BB) *** ASV Quicksilva Dig. CDQS 6092. Osorio, RPO, Bátiz – FRANCK: *Symphonic variations* **(*); RAVEL: *Left-hand concerto* ***; SCHUMANN: *Concerto.* **(*)

A delightfully lightweight performance of Saint-Saëns's frothy but engaging *morceau de concert*, infectious and sparkling. Nicely recorded, too.

CHAMBER MUSIC

Bassoon sonata, Op. 168; Clarinet sonata, Op. 167; Caprice on Danish and Russian airs for flute, oboe, clarinet and piano, Op. 79; Feuillet d'album, Op. 81 (arr Taffanel); *Oboe sonata, Op. 166; Odelette for flute and piano, Op. 162; Romance in D flat for flute and piano, Op. 37; Tarantelle for flute, clarinet and piano, Op. 6.*
(B) *** Cala Dig. CACD 1017 (2) [id.]. William Bennett, Nicholas Daniel, James Campbell, Rachael Gough, & Ens. – DEBUSSY: *Chamber music.* ***

The *Sonatas for clarinet*, *for oboe* and *for bassoon*, Opp. 166–168, are elegantly finished but surprising pieces, with an unaccustomed depth of feeling. The *Caprice* is a diverting kind of pot-pourri, inspired by the composer's visit to Russia in 1876, when he met Tchaikovsky and returned to Paris with the score of *Boris Godunov*, thus kindling the flame of interest in Mussorgsky that burned so brightly in later years. Paul Taffanel's arrangement of the *Feuillet d'album*, Op. 81, for flute, oboe and two each of clarinets, bassoons and horns, is a first recording and, like almost everything on this record, refreshing and elegant. That goes for the performances too, which are well recorded though the piano is occasionally overpowering. Strongly recommended – and outstanding value, considering that one gets two CDs for the price of one, economically packaged and liberally annotated.

Carnival of the animals (chamber version); *Piano trio in F, Op. 18; Septet in E flat for trumpet, strings and Piano, Op.65.*
(N) (BB) *** Virgin Classics Double Dig. VBD5 61516-2 [CDVB 61516] (2) Nash Ens. – DVORAK: *Piano quintet, Op. 81; Piano trio No. 4 (Dumky).* ***

In the sparkling Nash chamber version of the *Carnival of the animals*, Ian Hobson is joined by Susan Tomes. Its humour is nicely captured without clumsiness, and these players make sure the listener does not miss the composer's witty quotations, with delightful results. The *Septet* too is presented with a similar geniality and lightness of touch, and the account of the first of Saint-Saëns's two piano trios is similarly persuasive. The acoustic has warmth and the balance between the instruments, particularly in the *Grand fantaisie zoologique*, is admirably judged. Coupled with fine performances of two of Dvořák's most appealing chamber works, this inexpensive Virgin Double is self-recommending.

Piano trios Nos. 1 in F, Op. 18; 2 in E min., Op. 92.
(BB) *** Naxos Dig. 8.550935 [id.]. Joachim Trio.

These trios are separated by almost 30 years; the *F major*, Op. 18, comes from 1863, some four years after the *A minor Symphony* (No. 2) and the *First Piano concerto*, and the five-movement *E minor* is from 1892. No quarrels with the playing of the Joachim Trio (Rebecca Hirsch, Caroline Dearnley and John Lenehan). The pianist in particular has elegance and charm. This is delightful and inventive music, well recorded - and well worth the money.

Piano trio No. 1 in F, Op. 18.
(*) Ara. Dig. Z 6643 [id.]. Golub–Kaplan–Carr Trio – DEBUSSY **(*); FAURE: *Trios.* *

David Golub, Mark Kaplan and Colin Carr give a very good account of themselves in the *Piano trio in F major*. They are intelligent and imaginative, though in the variation movement Kaplan is not as commanding or full-bodied tonally as his opposite number in the Beaux Arts Trio (currently withdrawn). The piano dominates in the right way, and David Golub makes a particularly strong and vital impression. They are very well recorded too.

String quartets Nos. 1 in E min., Op. 112; 2 in G, Op. 153.
(N) *** Conifer Dig. 75605 51291-2 [id.]. Miami Qt. – FAURE: String quartet. ***
(N) ** Koch Schwann Dig. 364842 [id.]. Medici Qt.

The quartets are products of Saint-Saëns's maturity: the *E minor* dating from 1899, when he was well into his 60s, and the *G major* coming two decades later. They are both splendidly fashioned, the product of a cultured musical mind, though his invention, always fertile and finely shaped, is not quite as distinguished here as in his very best music. Of the two ensembles, the Miami Quartet score both in terms of polish and technical finesse, and musical insight, though the Medici play very well and are accorded excellent sound, rich and well balanced. The Miami score in also giving us an excellent bonus, Fauré's glorious *E minor Quartet*.

Violin sonatas Nos. 1 in D min., Op. 75; 2 in E flat, Op. 102; Berceuse, Op. 38; Introduction and Rondo capriccioso, Op. 28 (arr. Bizet).
** ASV Dig. CDDCA 892 [id.]. Xue-Wei, John Lenehan.

Of Saint-Saëns's two *Violin sonatas* the second is the more appealing with its simple *Andante* and closing *Allegro grazioso*, in which Xue-Wei seems thoroughly at home. He is also delightfully nimble in the Scherzo (as is his fine partner, John Lenehan) and he manages the *moto perpetuo* finale of the *First sonata* with equal facility. Before that comes the lovely *Berceuse* which shows Xue-Wei's tone at its most appealing, but in the opening *Introduction and Rondo capriccioso*, played with real sparkle, the close microphones are unflattering to the violin's upper range.

Violin sonata No. 1 in D min., Op. 75.
*** Essex CDS 6044 [id.]. Accardo, Canio – CHAUSSON: *Concert.* ***
(N) (BB) *** Arte Nova Dig. 74321 59233-2 [id.]. Mirijam Contzen, Valéry Rogatchev – DEBUSSY; FRANCK: *Violin sonatas.* ***

The performance by Accardo and Canio is marvellously played, selfless and dedicated. The recording too is very good, and this can be recommended strongly, if the coupling is suitable.

Not only does the young German violinist, Mirijam Contzen, give purposeful, idiomatic readings of Debussy and Franck, she is just as persuasive in a work too easily under-appreciated. In this Saint-Saëns sonata she uses her rich, warm tone to give a compelling, purposeful performance, passionate in the first movement, poised and intense in the inner meditation of the second, light and sparkling in the Scherzo and brilliant in the exuberant finale. With sensitive accompaniment this makes an outstanding bargain, very well recorded.

VOCAL MUSIC

Choral songs: *Calme des nuits; Des pas dans l'allée; Les fleurs et les arbres.*
*** Ph. Dig. 438 149-2 [id.]. Monteverdi Ch., O Révolutionnaire et Romantique, Gardiner – FAURE: *Requiem*; DEBUSSY; RAVEL: *Choral works.* ***

Three charming examples of Saint-Saëns's skill and finesse in drawing inspiration from early sources in a way remarkable at the time he was writing. Gardiner and his team give ideal performances, adding to the valuable list of rarities which he provides as coupling for the Fauré *Requiem*.

OPERA

Samson et Dalila (opera): complete.
*** EMI CDS7 54470-2 (2) [Ang. CDCB 54470]. Domingo, Meier, Fondary, Courtis, L'Opéra-Bastille Ch. & O, Myung-Whun Chung.
(M) **(*) DG 413 297-2 (2) [id.]. Obraztsova,

Domingo, Bruson, Lloyd, Thau, Ch. & O de Paris, Barenboim.

(M) (**(*)) EMI Classics (SIS) mono CMS5 65263-2 (2). Luccioni, Bouvier, Cabanel, Cambon, Medus, Paris Opéra Ch. & O, Fourestier.

In the newer, EMI set, Domingo with Chung gives a deeper, more thoughtful performance than on DG, broader, with greater repose and a sense of power in reserve. When the big melody appears in Dalila's seduction aria, *Mon cœur s'ouvre*, Chung's idiomatic conducting encourages a tender restraint, where others produce a full-throated roar. Meier may not have an ideally sensuous voice for the role, with some unwanted harshness in her expressive account of Dalila's first monologue, but her feeling for words is strong and the characterization vivid. Generally Chung's speeds are on the fast side, yet the performance does not lack weight, with some first-rate singing in the incidental roles from Alain Fondary, Samuel Ramey and Jean-Philippe Courtis. Apart from backwardly placed choral sound, the recording is warm and well focused.

Barenboim proves as passionately dedicated an interpreter of Saint-Saëns here as he did in the *Third Symphony*, sweeping away any Victorian cobwebs. It is important, too, that the choral passages, so vital in this work, be sung with this sort of freshness, and Domingo has rarely sounded happier in French music, the bite as well as the heroic richness of the voice well caught. Renato Bruson and Robert Lloyd are both admirable too; sadly, however, the key role of Dalila is given an unpersuasive, unsensuous performance by Obraztsova, with her vibrato often verging on a wobble. The recording is as ripe as the music deserves.

EMI's 1946 recording from the Paris Opéra provides a formidable showcase for outstanding singers, little known outside France, who represented a singing tradition that largely fell into ruins in following decades. José Luccioni was a favourite in Paris, his voice combining lyric beauty with heroic timbre that made him an outstanding choice as Samson. His diction and command of style are as sure as his vocal production, and so it is with Hélène Bouvier, boasting a rich mezzo, rock-steady throughout its range, and again a perfect command of style. Sadly, her career was cut short by polio. Paul Cabanel as the High Priest was also at the end of his career but is impressive too. Choral singing and orchestral playing are often ragged, and the sound from 78-r.p.m. discs is very limited; but this is a performance with plenty of feeling, well worth investigating.

Salieri, Antonio (1750–1825)

Double concerto in C for flute and oboe.

*** Chandos Dig. CHAN 9051 [id.]. Susan Milan, David Theodore, City of L. Sinf., Hickox – MOZART: *Flute and harp concerto; Oboe concerto.* ***

Salieri's innocently insubstantial *Double concerto* is quite transformed by the charisma and sheer style of the solo playing from Susan Milan and David Theodore. The catchy little triplet figure which dominates the first movement is articulated with engaging crispness, and a dialogue which can too easily sound garrulous here is full of charm. The exquisite playing of Theodore in the simple melody of the *Largo* and the perfect blending of the two soloists turns it into a really memorable slow movement, and the flute and oboe chase each other round engagingly in their winning decorations of the nicely poised Minuet finale. Hickox's accompaniment is both polished and genial, and the recording casts a pleasing glow over the whole proceedings.

Falstaff or *The Three Tricks* (complete).

(N) *** Chandos Dig. CHAN 9613 (2) [id.]. Romano Franceschetto, Lee Myeounghee, Giuliano de Filippo, Chiara Chialli, Fernando Luis Ciuffo, Filippo Bettoschi, Natalia Valli, Milan Madrigalists & Guido Cantelli, O, Alberto Veronesi.

Like Verdi, Salieri and his librettist ignore the Falstaff of the histories. They tell the story within the framework of the conventional two-act opera of the period with crisp and brief numbers leading to extended finales. Though Fenton and Anne (Nannetta) are omitted, Mistress Page (here renamed Slender) is given her husband. Though it never comes near to matching Mozart, it is all great fun, particularly in performances as fresh and lively as these. The Chandos version takes priority over the Hungaroton (HCD 21789/91) – which in any case is currently not easily obtainable – when thanks to the brisk, alert pacing of Veronesi the opera is squeezed on to two discs instead of three. Though Romano Franceschetto in the title-role is not so firmly commanding as Joszef Gregor in the Hungarian performance, he does sing characterfully. As for the rest, the Italian cast on Chandos is fresher and more idiomatic than the Hungarian, with fuller sound an added advantage.

Sallinen, Aulis (born 1935)

(i) *Violin concerto, Op. 18;* (ii) *Nocturnal dances of Don Juanquixote, Op. 58; Some aspects of Peltoniemi Hintrik's funeral march, Op. 19; Variations for orchestra (Juventas variations), Op. 8.*

*** BIS Dig. CD 560 [id.]. (i) Koskinen; (ii) Thedéen; Tapiola Sinf., Vänskä.

The *Variations for orchestra* is an imaginative and inventive piece which shows remarkable command of the orchestra. It is tonally ambiguous without being serial; indeed at one point there is a reminder of Britten. The *Violin concerto* is also rewarding and in the slow movement often beautiful but its lyrical impulse is not strong enough for it to enter the standard repertoire. It has a powerful advocate in Eeva Koskinen. *Some aspects of Peltoniemi Hintrik's funeral march* is a transcription for full strings of his *Third Quartet*, a one-movement work in five variations; emphatically not one of his strongest works, any more than are *The Nocturnal Dances of Don Juanquixote*. Excellent playing from Torleif Thedéen and the Tapiola Sinfonietta under Osmo Vänskä and a vivid, well-lit but not overbright BIS recording.

(i) *Symphonies Nos. 1; 3;* (ii) *Chorali;* (iii) *Cadenze for solo violin;* (iv) *Elegy for Sebastian Knight;* (v) *String quartet No. 3.*
*** BIS CD 41 [id.]. (i) Finnish RSO, Kamu; (ii) Helsinki PO, Berglund; (iii) Paavo Pohjola; (iv) Frans Helmerson; (v) Voces Intimae Qt.

The *First Symphony*, in one movement, is diatonic and full of atmosphere, as indeed is the *Third*, a powerful, imaginative piece which appears to be haunted by the sounds and smells of nature. The performances under Okko Kamu are excellent. *Chorali* is a shorter piece, persuasively done by Paavo Berglund; and there are three chamber works, albeit of lesser substance. The recordings are from the 1970s and are all very well balanced. Highly recommended.

Symphonies Nos. 2 (Symphonic dialogue for solo percussion player and orchestra), Op. 29; 6 (From a New Zealand Diary), Op. 65; Sunrise Serenade, Op. 63.
*** BIS Dig. CD 511 [id.]. Malmö SO, Okko Kamu.

The *Second Symphony*, like the *First*, is a one-movement affair lasting a quarter of an hour. Its sub-title, *Symphonic dialogue for solo percussion player and orchestra*, gives an accurate idea of its character, pitting the fine soloist, Gerd Mortensen, against the remaining orchestral forces. The main work is the ambitious *Sixth Symphony*. Like the *Third Symphony*, it is powerfully evocative of natural landscape; indeed it is one of the strongest and most imaginative of all Sallinen's symphonies. Okko Kamu gets very responsive playing from the Malmö Symphony Orchestra in both symphonies and in the slight but effective *Sunrise Serenade*. The recording is excellent.

Symphonies Nos. 4, Op. 49; 5 (Washington mosaics), Op. 57; Shadows (Prelude for orchestra), Op. 52.
*** BIS Dig. CD 607 [id.]. Malmö SO, James DePreist.

Suffice it to say that these new performances by the Malmö Symphony Orchestra under James DePreist are every bit as good as the Helsinki rivals listed above and below; if anything, the recording has more impressive range and definition.

Chamber music Nos. I, Op. 38; (i) *II, for alto flute and strings, Op. 41;* (iii) *III, for cello and strings (The Nocturnal dances of Don Juanquixote), Op. 58. Some aspects of Peltoniemi Hintrik's funeral march* (*Quartet No. 3* arr. for strings); *Sunrise serenade for 2 trumpets, piano and strings, Op. 63.*
(BB) *** Naxos Dig. 8.553747 [id.]. Finnish CO, Kamu, with (i) Hanna Juutilainen; (ii) Mats Rondin.

Aulis Sallinen has composed a number of works for string orchestra which are widely admired in his home country. His music is tonal and accessible ('audience friendly'), and the present pieces are in no way forbidding. However, they strike the present writer as all too insubstantial, the invention thin and repetitive. They are given dedicated performances by the exemplary soloists and Okko Kamu and the Finnish Chamber Orchestra. Others may respond more warmly to this music, and those who do will find the playing and recording very good indeed.

Kullervo (opera).
*** Ondine Dig. ODE 780-3T. Hynninen, Sallinen, Jakobsson, Silvasti, Vihavainen, Finnish Nat. Op. Ch. & O, Ulf Söderblom.

Although the theme will be familiar from Sibelius's early symphony of the same name, Sallinen has based his *Kullervo* on the play by Aleksis Kivi and he wrote the libretto himself. The plot emerges from a mixture of narration, in which the chorus plays a central role, and dreams. The opera is a compelling musical drama, far more atmospheric and musically effective than its immediate predecessor, *The King goes forth to France*. Sallinen's musical language has debts to composers as diverse as Britten (shadows of the 'Sunday morning' interlude in *Peter Grimes* briefly cross the score in Kullervo's Dream at the beginning of Act II), Puccini, Debussy even, though they are synthesized into an effective vehicle for a vivid theatrical imagination. There is impressive variety of pace and atmosphere, and the black voices of the Finnish Opera Chorus resonate in the memory. So, too, do the impressive performances of Jorma Hynninen as Kullervo and Anna-Lisa Jakobsson as the smith's young wife and, indeed, the remainder of the cast and the Finnish National Opera Orchestra under Ulf Söderblom. While *Kullervo* may not be a great opera, it is gripping and effective musical theatre, and the Ondine recording has excellent presence and detail.

Sammartini, Giovanni Battista
(1700–75)

Symphonies in D; G; String quintet in E.
(B) *** HM Musique d'Abord HMA 1901245 [id.]. Ens. 415, Banchini – Giuseppe SAMMARTINI: *Concerti grossi*, etc. ***

Giovanni Battista was the younger of the two Sammartini brothers; he spent his whole life in Milan. On this record, the Ensemble 415, led by Chiara Banchini, offer two of his symphonies; although neither attains greatness, they have genuine appeal. Good recording.

Sammartini, Giuseppe (*c.* 1693–1750)

Concerti grossi Nos. 6 & 8; (i) *Recorder concerto in F.*
(B) *** HM Musique d'Abord HMA 901245 [id.]. (i) Conrad Steinmann; Ens. 415, Banchini – Giovanni SAMMARTINI: *Symphonies*, etc. ***

Giuseppe settled in England in the 1720s and he was a refined and inventive composer. The Ensemble 415 is a period-instrument group; they produce a firmly focused sound, even though the textures are light and the articulation lively. Excellent playing from Conrad Steinmann in the *Recorder concerto*.

Santos, Joly Braga (1924–88)

Symphonies Nos. 3 and 6.
(N) *** Marco Polo Dig. 8.225087 [id.]. Ana Ester Neves, São Carlos Theatre Ch., Portuguese SO, Alvaro Cassuto.

José Manuel Joly Braga Santos is the leading Portuguese symphonist of his day. His *Third Symphony* composed in 1949, when he was in his mid 20s, is strongly modal in idiom, with a strong sense of forward movement and a powerful feeling for architecture. It is imaginatively scored and at times suggests Vaughan Williams, and even at one point in the slow movement (about two and a half minutes in) the Shostakovich of the *Fifth Symphony*. The *Sixth Symphony* (1972) is a one-movement work with a closing choral section. The first two-thirds are purely orchestral and more expressionist in its musical language, non-tonal but without being dodecaphonic, the choral part being tonal. Very good performances and recordings.

Sarasate, Pablo (1844–1908)

'*Música española*': (i; vi) *Capricho vasco, Op. 24; Introducción y tarantela, Op. 43*; (ii; iv) *8 Danzas españolas, Op. 22/1–2; Op. 22/1–2; Op. 23/1–2; Op. 26/1–2*; (i; v) *Jota aragonesa, Op. 27; (ii; iii; iv) Navarra for 2 violins, Op. 33.*
(N) (B)*** Decca Double stereo/mono 433 938-2 (2) [id.]. (i) Ruggieri Ricci; (ii) Campoli; (iii) Belinda Bunt; (iv) Daphne Ibbott; (v) Ernest Lush; (vi) Louis Persinger – (with Marisa Robles Instrumental recital); RODRIGO: *Concierto de Aranjuez.* ***

One of the most attractive of Decca's '*Música española*' series, this restores to the catalogue Campoli's charismatic set of Sarasate's *Danzas españolas*, plus *Navarra* in which he is joined by Belinda Blunt. Campoli is in excellent form and he has never been so truthfully recorded. With the art that disguises art he makes these dances sound effortless yet brilliant, and infinitely stylish. Ricci takes over for three other genre pieces and plays with stunning bravado in the *Tarantella*, Op. 43. This and the *Capricho* are mono but one would hardly guess. Popular light music this may be, but it is all so thoroughly enjoyable when the playing is of this quality. The recording is at times rather close (especially the Ricci items), but never troubling.

Carmen fantasy, Op. 25.
✿ *** EMI CDC7 47101-2 [id.]. Itzhak Perlman, RPO, Foster – PAGANINI: *Concerto No. 1.*** ✿

Played like this on EMI, with superb panache, luscious tone and glorious recording, Sarasate's *Fantasy* almost upstages the concerto with which it is coupled. The recording balance is admirable, with the quality greatly to be preferred to many of Perlman's more recent digital records.

Zigeunerweisen, Op. 20.
*** DG Dig. 431 815-2 [id.]. Gil Shaham, LSO, Lawrence Foster – WIENIAWSKI: *Violin concertos Nos. 1 & 2*, etc. ***
(M) (***) RCA Heifetz Collection mono 09026 61753-2 [id.]. Heifetz, RCA Victor SO, Steinberg – CHAUSSON: *Poème* **(*); LALO: *Symphony espagnole* (**(*)); SAINT-SAENS: *Havanaise*, etc. (***)
(***) EMI mono CDH7 64251-2 [id.]. Heifetz, LPO, Barbirolli – SAINT-SAENS: *Havanaise*, etc.; VIEUXTEMPS: *Concerto No. 4;* WIENIAWSKI: *Concerto No. 2.* (***)
(B) **(*) [EMI Red Line Dig. CDR5 69861]. Mutter, O Nat. de France, Ozawa – BIZET: *Carmen: suites*, etc; LALO: *Symphonie espagnole.* **(*)

Gil Shaham plays Sarasate's sultry and dashing gypsy confection with rich timbre, languorous ardour and a dazzling display of fireworks at the close.

What can one say about the Heifetz performances except that they are unsurpassed: they are dazzling in the fireworks and with the most luscious tone and sophisticated colouring in the lyrical melody. The recording is dry but faithful. This is a marvellous disc.

A sparkling performance of Sarasate's gypsy pot-pourri from Anne-Sophie Mutter, given good support from Ozawa. There are some dazzling fireworks, but some may feel her playing in the famous principal lyrical melody too chaste; others will enjoy the total absence of schmaltz. The balance places the solo violin well forward, and the timbre is very brightly lit.

Sarmanto, Heikki (born 1939)

'Meet the composer': (i–ii) *Kalevala Fantasy: Return to life*. (iii) *Max and the Enchantress; Sea of balloons;* (iv–v; ii) *Suomi (A symphonic jazz poem for orchestra);* (iii; vi) *The Traveller: Northern atmosphere*. (Instrumental): (iv; vii) *Distant dreams: Tender wind. Pan fantasy: The awakening; In the night*. (Vocal) (viii) *Carrousel;* (ix) *Light of love;* (x) *New England images;* (xi; iii) *New Hope Jazz Mass: Have mercy on us*. (x) *Northern pictures*.

(B) ** Finlandia/Warner Dig. Double 0630 19809-2 (2). (i) UMO Jazz O; (ii) dir. composer; (iii) Heikki Sarmanto Ens.; (iv) with Juhani Aaltonen; (v) with O; (vi) with Vasile Pantir, Tom Rainey; (vii) composer (keyboards); (viii) Helen Merrill, Tapiola Sinf., Torrie Zito; (ix) Karen Parks, Samuel McKelton, Opera Ebony, Kyösti Haatanen; (ix–x) Sarmanto Jazz Ens.; (x) Finnish Chamber Ch., Eric-Olof Söderström; (xi) Maija Hapuoja, Gregg Smith Vocal Qt, Long Island Symphonic Choral Assoc., Gregg Smith.

Heikki Sarmanto firmly 'eludes all attempts at categorization', writes Antti Suvanto in his original notes for this set. Sarmanto was a theory pupil of Joonas Kokkonen and he went on to further studies in the United States. The main influence on the music that represents him here is Duke Ellington, though few of the pieces here rival his model. He is accomplished and inventive, though the choral pieces really do strike us as having more facility than taste. There is some good playing from the various artists involved, and Sarmanto is obviously a skilled as well as a prolific musician. On the whole, however, his music strikes us as deeply unappealing.

Sarum Chant

Missa in gallicantu; Hymns: A solis ortus cardine; Christe Redemptor omnium; Salvator mundi, Domine; Veni Redemptor omnium.

*** Gimell/Ph. Dig. 454 917-2 [id.]. Tallis Scholars, Peter Phillips.

Filling in our knowledge of early church music, the Tallis Scholars under Peter Phillips here present a whole disc of chant according to the Salisbury rite – in other words *Sarum chant* – which, rather than the regular Gregorian style, was what churchgoers of the Tudor period and earlier in England heard at their devotions. The greater part of the record is given over to the setting of the First Mass of Christmas, intriguingly entitled *Missa in gallicantu* or *Mass at cock-crow*. Though this is simply monophonic (the men's voices alone are used), it is surprising what antiphonal variety there is. The record is completed with four hymns from the Divine Offices of Christmas Day. The record is warmly atmospheric in the characteristic Gimell manner.

Satie, Erik (1866–1925)

Les aventures de Mercure (ballet); *La belle excentrique: Grand ritournelle. 5 Grimaces pour 'Un songe d'une nuit d'été'; Gymnopédies Nos. 1 & 3; Jack-in-the-box* (orch. Milhaud); *3 Morceaux en forme de poire; Parade* (ballet); *Relâche* (ballet).

(M) **(*) Van. 08.4030.71 [OVC 4030]. Utah SO, Maurice Abravanel.

A generous mid-priced collection of Satie's orchestral music, well played and given full, vivid recording from the early 1970s; if Abravanel fails to throw off some of the more pointed music with a fully idiomatic lightness of touch, these are still enjoyable performances; the ballet scores have plenty of colour and rhythmic life.

Gymnopédies Nos. 1 & 3 (orch. Debussy).

(B) *** Sony SBK 63056 [id.]. (i) Cleveland O, Louis Lane – DEBUSSY: *Petite suite;* RAVEL: *Introduction and allegro* etc. ***

Satie's *Gymnopédies*, heard in Debussy's orchestration, are beautifully played by the excellent Cleveland band. Louis Lane has the full measure of the languorous melancholy of these haunting pieces, and his chosen tempi are admirably judged. The sound too is warmly atmospheric.

Parade.

(M) *** Mercury (IMS) 434 335-2 [id.]. LSO, Dorati – AURIC: *Overture;* FETLER: *Contrasts;* FRANCAIX: *Piano concertino;* MILHAUD: *Le bœuf sur le toit.* ***

Satie's *Parade* is the most audacious piece in an excellent Mercury compilation of (mostly) twentieth-century French music, its scoring including several extra-musical effects. Dorati makes it all fit together wittily and entertainingly, and the LSO make the most of the vivid scoring, with the brass obviously relishing their slightly vulgar theme which is somewhat reminiscent of Kurt Weill. The necessary atmosphere and colour are given to the more restrained sections of the score, and the Mercury recording team excel themselves in presenting Satie's kaleidoscopic circus colours with the utmost vividness.

PIANO MUSIC

Piano, 4 hands: (i) *La Belle excentrique; 3 Morceaux en forme de poire.* Solo piano: *Caresse; Croquis et agaceries d'un gros bonhomme en bois; Danse de travers; Descriptions automatiques; Fantaisie valse; Passacaille; Les pantins dansent; 1ère Pensée Rose Croix; Petite ouverture à danser; Pièces froides I: Airs à faire fuir. II: Danse de travers. Poudre d'or; Prélude de la porte héroïque du ciel; Prélude en tapisserie; Valse ballet; 3 Valses distinguées du précieux dégoûté.*
*** Virgin/EMI VC7 59296-2. Anne Queffélec; (i) with Catherine Collard.

Although we think Pascal Rogé is very special in this repertoire, Anne Queffélec has strong claims too. She can be quirky, as in the opening *Croquis et agaceries d'un gros bonhomme en bois* or, more particularly, the satirical *Valse ballet*; she is engagingly cool in the *Pièces froides*; her accounts of the *Caresse* and *Les pantins dansent* are quite haunting, while the *Petite ouverture à danser* has much charm. In the *Trois morceaux en forme de poire* and the lively *La Belle excentrique* she is partnered by the late lamented Catherine Collard, and how brilliantly they end the concert with that final quartet of sparkling vignettes, opening with the dazzling *Grande ritournelle* and ending with the irrepressible *Can-can 'grand-mondain'*. The recording is excellent and, although this collection omits the famous *Gymnopédies* and *Gnossiennes*, they are readily available elsewhere and on Rogé's fine Decca recitals (410 220-2, 421 713-2 & 455 370-2).

Aperçus désagréables; La belle excentrique (fantaisie sérieuse) (both for 4 hands); *Croquis et agaceries d'un gros bonhomme en bois; Descriptions automatiques; Embryons desséchés; En habit de cheval* (for 4 hands); *Le fils des étoiles, wagnerie kaldéenne du Sar Peladan; 6 Gnossiennes; 3 Gymnopédies; Jack-in-the-box; 3 Mouvements en forme de poire* (for 4 hands); *3 Nocturnes; Peccadilles importunes; 3 Petites pièces montées* (for 4 hands); *Pièces froides; Préludes flasques (pour un chien); Première pensée et sonneries de la Rose Croix; 3 Sarabandes; Sonatine bureaucratique; Sports et divertissements; 3 Valses distinguées du précieux dégoûté.*
(B) **(*) EMI Rouge et Noir (SIS) CZS5 68994-2 (2) [CDZB 672822]. Aldo Ciccolini.

Although Satie's achievement is sometimes overrated by his admirers, about much of this music there is a desperate melancholy and a rich poetic feeling which are altogether unique. Aldo Ciccolini is widely praised as a Satie interpreter and he plays here with unaffected sympathy. He certainly understands the *douloureux* feeling of the famous *Gymnopédies* and finds the '*conviction et tristesse rigoureuse*' of the *Gnossiennes. La belle excentrique* is thrown off with great dash and élan. In the works where (by electronic means) Ciccolini provides all four hands, the percussive edge of the pianism seems somewhat accentuated by the recording, but generally the piano recording is very acceptable, and the CD transfer has plenty of colour and sonority.

Avant-dernières pensées; Chapitres tournés en tous sens; Croquis et agaceries d'un gros bonhomme en bois; Descriptions automatiques; Deux rêveries nocturnes; Heures séculaires et instantanées; Nocturnes Nos. 1–3, 5; Nouvelles pièces froides; Pièces froides; Prélude de la porte héroïque du ciel; Les trois valses distinguées du précieux dégoûté; Véritables préludes flasques.
*** Decca Dig. 421 713-2 [id.]. Pascal Rogé.

Pascal Rogé's choice of repertoire on this well-filled disc ranges from the Rose-Croix pieces through to the *Nocturnes*. As with the earlier recital (see below), his playing has an eloquence and charm that are altogether rather special, and the recorded sound is very good indeed.

(i) *Avant-dernières pensées; Embryons desséchés; Gnossiennes Nos. 1–5; Gymnopédies Nos. 1–3; Nocturne No. 1; Sarabandes Nos. 1–3; Sonatine bureaucratique; 3 Valses distinguées du précieux dégoûté;* (ii) *Croquis et agaceries d'un gros bonhomme en bois; Descriptions automatiques; Je te veux; Poudre d'or.*
(B) **(*) Sony SBK 48283 [id.]. (i) Daniel Varviso; (ii) Philippe Entremont.

Both recitals here were recorded in 1979. Daniel Varviso has the measure of these pieces and plays admirably. Perhaps the first of the *Embryons desséchés* could have greater delicacy and wit, and there could be greater melancholy in the second of the *Gymnopédies*. But one's main reservation concerns the closely balanced recording of the piano and the slightly dry sound. Entremont, too, is placed forwardly, but he brings some charm to *Je te veux* and *Poudre d'or*, while the *Descriptions automatiques* are engagingly crisp and witty.

Avant-dernières pensées; Embryons desséchés; 6 Gnossiennes; 3 Gymnopédies; Pièces froides; Sarabande No. 3; Sonatine bureaucratique; 3 Valses distinguées du précieux dégoûté; 3 Véritables préludes flasques (pour un chien).
*** BIS Dig. CD 317 [id.]. Roland Pöntinen.

Roland Pöntinen was still in his early 20s when this recording was made. He seems perfectly in tune with the Satiean world, and his playing is distinguished by sensibility and tonal finesse. He is very well recorded too.

Berceuse; Caresse; 6 Gnossiennes; 3 Gymnopédies; Nocturne No. 4; 2 Oeuvres de jeunesse; Peccadilles importunes; Petit prélude à la journée; Le Piccadilly; Poudre d'or; Prélude de la porte héroïque du ciel; Rêverie du pauvre; Sonatine bureaucratique.
(N) *** Decca Dig. 458 105-2 [id.]. Pascal Rogé.

This generous compilation, taken from Rogé's uniquely distinguished Decca coverage of Satie's piano music, is entitled (reasonably enough) '*Piano dreams*'. The selection concentrates on the composer's gentler, haunting evocations, including – besides the *Gymnopédies* and *Gnossiennes* – several highlights from the third disc, which we especially enjoyed. The mood livens up towards the close, with the ragtime valse from *Les Oeuvres de jeunesse*, and finally the cakewalk, *Le Piccadilly*. With first-class recording, this could well be a first choice for those wanting a single-disc Satie collection.

Caresse; Carnet d'esquisses et de croquis; Danse de travers; La Diva de l'Empire; Enfantillages pittoresques; Esquisses et Sketch montmartroise; Le Fils des étoiles: Preludes to Acts I & II. 2 Oeuvres de jeunesse; Les pantins dansent; Peccadilles importunes; Petite musique de clown triste; Petite ouverture à danser; Le Piège de Méduse; Première pensée Rose Croix; Rêverie du pauvre; Sports et divertissements.
(N) *** Decca Dig. 455 370-2 [id.]. Pascal Rogé.

This third CD in Pascal Rogé's ongoing survey is if anything even finer than its predecessors, with much of the music here comparatively unfamiliar. There is some exquisite playing, particularly in the *Enfantillages pittoresques*, the delicately sensuous and infinitely brief *Caresse*, and the two serene *Préludes* for *Le Fils des étoiles*. The waltzes of *Deux Oeuvres de jeunesse* and the little dance movements of *Le Piège de Méduse* are delectably pointed, and there is both wit and charm in *L'Esquisses et Sketch montmartroise* and the 20 snippets which make up the *Sports et divertissments* after the opening *Choral inappétissant*. The final piece here, *Rêverie du pauvre,* has a haunting stillness. The recording, in an ideal acoustic, could not be more real.

Embryons desséchés; 6 Gnossiennes; 3 Gymnopédies; Heures séculaires et instantanées; Nocturnes Nos. 1–5; Sonatine bureaucratique; Sports et divertissements.
*** Hyperion Dig. CDA 66344 [id.]. Yitkin Seow.

The Singapore-born pianist Yitkin Seow is a good stylist; his approach is fresh and his playing crisp and marked by consistent beauty of sound. Seow captures the melancholy of the *Gymnopédies* very well and the playing, though not superior to Rogé or Queffélec in character or charm, has a quiet reticence that is well suited to this repertoire. The recording is eminently truthful.

Embryons desséchés; 6 Gnossiennes; 3 Gymnopédies; Je te veux; Nocturne No. 4; Le Picadilly; 4 Préludes flasques; Prélude en tapisserie; Sonatine bureaucratique; Vieux séquins et vieilles cuirasses.
*** Decca Dig. 410 220-2. Pascal Rogé.

Rogé has real feeling for this music and conveys its bitter-sweet quality and its grave melancholy as well as he does its lighter qualities. He produces, as usual, consistent beauty of tone, and this is well projected by the recording. Very well recorded, this remains the primary recommendation on CD for this repertoire, together with its companion above.

Sauer, Emil von (1862–1942)

Piano concerto No. 1 in E min.
*** Hyperion Dig. CDA 66790 [id.]. Stephen Hough, CBSO, Lawrence Foster – SCHARWENKA: *Piano concerto No. 4.* ***

Winner not only of the *Gramophone*'s Concerto Award, but also voted Record of the Year in 1996, this potent coupling of Sauer and Scharwenka surely combines every feature of the 'Romantic concerto', from flamboyant display to beguiling lyricism. As a greatly admired virtuoso, Emil von Sauer was an able exponent of the Scharwenka concerto; and his own work, although lighter in feeling, makes comparable demands on the dexterity of the soloist. Its delightful melodic vein and style have much in common with Saint-Saëns, especially in the Scherzo, although the touching *Larghetto amoroso* also evokes the poetic atmosphere of Chopin. The good-natured finale is relished here by soloist and orchestra alike, and Stephen Hough sparkles his way through its glittering upper tessitura. Altogether this makes a perfect foil for the more ambitious concerto with which it is paired. Splendid recording, with a nice sense of scale.

Sauguet, Henri (1901–89)

Mélodie concertante for cello and orchestra.
*** Russian Disc RDCD 11108 [id.]. Rostropovich, USSR SO, composer – BRITTEN: *Cello Symphony.* **(*)

Sauguet belongs at the heart of the Gallic tradition, and the opening of his *Mélodie concertante* has a dream-like, pastoral quality that is reminiscent of the Honegger *Cello concerto*. Its source of inspiration was an old, persistent memory of a young cellist from Bordeaux, and the 'warm, urgent sonorities with which she sought to interpret Debussy's music'. It is an extended improvisation, based on a haunting, introspective theme heard at the beginning of the piece. The performance is, of course, authoritative in every way, and the 1964 analogue recording sounds every bit as good as it did in its fine LP format.

Saxton, Robert (born 1953)

(i) *Chamber symphony (Circles of light);* (ii) *Concerto for orchestra; The Ring of eternity;* (i) *The Sentinel of the rainbow.*

(M) *** EMI Dig. CDM5 66530-2. (i) L. Sinf.; (ii) BBC SO; Knussen.

Robert Saxton is one of the most immediately communicative of the younger generation of British composers, using the orchestra with a panache that plainly reflects his own pleasure in rich and colourful sound. These four works, all written between 1983 and 1986, bring fine examples, notably the *Concerto for orchestra*, first given at the Proms in 1984. Its four linked sections broadly follow a symphonic shape, as do those of the *Chamber symphony* of 1986, which uses smaller forces, with solo strings. That later work has the title *Circles of light* and was inspired by a quotation from Dante, when in the *Divine Comedy* he looks into the eyes of his beloved, Beatrice, and links what he sees to the movement of the heavens. The other two works, both lasting around 15 minutes, also have evocative titles and are linked in the composer's mind to the *Concerto for orchestra* to form a sort of trilogy. Oliver Knussen draws intense, committed playing both from the BBC Symphony Orchestra in the *Concerto for orchestra* and *The Ring of eternity*, and from the London Sinfonietta in the chamber-scale works. Full, warm recording.

Scarlatti, Alessandro (1660–1725)

Concerti grossi Nos. 1 in F min.; 2 in C min.; 3 in F; (i) *Sinfonie di concerti grossi for flute and strings Nos. 7 in G min.; 8 in G; 9 in G min.; 10 in A min.; 11 in C; 12 in C min.*

(M) *** Ph. (IMS) Dig./Analogue 434 160-2. (i) William Bennett; I Musici.

These noble and elevated works, though not radical in style, have invention of real quality to commend them. I Musici give performances of much eloquence and warmth and great transparency; the latter is welcome in the fugal movements, especially as the 1979 analogue recording is of the very first rank. The *Sinfonie di concerti grossi* feature a flute soloist, in this instance the excellent William Bennett, who plays fluently and in fine style. The performances are lively and attractive, and eminently freshly recorded in Philips's best digital sound.

Cantatas: *Clori e Mirtillo; E pur vuole il cielo e amore; Ero e Leandro; Filli che esprime la sua fede a Fileno; Marc'Antonio e Cleopatra; Questo silenzio ombroso.*

*** Virgin/Veritas/EMI Dig. VC5 45126-2. Gérard Lesne, Sandrine Piau, Il Seminario Musicale.

These six cantatas bring together Gérard Lesne and his well-matched partner, Sandrine Piau. Each has a solo item, but the most striking works are those in which they join together. As so often with this repertoire, the texts dramatize the problems of lovers who are unable to be together or who destiny insists must part. The most dramatic of these is the dialogue between Antony and Cleopatra at the moment when he has to leave for Rome. The opening, much shorter, pastoral cantata here, *Questa silenzio ombroso* ('This shady quietude'), is a deeply expressive duet which lightens as the soprano line describes the sweetly lamenting nightingale. *Filli che esprime la sua fede a Fileno*, an expression of steadfast love, has a long instrumental introduction for violin and flute which comes off well, as does the skipping closing section; but in the melancholy central aria there is a watery obbligato flute and, although the timbre is perfectly matched to Lesne's vocal line, some listeners may regret that the flautist is unable to offer reliable intonation. Both vocal artists are on top form, and the simple continuo accompaniments are admirably played by Il Seminario Musicale. This is specialized repertoire, perhaps not to all tastes; but Lesne and Piau are exceptional artists.

Cantata per la Notte di Natale: Abramo, il tuo sembiante (Christmas Eve cantata).

(N) *** Opus 111 Dig. OPS 30-156 [id.]. Rossana Bertini, Elena Fedi, Claudio Cavina, Sandro Naglia, Sergio Foresti, Concerto Italiano, Alessandrini (with CORELLI: *Christmas Concerto grosso in G min., Op. 6/ 8.* ***)

This delightful semi-operatic cantata was designed for performance at the Apostolic Palace in Rome, on Christmas Eve 1705, to an audience of cardinals and including the Pope. With a text by Silvio Stampiglia, most original in conception, it presents the Nativity through the eyes of five figures from the Old Testament, Abraham (bass), Ezekiel (soprano), Isaiah (tenor), Jeremiah (alto) and Daniele (soprano), who are all together in Limbo, where they await the Messiah. It is Daniele who has two of the most joyful arias to sing, *Pargoletto in rozze fasce* and *Senti, che lieti intorno al bel presepe*, both in 12/8 time. The second soprano (Ezekiel) also has a spectacular aria, *Se togli dall'alma*, just before the exultant closing chorus. But there is splendid music for all the solosts, and especially the excellent male alto, Claudio Cavina who as Jeremiah foresees and laments the coming suffering and death of Christ.

The whole performance bursts with life under Rinaldo Alessandrini, and makes a fine entertainment, touching, but never solemn. Corelli's most famous concerto grosso, with its *Pastorale* closing movement, is used as a vivacious introduction. The recording sparkles and this is very highly recommended.

Missa, Ad usum Capellae Pontificale. Motets: *Ad te, Domine, levavi; Domine vivifica me; Exaltabo e Domine quoniam; Exultate Deo adjutori; Intellige clamorem meum; Salvum fac populum tuum.*
(M) **(*) Erato/Warner 0630 11229-2. Lausanne Vocal Ens., Michel Corboz.

The *Missa, Ad usum Capellae Pontificale* is a fine example of Scarlatti's ready homage to the *stilo antico*. Written in Rome, it was dedicated to Pope Innocent XIII in 1721. The atmosphere is restrained, never overtly dramatic. The polyphony is in four parts; in the *Sanctus* there is a homophonic section, while the brief *Benedictus*, like the melismatic closing *Agnus Dei*, is made simple by the composer's restricting himself to two-part writing throughout. Overall, if not ambitious, the Mass is a moving work, never austerely withdrawn, and Corboz's refined performance catches its restrained mood; even if perhaps he could have produced more dramatic contrast at times, the peaceful atmosphere is very affecting. Each of the six *a cappella* motets is short (between two and four minutes); they were also almost certainly written in Rome in the first decade of the eighteenth century. The first four, with their gentle linear flow and serene atmosphere, are again very much in the inherited Palestrina tradition. In the fifth, *Ad te, Domine, levavi*, the composer more strongly asserts his own harmonic style; but all five are beautiful and Corboz's performances are worthy of them. The final motet, *Exultate Deo adjutori*, understandably brings a change of mood, and the result is quite light-hearted, very like a madrigal. The reissue is well documented, but it is a pity there are no translated texts.

Motets: *De tenebroso lacu; Infirmata, vulnerata;* (i) *Salve Regina. Totus amore languens.*
(M) *** Virgin Veritas/EMI (SIS) VC5 45103-2 [id.]. Gérard Lesne; (i) Véronique Gens; Il Seminario Musicale.

The remarkably gifted alto, Gérard Lesne, together with the refreshingly stylish instrumental group, Il Seminario Musicale, are rediscovering virtually forgotten baroque repertoire. Lesne has already given us an outstanding collection of motets of Baldassare Galuppi (see above); now he turns to Alessandro Scarlatti, who wrote about a hundred such works. Often strikingly original, in many ways they are like vocal concerti grossi, contrasting slow and fast movements to suit the text; at the same time they combine an Italianate expressive melodic cantilena with an operatic feeling for drama. *De tenebro lacu* evokes a vision of souls in hell and the highly imaginative string introduction (a simple but spiky falling arpeggio) creates the mood for the opening words, 'From the depths of the dark lake'. The profound melancholy of *Infirma, vulnerata* is revealed with touching eloquence. Lesne is right inside the music's expressive world and it is difficult to imagine this being better sung. In the setting of *Salve Regine* he is joined by Véronique Gens, and their voices blend admirably. Throughout the accompaniments are creative, vital and warmly supportive – stimulating and beautiful in their own right. This is period-instrument performance at its most revealing. The recording is vivid, yet has just the right degree of warmth and spaciousness. Full translations are provided.

Motets: *Domine, refugium factus es nobis; O magnum mysterium.*
(B) *** Decca Double 443 868-2 (2) [id.]. Schütz Ch. of L., Roger Norrington – BONONCINI: *Stabat Mater* ***; PERGOLESI: *Magnificat in C; Stabat Mater* **(*); D. SCARLATTI: *Stabat Mater;* CALDARA: *Crucifixus;* LOTTI: *Crucifixus.* ***

These two motets are fine pieces that show how enduring the Palestrina tradition was in seventeenth-century Italy. They are noble in conception and are beautifully performed here and, given first-class sound, make a fine bonus for this enterprising Double Decca collection of Italian baroque choral music.

St. Cecilia mass.
(N) (B) *** Decca Double 458 370-2 (2) [id.]. Harwood, Eathorne, Cable, Eans, Keyte, St John's College Ch., Wren O, Guest – C. P. E. BACH: *Magnificat;* J. S. BACH: *Magnificat.* ***

This is far more florid in style than Scarlatti's other Masses and it receives from Guest a vigorous and fresh performance. The soloists cope with their difficult fioriture very confidently and they match one another well. This now comes as part of a Decca Double offering excellent accounts of *Magnificats* by Bach, father and son.

Stabat Mater.
(N) *** Opus 111 Dig. OPS 30-160 [id.]. Gemma Bertagnolli, Sara Mingardo, Concerto Italiano, Rinaldo Alessandrini – PERGOLESI: *Stabat Mater.* *** ✿

If somewhat less theatrical than Pergolesi's setting, Scarlatti's music brings continual bursts of vitality to contrast with the rich flowing polyphonic lines when the soprano and alto voices are combined. There are memorably expressive solos for both singers and, as in the companion work, they combine touchingly for the work's closing benediction before the tension lifts at the coda. Once again both the radiant soprano, Gemma Bertagnolli, and the dark-voiced contralto, Sara Mingardo, rise fully to the challenge of this remarkable music, and Alessandrini's instrumental support could not be more persuasive or authentic.

Scarlatti, Domenico (1685–1757)

The Good-humoured ladies (ballet suite; arr. Tommasini).
(M) *** EMI CDM5 65911-2. Concert Arts O, Robert Irving – GLAZUNOV: *The Seasons;* WALTON: *Wise virgins.* ***
(B) **(*) Sony SBK 60311 [id.]. Cleveland O, Louis Lane – RESPIGHI: *The Birds; Church windows.* **(*)

Scarlatti's music in Tommasini's witty arrangement chatters along very like a group of dear old ladies gossiping over tea. Irving points this up most beautifully and (especially in the finale) offers some very brilliant orchestral playing, while the *Andante* (from the *Sonata in B minor*, Kk 87) is touchingly tender. The recording is first class and completely belies its age (1961).

Louis Lane directs freshly an enjoyable account of this delightfully light-hearted music, so wittily scored. The Clevelanders respond with style and delicacy, and the 1970 Severance Hall recording is warm and pleasing, even if ideally it could be a little more transparent. However, the so-called '*Cats' fugue*' is neatly and clearly articulated, and Lane scores a bonus point by including the *Overture*.

Keyboard sonatas (complete).
*** Erato/Warner 2292 45309-2 (34) [id.]. Scott Ross, Huggett, Coin, Henry, Vallon.

The tercentenary of Domenico Scarlatti's birth prompted the production of an integral recording of Scarlatti's 555 *Keyboard sonatas*, including the three intended for organ, others for violin and continuo, and two for the unlikely combination of violin and oboe in unison. Scott Ross, who, with the participation of Monica Huggett (violin), Christophe Coin (cello), Michel Henry (oboe) and Marc Vallon (bassoon), is primarily responsible, plays five different harpsichords plus the organ, and he is very well recorded throughout in varying acoustics. Scarlatti's invention shows an inexhaustible resourcefulness, and Ross's playing is fully worthy: he is lively, technically assured, rhythmically resilient and, above all, he conveys his enjoyment of the music, without eccentricity. We cannot claim to have heard all 34 CDs, but all the evidence of sampling suggests that for the Scarlatti addict they will prove an endless source of satisfaction. The documentation is ample, providing a 200-page booklet about the composer, his music and the performers. The overall cost of this set is somewhere in the region of £200.

Keyboard sonatas, Kk. 1, 3, 8–9, 11, 17, 24–5, 27, 29, 87, 96, 113, 141, 146, 173, 213–14, 247, 259, 268, 283–4, 380, 386–7, 404, 443, 519–20, 523.
*** Virgin/EMI Dig. VCD5 45123-2 (2) [ZDCB 45123]. Mikhail Pletnev (piano).

What a happy idea to record a carefully chosen selection of some of Scarlatti's finest and most adventurous sonatas, stretching over two CDs, giving the fullest opportunity to demonstrate the extraordinary range of this music in a recital-length programme playing for 140 minutes. In the opening *D major Sonata*, Kk. 443, Pletnev establishes a firm pianistic approach, yet the staccato articulation reminds us that the world of the harpsichord is not so far away. However, in the *G major Sonata*, Kk. 283, and in the following Kk. 284 his fuller piano sonority transforms the effect of the writing. The second CD opens with the almost orchestral Kk. 96 *in D*, with its resonant horn calls, and later the lovely, flowing *C minor Sonata* and the even more expressive Kk. 11 *in F sharp minor* bring a reflective poetic feeling, which could not have been matched in colour by the plucked instrument. The performances throughout are in the very front rank, and excited comparisons with Horowitz at the time. Small wonder that it won a Gramophone magazine Award in the year of its issue.

Keyboard sonatas, Kk. 1, 8–9, 11, 13, 20, 87, 98, 119, 135, 159, 380, 450, 487 & 529.
*** DG Dig. 435 855-2 [id.]. Ivo Pogorelich (piano).

Pogorelich plays with captivating simplicity and convinces the listener that this is music which sounds far more enjoyable on the piano than on the harpsichord. His dazzlingly execution, using the lightest touch, consistently enchants the ear with its subtle tonal colouring, and the music emerges ever sparkling and fresh. These performances can be measured against those of Horowitz and not found wanting. Moreover Pogorelich is beautifully recorded in an ideal acoustic, and the hour-long programme is admirably chosen to provide maximum variety.

Keyboard sonatas: Kk. 1, 9, 30, 69, 113, 127, 132–3, 141, 159, 175, 215, 380, 430, 481, 492 & 502.
*** Collins Dig. 1322-2 [id.]. Joanna MacGregor (piano).

Joanna MacGregor has a lively intelligence and exemplary taste; she plays all these sonatas with flawless technical address and flair. Pianistic narcissism seems foreign to her nature and her interpretations are quite properly conceived in pianistic terms and do not strive to imitate the terrace dynamics of the harpsichord. Moreover she is very well recorded.

Keyboard sonatas, Kk. 3, 52, 184–5, 191–3, 208–9, 227, 238–9, 252–3.
(B) *** Sony Seon SBK 60099 [id.]. Gustav Leonhardt (harpsichord).

Very distinguished playing from Gustav Leonhardt, who often plays with dash and exuberance, as in the first sonata here, Kk. 3 *in A minor*. He uses a copy of a Dulcken harpsichord, and these are consistently characterful performances which project direct to the listener in well-focused, clean sound, recorded in a pleasant acoustic.

Keyboard sonatas, Kk. 7, 33, 49, 54, 87, 96, 105–7, 159, 175, 206–7, 240–41, 347–8, 380–81, 441–4, 518–19, 524–5.
(B) *** HM HMP 90 1164/5 [(M) id.]. Rafael Puyana (harpsichord).

Rafael Puyana gives eminently red-blooded performances of these *Sonatas*, which are refreshing and invigorating. He uses a three-manual harpsichord from 1740 by Hass of Hamburg, restored by Andrea Goble, which makes a splendidly rich sound, present and lively. Authoritative playing, though he tends, with some exceptions, to concentrate on the more outgoing and brilliant rather than the inward-looking *Sonatas*.

Complete Keyboard Sonatas, Volume 1: *Kk. 8, 13, 44, 184, 246, 402, 421, 427, 430, 434, 446, 450, 487, 523, 531, 533, 544.*
(N) (BB) *** Naxos Dig. 8.553061 [id.]. Eteri Andjaparidze (piano).

This first CD in a proposed complete survey on Naxos is very promising indeed. Eteri Andjaparidze, born in Soviet Georgia, was the youngest artist to win an award in the 1974 Moscow International Tchaikovsky Piano Competition, and she went on to take the Grand Prix at the similar event in Montreal two years later. She is an immensely gifted and musical player, and plays Scarlatti with a winning combination of poised elegance and depth of feeling. She draws on the wide range of dynamic and colouring a modern concert grand piano will afford, and opens (with K.487 in C major) in a boldly rhythmic style that immediately conjures up an impression of a two manual harpsichord. Yet so much of her articulation is pianistic, delicate and intimate, and this gentle playing can be infinitely touching. The thoughtful melancholy in the *D minor*, and *G minor Sonatas*, K. 434 and K.8, in some ways reminds one of J. S. Bach; and yet there is much that is joyful too, not least the brilliant skipping *G major*, K.523. Beautifully recorded, this is a treasurable disc, well documented, which can compete on equal terms with almost any of the more expensive collections listed above and below.

Keyboard sonatas, Kk. 8, 20, 32, 107, 109, 124, 141, 159, 234, 247, 256, 259, 328, 380, 397, 423, 430, 440, 447, 481, 490, 492, 515 & 519.
❁ (***) EMI (SIS) mono CHS7 64934-2 [id.]. Wanda Landowska (harpsichord).

Landowska led the revival of interest in the harpsichord at a time when it was a relative rarity both in the recital room and in the recording studio. She used a thunderous Pleyel that was specially built to withstand the rigours of 1920s and '30s travel; but her playing has more character than most other modern players put together; it is electrifying in its sheer vitality and imagination. Lionel Salter's excellent notes quote her as saying she was 'sensitive to Scarlatti's bucolic mind, his rustic jauntiness . . . the elemental strength, the richness of his rhythmical power, as well as all that is Moorish in them. He has the genuine nobility, the heroism and the audacity of Don Quixote.' The first batch of sonatas was recorded in 1934 and the others in 1939 and 1940. Indispensable.

Keyboard sonatas, Kk. 9, 27, 33, 69, 87, 96, 159, 193, 247, 427, 492, 531; Fugue in G min., K.30.
(M) *** Erato/Warner 4509 96960-2. Anne Queffélec (piano).

Anne Queffélec employs a modern Steinway with great character and apomb. She immediately captures the listener in the dashing opening of the *D major Sonata*, Kk. 96, with its lively fanfares and, in the gentler *B minor*, Kk. 27, her rippling passagework is Bach-like in its simplicity. She alternates reflective works with those sonatas calling for sparkling bravura and her choice is unerringly effective. The recital closes with a *Fugue* which unfolds with calm inevitability. The 1970 recording is first class; the piano is naturally focused and has plenty of space, without any resonant blurring.

Keyboard sonatas, Kk. 25, 33, 39, 52, 54, 96, 146, 162, 197–198, 201, 303, 466, 474, 481, 491, 525, 547.
**(*) Sony SK 53460 [id.]. Vladimir Horowitz (piano).

Provided you are prepared to accept sometimes less than flattering and often rather dry recorded sound, this is marvellous playing which sweeps away any purist notions about Scarlatti having to be played on the harpsichord. The 18 sonatas were chosen by Horowitz after he had recorded nearly twice as many throughout 1964. The very opening, staccato *D major*, Kk. 33, is made to sound very brittle by the close balance, but in the following *A minor*, Kk. 54, the pianist's gentle colouring is fully revealed. Here, as in the two slow *F minor sonatas*, Kk. 466 and Kk. 481, the music is particularly beautiful in a way not expected of Scarlatti. The playing time has been extended to 72 minutes by the addition of six more sonatas to the content of the original CD.

Keyboard sonatas, Kk. 32, 64, 69, 87, 133, 146, 160, 198, 208, 213, 380, 429, 466, 481, 511, 517; Toccata in D min.
(B) **(*) Cal. Approche CAL 6670 [id.]. Inger Södergren.

Inger Södergren gives an appealing recital of 16 well-contrasted *Sonatas* plus a brilliant account of the highly individual *Toccata in D minor*. Some might feel that her gentle, almost wistful treatment of the lyrical sonatas errs towards being too romantic but her keen sensitivity and crisp articulation in the lively pieces are unimpeachable, and she is very well recorded.

Keyboard sonatas, Kk. 46, 87, 99, 124, 201, 204a, 490–92, 513, 520–21.
(M) *** CRD CRD 3368; *CRDC 4068* [id.]. Trevor Pinnock (harpsichord).

No need to say much about this: the playing is first rate and the recording outstanding in its presence and clarity. There are few better anthologies of Scarlatti in the catalogue, although the measure is not particularly generous.

Keyboard sonatas, Kk. 108, 118–19, 141, 198, 203, 454–5, 490–92, 501–2, 516–19.
*** HM/BMG Dig. RD 77224 [77224-2]. Andreas Staier (harpsichord).

Andreas Staier characterizes each of these Scarlatti sonatas vividly and with real imagination. Playing (and recording) of this quality has no need to fear even the most exalted comparisons. A strongly recommended issue.

Keyboard sonatas: Kk. 115–16, 144, 175, 402–3, 449–50, 474–5, 513, 516–17, 544–5.
**(*) Decca Dig. 421 422-2. András Schiff (piano).

Exquisite and sensitive playing, full of colour and delicacy. As always, András Schiff is highly responsive to the mood and character of each piece. At times one wonders whether he is not a little too refined: in some, one would have welcomed more abandon and fire. However, for the most part this is a delightful recital, and the Decca recording is exemplary in its truthfulness.

Keyboard sonatas, Kk. 213–14; 318–19; 347–8; 356–7; 380–81; 454–5; 478–9; 524–7.
(B) *** DG 439 438-2 [id.]. Ralph Kirkpatrick (harpsichord).

At the beginning of the 1970s, when this recital first appeared on LP, Ralph Kirkpatrick's monumental study of Domenico Scarlatti was the standard work on the subject, and still remains enormously readable and erudite. These performances, paired according to his theory, have all the panache and scholarship one would expect from this artist, in addition to a welcome degree of freedom and poetry. Some of his Bach playing has seemed pedantic, so it is a pleasure to welcome this brightly recorded bargain collection back to the catalogue without reservation.

Keyboard sonatas, Kk. 159, 175, 208, 213, 322 & 380 (arr. for guitar).
(B) *** Sony SBK 62425 [id.]. John Williams (guitar) – GIULIANI: *Variations on a theme by Handel;* PAGANINI: *Caprice; Grand sonata;* VILLA-LOBOS: *5 Preludes.* ***

Guitar arrangements of Scarlatti sonatas have their charms when played by an artist as imaginative as John Williams. He manages by percussive plucking to sound at times almost like a harpsichord, while his gentle playing is always beguiling, especially in the delightful *D major Sonata*, Kk 159. The recording is faithful, somewhat close and larger than life, but never unacceptably so. This diverse and well-planned recital (76 minutes) is very enjoyable indeed.

Dixit Dominus.
*** DG Dig. 423 386-2 [id.]. Argenta, Attrot, Denley, Ashley Stafford, Varcoe, Ch. & E. Concert, Pinnock – VIVALDI: *Gloria.* ***

Pinnock, as so often, inspires his performers to sing and play as though at a live event. This Scarlatti Psalm-setting, very well recorded, makes an attractive coupling for the better known of Vivaldi's settings of the *Gloria*.

Stabat Mater.
(B) *** Decca Double 443 868-2 (2) [id.]. Schütz Ch. of L., Roger Norrington – BONONCINI: *Stabat Mater* ***; PERGOLESI: *Magnificat in C; Stabat Mater* **(*); A. SCARLATTI: *Domine, refugium factus es nobis; O magnum mysterium;* CALDARA: *Crucifixus;* LOTTI: *Crucifixus.* ***
(B) **(*) Sony SBK 48282 [id.]. BBC Singers, John Poole – VIVALDI: *Stabat Mater; Dixit Dominus.* **(*)

Norrington's performance is admirable, though not always impeccable in matters of tonal balance; and the recording is very good. Overall this well-designed Double Decca set combines three fine *Stabat Mater* settings with other comparable baroque choral music, all well performed and impressively recorded.

A thoroughly musical, if not distinctive, performance from the BBC Singers, who blend well together and are realistically recorded. An attractive coupling for two enjoyable period performances of Vivaldi.

Scharwenka, Franz Xaver
(1850–1924)

Piano concerto No. 4 in F min., Op. 82.
*** Hyperion Dig. CDA 66790 [id.]. Stephen

Hough, CBSO, Lawrence Foster – SAUER: *Piano concerto No. 1.* ***

Scharwenka, famous virtuoso pianist as well as composer and teacher (admired by Busoni and Liszt), wrote four piano concertos; this, his finest, dates from 1908. It was very famous in its time and its composer was later to play it triumphantly in New York (in 1910) with Gustav Mahler conducting. It is ambitiously flamboyant and on the largest scale: in four movements, with the first lasting nearly 19 minutes. Its invention, which manages a potent mix of bravura and lyricism, readily holds the attention, with plenty of interest in the bold orchestral tuttis. The second-movement *Allegretto* has much charm and is very deftly scored; a full flood of romanticism blossoms in the *Lento* slow movement. The stormy *con fuoco* finale combines a touch of wit and more robust geniality with glittering brilliance and power; and all four movements make prodigious technical and artistic demands on the soloist, to which Stephen Hough rises with great technical aplomb and consistent panache; he also plays with fine poetic sensibility. He is given vigorously committed support by Lawrence Foster and the CBSO and a first-class Hyperion recording. Winner not only of the *Gramophone* Concerto Award, this was also that magazine's Record of the Year in 1996, and deservedly so.

Scheidt, Samuel (1587–1654)

Ludi musici (Hamburg, 1621): excerpts.
*** Audivis Astrée Dig. ES 8559 [id.]. Hespèrion XX, Jordi Savall.

Although he studied briefly under Sweelinck in Amsterdam in 1608–9, Samuel Scheidt spent his life in Halle, both as organist and for five years as Kapellmeister. He published four collections of instrumental music between 1621 and 1624 under the title *Ludi musici* but only the First Book survives, and all these pieces are drawn from it. For all its good nature, his music has a melancholy streak. It is immediately striking in the touchingly expressive extended opening of the *Paduan à 4* (from Cantus IV) with its gentle, lyrical flow and passing dissonances. The later *Paduan* (from Cantus V) is also very touching, and has much in common with Dowland's *Lachrimae*. Scheidt actually draws on Dowland in his spirited *Battle galliard*, so characteristic of its time. Other English tunes are featured in his canzons, notably in the delightful five-part *Canzon* (from Cantus XXVI). All this music is played with characteristic finesse, nicely judged espressivo and plenty of vitality by the superb Jordi Savall and Hespèrion XX, and the viol sound is smooth and pleasingly natural, with none of that scratchiness which comes from too close microphones.

Schein, Johann Hermann (1586–1630)

Banchetto musicale (1617): *Nos. 2, Suite a 5 in D; 6, Suite a 5 in D; 16, Suite a 5 in A; 20, Suite a 5 in E; 26, Canzon a 5 in A (Corollarium).* *Venus Kräntzlein* (1609): *Nos. 17, Intrada a 5 in D; 20, Intrada a 5 in G; 22, Gagliarda a 5 in D; 23, Canzon a 5 in A.*
(M) *** Virgin Veritas/EMI Dig. VM5 61399-2 [CDM 61399]. Hespèrion XX, Jordi Savall.

Johann Hermann Schein was one of Bach's predecessors as Cantor of St Thomas's Church in Leipzig. His instrumental music has much in common with that of his Italian contemporary, Giovanni Gabrieli, although the interplay between various groups, usually brass and strings (or recorder), is much less spectacular. The *Canzon in A major* (*Corollarium*), however, is a more ambitious piece, very much in the contrapuntal Gabrieli manner. The *Banchetto musicale* is (like Telemann's *Tafelmusik*) intended as a background for meals, although the sonorous brass writing with occasional bravura roulades would suggest that the banqueting hall would have needed to be very spacious. However, the very pleasing expressive music (especially the *Padouanas*) invites lower dynamic levels. The *Intradas* open with a drum-beat, suggesting the musicians marching in to the feast. The performances here are stylish and pleasing, responding to the music's dolorousness. Perhaps they could have been more robust, but the result is very suitable for domestic listening and is very well recorded.

Schickele, Peter (born 1935)

Oboe concerto.
(M) *** Carlton Fanfare Dig. 30366 0065-2 [id.]. Pamela Pecha, Moscow PO, Paul Freeman – VAUGHAN WILLIAMS: *Oboe concerto;* R. STRAUSS: *Oboe concerto.* ***

Peter Schickele (also known as P. D. Q. Bach) is a professional American musical joker, though his humour is pretty feeble. He studied composition under Milhaud, so it is not surprising that his well-crafted and highly spontaneous concerto has its exotic side, especially in its central *Chant*. But Schickele's invention throughout the piece is ear-tickling and this work is in every way winning, ending with a touching *Epilogue*. It is a pity that the very sparse notes provided with this CD do not provide more information about its gestation, but they do tell us that the present performer is its dedicatee, and she gives it a performance of great character and immediate appeal. She is both well accompanied and vividly recorded.

Schillings, Max von (1868–1933)

(i) Violin concerto, Op. 23. King Oedipus (tone-poem), *Op. 11; Moloch: Harvest festival scene.*
*** Marco Polo Dig. 8.223324 [id.]. (i) Ernö Rozsa; Czecho-Slovak RSO (Bratislava), Alfred Walter.

Max von Schillings's *Violin concerto* is a beautifully crafted and highly accomplished score in the post-Romantic idiom with echoes of Wagner, Richard Strauss, Reger and Pfitzner. It is a long work whose first movement alone runs to 23 minutes. Although it reveals no strong individuality, it has a certain rhetorical command and lyrical warmth to commend it, and its masterly handling of the orchestra will make a strong appeal to those with a taste for turn-of-the-century music. Its attractions are considerable and they are well conveyed in this passionate and committed performance. The eloquent soloist is the twenty-year-old Romanian-born Hungarian, Ernö Rozsa, who plays marvellously and inspires the Kosice Orchestra under Alfred Walter to great heights. Neither the excerpt from the opera *Moloch* (1906) nor the *Symphonic Prologue to the Oedipus Tyrannus of Sophocles* (1900) makes anywhere near as strong an impression. The Marco Polo recording is very well detailed and has plenty of warmth and presence.

Schmelzer, Johann (c. 1620–80)

Balletto di centauri, ninfe e salvatici; Balletto di spiritelli; Sacro-Profans concentus musicus: Sonata I a 8; Sonata a 7 flauti; Sonata con arie der kaiserlichen Serenade.
(N) (B) *** Decca Double 458 081-2 (2) [id.]. New L. Consort, Pickett – BIBER: *Ballettae; Sonate; Serenade; Requiem.* ***

Johann Schmelzer made his reputation initially as a virtuoso violinist (the famous and nearly most distinguished in all Europe', suggested a contemporary accolade); as a climax to his career, he was apppointed Vice-Kapellmeister to the Viennese Imperial Court, and in 1679 he became Kapellmeister – almost too late, for he died of the plague a year later. One of his tasks was the provision of ballet music for use in pageants, and much of this survives. The two brief scores included here last for about five minutes each, with an average of a movement per minute, but these vignettes have considerable charm. The *Balletto di spiritelli* is scored for recorders and curtal (an ancestor of the bassoon), violins and viols, and the *Balletto di centauri* uses cornets and sackbuts, as well as recorders, strings and continuo. The even more robust *Sonata con arie zu der kaiserlichen Serenada* (with three trumpets, timpani plus a string ensemble and continuo) has six movements, including two *Arias* and a *Canario*, but still only lasts seven minutes. Philip Pickett himself leads the consort of recorders in the *Sonata a 7*, which is a fairly ambitious continuous piece, longer than either of the ballets, and the *Sonata a 8* highlights a trumpet duo against a group of violins and viols. This is agreeably inventive music, which is brought refreshingly to life by Pickett's instrumetal ensemble, using original instruments to persuasive effect. The recording is both clear and spacious. Generously coupled with comparable instrumental music by Biber plus the *F minor Requiem*, this is one of the very finest of the Decca Doubles deriving from the Oiseau-Lyre catalogue.

Sonata natalitia a 3 chori; Sonata II a 8 chori; 3 Sonatas a 3; Sonata a 4; Sonata a 5; Sonata IV a 6; Sonata I a 8.
(M) ** Teldec/Warner 4509 95989-2 (2) [id.]. VCM, Harnoncourt (with FUX: *Concentus musico instrumentis.* ***)

While the *Sonata natalitia*, using recorders, piffari (early oboes), trombones and strings, certainly creates aurally fascinating and intricate textures, some of the other works, especially those for brass (where the clarinos produce a curious throttled tone), are less successful. It is when we come to the *Sonata IV a 6* (for two violins, three viols and continuo), the *Sonata a 3* (for violin, viola (violetta), viol and continuo), and the *Sonata a 3* (for three violins and continuo) that the composer begins really to stimulate the listener properly, and it is a pity that these were not added on to the Fux programme to make a single CD instead of giving Schmelzer a 48-minute disc to himself. No complaints about the recording, which is excellent.

Schmidt, Franz (1874–1939)

Symphonies Nos. 1 in E; 2 in E flat; 3 in A; 4 in C.
(N) *** Chandos Dig. CHAN 9568 (4) [id.]. Detroit SO, Neeme Järvi.

Chandos have now boxed their individual releases of the symphonies into a 4-CD set, discarding the fill-ups. The *First Symphony* was composed during Schmidt's early to mid 20s and, as one might expect, is derivative. He was fleetingly a pupil of Bruckner, before passing into the hands of Robert Fuchs, who taught such dissimilar figures as Mahler, Sibelius and Hugo Wolf. He was for many years first cello in the Vienna Philharmonic, and as one might expect, his orchestration is masterly. Right from the start, one is left in no doubt that Schmidt is a born symphonic composer with a real feeling for the long-breathed line and the natural growth flow of ideas. He began work on the *Second Symphony* on leaving the Vienna Philharmonic in 1911 and finished two years later. The *Third* (1927–8) was entered in the 1928 Schubert Centenary Competition, sponsored by the Columbia Graphophone Company and though the first prize went to Atterberg's *Sixth Symphony*, the Schmidt was judged the finest Austrian entry. It is a richly imaginative score in the romantic tradition, though it yields pride of place among the symphonies to the elegiac, valedictory *Fourth* (1933–4) whose nobility and depth of feeling shines through every bar. The Detroit Symphony Orchestra under Neeme Järvi play with a freshness and enthusiasm which is totally persuasive. They almost sound Viennese and the recording is very good indeed.

Symphony No. 2 in E flat.
(N) (**) Music & Arts mono CD 991 [id.]. VPO, Dmitri Mitropoulos – SCHOENBERG: *Verklärte Nacht, Op. 4.* (**)

Mitropoulos's account of the *Second Symphony* with the Vienna Philharmonic comes from a concert he conducted a year or so before his death. It makes a valuable appendix for the Järvi set and leaves no doubts as to his interpretative stature. Here was a conductor who more than deserves his legendary reputation. The fine playing, alas, is not matched by good recording and some tolerance has to be extended – and is worth extending.

Symphony No. 4 in C.
(B) *** Decca 440 615-2 (2) [id.]. VPO, Zubin Mehta – MAHLER: *Symphony No. 2 (Resurrection).* ***

Symphony No. 4 in C min.; Variations on a Hussar's song.
*** EMI Dig. CDC5 55518-2. LPO, Welser-Möst.

One of Schmidt's greatest and most personal works, coupled with one of his most genial. This neglected symphony is in one long movement, whose material all derives from the inspired, long-breathed trumpet theme with which it opens. Schmidt's music has an elegiac feel to it and a nobility of utterance which places him almost as the natural successor to Bruckner. The orchestration is masterly and the chromaticism, though occasionally reminiscent of Reger, is never cloying. Mehta's impressive recording of it with the Vienna Philharmonic from the early 1970s, easily one of his most memorable discs, has recently been reissued by Decca as the coupling for his Mahler *Second* (see above); but the EMI set from the LPO and Franz Welser-Möst completely supersedes it. Like many Austrians, Welser-Möst obviously has great feeling for the composer and manages to convey this to his players. The delightful *Variations on a Hussar's song*, written two years before the symphony in 1931, comes off with equal conviction.

(i) *Quintet in B flat for clarinet, piano and strings*; (ii) *3 Fantasy pieces on Hungarian National melodies*. (Piano) *Romance in A; Toccata in D min.*.
(N) ** Marco Polo Dig. 8.223415 [id.]. Daniela Ruso with (i) Aládár Janoska, Frantisek Török, Alexander Lakatos; (i; ii) Ján Slávik.

The *Quintet for clarinet, piano, violin, viola and cello* of 1932, like so much of Schmidt's music with piano, was composed with the left-handed pianist Paul Wittgenstein (brother of the philosopher) in mind. The piano part was subsequently rearranged for two hands by Friedrich Wührer. Despite the advantage of its relative brevity, this quintet is neglected in the recital room. Its character is predominantly elegiac; it was composed after the death of Schmidt's daughter, and can best be described as having something of the autumnal feeling of late Brahms, the subtlety of Reger, and the dignity and nobility of Elgar or Suk. The players sound pretty tentative at the very start but soon settle down, though their tempo could with advantage have been slower. All the same it is a thoroughly sympathetic, recommendable account. The *Drei Phantasiestücke* and the two piano pieces, the *Romance* and the *D minor Toccata*, are earlier and less interesting, though they are well enough played.

Clarinet quintet No. 2 in A (for clarinet, piano & strings).
*** Marco Polo Dig. 8.223414 [id.]. Jánoska, Mucha, Lakatos, Slávik, Ruso.

The *Quintet in A major for clarinet, piano and strings* is unusual: it begins like some mysterious other-worldly scherzo which immediately introduces a pastoral idea of beguiling charm. The second movement is a piano piece in ternary form; there is a longish scherzo, full of fantasy and wit, and there is an affecting trio, tinged with the melancholy of late Brahms. The fourth movement sets out as if it, too, is going to be a long, meditative piano piece, but its nobility and depth almost put one in mind of the Elgar *Quintet*. The fifth is a set of variations on a theme of Josef Labor, and is sometimes played on its own. In all, the piece takes an hour and, of the two performances now before the public, the Slovak account on Marco Polo is the one to go for. The recording has freshness and bloom, though it could benefit from a bigger recording venue. This is a glorious work.

String quartets Nos 1 in A; 2 in G.
(N) *** Nimbus Dig. NI 5467 [id.]. Franz Schubert Qt. of Vienna.

The Schmidt quartets come from 1925 and 1929 respectively, and inhabit much the same world as Reger, early Schoenberg and Strauss. The Franz Schubert Quartet of Vienna succeed in handling the dense chromatic part-writing that opens the *Second quartet* with rock-steady intonation. Those who respond to the *Fourth Symphony* will find much to delight them here and the recording is lifelike and well balanced.

Quintet for two violins, viola, cello and piano left hand.

(N) *** Sony Dig. SK 48253 [id.]. Leon Fleischer, Joseph Silverstein, Joel Smirnoff, Michael Tree, Yo-Yo Ma – KORNGOLD: *Suite for two violins, cello and piano left hand, Op. 23.* ***

An impressive account in every way which in most respects supersedes the 1992 Orfeo version (now withdrawn). The present version is aptly coupled with the Op. 23 *Korngold Suite*, also written for Paul Wittgenstein. All in all an unusual and stimulating disc.

Das Buch mit sieben Siegeln (The Book with 7 seals).

(N) *** EMI Dig CDS5 56660-2 [CDCB 56660]. Christiane Oelze, Cornelia Kallisch, Stig Andersen, Lothar Odinius, René Pape, Alfred Reiter, Bav. Rad. Ch & SO, Franz Welser-Möst, Friedemann Winkelhoger (organ).

**(*) Calig Dig. CAL 50 978/9 [id.]. Fontana, Hintermeier, Azesberger, Büchner, Holl, Hollzer, V. Singverein, VSO, Stein; Martin Haselböck (organ).

(M) (***) Sony mono SM2K 68442 (2) [id.]. Gueden, Malaniuk, Dermota, Wunderlich, Berry, V. Singverein, VPO, Mitropoulos; Alois Forrer (organ).

After finishing the *Fourth Symphony* in 1933, Schmidt devoted his remaining creative years to this setting of the *Revelation of St John the Divine*, completing it in 1937. The newest version was recorded by EMI in the Herkulessaal, Munich, and is played by the magnificent Bavarian Radio Orchestra under Franz Welser-Möst, who shows great sympathy for the score. This supplants the Calig version recorded live at the Grosser Musikvereinsaal in Vienna in May 1996, which also has the advantage of modern recorded sound.

The mid-price Sony version comes from Austrian Radio tapes of a live performance given as part of the Salzburg Festival in August 1959, with an illustrious line-up and under the legendary Dmitri Mitropoulos. The Sony is a mono recording but given the eloquence and dedication of Mitropoulos's conducting, any sonic limitations are soon forgotten. Under his inspired direction every phrase means something. There is nothing routine and much that is inspired – certainly the singing of Anton Dermota, who took part in the first performance in 1938 and thus brings special authority to the role. It is difficult to grade these recordings. Given its fervour and intensity the Mitropoulos cannot have fewer than three stars despite the mono sound. Horst Stein's 1996 performance (on Calig) is impressive but the recording does not match the newcomer in transparency: the sound is not of the very highest order though it is perfectly acceptable.

Schmitt, Florent (1870–1958)

Symphony No. 2, Op. 137; La danse d'Abisag, Op. 75; (i) *Habeyssée* (suite for violin and orchestra), *Op. 110. Rêves, Op. 65.*

*** Marco Polo Dig. 8.223689 [id.].(i) Hannele Segerstam; Rheinland-Pfalz PO, Leif Segerstam.

La danse d'Abisag, like the much earlier *Tragédie de Salomé*, has a biblical theme: unlike Salome, Abisag, despite her erotic dancing, fails to arouse the ageing monarch (King David). The *Symphony No. 2*, Op. 137, so numbered to distinguish it from the *Symphonie concertante for piano and orchestra*, was a work of Schmitt's advanced age – and no mean achievement for a composer in his 88th year! In terms of orchestral expertise and flair, it is second to none, and the opulence of its palette and imaginative vitality is remarkable. *Rêves* is an early piece, inspired by a poem by Léon-Paul Fargue and appropriately atmospheric; and *Habeyssée*, said to be inspired by an Islamic legend, is a three-movement suite for violin and orchestra. This is a rewarding issue which offers some good playing from the Rheinland-Pfalz Orchestra under Segerstam, who excels in this repertoire. Good recording too.

Piano trio: Très lent.

(BB) **(*) Naxos Dig. 8.550934 [id.]. Joachim Trio – DEBUSSY; RAVEL: *Piano trios.* **(*)

This three-minute fragment, about which the notes are uninformative, is rather haunting and, like the rest of the programme, beautifully played and recorded.

La tragédie de Salomé (ballet; complete).

*** Marco Polo Dig. 8.223448 [id.]. Fayt, Rheinland-Pfalz PO, Davin.

The full score of the original hour-long ballet now emerges from its long slumber to make its first appearance since 1907. Although the scoring is for fewer players, Schmitt's skill as an orchestrator is such that the heady, exotic draft he prepared is hardly less potent than the more sumptuously scored, 1908 version. The piece is as long again as the more familiar ballet, and much of the music that was lost in the process is every bit as atmospheric and colourful. Patrick Davin and the Rheinland-Pfalz Philharmonic Orchestra cast a strong spell, and Marie-Paule Fayt is the off-stage nymphet. The Marco Polo recording has a good, spacious acoustic and plenty of detail. This is a valuable addition to the catalogue, almost worthy of a Rosette insofar as the music really deserves to be heard and appreciated, and these performers do it justice. The documentation is of unusual interest and gives a detailed account of the action of the ballet.

Schnittke, Alfred (born 1934)

Concerto grosso No. 1; Quasi una sonata; Moz-Art à la Haydn; A Paganini.
(M) *** DG Dig. (IMS) 445 520-2 [id.]. Kremer, Smirnov, Grindenko, COE, Schiff.

If you want to jump in at the deep end of the Schnittke repertoire, the present collection offers the formidable, at times even ferocious, *Quasi una sonata* with its extraordinary scratchings and abrasions, the pastiche *Moz-Art à la Haydn*, which is almost humorous, and the virtuoso solo violin piece, *A Paganini*. The performances here are expert, very committed and brilliantly recorded.

(i) *Cello concerto No. 2. In memoriam . . .*
*** Sony Dig. SK 48241 [id.]. (i) Rostropovich; LSO, Ozawa.

Schnittke has a strong feeling for the cello, and his *Second Cello concerto* is conceived on a large scale, the main emotional weight residing in the fifth and last movement, a passacaglia lasting a quarter of an hour. Its powerful, concentrated atmosphere resonates long in the mind and leaves what one could describe as a strong aftertaste. So, for that matter, does *In memoriam. . .*, a transcription and reworking of the *Piano quintet*, written on the death of his mother. Something of the very private grief and spare, hollow textures of the quintet is lost but there are gains in colour in the highly imaginative use of the orchestra. The recording has exceptional richness, detail and depth and the performance of the concerto has all the authority and panache one might expect.

Violin concertos Nos. 1–2.
*** BIS Dig. CD 487 [id.]. Mark Lubotsky, Malmö SO, Eri Klas.

The *First Violin concerto* inhabits a post-romantic era. Its lyricism is profoundly at variance with its successor of 1966, commissioned by Mark Lubotsky, the soloist on this record. Here the central concept is what Schnittke calls 'a certain drama of tone colours', and there is no doubt that much of it is vividly imagined and strongly individual. The double-bass is assigned a special role of a caricatured 'anti-soloist'. There is recourse to the once fashionable aleatoric technique, but this is all within carefully controlled parameters. The Malmö orchestra under Eri Klas play with evident feeling in both works and are very well recorded. This is an altogether highly satisfactory coupling.

(i) *Gogol suite* (compiled Rozhdestvensky); *Labyrinths*.
*** BIS Dig. CD 557 [id.]. Malmö SO, Lev Markiz; (i) with Anton Kontra.

There is a surrealistic quality to the *Gogol suite* reminiscent of Gogol's own words quoted in Jürgen Köchel's note, 'The world hears my laughter; my tears it does not see nor recognise.' *Labyrinths* is a ballet score composed in 1971, thin in development and musical ideas but sufficiently strong in atmosphere to survive the transition from stage to concert hall. The Malmö Orchestra under Lev Markiz play very well and the recording is in the demonstration class.

Cello sonata.
*** BIS Dig. CD 336 [id.]. Torleif Thedéen, Roland Pöntinen – STRAVINSKY: *Suite italienne;* SHOSTAKOVICH: *Sonata.* ***

The *Cello sonata* is a powerfully expressive piece, its avant-garde surface enshrining a neo-romantic soul. Torleif Thedéen is a refined and intelligent player who gives a thoroughly committed account of this piece with his countryman, Roland Pöntinen.

Symphony No. 1.
*** Chandos Dig. CHAN 9417 [id.]. Russian State SO, Gennady Rozhdestvensky.

Schnittke's *First Symphony* dates from 1969–72 and is a huge radical canvas lasting some 68 minutes. In his essay on 'The Symphony in the Soviet Union' in *A Guide to the Symphony*, David Fanning writes that it 'contains a whole lexicon of advanced devices – the theatricality of American happenings with the players entering one by one and leaving at the end only to enter again as if to restart the whole process, the aleatory (chance) elements of the Polish school, and the multiple quotations of Berio's *Sinfonia* plus a cadenza for jazz violin'. As for the aleatory elements, one is reminded of Hans Keller's remark: 'If there are no wrong notes, then how can there be right ones?' It is essentially a musical gesture, a tirade rather than a symphony of protest and anger, that must have set off powerful resonances in the 1970s Soviet scene, in much the same way as did Solzhenitzyn's writings, but which sounds pretty thin a quarter of a century on. Rozhdestvensky's performance is committed, and the recording, made at a public performance in the Moscow Conservatoire in 1988, is well detailed. There is more rhetoric than substance here. The three stars are allotted for the performance and recording; for the composition the stars can be aleatoric!

(i) *Symphony No. 4;* (ii) *3 Sacred Hymns.*
*** Chandos Dig. CHAN 9463 [id.]. (i) Jaroslav Zdorov, Dmitri Pianov; (i–ii) Russian State Symphonic Cappella; (i) Russian State SO; Valery Polyansky.

The *Fourth Symphony* draws on Christian (Catholic,

Lutheran and Russian Orthodox) and Jewish chant and is avowedly religious in programme, reflecting episodes in the life of the Virgin Mary. It lasts 40 minutes and is scored for two singers, one a counter-tenor, chorus and orchestra; it also makes inventive and colourful use of keyboard sonorities. Readers with a keen interest in Schnittke will find both the performance and the recording to be of high quality. Others may share our less enthusiastic response to the piece: it seems too concerned with gesture and essentially empty of musical substance. The *Three Sacred Hymns* for *a cappella* choir from 1983 are both eloquent and beautiful.

Prelude in memoriam Shostakovich (for 2 solo violins).
*** Chandos Dig. CHAN 8988 [id.]. Mordkovitch, Young – PROKOFIEV; SHOSTAKOVICH: *Violin sonatas*. ***

The Schnittke *Prelude* for two solo violins is the shortest of the works on Lydia Mordkovitch's excellent disc of Soviet violin music, but it is among the most moving in its intense, elegiac way. She is well matched by her partner, Emma Young.

String quartet No. 2.
**(*) Collins Dig. 1450-2 [id.]. Duke Qt – SHOSTAKOVICH: *String quartet No. 8;* TCHAIKOVSKY: *String quartet No. 1.* **(*)

Schnittke's *First Quartet* dates from 1966, but he waited 14 years before returning to the medium in 1980. It was written as a memorial to the film director Larissa Shepitko, who died in a car accident the previous year. Its four movements convey pain and anguish and, even for those who find Schnittke's music more shadow than substance, it makes a strange and disturbing impact. The recording is a bit too closely balanced to warrant a full three-star recommendation but artistically this is a success.

Violin sonata No. 1; Sonata in the olden style.
*** Chandos Dig. CHAN 8343 [id.]. Dubinsky, Edlina – SHOSTAKOVICH: *Violin sonata.* ***

Schnittke's *First sonata* is a well-argued piece that seems to unify his awareness of the post-serial musical world with the tradition of Shostakovich. On this version it is linked with a pastiche of less interest, dating from 1977. Excellent playing from both artists, and very good recording too.

Piano sonata.
*** Chandos Dig. CHAN 8962 [id.]. Boris Berman – STRAVINSKY: *Serenade*, etc. ***

Berman gives as persuasive an account of Schnittke's *Piano sonata* as it is possible to imagine. He is very well recorded, too, and the three Stravinsky pieces with which it comes are also given with great pianistic elegance.

Piano trio.
(N) *** Nimbus Dig. NI 5572 [id.]. V. Piano Trio – SHOSTAKOVICH: *Trios, Opp. 8 & 67.* ***

Schnittke's *Piano trio* has its origins in a string trio written in 1985. In 1987 it was transcribed as the *trio sonata for chamber orchestra* and then in 1992 put into its present form. The Vienna Piano Trio give as convincing a performance as you are ever likely to hear, and they certainly get superb recorded sound.

OPERA

Leben mit einem Idioten (Life with an idiot): complete.
*** Sony Dig. S2K 52495 (2) [id.]. Duesing / Bischoff, Ringholz, Haskin, Zimnenko, Leggatte, Vocal Ens. & Rotterdam PO, Rostropovich.

This is a live recording, with Mstislav Rostropovich conducting, of the world première production of Schnittke's first opera, *Life with an idiot*, staged by Netherlands Opera in Amsterdam in the spring of 1992. Predictably, the piece defies operatic convention, which means that it is at least as effective on disc as when seen in the theatre. This is an adaptation not of Dostoevsky but of a story by a fellow dissident, Victor Erofeyev, who like Schnittke spent some of his youth in the West. It is an allegory of Soviet oppression. As an opera it hardly works, but Schnittke's often violent, always energetic score characteristically heightens nerve-jangling situations to make it an involving personal cantata, with incidental musical echoes of Stravinsky's comparably stylized domestic cantata, *The Wedding*. Rostropovich draws a vigorous performance from the Rotterdam Philharmonic, with Dale Duesing and Teresa Ringholz as the central character and his wife, both excellent, and with Howard Haskin providing peremptory interjections as the central character, Vova.

Schoeck, Othmar (1886–1957)

(i) *Horn concerto, Op. 65. Prelude for orchestra, Op. 48;* (ii) *Serenade for oboe, cor anglais and strings, Op. 27. Suite in A flat for strings.*
** CPO Dig. CPO 999 337-2 [id.]. (i) Bruno Schneider; (ii) Silvia Zabarella, Martin Zuchner; Coll. Musik, Winterthur, Werner Andreas Albert.

The major work here is the five-movement *Suite in A flat for strings*, which Schoeck composed in 1945. Although it is not quite as poignant as *Sommernacht*, there is some imaginative and expressive writing. The second movement, *Pastorale tranquillo*, has that sense of melancholy and nostalgia so characteristic of Schoeck. In it he imagined 'the peace and deep stillness of the forests'. The slightly later *Con-*

certo for horn and strings (1951) is well played by Bruno Schneider and is an appealing piece that will strike a responsive chord among all who care for late Strauss. The *Serenade for oboe, cor anglais and strings* is a five-minute interlude which Schoeck composed for a much-truncated production of his opera, *Don Ranudo*, at Leipzig in 1930. The *Prelude for orchestra* (1930) is new to records and serves as a reminder that Schoeck was at one time a pupil of Reger. Its textures lack transparency, but this is in part due to the rather opaque recording, made in a radio studio. It is perfectly acceptable, but the strings could do with more bloom and tuttis need to open out a little more.

Violin sonatas: in D, Op. 16; in E, Op. 46; in D, WoO22; Albumblatt, WoO70.
(N) ** Guild Dig. GMCD7142 [id.]. Paul Barritt, Catherine Edwards.

The two *D major Violin sonatas* come from the first decade of the present (soon to be last) century. The student essay of 1905 is of lesser interest, but Op. 16 was composed four years later at the time of Schoeck's infatuation with Stefi Geyer who also inspired his *Violin concerto* (1912) and the first concerto of Bartók. It has a strong vein of lyricism and a characteristic warmth of invention. The *Sonata in E major, Op. 46*, of 1931 inhabits a totally different world: it comes after *Penthesilea* and is closer in spirit to the *Notturno* for baritone and string quartet which it predates. Its musical language is less immediate, and in this respect could possibly be compared with late Fauré, though there is no resemblance in idiom. Paul Barritt and Catherine Edwards give very capable and sensitive performances and were the recording a little more spacious and less forward, this would gain the three stars.

Elegie (song cycle), *Op. 36.*
(N) ❀ *** CPO Dig. CPO 999 472-2 [id.]. Andreas Schmidt, Winterthur Music Collegium, Werner Andreas Albert.

This CD will be a revelation to those who doubt Schoeck's stature as one of the major twentieth-century masters of song. It is a work of astonishing beauty and imagination. The *Elegie, Op. 36*, is the first of his song cycles, and dates from 1922. It has been described as 'a narrative of a dying love' and to some extent charts the turbulent course of the composer's affair with the pianist Mary de Senger. The cycle comprises 24 short but concentrated settings of poems by Lenau and Eichendorff, and is for baritone and a small instrumental ensemble, used with great subtlety and resource. The songs are powerfully evocative and beautifully fashioned; each one immediately establishes its own atmosphere within a bar or two, and draws the listener completely into its world. Almost any would serve as an example but particularly potent is the third, *Stille Sicherheit*, which is extraordinarily concentrated in feeling, or the wonderfully haunting *Vesper*, with its tolling bells and almost tangible halflights. This is deeply felt music with a wonderful sense of line, and Andreas Schmidt sings with tremendous conviction. Werner Andreas Albert gets very sensitive and supportive playing from the Winterthur ensemble and the CPO recording is first class.

3 Lieder, Op. 35; 6 Lieder, Op. 51; Das Wandsbecker Liederbuch, Op. 52; Im Nebel; Wiegenlied.
** Jecklin Dig. JD677-2 [id.]. Juliane Banse, Dieter Henschel, Wolfram Rieger.

Das Wandsbecker Liederbuch is a latterday equivalent of the Hugo Wolf Songbooks; they offer a portrait of a poet (in this case Mathius Claudius) rather than a thematically connected cycle, and the songs, though highly conservative in idiom, are full of subtleties and depth, as indeed are the remaining songs on this CD. They are decently sung and recorded, and admirers of Schoeck's art need not hesitate.

Der Sänger (The Singer), Op. 57.
** Koch-Schwann Dig. 310921 [id.]. Frieder Lang, Ruth Lang-Oester.

Der Sänger is a setting of 26 poems by the 19th-century Swiss poet, Heinrich Leuthold, to whose work Schoeck's friend, Hermann Hesse, had introduced him. Its sentiment harmonized with Schoeck's own feelings of melancholia and the feeling that he had been denied the recognition to which his talents entitled him. Like the other late song-cycles *Unter Sternen* (*Under the stars*) and *Das stille Leuchten* (*The silent light*) it contains songs of great beauty.

OPERA

Venus (complete).
*** MGB Musikszene Schweiz CD 6112 (2) [id.]. Lang, Popp, O'Neal, Fassbender, Skovhus, Alföldi, Heidelberg Kammer Ch., Basle Boys' Ch., Swiss Youth PO, Venzago.

Venus is based on a libretto by Schoeck's school-friend, Armin Rüeger, who drew on two sources for his text: Prosper Mérimée's *La Vénus d'Ille* and a short story by Eichendorff called *Das Marmorbild*. The basic argument is simple and comes from Ovid, though Rüeger sets the action in a country castle in the south of France. The tenor role is particularly demanding and may have hampered the work reaching the international stage. Venzago's conducting radiates total dedication, and so does the playing of the young Swiss orchestra. The opening scene almost prompts one's thoughts to turn to the Strauss of *Ariadne*, but as the opera unfolds Venzago's view of the work as partly 'an enormous orchestral poem (exposition, development, Scherzo and recapitulation) with obbligato voices' seems more and more valid. The sheer quality of the invention is notable amd many of the ideas, particularly the Venus motive, have great tenderness and delicacy. Schoeck's scoring is superb, and those who know *Penthesilea* should lose no time in acquiring this glorious score. The performance may not be absolutely ideal vocally, but it is worth putting up with that for the sake of such beautiful music. Good and atmospheric recording.

Schoenberg, Arnold (1874–1951)

'*Arnold Schoenberg Exposition*'.
(M) **(*) Sony SM4K 62364 (4).

This four-CD survey gives the listener an opportunity to investigate Schoenberg's development and also to make an assessment of his atonal explorations. In making a powerful contribution to the influence of the Second Viennese School, Schoenberg left a trail of wreckage behind in the field of traditional writing. Other composers, less individually suited to the straitjacket of the atonal system, climbed aboard the bandwagon, often with disastrous results (for them and us), and the onward progress of tonal diatonic writing was forced into a musical backwater. Fortunately times are changing, and it will be interesting to see how much of Schoenberg's output survives to become part of the major repertoire of the twenty-first century.

'*The Early tonal years*': (i) *Chamber symphony No. 1, Op. 9;* (ii) *Verklaerte Nacht (String sextet), Op. 4;* (iii) *Friede auf Erden, Op. 13;* (iv) *Gurrelieder: Song of the wood-dove.*
(M) *** Sony SMK 62019. (i) Marlborough Festival O (members); (ii) Trampler, Ma, Juilliard String Qt; (iii) BBC Singers; (iv) Jessye Norman, Ens. InterContemporain (members), Boulez.

The first disc, not unexpectedly, opens with Schoenberg's post-Wagnerian *Verklaerte Nacht* with its erotically potent, Tristanesque chromaticism, written in 1902. The Juilliard performance of what is in effect a symphonic poem for string sextet is highly charged but rather over-characterized. The composer's volatile but seamless, sensuous flow does not proceed as evenly as would be ideal. Nevertheless, technically it is marvellously played and richly and atmospherically recorded. In 1906 Schoenberg took a new path with the polyphonically complex *First Chamber Symphony* for 15 instruments. The Marlborough performance is committed and highly spontaneous. *Friede auf Erden* ('Peace on earth') for unaccompanied chorus was written the following year, its part-writing even more thornily complex. Here its vocal difficulties, which inhibited early performances, are readily surmounted by the BBC Singers under Boulez and they make it sound almost mellifluous. In the lovely *Lied der Waldtaube* ('Song of the wood dove') from *Gurrelieder*, Jessye Norman is a radiant soloist, crowning her performance with a thrilling top B flat.

'*The Expressionist years*': (i) *String quartet No. 2 in F sharp min., Op. 10;* (ii) *6 Small pieces for piano, Op. 19;* (iii) *Pierrot lunaire, Op. 21;* (iv) *Die glückliche Hand, Op. 18.*
(M) **(*) Sony SMK 62020. (i) Valente, Juilliard String Qt; (ii) Glenn Gould; (iii) Yvonne Minton (reciter), Debost, Pay, Zukerman, Harrell, Barenboim; (iv) Nimsgern, BBC Singers and SO; (iii; iv) Boulez.

The *Second String quartet* (1907–8) is individual and powerful; its last two movements (both slow) are intensified by the contribution of the soprano Benita Valente. The Juilliards are less sympathetic than they were in *Verklaerte Nacht*: there is no lack of intensity but there is a want of real *pianissimo*, intensified by the close balance. Glenn Gould displays a ready grasp of the six minuscule piano *Pieces* (1911). But the key work here is *Pierrot lunaire* (1912), a setting of 21 poems by Albert Giraud for recitalist and modest-sized instrumental ensemble, which brings many technical and interpretative problems. As can be seen from the cast-list here, the performance gathers together a distinguished group of instrumentalists, but the result is lacking in the expressive intensity one expects of Boulez in this music. With Yvonne Minton eschewing sing-speech, the vocal line is too precisely pitched. Boulez's approach places Schoenberg's score within the mainstream of vocal writing, and many listeners will relish the comparative lack of difficulty in coming to terms with its highly original language. *Die glückliche Hand* (which the composer translated as 'The hand of Fate') is much more successful, with Nimsgern an impressive bass soloist. The disc ends with a six-minute interview with Halsey Stephens, 'Schoenberg the painter', recorded in 1949.

'*Dodecaphony*': (i) *Variations for orchestra, Op. 31;* (ii) *Suite for piano, Op. 25;* (iii) *Moses und Aron: Act II, scene 3.*
(M) ** Sony SMK 62021. (i; iii) BBC SO, Boulez; (ii) Glenn Gould; (iii) Palmer, Knight, Manning, Watts, Cassilly, Winfield, Hermann, Orpheus Boys' Ch.

Boulez's strong, compulsive account of the orchestral *Variations* is also available coupled with a matching orchestral version of *Verklaerte Nacht* (see below). Here it is supplemented by a recorded talk by the composer, made by Radio Frankfurt in 1931. Gould's 1964 recording of the piano *Suite*, Op. 25, has the expected concentration. But it was a curious idea to select just the third scene of the second Act of *Moses and Aron* (1932), effective though it is, when the complete recording of the opera from which it comes is readily available. It is certainly well performed and recorded.

'*Schoenberg in America*': (i) *Piano concerto in C, Op. 42;* (ii) *Phantasy for violin with piano accompaniment, Op. 47;* (iii) *String trio, Op. 45;* (iv) *Dreimal tausand Jahre, Op. 50a;* (v) *Kol Nidre, Op. 39;* (vi) *Psalm 130, Op. 50b;* (vii) *A survivor from Warsaw, Op. 46.*

(M) *** Sony SMK 62022. (i) Ax, Philh. O, Salonen; (ii) Menuhin, Gould; (iii) Juilliard Qt (members); (iv; vi) BBC Singers; (vii) Günther Reich; (v; vii) Shirley-Quirk, BBC Ch. & SO; (iv–vii) Boulez.

With Schoenberg's *Piano concerto* we take a jump of a decade to 1942. It is a work which consciously echoes the world of the romantic concerto in 12-note serial terms, but the thick and (at times) glutinous textures favoured by the composer tend to obscure the focus of the argument rather than making it sweeter on the ear. The soloist, Emanuel Ax, immediately displays an engaging lyrical feeling at the opening, and his performance is warmly sympathetic (the *Giocoso* finale very attractively handled). But despite flatteringly luminous (1992) recording, made in Watford Town Hall, Salonen does not convince the listener that the work is orchestrally a complete success. Of Schoenberg's final two chamber works, the intractable *String trio* was begun in 1946 when the composer was in hospital, recovering from a heart attack; Schoenberg suggested that its restless progress reflected the course of his illness, treatment and convalescence. It is confidently played by the Juilliard group and the 1985 recording is very well balanced. The *Phantasy for violin and piano* (1949), though not opening very invitingly, is perhaps marginally more approachable. This distinguished account by Menuhin and Gould is a mono recording from 1965, made by CBC in Toronto, and it is of first-class quality. But perhaps the most striking music here, apart from *A survivor from Warsaw* with its extraordinary opening so vividly and dramatically projected, is the remaining triptych of vocal pieces from the BBC Singers. In such choral works, particularly when inspired by a Jewish theme, as in the magnificent *Kol Nidre* of 1938 for narrator, mixed chorus and orchestra, the composer's full romanticism broke out. Fine performances and excellent sound.

(i) *Accompaniment to a motion picture scene, Op. 34;* (ii) *Chamber symphony No. 1, Op. 9;* (i; iii) *Die Jakobsleiter* (oratorio fragments, completed Zillig).

(M) *** Sony SMK 48462 [id.]. (i) BBC SO; (ii) Ens. InterContemporain (members); (iii) Nimsgern, Bowen, Partridge, Hudson, Shirley-Quirk, Rolfe Johnson, Wenkel, Mesplé, BBC Singers; Boulez.

It is good to see the reappearance of Boulez's first Schoenberg survey on Sony at mid-price, even if, as seems likely, he re-records the repertory. The performance of the film scene is as atmospheric as one would expect, if not as emotionally involved as the *Chamber Symphony*, given a strong, warmly enjoyable account. (The second *Chamber Symphony* is coupled with *Moses und Aron* – see below.) *Die Jakobsleiter* is an ambitious oratorio, which he left fully sketched out. It was completed and orchestrated by Winifried Zillig, revealing an exceptionally powerful piece. Strongly cast, the performance has passion and commitment and the recording projects it vividly.

Chamber Symphonies Nos. 1–2; (i) *Piano concerto, Op. 42.*

*** Ph. Dig. 446 683-2 [id.]. (i) Alfred Brendel; SW German RSO, Baden-Baden, Michael Gielen.

Alfred Brendel has been a lifelong champion of the *Piano concerto*: this is his third recording and it is undoubtedly the most telling, partly because the knotty orchestral textures are brightly revealed in a recording which is admirably clear yet does not lack fullness, while the balance with the piano is admirable. The performance is strong, impassioned in the *Adagio*, with the mixtures of *grotesquerie* and *giocoso* nicely juxtaposed in the finale, where Brendel's contribution is quite brilliant. Michael Gielen is a committed partner, subtle in his rhythmic inflexions and bringing plenty of vitality to the accompaniment, matching Brendel's dash in the last movement. The choice of coupling seems apt when the two *Chamber Symphonies* have never been more enjoyable on record, their diverse moods and amazing range of colouring caught with lyrical warmth and detail finely and affectionately observed. The orchestral playing is of the very highest calibre. Indeed Gielen finds both charm and gaiety (rare commodities with Schoenberg) in the *con fuoco* finale of No. 2, although of course the movement ends in dark melancholy. Again first-rate recording. A major addition to the Schoenberg discography.

(i) *Chamber Symphony No. 1 , Op. 9;* (ii) *5 Pieces for orchestra;* (i) *Variations, Op. 31; Verklaerte Nacht;* (iii) *Erwartung, Op. 17; 6 Songs, Op. 8.*

(B) **(*) Double Decca Analogue/Dig. 448 279-2 (2). (i) LAPO, Mehta; (ii) Cleveland O, or (iii) VPO, with Anja Silja, Dohnányi.

It was to Los Angeles that Schoenberg moved to live out his last years, and it would have gladdened him that his local orchestra had achieved a degree of brilliance to match that of any orchestra in America. The *First Chamber Symphony* is given a rich performance under Mehta, arguably too fast at times but full of understanding for the romantic emotions which underlie much of the writing. The Op. 31

Variations, among the most taxing works Schoenberg ever wrote, somehow reveal their secrets and their unmistakable greatness more clearly when the performance has such a sense of drive. Mehta's *Verklaerte Nacht* has warmth and intensity yet is free of schmalz; it is sympathetically recorded and the Los Angeles strings play with great virtuosity and opulence of tone. The Cleveland Orchestra are comparably at home in Schoenberg's seminal *Five Pieces*. Their perfection of ensemble goes with a remarkable depth of feeling, and the digital recording, full, rich and weighty, is of demonstration standard, not as brightly lit as the quality the Decca engineers provide for Mehta. Schoenberg's searingly intense monodrama, *Erwartung*, makes an apt bonus. Silja is at her most committed. The sound under pressure may be raw, but the self-tortured questionings of the central character come over grippingly; again the digital sound is outstandingly vivid.

(i) *Chamber Symphony No. 1, Op. 9;* (ii; iii) *Erwartung;* (iii) *Variations for orchestra, Op. 31.*
*** EMI Dig. CDC5 55212-2. (i) Birmingham Contemporary Music Group; (ii) Bryn-Julson; (iii) CBSO; Sir Simon Rattle.

With Rattle there is no question of missing the heart behind the composer's severe intellectual argument. In the *Chamber Symphony No. 1* Rattle, with 15 players from the Birmingham Contemporary Music Group, springs rhythms infectiously, relaxedly bringing out the thrust of argument. The playing may not be as bitingly crisp as in some rival versions but it has far more character, thanks to both conductor and players. By contrast, he is daringly expansive in the *Variations* of 1928, even more so than Karajan in his classic recording with the Berlin Philharmonic. The Birmingham players may not always be quite so refined as the Berliners, but they play with even greater emotional thrust and with a keener sense of mystery, while heightened dynamic contrasts add to the dramatic bite. Equally in Schoenberg's taxing atonal vocal lines, Phyllis Bryn-Julson sings with a clarity and definition to coax the ear instead of assaulting it. She may not be as dominant or powerful as Jessye Norman in her Philips recording (see below), but, bright and clear, she gives a more vulnerable portrait, tender and compelling, with Rattle more urgent than James Levine for Norman. Superb sound.

Piano concerto, Op. 42.
*** Chandos Dig. CHAN 9375. Malling, Danish Nat. RSO, Schønwandt (with SCHUMANN: *Piano concerto*. *(*))

Amalie Malling proves an intelligent and sympathetic soloist who, if not more persuasive than some of her better-known rivals such as Pollini and Brendel, is every bit as convincing. Michael Schønwandt gets very good results from the Danish orchestra and the texture is lucid and transparent, and splendidly recorded. The coupling is, however, not completely logical or particularly successful. This needs a reissue with the pairing better thought out.

(i; ii) *Piano concerto, Op. 42*; (ii; iii) *Violin concerto, Op. 33*; (iv) *Pelleas und Melisande, Op. 5*; *Variations, Op. 31*.
(N) (B) *** Erato/Warner/Ultima Dig. 3984 24241-2 (2) [id.]. (i) Peter Serkin, (ii) LSO; (iii) Pierre Amoyal; (iv) Chicago SO; Pierre Boulez.

A good and inexpensive introduction to Schoenberg ranging from the early, lush *Pelleas und Melisande* to the intractable yet rewarding *Violin concerto* and the masterly *Variations for orchestra*, in authoritative performances and exemplary recordings.

Concerto for string quartet and orchestra after Handel's Concerto grosso, Op. 6/7.
(N) *** Arabesque Dig. Z 6723 [id.]. San Francisco Ballet O, Lark Qt., Jean-Louis Le Roux – HANDEL: *Concerto grosso in B flat, Op. 6/7.* ELGAR: *Introduction and allegro for strings*; SPOHR: *Concerto for string quartet and orchestra*. ***

In his extraordinarily bizarre pastiche, Schoenberg (in 1933) virtually recomposed Handel's Op. 6/7 for string quartet and large modern orchestra, adding a plentiful spicing of dissonance and special effects, even string harmonics. The result, inflated to nearly twice the length of the original, is at times grotesque, but always aurally fascinating and entertaining, for Handel's underlying tunefulness keeps bursting through. The performance has plenty of edge, vitality and colour and it was a bright idea to include also Handel's original (in a performance for full modern strings) so the listener can switch back and forth between the two utterly different sound worlds.

Pelleas und Melisande (symphonic poem), *Op. 5*.
(N) (***) Music & Arts mono CD 967 [id.]. VPO, Dmitri Mitropoulos – SCRIABIN: *Prometheus*. (***)
(N) *(*) Koch Dig. 3-7316-2 [id.]. Houston SO, Eschenbach – WEBERN: *Passacaglia*. *(*)

It was Richard Strauss who suggested to Schoenberg the subject of Maeterlinck's drama as an opera. Schoenberg opted for a Straussian symphonic poem, and this he completed before he ever knew that Debussy had turned the same subject into an opera.

A remarkable document from Mitropoulos with the Vienna Philharmonic Scriabin. The sound calls for some considerable tolerance but the performance of *Pelleas und Melisande* has great eloquence and fervour.

Christoph Eschenbach and the Houston Symphony were recorded at concert performances but strangely enough they sound curiously cautious and careful.

Pelleas und Melisande, Op. 5; Variations for orchestra, Op. 31; Verklaerte Nacht (orchestral version), *Op. 4*.
(M) *** DG 427 424-2 (3). BPO, Karajan – BERG: *Lyric suite; 3 Pieces;* WEBERN: *Collection*. ***

The Straussian opulence of Schoenberg's early symphonic poem has never been as ravishingly presented as by Karajan and the Berlin Philharmonic in this splendidly recorded version. The gorgeous tapestry of sound is both rich and full of refinement and detail, while the thrust of argument is powerfully conveyed. These are superb performances which present the emotional element at full power but give unequalled precision and refinement. The Op. 31 *Variations*, the most challenging of Schoenberg's orchestral works, here receives a reading which vividly conveys the ebb and flow of tension within the phrase and over the whole plan. Superb recording, excellently remastered.

Pelleas und Melisande (symphonic poem), *Op. 5; Verklaerte Nacht, Op. 4*.
(M) *** DG 457 721-2 [id.]. BPO, Karajan.
*** DG Dig. (IMS) 439 942-2. Philh. O, Sinopoli.

Karajan's unsurpassed performances of these two early Schoenberg masterpieces, taken from the above set, makes an ideal candidate for separate reissue in DG's series of Originals.

In *Pelleas* Sinopoli, broad and expansive, cannot quite match the biting passion and sharp characterization of Karajan in his superb Berlin performance, but he finds an impressionistic beauty in this richly varied score which for once relates it to the Debussy masterpiece on the same subject. In *Verklaerte Nacht* Sinopoli does not draw such weight of sound from the Philharmonia strings as do some other versions which use the 1943 string orchestra score, but in his refinement he relates it more clearly to the chamber scale of the original sextet. Glowing sound to match.

(i) *Pelleas and Melisande (symphonic poem), Op. 5*; (ii) *Verklaerte Nacht, Op. 4* (string sextet version).
(N) (B) **(*) Ph. Double 462 309-2 (2). (i) Rotterdam PO, Zinman; (ii) augmented New Vienna Qt. – FAURE: *Pelléas et Mélisande; Pavane, Op. 50* ***. SIBELIUS *Pelléas et Mélisande; Swan of Tuonela*. **(*)

In a useful anthology of music inspired by Maeterlinck's play, Zinman's reading of Schoenberg's somewhat inflated symphonic poem is strongly characterized and very well played, finding warmth and refinement as well as passion. If the Rotterdam Orchestra cannot quite match Karajan's Berlin Philharmonic version, they are richly recorded in a glowing acoustic which flatters Schoenberg's sometimes pungent scoring. The inclusion of Schoenberg's other most famous early work seems apt, as it was written in 1899, three years before the symphonic poem. The choice of the string sextet rather than the orchestral version is perhaps less appropriate, but it is passionately played, and though the matching of the members of the augmented New Vienna Quartet is not flawless, they produce a full body of tone and the performance remains very persuasive.

3 Pieces for chamber orchestra (1910); *Suite, Op. 29; Verklaerte Nacht* (string sextet version), *Op. 4*.
(M) *** Sony Analogue/Dig. SMK 48465 [id.]. Ens. InterContemporain (members), Boulez.

Boulez first recorded *Verklaerte Nacht* in the version for full strings – see below – but this beautifully played account for solo strings is even more impressive. The neo-classical *Suite* – with Boulez this time conducting a mere seven players – reveals a totally different side of the composer, a spiky piece presented at its sharpest in this reading. There is no lack of intimacy and expressive feeling, and the CBS recording is first class. The *Three Pieces for chamber orchestra* were found after Schoenberg had died and date from 1910. They are atonal and the third piece was unfinished. This is an earlier analogue recording but of good quality.

(i) *5 Pieces for orchestra, Op. 16;* (ii) *Ode to Napoleon Buonaparte, Op. 41* (for string quartet, piano and reciter); (iii) *Serenade, Op. 24* (for clarinet, bass clarinet, mandolin, guitar, violin, viola, cello and bass voice).
(M) *** Sony SMK 48463 [id.]. (i) BBC SO; (ii) David Wilson-Johnson; (iii) John Shirley-Quirk; (ii; iii) Ens. InterContemporain (members), Boulez.

With Boulez, the *Five Pieces for orchestra* emerge as colourfully expressive, hardly more elusive than Debussy when played as strongly as this. The Abbey Road recording has plenty of body and atmosphere. The *Serenade* finds Schoenberg in rather crustily neo-classical mood, and even Boulez with his team (including Shirley-Quirk) cannot bring out all the lightness the composer seems to have intended. With David Wilson-Johnson a characterfully ironic narrator, the Byron setting of the *Ode to Napoleon* is more warmly memorable. Both are very clearly recorded and, if the balance is close, there is plenty of ambient warmth.

Variations for orchestra, Op. 31.
(N) (**) Orfeo C 488 981 B [id.]. BPO, Mitropoulos – DEBUSSY: *La Mer* (**); MENDELSSOHN: *Symphony No. 3*. (**)

This was recorded at the Salzburg Festival in 1960

and is obviously a performance of stature. Indeed, listening through the execrable recording, it is clear that Mitropoulos is producing great beauty of sound, as Karajan did in his DG recording with the same orchestra. But the frequency range is narrow and the tone is shrill and strident. Austrian Radio recordings of this period were not of good quality, and this calls for considerable tolerance.

Variations for orchestra, Op. 31; Verklaerte Nacht, Op. 4.
✿ *** DG 415 326-2. BPO, Karajan.

(i) *Variations for orchestra, Op. 31;* (ii) *Verklaerte Nacht, Op. 4;* (i; iii) *Die glückliche Hande, Op. 18.*
(M) **(*) Sony SMK 48464 [id.]. (i) BBC SO; (ii) NYPO; (iii) Siegmund Nimsgern, BBC Singers; Boulez.

Karajan's version of *Verklaerte Nacht* is altogether magical and very much in a class of its own. There is a tremendous intensity and variety of tone and colour: the palette that the strings of the Berlin Philharmonic have at their command is altogether extraordinarily wide-ranging.

Boulez's BBC account of the *Variations* and the New York performance of *Verklaerte Nacht* may lack the warmth, final polish and subtlety of Karajan's celebrated versions, but Boulez's earthiness, unrelentingly forceful, is compelling in the former, while in the latter he has the full measure of Schoenberg's poetry and secures responsive playing from the New York strings. The Sony recording is vivid but not as richly beautiful as the Berlin sound. There is also a bonus here in the 'psychological pantomime', *Die glückliche Hande*, which is sharply observed, with Nimsgern a fine soloist.

Verklaerte Nacht.
(BB) *** RCA Navigator 74321 29243-2. Georgian State CO, Liana Isakadze – BERG: *Violin concerto*; WEBERN: *Passacaglia for orchestra.* ***
(N) (**) Music & Arts mono CD991 [id.]. VPO, Dmitri Mitropoulos – SCHMIDT: *Symphony No. 2.* (**)

On the evidence of this CD, the Georgian State Chamber Orchestra have a first-class string section, and they play Schoenberg's sensuous string work with a uniquely Slavonic ardour to grip the listener in the intensity of the final climax. Isakadze controls the emotional ebb and flow unerringly, and there is refinement here as well as passion. The recording is admirably full and vivid, and this comes at the lowest possible price with two other key twentieth-century works.

Mitropoulos's account of *Verklärte Nacht* with the Vienna Philharmonic strings comes from a concert he conducted a year or so before his death. It must rank among the finest of its period – including the superb commercial recording he made with the New York Philharmonic. Here is a conductor who is really made of music and deserves his reputation. The wonderful playing, alas, is not matched by wonderful recording.

(i) *Verklaerte Nacht, Op. 4; 5 Orchestral pieces, Op. 16;* (ii) (Piano): *3 Pieces, Op. 11; 6 Little Pieces, Op. 19.* arr. BUSONI: *Piece, Op. 11/2 (Konzertmässige interpretation).*
*** Teldec/Warner Dig. 4509 98256-2. (i) Chicago SO, Barenboim; (ii) Barenboim (piano).

Barenboim's Teldec reading of *Verklaerte Nacht* in the 1943 string orchestra version is weighty and passionate, with the Chicago strings playing superbly, while the *Five Orchestral pieces* are comparably purposeful and sharply characterized. They lead naturally to the miniatures for piano, which Barenboim interprets with persuasive warmth, treating them rather like Brahms 'with the wrong notes'. He concludes with a fascinating rarity, an elaborate rearrangement of the second of the Op.11 *Pieces* which Busoni made in 1909, turning it into something close to late Liszt. The notes are excellent, with copious musical illustrations. Warm sound, if not ideally detailed in the orchestral works.

Verklaerte Nacht, Op. 4 (string sextet version).
✿ (***) Testament mono SBT 1031 Hollywood Qt, with Alvin Dinkin, Kurt Reher – SCHUBERT: *String quintet.* (***) ✿
*** Hyperion Dig. CDA 66425 [id.]. Raphael Ens. – KORNGOLD: *Sextet.* ***

The 1950 Hollywood account was the first version of *Verklaerte Nacht* in its original sextet form ever to appear on records, and arguably it remains unsurpassed and possibly unequalled. This almost flawless performance enjoyed the imprimatur of Schoenberg himself, who supplied the sleeve-note for it (reproduced in the excellent booklet), the only time he ever did so. The sound is remarkably good and very musical. Recommended with enthusiasm.

For those wanting a modern, digital version, the Raphael Ensemble have the advantage of very good recorded sound and give a fine account of Schoenberg's score. They also have the advantage of a rarity in their coupling, the youthful *Sextet* of Korngold.

(i) *Verklaerte Nacht* (string sextet version), *Op. 4;* (ii) *String quartet No. 2 in F sharp min., Op. 10.*
(B) **(*) DG Classikon 439 470-2. LaSalle Qt, with (i) McInnes and Pegis; (ii) Margaret Price – WEBERN: *6 Bagatelles* etc. ***

For those who feel that Schoenberg's *Verklaerte Nacht* is best served by the version for solo strings, the LaSalle Quartet give a virtuosic account with no lack of expressive feeling. At times they are inclined to rush things, but the digital recording, if rather bright, is faithful enough. It is good also to have on this bargain disc, not just the chamber version of the post-Wagnerian symphonic poem, but also the rather later *Second Quartet*. Its last two movements (both slow) are intensified by the contribution of a soprano, here the secure and sympathetic Dame Margaret Price. Unfortunately the back-up notes (which are otherwise adequate) omit the words of her two songs, settings of poems by Stefan George – *Litanei* and *Entrückung* ('Transport') – particularly as they are important in establishing the composer's intentions. The 1969 analogue recording, however, cannot be faulted, and the couplings are well chosen and generous.

OTHER CHAMBER MUSIC

String quartets Nos. 1 in D min., Op. 7; (i) *2 in F sharp min., Op. 10. 3, Op. 30; 4, Op. 37.*
(***) Archiphon ARC mono 103/4 [id.]. Kolisch Qt, (i) with C. Gifford.

No quartet has ever been more closely associated with these pieces than the Kolisch, and the present recordings were made at the turn of 1936–7. The Hollywood composer, Alfred Newman, who was studying with Schoenberg at the time, brought the quartet into the film studio and recorded the whole cycle as a present for the composer. They were straight performances with no re-takes, though the Kolisch always played these works (and other repertoire) by heart – with the exception of the *Fourth*, which was new. They recorded this work just before giving its première. It is well worth putting up with surface noise (which one soon barely notices anyway) for the sake of *real* music-making. Indeed, given phrasing of this quality, one is tempted to say that even the sceptic will be persuaded that there is more to the rigorously disciplined *Third* and *Fourth Quartets* than later ensembles have found; and never have the two earlier *Quartets* sounded so eloquent. The set contains a short speech of thanks by Schoenberg.

Piano music: *3 Pieces, Op. 11; 6 Small Pieces, Op. 19; 5 Pieces, Op. 23; 3 Pieces, Op. 33a & b; Suite, Op. 25.*
(M) *** DG (IMS) 423 249-2. Maurizio Pollini.

This CD encompasses Schoenberg's complete piano music. Pollini plays with enormous authority and refinement of dynamic nuance and colour, making one perceive this music in a totally different light from other performers. He is accorded excellent sound (very slightly on the dry side), extremely clear and well defined.

VOCAL MUSIC

Music for chorus: *2 Canons; 3 Canons, Op. 28; Dreimal Tausend Jähre, Op. 50a; Friede auf Erden, Op. 13; 3 Folksongs, Op. 49; 3 German folksongs; Kol Nidrei, Op. 39; 4 Pieces, Op. 27; 6 Pieces, Op. 35; Psalm 130, Op. 50b; Modern Psalm No. 1, Op. 50 C; A Survivor from Warsaw, Op. 46.*
(M) *** Sony S2K 44571 (2) [id.]. John Shirley-Quirk, Günther Reich, BBC Singers, BBC SO, Pierre Boulez.

With passionately committed performances from the BBC Singers, this superb collection of choral music explodes any idea that Schoenberg was a cold composer. His adoption of an idiom far removed from abrasive atonality in most of these pieces makes this one of the most approachable of Schoenberg sets, with the use of a narrator in three of the works adding spice to the mixture. The later works, written in America, use 12-note technique with astonishingly warm, rich results. First-rate recording. Translations are given of the full texts.

Choral works: *Dreimal Tausend Jahre, Op. 50a; 3 Folksongs, Op. 49; Friede auf Erden Op. 13; 4 Pieces, Op. 27; 6 Pieces, Op. 35; Psalm 130, Op. 50b; 3 Satires, Op. 28.*
(BB) *** Arte Nova/BMG Dig. 74321 27799-2 [id.]. South German R. Ch., Stuttgart, Huber.

Though this disc does not – as is claimed on the cover – contain the complete choral works, omitting those with orchestra for example, it offers most of the finest in superlative performances, beautifully recorded. Comparing these readings with those of Pierre Boulez in his pioneering recordings for Sony with the BBC Chorus, the Stuttgart choir is consistently crisper in ensemble and more clearly confident in matching and pitching. So much so that Rupert Huber, the conductor, can readily and without serious problem adopt faster, more flowing speeds, which give the performances greater impact. It is astonishing to find the early *Friede auf Erden* ('Peace on earth'), once thought to be unperformable, sung here with an expressive ease and confidence such as you might find in a Bach performance. At super-bargain price, an issue to suggest to anyone hitherto daunted by this bogeyman composer, as well as to his regular admirers.

Erwartung, Op. 17.
*** Decca Dig. 417 348-2 (2) [id.]. Anja Silja, VPO, Dohnányi – BERG: *Wozzeck.* ***
(M) (**(*)) Sony Heritage mono MH2K 62759 (2) [id.]. Dow, NYPO, Mitropoulos – BERG: *Wozzeck*; KRENEK: *Symphonic elegy.* (***)

Schoenberg's searingly intense monodrama makes an apt and generous coupling for Dohnányi's excellent version of Berg's *Wozzeck*. As in the Berg, Silja is at her most passionately committed, and the digital sound is exceptionally vivid.

Mitropoulos recorded Schoenberg's sinister monodrama in 1951, the same year as his recordings of *Wozzeck* and the Krenek piece. Unlike the Berg opera, this was recorded in the studio and, though the performance does not crackle with quite such high-voltage electricity, it has similar clarity and purposefulness. Dorothy Dow tackles the formidable vocal line with freshness and clarity, though the timbre of her voice, firm but with a hint of flutter, does not provide quite enough variety to bring out the full emotional weight of the central character's soul-searching on finding the body of her lover. The result is not as chilling as it can be, though satisfying musically. As with the Berg, full libretto and translations are provided, but this CD is comparatively expensive.

(i) *Erwartung*. (ii) Cabaret songs: *Arie aus dem Spiegel von Arcadien; Einfältiges Lied; Galathea; Der genügsame Liebhaber; Jedem das Seine; Mahnung; Nachtwandler* (with trumpet, piccolo & snare drum).

*** Ph. (IMS) Dig. 426 261-2. Jessye Norman; (i) Met. Op. O, Levine; (ii) James Levine (piano).

The monodrama, *Erwartung* – 'Expectation' – may be among the least appealing of Schoenberg's formidable *œuvre*, but Jessye Norman and James Levine present it on a Philips disc which could well win the composer more friends than any ever issued before. She herself has said that *Erwartung* is 'technically the most difficult thing I have ever sung' but that, having learnt it, she found it 'immensely singable'. That clearly accounts for the warmth, intensity, range of expression and sheer beauty that she and Levine bring to this score. Levine draws ravishing sounds from the Metropolitan Opera Orchestra; Jessye Norman's singing, beautiful and totally secure over the widest range of expression and dynamic, is a revelation too. Compare this with Anja Silja, accompanied by Christoph von Dohnányi on their fine Decca issue, and the extra depth, range of emotion and refinement of the New York performance come out at every point. The impact of this *Erwartung* is brilliantly heightened by the total contrast of the Schoenberg coupling. Accompanied by Levine at the piano – a sparkily individual partner – Jessye Norman sings all eight of the cabaret songs that Schoenberg wrote when he was working in Berlin. In these witty, pointed, tuneful songs Schoenberg was letting his hair down in a way that to his detractors must be almost unimaginable. These are art-songs that yet completely belong to the half-world of cabaret and Jessye Norman projects her personality as masterfully as a latterday Marlene Dietrich.

(i) *Erwartung, Op. 17*; (ii) *Pierrot Lunaire, Op. 21*.

(N) ** Teldec/Warner Dig. 3984 22901-2 [id.]. (i) Luisa Castellani, Andrea Lucchesini, members of Dresden State O; (ii) Alessandra Marc; Dresden State O, Sinopoli.

Sinopoli, a sympathetically persuasive interpreter of Schoenberg, who brings out any underlying romanticism, offers an apt coupling not otherwise available – but the results are flawed. The live recording of *Erwartung* has Alessandra Marc as a warm-toned soloist with a rich chest register, who sings well, but conveys little of the horror behind this monodrama. Luisa Castellani in *Pierrot lunaire* is intimately confidential in her sing-speech recitations, but too often is masked by the instruments, which are balanced too far forward.

Gurrelieder.

(N) *** Teldec Dig. 4509-98424-2(2). Moser, Voigt, Larmore, Weikl, Riegel, Brandauer, Saxon State Op. Ch., Dresden, Leipzig R. Ch., Prague Male Ch., Dresden State O, Sinopoli.

*** DG Dig. 439 944-2 (2). Sweet, Jerusalem, Lipovšek, Wekler, Langridge, Sukowa, Vienna State Op. Ch., Schoenberg Ch., Slovak Phil Ch., BPO, Abbado.

*** Decca Dig. 430 321-2 (2) [id.]. Jerusalem, Dunn, Fassbaender, Brecht, Haage, Hotter, St Hedwig's Cathedral Ch., Berlin, Düsseldorf State Musikverein, Berlin RSO, Chailly.

(i) *Gurrelieder;* (ii) *4 Orchestral songs*.

(M) *** Sony SM2K 48459 (2) [id.]. (i) Jess Thomas, Napier, Nimsgern, Bowen, Reich, BBC Singers & Ch. Soc., Goldsmith's Ch. Union, Men's voices of LPO Ch.; (i; ii) Yvonne Minton, BBC SO; Boulez.

In his highly compelling live recording, Sinopoli conducts the most sensuous reading of *Gurrelieder* on record, bringing out all its high romantic voluptuousness. Speeds are spacious, thanks in part to his expressive freedom, and anyone who has ever thought of Schoenberg as cold should certainly hear this, magnetic from first to last, helped by rich, immediate sound. The soloists are excellent, even if Thomas Moser as Waldemar is gritty at times in a Wagnerian way. While the Abbado and Chailly versions are by no means upstaged (the latter with a superb Decca recording) and Boulez, too, has his own special insights to offer, this new Sinopoli set could well be first choice for many collectors.

Recorded live in the Philharmonie, Berlin, Abbado's version begins magnetically with the most delicate tracery of sound, immediately capturing both atmosphere and dramatic intensity. Though Siegfried Jerusalem as Waldemar is not quite as firmly focused as he was on Riccardo Chailly's Decca set, he conveys more passion, and regularly Abbado's reading is freer and more volatile than Chailly's, with a sense of wonder enhanced by the very atmosphere of a concert. Susan Dunn as Tove in Chailly's version is firmer and truer than Abbado's Sharon Sweet, whose tight vibrato is often intrusive, but this is a strong, characterful reading, and Marjana Lipovšek is deeply moving as the Wood-dove, with the hushed tension behind her big solo tellingly conveyed. Philip Langridge is outstanding as Klaus-Knarr and Hartmut Welker makes a bluff if slightly unsteady Peasant. The only soloist who is controversial is the woman speaker, Barbara Sukowa, whose use of sliding *Sprech-Stimme*, chattering in the style of *Pierrot lunaire*, comes near to being comic. With the Berlin Philharmonic's playing richly and atmospherically caught, this must now stand as a first choice among live recordings, though the extra weight and detail of the sound in Chailly's studio version will for many make that still preferable.

Chailly's magnificent recording of Schoenberg's massive *Gurrelieder* remains highly recommendable. Siegfried Jerusalem as Waldemar is not only warm and firm of tone, but imaginative too. Susan Dunn makes a sweet, touchingly vulnerable Tove, while Brigitte Fassbaender gives darkly baleful intensity to the message of the Wood-dove. Hans Hotter is a characterful Speaker in the final section. The impact of the performance is the more telling with sound both atmospheric and immediate, bringing a fine sense of presence, not least in the final choral outburst.

Boulez's warm, expressive style using slow, luxuriating tempi brings out the operatic quality behind Schoenberg's massive score. With Boulez, the Wagnerian overtones are richly expressive and, though Marita Napier and Jess Thomas are not especially sweet on the ear, they show the big, heroic qualities which this score ideally demands, while Yvonne Minton is magnificent in the *Song of the Wood-dove*. Boulez builds that beautiful section to an ominous climax and, at mid-price, remains competitive, for the CBS/Sony recording has attractively vivid and atmospheric sound, and this set also offers a generous coupling of Yvonne Minton's fine account of the *Orchestral songs*.

Pierrot lunaire, Op. 21 (see also above, under *The Book of the Hanging Gardens*).

(M) *** Chandos CHAN 6534 [id.]. Jane Manning, Nash Ens., Rattle – WEBERN: *Concerto*. ***

Jane Manning is outstanding among singers who have tackled this most taxing of works, steering a masterful course between the twin perils of, on the one hand, actually singing and, on the other, simply speaking; her sing-speech brings out the element of irony and darkly pointed wit that is an essential. Rattle draws strong, committed performances from the members of the Nash Ensemble and, apart from some intermittently odd balances, the sound is excellent.

(i) *Pierrot lunaire, Op. 21; Herzgewächse, Op. 20*. (ii) *Ode to Napoleon Buonaparte, Op. 41*.

(N) *** DG Dig. 457 630-2 [id.]. (i) Christine Schäfer; (ii) David Pittman-Jennings; Soloists of Ensemble Intercontemporain, Boulez.

For *Pierrot lunaire*, Boulez imaginatively chooses a sweet-toned soprano and the result is the more revealing, in an element of beauty and mystery usually missing while the dramatic point of this cabaret-like sequence is never underplayed. Balance is excellent, with the Ensemble Intercontemporain playing with warmth and brilliance, as they do in the brief *Herzgewächse* (Schäfer again radiant) and in the *Ode to Napoleon*. David Pittman-Jennings takes an idiosyncratic view of the narration, reciting in a stylized way as though English is a foreign language, but it is good to have this neglected work so well played and recorded.

OPERA

Moses und Aron.

*** Decca (IMS) Dig. 414 264-2 (2) [id.]. Mazura, Langridge, Bonney, Haugland, Chicago Ch. and SO, Solti.

(i) *Moses und Aron* (complete); (ii) *Chamber Symphony No. 2, Op. 38*.

(M) *** Sony SM2K 48456 (2). (i) Reich, Cassilly, Palmer, Knight, BBC Singers, Orpheus Boys' Ch., BBC SO; (ii) Ens. InterContemporain; Boulez.

Solti gives Schoenberg's masterly score a dynamism and warmth which set it firmly – if perhaps surprisingly – in the grand romantic tradition, yet finds an element of fantasy and, in places – as in the *Golden Calf* episode – a sparkle such as you would never expect from Schoenberg. The Moses of Franz Mazura may not be as specific in his sing-speech as was Gunter Reich in the two previous versions – far less sing than speech – but the characterization of an Old Testament patriarch is the more convincing. As Aaron, Philip Langridge is lighter and more lyrical, as well as more accurate, than his predecessor with Boulez, Richard Cassilly. Aage Haugland with his firm, dark bass makes his mark in the small role of the Priest; Barbara Bonney too is excellent as the Young Girl. Above all, the brilliant singing of the Chicago Symphony Chorus matches the playing of the orchestra in virtuosity. More than ever the question-mark concluding Act II makes a pointful close, with no feeling of a work unfinished. The brilliant recording has an even sharper focus on CD.

Pierre Boulez is helped not just by the passionately committed singing and playing (with Günter Reich expansive in his fully rounded characterization of Moses) but also by the rich, atmospheric recording, so that the operatic qualities are allowed to blossom. It is typical of Boulez that in the final scene Moses' mounting frustration in the face of the glib, articulate Aaron is superbly built up, so that the final words – *O Wort, du Wort das mir fehlt* – come with a compelling sense of tragedy. Though the composer planned a third Act, such a moment makes a telling conclusion. Richard Cassilly makes a big-scaled Aaron, a worthy brother-adversary to the central tragic figure. The *Second Chamber Symphony*, given an equally committed performance, follows the end of the opera to make a good bonus on the second CD.

Schreker, Franz (1878–1934)

(i) *Chamber symphony for 23 solo instruments;* (ii) *Nachtstück;* (i) *Prelude to a drama;* (ii) *Valse lente.*

**(*) Koch Int. Dig. CD 311 078. Berlin RSO, (i) Gielen, (ii) Rickenbacher.

Schreker's *Chamber symphony* is quite magical, scored with great delicacy and feeling for colour. The other works are not quite so seductive but they, too, have a heady art-nouveau atmosphere. A most rewarding disc, with good performances and very acceptable, though not out of the ordinary, recording. But don't miss this issue.

Der Geburtstag der Infantin.

(N) ** Edition Abseits Dig. ED A013-2 [id.]. Berlin Kammersymphonie, Jürgen Bruns – TOCH: *Tanz-Suite, Op. 30.* **

This is a first recording of the original 1910 version of Schreker's dance pantomime on Oscar Wilde's short story, *The birthday of the Infanta*. Schreker subsequently made a concert suite for full orchestra in 1923, and the original chamber orchestra version was believed lost. It surfaced during the 1980s in a Vienna Archive, having been misfiled. Good playing and recording.

Die Gezeichneten (opera): complete.

*** Decca (IMS) Dig. 444 442-2 (3) [id.]. Kruse, Connell, Pederson, Muff, Berlin R. Ch. & O, Zagrosek.

*(*) Marco Polo Dig. 8.223328/30 [id.]. Soloists, Dutch R. & TV Ch. & O, De Waart.

The opening prelude of this opera with its magic, shimmering sounds, using the most exotic orchestration, establishes the hothouse atmosphere of a story which in its melodrama can indeed be regarded as decadent, if hardly more so than Strauss's *Salome*. What Zagrosek's gloriously recorded version demonstrates is the range of atmospheric beauty in the score. Ripe echoes of composers from Scriabin to Puccini intensify the story of a dying woman painter, Carlotta, who deserts her faithful, ugly lover, Alviano, in favour of the physical love of Tamare, finally giving herself to him with fatal consequences. The Decca cast has no weak link, with Heinz Kruse fresh and clear-toned in the taxing tenor role of Alviano and Elizabeth Connell conveying with sharp clarity the positive yet vulnerable character of the heroine. Monte Pederson in cleanly focused singing conveys the animal quality of Tamare, while Alfred Muff is well contrasted as the older figure of Duke Adorno. Zagrosek draws dedicated playing and singing from the massive ensemble, and the beautifully balanced sound is of demonstration quality.

Irrelohe (opera; complete).

*** Sony Dig. S2K 66850 (2) [id.]. Pabst, DeVol, Randová, V. Singverein, VSO, Gülke.

Ten years ago Schreker was barely represented on record, but now *Die Gezeichneten* and *Der Schatzgräber* are both available on CD. *Irrelohe* comes immediately after *Der Schatzgräber*, being first produced in 1924. Hailed after the First World War as the finest musical-dramatist after Wagner, Schreker was subjected to increasing denigration. His musical language is lush and overripe in the manner of Strauss and Puccini. The idiom is a cross between the Strauss of *Elektra* and Korngold. *Irrelohe* was attacked by the press, but this was as much the result of resentment at his success and of growing anti-semitism. The opera is set in the eighteenth century. Count Heinrich (Michael Pabst) lives as a recluse in Irrelohe castle, fearing hereditary madness should he give way to sexual passion. His love for Eva (Luana DeVol) inspires the jealousy of her suitor, Peter, as well as the enmity of Christobald, whose own fiancée had been raped by Heinrich's father. Peter attempts to prevent their wedding but is killed in the ensuing struggle; in the meantime, Christobald sets fire to Irrelohe. (Echoes of Valhalla's fate in *Götterdämmerung*.) Eva finally sings of the redemptive power of love. Although Wolfgang Molkow's note speaks of it having 'quite an inventory of horror-film clichés', *Irrelohe* holds the listener almost from start to finish. The characters and the vocal lines are finely drawn and the orchestral sound is sumptuous. It is imaginative music, highly sophisticated in its use of the orchestra, but in a succession of effectively realized atmospheres rather than being strongly melodic in inspiration. There are inspired passages – the Prelude to Act III is one, though the Act is probably the least interesting musically. The performance under Peter Gülke is thoroughly committed and the cast is strong. The set derives from a concert performance at the Grosser Musikvereinsaal in Vienna and, although the singers are a bit forward, there is excellent orchestral detail. The break at the end of the first CD (in the middle of Act II, scene 8) is ugly. Those who know *Der Schatzgräber* will need no prompting to investigate this set. This is gripping and masterly stuff, and Schreker's score is well served by the cast, orchestra and all involved in this production.

Der Schatzgräber (opera): complete.

**(*) Capriccio Dig. 60010-2 (2) [id.]. Protschka, Schnaut, Stamm, Haage, Hamburg State O, Gerd Albrecht.

The attractions of Schreker's sweet-sour treatment of a curious morality fairy-story are fairly well conveyed in this first recording, made live at the Hamburg State Opera in 1989, though there are very few signs of the audience's presence, with no applause, even at the end. Josef Protschka sings powerfully as Elis, hardly ever over-strenuous, but Gabriele Schnaut finds it hard to scale down her very bright and powerful soprano and seems happiest when she is scything your ears with loud and often unsteady top notes; yet she is certainly dramatic in this equivocal role. Outstanding among the others is Peter Haage as the court jester. *Der Schatzgräber* may be hokum, but it is enjoyable hokum, and, with Albrecht drawing committed performances from the whole company, this well-made recording is most welcome.

Schubert, Franz (1797–1828)

ORCHESTRAL MUSIC

(i) *Konzertstück in D, D.345; Rondo in A for violin and strings, D.438;* (ii) *Duo in A, D.574; Fantasy in C, D.934.*
(B) *** DG analogue/Dig. 453 665-2 [id.]. Gidon Kremer, with (i) LSO, Emil Tchakarov; (ii) Valery Afanassiev.

This is not only one of Kremer's most impressive records, it happily fills a gap in the catalogue in combining two of Schubert's most engaging concertante pieces with two of his finest works for violin and piano, the *Duo* from 1817 and the *Fantasy* from a decade earlier. All four have that freshness and (at times) innocence of invention which make Schubert's instrumental music so engaging, yet Kremer and Afanassiev (a splendid partnership) treat the *Duo* as a major sonata by observing the first-movement exposition repeat. They also show imaginative flair in the *Fantasy*, especially in its chimerical *Allegretto*. The concertante pieces are equally successful, the recording is excellent, and this was an excellent choice for including within DG's special bicentenary collection.

Rondo in A for violin and strings, D.438.
*** EMI Dig. CDC7 49663-2 [id.]. Kennedy, ECO, Tate – BRUCH; MENDELSSOHN: *Concertos*. ***

The ideas in Schubert's *Rondo* flow very sweetly with Kennedy, making this an attractive bonus to the usual Bruch–Mendelssohn coupling.

Rosamunde Overture (Die Zauberharfe, D.644) and incidental music, D.797 (complete).
*** DG Dig. 431 655-2 [id.]. Anne Sofie von Otter, Ernst Senff Ch., COE, Abbado.

Abbado and COE give joyful performances of this magical incidental music. It is a revelation to hear the most popular of the entr'actes played so gently: it is like a whispered meditation. Even with a slow speed and affectionate phrasing, it yet avoids any feeling of being mannered. Glowing recording to match. Anne Sofie von Otter is an ideal soloist.

Symphonies Nos. 1–6; 8–9.
*** RCA Dig. 09026 62673-2 (4) [id.]. Dresden State O, Sir Colin Davis.
(BB) *** Arte Nova Dig. 74321 54458-2 (4) [id.]. Putbus Festival O, Wilhelm Keitel.
(N) (B) **(*) IMG Artists GIB 7905-2 (5). Sinfonia Varsovia, Lord Menuhin. (Disc 5 includes conversation in German – Menuhin/Jurgen Seeger).
**(*) Teldec/Warner Dig. 4509 91184-2 (4) [id.]. Concg. O, Harnoncourt.
(B) **(*) Nimbus Dig. NI 5270/3 [id.]. Hanover Band, Roy Goodman.

Symphonies Nos. 1–6; 8–9; Grand Duo in C, D.812 (orch. Joachim); *Rosamunde overture (Die Zauberharfe), D.644.*
*** DG Dig. 423 651-2 (5) [id.]. COE, Abbado.

Symphonies Nos.1–6.
(N) (B) **(*) EMI double fforte CZS5 73359-2 (2) [CDFB 73359]. Menuhin Festival O, Lord Menuhin.

Symphonies Nos. 8 (Unfinished); 9 (Great); Overtures: Alfonso and Wstrella; in C and in D in the Italian style; Die Zwillingsbüder.
(N) (B) **(*) EMI double fforte CZS5 73362-2 (2) [CDFB 73362]. Menuhin Festival O, Lord Menuhin.

Symphonies Nos. 1–6; 8 (Unfinished); 9 (Great); Overtures: Fierabras; In the Italian style in C; Des Teufels Lustschloss.
(B) **(*) Decca 430 773-2 (4). VPO, István Kertész.

Symphonies Nos. 1–6; 8 (Unfinished); 9; Rosamunde: Overture (Die Zauberharfe) & ballet music.
(M) **(*) EMI CMS5 66114-2 (4). BPO, Karajan (with WEBER: *Der Freischütz: Overture* **(*)).

Symphonies Nos. 1 in D, D.82; 2 in B flat, D.125.
(M) **(*) EMI CDM5 66102-2 [id.]. BPO, Karajan (with WEBER: *Der Freischütz: Overture* **(*)).

Symphonies Nos. 3 in D, D.200; 4 in C min. (Tragic), D.417; Rosamunde: Ballet music 1–2.
(M) ** EMI CDM5 66103-2 [id.]. BPO, Karajan.

Symphonies Nos. 5 in B flat, D.485; 6 in C, D.589; Rosamunde: Overture (Die Zauberharfe), D.644.
(M) **(*) EMI CDM5 66104-2 [id.]. BPO, Karajan.

Symphonies Nos. 8 in B min. (Unfinished), D.759; 9 in C (Great), D.944.
(M) **(*) EMI CDM5 66105-2 [id.]. BPO, Karajan.

Symphonies Nos. 1 in D, D.82; 2 in B flat, D.125; Rosamunde: Overture (Die Zauberharfe), D.644.
(B) **(*) DG 453 661-2. BPO, Boehm.

Symphonies Nos. 3 in D, D.200; 4 in C min. (Tragic), D.417; Rosamunde: Ballet music Nos. 1–2, D.797.
(B) ** DG 453 662-2. BPO, Boehm.

Symphonies Nos. 5 in B flat, D.485; 6 in C, D.589.
(B) *** DG 453 663-2. BPO, Boehm.

Symphonies Nos. 8 in B min. (Unfinished), D.759; 9 in C (Great), D.944.
(B) *** DG 453 664-2. BPO, Boehm.

Symphonies Nos. 1 in D, D.82; 4 in C (Tragic), D.417; Overture in the Italian style in C, D.591.
*** Teldec/Warner Dig. 4509 97509-2. Concg. O, Harnoncourt.

Symphonies Nos. 2 in B flat, D.125; 6 in C, D.589.
** Teldec/Warner Dig. 4509 97510-2. Concg. O, Harnoncourt.

Symphonies Nos. 3 in D, D.200; 5 in B flat, D.485; 8 in B min. (Unfinished).
*** Teldec/Warner Dig. 4509 97511-2. Concg. O, Harnoncourt.

Symphony No. 9 in C (Great), D.944.
**(*) Teldec/Warner Dig. 4509 97512-2. Concg. O, Harnoncourt.

Abbado's is an outstanding set. Rarely has he made recordings of the central Viennese classics which find him so naturally sunny and warm in his expression. Speeds are often on the fast side but never feel breathless, and the recording is refined, with fine bloom on the string-sound. Textually too, the Abbado set takes precedence over its rivals and there are certain fascinating differences from what we are used to. The five CDs are now also available separately – see below.

Sir Colin Davis's Dresden cycle of the Schubert symphonies, neatly fitted on four discs (offered for the price of three) despite observing all repeats, was issued to celebrate the Schubert bicentenary in 1997. It makes a glowing tribute that regularly reveals Davis drawing magnetic and intense playing from the Dresden orchestra, with the polish of the ensemble adding to the impact, never making the results sound self-conscious. In the youthful symphonies, Nos. 1–3, Davis does not forget that these were written soon after Beethoven's *Seventh* and *Eighth*, refusing to regard them as just elegantly Mozartian, but genuinely Schubertian. In the middle symphonies Davis seems happier bringing out the elegance and charm, but then crowns the cycle with a radiant reading of the *Unfinished*, marked by high dynamic contrasts. In the *Great C major* Davis observes every repeat, and tensions are not quite so keen. This is a most distinguished cycle, helped by glowing sound. Abbado's superb, keenly concentrated cycle with the COE still is not surpassed, using a smaller ensemble in a drier acoustic. But his set, which includes the *Grand Duo*, runs to five premium-priced discs and so costs considerably more. When the four Davis discs are made available separately, the first one (coupling Nos. 1, 3 and 8) will make an excellent and generous sampler. The Abbado series is already available on separate discs, all highly recommendable, and the *Ninth* particularly so.

In full, immediate, yet open sound the Arte Nova performances are as fresh and direct as any you will find. Springing rhythms persuasively to avoid any sense of excessive haste, Keitel follows period practice to the extent of favouring fast speeds, whether in allegros or andantes. Light, crisp articulation also helps to bring transparent textures, with dynamic contrasts dramatically brought out and Scherzo-like Minuets given extra bite, thanks to sharp observance of accented cross-rhythms. If the earlier symphonies up to No. 6 are remarkable above all for their freshness, the *Unfinished* then brings the one idiosyncratic interpretation, with the first movement taken very slowly and steadily. The *Great C major Symphony* – with all repeats observed – brings steady speeds, again on the brisk side, and a fresh, direct manner.

Karajan presents a most polished and beautiful set of Schubert symphonies. Now reissued as part of EMI's Karajan Edition, they were recorded in the latter part of the 1970s in the Philharmonie. The point and elegance of the Berliners' playing in the early symphonies is most persuasive, yet the results are never mannered. The reverberant acoustic gives the impression of a band rather large for Schubert, lacking in brightness and transparency, and the *Fourth Symphony*, the *Tragic*, finds Karajan less compelling. The *Unfinished*, dating from 1975, with Berlin refinement at its most ethereal, has an otherworldly quality, rapt and concentrated. The *Great C major* (1977) is also compelling, but here some may find that the reverberant acoustic gives the impression of too much weightiness. The disc which includes the first two symphonies opens with a weightily dramatic performance of Weber's *Der Freischütz overture*, recorded digitally in 1981.

Boehm's cycle of the Schubert symphonies was recorded over a decade between 1963 and 1973, and the Berlin Philharmonic plays with striking warmth and finesse throughout. Boehm does not smile as often as Schubert's music demands – especially by the side of Beecham in Nos. 3 and 5, but he is always sympathetic. Certainly the Berlin wind are a joy to listen to, and it is only in the early symphonies that he does not quite capture the youthful sparkle of these delightful scores, although in its way No. 1 is brightly and elegantly done and No. 2 also is characteristically strong; both are classical in spirit. No. 4 offers splendidly disciplined playing, but this is not one of the more characterful interpretations of the set. Boehm's warmly graceful account of No. 5 and the glowing performance of No. 6, coupled together, show Boehm at his best, taking an easy-going view, with relaxed tempi that never grow heavy. The remastered sound is remarkably fine, fresher and clearer and without loss of bloom, although the focus in No. 6 is not absolutely sharp. Boehm capped his series with an outstanding account of the *Unfinished Symphony* and one of the finest of all recorded performances of the *Great C major*, to make an excellent coupling. The recording is very good indeed and in its CD transfer sounds fresh, warm and full.

Kertész began his Schubert cycle with Nos. 8 and 9 and the overtures, and these two symphonies are the finest performances in the cycle. The *Ninth* is fresh, dramatic and often very exciting, the *Unfinished* highly imaginative and comparably dramatic in its wide dynamic contrasts. In the two early symphonies Kertész scores with the spirited VPO playing and a light touch, and this also applies to Nos. 3 and 6, even if they are without the last ounce of character and distinction. The playing of the VPO is beyond reproach throughout, and it has a pervading freshness, helped by the transparent yet full Decca sound.

It is a pity that Harnoncourt in his Schubert cycle did not turn, like Abbado, to the Chamber Orchestra of Europe instead of to the Concertgebouw. As it is, Harnoncourt takes a relatively severe view, and significantly he is at his finest in the darkness of the *Tragic Symphony*. There is little of Schubertian charm here, with his eccentrically slow tempo for the finale of No. 6 in its lumbering gait missing the pure sunlight of the piece. Echoing period practice, Harnoncourt's preference for short phrasing also tends to make slow movements less songful, though equally it adds to the bite and intensity of other movements, notably Scherzos with their sharp cross-rhythms. Not that any reservations detract seriously from a most refreshing cycle, direct and unmannered. Though the reverberance of the Amsterdam Concertgebouw hall obscures detail in tuttis, as well as reinforcing the weight of sound, the recording is warm and otherwise helpful. Harnoncourt, like Abbado, has used specially prepared texts, but they avoid the radical changes that spice the Abbado set. The two Harnoncourt discs to go for are the pairing of the *Tragic* with No. 1 and the generous triptych of Nos. 3, 5 and the *Unfinished*.

As in his Beethoven cycle, also recorded for Nimbus, Goodman draws lively, beautifully sprung performances of the Schubert symphonies from the players of the Hanover Band. For anyone wanting period performances of these works, they can be warmly recommended as a mid-priced set, with the reservation that the characteristic Nimbus balance is more damaging here than it is in Beethoven. The strings are attractively caught in a warm acoustic, but the reverberation tends to obscure detail in tuttis, with the woodwind set so far backwards that it is often barely audible, and even the rasp of the natural horns is underplayed. Nos. 1 and 4 (*Tragic*) have also been issued separately on NI 5158, and the *Unfinished* is available coupled with the *Overture and incidental music from Rosamunde* (NI 5274), both at full price.

Menuhin's earlier EMI set dates from the end of 1960s, and in many ways his approach anticipates that of the later set of three decades later. Youthful ardour burns in most of these performances. Some will find them too thrustful, not gentle enough, but the result is always refreshing. Beecham made No, 3 sparkle far more than Menuhin does, but at least the Menuhin approach shows the music's underlying strength, and although the gaiety in the early symphonies sometimes becomes a little relentless the string playing is graceful, and the energy is never in doubt. The approach to Nos. 4 and 5 is unsentimental and direct, although the finale of No. 5 is comparatively leisurely; a greater degree of expressiveness in slow movements would have been welcome. No. 6 is a delicious performance, of the kind that Beecham used to give, and the affectionate touch in the *Andante* brings a glow of warmth. The *Unfinished* returns to the mood of Nos. 4 and 5, and here a little more relaxation would have been ideal. But, as in the overtures which are offered as a sizeable bonus, the playing is unmannered and fresh. With No. 9 the forward, clear recorded quality which is characteristic of the set as a whole means that there is no feeling of a large orchestra in the concert hall. Menuhin has preferred to retain the smaller (and authentic) scale. The performance has plenty of character; brisk, lightweight and refreshing, it is very enjoyable in its way, even though it leaves one remembering more searching interpretations. The CD transfers are most musically done, retaining the analogue warmth and bloom, yet with the extra clarity adding to the bite of the music-making.

Menuhin's second, more recent IMG cycle of the Schubert symphonies offers performances electrically tense, generally at brisk speeds, with an easy feeling for Schubertian lyricism, helped by alert, warmly responsive playing from this leading Polish chamber orchestra and full, immediate recording. With Menuhin there is no question of the early symphonies – boyhood works often described as Haydnesque – being mistaken for eighteenth-century music. Modest in scale, these are interpretations that yet bite home with Beethovenian power. With the last two symphonies the approach is equally fresh, with fast, steady speeds and high contrasts. Most radical of all is the *Great C major*, brisk and urgent. The disappointment is that the supplementary disc offers Menuhin's conversation in German only.

Symphonies Nos. 1–3; 4 (Tragic); 5–7; 8 (Unfinished); 9 in C (Great); 10 in D, D.936a; Symphonic fragments in D, D.615 and D.708a (completed and orch. Newbould).
*** Ph. Dig. 412 176-2 (6) [id.]. ASMF, Marriner.

Marriner's excellent set gathers together not only the eight symphonies of the regular canon but two more symphonies now 'realized', thanks to the work of Professor Brian Newbould of Hull University. For full measure, half a dozen fragments of other symphonic movements are also included, orchestrated by Professor Newbould. The set brings sparkling examples of the Academy's work at its finest, while the bigger challenges of the *Unfinished* (here completed with Schubert's Scherzo filled out and the *Rosamunde B minor Entr'acte* used as finale) and the *Great C major* are splendidly taken. These are fresh, direct readings, making up in rhythmic vitality for any lack of weight. The recordings, all digital, present consistent refinement and undistractingly good balance. But this set now seems expensive.

Symphonies Nos. 1 in D, D.82; 2 in B flat, D.125.
*** DG (IMS) Dig. 423 652-2 [id.]. COE, Abbado.
(BB) **(*) Naxos Dig. 8.553093 [id.]. Failoni O of Budapest, Michael Halász.
(N) (B) ** Carlton Dig. 3036 601132 [id.]. Budapest SO, Tamas Vásáry.

The coupling of the two earliest *Symphonies* on DG brings bright and sparkling performances, reflecting the youthful joy of both composer and players. Abbado brings out the sunny relaxation of the writing, most exhilaratingly of all in the light-hearted finales. The recording of both captures the refined playing of the COE very vividly.

Michael Halász and the Failoni Orchestra are affectionately easy-going rather than overtly dramatic, but they play both these works most winningly, finding all the delicacy of Schubert's inspiration. The recording too is full and naturally balanced, and one's only reservation is that the resonance of the Italian Institute in Budapest makes the tuttis spread and lose some of the sharpness of focus. But this is a most enjoyable disc nevertheless and well worth its modest cost.

Vásáry's live recordings offer crisp and fresh readings of these teenage works, which may be short on charm but which convey the urgency of youth. He particularly relishes the *Second Symphony* with its extended and adventurous first movement and feather-light finale. Full, warm recording not always clear on inner detail.

Symphonies Nos. 1 in D, D.82; 5 in B flat; Overture in the Italian style in D, D.590; Overture Des Teufels Lustschloss, D.84.
(M) *** Carlton Dig. 30367 01272 [id.]. E. Sinfonia, Sir Charles Groves.

This coupling of the *First* and *Fifth Symphonies* gets Groves's cycle off to an excellent start. First-movement *Allegros* have weight, yet rhythms are nicely sprung. Both *Andantes* are gracious and well paced, and the finale of No. 1 dances airily. The Minuet/Scherzo of No. 5 is particularly attractive; the Trio with its glowing horns flows agreeably. The two *Overtures* are a distinct asset: the piece in Italian style is relaxed and sunny, while the drama and pathos of *Des Teufels Lustschloss* ('The Devil's Pleasure Castle') are well caught with some fine, sonorous brass. First-rate Abbey Road recording, which has both body and glowing detail.

Symphony No. 3 in D, D.200.
*** RCA Dig. 09026 61876-2. N. German RSO, Wand – SCHUMANN: *Symphony No. 3.* ***

Günter Wand's Schubert *D major* is most attractive: very well played and vital, though 56 minutes for a full-price CD is not particularly generous these days. The recording, made at the Musikhalle in Hamburg, has warmth and presence.

Symphonies Nos. 3 in D, D.200; 4 in C min. (Tragic), D.417.
*** DG Dig. 423 653-2 [id.]. COE, Abbado.
(N) (M) *(*) Carlton Dig. 3036 601032 [id.]. Budapest SO, Tamas Vásáry

Crisp, fast and light, No. 3 is given a delectable performance by Abbado. In No. 4, the *Tragic*, Abbado makes the slow C minor introduction bitingly mysterious before a clean, elegant *Allegro*, and with this conductor the other movements are also elegant and polished as well as strong. Textually, No. 4 eliminates the extra bars in the slow movement which had been inserted originally by Brahms. The slow movement is outstandingly beautiful, with the oboe solo – presumably COE's Douglas Boyd – most tenderly expressive.

Like his coupling of Nos 1 and 2, Vásáry's disc of Nos 3 and 4 offers live recordings. No. 4 opens with very dim sound, which improves only as the first movement progresses. Tuttis remain a little clouded, but No. 3 offers better sound, if not ideal. The readings are plain and direct, lacking exposition repeats in the first movements and with generally fast speeds rarely capturing the sparkle or charm of the music.

Symphonies Nos. 3 in D, D.200; 4 in C min. (Tragic), D.417; Overtures: Der häusliche Krieg, D.787; In the Italian style in C, D.591; Der Teufel als Hydraulicus, D.4.
(M) **(*) Carlton Dig. 30367 01292 [id.]. E. Sinfonia, Sir Charles Groves.

Groves is in good form in this extremely generous anthology. First movements are a little lacking in rhythmic point, but the *Allegretto* of No. 3 has plenty of charm and the *Andante* of the *Tragic* is gentle and gracious; both finales are vivaciously done. The two unknown overtures are a real bonus. *Der häusliche Krieg* (only rediscovered in the early 1960s) opens with an attractive horn chorale and later becomes quite jolly; *Der Teufel als Hydraulicus* is only half its length but is agreeable enough. It is the earliest of Schubert's orchestral works, written when the composer was 14. The *Italian overture* is also affectionately done.

Symphonies Nos. 3 in D, D.200; 5 in B flat, D.485; 6 in C, D.589.
❁ (M) *** EMI CDM5 66984-2 [CDM5 66999]. RPO, Beecham.

Beecham's are magical performances in which every phrase breathes. There is no substitute for imaginative phrasing and each line is shaped with affection and spirit. The *Allegretto* of the *Third Symphony* is an absolute delight. The delicacy of the opening of the *Fifth* is matched by the simple lyrical beauty of the *Andante*, while few conductors have been as persuasive as Beecham in the *Sixth* 'little' *C major Symphony*. The sound is now just a shade drier in Nos. 3 and 6 than in their last LP incarnation but is generally faithful and spacious. This is an indispensable record for all collections and a supreme bargain in the Schubert discography, now rightly reissued as one of EMI's 'Great recordings of the century'.

Symphonies Nos. 3 in D, D.200; 6 in C, D.589.
(BB) *** Naxos Dig. 8.553094 [id.]. Failoni O of Budapest, Michael Halász.

These are delightful performances, fully capturing the innocent charm of these youthful symphonies. The Failoni strings play with airy grace and the woodwind bring a similar delicacy of colour to their solos and gentle chording. Michael Halász is most sensitive and in the *Allegretto* second movement of No. 3 – Schubert at his most endearingly ingenuous – the conductor's style is Beechamesque in its affectionate elegance. The economy of Schubert's scoring means that the resonant acoustic affects the clarity of the tuttis only marginally and it certainly lends an attractive bloom to the proceedings.

Symphonies Nos. 3 in D, D.200; 8 in B min. (Unfinished), D.759.
(M) **(*) DG 449 745-2 [id.]. VPO, Carlos Kleiber.

Carlos Kleiber's 1979 Schubert coupling has been greatly admired in some quarters, so it is not surprising that DG have chosen it for reissue in their series of 'Originals'. Kleiber is a refreshingly unpredictable conductor, turning at times towards quirkiness, as in the slow movement of No. 3, which is rattled through jauntily at breakneck speed. The Minuet too becomes a full-blooded Scherzo, and there is little rest in the outer movements. The *Unfinished* brings a more compelling performance, but there is unease in the first movement, where first and second subjects are not fully co-ordinated, the contrasts sounding a little forced. The recording brings out the brass sharply, and is of wide range.

Symphony No. 4 in C min. (Tragic), D.417.
(M) (***) DG mono 457 705-2 [id.]. BPO, Igor Markevitch – BERWALD: *Symphonies Nos. 3 & 4.* (***)

Although it derives from a (very fine) mono LP, first issued in the mid 1950s, Markevitch's remains a hotly competitive version, perhaps not as introspective as might be – but then, despite the label 'Tragic', this is a fresh, early work. The Berlin Philharmonic plays with its characteristic warmth and brilliance, and the reverberant recording hardly sounds its age at all.

Symphony Nos. 4 in C min. (Tragic); 6 in C.
(N) ** EMI Dig. CDC7 54210-2 [id.]. London Classical Players, Roger Norrington.

Norrington's period performances are consistently clean, fresh and transparent in very much the same style as his Beethoven. Speeds are fast, often very fast, but the crisp articulation of the London Classical Players prevents them from sounding breathless, allowing a spring to the rhythms. No. 6 works better than No. 4, where the sourness of period violins and woodwind is at times obtrusive. Well-balanced sound. But at full price this is only really recommendable to admirers of these artists.

Symphony No. 4 in C min. (Tragic), D.417; Grand duo in C, D.812 (orch. Joachim).
(BB) **(*) Naxos 8.553095 [id.]. Failoni O of Budapest, Michael Halász.

Halász presents the *Tragic Symphony* – Schubert himself gave the work its title – sympathetically and, though this is not a strongly dramatic reading, the resonant acoustic adds a certain weight, and the *Andante* is warmly and expressively played. This inexpensive disc is valuable for its coupling, the orchestration of the large-scale *Grand Duo* for piano duet, written in 1824 and orchestrated by the violinist Josef Joachim. The work is convincingly played, with gravitas and freshness nicely balanced. The warm resonancy of the Budapest Italian Institute suits this work very well.

Symphony No. 5 in B flat, D.485.
(M) *** DG 447 433-2 [id.]. VPO, Boehm – BEETHOVEN: *Symphony No. 6.* ***
(M) *** RCA 09026 61793-2 [id.]. Chicago SO, Fritz Reiner (with MENDELSSOHN: *Hebrides overture* ***) – BRAHMS: *Symphony No. 3.* ***
(N) **(*) BBC Legends BBCL 4003-2 [id.]. BBC SO, Rudolf Kempe – BRAHMS: *Symphony No. 4.* **(*)

Boehm's recording of the *Fifth Symphony* dates from the very end of his career. In his 80s he preferred a tauter, more incisive view than he had given in his 1967 Berlin performance, weightier, but still with a light rhythmic touch, while the slow movement is not lacking grace. The finale is strong and purposeful and this is Boehm at his finest, with superbly polished and responsive VPO playing in repertoire they know and love. The 1980 recording is full and warm, taken from a live performance at the Hohenems Schubertiade, and rightly reissued now in DG's 'Legendary Recordings' series of 'Originals'.

Reiner's is a most attractive performance, brightly and clearly recorded, yet with a glowing ambience. This reading of No. 5, essentially sunny and with an easy-going *Andante*, brings a strongly vigorous finale, following a third movement where Reiner indulges the trio with an affectionate rallentando. Mendelssohn's Hebrides overture comes as an exciting encore: its storm has seldom sounded more dramatic, yet the lyrical warmth is not missed. Again, fresh sound.

Kempe's *Fifth Symphony* comes as a makeweight to an excellent 1974 concert performance of the Brahms *Fourth*. The Schubert was recorded at a Promenade Concert three years earlier, and is a delight from start to finish. Very musicianly, enjoyable, natural and full of life. Small wonder that Beecham thought so highly of Kempe. Very decent sound too.

Symphonies Nos. 5 in B flat, D.485; 6 in C, D.589.
*** DG Dig. 423 654-2. COE, Abbado.

Abbado brings out the happy songfulness of the slow movements in these works, as well as the rhythmic resilience of the *Allegros*. As in No. 4, so also in No. 6 Abbado eliminates the extra bars added by Brahms in his original Schubert Edition. Excellent recording, with fine bloom and good, natural contrasts.

Symphonies Nos. 5 in B flat, D.485; 8 in B min. (completed by Brian Newbold).
**(*) Virgin Veritas/EMI (SIS) Dig. VER5 61305-2 [CDM 61305]. OAE, Mackerras.

Though not as magnetic as his account of No. 9, Mackerras's performance of No. 5 has comparable qualities of freshness and resilience. Tempi are only marginally brisker than traditional performances, and the slow movement has grace if not quite the degree of warmth that Boehm and Walter find. The special claims of the Veritas reissue is that the '*Unfinished' Symphony* is here heard as finished by Brian Newbold. He opens in the mysterious depths with the darkest *pianopianissimo*, and the plangent period timbres bring a real sense of *Sturm und Drang*, with powerful contrasts and strong, forceful accents in the second movement. Excellent recording. A stimulating coupling.

Symphonies Nos. 5 in B flat, D.485; 8 in B min. (Unfinished).
(M) *** Sony Bruno Walter Edition SMK 64487 [id.]. Columbia SO or NYPO, Walter (with: BEETHOVEN: *Overture Leonora No. 3* ***).
(B) *** EMI CfP CD-CFP 6036. LPO, Sir John Pritchard.

Bruno Walter brings special qualities of warmth and lyricism to the *Unfinished*. Affection, gentleness and humanity are the keynotes of this performance; while the first movement of the *Fifth* is rather measured, there is much loving attention to detail in the *Andante*. The 1961 recording emerges fresh and glowing in its CD format and, like the rest of the Walter series, completely belies its age. The sound is richly expansive as well as clear, and the CD is in every way satisfying.

Pritchard's performances are most refreshing. In the *Fifth Symphony* his simplicity of approach is disarming and his directness allows for nudging delicacy, as at the very start, while the playing of the LPO is beautifully refined; the slow movement, too, is both serene and warm. The reading of the *Unfinished* is magnetic, unusually direct, establishing the first movement as a genuine symphonic allegro but with no feeling of breathlessness, even in the melting lyricism of the incomparable second subject. The high dramatic contrasts are fearlessly presented, and the second movement brings purity and freshness too. The 1980 recording is very naturally balanced.

Symphonies Nos. 5 in B flat, D. 485; 8 in B min. (Unfinished), D. 759; 9 in C (Great), D. 944.
(B) *** Decca Double Dig. 448 927-2 (2). VPO, Solti.
(N) (M) (**(*)) RCA mono 74321 59480-2 (2) [id.]. NBC SO, Toscanini – MENDELSSOHN: *Symphonies Nos. 4–5.* (**(*))

This Double Decca coupling three favourite Schubert symphonies is one of the most attractive of all Solti's many reissues on the Decca label. There have been more charming versions of No. 5 but few that so beautifully combine freshness with refined polish. The *Unfinished* has Solti adopting measured speeds but with his refined manner keeping total concentration. The *Great C major Symphony* is an outstanding version, among the very finest, beautifully paced and sprung in all four movements, and superbly played. It has drama as well as lyrical feeling, but above all it has a natural sense of spontaneity and freshness. The recordings all confirm the Vienna Sofiensaal as an ideal recording location, and the glowing detail, especially in No. 9, is a source of consistent pleasure.

To have all three of the Schubert symphonies that Toscanini recorded, in a single package, makes an attractive bargain, particularly when the new transfer gives extra body to the sound, with the original dry acoustic given fair ambience. Toscanini's Schubert may lack charm, but the symphonic power is made all the clearer.

Symphonies Nos. 5 in B flat, D.485; 9 in C, D.944 (The Great).
(N) (M) *** Penguin Classics Decca 460 634-2 [id.]. VPO, Kertész.
(M) (**) RCA mono GD 60291 [60291-2-RG]. NBC SO, Toscanini.

A good choice for a Penguin Classics coupling from the Kertész/VPO series. No. 5 offers attractive, stylish playing. Kertész does not always find the smile in Schubert's writing, but here he is at his freshest, and the playing of the Vienna Philharmonic is exemplary. The *Ninth* is perhaps the finest performance in the whole cycle. Like the *Fifth*, it is remarkably well recorded, with an appealing overall warmth yet plenty of bite and clarity. One is made conscious that the symphony is scored for trombones as well as horns, something that does not emerge clearly in some recordings. The performance is fresh, dramatic and often very exciting. Kertész's springlike approach counteracts any feeling that each movement is just a shade too long.

In his 1947 performance of No. 9, Toscanini is tauter and faster than in either his earlier or later recordings. A useful antidote for it serves to remind one that Schubert was still a young man when this was composed with what was a bright future ahead and that the valedictory halo which came to surround it was a nineteenth-century phenomenon.

Symphonies Nos. (i) *6 in C;* (ii) *9 in C (Great).*
(M) **(*) Mercury [434 354-2]. (i) LSO, Schmidt-Isserstedt; (ii) Minneapolis SO, Skrowaczewski.

A unique coupling of the two C major symphonies – each completely different in character – and two most interesting readings. The *Sixth* with Schmidt-Isserstedt is a little matter-of-fact, but helped by the warm, glowing ambience of Watford Town Hall, he underlines the bubbling gaiety of the work. All is joy until the finale, when the *Allegro moderato* is a little too moderate. In the *Ninth* Skrowaczewski is attractively straightforward and animated. He manages to maintain a steady speed through the whole of the coda in the first movement without sounding ruthless and, after a sympathetic *Andante*, the Scherzo and finale have compelling impetus. The 1961 Minneapolis recording is full-bodied but (as so often in the Northtrop Auditorium) the violins are made to sound fierce.

'*The essential Schubert*': (i) *Symphonies Nos. 8 in B min. (Unfinished), D.759; 9 in C (Great) D.944;* (ii; iii) *Piano quintet in A (Trout), D.667;* (ii) *Impromptu in G flat, D.899/3; Moment musical, D.780/3; Rosamunde:* (iv) *Jägerchor; Ballet music in G.* Lieder: (v) *An Sylvia;* (vi) *Ave Maria;* (vii) *Die Forelle;* (v) *Heidenröslein.*
(B) *** Decca Double Analogue/Dig. 444 546-2 (2). (i) VPO, Solti; (ii) Clifford Curzon; (iii) V. Octet (members); (iv) V. State Op. Ch., VPO, Münchinger; (v) Hermann Prey, Karl Engel; (vi) Leontyne Price, VPO, Karajan; (vii) Gabriele Fontana, György Fischer.

Whatever constitutes the 'essential' Schubert (and there is a great deal more of it than can be included on a pair of CDs), the *Unfinished* and *Great C major Symphonies* are certainly indispensable, and Solti does these marvellous works full justice. Both bring superb VPO playing. The *Unfinished* has great concentration and atmosphere and there are few accounts of No. 9 that are more glowingly resilient, lyrically fresh and sunny, yet with plenty of drama. The Decca recording too is outstanding in its richness and detail. Clifford Curzon's vintage recording of the *Trout* is hardly less distinguished, a good-natured reading with an admirable rapport between the pianist and the excellent Viennese players. Again vigour and freshness go hand in hand. The recording is beautifully balanced and has a pleasingly warm ambience. Curzon's performances of the most beautiful of Schubert's *Impromptus* and a favourite *Moment musical* are hardly less winning, while Hermann Prey and Gabriele Fontana (who is delightfully innocent-sounding in *Die Forelle*) give fine accounts of three famous songs. The inclusion of the *Hunting chorus* from *Rosamunde* alongside the familiar *Ballet music* is a pleasant surprise and, if so much else is missing (notably the *String quintet* and great final *Piano sonata in B flat*), this is still a thoroughly worthwhile set, playing for 148 minutes.

Symphony No. 8 in B min. (Unfinished), D.759.
✿ (M) *** DG Dig. 445 514-2 [id.]. Philh. O, Sinopoli – MENDELSSOHN: *Symphony No. 4 (Italian).* ***

Sinopoli secures the most ravishingly refined and beautiful playing; the orchestral blend, particularly of the woodwind and horns, is magical. It is a deeply concentrated reading of the *Unfinished*, bringing out much unexpected detail, with every phrase freshly turned in seamless spontaneity. The contrast, as Sinopoli sees it, is between the dark tragedy of the first movement, relieved only partially by the lovely second subject, and the sunlight of the closing movement, giving an unforgettable, gentle radiance. The exposition repeat is observed, adding weight and substance. Warmly atmospheric recording, made in Kingsway Hall.

Symphony No. 8 in B min. (Unfinished); Grand Duo in C, D.812 (orch. Joachim).
*** DG (IMS) Dig. 423 655-2. COE, Abbado.

Abbado's outstandingly refined and sensitive version comes with an unusual and valuable coupling, the orchestral arrangement of the piano-duet *Grand Duo* made by Joachim, once erroneously thought to be the missing *Symphony No. 7*. The second subject in the *Unfinished* brings some slightly obtrusive agogic hesitations at the beginning of each phrase; but with such responsive playing they quickly sound fresh and natural.

Symphonies Nos. 8 (Unfinished); 9 in C (Great).
(M) *** Decca 452 892-2. (i) VPO; (ii) LSO; Josef Krips.
(B) *** RCA Twofer Dig. 09026 68314-2 (2) [id.]. BPO, Günter Wand.
(N) *** Telarc Dig. CD 80502 [id.]. Scottish CO, Mackerras.
(B) *** DG 439 475-2 [id.]. BPO, Karl Boehm.
(B) **(*) Sony SBK 48268 [id.]. Cleveland O, Szell.
(M) **(*) Erato/Warner Dig. 2292 45986-2 (2). Lyon Op. O, Gardiner.

Krips recorded the *Unfinished* in the very early days of mono LP, a gentle, glowing performance; and here in 1969 with the LSO he directs an unforced, flowing and wonderfully satisfying account, helped by excellent playing and splendid Sofiensaal recording, produced by Christopher Raeburn. This makes a splendid coupling for Krips's much earlier LSO recording of the *Ninth*, which has long been counted by us as one of his very finest records, perhaps *the* finest. The performance similarly has a direct, unforced spontaneity which shows Krips's natural feeling for Schubertian lyricism at its most engaging.

In a two-disc format, two for the price of one, Günter Wand offers visionary performances of both works, superbly played in live Berlin performances and glowingly recorded. Wand's magnetism, the dedication he conveys, depends not on any self-consciously expressive gestures but on direct response to the music and to Schubert's detailed markings. Consistently he makes the playing sound spontaneous, even in the tricky problems of speed-changes in the *Great C major*. In the manner of his generation he does not observe exposition repeats in the outer movements or second-half repeats in the Scherzo, but this is a beautifully co-ordinated, strong and warm reading. The *Unfinished* is just as magnetic, again with no exaggeration, but with every interpretative problem solved as though it did not exist. An outstanding issue if you want this coupling.

Having earlier recorded both these symphonies for Virgin with the period instruments of the OAE, Mackerras here gives his revised thoughts using modern instruments. The results are both intense and refreshing, with the benefits of period performance consistently apparent in the clarity of texture, but with warmer, sweeter string sound, which yet on a chamber-scale has the necessary freshness. In the finale of the *Great C major* this time the sound is even more transparent, but where in the Scherzo he omits second-half repeats this time, he does include the exposition repeat in the finale, omitted before. Broadly, Mackerras's readings remain the same – fresh, alert and beautifully sprung, generally at speeds on the fast side – but with more of the mystery of the *Unfinished* revealed than before. A highly recommendable version of this ideal and generous coupling.

Boehm's mid-1960s version of the *Unfinished Symphony* with the Berlin Philharmonic combines deep sensitivity and great refinement, and the points of detail as well as the overall warmth keep this version among the very finest on record. The opening of the development – always a key point – is magically done, and, throughout, the superb recording quality gives unusual clarity while allowing the Berlin Philharmonic ensemble its natural opulence. Boehm's performance of the *Ninth*, recorded three years earlier, stands in the lyrical Furtwängler tradition rather than in the forceful Toscanini stream, but it is the balance between the conflicting interests in this symphony which distinguishes Boehm's reading. The recording is very good indeed and in its CD transfer sounds fresh, warm and full. At Classikon price a fine bargain.

Szell's, too, is a splendid performance of the *Unfinished*, strong yet sensitive. Phrasing and general discipline are so immaculate, one would expect the result to seem cold but, on the contrary, Szell never lacks warmth here, and drama and beauty walk hand in hand in the second movement. Apart from the lack of a real *pianissimo*, the 1960 recording is very good for its time. The *Ninth* dates from the previous year. Szell's control of tempo in the first movement brings a convincing onward flow, and the performance is notable for the alertness and rhythmic energy of the playing, yet there is no lack of resilience in the *Andante*. In the brilliant finale few rivals can match the precision of the hectic triplet rhythms. The sound is fuller in this remastered form than it was originally on LP.

Gardiner made these recordings in 1986 and 1987, with modern instruments. In the opening movement of the *Great C major* he negotiates all the problems inherent in the tempo changes with consummate ease: indeed the coda of the first movement is particularly satisfying. The *Andante* is certainly *con moto* but is elegantly handled, and it is surprising, considering that the performance was recorded live, that the reading overall lacks the last degree of compulsive zest, although the warm acoustic does tend to blunt some of its attack and the bite of the modern string instruments. The resonance suits the *Unfinished*, which is most impressive and dramatic, yet with the second movement glowingly lyrical.

Symphony No. 9 in C (Great), D.944.
✪ (M) *** Decca Legends Dig. 460 311-2 [id.]. VPO, Solti – WAGNER: *Siegfried Idyll.* ***
(M) *** Virgin Veritas/EMI Dig. VER5 61245-2 [CDM 61245]. O of Age of Enlightenment, Mackerras.
(M) (***) DG mono 447 439-2 [id.]. BPO, Furtwängler – HAYDN: *Symphony No. 88.* (***) ✪
(B) *** EMI forte CZS5 69364-2 (2) [CDFB 69364]. Cleveland O, George Szell – BEETHOVEN: *Symphony No. 7* *** ✪; ROSSINI: *Overtures.* **(*)
(B) *** EMI CfP CD-CFP 6037. LPO, Sir John Pritchard.
(M) **(*) Ph. Dig. 442 646-2. ASMF, Marriner.

Symphony No. 9 in C (Great); Rosamunde: Overture (Die Zauberharfe), D.644.
*** DG Dig. 423 656-2 [id.]. COE, Abbado.

Symphony No. 9 in C (Great); Rosamunde: Overture; Ballet music; Entr'acte No. 3.
(M) **(*) Bruno Walter Edition: Sony SMK 64478 [id.]. Columbia SO, Bruno Walter.

Symphony No. 9 in C (Great); Rosamunde: Overture; Entr'acte No. 2; Ballet No. 2.
(M) **(*) DG (IMS) Dig. 445 559-2. Chicago SO, James Levine.

Symphony No. 9 in C (Great); Rosamunde: Ballet music Nos. 1–2.
(B) (***) Dutton Lab. mono CDEA 5003 [id.]. LSO, Bruno Walter – HAYDN: *Symphony No. 92.* (***)

Symphony No. 9 in C (Great); (i) *Gesang der Geister über den Wassern.*
(N) *** DG Dig. 457 648-2 [id.]. VPO, John Eliot Gardiner; (i) with Monteverdi Ch.

Solti's superb recording with the VPO (one of his finest records) is also available as part of a Decca Double, which includes Nos. 5 and 8 (see above). Decca have rightly chosen it for reissue in their Legends series, coupled with Wagner's *Siegfried Idyll.* Both performances have comparable distinction and show that Solti could relax in music which he loved, without sacrificing concentration and drama.

Though the COE is by definition an orchestra of chamber scale, the weight of Abbado's version, taken from his complete cycle, is ample, while allowing extra detail to be heard, thanks also to the orchestra's outstandingly crisp ensemble. Speeds are very well chosen, and the expressive detail is consistently made to sound natural. This version is important too for including textual amendments, and the Scherzo has four extra bars that were originally cut by Brahms in his early edition. The sound is beautifully refined, to match the point and polish of the playing. The *Rosamunde* (*Zauberharfe*) *overture* makes a valuable and generous fill-up.

Gardiner's reading was recorded live at the Salzburg Festival in 1997, representing a most refreshing meeting-point between period performance and traditional Viennese. The result is strong and weighty, with expressive rubato encouraged, but within a tauter frame than usual in this orchestra's performances, and with generally fast speeds. Clarity is here combined with sweetness, and that also applies to the dedicated performance of the beautiful motet, which was given at the same concert with Gardiner's Monteverdi Choir imported for the occcasion. Highly recommendable with good, clear sound, and far finer than Gardiner's earlier recording of the *Great C major* for Erato.

In his pioneering version with period instruments, Sir Charles Mackerras and the Orchestra of the Age of Enlightenment on the Virgin Classics label give a winning performance, one that will delight both those who prefer conventional performance and devotees of the new authenticity. The characterful rasp and bite of period brass instruments and the crisp attack of timpani are much more striking than any thinness of string-tone. It is a performance of outstanding freshness and resilience. With every single repeat observed, the heavenly length is joyfully as well as powerfully sustained and the warm, atmospheric recording gives a fine sense of presence. Now at mid-price, it is even more recommendable.

Coupled with a unique version of Haydn's *Symphony No. 88*, also recorded in the Jesus-Christus-Kirche in Berlin, Furtwängler's version makes a perfect candidate for reissue in DG's 'Legendary Performances' series. As with the Haydn, he gives the *Great C major* a glowing performance, if a highly individual one. The first movement brings an outstanding example of his wizardry, when he takes the recapitulation at quite a different speed from the exposition and still makes it sound convincing. In the beautifully played *Andante*, his very slow tempo is yet made resilient by fine rhythmic pointing. The mono recording dates from 1951 and the sound is remarkably fresh and very well balanced, with the dynamic range in the slow movement strikingly wide.

Szell's Cleveland account was his second in stereo with that orchestra (the first is discussed above, paired with the *Unfinished*). It was made in Severance Hall by an EMI team led by Peter Andry and – although subsequently issued on the CBS Epic label – it has the hallmarks of an HMV recording from the beginning of the 1970s, with a wider dynamic range than Szell usually enjoyed and better overall balancing. It sounds remarkably good in this new CD transfer. Szell's powerful reading provides a reminder that the parallels between him and another great disciplinarian conductor, Toscanini, were sometimes significant. Szell's approach is similarly direct, but lyrical feeling underlies the surface brightness and the crisply sprung rhythms are exhilarating. In the hectic triplets of the finale the orchestra is unmatched in precision, with a sparkling lightness of articulation that is a joy to the ear.

Bruno Walter's classic account of the *Great C major*, recorded in London in September 1938, enjoyed great celebrity in the 1940s and early 1950s, and is in many respects a more vital performance than his later version for CBS/Sony, enjoyable though that is. The cosily charming Walter glows from the *G major Rosamunde ballet*, but the vitality and resilience of *Allegros* in the *Great C major* are what really strike the listener. Walter's relaxed tempos and expressive phrasing in the slow movement seem just right, with the speed variations in the first movement far less free than with many conductors since. Excellent transfers. A fine addition to the Dutton bargain-price series.

As in *Symphonies Nos. 5* and *8*, Sir John Pritchard gives a superbly fresh account of the *Great C major Symphony* and one which is as vital as it is refreshing. As in the *Unfinished*, the tempi are on the fast side and the manner is direct, but the results are never breathless. It is always a significant sign when one welcomes repeats observed in this already long symphony, and at the time he made this recording (1975) Pritchard observed repeats more than anyone else on record. Only the exposition repeat in the finale is omitted. The very opening brings a slightly square account of the introductory horn-theme, but after that the resilience of the LPO playing is consistent, with the players often keenly challenged by the fast tempo and later able to relax into the lyricism of the slow movement.

Taken from his collected edition of Schubert symphonies, Sir Neville Marriner's account of the *Great C major* makes up for any lack of weight with the fresh resilience of the playing, consistently well sprung. All repeats are observed, bringing the timing of the *Symphony* to over an hour; however, the fill-up offered with the full-priced issue (a two-movement fragment, D.615, written just after the *Sixth Symphony* and orchestrated by Brian Newbold) has now been omitted and, although the recording is first rate, this makes the present reissue much less tempting in a competitive market-place.

Bruno Walter's 1959 CBS recording has been impressively enhanced on CD; the warm ambience of the sound – yet with no lack of rasp on the trombones – seems ideal for his very relaxed reading. The performance has less grip than Furtwängler's, while Solti shows greater spontaneity; but in the gentler passages there are many indications of Walter's mastery, not least in the lovely playing at the introduction of the second subject of the *Andante*. There is much to admire, even if this never quite achieves the distinction of the conductor's earlier recordings of this symphony. The *Rosamunde* music makes an endearing bonus.

Levine conducts a refined performance, beautifully played and excellently recorded, which is commendably free from mannerism yet which may on that account seem under-characterized. He omits the exposition repeats in the outer movements (just as was universally done until recently). Conversely, all the repeats in the Scherzo are observed, which unbalances the structure.

Symphonies No. 10 in D, D.936A; in D, D.615; D, D.708A (arr. Brian Newbould).

(N) *** Hyperion Dig. CDA 67000 [id.]. SCO, Mackerras.

Though there are no Schubert masterpieces here, it is fascinating to hear Brian Newbould's sensitive and scholarly realizations of these symphonic fragments. Yet it is tantalizing to find the first fragment of D.615 cut off after an introduction and exposition that promise a fine structure, and in D.708A there are four movements in embryo, with the first veering off into unexpected keys, so that the second subject comes in A flat, the remotest key from D. Most illuminating of all is the *Symphony No. 10*, which appears to have been the very last work that Schubert composed in the weeks before his death. Enough of that has survived for Newbould to piece together the three full movements that Schubert planned, with the spareness of the central slow movement even pointing forward to Mahler. Dedicated performances and warm recording.

CHAMBER AND INSTRUMENTAL MUSIC

Arpeggione sonata, D.821 (arr. for cello) (see also under *Trout quintet*).

*** Ph. (IMS) Dig. 412 230-2 [id.]. Maisky, Argerich – SCHUMANN: *Fantasiestücke* etc. ***

(BB) *** Naxos Dig. 8.550654 [id.]. Maria Kliegel, Kristin Merscher – SCHUMANN: *Adagio and allegro* etc. ***

(M) **(*). Decca 443 575-2. Rostropovich, Britten – BRIDGE: *Cello sonata*. ***

(N) (M) **(*) Decca Legends 460 974-2 [id.]. Rostropovich, Britten (as above) – DEBUSSY: *Sonata*: SCHUMANN: *5 Stücke in Volkston*. ***

(*) EMI Dig. CDC5 55166-2. Caussé, Duchable – BEETHOVEN: *Notturno;* REINECKE: *Fantasiestücke*. *

Mischa Maisky and Martha Argerich make much more of the *Arpeggione sonata* than any of their rivals. Their approach may be relaxed, but they bring much pleasure through their variety of colour and sensitivity. The Philips recording is in the very best traditions of the house.

At super-bargain price, Maria Kliegel and Kristin Merscher are highly competitive. The performances are well shaped and sensitive, though perhaps lacking the last ounce of distinction and character you find in, say, the Rostropovich–Britten account. All the same, neither the Schubert nor the Schumann coupling will disappoint at this price, given the general high standard of playing and recording.

Rostropovich gives a curiously self-indulgent interpretation of Schubert's amiable *Arpeggione sonata*. The playing of both artists is eloquent and it is beautifully recorded, but it will not be to all tastes. However, the 1968 recording is particularly valuable for its coupling of the Bridge *Sonata*. The reissue is part of Decca's Classic Sound series, and there is an alternative coupling with Debussy and Schumann in Decca's Legend series.

Gérard Caussé gives a refined account of the *Arpeggione sonata* with François-René Duchable. His viola sounds closer to the original instrument than does the modern cello. Though he is sensitive, Duchable is not always the most imaginative partner.

Arpeggione sonata in A min., D.821; Cello sonatinas Nos. 1–3, D.384–5 & D.408.
*** Channel Classics Dig. CCS 9696 [id.]. Pieter Wispelwey, Paolo Giacometti.

The simple charms of Schubert's *Arpeggione sonata* are often elusive, but not here. The highly musical Pieter Wispelwey has the full measure of Schubert's innocent lyricism, and the pianist's light touch in the finale is especially persuasive. Paolo Giacometti makes a most convincing case for the use of the fortepiano in Schubert, and the restored instrument itself, originally built by Salvatore Lagrassa around 1815, has a remarkable range of colour. Pieter Wispelwey's tone, using gut strings, always sings and, even using a minimum of vibrato, he constantly cajoles the ear, while his phrasing has an appealing simplicity. Thus the three violin *Sonatinas* are made to sound convincing in these cello transcriptions, especially the *G minor*, D.408, in which the *Andante* and finale are endearing. The recording is forwardly but truthfully balanced. Recommended.

(i) *Arpeggione sonata, D.821;* (ii) *Piano quintet in A (Trout), D.667. Adagio in E flat ('Notturno')* (for piano trio), *D.897.*
(B) **(*) DG 453 667-2. (i) Pierre Fournier, Jean Fonda; (ii) Christoph Eschenbach, Koeckert Qt.

Pierre Fournier made one of the key modern arrangements of the *Arpeggione sonata* for cello (also used by Tortelier) and he gives this a wholly persuasive account. He is beautifully balanced and recorded. Alongside it comes an enjoyably alert performance from Christoph Eschenbach and members of the Koeckert Quartet of the *Trout*. The variations are given plenty of individual interest, the outer movements striking momentum, with Eschenbach playing elegantly. The recording acoustic is clear and rather dry. The *Notturno* has the advantage of a warmer acoustic and is played most sympathetically.

Arpeggione sonata, D.821 (arr. in G min. for clarinet & piano).
*** Chandos Dig. CHAN 8506 [id.]. Gervase de Peyer, Gwenneth Pryor – SCHUMANN: *Fantasiestücke; 3 Romances;* WEBER: *Silvana variations.* ***

So persuasive is the performance of Gervase de Peyer and Gwenneth Pryor that the listener is all but persuaded that the work was actually written for this combination.

(i) *Fantasy in C, D.934;* (i; ii) *Piano trio No. 2 in E flat, D.929;* (iii) *String quartets Nos. 8 in B flat, D.112 (Op. 168); 14 in D min. (Death and the Maiden), D.810; 15 in G, D.887 (Op. 161).*
(***) Pearl mono GEMMCDS 9141 (2) [id.]. (i) Adolf Busch, Rudolf Serkin; (iii) with Hermann Busch; (iii) Busch Qt.

Some have spoken of the Busch Quartet's Schubert as the greatest ever committed to disc. Certainly the *G major Quartet* has never had so searching and powerful a reading, and the early *B flat Quartet*, which used to be known as Op. 168, sounds every bit as captivating as one remembers it from the days of shellac. The *E flat Trio* and the *C major Fantasy* are also in the highest class, and the Pearl transfers are very good indeed. These two CDs, packed economically in one jewel-case, encompass three LPs and are really excellent value for money. A lovely set.

Flute quartet (after Matiegka, for flute, guitar, viola and cello).
(N) *** Koch Dig. 3-7404-2. Still, Falletta, Neubauer, Thomas – BEETHOVEN: *Serenade, Op. 8;* KREUTZER: *Grand trio.* ***

Schubert himself played the guitar, and the present quartet is a reworking of a *Notturno* by Matiegka, originally for flute, viola and guitar, with a cello part added for Schubert's father to play. However, only two and a half variations (out of eight) were completed of Matiegka's finale. Much later, the guitarist JoAnn Falletta returned to Matiegka's original and finished off the transcription – very effectively, as can be heard here. The result is charmingly ingenuous, and with fine playing and recording makes very agreeable lightweight listening.

5 German dances with 7 trios and coda; 5 Minuets and 6 Trios, D.89.
(N) *(*) Finlandia/Warner 0630 17674-2 [id.]. Ostrobothnian CO, Juha Kangas – MOZART: *Divertimenti for strings Nos. 1–3.* *(*)

Where in early Mozart Kangas is painfully hectic, in early Schubert he is too heavy-handed, making the *Minuets* big and bluff rather than charming, even if the *German dances* fare better. The Ostrobothnian Orchestra plays well.

Octet in F, D.803.
*** Chandos Dig. CHAN 8585 [id.]. ASMF Chamber Ens.
*** ASV Dig. CDDCA 694 [id.]. Gaudier Ens.
(N) ** Sony Dig. SK 66264 [id.]. Mozzafiato & L'Archibudelli.

Octet in F, D.803; Eine kleine Trauermusik (for wind nonet), D.79.
*** Praga Dig. PR 250 087 [id.]. Czech Nonet.

(i) *Octet in F, D.803;* (ii) *Minuet and Finale in F for wind octet, D.72.*
✿ (B) *** Decca Eclipse Dig. 448 715-2 [id.]. (i) Vienna Octet; (ii) Vienna Wind Soloists.

As a companion disc to their equally delectable version of the Beethoven *Septet*, the Vienna Octet give a gloriously warm-hearted and sparkling account of Schubert's *Octet*. The *Andante with variations* has great charm and the high spirits of the finale are bucolic in their joy, with the coda managed superbly. This is irresistible, and the two charming miniatures from Schubert's youth make a delightful encore. Demonstration sound-quality and the lowest possible price take this straight to the top of the list.

The Chandos version brings a performance just as delightful as the earlier one by the ASMF, less classical in style, a degree freer in expression, with Viennese overtones brought out in Schubert's sunny invention. It has the benefit of excellent modern digital sound, cleaner on detail than before.

The members of the Czech Nonet give an engagingly infectious performance, never more so than in the finale which, after a dramatic opening, continues with rustic high spirits, often winningly bucolic in feeling. But the playing throughout combines refinement of blending and ensemble with spirited warmth. The *Trauermusik*, which opens with solemn horns, makes an unusual prelude for the main work. The recording is beautifully balanced within a spacious but not over-resonant acoustic.

The Gaudier Ensemble give an entirely winning account of the *Octet*, essentially spontaneous yet very relaxed and catching all the ingenuous Schubertian charm. Excellent sound, vivid yet well balanced within a pleasing acoustic which gives a feeling of intimacy. An ideal record for a warm summer evening.

On Sony Mozzafiato & L'Archibudelli join forces with their period instruments and achieve a certain *gemütlisch*. But only at the expense of a degree of slackness, especially in the *Adagio*, and this performance fails to sparkle.

(i) *Octet in F, D.803;* (ii) *Introduction and variations for flute and piano on 'Trock'ne Blumen'* from *Die schöne Müllerin, D.802.*
(B) *** DG 453 666-2. (i) V. Chamber Ens.; (ii) Aurèle Nicolet, Karl Engel.

The Vienna Chamber Ensemble do not overlap in personnel with the New Vienna Octet, who have recorded this work for Decca, though their performance has a similar polish and urbane Viennese warmth. This is mellifluous Schubert, and very engaging it is: fresh and elegant. This dates from 1980, and the CD transfer maintains the smoothness and realism of the LP. Very enjoyable. The innocent set of variations on a melancholy little tune makes a slight but pleasing encore.

Octet in F, D. 803; Wind octet, in F. D.72.
(N) (BB) **(*) Naxos Dig. 8.550389 [id.]. Budapest Schubert Ensemble.

A vivacious-enough account from the Schubert Ensemble on Naxos provides a more than viable super-bargain version, particularly as the bonus, a little *Wind octet* in the same key, has a particularly winning finale. Good playing and lively recording ensure that this disc gives pleasure, although it is worth paying the extra money for the Decca Vienna version.

(i) *Octet in F, D.803;* (i–ii) *Piano quintet in A (Trout), D.667;* (iii) *Violin sonatinas Nos. 1–3, D.384/5 & D.408.*
(B) *** O-L Dig./Analogue Double 455 724-2 (2) [id.]. (i) AAM Chamber Ens.; (ii) Stephen Lubin (fortepiano); (iii) Jaap Schröder, Christopher Hogwood (fortepiano).

We have long praised the Academy's 1988 recording of the *Octet* using period instruments for bringing out the open joyfulness of Schubert's inspiration, with excellent matching and vivid recording. The reading is not at all stiff or pedantic, but personal and relaxed. Lightness is the keynote, with speeds never eccentrically fast. The vibrant account of the *Trout*, from three years later, is even more successful. At first the opening tempo may seem brisk, but the lyrical flow is impetuous rather than hurried. Stephen Lubin leads zestfully from his fortepiano and there is also a nice rhythmic spring in the *Andante*, while the variations bring the most engaging and sparkling pianism of all. The recording, made in the Henry Wood Hall, is perfectly balanced, the sound both warm and transparent, so that the ear relishes the interplay and never seeks the fuller sonority of a modern piano. The present pairing makes a clear choice for those wanting these favourite works played on period instruments, and the three *Violin sonatinas*, which (with repeats included) offer a further 55 minutes of Schubertian delights. Jaap Schröder uses a Stradivarius and Christopher Hogwood a fortepiano from about 1825 by Georg Haschka. Schröder plays with fine artistry, and both artists are truthfully recorded (in 1978). The CD transfers cannot be faulted.

Piano quintet in A (Trout), D.667.
(N) *** BBC Legends BBCL 4009-2 (2) [id.].

Clifford Curzon, Amadeus Qt, James Merret – BRAHMS: *Piano quintet in F min., Op. 34.* ***
*** Ph. Dig. 446 001-2 [id.]. Alfred Brendel, Thomas Zehetmair, Tabea Zimmermann, Richard Duven, Peter Riegelbauer – MOZART: *Piano quartet No. 1.* ***
(BB) *** Belart 450 056-2 [(M) id. import]. Ingrid Haebler, Arthur Grumiaux, Georges Janzer, Eva Czako, Bernard Cazauran – MOZART: *Clarinet quintet.* **(*)
(M) *** Decca 448 602-2 [id.]. Curzon, Vienna Octet (members) – DVORAK: *Piano quintet.* ***
(B) **(*) Hyperion Dyad Dig. CDD 22008 (2) [id.]. Schubert Ens. of L. – HUMMEL: *Piano quintet;* SCHUMANN: *Piano quintet; Piano quartet.* **(*)
(N) **(*) Decca Dig. 460 034–2 Andreas Haefliger, Takács Qt (with MOZART: *Serenade: Eine kleine Nachtmusik* **; WOLF: *Italian serenade* **(*)).

Piano quintet in A (Trout); Adagio and rondo concertante in F, D.487.
(BB) **(*) Naxos Dig. 8.550658 [id.]. Jenö Jandó, Kodály Qt, with István Tóth.

Piano quintet in A (Trout); Adagio and Rondo concertante, D.487; Notturno in E flat for piano trio, D.897.
(N) (M) **(*) Classic fm Dig. 75605 570062. Boris Berezovsky, Soloists of ROHOCG.

(i; ii; iii) *Piano quintet in A (Trout);* (i; iii) *Arpeggione sonata, D.821*; (iv; i). *Die Forelle.*
**(*) Sony Dig. SK 61964 [id.]. (i) Ax; (ii) Frank, Young, Meyer; (iii) Ma; (iv) Barbara Bonney.

(i) *Piano quintet in A (Trout);* (ii) *String quartet No. 14 (Death and the Maiden).*
(M) *** Ph. 442 656-2. (i) Beaux Arts Trio with Samuel Rhodes & Georg Hörtnagel; (ii) Italian Qt.
(B) **(*) Sony SBK 46343 [id.]. (i) Horszowski, Budapest Qt (members), Julius Levine; (ii) Juilliard Qt.
(M) **(*) DG Originals 449 746-2 [id.]. Amadeus Qt, with (i) Gilels, Zepperitz.

(i) *Piano quintet in A (Trout);* (ii) *Die Forelle;* (iii) *Der Hirt auf dem Felsen.*
**(*) ASV Dig. CDDCA 684 [id.]. (i) Yitkin Seow, Prometheus Ens.; (ii; iii) Ann Mackay; (iii) Christopher Craker.

(i) *Piano quintet in A (Trout); Fantasia in C (Wanderer), D.760.*
(B) *** [EMI Red Line Dig. CDR5 72567]. Sviatoslav Richter, (i) with Borodin Qt.

(i) *Piano quintet in A (Trout), D.667. Moments musicaux, D.780.*
(N) (M) *** Decca Dig. 458 608-2 [id.]. András Schiff; (i) Hagen Qt.

(i) *Piano quintet in A (Trout);* (ii) *Der Hirt auf dem Felsen.*
(B) **(*) Carlton IMP Dig. 30367 01822 [(M) id.]. (i–ii) Ian Brown; (i) Nash Ens.; (ii) Felicity Lott, Michael Collins.

András Schiff and the Hagen Quartet give a delectably fresh and youthful reading of the *Trout quintet*, full of the joys of spring, but one which is also remarkable for hushed concentration, as in the exceptionally dark and intense account of the opening of the first movement. The Scherzo brings a light, quick and bouncing performance, and there is extra lightness too in the other middle movements. Alongside Brendel (but no other current rivals), this version observes the exposition repeat in the finale, and with such a joyful, brightly pointed performance one welcomes that. The *Moments musicaux* are also beautifully played and recorded, and make a considerable bonus.

The later Brendel performance is superbly recorded, the imagery rich and tangible, especially the piano, with Thomas Zehetmair's violin sweetly caught and the string bass gently resounding at the bottom. Like Brendel's previous Cleveland performance, which it easily displaces, this lacks something in traditional Viennese charm, but it has a compensating warmth and weight and certainly plenty of natural impetus, with Brendel consistently persuasive. The inclusion of a substantial Mozart coupling gives this Philips account quite an advantage.

Like the Brahms *quintet*, with which it is coupled on a bonus disc, Curzon's live recording of the *Trout quintet* with the augmented Amadeus Quartet, made at the Royal Festival Hall in 1971, amply compensates in warmth and power for what it may lack in high studio polish, with all five artists at their most spontaneous. The *Trout* variations may be on the slow side, but the rhythmic pointing is a delight. Good radio sound, smoother on top than Curzon's famous Decca version.

From the augmented Beaux Arts Trio comes one of the most delightful and fresh *Trouts* now available. Every phrase is splendidly alive, there is no want of vitality and sensitivity, and a finely judged balance and truthful (1976) recording make it a most desirable version. The Italian Quartet's version of the *Death and the Maiden* dates from a decade earlier, but the recording was first class in its day, and this sounds every bit as good as the *Trout*. The performance remains one of the finest available. The slow movement is particularly eloquent.

Richter dominates the EMI digital recording of the *Trout quintet*, not only in performance but in balance. Yet this account has marvellous detail, with many felicities drawn to the attention that might have gone unnoticed in other versions. The first movement is played very vibrantly indeed, while the second offers a complete contrast, gently lyrical, and the variations have plenty of character. This is very satisfying, even though other versions are stronger on Schubertian charm. The performance of the *Wanderer fantasia* comes from as long ago as 1963 but still sounds well. It is very distinguished indeed and makes a superb bonus, even if the piano-timbre is a shade hard.

Clifford Curzon's 1958 Decca recording of the *Trout* reveals its age in the thin violin-timbre, although the piano tone has plenty of colour. It remains a classic performance, with a distinguished account of the piano part and splendidly stylish support from the Vienna players impressively remastered, coupled to Dvořák's Op. 81 *Piano quintet* in Decca's Classic Sound series.

There is some admirably unassertive and deeply musical playing from Ingrid Haebler and from the incomparable Grumiaux. These artists do not try to make 'interpretative points' but are content to let the music speak for itself. The quality of the recorded sound is good. This is available on Belart attractively coupled with Mozart's *Clarinet quintet*.

Horszowski's contribution to the *Trout* is most distinguished and his clean, clear playing dominates the performance which, although full of imaginative detail, is a little on the cool side – though refreshingly so, for all that. The Juilliard Quartet are far from cool in the *Death and the Maiden quartet*, the unanimity of ensemble consistently impressive. In both works the sound is a little dry, but not confined.

In the 1975 DG recording of the *Trout* there is a masterly contribution from Gilels, and the Amadeus play with considerable freshness. The approach is very positive, not as sunny and spring-like as in some versions, but rewarding in its seriousness of purpose. The recording balance is convincing and the remastering creates a firm and vivid sound-image. The Amadeus's account of the *Death and the Maiden quartet* was their first analogue recording of this work in 1959. The unanimity of ensemble is remarkable. The quartet play as one in dealing with the finer points of phrasing, for example at the very beginning of the variations. The early DG stereo, too, is very good.

On Classic fM, Boris Berezovky leads a direct, spontaneous account, in which he makes a memorable contribution to the famous variations. If the performance (which includes the exposition repeat) had been imbued with the added expressive intensity which appears at the beginning of the *Adagio and Rondo concertante*, it would have been even more recommendable; but it is certainly fresh and well recorded. The *Notturno* also opens (and closes) with rapt concentration (and one recalls the slow movement of the *String quintet*), but the playing is also just a little mannered.

The account by the Nash Ensemble on Carlton also brings a fill-up in the shape of *The Shepherd on the rock*. They are rather forwardly recorded here and their account is just a little wanting in the spontaneity that distinguishes the finest of the current versions. Ian Brown is, as always, a sensitive artist.

A lively, immediate account from the Schubert Ensemble of London, strongly led by the pianist, William Howard. The first movement is brisk but committed, and the famous variations are well characterized. There are more touching accounts on record but few more vivaciously spontaneous, with a vivid recording to match.

Emanuel Ax leads an impressive ensemble in this invigorating Sony account of the *Trout quintet* which opens every bit as freshly as the later Brendel version. But, alas, there is a constant tendency to move onwards too quickly. This does not affect the famous theme and variations, which is done most imaginatively, but the Scherzo is very fast indeed, and the finale sounds rushed. A pity, as Yo-Yo Ma's performance of the *Arpeggione sonata* is totally endearing, with all the warmth, joy and innocent Schubertian charm one could ask for. To include the song associated with Schubert's quintet is always a happy idea, even if Barbara Bonney's account is direct rather than innocently beguiling. No complaints about the recording balance or the generous measure.

The Jandó/Kodály Trout is above all bracing. The first movement is soon moving along briskly and at a concert one could well be swept along by the momentum of the performance, for there is relaxation in the *Andante* and the famous *Variations* are mellow and strongly characterized. The polish and impetus of this playing is never in doubt and the recording is excellent, but this account obviously comes from east of Vienna. The *Adagio and Rondo concertante* sounds a stronger work here than usual and the *Rondo* is spirited and jolly.

Andreas Haefliger joins the Takács Quartet for one of the breeziest accounts of the *Trout quintet* on record, with the first-movement exposition repeat made an integral part of the forward flow. The sense of briskness comes as much from the players' style as the actual tempi, although the finale certainly wings its way along with an irresistible impulse. Some of the music's relaxed charm is lost, partly the effect of the recording balance which makes the violin timbre sound somewhat thin. Mozart's *Eine kleine Nachtmusik* is effective enough, though not memorable, but the Wolf *Italian serenade* certainly doesn't lack sparkle.

(i; ii) *Piano quintet in A (Trout);* (i; iii) *Piano trios Nos. 1 in B flat, D.898; 2 in E flat, D.929; Notturno in E flat, D.897; Sonata in B flat, D.28* (both arr. for piano trio).

(B) **(*) EMI (SIS) CZS7 62742-2 (2). (i) Hephzibah Menuhin; (ii) Amadeus Qt, J. Edward Merrett; (iii) Lord Menuhin & Maurice Gendron.

The 1958 Hephzibah Menuhin/Amadeus *Trout* has a pleasingly domestic sense of scale and considerable charm, even though the bright recording creates a balance in favour of the upper register of the piano and the upper strings. The Amadeus Quartet play with nicely judged feeling. Intimacy is also the keynote of the works for piano trio, and in the *Trios* Menuhin relaxes with his pianist sister and cellist friend to produce delightfully spontaneous-sounding performances. The atmosphere of the *Second Trio* is well caught, and the unassertive music-making captures the music's spirit very appealingly. These recordings are cleanly remastered; the sound lacks something in fullness but the focus is natural and the balance realistic.

(i) *Piano quintet in A (Trout), D. 667. String quartets Nos. 13 in A min., D.804; 14 in D min. (Death and the Maiden), D.810; 15 in G, D.887;* (ii) *String quintet in C, D.956.*
(M) ** EMI (SIS) CMS5 66144-2 (4). Alban Berg Qt, with (i) Leonskaja, Hörtnagel; (ii) Heinrich Schiff.

Compilations of this kind always bring the inherent danger that a single performance may be much less successful than the rest and so reduce the appeal of the set as a whole. If EMI had included just the string works here, this box would have been very attractive. But the *Trout* (in which the quartet are joined by Elisabeth Leonskaja and Georg Hörtnagel) brings keen disappointment. Despite the excellence of the recording and some incidental beauties, it remains a curiously uninvolving performance with routine gestures.

The *A minor Quartet*, however, is beautifully managed, though the slow movement (with the theme of the *Rosamunde Entr'acte*) is very fast indeed. The exposition repeat is omitted in the first movement of *Death and the Maiden* but otherwise this, too, is a very impressive performance. The playing is breathtaking in terms of tonal blend, ensemble and intonation throughout both these works; if one is not always totally involved, there is much to relish and admire. In the *G major* the Alban Berg players are most dramatic. They are strikingly well recorded, and beautifully balanced; but the sense of over-projection somehow disturbs the innocence of some passages.

In the great *C major Quintet*, where they are joined by Heinrich Schiff, they produce a timbre which is richly burnished and full-bodied. Once more there is no first-movement exposition repeat, but theirs is still a most satisfying account, strongly projected throughout. Given the sheer polish and gorgeous sound that distinguishes such playing, this account ranks high among current recommendations and the recording is admirable. But as a collection a mixed success.

Piano trios Nos. 1 in B flat, D.898; 2 in E flat, D.929.
**(*) Sony Dig. SK 62695 [id.]. Jos van Immersel, Vera Beths, Anner Bylsma.
(N) (B) **(*) Decca Dig 455 685-2 (2) [id.]. Ashkenazy, Zukerman, Harrell.

Piano trios Nos. 1–2; Adagio in E flat ('Notturno') (for piano trio), *D.897; Sonata in B flat* (for piano trio), *D.28.*
(M) *** Teldec/Warner Dig. 0630 12337-2 (2). Haydn Trio of Vienna.
**(*) Teldec/Warner 4509 94558-2 (2). Trio Fontenay.

(i) *Piano trios Nos. 1–2; Adagio in E flat ('Notturno')* (for piano trio), *D.897; Sonata in B flat* (for piano trio), *D.28;* (ii) *String trios: in B flat* (in one movement), *D.471; in B flat, D.581.*
(B) *** Ph. Duo 438 700-2 (2) [id.]. (i) Beaux Arts Trio; (ii) Grumiaux Trio.

The Beaux Arts set of the Schubert *Piano trios* from the late 1960s is another of the extraordinary bargains now offered on the Philips Duo label. The performances provide impeccable ensemble, with the pianist, Menahem Pressler, always sharply imaginative and the cellist, Bernard Greenhouse, bringing simple dedication to such key passages as the great slow-movement melody of the *Trio No. 2 in E flat*. The *Notturno*, played here with great eloquence, recalls the rapt, hushed intensity of the glorious slow movement of the *String quintet*. What makes the set doubly attractive is the inclusion of the two much rarer *String trios*, also early works from 1816/17. Given such persuasive advocacy, both pieces cannot fail to make a strong impression.

The Haydn Trio of Vienna are a highly musical and well-integrated group who are at one with the Schubertian spirit. Their playing is full of vigour and their characterization is strong and often robust, yet with a balancing intimacy. Both slow movements are beautifully yet simply played, while the Scherzo of No. 2 sparkles lightly as it should: here the excellent pianist, Heinz Medjimorec, is delectably nimble. In the *Notturno* the contrast is very marked between the hushed opening and the assertive middle section. With excellent, well-balanced, modern digital recording this stands high among current lower-priced recommendations, although one regrets that the accompanying documentation is inadequate.

There are many felicities of detail in the performances from the Trio Fontenay and their affectionate lyricism certainly does not lack warmth. But at times they over-dramatize and at others there is a feeling that phrasing is indulgent, as for instance with Niklas Schmidt's beautifully timbred yet almost sensuous cello solo in the *Andante* of the *B flat Trio*. The rapt opening of the *Notturno* needs a greater feeling of Schubertian innocence: a serenity without too much *espressivo*. The first movement of the *B flat Trio* has a strong impulse, and the Scherzo is treated as an opportunity for extrovert virtuosity. Excellent recording, but these performances lack the springlike freshness of the competing Viennese group, or indeed the famous Beaux Arts set on Philips.

Those wanting period performances of the Schubert *Piano trios* will find Immersel, Beths and Bylsma attractively characterful, although textures are lean and the approach is less strong on charm than it is on vigour and drama. There could be more lyrical give-and-take in the slow movement of the *B flat Trio*; however, there is nicely judged delicacy of feeling and plenty of concentration for the delightful *Andante con moto* slow movement of the *E flat Trio*, and the Scherzo which follows has an attractively light touch (as indeed does the Scherzo of D.898). The recording is well balanced and realistic.

Ashkenazy, Zukerman and Harrell give strong performances of both works, full of impetus and there is much subtlety of detail. But although the concentration of the playing in the slow movement of the *E flat Trio* is in no doubt and Ashkenazy produces scintillating passage work, in the last resort the innocent charm which informs Schubert's inspiration is all but missed. The players are not helped by a vividly forward recording which tends to sound aggressive in *fortissimos*, though some reproducers will register this more strikingly than others. These are new digital recordings but the two discs are offered as a Decca Double.

Piano trio No. 1 in B flat, D.898.
(B) *** EMI forte CZS5 69367-2 (2) [CDFB 69367]. David Oistrakh, Sviatoslav Knushevitzky, Lev Oborin – BEETHOVEN: *Archduke trio* ***; BRAHMS: *Violin sonatas Nos. 1–2.* **(*)

Schubert's music needs warmth and humanity, and this well-integrated Russian team on the bargain Forte reissue give both these qualities in abundance. They strive for beauty of tone and accuracy of ensemble (both of which they achieve with apparent ease) and imbue the music with just that essence of clarity and warmth that it demands by right. The tempi are sensitively chosen, and the Scherzo is handled in masterly fashion by all three players. Excellent piano-tone and a good round sound from the strings. The encores are beautifully played and, if the couplings are suitable, this makes a fine bargain.

Piano trio No. 1 in B flat; Sonata movement in B flat.
(BB) **(*) Naxos Dig. 8.550131; *4550131* [id.]. Stuttgart Piano Trio.

The Stuttgart Piano Trio may be at budget price but this is not a bargain-basement performance; the playing is musicianly and intelligent and there are many sensitive touches. Although the sound is somewhat less than ideal, there is a reasonable amount of air round the three instruments.

String quartets

String quartets Nos. 1–15.
(M) ** DG 419 879-2 (6). Melos Qt of Stuttgart.

The early quartets have a disarming grace and innocence, and some of their ideas are most touching. The Melos are an impressive body whose accounts of this repertoire are unmannered and on the whole sympathetic. They are let down by the undifferent recording quality, but the remastering has brought added presence.

String quartets Nos. 1 in G min./B flat, D.18; 2 in C, D.32; 3 in B flat, D.36; 4 in C, D.46; 5 in B flat, D.68; 9 in G min., D.173; 10 in E flat, D.87; 12 in C min. (Quartettsatz), D.703; 15 in G, D.887; in C min. (Overture), D.8a.
(N) *** CPO Dig. CPO 999 410-2 (3) [id.]. Auryn Qt.

String quartets Nos. 6 in D, D.74; 7 in D, D.94; 8 in B flat, D.112; 11 in E, D.353; 13 in A min., D.804; 14 in D min. (Death and the Maiden), D.810. 5 Minuets and 5 German dances, D.89.
(N) **(*) CPO Dig. CPO 999 409-2 (3) [id.]. Auryn Qt.

The Auryn Quartet give eminently satisfactory accounts of the Schubert quartets adding also some early minuets and trios, D.89. They are at their happiest in the earlier quartets which they play with an unforced fluency which will delight listeners. They may not always penetrate the depths of the *G major*, D.887, as some of their rivals do, but generally speaking both performances and recordings are more than just serviceable. The package is far more economical than the Leipzig Quartet on Dabringhaus and Grimm, which stretches to nine CDs – and just as comprehensive. Those looking for a complete ready-made Schubert quartet cycle could find this a worthwhile investment. Not every performance is competitive with the finest, but they are all eminently musical.

String quartets Nos. 1 in G min., D.18; 13 in A min., D.804; Overture in B flat (fragment), *D.470.*
*** MDG Dig. MDG 307 0602-2 [id.]. New Leipzig Qt.

String quartets Nos. 2 in C, D.32; 11 in E, D. 353; Overture in C min. (for string quintet), *D.8; Fragment, D. 87a.*
(N) *** MDG Dig. MDG 307 0609-2 [id.]. New Leipzig Qt.

String quartets Nos. 4 in C, D.46; 5 in B flat, D. 68 (including 1st & 2nd versions of *Allegro maestoso*); *2 Ländler for 2 violins in D, D.354.*
(N) *** MDG Dig. MDG 307 0608-2 [id.]. New Leipzig Qt.

String quartets Nos. 5 in B flat, D.68; 10 in E flat, D.87; in C min. (fragment), *D.103.*
*** MDG Dig. MDG 307 0605-5 [id.]. New Leipzig Qt.

String quartets Nos. 6 in C, D.74; 8 in B flat, D.112; in B flat (fragment), *D.470.*
*** MDG Dig. MDG 307 0606-5 [id.]. New Leipzig Qt.

String quartets Nos. 7 in D, D.94; 9 in G min., D.173; Quartet movement in C min., D. 703.
(N) *** MDG Dig. MDG 307 0607-2 [id.]. New Leipzig Qt.

String quartet No. 14 in D min. (Death and the Maiden), D.810; Minuet, D.86; Minuets and German dances, D.89.
*** MDG Dig. MDG 307 0604-2 [id.]. New Leipzig Qt.

String quartet No. 15 in G, D.887; Fragment, D.2c; String trio, D.472.
*** MDG Dig. MDG 307 0601-2 [id.]. New Leipzig Qt.

(i) *String quintet in C, D.956. Fragment, D.3; Overture, D.8a.*
*** MDG Dig. MDG 307 0603-2 [id.]. (i) Michael Sanderling; New Leipzig Qt.

The New Leipzig Quartet offer an ideal approach. They have great sweetness of tone, yet they are not sugary; they give us a wide dynamic range without drawing attention to themselves, and they seem totally inside the Schubert tradition. They have much greater warmth than the Melos of Stuttgart on DG and are far removed from the overpowering jet-setting quartet-machines. Theirs is humane music-making which conveys some sense of period and naturalness of expression. The *Quintet* may not be as intense as some versions but it is still very rewarding. The recordings are very good and the set has the merit of including various less familiar fragments. A thoroughly musical and well-recorded series.

String quartets Nos. 4 in C, D.46; 14 in D min. (Death and the Maiden), D.810.
*** RCA Dig. RD 87990 [id.]. Tokyo Qt.

Among newer recordings, the Tokyo give a keenly felt and beautifully phrased account of *Death and the Maiden*, and they are persuasive advocates of the charming, early *C major Quartet*; moreover the RCA recording is first class. They make a very beautiful sound (which some might find too sweet) and in this respect are to be preferred to the Lindsays, though the latter go deeper into the music. This is well worth ranking among the top recommendations, for those looking for a modern version.

String quartet No. 8 in B flat, D.112.
(M) (***) EMI mono CHS5 65308-2 (4) [id.]. Busch Qt (with MENDELSSOHN: *Capriccio in E min.*) – BEETHOVEN: *String quartets.* *** ✪

The excellence and lightness of spirit the Busch communicate in this quartet is exhilarating. There is an alternative transfer available on Pearl (see above).

String quartets Nos. 8 in B flat, D.112; 13 in A min., D.804.
*** ASV Dig. CDDCA 593 [id.]. Lindsay Qt.

In the glorious *A minor* the Lindsays lead the field. It would be difficult to fault their judgement in both these works on tempi and expression, and dynamics are always the result of keen musical thinking. Excellent recording.

String quartets Nos. 9 in G min., D.173; 13 in A min., D.804.
(B) *** Teldec/Warner 3984 21968-2. Alban Berg Qt.

Here is another vintage disc from the Alban Berg Quartet to match their splendid coupling of Haydn's Op. 74/3 and Op. 76/3, and this superb playing can only add to their laurels: finely integrated ensemble matched to depth of feeling. The *A minor Quartet* has its slow movement based upon Schubert's famous *Rosamunde* melody, and the eloquence here is gloriously natural and unforced. The *Andantino* of the *G minor* is also memorably done, and the crisp articulation in the finale is a joy. The recording is admirably balanced and truthful.

String quartets Nos. 10 (7) in E flat, D.87; 13 in A min., D.804.
✪ *** Audivis Astrée Dig. E 8580 [id.]. Mosaïques Qt.

The splendid period-instrument Mosaïques Quartet, having been hugely successful in Haydn and highly rewarding in Mozart, here move on to Schubert with equally impressive results. Above all these performances, so notable for their points of closely observed detail, are highly spontaneous. The very opening of the *E flat Quartet* (published posthumously as No. 10, but actually the seventh in order of composition, and written in 1816) is warmly inviting, and the players have the full measure of the songful serenity of its lovely *Adagio*. The profundities of the *A minor* are fully understood by this highly sensitive group, and the recapitulation is particularly memorable. There is dramatic intensity as well as charm in the famous ('*Rosamunde*') *Andante*, and the subtleties of the Minuet are nicely caught, with the finale following gracefully: the delicacy of the shading of the playing here is a marvel. A superb disc, beautifully recorded.

String quartets Nos. 12 in C min. (Quartettsatz), D.703; 13 in A min., D.804; 14 in D min. (Death and the Maiden); 15 in G, D.887.
(B) *** Ph. Duo 446 163-2 (2) [id.]. Italian Qt.

The Italian Quartet's 1965 coupling of the *Quartettsatz* and the *Death and the Maiden quartet* was counted the finest available in its day, with the famous variations played with great imagination and showing a notable grip in the closing pages. Technically the playing throughout is remarkable. There is just a hint of edge on the sound at times, but the original recording was very well balanced, and the CD adds to the immediacy. These players' understanding of Schubert is equally reflected in their performance of the *A minor Quartet*, recorded a decade later. Originally the long exposition repeat was omitted to get the work on a single LP side; now it has been restored. The familiar '*Rosamunde*' slow movement is beautifully paced, with an impressive command of feeling. The 1976 sound, too, is first class. The *G major Quartet* is, if anything, even finer. The conception is bold, the playing is distinguished by the highest standards of ensemble, intonation and blend, and the recording is extremely vivid, making this one of the most thought-provoking accounts of the *Quartet* ever. The 1977 recording still sounds remarkably real and present. Excellent CD transfers throughout.

String quartets Nos. 12 in C min. (Quartettsatz), D.703; 13 in A min., D.804; 14 in D min. (Death and the Maiden), D.810; 15 in G, D.887; (i) *String quintet in C, D.956.*

(N) **(*) DG Dig. 459 151-2 (3) [id.]. Emerson Qt. with (i) Rostropovich.

The Emersons certainly have an amazing technical address and are among the finest quartets playing now. Their attack and ensemble are impeccable; their tonal blend and finesse disarm criticism. Their approach is distinctly late twentieth-century Manhattan, rather than early nineteenth-century Europe with its gentler colours. Yet at the same time, it would be just as wrong to dismiss them – they spring from a different culture and have no want of intelligence and insight. There is tenderness at times and, in the *C major Quintet* with Rostropovich as second cello, an abundant eloquence. Good recording.

String quartets Nos. 12 in C min. (Quartettsatz), D.703; 14 in D min. (Death and the Maiden), D.810.

*** ASV Dig. CDDCA 560 [id.]. Lindsay Qt.

(BB) **(*) Naxos Dig. 8.550221 [id.]. Mandelring Qt.

The Lindsays' intense, volatile account of the *Death and the Maiden quartet* is played with considerable metrical freedom and the widest range of dynamic, and the *Quartettsatz*, which acts as the usual filler, is unusually poetic and spontaneous in feeling. The recording is excellent.

The Mandelring Quartet are very good indeed. The performances are sensitively and sensibly played and very decently recorded, and anyone tempted by this Naxos disc will not be disappointed for so modest an outlay.

String quartets Nos. 12–15; (i) *String quintet in C, D. 956.*

(M) *** Nimbus Dig. NI 1770 [id.]. Brandis Qt, (i) with W.-S. Yang.

This is a first-class set in every way and an excellent recommendation for those wanting digital recordings of the late *Quartets* plus the *Quintet* in a mid-priced box. The Brandis Quartet, a fine Central European group, have warmth and they bring a natural eloquence to all these quartets which are all the more potent for being free of interpretative point-making. In the great *C major Quintet*, with beautiful matching, they again convey spontaneous expressiveness, and they are not afraid to linger a little over the first movement's lovely second-subject melody. Their slow movement, played freely, has rapt tension but, again, also conveys warmth, rather an ethereal, withdrawn atmosphere which communicates in a quite individual way. They are very naturally recorded.

String quartets Nos. 13 in A min., D.804; 14 in D min. (Death and the Maiden), D.810.

(B) *** Ph. Virtuoso 426 383-2. Italian Qt.

This separate bargain issue, taken from the above Duo, is most welcome. The sound is excellent.

String quartet No. 14 in D min. (Death and the Maiden).

(BB) *** CfP Silver Double CDCFPSD 4772 (2) [id.]. Gabrieli Qt – BORODIN: *String quartet No. 2* ***; BRAHMS: *Clarinet quintet* **(*); DVORAK: *String quartet No. 12.* ***

Like the other performances on this Classics for Pleasure Silver Double, the Gabrielis give a direct, sensitive and polished account of Schubert's great *D minor Quartet*, not wearing their hearts on their sleeves but genuinely touching in the slow movement. The recording, from the beginning of the 1970s, is first class and has been smoothly transferred to CD. For those collectors wanting all four works, this is excellent value.

String quartets Nos. 14 in D min. (Death and the Maiden); 15 in G.

(***) EMI (mono) CDH7 69795-2 [id.]. Busch Qt.

The Busch Quartet's account is more than 50 years old, but it brings us closer to the heart of this music than almost any other. The slow movement of the *Death and the Maiden quartet* is a revelation, and the same must be said of the *G major*, which has great depth and humanity. For its age, the sound is still amazing.

String quartet No. 15 in G, D.887; (i) *Notturno for piano trio, D. 897.*

*** Decca Dig. 452 854-2 [id.]. Takács Qt, (i) with Andreas Haefliger.

As in their performance of the *String quintet* (see

below), the Takács Quartet play very freely, using the widest range of dynamic, with the leader often dropping to a withdrawn *pianissimo* with seeming spontaneity, so that the result does not seem mannered or self-conscious. The opening of the *Andante* brings the most delicate entry from the cello, gentle and restrained, and the Scherzo, too, opens with a gossamer touch, while the finale dances with joyful vigour. In the *Notturno* Andreas Haefliger weaves his piano figurations with comparable finesse. The top-quality recording has fine presence, yet the quartet image is set slightly back.

String quintet in C, D.956.
*** ASV Dig. CDDCA 537 [id.]. Lindsay Qt, Douglas Cummings.
(N) (M) *** EMI CDM5 66890-2 [CDM5 66942]. Alban Berg Qt with Heinrich Schiff.
❁ (***) Testament mono SBT 1031 Hollywood Qt, Kurt Reher – SCHOENBERG: *Verklaerte Nacht.* (***) ❁
(B) *** EMI CfP CD-CFP 6038 [id.]. Chilingirian Qt, Jennifer Ward Clarke.
*** Channel Classics Dig. CCS 6794 [id.]. Orpheus Qt, Peter Wispelwey.
*** Teldec/Warner Dig. 4509 94564-2 [id.]. Borodin Qt, Misha Milman.
(***) Biddulph mono LAB 093 [id.]. Pro Arte Qt, Anthony Pini – BRAHMS: *String sextet No. 1.* (***)
(B) **(*) DG 453 668-2 [415 373-2]. Melos Qt, Mstislav Rostropovich.
(B) (***) Millennium mono MCD 80124 [id.]. V. Konzerthaus Qt.

(i) *String quintet in C; String quartet No. 12 (Quartettsatz), D.703.*
*** Decca Dig. 436 324-2. Takács Qt, (i) with Miklós Perényi.

String quintet in C; String trio in B flat, D.581.
(BB) *** ASV Quicksilva Dig. CDQS 6207 [(M) id.]. Locrian Ens.
(BB) *** Naxos Dig. 8.550388. Villa Musica Ens.

(i) *String quintet in C, D.956;* (ii) *Auf der Strom, D.943;* (iii) *Gretchen am Spinnrade; Nacht und Träume; Rastlose Liebe.*
(M) *** Sony Theta Dig. SMK 60032 [id.]. (i) Cleveland Qt, Yo-Yo Ma; (ii) Benita Valente, Myron Bloom, Rudolf Serkin; (ii) Kiri Te Kanawa, Richard Amner.

The Lindsay version gives the impression that one is eavesdropping on music-making in the intimacy of a private concert. They observe the first-movement exposition repeat and the effortlessness of their approach does not preclude intellectual strength. In the ethereal *Adagio* they effectively convey the sense of it appearing motionless, suspended, as it were, between reality and dream, yet at the same time never allowing it to become static. Their reading must rank at the top of the list; it is very well recorded.

The Cleveland Quartet and Yo-Yo Ma have won golden opinions for their account of the *Quintet* on Sony. They are scrupulous in observing dynamic markings (the second subject is both restrained and *pianissimo*) and they also score by observing all repeats. Their performance has feeling and eloquence, as well as a commanding intellectual grip. Moreover they are admirably recorded and thus present a strong challenge at mid-price. For the reissue, some Schubert Lieder have been added. A fine performance from Benita Valente of Schubert's extended scena evoking a lover's departure, *Auf der Strom* ('On the river'), which has both passion and charm, is made memorable by Myron Bloom's glorious horn obbligato. Of the following three songs from Kiri Te Kanawa, *Gretchen am Spinnrade* has a delightful simplicity and *Nacht and Träume* is tonally ravishing. So this vocal music makes a considerable bonus.

Few ensembles offer timbre as full-bodied or as richly burnished as that produced by the Alban Berg and Heinrich Schiff, whose recording has impressive sonority, although there is just a touch of digital fierceness on top. This group has the advantage of wonderfully homogeneous tone, even in their raptly sustained *pianissimo* in the *Adagio*. Given the sheer polish and full sound that distinguishes their playing, this must rank high among current recommendations. The performance is strongly projected and excellently balanced by the recording engineers. However, unlike the Lindsays, they do not observe the first movement exposition repeat. This CD now returns to the catalogue in EMI's 'Great recordings of the century' series.

The Hollywood Quartet's 1951 version of the *Quintet* with Kurt Reher as second cello stands apart. Over 40 years on, its qualities of freshness and poetry, as well as an impeccably confident technical address, still impress as deeply as ever. This is the product of consummate artistry and remains very special indeed.

However, the new recording of the *Quintet* on ASV Quicksilva by members of the Locrian Ensemble must also be given the strongest recommendation. It is for the 1990s what the famous old Saga version was for the 1960s. It has polish, warmth (particularly in the lovely secondary theme of the first movement) and deep feeling. The hushed *pianissimo* playing in the *Adagio* is magnetic, rapt in its intensity, and the players have the advantage of a silent background and excellent, truthful recording in a pleasing acoustic. The lighter, single-movement *Trio in B flat* is also played most persuasively, its nostalgic feeling nicely caught.

The Takács Quartet with Miklós Perényi on Decca (very well recorded), taking a freely expressive view and sounding spontaneous, regularly find Schubertian magic, as when the leader plays with the most withdrawn half-tone at the start of the *Adagio* slow movement. Particularly when the Takács disc also offers the *Quartettsatz* as a bonus, the Decca issue remains competitive, with the jollity of the Scherzo and finale set against the spacious strength of the first two massive movements.

Vividly recorded (in 1980), with clear placing of instruments in a smallish but not dry acoustic (in fact a chapel), the Chilingirian version presents a most compelling account, totally unmannered and direct in style but full of concentration and spontaneity. So one has the consistent sense of live performance, and the great melody of the first movement's second subject emerges without any intrusive nudging or overexpressiveness. The slow movement too has natural intensity, though the closeness of the recording prevents one from observing a really soft *pianissimo*. Throughout, the string-timbres and blending are most natural.

The Villa Musica players tackle the great *C major Quintet* with a freshness and concentration that are consistently compelling, even if the finale is neat and clean rather than urgently dramatic. The little *String trio* makes an attractive and generous fill-up, another assured and stylish performance. With clear, well-balanced recording this super-budget issue makes an outstanding bargain.

The Orpheus Quintet offer a performance of communicated warmth and feeling, both in the slow movement and in the remarkable *Andante* central section of the Scherzo. The playing is fresh and feels alive, and the recording has striking body and realism.

On Teldec, the augmented Borodin Quartet command the listener's rapt attention throughout a performance which demonstrates both their emotional involvement and their almost unique unanimity of ensemble. The *Adagio* is beautifully played, but its special, almost unearthly intensity is not experienced to the full, as the players strive – with great success – to create the most beautifully blended sound. The recording is superbly balanced, and it is impossible for the listener not to respond to music-making of this calibre.

Rostropovich plays as second cello in the Melos performance, and no doubt his influence from the centre of the string texture contributes to the eloquence of the famous *Adagio* which, like the performance as a whole, is strongly, even dramatically, characterized. The emphasis on the rhythmic articulation of the outer movements leaves no doubt as to the power of Schubert's writing, and there is no lack of atmosphere in the opening and closing sections of the slow movement. The recording is live and immediate. A fine version, but not a first choice.

The Pro Arte Quartet's 1935 account of the Schubert *Quintet*, with Anthony Pini as second cello, dominated the pre-war catalogues. Its humanity and warmth still tell, particularly in the slow movement. It comes with a fine account of the Brahms *B flat Sextet*, made in the same year. Needless to say, some allowance has to be made for the recording, eminently well transferred though it is.

The Vienna Konzerthaus Quartet are right inside this music and they give a simple, direct and refreshingly unexaggerated reading of great appeal. There is real tension here, and it is a pity that the early recording-balance prevents a real *pianissimo* registering in the slow movement where there is no lack of intensity; otherwise the sound is excellent and, even as it stands, this is a most rewarding version.

Violin sonatinas, Nos. 1–3; Fantasy in C, D.934.
(BB) *(**) Naxos Dig. 8.550420 [id.]. Dong-Suk Kang, Pascal Devoyon.

Korean-born Dong-Suk Kang plays with style and panache and is given excellent support by Pascal Devoyon. Neither is well served by the recording, however, made in a cramped studio that robs the piano-tone of some of its timbre, while the close balance does less than complete justice to the sound this fine violinist makes in the flesh. Nevertheless it still gives pleasure. Performances three stars; the recording one.

Violin sonatinas Nos. 1–3; Rondo in B min. (Rondeau brillant), D.895; Duo in A (Grand duo), D.574; Fantasie in C, D.934.
(M) *** Sony Stern Edition IV Dig./Analogue SM2K 64528 (2) [id.]. Isaac Stern, Daniel Barenboim (with: HAYDN: *Violin concerto in C, Hob VIIa/1* with Chamber O **).

It is good to have these 1988 Stern recordings reissued at mid-price. The performances have a natural warmth and plenty of character, yet there is an unaffected simplicity and directness of style which suits the three early *Sonatinas*, written in 1816 but not published until two decades later. One has only to sample the *Andante* of the *G minor*, D.408, or the sturdy opening of the *Allegro* of the *Rondo brillant* to appreciate the affinity these artists have with Schubert's muse. The *Grand duo* (the title was invented by Diabelli for the work's posthumous publication) dates from little more than a year later, but both artists provide the necessary added flair (especially in the Scherzo) for this rather more ambitious piece. The gentle, mysterious opening of the *Fantasie* is superbly caught and the lilting *Allegretto* makes a perfect foil for the songful *Andantino* (which readily takes wing on Stern's bow). The finale is a joy. The Haydn *Concerto*, excellently recorded in mono in 1947, is a very acceptable bonus. Stern directs the work himself and the highlight of the performance is his touching account of the *Adagio*, although the accompanying guitar-like orchestral pizzicatos could ideally have had a lighter touch. A superb set just the same.

PIANO MUSIC

Piano music for four hands

Allegro in A min. (Lebensstürme), D.947; Divertissement à la Française in E min., D.823; Divertissement à la Hongroise in G min., D.818; Fantasia in F min., D.940; Grand duo in C, D.812; 4 Ländler, D.814.

(B) *** EMI forte CZS5 69770-2 (2) [CDFB 69770]. Christoph Eschenbach and Justus Frantz.

German dance in G min., D.818; Grande marche funèbre, D.859; Grande marche héroïque, D.885; 6 Grandes marches et trios, D.819; Grand Rondeau (Allegretto quasi andantino), D.951; Kindermarsch in G min., D.928; 2 Ländler in E, D.618; 2 Marches caractéristiques, D.886; 2 Marches héroïques, D.602; 3 Marches militaries, D.733.

(B) *** EMI forte CZS5 69764-2 (2) [CDFB 69764]. Christoph Eschenbach and Justus Frantz.

Cristoph Eschenbach and Justus Frantz made their extensive survey of Schubert's four-handed piano music in 1978 and 1979, and the Abbey Road recording was of high quality. The CD transfers occasionally bring a touch of hardness in the treble, but the underlying sound is full and well rounded and has plenty of colour. The first collection listed includes the finest work ever written in the genre, the *F minor Fantasia*. The opening here may suggest that the performances is too reticent, but that is deceptive and this is as powerful a reading as any available with its rhythms well sprung; and the same comment applies to *Grand Duo*, while the wide range of mood in the *Lebensstürme* (a title almost certainly not Schubert's own) is encompassed impressively. The delicate interplay between the two pianists is a constant delight, whether in the simple *Ländler*, the charming central *Andantino varié* of the *Divertissement à la Française* or the cimbalom imitations in the companion Hungarian-style *Divertissement*, both extended three-movement works showing the composer at his most felicitously inventive and presented here joyfully.

The second collection includes a great many marches, but their expressive range is very much wider than might be expected. Much of it is jolly and extrovert, but there is delicacy and lyricism too, as in the fifth *Grand march and trio* of D.819 *in E flat minor*, which is quite dolorous, while the sixth has a brio to match the most famous *Marche militaire*. In the hands of Eschenbach and Frantz the third *Marche héroïque* of D.602 is quite charming, more like an impromptu. The *German dance in G minor* opens with appealing restraint and the *Kindermarsch* brings a delightful, child-like simplicity, while the two *Marches caractéristiques* sparkle with brilliance. Most remarkable of all are the *Grandes marches funèbre et héroïque*, written to mark, first, the death of Tsar Alexander I of Russia in 1825 and then the coronation of his successor, Nicholas I. The first is highly eloquent, but it is the second, in A minor, which is the more extended (17 minutes), with a characteristic lyrical strain as its centrepiece. The closing *Grand rondeau*, most touchingly played, was written in June 1828, only five months before the composer's death at the age of thirty-one. Choice in this instance will depend on how much of this repertoire you want in your collection, for the playing of Anne Queffélec and Imogen Cooper on the competing Erato set is no less eloquent than their rivals, and they are very well recorded. At times Escenbach and Frantz score in sheer freshness, but the EMI sound has a brighter edge.

Allegro in A min., (Lebenstürme), D.947; Divertissement, D.823; Grandes marches, D.819; 4 Polonaises, D.599; Rondo in A, D.951; Variations in E min. on a French song, D.624.

*** Sony S2K 66256 (2) [id.]. Tal, Groethuysen.

Tal and Groethuysen are about the best duo-partnership currently before the public and almost any of their records can be recommended to those who care for intelligent and sensitive playing. This set is no exception and brings much pleasure. They play with a genuine Schubertian sensibility and the widest range of dynamic: the delicacy of their *pianissimos* is most impressive. Their opening *Lebenstürme* ('Storms of life') is appropriately volatile, and the *Variations on a French song* are most engaging. The recording is resonant, but they are not too closely balanced.

Allegro moderato and Andante, D.968; Fantasy in G min., D.9; 3 Marches Militaires D.733; 4 Polonaises, D.599; Variations on 'Marie' by Herold.

(N) (BB) **(*) Naxos Dig. 8.553441 [id.]. Jandó, Kollar.

This disc of some of Schubert's lesser works for piano duet begins most temptingly with the most famous of his *Marches militaires*, played by the Hungarian duo with crispness and vigour. Ranging from the very early *Fantasy* to the late *Allegro and Andante*, this well-recorded collection may be a little short on charm, but is winningly fresh throughout.

Andantino varié in B min., D.823; Duo in A min., D.947; Fantasia in F min., D.940; Grand duo sonata in C, D.812; 3 Marches militaires, D.733; 6 Polonaises, D.824; Rondo in A, D.951; Variations on an original theme in A flat, D.813.

(M) *** Erato/Warner 0630 11231-2 (2). Anne Queffélec & Imogen Cooper.

It is good to have a thoroughly recommendable mid-priced set of Schubert's music for piano/four hands, including the greatest work ever written for the genre, the *F minor Fantasia*. Some of this music (including that piece) has also been recorded by Gilels and his daughter Elena for DG, and that shorter survey will no doubt resurface before too long; but the playing of Anne Queffélec and Imogen Cooper is hardly less eloquent than their rivals', and they also offer a commanding account of the *Grand duo sonata*. The slighter pieces also come off well: the *Variations* are beautifully played and have an engaging innocence, while the most famous *Marche militaire* sparkles. Its two lesser-known companions are also worth having on disc when played (like the six *Polonaises*) so brightly and spontaneously. The 1978 analogue recording is well balanced, clear and natural, the acoustic neither over-reverberant nor too confined.

Divertissement à l'hongroise in G min., D.818; Fantaisie in F min., D.940; Introduction and 4 variations on an original theme and finale in B flat, D.603; 3 Marches héroïques, D.602; Overture in F, D.675; 6 Polonaises, D.824; 8 Variations on a theme from Hérold's opera Marie in C, D.908.
**(*) Sony S2K 58955 [id.]. Duo Tal and Groethuysen.

This is interesting and rare repertoire, and the Duo Tal and Groethuysen play it with lively vigour. They are at their best in the glorious *Fantaisie in F minor*, and they find charm in the *Introduction and four variations on an original theme*. But elsewhere they often seem too loud, in the *Overture* for instance and in the *Divertissement* (and the recording is not entirely flattering to their *fortissimos*).

Fantasia in F min., D.940.
*** Sony Dig. SK 39511 [id.]. Murray Perahia, Radu Lupu – MOZART: *Double piano sonata.* ***
*** Chandos Dig. CHAN 9162 [id.]. Lortie, Mercier – MOZART: *Andante with variations* etc. ***

Recorded live at The Maltings, the performance of Lupu and Perahia is full of haunting poetry, with each of these highly individual artists challenging the other in imagination. Warmly atmospheric recording.

The Louis Lortie–Hélène Mercier partnership is as impressive here as it is elsewhere. The Schubert holds its own even against such illustrious competition as the Lupu–Perahia recording on Sony, also coupled with Mozart. Very good recording.

(i) Piano duet: *Fantasy in F min., D.940; Introduction and variations on an original theme in B flat, D.603; 2 Marches caractéristiques in C, D.886; Rondo* (for piano duet) *in D, D.608.* (Piano) *6 German dances, D.783; Impromptus Nos. 1–4, D.899; 5–8, D.935; 6 Moments musicaux, D.780; Piano sonatas Nos. 3 in E, D.459; 4 in A min., D.537; 7 in E flat, D.568; 9 in B, D.575; 13 in A, D.664; 14 in A min., D.784; 16 in A min., D.845; 17 in D, D.850; 18 in G, D.894; 19 in C min., D.958; 20 in A, D.959; 21 in B flat, D.960.*
(B) **(*) Ph. 456 367-2 (7). Ingrid Haebler, (i) with Ludwig Hoffmann.

To quote *New Grove*, Ingrid Haebler's 'piano style is essentially feminine and unassertive and she has been criticized for reticent playing. But she has qualities which make her a distinguished and faithful interpreter of Schubert.' Her *Moments musicaux* can be ranked with the finest available. Her stereo survey of the *Sonatas* was incomplete and somewhat uneven but she has special insights to offer, and the disarming simplicity of her Schubertian style cannot fail to give pleasure when she is so well recorded. The music for piano duet was among the first to be recorded (in 1961) but one would not guess this from the excellent quality with which it reproduces. The playing is very good indeed and finds Miss Haebler and her partner in top form. As is immediately apparent at the sensitive opening of the *F minor Fantasy*, this is relaxed and spontaneous playing that should give much pleasure.

Solo piano music

Allegretto, D.915; Impromptus Nos. 1–4, D.899; 5–8, D.935; 3 Klavierstücke, D.946.
(N) **(*) DG Dig. 457 550-2 (2) [id.]. Maria João Pires.

Maria João Pires proves as impressive a Schubertian as she is a Mozart interpreter, though there are some fussy touches that may not wear well. The set is mysteriously entitled '*Le voyage magnifique*' and is imaginatively presented, portraying Mme Pires bestriding rocky landscapes in the mist. The presentation reproduces various quotes from Goethe and does not tell us too much about Schubert, but Pires does! Despite the odd touch of prettification, this is satisfying playing and eminently well recorded. However the set is uneconomically laid out on a pair of full-priced CDs, the first of which only plays for 35 minutes 20 seconds!

Allegretto in C min., D.915; Moments musicaux Nos. 1–6, D.780; 2 Scherzi, D.593; 12 Valse nobles, D.969.
(M) **(*) DG (IMS) 435 072-2. Daniel Barenboim.

Some of the finest playing here comes in the two *Scherzi*. The *Allegretto in C minor* is given an effective, improvisatory quality, but the 12 *Valses nobles* are played too forcefully for their full charm to be revealed. In the *Moments musicaux* there is much to admire, yet there is an element of calculation that robs the impact of freshness. The piano-tone on DG has impressive presence and weight.

Fantasia in C (Wanderer), D.760.
*** Sony Dig. MK 42124 [id.]. Murray Perahia – SCHUMANN: *Fantasia in C.* ***
*** EMI CDM5 66895-2. Sviatoslav Richter – DVORAK: *Piano concerto.* ***
(M) *** Ph. 420 644-2. Alfred Brendel – *Sonata No. 21.* ***
(M) *** DG 447 451-2 [id.]. Maurizio Pollini – SCHUMANN: *Fantasia, Op. 17.* ***
(M) **(*) DG Dig. 445 562-2 [id.]. Yevgeny Kissin – BRAHMS: *Fantasias* **(*); LISZT: *Concert paraphrases of Schubert Lieder*, etc. ***

Murray Perahia's account of the *Wanderer* stands alongside the finest. In his hands it sounds as fresh as the day it was conceived, and its melodic lines speak with an ardour and subtlety that breathe new life into the score. The recording is more than acceptable.

Richter's 1963 performance (now reissued as one of EMI's 'Great recordings of the Century') is masterly in every way. The piano-timbre is real and the remastering gives the great pianist a compelling presence; the coupling is hardly less outstanding.

Brendel's playing is of a high order, and he is truthfully recorded and coupled with what is perhaps Schubert's greatest Sonata, so this is excellent value at mid-price.

Pollini's account is outstanding and, though he is not ideally recorded and the piano-timbre is shallow, the playing still shows remarkable insights. Moreover the Schumann coupling is equally fine.

Kissin, the amazing young Russian, gives a fine account of the *Wanderer*, though it is not quite as persuasive (perhaps he himself is not quite as persuaded by the music) as the finest rivals. Of course there is some very fine pianism, but other artists, Kempff for instance, find greater depths. Good DG recording.

Fantasia in C (Wanderer), D.760; Andante in A, D.604; Allegretto in C min., D.915; 3 Klavierstücke (Impromptus), D.946; Scherzo in B flat, D.593/1; 13 Variations on a theme by Anselm Hüttenbrenner in A min., D.576.
(M) *** DG (IMS) 453 289-2. Wilhelm Kempff.

Although there is no lack of strength in the *Wanderer fantasia*, the high drama which such a pianist as Sviatoslav Richter finds is missing; but the result with Kempff is equally compelling, with a moulding of the structure which gives the illusion of spontaneity. Kempff then injects all his habitual magic into the other often deceptively simple pieces. His playing is utterly disarming in the second of the three *Klavierstücke*, which were written in the last year of Schubert's life, easy, happy inspirations that wear greatness easily. Whatever the tone of Schubert's voice, Kempff's crystal touch and natural intensity make for pure delight. Excellent analogue recording (from 1967–71) naturally transferred.

Impromptus Nos. 1–4, D.899; 5–8, D.935; 3 Klavierstücke, D.946; Moments musicaux Nos. 1–6, D.780; Allegretto in C min., D.915; 6 German dances, D.820; Grazer Galopp, D.925; Hungarian melody in B min., D.817; 12 Ländler, D.790.
(B) *** Decca Double Dig. 458 139-2 (2) [id.]. András Schiff.

Impromptus Nos. 1–4, D.899; 5–8, D.935; 3 Klavierstücke (Impromptus), D.946; 6 Moments musicaux, D.780; 12 German dances, D.790; 16 German dances, D.783.
❁ (B) *** Ph. Duo 456 061-2 (2). Alfred Brendel.

Brendel's analogue set of the *Impromptus* is magical, and the *Moments musicaux* are among the most poetic in the catalogue. It is difficult to imagine finer Schubert playing than this; to find more eloquence, more profound musical insights, one has to go back to Edwin Fischer – and even here comparison is not always to Brendel's disadvantage. The *Klavierstücke* are searching, and in his hands the *German dances*, although retaining their underlying charm, sound anything but trivial. The recordings date from the early 1970s and offer Philips's very finest analogue quality; the remastering is expert and the focus is very slightly cleaner, without any loss of bloom.

It was with this pair of 1990 discs that András Schiff laid the foundations for his Schubertian odyssey. The playing is idiomatic, intelligent and humane, and the recording is more than acceptable. It is impossible to recommend his *Impromptus* in preference to those of Brendel, but no one will be disappointed with them. We had hoped the arrangement of repertoire would have been reordered by Decca so that (as with major competitors) the eight *Impromptus* would have been placed on a single CD. However, their reissue as a Double means that all this music is easily accessible, and Schiff has the advantage of very natural digital recording, the effect lighter-textured than with Brendel.

Impromptus Nos. 1–4, D.899; 5–8, D.935; Moments musicaux Nos. 1–6, D. 780; Piano sonatas Nos. 13 in A, D.664; 21 in B flat, D.960.
(N) ❁ (B) *** DG Double 459 412-2 [id.]. Wilhelm Kempff.

Kempff's set of *Impromptus* were the first of this collection to be recorded (in 1965) and the sound has a touch of hardness, although the remastering has improved the quality, which is now noticeably fuller and warmer. Predictably fine playing, of course, and the magic is obvious from the gentle opening of the first *C major* work. The D.899 set is beautifully done, with all the pieces perceptively characterized: the *G flat major* is wonderfully intimate and ruminative; the equally famous *A flat major* of D.935 is quite lovely, and the *Rosamunde* theme with variations has an engaging innocence. The two *Sonatas* followed in January 1967 and are cherishable: neither performance has been surpassed and here the piano-timbre is richer, fully coloured and resonant in the bass. It is a tribute to Kempff's artistry that with the most relaxed tempi he conveys such consistently compulsive intensity. Hearing the opening of D.960, one might feel that this is going to be a lightweight account of Schubert's greatest sonata, but in fact the long-breathed expansiveness is hypnotic so that here, quite as much as in the *Great C major Symphony*, one is bound by the spell of heavenly length. Rightly, Kempff repeats the first-movement exposition repeat, with the important nine bars of lead-back, and though the overall manner is less obviously dramatic than is common, the range of tone-colour is magical, with sharp terracing of dynamics to plot the geography of each movement. Though very much a personal utterance this interpretation is no less great for that. Both this and the equally warm and concentrated account of the *A Major*, again with a hauntingly rapt *Andante*, belong to a tradition of pianism that has almost disappeared, and we must be eternally grateful that its expression has been so glowingly captured here. The *Moments musicaux* were recorded in the summer of the same year and the sound is very good, if not so full in timbre as the sonatas. Kempff characteristically gives intimate performances of pieces which range so much farther than one expects from their name and scale. Kempff's allegros are never very fast and the results sing in the most relaxed way. All in all this is a treasurable set, indispensable to any collector who cares about Schubert or indeed the art of the piano.

Impromptus Nos. 1–4, D. 899; 5–8, D.935.
*** Sony Dig. SK 37291 [id.]. Murray Perahia.
(N) (M) *** Decca Legends Dig. 460 975-2 [id.]. Radu Lupu.
(BB) **(*) Naxos Dig. 8.550260 [id.]. Jenö Jandó.

Perahia's account of the *Impromptus* is very special indeed. Directness of utterance and purity of spirit are of the essence here, with articulation of sparkling clarity. The CBS recording is very good, truthful in timbre.

Lupu's account of the *Impromptus* is of the same calibre as the Brendel analogue version, and he is most beautifully recorded on CD. Indeed, in terms of natural sound this is a most believable image. This version now has a considerably price advantage in Decca's Legend series.

Though his set of the *Impromptus* is not ideally recorded (the microphones are rather too close, with unpleasing results in *fortissimo* passages), Jandó has been worse served by the engineers. He is a very musical player and his unaffected (and often perceptive) readings are more than acceptable.

4 Impromptus, D.899; Klavierstuck in A, D.604; 6 Moments musicaux, D.780; 13 Variations on a theme by Huttenbrenner, D.756.
(N) (B) ** Carlton Dig. 30367 01832 [id.]. Dirk Joerles.

Dirk Joerles is a highly musical Schubertian, but at times a little cool, and the *Variations* lack charm. However, the *Impromptus* are a distinct success, particularly the *G flat* and *A flat* (Nos. 3 & 4), and it is a pity he did not record the complete set. The recording is pleasingly natural.

Impromptus Nos. 1–4, D.899; Piano sonata No. 21 in B flat, D.960.
*** Calliope Dig. CAL 9689 [id.]. Inger Södergren.

Inger Södergren's account of the first four *Impromptus* belongs in exalted company, and the *B flat Sonata* is hardly less fine. Her playing is marked throughout by sensitivity and a selfless and unostentatious dedication to Schubert. The recording is acceptable rather than outstanding.

4 Impromptus, D.899; Impromptu in B flat, D.935/3; Moments musicaux, D.780/1, 2 & 6.
(B) *** LaserLight Dig. 15609 [id.]. Jenö Jandó.

Jenö Jandó is here heard recorded in an acoustic that does justice to his talent. The sound, at least in the opening *B flat major Impromptu* of D.935, is fresh and truthful, the ambience is warm, and the playing is very good. The balance is not as good in the three *Moments musicaux* or in the D.899 *Impromptus*: it is closer and marginally drier.

Moments musicaux Nos. 1–6, D.780; 3 Klavierstücke, D. 946.
(M) *** Virgin Veritas/EMI Dig. VER5 61161-2. Melvyn Tan (fortepiano) – BEETHOVEN: *Allegretto in C min*, etc. ***

These pieces sound very effective indeed on Melvyn Tan's fortepiano (a modern instrument by Derek Adlam, modelled on an 1814 Viennese instrument). Tan finds a remarkable range of colour and, though the effect is less mellow than with a modern instrument, one's ears adjust almost immediately, so strongly does his playing project. With textures clear but not bare, the music's inner emotional feeling is conveyed the more readily, while the perky *No. 3 in F minor* has a most engaging character when articulated with such precison.

Moments musicaux Nos. 1–6, D.780; 3 Klavierstücke, D.946; Allegretto in C min., D.915.
(BB) **(*) Naxos Dig. 8.550259 [id.]. Jenö Jandó.

Though the venue is the Italian Institute in Budapest, Jandó is much better recorded here than he often has been. He proves a thoroughly sympathetic and sensitive Schubertian, but he is still too upfront. The opening of the *Drei Klavierstücke* is a shade too fast (Jandó does not completely convey its dark, disturbing overtones) but the middle section is beautifully judged. Thoughtful and intelligent music-making, acceptably recorded, and very good value for money.

Moments musicaux, D.780; 2 Scherzi, D.593; Piano sonata No. 14 in A min., D.784.
*** DG Dig. 427 769-2. Maria João Pires.

Maria João Pires gives masterly accounts of the *Moments musicaux* and the *A minor Sonata*, distinguished throughout by thoughtful and refined musicianship, and she is fully aware of the depth of feeling that inhabits the *Moments musicaux*, without ever indulging in the slightest expressive exaggeration. The digital recording is exceptionally present and clear.

Piano sonatas

Piano sonatas Nos. 1 in E, D.157; 2 in C, D.279; 3 in E, D.459; 4 in A min., D.537; 5 in A flat, D.557; 6 in E min., D.566; 7 in E flat, D.568; 9 in B, D.575; 11 in F min., D.625; 13 in A, D.664; 14 in A min., D.784; 15 in C, D.840 (Relique); 16 in A min., D.845; 17 in D, D.850; 18 in G, D.894; 19 in C min., D.958; 20 in A, D.959; 21 in B flat, D.960.
(M) *** EMI Eminence Dig. CDBOX FS1 (8) (also available separately). Martino Tirimo.
(M) *** DG 423 496-2 (7) [id.]. Wilhelm Kempff.
(M) *** Decca Dig. 448 390-2 (7). András Schiff.

It is a far cry from the geographical certainty of Beethoven's great cycle of 32 piano sonatas to the haphazard, fragmented series of sonatas which Schubert left behind on his premature death at the age of 31. Yet viewed as a whole, with the culminating works of his final years providing a sublime equivalent to the late Beethoven works, the Schubert series is just as revealing of a supreme master, here more than ever in this new recorded cycle.

Martino Tirimo, scholar and musical thinker as well as virtuoso, in these eight magnificent discs fills an important gap. As he says in his note to the last of the series, 'It is surely extraordinary that we have had to wait until 200 years after Schubert's birth for an edition to present all 21 sonatas in their complete form and in chronological order, and for a recording of them all which includes every movement of each work.' These discs superbly supplement his printed *Urtext* edition, already established as a new authority.

One has to remember how relatively recently it is that Schubert's sonatas have been appreciated at all. Even the great Artur Schnabel, as a pioneer, concentrated on a select few, and it is much more recently that pianists like Wilhelm Kempff, Alfred Brendel and András Schiff have sought to give us complete cycles. Yet even they have baulked at the works left incomplete, only occasionally – as Schiff does – including a fragment of a movement, finishing the music in mid-air.

Tirimo here uses his own completions in eight substantial movements. As he says, the evidence is that Schubert left them incomplete – generally cut off at the start of the recapitulation, with all the material already assembled – fully intending to round them off later, obviously not intending to reject them. It is a fair justification, and Tirimo's texts, imaginative as they are, prove revelatory, not intrusive.

Almost all the discs include one of the late sonatas, and most also have works previously left incomplete. All can be recommended warmly but, if a first choice has to be made, the third disc makes an excellent recommendation. In addition to the late *C minor Sonata* – the least known of the three masterpieces Schubert wrote in the year of his death – it has an amazing four-movement work in F sharp minor, previously left as a single-movement torso. The opening is astonishing, poetic and visionary, looking far beyond the early nineteenth century, with a haunting idea very close to the wonderful first theme of Schubert's *F minor Fantasy* for piano duet. Anyone who doubts that here is a master to bracket with the great Schubertians of our time should hear the final disc, with its searching account of the last masterpiece in B flat, in which the *Adagio* slow movement matches the finest versions of the past in its rapt, hushed intensity.

Wilhelm Kempff's cycle was recorded over a four-year period (1965–9) and elicited much admiration in our earlier editions. DG has now collected the sonatas into a seven-CD box and those wanting a comprehensive survey of this repertoire will find much refreshment here. There have been performances of comparable stature: Gilels in the *A minor*, D.784, and *D major*, D.850, Lupu (*G major*, D.894), Perahia (*A major*, D.960) and Richter, but before the arrival of the Tirimo Edition there was no individual overview of the whole cycle that was as consistently satisfying as Kempff's. The recordings are not state of the art (there is an occasional hint of shallowness) but there is a wisdom about his playing which puts it in a special category.

With Schiff's collection (like Kempff's survey) including the *First Sonata*, D.157 (written when the composer was eighteen), and also the fragment of the *Eighth* (which Kempff omits), Schiff sets the seal on his seven-CD survey for Decca which has excited golden opinions. In his note he calls them 'among the most sublime contributions written for the piano' – and he plays them as if they are, too. Yet Schiff's is a survey that blends pianistic finesse with keen human insights. He has a good feeling for the architecture of these pieces and he invests detail with just the right amount of feeling. Good modern, digital recordings, made in the Brahms-Saal of the Musikverein in Vienna. The CDs come conveniently packaged in a mid-priced box.

Tirimo Complete Sonata Edition

Piano sonatas, Vol. 1: *Nos. 3 in E, D.459; 5 in A flat, D.557; 18 in G, D.894.*
(B) *** EMI Eminence Dig. CD-EMX 2278 [id.]. Martino Tirimo.

In this repertory there are few more thoughtful pianists than Tirimo. This is the first disc in a uniquely complete recorded cycle. Tirimo not only reveals new textual points but consistently matches great Schubertians in readings marked by delicate phrasing and bold choice of speeds. So in the late *G major Sonata* Tirimo is initially gentler than his rivals, both in the expansive first movement and in the lyrical *Andante*, playing with a velvet legato; but then in fast speeds for the *Allegro* Minuet and the *Allegretto* finale, he heightens the drama. Most impressive too is the natural weight and gravity he brings to the central *Adagio* in the five-movement *Sonata No. 3 in E*, a problematic work which Tirimo discusses most illuminatingly in his notes.

Piano sonatas, Vol. 2: *Nos. 2 in C, D.279; 17 in D, D.850.*
(B) *** EMI Eminence Dig. CD-EMX 2279. Martino Tirimo.

This second disc in Tirimo's cycle closely follows the first, both in the authority of the playing and – rather less happily – in the reverberant recording. Here too there is a late sonata, the great *D major*, with Tirimo bringing out the dramatic contrasts, springing rhythms persuasively and illuminating new textual points, notably in the second-movement *Andante*. *No. 2 in C*, a striking teenage inspiration, is the more impressive when it comes in a version with the witty *Allegretto* finale completed by Tirimo. He also includes an alternative version of the Minuet, with a different Trio.

Piano sonatas, Vol. 3: *Nos. 1 in E, D.157; 9 in F sharp min., D.571* (completed Tirimo); *19 in C min., D.958.*
(B) *** EMI Eminence Dig. CD-EMX 2280. Martino Tirimo.

The *Sonata in F sharp minor* (No. 9) opens hauntingly. It was written in 1817, and the unfinished first movement became separated from the *Allegro* (finale) and Scherzo, which existed independently; more musical detective work isolated the slow movement, and the work has now been put together and completed most successfully by Tirimo: it is one of the illuminating performances here. The trickling theme of its Scherzo is charmingly Schubertian. The *First (E major) Sonata* was written soon after the composer's 18th birthday. The opening is boldly classical, but Schubertian fingerprints appear in the lilting secondary material, and the disconsolate *Andante in E minor* is very touching in Tirimo's hands. The recording remains truthful and one soon adjusts to the resonance.

Piano sonatas, Vol. 4: *Nos. 4 in A min., D.537; 11 in C, D.613* (completed Tirimo); *20 in A, D.959.*
(B) *** EMI Eminence Dig. CD-EMX 2281. Martino Tirimo.

The *Sonata in C*, D.613, dates from the year after the *F sharp minor* (on the previous disc). The *Adagio* was the only completed movement of the three and was published independently in 1869. It is one of Schubert's finest and is played very winningly here. The other two movements had to wait 28 years before being printed in the complete edition of Schubert's works. Tirimo successfully completed the first movement (which the composer left at the end of the development section) and the engaging *Allegretto* finale. His veiled tone in the touching *Andantino* of the *A major Sonata* is matched by the sparkling, light-hearted Scherzo. Excellent if noticeably resonant sound.

Piano sonatas, Vol. 5: *Piano sonatas Nos. 15 in C (Reliquie), D.840; 16 in A min., D.845.*
(B) *** EMI Eminence CD-EMX 2282. Martino Tirimo.

In the fifth volume of his Schubert cycle, Tirimo strikingly couples the great *A minor Sonata* (dedicated to Archduke Rudolf, Beethoven's patron, and one of only three published in the composer's lifetime) with the unfinished *Sonata in C*, to which a publisher gave the sentimental title, *Relique*. The first of the two completed movements is among the most powerful and ambitious that Schubert ever wrote, here masterfully interpreted, but Tirimo's completion of the last two movements – the finale presenting formidable problems – satisfyingly sets that towering movement in a full four-movement structure to match the *A minor* work in achievement.

Piano sonatas, Vol. 6: *Piano sonatas Nos. 7 in D flat, D.567; 12 in F min., D.625; 14 in A min., D.784.*
(B) *** EMI Eminence CD-EMX 2283. Martino Tirimo.

The *Sonata in D flat* – a rare key for a sonata in Schubert's time – is an alternative version of the *E flat Sonata*, D.568, sufficiently different to justify its inclusion as a separate work. The *F minor Sonata*, unlike most of the fragmentary ones, was left with its first movement incomplete, a broodingly dark movement with some strikingly original piano writing, making its completion most welcome. The *A minor*, D.784, much more compact than the later *A minor*, is the first of what might be counted as Schubert's late sonatas, with a slow movement weightier than its length might suggest and a haunting *moto perpetuo* finale. As in the rest of the cycle, Tirimo offers dedicated performances, and the warm recording is eminently truthful.

Piano sonatas, Vol. 7: *Piano sonatas Nos. 8 in E flat, D.568; 10 in B, D.575; 13 in A, D.664.*
(B) *** EMI Eminence CD-EMX 2284. Martino Tirimo.

The penultimate disc of Tirimo's outstanding Schubert cycle couples the one sonata which throughout a century or so of neglect remained a popular work with pianists, the *A major*, D.664, blissfully lyrical throughout. It is a measure of Tirimo's insight that he brings out searching qualities behind the happiness of inspiration. The other works on the disc are two of the seven sonatas that Schubert wrote in 1817, the *E flat* with a G minor slow movement darker than the rest (originally conceived for another work) and a leisurely Minuet like a slow polonaise. The *B major* too brings strikingly experimental writing. Performances and recording well up to standard.

Piano sonatas, Vol. 8: *Piano sonatas Nos. 6 in E min., D.566; in C sharp min.* (fragment), *D.655; in E min.* (fragment), *D.769a; 21 in B flat, D.960.*
(B) *** EMI Eminence CD-EMX 2285. Martino Tirimo.

Martino Tirimo impressively rounds off his Schubert cycle – the most comprehensive yet recorded – with a deeply dedicated account of the last and greatest of the sonatas, that in B flat. He contrasts the spacious, visionary music of the first two movements sharply against the crisply rhythmic writing of the last two, bringing out the lilting lightness while firmly establishing their relationship with the earlier movements. The extra items make a valuable supplement, two tantalizing fragments from minor-key first movements that incomprehensibly failed to get completed, and the *E minor Sonata* of 1817, which had all four movements finally assembled as recently as 1948, with the second-movement *Allegretto* and the finale easily flowing in Schubert's most winning manner.

Other sonata recordings

Piano sonatas Nos. 14–21; German dances; Impromptus; Moments musicaux; Wanderer fantasia.
*** Ph. Dig. 426 128-2 (7). Alfred Brendel.

Piano sonatas Nos. 14 in A min., D.784; 17 in D, D.850.
*** Ph. Dig. 422 063-2. Alfred Brendel.

Piano sonatas Nos 15 in C (Relique), D.840; 18 in G, D.894.
*** Ph. Dig. 422 340-2. Alfred Brendel.

Piano sonata No. 16 in A min., D.845; 3 Impromptus, D.946.
*** Ph. Dig. 422 075-2. Alfred Brendel.

Piano sonata No. 19 in C min., D.958; Moments musicaux Nos. 1–6, D.780.
*** Ph. Dig. 422 076-2. Alfred Brendel.

Piano sonata No. 20 in A, D.959; Allegretto in C min., D.915; 16 German dances, D.783; Hungarian melody in B min., D.817.
**(*) Ph. Dig. 422 229-2. Alfred Brendel.

Piano sonata No. 21 in B flat, D.960; Wanderer fantasia, D.760.
*** Ph. Dig. 422 062-2. Alfred Brendel.

Brendel's later digital set is more intense than his earlier cycle of recordings for Philips, though there was a touching freshness in the earlier set, and he has the benefit of clean, well-focused sound. These are warm performances, strongly delineated and powerfully characterized, which occupy a commanding place in the catalogue. They are separately available, and all of them can be confidently recommended to Brendel's admirers.

'The last six years, 1823–1828', Vol. 1: Piano sonatas Nos. 14 in A min., D.784; 18 in G, D.894; 12 German dances (Ländler), D.790.
*** Priory/Ottavo Dig. OTR C68608 [id.]. Imogen Cooper.

Vol. 2: *Piano sonatas Nos. 15 in C, D.840; 20 in C, D.959; 11 Ecossaises, D.781.*
*** Priory/Ottavo Dig. OTR C58714 [id.]. Imogen Cooper.

Vol. 3: *Piano sonata No. 16 in A min., D.845; 4 Impromptus, D.935.*
*** Priory/Ottavo Dig. OTR C88817 [id.]. Imogen Cooper.

Vol. 4: *Piano sonata No. 17 in D, D.850; 6 Moments musicaux, D.780.*
*** Priory/Ottavo Dig. OTR C128715 [id.]. Imogen Cooper.

Vol. 5: *Piano sonata No. 21 in B flat, D.960; Allegretto in C min., D.915; 3 Impromptus (Klavierstücke), D.946.*
*** Priory/Ottavo Dig. OTR C88821 [id.]. Imogen Cooper.

Vol. 6: *Piano sonata No. 19 in C min., D. 958; 4 Impromptus, D.899.*
*** Priory/Ottavo Dig. OTR C78923 [id.]. Imogen Cooper.

Imogen Cooper, in her outstanding set on the Dutch Ottavo label, has a true Schubertian sensibility; her feeling for this composer's special lyricism is second to none, yet her playing has both strength and a complete understanding of the music's architecture. The recordings were made in the London Henry Wood Hall over a period of three years, between June 1986 and July 1989, using a Steinway for the first three volumes and a fine-sounding Yamaha for the later records. The balance is admirable and the sound full, with a convincing natural resonance. The playing has the spontaneity of live music-making, and the warm colouring and fine shading of timbre are as pleasing to the ear as the many subtle nuances of phrasing, which are essentially based on a strong melodic line. These performances can be recommended alongside those by artists with the most illustrious names, and they do not fall short. With their fine, modern, digital recording these CDs will give much delight and refreshment.

Piano sonatas Nos. 1 in E, D.157; 14 in A min., D.784; 20 in A, D.959.
(M) *** Decca 425 033-2. Radu Lupu.

Lupu is sensitive and poetic throughout. In the *A major* work he strikes the perfect balance between Schubert's classicism and the spontaneity of his musical thought, and at the same time he leaves one with the impression that the achievement is perfectly effortless, with an inner repose and depth of feeling that remain memorable long after the record has ended. Excellent vintage Decca recording, made in the Kingsway Hall in the late 1970s.

Piano sonata No. 4 in A min., D.537.
** DG (IMS) Dig. 400 043-2. Michelangeli – BRAHMS: *Ballades*. ***

Michelangeli's Schubert is less convincing than the Brahms coupling. His playing, though aristocratic and marvellously poised, is not free from artifice, and the natural eloquence of Schubert eludes him. Splendid recording.

Piano sonatas Nos. 4 in A min., D.537; 13 in A, D.664; 14 in A min., D.784; 15 in C (Relique), D.840; 16 in A min., D.845; 19 in C min., D.958; 20 in A, D.959; 21 in B flat, D.960; Allegretto in C min., D.915; 11 Ecossaises, D.781; Fantasia in C (Wanderer), D.760; 12 German dances, D.790; 16 German dances, D.783; Hungarian melody in B min., D.817; 6 Moments musicaux, D.780.
(M) *** Ph. Brendel Edition Analog/Dig. 446 923-2 (5). Alfred Brendel.

Four out of the five records here come from Brendel's earlier, analogue set of Schubert recordings, but the first, pairing Nos. 4 and 13, is digital. Here Brendel's account of the *A minor Sonata*, D.537, sounds a little didactic: the gears are changed to prepare the way for the second group, and this sounds unconvincing on the first hearing and more so on the repeat. He also broadens on the modulation to F major towards the end of the exposition, only to quicken the pulse in the development. The result is curiously inorganic. The *A major*, D.664, is also given with less simplicity and charm than one expects from this great artist. Both in *Sonatas 14 in A minor* and *15 in C major* he manages to convey romantic feeling within a relatively taut framework; indeed in the *C major* his eloquence and poetry leave nothing to be desired. No. 16, D.845, is one of the very finest of the series, with a searching reading of the first movement, free in expression, but direct too. The variations of the slow movement are given heavenly length, while the Scherzo and finale have strength and urgency. *No. 20 in A major*, however, suffers from rather more agogic changes than is desirable, and the *C minor Sonata*, D.958, is also not free from this charge. Brendel's performance of the final *B flat major Sonata* is as impressive and full of insight as one would expect; his playing of the *Wanderer fantasia* is also of a high order, and throughout he is truthfully recorded. The *German dances* are delightful and particularly beautifully played, while the *Moments musicaux* are given wonderfully poetic performances and rank very highly indeed in Brendel's Schubert discography. The slightly soft-grained recording is exemplary.

Piano sonata No. 5 in A flat, D.557; 2 Scherzi, D.593.
(M) *** Decca 448 129-2. Radu Lupu – BRAHMS: *Piano sonata No. 3*. ***

In the little three-movement *A flat Sonata* Lupu strikes the perfect balance between Schubert's classicism and the spontaneity of his musical thought, and at the same time he leaves one with the impression that this achievement is perfectly effortless. The *Andante* unfolds with appealing delicacy and the finale combines delicacy with strength. The two *Scherzi* are hardly less successful, the first particularly light and charming, the second rather more quixotic in mood. The analogue recording from the mid 1970s is as natural and fresh as the performances themselves.

Piano sonatas Nos. 9 in B, D.575; 11 in F min., D.625; 13 in A, D.664; Moment musical, D.780/1.
(N) *** BBC Legends BBCL 4010-2 [id.]. Sviatoslav Richter.

This disc comprises a Schubert recital Richter gave at the Royal Festival Hall in 1979, and though the BBC microphone was slightly too close to the instrument (no doubt to minimize audience noise), the dryish sound is perfectly acceptable. Richter recorded all three sonatas for EMI in Japan three years later, and there is little significant difference in approach between the two accounts. As always his playing is magisterial and eloquent. Thoroughly recommendable.

Piano sonatas Nos. 13 in A, D.664; 14 in A min., D.784; Hungarian melody, D.817; 12 Waltzes, D.145.
✿ (M) *** Decca 443 579-2 [id.]. Ashkenazy.

A magnificent record in every respect. Ashkenazy is a great Schubertian who can realize the touching humanity of this giant's vision as well as his strength. There is an astonishing directness about these performances and a virility tempered by tenderness. This matches Ashkenazy's own high standards, and Decca have risen remarkably to the occasion. The 1966 analogue recording, reissued in Decca's Classic Sound series, has splendid range and fidelity.

Piano sonatas Nos. 13 in A, D.664; 21 in B flat, D.960.
*** Decca (IMS) Dig. 440 295-2 [id.]. Radu Lupu.
**(*) Conifer Dig. 75605 51254-2 [id.]. Mikhail Kazakevich.

Notwithstanding their series of Schubert Sonatas from András Schiff, Decca celebrated Radu Lupu's first return to the studios in over a decade with new recordings of two Schubert Sonatas. It is one of the most searching of all new Schubert recordings and finds this masterly pianist at his most eloquent and thoughtful. Not as well recorded as Schiff.

Mikhail Kazakevich is also an impressive Schubertian, playing these two masterpieces with thoughtful understanding and the great *B flat Sonata* (in which he includes the exposition repeat) with commanding boldness. He is very well recorded. At a recital this performance would certainly be very well received, but in terms of recording he faces considerable competition and it must be conceded that Ashkenazy and Schiff both bring a finer sensibility to the *A major*, while for the *B flat* one would more readily turn to Kovacevich or Kempff (among others).

Piano sonata No. 14 in A min., D784; Moments musicaux, D789; 12 Grazer Walzer, D924.
(N) *** Erato/Warner Dig. 0630-17869-2 [id.]. Till Fellner.

Till Fellner more than justifies his growing reputation in this fine Schubert recital. His playing is totally unaffected and completely natural, and at the same time is distinguished by great finesse and sensitivity. He never fusses over detail and shows both a freshness and spontaneity of feeling and a command of the architecture of the music. One of the finest Schubert recitals in the current lists.

Piano sonatas Nos. 15 in C (Relique), D.840; 18 in G, D.894.
(N) *** Philips Dig. 454 453-2 [id.]. Mitsuko Uchida.

The unfinished torso of the *Relique sonata* is given an eloquent, inward-looking reading of great tonal beauty. The *G major sonata* is masterly, combining careful thought with emotional depth. One of the best Schubert sonata discs of the last two or three years. The Philips recording is excellent in every way.

Piano sonatas Nos. 15 in C (Unfinished), D.840; 19 in C min., D.958; 16 German Dances, D.783.
(M) *** Van. 08.4026.71 [OVC 4026]. Alfred Brendel.

Brendel was at his finest and most spontaneous in the 1960s. The *C minor Sonata* is particularly fine, with a thoughtful, improvisatory feeling in the slow movement which is consistently illuminating. The two-movement *C major Sonata* also has a memorable *Andante*, and the *German Dances* are an endless delight. The recording is full and bold.

Piano sonata No. 17 in D, D.850.
(M) *** RCA 09026 61614-2 [id.]. Emil Gilels – LISZT: *Sonata.* ***

Like the Liszt *Sonata* with which it is coupled, Gilels's highly perceptive account captures the music's Schubertian spirit in a somewhat similar way to Curzon's very persuasive account. If in his own way Gilels is authoritative and commanding, like Curzon he finds a special magic to engage the ear in the delightful finale.

Piano sonata No. 17 in D, D.850; Impromptus in A flat; in G flat, D.899/3–4; Moments musicaux Nos. 1–6, D. 780.
(M) *** Decca 443 570-2 [id.]. Clifford Curzon.

Some who know more forceful interpretations may find this too wayward, but Schubert surely thrives on some degree of coaxing. Curzon could hardly be more convincing – the spontaneous feeling of a live performance captured better than in many earlier discs. Curzon also gives superb performances of the *Moments musicaux*. These readings are among the most poetic in the catalogue, and the recording throughout is exemplary. The *Impromptus* make an attractive bonus (the *G flat major* particularly magical) in this reissue in Decca's Classic Sound series, and they too are beautifully played. The recording remains of Decca's finest analogue quality.

Piano sonatas Nos. 17 in D, D.850; 20 in A, D.959; 21 in B flat, D.960; March in E, D.606; Moments musicaux, D.780.
(M) (***) EMI mono CHS7 64259-2 (2) [ZDHB 64259: *Sonatas Nos. 20 & 21* only]. Artur Schnabel.

It was thanks to Schnabel's championship that the *Piano sonatas* re-entered the repertory for they were rarities in the recital rooms of the 1920s and early 1930s. Both the *A major* and *B flat Sonatas* sound as well as they are ever likely to, for neither was state-of-the-art piano-sound. The *Moments musicaux* sound remarkably full-bodied. The playing is full of characteristic insights, though it must be admitted that later recordings of the *B flat* from Kempff and Curzon surpassed Schnabel technically. But as always with this artist there is imagination of a remarkable order. These recordings are now 50 years old, but some of the playing Schnabel offers – at the opening of the *B flat* and in the slow movements of all three Sonatas – will never be less than special.

Piano sonata No. 19 in C min., D.958; Moments musicaux Nos. 1–6, D.780.
(M) *** Decca Dig. 417 785-2. Radu Lupu.

Lupu's performance has a simple eloquence that is

most moving. His *Moments musicaux* are very fine indeed. The Decca recording is very natural and, at mid-price, this is extremely competitive.

Piano sonatas Nos. 19 in C min., D.958; 20 in A, D.959.
(B) *** DG 453 673-2. Wilhelm Kempff.

Kempff is never less than illuminating in Schubert, and these highly spontaneous performances are nicely turned and well shaped, as one would expect from so authoritative a Schubertian, and there are numerous imaginative insights. The recording gives pleasingly realistic sound, even if it is not of DG's very finest.

Piano sonatas Nos. 19 in C min., D.958; 20 in A, D.959.
*** DG (IMS) Dig. 427 327-2 [id.]. Maurizio Pollini.

Piano sonata No. 21 in B flat, D.960; Allegretto in C min., D.915; Klavierstücke, D.946.
*** DG (IMS) Dig. 427 326-2 [id.]. Maurizio Pollini.

In Pollini's hands these emerge as strongly structured and powerful sonatas, yet he is far from unresponsive to the voices from the other world with which these pieces resonate. Perhaps with his perfect pianism he does not always convey a sense of human vulnerability, as have some of the greatest Schubert interpreters.

Piano sonatas Nos. 19 in C min., D. 958; 20 in A, D. 959; 21 in B flat, D. 960; 3 Impromptus (Klavierstücke), D. 946/1–3.
(B) **(*) Ph. Duo 438 703-2 [id.]. Alfred Brendel.

Brendel's analogue recordings of the Schubert late Sonatas were among the finest of his records made in the early 1970s and would seem an obvious recommendation on Philips's Duo bargain label. But the *A major* suffers from interferences with the flow of the musical argument which are a little too personal. The *C minor Sonata* is not free from this problem but it remains an impressive performance. Brendel's account of the *B flat Sonata* is both serious and introspective, and he is not unduly wayward; moreover he is at his very finest in the *Klavierstücke*. This is eloquent and profoundly musical playing. Throughout, the recording is well up to Philips's high standard of realism and the CD transfers are impeccable, with little background hiss.

Piano sonata No. 20 in A, D.959.
*** Sony Dig. MK 44569 [id.]. Murray Perahia – SCHUMANN: *Piano sonata No. 2*. ***

Perahia's combination of intellectual vigour and poetic insight shows that awareness of proportion and feeling for expressive detail which distinguish the greatest interpreters. As always with this artist, every phrase speaks and each paragraph breathes naturally.

Piano sonatas Nos. 20 in A, D.959; 21 in B flat, D.960.
(M) *** Virgin Veritas/EMI VER5 61272-2. Melvyn Tan (fortepiano).

Melvyn Tan uses a fortepiano that was much admired by Beethoven. He is a compelling artist of keen musical intelligence who makes you listen, even when you might not agree with every expressive or agogic hesitation. Generally speaking, tempi are well judged, though the *Andantino* of the *A major* and the slow movement of the *B flat* are far too fast, if surprisingly persuasive. His account of this sonata is very impressive: there is depth of feeling as well as many felicities of sonority. These performances will make you think afresh about this music. The recording is first class.

Piano sonata No. 21 in B flat, D.960.
(M) *** Decca 448 578-2 [id.]. Clifford Curzon – BRAHMS: *Piano sonata No. 3* etc. ***
(M) *** Ph. 420 644-2. Alfred Brendel – *Wanderer fantasia*. ***

Curzon's is among the finest accounts of the *B flat Sonata* in the catalogue. Tempi are aptly judged and everything is in fastidious taste. Detail is finely drawn but never emphasized at the expense of the architecture as a whole. It is beautifully recorded, and the piano sounds very truthful in timbre. For the reissue in Decca's 'Classic Sound' series, the Brahms *F minor Sonata* has been added, an equally perceptive account, plus a pair of *Intermezzi*, to make this quite outstanding value.

Brendel's earlier analogue performance is as impressive and full of insight as one would expect. He is not unduly wayward, for his recording has room for the *Wanderer fantasy* as well, and he is supported by excellent Philips sound.

Piano sonata No. 21 in B flat, D.960; Allegretto in C min., D.915; 12 Ländler, D.790.
✽ *** EMI Dig. CDC5 55359-2 [id.]. Kovacevich.

Stephen Kovacevich made a memorable recording of the great *B flat major Sonata* for Hyperion which (in our 1988 edition) we called 'one of the most eloquent accounts on record of this sublime sonata and one which is completely free of expressive point-making. It is an account which totally reconciles the demands of truth and the attainment of beauty.' One could well say the same of the present version, though, if anything, it explores an even deeper vein of feeling than its predecessor. With excellent, truthful recording, it earns the strongest and most enthusiastic recommendation.

Piano sonata Nos. 21 in B flat, D.960; Drei Klavierstücke, D.946.
(N) *** Philips Dig. 456 572-2 [id.]. Mitsuko Uchida.

Mitsuko Uchida couples the last Sonata with the *Drei Klavierstücke*. Hers is a performance of considerable stature; she allows Schubert to speak for himself. There is a rapt concentration and an almost other-worldly quality about her playing that will repay the attentive listener. Some may feel that she lingers a little too long in the slow movement and allows the onward flow of the music to stagnate – and they will doubtless prefer Curzon or Brendel. In any event there is no doubt whatever as to the excellence of the Philips recording.

VOCAL MUSIC

Lieder on record (1898–1952): Volume 1, 1898–1939 (all with piano unless otherwise indicated): *Ave Maria* (1898) Edith Clegg; sung in English. *Ungeduld* (1901) Paul Knüpfer. *Heidenröslein* (1902) Minnie Nast. *Litanei* (1901); *Ständchen: Zögernd leise* – with Hofoper Ch. & O, Bruno Seidler (1908) both Marie Götze. *Ständchen* (sung in English): *Hark, hark! the lark* (1902) David Bispham. *Die schöne Müllerin: Der Neugierige* (1902) Franz Naval. *Rastlose Liebe* (1902); *Die Allmacht* (1910) both Edyth Walker. *Erlkönig* (1906); *Du bist die Ruh'; Die Liebe* (1907) all three Lilli Lehmann. *Der Wanderer* (1902) Ernst Wachter. *Schwanengesang: Abschied* (1904); *Winterreise: Der Leiermann* (1934) both Harry Plunket-Greene; sung in English. *An die Leier* (1909) Pauline Cramer. *Die Forelle* (1902) Leopold Demuth. *Schwanengesang: Am Meer* (1904) Gustav Walter. *Die junge Nonne* (1907) Susan Strong (with orchestra). *Der Wanderer* (1906); *Schwanengesang: Aufenthalt* (1912); *Winterreise: Der Leiermann* (1910) all three Lev Sibiriakov; sung in Russian. *Frühlingsglaube* (1910) Heinrich Hensel. *Der Kreuzzug* (1905) Wilhelm Hesch. *Schwanengesang: Ständchen* (1907 with orchestra) & *Liebesbotschaft* (1909) both Leo Slezak. *An die Musik; Du bist die Ruh'* (1911 – both with Arthur Nikisch, piano); *Suleika II* (1929 – with Coenraad V. Bos, piano); *Ellens Gesang* (1939 – with Gerald Moore, piano) all four Elena Gerhardt. *Die schöne Müllerin: Das Wandern* (1914); *Winterreise: Der Leiermann* (1928) both Sir George Henschel (accompanying himself on the piano). *Die schöne Müllerin: Der Müller und der Bach* (1911) Elise Elizza. *An die Musik; Gruppe aus dem Tartarus* (1910) both Ottilie Metzger. *Sei mir gegrüsset* (1921) Friedrich Brodersen. *Die schöne Müllerin: Undgeduld & Wohin?* (1922–3) both Frieda Hempel. *Gruppe aus dem Tartarus* (1924); *Erlkönig* (1936, with Gerald Moore) both Alexander Kipnis. *Du bist die Ruh* (1924); *Die Liebe hat gelogen* (1927, with Edwin Schneider) both John McCormack. *Im Abendrot; Verklärung* (1929) both Aaltje Noordewier-Reddingius. *Winterreise: Rückblick; Frühlingstraume & Mut!* (1927) all three Richard Tauber, with Mischa Spoliansky. *Gretchen am Spinnrade; Mignon II* (1928) both Meta Seinemeyer, with O, Frieder Weissmann. *Die Forelle; Lachen und Weinen* (1928); *Winterreise: Der Lindenbaum* (1931) all three Vanni Marcoux, with Piero Coppola; sung in French. *An die Musik* (1926) Ursula van Diemen, with Arpád Sándor. *Memnon* (1932) Harold Williams, with Herbert Dawson. *Das Lied im Grünen* (1930) Sigrid Onegin, with Clemens Schmalstich. *Schwanengesang: Der Doppelgänger. Der Tod und das Mädchen* (1930 with O, Eugene Goossens) both Feodor Chaliapin (sung in Russian). *Schwanengesang: Aufenthalt; Ihr Bild. Die schöne Müllerin: Pause* (1928) all three Hans Duham, with Ferdinand Foll. *Sei mir gegrüsset; Auf dem Wasser zu singen; Geheimes* (1927) all three Lotte Lehmann with O, Manfred Gurlitt. *Winterreise: Der Lindenbaum. Der Tod und das Mädchen* (1926) both Julia Culp, with Fritz Lindemann.
(M) (***) EMI mono CHS5 66150-2 (3).

The first item in this fascinating historical survey offers a frisson to the listener, even though it is a very swoopy account of *Ave Maria* sung in English. It is what is thought to be the very first recording of a Schubert song, delivered in 1898 by Edith Clegg, a contralto known only for having sung at Covent Garden in 1909. From then on the focus grows ever clearer, both in sound and in vocal technique, with even the second item, *Ungeduld* from *Die schöne Müllerin*, recorded by the German bass, Paul Knüpfer, in 1901 with a forwardness and clarity that defy the years.

Each item brings its revelations, with the American David Bispham singing *Hark, hark! the lark* in 1902 in a prim D'Oyly Carte English accent; the soprano Lilli Lehmann, in 1906 giving an intensely dramatic account of *Erlkönig*; Harry Plunket-Greene (born 1865), vivid in 1934 electrical recording, characterfully giving *Der Leiermann* from *Winterreise* in English, every word clear, but with an Irish accent, the narrative effect like a folk-song; Lev Sibiriakov transforming the same song to become intensely Russian (again extraordinarily vivid recording, made in St Petersburg by Fred Gaisberg); and Sir George Henschel (born 1850) at 78 recording that same song in the original German with a firmness and point for any modern singer to envy. It is amazing to think that the tenor Gustav Walter, who was recorded in a ringing account of *Am Meer* at the age of 70, was born in 1834, within six years of Schubert's death.

It is a set which telescopes history and tells, among much else, what store all these vintage singers set by firm, clear delivery with not a hint of a wobble among them. Quite apart from such starry names as Chaliapin, Tauber and McCormack, Alexander Kipnis (who gives another memorable account of *Erlkönig*), the brilliant Frieda Hempel and the golden-toned Meta Seinemeyer demand special mention. Anyone listening to these 65 items, lasting three hours, will be amazed at the riches, with freshness the keynote, stylistically flawed only occasionally in sentimental *rallentandos*. Texts are given in the booklet but, alas, none of the potted biographies from the original LP set nor (worse still) an index of songs. Unmissable just the same.

Lieder on record, 1898–1952: Volume 2, 1927–52: *Schwanengesang: Der Atlas* (1930); *Erlkönig* (orch. Berlioz); *Schwanengesang: Der Doppelgänger* (1934) all three Charles Panzéra, with O, Piero Coppola (sung in French). *Die Forelle* (1927); *Der Hirt auf dem Felsen* (1929) both Lotte Schöne, the second with Berlin State Op. O, Leo Blech); *Schwanengesang: Am Meer* (1929) Friedrich Schorr, with Robert Jäger. *Gretchen am Spinnrade* (1929) Dusolinna Giannini, with Michael Raucheisen. *Erlkönig* (1930) Georges Thill, with Henri Etcheverry (baritone), C. Pascal (treble) & O. *Der Tod und das Mädchen* (1929) Maria Oiszewska, with George Reeves. *Nachtviolen; An die Geliebte; Das Heimweh* (1938) all three Elisabeth Schumann, with Leo Rosenek. *Der Jüngling an der Quelle* (1936) Elisabeth Schumann, with Elizabeth Coleman. *An die Nachtigall* (1933); *Der Schmetterling* (1937) both Elisabeth Schumann, with George Reeves. *Der Musensohn* (1932) Therese Behr-Schnabel, with Artur Schnabel. *An die Laute; Am See* (1932); *Der Wanderer an den Mond* (1937) all three Karl Erb, with Bruno Seidler-Winkler. *Schwanengesang: Frühlingssehnsucht* (1937) Karl Erb, with Gerald Moore. *Auflösung; Schwanengesang: Liebesbotschaft* (1935); *Wiegenlied: Schlafe, schlafe; Wiegenlied: Wie sich der Auglein* (1933) all five Ria Ginster, with Gerald Moore. *Ganymed; Rosamunde: Der Vollmond strahlt. Winterreise: Das Wirthaus* (1938); *Schwanengesang: Kriegers Ahnung* (1937) all four Herbert Janssen, with Gerald Moore. *Mignon I; Nachtstücke; Die junge Nonne* (1937) all three Susan Metcalfe-Casals, with Gerald Moore. *Erlkönig* (1937) Marta Fuchs, with Michael Raucheisen. *Schwanengesang: Die Taubenpost* (1937) both Gerhard Hüsch, with Gerald Moore. *Lied eines Schiffers; Widerschein* (1939) both Gerhard Hüsch, with Hanns Udo Müller. *Auf dem Wasser zu singen* (1943) Frida Leider, with Michael Raucheisen. *Die schöne Müllerin: Halt!; Eifersucht und Stolz* (1945); *Schäfers Klagelied* (1949) all three Aksel Schiotz, with Gerald Moore. *Die Vögel; Liebhaber in allen Gestalten* (1948) both Elisabeth Schwarzkopf, with Gerald Moore; *Seligkeit* (1946) Elisabeth Schwarzkopf, with Karl Hudez. *Im Frühling; Auf der Bruck* (1950) both Peter Pears, with Benjamin Britten. *Der Hirt auf dem Felsen* (1947) Margaret Ritchie, with Reginald Kell (clarinet) & Gerald Moore. *Schwanengesang: Ihr Bild* (1947) Julius Patzak, with Hermann von Nordberg. *Auf dem Wasser zu singen* (1948) Irmgard Seefried, with Gerald Moore. *Heidenröslein* (1947) Irmgard Seefried, with Hermann von Nordberg. *Am Bach im Frühling; Gruppe aus dem Tartarus; Meerstille; Wandrers Nachtlied I–II* (1949) all five Hans Hotter, with Gerald Moore. *An die Leier* (1949) Flora Nielsen, with Gerald Moore. *Prometheus* (1949) Bernhard Sönnerstedt, with Gerald Moore. *Aus Heliopolis I* (1949) Endré Koréh, with Hermann von Nordberg. *Die schöne Müllerin: Am Feierabend; Trock'ne Blumen. Nacht und Träume. Schwanengesang: Das Fischermädchen* (1951) all four Dietrich Fischer-Dieskau, with Gerald Moore. *Die Allmacht; Frühlingsglaube; Wandrers Nachtlied II* (1952) Kirsten Flagstad, with Gerald Moore.
(M) (**(*)) EMI mono CHS5 66154-2 (3).

This second volume in EMI's historic survey of Schubert song on record brings almost comparable delight, even if there are fewer surprises when many, if not most, of the singers are already familiar from their recordings. The 64 items lead up to the two great exponents of Lieder in our time, Schwarzkopf and Fischer-Dieskau, here both vividly characterful at the start of their recording careers. In timbre the charming Lotte Schöne might almost be mistaken for the even more sparkling Elisabeth Schumann, here represented in five brief songs. Naturally German singers predominate, but some of the most cherishable items are from non-German singers: Charles Panzéra and Georges Thill from France (heard in a version of *Erlkönig*, sung very dramatically in French as a trio with Henri Etcheverry and a boy treble), Peter Pears and Margaret Ritchie from Britain, as well as transatlantic singers like Dusolina Giannini (fresh and powerful in *Gretchen am Spinnrade*), Flora Nielsen and Susan Metcalfe-Casals, whose very rare recordings, privately made for her by EMI, are a revelation. The only disappointments are the recordings of Therese Behr-Schnabel (accompanied by her husband), recorded when she was 58, and Herbert Janssen, whose rapid flutter in the voice is distracting among performances of immaculate firmness. The programme ends with three songs from Kirsten Flagstad, in 1953 past her prime but still commanding. Excellent transfers, as in the first volume, with the same reservations over documentation.

Dietrich Fischer-Dieskau: The EMI Recordings

The First Recital (1951): *Der Atlas; Ihr Bild; Fischermädchen; Die Stadt; Am Meer; Der Doppelgänger; Erlkönig; Nacht und Träume; Du bist die Ruh; Ständchen.*

Volume I (1955): *Der Wanderer an den Mond; Uber Wildemann; Der Einsame; Auflösung; Der Kreuzzug; Totengräbers Heimweh; Nachtviolen; Frühlingssehnseht; Geheimnes; Rastlose Liebe; Liebesbotschaft; Im Abendrot; Abschied.*

Volume II (1957): *Dem Unendlichen; Die Sterne; An die Musik; Wehmut; Kriegers Ahnung; Der Zwerg; Der Wanderer; Frühlingsglaube; Die Taubenpost; An Silvia; Im Frühling; Auf der Bruck.*

Volume IIIa (1958): *Ständchen; Alinde; Nähe des Geliebten; Normanns Gesang; In der Ferne.*

Volume IIIb (1958): *Aufenthalt; Lied des gefangenen Jägers; Greisengesang; Erlkönig; Nachtstück.* (all with Gerald Moore).

Volume IV (1959): *Gruppe aus dem Tartarus; Die Götter Griechenlands; Ewartung; Sehnsucht; Der Taucher.*

Volume V (1959): *Der Sänger; Die Bürgschaft; Der Fischer; Einsamkeit.*

Volume VIa (1959): *Am Strome; Der Alpenjäger; Erlafsee; Wie Ulfru fischt; Beim Winde; Trost; Auf der Donau* (1959).

Volume VIb (1959): *Abendstern; Liedesend; Sehnsucht; Heliopolis; Zum Punsche; Der Sieg; An die Freunde.*
(Volumes IV–VIb with Karl Engel).

Volume VII (1962): *Der Atlas; Ihr Bild; Das Fischermädchen; Die Stadt; Am Meer; Der Doppelgänger; Lachen und Weinen; Dass sie hier gewesen; Sei mir gegrüsst; Du bist die Ruh; Im Walde (Waldesnacht).*

Volume VIII (1965): *Seligkeit; Heidenröslein; Ständchen; Des Fischers Liebesglück; Fischerweise; Der Jüngling an der Quelle; An die Laute; Die Forelle; Auf der Riesenkoppe.*

Volume IX (1965): *An die Entfernte; Auf dem Wasser zu singen; Der Schiffer; Der Wanderer; Nachtgesang; Das Zügenglöcklein; Der Jüngling und der Tod; Das Heimweh; Das Lied im Grünen; Der Tod und das Mädchen; Der Winterabend; Der zürnende Barde; Der Strom; Litanei auf das Fest Aller Seelen.*
(all with Gerald Moore).

(M) *** EMI mono/stereo CMS5 65670-2 (6). Dietrich Fischer-Dieskau, Gerald Moore or Karl Engel.

This HMV set makes an admirable survey of Fischer-Dieskau's Schubert recordings for EMI over a decade and a half before he moved to Deutsche Grammophon to make the extensive survey listed below. It is particularly interesting to compare the earliest recordings (the first in mono), with the voice and manner still youthfully fresh, to the second generation, again with Gerald Moore but also with Karl Engel. The contrast is fascinating, with the voice still younger than on DG. The transfers are superbly managed and full translations are provided to make this an indispensable supplement to the DG sets.

Lieder, Volume 1 (1811–17); Volume 2 (1817–28); Song cycles: *Die schöne Müllerin; Schwanengesang; Winterreise.*

(B) *** DG 437 214-2 (21). Fischer-Dieskau, Gerald Moore (as below).

Fischer-Dieskau's monumental survey of all the Schubert songs suitable for a man's voice (some of the longer ones excepted) was made over a relatively brief span, with the last 300 songs concentrated on a period of only two months in 1969, yet there is not a hint of routine. The two big boxes of nine discs come at bargain price, whereas the smaller box, containing the song-cycles, comes at mid-price. Nor has the background information been skimped. Each box contains complete German texts and English translations (plus summaries in French) as well as introductory essays. The one serious omission is an alphabetical list of titles. It makes it unnecessarily hard to find a particular song – much the most likely way of using so compendious a collection.

This collection of 21 CDs is offered at bargain price, as are the two separate nine-disc collections of Lieder listed below. The three great song-cycles, also included here, cost more if purchased separately.

Lieder, Volume I (1811–17): *Ein Leichenfantasie; Der Vatermörder* (1811); *Der Jüngling am Bache* (1812); *Totengräberlied; Die Schatten; Sehnsucht; Verklärung; Pensa, che questo istante* (1813); *Der Taucher* (1813–15); *Andenken; Geisternähe; Erinnerung; Trost, An Elisa; Die Betende; Lied aus der Ferne; Der Abend; Lied der Liebe; Erinnerungen; Adelaide; An Emma; Romanze: Ein Fräulein klagt' im finstern Turm; An Laura, als sie Klopstocks Auferstehungslied sang; Der Geistertanz; Das Mädchen aus der Fremde; Nachtgesang; Trost in Tränen; Schäfers Klagelied; Sehnsucht; Am See* (1814); *Auf einen Kirchhof; Als ich sie erröten sah; Das Bild; Der Mondabend* (1815); *Lodas Gespenst* (1816); *Der Sänger* (1815); *Die Erwartung* (1816); *Am Flusse; An Mignon; Nähe des Geliebten; Sängers Morgenlied; Amphiaraos; Das war ich; Die Sterne; Vergebliche Liebe; Liebesrausch; Sehnsucht der Liebe; Die erste Liebe; Trinklied; Stimme der Liebe; Naturgenuss; An die Freude; Der Jüngling am Bache; An den Mond; Die Mainacht; An die Nachtigall; An die Apfelbäume; Seufzer; Liebeständelei; Der Liebende; Der Traum; Die Laube; Meeres Stille;*

Grablied; Das Finden; Wandrers Nachtlied; Der Fischer; Erster Verlust; Die Erscheinung; Die Täuschung; Der Abend; Geist der Liebe; Tischlied; Der Liedler; Ballade; Abends unter der Linde; Die Mondnacht; Huldigung; Alles um Liebe; Das Geheimnis; An den Frühling; Die Bürgschaft; Der Rattenfänger; Der Schatzgräber; Heidenröslein; Bundeslied; An den Mond; Wonne der Wehmut; Wer kauft Liebesgötter? (1815); *Der Goldschmiedsgesell* (1817); *Der Morgenkuss; Abendständchen: An Lina; Morgenlied: Willkommen, rotes Morgenlicht; Der Weiberfreund; An die Sonne; Tischlerlied; Totenkranz für ein Kind; Abendlied; Die Fröhlichkeit; Lob des Tokayers; Furcht der Geliebten; Das Rosenband; An Sie; Die Sommernacht; Die frühen Gräber; Dem Unendlichen; Ossians Lied nach dem Falle Nathos; Das Mädchen von Inistore; Labetrank der Liebe; An die Geliebte; Mein Gruss an den Mai; Skolie – Lasst im Morgenstrahl des Mai'n; Die Sternenwelten; Die Macht der Liebe; Das gestörte Glück; Die Sterne; Nachtgesang; An Rosa I: Warum bist du nicht hier?; An Rosa II: Rosa, denkst du an mich?; Schwanengesang; Der Zufriedene; Liane; Augenlied; Geistes-Gruss; Hoffnung; An den Mond; Rastlose Liebe; Erlkönig* (1815); *Der Schmetterling; Die Berge* (1819); *Genügsamkeit; An die Natur* (1815); *Klage; Morgenlied; Abendlied; Der Flüchtling; Laura am Klavier; Entzückung an Laura; Die vier Weltalter; Pflügerlied; Die Einsiedelei; An die Harmonie; Die Herbstnacht; Lied: Ins stille Land; Der Herbstabend; Der Entfernten; Fischerlied; Sprache der Liebe; Abschied von der Harfe; Stimme der Liebe; Entzückung; Geist der Liebe; Klage: Der Sonne steigt; Julius an Theone; Klage: Dein Silber schien durch Eichengrün; Frühlingslied; Auf den Tod einer Nachtigall; Die Knabenzeit; Winterlied; Minnelied; Die frühe Liebe; Blumenlied; Der Leidende; Seligkeit; Erntelied; Das grosse Halleluja; Die Gestirne; Die Liebesgötter; An den Schlaf; Gott im Frühling; Der gute Hirt; Die Nacht; Fragment aus dem Aeschylus* (1816); *An die untergehende Sonne* (1816/17); *An mein Klavier; Freude der Kinderjahre; Das Heimweh; An den Mond; An Chloen; Hochzeitlied; In der Mitternacht; Trauer der Liebe; Die Perle; Liedesend; Orpheus; Abschied; Rückweg; Alte Liebe rostet nie; Gesänge des Harfners aus Goethes Wilhelm Meister: Harfenspieler I: Wer sich der Einsamkeit ergibt; Harfenspieler II: An die Türen will ich schleichen; Harfenspieler III: Wer nie sein Brot mit Tränen ass. Der König in Thule; Jägers Abendlied; An Schwager Kronos; Der Sänger am Felsen; Lied: Ferne von der grossen Stadt; Der Wanderer; Der Hirt; Lied eines Schiffers an die Dioskuren; Geheimnis; Zum Punsche; Am Bach im Frühling* (1816); *An eine Quelle* (1817); *Bei dem Grabe, meines Vaters; Am Grabe Anselmos; Abendlied; Zufriedenheit; Herbstlied; Skolie: Mädchen entsiegelten; Lebenslied; Lieden der Trennung* (1816); *Alinde; An die Laute* (1827); *Frohsinn; Die Liebe; Trost; Der Schäfer und der Reiter* (1817); *Lob der Tränen* (1821); *Der Alpenjäger; Wie Ulfru fischt; Fahrt zum Hades; Schlaflied; Die Blumensprache; Die abgeblühte Linde; Der Flug der Zeit; Der Tod und das Mädchen; Das Lied vom Reifen; Täglich zu singen; Am Strome; Philoktet; Memnon; Auf dem See; Ganymed; Der Jüngling und der Tod; Trost im Liede* (1817).

(B) *** DG 437 215-2 (9). Dietrich Fischer-Dieskau, Gerald Moore.

This remarkable project, with Volume 1 recorded between 1966 and 1968 and Volume 2 over two months of intensive sessions in 1969, is an astonishing achievement in bringing together the greatest Schubertian of our time and the finest accompanist in a wide survey of the Lieder for solo voice. Already in 1811, as a boy in his early teens, Schubert was writing with astonishing originality, as is shown in the long (19 minutes) opening Schiller setting, a *Funeral Fantasy* with its rough, clashing intervals of a second and amazing harmonic pointers to the future. Drama comes very much to the fore in the second song here, *Der Vatermörder* ('A father died by his son's hand'), while the composer's endearing, flowing lyricism makes both *Der Jüngling am Bache* and *Die Schatten* sound remarkably mature. *Totengräberlied* ('Dig, spade, dig on!') brings a characteristically light touch to a gravedigger's soliloquy as he reflects that rich and poor alike, handsome and noble, are all in the end reduced to bones. Throughout these nine well-filled CDs the diversity of Schubert's imagination holds the listener, and his melodic gift almost never disappoints, especially when the performances are so completely at home with the music. The songs are presented in broadly chronological order and the arrangement of items ensures that each disc of the nine makes a satisfying recital in its own right. The CD transfers are impeccable, adding a little in presence to what were originally very well-balanced recordings.

Lieder, Volume II (1817–28): *An die Musik; Pax vobiscum; Hänflings Liebeswerbung; Auf der Donau; Der Schiffer; Nach einem Gewitter; Fischerlied; Das Grab; Der Strom; An den Tod; Abschied; Die Forelle; Gruppe aus dem Tartarus; Elysium; Atys; Erlafsee; Der Alpenjäger; Der Kampf; Der Knabe in der Wiege* (1817); *Auf der Riesenkoppe; An den Mond in einer Herbstnacht; Grablied für die Mutter; Einsamkeit; Der Blumenbrief; Das Marienbild* (1818); *Litanei auf das Fest Allerseelen* (1816); *Blondel zu Marien; Das Abendrot; Sonett I: Apollo, lebet noch dein Hold verlangen; Sonett II: Allein, nachdenken wie gelähmt vom Krampfe; Sonett III: Nunmehr, da*

Himmel, Erde schweigt; Vom Mitleiden Mariä (1818) ; *Die Gebüsche; Der Wanderer; Abendbilder; Himmelsfunken; An die Freunde; Sehnsucht; Hoffnung; Der Jüngling am Bache; Hymne I: Wenige wissen das Geheimnis der Liebe; Hymne II: Wenn ich ihn nur hab; Hymne III: Wenn alle untreu werden; Hymne IV: Ich sag es jedem; Marie; Beim Winde; Die Sternennächte; Trost; Nachtstück; Prometheus; Strophe aus Die Götter Griechenlands* (1819); *Nachthymne; Die Vögel; Der Knabe; Der Fluss; Abendröte; Der Schiffer; Die Sterne; Morgenlied* (1820); *Frühlingsglaube* (1822); *Des Fräuleins Liebeslauschen* (1820); *Orest auf Tauris* (1817); *Der entsühnte Orest; Freiwilliges Versinken; Der Jüngling auf dem Hügel* (1820); *Sehnsucht* (1817); *Der zürnenden Diana; Im Walde* (1820); *Die gefangenen Sänger; Der Unglückliche; Versunken; Geheimnes; Grenzen der Menschheit* (1821); *Der Jüngling an der Quelle* (1815); *Der Blumen Schmerz* (1821); *Sei mir gegrüsst; Herr Josef Spaun, Assessor in Linz; Der Wachtelschlag Ihr Grab; Nachtviolen; Heliopolis I: Im kalten, rauhen Norden; Heliopolis II: Fels auf Felsen hingewälzet; Selige Welt; Schwanengesang: Wie klage'ich's aus; Du liebst mich nicht; Die Liebe hat gelogen; Todesmusik; Schatzgräbers Begehr; An die Leier; Im Haine; Der Musensohn; An die Entfernte; Am Flusse; Willkommen und Abschied* (1822); *Wandrers Nachtlied: Ein Gleiches; Der zürnende Barde* (1823); *Am See* (1822/3); *Viola; Drang in die Ferne; Der Zwerg; Wehmut; Lied: Die Mutter Erde; Auf dem Wasser zu singen; Pilgerweise; Das Geheimnis; Der Pilgrim; Dass sie hier gewesen; Du bist die Ruh; Lachen und Weinen; Greisengesang* (1823); *Dithyrambe; Der Sieg; Abendstern; Auflösung; Gondelfahrer* (1824); *Glaube, Hoffnung und Liebe* (1828); *Im Abendrot; Der Einsame* (1824); *Des Sängers Habe; Totengräbers Heimwehe; Der blinde Knabe; Nacht und Träume; Normans Gesang; Lied des gefangenen Jägers; Im Walde; Auf der Bruck; Das Heimweh; Die Allmacht; Fülle der Liebe; Wiedersehn; Abendlied für die Entfernte; Szene I aus dem Schauspiel Lacrimas; Am mein Herz; Der liebliche Stern* (1825); *Im Jänner 1817 (Tiefes Leid); Am Fenster; Sehnsucht; Im Freien; Fischerweise; Totengräberweise; Im Frühling; Lebensmut; Um Mitternacht; Uber Wildemann* (1826); *Romanze des Richard Löwenherz* (1827); *Trinklied; Ständchen; Hippolits Lied; Gesang (An Silvia); Der Wanderer an den Mond; Das Zügenglöcklein; Bei dir allein; Irdisches Glück; Wiegenlied* (1826); *Der Vater mit dem Kind; Jägers Liebeslied; Schiffers Scheidelied; L'incanto degli occhi; Il traditor deluso; Il modo di prender moglie; Das Lied im Grünen; Das Weinen; Vor meiner Wiege; Der Wallensteiner Lanznecht beim Trunk; Der Kreuzzug; Das Fischers Liebesglück* (1827); *Der Winterabend; Die Sterne; Herbst; Widerschein* (1828); *Abschied von der Erde* (1825/6).

(B) *** DG 437 225-2 (9). Dietrich Fischer-Dieskau, Gerald Moore.

Volume II of this great project brings the mature songs; performances and recording are just as compelling as in Volume 1. In their Berlin sessions Fischer-Dieskau and Moore adopted a special technique of study, rehearsal and recording most apt for the project. The sense of spontaneity and new discovery is unfailing, since each take was in fact a performance. On a later occasion, both artists might have taken a different view but, using the ease of access possible with CD, this collection is a unique way of sampling the many different aspects of Schubert's genius. The collection opens appropriately with *An die Musik* of 1817 and, as before, the songs in this volume are laid out chronologically with certain obvious exceptions – on disc 4, for instance, *Orest auf Tauris* (1817) is placed alongside the highly contrasted *Der entsühnte Orest*, 'Orestes purified' (1820) – and the closing recital on disc 9 is suitably concluded with *Abschied von der Erde* ('Farewell to the Earth'), dating from 1825/6. Once again there is much unfamiliar repertory to discover: the four *Hymnes* grouped together on the second disc are little known but show the composer's imaginative diversity in a specifically religious connotation, while the unexpected song dedicated to *Herr Josef Spaun, Assessor in Linz*, which closes the fourth CD, is strikingly operatic. Both booklets offer full translations and each includes also brief essays by Fischer-Dieskau and Walther Dürr on the composer.

Lieder, Volume III: Song-cycles: *Die schöne Müllerin; Schwanengesang; Die Winterreise.*

(M) *** DG 437 235-2 (3). Dietrich Fischer-Dieskau, Gerald Moore.

Fischer-Dieskau and Moore had each recorded these great cycles of Schubert several times already before they embarked on this set in 1971/2 as part of DG's Schubert song series. It was no mere repeat of earlier triumphs. If anything, these performances – notably that of the darkest and greatest of the cycles, *Winterreise* – are even more searching than before, with Moore matching the hushed concentration of the singer in some of the most remarkable playing that even he has put on record. As in the extensive recitals listed above, Fischer-Dieskau is in wonderfully fresh voice, and the transfers to CD have been managed very naturally.

Lieder: *Abendbilder; Am Fenster; Auf der Bruck; Auf der Donau; Aus Heliopolis; Fischerweise; Im Frühling; Liebeslauschen; Des Sängers Habe; Der Schiffer; Die Sterne; Der Wanderer; Wehmut; Das Zügenglöcklein.*

(M) *** DG (IMS) 445 717-2 [id.]. Dietrich Fischer-Dieskau, Sviatoslav Richter.

Recorded live in 1977, this beautifully balanced selection of Schubert songs displays the singer's enormous range of expression, as well as the acute sensitivity of the pianist in responding. The songs have been grouped almost in a cycle, starting with a biting expression of self-torment (*Des Sängers Habe*). This is sung aggressively here (understandably so) but gradually the mood lightens from melancholy (*Wehmut*) to brighter thoughts (*Das Zügenglöcklein* – 'The little bell'). Not many of these songs are well known, but it is a programme to delight aficionado and newcomer alike, atmospherically recorded with remarkably little interference from audience noises.

Elly Ameling collection ('The early years'): Disc 1: *An die Laute; An die Nachtigall* (2 settings); *An Sylvia; Der Blumenbrief; Du bist die Ruh'; Du Liebst mich nicht; Das Lied im Grünen; Der Einsame; Fischerweise; Die Gebüsche; Im Abendrot; Im Freien; Im Haine; Die Liebe hat gelogen; Der liebliche Stern; Das Mädchen; Die Männer sind méchant; Minnelied; Nacht und Träume; Nachtviolen; Rosamunde: Romanze. Schlummerlied; Der Schmetterling; Seligkeit; Die Sterne; Die Vögel; Der Wachtelschlag.* Disc 2: *Ave Maria; Gretchen am Spinnrade; Gretchens Bitte; Heidenröslein; Jäger, ruhe von der Jagd; Der König in Thule; Die junge Nonne; Die Liebende schreibt; Liebhabner in allen Gestalten; 4 Mignon Lieder (Kennst du das Land; Nur wer die Sehnsucht kennt; Heiss mich nicht reden; So lass mich scheinen); Nähe des Geliebten; Raste, Krieger!; Scene aus Faust; Suleika I & II.* Disc 3: *Abendbilder; An die Musik; An den Mond; Bertas Lied in der Nacht; Die Blumensprache; Erster Verlust; Frülingssehnsucht; Der Knabe; Nachthymne; Schwestergruss; Sei mir gegrüsst; Die Sterne; Wiegenlied.* Disc 4: *Am Bach im Frühling; An den Tod; An die Entfernte; An die untergehende Sonne; Auf dem Wasser zu singen; Die Forelle; Fülle der Liebe; Ganymed; Die Götter Griechenlands; Im Abendrot; Im Frühling; Der Musensohn; Der Schiffer; Schwanengesang: Sehnsucht; Sprach der Liebe.*
(M) *** Ph. Analogue/Dig. 438 528-2 (4). Elly Ameling, Dalton Baldwin (CDs 1–3); Rudolf Jansen (CD 4).

Elly Ameling appeared on the international scene in the mid 1960s. These records cover her period of maturity from 1972 until 1984. Her lovely voice with its diamond purity is consistently appealing and she is a persuasive interpreter, whether in the engaging *Mignon* songs or in the most familiar favourites: the poised freshness of *Nacht und Träume*, the innocence of *Nachtviolen* or the more emotionally fraught *Die Liebe hat gelogen*. These, like so much else, are most affecting; the analogue recordings on the first two discs show her at the peak of her form, with Dalton Baldwin most sensitive in support. The third disc, digitally recorded in 1982, had the distinction of being the first Lieder recital to appear on compact disc and readily deserved its accolade. It is a typically characterful and enchanting collection, starting with *An die Musik* and including other favourites like the *Cradle song* as well as lesser-known songs that admirably suit the lightness and sparkle of Ameling's voice. The fourth CD offers a 1984 digital recital with Rudolf Jansen accompanying. It brings more delights, even if the voice is not quite as fresh and agile as in the earlier collections, notably the 1972 recordings included on the second disc. Yet she is able to bring new depths to such a song as *An die Entfernte* and her breath control remains immaculate – as in the opening *Ganymed* – while she still brings delightful bounce to the ever-popular *Der Musensohn*. Her voice is caught naturally by the engineers and the balance is excellent. A treasurable collection, marred only by the absence of translations: only the German texts are given.

The Graham Johnson Schubert Lieder Edition

When it comes to background information, Graham Johnson's Schubert Lieder Edition for Hyperion – using some of the greatest singers of the day – is unmatchable. With each disc devoted to a group of songs on a particular theme, Johnson provides notes that add enormously to the enjoyment, heightening the experience of hearing even the most familiar songs.

Lieder Vol. 1: *Der Alpenjäger; Amalia; An den Frühling; An den Mond; Erster Verlust; Die Ewartung; Der Fischer; Der Flüchtling; Das Geheimnis; Der Jüngling am Bache; Lied; Meeres Stille; Nähe des Geliebten; Der Pilgrim; Schäfers Klagelied; Sehnsucht; Thekla; Wanderers Nachtlied; Wonne der Wehmut.*
*** Hyperion Dig. CDJ 33001 [id.]. Dame Janet Baker, Graham Johnson.

Hyperion's complete Schubert song edition, masterminded by the accompanist, Graham Johnson, this first volume sets the pattern of mixing well-known songs with rarities. Dame Janet's whole collection is devoted to Schiller and Goethe settings, above all those he wrote in 1815, an exceptionally rich year for the 18-year-old; one marvels that, after writing his dedicated, concentrated setting of *Wanderers Nachtlied*, he could on that same day in July write two other equally memorable songs, *Der Fischer* and *Erster Verlust* (*First loss*). Dame Janet is in glorious voice, her golden tone ravishing in a song such as *An den Mond* and her hushed tone caressing the ear in *Meeres Stille* and *Wanderers Nachtlied*. Presented like this, the project becomes a voyage of discovery.

Lieder Vol. 2: *Am Bach im Frühling; Am Flusse; Auf der Donau; Fahrt zum Hades; Fischerlied* (two settings); *Fischerweise; Der Schiffer; Selige Welt; Der Strom; Der Taucher; Widerschein; Wie Ulfru fischt*.
*** Hyperion Dig. CDJ 33002 [id.]. Stephen Varcoe, Graham Johnson.

Graham Johnson, with the baritone Stephen Varcoe, devises a delightful collection of men's songs, culminating in the rousing strophic song, *Der Schiffer*, one of the most catchily memorable that Schubert ever wrote, here exhilaratingly done. Otherwise the moods of water and wave, sea and river, are richly exploited. The last 28 minutes of the collection are devoted to the extended narrative, *Der Taucher* (*The Diver*), setting a long poem of Schiller which is based on an early version of the Beowulf saga. Varcoe and Johnson completely explode the long-accepted idea that this is overextended and cumbersome, giving it a thrilling dramatic intensity.

Lieder Vol. 3: *Abschied; An die Freunde; Augenlied; Iphigenia; Der Jüngling und der Tod; Lieb Minna; Liedesend; Nacht und Träume; Namenstagslied; Pax vobiscum; Rückweg; Trost im Liede; Viola; Der Zwerg*.
*** Hyperion Dig. CDJ 33003 [id.]. Ann Murray, Graham Johnson.

This is one of Ann Murray's finest records, with the intimate beauty of the voice consistently well caught and with none of the stress that the microphone exaggerates on record. Like the songs that Johnson chose for Ann Murray's husband, Philip Langridge, these too represent Schubert in his circle of friends, with their poems his inspiration, including a long flower ballad, *Viola*, by his close friend, Franz von Schober, which Murray and Johnson sustain beautifully.

Lieder Vol. 4: *Alte Liebe rostet nie; Am See; Am Strome; An Herrn Josef von Spaun (Epistel); Auf der Riesenkoppe; Das war ich; Das gestörte Glück; Liebeslauschen; Liebesrausch; Liebeständelei; Der Liedler; Nachtstück; Sängers Morgenlied* (2 versions); *Sehnsucht der Liebe*.
*** Hyperion Dig. CDJ 33004 [id.]. Philip Langridge, Graham Johnson.

Philip Langridge brings a collection to illustrate Schubert's setting of words by poets in his immediate circle, ending with *Epistel*, a tongue-in-cheek parody song addressed to a friend who had left Vienna to become a tax collector, extravagantly lamenting his absence. It is Johnson's presentation of such rarities that makes the series such a delight. Langridge has rarely sounded so fresh and sparkling on record.

Lieder Vol. 5: *Die Allmacht; An die Natur; Die Erde; Erinnerung; Ferne von der grossen Stadt; Ganymed; Klage der Ceres; Das Lied im Grünen; Morgenlied; Die Mutter Erde; Die Sternenwelten; Täglich zu singen; Dem Unendlichen; Wehmut*.
*** Hyperion Dig. CDJ 33005 [id.]. Elizabeth Connell, Graham Johnson.

Thanks in part to Johnson's choice of songs and to his sensitive support at the piano, Connell has rarely sounded so sweet and composed on record, yet with plenty of temperament. The collection centres round a theme – this one, Schubert and the countryside, suggested by the most popular song of the group, *Das Lied im Grünen*. As ever, the joy of the record is enhanced by Johnson's brilliant, illuminating notes.

Lieder Vol. 6: *Abendlied für die Entfernte; Abends unter der Linde* (two versions); *Abendstern; Alinde; An die Laute; Des Fischers Liebesglück; Jagdlied; Der Knabe in der Wiege (Wiegenlied); Lass Wolken an Hügeln ruh'n; Die Nacht; Die Sterne; Der Vater mit dem Kind; Vor meiner Wiege; Wilkommen und Abschied; Zur guten Nacht*.
*** Hyperion Dig. CDJ 33006 [id.]. Anthony Rolfe Johnson, Graham Johnson (with chorus).

The theme of Anthony Rolfe Johnson's contribution is 'Schubert and the Nocturne'. Two items include a small male chorus, a group of individually named singers. *Jagdlied* is entirely choral, and the final *Zur guten Nacht*, a late song of 1827, has the 'Spokesman' answered by the chorus, ending on a gentle *Gute Nacht*. Rolfe Johnson's voice has never sounded more beautiful on record, and the partnership of singer and accompanist makes light even of a long strophic song (using the same music for each verse) like *Des Fischers Liebesglück*, beautiful and intense.

Lieder Vol. 7: *An die Nachtigall; An den Frühling; An den Mond; Idens Nachtgesang; Idens Schwanenlied; Der Jüngling am Bache; Kennst du das Land?; Liane; Die Liebe; Luisens Antwort; Des Mädchens Klage; Meeres Stille; Mein Gruss an den Mai; Minona oder die Kunde der Dogge; Naturgenuss; Das Rosenband; Das Sehnen; Sehnsucht* (2 versions); *Die Spinnerin; Die Sterbende; Stimme der Liebe; Von Ida; Wer kauft Liebesgötter?*.
*** Hyperion Dig. CDJ 33007 [id.]. Elly Ameling, Graham Johnson.

An extraordinarily rewarding sequence of 24 songs, all written in the composer's *annus mirabilis*, 1815. With Ameling both charming and intense, Johnson's robust defence in his ever-illuminating notes of the first and longest of the songs, *Minona*, is amply confirmed, a richly varied ballad. Here too is a preliminary setting of *Meeres Stille*, less well-known than the regular version, written a day later, but just as clearly a masterpiece, sung by Ameling in a lovely intimate half-tone at a sustained *pianis-*

simo. It is fascinating too to compare the two contrasted settings of Mignon's song, *Sehnsucht*, the first of five he ultimately attempted.

Lieder Vol. 8: *Abendlied der Fürstin; An Chloen; An den Mond; An den Mond in einer Herbstnacht; Berthas Lied in der Nacht; Erlkönig; Die frühen Gräber; Hochzeitslied; In der Mitternacht; Die Mondnacht; Die Nonne; Die Perle; Romanze; Die Sommernacht; Ständchen; Stimme der Liebe; Trauer der Liebe; Wiegenlied.*
*** Hyperion Dig. CDJ 33008 [id.]. Sarah Walker, Graham Johnson.

For Sarah Walker, with her perfectly controlled mezzo at its most sensuous, the theme is 'Schubert and the Nocturne', leading from the first, lesser-known version of the Goethe poem, *An den Mond*, to two of the best-loved of all Schubert's songs, the delectable *Wiegenlied*, 'Cradle-song', and the great drama of *Erlkönig*, normally sung by a man, but here at least as vividly characterized by a woman's voice.

Lieder Vol. 9: *Blanka; 4 Canzonen, D.688; Daphne am Bach; Delphine; Didone abbandonata; Gott! höre meine Stimme; Der gute Hirt; Hin und wieder Fliegen Pfeile;* (i) *Der Hirt auf dem Felsen. Ich schleiche bang und still (Romanze). Lambertine; Liebe Schwärmt auf allen Wegen; Lilla an die Morgenröte; Misero pargoletto; La pastorella al prato; Der Sänger am Felsen; Thekla; Der Vollmond strahlt (Romanze).*
*** Hyperion Dig. CDJ 33009 [id.]. Arleen Augér, Graham Johnson; (i) with Thea King.

'Schubert and the theatre' is the theme of Arleen Augér's contribution, leading up to the glories of his very last song, the headily beautiful *Shepherd on the rock*, with its clarinet obbligato. The *Romanze, Ich schleiche bang* – adapted from an opera aria – also has a clarinet obbligato. Notable too are the lightweight Italian songs that the young Schubert wrote for his master, Salieri, and a lovely setting, *Der gute Hirt* ('The good shepherd'), in which the religious subject prompts a melody which anticipates the great staircase theme in Strauss's *Arabella*.

Lieder Vol. 10: *Adelwold und Emma; Am Flusse; An die Apfelbäume, wo ich Julien erblickte; An die Geliebte; An Mignon; Auf den Tod einer Nachtigall; Auf einen Kirchhof; Harfenspieler I; Labetrank der Liebe; Die Laube; Der Liebende; Der Sänger; Seufzer; Der Traum; Vergebliche Liebe; Der Weiberfreund.*
*** Hyperion Dig. CDJ 33010 [id.]. Martyn Hill, Graham Johnson.

Graham Johnson here correlates the year 1815 with what has been documented of his life over those 12 months, which is remarkably little. So the songs here form a kind of diary. The big item, overtopping everything else, is the astonishing 38-stanza narrative song, *Adalwold and Emma*, with Hill ranging wide in his expression. It is almost half an hour long, from the bold march-like opening to the final happy resolution.

Lieder Vol. 11: *An den Tod; Auf dem Wasser zu singen; Auflösung; Aus 'Heliopolis' I & II; Dithyrambe; Elysium; Der Geistertanz; Der König in Thule; Lied des Orpheus; Nachtstück; Schwanengesang; Seligkeit; So lasst mich scheinen; Der Tod und das Mädchen; Verklärung; Vollendung; Das Zügenglöcklein.*
*** Hyperion Dig. CDJ 33011 [id.]. Brigitte Fassbaender, Graham Johnson.

Starting with a chilling account of *Death and the maiden*, the theme of Brigitte Fassbaender's disc is 'Death and the composer'. Fassbaender's ability precisely to control her vibrato brings baleful tone-colours, made the more ominous by the rather reverberant, almost churchy, acoustic. So in *Auf dem Wasser zu singen* the lightly fanciful rippling-water motif presents the soul gliding gently 'like a boat' up to heaven, and the selection ends astonishingly with what generally seems one of the lightest of Schubert songs, *Seligkeit*. This, as Johnson suggests, returns the listener from heaven back to earth. In this, as elsewhere, Fassbaender sings with thrilling intensity, with Johnson's accompaniment comparably inspired.

Lieder, Vol. 12: *Adelaide; An Elise; An Laura, als sie Klopstocks Auferstehungslied sang; Andenken; Auf den Sieg der Deutschen; Ballade; Die Betende; Don Gayseros I, II, III; Der Geistertanz; Lied an der Ferne; Lied der Liebe; Nachtgesang; Die Schatten; Sehnsucht; Trost; Trost in Tränem; Der Vatermörder.*
** Hyperion Dig. CDJ 33012 [id.]. Adrian Thompson, Graham Johnson.

Adrian Thompson's disc brings the only disappointment in Graham Johnson's outstanding Schubert series. As recorded, the voice sounds gritty and unsteady, with the tone growing tight and ugly under pressure, yet this collection of early songs, all teenage inspirations, still illuminates the genius of Schubert at this earliest period of his career.

Lieder, Vol. 13: (i) *Eine altschottische Ballade. Ellens Gesang I, II & III (Ave Maria); Gesang der Norna; Gretchen am Spinnrade; Gretchens Bitte; Lied der Anna Lyle; Die Männer sind méchant; Marie; Das Marienbild;* (i) *Normans Gesang; Szene aus Faust. Shilrik und Vinvela; Die Unterscheidung.*
*** Hyperion Dig. CDJ 33013 [id.]. Marie McLaughlin, Graham Johnson; (i) with Thomas Hampson.

The theme for Marie McLaughlin's contribution to

the Hyperion Schubert edition is broadly a survey of Schubert's inner conflicts and contradictions. The Goethe settings are crowned by one of the most celebrated of all Schubert songs, *Gretchen am Spinnrade*. McLaughlin gives a fresh and girlish portrait, tenderly pathetic rather than tragic. Fascinatingly the selection also includes *Gretchens Bitte*, an extended song that Schubert left unfinished and for which Benjamin Britten in 1943 provided a completion of the final stanzas. The translations of Scottish ballads cover a wide range. *Eine altschottische Liede* is one of the three dramatic items involving the baritone Thomas Hampson, which also include a sinister dialogue for Gretchen and an evil spirit, *Szene aus Faust*. McLaughlin's voice comes over sweetly, with brightness and much charm.

Lieder, Vol. 14: *Amphiaraos; An die Leier;* (i) *Antigone und Oedip. Der entsühnte Orest; Freiwilliges Versinken; Die Götter Griechenlands; Gruppe aus dem Tartarus; Fragment aus dem Aeschylus;* (i) *Hektors Abschied. Hippolits Lied; Lied eines Schiffers an die Dioskuren; Memnon; Orest auf Tauris; Philoktet; Uraniens Flucht; Der Zürnenden Diana.*
*** Hyperion Dig. CDJ 33014 [id.]. Thomas Hampson, Graham Johnson; (i) with Marie McLaughlin.

Thomas Hampson's theme here is 'Schubert and the classics', mainly Ancient Greece. Matching the hushed intensity of the opening song, *Die Götter Griechenlands*, singer and accompanist give a rapt performance, and Hampson's ecstatically sweet tone, with flawless legato, contrasts with the darkly dramatic timbre – satisfyingly firm and steady – that he finds for later songs and dialogues, including the finale *Hektors Abschied*. In that dialogue Marie McLaughlin sings the part of Andromache to Hampson's Hector.

Lieder, Vol. 15: *Am Fenster; An die Sonne; An die untergehende Sonne; Der blinde Knabe; Gondelfahrer; Im Frieien; Ins stille Land; Die junge Nonne; Klage an den Mond; Kolmas Klage; Die Mainacht; Der Mondabend; Der Morgenkuss; Sehnsucht; Der Unglückliche; Der Wanderer an den Mond; Der Winterabend.*
❁ *** Hyperion Dig. CDJ 33015 [id.]. Dame Margaret Price, Graham Johnson.

In the fifteenth disc of his Hyperion series, Graham Johnson, accompanying Dame Margaret Price in songs on the theme of 'Night', achieves a new peak. One winning rarity is *Klage an den Mond* ('Lament to the Moon'), gloriously fresh and lyrical. Price and Johnson find here a distinctive magic so that its simple melody rings through the memory for hours. The other Holty setting on Margaret Price's disc is of *Die Mainacht*, much better known in Brahms's raptly beautiful setting. The young Schubert simply lets his lyricism flower as no one else could. Johnson and Dame Margaret match that with folk-like freshness, concealing art. In the best-known song, *Der Wanderer an den Mond*, Price is light and crisp, but she finds extra mystery in the moonlight scene of *Am Fenster*, poignantly reflecting the lover's sadness.

Lieder, Vol. 16: *An die Freude; An Emma; Die Bürgschaft; Die Entzückung an Laura I & II; Das Geheimnis; Der Jüngling am Bache; Laura am Clavier; Leichenfantasie; Das Mädchen aus der Fremde; Die vier Weltalter; Sehnsucht; Der Pilgrim.*
*** Hyperion Dig. CDJ 33016 [id.]. Thomas Allen, Graham Johnson.

Following the pattern of Graham Johnson's unique Schubert series, Thomas Allen in Schiller settings is challenged to some of his most sensitive singing, using the widest tonal range. They include two extended narrative songs that are a revelation, one of them, *Leichenfantasie* ('Funereal fantasy'), written when Schubert was only 14. As before, Johnson's notes and commentaries greatly heighten one's understanding both of particular songs and of Schubert generally.

Lieder, Vol. 17: *Am Grabe Anselmos; An den Mond; An die Nachtigall; An mein Klavier; Aus 'Diego Manazares' (Ilmerine); Die Einsiedelei; Frühlingslied; Geheimnis; Der Herbstabend; Herbstlied; Die Herbstnacht; Klage; Klage um Ali Bey; Lebenslied; Leiden der Trennung; Lied; Lied in der Absehenheit; Litanei; Lodas Gespenst; Lorma; Minnelied; Pflicht und Liebe; Phidile; Winterlied.*
*** Hyperion Dig. CDJ 33017 [id.]. Lucia Popp, Graham Johnson.

It was fitting that one of the last recordings which Lucia Popp made, only months before her tragic death in the autumn of 1993, was her contribution to Graham Johnson's Schubert series. These songs, written in 1816 and almost all of them little known, inspire all her characteristic sweetness and charm. They include an extended narrative song to a text from Ossian, *Lodas gespent*, which, like others resurrected by the indefatigable Johnson, defies the idea that long equals boring. She also relishes two of Schubert's rare comic songs, pointing them deliciously. As ever, Johnson's notes are a model of fascinating scholarship.

Lieder, Vol. 18: *Abendlied; An den Schlaf; An die Erntferne; An die Harmonie; An mein Herz; Auf den Tod einer Nachtigall; Auf der Bruck; 'Die Blume und der Quell'; Blumenlied; Drang in die Ferne; Erntelied; Das Finden; Das Heimweh* (2 versions); *Im Frühling; Im Jänner 1817 (Tiefes Lied); Im Walde; Lebensmut; Der Liebliche*

Stern; Die Nacht; Uber Wildemann; Um Mitternacht.
*** Hyperion Dig. CDJ 33018 [id.]. Peter Schreier, Graham Johnson.

This 18th disc in Graham Johnson's masterly series represents the halfway point, with Peter Schreier providing a keenly illuminating supplement to his prize-winning recordings with András Schiff of the great Schubert song-cycles for Decca. The challenge is just as great here, when this particular group centres on strophic songs. The first nine songs are all early ones, dating from 1816, leading to just one extended non-strophic song, *Das Heimweh*, D.851, of 1825. Its weight and complexity come over the more powerfully after such a preparation. Johnson then delivers a master-stroke by devising for Schreier what amounts to a new Schubert song-cycle, presenting in sequence ten settings of poems from the *Poetisches Tagebuch* ('Poetic Diary'), by the obsessive, unstable poet, Ernst Schulze, all written in 1825 and 1826. Quoting the first song, Johnson calls the cycle *Auf den wilden Wegen* ('On the wild paths'), with the sequence following the poet's madly fanciful love-affair with a beloved who in real life rejected him as a mere stranger. Schreier and Johnson in their imaginative treatment present clear parallels with *Winterreise*, offering one momentary haven of happiness, instantly shattered. That comes in the best-known song, *Im Frühling*, among the most haunting that even Schubert ever wrote. Johnson's comprehensive notes, as in previous discs of the series, intensify enjoyment enormously.

Lieder, Vol. 19: *Abendlied; Am See; Auf dem See; Auf dem Wasser zu singen; Beim Winde; Der Blumen Schmerz; Die Blumensprache; Gott im Frühling; Im Haine; Der liebliche Stern; Nach einem Gewitter; Nachtviolen; Die Rose; Die Sterne; Suleika I & II; Die Sternennächte; Vergissmeinicht.*
*** Hyperion Dig. CDJ 33019 [id.]. Felicity Lott, Graham Johnson.

Graham Johnson's theme for Felicity Lott's disc is 'Schubert and flowers', prompting a sequence of charming, ever-lyrical songs, mostly neglected but including such a favourite as *Nachtviolen* (raptly sung) and – less predictably – *Auf dem Wasser zu singen*, all enchantingly done. Lott's soprano is not caught quite at its purest, but the charm and tender imagination of the singer consistently match the inspired accompaniments. In his detailed notes Johnson manages to include a 'Schubertian florilegium', listing several hundred of the songs inspired by particular flowers.

Lieder, Vol. 20: '*Schubertiad*' (1815) Songs and part-songs: *Abendständchen (An Lina); Alles um Liebe; Als ich sie errötten sah; Begräbnislied; Bergknappenlied; Der erste Liebe; Die Frölichkeit; Geist der Liebe; Grablied; Heidenröslein; Hoffnung; Huldigung; Klage um Ali Bey; Liebesrausch; Die Macht der Liebe; Das Mädchen von Inistore; Der Morgenstern; Nachtgesang; Ossians Lied nach dem Falle Nathos; Osterlied; Punschlied (Im Norden su singen); Schwertlied; Schwangesang; Die Tauschung; Tischerlied; Totenkranz für ein Kind; Trinklied* (2 versions); *Trinklied vor der Schlacht; Wiegenlied; Winterlied; Der Zufriedene.*
*** Hyperion Dig. CDJ 33020 [id.]. Patricia Rozario, John Mark Ainsley, Ian Bostridge, Michael George, Graham Johnson; L. Schubert Chorale, Stephen Layton.

The 20th volume of the Hyperion Schubert series brings a different kind of recital disc, with a range of singers performing no fewer than 32 brief songs and ensemble numbers, all written in 1815. Johnson conceives that this might well have been the sort of Schubertiad to take place towards the end of that year and, aptly for the opening and closing numbers, chooses drinking songs. In between, the vigorous and jolly songs are effectively contrasted with a few darker ones, such as a burial song. The team of singers has the flair one expects of Johnson as founder of the Songmakers' Almanac, with the young tenor, Ian Bostridge, appearing in one of his first recordings. More Schubertiads are planned for later on in the Hyperion series.

Lieder, Vol. 21: Songs from 1817–18: *Die abgeblühte Linde; Abschied von einem Freunde; An die Musik; An eine Quelle; Erlafsee; Blondel zu Marien; Blumenbrief; Evangelium Johannes; Der Flug der Zeit; Die Forelle; Grablied für die Mutter; Häbflings Liebeswerbung; Impromptu; Die Liebe; Liebhaber in allen Gestalten; Lied eines Kind; Das Lied vom Reifen; Lob der Tränen; Der Schäfer und der Reiter; Schlaflied; Schweizerlied; Sehnsucht; Trost; Vom Mitleiden Mariä.*
*** Hyperion Dig. CDJ 33021 [id.]. Edith Mathis, Graham Johnson.

Instead of adopting a particular theme for this sequence, sung with characteristic sweetness by the Swiss soprano, Edith Mathis, Graham Johnson has devised a delectable group of 24 songs written in 1817–18, including a high proportion of charmers. Two of them are among the best known of all Schubert's songs, *Die Forelle* ('The trout') and *An die Musik*, here sung with disarming freshness and given extra point through Johnson's inspired playing. The songs in swinging compound or triple time are particularly delightful, as are the often elaborately decorative accompaniments which Johnson points with winning delicacy.

Lieder, Vol. 22: '*Schubertiad II*': *Der Abend; Das Abendroth; An die Sonne; An Rosa I & II; An Sie; Das Bild; Cora an die Sonne; Cronnan;*

Die drei Sänger; Die Erscheinung; Furcht der Geliebten; Gebet wahrend der Schlacht; Genugsamkeit; Das Grab; Hermann und Thusnelda; Das Leben ist ein Traum; Lob des Tokayers; Lorma; Das Mädchen aus der Fremde; Morgenlied; Punschlied; Scholie; Selma und Selmar; Die Sterne; Trinklied; Vaterlandslied.
*** Hyperion Dig. CDJ 33022 [id.]. Lorna Anderson, Catherine Wyn-Rogers, Jamie MacDougall, Simon Keenlyside; Graham Johnson.

The year 1815 was an *annus mirabilis* for Schubert, and Graham Johnson here, from the wealth of songs written in those 12 months, devises a sequence such as the composer might have performed with friends in an intimate Schubertiad. So the solo items are punctuated by three male-voice quartets and one trio for female voices in which the main soloists, listed above, are joined by four other distinguished singers: Patricia Rozario, Catherine Denley, John Mark Ainsley and Michael George. Though most of the 28 items are brief, they include one more-extended song, *Die drei Sänger* ('The three minstrels'), in which Schubert adventurously illustrates the narrative in an almost operatic way. The final page is missing from the manuscript, which is here sensitively completed by Reinhard von Hoorickx.

Lieder, Volume 23: Songs from 1816: *Abendlied; Abschied von der Harfe; Am ersten Maimorgen; An Chloen; Bei dem Grabe meines Vater; Edone; Der Entfernten; Freude der Kinderjahre; Die frühe Liebe; Geist der Liebe; Gesänger des Harfners aus 'Wilhelm Meister' (Wer sich der Einsamkeit ergibt; Wer nie sein Brot mit Tränen ass; An die Türen will ich schleichen); Das Grab; Der Hirt; Julius an Theone; Der Jüngling an der Quelle; Klage; Die Knabenzeit; Der Leidende* (2 versions); *Die Liebesgötter; Mailied; Pflügerlied; Romanze; Skolie; Stimme der Liebe; Der Tod Oscars; Zufriedenheit.*
*** Hyperion Dig. CDJ 33023 [id.]. Christoph Prégardien, Graham Johnson.

The German lyric tenor Christoph Prégardien uses his lovely voice with its honeyed tone-colours through a wide expressive range in a very varied selection of songs from 1816. It is his artistry as well as Johnson's that makes the opening item so riveting, a long narrative song to words by Ossian in translation, which Prégardien's feeling for word-meaning helps to bring to life. That is followed by a brief chorus, *Der Grab*, sung by the London Schubert Chorale, which Johnson intends as a comment on that narrative. The poet is Johann von Salis-Seewis, who is also represented by four solo songs, including the ravishing *Der Jungling an der Quelle*, one of the most haunting that Schubert ever composed. In that year Schubert was expanding the range of poets he chose to set, including Johann Mayrhofer for the first time, here represented by the little-known *Der Hirt* ('The shepherd'). The selection of 19 items is rumbustiously rounded off by a drinking-song, *Skolie*.

Lieder, Vol. 24: *Goethe Schubertiad: An Mignon; An Schwager Kronos; Bundeslied; Erlkönig; Ganymed; Geistes-Gruss; Gesang der Geister über den Wassern* (2 versions); *Der Goldschmiedsgesell; Der Gott und die Bajadere; Hoffnung; Jägers Abendlied* (2 versions); *Mahomets Gesang; Mignon (So lasst mich scheinen); Rastlose Liebe; Der Rattenfänger; Schäfers Klagelied; Der Schatzgräber; Sehnsucht* (2 versions); *Sehnsucht (Nur wer die Sehnsucht kennt); Tischlied; Wer nie sein Brot mit Tränen ass.*
*** Hyperion Dig. CDJ 33024 [id.]. Christine Schäfer, John Mark Ainsley, Simon Keenlyside, Michael George, L. Schubert Chorale, Stephen Layton; Graham Johnson.

This collection, drawn from Schubert's many settings of Goethe, aims to celebrate the important role the poet's works played in the composer's life. Graham Johnson in his notes makes high claims: 'It was the collaboration between Schubert and Goethe which allowed song with piano to become an enduring and valid means of musical expression on a large emotional scale.' Sadly, Goethe himself was indifferent to the inspired efforts of this then-obscure composer, but it did not affect the intensity of Schubert's response to the words. This selection, like that of Volume 28, devoted to Schiller, is related to the life of the poet and includes many fascinating items, not least those in which Schubert set a text more than once. There are half a dozen of them here, including two quite different settings of *The Song of the Spirits over the Waters*, each completed by other hands. The second, for male chorus, is particularly powerful. Also fascinating is the version of *Erlkönig* here, with three singers taking part, characterizing the different voices in the story, a practice which Schubert himself sanctioned. (This is also included in Volume 2 of EMI's historical Lieder collection, with Georges Thill leading a performance in French.) All the singers here are ideally responsive, with Michael George reining in a voice weightier than the rest.

Lieder, Vol. 25: (i) *Die schöne Müllerin* (song-cycle); (ii) with additional poems by Wilhelm Müller.
❁ *** Hyperion Dig. CDJ 33025 [id.]. (i) Ian Bostridge, Graham Johnson; (ii) read by Dietrich Fischer-Dieskau,

For this first of the big song-cycles in his comprehensive Schubert edition for Hyperion, Graham Johnson could not have chosen his singer more shrewdly. It is a delight to have in Ian Bostridge a tenor who not only produces youthfully golden tone for this young man's sequence but who also gives an eagerly detailed account of the 20 songs, mesmeric at the close, to match even the finest rivals. With the help of Johnson's keenly imaginative accompaniment, Bostridge's gift for changing face and conveying mood makes the story-telling exceptionally fresh and vivid. The bonus is also to have Dietrich Fischer-Dieskau (now retired from singing) reciting the Müller poems which Schubert failed to set. Johnson is at his most inspired too in his detailed notes, which will be a revelation even to experienced Schubertians.

Lieder, Vol. 26: *'An 1826 Schubertiad': 2 Scenes from Lacrimas* (*Schauspiel*); *4 Mignon Lieder* of Wilhelm Meister. Lieder: *Abschied von der Erde; An Sylvia; Das Echo; Der Einsame; Grab und Mond; Mondenschein; Nachthelle; Des Sängers Habe; Ständchen; Totengräberweise; Trinklied; Der Wanderer an den Mond; Widerspruch; Wiegenlied.*

*** Hyperion Dig. CDJ 33026 [id.]. Christine Schäfer, John Mark Ainsley, Richard Jackson. L. Schubert Chorale, Layton; Graham Johnson.

Starting with *Der Einsame*, sung by Richard Jackson, one of the most haunting of Schubert songs, here is a Schubertiad that brings its measure of darkness, relying entirely on Lieder which Schubert wrote in 1825 and 1826. By then he was writing fewer songs than before, but was hitting the mark every time. It ends in sombre tones with *Abschied von der Erde* ('Farewell to the Earth'), not a song at all but a melodrama for reciter and piano, which Richard Jackson narrates as effectively as one could imagine. Christine Schäfer and Richard Jackson between them perform most of the programme, with John Mark Ainsley contributing just one or two, including *To Sylvia*. That is one of the three Shakespeare settings which come as a lightweight interlude. Schäfer's contributions shine the most brightly, not least the hypnotic *Wiegenlied*, to words by Seidl. Graham Johnson's notes include a survey of Schubert's career in 1825–6, a list of the songs written then, and his brilliant analysis of each item.

Lieder, Vol. 27: *Abendröte cycle of Friedrich von Schlegel* (complete). Other settings of Friedrich von Schlegel: *Blanka; Fülle der Liebe; Im Walde; Der Schiffer*. Settings of August von Schlegel: *Lebensmelodien; Lob der Tränen; Sonnets I–III; Sprache der Liebe; Wiedersehn.*

*** Hyperion Dig. CDJ 33027 [id.]. Matthias Goerne, Christine Schäfer, Graham Johnson.

When the young German baritone Matthias Goerne, made his début at Wigmore Hall, deputizing on a gala occasion, it was instantly obvious that here was a major new Lieder singer. He makes an inspired choice for this fine disc in Graham Johnson's collected edition of the Schubert songs, firmly established as one of the most important recording projects of the nineties. With a masterly feeling for words and vocal line Goerne brings out the full charm of these settings of poems by the von Schlegel brothers, Friedrich as well as August, the translator of Shakespeare. The seven songs to words by August are rounded off with three settings of his translations of Petrarch sonnets, while Johnson, prompted by circumstantial evidence, has ingeniously assembled a cycle of 11 Friedrich von Schlegel settings, *Abendröte* ('Sunset'), with Christine Schäfer as soloist in three of them, though not in the best-known of them, *Die Vogel* ('The Bird'), a favourite with both Elisabeth Schumann and Elisabeth Schwarzkopf. Görne and Johnson regularly demonstrate what masterpieces even some of the least known and briefest songs are. Johnson's notes are, as ever, a model, explaining why belated publication of particular songs has unfairly brought about neglect.

Lieder Vol. 28: 'Schubertiad' (1822): *Am Flusse; An die Entfernte!; Du liebst mich nicht; Frülingsgesang; Geheimes; Geist der Liebe; Ihr Grab; Im Gegenwärtigen Vergangenes; Johanna Sebus; Die Liebe hat gelogen; Mahomets Gesang; Mignon (Heiss mich nicht reden); Der Musensohn; Die Nachtingall; Schatzgräbers Begehr; Sei mir gegrüsst!; Selige Welt; Des Tages Weihe; Todesmusik; Versunken; Der Wachtelschlag; Willkommen und Abschied.*

(N) *** Hyperion Dig. CDJ 33028 [id.]. Christine Schäfer, John Mark Ainsley, Maarten Koningsberger, Ch., Graham Johnson.

Described as an 1822 Schubertiad, this volume offers an attractively varied collection of items, not just songs from the principal tenor and baritone, both sensitive singers, but concerted numbers, ending with a solemn quartet, a miniature cantata, *Des Tages Weihe*. Settings of Goethe predominate, with Christine Schäfer a very welcome contributor in the first version of *Der Musensohn*, made to sparkle in a higher key than usual. The sound between items is not always consistent, when the chorus is set in a more reverberant acoustic.

Lieder Vol. 29: *Abendbilder; Blondel zu Marien; Einsamkeit* (cantata); *Frühlingsglaube; Himmelsfunken; Hoffnung; Hymne I – IV; Im Walde (Waldesnacht); Der Jüngling auf dem Hügel; Die Liebende schreibt; Morgenlied; Nachthymne; Trost.*

(N) *** Hyperion Dig. CDJ 33029 [id.]. Marjana Lipovšek, Nathan Berg, Graham Johnson.

Though Marjana Lipovšek with her warm, velvety mezzo, is the central soloist in this collection of songs from 1819 and 1820, the young Canadian baritone, Nathan Berg, takes on the biggest challenge here. That is the cantata, *Einsamkeit*, in 12 sections, setting words by Mayrhofer, with whom Schubert at that time shared a small room. The beauty and range of tone, with flawless legato, make one want to hear more of Berg, but Lipovšek's contribution is equally persuasive in a wide range of songs including five settings of metaphysical poems by Novalis, distinctive in Schubert's oeuvre. Like his playing, Johnson's sleeve notes are revelatory, both on the music and Schubert's life and character.

Lieder, Vol. 30: *Winterreise* (song cycle), *D.911.*
(N) *** Hyperion Dig. CDJ 33030 [id.]. Matthias Goerne, Graham Johnson.

For this greatest of song-cycles Graham Johnson has boldly turned not to a staid, long-experienced artist but to Matthias Goerne, the young baritone who is rapidly proving himself the most exciting and inspired Lieder-singer since Dietrich Fischer-Dieskau. Goerne movingly brings out the point that this is the tragedy of a young lover, not an old one. He sings not just with velvety beauty of tone in every register but with a rapt dedication that forces you to rethink each poem in the cycle, ending with a chill that is all-involving. At every point Graham Johnson heightens the experience with his subtly pointed playing. His commentary in a massive booklet not only illuminates the musical inspiration, but invaluably puts the work in its historical context, showing how profoundly Schubert's reordering of the songs, different from that of the poet, Müller, heightens their tragic impact.

Lieder, Vol. 31: *Die Allmacht* (2nd version for chorus); *Die gestirne; Hagars Klage; Himmelsfunken; Im Abendrot; Das Mädchens Klage* (1st version); *Mirjams Siegergesang; Psalms Nos. 13; 23* (both trans. Mendelssohn); *Psalm 92* (unaccompanied in Hebrew); *Dem Unendlichen.*
(N) *** Hyperion Dig. CDJ 33031 [id.]. Christine Brewer, Holst Singers, Stephen Layton; Graham Johnson.

In Graham Johnson's superb series covering all of Schubert's songs, this disc devoted to sacred songs is quite distinct from previous issues, offering not only those for solo voice, but some with chorus too. With the sensitive and powerful American soprano, Christine Brewer, as the central soloist, joined by the Holst singers and other soloists in the concerted numbers, this provides a fascinating survey of Schubert's equivocal approach to religious inspiration, too individual to follow Catholic dogma precisely. Schubert may not have been devout, but the plight of Hagar and Ishmael in the desert, as told in Genesis, led him as a mere 14-year-old to write an extended 16-minute sequence. It is good to have this big religious narrative piece – *Hagars Klage* and *Mirjams Siegesgesang*, a cantata on the Exodus story of Miriam, from the last year of his life – so strongly and persuasively performed, defying length. There is also some electrifying chorus work from the Holst Singers in the Psalm settings. The first two come in translations by Moses Mendelssohn, grandfather of the composer, while Schubert set the third in the original Hebrew, responding sensitively to a commission from a Jewish friend. The solo songs, often simple and hymn-like, are also beautifully sung by the rich-toned mezzo, Christine Brewer. As ever in this series, Johnson's brilliant notes are an inspiration.

Lieder, Vol. 32: *'An 1816 Schubertiad': An die Sonne; Beitrag zur Fünfzigjährigen Jubelfeier des Herrn von Salieri: Der Entfernten; Entzückung; Der Geistertanz; Gott der Weltschöpfer; Gott im Ungewitter; Grablied auf einen Soldaten; Das grosse Halleluja; Licht und Liebe; Des Mädchens Klage; Naturgenuss; Ritter Toggenburg; Schlachtgesang; Vedi quanto adoro (Dido Abbandonata); Die verfehlte Stunde; Der Wanderer; Das war ich; Zufriedenheit; Zum Punsche.*
(N) *** Hyperion Dig. CDJ 33032 [id.]. Dawson, Schäfer, Murray, Mark Ainsley, Daniel Norman, Prégardien, Schade, Spence, Maltman, Varcoe, L. Schubert Chorale & Soloists, Stephen Layton; Graham Johnson.

With the exception of *Der Wanderer*, few items in this '*1816 Schubertiad*' are well known, yet it makes for fascinating listening, with Graham Johnson's illuminating notes providing an ideal commentary. Solitary but substantial contributions from such artists as Christine Schäfer and Christoph Prégardien come as bonuses from earlier sessions in the series, and the collaboration of various artists on ensemble pieces brings just the right atmosphere for a Schubertiad. A trivial but charming sequence of four items was written in celebration of the 50th anniversary of the arrival in Vienna of Schubert's evidently much-loved teacher, Salieri. The brief, trivial canon, *Unser aller Grosspapa* is a special delight. Full, warm sound.

Hyperion Schubert Edition sampler. Lieder: (i) *Die Allmacht;* (ii) *Alinde;* (iii) *Als ich sie erröten sah;* (iv) *Am Bach im Frühling;* (v) *Am See;* (vi) *Am Strome;* (vii) *An den Frühling;* (viii) *An die Sonne;* (ix) *An Emma;* (x) *An Silvia;* (xi) *Auflösung;* (xii) *Blondel zu Marien;* (xiii) *Erlkönig;* (xiv) *Jüngling an der Quelle;* (xv) *Der liebliche Stern;* (xvi) *Lied, D.284;* (xvii) *Lied eines Schiffers an die Dioskuren;* (xviii) *Lob der Tränen;* (iii) *Mein;* (xix) *Romanze;* (xx) *Rückweg;* (xxi) *Sehnsucht;* (xxii) *Seufzer;* (xiii) *Ständchen;* (xxiii) *Tost im Tränen;* (xxiv) *Unterscheidung.*
(BB) *** Hyperion Dig. HYP 200 [id.]. (i) Elizabeth Connell; (ii) Anthony Rolfe Johnson; (iii) Ian Bostridge; (iv) Stephen Varcoe; (v) Felicity Lott; (vi) Philip Langridge; (vii) Elly Ameling; (viii) Margaret Price; (ix) Thomas Allen; (x) John Mark

Ainsley; (xi) Brigitte Fassbaender; (xii) Edith Mathis; (xiii) Sarah Walker; (xiv) Christoph Prégardien; (xv) Peter Schreier; (xvi) Janet Baker; (xvii) Thomas Hampson; (xviii) Matthias Görne; (xix) Arleen Augér, Thea King; (xx) Ann Murray; (xxi) Christine Schäfer; (xxii) Martyn Hill; (xxiii) Adrian Thompson; (xxiv) Marie McLaughlin; all with Graham Johnson.

This is a delightful sampler, featuring the widest range of the fine Lieder singers whom Graham Johnson has assembled for his magnificent project, which is covered in depth in our main *Guide*. Dame Janet Baker, Dame Margaret Price and Dame Felicity Lott are on the list, with Peter Schreier, Christoph Prégardien, Brigitte Fassbaender, Elly Ameling and the late Arleen Augér among the distinguished singers from outside Britain. Inspired newcomers include Christine Schäfer, Matthias Goerne and, in some ways most striking of all, Ian Bostridge, who contributes three songs. Sarah Walker has the longest item, a serenade, *Ständchen*, quite different from the famous one, with male chorus as backing. What – understandably – are missing are the texts and detailed notes which Johnson provides for the individual discs, but the booklet includes full details of each of the first 27 discs.

'The Songmakers' Almanac Schubertiade': I, *'Lebensmut': Die junge Nonne; Der zürnende Diana; Vom Mitleiden Mariä; Lachen und Weinen; Selige Welt; Mignon und der Harfner; Auflösung; Lebensmut; Weilkommen und Abscheid.* II, *'Nacht und Träume': An die Laute; Wiegenlied; Ellens Gesang II; Nacht und Träume; Licht und Liebe; Ständchen (Horch! horch! die Lerch); Der Tod und das Mädchen; Der Winterabend; Abschied von der Erde.* III, *'Das Lied im Grünen': Fischerweise; Das Lied im Grünen; Der Schiffer; Nähe des Geliebten; Frühlingsglaube; Wandrers Nachtlied; Im Frühling; Wehmut; Auf der Bruck.* IV, *'An mein Klavier': An mein Klavier; Zum Punsche; Geheimnis; Viola; Der Hochzeitsbraten.*

(B) **(*) Hyperion Dyad CDD 22020 (2) [id.]. Felicity Lott, Ann Murray, Anthony Rolfe Johnson, Richard Jackson; Graham Johnson.

Recorded in 1983, this two-disc collection in Hyperion's two-for-the-price-of-one Dyad series presents over two hours of songs arranged by related groups – 'The romantic struggle', 'Serenades and lullabies', 'Nature and love', 'At home with the Schubertians'. That was the way Graham Johnson devised his immensely popular Songmakers' Almanac concerts, making this a forerunner of his brilliantly conceived recorded edition of the complete songs. Johnson's notes, including comments on individual items and full texts, observe a similar pattern to that adopted in the main edition, though a song like the Seidl *Wiegenlied* is allowed only three of its stanzas, not all five. The analogue recording, given an AAD transfer to CD, is not quite as clean as in the main edition, not quite sharply focused enough. Such inspired performances give a delightful impression of just such live events as the original Schubertiads. Left to the end are the two items which are by far the longest: the poignant *Viola*, a ballad telling of an abandoned flower, with Ann Murray a charming soloist, and the convivial *Hochzeitsbraten* ('Wedding dish'), featuring the other three soloists. All four singers are at their freshest, with Ann Murray in particularly fine voice, taking on many of the most challenging songs.

Secular vocal music

Secular vocal music and Part-songs: *Die Advocaten; An den Frühling; Andenken; Bardengesang; Bergknappenlied; Bootsgesang; Coronach; Die Entfernten; Dessen Fahne; Donnerstürme wallte; Das Dörfchen; Dreifach ist der Schritt der Zeit* (2 versions); *Ein jugendlicher Maienschwung; Eisiedelei; Erinnerungen; Ewige Liebe; Fischerlied; Flucht; Frisch atmet des Morgens lebendiger Hauch; Frühlingsgesang; Frühlingslied* (2 versions); *Geist der Liebe; Der Geistertanz; Gesang der Geister über den Wassern; Goldner Schein; Der Gondelfahrer; Gott in der Natur; Grab und Mond; Hier strecket; Hier unarmen sich getreue Gatten; Im Gegenwärtigen Vergangenes; Jünglingswonne; Klage um Ali Bey; Lacrimosa son io* (2 versions); *Leise, leise, lasst uns singen; Liebe; Liebe säusein die Blätter; Lied im Freien; Lutzows wilde Jagd; Mailied* (3 versions); *Majestät'sche Sonnenrose; Mirjams Siegesgesang; Mondenschein; Der Morgernstern; Die Nacht; Nachtgesang im Walde; Nachthelle; Die Nachtigall; Nachtmusik; Naturgenuss; Nur wer die Sehnsucht kennt; La Pastorella al prato; Punschlied; Räuberlied; Ruhe, schönstes Glück der Erde; Schlachtegesang; Der Schnee zerrinnt; Selig durch die Liebe; Ständchen (Zögernd leise); Das stille Lied; Thronend auf erhab'nem Sitz; Totengräberlied; Trinklied* (4 versions); *Trinklied aus dem 16 (Jahrhundert); Trinklied im Mai; Trinklied im Winter; Unendliche Freude* (2 versions); *Vorüber die stöhnende Klage; Wehmut; Wein und Liebe; Wer die steile Sternenbalm; Widerhall; Widerspruch; Wilkommen, lieber schöner Mai; Zum Rundetanz; Zur guten Nacht; Die zwei Tugendwege.*

(M) *** EMI (SIS) CMS5 66139-2 (4). Hildegard Behrens, Brigitte Fassbaender, Peter Schreier, Dietrich Fischer-Dieskau, Capella Bavariae, Bav. R. Ch. & SO, Sawallisch.

Schubert's part-songs make up a sizeable proportion of his total output, and this outstanding four-disc collection, superbly performed and recorded with Sawallisch the most understanding guide, both as pianist and conductor, brings out many rare treasures. Many are jolly ballads to celebrate life's simple pleasures, like the opening 'Song in the open air'; others are more expressively eloquent, such as *Ruhe, schönstes Glück der Erde* ('Rest, greatest earthly blessing'), the joyous *Gott in der Natur*, and the evocative male-voice chorale, *Nachtmusik*. On the other hand, *Die Advocaten* is a light-hearted trio in which a pair of lawyers wonder whether their fees are going to be paid; their client, Mr Sempronius, then arrives to do so, if reluctantly, and they are all bewitched by the clink of coins. The longest item, *Miriam's Song of triumph, on a Biblical subject*, is almost a miniature oratorio. Two striking Psalm-settings and the *Hymn to the Holy Ghost* (with brass accompaniment) have been omitted from the original LP collection but are now included on Sawallisch's EMI set of Schubert's religious music. Another substantial piece to cherish here is the version of *The Song of the Spirits over the Waters* with eight-part chorus and strings, as well as the atmospheric *Nachtgesang im Walde*, with horns accompanying a male-voice ensemble. Not surprisingly, horns also provide a lively opening for the gleeful and much briefer *Lützows wilde Jagd*, which begins the fourth disc. The highly imaginative setting of *Wehmut*, which comes near the end of the collection, has a haunting tolling bell effect, achieved in the voices alone. The tiny songs designed for Schubert and his friends to sing together, many of them drinking songs, add to the delight of the collection. Highly recommended to any Schubertian eager for new discovery. The transfers to CD could hardly have been managed more naturally, and the singers are given a fine presence.

Miscellaneous vocal recitals

Abendlied der Fürstin; An die Nachtigall; An die Sonne; Blanca (Das Mädchen); Du bist die Ruh'; Ellens Gesang I, II & III; Gesang der Norna; Gretchen am Spinnrade; Im Freien; Der Hirt auf dem Felsen; Die junge Nonne; Klage der Ceres; Klaglied; Die Liebende schreibt; Lied de Anne Lyle; Lied der Mignon I, II & III; Das Mädchens Klage; Die Männer sind méchant; Mignons Gesang; Suleika I & II; Wiegenlied.

(B) *** DG Double 453 082-2 (2) [id.]. Gundula Janowitz, Irwin Gage.

This attractive DG Double is self-recommending. Many of the songs here are favourites, although there are some novelties. They come from a comprehensive survey of Lieder suitable for female voice, originally issued on five LPs and recorded in 1976–7. They receive persuasive handling from Janowitz and, with a voice so naturally beautiful and used with such musical intelligence, the results are consistently compelling, helped by the sympathetic, concentrated accompaniments of Irwin Gage. If *Gretchen am Spinnrade*, which comes near the beginning of the recital, is somewhat idiosyncratic in its speed variations, Janowitz makes it very much her own, and her *Die junge Nonne*, which opens the second CD, is similarly appealing. Perhaps the most ravishing singing comes in the *Wiegenlied* and *Du bist die ruh* and, most memorably of all, the first Suleika song (*Was bedeutet die Bewegung?*) with its gentle closing *pianissimo* as the singer reflects that the soft whisper of the wind suggests the breath of love. The recital ends with the famous *Shepherd on the rock* with its clarinet obbligato well played by Ulf Rodenhäuser, although it has been presented more seductively elsewhere. The recording is first rate and full translations are included.

'A Schubert evening': (i) *Abendstern; Am Grabe Anselmos; An die Nachtigall; An die untergehende Sonne'; Berthas Lied in der Nacht; Delphine; Ellen's Gesang* from *The Lady of the Lake (Raste Krieger; Jäger von der Jagd; Ave Maria); Epistel an Herrn Josef von Spaun; Gondelfahrer; Gretchen am Spinnrade; Hin und wieder; Iphigenia; Die junge Nonne; Kennst du das Land; Liebe schwärmt; Das Mädchen; Das Mädchens Klage; Die Männer sind méchant; Mignon Lieder I–III (Heiss mich nicht reden; So lasst mich scheinen; Nur wer die Sehnsucht kennt); Schlummerlied; Schwestergruss; Strophe von Schiller (Die Götter Griechenlands); Suleika songs I–II (Was bedeutet die Bewegung; Ach, um deine feuchten Schwingen); Wiegenlied; Wiegenlied (Schlafe, schlafe)*. 'Favourite Lieder': (ii) *An die Musik; An Sylvia; Auf dem Wasser zu singen; Du bist die Ruh'; Die Forelle; Frühlingslaube; Heidenröslein; Litanei; Der Musensohn; Nacht und Träume; Rastlose Lied; Der Tod und das Mädchen.*

✿ (B) *** EMI CZS5 69389-2 (2) [CDMB 69389]. Dame Janet Baker, with (i) Gerald Moore; (ii) Geoffrey Parsons.

This very generous collection, offered on EMI's two-for-the-price-of one forte label, combines a pair of recitals recorded by Dame Janet at two different stages in her career, in 1970 and a decade later. The first collection ranges wide in an imaginative *Liederabend* of Schubert songs that includes a number of comparative rarities. They move from the delectably comic *Epistel* to the ominous darkness of *Die junge Nonne*. The two cradle songs are irresistible, the Seidl setting even more haunting than the more famous one; and throughout Baker consistently displays the breadth of her emotional mastery and her range of tone-colour. With Gerald Moore (who returned to the studio out of retirement especially for the occasion) still at his finest, this is a rarely satisfying collection. Only the opening *Gretchen am Spinnrade* brings a performance which one feels Baker could have intensified on repetition, but the rest could not be more treasurable. A very high proportion of favourite Schubert songs is included in the 1980 group. With a great singer treating each with loving, detailed care, the result is a charmer of a recital. The very first item, Dame Janet's strongly characterized reading of *Die Forelle*, makes it a fun song, and similarly Parsons's naughty, springing accompaniment to *An Sylvia* (echoed later by the singer) gives a twinkle to a song that can easily be treated too seriously. One also remembers the ravishing *subito piano* for the second stanza of *An die Musik*. The later recording is of fine EMI vintage and catches the more mature voice naturally and with rather more presence than a decade earlier. It is a pity that, because the set is so economically priced, there are no translations, but this remains an unmissable reissue.

Lieder: *Alinde; Am Tage aller Seelen; An die Entfernte; An die Laute; Auf dem Wasser zu singen; Auf der Riesenkoppe; Die Bürgschaft; Du bist die Ruh'; Der Fischer; Der Fischers Liebesglück; Fischerweise; Die Forelle; Die Götter Griechenlands; Greisengesang; Heidenröslein; Das Heimweh; Im Walde; Der Jüngling an der Quelle; Der Jüngling und der Tod; Lachen und Weinen; Lied des gefangenen Jägers; Das Lied im Grünen; Nachtgesang; Nachtstück; Nähe des Geliebten; Normans Gesang; Der Schiffer; Sei mir gegrüsst; Seligkeit; Das sie hier gewesen; Ständchen; Strophe aus Die Götter; Der Strom; Der Tod und das Mädchen; Der Wanderer; Der Winterabend; Das Zügenglöcklein; Der zürnende Barde.*
(M) *** EMI (SIS) CMS7 63566-2 (2) [Ang. CDMB 63566]. Dietrich Fischer-Dieskau, Gerald Moore; Karl Engel.

Dating from 1965, most of the items in this collection of Schubert songs superbly represent the second generation of Fischer-Dieskau recordings with Gerald Moore, deeper and more perceptive than his mono recordings, yet with voice and manner still youthfully fresh. The contrast is fascinating, if subtle, between that main collection and the last nine songs on the second disc: they were recorded six years earlier, with three of them accompanied by Karl Engel, and with the voice still younger but presented in drier sound.

Lieder: *Die Allmacht; An die Natur; Auf dem See; Auflösung; Erlkönig; Ganymed; Gretchen am Spinnrade; Der Musensohn; Rastlose Liebe; Suleika I; Der Tod und das Mädchen; Der Zwerg.*
*** Ph. (IMS) Dig. 412 623-2. Jessye Norman, Philip Moll.

Jessye Norman's characterization of the four contrasting voices in *Erlkönig* is powerfully effective, with none of the reticence which marked her Lieder singing early in her recording career. The poignancy of *Gretchen am Spinnrade* is exquisitely touched in, building to a powerful climax; throughout, the breath control is a thing of wonder, not least in a surpassing account of *Ganymed*. Fine, sympathetic accompaniment from Philip Moll, and first-rate recording.

Lieder: *An den Mond; An die Musik; Auf dem Wasser zu singen; Du bist die Ruh'; Erlkönig; Erster Verlust; Der Fischer; Fischerweise; Die Forelle; Ganymed; Frühlingsglaube; Heidenröslein; Im Frühling; Im Haine; Litanei auf das Fest Allerseelen; Der Musensohn; Nacht und Träume; Seligkeit; An Silvia; Wandrers Nachtlied I & II; Der Zwerg.*
(N) *** EMI Dig. CDC5 56347-2 [id.]. Ian Bostridge, Julius Drake.

Few discs of favourite Schubert songs match this for sheer beauty. As in his prizewinning recording of *Die schöne Mullerin* for Hyperion, Ian Bostridge here not only sings with ravishing tenor tone but, with German words heightened, offers fresh revelation in even the best-known songs. So, with Julius Drake matching him in insight, *Die Forelle* ('The Trout'), opens the sequence in youthful eagerness, light and brisk, and lightness is also the keynote in such songs as *Heidenroslein*. The contrast is all the keener when in darker songs such as *Wandrers Nachtlied*, Bostridge sings with such rapt intensity, the legato lines perfectly sustained on a mere thread of sound.

Goethe Lieder:(i) *An den Mond; An schwager Kronos; Auf dem See; Erster Verlust; Ganymed; Gesänge des Harfners: Harfenspieler I, II, & III Jägers Abendlied; Meeres Stille; Der Musensohn; Prometheus; Wandrers Nachtlied I & II.* (ii) *Am Flüsse; Erlkönig; Geheimes; Grenzen des Menschheit; Heidenröslein; Der König in Thule; Nähe des Geliebten; Rastlose Liebe; Wilkommen und Abscheid.*
(N) (M) *** DG 457 747-2 [id.]. Dietrich Fischer-Dieskau; (i) Joerg Demus; (ii) Gerald Moore.

This reissued collection draws on three sets of recordings: Fischer Dieskau's first stereo DG Goethe LP, recorded with Demus in 1960, and two subsequent groups with Gerald Moore dating from a decade later. Some of the very finest Goethe settings are here and Fischer-Dieskau is on top of his form, but the partnership with Demus is less than ideal. He proves a capable but not highly imaginative accompanist, although his artistry is not to be denied. But as for the singing, the spectrum of emotion takes on a new glow as each song begins. The two settings of *Wandrers Nachtlied* are particularly fine, as are the joyous *Der Musensohn* and the fiery *An schwager Kronos*. Needless to say the partnership with Gerald Moore is much more of a symbiosis, and these later performances are outstanding in every way. The recording too, is warmer and has a more pleasing ambience. A treasurable disc, just the same, well worthy of DG's Originals.

Goethe Lieder: *An den Mond; An die Türen; An Mignon; Auf dem See; Erster verlust; Erlkönig; Der Fischer; Ganymed; Heidenröslein; Meeres Stille; Der Musensohn; Nachtgesang; Nahe des Gelibten; Prometheus; Rastlose Liebe; Schäfers Klaglied; Schwager Kronos; Versunken; Wandrers Nachtlied; Wer nie sein Brot mit Tränen ass; Wer sich der Einsamkeit ergibt.*
(N) *** Decca Dig. 452 917-2 [id.]. Matthias Goerne, Andreas Haefliger.

Matthias Goerne here confirms his mastery as a Lieder-singer, already revealed in his account of *Winterreise* and other Schubert songs in Graham Johnson's collected edition on Hyperion. With Andreas Haefliger a deeply understanding accompanist – challenging as well as matching his partner – Goerne here tackles a beautiful sequence of Goethe settings, thrillingly powerful in *Prometheus*, youthfully exuberant in such a favourite as *Der Musensohn*, finding a rapt gravity rare in a young singer in such visionary songs as *Meeres Stille*. Even the understatement of his *Erlkönig* brings bonuses in extra beauty. Outstanding in every way.

(i) *Am grabe Anselmos; An die Musik; An die Nachtigall; An Sylvia; Auf dem See; Auf dem Wasser zu singen; Dass sie hier gewesen; Die Forelle; Die junge Nonne; Du bist die Ruh'; Ganymed; Geheimes; Gretchen am Spinnrade; Heidenröslein; Lachen und Weinen; Der Musensohn; Rastlose Liebe; Sei mir gegrüsset; Seligkeit; Ständchen; Suleika I & II; Wiegenlied.* (ii) *Winterreise* (song-cycle), *D.911*.
(BB) **(*) Virgin Classics Dig. Double VBD5 61457-2 (2) [(B) CDVB 61457]. (i) Arleen Augér, Lambert Orkis (fortepiano); (ii) Thomas Allen, Roger Vignoles (piano).

This Virgin Double joins up Arleen Augér's collection of favourite Lieder with Thomas Allen's *Winterreise*, dating from 1991 and 1994 respectively. The distinctive point about Arleen Augér's collection of Schubert songs – which includes a high proportion of favourites – is that the accompaniment is played by Lambert Orkis on a fortepiano. Though Augér's voice is caught most beautifully, with the tone consistently sweet and pure, the scale of the accompaniment intensifies a lightweight feeling, with beauty of tone given higher priority than word-meaning. Though in intensity and concern for detail this cannot match Augér's fine full-priced disc in Graham Johnson's Schubert series for Hyperion (CDJ 33009), it clearly has its place.

On the second disc Thomas Allen, understandingly supported by Roger Vignoles, tackles this Everest of the Lieder repertory with a beauty of tone and line that sets his reading apart. Allen's concentration on purely musical qualities, far from watering down word-meaning, is used to intensify the tragic emotions of the wandering lover. Allen uses a wider dynamic range than most of his direct rivals, shading the voice down to a half-tone for intimate revelations, then expanding dramatically, using the art of the opera-singer. In the two final songs, *Die Nebensonnen* and *Der Leiermann*, he is very restrained, keeping them hushed instead of underlining expressiveness. The poignancy of Schubert's inspiration is allowed to speak for itself. The one serious reservation here is the lack of translations.

Lieder: *An die Laute; An die Leier; An die Musik; An Silvia; Auf der Bruck; Du bist die Ruh'; Erlkönig; Das Fischermädchen; Die Forelle; Ganymed; Gruppe aus dem Tartarus; Heidenröslein; Lachen und Weinen; Litanei auf das Fest; Meeres Stille; Der Musensohn; Rastlose Liebe; Schäfers Klagelied; Ständchen; Die Taubenpost; Der Tod und das Mädchen; Der Wanderer; Wandrers Nachtlied.*
*** DG Dig. 445 294-2. Bryn Terfel, Malcolm Martineau.

Bryn Terfel's DG disc of Schubert was one of his first recordings to confirm his exceptional gift of projecting his magnetic personality with keen intensity, in Lieder, not just in opera. Terfel emerges as a positive artist, giving strikingly individual and imaginative readings of these 23 favourite songs. As you immediately realize in three favourite songs common to both collections, *Heidenröslein, An Silvia* and *Du bist die Ruh*', Terfel is daring in confronting you face to face, very much as the young Fischer-Dieskau did, using the widest range of dynamic and tone. You might argue that Terfel's characterization of the different characters in *Erlkönig* is too extreme, but it is a measure of his magnetism that the result is so dramatically compelling. Full, firm sound.

An die Laute; An die Musik; An Silvia; Der Einsame; Im Abendrot; Liebhaber in allen Gestalten; Lied eines Schiffers an die Dioskurern; Der Musensohn; Ständchen (Leise flehen meine Lieder).
(M) *** DG Originals 449 747-2 [id.]. Fritz Wunderlich, Hubert Giesen – BEETHOVEN: *Lieder;* SCHUMANN: *Dichterliebe*. ***

Few tenors have matched the young Wunderlich in the freshness and golden bloom of the voice. The open manner could not be more appealing here in glowing performances, well coupled with other fine examples of this sadly short-lived artist's work. A very apt addition to DG's series of 'Legendary performances'.

Lieder: *An die Musik; An Sylvia; Auf dem Wasser zu singen; Ave Maria; Du bist die Ruh'; Die Forelle; Ganymed; Gretchen am Spinnrade;*

Heidenröslein; Im Frühling; Die junge Nonne; Litanei; Mignon und der Harfner; Der Musensohn; Nacht und Träume; Sei mir gegrüsst; Seligkeit.
(M) *** Carlton Classics Dig. PCD 2016 [id.]. Felicity Lott, Graham Johnson.

At mid-price, Felicity Lott's collection brings an ideal choice of songs for the general collector. With Graham Johnson always the most imaginative accompanist, even the best-known songs emerge fresh and new, and gentle songs like *Litanei* are raptly beautiful.

Lieder: *An die Musik; An Sylvia; Auf dem Wasser zu singen; Ganymed; Gretchen am Spinnrade; Im Frühling; Die junge Nonne; Das Lied im Grünen; Der Musensohn; Nachtviolen; Nähe des Geliebten; Wehmut.*
(***) EMI mono CDH7 64026-2 [id.]. Elisabeth Schwarzkopf, Edwin Fischer.

Schwarzkopf at the beginning of her recording career and Fischer at the end of his make a magical partnership, with even the simplest of songs inspiring intensely subtle expression from singer and pianist alike. Though Fischer's playing is not immaculate, he left few records more endearing than this, and Schwarzkopf's colouring of word and tone is masterly.

Choral songs: *An die sonne; Gebe; Gesang der geister über den wassern; Gondelfahrer; Gott in der naur; Mondenschein; Nachtgesang im walde; Nachthelle; Die 23 psalm; Sehnsucht; Ständchen; Des tages weihe.*
(N) *** Ph. Dig. Monteverdi Ch., John Eliot Gardiner.

In a wide-ranging and illuminating choice of choral songs from deeply philosophical to trivial, Gardiner and his Monteverdi Choir offer performances at once immaculate and intense, using the widest range of tone and dynamic. Period accompaniments on the fortepiano from Malcolm Bilson, with a fine quintet of horns accompanying *Nachtgesang im Walde* and with accompaniment for lower strings in the longest item, *Gesang der Geister uber den Wassern*. Refined recording to match.

(i; ii) Duets: *Antigone und Oedip; Cronnan; Hektors Abschied; Hermann und Thusnelda; Licht und Liebe (Nachtgesang); Mignon und der Harfner; Selma und Selmar; Sing-Ubungen;* (vi) *Szene aus Goethes Faust.* (ii; iii; iv; v) Trios: *Die Advokaten; Gütigster, Bester, Weisester; Die Hochzeitsbraten; Kantata zum Geburtstag des Sängers Johann Michael Vogl; Punschlied; Trinklied; Verschwunden sind die Schmerzen (a cappella).* (i–iv) Quartets: *An die Sonne; Gebet; Die Geselligkeit (Lebenslust); Gott der Weltschöpfer; Gott im Ungewitter; Hymne an den Undenlichen; Nun lasst uns den Leib begraben (Begräbnislied); Des Tages Weihe; Der Tanz.*
(M) *** DG (IMS) 435 596-2 (2). (i) Dame Janet Baker; (ii) Fischer-Dieskau; (iii) Ameling; (iv) Schreier; (v) Laubenthal; Gerald Moore; (vi) with Berlin RIAS Chamber Ch.

Not all these duets are vintage Schubert – some of the narrative pieces go on too long – but the artistry of Baker and Fischer-Dieskau makes for magical results. Gerald Moore, who is at his finest throughout the set, relishes the magic too. The trios are domestic music in the best sense. Specially delightful are the two contrasted drinking songs, but *The wedding feast (Die Hochzeitsbraten)* is even more remarkable, a 10-minute scena in the style of *opera buffa*. The quartets, like the trios, were written for various domestic occasions, but the use of four voices seems to have led the composer regularly to serious or religious subjects. These are sweet and gentle rather than intense inspirations, but one could hardly ask for more polished and inspired performances than these. Fine recording from 1973/4, giving the singers a vivid presence on CD.

Lieder: *Auf dem Wasser zu singen; Ave Maria; Die Forelle; Du bist die Ruh'; Ganymed; Gretchen am Spinnrade; Gretchens Bitte; Heidenröslein; Heiss mich nicht reden;* (i) *Der Hirt auf dem Felsen. Im Abendrot; Kennst du das Land; Liebhaber in allen Gestalten; Nahe des Geliebten; Nur wer die Sehnsucht kennt; So lasst mich scheinen; Ständchen.*
*** Teldec/Warner Dig. 4509 90873-2 [id.]. Barbara Bonney, Geoffrey Parsons; (i) with Sharon Kam.

Barbara Bonney here is at her freshest, and who better to accompany her than Geoffrey Parsons? The generous programme (well over an hour) includes many firm favourites, and Bonney not only sings with much beauty of tone and a flowing Schubertian line but with keen concern for word-meanings. Songs like *Die Forelle*, *Auf dem Wasser zu singen* and the lovely *So lasst mich scheinen* sound especially fresh; and it is always good to have 'The shepherd on the rock' (*Der Hirt auf dem Felsen*) with its fluid obbligato clarinet (here the persuasive Sharon Kam). Spontaneous-sounding expressiveness in a natural partnership between fine artists.

Auf der Riesenkoppe; Der blinde Knabe; Du bist die Ruh'; Die Forelle; Das Geheimnis; Gretchen am Spinnrade; Heidenröslein; (i) *Der Hirt auf dem Felsen; Der König in Thule; La Pastorella; Schwanengesang; Die Wehmut.*
(B) **(*) EMI CfP CD-CFP 6040 [id.]. Dame Margaret Price, James Lockhart; (i) with Brymer.

Dame Margaret Price was in fine voice when she made this record in 1971. Her singing of Schubert is full-throated in style, although she successfully fines down the tone for a song like *Du bist die Ruh'*. The opening recitative of *Auf der Riesenkoppe* takes us straight into the opera house; *La Pastorella* (a charming song) reminds us of Rossini, and in *The Shepherd on the rock* the sheer breadth of the singing tends to dwarf even Jack Brymer's beguiling clarinet obbligato. *Die Forelle* is very attractively done, and *Der König in Thule* is serenely beautiful. *Heidenröslein* has a simple, affecting charm and in *Gretchen am Spinnrade* the soaring line is sensitively controlled, but Price's involvement is obvious. James Lockhart accompanies most sensitively but, maybe because of the recording balance, like Brymer he tends to be dwarfed by the voice. No translations are provided, but the notes give a synopsis of each song. Short measure at 47 minutes.

Lieder: *Berthas Lied in der Nacht; Fischerweise; Der Fluss; Die Forelle; Die gefangenen Sanger; Gretchen vor der Mater dolorosa; Hagars Klage; Heimliches Lieben; Im Frühling; Iphigenia; Kolmas Klage; Der König in Thule; Lambertine; Liebe schwarmt auf allen Wegen; Lilla an die Morgenrote; Des Mädchens Kläge* (2 versions); *Die Rose; Schwestergruss; Szene der Delphine; Thekla, eine Geisterstimme; Vergissmeinnicht; Vom Mitleiden Marias; Wiegenlied.*

(B) *** DG Double 453 139-2 (2) [id.]. Gundula Janowitz, Irwin Gage.

This second collection from Janowitz and Gage, taken from their 1976–7 survey, starts with what is probably Schubert's first vocal work, written when he was 14, *Hagars Klage*. Many of the earlier items are extended works, complete scenas or songs of many stanzas. They require persuasive handling, and Janowitz is greatly helped by the sympathetic, concentrated accompaniments of Irwin Gage. With a voice so naturally beautiful, and used with such easy musical intelligence, the results are consistently compelling, whether in the rarities or the popular songs such as *Die Forelle*. The recording is first rate.

Italian Songs: *Da quel sembiante appresi; Guarda, che bianca luna; Io vuo'cantar di Cadmo; Mi batte'l cor!; Mio ben ricordati; Non t'accostar all'urna; La pastorella; Pensa, che questo istante; Se dall'Etra; Vedi quanto adoro ancora ingrato!.*

*** Decca Dig. 440 297-2 [id.]. Cecilia Bartoli, András Schiff – BEETHOVEN: *Che fa il mio bene?* etc.; HAYDN: *Arianna a Naxos;* MOZART: *Ridente la calma.* ***

Bartoli is at her finest here in *Dido's lament*, but the other rare songs are also fresh and enjoyable, helped by sensitive accompaniments from András Schiff.

Church music

6 Antiphons for the Blessings of the Branches on Psalm Sunday; Auguste jam coelestium in G, D.488; Deutsche Messe, D.872 (with Epilogue, The Lord's Prayer); Graduale in C, D.184; Hymn to the Holy Ghost, D.964; Kyries: in D min., D.31; F, D.66; Lazarus, D.689; Magnificat in C, D.486; Offertorium (Totus in corde) in C, D.136; Offertorium (Tres sunt) in A min., D.181; 2 Offertoriums (Salve Regina) in F, D.223 & A, D.676; Psalm 23, D.706; Psalm 92, D.953; Salve Reginas: in B flat, D.106; in C, D.811; Stabat Mater in G min., D.175; Tantum ergo (3 settings) *in C, D.460/1 & D.739; Tantum ergo in D, D.750.*

(M) *** EMI (SIS) Dig./Analogue CMS7 64783-2 (3). Popp, Donath, Rüggerberg, Venuti, Hautermann, Falk, Fassbaender, Greindl-Rosner, Dallapozza, Araiza, Protschka, Tear, Lika, Fischer-Dieskau, Capella Bavariae, Bav. R. Ch. & SO, Sawallisch.

Volume two of Sawallisch's great and rewarding Schubertian survey has much glorious music, sung with eloquence and richly recorded in the Munich Hercules Hall. Even some of the shortest items – such as the six tiny *Antiphons*, allegedly written in half an hour – have magic and originality in them. Plainer, but still glowing with Schubertian joy, is the so-called *Deutsche Messe*. The *Magnificat*, too, is a strongly characterized setting, and even the three settings of St Thomas Aquinas's *Tantum ergo* (all in C) have their charm. There are other surprises. The lovely setting of the *Offertorium in C (Totus in corde)* is for soprano, clarinet and orchestra, with the vocal and instrumental lines intertwining delectably, while the no less appealing *Auguste jam coelestium* is a soprano–tenor duet. The *Salve Regina in C*, D.811, is written for four male voices, *a cappella*, and they again contribute to the performance of *Psalm 23*, where Sawallisch provides a piano accompaniment. The religious drama, *Lazarus*, has the third CD to itself. Schubert left it unfinished and, though no more dramatic than his operas, it contains much delightful music. With Robert Tear in the name-role, Helen Donath as Maria, Lucia Popp as Jemima, Maria Venuti as Martha, Josef Protschka as Nathanael and Fischer-Dieskau as Simon, it is very strongly cast and the performance is splendid; the singing is outstanding from chorus and soloists alike throughout this set. Warm, well-balanced recording.

Choruses: *Chor der Engel, D.440; Das Dörfchen, D.598; Gesang der Geister über den Wassern, D.714; Glaub, Hoffnung und Liebe, D.954; Gondelfahrer, D.809; Jägerlied, D.201; Kantate für Irene Kiesewetter, D.936; Klage um Ali Bey, D.140; Lützows wilde Jagd, D.205; Die Nacht,*

D.983C; Die Nachtigall, D.724; 23rd Psalm, D.706; (i) *92nd Psalm, D.953.*

(B) **(*) DG 453 679-2. Austrian R. Ch., ORF SO (members), Gottfried Preinfalk, with (i) Rudolph Katzböck.

An enjoyable and well-planned programme of Schubert's shorter choral works, including the engaging *Song of the Spirits over the waters*, the *Jägerlied* and *Lützows wilde Jagd* (complete with horns) and a pair of fine Psalm settings. Sympathetic if not distinctive performances, flattered by the warm recording acoustic.

Magnificat, D.486; Offertorium, D.963; Stabat Mater, D.383.

(M) *** Erato/Warner 4509 96961-2. Armstrong, Schaer, Ramirez, Huttenlocher, Goy, Lausanne Vocal Ens. & CO, Corboz.

Schubert's strikingly fresh setting of the *Stabat Mater* dates from the composer's 19th year, yet it shows him at the height of his early powers and has many anticipations of later music, especially in the Terzetto for soprano, tenor, bass and chorus (No. 11) and the fine chorus, *Wer wird Zähren sanflen Mitleids* (No. 5), with its superb horn-writing. There is a lovely, Bach-like tenor aria, with oboe obbligato, stylishly sung by Alejandro Ramirez, and a bass aria, *Sohn des Vaters*, recalling the Mozart of *Die Zauberflöte*, sung by Philippe Huttenlocher. The chorus is incisive, both in counterpoint in Schubert's lively fugues, and in the simple chordal writing. The other, lesser pieces make a good coupling, also persuasively directed by Corboz, and the recording, although not crystal clear, has transferred vividly.

Masses Nos. 1–6 (complete); *Kyries in B flat, D.45; D min., D.49; Offertorium in B flat, D.963; Salve Reginas: in F, D.379; in B flat, D.386; Stabat Mater in F min., D.383; Tantum ergo in E flat, D.962.*

(M) *** EMI (SIS) Dig./Analogue CMS7 64778-2 (4). Popp, Donath, Fassbaender, Dallapozza, Schreier, Araiza, Protschka, Fischer-Dieskau, Bav. R. Ch. & SO, Sawallisch.

Sawallisch's highly distinguished survey of Schubert's church music was recorded in the early 1980s. This first volume is centred on his major Mass settings, especially his masterpiece in this form, the *E flat Mass*. Though the chorus is not flawless here, the performances are warm and understanding. The earlier Mass settings bring superb, lively inspirations, not to mention the separate *Kyries* and *Salve Reginas*. Excellent, cleanly focused sound, for the most part digital, with the benefit of the ambience of the Munich Herkules-Saal.

Masses Nos. 1–6 (complete); *Deutsche Messe.*

*** Sony S4K 62778 (4) [id.]. Alexander Nader, Thomas Puchegger, Georg Leskovich, Jörg Hering, Kurt Azesberger, Harry van der Kamp, Belà Fischer, Albin Lenzer, Benjamin Schmidinger, treble soloists from V. Boys' Ch., Ch. Viennensis, OAE, Weil.

Masses Nos. 1 in F, D.105; 2 in G, D.167.

*** Sony Dig. SK 68247 [id.]. Nader, Puchegger, Leskovich, Hering, Azesberger, Van der Kamp, V. Boys' Ch., Ch. Viennensis, OAE, Bruno Weil.

Masses Nos. 3 in B flat, D.324; 4 in C, D.452.

*** Sony Dig. SK 68248 [id.]. Nader, Puchegger, Leskovich, Fischer, Hering, Van der Kamp, V. Boys' Ch., Ch. Viennensis, OAE, Bruno Weil.

(i) *Mass No. 5 in A flat, D.678* (2nd version); *Deutsche Messe, D.872.*

*** Sony Dig. SK 53984 [id.]. (i) Treble soloists from V. Boys' Ch. (Stefan Preyer, Thomas Weinnhappel), Hering, Van der Kamp; V. Boys' Ch., Ch. Viennensis, OAE, Bruno Weil.

Mass No. 6 in E flat, D.950.

*** Sony Dig. SK 66255 [id.]. Schmidinger, Lenzer, Hering, Azesberger, Van der Kamp, V. Boys' Ch., Ch. Viennensis, OAE, Bruno Weil.

Bruno Weil draws incandescent performances of all six of Schubert's *Masses* from his fine team, helped by sound that is clearer and more detailed than on direct rival recordings. The combination of Viennese choirs – with the trebles of the Vienna Boys' Choir outstandingly full and fresh – and a British period orchestra works superbly, making one appreciate, even more than with the Sawallisch versions, how seriously this area of Schubert's œuvre has been underappreciated, both in the early works and in the two mature masterpieces in A flat and E flat. In the earlier *Masses* and in the simple chordal writing of the *Deutsche Messe* the presence of boys adds to the impression of liturgical performances, fresh and dedicated. In the *Sixth Mass in E flat*, with his direct manner and brisk speeds, Weil reinforces the originality of Schubert's inspiration in this last and greatest of his Mass settings, written in the last year of his life. A set to recommend enthusiastically, not least to those who have dismissed Schubert's religious writing as uninspired. The recordings, realistically balanced, were made (unexpectedly) in Vienna's Casino Zögernitz (SK 68247/8), the Haydn-Saal of the Schloss Esterházy, Eisenstadt (SK 66255) and the Schloss Grafenegg, Reitschule, Austria (SK 53984). The one snag is the relatively short measure compared with the Sawallisch set, but for such music-making that is relatively unimportant.

The CDs are available separately, and those looking for a place to start might choose SK 53984, which couples the delightful *Deutsche Messe*, with its simple chordal settings of German words, with the A flat masterpiece which is Schubert's *Missa*

Solemnis. It helps that Weil uses the second version of the work, with the *Credo* more compact. As ever, he draws inspired playing and singing from his Austro-British team, with the bright, full treble sound of the Vienna Boys cleanly set against the period instruments of the Orchestra of the Age of Enlightenment, both beautifully balanced in a recording with plenty of bloom on the sound, yet with good detail.

Masses Nos. (i–iv) *4 in C, D.452;* (ii; iv–vi) *5 in A flat, D.678; 6 in E flat, D.950.* (iii; vii) *Offertorium, D.963;* (i–ii; iv; vii) *Tantum ergo, D.962.*

(N) (B) *** EMI double fforte Analogue/Dig. CZS5 73365-2 (2) [CDFB 73365]. (i) Popp; (ii) Fassbaender; (iii) Dallapozza; (iv) Fischer-Dieskau; (v) Donath; (vi) Araiza; (vii) Schreier; Bav. R. Ch. & SO, Sawallisch.

This inexpensive reissue from Sawallisch's excellent choral series combines three settings of the Mass including the two finest, *in A flat* and the masterly work *in E flat*; while the *Tantum ergo* (*in C*) also undoubtedly has its charm. These performances have stood the test of time, containing some outstanding singing from soloists and chorus, although the latter is not flawless in D.950. Sawallisch proves to be a warmly understanding Schubertian and the recordings are both vivid and atmospheric.

Mass No. 6 in E flat, D.950.

(B) **(*) DG Dig. 453 680-2. Mattila, Lipovšek, Hadley, Pita, Holl, V. State Op. Ch., VPO, Abbado.

Abbado takes a spacious rather than a dramatic view of Schubert's most popular setting of the Mass, making the music look forward to Bruckner. This is quite unlike the performance from Bruno Weil on Sony (see below) but is intriguing in its way. With first-rate singing from soloists and chorus it is certainly stimulating, with well-balanced digital sound, but it would not be a prime choice.

Song-cycles

Die schöne Müllerin (song-cycle), *D.795* (see also above, under Graham Johnson Schubert Lieder Edition, Volume 25).

*** DG 415 186-2 [id.]. Dietrich Fischer-Dieskau, Gerald Moore.

*** Decca (IMS) Dig. 430 414-2 [id.]. Peter Schreier, András Schiff.

*** Capriccio Dig. 10 082 [id.]. Josef Protschka, Helmut Deutsch.

(N) (BB) *** Belart 461 522-2. Gérard Souzay, Dalton Baldwin.

Fischer-Dieskau's classic 1972 version on DG remains among the very finest ever recorded, combining as it does his developed sense of drama and story-telling, his mature feeling for detail and yet spontaneity too, helped by the searching accompaniment of Gerald Moore. It is a performance with premonitions of *Winterreise*.

András Schiff brings new illumination in almost every phrase, to match the brightly detailed singing of Schreier, here challenged to produce his most glowing tone. Schreier, matching his partner as he did in their earlier, prize-winning recording of *Schwanengesang* (see below), transcends even his earlier versions of this favourite cycle, always conveying his response so vividly that one clearly registers his changes of facial expression from line to line. Outstandingly warm and well-balanced recording.

Josef Protschka gives an intensely virile, almost operatic reading, which is made the more youthful-sounding in the original keys for high voice. As recorded, the voice, often beautiful with heroic timbres, sometimes acquires a hint of stridency, but the positive power and individuality of the performance make it consistently compelling, with all the anguish behind these songs caught intensely. The timbre of the Bösendorfer piano adds to the performance's distinctiveness, well if rather reverberantly recorded.

Souzay's easy style is particularly suited to *Die schöne Müllerin*, the most sunny of song-cycles. Fischer-Dieskau may find more drama in the poems, but Souzay's concentration on purely musical values makes for one of the most consistently attractive versions, with the words never neglected and Dalton Baldwin giving one of his most imaginative performances on record. The 1964 sound is clear and well balanced, a trifle dry.

Die schöne Müllerin (complete); *Die Forelle; Frühlingsglaube; Heidenröslein.*

(M) ** DG 447 452-2 [id.]. Fritz Wunderlich, Hubert Geisen.

Fritz Wunderlich's recording was made in 1966 and here reappears as one of DG's 'Legendary Originals'. Wunderlich had one of the most headily beautiful voices among German tenors and that alone makes his record cherishable. But when he recorded the cycle (and the three favourite songs which are also included here), he had still to develop as a Lieder singer, and for so subtle a cycle the performance lacks detail. He was not helped either by a rather unimaginative accompanist, and the recording is unflattering to the piano.

Die Schöne Müllerin, D.795 (with spoken Prologue and Epilogue), D.795.

(N) (M) *(**) EMI CDM5 66907-2 [CDM5 66959]. Dietrich Fischer-Dieskau, Gerald Moore.

EMI have understandably chosen Fischer-Dieskau's 1961 recording of *Die Schöne Müllerin* (which includes spoken versions in German of the *Prologue* and *Epilogue*) for their 'Great recordings of the century' series. But alas, all their current remastering skill has not been able to improve the sound: the voice remains unpleasingly edgy. The later DG recording (also with Gerald Moore) remains far preferable.

Die schöne Müllerin, D.795; An die Musik; Du bist die Ruh; Erlkönig; Heidenröslein; Der Musensohn.
❀ (B) *** DG 453 676-2. Dietrich Fischer-Dieskau, Gerald Moore.

With the transfer barely giving an indication of its analogue source back in 1972, Fischer-Dieskau's classic version of *Die schöne Müllerin* remains among the very finest ever recorded. Though he had made several earlier recordings, this is no mere repeat of previous triumphs, now combining his developed sense of drama and story-telling, his mature feeling for detail and yet spontaneity too, helped by the searching accompaniment of Gerald Moore. It is a performance with premonitions of *Winterreise*. With extra Lieder added to fill out the recital, this is one of the most cherishable of Fischer-Dieskau's many superb Schubert CDs.

Song-cycles: *Die schöne Müllerin, D.795; Schwanengesang, D.957; Winterreise, D.911.* Lieder: *Du bist die Ruh'; Erlkönig; Nacht und Träume.*
(M) (***) EMI (SIS) mono CMS7 63559-2 (3) [id.]. Dietrich Fischer-Dieskau, Gerald Moore.

Fischer-Dieskau's early mono versions may not match his later recordings in depth of insight, but already the young singer was a searching interpreter of these supreme cycles. Gerald Moore was, as ever, the most sympathetic partner.

Song-cycles: (i) *Die schöne Müllerin, D.795* (with spoken *Prologue* and *Epilogue*); *Schwanengesang, D.957; Winterreise, D.911.* (ii) *Einsamkeit, D.620.*
(M) **(*) EMI (SIS) CMS5 66146-2 (3). Dietrich Fischer-Dieskau, (i) Gerald Moore; (ii) Karl Engel.

Fischer-Dieskau's EMI recordings of the three song-cycles were made in 1961–2, around the time of the great baritone's 40th birthday, and they represent the second wave of his Schubert interpretations. He was to re-record them, again with Gerald Moore, for DG with even greater thought and refinement, but the direct power of expression here is superb, too. For *Die schöne Müllerin*, he also included spoken versions of the *Prologue* and *Epilogue* (taken from the songs in Wilhelm Müller's cycle) which Schubert did not set. The snag is that in the case of *Die schöne Müllerin* the 1985 digital remastering has caused the voice to sound edgy and peaky at climaxes, although the other cycles, transferred later, are altogether smoother.

As an added bonus, following after *Schwanengesang*, we are offered a rarity: Schubert's 1818 setting of Johann Mayrhofer's poem in 12 stanzas, *Einsamkeit* ('Solitude'). At nearly 19 minutes, this is almost a mini-cycle in itself. Moving on from its thoughtful opening, Fischer-Dieskau follows the poet's mood-changes dramatically and with characteristic sensitivity, and the listener is thoroughly involved. The sound is excellent, and it is a pity that for this reissue EMI did not cue the individual verses. However, full translations are included.

Song-cycles: *Die schöne Müllerin; Schwanengesang* (with also: *Im Freien; Der Wanderer an den Mond; Das Zügenglöcklein*); *Winterreise.* Lieder: *Alinde; An den Monde; An die Leier; An die Laute; An die Musik; An Silvia; Dass sie hier gewesen; Der Einsame; Die Forelle; Frühlingsglaube; Im Frühling; Der Schiffer; Schwanengesang; Sei mir gegrüsset.* Goethe Lieder: *Ganymed; Geheimes; Heidenröslein; Liebhaber in allen Gestalten; Der Musensohn; Rastlose Liebe; Wandrers Nachtlied.*
(M) *** EMI CMS5 66145-2 (4). Olaf Bär, Geoffrey Parsons.

Die schöne Müllerin was the first of the cycles which Olaf Bär recorded, in 1986 in Dresden, with the voice fresher and more velvety than later. The tone is all the better suited to this young man's cycle, even more when contrasted with Fischer Dieskau's in the companion box of EMI's Schubert Edition, especially when the digital recording is so flattering to Bär's warmly beautiful lyrical flow. In *Winterreise*, recorded two years later, again with Geoffrey Parsons a masterful accompanist, Bär again finds a winning beauty of line and tone in singing both deeply reflective and strongly dramatic, if without quite the power of Fischer-Dieskau's poetic projection or the sheer intensity of Britten and Pears (see above). The third disc, recorded in 1989, amplifies the collection of late songs, posthumously published as *Schwanengesang*, with three well-chosen extra items from the same period, notably *Der Wanderer an den Mond*, where Bär brings out the agony and weariness of the traveller addressing the moon. The singing throughout is characteristically sensitive and dramatic, with *Ständchen* strong and passionate rather than light and charming. The fourth disc offers 21 miscellaneous songs, most of them favourites, including 7 Goethe settings. Recorded in 1991–2, they show the voice grittier than earlier, but still searchingly expressive, with Geoffrey Parsons again the most understanding accompanist.

Schwanengesang, D.957; Lieder: Am Bach in Frühling; An die Musik; Geheimes; Gruppe aus dem Tartarus; Im Abendrot; Im Frühling; Meerstille; Sei mir gegrüsst; Wandrers Nachtlied I & II.
(***) EMI mono CDH5 65196-2. Hans Hotter, Gerald Moore.

(i) *Schwanengesang* (song-cycle), *D.957;* (ii) Lieder: *An die Laute; An die Musik; An Silvia; Auflösung; Der Einsame; Fischerweise; Die Forelle; Der Schiffer; Der Wanderer an den Mond; Wandrers Nachtlied.*
(BB) *** ASV Quicksilva CDQS 6171 [(M) id.].
(i) John Shirley-Quirk, Steuart Bedford; (ii) Ian Partridge, Jennifer Partridge.

Schwanengesang (Lieder collection), *D.957;* Lieder: *An die Musik; An Sylvia; Die Forelle; Heidenröslein; Im Abendrot; Der Musensohn; Der Tod und das Mädchen.*
*** DG 415 188-2. Dietrich Fischer-Dieskau, Gerald Moore.

Schwanengesang. Am Fenster; Bei dir allein; Herbst; Der Wanderer an den Mond.
*** Decca Dig. 425 612-2. Peter Schreier, András Schiff.

Schwanengesang; 5 Lieder: *Am Fenster; Herbst; Sehnsucht; Der Wanderer an den Mond; Wiegenlied, D.867.*
❁ *** DG (IMS) Dig. 429 766-2. Brigitte Fassbaender, Aribert Reimann.

Brigitte Fassbaender gives a totally distinctive and compelling account of *Schwanengesang*, proving stronger and more forceful than almost any rival. She turns what was originally a relatively random group of late songs into a genuine cycle, by presenting them in a carefully rearranged order and adding five other late songs. Her magnetic power of compelling attention is intensified by the equally positive accompaniment of Aribert Reimann. The celebrated Schubert *Serenade* to words by Rellstab is far more than just a pretty tune, rather a passionate declaration of love; and Fassbaender builds her climax to the cycle round the final Heine settings, heightening their dramatic impact.

Fischer-Dieskau's DG version with Moore, though recorded ten years before his CD with Brendel (currently withdrawn), brings excellent sound in the digital transfer, plus the positive advantages, first that the voice is fresher, and then that the disc also contains seven additional songs, all of them favourites.

Schreier's voice may no longer be beautiful under pressure, but the bloom on this Decca recording and the range of tone and the intensity of inflexion over word-meaning make this one of the most compelling recordings ever of *Schwanengesang*. Enhancing that are the discreet but highly individual and responsive accompaniments of András Schiff. Like Bär on his fine EMI version, Schreier makes up a generous CD-length by including not just the 14 late songs published together as *Schwanengesang*, but four more, also from the last three years of Schubert's life. The recording is vividly real.

As in his darkly searching account of *Winterreise*, also recorded in mono with Gerald Moore in the 1950s, this Schubert collection coupling *Schwanengesang* with other favourite songs reveals Hotter at his peak. The voice as recorded may not always be beautiful, but the gravity and intensity of the singing reveal a master Lieder-singer, as commanding here as in his Wagner interpretations.

The ASV reissue happily combines Schubert interpretations from two fine British artists, John Shirley-Quirk and Ian Partridge, recorded in the late 1970s. *Schwanengesang*, containing some of Schubert's last and most memorable songs, presents the interpreter with an insuperable problem in that no single voice is suited to every one of them. John Shirley-Quirk's special success is in creating a feeling of unity over the whole group. Steuart Bedford provides equally imaginative accompaniments and the recording gives the artists good presence and an excellent balance. Ian Partridge then takes over for a well-chosen group of ten of the composer's most popular songs, and the fresh lyrical flow of his tenor voice gives much pleasure, making a pleasing change of vocal colour, matched by a comparable feeling for the Schubertian phrase. The intelligence of the interpretations complements the tonal beauty of the voice, with Jennifer Partridge a sensitive accompanist. The one drawback to this otherwise enjoyably generous (77-minute) collection is the absence of texts with translations – but they *are* available on request and without charge by writing to ASV.

Winterreise (song-cycle), *D.911.*
*** DG 415 187-2 [id.]. Dietrich Fischer-Dieskau, Gerald Moore.
*** Ph. Dig. 411 463-2. Dietrich Fischer-Dieskau, Alfred Brendel.
(N) *** Hyperion Dig. CDJ 33030 [id.]. Matthias Goerne, Graham Johnson.
*** Ph. Dig. 446 407-2 [id.]. Wolfgang Holzmair, Imogen Cooper.
(M) *** DG 447 421-2 [id.]. Dietrich Fischer-Dieskau, Joerg Demus.
❁ (M) *** Decca Legends 466 382-2 [id.]. Peter Pears, Benjamin Britten.
(N) *** RCA Dig. 09026 63147-2 [id.]. Thomas Quasthoff, Charles Spencer.
(B) *** DG Classikon 439 432-2. Fischer-Dieskau, Barenboim.
**(*) Decca (IMS) Dig. 436 122-2 [id.]. Peter Schreier, András Schiff.
*** EMI Dig. CDC7 49846-2. Brigitte Fassbaender, Aribert Reimann.
(M) **(*) DG (IMS) Dig. 445 521-2 [id.]. Christa Ludwig, James Levine.
(***) EMI mono CDM5 66985-2. Hans Hotter, Gerald Moore.
(M) **(*) DG (IMS) Dig. 453 987-2. Andreas Schmidt, Rudolf Jansen.

(N) ** EMI Dig. CDC5 56445-2 [id.]. Thomas Hampson, Wolfgang Sawallisch.

In the early 1970s Dietrich Fischer-Dieskau's voice was still at its freshest, yet the singer had deepened and intensified his understanding of this greatest of song-cycles to a degree where his finely detailed and thoughtful interpretation sounded totally spontaneous, and this DG version is now freshened on CD. However, the collaboration of Fischer-Dieskau with one of today's great Schubert pianists, Alfred Brendel, brings endless illumination in the interplay and challenge between singer and pianist, magnetic from first to last. With incidental flaws, this may not be the definitive Fischer-Dieskau reading, but in many ways it is the deepest and most moving he has ever given. The recording is excellent.

Matthias Goerne's outstanding performance is discussed above as Volume 30 of Graham Johnson's Schubert Lieder Edition and is among the most magnetically perceptive of recent versions.

Wolfgang Holzmair gives an exceptionally beautiful reading of this most taxing song-cycle, using his fresh, firm, youthful voice to present a vivid portrait of the tragic lover strikingly different from those which find weight and darkness from the start. Here, with the songs flowing more freely than usual, the traveller sets out in hope and eagerness, only later finding disillusion. The last two songs, *Die Nebensonnen* and *Der Leiermann*, are then the more moving for being understated, presented with daring simplicity, to make this a young man's tragedy. Imogen Cooper proves the most sympathetic accompanist, searching and imaginative.

There are those who regard Fischer-Dieskau's third recording of *Winterreise* as the finest of all, such is the peak of beauty and tonal expressiveness that the voice had achieved in the mid-1960s, and the poetic restraint of Demus's accompaniment. The recording still sounds well, and as a mid-price reissue in DG's Legendary Recordings series it certainly makes an excellent alternative recommendation.

What is so striking about the Pears performance is its intensity. One continually has the sense of a live occasion and, next to it, even Fischer-Dieskau's beautifully wrought singing sounds too easy. As for Britten, he re-creates the music, sometimes with a fair freedom from Schubert's markings, but always with scrupulous concern for the overall musical shaping and sense of atmosphere. The sprung rhythm of *Gefror'ne Tränen* is magical in creating the impression of frozen teardrops falling, and almost every song brings similar magic. The recording and the CD transfer are exceptionally successful in bringing a sense of presence and realism, and this is certainly a proper candidate for reissue on Decca's Legends label.

Thomas Quasthoff follows up his other fine discs for RCA with one of the most powerful accounts in years of this greatest of song-cycles. It confirms him as one of the outstanding new generation of Lieder-singers, alongside Matthias Goerne and Ian Bostridge. If Quasthoff cannot quite match Goerne in conveying the pathos of the final songs, the voice is even more beautiful, darker, with not a hint of roughness, and with an astonishing range of dynamic and tone. The words too come over with a clarity and bite rarely matched.

Fischer-Dieskau's fifth recording of Schubert's greatest cycle, made in 1979, has now appeared on DG's Classikon bargain label, with the voice still in superb condition. Prompted by Barenboim's spontaneous-sounding, almost improvisatory accompaniments, it is highly inspirational. In expression this is freer than the earlier versions, and though some idiosyncratic details will not please everyone the sense of concentrated development is irresistible. The recording is very natural and beautifully balanced, and full translations are included.

As in *Die schöne Müllerin* and *Schwanengesang*, the partnership of Schreier and Schiff brings much new revelation, with the pianist as individual in his imagination as the singer, rather as Britten is with Pears. Schreier's voice is not always perfectly steady, but the focus is clean, and only occasionally is there a roughening of tone, and that to intensify the drama. With Schreier's facial expression instantly apparent, this is an intensely involving reading, with changes of mood vividly conveyed, positive, electrifying, often confidential, though the full, immediate recording does not help *pianissimos*.

Brigitte Fassbaender gives a fresh, boyishly eager reading of *Winterreise*, marked by a vivid and wide range of expression; she demonstrates triumphantly why a woman's voice can bring special illumination to this cycle, sympathetically underlining the drama behind the tragic poet's journey rather than the more meditative qualities. Reimann, at times a wilful accompanist, is nevertheless spontaneous-sounding like the singer. Excellent sound.

With James Levine a concentrated and often dramatic accompanist, consistently adding to the sense of spontaneous and immediate communication, Christa Ludwig gives a warmly satisfying performance, making use of the mature richness of the voice rather than bringing any striking new insights. Though the different sections of *Frühlingstraum*, for example, are beautifully contrasted, it is the extra darkness of the piano in low keys that adds most to the tragedy. Full, natural recording.

Hans Hotter's 1954 mono recording of *Winterreise* has been reissued as one of EMI's 'Great recordings of the century'. It brings an exceptionally dark, even sepulchral performance, lightened by the imagination of Gerald Moore's accompaniment. Hotter scales down his great Wagnerian baritone so that only occasionally is the tone gritty. His concern for detail brings many moments of illumination, but the lack of animation makes this an unrelievedly depressing view.

Andreas Schmidt with Rudolf Jansen offers a beautifully sung, thoughtfully presented version of the greatest and most demanding of all song-cycles. With forwardly balanced sound on this 1990 digital recording, words are strikingly clear, enhancing Schmidt's use of dramatic contrast, with the voice, generally smooth and even, acquiring the necessary bite at climaxes. Everything is perfectly controlled, almost too much so: it means that the poignant dénouement at the end, conveying even greater tragedy than on the surface it seems, is to a degree underplayed, leaving one dry-eyed.

Though Thomas Hampson produces a stream of distinctively velvety tone, his account of this challenging song-cycle is too easy and undetailed, even bland, with Wolfgang Sawallisch uncharacteristically square and unimaginative in his playing. The experience is observed in detachment, where above all it should be involving.

(i) *Winterreise* (complete); Lieder: (ii) *An die Musik; An Sylvia; Auf dem See; Auf dem Wasser zu singen; Der Einsame;* (iii–iv) *Ellens Gesang III (Ave Maria);* (ii) *Erster verlust;* (iii–iv) *Die Forelle;* (ii) *Frühlingsglaube;* (iii–iv) *Ganymed;* (ii) *Gretchen am Spinnrade;* (iii; v–vi) *Der Hirt auf dem Felsen;* (iii; v) *Der Jüngling und der Tod;* (ii) *Der König in Thule; Lachen und Weinen; Der Musensohn; Nähe des Geliebten; Rastlose Liebe; Seligkeit;* (iii–iv) Ständchen; (ii) *Die Sterne.*

(B) **(*) EMI Rouge et Noir CZS5 72004-2. (i) Gérard Souzay, Dalton Baldwin; (ii) Brigitte Fassbaender, Erik Werba; (iii) Elly Ameling; (iv) Jorg Demus; (v) Irwin Gage; (vi) with George Pieterson.

There are splendid things here. Souzay's 1976 account of the *Winterreise* does not find him in such fresh voice as his earlier (1962) version on Philips. But Souzay is still an imaginative artist, and the Fassbaender and Ameling interpretations are memorable.

OPERA

Alfonso und Estrella (complete).
*** Berlin Classics BC2156-2 (3) [id.]. Schreier, Mathis, Prey, Adam, Fischer-Dieskau, Berlin R. Ch. & State Op. O, Suitner.

It is strange that Schubert, whose feeling for words in lyric poetry drew out emotions which have natural drama in them, had little or no feeling for the stage. Had his operas been produced, no doubt he would have learnt how to use music more positively; as it is, this tale of royal intrigue in medieval times never quite captures the listener as an opera should. Even so, it contains a stream of delightful music, Schubert at his most open and refreshing; under Suitner's direction it here receives a sparkling performance, excellently cast. Edith Mathis makes a sweet heroine, and Peter Schreier sings radiantly, as if in an orchestrated *Schöne Müllerin*. The reconciliation of the two principal male characters, Froila and Mauregato, is most touching as sung by Fischer-Dieskau and Prey. The recording is richly atmospheric and is splendidly transferred to CD. A full translation is included.

Fierrabras (complete).
*** DG (IMS) Dig. 427 341-2 (2) [id.]. Protschka, Mattila, Studer, Gambill, Hampson, Holl, Polgár, Schoenberg Ch., COE, Abbado.

Few operas by a great composer have ever had quite so devastatingly bad a press as *Fierrabras*. Schubert may often let his musical imagination blossom without considering the dramatic effect, but there are jewels in plenty in this score. Many solos and duets develop into delightful ensembles, and the influence of Beethoven's *Fidelio* is very striking, with spoken melodrama and offstage fanfares bringing obvious echoes. A recording is the ideal medium for such buried treasure, and Abbado directs an electrifying performance. Both tenors, Robert Gambill and Josef Protschka, are on the strenuous side, but have a fine feeling for Schubertian melody. Cheryl Studer and Karita Mattila sing ravishingly, and Thomas Hampson gives a noble performance as the knight, Roland. Only Robert Holl as King Karl (Charlemagne) is unsteady at times. The sound is comfortably atmospheric, outstanding for a live recording.

Die Verschworenen (complete).
(M) *** CPO/EMI CPO 999 554-2. Eda Moser, Fuchs, Dallapozza, Schary, Moll, Finke, Bav. R. Ch., Munich RO, Wallberg.

Die Verschworenen ('The Conspirators') originally had to have that title changed to 'Domestic Warfare' from fear of the censors; but in fact it is a harmless variant on the old theme of Aristophanes' *Lysistrata*, with the wives of returning crusaders withholding their favours from their menfolk. Though the heroine's lovely minor-key *Romance* near the beginning with clarinet obbligato points to serious emotions, and there is a Weber-like storm sequence, this is predominantly light-hearted, with ensemble passages which for the Anglo-Saxon listener will recall Gilbert and Sullivan, as in the fourth number, a chorus in which men are set against women. Much the longest number is the extended finale, structured like a Mozart operatic finale and here, as in Schubert's other one-act operas, there are hints that he had studied Beethoven's *Fidelio*. In this very well-made recording there is no weak link in the Munich cast, with the bass, Kurt Moll, outstanding as Count Heribert. As in other issues in this CPO series of recordings originally made by EMI, there is no libretto but a good synopsis linked to the CD tracks.

Der vierjährige Posten (complete).
(M) *** CPO/EMI CPO 999 553-2. Donath, Schreier, Fischer-Dieskau, Brokmeier, Lenz, Bav. R. Ch. & O, Wallberg.

Schubert wrote this one-act piece ('The Four-year Post') in 1815 at the age of 18. With little more than half an hour of music, including a substantial overture, its eight numbers have many characteristically Schubertian touches, not just in the flowing tunes but in foretastes of the *Rosamunde* music. More intriguingly, in this rather slight story set in a border village threatened by war, they suggest that Schubert had already heard and studied Beethoven's *Fidelio*, first given in its final form in Vienna the previous year. The similarity of the military music is particularly striking. Apart from the overture, the only extended number (and the only real aria) is the prayer of Kätchen, the heroine, which in its calm beauty seems to anticipate Agathe's aria, *Und ob die Volke*, in Weber's *Der Freischütz* of six years later. The cast in this recording, originally made by EMI–Electrola, is an outstanding one, with star singers forming a splendid team. Highly recommended, though the piece offers short measure for a whole disc. No libretto is provided, only a synopsis.

Die Zwillingsbrüder (complete).
(M) *** CPO/EMI CPO 999 556-2. Donath, Gedda, Moll, Fischer-Dieskau, Munich State Op. Ch., Bav. RSO, Sawallisch.

Die Zwillingsbrüder ('The Twin brothers'), completed in 1819, deftly tells the story of twin brothers, strikingly contrasted, both returning from serving in the army, the one a rough-diamond of a soldier, the other – thought to be dead – the devoted lover. Inevitably this leads to confusion, resolved only at the end in a conventional but winning way. When Fischer-Dieskau takes the roles of both twins – who never appear on stage together – the result is delightful, with Schubert inspired to sparkling music, and with the brothers' contrasting characters well conveyed in their respective arias. With Sawallisch drawing superb playing and singing from the whole team, this comes near to being an ideal performance, not just starrily cast but very well recorded.

Schulhoff, Erwin (1894–1942)

Flammen (opera; complete).
*** Decca (IMS) Dig. 444 630-2 (2). Westi, Eaglen, Vermillion, Prein, Wolff, Soloists, Berlin RIAS Chamber Ch., Deutsches SO, Berlin, John Mauceri.

Flammen is another impressive offering in Decca's remarkable Entartete Musik series of works condemned by the Nazis, this time featuring the Czech-Jewish composer, Erwin Schulhoff, who died in internment in 1942. First heard in Brno in 1932 with the Czech title, *Plameny*, this opera is a curiosity, a rich and exotic score inspired by a stylized story and characters, with long, purely instrumental passages which in a stage presentation would involve ballet and mime. The central figure is Don Juan, condemned to eternal life amid the hell-flames of the title, loved by the symbolic figure of Death (a woman) who is yet unable to claim him. The other principal women's roles are taken by a single singer (here the rich-voiced and formidable Jane Eaglen), with Donna Anna turning into Margarethe when the stylized story implies that Don Juan and Faust are linked. Dramatically, it is variably successful, but the concluding scenes are most moving. The performance is outstanding in every way, with John Mauceri drawing bitingly intense playing and singing from his excellent team. Kurt Westi is superb in the central role of Don Juan, clear, firm and fresh, and both Jane Eaglen and Iris Vermillion as Death sing with power and passion. Recording of demonstration quality.

Schulz, Johann Abraham
(1747–1800)

(i; ii; iii) *The Death of Christ (Christe Dod). Overture, The Harvest festival (Höstgilder)*. (iii) (Keyboard): *Allegretto in C; Andante sostenuto in A, Op. 1/1*. (i; iv) Songs: *Abendlied; An die Natur; Mailied; Neujahrslied*. (ii; iii) Motet: *Denk ich Gott an deine Güte* (arr. from Haydn's *Symphony No. 104*).
(N) *** Chandos Dig. CHAN 9553 [id.]. (i) Dam-Jensen, Halling, Zachariassen, Mannov; (ii; iii) Danish National Ch. & RSO, Hogwood; (iv) Hogwood (fortepiano).

Born in north Germany in 1747, Johann Abraham Peter Schulz established himself in Copenhagen as the pioneer of Danish national music, dying in 1800. *The Death of Christ* is a 35-minute cantata, both moving and dramatic, which in its linked sequence of 13 sections moves from total darkness, mourning Christ's death, to blazing light in the exhilarating final chorus,'*He lives!*' In style Schulz echoes both Haydn and C. P. E. Bach with a fascinating anticipation of Beethoven's *Pastoral Symphony* in the storm music. Excellent performance under Hogwood, who also plays two fortepiano pieces as interludes. Inger Dam-Jensen, Cardiff Singer of the World, is outstanding among the soloists, both in the cantata and in the songs *Abendlied* and *Mailied*.

Schuman, William (1910–92)

American festival overture.
(N) (B) *** DG Classikon 445 129-2. LAPO, Bernstein – BARBER: *Adagio for strings.* BERNSTEIN: *Candide overture;* COPLAND: *Appalachian spring;* ***

Schuman's *overture* is the least known of the four representative works making up this attractive Classikon disc. It is rather like a Walton comedy overture with an American accent, and is played here with tremendous panache. Close, bright, full recording.

In praise of Shahn (Canticle for orchestra); (i) *To thee old cause (Evocation for oboe, brass, timpani, piano and strings).*
(M) *** Sony SMK 63088 [id.]. (i) Gomberg (oboe); NYPO, Bernstein – BARBER: *Adagio for strings; Violin concerto.* ***

Both of these works are commemorative. *To thee old cause* is dedicated to the memory of Dr Martin Luther King, and the score quotes from Walt Whitman ('*Thou peerless, passionate, good cause, Thou stern, remorseless, sweet idea*'). It features an oboe obbligato within its string textures which are reinforced by brass sonorities. In a single movement, its *Largissimo* opening is intense and evocative; thereafter there are frequently shifting moods, although poignant lyrical feeling predominates, and the final gentle resolution suggests an acceptance of the human condition. *In praise of* (Ben) *Shahn* remembers the New York artist. It is in two sections, marked *Vigoroso* and *Lento*, although both (drawing on Eastern European Jewish folk material) include dynamic and expressive writing. This is music which in its atmosphere and use of dissonance often looks back to Charles Ives, although Schuman's own individual voice is never submerged. Bernstein is in his element and neither piece could receive more passionate advocacy. The (1970) Avery Fisher Hall recording is very immediate but has plenty of atmosphere too.

Judith; New England triptych; Symphony for strings; Variations on America.
*** Delos Dig. DE 3115 [id.]. Seattle SO, Gerard Schwarz.

The composer himself heard these performances and spoke of their combination of 'intellectual depth, technical superiority and emotional involvement' – and who are we to dissent! The *Symphony for strings*, his Fifth, is one of his strongest and most beautiful works. This Seattle account has the advantage of fresh recorded sound. The ballet, *Judith*, was written for Martha Graham. Powerful and atmospheric music, here given a performance with both these qualities. The *New England triptych* makes use of New England themes by the Bostonian William Billings (1746–1800), whose music served to fuel the cause of the American Revolution. This present account is superior to the version by Howard Hanson on Mercury.

New England triptych.
(M) *** Mercury [432 755-2]. Eastman-Rochester O, Howard Hanson – IVES: *Symphony No. 3* etc. *** (with MENNIN: *Symphony No. 5.* **(*))

William Schuman is not as outrageously original as Ives, but his sound-world is individual and wholly American. Each of the three pieces is an orchestral anthem, the first a thrustingly vibrant *Hallelujah*; the second is in the form of a round, and the finale features a marching song. Splendidly alive playing and excellent (1963) Mercury recording, admirably transferred to CD.

Symphonies Nos. 3; 5 (for strings); 8.
(N) (M) *** Sony SMK 63163 [id.]. NYPO, Leonard Bernstein.

The three symphonies on this disc were all recorded during Bernstein's time with the New York Philharmonic in the 1960s, but were never released here up till now. During his youth WilliamSchuman had been a keen jazz musician, and led his own group, the rather sedately named (as it seems from the vantage point of the late 1990s) 'Billy Schuman and His Alamo Society Orchestra'. Nothing could be further removed from the austere world of his *Third quartet* or the concentration and rigour of the symphonies. These performances, all by the New York Philharmonic, are powerfully conceived and superbly executed. The commanding sense of line, rhythmic momentum and harmonic vocabulary of the *Third* show that Schuman's studies with Roy Harris were not wasted. Schuman suppressed his first two symphonies. He was fond of quoting the radio listener who wrote to him after a Boston Symphony broadcast of the *Second*, saying that it made him 'lose faith in the power of aspirin tablets'. The *Third* (1941) is (to quote Bernstein) 'alive, radiant and optimistic', and it is without question a masterpiece. It has the sweep and power of Harris, the freshness of Copland and an entirely individual and compelling atmosphere. Bernstein's 1960 performance is superb, and superior to his later remake for DG. The *Symphony for strings* comes from 1943 and is consistently imaginative, with a highly developed and sophisticated harmonic vocabulary. The *Eighth Symphony*, on the other hand, was commissioned by the New York Philharmonic in 1962. Its inspiration gives the impression of being manufactured rather than composed, except in the impressive and beautiful *Largo* movement; but make no mistake, its two companions on this record are among the finest symphonies to come out of America. The performances are terrific and the recordings, all emanating from the 1960s, are expertly restored, sounding much fresher and better defined than the LP originals.

Symphony No. 10 (American Muse); American Festival overture; New England triptych. IVES, arr. SCHUMAN: *Variations on America.*
*** RCA Dig. 09026 61282-2 [id.]. St Louis SO, Slatkin.

Schuman's *Tenth Symphony* was composed in 1975 for the United States Bicentennial; it is a three-movement piece whose centre of gravity resides in its big, contemplative middle movement with the usual polytonal choral harmonies. But splendid though much of it is, Schuman's inspiration is touched a little by routine, the gestures sound just a little too much like self-imitation when put alongside the more spontaneous eloquence of symphonies 3–6. There is plenty of excitement in the outer movements and the St Louis orchestra play with enormous conviction. Their performance of the *American Festival overture* is pretty dazzling, too, and yields little to Bernstein's DG account. Both the *New England triptych* and the Ives transcription, *Variations on America*, fare equally well.

String quartets Nos. 2, 3 & 5.
*** HM Dig. HMU 907114 [id.]. Lydian String Qt.

The *Third Quartet* (1939) serves as a reminder of what a powerful composer William Schuman is. Less accessible, perhaps, than Aaron Copland or his exact contemporary, Samuel Barber, Schuman's music has sinew and a toughness that is bracing. It demands persuasive and committed playing from its interpreters, which it receives from the fine Lydian Quartet, and concentration from its listeners. The *Second Quartet* (1937) is slighter than the *Third* but is a strong piece nevertheless. The latter has something of the volcanic energy and drive of the *Third Symphony*, Schuman's best-known work, as well as its sense of line and momentum; it is one of the great American quartets. The *Fifth Quartet* is a relatively late piece, coming from 1987, and its opening is among Schuman's most inward and searching inspirations. Some may find his quartets a hard nut to crack but they are well worth taking trouble over. All three are beautifully played and recorded.

Schumann, Clara (1819–96)

Piano trio in G min., Op. 17.
*** Hyperion Dig. CDA 66331 [id.]. Dartington Piano Trio – Fanny MENDELSSOHN: *Trio.* ***

Clara's *Piano trio* moves within the Mendelssohn–Schumann tradition with apparently effortless ease and, when played as persuasively as it is here, makes a pleasing impression. If it does not command the depth of Robert, it has a great deal of charm to commend it. Excellent recording.

Schumann, Robert (1810–56)

Cello concerto in A min., Op. 129.
*** BIS Dig. CD 486 [id.]. Torleif Thedéen, Malmö SO, Markiz – ELGAR: *Concerto.* ***
(M) **(*) Mercury (IMS) 432 010-2 [id.]. Janos Starker, LSO, Skrowaczewski – LALO: *Concerto* **(*); SAINT-SAENS: *Concerto.* ***
*** RCA Dig. 09026 68027-2 [id.] Starker, Bamberg SO, Russell Davies – HINDEMITH: *Cello concerto.* ***
(BB) *** Naxos Dig. 8 550 938 [id.]. Maria Kliegel, Nat. SO of Ireland, Andrew Constantine – BRAHMS: *Double concerto.* ***
(B) *** Decca Eclipse Dig. 448 712-2; *448 712-4* [(M) id. import]. Lynn Harrell, Cleveland O, Marriner – LALO; SAINT-SAENS: *Concertos.* ***
(M) *** Sony Dig. SMK 60151 [id.]. Ma, Bav. RSO, Sir Colin Davis – DVORAK: *Cello concerto.* ***
(N) (M) *(*) EMI CDM5 66913-2 [CDM5 66965]. Rostropovich, O Nat. de France, Bernstein – R. STRAUSS: *Don Quixote.* ***

The young Swedish virtuoso, Torleif Thedéen, is splendidly recorded on BIS, and the Malmö orchestra give him sympathetic support. He plays with a refreshing ardour, tempered by nobility and a reticence that is strongly appealing. He couples it with an account of the Elgar that is every bit as attuned to the latter's sensibility as any in the catalogue. Strongly recommended.

Janos Starker gives a persuasive account of it that is thoroughly sensitive to the letter and spirit of the score. Skrowaczewski accompanies with spirit and without the rather explosive, clipped tutti chords that somewhat disfigure the Lalo with which it is coupled. The 1962 recording is amazing for its age: people make great claims for these early Mercury recordings and, judging from this expertly engineered disc, rightly so!

On RCA, playing of finesse from Starker, who has recorded the Schumann *Concerto* many times. He is well accompanied by Russell Davies and the Bambergers, and very decently recorded. For those wanting a hybrid coupling this can be recommended, but the Hindemith may not be a first choice of coupling for those primarily interested in Schumann, and Starker's earlier, Mercury version will seem a better choice for most of his admirers, particularly as it is offered at mid-price.

The Schumann *Cello concerto* makes an apt coupling for the Brahms *Double concerto* and is the more attractive for coming on the Naxos super-budget label in a warmly spontaneous-sounding performance, very well recorded. Kliegel takes a spacious, lyrical view of the first movement, using a soft-grained tone at the start, with wide vibrato. The simple, dedicated approach to the central *Langsam* also brings dedicated playing, while the finale is wittily pointed, not least in the second subject.

Harrell's is a big-scale reading, strong and sympathetic, made the more powerful by the superb accompaniment from the Cleveland Orchestra. Its controversial point is that he expands the usual cadenza with a substantial sequence of his own. The digital recording is outstandingly fine.

As always, Yo-Yo Ma's playing is distinguished by great refinement of expression, and his account of the *Concerto* is keenly affectionate, although at times he carries tonal sophistication to excess and drops suddenly into *sotto voce* tone and near-inaudibility. Both he and Sir Colin Davis are thoroughly attuned to the sensibility of this composer. The balance, both between soloist and orchestra and within the various departments of the orchestra, blends perfectly.

Except in the finale where energy triumphs, the collaboration of Rostropovich and Bernstein sounds disappointingly self-conscious. The great Russian cellist is at his most indulgent, not least in the lovely slow section, which is pulled about wilfully at a very slow basic tempo. The Strauss coupling is in an altogether different class, so this is a strange choice for EMI's 'Great recordings of the century' series.

(i) *Cello concerto in A min.;* (ii) *Piano concerto in A min.*

(M) **(*) DG (IMS) 449 100-2. (i) Rostropovich, Leningrad PO, Rozhdestvensky; (ii) Argerich, Nat. SO of Washington, Rostropovich.

Rostropovich's DG performance of the *Cello concerto* is superbly made, introspective yet at the same time outgoing, with a peerless technique at the command of a rare artistic imagination. The sound is vivid. In the *Piano concerto* Rostropovich moves to the rostrum and Argerich takes on the role of soloist. The partnership produces a performance which is full of contrast – helped by a recording of wide dynamic range – and strong in temperament. There is an appealing delicacy in the *Andantino* and the outer movements have plenty of vivacity and colour. Yet in the last analysis the work's special romantic feeling does not fully blossom here, although the playing is not without poetry. The recording is admirably lifelike and well balanced.

Piano concerto in A min., Op. 54.

(M) *** Ph. 446 192-2. Kovacevich, BBC SO, Sir Colin Davis – GRIEG: *Concerto; Sonata.* ***

*** EMI Dig. CDC7 54746-2. Lars Vogt, CBSO, Rattle – GRIEG: *Concerto.* ***

*** Sony Dig. SK 44899 [id.]. Perahia, Bav. RSO, Colin Davis – GRIEG: *Concerto.* ***

(M) *** RCA [60420-2-RG]. Van Cliburn, Chicago SO, Reiner – MACDOWELL: *Concerto No. 2.* **(*)

(M) *** RCA 09026 62691-2 [id.]. Van Cliburn, Chicago SO, Reiner – PROKOFIEV: *Piano concerto No. 3.* **(*)

*** Ph. 412 251-2. Brendel, LSO, Abbado – WEBER: *Konzertstück.* ***

(M) (**(*)) EMI CDM5 66597-2. Walter Gieseking, Phil. O, Karajan – FRANCK: *Symphonic variations;* GRIEG: *Piano concerto.* (**(*))

(M) **(*) Decca Legends 466 383-2 [id.]. Radu Lupu, LSO, Previn – GRIEG: *Concerto.* **(*)

(B) **(*) Decca 433 628-2 [id.]. Gulda, VPO, Andrae – FRANCK: *Symphonic variations* *** ✿; GRIEG: *Concerto.* ***

(B) **(*) [EMI Red Line Dig. CDR5 69859]. Cécile Ousset, LPO, Masur – GRIEG: *Piano concerto.* **(*)

(BB) **(*) ASV Quicksilva Dig. CDQS 6092. Osorio, RPO, Bátiz – FRANCK: *Symphonic variations* **(*); RAVEL: *Left-hand concerto* ***; SAINT-SAENS: *Wedding-cake.* ***

(i; ii) *Piano concerto in A min.;* (i; iii) *Introduction and allegro appassionato, Op. 92. Novellette in F, Op. 21/1; Toccata in C, Op. 7; Waldszenen, Op. 82.*

(M) **(*) DG stereo/mono 447 440-2 [id.]. Sviatoslav Richter, with (i) Warsaw Nat. PO, (ii) Witold Rowicki, (iii) Stanislaw Wislocki.

(i) *Piano concerto in A min. Arabeske; Etudes symphoniques, Op. 13.*

(M) *** RCA 09026 61444-2 [id.]. Rubinstein; (i) RCA Victor SO, Krips.

(M) **(*) DG (IMS) Dig. 445 522-2 [id.]. Pollini; (i) BPO, Abbado.

(i) *Piano concerto in A min.; Carnaval; Kinderszenen (Scenes from childhood), Op. 15.*

(B) **(*) DG Classikon 439 476-2 [id.]. Wilhelm Kempff; (i) Bav. RSO, Kubelik.

Our primary recommendation for this favourite Romantic concerto remains with the successful symbiosis of Stephen Kovacevich and Sir Colin Davis, who give an interpretation which is both fresh and poetic, unexaggerated but powerful in its directness and clarity, and the spring-like element of the outer movements is finely presented by orchestra and soloist alike. This is even more attractive at mid-price.

Lars Vogt was the Second Prize winner at the 1990 Leeds International Piano Competition when he impressed by his sensitivity and innate sense of style. Both these attributes, and a keen imagination, are strongly in evidence in this account of the Schumann, in which he is well supported by Simon Rattle and the CBSO. There is stiff competition, of course, but among modern recordings Vogt acquits himself with honour.

Perahia's 1988 version benefits from having the guiding hand of Sir Colin Davis directing the orchestra. The recording is live. Perahia is never merely showy, but here he enjoys displaying his ardour and virtuosity as well as his ability to invest a phrase with poetry and magic. With its full and spacious sound, the Perahia is among the finest digital versions of this favourite coupling.

It is good to have Rubinstein's 1958 New York Manhattan Center recording of the *A minor Piano concerto* back as it is clearly preferable to his Chicago version, which suffered from a more restricted dynamic range: few apologies need be made for the sound. Rubinstein takes the *Allegros* of these two interconnected movements (separated by the charming *Intermezzo*) at comparatively modest speeds and he achieves the ideal compromise between an impression of spontaneous poetry in quieter passages (his rubato is marked but most natural) and a firm overall control. It is interesting that the conductor here, Josef Krips, was also the conductor on Kempff's old mono recording, which was also notable for its relaxed *Allegros*, and one wonders what influence he had in the matter. As couplings, we are offered Rubinstein's 1969 recording of the *Arabeske*, aristocratic in feeling and the *Etudes symphoniques*, recorded at a live recital in Carnegie Hall in 1961. Commanding playing.

Kempff, after a rather positive account of the opening chords of the *Piano concerto*, proceeds characteristically to produce an unending stream of poetry. The dialogue of the *Intermezzo* is like an intimate conversation overheard. Tempi are generally leisurely, notably so in the finale where there is fine support from the Bavarian Radio Orchestra under Kubelik. Good early-1970s recording. But of the solo recordings neither is among Kempff's more compelling Schumann performances.

Van Cliburn's performance is very persuasive, the first movement rhapsodical in feeling, certainly poetic but exciting too. The *Intermezzo* is pleasingly fresh and the finale admirably buoyant and spirited. Altogether this is most attractive, and so is the unusual MacDowell coupling. It also comes with an alternative coupling of Prokofiev No. 3.

Brendel's is a thoroughly considered, yet fresh-sounding performance, with meticulous regard to detail. There is some measure of coolness, perhaps, in the slow movement, but on the whole this is a distinguished reading.

Gieseking's 1953 recording with Karajan and the Philharmonia was overshadowed at the time by Lipatti's version. There is much to relish in Gieseking's refined performance – and in particular the exquisite *Intermezzo*. It is well worth reviving, and Andrew Walter's transfer is first class.

Lupu's clean boldness of approach to the first movement is appealingly fresh, but the fusing together of the work's disparate masculine and feminine Romantic elements has not been entirely solved. The digital CD transfer is especially telling in the quieter moments, but tuttis are less transparent.

Gulda's account is refreshingly direct yet, with light, crisp playing, never sounds rushed. The *Intermezzo* remains delicate in feeling, with nicely pointed pianism. The finale is just right, with an enjoyable rhythmic lift, and the early stereo (1956), though a little dated, is fully acceptable.

Cécile Ousset, with sympathetic support from Masur, gives a spirited account of the Schumann *Concerto*, like the Grieg coupling rather weightier than one might have expected but not lacking sparkle, while the central dialogue with the orchestra is delightfully done.

Pollini's account of the concerto is not without tenderness and poetry, but he is at times rather business-like and wanting in freshness. He is handicapped by rather unventilated recording and an inconsistent balance. (The piano seems much further back in the slow movement by comparison with the first.) The coupling is every way successful: the *Symphonic studies* has a symphonic gravitas and concentration; it also has the benefit of excellent recorded quality.

Richter's reissue in DG's 'Originals' series does not always represent him at his very finest. The concerto is not as interesting or personal as one would have expected. Perhaps the sluggishness of the orchestral playing affected his concentration. Not that the concerto or the *Introduction and allegro appassionato* lack style but the tension could be greater. The focus of the late-1950s Polish recording has been improved in the concerto but in Opus 92 remains a little fuzzy around the edges, not quite up to the standard one expects from DG. The *Novellette* and *Toccata* are fabulous performances, full of hair-raising virtuosity, but shaped with an unerring sense of style and musical as well as technical control. The piano tone is dry but clear. The *Waldszenen* is a mono recording from 1956 and beautifully played, Richter very much the poet of the forest, and the mono sound gives no cause for complaint.

Jorge Federico Osorio's account of the Schumann *Concerto* is boldly romantic yet in no way lacking in poetry. The central *Intermezzo* is beautifully in scale, but in the first movement, with Bátiz bringing strong support in the tuttis, he presses on impulsively, and the finale has similar urgency. Some may prefer a more relaxed romanticism, but there is no lack of spontaneity here and the result is undoubtedly fresh and involving. Excellent recording and recommendable couplings make this disc a genuine bargain.

(i) *Piano concerto in A min., Op. 54;* (ii) *Abendlied, Op. 85/12; Adagio and Allegro in A flat, Op. 70; Fantasiestücke, Op. 73; 3 Romances, Op. 94; 5 Stücke im Volkston, Op. 102.* (Piano) *Etudes symphoniques, Op. 13. Fantasia in C, Op.*

17; Fantasiestücke, Op. 12; Kinderszenen, Op. 15; Kreisleriana, Op. 16.

(M) *** Ph. Brendel Edition Analogue/Dig. 446 925-2 (5). Alfred Brendel, with (i) LSO, Abbado; (ii) Heinz Holliger – BRAHMS: *Piano concertos; Ballades*, etc. ***

Brendel's is a fresh, thoughtful account of the *Piano concerto*, though missing something of the work's delicate romantic feeling in the slow movement. Neither the orchestral response under Abbado nor the Philips recording will seriously disappoint. It was a curious idea to include the series of pieces with oboe, beautifully though Holliger plays. They are available separately – see below. But the piano music is all well chosen. The very opening of the *Fantasiestücke*, Op. 12, demonstrates magically spontaneous playing; both this and the *Fantasia in C* are full of imaginative touches of colour, strong as well as poetic. The digital sound is rather more forward than one would encounter in the recital room, but it serves Brendel well and truthfully conveys the depth of timbre. *Kinderszenen* and *Kreisleriana* bring more thoughtful and poetically characterized playing from Brendel, and he is again very well recorded, while the *Etudes symphoniques* are ardent and yet beautifully controlled, again given first-class digital sound.

Violin concerto in D min.

*** Decca Dig. 444 811-2 [id.]. Joshua Bell, Cleveland O, Christoph von Dohnányi – BRAHMS: *Violin concerto.* ***

With Dohnányi and the Cleveland Orchestra adding to the weight and drama, Joshua Bell in a commanding performance defies the old idea of this concerto as flawed: he brings out its charm as well as power. The central slow movement has rapt intensity and the dance-rhythms of the finale have fantasy as well as jauntiness and jollity. Full-bodied, well-balanced recording.

Violin concerto in D (edited Schunemann and Kulenkampff).

(B) (***) Dutton Lab. mono CDEA 5018 [(M) id.]. Georg Kulenkampff, BPO, Hans Schmidt-Isserstedt (with MOZART: *Adagio* from *Violin concerto in A, K.219* (***)) – BEETHOVEN: *Violin concerto.* (***) ✿

This recording was made in 1937, and the score includes an extensive revision of the solo violin part made by the soloist. Kulenkampff plays it with radiant lyricism, and the recording in this new Dutton transfer sounds astonishingly good for its age, if not quite as impressive as the Beethoven coupling. The Mozart *Adagio* makes an exquisite final encore.

Introduction and Allegro appassionato in G, Op. 92.

(B) **(*) Sony SBK 48166 [id.]. Rudolf Serkin, Phd. O, Ormandy – BRAHMS: *Concerto No. 1* **(*); MENDELSSOHN: *Capriccio brillant.* **

The *Introduction and Allegro appassionato in G major* brings the full flowering of Schumann's romanticism.

Serkin plays with his accustomed panache and he is given excellent support from Ormandy. The piano-tone could be fuller in timbre but the overall effect has considerable warmth, and those looking for a recording of this relatively unfamiliar piece will find much here to arrest them. The Brahms coupling shows Serkin at his finest.

Symphony in G min. (Zwickau); Symphonies Nos. 1 in B flat (Spring), Op. 38; 2 in C, Op. 61; 3 in E flat (Rhenish), Op. 97; Symphony No. 4 in D min.: original 1841 version and revised 1851 version, *Op. 120*; (i) *Konzertstück for 4 horns and orchestra in F, Op. 86.*

(N) ✿ *** DG Dig. 457 591-2 (3) [id.]. ORR, John Eliot Gardiner.

Gardiner seeks to validate the claim of nineteenth-century commentators that Schumann's symphonies were the most significant addition to the repertory since Beethoven. With his brilliant orchestra of period instruments Gardiner offers not just the four regular symphonies but a complete survey of Schumann as symphonist. He seeks specifically to explode the myth that Schumann was a poor orchestrator, pointing out how quick he was to learn from his own mistakes. Gardiner makes an exception over the 1851 revision of the *Fourth Symphony*, in which Schumann thickened the woodwind writing with much doubling. Illuminatingly, both versions of that symphony are included, with the contrasts well brought out. Gardiner himself, like Brahms, prefers the slimmer, more transparent first version, suggesting that the 1851 changes made it safer and less original. Yet paradoxically, in performance Gardiner is even more inspired in the later version, which here emerges as bitingly dramatic, working up to a thrilling coda. Like other cycles this one offers the *Overture*, *Scherzo* and *Finale* of 1841 as a necessary extra, but still more fascinating is the *Konzertstück* of 1849 for four horns, with the ORR soloists breathtaking in their virtuosity on nineteenth-century instruments. Also included is the early, incomplete *Symphony in G minor* of 1832 (named after Schumann's home town of Zwickau). Under Gardiner the two completed movements emerge as highly original in their own right. Though Roy Goodman's rival RCA set offers rather warmer performances, Gardiner is even more incisive and refreshing, and his inclusion of so much extra material confirms the preference.

Symphonies Nos.1 in B flat (Spring), Op. 38;2 in C, Op. 61;3 in E flat (Rhenish), Op. 97; 4 in D min., Op. 120 (original version).

(N) **(*) Teldec Dig. 0630 12674-2(2) [id.]. COE, Harnoncourt.

Typically, Harnoncourt takes a distinctive view of Schumann in his symphony cycle, drawing fine playing from the COER, even though the slightly distanced recording with a relatively small string band reduces the impact. Those devoted to Harnoncourt's rethinking will find much to admire, not least in the original version of No. 4, but too often his point-making draws attention to itself distractingly, with fussy detail in obtrusive rallentandos or a reluctance to phrase over a melody as in the slow movement of No. 1. It is surprising too to find him trivializing the Cologne Cathedral fourth movement of the *Rhenish*.

Symphonies Nos. 1 in B flat (Spring); 2 in C; 3 (Rhenish); 4 in D min. (original Leipzig version); *Overture, scherzo and finale, Op. 52.*
*** RCA Dig. 09026 61931–2 (2) [id.]. Hanover Band, Goodman.

Few period performances of nineteenth-century works can match Roy Goodman's refreshing accounts, either for the vigour and electricity of the playing or for the new perceptions given. Convincingly Goodman shows how these works are far more cohesive in their often volatile inspiration than many used to think. Textures are clarified, but never to reduce the impact of the music, rather to give them exceptionally clean-cut terracing of sound, thanks also to the satisfyingly beefy recording. Most thrilling are the antiphonal contrasts of the brass choirs, setting the braying timbre of period horns (two of the four natural valveless instruments in Nos. 1 and 4, as the composer wanted) against the brightness of the trumpets. The sharp accenting of woodwind comment, often syncopated, is also enhanced, with Goodman securing superb ensemble. The strings are naturally thinner, with violins and cellos unable to expand over the wide dynamic range of modern instruments, but Goodman compensates in encouraging a warmly espressivo style in slow movements, with *Andantes* flowing easily, never trivialized. The first disc contains the three works dating from 1841, not just the *Spring Symphony* (No. 1) and the *Overture, scherzo and finale* but the original Leipzig version of the *Symphony No. 4*, usually heard in the revision of ten years later. Not only is the scoring lighter, the slow transitions into the *Allegros* of the outer movements are both more compact, with each sequence made very convincing by Goodman, particularly the big crescendo into the finale. Brahms preferred this earlier version, and here one registers why.

Symphonies Nos. 1–4.
(M) *** DG 429 672-2 (2). BPO, Karajan.
*** DG (IMS) Dig. 439 923-2 (2). Dresden State O, Sinopoli.
(B) *** RCA 74321 20294-2 (2). Phd. O, James Levine.
(B) **(*) DG Double Dig. 453 049-2 (2) [id.]. VPO, Bernstein.

Symphonies Nos. 1–4: Manfred overture, Op. 115.
(M) **(*) Sony MH2K 62349 (2) [id.]. Cleveland O, George Szell.

Symphonies Nos. 1 in B flat (Spring), Op. 38; 2 in C, Op. 61.
(B) *** Sony SBK 48269 [id.]. Bav. RSO, Kubelik.

Symphonies Nos. 3 in E flat (Rhenish), Op. 97; 4 in D min., Op. 120; Overture Manfred, Op. 115.
(B) *** Sony SBK 48270 [id.]. Bav. RSO, Kubelik.

Symphonies Nos. 1–4; Overture, scherzo and finale, Op. 52.
(M) *** EMI (SIS) CMS7 64815-2 (2) [id.]. Dresden State O, Sawallisch.

Symphonies Nos. 1–4; Overture: Julius Caesar, Op. 128; Overture, scherzo and finale, Op. 52.
(N) (B) **(*) Decca Double 448 030-2 (2) [id.]. VPO, Solti.

The Dresden CDs of the Schumann *Symphonies* under Sawallisch are as deeply musical as they are carefully considered; the orchestral playing combines superb discipline with refreshing naturalness and spontaneity. Sawallisch catches all Schumann's varying moods, and his direction has splendid vigour. These recordings have dominated the catalogue, alongside Karajan's, for some years. Although the reverberant acoustic brought a degree of edge to the upper strings, the sound-picture has the essential fullness which the Karajan transfers lack, and the remastering has cleaned up the upper range to a considerable extent. The set now appears in a mid-priced box.

Otherwise Karajan's interpretations of the Schumann *Symphonies* stand above all other recordings on modern instruments. No. 1 is a beautifully shaped performance, with orchestral playing of the highest distinction; No. 2 is among the most powerful ever recorded, combining poetic intensity and intellectual strength in equal proportions; and No. 3 is also among the most impressive versions ever commited to disc: its famous fourth-movement evocation of Cologne Cathedral is superbly spacious and eloquent, with quite magnificent brass playing. No. 4 can be classed alongside Furtwängler's famous record, with Karajan similarly inspirational, yet a shade more self-disciplined than his illustrious predecessor. However, the reissued complete set brings digital remastering which – as with the Brahms symphonies – has leaner textures than before, while in tuttis the violins above the stave may approach shrillness.

In vivid sound, warm yet finely detailed, Sinopoli directs the Dresden Staatskapelle in powerful, immediately compelling performances of all four symphonies, No. 2 being taken from a live performance. Sinopoli's way of moulding phrases and varying tempi is here consistently convincing, with the Dresden players responding warmly. Speeds are extreme at times in both directions – weighty and slow in the Scherzo of No. 4, athletically brisk in the finale – but the conviction of each reading is never in doubt, and the recording is particularly rich and full on brass, most important in the outer movements of the *Rhenish*. There is no finer digital cycle using modern instruments, though Roy Goodman's RCA version on period instruments is even more revelatory.

The RCA bargain 'Symphony Edition' brings a splendid set of Schumann to cap the series. Recorded in a glowingly warm acoustic, the Philadelphia Orchestra has seldom sounded so rich-textured over recent years. The performances are as vital as they are warm, and Levine usually produces accelerandos at the ends of outer movements to increase the excitement. The two discs are available separately at mid-price: *Symphonies Nos. 1* and *3* (74321 20295-2) and *Symphonies Nos. 2* and *4* (74321 20296-2).

Kubelik's fine Sony set also remains fully competitive. The recording was made in the Hercules-Saal, Munich, in 1979, and the advantages of that glowing acoustic can be felt throughout. The orchestral playing is generally very fine (if not quite as polished as the Berlin Philharmonic in his earlier DG set – now deleted) and is especially eloquent in the spacious slow movements. These are strongly characterized readings with plenty of vitality which display the same bright and alert sensitivity to Schumann's style as did his earlier set for DG. But the Sony recording is obviously more modern, and the latest CD transfer brings plenty of body to the sound and a better focus to the violins than in the Sawallisch set. Many will count the *Manfred Overture* a desirable additional bonus.

Szell's set of Schumann symphonies was recorded in pairs, in 1958 (Nos. 1–2) and 1960 (Nos. 3–4). Over the years the individual works have been available only very sporadically in the UK and we cannot trace making a previous assessment of No. 2, with which Szell began his cycle in October 1958. It proves to be a thrilling performance of great power and strong forward thrust, yet the eloquent *Adagio* expands gloriously and brings the most ardent response from the Cleveland strings. Szell is at his most incisive and the orchestra are at their warmest in No. 1, truly a *Spring Symphony* in this exhilarating yet romantic reading. The account of the *Rhenish* is even finer, marvellously full of life. The playing is breathtaking, with the horns gloriously full-blooded. No. 4 is strong and dramatic, not as weighty as some, but equally convincing. Szell proves himself an outstanding exponent of Schumann, able to stand alongside the finest interpreters of his day, and, were it not for the reduced range of dynamic, this set would have earned a Rosette. The two discs are packaged in an attractive stiff cardboard container, opening up like a book, with fine documentation.

Bernstein's VPO recordings from 1984–5 have the extra voltage which comes with live music-making at its most compulsive, though he seems reluctant to let the music speak for itself. The first movement of the *Spring Symphony* is pushed very hard, and the *Second Symphony* also brings the same larger-than-life projection. Slow movements are obviously deeply felt and have both warmth and humanity. In the *Rhenish Symphony* Bernstein's expressive indulgences are by no means as disruptive as some reviews have indicated. The outer movements of the *Fourth* are not allowed to move forward at a steady pace, but the *Romanze* has warmth and charm, even if the phrasing at the opening has an element of self-consciousness. Even so, with splendid orchestral playing and much engaging detail, there is a great deal to admire throughout these performances, and the resonant acoustic of the Grossersaal of the Musikverein gives the music-making a robust immediacy.

Solti's Schumann interpretations are full of his personal brand of lyrical intensity. The most compelling performance of the cycle is the *Second Symphony*, with its passionate slow movement. But throughout the work, with unwanted tensions removed and with a feeling of spontaneous lyricism paramount, this is a most compellingly individual reading. The performance of the *Spring Symphony* does not quite match this degree of ardent inspiration. It is played well enough but is just a shade disappointing. However the *Rhenish* is another memorable performance. Here Solti's sense of rhythm is strikingly alert so that the first movement hoists one aloft on its soaring melodies and comparably, the drama of the *Fourth Symphony* is given full force without ever falling into excessive tautness: there is always room to breathe. The *Julius Caesar overture* is no masterpiece, but makes an enjoyable bonus and the *Overture, scherzo and finale* is very successful. The late 1960s recordings are slightly dry, bright and forward, but one cannot complain that Schumann's scoring sounds too thick!

Symphony No. 1 in B flat (Spring), Op. 38.
(M) *** DG 447 408-2 [id.]. BPO, Karajan – BRAHMS: *Symphony No. 1.* ***

Karajan is totally attuned to Schumann's sensibility and he provides a strong yet beautifully shaped performance of the *Spring Symphony*. The very opening is electrifying with the Berlin Philharmonic giving of their finest, and this unsurpassed reading makes a highly appropriate coupling with Brahms in DG's Legendary Performances series of 'Originals'. The sound is an obvious improvement on the previous CD incarnation of this well-balanced analogue recording from the early 1970s, adding body and weight to the clear, fresh detail.

Symphonies Nos. 1; 3 in E flat (Rhenish), Op. 97.
(BB) *** ASV Quicksilva Dig. CDQS 6073 [id.]. RLPO, Janowski.

Janowski's pairing of the *Spring* and *Rhenish Symphonies* is particularly successful. The pacing throughout both symphonies is most convincing, with a good deal of the inspirational pull that makes the Karajan readings so telling. In the Cologne Cathedral evocation of the *Rhenish*, the Liverpool brass rise sonorously to the occasion and the recording is altogether first class, bright, clear and full, with a concert hall ambience. At super-bargain price, this is strongly competitive.

Symphonies Nos. 1; 4 in D min.
(M) *** DG (IMS) 445 718-2 [id.]. BPO Karajan.

As we go to press, Karajan's recording of the *Spring Symphony* is additionally available coupled with the splendid account of the *Fourth Symphony* at mid-price, in which the current transfer seems somewhat fuller than in the boxed set.

Symphony No. 2 in C, Op. 60; Konzertstück for four horns; Manfred Overture, Op. 115.
(N) *(*) DG Dig. 453 480-2 [id.]. Philh. O, Christian Thielemann.

Christian Thielemann is obviously a major talent, and made a strong impression both at the Met and at Covent Garden when he conducted Richard Strauss's *Elektra* and Pfitzner's *Palestrina*. Alas, his Schumann proves a great disappointment. He produces a superb sound from the Philharmonia but he pulls the *Second Symphony* mercilessly. The sublime slow movement is never allowed to speak for itself. The same goes for the *Manfred Overture*, though he is less intrusive in the *Konzertstücke*. Good recording but a write-off all the same.

Symphonies Nos. 2 in C, Op. 61; 3 in E flat (Rhenish), Op. 97.
*** DG (IMS) Dig. 423 625-2. BPO, Levine.
(B) **(*) DG Classikon 439 455-2. Chicago SO, Barenboim.

Levine conducts warm and positive readings of both symphonies, drawing superb playing from the Berlin Philharmonic. Though the Berlin recording is warm and full to match – allowing thrilling crescendos in the Cologne Cathedral movement of the *Rhenish* – the inner textures are not ideally clear. The compensation is that the modern digital recording gives a satisfyingly full body to the sound.

Barenboim takes an overtly romantic view of these symphonies. His are weighty performances which yet bring out the lyrical, poetic warmth, underlining dramatic contrasts. The Chicago orchestra plays with extrovert brilliance, but the recording is variably successful in bringing that out.

Symphony No. 3 in E flat (Rhenish), Op. 97.
(M) *** DG (IMS) Dig. 445 502-2 [id.]. LAPO, Giulini – BEETHOVEN: *Symphony No. 5.* ***
*** RCA Dig. 09026 61876-2. N. German RSO, Wand – SCHUBERT: *Symphony No. 3.* ***

Giulini's *Rhenish* is completely free of interpretative exaggeration and its sheer musical vitality and nobility of spirit are beautifully conveyed. The Los Angeles players produce a very well-blended, warm and cultured sound that is a joy to listen to in itself. The 1980 recording is also extremely fine and, with its superb Beethoven coupling, this is very highly recommendable.

Günter Wand's account of the *Rhenish* has integrity; it is straightforward and direct and in the Cologne Cathedral movement has no want of dignity. Wand is in excellent form, and the recordings are both spacious and present. Recommendable but not a first choice.

Symphony No. 4 in D min., Op. 120.
❁ (M) (***) DG mono 457 722-2 (2) [id.]. BPO, Furtwängler – FURTWANGLER: *Symphony No. 2.* (***)

Furtwängler's legendary account of the *Fourth Symphony* with the Berlin Philharmonic comes from 1953, the year before his death. It has long enjoyed classic status, and deservedly so. It is a really great performance and conveys the illusion that the musicians are spontaneously composing or improvising this music. The 'Wagnerian' preparation for the finale is quite electrifying, yet at the same time there is a commanding musical grip on the proceedings. The sound is remarkably warm and vivid for its period.

CHAMBER MUSIC

Abendlied, Op. 85/2; Adagio and allegro in A flat, Op. 70; Fantasiestücke, Op. 73; 3 Romances, Op. 94; 3 Pieces in Folk style, Op. 102/2–4.
(M) *** Ph. (IMS) 426 386-2. Heinz Holliger, Alfred Brendel.

The three *Romances* are specifically for oboe, but Holliger suggests that the others too are suitable for oboe, since the composer himself gave different options. One misses something by not having a horn in the *Adagio and allegro*, a cello in the folk-style pieces, or a clarinet in the *Fantasiestücke* (the oboe d'amore is used here); but Holliger has never sounded more magical on record and, with superbly real recording and deeply imaginative accompaniment, the result is an unexpected revelation.

Adagio & allegro, Op. 70; Fantasiestücke, Op. 73; 5 Stücke im Volkston, Op. 102.
(BB) *** Naxos Dig. 8.550654 [id.]. Maria

Kliegel, Kristin Merscher – SCHUBERT: *Arpeggione sonata.* ***

Maria Kliegel and Kristin Merscher couple these charming Schumann miniatures with the Schubert *Arpeggione*, though Sony also throw in the Mendelssohn *Variations concertantes*, written for his amateur cellist brother, Paul, and one of the *Songs without words* for good measure. Kliegel and Merscher turn in fresh and musical performances and are recorded in very clean and well-focused sound.

Fantasiestücke, Op. 73.
*** Decca Dig. 430 149-2 [id.]. Cohen, Ashkenazy – BRAHMS: *Clarinet sonatas.* ***

Fantasiestücke, Op. 73; 3 Romances, Op. 94.
*** Chandos Dig. CHAN 8506 [id.]. Gervase de Peyer, Gwenneth Pryor – SCHUBERT: *Arpeggione sonata;* WEBER: *Silvana variations.* ***

With warmth of tone and much subtlety of colour, Gervase de Peyer gives first-class performances and is well supported by Gwenneth Pryor. The recording is most realistic.

A thoroughly recommendable alternative account by Franklin Cohen and Vladimir Ashkenazy of these lovely pieces; if you want them on clarinet, this version is as good as any. It is well recorded, too.

Fantasiestücke, Op. 73; 5 Stücke in Volkston, Op. 102.
*** Ph. (IMS) Dig. 412 230-2 [id.]. Maisky, Argerich – SCHUBERT: *Arpeggione sonata.* ***

Mischa Maisky and Martha Argerich give relaxed, leisurely accounts of these pieces that some collectors will find a bit self-indulgent. Others will luxuriate in the refinement and sensitivity of their playing.

Märchenbilder, Op. 113.
*** Virgin/EMI (SIS) Dig. VC7 59309-2. Lars Anders Tomter, Leif Ove Andsnes – BRAHMS: *Viola sonatas.* *** ✽
**(*) Chandos Dig. CHAN 8550 [id.]. Imai, Vignoles – BRAHMS: *Viola sonatas.* **(*)

The young Norwegian duo bring great sensitivity and freshness to bear on the *Märchenbilder*, and their playing gives great pleasure, as does the Brahms coupling.

The *Märchenbilder* are pleasing miniatures, persuasively played here by Nobuko Imai and Roger Vignoles. The recording acoustic is not ideal, but this does not seriously detract from the value of this coupling.

Piano quartet in E flat, Op. 47; Piano quintet in E flat, Op. 44.
(B) **(*) Hyperion Dyad Dig. CDD 22008 (2) [id.]. Schubert Ens. of L. – HUMMEL: *Piano quintet;* SCHUBERT: *Trout quintet.* **(*)
(M) **(*) CRD CRD 3324; *CRDC 4024* [id.]. Rajna, members of the Alberni Qt.

Lively, committed performances from the Schubert Ensemble of London led by their excellent pianist, William Howard, There are more individual versions of both works but if this inexpensive Dyad compilation seems tempting, the overall standard of musicianship is commendable and their playing enjoyable. Good if not outstanding recording. The Beaux Arts Philips CD remains first choice.

Though not flawlessly polished in their playing, Thomas Rajna and the Alberni give performances that in their way are as urgent and enjoyable as those on the Philips duo. The recording is brighter and crisper, which gives an extra (and not unlikeable) edge to the performances.

Piano quartet in E flat, Op. 47; Piano quintet in E flat, Op. 44; Adagio and allegro in A flat, Op. 70; Andante & variations in B flat, Op. 46; Fantasiestücke, Op. 73; Märchenbilder, Op. 113; Violin sonata No. 2 in D min., Op. 121.
*** EMI (SIS) Dig. CDS5 55484-2 (2). Argerich, Schwarzenberg, Hall, Imai, Maisky, Neunecker, Gutman, Rabinovitch.

These recordings were made at a series of informal concerts at Nijmegen, and they radiate a spontaneity and life that are more difficult to capture under studio conditions. The *Piano quintet* with Argerich, Dora Schwarzenberg, Lucy Hall, Nobuko Imai and Mischa Maisky must be numbered among the most vibrant on record, and the *Piano quartet*, with Natalia Gutman replacing Maisky and with Alexandre Rabinovitch at the piano, is hardly less fine. Although this is an arbitrary collection, those whose needs are met by this particular compilation will not be disappointed.

(i) *Piano quartet in E flat, Op. 47; Piano quintet in E flat, Op. 44. Piano trios Nos. 1 in D min., Op. 63; 2 in F, Op. 80; 3 in G min., Op. 110.*
(B) *** Ph. Duo 456 323-2 (2) [id.]. Beaux Arts Trio, (i) with Dolf Bettelheim and Samuel Rhodes.

Once again Philips have compiled a particularly generous measure for this Duo of Beaux Arts Schumann performances from the 1970s. This illustrious trio (with associates) give splendid readings of the *Piano quartet* and *quintet*. The vitality of inspiration is brought out consistently, and with that goes their characteristic concern for fine ensemble and refined textures. They are also probably the safest bet for the three *Piano trios*. Throughout, the set offers cultured and concentrated music-making, matched by truthful and present analogue recording.

Piano quintet in E flat, Op. 44.
(BB) *** Naxos Dig. 8.550406; *4550406* [id.].

Jenö Jandó, Kodály Qt – BRAHMS: *Piano quintet*. ***
(***) Testament mono SBT 3063 [id.]. Victor Aller, Hollywood Qt – BRAHMS: *Piano quartets* etc. (***)
(BB) **(*) ASV Quicksilva Dig. CDQS 6217 [id.]. Suzanne Bradbury, Silvestri String Qt – BARTOK: *Piano quintet*. **(*)

A strongly characterized performance of Schumann's fine *Quintet* from Jenö Jandó and the Kodály Quartet. This is robust music-making, romantic in spirit, and its spontaneity is well projected by a vivid recording, made in an attractively resonant acoustic. An excellent bargain.

Exhilarating and masterly, the Hollywood Quartet and Victor Aller on Testament comes from the compilation of Brahms chamber music, recorded in the mid 1950s. A performance of some stature which transcends sonic limitations.

Suzanne Bradbury and the Silvestri Quartet give eminently satisfactory performances of the Schumann *Quintet* and, although they would not necessarily be a first choice, they deserve a recommendation, not least on account of the enterprising Bartók coupling.

Piano trios Nos. 1–3; Fantasiestücke in A min., Op. 88.
*** Ph. (IMS) Dig. 432 165-2 (2). Beaux Arts Trio.
**(*) Chandos Dig. CHAN 8832/3 (2) [id.]. Borodin Trio.

Piano trio No. 1 in D min., Op. 63.
(M) **(*) CRD CRD 3433; *CRDC 4133* [id.]. Israel Piano Trio – BRAHMS: *Piano trio No. 2*. **(*)

Piano trios Nos. 2 in F, Op. 80; 3 in G min., Op. 110; Fantasiestücke, Op. 88.
(M) ** CRD Dig. CRD 3458 [id.]. Israel Piano Trio.

The Beaux Arts are probably the safest bet in this repertoire, an instance of the most obvious recommendation being the best. Not that competition is exactly legion, but none that we have heard can outclass them in terms of musicianship and finesse. Cultured playing, matched by truthful and present recording.

On Chandos are full-hearted performances that give undoubted pleasure – and would give more, were it not for some swoons from Rostislav Dubinsky who, at the opening of the *D minor Trio*, phrases with a rather ugly scoop. While too much should not be made of this, greater reticence would have been more telling throughout. The Chandos recording is vivid and faithful.

The Israel Piano Trio give a powerfully projected account of the *D minor Trio*; the pianist is at times rather carried away, as if he were playing a Brahms concerto. There are, however, some sensitive and intelligent touches, and the recording is first class. Nos. 2 and 3 are much the same: lively, articulate playing with a sometimes over-forceful pianist.

Piano trios Nos. 1 in D min., Op. 63; 2 in F, Op. 80.
(M) **(*) Virgin/EMI Dig. CUV5 61313-2 [CDVB 61442 with Mendelssohn *Trios* ***]. Grieg Trio.

These mid-price accounts of the first two Schumann *Trios* are new recordings and not reissues, as is the case of their 1992 Brahms *Trios* on the same label. Their approach to Schumann is admirably forthright and well characterized. The pianist Vebjørn Anvik is a commanding player (sometimes open to the criticism of being too assertive) but always intelligent. His partners have splendid spirit and sensitivity though the recording is a shade lacking in transparency in the middle and lower register. The Beaux Arts offering on two CDs of all three *Piano trios* plus the *Fantasiestücke*, Op. 88, remains a first recommendation, but the Griegs are to be preferred to the overbright Fontenay on Teldec.

String quartet No. 1 in A min., Op. 41/1.
*** RCA Dig. 09026 61438-2 [id.].Vogler Qt – BRAHMS: *String quartet No. 3*. ***

String quartet No. 3 in A, Op. 41/3.
*** RCA Dig. 09026 61866-2 [id.]. Vogler Qt – BRAHMS: *String quartet No. 2*. ***

Fine accounts of both *Quartets* from the Vogler, an extremely fine quartet who have recently recorded the quartets of both Brahms and Schumann. If the coupling meets your particular needs, it would really be difficult to improve on them. They have the advantage of a rich and beautifully blended sonority and refined musicianship. Moreover the RCA recording is very good indeed.

String quartets Nos. 1 in A min.; 2 in F, Op. 41/1–2.
(M) *** CRD CRD 3333; *CRDC 4033* [id.]. Alberni Qt.

These well-recorded and sympathetic performances by the Alberni Quartet have plenty of finesse and charm and are guided throughout by sound musical instinct.

Violin sonatas Nos. 1 in A min., Op. 105; 2 in D min., Op. 121.
*** DG (IMS) Dig. 419 235-2 [id.]. Gidon Kremer, Martha Argerich.

The *Violin sonatas* both date from 1851 and are 'an oasis of freshness' in Schumann's last creative period. Kremer and Argerich are splendidly reflective and mercurial by turn and have the benefit of an excellent recording.

Fünf Stücke in Volkston (for cello and piano).
(M) *** Decca 452 895-2 [id.]. Rostropovich,

Britten – BRITTEN: *Sonata;* DEBUSSY: *Cello sonata in D min.* ***
(N) (M) *** Decca Legends 460 974-2 [id.]. Rostropovich, Britten (as above) – DEBUSSY: *Sonata* ***; SCHUBERT: *Arpeggione sonata.* **(*)

Though simpler than either the Britten or Debussy sonatas with which it is coupled, this is just as elusive a work. Rostropovich and Britten show that the simplicity is not as square and solid as might at first seem and that, in the hands of masters, these *Five Pieces in folk style* have a rare charm, particularly the last with its irregular rhythm. The excellent recording justifies the reissue under the Classic Sound logo, and is also available with Schubert instead of Britten in Decca's Legend series.

PIANO MUSIC

Abegg variations, Op. 1; Davidsbündlertänze, Op. 6.
*** Ottavio Dig. OTRC 39027 [id.]. Imogen Cooper – BRAHMS: *Fantasias, Op. 116.* ***

Imogen Cooper plays the *Abegg variations* with a rare combination of iridescent brilliance and poetic feeling, and she characterizes the *Davidsbündlertänze* with consistent imagination and colour. Her playing is spontaneous from first to last, and the recording most realistic.

Albumblätter, Op. 99; Arabeske, Op. 18; Etudes symphoniques, Op. 13.
(BB) *** Naxos Dig. 8.550144 [id.]. Stefan Vladar.

Stefan Vladar intersperses the additional studies that Schumann published as an appendix into the *Etudes symphoniques*. His account is quite simply superb in every respect and deserves recording of comparable excellence. The *Albumblätter* is hardly less masterly. Artistically this rates three stars, with the compelling quality of the playing transcending the sonic limitations of the recording.

Arabeske in C, Op. 18; Blumenstück, Op. 19; Carnaval, Op. 9; Davidsbündlertänze, Op. 6; Fantasia in C, Op. 17; 8 Fantasiestücke, Op. 12; 3 Fantasiestücke, Op. 111; Faschingsschwank aus Wien, Op. 26; Humoresque in B flat, Op. 20; Kinderszenen, Op. 15; 4 Nachtstücke, Op. 23; Novelletten, Op. 21; Papillons, Op. 2; 3 Romances, Op. 28; Piano sonatas Nos. 1 in F sharp min., Op. 11; 2 in G min., Op. 22; Waldszenen, Op. 82.
(M) **(*) Ph. (IMS) 432 308-2 (7). Claudio Arrau.

Claudio Arrau's playing has warmth, poise and the distinctive, aristocratic finesse that graced everything this artist touched. Arrau has the measure of Schumann's impulsive temperament and is almost always perfectly attuned to his sensibility. Not all the rubati ring true and there are moments that seem a little self-conscious. But there is a very great deal to admire in this compilation, and few collectors will be greatly disappointed.

Arabesque in C, Op. 18; Carnaval, Op. 9; Humoresque in B flat, Op. 20; Toccata in C, Op. 7.
(N) *** BIS Dig. CD-960 [id.]. Freddy Kempf.

A debut recital from Freddy Kempf who caused such a stir at the 1998 Tchaikovsky Competition in Moscow. British viewers will remember him from the BBC Musician of the Year competition some years ago as an artist of quality. His Schumann blends the right amount of intelligence and intuitive feeling. He is at his best in the reflective and inward moments and his *Humoresque* is particularly successful. He has remarkable technical prowess and refined musicianship. The recorded sound is very lively and natural, and the disc as a whole gives much satisfaction.

Arabeske in C, Op. 18; Etudes symphoniques, Op. 13.
**(*) Decca (IMS) Dig. 444 338-2 [id.]. Thibaudet – BRAHMS: *Paganini variations.* **(*)

Jean-Yves Thibaudet is a cultured player who offers good taste and refined pianism. His technical command is second to none, but in terms of poetic insight he must yield to Vladar in the *Arabesque* and the *Symphonic studies*. Those who invest in this disc will find much to satisfy them but, despite good Decca sound, there is not enough to disturb earlier recommendations.

Arabeske, Op. 18; 3 Romanzen; Faschingsschwank aus Wien; Waldszenen.
**(*) DG (IMS) Dig. 437 538-2. Maria João Pires.

Maria João Pires is an artist of insight and temperament. Her Schumann recital is well worth hearing. She is a musician of intuition who is thoroughly inside Schumann's world and though in none of these pieces would her version be a first choice, it is still deserving of recommendation.

Bünte Blätter, Op. 99; Nachstücke, Op. 23; 3 Romanzen, Op. 28.
(N) ** Decca Dig. 452 855-2. Vladimir Ashkenazy.

Ashkenazy's art never falls below a certain level of excellence and often rises to great heights. This beautifully recorded disc, however, rarely takes off and is relatively unexceptional and unmemorable.

Carnaval; Faschingsschwank aus Wien, Op. 26; Kinderszenen, Op. 15.
(B) *** DG Classikon 449 855-2. Daniel Barenboim.

Barenboim's 1979 reading of *Carnaval* is one of

his finest recording achievements as a pianist. His lively imagination lights on the fantasy in this quirkily spontaneous sequence of pieces and makes them sparkle anew. *Carnival jest from Vienna* is more problematic, but the challenge inspires Barenboim, and here too he is at his most imaginative and persuasive, bringing out the warmth and tenderness, as well as the brilliance. The recording is bold and truthful.

Davidsbündlertänze, Op. 6; Sonata No. 2 in G min., Op. 22; Toccata, Op. 7.
*** Teldec/Warner Dig. 9031 77476 [id.]. Boris Berezovsky.

Boris Berezovsky is a keyboard lion of the first order. Everything we have so far heard of his has been of exceptional artistry and great finesse. His formidable musicianship is allied to a technique of magisterial calibre, and this coupling is very impressive indeed.

5 Etudes, Op. posth.; Etudes symphoniques, Op. 13; Papillons, Op. 2.
**(*) Sony [MK 34539]. Murray Perahia.

Murray Perahia has a special feeling for the *Symphonic studies*. He also plays the additional five studies, which Schumann omitted from the published score, as an addendum. The *Papillons* are unlikely to be surpassed but the engineers give Perahia too close a balance to be ideal.

Etudes symphoniques.
(B) *** EMI (SIS) forte Dig. CZS5 69521-2 (2) [CDFB 69521]. Alexeev – BRAHMS: *Fantasias*, etc. ***

Dimitri Alexeev combines the virtuoso technique which the work demands with supreme musicality and poetic feeling, the performance providing a structural cohesion not always in evidence. The digital recording, made several years later than that of the coupling, is excellent in bringing out the warmth of the piano-tone. A first-rate bargain.

Etudes symphoniques, Op. 13; Fantasie in C, Op. 17.
(M) *** Van. 08 9165 72 (2). Brendel (with SCHUBERT: *Piano sonatas Nos. 15 & 19* etc.)

Brendel's opening phrase of the *Symphonic studies* is immediately individual, and yet in essence these readings from the 1960s are not wayward, even though they are strongly personalized. There are other ways of approaching Schumann, but in Brendel's hands the music's structure emerges anew and has the emotional grip one associates with Beethoven. Excellent recording to match the playing.

Etudes symphoniques, Op. 13; Intermezzi, Op. 4; Sonata No. 2 in G min., Op. 22; Toccata, Op. 7.
*** Conifer Dig. 75605 51227-2 [id.]. Mikhail Kazakevich.

Mikhail Kazakevich has a natural feeling for both the virtuosic pianism and the fervour of Schumann together with inwardness and poetic insight. Indeed his is one of the finest accounts of the *G minor Sonata* and the *Etudes symphoniques* to have appeared in recent years. In terms of technical address and subtlety of colouring, Kazakevich is most impressive. The recording is good though just a trifle shallow at times.

Fantasia in C, Op. 17.
(M) *** DG 447 451-2 [id.]. Maurizio Pollini – SCHUBERT: *Wanderer fantasia.* ***
*** Sony Dig. MK 42124 [id.]. Murray Perahia – SCHUBERT: *Wanderer fantasia.* ***

This is among the most distinguished Schumann performances in the catalogue. Pollini's playing throughout has a command and authority on the one hand and deep poetic feeling on the other that hold the listener spellbound. The recording is good but not outstanding. A welcome mid-priced reissue in DG's series of 'Originals'.

Murray Perahia's account of the *C major Fantasy* is a performance of vision and breadth, immaculate in its attention to detail and refinement of nuance. The recording is good, even if it does not wholly convey the fullest range of sonority and dynamics.

Fantasia in C, Op. 17; Faschingsschwank aus Wien (Carnival jest from Vienna), Op. 26; Papillons, Op. 2.
(M) *** EMI (IMS) CDM7 64625-2 [id.]. Sviatoslav Richter.

Richter's 1961 account of the *C major Fantasy* is a wonderfully poetic performance. Richter's phrasing, his magnificent control of dynamics, his gift for seeing a large-scale work as a whole – all these contribute towards the impression of unmatchable strength and vision. The recording is faithful, with genuine presence. The other two works included on this CD were recorded live during Richter's Italian concert tour a year later. The piano sound inevitably is somewhat less sonorous, shallower at *fortissimo* level, but fully acceptable. The account of *Papillons* is beguilingly subtle in control of colour.

Fantasia in C, Op. 17; Kreisleriana, Op. 16.
(M) *** RCA 09026 61264-2 [id.]. Artur Rubinstein.

Rubinstein's account of the *C major Fantasy* is wonderfully subtle in its control of tempo and colour: the poetry of the outer sections is quite magical. In spite of the close balance, Rubinstein achieves exquisite gradations of tone; the recording, made in 1965, is among the best he received during this period. *Kreisleriana* is hardly less compelling, with the great pianist at his most aristocratic, although the recording is a bit shallow.

Fantasiestücke, Op. 12; Kinderszenen, Op. 15; Kreisleriana, Op. 16.
(M) *** Ph. Dig. 434 732-2. Alfred Brendel.

Fantasiestücke is strong as well as poetic. The *Kinderszenen* is also one of the finest performances of the 1980s and is touched with real distinction. Brendel's *Kreisleriana* is intelligent and finely characterized. He is better recorded (in 1981/2) than most of his rivals and, though certain details may strike listeners as less spontaneous, the overall impression is highly persuasive.

Fantasia in C, Op. 17; Piano sonata No. 1 in F sharp min., Op. 11.
(N) ❁ *** EMI Dig. CDC5 56414-2 [id.]. Leif Ove Andsnes.

The young Norwegian pianist gives us the freshest and most vibrant account of the *C major Fantasy* since Murray Perahia, coupled with as fine an account of the *F sharp minor Sonata* as you could find. It is beautifully paced and shaped. This is both magisterial and subtle playing, and well served by the engineers.

Humoreske in B flat, Op. 20.
(BB) **(*) Naxos Dig. 8.550469 [id.]. Wolf Harden – REGER: *Variations.* **(*)

Wolf Harden's performance of the Schumann *Humoreske* is highly imaginative, idiomatic and full of sensitive touches. There is plenty of air round the aural image.

Humoreske, Op. 20; Kinderszenen, Op. 15; Kreisleriana, Op. 16.
*** Decca Dig. 440 496-2 [id.]. Radu Lupu.

Schumann playing of quite exceptional insight and naturalness. Lupu is one of the few artists whose understanding of the composer can be measured alongside that of Murray Perahia. His account of the *Humoreske*, Op. 20, is the most poetic and spontaneous since the famous Richter version (issued over here in the 1950s on Parlophone), and the *Kreisleriana* are hardly less magical. This is playing of great poetry and authority. The recording is excellent, albeit resonant, and although there are odd occasions where twangy notes disturb they are of small moment in playing of such distinction.

Kinderszenen, Op. 15; Kreisleriana, Op. 16; Novellette in F, Op. 21/1.
(M) *** DG Dig. 445 599-2. Vladimir Horowitz.

The subtle range of colour and articulation in *Kreisleriana* is remarkable, but then Horowitz plays in the studio just as if he were in front of a live audience, and the freshness and accuracy would be astonishing if we had not heard him repeating the trick. He was over 80 when he recorded the *Novellette* but the playing betrays remarkably little sign of frailty, and the recording given him by the DG engineers was among the finest he ever received. *Kinderszenen*, however, comes from a live recital, recorded in the Vienna Musikverein in 1987, a delightfully innocent performance never making pianistic points but letting the music speak for itself. The recording is good, but the audience's bronchial afflictions are inevitably a nuisance, even during the early spring of the year! An unmissable collection, just the same.

Kinderszenen, Op. 15; Sonata No. 1 in F sharp min., Op. 11; Waldszenen, Op. 82.
*** Decca (IMS) Dig. 421 290-2 [id.]. Vladimir Ashkenazy.

Ashkenazy has his finger(s) on the pulse of Schumann's inspiration. The playing is very natural and all the more impressive for that. He proves a sound guide in the *Waldszenen*, and his *Kinderszenen* has a naturalness and directness that are attractive. Good Decca recording.

Piano sonata No. 2 in G min., Op. 22.
*** Sony Dig. MK 44569 [id.]. Murray Perahia – SCHUBERT: *Piano sonata No. 20.* ***

Perahia's account of the Schumann *G minor Sonata* is fresh, ardent and vital; every phrase is beautifully moulded yet somehow seems spontaneous in feeling – and spontaneity was the essence of Schumann's youthful genius. The recording places the listener fairly near the piano but is eminently truthful.

ORGAN MUSIC

4 Sketches, Op. 58 (ed. Bate).
(BB) *** ASV Quicksilva CDQS 6127 [id.]. Jennifer Bate (Royal Albert Hall organ) – LISZT: *Organ music.* ***

The *Four Sketches* were originally written for a piano with pedal attachment and are here arranged for organ by E. Power Biggs. Each of the pieces is in 3/4 time, but the writing is attractively diverse; they are pleasant trifles. Rich, atmospheric recording with fair detail, impressively transferred to CD. Generously coupled with Liszt's three major organ warhorses, this makes a very tempting superbargain reissue.

VOCAL MUSIC

The Graham Johnson Lieder Edition

Following up his monumental Schubert song series for Hyperion, Graham Johnson here sets out on his parallel Schumann project with the same inspired combination of scholarship and artistry.

Lieder Vol. 1: *6 Gedichte und Requiem, Op. 90; 6 Gesänge, Op. 107. Aufträge; Die Blume der Ergebung; Er ist's; Heiss'mich nicht reden; Ihr Stimme; Mädchen-Schwermut; Melancholie; Die Meerfee; Mignon (Kennst du das Land?); Nachtlied; Nur wer die Sehnsucht kennt; Röslein,*

Röslein!; Sängers Trost; Singet nicht in Trauertönen; So lasst mich scheinen; Das verlassene Mägdelein; Warnung; Zigeunerliedchen I & II.
(N) *** Hyperion Dig. CDJ 33101 [id.]. Christine Schäfer, Graham Johnson.

For Volume 1, Christine Schäfer is chosen to sing a collection of late songs, written between 1849 and 1852, which reflect the increasing disturbance of the composer's mind in bouts of depression. Though these songs – generally with writing more chromatic than earlier – have been seriously neglected, Schäfer and Johnson consistently show that Schumann's inspiration remained undiminished. The recording, forward and well-balanced, does not always bring out the full sweetness of Schäfer's voice, though the subtlety and beauty of her tonal shading is faithfully caught, in unfailingly sensitive response to word-meaning.

Lieder Vol. 2: *3 Gedichte von Emanuel Geibel, Op. 30; 12 Gedicht von Justinus Kerner, Op. 35; 4 Husarenlieder, Op. 117; An die Türen will ich schleiden; Ballade des Harfners; Die Löwenbraut; Wer nie sein Brot mit Tränen ass; Wer sich der Einsamkeit ergibt.*
(N) *** Hyperion Dig. CDJ 33102 [id.]. Simon Keenlyside, Graham Johnson.

The virility of Simon Keenlyside's strongly projected singing is thrilling. This selection of songs concentrates on four poets, starting with four powerful settings of Goethe from late in Schumann's career, contrasting with light, ballad-like *Hussar songs* also late, to words by Lenau. The other two groups are of early songs, including *Der Hidalgo* to words by Geibel, with sparkling Spanish dance rhythms, and the substantial set of 12 settings of Justinus Kerner, a figure who links the other three poets. Johnson's notes as ever, like his playing, could not be more illuminating.

Lieder Vol. 3: *Frauenliebe und Leben, Op. 42* with poem: *Traum der eignen Tage, 7 Lieder of Elisabeth Kulmann, Op. 104; Songs of Mary Queen of Scots, Op. 135.* Lieder: *Blonde Lied; Geisternähe; Gesungen!; Himmel und Erde; Jasminenstrauch; Die Kartenlegerin; Loreley; Sag'an, o lieber Vogel mein; Schneeglöckchen; Die Soldatenbraut; Stiller Vorwurf.*
(N) *** Hyperion Dig. CDJ 33103 [id.]. Juliane Banse, Graham Johnson.

The young German soprano Juliane Banse, with her warm, vibrant voice beautifully controlled, makes an imaginative choice of artist for this third volume of Graham Johnson's Schumann series. The selection concentrates mainly on songs on the subject of women's life and loves, not just in the ever-popular *Frauenliebe und Leben*. In that cycle, the strong tonal contrasts in Banse's singing heighten the drama throughout, but most of all in the final tragic song. As an epilogue, Banse recites the final poem in Chamisso's cycle, which wisely Schumann did not set. She also reads the composer's superscriptions before the touching songs to poems by Elisabeth Kulmann, a poet who died tragically at 17. Rounding off the disc is the late set of five poems to words by Mary Queen of Scots – as Johnson points out, another 'Frauenliebe' without the 'Leben'. Fine recording and excellent notes.

Lieder from *Album für die Jugend, Op. 79; Gedichte der Königen Maria Stuart, Op. 135; Myrthen Lieder, Op. 25:* excerpts. *Abends am Strand; Die Kartenlegerin; Ständchen; Stille Tränen; Veratine Liebe.*
(M) *** CRD CRD 3401; *CRDC 4051* [id.]. Sarah Walker, Roger Vignoles.

Sarah Walker's 1982 Schumann collection is most cherishable, notably the five Mary Stuart songs which, in their brooding darkness, are among Schumann's most memorable. With superb accompaniment and splendid recording, this is an outstanding issue.

Dichterliebe, Op. 48.
(M) *** DG Originals 449 747-2 [id.]. Fritz Wunderlich, Hubert Giesen – BEETHOVEN; SCHUBERT: *Lieder.* ***

Wunderlich, had he lived, would no doubt have surpassed this early recording of a favourite Schumann song-cycle but, even with an often unimaginative accompanist here, his freshness is most endearing, irresistible with so golden a voice.

Dichterliebe, Op. 48; Liederkreis, Op. 39.
*** Ph. (IMS) Dig. 416 352-2 [id.]. Dietrich Fischer-Dieskau, Alfred Brendel.

Fischer-Dieskau, in inspired collaboration with Alfred Brendel, brings an angry, inconsolable reading, reflecting the absence of fulfilment in the poet's love. The Op. 39 *Liederkreis* also brings inspired, spontaneous-sounding performances, with the voice here notably fresher.

Dichterliebe (song-cycle), *Op. 48; Liederkreis* (song-cycle), *Op. 39; Myrthen Lieder, Op. 25.*
*** DG 415 190-2. Dietrich Fischer-Dieskau, Christoph Eschenbach.

An outstandingly fine *Dichterliebe* plus the magnificent Op. 39 *Liederkreis*, made the more attractive on CD by the generous addition of seven of the *Myrthen* songs. Eschenbach is imaginative without ever being intrusive. Very good sound for the period.

Dichterliebe, Op. 48; Liederkreis, Op. 24. Lieder: *Der arme Peter (I; II; III); Du bist wie eine Blume; Lehn deine Wang'; Die Lotusblume; Mein Wagen rollet langsam; Tragödie (I; II); Was will die einsame Träne.*
*** Ph. Dig. 446 086-2 [id.]. Wolfgang Holzmair, Imogen Cooper.

Holzmair, with his light, tenorish baritone, proves a perfect poet in *Dichterliebe*. Not many recordings so happily combine consistent beauty of tone over a wide range with such ardour, intensity and fine detail, and Imogen Cooper is an inspired accompanist. In the other Heine cycle, the *Liederkreis*, Op. 24, as well as the other songs, Holzmair proves a masterly interpreter, alert and intense but finely controlled. Excellent sound.

Frauenliebe und Leben, Op. 42; 5 Lieder, Op 40 (Märzveilchen; Muttertraume; Der Soldat; Der Spielmann; Verratene Liebe). Lieder: *Abendlied; Dein Angesicht; Die Kartenlegerin; Die Löwenbraut; Lust der Sturmnacht; Mein schöner Stern; Die Meersee; Rose, Meer und Sonne; Der Schatzgräber Schneeglöckchen; Des Sennen Abscheid; Die Soldatenbraut; Stille Liebe; Volksliedchen; Vom Schlaraffenland.*
*** DG Dig. 445 881-2 [id.]. Anne Sofie von Otter, Bengt Forsberg.

Anne Sofie von Otter characterizes the contrasting songs in *Frauenliebe* with exceptional intensity, presenting a character, as in an opera, developing from youthful, eager girl to bereaved widow. By creating a character outside herself, von Otter may for some seem a shade detached compared with other, more personally involved singers, but that strengthens the cycle, minimizing the sentimentality of the poems. This is an exceptionally generous recital (79 minutes) and other songs on the disc are then characterized commandingly, with dramatic contrasts heightened. Try the beautiful Heine setting, *Dein Angesicht* ('Your face'), sung with poise and flawless legato. Excellent sound and fine accompaniment from Forsberg. Highly recommended.

Frauenliebe und Leben, Op. 42; Liederkreis, Op. 39; Aus den östlichen Rosen; Kennt du das Land; Meine rose; Der Nussbaum; Requiem; Die Soldatenbraut; Widmung.
(M) *** Carlton Classics Dig. 30367 02022 [id.]. Felicity Lott, Graham Johnson.

There are several versions of Schumann's *Frauenliebe und Leben* that command our allegiance, yet Felicity Lott and Graham Johnson are highly distinguished. Felicity Lott is a connoisseur's artist, far greater than many more illustrious and publicized rivals, and she sings here with great poise and a completely unaffected artistry. The recording comes from 1990 and is not new, but the finesse and musicianship of this partnership, as well as the intelligence which guides everything they do, make it treasurable. The sound, too, is very good indeed.

12 Gedichte, Op. 35; Liederkreis, Op. 39.
(N) *** Decca Dig. 460 797-2 [id.]. Matthias Goerne, Eric Schneider.

Matthias Goerne's earlier Schubert recital with Ashkenazy was much and widely admired and this coupling of the Op. 39 *Liederkreis* and the 12 songs of Op. 35 is hardly less fine. Goerne's silken, soft-grained tone and his elegant phrasing will win him and his partner Eric Schneider many new friends. There are times when some may feel he underprojects, favouring an almost whispered delivery but his intelligence and discernment are never in doubt. Good Decca recording.

Liederkreis, Op. 39; 12 Kerner Lieder, Op. 35.
(B) *** Hyperion Helios Dig. CDH 55011 [id.]. Dame Margaret Price, Graham Johnson.

As a spin-off from Graham Johnson's Schubert recording with Dame Margaret Price (No. 15 in the series), Johnson partners her here in a superb Schumann disc, coupling the sequence of *12 settings of Justinus Kerner*, Op. 35, with the Eichendorff *Liederkreis*, Op. 39. The singer's presence, magnetism and weight of expression are superbly caught, and the tonal beauty and immaculate sense of line go with detailed imagination in word-pointing. Price may underplay the horror of such a song from Opus 39 as *Waldesgesprach* about meeting the Lorelei, but the moment of confrontation is sharply pointed when legato is suddenly abandoned. The lesser-known *Kerner Lieder* also contain many treasures. First-rate sound. Full notes and texts with translations are included in this bargain reissue.

Das Paradies und die Peri.
(B) *** RCA Twofer Dig. 74321 34173-2 (2) [id.]. Büchner, Schmil, Kaufmann, Planté, Schopper, Sweet, Schmiege, Subrata, Titus, Schopper, Bamberg Ch. & SO, Kuhn.

Though Clara Schumann described this secular oratorio as the most beautiful work that her husband had yet written, it cannot match the songs that he was writing at the same time. Even so, this morality on the theme of salvation has many beauties.

The RCA Twofer derives from the Eurodisc catalogue. Gustav Kuhn offers a fine team of soloists and bright, well-balanced recording. The two most important soloists are certainly characterful, Sharon Sweet powerful if not always ideally firm as the Peri and Eberhard Büchner clear, fresh and keenly idiomatic as the first tenor.

(i) *Requiem in D flat, Op. 148;* (ii) *Requiem für Mignon, Op. 98b.*
(B) *** EMI Dig. CZS7 67819-2 (2). (i) Helen Donath, Doris Soffel, Nicolai Gedda; (i; ii) Dietrich Fischer-Dieskau; (ii) Brigitte Lindner, Andrea Andonian, Mechthild George, Monika Weichhold; Düsseldorf Musical Soc. Ch., Düsseldorf SO, Klee – BRAHMS: *German Requiem.* **(*)

Like Mozart, Schumann was unable to shake off the

conviction that the *Requiem* was for himself. The opening *Requiem aeternam* is affecting and dignified, and the final *Benedictus* has a haunting eloquence. Bernhard Klee extracts a very sympathetic response from his distinguished team of soloists and the fine Düsseldorf chorus and orchestra. They also give an attentive and committed account of the 1849 *Requiem for Mignon*, Op. 98b. The EMI recording is natural and well balanced. This now comes in harness with Tennstedt's impressively spacious account of the Brahms *Requiem*.

Der Rose Pilgerfahrt, Op. 112.
*** Chandos Dig. CHAN 9350 [id.]. Inga Nielsen, Deon van der Walt, Annemarie Møller, Guido Paevatalu, Danish Nat. R. Ch. and SO, Gustav Kuhn.

Schumann wrote his cantata, *Der Rose Pilgerfahrt* ('The Pilgrimage of the rose'), in 1851 towards the end of his career, and the pity is that such a charming, fresh inspiration is so little known, for it defies the usual verdict that Schumann's later music lacks the spark which fired him earlier. The very opening has the lyrical openness of Schubert, its freshness enhanced by the interplay of solo voices and women's chorus. The idiom, as well as recalling Schubert, often suggests the folk-based writing of Humperdinck in *Hänsel und Gretel*, similarly innocent-seeming, but in fact subtle. Gustav Kuhn conducts an aptly bright and atmospheric performance, very well recorded, with Inga Nielsen and Deon van der Walt in the two principal roles. The chorus and orchestra are first rate and the recording, sponsored by Danish Radio, is full-bodied and atmospheric. A valuable rarity. Sadly, the booklet contains no translation alongside the German text, though Richard Wigmore's note and summary are very helpful.

Scenes from Goethe's Faust.
❁ (M) *** Decca (IMS) 425 705-2 (2). Harwood, Pears, Shirley-Quirk, Fischer-Dieskau, Vyvyan, Palmer, Aldeburgh Festival Singers, ECO, Britten.
**(*) Sony Dig. SK 66308 (2) [id.]. Terfel, Mattila, Rootering, Bonney, Wottrich, Vermillion, Poschner-Klebel, Graham, Blochwitz, Peeters, BPO, Abbado.

Though the episodic sequence of scenes is neither opera nor cantata, the power and imagination of much of the music, not least the delightful garden scene and the energetic setting of the final part, are immensely satisfying. In 1972, soon after a live performance at the Aldeburgh Festival, Britten inspired his orchestra and his fine cast of singers to vivid performances, which are outstandingly recorded against the warm Maltings acoustic. This is magnificent music, and readers are urged to explore it – the rewards are considerable.

Abbado's recording was taken live from concert performances in June 1994, using a cast, headed by Bryn Terfel in the title-role and with Karita Mattila as Gretchen, that could hardly be bettered at the time. Abbado's direction is strong and sympathetic, and the singing good; but one has only to go back to Benjamin Britten's inspired Decca recording of 1972 to find even keener imagination, not just in the conducting but in the singing too. Bryn Terfel is thoughtful and expressive as Faust, but Fischer-Dieskau was far more illuminating and detailed; Elizabeth Harwood as Gretchen sang even more radiantly than Mattila, bringing out the heroine's tenderness and vulnerability; and Jan-Hendrik Rootering as Mephistopheles is not as characterful as John Shirley-Quirk. The analogue 1972 sound is also rather cleaner than the 1994 digital, but, were the Decca set to become unavailable, this Sony will always provide a most enjoyable recording of an all-too-rare work.

Schurmann, Gerard (born 1928)

6 Studies of Francis Bacon for large orchestra; Variants for small orchestra.
*** Chandos CHAN 9167 [id.]. BBC SO, composer.

Inspired by the fantastic, often violent or painful paintings of Francis Bacon, Schurmann here writes a virtuoso orchestral showpiece, full of colourful effects. The vigour of the writing is admirably caught both in this performance and in the often spiky writing of the *Variants* for a rather smaller orchestra, set against passages of hushed beauty. First-rate 1979 recording, made in the warm acoustics of All Saints', Tooting, and admirably transferred to CD.

Schütz, Heinrich (1585–1672)

Christmas story (Weihnachthistorie).
(M) *** Virgin Veritas/EMI (SIS) VM5 61353-2. Kirkby, Rogers, Thomas, Taverner Cons., Taverner Ch., Taverner Players, Parrott – PRAETORIUS: *Christmas motets.* ***

Christmas story (Weihnachthistorie); 3 Cantiones sacrae (1625); Psalm 100.
(BB) *** Naxos Dig. 8.553514 [id.]. Agnew, Crookes, MacCarthy, Oxford Camerata, Summerly.

The reissued EMI version of Schütz's *Christmas story*, now on Virgin Veritas, has the advantage of three first-class soloists, all of whom are in excellent voice. One is soon gripped by the narrative and the beauty and simplicity of the line. There is no sense of austerity here, merely a sense of purity, with the atmosphere of the music beautifully captured by these forces under Andrew Parrott. Apart from a rather nasal edge on the violin tone, it is difficult to fault either this moving performance or the well-balanced and refined recording.

Summerly with his talented group of 10 singers – two of them doubling as soloists – give a compelling reading of Schütz's vivid and compact telling of the *Christmas story*. Aptly austere in its overall manner, with clear instrumental accompaniment, it yet brings out the beauty and vigour of the numbers depicting the different groups, in turn the angels, the shepherds and the wise men. The scholarly credentials are impeccable, with excellent notes provided, and the recording, made in Hertford College, Oxford, is full and vivid. The motets and the psalm-setting make a welcome fill-up.

Christmas story; Easter oratorio (Historia der Auferstehung Jesus Christi).
*** Sony Dig. SK 45943 [id.]. Prégardien, Van der Sluis, Egeler, Kendall, Müller, Robson, Spägele, Stuttgart Chamber Ch., Cologne Musici Fiata, Stuttgart Bar. O, Bernius.

Bernius's fine account of the *Christmas story* on Sony is certainly as good as any available, if not better, and enjoys the advantage of another major Schütz coupling, the *Historia der Auferstehung Jesus Christi*, a performance of exceptionally gripping quality. Schütz's second liturgical work after *The Psalms of David*, this *Easter oratorio* dates from 1623 and draws on both the text and the musical procedures of the *Easter Historia* by Antonio Scandello, one of Schütz's predecessors at Dresden. The work is one of grave, expressive beauty and a moving purity of utterance, and the performance here is excellent. It is more strongly projected than the inward and reposeful performance by René Jacobs and the Concerto Vocale on Harmonia Mundi (HMC 90 1311). On Sony Christopher Prégardien is an excellent Evangelist and Frieder Bernius has the advantage of first-rate soloists in Mieke van der Sluis, Andrea Egeler and Mona Spägele. Christoph Robson's Jesus is also moving. Bernius maintains an excellent sense of pace through both works and the instrumentalists are excellently balanced and recorded. Artistically and as a recording, this is among the finest of Schütz issues.

Deutsche Magnificat; Musikalische Exequien; Motets: Herr, nun lässest du deinen Diener (3 settings); *Vater unser, der du bist im Himmel.*
(N) *** Collins Dig. 1530-2 [id.]. The Sixteen, Symphony of Harmony and Invention, Harry Christophers.

To have the splendid *Deutsche Magnificat*, Schütz's last work, appropriately coupled with the extraordinary *Musikalische Exequien*, spectacularly conceived for double choir, and using the *Nunc dimittis* dramatically in the closing section, is marvellous. As a makeweight, three further settings of the latterpiece are included, one for solo bass and and the remaining pair for six-part ensemble, plus Schütz's very individual setting of *The Lord's Prayer*. The Sixteen are well up to their highest standard and the performances here beautifully recorded in St Augustin's Church, Kilburn.

Italian Madrigals (complete).
(B) *** HM HMA 1901162 [id.]. Concerto Vocale, René Jacobs.

Schütz's first and only *Book of Italian Madrigals* reflects his encounter with the music of Giovanni Gabrieli and Monteverdi. The Concerto Vocale, led by the counter-tenor, René Jacobs, employ a theorbo which provides added variety of colour, and at times they offer great expressive and tonal range. They omit the very last of the madrigals, the eight-part *Vasto mar*.

Motets: *Auf dem Gebirge; Der Engel sprach; Exultavit cor meum; Fili mi Absolon; Heu mihi Domine; Hodie Christus natus est; Ich danke Dir, Herr; O quam tu pulchra es; Die Seele Christi, helige mich; Selig sind die Todten.*
(BB) *** ASV Quicksilva CDQS 6105 [id.]. Pro Cantione Antiqua, L. Cornett & Sackbut Ens., Restoration Ac., Edgar Fleet.

An eminently useful and well-recorded super-bargain anthology of Schütz motets that offers such masterpieces as *Fili mi Absolon* (for bass voice, five sackbuts, organ and violone continuo) and the glorious *Selig sind die Todten* in well-thought-out and carefully prepared performances under Edgar Fleet. These accounts have a dignity and warmth that make them well worth considering. Moreover the CD transfer is excellently managed, the sound rich and clear.

Musicalische Exequien. Motets: *Auf dem Gebirge; Freue dich des Weibes Jugend; Ist nicht Ephraim mein teurer Sohn; Saul, Saul, was verfolgst du mich.*
*** DG (IMS) Dig. 423 405-2 [id.]. Monteverdi Ch., E. Bar. Soloists, His Majesties Sackbutts & Cornetts, Gardiner.

Schütz's *Musical Exequien* contains music that is amazing for its period. The Monteverdi Choir responds with fiery intensity, making light of the complex eight-part writing in the second of the three *Exequien*. Four more superb motets by Schütz make an ideal coupling, with first-rate recorded sound.

O bone Jesu, fili Mariae.
(M) *** DG Dig. 447 298-2. Monteverdi Ch., E. Bar. Soloists, Gardiner – BUXTEHUDE: *Membra Jesu nostri.* ***

A wonderfully eloquent performance of this *Spiritual concerto* by one of the greatest of baroque masters. Schütz juxtaposes stanzas of a poem ascribed to St Bernard of Clairvaux with prose passages of Latin devotional literature, treating the latter as recitative and the former set homophonically, and ending the cantata in *concertato* style. Beautifully recorded.

The Psalms of David (Psalmen Davids).
*** Sony Dig. S2K 48042 (2) [id.]. Stuttgart Chamber Ch. & Soloists, Cologne Musica Fiata, Wilson & Bernius.

The Psalms of David (1619) was the first work Schütz composed on his return to northern Europe after his years in Venice with Giovanni Gabrieli. The Sony version, recorded in 1991, is complete and the Stuttgart Chamber Choir and the Musica Fiata Köln under Frieder Bernius give both lively and expressive accounts; all the pieces were recorded in the course of a few days and the performances in some cases are a little routine. For the most part, however, this is a very fine and recommendable set, very thoroughly annotated and a considerable advance over the Archiv set made in 1971–2 by the Regensburger Domspätzen and the Hamburger Bläserkreis under Hans Martin Schneidt.

Psalm 150.
(B) **(*) EMI (SIS) forte CZS5 68631-2 (2) [CDFB 68631]. Cambridge University Musical Soc., Bach Ch., King's College Ch., Wilbraham Brass Soloists, Willcocks – G. GABRIELI: *Motets* etc. **(*) (with MONTEVERDI: *Vespers*. *(*))

Schütz's setting of *Psalm 150* is for double choirs and soloists, each used in juxtaposition against the others, with built-in antiphony an essential part of the composer's conception. The majesty of Schütz's inspiration certainly comes over vividly here, the closing *Alleluja* having remarkable weight and richness, though the overall focus of the recording is not absolutely clean. In the coupled Monteverdi *Vespers* there is actual distortion and the performance is disappointing.

The Resurrection (Easter oratorio); Meine Seele erhebt den Herren.
(M) *** HM Dig. HMT 7901311 [id.]. Concerto Vocale, René Jacobs.

René Jacobs's account of Schütz's *Historia der Auferstehung Jesu Christi* with the Concerto Vocale is a performance of great accomplishment and taste, and quite beautifully recorded. This performance still gives great pleasure, as does the lively account of *Meine Seele erhebt den Herren* from the second Book of the *Symphoniae sacrae* (1647). This makes a fine mid-priced alternative to Bernius's excellent Sony version, which includes also the *Christmas story* (SK 45943).

Sacred choral music (1648).
(M) **(*) HM/BMG Dig. GD 77171 (2) [id.]. Knabenchor Hannover, Heinz Hennig.

The Hanover recording of the Schütz *Geistliche Chormusik* comes from the early 1980s. It is of particular value in that it offers not only all 29 motets of the collection but also alternative versions of seven of them, two in more than one form. The notes are scholarly and helpful, and at mid-price it remains an attractive proposition. On the whole the singing is very good, though the tone of the Knabenchor of Hanover is not always perfectly focused; the recording, while generally acceptable, is at times a little opaque.

Der Schwanengesang (Opus ultimum; reconstructed by Wolfgang Steude).
(M) *** Virgin Veritas/EMI (SIS) VED5 61306-2 (2). Hannover Knabenchor, Hilliard Ens., L. Bar., Heinz Hennig.

Schütz's *Opus ultimum* is a setting of Psalm 119, the longest psalm in the psalter, which he divides into 11 sections. He finishes off this 13-part motet cycle with his final setting of Psalm 100, which he had originally composed in 1662, and the *Deutsches Magnificat*. Wolfram Steude's note recounts the history of the work, parts of which disappeared after Schütz's death; and his reconstruction of two of the vocal parts is obviously a labour of love. The performance is a completely dedicated one, with excellent singing from all concerned and good instrumental playing, and the conductor, Heinz Hennig, secures warm and responsive singing from his Hannover Knabenchor. The acoustic is spacious and warm and the recording balance well focused. The sound is firm, clear and sonorous.

Sinfoniae sacrae, Op. 66/2–13, 15, 17–19 (SWV 258–269, 271, 273–5).
(M) *** Erato/Warner Dig. 4509 96964-2. Dietschy, Bellamy, Laurens, Zaepfel, Elwes, De Mey, Fabre-Garrus, Les Saqueboutiers de Toulouse.

Schütz's 20 *Sinfoniae sacrae* of 1629, of which 16 are included here, are the result of the Dresden composer's second visit to Italy in 1628, when he was strongly influenced by Monteverdi and the Italian *concertato* style. These pieces fascinatingly combine voices and instruments in a single texture, usually with an interweaving interplay, and rarely with the instruments acting just as an obbligato. The performances are eminently stylish and freshly spontaneous, and the instrumentalists are expert – and, moreover, play in tune. The balance is beautifully judged, with voices and instruments within the same perspective, and the digital recording is wholly realistic.

Scriabin, Alexander (1872–1915)

(i) *Piano concerto in F sharp min., Op. 20;* (ii) *Poème de l'extase, Op. 54;* (i) *Prometheus – The poem of fire, Op. 60.*

*** Decca 417 252-2 [id.]. (i) Ashkenazy, LPO; (ii) Cleveland O; Maazel.

Ashkenazy plays the *Piano concerto* with great authority. *Prometheus* too, powerfully atmospheric and curiously hypnotic, is given a thoroughly poetic and committed reading and Ashkenazy copes with the virtuoso obbligato part with predictable distinction. Maazel's 1979 Cleveland recording of *Le Poème de l'extase* is a shade too efficient to be really convincing. The playing is often brilliant and the recording is very clear but the trumpets are rather forced and strident. However, it can be regarded as a bonus for the other two works.

Symphonies Nos. 1–3; Poème de l'extase; (i) *Prometheus.*

*** EMI CDS7 54251-2 (3) [CDC 54251]. Toczyska, Myers, Westminster Ch. (in *No. 1*), Phd. O, Muti, (i) with Alexeev.

Muti's complete set of the Scriabin symphonies can be recommended almost without reservation; overall the sound is as vivid and richly coloured as the performances. With the two later symphonies-cum-symphonic poems (*Le Poème de l'extase* white-hot with passionate intensity, yet masterfully controlled) now added, this is an impressive achievement.

(i) *Symphonies Nos. 2 in C min., Op. 29;* (ii) *3 in C min. (Le divin poème);* (iii) *Le poème de l'extase, Op. 54;* (i) *Rêverie, Op. 24.*

(N) (B) *** Chandos 2-for-1 Dig. CHAN 241-5 (2) [id.]. (i) RSNO; (ii) Danish Nat. RSO; (iii) Chicago SO; Neeme Järvi.

Although it is less amorphous than its predecessor, the *Second Symphony* needs the most fervent advocacy if the listener is to be persuaded. The splendid account from Järvi, with its richly detailed recording, can be recommended strongly. The mammoth *Third Symphony* calls for vast forces, but there is no doubt that it is original, both in layout and in substance. There is something refreshingly unforced and natural about Järvi's version, which puts this score in a far better light than those conductors who play it for all they are worth. Järvi's version of *Le poème de l'extase*, played superbly and recorded vividly and resonantly in Chicago's Orchestral Hall, emphasizes Scriabin's primary colours, with the trumpet solo penetrating boldly through the voluptuous texture and skirting vulgarity by a small margin. There have been more subtle performances, but this one certainly makes a strong impact.

Symphony No. 3 (Le divin poème); Le Poème de l'extase, Op. 54; Rêverie, Op. 24.

*** Decca (IMS) Dig. 430 843-2. Berlin RSO, Ashkenazy.

Vladimir Ashkenazy has the advantage of an all-Scriabin programme, and good engineering from the Decca team. The Berlin Radio forces are very good and there is a highly charged feel to the performances, particularly that of *Le Poème de l'extase.*

Le Poème de l'extase, Op. 54.

(M) *** Sony SM2K 64100 (2) [id.]. NYPO, Boulez – BARTOK: *Wooden Prince* etc. **(*)

(M) **(*) Decca (IMS) Phase 4 443 898-2 [id.]. Czech PO, Stokowski – MUSSORGSKY: *Pictures at an exhibition* **; STRAVINSKY: *Firebird suite; Pastorale.* **(*)

Boulez's electrifying account of *Le Poème de l'extase* (not previously released) has great ardour and splendid control. The all-important trumpet part emerges from within a texture that is inherently voluptuous, even if the sound-quality itself could be more alluring. This needs to be recoupled more appropriately on a single CD.

Stokowski's version of the *Poème de l'extase* was recorded live when the nonagenarian conductor visited Prague. The result, carefully edited from more than one performance, has all the passionate commitment of a concert-hall performance, with the ebb and flow of tension and the flexibiity of phrasing the more compellingly captured. The Phase Four recording highlights individual instruments, but not disastrously so.

Prometheus (The poem of fire), Op. 60.

(N) *** Ph. Dig. 446 715-2 [id.]. Alexander Toradze, Kirov Op. Ch & O., Valery Gergiev – STRAVINSKY: *Firebird* (complete ballet). ***

(N) (***) Music & Arts mono CD 967 [id.]. VPO, Dmitri Mitropoulos – SCHOENBERG: *Pelleas und Melisande, Op. 5a.* (***)

On Philips an *echt*-Russian account of *Prometheus,* with a suitably inflammable pianist in the person of Alexander Toradze. This is the only current recording by a Russian orchestra and under Gergiev's masterly direction they given an outstanding account of this voluptuous and gloriously decadent score. The recording, too, is in the demonstration class even if the pianist is perhaps slightly too forwardly placed in the aural picture. It comes with an appropriately incandescent *Firebird,* marvellously played and recorded.

The Mitropoulos is a fine account not quite as well recorded as his New York version. Despite its sonic limitations, this is well worth considering.

PIANO MUSIC

Etudes, Op. 8/7 & 12; Op. 42/5. Preludes, Op. 11/1, 3, 9, 10, 13, 14, 16; Op. 13/6; Op. 15/2; Op. 16/1 & 4; Op. 27/1; Op. 48/3; Op. 51/2; Op. 59/2; Op. 67/1. Sonatas Nos. 3, Op. 23; 5, Op. 53.

(M) (***) RCA mono/stereo GD 86215 [6215-2-RC]. Vladimir Horowitz.

The RCA engineers have done wonders to these

recordings from the 1950s though some of the original shallowness and clatter remains. The *Preludes* and the legendary account of the *Third Sonata* come from 1956. The *Fifth* is much later, coming from the mid 1970s, and has more bloom. The performances form an essential part of any good Horowitz collection.

Mazurkas, Op. 3/1–10; Op. 25/1–9; Op. 40/1–2.
*** Collins Dig. 1394-2 [id.]. Artur Pizarro.

Apart from Chopin, Scriabin is the only composer to have raised the mazurka to an art-form. These are often exquisite miniature tone-poems, and they are splendidly played and recorded. Artur Pizarro is a Leeds Competition Prizewinner, and listening to this record one sees why his artistry was so much admired.

24 Preludes, Op. 11
(N) *** Collins Dig. 1496-2 [id.]. Artur Pizarro – SHOSTAKOVICH: *24 Preludes, Op. 34.* ***

Pizarro is totally attuned to the sensibility of early Scriabin and his performance of the Op. 11 *Preludes* can scarcely be flawed at any point. Nor can the recording. A distinguished issue.

Piano sonatas Nos. 1–10; Sonate-fantaisie in G sharp min.
*** Hyperion Dig. CDA 67131/2 [id.]. Marc-André Hamelin.

Piano sonatas Nos. 1–10; Etude in C sharp min., Op. 2/1; Feuillet d'album, Op. 58; 2 Morceaux, Op. 57; 2 Poèmes, Op. 63; 4 Preludes, Op. 48; 5 Preludes, Op. 64; 2 Preludes, Op. 67; Vers la flamme, Op. 72.
(B) *** EMI forte CZS5 72652-2 (2) [id.]. John Ogdon.

Piano sonatas Nos. 1–10; 2 Danses, Op. 73; 4 Morceaux, Op. 51; 4 Morceaux, Op. 56; 2 Poèmes, Op. 32.
(B) *** Decca Double Analogue/Dig. 452 961-2 (2) [id.]. Vladimir Ashkenazy.

Marc-André Hamelin commands the feverish intensity, the manic vision, wide dynamic range and fastidious pedalling that Scriabin must have. There are other fine Scriabin cycles and, of course, celebrated accounts of single sonatas from Horowitz, Richter and Donna Amato, but of newer cycles Hamelin's must now be a first recommendation.

Ogdon is nothing if not persuasive, and the only reservation one need feel about his playing is an occasional tendency to be less than scrupulous in observing dynamic indications and a certain lack of finish. His account of the *Tenth Sonata*, however, is particularly fine, and if in the *Ninth* (*The Black Mass*) he does not match the demonic fury and power of Horowitz (and who, for that matter, does?) his is still a thoroughly felt and vividly realized reading. The shorter pieces are particularly appealing (the richly coloured *Etude in C sharp minor* which opens the first disc should tempt anyone to explore further). The piano is very well recorded throughout (at Abbey Road in 1971).

Ashkenazy's Scriabin set was reissued on a Double Decca to celebrate his sixtieth birthday. The recordings were made over a decade between 1972 and 1984 in the Kingsway Hall, Walthamstow, or All Saints', Petersham, but the sound is remarkably consistent. Ashkenazy is clearly attuned to this repertoire: he is as thoroughly at home in the miniatures as in the sonatas, readily finding their special atmosphere and colour. If he is at his very finest in the earlier sonatas, the last three are given with brilliance and vision, and there is no lack of awareness of the demonic side of Scriabin's personality.

Piano sonata No. 3 in F sharp min., Op. 23; 2 Poèmes, Op. 32; Vers la flamme, Op. 72.
**(*) Kingdom Dig. KCLCD 2001. Gordon Fergus-Thompson – BALAKIREV: *Piano sonata.* **(*)

Gordon Fergus-Thompson here gives a splendid account of Scriabin's overheated *F sharp minor Sonata* and sensitive, atmospheric performances of the other pieces here. A reverberant but good recording.

Piano sonatas Nos. 8, Op. 66; 9, Op. 68; 10, Op. 70; 2 Danses, Op. 73; 2 Poèmes, Op. 69; 2 Poèmes, Op. 71; 2 Preludes, Op. 67; 5 Preludes, Op. 74; Vers la flamme, Op. 72.
*(**) Altarus Dig. AIR-CD 9020 [id.]. Donna Amato.

Donna Amato seems wholly attuned to Scriabin's sensibility and plays all his late music (Opp. 66–74), including the last three Sonatas, to the manner born. Scriabin's world is claustrophobic – but unfortunately so is the recording, which sounds as if it was made in a small acoustic environment but with some echo added. The sound-quality diminishes the pleasure this CD gives but not of course Amato's artistry.

Sculthorpe, Peter (born 1929)

(i) *Nourlangie* (for solo guitar, strings and percussion). *From Kakadu; Into the dreaming.*
*** Sony Dig. SK 53361 [id.]. John Williams; (i) Australian CO, Richard Hickox – WESTLAKE: *Antarctica suite.* ***

Peter Sculthorpe, born in Tasmania, finds much of his inspiration in the Australian landscape. *Nourlangie* is an extraordinarily imaginative and evocative piece, inspired by the composer's first sight of the enormous monolithic rock of that name in the Kakadu National Park. The music fuses evocation (the opening, with sounding gongs, is very compelling) and local dance song, which are effectively and naturally integrated into the texture to give a strong underlying melodic vein. The performance here is superb, with John Williams's guitar heard in a concertante role, admirably balanced within the overall sound-picture. The other two pieces are for solo guitar. *From Kakadu* is an intimate, improvisatory piece, somewhat minimalist in conception, in four changing sections. *Into the dreaming* opens mystically but generates much energy in its central section before returning to the restrained mood of the opening. John Williams plays both pieces with total spontaneity and complete improvisational freedom. He is most naturally, if forwardly, recorded. Highly recommendable.

Searle, Humphrey (1915–82)

Symphonies Nos. 1, Op. 23; 4, Op. 38; Night music, Op. 2; Overture to a drama, Op. 17.
(N) *** CPO Dig. CPO 999 541-2 [id.]. BBC Scottish SO, Alun Francis.

Although he was a pupil of Webern, Humphrey Searle could think in long paragraphs as these symphonies show. The *First*, composed in 1952–3, is the more familiar as it was recorded in 1960 by Sir Adrian Boult and the LPO. The basic 12-note series is drawn from Webern's Op. 28 *Quartet*, but the overall musical character is far from the doctrinaire serialism of the 1950s and 1960s. There is an impressive breadth and concentration, and a powerful sense of menace. The *Fourth Symphony* (1960–62) is stark and severe, again intensely concentrated, and far from easily assimilated – but then why should everything be 'accessible'? It is a tough nut to crack but one worth taking trouble with. Two earlier pieces – the *Night music* (1943), a tribute to Webern on his 60th birthday, and the *Overture to a drama* (1949) – complete a disc that makes a representative introduction to this fine composer. Excellent playing and recording.

Seiber, Mátyás (1905–60)

Clarinet concertino.
*** Hyperion Dig. CDA 66215 [id.]. Thea King, ECO, Litton – BLAKE: *Concerto;* LUTOSLAWSKI: *Dance preludes.* ***

Mátyás Seiber's highly engaging *Concertino* was sketched during a train journey (in 1926, before the days of seamless rails) and certainly the opening *Toccata* has the jumpy, rhythmic feeling of railway line joints and points. Yet the haunting slow movement has a touch of the ethereal, while the Scherzo has a witty jazz element. Thea King has the measure of the piece; she is accompanied well by Andrew Litton, and very well recorded.

Four French folk songs: Réveillez-vous; J'ai descendu; Le Rossignol; Marguerite, elle est malade.
(M) *** RCA 09026 61601-2. Peter Pears, Julian Bream (guitar) – BRITTEN: *Songs from the Chinese*, etc; WALTON: *Anon in love.* ***

Mátyás Seiber's arrangements of four French folk-songs are enchantingly simple and, as Bream says, the accompaniments 'use the guitar adroitly'. They bring ravishing tone and line from Pears. Vivid recording, made by a Decca team, but it was unconscionable of RCA not to provide translations, even if one can enjoy the songs without them.

Seixas, Carlos de (1704–42)

Harpsichord concerto in A; Sinfonia in B flat; Keyboard sonatas Nos. 1, 16, 32–3, 42, 46–7, 57, 71 & 79.
*** Virgin Veritas/EMI (SIS) Dig. VC5 45114-2. Ketil Haugsand, Norwegian Bar. O.

The Portuguese composer Carlos Seixas spent his life as an organist in Lisbon, also teaching harpsichord at the Court. He is revealed here as having a distinct musical personality, and the jolly outer movements of his *A major Concerto* – separated by only a brief Adagio – are enjoyably spirited in the hands of Ketil Haugsand, who also conducts the excellent period orchestral group. The *Sinfonia* is essentially an Italian overture with a fast closing minuet, and the *Keyboard sonatas* also show Italian influences. The earlier works are in a single movement, but the last three are more ambitious. This is not great music but always inventive and very personable, and it is effectively presented here and very well recorded.

Motets: *Adebat Vincentius; Tantum ergo.*
(M) *** DG Codex 453 182-2. Jennifer Smith, Magali, Schwartz, Fernando Serafim, Gulbenkian Chamber Ch. & O, Michel Corboz – ALMEIDA: *Beatus vir*, etc.; CARVALHO: *Te Deum;* TEIXEIRA: *Gaudate, astra.* ***

Carlos de Seixas was a contemporary of Almeida and Teixeira, with whom he is joined in this stimulating collection of motets used to back up the Carvalho *Te Deum*. *Adebat Vincentius* brings a lively interplay within the double chorus, juxtaposed with a soprano/contralto duet, and thus makes a fine contrast with the serenely beautiful setting of *Tantum ergo*. Fine singing and first-class recording enhance the appeal of this eloquent music.

Serly, Tibor (1901–78)

Rhapsody for viola and orchestra.
(N) (BB) *** Naxos Dig. 8.554183 [id.]. Hong-Mei Xiao, Budapest PO, Kovacs – BARTOK: *Viola concerto (2 versions; ed. Bartok & ed. Serly); Two pictures.* ***

Tibor Serly, friend of Bartók and first editor of the unfinished *Viola concerto*, here offers a closely related work, less individual than Bartók's own, but well worth hearing. Beautifully played by the Chinese viola-player, Hong-Mei Xiao, it provides a good makeweight for the disc containing both editions of the Bartók concerto.

Sessions, Roger (1896–1985)

Concerto for orchestra.
*** Hyperion Dig. CDA 66050 [id.]. Boston SO, Ozawa – PANUFNIK: *Symphony No. 8.* ***

Sessions's *Concerto for orchestra* finds him at his thorniest and most uncompromising, with lyricism limited to fleeting fragments of melody; but the playful opening leads one on finally to a valedictory close, sharply defined. Ozawa makes a powerful advocate, helped by superb playing from the Boston orchestra.

Symphony No. 4; Symphony No. 5; Rhapsody for orchestra.
*** New World Dig. NW 345 [id.]. Columbus SO, Badea.

Roger Sessions shares with Walter Piston, his tonal contemporary, a highly developed sense of structure and an integrity that remained unshaken by changes of fashion. His musical language is dense and his logic is easier to sense than to follow. The performances by the Columbus Symphony Orchestra under Christian Badea appear well prepared, and there is no doubt as to their commitment and expertise. The sound ideally needs a larger acoustic, but every strand in the texture is well placed and there is no feeling of discomfort.

Shapero, Harold (born 1920)

Symphony for classical orchestra; Nine-minute overture.
**(*) New World Dig NW 373-2 [id.]. LAPO, Previn.

Harold Shapero's *Symphony for classical orchestra* has a propulsive energy and moves with complete assurance. This work seems to derive its inspiration from Beethoven and Stravinsky's *Symphony in C* and is a highly stimulating piece. Previn gets good results from the Los Angeles orchestra but does not bring the sheer vitality that distinguished Bernstein's pioneering record.

Shchedrin, Rodion (born 1933)

(i) *Carmen* (ballet; arr. from Bizet): *suite; Concerto for orchestra (Naughty limericks).*
(BB) **(*) Naxos Dig. 8.553038 [id.]. Ukrainian State O, Theodor Kuchar.

(i) *Carmen* (ballet; arr. from Bizet): *suite; Humoresque. In imitation of Albéniz; Stalin cocktail.*
*** Chandos Dig. CHAN 9288 [id.]. I Musici de Montréal, Yuli Turovski; (i) with Ens. Répercussion – TURINA: *La oración del torero.* ***

Rodion Shchedrin's free adaptation of Bizet's *Carmen* music uses Bizet's tunes, complete with harmony, and reworks them into a new tapestry using only strings and percussion (including vibraphone). The whole thing is brilliantly done and wears surprisingly well. There have been previous recordings of Shchedrin's score but this new Chandos version by I Musici de Montréal sweeps the board. Recorded in the richly resonant acoustic of the Eglise de la Nativité de la Sainte-Vierge, La Prairie, Quebec, the sound is very much in the demonstration bracket, with glittering percussion effects (marimba and vibraphone particularly well caught) and dramatic use of side drum snares. Yuli Turovski's performance opens evocatively and is highly dramatic, winningly expressive and subtle in its use of the wide range of string colour and dynamic. The pastiche, *In imitation of Albéniz*, and the grotesque, Shostakovich-like *Humoresque* are offset by a malignant parody-evocation of Stalin, full of creepy special effects and with a shout of horror at the end. They are very well presented here, but one would not want to return to them very often.

Kuchar's version is also vividly played, with wit as well as high drama and atmosphere. The Naxos recording is excellent. The brief *Concerto for orchestra* with its curious subtitle is a kaleidoscopic scherzando, a whirlwind presentation of Russian folk-motives over a minimalist ostinato. It is played with great verve but rather outstays its welcome.

Stalin cocktail.
*** RCA 09026 68061-2 [id.]. Moscow Virtuosi, Vladimir Spivakov – SHOSTAKOVICH: *Chamber symphony No. 2;* PART: *Collage on B-A-C-H* etc.; DENISOV: *Variations.* ***

Shchedrin's *Stalin cocktail* was written as a celebratory encore piece for Spivakov and his excellent chamber group. A nightmare-like presentation of a very famous Russian folksong cocks a snook at Stalin for whom the tune was once adapted with sycophantic lyrics. The cocktail is dashed to the ground at the close with a piercing vocal splash from all members of the orchestra.

Stihira.
(N) *** Erato/Warner Dig. 0630 17722-2 [id.]. Nat. SO, Mstislav Rostropovich – GLAZUNOV: *Violin concerto in A min., Op. 82;* PROKOFIEV: *Violin concerto No. 1 in D, Op. 19.* ***

Shchedrin here celebrates the millennium of the introduction of Christianity into Russia with a measured passacaglia-like piece based on Russian Orthodox chant, which builds up to a central climax of Mussorgskian splendour. The recording, made in the Kennedy Center, Washington, DC, is more airy and spacious than many from this venue.

Shebalin, Vissarion (1902–63)

(i) *Concertino for violin and orchestra, Op. 14/1;* (ii) *Concertino for horn and orchestra, Op. 14/2;* (iii) *Sinfonietta on Russian Folk Themes, Op. 43;* (iv) *Symphony No. 5, Op. 56.*

(N) ** Olympia Dig. stereo/mono OCD 599 [id.]. (i) Boris Shulgin, USSR Academic SO Ens., Gennady Provatorov; (ii) Boris Afanasiev, USSR Radio and TV SO, Nikola Anosov; (iii) USSR Radio and TV SO, Alexander Gauk; (iv) USSR State SO, Yevgeny Svetlanov.

Essentially a compilation disc. The most important work here is the well-structured and finely crafted *Fifth Symphony*, composed in the last year of Shebalin's life. It is well worth investigating, though his is not a strongly individual voice, even if his music is cultured and thoughtful. (Shostakovich had three photos of composers in his room – Shebalin was one, Mussorgsky and Mahler the others.) Svetlanov's is a live performance from 1963 recorded in mono. The two Op. 14 *Concertinos* come from the turn of the 1920s and 30s, and reflect the more outward-looking spirit of Soviet music at the time – there are reminders of Hindemith and contemporary French music. These are both stereo recordings, well played, though the solo horn has an obtrusive rubato. The horns produce a pretty blowsy sonority in the *Sinfonietta*, here heard in a 1954 mono recording. Composed in 1949–51 after the Zhdanov affair (as a result of which Shebalin was stripped of his official appointment as director of the Moscow conservatory), it is a perfunctory, second-rate piece. An interesting issue just the same.

Symphonies Nos. (i) *1 in F min., Op. 6;* (ii) *3 in C, Op. 17.*

**(*) Olympia OCD 577 [id.]. USSR RSO, (i) Mark Ermler; (ii) Valery Gergiev.

Shebalin made his symphonic debut in 1925, the same year as Shostakovich. His *First Symphony in F minor*, Op. 6, is heavily indebted to his mentor, Miaskovsky, and there are strong echoes of the latter's *Sixth Symphony*, composed two years earlier. Shebalin's craftsmanship is hardly less distinguished than Miaskovsky's: the orchestral writing is assured and the thematic invention is intelligent though not as memorable and characterful as in Shostakovich's No. 1. The *Third Symphony*, Op. 17, which comes from the 1930s, was dedicated to Shostakovich but, for all its moments of eloquence and undoubted expertise, its substance does not quite sustain its length. But both symphonies are well worth investigating. Good performances and decent 1970s recordings.

Sheppard, John (*c.* 1515–*c.* 1559)

Aeterne rex altissime; Audivi vocem de coelo; Beata nobis gaudia; Dum transisset Sabbatum (1st & 2nd settings); *In manus Tuas* (2nd & 3rd settings); *Gaude, gaude, gaude Maria; Hostis Herodes impie; Impetum fecerunt unanimes; In manus Tuas* (3rd setting); *Libera nos, salva nos* (2nd setting); *Sacris solemniis; Sancte Dei pretiose; Spiritus sanctus procedens* (2nd setting). Second Service: *Magnificat; Nunc dimittis. Te Deum laudamus.*
Western Wynde mass.

(B) *** Hyperion Dyad Dig. CDD 22022 (2) [id.]. The Sixteen, Harry Christophers.

Ave maris stella. Cantate mass. Motets: *Deus tuorum militum* (1st setting); *Filiae Hierusalem venite; Haec dies; In manus Tuas Domine* (1st setting); *In pacem in idipsum; Jesu salvator saeculi, redemptis; Jesu salvator saeculi verbum; Justi in perpetuum vivent; Laudem dicite Deo; Libera nos, salva nos* (1st setting); *Paschal Kyrie; Regis Tharsis et insulae; Salvator mundi, Domine; Spiritus sanctus procedens* (1st setting); *Verbo caro factus est.*

✿ (B) *** Hyperion Dyad Dig. CDD 22021 (2) [id.]. The Sixteen, Harry Christophers.

All the music here is of such high quality and it is so superbly sung and recorded that it seems only sensible to consider these two Dyad reissues together. The first collection listed (CD 22022) will be especially attractive as it includes Sheppard's *Western Wynde mass*. However, this is a less elaborate setting of this famous theme than some others, notably that of John Taverner, for until the closing *Agnus Dei* Sheppard consistently places the melodic line on top, whereas Taverner moves the tune about within the lower parts. Nevertheless Sheppard's setting has an appealingly simple beauty, while the extended *Te Deum laudamus* is even richer in its harmonic progressions. The soaring second version of *Dum transisset Sabbatum* and the third version of the sombre *In manus Tuas* (with their characteristic dissonances) are also memorable. The set includes ten more responsories, all of high quality and offering considerable variety, from the flowing antiphon, *Libera nos, salva nos* to the gently serene second setting (for Palm Sunday) of *In manus Tuas Domine.*

However, we have given our Rosette to the companion set (CD 22021), for it includes Sheppard's glorious six-voiced *Cantate mass*, much more complex than *Western Wynde* and, with its glowingly textured polyphony, surely among his most inspired works. There are also eleven responsories, all showing the composer at his most concentrated in inspiration. The Sixteen consistently convey the rapturous beauty of Sheppard's writing, above all in the ethereal passages in the highest register, very characteristic of him. Even there, the Sixteen's sopranos seem quite unstressed by the tessitura. There are not many more beautiful examples of Tudor polyphony than this.

Mass 'Cantate'; Respond: 'Spiritus Sanctus'.
(B) *** Cal. Approche CAL 6621 [id.]. The Clerkes of Oxenford, Wulstan – GIBBONS: *Hymns.* ***

John Sheppard's *Cantate Mass* appears in the Hyperion Dyad collection, above; but for those looking for a less expensive way of examining his claims to musical mastery, the present Calliope Approche bargain reissue is ideal. The *Mass*, sung here a third higher than the manuscript indicates, and involving the sopranos in formidable problems of tessitura, is among the most distinctive of Sheppard's works, presenting surprises in a way uncommon in civilized polyphonic writing. The textures here are refreshingly clear, helped by the superb performances of the Clerkes of Oxenford. The five-part *Spiritus Sanctus* is less striking but makes an excellent bonus, equally well recorded.

Christe Redemptor omnium; In manus tuas; Media vita; Reges Tharsis; Sacris solemniis; Verbum caro.
*** Gimell Ph. Dig. 454 916-2 [id.]. Tallis Scholars, Peter Phillips.

All the music here is based on chant, and much of it is for the six-part choir, which produces a particularly striking sonority. The *Media vita* ('In the midst of life we are in death') is a piece of astonishing beauty, and it is sung with remarkable purity of tone by the Tallis Scholars under Peter Phillips. Glorious and little-known music: the recording could hardly be improved on.

Motets: *Gaude, gaude, gaude Maria; In manus tuas* (1st setting); *Laudem dicite Deo; In pace; Verbum caro.*
(B) **(*) CfP CD-CFP 4638 [id.]. Clerkes of Oxenford, David Wulstan – TALLIS: *Motets.* **(*)

The performances by the Clerkes of Oxenford under David Wulstan are full of fervour, particularly in the inspired *Gaude, gaude, gaude Maria* and the closing *Verbum caro*. Wulstan presses on very strongly, and some might feel there is a lack of contrasting repose and not enough subtlety in the sheer thrust of his direction. But the commitment of the singing will surely convince anyone who buys this CD on impulse that this is great music and that its composer's name should be more familiar. The 1978 analogue recording has plenty of body and atmosphere.

Shostakovich, Dmitri (1906–75)

The Adventures of Korzinkina (film music): *suite, Op. 59; Alone* (film music): *suite, Op. 26; The Bug* (incidental music): *suite, Op. 19; The Golden Hills* (film music): *suite, Op. 30a*; (i) *Jazz band suite No. 1; Scherzos: in F sharp min., Op. 1; in E flat, Op. 7; The Tale of the Priest and his servant, Balda (suite), Op. 36; Theme with variations in B, Op. 7.* Orchestral transcriptions: D. SCARLATTI: *Pastorale & Capriccio.* Johann STRAUSS Jnr. *Vergnügungszug polka.* YOUMANS: *Tahiti trot (Tea for two).* Vocal transcriptions: BEETHOVEN: *Es war einmal ein König.* RIMSKY-KORSAKOV: *Ya dolgo zhdal Tebya (I waited for you).* (ii) *2 Fables after Ivan Krylov, Op. 4; Romance on Pushkin's poem, Spring, Op. 128. Big Lightning* (comic opera): excerpts.
(N) (B) *** BMG/Melodiya 74321 59058-2 (2) [id.]. USSR MoC SO & Chamber Ch., or USSR SO; or Moscow PO or Leningrad PO, with Soloists, or (i) Soloists Ens. or (ii) Moscow Conservatory Chamber Ch., Rozhdestvensky.

None of the music included in this highly recommendable Melodiya 'Twofer' is familiar or without interest to admirers of this composer, and most of it – tuneful and colourfully scored – has a wide general appeal. Much of it appears for the first time here on CD, and the anthology includes some of the composer's earliest music. The *Scherzo in F sharp minor* (1919) and *Theme and variations* (1922) are uncharacteristic, although the *Variations* has a burst of Russian flamboyance towards the close. The companion *E flat major Scherzo* is more individual – it includes a prominent part for the piano and there is already evidence of Shostakovich's special kind of wit, which certainly resurfaces in the film scores, which are from the 1930s and, whilst uncovering no masterpieces, bring much to relish. The *Golden Hills suite* includes an extraordinary extended organ *Fugue* to which the orchestra adds plangent dissonance at the climax. Perhaps the most engaging of these suites is the quixotic *Tale of the Priest and his servant, Balda*, originally written for an animated children's cartoon. The two Krylov fables are also early (1922): the first (*The Dragonfly and the ant*) most characterfully sung by Galina Borisova, the second is a more ambitious choral setting of *The Ass and the nightingale*. Shostakovich's satirical talent comes well to the fore in *The Bug*: the orchestra includes a flexotone and *Scene on the Boulevard* is a bizarre highlight. But the most remarkable find here is the 1932 score for the comic opera, *The Big Lightning*. Never staged, it describes the experiences of a Soviet citizen in a fictitious capitalist country and, vigorously sung, it is full of witty, even riotous pastiche. The little *Jazz suite* makes a delightful interlude with its *Waltz*, *Polka* and *Foxtrot*, as do the two charming Scarlatti woodwind arrangements and the exuberant *Excursion train polka* of Johann Strauss. But among the transcriptions it is Beethoven's *Song of the flea* which stands out (superbly sung by Nesterenko and sounding for all the world like a Russian folk-song) alongside the irrepressible *Tahiti trot*, Shostakovich's exhilarating version of Vincent Youmans's *Tea for two*.

'The Film album': Alone, Op. 26 (extended excerpts). *The Counterplan, Op. 33* (excerpts.). *The Gadfly: Romance. The Great Citizen, Op. 55: Funeral march. Hamlet, Op. 116* (excerpts). *Pirogov, Op. 76a: Scherzo & Finale. Sofia Perovskaya, Op. 132: Waltz. The Tale of the silly little mouse, Op. 56* (arr. Andrew CORNALL).
(N) *** Decca Dig. 460 792-2 [id.]. Concg. O, Chailly.

A winning companion to Chailly's 'Dance album'. Shostakovich's ready find of melody, and exotic orchestral palette spiced with touches of wit, make here for a kaleidoscope of memorable vignettes. The delightful opening *Presto* of the music from *The Counterplan* leads to a wistful romantic concertante violin episode, not unlike the more famous *Romance* from *The Gadfly*, which is also included. The continuous sequence illustrating *The Tale of the silly little mouse* (an animated cartoon) is full of delicate charm; the engaging *Valse* from *Pirogov* is rather more robust, and *Hamlet* brings music of more pungency and dramatic power. But the most substantial set of excerpts is taken from the composer's second film score, *Alone* (1930). It opens roisterously, follows up with a Kabalevsky-like *Galop*, and the other numbers, with avant-garde flair, bring a wide range of picaresque and touching evocations, describing a barrel organ, schoolchildren, a tempest, and ending with an eerie calm after the storm. First-rate Concertgebouw playing and the most vivid Decca recording ensure the success of this entertaining collection.

Ballet suites Nos. 1–5; Festive overture, Op. 96; Katerina Ismailova: suite.
*** Chandos Dig. CHAN 7000/1 [id.]. RSNO, Järvi.

This highly entertaining set generally represents Shostakovich in light-hearted, often ironic mood, throwing out *bonnes-bouches* like fireworks and with a sparkling vividness of orchestral colour. The *Ballet suites* re-use material from earlier works: the *Fifth suite* draws entirely on music from the 1931 ballet, *The Bolt* (see below). This is the most extended of the five suites, and typical of the young Shostakovich. The *Suite* from *Katerina Ismailova* (*Lady Macbeth of Mtsensk*) consists of entr'actes from between the scenes which effectively act as emotional links. Järvi is entirely at home in all this music and clearly relishes its dry humour. The recording is spectacular and resonantly wide-ranging in the Chandos manner.

The Bolt (ballet; complete recording).
*** Chandos Dig. CHAN 9343/4 (2) [id.]. Royal Stockholm PO, Stockholm Transport Band, Rozhdestvensky.

The Bolt dates from 1931 and in its original form sank without trace, largely thanks to the feeble, cumbersome propagandist libretto. Yet the dances are so sharp and colourful in their inspiration that over the years suites of movements have been heard, and now Rozhdestvensky in this vivid, full-blooded recording resurrects the complete score of 43 movements, lasting two and a half hours. Even if it is no masterpiece it demonstrates how dazzlingly inventive the young Shostakovich was, even when faced with an indifferent subject. Rozhdestvensky plainly believes passionately in this score, and he draws an electrifying performance from the Swedish orchestra. Demonstration sound.

Chamber symphony No. 2.
*** RCA Dig. 09026 68061-2 [id.]. Moscow Virtuosi, Vladimir Spivakov – DENISOV: *Variations*. PART: *Collage on B-A-C-H* etc. SHCHEDRIN: *Stalin cocktail*. ***

Vladimir Milman's arrangement of the *Third String quartet* as the *Chamber symphony No. 2* is every bit as effective as No. 1, transcribed by Barshai from the *Eighth*. The *F major Quartet* ranges enigmatically wide in mood, opening skittishly in folk-song style and with a strongly rhythmic Scherzo. At its heart is a powerful *Adagio* passacaglia which is to return to cap the passionate climax of the finale, which then moves towards a final *pianopianissimo* of bleak oblivion. The piece is played marvellously here, and the bright yet spacious recording seems just right.

Cello concerto No. 1 in E flat, Op. 107.
*** Sony Dig. MK 37840 [id.]. Yo-Yo Ma, Phd. O, Ormandy – KABALEVSKY: *Cello concerto No. 1*. ***
*** Chandos Dig. CHAN 8322 [id.]. Raphael Wallfisch, ECO, Geoffrey Simon – BARBER: *Cello concerto*. ***

(i) *Cello concerto No. 1 in E flat, Op. 107;* (ii) *Symphony No. 5 in D min., Op. 47.*
(M) *** Sony Dig. MYK 44903 [id.]. (i) Yo-Yo Ma, Phd. O, Ormandy; (ii) NYPO, Bernstein.

Yo-Yo Ma plays with an intensity that compels the listener, and the Philadelphia Orchestra give eloquent support. This has been reissued at mid-price, and coupled with Bernstein's exciting, high-voltage account of the *Fifth Symphony*, recorded in Tokyo in 1979 when the New York Philharmonic were on tour. On CD the bass is made to sound full and rich, and the slight distancing of the sound places the orchestra within a believable ambience.

Wallfisch handles the first movement splendidly, though there is not quite the same sense of momentum as in Yo-Yo Ma's account. However, he gives a sensitive account of the slow movement and has thoughtful and responsive support from the ECO. The Chandos recording is outstandingly fine.

Cello concertos Nos. 1 in E flat, Op. 107; 2 in G, Op. 126.

*** Ph. Dig. 412 526-2 [id.]. Heinrich Schiff, Bav. RSO, Maxim Shostakovich.

(BB) *** Naxos Dig. 8.550813 [id.]. Maria Kliegel, Polish Nat. RSO (Katowice), Antoni Wit.

**(*) BIS Dig. CD 626 [id.]. Torleif Thedéen, Malmö SO, James DePreist.

**(*) Virgin/EMI Dig. VC5 45145-2 [CDC 45145]. Truls Mørk, LPO, Jansons.

(BB) **(*) Arte Nova/BMG 74321 49688-2 [id.]. Kyrill Rodin, Russian PO, Konstantin Krimets.

Schiff's superbly recorded account does not displace Yo-Yo Ma in the *First*, but it can hold its own. The *Second Concerto* is a haunting piece, essentially lyrical; it is gently discursive, sadly whimsical at times and tinged with a smiling melancholy that hides deeper troubles. The recording is enormously impressive.

Maria Kliegel and the Polish National Radio Orchestra at Katowice under Antoni Wit give a very good account of both concertos that can be confidently recommended at this price. It can hold its own alongside the splendid full-priced Schiff account (Philips), as well as Torleif Thedéen (BIS) and Truls Mørk (Virgin), and on all counts is well worth considering.

The fine Swedish cellist, Torleif Thedéen, has a lot going for him and his passionately committed performances would honour any collection. He has the advantage of excellent engineering, which gives a very alive sound, plus good orchestral support from the Malmö Orchestra under James DePreist.

Truls Mørk, is an eminently forthright Shostakovich interpreter, and his account of both concertos also ranks among the very best. He is not afraid of allowing the music to speak for itself, and the amazingly present and vivid recording weighs heavily in Virgin's favour.

Kyrill Rodin enters hotly contested terrain and is obviously a highly accomplished artist. He dispatches the *First Concerto* with effortless élan and no mean eloquence. The important solo horn part does not have quite the same virtuosity as the Philadelphia Orchestra's Mason Jones in Rostropovich's pioneering version (now on Sony, coupled with Bernstein's account of the *Second Piano concerto* and André Previn's of the *First*). In the slow movement his vibrato may possibly trouble some listeners. The searching opening to the *Second Concerto* is beautifully characterized and the orchestral playing is spirited and sensitive, though the strings are perhaps not quite weighty enough. The recordings are a trifle bright at the treble end of the spectrum but are generally very well balanced. Impressive performances which have much going for them.

(i) *Cello concerto No. 1 in E flat, Op. 107; Piano concertos Nos.* (ii) *1 in C min., Op. 35;* (iii) *2 in F, Op. 102.*

(M) *** Sony MPK 44850. (i) Rostropovich, Phd. O, Ormandy; (ii) Previn; (iii) Bernstein; NYPO, Bernstein.

(BB) *** RCA Navigator 74321 29254-2. USSR RSO, with (i) Mikhail Khomitser, cond. Rozhdestvensky; (ii) Eugene List, cond. Maxim Shostakovitch.

Rostropovich made this recording of the *Cello concerto No. 1* within a few months of the first performance in Russia. Shostakovich himself attended the recording session in Philadelphia and gave his approval to what is a uniquely authoritative reading. Sony have now shrewdly made an attractive triptych for CD by including Bernstein's radiant account of the *Second Piano concerto*, along with Previn's equally striking account of No. 1. Though these New York performances bring somewhat dated recording, both pianists have a way of turning a phrase to catch the imagination, and a fine balance is struck between Shostakovich's warmth and his rhythmic alertness.

Eugene List plays the *First Piano concerto* with splendid dash and brilliance, underlining its brittle sonorities and brash swagger. He opens the *Second* with comparably crisp, rhythmic vigour and takes the finale very much up to speed; throughout there is plenty of character and spirit. Though the sound is vivid, the strings of the USSR Radio Symphony Orchestra are somewhat wanting in bloom. But both slow movements have plenty of atmosphere and List has the advantage of the authority of Maxim Shostakovich's direction. Rostropovich notwithstanding, his Russian colleague Mikhail Khomitser is a formidable soloist in the *Cello concerto*. The forward balance means that he dominates the performance, yet Rozhdestvensky provides a strong, concentrated backing. The orchestral recording could ideally be more refined but there is no lack of atmosphere. A real bargain,.

(i) *Cello concerto No. 1 in E flat, Op. 107;* (ii) *Violin concerto No. 1 in A min., Op. 99.*

(N) ❁ (M) *** Sony stereo/mono MHK 63327 [id.]. (i) Rostropovich, Phd. O, Ormandy; (ii) David Oistrakh, NYPO, Mitropoulos.

Rostropovich's recording première of the Shostakovich *First cello concerto* was made in 1959 and has for long enjoyed legendary status. It has probably not been surpassed, even by Rostropovich himself in subsequent recordings. David Oistrakh's mono recording of the *Violin concerto* with Mitropoulos conducting the New York Philharmonic still sounds stunning. The presentation brings alive memories of the original issues and induces much nostalgia. This reissue is comparatively expensive but well worth it.

Cello concerto No. 2, Op. 126.
(B) *** DG Double 437 952-2 (2) [id.]. Rostropovich, Boston SO, Ozawa – BERNSTEIN: *3 Meditations*, etc.; BOCCHERINI: *Cello concerto No. 2;* GLAZUNOV: *Chant du Ménestrel;* TARTINI: *Cello concerto;* TCHAIKOVSKY: *Andante cantabile*, etc.; VIVALDI: *Cello concertos.* ***

Rostropovich plays with beautifully controlled feeling, and Seiji Ozawa brings sympathy and fine discipline to the accompaniment, securing admirably expressive playing from the Boston orchestra. The analogue recording is first class. As can be seen, this is part of a remarkably generous DG Double anthology, showing Rostropovich's art over the widest range.

Piano concertos Nos. (i) *1 in C min. for piano, trumpet and strings, Op. 35;* (ii) *2 in F, Op. 102.*
(M) *** SMK 47618-2. [id.]. (i) André Previn, William Vacciano; (ii) Leonard Bernstein; NYPO, Bernstein (with: POULENC: *Double piano concerto:* Arthur Gold & Robert Fizdale (pianos) ***).

Piano concertos Nos. 1–2; The Unforgettable year 1919, Op. 89; The Assault on beautiful Gorky (for piano and orchestra).
(B) *** CfP Dig. CD-CFP 4547. Alexeev, Philip Jones, ECO, Maksymiuk.

Alexeev is a clear first choice in both Concertos, and his record would sweep the board even at full price. The digital recording is excellent in every way and scores over its rivals in clarity and presence. There is a fill-up in the form of a miniature one-movement Concerto from a film-score called *The Unforgettable year 1919.*

This shrewd pairing of Bernstein's radiant account of the *Second Concerto* with Previn's equally striking reading of No. 1 makes an attractive disc when coupled with a spiky yet genial version of the Poulenc *Double concerto*. The Shostakovich recordings are far from recent but sound most vivid. The Poulenc concerto, too, is both witty and abrasive, with an excellent contribution from the piano duo, Arthur Gold and Robert Fizdale. It was recorded at about the same time (1961) and the CD transfer of a not particularly smooth original is thoroughly satisfactory. This is one of the most winning discs in the Bernstein Royal Edition.

Piano concerto No. 1 in C min. for piano, trumpet and strings, Op. 35.
(M) *** Decca 448 577-2 [id.]. John Ogdon, John Wilbraham, ASMF, Marriner – BARTOK: *Divertimento; Music for strings, percussion and celesta.* ***

Ogdon, on top form, gives a clean, stylish performance which encompasses both the humour and the hints of romanticism in the *First Concerto*. He remains a little more detached than his accompanists in the tender slow movement, and the trumpet playing of John Wilbraham is masterly. In addition, the early 1970s recorded quality is most vivid. The comparatively backward balance of the strings gives the work a chamber quality to match that of the Bartók works, an unexpected but attractive coupling. The result is fully worthy of Decca's Classic Sound series, even if the recordings were all originally made by an Argo team!

Violin concertos Nos. 1 in A min., Op. 99; 2 in C sharp min., Op. 129.
(BB) *** Virgin/EMI (SIS) Dig. VBD5 61633-2 (2). Sitkovetsky, BBC SO, Andrew Davis – PROKOFIEV: *Violin Concertos* 1–2. ***
*** Chandos Dig. CHAN 8820. Lydia Mordkovitch, SNO, Järvi.
(BB) *** Naxos Dig. 8.550814 [id.]. Kaler, Polish Nat. RSO (Katowice), Wit.

Virgin's coupling by Sitkovetsky and the BBC Symphony Orchestra under Andrew Davis is impressive and intense; there is no doubt as to its excellence, it has tremendous bite. It is also splendidly recorded, and takes its place at the top of the list. Now on a Virgin Double, it comes with equal recommendations.

Mordkovitch's concentrated reading of No. 2 is matched by Järvi and the orchestra in their total commitment. She even outshines the work's dedicatee and first interpreter, David Oistrakh, in the dark reflectiveness of her playing, even if she cannot quite match him in bravura passages. In the better-known concerto (No. 1) the meditative intensity is magnetic, with a fullness and warmth of tone that have not always marked her playing on record before.

Here is another bargain issue from Naxos that vies with the best available, both in performance and in recording. Ilya Kaler, born in Moscow in 1963, a pupil of Leonid Kogan and winner of the Moscow Tchaikovsky Competition, already has some other impressive recordings for Naxos available. The technique is flawless, with playing that is not only brilliant but consistently beautiful tonally. The *Second Violin concerto* is particularly fine, the more wayward, more problematic work, in which Kaler relishes the key role given to the cadenzas. The haunting beauty of the performance may be measured by the gentle cadenza and final ghostly coda of the first movement, leading to a wonderfully rarefied account of the central *Adagio* and a mercurial, quicksilver one of the finale. If in the better-known *First concerto* Kaler's performance does not quite have the same intensity, that is partly a question of the marginally less taut orchestral accompaniment and of the recording balance.

Violin concerto No. 1 in A min., Op. 99.
*** Teldec/Warner Dig. 4509 92256-2 [id.]. Maxim Vengerov, LSO, Rostropovich – PROKOFIEV: *Violin concerto No. 1.* ***
(N) *** Sony Dig. SK 68338 [id.]. Midori, BPO, Abbado – TCHAIKOVSKY: *Violin concerto.* ***
*** EMI (SIS) Dig. CDC7 49814-2 [id.]. Perlman, Israel PO, Mehta – GLAZUNOV: *Violin concerto.* ***
(N) **(*) Simax Dig. PSC 1159 [id.]. Tellefsen, RPO, Berglund – BACH: *Violin concerto No. 2.* **(*)

Maxim Vengerov's pairing of Shostakovich with Prokofiev was the *Gramophone*'s 1995 Record of the Year. Vengerov comes into direct competition with Perlman in Shostakovitch's *A minor Concerto*, yet his playing can dazzle the ear equally tellingly; he also really gets under the skin of the concerto and finds an added depth of poetic feeling, while fully retaining all the music's thrust and spontaneity. Rostropovich and the LSO give splendid support, and this Teldec disc becomes a first recommendation, except for those wanting both Shostakovich concertos together on a single CD.

Having the Tchaikovsky concerto together with this twentieth-century Russian masterpiece brings out the parallels between the two, a point enhanced by Midori's readings, recorded live, with rhythm and phrasing freely expressive. At the start of the *Moderato* first movement of the Shostakovich her tone is so withdrawn that one has to prick the ears, and in the *Passacaglia* third movement she also conveys an ethereal poignancy in her *pianissimo* playing. Abbado is a powerful and sympathetic, yet discreet accompanist, with recording that is both warm and well detailed.

Perlman's version of the Shostakovich *First Violin Concerto* was recorded live in the Mann Auditorium in Tel Aviv. There is no violinist in the world who in sheer bravura can quite match Perlman, particularly live, and the ovation which greets his dazzling performance of the finale is richly deserved. Yet some of the mystery and the fantasy which Russian interpreters have found – from David Oistrakh onwards – is missing, and the close balance of the solo instrument, characteristic of Perlman's concerto recordings, undermines hushed intensity.

Arve Tellefsen gives a fine account of the concerto and brings fine musicianship and no lack of passion to it. Berglund proves a supportive accompanist and the RPO play well for him. Moreover the sound is very well balanced. But this is not a first choice.

'The Dance album': The Bolt: ballet suite, Op. 27a (1934 version); *The Gadfly* (extended excerpts from the film score), *Op. 97* (original orchestration); *Moscow-Cheryomushki* (suite from the operetta), *Op. 105.*
*** Decca Dig. 452 597-2 [id.]. Phd. O, Riccardo Chailly.

André Kostelanetz has already offered us a vivacious sampler of Shostakovich's entertainment music (see below), but surprisingly little of it is duplicated here. Chailly in fact offers 13 items from *The Gadfly* and reveals it to be far finer music than hitherto suspected, partly by using the original scoring. Erez Ofer, the Concertmaster of the Philadelphia Orchestra, plays the violin solo, the famous *Romance*, with delectable delicacy of feeling. For all his sophistication of detail and expressive expansiveness, Chailly doesn't miss out on the witty audacity. The opening number of *Moscow-Cheryomushki, A spin through Moscow* (when the chauffeur borrows the boss's car), has great energy and élan, the *Polka* from *The Bolt* combines wit with narrowly avoided vulgarity, and the boisterous opening of the following *Variations* will disappoint nobody. But, apart from the tunefulness, what one remembers most here is the superb playing of the Philadelphia Orchestra: the sonorous brass and vivid woodwind, while the strings haven't sounded like this in decades. The Decca team have found a new recording venue in New Jersey, and it is a joy to hear the luscious violins in *The Tango* from *The Bolt*, or *Montanelli* from *The Gadfly*; while the full body of tone in melancholy response to *The slap in the face* and the soft-voiced cellos and violas in *Gemma's room* recall the Stokowskian era.

The Gadfly (suite), *Op. 97a; Hamlet* (film incidental music), *Op. 116:* excerpts; *King Lear* (suite), *Op. 58a.*
**(*) Koch Dig. 3-7274-2. [id.]. Korean Broadcasting System SO, Vakhtang Jordania.

The Korean Radio forces offer *The Gadfly* and *King Lear* suites and the first, third and fourth movements of the *Hamlet* music. The Koch disc is to be preferred to other competitors for the greater intensity and discipline of the orchestral response, and the three movements from *Hamlet* are keenly felt. Both are eminently recommendable discs.

The Golden Age (ballet; complete).
**(*) Chandos Dig. CHAN 9251/2 [id.]. Royal Stockholm PO, Rozhdestvensky.

This is the first complete recording of Shostakovich's first ballet, with its extraordinary plot of Soviet and capitalist sportsmen and women. The famous *Polka* is meant to satirize a disarmament meeting in Geneva. The music as a whole is remarkably potent and full of succulent ideas (even *Tea for two* arrives during Act II) and with the big set-pieces expansively and sometimes darkly symphonic. The score is well played in Stockholm, but the warm orchestral style does not always readily bring out the music's plangent character and moments of barbed wit.

Hamlet (1932 production; complete incidental music), *Op. 32;* (1954 production; incidental music); *King Lear* (1941 production; complete incidental music), *Op. 58a.*
*** Cala Dig. CACD 1021 [id.]. Winter, Wilson-Johnson, CBSO, Mark Elder.

An enterprising release, which offers Shostakovich's music for Nikolai Akimov's 1932 production of *Hamlet*. Akimov altered and extended Shakespeare's conception, even interpolating bits of Erasmus; Hamlet appeared as 'an obese glutton who in outward appearance resembled Falstaff, Claudius was a timorous neurasthenic, and Ophelia was a dissolute, tipsy wench'. The play lasted five hours, and a whole hour had to be cut after the dress rehearsal. Shostakovich's score has many biting and sarcastic episodes, and listening to the 30 short numbers – some only a few seconds long – makes for unsettled listening. There are spoken interpolations from the player-king and queen. Also included here is a a Gigue and finale from a 1954 production of *Hamlet*, and the Fool's songs, brilliantly sung by David Wilson-Johnson, from a 1941 production of *King Lear*, full of inventive things. This is not top-drawer Shostakovich, but congratulations are in order for Cala's enterprise in recording all this and to the City of Birmingham Orchestra under Mark Elder for the vital and alert performances. The recording too is expertly and tastefully balanced.

The Limpid stream (complete ballet; revised Rozhdestvensky).
(N) ** Chandos Dig. CHAN 9423 [id.]. Royal Stockholm PO, Rozhdestvensky.

Shostakovich's ballet enjoyed much the same fate as *Lady Macbeth of the Mtsensk District* for, after a successful run of eight months, *The Limpid stream* was denounced in Pravda. It is not vintage Shostakovich nor complete, for as presented here it is a revision by Rozhdestvensky. Some of the numbers are familiar from *The Bolt* but there is nothing that is as good as, say, the *Polka* from *The Age of Gold*. Good recording and the playing is very good if a little wanting in abandon.

New Babylon (film score). (i) *From Jewish folk poetry* (song-cycle).
(N) *** Chandos Dig. CHAN 9600 [id.]. Russian State SO, Valeri Polyansky with (i) Tatiana Sharova, Ludmila Kuznetsova, Alexei Martynov.

It makes an unusual and revealing coupling having Shostakovich's long-buried music for the satirical silent film, *New Babylon*, paired with the moving sequence of Jewish song-settings. Polyansky and an excellent trio of soloists bring out the expressive depth of these deceptively simple, lyrical songs, regularly reflecting the composer's sympathy with the suffering of the Jews. *New Babylon* was the composer's very first film-score, with sharp parodies, 1920s-style, of French models reflecting the Parisian background of the story. Colourful, atmospheric orchestration beautifully caught in full-bodied, well-balanced sound.

Symphonies Nos. 1–15; (i; ii) *From Jewish folk poetry;* (ii) *6 Poems of Marina Tsvetaeva.*
(B) *** Decca Dig./Analogue 444 430-2 (11). Varady, Fischer-Dieskau, Rintzler; (i) Söderström, Karczykowski; (ii) Wenkel; Ch. of LPO or Concg. O; LPO or Concg. O, Haitink.

No one artist or set of performances holds all the insights into this remarkable symphonic canon, but what can be said of Haitink's set is that the playing of both the London Philharmonic and the Concertgebouw orchestras is of the highest calibre and is very responsive; moreover the Decca recordings, whether analogue or digital, are consistently of this company's highest standard, outstandingly brilliant and full. If without the temperament of a Mravinsky, Haitink proves a reliable guide to this repertoire, often much more than that, and sometimes inspired. All in all, a considerable achievement. The 11 discs are now offered together at bargain price, but they also remain available separately at mid-price – see below.

Symphonies Nos. 1–15.
(B) **(*) BMG/Melodiya 74321 19952-2 (10) [id.]. Soloists, Russian Republic Ch., Moscow PO, Kondrashin.

Symphonies Nos. 1 in F min., Op. 10; 12 in D min. (The Year 1917), Op. 112.
(M) ** BMG/Melodiya 74321 19848-2 [id.]. Moscow PO, Kondrashin.

Symphonies Nos. (i) *2 in B (October Revolution), Op. 14;* (ii) *14 in G min., Op. 135.*
(M) *** BMG/Melodiya 74321 19844-2 [id.]. (i) Russian Republic Ch.; (ii) Tselovalnik, Nestorenko; Moscow PO, Kondrashin.

Symphonies Nos. (i) *3 in E flat (The First of May), Op. 20; 5 in D min., Op. 47.*
(M) ** BMG/Melodiya 7432 119845-2 [id.]. (i) Russian Republic Ch.; Moscow PO, Kondrashin.

Symphony No. 4 in C min., Op. 43.
(M) *** BMG/Melodiya 74321 19840-2 [id.]. Moscow PO, Kondrashin.

Symphonies Nos. 6 in B min., Op. 54; 10 in E min., Op. 93.
(M) *(*) BMG/Melodiya 74321 19847-2 [id.]. Moscow PO, Kondrashin.

Symphony No. 7 in C (Leningrad), Op. 60.
(M) ** BMG/Melodiya 74321 19839-2 [id.]. Moscow PO, Kondrashin.

Symphony No. 8 in C min., Op. 65.
(M) *(*) BMG/Melodiya 74321 19841-2 [id.]. Moscow PO, Kondrashin.

Symphonies Nos. 9, Op. 70; 15 in A, Op. 103.
(M) **(*) BMG/Melodiya 74321 19846-2 [id.]. Moscow PO, Kondrashin.

Symphony No. 11 (The Year 1905), Op. 103.
(M) ** BMG/Melodiya 74321 19843-2 [id.]. Moscow PO, Kondrashin.

Symphony No. 13 in B flat min. (Babi Yar), Op. 113.
(M) *** BMG/Melodiya 74321 19842-2 [id.]. Eisen, Russian Republic Ch., Moscow PO, Kondrashin.

Kirill Kondrashin's cycle was made over a long period of time: the *Fourth Symphony* dates from 1962, not long after its first performance, while the last to appear were in the mid 1970s (Nos. 7, 14 and 15). The set is of importance in that Shostakovich himself expressed confidence in this conductor, and it is clear that in many instances he comes closer than most to the spirit of this music. Not all the performances strike us as *sans pareil*. In none of them is the playing of the Moscow Philharmonic as distinguished or as finely disciplined as in many rival accounts. Nor, to be fair, are Kondrashin's insights deeper than those of Mravinsky or (in the case of Nos. 5, 6, 7 and 11) Stokowski. It is rare to find one cycle that fulfils the aspirations with which it embarks and, although Haitink and the Concertgebouw have strong merits, there is no single survey that is absolutely ideal in every respect. Nos. 4, 13 and 14 make the strongest impression in Kondrashin's hands. Despite the sonic limitations inevitable over the course of nearly 40 years, the *Fourth* is almost indispensable. It has that sense of discovery, raw intensity and sheer eloquence which silence criticism – or should do. And the 1967 account of the *Thirteenth* has an authentic feel to it that makes its claims on the collector strong. Both the *Fourteenth*, song-cycle-cum-symphony, and the enigmatic *Fifteenth Symphony* have much to recommend them.

Elsewhere the cycle is less even. The brisk tempi Kondrashin adopts for the first movement of both the *Sixth* and *Eighth Symphonies* diminish their intensity of feeling and directness of effect and, though he makes out a stronger case for the *Third* than some rivals, he is no match for Mravinsky in the *Twelfth*. The Moscow Philharmonic strings are by no means as sumptuous as those of the USSR State Academic Symphony (or the 'USSR Symphony' as it was known at one time); and they do not sound quite as warm or smooth as on the LP. It is difficult to generalize, but the bass is sometimes firmer and definition is keener. There are roughnesses on the originals that are not quite smoothed out.

Symphony No. 1 in F min., Op. 10; (i) *Piano concerto No. 1 in C min., Op. 35.*
*** EMI (SIS) Dig. CDC5 55361-2. (i) Mikhail Rudy; BPO, Jansons.

Drawing superb playing from the Berlin Philharmonic, Jansons conducts a finely detailed reading of the *First Symphony* which is both precise and intense. So the second-movement scherzando, despite a very fast speed, is never breathless, and the oboe solo at the start of the slow movement could not be more tender in its refinement, while even the hectic close is perfectly controlled, both exciting and sharply focused. Mikhail Rudy in the concerto brings out new poetry, and the *Lento* slow movement has rarely been so yearningly beautiful, with the Berlin strings radiant. If in the outer movements Rudy does not bite as sharply as some pianists, his sensitivity is heightened by Jansons's idiomatic conducting, full of humour in the finale. Excellent sound.

(i) *Symphony No. 1 in F min., Op. 10;* (ii) *Festive overture, Op. 96.* Collection: *The Age of gold, Op. 22: Polka. Ballet suite No. 1: Galop; Music-box waltz; Dance. Ballet suite No. 2: Polka; Galop. The Gadfly, Op. 97a: Introduction; Barrel organ waltz; Nocturne; Folk festival; Galop. Moscow-Cheryomushki: Overture waltz; Galop.*
✽ (B) *** Sony SBK 62642 [id.]. (i) Phd. O, Ormandy; (ii) Columbia SO, André Kostelanetz.

Ormandy and the Philadelphia Orchestra recorded this version of the *First Symphony* in the presence of the composer in 1959, and their endeavours have never been surpassed. It is a beautifully proportioned, tense and vivid account, with everyone doing their utmost to get things right. The sound, too, is excellent. Still, after 40 years, a front-runner in spite of some excellent successors. The coupling could not have been better chosen: a suite of Shostakovichian orchestral lollipops selected by Kostelanetz, a dab hand at this kind of audacious light music. Readers who know the *Polka* from *The Age of gold* will know what to expect. Kostelanetz opens with a fizzing account of the *Festive overture*, Op. 96. Then comes the series of miniatures – mixed up to provide maximum contrast. Many of the pieces were virtually unknown when these performances first appeared in 1965, and even today few of them are familiar to the wider public. The fast numbers (like the Offenbachian *Galop* from *The Gadfly*) are redeemed from vulgarity by momentum and brilliant scoring, many of them suggesting the composer thumbing his nose at the Soviet authorities, and there is no better example than the *Moscow-Cheryomushki Overture waltz* with its trombone glissandi accompanying a very Russian dance-accelerando, followed by the equally infectious pot-pourri called *Folk festival*. But the gentler pieces are more memorable still: the hauntingly tender *Nocturne* from *The Gadfly* and the delicious *Barrel organ waltz* from the same source, matched by the *Music-box waltz* from the *Ballet suite No. 1*. Kostelanetz plays this music for all it's worth, and if again the recording is brash, this time it fits the music like a glove.

Symphonies Nos. 1 in F min., Op. 10; 3 (The First of May), Op. 20.
(M) *** Decca Dig. 425 063-2. LPO Ch., LPO, Haitink.

In this coupling, Haitink still leads the field, when the Decca recording is outstandingly clear and brilliant. His account of No. 1 is strong and very well played. It may lack something in youthful high spirits but not in concentration. No. 3 is not one of Shostakovich's finest works but is worth having when played as commitedly as here.

Symphonies Nos. 1 in F min., Op. 10; 5 in D min., Op. 47; (i) *7 in C, Op. 60; Prelude No. 14 in E flat min., Op. 34* (arr. Stokowski).
(***) Pearl mono GEMM CDS9044 [id.]. Phd. O; (i) NBC SO, Stokowski.

Stokowski's *First Symphony* was recorded in 1934, less than a decade after its première under Malko. The sound is dryish and, among the perfect ensemble and attack, the playing has one or two slight blemishes. But there is tremendous atmosphere and concentration, and the transfers are excellent. Stokowski's (1939) pioneering *Fifth* is an electrifying performance, impeccably played and splendidly transferred. The slow movement has a gripping intensity that is quite exceptional. But this is now available in a superior Dutton transfer, coupled with the *Sixth Symphony* (see below). The famous transcription of the *E flat minor Prelude*, Op. 34, has a brooding, Mussorgskian menace all its own, while Stokowski's *Leningrad Symphony* is hardly less gripping. This *Leningrad* for all its sonic defects makes for exciting listening.

Symphonies Nos. 1 in F min.; 6 in B min., Op. 54.
*** Chandos Dig. CHAN 8411 [id.]. SNO, Järvi.

Järvi's account of the *First Symphony* is more volatile than Haitink's in the outer movements – there is no lack of quirkiness in the finale, while the *Largo* is intense and passionate. The *Sixth* has comparable intensity, with an element of starkness in the austerity of the first movement. The Scherzo is skittish at first but, like the finale, has no lack of pungent force.

Symphonies Nos. 1 in F min., Op. 10; 9 in E flat, Op. 70.
*** Teldec/Warner Dig. 4509 90849-2 [id.]. Nat. SO of Washington, Rostropovich.

In Rostropovich's hands the youthful *First Symphony* begins very promisingly indeed and continues well. Indeed there is plenty of fulfilment. This *First* is a very good account, free from exaggeration, even if he rushes the Scherzo off its feet. Rostropovich is also given a decently balanced recording. The *Ninth*, too, is well served; fears that the slow movement might be pulled out of shape prove generally groundless, though there is one moment of agogic exaggeration. Generally, this can be recommended to those looking for this particular coupling.

Symphonies Nos. 2 in B (October Revolution), Op. 14; 3 in E flat (The First of May), Op. 20.
*** Teldec/Warner Dig. 4509 90853-2 [id.]. London Voices, LSO, Rostropovich.

Although Rostropovich is often prone to excessive expressive vehemence and tends on occasion to italicize and point-make, these two performances, like his accounts of the *First* and *Ninth*, have a natural eloquence that is very persuasive. The LSO respond to his playing with real fervour; everything is well prepared and well thought out, and he has the advantage of very well-engineered sound.

(i) *Symphonies Nos. 2 in B (October Revolution); 3 in E flat (The First of May), Op. 20; 4 in C min., Op. 43*; (ii) *Hamlet (suite), Op. 32*; (iii) *Overture Poor Columbus, Op. 23*.
(N) (B) **(*) BMG/Melodiya Dig./Analogue Twofer 74321 63462-2 (2) [id.]. (i) Russian State Academic Ch. Cappella, USSR MoC SO; (ii) Moscow PO; (iii) Leningrad PO, Rozhdestvensky.

The *Second Symphony*, a curious example of Shostakovich's quirky development as a young composer, is nevertheless made to sound convincing in Rozhdestvensky's hands with its eerily sombre opening and the Russian chorus at the end launching into a brief but potently ardent choral peroration, rather fiercely recorded. The *Third* opens with a melancholy clarinet solo over a gentle march rhythm in the lower strings, seductively atmospheric, before the main *Allegro* sets off more aggressively. Rozhdestvensky catches its chimerical, often violent mood changes, then finds a central core of serenity before the spiky, belligerent closing section leads to another dynamically exuberant chorus. The orchestra plays brilliantly and is vividly if coarsely recorded in the Soviet digital manner of the 1980s. In the equivocal *Fourth Symphony*, the ironic humour, as well as the concentrated power of the work, come over tellingly even if in the first movement Rozhdestvensky does nothing to mitigate rhythmic squareness, and the playing is not ideally refined. The second movement also has its slack moments but the result is highly idiomatic, as is the slow Mahlerian funeral march of the finale, one of the longest movements that Shostakovich ever wrote. As a bonus come 15 extremely diverse movements from the *Hamlet incidental music*, and a brief but characteristically quirky *Christopher Columbus overture*. In Russian eyes Columbus was an unheroic figure, an adventurer lured by gold. Again, strongly characterized brilliant performances, projected in bold, brightly lit sound.

Symphonies Nos. 2 (October Revolution), Op. 14; 10 in E min., Op. 93.
(M) **(*) Dig./Analogue 425 064-2. LPO Ch., LPO, Haitink.

Haitink's performance of No. 2 is admirable, and it is given excellently balanced sound with great presence and body. No. 10 is a masterpiece, and Haitink really has the measure of the first movement, whose climaxes he paces with an admirable sense of architecture. He secures sensitive and enthusiastic playing from the LPO, both here and in the malignant Scherzo. In the third movement he adopts a slower tempo than usual, which would be acceptable if there were greater tension or concentration of mood; but here and in the slow introduction to the finale the sense of concentration falters. The 1977 analogue recording (like the digital *Second*, made in the Kingsway Hall) is outstandingly realistic.

Symphony No. 4 in C min., Op. 43.
*** EMI Dig. CDC5 55476-2. CBSO, Rattle (with BRITTEN: *Russian funeral* ***).
*** Chandos Dig. CHAN 8640 [id.]. RSNO, Järvi.
(N) **(*) Teldec/Warner Dig. 9031 76261-2 [id.]. Nat. SO, Rostropovich.
(M) **(*) Decca 425 065-2. LPO, Haitink.

Rattle conducts his Birmingham orchestra in a revelatory performance of the elusive *Fourth Symphony*, sustaining the expansive movements masterfully, bringing out the biting irony and humour of much of the writing, presented with Russian swagger, while never forgetting the underlying darkness. Above all, the orchestra plays incandescently, with an unstoppable thrust to convey the impression of a live, tensely dramatic event, with the full-bodied sound (recorded in Birmingham's Symphony Hall) adding to the weight and impact. The rare Britten piece is a valuable and generous makeweight.

Järvi draws from the SNO playing which is both rugged and expressive, consistently conveying the emotional thrust of the piece and making the enigmatic ending, with its ticking rhythm, warmer than usual, as though bitterness is finally evaporating. He is helped by exceptionally rich, full recording.

Rostropovich's powerful account of the *Fourth Symphony* is among the most convincing of his Shostakovich cycle. He holds the score together admirably and avoids expressive excesses and heavy-handedness. Although this is not a first recommendation, it has a good deal going for it.

Haitink brings out an unexpected refinement in the *Symphony*, a rare transparency of texture. He is helped by recording of Decca's finest quality, vividly remastered. Detail is caught superbly; yet the earthiness and power, the demonic quality which can make this work so compelling, are underplayed.

Symphonies Nos. 4 in C min., Op. 43; 5 in D min., Op. 47.
(B) **(*) EMI forte CZS5 72658-2 (2) [CDFB 72658]. Chicago SO, Previn – BRITTEN: *Sinfonia da requiem*, etc. *** ❁

Previn's is an eminently straightforward, superlatively played and vividly recorded account of the *Fourth Symphony*. Orchestral playing is also of the highest quality in the *Fifth Symphony*, but here there is little sense of momentum, freshness and urgency. The recorded sound is extremely impressive.

Symphonies Nos. 4 in C min., Op. 43; 10 in E min., Op. 93.
(B) *** Sony SB2K 62409 (2) [id.]. Phd. O, Ormandy.

The *Fourth* was the symphony which Shostakovich withdrew on the eve of its première, to be replaced later by the *Fifth* as 'a Soviet artist's reply to just criticism'. Ormandy pioneered the work in the West. His reading of this strange and powerful symphony is less subtle than Kondrashin's Russian account, less refined than Haitink, but it is thoroughly convincing and has the Philadelphia Orchestra playing both brilliantly (witness the frenzied string passage at the climax of the first movement) and with real depth of feeling. The combination of irony, anguish and plangent lyricism, as in the central *Moderato*, is strongly characterized, while the curiously subdued atmosphere of the march which opens the finale is remarkably well caught. The 1963 recording, made in Philadelphia Town Hall, is spaciously full and vivid; it sounds excellent in the current CD transfer.

Ormandy went on to record No. 10 with equal success in the same venue in 1968, and again he makes a case for treating the work with a passion that is apt for Tchaikovsky. The result is not as refined in its effect as Karajan's DG version, but it still makes a compelling, indeed massive, impact, notably in the long first and third movements. Ormandy's control of string phrasing is again immaculate and his great orchestra is never less than convincing and is often superbly brilliant in the precision of its virtuosity. This makes a thoroughly worthwhile bargain coupling.

Symphony No. 5 in D min., Op. 47 (see also under *Cello concerto No. 1*).
*** EMI (SIS) Dig. CDC7 49181-2 [id.]. Oslo PO, Jansons.
(M) *** Erato/Warner 2292 45752-2 [id.]. Leningrad PO, Mravinsky.
**(*) Everest EVC 9030 [id.]. NY Stadium SO, Stokowski.

(M) **(*) Mercury (IMS) 434 323-2 [id.]. Minneapolis SO, Skrowaczewski – KHACHATURIAN: *Gayaneh ballet suite*. **(*)
**(*) Decca Dig. 440 476-2 [id.]. VPO, Solti – MENDELSSOHN: *Symphony No. 4*. **(*)

Symphony No. 5; Age of gold: Polka.
(B) **(*) Sony SBK 53261 [id.]. Phd. O, Ormandy – PROKOFIEV: *Love for 3 oranges: suite*. **

(i) *Symphony No. 5;* (ii) *Hamlet* (film incidental music), *suite, Op. 116*.
(BB) *** RCA Navigator 74321 24212-2 [Basic 100: 09026 68456-2]. (i) LSO, Previn; (ii) Belgian RSO, José Serebrier.

Previn's RCA version, dating from early in his recording career (1965), remains at the top of the list of bargain recommendations. This is one of the most concentrated and intense readings ever, superbly played by the LSO at its peak. In the third movement he sustains a slower speed than anyone else, making it deeply meditative in its dark intensity, while his build-up in the central development section brings playing of white heat. Only in the hint of analogue tape-hiss and a slight lack of opulence in the violins does the sound fall short of the finest modern digital recordings – and it is more vividly immediate than most. The new coupling (on the Navigator CD only) is appropriate. *Hamlet* obviously generated powerful resonances in Shostakovich's psyche and produced vivid incidental music. The playing of the Belgian Radio Orchestra under Serebrier is eminently serviceable without being really distinguished, but with atmospheric recording this 28-minute suite makes a considerable bonus.

Jansons's EMI version with the Oslo orchestra on top form brings a tautly incisive, electrically intense reading, marked by speeds notably faster than usual that yet have the ring of authenticity. The development section in the first movement, for example, builds up bitingly into a thrilling climax, with the accelerando powerfully controlled. Not a first choice, but an exciting one.

Mravinsky conducted the première of the *Fifth Symphony* in 1937, and so brings a special authority to this work. The present version is not free from the odd untidiness but there is still evidence of a commanding personality, and even though the recording itself is not in the luxury bracket, this CD must figure high on any list.

The Philadelphia Orchestra made the very first recording of the *Fifth Symphony* (under Stokowski), and they play it marvellously for Ormandy: the strings produce the most opulent tone and generate considerable eloquence in the slow movement; the solo flute, too, makes a highly distinguished contribution. Ormandy has always shown a special feeling for Shostakovich and he is direct and straightforward, but neither here (in 1965) nor in his later, RCA disc does one sense the degree of commitment that marked his earlier recording of the *First Symphony*. *The Age of gold Polka* makes a witty encore after the Prokofiev coupling.

The Stadium Symphony Orchestra of New York is neither as flexible nor as virtuosic an ensemble as the superb instrument Stokowski created in Philadelphia during the first decade of electric recording, but the Stokowski electricity is here as intensely as ever and it makes this performance an unforgettable experience. There is less subtlety in the individual wind solos than in the old 78 set, but the strings re-create that 'drenched radiance' of texture in the upper register that Stokowski made his own and which makes the lyrical climaxes of the first and third movements so memorable. The sound itself is surprisingly good, though there is background hiss.

Skrowaczewski's Minneapolis account of Shostakovich's *Fifth* was one of the first really successful stereo recordings, with great concentration in the *pianissimo* string-playing in the *Largo* and a finale which, after an exhilarating *Allegro*, brings a trenchant, ponderous coda, anticipating much later performances, after the composer had revealed that his closing section was not intended to be an ingenuous triumphant celebration. The first movement has a fast opening speed, but the conductor understands Shostakovich's melodic line and, although this is a wilful reading, it is also an exciting one. The recording was made in the Northrop Auditorium in 1961 and is full yet astonishingly clear, but the upper strings have that curious thinness which was characteristic of Mercury's Minneapolis ventures at that time. However, the ear soon adjusts, and this performance is very compelling.

In Shostakovich's *Fifth Symphony* Solti adopts a more espressivo style than in his previous Shostakovich recordings, with the *Largo* slow movement beautifully moulded at a flowing speed, conveying warmth in a movement which is often treated with emotional reserve. The great soaring second-subject theme of the first movement too is given the warmth of the Vienna strings, and in both the Scherzo and finale Solti brings out Shostakovich's wry humour rather than his more brutal qualities. The live recording, made in the Musikverein, is not very full-bodied, so this is hardly a first choice, but provides a welcome slant on the work itself and on the conductor.

Symphonies Nos. 5 in D min.; 6 in B min., Op. 54.
❁ (B) (***) Dutton Lab mono CDAX 8017 [id.]. Phd. O, Stokowski.

Stokowski's electrifying première of the *Fifth* has never been surpassed on record, notably for the intensity and beauty of the string-playing in the first and third movements. The new Dutton transfer is little short of miraculous in its vividness and presence, and the quality of the recording is astonishing.

Stokowski's *Sixth* was made in 1940, only a few months after the work was premièred, and it brings one face to face not only with this symphony but also with the bleak, harsh times during which it came into being. It is powerfully atmospheric, the lines wonderfully sustained and the playing at times frighteningly intense. This performance has a special ring of authenticity.

Symphonies Nos. 5 in D min.; 9 in E flat, Op. 70.
(M) *** Decca Dig. 425 066-2. (i) Concg. O; (ii) LPO, Haitink.
(BB) *** Naxos Dig. 8.550427 [id.]. Belgian R. & TV O, Alexander Rahbari.

In No. 5 Haitink is eminently straightforward, there are no disruptive changes in tempo, and the playing of the Concertgebouw Orchestra and the contribution of the Decca engineers are beyond praise. There could perhaps be greater intensity of feeling in the slow movement but, whatever small reservations one might have, it is most impressive both artistically and sonically. The coupled No. 9 is superb. Without inflation Haitink gives it a serious purpose, both in the poignancy of the waltz-like second movement and in the equivocal emotions of the outer movements. The recording is outstanding in every way.

Both in the hushed intensity of the lyrical passages and in the vigour and bite of Shostakovich's violent *allegros* Rahbari's reading is most convincing, with dramatic tensions finely controlled in a spontaneous-sounding way. In No. 9 Rahbari opts for a controversially slow *Moderato* second movement but sustains it well, and the outer movements are deliciously witty in their pointing. The playing of all sections is first rate, and the sound is full and brilliant. An outstandingly generous coupling makes this a most attractive issue, even with no allowance made for the very low price.

(i) *Symphonies Nos. 6 in B min., Op. 54;* (ii) *9 in E flat, Op. 70.*
**(*) DG (IMS) Dig. 419 771-2. VPO, Bernstein.
**(*) EMI (SIS) Dig. CDC7 54339-2 [id.]. Oslo PO, Mariss Jansons.
**(*) Everest EVC 9005 [id.]. (i) LPO, Boult; (ii) LSO, Sargent.

Perversely slow as Bernstein is in most movements of both symphonies, with the first movement of No. 6 and the *Moderato* (more like *Adagio*) of No. 9 minutes longer than any rival, the performances, recorded live, are electrifying, rhythmically alert to counter any slowness, helped by superb playing and spectacular recording.

Jansons in No. 6 is purposeful and strong, if emotionally restrained in the first movement, lithe and resilient in the Scherzo and finale, consistently adopting speeds on the fast side. No. 9 is then light and resilient, again with speeds on the fast side and with brilliant playing from the Oslo orchestra. Full, well-balanced recording, not as forward as the sound for most other Jansons Shostakovich discs.

Boult secures very good playing from the LPO and the late-1950s Walthamstow recording is excellent. But he is wanting a little in intensity. Sargent's account of the *Ninth* is lyrical and attractive, with infectious vitality in the odd-numbered of the five movements. Again the recording is very good indeed, approaching the demonstration class. This is undoubtedly an enjoyable coupling. However, these accounts are upstaged by Previn's *Sixth* and Haitink's *Ninth* – both differently coupled.

Symphonies Nos. 6 in B min., Op. 54; 12 in D min. (The Year 1917), Op. 112.
(M) *** Decca Dig. 425 067-2. Concg. O, Haitink.

Haitink's structural control, coupled with his calm, taut manner, is particularly impressive in the slow movement of No. 6. As a work, No. 12 is more problematic. There is much of the composer's vision and grandeur here but also his crudeness. However, the sheer quality of the sound and the superb responsiveness and body of the Concertgebouw Orchestra might well seduce many listeners. As with the *Sixth* the slow movement has a marvellous sense of atmosphere, which is well conveyed in this Decca performance; the Amsterdam orchestra play as if they believe every crotchet and, though not even their eloquence can rescue the finale, overall the performance is very successful.

Symphony No. 7 in C (Leningrad), Op. 60.
*** Chandos Dig. CHAN 8623 [id.]. SNO, Järvi.
(M) **(*) Decca Dig. 425 068-2. LPO, Haitink.
(M) **(*) Sony SMK 47616-2. NYPO, Bernstein.
(M) (***) RCA mono GD60293 [60293-2-RG]. NBC SO, Toscanini.

Järvi's is a strong, intense reading, beautifully played and recorded, which brings out the full drama of this symphony in a performance that consistently gives the illusion of spontaneity in a live performance, as in the hushed tension of the slow, expansive passages. There have been more polished versions than this, but, with its spectacular Chandos sound, it makes an excellent choice as a single-disc version.

Haitink is here eminently straightforward. There could perhaps be greater intensity of feeling in the slow movement, and the long first-movement *ostinato* is not presented histrionically; but the deep seriousness which Haitink finds in the rest of the work challenges comparisons with the other wartime symphony, the epic *Eighth*. The playing of the Concertgebouw Orchestra is beyond praise, and the splendid contribution of the Decca engineers ensures the success of this CD.

Bernstein brings a certain panache and fervour to his reading, particularly in the inspired slow movement, so that one is tempted to look indulgently at its occasional overstatements.

Toscanini and the NBC orchestra bring an urgency and fervour that is altogether special and an intensity that shines through the primitive recorded sound. There is a special feeling of authenticity that conveys the flavour of the period and the vividness of the experience more effectively than many modern recordings. Be warned, however, the 1942 sound does call for some tolerance.

Symphonies Nos. 7 in C (Leningrad), Op. 60; 8 in C min., Op. 65; King Lear (incidental music): (i) *Introduction and Cordelia's ballad;* (ii) *10 Buffoon's songs, Op. 58a.*

(B) **(*) BMG/Melodiya Twofer Dig. 74321 53457-2 (2) [id.]. USSR MoC SO, Rozhdestvensky; with (i) Natalia Burnasheva; (ii) Evgeni Nesterenko.

Rozhdestvensky's view of the *Leningrad Symphony*'s controversial first movement is unusually broad. It is undeniably powerful but runs the risk of overplaying the element of banality in the notorious *ostinato*. Many will prefer a brisker and more polished reading, but the ruggedness here is certainly authentic; the other movements also bring warmly expressive, spontaneous-sounding performances which lack only the last degree of subtlety. Rozhdestvensky then follows with a thrustful and incisive reading of the *Eighth*, with electrically intense playing that both holds the enormous structure together and brings out the element of fantasy which literal performances underplay. The spontaneity Rozhdestvensky regularly conveys in his recordings is here combined with sharpness of focus. In both symphonies the digital recording is full-bodied and wide-ranging with a full depth of string-tone, but it grows coarse in the biggest climaxes. The songs for Shakespeare's *King Lear* are an additional asset to the set. Natalia Burnasheva sings Cordelia's touching lyrical ballad eloquently and Nesterenko characterizes strongly the ten brief *Buffoon's songs* (most less than a minute in length) with their typical Shostakovian amalgam of grotesquerie and irony. No translations are offered, but there are good notes.

Symphony No. 8 in C min., Op. 65.

(N) **(*) BBC Legends BBCL4002-2 [id.]. Leningrad PO, Yevgeni Mravinsky (with MOZART: *Symphony No. 33 in B flat, K.319.* **)

(M) *** Decca Dig. 425 071-2. Concg. O, Haitink.

*** Teldec/Warner Dig. 9031 74719-2 [id.]. Nat. SO of Washington, Rostropovich.

**(*) Ph. (IMS) Dig. 446 062-2 [id.]. Kirov O, Gergiev.

Mravinsky's BBC recording comes from the Festival Hall Concert given on the Leningrad Orchestra tour in 1960 at which Shostakovich himself was present. It is billed as the UK première (Sir Henry Wood's Prom performance in 1944 took place in a makeshift BBC studio in Bedford because of the V2 bombs, and Sir Malcolm Sargent's 1959 performance at the Maida Vale studios was not a public concert; apart from a broadcast from Italy, it was not heard in the intervening years!). No one who was present will ever be likely to forget it. The performance was briefly issued in mono on Melodiya LPs (the coughs, which are not unduly intrusive, coincide exactly with off-air tapes) but this transfer reproduces the occasion with great realism and a wide dynamic range. This reading has tremendous intensity and authenticity of feeling; indeed it rivals the 1947 account included in the BMG/Melodiya box. It comes with a bonus – the first half of the concert, which was given over to an elegant performance of the Mozart *Symphony No. 33.* Even among modern recordings this more than holds its own and the sound is very good indeed. Mandatory listening.

Haitink characteristically presents a strongly architectural reading of this war-inspired symphony, at times direct to the point of severity. After the massive and sustained slow movement which opens the work, Haitink allows no lightness or relief in the Scherzo movements, and in his seriousness in the strangely lightweight finale (neither fast nor slow) he provides an unusually satisfying account of an equivocal, seemingly uncommitted movement.

With Rostropovich, his intensity and that of his players does not spill over into excess. This is a gripping account that can rank alongside the best performances one has heard on or off record – Mravinsky, Rozhdestvensky, Kondrashin and the excellent Haitink – and it is very well recorded too.

Recorded in Holland in 1994, Gergiev's reading is remarkable for its concentration, with the massive span of the first movement held firmly together, leading to towering climaxes. Though the third-movement Scherzo is warmer and less tough than it might be, it erupts thrillingly when the brilliant trumpet solo enters and then resolves after the climax at the end on to a very slow, sustained *Largo*. The culminating resolution is tenderly achieved on the seemingly inevitable transition into the relative ease of the last, hushed movement. The sound is full-bodied but slightly cloudy, not as vivid and immediate as in such outstanding versions as Haitink's, now at mid-price.

Symphony No. 9 in E flat, Op. 70; Festive overture, Op. 96; Katerina Ismailova (Lady Macbeth of Mtsensk): 5 Entr'actes. Tahiti trot (arr. of Youmans's *Tea for two*), *Op. 16.*

*** Chandos Dig. CHAN 8567 [id.]. RSNO, Järvi.

Järvi's version of the *Ninth* brings a warmly expressive, strongly characterized reading in superb, wide-ranging sound. The point and wit of the first movement go with bluff good humour, leading on to an account of the second-movement *Moderato* that is yearningly lyrical yet not at all sentimental, contrasted with the fun and jokiness of the final *Allegretto*. The mixed bag of fill-up items is both illuminating and characterful, ending with the jolly little chamber arrangement that Shostakovich did in the 1920s of Vincent Youmans's *Tea for two*, the *Tahiti trot*.

Symphonies Nos. (i) *9 in E flat;* (ii) *10 in E min.*
❀ (M) (***) Sony mono MPK 45698 [id.].
NYPO, (i) Efrem Kurtz; (ii) Dmitri Mitropoulos.

Dmitri Mitropoulos's pioneering account of the *Tenth Symphony* with the New York Philharmonic penetrates more deeply into the heart of this score than any newcomer; only Karajan's mid-1960s version can be put alongside it. It comes with Efrem Kurtz's 1949 version of the *Ninth* with the same orchestra, playing with great virtuosity. The sound is remarkably good for its period (an edit has removed one note from the opening phrase of the scherzo), but apart from that hiccup this is a stunning performance.

Symphony No. 10 in E min., Op. 93.
*** DG Gold Dig. 439 036-2 [id.]. BPO, Karajan.
*** EMI Dig. CDC5 55232-2. Phd. O, Jansons – MUSSORGSKY: *Songs and dances of death.* ***
(B) *** Carlton IMP Dig. PCD 2043 [id.]. Hallé O, Skrowaczewski.
(M) ** EMI Dig. CDM7 64870-2. Philh. O, Simon Rattle – BRITTEN: *Sinfonia da Requiem.* ***

Symphony No. 10 in E min., Op. 93; Ballet suite No. 4.
*** Chandos Dig. CHAN 8630 [id.]. RSNO, Järvi.

Already in his 1967 recording Karajan had shown that he had the measure of this symphony; this newer version is, if anything, even finer. In the first movement he distils an atmosphere as concentrated as before, bleak and unremitting, while in the *Allegro* the Berlin Philharmonic leave no doubts as to their peerless virtuosity. Everything is marvellously shaped and proportioned, and the early (1981) digital sound is made firmer by this 'original-image' bit re-processing.

Mariss Jansons's account of the *Tenth Symphony* is the finest of his series and the best version of this work we have had for some time. He draws a splendid response from the Philadelphia Orchestra, and the playing has tremendous fervour. Karajan's interpretation remains pre-eminent, but the EMI sound is generally preferable and Jansons offers a substantial coupling.

Järvi, too, conducts an outstandingly strong and purposeful reading in superb sound, full and atmospheric. In the great span of the long *Moderato* first movement he chooses an ideal speed, which allows for moments of hushed repose but still builds up relentlessly. The curious little *Ballet suite No. 4*, with its sombre *Prelude* leading to a bouncy *Waltz* and a jolly *Scherzo tarantella*, makes a delightful bonus.

Recorded in full, brilliant and weighty sound, Skrowaczewski's version of the *Tenth* is also a top recommendation. Above all, the spacious *moderato* of the long first movement has a natural power and concentration which put it among the finest versions, with the Hallé brass superbly focused at the climaxes.

Rattle's Philharmonia version is curiously wayward in the two big slow movements, first and third in the scheme. In the first, Rattle is exceptionally slow, and tension slips too readily. So too in the third movement. The Scherzo and energetic finale are much more successful. The recording does not help, with the strings sounding thin and lacking body.

(i) *Symphony No. 10 in E min., Op. 93* (arr. for piano duet); (ii) *Four Preludes from Op. 34* (arr. for violin & piano).
(M) (***) Revelation mono RV 70002 [id.].
Dmitri Shostakovich, with (i) Moisei Vainberg; (ii) Leonid Kogan.

The recording may be primitive but this is of great documentary interest, capturing Shostakovich and his fellow-composer Moisei Vainberg playing the *Tenth Symphony* in a piano-duet arrangement only a few months after its completion and not long before Mravinsky made the première recording. They play with great fervour and strain the instrument to the limit. The performance is surprisingly brisk (47 minutes as opposed to the usual 50) and completely involving. The transcriptions of the *Preludes* are wonderfully played by Kogan and the composer, and there are also a few bars from *The Gadfly* too.

Symphonies Nos. 10 in E min., Op. 93; 11 in G min. (The Year 1905), Op. 103; (i) *4 monologues on poems by Pushkin, Op. 91 (orch. Rozhdestvensky)*; (ii) *Poor Columbus: Finale, Op. 23.*
(N) (B) **(*) BMG/Melodiya Dig./Analogue Twofer 74321 63461-2 (2) [id.]. USSR MoC SO, Rozhdestvensky; with (i) Anatole Safiulio; (ii) MoC Chamber Ch.

Following the pattern of his Melodiya Shostakovich series, Rozhdestvensky conducts a strong and spontaneous-sounding reading of the *Tenth*, not as portentous or intense as some but with a vein of spikiness that is totally idiomatic. Though the digital sound is full and bright (appropriately fierce in the second movement), the bass seems to be boomy and rather vague in the opening movement, and internal textures are somewhat coarsened at climaxes. Rozhdestvensky takes an exceptionally spacious view of the opening *Adagio* movement of No. 11 (*The Palace Square*). But overall his reading is red-blooded, and if not as bitingly intense as some, he consistently draws warmly expressive phrasing from his young players. Only in the finale does he adopt a speed that is faster than usual, losing something in weight. Like the others in the series the sound is full-bodied but coarsens somewhat at climaxes. The *Four Pushkin monologues* (1952) are heard here in an orchestration by the conductor. Closing with a resigned *Farewell* (to life), they are concerned with fear and political oppression in the Tsarist era, but the contemporary implications are obvious. No texts or translations are included. The *Poor Columbus Finale* is the second of the two pieces Shostakovich wrote in 1929 to frame an opera by a German composer, Erwin Kessel, when the work was given an avant garde staging in Leningrad. It is a bizarre epilogue written to accompany a cartoon film, a lampoon of the USA, which in the section describing the 'Arrival of the Yankees' introduces the trumpet tune familiar in the finale of *First piano concerto*, while also interpolating a briefly passionate choral appeal for international peace.

Symphonies Nos. 10 in E min.; (i) *13 in B flat min. (Babi-Yar), Op. 113.*

(N) (B) *** EMI double fforte Dig./Analogue CZS5 73368-2 (2) [CDFB 73368]. LSO, Previn; (i) with Dimiter Petrov, LSO Ch.

Previn's is a strong and dramatic reading of No. 10, marked by a specially compelling account of the long first movement, which steers an ideal course between expressive warmth and architectural strength. At marginally slower speeds than usual, Previn's rhythmic lift both in the scherzo and in the finale brings exhilarating results, sparkling and swaggering. The digital recording is early (1982), but strikingly firm and full, less aggressive-sounding than Karajan's analogue version. The *Thirteenth Symphony*, inspired by the often angry poems of Yevtushenko, is presented at its most stark and direct. Previn takes a relatively literal view of the sprung rhythms in the ironic second movement, *Humour*, and makes the picture of peasant women queueing for food in the snow less atmospheric than it sometimes is. The result is that the work becomes a genuine symphony, rather than an orchestral song cycle, but ending in wistfulness on a final Allegretto, *A Career*, with weaving flutes and gentle lolloping pizzicato rhythms. Playing and analogue recording are superb, among the very finest from this source, making this a very attractive pairing on all counts.

Symphony No. 11 (The Year 1905), Op. 103.

*** Delos Dig. D/CD 3080 [id.]. Helsinki PO, James DePreist.

(N) *** Decca Dig. 448 179-2 [id.]. St. Petersburg PO, Ashkenazy.

(M) *** Decca Dig. 425 072-2. Concg. O, Haitink.

*** Testament SBT 1099 [id.]. Fr. R. O, André Cluytens.

1905 was the year of the first Russian uprising, which foreshadowed the revolution to come rather more than a decade later. The result is a programme symphony conceived on a fairly large scale and, as in the *Leningrad Symphony*, its style is sometimes repetitive. The DePreist version won golden opinions: it certainly has the benefit of magnificent recording. The Helsinki orchestra may lack the weight and richness of sonority of the greatest orchestras but it plays with great intensity and feeling. A performance that has striking atmosphere and expressive power.

Ashkenazy's Shostakovich readings never fall below a high standard of accomplishment. The recording here is extremely vivid and finely detailed. Nor is there any lack of intensity and atmosphere, so no one acquiring this version is likely to feel let down. All the same, the early accounts by Mravinsky and Stokowski have an extra special concentration and power that resonate longer in the memory.

Haitink's sense of architecture is as impressive as always, even if at times he seems almost detached, lacking the last degree of tension. However, the Concertgebouw Orchestra plays superbly, and the Decca sound is as brilliant and realistic as ever.

Cluytens's recording of the *Eleventh Symphony* was made only a few months after its première and was recorded in Paris in the presence of the composer, a day or so after he had recorded the two *Piano concertos* with the same artists. It was issued in mono on three sides, the fourth being left blank and, thanks to its uncompetitive format, did not survive long in the catalogue. It appears now in stereo for the very first time and sounds quite astonishing. Indeed it stands up to modern competition very well. Shostakovich called the *Eleventh* his 'most Mussorgskian work' and, as emerges in Elisabeth Wilson's *Shostakovich: A Life Remembered*, it was clear to Soviet audiences that its 'sub-text' was not so much the abortive February rebellion of the title as the events in Budapest, where the Soviet Union had just suppressed the Hungarian uprising.

Symphonies Nos. 11 (The Year 1905), Op. 103; 12 (The Year 1917), Op. 112; Age of Gold (suite), Op. 22; Hamlet (suite), Op. 32a; October (symphonic poem), Op. 131; Overture on Russian and Kirghiz folk themes, Op. 115.

(N) (B) **(*) DG Double Dig. 459 415-2 (2) [id.]. Gothenburg SO, Neeme Järvi.

This is a generous package and besides the appropriately paired symphonies this DG Double has four additional inducements which are all brought off impressively. Neeme Järvi's account of the *Eleventh*

Symphony too, has much to recommend it, including good orchestral playing and very fine recorded sound. However, good though it is, the performance misses the last ounce of intensity, and the same comments must apply to Järvi's performance of No. 12 (even though here the recording has rather less transparency and sharpness of focus). If this symphony is to come off it has to be played with 200 per cent conviction and panache, and Järvi's performance does not really challenge Mravinsky.

Symphony No. 12 in D min. (The Year 1917), Op. 112.
(M) *** Erato/Warner 2292 45754-2 [id.]. Leningrad PO, Mravinsky.

The *Twelfth Symphony* is one of Shostakovich's more problematic essays in the genre. However, when a conductor of Mravinsky's quality is at the helm and drawing playing of electrifying intensity from the Leningrad Philharmonic, that impression is almost dispelled. Mravinsky's first version appeared in the early 1960s and long reigned supreme, but this Erato account, taken from a concert performance in 1984, is even higher in voltage, and the recording does ample justice to their playing.

(i) *Symphonies Nos. 12 in D min. (The Year 1917), Op. 112*; (i; ii) *13 in B flat min. (Babi-Yar), Op. 113*; (iii) *Cello concerto No. 1 in E flat, Op. 107; 8 Preludes from Op. 34* (orch. Kelemen).
(N) (B) **(*) BMG/Melodiya Dig./Analogue Twofer 74321 63460-2 [id.]. (i) USSR MoC SO; (ii) with Anatoli Safiulin, Russian State Academy Male Ch.; (iii) Mikhail Khomitser, USSR Large SO; Rozhdestvensky.

Rozhdestvensky is most persuasive in the out-and-out programme symphony, No.12, bringing out the atmosphere and drama in its picture of events of the 1917 revolution. The rugged strength of the writing – not merely illustrative – comes over powerfully. The bright, sometimes coarse recording is typical of the series. *Babi-Yar* is dramatically impressive too, a performance of genuine eloquence. The bass soloist Anatoli Safiulin is responsive to the music's combination of anguish and irony, and the Russian State Academy Male Choir make a comparably impressive contribution. This is worthwhile in its own right and the recording is one of the best in the series. Though Kondrashin's version (also available on Melodiya) is even finer, this 'Twofer' remains excellent value. Mikhai Khomitser's fine version of the *First Cello concerto* (also available on RCA Navigator, coupled with the two piano concertos – see above) is a considerable bonus, as are the eight *Preludes*, felicitously orchestrated by Milko Kelemen. They act as a final encore, often featuring the piano in concertante style. Wry cheekiness alternates with dance rhythms and a gentle *Largo* (No. 17 in the piano original), while No. 14 brings a plangent central *Adagio* (here given to the trombones) which Stokowski also orchestrated. They are beautifully played and recorded.

Symphony No. 13 in B flat min. (Babi-Yar), Op. 113.
(M) *** Decca Dig. 425 073-2. Marius Rintzler, Concg. Male Ch. & O, Haitink.
*** Sup. SU 0160-2 231. Peter Mikuláš, Prague Philharmonic Ch., Prague SO, Maxim Shostakovich.
*** Teldec/Warner Dig. 2292 45349-2 [90848]. Yevtushenko, Leiferkus, New York Ch. Arts, NYPO, Masur.

The often brutal directness of Haitink's way with Shostakovich works well in the *Thirteenth Symphony*, particularly in the long *Adagio* first movement, whose title, *Babi-Yar*, gives its name to the whole work. That first of five Yevtushenko settings, boldly attacking anti-semitism in Russia, sets the pattern for Haitink's severe view of the whole. Rintzler with his magnificent, resonant bass is musically superb but, matching Haitink, remains objective rather than dashingly characterful. The resolution of the final movement, with its pretty flutings surrounding a wry poem about Galileo and greatness, then works beautifully. Outstandingly brilliant and full sound, remarkable even for this series.

Maxim Shostakovich's Supraphon version, with sound so vivid you hear some alien noises, is menacingly atmospheric, one of the finest of his recordings of his father's symphonies. Helped by the immediate sound, he sustains each movement with fine concentration, with each movement heightened by characterful singing from the superb Czech bass, Peter Mikuláš, even more individual than in his Naxos recording. So in the second movement, '*Humour*', brutal and tense, he conveys a gleam of manic menace in the music and brings out the full chilling horror of the third movement with its picture of women queueing. The chorus with its Slavonic timbres sounds totally idiomatic too, not balanced too close, making this one of the most convincing versions of this moving and atmospheric song-cycle symphony.

Kurt Masur's reading of the *Babi-Yar Symphony* is very powerful indeed, full of atmosphere and intensity. It has the benefit of Sergei Leiferkus and the Men of the New York Choral Artists and very clean and well-focused recording. Another point of interest is Yevtushenko's readings which flank the performance. It does not sweep the board, but it is certainly among the best versions we have had to date.

Symphony No. 14 in G min., Op. 135.
(BB) *** Naxos Dig. 8.550631 [id.]. Hajóssyová, Mikuláš, Slovak RSO (Bratislava), Ladislav Slovák.

(M) **(*) Sony SMK 47617-2. Teresa Kubiak, Isser Bushkin, NYPO, Bernstein.

(M) **(*) Teldec/Warner 0630 17514-2. Vishnevskaya, Reshetin, Moscow Academic SO (members), Rostropovich.

(i) *Symphony No. 14, Op. 135;* (ii) *6 Poems of Marina Tsvetaeva, Op. 143a.*

(M) *** Decca Dig. 425 074-2. (i) Varady, Fischer-Dieskau; (ii) Wenkel; Concg. O, Haitink.

The *Fourteenth* is Shostakovich's most sombre and dark score, a setting of poems by Lorca, Apollinaire, Rilke, Brentano and Küchelbecker, all on the theme of death; Haitink's version gives each poem in its original language. It is a most powerful performance, and the outstanding recording is well up to the standard of this fine Decca series. The song-cycle, splendidly sung by Ortrun Wenkel, makes a fine bonus.

Slovák's account of No. 14 is one of the finest in his Shostakovich series for Naxos, strongly characterized in each of the 11 contrasted movements with the help of two superb soloists. Mikuláš is just as strong and individual as in No. 13, and Hajóssyová with her firm, Slavonic mezzo is equally idiomatic. Regularly, Slovák and his performers bring out the menace behind the composer's inspiration on the theme of death, with the fourth song, '*The Suicide*', particularly moving in its tenderness. The booklet gives a summary of each poem, but no texts or translations. Full, immediate sound.

Rostropovich's performance dates from 1973 and has the advantage of a very clear, analogue recording. Detail is reproduced with striking presence and definition within a good orchestral perspective. The soloists are too close but the result is arrestingly vivid. The performance is dark and intense, with expressive detail sometimes underlined. Vishnevskaya may not be to all tastes (she can sing touchingly but can also sound shrill above the stave). Reshetin, however, is consistently impressive.

Bernstein's version with Teresa Kubiak and Isser Bushkin, recorded in 1976, does not have the benefit of such excellent sound as the Haitink, yet, taken in its own right, it is perfectly acceptable and the performance is both powerful and deeply felt without underlining expressive points to excess. Shostakovich's bleak ruminations on the theme of death exercise a compelling fascination, for Bernstein gets good playing from the New Yorkers and there is a Mussorgskian atmosphere here which eludes the Decca performance. A pity there is no coupling: this plays for only 51 minutes.

(i; ii) *Symphonies Nos. 14, Op. 135; 15 in A, Op. 141*; (ii) *4 Romances after Pushkin* (orch. Rozhdestvensky); (ii) *6 Romances to texts by British poets*. (iii) *6 Romances to texts by Japanese poets*; (iv) *8 English and American folk songs*.

(N) (B) *** BMG/Melodiya Dig./Analogue Twofer 74321 59057-2 (2) [id.]. USSR MoC SO, Rozhdestvensky; with (i) Makvala Kasrashvill, (ii) Anatoly Saifulin; (iii) Alexei Maslennikov; (iv) Elena Ivanova; Sergei Yakovenko.

In the *Fourteenth Symphony*, the Ministry of Culture Symphony Orchestra is magnetic in drawing Shostakovich's chosen sequence of poems together; sadly however, the booklet does not include texts, only a summary of each poem (and that applies to the other song cycles included here). The full, bright digital sound is more atmospheric than some in the Melodiya series, and though the voices are balanced close, their characterful Slavonic timbre will delight rather than offend Russian ears. As an instinctive interpreter of Shostakovich, Rozhdestvensky is very good at tapping the vein of wry humour in all the symphonies, a quality which comes to the fore in the equivocal *Fifteenth*. Again with vividly full-bodied sound this is another of the most recommendable of his Melodiya series, particularly when the additional couplings are so generous. On the first disc the darkly ambivalent passion of the Japanese love poems matches the lack of optimism in the Pushkin *Romances,* and on the second the Russian melancholy and resignation to Fate again imbues the six British settings (drawing on both Robert Burns and Shakespeare), especially when both singers are so involved and so persuasive. If the clouds finally lift for many of the closing group of English and American folk-songs, sadness still goes hand in hand with high spirits. They are all sung in Russian, opening with *The sailor's bride* (more familiar as '*Blow the wind southerly*'), and both this and '*Coming through the rye*' are very engaging in the Slavic tongue. The first seven are sung quite delightfully by Elena Ivanova, then Sergei Yakovenko's vibrant baritone gives a curious new slant to *Johnny will come marching home again*.

Symphony No. 15 in A, Op. 141.

(N) ** Teldec/Warner Dig. 9031 74560-2 [id.]. LSO, Rostropovich.

Rostropovich tends to underline and italicize too readily and the overall effect can be all too heavy. The LSO do not sound at their best in this 1992 recording and to offer its 45 minutes at full price in current trading conditions is distinctly uncompetitive.

(i) *Symphony No. 15 in A, Op. 141;* (ii) *From Jewish folk poetry* (song-cycle), *Op. 79*.

✿ (M) *** Decca Analogue/Dig. 425 069-2. (i) LPO; (ii) Söderström, Wenkel, Karczykowski, Concg. O; Haitink.

Early readings of the composer's last symphony seemed to underline the quirky unpredictability of the work, with the collage of strange quotations – above all the *William Tell* galop, which keeps recurring in the first movement – seemingly joky rather than profound. Haitink by contrast makes the first movement sound genuinely symphonic, bitingly urgent. He underlines the purity of the bare lines of the second movement; after the Wagner quotations which open the finale, his slow tempo for the main lyrical theme gives it heartaching tenderness, not the usual easy triviality. The playing of the LPO is excellent, with refined tone and superb attack, and the recording is both analytical and atmospheric. The CD includes a splendidly sung version of *From Jewish folk poetry*, settings which cover a wide range of emotions including tenderness, humour and even happiness as in the final song. Ryszard Karczykowski brings vibrant Slavonic feeling to the work which, with its wide variety of mood and colour, has a scale to match the shorter symphonies.

CHAMBER AND INSTRUMENTAL MUSIC

Cello sonata in D min., Op. 40.

(N) *** Virgin/EMI Dig. VC5 45274-2 [id.]. Truls Mørk, Lars Vogt – PROKOFIEV: *Cello sonata in C, Op. 119.* STRAVINSKY: *Suite Italienne.* ***

*** Chandos Dig. CHAN 8340 [id.]. Turovsky, Edlina – PROKOFIEV: *Sonata.* ***

*** BIS Dig. CD 336 [id.]. Thedéen, Pöntinen – SCHNITTKE: *Sonata;* STRAVINSKY: *Suite italienne.* ***

(BB) *** ASV Quicksilva Dig. CDQS 6218 [(M) id.]. Bernard Gregor-Smith, Yolande Wrigley – MARTINU: *Variations;* JANACEK: *Pohádka;* PROKOFIEV: *Cello sonata.* ***

(BB) **(*) Arte Nova Dig. 74321 27805-2 [id.]. Emil Klein, Cristian Beldi – PROKOFIEV: *Cello sonata.* **(*)

Of the many accounts of Shostakovich's fine *Sonata* listed in the catalogue, this newcomer from Truls Mørk and Lars Vogt can more than hold its own with the best. The performances are very vital and intelligent, and eminently well recorded. The booklet is carelessly edited: it twice speaks of this as the '*Cello Sonata No. 2*'.

Yuli Turovsky and Luba Edlina play the *Cello sonata* with great panache and eloquence, if in the finale they almost succumb at times to exaggeration in their handling of its humour – no understatement here.

The Swedish cellist, Torleif Thedéen, has a real feeling for its structure and the vein of bitter melancholy under its ironic surface. Roland Pöntinen gives him excellent support and the BIS recording does justice to this partnership.

Both the alternative bargain performances are very serviceable and are unlikely to disappoint. Bernard Gregor-Smith and Yolande Wrigley have the benefit of a recording with greater bloom and a more lively acoustic, though the piano is sometimes more dominant in the aural picture than is ideal.

Emil Klein and Cristian Beldi, both Romanian born, give a very well-characterized account of the *Sonata*, tautly held together and vital in feeling, though the sound is a bit dryish. The balance between cello and piano is very well judged, even if the timbre of the latter is less realistic than ASV's. Artistically there is not a great deal to choose between them. On balance, the ASV would be the one to have on account of the fresher sound and the additional Martinů and Janáček items.

Piano quintet in G min., Op. 57.

(***) Testament mono SBT 1077 [id.] Victor Aller, Hollywood Qt – FRANCK: *Piano quintet.* (***)

(M) **(*) CRD CRD 3351; *CRDC 4051* [id.]. Clifford Benson, Alberni Qt – BRITTEN: *Quartet No. 1.* ***

Piano quintet, Op. 57; Piano trio No. 2 in E min., Op. 67.

**(*) Chandos Dig. CHAN 8342; *ABTD 1088* [id.]. Borodin Trio, Zweig, Horner.

Piano quintet in G min.; Piano trio No. 2; 4 Waltzes for flute, clarinet & piano.

*** Virgin/EMI (SIS) Dig. VC7 59312-2 [id.]. Nash Ens. (members).

The Nash Ensemble on Virgin offer the ideal coupling – plus an interesting makeweight – of two of Shostakovich's key chamber works, written before his quartet series developed, when he completed only the first, relatively trivial work. The *Piano trio* is a particularly painful and anguished work, dedicated to the memory of a close friend, Ivan Sollertinsky, who died in the year of its composition. The Nash players bring out the dedicated intensity in this very personal writing, with refined readings which can be warmly recommended, even if they are not quite as characterfully individual as the very finest.

On Testament a magisterial account of the *Piano quintet* if ever there was one, this belongs among the finest of interpretations. Its praises were sung by the authors of *The Record Guide* in the mid 1950s when they spoke of it in their down-to-earth manner as 'a dazzling performance and their tone, though often extremely delicate, is never skinny'. Readers who care about Shostakovich should find it an indispensable issue and need make few allowances for the 1952 sound.

The Chandos version is bold in character and concentrated in feeling. Alternatively, there is a vigorous and finely conceived account from Clifford Benson and the Alberni Quartet, vividly recorded; if the Britten coupling is wanted, this will be found fully satisfactory.

Piano trios Nos. 1, Op. 8; 2, Op. 67.
(N) *** Nimbus Dig. NI 5572 [id.]. V. Piano Trio – SCHNITTKE: *Trio*. ***

The Vienna Piano Trio on Nimbus give cogently argued and finely paced accounts of both the Shostakovich *Trios*. The Vienna is among the best and are naturally and vividly recorded. If the 1985 Schnittke *Trio* appeals as a coupling, this is an eminently desirable recommendation.

Piano trio No. 2 in E min., Op. 67.
(N) *** Erato/Warner Dig. 0630 17875-2 [id.]. Repin, Berezovsky, Yablonsky – TCHAIKOVSKY: *Piano trio*. ***
(N) *** Decca Dig. 452 899-2 [id.]. Olli Mustonen, Joshua Bell, Steven Isserlis – MESSIAEN: *Quatuor pour la fin du temps*. ***

Vadim Repin, Boris Berezovsky and Dmitri Yablonsky give an eminently satisfying account of the *E minor Trio*, though the finale has some idiosyncratic touches that diminish pleasure. All the same there is a great deal to admire here. It is superbly recorded and comes with an outstanding account of the Tchaikovsky *Trio*.

The Decca is a marvellously telling and perceptive account of Shostakovich's masterpiece, and is very truthfully balanced. The only snag is the very wide dynamic range of the recording. The opening *pianopianissimo* has ethereal concentration, but registers so quietly that the listener is tempted to turn up the volume. If one does, the *fortissimos* are not quite comfortable, for the microphones are fairly close. But it is possible to get it right, and then the rewards of the playing are very considerable.

2 Pieces for string octet, Op. 11.
*** Chandos Dig. CHAN 9131 [id.]. ASMF Chamber Ens. – ENESCU: *Octet in C*; R. STRAUSS: *Capriccio: Sextet*. ***

The Academy of St Martin-in-the-Fields Chamber Ensemble play splendidly and with conviction; they are beautifully recorded and also offer a highly recommendable version of the Enescu *Octet*.

String quartets

String quartets Nos. 1–15.
(M) *** Decca 433 078-2 (6). Fitzwilliam Qt.

String quartets Nos. 1–15; (i) *Piano quintet in G min.* (ii) *2 Pieces for string octet, Op. 11.*
(M) *** BMG/Melodiya 74321 40711-2 (6) [id.]. Borodin Qt; with (i) Sviatoslav Richter; (ii) Prokofiev Qt.

The Shostakovich *Quartets* thread through his creative life like some inner odyssey and inhabit terrain of increasing spiritual desolation. The Fitzwilliam Quartet played to Shostakovich himself and gave the UK premières of his last three quartets, and they bring to the whole cycle complete and total dedication. One has only to sample the first two quartets to discover the sustained and often hushed intensity and spontaneity of this playing. They are given first-class recording too, with great presence and natural body. The recordings were made in All Saints' Church, Petersham, Surrey between 1975 and 1977; a rather forward balance was chosen, perhaps because of the ecclesiastical acoustic, and this is slightly emphasized by the CD transfer, yet there is a natural transparency and a firm focus throughout. There are minor criticisms, but they are too trivial to weigh in the balance, for this set is by any standards a formidable achievement.

Originally issued on EMI and now reappearing on BMG/Melodiya, the Borodin Quartet's second recording of Shostakovich's complete *String quartets* is an economical investment when purchased complete. The present recordings are made in a generally drier acoustic than their predecessors, and Nos. 3 and 5 suffer noticeably in this respect. However, the ears quickly adjust and the performances can only be described as masterly. The Borodins possess enormous refinement, an altogether sumptuous tone and a perfection of technical address that is almost in a class of its own – and what wonderful intonation! These and the Bartók six are the greatest quartet cycles produced in the present century and are mandatory listening. The *Piano quintet* was recorded at a public concert at the Moscow Conservatoire, and it goes without saying that with Richter at the helm the account is a powerful one, although the quality of the sound here is noticeably dry and forward. The *Two Pieces for string octet* are now added to the second CD.

String quartets Nos. 1–15. 2 Pieces for string quartet, Op. 36.
**(*) Olympia OCD 5009(5) [id.]. Shostakovich Qt.

String quartets Nos. 1 in C, Op. 49; 3 in F, Op. 73; 4 in D, Op. 83; 2 Pieces for string quartet, Op. 36.
(N) *** Olympia OCD 531 [id.]. Shostakovich Qt.

String quartets Nos. 10 in A flat, Op. 118; 11 in F min., Op. 122; 15 in E flat min, Op. 144.
(N) *** Olympia OCD 534 [id.]. Shostakovich Qt.

String quartets Nos. 2 in A, Op. 68; 5 in B flat, Op. 92; 7 in F sharp min., Op. 108.
*** Olympia OCD 532 [id.]. Shostakovich Qt.

String quartets Nos. 6 in G, Op. 101; 8 in C min., Op. 110; 9 in E flat, Op. 117.
*** Olympia OCD 533 [id.]. Shostakovich Qt.

String quartets Nos. 12 in D flat, Op. 133; 13 in B flat min., Op. 138; 14 in F sharp, Op. 142.
*** Olympia OCD 535 [id.]. Shostakovich Qt.

The eponymous Shostakovich quartet recorded a cycle over the period 1978 to 1985 and bring a special intensity to this repertoire as well as effortless technical address, and a tonal blend that gives their readings a strong claim on the collector's allegiance. We have responded to their cycle with appreciation; theirs are the kind of performances one would be perfectly happy with if they were the only ones available; and the recordings are very satisfactory indeed. The complete set is also available in a box. It is no longer possible to talk of an out-and-out first choice in this repertoire.

String quartets Nos. 1 in C, Op. 49; 2 in A, Op. 68; 4 in D, Op. 83.
(***) Koch/Consonance mono 81-3005 [id.]. Beethoven Qt.

String quartets Nos. 3 in F, Op. 73; 6 in G, Op. 101.
*** Koch/Consonance 81-3007 [id.]. Beethoven Qt.

String quartets Nos. 7 in F sharp min., Op. 108; 8 in C min., Op. 110; 15 in E flat min., Op. 144.
*** Koch/Consonance 81-3006 [id.]. Beethoven Qt.

String quartets Nos. 9, in E flat, Op. 117; 10 in A flat, Op. 118; 11 in F min., Op. 122.
*** Koch/Consonance 81-3009 [id.]. Beethoven Qt.

String quartets Nos. 12 in D flat, Op. 133; 13 in B flat min., Op. 138; 14 in F sharp, Op. 142.
*** Koch/Consonance 81-3008 [id.]. Beethoven Qt.

Right from the *First Quartet* of 1938 through to the last, finished not long before his death, the Beethoven Quartet were closely associated with the composer and gave the first performances of nearly all the quartets. Since they collaborated so closely with him, their view of this cycle carries special authority. Collectors who were lucky enough to get the old Melodiya LPs from the 1950s and 1960s and who still treasure them, will welcome their reappearance in this cleaned-up form. With a few exceptions (Nos. 8, 10 and 13), theirs were also first recordings – and no other group was closer to Shostakovich's mind. Nos. 9, 10 and 11, for example, were made in 1965 and 1969, when the works were fresh from the composer's pen. Even if you have the fine cycles by the Borodins and the Fitzwilliams, this set is an important documentary record. In some of the earlier recordings allowances must be made for the sound; No. 3 is a later performance (1960) than the old mono LP, which used to be coupled to the *Piano quintet* on Parlophone.

String quartets Nos. 1 in C, Op. 49; 8 in C min., Op. 110; 9 in E flat, Op. 117.
(BB) *** Naxos Dig. 8.550973 [id.]. Eder Qt.

If the Naxos disc is not necessarily a first choice, no one investing in it need fear they are getting short-changed. The Eder Quartet is a very distinguished ensemble and have a very good feeling for this repertoire. They are actually better recorded than the Borodins on EMI, and those for whom economy is a primary concern should consider this.

String quartets Nos. 2 in A, Op. 78; 3 in F, Op. 73; 7 in F sharp min., Op. 108; 8 in C min., Op. 110; 12 in D flat, Op. 133.
(BB) *** Virgin 2x1 Dig. YBD5 61630-2 (2). Borodin Qt.

String quartets Nos. 3 in F, Op. 73; 7 in F sharp min., Op. 108; 8 in C min., Op. 110.
*** Virgin/EMI Dig. VC7 59041-2 [id.]. Borodin Qt.
(N) *** BIS Dig. CD 913 [id.]. Yggdrasil Qt.

The new Borodin accounts now on a Virgin Double have the benefit of far better and more refined recording than their earlier, Melodiya versions on RCA. The sound is richer and cleaner and has a pleasing bloom, as one would expect from the Snape Maltings. As far as the performances are concerned, some things come off better than others so that on balance there is little to choose between the earlier and newer sets; those who have the former need not make a change. This is one of the greatest quartets now before the public and they are completely inside this music. Those coming new to these works will probably opt for the newer, Virgin, digital versions.

The Yggdrasil are a young Swedish group who have already made a positive impression with the three Berwald *Quartets* and are now embarking on a Shostakovich cycle. This first issue is an auspicious start with a bold and searching account of the autobiographical *Eighth*, and intelligent and satisfying readings of its companions. Both the Borodin and Fitzwilliam sets have done sterling service (and in lesser prominence the eponymous *Shostakovich quartet*) but there is always room for newcomers that promise as much as this.

String quartets Nos. 2 in A, Op. 68; 12 in D flat, Op. 133.
(BB) *** Naxos Dig. 8.550975 [id.]. Eder Qt.

If anything, the Eder coupling of Nos. 2 and 12 is even more impressive than their first disc. The account of the third-movement *Adagio: Recitativo and Romance* of No. 2 with its intense, improvisatory feeling is particularly fine, and the closing *Theme and variations* is strongly characterized. Similarly the extended *Allegretto* second movement of No. 12 is powerfully argued and these performances have compelling concentration throughout. The recording too is excellent.

String quartets Nos. 4 in D, Op. 83; 6 in G, Op. 101; 7 in F sharp min., Op. 108.
(BB) *** Naxos Dig. 8.550972 [id.]. Eder Qt.

Quite apart from its cost, this series by Hungary's Eder Quartet is emerging as one of the most competitive of the newer versions of this powerful music. The recorded sound is superior to the Melodiya Borodins and offers a serious challenge to them.

String quartets Nos. 4 in D, Op. 83; 8 in C min., Op. 110; 11 in F min., Op. 122.
*** ASV Dig. CDDCA 631 [id.]. Coull Qt.

The *Fourth quartet* is a work of exceptional beauty and lucidity, one of the most haunting of the cycle; the *Eleventh Quartet* is a puzzling, almost cryptic work in seven short movements. The Coull are among the most gifted of the younger British quartets and give eminently creditable accounts of all three pieces. Good if slightly overlit recording.

String quartets Nos. 4 in D, Op. 83; 11 in F min., Op. 122; 14 in F sharp, Op. 142.
*** DG (IMS) Dig. 445 864-2. Hagen Qt.

The Hagen Quartet is as impeccable an ensemble as any now before the public, and if the appearance of this disc heralds a complete cycle it is very good news. There is a stark austerity about the Beethoven Quartet's versions that the newcomers do not always achieve but, generally speaking, these belong among the most beautifully played and thoughtful readings of these *Quartets*.

String quartet No. 8, Op. 110.
❁ *** Koch Dig. 3-6436-2 [id.]. Medici Qt – BRITTEN: *Quartet No. 3;* JANACEK: *Quartet No. 1;* RAVEL: *Quartet;* SMETANA: *Quartet No. 1.* *** ❁
(M) *** Classic fM Dig. 75605 57027-2. Chilingirian Qt – BORODIN: *Quartet No. 2;* DVORAK: *Quartet in F, Op. 96.* ***
(M) **(*) Decca 425 541-2. Borodin Qt – BORODIN; TCHAIKOVSKY: *Quartets.* **(*)
**(*) Collins Dig. 1450-2 [id.]. Duke Qt – SCHNITTKE: *String quartet No. 2;* TCHAIKOVSKY: *String quartet No. 1.* **(*)

Immediately creating a powerful atmospheric spell at the opening, attacking the second movement with great ferocity and finding a bleak emptiness of constituents for the other-worldly closing obituary, this Medici account is a performance of rapt dedication and concentration, given a recording which achieves a remarkably natural presence.

On Classic fM the Chilingirians also give a tautly controlled performance, not as flexible as some but with the power enhanced by the rich, immediate digital recording.

The Borodins' Decca performance is outstanding and the recording real and vivid, although the balance means that in the CD transfer the effect is very forward, almost too boldly immediate.

The Duke Quartet are unquestionably a fine ensemble with keen, alert responses and remarkable unanimity of mind. As with their earlier CD, the upfront balance does not do them any favours and brings the listener uncomfortably near (sometimes it seems one is actually on) the platform. With this proviso, if the coupling meets your needs, you can invest in it with some confidence.

String quartets Nos. (i) *14, Op. 142;* (ii) *15, Op. 144.*
*** HM/Praga PR 254043 [id.]. (i) Glinka String Qt; (ii) Beethoven Qt.
(BB) *** Naxos Dig. 8.550976 [id.]. Eder Qt.

The Praga recordings date from 1976–7 and come from the Czech Radio archives. The Glinka Quartet is a first-rate ensemble and their intense account of the *Fourteenth Quartet*, recorded only a year after the composer's death, is deeply felt. The Beethoven Quartet's account of the *Fifteenth* (they also recorded it commercially for Melodiya) penetrates deeply into this death-haunted music.

Cultured and finely shaped performances of two of Shostakovich's bleakest works on Naxos. As quartet playing goes, the Eder are second to none, and they have the benefit of very good recording. Certainly worth the money.

Violin sonata, Op. 134.
*** Chandos Dig. CHAN 8988 [id.]. Mordkovitch, Benson – PROKOFIEV: *Sonatas;* SCHNITTKE: *In memoriam.* ***
*** Chandos Dig. CHAN 8343 [id.]. Dubinsky, Edlina – SCHNITTKE: *Sonata No. 1* etc. ***

The *Violin sonata* can seem a dry piece, but Mordkovitch's natural intensity, her ability to convey depth of feeling without sentimentality, transforms it. Clifford Benson is the understanding pianist. In first-rate sound it makes a fine central offering for Mordkovitch's well-planned disc of Soviet violin music.

Rostislav Dubinsky's account is undoubtedly eloquent, and Luba Edlina makes a fine partner. The recording is excellent too, although it is balanced a shade closely.

PIANO MUSIC

24 Preludes, Op. 34.
*** Decca (IMS) Dig. 433 055-2 [id.]. Olli Mustonen – ALKAN: *25 Preludes.* ***
(N) *** Collins Dig. 1496-2 [id.]. Artur Pizarro – SCRIABIN: *24 Preludes, Op. 11.* ***

Of the recordings of the Shostakovich *Preludes* Op. 34 currently listed in the catalogue, the Decca version by the young Finnish pianist, Olli Mustonen, is the strongest contender both artistically and technically. This is the best record of the *Preludes* since Menahem Pressler's old LP from the 1950s.

Like Mustonen, Pizarro characterizes the Shostakovich *Preludes, Op. 34* splendidly. They can scarcely be flawed at any point and this distinguished issue can be recommended alongside the Decca CD, with a choice of couplings – Alkan or Scriabin.

24 Preludes, Op. 34; Piano sonata No. 2, Op. 61
(N) ** Cyprès Dig. CYP2622 [id.]. Johan Schmidt.

Johan Schmidt is a young Belgian pianist with good fingers and clean articulation. He is fluent and intelligent but is let down by the synthetic sounding recording which is very two-dimensional. The piano is too close and the acoustic dry.

24 Preludes, Op. 34; Piano sonata No. 2, Op. 61; 3 Fantastic dances, Op. 5.
*** Hyperion Dig. CDA 66620 [id.]. Tatiana Nikolayeva.

Here are the most important Shostakovich piano works *not* inspired by Tatiana Nikolayeva, played by one of the composer's most trusted exponents and very well recorded indeed. She is one of the authentic advocates of Shostakovich, and her CD will be a must for most collectors. Recommended alongside Mustonen.

24 Preludes and fugues, Op. 87.
❁ (M) *** BMG/Melodiya 74321 19849-2 (3) [id.]. Tatiana Nikolayeva.
*** Hyperion Dig. CDA 66441/3 [id.]. Tatiana Nikolayeva.
(N) *** Decca Dig. 466 066-2 [id.]. Vladimir Ashkenazy.

In this repertoire, the first choice must inevitably be Tatiana Nikolayeva, 'the onlie begetter', as it were, of the *Preludes and fugues*. Her reading has enormous concentration and a natural authority that is majestic. There is wisdom and humanity here, and she finds depths in this music that have eluded most other pianists who have offered samples. No grumbles about the Hyperion recording, which is very natural. However, her Melodiya set, made in 1987, is if anything cleaner and better focused (if a bit dry). In neither reading will readers be disappointed.

Ashkenazy's set has the advantage of good Decca sound; there is a pleasing ambience and great clarity and warmth. His playing is very fine – that goes almost without saying – though he traverses the cycle in 141 minutes as opposed to Nikolayeva's 168. In comparing individual pieces, Nikolayeva always seems to find so much more in this music. She has been inside it and it shows in the subtlety of her colouring and depth of tone, and the sense of space. On its own terms the Ashkenazy is recommendable but he does not perhaps tell the whole story.

Preludes and fugues, Op. 87, Nos. 1 in C; 5 in D; 24 in D min.
(***) Testament mono SBT 1089 [id.]. Emil Gilels – CHOPIN: *Sonata No. 2;* MOZART: *Piano sonata No. 17.* (***)

These three *Preludes and fugues* were recorded in New York in 1955. The sound is a little dry and close, but the playing is magisterial.

24 Preludes and fugues, Op. 87, Nos. 2–4, 8–10, 14–16, 20–22.
(N) *(*) RCA Dig. 74321 61446-2 (2) [id.]. Olli Mustonen – BACH: *Preludes and fugues.* *(*)

Olli Mustonen has chosen a dozen of the Shostakovich Op. 87 set of *Preludes and Fugues*, composed for Tatiana Nikolayeva in 1950, and juxtaposes them with half of *Book I* of the Bach *Well-Tempered Clavier*. This is an idea that might work well in the concert hall or in a broadcast but will not necessarily meet the needs of collectors. His considerable technical prowess and command of part-writing are a vehicle for his own rather than Shostakovich's art. The eccentricities – exaggerated staccatos picked from the keyboard – and his narcissistic attention-seeking detract from the half of Shostakovich he does give us.

VOCAL MUSIC

Song of the forests, Op. 81.
(N) *** RCA Dig. 09026 68877-2 [id.]. Kisseliev, Bezzubenko, Glinka College Boys' Ch., St Petersburg Ch. & PO, Temirkanov – PROKOFIEV: *On guard for peace.* ***

The *Song of the forests*, unashamedly written as a Soviet propaganda piece, has regularly been dismissed as a potboiler but this fine recording under Temirkanov demonstrates that though Shostakovich deliberately simplified his idiom, the ideas are consistently fresh and memorable, not at all platitudinous. Solo and choral singing is first-rate, helped by full, atmospheric sound. Aptly and imaginatiovely coupled with the comparable Prokofiev propaganda piece.

OPERA

(i) *The Gamblers* (complete);(ii) *The Nose* (complete).
(N) (M) *** BMG/Melodiya 74321 60319-2 (2) [id.]. (i) Vladimir Rybasenko, Vladimir Tarkhov, Valery Belykh, Leningrad PO; (ii) Eduard Akimov, Valery Belykh, Nina Sasulova, Alexander Lomonosov, Lyudmila Sapegina, Moscow Chamber Theatre Ch. & O, (i & ii) Rozhdestvensky.

These two works, both based on Gogol, make an ideal coupling, each of them drawing on the satirical vein in the composer's personality. *The Gamblers* is only a fragment, written at the height of the Second World War in the same year as the *Leningrad Symphony*. As an attack on those who cheat society, its theme could be taken as both national (against Hitler) and domestic (against bureaucracy), and it is sad that it was never completed. In very immediate sound, with voices very clear, this is a live recording of the world première in Leningrad Philharmonic Hall in 1978, very well played and sung. *The Nose* dates from 1930, an even sharper attack on bureaucracy, and represents a full flowering of the Soviet avant-garde movement of the 1920s, soon to be suppressed. The singers and players of the Moscow Chamber Theatre give it a brilliantly idiomatic performance, vividly recorded, with Rozhdestvensky again the vigorous and colourful advocate. No librettos are provided, but the synopses are nicely detailed and linked to the copious index points, very necessary if the humour is to come over.

Lady Macbeth of Mtsensk (complete).
❁ *** EMI CDS7 49955-2 (2) [Ang. CDCB 49955]. Vishnevskaya, Gedda, Petkov, Krenn, Amb. Op. Ch., LPO, Rostropovich.
*** DG Dig. 437 511-2 (2) [id.]. Ewing, Haugland, Larin, Langridge, Kristine Ciesinski, Moll, Kotcherga, Zednik, Paris Bastille Op. Ch. & O, Myung-Whun Chung.

Rostropovich, in his finest recording ever, proves with thrilling conviction that this first version of Shostakovich's greatest work for the stage is among the most original operas of the century. Vishnevskaya is inspired to give an outstanding performance and provides moments of great beauty alongside aptly coarser singing; and Gedda matches her well, totally idiomatic. As the sadistic father-in-law, Petkov is magnificent, particularly in his ghostly return, and there are fine contributions from Robert Tear, Werner Krenn, Birgit Finnilä and Alexander Malta.

If ever Rostropovich's classic EMI recording of this opera is unavailable, then Chung's provides an alternative not quite so violent or powerful, but even more moving. The sound is more atmospheric, not quite so immediate, which enhances the gentler, lyrical approach that Chung takes in many passages from the very start. The biggest contrast comes in the portrayal of the heroine. Where Vishnevskaya makes her a ravening fire-eater, with the voice abrasive and aggressive, Maria Ewing's portrait is much more vulnerable, with moods and responses subtly varied, her feminine charms more vividly conveyed in singing far more sensuous, with the beauty of hushed *pianissimos* most tenderly affecting. Sergei Larin as Katerina's labourer-lover equally gains over his EMI rival, Nicolai Gedda, by sounding more aptly youthful, with his tenor both firm and clear yet Slavonic-sounding. His touch is lighter than Gedda's, with a nice vein of irony. Aage Haugland is magnificent as Boris, Katerina's father-in-law, and Philip Langridge sings sensitively as her husband, Zinovi, while Kurt Moll as the Old Convict provides an extra emotional focus in his important solo at the start of the last Act.

Sibelius, Jean (1865–1957)

Andante festivo; Finlandia, Op. 26; Karelia suite, Op. 11; King Christian II (suite); (i) *Luonnotar, Op. 70. The Oceanides, Op. 73.*
*** DG Dig. 447 760-2. (i) Soile Isokoski; Gothenburg SO, Neeme Järvi.

This magnificent, impeccably recorded Sibelius anthology brings one of the best accounts of *The Oceanides* we have had since the celebrated Beecham version, made at the composer's own request, and a first-class *Luonnotar* – again, one of the best ever made. The remaining pieces are hardly less satisfying. The engineering is by the usual Gothenburg team that serviced this orchestra's BIS recordings.

Autrefois (Scène pastorale), Op. 96b; The Bard, Op. 64; Presto in D for strings; Spring song, Op. 16; Suite caractéristique, Op. 100; Suite champêtre, Op. 98b; Suite mignonne, Op. 98a; Valse chevaleresque, Op. 96c; Valse lyrique, Op. 96a.
*** BIS Dig. CD 384 [id.]. Gothenburg SO, Järvi.

A mixed bag. *The Bard* is Sibelius at his greatest and most powerful, and it finds Järvi at his best. The remaining pieces are all light: some of the movements of the *Suite mignonne* and *Suite champêtre* could come straight out of a Tchaikovsky ballet, and Järvi does them with great charm. The last thing that the *Suite*, Op. 100, can be called is *caractéristique*, while the three pieces, Op. 96, find Sibelius in Viennese waltz mood. The rarity is *Autrefois*, which has a beguiling charm and is by far the most haunting of these pastiches. Sibelius introduces two sopranos and their *vocalise* is altogether captivating. The *Presto in D major for strings* is a transcription – and a highly effective one – of the third movement of the *B flat Quartet*, Op. 4. Excellent recording, as one has come to expect from BIS.

Belshazzar's Feast (suite), Op. 54; Dance intermezzo, Op. 45/2; The Dryad, Op. 45/1; Pan and Echo, Op. 53; Swanwhite, Op. 54.
*** BIS Dig. CD 359 [id.]. Gothenburg SO, Neeme Järvi.

Belshazzar's Feast, a beautifully atmospheric piece of orientalism, and the incidental music for Strindberg's *Swanwhite* may not be Sibelius at his most powerful but both include wonderful things. Neeme Järvi's collection with the Gothenburg orchestra is first class in every way.

Cassazione, Op. 6; Preludio; The Tempest: Prelude & suites 1–2, Op. 109; Tiera.
*** BIS Dig. CD 448 [id.]. Gothenburg SO, Järvi.

Järvi's recording of Sibelius's incidental music to *The Tempest* is among the most atmospheric since Beecham and, though it does not surpass the latter in pieces like *The Oak-tree* or the *Chorus of the winds*, it is still very good. The *Cassazione* resembles the *King Christian II* music in character, but it is well worth having on disc. Neither *Tiera* nor the *Preludio*, both from the 1890s, is of great interest or particularly characteristic.

Violin concerto in D min. (1903–4 version); *Violin concerto in D min., Op. 47* (1905; published version).

*** BIS Dig. CD 500 [id.]. Leonidas Kavakos, Lahti SO, Osmo Vänskä.

The first performance of the *Violin concerto* left Sibelius dissatisfied and he immediately withdrew it for revision. This CD presents Sibelius's initial thoughts so that for the first time we can see the familiar final version struggling to emerge from the chrysalis. Comparison of the two concertos makes a fascinating study: the middle movement is the least affected by change, but the outer movements are both longer in the original score, and the whole piece takes almost 40 minutes. The Greek violinist, Leonidis Kavakos, proves more than capable of handling the hair-raising difficulties of the 1904 version and is an idiomatic exponent of the definitive concerto. The Lahti orchestra under Osmo Vänskä give excellent support and the balance is natural and realistic. An issue of exceptional interest and value.

Violin concerto in D min., Op. 47.

✿ *** Sony Dig. SK 44548 [id.]. Cho-Liang Lin, Philh. O, Salonen – NIELSEN: *Violin concerto.* *** ✿

(M) *** Decca 425 080-2 [id.]. Kyung-Wha Chung, LSO, Previn – TCHAIKOVSKY: *Violin concerto.* ***

(M) *** RCA 09026 61744-2 [id.]. Heifetz, Chicago SO, Hendl – GLAZUNOV: *Concerto;* PROKOFIEV: *Concerto No. 2.* ***

(N) *** EMI Dig. CDC5 56418-2 [id.]. Sarah Chang, BPO, Mariss Jansons – MENDELSSOHN: *Violin concerto in E min.* ***

*** EMI CDC5 56150-2 [id.]. Perlman, Pittsburgh SO, Previn – TCHAIKOVSKY: *Violin concerto.* ***

(M) *** Sony Stern Edition I SMK 66829 [id.]. Stern, Phd. O, Ormandy – TCHAIKOVSKY: *Violin concerto.* ***

(M) *** EMI Dig. CD-EMX 2203. Little, RLPO, Handley – BRAHMS: *Violin concerto.* ***

*** EMI Dig. CDC7 54127-2 [id.]. Kennedy, CBSO, Rattle (with TCHAIKOVSKY: *Concerto.* **(*))

*** Erato/Warner Dig. 4509-98537-2 [id.]. Vadim Repin, LSO, Emmanuel Krivine – TCHAIKOVSKY: *Violin concerto.* ***

(***) EMI mono CDH7 61011-2. Ginette Neveu, Philh. O, Susskind – BRAHMS: *Concerto.* (***)

(BB) *** Naxos Dig. 8.550329; *4550329* [id.]. Dong-Suk Kang, Slovak (Bratislava) RSO, Adrian Leaper – HALVORSEN: *Air Norvégien* etc.; SINDING: *Légende;* SVENDSEN: *Romance.* ***

(**) EMI mono CDH7 64030-2 [id.]. Heifetz, LPO, Beecham – GLAZUNOV: *Violin concerto* (***) ✿; TCHAIKOVSKY: *Violin concerto.* (***)

Violin concerto; 2 Serenades, Op. 69; Humoresque No. 1 in D min., Op. 87/1.

*** DG Dig. 447 895-2. Anne-Sophie Mutter, Dresden State O, André Previn.

(i) *Violin concerto; Serenade No. 2 in G min., Op. 69. En Saga, Op. 9.*

*** Sony Classical SK 53272 [id.]. (i) Julian Rachlin; Pittsburgh SO, Lorin Maazel.

Cho-Liang Lin's playing is distinguished not only by flawless intonation and an apparently effortless virtuosity but also by great artistry. He produces a glorious sonority at the opening, which must have been exactly what Sibelius wanted, wonderfully clean and silvery, and the slow movement has tenderness, warmth and yet restraint with not a hint of over-heated emotions. Lin encompasses the extrovert brilliance of the finale and the bravura of the cadenza with real mastery. The Philharmonia Orchestra rise to the occasion under Esa-Pekka Salonen, and the recording is first class.

Kyung Wha Chung has inimitable style and an astonishing technique, and her feeling for the Sibelius *Concerto* is second to none. André Previn's accompanying cannot be praised too highly: it is poetic when required, restrained, full of controlled vitality and well-defined detail. The 1970 Kingsway Hall recording is superbly balanced and produces an unforced, truthful sound. This is a most beautiful account, poetic, brilliant and thoroughly idiomatic, and must be numbered among the finest versions of the work available.

Heifetz's stereo performance of the Sibelius *Concerto* with the Chicago Symphony Orchestra under Walter Hendl set the standard by which others have come to be judged. It is one of his finest recordings; in remastered form the sound is vivid, the Chicago ambience making an apt setting for the finely focused violin line.

In her live recording, made at a concert in the Philharmonie, Sarah Chang gives an astonishingly mature reading of the Sibelius. She may not be as passionate as her fellow-Korean, Kyung-Wha Chung, but with sweet, refined tone the thoughtfulness and spontaneous poetry of the playing make her comparably magnetic. Warm, atmospheric sound.

Itzhak Perlman plays the work as a full-blooded virtuoso showpiece and the Pittsburgh orchestra under André Previn him excellent support. He makes light of all the fiendish difficulties in which the solo part abounds and takes a conventional view of the slow movement, underlining its passion, and he gives us an exhilarating finale. The sound is marvellously alive and thrilling, though the forward balance is very apparent. This has now been recoupled with the Tchaikovsky concerto, but still at full price.

Julian Rachlin's account of the Sibelius *Concerto* is pretty stunning; indeed it has a purity of tone and intonation which is remarkable and a silvery, aristocratic quality that is entirely in harmony with Sibelius's conception. There are however some idiosyncratic touches in the first cadenza, and the music almost grinds to a halt at one point. His slow movement is strikingly fine and free from *zigeuner*-like sentiment and he understands the poignancy of the beautiful *G minor Serenade*, and it is a pity that he did not find room for its companion. Maazel gives excellent support throughout, and his *En Saga* is atmospheric but a bit brisk. The Sony engineers strike an excellent balance between soloist and orchestra, and the recording has great warmth, even if the upper strings could have greater transparency.

Where most violinists treat the opening as a deep meditation, Mutter makes it tougher than usual, less beautiful, using momentarily a vibratoless slightly steely tone. Like Perlman (among others), she relates this to the Tchaikovsky concerto, giving a performance of extremes, launching into the cadenza for example with rare fierceness. Not that her reading lacks inner qualities for, despite the close balance, the opening of the slow movement finds Mutter playing in rapt meditation on a half-tone. In the finale, taken fast, power is again the keynote. Previn draws a committed performance from an orchestra not noted for playing Sibelius. The all-Sibelius coupling is apt if (at 49 minutes) hardly generous. In the two *Serenades*, Mutter at her most inspired beautifully captures the wayward, quasi-improvisatory quality of these pieces.

Stern's 1969 recording has real passion yet, as the very opening demonstrates, there is no lack of feeling for the work's special atmosphere. Poetry is never in short supply, especially towards the close of the first movement. Ormandy provides a splendid accompaniment and the Philadelphia Orchestra matches Stern's virtuosity and warmth. The violin is forwardly placed, but the balance is much more satisfactory than some recordings from this source, while the remastering has greatly improved the sound: it has plenty of body and resonance.

Tasmin Little's hushed and mysterious account of the opening theme leads to a performance that is both poised and purposeful, magnetic in her combination of power and poetry. Her virtuosity culminates in an account of the finale in which, as in the Brahms, she finds an element of wit in the pointing of insistent dance rhythms. Throughout she is splendidly matched by the colourful playing of the RLPO under Vernon Handley.

Throughout, Nigel Kennedy's intonation is true and he takes all the technical hurdles of this concerto in his stride. There is a touch of the *zigeuner* throb in the slow movement, but on the whole he plays with real spirit and panache. This can be confidently recommended if the coupling with the Tchaikovsky, a rather more indulgent performance, is suitable. The playing of the Birmingham orchestra is excellent throughout as, indeed, is the EMI recording.

The purity and refinement of Vadim Repin's playing are what strike one first. The withdrawn darkness at the very start quickly opens out thrillingly to reveal his total command, the tautness of his control, with tone sharply focused. Here is a young artist who, for all the brilliance of his virtuosity, regularly keeps a degree of emotion in reserve, his very restraint adding to the intensity. The speed in the finale is thrillingly fast, yet Repin with light attack brings out the scherzando element as well as the passion.

The magnetism of Neveu in this, her first concerto recording, is inescapable from her opening phrase onwards, warmly expressive and dedicated, yet with no hint of mannerism. The EMI transfer is not as impressive as Dutton's (see below).

Dong-Suk Kang chooses some popular Scandinavian repertoire pieces, such as the charming Svendsen *Romance in G*, as makeweights. His version of the concerto is very fine, though the slow movement could do with more tenderness as opposed to passion. There is splendid virtuosity and authoritative in the outer movements. The orchestral playing is very acceptable too. In the bargain basement, this enjoys a strong competitive advantage, but even if it were at full price it would feature quite high in the current lists.

Although many first recordings have something special that stands out, the Heifetz/Beecham Sibelius *Violin concerto*, marvellous though it is, excites admiration rather than affection. And despite Sir Thomas's direction, Heifetz gave the more powerful account of it in his later, Chicago recording with Walter Hendl in the early days of stereo. (The reverse was the case with the Glazunov.) A good transfer nevertheless, and well worth having.

(i) *Violin concerto in D min., Op. 47;* (ii) *Symphony No. 7 in C, Op. 105; Tapiola, Op. 112.* (***) Ondine mono ODE 809-2 [id.]. (i) David Oistrakh, Finnish RSO, Nils-Eric Fougstedt; (ii) Helsinki PO, Beecham.

David Oistrakh's account of the *Violin concerto* has a marvellous strength and nobility, as well as an effortless virtuosity that carries all before it. His artistry inspires a warm response from the Finnish Radio Orchestra under Nils-Eric Fougstedt, who give magnificent support. There was always a special sense of occasion, too, at any Beecham concert and the opening of the *Seventh Symphony* is more highly charged than his EMI commercial recording with the RPO. *Tapiola* also has great intensity, though the orchestral playing does not have the finesse, magic and tonal subtlety of the RPO recording. Subfusc recording, but a coupling well worth investigating all the same.

(i) En Saga, Op. 9; Finlandia, Op. 26; (ii) *Karelia suite, Op. 11;* (i) *Legend: The Swan of Tuonela, Op. 22/2; Tapiola, Op. 112.*

(M) **(*) EMI Analogue/Dig. EMI CDM7 64331-2 [id.]. BPO, Karajan.

(BB) *** Belart 450 018-2 (without *Tapiola*). (i) SRO, Horst Stein; (ii) VPO, Maazel – GRIEG: *Peer Gynt.* ***

Karajan's *En Saga* is more concerned with narrative than with atmosphere to start with; the climax is very exciting and the *lento assai* section and the coda are quite magical. *Tapiola* is broader and more expansive than the first DG version; at the storm section, the more spacious tempo is vindicated and the climax is electrifying. *The Swan of Tuonela* is most persuasively done. These recordings date from 1977. The later, digital recording of *Karelia* has been added for the current reissue.

Horst Stein shows a gift for the special atmosphere of Sibelius, and these distinguished and poetic performances offer some of the finest playing we have had from the Suisse Romande Orchestra. Moreover Decca's 1972 recording approaches the demonstration class, especially in *En Saga*. Maazel's *Karelia* is also first rate.

(i) *En saga, Op. 9; Finlandia, Op. 26; Karelia suite, Op. 11;* (ii) *4 Legends, Op. 22;* (i; iii) *Luonnotar, Op. 70;* (ii) *Night ride and sunrise, Op. 55; Pohjola's daughter, Op. 49;* (i) *Tapiola, Op. 112.*

(B) *** Decca Double 452 576-2 (2). (i) Philh. O, Ashkenazy; (ii) SRO, Horst Stein; (iii) with Elisabeth Söderström.

This Double Decca combines Ashkenazy's first-class mid-priced digital collection from the 1980s with more distinguished and finely calculated performances from Horst Stein. *Night ride and sunrise* and *Pohjola's daughter* date from 1971. At the time, we thought they showed the Suisse Romande Orchestra in much better form than usual, and the *Legends*, too, are impressive, with a hell-for-leather account of *Lemminkäinen's return*. The 1980 analogue sound is again first class, having fine weight and definition. Again the Suisse Romande Orchestra plays very well. Even if the body of string tone does not match that of the Philharmonia, the brooding atmosphere of *The Swan of Tuonela* is well caught, and both the first and third *Legends* are well shaped and exciting. All in all, excellent value.

En Saga, Op. 9; Scènes historiques, Opp. 25, 66.

*** BIS Dig. CD 295 [id.]. Gothenburg SO, Järvi.

Järvi has the advantage of modern digital sound and the Gothenburg orchestra is fully inside the idiom of this music and plays very well indeed. Järvi's *En Saga* is exciting and well paced.

Finlandia, Op. 26; Karelia suite, Op. 11; Kuolema: Valse triste, Op. 44/1; Nightride and sunrise, Op. 55; The Oceanides, Op. 73; Tapiola, Op. 112.

(N) *** RCA 09026 68770-2 [id.]. LSO, Sir Colin Davis.

The two performances of special interest here are *Nightride and sunrise* and *The Oceanides*, neither of which Sir Colin has recorded before. *The Oceanides* holds up alongside the celebrated Beecham in atmosphere and poetic feeling and *Nightride and sunrise*, with its difficult transition from the trochaic ride to the stillness and grandeur of sunrise, is splendidly realized. Sir Colin's account of *Tapiola* is even more impressive and terrifying than his earlier Boston version. Very good sound.

Finlandia, Op. 26; Kuolema: Valse triste, Op. 44; Legend: The Swan of Tuonela, Op. 22/2.

*** DG Gold Dig. 439 010-2. BPO, Karajan – GRIEG: *Holberg suite* etc. ***

Coupled with Grieg, this is Karajan at his very finest in the early 1980s, and the remastered digital recording is impressively real and present, particularly in the languorous *Valse triste* and in *The Swan*, Karajan's third and final account on record, powerful in its brooding atmosphere. There is a touch of brashness in the brass in *Finlandia*, but generally this Berlin/Karajan partnership has never been surpassed.

(i) *6 Humoresques, Opp. 87 & 89; 2 Serenades, Op. 69; 2 Serious melodies, Op. 79; Ballet scene* (1891); *Overture in E* (1891).

*** BIS Dig. CD 472 (i) Dong-Suk Kang, Gothenburg SO, Neeme Järvi.

The *Humoresques* are among Sibelius's most inspired smaller pieces. They are poignant as well as virtuosic and have a lightness of touch, a freshness and a sparkle. The two *Serenades* have great poetic feeling and a keen Nordic melancholy. They are wonderfully played by this distinguished Korean artist, who is beautifully accompanied. The two orchestral works are juvenilia which predate the *Kullervo Symphony*. There are some characteristic touches, but Sibelius himself did not think well enough of them to permit their publication. All the violin pieces, however, are to be treasured, and the recording is top class.

King Christian II (suite), *Op. 27; Pelléas et Mélisande* (suite), *Op. 46; Swanwhite* (suite: excerpts), *Op. 54.*

*** Chandos Dig. CHAN 9158 [id.]. Iceland SO, Petri Sakari.

The *King Christian II* music is a winner and full of the most musical touches. It also includes a previously unrecorded *Minuet* and the *Fool's song*, excellently sung by Sauli Tiilikainen. Although the *Pelléas et Mélisande* suite does not displace either Beecham or Karajan, it makes a useful alternative to either – and that is praise indeed! It has plenty of atmosphere and, though tempi are on the slow side, there is always plenty of inner life. The *Swanwhite* (five movements only) is attentive to refinements of phrasing and dynamics and at the same time free from the slightest trace of narcissism. Beautifully natural recording, warm and well balanced.

4 Legends from the Kalevala (Lemminkäinen suite), Op. 22. Lemminkäinen and the Maidens of Saari; Lemminkäinen's homeward journey (1896 versions); Second ending of *Lemminkäinen's homeward journey* (1897 version); Excerpt from *Lemminkäinen in Tuonela* (1896 version).
(N) *** BIS Dig. CD 1015 [id.]. Lahti SO, Osmo Vänskvä.

As is well known, the *Four Legends* that comprise the *Lemminkäinen suite* (1895/6) were revised twice – in 1897 and then in 1900 – and, in the case of *Lemminkäinen and the Maidens of Saari* and *Lemminkäinen in Tuonela*, retouched for publication in 1939. BIS continues its exploration of the first versions of Sibelius's orchestral scores by bringing us the 1896 version of the former and also the first, much longer score of *Lemminkäinen's homeward journey*. This is very nearly twice as long as the definitive version and considerably less effective. The first Legend underwent a particularly fascinating transformation. The disc also offers the alternative 1897 ending of *Lemminkäinen's homeward journey* and an excerpt from *Lemminkäinen in Tuonela* which Sibelius excised. The finished work is played in exemplary fashion by Osmo Vanskä and his Lahti Orchestra and superbly recorded. *The Swan of Tuonela* is highly evocative and way up there among the best.

4 Legends, Op. 22 (Lemminkäinen and the maidens of Saari; The Swan of Tuonela; Lemminkäinen in Tuonela; Lemminkäinen's return).
*** BIS Dig. CD 294 [id.]. Gothenburg SO, Järvi.

4 Legends, Op. 22; The Bard, Op. 64; (i) *Luonnotar, Op. 70.*
(M) *** Chandos CHAN 6586 [id.]. SNO, Gibson, (i) with Phyllis Bryn-Johnson.

4 Legends, Op. 22; Tapiola, Op. 112.
*** Ondine ODE 852-2 [id.]. Helsinki PO, Leif Segerstam.

Although Segerstam perversely ignores Sibelius's instructions about the order of the *Legends* (so, for that matter, did Salonen) this is of little moment, given the fact that collectors can easily re-programme the disc. The performances of both the *Legends* and *Tapiola* are first class and are infinitely preferable to the symphony cycle Segerstam recorded in Copenhagen for Chandos. This is now a first recommendation for the *Legends*, while *Tapiola* is the best since Karajan.

Järvi has the advantage of fine, modern digital sound and a wonderfully truthful balance. Järvi gives a passionate and atmospheric reading of the first *Legend* and his account of *The Swan of Tuonela* is altogether magical, one of the best in the catalogue. He takes a broader view of *Lemminkäinen in Tuonela* than many of his rivals and builds up an appropriately black and powerful atmosphere. The disappointment is *Lemminkäinen's homeward journey* which lacks the possessed, manic quality of Beecham's very first record, which sounded as if a thousand demons were in pursuit.

Gibson comes at mid-price and offers sensitive performances of *The Bard*, and *Luonnotar*, where the soprano voice is made to seem like another orchestral instrument. The Scottish orchestra play freshly and with much commitment. *The Swan of Tuonela* has a darkly brooding primeval quality, and there is an electric degree of tension in the third piece, *Lemminkäinen in Tuonela*. The two outer *Legends* have ardent rhythmic feeling, and altogether this is highly successful. The recorded sound is excellent.

The Oceanides, Op. 73; Nightride and Sunrise, Op. 55; The Tempest (suites Nos. 1 & 2), Op. 111.
(N) **(*) Ondine Dig. ODE 914-2 [id.]. Helsinki PO, Leif Segerstam.

This is Segerstam's second recording of the first suite from *The Tempest* music, his earlier version on Chandos came as a fill-up to the *Fourth Symphony*. The newcomer is very fine indeed, full of atmosphere and power, and free from expressive exaggeration. *The Oceanides* is another matter: a generally rushed and breathless main section preceded by an insufferably slow opening. *Nightride and sunrise* is much finer: it is difficult to bring off well, but Segerstam paces it convincingly. State-of-the-art recording.

(i) *Pelléas et Mélisande* (incidental music; complete), *Op. 46*; (ii) *Legends: The Swan of Tuonela.*
(N) (B) **(*) Ph. Double 462 309-2 (2) [id.]. (i) Rotterdam PO, Zinman; (ii) Boston SO, Sir Colin Davis *** – FAURE: *Pelléas et Mélisande; Pavane, Op. 50* ***; SCHOENBERG: *Pelleas und Melisande; Verklaerte Nacht.* **(*)

The complete score is offered here (including *At the seashore*) and the orchestral playing is of high quality. Zinman is undoubtedly warmly sympathetic, but the music is just a shade undercharacterized. Nevertheless the recording is pleasingly warm and natural, and the couplings are pertinent (although not all lovers of Fauré and Sibelius are likely to respond to Schoenberg). A quite attractive package, just the same, for Sir Colin Davis's performance of *The Swan of Tuonela* is memorably atmospheric.

Rakastava (suite), *Op. 14; Scènes historiques, Opp. 25, 66; Valse lyrique, Op. 96/1.*
(M) *** Chandos CHAN 6591 [id.]. RSNO, Gibson.

Derived from music for a patriotic pageant, the first set of *Scènes historiques* are vintage Sibelius. In the *Love song* Gibson strikes the right blend of depth and reticence, while elsewhere he conveys a fine sense of controlled power. Convincing and eloquent performances that have a natural feeling for the music. Gibson's *Rakastava* is beautifully unforced and natural, save for the last movement which is a shade too slow. The *Valse lyrique* is not good Sibelius, but everything else certainly is. Gibson plays this repertoire with real commitment, and the recorded sound is excellent, with the orchestral layout, slightly distanced, most believable. At mid-price this is a specially desirable collection.

Scaramouche, Op. 71; The Language of the birds: Wedding march.
*** BIS Dig. CD 502 [id.]. Gothenburg SO, Neeme Järvi.

Scaramouche is Sibelius's only ballet and scored for relatively small forces, including piano (not unlike Strauss's music for *Le bourgeois gentilhomme*); at its best it reminds one of the luminous colourings of the *Humoresques* of five years later. A wistful, gentle and haunting score, often inspired though slightly let down by its uneventful second Act. Sibelius did not think highly enough of the *Wedding march* to Adolf Paul's play, *The Language of the birds*, to give it an opus number but it is in fact quite an attractive miniature. The playing of the Gothenburg orchestra under Neeme Järvi is altogether excellent and so, too, is the BIS recording.

SYMPHONIES

Symphonies Nos. 1–7.
(M) **(*) Chandos Dig. CHAN 6559 (3) [id.]. RSNO, Sir Alexander Gibson.

Symphonies Nos. 1, 2 & 4; Finlandia; Karelia suite.
(B) *** Decca Double Dig. 455 402-2 (2) [id.]. Philh. O, Vladimir Ashkenazy.

Symphonies Nos. 3, 5, 6 & 7; En Saga; Tapiola.
(B) *** Decca Double Dig. 455 405-2 (2) [id.] Philh. O, Vladimir Ashkenazy.

Symphonies Nos. 1 in E min., Op. 39; 4 in A min., Op. 63.
(BB) *** Belart 461 325-2. VPO, Maazel.

Symphonies Nos. 2 in D, Op. 43; 3 in C, Op. 32.
(BB) **(*) Belart 461 321-2. VPO, Maazel.

Symphonies Nos. 5 in E flat, Op. 82; 6 in D min., Op. 104; 7 in C, Op. 105.
(BB) *(**) Belart 461 323-2. VPO, Maazel.

(i) *Symphonies Nos. 1–7;* (ii) *Night ride and sunrise;* (i) *The Oceanides; Scene with cranes.*
(M) **(*) EMI CMS7 64118-2 (4). (i) CBSO, (ii) Philh. O, Simon Rattle.

Symphonies Nos. 1–7; Nightride and sunrise, Op. 55; Pelléas et Mélisande: suite, Op. 46; Pohjola's daughter, Op. 49.
(M) (***) Beulah mono 1–4PD 8 (4) [id.]. LSO, Collins.

Ashkenazy's Sibelius cycle has now been issued on a pair of Double Deccas, with four tone-poems added for good measure. It thus competes directly with Sir Colin Davis's series, similarly reissued on a pair of Philips Duos, and also including the *Violin concerto*. Even so, the Ashkenazy set takes precedence, partly because of the generally superior digital recording; but on performance grounds, too, these readings are very rewarding. A rich and strong, consistently enjoyable cycle. Ashkenazy by temperament brings out the expressive warmth, colour and drama of the composer rather than his Scandinavian chill, reflecting perhaps his Slavonic background. The recordings – made between 1979 and 1984, either at Walthamstow or in the Kingsway Hall – are full and rich as well as brilliant, most of them still of demonstration quality. For those wanting a complete set, they make a most attractive first recommendation, although for R. L. the newest cycle from Sir Colin Davis and the LSO on RCA takes pride of place at premium price, and this series will almost certainly appear in a box during the lifetime of this book.

Simon Rattle's performances with the City of Birmingham Symphony Orchestra are available both as a four-CD boxed set and as individual discs. The best advice is probably to opt for the individual disc for the *Fourth* and *Sixth*, coupled together. They are both impressive, as is his *Seventh*, coupled with the *Fifth* and the highly atmospheric *Scene with cranes*. As a set the box is worth considering, but it would not be first choice.

Sibelians should note that Collins's highly distinguished accounts of the symphonies (with the fill-ups) make a four-disc set in a slip-case at a saving on the price of the individual records.

The finest of Lorin Maazel's performances, which originated on the Decca label in the 1960s, are the *First* and *Fourth Symphonies*. The *First* has freshness and power to commend it, along with careful attention to both the letter and the spirit of the score; the *Fourth* brings comparable concentration: the first movement is as cold and unremitting as one could wish, and throughout the work Maazel identifies with the atmosphere and mystery of this music. In both symphonies the Vienna Philharmonic responds with enthusiasm and brilliance and the Decca engineers produce splendid detail, while the overall sound has fine body. The *Second* is excellent too and is beautifully played. Maazel's reading, however, leans more to the romantic view of the work: the Tchaikovskian inheritance is stressed rather than the classical forebears. The finale with ripe, vintage Decca recording is sumptuously gripping. The *Third* has a very good first movement, but the second is faster than ideal; it is not quite poetic or reflective enough. Even so, Maazel keeps a firm grip on the outer movements, and his build-up in the finale is most impressive. The *Fifth* and, more particularly, the *Sixth* do not come off so well. Maazel sounds relatively uninvolved in both works. His *Seventh Symphony*, however, proved another landmark in the Sibelius discography: it has great majesty and breadth. These three records together now cost little more than the price of a single premium-priced disc and represent the least expensive way to survey this repertoire. Certainly the first two discs are genuine bargains.

Sir Alexander Gibson's Sibelius cycle is impressive, both musically and from an engineering point of view; there are no weak spots anywhere. (Indeed, one respected critic chose Gibson's version of No. 1 as his first choice on a BBC 'Record Review' some years ago.) At the same time it must be conceded that the peaks do not dwarf, say, the Maazel *Fourth* or *Seventh*. The performances are eminently sane, sound and reliable, and no one investing in the set is likely to be at all disappointed. Taken individually, none would be an absolute first choice.

Symphonies Nos. 1 in E min., Op. 39; 2 in D, Op. 43; 4 in A min., Op. 63; 5 in E flat, Op. 82.
(B) *** Ph. Duo 446 157-2 (2) [id.]. Boston SO, Sir Colin Davis.

Symphonies Nos. 3 in C, Op. 52; 6 in D min., Op. 104; 7 in C, Op. 105; (i) *Violin concerto in D min., Op. 47. Finlandia, Op. 26; Legends: The Swan of Tuonela, Op. 22/2; Tapiola, Op. 112.*
(B) *** Ph. Duo 446 160-2 (2) [id.]. (i) Salvatore Accardo; Boston SO, Sir Colin Davis.

Sir Colin Davis's set of the symphonies, recorded during the second half of the 1970s, is undoubtedly among the finest of the collected editions, and now it is not only very economical (offered for the cost of two premium-price CDs) but three tone-poems and an estimable account of the *Violin concerto* are thrown in for good measure. Indeed Accardo's performance of the latter is very high on the recommended list. *Tapiola*, too, is atmospheric and superbly played. Nos. 1, 2, 5 and 7 were the first to be recorded in (1975/6). The idiomatic playing Davis secures from the Boston orchestra is immediately apparent. Tempi are well judged and there is a genuine sense of commitment and power though the recording is not quite as fine as Ashkenazy's on Decca. However, the remastering has undoubtedly improved its overall depth. Davis's accounts of the *Third*, *Fourth* and *Sixth Symphonies* are among the best on disc and they are excellently recorded. In the *Third* Davis judges the tempi in all three movements to perfection; no conductor has captured the elusive spirit of the slow movement or the power of the finale more effectively. The *Fourth* is arguably the finest of the cycle; there is a powerful sense of mystery, and the slow movement in particular conveys the feeling of communication with nature that lies at the heart of its inspiration. The *Fifth* is a little lacking in atmosphere; it is no match for Karajan. Here Davis is idiomatic and unfussy, as in the *Seventh*. Moreover the recording of these two works is again slightly two-dimensional, although this is less noticeable now than it was on LP. The *Sixth* is altogether more impressive and much more vivid as sound.

Symphonies Nos. 1–3; 5; Belshazzar's Feast (incidental music), *Op. 51; Karelia suite; Pohjola's daughter, Op. 49; Tapiola, Op. 112.*
(M) (***) Finlandia/Warner mono 4509 95882-2 (3). LSO, Robert Kajanus.

When the Finnish government sponsored recordings of the first two symphonies in 1930, Sibelius insisted on having Kajanus as the most authentic interpreter. These performances were all made in 1930 and 1932 and sound amazingly good for the period. The celebrated storm in *Tapiola*, taken at a much slower and more effective tempo than is now usual, still has the power to terrify despite the inevitable sonic limitations, and no conductor has ever given a more spell-binding and atmospheric account of the suite from *Belshazzar's Feast*. The broader, more leisurely view Kajanus takes of the *Third Symphony* comes as a refreshing corrective to the later, more hurried accounts by Anthony Collins and Lorin Maazel. No performer, save Beecham and Karajan, came closer to Sibelius's intentions. Essential listening for all Sibelians.

Symphony No. 1 in E min.; Finlandia, Op. 26; Karelia suite, Op. 11.
❁ *** EMI Dig. CDC7 542732 [id.]. Oslo PO, Mariss Jansons.

Mariss Jansons's account of the *First Symphony* is the finest to have appeared since Maazel's in the 1960s. The Oslo Philharmonic is on peak form, playing with thrilling virtuosity both in the *Symphony* and *Finlandia* and in the *Karelia suite*. Tempi are well judged, the players are responsive to every dynamic nuance, phrasing is beautifully shaped and the overall architecture of the piece is splendidly realized. A very exciting performance, which has you on the edge of your seat, and very vividly recorded too.

Symphonies Nos. 1 in E min.; 3 in C, Op. 52.
(***) Testament mono SBT 1049 [id.]. Philh. O, Kletzki.
(N) (BB) *** Naxos Dig. 8.554102 [id.]. Iceland SO, Petri Sakari.

Kletzki's account of the *First Symphony* has never been reissued since it first appeared on mono LP in

1954, while his *Third Symphony* is new to the UK. It is very different in approach from the Anthony Collins LP, which takes a somewhat racy view of both the first and second movements. Kletzki is tauter than the traditional Kajanus school yet far less headlong (or headstrong) than Collins. In both scores he and the Philharmonia Orchestra strike the right balance between the romantic legacy of the nineteenth century and the more severe climate of the twentieth. The recordings are beautifully balanced and have great warmth, and they come up splendidly in these transfers. A valuable addition to the Sibelius discography and strongly recommended.

Petri Sakari proves a sound and straightforward interpreter. There is no trace of expressive exaggeration but there is plenty of character. The playing of the Iceland Orchestra in both symphonies is spirited and vital, even if they do not command the virtuosity and polish of the major international ensembles. The *Third Symphony* is very well paced indeed and the playing has conviction. The recording, too, is natural and vivid with a good balance between the various sections of the orchestra. In any event good value for money.

Symphonies Nos. 1 in E min., Op. 39; 4 in A min., Op. 63.
(N) *** BIS Dig. BIS CD861 [id.]. Lahti SO, Osmo Vänskä.

In the *First Symphony* the Finnish conductor, Vänskä, secures a marvellously controlled and splendidly executed performance from his dedicated players. There is that sense of inevitability and of an irresistible forward movement throughout, though never at the expense of incidental beauty. The scherzo is among the most exciting on disc, very fast and full of controlled abandon. The *Fourth Symphony* receives a perceptive and deeply intelligent reading. The Lahti Orchestra play with keen concentration and intensity and though tempi are very slow (perhaps too much so in the case of the slow movement), the performance is marvellously sustained. As with Karajan and Sir Colin Davis, you feel a sense of authenticity: that you are completely inside the Sibelian landscape. The recording is natural and eminently well balanced. A distinguished issue.

Symphonies Nos. (i) *1 in E min.;* (ii) *5 in E flat;* (iii) *Romance in C for strings, Op. 42.*
(B) **(*) Sony Classical SBK 63060 [id.]. (i) Phd. O, Ormandy; (ii) NYPO, Bernstein; (iii) Cleveland Sinfonietta, Lane.

Ormandy's Sony account of the *First Symphony* with the Philadelphia Orchestra comes from 1961 and is first rate, while Bernstein's *Fifth* from the mid-1960s is arguably the finest of his Sibelius cycle when memories of his mentor, Koussevitzky, were still vivid. There is a small bonus in the form of Louis Lane's account of the *Romance for strings*. No one attracted by this coupling need hesitate.

Symphonies Nos. 1 in E min., Op. 39; 6 in D min., Op. 104.
(BB) *** Arte Nova Dig. 74321 49705-2 [id.]. Gran Canaria PO, Adrian Leaper.

The orchestra of the Gran Canaria is fine in every department. The strings are opulent and the wind too are first class. Adrian Leaper is an *echt*-Sibelian with both a command of the overall architecture and a feeling for the atmosphere. The *Sixth Symphony* is gripping, not perhaps in the same league as the Karajan, Davis and Ashkenazy but not far off. Although the *First Symphony* is very good, it does not represent the same challenge to existing recommendations. All the same, the disc is worth having, for both performances are good and the *Sixth* is magnificent. Excellent recording quality.

Symphonies Nos. 1 in E min.; 7 in C, Op. 105.
*** Decca (IMS) Dig. 444 541-2. San Francisco SO, Blomstedt.
✪ (***) Beulah mono IPD 8 [id.]. LSO, Anthony Collins.

To adapt a cocktail metaphor, Herbert Blomstedt and the San Francisco Symphony Orchestra give us Sibelius absolutely ice-cold and straight-up. Blomstedt is faithful to the spirit (and, mostly, the letter) of these scores, and the results that he and his players achieve are remarkably imposing. The *First Symphony* is one of the best we have had in recent years: it can be recommended alongside the Ashkenazy and Jansons. The *Seventh Symphony* has great strength – it is carefully built up, spacious and dignified; and in both symphonies there is no playing to the gallery. Good recorded sound.

There are those who (justly) count Anthony Collins's magnificent account of the *First Symphony* of 1952, with its haunting, other-worldly opening clarinet solo, as the finest ever put on disc, for the tension throughout the performance is held at the highest level. The closely integrated *Seventh* is also well understood by Collins, and once again the closing moments of the symphony are drawn together very impressively. The Decca recording remains remarkably vivid and, if the fortissimos are more one-dimensional than we expect today and the massed violins could ideally be fuller, the brass certainly makes a fine impact. There is no lack of underlying fullness, and a little paring of the upper range works wonders. The comparatively rare *Karelia overture*, which was recorded later (1955), makes a brief bonus.

Symphony No. 2 in D, Op. 43.
(M) ** Mercury (IMS) 434 317-2 [id.]. Detroit SO, Paray – DVORAK: *Symphony No. 9 (From the New World).* ***

Symphony No. 2 in D; Andante festivo; Kuolema: Valse triste, Op. 44/1; Legend: The Swan of Tuonela, Op. 22/2.
*** EMI (SIS) Dig. CDC7 54804-2 [id.]. Oslo PO, Jansons.

Symphony No. 2 in D; Finlandia; Kuolema: Valse triste. Legend: The Swan of Tuonela, Op. 22/3.
(M) **(*) [RCA Basic 100 09026 61856-2]. Phd. O, Ormandy.

Symphony No. 2 in D; Finlandia, Op. 26; Kuolema: Valse triste, Op. 44/1; Romance in C, Op. 42.
*** Decca (IMS) Dig. 436 566-2 [id.]. Boston SO, Ashkenazy.

Symphony No. 2 in D, Op. 43; Finlandia, Op. 26; Legends, Op. 22: Lemminkäinen's return; The Swan of Tuonela; Pohjola's daughter, Op. 49.
(N) (BB) (**) Naxos mono 8.110810 [id.]. NBC SO, Toscanini.

(i) *Symphony No. 2 in D;* (ii) *Karelia suite, Op. 11.*
(B) **(*) DG Classikon 439 499-2. (i) BPO; (ii) Helsinki RSO; Okko Kamu.

Symphony No. 2 in D; Romance for strings in C, Op. 42.
*** BIS Dig. CD 252 [id.]. Gothenburg SO, Järvi.

A very well shaped performance from Ashkenazy in Boston. There is an impressive sense of line throughout and yet no feeling that Sibelius's muse is held on too taut a rein. Ashkenazy's approach to the first movement is more measured than earlier maestros (Kajanus, Beecham – and, in more recent times, Järvi). However, many paths lead to the truth and Ashkenazy's performance is even finer than his earlier account for Decca. It is musically very satisfying – and recorded in a very natural concert-hall perspective. The Boston strings respond very ardently but with aristocratic poise in the *Romance in C* and in the remaining works in the programme. Strongly recommended.

Even in a highly competitive field the Oslo Philharmonic account of the *Second Symphony* under Mariss Jansons is a force to be reckoned with. If it lacks something of the high voltage that charged his reading of the *First Symphony*, it has no lack of excitement; it is superbly controlled and tautly held together, with no playing to the gallery in the finale. There is an aristocratic feel to it, and this extends to *The Swan* and the *Andante festivo*, which is distinguished by string playing of great intensity. Jansons whips *Valse triste* into something of a frenzy towards the climax, but elsewhere these performances are totally free from exaggeration. Excellent recording.

Järvi is very brisk in the opening *Allegretto*: this Gothenburg version has more sinew and fire than its rivals, and the orchestral playing is more responsive and disciplined than that of the SNO on Chandos (see below). Throughout, Järvi has an unerring sense of purpose and direction and the momentum never slackens. Of course, there is not the same opulence as with the Boston Symphony under Ashkenazy on EMI, but the BIS performance is concentrated in feeling and thoroughly convincing. The *Romance for strings* is attractively done.

In Ormandy's 1972 account of the *Second Symphony* the sound is undoubtedly spacious, although the violin-timbre lacks something in refinement because of the close microphones. But they play marvellously, and the superbly disciplined response of the whole orchestra cannot fail to hold the listener. Although Ormandy's reading rarely sheds new light on this wonderful score, there is no doubt that the rich sweep of the Philadelphia strings in the big tune of the finale – underpinned by the power and sonority of the brass – is compulsive in its intensity. The other pieces are played with considerable flair.

The Berlin Philharmonic give Kamu excellent support and rich sonority in his 1970 account of the *Second Symphony*, recorded not long after he won the Karajan conducting competition. One or two minor exaggerations apart, he gives a straightforward and dedicated account of the work. The fill-up in the form of the *Karelia suite* is expertly by the Helsinki Radio Orchestra.

In December 1940, at the time of the Russian invasion of Finland, Toscanini conducted these Sibelius performances, tautly controlled but emotional too, reflecting corporate feelings of the time. The first movement of the symphony is unusually fast, a true allegro, and speeds are never leisurely, yet more than was usual for him. Toscanini allows expressive freedom to his orchestral soloists, notably the cor anglais in the *Swan of Tuonela*. Dry, limited sound, transferred better than with some in this series.

Paray's account has plenty of tension – indeed one is immediately gripped by the excitement of the opening movement. The *Andante*, however, does not bring enough contrast and its histrionics seem episodic. The Scherzo has great energy and the finale develops a full head of steam, but overall, in spite of excellent early (1959) Mercury stereo, this reading with its impulsiveness fails to create the feeling of an organic whole.

Symphonies Nos. 2 in D; 3 in C, Op. 52.
(M) *** EMI CDM7 64120-2. CBSO, Sir Simon Rattle.
(N) **(*) BIS Dig. CD 862 [id.]. Lahti SO, Osmo Vänskä.

In No. 2 the CBSO play with fervour and enthusiasm except, perhaps, in the first movement where the voltage is lower – particularly in the development, which is not easy to bring off; however, the transition to the finale is magnificent and Rattle finds the *tempo giusto* in this movement. The Birmingham strings produce a splendidly fervent unison both here and elsewhere. Rattle's account of the *Third* is vastly superior to his *First* and *Second*. He penetrates the landscape of the slow movement completely, and the way in which he builds up the finale is masterly and sure of instinct. The recording, made in the Warwick Arts Centre, sounds very well balanced, natural in perspective and finely detailed.

Osmo Vänskä's accounts of the *Second* and *Third Symphonies* are as thought-provoking as his remarkable pairing of Nos. 1 and 4, though they are not quite deserving of the same star-rating. The dynamic markings are sometimes a little too extreme, the second theme of the slow movement marked *pianopianissimo* is almost whispered rather than played, and to readers playing the disc at less than full-room volume, it will be barely audible. It is just a shade self-conscious. Everything is carefully thought out, and the general effect is impressive. The *Third Symphony* is generally well paced and has the right atmosphere. Those following the series will not be disappointed. Very wide-ranging but expertly balanced sound.

Symphonies Nos. 2 in D; 5 in E flat, Op. 82.
(M) *** Chandos Dig. CHAN 6556 [id.]. RSNO, Sir Alexander Gibson.

The *Second* is among the best of Gibson's cycle and scores highly, thanks to the impressive clarity, fullness and impact of the 1982 digital recording. Gibson's reading is honest and straightforward, free of bombast in the finale. Tempos are well judged: the first movement is neither too taut nor too relaxed: it is well shaped and feels right. Overall this is most satisfying, as is the *Fifth*, which has similar virtues: at no time is there any attempt to interpose the personality of the interpreter, and the finale has genuine weight and power.

Symphonies Nos. 2 in D; 6 in D min., Op. 104.
*** RCA Dig. 09026 68218-2 [id.]. LSO, Sir Colin Davis.
(N) (M) (***) Dutton Lab. mono CDLX 7033 [id.]. RPO, Sir Thomas Beecham.
(***) Beulah mono 2PD 8. LSO, Anthony Collins.

The *Sixth* is a work for which Colin Davis has always shown a special affinity and understanding. Its purity of utterance and harmony of spirit give it a special place in the canon. Sir Colin's earlier recording with the Boston orchestra (see above) was one of the best in that magisterial cycle, and this newcomer is if anything even finer. There is 'nothing of the circus' (to quote the composer's own words *à propos* the *Fourth Symphony*) in his reading of the *Second*, and no playing to the gallery. There is a grandeur and a natural distinction about the playing.

Both Beecham's performances come from 1947 and the *Sixth Symphony* long enjoyed (and indeed still enjoys) classic status. (Sibelius's eldest daughter told R. L. in 1959 that it was the composer's own favourite version of any of his symphonies.) The *Second* was never issued in Britain – though catalogue numbers were allocated and it is listed in Clough & Cuming's World Encyclopaedia of Recorded Music. It has less fire and its tempi is generally less impetuous than Beecham's later public account with the BBC Symphony Orchestra but is still well worth having. Exemplary transfers, and in the *Sixth* a much more vivid sound than the previous EMI reissue, coupling it with Beecham's *Fourth*. This must be snapped up by all Sibelians.

The Decca sound in Collins's 1953 recording of the *Second Symphony* is fuller than in the *First Symphony*. The performance is superb, held together with a tension that carries the listener through from the first bar to the last. The closing pages of the finale, with the timpani again making a telling contribution, are particularly satisfying. The *Sixth* was recorded in 1955, and again the ear notices a further improvement in the sound, particularly at the radiant pastoral opening. The LSO play with much sensitivity, and woodwind and string detail is ever luminous; the conductor's special feeling for Sibelian colour and atmosphere is especially apparent in this work, with the beautiful final coda sustained with moving simplicity. Altogether a lovely performance.

Symphonies Nos. 2 in D; 7 in C, Op. 105.
(B) *** Sony SBK 53509 [id.]. Phd. O, Ormandy.

Ormandy was not so much underrated as taken for granted in an age which had the good fortune to have so many great conductors. The 1957 sound is far better than you might expect and the strings (and practically every other department) are much more sumptuous and responsive than they seem to be in Philadelphia nowadays. The *Second* gets a powerful (and, in the finale, rousing) performance, and the architecture is held together well throughout. The *Seventh*, recorded in 1960, is very impressive indeed: marvellously paced, intense and felt.

Symphony No. 3 in C; King Kristian II (suite), Op. 27.
*** BIS Dig. CD 228 [id.]. Gothenburg SO, Järvi.

With the *Third Symphony* there is a sense of the epic in Järvi's hands and it can hold its own with any in the catalogue. In Gothenburg, the slow movement is first class and the leisurely tempo adopted here by the Estonian conductor is just right. Järvi's coupling is the incidental music to *King Christian II*. This is very beautifully played and recorded.

Symphony No. 3 in C; Nightride and sunrise, Op. 55; Pelléas et Mélisande: suite, Op. 46; Pohjola's daughter, Op. 49.
(***) Beulah mono 3PD8. LSO, Anthony Collins.

More outstanding performances from Anthony Collins: only *Nightride and sunrise*, although dramatically effective, is slightly less memorable than the other works here. The other reservation concerns the tempo for the second movement, of the symphony. Some listeners find it too fast, but the playing has much delicacy of feeling and texture; Collins's approach matches the whole reading, which has a strong momentum overall, and the build-up of tension to the work's climax is satisfyingly controlled. The account of *Pohjola's daughter* is imaginative and colourful, and the excerpts from the incidental music to *Pelléas et Mélisande* are beautifully played. All the recordings, except *Nightride* (1955), were made in the Kingsway Hall in 1954 and absolutely no apologies need be made for the mono sound, which in this admirable CD transfer is remarkable for its vivid immediacy and fullness.

Symphonies Nos. 3 in C, Op. 52; 5 in E flat, Op. 82.
*** RCA Dig. 09026 61963-2 [id.]. LSO, Sir Colin Davis.
*** EMI (SIS) Dig. CDC5 55533-2. Oslo PO, Jansons.

Sir Colin Davis's account of the *Third Symphony* has a majesty and power that have few rivals. His *Fifth*, too, has tremendous grandeur as well as a feeling for the natural symphonic current that flows in these wonderful works. The recording has a splendour worthy of the music and the players. Both performances (and especially the *Fifth*) offer a marked advance on Davis's earlier, Boston versions – see above.

Mariss Jansons and the Oslo Philharmonic challenge Colin Davis and the LSO on exactly the same ground. It is a logical couping in that both symphonies include some of Sibelius's most innovative formal experiments, the finale of the *Third* and the first movement of the *Fifth*. The Oslo orchestra can certainly hold its own with the LSO in terms of beauty and weight of sonority. Their *Third* is wonderfully lithe and virile, though Sir Colin's broader tempo is perhaps better judged. But everything is marvellously alive and youthful. The *Fifth* is impressive, too, though the transition into the scherzo section of the first movement may strike some listeners used to Karajan, Sargent and Rattle's Philharmonia version as a shade precipitate. Strongly recommended – alongside but not in preference to Sir Colin's classic RCA version.

Symphonies Nos. 3 in C; 6 in D min.; 7 in C, Op. 105.
(M) *** Chandos CHAN 6557 [id.]. RSNO, Sir Alexander Gibson.

With three symphonies offered, some 74 minutes overall, this is a fine bargain and an excellent way to experience Gibson's special feeling for this composer. The SNO is in very good form. The first movement of the *Third* has real momentum. The *Andantino* is fast, faster than the composer's marking. Such a tempo, while it gives the music-making fine thrust, means that Gibson, like Collins before him, loses some of the fantasy of this enigmatic movement. But there is more here to admire than to cavil at. The *Sixth* is impressive too, with plenty of atmosphere and some radiant playing from the Scottish violin section; the *Seventh* has a rather relaxed feeling throughout, but it does not lack warmth and, as in No. 1, Gibson draws the threads together at the close with satisfying breadth.

Symphonies Nos. 4 in A min.; 5 in E flat, Op. 82.
*** Decca Dig. 425 858-2 [id.]. San Francisco SO, Herbert Blomstedt.
(***) Beulah mono 4PD 8 [id.]. LSO, Anthony Collins.

Blomstedt allows the music to unfold naturally and conveys a real sense of space. The *Fourth Symphony* has the intimacy of chamber music and yet communicates a strong feeling of the Nordic landscape. Blomstedt is particularly attentive to dynamic shading and gets playing of great tonal refinement from the San Francisco orchestra; no one makes the closing bars of the finale sound more affecting. The *Fifth Symphony* is also wonderfully spacious. Some may find the accelerando between the two sections of the first movement a shade steep, but there is a powerful sense of mystery in the development section.

Collins's opening to the *Fourth Symphony* with its desolate, Nordic atmosphere is remarkably restrained, yet the work as a whole has extraordinary underlying intensity. With Collins, every phrase breathes naturally and the lightening of mood in the Scherzo, with wind and string playing of great delicacy, is merely an interlude, before the powerfully sombre feeling of the *Il tempo largo* gives birth to a climax of compulsive power. In the finale the flux of mood and feeling that comes with its surge of animation is handled with great subtlety. The performance of the *Fifth Symphony* carries all before it, with the reading moving forward in a single sweep. In both symphonies the LSO is marvellously responsive. The 1954/5 Kingsway Hall mono recordings were among the finest in terms of balance and truthfulness that Decca made throughout the mono LP era, and this CD reproduces superbly.

Symphonies Nos. 4 in A min.; 5 in E flat; 6 in D min.; 7 in C; Legend: The Swan of Tuonela; Tapiola.
(N) (M) *** DG 457 748-2 (2) [id.]. BPO, Karajan.

This set (two discs at mid-price – issued as 'Originals') is a convenient way of collecting Karajan's splendid DG performances of Sibelius's last four symphonies, including his outstanding version of the *Fourth*. All but the *Sixth* are available separately in other formats (see below) and his glorious 1967 account of the latter remains almost unsurpassed by more recent accounts. So with a brooding *Swan of Tuonela* and a thrilling *Tapiola* thrown in for good measure, this can be strongly recommended. The Berlin Philharmonic are on their finest form and DG have obviously taken great care over these vivid new transfers.

Symphonies Nos. 4 in A min., Op. 63; 5 in E flat, Op. 82; Finlandia, Op. 26.
(M) (***) EMI mono CDM5 66600-2 [id.]. Philh. O, Karajan

Symphonies Nos. 6 in D min., Op. 104; 7 in C, Op. 105; Tapiola, Op. 112.
(M) (***) EMI mono CDM5 66602-2 [id.]. Philh. O, Karajan.

These mono performances with Karajan and the Philharmonia Orchestra are of special interest. Erik Tawaststjerna (*Sibelius Vol. 3*) notes that when Sir Thomas Beecham telephoned in response to a number of detailed criticisms that the composer had made of his 78s of the *Fourth Symphony* in 1937, Sibelius was overwhelmed by the flood of English which he only dimly grasped. He hastily agreed the Beecham recording. Walter Legge, however, showed Sibelius's tempo and other suggestions to Karajan before he made his 1954 recording. After hearing it, Sibelius drafted a telegram speaking of Karajan's 'deep insights and great artistic grip' and went so far as to tell Legge that 'Karajan is the only one who really understands my music.' Certainly these performances are of stature and carry the composer's imprimatur. The *Fourth* was always a favourite of Karajan's, and in some ways this is even finer than the subsequent Berlin accounts – the sound is leaner and more spare and conveys the sense of desolation at the core of its bleak, wintry terrain.

The *Fifth*, recorded in 1952, has not been issued on CD before. Earlier releases have chosen Karajan's 1960 Philharmonia account, but the breadth and majesty of the earlier issue are difficult to surpass. It does not quite match the achievement of the third and greatest of his four recordings, but it is a superbly realized and impressive reading. The *Sixth* and *Seventh* are hardly less fine, even if the latter concentrates more on the seamlessness of the structure than its power. As with the *Fourth Symphony*, Karajan recorded *Tapiola* no fewer than four times – and this is a dark, chilling version to rank with the best.

Symphonies Nos. 4 in A min.; 6 in D min.
(M) *** EMI CDM7 64121-2. CBSO, Sir Simon Rattle.

Simon Rattle's account of the *Fourth* invokes a powerful atmosphere in its opening pages: one is completely transported to its dark landscape with its seemingly limitless horizons. The string-tone is splendidly lean without being undernourished and achieves a sinisterly whispering pianissimo in the development. The slow movement is magical and the finale is hardly less masterly. Rattle's account of the *Sixth* is almost equally fine. It is still a *Sixth* to reckon with and its closing bars are memorably eloquent.

Symphonies Nos. (i) *4 in A min.;* (ii) *6 in D min., Op. 104;* (i) *The Bard, Op. 64; Lemminkäinen's return, Op. 22/4; The Tempest: Prelude.*
❁ (M) (***) EMI mono CDM7 64027-2. (i) LPO, (ii) RPO, Sir Thomas Beecham.

In its colour Beecham's 1947 account of the *Fourth Symphony* reflects his feeling that, far from being an austere work, as is often claimed, it is ripely romantic. No performance brings one closer to the music, while the recording, made over fifty years ago, sounds astonishingly fresh and bleak in this excellent transfer, and there is a concentration, darkness and poetry that few rivalled. Its eloquence is no less impressive. In the three shorter works on the disc Beecham's rhythmic sharpness and feeling for colour vividly convey the high voltage of Sibelius's strikingly original writing. *Lemminkäinen's homeward journey* is positively electrifying, while the *Prelude* to *The Tempest* is every bit as awesome an evocation of a storm as we had remembered. All these performances except the *Sixth Symphony* come from the late 1930s, but few allowances need be made, for they spring vividly to life in these remarkable transfers. Indispensable for all Sibelians.

Symphonies Nos. 4 in A min.; 7 in C; Kuolema: Valse triste.
❁ (M) *** DG 439 527-2. BPO, Karajan.

Karajan's celebrated 1965 account of the *Fourth Symphony* wears well. For many it remains the finest version of the *Fourth* on record, and it certainly ranks along with the Beecham as among the most insightful. The plush sonority of the Berlin Philharmonic at first deceives one into thinking that Karajan has beautified the symphony's landscape, but he comes closer to the spirit of the score than most others. (The symphony meant a great deal to him: he insisted on playing it alongside Beethoven in 1960 at his inaugural concert as the life-conductor of the orchestra at a time when Sibelius was held in the lowest esteem in Germany.) It is a performance of great concentration, deep thought and feeling. Although the new DG transfer of the recording does not have quite the body of violin-tone of the finest digital recordings, the acoustics of the Jesus-Christus-Kirche give weight and depth and a fine resonance to the bass. The performance is undoubtedly a great one. The *Seventh Symphony* is perhaps less successful though it comes off better than in Karajan's Philharmonia version, and the *Valse triste* is seductive. An indispensable record.

Symphony No. 5 (1915 version); *En Saga* (1892 version).
*** BIS Dig. CD 800 [id.]. Lahti SO, Vänskä.

Not long after Sibelius's death, the orchestral material for the first version of the *Fifth Symphony* was discovered in the attic at Ainola. To reconstruct the actual score was a simple matter (R. L. was shown the score in the mid-1960s). However, Sibelius's heirs opposed it entering the public domain in the conviction that it would have been against the composer's wishes. The next generation have now reconsidered the position and have allowed BIS to proceed with a recording. It offers an invaluable insight into the workings of the creative process and is testimony to Sibelius's refusal to rest content until he had fully realized his vision. The work is in four (not three) movements, the opening horn-call is yet to be discovered; and there are no final hammer-blow chords. But there is much else that is different, and to study these differences offers an endless source of fascination. The *En Saga* we know comes from 1901, when it was extensively revised for Busoni to conduct in Berlin. There are some Brucknerian touches in one or two places, as there were in *Kullervo*, composed earlier the same year, and the orchestration is less expert. Totally dedicated performances which the orchestra committed to tape before the family had actually given permission to release (as opposed to record) them. An essential disc for all Sibelians, and magnificently recorded into the bargain.

Symphony No. 5 in E flat (1915 version & definitive 1919 version).
(N) *** BIS Dig. CD 863 [id.]. Lahti SO, Osmo Vänskä.

BIS have now recoupled the original 1915 four-movement version of the *Fifth Symphony* with the definitive 1919 version, as part of their ongoing cycle from Osmo Vänskä and the Lahti Orchestra. Vänskä has a great feeling for the general architecture of the piece and paces it superbly. Our only reservation is his penchant for extreme *pianissimos* – the development section in the finale drops beyond a whisper to virtual inaudibility.

Symphony No. 5 in E flat, Op. 82.
(M) *** EMI CDM7 64737-2. Philh. O, Rattle – NIELSEN: *Symphony No. 4* etc. ***

Symphony No. 5; Finlandia; Kuolema: Valse triste. Tapiola, Op. 112.
(B) *** DG Classikon 439 418-2. BPO, Karajan.

Such is the excellence of the classic Karajan DG *Fifth* that few listeners would guess its age. It is a great performance, and this 1964 version is indisputably the finest of the four he made. The fillers are familiar performances, also from the mid-1960s. *Tapiola* is a performance of great intensity and offers superlative playing; *Finlandia* is also one of the finest accounts available, but *Valse triste* is played very slowly and in a somewhat mannered fashion.

Rattle's account of the *Fifth Symphony* with the Philharmonia was to the 1980s what Karajan's Berlin account was to the 1960s. It collected numerous prizes, even the *Deutscheschallplattenpreis* – and rightly! Everything about it feels right: the control of pace and texture and the balance of energy and repose. The development of the first movement has a compelling sense of mystery and the transition to the Scherzo section is beautifully judged. The Philharmonia Orchestra play splendidly and the EMI recording is very good indeed.

Symphonies Nos. 5 in E flat, Op. 82; 6 in D min., Op. 104; Legend: The Swan of Tuonela, Op. 22/3.
(M) *** DG 439 982-2. BPO, Karajan.

Karajan's 1964 *Fifth* is already available on DG's Classikon bargain label, coupled with short orchestral pieces. The new mid-priced reissue is obviously even more attractive, coupled with his glorious 1967 account of the *Sixth*, which remains almost unsurpassed by more recent accounts. The brooding *Swan of Tuonela* is placed between the two symphonies and is played just as admirably by the Berlin Philharmonic on their finest form. The CD transfers are miraculously managed so that the recordings show little sign of their age.

Symphonies Nos. 5 in E flat; 7 in C; Kuolema: Scene with cranes. Night ride and sunrise.
(M) *** EMI CDM7 64122-2. CBSO, Sir Simon Rattle.

In the *Fifth Symphony* Rattle is scrupulous in observing every dynamic nuance to the letter and, one might add, spirit. What is particularly impressive is the control of the transition between the first section and the Scherzo element of the first movement. There is a splendid sense of atmosphere in the development and a power unmatched in recent versions, save for the Karajan. The playing is superb, with recording to match. The *Seventh* is hardly less powerful and impressive: its opening is slow to unfold and has real vision. With the addition of an imaginative and poetic account of the *Scene with cranes* from the incidental music to *Kuolema*, this is the finest single disc in Rattle's Birmingham cycle.

Symphonies No. 6 in D min., Op. 104; 7 in C, Op. 105; Tapiola, Op. 112.
(N) *** BIS Dig. CD 864 [id.]. Lahti SO, Osmo Vänskä.

Osmo Vänskä's account of the *Sixth* and *Seventh Symphonies* brings his cycle to a fitting climax. The *Sixth* is serene yet taut, and the *Seventh* particularly fine both in pacing and character. Vänskä's reading of *Tapiola* has a thrilling intensity and if it is not the equal of Karajan or Beecham, it is certainly among the very best of the others. The Lahti

Orchestra always plays with enthusiasm and fire, and the BIS recording is first class.

Symphony No. 7 in C, Op. 105; Canzonetta, Op. 62a; Kuolema: Valse triste; Scene with cranes, Op. 44; Night ride and sunrise, Op. 55; Valse romantique, Op. 62b.
*** BIS Dig. CD 311 [id.]. Gothenburg SO, Järvi.

Neeme Järvi and the Gothenburg orchestra bring great energy and concentration to the *Seventh Symphony*. The only disappointment is the final climax, which is perhaps less intense than the best versions. However, it is a fine performance, and the music to *Kuolema* is splendidly atmospheric; *Night ride* is strongly characterized. The recording exhibits the usual characteristics of the Gothenburg Concert Hall and has plenty of body and presence.

Tapiola, Op. 112.
(M) *** DG (IMS) Dig. 445 518-2 [id.]. BPO, Karajan – NIELSEN: *Symphony No. 4.* ***

This is Karajan's fourth and undoubtedly greatest account of *Tapiola*, for he has the full measure of its vision and power. Never has it sounded more mysterious or its dreams more savage; nor has the build-up to the storm ever struck such a chilling note of terror: an awesomely impressive musical landscape; while the wood-sprites, weaving their magic secrets, come vividly to life.

The Wood nymph (tone-poem), *Op. 15;* (i) *The Wood nymph* (melodrama) (1895); *A lonely ski-trail; Swanwhite, Op. 54.*
*** BIS Dig. CD 815 [id.]. (i) Lasse Pöysti; Lahti SO, Vänskä.

Sibelius composed *The Wood nymph* in 1894–5 when the four *Lemminkäinen Legends* were taking shape in his mind. It is a re-working of the melodrama written for two horns, piano and strings to accompany the recitation of verses by the mainland Swedish poet, Viktor Rydberg. It is a substantial piece, as long as *En Saga* or the *Seventh Symphony*, though not of comparable quality. Sibelius thought well enough of it to programme it alongside the *First Symphony* at its première in 1899, but he never revised it. It is stirring stuff and begins with echoes of the *Karelia* music and in places comes close to both the first of the *Legends* and *Lemminkäinen's homeward journey*. It improves with every hearing: its main ideas haunt the listener and are difficult to dislodge from the brain! *A lonely ski-trail* is slight, but *The Wood nymph* melodrama is imaginative and highly unusual. The original music to *Swanwhite* has some poetic ideas that did not find their way into the suite, though for the most part there is not a great deal that is unfamiliar. Superb playing from the Lahti orchestra under Osmo Vänskä, and spacious, impeccably balanced recording.

CHAMBER MUSIC

(i) *Adagio in D min;* (ii, iii) *Duo in C for violin and viola;* (i) *Fugue for Martin Wegelius;* (iii, iv, v) *Piano trio in C (Lovisa)*; (vi, vii) *Suite in E for violin and piano;* (iii, iv) *Water drops for violin and cello.*
(N) *** Ondine Dig. ODE 850-2 [id.]. (i) Jean Sibelius Qt.; (ii) Matti Hirvikangas; (iii) Seppo Kimangen; (iv) Yoshiko Arai; (v) Juhani Lagerspetz; (vi) Pekka Kuusisto; (vii) Raija Kerppo.

These are all slight pieces from Sibelius's youth and student years: *Water drops* was written when he was ten and is of no artistic interest. The *Fugue* for his teacher, *Martin Wegelius* of 1888, was originally intended as the finale for his *A minor Quartet*, just as the *Adagio in D minor* (1890) was probably to have formed part of the *B flat Quartet*, Op. 4. This is the most individual of the pieces on this well-played and well-recorded set. With the exception of the *Lovisa Trio* of 1888, these are all first recordings.

(i) *Piano quartet in C min.* (for piano, two violins and cello); (ii) *String trio in G min.; Suite in A for string trio;* (iii) *Violin sonata in F.*
*** Ondine Dig. ODE 826-2 [id.]. (i) Novikov, Quarta, Miori, Rousi; (ii) Söderblom, Angervo, Gustafsson; (iii) Kovacic, Lagerspetz.

These are all early and uncharacteristic works. The *Violin sonata in F major* (1889) shows Sibelius still under the spell of Grieg. Only three movements of the *Suite in A major* for string trio (1888) survive (these artists give us what remains of the fourth movement, a *Gigue*); and its companion, the *String trio in G minor*, is also unfinished. Only the *Lento* survives intact, though the disc also gives a realization of what remains of the sketches of two other movements. The *Quartet in C minor* for piano, two violins and cello is a set of variations from the composer's Vienna year, 1891. All this is largely uncharacteristic and, save for the opening of the *A major Suite*, offers few glimpses of the mature Sibelius. The performances are dedicated and beautifully recorded.

(i) *Piano quintet in G min.; Piano trio in C (Lovisa); String quartet in E flat.*
*** Finlandia/Warner 4509 95858-2 [id.]. Sibelius Ac. Qt, (i) with Tawaststjerna.

(i) *Piano quintet in G min.; String quartet in D min. (Voces intimae), Op. 56.*
*** Chandos Dig. CHAN 8742 [id.]. (i) Anthony Goldstone; Gabrieli Qt.

The *Piano quintet* is a long and far from characteristic piece in five movements. Anthony Goldstone and the Gabrielis reverse the order of the second and third movements so as to maximize contrast. The first movement is probably the finest and Anthony Goldstone, an impressive player by any standards, makes the most of Sibelius's piano writing to produce a very committed performance. The *Voces intimae Quartet* is given a reflective, intelligent reading, perhaps at times wanting in momentum but finely shaped. Good recording.

The early *Quartet in E flat* is Haydnesque and insignificant, and the *Lovisa trio*, so called because it was written in that small town in the summer of 1888, offers only sporadic glimpses of things to come. The *Piano quintet* is given a fine performance on Finlandia, and there is little to choose between it and the more expansive Goldstone/Gabrieli account on Chandos.

String quartets: in E flat (1885); *A min.* (1889); *B flat, Op. 4* (1890); *D min. (Voces intimae), Op. 56.*
(M) *** Finlandia/Warner Dig./Analogue 4509 95851-2 (2). Sibelius Ac. Qt.

The *A minor Quartet* proves a delightful surprise with something of the freshness of Dvořák and Schubert. Sibelius obviously had ambivalent feelings towards the *B flat Quartet* and discouraged its performance. Its second movement bears a slight resemblance to a theme from *Rakastava*. Both are well worth resurrecting even if they do not, of course, match the mature *Voces intimae quartet* in artistry. The playing of the Sibelius Academy Quartet is exemplary and the recordings good: three are digital; *Voces intimae* dates from 1980 and is analogue.

String quartet in D min. (Voces intimae), Op. 56.
(N) *** Finlandia Dig. 3984 21445-2 [id.]. New Helsinki Qt. – GRIEG: *Quartet in G min. Op. 56.* ***
(***) Biddulph mono LAB 098 [id.]. Budapest Qt – GRIEG: *Quartet;* WOLF: *Italian serenade.* (***)

The most recent recording comes from the New Helsinki Quartet who couple *Voces intimae* with the Grieg *Quartet in G minor*. The disc is entitled 'Inner Voices', probably a better translation of *Voces intimae* than the usual 'intimate voices'. The performance is finely shaped and vital, yet full of sensitivity. It would be a very satisfying first recommendation among modern recordings, assuming price is no consideration. Apart from the excellence of the playing, the recording is also very present and well detailed.

A welcome transfer – the first on CD – of the 1933 pioneering *Voces intimae*, still unbeaten. It briefly appeared on LP (on the World Record label) and is newly (and well) transferred here by Ward Marston. Sibelians will need no reminders of its excellence – and the same goes for the couplings.

Music for violin and piano

5 Danses champêtres, Op. 106; Novellette, Op. 102; 5 Pieces, Op. 81; 4 Pieces, Op. 115; 3 Pieces, Op. 116.
*** BIS Dig. CD 625 [id.]. Nils-Erik Sparf, Bengt Forsberg.

Many of the items here, such as the delightful *Rondino* from Op. 81, are little more than salon music, but some of the others are rewarding pieces. Indeed the first of the *Danses champêtres* almost suggests the music to *The Tempest*, written at much the same time. Both the Opp. 115 and 116 pieces contain music of quality. As in the companion disc, Nils-Erik Sparf and Bengt Forsberg prove as imaginative as they are accomplished, and the only marginal criticism concerns the balance, which tends to favour the piano, whose tone sounds a little thick at the bass end of the aural spectrum.

2 Pieces, Op. 2 (2 versions); *Scaramouche: Scène d'amour. 2 Serious melodies, Op. 77; 4 Pieces, Op. 78; 6 Pieces, Op. 79; Sonatina in E, Op. 80.*
*** BIS Dig. CD 525 [id.]. Nils-Erik Sparf, Bengt Forsberg.

This CD offers the first recording of the 1888 versions of the *Grave* and the *Perpetuum mobile*, the two pieces which Sibelius assigned to Opus 2, together with the 1911 versions, in which the former was revised as *Romance in B minor* and the latter overhauled as *Epilogue*. The former bears a certain affinity to the slow movement of the *Violin concerto* and the prevalence of the tritone in the latter acts as a reminder that it was reworked in the wake of the *Fourth Symphony*. Exemplary performances of the later pieces, including *Laetare anima mea* and the 1915 *Sonatina*, Op. 80.

PIANO MUSIC

Autrefois, Op. 96b; 5 Esquisses, Op. 114; Finlandia, Op. 26; 8 Pieces, Op. 99; 5 Pieces, Op. 101; 5 Pieces, Op. 103; Valse chevaleresque, Op. 96c; Valse lyrique, Op. 96a.
*** Olympia Dig. OCD 635 [id.]. Annette Servadei.

6 Bagatelles, Op. 97; Melody for the Bells of Berghäll Church, Op. 65b; 5 Pieces, Op. 75; 13 Pieces, Op. 76; 5 Pieces, Op. 85; 6 Pieces, Op. 94.
*** Olympia Dig. OCD 634 [id.]. Annette Servadei.

10 Bagatelles, Op. 34; 6 Impromptus, Op. 5; 10 Pieces, Op. 24.
*** Olympia Dig. OCD 631 [id.]. Annette Servadei.

6 Finnish folksongs; Kavaljeren; Mandolinato; Morceau romantique; Pensées lyriques, Op. 40; 10 Pieces, Op. 58; Spagnuolo; Till trånaden; Valse triste, Op. 44/1.
*** Olympia Dig. OCD 632 [id.]. Annette Servadei.

Kyllikki, Op. 41; 4 Lyric Pieces, Op. 74; 2 Rondinos, Op. 68; Sonata in F, Op. 12; Sonatinas

Nos. 1 in F sharp min., 2 in E; 3 in B flat min., Op. 67/1–3.
*** Olympia Dig. OCD 633 [id.]. Annette Servadei.

By the exalted standards he set elsewhere, Sibelius's contribution to the keyboard seems limited in inventive resource. The *Melody* he wrote for the bells of Berghäll Church is slight but charming. There are some echoes of the *First Sonatina* in *Aquileja,* and pieces like *När rönnen blommar* ('When the rowan blossoms'), from the Op. 75 set, and *Berger et bergerette* have a certain charm. *Finlandia*, the *Valse lyrique*, *Autrefois* and *Valse chevaleresque* are all transcriptions of orchestral pieces. These were, of course, made when the piano arrangement served to give this music wider currency, a function long overtaken by the gramophone. No pianist, however imaginative and sensitive, could possibly convey the charm of *Autrefois*. The sonatinas attracted the admiration both of Kempff, who never recorded them, and of Glenn Gould, who did. Annette Servadei is a sympathetic and sensitive guide to this repertoire, and on the whole she is well recorded. She produces a wide range of keyboard colour and a good dynamic range. At times she is rather too closely observed by the microphone with a result that *forte* or *fortissimo* passages are insufficiently transparent. But on the whole the Olympia set makes a clear first choice in this repertoire.

3 Lyric pieces, Op. 41; 5 Characteristic impressions, Op. 103; 6 Impromptus, Op. 5; 5 Pieces, Op. 75; 5 Pieces, Op. 85; Finlandia (arr. composer).
(BB) *** Naxos Dig. 8. 553661 [id.]. Risto Lauriala.

Perfectly good playing and decent recording make this a useful alternative to the complete survey by Annette Servadei. Its price advantage will incline some readers to give it preference, and it also enjoys the benefit of decent recorded sound.

VOCAL MUSIC

(i) *Belshazzar's Feast* (complete score), *Op. 51; The Countess's Portrait (Grefvinnans konterfej);* (ii) *Jedermann (Everyman)* (incidental music), *Op. 83.*
*** BIS Dig. CD 737 [id.]. (i) Passikivi; Lahti SO, Vänskä; (ii) with Lehto, Tiilikainen, Pietiläinen, Lahti Chamber Ch.

BIS is coming up with repertoire which is completely unknown even to keen Sibelians. All three works on this disc are new to the catalogue. The incidental music to Hugo von Hofmannsthal's morality play, *Everyman*, comes from the autumn of 1916, when Sibelius was also working on the second version of his *Fifth Symphony*. The score runs to 16 numbers and takes 40 minutes. Although it was written at the height of the First World War, the theatre was able to muster considerable forces. A lot of the music is fragmentary, wisps of sound; all of it is atmospheric and the best of it (the *Largo* section from track 12 onwards) finds Sibelius at his most inspired. The complete score for Hjalmar Procopé's *Belshazzar's Feast* brings us some seven minutes of extra music. The scoring is different from and less effective than the concert suite. There is, for example, no oboe in the original; the seductive descending oboe theme in *Khadra's dance* is assigned to the clarinet. *Grefvinnans konterfej* (*The Countess's Portrait*) is a short, wistful piece for strings which comes from 1906 and was originally designed to accompany a recitation of *Porträtterna*, a poem by the mainland Swedish poet, Anna-Maria Lenngren. Dedicated, sensitive performances from the Lahti Symphony Orchestra and excellent recording. An indispensable disc for all Sibelians.

(i) *Karelia* (complete incidental music); (ii) *Kuolema, Op. 44; Valse triste* (1904 version).
(N) *** BIS Dig. CD 915 [id.]. (i) Heikki Laitinen, Taito Hoffgren; (i & ii) Raimo Laukka; (ii) Kirsi Tilhonen; Lahti SO, Osmo Vänska.

Although the *Karelia suite* is familiar enough, no one will have heard the complete score. It has only recently been put into performable shape. When it was originally performed in 1893, it ran to eight tableaux and portrayed various episodes in Karelian history. During the 1940s Sibelius destroyed the bulk of it, sparing only the overture, the movements familiar from the suite and the opening section, *A Karelian home - News of war*. However, a set of parts survived, albeit incomplete, and the composer, Kalevi Aho has prepared an edition which Osmo Vänskä and his musicians use for this score. Some things are disconcerting: the familiar cor anglais melody in the *Ballade* is given to a tenor, and the movement is far too long. But there is much of interest here that makes this essential listening for Sibelians. The incidental music to *Kuolema* (Death), written ten years later, was revised the following year (1904) and re-scored. The original second section, *Paavali's song*, is quite inspired, though Sibelius was quite right to add wind to represent the bird cries in the following scene (he conflated scenes 3 and 4 to form *Scene with cranes*). The disc also affords an opportunity to contrast the 1903 and 1904 versions of *Valse triste*, the differences will bring you up with a start. Superb playing and recording.

(i) *Karelia suite, Op. 11* (original scoring); (ii) *King Christian II, Op. 27* (complete original score); (iii) *Pelléas et Mélisande* (original scoring).
(N) *** BIS Dig. CD 918 [id.]. (i & ii) Raimo Laukka; (iii) Anna-Lisa Jakobsson; Lahti SO, Osmo Vänska.

BIS continues its exploration of Sibelius scores that are not in the public domain. The original score to Adolf Paul's play *King Christian II* was written in 1898, four movements at the beginning of the year, and the remaining three were composed during the summer for its revival that autumn. Sibelius re-scored them for larger forces when he made his concert suite the following year, his first orchestral work to be published. It is particularly good to hear the *Musette* in such a characterful form – just for wind. The changes in the score Sibelius composed for Bertel Gripenberg's Swedish translation of Maeterlinck's *Pelléas et Mélisande* are less extensive but we do have an additional section that have never been published. The *Karelia suite* comes is drawn from BIS CD 915. A highly successful issue of great interest to all Sibelians.

Kullervo Symphony, Op. 7.

*** Finlandia/Warner Dig. 0630 14906-2 [id.]. Groop, Hynninen, Polytech Ch., Finnish RSO, Jukka-Pekka Saraste.

*** Sony Dig. SK 52563 [id.]. Marianna Rørholm, Jorma Hynninen, Helsinki University Ch., LAPO, Salonen.

(i) *Kullervo Symphony, Op. 7; Symphony No. 7 in C, Op. 105; En saga, Op. 9; Rakastava, Op. 14.*

(N) *** RCA Dig. 09026 68312 [id.]. (i) Hillevi Martinpelto, Karl-Magnus Fredriksson, LS Ch.; LSO, Sir Colin Davis.

Sir Colin's account of the *Kullervo Symphony* is more spacious and commanding than most of the other listings, and it has been well worth waiting for. Although he takes over eighty minutes (and as a result runs to a second disc), it seems shorter than most of its rivals, though the work emerges as bigger. It is a superb performance and very well recorded too. The two soloists, both Swedish, are very good though they are not superior to such rivals as Groop, Isokoski and Hynninen. However this is a performance of real stature; Davis understands Sibelius as do few living conductors and no serious collector should neglect it. As well as Sibelius's earliest symphonic venture, he gives us the last – and a very impressive reading it is too. The work unfolds with a natural authority and there is space, power and serenity when required. Sir Colin recorded *En saga* in the early 1980s during his Boston years – very successfully – and this is hardly less fine. *Rakastava* for strings and percussion is a touching work, all the more affecting for its unforced eloquence. The last movement may strike some as a bit too slow. All in all, however, an outstanding set, which sets the seal on a triumphant and magisterial survey.

Sibelius's early symphony has been well served on CD, but Jukka-Pekka Saraste's performance with Finnish Radio forces is among the best of the current bunch. It has a more urgent sense of movement and a greater dramatic intensity than those by his countrymen, Paavo Berglund (EMI) and Leif Segerstam (Chandos), and it has a rougher, tougher centre and seems more in tune with the essential character of the work than Salonen's (Sony). Jorma Hynninen is common to all these performances save Segerstam and, though his voice has lost some of the bloom of his first recording of the piece, he remains pretty commanding. Monica Groop is also in excellent voice. Saraste, whose recent set of the symphonies, recorded in St Petersburg with the same orchestra, was nothing special, produces altogether excellent results here. He shares the same venue (the Cultural House in Helsinki) with Berglund's 1985 recording but, although the sound is not as transparent or well ventilated as the EMI nor the choral singing as well focused, everything is so much more musically alive.

Esa-Pekka Salonen's account of Sibelius's early *Kullervo Symphony* is gripping and held together tautly. It has a sweep and momentum that eluded Salonen's less-than-overwhelming Nielsen cycle. The Los Angeles orchestra, to whom this score must have been new, play with the enthusiasm of fresh discovery and Marianna Rørholm proves a worthy companion to the ubiquitous Hynninen. The first movement is taut, brisk and dramatic – very much as Sibelius's son-in-law took it at its first performance in recent times; the fifth is very imaginatively done, and only the fourth is perhaps a bit too fast, almost headlong.

The Tempest (incidental music), *Op. 109* (complete).

*** BIS Dig. CD 581 [id.]. Tiihonen, Passikivi, Hirvonen, Kerola, Heinonen, Lahti Opera Ch. & SO, Osmo Vänskä.

The familiar two suites from *The Tempest* plus the *Prelude* have been recorded many times (most notably and magically by Sir Thomas Beecham) but Sibelius's original score for the 1926 Copenhagen production of Shakespeare's play is extensive: it runs to some 34 numbers in all for soloists, mixed chorus, harmonium and orchestra, and takes about 65 minutes. There are some unfamiliar effects here: the muted strings with which we are familiar in the *Berceuse* were an afterthought. In the original, their music is allotted to the harmonium; and although this is at first startling, the effect is other-worldly in a completely unexpected way. There are other master-strokes that are missing (the insinuating bass clarinet in *The Oak-tree*) but much else that will be new. The *Chorus of the winds* with a real chorus is also quite magical – in fact the vocal writing is often highly imaginative – and the singers on the BIS CD are all good. The atmosphere is very strong and puts one completely under its spell. The BIS recording, though good, needs to be reproduced at a higher than usual level setting: some may find it too recessed and there is at the bottom end of the spectrum a certain want of transparency.

Songs

7 Songs, Op. 13; 6 Songs, Op. 50; 6 Songs, Op. 90; Resemblance (Likhet); A Song (En visa); Serenade (1888); Skogsrået (Wood-nymph) (1889); The Jewish girl's song (Den judiska flickans sång); (i) *The thought (Tanken) (1915).*
*** BIS Dig. CD 757 [id.]. Anne Sofie von Otter, Bengt Forsberg, (i) with Monica Groop.

We welcomed Anne Sofie von Otter's first recital (BIS CD 457), and this is hardly less successful. The Opp. 13 and 90 songs are all settings of Runeberg, Sibelius's favourite poet, but there are rarities such as *Skogsrået* ('The Wood-Nymph') – totally unrelated, by the way, to the melodrama and tone-poem of the same name which he wrote in the early 1890s – and never before recorded. Also new are the duet, *Tanken* ('The thought'), *Resemblance* and *A Song*. Von Otter and her partner characterize each song with the consummate artistry one expects from them, and the only possible reservation concerns the balance, which in some of the early songs favours the piano.

Six songs, Op. 36.
(N) *** Virgin Classics Dig. VC5 45273-2 [id.]. Solveig Kringelborn, Malcolm Martineau – GRIEG, NIELSEN, RANGSTROM: *Songs.* ***

Solveig Kringelborn's anthology takes its name, '*Black roses*', from the famous Sibelius song in this set. In some ways her recordings of Sibelius are the least satisfactory of the items in this welcome recital. She produces a beautiful sound throughout but her characterization, particularly in the setting of Fröding's *Tennis vid Trianon*, is less searching. All the same there is too much here that gives pleasure and her pianist Malcolm Martineau is superb throughout. Excellent recorded sound too.

Songs with orchestra: *Arioso; Autumn evening (Höstkväll); Come away, Death! (Kom nu hit, död!); The diamond on the March snow (Diamanten på marssnön); The fool's song of the spider (Sången om korsspindeln); Luonnotar, Op. 70; On a balcony by the sea (På verandan vid havet); The Rapids-rider's brides (Koskenlaskian morsiammet); Serenade; Since then I have questioned no further (Se'n har jag ej frågat mera); Spring flies hastily (Våren flyktar hastigt); Sunrise (Soluppgång).*
*** BIS CD 270 [id.]. Jorma Hynninen, Mari Anne Häggander, Gothenburg SO, Panula.

Jorma Hynninen is a fine interpreter of this repertoire: his singing can only be called glorious. Mari-Anne Häggander manages the demanding tessitura of *Arioso* and *Luonnotar* with much artistry, and her *Luonnotar* is certainly to be preferred to Söderström's. Jorma Panula proves a sensitive accompanist and secures fine playing from the Gothenburg orchestra. In any event, this is indispensable.

Arioso, Op. 3; Narcissus; Pelléas et Mélisande: The three blind sisters. 7 Songs, Op. 17; 6 Songs, Op. 36; 5 Songs, Op. 37; 6 Songs, Op. 88. Souda, souda, sinisorsa.
*** BIS Dig. CD 457 [id.]. Anne Sofie von Otter, Bengt Forsberg.

This lovely recital by Anne Sofie von Otter marked the start of the BIS project to record all the songs. Miss von Otter always makes a beautiful sound, but she has a highly developed sense of line and brings great interpretative insight to such songs as *My bird is long in homing* and *Tennis at Trianon*, which has even greater finesse than Söderström's. And what a good accompanist Bengt Forsberg is. The recording is good if a bit reverberant.

OPERA

The Maiden in the tower (opera). *Karelia suite, Op. 11.*
*** BIS Dig. CD 250 [id.]. Häggander, Hynninen, Hagegård, Kruse, Gothenburg Ch. and SO, Järvi.

The Maiden in the tower falls into eight short scenes. The orchestral interlude between the first two scenes brings us the real Sibelius, and the second scene is undoubtedly impressive; there are echoes of Wagner, such as we find in some of the great orchestral songs of the following decade. All the same, it lacks something we find in all his most characteristic music: quite simply, a sense of mastery. Yet there are telling performances here from Mari-Anne Häggander and Jorma Hynninen and the Gothenburg orchestra. Neeme Järvi's account of the *Karelia suite* is certainly original, with its *Intermezzo* too broad to make an effective contrast with the ensuing *Ballade*.

Signoretti, Aurelio (1597–1635)

Missa Looquebantur variis linguis apostoli in die Pentecoster; Vesperitina Psalmodia in Festas B.V. Bariae (Venice, 1639).
(N) *** Tactus Dig. TC 561901 [id.]. La Stagione Armonica, Sergio Balestracci (with PORTA: *Sonata detta La Porta a 4*; VIADANA: Sinfonia detta La Reggiana ***).

Here is another composer brought back to us from the seventeenth century by the enterprising Tactus label, this time from Venice. His four-part parody mass is based on a motet by Palestrina. It has a pleasing simplicity and eloquence and is presented here as a missa brevis, together with the Propers appropriate for the Feast of Pentecost (with the chants particularly pleasingly sung). Signoretti's remarkable collection of 1629 includes eighteen psalm settings plus three of the *Magnificat*. They are given here in an order to form Vespers for the Virgin Mary, including the appropriate antiphons and hymns, and are sung with great freshness and spontaneity. Two instrumental pieces of the same period act as prelude and postlude (the latter scored for brass). Altogether this is a thoroughly worthwhile enterprise, admirably thought out and impressively carried through. The recording is excellent.

Simpson, Robert (1921–97)

Energy; Introduction & allegro on a theme by Max Reger; The Four Temperaments; Volcano; Vortex.
*** Hyperion Dig. CDA 66449 [id.]. Desford Colliery Caterpillar Band, James Watson.

The Four Temperaments is a four-movement, 22-minute symphony of great imaginative power, and ingeniously laid out for the band. The *Introduction and allegro on a theme by Max Reger* is awesome and impressive. Together with *Volcano* and his most recent piece, *Vortex*, it makes up his entire output in this medium. The Desford Colliery Caterpillar Band under James Watson play with all the expertise and virtuosity one expects, and the recording has admirable clarity and body, though the acoustic is on the dry side.

Symphonies Nos. 1; 8.
*** Hyperion Dig. CDA 66890 [id.]. RPO, Vernon Handley.

Robert Simpson's *First Symphony* is a one-movement work, albeit in three sections, powerfully constructed and forcefully argued. It holds up to the test of time remarkably well and better than much other music of the 1950s. One critic has pointed to the *Eighth* as seeming to embody some 'colossal inner rage' and, like the *Fifth*, it undoubtedly has a combative tumult that rarely passes into tranquillity. Handley makes out a strong case for both scores, and the sound is absolutely first class. An indispensable issue for anyone who cares about the post-war symphony in Britain.

Symphonies Nos. 2; 4.
*** Hyperion Dig. CDA 66505 [id.]. Bournemouth SO, Vernon Handley.

The *Second*, composed in 1956 for Anthony Bernard's London Chamber Orchestra, is one of the very best; a work of enduring quality, music that is both accessible yet of substance. The *Fourth Symphony* is the more extended piece. Powerful and inspiriting music in totally dedicated performances by Vernon Handley, and excellent recording quality.

Symphonies Nos. 3 (1961); *5* (1971).
*** Hyperion Dig. CDA 66728 [id.]. RPO, Handley.

Vernon Handley brings us the première recording of the *Fifth Symphony*, a work of striking power and range. No admirer of the composer – and no one who cares about twentieth-century music in general – should pass these performances by, for it is music of a vital and forceful eloquence. Fine playing by the RPO under Handley, and exemplary recording.

Symphonies Nos. 6; 7.
*** Hyperion Dig. CDA 66280 [id.]. RLPO, Handley.

The *Sixth* is inspired by the idea of growth: the development of a musical structure from initial melodic cells in much the same way as life emerges from a single fertilized cell in nature. The *Seventh*, scored for chamber orchestral forces, is hardly less powerful in its imaginative vision and sense of purpose. Both scores are bracingly Nordic in their inner landscape and exhilarating in aural experience. The playing of the Liverpool orchestra under Vernon Handley could hardly be bettered, and the recording is altogether first class.

Symphony No. 9.
❁ *** Hyperion Dig. CDA 66299 [id.]. Bournemouth SO, Vernon Handley (with talk by the composer).

What can one say about the *Ninth* of Robert Simpson, except that its gestures are confident, its control of pace and its material are masterly? The CD also includes a spoken introduction to the piece that many listeners will probably find helpful. It is played superbly by the Bournemouth Symphony Orchestra under Vernon Handley, and is no less superbly recorded.

Symphony No. 10.
*** Hyperion Dig. CDA 66510 [id.]. RLPO, Handley.

The *Tenth Symphony* (1988) will be a tough nut to crack for many collectors. Its musical argument is unfailingly concentrated. Like its predecessor, it has a Beethovenian strength and momentum. But make no mistake: it is a work of stature, and it is very well played and recorded here.

(i) *Canzona for brass* (i & ii) *Media morte in vita sumus*; (ii) *Tempi*; (iii) *Eppur si muove*.
(N) *** Hyperion Dig. CDA 67016 [id.]. (i) Corydon Brass Ens. (ii) Corydon Singers, Matthew Best; (iii) Iain Quinn.

The *Canzona for brass* from 1957 has never sounded more impressive on CD. It has the dignity and grandeur of Gabrieli. The *Media morte in vita sumus* ('In the midst of death we are in life') has a depth and eloquence completely at variance with so much contemporary music. *Tempi* (1988) is a setting for *a cappella* choir of various Italian tempo indications, written for a choral competition in the composer's adopted Eire. Such is its beauty that it makes one regret that it is Simpson's only contribution to the medium. *Eppur si muove* (1988), an imposing 30-minute piece for organ, not dissimilar in scope and ambition to Nielsen's *Commotio*. Iain Quinn plays it with consummate mastery on the organ of Winchester Cathedral. The brass playing is superb and the Corydon Singers cope with Simpson's demanding vocal writing admirably even if the sopranos are obviously taxed at times above the stave. State-of-the-art recording. Not to be missed.

Horn quartet (for horn, violin, cello & piano); *Horn trio* (for horn, violin & piano).
*** Hyperion Dig. CDA 66695 [id.]. Richard Watkins, Pauline Lowbury, Christopher Green Armytage, Caroline Dearnley.

The *Quartet for horn, violin, cello and piano* of 1976 is of unfailing quality and imagination, and its development magnificently sustained. The composer draws some extraordinary sounds from these four instruments. In some ways this is one of his most deeply original and compelling works. These are most impressive pieces, and the performances are completely dedicated and highly imaginative. Excellent recording too.

String quartets Nos. 1–3.
(N) (**) Pearl mono GEM 0023 [id.]. Element Qt.

These are off-air recordings from the composer's own collection of the première broadcast performances in the Third Programme in the 1950s. They have a certain gutsy quality, a total and impassioned commitment that more than compensates for the odd rough edges.

String quartets Nos. 1; 4.
*** Hyperion Dig. CDA 66419 [id.]. Delmé Qt.

The *First Quartet* opens in as innocent a fashion as the Haydn *Lark Quartet* or Nielsen's *E flat*, but the better one comes to know it the more it is obvious that Simpson is already his own man. The second movement is a palindrome (most modern composers do not know how to write forwards, let alone backwards as well) but its ingenuity is worn lightly. The *Fourth* is part of the trilogy which Simpson conceived as a kind of commentary on Beethoven's *Rasumovsky quartets*. Yet they live very much in their own right. Excellent performances from the Delmé, and fine recording too.

String quartets Nos. 2; 5.
*** Hyperion Dig. CDA 66386 [id.]. Delmé Qt.

The *Second Quartet* is thought-provoking and full of character. The *Fifth*, composed over 20 years later in 1974, is one of the three modelled on Beethoven's *Rasumovsky Quartets* – in this case, Op. 59, No. 2 – and even emulates the phrase structure of the Beethoven. It is a long and powerfully sustained piece, which receives expert advocacy from the Delmé Quartet and excellent Hyperion sound.

String quartets Nos. 3 and 6; String trio (Prelude, Adagio & fugue).
*** Hyperion Dig. CDA 66376 [id.]. Delmé Qt.

The *Third Quartet* is a two-movement piece. Its finale is a veritable power-house with its unrelenting sense of onward movement which almost strains the medium. Its first movement is a deeply felt piece that has a powerful and haunting eloquence. The *Sixth* is further evidence of Simpson's remarkable musical mind. The *String trio* is a marvellously stimulating and thoughtful piece. Dedicated performances and excellent recording.

String quartets Nos. 7 and 8.
*** Hyperion Dig. CDA 66117 [id.]. Delmé Qt.

The *Seventh Quartet* has a real sense of vision and something of the stillness of the remote worlds it evokes, 'quiet and mysterious yet pulsating with energy'. The *Eighth* turns from the vastness of space to the microcosmic world of insect-life, but, as with so much of Simpson's music, there is a concern for musical continuity rather than beauty of incident. Excellent playing from the Delmé Quartet, and very good recorded sound too.

String quartet No. 9 (32 Variations & fugue on a theme of Haydn).
*** Hyperion Dig. CDA 66127 [id.]. Delmé Qt.

The *Ninth Quartet* is a set of thirty-two variations and a fugue on the minuet of Haydn's *Symphony No. 47*. Like the minuet itself, all the variations are in the form of a palindrome. A formidable achievement in any age, and a rarity in ours. The Delmé Quartet cope with its difficulties splendidly, and the performance carries the imprimatur of the composer.

String quartets Nos. 10 (For Peace); 11.
*** Hyperion Dig. CDA 66225 [id.]. Coull Qt.

The subtitle, *For Peace*, of No. 10 refers to 'its generally pacific character' and aspires to define 'the condition of peace which excludes aggression but not strong feeling'. Listening to this *Quartet* is like hearing a quiet, cool voice of sanity that refreshes the troubled spirit after a long period in an alien, hostile world. The one-movement *Eleventh* draws on some of the inspiration of its predecessor. It is a work of enormous power and momentum. Excellent performances and recording.

String quartet No. 12 (1987); (i) *String quintet* (1987).
*** Hyperion Dig. CDA 66503. Coull Qt, (i) with Roger Bigley.

Robert Simpson's *Twelfth Quartet* is a masterly and absorbing score. His *String quintet* is another work of sustained inventive power. The intonation and tone of the leader is not always impeccable, but the playing has commitment and intelligence.

Piano sonata; Michael Tippett, his mystery;

Variations and finale on a theme by Beethoven; Variations and finale on a theme by Haydn.
*** Hyperion Dig. CDA 66827 [id.]. Raymond Clarke.

The *Piano sonata* is a concentrated, craggy, powerfully argued piece, not obviously pianistic but bristling with challenges and difficulties. The *Variations and finale on a theme of Haydn* (1948) evince Simpson's lifelong interest in the palindrome. The short piece written for Tippett was a contribution to a birthday tribute. The *Variations and finale on a theme of Beethoven* are based on a little-known *Bagatelle*, WoO 61a. The performances are authoritative and, apart from a certain over-resonance, the recording satisfactory.

Sinding, Christian (1856–1941)

Légende, Op. 46.
(BB) *** Naxos Dig. 8.550329 [id.]. Dong-Suk Kang, Slovak (Bratislava) RSO, Adrian Leaper – HALVORSEN: *Air Norvégien* etc.; SIBELIUS: *Violin concerto;* SVENDSEN: *Romance.* ***

Dong-Suk Kang plays Sinding's *Légende* with great conviction and an effortless, songful virtuosity. It is by no means as appealing as the Halvorsen and Svendsen pieces but makes a good makeweight for an excellent collection in the lowest price range.

Suite (for violin and orchestra), *Op. 10.*
(M) *** EMI (IMS) CDM5 66060-2. Perlman, Pittsburgh SO, Previn – BARTOK: *Violin concerto No. 2;* CONUS: *Violin concerto.* ***

Heifetz recorded this dazzling piece in the 1950s, and it need only be said that Perlman's version is not inferior. The velocity of Perlman's first movement is little short of amazing.

Sirmen, Maddalena Lombardini (1735–99)

String quartets Nos. 1 in E flat; 2 in B flat; 3 in G min.; 4 in B flat; 5 in F min.; 6 in E.
*** Cala Dig. CACD 1019 [id.]. Allegri Qt.
(N) *** Tactus Dig. TC 731201 [id.]. Accademia della Magnifica Cuminità, Enrico Casazza.

Maddalena Lombardini was born in Venice and became a student at one of the *Mendicanti ospedale* (orphanages), the Italian ancestors of our present academies of music. She proved so talented that the governors sent her to continue her studies with Tartini and it was primarily as a violinist, in his view 'absolutely without equal', that she first made her reputation, although she also trained as a singer. Madame Sirmen travelled through Europe as a successful virtuoso, and by 1771 she was in London playing at the concerts organized by Abel and J. C. Bach. When her style of fiddling became outmoded (as speed came to be considered more desirable than polish and elegance), she turned to singing and secured a well-paid five-year appointment at the Dresden Opera, then moving on to St Petersburg. Finally Madame Sirmen returned home to Italy, where she spent the last 30 years of her life as teacher rather than performer.

Her *String quartets* (plus a similar batch of string trios and six violin concertos) date from her years at the orphanage and were published in Paris in 1769 by another enterprising woman, Madame Berault. The string quartet medium was at that time in its infancy (the present contribution is approximately contemporary with Haydn's Opus 9 set) and thus her easy skill in handling the medium is the more remarkable. There are two movements to each quartet, but the structure often subdivides into sections using different tempi. Most striking of all, *No. 5 in E minor* introduces a touching *Larghetto* which (within a span of eight minutes) returns after the central allegro. *No. 1 in E flat* is thematically and structurally a more interesting work, and it has a particularly striking second-movement *Allegretto* which is worthy of the young Mozart. The vivacious finale of the *Second Quartet*, which is used to end the disc, is comparable with Haydn. The Allegri Quartet obviously lived with this music for some time before this record was made, and they play it with much style and conviction, conveying their own pleasure in part-writing which is obviously enjoyable to play. With excellent recording, admirably present but naturally balanced, this is very much worth exploring.

Confusingly, the excellent Tactus alternative recording is documented under Maddalena's maiden name, Lombardini, which is reasonable enough as the *Quartets* were written while she was single. The six works are played simply, freshly and pleasingly. Even though a conductor is listed, they are given with one instrument to each part, and one is not aware of any 'interpretative' interference with the music's flow. The recording is excellent and this disc can be recommended alongside the Cala version: it is equally enjoyable, if not more so, and the players are given a strikingly natural presence.

Skoryk, Myroslav (born 1938)

Carpathian concerto: Hutsul triptych.
** ASV Dig. CDDCA 963 [id.]. Odessa PO, Hobart Earle – KOLESSA: *Symphony No. 1.* **

Myroslav Skoryk is now in his late fifties, a pupil of the veteran Ukrainian composer Mykola Kolessa, with whose *First Symphony* (1950) his pieces are coupled. Skoryk teaches composition at Lvov and has a considerable output to his credit, including two piano concertos, two violin concertos and a good deal of music for the theatre. The *Hutsul triptych* (1965) derives from a score Skoryk composed for the film, *Shadows of forgotten ancestors*, by Sergei Paradhzhanov. It is colourful, often atmospheric and inventive, not unlike some Shchedrin. The *Carpathian concerto* (1972) is an expertly scored orchestral piece with strong folkloric accents – and some cheap orientalism. Not a good piece nor strongly individual, but the centrepiece of the *Hutsul triptych* is worth hearing.

Skroup, František (1801–62)

The Tinker overture.

(**) Sup. mono SU 1914 011. Czech PO, Karel Sejna (with DVORAK: *The Cunning peasant overture* (**); SMETANA: *Festive Symphony* etc. (***))

Neither František nor his brother, Jan Nepomuk Skroup, has more than a peripheral hold on the current record catalogue. The author of the sleeve-note speaks of 'the stunning melodic spontaneity' of Skroup's *Overture* to *The Tinker*, which is no small claim. It is not a bad piece, but its melodic invention, while pleasant, is far from stunning. Sejna's performance is marvellously spirited, but the recording was made in 1951 and is rather thin on top!

Smetana, Bedřich (1824–84)

Má Vlast (complete).

*** Sup. Dig. 11 1208-2 [id.]. Czech PO, Kubelik.

(BB) *** Naxos Dig. 8.550931 [id.]. Polish Nat. RSO (Katowice), Antoni Wit.

*** Telarc CD 80265 [id.]. Milwaukee SO, Macal.

*** Chandos Dig. CHAN 9366 [id.]. Detroit SO, Neeme Järvi.

(M) *** Ph. Dig. 442 641-2. Concg. O, Antal Dorati.

(M) *** Virgin/EMI Dig. CUV5 61223-2. RLPO, Pešek.

*** DG Dig. 431 652-2 [id.]. VPO, Levine.

In 1990 Rafael Kubelik returned to his homeland after an enforced absence of 41 years to open the Prague Spring Festival with this vibrant performance of *Má Vlast*. He had recorded the work twice before in stereo, but this Czech version is special, imbued with passionate national feeling, yet never letting the emotions boil over. At the bold opening of *Vyšehrad*, with the harp strongly profiled, the intensity of the music-making is immediately projected, and the trickling streams which are the source of *Vltava* have a delicacy almost of fantasy but, after the relaxation for the moonlit sequence, one realizes that the return of the chorale as the river flows past Vyšehrad is a key point in Kubelik's reading. *Sárka*, with its bloodthirsty tale of revenge and slaughter, is immensely dramatic, contrasting with the pastoral evocations of the following piece; the Slavonic lilt of the music's lighter moments brings the necessary contrast and release. The recording is vivid and full but not sumptuous, yet this suits the powerful impulse of Kubelik's overall view, with the build-up to the exultant close of *Blaník* producing a dénouement of great majesty.

Antoni Wit and his excellent Polish National Radio Orchestra give us a superbly played and consistently imaginative account of Smetana's *Má Vlast*, whose patriotic aspirations can so readily turn into rhetoric. Not here, however. The spacious opening of *Vyšehrad*, marginally slower than usual, glows with romantic evocation; equally the flutes, trickling down from the sources of the *Vltava*, captivate the ear and the famous string-tune is unusually gracious and relaxed. The opening of *Sárka* brings tingling melodrama, which subsides naturally for the jaunty theme which follows. *From Bohemia's woods and fields* opens with opulent expansiveness, and later the ethereal high string entry is exquisitely made. The opening horn-call of *Tábor* emerges atmospherically from the mists of the past and the music develops great weight and gravitas. The warm resonance of the Concert Hall of Polish Radio in Katowice seems right for this very individual reading, full of fantasy, which goes automatically to the top of the list alongside Kubelik's distinguished, and justly renowned, 1990 Czech Philharmonic version on Supraphon, which is rather special.

Macal's Telarc version offers the finest recording of all; indeed it approaches the demonstration bracket. As with his version of Dvořák's *New World Symphony*, he provides a highly spontaneous and enjoyable performance, imaginatively conceived and convincingly paced. The very opening of *Vyšehrad*, with its relatively gentle harp roulades, sets the atmospheric mood of the reading; other accounts, notably Kubelik's, have greater Slavic fire and find a more red-bloodedly patriotic feeling, but the excellent orchestral playing is responsive to his less histrionic view. *Sárka* has a folksy flavour, the melodrama good-humoured, while in *From Bohemia's woods and fields*, after the radiant high string passage, the horns steal in magically with their chorale. Throughout the brass are full and sonorous, mitigating any rhetorical bombast in the last two symphonic poems; and Macal's Czech nationality ensures that the performance has idiomatic feeling.

Järvi's, too, is an enjoyably vivid performance, and he has the double advantage of first-class playing from the highly committed Detroit orchestra and the splendid acoustics of Symphony Hall. The romantic *Vyšehrad* is fresh and immediate, and the mountain streams of *Vltava* gleam brightly in the sunlight before the string-tune arrives and moves on with plenty of lyrical impetus. The jaunty village wedding is followed by an evocation of lovely, ethereal moonlight (matched by the high strings in *From Bohemia's woods and fields*) and the rapids bring high drama. *Sárka* is very dramatic indeed, with great melodramatic gusto and a heartfelt response from the strings. The opening of *Tábor* is tellingly ominous, and the weight of the Detroit brass makes a powerful contribution to both of the final two sections of the score; the zest of the Detroit music-making is always compelling, and the culminating climax is thrilling rather than expansively grandiloquent.

Dorati's is an extremely fine account of Smetana's cycle, avoiding most of the pitfalls with a reading which brings both vivid drama and orchestral playing of the finest quality. The music-making has a high adrenalin level throughout, yet points of detail are not missed. The accents of *Vyšehrad* may seem too highly stressed to ears used to a more mellow approach to this highly romantic opening piece, and *Vltava* similarly moves forward strongly. In the closing *Blaník*, Dorati finds dignity rather than bombast and the pastoral episode is delightfully relaxed, with a fine rhythmic bounce to the march theme. The Philips sound is splendid, with a wide amplitude and a thrilling concert-hall presence, and this reissue on the Philips Solo label makes an obvious recommendation in the mid-price range.

Pešek's reading does not miss the music's epic patriotic feeling, yet never becomes bombastic. There is plenty of evocation, from the richly romantic opening of *Vyšehrad* to the more mysterious scene-setting in *Tábor*, while the climax of *Sárka*, with its potent anticipatory horn-call, is a gripping piece of melodrama. The two main sections of the work, *Vltava* and *From Bohemia's woods and fields*, are especially enjoyable for their vivid characterization, while at the very end of *Blaník* Pešek draws together the two key themes – the *Vyšehrad* motif and the Hussite chorale – very satisfyingly.

Levine is upstaged by Dorati on Philips, who has a considerable price advantage plus the glorious acoustic of the Concertgebouw. Levine's performance is full of momentum and thrust, with much imaginative detail and most beautifully played. In *Tábor* and *Blaník* the VPO play with great vigour and commitment, and these patriotic pieces have both fervour and plenty of colour. The sound is full-bodied, with a wide amplitude and range, but it is less sumptuous and slightly less atmospheric than the Philips version.

Má Vlast: Vltava.

(B) *** Sony SBK 48264 [id.]. Cleveland O, Szell – BIZET: *Symphony;* MENDELSSOHN: *Midsummer Night's Dream.* ***

**(*) DG Gold Dig. 439 009-2. VPO, Karajan – DVORAK: *Symphony No. 9 (New World).* **(*)

(M) (**) RCA GD 60279 [60279-2-RG]. NBC SO, Toscanini – DVORAK: *Symphony No. 9;* KODALY: *Háry János suite.* (***)

The Clevelanders play *Vltava* superbly, from the opening trickle, through the village wedding and the moonlight sequence, to the climax at St John's rapids. The effect is both vivid and dramatic and the dynamic range not too restricted to spoil the element of contrast.

Karajan's VPO performance is characteristically well structured, and the recorded sound sounds quite expansive in this remastered format, even if the balance is not quite natural.

Recorded several years earlier than the other two items on Toscanini's disc, *Vltava* has painfully dry and close sound; but the intensity of Toscanini's performance still makes it a valuable document.

(i) *Má Vlast;* (ii) *Hakon Jarl, Op. 16;* (iii) *The Bartered Bride: Overture; Polka; Furiant.*

(B) ** Decca Double 443 015-2 (2) [id.]. (i) Israel PO, cond. Weller or (iii) Kertész; (ii) Detroit SO, Dorati – DVORAK: *Czech suite* etc. ***

Walter Weller's 1978 recording of *Má Vlast* is of Decca's vintage analogue quality, but the opening of *Vyšehrad* is curiously unevocative and, while Weller provides excellent detail in *Vltava*, the Israel Philharmonic's strings fail to captivate the ear in the glorious theme which spaciously represents the river. Weller is at his best in the later, more melodramatic pieces, and he secures generally good orchestral playing. There are no complaints about *Hakon Jarl* and under Kertész the pieces from *The Bartered Bride* are exceptionally vivid with the separate entries in the overture clearly positioned by the stereo.

(i) *Má Vlast* (complete); (ii) *Hakon Jarl, Op. 16; Prague Carnival; Richard III, Op. 11; Wallenstein's Camp, Op. 14*; (iii) *The Bartered Bride: Overture & 3 dances.*

(N) (B) *** DG Double Analogue/Dig. 459 418-2 (2) [id.]. (i) Boston SO; (ii) Bav. RSO, both cond. Kubelik; (iii) VPO, James Levine.

Kubelik's 1971 recording of *Má Vlast* with the Boston Symphony Orchestra has much in its favour, even if it is not as inspired as his later Supraphon version with the Czech Philharmonic.

Smetana's four symphonic poems can also be recommended to those who are attracted to the *Má Vlast* cycle. The jolly *Carnival in Prague*, the composer's last work, was written in 1883; the others are more melodramatic, dating from around 1860. The music has a flavour of Dvořák, if without that master's melodic and imaginative flair. The most spectacular is *Wallenstein's Camp* with its opportunities for offstage brass fanfares – very like Liszt's *Mazeppa* – well managed here. This is very enjoyable in its ingenuous way; but perhaps the most distinguished piece here is *Håkon Jarl*, which has a strong vein of full-blooded romanticism. The playing is first class throughout, the conductor's approach is fresh and committed, and the recording has good body and atmosphere, with the bass response now much more expansive than in the previous CD transfer.

Levine's *Bartered Bride Overture* and *dances*, which are used as makeweight are marvellously played and highly infectious. They were recorded digitally in the Musikverein in 1987. Levine offers the usual numbers plus the *Skočná*. The sound is full-bodied and vivid with a wide amplitude and range to give the music plenty of atmosphere – in the *Overture* the stabbing string fugato interchanges are splendidly caught by the stereo.

Piano trio in G min., Op. 15.
*** Chandos Dig. CHAN 8445 [id.]. Borodin Trio – DVORAK: *Dumky trio*. ***
*** Ara. Dig. Z6661 [id.]. Golub–Kaplan–Carr Trio – TCHAIKOVSKY: *Piano trio*. ***
*** Ph. (IMS) Dig. 432 125-2 [id.]. Beaux Arts Trio – MENDELSSOHN: *Piano trio No. 2*. ***
**(*) MDG MDGL 3247 [id.]. Trio Parnassus – ARENSKY: *Piano trio in D min*. **(*)

Writing the *Trio* was a cathartic act, following the death of the composer's four-year-old daughter, so it is not surprising that it is a powerfully emotional work. The writing gives fine expressive opportunities for both the violin and cello, which are taken up eloquently by Rostislav Dubinsky and Yuli Turovsky, and the pianist, Luba Edlina, is also wonderfully sympathetic. In short, a superb account, given a most realistic recording balance. Highly recommended.

Although the balance may place the listener a bit too close to the players for some tastes, the Arabesque CD offers a perfectly pleasing sound and the performance is eminently musical and unaffected. This is the kind of chamber-music playing to inspire confidence in the future: nothing overdriven, mechanized or attention-seeking. While it does not necessarily displace the Borodin Trio, it can be ranked among the best and is the only recording to offer so substantial a partner as the Tchaikovsky Trio – completely uncut, too.

The Beaux Arts account is not to be confused with the 1972 recording which they coupled with the Chopin *Trio* in the same key. It is the top recommendation for those wanting this coupling. They are very well recorded and are more restrained than their rivals on MDG.

The Trio Parnassus play very much in the nineteenth-century manner and tend to underline and italicize, but they give a likeable and convincing performance, very alive and vivid. Their coupling, the Arensky *D minor Trio*, may well sway some readers in their favour.

String quartet No. 1 in E min. (From my life).
✿ *** Koch Dig. 3-6436-2 [id.]. Medici Qt – BRITTEN: *Quartet No. 3;* JANACEK: *Quartet No. 1;* RAVEL: *Quartet;* SHOSTAKOVICH: *Quartet No. 8*. *** ✿
*** Sony Dig. SK 53282 [id.]. Artis Qt – DVORAK: *String quartet No. 14*. ***
*** Decca Dig. 452 239-2 [id.]. Takács Qt – BORODIN: *Quartet No. 2*. ***
*** EMI (SIS) Dig. CDC7 54215-2 [id.]. Alban Berg Qt – DVORAK: *String quartet No. 12*. ***
(***) Testament mono SBT 1072 [id.]. Hollywood Qt – DVORAK; KODALY: *Quartets*. (***)
(M) **(*) DG (IMS) 437 251-2. Amadeus Qt – DVORAK: *String quartet No. 12*. **(*)

Smetana's masterly autobiographical *Quartet* brings a performance of dramatic intensity and spontaneous warmth from the Medici, who are in inspired form throughout all five works in this outstanding set. They capture the touch of irony as well as the high spirits in the Scherzo and move us greatly in their deeply felt response to the beautiful, valedictory *Largo sostenuto*, while the sudden, violent change of mood in the finale is profoundly affecting. The recording has remarkable presence and realism.

The Artis Quartet also give one of the finest accounts of the *First Quartet*: imaginative, dramatic, ardent and sensitive. It is what one might call a narrative performance in that it holds one completely throughout without ever indulging in expressive overstatement. The Sony recording is in every way first class.

The Takács Quartet play Smetana's autobiographical work with great ardour; indeed it is impossible not to become caught up in the vibrant feeling of this playing. This makes a distinguished alternative to the Artis coupling on Sony for those preferring the (first-class) Borodin coupling. The Decca recording gives the players a very striking presence. However, one can't help reflecting that there was room for more music here.

By the side of the Artis account, the Alban Berg Quartet sound just a shade polished and professional. There is not quite enough spontaneity by comparison with the Artis, who carry one onwards with greater freshness and impulsiveness. All the same, there is much more to admire in the Alban Berg's reading than to cavil at: the first movement comes off well, and the EMI recording is very truthful and present. There is no cause to withhold a third star, particularly as their Dvořák is very successful.

This Hollywood Quartet recording was never issued in the UK in the 1950s when it was made. It is a performance of tremendous fire and passion, with an exhilarating rhythmic drive and a powerful sense of momentum. Yet everything sounds perfectly natural and not overdriven. Great quartet playing – and perfectly acceptable sound, given the mid-1950s date.

A strongly felt and purposeful account from the Amadeus who are on top form: their ensemble, matching of timbre and unanimous of attack, is peerless. At times one feels that Norbert Brainin's lyrical vibrato is not entirely suitable for this very personal utterance: he wears his heart too openly on his sleeve; but there is no doubt that the performance overall is gripping, and the 1977 recording vividly realistic.

String quartet No. 1 (From my life) – orchestral version by George Szell. *The Bartered Bride: Overture and dances.*
*** Chandos Dig. CHAN 8412 [id.]. LSO, Geoffrey Simon.

The Czech feeling of Szell's scoring is especially noticeable in the *Polka*, but overall there is no doubt that the fuller textures add a dimension to the music, though inevitably there are losses as well as gains. The powerful advocacy of Geoffrey Simon and the excellent LSO playing, both here and in the sparkling excerpts from *The Bartered Bride*, provide a most rewarding coupling. The recording is well up to the usual high Chandos standards.

String quartets Nos. 1 in E min. (From my life); 2 in D min.
*** ASV Dig. CDDCA 777 [id.]. Lindsay Qt (with DVORAK: *Romance; Waltzes Nos. 1–2* ***).
*** Collins Dig. 1323-2 [id.]. Talich Qt (with SUK: *Meditations on the St Wenceslas chorale* ***).

The Lindsay Quartet bring dramatic intensity to the *E minor Quartet* and play with great fire and vitality. Their (perhaps slightly forward) recording is very good indeed, and readers wanting both the Smetana *Quartets* together need look no further than them or the Talich Quartet on Collins.

The Talich Quartet have no want of drama or fire either. This is cultured playing, and moreover they are better served by their recording engineers than they were in their earlier, Calliope version. There is not a great deal to choose between the Talich and the Lindsays, and readers can invest in either with confidence. In each case there are attractive bonuses.

OPERA

The Bartered Bride: overture.
(M) *** RCA 09026 62587-2 [id.]. Chicago SO, Fritz Reiner – DVORAK: *Symphony No. 9* etc.; WEINBERGER: *Schwanda: polka and fugue.* ***

The easy, bustling virtuosity of the Chicago strings makes this vivacious performance of Smetana's famous overture hard to beat when the recording, too, is full yet has clear inner detail.

The Bartered Bride (complete, in Czech).
*** Sup. Dig. 10 3511-2 (3) [id.]. Beňačková, Dvorský, Novák, Kopp, Jonášová, Czech Philharmonic Ch. and O, Košler.

The digital Supraphon set under Košler admirably supplies the need for a first-rate Czech version of this delightful comic opera. The performance sparkles from beginning to end, with folk rhythms crisply enunciated in an infectiously idiomatic way. The cast is strong, headed by the characterful Gabriela Beňačková as Mařenka and one of the finest of today's Czech tenors, Peter Dvorský, as Jeník. Miroslav Kopp in the role of the ineffective Vašek sings powerfully too. As Kecal the marriage-broker, Richard Novák is not always steady, but his swaggering characterization is most persuasive. The CDs offer some of the best sound we have yet had from Supraphon, fresh and lively. The discs are fairly generously banded, but this could now be fitted on a pair of CDs, so the set is unnecessarily expensive. The libretto, however, has been improved and is clear and easy to use.

The Bartered Bride: highlights.
(M) **(*) Sup. 112251-2 [id.] (from above recording, with Beňačková, Dvorský; cond. Košler).

A well-made if not strikingly generous set of highlights from Košler's sparkling complete set. But the documentation includes only a list of excerpts unrelated to any synopsis, and there is no translation.

The Brandenburgers in Bohemia (complete).
**(*) Sup. 11 1804-2 (2) [id.]. Zídek, Otava, Subrtová, Kalaš, Joran, Vich, Prague Nat. Theatre soloists, Ch. & O, Jan Hus Tichý.

Smetana was forty before he wrote this, his first opera, understandably a mixture of strong, confident musical gestures and dramatic ineffectiveness. Though much of the drama centres on the fate of the heroine, Liduše, abducted by a Prague burgher with the mercenary Germanic name of Tausendmark, the love interest which must sustain any romantic opera is sketched in only cursorily. The main duet between Liduše and her beloved, Junoš, is charming and jolly rather than heartfelt, an opportunity missed. Nevertheless there is much to enjoy in a performance as lively as this, with stirring patriotic choruses sung with a will, even if their melodic invention is hardly distinguished. The recording was made as long ago as 1963, but it sounds well in the CD transfer, with the three Acts squeezed on to two very well-filled discs. Milada Subrtová sings with appealingly sweet, firm tone as Liduše, and the young Ivo Zídek makes a fresh-voiced hero, strained only a little on top. Tausendmark is sung by a stalwart veteran, Zdeněk Otava, making up in bite what he lacks in vocal quality. A collector's item.

Dalibor (complete).
*** Sup. 11 2185-2 (2) [id.]. Přibyl, Kniplová, Jindrák, Svorc, Horáček, Prague Nat. Theatre Ch. & O, Jaroslav Krombholc.

Smetana was at the peak of his creative powers when he wrote *Dalibor*, conceiving it while he was still writing *The Bartered Bride*. The contrast of mood and subject is extreme between that peasant comedy and this Gothic historical tragedy. Yet in the development of the plot, when the imprisoned hero's lover is disguised as the gaoler's assistant, *Dalibor* readily evokes associations with *Fidelio* and the subject prompted Smetana to write some of his most inspired music. Where in his first opera, *The Brandenburgers in Bohemia*, the patriotic choruses are conventional, here the opening chorus brings a stirring and measured number in triple time and a minor key. The confrontations between hero and heroine also inspire Smetana to some glorious writing, richly lyrical, most notably the love duet in the prison scene of Act II. This vintage set of 1967, sounding more vivid and full-blooded than many more recent recordings, features in those roles two of the most distinguished Czech singers of their time, both in their prime, the tenor Vílém Přibyl and the dramatic soprano, Nadezda Kniplová. The other principals are not so consistent, but Krombholc proves a most persuasive advocate, consistently bringing out the red-blooded fervour of the writing. Highly recommended to anyone who wants to investigate beyond *The Bartered Bride*. A full translation is provided.

Libuše.
**(*) Sup. Dig. 11 1276-2 633 (3) [id.]. Beňačková, Zítek, Svorc, Vodička, Děpoltová, Prague Nat. Theatre Ch. & O, Košler.

Recorded live at the Prague National Theatre in 1983, this performance vividly communicates the fervour of nationalist aspirations, more intense when shared with an audience. The cast here is even stronger than that of the previous recording under Krombholc, with Gabriela Beňačková-Cápová as Libuše memorable in her prophetic aria in Act III. Václav Zítek as Přemysi, her consort, provides an attractive lyrical interlude in Act II which, with its chorus of harvesters, has affinities with *The Bartered Bride*. In Act I there is some Slavonic wobbling, notably from Eva Děpoltová as Krasava, but generally the singing is as dramatic as the plot-line will allow. Košler directs committedly; with the stage perspectives well caught, an unintrusive audience and no disturbing stage-noises with such a static plot, the recording is very satisfactory. The cues still provide poor internal access for an opera playing for not far short of three hours. Twelve extra index points have been added to the 14 bands – not nearly enough for a work of this kind.

The Two Widows (complete).
** Sup.11 2122-2 (2) [id.]. Sormová, Machotková, Zahradníček, Horáček, Prague Nat. Theatre Ch. & O, Jílek.
** Praga/Chant du Monde PR 250 022/3 (2) [id.]. Jonášová, Machotková, Svejda, Jedlička, Prague RSO, Krombholc.

Starting with a jolly chorus, *The Two Widows* gives promise of rivalling in brightness Smetana's earlier comic masterpiece, *The Bartered Bride*. But this is a tale of country life in the big house rather than among the peasantry, with the plot centring on two cousins, both widows, and inconsequential confusions over which of them is going to marry the hero, Ladislav. That said, Smetana offers much delightful music and, if one regrets having choral contributions only at the very beginning and at the ends of each of the two Acts, there are some charming numbers in between, not least an aria for the hero, '*When Maytime arrives*', at the beginning of Act II. Jiří Zahradníček is at his best there, singing lustily, though in gentler moments Slavonic unsteadiness develops. Jaroslav Horáček is effective in the *buffo* bass role of Mumlal but, sadly, the casting of the two widows, both sopranos, involves the major role of Karolina going to the shrill and wobbly Naďa Sormová, while Marcela Machotková, who is altogether sweeter and firmer, with a mezzo-ish quality, is consigned to the role of Anežka with far less to sing, even though it is she who gets the hero. Recorded in 1975, this lively performance under Frantisek Jílek is on the whole well transferred to CD, though in a dry-ish acoustic the Prague Theatre violins sound undernourished. The libretto includes a very necessary translation.

Recorded in 1974, only eighteen months earlier than the Supraphon version, the Praga set, as transferred to CD by Chant du Monde, offers a more genial performance, a degree more expansive but in sound that is rougher and edgier, with less sense of presence. In the role of Ladislav, Miroslav Svejda has a more pleasing lyric tenor than his opposite number and is far more headily beautiful in the hero's aria. Jana Jonášová as Karolina is steadier than Sormová but, if anything, even shriller, not so warmly expressive in her Act II monologue. Again Machotková is excellent as Anežka, and Dalibor Jedlička is a first-rate *buffo* bass. Two balancing points against the Praga set are that Act II starts on the first disc, where Supraphon has one disc per Act, and that Praga offers only an English translation with no Czech text.

Smyth, Ethel (1858–1944)

(i) *Concerto for violin, horn & orchestra. Serenade in D.*
*** Chandos Dig. CHAN 9449 [id.]. (i) Sophie Langdon, Richard Watkins; BBC PO, Odaline de la Martinez.

The *Concerto for violin, horn and orchestra* was one of Dame Ethel's last works, written in 1927. It is a highly successful piece in every respect. The first movement begins with an ambitious string melody, then the soloists enter alternately with the endearing secondary idea (one of the composer's very best tunes), which is imaginatively developed in a free fantasia of flowing and dancing melody and varying moods; only at the recapitulation do the soloists share the opening theme. The romantic central *Elegy* brings a touchingly beautiful and nostalgic exchange between the two soloists.

The *Serenade in D major*, Smyth's first orchestral work (1890), might well be Brahms's *Third*! Not only does the rich string writing of the first movement have a glorious sweep, but the harmonic thinking and progressions are *echt*-Brahms. Yet Smyth's invention is of high quality, for all its eclecticism. With superb performances (clearly they are all enjoying themselves, including the first-rate soloists in the *Double concerto*) and warm, sumptuous recording, both these colourful and tuneful works will give great pleasure. This is easily the most impressive Smyth offering yet to have appeared on CD, conducted with understanding and commitment by a highly experienced advocate who has already given us a fine account of *The Wreckers*.

String quartet in E min.; (i) String quintet in E, Op. 4.
*** CPO Dig. CPO 999352-2 [id.]. Mannheimer Qt, with (i) Griesheimer.

These two works, given warmly expressive performances by a fine German quartet, represent Dame Ethel Smyth at opposite ends of her composing career. The *Quintet* of 1884 may suggest Dvořák's *American Quartet* and *New World Symphony* in its first movement, but the Smyth *Quintet* was written before either of those works, a strongly built piece with substantial outer movements framing three interludes, including a brief, magical *Adagio* which breathes the air of late Beethoven. Even more delightful and refreshing is the *Quartet*, begun in 1902 but not completed until ten years later. You could never imagine this often jaunty, amiable music coming from such a firebrand campaigner for women's rights. Instead of an allegro first movement, Smyth opts for an easy-going *Allegretto*, while the beautiful, peacefully lyrical slow movement equally belies the composer's political image.

COMPLETE PIANO MUSIC

Piano sonatas Nos. 1 in C; 2 in F sharp min.; 3 in D; 2 Canons; Aus der Jugendzeit! (To Youth!); 4 Four-part dances; Invention in D; Piece in E; Preludes and fugues: in F sharp; in C. Suite in E; Variations in D flat on an original theme.
** CPO Dig. CPO 999 327-2 (2) [id.]. Liana Serbescu.

Almost all this music dates from between 1877 and 1890, and the *C major Sonata* was Dame Ethel's first composition when she arrived to study in Leipzig in July 1877. It is a promising work, opening agreeably and with a gentle funeral march for its *Adagio* slow movement, which Liana Serbescu plays touchingly. The *Second Sonata* also has a pleasing but less distinctive *Andante*, and the *Third* is notable for its lively closing Scherzo. However, it cannot be said that any of these works are very distinctive, although the neo-classical *Suite* is jolly, with an engagingly soft-centred Minuet. The extended *Variations*, 'of an exceedingly dismal nature' according to the composer, are indeed rather heavy-going, although the theme itself is agreeable enough. There are immediate reminders of Brahms in the third and fourth of the *Four-part dances* which open the collection, and the two very successful *Preludes and fugues* which close the second CD successfully evoke the world of Mendelssohn. All this music is played sympathetically and is well recorded, but none of it is likely to re-enter the repertoire.

The Wreckers: Overture.
(B) *** CfP CD-CFP 4635 [id.]. RSNO, Gibson – GERMAN: *Welsh rhapsody;* HARTY: *With the wild geese;* MACCUNN: *Land of the Mountain and Flood.* ***

Ethel Smyth's *Overture* for her opera, *The Wreckers* (first performed in England in 1909), is a strong, meaty piece which shows the calibre of this remarkable woman's personality for, while the material itself is not memorable, it is put together most compellingly and orchestrated with real flair. The recording is full and the CD has refined detail. This CD makes a genuine bargain.

The Wreckers (opera): complete.
**(*) Conifer Dig. 75605 51250-2 (2) [id.]. Sidhom, Owens, Lavender, Wilson-Johnson, Bannatyne-Scott, Roden, Sand, Huddersfield Ch. Soc., BBC PO, Odaline de la Martinez.

Recorded live at the 1994 Proms in a concert performance at the Royal Albert Hall, the Conifer set of *The Wreckers* fills an important gap in the catalogue. The colourful overture has remained reasonably well known, but in melodic invention the rest of the opera hardly lives up to that opening. The plot is strong and sharply conceived, set in Cornwall and culminating in the drowning of the hero and heroine, trapped in a cave by vengeful villagers. The ending, which brings some of the most powerful writing in the opera, has been described fairly enough as 'Aida-on-sea'. Nevertheless, with Odaline de la Martinez directing a committed performance, this high-romantic melodrama makes an enjoyable piece, for all the lack of hummable tunes. One problem of the casting is that the role of the heroine is given to a mezzo soprano, and Anne-Marie Owens copes valiantly with the extreme range required. Justin Lavender makes a clear-toned hero, ostensibly too light for the role but sounding well on record. The others are stronger – David Wilson-Johnson characterful as the lighthouse keeper, Judith Howarth sweet-toned as the hero's jilted girlfriend and Peter Sidhom most powerful of all as the minister, suggesting that voices of Wagnerian strength might make a difference. Sadly, here the chorus is too backwardly balanced.

Soler, Antonio (1729–83)

(i) *Concertos for 2 organs Nos. 1–6;* (ii) *Fandango in D min.; Harpsichord sonatas Nos. 12 in G; 15 in D min.; 49 in D min.; 54 in C; 56 in F; 69 in F; 76 in F; 84 in D; 90 in F sharp.*
(N) (B) *** Erato/Warner Dig. Ultima Double 3984 27005-2 (2) [id.]. (i) Tini Mathot & Ton Koopman (organ); (ii) Scott Ross (harpsichord).

Soler is an individual composer who has a large quantity of keyboard music to his credit, much influenced by Domenico Scarlatti. He has less character than his illustrious model, and is in many respects more conventional, but he still has the capacity to offer surprising and original touches. This Ultima Double makes a useful and inexpensive entry into his world. The concertos (written for the Infante Gabriel of the Spanish Royal family) are not here played on a pair of organs but on a single instrument whose sounds emanate over a fairly wide spectrum, so that the ear often enjoys the effect of a stereo interplay. The instrument itself, in the Basilica della Misericordia, San Elpidio a Mare, Italy, has some piquant stops, one very like a crumhorn, and the two players here register imaginatively. The music itself is ingenuous, but appealingly so. The collection is framed by No. 3 *in G major* which has a striking opening *Andantino* and No.1 *in C* which ends with a characterful Minuet. Scott Ross then follows with the celebrated *Fandango* (uncut, though it is very repetitive), and ten well-chosen and diverse *Sonatas*, which cover the entire compositional period of Soler's life. No. 4 *in D minor* is appealingly lyrical, No. 59, with its glissando flourishes, is most like Scarlatti. The two closing works, Nos. 84 and 90 also demand and receive sparkling bravura. Indeed these performances are full of life and character and are, like the organ works, very well recorded.

KEYBOARD WORKS

Keyboard works: *Sonatas Nos. 1 in A; 3 in B flat; 24–5 in D min.; 28–9 in C; 30–31 in G; 96 in E flat; 118 in A min. Prelude No. 1 in D min.*
** Astrée Dig. E 8768 [id.]. Bob van Asperen (harpsichord).

Sonatas Nos. 2 in E flat; 65 in A min.; 105 in E flat; 111 in D; 117 in D min.; 124 in C; 125 in C; 126a and 126b in C min.; 127 in D; 128 in E min.; 130 in G min.; 131 in A.
** Astrée Dig. E 8779 [id.]. Bob van Asperen (harpsichord).

Sonatas Nos. 4 in G; 5 in F; 6 in F; 49 in D min.; 55 in F; 69 in F; 72 in F min.; 99 in C; 101 in F; 110 in D flat; 114 in D min.; 115 in D min.; 120 in D min.; Prelude No. 4 in F min.
** Astrée Dig. E 8777 [id.]. Bob van Asperen (harpsichord).

Sonatas Nos. 7–9 in C; 20–21 in C sharp min.; 95 in A. Prelude No. 3 in C.
** Astrée Dig. E 8769 [id.]. Bob van Asperen (harpsichord).

Sonatas Nos. 8 in C; 35 in G; 38 in C; 70; 71 in A min.; 77 in F sharp min.; 78 in F sharp min.; 79 in F sharp min.; 82 in G; 83 in F; 113 in E min.; 116 in G; Prelude No. 8 in F.
** Astrée Dig. E 8776 [id.]. Bob van Asperen (harpsichord).

Sonatas Nos. 10 in B min.; 11 in B; 12–14 in G; 52 in E min.; 73–4 in D; 92 in D (Sonata des clarines); 106 in E min.; Allegro pastoril; Prelude No. 6 in G.
** Astrée Dig. E 8770 [id.]. Bob van Asperen (harpsichord).

Sonatas Nos. 15 in D min.; 22 in D flat; 23 in D flat; 54 in D min.; 61 in C; 75 in F; 76 in F; 80 in G min.; 81 in G min.; 84 in D; 86 in D.
*(*) Astrée Dig. E 8772 [id.]. Bob van Asperen (harpsichord).

Sonatas Nos. 16 in E flat; 17 in E flat; 32 in G min.; 33 in G; 39 in D min.; 41 in F; 53 in A; 57 in G min.; 60a in C min.; 60b in C min.; 89 in F; Prelude No. 7 in C min.
** Astrée Dig. E 8775 [id.]. Bob van Asperen (harpsichord).

Sonatas Nos. 18 in C min.; 19 in C min.; 26 in E min.; 27 in E min.; 36 in C min.; 85 in F sharp min.; 90 in F sharp min.; 91 in D; 94 in G.
** Astrée Dig. E 8773 [id.]. Bob van Asperen (harpsichord).

Sonatas Nos. 35 in G; 38 in C; 70 in A min.; 71 in A min.; 77 in F sharp min.; 78 in F sharp min.; 79a & 79b in F sharp min.; 82 in G; 83 in F; 113 in E min.; 116 in G; Prelude No. 8 in F.

** Astrée Dig. E 8776 [id.]. Bob van Asperen (harpsichord).

Sonatas Nos. 37 in D; 46 in D; 56 in F; 98 in B flat min.; 100 in C min.; 103 in C min.; 108 in C; 109 in F; 112 in D; Fandango No. 146; Prelude No. 5 in D.

** Astrée Dig. E 8771 [id.]. Bob van Asperen (harpsichord).

Sonatas Nos. 42 in G min.; 43 in G; 47 in C min; 48 in C min.; 50 in C; 58 in G; 59 in F; 62 in E flat; 87 in G min.; 102 in D min.; 104 in D min.; 107 in F; 149 in F; Prelude No. 2 in G min.

** Astrée Dig. E 8778 [id.]. Bob van Asperen (harpsichord).

Sonatas Nos. 45 in C (por la Princesa de Asturias); 51 in C; 88 in D sharp; 93 in F; 97 in A; 119 in B flat; 132 in B flat; 154 in D sharp.

** Astrée Dig. E 8774 [id.]. Bob van Asperen (harpsichord).

An ambitious venture to record the complete keyboard output of Antonio Soler with Bob van Asperen is let down by insensitive engineering. He plays with plenty of vitality but the value of the enterprise is diminished by the oppressively close balance of the recording. Throughout, he uses either a copy of a 1764 Taskin (made by Michael Johnson two centuries later) or a copy of a 1745 Dülcken, made by Rainer Schülze in Heidelberg in 1969. However ingenious and varied in colour the registration of the distinguished Dutch harpsichordist, the effect is reduced to an unrelieved and uniform dynamic level which produces aural fatigue. The music is so characterful and the playing so fresh that these discs must be recommended, but readers will want to listen at low level and to only one or two pieces at a time. Moreover the documentation is too generalized for such an important project, with essays about the composer, the performer, the project research, and a cursory discussion of the music, repeated with each CD. Information is not given about individual works and no attempt is made to differentiate between the single-movement sonatas and the occasional more ambitious three- and four-movement combinations, like Nos. 92 and 98, in which Soler created composite works from movements of the same tonality but diverse character. The spectacular thirteen-minute *Fandango* which opens the fourth disc is presented without comment. Some of these works have no indication of tempo, but Bob van Asperen's judgement in this matter seems impeccable. The recording balance apart, this is an impressive achievement.

Harpsichord sonatas Nos. 1 in A; 15 in D min.; 18 in C min.; 19 in C min.; 43 in G; 54 in D min.; 85 in F sharp; 90 in F sharp; 91 in C. Op. 4/1; 101 in F; 110 in D flat.

(N) (BB) ** Naxos Dig. 8.553462 [id.]. Gilbert Rowland (harpsichord).

Harpsichord sonatas Nos. 16 in E flat; 17 in E flat; 35 in G; 42 in G min.; 46 in C; 52 in E min.; 83 in F; 87 in G min.; 92 in D, Op. 4/2; 106 in E min.; 116 in G.

(N) (BB) ** Naxos 8. 553463 [id.]. Gilbert Rowland (harpsichord).

Harpsichord sonatas Nos. 28 in C; 29 in C; 32 in G min.; 33 in G; 34 in E; 50 in C; 55 in F; 57 in G min.; 69 in F; 93 in F, Op.4/3 117 in D min.

(N) (BB) ** Naxos 8. 553463 [id.]. Gilbert Rowland (harpsichord).

A new series of the Soler Keyboard sonatas now arrives from Naxos, played with sensibility and often real panache by Gilbert Rowland on a modern copy of French two-manual harpsichord. The snag is that while he is truthfully and not too forwardly recorded, the acoustic of Epsom College Concert Hall (Surrey) is over-resonant and spreads the sound somewhat uncomfortably in the fast bravura passages. In the more reflective minor key works (*17 in D minor*; *52 in E minor*, for instance) there are no grumbles, and often the brilliance of the playing (as in the romping *No. 43 in G*, the sparkling *No.69 in F* and *106 in E minor*, with its crisp articulation) projects through the resonance. The discs have really excellent documentation, describing each individual work in detail.

Keyboard sonatas Nos. 15, 21, 42, 84–7, 89.

(N) (B) *** Decca Double 433 920-2 (2) [id.]. Alicia de Larrocha, Mateo – ALBENIZ: *Sonata*; GRANADOS: *Escenas románticas; Goyescas* etc. ***

Like the music of Scarlatti, with an advocate of this calibre these works are quite as pleasing heard on the piano as on the harpsichord. The performances are characteristically vital and the 1981 recording is excellent.

Keyboard sonatas Nos. 18 in C min.; 19 in C min.; 41 in E flat; 72 in F min.; 78 in F sharp min.; 84 in D; 85 in F sharp min.; 86 in D; 87 in G min.; 88 in D flat; 90 in F sharp; Fandango.

(M) *** Virgin Veritas/EMI VER5 61220-2. Maggie Cole (harpsichord or fortepiano).

Maggie Cole plays a dozen Soler pieces, eleven *Sonatas* and the celebrated *Fandango*, half of them on the harpsichord and the remainder on the fortepiano; she gives altogether dashing performances on both. Good pieces to sample are *No. 87 in G minor* (track 5) and, on the harpsichord, *No. 86 in D major* (track 9) or the *Fandango* itself. The playing is all very exhilarating and inspiriting. Played at a normal level-setting, both instruments sound a bit thunderous, but played at a lower level the results are very satisfactory.

Sor, Fernando (1778–1839)

Fantasia, Op. 30; Fantasia, Op. 7; Variations on a theme of Mozart, Op. 9.
(M) **(*) RCA Dig. 09026 61607-2. Julian Bream (guitar) – AGUADO: Collection. **(*)

Both Sor *Fantasias* are ambitious and each has a central set of variations. Bream's approach is spacious and his deliberation – for all the variety and skill of the colouring – means that the listener is conscious of the music's length, although it is all agreeable enough. The more concise Mozartian *Variations* remain Sor's most famous piece, and the variety and flair of the playing demonstrate why. The studio recording, made in New York, is eminently truthful.

'*Classic guitar': Grand solo (Introduction and allegro), Op. 14. Sonata in C, Op. 25.*
(M) **(*) RCA 09026 61593-2. Julian Bream (guitar) – GIULIANI: *Grand overture, Op. 61* etc.; DIABELLI: *Sonata in A*. **(*)

Sor's *Grand solo* is quite an attractive piece, with an *Andante largo* introduction instead of a slow movement, and it includes the theme and variations seemingly obligatory to this composer. The *Sonata in C*, however, is extremely inconsequential and easily forgettable. But all the music is beautifully played and immaculately recorded.

Sorabji, Khaikhosru (1892–1988)

Fantaisie espagnole.
(N) *** Altarus Dig. AIR-CD 9022 [id.]. Donna Amato.

Sorabji's *Fantaisie espagnole* comes from 1919 and shows his preoccupation with exotic, Szymanowskian keyboard textures and voluptuous Ravel-like harmonies. Donna Amato seems completely attuned to the idiom. It is a short work (just under eighteen minutes) and is brilliantly played and recorded on this Altarus single.

Sousa, John Philip (1854–1932)

Marches: *The Ancient and Honorable Artillery Company; The Black Horse Troop; Bullets and bayonets; The Gallant Seventh; Golden jubilee; The Glory of the Yankee Navy; The Gridiron Club; High school cadets; The Invincible eagle; The Kansas Wildcats; The Liberty Bell; Manhattan Beach; The National game; New Mexico; Nobles of the mystic shrine; Our flirtation; The Picadore; The Pride of the Wolverines; Riders for the flag; The Rifle Regiment; Sabre and spurs; Sesqui-centennial exposition; Solid men to the front; Sound off.*
(M) *** Mercury 434 300-2 [id.]. Eastman Wind Ens., Frederick Fennell.

Fennell's collection of 24 Sousa marches (73 minutes) derives from vintage Mercury recordings of the early 1960s. The performances have characteristic American pep and natural exuberance; the zest of the playing always carries the day. One of the more striking items is *The Ancient and Honorable Artillery Company*, which incorporates *Auld lang syne* as its middle section. The sound is, of course, first class.

Spohr, Ludwig (1784–1859)

Clarinet concerto No. 1 in C min., Op. 26.
(M) *** Classic FM Dig. 75605 57019-2. Colin Lawson, Hanover Band, Goodman – WEBER: *Clarinet concertos 1–2* etc. ***

The first of Spohr's *Clarinet concertos* may not have the memorability of the three Weber works with which it is coupled, but it provides a generous bonus on an outstanding disc. Colin Lawson, principal clarinet of the Hanover Band, plays most imaginatively with attractively reedy tone to match the period instruments of his colleagues. Full and vivid sound.

Concerto for string quartet and orchestra in A min., Op.131.
(N) *** Arabesque Dig. Z 6723 [id.]. San Francisco Ballet O, Lark Qt., Jean-Louis Le Roux – HANDEL: *Concerto grosso in B flat, Op. 6/7.* SCHOENBERG: *Concerto for string quartet and orchestra after Handel's Concerto grosso, Op. 4/7.* ELGAR: *Introduction and allegro for strings.* ***

This is a consistently engaging work (Spohr's very last concerto), inventive and tuneful – the slow movement is particularly fine – using the players in the solo quartet individually as well as in consort. It is very persuasively played, and with the proviso that the solo group are balanced rather forwardly, the recording is very good too. With imaginative couplings this is very much worth trying.

Symphonies Nos. 1 in E flat, Op. 20; 5 in C min., Op. 102.
**(*) Marco Polo Dig. 8.223363 [id.]. Slovak State PO (Košice), Alfred Walter.

Spohr wrote ten symphonies in all: the *First* when he was in his mid-twenties and still in thrall to Mozart; the *Fifth* comes from the late 1830s and was much admired by Schumann. The latter is certainly a better piece, but there is always a certain blandness about Spohr's invention even when he is at his best. Although he is no great symphonist, Spohr is an eminently civilized composer, and the case for him is well put by Alfred Walter and the Košice orchestra, who are decently served by the engineers.

Symphonies Nos. 2 in D min., Op. 49; 9 in B min.(The Seasons), Op. 143.
(N) ** Marco Polo Dig. 8.223454 [id.]. Slovak State PO (Košice), Alfred Walter.

The *Second Symphony* (1820) has dramatic undertones, but emerges here an amiable, Mendelssohnian work with a neat Scherzo and much Schubertian charm in the finale. Walter's performance is warm and polished, but one feels the music could be given a stronger profile. At the opening of *The Seasons*, written three decades later, the Schumanesque depiction of *Winter* entirely lacks icicles, but the '*Transition to Spring*' brings some delightful birdsong and leads to a charming Ländler which later becomes more animated. *Summer* is hazily somnulent with 'distant sounds of thunder', then simple horn calls lead into the more exuberant hunting and drinking scene of autumn, with some colourful orchestral effects. In imaginative force this is not a patch on Haydn, but one feels a really strongly characterized performance could make more of it than does the rather literal-minded Alfred Walter.

Symphonies Nos. 3 in C minor, Op. 78; 6 in G (Historical Symphony in the style and taste of four different periods), Op. 116.
(N) *** Marco Polo Dig. 8.223349 [id.]. Slovak State PO (Košice), Alfred Walter.

This coupling which so far is the best of the Walter–Spohr series, is well worth getting. The *Historical Symphony* is a fascinating pastiche, and the *C minor* is one of the finest of Spohr's early symphonies inspiring Walter to give one of his most vigorous and committed performances. The first movement opens with an eloquent *Grave*, and the two main ideas of the *Allegro* are emotionally well contrasted, and worked out most satisfyingly. The *Larghetto* has genuine depth, and the Scherzo, although spirited, is also romantic in feeling. But the most ambitious movement is the highly inventive finale, both life-enhancing and energetic, and with plenty of contrapuntal interest, including a full-scale central fugue. It is very well played indeed. The *Historical Symphony* is most endearing in its respect for the great masters. It opens with a solemn, full-orchestral treatment of the *C major fugue* from Book I of Bach's '48', and also introduces pastoral reminders of Handel's *Messiah*, including an allusion to 'He shall feed his flock'. The slow movement, richly scored, remembers both Mozart's *39th* and *Prague Symphonies*, and in the curiously lyrical scherzo. the timpani (rather too muted here) recall the Beethoven of the *Seventh Symphony*, which Spohr greatly admired, having taken part in its première under the composer. The inappropriately but agreeably frivolous finale, 'the latest of the new', then bursts with energy, drawing on the vivacious ideas of Adam and Auber, in particular the *Muette de Portici overture*. Walter is a convincing exponent of this curiously balanced work and his orchestra respond with enthusiasm.

Symphonies Nos. 7 in C (The Earthly and Divine in human life), Op. 121; 8 in G, Op. 137.
(N) ** Marco Polo Dig. 8.223432 [id.]. Slovak State PO (Kosice), Alfred Walter.

Programme symphonies are sometimes a doubtful proposition, for they seldom deliver quite what the listener expects from the titles. In contrasting his *Irdisches und Göttlisches im Menschenleben*, Spohr uses the concerto grosso principle, with an eleven-piece concertino representing the 'divine', while the full orchestra are the 'earthly'; here both elements are fairly fully integrated. He charmingly and successfully depicts *The world of childhood*, but the profounder sentiments of *The Age of Passion* defeat him, and the '*Final triumph of the heavenly*', moves from melodrama to a serene but complacent sentimentality. The *Eighth Symphony*, although conservative, is an altogether better proposition. Commissioned by the Philharmonic Society of London, it was premièred there in 1847. The work is fully scored: its kernel is a fine, sombre *Poco Adagio*, with the strings effectively underpinned by trombone sonorities. The Scherzo opens with a romantic horn call and features an obbligato solo violin in the Trio. Together with the engagingly songful finale, it almost turns the symphony into a serenade. Alfred Walter is clearly more at home here than in the programme work and the Slovak Orchestra creates a Bohemian bonhomie in the two final movements. Good, smooth, warm sound

CHAMBER MUSIC

Double quartet in D min., Op. 65.
(M) ** EMI CDM5 65995-2. Gervase de Peyer, Melos Ens. – BERWALD: *Septet* ***; WEBER: *Clarinet quintet*. **(*)

The Melos performance has plenty of character, but the recording, though clear and quite full, sounds a little edgy in the present transfer.

Double quartets Nos. 1 in D min., Op. 65; 2 in E flat, Op. 77; 3 in E min., Op. 87; 4 in G min., Op. 136.
(N) *** Hyperion Dig. Dyad CDD 22014 (2) [id.]. ASMF Chamber Ens.

The opening of the first *Double quartet* is inviting (as again is the rather solemn introduction of the *Third*, which then lightens, yet retains its nostalgic feeling). While this is all essentially amiable music, the standard of Spohr's invention is quite high throughout all four works, and the scoring cleverly makes the most of the antiphony between the two groups. So does the recording here, with a natural interplay within a pleasingly warm acoustic. The playing is predictably fluent and spontaneous-sounding, well blended and polished.

Nonet in F, Op. 31; Octet in E, Op. 32.
*** Hyperion Dig. CDA 66699 [id.]. Gaudier Ens.
(M) *** CRD CRD 3354; *CRDC 4054* [id.]. Nash Ens.

Spohr's *Octet* is a work of great charm; the variations on Handel's *Harmonious blacksmith* which form the third movement offer that kind of naïveté which, when played stylishly, makes for delicious listening. Here the Gaudier Ensemble give us a performance as imaginative as it is spontaneous, and the work's finale with its lolloping main theme is joyously spirited. The *Nonet* is also very attractive. Spohr's invention is again at its freshest and his propensity for chromaticism is held reasonably in check. The Hyperion recording is fresh and warm, clearly detailed against a resonant acoustic, although this means that the first violin is given a fractional hint of wiriness by the fairly close microphones.

The sound on the competing CRD disc is that bit more mellifluous, yet it remains natural and lifelike; some may prefer the greater suavity of the analogue tonal blend in this urbane music. The Nash Ensemble play both works with much elegance and style, and these performances are very civilized and hardly less spontaneous. They are well worth considering alongside their Hyperion competitors.

Piano trios Nos. 1 in E min., Op. 119; 2 in F, Op. 123; 3 in A min., Op. 124; 4 in B flat, Op. 133; 5 in G min., Op. 142.
*** CPO Dig. CPO 999 246-2 (3) [id.]. Ravensburg Beethoven Trio.

Piano trios Nos. 3 in A min., Op. 124; 4 in B flat, Op. 133.
**(*) Chandos Dig. CHAN 9372 [id.]. Borodin Trio.

Piano trios Nos. 1–5; (i) *Piano quintet in D, Op. 130.*
(N) (BB) ** Naxos Dig. 8.553206 (No. 1 & Quintet); 8.553205 (Nos. 2 & 4); 8.553164 (Nos. 3 & 5). Hartley Piano Trio; (i) with M. Outram.

Spohr's five *Piano trios* are among his freshest, most appealing chamber works, full of attractive ideas and fine craftsmanship. They are late works, the first three composed in 1841–2 and the remaining pair in 1846 and 1849 respectively. The Ravensburg Trio give fine performances, mellower, with slightly more gravitas than sparkle, although they too have an excellent pianist in Inge-Susann Römchild, whose touch is often pleasingly light. The CPO recording is warmer and fuller to suit the playing. In their different way these readings are almost equally enjoyable; indeed some listeners may prefer their more serious mood. The five *Trios* are just too long to fit on a pair of CDs, and the third plays for only 31 minutes.

The Borodin Trio offers plenty of life and the Chandos recording is pleasingly open and vivid. But Luba Edlina's vibrant temperament and timbre do not so readily match Spohr's relatively suave writing, and this coupling is less enjoyable than either of the complete sets.

The Naxos acccounts (available separately) are well played and serviceable, and have the advantage of including the *Piano quintet* which has a remarkable, sparkling scherzo, changing mood in the Trio. Its pensive *Adagio* is one of the composer's most expressively telling, and the finale then trips along gaily. The bravura piano writing (especially in the Scherzo) makes this seem like a concertante work with strings and the pianist here, Caroline Clemmov generally rises to the occasion. The recording is fully acceptable and this first disc of the three is worth sampling, and after that the third (with Nos. 3 and 5) for these players, if not having a particularly strong collective personality, are thoroughly musical and at home in this composer's idiom.

Piano and wind quintet in C min., Op. 52; Septet in A min. for flute, clarinet, horn, bassoon, violin, cello and piano, Op. 147.
(M) *** CRD CRD 3399; *CRDC 4099* [id.]. Ian Brown, Nash Ens.

These two pieces are among Spohr's most delightful, both the sparkling *Quintet* and the more substantial but still charmingly lighthearted *Septet*. Ian Brown at the piano leads the ensemble with flair and vigour, and the recording quality is outstandingly vivid.

String quartets Nos. 1 in C; 2 in C min., Op. 4/1–2; 5 in D, Op. 15/2.
(N) *** Marco Polo Dig. 8.223253 [id.]. New Budapest Qt.

If you enjoy the earlier and middle-period Haydn Quartets, you might well try Spohr. He seems also to have an almost inexhaustible fund of ideas and writes enjoyably smooth, well-crafted works, which every so often produce a movement which is quite memorable – like the gentle *Adagio* of his very first essay in the medium, strikingly fresh, written when the composer had just turned twenty. Op.4/2 has an opening movement which is worthy of Haydn and the *Poco Adagio* is just as thoughtful as its predecessor. The Rondo finale, with its dotted main theme is very catchy. Op. 15/2 is without a slow movement, which the composer probably excised after criticism at its first performance. However the accomplished fugal finale has a brief *Adagio* introduction. The performances here are always persuasive and well recorded too: it is a pity this series does not appear on the Naxos label, when it would be even more recommendable. However praise is due for the excellent documentation.

String quartets Nos. 7 in E flat; 8 in C, Op. 29/1–2.

**(*) Marco Polo Dig. 8.22355 [id.]. New Budapest Qt.

The Op. 29 *Quartets* are associated with Johann Tost (dedicatee of Haydn's Opp. 54/5 and 65). Both are written in Spohr's friendly, accomplished style; the first ingeniously bases its opening movement on a two-note motto theme and has an outstanding set of variations for its slow movement, surely worthy of Haydn. The tender *Adagio* of the *C major* is even finer, daring in its expressive chromaticism. Both performances are spontaneous and the players seem inside the music. If the very last ounce of finesse is missing, this is still vibrant, felt quartet-playing, without artifice, and the recording is lively and present.

String quartets Nos. 11 in E (Quatuor brillant), Op. 43; 12 in C, Op. 45/1.
(N) **(*) Marco Polo Dig. 8.223257 [id.]. New Budapest Qt.

String quartets Nos. 13 in E min.; 14 in F min., Op. 45/2–3.
(N) *** Marco Polo Dig. 8.223258 [id.]. New Buda pest Qt.

The *Quatuor brillant* dates from 1817, and its subtitle is deceptive, for, as its engaging opening suggests, it is essentially a lyrical work, although the closing Minuet sparkles brightly enough. The Op. 45 Quartets are more romantic in feeling, more suave in texture, moving further away from the classical Haydn idiom. However the rapt *Larghetto* of No. 13 is memorable, with a gentle staccato idea contrasting with the richly textured principal theme. A mellow but imaginatively varied Minuet follows, and the dotted finale is endearingly ingenuous, with a charmingly tapered coda. The melancholy introduction to the *F minor Quartet* certainly catches the listener up, but the clouds lifts with the key change to *A major* and the first movement is essentially amiable, although the hymn-like *Adagio* returns to the mood of the opening. The 'fantasy' scherzo is then most welcome, and the brilliant finale soon produced a lollipop lyrical idea, which then dominates the movement. The Budapest players are at their very best in these two fine works.

String quartets Nos. 15 in E flat; 16 in A, Op. 58/1–2.
(N) *** Marco Polo Dig. 8.23256 [id.]. New Budapest Qt.

The two Op. 58 *Quartets* written in 1821 show a new maturity, especially the noble *Adagio* of the *E flat major*, which reminds one of Mozart, after a cheerful first movement laced with effective pizzicatos. The light-hearted Scherzo, with its Viennese, Ländler influenced Trio, has much charm, and the work is capped by a springy closing Rondo. A splendid disc in every way.

String quartets Nos. 20 in A min; 21 in B flat, Op. 74/1–2.
(N) *** Marco Polo Dig. 8.223259 [id.]. New Budapest Qt.

The Opus 74 *Quartets*, dating from 1826, are further evidence of Spohr's increasingly deft integration of his ideas in finely argued first movements, essentially lyrical but not lacking dramatic elements. The *Larghetto con moto* of the *A minor*, shows him at his most songful; in the equally appealing Rondo finale a certain wistful mood persists until the brief, very positive coda. The opening *Allegro vivace* of the *B flat major* is gracefully light-hearted, although the *Larghetto* has more pathos. The third movement is a charming upbeat *Allegretto con variazioni*, but in the closing Rondo a delicate minor key feeling persists until, as in its predecessor, Spohr makes a sudden very definite close. The players here again respond very sympathetically to these attractive quartets and capture their spirit admirably. Fine, natural recording.

String quartets Nos. 27 in D min.; 28 in A flat, Op. 84/1–2.
**(*) Marco Polo Dig. 8.223251 [id.]. New Budapest Qt.

These two works, written in 1831–2, exemplify Spohr's smooth, finely integrated quartet-writing at its most characteristic. The slow movement, sustaining a mood of serene simplicity, is the most memorable in each case, although the lyrical finale of the *A flat major Quartet* is also rather appealing. Good performances, lively enough, but capturing the suaveness of the idiom. The recording is truthful.

String quartets Nos. 29 in B min., Op. 84/3; 30 (Quatuor brillant) in A, Op. 93.
**(*) Marco Polo Dig. 8.223252 [id.]. New Budapest Qt.

In many ways *No. 29 in B minor* is the finest of the Op. 84 set, with its touch of melancholy in the first movement, a lively minuet and a pensive slow movement. Op. 93, written in 1835, is more extrovert in atmosphere in the first movement (after a sombre introduction), but it offers another thoughtfully intense slow movement and a very jolly finale. It brings out the best in these players – and there is plenty of bravura for the first violin – and, again, good tonal matching plus a smooth, warm recording combine effectively for this slightly suave music.

String quintets Nos. 1 in E flat; 2 in G, Op. 3/1–2.
(N) **(*) Marco Polo Dig. 8.223597 [id.]. Augmented Danubius Qt.

String quintets Nos. 3 in B min., Op. 69; 4 in A min., Op. 91.
(N) **(*) Marco Polo Dig. 8.223599 [id.]. Augmented Danubius Qt.

Spohr's *String quintets* feature a second viola, which gives them a characteristically full, slightly bland texture. The first two date from 1813–14 and were composed in reverse order to their published listing. The suave opening theme of the *E flat major* is deceptive, for it is strong enough to influence the two following movements including the near-melancholy *Larghetto*, and the attractive Minuet and trio. In the *G major* work, a similarly mild opening theme is to dominate. An engaging Scherzo follows and then a winning *Andante* with variations, before the finale which is half-melancholy, half-cheerful. The two minor-key works which followed, No. 3 a decade later in 1826 and No. 4 in 1833–4, have even more of the wistful mood for which the composer is noted, especially the *Adagio* of the *B minor*, and its rather memorable, rocking barcarolle finale. The first movement of the *A minor* is slightly more ambivalent, but the slow movement has much in common with that of its predecessor, and even the *Presto* finale fails to chase away the clouds. The quality of Spohr's invention is well maintained throughout all four works, which are warmly and sympathetically played by the Danubius Quartet and smoothly and pleasingly recorded.

String quintet No. 4 in A min., Op. 91; String sextet in C, Op. 140; Pot-pourri on themes of Mozart, Op. 22.

**(*) Chandos Dig. CHAN 9424 [id.]. ASMF Chamber Ens.

String octet (Double quartet) in D min., Op. 65; String quintet No. 2 in G, Op. 3/2; String sextet in C, Op. 140.

*** Sony Dig. SK 53370 [id.]. L'Archibudelli & Smithsonian Chamber Players.

To be candid, the *A minor String quintet*, although as always with this composer well crafted, is rather bland, a characteristic the well-rehearsed ASMF performance does very little to counteract. The Mozartian potpourri is much more entertaining. The fine *String sextet in C major*, one of the composer's last chamber works, from 1848, has a particularly endearing Brahmsian main theme in the first movement, a hymn-like slow movement and a brilliant finale. The ASMF Chamber Ensemble give a fine, polished account of it, well recorded.

However, the period-instrument performance from L'Archibudelli combined with the Smithsonian Chamber Players is even finer: here is authenticity with much character, giving the *Larghetto* a grave nobility and finding a ready sparkle in the light-textured finale. There is an even more vivacious finale in the *Octet* to which these players respond with virtuosity and the lightest touch. The *G major String quintet* (with two violas) is hardly less striking in its variety of invention, especially the *Andante* (with very florid variations) and the unusual last movement with its ambivalent atmosphere and strain of nostalgia. (The composer – rightly – thought highly of this work.) There are few recordings on period instruments in which the ear is as consistently beguiled by the transparency of texture and the combination of bravura and warm tonal blending. Highly recommended.

Spontini, Gasparo (1774–1851)

Olympie (opera): complete.

**(*) Orfeo Dig. C 137862H (3) [id.]. Varady, Toczyska, Tagliavini, Fischer-Dieskau, Fortune, Berlin RIAS Chamber Ch., German Op. Male Ch., Berlin RSO, Albrecht.

In Spontini's *Olympie*, based on a historical play by Voltaire about the daughter of Alexander the Great, the writing is lively and committed and, despite flawed singing, so is this performance. Julia Varady is outstanding in the name-part, giving an almost ideal account of the role of heroine, but Stefania Toczyska is disappointingly unsteady as Statire and Franco Tagliavini is totally out of style as Cassandre. Even Dietrich Fischer-Dieskau is less consistent than usual, but his melodramatic presentation is nevertheless most effective. The text is slightly cut.

Stamitz, Carl (1745–1801)

Clarinet concertos Nos. 3 in B flat; 10 in B flat; 11 in E flat.

(N) *** EMI Dig. CDC7 54842-2 [id.]. Sabine Meyer, ASMF, Iona Brown – Johann STAMITZ: *Concerto in B flat.****

Clarinet concertos Nos 7 in E flat; 8 in B flat (Darmstadt Nos. 1–2); 10 in B flat; 11 in E flat.

(N) (BB) *** Naxos 8.554339 [id.]. Kálmán Berkes, Nicholas Esterházy Sinfonia.

Clarinet concerto No. 10 in B flat.

*** EMI Dig. CDC5 55155-2. Sabine Meyer, ASMF, Iona Brown – MOZART: *Clarinet concerto* etc.; WEBER: *Clarinet concerto No. 1.* ***

Sabine Meyer's performances are highly musical and she is given characteristically polished and elegant accompaniments by Iona Brown and the Academy. However Kálmán Berkes on Naxos is by no means a lesser soloist. He finds a Bohemian sense of fun in the closing Rondos which is less obvious with Meyer, although she still plays them lightheartedly and her collection remains very enjoyable. The accompaniments on Naxos are also warm and stylish and the recording excellent.

The slow movement of No. 10 is plain beside that of its Mozart coupling, but Sabine Meyer presents it persuasively and makes much of the genial passage-work of the outer movements, and especially the roulades of the dancing finale. She is stylishly accompanied and excellently recorded.

Sinfonias concertantes: (i) *in C for 2 violins and orchestra;* (ii) *in D for violin, viola and orchestra.*
(BB) **(*) ASV Quicksilva Dig. CDQS 6140 [id.]. Richard Friedman, L. Festival O, Ross Pople; with (i) Steven Smith; (ii) Roger Best – HAYDN: *Sinfonia concertante.* **(*)

Stamitz may not match Mozart but he is a personality in his own right and such a work as the *Sinfonia concertante in C for two violins*, here projected with fine spontaneity, brings a slow movement where one of the two soloists, playing alone, presents a 'singing' cantilena almost worthy of his greater contemporary. This *Andante* is also felicitously scored, with effective writing for the horns. The first movement has some good ideas too, and it is only the *Minuet* finale that lapses into conventionality; even so, like the first movement, the writing for the two soloists is inventively conceived. The companion *Sinfonia concertante for violin and viola*, if not quite so interesting in its material, has a historic link with Mozart's work for the same combination; as such, it makes fascinating listening. However, although the two soloists here play freshly and stylishly, they lack individuality of profile. Ross Pople directs the orchestra strongly, with tenderness in the central *Romance*, the earlier CBS/Sony account of this work by Stern and Zukerman (with the ECO under Barenboim) has far more personality.

Sinfonia concertante in D for violin, viola and orchestra.
(M) *** Sony Stern Edition I SM2K 66472 (2) [id.]. Stern, Zukerman, ECO, Barenboim – VIVALDI: *Concertos.* **(*)

This Stern/Zukerman performance was originally recorded (in 1971) quadraphonically at the EMI Abbey Road No. 1 Studio and was more appropriately coupled with Mozart's much greater *Sinfonia concertante*, featuring the same solo instruments. Stamitz's work is relatively lightweight, but again it gives these vital artists a chance to strike sparks off each other. The recording has plenty of atmosphere but the soloists are balanced unnaturally forward.

Symphonies: in D (La Chasse); in C & G Op. 13/16, No.4 & 5; in F, Op. 24/3.
(N) *** Chandos Dig. CHAN 9358 [id.]. L. Mozart Players, Matthias Bamert.

Carl Stamiz wrote over fifty symphonies and the present examples are most attractive examples of his three-movement 'Italian overture' style. His slow movements are Haydnesque and quite gracious; his finales are witty: that for the *F major* work is particularly catchy. *La Chasse* is the earliest work here and the outer movements have plenty of energy and whooping horn calls, with a rather wistful *Andante* to separate them. Excellent performances, very well played and recorded.

Stamitz, Johann (1717–57)

Clarinet concerto No. 1 in F; (i) *Double Clarinet concerto in B flat;* (ii) *Double concerto for clarinet and bassoon in B flat.*
(BB) *** Naxos Dig. 8.553584 [id.]. Kalman Berkes, with (i) Tomoko Takashima; (ii) Koji Okazaki; Nicholas Esterhazy Sinfonia.

Stamitz wrote no fewer than 11 clarinet concertos as well as the two double concertos on this first disc of a collected edition from Naxos. The *F major* solo *Concerto* is a delightful work with a vigorous first movement leading to a lyrical minor-key Andante and a jig finale. The double concerto was a favourite form with Stamitz, with long opening tuttis in the slow movements as well as the first. Both works are linked to the sinfonia concertante format as well as to the earlier form of the concerto grosso with its strongly contrasted, lightly scored passages for the solo instruments. Both are built on attractive material, but the work for clarinet and bassoon is the more successful, with instruments sharply contrasted. As soloist as well as director, Berkes with his reedy clarinet tone is well matched by his Japanese partners, helped by full, open recording.

Clarinet concerto in B flat.
(N) *** EMI Dig. CDC7 54842-2 [id.]. Sabine Meyer, ASMF, Iona Brown – Carl STAMITZ: *Concerto in B flat.* ***

Johann Stamitz's *concerto* has a rather fine slow movement and an elegantly good-natured closing rondo. It is most persuasively played here and excellently recorded.

Trumpet concerto in D (arr. Boustead).
*** Ph. Dig. 420 203-2 [id.]. Hardenberger, ASMF, Marriner – HAYDN; HUMMEL: *Concertos* *** ✿; HERTEL: *Concerto.* ***

This concerto was written either by Stamitz or by a composer called J. G. Holzbogen. The writing lies consistently up in the instrument's stratosphere and includes some awkward leaps. It is quite inventive, however, notably the finale, which is exhilarating on the lips of Håkan Hardenberger. There is no lack of panache here and Marriner accompanies expertly. Good if reverberant recording, with the trumpet given great presence.

Stanford, Charles (1852–1924)

(i) *Concert piece for organ and orchestra;* (ii) *Clarinet concerto in A min., Op. 80; Irish rhapsodies Nos. 1 in D min., Op. 78; 2 in F min. (Lament for the Son of Ossian), Op. 84;* (iii) *3 for cello and orchestra, Op. 137; 4 in A min. (The fisherman of Loch Neagh and what he saw); 5 in G min., Op. 147;* (iv) *6 for violin and orchestra, Op. 191; Oedipus Rex prelude, Op. 29.*

*** Chandos Dig. CHAN 7002/3 [id.]. (i) Gillian Weir; (ii) Janet Hilton; (iii) Raphael Wallfisch; (iv) Lydia Mordkovitch; Ulster O, Vernon Handley.

Stanford's set of *Irish rhapsodies* (two of them concertante pieces with highly responsive soloists) are the more impressive when heard as a set. They originally appeared coupled with the symphonies but sometimes seemed stronger and more concentrated than these more ambitious works. They are splendidly played and recorded. Gillian Weir makes a first-class soloist in the *Concert piece for organ and orchestra* and Janet Hilton is hardly less appealing in the work for clarinet. An essential supplement for those who have already invested in the four-CD box of the symphonies.

Clarinet concerto in A min., Op. 80.
*** Hyperion CDA 66001 [id.]. King, Philh. O, Francis – FINZI : *Concerto.* ***

(i) *Clarinet concerto in A min.* (for clarinet and strings) *Op. 80;* (ii) *3 Intermezzi* (for clarinet and piano).
*** ASV Dig. CDDCA 787 [id.]. Emma Johnson; (i) RPO, Groves; (ii) Martineau – FINZI: *Clarinet concerto* etc. ***

The Stanford *Clarinet concerto* finds Emma Johnson inspired, even freer and more fluent than Thea King on the rival Hyperion disc. It is a delight how Johnson can edge into a theme with extreme gentleness. So her first entry in the slow movement, taxingly high, seems to emerge ethereally from nowhere, while Thea King's firmer, sharper attack is less poetic. In the finale too King is strong and forthright, but Johnson is warmer and more personal with her cheekily witty treatment of the first solo. Sir Charles Groves and the RPO are warmly sympathetic accompanists, very well recorded, though the solo instrument is rather too close.

Piano concerto No. 1 in G, Op. 59.
*** Hyperion Dig. CDA 66820 [id.]. Piers Lane, BBC Scottish SO, Martyn Brabbins – PARRY: *Piano concerto.* ***

Written in 1894, the first of Stanford's two piano concertos brings even clearer Brahmsian echoes than usual, but the finesse of the writing and the ravishing beauty of the slow movement make it almost as enjoyable as the second and better-known concerto, particularly in a performance by turns as brilliant and poetic as Piers Lane's. Full, warm sound.

Piano concerto No. 2 in C min., Op. 126. Concert variations on an English theme: 'Down among the dead men', Op. 21.
(M) *** Chandos Dig. CHAN 7099 [id.]. Margaret Fingerhut, Ulster O, Vernon Handley.

(i) *Piano concerto No. 2 in C min., Op. 126;* (ii) *Becket, Op. 48: The Martyrdom (Funeral march);* (iii) *The Fisherman of Lough Neagh and what he saw (Irish rhapsody No. 4), Op. 141.*
*** Lyrita SRCD 219 [id.]. (i) Malcolm Binns, LSO; (ii–iii) LPO; (i; iii) Nicholas Braithwaite; (ii) Sir Adrian Boult.

Stanford's *Second Piano concerto*, although in three rather than four movements, is a work on the largest scale, recalling the Brahms *B flat Concerto*. Yet Stanford asserts his own melodic individuality and provides a really memorable secondary theme for the second movement. Margaret Fingerhut is a first-rate soloist both here and and in the apt and entertaining coupling, for Stanford was a dab hand at the variations format. Handley and his Ulster Orchestra are completely at home in this repertoire, and the Chandos recording is well up to the usual high standards of the house.

Malcolm Binns too plays with spontaneous freshness. The Lyrita recording is surely a demonstration of just how a piano concerto should be balanced. The *Funeral march* comes from incidental music commissioned at the request of Tennyson for Irving's production of his tragedy, *Becket*. It has an arresting opening but otherwise is a fairly straightforward piece, strongly melodic in a Stanfordian manner. Like the more familiar *Irish rhapsody*, it is splendidly played and recorded.

Symphonies Nos. 1–7.
*** Chandos Dig. CHAN 9279/82 (4) [id.]. Ulster O, Handley.

Now available in a box of four CDs, with the fill-ups which accompanied the original CDs now put aside for separate reissue, this is obviously the most attractive way to approach this generally impressive if uneven British symphonic canon. Handley and his Ulster Orchestra are completely at home in this repertoire, and the Chandos recording is consistently of this company's best quality.

Symphony No. 1 in B flat., Op. 78; Irish rhapsody No. 2: The Lament for the Son of Ossian, Op. 84.
*** Chandos Dig. CHAN 9049 [id.]. Ulster O, Handley.

Stanford's mature musical studies had been in Berlin and Hamburg, and he came back to England profoundly influenced by the German symphonic style (the Scherzo of the *First Symphony* (1876) even has the character of a Laendler). His work was duly performed and then, like the *Second*, put in a cupboard. Now we can discover for ourselves that, although he could assemble a convincing structure, his melodic invention was not yet strong enough to achieve real memorability. Handley and the Ulster Orchestra do their persuasive best for a piece which is certainly not a silk purse. The *Irish rhapsody* has distinctly more melodramatic flair. Excellent recording.

Symphony No. 2 in D min. (Elegiac); (i) *Clarinet concerto in A min., Op. 80.*
*** Chandos Dig. CHAN 8991 [id.]. Ulster O, Handley; (i) with Janet Hilton.

The *Second Symphony* has until now lain neglected for over a century. The influences of German masters are strong but the work still has its own individuality, for the most part in the scoring. The delightful *Clarinet concerto* makes a splendid coupling, with Janet Hilton at her most seductive, both in timbre and in warmth, and articulating with nimble expertise. A delightful performance.

Symphony No. 3 in F min. (Irish), Op. 28.
(M) *** EMI CDM5 65129-2. Bournemouth Sinf., Norman Del Mar – ELGAR: *Scenes from the Bavarian highlands.* ***

Symphony No. 3 in F min. (Irish), Op. 28; Irish rhapsody No. 5, Op. 147.
*** Chandos Dig. CHAN 8545 [id.]. Ulster O, Handley.

This *Third* and most celebrated of the seven symphonies of Stanford is a rich and attractive work, none the worse for its obvious debts to Brahms. The ideas are best when directly echoing Irish folk music, as in the middle two movements, a skippity jig of a Scherzo and a glowing slow movement framed by harp cadenzas. The *Irish rhapsody No. 5* dates from 1917, reflecting perhaps in its martial vigour that wartime date. Even more characteristic are the warmly lyrical passages, performed passionately by Handley and his Ulster Orchestra, matching the thrust and commitment they bring also to the *Symphony*.

Norman Del Mar directs an equally ripe performance, noting that the finale gives an attractive forward glance to Stanford's pupils, Holst and Vaughan Williams. The EMI recording is warm and well defined.

Symphony No. 4 in F, Op. 31; Irish rhapsody No. 6 for violin and orchestra, Op. 191; Oedipus Rex Prelude, Op. 29.
*** Chandos Dig. CHAN 8884 [id.]. Ulster O, Vernon Handley, (i) with Lydia Mordkovitch.

The *Fourth Symphony*, like the *Third*, is a highly confident piece and an effective symphony, even if it runs out of steam before the close of the finale despite attractive invention. The *Irish* concertante *rhapsody* is a much later work, its nostalgia nicely caught by the soloist here, Lydia Mordkovitch, who is obviously involved. Handley, as ever, takes the helm throughout with ardent commitment and makes the most of the many nice touches of orchestral colour. Excellent recording.

Symphony No. 5 in D (L'Allegro ed il Penseroso), Op. 56; Irish rhapsody No. 4 in A min. (The Fisherman of Lough Neagh and what he saw), Op. 141.
*** Chandos Dig. CHAN 8581 [id.]. Ulster O, Handley.

Stanford's *Fifth Symphony* is colourfully orchestrated and full of easy tunes, illustrating passages from Milton's *L'Allegro* and *Il Penseroso*. The last two movements readily live up to Stanford's reputation as a Brahmsian, representing the *Penseroso* half of the work, and the slow epilogue brings reminders of Brahms's *Third*. The *Irish rhapsody* is more distinctive, bringing together sharply contrasted, colourful and atmospheric Irish ideas under the title *The Fisherman of Lough Neagh and what he saw*. Excellent recording of the finest Chandos quality.

Symphony No. 6 in E flat (In memoriam G. F. Watts), Op. 94; Irish rhapsody No. 1 in D min., Op. 78.
*** Chandos Dig. CHAN 8627 [id.]. Ulster O, Vernon Handley.

Stanford's *Sixth Symphony* is not the strongest of the set, but it has a rather lovely slow movement, with a pervading air of gentle melancholy. The first movement has some good ideas but the finale is too long, in the way finales of Glazunov symphonies tend to overuse their material. Nevertheless Vernon Handley makes quite a persuasive case for the work and an even better one for the enjoyable *Irish rhapsody No. 1*, which features and makes rather effective use of one of the loveliest of all Irish tunes, the *Londonderry air*. Excellent sound.

Symphony No. 7 in D min., Op. 124; (i) *Concert piece for organ and orchestra, Op. 181;* (ii) *Irish rhapsody No. 3 for cello and orchestra, Op. 137.*
*** Chandos Dig. CHAN 8861 [id.]. Ulster O, Handley; with (i) Gillian Weir; (ii) Raphael Wallfisch.

The *Seventh Symphony* sums up its composer as a symphonist – structurally sound, yet not now so heavily indebted to Germany, and with the orchestration often ear-catching. It is not a masterpiece, but it could surely not be presented with more conviction than here by Handley and his excellent orchestra. The *Irish rhapsody* is very Irish indeed and makes the use of several good tunes. It is most sensitively played by Wallfisch, and Gillian Weir makes a strong impression in the *Organ 'concertino'*, where the composer uses only brass, strings and percussion in the accompaniment. The music has a touch of the epic about it.

Serenade (Nonet) in F, Op. 95.
*** Hyperion CDA 66291 [id.]. Capricorn – PARRY: *Nonet.* ***

Like the Parry *Nonet*, with which it is coupled, the *Serenade* is an inventive and delightful piece, its discourse civilized and the Scherzo full of charm. Capricorn play this piece with evident pleasure and convey this to the listener. The recording is very natural and truthfully balanced.

Violin sonatas Nos. 1 in D, Op. 11; 2 in A, Op. 70; Irish fantasy No. 1 (Caoine), Op. 54 No. 1; 5 Characteristic pieces, Op. 93.
(N) *** Hyperion Dig. CDA 67024 [id.]. Paul Barritt, Catherine Edwards.

One expected these to be enjoyably well-crafted works but they are a great deal more than that, teeming with memorable ideas, to make consistently delightful listing. Paul Barritt and Catherine Edwards play all this music with a spring-like freshness, and obviously enjoy every bar. They are beautifully recorded.

PIANO MUSIC

24 Preludes, Set 1, Op. 163; 6 Characteristic pieces, Op. 132.
*** Priory Dig. PRCD 449 [id.]. Peter Jacobs.

This collection comes as a pleasant surprise: one does not think of Stanford as a composer for the piano, and indeed his 24 *Preludes* are not bravura works like those of Chopin and Rachmaninov. Written in 1918, their chromatic key-sequence would suggest that they are more readily associated with Bach's *Well-tempered Clavier*, and the composer's following set in 1920 (to make a total of 48) seems to emphasize that parallel. The variety of Stanford's invention brings a continuing freshness throughout the set, which can be enjoyed as a progression as well as by selecting individual items. The *Characteristic pieces* were written six years earlier and are also of high quality, with the engaging *Rondel* (No. 4) dedicated to the Schumann of *Kinderszenen*. Peter Jacobs almost never disappoints and his performances here are accomplished, stylish, spontaneous and thoroughly sympathetic, while the recording is first class.

VOCAL MUSIC

3 Motets, Op. 38: Beati quorum via; Cœlos ascendit; Justorum animae. Anthems: *For lo, I raise up; Glorious and powerful God; How beautiful are their feet; If ye then be risen with Christ; The Lord is my Shepherd; Ye choirs of new Jerusalem; Ye holy angels bright.* (Organ) *Preludes and fugues in B and C, Op. 193/2–3.*
(M) *** CRD Dig. CRD 3497 [id.]. New College, Oxford, Ch., Higginbottom; Paul Plummer or Andrew Smith (organ).

Edward Higginbottom and his splendid choir never made a finer record than this. All this music shows Stanford at his most confidently inspired, readily carrying the listener with him, when the performances are so secure and committed and superbly recorded in the Chapel of New College, Oxford.

3 Motets, Op. 38: Beati quorum via; Cœlos ascendit; Justorum animae. Anthems: *For lo, I raise up, Op. 145; The Lord is my Shepherd. Bible songs: A song of peace; A song of wisdom, Op. 113/4 & 6.* Hymns: *O for a closer walk with God; Pray that Jerusalem. Magnificat for double chorus, Op. 164; Morning, Communion and Evening services in G, Op. 81: Magnificat and Nunc dimittis. Morning, Communion and Evening services in C, Op. 115: Magnificat and Nunc dimittis.* (Organ) *Postlude in D min.*
(M) *** EMI Dig. CDC5 55535-2. John Mark Ainsley, King's College, Cambridge, Ch., Stephen Cleobury (organ); James Vivian (organ accompaniments).

Framed by eloquently beautiful settings of the *Magnificat* and *Nunc dimittis* from 1902 and 1909 respectively (Alastair Hussain the radiantly secure treble soloist in the former), this 75-minute collection – the hundredth issue in EMI's distinguished British Music series – celebrates Stanford's remarkable achievement within the Anglican tradition over a quarter of a century. James Vivian, the current organ scholar, impressively provides some of the accompaniments which are usually important in their own right and make bravura demands on the player. Highly recommended alongside the CRD collection above. Both CDs are well worth having, even though some duplication is involved.

Magnificat in B flat, Op. 164; 3 Motets, Op. 38; Motet: Eternal Father, Op. 135.
*** Conifer Dig. 75605 51155-2 [id.]. Trinity College, Cambridge, Ch., Marlow – PARRY: *Songs of farewell.* ***

The *Three Motets*, early works, are settings of Latin hymns; *Eternal Father* is an elaborate setting of Robert Bridges; while the big-scale unaccompanied *Magnificat* for double choir makes a magnificent culmination. Immaculate performances and beautifully balanced, atmospheric recording.

(i) *Requiem, Op. 63;* (ii) *The Veiled Prophet of Khorassan* (excerpts).
*** Marco Polo 8.223580/1 [id.]. (i) Frances Lucy, Colette McGahon, Peter Kerr, Nigel Leeson-Williams, RTE Philharmonic Ch.; (ii) Virginia Kerr; Nat. SO of Ireland, cond. (i) Adrian Leaper; (ii) Colman Pearce.

Stanford's magnificent *Requiem* (1897) was composed in honour of the painter, Lord Leighton, who died in 1896. It is a powerfully conceived and moving work, integrating the soloists as a team with the choir in a particularly satisfying way. The contrasts of the writing, from the ethereal opening of the *Kyrie* to the blazing fortissimo of the *Tuba mirum*, are superbly caught here, the best recording we have had from Marco Polo and surely in the demonstration bracket. With fine solo singing to match the fervour of the chorus, Adrian Leaper can be congratulated on the great success of the first recording of a work that should surely be in the general choral repertoire. The exotic suite from Stanford's first opera, *The Veiled Prophet of Khorassan*, makes an agreeable if not distinctive encore. It is a pity that the *Requiem* is just a minute or so too long to fit on a single CD.

Songs of the Fleet, Op. 117; Songs of the sea, Op. 91.
(M) **(*) EMI CDM5 65113-2. Benjamin Luxon, Bournemouth SO & Ch., Del Mar – DELIUS: *Sea drift.* **

This is a very welcome coupling of Stanford at his most uninhibitedly vigorous. The four *Songs of the sea* are more immediately memorable in their boisterous way, with *The Old Superb* a real hit; but the *Songs of the Fleet* (also setting Newbolt poems, but with SATB chorus) make a pleasant sequel. Luxon's voice is quite well caught by the microphones, but the resonance takes some of the bite from the words of the chorus. Yet Del Mar's understanding of the idiom makes for lively and enjoyable results.

(i) *Stabat Mater, Op. 96; Te Deum* (from *Service in B flat, Op. 10)*; (ii) *6 Bible songs, Op. 113.*
(N) *** Chandos Dig. CHAN 9548 [id.]. (i) Attrot, Stephen, Robson; (i; ii) Varcoe; (ii) Watson; Leeds Philharmonic Ch., BBC PO, Hickox.

Sir Charles Villiers Stanford, Irish to the core, here offers a Protestant setting of the deeply Catholic text of the *Stabat Mater*. In its directness and vigour, this relates to Stanford's healthily Anglican church music on the one hand and to his symphonic writing on the other. Like his *Requiem*, this is a piece, long-neglected, that richly deserves revival, and Hickox with his excellent forces directs a performance, atmospherically recorded, that demands its return to the repertory. The six settings of Biblical texts for baritone and organ (warmly done by Stephen Varcoe and Ian Watson) are fresh and forthright, leading to the stirring *Te Deum in B flat*, one of the glories of English church music.

Stanley, John (1712–86)

6 Organ concertos, Op. 10.
(M) *** CRD CRD 3365; *CRDC 4065* [id.]. Gifford, N. Sinfonia.

These bouncing, vigorous performances, well recorded as they are on the splendid organ of Hexham Abbey, present these *Concertos* most persuasively. No. 4, with its darkly energetic C minor, is particularly fine. The recording is natural in timbre and very well balanced.

Concertos for strings, Op. 2/1–6.
(N) *** Chandos Dig. CHAN 0638 [id.]. Coll. Mus. 90, Standage.

These six highly engaging *Concertos for strings* by the almost blind English composer John Stanley, were published in 1742 and are concerti grossi in the style of Corelli and most closely Handel. For Stanley shares the latter's gift for a noble melodic contour. No. 3 is a fine example and also has a buoyant fugue of the kind Handel would have written. No. 2 is equally memorable and brings a solo cello contribution in the second movement. The period-instrument performances here are wonderfully spirited – vitality without abrasive edge – as well as bringing the right degree of expressive warmth. The recording is first class.

Stenhammar, Wilhelm (1871–1927)

(i) *Piano concerto No. 1 in B flat min., Op. 1. Symphony No. 3* (fragment).
*** Chandos Dig. CHAN 9074 [id.]. (i) Widlund; Royal Stockholm PO, Rozhdestvensky.

(i) *Piano concerto No. 1 in B flat min., Op. 1;* (ii) *Florez och Blanzeflor, Op. 3;* (iii) *Two Sentimental Romances, Op. 28.*
*** BIS Dig. CD 550 [id.]. (i) Love Derwinger; (ii) Peter Mattei; (iii) Ulf Wallin, Malmö SO, Paavo Järvi.

Stenhammar's *First Piano concerto* is full of beautiful ideas and the invention is fresh. Love Derwinger proves an impressive and sympathetic intepreter and gets good support from Järvi *fils*. The early *Florez och Blanzeflor* ('Flower and White-flower'), a ballad by Oscar Levertin, brings a certain Wagnerian flavour but has a charm that is sensitively sung by the young Swedish baritone Peter Mattei.

Chandos offer the less substantial coupling, a three-minute fragment from the *Third Symphony*, on which Stenhammar embarked in 1918–19. In itself it is too insignificant a makeweight to affect choice. But in the *Concerto* Mats Widlund proves the more imaginative soloist and brings just that little bit more finesse to the solo part. Rozhdestvensky gives excellent support and the Stockholm orchestra (and in particular their strings) have greater richness of sonority. The Chandos recording also has the edge on its BIS competitor in terms of depth and warmth.

(i) *Symphonies Nos. 1 in F; 2 in G min., Op. 34; Serenade for orchestra, Op. 31* (with *Reverenza* movement); *Excelsior Overture, Op. 13; The Song (Sången): Interlude, Op. 44; Lodolezzi sings (Lodolezzi sjunger): suite;* (ii) *Piano concertos Nos. 1 in B flat min., Op. 1;* (iii) *2 in D min., Op. 23;* (iv) *Ballad: Florez och Blanzeflor;* (v) *2 Sentimental Romances;* (vi) *Midwinter, Op. 24; Snöfrid, Op. 5.*

(M) *** BIS Dig. BIS CD 714/716 [id.]. (i) Gothenburg SO, Neeme Järvi; (ii) Love Derwinger; (iii) Cristina Ortiz; (iv) Peter Matthei; (v) Ulf Wallin; (vi) Gothenburg Ch.; (ii–v) Malmö SO, Paavo Järvi.

Järvi's performances are now repackaged at a distinctly advantageous price. Special points to note are: first, that this is the only version of the *Serenade for orchestra* (apart from Järvi's) to include the *Reverenza* movement which Stenhammar subsequently withdrew; secondly, that the *First Piano concerto* makes use of Stenhammar's own orchestration, which came to light only recently in America; and, thirdly, this is the most comprehensive compilation of Stenhammar's orchestral music now on the market. All the performances and recordings are of high quality, and the only serious criticism to make affects the first movement of the *Second Symphony*, which Järvi takes rather too briskly. In the *Second Piano concerto* Janos Solyom has a slight edge over the Ortiz, but hers is a good account, all the same. All the recordings are digital save for that of the *First Symphony*, which comes from a 1982 concert performance and has great warmth and transparency.

Symphony No. 1 in F.
*** BIS Dig. CD 219 [id.]. Gothenburg SO, Järvi.

The *First Symphony* displays sympathies with such composers as Brahms, Bruckner, Berwald and, in the slow movement, even an affinity with Elgar. Nevertheless there is plenty of originality in it. The recording has complete naturalness, and on CD there is additional presence and range, particularly at the bottom end of the register.

Symphony No. 2 in G min., Op. 34.
*** Cap. CAP 21151 [id.]. Stockholm PO, Westerberg.
(N) ** Swedish Soc. SCD 1014 [id.]. Stockholm PO, Tor Mann.

Symphony No. 2; Overture, Excelsior!, Op. 13.
*** BIS CD 251 [id.]. Gothenburg SO, Järvi.
(BB) **(*) Naxos Dig. 8.553888 [id.]. Royal SNO, Petter Sundkvist.

This is a marvellous symphony. It is direct in utterance; the melodic invention is fresh and abundant, and the generosity of spirit it radiates is heartwarming. The Stockholm Philharmonic under Stig Westerberg play with conviction and eloquence; the strings have warmth and body, and the wind are very fine too. The recording is vivid and full-bodied even by the digital standards of today: as sound, this record is absolutely first class.

Tor Mann's performance originally appeared on RCA in Sweden. It is an admirable performance, well held together and very sympathetic. All the same it is unrealistic to ask full price for a 1959 recording running to only 46 minutes. Stig Westerberg or Neeme Järvi are the ones to go for.

Neeme Järvi takes an altogether brisker view of the first movement than Westerberg, but the playing is spirited and the recording very good indeed, though not quite as distinguished as on the Caprice rival. The special attraction of this issue, however, is the *Overture, Excelsior!* It is an opulent but inventive score in the spirit of Strauss and Elgar and is played with enormous zest.

Petter Sundkvist's account of Stenhammar's glorious *Second Symphony* is absolutely first class interpretatively, though it is rather let down by the quality of sound, which does not match that of his Gothenburg rivals. It is a meticulous, dedicated account which radiates an understanding of and love for this music. The Royal Scottish National Orchestra respond with enthusiasm. A safe recommendation at the price, but the sound is not three-star.

CHAMBER MUSIC

(i) *Allegro brillante in E flat; Allegro ma non tanto;* (ii; iii) *Violin sonata in A min., Op. 19*; (iii) *Piano sonata in A flat, Op. 12.*
** BIS Dig. CD 764 [id.]. (i) Tale Qt (members); (ii) Tale Olsson; (iii) Lucia Negro.

All this music comes from the 1890s, before Stenhammar's personality was fully formed. The *A flat Sonata*, written in the same year (1895) as the better-known and somewhat Brahmsian *Three Fantasies*, Op. 11, was criticized by Nielsen as being too indebted to Beethoven and Mendelssohn; though derivative, it has some pleasing invention and a good feeling for form. Lucia Negro recorded it way back in the early 1980s but she plays it with even greater authority and sensitivity now. The *Violin sonata* comes from 1899 and was written for Stenhammar's chamber-music partner, the composer Tor Aulin. The *Allegro ma non tanto* is the first movement of a projected piano trio (1895); and little is known about the even earlier *Allegro brillante* fragment. The pianist, who is unfailingly responsive, rather swamps her partners here and in the *Violin sonata*, thanks to a less than satisfactory balance.

String quartets Nos. (i) *1 in C, Op. 2;* (ii) *2 in C min., Op. 14;* (iii) *3 in F, Op. 18; 4 in A min., Op. 25;* (i) *5 in C (Serenade), Op. 29;* (ii) *6 in D min., Op. 35.*
(M) *** Cap. CAP 21536 (3) [id.]. (i) Fresk Qt; (ii) Copenhagen Qt; (iii) Gotland Qt.

The *First Quartet* shows Stenhammar steeped in the chamber music of Beethoven and Brahms, though there is a brief reminder of Grieg; the *Second* is far more individual. By the *Third* and *Fourth*, arguably the greatest of the six, the influence of Brahms and

Dvořák is fully assimilated, and the *Fourth* reflects that gentle melancholy which lies at the heart of Stenhammar's sensibility. The *Fifth* is the shortest; the *Sixth* comes from the war years when the composer was feeling worn out and depressed, though there is little evidence of this in the music. Performances are generally excellent, as indeed is the recording, and it is good to have this thoroughly worthwhile set at mid-price.

PIANO MUSIC

Allegro con moto ed appassionato; 3 Fantasies, Op. 11; Impromptu; Impromptu-Waltz; Late summer nights, Op. 33; 3 Small piano pieces.
*** BIS Dig. CD 554 [id.]. Lucia Negro.

Although he was by all accounts a wonderful pianist, Stenhammar wrote relatively little piano music of real quality – with the exception of the *Sensommarnätter* (*Late summer nights*). Brahms is a dominant influence in the early *Allegro con moto ed appassionato* and in the Op. 11 *Fantasies*, but there is a strong individual personality at work too, and the *Sensommarnätter* ('Late summer nights'), which come from the period of the *Serenade for orchestra*, are wonderfully thoughtful and atmospheric pieces that inhabit a wholly personal world. Lucia Negro is thoroughly at home in this repertoire and plays with an effortless assurance and elegance that is very persuasive, and the BIS recording is altogether first rate.

3 Fantasies, Op. 11; Impromptu in G flat; Late summer nights, Op. 33; 3 Small piano pieces; Sonata in G min.
(BB) *** Naxos Dig. 8.553730 [id.]. Niklas Sivelöv.

Niklas Sivelöv proves a thoroughly idiomatic interpreter and is as much at home in the quasi-impressionistic third movement of the *Late summer nights* and the delicate *Poco allegretto* as he is in the virtuosic, big-boned, penultimate movement. He is very well served by the recording engineers. Well worth the money.

Piano sonatas Nos. 1 in C; 2 in C min.; 3 in A flat; 4 in G min.; Fantasie in A min.
**(*) BIS Dig. CD 634 [id.]. Lucia Negro.

The *Fantasie in A minor* and the *First Sonata* were written when Stenhammar was nine and were followed a year later by another sonata. The *A flat Sonata* comes from 1883 when he was twelve (not two years later as stated on the sleeve-note). All these juvenilia are in the style of Mozart, Weber and Mendelssohn – and it is puzzling why they should be thought worth recording. The *Sonata No. 4 in G minor* is another matter, and in it one recognizes the profile of the real Stenhammar. It comes from 1890, when he was nineteen, and has the breadth and scale of the mature composer. The ideas are long-breathed and the piano writing far more virtuosic and big-boned. The performances could not be more beguiling. Lucia Negro brings great charm and intelligence to the smaller pieces, which have a certain touching innocence, and she gives the *G minor Sonata* with total conviction. Good recording too. One is hardly likely to play the juvenilia more than once – hence the limitation on the fullest recommendation – despite the excellence of both the playing and recording.

VOCAL MUSIC

Lodolezzi sings: suite, Op. 39; (i) *Midwinter, Op. 24;* (ii) *Snöfrid, Op. 5; The Song* (interlude).
*** BIS Dig. CD 438 [id.]. (i; ii) Gothenburg Concert Hall Ch., (ii) with Ahlén, Nilsson, Zackrisson, Enoksson; Gothenburg SO, Järvi.

Snöfrid is an early cantata. The young composer was completely under the spell of Wagner at this time and it offers only occasional glimpses of the mature Stenhammar. *Midwinter* is a kind of folk-music fantasy or pot-pourri on the lines of Alfvén's *Midsummer vigil*, though not quite so appealing. *Lodolezzi sings* has much innocent charm. None of this is great Stenhammar but it is well worth hearing; the performances under Neeme Järvi are very sympathetic, and the recording is natural and present.

(i) *The Song (Sången), Op. 44;* (ii) *Two sentimental romances, Op. 28;* (iii) *Ithaca, Op. 21.*
*** Cap. CAP 21358 [id.]. (i) Sörenson, von Otter, Dahlberg, Wahlgren, State Ac. Ch., Adolf Fredrik Music School Children's Ch., (ii) Arve Tellefsen, (iii) Håkan Hagegård, Swedish RSO; (i) Blomstedt; (ii) Westerberg; (iii) Ingelbretsen.

The first half of *The Song* has been described as 'a great fantasy' and is Stenhammar at his best and most individual: the choral writing is imaginatively laid out and the contrapuntal ingenuity is always at the service of poetic ends: the second half is less individual. The solo and choral singing is superb and the whole performance has the total commitment one might expect from these forces. The superbly engineered recording does them full justice. The *Two sentimental romances* have great charm and are very well played, and Hagegård is in fine voice in another rarity, *Ithaca*.

30 Songs.
*** Caprice MSCD 623. Von Otter, Hagegård, Forsberg, Schuback.

These songs cover the whole of Stenhammar's career: the earliest, *In the forest*, was composed when he was sixteen, while the last, *Minnesang*, was written three years before his death. The songs are unpretentious and charming, fresh and idyllic, and nearly all are strophic. Hagegård sings the majority of them with his usual intelligence and artistry, though there is an occasional hardening of timbre. Anne Sofie von Otter is in wonderful voice and sings with great sensitivity and charm. Bengt Forsberg and Thomas Schuback accompany with great taste, and the recording is of the highest quality.

Sterndale Bennett, William
(1816–75)

Piano concertos Nos. 1 in D min., Op. 1; 3 in C min., Op. 9.
✽ *** Lyrita Dig. SRCD 204 [id.]. Malcolm Binns, LPO, Nicholas Braithwaite.

Perhaps it was hearing Mendelssohn play his *G minor Concerto* in 1832 that prompted the sixteen-year-old Sterndale Bennett to write his Opus 1, a concerto in D minor and a work of extraordinary fluency and accomplishment. David Byers, who has edited the concertos, speaks of Bennett's 'gentle lyricism, the strength and energy of the orchestral tuttis'; and they are in ample evidence, both here and in the *Third Piano concerto*, composed when he was eighteen. No praise can be too high for the playing of Malcolm Binns whose fleetness of finger and poetic sensibility are a constant source of delight, and for the admirable support he receives from Nicholas Braithwaite and the LPO. The engineers produce sound of the highest quality. A most enjoyable disc.

Piano concertos Nos. 2 in E flat, Op. 4; 5 in F min.; Adagio.
*** Lyrita Dig. SRCD 205 [id.]. Malcolm Binns, Philh. O, Nicholas Braithwaite.

The *Second concerto* proves to be another work of great facility and charm. It takes as its model the concertos of Mozart and Mendelssohn, and the brilliance and delicacy of the keyboard writing make one understand why the composer was so highly regarded by his contemporaries. The *F minor concerto* of 1836 is eminently civilized music with lots of charm; the *Adagio*, which completes the disc, is thought to be an alternative slow movement for Bennett's *Third Concerto* (1837). Malcolm Binns plays with great artistry, and the accompaniment by the Philharmonia Orchestra and Nicholas Braithwaite is equally sensitive. First-class recording.

(i) *Piano concerto No. 4 in F min.; Symphony in G. min.;* (i) *Fantasia in A, Op. 16.*
(M) *** Unicorn Dig. UKCD 2032. (i) Binns; Milton Keynes CO, Hilary Davan Wetton.

William Sterndale Bennett's eclectic *Fourth Piano concerto* reflects Chopin rather more than Mendelssohn and is agreeable and well structured. Its slow movement, an engaging *Barcarolle*, is a winner. The *Symphony* is amiable, not unlike the Mendelssohn string symphonies, slight but enjoyable. Malcolm Binns is a persuasive advocate of the *Concerto*, while Hilary Davan Wetton paces both works admirably and clearly has much sympathy for them. Excellent sound and a good balance.

Stevens, Bernard (1916–83)

(i) *Cello concerto; Symphony of liberation.*
*** Mer. CDE 84124. (i) Baillie, BBC PO, Downes.

Bernard Stevens came to wider notice at the end of the war when his *Symphony of liberation* won a *Daily Express* competition. What a fine work it proves to be, though the somewhat later *Cello concerto* is even stronger. Dedicated performances from Alexander Baillie and the BBC Philharmonic. Good recording.

(i) *Violin concerto; Symphony No. 2.*
*** Mer. CDE 84174 [id.]. (i) Ernst Kovacic; BBC PO, Downes.

The *Violin concerto* is a good piece and well worth investigating. Stevens is a composer of real substance, and the *Second Symphony* (1964) is impressive in its sustained power and resource. Ernst Kovacic is persuasive in the *Concerto* and Downes and the BBC Philharmonic play well. Good (but not spectacular) recording.

Still, William Grant (1895–1978)

Symphony No. 2 (Song of a new race) in G min.
*** Chandos Dig. CHAN 9226 [id.]. Detroit SO, Neeme Järvi – DAWSON: *Negro Folk Symphony;* ELLINGTON: *Harlem.* ***

Stokowski conducted the première of this attractive piece in 1937, seven years after the composer's *First Symphony* had been the first work by an Afro-American composer to be played by a major orchestra (the NYPO). Still worked as an arranger, so he knew how to score, and he had a fund of tunes: the slow movement is haunting, the high-spirited Scherzo whistles along like someone out walking on a spring morning. The idiom is totally American and, if the score is more a suite than a symphony, it remains very personable. It is played most persuasively here and is given a richly expansive recording.

Stockhausen, Karlheinz (born 1928)

(i) *Mikrophonie 1; Mikrophonie 2;* (ii) *Klavierstücke 1–11.*
(M) *** Sony S2K 53346 (2). (i) Members of W. German R. Ch. & Studio Ch. for New Music, Cologne, Kontarsky, Alings, Fritsch, Bojé, cond. Herbert Schernus; supervised by composer; (ii) Aloys Kontarsky (piano).

This reissue combines two important Stockhausen

recordings from the mid-1960s. *Mikrophonie 1* is electronic music proper; *Mikrophonie 2* attempts a synthesis of electronic music and choral sounds, and it is the vocal work that is the more immediately intriguing. It may be in dispute just how valid performances like these are when the composer's score allows many variables, but at least it is the composer himself who is supervising the production. Outstanding recording-quality for its time – as of course it should be with so many musician-engineers around in the Cologne studios.

The *Klavierstücke* provide a stimulating coupling. Aloys Kontarsky plays these eleven pieces – arguably the purest expression yet of Stockhausen's musical imagination – with a dedication that can readily convince even the unconverted listener. Seven of the pieces are very brief epigrammatic utterances, each sharply defined. The sixth and tenth pieces (the latter placed separately on the second disc) are more extended, each taking over 20 minutes. The effect at the begining of the ninth piece provides a clear indication of Stockhausen's aural imagination. The pianist repeats the same, not very interesting discord no fewer than 228 times, and one might dismiss that as merely pointless. What emerges from sympathetic listening is that the repetitions go nagging on so that the sound of the discord seems to vary, like a visual image shimmering in heat-haze. The other pieces, too, bring similar extensions of musical experience, and all this music is certainly communicative. Excellent if forward recording and extensive back-up notes. A good set on which to sharpen avant-garde teeth.

Stimmung (1968).
*** Hyperion CDA 66115 [id.]. Singcircle, Gregory Rose.

Gregory Rose with his talented vocal group directs an intensely beautiful account of Stockhausen's 70-minute minimalist meditation on six notes. Though the unsympathetic listener might still find the result boring, this explains admirably how Stockhausen's musical personality can hypnotise, with his variety of effect and response, even with the simplest of formulae. Excellent recording.

Stradella, Alessandro (1644–82)

Christmas cantatas: (i) *Ah, ah, troppo è ver;* (ii) *Si apra al riso* (both *per Il Santissimo natale*).
(BB) *** BMG/DHM Baroque Esprit Dig. 05472 77463 2 [id.]. (i) Mechthild Bach, Ruth Ziesak, Christoph Prégardien, (i–ii) Kai Wessel, Michael Schopper; (ii) Barbara Schlick; La Stagione Frankfurt, Michael Schneider.

With a freshness and originality one expects from the composer of *San Giovanni Battista*, Stradella's Christmas cantata, *Ah, ah, troppo è ver*, is a great deal more than a serene pastorella. Lucifer (Michael Schopper) appears at the very opening, strenuously to interrupt the good-natured *Sinfonia*, to announce his determination to thwart the influence of the Christ child. Then come three scenas, in turn depicting the Annunciation, the Nativity and the Adoration of the Magi with the Angel and Mary (Mechthild Bach), followed by the Shepherd (Ruth Ziesak), each given beautiful narrative arias, all of which are sung ravishingly here. Joseph (Christoph Prégardien) then rounds off the story-telling, and the work closes with an engagingly happy madrigal in which all participate. *Si apra al riso* is less dramatic but musically just as inspired, with two duets and a madrigal trio interspersed among the solo numbers, here with Barbara Schlick standing out from her excellent colleagues. Michael Schneider paces the music admirably and the instrumental playing is first class. Vivid recording in a pleasing acoustic completes the listener's pleasure. A real bargain.

Motets: *Benedictus Dominus Deo; Chare Jesu suavissime; Crocifissione e morte di N. S. Giesù Christo; Lamentatione il Mercoledì Santo; O vos omnes qui transitis*.
*** Virgin/Veritas/EMI VC5 45175-2. Gérard Lesne, Sandrine Piau, Il Seminario Musicale.

Throughout his life, Alessandro Stradella was associated with scandals, both financial and sexual, and he was finally murdered, although the reasons for this are obscure. He wrote church music which combined drama with remarkable serenity and expressive beauty. *Benedictus Dominus Deo* is a particularly beautiful duet cantata in which God is thanked for sending his son to earth to redeem mankind. *O vos omnes*, a solo cantata, is shorter but no less potent. The text first expresses a languishing adoration of Jesus, with sensuous use of descending chromatics, and the work ends with lively *Alleluias*. Lesne is a master of this repertoire, and in the former cantata he is radiantly joined by Sandrine Piau, who then goes on to dominate the joyously lyrical *Chare Jesu suavissime*, sweetly praising Saint Philip Neri. These works are framed by the more austere *Crocifissione e morte di N. S. Giesù Christo* (which has a memorably eloquent instrumental introduction, after which the solo line is both grave and plaintive) and the closing *Lamentatione for Ash Wednesday*, which is also restrained but touching beautiful. The accompaniments, by a small, authentic-instrument group, are very sensitive indeed. This is perhaps specialist repertoire, but Gérard Lesne has made it his own and his artistry is unsurpassed.

San Giovanni Battista (oratorio).
✿ *** Erato/Warner Dig. 2292 45739-2. Bott, Batty, Lesne, Edgar-Wilson, Huttenlocher, Musiciens du Louvre, Minkowski.

Stradella's oratorio on the Biblical subject of John

the Baptist and Salome is an amazing masterpiece and offers unashamedly sensuous treatment of the story. Insinuatingly chromatic melodic lines for Salome (here described simply as Herodias's daughter) are set against plainer, more forthright writing for the castrato role of the saint, showing the composer as a seventeenth-century equivalent of Richard Strauss. There is one amazing phrase for Salome, gloriously sung here by Catherine Bott, which starts well above the stave and ends after much twisting nearly two octaves below with a glorious chest-note, a hair-raising moment. Herod's anger arias bring reminders of both Purcell and Handel, and at the end Stradella ingeniously superimposes Salome's gloating music and Herod's expressions of regret, finally cutting off the duet in mid-air as Charles Ives might have done, bringing the whole work to an indeterminate close. Quite apart from Catherine Bott's magnificent performance, at once pure and sensuous in tone and astonishingly agile, the other singers are most impressive, with Gerard Lesne a firm-toned counter-tenor in the title-role and Philippe Huttenlocher a clear if sometimes gruff Herod. Marc Minkowski reinforces his claims as an outstanding exponent of period performance, drawing electrifying playing from Les Musiciens du Louvre, heightening the drama. Excellent sound. Not to be missed!

Straus, Oscar (1870–1954)

Marches: *Einzugs; Bulgaren; Die Schlossparade. Menuett à la cour*. Polka: *G'stellte Mäd'ln. Rund um die Liebe* (Overture); Waltzes: (i) *L'Amour m'emporte. Alt-Wiener Reigen; Eine Ballnacht; Der Reigen; Didi;* (i) *Komm, komm, Held meiner Träume; Tragante; Valse lente; Walzerträume*.
*** Marco Polo Dig. 8.223596 [id.]. (i) Veronika Kincses; Budapest Strauss SO, Alfred Walter.

It is good to have Oscar Straus (with one 's') represented in the Marco Polo series of Viennese dance music; even though he is no relation to the famous Strauss family, his style of writing echoed theirs, also absorbing influences from Lehár. His great hit was the operetta, *A Waltz Dream* (1907), which had a first run in Vienna of 500 performances. His *Walzerträume* is deftly based on the main theme from the operetta, and the *Einzugs-Marsch* comes from the same source. But he could also manage a neat polka and score it very prettily, as is instanced by *G'stellte Mäd'ln*, while the *Alt-Wiener Reigen waltz* is also full of charm and is played here very seductively. *Komm, komm, Held meiner Träume* is of course the famous 'Come, come, my hero', which comes from a parody operetta based on George Bernard Shaw's *Arms and the Man*. In 1908 it was a flop in Vienna, under its title *Der tapfere Soldat* ('The brave soldier') but was a resounding success in England and the USA later, when its title was changed to *The Chocolate Soldier* and its hit song took the world by storm. It is nicely sung here in soubrette style by Veronika Kincses. When the Second World War broke out, the now-world-renowned composer fled, first briefly to Paris, then to America. But he returned home when peace was resumed and wrote an engaging hit, sung first by Danielle Darrieux in a 1952 French film, *Madame de. . .*, and here by Veronika Kincses, and he capped his movie career with a Parisian-style waltz, *Der Reigen*, for the famous Max Ophüls film, *La Ronde*, the song eventually becoming better-known than the movie. The programme opens with a pot-pourri overture irresistibly full of sumptuous and light-hearted melody. It is infectiously played here, like the rest of the programme, by the first-class Budapest Strauss Symphony Orchestra, conducted with affection and great élan by Alfred Walter – easily the best CD he has made so far. The recording, too, is gorgeously sumptuous, and this is a marvellous disc to cheer you up on a dull day. Highly recommended.

Strauss, Franz (1822–1905)

Horn concerto in C min., Op. 8.
(N) (B) **(*) Decca Double 460 296 (2) [id.]. Tuckwell, LSO, Kertész – Richard STRAUSS: *Concertos*. **(*)

This concerto by Franz Strauss, Richard's father, at times half-anticipates the lyrical style his son was to favour a generation later. But the quality of the musical material is undistinguished, and with its florid ornamentation the writing shows a tendency to fall into the manner of the cornet air with variations. Tuckwell's performance is responsive and secure, but fails to convince the listener that the work should not be put back in the attic where it rightly belongs.

The Strauss family

Strauss, Johann Sr (1804–49) Strauss, Johann Jr (1825–99) Strauss, Josef (1827–70) Strauss, Eduard (1835–1916)

(all music listed is by Johann Strauss Jr unless otherwise stated)

Johann Strauss Jnr: The Complete Edition

Volume 1: Mazurka: *Veilchen, Mazur nach russischen motiven*. Polkas: *Fledermaus; Herzenslust; Zehner*. Quadrilles: *Debut; Nocturne*. Waltzes: *Bei uns z'Haus; Freuet euch des Lebens; Gunstwerber; Klangfiguren; Maskenzug française; Phönix-Schwingen*.

**(*) Marco Polo Dig. 8.223201-2 [id.]. CSSR State PO (Košice), Alfred Walter.

Volume 2: *Kaiser Franz Josef I, Rettungs-Jubel-Marsch*. Polkas: *Czechen; Neue Pizzicato; Satanella; Tik-Tak*. Polka-Mazurka: *Fantasieblümchen*. Quadrilles: *Cytheren; Indra*. Waltzes: *Die jungen Wiener; Solonsprüche; Vermälungs-Toaste; Wo die Zitronen blüh'n*.
** Marco Polo Dig. 8.223202-2. CSSR State PO (Košice), Alfred Walter.

Volume 3: Polkas: *Aesculap; Amazonen; Freuden-Gruss; Jux; Vergnügungszug*. Quadrilles: *Dämonen; Satanella*. Waltzes: *Berglieder; Liebeslieder; Lind-gesänge; Die Osterreicher; Wiener Punsch-lieder*.
**(*) Marco Polo Dig. 8.223203-2 [id.]. CSSR State PO (Košice), Alfred Walter.

Volume 4: Polkas: *Bürger-Ball; Hopser; Im Krapfenwald'l (polka française); Knall-Kügerin; Veilchen*. Marches: *Austria; Verbruederungs*. Quadrille: *Motor*. Waltzes: *Dividenden; O schoener Mai!; Serail-taenze*.
**(*) Marco Polo Dig. 8.223204-2 [id.]. CSSR State PO (Košice), Richard Edlinger.

Volume 5: *Russischer Marsch Fantasie*. Polkas: *Elisen (polka française); Heiligenstadt rendezvous; Hesperus; Musen; Pariser*. Quadrille: *Sur des airs français*. Waltzes: *Italienischer; Kennst du mich?; Nachtfalter; Wiener Chronik*.
*** Marco Polo Dig. 8.223205-2 [id.]. CSSR State PO (Košice), Oliver Dohnányi.

Volume 6: *Caroussel Marsch*. Polkas: *Bluette (polka française); Camelien; Warschauer*. Quadrilles: *Nach themen französischer Romanzen; Nordstern*. Waltzes: *Concurrenzen; Kuss; Myrthen-Kränze; Wellen und wogen*.
** Marco Polo Dig. 8.223206-2 [id.]. CSSR State PO (Košice), Oliver Dohnányi.

Volume 7: *Deutscher krieger Marsch; Kron marsch*. Polkas: *Bacchus; Furioso; Neuhauser*. Polka-Mazurka: *Kriegers liebchen*. Quadrille: *Odeon*. Waltzes: *Ballg'schichten; Colonnen; Nordseebilder; Schnee-Glöckchen; Zeitgeister*.
**(*) Marco Polo Dig. 8.223207-2 [id.]. Polish State PO, Oliver Dohnányi.

Volume 8: *Banditen-Galopp; Erzherzog Wilhelm genesungs marsch*. Polkas: *Leichtes blut; Wiedersehen; Pepita*. Quadrilles: *Nach motiven aus Verdi's 'Un ballo in maschera'; Saison*. Waltzes: *Cagliostro; Carnevals-Botschafter; Lagunen; Die Sanguiniker; Schallwellen*.
**(*) Marco Polo Dig. 8.223208-2 [id.]. Polish State PO, Oliver Dohnányi.

This extraordinary Marco Polo enterprise – to record the entire output of the Strauss family – began in 1988. Much of the music is here being put on disc for the first time and indeed the excellent back-up documentation tells us that three items on the first CD were part of the young Johann's first concert programme: the *Gunstwerber* ('Wooer of favour') *Waltz*, *Herzenslust* ('Heart's desire') polka and, even more appropriately, the *Debut-Quadrille*, so that makes Volume 1 of the series something of a collector's item, while Volume 3 also seems to have above-average interest in the selection of its programme.

Evaluation of these recordings has not been easy. The first three CDs were made by the Slovak State Philharmonic under Alfred Walter. The mood is amiable and the playing quite polished. With the arrival of Richard Edlinger and Oliver Dohnányi on the scene, the tension seems to increase, and there is much to relish. Of this second batch we would pick out Volumes 5, 7 and 8, all representing the nice touch of Oliver Dohnányi, with Volume 5 perhaps a primary choice, although there are many good things included in Volume 8.

Volume 9: *Habsburg Hoch! Marsch; Indigo marsch*. Polkas: *Albion; Anen; Lucifer*. Polka-Mazurka: *Nachtveilchen*. Quadrille: *Festival quadrille nach englischen motiven*. Waltzes: *Carnevalsbilder; Gedanken auf den Alpen; Kaiser*.
** Marco Polo Dig. 8.223209-2 [id.]. Polish State PO, Johannes Wildner.

Volume 10: *Pesther csárdás*. Polkas: *Bauern; Blumenfest; Diabolin; Juriston Ball*. Quadrille: *Nach beliebten motiven*. Waltzes: *Feuilleton; Morgenblätter; Myrthenblüthen; Panacea-klänge*.
** Marco Polo Dig. 8.223210-2 [id.]. Polish State PO (Katowice), Johannes Wildner.

Volume 11: *Revolutions Marsch*. Polkas: *Frisch heran!; Haute-volée; Herrmann; Patrioten*. Polka-Mazurka: *Waldine*. Quadrilles: *Die Afrikanerin; Handels-élite*. Waltzes: *Aus den bergen; Donauweibchen; Glossen; Klänge aus der Walachei*.
**(*) Marco Polo Dig. 8.223211-2 [id.]. CSSR State PO (Košice), Alfred Walter.

Volume 12: *Krönungs Marsch*. Polkas: *Aurora; Ella; Harmonie; Neues leben (polka française); Souvenir; Stürmisch in lieb' und tanz*. Quadrille: *Fest*. Waltzes: *Die Gemüthlichen; Hofballtänze; Man lebt nur einmal!; Wiener frauen*.
** Marco Polo Dig. 8.223212-2 [id.]. CSSR State PO (Košice), Alfred Walter.

Volume 13: *Egyptischer Marsch; Patrioten marsch*. Polkas: *Demolirer; Fidelen; Nur fort!; Tanzi-bäri; Was sich liebt, neckt sich (polka française)*. Quadrilles: *Nach motiven aus der oper 'Die Belagerung von Rochelle'; Neue melodien*. Waltzes: *Sirenen; Thermen; Die Zillerthaler*.
**(*) Marco Polo Dig. 8.223213-2 [id.]. CSSR State PO (Košice), Alfred Walter.

Volume 14: *Romance No. 1 for cello and orchestra*. Polkas: *Champagne; Geisselhiebe;*

Kinderspiele (polka française); Vöslauer. Quadrilles: *Bal champêtre; St Petersburg (quadrille nach russischen motiven).* Waltzes: *Du and du; Ernte-tänze; Frohsinns-spenden; Grillenbanner; Phänomene.*
**(*) Marco Polo Dig. 8.223214-2 [id.]. CSSR State PO (Košice), Alfred Walter.

Volume 15: *Jubelfest-Marsch.* Polkas: *Bijoux; Scherz.* Polka-Mazurkas: *Lob der frauen; La Viennoise.* Quadrilles: *Alexander; Bijouterie.* Waltzes: *Die Jovialen; Kaiser-Jubiläum; Libellen; Wahlstimmen.*
** Marco Polo Dig. 8.223215-2 [id.]. CSR SO (Bratislava), Johannes Wildner.

Volume 16: *Fürst Bariatinsky-Marsch.* Polkas: *Brautschau* (on themes from *Zigeunerbaron*); *Eljen a Magyar!; Ligourianer Seufzer; Schnellpost; Studenten. La berceuse quadrille; Zigeuner-Quadrille* (on themes from Balfe's *Bohemian Girl*). Waltzes: *Bürgerweisen; Freuden-Salven; Motoren; Sangerfährten.*
**(*) Marco Polo Dig. 8.223216 [id.]. CSSR State PO (Košice), Alfred Walter.

With Volume 9, we move to Poland and a new name, Johannes Wildner. He has his moments, but his approach seems fairly conventional. He does not make a great deal of the famous *Emperor Waltz* which closes Volume 9, although he does better with *Gedanken auf den Alpen*, another unknown but charming waltz. Alfred Walter – who began it all – then returns for Volumes 11–14. Of this batch, Volume 11 might be singled out, opening with the jolly *Herrmann-Polka*, while the *Klänge aus der Walachei, Aus den Bergen* ('From the Mountains') and *Donauweibchen* ('Nymph of the Danube') are three more winning waltzes; but the standard seems pretty reliable here, and these are all enjoyable discs. Volume 16 has another attractive batch of waltzes, at least two winning polkas and a quadrille vivaciously drawing on Balfe's *Bohemian Girl*. It also includes the extraordinary *Ligourian Seufzer polka*, in which the orchestra vocally mocks the Ligourians, a despised Jesuitical order led by Alfonso Maria di Ligouri. Another good disc.

Volume 17: *Kaiser Franz Joseph Marsch.* Polkas: *Armen-ball; 'S gibt nur a Kaiserstadt! 'S gibt nur a Wien; Violetta (polka française).* Quadrille: *Melodien.* Waltzes: *Adelen; Bürgersinn; Freiheits-lieder; Windsor-klänge.*
*** Marco Polo Dig. 8.223217-2 [id.]. CSR SO (Bratislava), Alfred Eschwé.

Volume 18: *Alliance-Marsche; Studenten-Marsch.* Polkas: *Edtweder-oder!; Invitation à la polka mazur; Leopoldstädter; Stadt und Land; Cagliostro-Quadrille.* Waltzes: *Grössfürstin Alexandra; Lava-Ströme; Patronessen; Die Pulizisten; Rathausball-Tänz.*
**(*) Marco Polo Dig. 8.223218-2 [id.]. CSSR State PO, Alfred Walter.

Volume 19: *Hoch Osterreich! Marsch.* Polkas: *Burschenwanderung (polka française), Electro-magnetische; Episode (polka française).* Quadrilles: *Le premier jour de bonheur, Opéra de Auber; Seladon.* Waltzes: *Dorfgeschichten (im Ländlerstyle); Novellen; Rosen aus dem Süden; Seid umschlungen, Millionen; Studentenlust.*
**(*) Marco Polo Dig. 8-223219-2 [id.]. Czecho-Slovak State PO (Košice), Alfred Walter.

Volume 20: *Dinorah-quadrille nach motiven der oper, 'Die Wallfahrt' nach Meyerbeer. Kaiser-Jäger Marsch. Slovianka-quadrille, nach russischen melodien.* Polkas: *Auf zum tänze; Herzel.* Polka-Mazurkas: *Ein herz, ein sinn; Fata Morgana.* Waltzes: *Aurora-ball-tänze; Erhöhte pulse; Flugschriften; Märchen aus dem Orient; Schwärmereien* (concert waltz).
** Marco Polo Dig. 8.223220-2 [id.]. Czecho-Slovak State PO (Košice), Alfred Walter.

Volume 21: *Ottinger Reiter Marsch.* Polkas: *Figaro (polka française); Patronessen (polka française); Sans-souci.* Polka-Mazurka: *Tändelei.* Quadrilles: *Orpheus; Rotunde.* Waltzes: *Cycloiden; G'schichten aus dem Wienerwald; Johannis-Käferin.*
** Marco Polo Dig. 8.223221-2 [id.]. Czecho-Slovak State PO (Košice), Johannes Wildner.

Volume 22: *Klipp-Klapp Galopp. Persischer Marsch.* Polkas: *L'Inconnue (polka française); Nachtigall.* Polka-Mazurka: *Aus der Heimat.* Quadrilles: *Carnevals-spektakel; Der lustige Krieg.* Waltzes: *Controversen; Immer heiterer (im Ländlerstyle); Maxing-tänze; Ninetta.*
** Marco Polo Dig. 8.223222-2 [id.]. Czecho-Slovak State PO (Košice), Johannes Wildner.

Volume 23: *Deutschmeister-Jubiläumsmarsch.* Polkas: *Maria Taglioni; Die Pariserin (polka française); Rasch in der tat!.* Polka-Mazurka: *Glücklich ist, wer vergisst.* Quadrilles: *Le beau monde; Indigo.* Waltzes: *Gross-Wien; Rhadamantus-klänge; Telegramme; Vibrationen; Wien, mein Sinn!*
** Marco Polo Dig. 8.223223-2 [id.]. Czecho-Slovak State PO (Košice), Johannes Wildner.

Volume 24: *Gavotte der Königin. Viribus unitis, Marsch.* Polkas: *Demi-fortune (polka française); Heski-Holki; Rokonhangok (sympathieklänge); So ängstlich sind wir nicht!.* Polka-Mazurka: *Licht und Schatten.* Quadrille: *Streina-terrassen.* Waltzes: *Idyllen; Jux-brüder; Lockvögel; Sinnen und Minnen.*

** Marco Polo Dig. 8.223224-2 [id.]. Czecho-Slovak State PO (Košice), Alfred Walter.

Volume 17 introduces another new name, Alfred Eschwé, and a particularly good collection, one of the highlights of the set, and it is beautifully played. Volume 18 brings back Alfred Walter and another very good mix of waltzes and polkas. Johannes Wildner then directs Volumes 21–3, and it must be said that the middle volume shows him in better light than the other two, and with a well-chosen programme.

Volume 25: *Grossfürsten Marsch*. Polkas: *Bonbon (polka française); Explosions; Lustger Rath (polka française); Mutig voran!* Polka-Mazurka: *Le Papillon*. Quadrilles: *Künstler; Promenade*. Waltzes: *Frauen-Käferin; Krönungslieder; Spiralen; Ins Zentrum!*
** Marco Polo Dig. 8.223225-2 [id.]. Czecho-Slovak State PO (Košice), Johannes Wildner.

Volume 26: *Es war so wunderschön Marsch*. Polkas: *Elektrophor; L'Enfantillage (polka française); Gut bürgerlich (polka française); Louischen (polka française); Pásmán*. Quadrilles: *Industrie; Sofien*. Waltzes: *Juristen-ball-tänze; Künstlerleben; Pasman; Singgedichte*.
*** Marco Polo Dig. 8.223226-2 [id.]. Austrian RSO, Vienna, Guth.

Volume 27: *Spanischer Marsch*. Polkas: *Drollerie; Durch's telephon; Express; Gruss an Wien (polka française)*. Polka-Mazurka. *Annina*. Quadrilles: *Künstler; Sans-souci*. Waltzes: *Aeolstöne; Souvenir de Nizza; Wein, Weib und Gesang; Frühlingsstimmen*.
✿ *** Marco Polo Dig 8.223227-2 [id.]. Austrian RSO, Vienna, Guth.

Volume 28: *Freiwillige vor! Marsch (1887). Frisch in's feld! Marsch*. Polkas: *Unter Donner und Blitz; Pappacoda (polka française)*. Polka-Mazurkas: *Concordia; Spleen*. Quadrille: *Tête-à-tête*. Waltzes: *Einheitsklänge: Illustrationen; Lebenswecker; Telegraphische depeschen*.
** Marco Polo Dig. 8.223228-2 [id.]. Czecho-Slovak State PO (Košice), Johannes Wildner.

Volume 29: *Brünner-Nationalgarde-Marsch. Der lustige Krieg, Marsch*. Polkas: *Die Bajadere; Hellenen; Secunden (polka française)*. Polka-Mazurka: *Une Bagatelle*. Quadrille: *Waldmeister*. Waltzes: *Deutsche; Orakel-Sprüche; Schatz; Tausend und eine Nacht; Volkssänger*.
** Marco Polo Dig. 8.223229-2 [id.]. Czecho-Slovak State PO (Košice), Alfred Walter.

Volume 30: *Fest-Marsch. Perpetuum mobile*. Polkas: *Alexandrinen; Kammerball; Kriegsabenteuer; Par force!* Quadrille: *Attaque*. Waltzes: *Erinnerung an Covent Garden; Kluh Gretelein; Luisen-sympathie-Klänge; Paroxysmen; Reiseabenteuer*.
** Marco Polo Dig. 8.223230-2 [id.]. Czecho-Slovak State PO (Košice), Alfred Walter.

Volume 31: *Napoleon-Marsch*. Polkas: *Husaren; Taubenpost (polka française); Vom Donaustrande*. Polka-Mazurka: *Nord und Süd*. Quadrilles: *Bonvivant; Nocturne*. Waltzes: *Gambrinus-tänze; Die ersten Curen; Hochzeitsreigen; Die Unzertrennlichen; Wiener bonbons*.
** Marco Polo Dig. 8.223231-2 [id.]. Czecho-Slovak State PO (Košice), Alfred Walter.

Volume 32: *Wiener Jubel-Gruss-Marsch*. Polkas: *Auf der Jagd; Olge; Tritsch-tratsch*. Polka-Mazurka: *An der Wolga*. Quadrilles: *Methusalem; Hofball*. Waltzes: *Fantasiebilder; Ich bin dir gut!; Promotionen. Wiener Blut*.
** Marco Polo Dig. 8.223232-2 [id.]. Czecho-Slovak State PO (Košice), Johannes Wildner.

Volume 26 brings another fresh name, and fresh is the right word to describe this attractive programme. From the bright-eyed opening *Elektrophor Polka schnell* this is winningly vivacious music-making and the waltz that follows, *Sinngedichte*, makes one realize that there is something special about Viennese string-playing, for this is the Orchestra of Austrian Radio. Volume 27 features the same orchestra and conductor and opens with the delectable *Künster-Quadrille*. After the aptly named *Drollerie* polka comes the *Aeolstöne* waltz with its portentous introduction, and the waltz itself is heart-warming. The *Souvenir de Nizza* waltz is hardly less beguiling and *Wine, women and song* and, to end the disc, *Frühlingsstimmen* – two top favourites – simply could not be better played. These two Peter Guth CDs are the finest of the series so far, and we award a token Rosette to the second of the two, although it could equally apply to its companion. After those two marvellous collections it is an anticlimax to return to the following volumes. There is much interesting music here, but the performances often have an element of routine.

Volume 33: *Saschen-Kürassier-Marsch*. Polkas: *Etwas kleines (polka française); Freikugeln*. Polka-Mazurka: *Champêtre*. Quadrilles: *Bouquet; Opern-Maskenball*. Waltzes: *Abschieds-Rufe; Sträusschen; An der schönen blauen Donau; Trau, schau, wem!*.
** Marco Polo Dig. 8.223233-2 [id.]. Czecho-Slovak State PO (Košice), Wildner.

Volume 34: (i) *Dolci pianti* (Romance for cello and orchestra). *Im russischen Dorfe, Fantasie*

(orch. Max Schönherr). *Russischer Marsch. Slaven-potpourri*. Polkas: *La Favorite (polka française); Niko*. Polka-Mazurka: *Der Kobold*. Quadrille: *Nikolai*. Waltzes: *Abschied von St Petersburg; Fünf paragraphen*.
*** Marco Polo Dig. 8.223234-2 [id.]. Slovak RSO (Bratislava), Dittrich, (i) with Jozef Sikora.

Volume 35: *Zivio! Marsch*. Polkas: *Jäger (polka française); Im Sturmschritt!; Die Zeitlose (polka française)*. Polka-Mazurka: *Die Wahrsagerin*. Quadrilles: *Der blits; Der liebesbrunnen*. Waltzes: *Accelerationen; Architecten-ball-tänze; Heut' ist heut' Königslieder*.
** Marco Polo Dig. 8.223235-2 [id.]. Slovak State PO (Košice), Wildner.

Volume 36: *Matador-Marsch*. Polkas: *Bitte schön! (polka française); Diplomaten; Kreuzfidel (polka française); Process*. Polka-Mazurka: *Der Klügere gibt nach*. Quadrilles: *Elfen; Fledermaus*. Waltzes: *D'Woaldbuama (im Ländlerstil)* (orch. Ludwig Babinski); *Extravaganten; Mephistos Höllenrufe; Neu-Wien*.
** Marco Polo Dig. 8.223236-2 [id.]. Slovak State PO (Košice), Alfred Walter.

Among the following batch, the CD that stands out features another new name, Michael Dittrich; working with the Slovak Radio Symphony Orchestra, he produces a splendid collection to make up Volume 34. The flexible handling of the *Slav Potpourri* shows his persuasive sympathy for Strauss, while the *Fünf Paragraphen* waltz has an equally delectable lilt. There is great charm in the elegant *La Favorite* polka and the *Abschied von St Petersburg* waltz has a nicely beguiling opening theme.

Volume 37: *Triumph-Marsch* (orch. Fischer). Polkas: *Das Comitat geht in die Höh!; Sonnnenblume; Tanz mit dem Besenstiel!* (all arr. Pollack); (i) *Romance No. 2 in G min. for cello and orchestra, Op. 35* (arr.Schönherr); Quadrilles: *Die Königin von Leon* (arr. Pollack); *Spitzentuch. Neue Steierische Tänze* (orch. Pollack); *Traumbild II;* Waltzes: *Jugend-Träume* (orch. Pollack); *Schwungräder*.
*** Marco Polo Dig. 8.223237 [id.]. Slovak State PO (Košice), Christian Pollack; (i) with Regina Jauslin.

Volume 37 is among the most interesting and worthwhile issues so far. It includes the waltz with which the nineteen-year-old Johann Junior created his first sensation at Zum Sperlbauer in Vienna. Particularly delectable is the set of *New Styrian dances*, seductively written in the Ländler style of Lanner's *Steierische Tänze*. While the *Romance for cello and orchestra* is agreeably slight, the other striking novelty here is *Traumbild II*, a late domestic work in two sections, the first of which is a gentle and charming 'dream-picture' of Strauss's wife, Adèle; the second shows the other side of her nature – more volatile and capricious. Both are in waltz time. Christian Pollack is not just a scholar but an excellent performing musician, and the playing here is polished, relaxed and spontaneous in an agreeably authentic way.

Volume 38: *Wiener Garnison-Marsch* (orch. Babinsky); *Ninetta-Galopp;* Polkas: *Damenspende; Lagerlust; Maskenzug* (2nd version); *Nimm sie hinn!; Zehner* (2nd version); Quadrilles: *Eine Nacht in Venedig; Serben* (orch. Babinski); Waltzes: *An der Elbe; Faschings-Lieder* (orch. Kulling); *Leitartikel*.
**(*) Marco Polo Dig. 8.223238 [id.]. Slovak State PO (Košice), Alfred Walter.

An der Elbe is a real find among the waltzes, a charming melodic sequence with a striking introduction. But the *Ninetta-Galopp* with its perky main theme and swirling woodwind answer has the potential to become a Strauss lollipop, while the more sedate *Maskenzug-Polka française* closes the programme engagingly. This is one of Alfred Walter's better programmes, nicely played and well recorded.

Volume 39: *Ninetta-Marsch*. Polkas: *I Tipferl; Sylphen; Unparteiische Kritiken;* Quadrilles: *Jabuka; Slaven-Ball* (both orch. Pollack); Quodlibet: *Klänge aus der Raimundzeit;* Waltzes: *Abschied; Irenen* (orch. Babinski); *Hell und voll*.
**(*) Marco Polo Dig. 8.223239 [id.]. Slovak State PO (Košice), Christian Pollack.

The two most interesting items here both date from Johann's last years, the *Abschied* (Farewell) *waltz* and the *Klänge aus der Raimundzeit* (1898), an affectionate *pot-pourri* including tunes by Johann Senior and Lanner. Johann originally called this good-humoured quodlibet 'Reminiscenz. Aus der guter alten Zeit' ('From the good old days'). The score of the waltz is written in the composer's own handwriting; his widow, Adèle, offered it to be performed posthumously in 1900. The *I Tipferl-Polka française* is based on a popular comic song from Strauss's *Prinz Methusalem*, and the couplet: 'The man forgot – the little dot, the dot upon the i!' is wittily pointed in the music. Christian Pollack directs excellent performances of all the music here which, although of varying quality, is never dull.

Volume 40: *Hochzeits-Praeludium;* Polkas: *Herzenskönigin; Liebe und Ehe; Wildfeuer;* Quadrilles: *Ninetta; Wilhelminen* (orch. Babinski); Waltzes: *Heimats-Kinder* (orch. Babinski); *The Herald* (orch. Schönherr); *Irrlichter; Jubilee* (orch. Cohen).
*(*) Marco Polo Dig. 8.223240 [id.]. Slovak RSO (Bratislava), Bauer-Theussl.

Volume 41: March: *Wo uns're Fahne weht;* Polkas: *Newa; Shawl;* Quadrilles: *Martha; Vivat!;*

Waltzes: *Burschen-Lieder; Gedankenflug; Lagunen. Traumbild* (symphonic poem). *Aschenbrödel (Cinderella): Prelude to Act III.*
** Marco Polo Dig. 8.223241 [id.]. Slovak RSO (Bratislava), Michael Dittrich.

Volume 42: *Hommage au public russe;* March: *Piccolo;* Polkas: *An der Moldau; Auroraball; Grüss aus Osterreich; Sängerlust; Soldatespiel;* Waltzes: *Gartenlaube; Hirtenspiele; Sentenzen.*
**(*) Marco Polo Dig. 8.223242 [id.]. Slovak State PO (Košice), Christian Pollack.

As it turns out, the music-making in Volume 40 under Bauer-Theussl immediately proves heavy-handed in the opening waltz, and the feeling throughout is that he is conducting for the commercial ballroom rather than the concert hall. As Pollack demonstrates in Volume 42, much more can be made of relatively strict tempo versions than Bauer-Theussl does with the *Irrlichter* and *Herald waltzes*.

Without being exactly a live wire, Michael Dittrich makes a good deal more of Volume 41. He is able to relax and at the same time coax the orchestra into phrasing with less of a feeling of routine and does very well indeed by the *Traumbild I* ('Dream picture No. 1'), a warmly relaxed and lyrical evocation, quite beautifully scored.

But when we come to Volume 42, so striking is the added vivacity that it is difficult to believe that this is the same orchestra playing. The *Gartenlaube-Walzer* is a real find; it has a charming introduction with a neat little flute solo, then the opening tune, lightly scored, is very engaging indeed. It is a great pity that Marco Polo did not hire the services of Christian Pollack much earlier in the series. Even the recording sounds better-focused here.

Volume 43: *Auf dem Tanzboden* (arr. Pollack); *Reitermarsch.* Polkas: *Herrjemineh; Postillon d'amour; Die Tauben von San Marco.* Quadrilles: *Simplicius; Des Teufels Antheil* (arr. Pollack); Waltzes: *Trifolien; Walzer-Bouquet No. 1; Wilde Rosen* (arr. Babinski & Kulling).
**(*) Marco Polo Dig. 8.223243 [id.]. Slovak State PO (Košice), Christian Pollack.

Volume 44: Polkas: *Auf freiem Fusse; Nur nicht mucken* (arr. Peak); *Von der Börse.* Quadrilles: *Hinter den Coulissen; Monstre* (with Josef STRAUSS). *Maskenfest; Schützen* (with Josef and Eduard STRAUSS). Waltzes: *Altdeutscher* (arr. Pollack); *Aschenbrödel (Cinderella); Strauss' Autograph Waltzes* (arr. Cohen).
** Marco Polo Dig. 8.223244 [id.]. Slovak State PO (Košice), Christian Pollack.

Volume 45: Ballet music from *Der Carneval in Rom* (arr. Schönherr); *Ritter Pásmán. Fest-Marsch. Pásmán-Quadrille* (arr. Pollack); *Potpourri-Quadrille; Zigeunerbaron-Quadrille.* Waltzes: *Eva; Ischler.*
**(*) Marco Polo Dig. 8.223245 [id.]. Slovak State PO (Košice), Alfred Walter.

With Christian Pollack directing with his usual light touch, Volume 43 is one of the best of the more recent Marco Polo issues, even if the *Walzer-Bouquet* is less winningly tuneful than its title suggests. *Wilde Rosen* is rather better, though not really memorable like *An dem Tanzboden* ('On the dance floor'), which was inspired by a painting. It is a real lollipop with a charming introduction (with clarinet solo) and matching postlude.

Volume 44 includes the brief (three-minute) but pleasant *Altdeutscher Waltz*, arranged by the conductor, and the relatively familiar *Aschenbrödel*, which is attractive but not one of Strauss's vintage waltzes. As usual with Pollack, the various quadrilles and polkas are agreebly relaxed but never dull, and the recording is up to standard.

Alfred Walter returns to conduct Volume 45, and he is at his finest in the lively and tuneful waltz which is the central movement of the *Ritter Pásmán ballet*. The other ballet music, from *Der Carneval in Rom*, is scored by Schönherr – and very vividly too. The *Eva waltz* is brief but delightfully graceful; *Ischler*, however, is more conventional. The quadrilles are nicely managed and the sound is very good.

Volume 46: March: *Vaterländischer.* Polkas: *Pawlowsk; Pizzicato* (with Josef); *Probirmamsell.* Quadrilles: *Marien; Annika.* Romance: *Sehnsucht.* Waltzes: *Cagliostro; Engagement; Greeting to America.* (i) Gradual: *Tu qui regis totum orbem.* SCHUMANN, arr. Johann STRAUSS: *Widmung.*
*** Marco Polo Dig. 8.223246 [id.]. Slovak RSO (Bratislava), Michael Dittrich; (i) with Slovak Philh. Ch. (members).

Michael Dittrich is on top form in Volume 46 of this ongoing series, opening vivaciously with a musical switch in march form, beginning with the *Radetzky* 'fanfare' and proceeding to quote intriguing snippets from all kinds of sources, including the Austrian national anthem. The *Greeting to America waltz* has a very appropriate and recognizable introduction and is as attractive as the delightfully scored *Engagement waltz*, also written for America. The Gradual, *Tu qui regis totum orbem* ('Thou who rulest the whole world'), is a surprise inclusion from the eighteen-year-old composer – an offertory sung in conjunction with the performance of a Mass by his teacher, Professor Dreschler – and very pleasing it is. The concert ends with one of the deservedly better-known waltzes, taken from the operetta *Cagliostro in Wien* and played in an elegantly vivacious but nicely flexible style, like the rest of this very appealing programme, one of the very best of the Marco Polo series. The recording is excellent.

Volume 47: Ballet music from *Die Fledermaus;* from *Indigo und die vierzig Räuber* (arr.

Schönherr). *Eine Nacht in Venedig: Processional march.* GOUNOD, arr. Johann STRAUSS: *Faust (Romance). Quadrille on themes from Faust.* Marches: *Kaiser Alexander Huldinungs; Kaiser Frans Joseph Jubiläums; Der Zigeunerbaron.* Waltzes: *Coliseum waltzes; Farewell to America; Sounds from Boston.*

*** Marco Polo Dig. 8.223247 [id.]. Bratislava City Ch., Slovak RSO (Bratislava), Johannes Wildner.

This is another very attractive compilation with many beguiling novelties. After the brief but lively march from *Der Zigeunerbaron* comes *Farewell to America*, an agreeable pastiche waltz which waits until its coda to quote *The Star-spangled Banner*. The engaging *Coliseum waltzes* uncannily anticipate the *Blue Danube*, complete with an opening horn theme. *Sounds from Boston*, written for the composer's Boston visit in 1872, is another pastiche waltz of considerable charm. All this music is liltingly and sparklingly presented by the Slovak Radio Orchestra, and no one could accuse the conductor, Johannes Wildner, of dullness.

Volume 48: Complete Overtures, Volume 1: *Concert overture: Opéra comique* (arr. Pollack). *Intermezzo* from *Tausend und eine Nacht.* Overtures: *Blindekuh; Cagliostro in Wien; Der Carneval in Rom; Die Fledermaus; Indigo und die vierzig Räuber. Prince Methusalem; Das Spitzentuch der Königen.*

**(*) Marco Polo Dig. 8.223248 [id.]. Slovak State PO (Košice), Alfred Walter.

Collections of operetta overtures are almost always entertainingly tuneful, and this one is no exception. It begins with a curiosity that may or may not be authentic, an *Overture comique* written by the young Johann Jr for large harmonium (a kind of orchestrion) and piano, and afterwards arranged by the Strauss scholar, Fritz Lange, for violin and piano. None of the ideas it contains can be traced to the composer's notebooks, but the piece is attractive and is well put together in the form of a concert overture. It is heard here in a new arrangement (following the Lange manuscript) by Christopher Pollack. Walter conducts the other overtures very agreeably and makes the most of their pretty scoring yet one feels that some of the livelier ideas might have been given a bit more zip.

Volume 49: Complete overtures, Volume 2: *Aschenbrödel (Cinderella): Quadrille.* Overtures: *Die Göttin der Vernunft (The Goddess of reason); Der lustige Krieg. Jabuka: Prelude to Act III. Eine Nacht in Venedig: Overture* and *Prelude to Act III.* Overtures: *Simplicius; Waldmeister; Der Zigeunerbaron.*

**(*) Marco Polo Dig. 8.223275 [id.]. Slovak State PO (Košice), Alfred Walter.

Alfred Walter's second collection of overtures has distinctly more sparkle than the first. What one rediscovers on listening through this pair of discs is not only the fecundity of Johann's invention and the charm of his orchestration, but also the felicitous way he turns a pot-pourri into a naturally spontaneous sequence of ideas. The recording throughout both collections is first class, spacious and with a ballroom warmth.

Volume 50: (i) *Am Donaustrand;* (i) *Erste Liebe (Romanze); Erster Gedanke;* (i) *Ein gstanzi von Tanzl; Die Fledermaus: Csárdás and New Csárdás. Frisch gewagt* (Galop); *Da nicken die Giebel* (Polka-Mazurka); *Die Göttin der Vernunft* (Quadrille); (i) *Dolci pianti;* Waltzes: (i) *Frühlingsstimmen;* (i) *King Gretelein; Nachgelassener; Odeon-Waltz;* (i) *Wo die Citronen blüh'n;* (i) *Wenn du ein herzig Liebchen hast.*

*** Marco Polo Dig. 8.223276 [id.]. (i) Marilyn Hill Smith; Slovak RSO (Bratislava), Christian Pollack.

Marilyn Hill Smith sings a number of items, and her light soubrette is just right for this repertoire. She presents *Wo die Citronen blüh'n* with much vivacity and is hardly less sparkling in the famous *Voices of spring*. Pollack makes the most of the waltzes and is especially characterful in the polka-mazurka, *Da nicken die Giebel*, which sounds a bit like a slow waltz with extra accents. Again, first-rate recording.

Volume 51: *Auf der Alm* (Idyll); *Fürstin Ninetta* (Entr'acte); Galop: *Liebesbotschaft;* (i) Choral polka: *Champêtre (Wo klingen die Lieder).* Polka-mazurka: *Promenade-Abenteuer.* (ii) *Romance No. 2 for cello and orchestra.* Choral waltz: (i) *An der schönen, blauen Donau.* Waltzes: *Centennial; Enchantment; Engagement; Farewell to America; Manhattan; Tauben.* Songs: (iii) *Bauersleut' im Künstlerhaus; D'Hauptsach* (both arr. Rott).

✿ *** Marco Polo Dig. 8.223279 [id.]. Slovak RSO (Bratislava), Jerome Cohen; with (i) Slovak Philharmonic Ch.; (ii) Ivan Tvrdik; (iii) Adrian Eröd.

It is rather appropriate that Volume 51 should be special, and so it is. It opens with the enchanting choral *Polka mazurka champêtre*, introduced by the horns and gloriously sung by a male chorus with a nicely managed diminuendo at the coda. And it ends with Strauss's masterpiece, the *Blue Danube*, also for male-voice choir and sung with an infectious lilt, to leave the listener in high spirits. All the other half-dozen waltzes here are virtually unknown, and every one is delightful. Of the two brief baritone solos the second, *D'Hauptsach*, has a most pleasing melody. No other record in the series so far offers such a fine package of unexpected delights or more hidden treasure, and there could be no better advocate than the present conductor, Jerome Cohen. He has the advantage of spacious, naturally balanced recording. A Rosette then for the sheer enterprise of the first half-century of this series and also for the special excellence of this collection with its discovery of six remarkably fine waltzes.

Potpourris, Volume 1: *Cagliostro in Wien; Indigo und die vierzig Räuber; Der lustige Krieg; Eine Nacht in Venedig; Prinz Methusalem; Das Spitzentuch der Königin.*
(N) *(*) Marco Polo Dig. 8.225074 [id.]. Slovak State PO (Kosice), Christian Pollack.

Potpourris, Volume 2: *Fürstin Ninetta; Die Göttin der Vernunft; Jabuka (Das Apfelfest); Ritter Pásmán; Simplicius.*
(N) *(*) Marco Polo Dig. 8.225075 [id.]. Slovak State PO (Kosice), Christian Pollack.

Even today, selections from musical shows are the mainstay of the bandstand, and so it was in the days of the Strauss family. However, although they include a fair smattering of good tunes, some of the pot-pourris here outlast their welcome (*Indigo und die vierzig Räuber* runs for over 18 minutes) and the scoring of the vocal numbers is seldom very imaginative. Curiously even Christian Pollack, usually an inspired Straussian, is below his best form, and he fails to make a case for them. In the end this becomes nothing more than wallpaper music. So this pair of discs, although well enough played, is of documentary interest only.

Boskovsky Strauss Edition

Galops: *Aufs Korn; Banditen*. Marches: *Egyptischer; Franz Joseph I Rettungs-Jubel; Napoleon; Persischer; Russischer; Spanischer. Perpetuum mobile*. Polkas: *Annen; Auf der Jagd; Bitte schön!; Champagner; Demolirer; Eljen a Magyar; Explosionen; Freikugeln; Im Krapfenwaldl; Leichtes Blut; Lob der Frauen; Ohne Sorgen; Pizzicato* (with Josef); *Neue Pizzicato; So ängst sind wir nicht; 'S gibt nur a Kaiserstadt, 's gibt nur a Wien!; Stürmisch in Lieb' und Tanz; Tik-Tak; Tritsch-Tratsch; Unter Donner und Blitz (Thunder and lightning); Vernügungszug*. Quadrilles: *Fledermaus; Orpheus; Schützen* (with Josef & Eduard). Waltzes: *Accelerationen; An der schönen Blauen Donau (Blue Danube); Bei uns z'Haus; Carnavals-Botschafter; Du und Du; Errinerung an Covent-Garden; Freuet euch des Lebens; Frühlingsstimmen (Voices of spring); Geschichten aus dem Wienerwald (Tales from the Vienna Woods); Kaiser (Emperor); Künsterleben (Artist's life); Lagunen; Liebeslieder; Mephistos Höllenrufe; Morgenblätter (Morning papers); Nordseebilder; Rosen aus dem Süden (Roses from the South); Seid umschlungen, Millionen!; Schneeglöckchen; 1001 Nacht; Wein, Weib und Gesang (Wine, women and song); Wiener Blut (Vienna blood); Wiener Bonbons; Wo die Citronen blüh'n!*. Johann STRAUSS Sr: Galops: *Sperl; Wettrennen. Radetzky march*. Polka: *Piefke und Pufka*. Waltz: *Loreley-Rhein-Klänge*. Josef STRAUSS: Polkas: *Auf Ferienreisen; Brennende Liebe; Eingesendt; Die Emancipirte; Extempore; Feuerfest; Frauenherz; Heiterer Mut; Im Fluge; Jokey; Die Libelle; Moulinet; Rudolfsheimer; Die Schwätzerin*. Waltzes: *Aquarellen; Delirien; Dorfschwalben aus Osterreich (Village swallows); Dynamiden; Mein Liebenslauf ist Lieb und Lust; Sphärenklänge (Music of the spheres); Transactionen*. Eduard STRAUSS: Polkas: *Bahn Frei!; Mit Extrapost*. Waltz: *Fesche Geister*.
(B) **(*) Decca 455 254-2 (6) [id.]. VPO, Willi Boskovsky.

These six vintage CDs (offering 86 titles) span Willi Boskovsky's long (analogue) recording career for Decca, stretching over two decades from the late 1950s onwards, when his records dominated the LP discography in the Strauss family repertoire.

Even so, Boskovsky's achievement in this repertoire remains unique, both in its range – the output of Josef, particularly his polkas, is notably well covered – and the almost unfailing sparkle of the performances. The present CD transfers are very vivid and immediate, and their brightness has also served to add a hint of coarseness to some of the lively music (for instance the engaging quadrilles on disc 6). The ear adjusts, however, when the music-making is so zestful and alive: in spite of such reservations, there is no finer or more all-embracing collection of the best of the output of the Strauss family than in this box.

New Year's Day concert in Vienna (1979): Polkas: *Auf der Jagd* (with encore); *Bitte schön! Leichtes Blut; Pizzicato* (with Josef); *Tik-Tak*. Waltzes: *An der schönen blauen Donau; Bei uns zu Haus; Loreley-Rheine-Klänge; Wein, Weib und Gesang*. Josef STRAUSS: *Moulinet polka; Die Emanzipierte polka-mazurka; Rudolfsheimer-Polka; Sphärenklänge waltz*. Johann STRAUSS, Snr: *Radetzky march*. Eduard STRAUSS: *Ohne Bremse polka* (with ZIEHRER: *Herreinspaziert! waltz;* SUPPE: *Die schöne Galathée overture*).
(B) *** Decca 448 572-2 (2). VPO, Willi Boskovsky.

Decca chose to record Boskovsky's 1979 New Year's Day concert in Vienna for their very first digital issue on LP. The clarity, immediacy and natural separation of detail are very striking throughout, and the strings of the Vienna Philharmonic are brightly lit. The music-making itself is another matter. It reaches its peak when the side-drum thunders out the introduction to the closing *Radetzky march*, a frisson-creating moment which, with the audience participation, is quite electrifying.

'1987 New Year Concert in Vienna': Overture: *Die Fledermaus*. Polkas: *Annen; Pizzicato* (with Josef); *Unter Donner und Blitz; Vergnügungszug*. Waltzes: *An der schönen blauen Donau;* (i) *Frühlingsstimmen*. J. STRAUSS Snr: *Beliebte Annen* (polka); *Radetzky march*. Josef STRAUSS: *Ohne Sorgen polka;* Waltzes: *Delirien; Sphärenklänge*.
*** DG Dig. 419 616-2 [id.]. VPO, Karajan; (i) with Kathleen Battle.

In preparation for this outstanding concert, which was both recorded and televised, Karajan re-studied the scores of his favourite Strauss pieces; the result, he said afterwards, was to bring an overall renewal to his musical life beyond the scope of this particular repertoire. The concert itself produced music-making of the utmost magic; familiar pieces sounded almost as if they were being played for the first time. Kathleen Battle's contribution to *Voices of spring* brought wonderfully easy, smiling coloratura and much charm. *The Blue Danube* was, of course, an encore, and what an encore! Never before has it been played so seductively on record. In the closing *Radetzky march*, wonderfully crisp yet relaxed, Karajan kept the audience contribution completely in control merely by the slightest glance over his shoulder. This indispensable collection makes an easy first choice among Strauss compilations. Unfortunately the current presentation is without proper musical documentation, which is a disgrace. We have consequently removed our Rossette.

'1989 New Year Concert in Vienna': Overture: *Die Fledermaus*. Csárdás: *Ritter Pásmán*. Polkas: *Bauern; Eljen a Magyar!; Im Krapfenwald'l; Pizzicato* (with Josef). Waltzes: *Accelerationen; An der schönen blauen Donau; Frühlingsstimmen; Künstlerleben*. Josef STRAUSS: Polkas: *Jockey; Die Libelle; Moulinet; Plappermäulchen*. Johann STRAUSS, Snr: *Radetzky march*.
**(*) Sony/CBS CD 45938 [id.]. VPO, Carlos Kleiber.

Kleiber's pursuit of knife-edged precision prevents the results from sounding quite relaxed enough, with the Viennese lilt in the waltzes analysed to the last micro-second instead of just being played as a dance. In the delicious polka, *Im Krapfenwald'l*, the cheeky cuckoo-calls which comically punctuate the main theme are made to sound beautiful rather than rustic, and fun is muted elsewhere too. But in one or two numbers Kleiber really lets rip, as in the Hungarian polka, *Eljen a Magyar!* ('Hail to Hungary!'), and in the *Ritter Pásmán Csárdás*. This concert now reappears on a single full-price disc, playing for 76 minutes and omitting just one waltz, *Bei uns zu Haus*. Not everyone responds positively to Kleiber's rather precise style with Viennese rhythms, but this is still an enjoyably spontaneous concert, made the more attractive by the warm, full recording, with the presence of the audience nicely implied without getting in the way.

'1990 New Year Concert': *Einzugsmarsch* (from *Der Zigeunerbaron*). Polkas: *Explosionen; Im Sturmschritt; Tritsch-tratsch*. Waltzes: *An der schönen blauen Donau; Donauweibchen; G'schichten aus dem Wienerwald; Wiener Blut*. Josef STRAUSS: Polkas: *Eingesendet; Die Emancipitre; Sport; Sympathie*. Johann STRAUSS Snr: *Indianer galop. Radetzky march*.
*** Sony Dig. SK 45808. [id.]. VPO, Zubin Mehta.

A worthy successor to Karajan's wonderful 1987 concert, not *quite* its equal but offering a programme of mainly novelties. This was Mehta's finest record for years; he conjures a magical response from the VPO and is just as persuasive in the famous waltzes. The recording is superb.

'1992 New Year Concert': Overture: *Der Zigeunerbaron*. Polkas: *Neue pizzicato; Stadt und Land; Tritsch-Tratsch; Unter Donner und Blitz; Vergnügungszug*. Waltzes: *An der schönen blauen Donau; Tausend und eine Nacht. Persischer march*. J. STRAUSS Snr: *Radetsky march*. Joseph STRAUSS: Waltzes: *Dorfschwalben aus Osterreich; Sphärenklänge* (with NICOLAI: Overture: *The Merry Wives of Windsor*).
**(*) Sony Dig. SK 48376 [id.]. VPO, Carlos Kleiber.

As with his earlier (1989) concert, Kleiber is very precise, and occasionally one wishes for a degree more relaxation. He opens his programme with a beautifully played account of Nicolai's *Merry Wives of Windsor overture*, and the introductions for *1001 Nights* and Josef's so-called '*Village swallows*' and '*Music of the spheres*' are nicely managed and attractively atmospheric. There is plenty of dash in the polkas; but at times elsewhere rubato seems just a trifle calculated, especially so in the *Blue Danube*. The playing and recording are well up to standard, and admirers of the Kleiber Strauss style, which certainly does not lack vitality, will be well pleased. All Straussians will find much to enjoy here.

'1994 New Year's Day Concert': *Caroussel-Marsch; Lieder-Quadrille, nach beliebten Motiven*. Polkas: *Ein Herr und ein Sinn; Enfantillage; Luzifer*. Waltzes: *Accelerationen; An der schönen blauen Donau; G'schichten aus dem Wienerwald; Die Fledermaus: Csárdás*. Johann STRAUSS Snr: *Radetzky march*. Josef STRAUSS: Polkas: *Aus der Ferne; Feuerfest!; Ohne Sorgen*. Eduard STRAUSS: *Mit Chic polka*. with LANNER: *Die Schönbrunner* (waltz).
*** Sony Dig. SK 46694 [id.]. VPO, Lorin Maazel.

Lorin Maazel makes the 1994 New Year concert one of the most effervescent ever, relaxing in a jovial way that one would hardly have expected. His triumph is crowned when in *Tales from the Vienna Woods* he takes up the violin and with Werner Hink from the orchestra plays the slinky duet sections at the beginning and end in an *echt*-Viennese manner. Curiously, the disc fails to mention Maazel's other extra contribution: in the quick polka by Josef Strauss, *Ohne Sorgen* ('Without a care'), Maazel – using an instrument at his elbow, as the television relay revealed – provides decorations on the glockenspiel. Aptly the recording highlights the glockenspiel notes. That polka is just one of the sparkling rarities in the collection – ten of them out of a total of 15 items. The *Schönbrunner waltz* of Joseph Lanner is a first-ever recording, light and charming if not specially characterful, but other rare delights include the French polka *Feuerfest* by Josef Strauss with its clanging hammers and anvils, the *Lucifer polka* with bangs on the drum, and the galumphing *Caroussel march*, both by Johann Strauss Junior. Applause has been tactfully edited, but some may find there is still too much.

'1995 New Year's Day concert': An der schönen blauen Donau; Mephistos Höllenrufe; Morgenblätter; Perpetuum mobile; Process; Reitermarsch; Russische Marsche-Phantasie; Schützen; Josef STRAUSS: *Arm in Arm; Auf Ferienreisen; Mein Lebenslauf ist Lieb' und Lust; Thalia.* Eduard STRAUSS: *Electrisch polka;* Johann STRAUSS Snr: *Alice polka; Radetzky march.*
*** Sony SK 66860 [id.]. VPO, Zubin Mehta (with LANNER: *Favorit-Polka*).

Even more than usual, the 1995 New Year Concert reflected the personality of its conductor, Zubin Mehta, a bluff and jolly master of ceremonies. In the programme there is a high proportion of rarities, including two total novelties, buried for a century in some archive in Coburg. The slinky and lyrical Mazurka polka, *Thalia*, by Josef Strauss is particularly delightful, and Eduard Strauss's *Electrisch polka* is as breezily energetic as one would expect. Other rare charmers include the *Alice polka* with Czech overtones, by Johann Strauss the elder, dedicated to Princess Alice, daughter of Queen Victoria, and the *Russian March-fantasy* by Johann Strauss the younger, even more Slavonic in flavour. Lanner's *Favorit polka* includes an authentic Rossini crescendo, and even in this context the swinging waltz, *Mephistos Höllenrufe* (*Mephisto's calls from Hell*), might win a prize for oddity of title. *Morgenblätter* (*Morning Papers*) remains well known, but it is odd, when its main tune is so haunting, that Josef Strauss's waltz, *Mein Lebenslauf ist Lieb' und Lust*, is not played much more. If Mehta's traditional rounding off for the *Perpetuum mobile* polka comes in a little too quickly, and the audience starts clapping in the *Radetzky march* too soon (remember the way Karajan controlled them!), that plainly reflects the exuberance of the occasion, well caught on a very well-filled disc.

'1996 New Year Concert': Fest-Marsch; Overtures: *Göttin der Vernunft; Waldmeister.* Polkas: *Blumenfest; Furioso Secunden.* Waltzes: *An der schönen blauen Donau; Kaiser; Lagunen; Phönix-Schwingen.* Johann STRAUSS Sr: *Radetzky march.* Eduard STRAUSS: *Mit Vergnügen* (polka). Josef STRAUSS: Polkas: *Jokey; Die Nasswalderin; Die tanzende Muse.*
*** RCA Dig. 09026 68421-2 [id.]. VPO, Maazel (with ZIEHRER: *Wiener Burger*).

Very vividly recorded, for the first time by RCA, the 1996 New Year concert is exceptional for the number of novelties included in the programme. It is amazing how this annual event changes Lorin Maazel from a scowling figure to that of a cosy Viennese: he is pictured on the sleeve, violin in hand, grinning with delight; and the performances, relaxed and idiomatic, consistently reflect his ease. He plays the violin solo in Strauss's little-known *Goddess of Reason Overture*, one of half a dozen delightful rarities that he has unearthed, never before heard at the New Year concerts. Others include the jaunty *Blumenfest polka* and the *Wings of the phoenix waltz*, with one theme like 'Chopsticks' transformed. A free supplementary CD has the encores, the *Furioso polka* and, of course, the *Radetzky march.*

'New Year's concert '97': March: *Russischer.* Polkas: *Die Bajadere; Bluette; Fata Morgana; Neue Pizzicato; Patronessen; 's gibt nur a Kaiserstadt, 's gibt a Wien!.* Waltzes: *An der schönen, blauen Donau; Freuet euch des Lebens; Hofballtänze; Motoren.* Josef STRAUSS: Polkas: *Carrière; Eingesendet; Frauenherz; Vorwärts!.* Waltz: *Dynamiden.* STRAUSS, Johann Sr: *Radetzky march* (with SUPPE: *Light cavalry overture.* HELLMESBERGER: Polka: *Leichtfüssig*).
*** EMI Dig. CDC5 56336-2 (2) [id.]. VPO, Riccardo Muti.

Riccardo Muti here breaks away from his more usual severity into music-making wreathed in smiles. In the subtlety of his rhythmic pointing he transcends even what we expect of the Vienna Philharmonic in waltz-time. Muti in his approach to this repertory regularly concentrates on the refinement of the writing, bringing out inner strands, graduating pianissimos, encouraging the Vienna Philharmonic's reputation as the most refined orchestra in the world. In recent years the programmes have been including more and more rarities from the countless scores in the Strauss archives, yet this programme goes further than ever before. In its 100 or so minutes the rarities vastly outnumber the well-known favourites, making this an issue to attract far more than the usual devotees of the

Viennese New Year. There are no fewer than eight Strauss items entirely new to these concerts, and it is only at the end, as the traditional second encore, when Muti (with a spoken greeting) introduces the *Blue Danube*, that we are on familiar ground. Add to that Suppé's *Light cavalry overture*, transformed from its military band associations, and you have a mixture guaranteed to delight, helped by vivid recording with plenty of air round the sound.

'1998 New Year Concert': *Wo uns're Fahne marsch*. Overture: *Prinz Methusalem*. Polka: *Trisch-Tratsch*. Polka schnell: *Nur fort!*. Waltzes: *An der schönen blauen Donau; Nachtfalter; Nordseebilder; Rosen aus dem süden; Wiener bonbons*. Josef HELLMESBERGER: *Kleiner galop*. Josef STRAUSS: Polkas Mazur: *Die Schwebenda; In der Heimat!*. Polkas schnell: *Jocas; Plappermäulchen*. Quadrille: *Neue melodien*. Johann STRAUSS Snr: *Annen-Polka; Radetzky marsch; Marianka-Polka*. Eduard STRAUSS: *Polka schnell: Bahn frei!*.
(N) (B) *** RCA Dig. Double 09026 63144-2 (2) [id.]. V. Boys' Ch., VPO, Zubin Mehta.

Zubin Mehta, trained in Vienna, lives up to tradition in this his third 'New Year's Concert', mixing novelties – no fewer than eight items totally new to the event – with old favourites, all immaculately presented. It is a novelty too having the Vienna Boys choir adding sparkle to two of the well-known polkas. The two-disc format at no extra charge allows the whole concert to be included, traditional encores and all.

'1999 New Year Concert': *Banditen-Galopp; Perpetuum mobile*; Polkas: *Hopser*; (i) *Scherz* (for violin and orchestra); *Tritsch-Tratsch; Unter Donner und Blitz*; Waltzes: *An der schönen blauen Donau; Donauweibchen; Geschichten aus dem Wiener Wald; Künsterleben; Sinngedichte*. Johann STRAUSS Snr: *Furioso-Galopp* (after Liszt); *Radetzky-Marsch; Walzer à la Paganini* (for violin and orchestra).
(N) *** RCA Dig. 74321 61687-2 [id.]. VPO, Lorin Maazel (i) violin; & cond.

Lorin Maazel in this, his tenth New Year's Concert in Vienna, consistently captures the right atmosphere, boldly taking up his solo violin in the *Scherz-Polka* and *Walzer à la Paganini*, entering into the fun in a way to lighten his once severe image. To mark the centenary of the death of the younger Johann, the programme starts with the very first of his hundreds of opuses, the '*Epigram Waltz*', *Sinngedichte*, just as winningly lyrical as many later favourites. Some New Year's Concerts take you by storm with their bite and energy, but this one makes its point above all by charming, whether in the languorous introduction to *Tales from the Vienna Woods* or such rarities as the late *Donauweibchen* ('*Little Woman of the Danube*), the waltz on themes from the operetta, *Simplicius*, and the insinuating *Hopser-Polka*. The uproarious *Banditen-Polka* with its police-whistles and gunshots then raises the temperature, before the final traditional jamboree.

Marches: *Egyptischer; Persischer*. Polkas: *Auf der Jagd; Pizzicato* (with Josef); *Unter Donner und Blitz; Postillon d'amour; Leichtes Blut*. Waltzes: *G'schichten aus dem Wienerwald; Morgenblätter; Wiener Blut*. Josef STRAUSS: *Sphärenklänge*.
(M) *** DG 449 768-2 [id.]. BPO, Karajan.

Karajan was almost always a persuasive conductor of Strauss waltzes and polkas, if not as consistently reliable as Boskovsky. But in making a selection for the 'Originals' series the DG producers have perceptively chosen the present collection, based on an LP originally published in 1971. A few prize items have been added, notably the engaging *Postillon d'amour polka*, which is bounced in true dance rhythm, and Josef's *Sphärenklänge*, which Karajan shapes most affectionately, particularly the lovely opening. But the original disc is most notable for the central section of the *Egyptian march* when, after opening boldly and providing some delightfully colourful detail, Karajan pulls back so that the Berlin orchestral players can make a robust vocal contribution to the middle section. The piece is then charmingly pared down, like a patrol disappearing into the distance. The *Pizzicato polka* is played very gently, as a foil to the more lively items which surround it. Of the waltzes, *Wiener Blut* lilts attractively, and *Tales from the Vienna woods* is coaxed most seductively with a particularly delicate zither solo. The sound is excellent, and altogether this is the best Karajan Johann Strauss disc in the DG catalogue, apart from his famous 1987 New Year concert in Vienna, which is unsurpassable.

Napoleon-Marsch. Polkas: *Annen; Explosionen; Tritsch-Tratsch*. Waltzes: *An der schönen blauen Donau; Morgenblätter; 1001 Nights; Wein, Weib und Gesang; Wiener Bonbons*. Josef STRAUSS: *Dorfschwalben aus Osterreich*. Johann STRAUSS Snr: *Radetzky march*.
(B) *** Decca 433 609-2. VPO, Willi Boskovsky.

A particularly enjoyable concert of Boskovsky repertoire, chosen and ordered with skill, opening with the *Blue Danube* and closing with the rousing *Radetzky march*. The VPO are on their toes throughout. The recording dates range from 1958 to 1976; some are spikier than others in the upper range, but the warm Sofiensaal ambience is always flattering.

(i) *Overture: Die Fledermaus*. Waltzes: (ii) *An der schönen blauen Donau; Carnavals-Botschafter; Donauweibchen; Du and du; Feuilleton; Flugschriften;* (i) *Geschichten au dem Wienerwald; Kaiser;* (ii) *Die Leitartikel;*

Morgenblätter; (i) *1001 Nacht;* (ii) *Wein, Weib und Gesang; Wiener Frauen.* Polkas: (i) *Im Krapfenwald'l; Leichtes Blut.* Josef STRAUSS: Waltzes: *Dynamiden; Sphärenklänge.* Johann STRAUSS Sr: *Radetzky march.*

(BB) *** EMI Seraphim Dig./Analogue CES 68535-2 (2) [CDEB 68535]. (i) VPO, Rudolf Kempe; (ii) J. Strauss O of V., Willi Boskovsky.

A fascinating juxtaposition of two quite different styles of Johann Strauss performance. From the very opening of the *Blue Danube*, the playing of Boskovsky's Johann Strauss Orchestra balances an evocative Viennese warmth with vigour and sparkle; he is at his very best exploring the novelties – *Donauweibchen* and *Wiener Frauen* are particularly winning – with a few familiar numbers like the vivacious *Morgenblätter*, *Du and du* and *Wein, Weib und Gesang* thrown in. The latter, incidentally, has an abbreviated introduction. The digital recording from the early 1980s is excellent. Kempe opens the second disc with a vivaciously volatile account of the *Die Fledermaus overture*, but in the waltzes he is unashamedly indulgent, especially in the introductions of the two Josef Strauss items, and *1001 Nacht*. With quite gorgeous playing from the VPO strings this is almost decadently voluptuous, moving to a sumptuous climax. Both polkas are infectious and *Im Krapfenwald'l*, with its cuckoo calls, brings an affectionate smile. The recordings, from 1958 and 1961, sound amazingly good. With a playing time of nearly 143 minutes, this is outstanding value.

Overtures: *Die Fledermaus; Der Zigeunerbaron.* Waltzes: *An der schönen blauen Donau; Geschichten aus dem Wiener Wald; Kaiser; Wiener Blut.*

(M) (***) Bruno Walter Edition: Sony mono SMK 64467 [id.]. Columbia SO, Bruno Walter (with BRAHMS: *Hungarian dances Nos. 1, 3, 10 & 17* (***); SMETANA: *Vltava.* (**))

It is good to have a reminder of Bruno Walter's way with Johann Strauss, full of vivacity, and with *Wiener Blut* obviously the conductor's favourite among the waltzes here, as he coaxes the opening beguilingly and then draws some ravishing playing from the violins. The two overtures are bright and volatile. No apologies whatsoever about the 1956 mono recording, which is warm and spacious and sounds almost like early stereo.

Pappacoda polka; Der lustige Kreig (quadrille); *Klug Gretelein* (waltz). Josef STRAUSS: *Defilir marsch;* Polkas: *Farewell; For ever.* Eduard STRAUSS: *Weyprecht-Payer marsch;* Polkas: *Mädchenlaune; Saat und Ernte;* Waltzes: *Die Abonnenten; Blüthenkranz Johann Strauss'scher.* J. STRAUSS III (son of Eduard): *Schlau-Schlau polka.*

*** Chandos Dig. CHAN 8527. Johann Strauss O of V., Rothstein, with M. Hill-Smith.

This programme is admirably chosen to include unfamiliar music which deserves recording; indeed, both the *Klug Gretelein waltz*, which opens with some delectable scoring for woodwind and harp and has an idiomatic vocal contribution from Marilyn Hill-Smith, and *Die Abonnenten* (by Eduard) are very attractive waltzes. *Blüthenkranz Johann Strauss'scher*, as its title suggests, makes a potpourri of some of Johann's most famous melodies. The polkas are a consistent delight, played wonderfully infectiously; indeed, above all this is a cheerful concert, designed to raise the spirits; the CD sound sparkles.

Perpetuum mobile. Polkas: *Annen; Auf der Jagd; Pizzicato* (with Josef); *Tritsch-Tratsch; Unter Donner und Blitz.* Waltzes: *An der schönen blauen Donau; G'schichten aus dem Wienerwald; Kaiser; Wiener Blut.* Josef STRAUSS: *Delirien waltz.*

(M) **(*) DG (IMS) 437 255-2 [id.]. BPO, Karajan.

Here is a selection taken from two analogue LPs which Karajan made in 1966 and 1969 respectively. The performances have characteristic flair and the playing of the Berlin Philharmonic has much ardour as well as subtlety, with the four great waltzes of Johann II all finely done (the *Emperor* has a particularly engaging closing section) and the polkas wonderfully vivacious. The current remastering is satisfactory, brightly lit, but with the Jesus-Christus Kirche providing ambient fullness.

Polkas: *Fledermaus* (from *Die Fledermaus*); *Kreigsabenteur* (from *Der Zigeunerbaron*); *Pizzicato* (with Josef); *Unter Donner und Blitz.* Waltzes: *Accelerationen; Rosen aus dem Süden; 1001 Nacht; Wo die Zitronen blüh'n.* Eduard STRAUSS: Polka: *Bahn frei.* Waltz: *Doktrinen.* Josef STRAUSS: Waltzes: *Dynamiden; Sphärenklänge.*

✿ (M) *** RCA 09026 61688-2 [id.]. Boston Pops O, Arthur Fiedler.

Arthur Fiedler, the doyen of the Boston Pops, never made a better record than this. He shapes the introductions to these famous walzes with captivating charm. Strauss records don't come any better than this, and the warm Boston acoustics, superbly caught in the early days of stereo (1956–9), add a special allure to all this music-making.

Polkas: *Czech; Pizzicato* (with Josef). Waltzes: *Kaiser; Rosen aus dem Süden; Sängerlust; Wiener Blut; Wiener Bonbons.* J. STRAUSS Sr: *Radetzky march.* Josef STRAUSS: Polkas: *Feuerfest; Ohne Sorgen.*

(BB) **(*) ASV CDQS 6020 [(M) id. import]. LSO, leader Georgiadis (violin).

The LSO is on top form and the rhythmic feel of the playing combines lilt with polished liveliness. There is delicacy (the *Czech polka* is enchanting) and boisterousness, as in the irresistible anvil effects in the *Feuerfest polka*. The closing *Radetzky march* is as rousing as anyone could wish, while the waltzes combine vitality and charm. With good recording in a suitably resonant acoustic, which tends to emphasize the bass, this is recommendable, especially at budget price.

Polka: *Unter Donner und Blitz;* Waltzes: *An der schönen blauen Donau; Kaiser; Morgenblätter; Rosen aus dem Süden; Schatz; Wiener Blut.* Josef STRAUSS: Waltz: *Dorfschwalben aus Osterreich.*
(M) **(*) RCA 09026 68160-2 [id.]. Chicago SO, Fritz Reiner (with: Richard STRAUSS: *Der Rosenkavalier: Waltzes;* WEBER/BERLIOZ: *Invitation to the dance* ***).

Reiner's collection was recorded in 1957 and 1960, and some of the voluptuousness of the Chicago ambience has disappeared in this fresh remastering. Although the *Thunder and lightning polka* has an unforgettable explosive exuberance, these performances are memorable for their Viennese lilt, especially the *Emperor waltz* (affectionate rather than seeking nobility of outline) and Josef's *Village swallows*. Reiner is especially persuasive in the introductory interchanges of Weber's *Invitation to the waltz* which, like the Richard Strauss *Rosenkavalier* sequence, has been added for the present reissue. The latter shows Reiner at his finest, and here the string-sound has added opulence.

Waltzes: *Accelerationen; An der schönen blauen Donau (Blue Danube); Du und Du; Frühlingstimmen (Voices of spring); Geschichten aus dem Wiener Wald (Tales from the Vienna Woods); Kaiser (Emperor); Künsterleben (Artist's life); Liebeslieder; Morgenblätter (Morning papers); Rosen aus dem Süden (Roses from the South); 1001 Nacht; Wein, Weib und Gesang (Wine, women and song); Wiener Blut (Vienna blood); Wiener Bonbons; Wo die Zitronen blühn (Where the lemon trees bloom).* Josef STRAUSS: *Dorfschwalben aus Osterreich; Sphären-klange (Music of the spheres).*
(B) *** Decca Double 443 473-2 (2). VPO, Willi Boskovsky.

These recordings span Willi Boskovsky's long recording career with the VPO for Decca, stretching over two decades, when his records dominated the LP discography in the Strauss family repertoire. The first group to be recorded (*Liebeslieder*, ending disc 1, *Wiener Blut*, *Wiener Bonbons* and *Artist's life*, which open disc 2) are particularly 'live' and fresh, dating from 1958; and the last, a charmingly lilting performance of Josef Strauss's *Village swallows*, comes from 1976. One might think that such a succession of Strauss waltzes spread over two discs might produce a degree of listening fatigue, but that is never the case here, such is Johann's resource in the matter of melody and freshness of orchestration. The earliest recordings show their age a bit in the violin tone, but Decca set high technical standards from the beginning, and from the 1960s onwards the strings are tonally more expansive, while the glorious Viennese ambient glow is consistent throughout. Indeed on CD it is remarkable just how well these vintage recordings sound. With 145 minutes of music offered on a Double Decca reissue (two discs for the price of one), this is excellent value.

VOCAL MUSIC

Vocal waltzes

(i) *Auf's Korn! Bundesschützen-Marsch.* (ii) *Hoch Osterreich! Marsch.* Polkas: (i) *Burschenwanderung (polka française); 's gibt nur a Kaiserstadt! 's gibt nur ein Wien!;* (ii) *Sängerslust.* Waltzes: *An der schönen blauen Donau;* (i) *Bei uns z'Haus;* (ii) *Gross-Wien;* (i) *Myrthenblüthen;* (ii) *Neu-Wien; Wein, weib und gesang!*
**(*) Marco Polo Dig. 8.223250-2. Wiener Männergesangverein, Czecho-Slovak RSO (Bratislava), (i) Gerhard Track; (ii) Johannes Wildner.

A most enjoyable collection. Wildner is occasionally a bit strong with the beat, but the *Blue Danube* with chorus is much more enjoyable than his performance with orchestra alone. The singers are Viennese, so they have a natural lilt, and the recording has an ideal ambience.

OPERA

Die Fledermaus (complete).
*** Ph. Dig. 432 157-2 (2) [id.]. Kiri Te Kanawa, Gruberová, Leech, Wolfgang Brendel, Bär, Fassbaender, Göttling, Krause, Wendler, Schenk, V. State Op. Ch., VPO, Previn.
(BB) *** CfP Silver Double CDCFPSD 4793 (2) [id.]. Scheyrer, Lipp, Dermota, Berry, Ludwig, Terkal, Waechter, Kunz, Philh. Ch & O, Otto Ackermann.
(N) (M) *** EMI CMS5 66223-2 (2). Rothenberger, Holm, Gedda, Dallapozza, Fischer-Dieskau, Fassbaender, Berry, V. State Op. Ch., VSO, Boskovsky.
(M) (***) EMI mono CMS5 67074-2 (2). Schwarzkopf, Streich, Gedda, Krebs, Kunz, Christ, Philh. Ch. & O, Karajan.
(N) (M) (**) RCA mono 74321 61949-2 [id.]. Gueden, Streich, Waechter, Zampieri, Berry, Stolze, Kunz, Klein, Ott, Meinrad, V. St. Op. Ch. & O, Karajan.

André Previn here produces an enjoyably idiomatic

account of Strauss's masterpiece, one which consistently conveys the work's exuberant high spirits. Dame Kiri Te Kanawa's portrait of Rosalinde brings not only gloriously firm, golden sound but also vocal acting with star quality. Brigitte Fassbaender is the most dominant Prince Orlofsky on disc. Singing with a tangy richness and firmness, she emerges as the genuine focus of the party scene. Edita Gruberová is a sparkling, characterful and full-voiced Adèle; Wolfgang Brendel as Eisenstein and Olaf Bär as Dr Falke both sing very well indeed, though their voices sound too alike. Richard Leech as Alfred provides heady tone and a hint of parody. Tom Krause makes a splendid Frank, the more characterful for no longer sounding young. Anton Wendler as Dr Blind and Otto Schenk as Frosch the jailer give vintage Viennese performances, with Frosch's cavortings well tailored and not too extended. This now goes to the top of the list of latterday *Fledermaus* recordings, though with one serious reservation. The Philips production in Act II adds a layer of crowd noise as background throughout the Party scene, even during Orlofsky's solos. Strauss's gentler moments are then seriously undermined by the sludge of distant chatter and laughter, as in the lovely chorus *Bruderlein und Schwesterlein*, yearningly done. Otherwise the recorded sound is superb, with brilliance and bite alongside warmth and bloom, both immediate and well balanced. Like Kleiber on DG, Previn opts for the *Thunder and lightning polka* instead of the ballet.

On a CfP Silver Double, with a synopsis rather than a libretto, comes a vintage *Fledermaus* from 1960. It makes a superb bargain, for the singing is consistently vivacious. Gerda Scheyrer's Rosalinde brings the only relative disappointment, for the voice is not ideally steady; but Wilma Lipp is a delicious Adèle and Christa Ludwig's Orlofsky is a real surprise, second only to Brigitte Fassbaender's assumption of a breeches role that is too often disappointing. Karl Terkal's Eisenstein and Anton Dermota's Alfred give much pleasure, and Erich Kunz's inebriated Frosch in the finale comes off even without a translation. Ackermann's direction has not the subtlety of Karajan, but the final result is lively and polished, with a real Viennese flavour. The sound has come up remarkably vividly – there is a nice combination of atmosphere and clarity.

For those wanting a fairly modern, mid-priced version should consider EMI's mid-priced Boskovsky set. Though he sometimes fails to lean into the seductive rhythms as much as he might, his is a refreshing account of a magic score. Rothenberger is a sweet, domestic-sounding Rosalinde, relaxed and sparkling if edgy at times, while, among an excellent supporting cast, the Orlovsky of Brigitte Fassbaender must again be singled out as the finest on record, tough and firm. The entertainment has been excellently produced for records, with German dialogue inserted, though the ripe recording sometimes makes the voices jump between singing and speaking. The remastering is admirably vivid.

The mono recording of Karajan's 1955 version (now reissued as a 'Great recording of the Century') has great freshness and clarity, along with the polish which for many will make it a first favourite. Schwarzkopf makes an enchanting Rosalinde, not just in the imagination and sparkle of her singing but also in the snatches of spoken dialogue (never too long) which leaven the entertainment. As Adèle, Rita Streich produces her most dazzling coloratura; Gedda and Krebs are beautifully contrasted in their tenor tone, and Erich Kunz gives a vintage performance as Falke. The original recording, crisply focused, has been given a suitable facelift.

Recorded live by Austrian Radio at the Vienna State Opera on New Year's Eve, 1960, the RCA set gives a vivid picture of the event, warts and all. For the non-German speaker, the acres of dialogue will be a serious deterrent, notably in Act III with only 15 minutes of music out of 40. The performance too in the excitement of the occasion has nothing like the polish of either of Karajan's studio recordings, and the recorded sound is far more limited, though the voices come over well. This is still a cherishable issue for capturing the atmosphere and special flavour of a great Viennese occasion, with Karajan taking a more relaxed view here than in the studio, with the singers freer and less disciplined. Hilde Gueden is the complete charmer (as on her early Decca set, a very Viennese heroine), with Walter Berry as Falke, Giuseppe Zampieri as Alfred and Peter Klein as Dr Blind, also relishing the comedy all the more. The party junketings in Act II include not just Erich Kunz singing the *Fiakerlied* by Gustav Pick, but a special guest, Giuseppe di Stefano, singing *O sole mio* and Lehár's *Dein ist mein ganzes Herz* (Italy's tribute to Vienna, prompting wild cheering). Also a 10-minute ballet, *Schottisch, Russisch Hungarisch and Polka*.

A Night in Venice (Eine Nacht in Venedig): complete.

(***) EMI mono CDH7 69530-2. Schwarzkopf, Gedda, Kunz, Klein, Loose, Dönch, Philh. Ch. & O, Ackermann.

A Night in Venice, in Erich Korngold's revision, is a superb example of Walter Legge's Philharmonia productions, honeyed and atmospheric. As a sampler, try the jaunty little waltz duet in Act I between Schwarzkopf as the heroine, Annina, and the baritone Erich Kunz as Caramello, normally a tenor role. Nicolai Gedda as the Duke then appropriates the most famous waltz song of all, the *Gondola song* but, with such a frothy production, purism would be out of place. The digital remastering preserves the balance of the mono original admirably.

Wiener Blut (complete).

(***) EMI mono CDH7 69529-2. Schwarzkopf,

Gedda, Köth, Kunz, Loose, Dönch, Philh. Ch. & O, Ackermann.
(M) **(*) EMI CMS7 69943-2 (2). Rothenberger, Gedda, Holm, Hirte, Putz, Cologne Op. Ch., Philh. Hungarica, Boskovsky.

To have Schwarzkopf at her most ravishing, singing a waltz song based on the tune of *Morning Papers*, is enough enticement for this Philharmonia version of the mid-1950s, showing Walter Legge's flair as a producer at its most compelling. Schwarzkopf was matched by the regular team of Gedda and Kunz and with Emmy Loose and Erika Köth in the secondary soprano roles. The original mono recording was beautifully balanced, and the facelift given here is achieved most tactfully.

The EMI set conducted by Willi Boskovsky makes a delightful entertainment, the performance authentic and with a strong singing cast. The recording is atmospherically reverberant, but there is no lack of sparkle. However, for some there will be too much German dialogue, which also involves two CDs.

Der Zigeunerbaron (The Gipsy Baron): complete.
(***) EMI mono CDH7 69526-2 (2).
Schwarzkopf, Gedda, Prey, Kunz, Köth, Sinclair, Philh. Ch. & O, Ackermann.

This superb Philharmonia version of *The Gipsy Baron* from the mid-1950s, now restored to the catalogue, has never been matched in its rich stylishness and polish. Schwarzkopf as the gipsy princess sings radiantly, not least in the heavenly Bullfinch duet (to the melody made famous by MGM as *One day when we were young*). Gedda, still youthful, produces heady tone, and Erich Kunz as the rough pig-breeder gives a vintage *echt*-Viennese performance of the irresistible *Ja, das schreiben und das lesen*. The CD transcription from excellent mono originals gives fresh and truthful sound, particularly in the voices.

Der Zigeunerbaron (arr. Harnoncourt; Linke: complete).
*(**) Teldec/Warner Dig. 4509 94555-2 (2) [id.].
Coburn, Lippert, Schasching, Hamari, Holzmair, Oelze, Von Magnus, Lazar, Arnold Schoenberg Ch., VSO, Harnoncourt.

When *Zigeunerbaron*, second only to *Fledermaus* among Strauss operettas, has been so neglected on disc, this new Teldec set, offering a more expanded text than ever before, fills an important gap. Harnoncourt, as a Viennese and with a Viennese orchestra, ensures that the Strauss lilt is winningly and authentically observed from the *pot-pourri* overture onwards, and Harnoncourt's concern (as a period specialist) for clarity of texture gives the whole performance a sparkling freshness. Sadly, the casting is seriously flawed, when the central character of the gypsy princess, Saffi, is taken by a soprano, Pamela Coburn, who, as recorded, sounds strained and unsteady. She projects little of the glamour needed, the quality that Elisabeth Schwarzkopf so radiantly displays on the classic EMI mono set of 1954. The others are better, with Rudolf Schasching catching the fun behind the comic role of the pig-breeder, Zsupán, authentically but without exaggeration, and the light tenor, Herbert Lippert, is charming as the hero, Barinkay. Among the rest, the mezzo, Elisabeth von Magnus, sings in cabaret style in the supporting role of Mirabella, given a major point-number here, often omitted. Christiane Oelze as Arsena, the girl who does not get the hero, sings far more sweetly than Coburn, and Julia Hamari as Saffi's foster-mother, Czipra, sounds younger than her daughter. The recording is full and vivid, but many will feel that there is too much German dialogue – largely accounting for the extended length of two and a half hours.

Strauss, Josef (1827–70)

Josef Strauss: The Complete Edition

Volume 1: Polkas: *Angelica; Bauern; Eislauf; Etiquette; Moulinet; Thalia*. March: *Galenz*. *Kakadu-quadrille*. Waltzes: *Fantasiebilder; Marien-Klänge; Wiegenlieder*.
** Marco Polo Dig. 8.223561 [id.]. Budapest Strauss SO, Alfred Walter.

Volume 2: *Amazonen-Quadrille*. Polkas: *Arabella; Diana; Genien; Stiefmütterchen; Sturmlauf; Sympathie*. *Schottischer Tanz*. Waltzes: *Petitionen; Tranz-Prioriräten*: Arr. of SCHUMANN: *Träumerei*.
** Marco Polo Dig. 8.223562 [id.]. Slovak State PO (Košice), Alfred Walter.

Volume 3: *Avantgarde march*. Polkas: *Gnomen; Die Lachtaube; Die Naïve; Ohne Sorgen; Sport*. Quadrilles: *Caprice; Flick-flock*. Waltzes: *Assoziationen; Ernst und Humor; Mai-Rosen*.
** Marco Polo Dig. 8.223563 [id.]. Slovak State PO (Košice), Alfred Walter.

It is good to see Marco Polo now exploring the output of Josef Strauss, of which we know remarkably little. Indeed almost all the items in this first volume are completely unfamiliar. Alfred Walter's easy-going style permeates the whole programme, and most of the polkas are left badly needing a more vital pacing. The waltzes are lilting in a lazy way, and this well-recorded disc has great documentary interest, while the back-up notes are equally praiseworthy.

In Volume 2, Walter introduces two more waltzes which are fully worthy of Johann Jnr; *Petitionen* is particularly inventive. The polkas are amiable, with *Diana* aptly introduced by the horns.

Volume 3 opens with a sprightly march (not too heavily articulated), but the highlights are the *Assoziationen* and *Ernst und Humor* waltzes and the *Sport polka*, played here with with great spirit, and the closing (and justly renowned) *Ohne Sorgen polka*, which the Slovak players present with much enthusiasm, including the vocal interpolations. Excellent recording.

Volume 4: March: *Osterreichscher Kronprinzen;* Polkas: *La Chevaleresque; Jockey; Schlarffen; Titi; Wiener Leben;* Quadrilles: *Genovefa; Turner. Ständchen;* Waltzes: *Freudengrüsse; Frohes Leben; Vereins-Lieder*.
**(*) Marco Polo Dig. 8.223564 [id.]. Slovak RSO (Bratislava), Michael Dittrich.

Josef usually proves most reliable in his polkas, and *Schlarffen* is one of his finest, while the *Titi polka* is delicious, with the portrait of that pretty bird implied in the scoring rather than with any imitations. Both are very infectious as presented here by the excellent Michael Dittrich, and the better-known *Jockey* bursts with vivacity. The programme ends with a simple *Serenade* that might or might not have been intended as a tribute to Wagner.

Volume 5: *Defilier* (March); Polkas: *Die Gazelle; Maiblümchen; Die Marketenderin; Mignon; Vorwärts;* Quadrilles: *Csikos; Die Grossherzogin von Gerolstein;* Waltzes: *Dynamiden (Geheime Anziehungskräfte); Flammen; Huldigungslieder*.
**(*) Marco Polo Dig. 8.223565 [id.]. Slovak State PO (Košice), Christian Pollack.

The very fetching *Die Grossherzogin quadrille* gets this programme off to a good start. Pollack (as elsewhere) chooses a dancing tempo and one wants to get up and join in. Of the three waltzes included here, there is one masterpiece: *Dynamiden*, with its ravishing cantabile is fully worthy of Johann, and it is beautifully played. Pollack takes the polka-mazurkas at dance tempi with a strong accent on the first beat, which is obviously authentic; but for concert perfomance a slightly faster tempo might have been more effective, and this especially applies to *Maiblümchen*, which closes the concert. Nevertheless this is one of the most rewarding Josef Strauss collections so far in the series.

Volume 6: March: *Victor*. Polkas: *Carrière; Causerie; Figaro; Joujou; Tanz-Regulator; Waldröslein. Musen quadrille*. Waltzes: *Die Industriellen; Krönungslieder; Nilfluthen*.
**(*) Marco Polo Dig. 8.223566 [id.]. Slovak State PO (Košice), John Georgiadis.

Of the three waltzes here, the first, *Die Industriellen*, is marginally the most beguiling, and Georgiadis has its measure, both at the lilting opening tune and in its engaging secondary scalic figure that rises and falls in a busy little group of notes. Of the polkas, the *Causerie* ('Chatting') is the most ingenuously charming, while *Carrière* is one of Josef's most infectious galops. John Georgiadis is thoroughly at home here, and this music is all stylishly presented and again very well recorded.

Volume 7: March: *Erzherzog Karl;* Polkas: *Bouquet; Frohsinn; Irenen; Jucker;* Polka mazurs:*Die Idylle; Minerva;* Quadrille: *Parade;* Waltzes: *Friedenspalmen; Hesperus-Bahnen; Streichmagnete*.
(N) ** Marco Polo Dig. 8.223567 [id.]. Slovak State PO (Kosice), Mika Eichenholz.

Volume 7 opens winningly with the *Jockey polka*, and the hardly less engaging *Parade quadrilles*. Here Mika Eichenholz displays a light rhythmic touch and the Slovak State Philharmonic continue to be thoroughly at home. If he is less impressive in the two Polka mazurs which tend to hang fire, the *Irenen poka* which ends the programme is delightfully pert.

Volume 8: Polkas: *Die Amazone; Arm in arm; En passant; Mailust; Saus und Braus; Seraphinen; Sylphide;* Quadrille: *Debardeurs;* Waltzes: *Die Clienten; Expensnoten; Wiener Stimmen*.
(N) ** Marco Polo Dig. 8.223568 [id.]. Slovak State PO (Kosice), Mika Eichenholz.

This collection is mainly of documetary interest. The various Polkas proceed in leisurely fashion, and it is not until the waltzes, *Die Clienten* and *Expensnoten*, that the music rises much above routine formulas. Eichendorf indulges them in his casual manner, and also the seductive *Arm in arm* polka masur, which follows, while *Wiener Stimmen* lilts most engagingly of all, with the main theme nicely lifted. Any of these items could be very impressive in the hands of a great conductor.

Volume 9: March: *Deutscher Union;* Polkas: *Adamira; Eingesendet; Lieb' und Wein; Masken; Die Spinnerin; Zephir;* Quadrille: *Bivouac;* Waltzes: *Deutsche Sympathien; Rudolphsklänge; Studentenräume*.
(N) Marco Polo Dig. 8.223569 [id.]. Slovak State PO (Kosice), Christian Pollack.

Not surprisingly, with Christian Pollack in charge, this is one of the best if not *the* best of Marco Polo's Josef Strauss series. The opening *Adamira polka* sparkles with life and the following *Bivouac-Quadrille* bounces along infectiously. These performance are in a completely different class to those directed by Mika Eichenholz, and all three waltzes glow with rhythmic and melodic life. Splendid playing and first-class rcording makes this a disc to treasure.

Volume 10: Polkas: *Abendstern; For ever; Gruss an München; Harlekin; Heiterer Muth; Herzbleamerl; Nachtschatten;* Quadrille: *Touristen;* Waltzes: *Herztöne; Wiener Fresken; Wiener Kinder*.
(N) *** Marco Polo Dig. 8.223570 [id.]. Slovak State PO (Kosice), Christian Pollack.

The performances on Volume 10 are just as vivacious as those in Volume 9. Everything is played with affection and strong rhythmic character.

Volume 11: Polkas: *Bon-bon; Die Emancipirte; Lust-Lager; Schwalbenpost; Die Schwätzerin; Victoria;* Quadrilles: *Dioscuren; Les Géorgiennes;* Waltzes: *Gedenkblätter; Hochzeits-Klänge; Maskengeheimnisse.*
(N) **(*) Marco Polo Dig. 8.223571 [id.]. Razumovsky SO, Alfred Eschwé.

There is nothing that really stands out in Volume 11, although the *Schwalbendpost polka* is jolly enough, and there are some nice touches of orchestral colour throughout (notably in the *Schwätzerin polka masur*). Eschwé is a more flexibly imaginative conductor than Eichenholz, but does not have the natural flair of Pollack.

Volume 12: March: *Schützen;* Polkas: *Allerlei; Amaranth; Frisch auf!; Laxenburger; Une pensée; Schabernack;* Quadrille: *Herold;* Waltzes: *Helenen; Schwert und Leyer; Tanzadressen an die Preisgekrönten.*
(N) *** Marco Polo Dig. 8.223572 [id.]. Slovak State PO (Kosice), Christian Pollack.

Christian Pollack returns for Volume 12, as is immediately obvious from the spirited and vivid opening, *Herold-Quadrille*, which is fully worthy of Johann and very elegantly scored. Pollack also again brings a lilting sweep to the string tunes in all three waltzes. *Schwert and Leyer* opens melodramatically, but then a very seductive melody steals in on the strings. *Tanzadressen an die Preisgekrönten* is another of Josef's best, and *Helenen* with its chattering opening flutes is a real charmer.

Volume 13: *Phönix-Marsch*. Polkas: *Extempore; Farewell; Matrosen; Wiener*. Polka-Mazurka: *Die Galante*. Quadrilles: *Toto; Turnier*. Waltzes: *Deutsche Grüsse; Herbstrosen; Wintermärchen.*
(N) ** Marco Polo Dig. 8.223573 [id.]. Slovak State PO (Kosice), Michael Dittrich.

Michael Dittrich brings zest to the opening march and sparkle to the polkas and he shapes the three waltzes affectionately. But he is just a little bit too relaxed to realize their full potential, even though they are beautifully played, and the recording is well up to the usual standard of this fine series. The closing *Turnier-Quadrille* is an infectious highlight.

Volume 14: Polkas: *Auf Ferienreisen; Bellona; Künstler-Gruss; Neckerei; La simplicité; Springinsfeld; Die Tänzerin;* Quadrille: *Blaubart;* Waltzes: *Disputationen; Die guten, alten Zeiten; Die Zeitgenossen.*
(N) ** Marco Polo Dig. 8.223574 [id.]. Slovak State PO (Kosice), Michael Dittrich.

Volume 14 opens with a vivacious account of the spirited *Auf Ferienreisen polka* and is also notable for the Bluebeard-Quadrille, an engaging Offenbach pot-pourri, neatly scored, with plenty of familiar tunes, where Dittrich too, is at his best. But again he makes too little of the three waltzes, being content to play them through *a tempo*.

Volume 15: *Hesperus-Ländler*. March: *Ungarischer Krönungsmarsch*. Polkas: *Amouretten; Gedenke mein!; Plappermäulchen; Winterlust*. Polka-Mazurkas: *Die Nasswalderin; Vielliebchen*. Quadrille: *Theater*. Waltzes: *Combinationen; Lustschwärmer*.
(N) ** Marco Polo Dig. 8.223575 [id.]. Slovak State PO (Kosice), Arthur Kulling.

Two famous numbers stand out here: the *Plappermäulchen polka*, played here with considerable gusto and the waltz, *Mein Lebenslauf ist Lieb' und Lust* which is given a routine performance. Indeed Arthur Kulling is another conductor who is at his best in the bright work, rather than in coaxing the waltzes. The very agreeable Ländler is also rather heavily presented. The *Theatre Quadrille* includes melodies from operas and operettas by Verdi, Suppé and Meyerbeer, among others, and as usual is nicely orchestrated. But Kulling does not make a great deal of it.

Volume 16: March: *Schwarzenberg-Monument*. Polkas: *Fashion; Freigeister; In der Heimat; Punsch; Die Schwebende; Wilde Rose;* Waltzes: *Ball-Silhouetten; Frauenwürde; Wiener Couplets.* Quadrilles: *Lancer; Schäfer*.
(N) ** Marco Polo Dig. 8.223618 [id.]. Slovak State PO (Košice), Arthur Kulling.

Kulling opens with a rhythmically buoyant account of the march, the Polkas have life and charm, and the two Quadrilles are elegant enough. All three waltzes here are among Josef's most appealing (often with a strong whiff of Johann) and *Frauenwirde* has a most enticing opening. They are well played, have a relaxed rhythmic feeling, and lilt warmly, but Pollack would surely have given them even more personality. As always in this series the recording ambience is very pleasing.

Volume 17: March: *Wallonen*. Polkas: *Edelweiss; Feurfest!; Jocus; Die Sirene; Tag un Nacht; Verliebte Augen*. Quadrille: *Polichinello*. Waltzes: *Dorfschwalben aus Osterreich (Village swallows); Perlen der Liebe; Sphärenklange (Music of the spheres).*
(N) ** Marco Polo Dig. 8.223619 [id.]. Slovak State PO (Košice), Ernst Märzendorfer.

Ernst Märzendorfer presents all the polkas here pleasingly enough. The opening *Die Sirene* is charming, and the famous *Feuerfest!* has gusto. The *Policinello–Quadrille* (complete with a brief chorus near the end) is winningly sprightly, and he also finds a nice bouncy rhythm for the *Wallonen-Marsch*, which is really a lilting two-step. But although the two great waltzes, *Music of the spheres* and the chirping *Village swallows* are nicely introduced, once the music gets underway, routine sets in, and *Perlen de Liebe* is at times mannered. Good playing and excellent recording.

Volume 17: March: *Armee.* Polkas: *Brennende Liebe; Gurli; Im Fluge; Die Libelle; Rudolfsheimer;* Quadrilles: *Colosseum. Sturm;* Waltzes: *Aquarellen; Die Ersten nach den Letzten; Normen.*
(N) *** Marco Polo Dig. 8.223620 [id.]. Slovak State PO (Košice), Karl Albert Geyer.

There is an engaging story about the composition of *Die Ersten nach den Letzten*, one of Josef's best waltzes, and a real find. in August 1853 'Pepi' Strauss, as he was affectionately known, found himself obliged to direct the orchestra for the first time, because his brother was recuperating after a serious illness. For the same reason he had also to provide a waltz for the occasion. Determined that his substitute musical directorship should not be permanent, he called the waltz *Die Ersten und Letzen* ('The first and the last'). But the piece, published as his Op. 1, enjoyed considerable success, and he was unable to maintain his resolve. Thus, with a hint of irony, but also with a twinkle, he called his Opus 12 (above), '*The first after the last*'. *Normen* ('Standards') is also a very attractive piece, with a chirruping main theme and plenty of good ideas. Geyer is a much more persuasive advocate than many of his colleagues, and with some perky polkas (*Gurli*, the lilting *Rudolfsheimer*, and *Im Fluge* among the most characteristic), the justly celebrated *Aquarellen*, and a pair of attractive Quadrilles, this is one of the best discs in the series.

Strauss, Richard (1864–1949)

Symphonic poems: *An Alpine Symphony, Op. 64; Death and transfiguration, Op. 24; Don Juan, Op. 20; Ein Heldenleben, Op. 40.*
(M) *** Chandos Dig. CHAN 7009/10 [id.]. Royal SNO, Neeme Järvi.

Symphonic poems: *Also sprach Zarathustra, Op. 30;* (i) *Don Quixote, Op. 35. Macbeth, Op. 23; Symphonia domestica, Op. 53; Till Eulenspiegel, Op. 38.*
(M) *** Chandos Dig. CHAN 7011/12 [id.]. Royal SNO, Järvi; (i) with Raphael Wallfisch.

Järvi's generally distinguished survey of the Strauss symphonic poems was recorded in the sumptuous acoustics of the Caird Hall, Dundee, between 1986 and 1989. If occasionally the resonance prevents the sharpest internal clarity, the skilled Chandos engineering ensures that the orchestral layout is very believable, heard within a natural perspective. The account of *An Alpine Symphony* is ripely enjoyable, with the reverberant acoustic here very helpful. Järvi seeks to present a general scenic view within a performance that is not as electrically taut or crisp of ensemble as, say, Karajan's but which is very effective in giving a genial description of the changing landscapes. *Death and transfiguration* shows the orchestra at its finest and here detail is revealed well, within a reading which has impressive control. *Don Juan* is portrayed as a bluff philanderer and the reading seeks sentience and amplitude rather than searing brilliance. *Ein Heldenleben* is strongly characterized and warmly sympathetic from first to last, marked by powerful, thrustful playing, lacking only the last degree of refinement in ensemble.

Järvi's *Symphonia domestica* is particularly successful, as indeed is his joyful portrait of *Till. Macbeth*, less than a masterpiece, is also presented very persuasively; few if any recorded performances make a better case for it. *Don Quixote* then takes a rather leisurely journey, although an amiable one. Raphael Wallfisch, the solo cellist, plays splendidly but, like the excellent violist, John Harrington, is very forwardly balanced, while inner orchestral detail is less than ideally clear. *Also sprach Zarathustra*, which closes the programme, is the least successful of the series, with the reverberant acoustic rather muddying the sound, without bringing compensating richness; moreover the organ pedal at the opening is much too dominant. At mid-price they are undoubtedly competitive, particularly for collectors who enjoy Chandos's rich tapestries of sound.

An Alpine Symphony, Op. 64; Macbech, Op. 23 (74321 57128-2). *Also sprach Zarathustra, Op. 30; Der Rosenkavalier* (orchestral suite); *Don Juan, Op. 20* (09026 68225-2). *Death and transfiguration, Op. 53; Symphonia domestica, Op. 52* (09026 68221-2). *Ein Heldenleben, Op. 40; Till Eulenspiegel, Op. 28* (09026 68775-2).
(N) *** RCA Dig. 09026 63265-2 (4) [id.]. Bavarian RSO, Lorin Maazel.

We have observed before that Lorin Maazel's interpretative instinct is usually transformed when he records in Vienna, and here it proves equally true in Munich. Of course he has the advantage of the Bavarian Radio Symphony Orchestra – a magnificent body, who have a natural affinity with Richard Strauss. But one is also struck by the conductor's own freshness of approach and his imaginative insights in all of these wonderful scores. The opening of *Also sprach Zarathustra*, taken very spaciously, must now be the most spectacularly recorded on record, crystal clear over the sustained pedal with blazing brass. But then the slow tempo is maintained, and the very wide dynamic range of the recording underlined by the delicacy of his portrayal of the 'Dwellers in the world beyond'. There is explosive passion later, but the 'Science' evocation has great atmosphere and the 'Tanzlied' much delicacy. Similarly in the *Rosenkavalier suite*, which opens and closes with enormous verve, the music for the lovers and the 'Silver rose presentation' is exquisitely tender, with lovely oboe playing. Of Strauss's two great fictional heroes, *Don Juan* is portrayed with a throbbing virility and energy: the strings thrillingly ardent, particularly in their final reprise after the superb horn re-entry. The closing moments of utter disillusionment are then the more telling. *Till* is equally strongly characterized, portrayed as a robustly dynamic figure, unrepentently humorous, who comes to a really spectacular end, and then endearingly floats off to the next world without any regrets. *Death and transfiguration* is better recorded than Maazel's 1983 DG version, and the orchestral playing is equal in every way to the emotional and virtuosic demands of the score. Maazel's approach to the underrated *Symphonie domestica* is both subtle and refined and attractively free of any overblown exaggeration. These same qualities inform *Ein Heldenleben*, which has plenty of impetus and intensity, yet is splendidly detailed. *Macbeth* is remarkably successful too, but the most vivid pictorialization comes in the eventful *Alpine Symphony*, with the offstage hunting horns perhaps more thrilling here than on any other record. In short these are first-class performances, the interpretations as sound as they are resourceful. Of course Karajan, Kempe and Haitink all have something very special to say in this repertoire, but anyone wanting spectacular modern digital sound will find much to admire in Munich, with the ambience of the Herkulessaal adding an allure to three out of the four discs. *Ein Heldenleben* and *Till* were made in the studio, but certainly do not lack ambience. The one snag is that the microphones have given a degree of unnatural digital brightness to the *fortissimo* high violins, but this can be tempered with flexible controls. The four discs (which come in a slipcase) are each available separately but, ungenerously, RCA offer no saving if you buy the complete set.

An Alpine Symphony, Op. 64.
*** DG Gold Dig. 439 017-2 [id.]. BPO, Karajan.
*** Ph. (IMS) Dig. 416 156-2. Concg. O, Haitink.

An Alpine Symphony, Op. 64; Don Juan, Op. 20.
(N) (M) *** Decca Dig. 466 423-2 [id.]. San Francisco SO, Blomstedt.

Blomstedt has developed into a conductor of real stature who knows how to control and pace a work and relate climaxes to one another. His *Alpine Symphony* is superbly shaped and has that rare quality of relating part to whole in a way that is totally convincing as is the reading of *Don Juan*. Throughout he gets scrupulously attentive playing from the San Francisco Orchestra and a rich, well-detailed Decca recording.

This DG reissue in the Karajan Gold series is one of the most remarkable in its improvement of the sound over the original CD issue. The acoustic boundaries of the sound seem to have expanded. Detail is not analytically clear, but the sumptuous body of tone created by the orchestra is glorious, with the violins glowing and soaring as they enter the forest. Undoubtedly this performance is very distinguished, wonderfully spacious and beautifully shaped – the closing *Night* sequence is very touching – and played with the utmost virtuosity.

Haitink's account on Philips is a splendid affair, a very natural-sounding recording and strongly characterized throughout. The perspective is excellent, and there is plenty of atmosphere, particularly in the episode of the calm before the storm. Above all, the architecture of the work as a whole is impressively laid out and the orchestral playing is magnificent. This can hold its own with the best.

An Alpine Symphony, Op. 64; Aus Italien, Op. 16; Dance suite from pieces by François Couperin; (i) *Don Quixote, Op. 35. Macbeth, Op. 23; Metamorphosen for 23 solo strings.*
(M) *** EMI (SIS) CMS7 64350-2 (3) [EMIC 64350]. (i) Paul Tortelier; Dresden State O, Kempe.

This is the third of the three boxes of Richard Strauss's orchestral and concertante music, recorded during the first half of the 1970s. The Dresden orchestra is a magnificent body and the strings produce gloriously sumptuous tone, which is strikingly in evidence in *Metamorphosen*. Rudolf Kempe had recorded the *Alpine Symphony* before with the RPO, and there is little to choose between the two so far as interpretation is concerned: he brings a glowing warmth to this score. His *Aus Italien* is more convincing than any previous version: the sound with its finely judged perspective is again a decisive factor here. He gives a most musical account of the delightful *Dance suite* based on Couperin keyboard pieces, although here some might wish for more transparent textures. Perhaps one could also quarrel with the balance in *Don Quixote*, which gives Tortelier exaggerated prominence and obscures some detail. The performance, however, is another matter and must rank with the best available. *Macbeth* also is convincing, and well paced.

(i) *An Alpine Symphony, Op. 64;* (ii) *Also sprach Zarathustra, Op. 30; Don Juan, Op. 20;* (iii) *Ein Heldenleben, Op. 40;* (ii) *Till Eulenspiegel, Op. 28.*
(B) *** Double Decca 440 618-2 (2) [id.]. (i) Bav. RSO; (ii) Chicago SO; (iii) VPO; Solti.

The Bavarian Radio Orchestra recorded in the Herculessal in Munich could hardly sound more opulent in the *Alpine Symphony* and the superb quality of the 1979 analogue recording tends to counterbalance Solti's generally fast tempi. The performances of *Also sprach Zarathustra*, *Don Juan* and *Till Eulenspiegel* come from analogue originals, made in

Chicago a few years earlier. Solti is ripely expansive in *Zarathustra*, and throughout all three symphonic poems there is the most glorious playing from the Chicago orchestra in peak form. For *Ein Heldenleben* Solti went (in 1977–8) to Vienna, and this is another fast-moving performance, tense to the point of fierceness in the opening tutti and elsewhere. It underlines the urgency rather than the opulence of the writing but Solti is at his finest in the final coda after the fulfilment theme, where in touching simplicity he finds complete relaxation at last, helped by the exquisite playing of the Vienna Philharmonic concertmaster, Rainer Küchl. The Decca recording is formidably wide-ranging to match this high-powered performance and, as with the rest of the programme, the transfers to CD are full-bodied and vividly detailed.

Also sprach Zarathustra, Op. 30; Le bourgeois gentilhomme (suite of incidental music for Molière's play), *Op. 60;* (i) *Violin concerto in D min., Op. 8. Death and transfiguration, Op. 24; Josephslegende, Op. 63; Schlagobers* (waltz), *Op. 70; Symphonia domestica, Op. 53; Der Rosenkavalier: Waltz sequence; Salome: Dance of the 7 veils.*
(M) *** EMI (SIS) CMS7 64346-2 (3) [EMIC 64346]. (i) Ulf Hoelscher; Dresden State O, Kempe.

Ulf Hoelscher's eloquent account of this attractive early *Violin concerto* is more than welcome, as is the *Symphonia domestica*. Kempe's version of this work is no less desirable than Karajan's, a little more relaxed without being in any way less masterly. His *Also sprach Zarathustra* is completely free of the sensationalism that marks so many newer performances. The rest of the programme is well worth having, particularly *Le bourgeois gentilhomme*. Recording and CD transfers are well up to standard.

Also sprach Zarathustra, Op. 30; Le bourgeois gentilhomme: Suite, Op. 60. Der Rosenkavalier: Waltzes.
(M) *** RCA 09026 60930-2 [60930-2]. Chicago SO, Reiner.

Reiner's 1954 account of *Also sprach Zarathustra* with its impressive feeling of space is a wonderful performance that ranks alongside the very best ever committed to disc. The same goes for the suite from *Le bourgeois gentilhomme* – possibly the finest ever, and sounding marvellously fresh considering its date (1956). Incandescent music-making, transferred to CD with stunning success.

Also sprach Zarathustra; (i) *Burleske for piano and orchestra. Don Juan, Op. 20.*
*** EMI Dig. CDC5 56364-2 [id.]. (i) Emanuel Ax; Phd. O, Sawallisch.

The new Philadephia Orchestra recording of *Also sprach Zarathustra* is a different matter. One of Sawallisch's finest recordings with this orchestra, it is passionate yet nobly contoured, and the famous opening is extremely spectacular and expansive. The recording was made in the New Jersey Studios at Collingswood (where Decca followed on with their splendid Shostakovich sessions). It is good, too, to have a fine, modern version of the witty *Burleske*, with Emanuel Ax giving a sparkling account of the solo piano part. This was originally premièred only seven months after *Don Juan* was first heard under the composer's baton, so the coupling is apt. Sawallisch's view of the latter is spacious rather than hard-driven, but the climax is thrilling, with the orchestra again giving of their best.

Also sprach Zarathustra; Death and transfiguration, Op. 24; Don Juan, Op. 20.
*** DG (IMS) Gold Dig. 439 016-2. BPO, Karajan.
*** Telarc Dig. CD 80167 [id.]. VPO, Previn.

As a performance the 1983 Karajan *Also sprach Zarathustra* (coupled with an exciting account of *Don Juan*) will be hard to beat and could very well be first choice. And the newly remastered CD in the Karajan Gold series has great dynamic range and presence, particularly at the extreme bass and treble, and the massed violins produce wonderfully radiant textures, as in the section marked *Von der grossen Sehnsucht* ('of the great longing'). The soaring main theme of *Don Juan* is hardly less sumptuous and the playing is electrifying in its energy. In Strauss, Karajan has no peer and this is one of his finest records from the early 1980s.

Previn draws magnificent playing from the Vienna Philharmonic in powerful, red-blooded readings of the symphonic poems, and the recording is among Telarc's finest. Strongly recommended for anyone wanting this particular coupling, and enjoying spectacularly voluptuous sound-quality.

Also sprach Zarathustra, Op. 30; (i) *Burleske for piano and orchestra Der Rosenkavalier: 1st & 2nd Waltz sequences. Der Liebe de Danae (symphonic fragment); Metamorphosen for 23 solo strings.*
(N) (B) *** Delos Double Dig. DE 3707 (2) [id.]. (i) Carol Rosenberger; Seattle Symphony, Gerard Schwarz.

Throughout this programme the Seattle Orchestra plays splendidly, with warmth, passion and finish, and the concert hall acoustic is just right for this richly scored music. With no loss of definition, there is a degree of sumptuousness and bloom here missing in Lorin Maazel's otherwise technically impressive RCA Bavarian CDs (see above). Gerard Schwarz's earlier recordings have already proved him a dedicated and idiomatic Straussian. His version of *Metamorphosen* (see below) is sustained at a very spacious tempo indeed. But it is unfailingly eloquent and holds the listener in its grip throughout. So does *Also sprach Zarathustra*, which has a fine forward sweep but plenty of imaginative detail. The *Burleske* is an affectionately fanciful performance, rather loosely held together, but with Carol Rosenburger an endearingly nimble and romantic soloist. The two *Waltz sequences* from *Der Rosenkavalier* are spirited enough, but add up to nearly 22 minutes and would outstay their welcome if not cued into two separate groups. However, the *symphonic fragment* from *Die liebe der Danae*, Strauss's penultimate opera, is sombrely and movingly powerful and makes an excellent foil for the seductive *Salome's dance*, as voluptuously involving an account as any on record, closing with thrilling abandon. With such fine playing and superb sound this pair of discs, offered for the cost of one, is worthy any collector's outlay.

(i) *Also sprach Zarathustra; Death and transfiguration; Don Juan; Ein Heldenleben; Till Eulenspiegel;* (ii) *Der Rosenkavalier: Waltz sequence.*
(B) *** Ph. Duo Dig./Analogue 442 281-2 (2). Concg. O, (i) Haitink; (ii) Jochum.

Haitink's performances are undoubtedly distinguished, superbly played, persuasively and subtly characterized. He finds added nobility in *Death and transfiguration*, while there is no lack of swagger in the accounts of both the *Don* and *Till*. The easy brilliance of the orchestral playing is complemented by the natural spontaneity of Haitink's readings, seamless in the transition between narrative events, without loss of the music's picaresque or robust qualities. Haitink's 1974 *Also sprach Zarathustra* was often spoken of in the same breath as Karajan's analogue alternative, issued in the same year. There is no lack of ardour from the Concertgebouw players and the reading has breadth and nobility. The 1970 *Ein Heldenleben* is also one of Haitink's finest records. He gives just the sort of performance, brilliant and swaggering but utterly without bombast, which will delight those who normally resist this rich and expansive work. The Philips sound here is admirably faithful and skilfully remastered. For good measure Jochum's *Waltz sequence* from *Rosenkavalier* has been added, though here the recording, though good for its age (the early 1960s), has not quite the opulence of the Haitink recordings. One of the finest of all the Duo bargains.

Also sprach Zarathustra; Death and transfiguration; Till Eulenspiegel.
(B) *** Decca Eclipse Dig. 448 224-2. Cleveland O, Ashkenazy.

Glorious Decca Cleveland sound in this triptych and marvellously reponsive playing from the orchestra. As sound, this is in the demonstration bracket; but other readings, notably those of Karajan, are just that bit more characterful.

Also sprach Zarathustra; Don Juan; Till Eulenspiegel; Salome: Dance of the 7 veils.
(M) *** Decca Legends 466 388-2 [id.]. VPO, Karajan.

Karajan's Decca version of *Also sprach Zarathustra* was a famous early stereo demonstration disc in its day (1959), with its wide dynamic range and thrilling orchestral virtuosity; all its tonal opulence is restored in the CD transfer. The other works were recorded a year later and sound freshly minted, amazingly full and sharply detailed. *Till* is irrepressibly cheeky and full of wit, and *Salome's dance* is decadently sensuous. *Don Juan* brings a similar, richly voluptuous response from the Vienna strings. Again the playing is superb, as beguiling in the love music as it is exhilarating in the chase. An admirable candidate for Decca's Legends series.

Also sprach Zarathustra, Op. 30; (i) *Don Quixote, Op. 35.*
(B) **(*) Sony SBK 47656 [id.]. Phd. O, Ormandy; (i) with Lorne Munroe.

Ormandy's 1963 Sony *Also sprach Zarathustra*, if not as overwhelming as his later, EMI version, has much virtuoso orchestral playing to commend it and many felicities of characterization. His (1961) *Don Quixote* will also give considerable pleasure. There is some marvellous orchestral playing and the two soloists play splendidly with plenty of character but without the 'star soloist' approach favoured by so many record companies. A very competitive coupling.

Also sprach Zarathustra, Op. 30; Ein Heldenleben.
✽ (M) *** RCA 09026 61494-2 [Basic 100 09026 61709-2]. Chicago SO, Fritz Reiner.
(M) *** Ph. (IMS) Dig. 442 645-2 [id.]. Boston SO, Ozawa.

These were the first stereo sessions the RCA engineers arranged with Fritz Reiner, after the company had taken over the Chicago orchestra's recording contract from Mercury. It must be said – to their enormous credit – that the RCA recording team 'got it right' from the very beginning, and the series of records they made with Reiner and his players in Orchestra Hall remain a technical peak in the history of stereo recording and the impressive feeling of space it conveyed. Later reissues have improved on its definition but none has done so with the stunning success of the present transfer. *Ein Heldenleben* shows Reiner in equally splendid form. There have been more incisive, more spectacular and more romantic performances, but Reiner achieves an admirable balance and whatever he does is convincing. If anything, the recording sounds even better than *Also sprach* and the warm acoustics of Orchestra Hall help convey Reiner's humanity in the closing pages of the work.

Ozawa's 1981 recording of *Also sprach Zara-*

thustra became one of the first demonstration records for compact disc, and even for today's ears the depth and unforced firmness of the organ pedal sound leading on to an extraordinary crescendo cannot fail to bring a shiver to the nape of the listener's neck. The solo strings are balanced rather close, but otherwise this is a wonderfully warm and natural sound, with both a beguiling bloom and fine inner clarity. Ozawa as a Strauss interpreter goes for seductive phrasing and warmth rather than high drama or nobility, but this remains one of his finest achievements at Boston.

Also sprach Zarathustra, Op. 30; Don Juan, Op. 20; Till Eulenspiegel, Op. 28; Salome: Salome's dance.
(M) *** DG 447 441-2 [id.]. BPO, Karajan.

Karajan's 1974 DG analogue version of *Also sprach Zarathustra* is coupled with his vividly characterized performance of *Till Eulenspiegel* and a thrillingly ebullient *Don Juan*, plus his powerfully voluptuous account of *Salome's dance*. The Berlin Philharmonic plays with great fervour (the timpani strokes at the very opening are quite riveting) and creates characteristic body of tone in the strings, although the digital remastering has thrown a much brighter light on the violins.

Aus Italien, Op. 16; Die Liebe der Danae (symphonic fragment); *Der Rosenkavalier: waltz sequence No. 2.*
(BB) *** Naxos Dig. 8.550342 [id.]. Slovak PO, Zdenék Košler.

On Naxos, a very well-recorded and vividly detailed account of *Aus Italien* with an excellent sense of presence. The orchestra plays very well for Zdenék Košler both here and in the ten-minute symphonic fragment Clemens Krauss made from *Die Liebe der Danae* and in the *Rosenkavalier* waltz sequence. The Slovak Philharmonic is a highly responsive body, with cultured strings and wind departments and, given the quality of the recorded sound, this represents a real bargain.

Le bourgeois gentilhomme: suite; Dance suite after Couperin, Op. 60.
(N) *** Ph. Dig. 446 696-2. ASMF, Marriner.

Marriner keeps a classical poise in these charming examples of eighteenth-century pastiche from an arch late-romantic. The *Le bourgeois gentilhomme* suite was salvaged from the incidental music Strauss wrote for the Molière play, when the first version of *Ariadne auf Naxos* – for which Molière provided the introduction – proved too cumbersome. Winningly stylish, Marriner is helped by clear, well-balanced recording The *Dance suite* – based on harpsichord pieces – dates from 1920, with Strauss again writing happily in a style he described as being 'with his left hand'. Marriner keeps a perfect balance between romantic expressiveness and classical precision, with rhythms light and pointed, with crisp ensemble, generally at flowing speeds. There is lightness of touch and the requisite finesse and charm.

Le bourgeois gentilhomme (suite), *Op. 60; Symphonia domestica, Op. 53.*
(M) *** RCA 09026 68637-2 [id.]. Chicago SO, Fritz Reiner.

Reiner's account of *Le bourgeois gentilhomme* is superbly done – possibly the finest ever – and sounding marvellously fresh, considering its date (1956). The *Symphonia domestica* comes from two years later and is another wonderful performance, a reading of stature worthy to rank alongside the best; and the CD transfer brings splendidly vivid sound-quality.

(i) *Burleske in D min. for piano and orchestra.* (ii) *Duet-concertino for clarinet, bassoon and strings.* (iii) *Horn concertos Nos. 1–2.* (iv) *Oboe concerto in D. Don Juan, Op. 20; Ein Heldenleben, Op. 40.* (v) *Panathenäenzug for piano (left hand) and orchestra; Parergon on Symphonia domestica for piano (left hand) and orchestra. Till Eulenspiegel, Op. 28.*
(M) *** EMI CMS7 64342-2 (3) [EMIC 64342]. (i) Malcolm Frager; (ii) Manfred Weise, Wolfgang Liebscher; (iii) Peter Damm; (iv) Manfred Clement; (v) Peter Rösel; Dresden State O, Kempe.

Volume 1 of the Kempe/EMI Strauss series includes all the major concertante works except the *Violin concerto*. Most collectors will already have a *Don Juan*, which is perhaps the least electrifying of Kempe's symphonic poems, and the same surely applies to *Till Eulenspiegel*, although it is an excellent performance. The *Burleske* is well worth having (it is beautifully recorded) and there are few satisfactory alternatives in the *Parergon* to the *Symphonia domestica* or the *Panathenäenzug*, both written for the one-armed pianist, Paul Wittgenstein, and played impressively here. Peter Damm's performances of the *Horn concertos* are first class. Similarly, while Manfred Clement's *Oboe concerto* is a sensitive reading, his creamily full timbre may not appeal to those brought up on Goossens. There can be no reservations whatsoever about the *Duet concertino*, where the sounds from bassoon and clarinet are beguilingly succulent, while the intertwining of both wind soloists with the dancing orchestral violins of the finale has an irresistible, genial finesse. Throughout, the superb playing of the Dresden orchestra under Kempe adds an extra dimension to the music-making.

Burleske for piano and orchestra.
(N) *** RCA Dig.9026 68028-2 [id.]. Barry Douglas, Radio France PO, Janowski – REGER: *Piano concerto.* ***

(BB) **(*) RCA Navigator 74321 21286-2. Byron Janis, Chicago SO, Reiner – MAHLER: *Symphony No. 4.* **(*)
(B) *(**) Sony SBK 53262 [id.]. Rudolf Serkin, Phd. O, Ormandy – BRAHMS: *Piano concerto No. 2.* **(*)

(i) *Burleske;* (ii) *Don Quixote, Op. 35.*
(M) *** RCA 09026 61796-2 [id.]. (i) Byron Janis; (ii) Janigro; Chicago SO, Fritz Reiner.

Burleske; Parergon, Op. 73; Stimmungsbilder, Op. 9.
**(*) Ara. Dig. Z 6567 [id.]. Ian Hobson, Philh. O, Del Mar.

(i) *Burleske; Symphonia domestica, Op. 53.*
*** Sony MK 42322 [id.]. (i) Barenboim; BPO, Mehta.

Barry Douglas gives a very brilliant and persuasive account of the Strauss, of which Serkin – also a champion of the Reger *concerto* – was a keen exponent. This is arguably his best record to date.

The *Burleske* for piano and orchestra is also given with great brilliance and panache by Daniel Barenboim in a beautifully balanced recording, while Mehta's version of the *Symphonia domestica* is humane and relaxed and has great warmth; he certainly gets pretty sumptuous playing from the Berlin Philharmonic and has the advantage of very good sound. A highly recommendable disc.

The brilliance of the *Burleske* is again brought out well by Byron Janis, who does not miss the music's witty or lyrical side. Even at full price, Reiner's *Don Quixote* was a top recommendation. Reiner was a masterly Straussian and this 1959 version was one of the very finest of RCA's Chicago Hall recordings. Antonio Janigro plays stylishly and with assurance. The recording of *Burleske* is somewhat shallower than that of the tone-poem (though a considerable improvement on the original LP), but this helps to ensure that Strauss's youthful writing does not sound too sweet. On the bargain-price Navigator alternative, the recording gives a brilliantly sparkling, somewhat dry piano-image, and the orchestra too is brought forward by the comparatively close microphones (although there is no lack of ambience).

Ian Hobson's account of the *D minor Burleske*, on its own terms, is eminently satisfactory, and he is well supported by Norman Del Mar and the Philharmonia, and is well recorded. The *Parergon* for left hand is again very well played. The *Stimmungsbilder* are early, rather Schumannesque pieces, written in 1884: Hobson gives a rather touching account of *Träumerei*, and though one can imagine a performance of the *Intermezzo* with greater charm, there is still much to admire here. Decent recording.

The Sony alternative is a generally excellent performance of what is still a comparative rarity on disc. Serkin plays with great brilliance, and the music's lyrical side – uncharacteristic but winning – is well understood. The current remastering is an improvement on the original, but the piano timbre is bright and somewhat clattery and the orchestral textures are made somewhat two-dimensional by the close microphones. Nevertheless this is an arresting performance.

(i; ii; iii) *Burleske for piano and orchestra;* (iv; v) *Duet concertino for clarinet and bassoon;* (vi; ii; vii) *Horn concertos Nos. 1 in E flat, Op. 11; 2 in E flat;* (viii; v) *Oboe concerto;* (ix; v) *Violin concerto in D min., Op. 8.*
(N) (B) **(*) Decca Double mono/stereo Analogue/Dig. 460 296-2 (2). (i) Gulda; (ii) LSO; (iii) Collins; (iv) Dmitri Ashkenazy, Kim Walker; (v) Berlin RSO, Vladimir Ashkenazy; (vi) Barry Tuckwell; (vii) Kertész; (viii) Gordon Hunt; (ix) Boris Belkin – Franz STRAUSS: *Horn concerto.* **(*)

An interesting, if not entirely successful collection, which yet remains value for money at Double Decca price. For the *Burleske*, Decca have turned back to a first rate 1954 mono performance in which Gulda, on top form, is vivaciously partnered by Anthony Collins. They respond readily to its scherzando wit, while the muted ending is quite touching. The recording is very good for its period, although with Strauss one ideally needs more opulence in the orchestral violin tone. The *Duet concertino* is an elusive work and here the timbres of the clarinet and bassoon soloists are rather too sharply individual to gel, and the conductor holds the orchestral reins rather slackly: the result is characterful but lacks an ongoing fluency and grip. Barry Tuckwell's essentially lyrical approach to the two horn concertos also misses some of the music's character. One can play the *First concerto* as a successor to Mozart, and yet bring out the moments of *Don Juan* boldness, as Dennis Brain has demonstrated. Tuckwell's approach falls between the two styles, and the more florid *Second concerto* also needs a stronger impulse, although the finale brings engaging light-hearted bravura. Boris Bekin's performance of the *Violin concerto* isn't technically flawless, yet is distinctly enjoyable (see below). But the highlight of the set is Gordon Hunt's superb account of the *Oboe concerto*. His creamy tone is ideally suited to Strauss's songful late masterpiece, and its technical hazards are surmounted with easy aplomb. There is no finer version.

Horn concerto No. 1 in E flat, Op. 11.
(M) *** EMI Dig. CDM7 64851-2. Radovan Vlatkovič, ECO, Tate – MOZART: *Horn concertos Nos. 1–4* etc. ***

Radovan Vlatkovič gives a superb account of the *First Concerto* which, although ripely romantic, has so much in common with the spirit of the Mozart concertos with which it is coupled. He is particularly good in the bold central episode of the *Andante* and caps his performance with an exhilaratingly nimble account of the finale. Tate accompanies admirably and the rich, natural, Abbey Road recording could hardly be better balanced.

Horn concertos Nos. 1 in E flat, Op. 11; 2 in E flat.

❁ (***) EMI mono CDC7 47834-2 [id.]. Dennis Brain, Philh. O, Sawallisch – HINDEMITH: *Horn concerto.* (***)

(N) **(*) EMI Dig. CDC5 56183-2. Marie Luise Neunecker, Bamberg SO, Metzmacher – BRITTEN: *Serenade.* **(*)

Dennis Brain's performances are incomparable and almost certainly will never be surpassed. Sawallisch gives him admirable support, and fortunately the latest EMI CD transfer captures the full quality of the 1956 mono recording. The orchestra is a bit backward, but Brain's glorious melodic line soars aloft ravishingly.

Marie-Luise Neunecker is a young German musician who plays with extraordinary flair and agility, relishing the virtuoso demands of both of Strauss's horn concertos in playing of winning freedom and spontaneity. The Britten *Serenade* makes an unusual and attractive coupling, though in all three works the orchestra is recorded relatively thinly.

(i) *Horn concertos Nos. 1 in E flat, Op. 11; 2 in E flat;* (ii) *Duet concertino for clarinet and bassoon. Wind serenade in E flat, Op. 11.*

(N) (B) *** CfP Dig. 573 5132 [id.]. (i) David Pyatt; (ii) Joy Farrall, Julie Andrews; Britten Sinfonia, Nicholas Cleobury.

David Pyatt gives a ripely exuberant performance of the first of Strauss's two *Horn concertos*, which is very much in the spontaneous style of the Mozart concertos. The more elusive first movement of the *Second Concerto* is shaped – often quite subtly – in an attractively rhapsodical style; the ecstatic solo line of the *Andante*, gently introduced by the oboe, is beautifully played while the finale brings heady, lightly tongued bravura. The outer movements of the gently rapturous *Duet concertino* (a late masterpiece, written the year before the *Vier letzte Lieder*) are presented with enticing delicacy of texture, and the slow movement again brings a most touchingly doleful opening solo, this time from the bassoonist, Julie Andrews. Cleobury and the Britten Sinfonia give sensitive support throughout, and the early *Serenade* is also made the more attractive by the lightness of touch of the wind blending, its sonorities always fresh, never congealing, helped by the naturally balanced recording, made in the Henry Wood Hall, Southwark. For those who want a change from the Dennis Brain Philharmonia accounts of the *Horn concertos* from the 1950s, this would be a distinct contender.

(i) *Horn concertos Nos. 1 in E flat, Op. 11;* (ii) *2 in E flat*; (iii) *Oboe concerto*; (iv) *Duet concertino for clarinet and bassoon.*

(N) *** DG Dig. 453 483-2. (i) Ronald Janezic, (ii) Lars-Michael Stransky; (iii) Martin Gabriel; (iv) Peter Schmidl, Michael Werba; VPO, André Previn.

Here is some glorious music-making, relaxed, unforced and full of expressive delights. The virtuosity is at no time self-regarding and everybody appears to be enjoying themselves. The sound, too, is as natural as the music-making. A most welcome addition to the catalogue.

(i) *Horn concerto No. 1. Don Juan, Op. 20*; (ii) *Don Quixote, Op. 35.*

(N) *** Sony MHK 63123 [id.]. (i) Myron Bloom; (ii) Pierre Fournier; Cleveland O, Szell.

Just how masterly Szell was as a Straussian comes out in all three of these items, recorded in 1960 and 1961. By then Szell had built the Cleveland Orchestra into what was regularly described as the finest in America. These performances bear out not just what tautness and precision of ensemble the orchestra was achieving, but their thrusting emotional intensity. Myron Bloom, one of the greatest of American horn-players, provides an illuminating note on Szell, whom he reveres. In the *Horn concerto No. 1* he plays with a thrilling range of dynamic and tone colour. This version of *Don Quixote* – which Fournier recorded several years before the one with Karajan in Berlin – is, surprisingly, freer in rubato, as well as more urgent. A most welcome historic reissue, very well transferred, with sound both warm and detailed, though it is a pity the price is so high, apparently because of the elaborate packaging of this series.

Oboe concerto.

*** Nimbus Dig. NI 5330 [id.]. John Anderson, Philh. O, Simon Wright – FRANCAIX: *L'horloge de flore;* MARTINU: *Concerto.* ***

(M) *** Carlton Dig. 30366 0065-2 [id.]. Pamela Pecha, Moscow PO, Paul Freeman – VAUGHAN WILLIAMS: *Oboe concerto*; SCHICKELE: *Oboe concerto.* ***

*** ASV Dig. CDCOE 808 [id.]. Douglas Boyd, COE, Berglund – MOZART: *Oboe concerto.* ***

(i) *Oboe concerto. Metamorphosen for 23 solo strings.*

**(*) Ph. Dig. 446 105-2. Heinz Holliger, COE.

John Anderson, principal oboe of the Philharmonia, gives a ravishing acount of Strauss's delectable concerto, his timbre slightly riper than that of Holliger, and the Nimbus digital recording is better integrated.

Pamela Pecha was co-principal of the Cleveland Orchestra for 12 years, the first woman in the orchestra's wind section, and she also gives a completely persuasive account of the Strauss *Concerto*, the opening easily flexible and the slow movement warmly songful. Paul Freeman and the Moscow Philharmonic Orchestra provide an accompaniment which does not miss the work's essential mellow dimension, and the recording has a glowing ambience which suits the music far better than the rather cool effect of the Philips sound-balance for Holliger. Moreover the Carlton couplings are particularly attractive.

Douglas Boyd winningly brings out the happy glow of Strauss's inspiration of old age, and his warm oboe tone, less reedy than some, brings out the *Rosenkavalier* element in this lovely concerto. With warm, well-balanced recording, the gentle contrast of romantic and classical in this work is conveyed delectably.

Holliger is never less than masterly and the assurance of his playing is remarkable. But, as with his earlier, analogue recording, there is a hint of efficiency at the expense of ripeness, and in the slow movement he fails to convey a sheer love for the music in its most absolute sense. He is not helped by being balanced rather too closely and the effect is not flattering to his timbre. As an apt coupling he takes up the baton and directs a very well-controlled and thoughtfully shaped performance of the *Metamorphosen*, but once again there is an absence of ripeness, and the recording, while it reveals every strand of detail, brings a degree of excess digital definition to the climax.

(i) *Oboe concerto in D.* (ii) *Serenade for wind, Op. 7; Sonatine No. 1 in F for wind (From an invalid's workshop); Suite in B flat for 13 wind instruments, Op. 4; Symphony for wind (The happy workshop).*

(B) *** Ph. Duo 438 733-2 (2) [id.]. (i) Heinz Holliger, New Philh. O; (ii) Netherlands Wind Ens.; Edo de Waart.

The *Serenade* is beautifully played, warm and mellifluous, and so is the *Sonatina*, a late work, written while Strauss was recovering from an illness and appropriately subtitled. It is a richly scored piece, as thoroughly effective as one would expect from this master of wind writing. Both this and the *B flat Suite*, delightful pieces, are given beautifully characterized accounts here, while the performance of the *Symphony for wind instruments* is crisp and alert. Throughout this music-making, the ear is struck by the Netherlanders' beautifully homogeneous tone, and their phrasing is splendidly alive. The recordings made between 1970 and 1972 are full, well-detailed and truthful. As if this were not bounty enough, Holliger's earlier (1970) version of the *Oboe concerto* is thrown in for good measure. The playing is masterly, an assured, stylish account, and Edo de Waart accompanies persuasively. Again very good recording.

Violin concerto in D min., Op. 8.

*** ASV Dig. CDDCA 780 [id.]. Xue Wei, LPO, Glover – HEADINGTON: *Violin concerto.* *** ✿

(B) **(*) Decca Eclipse Dig. 448 988-2. Boris Belkin, Berlin RSO, Ashkenazy – BRAHMS: *Violin concerto.* ***

With Jane Glover and the LPO warmly sympathetic accompanists, Xue Wei makes a very persuasive case for this very early work of Strauss, with its echoes of Mendelssohn and Bruch.

Though not quite a match for Xue Wei, partly because just occasionally his intonation is not absolutely immaculate, Belkin finds much charm in the Mendelssohnian second group of the opening movement, and he plays the *Lento* with an appealing fragile tenderness, then following with fairy-light articulation in the dancing finale. Ashkenazy provides a gracefully supportive accompaniment and the Decca sound is excellent, although perhaps the soloist is a trifle too closely miked – perhaps because the recording was made in the Berlin Jesus-Christus Kirche.

Death and transfiguration, Op. 24.

(M) (***) RCA mono GD 60312. Phd. O, Toscanini – TCHAIKOVSKY: *Symphony No. 6.* (***)

Toscanini's characteristically taut control of tension goes with what was for him a more warmly expressive style than usual, thanks to the influence of the Philadelphia Orchestra. With the transfer giving good body to the limited sound, it is comparable with his equally intense reading of Tchaikovsky's *Pathétique* from the same period.

Death and transfiguration, Op. 24; Don Juan, Op. 20; Till Eulenspiegel, Op. 28; Salome: Dance of the 7 veils.

(M) *** EMI CDM5 66823-2 [id.]. Philh. O, Klemperer.

Although it is a pity that the *Metamorphosen* could not have been included, this compilation, reissued as part of EMI's 'Klemperer Legacy', admirably reassembles the conductor's other key Richard Strauss recordings. In his hands it is *Death and transfiguration* that excites the greatest admiration, invested with a nobility too rarely heard in this work. But not everyone will respond to his teatment of the other two symphonic poems. *Don Juan* is clearly seen as 'the idealist in search of perfect womanhood' (even if his primary test is made between the sheets). Yet both here and in *Till Eulenspiegel* the all-important feeling of spontaneity is not always present. The account of *Salome's dance*, however, is splendidly sensuous and, with marvellous Philharmonia playing and a superb new transfer of a recording made in the Kingsway Hall in 1960–61, this collection is certainly not lacking in strength of characterization.

Death and transfiguration, Op. 24; Don Quixote, Op. 35.
(M) (**(*)) RCA mono GD 60295 [60295-2-RG]. NBC SO, Toscanini.

Toscanini's account of *Don Quixote* from 1953, electrifying and masterly, with a superb soloist in Frank Miller, sounds a shade overdriven. It does not have quite the humanity or expressive flexibility of the Reiner reading. However, his 1952 *Tod und Verklärung* is quite simply stunning.

Death and transfiguration; Metamorphosen for 23 solo strings.
✿ *** DG Dig. 410 892-2 [id.]. BPO, Karajan.

Death and transfiguration; Metamorphosen for 23 solo strings; (i) *Vier letzte Lieder (4 Last songs).*
(M) **(*) DG 447 422-2 [id.]. BPO, Karajan, (i) with Gundula Janowitz.

Karajan's digital account of *Metamorphosen* has even greater emotional urgency than the 1971 record he made with the Berlin Philharmonic and there is a marginally quicker pulse. The sound is fractionally more forward and cleaner but still sounds sumptuous, and the account of *Death and transfiguration* is quite electrifying. It would be difficult to improve on this coupling by the greatest Strauss conductor of his day.

Karajan surpassed his analogue recordings of both *Death and transfiguration* and the *Metamorphosen* when he re-recorded them digitally, but the earlier versions offered here are still powerful and convincing In the *Four last songs*, Janowitz produces a beautiful flow of creamy tone while leaving the music's deeper and subtler emotions under-exposed. The transfers are very impressive, and *Death and transfiguration* can still be regarded as a showpiece among Karajan's earlier Berlin recordings.

(i) *Death and transfiguration; Symphonia domestica, Op. 53;* (ii) *Salome's dance of the seven veils.*
(B) *** Sony SBK 53511 [id.]. (i) Cleveland O, Szell; (ii) Phd. O, Ormandy.

Szell's *Death and transfiguration* dates from 1957 and it is still unsurpassed. The opening has the most compelling atmosphere and the triumphant closing pages are the more effective for Szell's complete lack of indulgence. The recording has been vastly improved in the present transfer, with Cleveland's Masonic Temple providing a richly expansive ambience. The *Symphonia domestica*, recorded in 1964, is less naturally balanced: the engineers seem more concerned with making every detail tell, but the performance brings such powerful orchestral playing, with glorious strings especially in the passionate *Adagio*, that criticism is disarmed: there is certainly no lack of body here. The programme ends with an extraordinarily voluptuous Philadelphia performance of *Salome's dance*, which conjures up a whole frieze of naked female torsos. Ormandy directs with licentious abandon, and the orchestra responds with tremendous virtuosity and ardour, unashamedly going over the top at the climax. Here the sound is a bit glossy but, with playing like this, one can certainly adjust.

Don Juan, Op. 20.
(N) (M) *** RCA 09026 63301-2 [id.]. Chicago SO, Fritz Reiner – WAGNER: *Götterdämmerung & Meistersinger*: excerpts. **(*)
*** Decca Dig. 444 458-2 [id.]. Carnegie Hall Project O, Solti – BRAHMS: *Variations on a theme of Haydn* **(*); SHOSTAKOVICH: *Symphony No. 9* (with Concert **(*)).

Reiner's performance of this great Strauss showpiece is among the finest ever, with a superbly thrilling climax when the great horn theme leaps out unforgettably, to be followed by a closing atmosphere of sombre sentience and disillusion. The new transfer of the 1960 recording is impressive in catching the full Chicago amplitude and brilliance.

The Decca version was recorded at the end of a special workshop in which gifted instrumentalists were assembled in Carnegie Hall and given the opportunity to work with Sir Georg Solti. His *Don Juan* is the best thing on the disc. The playing is very good indeed and Sir Georg gets highly exhilarating results. Both the Brahms and the Shostakovich may seem a little too highly charged for some tastes, but there is no doubt about the electricity Solti engenders.

(i) *Don Juan, Op. 20;* (ii) *Ein Heldenleben, Op. 40;* (i) *Till Eulenspiegel, Op. 28.*
(M) *** Sony SBK 48272 [id.]. (i) Cleveland O, Szell; (ii) Phd. O, Ormandy.

Szell's *Don Juan*, sounding really impetuous yet never rushed, delights ear and senses by its forward surge of passionate lyricism, the whole interpretation founded on a bedrock of virtuosity from the remarkable Cleveland players. *Till* is irrepressibly cheeky (the characterization again created from the most polished orchestral response) and here the recording acoustic is almost perfect, with a warm glow on the tone of the players and every detail – and Szell makes sure one can hear every detail – crystal clear, without any loss of momentum or drama.

Ormandy's *Ein Heldenleben* is a really big conception. It is an engulfing performance, and the composite richness of tone and the fervour of the playing, from the Battle section onwards, bring the highest possible level of orchestral tension, finally relaxing most touchingly for the fulfilment sequence and closing with a sonorous brass cadence that is made to sound inevitable. The 1960 recording is more two-dimensional, less full, than the Cleveland recordings (which, surprisingly, were made as early as 1957) but is still appropriately spacious.

Don Juan; Till Eulenspiegel; Salome: Dance of the seven veils.
*** Everest EVC 9004 [id.]. NY Stadium SO, Stokowski – CANNING: *Fantasy on a hymn tune*. ***

A justly famous Stokowski triptych from the late 1950s, with the spacious recording now cleaned up and sounding very well indeed. Not surprisingly with the old magician in charge, Salome is made to languish more voluptuously than ever before, and even *Till* in his posthumous epilogue has a languishing mood on him. *Don Juan* indulges himself with rich sensuality, yet leaps off into the fray with undiminished vitality, while the great unison horn-call is held back with a compellingly broadened thrust. As ever, Stokowski is nothing if not convincing, and those looking for really ripe versions of these pieces need not hesitate. The Canning coupling is also worth having.

Don Quixote.
(M) *** EMI (SIS) CDM5 66106-2 [id.]. Rostropovich, BPO, Karajan – WAGNER: *Die Meistersinger: Overture; Tannhäuser: Overture and Venusberg music*. ***
(N) (M) *** EMI CDM5 66913-2. Rostropovich, BPO, Karajan – SCHUMANN: *Cello concerto*. ***
(N) (BB) *** Virgin Classics Dig. VBD5 61490-2 [CDVB 61490]. Steven Isserlis, Minnesota O, Edo de Waart – BLOCH: *Schelomo*. ELGAR: *Cello concerto*; KABALEVSKY: *Cello concerto No. 2*; TCHAIKOVSKY: *Rococo variations* etc. ***
✿ *** EMI CDC5 55528-2 [id.]. Jacqueline du Pré, New Philh. O, Boult – LALO: *Cello concerto in D min*. ***

(i) *Don Quixote, Op. 35. Don Juan, Op. 20.*
(M) *** RCA 09026 68170-2 [id.]. Chicago SO, Fritz Reiner, (i) with Antonio Janigro.

(i) *Don Quixote. Till Eulenspiegel.*
**(*) DG (IMS) Dig. Gold 439 027-2 [id.]. (i) Meneses; BPO, Karajan.

The Karajan/Rostropovich account of *Don Quixote* is predictably fine. The recorded sound (1975) is impressively remastered, spectacular in its realism, with well-defined detail, superb warmth and body, and fine perspective, its only failing a tendency for Rostropovich to dominate the aural picture. He dominates artistically, too. His Don is superbly characterized, and the expressiveness and richness of tone he commands are a joy in themselves. There are moments when one wonders whether the intensity of his response does not lead to over-emphatic tone, but in general both the cello and viola soloists and the Berlin orchestra under Karajan silence criticism. Even if you already have Karajan's earlier (1969) version with Fournier for DG, which is in some ways subtler, this EMI version is not to be missed, and the Wagner couplings are also of the highest calibre.

The superb Karajan/Rostropovich account of *Don Quixote* also comes re-coupled with Schumann's *Cello concerto* as one of EMI's 'Great recordings of the century' series, which the latter performance (with Bernstein) certainly is not. A sad mismatching!

Steven Isserlis, too, gives a firmly characterized account of the solo part, and although Edo de Waart and the Minnesota Orchestra may not succeed in producing the same refinement of texture as such Straussians as Kempe, Reiner and Karajan, the orchestral playing is generally very good indeed. The sound has both depth and clarity, and the couplings are both incredibly generous and finely played.

Even at full price, Reiner's *Don Quixote* was a top recommendation. Reiner was a masterly Straussian and this 1959 version was one of the very finest of RCA's Chicago Hall recordings. The recording has been freshly remastered for its new coupling with *Don Juan* and detail seems even more refined, though there is no loss of amplitude in climaxes: the ride through the air (track 10) is remarkly expansive. *Don Juan* dates from the earliest days of stereo (1959) and is most famous for its superbly thrilling climax in which the great horn-theme leaps out unforgettably, thrustfully echoed by the strings. But the lustre of the strings is hardly less remarkable, and again John Pfeiffer's new transfer is enormously improved over its first presentation on CD, with greater transparency not achieved at the expense of body of tone.

Over 20 years after her playing career was cut short so tragically, Jacqueline du Pré's recorded repertory is thrillingly expanded in previously unpublished recordings of Strauss and Lalo. *Don Quixote* comes in a studio recording, dating from 1968, which has been lovingly pieced together from long-buried tapes. The recording producer, Andrew Keener, discovered in the EMI archive not only session-tapes of *Don Quixote* with Klemperer and the New Philharmonia, but a complete take (except for the first bar) of the whole work, recorded two days later with Boult taking over after Klemperer withdrew. From the Klemperer session Keener was able to restore that first bar and to insert other tiny patches, so putting together a complete performance. One wants to echo Boult's instant cry of 'Bravo!' at the end. No doubt Jacqueline du Pré with more time would have sharpened up some of the bravura passages, but in its tenderness and poignancy this reading is unsurpassed. The lyrical dialogue between Sancho Panza and Quixote in the third variation has a heartfelt warmth, with Herbert Downes a fine partner on the viola. Above all, the final death scene is more yearningly tender than on any rival recording, a magical example of her art. Excellent background notes are provided by Tully Potter as well as by Andrew Keener.

Karajan's digital recording with Antonio Meneses and Wolfram Christ has been given the 'original image bit re-processing' treatment and there is some improvement in the sound. But the perspective remains far from natural and neither the performance nor the recording is a patch on his earlier versions with Rostropovich (EMI) or the late Pierre Fournier, which latter version remains available at mid-price.

(i) *Don Quixote, Op. 35;* (ii) *Horn concerto No. 2 in E flat.*

(N) (M) *** DG 457 725-2 [id.]. (i) Fournier; (ii) Norbert Hauptmann; BPO, Karajan.

Fournier's partnership with Karajan is outstanding and so is the 1966 recording. It is of DG's very finest quality, with remarkable transparency, yet plenty of warmth and a believable perspective. The great cellist brings infinite subtlety and (when required) repose to his part and Karajan's handling of the orchestral detail is quite splendid. The finale and Don Quixote's death are very moving. While this is justly reissued as one of DG's Originals, the new coupling seems less appropriate than its predecessor (Karajan's superlative 1973 analogue version of *Death and transfiguration*). Nevertheless Norbert Hauptmann's account of the more florid of Strauss's two horn concertos is ripely assured with a most eloquent and touching *Andante*.

Ein Heldenleben, Op. 40.

(M) *** EMI (SIS) CDM5 66108 [id.]. BPO, Karajan – WAGNER: *Der fliegende Holländer: Overture; Parsifal: Preludes.* ***

(M) *** DG 449 725-2 [id.]. BPO, Karajan – WAGNER: *Siegfried idyll.* ***

(B) *** EMI forte CZS5 69349-2 (2) [CDFB 69349]. LSO, Barbirolli – MAHLER: *Symphony No. 6.* **(*)

Ein Heldenleben; Death and transfiguration, Op. 24.

**(*) DG Dig. Gold 439 039-2 [id.]. BPO, Karajan.

The 1974 EMI Karajan *Heldenleben* is superlatively recorded. The performance shows a remarkable consistency of approach on Karajan's part and an equal virtuosity of technique and even greater sumptuousness of tone on the part of the Berlin Philharmonic than the earlier, DG performance; indeed the sound is remarkably vivid. Some have found the playing marginally less spontaneous, but it is gloriously ardent and, listening to it objectively, there seems little difference between the two readings. Couplings might dictate a choice; both discs offer the music of Wagner; the EMI is the more generous: an electrifying *Flying Dutchman overture*, and glorious playing (and recording) in the two *Parsifal Preludes*.

Although Karajan's 1959 *Heldenleben* cannot quite match his later EMI version in sumptuousness it still sounds remarkably impressive. Its selection for reissue in DG's series of 'Originals' seems particularly apt, since this was not only the first post-war recording Karajan made for DG but also his very first in stereo. It is a superb performance. Playing of great power and distinction emanates from the Berlin Philharmonic and, in the closing section, an altogether becoming sensuousness and warmth. The remastering makes the most of the ambient atmosphere and, while not losing body, firms up the orchestral detail. The new coupling of Wagner's *Siegfried idyll*, in which Karajan was unsurpassed, could not be more appropriate.

Barbirolli recorded *Ein Heldenleben* at Abbey Road in 1969, not long before his death. By a strange coincidence, Beecham similarly devoted some of his last recording sessions to this 'hero's life'. The vigour, nobility and richness of the Beecham version seemed to sum up his achievement over the years, and here Barbirolli sets the seal on his Indian summer in the recording studio. All the tempi are slow, even by his latter-day standards. He luxuriates in every moment of this opulent score (his occasional groans of pleasure sometimes punctuating the score) and the LSO, in superb form, follows him with warmth and ardour through every expressive rallentando. The result is inevitably controversial but, with full-bodied Abbey Road recording and the inescapable electricity of a great occasion, this is a performance which many will relish. The CD transfer has lost some of the original opulence, but there was enough and to spare, and the sound now has greater focus and detail.

Karajan's digital *Heldenleben* has tremendous sweep and all the authority and mastery we have come to expect – and indeed to take for granted. Nor is the orchestral playing anything other than glorious – indeed, in terms of sheer virtuosity, the Berlin players have never surpassed this. There is also a dramatic fire and virtuosity that are quite electrifying. However, in spite of the 'original-image bit re-processing' the early (1983) digital recording falls short of the highest present-day standards. Since Karajan's superb *Death and transfiguration* (recorded only three years later) has been added to it, the ear is drawn to notice that *Ein Heldenleben*, although firmly focused, has less warmth and the strings by comparison lack bloom, while the violins have a certain glassiness in the high treble, characteristic of the early digital era.

Ein Heldenleben, Op. 40; Feuersnot: Liebszene; Intermezzo: Träumerei am Kamin; Salome: Dance of the Seven Veils.

(N) (***) Testament mono SBT 11147 [id.]. RPO, Sir Thomas Beecham.

Many of the authors' generation got to know *Ein Heldenleben* from Beecham's 1947 account – and how fortunate we were, for it remains a model of its kind; authoritative, marvellously paced and beautifully transparent in its textures. It was recorded in connection with the famous Strauss festival that year when the great composer visited London at the end of the war, and the newly formed RPO and Sir Thomas were at the beginning of their long and flourishing partnership. A glorious performance which long held sway (though HMV never issued it on LP on this side of the Atlantic) until Karajan's 1959 account came along. The other Strauss excerpts were recorded in the late 1940s before the advent of the mono LP.

Intermezzo: Symphonic interludes.
*** Chandos Dig. CHAN 9357 [id.]. Detroit SO, Neeme Järvi – SCHMIDT: *Symphony No. 1.* ***

Neeme Järvi is an underrated Straussian and here he proves equal to the very best. He and his Detroit musicians give a thoroughly persuasive account of the interludes Strauss extracted from *Intermezzo*, and this comes as a generous fill-up to Schmidt's derivative but delightful *First Symphony*. Strongly recommended.

Josephslegende (ballet): *suite, Op. 63; Symphonia domestica, Op. 53.*
**(*) Delos Dig. DE 3082 [id.]. Seattle SO, Gerard Schwarz.

Strauss composed the *Josephslegende* for Diaghilev on the grandest scale for large orchestra. Gerard Schwarz gives us the suite from the ballet in addition to a very idiomatic account of the *Symphonia domestica*. There is very good playing from the Seattle orchestra: cultured, thoroughly idiomatic and with splendid sweep; the recording, too, is splendidly detailed, if perhaps just a bit too brightly lit to be ideal.

Metamorphosen for 23 solo strings.
(N) *** Chandos Dig. CHAN 9708 [id.]. Norwegian CO, Iona Brown – TCHAIKOVSKY: *Souvenir de Florence.* ***
(N) (M) *** EMI CMS5 67036-2 (2). [id.]. Philh. O, Klemperer – MAHLER: *Symphony No. 9;* WAGNER: *Siegfried idyll.* ***
(N) *** EMI Dig. CDS5 56580-2 [id.]. VPO, Sir Simon Rattle – MAHLER: *Symphony No. 9.* ***
*** DG Dig. 447 744-2. Dresden State O, Sinopoli – BRUCKNER: *Symphony No. 8.* ***
*** Delos Dig. DE 3121 [id.]. Seattle SO, Gerard Schwarz – HONEGGER: *Symphony No. 2;* WEBERN arr. SCHWARZ: *Langsamer satz.* ***
(B) **(*) EMI CZS5 69252-2 (2). New Philh. O, Barbirolli – MAHLER: *Symphony No. 6.* **(*)

Iona Brown's performance has a powerfully passionate impetus that is wholly spontaneous, with intense valedictory feeling in the shading down of the closing pages, which has wonderful concentration. The Chandos recording is outstandingly fine.

With Klemperer, *Metamorphosen* has a ripeness that exactly fits Strauss's last essay for orchestra, helped by the superb Philharmonia string-playing, rich in texture but with striking refinement of detail. The remastering of the 1961 Kingsway Hall recording for the 'Klemperer Legacy' is very impressive.

In Sinopoli's hands, *Metamorphosen* has a simplicity of utterance and a natural, unforced quality that is most impressive. The strings of the Staatskapelle Dresden produce a magnificent sonority and the DG engineers do them proud.

Rattle with the Vienna Philharmonic, producing string sounds of magical beauty, brings out the visionary intensity behind this late flowering of Strauss's genius, sustaining its long span masterfully. Warm, atmospheric sound. An excellent coupling for Mahler's *Ninth*.

Gerard Schwarz's account of Strauss's elegiac threnody is sumptuously recorded. Indeed this *Metamorphosen* is as deeply felt and dignified as it is unhurried, and it should be heard. The listener is completely drawn into its world and, although it does not supersede the Kempe or any of the Karajan accounts except perhaps in terms of recorded realism, it deserves to be recommended alongside them. At 32 minutes it may be the slowest *Metamorphosen* on disc, but it is certainly one of the best.

Barbirolli's version of the *Metamorphosen* is a fine one, with a warm glow and an intense, valedictory feeling, and the playing of the NPO strings is most eloquent. The 1967 Abbey Road recording still sounds well; however, although it still has weight, the present CD transfer has lost some of its original bloom and opulence.

Serenade for wind, Op. 7; Sonatine No. 1 in F for wind (From an invalid's workshop); Suite in B flat for 13 wind instruments, Op. 4; Symphony for wind (The happy workshop).
(B) *** Hyperion Dyad Dig. CDD 2015 (2) [id.]. London Winds, Michael Collins.

The London Winds on Hyperion are fairly closely observed by the microphone-balance and the effect is clearly defined and dramatic. The playing has the strongest impulse, the autumnal feeling less apparent in the *Serenade*. But one cannot help being caught up by playing that is so vividly robust and vital, and by no means lacking in warmth and affection. Even if there is a touch of over-projection, inner detail is clear and many will like the extra bite on the sound.

Symphonia domestica, Op. 53; Death and transfiguration, Op. 24.
(M) *** EMI CDM5 66107-2 [id.]. BPO, Karajan – WAGNER: *Lohengrin: Preludes; Tristan und Isolde: Prelude & Liebestod.* ***

Symphonia domestica, Op. 53; Festliches Praeludium; Till Eulenspiegel, Op. 28.
*** EMI Dig. CDC5 55185-2. Phd. O, Sawallisch.

Symphonia domestica, Op. 53; (i) *Parergon zur Symphonia domestica, Op. 73.*
*** DG Dig. 449 188-2. (i) Gary Graffman; VPO, Previn.

Strauss's *Symphonia domestica* is quite admirably served by Karajan's mid-priced 1973 recording, which now re-emerges as part of EMI's Karajan Edition, coupled with some superb Wagner performances. The playing is stunningly good and the sumptuous Berlin strings produce tone of great magnificence. EMI provide a recording (made in the Salle Wagram, Paris, in 1973) not quite as sumptuous as the Berlin recordings mentioned above but of wide range, superbly focused detail and warm ambience.

Wolfgang Sawallisch's *Symphonia domestica* is *echt*-Strauss, unexaggerated and civilized. He draws excellent playing from the Philadelphia Orchestra and gives a performance that reveals this score for what it is: one of the finest of Strauss's works. This is easily the best *Symphonia domestica* since the Karajan version of the 1970s, and it is accorded refined and well-detailed sound.

André Previn has the more logical and useful coupling in the 1924 *Parergon* on themes from the symphony that Strauss composed for the one-armed Paul Wittgenstein. Previn gives the Vienna Philharmonic its head in repertoire that they know inside out. A thoroughly musical and enjoyable account, enhanced by the *Parergon*, in which Gary Graffman proves an eloquent soloist. It is a strong work given with great character here, and more convincing than Malcolm Frager's for Kempe. Neither version is to be preferred to the Karajan, but both are thoroughly enjoyable.

Symphony in F min, Op.12;Symphony in D min.
(N) *** Koch Dig. 3-6532-2 [id.]. Berlin RSO or Bavarian RSO, Karl Anton Rickenbacher.

Like Korngold a generation later, Strauss was a composing prodigy. These two early symphonies, the one written when he was barely 16, the other at 19, may give little idea of the mature composer's style, but the skill of the writing is astonishing, not least the instrumentation. The *D minor* has many Mendelssohnian echoes, strikingly so in the first movement, while Opus 12 brings an admixture of Brahms, with just occasional Wagnerian hints. Clean-cut performances and recording. A welcome addition to Koch's series,'The Unknown Richard Strauss'.

Till Eulenspiegel.
(N) (B) (***) Dutton Lab. mono CDEA 5013 [id.]. Boston SO, Serge Koussevitzky – BERLIOZ: *Harold in Italy.*(**(*))

Till Eulenspiegel, recorded in 1945, makes a spectacular fill-up to Koussevitzky's pioneering account of the Berlioz, another fizzing performance, both warm and brilliant, very well-transferred in sound both full-bodied and airy.

CHAMBER MUSIC

Capriccio, Op. 85: String sextet.
*** Hyperion Dig. CDA 66704 [id.]. Raphael Ens. – BRUCKNER: *String quintet.* ***
*** Chandos Dig. CHAN 9131 [id.]. ASMF Chamber Ens. – ENESCU: *Octet in C;* SHOSTAKOVICH: *2 Pieces for string octet.* ***

The opening sextet from Strauss's last opera, *Capriccio*, makes an excellent fill-up to the Bruckner *String quintet*. Obviously readers are unlikely to buy the Bruckner for the sake of such a short work, even though it is of great beauty, but those who do will be rewarded by some fine music-making and recording.

The autumnal preface to *Capriccio* is also the expertly played fill-up to Enescu's remarkable *Octet*; very well recorded it is, too.

String quartet in A, Op. 2.
(N) (B) **(*) Hyperion Helios Dig. CDH 55012 [id.]. Delmé Qt – VERDI: *Quartet.*

The Strauss *Quartet* is early and derivative, as one might expect from a sixteen-year-old, but it is amazingly assured and fluent. The Delmé version is well played; however, although the basic acoustic is pleasing, the sound-balance remains a little on the dry side.

Violin sonata in E flat, Op. 18.
(N) (M) *** DG Dig 457 907-2 [id.]. Kyung Wha Chung, Krystian Zimerman – RESPIGHI: *Sonata.* ***
(M) (***) RCA mono 09026 61763-2 [id.]. Heifetz, Brooks Smith – BRAHMS: *Piano trio No. 1;* DOHNANYI: *Serenade.* (***)

Among modern versions Kyung Wha Chung is *primus inter pares*, and her version of the Strauss scores over rivals also in the power and sensitivity of Krystian Zimerman's contribution and the excellence of the DG recording. There is, however, a cut of 42 bars in the coda of the first movement (Universal Edition) which appears to be sanctioned, as Heifetz also observes it in his recording.

Heifetz's legendary recording of the Strauss *Sonata* with Brooks Smith, which has never been surpassed, was made in 1954 and comes with his 1941 recordings of the Brahms *B major Trio* with Rubinstein and Feuermann and a masterly account with Primrose and Feuermann of the Dohnányi *Serenade for string trio*. Self-recommending.

Piano sonata in B min., Op. 5; 5 Pieces, Op. 3; (i) *Enoch Arden, Op. 38;* (ii) *Ophelia Lieder, Op. 67.*
(M) ** Sony SM2K 52657 (2) [S2K 52657]. Glenn Gould; with (i) Claude Rains; (ii) Elisabeth Schwarzkopf.

Neither the early Op. 3 *Pieces* nor the *Piano sonata in B minor* are top-drawer Strauss, but Glenn Gould plays with such intensity that he almost convinces you that they are. Moreover the intensity is not overstated, and eccentricity surfaces only in his accompaniments for Elisabeth Schwarzkopf's *Ophelia Lieder*. Strauss's mélodrame to Tennyson's *Enoch Arden* is hardly one of the composer's success stories, but it has a certain period fascination that makes this disc worth collecting. Unfortunately, the sound is dry and the balance almost claustrophobic.

VOCAL AND CHORAL MUSIC

Choral music: *Der Abend; Hymne, Op. 34/1–2; Deutsche Motette, Op. 62.*
(B) *** Decca Double 455 035-2 (2) [id.]. Jessica Cash, Jean Temperley, Wynford Evans, Stephen Varcoe, Schütz Choir of L., Norrington – BRUCKNER: *Mass No. 2* etc. **

Strauss, usually the most business-like and practical of composers, made these unaccompanied choral pieces so difficult for any choir to sing that they have been almost totally ignored. The *German Motet*, with 16 choral lines plus soloists, has the sopranos soaring to top D flat and staying there, while the basses at one point go down to bottom B, and the shifting harmonies make one's head reel. But what matters is that in superb performances like these the music is richly poetic, quite distinct within the whole choral repertoire, with glowing reminders of Strauss's loveliest music, from the *Rosenkavalier Trio* and *Ariadne* to the *Four Last songs*. *Der Abend* might be a direct tribute to the heaven-vision of Strauss's friend, Mahler. The (originally Argo) recording is gloriously resonant and clear.

Choral music: (i) *An den Baum Daphne;* (ii) *Der Abend; Hymne, Op. 34/1–2;* (iii) *Deutsche Motette, Op. 62;* (iv) *Die Göttin im Putzzimer.*
*** Chandos Dig. CHAN 9223 [id.]. (i) Marianne Lund, Christian Lisdorf, Copenhagen Boys' Ch.; (iii) Tina Kiberg, Randi Stene, Gert Henning-Jensen, Ulrik Cold; (i–iv) Danish Nat. R. Ch., Stefan Parkman.

Although Stefan Parkman's account of the *Deutsche Motette* does not eclipse memories of the magical singing of the Swedish Radio Choir under Eric Ericson, this disc brings very good performances of some very beautiful and curiously little-known music. The engineers produce a realistic sound too.

8 Lieder, Op. 10; 5 Lieder, Op. 15; 6 Lieder, Op. 17; 6 Lieder, Op. 19; Schlichte Weisen, Op. 21; Mädchenblumen, Op. 22; 2 Lieder, Op. 26; 4 Lieder, Op. 27; Lieder, Op. 29/1 & 3; 3 Lieder, Op. 31; Stiller Gang, Op. 31/4; 5 Lieder, Op. 32; Lieder, Op. 36/1–4; Lieder, Op. 37/1–3 & 5–6; 5 Lieder, Op. 39; Lieder, Op. 41/2–5; Gesänge älterer deutscher Dichter, Op. 43/1 & 3; 5 Gedichte, Op. 46; 5 Lieder, Op. 47; 5 Lieder, Op. 48; Lieder, Op. 49/1 & 2; 4–6; 6 Lieder, Op. 56; Krämerspiegel, Op. 66; Lieder, Op. 67/4–6; Lieder, Op. 68/1 & 4; 5 kleine Lieder, Op. 69; Gesänge des Orients, Op. 77; Lieder, Op. 88/1–2; Lieder ohne Opuszahl.
(M) *** EMI CMS7 63995-2 (6) [EMIC 63995]. Dietrich Fischer-Dieskau, Gerald Moore.

Fischer-Dieskau and Moore made these recordings of the 134 Strauss songs suitable for a man's voice between 1967 and 1970, tackling them in roughly chronological order. With both artists at their very peak, the results are endlessly imaginative, and the transfers are full and immediate, giving fine presence to the voice.

Lieder: *Ach, weh mir unglückhaftem Mann; All meine Gedanken; Breit' über mein Haupt; Freundliche Vision; Heimliche Aufforderung; Ich liebe dich; Mein Auge; Morgen; Die Nacht; Nachtgang; Nichts; Ruhe, meine Seele; Ständchen; Traume durch die Dämmerung; Wie solten wir geheim sie halten; Wozu noch, Mädchen; Zueignung.*
(M) *** Ph. (IMS) 442 744-2 (2). Gérard Souzay, Dalton Baldwin – WOLF: *Italienisches Liederbuch.* ***

In subtlety of phrasing and beauty of line Souzay is here at his finest, and songs like *Ich liebe dich* or the delightful *Serenade* sound freshly minted. There is also a superb lightness of touch when called for. The accompaniments are characteristically sensitive and perceptive, and the recording is well balanced. But why did this have to come in harness with the *Italian Lieder Book* (as part of the Philips Early Years series), rather than be available separately?

Lieder: *Allerseelen; Ach Lieb ich muss nun Scheiden; Befreit; Du meines Herzens Krönelein; Einerlei; Heimliche Aufforderung; Ich trage meine Minne; Kling!; Lob des Leidens; Malven; Mit deinen blauen Augen; Die Nacht; Schlechtes Wetter; Seitdem dein Aug; Ständchen; Stiller Gang; Traume durch die Dämmerung; Wie sollten wir geheim; Wir beide wollen springen; Zeltlose.*
*** Ph. (IMS) Dig. 416 298-2 [id.]. Jessye Norman, Geoffrey Parsons.

Jessye Norman's recital of Strauss brings heartfelt, deeply committed performances, at times larger than life, which satisfyingly exploit the unique glory of the voice. The magnetism of the singer generally silences any reservations, and Geoffrey Parsons is the most understanding of accompanists, brilliant too. Good, natural recording.

Lieder: *Allerseelen; All' mein' Gedanken; Befreit; Cäcilie; Efeu; Heimliche Aufforderung; Herr Lenz; Hochzeitlich; Junggesellenschwur; Liebeshymnus; Mein Auge; Meinem Kinde; Nachtgang; Nichts; Das Rosenband; Sehnsucht; Ständchen; Traum durch die Dämmerung; Waldseligkeit; Wasserrose; Weihnachtsgefühl; Winternacht.*
(M) *** EMI Eminence Dig. CD-EMX 2250 [id.]. Simon Keenlyside, Malcolm Martineau.

Keenlyside follows up the success of his fine Schubert recital, also for EMI Eminence (currently withdrawn), with this excellent collection of Strauss Lieder, beautifully sung, again with Malcolm Martineau a most sensitive accompanist. Try the highly distinctive, intimate reading of *Ständchen* ('Serenade'), with Keenlyside singing almost in a half-tone and with Martineau playing magically. The fine-spun legato of *Waldseligkeit* and the poise of *Meinem Kinde* are equally impressive. Keenlyside uses a head voice for the gentle top notes of *Allerseelen* ('All Saints' Day'), but then finds plenty of power, sharply focused, in songs like *Befreit*. The sequence is rounded off with two exhilarating songs, *Cäcilie* and *Herr Lenz* (with its pun on the name Strauss – nosegay). Though this comes at mid-price, text and translations are provided. Excellent EMI sound.

Lieder: *Befreit; Hat gesagt, bleibt's nicht dabei; Ich trage meine Minne; Meinem Kinde; Der Rosenband; Die sieben Siegel; Wie sollten wir geheim sie halten.*
*** DG 437 515-2. Anne Sofie von Otter, Bengt Forsberg – BERG: *Early Lieder*. KORNGOLD: *Lieder*. ***

Anne Sofie von Otter and Bengt Forsberg follow up their prize-winning disc of Grieg songs with another inspired set of performances. Though they are even more illuminating in Berg and Korngold, the imaginative selection of seven Strauss songs brings warm, intense singing and sensitive accompaniments.

Lieder: *Des Dichters Abendgang; Freundliche Vision; Heimliche Aufforderung; Ich trage meine Minne; Liebeshymnus; Morgen!; Das Rosenband; Ständchen; Traum durch die Dämmerung; Verführung; Waldseligkeit; Zueignung.*
(N) (B) **(*) Ph. Virtuoso Dig. 432 614-2. Siegfried Jerusalem, Leipzig, GO, Masur.

Starting with an account of *Heimliche Aufforderung* that is both heroic and glowingly beautiful, Siegfried Jerusalem's collection of Strauss Lieder in orchestral arrangements provides a male counterpart to Jessye Norman's magnificent disc, also recorded with Masur and the Leipzig Gewandhaus Orchestra. The shading of tone which Jerusalem commands is most sensitive, as in *Morgen* or a delicate rendering of *Ständchen*. Naturally balanced recording, warmly reverberant to bring out the ravishing beauty of Strauss's orchestrations. However, the reissue has no documentation whatsoever apart from a list of titles. How can a major company like Philips allow this to happen?

Four last songs; Lieder: *Allerseelen; Freundliche Vision; Geduld; Die Georgine; Meinem Kinde; Morgen!; Muttertändelei; Die Nacht; Nichts; Das Rosenband; Ruhe, meine Seele!; Die Verschwiegenen; Wiegenlied; Die Zeitlose; Zueignung.*
(N) **(*) Decca Dig. 460 812-2 [id.]. Barbara Bonney, Malcolm Martineau.

Barbara Bonney uses her creamy soprano with great sensitivity and concern for detail in this generous selection of Strauss Lieder, even if the tonal range could be wider. With a high proportion of favourite songs, the disc can be fairly warmly recommended, though the *Four Last songs* are not entirely successful with piano instead of orchestral acompaniment. Even the keenly imaginative Malcolm Martineau cannot conceal the problems in the last two songs, which cry out for a sustained legato beyond anything possible on the piano, notably in the long link between stanzas in *Beim schlafengehen*. Warm, well-balanced sound.

Four Last songs; Lieder: *Das Bächlein; Befreit; Cäcilie; Freundliche Vision; Die heiligen drei Könige aus Morgenland; Mein Auge; Meinem Kinde; Morgen; Muttertändelei; Ruhe, meine Seele!; Waldseligkeit; Wiegenlied.*
**(*) Chandos Dig. CHAN 9054 [id.]. Felicity Lott, RSNO, Järvi.

Drei Hymnen, Op. 71. Orchestral songs: *Des Dichters Abendgang; Frühlingsfeier; Gesang der Apollopriesterin; Liebeshymnus; Das Rosenband; Verführung; Winterliebe; Winterweihe; Zueignung.*
*** Chandos Dig. CHAN 9159 [id.]. Felicity Lott, RSNO, Järvi.

Felicity Lott's two discs bring together a whole series of recordings of Strauss songs in their orchestral versions which originally appeared as couplings for Järvi's discs of the Strauss symphonic poems. She sings them beautifully, though the voice is not always caught at its most golden, notably in the *Four Last songs* which yet are movingly done. The second CD includes the first recording of *Drei Hymnen*, Holderlin settings composed in 1921, pantheistic poems about love of nature which are full of ardour and are provided with the most opulent accompaniments. Lott's voice, for the most part well focused, rides over the rich orchestral textures impressively, and throughout both discs there is agreeably warm, full, orchestral sound.

Four Last songs; Orchestral Lieder: *Das Bächlein; Freundliche Vision; Die heiligen drei Könige; Meinem Kinde; Morgen; Muttertändelei; Das Rosenband; Ruhe, meine Seele; Waldseligkeit; Wiegenlied; Winterweihe; Zueignung.*
❁ *** EMI CDM5 66908-2 [CDM 66960]. Elisabeth Schwarzkopf, Berlin RSO or LSO, Szell.

(i) *Four Last songs;* Orchestral Lieder: *Befreit; Cäcilie; Muttertändelei; Waldseligkeit; Wiegenlied. Der Rosenkavalier: suite.*
**(*) RCA Dig. 09026 68539-2 [id.]. (i) Renée Fleming; Houston SO, Eschenbach.

Four Last songs; Lieder: *Befreit; Morgen; Muttertändelei; Ruhe, meine Seele; Wiegenlied; Zueignung.*
(M) **(*) Sony SMK 76794 [id.]. Kiri Te Kanawa, LSO, Andrew Davis.

Four Last songs; Lieder: *Cäcilie; Meinem Kinde; Morgen; Ruhe, meine Seele; Wiegenlied; Zueignung.*
❁ *** Ph. Dig. 411 052-2 [id.]. Jessye Norman, Leipzig GO, Masur.

(i) *Four Last songs*. (ii) *Arabella* (opera): excerpts. (i) *Capriccio* (opera): Closing scene.
(***) EMI mono CDH7 61001-2 [id.]. Elisabeth Schwarzkopf, (i) Philh. O, Ackermann; (ii) Metternich, Gedda, Philh. O, Von Matačić.

Four Last songs; Die heiligen drei Könige. Capriccio (opera): *Moonlight music and monologue* (closing scene); *Metamorphosen for 23 solo strings.*
(M) *** DG Dig. 445 599-2. Anna Tomowa-Sintow, BPO, Karajan.

Strauss's publisher Ernest Roth says in the score of the *Four Last songs* that this was a farewell of 'serene confidence', which is exactly the mood Jessye Norman conveys. The start of the second stanza of the third song, *Beim Schlafengehen*, brings one of the most thrilling vocal crescendos on record, expanding from a half-tone to a gloriously rich and rounded forte. In concern for word-detail Norman is outshone only by Schwarzkopf, but both in the *Four Last songs* and in the orchestral songs the stylistic as well as the vocal command is irresistible, with *Cäcilie* given operatic strength. The radiance of the recording matches the interpretations.

For the reissued CD version of Schwarzkopf's raptly beautiful recording of the *Four Last songs*, EMI have added not just the old coupling of Strauss orchestral songs but also the extra seven which she recorded three years later in 1969, also with George Szell conducting, but with the LSO instead of the Berlin Radio Symphony Orchestra. There are few records in the catalogue which so magnetically capture the magic of a great performance, with the intensity of Schwarzkopf's singing in all its variety of tone and meaning perfectly matched by inspired playing. The current remastering seems to add even more lustre to voice and orchestra alike, and this CD is one of the highlights of EMI's 'Great recordings of the century' series.

Schwarzkopf's 1953 version of the *Four Last songs* comes with both its original coupling, the closing scene from *Capriccio*, also recorded in 1953, and the four major excerpts from *Arabella* which she recorded two years later. The *Four Last songs* are here less reflective, less sensuous, than in Schwarzkopf's later version with Szell, but the more flowing speeds and the extra tautness and freshness of voice bring equally illuminating performances. Fascinatingly, this separate account of the *Capriccio* scene is even more ravishing than the one in the complete set, and the sound is even fuller, astonishing for its period.

Before he made this recording of the closing scene from *Capriccio* with Anna Tomowa-Sintow, Karajan, supreme Straussian, had never previously conducted Strauss's last opera. It is a ravishing performance with one of his favourite sopranos responding warmly and sympathetically; if lacking the final touch of individual imagination that such inspired music cries out for, one senses the close rapport between conductor and singer. Similarly in the other late, great masterpiece, the *Four Last songs*, Tomowa-Sintow's lovely, creamy-toned singing tends to take second place in the attention, almost as if the voice was a solo instrument in the orchestra, and the result is undoubtedly very touching. The orchestral version of Strauss's nativity-story song makes an attractive extra item. The recording is warm, lacking a little in a sense of presence, but compensating in atmosphere. For this reissue Karajan's 1980 digital account of *Metamorphosen* has been added; it has even greater emotional urgency than his earlier, analogue version, recorded in 1971, and there is a marginally quicker pulse. Here the digital recording is rather more sumptuous.

Dame Kiri Te Kanawa gives an open-hearted, warmly expressive reading of the *Four Last songs*. If she misses the sort of detail that Schwarzkopf uniquely brought, her commitment is never in doubt. Her tone is consistently beautiful, but might have seemed even more so if the voice had not been placed rather too close in relation to the orchestra. The orchestral arrangements of other songs make an excellent coupling and Andrew Davis directs most sympathetically. A splendid mid-price recommendation.

Renée Fleming with her rich, mature soprano gives warmly sympathetic readings of the *Four Last songs*, thrilling in climaxes as the voice is allowed to expand, and full of fine detail, even if these readings lack the variety of a Schwarzkopf. The five separate orchestral Lieder also bring a wide expressive range, with *Waldseligkeit* beautifully poised, and ending boldly on *Cäcilie*. The singer is not helped by the way that Eschenbach makes the accompaniments seem a little sluggish, polished though the playing is. Something of the same lack of thrust marks his account of Strauss's own arrangement of the *Rosenkavalier* excerpts, despite beautiful playing from the Houston orchestra. How much more welcome would it have been to have had extra items from the singer.

OPERA

Die Aegyptische Helena (complete).

(M) **(*) Decca (IMS) 430 381-2 (2) [id.]. Dame Gwyneth Jones, Hendricks, Kastu, Detroit SO, Dorati.

Dorati, using the original Dresden version of the score, draws magnificent sounds from the Detroit orchestra, richly and forwardly recorded. The vocal sounds are less consistently pleasing. Gwyneth Jones has her squally moments as Helen, though it is a commanding performance. Matti Kastu manages as well as any Heldentenor today in the role of Menelaus, strained at times but with a pleasing and distinctive timbre.

Arabella (complete).

*** Decca 460 232-2 (2) [id.]. Della Casa, Gueden, London, Edelmann, Dermota, V. State Op. Ch., VPO, Solti.

*** Decca Dig. 417 623-2 (3) [id.]. Te Kanawa, Fontana, Grundheber, Seiffert, Dernesch, Guttstein, ROHCG Ch. & O, Tate.

(M) (***) DG mono 445 342-2 (3). Reining, Hotter, Della Casa, Taubmann, VPO, Boehm.

Della Casa soars above the stave with the creamiest, most beautiful sounds and constantly charms one with her swiftly alternating moods of seriousness and gaiety. Perhaps Solti does not linger as he might over the waltz rhythms, and it may be Solti too who prevents Edelmann from making his first scene with Mandryka as genuinely humorous as it can be. Edelmann otherwise is superb, as fine a Count as he was an Ochs in the Karajan *Rosenkavalier*. Gueden, too, is ideally cast as Zdenka and, if anything, in Act I manages to steal our sympathies from Arabella, as a good Zdenka can. George London is on the ungainly side, but then Mandryka is a boorish fellow anyway. Dermota is a fine Matteo, and Mimi Coertse makes as much sense as anyone could of the ridiculously difficult part of Fiakermilli, the female yodeller. The sound is brilliant. It has now been impressively remastered on to two discs with the break coming just before Milli begins her yodelling song.

Dame Kiri Te Kanawa, in the name-part, gives one of her very finest opera performances on record. It is a radiant portrait, languorously beautiful, and it is a pity that so unsuited a soprano as Gabriele Fontana should have been chosen as Zdenka next to her, sounding all the more shrill by contrast. Franz Grundheber makes a firm, virile Mandryka, Peter Seiffert a first-rate Matteo, while Helga Dernesch is outstandingly characterful as Arabella's mother. Tate's conducting is richly sympathetic and the Decca recording is first class.

Recorded live in August 1947 at the Salzburg Festival, the Boehm recording was issued in 1994 to celebrate the centenary of his birth, a radiant account with an outstanding cast. Maria Reining is here in firm, true voice, conveying not just the dignity of the heroine but the depth of feeling behind her often imperious manner. Hans Hotter too in his early maturity is in splendid voice, a superb Mandryka, characterful and well focused. Lisa della Casa, destined to make the role of Arabella a speciality, is here a charming Zdenka, fresh and girlish; and the rest of the cast includes many Viennese stalwarts of the period. Despite the limitations of the orchestral sound and some very rough playing, it is a most cherishable set.

Ariadne auf Naxos (complete).

(N) ❁ (M) (***) EMI mono CMS5 67077-2 (2) [CMS5 67156]. Schwarzkopf, Schock, Rita Streich, Dönch, Seefried, Cuénod, Philh. O, Karajan.

*** Ph. Dig. 422 084-2 (2) [id.]. Jessye Norman, Varady, Gruberová, Asmus, Bär, Leipzig GO, Masur.

**(*) Decca 460 233-2 (2). Leontyne Price, Troyanos, Gruberová, Kollo, Berry, Kunz, LPO, Solti.

(B) **(*) DG Double Dig. 453 112-2 (2). Anna Tomowa-Sintow, Kathleen Battle, Agnes Baltsa, Gary Lakes, Kurt Rydl, Hermann Prey, Heinz Zednik, VPO, James Levine.

(M) **(*) EMI CMS7 64159-2 (2). Janowitz, Geszty, Zylis-Gara, King, Schreier, Prey, Dresden State Op. O, Kempe.

Elisabeth Schwarzkopf makes a radiant, deeply moving Ariadne, giving as bonus a delicious little portrait of the Prima Donna in the Prologue. Rita Streich was at her most dazzling in the coloratura of Zerbinetta's aria and, in partnership with the harlequinade characters, sparkles engagingly. But it is Irmgard Seefried who gives perhaps the supreme performance of all as the Composer, exceptionally beautiful of tone, conveying a depth and intensity rarely if ever matched. Rudolf Schock is a fine Bacchus, strained less than most, and the team of theatrical characters includes such stars as Hugues Cuénod as the Dancing Master. The fine pacing and delectably pointed ensemble add to the impact of a uniquely perceptive Karajan interpretation – truly a 'Great Recording of the Century'. Though in mono and with the orchestral sound a little dry, the voices come out superbly.

Jessye Norman's is a commanding, noble,

deeply felt performance, ranging extraordinarily wide; she provides the perfect focus for a cast as near ideal as anyone could assemble today. Julia Varady as the Composer brings out the vulnerability of the character, as well as the ardour, in radiant singing. The Zerbinetta of Edita Gruberová is a thrilling performance and, even if the voice is not always ideally sweet, the range of emotions Gruberová conveys, as in her duet with the Composer, is enchanting. Paul Frey is the sweetest-sounding Bacchus on record yet, while Olaf Bär as Harlekin and Dietrich Fischer-Dieskau in the vignette role of the Music-Master are typical of the fine team of artists here in the smaller character parts. Masur proves a masterly Straussian and he is helped by the typically warm Leipzig recording.

Brilliance is the keynote of Solti's set of *Ariadne*. What the performance is short of is charm and warmth. Everything is so brightly lit that much of the delicacy and tenderness of the writing tends to disappear. Nevertheless the concentration of Solti in Strauss is never in doubt, and Leontyne Price makes a strong central figure, memorably characterful. Tatiana Troyanos is affecting as the composer, and Edita Gruberová establishes herself as the unrivalled Zerbinetta of her generation, though here she is less delicate than on stage. René Kollo similarly is an impressive Bacchus. The new Decca CD transfer is characteristically vivid, although it is not wanting in warmth and atmosphere. However, like *Arabella*, this set is now at premium price.

James Levine conducts a spacious, sumptuously textured reading of *Ariadne* which almost makes you forget that it uses a chamber orchestra. As Ariadne herself, Tomowa-Sintow with her rich, dramatic soprano adds to the sense of grandeur and movingly brings out the vulnerability of the character. But ultimately she fails to create as fully rounded and detailed a character as her finest rivals, and the voice, as recorded, loses its bloom and creaminess under pressure, marring the big climaxes. Both Agnes Baltsa as the Composer and Kathleen Battle as Zerbinetta are excellent: the one tougher than most rivals with her mezzo-soprano ring, little troubled by the high tessitura, the other delectably vivacious, dazzling in coloratura, but equally finding the unexpected tenderness in the character, the underlying sadness clearly implied in the Prologue duet with the Composer. She brings home just why the boy is so enamoured. The *commedia dell'arte* characters and the attendant theatrical team are strongly taken by stalwarts of the Vienna State Opera, among them Kurt Rydl, Hermann Prey and Heinz Zednik, while the Heldentenor role of Bacchus, always hard to cast, is strongly taken by Gary Lakes, clear-toned and firm, at times pinched but never strained. The very reasonable cost of this set should tempt many collectors to sample this very rewarding opera, particularly when the recording is so warmly flattering to both singers and orchestra.

Kempe's relaxed, languishing performance of this most atmospheric of Strauss operas is matched by opulent recording, warmly transferred to CD. Gundula Janowitz sings with heavenly tone-colour (marred only when hard-pressed at the climax of the Lament), and Teresa Zylis-Gara makes an ardent and understanding Composer. Sylvia Geszty's voice is a little heavy for the fantastic coloratura of Zerbinetta's part, but she sings with charm and assurance. James King presents the part of Bacchus with forthright tone and more taste than do most tenors. Compared with Karajan's mono set with Schwarzkopf, this is less than ideal, but that has rather dry mono sound and here there is warmth and atmosphere in plenty, and there is a price advantage over the Philips digital stero set with Jesseye Norman.

'Vienna State Opera live': Volume 23: *Ariadne auf Naxos* (complete).

(M) (***) Koch 3-1473-2 (2). Reining, Seefried, Noni, Lorenz, Schoeffler, Vienna State Op. O, Boehm (with WAGNER: *Meistersinger:* excerpts. (**))

Recorded live in June 1944, *Ariadne* is here presented in sound that is astonishingly full-bodied for the period. The sense of presence on the voices is most compelling, and it is fascinating to hear Seefried in the first of her three magnificent recorded performances, singing with, if anything, even more passion than later, in full, firm sound. Maria Reining makes a warm, touching Ariadne, and Max Lorenz as Bacchus has rarely been matched in subsequent recordings, sweeter and less strenuous than most Heldentenoren. Alda Noni makes a bright, mercurial Zerbinetta, not always note-perfect in her coloratura but with plenty of sparkle, and Paul Schoeffler is warm and wise as the Music-master. With 40 minutes of *Meistersinger* excerpts as filler, it is a historic set for non-specialists to consider.

(i) *Ariadne auf Naxos* (excerpts). Lieder: (ii) *Befreit; Einerlei; Hat gesagt; Morgen!; Schlechtes Wetter; Seit dem dein Aug'; Waldseligkeit.*

*** Testament SBT 1036 [id.]. Lisa della Casa, with (i) Rudolf Schock, BPO, Erede; (ii) Sebastian Peschko.

The 1959 stereo recording is full and immediate, bringing out the glories of Della Casa's creamy soprano but failing to convey the full, atmospheric beauty of the music, notably in the echo chorus of Naiads. Della Casa had earlier recorded *Ariadne's Lament* for Decca, but this is even more powerful. The first excerpt is of the opening of the entertainment from the overture through to Ariadne's first solo. There follow her second solo, *Ein Schönes war*, and the *Lament*, while the last extended excerpt has the whole of the final scene from the entry of Bacchus. Rudolf Schock sings nobly, and Erede brings out the lyrical warmth of the writing. Della Casa is less imaginative in the Strauss Lieder but still sings very beautifully and persuasively. The faithful and full Testament transfers bring out the wide range of the recording, tending to emphasize sibilants in the singing.

Capriccio (complete).
(***) EMI mono CDS7 49014-8 (2) [Ang. CDCB 49014]. Schwarzkopf, Waechter, Gedda, Fischer-Dieskau, Hotter, Ludwig, Moffo, Philh. O, Sawallisch.

In the role of the Countess in Strauss's last opera, Elisabeth Schwarzkopf has had no equals. This recording, made in 1957 and 1958, brings a peerless performance from her, full of magical detail both in the pointing of words and in the presentation of the character in all its variety. Not only are the other singers ideal choices in each instance, they form a wonderfully co-ordinated team, beautifully held together by Sawallisch's sensitive conducting. As a performance this is never likely to be superseded. The mono sound presents the voices with fine bloom and presence, but the digital transfer makes the orchestra a little dry and relatively backward by comparison.

Capriccio: Prelude. Feuersnot: Love scene. Guntram: Prelude.
*** DG Dig. 449 571-2 [id.]. German Opera, Berlin, O, Thielemann – PFITZNER: *Das Herz* etc. **(*)

These Strauss items, two of them rare, make an excellent coupling for the Pfitzner which Thielemann chose for his début recording with DG. Though in the *Feuersnot* Love scene the orchestra of the Deutsches Opera in Berlin is not quite as poised or refined as the Staatskapelle in Dresden for Sinopoli, the thrust and passion are even greater, with a freer expressiveness. Excellent sound.

Elektra (complete).
✿ *** DG Dig. 453 429-2 (2) [id.]. Marc, Schwarz, Voigt, Jerusalem, Ramey, V. State Op. Konzertvereinigung, VPO, Sinopoli.
*** Decca 417 345-2 (2) [id.]. Nilsson, Collier, Resnik, Stolze, Krause, V. State Op. Ch., VPO, Solti.

Sinopoli directs an incandescent performance of *Elektra*, at once powerful and sensuous, vividly recorded in full-bodied sound, and with a team of principals unmatched since Solti's classic recording with Birgit Nilsson. Alessandra Marc, a fine Chrysothemis in the Barenboim version, is here much more aptly cast in the title-role, instantly establishing her command in the opening monologue, magnetically done. Where she scores even over Nilsson is in the warmth and beauty of tone. Not only are the dramatic outbursts thrillingly projected with firmly focused tone, she is just as compelling in gentler moments, whether reflecting the creepily sinister side of Elektra's character or in her radiant ecstasy following her recognition of her brother, Orest. The glorious solo ending with the rapturous cry of '*Seliger*' ('happier') has never been caught so seductively on disc as here, with Sinopoli drawing glowing playing from the Vienna Philharmonic, if anything even more persuasive than he was in his recording of *Salome*. Deborah Voigt as Chrysothemis is clear and firm too, well contrasted, and Hanna Schwarz is a powerful Klytemnestra, with bitingly well-focused tone. Having such a fine, heroic tenor as Siegfried Jerusalem in the small role of Aegist is another tribute to the casting, crowned by the choice of Samuel Ramey as a warm and strong Orest, a perfect foil for Alessandra Marc. The performance is rounded off with a thrilling account of the final scene, capturing Elektra's hysterical joy with rare intensity.

Nilsson is almost incomparable in the name-part, with the hard side of Elektra's character brutally dominant. Only when – as in the Recognition scene with Orestes – she tries to soften the naturally bright tone does she let out a suspect flat note or two. As a rule she is searingly accurate in approaching even the most formidable exposed top notes. One might draw a parallel with Solti's direction – sharply focused and brilliant in the savage music which predominates, but lacking the languorous warmth one really needs in the Recognition scene, if only for contrast. The brilliance of the 1967 Decca recording is brought out the more in the newest digital transfer on CD, aptly so in this work. The fullness and clarity are amazing for the period.

(i) *Elektra: Soliloquy; Recognition scene; Finale. Salome: Dance of the seven veils; Finale.*
(M) *** RCA 09026 68636-2 [id.]. Inge Borkh, Chicago SO, Fritz Reiner; (i) with Schoeffler, Yeend, Chicago Lyric Theatre Ch.

With Borkh singing superbly in the title-role alongside Paul Schoeffler and Francis Yeend, this is a real collectors' piece. Reiner provides a superbly telling accompaniment; the performance of the Recognition scene and final duet are as ripely passionate as Beecham's old 78-r.p.m. excerpts and outstrip the complete versions. The orchestral sound is thrillingly rich, the brass superbly expansive. For the reissue, Reiner's full-blooded account of *Salome's dance* has been added, and Borkh is comparably memorable in the finale scene. No Straussian should miss this disc.

Feuersnot (complete).
(N) (B) *** Arts Dig. 47546-2 (2) [id.]. Julia Varady, Bernd Weikl, Helmut Bergere–Tuna, Tölz Boys' Ch., Bav. R. Ch., Munich RO, Heinz Fricke.

Feuersnot, Strauss's second opera,which was first given in 1901, is an allegory with an element of satire, set in medieval times. Like his first (*Guntram*) it is opulently scored, and in three compact Acts tells its story of Kunrad, a young sorcerer who, when rejected and ridiculed, puts a curse on the town, extinguishing all fire and light. This Bavarian Radio recording made in 1985 fills an important gap and is the more welcome on a bargain label. The performance is a fine one, with Bernd Weikl as Kunrad and Julia Varady as Dimut, his beloved, the Mayor's daughter – both outstanding. Heinz Fricke directs a warmly expressive performance in well-balanced digital radio sound. Recommended.

Feuersnot: Love scene. Die Frau ohne Schatten: Symphonic fantasy. Salome: Dance of the seven veils.

*** DG Dig. 449 216-2. Dresden State O, Sinopoli – WEBER: *Overtures: Der Freischütz; Oberon*. ***

Sinopoli has already shown us in his complete recording of *Salome* for DG, made in Berlin, how warmly sympathetic he is to Strauss's operatic music. With his Dresden orchestra the results are, if anything, even more sensuous, not least in *Salome's dance*, when ravishing string-tone is perfectly married to Sinopoli's moulded and flexible style. The Love scene from Strauss's very first opera, *Feuersnot*, is drawn from the closing pages of the opera, a delectable lollipop that ought to be much better known. Much the longest piece on the disc is the *Symphonic fantasy* from *Die Frau ohne Schatten*, which Strauss put together in 1946 at a time when complete performances of this favourite of his among his operas looked unlikely. Again Sinopoli's concentration and the gorgeous playing of the orchestra, sumptuously recorded, give cohesion to an obviously sectional piece. Odd as the coupling with Weber overtures is, the results are equally superb.

Die Frau ohne Schatten.

✽ *** Decca Dig. 436 243-2 (3) [id.]. Behrens, Varady, Domingo, Van Dam, Runkel, Jo, VPO, Solti.

In the Heldentenor role of the Emperor, Plácido Domingo, the superstar tenor, gives a performance that is not only beautiful to the ear beyond previous recordings but which has an extra feeling for expressive detail, deeper than that which was previously recorded. Hildegard Behrens as the Dyer's wife is also a huge success. Her very feminine vulnerability is here a positive strength, and the voice has rarely sounded so beautiful on record. Julia Varady as the Empress is equally imaginative, with a beautiful voice, and José van Dam with his clean, dark voice brings a warmth and depth of expression to the role of Barak, the Dyer, which goes with a satisfyingly firm focus. Reinhild Runkel in the key role of the Nurse is well in character, with her mature, fruity sound. Eva Lind is shrill in the tiny role of the Guardian of the Threshold, but there is compensation in having Sumi Jo as the Voice of the Falcon. With the Vienna Philharmonic surpassing themselves, and the big choral ensembles both well disciplined and warmly expressive, this superb recording is unlikely to be matched, let alone surpassed, for many years. Solti himself is inspired throughout.

Guntram (complete)

(N) (BB) ** Arte Nova Dig. 74321 61339-2 (2) [id.]. Alan Woodrow, Elisabeth Wachutka, Ivan Konsulov, Hans-Peter Scheidegger, Marchigiana PO, Gustav Kuhn.

Strauss's very first opera, set in the age of chivalry, is an opulent piece, unashamed in its high romanticism. On the Arte Nova label Gustan Kuhn conducts a warm, thrustful performance, recorded live at Garmisch-Partenkirchen, with the rich orchestral tapestries beautifully caught in open, refined sound, only occasionally disturbed by audience noises. Alan Woodrow makes a strong Guntram, with his firm Heldentenor tone only occasionally strained. Elisabeth Wachutka with her fruity soprano sounds too mature for the heroine, Freihild, and none of the other singers quite matches those in the currently withdrawn rival version on Sony, but this makes an excellent super-bargain set for those wanting to sample this opera inexpensively, although we hope the preferable CBS/Sony set will soon return to the catalogue.

Intermezzo (complete).

*** EMI CDS7 49337-2 (2). Popp, Brammer, Fischer-Dieskau, Bav. RSO, Sawallisch.

The central role of *Intermezzo* was originally designed for the dominant and enchanting Lotte Lehmann; but it is doubtful whether even she can have outshone the radiant Lucia Popp, who brings out the charm of a character who, for all his incidental trials, must have consistently captivated Strauss and provoked this strange piece of self-revelation. The piece inevitably is very wordy, but with this scintillating and emotionally powerful performance under Sawallisch, with fine recording and an excellent supporting cast, this set is as near ideal as could be, a superb achievement. The CD transfer is well managed but – unforgivably in this of all Strauss operas – no translation is given with the libretto, a very serious omission.

Der Rosenkavalier (complete).

✽ *** EMI CDS5 56242-2 (3) [EMIC 56242]. Schwarzkopf, Ludwig, Stich-Randall, Edelmann, Waechter, Philh. Ch. & O, Karajan.

*** EMI Dig. CDS7 54259-2 (3). Kiri Te Kanawa, Anne Sofie von Otter, Rydl,

Grundheber, Hendricks, Dresden Op. Ch., Dresden Boys' Ch., Dresden State O, Haitink.

(N) **(*) Decca 417 493-2 (3) [id.]. Crespin, Minton, Jungwirth, Donath, Wienr, V. State Op. Ch., VPO, Solti.

(N) (B) (**) Naxos mono 8.110034/36 (3) [id.]. Lotte Lehmann, Risë Stevens, Marita Farrell, Emanuel List, Friedrich Schorr, Met. Op.Ch. & O, Artur Bodanzky. (with Lieder Recital of 5/8/1948): Lotte Lehmann with Phd. O, Ormandy: *Allerseelen; Morgen; Traum durch die Dämmerung; Zueignung*. (Commentary: Jack Little). SCHUBERT: *Ständchen*. BRAHMS: *Wiegenlied* (both with piano)).

The glory of Karajan's 1956 version, one of the greatest of all opera recordings, shines out the more delectably on CD. Though the transfer in its very clarity exposes some flaws in the original sound, the sense of presence and the overall bloom are if anything more compelling than ever. As to the performance, it is in a class of its own, with the patrician refinement of Karajan's spacious reading combining with an emotional intensity that he has rarely equalled, even in Strauss, of whose music he remains a supreme interpreter. Matching that achievement is the incomparable portrait of the Marschallin from Schwarzkopf, bringing out detail as no one else can, yet equally presenting the breadth and richness of the character, a woman still young and attractive. Christa Ludwig with her firm, clear mezzo tone makes an ideal, ardent Octavian and Teresa Stich-Randall a radiant Sophie, with Otto Edelmann a winningly characterful Ochs, who yet sings every note clearly.

Vocally the biggest triumph of Haitink's beautifully paced reading is the Octavian of Anne Sofie von Otter, not only beautifully sung but acted with a boyish animation to make most rivals sound very feminine by comparison. If the first great – and predictable – glory of Dame Kiri's assumption of the role of the Marschallin is the sheer beauty of the sound, the portrait she paints is an intense and individual one, totally convincing. The portrait of Sophie from Barbara Hendricks is a warm and moving one, but less completely satisfying, if only because her voice is not quite so pure as one needs for this young, innocent girl. Kurt Rydl with his warm and resonant bass makes a splendid Baron Ochs, not always ideally steady, but giving the character a magnificent scale and breadth. Whatever the detailed reservations over the singing, it is mainly due to Bernard Haitink, and his long experience conducting this opera at Covent Garden and elsewhere, that this is the most totally convincing and heartwarming recording of *Rosenkavalier* since Karajan's 1956 set. This recording, unlike the Karajan, opens out the small stage cuts sanctioned by the composer.

The current remastering of the Solti *Der Rosenkavalier* from the late 1960s has brought the most striking improvement in the sound among all the Decca reissues of his Strauss opera series. The brilliance of the original recording remains, though without unnatural emphasis and there is now a compensating body and ambient warmth, so essential for this gloriously ripe score. The VPO strings have a lovely sheen, yet inner detail is glowingly clear. Crespin is here at her finest on record, with tone well focused; the slightly maternal maturity of her approach will appear for many ideal. Manfred Jungwirth makes a firm and virile, if not always imaginative Ochs, Yvonne Minton a finely projected Octavian and Helen Donath a sweet-toned Sophie. Solti's direction is fittingly honeyed, with tempi even slower than Karajan in the climactic meoments. The one serious disappointment is that the great concluding Trio does not quite lift one to the tear-laden height one ideally wants. Even so this *Rosenkavalier* offers much to ravish the ear.

Here with a live performance, recorded at the Met in 1939 on acetate discs, Naxos fill in many of the gaps in EMI's classic recording of Lehmann as the Marschallin, made earlier in Vienna. The orchestral sound is thin and variable, the swishing surface noise often intrusive, but the voices are surprisingly well caught, with Lehmann rich, firm and true, giving a commanding performance, cherishable in every detail. Risë Stevens at the beginning of her career makes a clear; positive Octavian, an excellent foil, characterizing well, and Marita Fareli as Sophie is bright and clear. The presentation of the silver rose scene is clean and accurate, with fine attack, but remains dry-eyed, lacking tenderness. Emanual List is a splendid Ochs, never letting the comedy undermine vocal lines, even if he is challenged at both top and bottom of the range. Friedrich Schorr is a commanding Faninal – luxury casting. Artur Bodzansky is an efficient conductor, opting for fastish speeds. In the manner of the day the score is savagely cut, with even the big ensemble reprise of the main waltz-theme omitted before the final scene. Lotte Lehmann adds a brief Lieder recital as a bonus.

(i) *Der Rosenkavalier* (abridged version); Lieder: (ii) *All' mein Gedanken; Freundliche Vision; Die Heiligen drei Könige; Heimkehr; Ich schwebe; Des Knaben Wunderhorn: Hat gesagt . . .; Morgen; Muttertändelei; Schlechtes Wetter; Ständchen* (2 versions); *Traum durch die Dämmerung;* (iii) *Mit deinen blauen Augen; Morgen; Ständchen; Traum durch die Dämmerung*.

(M) (***) EMI mono CHS7 64487-2 (2). (i) Lehmann, Schumann, Mayr, Olszewska, Madin, V. State Op. Ch., VPO, Robert Heger; (ii) Elisabeth Schumann; (iii) Lotte Lehmann (with var. accompanists).

It is good to have a fresh CD transfer, immaculate

in quality, of this classic, abridged, early recording of *Der Rosenkavalier*, containing some 100 minutes of music, made in 1933 in Vienna. Lotte Lehmann as the Marschallin and Elisabeth Schumann as Sophie remain uniquely characterful and, though 78-r.p.m. side-lengths brought some hastening from Heger, notably in the great trio of Act III, the passion of the performance still conveys a sense of new discovery, a rare Straussian magic. There is no libretto, but a synopsis is cued with each excerpt. As a bonus we are offered a glorious Lieder recital, featuring both the principal sopranos, and demonstrating Lehmann's darker timbre, the richness immediately noticeable at her first song, the lovely *Mit deinen blauen Augen*. Versions of *Traume durch die Dämmerung* and the soaring *Ständchen* are sung by both artists, and two different Schumann performances are included of the latter: one (from 1927) fresh and lilting, the other (from 1930) faster and with much clearer sound. *Heimkehr* (1938) is ravishing, and *Die Heiligen drei Könige*, from ten years earlier, with a remarkably well-recorded orchestral accompaniment, is also memorable. No song translations are included, but again the CD transfers are well managed.

Der Rosenkavalier: highlights.
(M) *** EMI CDM5 65571-2 [ZDM 634522]. Schwarzkopf, Ludwig, Stich-Randall, Edelmann, Waechter, Philh. Ch. & O, Karajan.
(M) *** Decca 452 730-2 [id.]. Régine Crespin, Elisabeth Söderström, Hilde Gueden, Heinz Holecek, V. State Op. Ch., VPO, Silvio Varviso.

On EMI we are offered the Marschallin's monologue to the end of Act I (25 minutes); the Presentation of the silver rose and finale from Act II; and the Duet and Closing scene, with the Trio from Act III, flawlessly and gloriously sung and transferred most beautifully to CD. A superb disc in every way.

This Decca set of highlights, gorgeously recorded in the Sofiensaal in 1964, is a collector's item. Régine Crespin was to go on to record the complete opera very successfully with Solti, but Varviso is hardly less sympathetic here. The present 62-minute selection was a trial run – and very successful it was. Crespin's portrayal of the Marschallin may be plainer than Schwarzkopf's and the projection of character less intense, but it is gloriously sung and remains very affecting indeed: Crespin rarely if ever made a better record. She is beautifully supported by Söderström and Gueden. The selection is admirably chosen to include the Introduction and opening scene, and the Marschallin's monologue, duet and closing scene from Act I (35 minutes in all). Then comes the Presentation of the Silver Rose from Act II (which ends without a tailoring cadence) and lastly, from Act III, the Marschallin's meeting with Sophie, the great Trio and final Duet between the two lovers. Not to be missed.

Der Rosenkavalier: highlights (in English).
(M) **(*) Chandos Dig. CHAN 3022 [id.]. Yvonne Kenny, Diana Montague, Rosemary Joshua, John Tomlinson, Andrew Shore, Mitchell Ch., Kay Children's Ch., LPO, David Parry.

This generous 80-minute selection from *Der Rosenkavalier* sung in English, reflects the strength of English National Opera's highly successful stage production. David Parry paces the score most persuasively, and the orchestral sound is aptly sumptuous, if a little clouded on detail. The selection of items, concentrating on the beginnings and endings of Acts, cannot be faulted, except that Tomlinson's strongly characterized Baron Ochs – with nobility part of the mixture – is represented only by the end of Act II, with its great Waltz theme. One snag is that the recording tends to exaggerate the singers' vibratos, intrusively so only with Yvonne Kenny as the Marschallin. She is strong but not very warm with such a noticeable flutter in the voice. On the other hand, Diana Montague is a winningly expressive Octavian, and Rosemary Joshua a sweet-toned Sophie. The booklet includes full text in the English version of Alfred Kalisch.

Salome (complete).
*** DG. Dig. 431 810-2 (2) [id.]. Studer, Rysanek, Terfel, Hiestermann, German Opera, Berlin, Ch. & O, Sinopoli.
(N) *** Chandos CHAN 9611 (2) [id.]. Inga Nielsen, Robert Hale, Reiner Goldberg, Anja Silja, Danish National RSO, Michael Schonwandt.
*** Decca 414 414-2 (2) [id.]. Nilsson, Hoffman, Stolze, Kmentt, Waechter, VPO, Solti.
(N) *** EMI CMS5 67080-2 (2) [CMS5 67159]. Behrens, Bohme, Baltsa, Van Dam, VPO, Karajan.
*** Decca Dig. 444 178-2 (2) [id.]. Malfitano, Terfel, Riegel, Schwarz, Begley, VPO, Christoph von Dohnányi.

The glory of Sinopoli's DG version is the singing of Cheryl Studer as Salome, producing glorious sounds throughout. Her voice is both rich and finely controlled, with delicately spun pianissimos that chill you the more for their beauty, not least in Salome's attempted seduction of John the Baptist. Sinopoli's reading is often unconventional in its speeds, but it is always positive, thrusting and full of passion, the most opulent account on disc, matched by full, forward recording. As Jokanaan, Bryn Terfel makes a compelling recording début, strong and noble, though the prophet's voice as heard from the cistern sounds far too distant. Among modern sets this makes a clear first choice, though Solti's vintage Decca recording remains the most firmly focused, with the keenest sense of presence, especially in the newly remastered version.

With an outstanding cast, the Chandos version, recorded in cooperation with the Danish Broadcasting Corporation, stands out among modern digital versions for its purposeful strength, intensely dramatic and warmly expressive from first to last. The involvement is made all the stronger by the rich, full recording, which balances voices relatively close, so that every word is audible, but gives comparable weight to the opulent orchestral sound. Inga Nielsen is a superb Salome, pingingly precise in her vocal attack, with an apt hint of acid in the voice but always firm, with no shrillness. The result is a portrayal with all the strength needed, not least for the unrelenting malevolence at the end, but leaving one with the impression of a character still young. Robert Hale is a characterful and expressive, if at times gruff, Jokanaan, and the Heldentenor, Reiner Goldberg, and the veteran Anja Silja, make an exceptionally strong, well-characterized duo as Herod and Herodias. Smaller roles are also well cast. A strong competitor for Sinopoli's comparably purposeful version with Cheryl Studer on DG.

Birgit Nilsson is splendid throughout; she is hard-edged as usual but, on that account, more convincingly wicked: the determination and depravity are latent in the girl's character from the start. Of this score Solti is a master. He has rarely sounded so abandoned in a recorded performance. Waechter makes a clear, young-sounding Jokanaan. Gerhardt Stolze portrays the unbalance of Herod with frightening conviction, and Grace Hoffman does all she can in the comparatively ungrateful part of Herodias. The vivid CD projection makes the final scene, where Salome kisses the head of John the Baptist in delighted horror (*I have kissed thy mouth, Jokanaan!*), all the more spine-tingling, with a close-up effect of the voice whispering almost in one's ear.

Hildegard Behrens is also a triumphantly successful Salome. The sensuous beauty of tone is conveyed ravishingly, but the recording is not always fair to her fine projection of sound, occasionally masking the voice. All the same, the feeling of a live performance has been captured well, and the rest of the cast is of the finest Salzburg standard. In particular José van Dam makes a gloriously noble Jokanaan, and in the early scenes his offstage voice from the cistern at once commands attention. Karajan – as so often in Strauss – is at his most commanding and sympathetic, with the orchestra, more forward than some will like, playing rapturously. This is a performance which, so far from making one recoil from perverted horrors, has one revelling in sensuousness. However, whether it is one of the 'Great Recordings of the Century' is open to question.

Dohnányi's is a clear, sharply focused reading, in full-ranging sound more refined than any. With the orchestra set further behind the voices than usual in Decca opera recordings, the violence is to a degree underplayed and the chamber quality of the score (intended by Strauss) enhanced. Catherine Malfitano brings out the girlish element in Salome, while also bringing out her malevolence. The beat in her voice can be distracting, occasionally turning into a wobble, but she rises superbly to the final scene, with full power and precision, a thrilling climax. As Jokanaan, Bryn Terfel is even finer than he was for Sinopoli, rich and firm, with the voice of the prophet from the cistern clearly focused. Kenneth Riegel as a neurotic Herod, Hanna Schwarz as a powerful, sharply dramatic Herodias and Kim Begley as a ringing Narraboth are all outstanding.

Die schweigsame Frau (complete).

(M) (***) DG (IMS) mono 445 335-2 (2) [id.]. Gueden, Wunderlich, Prey, Hotter, VPO, Boehm.

(M) **(*) EMI (SIS) CMS5 66033-2 (3). Adam, Scovotti, Burmeister, Trudeliese Schmidt, Dresden State Op. Ch. & State O, Janowski.

With a cast that could hardly be bettered, Boehm masterfully relishes the high spirits as well as the classical elegance of this late Strauss opera and, though the acoustic is dry and stage noises are often fearsomely intrusive, the sense of presence on the voices makes it consistently involving. Based on Ben Jonson's *Epicoene* but updated to 1780 by the librettist, Stefan Zweig, this comic opera about an old bachelor who hates noise is above all centred on lively, sharply pointed ensembles, and the starry cast is here splendidly drilled to bring out the humour. Hans Hotter in his prime makes a wonderfully bluff curmudgeon, pointing every word characterfully. Hilde Gueden – greeted with wild applause on her first entry along with Fritz Wunderlich – is a deliciously minx-ish heroine, using her distinctive golden tone, while the young Wunderlich gives a glorious performance. As the barber who aids the conspiratorial young couple against the old man, Hermann Prey has rarely sounded stronger or more beautiful on disc.

Janowski conducts an efficient rather than a magical performance, and Theo Adam's strongly characterized rendering of the central role of Dr Morosus is marred by his unsteadiness. Jeanette Scovotti is agile but shrill as the Silent Woman, Aminta. A valuable set of mixed success. The CD transfer brings the usual advantages but underlines the oddities of the recording. The reissue (unlike the previous full-priced set) includes a libretto/booklet with full English translation.

Arias from: *Die Aegyptische Helena; Ariadne auf Naxos; Die Frau ohne Schatten; Guntram; Der Rosenkavalier; Salome.*

(M) *** RCA GD 60398 [60398-2-RG]. Leontyne

Price, Boston SO or New Philh. O, Leinsdorf; LSO, Cleva.

Leontyne Price gives generous performances of an unusually rich collection of Strauss scenes and solos, strongly accompanied by Leinsdorf (or Cleva in *Ariadne*), always at his finest in Strauss. Recorded between 1965 and 1973, Price was still at her peak, even if occasionally the voice grows raw under stress in Strauss's heavier passages. It is particularly good to have rarities as well as such regular favourites as the Empress's awakening from *Die Frau ohne Schatten*, one of the finest of all the performances here.

Stravinsky, Igor (1882–1971)

The Stravinsky Edition: Volume 1, Ballets, etc.: (i) *The Firebird;* (i) *Fireworks;* (iii) *Histoire du soldat;* (i) *Petrushka;* (iv, iii) *Renard the fox;* (i) *The Rite of spring;* (i) *Scherzo à la russe;* (ii) *Scherzo fantastique;* (v) *The Wedding* (*Les Noces)* (SM3K 46291) (3) [id.].

Volume 2, Ballets etc.: (vi) *Agon;* (i) *Apollo;* (i) *Le baiser de la fée;* (i) *Bluebird (pas de deux);* (vii) *Jeu de cartes;* (viii) *Orphée;* (ix, i) *Pulcinella;* (ii) *Scènes de ballet* (SM3K 46292) (3) [id.].

Volume 3, Ballet suites: (i) *Firebird; Pétrouchka; Pulcinella* (SMK 45293) [id.].

Volume 4, Symphonies: (i) *Symphony in E;* (ii) *Symphony in C;* (i) *Symphony in 3 movements;* (x, ii) *Symphony of Psalms;* (i) Stravinsky in rehearsal: *Apollo; Piano concerto; Pulcinella; Sleeping beauty; Symphony in C; 3 Souvenirs* (SM2K 46294) [id.].

Volume 5, Concertos: (xi, i) *Capriccio for piano and orchestra* (with Robert Craft); *Concerto for piano and wind;* (xii, i) *Movements for piano and orchestra;* (xiii, i) *Violin concerto in D* (SMK 46295) [id.].

Volume 6, Miniatures: (i) *Circus polka; Concerto in D for string orchestra; Concerto for chamber orchestra, 'Dumbarton Oaks';* (ii) *4 Etudes for orchestra;* (i) *Greeting prelude;* (ii) *8 Instrumental miniatures; 4 Norwegian moods; Suites Nos. 1–2 for small orchestra* (SMK 46296) [id.].

Volume 7, Chamber music and historical recordings: (iii) *Concertino for 12 instruments;* (xiv, xv) *Concerto for 2 solo pianos;* (xv, xvi) *Duo concertante for violin and piano;* (xvii, xviii) *Ebony Concerto (for clarinet and big band);* (iii) *Octet for wind;* (xix, iii) *Pastorale for violin and wind quartet;* (xv) *Piano rag music;* (xviii) *Preludium;* (xx, iii) *Ragtime* (for 11 instruments); (xv) *Serenade in A;* (iii) *Septet;* (xii) *Sonata for piano;* (xxi) *Sonata for 2 pianos;* (xviii) *Tango;* (xxii) *Wind symphonies* (SM2K 46297) [id.].

Volume 8, Operas and songs: (xxiii, iii) *Cat's cradle songs;* (xxiii, xxiv) *Elegy for J. F. K.;* (xxv, ii) *Faun and shepherdess;* (xxvi,iii) *In memoriam Dylan Thomas;* (xxvii, iii) *3 Japanese Lyrics* (with Robert Craft)*;* (xxvii, xxix) *The owl and the pussycat;* (xxvii, iii) *2 poems by K. Bal'mont;* (xxx, i) *2 poems of Paul Verlaine;* (xxiii,i) *Pribaoutki (peasant songs);* (xxiii, i) *Recollections of my childhood;* (xxviii, xxxi) *4 Russian songs;* (xxxvii) *4 Russian peasant songs;* (xxiii, iii) *3 songs from William Shakespeare;* (xxvii, i) *Tilim-Bom (3 stories for children);* (xxxii) *Mavra;* (xxxiii) *The Nightingale* (SM2K 46298) [id.].

Volume 9: (xxxiv) *The Rake's progress* (SM2K 46299) [id.].

Volume 10, Oratorio and melodrama: (xxxv, i) *The Flood* (with Robert Craft); (i) *Monumentum pro Gesualdo di Venosa (3 madrigals recomposed for instruments);* (vii) *Ode;* (xxxvi) *Oedipus Rex;* (xxxvii, xxxviii, i) *Perséphone* (SM2K 46300) [id.].

Volume 11, Sacred works: (x) *Anthem (the dove descending breaks the air);* (x) *Ave Maria;* (xxxix, x, i) *Babel;* (xxviii, xxvi, x, iii) *Cantata;* (xl) *Canticum sacrum;* (x, ii) *Credo;* (x, iii) *Introitus (T. S. Eliot in Memoriam);* (xli) *Mass;* (x, i) *Pater noster;* (xlii, i) *A Sermon, a narrative & a prayer;* (xliii, i) *Threni;* (x, i) *Chorale: Variations on: Vom Himmel hoch, da komm ich her* (arr.); *Zvezdoliki* (SM2K 46301) [id.].

Volume 12, Robert Craft conducts: (xliv, i) *Abraham and Isaac;* (iii) *Danses concertantes;* (xlv) *Double canon: Raoul Dufy in memoriam;* (xlvi) *Epitaphium;* (i) *Le chant du rossignol* (symphonic poem); (i) *Orchestral variations: Aldous Huxley in memoriam;* (xlvii) *Requiem canticles;* (i) *Song of the nightingale* (symphonic poem) (SM2K 46302) [id.].

Complete Stravinsky Edition.

(B) *** Sony SX22K 46290 (22) [id.]. (i) Columbia SO; (ii) CBC SO; (iii) Columbia CO; (iv) Shirley, Driscoll, Gramm, Koves; (v) Allen, Sarfaty, Driscoll, Samuel Barber, Aaron Copland, Lukas Foss, Roger Sessions, American Chamber Ch., Hills, Columbia Percussion Ens.; (vi) Los Angeles Festival SO; (vii) Cleveland O; (viii) Chicago SO; (ix) Jordan, Shirley, Gramm; (x) Festival Singers of Toronto, Iseler; (xi) Philippe Entremont; (xii) Charles Rosen; (xiii) Isaac Stern; (xiv) Soulima Stravinsky; (xv) Igor Stravinsky; (xvi) Szigeti; (xvii) Benny Goodman; (xviii) Columbia Jazz Ens.; (xix) Israel Baker; (xx) Tony Koves; (xxi) Arthur Gold, Robert Fizdale; (xxii) N. W. German RSO; (xxiii) Cathy Berberian; (xxiv) Howland, Kreiselman, Russo; (xxv) Mary Simmons;

(xxvi) Alexander Young; (xxvii) Evelyn Lear; (xxviii) Adrienne Albert; (xxix) Robert Craft; (xxx) Donald Gramm; (xxxi) Di Tullio, Remsen, Almeida; (xxxii) Belinck, Simmons, Rideout, Kolk; (xxxiii) Driscoll, Grist, Picassi, Smith, Beattie, Gramm, Kolk, Murphy, Kaiser, Bonazzi, Washington, D. C., Op. Society Ch. & O; (xxxiv) Young, Raskin, Reardon, Sarfaty, Miller, Manning, Garrard, Tracey, Colin Tilney, Sadler's Wells Op. Ch., John Baker, RPO; (xxxv) Laurence Harvey, Sebastian Cabot, Elsa Lanchester, John Reardon, Robert Oliver, Paul Tripp, Richard Robinson, Columbia SO Ch., Gregg Smith; (xxxvi) Westbrook (nar.), Shirley, Verrett, Gramm, Reardon, Driscoll, Chester Watson Ch., Washington, D. C., Op. Society O; (xxxvii) Gregg Smith Singers, Gregg Smith; (xxxviii) Zorina, Molese, Ithaca College Concert Ch., Fort Worth Texas Boys' Ch.; (xxxix) John Calicos (nar.); (xl) Robinson, Chitjian, Los Angeles Festival Ch. & SO; (xli) Baxter, Albert, Gregg Smith Singers, Columbia Symphony Winds & Brass; (xlii) Verrett, Driscoll, Hornton (nar.); (xliii) Beardslee, Krebs, Lewis, Wainner, Morgan, Oliver, Schola Cantorum, Ross; all cond. composer. (xliv) Richard Frisch; (xlv) Baker, Igleman, Schonbach, Neikrug; (xlvi) Anderson, Bonazzi, Bressler, Gramm, Ithaca College Concert Ch., Gregg Smith; cond. Robert Craft.

On these 22 bargain-price discs (each volume also available separately at mid-price) you have the unique archive of recordings which Stravinsky left of his own music. Presented in a sturdy plastic display box that enhances the desirability of the set, almost all the performances are conducted by the composer, with a few at the very end of his career – like the magnificent *Requiem canticles* – left to Robert Craft to conduct, with the composer supervising. In addition there is a handful of recordings of works otherwise not covered, mainly chamber pieces. With some recordings of Stravinsky talking and in rehearsal (included in the box devoted to the symphonies) it makes a vivid portrait.

Of the major ballets, *Petrushka* and *The Firebird* are valuable, but *The Rite* is required listening: it has real savagery and astonishing electricity. (It is also available in a separate issue – see below). The link between *Jeu de cartes* from the mid-1930s and Stravinsky's post-war opera, *The Rake's Progress*, is striking, and Stravinsky's sharp-edged conducting style underlines it, while the *Scènes de ballet* certainly have their attractive moments. If *Orpheus* has a powerful atmosphere, *Apollo* is one of Stravinsky's most gravely beautiful scores, while *Agon* is one of the most stimulating of Stravinsky's later works, and here the orchestra respond with tremendous alertness and enthusiasm to Stravinsky's direction. The recording of *Le baiser de la fée* is a typical CBS balance with forward woodwind. However the splendid performance overcomes such a technical drawback. Stravinsky's recording of *Pulcinella* includes the vocal numbers, while in the orchestra the clowning of the trombone and the humour generally is strikingly vivid and never too broad. Similarly with the chamber scoring of the suite from *The Soldier's tale*, the crisp, clear reading brings out the underlying intense emotion of the music with its nagging, insistent little themes. There is a ruthlessness in the composer's own reading of *Les Noces* which exactly matches its primitive Russian feeling, and as the performance goes on so one senses the added alertness and enthusiasm of the performers. *Renard* is a curious work, a sophisticated fable which here receives too unrelenting a performance. The voices are very forward and tend to drown the instrumentalists.

In the early *Symphony in E flat*, Op. 1, the young Stravinsky's material may be comparatively conventional, but in this definitive performance the music springs to life. Each movement has its special delights to outweigh any shortcomings, while in the *Symphony in three movements* Stravinsky shows how, by vigorous, forthright treatment of the notes, the emotion implicit is made all the more compelling. The Columbia Symphony plays superbly and the recording is full and brilliant. Stravinsky never quite equalled the intensity of the pre-war 78-r.p.m. performance of the *Symphony of Psalms*, but the later, stereo version is still impressive. It is just that, with so vivid a work, it is a shade disappointing to find Stravinsky as interpreter at less than maximum voltage. Even so, the closing section of the work is very beautiful and compelling. The CD transfers of the American recordings are somewhat monochrome by modern standards but fully acceptable.

The iron-fingered touch of Philippe Entremont has something to be said for it in the *Capriccio for piano and wind*, but this performance conveys too little of the music's charm. The *Movements for piano and orchestra* with the composer conducting could hardly be more compelling. Stern's memorable account of the *Violin concerto in D* adds a romantic perspective to the framework. But an expressive approach to Stravinsky works marvellously when the composer is there to provide the bedrock under the expressive cantilena.

The *Dumbarton Oaks concerto* with its obvious echoes of Bach's *Brandenburgs* is one of the most warmly attractive of Stravinsky's neo-classical works, all beautifully played and acceptably recorded. The *Octet for wind* of 1924 comes out with surprising freshness and if the *Ragtime* could be more lighthearted, Stravinsky gives the impression of knowing what he wants. The *Ebony concerto*, in this version conducted by the composer, may have little of 'swung' rhythm, but it is completely faithful to Stravinsky's deadpan approach to jazz.

In *Le rossignol* the singing is not always on a par with the conducting, but it is always perfectly adequate and the recording is brilliant and immediate. *Mavra* is sung in Russian and, as usual, the soloists – who are good – are too closely balanced, but the performance has punch and authority and on the whole the CD quality is fully acceptable. The songs represent a fascinating collection of trifles, chips from the master's workbench dating from the earliest years. There are many incidental delights, not least those in which the magnetic Cathy Berberian is featured.

The Rake's Progress has never since been surpassed. Alexander Young's assumption of the title-role is a marvellous achievement, sweet-toned, accurate and well characterized. In the choice of other principals, too, it is noticeable what store Stravinsky set by vocal precision. Judith Raskin makes an appealing Anne Trulove, John Reardon is remarkable more for vocal accuracy than for striking characterization, but Regina Sarfaty's Baba is marvellous on both counts. The Sadler's Wells Chorus sings with great drive under the composer, and the Royal Philharmonic play with warmth and a fittingly Mozartian sense of style to match Stravinsky's surprisingly lyrical approach to his score. The CDs offer excellent sound.

The *Cantata* of 1952 is a transitional piece between Stravinsky's tonal and serial periods. However, of the two soloists, Alexander Young is much more impressive than Adrienne Albert, for her voice brings an unformed choirboy sound somehow married to wide vibrato. The *Canticum sacrum* includes music that some listeners might find tough (the strictly serial choral section). But the performance is a fine one and the tenor solo from Richard Robinson is very moving. The Bach *Chorale variations* has a synthetic modernity that recalls the espresso bar, though one which still reveals underlying mastery. The *Epitaphium* and the *Double canon* are miniatures, dating from the composer's serial period, but the *Canon* is deliberately euphonious.

The *Mass* is a work of the greatest concentration, a quality that comes out strongly if one plays this performance immediately after *The Flood*, with its inevitably slack passages. As directed in the score, trebles are used here, and it is a pity that the engineers have not brought them further forward: their sweet, clear tone is sometimes lost among the lower strands. In *The Flood*, originally written for television, it is difficult to take the bald narrations seriously, particularly when Laurence Harvey sanctimoniously keeps talking of the will of 'Gud'. The performance of *Oedipus Rex*, too, is not one of the highlights of the set. *Perséphone*, however, is full of that cool lyricism that marks much of Stravinsky's music inspired by classical myths. As with many of these vocal recordings, the balance is too close, and various orchestral solos are highlighted.

Of the items recorded by Robert Craft, the *Requiem canticles* stands out, the one incontrovertible masterpiece among the composer's very last serial works and one of the most deeply moving works ever written in the serial idiom. Even more strikingly than in the *Mass* of 1948, Stravinsky conveys his religious feelings with a searing intensity. The *Aldous Huxley variations* are more difficult to comprehend but have similar intensity. Valuable, too, is the ballad *Abraham and Isaac*.

OTHER RECORDINGS

Apollo (*Apollon musagète;* complete ballet); (i) *Capriccio for piano and orchestra. Pulcinella* (ballet): *suite.*
(M) *** Decca (IMS) 443 577-2. (i) John Ogdon; ASMF, Marriner.

In the *Pulcinella* suite, where the sharp separation of instruments (for example, double-basses against trombones in the *Vivo*) makes for wonderful stereo, the precision of the playing outshines that of almost all rival versions. The ethereal string-tones of *Apollo* make an ideal coupling, with the elegantly polished response of the Academy players comparing impressively with the outstanding Karajan version. Again the neo-classical quality of the *Capriccio*, a charming work, is beautifully underlined, while the soloist, John Ogdon, provides the contrasting element of sinewy toughness. An outstanding 'Classic sound' disc in every way, very well transferred to CD.

(i) *Apollo (Apollon musagète)* (ballet): complete; *Circus polka;* (ii) *Petrushka* (ballet: 1911 score): complete.
(B) *** DG Classikon 439 463-2. (i) BPO, Karajan; LSO, Dutoit.

Apollo is a work in which Karajan's moulding of phrase and care for richness of string texture make for wonderful results, especially in the glorious *Pas de deux*. The 1972 recording is of DG's highest quality and in no way sounds its age. The *Circus polka* is played with comparable panache. The coupling is Charles Dutoit's first recorded *Petrushka*, made for DG in the Henry Wood Hall in 1975/6. The result is triumphantly spontaneous in its own right, with rhythms that are incisive yet beautifully buoyant, and a degree of expressiveness in the orchestral playing that subtly underlines the dramatic atmosphere. Excellent value.

(i) *Apollo;* (ii) *The Firebird; Petrushka* (1911 score); *The Rite of spring* (complete ballets).
❁ (B) *** Ph. Duo 438 350-2 (2) [id.]. (i) LSO, Markevitch; (ii) LPO, Haitink.

Markevitch's gravely beautiful reading of *Apollon musagète* comes here with Haitink's strikingly refined account of the other key ballets. In *The Firebird* the sheer savagery of *Katshchei's dance* may be a little muted, but the sharpness of attack and clarity of detail make for a thrilling result, while the magic and poetry of the whole score are given a hypnotic beauty. In *Petrushka* the rhythmic feeling is strong, especially in the Second Tableau and the finale, where the fairground bustle is vivid. The natural, unforced quality of Haitink's *Rite* also brings real compulsion. Other versions may hammer the listener more powerfully, thrust him or her along more forcefully; but the bite and precision of the LPO playing here are most impressive, as throughout the set, while the recording's firm definition and the well-proportioned and truthful aural perspective make it a joy to listen to. Outstanding value.

Apollo (complete ballet; revised 1947 version); *Firebird* (ballet) *suite* (1945); *Scherzo fantastique*.
(N) **(*) Decca Dig. 458 142-2 [id.]. Concg.O, Chailly.

With superb demonstration-worthy Decca recording, and wonderfully delicate orchestral textures, Chailly achieves glowingly diaphonous sounds in Stravinsky's early *Scherzo fantastique* and then he revels in the rich Rimskyan colours of the extended 1945 *Firebird suite*, which includes the three delectable *Pantomimes*. Bold dramatic contrast comes with the explosive *Katschei's Danse infernale* and in the more expansive finale. A similar warm sensuousness pervades Chailly's somewhat indulgent reading of *Apollo*, where the score's refined neo-classicism is muted in favour of opulent warmth. Some of the ballet's rhythmic profile is lost, especially in the celebrated *Pas de deux*, which is far more voluptuous here than with Karajan. But with such gorgeous sound this is easy to enjoy.

Apollo; Orpheus (ballets).
*** ASV CDDCA 618 [id.]. O of St John's, Lubbock.

The ASV issue offers an ideal coupling, with refined performances and excellent recording. The delicacy of the rhythmic pointing in *Apollo* gives special pleasure, and there is a first-rate solo violin contribution from Richard Deakin. This is one of Stravinsky's most appealing later scores, as readily accessible as the more famous ballets of his early years.

(i–ii) *Le baiser de la fée* (ballet; complete); (i; iii) *Ode;* (iv) *Symphonies of wind instruments;* (i; ii) *Symphony in E flat, Op. 1*; (i; iii) *Symphony in C*; *Symphony in three movements*.
(N) (B) *** Chandos 2-for-1 Analogue/Dig. CHAN 241-8 (2) [id.]. (i) RSNO; (ii) Neeme Järvi; (iii) Gibson; (iv) Nash Ens., Rattle.

Strauss's deft scoring of *Le baiser de la fée* is here a constant delight, much of it on a chamber-music scale; and its delicacy, wit and occasional pungency are fully appreciated by Järvi, who secures a wholly admirable response from his Scottish orchestra. The ambience seems exactly right, bringing out wind and brass colours vividly. As for the symphonies, even when compared with the composer's own versions, the performances by the Royal Scottish Orchestra – in excellent form under Sir Alexander Gibson – stand up well, with Järvi directing the early *E flat* work equally impressively. The vivid naturalness of the splendid 1982 digital recordings compensates for any slight lack of bite. The cool, almost whimsical beauty of the *Andante* of the *Symphony in three movements* is most subtly conveyed, and the inner movements of the *Symphony in C* are beautifully played. Moreover the Nash Ensemble's perceptive account of the *Symphonies of wind instruments* under Rattle does not let the side down. It is good to have also as a bonus the *Ode* in memory of Natalia Koussevitzky, which has an extrovert, rustic scherzo section framed by short elegies.

Le baiser de la fée (ballet; complete). TCHAIKOVSKY, arr. STRAVINSKY: *Sleeping Beauty: Bluebird pas de deux*.
*** Sony Dig. SK 58949. [id.]. La Scala, Milan, PO, Muti (with BARTOK: *2 Pictures*. ***)

Muti gives the *Baiser de la fée* a performance of great elegance and finesse that is as good as any of its rivals. The recording is admirably detailed and the perspective well judged. If the Bartók coupling is suitable, this is very recommendable.

(i) *Le baiser de la fée (Divertimento);* (ii) *Petrushka:* excerpts: *(Danse russe; Chez Petrushka; La fête populaire);* (i) *Pulcinella: suite;* (ii) *The Rite of spring* (complete ballet).
(B) (***) EMI Rouge et Noir mono CZS5 69674-2 (2). (i) French Nat. R. O; (ii) Philh. O, Markevitch – PROKOFIEV: *Love for three oranges* etc. (**)

Markevitch's electrifying 1959 recording of *The Rite of spring* has long been famous, even though the documentation suggests that it is mono. The Philharmonia playing is superbly exciting, and the conductor's rhythmic vitality and ruthless thrust are matched by an amazingly spectacular recording which hardly sounds dated even now. In the elegant *Divertimento*, which Stravinsky culled from his Tchaikovskian ballet *Le baiser de la fée*, the French orchestral playing here has both finesse and flair. The three excerpts from *Petrushka* are similarly lively and colourful, and only *Pulcinella* is slightly disappointing: the trombones blow raspberries in their famous *Vivo* duet with the double basses, and elsewhere Markevitch dilutes the music's charm by his forcefulness. However this is certainly value for money.

(i, v) Le baiser de la fée (complete); *Pulcinella* (complete); *Symphony in C;* (ii, iii, v) *L'histoire du soldat: suite;* (ii, iv, v) *Octet for wind instruments.*

(N) (M) (***) Sony mono MH2K 63325 (2) [id.]. (i) Cleveland O; (ii) Oppenheim, Glickman, Nagel, Price; (iii) Howard, Schneider, Levine; (iv) Baker, Deutscher, Weis, Hixson; (v) composer.

The Cleveland Orchestra was apparently Stravinsky's favourite American Orchestra and he made these recordings with them in the early 1950s. Generally speaking, the performances have a greater polish and style than the later versions Stravinsky made in stereo with the CBC (Toronto) or the Columbia Symphony. The *Symphony in C* and *Le baiser de la fée* are particularly good. As always with their Heritage series, Sony give us handsome presentation and documentation. But they are priced at the very top-end of the mid-range.

Canon on a Russian popular tune; Firebird (ballet) suite (1945 version); Scherzo à la Russe; Symphony in E flat.

(N) ** DG Dig. 453 434-2 [id.]. Russian Nat. O, Pletnev.

A disappointment. Of course Pletnev is attentive to dynamic nuance and many other subtleties, but his *Firebird suite* is completely lacking in atmosphere. The *Scherzo à la Russe* and the early *Symphony in E flat* fare better. A mixed bag but very well recorded.

Capriccio for piano and orchestra; Concerto for piano and wind instruments; Movements for piano and orchestra; Symphonies of wind instruments.

*** Sony Dig. SK 45797 [id.]. Paul Crossley, L. Sinf., Salonen.

This is the sort of repertoire in which Esa-Pekka Salonen excels and in which Paul Crossley is also expert. All three performances can hold their own with the best, as indeed can the *Symphonies of wind instruments*. It is good to make the acquaintance of this CD, which can be confidently recommended to all lovers of the composer. Excellent digital recording too.

Le chant du rossignol (Song of the nightingale): symphonic poem.

✿ (M) *** DG 449 769-2 (2) [id.]. Berlin RSO, Lorin Maazel – RAVEL: *L'heure espagnole; L'enfant et les sortiléges;* RIMSKY-KORSAKOV: *Capriccio espagnol.* ***

(M) *** RCA 09026 68168-2 [id.]. Chicago SO, Fritz Reiner – RIMSKY-KORSAKOV: *Scheherazade* ***

Le chant du rossignol, which Stravinsky made from the material of his opera, deserves a much more established place in the concert repertoire. Maazel's justly famous version dates from 1958, slightly later than Reiner's. Maazel is nothing if not dramatic, but above all he revels in the glittering orchestral detail and the marvellous atmosphere this score commands. The Berlin Radio Orchestra produces a feast of chimerical glowing colours and the DG engineers of the time surpassed themselves. For today's ears the recording sounds as if it might have been made yesterday instead of 40 years ago, ideally selected for DG's 'Originals', and well coupled with Ravel's two delightful neo-classical operas and Maazel's superb Berlin Philharmonic version of Rimsky-Korsakov's *Capriccio espagnol* from the same period.

Reiner's version of 1956 in its currently remastered form also brings astonishingly full and vivid sound, full of presence, an excellent coupling for his strong and dramatic reading of *Scheherazade*. Reiner's virile, sharply focused reading relates it more clearly than usual to the *Rite of spring*.The virtuosity of the playing and the clarity of its direction are arresting, yet the refined and glittering detail of the orchestral palette is most evocative.

(i; ii) *Le chant du rossignol;* (iv; v) *L'histoire du soldat (The Soldier's tale)*; (i; iii) *Pulcinella* (complete ballet); (iv; vi) *Renard* (burlesque).

(N) (B) **(*) Erato/Warner Ultima 3984 24246-2 (2). (i) O Nat. de France, (ii) Boulez; (iii) Ens. Intercontemporain, with Murray, Rolfe Johnson, Estes; (iv) Instrumental Ens., Dutoit; (v) with Simon, Berthet, Carrat; Huttenlocher, Bastin; (vi) Tappy, Blazer, Huttenlocher, Bastin.

The two discs included in this Ultima Double make a particularly apt pairing, as the four works assembled here date from a notable period in Stravinsky's development when, shortly after composing *The Rite of Spring*, he moved from his Russian style into neo-classical mode. The symphonic poem which he created in 1917 from the material of his opera *Le Rossignol* (1914), with its extraordinary rich fantasy and vividness of colouring, marks the crossover, while *Pulcinella* draws on the music of Pergolesi. Here Boulez secures superb playing from the Ensemble Intercontemporain and his singers are first class in every way. His is a fine performance, but his pacing is more extreme than some versions with contrasts between movements almost over-characterized, helped with periodic added edge in the timbre.

The remaining two works are directed no less admirably by Dutoit, who brings out all their wit and irony, and in *L'histoire du soldat* the underlying melancholy. He is helped by splendid casts (Gérard Carrat a lively narrator and François Simon a cunning devil in the latter, with characterful violin solos from Nicolas Chumachenco, and Eric Tappy particularly impressive in the bizarre animal burlesque, *Renard)*. The ensemble playing, too, is crisp and plangent. Excellent recording. The one snag, and it is serious, is that while the use of the French language is a stimulating choice, the complete absence of librettos with translations is not – and there is a great deal of spoken dialogue in *L'histoire du soldat*.

Concerto for strings in D, 'Dumbarton Oaks'; 8 Instrumental miniatures; (i) *Ebony concerto.*

(M) *** DG 447 405-2. (i) Michel Arrignon; Ens. InterContemporain, Pierre Boulez – BERG: *Chamber concerto.* ***

A highly suitable coupling for the Berg in DG's 'Originals' series. The close sound is never two-dimensional and lacking in ambient colour. The playing of the Ensemble InterContemporain is very brilliant indeed. There is much to enjoy in these performances, which are spiced with the right kind of wit and keenness of edge, and even those who do not normally respond to Boulez's conducting will be pleasantly surprised with the results he obtains here.

Concerto for strings in D, 'Dumbarton Oaks'; Pulcinella (suite).

(M) *** DG (IMS) Dig. 445 541 [id.]. Orpheus CO – BARTOK: *Divertimento for strings* etc. **(*)

Remarkably fine playing from this conductorless group. Their ensemble in the *Pulcinella suite* is better than that of most conducted orchestras, and the overall impression they convey is one of freshness and spontaneity. Much the same must be said of *Dumbarton Oaks*, which has great zest and brilliance. The DG recording is clean and lifelike and the perspective very natural. While this disc does not eclipse memories of all rivals, it can more than hold its own with most competition, past and present.

Concerto for strings in D.

(M) *** DG 447 435-2 [id.]. BPO, Karajan – HONEGGER: *Symphonies Nos. 2 & 3* *** ✿

Karajan's version of the *Concerto in D for strings* – written within a few months of the Honegger *Symphonie Liturgique*, with which it is coupled – may strike some listeners as not quite acerbic or biting enough, but the finesse and lightness of touch of the Berlin strings and their rhythmic legerdemain are a delight. The recording is first class.

Ebony concerto.

*** RCA Dig. 09026 61360-2 [id.]. Stoltzman, Woody Herman's Thundering Herd – BERNSTEIN: *Prelude, fugue and riffs;* COPLAND; CORIGLIANO: *Concertos.* ***

Richard Stoltzman follows Benny Goodman before him in offering a suitably cool, yet lively and entirely idiomatic account of Stravinsky's *Ebony concerto*, coupled with Bernstein's *Prelude, fugue and riffs* and Copland's *Concerto*. Stolzman has the advantage of modern digital sound, and he also includes a fine account of John Corigliano's *Concerto*.

(i; ii) *Ebony Concerto;* (iii) *Violin concerto;* (iv) *Symphony in C; Symphony in three movements;* (ii) *Symphonies for wind instruments;* (v) *Symphony of Psalms.*

(B) **(*) Ph. Duo 442 583-2 (2). (i) Pieterson; (ii) Netherlands Wind Ens., Edo de Waart; (iii) Grumiaux, Concg. O, Bour; (iv) LSO, C. Davis; (v) Russian State Ac. Ch. & SO, Markevitch.

A lithe, refined, yet vital account of the *Violin concerto* from Grumiaux and the Concertgebouw Orchestra. The 1967 recording is just a little dated but well balanced. George Pieterson's version of the *Ebony concerto* with the Netherlands Wind Ensemble is not as overtly jazzy as some but its dry, sardonic wit and the dark sonorities of the finale make it individual. The *Symphonies for wind instruments* also show the controlled blend of colour for which this Dutch wind group are famous. Sir Colin Davis's account of the *Symphony in C* is splendidly alert, well played and stimulating. The performance of the *Symphony in three movements* is also lively, but compared with Stravinsky's own it is over-tense. Markevitch's 1964 Russian performance of the *Symphony of Psalms* is as vibrantly Slavonic as one could wish, yet the closing 'Alleluias' still bring a frisson in their raptly gentle expressive feeling. The sound is brightly vivid but not harsh.

Violin concerto in D.

(M) *** Decca (IMS) 425 003-2 [id.]. Kyung-Wha Chung, LSO, Previn – PROKOFIEV: *Concertos Nos. 1–2.* ***

*** Sony Dig. SK 53969 [id.]. Cho-Liang Lin, LAPO, Esa-Pekka Salonen – PROKOFIEV: *Violin concertos Nos. 1 & 2.* *** ✿

(N) *** Teldec Dig. 4509 98255-2 [id.]. Itzhak Perlman, Chicago SO, Barenboim – PROKOFIEV: *Violin concerto No. 2.* ***

(M) *** DG 447 445-2 [id.]. Itzhak Perlman, Boston SO, Ozawa – BERG: *Concerto;* RAVEL: *Tzigane.* ***

(N) *** Ph. Dig. 456 542-2 [id.]. Viktoria Mullova, LAPO, Esa-Pekka Salonen – BARTOK: *Violin concerto No. 2.* **

(M) (***) Sony mono SMK 64505 [id.]. Stern, Columbia SO, composer (with ROCHBERG: *Violin concerto.* *(**))

Kyung-Wha Chung is at her most incisive in the spikily swaggering outer movements which, with Previn's help, are presented here in all their distinctiveness; tough and witty at the same time. In the two movements labelled *Aria*, Chung brings fantasy as well as lyricism, less overtly expressive than Perlman but conveying instead an inner, brooding quality. Brilliant Decca recording, the soloist diamond-bright in presence but with plenty of orchestral atmosphere.

As in the two Prokofiev concertos, so in the Stravinsky Lin plays with power and warmth, while Salonen terraces the accompaniment dramatically, with woodwind and brass bold and full. The Prokofiev coupling is outstanding.

Though Perlman's coupling of the Stravinsky *concerto* and Prokofiev No. 2 on Teldec is most ungenerous, this performance, recorded live in 1994, is more compelling than his earlier studio recording, with Barenboim adding to the urgency and energy. Far more Stravinskian wit is conveyed in the outer movements, with rhythms more bouncy and with phrasing more seductively individual. In the two slow inner movements, Arias I and II, Perlman opts for speeds marginally more flowing, with Aria II more inward than before, more reflective even at a faster speed.

Perlman's precision, remarkable in both concertos on the DG disc, underlines the neo-classical element in the outer movements of the Stravinsky, while the two *Aria* movements are more deeply felt and expressive. The balance favours the soloist, but no one will miss the commitment of the Boston orchestra's playing, vividly recorded. The Ravel *Tzigane* has now been added for good measure.

The Stravinsky *concerto* suits Viktoria Mullova and her brilliant partners in Los Angeles rather better than does the Bartók coupling, and this version can certainly be put in our recommended list. The Philips recording is first rate in every respect.

Stern's 1951 mono recording with the composer has never been surpassed and seldom approached. The outer movements have an exhilarating combination of rhythmic bite and wit, and the two central arias bring a very special subtlety of colour and feeling. The sound is of the highest quality: no apologies whatsoever need be made for it. Listening to the record lifts the spirits, and we would have given it a Rosette were it not for the Rochberg coupling, which (as music) is very much of the second grade, even if Stern's performance is not.

Danses concertantes; Orpheus (complete ballet).
(N) *** DG Dig. 459 644-2 [id.]. Orpheus CO.

One continues to marvel at the sophistication and the seeming spontaneity of the playing from this unique conductorless chamber orchestra. The refined colouring and feeling for atmosphere at the opening of *Orpheus* and the sharp rhythmic bite of the later *Pas d'action*, is matched by the wit of the *Pas de deux* of the *Danses concertantes*, and the delicacy distilled in the *Thème varié*, with the closing sections of both works particularly satisfying. These performances are unsurpassed, and the recording is of DG's finest, very much in the demonstration bracket for ambient warmth, clear detail and natural balance.

The Firebird (ballet): complete (with rehearsal).
(M) *** Decca (IMS) 443 572-2 [id.]. New Philh. O, Ernest Ansermet.

The Firebird (ballet: complete).
(N) *** Ph. Dig. 446 715-2. Kirov O., Valery Gergiev – SCRIABIN: *Prometheus*. ***
(B) **(*) EMI forte CZS5 72664-2 (2) [CDEB 72664]. O de Paris, Seiji Ozawa – BARTOK: *Concerto for orchestra* **(*); JANACEK: *Sinfonietta* ***; LUTOSLAWSKI: *Concerto for orchestra*. **(*)

The Firebird (complete); *Le chant du rossignol; Fireworks; Scherzo à la russe.*
❁ (M) *** Mercury 432 012-2 [id.]. LSO, Dorati.

The CD transfer of Dorati's electrifying, 1960 Mercury version of *The Firebird* with the LSO makes the recording sound as fresh and vivid as the day it was made; the brilliantly transparent detail and enormous impact suggest a modern digital source rather than an analogue master made over 30 years ago. The performance sounds completely spontaneous and the LSO wind playing is especially sensitive. Only the sound of the massed upper strings reveals the age of the original master, although this does not spoil the ravishing final climax; the bite of the brass and the transient edge of the percussion are thrilling. The recording of Stravinsky's glittering symphonic poem, *The song of the nightingale*, is hardly less compelling. Dorati's reading is urgent and finely pointed, yet is strong, too, on atmosphere. The other, shorter pieces also come up vividly.

Ansermet came to London in November 1968 to re-record the complete *Firebird* in the Kingsway Hall, only a few months before he died, and achieved more polished playing than in his earlier version with his own Suisse Romande Orchestra; yet the interpretations are amazingly consistent. The first-class transfer readily demonstrates the atmosphere and vividly dramatic detail for which this conductor's records were justly famous.

The complete *Firebird* has been well served on CD in recent years but strangely enough this is its first recording (on Philips) by Russian artists. It has, as one might expect, a strong sense both of atmosphere and theatre, and Valery Gergiev manages the transitions between sections, dramatic characterization and contrasts with consummate mastery. The orchestra play with effortless virtuosity and are recorded with remarkable realism and definition. Although it is difficult to speak of a first choice in so hotly contested a field, Gergiev's would be a viable contender. The coupling, Scriabin's *Prometheus*, can hold its own alongside most rivals.

Ozawa's first (1972) recording with the Orchestre de Paris is a *Firebird* of luxurious and exotic plumage. True, in one or two pianissimo string passages there could be greater mystery and more tenderness, but for the most part this is very well played indeed. In its CD transfer the upper range now has that added digital sharpness of focus that is not quite natural.

(i) *The Firebird* (complete); (ii) *The Rite of spring* (complete).
❁ (M) *** Sony Theta SMK 60011 [id.]. Columbia SO, composer.
(BB) *** ASV Quicksilva CDQS 6031 [(M) id.]. (i) RPO, Dorati; (ii) Nat. Youth O of Great Britain, Sir Simon Rattle.
(B) *** Decca Eclipse Dig. 448 226-2. Detroit SO, Antal Dorati.

Stravinsky's own (1961) version of *Firebird* is of far more than documentary interest, when the composer so tellingly relates it to his later work, refusing to treat it as merely atmospheric. What he brings out more than others is the element of grotesque fantasy, the quality he was about to develop in *Petrushka*, while the tense violence with which he presents such a passage as *Katschei's dance* clearly looks forward to *The Rite of spring*. That said, he encourages warmly expressive rubato to a surprising degree, with the line of the music always held firm. But the revelatory performance here is *The Rite of spring*, for Stravinsky's own (1960) reading has never been surpassed as an interpretation of this seminal twentieth-century score. Over and over again, one finds passages which in the balancing and pacing (generally fast) give extra thrust and resilience, as well as extra light and shade. The digital transfer may be on the bright side, but brass and percussion have thrilling impact, sharply terraced and positioned in the stereo spectrum. This is a CD that should be in every basic collection.

On ASV Dorati's tempi in the *Firebird* are comparatively fast. But this matches his dramatic approach, as does a recording balance which is rather close, although there is no serious lack of atmosphere. Not surprisingly with Simon Rattle at the helm, the performance of the *Rite* by the National Youth Orchestra is not just 'good considering', but 'good absolute'; the youngsters under their young conductor (the recordings here date from 1976/7) produce warm and spontaneous playing, and the penalty of having a few imprecisions and errors is minimal. The sound here is slightly more atmospheric than in the coupling, but again there is plenty of bite and the timpani make a fine effect.

Dorati's Detroit version of *The Firebird* has the benefit of spectacular digital recording. The clarity and definition of dark, hushed passages are amazing. There is plenty of space round woodwind solos, and only the concertmaster's violin is spotlit. Although Dorati's reading has changed little from his previous versions with London orchestras, there is just a little more caution. Individual solos are not so characterful and *Katschei's dance* lacks just a degree in excitement; but overall this is a strong and beautiful reading, even if the Mercury LP account (see above), is not entirely superseded. Similarly, in terms of recorded sound, Dorati's *Rite* with the Detroit orchestra scores over almost all its rivals. This has stunning clarity and presence, exceptionally lifelike and vivid sound, and the denser textures emerge more cleanly than ever before. It is a very good performance too, generating plenty of excitement. The only let-down is the final *Sacrificial dance*, which needs greater abandon and higher voltage. However the performance is so vivid that it belongs among the very best.

The Firebird: suite (1919 version).
*** DG (IMS) Dig. 437 818-2 [id.]. O de l'Opéra Bastille, Chung – RIMSKY-KORSAKOV: *Scheherazade*. ***

Myung-Whun Chung gets very musical results from his players and there are many imaginative touches. The sound has great warmth and richness, but the perspective is absolutely right too.

Ballets: *The Firebird* (suite; 1919 version); *Jeu de cartes; Petrushka* (1911 version); (i) *Pulcinella* (1947 version); *The Rite of spring*.
(B) *** DG Double 453 085-2 (2) [id.]. LSO, Abbado; (i) with Teresa Berganza, Ryland Davies, John Shirley-Quirk.

(i) *Pulcinella* (ballet; complete); *The Rite of spring*.
(B) *** DG Classikon 439 433-2.

(i) Berganza, Ryland Davies, Shirley-Quirk; LSO, Abbado.

The highlight on this DG Double here is *Petrushka*, while both the *Firebird suite* and *Jeux de cartes* are given stunning performances. The LSO plays with superb virtuosity and spirit. The neo-classical score of *Pulcinella* is given a surprisingly high-powered reading, and not just the playing but the singers too are outstandingly fine. Abbado's feeling for atmosphere and colour is everywhere in evidence, heard against an excellently judged perspective. There is a degree of detachment in Abbado's reading of *The Rite of spring*, although his observance of markings is meticulous and the orchestra obviously revels in the security given by the conductor's direction. The recording here is multi-miked, and the effect is less exciting than one would have expected. Nevertheless this is a worthwhile investment if taken as a whole. As can be seen, *Pulcinella* and *The Rite of spring* are also available separately on a bargain Classikon CD.

Firebird suite; Pastorale.
(M) **(*) Decca Phase Four 443 898-2 [id.]. Czech PO, Stokowski – MUSSORGSKY: *Pictures at an exhibition* **; SCRIABIN: *Poème de l'extase*. **(*)

Tremendously sumptuous sound from Stokowski,

while some of the relatively quiet music (the dynamic range is limited by the forward balance) shows the wonderful luminosity he could uniquely command from the orchestra. Rich-textured violins dominate the beginning of the final climax, which is powerfully inflated. *The Pastorale*, a 'song without words' written in 1908, makes a pleasant and unusual bonus. It is warmly played and, again, sumptuously recorded.

Jeu de cartes.
(M) (**) EMI mono CDM5 66601-2. Philh. O, Karajan – BRITTEN: *Variations on a theme of Frank Bridge;* VAUGHAN WILLIAMS: *Fantasia on a theme by Thomas Tallis.* (***) ✿

First-class Philharmonia playing, of course, but Karajan's approach to Stravinsky's ballet rhythms is too suave to give satisfaction. This is music which, above all, needs at least a degree of bite – and that is not forthcoming here. But the Britten and Vaughan Williams couplings are a different matter; indeed, they more than justify the cost of this CD as an essential purchase.

Petrushka (ballet): complete.
(N) (***) Testament mono SBT 1139 [id.]. Philh. O, Stokowski – RIMSKY-KORSAKOV: *Scheherazade.* (**)

Stokowski's *Petrushka* with the Philharmonia Orchestra is superb. The orchestral playing is exciting and full of colour. It is almost as impressive as his famous pre-war set with the Philadelphia Orchestra – and that is saying something. It is coupled, however, with a somewhat idiosyncratic *Scheherazade.*

Petrushka (1911 original version).
(N) (M) *** RCA mono 09026 63303-2 [id.]. Boston SO, Monteux – FRANCK: *Symphony in D min.**** ✿

As he conducted the ballet's première, it is good to have Monteux's 1951 Boston recording at last satisfactorily remastered, with the sound now vivid and the Boston ambience more of an advantage than a drawback. The performance has undoubted flair and is very well played.

Petrushka (1911 version; complete). *The Firebird: suite* (1919). *Fireworks; Pastoral* (arr. Stokowski).
✿ (***) Dutton Lab. mono CDAX 8002 [id.]. Phd. O, Stokowski (with SHOSTAKOVICH: *Prelude in E flat min., Op. 34/14,* arr. Stokowski (***)).

Stokowski's 1937 version of *Petrushka* is very special indeed, the sound tremendously present and amazingly detailed for its period – high fidelity even by today's standards – and the performance is marvellously characterized and full of atmosphere: indeed it is difficult to think of a portrayal of Petrushka himself that is more poignant, keenly felt or brilliantly coloured. The playing of the Philadelphia Orchestra is quite stunning, and the Dutton transfer gets far more detail on to CD than the RCA rival; it is also smoother on top. The 1935 *Firebird suite* (its ending cut, to fit on a 78-r.p.m. side) takes wing too – equally strongly characterized and full of atmosphere. The shorter pieces are rarities. A marvellous collection – indeed, a desert island disc.

Petrushka (complete; 1947 version).
(N) (M) *** Carlton Dig. 30366 01002 [id.]. Boston PO, Benjamin Zander – RAVEL: *Piano concerto in G.* ***

Benjamin Zander conducts a remarkably compelling account of *Petrushka* which is extraordinarily vivid in detail, yet everything is placed within a natural perspective. There is no highlighting, and Stravinsky's score glows in its natural colours. The Boston playing is refined, yet the ballet's narrative is most atmospherically conveyed. The result is uncommonly satisfying and, if the unusual coupling is suitable, this is well worth considering.

Petrushka (1947 version); (i) *Pulcinella* (complete ballets).
*** Decca (IMS) Dig. 443 774-2 [id.]. Concg. O, Chailly; (i) with Anna Caterina Antonacci, Pietro Ballo; William Shimell.

A splendid digital *Petrushka* from Chailly, vividly characterized and with genuine pathos in Petrushka's cell scene. The orchestral playing is superb and the Decca engineers have pulled out all the stops, providing glittering detail, yet making full use of the warm Concertgebouw ambience. *Pulcinella* is equally winning, perhaps not as high-powered as the Abbado version, but with some splendidly incisive string-playing and plenty of rhythmic lift. Again the recording is in the demonstration bracket.

(i) *Petrushka* (complete 1911 score); (ii) *The Rite of spring.*
(M) **(*) Sony SMK 64109 [id.]. (i) NYPO; (ii) Cleveland O; Pierre Boulez.

There is a controlled intensity about Boulez's 1971 New York performance of *Petrushka*, and it is a pity that the 1971 recording, made in the Avery Fisher Hall, becomes fierce at higher dynamic levels. In *The Rite of spring*, recorded two years earlier in Severance Hall, Cleveland, Boulez is less lyrical than the composer but compensates with relentless rhythmic urgency. The massive vividness of sound matches the monolithic quality of the interpretation.

(i) *Petrushka* (1947 score); *The Rite of spring;* (ii) *4 Etudes for orchestra.*
(M) **(*) Mercury 434 331-2 [id.]. (i) Minneapolis SO; (ii) LSO; Dorati.

Dorati's famous (1959) Mercury recording of *Pet-*

rushka is exceptionally clean and vivid, with the semi-clinical Minneapolis recording bringing stereoscopic detail in the two central tableaux. There is plenty of drama too, and the final scene is touchingly done. Inevitably the sound is dated, with the bright upper range as caught by the Telefunken microphones not quite natural, but this adds a sharp cutting edge and impact to Dorati's extremely violent performance of *The Rite of spring*. His speeds are fast – sometimes considerably faster than is indicated in the score – but the LSO players carry complete conviction, the tautness of the work the more clearly revealed. The orchestral *Etudes* were recorded later (1964) in Watford, and have a fuller ambience.

Petrushka (1947) score; *The Rite of spring; Fireworks, Op. 4.*
(N) (M) ** RCA 09026 63311-2 [id.]. (i) Boston SO; (ii) Chicago SO, Seiji Ozawa.

Recorded in 1968 and 1969 respectively, and effectively remastered for RCA's new High Performance series, Ozawa's accounts of *Petrushka* and the *Rite of spring* are unequal in appeal. *Petrushka* is a lightweight interpretation in the best sense with Ozawa's feeling for the balletic quality of the music coming over, sometimes at the expense of dramatic emphasis. However, he is at times too dainty, and the underlying tension suggesting the strong feelings of the puppet characters is not always apparent. There are certainly more earthy accounts of the *Rite of spring* available, even if the Chicago acoustic adds to the weight of the performance. Curiously, the early *Fireworks*, which one would have thought suited Ozawa's talents best of all, sounds rather aggressive.

(i) *Pulcinella* (complete); *Renard. Ragtime; Octet.*
*** Sony Dig. SK 45965 [id.]. (i) Kenny, Aler, Tomlinson, Robson, Wilson-Johnson; L. Sinf., Esa-Pekka Salonen.

Salonen may be less objective than some rivals, but not only is the fun behind much of this music delightfully brought out, he moulds it sufficiently to suggest a warmth behind neo-classical forms and, frequently, a debt to jazz. That is so not just in *Ragtime* but also in such a work as the delightful *Octet* of 1922–3. When *Pulcinella* is here given with voices, it is good to have another early example of music-theatre in *Renard*, necessarily a rarity in concert, with the Russian folk-tale presented with bluff good humour. Warm recording to match.

(i) *Pulcinella* (complete); *Danses concertantes.*
(BB) *** Naxos Dig. 8.553181 [id.]. (i) Fiona James, Ian Bostridge, Henry Herford; Bournemouth Sinf., Stefan Sanderling.

The complete *Pulcinella ballet* is fresh and alert and with the impact of the crisp, clean ensemble reinforced by full and immediate sound on an apt chamber scale. This was one of the very first recordings made (in 1993) by the tenor, Ian Bostridge, and the heady beauty of his voice is superbly caught in such vocal numbers as the *Serenata*. The other soloists are also good. A full text and English translation are given, and it is good to have the far later *Danses concertantes* (1941–2) as a valuable makeweight, done with equal point and polish. Strongly recommended.

The Rite of spring (complete ballet) (see also above, under *Petrushka*).
(M) *** EMI Dig. CDM7 64516-2. Phd. O, Muti – MUSSORGSKY: *Pictures.* ***

Muti generally favours speeds a shade faster than usual, and arguably the opening bassoon solo is not quite flexible enough, for metrical precision is a key element all through, and the performance presents the violence with a red-blooded forcefulness that is very compelling. The recording, not always as analytically clear as some rivals, is strikingly bold and dramatic, with brass and percussion caught exceptionally vividly. At mid-price, coupled with an equally outstanding version of Mussorgsky's *Pictures*, this is very competitive indeed.

The Rite of spring (orchestral and pianola versions).
(N) (M) *** Carlton Dig. 30366 00992 [id.]. Boston PO, Zander; Rex Lawson (pianola).

Zander's live recording with the Boston Philharmonic brings a hard-hitting colourful performance, directly related to the pianola version with which it is paired. Stravinsky himself in the 1920s supervised the original Pleyela piano-roll recording, which Rex Lawson 'plays' very effectively on a resonant Bösendorfer Imperial. With this pianola system (unlike the reproducing rolls which captured the actual playing of a concert pianist) the piano roll represented a form of transcription of the printed score, accurate in note lengths and time values. The pianolist playing the score back uses pedals to create dynamic levels and accents, and levers to phrase and sustain, and bring the music back to life. The speeds at which everything is presented remain predetermined and unalterable; and here the most striking point on speed is the very fast tempo for the opening of the final *Sacrificial dance*, markedly faster than Stravinsky's own last – and finest – of his three recordings. Zander suggests (and he offers additional documentary evidence from Marie Lambert, the Russian ballerina, quoting comments made by the composer at the orginal dance rehearsals of the ballet) that Stravinsky intended this faster tempo for the ballet's finale and that he modified the tempo only when he discovered that orchestras could not cope with the music at his intended speed (even his own 1960 recording contains inaccuracies). There is no doubt that played up to this faster tempo, the *Danse sacrale* is electrifying, capping a performance which now projects rhythms with biting confidence that defeated professionals three-quarters of a century earlier. The recording is full and vivid if not always as sharply defined as the playing.

The Rite of spring; Circus polka; Fireworks, Op. 4; Greeting prelude (Happy birthday).
(N) (BB) **(*) CfP 573 4412. LPO, Mackerras.

Mackerras's version brings a powerful, often spacious performance, recorded in opulent and finely textured, if slightly distanced sound. The weight of the recording adds powerfully to the dramatic impact, though it is a pity that timpani are backward and less sharply focused than they might be. Though short measure, the three little orchestral trifles are done by Mackerras with delectable point and wit.

The Soldier's tale (*L'histoire du soldat;* complete).
*** Nimbus Dig. NI 5063 [id.]. Christopher Lee, SCO, Lionel Friend
*** Chandos Dig. CHAN 9189 [id.]. Aage Haugland, SNO, Järvi.

With the actor Christopher Lee both narrating and taking the individual parts, bringing out the sinister side of the story, the Nimbus issue brings an attractively strong and robust reading, lacking the last degree of refinement but with some superb solo playing – from the violinist, for example. The recording is vivid and full of presence, with the speaking voice related to instruments far better than is usual. For a version in English, it makes an excellent investment.

The Chandos version provides an excellent alternative. Aage Haugland takes a more forthright view than Lee, with the Soldier less of a Cockney and with the Devil given a crypto-French accent as a very oily character. Where the Chandos scores is in the sharper focus of the performance, generally brisker and tauter at faster speeds, helped by a close recording which yet has plenty of air round the sound.

The Soldier's tale (suite).
(M) *** Van. 08.8013.71 [OVC 8013].
Instrumental Ens., Leopold Stokowski – THOMSON: *Film scores.* ***

Stokowski works his magic upon this surprisingly neglected score, making the most of its lyrical warmth as well as the more abrasive Devil's music, which has plenty of rhythmic bite. The septet of expert instrumentalists is naturally recorded in a studio acoustic, but one which has plenty of ambience.

(i) *The Soldier's Tale* (English version; complete); (ii) *Dumbarton Oaks concerto in E flat.*
(N) (BB) *** Naxos Dig. 8.55366-2 [id.]. (i) David Thomas, Benjamin Soames, Jonathan Keeble, & Instrumental Ens.; (ii) Northern Ch. O.; Nicholas Ward.

With recording ideally balanced, intimate but not too dry, with fair bloom on voices and instruments, Nicholas Ward on Naxos offers a crisp and well-lifted account of the complete *Soldier's Tale*, with seven stylish players from the Northern Chamber Orchestra. Using the idiomatic English version of Michael Flanders and Kitty Black, the three actors characterize well without exaggeration. From the full chamber orchestra the *Dumbarton Oaks concerto* makes a generous and apt coupling, similarly crisp and persuasive.

CHAMBER AND INSTRUMENTAL MUSIC

(i) *Divertimento* (from *Le baiser de la fée*); *Duo concertante; Suite italienne;* (ii) *Mavra: Chanson russe.*
(M) *** EMI Analogue/Dig. CDM5 66061-2. Itzhak Perlman, with (i) Bruno Canino; (ii) Samuel Sanders (with RACHMANINOV: *Vocalise, Op. 34/14;* Songs: *It's peaceful here* (arr. Heifetz); *Daisies* (arr. Kreisler) ***; TCHAIKOVSKY: *Andante cantabile* from *Op. 11; Chanson sans paroles* (arr. Kreisler); *Souvenir d'un lieu cher: Mélodie, Op. 42/2* (arr. Flesch) **).

The *Italian suite* was arranged from the Pergolesi-based ballet, *Pulcinella*, while the *Duo concertante* was written after the *Violin concerto* and for the same artist, Samuel Dushkin. The *Divertimento* is arranged from movements of the Tchaikovsky-derived ballet, *The fairy's kiss*. Perlman plays all this music with warmth and understanding, and his achievement in the *Duo concertante*, which has often seemed a dry work, is particularly remarkable. Bruno Canino makes a sympathetic partner and the 1974 recording, originally excellent, has been clearly and cleanly transferred to CD, the sound more strongly etched than on LP. Perlman's seductively slinky account of the *Chanson russe* from *Mavra* was recorded four years later, and the two Rachmaninov songs, which are played with a delightful flowing lyricism, are digital; but in all these encores the sound is warmer and smoother. Samuel Sanders gives admirable support, although he is made to sound a little self-effacing by the recording balance.

3 Pieces for string quartet.
*** ASV Dig. CDDCA 930 [id.]. Lindsay Qt – DEBUSSY; RAVEL: *Quartets.* **(*)

A vital, finely etched performance of these delightful pieces from the Lindsays. A good fill-up to thoughtful and vigorous accounts of the Debussy and Ravel *Quartets*. Good recordings.

Suite Italienne for cello and piano.
(N) *** Virgin/EMI Dig. VC5 45274-2 [id.]. Truls Mørk, Lars Vogt – PROKOFIEV: *Cello sonata in C, Op. 119.* SHOSTAKOVICH: *Cello sonata.*

Truls Mørk and Lars Vogt give a very lively account of Stravinsky's delightful *Suite italienne*, the transcription made in collaboration with Piatigorsky of five numbers from *Pulcinella*. It is a welcome makeweight for their eloquent accounts of the Shostakovich and Prokofiev sonatas.

Suite italienne.
*** BIS Dig. CD 336 [id.]. Torleif Thedéen, Roland Pöntinen – SCHNITTKE: *Sonata;* SHOSTAKOVICH: *Sonata.* ***

Stravinsky made several transcriptions of movements from *Pulcinella*, including the *Suite italienne* for violin and piano. The performances by Torleif Thedéen and Roland Pöntinen, Swedish artists both in their mid-twenties, are felicitous and spontaneous, and they are afforded strikingly natural recording.

PIANO MUSIC

Piano duet

Rite of spring (arr. composer).
(BB) **(*) Arte Nova Dig. 74321 51638-2 (2) [id.]. Irina Tchernoussova, Elisabeth Romanovskaya – RACHMANINOV: *Suites Nos. 1–2* etc. **(*)

This splendid Russian duo plays Stravinsky's own piano-duet version of the *Rite of spring* with superb precision and clarity, aerating the complex textures. If the result is light and clear rather than barbaric, it certainly provides an illuminating view of this masterpiece, a generous and apt coupling for the Rachmaninov duets making up this two-disc issue.

Solo piano music

Circus polka; 4 Etudes, Op. 7; Piano-rag-music; Scherzo; Serenade in A; Sonata in F sharp min.; Sonata (1924); Tango.
*** Collins Dig. 1374-2 [id.]. Victor Sangiorgio.

Victor Sangiorgio plays with great character and virtuosity, and in some pieces is more successful and more thoughtful than his previous rivals. He also benefits from vivid and present recording. Thoroughly recommendable.

3 movements from Petrushka.
(M) *** DG 447 431-2 [id.]. Maurizio Pollini – *Recital.* ***

Staggering, electrifying playing from Pollini, creating the highest degree of excitement. This is part of an outstandingly generous recital of twentieth-century piano music.

Piano sonata; Piano-rag music; Serenade in A.
*** Chandos Dig. CHAN 8962 [id.]. Boris Berman – SCHNITTKE: *Sonata.* ***

Boris Berman is an artist of powerful intelligence who gives vivid and alertly characterized accounts of all these pieces. Excellent piano sound, too, from the Chandos engineers. Strongly recommended.

VOCAL MUSIC

(i) *Mass;* (ii) *Les Noces.*
(M) *** DG (IMS) 423 251-2 [id.]. (i) Trinity Boys' Ch., E. Bach Festival O; (i, ii) E. Bach Festival Ch.; (ii) Mory, Parker, Mitchinson, Hudson; Argerich, Zimerman, Katsaris, Francesch (pianos), percussion; cond. Bernstein.

In the *Mass* the style is overtly expressive, with the boys of Trinity Choir responding freshly, but it is in *Les Noces* that Bernstein conveys an electricity and a dramatic urgency which give the work its rightful stature as one of Stravinsky's supreme masterpieces, totally original and – even today – unexpected, not least in its black-and-white instrumentation for four pianos and percussion. The star pianists here make a superb, imaginative team.

(i) *Perséphone. The Rite of spring.*
(M) *** Virgin/EMI Dig. VMD5 61249-2 (2). (i) Anne Fournet, Rolfe Johnson, Tiffin Boys' School Ch., LPO Ch.; LPO, Kent Nagano.

Where Stravinsky himself – at speeds consistently more measured than Nagano's – takes a rugged, square-cut view of *Perséphone*, Nagano, much lighter as well as more fleet, makes the work a far more atmospheric evocation of spring. The narration of Anne Fournet brings out all the beauty of Gide's words, with Anthony Rolfe Johnson free-toned in the taxing tenor solos. Nagano's reading of *The Rite of spring* has similar qualities. If it is less weightily barbaric than many, the springing of rhythm and the clarity and refinement of instrumental textures make it very compelling, with only the final *Danse sacrale* lacking something in dramatic bite.

OPERA

Oedipus Rex (opera-oratorio).
*** Sony Dig. SK 48057 [id.]. Cole, Von Otter, Estes, Sotin, Gedda, Chéreau, Eric Ericson Chamber Ch., Swedish RSO & Ch., Salonen.

Salonen with his Swedish forces and an outstanding cast offers an ideal combination of rugged power and warmth, delivered expressively but without sentimentality. The pinpoint precision of ensemble of the choruses does more than anything else to punch home the impact of this so-called opera-oratorio, with its powerful commentary, Greek-style. The singing of the two principals, Vinson Cole as Oedipus and Anne Sofie von Otter as Jocasta, then conveys the full depth of emotion behind the piece. Simon Estes as Creon and Hans Sotin as Tiresias are both firm and resonant, with Nicolai Gedda still strong as the Shepherd. With recorded sound both dramatically immediate and warm, and with splendid narration in French from Patrice Chéreau, this displaces all rivals, even the composer's own American version.

Stravinsky Edition, Volume 9: *The Rake's progress* (complete).
(M) *** Sony SM2K 46299 (2) [id.]. Young, Raskin, Reardon, Sarfaty, Miller, Manning, Sadler's Wells Op. Ch., RPO, composer.

The Rake's progress (complete).
(N) *** DG Dig. 459 648-2 (2) [id.]. Ian Bostridge, Deborah York, Bryn Terfell, Martin Robson, Anne Howells, Anne Sofie von Otter, Monteverdi Ch., Gardiner.
*** Erato/Warner Dig. 0630 12715-2 (2). Hadley, Upshaw, Lloyd, Ramey, Collins, Bumbry, Lyon Opera Ch. & O, Kent Nagano.

It was a splendid idea to get Stravinsky to come to London to record *The Rake's progress* in what has many elements of the original Sadler's Wells production – which incidentally the composer attended some time earlier. The casting is uniformly excellent with the Rake of Alexander Young dominating but Judith Raskin an attractive heroine. Regina Sarfaty's Baba is superbly characterized and her anger at being spurned just before the 'squelching' makes a riveting moment. The composer conducts with warmth as well as precision, both chorus and orchestra respond persuasively, and the CD transfer is excellent.

With two such characterful singers in the central roles of Tom and Nick Shadow, Gardiner's DG set instantly establishes its individuality, and Gardiner's incisive direction, with brilliant, polished playing from the LSO confirms this as the finest of modern versions. It even outshines the composer's own vintage version, equally well cast, when Gardiner, at speeds often faster than usual, brings extra sparkle to the rhythmic neo-classical writing and conveys a hushed intensity in the many tender moments of this moral tale. Bostridge's lyric tenor might seem too light for the role of Tom, but with fine pointing of words he underlines the Rake's vulnerability, the ease with which he gives way to temptation. Terfel makes a seductive Nick Shadow, strong and sardonic, singing superbly, and the young American, Deborah York, sings with golden tone and dazzling flexibility as Anne, untroubled by high tessitura. The rest of the team is equally strong, with Anne Sofie von Otter making Baba the Turk the most eloquent nagger. Well-balanced recording – the point on which other modern versions fall short – with well-defined sound staging.

Kent Nagano, with his Lyon Opera forces and an outstanding cast of soloists, directs a fresh and crisp account. In the title-role Jerry Hadley, with his fresh, clear tone, is aptly youthful-sounding and brings out the pathos of the final scenes when struck insane by Nick Shadow. Samuel Ramey is powerful and sinister in that devilish role, as he was in the earlier, Chailly version, and Dawn Upshaw makes a tenderly affecting Anne Trulove, bringing out the heroine's vulnerability. Robert Lloyd as Trulove and Anne Collins as Mother Goose are both very well cast, and the veteran, Grace Bumbry, makes a fruity Baba the Turk. Excellent ensemble from the Lyon Opera chorus, though the balance is a little backward. Otherwise first-rate sound, making this a good, modern, digital alternative to the composer's own version.

Le rossignol (complete).
(N) ❁ (***) Testament mono SBT 1135 [id.]. Janine Micheau, Geneviève Moizan, Jean Giraudeau, Lucien Lovano, Michel Roux; French R. Ch. & O., André Cluytens – DELAGE: *Quatre Poèmes hindous*. ***

Le rossignol was begun before *Firebird* and finished after *The Rite of spring* and remains one of Stravinsky's most magical and imaginative creations. By comparison with his other masterpieces it has been curiously neglected on record. Apart from Stravinsky himself and Boulez ('that arch-opportunist', as Stravinsky once called him), André Cluytens's pioneering mono account completes its discography. The performance comes from 1954 and those who purchased it at the time (as did R. L.) have subsequently found their allegiance unchallenged by its successors. Apart from the powerful atmosphere that Cluytens evokes from his fine orchestra, the performance is unforgettable on account of the superlative singing of Janine Micheau in the title role and the general excellence of the other soloists. It has something of the same quality of sheer perfection that distinguished Ernest Bour's recording of Ravel's *L'Enfant et les sortilèges*, which Testament restored to circulation some years ago.

Strozzi, Barbara (c. 1619–64)

Sacri musicali affetti, Libro I, *Op. 5* (extracts): *Erat Petrus; Hodie oritur; Mater Anna; Nascente Maria; O, Maria; Parasti cor meum; Salve Regina; Salve sancta caro.*
❁ *** HM Dig. ED 13048 [id.]. Maria Cristina Kiehr, Concerto Soave (with: GIANONCELLI: *Tastegiatas 1–2;* BIAGIO MARINI: *Sonate da chiesa e da camera; Sinfonia secondo tuono;* TARQUINIO MERULA: *Capriccio cromatico; Canzon* ***).

Born in about 1619, Barbara Strozzi was the adopted daughter of the poet Giulio Strozzi, librettist for

Monteverdi and Cavalli, and she became a highly regarded pupil of the latter composer. She initially made her name both as a singer and as a woman of great beauty, and her writing combines purity of feeling and line with a sensuous spiritual ecstasy that is uniquely feminine.

The opening *Salve Regina* with its sighing phrases and melancholy descending scale is wonderfully tender, yet the music has a life-celebrating vitality too. The motet *Erat Petrus* (the Gospel story of Peter set free from prison) is virtually an operatic scena, set with great rhythmic variety and using a dialogue device between 'two' voices with aplomb. The melodic line of *Mater Anna* is simple but quite lovely, and here it is a rising scale which brings a ravishing frisson. Perhaps most remarkable of all is the ravishing F minor *Parasti cor meum*, bringing sliding chromatic glissandi – surely a perfect illustration of the Italian word, *affetti*. Maria Kiehr's singing here is unforgettable, as is her bravura decorative flair; indeed her ornamentation is a model of expressive understanding throughout. She is beautifully accompanied by the appropriately named Concerto Soave. To make the programme even more enjoyable, the vocal items are interspersed with admirably chosen intrumental pieces by Strozzi's contemporaries. The recording is admirably balanced and very natural. This is a treasurable collection and a musical revelation.

'To the unknown goddess': Cantate, ariette e duetti, Op. 2: L'amante segreto . . . Voglio, voglio morire; Amor dormiglione . . . Amor, non dormir più; La fanciuletta semplice . . . Spesso per entro al petto; Gite o giorni dolenti; Giusta negativa . . . Non mi dite ch'io canti; La sol, fa, mi, re do . . . La mia donna perchè canta. Cantate ariete a una, due e tre voci, Op. 3: Ardo in tacito foco. Diporti di Euterpe, Op. 7: Appresso ai molli argenti; Lagrime mie . . . Lagrime mie, a che vi trattenete; Pensaci ben mio core; Tradimento.
(M) *** Carlton Dig. 30366 00412 [id.].
Catherine Bott, Paula Chateauneuf; Timothy Roberts; Frances Kelly.

This Carlton CD turns from Barbara Strozzi's religious music to her secular love songs. The very first in this recital, *Ardo in tacito foco* ('The heart forbids the tongue to pronounce the beloved's name') immediately displays her characteristic languishing musical device of a chromatically inclined downward scale, while the opening of the Lamento, *Lagrime mie, a che vi trattenete* ('My tears, why do you hold back'), with its equally luscious chromatic sighs, is just as affecting. Catherine Bott revels in its yearning line, with her embellishments adding to the languor. But there is considerable variety of mood here. *La fanciuletta semplice* ('The simple girl') and *Amor dormiglione* are both charmingly fresh and uncomplicated. Most eloquent of all is the closing *Appresso ai molli argenti* ('Close to the soft banks of a murmuring stream') with its remarkable word-imagery set with real imaginative flair. Catherine Bott encompasses its florid upper tessitura with freshness and ease, she responds readily to moments of sensuality, and her bravura decorated runs are remarkably secure. The small accompanying group (archlute or guitar, harpsichord and double harp) is just right, and so is the recording balance. Strongly recommended, especially if you have already tried the Harmonia Mundi disc.

Suk, Josef (1874–1935)

Asrael Symphony, Op. 27.
✿ *** Chandos Dig. CHAN 9042 [id.]. Czech PO, Bělohlávek.
(M) *** EMI CDM5 73480-2 [id.]. RLPO, Pešek.

Jiří Bělohlávek, the principal conductor of the Czech Philharmonic, draws powerfully expressive playing from the orchestra in a work which in its five large-scale movements is predominantly slow. Next to Pešek's fine Liverpool performance, the speeds flow a degree faster and more persuasively, and the ensemble, notably of the woodwind, is even crisper, phenomenally so. It helps too that the sound is warmer, closer and more involving than the refined but more distant Virgin recording.

Pešek's Liverpool version has altogether greater sensitivity and imagination than the earlier Supraphon account from Vaclav Neumann, and the sympathy of the Liverpool players is very apparent, but there is no doubt that Bělohlávek's gutsier Czech performance has a greater sense of thrust and power, and for those coming new to this fine work it will be a revelation.

A Fairy-tale, Op. 16; Praga (symphonic poem), Op. 26.
*** Sup. Dig. 10 3389-2 [id.]. Czech PO, Libor Pešek.

Suk's *A Fairy-tale* is full of charm and originality, and it is persuasively played here. It is coupled with *Praga*, a patriotic tone-poem reflecting a more public, out-going figure than *Asrael*, which was to follow it. Libor Pešek secures an excellent response from the Czech Philharmonic; the recordings, which date from 1981–2, are reverberant but good.

A Fairy-tale, Op. 16; Serenade for strings in E flat, Op. 6.
*** Chandos Dig. CHAN 9063 [id.]. Czech PO, Jiří Bělohlávek.

This new Chandos account of the unfailingly fresh *Serenade for strings* is probably the most captivating since the days of Talich, and the Czech Philharmonic strings play with their customary warmth and eloquence. *A Fairy tale* (*Pohádka*) is beautifully played and certainly better recorded than in the earlier version Bělohlávek made with the Prague Symphony for Supraphon.

Fantasy in G min. (for violin and orchestra), *Op. 24.*
(M) *** Sup. SU 1928-2 011 [id.]. Josef Suk, Czech PO, Karel Ančerl – DVORAK: *Violin concerto* etc. ***
(N) *** Decca 460 316-2 [id.]. Pamela Frank, Czech PO, Mackerras – DVORAK: *Violin concerto; Romance in F min.* **

Suk's *Fantasy* is a brilliant piece which relates to the traditional essays in violin wizardry as well as to the Czech nationalist tradition. Suk's playing is refreshing and the orchestral accompaniment under Ančerl is no less impressive. Good remastered 1960s sound.

Pamela Frank's is a really exceptional performance of the rare Suk *Fantasy*, at 24 minutes longer than many romantic violin concertos. Under Sir Charles Mackerras the Czech Philharmonic launch into the opening with a bite and fire which prepares one well for the soloist's concentrated passion, using the widest range of expression, dynamic and tone. In a performance such as Frank's, with this conductor and orchestra, this episodic piece could hardly be more dramatic or involving. The sound is superb, markedly fuller than that given to the two Dvořák works, which are relatively disappointing.

Fantastic Scherzo, Op. 25.
*** Chandos Dig. CHAN 8897 [id.]. Czech PO, Bělohlávek – MARTINU: *Symphony No. 6;* JANACEK: *Sinfonietta.* ***

This captivating piece brings playing from the Czech Philharmonic under Bělohlávek which is even finer than any of the earlier performances and it cannot be too strongly recommended, particularly in view of the excellence of the coupling.

Praga, Op. 28; (i) *Ripening, Op. 34* (symphonic poems).
*** Virgin/EMI Dig. VC7 59318-2. (i) RLPO Ch.; RLPO, Pešek.

Ripening came after the *Asrael Symphony* and *A Summer tale* and there is no doubt as to its imaginative resource and richness of invention. Libor Pešek and his Liverpool forces give as dedicated an account of this as one could possibly wish. *Prague*, an earlier piece from 1904, is not quite in the same league but it is still an admirable makeweight and is played with exemplary commitment. Very good recorded sound too.

Serenade for strings in E flat, Op. 6.
(BB) *** ASV Quicksilva CDQS 6094. Polish R. CO, Duczmal – TCHAIKOVSKY: *Serenade* ***; GRIEG: *2 Elegiac melodies; Holberg suite.* **(*)
(BB) *** Naxos 8.550419 [id.]. Capella Istropolitana, Kr(e)chek – DVORAK: *String serenade.* **(*)
(M) **(*) Virgin/EMI Dig. CUV5 61144-2. LCO, Christopher Warren-Green – DVORAK: *Serenade.* **(*)

Serenade for strings in E flat, Op. 6; Meditation on an old Czech hymn (St Wenceslas), Op. 35a.
(B) **(*) Discover Dig. DICD 920234 [id.]. Virtuosi di Praga, Oldřich Vlček – JANACEK: *Suite.* ***

Suk's *Serenade* is a gorgeous work and it receives a lovely performance from the Polish Radio Chamber Orchestra under Agnieszka Duczmal. This is altogether first rate, and the recording is full-textured and well balanced, bringing out Duczmal's many fine shadings of colour. This inexpensive version is second only to the full-priced Chandos account above from Belohlávec coupled with *A Fairy-tale* (see above).

On Naxos another entirely delightful account of Suk's *Serenade*. The innocent delicacy of the opening is perfectly caught and the *Adagio* is played most beautifully and then, with a burst of high spirits (and excellent ensemble), the finale bustles to its conclusion with exhilarating zest. The recording is first class, fresh yet full-textured, naturally balanced and transparent.

Warren-Green and his LCO also give a wonderfully persuasive account of Suk's *Serenade*, making obvious that its inspiration is every bit as vivid as in the comparable work of Dvořák. The recording, made in All Saints', Petersham, is fresh, full and natural without blurring from the ecclesiastical acoustic. However, the original CD also included the Tchaikovsky *Serenade*, which is now missing, so even at mid-price this is not such a bargain as it looks, with only 52 minutes' playing time.

The Prague Virtuosi create a richly full-bodied sonority here and play this music idiomatically and with ardent, expressive feeling. Some might feel that the *Serenade* benefits from a slightly more subtle and less extrovert approach, but the passionately gripping account of the *Wenceslas meditation* brings an entirely appropriate emotional intensity. Splendidly vivid recording,

String quartets Nos. 1 in B flat, Op. 11; 2, Op. 31; Ballade; Barcarolle; Meditation on the Czech choral, St Wenceslas, Op 35a; Minuet.
❁ (M) *** CRD Dig. CRD 3472 [id.]. Suk Qt.

The early *B flat Quartet* is essentially a sunny work, yet its *Adagio* has a remarkable potency of elegiac feeling, which is very affecting in a performance as ardently responsive as that by the eponymous Suk Quartet on CRD. They also catch the light-hearted delicacy of the opening movement and the blithe gaiety of the closing *Allegro giocoso* to perfection. The *Second Quartet* is far more concentrated than its predecessor, and its expressive opening (a series of descending chords), which runs through the whole work, was originally intended for a piece called *Mysterium*; its thematic material is curiously haunting and in some ways its boldness and forward-looking writing suggest that Janáček's quartets are just around the corner. The performance here is not only deeply moving and seemingly spontaneous, it is wonderfully full of observed detail. Of the other works here the simple *Meditation* is played very touchingly, while the *Barcarolle* is a charming piece of juvenilia, a real lollipop, to show the composer's ready melodic facility. CRD have never made a better record than this superb collection. The beauty and internal transparency of string texture is matched by the natural presence of the group itself.

PIANO MUSIC

About Mother, Op. 28; Lullabies, Op. 33; 4 Piano pieces, Op. 7; Spring, Op. 22a; Summer, Op. 22b; Things lived and dreamed, Op. 30.
*** Chandos Dig. CHAN 9026/7 [id.]. Margaret Fingerhut.

It is striking how the earliest works here have a carefree, sweetly lyrical character, gentler than Dvořák but typically Czech. Then, after the death in 1904 and 1905 of his mentor, Dvořák, and his wife (Dvořák's daughter), even these fragmentary inspirations, like the massive *Asrael Symphony*, become sharp, sometimes even abrasive. The second disc brings the finest and most ambitious of the suites in which Suk generally collected his genre pieces, *Things lived and dreamed*. Margaret Fingerhut proves a devoted advocate, playing with point and concentration, helped by full-ranging Chandos sound.

Sullivan, Arthur (1842–1900)

Ballet music

L'Ile enchantée (complete ballet); *Thespis*: suite.
**(*) Marco Polo 8.2234560 [id.]. RTE Concert O, Dublin, Andrew Penny.

L'Ile enchantée was written to be fitted into a Covent Garden production of Bellini's *La Sonnambula* in 1864. Its somewhat Verdian style, using lyrical brass solos as well as engaging woodwind (as in the *Mazurka* variation, which is Delibesian), would have fitted well into its Bellinian slot, and the score is quite lively, with a splendid final *Galop*. *Thespis* was an early Gilbert and Sullivan creation which did not survive, and the very introduction of the ballet suite unmistakably establishes the jolly rhythmic pattern we associate with the Savoy Operas, while its closing *Galop* has a character which draws on both influences. Andrew Penny changes from Malcolm Arnold to Sullivan with equally sympathetic results. He secures bold, lively playing from the Dublin orchestra, and the resonant recording is very suitable, if without the lustrous glow we associate with Decca's ballet records.

King Arthur (incidental music): suite; *Macbeth* (incidental music): suite; *The Merry Wives of Windsor* (incidental music): suite.
*** Marco Polo Dig. 8.223635 [id.]. Margaret MacDonald, RTE Chamber Ch. & Concert O Dublin, Andrew Penny.

This is perhaps the finest of the four Marco Polo records of Sullivan's music, showing the composer at his most pleasingly inventive and appealing. The opening *Chorus of Lake Spirits* in *King Arthur* might well have come out of *Patience* (they sound very much like lovesick maidens). But the following, more confident *Unseen spirits* would have fitted more readily into *Iolanthe*. The music for *Macbeth* brings a fine Overture with some striking brass writing, and the *Introduction to Act IV* has a rather good tune (though hardly with the flavour of Shakespearean tragedy). But easily the finest number is the deliciously fairy-like, Mendelssohnian *Chorus of the Spirits in the Air*, while the following *Chorus of Witches and Spirits* sounds more like the opening of the Act I finale to another Savoy Opera. All the music for *The Merry Wives of Windsor* sounds as if it were part of an operetta, and the closing *Dance* with chorus rounds the whole programme off in exhilarating fashion. Sullivan's flow of attractive ideas makes for a most enjoyable 50 minutes, and all the performers rise to the occasion. The recording is excellent.

(i) *Overtures: Cox and Box; Princess Ida; The Sorcerer;* (ii) *Overture in C (In Memoriam).*
(M) **(*) EMI CMS7 764409-2 (2) [Ang. CDMB 64409]. (i) Pro Arte O, Sargent; (ii) RLPO, Groves – *The Pirates of Penzance*. ***

This collects together the overtures from the operas not recorded by Sargent in his EMI series. The performances are characteristically bright and polished. *In Memoriam* is a somewhat inflated religious piece written for the 1866 Norwich Festival.

Overtures: *Di Ballo; The Gondoliers; HMS Pinafore; Iolanthe; Patience; The Pirates of Penzance; Princess Ida; Ruddigore; The Sorcerer; The Yeomen of the Guard* (all arr. Geoffrey Toye).
*** Nimbus Dig. NI 5066 [id.]. SCO, Alexander Faris.

A well-played and well-recorded collection of Sullivan overtures. Mostly they are little more than pot-pourris, but *The Yeomen of the Guard* is an exception, and the gay *Di Ballo* here shows Sullivan's scoring at its most felicitous.

Overtures: *Di ballo; HMS Pinafore; The Gondoliers; Iolanthe; The Mikado; Macbeth; Patience; The Pirates of Penzance; The Yeomen of the Guard.*

(N) (B) ** Ph. 434 916-2. ASMF, Marriner.

From the ASMF under Marriner comes playing of much elegance and finesse (the oboe solos are delightful), warmly and naturally recorded. There is much to admire, particularly in *Di ballo*, while the Gavotte in *The Gondoliers* is winningly stylish. But the absence of real sparkle is a drawback, and the more ambitious pieces like *The Yeomen of the Guard* and *The Tempest* lack a sense of theatrical drama.

Pineapple Poll (ballet; arr. Mackerras).
(M) *** Decca Dig. 436 810-2 (2). Philh. O, Mackerras – *Princess Ida*. ***
(B) *** CfP CD-CFP 4618. LPO, Mackerras – VERDI: *Lady and the fool*. ***

(i) *Pineapple Poll* (ballet; arr. Mackerras); (ii) Overtures: *Iolanthe; The Mikado; Ruddigore; The Yeomen of the Guard.*
(M) *** EMI CDM5 66538-2. (i) RPO; (ii) Philh. O; Sir Charles Mackerras.

On Decca Mackerras conducts with warmth as well as vivacity, and the elegantly polished playing of the Philharmonia Orchestra gives much pleasure. The record was made in the Kingsway Hall with its glowing ambience, and the CD transfer, though brightly vivid, has a pleasing bloom. Indeed the quality is in the demonstration bracket, with particularly natural string textures.

Mackerras's earlier (1960) Abbey Road recording is still striking for its sheer brio, while the playing has a real feeling of the ballet theatre, the recording is now freshly remastered and sounds splendidly vivid. What makes the reissue a collector's item is the group of four overtures, recorded by the Philharmonia at their peak in 1956. They are played with marvellous vivacity and sparkle and a delightful lilting flow in the lyrical melodies. The recording is excellent and does not betray its age.

Mackerras's LPO version of the suite on CfP, made in the London Henry Wood Hall in 1977, is also striking for its affection and vivacity. With an apt Verdi coupling, this is excellent value, very well transferred to CD.

Victoria and Merrie England (complete ballet).
*** Marco Polo 8.223677 [id.]. RTE Sinf., Dublin, Andrew Penny.

Victoria and Merrie England was not a ballet as we understand it today, but a uniquely British combination of mime to music, written to celebrate Queen Victoria's Diamond Jubilee and so was also well laden with patriotism. Essentially a historical cavalcade, its six principal scenes dealt in turn with Ancient Britain, May Day in Queen Elizabeth's time, The Legend of Herne the Hunter, Christmas revels in the time of Charles II, the Coronation of Queen Victoria and, finally, a celebration of Britain's Glory, with a military parade and the entrance of Britannia. The score and orchestral parts were lost; however, assiduous research sponsored by the Sullivan Society finally enabled the assembling of a complete score, edited by Roderick Spencer. It's engaging stuff, with plenty of allusions to the Savoy Operas. Sullivan's invention, if not always of his highest quality, maintains a pretty good standard, with plenty of jolly tunes and jaunty ideas. Whoever was responsible for the scoring, it works well. Sullivan used his *Imperial march* for the Coronation scene. But it is the final section, 'Britain's Glory', which is the most robustly enjoyable, with the entrance of English, Irish, Scottish and Colonial troops celebrated with a series of folk tunes, wittily climaxed with 'For he is an Englishman' borrowed from *HMS Pinafore* and sentimentally followed with *There's no place like home*, and finally a brassy version of the National Anthem. It's all very endearing, and Andrew Penny presents it with warm affection and much gusto. It isn't great music but it is good fun.

OPERAS

The major Decca and EMI sets

(i) *Cox and Box* (libretto by F. C. Burnand) complete; (ii) *Ruddigore* (complete; without dialogue).
(M) *** Decca 417 355-2 (2) [id.]. (i) Styler, Riordan, Adams; New SO of L.; (ii) Reed, Round, Sandford, Riley, Adams, Hindmarsh, Knight, Sansom, Allister, D'Oyly Carte Op. Ch., ROHCG O, Godfrey.

The Gondoliers (complete; with dialogue).
(M) *** Decca 425 177-2 (2) [id.]. Reed, Skitch, Sandford, Round, Styler, Knight, Toye, Sansom, Wright, D'Oyly Carte Op. Ch., New SO of L., Godfrey.

The Gondoliers (complete; without dialogue).
(M) **(*) EMI CMS7 64394-2 (2) [Ang. CDMB 64394]. Evans, Young, Brannigan, Lewis, Cameron, Milligan, Monica Sinclair, Graham, Morison, Thomas, Watts, Glyndebourne Festival Ch., Pro Arte O, Sargent.

(i; ii) *The Grand Duke*. (ii) *Henry VIII: March & Graceful dance*. (iii) *Overture Di Ballo*.
*** Decca 436 813-2 (2) [id.]. (i) John Reed, Meston Reid, Sandford, Rayner, Ayldon, Ellison, Conroy-Ward, Lilley, Holland, Goss, Metcalfe, D'Oyly Carte Op. Ch.; (ii) RPO, Nash; (iii) Philh. O, Mackerras.

HMS Pinafore (complete; with dialogue).
❁ (M) *** Decca 414 283-2. Reed, Skitch, Round, Adams, Hindmarsh, Wright, Knight, D'Oyly Carte Op. Ch., New SO of L., Godfrey.

HMS Pinafore (complete; without dialogue); *Trial by Jury*.

(M) *** EMI CMS7 64397-2 (2) [Ang. CDMB 64397]. George Baker, Cameron, Lewis, Brannigan, Milligan, Morison, Thomas, M. Sinclair, Glyndebourne Festival Ch., Pro Arte O, Sargent.

HMS Pinafore: highlights.
(B) *** Decca 436 145-2 (from above D'Oyly Carte Opera recording; cond. Godfrey).

Iolanthe (complete; with dialogue).
(M) *** Decca 414 145-2; *414 145-4* (2). Sansom, Reed, Adams, Round, Sandford, Styler, Knight, Newman, D'Oyly Carte Op. Ch., Grenadier Guards Band, New SO, Godfrey.

Iolanthe (complete; without dialogue).
(M) *** EMI CMS7 64400-2 (2). George Baker, Wallace, Young, Brannigan, Cameron, M. Sinclair, Thomas, Cantelo, Harper, Morison, Glyndebourne Festival Ch., Pro Arte O, Sargent – *Di Ballo overture*. **

The Mikado (complete; without dialogue).
(M) *** Decca 425 190-2 (2). Ayldon, Wright, Reed, Sandford, Masterson, Holland, D'Oyly Carte Op. Ch., RPO, Nash.
(M) **(*) EMI CMS7 644403-2 (2) [Ang. CDMB 64403]. Brannigan, Lewis, Evans, Wallace, Cameron, Morison, Thomas, J. Sinclair, M. Sinclair, Glyndebourne Festival Ch., Pro Arte O, Sargent.

Patience (complete; with dialogue).
(M) *** Decca 425 193-2 (2). Sansom, Adams, Cartier, Potter, Reed, Sandford, Newman, Lloyd-Jones, Toye, Knight, D'Oyly Carte Op. Ch. & O, Godfrey.

The Pirates of Penzance (complete; with dialogue).
(M) *** Decca 425 196-2. Reed, Adams, Potter, Masterson, Palmer, Brannigan, D'Oyly Carte Op. Ch., RPO, Godfrey.

The Pirates of Penzance: highlights.
(B) *** Decca 436 148-2 [id.]. Reed, Adams, Brannigan, Masterson, Potter, Palmer, D'Oyly Carte Op. Co. Ch., RPO, Godfrey.

The Pirates of Penzance (complete; without dialogue).
(M) *** EMI CMS7 64409-2 (2) [Ang. CDMB 64409]. George Baker, Milligan, Cameron, Lewis, Brannigan, Morison, Harper, Thomas, Sinclair, Glyndebourne Festival Ch., Pro Arte O, Sargent – *Overtures*. **(*)

(i) *Princess Ida* (complete; without dialogue); (ii) *Pineapple Poll* (ballet; arr. Mackerras)
(M) *** Decca 436 810-2 (2) [id.]. (i) Sandford, Potter, Palmer, Skitch, Reed, Adams, Raffell, Cook, Harwood, Palmer, Hood, Masterson, D'Oyly Carte Op. Ch., RPO, Sargent; (ii) Philh. O, Mackerras.

(i) *The Sorcerer* (complete, without dialogue); (ii) *The Zoo* (libretto by Bolton Rowe).
*** Decca 436 807-2 (2) [id.]. (i) Adams, David Palmer, Styler, Reed, Christene Palmer, Masterson; (ii) Reid, Sandford, Ayldon, Goss, Metcalfe; nar. Geoffrey Shovelton; (i; ii) D'Oyly Carte Op. Ch., RPO; (i) Godfrey; (ii) Nash.

(i) *Utopia Ltd* (complete). Overtures: *Macbeth; Marmion. Victoria and Merrie England.*
**(*) Decca 436 816-2 (2) [id.]. (i) Sandford, Reed, Ayldon, Ellison, Buchan, Conroy-Ward, Reid, Broad, Rayner, Wright, Porter, Field, Goss, Merri, Holland, Griffiths, D'Oyly Carte Op. Ch.; RPO, Nash.

(i) *The Yeomen of the Guard* (complete; without dialogue); (ii) *Trial by Jury*.
(M) *** Decca 417 358-2. Hood, J. Reed, Sandford, Adams, Raffell; (i) Harwood, Knight; (ii) Round; D'Oyly Carte Op. Ch.; (i) RPO, Sargent; (ii) ROHCG O, Godfrey.

As can be seen, the two basic sets of recordings of the major Savoy Operas, nearly all from Godfrey (on Decca) and Sargent (on EMI), are available at mid-price, although the EMI sets of *Patience*, *Ruddigore* and *The Yeomen of the Guard* have been withdrawn. The Decca series usually has the advantage (or disadvantage, according to taste) of including the dialogue. Certain of the operas are available only in D'Oyly Carte versions, and of these the most fascinating is *Cox and Box.* This pre-Gilbertian one-Acter is based on a play (called *Box and Cox*) with the story of two men sharing the same rooms – one is a hatter, the other works on a newspaper at night – without knowing it, so that Bouncer, the unscrupulous landlord, can collect a double rent. It was written in 1867 and thus pre-dates the first G&S success, *Trial by Jury*, by eight years. One must notice the captivating *Bacon 'Lullaby'*, so ravishingly sung by Joseph Riordan. Later on, in Box's recitative telling how he 'committed suicide', Sullivan makes one of his first and most impressive parodies of grand opera, which succeeds also in being effective in its own right. The D'Oyly Carte performance is splendid in every way. It is given a recording which, without sacrificing clarity, conveys with perfect balance the stage atmosphere.

The Grand Duke, on the other hand, was the fourteenth and last of the Savoy Operas. In spite of a spectacular production and a brilliant first night on 7 March 1896, the work played for only 123 performances then lapsed into relative oblivion, although it has been revived by amateur societies. The present recording, the only complete version, came after a successful concert presentation in 1975, and the recorded performance has both polish and vigour, although the chorus does not display the crispness of articulation of ready familiarity. The recording is characteristically brilliant. The bonuses are well worth having, with Mackerras's account of the *Overture Di Ballo* showing more delicacy of approach than usual, though certainly not lacking sparkle.

Turning now to the major G&S successes, it seems sensible to consider the Decca and EMI alternatives together. EMI usually offer some orchestral bonuses and, in the case of *HMS Pinafore*, add *Trial by Jury* as well (as was the practice in the theatre in the heyday of the D'Oyly Carte Opera Company). Godfrey's Decca *Trial by Jury* is saved for inclusion with their outstanding *Yeomen of the Guard*. The Sargent version of *Trial by Jury* (with George Baker as the Judge) is by general consent the best there is, if only by a small margin, and the EMI version of *Pinafore* is wonderfully fresh too, beautifully sung throughout, while the whole of the final scene is musically quite ravishing.

But the 1960 Godfrey set of this opera is very special indeed, and *HMS Pinafore* is in our view the finest of all the D'Oyly Carte stereo recordings. While Owen Brannigan, on EMI, without the benefit of dialogue conveys the force of Dick Deadeye's personality remarkably strongly, Donald Adams's assumption of the role on Decca (which does have the dialogue) is little short of inspired, and his larger-than-life characterization underpins the whole piece. The rest of the cast make a splendid team: Jean Hindmarsh is a totally convincing Josephine – she sings with great charm – and John Reed's Sir Joseph Porter is a delight.

The D'Oyly Carte set of *The Gondoliers* has now been remastered and the quality brought up to Decca's usual high standard. The solo singing throughout is consistently good, the ensembles have plenty of spirit and the dialogue is for the most part well spoken. As a performance this is on the whole preferable to the Sargent account, if only because of the curiously slow tempo Sargent chooses for the *Cachucha*. However, on EMI there is still much to captivate the ear, and Owen Brannigan, a perfectly cast Don Alhambra, sings a masterly *No possible doubt whatever*. The age of the 1957 recording shows in the orchestra but the voices sound fresh and there is a pleasing overall bloom.

With *Iolanthe*, choice between the two alternatives is a case of swings and roundabouts. The 1960 Decca set was given added panache by the introduction of the Grenadier Guards Band into the *March of the Peers*. Mary Sansom is quite a convincing Phyllis, and if her singing has not the sense of style that Elsie Morison brings to the part, she is completely at home with the dialogue. Also Alan Styler makes a vivid and charming personal identification with the role of Strephon, an Arcadian shepherd, whereas John Cameron's dark timbre on EMI seems much less suitable for this role, even though he sings handsomely. However, on EMI the climax of Act I, the scene in which the Queen of the Fairies lays a curse on members of both Houses of Parliament, shows most excitingly what can be achieved with the 'full operatic treatment': this is a dramatic moment indeed. George Baker, too, is very good as the Lord Chancellor: the voice is fuller, more baritonal than John Reed's dryly whimsical delivery, yet he provides an equally individual characterization. Godfrey's conducting is lighter and more infectious than Sargent's in the Act I finale, but both performances offer much to delight the ear in the famous Trio of Act II with the Lord Chancellor and the two Earls.

The 1973 stereo remake of *The Mikado* by the D'Oyly Carte Company directed by Royston Nash is a complete success in every way and shows the Savoy tradition at its most attractive. It is a pity no dialogue is included, but the choral singing is first rate, and the glees are refreshingly done, polished and refined, yet with plenty of vitality. John Reed is a splendid Ko-Ko, Kenneth Sandford a vintage Pooh-Bah and Valerie Masterson a charming Yum-Yum. John Ayldon as the Mikado provides a laugh of terrifying bravura, and Lyndsie Holland is a formidable and commanding Katisha. The Sargent set, with its grand operatic style, brings some fine moments, especially in the finales to both Acts. Owen Brannigan is an inimitable Mikado and Richard Lewis sings most engagingly throughout as Nanki-Poo, while Elsie Morison is freshly persuasive as his young bride-to-be. All in all, there is much to enjoy here, but this remains very much a second choice.

Owen Brannigan was surely born to play the Sergeant of Police in *The Pirates of Penzance*, and he does so unforgettably in both the Decca and EMI sets. On Decca there is a considerable advantage in the inclusion of the dialogue, and here theatrical spontaneity is well maintained. Donald Adams is a splendid Pirate King. John Reed's portrayal of the Major General is one of his strongest roles, while Valerie Masterson is an excellent Mabel. Godfrey's conducting is as affectionate as ever, and one can hear him revelling in the many added touches of colour that are made possible when he has the RPO to play for him. Sargent's version is great fun, too. Its star is George Baker, giving a new and individual portrayal of the Major General. The opera takes a little while to warm up, but there is much to enjoy here. On balance, the Decca set is to be preferred, for Brannigan is especially vivid, and the dialogue undoubtedly adds an extra sense of the theatre.

Patience and *Ruddigore* were the two greatest successes of the Sargent series and it is sad that they have been deleted. However, the extra card in the D'Oyly Carte hand in *Patience* is the dialogue, so important in this opera above all, with its spoken poetry; if Mary Sansom does not give the strongest portrayal vocally, of the main role, both Bunthorne and Grosvenor are well played, while the military numbers, led by Donald Adams in glorious voice, have an unforgettable vigour and presence. The

D'Oyly Carte *Ruddigore* comes up surprisingly freshly, in fact better than we had remembered it, though it is a pity the dialogue was omitted. The performance includes *The battle's roar is over*, which is (for whatever reason) traditionally omitted. There is much to enjoy here (especially Gillian Knight and Donald Adams, whose *Ghosts' high noon* song is a marvellous highlight). Isidore Godfrey is his inimitable sprightly self and the chorus and orchestra are excellent. A fine traditional D'Oyly Carte set, then, brightly recorded.

Princess Ida is fake feminism with a vengeance. Elizabeth Harwood in the name-part sings splendidly, and John Reed's irritably gruff portrayal of the irascible King Gama is memorable; he certainly is a properly 'disagreeable man'. The rest of the cast is no less strong and, with excellent teamwork from the company as a whole and a splendid recording, spacious and immediate, this has much to offer, even if Sullivan's invention is somewhat variable in quality. The CD transfer is outstanding and the 1965 recording has splendid depth and presence. As a bonus we are offered Mackerras's vivacious and polished 1982 digital recording of his scintillating ballet score, *Pineapple Poll*.

The Sorcerer is the Gilbert and Sullivan equivalent of *L'elisir d'amore*, only here a whole English village is affected, with hilarious results. John Reed's portrayal of the sorcerer himself is one of the finest of all his characterizations. The plot drew from Sullivan a great deal of music in his fey, pastoral vein. By 1966, when the set was made, Decca had stretched the recording budget to embrace the RPO, and the orchestral playing is especially fine, as is the singing of the D'Oyly Carte chorus, at their peak. John Reed gives a truly virtuoso performance of his famous introductory song, while the spell-casting scene is equally compelling. The final sequence in Act II is also memorable. The sound is well up to Decca's usual high standard .

Both recordings of *The Yeomen of the Guard*, Decca's and EMI's deleted set, were conducted by Sir Malcolm Sargent. The later Decca account has marginally the finer recording and Sir Malcolm's breadth of approach is immediately apparent in the *Overture*. Both chorus and orchestra (the RPO) are superbly expansive and there is again consistently fine singing from all the principals (and especially from Elizabeth Harwood as Elsie). This Decca *Yeomen* is unreservedly a success, with its brilliant and atmospheric recording. In any case, the considerable bonus is the inclusion of Godfrey's immaculately stylish and affectionate *Trial by Jury* with John Reed as the Judge.

Utopia Ltd was first performed in 1893, ran for 245 performances and then remained unheard (except for amateur productions) until it was revived for the D'Oyly Carte centenary London season in 1974, which led to this recording. Its complete neglect is unaccountable. Royston Nash shows plenty of skill in the matter of musical characterization, and the solo singing is consistently assured. When Meston Reid as Captain FitzBattleaxe sings 'You see I can't do myself justice' in *Oh, Zara*, he is far from speaking the truth – this is a performance of considerable bravura. The ensembles are not always as immaculately disciplined as one is used to from the D'Oyly Carte, and *Eagle high* is disappointingly focused: the intonation here is less than secure. However, the sparkle and spontaneity of the performance as a whole are irresistible. The CD transfer shows the 1975 recording as being of Decca's best vintage quality. Of the fillers, the *Macbeth overture* is dramatic and brightly coloured but not inspired, and the *Marmion overture*, too, is not really memorable. The selection from *Victoria and Merry England*, includes some pleasing ideas. All are vividly played and brightly recorded.

The Zoo (with a libretto by Bolton Rowe, a pseudonym of B. C. Stevenson) dates from June 1875, only three months after the success of *Trial by Jury* – which it obviously seeks to imitate, as the music more than once reminds us. Although the libretto lacks the finesse and whimsicality of Gilbert, it is not without humour, and many of the situations presented by the plot (and indeed the actual combinations of words and music) are typical of the later Savoy Operas. As the piece has no spoken dialogue it is provided here with a stylized narration, well enough presented by Geoffrey Shovelton. The performance is first class, splendidly sung, fresh as paint and admirably recorded, and it fits very well alongside *The Sorcerer*. The CD transfer is more brightly lit than its companion, and the opera has animal noises to set the scene and close the opera.

Other complete recordings

The Gondoliers (complete; without dialogue); *Overture Di Ballo*.
*** That's Entertainment CD-TER2 1187; *ZCTED 1187* (2) [id.]. Suart, Rath, Fieldsend, Oke, Ross, Hanley, Woollett, Pert, Creasy, D'Oyly Carte Op. Ch. & O, John Pryce-Jones.

The That's Entertainment set of *The Gondoliers* was recorded at Abbey Road studios in 1991, offers very good sound and speaks well for the standards of the resuscitated D'Oyly Carte company. The men are very good indeed. Richard Suart's Duke of Plaza-Toro is as dry as you could wish, while the voice itself is resonant, and his duet in Act II with the equally excellent Duchess (Jill Pert), in which they dispense honours to the undeserving, is in the best Gilbertian tradition. Perhaps Gianetta (Lesley Echo Ross) and Casilda (Elizabeth Woollett) are less individually distinctive and slightly less vocally secure than their counterparts on the Godfrey and Sargent versions, but they always sing with charm. The chorus is first class – the men are especially virile at the opening of Act II. The orchestral playing is polished, and the ensembles are good, too; John Pryce-Jones conducts with vigour and an impressive sense of theatrical pacing. The finale brings an exhilarating closing *Cachucha* to round the opera off nicely. The acoustic of the recording has both warmth and atmosphere.

HMS Pinafore.
✽ *** Telarc Dig. CD 80374 [id.]. Suart, Allen, Evans, Schade, Palmer, Adams, Ch. & O of Welsh Opera, Mackerras.

Sir Charles Mackerras here gives an exuberant reading of the first operetta of the cycle. The lyricism and transparency of Sullivan's inspiration shine out with winning freshness. The casting is not just starry but inspired. Even such a jaunty number as the 'encore' trio, *Never mind the why and wherefore*, gains in point when so well sung and played as here, with Allen joined by Rebecca Evans as an appealing Josephine and Richard Suart as a dry Sir Joseph Porter. Michael Schade is heady-toned as the hero, Ralph Rackstraw, while among character roles Felicity Palmer is a marvellously fruity Little Buttercup, with Richard van Allan as Bill Bobstay and the veteran, Donald Adams, a lugubrious Dick Deadeye. As with the previous CDs of *Mikado* and *Pirates of Penzance*, Telarc squeezes the whole score on to a single CD, vividly recorded.

Iolanthe (complete; without dialogue). *Thespis* (orchestral suite).
**(*) That's Entertainment Dig. CD-TER2 1188 (2) [id.]. Suart, Woollett, Blake Jones, Richard, Creasy, Pert, Rath, Hanley, D'Oyly Carte Opera Ch. & O, Pryce-Jones.

After the success of the new D'Oyly Carte *Gondoliers*, this fresh look at *Iolanthe* is something of a disappointment. John Pryce-Jones obviously sees it as a very dramatic opera indeed, and he ensures that the big scenes have plenty of impact (the *March of the Peers*, resplendent with brass, quite upstages the Decca version incorporating a Guards band). But his strong forward pressure means that the music feels almost always fast-paced, and the humour is completely upstaged by the drama, especially in the long Act I Finale, which is certainly zestful. The Lord Chancellor's two patter songs in Act I, *The law is the true embodiment* and *When I went to the bar*, are very brisk in feeling, and Richard Suart, an excellent Lord Chancellor, is robbed of the necessary relaxed delivery so that the words can be relished for themselves. Jill Pert is certainly a formidable Queen of the Fairies, but elsewhere the lack of charm is a distinct drawback.

(i) *Iolanthe:* highlights; (ii) *The Mikado* (complete, without dialogue).
(B) *** CfP CD-CDPD 4730 (2) [id.]. (i) Shilling, Harwood, Moyle, Dowling, Begg, Bevan, Greene, Kern; (ii) Holmes, Revill, Wakefield, Studholme, Dowling, Allister, John Heddle Nash; Sadler's Wells Op. Ch. & O, Alexander Faris.

The Sadler's Wells *Iolanthe* is stylistically superior to Sargent's earlier EMI recording and is often musically superior to the Decca/D'Oyly Carte versions. Alexander Faris often chooses untraditional tempi. *When I went to the bar* is very much faster than usual, with less dignity but with a compensating lightness of touch. Eric Shilling is excellent here, as he is also in the *Nightmare song*, which is really *sung*, much being made of the ham operatic recitative at the beginning. The lovers, Elizabeth Harwood as Phyllis and Julian Moyle as Strephon, make a charming duo, and the Peers are splendid. Their entry chorus is thrilling and their reaction to the Fairy Queen's curse is delightfully, emphatically horrified, while the whole Act I finale (the finest in any of the operas) goes with infectious stylishness. All the solo singing is of a high standard and Leon Greene sings the Sentry song well. But one has to single out special praise for Patricia Kern's really lovely singing of Iolanthe's aria at the end of the opera. The recording has splendid presence and realism.

The Sadler's Wells *Mikado* is traditional in the best sense, bringing a humorous sparkle to the proceedings, which gives great delight. Clive Revill is a splendid Ko-Ko; John Heddle Nash is an outstanding Pish-Tush, and it is partly because of him that the *Chippy chopper* trio is so effective. Denis Dowling is a superb Pooh-Bah, and Marion Studholme a charming Yum-Yum. Jean Allister's Katisha is first rate in every way; listen to the venom she puts into the word '*bravado*' in the Act I finale. Even the chorus scores a new point by their stylized singing of *Mi-ya-sa-ma*, which sounds engagingly mock-Japanese. The one disappointment is John Holmes in the name-part. He sings well but conveys little of the mock-satanic quality. But this is a small point in an otherwise magnificent set, which has a vivacious new overture arranged by Charles Mackerras.

The Mikado (complete, but without Overture).
✽ *** Telarc Dig. CD 80284 [id.]. Donald Adams, Rolfe Johnson, Suart, McLaughlin, Palmer, Van Allan, Folwell, Welsh Nat. Op. Ch. and O, Mackerras.

With the overture omitted (not Sullivan's work) and one of the stanzas in Ko-Ko's 'little list' song (with words unpalatable today), the whole fizzing Mackerras performance is fitted on to a single, very well-filled disc. The cast has no weak link and Mackerras is electrically sharp at brisk speeds, sounding totally idiomatic and giving this most popular of the G&S operettas an irresistible freshness at high voltage. The tingling vigour of Sullivan's invention is constantly brought out, with performances from the WNO Chorus and Orchestra at once powerful and refined. With that sharpness of focus Sullivan's parodies of grand opera become more than just witty imitations. So Katisha's aria at the end of Act II, with Felicity Palmer the delectable soloist, has a Verdian depth of feeling. It is good too to hear the veteran Savoyard, Donald Adams, as firm and resonant as he was in his D'Oyly Carte recording made no less than 33 years earlier.

Ruddigore (complete recording of original score; without dialogue).
*** That's Entertainment CDTER2 1128; *ZCTED 1128* [MCA MCAD2 11010]. Hill Smith, Sandison, Davies, Ayldon, Hillman, Innocent, Hann, Ormiston, Lawlor, New Sadler's Wells Op. Ch. & O, Simon Phipps.

What is exciting about the New Sadler's Wells production of *Ruddigore* is that it includes the original finale, created by the logic of Gilbert's plot which brought *all* the ghosts back to life, rather than just the key figure. The opera is strongly cast, with Marilyn Hill Smith and David Hillman in the principal roles and Joan Davies a splendid Dame Hannah, while Harold Innocent as Sir Despard and Linda Ormiston as Mad Margaret almost steal the show. Simon Phipps conducts brightly and keeps everything moving forward, even if his pacing is not always as assured as in the classic Godfrey version. The recording is first class, with fine theatrical atmosphere.

The Yeomen of the Guard (complete; with dialogue).
(B) **(*) Ph. Duo 462 508-2 (2). Thomas Allen, Streit, Dean, Terfel, Mackie, McNair, Collins, Rigby, ASMF and Ch., Marriner.

(i) *The Yeomen of the Guard;* (ii) *Trial by Jury* (both complete; without dialogue).
*** Telarc 2CD 809404 (2) [id.]. (i) Mellor, Archer, Palmer (i; ii) Suart, Adams, Maxwell; (ii) Evans, Banks, Savidge; Welsh Nat. Op. Ch. and O, Mackerras.

Less starrily cast than Sir Neville Marriner's Philips set of *The Yeomen of the Guard*, this fourth Telarc issue of G&S is yet far more involving as a performance, conveying more exuberantly the sparkle as well as the emotional weight of this most serious of the canon. Alwyn Mellor makes a far more appealing heroine than Sylvia McNair on Philips, who was well below her best. Among the others, Felicity Palmer makes a delectably fire-snorting Dame Carruthers, and the veteran, Donald Adams, an incomparable Sergeant Meryll. (His cries of 'Ghastly, ghastly' when cornered by the Dame are wonderful.) Richard Suart as Jack Point may be far less effective vocally than Thomas Allen, but he characterizes vividly in authentic style, and the only weak link is the Fairfax of Neil Archer, who too often sounds strained. Even so, the final bringing-together of Fairfax and Elsie could not be more touching. The absence of spoken dialogue allows *Trial by Jury* to be included as a fill-up, with Suart even more aptly cast and Adams again incomparable as the Usher, while the WNO Chorus again sings with ideal clarity. Otherwise it involves different singers, with Rebecca Evans golden-toned as the Plaintiff and Barry Banks firm if light as the Defendant.

Sir Neville Marriner's version is cast from strength but fails to capture the exuberance and fun in the writing that Mackerras's WNO performance does. It is good to have Thomas Allen as Jack Point, singing beautifully and giving emotional weight to the rejected clown in love with the heroine. The excellent Mozart tenor, Kurt Streit, makes an impressive hero, and even the smallest roles are taken by singers of the calibre of Bryn Terfel, Neil Mackie and Judith Howarth. The big disappointment is the way Sylvia McNair's usually sweet soprano is caught in the role of Elsie: often sour with suspect intonation. Spoken dialogue is included, which for some will be a deciding factor.

Collections

Highlights from: *The Gondoliers; HMS Pinafore; Iolanthe; The Mikado; The Pirates of Penzance; The Yeomen of the Guard.*
(B) **(*) CfP CD-CFP 4238 [id.]. Soloists, Glyndebourne Festival Ch., Pro Arte O, Sargent.

An attractive selection of highlights offering samples of six of Sargent's vintage EMI recordings. There is some distinguished solo singing and, if the atmosphere is sometimes a little cosy, there is a great deal to enjoy. The recordings have transferred well.

'The very best of Gilbert and Sullivan': extracts from: (i; iv) *The Gondoliers; HMS Pinafore; Iolanthe.* (ii; v) *The Mikado.* (i; iv) *Patience.* (ii; iv) *The Pirates of Penzance.* (ii; vi) *Princess Ida; Ruddigore.* (ii; iv) *The Sorcerer.* (iii–iv) *Trial by Jury.* (ii; vi) *The Yeomen of the Guard.*
✿ (B) *** Decca Double 460 010-2 (2). John Reed, Valerie Masterson, Gillian Knight, Thomas Round, Donald Adams, Kenneth Sandford, Joyce Wright, Owen Brannigan, Jennifer Toye, Alan Styler and soloists, D'Oyly Carte Op. Ch., (i) New SO; (ii) RPO; (iii) ROHCG O; cond. (iv) Isidore Godfrey; (v) Royston Nash; (vi) Sir Malcolm Sargent.

If you are looking for a CD to cheer you up on a dull day, either of the pair which make up this Double Decca will serve admirably. The overall selection earns full marks for perception and variety. *The Mikado* is (understandably) the most generously treated, including ten items, and the only real miscalculation was to end the second disc with the trio,

This helmet I suppose from *Princess Ida*, which, following immediately after John Reed's delicious *Whene'er I spoke sarcastic joke*, comes as an anticlimax. The joyous trio, *If you go in, you're sure to win*, from *Iolanthe* (which comes earlier), would have been more effective or, better still, the Act I finale, which is omitted and for which there would have just about been room. Yet this is carping. The consistent wit of Gilbert's words, the delightful Sullivan melodies and the sparkle of Godfrey's conducting are a constant joy

Highlights from: (i; ii) *HMS Pinafore;* (iii; iv) *The Mikado;* (ii; iv; v) *The Pirates of Penzance;* (ii; vi) *Trial by Jury;* (vii) *The Yeomen of the Guard.*

*** Telarc Dig. CD 80431 [id.]. Richard Suart, with (i) Thomas Allen, Felicity Palmer; (ii) Rebecca Evans; (iii) Anthony Rolfe Johnson, Marie McLaughlin, Anne Howells, Janice Watson; (iv) Richard van Allan, Nicholas Folwell; (v) John Mark Ainsley, Julia Gossage; (vi) Barry Banks, Eric Garrett, Peter Savidge, Gareth Rhys Davies; (vii) Neil Archer, Alwyn Mellor, Pamela Helen Stephen; Welsh Nat. Op. Ch. & O, Mackerras.

Even with 76 minutes' playing time, this can be no more than a sampler of Mackerras's effervescent G&S series for Telarc, dominated by the dry-timbred Richard Suart in the key patrician roles. As can be seen, most of the other soloists change with each opera, but the standard remains extraordinarily high. The choice of excerpts is inevitably arbitrary with about half-a-dozen items from each of the two-Act operas and three from *Trial by Jury*. If you buy this, you will inevitably be tempted to go on to one or other of the complete sets. Nevertheless it is a splendid collection in its own right. Characteristically first-class Telarc sound.

Suppé, Franz von (1819–95)

Overtures: *Beautiful Galathea; Boccaccio; Light cavalry; Morning, noon and night in Vienna; Pique dame; Poet and peasant.*

(M) *** Mercury 434 309-2 [id.]. Detroit SO, Paul Paray – AUBER: *Overtures*. *** ❀

Listening to Paray, one discovers a verve and exhilaration that are wholly Gallic in spirit. His chimerical approach to *Beautiful Galathea* (with a wonderfully luminous passage from the Detroit strings near the very opening) is captivating, and the bravura violin playing in *Light Cavalry* is remarkably deft. With its splendid Auber coupling this is one of Mercury's most desirable reissues.

Overtures: Disc 1: *Beautiful Galathea; Jolly robbers (Banditenstreiche); Light cavalry; Morning, noon and night in Vienna; Pique dame; Poet and peasant.* Disc 2: *Fatinitza; Die Frau Meisterin; Der Gascogner; Die Irrfahrt um's Glück; Juanita; Das Modell; Wiener-Jubel.*

(B) *** RCA Twofer Dig. 74321 34174-2 (2) [(M) id. import]. RPO, Gustav Kuhn.

By joining up Gustav Kuhn's two separate collections in a Twofer, RCA have created the most comprehensive single grouping of Suppé overtures in the catalogue. The first disc assembles the six best known, including the four popular favourites, among which *Beautiful Galathea* stands out; the second, equally distinctive, offers seven hardly less memorable novelties. Kuhn lavishes much care over detail. Tempi are spacious, generally slower than usual, but the effect is not to rob the music of vitality, rather to add to its stature. In the lyrical sections he conjures the most beautiful, expansive playing from the RPO, yet he can be racy in the galops while not rushing the music off its feet. The second programme is especially valuable in offering CD débuts for three items. Kuhn is in his element in the powerfully solemn opening of *Die Irrfahrt um's Glück* with its magical/mystical portents; yet the more volatile introduction to *Donna Juanita* is hardly less telling, and very beautifully played. Throughout, Kuhn seeks to remove any suggestion of cheapness from the music, and these are performances of real breadth. While they do not have the unbuttoned gusto of some versions, the added gravitas more than compensates. Full, resonant recording of very high quality adds to this impression.

Overtures: *Die Frau Meisterin; Die Irrfahrt um's Glück; Light cavalry; Morning, noon and night in Vienna; Pique Dame; Poet and Peasant; Tantalusqualen; Wiener-Jubel (Viennese Jubilee).*

❀ *** EMI (IMS) Dig. CDC7 54056-2. ASMF, Marriner.

Marriner's collection of Suppé *Overtures* goes straight to the top of the list. It is expansively recorded and it produces the most spectacular demonstration quality. The performances have tremendous exuberance and style: this is one of Marriner's very best records. The novelties are delightful. *Die Irrfahrt um's Glück* – concerned with magical goings-on – has a massively portentous opening, superbly realized here; *Die Frau Meisterin* produces a deliciously jiggy waltz tune, and *Wiener-Jubel*, after opening with resplendent fanfares, is as racy as you could wish. Not to be missed.

Svendsen, Johan Severin
(1840–1911)

Romance in G, Op. 26.

(BB) *** Naxos Dig. 8.550329 [id.]. Dong-Suk Kang, Slovak (Bratislava) RSO, Adrian Leaper – HALVORSEN: *Air Norvégien* etc.; SIBELIUS: *Violin concerto;* SINDING: *Légende.* ***

Dong-Suk Kang plays Svendsen's once-popular *Romance in G* without sentimentality but with full-hearted lyricism. The balance places him a little too forward, but the recording is very satisfactory.

Symphonies Nos. 1 in D, Op. 4; 2 in B flat, Op. 15.
(N) (BB) *** Naxos Dig. 8 553898 [id.]. Bournemouth SO, Bjarte Engeset.
(N) **(*) Finlandia/Warner Dig. 0630-19055-2 [id.]. Norwegian Radio O, Ari Rasilainen.

Symphonies Nos. 1–2; 2 Swedish folk-melodies, Op. 27.
*** BIS Dig. CD 347 [id.]. Gothenburg SO, Neeme Järvi.

Svendsen excelled (where Grieg did not) in the larger forms and, as befits a conductor, was a master of the orchestra. The *D major Symphony* is a student work of astonishing assurance and freshness, in some ways even more remarkable than the *B flat*. Neeme Järvi is a splendid guide to this terrain; these are first-class performances, sensitive and vital, and the excellent recordings earn them a strong recommendation.

The neglect of these captivating symphonies is difficult to understand. They have never been championed by one of the great European or American orchestras yet they deserve to be drawn to the attention of the widest public. Järvi's recording is strongly challenged by Bjarte Engeset and the Bournemouth Orchestra. These players are obviously encountering this music with enthusiasm and they are well served by both the acoustic and the engineering. At the Naxos price it is a real bargain.

There is nothing wrong with the Finlandia version from the Norwegian Radio Orchestra under Ari Rasilainen either, though the recording is not as good as BIS for Neeme Järvi and the Gothenburg Orchestra, and at full price does not displace it.

Symphony No. 2 in B flat, Op. 15; Carnival in Paris, Op. 9; Norwegian Artists' Carnival, Op. 14; Norwegian Rhapsody No. 2, Op. 19; (i) *Romance in G, for violin and orchestra, Op. 26.*
(N) ** Chatsworth Dig. FCM 1002 [id.]. Stavanger SO, Grant Llewelyn; (i) with Marianne Thorsen.

Decent performances from Stavanger of the *Second Symphony* and other popular Svendsen pieces under the Welsh conductor, Grant Llewelyn. The strings do not have the depth of sonority of their immediate rivals, but the orchestra plays with freshness and enthusiasm.

Octet in A, Op. 3; (i) *Romance in G for violin and strings, Op. 26.*
(N) *** Chandos Dig. CHAN 9258 [id.]. ASMF Chamber Ens. (i) with Sillito – NIELSEN: *String quintet in G.* ***

(i) *Octet in A, Op. 3; String quartet in A min., Op. 1.*
(N) *** BIS Dig CD753 [id.]. Kontra Qt; with (i) Bjørnkjaer, Madsen, Rasmussen, Holm Johansen.

Svendsen's youthful *Octet, Op. 3* is a product of his student years at Leipzig, and was obviously inspired by Mendelssohn. But unlike Gade, it has a strong personality of its own and is full of lively and attractive invention. The scherzo is particularly delightful. The Kontra Quartet and their colleagues give a spirited account of it, coupling it with another student work, the *A minor Quartet, Op. 1*. A good well-balanced sound.

However, those primarily wanting the *Octet* should turn to the Academy of St Martin-in-the-Fields Chamber Ensemble whose leader, Kenneth Silito, plays the G major *Romance* as a fill-up. First-rate performances and recording.

Sweelinck, Jan (1562–1621)

Ballo del Granduca; Echo fantasia; Engelsche Fortuyn; Puer nobis nascitur.
*** Chandos Dig. CHAN 0514 [id.]. Piet Kee (organ of St Laurens Church, Alkmaar) – BUXTEHUDE: *Collection*. **(*)

Sweelinck lived during the Dutch Golden Age and was a contemporary of Rembrandt. His music is colourful and appealing, and it could hardly be better represented than in this engaging 'suite' of four contrasted pieces, three of which are based on melodies by others. Piet Kee is a very sympathetic advocate and he is given a recording of demonstration standard.

Cantiones sacrae (1619).
(N) *** Hyperion Dig. CDA 67103 (Nos. 1–21); CDA 67104 (Nos. 22–37).Trinity College Chapel Ch., Cambridge, Richard Marlow.

Celebrated during his lifetime as a keyboard virtuoso and teacher, the Dutch composer Jan Pieterszoon Sweelinck wrote a great deal of vocal music (though none in his own language), including French chansons and Psalm settings, and Italian madrigals. The 37 *Cantiones sacrae*, which date from 1691, are in Latin, for five-part choir, and surely represent him at a peak of inspiration. The range of texts is wide, but most pertain to major feasts of the liturgical year. The settings are predominantly homophonic, with an engaging antiphonal interplay of voices and fourteen of them end with jubilant extended Alleluias, often resplendently capping what has gone before. This pair of Hyperion discs (each available separately) offers glorious music, gloriously sung. The simplicity and underlying vitality of the very first piece, *Non omnis qui dicit mihi, Domine* captures the listener's ear, and the opening sequence of some half-a-dozen fairly serene settings is then interrupted by three exuberant motets of praise, *Ecce nunc benedicte Dominum, Cantata Domino* and the exultant *Venite exultemus Domino*. But the sequence which opens the second disc, beginning with *In illo tempore*, celebrating the naming of Jesus, is hardly less fine. The resonant acoustic is right for the music, but brings some distinct blurring of the upper focus. Nevertheless this is an outstanding set.

Szymanowski, Karol (1882–1937)

(i) *Violin concertos Nos. 1, Op. 35; 2, Op. 61. Concert overture, Op. 12.*
*** Chandos Dig. CHAN 9496 [id.]. (i) Lydia Mordkovitch; BBC PO, Sinaisky.

(i) *Violin concertos Nos. 1, Op. 35; 2, Op. 61;* (ii) *Romance, Op. 23; 3 Paganini caprices, Op. 40.*
*** EMI Dig. CDC5 55607-2 [id.]. Zehetmair, (i) CBSO, Rattle; (ii) Silke Avenhaus.

At long last these concertos are coming into their own and one can expect other musicians to take up their challenge. They will have to be good to dislodge Thomas Zehetmair's deeply felt versions with Rattle and the CBSO. Rattle conjures up the Szymanowskian sound-world with real flair, and the soloist characterizes each phrase with impeccable instinct. The engineers deliver first-rate sound in both works and in the four violin and piano makeweights, in which Zehetmair is well supported by the young German pianist, Silke Avenhaus.

Lydia Mordkovitch is also admirably suited, full-toned and red-blooded, for these exotic concertos, helped by playing, richly recorded, from the BBC Philharmonic under Vassily Sinaisky, the orchestra's Principal Guest Conductor. Both works are strongly contrasted with the early and extrovert *Concert overture*, an illuminating coupling.

(i) *Violin concerto No. 2, Op. 61;* (ii) *Symphonies Nos. 2, Op. 19;* (iii) *3 (Song of the night), Op. 27.*
(B) **(*) Decca Double Dig. 448 258-2 (2) [id.]. (i) Juillet, Montreal SO, Dutoit; (ii; iii) Detroit SO, Dorati; (iii) with Karczykowski, Jewell Ch. – LUTOSLAWSKI: *Concerto for orchestra* etc. **(*)

Chantal Juillet is a selfless and dedicated interpreter of the *Second Violin concerto* and she is truthfully balanced, for her small tone does not always sing through Szymanowski's opulently coloured textures. But the orchestral detail emerges with great fidelity and Dutoit's conducting is unfailingly sympathetic. So is Dorati in the two symphonies, and the Decca recording is better detailed than the competing EMI version, with the richness of Szymanowski's textures fully revealed and the chorus clear and well balanced in No. 3. If the Polish performances are in some ways more penetrating, there is no doubting the superiority of the Decca sound.

(i) *Harnasie (ballet pantomime), Op. 55;* (ii) *Mandragora (pantomime), Op. 43; Etude for orchestra in B flat min., Op. 3* (orch. Fitelberg).
(BB) *** Naxos Dig. 8.553686 [id.]. Polish State PO (Katowice), Karol Stryja; (i) with Henryk Grychnik, Polish State PO Ch.; Stanislaw Meus.

Harnasie, like the Op. 50 *Mazurkas*, is the fruit of Szymanowski's encounter with the Polish folk music of the Góral mountains, and its heady exoticism is quite captivating. Stryja's recording is a good one and, though not quite as intoxicating as the full-price Satanowski on Koch, runs it pretty close. Like its rival, it is coupled with *Mandragora*, a harlequinade for chamber forces from 1920 – not Szymanowski at his most fully characteristic but a cultivated and intelligent score. Worth the money.

Symphonies Nos. 1 in F min., Op. 15; 2 in B flat, Op. 19.
(BB) *** Naxos Dig. 8.553683 [id.]. Polish State PO (Katowice), Karol Stryja.

The two-movement *First Symphony* (1906–7) was first performed in 1909 and was received coolly. Alistair Wightman called it heavily overscored even by the standards of the period. The *Second* (1911) is heavily indebted to Reger, Scriabin and Strauss. It is overlong but it contains original and memorable passages. In its previous incarnation on the Marco Polo label this had two stars but, given the modest price asked and on the principle that it justifies the modest expense involved, it deserves upgrading.

Symphonies Nos. 2 in B flat, Op. 19; (i) *4 (Symphonie concertante).*
*** Chandos Dig. CHAN 9478 [id.]. (i) Howard Shelley; BBC PO, Vassily Sinaisky.

The *Second* and *Fourth Symphonies* are two decades apart. The soft-focus Chandos recording of No. 2 is less clearly defined than, say, Dorati's brightly lit, well-detailed account on Decca (see above), but it presents a more atmospheric aural picture. Vassily Sinaisky is a highly sympathetic interpreter of the piece, and this BBC version must be a prime recommendation. So, too, is the coupling, the *Symphonie concertante* (1932). Howard Shelley produces a quality of sound that is as luminous and every bit as refined and velvet-toned as the two rivals from Piotr Paleczny (on EMI and BBC). The balance between piano and orchestra is particularly well managed, and the lush orchestral textures are more lucid than we have heard them elsewhere.

Symphonies Nos. (i) *3 (Song of the night), Op. 27;* (ii) *4 (Symphonie concertante), Op. 60. Concert overture, Op. 12.*
(BB) *** Naxos Dig. 8.553684 [id.]. (i) Wieslaw Ochmann, Polish State Philharmonic Ch.; (ii)

Taduesz Zmudzinski; Polish State PO (Katowice), Karol Stryja.

Stryja's set of the *Song of the night* and the *Fourth Symphony* offers a well-filled disc that is worth its asking price. He uses a tenor in the *Third Symphony* and, although he does not produce the luxuriant and heady atmosphere of Witold Rowicki's (now deleted) version, it is well worth considering. Taduesz Zmudzinski is an effective soloist in the *Fourth Symphony* or *Symphonie concertante* for piano and orchestra. The performance of the Straussian and derivative *Concert overture* is as persuasive as it can be. The sound in the *Third Symphony* is good, in the remaining pieces rather less impressive but still acceptable.

(i) *Symphony No. 3 (Song of the night), Op. 27;* (ii) *Litania do Marii Pany, Op. 59;* (iii) *Stabat Mater, Op. 53.*
*** EMI Dig. CDC5 55121-2 [id.]. (i) Jon Garrison; (ii–iii) Elzbieta Szmytka; (iii) Florence Quivar, John Connell; CBSO Ch., CBSO, Rattle.

Szymanowski has that fastidious ear for texture and heightened sense of vision that distinguish mystics, and nowhere is atmosphere more potent than in the *Third Symphony*, the *Song of the night*. Sir Simon is equally committed and persuasive in the *Stabat Mater*, these days a standard coupling, and one of the unequivocally great choral works of the century. These are very good performances and the sumptuous and finely detailed recording is absolutely state-of-the-art.

Symphony No. 4 (Symphonie concertante).
** Koch 3-6414-2 [id.]. Ewa Kupiec, Bamberg SO, Judd – LUTOSLAWSKI: *Piano concerto.* ***

As she shows in her inspired account of the Lutoslawski concerto, with which this symphony is coupled, Ewa Kupiec is a pianist with a formidable technique, who conveys a feeling of spontaneous expressiveness even when taxed by bravura writing. Though this is not as purposeful a performance as that of the Lutoslawski coupling – largely a question of the orchestra not sounding so well attuned – this makes an unusual if rather ungenerous coupling of two concertante works for piano by Polish composers of successive generations. First-rate sound.

CHAMBER MUSIC

Mythes, Op. 30; Kurpian folk song; King Roger: Roxana's aria (both arr. Kochanski).
❁ (M) *** DG (IMS) 431 469-2. Kaja Danczowska, Krystian Zimerman – FRANCK: *Violin sonata.* ***

Kaja Danczowska brings vision and poetry to the ecstatic, soaring lines of the opening movement of *Mythes, The Fountains of Arethusa*. Her intonation is impeccable, and she has the measure of these other-worldly, intoxicating scores. There is a sense of rapture here that is totally persuasive, and Krystian Zimerman plays with a virtuosity and imagination that silence criticism. An indispensable reissue.

Violin sonata in D min., Op. 9; La Berceuse d'Aïtacho Enia, Op. 52; 3 Mythes, Op. 30; Notturno e Tarantella, Op. 28; Romance in D, Op. 23. arr.: *3 Paganini caprices, Op. 40.*
(BB) *** ASV Quicksilva Dig. CDQS 6215 [(M) id.]. Detlef Hahn, Mark Fielding.

Detlef Hahn and Mark Fielding survey Szymanowski's output for violin and piano in chronological order, starting with the early *D minor Sonata* of 1904, and ending with *La Berceuse d'Aïtacho Enia*, named after the villa in France in which Szymanowski spent a period of convalescence in 1925. With Hahn producing consistently rich, full tone, the warmth of the writing is brought out most persuasively, and the chronological arrangement of the pieces lets one appreciate the stylistic development of the composer from the *Sonata*, Brahmsian with Slavonic tinges, through to the highly imaginative writing of the later years from 1915 onwards. That was the watershed year which produced both the *Notturno e tarantella* and the three *Mythes*. Both artists have a good feel for Szymanowski as can be heard in that evocative piece. The sound is basically full, but the upper range is rather bright and there is at times a hint of glare. This is not enough to inhibit a strong recommendation, for the artists respond to the music with great sympathy and their playing gives much pleasure.

Violin sonata in D min., Op. 9; Mythes, Op. 30; Nocturne and tarantella, Op. 28.
**(*) Chandos Dig. CHAN 8747 [id.]. Lydia Mordkovitch, Marina Gusk-Grin.

Lydia Mordkovitch is ideally attuned to this sensibility and plays both the *Sonata* and the later works beautifully, and she is sensitively partnered by Marina Gusk-Grin. This can be recommended, though this account of the *Mythes* does not displace Danczowska and Zimerman, and the ASV CD above offers more music for less cost.

PIANO MUSIC

Complete piano music

Disc 1: *9 Preludes, Op. 1; Variations in B flat min., Op. 3; 4 Etudes, Op. 4; Sonata No. 1 in C min., Op. 8* (NI 5405).

Disc 2: *Variations on a Polish theme in B min., Op. 10; Fantasia in C min., Op. 14; Prelude and fugue in C sharp min., (1909); Sonata No. 2 in A, Op. 21* (NI 5406).

Disc 3: *Métopes (3 Poèmes), Op. 29; 15 Etudes,*

Op. 33; Masques, Op. 34; Sonata No. 3, Op. 36 (NI 5435).

Disc 4: *20 Mazurkas, Op. 50; 2 Mazurkas, Op. 62; 4 Polish pieces (1926); Romantic waltz* (1925) (NI 5436).

(B) *** Nimbus Dig. NI 1750 (4) [id.]. Martin Jones.

Martin Jones is thoroughly at home in this repertoire. Back in the 1970s he recorded an exploratory LP recital of Szymanowski's piano music for Argo, to which we gave a warm welcome. This complete Nimbus survey invites equal enthusiasm, particularly as the music is presented in historical sequence. The *Nine Preludes* of Op. 1, although published in 1906, were composed much earlier and are simple, romantic miniatures, with at times a flavour of Chopin. The two sets of *Variations* of Op. 3 and Op. 10, although appealingly inventive (in Op. 3 the *Andante tranquillo* theme closes the work as an *Allegro con fuoco*) are in the received German tradition; but the *Four Etudes* of Op. 4 and the opening movement of the impressive *First Sonata* already suggest Scriabin. All these works date from 1900–1904, but their moments of melancholia, also found in evocative *C major Fantasy*, already seem quite individual. The *Second sonata* (1910/11) is much more complex in both its structure and use of chromaticism. The first movement is rhapsodic and passionate, the second brings another set of variations, very considerably removed from Opp. 3 and 10. The later pieces, *Masques* and *Métopes*, written at about the time of the *First Violin concerto*, show Szymanowski responding to French influences and early Stravinsky, and evolving a sophisticated exoticism all his own. The beautiful and always imaginative *Etudes* (1916) draw on a whole range of styles, from Ravel and Debussy, and even Bartók, but they are well assimilated. The *Third sonata* (1917) is wholly impressionistic and Martin Jones manages its quixotic changes of mood and atmosphere most compellingly. The *Mazurkas*, from the 1920s, find Szymanowski seeking to create an authentic Polish idiom in contemporary terms. The advantage of listening to this rewarding music in sequence means that one senses the composer gradually forging his own individuality. Martin Jones is a consistently persuasive advocate and he is naturally recorded. A most rewarding set, the more attractive for being inexpensive.

4 Etudes, Op. 4; Fantasy, Op. 14; Masques, Op. 34; Métopes, Op. 29.

*** Hyperion Dig. CDA 66409 [id.]. Dennis Lee.

Dennis Lee not only encompasses the technical hurdles of *Masques* and *Métopes* with dazzling virtuosity but also provides the keenest artistic insights. His Hyperion CD is quite simply the finest record of Szymanowski's piano music to have appeared to date; he conveys the exoticism and hothouse atmosphere of these pieces; moreover he handles the early Chopinesque *Etudes* and the *Fantasy* with much the same feeling for characterization and artistry. The Hyperion sound is very good indeed.

4 Etudes, Op. 4; Mazurkas, Op. 50/1–4; Metopes, Op. 29; Piano sonata No. 2 in A, Op. 21.

(BB) *** Naxos Dig. 8.553016-2 [id.]. Martin Roscoe.

Fantasia in C, Op. 14; Masques, Op. 34; Mazurkas, Op. 50/5–12; Variations on a Polish theme, Op. 10.

(BB) *** Naxos Dig. 8.553300 [id.]. Martin Roscoe.

Martin Roscoe proves a perceptive and sensitive interpreter of Szymanowski and the first two discs augur well for this ongoing series. In the four *Mazurkas*, Op. 50, that open the first CD he shows real feeling and insight. He is equally persuasive in the early Chopinesque *Etudes*, Op. 4, and the refined impressionism of *Metopes*. The *Second Sonata* is a problematic piece, full of virtuosic hurdles, romantic gestures and Regerian ingenuity. The second disc gives us the *C major Fantasy*, Op. 14, and the Op. 10 *Variations*, in which the debts to Scriabin and Chopin have yet to be fully discharged. A fine account of the *Masques*, too. This is playing of quality. As far as recording is concerned, Martin Roscoe is well served.

Piano sonatas Nos. 1 in C min., Op. 8; 2 in A, Op. 21; 3, Op. 35; Prelude and fugue in C sharp min.

(N) *** Minerva Athene Dig. ATHCD 19 [id.]. Raymond Clark.

Readers who want to explore just the three piano sonatas and in so doing follow Szymanowski's output from 1904 through to the late sonata of 1917, should consider this excellently played offering. No less than Martin Jones, Raymond Clarke has an intuitive grasp of – and affinity with – Szymanowski's sound world. He is second to none in terms of sensibility and keyboard command. His version of the *First sonata* is particularly convincing. Good recording, though not in the demonstration class.

VOCAL MUSIC

(i) *Demeter, Op. 37b;* (ii) *Litany to the Virgin Mary;* (iii) *Penthesilea;* (iv) *Stabat Mater, Op. 53;* (v) *Veni Creator, Op. 57.*

(BB) *** Naxos Dig. 553687 [id.]. Polish State PO (Katowice), Karol Stryja, with (i) Anna Malewicz-Madej; (iii) Roma Owsinska; (iv) Jadwiga Gadulanka, Krystyna Szostek-Radkowa, Andrzej Hiolski; (v) Barbara Zogórzanka; (i–ii; iv–v) Polish State Ch., Katowice.

Szymanowski's *Stabat Mater* is not only one of his

greatest achievements but one of the greatest choral works of the present century. This welcome account has the advantage of highly sensitive conducting and an excellent response from the orchestra, but some of the solo singing is less distinguished, and Jadwiga Gadulanka's intonation is less than perfect. The *Litany to the Virgin Mary* is another late work of great poignancy; but *Demeter*, composed not long after the *Violin concerto* and the *Third Symphony*, has the same exotic, almost hallucinatory textures that distinguish these works. It is all heady and intoxicating stuff, and not to be missed by those with a taste for this wonderful composer.

(i) *3 Fragments of the poems by Jan Kasprowicz, Op. 5;* (ii) *Love songs of Hafiz, Op. 24;* (iii) *Songs of the fairy-tale princess, Op. 31;* (iv) *Songs of the infatuated muezzin, Op. 42.*
*** Schwann Dig. CD 314 001 [id.]. (i) Krystyna Szostek-Radkova; (ii) Krystyna Rorbach; (iii) Izabella Klosinska; (iv) Barbara Zagórzanka, Polish Nat. Op. O, Satanowski.

In the *Songs of the fairy-tale princess*, one feels that Szymanowski must have known Stravinsky's *Le Rossignol* – Izabella Klosinska certainly sings like one. All the singing is very good, but Barbara Zagórzanka in the imaginative *Songs of the infatuated muezzin* deserves special mention. Satanowski achieves marvellously exotic and heady atmosphere throughout, and the recording is excellent.

(i) *3 Fragments of the poems by Jan Kasprowicz, Op. 5;* (ii) *Love songs of Hafiz, Op. 24;* (iii) *Songs of the fairy-tale princess, Op. 31;* (iv) *Songs of the infatuated muezzin, Op. 42;* (v) *King Roger: Roxana's Song.*
(BB) **(*) Naxos Dig. 8.553688 [id.]. (i) Anna Malewicz-Madej; (ii & iv) Ryszard Minkiewicz; (iii) Jadwiga Gadulanka; (v) Barbara Zagórzanka; Katowice Polish State PO, Karol Stryja.

On Naxos, both the *Songs of the infatuated muezzin* and the *Love songs of Hafiz* are sung by a tenor (Ryszard Minkiewicz) with impressive insight, but the 1989 recording is very resonant and does not flatter him. Jadwiga Gadulanka is hardly less impressive than Klosinska in the extraordinary *Songs of the fairy-tale princess* and Barbara Zagórzanka sings the famous *Chant de Roxane* beautifully, and both she and Anna Malewicz-Madej in the Kasprowicz songs are very well balanced.

STAGE WORKS

(i) *Harnasie, Op. 55;* (ii) *Mandragora, Op. 43.*
*** Schwann Musica Mundi/Koch Dig. 311064. (i) Jozef Stépień; (ii) Paulus Raptus; (i) Polish Nat. Op. Ch.; Polish Nat. Op. O, Robert Satanowski.

Robert Satanowski's version of Szymanowski's choral ballet, *Harnasie*, is the best so far. It is an opulent score and, like the Op. 50 *Mazurkas*, is the product of the composer's encounter with the folk music of the Gorá mountains. It is richly coloured and luxuriant in texture and has a powerfully heady atmosphere. Full justice is done to its opulence and character in this excellent performance. *Mandragora* is a harlequinade for chamber forces, and the performance is persuasive. Both works are very well served by the engineers. A most valuable addition to the catalogue.

Takemitsu, Toru (1930–96)

To the edge of dream.
*** EMI Dig. CDC7 54661-2 [id.]. Julian Bream, CBSO, Rattle – RODRIGO: *Concierto de Aranjuez;* ARNOLD: *Guitar concerto.* ***

A highly sympathetic account of Takemitsu's hypnotically evocative concertante work, using a large orchestra with great economy so as never to overwhelm the soloist. The music is very atmospheric, texturally beautiful but essentially static. It could hardly be better recorded.

Tallis, Thomas (*c.* 1505–85)

Complete music, Volume 1: The Early works: *Alleluia: Ora pro nobis; Ave Dei patris filia; Ave rosa sine spinis; Euge celi porta; Kyrie Deus creatore; Mass Salve intemerata; Salve intemerata.*
(N) *** Signum Dig. SIG 001 [id.]. Chapelle du Roi, Alistair Dixon.

To match the comprehensive survey of the music of his contemporary, William Byrd, by the Cardinall's Musick on ASV, the London-based Chapelle du Roi is undertaking the recording of all the music of Tallis (over a series of nine CDs). The choir is made up of ten young singers, and was founded by Alistair Dixon in 1994, the year he was appointed a Gentleman in Ordinary at Her Majesty's Chapel Royal. The first disc augers extremely well for the project. The programme is framed by three Marian votive antiphons, the first two comparatively immature and rather similar: *Ave Dei patris filia* (in a reconstructed text), and *Ave rosa sine spinis*. Both are works which have simple beginnings and continue in a restrained but more complex polyphony; the second is rather more purposeful than the first. *Salve intemerata*, however, is masterly in its concisely integrated part writing (with some soaring treble solos, beautifully sung here). It can surely be compared with the famous *Spem in alium*, and becomes remarkably complex, and yet very succinct at the closing *Amen*. The mass sharing its name uses much of the same material: the *Gloria* and *Sanctus* are particularly fine. The *Alleluia* and *Eugi celi porta* are less ambitious, but still serenely beautiful, four-part plainchant settings used as part of the Ladymass. The standard of singing here is very high indeed, beautifully blended and secure, and Alistair Dixon's pacing is very convincing. The recording, made at St Augustine's Church, Kilburn (engineer Mike Hatch) is admirable in every way.

Complete music, Volume 2: Music at the Reformation: *Benedictus; Conditor kyrie; Hear the voice and prayer; If ye love me; Magnificat; Mass for four voices; A New commandment; Nunc dimittis; Remember not O Lord God; Sancte deus; Te deum for meanes.*
(N) *** Signum Dig. SIG 002 [id.]. Chapelle du Roi, Alistair Dixon.

Most, and possibly all, the music here dates from the 1540s and reflects the remarkable diversity of musical response that came directly from the profound change in reformed religious procedures which developed in England within a single decade. Tallis himself joined the new, non-monastic cathedral choir at Canterbury in 1540, and went on to become a lay Gentleman of the Chapel Royal (almost certainly working immediately as a composer) in 1543/4. Much liturgical music was still sung in Latin, notably the splendid *Magnificat* and the deeply felt *Sancte Deus*, but already there are settings in English, including three fine early anthems, an extended English *Benedictus* and a remarkable five-part *Te Deum*, all very different from the music on Volume 1 of this series. The surprisingly homophonic setting of the Latin *Mass* is forward-looking too, and very telling. The *Agnus Dei* is most beautiful. *If ye love me* resourcefully alternates chordal and immitative section. The sheer variety of the music here is remarkable and makes a stimulating second volume in this distinguished series.

Complete music, Volume 3: Music for Queen Mary: *Beati immaculati; Gaude gloriosa* (Votive antiphon); *Deus Creator (Kyrie); Mass Puer natus est nobis: Gloria. Sanctus, Benedictus & Agnus Dei* (with Introit): *Puer natus est nobis*; Alleluia: *Dies sanctificatus*; Sequence: *Celeste organum*; Gradual & Communion: *Viderunt omnes; Suscipe quaeso.*
(N) **(*) Signum Dig. SIG 003 [id.]. Chapelle du Roi, Alistair Dixon.

Volume 3 returns to the Latin rite and all the works here date from the reign of Mary Tudor (1553–8). The collection opens with the Psalm setting *Beati immaculati* and includes also the glorious, large-scale votive antiphon, *Gaude gloriosa*, magnificently sung. The key work, however, is the seven-part *Mass Puer natus est* which is incomplete. Here the *Gloria, Sanctus* and *Agnus Dei* are performed with the plainchant Propers for the third mass of Christmas. As usual the singing is splendid, but there is a good deal of monodic chant here, beautifully phrased certainly, but which will reduce the appeal of this volume for some collectors.

Absterge Domine; Candidi facti sunt; Nazareri; Derelinquat impius; Dum transisset sabbatum; Gaude gloriosa Dei Mater; Magnificat and Nunc dimittis; Salvator mundi.
(M) *** CRD CRD 3429; *CRDC 4129* [id.]. New College, Oxford, Ch., Higginbottom.

The performances by the Choir of New College, Oxford – recorded in the splendid acoustic of the College Chapel – are very well prepared, with good internal balance, excellent intonation, ensemble and phrasing. The *Gaude gloriosa* is one of Tallis's most powerful and eloquent works.

Audivi vocem; Ave Dei patris filia; Magnificat (4 vv); *Mass Puer natus est nobis.*
(N) *** Ph. Gimell Dig. 454 934-2 [id.]. Tallis Scholars, Peter Phillips.

The performance by the Tallis Scholars of the reconstructed Tallis Christmas mass has an appealing directness and simplicity and is well up to the standard of its competitors. The four-part *Magnificat* is an early work, but is again very impressively sung here and the programme is completed with two votive antiphons. *Ave Dei patris filia* is most appealing. It has a particularly striking soaring opening from the trebles emphasizing the word '*Ave*' which illuminates the music throughout its seven stanzas. Excellent recording, but there would have been room for more music here.

(i) *Audivi vocem;* (ii–iii) *Derelinquat impius;* (ii; iv) *Dum transisset sabbatum;* (ii–iii) *Ecce tempus idoneum;* (ii; iv) *Honor, virtus et potestas;* (ii–iii) *In ieiunio et fletu; In manus tuas; Lamentations of Jeremiah I and II;* (ii; iv) *Loquebantur variis linguis;* (ii–iii) *O nata lux de lumine; Salvator mundi; Sancte Deus; Spem in alium* (40-part motet); *Te lucis ante terminum* (2 settings); *Veni Redemptor gentium; Videte miraculum;* (i) *Te Deum.* (Organ) (v) *Clarifica me, pater; Fantasy; Iam lucis;* (vi) *Lesson.*
(B) **(*) Decca Double Analogue/Dig. 455 029-2 (2) [id.]. (i) St John's College, Cambridge, Ch., Guest; (ii) King's College, Cambridge, Ch.; (iii) Willcocks; (iv) Cleobury; (v) Peter White; (vi) Andrew Davis.

This fine collection bears out that the curiously dark melodic colouring of the theme used by Vaughan Williams in his Fantasia is typical, covering a wide range of his works. The King's College Choir are in their element in music mostly written for Waltham Abbey or the Chapel Royal, whether conducted by Willcocks or Cleobury. The highlight of their programme is the magnificent 40-part motet, *Spem in alium*, in which the Cambridge University Musical Society joins forces with King's. The *Lamenta-*

tions are performed authentically, using men's voices only. The motets, *Sancte Deus* and *Videte miraculum*, are for full choir, and here the balance gives slight over-prominence to the trebles. The choir of St John's College under George Guest sing well in the *Te Deum* but sound happier in their motet, *Audivi vocem*. Andrew Davis is an excellent advocate of the *Organ Lesson*; the other two organ pieces are musically less interesting but are well played by Peter White. The (originally Argo) recording is full and atmospheric throughout, although the choral focus is not always sharp.

Anthems: *Blessed are those that be undefiled; Christ, rising again; Hear the voice and prayer; If ye love me; A new commandment; O Lord, in Thee is all my trust; O Lord, give thy holy spirit; Out from the deep; Purge me; Remember not, O Lord God; Verily, verily I say: 9 Psalm Tunes for Archbishop Parker's Psalter.*
*** Gimell/Ph. Dig. 454 907-2 [id.]. Tallis Scholars, Phillips.

This disc collects the complete English anthems of Tallis and is thus a valuable complement to the discs listed above. Here women's voices are used instead of boys', but the sound they produce has boyish purity, and the performances could hardly be more committed or idiomatic. Strongly recommended.

Motets: *Ecce tempus idoneum; Gaude gloriosa Dei Mater; Loquebantur variis linguis; O nata lux de lumine; Spem in alium.*
(B) **(*) CfP CD-CFP 4638 [id.]. Clerkes of Oxenford, David Wulstan – SHEPPARD: *Motets*. **(*)

A useful issue, since it not only juxtaposes motets by Tallis against those of his great (but less familiar) contemporary, John Sheppard, but also gives us a strongly sung bargain version of the famous forty-part motet, *Spem in alium*. Here the resonance of Merton College Chapel means that definition could be more refined, and throughout the programme David Wulstan's tempi are somewhat brisk, while at times there is also some sense of strain among the women. Reservations notwithstanding, there are fine things on this inexpensive CD, and it can be recommended.

Gaude gloriosa; Loquebantur variis linguis; Miserere nostri; Salvator mundi, salva nos, I and II; Sancte Deus; Spem in alium (40-part motet).
✿ *** Gimell/Ph. 454 906-2 [id.]. Tallis Scholars, Phillips.

Within the ideal acoustics of Merton College Chapel, Oxford, the Tallis Scholars give a thrilling account of the famous 40-part motet, *Spem in alium*, in which the astonishingly complex polyphony is spaciously separated over a number of point sources, yet blending as a satisfying whole to reach a massive climax. The *Gaude gloriosa* is another much recorded piece, while the soaring *Sancte Deus* and the two very contrasted settings of the *Salvator mundi* are hardly less beautiful. The vocal line is beautifully shaped throughout, the singing combines ardour with serenity, and the breadth and depth of the sound are spectacular.

Lamentations of Jeremiah. Motets: *Absterge domine; Derelinquat impius; In jejunio et fletu; In manus tuas; Mihi autem nimis; O sacrum convivium; O nata lux de lumine; O salutaris hostia; Salve intemerata virgo.*
*** Gimell/Ph. Dig. 454 925-2 [id.]. Tallis Scholars, Peter Phillips.

This, the third of the Tallis Scholars' discs devoted to their eponymous composer, is centred on the two great settings of the *Lamentations*. They have often been recorded before, but never more beautifully than here, performances that give total security. As well as the eight fine motets, the collection also has a rare Marian antiphon, *Salve intemerata*, that is among Tallis's most sustained inspirations. Clear, atmospheric recording of striking tangibility.

Mass for four voices; Motets: *Audivi vocem; In manus tuas Domine; Loquebantur variis linguis; O sacrum convivium; Salvator mundi; Sancte Deus; Te lucis ante terminum; Videte miraculum.*
(B) *** Naxos Dig. 8.550576 [id.]. Oxford Camerata, Jeremy Summerly.

The Oxford Camerata with their beautifully blended timbre have their own way with Tallis. Lines are firm, the singing has serenity but also a firm pulse. In the *Mass* (and particularly in the *Sanctus*) the expressive strength is quite strongly communicated, while the *Benedictus* moves on spontaneously at the close. The motets respond particularly well to Jeremy Summerly's degree of intensity. The opening *Loquebantur variis linguis* has much passionate feeling, and this (together with the *Audivi vocem*, and especially the lovely *Sante Deus*) shows this choir of a dozen singers at their most eloquent. The recording, made in the Chapel of Wellington College, is very fine indeed. Excellent value.

Mass: Puer natus est nobis (for seven voices).
(M) *** EMI Dig. CDM5 65211-2. King's College, Cambridge, Ch., Ledger – BYRD: *Mass for 5 voices;* TYE: *Mass: Euge Bone.* ***

The magnificent seven-part writing in the *Mass* (a work assembled in recent years from a variety of sources – see below) contrasts well with the Byrd and Tye *Masses*, both masterpieces, with which it is coupled. The choir, at its finest, is beautifully recorded (digitally, in 1981, whereas the two couplings are analogue) against the ample acoustic of the King's Chapel.

Mass Puer natus est; Motets: *Salvatore mundi; Suscipe quaeso Dominus.*

❀ (M) *** Cal. CAL 6623 [id.]. Clerkes of Oxenford, David Wulstan – WHITE: *Motets*. *** ❀

An outstanding reissue, made the more desirable by the inclusion of the four beautiful motets by the neglected Elizabethan contemporary of Tallis, Robert White. The Tallis *Mass* was reconstructed by David Wulstan and Sally Dunkley, prompted by the researches and speculations of Joseph Kerman and Jeremy Noble. The *Credo* exists only as a fragment, but the results are intensely beautiful. The *Mass* is among the finest Tallis, and it is performed with dedication and authority. The analogue recording could hardly be bettered.

Taneyev, Sergei (1856–1915)

Suite de concert (for violin and orchestra), *Op. 28*.

(M) *** EMI CDM5 65419-2. David Oistrakh, Philh. O, Malko – MIASKOVSKY: *Cello concerto*. *** ❀

David Oistrakh's superb account of Taneyev's attractively diverse *Suite*, ranging from rhapsodic ardour in the first (of five movements) to sparkling virtuosity in the *Tarantella* finale, has been available only rarely, even on LP. The early (1956) stereo is of high quality and few would guess the age of the recording from the present CD transfer, which is full-bodied and admirable.

Symphony No. 4 in C min., Op. 12; Overture The Oresteia, Op. 6.

*** Chandos Dig. CHAN 8953 [id.]. Philh. O, Järvi.

The *Fourth Symphony*, sometimes known as the *First* as it was the first to be published in Taneyev's lifetime, is a long piece of 42 minutes. Though some of its gestures are predictable, the best movement is the delightful scherzo which betrays his keenness of wit. Elsewhere neither his ideas nor their working out are quite as fresh or as individual as in such pieces as, say, the *Piano quintet*. Neeme Järvi gets very good playing from the Philharmonia.

Piano quartet in E, Op. 20.

**(*) Pro Arte Dig. CDD 301 [id.]. Cantilena Chamber Players.

The *Piano quartet* is a finely wrought and often subtle work. With a superbly sensitive contribution from Frank Glazer, the performance is altogether first rate, though the acoustic in which it is recorded is not quite big enough.

Piano quintet in G min., Op. 30.

*** Ara. Dig. Z 6539 [id.]. Jerome Lowenthal, Rosenthal, Kamei, Thompson, Kates.

Not only is the *Piano quintet* well structured and its motivic organization subtle, its melodic ideas are strong and individual. It is arguably the greatest Russian chamber work between Tchaikovsky and Shostakovich. The recording is not in the demonstration bracket, but it is very good; and the playing, particularly of the pianist Jerome Lowenthal, is excellent. Strongly recommended.

Piano trio in D, Op. 22.

*** Chandos Dig. CHAN 8592 [id.]. Borodin Trio.

This *Trio* is a big, four-movement work. The invention is attractive – and so, too, is the excellent performance and recording. Strongly recommended.

Tansman, Alexandre (1897–1986)

Symphony No. 5 in D min.; 4 Movements for orchestra; Stèle in memoriam d'Igor Stravinsky.

**(*) Marco Polo Dig. 8.223379 [id.]. Slovak PO (Kosice), Meir Minsky.

The Polish-born Alexandre Tansman was a prolific composer, well-known for his music for guitar which Segovia popularized. Readers will recognize a certain affinity with his countryman Szymanowski; his craftsmanship is fastidious and his command of the orchestra impressive. His music is highly atmospheric, with shimmering textures enhanced by celeste, piano and vibraphones and sensitively spaced pianissimo string chords, plus poignant wind writing. The *Quatre mouvements pour orchestre* is impressive and resourceful. The *Fifth Symphony*, which dates from his Hollywood years, is less successful. The ideas are pleasing without being as memorable or as individual as the two companion works. The performances are very serviceable and the recordings decent.

Tarp, Svend Eric (born 1908)

(i) *Piano concerto in C, Op. 39;* (ii) *Symphony No. 7 in C min, Op. 81;* (iii) *The Battle of Jericho, Op. 51;* (iv) *Te Deum, Op. 33.*

**(*) Marco Polo Dacapo Dig. DCCD 9005 [id.]. Danish Nat. RSO, with (i) Per Solo; (i; iii) Schønwandt; (ii) Schmidt; (iv) Danish Nat. R. Ch., Nelson.

The only familiar work here is the neo-classical, Françaix-like *Piano concerto*, a light, attractive piece. There is a distinctively Danish feel to the *Te Deum*, though the piece is eclectic and owes a lot to Stravinsky and may even at times remind English listeners of Walton. The *Seventh Symphony* is neoclassical in feeling, very intelligent music, and only occasionally bombastic. The performances, which come from 1986–90, are enthusiastic and committed, and the recordings are serviceable without being top-drawer.

Tartini, Giuseppe (1692–1770)

Concerti grossi Nos. 3 in C; 5 in E min. (trans. by Giulietto Menghini from *Sonatas, Op. 1/3 & 5*); (i) *Cello concerto in D. Violin concertos:* (ii) *in A min.;* (iii) *in G.*

(B) *** HM Dig. HMX 290853.55 (3) [(M) id.]. (i) Roel Dieltiens; (ii) Enrico Gatti; (iii) Chiara Banchieri; Ens. 315 – CORELLI: *Trio sonatas, Op. 5/1–6.* VIVALDI: *Chamber sonatas.* ***

Here Banchieri's flexible Ensemble 315 expands to become a chamber orchestra (8;2;2;2) and in the *Cello concerto* horns are added. All three works have eloquent slow movements and they are played admirably, using period instruments very persuasively. The concertos are framed by a pair of *Concerti grossi* effectively arranged from two of Tartini's *Trio sonatas.* Warmly resonant sound ensures that orchestral textures are not wanting in body. The disc comes at bargain price in a slip case in harness with *Sonatas* of Corelli and Vivaldi.

Cello concerto in A.

(B) *** DG Double 437 952-2 (2) [id.]. Rostropovich, Zurich Coll. Mus., Sacher – BERNSTEIN: *3 Meditations;* BOCCHERINI: *Cello concerto No. 2;* GLAZUNOV: *Chant du Ménestrel;* SHOSTAKOVICH: *Cello concerto No. 2;* TCHAIKOVSKY: *Andante cantabile* etc.; VIVALDI: *Cello concertos.* ***

As with the other works in this fine 1978 collection, Rostropovich's view of Tartini's *A major Concerto* is larger than life; but the eloquence of the playing disarms criticism, even when the cellist plays cadenzas of his own that are not exactly in period. This is part of a first-class Double DG anthology which can be recommended almost without reservation.

(i; ii) *Cello concerto in A.* (iii; ii) *Violin concertos in D min., D.45; (iv; ii) in E min., D.56; in G, D. 82.* (iii; v) *Violin sonatas* (for violin & continuo): *in A; in G min.; in F, Op. 1/1, 10, & 12; in C, Op. 2/2; in G min.(Devil's Trill).*

(N) (B) *** Erato/Warner Ultima 3984 25601-2 (2). (i) Piero Toso; (ii) I Solisti Veneti.

Here is a collection to make the listener understand why Tartini was so admired in his day. Spanning both halves of the eighteenth century as he did, he possesses the lyrical purity of Corelli and Vivaldi with a forward-looking sensibility that is highly expressive. Indeed his invention is almost romantic at times and there are moments of vision which leave no doubt that he is underrated. The first work on the opening disc is the *Violin concerto in D minor,* D.45 which opens with a richly winning orchestral ritornello and has a very beautiful central *Grave* which Piero Toso plays exquisitely. The other concertos also have memorable slow movements to which Amoyal and Zannerini both respond persuasively. The orchestral playing is committed and the fresh, warm analogue recording from the 1970s is pleasingly transferred. Tartini's sonatas take their virtuosity for granted; even the *Devil's Trill* (said to have been dictated to the composer by the Devil in a dream) does not flaunt its bravura until the finale with its extended trills – considered impossibly difficult in his day. Instead these works call for playing of the greatest technical finesse and musicianship. Pierre Amoyal plays them superbly; he makes no attempt to adapt his style to period-instrument practice. Instead his performances have a sweetness of tone and expressive eloquence to commend them, and though he is forwardly placed, the (unimportant) harpsichord continuo just comes through to give support. The violin is beautifully recorded. A most desirable pair of CDs.

Cello concerto in D.

(N) *** Teldec/Warner Dig. 9031 77311-2. Rostropovich, Saint Paul CO, Hugh Wolff – C. P. E. BACH; VIVALDI: *Concertos.* ***

A commanding performance by Rostropovich of the Tartini concerto, originally written for viola da gamba and transcribed for cello in the late 1920s by Rudolf Hindemith and revised here by Hugh Wolff. It is a mellifluous and beautiful work, played with great eloquence not only by the distinguished soloist, but the fine Saint Paul Orchestra. Excellent recorded sound.

Violin concertos: in E min., D.56; in A, D.96; in A min., D.113.

(M) *** Erato/Warner 4509 92188-2. Uto Ughi, Sol. Ven.

Tartini is a composer of unfailing originality, and the three violin concertos on this record are all very rewarding. The *Concerto in A major,* which comes last on the disc, has an additional (probably) alternative slow movement, a *Largo Andante* which is particularly beautiful. Uto Ughi's performances are distinguished by excellent taste and refinement of tone, and I Solisti Veneti are hardly less polished. The harpsichord continuo is reticent, but otherwise the recording is exemplary. Highly recommended.

(Unaccompanied) *Violin sonatas: in A min., B:a3, in G min., (Sonata de Diavolo), B:g5 ; L'arte del arco, B:f11: 14 Variations on the Gavotte from Corelli's Op. 5/10; Pastorale for violin in scordatura, B:a16.*

(N) ❁ HM Dig. HMU 907213 [id.]. Andrew Manze (baroque violin).

'Andrew Manze fiddles like a man possessed,' said *Classic CD* of his performance of the famous *Devil's Trill sonata.* Indeed he plays those genuinely fiendish trills in the finale quite hair-raisingly. Although Tartini's most famous work was not discovered until thirty years after the composer's death, Manze recreates here the electrifying effect Tartini's playing must have had on his own generation. Manze calls the opening *Largo* an 'infernal siciliana' (yet presents it with great poise and refined espressivo), and the central movement (hardly less remarkable) becomes a 'demonic moto perpetuo'. Yet Corelli's gavotte is played with engaging delicacy, the bravura left for the variations. The *A minor Sonata* also includes a set of variations which again offers an amazing range of musical and technical opportunities, as does the colourful hurdy-gurdy finale of the *Pastorale* which ends so hauntingly. These works were left with a written bass line – omitted here because, according to Manze, this was the composer's stated 'true intention' and own practice. Manze's playing is totally compelling and certainly confirms that the music is 'complete' without a continuo. The recording is very real and immediate.

Tavener, John (born 1944)

Eternal memory.
*** RCA Single 09026 61966-2 [id.]. Steven Isserlis, Moscow Virtuosi, Spivakov – BLOCH: *From Jewish life.* ***

Those who have responded to Tavener's *Protecting veil* (from which the composer quotes in this shorter, more succinct evocation) will readily be drawn to the mystical, three-part structure of *Eternal memory*. Isserlis reaffirms his total identification with Tavener's muse, here bringing an alternation of life's disquieting alarms and its final serenity. The choice of presentation – a CD single – and an apt coupling should also make this a good sampler for those who have not yet ventured beneath *The Protecting veil.*

(i) *Eternal memory for cello and strings;* (ii) *The Hidden treasure* (for string quartet); (iii) *Svyati (O Holy one)* for cello and chorus; (iv) *Akhmatova songs* for soprano and cello. *Chant* for solo cello.
*** RCA Dig. 09026 68761-2 [id.]. Steven Isserlis; with (i) Moscow Virtuosi, Spivakov; (ii) Daniel Phillips, Krista Feeney, Todd Phillips; (iii) Kiev Chamber Ch., Mykola Gobdych; (iv) Patricia Rosario.

All this music is constructed simply (simplistically, some might say) and is based for the most part on a simple rising and falling scalic sequence, in the case of the *Svyati* and *Eternal memory* linked thematically. Their atmosphere is magnetic. *Eternal memory* moves on from *The Protecting veil* and the composer describes its evocation as 'the remembrance of death; the remembrance of Paradise lost': its serene outer sections frame a more troubled centrepiece, 'grotesque, dance-like and rough'. *The Hidden treasure* for string quartet still has a dominating cello role and might be described as a religious pilgrimage, closing with a mystical transformation. In the *Akhmatova songs* the rising and falling sequence is floridly ornamented, and the singer is required to soar up ecstatically to the top of her range, which Patricia Rosario manages confidently. *Svyati* returns to a simple but radiant dialogue, alternating cello soliloquy with a mystical choral response. Steven Isserlis has never made a finer record than this, and he gives the feeling of quiet improvisation (especially in his solo *Chant*); throughout, the singing and playing capture the music's atmosphere superbly. The beautiful recording has a natural presence.

(i) *The Protecting veil;* (ii) *The Last sleep of the Virgin (a veneration for strings and handbells).*
(N) **(*) Telarc Dig. CD 80487 [id.]. (i) France Springuel; (ii) Carlo Willems; I Flamminghi, Rudolf Werthen.

(i) *The Protecting veil* (for cello and orchestra); *Thrinos.*
*** Virgin/EMI Dig. VC7 59052-2 [id.]. Steven Isserlis, (i) LSO, Rozhdestvensky – BRITTEN: *Cello suite No. 3.* ***

(i) *The Protecting veil;* (ii) *Wake up... and die.*
(N) *** Sony Dig. SK 62821 [id.]. Yo-Yo Ma, with (i) Baltimore SO; (ii) with cellos of Baltimore SO, David Zinman.

(i) *The Protecting veil* (for cello and orchestra);
(ii) *In alium* (for soprano, tape and orchestra).
(N) (BB) *** Naxos Dig. 8.554388 [id.]. (i) Maria Kliegel; (ii) Eileen Hulse; Ulster O, Takuo Yuasa.

In the inspired performance of Steven Isserlis, dedicatedly accompanied by Rozhdestvensky and the LSO, *The Protecting veil* has an instant magnetism, at once gentle and compelling. Tavener's simplicity of idiom has you escaping at once into a spiritual world, sharing his visions. The 'protecting veil' of the title refers to the Orthodox Church's celebration of a tenth-century vision, when in Constantinople the Virgin Mary appeared and cast her protecting veil over the Christians who were being attacked by the Saracen armies. Tavener, himself a Greek Orthodox convert, echoes the cadences of Orthodox chant, ending each section with passages of heightened lyricism for the soloist. Each time that guides the ear persuasively on into the next section, leading at the end to the work's one sharply dramatic moment, when a sudden surge represents Christ's Resurrection. Much is owed to the performance, with Isserlis a commanding soloist. He is just as compelling in the other two works on the disc, not just the Britten but also the simple lyrical lament, *Thrinos*, which Tavener wrote especially for him. Excellent recording.

The magnetic qualities of *The Protecting veil*,

John Tavener's religious meditation inspired by the Virgin Mary, made Steven Isserlis's original recording a bestseller. Yo-Yo Ma, rather more withdrawn, is equally concentrated, daringly adopting an even slower tempo in the central section, *Lament of the Mother of God*. He is helped by the sympathetic accompaniment of David Zinman and the Baltimore Orchestra, with recording a degree more transparent than the original RCA. The fill-up is a new work, similarly visionary, commissioned from Tavener by Sony, in which, using a palindromic motif, the spacious cello solo is enhanced by cellos from the orchestra.

Using a warm, wide vibrato, Maria Kliegel gives a dedicated reading of John Tavener's visionary piece inspired by the Virgin Mary. With Yuasa drawing superb playing from the Ulster Orchestra, as he does in the equally recommendable Naxos issue of MacMillan, this is an unusually spacious reading that sustains its length well. What makes it specially attractive is the coupling, *In alium*, a piece for soprano, tape and orchestra which is at once devotional and sensuous. The layering of textures, with dramatic contrasts, is vividly caught in the excellent Naxos recording. Warmly recommended to anyone wanting to investigate the Tavener phenomenon.

The cello soloist in the Telarc version is relatively reticent emerging out of the orchestra, but the playing is beautiful in its gentle way. *The Last sleep of the Virgin*, written originally for string quartet in memory of Dame Margot Fonteyn, makes an apt coupling in the conductor's enriched version for string orchestra.

The Repentant thief.
*** Collins Dig. Single 2005-2. Andrew Marriner, LSO, Tilson Thomas.

In this memorable work for clarinet and orchestra (Andrew Marriner the keenly responsive soloist) Tavener creates a sharply defined structure, contrasting visionary intensity with rhythmic urgency in alternating *Dances*, *Laments* and *Refrains*.

String quartets: *The Hidden Treasure;* (i) *The Last sleep of the Virgin.*
*** Virgin/EMI Dig. VC5 45023-2. Chilingirian Qt, (i) with Iain Simcock (handbells) – PART: *Fratres; Summa.* ***

'Quiet and intensely fragile' is Tavener's guide to performances of *The Last sleep of the Virgin*, a work which might be described as an ethereal suggestion, using the simplest means (string quartet and tolling bell) to convey both the reality and the implications of the death and burial of 'the Mother of God'. *The Hidden Treasure* in its seeking for Paradise offers more violent contrasts (a brief cello cadenza-soliloquy a key factor) interrupting the flow of the spiritual journey. Tavener's world is all his own and the artists convey the music's logic with hypnotic concentration, helped by a resonant acoustic. The mystical close of *The Hidden Treasure* brings a shimmering *pianissimo-diminuendo* of remarkable intensity.

VOCAL MUSIC

The Akathist of Thanksgiving.
✿ *** Sony Dig. SK 64446 [id.]. Bowman, Wilson, Westminster Abbey Ch., BBC SO & Singers, Martin Neary.

Even among Tavener's many works inspired by his Greek Orthodox faith, *The Akathist of Thanksgiving* stands out for its concentrated intensity. The composer's personal response to the text by a monk in the Stalin era inspires striking atmospheric contrasts of motif and texture, with the main choir set against a phalanx of 16 soloists, mainly counter-tenors and basses, led by James Bowman and Timothy Wilson. The recording was taken live from the performance given in January 1994 at Westminster Abbey. The result on disc is both warmly atmospheric and well defined, with high dynamic contrasts involving not just choral forces but strings, heavy brass and percussion. Martin Neary proves an inspiring conductor, drawing incandescent tone from the choirs, thrillingly reinforced by the underlying weight of instrumental sound.

Annunciation; 2 Hymns to the Mother of God; (i) *Innocence; The Lamb;* (ii) *Little Requiem for Father Malachy Lynch; Song for Athene; The Tyger.*
*** Sony Dig. SK 66613 [id.]. Westminster Abbey Ch., Martin Neary; with (i) Patricia Rozario, Graham Titus, Leigh Nixon, Alice Neary (cello), Martin Baker (organ); (ii) ECO.

There is no finer disc than this to represent John Tavener as choral composer. With Martin Neary drawing incandescent singing from the Westminster Abbey Choir, it offers a sequence of Tavener's best-known short works – such as the Blake settings, *The Lamb* and *The Tyger*, and the *Hymns to the Mother of God* – as well as longer pieces in which he movingly exploits spatial effects. *Innocence*, specially written for Westminster Abbey, encapsulates in its 25-minute ritual what many of his more expansive pieces have told us, with multi-layered elements atmospherically contrasted, near and far, starting with apocalyptic organ-sounds and ending with a surging climax. The elegiac *Song for Athene*, heard at the funeral of Princess Diana, is also among Tavener's most beautiful and touching inspirations, a ritual inspired by Orthodox chant over a drone bass. The Sony recording vividly captures the Abbey acoustic, with extreme dynamics used impressively to convey space and distance.

(i) *Eternity's sunrise;* (ii) *Funeral canticle; Petra:*

A ritual dream; (i; iv) *Sappho: Lyrical fragments;* (i; v) *Song of the angel.*
(N) *** HM Dig. HMU 907231 [id.]. (i) Patricia Rozario, (ii) George Mosely, AAM Ch., (iv) Julia Gooding, (v) Andrew Manze; with AAM, Paul Goodwin.

Before the Academy of Ancient Music commissioned John Tavener to compose a 25th-anniversary piece for them, he had never thought of writing for period instruments. It proved revelatory. *Eternity's sunrise* is an elegiac setting of words by Blake in Tavener's rapt and intense style, with the soprano, Patricia Rozario, both pure and sensuous in singing the soaring cantilena. The final work on the disc, the *Funeral canticles* for baritone and chorus, is related in being written in memory of the composer's father; 'calm and mesmeric' as Paul Goodwin says in his note, over an extended span, one of the finest, most intense examples of Tavener's religious minimalism. Of the rest *Sappho* represents Tavener at an earlier period, grittier in expression, while *Petra* and the *Song of the angel* bring ethereal violin solos from Andrew Manze set against the voices. Radiantly atmospheric sound to match.

Funeral Ikos; (i) *Ikon of Light. Carol: The Lamb.*
*** Gimell/Ph. 454 905-2 [id.]. Tallis Scholars, (i) Chilingirian Qt (members), Phillips.

Ikon of Light is a setting of Greek mystical texts, with chant-like phrases repeated hypnotically. The string trio provides the necessary textural variety. More concentrated is *Funeral Ikos*, an English setting of the Greek funeral sentences, often yearningly beautiful. Both in these and in the brief setting of Blake's *The Lamb*, the Tallis Scholars give immaculate performances, atmospherically recorded in the chapel of Merton College, Oxford.

We shall see Him as He is.
*** Chandos Dig. CHAN 9128 [id.]. Rozario, Ainsley, Murgatroyd, Britten Singers, Chester Festival Ch., Hickox.

We shall see Him as He is is a sequence of what Tavener describes as musical ikons, setting brief, poetic texts based on the Epistle of St John, each inspired by a salient event in the life of Christ: His baptism, the Wedding Feast at Cana, the cleansing of the Temple, and on to the Last Supper, the Crucifixion and the Resurrection. Each ikon is punctuated by a choral Refrain, setting the words of the work's title in Greek. Though at first the inspiration may seem painfully thin, the simple ritual becomes magnetic, with its structured, highly atmospheric use of large-scale choral forces progressing towards rapt contemplation of the Resurrection, the ultimate ikon. The recording, with Richard Hickox conducting the BBC Welsh Symphony Orchestra, the Britten Singers and Chester Festival Chorus, was made live at a dedicated Prom performance. The tenor John Mark Ainsley in the central solo role of St John sings with deep feeling, while Patricia Rozario makes her brief, wide-ranging solo a soaring climax.

Mary of Egypt (complete).
*** Collins Dig. 7023-2 (2) [id.]. Rozario, Varcoe, Goodchild, Ely Cathedral Ch., Britten-Pears Chamber Ch., Aldeburgh Festival Ens., Lionel Friend.

Mary of Egypt was recorded live at the Aldeburgh Festival first performances in June 1992 and, characteristically, Tavener compels you to accept his slow pacing and paring down of texture. In many ways the disc works better than the live staging, when with the help of the libretto the developments in the bald, stylized plot can be more readily followed. The musical landmarks are sharply defined in clear-cut, memorable motifs, with moments of violence set sharply against the predominant mood of meditation. What is disconcerting is the disembodied voice representing the Mother of God, Chloe Goodchild, using weird Oriental techniques, sounding like a raw baritone. Under Lionel Friend the performance has a natural concentration, with Patricia Rozario as Mary and the baritone, Stephen Varcoe, as Zossima both outstanding. Their confrontation in Act III brings a radiant duet that acts as a climactic centrepiece to the whole work. A synopsis and libretto are provided, but instead of notes there is a 15-minute interview with the composer, informative but disconcertingly over-amplified.

Taverner, John (*c.* 1495–1545)

Missa gloria tibi Trinitas; Audivi vocem (responsory); ANON.: *Gloria tibi Trinitas.*
*** Hyperion CDA 66134 [id.]. The Sixteen, Harry Christophers.

Missa gloria tibi Trinitas; Dum transisset sabbatum; Kyrie a 4 (Leroy).
*** Gimell/Ph. Dig. 454 995-2 [id.]. Tallis Scholars, Phillips.

This six-voice setting of the Mass is richly varied in its invention (not least in rhythm) and expressive in a deeply personal way very rare for its period. Harry Christophers and The Sixteen underline the beauty with an exceptionally pure and clear account, superbly recorded and made the more brilliant by having the pitch a minor third higher than modern concert pitch.

Peter Phillips and the Tallis Scholars give an intensely involving performance of this glorious example of Tudor music. The recording may not be as clear as on the rival Hyperion version, but Phillips rejects all idea of reserve or cautiousness of expression; the result reflects the emotional basis of the inspiration the more compellingly. The motet,

Dum transisset sabbatum, is then presented more reflectively, another rich inspiration.

Missa Mater Christi; Motets: *Mater Christi; O Wilhelme, pastor bone.*
*** Nimbus Dig. NI 5218 [id.]. Christ Church Cathedral Ch., Stephen Darlington.

This is a liturgical reconstruction by Andrew Carwood for the Feast of the Annunciation of Our Lady, at Eastertide, which intersperses Taverner's *Missa Mater Christi* with the appropriate chant. The disc also includes the Motet *Mater Christi*, on which the Mass itself is built, and the antiphon, *O Wilhelme, pastor bone*. The singing under Stephen Darlington is first class, and the recording made, not at Christ Church, but at Dorchester Abbey, Oxfordshire, is difficult to fault: it is well focused and excellently balanced with a firm image.

Mass, O Michael; Dum transisset sabbatum; Kyrie a 4 (Leroy).
*** Hyperion Dig. CDA 66325 [id.]. The Sixteen, Harry Christophers.

The *Missa O Michael* is an ambitious six-part Mass lasting nearly 40 minutes which derives its name from the respond, *Archangeli Michaelis interventione*, which prefaces the performance. The chant on which the Mass is built appears no fewer than seven times during its course. The so-called Leroy *Kyrie* (the name thought to be a reference to *le roi* Henry) fittingly precedes it: the *Missa O Michael* has no Kyrie. The Easter motet, *Dum transisset sabbatum*, completes an impressive disc.

Missa Sancti Wilhelmi; Dum transisset Sabbatum; Ex eius tumba; O Wilhelme, pastor bone.
*** Hyperion Dig. CDA 66427 [id.]. The Sixteen, Harry Christophers.

The *Missa Sancti Wilhelmi* (known as 'Small Devotion' in two sources and possibly a corruption of *S. Will devotio*) is prefaced by the antiphon, *O Wilhelme, pastor bone*, written in a largely syllabic, note-against-note texture, and the second of his two five-part settings of the Easter respond, *Dum transisset Sabbatum*, and washed down, as it were, by the Matin responds for the Feast of St Nicholas, *Ex eius tumba*, believed to be the only sixteenth-century setting of this text. The singing of The Sixteen under Harry Christophers is expressive and ethereal, and the recording impressively truthful. Recommended with confidence.

Mass: The Western Wynde; Christe Jesu pastor bone; Dum transisset Sabbatum; Kyrie Le Roy; Mater Christie.
(B) *** Decca Double 452 170-2 (2) [id.]. King's College, Cambridge, Ch., Willcocks – BYRD: *Masses for 3, 4 and 5 voices* etc. ***

John Taverner's remarkable individuality is admirably shown by this excellent King's concert. The *Western Wynde Mass* (so called because of its use of this secular tune as a constantly recurring ground) is a masterpiece. Its lines soar to express rich expressive feeling, particularly in the *Sanctus*, and overall it is hauntingly memorable. The other music here also shows the composer's wide range of expressive power: the motets, works of great beauty, match the Mass in their inspiration. With first-class King's performances, appropriately more extrovert in feeling than the coupled music of Byrd, this makes an outstanding collection, with the highly evocative 1961 (originally Argo) recording giving the trebles an abundant body of tone.

Tchaikovsky, Peter (1840–93)

Andante cantabile for cello and orchestra, Op. posth; (i) *Variations on a rococo theme, Op. 33.*
(B) *** DG Double 437 952-2 (2) [id.]. Rostropovich, BPO; (i) cond. Karajan – BERNSTEIN: *3 Meditations;* BOCCHERINI: *Cello concerto No. 2;* GLAZUNOV: *Chant du Ménestrel;* SHOSTAKOVICH: *Cello concerto No. 2;* TARTINI: *Cello concerto;* VIVALDI: *Cello concertos.* ***

Rostropovich indulges himself affectionately in the composer's arrangement of the *Andante cantabile*, and the balance – all cello with a discreet orchestral backing – reflects his approach. Rostropovich's famous and much-praised account of the *Rococo variations* with Karajan (see below) has been added as part of a highly desirable anthology – a bargain in DG's Double-CD series with two discs offered for the price of one.

Andante cantabile, Op. 11; Nocturne, Op. 19/4; Pezzo capriccioso, Op. 62 (1887 version); *2 Songs: Legend; Was I not a little blade of grass; Variations on a rococo theme, Op. 33* (1876 version).
*** Chandos Dig. CHAN 8347 [id.]. Wallfisch, ECO, Simon.

Andante cantabile, Op. 11; Nocturne in D min., Op. 19/4; Pezzo capriccioso in B min., Op. 62; Variations on a rococo theme for cello and orchestra, Op. 33.
(M) **(*) BMG/Melodiya 74321 40724-2 [id.]. Valentin Feighin, Estonian State SO, Neeme Järvi – HAYDN: *Cello concerto.* **(*)

This delightful Chandos record gathers together all of Tchaikovsky's music for cello and orchestra – including his arrangements of such items as the famous *Andante cantabile* and two songs. The major item is the original version of the *Rococo variations* with an extra variation and the earlier variations put in a more effective order, as Tchaikovsky wanted. Geoffrey Simon draws lively and sympathetic playing from the ECO, with Wallfisch a vital if not quite flawless soloist. Excellent recording, with the

CD providing fine presence and an excellent perspective.

Jarvi's disc is one of a half-dozen devoted to his early recordings made in the USSR, issued by BMG/Melodiya to mark his sixtieth birthday. Most were made in the mid-1960s, but these are the last recordings he made in 1978 in Tallinn with the Estonian State Orchestra before he left for Sweden and the USA. It comprises Tchaikovsky's major output for cello and orchestra and features Valentin Feighin, a player of great naturalness and expressive eloquence, little known in the West. These are glorious performances, a worthy companion to Daniil Shafran's Haydn concerto with which they are coupled.

Andante cantabile, Op. 11; Nocturne, Op. 19/4 (both arr. for cello & orchestra); Pezzo capriccioso, Op. 62; Variations on a rococo theme, Op. 33 (original versions).

(N) (BB) *** Virgin Classics Dig. VBD5 61490-2 [CDVB 61490]. Steven Isserlis, COE, Gardiner – BLOCH: *Schelomo*. ELGAR: *Cello concerto*; KABALEVSKY: *Cello concerto No. 2*; R. STRAUSS: *Don Quixote*. ***

All lovers of the cello will be tempted by the extraordinarily generous collection offered on this bargain Virgin Double. Not only are all the performances of high quality, but Isserlis offers Tchaikovsky's original versions of both the *Pezzo capriccioso* and the *Rococo variations*. The solo playing has at times a slight reserve, but also an elegant delicacy, most noticeable in the *Andante cantabile*. Throughout, Gardiner provides gracefully lightweight accompaniments and the Virgin recording is faithfully balanced, fresh in texture and warm in ambience. Although there is some sparkling and flawless bravura in the variations, the performance here has less extrovert feeling than with Rostropovich, but many will feel that its lightness of touch has a special appeal.

Andante cantabile, Op. 11; Nocturne in C sharp min., Op. 19/4; Souvenir de Florence, Op. 70; Variations on a rococo theme, Op. 33; Eugene Onegin: Lensky's aria.

*** DG Dig. 453 460-2 [id.]. Mischa Maisky, Orpheus CO.

If in the central cello repertory Mischa Maisky can seem dangerously wilful, Tchaikovsky here suits him perfectly. Understandably, with him as star, the *Rococo variations*, not the longest work, get top billing, and they receive a warmly persuasive reading, at once impulsive and freely expressive. Long versed in conductorless playing, the brilliant Orpheus Chamber Orchestra follow him loyally, as they do in the other concertante items, as arranged by the composer. In the celebrated *Andante cantabile* Maisky uses full tone for the opening melody and then most beautifully begins the middle section in a hushed pianissimo. Paradoxically, much the longest work, the *Souvenir de Florence*, is the one which gives Maisky the least to do as soloist. The original string sextet version is here adapted for full strings, with Maisky coming to the fore only in the second movement. The playing is just as rich and persuasive, with finely polished ensemble. Excellent recording, warm and well balanced.

Capriccio italien, op. 45.

(N) ❁ (M) *** RCA 09026 63302-2 [id.]. RCA Victor SO, Kiril Kondrashin – KABALEVSKY: *The Comedians suite*; KHACHATURIAN: *Masquerade suite*. RIMSKY-KORSAKOV: *Capriccio espagnol*. ***

Kondrashin's 1958 recording of Tchaikovsky's *Capriccio italien* has never been surpassed. It was made in New York's Manhattan Center, with the orchestra inidentified, but probably the NYPO. They play superbly, and Kondrashin's reading has great flair and excitement. The arresting opening still surprises by its impact, the brass fanfares – first trumpets, then horns, then the full tutti – sonically riveting. The music is alive in every bar and a model of careful preparation, with the composer's dynamic markings meticulously terraced. Kondrashin's pacing throughout is absolutely right and the closing section is highly exhilarating. This is a stereo demonstration disc if ever there was one. And the couplings are pretty good too.

Capriccio italien, Op. 45; 1812 Overture, Op. 49; Fatum, Op. 77; Festive overture on the Danish National Anthem, Op. 15; Francesca da Rimini, Op. 32; Hamlet (fantasy overture), *Op. 67a; Romeo and Juliet* (fantasy overture); *The Tempest* (symphonic fantasy), *Op. 18.*

*** Olympia Dig. OCD 512 A/B (2) [id.]. SO of Russia, Dudarova.

This exciting two-disc Tchaikovsky compilation includes one of the finest performances of *The Tempest* ever recorded, structurally convincing, full of atmosphere. Veronika Dudarova cannot do quite so much for *Fatum*, which remains an obstinately clumsy structure. *Romeo and Juliet* has passion, excitement and a certain Slavonic reserve at the presentation of the love theme, which make for a very satisfying whole; and a spacious gravity informs *1812*, although it does not lack impetus, with the climax (using drums rather than cannon) bringing a gloriously expansive treatment of the Russian hymn. *Capriccio italien* is very Russian too, especially the nostalgic treatment of the broad string melody, but there is plenty of energy and spectacle, and the end is almost alcoholically rumbustious, with a not quite convincing sudden accelerando at the coda. *Francesca da Rimini* and *Hamlet* here can almost be spoken of in the same breath as the famous Stokowski versions. The former has some glorious playing in the middle section, full of rich woodwind colouring, and a ferociously demonic portrayal of the inferno and the lovers' final, cataclysmic punishment; the latter has a uniquely touching portrayal of Ophelia's onset of madness (a poignant oboe solo) and a passionately sombre close. The Symphony Orchestra of Russia is apparently a permanent pick-up group, formed from members of other Russian orchestras, who play with great ardour and virtuosity. The 1992 digital recording is spectacular to suit the music-making, yet not blatant.

(i) *Capriccio italien; 1812 overture; Romeo and Juliet;* (ii) Song: *None but the lonely heart; Eugene Onegin: Lensky's aria.*
(B) *** [EMI Red Line Dig. CDR5 69844]. (i) Philh. O, Domingo; (ii) Domingo, Philh. O, Behr.

Here we have Domingo in his latterday role as conductor giving heartfelt and individual readings of three popular orchestral favourites, with plenty of drama and with the passion worn on the sleeve. *1812* is ceremonially measured, with the organ adding breadth and spectacle at the close. The recording is appropriately spacious and resonant. Any lack of sharp co-ordination of ensemble is compensated for by the impact. The vocal items show that Domingo can still tug at the emotions in his more familiar role. The recording, made in All Saints', Tooting, is expansively resonant.

Capriccio italien, Op. 45; 1812 Overture; Marche slave, Op. 31; Romeo and Juliet (fantasy overture).
(BB) *** Naxos Dig. 8.550500; *4550500* [id.]. RPO, Adrian Leaper.

Adrian Leaper proves a natural Tchaikovskian: whether in the colourful extravagance of the composer's memento of his Italian holiday, the romantic ardour and passionate conflict of *Romeo and Juliet*, the sombre expansiveness of *Marche slave* with its surge of adrenalin at the close, or in the extrovert celebration of *1812*, he draws playing from the RPO that is spontaneously committed and exciting. The brilliantly spectacular recording, with plenty of weight for the brass, was made in Watford Town Hall, with realistic cannon and an impressively resonant imported carillon to add to the very exciting climax of *1812*.

Capriccio italien, Op. 45; Manfred Symphony, Op. 58; Romeo and Juliet (fantasy overture); Serenade for strings in C, Op. 48; The Tempest, Op. 18.
(B) *** BMG/Melodiya Twofer 74321 34164-2 (2). USSR SO, Svetlanov.

Svetlanov's recordings of the major Tchaikovsky orchestral works, made in the late 1960s, still stand up well to current competition; the remastering for CD is highly successful, retaining the vividness and colour and minimizing any coarseness. Their reissue on three 'Twofers' makes a good bargain. The key work here is *Manfred*, and Svetlanov provides a superb account, strong and uninhibited, among the finest available: the orchestral playing has splendid colour and urgency, with plenty of passion from the strings. The full-blooded Russian recording is entirely appropriate and, while the work's weaker moments are not totally disguised, this is altogether most satisfying.

Piano concertos Nos. 1–3; Concert fantasy, Op. 56.
(BB) **(*) Virgin Classics Dig. Double VBD5 61463-2 (2) [CDVB 61462]. Mikhail Pletnev, Philh. O, Fedoseyev.

Mikhail Pletnev's masterful account of the *First Concerto* has all the qualities we associate with his remarkable pianism. This high-voltage account, together with that of the *Concert fantasy*, is among the very finest of modern recordings in the catalogue. Vladimir Fedoseyev and the Philharmonia Orchestra give excellent support and the recording is exemplary. The *Second Concerto* brings comparably commanding playing from Pletnev, but it also brings a small but unncessary cut in the slow movement. It would be difficult to improve on the *Third Concerto*, which is characterized strongly and interestingly. The recording is very good, but not in the demonstration bracket. Admirers of this pianist will count this Virgin Double (two CDs for the cost of one mid-priced disc) an outstanding bargain.

Piano concerto No. 1 in B flat min., Op. 23.
*** Hänssler Dig. CD 98.932 [id.]. Garrick Ohlsson, ASMF, Marriner – RACHMANINOV: *Piano concerto No. 2.* ***
✿ (M) (***) RCA mono GD 60321. Horowitz, NBC SO, Toscanini – MUSSORGSKY: *Pictures.* (***)
*** Ph. 446 673-2 [id.]. Martha Argerich, Bavarian RSO, Kondrashin – RACHMANINOV: *Piano concerto No. 3.* ***
(M) *** RCA 09026 61961-2. Van Cliburn, RCA SO, Kondrashin – BEETHOVEN: *Piano concerto No. 5.* ***
*** Chesky CD-13 [id.]. Earl Wild, RPO, Fistoulari – DOHNANYI: *Variations on a nursery tune* etc. ***
(M) *** Decca 417 750-2 [id.]. Ashkenazy, LSO, Maazel – CHOPIN: *Concerto No. 2.* ***
(M) **(*) BMG/Melodiya 74321 40721-2 [id.]. Grigori Sokolov, USSR SO, Neeme Järvi – SAINT-SAENS: *Piano concerto No. 2.* **(*)
(M) (***) RCA mono GD 60449 [60449-2-RG]. Horowitz, NBC SO, Toscanini – MUSSORGSKY: *Pictures* etc. (***)
(M) (**) DG 447 420-2. Sviatoslav Richter, VSO, Karajan – RACHMANINOV: *Piano concerto No. 2.* ***

(i) *Piano concerto No. 1. The Seasons, Op. 37: January; February; April; May; August; October; November; December.*
(B) *** Tring. Dig. TRP 023 [id.]. Ronan O'Hora, (i) with RPO, James Judd.

(i) *Piano concerto No. 1. Theme and variations, Op. 19/6.*
(M) *** EMI (SIS) CDM7 64329-2 [id.]. Gavrilov, (i) Philh. O, Muti – BALAKIREV: *Islamey*; PROKOFIEV: *Concerto No. 1.* ***

It is good to have a really splendid, modern coupling of these two most popular romantic concertos from Ohlsson and Marriner that can measure up to the finest versions from the past, presented in naturally balanced, modern, digital recording of the very highest quality. The Tchaikovsky opens with a commanding melodic sweep, and the first-movement allegro is as full of poetic detail as it is exciting, leading on to the cadenza in the most spontaneous way. The *Andante semplice* is charmingly light-hearted and, after the scintillating centrepiece, is very tender at its reprise. The dancing finale brings all the bravura you could ask for, with weight and power as well as excitement.

Horowitz's famous record of the *B flat minor Concerto*, recorded at a concert in Carnegie Hall in 1943 with his father-in-law conducting, has achieved legendary status and has dwarfed almost every record of the work made since. The power of the playing means that within seconds the ear makes allowances for the sonic limitations. This performance has now been reissued as part of the Toscanini Edition with a more attractive coupling than in its last incarnation. A record not to be missed on any account. (Readers should note that this live concert version of the Tchaikovsky *Concerto* is still also available coupled with Horowitz's 1952 recording, conducted by Reiner, of Beethoven's *Emperor Piano concerto*, on RCA GD 87992.)

Argerich's Philips issue comes from a live performance given in October 1980, full of animal excitement, with astonishingly fast speeds in the outer movements. The impetuous virtuosity is breathtaking, even if passage-work is not always as cleanly articulated as in her superb studio performance for DG. That earlier version also brings more variety of tone; but you will find few more satisfying performances on record than either of these. The CD version clarifies and intensifies the already vivid sound, which is fuller than her DG version of nine years earlier (see below), and the new coupling with her even more sensational account of Rachmaninov's *Third Concerto* from earlier makes this a very desirable issue.

Van Cliburn and the Soviet conductor Kondrashin give an inspired performance with as much warmth as glitter. The 1958 recording is forward and could do with more atmosphere, but the digital remastering has brought a firmer orchestral image, and the piano timbre is also improved. Coupled with an outstanding version of the *Emperor concerto*, this is a very distinguished reissue, even if the piano timbre here is shallower than in the coupling.

Even in the shadow of Horowitz, the spectacular reissue by Earl Wild with the RPO under Fistoulari stands as one of the finest accounts ever of this much-recorded work and needs no apology for its sound, which is vintage quality of the early 1960s. From the first sweep of the opening the reading is distinguished by its feeling of directness and power, yet the lyrical side of the music (the first movement's second subject, the outer sections of the *Andantino*) brings a comparable sensitivity. The finale too, played with crackling bravura, again recalls the famous Horowitz/Toscanini live Carnegie Hall recording and Fistoulari makes a superb final climax.

Having already given us an outstanding version of the Grieg *Concerto*, Ronan O'Hora and James Judd repeat their success with a memorably fresh, new look at Tchaikovsky's *B flat minor Concerto*. The very opening is gloriously arresting, and then O'Hora sets off with a crisp, sparkling duplet rhythm for the main theme of the allegro, pulling back naturally and poetically for his gentle introduction of the lovely second group. The *Andante semplice* brings contrasting delicacy, and in the central section O'Hora's chimerical lightness is like a will-o'-the-wisp. Then the finale makes a fitting culmination, with the joyful spirit of Russian dance paramount. The whole performance has the spontaneous feel of a live occasion, and the recording balance is just about ideal, with a bold, natural piano-image set against a richly spacious orchestral tapestry. As with his Grieg record, the pianist chooses a coupling of solo pieces, eight out of the twelve 'months' which make up *The Seasons* presented with an agreeable, impulsive charm and plenty of colour.

Ashkenazy refuses to be stampeded by Tchaikovsky's rhetoric, and the biggest climaxes of the first movement are made to grow naturally out of the music. In the *Andantino* too, Ashkenazy refuses to play flashily. The finale is very fast and brilliant, yet the big tune is broadened at the end in the most convincing way. The remastering is highly successful: the piano sounds splendidly bold and clear while the orchestral balance is realistic.

Grigory Sokolov was only sixteen when he won the Tchaikovsky Piano Competition in 1966 with a dazzling account of the Saint-Saëns *G minor Concerto*, with which the Tchaikovsky *B flat minor Concerto* is coupled. The Tchaikovsky performance from the following year is no less remarkable, and not just for virtuosic display but also for poetic depth. Remarkable playing, not just from the young soloist but also from the USSR Symphony Orchestra and Neeme Järvi. The recording may be rough, but, given the excitement generated by this young performer, few will be worried.

Horowitz's earlier version, coupled with the Mussorgsky, was made in Carnegie Hall, in 1941, under studio conditions. The recording is altogether better balanced than the live performance by the same artists, and the orchestral sound is much fuller. Toscanini, forcing the pace throughout, creates enormous urgency, with his soloist responding readily. This is exhilarating, but the sense of occasion of the live performance makes that even more satisfying despite its sonic limitations.

Gavrilov is stunning in the finale of the *Concerto*; however, the final statement of the big tune is too broadened to be convincing. In the main Allegro contrasts of dynamic and tempo are extreme, in a performance that often sounds self-conscious. The recording is full and sumptuous. In the *Variations*, Op. 19, Tchaikovsky's, full of felicitous invention, Gavrilov's playing is stylishly sympathetic, and the Balakirev and Prokofiev couplings are dazzling.

The element of struggle for which this work is famous is all too clear in the Richter/Karajan performance; not surprisingly, these two musical giants do not always agree: each chooses a different tempo for the second subject of the finale and maintains it, despite the other. In both the dramatic opening and the closing pages of the work the approach is mannered and self-conscious, not easy to enjoy. The recording is full-blooded, with a firm piano image.

(i) *Piano concertos No. 1 in B flat min., Op. 23;* (ii) *2 in G, Op. 44* (arr. Siloti).
(N) (M) ** DG mono 457 751-2 [id.]. Cherkassky, BPO; (i) Leopold Ludwig; (ii) Richard Kraus.

Cherkassky's were famous performances in their day. Some might find the opening of the *First concerto* too slow and massive, but it is also impressively powerful. At the beginning of the main allegro the soloist indulges in some rather coy rubato, but the performance soon settles down to offer plenty of thrills and, in the second subject (and later in the slow movement), sensitive playing from all concerned. There is also the kind of spontaneity one enjoys at a live performance. The DG sound is clear and well balanced, with excellent piano image. The upper strings, however, are less smooth than usual.

The *Second concerto* was recorded before conductors had discovered that the first movement is in split common time, and meant to be taken at two-beats-in-a-bar. Richard Kraus plods along emphatically using four, and Tchaikovsky's opening is immediately bogged down. Cherkassky's playing in superb throughout, but he uses the truncated Siloti edition. Some will feel that his flair and poetry more than compensate but not the present writer. This recording comes in excellent mono sound.

(i) *Piano concerto No. 1;* (ii) *Violin concerto in D, Op. 35.*
(B) *** DG 439 420-2 [449 816-2]. (i) Martha Argerich, RPO, Dutoit; (ii) Milstein, VPO, Abbado.
(BB) *** RCA Navigator 74321 17900-2 [RCA 60491]. (i) John Browning; (ii) Erick Friedman; LSO, Ozawa.

Argerich's 1971 version of the *First Piano concerto* with Dutoit has long been among the top recommendations. The sound is firm, with excellent presence, and its ambience is more attractive than the later version. The weight of the opening immediately sets the mood for a big, broad performance, with the kind of music-making in which the personalities of both artists are complementary. Argerich's conception encompasses the widest range of tonal shading. Milstein's 1973 performance of the *Violin concerto* is equally impressive, undoubtedly one of the finest available, while Abbado secures playing of genuine sensitivity and scale from the Vienna Philharmonic, with a recording that is also well balanced.

Browning's mid-1960s interpretation of the solo role in the *Piano concerto* is remarkable, not only for power and bravura but for wit and point in the many *scherzando* passages, and in the finale he adopts a fast and furious tempo to compare with Horowitz. Erick Friedman, Heifetz's pupil, is a thoughtful violinist who gives a keenly intelligent performance of the companion work, imbued with a glowing lyricism and with a particularly poetic and beautiful account of the slow movement. Ozawa gives first-rate support to both soloists. The recording is excellent. Two outstanding performances offered in the lowest price-range.

(i) *Piano concerto No. 1 in B flat min., Op. 23; Symphony No. 6 in B min. (Pathétique), Op. 74.*
(N) (B)(**(*)) Naxos mono 8.110807 [id.]. (i) Vladimir Horowitz; NBC SO, Toscanini.

Horowitz's reading of the Tchaikovsky concerto with his father-in-law, Toscanini, is well known from RCA issues, but this is the 1941 performance given at Carnegie Hall, even faster and more exciting than the better-known 1943 version, The playing is not always immaculate, but it is wonderfully incisive in articulation. This version of the *Pathétique symphony* comes from the same concert, taut and urgently exciting rather than warmly emotional, marginally broader in the outer movements than his 1947 reading on RCA. Typically limited sound, not quite as dry as many from this source.

Piano concerto No. 2 in G (complete); *Piano sonata No. 1 in G (Grande sonate), Op. 37.*
*** Teldec/Warner Dig. 9031 72296-2. Elisabeth Leonskaja; (i) Leipzig GO, Kurt Masur.

Leonskaja gives a splendid performance of Tchaikovsky's *G major Piano concerto*, weighty, expansive and compelling. The red-blooded orchestral tuttis are matched by Leonskaja's bold, forwardly balanced pianism, and if in the slow movement she misses some of its delicacy, she is ardently lyrical. The finale, too, is not chimerical but forceful in its exuberance, powerful and exciting, and the rich Leipzig recording matches the style of the performance. The coupling of Tchaikovsky's *Grand Sonata* in the same key is surely an ideal one. Leonskaja has the full measure of its rhetoric, fresh and spontaneous in the *Andante*.

Piano concertos Nos. 2 in G, Op. 44; 3 in E flat, Op. 75.

✪ *** EMI Dig. CDC7 49940-2. Donohoe, Bournemouth SO, Barshai.

*** Ara. Dig. Z 6583 [id.]. Jerome Lowenthal, LSO, Comissiona.

Donohoe's much-praised recording of Tchaikovsky's *Second Piano concerto* is coupled with his excellent account of the *Third*. This superb recording of the full, original score of the *Second* in every way justifies the work's length and the unusual format of the slow movement, with its extended solos for violin and cello; these are played with beguiling warmth by Nigel Kennedy and Steven Isserlis. Barshai's pacing is perfectly calculated. The first movement goes with a splendid impetus, and the performance of the slow movement is a delight from beginning to end. Peter Donohoe plays marvellously and in the finale he is inspired to Horowitz-like bravura. The recording is spacious and very well balanced.

In an attractive coupling of two unjustly neglected works, the energy and flair of Lowenthal and Comissiona combine to give highly spontaneous performances, well balanced and recorded. If the *G major Concerto* has not quite the distinction of the EMI version, it is still satisfyingly alive; the soloist brings an individual, poetic response as well as bravura. With very good sound, this is well worth investigating, as the account of the *Third Concerto* is comparably spontaneous.

Piano concerto No. 3.

(*) Chandos Dig. CHAN 9130 [id.]. Geoffrey Tozer, LPO, Järvi – *Symphony No. 7.* *

It was a good idea to record the *Third Piano concerto* alongside the *Seventh Symphony*, on whose first movement it is based (see below). Geoffrey Tozer is an excellent soloist and, as in his Medtner performances for Chandos, plays with sympathy as well as powerful bravura. The playing of the London Philharmonic is not so consistent, with violin tone as recorded often thin, not opulent enough for big Tchaikovsky melodies.

Violin concerto in D, Op. 35.

*** Teldec/Warner Dig. 4509 90881-2. Vengerov, BPO, Abbado – GLAZUNOV: *Violin concerto.* ***

*** Erato/Warner Dig. 4509 98537-2. Vadim Repin, LSO, Emmanuel Krivine – SIBELIUS: *Violin concerto.* ***

(M) *** Decca 425 080-2 [id.]. Kyung-Wha Chung, LSO, Previn – SIBELIUS: *Violin concerto.* ***

*** Sony Dig. SK 66567 [id.]. Julian Rachlin, Moscow RSO, Vladimir Fedoseyev – PROKOFIEV: *Violin concerto No. 1.* ***

(N) *** Sony Dig. SK 68338 [id.]. Midori, Berlin PO, Abbado – SHOSTAKOVICH: *Violin concerto No. 1.* ***

*** EMI (SIS) Dig. CDC7 54753-2 [id.]. Sarah Chang, LSO, Sir Colin Davis – BRAHMS: *Hungarian dances.* ***

(N) ✪ (M) (***) Dutton Lab. mono CDK 1204 [id.]. Ida Haendel, Nat. SO, Basil Cameron – DVORAK: *Violin concerto*; SAINT-SAENS: *Introduction and rondo capriccioso.* (***)

*** EMI (SIS) CDC5 56150-2. Perlman, Phd. O, Ormandy – SIBELIUS: *Violin concerto.* ***

(BB) *** Naxos Dig. 8.550153; *4550153* [id.]. Takako Nishizaki, Slovak PO, Kenneth Jean – MENDELSSOHN: *Concerto.* ***

(B) *** DG Double 453 142-2 (2). Nathan Milstein, VPO, Abbado – BEETHOVEN: *Concerto* ***; BRAHMS: *Concerto* **(*); MENDELSSOHN: *Concerto.* ***

(N) (M) *** Penguin Classics DG 460 619-2 [id.]. Nathan Milstein, VPO, Abbado – MENDELSSOHN: *Concerto.* ***

*** Decca Dig. 421 716-2 [id.]. Joshua Bell, Cleveland O, Ashkenazy – WIENIAWSKI: *Violin concerto No. 2.* ***

(M) *** Sony Stern Edition I SMK 66829 [id.]. Stern, Phd. O, Ormandy – SIBELIUS: *Violin concerto.* ***

(***) Testament mono SBT 1038 [id.]. Ida Haendel, RPO, Goossens – BRAHMS: *Violin concerto.* (***)

(M) (***) EMI mono CDH7 64030-2 [id.]. Heifetz, LPO, Barbirolli – GLAZUNOV: *Violin concerto* (***) ✪; SIBELIUS: *Violin concerto.* (**)

(N) **(*) Globe Dig. GLO 5174. Lubotsky, Estonian Nat. SO, Volmer – ARENSKY: *Violin concerto;* RIMSKY-KORSAKOV: *Concert fantasy.* **(*)

Violin concerto in D; Sérénade mélancolique, Op. 26; Souvenir d'un lieu cher, Op. 42/3: Mélodie. Valse-scherzo, Op. 34.

*** ASV Dig. CDDCA 713 [id.]. Xue-Wei, Philh. O, Accardo.

Violin concerto in D; Sérénade mélancolique. String serenade: Waltz.

(M) **(*) RCA 09026 61743-2 [id.]. Heifetz, Chicago SO, Reiner – MENDELSSOHN: *Concerto.* **(*)

The two most popular romantic Russian violin concertos make an excellent and surprisingly rare coupling, and Vengerov gives inspired performances of both, with magic inspiration breathing new life into well-known music. This Tchaikovsky reading immediately establishes itself as a big performance, both in the daring manner and in the range of dynamic of the playing. For all his power and his youthfully eager love of brilliance, Vengerov is never reluctant to play really softly. The central *Canzonetta* is full of Russian temperament, and the finale is sparklingly light, with articulation breathtakingly clean to match the transparency of the orchestral textures.

Repin's withdrawn tone in moments of meditation and his fondness for the gentlest pianissimos are as remarkable as his purity and sharpness of focus in bravura. Many interpretative details like sudden pianissimos are remarkably similar to those in the Teldec version by his close colleague, Maxim Vengerov, but this is a tauter reading with tone, less fat. It brings many moments of magic, such as the gentle lead-in to the second subject and the whispered statement of the main theme in the central *Canzonetta*, enhanced by the natural balance of the soloist in refined and well-detailed Erato recording, making it a highly recommendable alternative to Chung and Mullova in this favourite coupling.

Chung's earlier recording of the Tchaikovsky *Concerto* with Previn conducting has remained one of the strongest recommendations for a much-recorded work ever since it was made, right at the beginning of her career. Although she recorded it later with Dutoit, anyone should be well satisfied with Chung's 1970 version with its Sibelius coupling. With Previn a most sympathetic and responsive accompanist, this has warmth, spontaneity and discipline, every detail is beautifully shaped and turned without a trace of sentimentality. The recording is well balanced and detail is clean. A welcome reissue in Decca's Classic Sound series.

As in the Prokofiev, Julian Rachlin gives an exceptionally characterful and distinctive reading, not conventionally high-powered but thoughtful and hushed in intensity, rare qualities in this concerto. He is helped by a natural balance for the solo instrument in these live recordings, made in the Moscow Conservatoire in February 1994. Rachlin uses echo effects – not always marked in the score – in the lyrical episodes of both the central *Canzonetta* and the finale, where he not only plays with yearning beauty but also gives sparkle to the main theme rather than thrusting on with sheer power. The volatile quality of this live recording sets problems for the orchestra, which is not always crisp in its ensemble.

In her live recording Midori, with the solo instrument naturally balanced, gives a reading which makes its impact as much in hushed poetry as in virtuoso display, with rhythms and phrasing freely expressive. Though the central Canzonetta is taken dangerously slowly, the rapt intensity is most compelling. As in the Shostakovich, Abbado and the Berlin Philharmonic give warm and powerful support, very well recorded. Midori adopts the tiny traditional cuts in the finale, arguably the preferable course.

Sarah Chang, here recorded in her teens, is an artist who, from her first note onwards, compels attention with her poetic and imaginative treatment of each phrase, always sounding spontaneous. Not only does she play with exceptionally pure tone, avoiding heavy coloration, her individual artistry does not demand the wayward pulling-about often found in this work. In that she is enormously helped by the fresh, bright and dramatic accompaniment provided by the LSO under Sir Colin Davis, always a sensitive and helpful concerto conductor, and here encouraging generally steady speeds. The snag is the ungenerous coupling, but Chang's performances of the four Brahms *Hungarian dances* are delectable.

The Dutton CD offers Ida Haendel's first orchestral recording for Decca, made in April 1945. She later re-recorded the work for EMI, but this first version has a very special magic and a natural warmth that is irresistible (in some ways comparable with Chung's first Decca account with Previn). The whole performance flows with a remarkably spontaneous freshness. Basil Cameron's accompaniment is professional and little more, but the orchestra obviously responded to their young soloist, and the wind playing in her ravishingly delicate *Canzonetta*, and in the secondary 'Russian-folk' material of the sparkling finale is richly hued. The admirably balanced recording is little short of amazing, as is the naturalness of the Dutton transfer. Almost immediately one totally forgets that the performance has a 78 shellac source (which brings a cut of the repeat in the first orchestral 'polacca' ritornello); one simply sits back and enjoys the wonderfully sympathetic playing. This surely ranks alongside the 78 rpm Heifetz/Barbirolli version as being one of the most memorable ever committed to disc.

Xue-Wei gives a warmly expressive reading of this lovely concerto, missing some of the fantasy and mystery. With rich, full tone, he brings out the sensuousness of the work, while displaying commanding virtuosity. The central *Canzonetta* is turned into a simple song without words, not over-romanticized. The coupling will be ideal for many, consisting of violin concertante pieces by Tchaikovsky, not just the *Sérénade mélancolique*, but the *Valse-scherzo* in a dazzling performance, and *Mélodie*, the third of the three pieces that Tchaikovsky grouped as *Souvenir d'un lieu cher*, freely and expressively done. The orchestral playing under another great violin virtuoso is warmly sympathetic but could be crisper, not helped for detail in tuttis by the lively acoustic.

There can be no real reservations about the sound

of the present remastering of Heifetz's 1957 stereo recording, both full and brilliant. Heifetz is closely balanced, but the magic of his playing can be fully enjoyed. There is some gorgeous lyrical phrasing, and the slow movement marries deep feeling and tenderness in an ideal performance. The finale is dazzling but is never driven too hard. Reiner always accompanies understandingly, producing fierily positive tuttis. The Mendelssohn coupling is equally desirable, and the *Sérénade mélancolique* makes a splendid bonus.

Taken from an analogue original of the late 1970s, Perlman's Philadelphia version sounds all the fuller and more natural in its CD format, with the soloist balanced less aggressively forward than usual. His expressive warmth goes with a very bold orchestral texture from Ormandy and the Philadelphia Orchestra, and anyone who follows Perlman – in so many ways the supreme violin virtuoso of our time – is not likely to be disappointed. The old coupling of just the *Sérénade mélancolique* has now been more generously replaced with the Sibelius concerto, but this disc remains at full price.

Takako Nishizaki gives a warm and colourful reading, tender but purposeful and full of temperament. As in the Mendelssohn with which this is coupled, the central slow movement is on the measured side but flows sweetly, while the finale has all the necessary bravura, even at a speed that avoids breathlessness. Unlike many, Nishizaki opens out the little cuts which had become traditional. With excellent playing and recording, this makes a first-rate recommendation in the super-bargain bracket.

Milstein's fine (1973) version with Abbado remains among the more satisfying recordings. It now comes as part of a DG Double with three other concertos, although it is Zukermann rather than Milstein who plays the Beethoven (and very impressively too). However this same Milstein–Tchaikovsky performance is also available on a single Penguin Classics CD, coupled with Mendelssohn, which some collectors may prefer. The author's note, by Jan Morris, concentrates on the Mendelssohn coupling.

Bell may not have quite the fantasy of a version like Chung's Decca performance, but it is an outstanding account, very recommendable if you fancy the unusual coupling of Wieniawski. Full, brilliant recording, with the soloist well balanced.

Stern was on peak form when he made his first stereo recording with Ormandy. It is a powerfully lyrical reading, rich in timbre and technically immaculate. The playing is poetic, but it is not helped by the very close balance of the soloist, so that *pianissimos* consistently become *mezzo fortes*. The orchestral sound is vivid but lacks amplitude.

Recorded in mono in 1953, Ida Haendel's red-bloodedly romantic EMI account is such a distinctive, positive and powerful reading, one is grateful to Testament for bringing back so unjustly neglected a recording, and in such a vivid transfer. With speeds on the broad side in the first two movements, and generally kept steady, Haendel's warmly expressive style is the more compelling, leading to a fast and muscular account of the finale. It is generously and ideally coupled with Haendel's masterly reading of the Brahms, similarly neglected.

Heifetz's first (mono) recording of the Tchaikovsky *Violin concerto*, made in 1937, has tremendous virtuosity and warmth. The sound is opaque by modern standards but the ear quickly adjusts, and the performance is special even by Heifetz's own standards. The transfer, too, is very good and, coming as it does with a classic account of the Glazunov and a fascinating Sibelius, this is a fine bargain.

Mark Lubotsky is perhaps best known for his recording of the Britten *concerto* with the composer conducting. His performance of the Tchaikovksy with Arvo Volmer and the fine Estonian National Orchestra is wonderfully musical and natural. Not perhaps as high-powered or flamboyant as many rivals but everything unfolds naturally and effortlessly. It comes with enterprising couplings including the endearing Arensky *concerto*.

(i) *1812 Overture; Capriccio italien.*

❁ (M) *** Mercury 434 360-2 [id.]. (i) Bronze French cannon, bells of Laura Spelman Rockefeller Memorial Carillon, Riverside Church, New York City; Minneapolis SO, Dorati (with separate descriptive commentary by Deems Taylor) – BEETHOVEN: *Wellington's victory*. *** ❁

Just as in our listing of this famous Mercury record we have placed *1812* first, so in the credits the cannon and the glorious sounds of the Laura Spelman Carillon take precedence, for in the riveting climax of Tchaikovsky's most famous work the effects completely upstage the orchestra. On this remastered CD the balance is managed spectacularly, with the 'shots' perfectly timed, while the Minneapolis orchestra clearly enjoy themselves both in *1812* and in the brilliant account of *Capriccio italien*. Deems Taylor provides an avuncular commentary on the technical background to the original recording.

1812 Overture; Hamlet (fantasy overture), *Op. 67; The Tempest, Op. 18.*

*** Delos Dig. D/CD 3081 [id.]. Oregon SO, James DePreist.

The Oregon orchestra show their paces in this vividly colourful triptych, and James DePreist is a highly sympathetic Tchaikovskian. In *1812*, the cannon are perfectly placed and their spectacular entry is as precise as it is commanding. The performance overall is highly enjoyable, energetic but with the pacing unforced. The performances of both *Hamlet* and *The Tempest* are passionately dramatic, the latter generating comparable intensity to (but more melodrama than) Dorati's Decca version.

(i) *1812 Overture;* (ii) *Marche slave.*
(M) **(*) Decca Phase Four 443 896-2 [id.]. (i) Welsh Nat. Op. Ch., Band of Grenadier Guards, RPO Ch., RPO; (ii) LSO; Stokowski – MUSSORGSKY: *Night on the bare mountain* etc. **; BORODIN: *Prince Igor: Polovtsian dances.* **

Stokowski's very eccentric *1812* certainly does not lack spectacle, although it is coarsely recorded. The pyrotechnic effects in the closing pages are accompanied by an overwhelmingly carillon, then suddenly the chorus appears out of nowhere to sing the Russian hymn. Similarly in *Marche slave* there are gross manipulations of balance to bring out certain instruments (the heavy brass especially) and effects. But it is a powerful performance with a whimsical beginning to the coda.

1812 Overture, Op. 49; Romeo and Juliet (fantasy overture); Serenade for strings, Op. 48; The Voyevoda, Op. 78.
(N) ** Decca Dig. 455 971-2. St. Petersburg PO, Vladimir Ashkenazy.

Good playing from the St Petersburg Philharmonic under Vladimir Ashkenazy and vivid sound from the Decca engineers. All the same there is nothing really special about this issue, nothing that resonates in the memory long afterwards. Although it is better than ordinary, it falls a long way short of extraordinary.

Festival overture on the Danish national anthem, Op. 15; (i) *Hamlet: Overture and incidental music, Op. 67 bis. Mazeppa: Battle of Poltava and Cossack dance; Romeo and Juliet* (fantasy overture; 1869 version); *Serenade for Nikolai Rubinstein's saint's day.*
*** Chandos Dig. CHAN 8310/11 [id.]. LSO, Simon, (i) with Janis Kelly, Hammond-Stroud.

Tchaikovsky himself thought his *Danish Festival overture* superior to *1812*, and though one cannot agree with his judgement it is well worth hearing. The *Hamlet* incidental music, however, shows the composer's inspiration at its most memorable. The music from *Mazeppa* and the tribute to Rubinstein make engaging bonuses, but the highlight of the set is the 1869 version of *Romeo and Juliet*. It is fascinating to hear the composer's early thoughts before he finalized a piece which was to become one of the most successful of all his works. The performances here under Geoffrey Simon are excitingly committed and spontaneous.

Francesca da Rimini.
(M) *** DG 453 988-2. Leningrad PO, Rozhdestvensky – SHOSTAKOVICH: *Symphony No. 5.* **(*)

Rozhdestvensky's *Francesca da Rimini* is a *tour de force* and can almost be spoken of in the same breath as Beecham's electrifying pre-war recording with the LPO (now available in a superb Dutton transfer – see Concerts, below). As with Beecham, the inferno music is breathtakingly done and the music for the lovers' passion, which with Beecham is deeply felt and poignant, is conveyed with enormous intensity by the Leningrad orchestra. The 1959 recording, made in Wembley Town Hall, is reverberant, with the Russian brass rather blatant in climaxes, but the excitement and spontaneity of the performance are dominant.

Francesca da Rimini; Hamlet (fantasy overture), *Op. 67a.*
✿ *** Everest EVC 9037 [id.]. NY Stadium O, Stokowski.

Stokowski's famous Everest coupling – one of his greatest records – is here remastered for CD with great success, with the sound cleaner and clearer, yet remarkably expansive in the bass in *Hamlet*. Stokowski's performance is inspired: he plays the central lyrical tune so convincingly that it conveys a sombre passion apt for a Shakespearean tragedy, even though Stokowski brings out how intensely Russian the music is, up to the moving funeral march at the end. *Francesca* is hardly less exciting: the opening whirlwinds have seldom roared at such tornado speeds before, the central section is played with beguiling care for detail and balance and, when the great polyphonic climax comes and the themes for the lovers' passion intertwine with music to suggest they are discovered, the tension is extreme. The New York Stadium Orchestra drew on the New York Philharmonic for its players and their deep commitment more than makes up for any slight imperfections of ensemble. An indispensable record for all Tchaikovskians.

(i) *Hamlet: Overture and incidental music, Op. 67 bis. Romeo and Juliet* (fantasy overture: original (1869) version).
*** Chandos Dig. CHAN 9191 [id.]. (i) Janis Kelly, Hammond-Stroud; LSO, Simon.

An admirable recoupling. The (1869) original version of *Romeo and Juliet*, a most enjoyable rarity, is very different from the 1880 revision we all know, with a completely different opening section. After a less well-organized development of the feud and love music, it ends sombrely but rather less tellingly than Tchaikovsky's final masterpiece. Geoffrey Simon is a committed advocate and the performances here are exciting and spontaneous. The *Hamlet incidental music* is hardly less valuable. The overture is a shortened version of the *Hamlet fantasy overture*, but much of the rest of the incidental music is unknown, and the engaging *Funeral march* and the two poignant string elegies show the composer at his finest. *Ophelia's mad scene* is partly sung and partly spoken, and Janis Kelly's performance is most sympathetic, while Derek Hammond-Stroud is suitably robust in the *Gravedigger's song*. A translation of the vocal music is provided, here sung in French as in the original production of *Hamlet* at St Petersburg. The digital recording has spectacular resonance and depth.

Manfred Symphony, Op. 58.

❀ *** Chandos Dig. CHAN 8535 [id.]. Oslo PO, Jansons.

*** Virgin/EMI Dig. VC7 59230-2. Bournemouth SO, Litton.

(***) Testament mono SBT 1048 [id.]. Philh. O, Paul Kletzki – BORODIN: *Symphony No. 2.* (***)

(N) **(*) BBC Legends BBCL 1007-2 [id.]. Bournemouth SO, Constantin Silvestri – RESPIGHI: *Pines of Rome*. ***

(N) *(*) Testament mono SBT 1129 [id.]. O. Nat de la Radiodiffusion Française, Constantin Silvestri – LISZT: *Tasso*. **(*)

Manfred Symphony; The Tempest, Op. 18.

*** DG (IMS) Dig. 439 891-2 [id.]. Russian Nat. O, Pletnev.

Since the coming of stereo there has never been a shortage of good recordings of *Manfred*, but Pletnev's tends to trump what has gone before. The actual sounds of the Russian orchestra, the wind as well as the ardent strings, bring a plangent colouring to Tchaikovsky's inspired scoring, but Pletnev identifies with the ongoing sweep of the work, yet he can relax glowingly in the pastoral evocation of the slow movement. In *The Tempest*, which is uneven in inspiration, Pletnev again carries the piece through on a wave of passionate romantic feeling. The recording is first class and this is one of his finest Tchaikovsky records.

Except in a relatively relaxed view of the *vivace* second movement, Jansons favours speeds flowing faster than usual, bringing out the drama but subtly varying the tensions to press each climax home to the full and always showing his mastery of Tchaikovskian rubato: his warmly expressive phrasing never sounds self-conscious when it is regularly given the freshness of folksong. The performance culminates in a thrilling account of the finale, leading up to the entry of the organ, gloriously resonant and supported by luxuriant string sound. The Chandos recording is among the finest in the Oslo series, atmospheric but with fine inner detail.

Litton and the Bournemouth orchestra are particularly successful in the delicate, poetic moments of *Manfred*. The Astarte theme in the first movement has rarely been moulded so affectionately, and Litton, after a relatively lightweight start, controls tension to bring out the narrative sequence of this programme work, the dramatic cohesion. Litton points the chattering semiquavers of the 'Alpine Fairy' Scherzo with engaging wit and fantasy, and his broad speed for the third-movement *Andante* allows the oboist to play his opening solo with tender expressiveness. The sound is clean-cut and well balanced, with a very dramatic organ entry at the end.

Like the Borodin with which it is coupled, *Manfred* is given a vintage Philharmonia performance from the mid-1950s. Though, in the manner of the time, Kletzki makes cuts and one or two amendments of orchestration, this is a reading which, far more than usual, carries you warmly and thrustfully through music which can seem unduly episodic. So the electricity which Kletzki generates in the central *Allegro con fuoco* section of the finale is remarkable, with the playing throughout marked by superfine clarity of articulation and subtle rubato. As to the recording and transfer, the brass and wind have thrilling immediacy, and the dynamic range is astonishing for the time.

Constantini Silvestri's years with the Bournemouth Orchestra were highly productive and this BBC CD of their broadcasts shows how excellent was their ensemble and discipline. The *Manfred Symphony* comes in a 1963 broadcast from the Winter Gardens. Silvestri does bring a highly charged emotional current to this score and much spontaneity of feeling, but the music is still pulled about in a way which will not enjoy universal acclaim. The recording is very good and the Respighi coupling outstanding.

In the earlier *Manfred* Symphony he recorded with the Orchestre National de France, Silvestri tarted up Tchaikovsky's orchestration, but it is not that as much as the moments of sour intonation and agogic distortion, that diminish the appeal of his recording. The Bournemouth broadcast is to be preferred but the Testament does have the benefit of a first-class fill-up in Liszt's *Tasso*.

The Nutcracker (ballet), *Op. 71* (complete).

(N) *** Ph. Dig. 462 114-2 [id.]. Kirov O & ch., Valery Gergiev.

*** Decca Dig. 433 000-2 (2) [id.]. Finchley Children's Music Group. RPO, Ashkenazy – GLAZUNOV: *Seasons*. ***

*** Telarc Dig. CD 8137 (2) [id.]. London Symphony Ch., LSO, Mackerras.

(B) *** BMG/Melodiya Twofer 74321 40067-2 (2). Bolshoi Theatre Children's Ch., Bolshoi Theatre O, Rozhdestvensky.

(M) *** CfP CD-CFPD 4706 (2) [Ang.CDCB 47267]. Amb. S., LSO, Previn.

(B) *** Decca Double 444 827-2 (2) [id.]. Nat. PO, Bonynge – OFFENBACH: *Le Papillon*. ***

**(*) EMI (SIS) Dig. CDS7 54600-2 (2) [Ang. CDQB 54649-2]. New L. Children's Ch., LPO, Jansons.

(i) *The Nutcracker* (complete); (ii) *Serenade for strings in C, Op. 48*.

(M) **(*) Mercury (IMS) 432 750-2 (2). (i) LSO; (ii) Philharmonia Hungarica, Antal Dorati.

(i) *The Nutcracker* (ballet): complete; (ii) *Sleeping Beauty* (ballet): highlights.
(B) *** Ph. Duo 442 562-2 (2) [id.]. (i) Concg. O, with boys' Ch., Dorati; (ii) LSO, Fistoulari.

The Nutcracker (complete); *The Sleeping Beauty: Aurora's Wedding.*
*** Decca Dig. 440 477-2 (2) [id.]. Face School Children's Ch., Montreal SO, Charles Dutoit.

The Nutcracker (complete); *Eugene Onegin: Introduction; Waltz; Polonaise.*
*** Ph. (IMS) Dig. 420 237-2 (2). BPO, Bychkov.

Gergiev's new complete recording tends to sweep the board. Not only is it on a single CD (over 81 minutes), but it is magnificently played and recorded. Tchaikovsky's inspired score emerges pristine and fresh as one of his most perfect masterpieces, glittering with colour and sweeping to a series of great climaxes notably the gloriously expansive *Journey through the pine forest* (here called '*In the Christmas tree*'). The great *Adagio* for the two principal dancers has a passionate Russian ardour. It might be suspected that Gergiev's tendency to brisk tempi was motivated by the desire to get his performance on a single disc. Whether or not that is so, the lively characteristic dances are simply bursting with slavonic fervour. If, alongside Ashkenazy, there is a certain want of magic and charm, Gergiev everywhere displays a keen ear for Tchaikovsky's vivid orchestral detail. The lighter characteristic numbers are delectably done, notably the humorous *Chinese dance*, while the *Waltz of the flowers* and the earlier *Waltz of the Snowflakes*, with its elfin chorus, are most elegantly played. There are no pauses between numbers in the *Divertissement*, and this may well be dictated by the single-disc format. But it also increases the feeling that the score overall is a composite whole, and this is emphasized by the sense of apotheosis in the finale. Unless you are looking for a more relaxed spacious approach, this can be highly recommended.

Ashkenazy's digital *Nutcracker* takes its place at the top of the list, ideally coupled with Glazunov's *Seasons*, in an equally enticing performance. It has the benefit of Walthamstow acoustics and state-of-the-art Decca digital sound, glowingly warm. The *Snowflakes* choral *waltz* has warmth as well as charm and the famous characteristic dances of the Act II Divertissement match elegance and character with a multi-hued palette of colour. Ideally the recording could be more generously cued, but for the music-making and recording there can only be the highest praise.

Dutoit's Decca recording comes into immediate competition with the Ashkenazy set. It is beautifully played, with much sophisticated detail, and the Montreal acoustic provides brilliance, vivid colouring and striking transparency of detail. The party scene has great zest and character and the famous characteristic dances of the Act II *Divertissement* are made to sound wonderfully fresh, as is the *Waltz of the Snowflakes*, with its charming chorus of children. The sound is less sumptuous than with Ashkenazy, but both recordings are of Decca's finest quality and each of the two sets has its own felicities. For a coupling Dutoit offers *Aurora's Wedding*, a truncated version of *The Sleeping Beauty* which swiftly encapsulates the storyline, then moves on to the last-Act *Divertissement*. It makes an agreeable set of highlights, especially when played as spiritedly and elegantly as it is here, and the Decca recording is most successful.

The Telarc set was recorded in Watford Town Hall, which adds glamour to the violins and a glowing warmth in the middle and lower range. When the magic spell begins, the spectacularly wide dynamic range and the extra amplitude make for a physical frisson in the climaxes, while the glorious climbing melody, as Clara and the Prince travel through the pine forest, sounds richly expansive. Before that, the battle has some real cannon-shots interpolated but is done good-humouredly, for this is a toy battle. The great *Pas de deux* brings the most sumptuous climax, with superb sonority from the brass on the Telarc version. The Telarc presentation is ideal, with a detailed synopsis.

Semyon Bychkov has the services of the Berlin Philharmonic, and they offer superlative playing, of striking flair and character. Although a concert-hall ambience is favoured, the strings seem more forward. There is some superbly stylish playing in the *Divertissement*, and there are many moments when the extra vividness of the Berlin recording is especially compelling. As a a modest bonus the *Eugene Onegin* excerpts are brilliantly done. The Philips notes are extensive but not well matched to the CD cues.

Dorati's 1975 complete *Nutcracker* with the Concertgebouw Orchestra makes a good first choice in the bargain category, very well coupled with Fistoulari's equally outstanding 1962 set of highlights from the *Sleeping Beauty*. In the former the playing of the Concertgebouw Orchestra is most refined as well as very dramatic. Its vitality is clear from the *Miniature overture* onwards with an engaging rhythmic spring and no forcing of accents. The Pine forest journey has seldom sounded more ardent and is built to a tremendous climax. Then the *Waltz of the Snowflakes* produces the most delightfully fresh choral quality from the Boys' Choir of St Bravo Cathedral, Haarlem. The CD transfer brings less sumptuous sound than on the old LPs, but the Concertgebouw ambience ensures body as well as vividness. Fistoulari's greatness as a ballet conductor is well celebrated by the *Sleeping Beauty* selection, which was extremely well recorded in its day and has transferred to CD with striking amplitude and brilliance. The selection is well made and satisfying, with plenty of charm and sparkling colours from the LSO wind players.

Rozhdestvensky's recording, originally issued on HMV in the mid-1970s, remains among the most vital accounts. It has a very strong Russian colouring, nowhere more strikingly different from a Western approach than in the *Waltz of the snowflakes*, with the children's voices singing lustily. The timbres of woodwind and brass are robustly textured, the colouring bold. The *March* has a more military brassiness than usual – and very arresting it is, quite unlike the more piquant stylization one normally expects. There is never the slightest hint of sentimentalizing the music, while the opening party scene conveys the rumbustious character of adults and children enjoying themselves. Every point of Tchaikovsky's music tells, and the vigour of the playing disarms any criticism. The excellent recording dates from 1960, given a lively projection on CD.

With Dorati's LSO *Nutcracker* the Mercury engineering has natural balance, warmly atmospheric with typically refined detail. Dorati relishes every detail, his characterization is strong, and the playing is full of life and elegance. The *Journey through the pine forest* expands magnificently while the choral delicacy of the *Waltz of the snowflakes* is full of charm. In Act II the characteristic dances have much colour and vitality. The *Serenade for strings* is less compelling. The slightly dry effect does not capture quite enough of the hall ambience, focusing closely on the Philharmonia Hungarica, who could at times be more polished. It is an affectionate performance, but not a very vital one.

Previn's earlier (1972) analogue set with the LSO has been freshly remastered. As in his later, digital version (only available combined with the other two ballets), the famous dances in Act II are given with refinement and point, and the orchestral playing throughout is of very high quality. With Act I sounding brighter and more dramatic than in its original LP format, this CfP reissue makes a fine bargain alternative.

Bonynge's set is made the more attractive by its rare and substantial Offenbach coupling. His approach is sympathetic and the orchestral playing is polished, even if in the opening scene he misses some of the atmosphere. With the beginning of the magic, as the Christmas tree expands, the performance becomes more dramatically involving and Bonynge is at his best in the latter part of the ballet, with fine passion in the Act II *Pas de deux* and plenty of colour in the characteristic dances. The Decca Kingsway Hall recording is brilliant on top, yet has a glowing ambient warmth.

Jansons's EMI version is highly dramatic, the histrionic effect emphasized by spectacular recording, especially of the brass which sounds almost Wagnerian at times. This is certainly lively and exciting, and it is stylishly played, but it has less warmth and magic than the Decca Ashkenazy digital recording. Moreover there is no coupling.

Nutcracker suite, Op. 71a.

(M) *** Decca Phase Four 455 154-2 [id.].
Boston Pops O, Fiedler (with J. STRAUSS: *Waltzes.* **)

(B) **(*) Sony SBK 46550 [id.]. Phd. O, Ormandy – CHOPIN: *Les Sylphides;* DELIBES: *Coppélia; Sylvia: Suites.* ***

Fiedler's Phase Four performance has marvellous spirit and vigour; the music is played with striking élan and colour, spirited and spontaneous-sounding. The vividly coloured recording helps to project the music-making. This is a demonstration of Phase Four at its very best.

The Philadelphia Orchestra made this wonderful music universally famous in Walt Disney's *Fantasia* and they know how to play it just as well under Ormandy in 1963 as they did under Stokowski. Perhaps there is less individuality in the characteristic dances, but the music-making has suitable moments of reticence (as in the neat *Ouverture miniature*) as well as plenty of flair. In the *Waltz of the flowers* Ormandy, with no justification, takes the soaring violin tune an octave up on its second appearance.

(i) *The Nutcracker; Sleeping Beauty; Swan Lake:* excerpts.

(B) **(*) EMI (SIS) CZS7 62816-2 (2) [id.].
LSO, André Previn, (i) with Amb. S.

By the use of two CDs, offering some 148 minutes of music, this EMI box (issued in the 'two for the price of one' series) covers a substantial proportion of the key numbers from all three ballets. *The Nutcracker* selection is particularly generous in including, besides virtually all the most famous characteristic dances, the 13-minute episode in Act I starting with the Battle sequence, continuing with the magical Pine forest journey and finishing with the delightful choral *Waltz of the snowflakes*. Previn and the LSO provide vivacious playing and the recording is full, bright and vivid. The remastering, however, loses some of the smoothness and refinement of focus of the original, analogue recordings. This remains very enjoyable and excellent value.

Nutcracker suite; Sleeping Beauty: suite; Swan Lake: suite.

❁ (M) *** DG 449 726-2 [id.]. BPO, Rostropovich.

(M) *** EMI (SIS) CDM7 64332-2. LSO, Previn.

(M) *** Decca Legends 466 379-2 [id.]. VPO, Karajan.

Rostropovich's triptych of Tchaikovsky ballet suites is very special. His account of the *Nutcracker suite* is enchanting: the *Sugar plum fairy* is introduced with ethereal gentleness, the *Russian dance* has marvellous zest and the *Waltz of the flowers* combines warmth and elegance with an exhilarating vigour. The *Sleeping Beauty* and *Swan Lake* selections are hardly less distinguished, and in the former the *Panorama* is gloriously played. The CD remastering (for DG's 'Legendary Recordings' series), which was always outstanding, now approaches demonstration standard, combining bloom with enhanced detail. Sixty-nine minutes of sheer joy, and at mid-price.

The digital remastering has been very successful on the EMI disc, freshening the sound of the excellent recordings, taken from Previn's analogue complete sets (which means that the *Dance of the sugar plum fairy* in *The Nutcracker* has the longer coda rather than the ending Tchaikovsky devised for the *Suite*). The performances are at once vivid and elegant, warm and exciting. Previn's *Panorama* from *Sleeping Beauty* is hardly less beguiling than Rostropovich's and the recording has comparable warmth. There is nearly 73 minutes of music here, and this version can be strongly recommended alongside the DG disc.

This triptych was made during Karajan's Decca period in the 1960s. As reissued in Decca's Legend series, the recording is very impressive indeed; tuttis are well focused by the digital transfer, and the glowing ambience of the Sofiensaal flatters the strings and adds to the woodwind colourings, particularly in the *Nutcracker suite*, which is less bland here than in Karajan's later re-recording with the BPO. Overall this disc offers very fine playing from the VPO and, although the atmosphere is generally relaxed (especially in *Sleeping Beauty*), there is a persuasive warmth.

Romeo and Juliet (fantasy overture and excerpt).

(N) (M) *** Classic fM Dig. 75605 57047. RPO, Daniele Gatti. PROKOFIEV: *Romeo and Juliet* (ballet): excerpts ***

Opening with a very gentle picture of Friar Lawrence, and following later with an exquisitely refined introduction of the great love theme, Daniele Gatti's performances could not be more highly charged romantically, and with a vividly passionate (if not always immaculate) response from the RPO, the climaxes are thrilling, with the horns and trumpets ringing out superbly at the climax of the duel sequence. The recording too is splendidly full and sumptuous, and the rare coupling with Prokofiev could not be more apt. This is one of Classic fM's finest issues so far.

Serenade for strings in C, Op. 48.

(BB) *** ASV Quicksilva CDQS 6094 [id.]. Polish R. CO, Duczmal – SUK: *Serenade* ***; GRIEG: *2 Elegiac melodies, Holberg suite* etc. **(*)

The Polish Radio Chamber Orchestra is a first-class body of players, and they give a highly individual reading, full of subtlety and grace. The conductor's imaginative nuancing of dynamic shading is most winning, and this account often finds a rare quality of tenderness alongside its vigour and expansiveness. The Waltz is relaxed and gentle, and there is a wistful delicacy in the *Elégie*. The finale is exquisitely prepared, then the allegro is off with the wind, very fast, light and balletic, again with engagingly crisp articulation. This is a performance to make one appreciate this as among the composer's greatest works, with its Mozartian elegance and perfection of form. The recording is excellent, full, transparent, yet with a fine bloom.

Serenade for strings; Souvenir de Florence, Op. 70.

(BB) *** Naxos Dig. 8.550404 [id.]. Vienna CO, Philippe Entremont.

Entremont's performances of Tchaikovsky's two major string works communicate above all a feeling of passionate thrust and energy. After the ardour of the *Elégie*, the finale steals in persuasively, with dance-rhythms bracing and strong. The unaccountably neglected *Souvenir de Florence* has comparable momentum and eagerness. The dashing main theme of the first movement swings along infectiously, while the wistful secondary idea also takes wing. Entremont brings out the charm in writing inspired by Russian folksong. The VCO are committed, persuasive advocates to make one wonder why the *Souvenir* does not have a more central place in the string repertoire.

Serenade for strings in C, Op. 48; Suite No. 4 in G (Mozartiana), Op. 61; (i) *Nocturne in C sharp min., Op. 19/4* (arr. for cello and orchestra); (ii) *Legend: Christ in his garden.*

(N) ** BBC Legends stereo/mono BBCB 8002-2 [id.]. ECO, Britten; with (i) Rostropovich; (ii) Peter Pears.

Britten's relaxed accounts of the *Serenade* and *Suite* are warmly persuasive but not distinctive: the string articulation in the second subject of the first movement of the former could be more stylishly pointed, yet the *Preghiera* in the latter (an arrangement of Mozart's *Ave verum*) is very appealingly done. The solo contributions from Rostropovich and Pears add to the character of the programme, but there are more memorable recordings available of both the major works.

The Sleeping Beauty (ballet), *Op. 66* (complete).

(N) ✿ *** DG Dig. 457 634-2(2) [id.] Russian Nat. O, Mikhail Pletnev.

(BB) *** Naxos Dig. 8.550490/2 [id.]. Slovak State PO (Košice), Andrew Mogrelia.

**(*) Ph. Dig. 434 922-2 (3). Kirov O (St Petersburg), Gergiev.

Pletnev's is a performance of individuality and high quality. It is a strongly narrative and dramatic account that has tenderness (as in the opening of the *Pas de six* in the Prologue) and much the same virtuosity that Pletnev exhibits at the keyboard (the coda that follows *Aurora's variation* in Act II or the *Diamond fairy* in Act III). The articulation is pretty dazzling throughout and the there is plenty of wit in the Act III Divertissement. Even though there are times when tempi seem too brisk for dancing, everything sounds fresh. The recording is very good, wide in dynamic range and well balanced – as indeed one expects when Wolfgang Mitlehner is in charge of the sound – though not in the demonstration bracket (perhaps wanting a shade in amplitude). DG accommodate the set on two CDs (of 79 and 80 minutes respectively).

Andrew Mogrelia conducts Tchaikovsky's score with an ideal combination of warmth, grace and vitality. Moreover the Slovak State Philharmonic prove to be an excellent orchestra for this repertoire, with fine wind-players and equally impressive string principals for the important violin and cello solos. Mogrelia relishes the orchestral detail – and there is much inspired Tchaikovskian scoring here – and he moves the music on with a natural sense of pacing and generates great excitement in the big set-pieces. The Naxos digital recording is full and brilliant without being overlit, and the acoustics of the House of Arts in Košice bring a spacious ambience, with vivid orchestral colours. A first choice among all available recordings, irrespective of cost.

The Kirov recording of Tchaikovsky's complete ballet is in every way satisfying. The playing – from an orchestra completely inside the music – is warmly sympathetic and vital, with no suggestion that familiarity has bred any sense of routine. Gergiev is a subtle interpreter, and his performance of the beautiful *Panorama* floats gently and radiantly over its rocking base. The Act III *Pas de quatre* for all four fairies is a highlight of the sparkling Act III *Divertissement*. The Philips recording is sumptuous without being cloudy and it expands magnificently for Tchaikovksy's rhetorically exciting climaxes without assaulting the ears.

(i) *Souvenir d'un lieu cher (Méditation), Op. 42/ 1;* (ii) *Sérénade mélancolique for violin and orchestra, Op. 26.*

(M) *** Sony Stern Edition I SMK 66830 [id.]. Isaac Stern, with (i) Nat. SO, Rostropovich; (ii) Columbia SO, Brieff – BRUCH: *Violin concerto No. 1*; WIENIAWSKI: *Violin concerto No. 2*. **(*)

Glorious playing from Stern. He is recorded too closely (as is the Columbia Symphony in the *Sérénade*) but his warm timbre is caught lusciously and he knows just how to convey the composer's nostalgic feeling. Both accompaniments are sympathetic.

Suites Nos.1 in D min., Op.43; 2 in C; 3 in G, Op. 55; 4 in G, (Mozartiana), Op. 55.

(N) *** Chandos Dig. CHAN 9676 (2) [id.]. Detroit SO, Järvi.

(N) (B) *** BMG/Melodiya Dig. Twofer 74321 59054-2 (2). USSR SO, Svetlanov.

(N) (B) *** Ph. Duo 454 253 (2) [id.]. New Phil. O, Dorati.

(N) (B) *** Naxos Dig. 8.550644 (1–2); **(*) 8.550728 (3–4) [id.]. Nat. SO of Ireland, Stefan Sanderling.

Tchaikovsky's four *Orchestral Suites*, for which the composer had a great affection, are full of good things and, as they are infrequently heard in the concert hall, make ideal gramophone fare. David Brown, in his definitive biography, thought highly of them, regarding them as 'something of a collective landmark in Tchaikovsky's evolution' suggesting further that (in special reference to the *Second suite*) the composer undertook a radical reassessment of his orchestration in devising these works. Their extraordinary range of colour demands recording of the very highest quality and that is just what Chandos for the most part provides, which gives Järvi's set a place at the top of the list, even though Svetlanov's Melodiya 'Twofer' remains very competitive indeed, and also has excellent sound.

Järvi generally adopts somewhat brisk tempi, especially in No. 1, but the Detroit orchestral response in both the two earliest suites is consistently winning. The melancholy bassoon which opens the *First*, the pensive clarinet in the second movement, and later the chattering flutes as the composer's mood lightens, are all most engaging, while the lyrical string playing in the doleful *Andante semplice* is found again in the lighthearted *Valse* of No. 2. Similarly, the light rhythmic touch in the Scherzo is matched by the joyous closing *Gavotte* and again in the *Scherzo burlesque* in No. 2, with its folksy accordions, and the crisper articulation in the *Danse baroque* 'in the style of Dargomizhsky' which ends this *Second Suite* so vigorously.

The performance of the *Fourth suite* also has an agreeable warmth, aptly Tchaikovskian even more than it is elegantly Mozartian, with the soaring melody of the *Preghiera* third movement (an arrangement of Mozart's *Ave verum*) made lovingly expressive rather than classically restrained; then Järvi brings out the robust jollity in the set of variations which makes up the finale. In No. 3, the most ambitious of the set, Järvi continues to draw warmly expressive playing from his Detroit musicians even if his treatment here is a little heavy-handed (as it is just occasionally in No. 2). The performance is well characterized – not least in the colourfully varied variations which make up the last and longest movement and which are given an ebullient finale – but lacks something in charm. In this the acoustic of the Detroit hall is not as helpful as it might be to high *fortissimo* violins. Järvi is most successful in the thrust of his conducting as he builds up to powerful climaxes.

Svetlanov and his Russian players have something to teach Järvi here. After opening warmly with delicate lyrical phrasing from the violins, the music steadily gathers passion as the whole orchestra takes up Tchaikovsky's flowing melody. Svetlanov treats the whole suite very flexibly and freely, supported by the most eloquent response from one of the premier Russian orchestras. In the *Theme and variations* some of his tempi are unexpected, and the final *Polacca* is less overwhelming than with Järvi, seeking to emphasize dance rhythms rather than be grandiose. Helped by some of the finest digital sound on the Melodiya label and a pleasingly warm acoustic, Svetlanov also gives the *First suite* a strong Russian feeling; even if the wind solos are perhaps slightly less beguiling than those in Detroit, the closing *Gavotte* is delightfully spirited. The account of the *Second* is truly inspirational, doubly distinctive for making the listener realize that this is a far more substantial work than was previously thought. In the closing *Danse baroque* the Russian energy of the performance bubbles right over. Svetlanov is hardly less successful in the *Fourth Suite* (*Mozartiana*), where Tchaikovsky's neat scoring is always respectful of the orginal music. The *Preghiera* is more restrained than with Järvi and the closing variations (where Mozart used Gluck's '*Unser dummer Pöbel meint*') are a delight.

Dorati's set, from the late 1960s with the New Philharmonia Orchestra, also has a lot going for it. The sound has some lack of transparency and ultimate vividness alongside the Detroit and Russian recordings, but it is pleasingly naturally balanced. Dorati was a masterly ballet conductor and he brings out the balletic feeling, in the first two suites especially, revelling in the infinitely inventive orchestral detail which shows the composer consistently seeking new orchestral colourings. *Mozartiana* is neatly and stylishly done. In the *Third suite* Svetlanov demonstrates more Russian temperament, but Dorati is thoroughly at home in the *Theme and variations*, capped by a splendid closing *Polacca*: the Philips recording expands impressively here and rises to the occasion.

On Naxos, Stefan Sanderling (son of Kurt) gives nicely turned performances of the first two suites, neatly characterized and with much charm and colour. The playing of the National Symphony Orchestra of Ireland is polished and naturally sympathetic to the Tchaikovskian ardour that regularly wells up in this music. The *Third* and *Fourth suites* are slightly less successful. Sanderling shows much delicacy of feeling, both in the opening *Gigue* of *Mozartiana* and in the *Elégie*, the first movement of the *Third suite*, and it is a pity that one has reservations about the sets of variations which Tchaikovsky uses for his final movements. In *Mozartiana* Sanderling is very romantic and his affectionate rubato affects the Mozartian directness of manner. The masterly *Theme and variations* which end the *Third suite* are splendidly done until the finale, which refuses to take off: Sanderling is that bit too grandiose and measured. Nevertheless with recording which is spacious yet allows orchestral detail to emerge vividly, this can certainly be considered at its modest cost, although the first disc is more successful than the second.

Swan Lake (ballet), *Op. 20* (complete).
*** Decca Dig. 436 212-2 (2) Montreal SO, Dutoit.
*** ROH Dig. 301/2 [id.]. ROHCG O, Mark Ermler.
(B) *** CfP Dig. CD-CFPD 4727 (2). Philh. O, John Lanchbery.

Dutoit offers the original score virtually complete, as Tchaikovsky conceived it. Into it he poured some of his finest melodic inspiration and colouristic orchestral skill, to provide just over two and a half hours of consistently appealing music in which there is not a single dull bar. The Montreal orchestra play it beautifully, rising to the plot's histrionic moments and (with the help of St Eustache acoustics and the Decca engineers) the final apotheosis, when the great Swan melody achieves its transformation into an exultant B major climax, is gloriously expansive. Dutoit's reading, without lack of drama, emphasizes the warmth and grace of the music, its infinite variety. Lanchbery's digital EMI set (not absolutely complete – see below) has a more exhilarating theatrical vitality, but the EMI sound is less glamorously full than the Decca recording.

Released from the Covent Garden pit to record in the warm acoustic of All Saints', Tooting, the players have responded to Ermler's deeply sympathetic direction with both refinement and red-blooded commitment, and one is constantly aware of the idiomatic feeling born of long acquaintance. The sound is exceptionally full and open, with the brass in particular giving satisfying weight to the ensemble without hazing over the detail. The set has now been reissued on a pair of CDs with the break coming in Act II after the *Dance of the little swans*. Ermler's broad speeds consistently convey, more than most rivals', the feeling of an accompaniment for dancing, as in the great andante of the Act I *Pas de deux*. This is a set to have you sitting back in new enjoyment.

Lanchbery's 1982 *Swan Lake* makes a superb bargain. The CfP reissue on a pair of CDs, which play for 79 minutes and 75 minutes respectively, accommodates Acts I and II on the first disc and Acts III and IV on the second. Though two numbers are cut, the set includes the extra music (a *Pas de deux*) which Tchaikovsky wrote to follow the *Pas de six* in Act III, when Siegfried dances with Odile, mistakenly believing her to be Odette. The EMI recording, made at Abbey Road, is very fine indeed: spacious, vividly coloured and full, with natural perspective and a wide dynamic range. The orchestral playing is first class, with polished, elegant string phrasing matched by felicitous wind solos. Lanchbery's rhythmic spring is a constant pleasure; everything is alert and there is plenty of excitement at climaxes.

Swan Lake (ballet), *Op. 20* (slightly abridged recording of the European score).
(B) **(*) Decca Double 440 630-2 (2) [id.]. SRO, Ansermet – PROKOFIEV: *Romeo and Juliet.* **

Returning to Ansermet's 1959 recording of *Swan Lake*, one is amazed by the vigour of the playing and the excellence of the recording. The Drigo version of the score, which Ansermet uses, dates from 1895; Drigo added orchestrations of his own, taken from Tchaikovsky's piano music (Op. 72), yet he left out some 1,600 bars of the original score. Ansermet offers the Act I introduction and Nos. 1–2, 4, 7 and 8; Act II, Nos. 10–13; Act III, Nos. 15, 17–18 and 20–23, with No. 5 (the *Pas de deux)* then interpolated before Nos. 28 and 29 from Act IV. Despite the obvious gaps, most of the familiar favourites are included here, and the music-making has such zest and colour that one revels in every bar. The solo wind playing is not always as sweet-timbred as in some other versions, but the violin and cello solos are well done. The transfer is well managed, full-blooded and bright. It was a happy idea to couple this on its Double Decca reissue with a selection of 15 items from the two suites from Prokofiev's *Romeo and Juliet* ballet, even if here the orchestral playing is less impressive.

SYMPHONIES

Symphonies Nos. 1–6.
(M) *** DG 429 675-2 (4) [id.]. BPO, Karajan.
*** DG Dig. 449 967-2 (5) [id.]. Russian Nat. O, Mikhail Pletnev.

Symphonies Nos. 1–3; Francesca da Rimini, Op. 32.
(B) **(*) BMG/Melodiya Twofer 74321 34163-2 (2) [id.]. USSR SO, Svetlanov.

Symphonies Nos. 4–6 (Pathétique); Andante cantabile in B flat, Op. 11; The Voyevoda, Op. 78.
(B) **(*) BMG/Melodiya Twofer 74321 40066-2 (2) [id.]. USSR SO, Svetlanov.

Symphonies Nos. 1–6; Capriccio italien; Manfred Symphony.
❀ (M) *** Chandos Dig. CHAN 8672/8 [id.]. Oslo PO, Jansons.

Jansons's Tchaikovsky series, which includes *Manfred*, is self-recommending. The full romantic power of the music is consistently conveyed and, above all, the music-making is urgently spontaneous throughout, with the Oslo Philharmonic Orchestra always committed and fresh, helped by the richly atmospheric Chandos sound. The seven separate CDs offered here are packaged in a box priced as for five premium discs.

Karajan offers the six symphonies fitted on to four mid-priced CDs, the only drawback being that Nos. 2 and 5 are split between discs. From both a performance and a technical point of view, the accounts of the last three symphonies are in every way preferable to his later, VPO digital versions; all offer peerless playing from the Berlin Philharmonic.

Pletnev's readings have all the innate aristocratic feeling Tchaikovsky could ask for, but at no time does Pletnev wear his heart on his sleeve. The wide dynamic spectrum and clarity of articulation that distinguish his pianism are clearly in evidence, but virtuosity, brilliance and colour are never there at the expense of artistic truth. Some may feel that the emphasis in the *First Symphony* is too much on the *rêveries* of the title, and Tchaikovsky's rhetoric might be handled more convincingly; but, for the most part, Pletnev's approach throughout the cycle is the reverse of the overblown. Indeed the highly charged, high-voltage sound which we associate with Mravinsky surfaces in the *Pathétique*, but otherwise he sets greater store by classicism, carefully balanced proportions and a masterly sense of line. DG have accorded the cycle very fine and well-detailed sound. The set comes with copious scholarly annotation by Richard Taruskin.

Svetlanov's are performances of much temperament and fire, though the orchestral playing is a little variable. With fast tempi in the outer movements the *First Symphony* comes fully alive, with the atmosphere of the Russian winter felt in the *Adagio*. The *Little Russian* has plenty of character too. Svetlanov takes the *Andantino* very slowly but retains the charm, and he does not let the finale get out of hand. The *Polish Symphony* is a performance of strong contrasts between the inner and outer movements. The *Fourth*, bold and direct, stands out among the last three symphonies, very well held together. In the finale Svetlanov makes no pause each time the second subject appears. The *Fifth*, while it has a fine lyrical impulse, is surprisingly undramatic. The *Pathétique* is much more convincing, with a beautifully moulded second subject. The Scherzo-march is somewhat relaxed but the finale is powerfully controlled and eloquent. The extra items are well worth having, especially the rare *Voyevoda*, while the middle section of *Francesca da Rimini* has a unique lyrical fervour. The sound throughout is bright and full-blooded to match the performances. An excellent bargain on two BMG/Melodiya Twofer issues.

Symphonies Nos. 1 (Winter daydreams); 2 (Little Russian); 3 (Polish).
❀ (B) *** Mercury Double 434 391-2 (2) [id.].

LSO, Dorati – ARENSKY: *Variations on a theme by Tchaikovsky.* *(*)

Dorati recorded the first three Tchaikovsky symphonies between the 26th and the 30th July 1965 in Watford Town Hall, not long before Mercury ceased to be an independent company. The set was briefly available in America but only the *First Symphony* was ever issued in the UK. Dorati had clearly thought deeply about each symphony, for each of his interpretations is individual and all three have a striking freshness. After its comparatively mellow beginning, the opening movement of the *First Symphony* generates great thrust and excitement, while the lovely, wistful *Adagio* expands romantically to its powerful climax on the horns, before the touchingly nostalgic closing section. The horn solo which introduces and closes the first movement of the *Little Russian Symphony* is not bold but hauntingly evocative, and the following allegro is crisp and energetic with a powerful recapitulation. Again in No. 3 Dorati catches the full character of the music's Russian melancholy which dominates the introduction, and he infuses the *Allegro vivo* with great thrust and rhythmic strength. The three central movements are the heart of the symphony and they are beautifully played, full of doleful colouring and nostalgia. The brilliant, spacious and full-blooded recording is just right for this music. There is a touch of fierceness at times, but it adds to the bite, and altogether these performances are remarkably satisfying. The Arensky coupling is apt, but in the event somewhat disappointing.

(i) *Symphonies Nos. 1 in G min. (Winter daydreams); 2 in C min. (Little Russian); 3 in D (Polish);* (ii) *Francesca da Rimini.*
(B) *** Ph. Duo 446 148-2 (2) [id.]. (i) LSO; (ii) New Philh. O; Markevitch.

Markevitch is a good Tchaikovskian and his readings have fine momentum and plenty of ardour. In the *First Symphony* he finds the Mendelssohnian lightness in his fast pacing of the opening movement, while there is real evocation in the *Adagio* and a sense of desolation at the reprise of the *Andante lugubre*, before the final rousing peroration. In the *Little Russian Symphony* the opening horn solo is full of character and the allegro tautly rhythmic. The *marziale* marking of the *Andantino* is taken literally, but its precise rhythmic beat is well lifted. The finale is striking for its bustling energy rather than its charm. The *Polish Symphony* has a comparably dynamic first movement, but the central movements are expansively warm, the ballet-music associations not missed. *Francesca da Rimini* is very exciting too, and there is some lovely wind playing from the New Philharmonia in the central section. Excellent sound, warmly resonant and full-bodied.

Symphony No. 1 in G min. (Winter daydreams), Op. 13.
*** Chandos Dig. CHAN 8402 [id.]. Oslo PO, Jansons.

Symphony No. 1 (Winter Daydreams); Hamlet (fantasy overture), *Op. 67.*
(BB) *** Naxos Dig. 8.550517 [id.]. Polish Nat. RSO, Adrian Leaper.

Refreshingly direct in style, Jansons with his brilliant orchestra gives an electrically compelling performance of this earliest of the symphonies. Structurally strong, the result tingles with excitement, most of all in the finale, faster than usual, with the challenge of the complex fugato passages taken superbly. The recording is highly successful.

Leaper conducts a taut and sympathetic reading of *Winter Daydreams*, with excellent playing from the Polish orchestra enhanced by vivid recording, fresh and clear, with plenty of body and with refined pianissimo playing from the strings in the slow movement. This is among the finest Tchaikovsky recordings on the Naxos list, with all four movements sharply characterized. The overture too comes in a tautly dramatic reading. An outstanding bargain.

Symphony No. 2 in C min. (Little Russian), Op. 17 (original (1872) score); *Festive overture on the Danish national anthem, Op. 15; Serenade for Nikolai Rubinstein's saint's day; Mazeppa: Battle of Poltava; Cossack dance.*
*** Chandos Dig. CHAN 9190 [id.]. LSO, Geoffrey Simon.

This is the first recording of Tchaikovsky's original score of the *Little Russian Symphony* and probably the first performance outside Russia. In 1879 Tchaikovsky retrieved the score and rewrote the first movement. He left the *Andante* virtually unaltered, touched up the scoring of the Scherzo, made minor excisions and added repeats, and made a huge cut of 150 bars (some two minutes of music) in the finale. He then destroyed the original. (The present performance has been possible because of the surviving orchestral parts.) Though this first attempt cannot match the reworked first movement, and the finale – delightful though it is – needs no extra bars, it is fascinating to hear the composer's first thoughts, and this is an indispensable recording for all Tchaikovskians. Geoffrey Simon secures a committed response from the LSO, and the recording is striking in its inner orchestral detail and freshness. The music from *Mazeppa*, the *Danish Festival overture* and the tribute to Rubinstein make engaging bonuses.

Symphony No. 2 in C min., Op. 17 (Little Russian)
(N) **(*) Finlandia Dig. 3984 228352-2 [id.].

Norwegian Radio. O, Ari Rasilainen. – BORODIN: *Symphony No. 1*. **(*)

A very enjoyable and recommendable account of the *Little Russian Symphony* from the Norwegian Radio Orchestra and their Finnish conductor. Not necessarily a first choice but it is well enough played and recorded, and gives pleasure.

Symphony No. 2 (Little Russian); Capriccio italien, Op. 45.
*** Chandos Dig. CHAN 8460 [id.]. Oslo PO, Jansons.

Like other conductors who learned their craft in the Soviet Union, Jansons prefers a fastish speed for the *Andantino* second movement, but what above all distinguishes this version is the joyful exuberance both of the bouncy Scherzo – fresh and folk-like in the Trio – and of the finale, and the final coda brings a surge of excitement, making most others seem stiff. The coupling is a fizzing performance of the *Capriccio italien*, bringing a gloriously uninhibited account of the coda with its deliberately vulgar reprise of the Neapolitan tune. With some edge on violin tone, this is not the finest of the Chandos Oslo recordings, but is still fresh and atmospheric.

Symphonies Nos. (i) *2 (Little Russian), Op. 17;* (ii) *4 in F min.*
❀ (B) *** DG 429 527-2. (i) New Philh. O; (ii) VPO, Claudio Abbado.

Abbado's coupling of Tchaikovsky's *Second* and *Fourth Symphonies* is one of the supreme bargains of the current catalogue. His account of the *Little Russian Symphony* is very enjoyable, although the first movement concentrates on refinement of detail. The *Andantino* is nicely pointed, and the Scherzo is admirably crisp and sparkling. The finale is superb, with fine colour and thrust and a memorably spectacular stroke on the tam-tam before the exhilarating coda. The 1967 recording still sounds excellent. This account of the *Fourth Symphony* is unsurpassed on record. Abbado's control of the structure of the first movement is masterly. The *Andantino*, with its gentle oboe solo, really takes wing in its central section, followed by a wittily crisp Scherzo, while the finale has sparkle as well as power. It was recorded in 1975 in the Musikverein and still sounds very good indeed.

Symphony No. 3 in D (Polish), Op. 29.
*** Chandos Dig. CHAN 8463 [id.]. Oslo PO, Jansons.

Tchaikovsky's *Third* is given a clear, refreshingly direct reading by Jansons, but it is the irresistible sweep of urgency with which he builds the development section of the first movement that sets his performance apart, with the basic tempo varied less than usual. The second movement is beautifully relaxed, the *Andante elegiaco* heartwarmingly expressive, tender and refined, and the Scherzo has a Mendelssohnian elfin quality; but it is the swaggering reading of the finale which sets the seal on the whole performance. Though the recording does not convey a genuinely hushed pianissimo for the strings, it brings full, rich and brilliant sound.

Symphonies Nos. (i) *4 in F min., Op. 36;* (ii) *5 in E min., Op. 64; 6 in B min. (Pathétique).*
(B) *** DG Double 453 088-2 [id.]. BPO, Karajan.
(B) *** Decca Double 443 844-2 (2). Philh. O, Ashkenazy.
(M) (***) DG mono 447 423-2 (2). Leningrad PO; (i) Kurt Sanderling; (ii) Mravinsky.
(B) **(*) Ph. Duo 438 335-2 (2) [id.]. LSO, Markevitch.

Who would have thought in the early days of CD that before long we should be offered Karajan's outstanding Berlin Philharmonic performances of the three last symphonies for the cost of one premium-priced CD. Karajan's 1977 analogue version of No. 4 (the most atmospherically recorded of the three) is more compelling than his previous recordings and also is preferable to the newer, digital, Vienna version. Similarly the 1976 reading of the *Fifth* stands out from his other recordings. The Berlin Philharmonic string-playing is peerless. Karajan had a special affinity with Tchaikovsky's *Pathétique symphony*, and of his five stereo versions this one from 1977 is the finest. The digital remastering of the analogue recordings is first rate.

Ashkenazy's set makes a fine alternative bargain on Double Decca, although the layout splits No. 5 across the two discs between the second and third movements. Apart from the emotional power and strong Russian feeling of the readings, the special quality which Ashkenazy conveys is spontaneity. The freshness of his approach, his natural feeling for lyricism on the one hand and drama on the other, is consistently compelling. The late-1970s Kingsway Hall recording quality is full and atmospheric. This could be a best buy for those wanting all three symphonies in modern stereo (but not digital) versions, as the sound is more sumptuous than that provided by DG for Karajan.

Mravinsky re-recorded the three last symphonies of Tchaikovsky with his Leningrad orchestra for DG in stereo, but these legendary earlier, mono performances (No. 4 conducted by Kurt Sanderling) from the mid-1950s were even more satisfying, and they sound marvellously vivid. The earlier readings, without loss of concentration, were less exaggeratedly histrionic, and Sanderling's speeds for the finale of the *Fourth Symphony* particularly, but also Mravinsky's for the *Fifth*, were not as frenetic as in the latter's stereo versions. The opening of the *Fifth* again brings an added dimension of Russian melancholy, and Mravinsky sustains a lyrical intensity throughout the symphony characteristic of all his Tchaikovsky readings. The slow movement brings a performance of great dramatic extremes, the only drawback for Western ears being the solo horn sounding like a euphonium. The emotional power of Mravinsky's *Pathétique* has never been surpassed. The climax of the first movement has tremendous passion, the Scherzo/march is brilliantly pointed yet has plenty of weight, and the finale is deeply eloquent, genuinely touching rather than hysterical, with a characterful rasp from the Russian trombones.

There are many collectors who count Markevitch's Philips recordings from the 1960s as having a similar distinction. Certainly Markevitch's *Fourth* is as exciting as almost any available. It has a superb thrusting first-movement Allegro, and Markevitch brings to the first movement of the *Fifth* a similarly forthright, highly charged approach. He makes no concessions to the second-subject group, which is presented with no let-up on the fast pace at which he takes the main *Allegro*. In the *Pathétique* Markevitch provides great intensity in his account of the first movement. The second movement has both warmth and elegance, and the march is treated broadly, providing suitable contrast before a deeply felt performance of the finale, where the second subject is introduced with great tenderness.

(i) *Symphonies Nos. 4–6 (Pathétique); Andante cantabile for strings; Marche slave, Op. 31; Romeo and Juliet (fantasy overture)*; (ii) *Serenade for strings, Op. 48*.

(N) (BB) *** Royal Classics HR 704032 (3). (i) Hallé O; (ii) LSO, Barbirolli.

Even more than the comparable Royal Classics bargain package of Barbirolli's late Dvořák symphonies, this very inexpensive Tchaikovsky set is self-recommending. The current EMI transfers have immeasurably improved the sound, mostly from the late 1950s, although the two string works come from the following decade. The power and drive of the outer movements of the *Fourth Symphony* is matched by the passionate romantic drama of the *Fifth*, while the *Pathétique* has the widest emotional range of all, opening rather gently but combining great ardour and sombre dignity in the finale. There is refinement of romantic feeling as well as excitement and passion in *Romeo and Juliet*. All these were originally Pye recordings, but the *String serenade* was made with the LSO at Abbey Road. It has all the expressive warmth one might expect, yet in the first movement Barbirolli pays homage to the composer's Mozartean inspiration in the neatly articulated steadiness of the secondary theme in the first movement. The *Andante cantabile* is also comparatively refined, balanced by a rumbustious *Marche slave*.

Symphony No. 4 in F min., Op. 36.

*** Chandos Dig. CHAN 8361 [id.]. Oslo PO, Jansons.

**(*) DG (IMS) Gold Dig. 439 018-2 [id.]. VPO, Karajan.

Symphony No. 4; Capriccio italien.

(M) *** DG 419 872-2. BPO, Karajan.

(i) *Symphony No. 4;* (ii) *Romeo and Juliet* (fantasy overture).

(M) *** Telarc Dig. CD 82002 [id.]. Cleveland O, Lorin Maazel.

(N) ** Teldec Dig. 0630-13698-2 [id.]. Chicago SO, Daniel Barenboim.

Jansons conducts a dazzling performance of the *Fourth*, unusually fresh and natural in its expressiveness, yet with countless subtleties of expression, as in the balletic account of the second-subject group of the first movement. The *Andantino* flows lightly and persuasively, the Scherzo is very fast and lightly sprung, while the finale reinforces the impact of the whole performance: fast and exciting, but with no synthetic whipping-up of tempo. That is so until the very end of the coda, which finds Jansons pressing ahead just fractionally as he would in a concert, a thrilling conclusion made the more so by the wide-ranging, brilliant and realistic recording.

Karajan's 1977 analogue version is more compelling than any of his other versions. It is the vitality and drive of the performance as a whole that one remembers above all, but also the beauty of the wind playing at the opening and close of the slow movement. The CD transfer is extremely vivid. The *Capriccio italien* makes a good filler.

Maazel's 1979 Telarc Cleveland recording is very similar to his very successful 1965 Decca record, and only in the finale does the new version differ markedly from the old, by seeking amplitude and breadth in preference to uninhibited, extrovert excitement. Maazel's approach generates a strong forward momentum in the first movement and is consistently involving in its directness. The slow movement, with a plaintive oboe solo, is most appealing, and in the finale the Cleveland Orchestra produces a thrilling sound. *Romeo and Juliet*, recorded two years later, is given a spaciously romantic performance, reaching a climax of considerable passion.

The *Fourth* is the most successful of the last three Tchaikovsky symphony recordings which Karajan made in 1985 in connection with the Telemondial video project. Although the playing of the Vienna orchestra does not match that of the Berlin Philharmonic in earlier versions, the performance itself has greater flexibility and more spontaneity. The freer control of tempo in the first movement brings a more relaxed second-subject group, while in the *Andantino* the phrasing is less calculated. The warmly resonant acoustic is attractive; even if detail is not absolutely clear, there is no lack of fullness, and Karajan admirers should not be disappointed.

From Barenboim on Teldec, good, well-prepared and spirited accounts of both the *Fourth*

Symphony and the *Romeo and Juliet overture*. At the same time, this does not challenge let alone displace prime recommendations. These are not the kind of performances that invite frequent re-hearing though neither the performance nor the recording could be called second rate.

Symphony No. 5 in E min., Op. 64.

(N) ❁ *** Ph. Dig. 462 905-2 [id.]. VPO, Valery Gergiev.

*** Chandos Dig. CHAN 8351 [id.]. Oslo PO, Jansons.

*** RCA Dig. 09026 68032-2. N. German RSO, Wand – MOZART: *Symphony No. 40.* ***

(N) (M) **(*) EMI CDM5 67032-2. [id.].Philh. O, Klemperer – HAYDN: *Symphony No. 98.* **

**(*) DG (IMS) Gold Dig. 439 019-2 [id.]. VPO, Karajan.

(M) **(*) Decca Phase Four 455 157-2 [id.]. New Philh. O, Stokowski (with GLAZUNOV: *Violin concerto.* **)

Symphony No. 5 in E min.; Francesca da Rimini, Op. 32.

(B) **(*) [EMI Red Line Dig. CDR5 69842]. Phd. O, Muti.

Symphony No. 5; Marche slave.

(M) *** DG 419 066-2. BPO, Karajan.

(i) *Symphony No. 5;* (ii) *Nutcracker suite, Op. 71a.*

(B) *** DG Classikon 439 434-2. (i) Leningrad PO, Mravinsky; (ii) BPO, Karajan.

Symphony No. 5; Serenade for strings in C, Op. 48.

(B) *** Sony SBK 46538 [id.]. Phd. O, Ormandy.

Symphony No. 5; (i) *Eugene Onegin: Tatiana's letter scene.*

(M) *** EMI Dig. CD-EMX 2187. LPO, Sian Edwards; (i) with Eilene Hannan.

Valery Gergiev and the Vienna Philharmonic were recorded at the 1998 Salzburg Festival and their account of the *Fifth Symphony* is really quite special. Those who take this great work for granted should lose no time in hearing this. It is a performance of real stature, entirely free of any playing to the gallery or wearing its heart on its sleeve but totally electrifying. No wonder the audience went wild at the end. It certainly belongs among the best *Fifths* on record. Some collectors will find full price a bit steep for 46 minutes, however marvellous the performance and excellent the recording, but it is worth remembering that even so it would have cost far more to get a ticket to the Grosses Festspielhaus! If you can put economy to one side, you will be rewarded with out-of-the-ordinary music-making.

Sian Edwards conducts an electrifying and warm-hearted reading of Tchaikovsky's *Fifth*, which matches any version in the catalogue, particularly when it comes with an unusual and exceptionally attractive fill-up, *Tatiana's letter scene* from *Eugene Onegin*. That is freshly and dramatically sung, in a convincingly girlish impersonation, by the Australian, Eilene Hannan. Sian Edwards's control of rubato is exceptionally persuasive, notably so in moulding the different sections of the first movement of the symphony, while the great horn solo of the slow movement is played with exquisite delicacy by Richard Bissell. The Waltz third movement is most tenderly done, while the finale brings a very fast and exciting allegro, challenging the orchestra to brilliant, incisive playing.

In the first movement, Jansons's refusal to linger never sounds anything but warmly idiomatic, lacking only a little in charm. The slow movement again brings a steady tempo, with climaxes built strongly and patiently but with enormous power, the final culmination topping everything. In the finale, taken very fast, Jansons tightens the screw of the excitement without ever making it a scramble, following Tchaikovsky's notated slowings rather than allowing extra rallentandos. The sound is excellent, specific and well focused within a warmly reverberant acoustic, with digital recording on CD reinforcing any lightness of bass.

Mravinsky's earlier stereo version of the *Fifth* with the Leningrad Philharmonic on DG would occupy a distinguished place in any collection. The performance is full of Slavonic vitality and the reading is romantic as well as red-blooded (the second subject of the first movement is both warm and graceful). The solo horn has a faint wobble in the famous solo in the slow movement, and the trumpets in the final peroration of an exhilaratingly fast finale also have a vibrato, but these details are unimportant when the reading has such fire and individuality. The recording, made in Watford Town Hall in 1960, is resonant and full, if not always absolutely clean in focus. By comparison Karajan's 1966 *Nutcracker suite* sounds a little cool, but it is marvellously polished and vivid, and the *Waltz of the flowers* is most elegant.

Unexpectedly and generously coupled with Mozart's *G minor Symphony*, Wand's live recording brings a unique reading of Tchaikovsky's *Fifth*, one which might be described as the vision of a great Brucknerian, not in any way dull or boring but refreshing and intense. His own delight shines out as each fresh idea appears. The rapt, devotional account of the slow movement with its opening horn solo brings *pianissimos* of breath-catching delicacy, a reading the more moving for its restraint. The waltz lilts easily and delicately, and then the finale brings at last a sense of release, brilliant and exciting, with the slow march of the coda flowing more easily than usual. In all this Wand owes much to the players of the North German Radio Orchestra, helped by the engineers, so that many details which are normally obscured are brought out with distinctive timbres – notably of the horns – set against a glowing acoustic.

Karajan's 1976 recording stands out from his

other recordings of the *Fifth*. The first movement is unerringly paced and has great romantic flair; in Karajan's hands the climax of the slow movement is grippingly intense, though with a touchingly elegiac preparation for the horn solo at the opening. The Waltz has character and charm too – the Berlin Philharmonic string playing is peerless – and in the finale Karajan drives hard, creating a riveting forward thrust. The remastered recording brings a remarkable improvement.

Ormandy's *Fifth*, splendidly recorded in the spacious acoustics of Philadelphia's Broadwood Hotel, is early (1959) stereo and is one of his very finest Tchaikovsky performances. There is not a suspicion of routine, and the Philadephia strings play gloriously, particularly in the *Andante cantabile*, which generates great passion. Again the weight of string-tone at the opening of the *Serenade* (recorded the following year) establishes the full-blooded character of Ormandy's approach. The finale opens delicately but soon generates great bustle. Overall this coupling is a magnificent demonstration of the Ormandy regime in Philadelphia at its very peak.

Klemperer's performance is surprisingly successful in a way one would not perhaps expect. There is an expanding emotional warmth in the treatment of the opening movement with the second subject blossoming in a ripely romantic way. The slow movement too, if not completely uninhibited, is played richly with a fine horn solo from Alan Civil. The Waltz is perhaps marginally disappointing but the Finale has splendid dignity. Good recording and an excellent transfer, but the Haydn coupling is less recommendable.

The oddity of Muti's Philadelphia version is that, though the first two movements have the disappointingly over-relaxed manners that marked his *Pathétique* earlier, often with surprisingly slack ensemble, the last two movements are played with the high voltage one expects of this conductor and orchestra at their finest. The fill-up is also played at white heat, a powerful performance. It makes a rare and worthwhile coupling. The sound, not as clear as it might be, has warmth and weight beyond most recent Philadelphia issues.

Karajan's last VPO version of the *Fifth* brings a characteristically strong and expressive performance; however, neither in the playing of the Vienna Philharmonic nor even in the recorded sound can it quite match his 1977 Berlin Philharmonic version for DG. Though the long takes have brought extra spontaneity, the recording of the strings in the Musikvereinsaal is inconsistent, with front-desk players sharply focused but not the whole body of strings behind them, and with woodwind set at a distance. After a disappointingly slack Waltz the finale goes especially well, with the Vienna brass biting superbly in the first reprise of the movement's main theme.

Stokowski is spectacularly recorded (in Stuttgart in 1966). But the conductor's concern with tonal grandeur has its drawbacks, and his cuts make the end result controversial. He tends to languish rather than press forward. The speeds for the main allegros of the first and last movements are spacious, with some sacrifice of vitality. Yet with the flick of the wrist, as it were, Stokowski can create some fine blazes of excitement, lighting up every detail of Tchaikovsky's inspired orchestration. However, there are a number of cuts (four bars, twice, in the first movement, two bars in the introduction to the finale, and a longer cut later), and Stokowski dispenses with the pause before the final coda.

Symphony No. 6 in B min. (Pathétique), Op. 74.

*** Chandos Dig. CHAN 8446 [id.]. Oslo PO, Jansons.

(N) (M) **(*) Penguin Classics DG 460 609-2 [id.]. BPO, Karajan.

(N) (***) Biddulph mono WHL 046 [id.]. Phd. O, Ormandy – MUSSORGSKY: *Pictures at an exhibition* (orch Cailliet). (***)

(M) (***) RCA mono GD 60312 [60312-2-RG]. Phd. O, Toscanini – R. STRAUSS: *Death and transfiguration*. (***)

Symphony No. 6 (Pathétique); Capriccio italien; Eugene Onegin: Waltz & Polonaise.

(B) **(*) Sony SBK 47657 [id.]. Phd O, Ormandy.

Symphony No. 6 (Pathétique); 1812 Overture.

(M) **(*) RCA 09026 61246-2 [id.]. Chicago SO, Reiner – LISZT: *Mephisto waltz*. ***

Symphony No. 6 (Pathétique); Marche slave, Op. 31.

❁ (BB) *** Virgin/EMI Dig. 2x1 VBD5 61636-2 (2) [CDBV 61636]. Russian Nat. O, Mikhail Pletnev – *The Seasons*, etc. ***

Symphony No. 6 (Pathétique); Nutcracker suite, Op. 71a.

(M) (**) RCA mono GD 60297. NBC SO, Toscanini.

Symphony No. 6 (Pathétique); Romeo and Juliet (fantasy overture).

(M) *** Virgin/EMI (SIS) Dig. CUV5 61267-2. Bournemouth SO, Andrew Litton.

(M) *** DG Masters Dig. 445 601-2. Philh. O, Sinopoli.

(M) **(*) Mercury 434 352-2 [id.]. LSO, Antal Dorati.

(i) *Symphony No. 6 (Pathétique);* (ii) *Swan Lake* (ballet): *suite*.

(B) *** DG 439 456-2. (i) Leningrad PO, Mravinsky; (ii) BPO, Karajan.

The *Pathétique* was Mikhail Pletnev's début on record as a conductor with the Russian National Orchestra that has been formed for him. There is no doubt that this is among the most vividly dramatic accounts of this symphony. The way in which Pletnev launches us into the development of the first movement still takes one aback, even when one knows what to expect. His hand-picked orchestra is as virtuosic as Pletnev himself can be on the keyboard, with a challengingly fast tempo for the Scherzo. There is a stirring account of *Marche slave* too, and a very fine recording, perfectly balanced, although the effect is a little recessed. This is now linked to Pletnev's *Seasons* on a Virgin Double – an astonishing bargain.

Mariss Jansons and the Oslo Philharmonic crown their magnetically compelling Tchaikovsky series with a superbly concentrated account of the last and greatest of the symphonies. It is characteristic of Jansons that the great second-subject melody is at once warm and passionate yet totally unsentimental, with rubato barely noticeable. The very fast speed for the third-movement *March* stretches the players to the very limit, but the exhilaration is infectious, leading to the simple dedication of the slow finale, unexaggerated but deeply felt. Fine, warm recording as in the rest of the series.

Litton's is an outstanding performance, full of temperament, not just fiery but tender too, arguably the finest of the whole Litton cycle. The Bournemouth playing has never been neater, with the sound bringing out the fine clarity of articulation. The only idiosyncrasy is that in the big second-subject melodies of the outer movements Litton prefers speeds broader than usual, but with no hint of self-indulgence in the finely moulded phrasing. With an account of *Romeo and Juliet* that builds up powerfully from a restrained start, the disc makes a splendid culmination to his Tchaikovsky series.

If one divides interpreters of this *Symphony* into those who tend to press ahead in stringendo and those who hold back in ritenuto, Sinopoli – perhaps surprisingly after his Elgar *Second* – is firmly in the former group. What is striking here is the passion of the playing of the Philharmonia, recorded with the most satisfying opulence. Sinopoli's reading of the opening movement is beautifully shaped, with the second subject introduced very tenderly. He adopts slow speeds for the middle two movements but sustains them well, with a moving and eloquent account of the finale. The big advantage that Sinopoli has in this mid-priced reissue is that it is generously coupled with *Romeo and Juliet*, which is also very exciting. Even if there is a hint of self-consciousness at the first entry of the love theme, there is plenty of uninhibited passion in the later repeats. In short this is one of the finest digital versions of the *Pathétique*. Excellent recording.

Mravinsky's very Russian (stereo) account of the *Pathétique* is justly renowned. It is deeply passionate, yet the second subject of the first movement is introduced with much tenderness. The last two movements are very fine indeed; the Scherzo/march is brilliantly pointed, yet has plenty of weight, and the finale is very moving without ever letting the control slip. The present transfer of the 1960 recording (made in Wembley Town Hall) maintains the agreeable ambience, even if at times the Russian brass comes over raucously. Karajan's *Swan Lake suite* is most exciting, with polished and brilliant BPO playing, and the recording, made a decade after the symphony, has rather less alluring string sound.

Karajan had a very special affinity with Tchaikovsky's *Pathétique Symphony*, and – remembering Furtwängler's famous 78 rpm set – so has the Berlin Philharmonic Orchestra. He has recorded it five times in stereo. For many, this 1977 version, now reissued on Penguin Classics, is the finest, and it is a pity that the CD transfer is brightly lit to the point of harshness in the loudest climaxes. And the brilliant recording is of the widest dynamic range (though it does not have a very sumptuous lower resonance). Yet the impact of Tchaikovsky's climaxes is tremendously powerful, the articulation of the Berlin players precise and strong. The climactic peaks generate tremendous tension and the effect on the listener is almost overwhelming. In the 5/4 movement Karajan allows the middle section to increase the elegiac feeling, against a background of remorseless but distanced drum-beats like a tolling bell. The finale has great passion and eloquence, with two gentle sforzandos at the very end to emphasize the finality of the closing phrase. The accompanying author's note is by Edmund White.

It was in 1936 that, having been music director of the Minneapolis Orchestra, Ormandy was appointed co-conductor in Philadelphia alongside Leopold Stokowski. This electrifying performance of the *Pathétique Symphony*, one of the fastest ever on disc, was Ormandy's first Philadelphia recording, begun in December of 1936 and completed the following month. So in the first movement Ormandy is more volatile than in his later recordings, tending to press on faster after setting a tempo. The result is very powerful and exciting, not at all sentimental. First-rate transfer.

Ormandy's fine 1960 performance is a reading of impressive breadth, dignity and power, with no suggestion of routine in a single bar. The orchestra makes much of the first-movement climax and plays with considerable passion and impressive body of tone in both outer movements; yet there is an element of restraint in the finale which prevents any feeling of hysteria. In short, this is most satisfying, a performance to live with; the CD transfer, while brightly lit, avoids glare in the upper range. Ormandy's panache and gusto give the *Capriccio italien* plenty of life without driving too hard, and the dances are rhythmically infectious.

Reiner is given full-blooded 1957 sound but his *Pathétique* – although it has some bursts of excitement in the first movement, and the Chicago ambience adds much to the lively Scherzo/march –

as a whole does not completely convince. The last movement is tender rather than producing the intensity and anguish inherent in a Russian performance. *1812* is without cannon but is very enjoyable none the less. What makes this reissue distinctive is Reiner's superb account of Liszt's *Mephisto waltz*, perhaps the finest on record.

Dorati's 1960 recording of the *Pathétique* is much better focused on CD than it was on LP, with brilliance underpinned by the weight and resonance of Watford Town Hall. The reading has plenty of dynamism in the first movement and the 5/4 movement, unusually brisk, is exhilarating, if hardly a conventional reading. There are some minor eccentricities of tempi in the Scherzo/march but the climax is thrilling, and the finale is finely done, volatile, but grippingly so. *Romeo and Juliet* opens with dignity, is tender in the love music and brings plenty of excitement at the climax.

Toscanini's Philadelphia version of the *Pathétique* glows with the special magic that developed between him and the orchestra over the winter season of 1941–2. Though far more disciplined than most readings, it is altogether warmer than his NBC recording, with the great second-subject melody of the first movement tender in its emotions, not rigid in its easy rubato. He even eases the tempo sympathetically for the fortissimo entries of the march in the third movement. Alongside a magnificent account of the Strauss – an apt link, with death the theme – it makes a superb historical document.

The 1947 NBC recording for Toscanini, dry and unhelpful, also has high 78 surface hiss, which detracts from a characteristically powerful and intense performance. Speeds are all on the fast side, but only in the first movement do the results ever sound perfunctory, and the middle movements are delectably pointed in rhythm, while the slow finale at a flowing speed is both noble and passionate. The sound for the *Nutcracker* is far clearer, a crisp, bright interpretation, even if the Sugar-Plum Fairy is heavy-footed.

Symphony No. 7 (arr. Bogatyryev).
*** Chandos Dig. CHAN 9130 [id.]. LPO, Neeme Järvi – *Piano concerto No. 3*. **(*)

Just over 30 years after Eugene Ormandy and the Philadelphia Orchestra first recorded Bogatyryev's completion of Tchaikovsky's *Symphony No. 7*, Neeme Järvi provided this valuable alternative, helpfully coupled with the one-movement *Piano concerto No. 3* which Tchaikovsky drew from the symphony's first movement. This reconstructed symphony, abandoned not long before Tchaikovsky wrote his culminating masterpiece in the *Pathétique Symphony*, may be no match for the regular canon, but it brings many Tchaikovskian delights. Having symphony and concerto side by side makes it very easy to compare Bogatyryev's reconstruction of the original version, in structure identical except for the central solo cadenza. In the *Symphony* Järvi, with speeds a degree more expansive than Ormandy in all four movements, finds more poetry, more fantasy, and the modern digital recording allows far more light and shade over a much wider dynamic range. Apart from the thinness on the upper strings, the recorded sound is satisfyingly full and warm. Geoffrey Tozer – see above – gives a fine performance of the *Concerto*.

Variations on a rococo theme for cello and orchestra, Op. 33.

❀ *** EMI Dig. CDC5 56126-2 [id.]. Han-Na Chang, LSO, Rostropovich – BRUCH: *Kol Nidrei;* FAURE: *Elégie;* SAINT-SAENS: *Cello concerto No. 1*. ***

(M) *** DG 447 413-2 [id.]. Rostropovich, BPO, Karajan – DVORAK: *Cello concerto*. *** ❀

(M) *** Carlton Dig. 30366 0011-2 [id.]. Tortelier, RPO, Groves – DVORAK: *Rondo in G min.* ***; ELGAR: *Cello concerto in E min.* **(*)

(BB) *** CfP Silver Double CDCFPSD 4775 (2). Robert Cohen, LPO, Macal – BEETHOVEN: *Triple concerto;* DVORAK: *Cello concerto;* ELGAR: *Cello concerto*. ***

(B) *** Sony SBK 48278; *SBT 48278* [id.]. Leonard Rose, Phd. O, Ormandy – BLOCH: *Schelomo* ***; FAURE: *Élégie* ***; LALO: *Concerto*. **(*)

(M) *** [RCA Basic 100 09026 68086-2; *68086-4*]. Ofra Harnoy, LPO, Mackerras – DVORAK: *Cello concerto*. ***

Han-Na Chang gives a memorably beautiful performance of the Tchaikovsky *Rococo variations*. This phenomenally gifted 13-year-old Korean-born cellist has the most ravishing tone and a wonderfully musical sense of line. Rostropovich as conductor sets the scene with an affectionate elegance, and then Chang introduces Tchaikovsky's theme with disarming simplicity, with the first variation following with a natural, spontaneous flow and the third generating just the right degree of energy. The fourth, *Andante grazioso*, introduced very gently, is quite ethereal and No. 6, where Tchaikovsky turns the melody into a nostalgic Russian folksong, even more touchingly seductive. The finale has the expected dash, and the crispest articulation. The LSO are inspired by Chang to give a wonderfully sensitive accompaniment, and the recording is in the demonstration class.

Like Chang, Rostropovich uses the published score rather than the original version which more accurately reflects the composer's intentions. But this account, with Karajan's glowing support, is so superbly structured in its control of emotional light and shade that one is readily convinced that this is the work Tchaikovsky conceived. The recording (made in the Jesus-Christus Kirche) is beautifully balanced and is surely one of the most perfect examples of DG's analogue techniques.

Tortelier's version on the Carlton label is warm and red-blooded, if technically not as flawless as his earlier reading, but the recording is pleasantly atmospheric, slightly distanced so that the tenderness of the performance is brought out the more.

Ofra Harnoy's scale is smaller, the style elegant, not missing the colour or ardour but never forgetting the word 'rococo' in the title. It is a considerable performance, stylish yet emotionally responsive, and Paul Freeman's accompaniment is first class. Ofra Harnoy's alternative coupling with Dvŏrák is available only in the USA.

Leonard Rose's warm and elegant – at times ardent – account of these splendid variations is balm to the senses, and Ormandy provides admirable support. The recording is forwardly balanced but the dynamic range remains reasonably wide, and the cello is firmly and realistically focused.

CHAMBER AND INSTRUMENTAL MUSIC

Piano trio in A min., Op. 50.

(N) *** Erato/Warner Dig. 0630 17875-2 [id.]. Repin, Berezovsky, Yablonsky – SHOSTAKOVICH: *Piano trio, Op. 67.* ***

*** Ara. Dig. Z6661 [id.]. Golub–Kaplan–Carr Trio – SMETANA: *Piano trio.* ***

**(*) EMI CDC7 47988-2. Ashkenazy, Perlman, Harrell.

**(*) Sony Dig. SK 53269 [id.]. Yefim Bronfman, Cho-Liang Lin, Gary Hoffman – ARENSKY: *Piano trio No. 1.* **(*)

An outstanding and involving account of the Tchaikovsky from Vadim Repin, Boris Berezovsky and Dmitri Yablonsky, is superbly recorded by the Erato team. This now makes a clear first choice for a splendid and highly characteristic work that is still undervalued by many Tchaikovskians. Moreover, it has a fine version of the wartime Shostakovich *Trio* as coupling.

The Golub/Kaplan/Carr account of the Smetana *G minor Piano trio* is well-matched in the Tchaikovsky, which has the merit of being completely uncut. The balance places the listener rather too close to the players, but the sound is perfectly pleasing and the performance refreshingly unaffected. Nothing is overdriven, mechanized or attention-seeking.

With the keyboard dominating, the first movement of Tchaikovsky's *Piano trio* can so easily sound too rhetorical, and that is not entirely avoided by Ashkenazy, Perlman and Harrell. The *Variations* which form the second part of the work are very successful, with engaging characterization and a great deal of electricity in the closing pages. Generally this group carry all before them, with their sense of artistic purpose and through their warmth and ardour. The sound is on the dry side, with the digital remastering increasing the sharpness of focus, not ideally atmospheric. This is still at full price and comes without a coupling.

The Sony account from Yefim Bronfman, Cho-Liang Lin and Gary Hoffman is a keenly lyrical and expressive performance of this work, which suffers from a less than ideally balanced recording. Yefim Bronfman is allowed to swamp the texture when the dynamic level rises, even though, as in the Arensky with which it is coupled, it is obvious that he is playing with delicacy. Both Cho-Liang Lin and Gary Hoffman are marvellous players whose refinement and purity give unfailing delight.

Souvenir de Florence, Op. 70.

(N) *** Chandos Dig. CHAN 9708 [id.]. Norwegian CO, Iona Brown – R. STRAUSS: *Metamorphosen.* ***

(N) *** Hyperion Dig. CDA 66648 [id.]. Raphael Ens. – ARENSKY: *String quartet in A min., Op. 35.* ***

*** Chandos Dig. CHAN 9878 [id.] ASMF Chamber Ens. – GLAZUNOV: *String quintet.* ***

** Mer. Dig. CDE 84211 [id.]. Arienski Ens. – ARENSKY: *String quartet No. 2* ***; BORODIN: *Sextet movements.* **

Iona Brown and the Norwegian Chamber Orchestra give us a splendid new account of the full orchestral version of Tchaikovsky's invigorating and captivating *Souvenir de Florence*, bouncingly rhythmic in the opening movement, and buoyantly exuberant in the swinging secondary theme of the finale. There is both warmth and subtlety in the inner movements. Iona Brown participated in Marriner's stereo première of the work for Argo in the 1970s and she matches its glowing sense of joy, fine pointing and precision of ensemble. That version, however, was cut to fit an LP side: this is complete and given one of Chandos's most brilliant and full-bodied recordings. The result is irresistible.

A first-rate performance of the *Souvenir de Florence* which can hold its own with the very best. The Raphael Ensemble play with total unanimity of ensemble and richness of tone. Their coupling, the Arensky *quartet with two cellos* is magnificently played. The recording may be a snag for some collectors – it is all a bit too forward and we are very much in the front row – but there is no reason to withhold a third star given its artistry and authority.

From the ASMF Chamber Ensemble, a very sympathetic and well-recorded account of *Souvenir de Florence* which deserves a warm recommendation as an alternative. Its coupling, which brings a Glazunov rarity, strengthens its claims.

A very good rather than a distinguished performance of Tchaikovsky's eloquent *Souvenir de Florence* on Meridian, very decently recorded. The strength of the issue lies in the interest of its coupling, an Arensky rarity, the *A minor Quartet*, from which the well-known *Variations on a theme of Tchaikovsky* derive, and two Mendelssohnian movements from the Borodin *Sextet*.

Souvenir d'un lieu cher, Op. 42; Valse scherzo in C, Op. 34 (orch. Glazunov).
(N) *** DG Dig. 457 064-2 [id.]. Gil Shaham, Russian Nat. O, Pletnev – GLAZUNOV & KABALEVSKY: *Concertos*. ***

Eloquent and dazzling playing of these Tchaikovsky pieces by Gil Shaham and the Russian National Orchestra under Pletnev are an additional inducement to get this fine disc of the Glazunov and Kabalevsky *concertos*.

String quartet in B flat; String quartets Nos. 1–3; (i) *Souvenir de Florence.*
(M) *** BMG/Melodiya 74321 18290-2 (2). Borodin Qt, (i) with Rostropovich, Talalyan.
*** Teldec/Warner Dig. 4509 90422-2 (2) [id.]. Borodin Qt, (i) with Yurov, Milman.

String quartets Nos. 1 in D, Op. 11; 3 in E flat, Op. 30.
*** Nimbus Dig. NI 5380 [id.]. Franz Schubert Qt.

String quartet No. 2 in F, Op. 22; (i) *Souvenir de Florence.*
*** Nimbus Dig. NI 5399 [id.]. Franz Schubert Qt, (i) with Flieder, Schultz.

In the mid-priced BMG/Melodiya set the *Souvenir de Florence* with Rostropovich and Talalyan comes from 1965, whereas the three *Quartets* plus the student *Quartet movement* that Tchaikovsky wrote in 1865 were all recorded at roughly the same time (1979–80). The Teldec set, made in 1993 in the Berlin Teldec studios, is digital and the sound is a shade drier: it also includes the early *B flat movement*. Both sets are superb, unassailable recommendations.

The two Nimbus discs have the advantage of being available separately. The two couplings, of *No. 1 in D major* and *No. 3 in E flat*, and the *F major quartet* and the *Souvenir de Florence*, offer good playing and the sound-balance offers one of the best chamber-music recordings Nimbus have given us. The Franz Schubert Quartet possess smooth, beautifully produced sound and good ensemble.

String quartet No. 1 in D, Op. 11.
(M) *** Cal. CAL 6202 [id.]. Talich Qt – BORODIN: *Quartet No. 2*. **(*)
(***) Testament mono SBT 1061 [id.]. Hollywood Qt – GLAZUNOV: *5 Novelettes;* BORODIN: *String quartet No. 2 in D*. (***)
(M) **(*) Decca 425 541-2. Gabrieli Qt – BORODIN; SHOSTAKOVICH: *Quartets*. **(*)
**(*) Collins Dig. 1450-2 [id.]. Duke Qt – SCHNITTKE: *String quartet No. 2;* SHOSTAKOVICH: *String quartet No. 8*. **(*)

A glorious account of Tchaikovsky's best-loved quartet from the Talich group. They play the opening movement with an unassertive, lyrical feeling that is quite disarming, while the famous *Andante cantabile* has never sounded more beautiful on record, shaped with a combination of delicacy of feeling and warmth that is wholly persuasive. The Scherzo has plenty of verve, and the finale winningly balances the music's joyful vigour and its underlying hint of melancholy with a typical lightness of touch. The 1987 digital recording is beautifully balanced. Highly recommended.

The Hollywood Quartet's LP first appeared in 1953 and their fervent account has a persuasive eloquence which still puts one under its spell. The sound has been improved, and the addition of the Glazunov, which is new to the catalogue, enhances its value. The disc runs to one second short of 80 minutes, and the sleeve warns that some older CD players may have difficulty in tracking it.

The Gabrielis give a finely conceived performance, producing well-blended tone-quality, and the 1977 recording is clean and alive; but ideally the upper range could be less forcefully projected.

An intelligent and expressive account of the *D major Quartet* from the Duke Quartet on Collins. If it is not a first choice, it is because of an upfront balance which does not enhance the quartet's beauty of tone. Readers with high-grade equipment will find this more worrying than others.

PIANO MUSIC

Solo piano music

Album for the young, Op. 39; Aveu passioné in E min.; Capriccio in G flat, Op. 8; Dumka, Op. 59; Impromptu in A flat; Impromptu-caprice in G; Military march in B flat; Momento Lyrico in A flat; 6 Morceaux composés sur un seul thème, Op. 21; 2 Morceaux, Op. 10; 3 Morceaux, Op. 9; 6 Morceaux, Op. 19; 6 Morceaux, Op. 51; 12 Morceaux, Op. 40; 18 Morceaux, Op. 72; 2 Pieces, Op. 1; Potpourri on themes from the opera 'Voyevoda'; Romance in F min., Op. 5; 3 Romances; (i) arr: *50 Russian folksongs. The Seasons, Op. 37b; Sonata No. 1 in C sharp min., Op. 80; (Grand) Sonata (No. 2 in G), Op. 37a; 3 Souvenirs de Hapsal, Op. 2; Theme and variations in A min.; Valse caprice in D, Op. 4; Valse-scherzo in A; Valse-scherzo in A, Op. 7.*
**(*) Erato/Warner Dig. 2292 45969-2 (7). Viktoria Postnikova, (i) Gennady Rozdestvensky.

Piano sonata No. 1 in C sharp min.; The Seasons, Op. 37b.
**(*) Erato/Warner Dig. 2292 45512-2 (from above). Viktoria Postnikova.

Almost every one of these pieces brings attractive melodic writing, but they need care in presentation. Viktoria Postnikova's imagination is patently caught by even the simplest inspirations. In her hands nothing sounds trivial. The *Grand sonata* has a comparable rhetoric to the first movements of the *Second Piano concerto* and the *Piano trio*, yet the result here is never hectoring and the slow movement is most sensitively played. The two most famous sets of genre pieces, *The Seasons* and the Op. 39 collection for young people, are affectionately characterized. Rozdestvensky joins her for Tchaikovsky's four-handed arrangements of the 50 Russian folksongs. The sixth is instantly familiar from its use in the second movement of the *Little Russian Symphony*. Similarly, the Scherzo of the *C sharp minor Sonata* which (in spite of its high opus number) is a student work, brings a reminder of the *Winter Daydreams Symphony*. This Schumannesque sonata is available separately, coupled to *The Seasons*. The *Theme and variations in A minor* is an engaging piece and the *Pot-pourri on themes from The Voyevoda* offers a fascinating sampler of ideas from a virtually unknown opera. In short, everything here is well worth having, and the last item on the very first disc of early pieces brings a *Humoresque* (Op. 10/2) which Stravinsky appropriated and scored for horns to produce one of the most memorable themes in his *Baiser de la fée* pastiche ballet score. The only snag is that the recording quality, while live and present, is sometimes hard on top.

Capriccioso in B flat, Op. 19/5; Chanson triste, Op. 40/2; L'espiègle, Op. 72/12; Humoresque in G, Op. 10/2; Méditation, Op. 72/5; Menuetto-scherzoso, Op. 51/3; Nocturne in F, Op. 10/1; Rêverie du soir, Op. 19/1; Romances: in F min., Op. 5; in F, Op. 51/5; The Seasons: May (White nights), June (Barcarolle), November (Troika); January (By the fireplace). Un poco di Chopin, Op. 72/15; Valse de salon, Op. 51/2; Waltz in A flat, Op. 40/8; Waltz-scherzo in A min., Op. 7.

*** Olympia Dig. OCD 334 [id.]. Sviatoslav Richter.

It is good to hear Richter (recorded in 1993 by Ariola-Eurodisc) given first-class, modern, digital sound and on top technical form, showing that he had lost none of his flair. These miniatures are invested with enormous character in playing of consistent poetry; there is never a whiff of the salon. The opening *Nocturne in F major*, the charming neo-pastiche called *Un poco di Chopin* and the haunting *Rêverie du soir* readily demonstrate Richter's imaginative thoughtfulness, while the apparently simple *Capriccioso in B flat* produces a thrilling burst of bravura at its centrepiece. They are all captivating, and the bolder *Menuetto-scherzoso* also shows Tchaikovsky at his most attractively inventive. With its very truthful sound-picture, this is a first recommendation for anyone wanting a single CD of Tchaikovsky's piano music.

The Seasons, Op. 37a.

**(*) Chandos Dig. CHAN 8349 [id.]. Lydia Artymiw.

(N) (**) Sony Dig. SK60689 [id.]. Yefim Bronfman. – BALAKIREV: *Islamey*. *

The Seasons, Op. 37b; 6 Pieces, Op. 21; Sleeping Beauty (excerpts) arr. Pletnev.

(BB) *** Virgin/EMI Dig. 2x1 VBD5 61636-2 [CDBV 61636] (2). Mikhail Pletnev – *Symphony No. 6*. *** ❁

Tchaikovsky's twelve *Seasons* (they would better have been called 'months') were written to a regular deadline for publication in the St Petersburg music magazine, *Nuvellist*. Mikhail Pletnev has exceptional feeling for Tchaikovsky, revealing depths that are hidden to most interpreters. He grips one from first note to last, not only in *The Seasons* but also in the charming and touching *Six morceaux*, Op. 21. Fresh and natural recorded sound.

This now comes together with the *Sleeping Beauty* excerpts (see below) and the *Pathétique Symphony* on a remarkably generous Virgin Double.

It is the gentler, lyrical pieces that are most effective in the hands of Lydia Artymiw, and she plays them thoughtfully and poetically. Elsewhere, she sometimes has a tendency marginally to over-characterize the music. The digital recording is truthful.

No quarrels with Yefim Bronfman's account of Tchaikovksy's endearing portraits of the months of the year. However his artistry is not matched by comparable recording. The sound is shallow, and closely balanced in a claustrophobic studio. It is a tribute to his sensitivity that even under such close microphone scrutiny he still gives some pleasure. However at less than 50 minutes' playing-time, this is a non-starter.

Sleeping Beauty (excerpts) arr. Pletnev.

❁ *** Virgin/EMI Dig. VC7 59611-2 [id.]. Mikhail Pletnev – MUSSORGSKY: *Pictures at an exhibition*. *** ❁

In the present transcription Pletnev gives us about 30 minutes of *The Sleeping Beauty* in a dazzling performance. In clarity of articulation and virtuosity this is most remarkable – also in poetry and depth of feeling. In every way a *tour de force*.

VOCAL MUSIC

4 Duets: *Dawn; Evening; In the garden by the river; Tears.*

(N) *** BBC Legends BBCB 8001-2 [id.]. Heather Harper, Dame Janet Baker, Benjamin Britten – BRAHMS: *Liebeslieder waltzes, Op. 52*. ROSSINI: *Soirées musicales*. ***

Heather Harper and Janet Baker, recorded at the Aldeburgh Festival in 1971, make a dream duet partnership in these tenderly sentimental duets, sung in English. Britten's inspired accompaniment adds poetry to Tchaikovsky's distinctive piano writing. No texts are given, but James Bowman writes movingly of such 'family music-making' at Aldeburgh.

The Liturgy of St John Chrysostom, Op. 41.
(N) (BB) **(*) Naxos Dig 8.553854.2 [id.]. Viktor Ovdiy, Pavlo Mezhulin, Kiev Chamber Ch., Mykola Hobdych.

In contrast with rival versions of this masterpiece of Russian orthodox music, which offer substantial couplings, the Naxos issue presents a liturgical performance complete with the priests' solos, almost 70 minutes long. Not all collectors will want such a format for repeated listening, but for those who prefer such an authentic course, this Naxos disc can be warmly recommended, strongly and idiomatically performed with fine solos, and atmospherically recorded in a church in Kiev.

Liturgy of St John Chrysostom, Op. 41; (ii) *9 Sacred pieces* (for unaccompanied chorus); (ii) *An angel crying.*
(N) *** Hyperion Dig. CDA 66948 [id.]. Corydon Singers, Matthew Best.

Liturgy of St John Chrysostum, Op. 41; 6 Sacred pieces: Blessed are they who Thou hast chosen; The hymn of the Cherubim; It is meet; Now the angels are with us; Our Father; To Thee we sing.
(N) (B) *** EMI forte (SIS) CZS5 68661-2 (2) [CDFB 68661]. Soloists, Bulgarian a Cappella Ch., Georgi Robev.

One does not think of Tchaikovsky as a composer of church music, yet listening to these ardent and moving performances of these sacred works, one realizes that like most Russians he found a religious dimension within himself and was deeply moved by the words he was setting, adopting a simpler, less exotic vocal style than usual. The a cappella *Liturgy of St John Chrysostom*, which dates from 1878, was not commissioned but written simply to reflect his devotion to the Russian Orthodox Church. Best and the Corydon Singers in their refined, dedicated performances bring out the freshness and energy in this inspired music, with basses cleanly focused down to subterranean depths, echoing authentic Russian examples. The disc also contains the sequence of *9 Sacred choruses* which Tchaikovsky wrote five or six years after the *Liturgy*, even simpler in style, but showing his ready melodic gift, and a separate piece, a dramatic Easter Day anthem, *An angel crying*, which is a miniature masterpiece. Warm, clear sound.

The alternative Bulgarian performances (although the cost is about the same) stretch to a pair of CDs, and include only six of the nine choruses. Yet the Bulgarian singing has an added idiomatic Slavonic colouring and great intensity of feeling, and aided by the cathedral acoustic, the effect is wonderfully spacious. Indeed this music could hardly be performed more convincingly and the recording is superb.

The Snow Maiden, Op. 12 (complete incidental music).
*** Chandos Dig. CHAN 9324 [id.]. Irina Mishura-Lekhman, Vladimir Girshko, Michigan University Choral Society, Detroit SO, Järvi.

Ostrovsky's play, *The Snow Maiden*, based on a Russian folk-tale, prompted Tchaikovsky to compose incidental music, no fewer than 19 numbers, lasting 80 minutes, a cherishable rarity. Much of it is vintage material, very delightful, bringing reminders of *Eugene Onegin* in the peasant choruses and some of the folk-based songs, and of the later Tchaikovskian world of *The Nutcracker* in some of the dances. He himself thought so well of the music that he wanted to develop it into an opera, but was frustrated when Rimsky-Korsakov wrote one first.

The consistent freshness and charm of invention comes out in Järvi's reading of the 19 numbers, lasting just under 80 minutes. It makes a delightful, undemanding cantata, very well played and sung, and is a clear first choice.

Songs: *Amid the noise of the ball; Behind the window; The canary; Cradle song; The cuckoo; Does the day reign?; Do not believe; The fearful minute; If only I had known; It was in the early spring; Last night; Lullaby in a storm; The nightingale; None but the lonely heart; Not a word, O my friend; Serenade; Spring; To forget so soon; Was I not a little blade of grass?; Why?; Why did I dream of you?*
*** Hyperion Dig. CDA 66617 [id.]. Joan Rodgers, Roger Vignoles.

The warmly distinctive timbre of Joan Rodgers's lovely soprano has been heard mainly in opera but she is equally compelling in this glowing disc of songs. Her fluency with Russian texts as well as the golden colourings of her voice make this wide-ranging collection a delight from first to last. Though the voice is not quite at its richest in the most celebrated song of all, *None but the lonely heart*, the singer's subtle varying of mood and tone completely refutes the idea that Tchaikovsky as a song-composer was limited. One of the finest discs issued to mark the Tchaikovsky centenary in 1993.

OPERA

Eugene Onegin (complete).
*** Decca 417 413-2 (2). Kubiak, Weikl, Burrows, Reynolds, Ghiaurov, Hamari, Sénéchal, Alldis Ch., ROHCG O, Solti.

**(*) DG Dig. 423 959-2 (2) [id.]. Freni, Allen, Von Otter, Schicoff, Burchuladze, Sénéchal, Leipzig R. Ch., Dresden State O, Levine.

Solti, characteristically crisp in attack, has plainly warmed to the score of Tchaikovsky's colourful opera, allowing his singers full rein in rallentando and rubato to a degree one might not have expected of him. The Tatiana of Teresa Kubiak is most moving – rather mature-sounding for the *ingénue* of Act I, but with her golden, vibrant voice rising most impressively to the final confrontation of Act III. The Onegin of Bernd Weikl may have too little variety of tone, but again this is firm singing that yet has authentic Slavonic tinges. The rest of the cast is excellent, with Stuart Burrows as Lensky giving one of his finest performances on record yet. Here, for the first time, the full range of expression in this most atmospheric of operas is superbly caught, with the Decca CDs vividly capturing every subtlety – including the wonderful off-stage effects.

The DG version brings a magnificent Onegin in Thomas Allen, the most satisfying account of the title-role yet recorded. It is matched by the Tatiana of Mirella Freni, even at a late stage in her career readily conveying girlish freshness in her voice. The other parts are also strongly taken. The tautened-nerves quality in the character of Lensky comes out vividly in the portrayal by Neil Shicoff, and Anne Sofie von Otter with her firm, clear mezzo believably makes Olga a younger sister, not too mature a character. Paata Burchuladze is a satisfyingly resonant Gremin and Michel Sénéchal, as on the Solti set, is an incomparable Monsieur Triquet. What welds all these fine components into a rich and exciting whole is the conducting of James Levine with the Dresden Staatskapelle: passionate, at times even wild in Slavonic excitement, yet giving full expressive rein to Tchaikovskian melody, allowing the singers to breathe. The Leipzig Radio Choir sings superbly as well. The snag is that the DG recording is dry and studio-bound, with sound close and congested enough to undermine the bloom on both voices and instruments. In every way the more spacious acoustic in the Solti set is preferable.

Eugene Onegin: highlights.
(M) **(*) DG Dig. 445 467-2 (from above set, with Allen, Freni, Von Otter, Shicoff, Burchuladze; cond. Levine).

Even though the Levine set is not a first choice for the complete opera, this 75-minute selection brings out the superb qualities of the singing. It includes the Letter scene (with Freni a freshly charming Tatiana), the Waltz and Polonaise scenes (with the excellent Leipzig Radio Chorus), also the Act II Duel scene and other key arias, all strongly characterized, and the entire closing scene (11 minutes). The recording, made in the Dresden Lukaskirche, is too closely balanced and unatmospheric.

Mazeppa (complete).
*** DG (IMS) Dig. 439 906-2 (3) [id.]. Leiferkus, Gorchakova, Larin, Kotscherga, Dyadkova, Stockholm Royal Op. Ch., Gothenburg SO, Neeme Järvi.

Full of magnificent music, *Mazeppa* – dating from 1884, five years after *Eugene Onegin* – has been sadly neglected on disc. Apart from a Russian set, briefly available, this is the first complete recording of the opera, and it satisfyingly fills an important gap with a performance thrillingly sung and vividly conducted. Sergei Leiferkus sings the title-role superbly, with his very Russian-sounding tone a little grainy and tight in the throat, and entirely apt for the character. There is no flaw either among the other principals. Sergei Larin, in what might seem the token tenor part of Andrey, sings with such rich, heroic tone and keen intensity that the character springs to life. Equally, the magnificent, firm-toned bass, Anatoly Kotscherga, father of the heroine, Maria, confirms the high impressions he created in his Boris recording with Abbado. As Maria, Galina Gorchakova also emerges as one of the latter-day stars among Russian singers, with her rich mezzo gloriously caught, even if the final lullaby for her dead lover, Andrei, could be more poignant. Järvi draws electric playing from the Gothenburg orchestra, not least in the fierce battle music which opens Act III. The only disappointment is that the opportunity was not taken of also recording the conventional finale to the opera which Tchaikovsky originally wrote.

The Queen of Spades (Pique Dame) (complete).
*** Ph. Dig. 438 141-2 (3) [id.]. Grigorian, Putilin, Chernov, Solodovnikov, Arkhipova, Gulegina, Borodina, Kirov Op. Ch. & O, Gergiev.
**(*) Sony Dig. S3K 45720 (3) [id.]. Dilova, Evstatieva, Toczyska, Konsulov, Ochman, Masurok, Bulgarian Nat. Ch., Sofia Festival O, Tchakarov.

When each new recording of this opera for many years has been flawed, it is good that Gergiev and his talented team from the Kirov Opera in St Petersburg have produced a winner. The very opening, refined and purposeful, sets the pattern, with Gergiev controlling this episodic work with fine concern for atmosphere and dramatic impact, unafraid of extreme speeds and telling pauses. Though the engineers fail to give a supernatural aura to the voice of the Countess when she returns as a ghost, the recorded sound is consistently warm and clear. It is good to have the veteran Irina Arkhipova singing powerfully and bitingly in that key role, while the other international star, Olga Borodina, is unforgettable as Pauline, singing gloriously with keen temperament. Otherwise Gergiev's chosen team offers characterful Slavonic voices that are yet well focused and unstrained, specially important with the tenor hero, Herman, here dashingly sung by Gegam Grigorian. As the heroine, Lisa, Maria Gulegina sings with warm tone and well-controlled vibrato, slightly edgy under pressure.

Tchakarov in his Sony series of Russian operas conducts a fresh, expressive and alert account of *Queen of Spades*, very well recorded. Wieslaw Ochman makes an impressive Herman, amply powerful and only occasionally rough. Yuri Masurok is a superb Yeletsky, and the duet of Lisa and her companion, Pauline, is beautifully done by Stefka Evstatieva and Stefania Toczyska, one of Tchaikovsky's most magical inspirations. As the old Countess, Penka Dilova has a characteristically fruity Slavonic mezzo, very much in character, if with a heavy vibrato. The Countess's famous solo is taken very slowly indeed but is superbly sustained. Ensembles and chorus work are excellent, timed with theatrical point.

Yolanta (complete).
*** Ph. Dig. 442 796-2 (2) [id.]. Gorchakova, Alexashkin, Hvorostovsky, Grigorian, Kirov Op. Ch. & O, Gergiev.
(M) **(*) Erato/Warner Dig. 2292 45973-2 (2) [id.]. Vishnevskaya, Nicolai Gedda, Groenroos, Petkov, Krause, Cortez, Tania Gedda, Anderson, Dumont, Groupe Vocale de France, O de Paris, Rostropovich.

Gergiev and his outstanding Kirov team give a warm, idiomatic reading of Tchaikovsky's charming fairy-tale opera of the blind princess. Bringing out the atmospheric beauty of the score, it completely outshines the existing Rostropovich version on Erato, where, quite apart from incidental flaws, Galina Vishnevskaya sounds far too mature for a young princess. Here, by contrast, Galina Gorchakova gives the most moving portrait of the heroine, tender and vulnerable, with words delicately touched in. As Vaudémont, the knight who falls in love with her, Gegam Grigorian sings with rather tight, very Russian tenor-tone, not always pleasing but with a fine feeling for the idiom and a natural ease in high tessitura. Dmitri Hvorostovsky sings nobly and heroically as Robert, his more vigorous friend and rival, while Sergei Alexashkin sings with dark, grainy – again very Russian – tone as King René, Iolanta's father. Above all, the exchanges between characters consistently convey the feeling of stage-experience. The recording, not ideally clear but well balanced, was made in the theatre but under studio conditions. The first disc, containing three-quarters of the music, takes the story to the end of the long Iolanta/Vaudémont duet.

The Erato performance offered here was recorded at a live concert performance in the Salle Pleyel in December 1984, with excellent, spacious sound. Rostropovich's performance has a natural expressive warmth to make one tolerant of vocal shortcomings. Though Vishnevskaya is far too mature for the role of a sweet young princess, she does wonders in softening her hardness of tone, bringing fine detail of characterization. Gedda equally by nature sounds too old for his role, but again the artistry is compelling and ugly sounds are few. More questionable is the casting of Dimiter Petkov as the King, far too wobbly as recorded. Now reissued on a pair of mid-priced CDs, this is still well worth exploring.

Arias from: *The Enchantress; Eugene Onegin; Iolantha; Mazeppa; The Queen of Spades*.
*** Ph. (IMS) Dig. 426 740-2. Dmitri Hvorostovsky, Rotterdam PO, Gergiev – VERDI: *Arias*. ***

Hvorostovsky presents an eager, volatile Onegin, a passionate Yeletski in *Queen of Spades* and an exuberant Robert in *Iolantha*. One can only hope that he will be guided well, to develop such a glorious instrument naturally, without strain.

Tcherepnin, Alexander (1899–1977)

Le Pavillon d'Armide (ballet; complete).
**(*) Marco Polo Dig. 8.223779 [id.]. Moscow SO, Henry Shek.

Le Pavillon d'Armide was the ballet with which Diaghilev opened his first *Ballets russes* season introducing Nijinsky. Its invention is fluent, owing much to Tcherepnin's teacher, Rimsky-Korsakov, and to Tchaikovsky. It is not as atmospheric or as interesting as *Le Royaume enchanté*, which Pletnev has recorded with the Russian National Orchestra, nor is it as well played. It runs to well over an hour and the inspiration is uneven. At its best, though, it has real charm, and the scoring is always full of colour. It is very well recorded.

Symphony No. 4, Op. 91; Romantic overture, Op. 67; Russian dances, Op. 50; Suite for orchestra, Op. 87.
*** Marco Polo Dig. 8.223380 [id.]. Czech-Slovak State PO (Košice), Wing-Sie Yip.

The *Fourth Symphony* is among Alexander Tcherepnin's finest works. Written in the mid-1950s, it is colourful and tautly compact, neoclassical in idiom, very well organized and full of lively and imaginative musical invention. The *Suite*, Op. 67, is less individual and in places recalls the Stravinsky of *Petrushka* and *Le chant du rossignol*. Like the much earlier *Russian dances*, it is uneven in quality but far from unattractive. The *Romantic overture* was composed in wartime Paris when taxis and private cars were forbidden and there was a return to horse-drawn traffic, which reminded Tcherepnin of his childhood in St Petersburg. Generally good performances, decently recorded too under the young Chinese conductor, Wing-Sie Yip, who draws a lively response from her players.

Tcherepnin, Nikolai (1873–1945)

Narcisse et Echo, Op. 40.

(N) *** Chandos Dig. CHAN 9670 [id.]. Hague Chamber Ch., & Residentie O, Rozhdestvensky.

When Diaghilev opened his first season of the Ballets Russes in Paris in 1909, his conductor was Nikolai Tcherepnin, who conducted his *Le Pavilion d'Armide*. Two years later, Tcherepnin, teacher of Prokofiev and father of Alexander Tcherepnin, composed this endearing and atmospheric choral ballet, *Narcisse et Echo*, for the company's season in Monte Carlo. Diaghilev then mounted it in Paris only a year before Ravel's *Daphnis et Chloë*. For much of the time it sounds more French than Russian, with fascinating anticipations of *Daphnis*, not least in obbligato choral passages. Other sections mirror what the young Stravinsky was writing, but toned down. There also is a lot of Rimsky-Korsakov in it, and if you respond to that Russian master as well as Scriabin and Ravel, you will like this. It is somewhat static and in the last part of the ballet Narcissus is simply absorbed in gazing at his own reflection. However, though it is emphatically not great music, there is much that enchants. Rozhdestvensky is the ideal advocate, helped by ripe Chandos sound.

La Princesse lointaine; Le royaume enchanté.

*** DG Dig. 447 084-2 [id.]. Russian Nat. O, Mikhail Pletnev – LIADOV: *Baba-Yaga* etc; RIMSKY-KORSAKOV: *Suite: Le Coq d'or*. ***

Like Liadov, Nikolai Tcherepnin was a pupil of Rimsky-Korsakov, whose opera, *Le Coq d'or*, he introduced to Parisian audiences. He was Diaghilev's conductor for the latter's very first Paris season, and he taught conducting for a time and numbered Prokofiev among his pupils. The two pieces recorded here inhabit the same world as Rimsky, and *Le royaume enchanté* ('The enchanted kingdom'), which gives its name to the whole record, blends his master's voice with that of French impressionism. It is based on the same fairy-tale as *Firebird*, and is prefaced by the words: 'A spellbound calm binds the kingdom of Kashchei.' It is quite magical, highly atmospheric and well worth resurrecting. It enjoys the most persuasive advocacy from Pletnev and the Russian National Orchestra, and good recording.

Teixeira, António (1707–after 1759)

Motet: *Gaudate, astra.*

(M) *** DG Codex 453 182-2. Jennifer Smith, Fernando Serafim, Calabrese, Ferreira, De Macedo, Fernandes – ALMEIDA: *Beatus vir* etc.; CARVALHO: *Te Deum*. SEIXAS: *Adebat Vincentius* etc. ***

Teixeira's non-liturgical, Italianate motet, *Rejoice, stars, rejoice*, alternates tenor recitative with a pair of delightful soprano arias, gracefully and – in the case of the second – brilliantly sung by Jennifer Smith. The continuo support here is excellent, and the recording is fresh and pleasing. Most enjoyable.

Te Deum.

*** Collins Dig. 1359-2 [id.]. The Sixteen Ch. & O, Christophers.

Here is another remarkable Portuguese composer who, courtesy of his king (João V), like his contemporary, Almeida – see above – was sent to study in Rome for a decade (only ten years old when he arrived). He returned in due course and in 1734 produced this spectacular work for diverse soloists, five choirs and a large orchestra, here involving the usual forces of The Sixteen augmented, with no lack of choral spectacle. For the most part Teixeira's invention matches his ambitious canvas, and like Handel's oratorios, the result lies somewhere between opera and oratorio. The soloists too respond to the challenge, to produce an aural feast. The recording is suitably spacious and wide-ranging.

Telemann, Georg Philipp (1681–1767)

Alster (Overture) suite; La Bouffonne suite; Triple horn concerto in D; Grillen-Symphonie.

*** Chandos Dig. CHAN 0547 [id.]. Coll. Mus. 90, Standage.

This collection offers some of Telemann's most colourful and descriptive music, often quite bizarrely scored. The *Triple horn concerto* opens the programme with the hand-horns rasping boisterously. Then comes *La Bouffonne suite* with its elegant *Loure* and the extremely fetching *Rigaudon*, while the work ends with a touchingly delicate *Pastourelle*, beautifully played here. The *Grillen-Symphonie* ('Cricket symphony') brings a piquant dialogue between upper wind and double-basses in the first movement, while the second has unexpected accents and lives up to its name *Tändelnd* (Flirtatious). The horns (four of them) re-enter ambitiously at the colourful *Overture* of the *Alster suite*, add to the fun in the *Echo* movement, and help to simulate the Hamburg glockenspiel which follows. The entry of the Alster Shepherds brings a piquant drone effect, but best of all is the wailing *Concerto of frogs and crows*, with drooping bleats from the oboe and then the principal horn. Apart from the special effects, the suite also has one of the composer's most tenderly fragile slow movements for muted strings (*Der ruhende Pan*). Standage and his group make the very most of Telemann's remarkable orchestral palette and play with great vitality as well as finesse. This is one of the most entertaining Telemann collections in the catalogue, and it is splendidly recorded.

Concertos: for 2 chalumeaux in D min.; for flute in D; for 3 oboes, 3 violins in B flat; for recorder & flute in E min.; for trumpet in D; for trumpet & violin in D.
*** DG Dig. (IMS) 419 633-2 [id.]. Soloists, Col. Mus. Ant., Goebel.

As Reinhard Goebel points out, Telemann 'displayed immense audacity in the imaginative and ingenious mixing of the colours from the palette of the baroque orchestra', and these are heard to excellent effect here. Those who know the vital *B flat Concerto* for three oboes and violins, from earlier versions, will find the allegro very fast indeed and the slow movement quite thought-provoking. The chalumeau is the precursor of the clarinet, and the concerto for two chalumeaux recorded here is full of unexpected delights. Marvellously alive and accomplished playing, even if one occasionally tires of the bulges and nudges on the first beats of bars.

Concerto for 2 chalumeaux in D min.; Sonata for two chalumeaux in F; G; Viola concerto in G; Overture des Nations anciens et modernes in G; Völker Overture (Suite in B flat).
(N) *** Chandos Dig. CHAN 0593 [id.]. Lawson, Harris, Standage, Coll. Mus. 90.

Colin Lawson and Michael Harris with their 'liquid' timbres find a delicate charm in the two works for chalumeax and the *Sonata* has a rather touching *Grave*, which is played very serenely. Standage himself takes the solo part with distinction and pleasingly full timbre in the famous *Viola concerto*, and his characterization of the *Ancient and modern Overture* is alert and strong, finding dignity in *Les allemands* and not overdoing the closing parody lament for *Les vieilles femmes*. He is equally positive in the so-called *'Folk' Overture*, played vibrantly. Its last five movements each draw on a different culture – Turkish, Russian and so on – but with their rhythms given a Western overlay. This continuing Standage series, using period instruments, is proving to be the most rewarding of current Telemann recordings but it is a lapse of the usual Chandos standards that the documentation omits the TWV numbers.

Horn concerto in D; Double horn concerto in D; Triple horn concerto in D; Suite in F for 2 horns and strings; Tafelmusik, Book 3: *Double horn concerto in E flat.*
*** Ph. Dig. (IMS) 412 226-2 [id.]. Baumann, Timothy Brown, Hill, ASMF, Iona Brown.

The *E flat Concerto* comes from the third set of *Tafelmusik* (1733) and is the best-known of the four recorded here. The playing here and in the other concertos is pretty dazzling, not only from Hermann Baumann but also from his colleagues, Timothy Brown and Nicholas Hill. Mention should also be made of the concertante contributions from the two violinists. Telemann's invention rarely fails to hold the listener, and the recording has warm ambience and excellent clarity.

Oboe concertos: in C min.; D (Concerto gratioso); E; E flat; F; Oboe d'amore concerto in G.
*** Unicorn Dig. DKPCD 9128 [id.]. Sarah Francis, L. Harpsichord Ens.

Oboe concertos in C min.; D min.; F min.; Oboe d'amore concertos in E; E min.; (i) *Triple concerto for oboe d'amore, flute and viola d'amore.*
*** Unicorn Dig. DKPCD 9131 [id.]. Sarah Francis; (i) Graham Mayer, Elizabeth Watson; L. Harpsichord Ens.

Sarah Francis's survey of Telemann's *Oboe* and *Oboe d'amore concertos* brings modern-instrument performances, which are a model of style. The *G major Oboe d'amore concerto* on the first disc is most gracious (with colouring dark-timbred like a cor anglais in the *soave* first movement). The *Concerto gratioso*, too, is aptly named. The *C minor Oboe concerto* begins with a *Grave*, then the main Allegro brings a witty dialogue between soloist and violins, with the theme tossed backwards and forwards like a shuttlecock. But it is the works for oboe d'amore that are again so striking. Most imaginative of all is the *Triple concerto* with its sustained opening *Andante* (rather like a Handel aria) and *Siciliano* third movement with the melody alternating between oboe d'amore and viola d'amore, and nicely decorated by flute triplets. The performances are full of joy and sparkle as well as expressive. They are beautifully recorded and make a very good case for playing this repertoire on modern instruments.

Oboe concertos: in D min.; E min.; F min.
(M) *** Virgin Veritas/EMI (SIS) Dig. VER5 61152-2. Hans de Vries, Alma Musica Amsterdam, Bob van Asperen – ALBINONI: *Concertos from Op. 9.* ***

Hans de Vries is a very fine player and he produces an attractively full yet refined timbre from his baroque oboe (which dates from 1735). Apart from the stylishness of his phrasing, there are absolutely no intonation problems and the bravura articulation in the *moto perpetuo Allegro molto* second movement of the *E minor Concerto* is astonishingly clean. The authentic accompaniments are alert and stylish and not in the least vinegary. The solo balance seems excessively forward, but that may be partly the result of the acoustic, and the accompanying strings remain well in the picture.

Concerto in B flat for 3 oboes and 3 violins; Concerto in E for flute, oboe d'amore & viola d'amore. Tafelmusik, Part I: *Concerto in A for flute, violin and cello;* Part II: *Concerto in F for 3 violins.*

(N) *** Chandos Dig. CHAN 0580 [id.]. Soloists, Coll. Mus. 90, Standage.

Another splendid Standage collection. The Triple concertos are all among the composer's most colourful works and the period wind instruments here are piquant in their mixed colours, the strings lithe, yet not abrasive. The opening of the *E major Concerto* (which comes last in the programme) tickles the ear engagingly with its opening *Andante* and the third movement *Siciliano* is equally diverting. The lively opening movement of the *Tafelmusik triple violin concerto* momentarily recalls Handel's *Queen of Sheba*, and it has a particularly eloquent *Largo*. First-class playing and recording throughout. It is a pity that again the documentation (otherwise good) does not identify the works with TWV catalogue numbers.

Concerto for 3 oboes & 3 violins in B flat, TWV 44:43; (i) *Concerto for recorder, bassoon & strings in F; Concerto for 4 violins in G, TWV 40:201; Overture (Suite) in F for 2 horns, violins & continuo, TWV 44:7.*

(M) *** Teldec/Warner 0630 12320-2. VCM, Harnoncourt, (i) with Frans Brüggen, Otto Fleischmann.

Another outstanding Telemann disc. The five-movement Overture or Suite featuring a pair of horns shows the composer at his most characteristic (natural horns are used), and the performances are most persuasive. The oboes also sound splendidly in tune, not easy with the baroque instrument, and phrasing is alive and sensitive. Only the *Concerto for recorder and bassoon* lets the disc down a little; it is also not as well played as the others. The quality is good and the digital remastering has not tried to clarify artificially what is basically a resonant recording with inner detail mellowed by the ambience. One would not guess that it dates from 1966.

Recorder concerto in C; (i) *Double concerto for recorder and bassoon.*

*** BIS Dig. CD 271 [id.]. Pehrsson, (i) McGraw; Drottningholm Bar. Ens. – VIVALDI: *Concertos.* ***

Clas Pehrsson and Michael McGraw are most expert players, as indeed are their colleagues of the Drottningholm Baroque Ensemble; the recordings are well balanced and fresh.

Double concerto in F, for recorder, bassoon & strings; Double concerto in E min., for recorder, flute & strings; Suite in A min., for recorder & strings.

*** Ph. Dig. (IMS) 410 041-2. Petri, Bennett, Thunemann, ASMF, Iona Brown.

The *E minor Concerto* for recorder, flute and strings is a delightful piece and is beautifully managed, even though period-instrument addicts will doubtless find William Bennett's tone a little fruity. The playing throughout is most accomplished and the *Suite in A minor*, Telemann's only suite for treble recorder, comes off beautifully. The orchestral focus is not absolutely clean, though quite agreeable.

(i–iii) *Double concerto in E min. for recorder and transverse flute;* (iv) *Viola concerto in G;* (i; v) *Suite in A min. for flute and strings;* (iii) *Overture des Nations anciens et modernes in G.*

(M) *** Teldec/Warner 9031 77620-2 [id.]. (i) Frans Brüggen, (ii) Franz Vester, (iii) Amsterdam CO, André Rieu; (iv) Paul Doctor, Concerto Amsterdam, Brüggen; (v) SW German CO, Friedrich.

All these works show Telemann as an original and often inspired craftsman. His use of contrasting timbres in the *Double concerto* has considerable charm; the *Overture des Nations anciens et modernes* is slighter but is consistently and agreeably inventive, and the *Suite in A minor*, one of his best-known works, is worthy of Handel or Bach. Frans Brüggen and Franz Vester are expert soloists and Brüggen shows himself equally impressive on the conductor's podium accompanying Paul Doctor, the rich-timbred soloist in the engaging *Viola concerto*. The sixties sound, splendidly remastered, is still excellent, with fine body and presence.

Concerto in A min. for 3 treble recorders and strings; Paris quartet No.6 in E min.; Quadro in G min.; Sonata in F (Corellisierende); Trio sonata in B flat.

(N) **(*) Channel Classics Dig. CCS 5093 [id.]. Florilegium.

Instead of recording groups of categorized works, Florilegium often prefer to take a varied cross-section of a composer's output and create an ongoing concert. This works pleasingly here, with a fair amount of instrumental variety, and playing which is sensitive and vigorous by turns. If the well-known *Triple concerto in A minor* sounds more effective with a larger ripieno, the *Quadro* with its whirlwind *allegros* and memorable central *Adagio* is very successful as is the opening Corellian pastiche. The group are very well recorded but this is not one of their more memorable collections.

Trumpet concerto in D; (i) *Double trumpet concerto in E flat;* (ii) *2 Concertos in D for trumpet, 2 oboes & strings;* (i; iii) *Concerto in D for 3 trumpets & strings.*

*** Ph. Dig. 420 954-2 [id.]. Hardenberger, with (i) Laird; (ii) Nicklin, Miller; (iii) Houghton; ASMF, Iona Brown.

The effortless playing of Hardenberger in the highest register and his admirable sense of style dominate a concert where all the soloists are expert and well blended by the engineers. The concertos with oboes offer considerable variety of timbre and have fine slow movements; there is for instance an engaging *Poco andante* where the oboes are given an *Aria* to sing over a simple but effective continuo, given here to the bassoon (Graham Sheen). That same work is structured unusually in five movements, with two short *Grave* sections to provide pivots of repose. Telemann is always inventive and, with such excellent playing and recording, this can be recommended to anyone who enjoys regal trumpet timbre.

(i) *Viola concerto in G;* (ii) *Suite in A min. for recorder and strings; Tafelmusik,* Part 2: (iii) *Triple violin concerto in F;* Part 3: (iv) *Double horn concerto in E flat.*

✿ (BB) *** Naxos Dig. 8.550156; *4550156* [id.]. (i) Kyselak; (ii) Stivín; (iii) Hoelblingova, Hoelbling, Jablokov; (iv) Z. & B. Tylšar, Capella Istropolitana, Richard Edlinger.

The Rosette is awarded for enterprise and good planning, as well as good music-making. It is difficult to conceive of a better Telemann programme for anyone encountering this versatile composer for the first time and coming fresh to this repertoire, having bought the inexpensive Naxos CD on impulse. Ladislav Kyselak is a fine violist and is thoroughly at home in Telemann's splendid four-movement concerto; Jiři Stivín is an equally personable recorder soloist in the masterly *Suite in A minor*; his decoration is a special joy. The *Triple violin concerto* with its memorable *Vivace* finale and the *Double horn concerto* also show the finesse which these musicians readily display. Richard Edlinger provides polished and alert accompaniments throughout. The digital sound is first class.

Darmstadt overtures (suites), TWV 55/C6 (complete).

(M) *** Teldec/Warner 4509 93772-2 (2). VCM, Harnoncourt.

What strikes one with renewed force while listening to these once again is the sheer fertility and quality of invention that these works exhibit. This is music of unfailing intelligence and wit and, although Telemann rarely touches the depths of Bach, there is no lack of expressive eloquence either. The performances are light in touch and can be recommended with real enthusiasm. This would make an excellent start to any Telemann collection.

Overture (Suite) in B flat (La Bourse); Suites in C and G.

(M) *** Vanguard/Passacaille Dig. 99710 [id.]. Il Fondamento, Paul Dombrecht.

Paul Dombrecht and Il Fondamento follow up the success of their *Water music* coupling with characterful period-instrument performances of three more of Telemann's suites. Each is in its usual form: French overture followed by various dances, sometimes given epithets. The *C major Suite* (which comes last on this CD) is one of the most sprightly and its third number (*Les étudiants galliards*) is something of a hit. There is also a fine *Sarabande*, while the penultimate *Canaries* and closing *Air Italien* also have much charm. The *Overture in B flat* is also a suite of dances, and every number is given a sobriquet, such as the charming *Le repos interrompu*, *La guerre en la paix* and, more remarkably, *L'Espérance de Mississippi*. Its overall title, *La Bourse*, is associated with the ground floor of the composer's mansion, where he lived between 1712 and 1721, which at that time housed the Hamburg Stock Exchange. Excellent recording.

Tafelmusik (Productions 1–3) complete.

(M) *** Teldec/Warner 4509 95519-2 (4). Concerto Amsterdam, Frans Brüggen.

*** DG Dig. (IMS) 427 619-2 (4). Col. Mus. Ant., Reinhard Goebel.

Brüggen's Teldec set was made in the mid-1960s. The playing is very good indeed, and the recorded quality, like so many of these Das Alte Werk reissues, is first rate, with the usual proviso that the balance is forward, reducing the range of dynamic. The solo playing is expert (Hermann Baumann and Adriaan van Woudenberg are the impressive horn players in the *Double concerto* in the Third Book). The performances have vitality throughout, the sound is full yet has a spicing of astringency, and this mid-priced reissue compares very favourably with the premium-priced sets.

The playing of the Musiqua Antiqua is distinguished by dazzling virtuosity and unanimity of ensemble and musical thinking. They also have the advantage of very vivid and fresh recording quality; the balance is close and present without being too forward and there is a pleasing acoustic ambience.

Tafelmusik, Production 3: *Overture in B flat; Quartet in E min.;* Production 2: *Concerto in F; Trio sonata in E flat; Solo (Violin) sonata in A; Conclusion in B flat.*

*** DG Dig. (IMS) 429 774-2 [id.] (from above set, directed Goebel).

For those not wanting a complete set, this arbitrary but well-chosen 75-minute selection may prove useful. The recording is faithful, though the edginess of Goebel's violin timbre will not suit all tastes.

Water music (Hamburger Ebb' und Fluth).

(M) *** Van./Passacaille Dig. 99713 [id.]. Il Fondamento, Paul Dombrecht – HANDEL: *Water music.* ***

(N) *** Hyperion Dig. CDA 66967 [id.]. King's Cons., Robert King – HANDEL: *Water music.* ***

Telemann's *Water music* is rightly one of his most popular works, and it is good to have a thoroughly recommendable period-instrument performance available at mid-price and aptly coupled with Handel. The playing is of a high standard and the reed instruments of Il Fondamento are characterful. Telemann's invention never fails him, not only in the lively numbers but also in the expressive writing: the Loure (*Der Verliebte Neptunes*) is most memorable. But most striking of all is the Gigue entitled *Ebbe und Fluth*, which ingeniously suggests the shifting currents of the Alster. The recording is excellent.

The King's Consort performance is comparably enjoyable. There is exhilarating playing from the oboes in the Overture and the following Sarabande (with recorders) is seductive, as is the later Minuet (*Der angeneheme Zephir*). In short this is excellent in every way and like the Vanguard disc, which we prefer by the smallest margin, similarly coupled with the *Water music* of Handel.

CHAMBER MUSIC

Essercizii musicale: Trio sonata in C min. for recorder, oboe and continuo, TWV 42:c2. Der getreue Musik-Meister: Sonata for recorder and violino piccolo, TWV 40:111. Quartets: in A min. for recorder, oboe, violin and continuo, TWV 43:a3; in G for recorder, oboe, violin and continuo, TWV 43:g6; in G min. for recorder, two violins and continuo, TWV 43:g3; in G min. for recorder, violin, viola and continuo, TWV 43:g4; Trio Sonatas: in A min. for recorder, violin and continuo, TWV 42:a1; in A min. for recorder, violin and continuo, TWV 42:a4; in A min. for recorder, oboe and continuo, TWV 42:a6; in C for recorder, pardessus de viole and continuo, TWV 42:c2; in C min. for recorder, oboe and continuo, TWV 42:c7; in D min. for recorder, pardessus de viole and continuo, TWV 42:d7; in D min. for recorder, violin and continuo, TWV 42:d10; in E min. for recorder, oboe and continuo, TWV 42:e6; in F for recorder, pardessus de viole and continuo, TGWV 42:f6; in F for recorder, violin and continuo, TWV 42:f8; in F for recorder, oboe & continuo, TWV 42:f9; in F for recorder, oboe and continuo, TWV 42:f15; in F min. for recorder, violin and continuo, TWV 42:f2; in G min. for recorder, pardessus de viole and continuo, TWV 42:g9.

(M) *** Teldec/Warner 4509 97455-2 (3). Kees Boeke, Walter van Hauwe, Hans de Vries, Alice Harnoncourt, Anita Mitterer, Woulter Möller, Bob van Asperen.

There is a great deal of music here, lasting for nearly three hours, but Telemann admirers will find nearly all of it fascinating. The works are cunningly selected to show the composer at his most inventive. As can be seen, there is considerable variety of texture, and within that there is a fair variety of style. Performances are expressive and lively and there is much unostentatious virtuosity; the demands of scholarship and authenticity do not inhibit the music-making. As with most Das Alte Werk reissues from the 1970s, the sound is closely balanced, which reduces the range of dynamic, although the playing itself is expert and has plenty of light and shade. As an ideal sampler, on the second disc there is an intriguing *Sonata for recorder and violino piccolo* (from *Der getreue Musik-Meister*) and the *Trio sonata* (for recorder, oboe and continuo), followed by two *Quartets*, all showing the composer at his finest.

12 Fantasias for unaccompanied violin (complete).

(M) *** Maya Dig. MCD 9302 [id.]. Maya Homburger.

Telemann's *12 Fantasias* for solo violin are a decade later than Bach's *Partitas* and *Sonatas,* and they are less ambitious and less demanding. Each is in either three or four movements, usually opening with a *Largo* or *Grave*, alternating with *Allegros*. With striking invention, they make very enjoyable listening, especially when played with such life and style. Maya Homburger uses a baroque violin and has joined in recordings with the Academy of Ancient Music, English Baroque Soloists and the English Concert. This is cheerful music and it would be difficult to imagine these works being played more freshly or with a more sensitive espressivo. Homburger is recorded most naturally against a warm but not too resonant acoustic, and there is not a trace of vinegar in her timbre.

6 Flute quartets or Trios (Hamburg, 1733). *Der Getreu Musikmeister: Cello sonata* (for cello and continuo) *in D.*

(N) **(*) Lyrichord Dig. LEMS 8028 [id.]. Mélomanie.

Telemann himself published his *Six Quatuors ou Trios*, ensuring their success by making them available for performance on various alternative combinations of flutes, violins, bassoon and cello, with a flexible continuo. This is their first complete recording. The collection divides into two groups. The first three works are three- or four-movement sonatas in an elegant conversational style; the last three each open with a slow movement followed by three unpredictable 'Divertimenti', showing the composer imaginatively trying out different dance forms. The four-movement *Cello sonata* offered as bonus also shows the composer at his best. It is very well played, as are the Quartets (favouring two period flutes – not always absolutely immaculate in tuning – cello and harpsichord).

Flute quartets, Book 4 (Paris c.1752): Sonatas Nos. 1–6.

(N) **(*) Globe Dig. GLO 5146 [id.]. Hazelzet, Stuurop, Wim tem Have, Ogg, Scheifes.

Although they are listed in the *New Grove*, there is some doubt about the authenticity of these simple, four-movement works, which the composer designated as *Sonatas*. They are not trivial, but pleasingly inventive, with a charming simplicity. If they are Telemann's, he probably wrote them earlier than the published date. Wilbert Hazelzet uses a modern copy of a mid-eighteenth-century flute, and his nimble playing, with immaculate tuning, and decorative flourishes (never overdone) readily tweak the ear. His supporting group provide a somewhat insubstantial (though not edgy) backing, but the solo playing is so adept and full of personality that one accepts Hazelzet's ready domination of the proceedings.

12 Paris (Flute) quartets: Nos. 1–6 (Hamburg, 1730); 7–12 (Nouveaux quatuors en six suites) (1738) (complete).

(N) *** Sony Vivarte Dig. S3K 63115 (3) [id.]. Barthold, Sigiswald and Wieland Kuijken, Gustav Leondardt.

In 1730 Telemann published in Hamburg a set of six quartets for violin, flauto traverso, viola da gamba and bass continuo, and these were sufficiently popular to be pirated by the French publishing house, Le Clerk, and reprinted in 1736 – without the composer's permission. Telemann learned by this experience: during a long and fruitful visit to Paris in 1737/8, by virtue of a Privilège du Roi, he was able himself to publish a new and even finer set, which he called *Nouveaux quatuors*. Here the invention, felicitous enough in the earlier works, is even more diverting, with the six-movement format giving greater variety of style and expression. The complete set by the Kuijken group is thoroughly recommendable, the playing always sympathetic, consistently fresh, alert, and sunny: these period instruments all emerge with pleasing countenance. The digital recording is beautifully clear and immediate within a most agreeable ambience.

(i) *6 Paris quartets (Nouveaux quatuors en six suites)* (1738): *Nos. 1 in D min.; 2 in A min.; 3 in G; 4 in B min.; 5 in A; 6 in E min.;* (ii) (Orchestral) *Suites: in E flat (La Lyra) for strings;* (iii) *in F for solo violin, 2 flutes, 2 oboes, 2 horns, strings & timpani.*

(M) *** Teldec/Warner 4509 92177-2 (2) [id.]. (i) Quadro Amsterdam (Frans Brüggen, Jaap Schröder, Anner Bylsma, Gustav Leonhardt); (ii) Concerto Amsterdam, Frans Brüggen; (iii) with Schröder.

These performances are of such virtuosity that they silence criticism, and Frans Brüggen in particular dazzles the listener. The recording too is first class, and the CD transfer is immaculate. To fill out the second CD, there are two orchestral suites. The *Suite in F* is the more ambitious and probably dates from the beginning of the 1730s; the autograph score was found in Dresden, and this was almost certainly one of the works '*per molti strumenti*' written (and not only by Telemann), for the local orchestra, so famous at the time. The *La Lyra Suite in E flat major* is much earlier, but its invention is hardly less resourceful and in the third movement, *La Vielle*, Telemann gives an imitation of a hurdy-gurdy.

Paris quartets (1730): Nos. 2, Concerto secondo in D; 3, Sonata prima in A; 4, Sonata seconda in G min.; 5, Première suite in E min. Fantasias: Nos. 5 in A for (solo) *violin; Nos. 7 in D for* (solo) *flute; 8 in G min. for harpsichord.*

(N) *** Channel Classics Dig. CCS 13598 [id.]. Florilegium.

Instead of providing a set, Florilegium have chosen four of the earlier quartets and set them in the context of a concert, interspersed with solo *Fantasias*. They play with affectionate warmth, readily bringing out shades of melancholy in slow movements, to contrast with the busy allegros, played with real virtuosity, with the tone of Ashley Solomon's period flute particularly enticing. But the timbre and clean articulation of the two string players, Rachel Podger (violin) and Daniel Yeadon (viola da gamba), are hardly less appealing, and the overall blend of tone in a warm but intimate acoustic could not be more attractive. These players convey a deeper expressive feeling than the Kuijkens.

Quadros (Quartets): in A min. for recorder, oboe, violin and continuo, TWV 43:a3; in G, for recorder, oboe, violin and continuo, TWV 43:g6; in G min. for oboe, violin, viola da gamba and continuo, TWV43:g92; in G min. for recorder, violin, viola da gamba, and continuo, TWV43:g94. Essercizii musici: Trio sonatas: in C min. for recorder, oboe and continuo, TWV 42:c2; in F for recorder, viola da gamba and continuo, TWV 42:f3. Trio sonata in D min. for recorder, violin and continuo, TWV 42:d10.

(N) *** Globe Dig. GLO 5154 [id.]. Ens. Senario.

These *Quadros* (or Quartets) are among Telemann's very finest chamber music, every bit as inventive and diverting as the more famous *Paris* quartets. Telemann writes parts of equal interest for all three of his solo instruments, and provides slow movements of considerable expressive intensity, framed by winningly virtuosic allegros. Perhaps finest of all is the *G major Quartet*, with its solemn central *Grave*, but the *G minor Quartet* (TWV 43:g94) which opens the programme, is hardly less seductive. Telemann subtitles the *A minor* work '*Concerto*', and indeed there is plenty of opportunity for virtuoso display here, and its four movements also include a pair of touching *Adagios*. The *Trio sonatas*, slighter in texture, are also very enjoyable when presented so freshly. Indeed the performances here could hardly be bettered. The brilliant recorder playing of Saskia Coolen, is well matched by the oboeist, Peter Frankenberg, and the group overall integrates splendidly. The balance and recording could hardly be improved on. This is one of the most delightful Telemann collections in the catalogue.

Sonatas Corellisante Nos.1–6; Canonic duos Nos. 1–4.
(N) ** Chandos Dig. CHAN 0549 [id.]. Standage, Comberti, Coe, Parle, Collegium Musicum 90.

The six (Trio) *Sonatas Corellisante* of 1735 are not transcriptions, as might be first expected, but original works 'in the Italian style', although it is essentially an overlay rather than intrinsic to Telemann's invention. Frankly this is too often routine, and fails to either sparkle or have the sunshine sonority of the real thing. Perhaps it might sound better on the fuller sound of modern instruments. These performances here are alert, but hardly beguiling, and the simpler *Canonic duos*, which are played with sprightly vivacity, completely upstage them.

Sonatas for two recorders Nos. 1–6; Duetto in B flat.
*** BIS Dig. CD 334 [id.]. Clas Pehrsson, Dan Laurin.

Canon sonatas Nos. 1–6; Duettos Nos. 1–6.
*** BIS Dig. CD 335 [id.]. Clas Pehrsson, Dan Laurin.

All the *Duet sonatas* are in four movements, the second being a fugue; the *Canon sonatas* are for two flutes, violins or bass viols. Needless to say, listening to two recorders for longer than one piece at a time imposes a strain on one's powers of endurance, however expert the playing – and expert it certainly is. The BIS versions can be recommended. However, although it is good to have the two treble recorders blending so well together, a clearer degree of separation would have helped in the imitative writing.

Sonatas for 2 flutes, TW 40: 130–35.
**(*) Lyrichord Dig. LEMS 8019 [id.]. Kimberley Reighley, Tom Moore.

Telemann wrote four sets of sonatas for two flutes, all designed for amateurs to play and enjoy, for they do not make too many bravura demands. However, this fourth series (which remained unpublished but which probably dates from the end of the 1730s or the beginning of the 1740s) uses keys which were more difficult for the one-keyed flute of that time, so these works were clearly aimed at players with fair performance skills. They are each in four movements, and the slow movement is usually marked *Dolce* or *Amoroso*. They are well presented here on period instruments although, amiable as it is, this is music to take in small doses.

Sonata Metodiche Nos. 1–6 (1728); *7–12* (1732).
*** Accent Dig. ACC 94104/5D (2) [id.]. Barthold and Wieland Kuijken, Roberts Kohnen.

Telemann's *Methodical sonatas* were written in two sets of six, the first designated 'for violin or flute', the second 'for flute or violin', which is a curious alternation of emphases, the more so as the second set sometimes uses keys which are less comfortable for the baroque flute. Not that this is apparent in these expert performances, lively and expressive by turns. All the sonatas of the first set are in four movements; four out of the second six add a fifth, and there is plenty of variety in the music itself. One of the purposes of these sonatas was to instruct amateurs in the art of ornamentation, so Telemann wrote out ornaments in the French style for each first movement, while mixing French and Italian styles in the writing itself. A worthwhile addition to the catalogue, very well recorded, though these are not works to be heard all at one go!

6 Trio Sonatas in the Italian style (Sonates en Trios dans le Goût Italien) TWV 42: g3; c1; a2; d2; e1; d4; Trio sonata in G, TWV 42: g12.
(N) *** Lyrichord Dig. LEMS 8035 [id.]. Tom Moore, David Myford, Donna Fournier, Janet Palumbo.

Telemann had altogether greater success with his *Trio Sonatas in the Italian style* than with his Corelli imitations. The basic set of six was published in Paris (between 1731 and 1733) from a stolen manuscript, and the seventh work (g3 and g12 are interchangeable) comes from a manuscript preserved in Darmstadt. They are pleasingly lightweight sunny works, played here with the second part authentically given to the violin rather than a flute. The *C minor* and *A major* works are particularly attractive, but the standard of invention is high, and particularly striking in the minor-key works. They are most felicitously played by this very musical period-instrument group, who know all about elegance, and very well balanced. Tom Moore's baroque flute has a most agreeably watery timbre that is wholly authentic.

VOCAL MUSIC

Cantatas for the first Sunday of Advent: Saget den verzagten Herzen, TWV 1:1233; Saget der Tochter Zion, TWV 1: 1235. Cantatas for the first day of Christmas: Auf Zion! Und lass in geheilgten Hallen, TWV 1: 109; Kündlich gross ist das Gottselige Geheimnis, TWV 1: 1020.
(N) *** CPO Dig. CPO 999 515-2 [id.]. Mields, Schwarz, Jochens, Schmidt, Magdeburg Chamber Ch., Michaelstein Telemann CO, Ludger Rémy.

This is marginally the finest of Rémy's series of Telemann's festive cantatas so far. Their date of composition is uncertain but they show Telemann in full flight of inspiration. The layout is similar to the cantatas of Bach, usually opening with a sinfonia, followed by a series of arias – often with wind obbligati – and a closing chorale; the accompaniments are deftly scored. The opening of *Saget den verzagten Herzen* brings a splendid interchange between soloists and chorus, and the following alto aria (marked *Affettuoso*) – *So komm den auch* – is touchingly eloquent, while the bass and tenor soloists both have lively arias to follow. The bravura bass aria, *Zerstreuet euch*, which opens *Saget de Tochter Zion*, has even more brilliant trumpet parts and the opening bass aria of *Auf, Zion*, decorated with flutes, is equally memorable. The Christmas story is then told in a series of brief recitatives and choruses, much more atmospheric and dramatic than the so-called 'Christmas oratorio' below. The second of the two Christmas Day cantatas, *Kündlich gross ist das Gottselige Geheimnis* is even more dramatic and has a remarkable soprano aria punctuated by trumpets and drums. The alto air *Göttlich Kind* is a Handelian alto and trumpet duet, and the trumpets stay for the bass aria. Rémy directs with flair, and with strikingly good male soloists, fine choral singing and first-rate playing from his period-instrument accompanying group, this is well worth seeking out. The documentation (as throughout the series) is impeccable, including full translations.

Christmas oratorio: Die Hirten on der Krippe zu Bethlehem, TWV 1:797; Christmas cantatas: Siehe, ich verkündige Euc (1761), TWV 1:1334; Der Herr hat offenbaret (1762): TWV 1: 262.

(N) **(*) CPO Dig. CPO 999 419-2 [id.]. Backes, George, Post, Mertens, Michaelstein Chamber Ch. & Telemann CO, Ludger Rémy.

Telemann composed his two-part so-called '*Christmas oratorio'* in his late 70s and the two Christmas cantatas in his early 80s. The oratorio opens with the chorale we know as '*In dulci jubilo'*, fully scored with trumpets, to the words, *O Jesu parvule* – and is simply structured and comparatively unambitious, with the chorus interleaving the arias with chorales. Flutes and trumpets are used to decorate the pastoral scenes. There is a fine bass aria welcoming the shepherds. But the cantatas are much more ambitious. The 1761 work opens arrestingly with a brilliant soprano aria when the angel sings those famous words '*Behold I bring you glad tidings'* with trumpets blazing, and she is answered dramatically by the choral heavenly host who return to praise God after fine contributions from both the tenor and bass. The 1762 cantata opens and closes with a chorus, and the following arias for soprano and bass (again using trumpets and futes) are both rather fine. Fortunately the soloists here are again excellent and if the conductor of the small period-instrument ensemble is at times rhythmically a bit emphatic in the oratorio, he keeps the music alive and flowing. The recording is excellent.

Cornett cantatas: *Cantata for the 2nd Sunday after Epiphany: Sehet an die Exempel der Alten, TWV 1: 1259; Cantata for Exaudi Sunday Ich halte aber dafür, TWV 1: 840; Cantata for Rogation Sunday: Erhöre mich, wenn ich rufe, TWV 1: 459.*

(N) *** CPO Dig. CPO 999 542-2 [id.]. Spägele, Vass, Jochens, Mertens, Leipzig Bläser Collegium, Michaelstein Telemann CO, Ludger Rémy.

These three cantatas (from 1717 and 1720/21) are remarkable for their orchestration which includes not only cornettino but three trombones, two oboes and strings, although a normal continuo is used for the recitatives. The rich textures Telemann creates are very much his own, not like Gabrieli, rather nearer to Schütz. In consequence he does not demand a chorus, and the chorales are sung by the soloists, never more effectively than at the end of *Epiphany cantata*, following a fine soprano aria. Telemann uses his colourful ripieno imaginatively throughout, and especially so in the *Rogation cantata* which is shared by tenor and bass. Wilfried Jochens and Klaus Mertens are in splendid form, and make the most of all their opportunities, especially their fine penultimate duet, richly embroidered by the brass and wind, *Herr, auf dein Wort verlass ich mich*, which is again followed by the closing chorale. The *cantata for Exaudi Sunday* opens with a spectacular polyphonic interplay, shared by singers and orchestra, and after an alto recitative the cornetti decorate the bass aria, while oboes are used later for the alto solo, and the work closes with a serene Martin Luther hymn. If the invention in these works is less dramatic than in the *Advent* and *Christmas cantatas*, many of the individual numbers are lyrically very persuasive, especially when they are so well sung, and so musically accompanied by this strikingly well-balanced period instrument ensemble under the excellent Ludger Rémy.

Secular cantatas: (i) *Die Landlust;* (ii) *Der Schulmeister;* (i) *Von geliebten Augen*; (iii) *Suite in D for viola and strings, TWV 55:D 6.*

(N) (M) *** DHM/BMG 05472 77817-2 [id.]. (i) Elisabeth Speiser; (ii) Siegmund Nimsgern, Stuttgart Hymnus-Chorknaben; (iii) Johannes Koch, Coll. Aur.

It is good to have this splendid triptych of secular cantatas from the 1960s back in the catalogue, with an agreeable concertante orchestral suite thrown in for good measure. *Der Schulmeister* is most diverting, about a schoolmaster teaching his class to sing. Indeed it is one of those rare musical works to make you smile, when Nimsgern leads his schoolboy pupils up the scale near the very beginning of the work. In a rumbustious sparkling performance he goes completely over the top. The other two cantatas, charmingly sung by Elizabeth Speiser, are lyrical, *Die Landlust* a lighter, pastoral piece and *Von geliebten Augen* a darker, more expressive work; both are well worth exploring, when the accompaniments from the Collegium Aureum are very lively, and the sound fresh, full and clear.

(i) *St Mark Passion*; (ii) *Magnificats in C & G*.
(N) (B) **(*) Ph. Duo 462 293-2 (2). Giebel, Malaniuk, Altmeyer, Rehfuss, Lausanne Youth Ch., Munich Pro Arte O, Kurt Redel; with (i) Günter; (ii) Reuter-Wolf.

Telemann was as prolific in his vocal music as in his instrumental and orchestral works and this setting of the *St Mark Passion* is one of many. It is an expressive piece, but only in places does the writing show real individuality. This performance, however, is an outstandingly good one, with fresh intelligent solo singing and thoroughly committed and understanding direction from Kurt Redel. The two settings of the *Magnificat* – one in Latin, one in German – then make a fascinating contrast, the German work altogether gentler than the Latin setting. Telemann may not match Bach in sublimity of inspiration, but the vigour of his choral writing is very refreshing here. Strong, well-tuned performances except for some unsteadiness from contralto and bass soloists. All three recordings come from the early 1960s and still sound well.

Thomas, Ambroise (1811–96)

Overtures: *Mignon; Raymond*.
(M) *** Mercury (IMS) 434 321-2. Detroit SO, Paray – BIZET: *L'Arlésienne; Carmen: suites*. **(*)

These justly famous overtures are almost never heard in the concert hall nowadays. *Mignon*, opening with a delightful series of lyrical ideas on flute, clarinet and then horn, is matched by the ebullience of *Raymond*, perhaps more of a bandstand piece. The Detroit orchestra play both with wonderful finesse and Gallic spirit: this is repertoire which Paray directs incomparably, like his Auber overtures on the same label. The excellent (1960) recording was made in the Cass Technical High School Auditorium.

Hamlet (complete).
*** EMI (SIS) Dig. CDS7 54820-2 (3) [Ang. CDCC 54820]. Hampson, Anderson, Ramey, Graves, Kunde, Garino, Le Roux, Trempont, Amb. S., LPO, Antonio de Almeida.
(M) *** Decca Dig. (IMS) 433 857-2 (3). Milnes, Sutherland, Morris, Winbergh, Conrad, Tomlinson, WNO Ch. & O, Bonynge.

Thomas's *Hamlet* may be an unashamed travesty of Shakespeare, complete with happy ending (in its original form), but it remains a strong and enjoyable example of French opera of its period. So much was evident from Richard Bonynge's 1983 Decca set. If the EMI set is even more strikingly successful, it is not just that it provides an unusually full text – with the tragic, so-called Covent Garden ending and the ballet music in an appendix – but that Thomas Hampson gives such a commanding performance in the title-role. Hampson's superb, finely shaded singing goes with Shakespearean power in the acting, and the character emerges as a young hero, ardent but vulnerable, endlessly self-questioning. One no longer finds the aria, *Etre ou ne pas être*, sounding conventional or trivial, and consistently Hampson magnetizes the attention the moment he begins to sing. June Anderson is not so happily cast as Ophelia. The voice is inclined to sound too edgy, and she is hardly more successful at sounding girlish than Sutherland at the end of her career, hardly matching her older rival in the Act III ballad, but the singing is felt and expressive. The rest of the cast may not be as starry as that in the Decca version, but there is no serious weakness. Almeida is understanding, and the presentation of the full text, conveniently, with trivia consigned to the appendix, and with a recently discovered duet for Claudius and Gertrude as a bonus, makes it invaluable.

On the Decca set, Ophélie has priority vocally in brilliant and beautiful numbers, with Sutherland taking all the challenges commandingly. Ophelia's famous Mad scene was one of the finest of her early recordings, and here, 24 years later, she still gives a triumphant display, tender and gentle as well as brilliant in coloratura. The heroine's primacy is reinforced when the role of Hamlet is for baritone, here taken strongly if with some roughness by Sherrill Milnes. Outstanding among the others is Gösta Winbergh as Laërte (in French without the final 's'), heady and clear in the only major tenor role. John Tomlinson as Le Spectre sings the necessary monotones resonantly, James Morris is a gruff Claudius and Barbara Conrad a fruity Gertrude. The compelling success of the whole performance of a long, complex opera is sealed by Bonynge's vigorous and sympathetic conducting of first-rate Welsh National Opera forces, brilliantly and atmospherically recorded. The layout, with Act I on the first CD and the other four Acts, two apiece, on the other two, is ideal, and the documentation is good.

Mignon (complete).
(N) (M) *** Sony SM3K 34590 (3) [id.]. Marilyn Horne, Alain Vanzo, Ruth Welting, Nicola Zaccaria, Frederica von Stade, Claude Méloni, André Battedou, Paul Hudson, Ambrosian Op. Ch., Philh. O, de Almeida.

It was admirably enterprising of CBS, now Sony, to record Thomas's once-popular adaptation of

Goethe. As old record catalogues bear witness, it has many vocal plums, and here a very full account of the score is given, with virtually all the alternatives which the composer devised for productions after the first – not least one at Drury Lane in London where recitatives were used (as here) instead of spoken dialogue; an extra aria was given to the soubrette Philine and other arias were expanded. The role of Frédéric was given to a mezzo-soprano instead of a tenor, and here the appropriately named Frederica von Stade is superb in that role, making one rather regret that she was not chosen as the heroine. However, Marilyn Horne is in fine voice and sings with great character and flair, even if she hardly sounds the frail figure of the ideal Mignon. None the less, with Alain Vanzo a sensitive Wilhelm, Ruth Welting a charming Philine, and colourful conducting from Almeida, this is an essential set for lovers of French opera. The 1977 recording has a pleasingly warm ambience and the voices are naturally caught in the present transfer. There is occasionally just a touch of fierceness in fortissimos, but otherwise the sound is very good indeed. A full libretto and translation are included.

Thompson, Randall (1899–1984)

Symphony No. 2 in E min.

(N) (BB) **(*) Sony SMK 60594 [id.]. NYPO, Bernstein – DIAMOND: *Symphony No. 4*; HARRIS: *Symphony No. 3*. **(*)

(N) *** Chan. Dig. CHAN 9439 [id.]. Detroit SO, Neeme Järvi – CHADWICK: *Tam O'Shanter etc.* ***

Randall Thompson's *Second Symphony* (1931) enjoyed a good deal of exposure in the 1940s though it does not have the strongly distinctive personality of Harris or Piston. Leonard Bernstein's New York recording comes from 1968 and has great vitality and momentum to commend it. Despite its star rating, the performance rates higher than the Järvi – good though that is – for it has stronger character and drive. The sound is good, too, but not in the same street as the Chandos.

Neeme Järvi and the Detroit Orchestra give an eminently satisfying account, and have a finely detailed and luxurious recording. Those for whom sound is very important can safely invest in this, for the Chadwick coupling is well worth having.

Thomson, Virgil (1896–1989)

Film music: *Louisiana Story: Arcadian songs and dances and suite. The plow that Broke the Plains: suite. Power among Men: Fugues and Cantilenas.*

(N) **(*) Hyperion Dig. CDA 66576 [id.]. New L. O, Ronald Corp.

Apart from his opera *Four Saints in Three Acts* (available on two separate recordings in the USA), Virgil Thomson is best known for his film score to Flaherty's *Louisiana Story*. Here we are offered both the four-movement suite and a series of brief vignettes, curiously called *Arcadian songs and dances*, of which the first (*Sadness*) and last (*The squeeze box*) are the most striking. The *Fugues and Cantilenas* from *Power among Men* are also not what one might expect from the titles, but are atmospheric and imaginatively scored. All this music is quite appealing, even if only very occasionally does one feel it is first rate. The performances by Ronald Corp and the New London Orchestra, are deft, evocatively played, and well recorded. But at times one would have liked a stronger profile to the characterization.

Film scores: *The Plow that broke the Plains; The River* (suites).

(M) *** Van. 08.8013.71 [OVC 8013]. Symphony of the Air, Leopold Stokowski – STRAVINSKY: *Soldier's Tale*. ***

Virgil Thomson's orchestral music may be sub-Copland (he too uses cowboy tunes like *Old paint*), but in Stokowski's charismatic hands these two film scores emerge with colours glowing and their rhythmic, folksy geniality readily communicating. The recording is resonantly atmospheric, but vivid too. Most enjoyable, and with a worthwhile coupling. This is at upper mid-price in the USA.

Ticheli, Frank (born 1958)

Postcard; Radiant voices.

*** Koch Dig. 3-7250-2 [id.]. Pacific SO, Carl St Clair - CORIGLIANO: *Piano concerto*. ***

Frank Ticheli, composer-in-residence to this Pacific orchestra largely made up of musicians from film studios, here offers two warm, unproblematic works, ingeniously and wittily argued, full of engaging echoes of composers from Bartók and Copland to John Adams, with a flavouring of Walton in the jazz rhythms. First-rate performances and sound. An attractive coupling for the ambitious, similarly communicative *Piano concerto* of John Corigliano.

Tippett, Michael (1905–98)

Concerto for orchestra; (i) *Triple concerto.*

*** Chandos Dig. CHAN 9384-2 [id.]. (i) Levon Chilingirian, Simon Rowland-Jones, Philip de Groote; Bournemouth SO, Hickox.

Hickox's coupling of these two major orchestral works is a fine supplement to his set of the four Tippett symphonies, also with the Bournemouth orchestra, warmly recorded in well-focused sound. Levon Chilingirian makes a powerful leader for the trio of soloists, heightening the sharp contrasts of the elliptical argument in Tippett's late return to lyricism. The *Concerto for orchestra*, written in very much the same vein as the opera, *King Priam*, is presented with similar concentration and concern for lyrical warmth.

(i) *Concerto for double string orchestra;* (ii–iv) *Piano concerto;* (i) *Fantasia concertante on a theme of Corelli; Little music for strings;* (v; iv) *Praeludium for brass, bells and percussion; Suite for the birthday of Prince Charles;* (vi; iii–iv) *Triple concerto for violin, viola, cello and orchestra;* (vii) *The blue guitar* (sonata for solo guitar). Vocal music: (viii–ix) *Bonny at morn* (Northumbrian folksong for unison voices and 3 recorders); (viii) *A Child of our time: 5 Negro spirituals.* (viii; x) *Crown of the year* (cantata); (viii) *Dance, Clarion air* (madrigal); (xi) *Evening canticles;* (viii) *Music* (unison song); *Plebs Angelica* (motet for double choir); *The weeping Babe* (motet for soprano and choir). *The Midsummer Marriage:* (v; iv) *Ritual dances;* (xii) *Sosostris's aria.*

(BB) *** Nimbus Dig. NI 1759 (4) [id.]. (i) English String O, William Boughton; (ii) Martino Tirimo; (iii) BBC PO; (iv) cond. composer; (v) E. N. Philh. O; (vi) Ernest Kovacic, Gerard Causé, Alexander Baillie; (vii) Craig Ogden; (viii) Christ Church Cathedral Ch., Oxford (members), Stephen Darlington; (ix) Michael Copley, Maurice Hodges, Evelyn Nallen; (x) Medici Qt, with wind soloists, Martin Jones (piano) and percussion; (xi) St John's College, Cambridge, Ch., George Guest; (xii) Alfreda Hodgson.

This bargain collection of Tippett, issued to commemorate the composer's death in 1998, is specially valuable for containing two discs of recordings made by Tippett himself. When he did them, he was already in his late eighties, and the performance of the *Ritual dances* from *A Midsummer marriage* is not as incisive as most other versions, but the warmth of expressiveness and the sense of occasion conveyed are most compelling, the more so in Alfreda Hodgson's rich and resonant performance of Sorostris's aria from the same opera, even though the voice is backwardly balanced. It is good too to have Tippett offering a rare example of his occasional music in the uncomplicated *Prince Charles suite*. Even more valuable is the concerto disc, again more relaxed at more spacious speeds than rival versions, but with outstanding soloists revealing Tippett at his most warmly magnetic. Martino Tirimo is particularly impressive in the elaborate figuration of the *Piano concerto* which can easily sound empty. Broad speeds, well sustained, also mark William Boughton's readings of the string pieces on the fourth disc; the *Guitar sonata*, tautly played by Craig Ogden, and *Evening canticles* sung by the St John's College Choir under George Guest (for whom they were written) make a splendid supplement. The choral singing from Christ Church Cathedral Choir on the second disc is also excellent, with the school cantata, *The Crown of the year*, revealing the composer at his most open and least enigmatic. Warm, atmospheric sound, characteristic of Nimbus.

Concerto for double string orchestra; Divertimento on 'Sellinger's round'; Little music for strings; (i) *The Heart's assurance* (orch. Meirion Bowen).

**(*) Chandos Dig. CHAN 9409 [id.]. City of L. Sinf., Richard Hickox, (i) with John Mark Ainsley.

Hickox draws warm and energetic performances from his chamber orchestra, opulently recorded with fine definition. The first movement of the *Concerto* may lack a little in bite, but the slow movement is ravishing and the finale fizzes with energy. The bonus is the first recording of the song-cycle, *The Heart's assurance*, in the orchestration prepared by Meirion Bowen with the composer's express approval. What with piano accompaniment can seem a gritty, uncompromising piece here emerges with warmth and beauty, thanks also to the fine singing of John Mark Ainsley.

Concerto for double string orchestra; Fantasia concertante on a theme of Corelli; (i) *Songs for Dov.*

(M) *** Virgin/EMI Ultraviolet Dig. CUV5 61326-2. SCO, composer, (i) with Nigel Robson.

It is particularly valuable to have the *Concerto for double string orchestra*, which Tippett had never previously recorded himself. Interpreting his own youthful inspiration, the nonogenarian gives delightfully pointed readings of the outer movements, bringing out the jazzy implications of the cross-rhythms, not taking them too literally, while the lovely melody of the slow movement has never sounded more warmly expressive. The Scottish Chamber Orchestra plays with comparable passion in the *Fantasia concertante*, a related work from Tippett's middle period, while Nigel Robson is a wonderfully idiomatic and convincing tenor soloist in the difficult vocal lines of the three *Songs for Dov*. Warm, full recording.

Little music for string orchestra.

(M) **(*) Chandos Dig. CHAN 6576 [id.]. Soloists of Australia, Ronald Thomas – BLISS: *Checkmate*; RUBBRA: *Symphony No. 5.* ***

Tippett's *Little music* was written in 1946 for the Jacques Orchestra. Its contrapuntal style is stimulating but the music is more inconsequential than the *Concerto for double string orchestra*. It receives a good if not distinctive performance here, truthfully recorded.

(i) *The Rose lake.* (ii) *The Vision of St. Augustine.*
(N) ✿ *** Conifer Dig. 75605 51304-2 [id.].
LSO (i) Sir Colin Davis. (ii) with John SHirley Quirk, LSO Ch., Composer.

No leading composer, not even Verdi, has had quite such an extended or fruitful Indian summer of creativity as Sir Michael Tippett. *The Rose lake* is his culminating masterpiece, first performed when he was 90, an extended half-hour piece, an orchestral song without words, as he described it. As Sir Colin Davis's superb recording with the LSO demonstrates from first to last, *The Rose lake* could not provide a richer conclusion, arguably the most beautiful of all his works. It was in 1990 on a visit to Senegal that the 85-year-old composer visited a lake, Le lac rose, where at midday the sun transformed its whitish-green colour to translucent pink. It led to this musical evocation of the lake from dawn to dusk, centred round the climactic mid-moment, when the lake is in full song. The twelve sections, sharply delineated, form a musical arch, with the lake-song represented in five of them on soaring unison strings in free variation form.

That culminating masterpiece is well coupled with Tippett's own 1971 recording, never previously available on CD, of his cantata, *The Vision of St Augustine*. First heard in 1965, it is a work which in its new sounds can now be seen as the beginning of his adventurous Indian Summer. His reading is expansively atmospheric rather than tautly drawn, bringing out the mystery of the piece.

Symphony No. 1; (i) *Piano concerto.*
*** Chandos Dig. CHAN 9333 [id.]. (i) Howard Shelley; Bournemouth SO, Richard Hickox.

Those who thought that Sir Colin Davis's pioneering recordings of the first three Tippett symphonies (which are currently withdrawn) were definitive will find fresh revelation in Richard Hickox's readings, not least in the *First Symphony*. Hickox may be less biting, but he gives an extra spring to the chattering motor rhythms at the start, and from then on the Bournemouth performance is regularly warmer and more expressive, as in the distinctive trumpet melody in the slow movement. In the last two movements too, Hickox finds more fun and jollity in Tippett's wild inspirations. The *Piano concerto*, with Howard Shelley a superb soloist, brings another revelatory performance, warm and affectionate but purposeful too, rebutting any idea that with their fluttering piano figurations these are meandering arguments. Warm, full, atmospheric sound, with the piano balanced within the orchestra instead of in front of it. This must now be a first recommendation.

Symphony No. 2; New Year (opera): *suite.*
*** Chandos Dig. CHAN 9299 [id.].
Bournemouth SO, Richard Hickox.

As in the *First Symphony*, Hickox with extra lift in the rhythms brings out the joy behind Tippett's inspirations without ever losing a sense of purpose. This may be a less biting performance than Sir Colin Davis's was on Decca, but it is consistently warmer, with extra fun and wit in the third-movement Scherzo. The coupling is also valuable, when Tippett's own suite from his last opera, *New Year*, brings out the colour and wild energy of this inspiration of his mid-eighties. If anything, the music seems the more telling for being shorn of the composer's own problematic libretto. The obbligato instruments – saxophones, electric guitars and kit drums – are most evocatively balanced in the warm, atmospheric recording.

(i) *Symphony No. 3. Praeludium for brass, bells and percussion.*
*** Chandos Dig. CHAN 9276 [id.].
Bournemouth SO, Richard Hickox; (i) with Faye Robinson.

In two long movements, each lasting nearly half an hour, the *Third Symphony* is not easy to hold together and, though Richard Hickox and the Bournemouth orchestra cannot match the original performers, Sir Colin Davis and the LSO, in power, they find more light and shade. Hickox gives wit to the Stravinskian syncopations in the first section and then dedicatedly carries concentration through the pauses of the slow second half of the movement. Though Faye Robinson's voice in the blues sections of the second movement is not as warm or firm as Heather Harper's was, she is more closely in tune with the idiom, helping to build the sequence to a purposeful conclusion in the long final scena. The recording is full and warm to match. The *Praeludium for brass, bells and percussion* was written in 1962 for the 40th anniversary of the BBC, a gruff, angular piece hardly suggesting celebration, but none the less welcome in a well-played performance.

Symphony No. 4; (i) *Byzantium.*
*** Decca Dig. 433 668-2. (i) Faye Robinson; Chicago SO, Solti.

Symphony No. 4; Fantasia concertante on a theme of Corelli; (i) *Fantasia on a theme of Handel* (for piano and orchestra).
*** Chandos Dig. CHAN 9233 [id.]. (i) Howard Shelley; Bournemouth SO, Hickox.

Byzantium, written to celebrate Sir Georg Solti's 30-year association with the Chicago orchestra, is an extended setting for soprano of the Yeats poem of that name. This is Tippett at his most exotic, responding vividly to the words; and the live recording (made in Carnegie Hall, New York, at one of the first performances) can hardly be faulted. Faye Robinson, taking over from Jessye Norman at the last minute, gives a radiant performance, triumphantly breasting the problems of the often stratospheric and angular vocal-line; equally, Solti draws brilliant, responsive playing from the orchestra. It is apt to have Tippett's *Symphony No. 4* as coupling, another work written for, and played by, Solti and the Chicago orchestra.

In the *Fourth Symphony* Richard Hickox and the Bournemouth Symphony are less weighty than the work's originators, but they are generally warmer and more atmospheric. In place of Solti's fiery brilliance, Hickox brings an element of wildness to the fast sections and he also finds a vein of tenderness in the meditative sections. The well-known *Corelli variations* have never sounded quite as sumptuous and resonant as here, and the disc is generously rounded off with a welcome rarity: the early *Handel Fantasia for piano and orchestra*. Howard Shelley is most convincing in the weighty piano-writing, like his accompanists giving the music warmth. Full-blooded sound to match.

String quartets Nos. 1–5.
*** ASV Analogue/Dig. CDDCS 231 (2) [id.]. Lindsay Qt.

String quartet No. 4.
*** ASV Dig. CDDCA 608 [id.]. Lindsay Qt – BRITTEN: *Quartet No. 3.* ***

String quartet No. 5.
*** ASV Dig. CDDCA 879 [id.]. Lindsay Qt (with BROWN: *Fanfare to welcome Sir Michael Tippett;* MORRIS: *Canzoni ricertati;* PURCELL: *3 Fantasias;* WOOD: *String quartet* ***).

This set neatly brings together the première recordings of Tippett's last two quartets, each written for the Lindsays, with the recordings the same players made in the 1970s for L'Oiseau-Lyre of the first three quartets in the series, long unavailable. Neatly fitted into a slim double jewel-case, this issue completely upstages the Collins set of the first four quartets. The notes include the composer's own commentary on the first three quartets, written for the original issue. He explains that he regards these works, written between 1935 and 1946, as a sequence, each developing out of the other. One of the most beautiful movements is the *Lento cantabile* of No. 1, written as a replacement for the original two central movements. No. 2 is the most classically balanced in four movements, while the five movements of No. 3, the longest and weightiest of these early works, reflect Tippett's experience of hearing the Bartók *Quartets*, not in idiom but in broad approach. There followed a long gap before hearing the Lindsays play led Tippett to write No. 4 in 1977–8, developing the birth-to-death theme he adopted in the *Symphony No. 4*. He followed that with No. 5 in 1990–91, using late Beethoven as a conscious model. The Lindsays give performances as near definitive as could be, making one realize why they inspired the composer so positively. The analogue sound for Nos. 1–3, as transferred, is brighter, with less body than the digital recordings for Nos. 4 and 5.

As can be seen, the *Fourth* and *Fifth Quartets* are also available separately, the *Fourth* well coupled with Britten's *Third*. The other varied items which come on CDDCA 879 with No. 5 are designed as a pendant to the Tippett, music by composers with whom he is associated, from Purcell, always a strong influence, to Christopher Brown from a young generation, paying tribute in a vigorous fanfare. R. O. Morris and Charles Wood were Tippett's teachers, both represented in beautifully crafted quartet pieces, the one a pair of contrasted fugal movements, the other a crisp, four-movement work with echoes of Irish folksong and dance-rhythms, a most attractive piece.

Piano sonatas Nos. 1 (Fantasy-Sonata); 2–3.
*** Chandos Dig. CHAN 9468 [id.]. Nicholas Unwin.

Piano sonatas Nos. 1 (Fantasy sonata); 2–4.
*** CRD Dig. CRD 34301; *CRDC 4130/1* (2) [id.]. Paul Crossley.

Paul Crossley has been strongly identified with the Tippett sonatas; he recorded the first three for Philips in the mid-1970s: indeed, No. 3 was written for him. The *Fourth* and last (1983–4) started life as a set of five bagatelles. Crossley contributes an informative and illuminating note on the sonata and its relationship with, among other things, Ravel's *Miroirs*; his performance has all the lucidity and subtlety one would expect from him. These masterly accounts are matched by truthful and immediate sound-quality on CD, with excellent chrome cassettes too.

Nicholas Unwin is an impressive player and has all the technical resources for these pieces at his command. He has an exceptionally wide range of colour, though at times Crossley has more subtlety and delicacy when Tippett's fantasy takes wing. The Chandos recording is superb. Crossley's set takes two CDs but, if you happen not to need or want the *Fourth*, this is a viable alternative.

VOCAL MUSIC

A Child of our time (oratorio).
*** Collins Dig. 1339-2. Robinson, Walker, Garrison, Cheek, CBSO Ch. & SO, composer.
*** Chandos Dig. CHAN 9123 [id.]. Haymon, Clarey, Evans, White, L. Symphony Ch., LSO, Hickox.

Sir Michael Tippett in his mid-eighties may not have secured the best-disciplined performance on record of this earliest of his oratorios, but it is generally the most moving. The spirituals which punctuate the story like chorales in a Bach Passion have a heart-easing expressiveness, warmly idiomatic, while the lightness and resilience of *Nobody knows* allows the syncopations to be pointed with winning jazziness. Next to Sir Colin Davis's taut, tough reading on Philips this may be relatively slack, taking a full five minutes longer overall, but the Collins sound is fuller and warmer than that of rival versions. The soloists are placed well forward, an outstandingly characterful team of singers specially associated with Tippett's music.

Hickox's version of Tippett's oratorio, *A Child of our time*, establishes its place against severe competition largely through the exceptionally rich recording and its distinctive choice of soloists, a quartet of black singers. Not only do Cynthia Haymon, Cynthia Clarey, Damon Evans and Willard White make the transitions into the spirituals (used in the way Bach used chorales) seem all the more natural, their timbres all have a very sensuous quality. The London Symphony Chorus, though not at its most incisive, sings well, responding to Hickox's warmly expressive style, often even more expansive than the composer himself on his recent recording.

(i) *A Child of our time* (oratorio); (ii) *The Knot Garden* (opera; complete).
*** Ph. 446 331-2 (2). (i) Norman, J. Baker, Cassilly, Shirley-Quirk, BBC Singers, BBC Ch. Soc. & SO; (ii) Herinx, Minton, Gomez, Barstow, Carey, Tear, Hemsley, ROHCG O; C. Davis.

Sir Colin Davis's superb recorded performance of *The Knot Garden* aptly coupled with Davis's 1975 recording of the oratorio, *A Child of our time*, comes on a pair of well-filled CDs at full price. *The Knot Garden* is a conversation-piece, set in a garden, to a libretto by the composer, very much in the style of a T. S. Eliot play. The brief central Act, called *Labyrinth*, has characters thrown together two at a time in a revolving maze, a stylized effect which contributes effectively to Tippett's process of psychiatric nerve-prodding. Recorded in vivid, if rather dry, sound, the message comes over if anything more effectively than on stage. The recording of *A Child of our time* is also cleanly defined, here suiting Davis's sharply focused performance. Speeds are on the fast side, both in the spirituals, which here take the place that Bach gave to chorales, and in the other numbers. Consistently Davis allows himself far less expressive freedom than the composer in his outstanding Collins version and he misses the tenderness which can make the setting of *Steal away* at the end of Part 1 so moving. He has a superb quartet of soloists; and their fine contribution, together with that of the chorus, matches this approach.

The Midsummer marriage (complete).
✽ *** Lyrita SRCD 2217 (2) [id.]. Remedios, Carlyle, Burrows, Herinx, Harwood, Watts, Ch. & O of ROHCG, Sir Colin Davis.

Originally on Philips, this 1970 recording of Tippett's first opera firmly establishes this as a warmly melodic, rich-textured work that should be in the standard repertoire, alongside Britten's *Peter Grimes*. That Tippett's visionary conception, created over a long period of self-searching, succeeds so triumphantly on record is a tribute above all to the exuberance of the composer's glowing inspiration, his determination to translate the beauty of his vision into musical and dramatic terms. There are few operas of any period which use the chorus to such effect, often in haunting offstage passages, and, with Sir Colin Davis a burningly committed advocate and with a cast that was inspired by live performances in the opera house, this is a set hard to resist, even for those not normally fond of modern opera. The so-called 'difficulties' of the libretto, with its mystical philosophical references, fade when the sounds are so honeyed in texture and so consistently lyrical, while the story – for all its complications – preserves a clear sense of emotional involvement throughout. The singing is glorious, the playing magnificent and the recording outstandingly atmospheric, and the Lyrita transfer intensifies the keen sense of realism, the feeling of sitting in the stalls inside an opera house with perfect acoustics.

King Priam (complete).
*** Chandos Dig. CHAN 9406/7 [id.]. Bailey, Harper, Allen, Palmer, Langridge, Minton, Tear, Roberts, L. Symphony. Ch., LSO, Atherton.

'The future of any twentieth-century opera depends quite a lot on recording,' Sir Michael Tippett said on the appearance of this superb set, and it is no exaggeration that it set the seal on the acceptance of a masterly work which yet seemed disconcerting when it first appeared in 1962. The dry fragmentation of texture and choppy compression of the drama then seemed at odds with an epic subject, particularly after the lyrical, expansive warmth of Tippett's preceding opera, *The Midsummer marriage*. With an outstanding cast of the finest British singers of the time, Atherton in this 1980 recording brings out the sharp cogency of the writing, the composer's single-mindedness in pursuing his own individual line. The Wagnerian, Norman Bailey, sounds agedly noble in the title-role, with Robert Tear a shiningly heroic Achilles and Thomas Allen a commanding Hector, illuminating every word. The digital recording, originally made by Decca, comes out brilliantly on CD, with each Act fitted conveniently on a single disc.

Tjeknavorian, Loris (b. 1937)

Piano concerto, Op. 4.
(N) *** ASV Dig. CD DCA 984 [id.]. Babakhanian, Armenian PO, composer – BABADZHANIAN: *Heroic ballade; Nocturne.* ***

A highly coloured work, very much in the tradition

of Khachaturian, but rather more dissonantly pungent, Tjeknavorian's *Fourth concerto* certainly makes an immediate impact on the listener. There is a central pianistic soliloquy at the centre of the first movement, sinuously Armenian in flavour, which leads to a huge climax, ridden by the pianist's thundering bravura, before the wildly obstreperous orchestra returns to add to the melée. Introduced by a yearning horn theme, the *Andante* wears its romantic heart on its sleeve, even though the soloist ruminates; and the rumbustious, syncopated finale also has a sinuous lyrical interlude, before the orchestra returns for the riotous race to the winning post. Babakhanian is an ideal soloist, producing explosions of virtuosity whenever needed, yet persuasively sensitive to the work's lyrical side. With the composer conducting, and the orchestra on their toes, the result surely is definitive, for the recording is extremely vivid.

Toch, Ernst (1887-1964)

5 Pieces for wind and percussion.
*** Virgin/EMI Dig. VC5 45056-2. Deutsche Kammerphilharmonie Wind – HINDEMITH: *Septet for Wind;* WEILL: *Violin concerto.* ***

The Viennese-born Ernst Toch is better known as a teacher than as a composer. While he was an influential figure in Germany in the 1920s and early '30s, he never really recovered the ground lost when he was forced out of Germany by the Nazis. These *Five Pieces for wind and percussion* of 1959 are charming, lyrical and full of imagination – as well as (in the third, *Night Music*) humour (as in the second, *Caprice*) and a gentle melancholy, as in the *Roundelay*. Beautiful playing and superbly life-like, well-balanced recording. Highly recommended.

Tanz-Suite, Op. 30.
(N) ** Edition Abseits EDA013-2 [id.]. Kammersymphonie Berlin, Jürgen Bruns – SCHREKER: *Der Geburtstag der Infantin.* **

Ernst Toch's *Dance suite* comes from 1923. It is an expertly crafted piece, inventive and resourceful. The playing of the Kammersymphonie Berlin under Jürgen Bruns is first rate and the recording eminently serviceable.

Tomkins, Thomas (1572–1656)

Music for viols: *Almain in F* (for 4 viols); *Fantasias 1, 12 & 14* (for 3 viols); *Fantasia* (for 6 viols); *Galliard: Thomas Simpson* (5 viols & organ); *In Nomine II* (for 3 viols); *Pavane in A min.* (for 5 viols & organ); *Pavane in F; Ut re mi (Hexachord fantasia)* (both for 4 viols); (Keyboard) (i) *Fancy for two to play. Pavan and galliard: Earl Strafford.* (Organ) *In nomine; Miserere; Voluntary;* Verse anthems: *Above the stars; O Lord, let me know mine end; Thou art my King.*
✿ (BB) *** Naxos Dig. 8.550602 [id.]. Rose Consort of Viols, Red Byrd; Thomas Roberts; (i) with John Bryan.

This well-planned Naxos programme is carefully laid out in two parts, each of viol music interspersed with harpsichord and organ pieces and ending with an anthem. It gives collectors an admirable opportunity to sample, very inexpensively, the wider output of Thomas Tomkins, an outstandingly fine Elizabethan musician whose music is still too little known. Born in Gloucester, he spent his career both as 'instructor choristarum' at Worcester Cathedral and as a member of the Chapel Royal, helping to supervise the music at the coronation of Charles I. But with the arrival of Cromwell he withdrew from public life. Though he is best known for his magnificent church music, it is refreshing to discover what he could do with viols, experimenting with different combinations of sizes of instrument, usually writing with the polyphony subservient to expressive harmonic feeling, as in the splendid and touching *Fantasia for 6 voices*. Perhaps the most remarkable piece here is the *Hexachord fantasia*, where the scurrying part-writing ornaments a rising and falling six-note scale (hexachord). The two five-part verse anthems and *Above the stars*, which is in six parts, are accompanied by five viols, with a fine counter-tenor in *Above the stars* and a bass in *Thou art my King*.

The Great service (No. 3); Anthems: *Know you not; Oh, that the salvation; O Lord, let me know mine end; Organ voluntaries: in A; in C; in G.*
*** CRD Dig. CRD 3467; *CRDC 4167* [id.]. New College, Oxford, Ch., Edward Higginbottom; David Burchell.

The Great service (No. 3); When David heard; Then David mourned; Almighty God, the fountain of all wisdom; Woe is me; Be strong and of a good courage; O sing unto the Lord a new song; O God, the proud are then risen against me.
*** Gimell/Ph. Dig. 454 924-2 [id.]. Tallis Scholars, Phillips.

Tomkins is a madrigalist and fluent contrapuntist in the Elizabethan manner who found his highest fulfilment in church music like the magnificent examples contained on this Gimell disc. The *Great Service*, in no fewer than ten parts, sets the four canticles – *Te Deum*, *Jubilate*, *Magnificat* and *Nunc dimittis* – with a grandeur rarely matched, using the most complex polyphony. The following motets bring comparable examples of his mastery. These complex pieces bring the flawless matching and even tone for which the Tallis Scholars are celebrated, and with recording to match.

Many will prefer the more direct and throatier style of the Choir of New College, Oxford; even if the choral sound (recorded in the chapel of New College) is less sharply defined, the effect is very satisfying and real. The service is given added variety by the inclusion of three organ voluntaries, well played by David Burchell. What makes this record especially attractive is the inclusion of three of Tomkins's most beautiful anthems. The treble solos in *Know you not* and *Oh, that the salvation* are ravishingly done, and the alto soloist in *O Lord, let me know mine end* is hardly less impressive.

Torelli, Giuseppe (1658–1709)

Concerti grossi, Op. 8/2–3, 6, 8, 9 & 12.

(N) *** Ph. Dig. 432 118-2 [id.]. Mariana Sirbu, (with Antonio Perez in Nos. 2, 3 & 6); I Musici.

Torelli's individual concerti grossi (and particularly the *Christmas concerto* – No. 6 of the present set) have been featured on various anthologies over the years, but this is the first CD to be devoted entirely to his Opus 8, and very rewarding it is. I Musici are on top form. Their playing is sunny, yet full of vitality. The twelve *Op. 8 Concerti grossi* are divided into six concertos featuring two violin soloists (Nos. 1–6) and six featuring a single concertante violin. The first concerto on the disc, No. 12, in three movements, brings a very demanding solo role, which Mariana Sirbu takes with distinction. No. 9 which follows is in five movements, with three *Allegros* separating two serene *Largo* slow movements, again played most beautifully. The justly renowned *Concerto in G minor* (No. 6) brings a radiant opening pastoral cradle song. Its rocking theme, played more spiritedly, also permeates the finale; in between comes a reflective shared soliloquy from the two soloists. Throughout, these splendid performances are matched by recording of the utmost naturalness. Highly recommended.

Tosti, Francesco (1846–1916)

Songs: *L'alba sepàra della luce l'ombra; Aprile; 'A vucchella; Chanson de L'adieu; Goodbye; Ideale; Malia; Marechiare; Non t'amo; Segreto; La serenata; Sogno; L'ultima canzone; Vorrei morire.*

(M) *** Ph. (IMS) 426 372-2. José Carreras, ECO, Muller.

Tosti (knighted by Queen Victoria for his services to music) had a gently charming lyric gift in songs like these, and it is good to have a tenor with such musical intelligence – not to mention such a fine, pure voice – tackling once-popular trifles like *Marechiare* and *Goodbye*. The arrangements are sweetly done, and the recording is excellent.

Tovey, Donald (1875–1940)

Piano concerto in A, Op. 15.

(N) *** Hyperion Dig. CDA 67023 Steven Osborne, BBC Scottish SO, Brabbins – MACKENZIE: *Scottish concerto.* ***

Hyperion in its imaginative series of Romantic piano concertos here offers two Scottish works. Sir Donald Tovey is best known for his analytical essays, and his *concerto*, if less distinctively Scottish, is the grander work with weighty textures and a strongly controlled structure. The young Scottish pianist, Steven Osborne, is a brilliant advocate.

Trunk, Richard (1879–1968)

7 Christmas Lieder, Op. 71: Advent; Weihnachten; Maria; In der Krippe; Die heiligen drei Könige; Idyll; Christbaum.

❁ *** EMI Dig. CDC5 56204-2 [id.]. Olaf Bär, Helmut Deutsch (with Recital: '*Christmas Lieder*' *** ❁).

These delightful Christmas settings by Richard Trunk are the surprise at the centre of Olaf Bär's superb collection of German Christmas songs. Trunk, a pupil of Rheinberger, lived in America for a period, returning to Germany after the outbreak of the First World War, and he established himself as conductor and academic in Cologne. His remarkable feeling for words and easy melodic lyricism are very much in the mainstream of German Lieder and, even if the style of the music is more eclectic, its invention is engagingly individual and never flags. Olaf Bär gives inspired performances, relishing the subtleties in the marriage of text and vocal line, especially in the dramatic tale of the meeting between the *Drei Könige* and Herod. The highlight is the masterly *Idyll*, picturing Mary beneath a lime tree rocking her son to sleep with four angels on guard overhead.

Truscott, Harold (1914–92)

Symphony in E; Elegy for string orchestra; Suite in G.

*** Marco Polo 8.223674 [id.]. Nat. SO of Ireland, Gary Brain.

Harold Truscott broadcast as a pianist for the BBC, specializing in Schubert, and this record suggests that his own music, for all its eclectic influences, has genuine individuality and power. The moving *Elegy* for strings, elliptical in structure, is a near-masterpiece, and the three-movement *Symphony*, which dates from the end of the 1940s, is a powerfully argued piece. The *Suite in G* has a *Molto Andante* which confirms the intensity of feeling the composer could create with string textures. Gary

Brain has an instinctive feel for all these works and holds together the turbulent moods of the first movement of the *Symphony* coherently, while the Dublin orchestra rise to the occasion and play with much conviction throughout. The recording is full-bodied, with the resonance at the service of the music but without clouding textures.

Tubin, Eduard (1905–82)

(i) *Balalaika concerto; Music for strings; Symphony No. 1.*
*** BIS Dig. CD 351 [id.]. (i) Sheynkman; Swedish RSO, Järvi.

The opening of the *First Symphony* has a Sibelian breadth, but for the most part it is a symphony apart from its fellows. The quality of the musical substance is high; its presentation is astonishingly assured for a young man still in his twenties, and the scoring is masterly. Emanuil Sheynkman's account of the *Balalaika concerto* with Neeme Järvi is first class, both taut and concentrated. Excellent recording.

(i) *Ballade for violin and orchestra;* (ii) *Double-bass concerto;* (i) *Violin concerto No. 2; Estonian dance suite; Valse triste.*
*** BIS Dig. CD 337 [id.]. (i) Garcia; (ii) Ehren; Gothenburg SO, Järvi.

Tubin's highly imaginative *Double-bass concerto* has an unflagging sense of momentum and is ideally proportioned; the ideas never outstay their welcome and one's attention is always held. The *Second Violin concerto* has an appealing lyricism, is well proportioned and has a strong sense of forward movement. The *Ballade* is a work of gravity and eloquence. *Valse triste* is a short and rather charming piece, while the *Dance suite* is the Estonian equivalent of the *Dances of Galánta*. Splendid performances from both soloists in the *Concertos* and from the orchestra under Järvi throughout, and excellent recording.

Symphonies Nos. 2 (The Legendary); 6.
*** BIS CD 304 [id.]. Swedish RSO, Järvi.

The opening of the *Second Symphony* is magical: there are soft, luminous string chords that evoke a strong atmosphere of wide vistas and white summer nights, but the music soon gathers power and reveals a genuine feeling for proportion and of organic growth. If there is a Sibelian strength in the *Second Symphony*, the *Sixth*, written after Tubin had settled in Sweden, has obvious resonances of Prokofiev – even down to instrumentation – and yet Tubin's rhythmic vitality and melodic invention are quietly distinctive. The Swedish Radio Symphony Orchestra play with great commitment under Neeme Järvi, and the recorded sound is magnificent.

Symphonies Nos. 3; 8.
*** BIS Dig. CD 342 [id.]. Swedish RSO, Järvi.

The first two movements of the wartime *Third Symphony* are vintage Tubin, but the heroic finale approaches bombast. The *Eighth* is his masterpiece; its opening movement has a sense of vision and mystery, and the atmosphere stays with you. This is the darkest of the symphonies and the most intense in feeling, music of great substance. Järvi and the Swedish orchestra play it marvellously and the recording is in the demonstration bracket.

Symphonies Nos. (i) *4 (Sinfonia lirica);* (ii) *9 (Sinfonia semplice); Toccata.*
❀ *** BIS Dig. CD 227 [id.]. (i) Bergen SO, (ii) Gothenburg SO, Järvi.

The *Fourth* is a highly attractive piece, immediately accessible, the music well argued and expertly crafted. The opening has a Sibelian feel to it but, the closer one comes to it, the more individual it seems. The recording comes from a concert performance with an exceptionally well-behaved audience. The *Ninth Symphony* is in two movements: its mood is elegiac and a restrained melancholy permeates the slower sections. Its musical language is direct, tonal and, once one gets to grips with it, quite personal. If its spiritual world is clearly Nordic, the textures are transparent and luminous, and its argument unfolds naturally and cogently. The playing of the Gothenburgers under Järvi is totally committed in all sections of the orchestra. The performances are authoritative and the recording altogether excellent.

Symphony No. 5 in B min.; Kratt (ballet suite).
*** BIS Dig. CD 306 [id.]. Bamberg SO, Järvi.

The *Fifth* makes as good a starting point as any to investigate the Tubin canon. Written after he had settled in Sweden, it finds him at his most neo-classical; the music is finely paced and full of energy and invention. The ballet suite is a work of much character, tinged with folk-inspired ideas and some echoes of Prokofiev.

Symphony No. 7; (i) *Concertino for piano and orchestra; Sinfonietta on Estonian motifs.*
*** BIS Dig. CD 401 [id.]. (i) Roland Pöntinen; Gothenburg SO, Järvi.

The *Seventh* is a marvellous work and it receives a concentrated and impressive reading. As always with Tubin, you are never in doubt that this is a real symphony which sets out purposefully and reaches its goal. The ideas could not be by anyone else and the music unfolds with a powerful logic and inevitability. Neeme Järvi inspires the Gothenburg orchestra with his own evident enthusiasm. The *Concertino for piano and orchestra* has some of the neo-classicism of the *Fifth Symphony*. Roland Pöntinen gives a dashing account of the solo part. The *Sinfonietta* is a fresh and resourceful piece, a

Baltic equivalent of, say, Prokofiev's *Sinfonietta*, with much the same lightness of touch and inventive resource. Superb recording.

Symphony No. 10; (i) *Requiem for fallen soldiers.*
*** BIS Dig. CD 297 [id.]. Gothenburg SO, (i) with Lundin, Rydell, Hardenberger, Lund Students' Ch., Järvi.

Tubin's *Requiem*, austere in character, is for two soloists (a contralto and baritone) and male chorus. The instrumental forces are merely an organ, piano, drums, timpani and trumpet. The simplicity and directness of the language are affecting and the sense of melancholy is finely controlled. The final movement is prefaced by a long trumpet solo, played here with stunning control and a masterly sense of line by the young Håkan Hardenberger. It is an impressive and dignified work, even if the choral singing is less than first rate. The *Tenth Symphony* is a one-movement piece that begins with a sombre string idea, which is soon interrupted by a periodically recurring horn call – which resonates in the mind long afterwards. The recordings are absolutely first class.

(i; iii) *Ballade; Capricci Nos. 1 & 2; The Cock's dance; Meditation; 3 Pieces; Prelude.* (i) *Sonata for unaccompanied violin.* (i; iii) *Violin sonatas Nos. 1 & 2; Suite of Estonian dance tunes; Suite on Estonian dances.* (ii; iii) *Viola sonata; Viola sonata* (arr. of *Alto saxophone sonata*).
*** BIS Dig. CD 541/542 (2) [id.]. (i) Leibur; (ii) Vahle; (iii) Rumessen.

Although the smaller pieces are finely wrought, Tubin seems to come into his own on a larger canvas. Particularly impressive are the *Second Violin sonata* (*In the Phrygian mode*), the visionary *Second Piano sonata*, and the two sonatas for viola, one a transcription of the alto-saxophone sonata with its foretaste of the *Sixth Symphony* (1954) in which that instrument plays a prominent, almost soloistic role, and the later *Viola sonata* (1965). As so often with Tubin's non-symphonic music, there is much of interest to reward the listener. Highly accomplished performances from Arvo Leibur and Petra Vahle, and exceptionally thorough documentation from the pianist Vardo Rumessen, with over 40 music-type examples. The recording is truthful, but the acoustic lends a shade too much resonance to the piano, which is often bottom-heavy.

Complete piano music: *Album leaf; Ballad on a theme by Maat Saar; 3 Estonian folk-dances; 4 Folksongs from my country; A little march for Rana; Lullaby; 3 Pieces for children; Prelude No. 1; 7 Preludes; Sonatas Nos. 1–2; Sonatina in D min.; Suite on Estonian shepherd melodies; Variations on an Estonian folk-tune.*
*** BIS Dig. CD 414/6 [id.]. Vardo Rumessen.

Tubin's first works for piano inhabit a world in which Scriabin, Ravel and Eller were clearly dominant influences but in which an individual sensibility is also to be discerned. The resourceful *Variations on an Estonian folk-tune* is a lovely work that deserves a place in the repertoire, as does the *Sonatina in D minor*, where the ideas and sense of momentum are on a larger scale than one would expect in a sonatina. The *Second Sonata* is a key work in Tubin's development. It opens with a shimmering figure in free rhythm, inspired by the play of the aurora borealis, and is much more concentrated than his earlier piano works. Vardo Rumessen makes an excellent case for it and it is impressive stuff. The performances are consistently fine, full of understanding and flair, and the recording is very natural.

OPERA

Barbara von Tisenhusen.
*** Ondine Dig. ODE776-2 (2). Raamat, Sild, Kuusk, Puurabar, Ants Kollo, Estonian Op. Company & O, Peeter Lilje.

Tubin's opera with its theme of illicit passion is not long, consisting of three Acts of roughly 30 minutes each. It has pace and variety of dramatic incident and musical textures, and the main roles in the action are vividly characterized. The musical substance of the opera is largely based on a chaconne-like figure of nine notes heard at the very outset, yet the theme changes subtly and skilfully to meet the constantly shifting dramatic environment so that the casual listener will probably not be consciously aware of the musical means Tubin is employing. All the singers are dedicated and serve the composer well and, though the orchestra is not first class, it too plays with spirit and enthusiasm under Peeter Lilje. The recording produces a sound comparable to that of a broadcast relay rather than the opulent sound one can expect from a commercial studio recording. A strong recommendation.

The Parson of Reigi; (i) *Requiem for fallen soldiers.*
*** Ondine Dig. ODE783-2 (2). Maiste, Eensalu, Tônuri, Kuusk, Estonian Op. Company & O, Paul Mägi; (i) Urve Tauts; Talevaldis Deksnis, Urmas Leiten; Rein Tiido, Rein Roos, Estonian Nat. Male Ch., Eri Klas.

After the success of *Barbara von Tisenhusen*, the Estonian Opera immediately commissioned Tubin to compose *The Parson of Reigi*, and it, too, concerns an illicit relationship. Tubin's music powerfully evokes the claustrophobic milieu of a small, closely knit fishing community and is particularly successful in conveying atmosphere. The dawn scene where the parson, Lampelius, blesses the departing fishermen is particularly imaginative, as is the evocation of the white summer nights in the Garden scene, where the heroine confesses her illicit passion. As in *Barbara von Tisenhusen*, Tubin's powers of characterization of both the major and supporting roles are striking, and there is a compelling sense of dramatic narrative as well as variety of pace. The performance of the three principal singers is very good – especially the parson, splendidly sung by the baritone, Teo Maiste – and the only let-down is in the quality of the orchestral playing, which is little more than passable.

The coupled *Requiem for Fallen Soldiers* is generally to be preferred to the rival account on BIS coupled with the *Tenth Symphony* (see above). The Estonian singers produce better focused and darker tone than their Swedish colleagues, though the BIS recording has some amazingly lyrical playing by Håkan Hardenberger. The Estonian player, Urmas Leiten, is very eloquent too. Strongly recommended.

Turina, Joaquin (1882–1949)

(i) *Danzas fantásticas, Op. 22; La oracion del torero, Op. 34;* (ii) *Rapsodia sinfónica, Op. 66.*
(N) (B) *** Decca Double Dig. 433 905-2 (2) [id.]. (i) SRO, López-Cobos; (ii) de Larrocha, LPO, Frühbeck de Burgos – ALBENIZ: *Iberia; Navarra; Rapsodia española; Suite española;* GRANADOS: *Andaluza; Goyescas: Intermezzo;* SARASATE: *Aires gitanos.* ***

López-Cobos secures sophisticated playing from the Suisse Romande Orchestra in the *La oracíon del torero* and the three *Danzas fantásticas*, which are given an unexpected subtlety of detail. Of course the splendid Decca recording helps, colourful and brilliant, yet comparatively refined.

La Oración del Torero (version for string orchestra).
*** Chandos Dig. CHAN 9288 [id.]. I Musici di Montréal, Yuli Turovsky – SHCHEDRIN: *Carmen ballet suite* etc. ***

The composer's string-orchestral version of the haunting *Oración del Torero* is warmly and sensitively played and very well recorded here, and if the quartet version is even more subtle (see below) this makes an enjoyable foil for Shchedrin's brilliant arrangement of music from Bizet's *Carmen*.

Rapsodia sinfónica (arr. Halfter).
(B) *** Decca Eclipse Dig. 448 243-2. Alicia de Larrocha, LPO, Frühbeck de Burgos – ALBENIZ: *Rapsodia española;* RODRIGO: *Concierto de Aranjuez* etc. ***
(M) (***) Dutton Lab. mono CDCLP 4000 [id. full price]. Moura Lympany, Philh. O, Susskind (with ALBENIZ: *Tango;* GRANADOS: *Goyescas No. 4;* CHOPIN: *Fantasie-Impromptu*) – MOZART: *Piano concertos Nos. 12 & 21.* (***)

Turina's *Rapsodia sinfónica* has been recorded by others, but in the hands of Alicia de Larrocha it is played with such éclat that it becomes almost memorable and thoroughly entertaining. Excellent, vivid sound.

Turina's *Rapsodia sinfonica* enjoyed great popularity in the days of 78-r.p.m. records, and far greater than its present-day profile would suggest. In her 1949 recording Moura Lympany despatches it with all the lightness and delicacy you could wish for. Her Albéniz, Chopin and Granados encores all come from 1953, when HMV were still issuing shellac records, and they have great charm and style. Excellent transfers.

CHAMBER MUSIC

La Oración del Torero.
*** Collins Dig. 1267-2 [id.]. Britten Qt – CHERUBINI; VERDI: *Quartets.* ***
(***) Testament mono SBT 1053 [id.]. Hollywood Qt – CRESTON: *Quartet;* DEBUSSY: *Danses sacrées;* RAVEL: *Intro and allegro;* VILLA-LOBOS: *Quartet No. 6.* (***)

Turina's seductively gentle evocation was conceived with lutes in mind, but quartet playing of this calibre makes the string medium seem exactly right for the music, and brings a refined ravishing of the senses. The performance is full of lush Andalusian atmosphere, yet has an element of restraint and never becomes over-ripe, helped by superb recording and a most sympathetic acoustic. The '*delicadísimo'* close is magical.

It is difficult to imagine Turina's famous piece being played with greater expressive eloquence or more perfect ensemble than by the incomparable Hollywood Quartet and it comes as part of a valuable and beautifully transferred anthology.

GUITAR MUSIC

Fandanguillo, Op. 36; Homenaje a Tarréga; Ráfaga, Op. 53; Sevillana (Fantasia), Op. 29; Sonata, Op. 61.
(M) *** EMI Dig. CDM5 66574-2 [id.]. Manuel Barrueco – ALBENIZ: *Suite española, Op. 47.* ***

It was Segovia who prompted Turina to write these vibrantly colourful pieces which are now central to any classical guitarist's repertoire. The *Fandanguillo* (its percussive thumping imitates the stamping feet of the zapateado) and *Sevillana* are vibrant with flamenco rhythms, while the spectacular and evocative *Ráfaga* translates as 'gust of wind'. They are played here with panache and glittering virtuosity. The *Sonata* requires a more subtle palette, and a sense of structure. Barrueco's account is masterly, seducing the ear in the gentle, seemingly improvisatory central *Andante* and then creating a flashing pulse for the chimerical finale. The recording is intimate, yet with a fine sense of presence.

Turnage, Mark-Anthony (born 1960)

(i) *Dispelling the fears;* (ii) *Night dances;* (iii) *Your Rockaby.*
*** Argo Dig. 452 598-2. (i) Hardenberger, Wallace, Philh. O, Harding; (ii) Hulse, Tunstall, Constable, Wallace, L. Sinf., Knussen; (iii) Robertson, BBC SO, Andrew Davis.

Turnage is a natural communicator who can happily draw on the widest range of influences and produce music that, for all its modernity, is immediately enjoyable to more than the specialist. These three works offer an impressive survey of his orchestral progress from 1981, when he wrote *Night dances*, to the mid-1990s, when he completed *Your Rockaby*. It helps that jazz and popular music provide an important strand in Turnage's writing. *Night dances* has a movement directly drawing on Miles Davis, and *Your Rockaby* is in effect a saxophone concerto, while the bluesy lyrical passage at the end of *Dispelling the fears* provides a welcome resolution to what is otherwise a tough piece. It is a mark of Turnage's genuine originality that the different sources of inspiration coalesce into a satisfying stylistic whole. With starry soloists, these are performances which consistently bring home the power and concentration of the music, helped by cleanly focused recording.

Greek (opera; complete).
*** Argo Dig. 440 368-2. Quentin Hayes, Richard Suart, Fiona Kimm, Helen Charnock, Greek Ens., Bernas.

Turnage's opera, *Greek*, is out to shock at all costs, beginning with a spoken introduction from the central character, Eddy, rich in vulgarities. This is the Oedipus myth freely adapted to the East End of London ('Eddy-pus' you might deduce). The colour and energy of Turnage's writing, violently dissonant with copious percussion, is brilliantly caught. The unprepared listener may resist at first, but Turnage with his echoes of popular music and his element of lyricism is a powerful communicator. What comes out less well than on stage is the humour, which seems heavy-handed, though the parody of a music-hall duet for Mum and Dad at the end of Act I has plenty of wit. Quentin Hayes has all the impact needed as the central rough diamond, with Richard Suart as Dad, Fiona Kimm as Wife and Helen Charnock as Mum all singing with bite and conviction, tackling not just those roles but incidentals too. On a single disc with libretto and notes, it can be strongly recommended to the adventurous.

Tye, Christopher (*c.* 1505–*c.* 1572)

Mass: Euge bone (in 6 parts).
(M) *** EMI CDM5 65211-2. King's College, Cambridge, Ch., Ledger – BYRD: *Mass for 5 voices;* TALLIS: *Mass: Puer natus est nobis.* ***

Christopher Tye's *Mass for six voices* is one of the glories of early Tudor music, amazingly rich and complex. This fine (1980) recording – attractively coupled with Byrd's masterpiece and the wonderfully reconstructed Tallis work – is well balanced between clarity and atmosphere, and the quality of the singing is a fine tribute to Ledger's work with this unique choir.

Masses *Euge bone; Peterhouse; Western Wind.*
(N) (M) *** ASV Gaudeamus Dig. CD GAU 190 (2) [id.]. Ely Cathedral Ch., Paul Trepte.

Chrisopher Tye spent most of his musical life in Cambridge and Ely, and became master of the chorus and organist at Ely Cathedral in 1543; he retired to take holy orders in 1560 but remained living near Ely. So the soaring acoustics of Ely Cathedral and performances by its present-day choir could not be more apt for his three greatest masses, of which the large-scale *Euge bone* is the most splendid. The passionate singing here is fully worthy, the choral sound glorious. With a playing time of 83 minutes, the three works would not fit on to a single CD, but the two discs are offered for the price of one.

Ullmann, Viktor (1898–*c.* 1944)

(i) *Der Kaiser von Atlantis* (opera; complete); (ii) *Hölderlin Lieder: Abendphantasie; Der Frühling; Wo bist du?*
*** Decca (IMS) Dig. 440 854-2 [id.]. (i) Kraus, Berry, Vermillion, Lippert, Mazura, Leipzig GO, Lothar Zagrosek; (ii) Vermillion, Alder.

In Decca's *Entartete Musik* series, *Der Kaiser von Atlantis* ('The Emperor of Atlantis') was a work written in a Nazi concentration camp. Sharp, Weill-like writing, with the chance availability of such instruments as organ and banjo heightening the flavour, is tempered by echoes of Zemlinsky and Berg. The result is a strongly drawn sequence involving not just the central character, Kaiser Overall, a caricature of Hitler, but the key figure of Death, Harlequin, a Drummer-girl and two soldiers, one of them, Bubikopf, sung by a soprano. The death theme from Suk's *Asrael Symphony* is the centre of a complex web of references intended for the Terezin audience, a cultural élite. The mixture of satire and poignancy is most moving, not least in the use of Luther's hymn, *Ein feste Burg*, in the finale. Zagrosek conducts an outstanding performance with a characterful, well-cast team of soloists, led superbly by the baritone, Michael Kraus, as Overall. The three settings of *Hölderlin*, written in the same year, are mellower in style, with Ullmann's admiration of Berg flowering in warmly romantic, tonal writing. They are beautifully sung by Iris Vermillion, accompanied at the piano by Jonathan Alder. Excellent recording. The single CD comes in a box with libretto, text and translations, plus copious notes.

Urbanner, Erich (born 1936)

String quartet No. 3.
(M) *** Teldec/Warner 3984 21967-2. Alban Berg Qt – BERG: *Lyric suite* etc.; WEBERN: *6 Bagatelles* etc. ***

Urbanner's avant-garde *Third Quartet* is expertly played, but its single-movement form, Schoenbergian in ancestry, does not yield music of real memorability. The Berg and Webern couplings are what make this finely recorded reissue a desirable acquisition.

Vachon, Pierre (1731–1803)

String quartets, Op. 5/2; Op. 7/2.
*** ASV Gaudeamus Dig. CDGAU 151 [id.]. Rasumovsky Qt – JADIN: *Quartets.* ***

Although none of the works on this disc are masterpieces, the music provides us with an interesting and enjoyable sampler of the French school of quartet writing at the end of the eighteenth century. Vachon, born in Arles, was a frequent visitor to London, playing in his own concertos at the Haymarket Theatre. He wrote his quartets in a *galant* style which the French called the *quatuor concertant ou dialogué*. Op. 5 and Op. 7 were both published in London during the composer's first visit, at the beginning of the 1770s. The performances here are polished and well recorded. Enjoyable in an innocuous way.

Vainberg, Moishei (1919–96)

Chamber Symphonies Nos. 1, Op. 145; 4, Op. 153.
(N) *** Olympia Dig. OCD 651 [id.]. Umeå SO, Thord Svedlund.

The chamber symphonies come from the last decade of his life: the *First* for string orchestra (1986) comes from the same year as the *Eighteenth Symphony*, and the *Fourth* for strings and clarinet (1992), was his penultimate work. The opening movement of the *First* is pastoral in character, closer in feeling to a divertimento or sinfonietta than a real symphony. The *Fourth* is a dark, bleak score that is as unremitting as late Shostakovich, and strongly valedictory in feeling. A haunting piece, music of real substance and well worth investigating. The Swedish orchestra play well and are decently recorded.

(i; ii) *Violin concerto in G min., Op. 67.* (iii) *Rhapsody on Moldavian Themes, Op. 47/1*; (ii) *Symphony No. 4 in A min., Op. 61.*
(N) **(*) Olympia OCD 622 [id.]. (i) Leonid Kogan; (ii) Moscow PO, Kirill Kondrashin; (iii) USSR Ac. SO, Yevgeni Svetlanov.

The *Fourth Symphony* was composed in 1957 but revised in 1961 when the order of the inner movements was reversed. It is an inventive and inspiring work with occasional reminders of Hindemith and Mahler. It is highly intelligent music, invigorating, with a powerful sense of inevitability and momentum – and touches of humour too. The *Violin concerto* was championed by Kogan and much admired by Shostakovich, whose spiritual kinship the work seems to record. It is one of the finest Russian concertos of the 1960s, and Kogan plays it wonderfully. The two performances appeared on the HMV Melodiya label in the early 1970s. Vainberg's mother came from Kishinyov in Moldavia, which may account for his choice for the *Rhapsody on Moldavian Themes* which is a much earlier piece (1949). In addition to the orchestral version, it exists in versions for violin and piano, and violin and orchestra, and was in David Oistrakh's repertoire. These performances are from the 1960s, save for the *Rhapsody* (1974) and make an ideal introduction to this interesting composer.

The Golden Key (ballet), *Op. 55: suites Nos. 1–3; suite 4:* excerpts.
*** Olympia OCD 473 [id.]. Bolshoi Theatre O, Mark Ermler.

The Golden Key is a full-length ballet dating from 1955, based on a story by Alexis Tolstoy. The scenario concerns a troupe of puppets with a Petrushka or Pierrot-like figure at the centre. This generous selection (not far short of 80 minutes) gives a good idea of the quality of Vainberg's invention and his skill in making telling character-studies. There is some arresting music here and it is well performed by Bolshoi forces under Mark Ermler, and decently recorded.

Symphony No. 2 for strings, Op. 30; Chamber symphony No. 2 for strings and timpani.
(N) *** Olympia Dig. OCD 652 [id.]. Umeå SO, Thord.

The lyrical *Second Symphony* (1945/6) is haunted by a restless melancholy which permeates the whole fabric, yet the result is in no way depressing. The *Chamber Symphony No. 2* is a relatively late work (1987) and although it is freely rhapsodic, the mood is more positive and often songful, with the timpani used sparingly in the opening movement. The nostalgic feeling returns in the central movement which is marked *Pesante*, but the atmosphere darkens in the long drawn *Andante sostennuto* finale, which reaches a passionately plangent climax before its quietly resigned coda, with a single timpani stroke to make a final resolution. Both symphonies are played with great eloquence, and are warmly and naturally recorded.

Symphonies Nos. (i) *6 in A min.;* (ii) *10 in A min.*
** Olympia mono/stereo OCD 471 [id.]. (i) Moscow Ch. School Boys' Ch., Moscow PO, Kondrashin; (ii) Moscow CO, Barshai.

The *Sixth Symphony* is a dark and powerful work, more satisfying than the *Tenth* for strings, in which the invention does not fully sustain its length. Both works are nevertheless worth exploring and, though the recordings are analogue (the *Sixth*, only in mono), they are very acceptable. The performances under Kirill Kondrashin and Rudolf Barshai are persuasive and authoritative.

Symphonies Nos. (i) *7, Op. 81;* (ii) *12, Op. 114 (In memory of Dmitri Shostakovich).*
**(*) Olympia OCD 472 [id.]. (i) Moscow CO, Barshai; (ii) USSR TV & R. SO, Maxim Shostakovich.

The present issue couples the *Seventh Symphony*, written for the unusual combination of strings and harpsichord and which comes from the early 1960s, and the *Twelfth*, which takes 52 minutes and was written in 1976 after Shostakovich's death. This inventive music is much indebted to, but never wholly overshadowed by, Shostakovich. Both the recordings are analogue and come from 1967 and 1979 respectively, but they reproduce well.

Vaňhal, Jan (1739–1813)

(i) *Double bassoon concerto in F; Sinfonias: in A min.; F.*
**(*) BIS CD 288 [id.]. (i) Wallin, Nilsson; Umeå Sinf., Saraste.

The best work here is the *Concerto*, an arresting and inventive piece, with the slow movement touching a deeper vein of feeling than anything else on the disc. It is not too fanciful to detect in some of the harmonic suspensions the influence of Gluck, with whose music Vaňhal came into contact in the late 1760s. The two *Sinfonias* are less musically developed but very interesting: the minuet of the *F major* has a '*Sturm und Drang*' feel to it: Vaňhal's symphonies may well have paved the way for Haydn at this period; they were certainly given by Haydn while Kapellmeister at the Esterhazy palace. The recording is good, as one has come to expect from this source, even if the acoustic is on the dry side. Very good playing of the Umeå ensemble.

Violin concerto in B.
(B) *** Discover Dig. DICD 920265 [id.]. Ivan Zenaty, Virtuosi di Praga, Oldrich Vlček – MYSLIVECEK: *Violin concerto.* ***

Like his Bohemian contemporary, Mysliveček, Vaňhal was born in Bohemia almost a generation before Mozart; he similarly wrote inventive, lively music, of which this violin concerto is an appealing example, with the central slow movement a nostalgic intermezzo. On this well-recorded bargain issue Ivan Zenaty with his clean, full tone proves an outstanding advocate, with the Virtuosi di Praga providing lively support on modern instruments. Excellent recording.

Varèse, Edgar (1883–1965)

Tuning up. Amériques (original version); Arcana; Dance for burgesses' (i) *Density 21.5 Déserts;* (ii) *Ecuatorial.* (iii; iv) *Un grand sommeil noir* (original version). (iii) *Un grand sommeil noir* (orch. Beaumont). *Hyperprism; Intégrales; Ionisation;* (v; vi) *Nocturnal. Octandre;* (v) *Offrandes. Poème électronique.*
(N) ✿ *** Decca Dig. 460 208-2 (2) [id.]. Concg O. or ASKO Ens., Chailly; with (i) Jacques Zoon, (ii) Kevin Deas, (iii) Mireille Delunsch & (iv) François Kardoncuff; (v) Sarah Leonard; (vi) Prague Philharmonic Male Ch.

Apart from Stravinsky, who directed his own edition for CBS/Sony, and Henze, so admirably served by DG, few modern composers have had almost their total musical output so convincingly and authoritatively performed in a single recorded anthology. Moreover, the present Varèse survey is overseen by Professor Chou Wen-Chung, the composer's pupil, and later also his editor. Varèse first came to public notice in the 1930s when Percy Scholes chose him to represent the last word in zany modernity in his 'Columbia History of Music', but his mockery backfired. *Octandre* (one movement then recorded) sounds as quirkily original now as it did then (it is marvellously played here). The witty opening *Tuning up* sets the mood for writing which is ever ready to take its own course regardless of tradition, and set new musical paths. *Amériques*, which follows, is heard in its original 1921 version, lavishly scored, with reminiscences of music by others, not least the Stravinsky of *The Rite of Spring*. It makes fascinating listening. *Ionisation*, less ear-catching, stands as a historic pointer towards developments in percussion writing. *Poème électronique* originated at the 1958 Brussels World Fair, where it was played through more than 400 loudspeakers inside the Philips pavilion. The montage of familiar and electronic sounds (machine noises, sonorous bells, etc) comes from the composer's own original four-track tape. But all the works here are sharply distinctive and show the composer as a true revolutionary, usually decades ahead of his time. The vocal pieces are among the most aurally fascinating, not least *Ecuatorial*, a setting in Spanish with bass soloist of a Maya prayer, brightly coloured and sharp with brass, percussion, organ, piano and ondes martenot. *Un grand sommeil noir* is a rare surviving early song, lyrically Ravellian in feeling, heard here in both the original version with piano, and in an orchestration by Antony Beaumont. *Nocturnal*, Varése's haunting last piece, was left unfinished. Completed by Professor Chou, it is as extravagant and uninhibited as ever, featuring male chorus and a solo soprano voice, used melodically to evoke a mysterious dream-world. All the performances here are superbly definitive and this set will be hard to surpass. What is most remarkable is the consistent level of tension which Chailly achieves, which holds through the moments of space which separate the musical phrases or percussive comments. The recording acoustic too, is open, yet everything is clear. This music may not be too everyone's taste, but few will resist its magnetism if taken a work at a time.

Arcana; Intégrales; Ionisation.
**(*) Decca 448 580-2 [id.]. LAPO, Mehta – KRAFT: *Concerto for 4 percussion soloists and orchestra* etc. **(*)

Decca's 1971 vintage stereo recording of these three key works with their unusual timbres and textures remains highly recommendable. The performances under Mehta have the easy expressiveness that comes from close and warm acquaintance by the players. However, the coupled music by William Kraft wears less well.

Vaughan Williams, Ralph
(1872–1958)

'*Portrait of Vaughan Williams*' (i–iii) *Oboe concerto;* (i–ii) *Fantasia on Greensleeves; Fantasia on a theme by Thomas Tallis; Five variants of Dives and Lazarus;* (iv) *The Lark ascending. The Wasps overture;* (v; vi) *Phantasy quintet;* (v) *String quartets Nos. 1–2;* (vii; viii; i) *Flos campi;* (vii) *Mass in G min.;* (vii; i) *O, clap your hands; The Old hundredth psalm tune;* (viii; i; ix) *An Oxford elegy;* (vii) *3 Shakespeare songs.* Sacred and secular songs: *Blessed Son of God; Lord, Thou hast been our refuge; No sad thought his soul affright; O taste and see; Valiant for truth;* (vii; i) *Te Deum.*
(N) (BB) *** Nimbus Dig. NI 1754 (4) [id.]. (i) English String O, (ii) William Boughton; (iii) with Maurice Bourge; (iv) Michael Bochman; (v) Medici Qt; (vi) with S. Rowland-Jones; (vii) Christ Church Cathedral Ch., Oxford, Stephen Darlington; (viii) with Roger Best; (ix) with Jack May (narrator).

This splendid super-budget Nimbus box-set offers a wonderfully illuminating cross-section of Vaughan Williams's music, showing its consistent inspiration, and both its diversity and its linkages. The orchestral and concertante music included here is all very familiar, but is most sympathetically played under William Boughton (with sensitive soloists) and presented amply and atmospherically, and with a rich amplitude of string tone. The chamber music shows a more intimate side of the composer: the special atmosphere of these works, with moments of haunting delicacy, are warmly and idiomatically caught, but with no lack of concentration and intensity. The Medici players were recorded in The Maltings, which means a sympathetic ambience, but also that the microphones are rather close. The glorious sonorities of the unaccompanied *Mass in G minor*, with its double choir and four soloists draw an immediate vocal parallel with the *Tallis fantasia*. The *Mass* opens with a *Kyrie* which looks back to the Elizabethan era and beyond, and then blossoms polyphonically in the *Gloria* and swaying *Sanctus* before the beautiful closing *Agnus Dei*. The *Oxford elegy* brings more fine music, but the narrative, confidently and clearly delivered here by Jack May, remains as intrusive as ever (its inclusion was not one of the composer's best ideas). With Roger Best a fine viola soloist, *Flos campi* is particularly successful, as are the *Te Deum* and the shorter unaccompanied choral songs, especially the three imaginative Shakespeare settings. All in all this is a cornucopia of musical joys, worth getting, even if you already have recordings of the better-known orchestral pieces.

Concerto grosso for strings; (i) *Concerto accademico for violin;* (ii) *Oboe concerto;* (iii) *Piano concerto in C;* (iv) *Tuba concerto. Two Hymn-tune Preludes;* (v) *The Lark ascending. Partita for double string orchestra;* (vi) *Towards the unknown region.*
*** Chandos Dig. CHAN 9262/3 [id.]. (i) Sillito; (ii) Theodore; (iii) Shelley; (iv) Patrick Harrild; (v) Michael Davis; (vi) LSO Ch.; LSO, Bryden Thomson.

Chandos offer here as a separate compendium the series of mostly concertante works that were used as fillers for Bryden Thomson's set of the *Symphonies*, and with generous measure and characteristically fine recording this pair of CDs is very attractive. With immaculate LSO string ensemble, the *Concerto grosso* under Thomson's persuasive direction shows how in glowing sound its easy, unforced inspiration brings it close to the world of the *Tallis fantasia*. While many performances of the *Concerto accademico* make the composer's neo-classical manner sound like Stravinsky with an English accent, Thomson and Sillito find a rustic jollity in the outer movements very characteristic of Vaughan Williams. David Theodore's plangent tones in the

Oboe concerto effectively bring out the equivocal character of this highly original work, making it far more than just another pastoral piece. Howard Shelley addresses the neglected *Piano concerto* with flair and brilliance, making light of the disconcerting cragginess of the piano writing and consistently bringing out both the wit and the underlying emotional power. The bluff good humour of the *Tuba concerto* is beautifully caught in Patrick Harrild's rumbustious account and this outstanding tuba soloist plays with wit and panache. Michael Davis makes a rich-toned soloist in *The Lark ascending*, presenting it as more than a pastoral evocation. The *Hymn-tune Preludes* are unashamedly pastoral in tone; then the *Partita* finds the composer in more abrasive mood, less easily sympathetic. *Towards the unknown region* is the only relative disappointment – a setting of Whitman that antedates the *Sea Symphony*. The choral sound is beautiful, but this early work really needs tauter treatment.

(i) *Concerto grosso for strings;* (i–ii) *Oboe concerto;* (i) *English folksongs suite* (trans. Gordon Jacob); *Fantasia on Greensleeves* (arr. GREAVES); (iii) *Fantasia on a theme by Thomas Tallis;* (i; iv) *The Lark ascending;* (iii) *Five variants of Dives and Lazarus; In the Fen Country; Norfolk rhapsody No. 1;* (v) *Partita for double string orchestra;* (i; vi) *Romance for harmonica, strings and piano.*

(N) (B) **(*) Decca Double Analogue/Dig. 460 357-2 (2) [id.]. (i) ASMF, Marriner; (ii) Nicklin; (iii) New Queen's Hall O, Wordsworth; (iv) Iona Brown; (v) LPO, Boult; (vi) Reilly.

This Decca Double offers a fascinating comparison in that the first disc offers modern-instrument recordings (from Marriner and his Academy) and the second a special kind of period-instrument performance, although it is Boult and the LPO who give us the *Partita*. With the ASMF, Celia Nicklin gives a most persuasive account of the elusive *Oboe concerto* while the *Concerto grosso* is lively and polished. The atmospheric *Romance*, although not one of the composer's most inspired works is still worth having, and the *Folksongs* could hardly be presented more breezily; *The Lark ascending* is superbly balanced and refined, with Iona Brown an inspirational soloist. The performances on the second disc are given by the re-formed New Queen's Hall Orchestra playing instruments in use at the turn of the century. *Portamento* is featured in the string style but here it is applied very judiciously, and for the most part the ear notices the fuller, warmer sonority of the violins, the treble less brilliant in attack. In works like the *Tallis fantasia* and *Dives and Lazarus* one can readily wallow in the richly refined textures, but Wordsworth's performance of *Tallis* misses the final degree of intensity at the climax, and the opening of *Dives and Lazarus* is also rather relaxed, even indulgent in relishing the sheer breadth of sonority achieved, though the closing pages are ethereally lovely. The performers are at their finest in the evocative opening of the *Norfolk rhapsody*, while *In the Fen Country* has a fine idyllic ardour, with some very sensitive playing from wind and brass in the coda. The Wordsworth recording, made in Walthamstow Assembly Hall, is splendidly expansive and natural.

Oboe concerto.

(M) *** Carlton Fanfare Dig. 30366 0065-2 [id.]. Pamela Pecha, Moscow PO, Paul Freeman – R. STRAUSS: *Oboe concerto;* SCHICKELE: *Oboe concerto.* ***

Pamela Pecha gives a most attractive account of this sometimes elusive concerto, playing its opening cantilena with pleasing spontaneity and revelling in its folksong element. The effect is both fresh and warm-hearted. She is very well accompanied, and the recording is glowingly atmospheric.

(i; ii) *Oboe concerto*; (i; iii) *Tuba concerto*; (iv) *Fantasia on Greensleeves; Five variants of Dives and Lazarus; Sinfonia antartica (No. 7); The Wasps: Overture.*

(N) (M) (***) EMI mono CMS5 66543-2 (2) [CDMB 66543]; (i) LSO; with (ii) Evelyn Rothwell; (iii) Philip Catelinet; (iii) Hallé O, Barbirolli – ELGAR: *Cockaigne; Introduction and allegro; Serenade.* (***)

Vividly transferred, this double-disc collection brings together Barbirolli's superb readings of Vaughan Williams and Elgar from the early 1950s. Strong and warmly expressive, these performances reflect the quality of the Hallé in the early 1950s, with the LSO equally responsive in the concertos. Central to the collection is the première recording of the *Sinfonia antartica*, made only five months after Barbirolli had conducted the first performance in January 1953. The thrust and power have never been surpassed, and the clear, immediate recording brings out the originality of the orchestration. Evelyn Rothwell, Lady Barbirolli, plays the *Oboe concerto* with heartfelt warmth and understanding, while the *Tuba concerto* is superbly characterized, bluff in the outer movements, tender in the slow movement. With the coupled Elgar items, an outstanding reissue.

(i) *Oboe concerto. Fantasia on Greensleeves;* (ii) *The Lark ascending.*

(M) *** DG 439 529-2. (i) Neil Black; (ii) Zukerman, ECO, Barenboim – DELIUS: *Aquarelles* etc.; WALTON: *Henry V.* ***

Neil Black's creamy tone is ideally suited to Vaughan Williams's *Oboe concerto* and he gives a wholly persuasive performance. Zukerman's account of *The Lark ascending* is full of pastoral rapture – not always quite idiomatic but totally ravishing. The recordings from the late 1970s are warmly atmospheric in the digital remastering.

Piano concerto in C.
*** Lyrita SRCD 211 [id.]. Howard Shelley, RPO, Handley – FOULDS: *Dynamic triptych.* ***
(M) *** EMI Dig. CD-EMX 2239 [id.]. Piers Lane, RLPO, Handley – DELIUS: *Piano concerto;* FINZI: *Eclogue.* ***

This was the first recording of the *Concerto* in solo form, not quite as originally written, because the definitive score, published not too long before this Lyrita record was made, opts for ending with a serene coda instead of the original brief dispatching coda of ten bars. The wonder is that, though the solo piano writing is hardly pianistic, the very challenge to as fine an exponent as Shelley brings out an extra intensity to a highly individual work, compared with VW's two-piano arrangement. Despite the thick textures, there is lightheartedness in much of the writing, whether the urgently chattering *Toccata* or the *Alla tedesca* which emerges out of the toughly chromatic fugue of the finale. Shelley has re-recorded the piece digitally for Chandos (see below), but that is coupled with the *Ninth Symphony*, and many may find the stimulating Foulds coupling on Lyrita even more enticing. The 1984 recording is very impressive in its remastered form.

Piers Lane defies the old idea of this as a grittily unpianistic work, giving it a powerful, refreshing reading, helped by fine playing from the RLPO under Handley, always a sympathetic Vaughan Williams interpreter. Though this hardly outshines Howard Shelley's Lyrita version, the apt and unusual coupling can be warmly recommended.

(i) *Piano concerto; Symphony No. 9 in E min.*
*** Chandos Dig. CHAN 8941 [id.]. (i) Howard Shelley, LPO, Bryden Thomson.

The most strikingly original of the three movements of the *Piano concerto* is the imaginative and inward-looking *Romanza*, which has some of the angularity of line one finds in *Flos campi*, while the finale presages the *Fourth Symphony*. The piece abounds in difficulties, which Howard Shelley addresses with flair and brilliance. He makes light of the disconcerting cragginess of the piano writing and consistently brings out both the wit and the underlying emotional power. Bryden Thomson conducts a powerful performance of the last of Vaughan Williams's symphonies. Though the playing may not be ideally incisive, it brings out an extra warmth of expression. Both performances are greatly helped by the richness and weight of the Chandos sound, warmly atmospheric but with ample detail and fine presence.

English folksongs suite; Fantasia on Greensleeves; In the Fen Country; (i) *The Lark ascending; Norfolk rhapsody No. 1;* (ii) *Serenade to music.*
(M) *** EMI CDM7 64022-2 [id.]. LPO, LSO or New Philh. O, Sir Adrian Boult; (i) with Hugh Bean; (ii) 16 soloists.

All the music here is beautifully performed and recorded. Hugh Bean understands the spirit of *The Lark ascending* perfectly and his performance is wonderfully serene. The transfers are fresh and pleasing; in the lovely *Serenade* (which Boult does in the original version for 16 soloists) the voices are given greater presence.

English folk songs suite; Flourish for wind band; Toccata marziale.
(N) *** Chandos Dig. CHAN 9697 [id.]. Royal Northern College of Music Wind O, Timothy Reynish – HOLST: *Hammersmith; Marching song; Military band suites* etc. ***

Vaughan Williams's music for wind band is less inspired than that of Holst, but the jaunty *English folk songs suite* certainly sounds more vivid in its original scoring than it does in the orchestral version. It could hardly be played more breezily than it is here, and the other two pieces also come off splendidly. Demonstration sound.

English folksongs suite; Toccata marziale.
(BB) *** ASV Quicksilvae CDQS 6021. London Wind O, Denis Wick – HOLST: *Military band suites* etc. ***

As in the Holst suites, the pace of these performances of the original scores is attractively zestful, and if the slow movement of the *English folksongs suite* could have been played more reflectively, the bounce of *Seventeen come Sunday* is irresistible.

Fantasia on Greensleeves; (i) *Fantasia on a theme of Thomas Tallis.*
✿ EMI CDC7 47537-2 [id.]. Sinfonia of L. (i) with Allegri Qt, Barbirolli – ELGAR: *Introduction and allegro* etc. *** ✿

The rich projection of the Tallis theme on which Vaughan Williams based his *Fantasia* when it first appears in full, after the pizzicato introduction, sets the seal on Barbirolli's quite outstanding performance of the *Tallis fantasia*, one of the great masterpieces of all music. The wonderfully ethereal and magically quiet playing of the second orchestra is another very moving feature of this remarkable performance. The remastered CD retains all the warmth, amplitude and bloom of the superb (1963) recording; it is beautifully focused, so that the gently radiant closing section is particularly moving. The *Greensleeves fantasia*, makes an irresistible bonus.

(i) *Fantasia on Greensleeves; Fantasia on a theme by Thomas Tallis;* (ii) *The Lark ascending.*
(M) *** Virgin/EMI Dig. CUV5 61126-2 [id.]. (ii) Christopher Warren-Green; (i–ii) LCO,

Warren-Green – ELGAR: *Introduction and allegro* etc. ***

(B) *** Sony SBK 62645 [id.]. (i) Phd. O, Ormandy; (ii) Rafael Druian; Cleveland Sinf., Louis Lane – DELIUS: *Brigg Fair; Dance Rhapsody No. 2* etc. ***

Christopher Warren-Green and his London Chamber Orchestra give a radiant account of *The Lark ascending*, in which Warren-Green makes a charismatic solo contribution, very free and soaring in its flight and with beautifully sustained true *pianissimo* playing at the opening and close. For the *Tallis fantasia*, the second orchestra (2.2.2.2.1) contrasts with the main group (5.4.2.2.1) and here, though the effect is beautifully serene, Warren-Green does not quite match the ethereal, other-worldly pianissimo that made Barbirolli's reading unforgettable. The performance overall has great ardour and breadth, almost to match the coupled *Introduction and allegro* of Elgar in its intensity. The recording, made at All Saints' Church, Petersham, ideal in its resonant warmth and atmosphere yet with sharp definition.

The excellent performances from 1963 on Sony demonstrate the special feeling American musicians can find for English music. In the *Tallis fantasia* Ormandy (like Barbirolli) characteristically underlines the drama of a work that is often regarded as delicate and atmospheric. The recording of *The Lark ascending* was made during the period when Louis Lane was a colleague of George Szell at Cleveland and the orchestra was at the peak of its form. Rafael Druian is the intensely poetic violin soloist, producing the most delicate sustained *pianissimos*, even though the balance is close. The orchestral playing, is both polished and characterful. The CD transfers have expanded the original sound most strikingly. With expressive Delius performances as coupling, this is one of the most desirable of Sony's 'Esssential Classics'.

Fantasia on Greensleeves; (i) *The Lark ascending.*

(B) *** DG Classikon 439 464-2. (i) Zukerman; ECO, Barenboim – BRITTEN: *Serenade*; DELIUS: *On hearing the first cuckoo in spring* etc. ***

This DG Classikon bargain CD makes a most attractive anthology. Zukerman's account of *The Lark ascending* has a uniquely rapturous pastoralism and it is beautifully played and recorded.

(i–ii) *Fantasia on Greensleeves;* (iii–iv) *2 Hymn-tune preludes;* Overtures: *The Poisoned kiss;* (v; ii) *The Wasps*: Overture; (vi) *Romance for harmonica and orchestra;* (iii–iv) *The Running set;* (iii–iv) *Sea songs* (march); (iii; vii; viii) *Suite for viola and orchestra;* (ix) *Six studies in English folksong;* (iii; vii; viii; x) *Flos Campi;* (xi) *Linden Lea;* (xii) *The House of Life: Love-sight; Silent noon; Heart's haven;* (ii; v) *Serenade to music.*

(N) (B) **(*) Chandos 2-for 1 Analogue/Dig. CHAN 241-9 (2) [id.]. (i) BBC PO; (ii) Handley; (iii) Bournemouth Sinf.; (iv) Hurst; (v) LPO; (vi) Reilly, ASMF, Marriner; (vii) Riddle; (viii) Del Mar; (ix) Hilton, Swallow; (x) Bournemouth Sinf. Ch.; (xi) Huddersfield Ch., Kay; (xii) Varcoe, City of L. Sinfonia, Hickox.

A generally attractive, if rather bitty anthology, including a fair proportion of lesser-known Vaughan Williams. Exceptionally well recorded and vividly impressive, Vernon Handley's readings of the *Wasps overture*, the *Greensleeves fantasia* and the *Serenade to music* in its orchestral version are most sympathetically done. The *Overture* to the opera *The Poisoned kiss* is merely a pot-pourri, but it is presented most persuasively here. *The Running set* is an exhilarating fantasy on jig rhythms. Fine performances under George Hurst, who also includes the two very characteristic *Hymn tune preludes*. The evocation of the Song of Solomon contained in *Flos campi* shows Vaughan Williams at his most rarefied and imaginative, while the *Suite for viola and orchestra* is lightweight but engagingly unpretentious music with its charming *Carol* and quirky *Polka mélancolique*. Frederick Riddle is an eloquent soloist, even if the playing is not always technically immaculate, and Norman Del Mar directs sympathetically. Tommy Reilley, with Marriner, gives a haunting account of the *Romance for harmonica and orchestra*, while the attractive arrangements for clarinet and piano of the *Folksong studies* are also played most sensitively by Janet Hilton and Keith Swallow. Roger Varcoe is the generally sympathetic soloist in three of the songs from the Rosetti cycle, *The House of life* (orchestrated by Maurice Johnson), of which the most famous is *Silent noon*. His vibrato is occasionally intrusive, but the warmth of Hickox's accompaniment is a considerable plus point. *Linden Lea* is heard in its choral arrangement, pleasingly sung a cappella by the Huddersfield Choral Society under Brian Kay.

Fantasia on Greensleeves; Five variants of Dives and Lazarus; Partita for double string orchestra.

(N) (M) **(*) Carlton Classics Dig. 30366 00602 [id.]. E. Sinf., John Farrer – IRELAND: *Concertino pastorale; A Downland suite; The Holy boy.* **(*)

Farrer's performances are warmly sympathetic and well played. Some may look for a larger body of strings both in the rich sonorities of *Dives and Lazarus* and in the *Partita*. However, in the latter case the work's original form was a sextet (called a Double trio), a chamber performance adds to the textural clarity, and the sounds here are by no means lacking fullness. The characterization is strong, particularly in the central movements.

Fantasia on a theme by Thomas Tallis.
(M) *** EMI CDM5 66760-2 [id.]. RPO, Stokowski – DVORAK: *String serenade;* PURCELL: *Dido and Aeneas: Dido's lament.* ***
✿ (M) (***) EMI mono CDM5 66601-2 [id.]. Philh. O, Karajan – BRITTEN: *Variations on a theme of Frank Bridge* (***) ✿; STRAVINSKY: *Jeu de cartes.* (**)
(N) (M) **(*) EMI Dig. CDM5 66761-2 [id.]. City of L. Sinf., Hickox – ELGAR: *Introduction and allegro for strings*; **(*); WALTON: *Sonata for strings.* ***

Stokowski's care with tonal balance brings radiant antiphonal effects as the various string-groups are contrasted. Surprisingly, the performance is unusually straightforward; there is less variation of speed than is common and there is little *stringendo* at the approach to the main climax. Stokowski is comparatively serene, yet his restraint does not in any way interfere with the music's forward momentum. He conjures the ripest string playing from the RPO and some lovely, refined instrumental solos. The 1975 Abbey Road sound has fine body and a wide dynamic range.

Karajan's version of the *Tallis fantasia*, coupled with Britten's *Variations on a theme of Frank Bridge*, is one of the outstanding records of the 1950s, sounding as fresh and sonorous today as it did then. Sonically it is little short of amazing, and artistically it is no less impressive. The playing of the Philharmonia strings is superlative, and the *Tallis fantasia* sounds both idiomatic and vivid, like a newly cleaned painting.

Although recorded in a church (St Augustine's, Kilburn) the comparatively close microphones bring a sound-picture less than ideally atmospheric for Richard Hickox's 1993 version of the *Tallis fantasia*. Fine playing and no lack of ardour, but the Barbirolli and Warren-Green versions are more evocative, to say nothing of Karajan and Stokowski.

Fantasia on a theme of Thomas Tallis; Five variants of Dives and Lazarus; In the Fen Country; Norfolk rhapsody.
*** Chandos Dig. CHAN 8502 [id.]. LPO, Bryden Thomson.

Boult recorded *In the Fen Country* and the *Norfolk rhapsody* successfully, but neither is otherwise available in modern digital sound. Bryden Thomson is a most persuasive guide in all this repertoire, and in the other two pieces more than holds his own with most of the opposition.

(i) *Fantasia on a theme by Thomas Tallis; Five variants of Dives and Lazarus; Norfolk rhapsody No. 1;* (ii) *In Windsor Forest;* (i; iii) *Toward the Unknown Region.*
(M) *** EMI CDM5 65131-2 [id.]. (i) CBSO; (ii) Bournemouth Symphony Ch. & Sinf.; (iii) with CBSO Ch.; Norman Del Mar.

Norman Del Mar's strong and deeply felt account of the *Tallis fantasia* is given a splendid digital recording, with the second orchestral group creating radiant textures. The direct approach, however, lacks something in mystery, and not all of the ethereal resonance of this haunting work is conveyed. The early (1907) cantata, *Toward the Unknown Region*, set to words of Walt Whitman, and *In Windsor Forest*, which the composer adapted from his Falstaff opera, *Sir John in love*, make a perfect coupling. Norman Del Mar directs warmly sympathetic performances, given excellent sound.

Film music: *Coastal Command* (suite); *Elizabeth of England: Three Portraits. 49th Parallel: Prelude. The Story of a Flemish Farm* (suite).
**(*) Marco Polo 8.223665 [id.]. RTE Concert O, Dublin, Andrew Penny.

Vaughan Williams's wartime film music was of the highest quality. The Powell/Pressburger movie *49th Parallel* (1941), made in the early years of the war, inspires a *Prelude* with a nostalgic patriotic feeling. *Coastal Command* (1942) was a dramatized documentary which centred on the romantic profiles of the Catalina flying-boats, resulting in warmly evocative music, with echoes from the composer's symphonic writing. The even more imaginative (1943) score for *The Story of a Flemish Farm* (a true story about personal sacrifice which enabled a wartime escape to England) brings similar resonances. The masterly evocation of *Dawn in the barn* clearly anticipates the *Sixth Symphony*, while the haunting sequence, *The Dead Man's Kit*, evokes the *Sinfonia antartica*. *Elizabeth in England* (1955–7), another documentary, narrated by Alec Clunes, has its Elizabethan hey-nonny flavour, but there is a haunting *Poet* sequence which introduces a magically gentle tune, also used in the *Sea Symphony*. Finally comes a celebration of *The Queen*, not just regal but thoughtful in restrained nobility. Andrew Penny is a splendid advocate in performances eloquent in their mood-painting. The recording is bright and full, if rather two-dimensional.

Job (A masque for dancing).
(N) (B) *** CfP Dig. CDCFP 4603 [id.]. LPO, Vernon Handley.

Job (A masque for dancing); (i) *The Lark ascending.*
(BB) *** Naxos Dig. 8.553955 [id.]. E. N. Philh., Lloyd-Jones, (i) with David Greed.

Job (A masque for dancing); The Wasps overture.
(BB) (***) Belart mono 461 122-2 [id.]. LPO, Boult.

*(**) Everest EVC 9006 [id.]. LPO, Boult (with ARNOLD: *4 Scottish dances*: cond. composer **(*)).

In this splendid account of Vaughan Williams's masterly ballet score, David Lloyd-Jones – at super-budget price on Naxos – upstages almost all competition. He gives a performance tingling with drama, yet with great delicacy. The opening scene is particularly atmospheric and the *Saraband of the Sons of God* brings a noble dignity, especially when it returns expansively on the full brass. There is much fine orchestral playing. The big climaxes bring a superb brass contribution, almost submerging the organ at the vision of Satan. The dance rhythms are caught superbly – bitingly so in *Satan's dance of triumph*, genially Holstian in the *Galliard of the Sons of the Morning*. The Epilogue is touchingly ethereal. The recording, made in Leeds Town Hall, has an ideal spaciousness, yet combines vivid detail with glowing textures. For an encore the orchestral leader, David Greed, provides an exquisitely delicate portrayal of *The Lark ascending*, with a beautifully sustained closing *pianissimo*.

Handley's performance too is outstandingly fine. His dedicated approach shows the composer's inspiration at its most deeply characteristic and at its most consistently noble. The breadth of dynamic range of the EMI recording is used to enormous effect to increase the drama: the organ entry representing Satan enthroned in heaven has even greater presence than with the Naxos version and is overwhelming in impact and power. Comparably the ravishingly luminous espressivo playing in the work's quieter lyrical pages is movingly beautiful, with the music's evocative feeling memorably captured. This is undoubtedly one of Handley's major achievements in his Vaughan Williams discography, ranking alongside the *Fifth Symphony*.

Of Boult's four LP recordings of *Job*, this Belart/Decca mono version has great warmth and freshness. The mono recording sounds fuller and more atmospheric than some early digital stereo discs, and the same comment might apply to the delightful incidental music for *The Wasps*, with the lovely string-tune in the *Overture* warm and spacious and the delicious *March past of the kitchen utensils* piquant.

The Everest performance of *Job* under the work's dedicatee was Boult's second LP of Vaughan Williams's ballet. It is sensitive and spontaneous but, unusually for this label, the recording is made aggressive at climaxes because of the close microphoning of the brass, which sound strident, while the massed strings are somewhat tight, reflecting the problems of recording in the Royal Albert Hall. *The Wasps overture* was done at Walthamstow and sounds full and unconfined. This outstanding performance sparkles, and has a very broad tempo for the beautiful secondary theme. Malcolm Arnold conducts his own *Scottish dances* with élan and is especially persuasive in the third with its glorious picture of the Highland scenery, which produced one of the loveliest tunes the composer ever wrote. The recording is expansive; otherwise the brightly vivid sound is not quite as smooth as the best Everest reissues.

The Lark ascending.

(N) *** EMI Dig. CDC5 56413-2 [id.]. Kennedy, CBSO, Rattle – ELGAR: *Violin concerto*.***

Kennedy provides a valuable and welcome fill-up to his fine remake of the Elgar *concerto* in this spacious and inspirational account of Vaughan Williams's evocative piece, beautifully recorded.

SYMPHONIES

Symphonies Nos. 1–8; Partita for double string orchestra.

(BB) (***) Belart mono 461 442-2 (5). Baillie, Cameron, Ritchie, Gielgud, LPO Ch., LPO, Boult.

In some ways Boult's mono set of the Vaughan Williams *Symphonies* (No. 8 is in stereo) is unsurpassed, and the recording still sounds amazingly realistic, especially in the *Sea Symphony*, a demonstration LP in its day. The composer was present at the recording sessions and the orchestral playing was notable for its inspirational intensity. The five discs are handsomely packaged in a strong cardboard box with an engaging portrait of the young composer on the front. A set which is as indispensable as it is inexpensive. The discs are all available separately. Boult's first recording of No. 9 is on Everest (EVC 9001).

Symphonies Nos. 1–9.

**(*) Chandos Dig. CHAN 9087/91 [id.]. LSO, Thomson (with Yvonne Kenny, Brian Rayner Cook in *No. 1*; Kenny in *No. 3*; Catherine Bott in *No. 7*; London Symphony Ch. in *Nos. 1* & *7*).

Symphonies Nos. 1–9 (complete); *Fantasia on Greensleeves; Fantasia on a theme of Tallis; Norfolk rhapsody No. 1; 5 Variants of Dives and Lazarus.*

(M) **(*) RCA 09026 61460-2 (6) [id.]. Philh. O, Slatkin.

Symphonies Nos. 1–9; (i) *Flos Campi; Serenade to music.*

(M) *** EMI Dig./Analogue CD-BOXVW 1 (6) [id.]. Soloists, Liverpool Philharmonic Ch., RLPO, Vernon Handley; (i) with Christopher Balmer.

Handley's set consists of the six individual CDs in a handsome blue slipcase, and it will especially suit those needing both economy and modern, digital sound; only the *Sinfonia Antartica* is analogue – and that is still a fine modern recording, offering also the orchestral version of the *Serenade to music* as a fill-up. In all his Vaughan Williams recordings Handley shows a natural feeling for expressive rubato and is totally sympathetic. Many of his performances are first or near-first choices and No. 5 is outstanding in every way. This disc also includes a very successful account of *Flos Campi*.

Leonard Slatkin, following in the footsteps of André Previn in the earlier VW cycle for RCA (now withdrawn), shows consistent sympathy for the idiom. Like the composer himself in his surviving recordings, Slatkin prefers speeds faster than usual, and that makes the central symphonies of the cycle less warmly expressive and less atmospheric than some rivals, but the earliest and, notably, the last symphonies find Slatkin at his finest. His achievement in this cycle is above all to demonstrate that the last three symphonies make a worthy conclusion, unconventionally but tellingly symphonic. Fine playing and generally full, atmospheric recording. The six CDs are offered for the price of four.

By omitting the various fillers, Chandos have fitted the nine Vaughan Williams symphonies on to five CDs; each work is offered without a break. However, Bryden Thomson's achievement is somewhat uneven through the cycle. In the *Sea Symphony* the chorus lacks the sharpest focus and the microphone is not kind to Brian Rayner Cook, the baritone soloist. In the *Pastoral Symphony* the orchestral sound is almost too tangible, losing some of the more gentle atmospheric feeling, and this applies also to the *Sinfonia Antartica*. Generally there is no lack of power, and the readings have both individuality and warmth as well as wide-ranging digital recording.

A Sea Symphony (No. 1).

(B) **(*) EMI Dig. CD-EMX 2142. Rodgers, Shimell, Liverpool PO Ch., RLPO, Handley.

(BB) (***) Belart mono 450 144-2. Baillie, Cameron, LPO Ch. & O, Boult.

*** EMI Dig. CDC7 49911-2 [id.]. Lott, Summers, LPO Ch., LPO, Haitink.

(M) *** EMI CDM7 64016-2 [id.]. Armstrong, Carol Case, LPO Ch., LPO, Boult.

*** RCA Dig. 09026 61197-2 [id.]. Benita Valente, Thomas Allen, Philh. Ch. & O, Leonard Slatkin.

Vernon Handley conducts a warmly idiomatic performance, which sustains relatively slow speeds masterfully. The reading is crowned by Handley's rapt account of the slow movement, *On the beach at night alone*, as well as by the long duet in the finale, leading on through the exciting final ensemble, *Sail forth*, to a deeply satisfying culmination in *O my brave Soul!* Joan Rodgers makes an outstandingly beautiful soprano soloist, with William Shimell drier-toned but expressive. The recording, full and warm, has an extreme dynamic range, placing the two soloists rather distantly.

As a performance, Boult's (early 1952) Decca mono recording with outstanding soloists and incisive and sympathetic singing from the LPO Choir has never been surpassed. This conveys the urgency as of a live performance, with the dramatic opening astonishingly vivid and real in the vintage sound. Boult was at his most inspired. This Belart CD makes the very most of the master tape, and only the lack of body of the massed upper strings betrays the age of the original. The choral sound is full and well focused and the Kingsway Hall acoustic spacious and warm; the closing section, *Away O soul*, is particularly beautiful.

As in the rest of his Vaughan Williams series, Bernard Haitink takes what to traditional English ears may seem a very literal view, not idiomatic but strong and forthright. Speeds are almost all unusually spacious, making this (at well over 70 minutes) the slowest version on record; but Haitink sustains that expansiveness superbly. It is the nobility of the writing, rather than its emotional warmth, that is paramount. The recording is the fullest and weightiest yet given to this work, with the orchestra well defined in front of the chorus. Felicity Lott and Jonathan Summers are both excellent.

Boult's stereo version demonstrates his affectionate style, drawing consistently expressive but never sentimental phrasing from his singers and players. John Carol Case's baritone does not sound well on disc with his rather plaintive tone-colour, but his style is right, and Sheila Armstrong sings most beautifully. The set has been remastered with outstanding success.

With Slatkin drawing passionate playing and singing from his Philharmonia performers and with Thomas Allen outstanding among the baritones who have tackled this role, the newer RCA version is a strong contender. Slatkin's ability to lift the folk-like rhythms of the early Vaughan Williams makes for idiomatically expressive results, though he cannot match Handley, for example, in conveying the mystery behind some of these Whitman settings. The bright, clear tones of the soprano soloist, Benita Valente, are marred by an intrusive vibrato, robbing the sound of purity. The recording of the chorus is full and bright, with soloists balanced relatively close.

A London Symphony (*No. 2;* original score).

(***) Biddulph mono WHL 016 [id.]. Cincinnati SO, Eugene Goossens – WALTON: *Violin concerto* (***) (with Concert (***)).

This is the only recording ever made of the 1920 version of Vaughan Williams's *London Symphony*. That involves three minutes of intensely poetic music, later excised in RVW's definitive 1936 edition. The sessions immediately followed the first recording of the Walton *Violin concerto* with Heifetz in 1941 in which Goossens and the Cincinnati orchestra provided the accompaniment. The coupling (together with other British music) is among the most valuable of all the reissues in the Biddulph catalogue, with excellent CD transfers.

A London Symphony (No. 2).
(M) **(*) EMI CDM5 65109-2. Hallé O, Barbirolli – IRELAND: *London overture*. ***

A London Symphony; Fantasia on a theme of Thomas Tallis.
(M) *** EMI CDM7 64017-2 [id.]. LPO, Boult.
*** EMI (SIS) CDC7 49394-2 [id.]. LPO, Haitink.

A London Symphony; Partita for double string orchestra.
(BB) *** Belart mono/stereo 461 008-2. LPO, Sir Adrian Boult.

A London symphony; The Wasps: Overture.
(BB) *** Naxos Dig. 8.550734. Bournemouth SO, Kees Bakels.

The Naxos version of Vaughan Williams's *London Symphony*, coupled with the *Wasps Overture*, is powerful and dedicated. Kees Bakels draws ravishing sounds from the Bournemouth Symphony Orchestra, notably the strings, with the Scherzo cleanly pointed and the slow movement both warm-hearted and refined, and with pianissimos that have you catching the breath. The problem is the extreme range of dynamic in the recording. A thrilling experience none the less.

The sound is spacious on Boult's splendid 1970 version and the orchestra produces lovely sounds in deeply committed playing. With Boult's noble, gravely intense account of the *Tallis fantasia* offered as a coupling, this remains a very viable option. The CD transfer is very successful indeed.

In jaunty themes, Haitink's straight manner at times brings an unexpected Stravinskian quality, and his expansively serene handling of the lovely melodies of the slow movement brings elegiac mobility rather than romantic warmth. In the *Tallis Fantasia*, the straight rhythmic manners make the result sensitively unidiomatic too but very powerful in its monumental directness. The recording has spectacular range.

In his 1968 EMI recording of the *London Symphony*, Barbirolli did not quite achieve the intensity of his earlier, Pye version (currently withdrawn), choosing a more relaxed and spacious approach. In many places this brings a feeling of added authority, as at the end of the first movement where the threads are drawn together with striking breadth. The slow movement gains from the fuller recording but has less passion, while the Scherzo, taken slowly, is more controversial, though the finale is powerful, with the Epilogue finely graduated in its dynamics. An impressive account.

Boult's 1952 recording of the *London Symphony* has great atmosphere and intensity. His later, EMI performance is warmer, but the voltage of this first LP version is very compelling, bringing the feeling of a live performance. The mono sound is spacious, but the violins sound very thin above the stave, and the remastering has not improved that. The *Partita* was recorded in the earliest days of stereo in 1956. It is not one of the composer's most striking works, but it is well played and the string sound is very agreeable.

(i) *A London Symphony (No. 2); Fantasia on Greensleeves; The Wasps Overture;* (ii) *Serenade to music.*
(M) (***) Dutton Laboratories mono CDAX 8004 [id.]. (i) Queen's Hall O; (ii) Isobel Baillie, Stiles Allen, Elsie Suddaby, Eva Turner, Margaret Balfour, Astra Desmond, Muriel Brunskill, Mary Jarred, Heddle Nash, Walter Widdop, Parry Jones, Frank Titterton, Roy Henderson, Robert Easton, Harold Williams, Norman Allin, BBC SO; Sir Henry Wood.

The historic Decca recording of Vaughan Williams's *London Symphony*, with the specially assembled group of musicians designated as the 'Queen's Hall Orchestra', conducted by Sir Henry Wood, brings a most striking discrepancy of pace with modern performances. The first movement alone takes over three minutes less than in most latter-day recordings. The not-so-slow introduction may lack mystery but there has never been a more passionate account of the work than this on record, and even with limited dynamic range – no true *pianissimo* is caught – the hushed intensity of the slow movement is tellingly conveyed. The *Symphony* comes coupled with shorter Vaughan Williams works, *The Wasps Overture*, *Greensleeves* and, best of all, the original (1938) Columbia recording of the *Serenade to music*, with the 16 soloists specified in the score, a stellar group. The gently soaring phrase 'of sweet harmony' has never sounded so sweetly angelic as when sung here by Isobel Baillie. The Dutton Laboratory transfers are outstandingly true to the originals.

A London Symphony (No. 2); Fantasia on a theme of Thomas Tallis; Norfolk rhapsody.
**(*) RCA Dig. 09026 61193-2 [id.]. Philh. O, Slatkin.

Characteristically, Slatkin takes a brisk view of many of the themes of the *London Symphony*, opting for a direct rather than a warmly expressive style. The result is less atmospheric than with many rivals but, more than most, he keeps the work tautly symphonic. The sound is refined but not as immediate as it might be, except with the opulent Philharmonia brass. The coupling is unusual and generous, offering a refined rather than weighty account of the *Tallis Fantasia*, as well as the rare and attractive *Norfolk rhapsody*.

(i) *A Pastoral Symphony (No. 3); Symphony No. 4 in F min.*
(M) *** EMI Dig. CD-EMX 2192. (i) Barlow; RLPO, Vernon Handley.

(i) *A Pastoral Symphony (No. 3); Symphony No. 4 in F min.; Fantasia on Greensleeves.*
**(*) RCA Dig. 09026 61194-2 [id.]. (i) Linda Hohenfield; Philh. O, Slatkin.

Although Vernon Handley's speeds are relatively fast – as those of his mentor, Boult, tended to be – he has the benefit of refined modern digital recording to help bring out the element of mystery in the *Pastoral Symphony*. Handley's approach to the *Fourth Symphony* is relatively light and not at all violent, but makes a good case for his alternative approach.

Taking his cue from the composer's own recording of the *Fourth Symphony*, Slatkin's speeds not just for the violent *Fourth Symphony* but for the elusive *Pastoral Symphony* are consistently on the fast side. In the *Pastoral* it tends to mean – as it did even with Boult – that mystery is lacking and, though the *Fourth* gains in power and urgency, the rhythms are sprung less infectiously. The recording is atmospheric but clearly focused, which helps the *Fourth* more than its predecessor.

(i) *A Pastoral Symphony (No. 3);* (ii) *Symphony No. 5 in D.*
(M) *** EMI CDM7 64018-2 [id.]. (i) Margaret Price, New Philh. O; (ii) LPO, Sir Adrian Boult.
(BB) (***) Belart mono 461 118-2. (i) Margaret Ritchie; LPO, Boult.
(N) ** Decca Dig. 458 357-2. LPO, Sir Roger Norrington.

On EMI, in the *Pastoral Symphony* Boult is not entirely successful in controlling the tension of the short but elusive first movement, although it is beautifully played. The opening of the *Lento moderato*, however, is very fine, and its close is sustained with a perfect blend of restraint and intensity. In a generous coupling Boult gives a loving and gentle performance of No. 5, easier and more flowing than most rivals', and some may prefer it for that reason, but the emotional involvement is a degree less intense, particularly in the slow movement. Both recordings have been very successfully remastered.

It is good to have Boult's earlier, Kingsway Hall recordings back in the catalogue. They were made in 1952/3 with the composer present; although some allowances have to be made for the lack of amplitude in the upper string climaxes, the CD transfer is impressively full and the recording luminous. The translucent textures Boult creates in the *Pastoral Symphony* with its ethereal opening, and his delicacy later are balanced by his intensity in the *Fifth*, where the climax of the first movement has wonderful breadth and passion. The LPO of the time play with great sympathy and warmth.

Norrington takes a cool view of these two symphonies. Textures are exceptionally clean, the playing of the LPO most refined, but Norrington's preference for a very steady beat, rarely allowing himself much rubato even at climaxes prevents these performances from having full emotional impact, a degree of restraint that might be approved by those who prefer an objective view. But there is a dimension missing here, especially in No. 5. Refined Decca sound to match.

A Pastoral Symphony (No. 3); Symphony No. 6 in E min.
(BB) **(*) Naxos Dig. 8.550733 [id.]. Bournemouth SO, Kees Bakels.

Kees Bakels' serenely expressive account of the *Pastoral* has moments of drama to heighten its quiet, atmospheric intensity. There is much lovely orchestral playing, with the soloists in the Bournemouth Symphony Orchestra very sympathetic to the music's subtle, lyrical resonance. The account of the *Sixth* does not catch the degree of underlying menace in the *Lento* second movement, but the performance has plenty of life and vigour, and Bakels sustains the epilogue with an ethereal, glowing *pianissimo*. First-rate Naxos recording in both works.

(i–ii) *Symphony No. 4 in F min.;* (ii–iv) *Oboe concerto;* (iii; v) *Fantasia on a theme of Tallis; The Wasps: Overture.*
(M) **(*) EMI CDM5 66539-2. (i) RPO; (ii) Berglund; (iii) Bournemouth SO; (iv) with John Williams; (v) Silvestri.

Berglund directs a rugged, purposeful account of the *Fourth Symphony*, one which refuses to relax even in the more lyrical passages. Berglund follows the composer himself in preferring an unusually fast speed in the first movement, while the second movement is superbly sustained at a very slow tempo. Any lack of polish in the playing of the RPO must be balanced against its extra bite. Silvestri's individual reading of the *Tallis Fantasia* is brilliant and not expansive, with keen tension in the opening and closing pages. His account of *The Wasps Overture* emphasizes the brio, with the great lyrical melody not allowed to interfere with the forward momentum. The vivacity of the playing is well projected in vivid recording. The *Oboe concerto*, beautifully played by the Bournemouth orchestra's principal in the mid-1970s, makes a charming pastoral interlude between the two major works.

Symphonies Nos. (i) *4 in F min.;* (ii) *5 in D.*
(M) (***) Dutton Lab. mono CDAX 8011 [id.]. (i) BBC SO, composer; (ii) Hallé O, Barbirolli.

In 1937 Vaughan Williams recorded his violent *Fourth Symphony* with the BBC Symphony

Orchestra, then at its pre-war peak, inspiring a bitingly urgent performance. This historic recording has been transferred to CD by Michael Dutton in astonishingly full-bodied sound, bringing out the high voltage of the playing, never quite matched since on record. Aiming to shock, RVW said he wasn't sure he liked the piece, but it was what he meant. After that, the *Fifth Symphony*, inspired by Bunyan, held no shocks; but, more than anyone, Sir John Barbirolli in this première recording of 1944, made in the year following its first performance, brings out a rare passion behind the seamless pastoral idiom. The great climaxes in the first and third movements are more red-blooded than in any recordings since. Though the string-playing of the wartime Hallé may not be as immaculate as one would expect today, this is a magnetic performance, vividly transferred.

Symphonies Nos. 4 in F min.; 6 in E min.
(M) **(*) EMI CDM7 64019-2. New Philh. O, Sir Adrian Boult.
(BB) (**(*)) Belart mono 461 117-2 [id.]. LPO, Boult (with speech by the composer).

Symphony Nos. (i) *4 in F min.;* (ii) *6 in E min.;* (i) *Fantasia on a theme by Thomas Tallis.*
(B) (***) Sony mono SBK 62754 [id.]. NYPO, (i) Mitropoulos; (ii) Stokowski.

The recordings of Vaughan Williams's two apocalyptic symphonies made by the New York Philharmonic – No. 4 conducted in 1956 by Dmitri Mitropoulos (in a reading approved by the composer himself) and No. 6 in 1949 by Stokowski (directing with unsentimental thrust) – make a fascinating coupling. As transferred to CD they sound far better than they ever did on LP. Both demonstrate what idiomatic power and brilliance American players could bring to the composer's two most abrasive symphonies. Stokowski's reading is the more controversial, disconcertingly fast in the slow movement and unpointed in the slow, visionary finale. Mitropoulos in a generous fill-up shows equal understanding of the rarefied *Tallis Fantasia*.

In the *Fourth Symphony* Sir Adrian draws from the New Philharmonia playing of the highest quality, and the slow movement is particularly successful. The recording, too, is first class, enhancing the sharp attack in the powerful first movement of the *Sixth Symphony*. Though the rarefied finale is played beautifully, atmospheric and mysterious, tension is too low.

On Belart, Boult shows himself to be a master interpreter of Vaughan Williams, but in the tearingly dramatic *Fourth Symphony* the age of the recording and its relative lack of amplitude blunt the work's impact. By contrast, in the *Sixth* Boult drew from the LPO some of the very finest and most committed playing in the whole cycle, unmatched in his later EMI cycle. After the ebullience of the first movement comes the frightening warning of the slow movement. The complete desolation of the hushed finale is wonderfully sustained. A spoken eulogy is included from the composer, who was present at the sessions. Impressive Decca mono recording.

Symphony No. 5 in D; (i) *Flos campi* (suite).
❁ (M) *** EMI Dig. CD-EMX 9512 [id.]. RLPO, Handley; (i) with Christopher Balmer & Liverpool Philharmonic Ch.

Symphony No. 5 in D; Hymn-Tune Prelude; Prelude & Fugue in C min.; (i) *The Pilgrim pavement; Psalm 23; Valiant for truth.*
(N) *** Chandos Dig. CHAN 9666 (i) Richard Hickox Singers; LSO, Hickox.

Symphony No. 5 in D; (i) *The Lark ascending; Norfolk rhapsody.*
*** EMI Dig. CDC5 55487-2. LPO, Haitink, (i) with Sarah Chang.

It was Hickox who at the Barbican in London was the first conductor to perform the Vaughan Williams symphonies as a cycle, and here with the LSO he captures a similar visionary fervour in this most characteristic of the series. Hickox's style is warmly expressive, moulding phrases and tempo affectionately, always sounding spontaneous, building climaxes with shattering power. The LSO respond with playing both rich and refined, helped by the wide-ranging Chandos sound. Equally, the rarities on the disc are most persuasively done, three of them première recordings. *The Pilgrim pavement* is a touchingly direct devotional motet written for the church of St John the Divine in New York, and the setting of *Psalm 23* for soprano is adapted from his opera, *The Pilgrim's progress*, while the *Prelude and fugue* is an amplification of an organ work of 1930, which anticipates the abrasive Vaughan Williams of *Job*.

Vernon Handley's disc is outstanding in every way, a spacious yet concentrated reading, superbly played and recorded, which masterfully holds the broad structure of this symphony together, building to massive climaxes. The warmth and poetry of the work are also beautifully caught. The rare and evocative *Flos campi*, inspired by the Song of Solomon, makes a generous and attractive coupling, equally well played if rather closely balanced. The sound is outstandingly full, giving fine clarity of texture.

Haitink's measured, dedicated view of VW, broad and steady in tempo, goes with beautiful playing from the LPO, notably in refined pianissimos from the string section. This may not be as passionate as some other versions in climaxes, but it compensates in monumental strength. After the measured speeds in earlier movements, the finale brings extra purposefulness in a flowing tempo. Haitink draws out comparable qualities in the rare *Norfolk rhapsody*, while Sarah Chang proves an intensely poetic soloist in *The Lark ascending*, volatile at the start in the bird-like fluttering motif and magnetically concentrated throughout. Full, atmospheric recording to match.

Symphonies Nos. 5 in D; 9 in E min.
(N) (BB) *** Naxos Dig. 8.550738 [id.]. Bournemouth SO, Kees Bakels.

Kees Bakels and the Bournemouth Symphony follow up their earlier issues with a superb coupling of No. 5, arguably the peak of the series, and the very last *symphony*, long underestimated. Drawing the most refined playing from the Bournemouth orchestra, not least the strings, he finds in a relatively direct reading an extra purity and nobility, pointing the big emotional climaxes of the first and third movements most tellingly. Speeds are on the fast side, but the visionary beauty is perfectly caught. No. 9, with its original structure flouting convention, emerges strong and fresh, with the *Andante tranquillo* finale bringing echoes of the comparable movement of No. 6. Clear, refined recording to match.

Symphony No. 6 in E min.; Fantasia on a theme of Thomas Tallis; (i) *The Lark ascending.*
*** Teldec/Warner Dig. 9031 73127-2 [id.]. (i) Tasmin Little; BBC SO, Sir Andrew Davis.

Andrew Davis's reading of the *Sixth* is taut and urgent, with emotions kept under firm control. The two shorter works which come as supplement are given more warmly expressive, exceptionally beautiful performances, with Tasmin Little an immaculate soloist in *The Lark ascending*. Teldec's wide-ranging sound, setting the orchestra at a slight distance, blunts the impact of the symphony in the first three movements, but then works beautifully in the chill of the hushed pianissimo meditation of the finale, as it does too in the fill-ups.

Symphonies Nos. 6 in E min.; 9 in E min.
(M) *** EMI Dig. CD-EMX 2230. RLPO, Vernon Handley.

Handley, with rich, full recording, gives warm-hearted readings of Nos. 6 and 9, two works that in their layout – both ending on measured, visionary slow movements – can be seen as related, quite apart from sharing the same key. Handley lacks some of the darker, sharper qualities implied. Though his speeds are consistently faster, his is a comparatively comfortable reading, and the recording adds to that impression. Handley's approach is a valid one, when the slow pianissimo finale, here presented as mysterious rather than desolate, was inspired not by a world laid waste by nuclear war, but by Prospero's 'cloud-capp'd towers' in Shakespeare's *The Tempest*.

Sinfonia Antartica (No. 7).
*** EMI Dig. CDC7 47516-2 [id.]. Sheila Armstrong, LPO Ch., LPO, Haitink.
(BB) *** RCA Navigator 74321 29248-2 [(M) id. import]. Heather Harper, Sir Ralph Richardson, London Symphony Ch., LSO, André Previn – WALTON: *Cello concerto.* ***

(i) *Sinfonia Antartica (No. 7); Five Variations of Dives and Lazarus; Sea songs* (Quick march).
**(*) RCA Dig. 09026 61195-2 [id.]. (i) Linda Hohenfield; Women of Philh. Ch.; Philh. O, Slatkin.

(i) *Sinfonia Antartica (No. 7); Serenade to music.*
(M) *** EMI Dig. CD-EMX 2173. (i) Alison Hargan; RLPO and Ch., Vernon Handley.

(i) *Sinfonia Antartica (No. 7); The Wasps* (incidental music): *Overture and suite.*
(M) **(*) EMI CDM7 64020-2 [id.]. (i) Sheila Armstrong; LPO, Sir Adrian Boult.

With exceptionally full and realistic recording, Haitink directs a revelatory performance of what has long been thought of as merely a programmatic symphony. Based on material from VW's film music for *Scott of the Antarctic*, the symphony is in fact a work which, as Haitink demonstrates, stands powerfully as an original inspiration in absolute terms. Only in the second movement does the 'penguin' music seem heavier than it should be, but even that acquires new and positive qualities, thanks to Haitink.

In the *Sinfonia Antactica* Previn's interpretation concentrates on atmosphere rather than drama in a performance that is sensitive and literal. Because of the recessed effect of the sound, the portrayal of the ice-fall (represented by the sudden entry of the organ) has a good deal less impact than on Vernon Handley's version. Before each movement Sir Ralph Richardson speaks the superscription written by the composer on his score. Previn's account of the *Eighth* brings no reservations, with finely pointed playing, the most precise control of dynamic shading, and a delightfully Stravinskian account of the bouncing Scherzo for woodwind alone. Excellent recording, which has been opened up by the digital remastering and made to sound more expansive. As can be seen, Previn's *Sinfonia Antartica* is also available coupled with Walton's *Cello concerto* – a real bargain on RCA's super-budget Navigator label.

As in his other Vaughan Williams recordings, Handley shows a natural feeling for expressive rubato and draws refined playing from the Liverpool orchestra. At the end of the epilogue Alison Hargan makes a notable first appearance on disc, a soprano with an exceptionally sweet and pure voice. In well-balanced digital sound it makes an outstanding bargain, particularly when it offers an excellent fill-up, the *Serenade to music*, though in this lovely score a chorus never sounds as characterful as a group of well-chosen soloists. This can be recommended alongside Haitink but costs much less.

Sir Adrian gives a stirring account and is well

served by the EMI engineers. The inclusion of Vaughan Williams's Aristophanic suite, *The Wasps*, with its endearing participation of the kitchen utensils plus its tuneful *Overture*, is a bonus, although in the *Overture* the upper strings sound a bit thin.

The Slatkin version offers an exceptionally strong and dramatic account of the *Sinfonia Antartica* which, thanks to speeds brisker than usual, notably in the first movement, is presented as a symphonic structure rather than just a series of atmospheric sound-pictures. The slow movement may not convey the same chill as other versions, with the cleanly focused recording dispelling mistiness, but the originality of instrumentation gives a tautness to the argument, not usually conveyed in this work. The soprano soloist could also sound more mysterious, but she sings with bright, clear tone. The couplings, idiomatically done, are unusual and attractive.

(i) *Sinfonia Antartica (No. 7); Symphony No. 8 in D min.*

(BB) *** Belart mono/stereo 461 116-2. LPO, Boult; (i) with Margaret Ritchie, LPO Ch.; superscriptions spoken by Sir John Gielgud.

(N) (BB) *** Naxos Dig. 8. 550737 [id.]. Bournemouth SO, Kees Bakels; (i) with Lynda Russell, Waynflete Singers; (superscriptions read by David Timson).

Boult's 1953 performance of the *Sinfonia Antartica* has never been surpassed; the atmospheric mono recording, with its translucent icy vistas and Margaret Ritchie's floating, wordless soprano voice sounding ethereal, remains a model of balancing. Boult and the LPO achieve keen concentration throughout, and the evocation of the frozen landscapes and the shifting ice-floes is as compelling as his control of the structure of a work that is never easy to hold together. Sir John Gielgud's superscriptions (from the score) act as moving preludes. The recording of the *Eighth Symphony* is early stereo (1956). Only the first and last movements make use of the full orchestra (which includes a remarkable array of tonal percussion) while the middle two movements are scored for wind instruments alone (Scherzo) and strings alone (*Cavatina*). The LPO plays beautifully, and the Decca engineers have relished the challenge of balancing the exotic sounds of glissando tubular bells, tuned gongs, vibraphone and xylophone. The string-tone sounds far fuller than it did when this recording last appeared, crowning this remarkably successful series of Belart super-bargain reissues.

Kees Bakels adds to his impressive series of Vaughan Williams recordings for Naxos with powerful, intense performances of two of the more problematic works, written towards the end of the composer's career, when he deliberately defied symphonic convention. The *Antartica* is particularly impressive, helped by vividly atmospheric recording which, with superb separation, clarifies textures – not least the percussion and wind-machine – and beautifully captures the ethereal sound of Lynda Russell singing off-stage. Bakels's fast speed for the opening movement tautly draws together a structure which can seem dangerously episodic, and the thrust is maintained through the other movements. Sensibly the superscriptions are included on separate tracks at the end of the disc. No. 8 is excellently done too, with an element of wildness brought out in the sharp contrasts of the first movement, bouncing humour in the Scherzo and refinement in the slow movement and finale.

Symphonies Nos. 8 in D min.; 9 in E min.

(M) *** EMI CDM7 64021-2 [id.]. LPO, Sir Adrian Boult.

Symphonies Nos. 8 in D min.; 9 in E min.; Flourish for Glorious John.

*** RCA Dig. 09026 61196 [id.]. Philh. O, Slatkin.

The concluding disc brings a deeply satisfying culmination to Slatkin's Vaughan Williams cycle, arguably the finest of all, brilliantly played and recorded. The *Flourish*, never previously recorded, is a 90-second work that says much more than its brevity might suggest, a tribute to Sir John Barbirolli that seems almost to present the composer's work in microcosm. Both the last two symphonies are seriously underestimated, and Slatkin's bitingly intense performances, adopting speeds faster than usual, give them a compelling tautness. So the finales of both symphonies prove exceptionally satisfying, not just the bell-like ostinatos of No. 8 but the elusive string-writing of No. 9, which here emerges as a close relation to the visionary slow finale of No. 6. Bright, immediate recording, with more presence than in most of the series, and splendid playing.

Boult's account of the *Eighth* may not be as sharply pointed as Slatkin's version, but some will prefer the extra warmth and lyricism. The *Ninth* contains much noble and arresting invention, and Boult's performance is fully worthy of it. He draws most committed playing from the LPO, and the recording is splendidly firm in tone. The digital remastering is well up to the high standard EMI have set with these reissues of Boult's recordings.

Symphony No. 9 in E min.

**(*) Everest EVC 9001 [id.]. LPO, Boult – ARNOLD: *Symphony No. 3.* **(*)

Boult's first stereo record of the *Ninth* on Everest is prefaced on CD by a brief speech from the conductor, regretting the composer's death seven months before the recording sessions. The sound was very good for its day with a wide dynamic range, and it sounds even better now, lacking only a little in warmth and lustre. Boult's interpretation changed very little over the years; this early version seems tauter than the later remake for EMI, but this may be partly the effect of the less expansive sound.

Symphony No. 9 in E min.; Job (A masque for dancing).
**(*) Teldec/Warner Dig. 4509 98463-2 [id.]. BBC SO, Sir Andrew Davis.

It was a promising idea to couple Vaughan Williams's early (1930) ballet score (intended for Diaghilev but rejected as being 'too English') with the last of his symphonies, written 27 years later. The 'Masque for dancing' (as the composer described it) vividly depicts the biblical narrative, while originally the symphony's atmosphere was inspired by the cathedral city of Salisbury, with direct reference in the second movement to the heroine's fate in the Thomas Hardy novel, *Tess of the D'Urbervilles*. The BBC Symphony Orchestra play both scores splendidly, and the recording is spacious. However, as in Davis's other Vaughan Williams records, the orchestra is set back and some of the impact is lost, especially in the nightmarish Scherzo. *Job* is very successful. The spectacular organ entry makes a huge impact, while Job's comforters are strongly characterized and the serene closing music.

CHAMBER MUSIC

Fantasia on Greensleeves; The Lark ascending; 2 Pieces; 6 Studies in English folksong (all for violin and piano); *Violin sonata*.
(M) *** Carlton Classics Dig. 30366 00132 [id.]. Lydia Mordkovitch, Julian Milford.

Vaughan Williams's violin-writing can seem wayward and elusive, but in Lydia Mordkovitch, always inspired in English music, it finds an ideal interpreter. It is especially good to have the rarely heard *Violin sonata* with Mordkovitch's warmth matched by Julian Milford. He also proves an outstanding accompanist in the deeply felt reading of *The Lark ascending*, given a new slant in its version with piano, rather than orchestra. Excellent, well-balanced recording.

(i) *Phantasy quintet* (for 2 violins, 2 violas & cello); *String quartet No. 2 in A min. (For Jean on her birthday);* (ii; iii) *6 Studies in English folk-song for cello and piano;* (iii; iv) *Violin sonata in A*.
(M) *** EMI CDM5 65100-2. (i) Music Group of London; (ii) Eileen Croxford; (iii) David Parkhouse; (iv) Hugh Bean.

This collection of relatively little-known chamber works, very well performed and recorded at Abbey Road in 1972/3, can be recommended strongly. The *Phantasy quintet* dates from the composer's full maturity in 1912. The ethereal opening of this compressed one-movement work is Vaughan Williams at his most ecstatic. The *Six studies in English folk-song* are highly characteristic too, while the *Violin sonata* (1954) is a relatively gawky work but one which, like much later Vaughan Williams, has a tangily distinctive flavour, especially in a performance as fine as this. The *Second quartet*, written between the *Fifth* and *Sixth Symphonies*, was offered as a birthday present to a viola player friend of the composer, Jean Stewart. It contains some strikingly original ideas, notably in the purposefully sombre but bleakly haunting *Largo*. The performances by the Music Group of London bring out the deeper qualities of both this and the richly scored *Quintet*.

6 Studies in English folk-song for clarinet and piano.
*** Chandos Dig. CHAN 8683 [id.]. Hilton, Swallow – BAX: *Sonata* **(*); BLISS: *Quintet*. ***

These *Folk-song studies*, which Vaughan Williams published in arrangements for the viola and cello, come from the mid-1920s and are very beautiful, most sensitively played by Janet Hilton and Keith Swallow.

Violin sonata in A min.
(M) **(*) EMI CDM5 66122-2. Yehudi Menuhin, Hephzibah Menuhin – ELGAR: *Sonata* **(*); WALTON: *Sonata*. (**)

The late Vaughan Williams *Sonata* is an unexpected piece for the Menuhins to record and, though in the first movement (as in the Elgar) their tempo is controversially slow, giving the music unexpected weight, the whole performance makes a fine illumination of an elusive piece, not least from the pianist, who copes splendidly with the often awkward piano-writing. The recording is first rate.

VOCAL MUSIC

Songs of travel; Linden Lea.
(BB) *** Belart 461 493-2. Robert Tear, Philip Ledger – PARRY: *English lyrics*. **(*)

Robert Tear's set of the nine *Songs of travel* plus the favourite among the others, *Linden Lea*, all of which are vividly sung and recorded, are available on a super-bargain Belart CD which couples them with 20 rarely heard songs of Parry.

Arr. of traditional carols: *As it fell one May morning (The holy well); Behold the great Creator (This endris night); Come all you faithful Christians (Hereford carol); From far away we come to you (Snow in the street); How far is it to Bethlehem? (Children's song of the nativity); It was on Christmas Day (All in the morning); Joseph dearest, Joseph mine (Song of the crib); Nowell, this is the salutation (Salutation carol); O little town of Bethlehem; Now blessed be thou, Christ Jesu (Coverdale's carol); Now is Christmas y-come (Golden carol); On Christmas night (Sussex carol); Rise up, rise up, you merry men all! (The miraculous harvest); Shepherds left*

their flocks a-straying (Quem pastores); Sweet baby, sleep! (Wither's rocking hymn); Sweet dreams, form a shade o'er my lovely infant's head (Blake's cradle song); This is the truth sent from above; Wassail (Gloucestershire Wassail).
(B) **(*) Carlton Dig. 30367 01212 [(M) id.]. Cardiff Festival Ch., Owain Arwel Hughes, Robert Court.

Many of Vaughan Williams's arrangements of traditional carols are designed for congregational use, admirably straightforward strophic settings with organ. There are obvious highlights. *Wither's rocking hymn* and *Coverdale's carol* are rightly famous, and the simplicity of *Blake's cradle song* is beautifully caught here, with trebles alternating with the fuller choir. VW remembered that early carols were often dance-songs and *Now is Christmas y-come*, and *Nowell, this is the salutation*, similarly treated, are rhythmically vigorous. The much more elaborate setting of the *Gloucestershire Wassail* is the obvious highlight, and the concert ends with a boldly extrovert *Susssex carol*, with a strong contribution from the organist, Robert Court. The singing is of high calibre and the recording warmly atmospheric, but with hymn-like settings predominant the collection lacks variety.

Dona nobis pacem; 4 Hymns; Lord, Thou hast been our refuge (Psalm 90); O clap your hands (Psalm 47); Toward the unknown region.
*** Hyperion Dig. CDA 66655 [id.]. Judith Howarth, John Mark Ainsley, Thomas Allen, Corydon Singers & O, Matthew Best.

Using a relatively small choir and orchestra, Best takes an intimate view of *Dona nobis pacem* but one which as a result is even sharper in focus, capturing the dramatic contrasts as a big performance would, with words unusually clear. The sweet-toned Judith Howarth and the warmly expressive Thomas Allen are ideal soloists. *Toward the unknown region* was VW's first big choral work, not as distinctive as his later music but with many typical fingerprints. Best brings out the beauty of the choral writing, as he does in the even rarer *Four Hymns* for tenor, viola and strings, which the composer intended as a counterpart to the *Five Mystical songs*. Ainsley is the clear tenor soloist, though strained a little at the top. The setting of *Psalm 90* is the more effective here for having, instead of a semi-chorus, the optional baritone soloist, with Allen again singing with deep dedication.

Dona nobis pacem; 5 Mystical songs.
*** Chandos Dig. CHAN 8590 [id.]. Wiens, Rayner Cook, LPO Ch., LPO, Bryden Thomson.

The *Dona nobis pacem* is well performed on this Chandos disc, with Edith Wiens and Bryan Rayner-Cook as soloists. The latter gives an eloquent account of the much earlier *Five Mystical songs*, with Bryden Thomson drawing committed playing from the LPO. The recording is warmly resonant, with clear orchestral detail.

(i; ii) *Dona nobis pacem;* (ii; iii) *Sancta civitas.*
*** EMI CDC7 544788-2 [id.]. (i) Yvonne Kenny; (ii) Bryn Terfel; (iii) Philip Langridge, St Paul's Cathedral Choristers; L. Symphony Ch., LSO, Hickox.

These two visionary masterpieces, both seriously neglected, both with Latin titles and both dating from the inter-war period, make an ideal and generous coupling. Drawing passionate performances from his choir and soloists (notably from Bryn Terfel in both works), Hickox brings out not only the visionary intensity and atmospheric beauty – as in the offstage trumpets and '*Alleluias*' near the start of *Sancta civitas* – but also the dramatic power. Both these works may be predominantly meditative, but they have moments of violence which relate directly to the dark side of VW, as expressed in the *Fourth Symphony*, such as the chorus, '*Beat! beat! drums!*', the second section of *Sancta civitas*. In that same work it is fascinating to have the words '*Babylon the great is fallen*' set as a hushed lament instead of as a shout of triumph, as in Walton's *Belshazzar's Feast*. Hickox is a degree broader in his speeds than previous interpreters on disc, but is all the warmer for it.

(i) *Epithalamion;* (ii) *Merciless beauty.*
(M) *** EMI Dig./Analogue CDM7 64730-2. (i) Roberts, Shelley, Bach Ch., LPO, Willcocks; (ii) Langridge, Endellion Qt – *Riders to the sea.* ***

Vaughan Williams's setting of *Epithalamion* began life as a masque in the late 1930s and, only a year before he died, he expanded it into the coolly lyrical cantata recorded here. Scored for baritone and small orchestra with piano (Howard Shelley superb) and solo parts for flute and viola, it is an eloquent and thoroughly characteristic piece. Stephen Roberts gives a beautiful account of it, and Philip Langridge is hardly less impressive in *Merciless beauty*, three much earlier settings for voice and string trio. *Riders to the sea* is also indispensable – see below. This reissue makes a most valuable addition to the Vaughan Williams discography. The first two works were recorded digitally; *Riders to the sea* is analogue (1970) but sounds equally vivid and well focused. Splendid performances throughout.

(i) *Fantasia on Christmas carols.* arr. of carols: *And all in the morning; Wassail song* (also includes: TRAD., arr. Warlock: *Adam lay y-bounden; Bethlehem down*).
(M) ** EMI CDM7 64131-2. Guildford Cathedral Ch., Pro Arte O, Barry Rose; (i) with Barrow – HELY-HUTCHINSON: *Carol Symphony;* QUILTER: *Children's overture.* **

Vaughan Williams's joyful *Fantasia on Christmas carols* is comparatively short. It was written for performance in 1912 in Hereford Cathedral, so the acoustic at Guildford Cathedral is apt. The performance here is suitably exuberant, and John Barrow is a good soloist, but not everyone will respond to his timbre and style, and the King's performance with Hervey Alan is marginally preferable (currently unavailable). But the Christmas carol arrangements are delightful, beautifully sung and recorded. Valuable couplings too.

(i) *Fantasia on Christmas carols;* (ii) *Flos Campi;* (i) *5 Mystical songs;* (iii) *Serenade to music.*
*** Hyperion Dig. CDA 66420 [id.]. (i) Thomas Allen, (ii) Imai & Corydon Singers; (iii) 16 soloists; ECO, Best.

This radiant record centres round the *Serenade to music* and, as in the original performance, 16 star soloists are here lined up; though the team of women does not quite match the stars of 1938, the men are generally fresher and clearer. Above all, thanks largely to fuller, modern recording, the result is much more sensuous than the original, with ensemble better matched and with Matthew Best drawing glowing sounds from the English Chamber Orchestra. The other items are superbly done too, with Nobuko Imai a powerful viola soloist in the mystical cantata, *Flos Campi*, another Vaughan Williams masterpiece. Thomas Allen is the characterful soloist in the five *Mystical songs*. Warmly atmospheric sound to match the performances.

(i) *Flos Campi; Household music (3 Preludes on Welsh hymn tunes).*
*** Chandos Dig. CHAN 9392 [id.]. (i) Philip Dukes, N. Sinfonia, Richard Hickox – *Riders to the sea.* ***

Philip Dukes proves a rich and eloquent viola soloist in *Flos Campi*, in which the Northern Sinfonia Chorus is balanced more forwardly and powerfully than usual, and this is a remarkably successful performance on all counts. The *Household music*, never recorded before, offers three delightful miniatures, written in 1941 as a wartime exercise, intended for amateur musicians as well as professionals.

Lord Thou hast been our refuge; Prayer to the Father of Heaven; A vision of aeroplanes.
*** Chandos Dig. CHAN 9019 [id.]. Finzi Singers, Spicer – HOWELLS: *Requiem* etc. ***

These three choral pieces make an apt coupling for the Howells choral works on the Finzi Singers' disc. *A vision of aeroplanes* improbably but most imaginatively uses a text from Ezekiel.

Mass in G min.
(M) *** EMI CDM5 65595-2. King's College, Cambridge, Ch., Willcocks – BAX; FINZI: *Choral music.* ***

Here, with the finest band of trebles in the country, Sir David Willcocks captures the beauty of the Vaughan Williams *Mass* more completely than any rival, helped by the fine, atmospheric, analogue recording. This is a work which, on the one hand, can easily seem too tense and lose its magic or, on the other, fall apart in a meandering style; Willcocks admirably finds the middle course. Although recorded two decades before the Bax and Finzi couplings, the remastered analogue sound is still full and fresh.

5 Mystical songs; O clap your hands.
(M) *** EMI CDM5 65588-2. John Shirley-Quirk, King's College, Cambridge, Ch., ECO, Willcocks – FINZI: *Dies natalis;* HOLST: *Choral fantasia; Psalm 86.* ***

In the *Five Mystical songs* to words by George Herbert, John Shirley-Quirk sings admirably, and the motet, *O clap your hands*, makes a fine bonus for a recommendable triptych of English vocal works.

(i) *5 Mystical songs*; (i; ii) *5 Tudor portraits.*
(N) (B) **(*) Hyperion Helios Dig. CDH 55004 [id.]. (i) Henry Herford; (ii) Sarah Walker; Guildford Choral Soc., Philh. O, Hilary Davan Wetton.

The contrast of religious pastoralism of the *Five Mystical songs* and the rumbustious vigour of the *Tudor portraits* is well understood by Hilary Davon Wetton. Henry Herford is the rather restrained but sympathetic soloist in the former (an early work, concurrent with the *Sea Symphony*); his vocal style is less well suited to the portrait of *Pretty Bess* in the latter, written a quarter of a century later. Sarah Walker touchingly sings her *Lament* for her pet sparrow (the victim of her cat), and although she is a little strained at the climax, the chorus opens up powerfully and then paints a touching epitaph. She also gives a robust picture of *The tunning of Elinor Running*. The chorus are boldly enthusiastic both here and in the burlesque *Epitaph on John Jayberd of Diss*. The Philharmonia play sensitively and enter fully into the spirit of the bawdy Elizabethan frolics, playing with colourful vigour in the brilliant closing scherzo, *Jolly Rutterkin*, with its lively cross-rhythms. Henry Herford, too is more vociferous here. The recording is truthful, although the chorus could have been given more bite, for the words are not ideally clear. Otherwise an enjoyable and recommendable bargain coupling, which supplies full texts and even a brief glossary of unfamiliar Elizabethan terms.

(i) *On Wenlock Edge;* (ii) *Songs of travel* (song-cycles).
(M) *** EMI Dig. CDM7 64731-2. (i) Robert

Tear; (ii) Thomas Allen, CBSO, Rattle – BUTTERWORTH; ELGAR: *Songs*. ***

Vaughan Williams's own orchestration of his Housman song-cycle, made in the early 1920s, has been curiously neglected. It lacks something of the apt, ghostly quality of the version for piano and string quartet, but some will prefer the bigger scale. The orchestral version brings home the aptness of treating the nine songs as a cycle, particularly when the soloist is as characterful and understanding a singer as Thomas Allen. The Housman settings in the other cycle are far better-known, and Robert Tear, as in his earlier recording with Vernon Handley, proves a deeply perceptive soloist. Warm, understanding conducting and playing, and excellent sound.

On Wenlock Edge (song-cycle from A. E. Housman's *A Shropshire Lad*); (i) *10 Blake songs for voice and oboe. 4 Hymns: (Lord, come away!; Who is this fair one?; Come love, come Lord; Evening hymn);* Songs: *Merciless beauty;* (ii) *The new ghost; The water mill.*

(M) *** EMI CDM5 65589-2. Ian Partridge, (i) Janet Craxton, Music Group of London; (ii) Jennifer Partridge.

The EMI mid-priced CD is an outstandingly beautiful record, with Ian Partridge's intense artistry and lovely individual tone-colour used with compelling success in Vaughan Williams songs both early and late. The Housman cycle has an accompaniment for piano and string quartet which can sound ungainly but which here, with playing from the Music Group of London, matches the soloist's sensitivity; the result is atmospheric and moving. The *Ten Blake songs* come from just before the composer's death: bald, direct settings that with the artistry of Partridge and Craxton are darkly moving. The tenor's sister accompanies with fine understanding in two favourite songs as a welcome extra. The other rare items make an attractive bonus, with the *Four Hymns* distinctively accompanied by viola and piano.

The Shepherds of the Delectable Mountains; 3 Choral hymns; Magnificat; A Song of thanksgiving; Psalm 100.

*** Hyperion Dig. CDA 66569 [id.]. Gielgud, Dawson, Kitchen, Wyn-Rogers, Ainsley, Bowen, Thompson, Opie, Terfel, Best, Corydon Singers, L. Oratory Junior Ch., City of L. Sinfonia, Best.

With Sir John Gielgud as narrator and Lynne Dawson as the sweet-toned soprano soloist, Best gives *A Song of thanksgiving* a tautness and sense of drama, bringing out the originality of the writing, simple and stirring in its grandeur, not for a moment pompous. The *Magnificat* brings more buried treasure, a massive setting designed not for liturgical but for concert use. With its haunting ostinatos it is closer to Holst's choral music than most Vaughan Williams. The *Three Hymns* and the setting of *Psalm 100* are comparably distinctive in their contrasted ways, and it is good to have a recording of the Bunyan setting, *The Shepherds of the Delectable Mountains*. Most of the solo singing is excellent, and the chorus is superb, helped by warmly atmospheric recording.

The Pilgrim's progress (incidental music, ed. Palmer).

*** Hyperion CDA 66511 [id.]. Sir John Gielgud, Richard Pasco, Ursula Howells, Corydon Singers, City of L. Sinfonia, Best.

Vaughan Williams had a lifelong devotion to Bunyan's great allegory, which fired his inspiration to write incidental music for a BBC radio adaptation of the complete *Pilgrim's Progress*. Much of the material, but not all, then found a place in the opera. Christopher Palmer has here devised a sequence of 12 movements, which – overlapping with the opera and the *Fifth Symphony* – throws up long-buried treasure. Matthew Best draws warmly sympathetic performances from his singers and players, in support of the masterly contributions of Sir John Gielgud, taking the role of Pilgrim as he did on radio in 1942, and Richard Pasco as the Evangelist.

(i) *5 Tudor portraits;* (ii) *Benedicite;* (iii) *5 variants of Dives and Lazarus.*

(M) **(*) EMI CDM7 64722-2. (i) Bainbridge, Carol Case, Bach Ch., New Philh. O; (ii) Harper, Bach Ch., LSO; (iii) Jacques O; Willcocks.

Ursula Vaughan Williams reports in her biography of the composer that the first performance of the *Five Tudor portraits* – in Norwich in 1936 – was remarkable for shocking many of the audience. The composer deliberately chose bawdy words by the early Tudor poet, John Skelton, and set them in his most rumbustious style. This is a good, strong performance, but the soloists are not earthy enough for such music. The digital remastering has brought splendid bite and projection to the chorus without losing too much of the original ambience. The *Benedicite* is another strong work, compressed in its intensity, too brief to be accepted easily into the choral repertory, but a fine addition to the RVW discography. *Five variants of Dives and Lazarus* is beautifully played and warmly recorded, bringing serenity after the vigour of the vocal works.

OPERA

A Cotswold romance (adapted by Maurice Jacobson in collaboration with the composer from *Hugh the Drover*); *Death of Tintagiles.*

(N) *** Chandos Dig. CHAN 9646 [id.]. Rosa Mannion, Thomas Randle, Matthew Brook, LPO Ch., LSO, Hickox.

This makes a splendid supplement to Hickox's outstanding recording of Vaughan Williams's last opera, *The Pilgrim's Progress*. Saddened towards the end of his life that his tuneful ballad opera, *Hugh the Drover*, was seriously neglected, he adapted some of the most winning sequences to produce this cantata, *A Cotswold romance* – never recorded before. Even though some striking items from the opera are omitted, it helps that the role of the chorus is expanded, with the colour and vigour of the original enhanced. *The Death of Tintagiles*, even more neglected, is drawn from Vaughan Williams's incidental music for a Maeterlinck play, six dark and spare fragments anticipating later Vaughan Williams works.

Hugh the Drover (complete).
*** Hyperion Dig. CDSA 66901/2 [id.]. Bonaventura Bottone, Rebecca Evans, Sarah Walker, Richard Van Allan, Alan Opie, Corydon Singers & O, Matthew Best.

Described as a ballad opera, *Hugh the Drover* uses folk-themes with full-throated Puccinian warmth. The Hyperion version in atmospheric digital sound offers a fresh, light view, resilient and urgent in the first Act, hauntingly tender in the second. Rebecca Evans is superb as the heroine, Mary, with Bonaventura Bottone an amiable Hugh, only occasionally strained, well supported by a cast of generally fresh young singers.

The Pilgrim's Progress (complete).
(N) ✿ *** Chandos Dig. CHAN 9825 (2) [id.]. Gerald Finley, and soloists, ROHCG Ch. & O, Hickox.
(M) *** EMI CMS7 64212-2 (2). Noble, Burrowes, Armstrong, Herincx, Carol Case, Shirley-Quirk, Keyte, LPO Ch., LPO, Boult.

Vaughan Williams called his Bunyan-inspired opera a 'Morality', but was very clear that he did not want it treated as an oratorio. Richard Hickox clearly registers that in a performance that glows from beginning to end. He not only brings out the visionary intensity of much of the writing – notably in the ideas drawn from the *Fifth Symphony* – but also the passion and urgency, pacing the music to bring out the underlying drama in heightened contrasts. As in his recording of that symphony, Hickox is masterly in moulding phrases to magnetize the ear, always a warm interpreter, reflected in the unfailing ardour of the Covent Garden Chorus and Orchestra. The big cast is a strong one, mainly of young singers, led by Gerald Finley as a firm, fresh-voiced Pilgrim, and with Peter Coleman-Wright introducing the opera strongly as John Bunyan. The Chandos recording is superb, spacious and atmospheric, with the many offstage effects beautifully balanced, yet with words always clear. It is one of the many delights of this opera to register the heightened moments when the libretto quotes a Psalm or other familiar sources. Vaughan Williams may not have been a practising Christian, but the depth of his humanitarian faith was never more powerfully demonstrated than here, supremely so in this overwhelming recording.

On EMI John Noble gives a dedicated performance in the central role of Pilgrim, and the large supporting cast is consistently strong. Vanity Fair may not sound evil here, but Vaughan Williams's own recoil is vividly expressed, and the jaunty passage of Mr and Mrs By-Ends brings the most delightful light relief. Boult underlines the virility of his performance with a fascinating and revealing half-hour collection of rehearsal excerpts, placed at the end of the second CD. The outstanding recording quality is confirmed by the CD transfer, which shows few signs of the passing of two decades.

Riders to the sea (opera) complete.
*** Chandos Dig. CHAN 9392 [id.]. Finnie, Daymond, Dawson, Attrot, Stephen, N. Sinfonia, Richard Hickox – *Flos Campi* etc. ***
(M) *** EMI CDM7 64730-2. Burrowes, M. Price, Watts, Luxon, Amb. S., L. O Nova, Meredith Davies – *Epithalamion; Merciless Beauty*. ***

The one-Act opera, *Riders to the sea*, is among Vaughan Williams's supreme masterpieces, a word-by-word setting of J. M. Synge's one-Act play which heightens an already darkly intense drama. As in other Vaughan Williams works, Hickox takes a broad, warmly idiomatic view, less urgent than the previous, EMI recording, more timeless and mysterious, helped by opulently atmospheric recording. He is helped too by an excellent cast. Even if Linda Finnie as the old woman, Maurya, who loses all her sons to the sea, cannot quite match Helen Watts on the original recording, her final monologue of lament and resignation provides a moving, deeply expressive culmination. Among the others, Karl Daymond as Bartley, the last son to drown, is a newcomer to note, as impressive here as he was in Hickox's recording of Purcell's *Dido*. The generous coupling adds to the disc's attractions.

The earlier, EMI disc offers a strong, clean-cut performance with Helen Watts giving one of her finest performances as the old woman Maurya. It is also beautifully recorded in wonderfully atmospheric sound, though the wind machine is too prominent. With its rare couplings, this can be strongly recommended alongside the Chandos version. All who care about this composer should investigate one or other of these records.

Sir John in Love (complete).
(M) *** EMI CMS5 66123 (2). Herincx, Bainbridge, Watts, English, Eathorne, Tear, John Alldis Ch., New Philh. O, Meredith Davies.

'He wrote it for his own enjoyment,' commented Ursula Vaughan Williams when talking of her husband's project to compose a Falstaff opera, fully appreciating the obvious comparisons with Verdi, not to mention Nicolai and Holst. That love comes out from first to last in a rich and delightful score, tricked out with musical plums in almost every scene, not just the famous arrangement of *Greensleeves*, but also in delectable settings of 18 Elizabethan lyrics, and folksong themes that are superbly integrated in the score. Though the libretto does not begin to match Boito's Verdi, it has its own felicities, and the minor characters are more fully presented. On record any dramatic weaknesses tend to be minimized, particularly in a vigorous and well-sung performance like this one, with Meredith Davies relishing the colourfulness of the score. Raimund Herincx is a positive and sympathetic Falstaff, and Helen Watts as Mrs Quickly and Elizabeth Bainbridge as Mrs Ford rise ripely to the occasion. Wendy Eathorne as Anne Page and Robert Tear as Fenton make a delightful pair of lovers, and such singers as Gerald English as Dr Caius add to the stylishness. The 1974 Abbey Road recording is vivid and warmly atmospheric and beautifully balanced.

Vecchi, Orazio (1550–1605)

L'Amfiparnaso (commedia harmonica); *Il Convito musicale* (musical banquet: excerpts): *O Giardiniero; Lunghi danni; Bando del asino*.
(B) *** HM Dig. HMC 90856.58 (3) [(M) id. import]. Ens. Clément Jannequin, Dominique Visse – BANCHIERO: *Barca di Venetia per Padova* ***; MARENZIO: *Madrigals* **(*); LASSUS: *Madrigal comedies*. ***

Orazio Vecchi is the least familiar of the four Italian composers represented in this three-disc collection of each of whom contributes a collection of (usually) dramatized madrigals. Unlike Lassus, Vecchi, although earning his living as a *maestro di capella* in the church, leaned in his own music towards the secular. *L'Amfiparnaso* is a series of linked scenas, sung rather than acted, involving conventional comedy characters. It is all slight but well crafted and is brought vividly to life by the solo and ensemble singing here. *Il Convito musicale* (of which we are given only excerpts) is an innocent pastoral sequence set in a garden. A touching lament, *Lunghi danni*, follows; but it is the closing section, with its engaging vocal imitations of instruments and animals croaking all together, which makes the piece memorable. The recording is first class and so is the documentation.

L'Amfiparnaso (madrigal comedy).
(BB) *** Naxos Dig. 8.553312 [id.]. Cappella Musicale di Petronio di Bologna, Vartolo.

Described as a 'madrigal comedy', Vecchi's *L'Amfiparnaso*, first performed in 1594, fascinatingly points forward to the development of opera as a new genre in the following decade. The text in a Prologue and three brief Acts develops a comic plot stocked with *commedia dell'arte* characters, but, instead of solo voices representing different characters, here each scene is set as a madrigal for a small group of voices. Each madrigal, three in the first Act, five in both the other two, is preceded by a brief spoken summary, the whole making up a taut entertainment that still sounds fresh and charming after 400 years. Much is owed to the liveliness of the Naxos performance, using a first-rate ensemble from Bologna under Sergio Vartolo. With splendidly crisp ensemble the singers consistently bring out the sharply rhythmic quality of Vecchi's writing, with clear, well-balanced sound. Full texts and an English translation are provided.

Veracini, Francesco Maria
(1690–1768)

Overtures (Suites) Nos. 1 in B flat; 2 in F; 3 in B flat; 4 in F; 6 in B flat.
*** DG (IMS) Dig. 439 937-2. Col. Mus. Ant., Goebel.

The flamboyant and eccentric Florentine composer, who spent almost the entire middle period of his life working away from home, successfully penetrated and then established himself at the Dresden court, and these concertos were composed for the Dresden court orchestra, probably around 1716. Their character brings a curious amalgam of Italian volatility and German weight, and they have something in common with the orchestral suites of Telemann. Yet Telemann loved instrumental light and shade, whereas Veracini favoured tutti scoring. The music is strong in personality and there is no shortage of ideas, but energy is more important than expressive lyricism, with usually a single brief sarabande to provide contrast as the centrepiece of up to half-a-dozen dance movements. Musica Antiqua of Cologne, often abrasive, seem custom-made for this repertoire, playing with consistent vitality and obvious enjoyment. The recording is first class, within a spacious acoustic.

12 Sonate accademiche, Op. 2.
*** Hyperion Dig. CDA 66871/3 (3). Locatelli Trio.

Alongside his fame as a composer, Veracini was renowned as a master of the violin: he boasted that there 'was but one God and one Veracini', so that even Tartini was initimidated by his prowess. The 12 *Sonate accademiche* date from 1744. They are much more Italianate than the overtures, though German influence remains strong. The writing has a rhapsodic exuberance and drive, and, as with the overtures, dance movements predominate. But there are touching lyrical interludes and some lovely slow movements. The last *Sonata* is masterly, opening with a descending minor scalic theme, which is first used for a *Passacaglia*, then for a *Capriccio cromatico*, and finally provides the basis for an ambitious closing *Ciaccona*. The Locatelli Trio, led by Elizabeth Wallfisch, are a first-class group and their authentic style, strongly etched, is full of joy in the music's vitality, while the composer's lyrical side is most persuasively revealed. Paul Nicholson's continuo is very much a part of the picture, especially in the works using an organ – which is very pleasingly balanced. The recording is vivid and immediate.

Verdi, Giuseppe (1813–1901)

(i) *Ballet music from: Aida (including Triumphal march); Macbeth; Otello*. (ii) Overtures: *Aroldo; La forza del destino; Giovanna d'Arco; Luisa Miller; Nabucco; Oberto, conte di San Bonifacio; I vespri siciliani*.

(B) *** Decca Eclipse Dig. 448 238-2. (i) Bologna Teatro Comunale O; (ii) Nat. PO; Chailly.

Chailly's version enjoys brilliant Decca recording. Besides the ballet music, which is presented with gusto and style, he offers the four most obviously desirable overtures plus three rarities, including the overture to Verdi's very first opera, *Oberto*, and the most substantial of the early ones, *Aroldo*. Crisp and incisive, Chailly draws vigorous and polished playing from the excellent National Philharmonic.

The Lady and the fool (ballet suite; arr. Mackerras).

(B) *** CfP CD-CFP 4618. LPO, Mackerras – SULLIVAN: *Pineapple Poll*. ***

Mackerras's arrangement of Verdi has not caught the public fancy in quite the way of the coupled *Pineapple Poll*, but the scoring is witty and the music vivacious, and it is very well played and recorded here.

Overtures and Preludes: *Aida* (Prelude); *Alzira; Aroldo* (Overtures); *Attila; Un ballo in maschera* (Preludes); *La battaglia di Legnano; Il Corsaro* (Sinfonias); *Ernani* (Prelude); *La forza del destino* (Overture); *Un giorno di regno; Giovanna d'Arco* (Sinfonias); *Luisa Miller* (Overture); *Macbeth; I Masnadieri* (Preludes); *Nabucco* (Overture); *Oberto, Conte di San Bonifacio* (Sinfonia); *Rigoletto; La Traviata* (Preludes); *I vespri siciliani* (Overture).

(B) *** DG Double 453 058-2 (2) [id.]. BPO, Karajan.

It is good to have Karajan's complete set of Overtures and Preludes back in the catalogue. The 1975 recording was one of the very best made in the Philharmonie: the sound combines vividness with a natural balance and an attractive ambience. The performances have an electricity, refinement and authority that sweep all before them. The little-known overtures, *Alzira*, *Aroldo* and *La battaglia de Legnano*, are all given with tremendous panache and virtuosity. Try the splendid *Nabucco* or the surprisingly extended (8-minute) *Giovanna d'Arco* to discover the colour and spirit of this music-making, with every bar spontaneously alive, while there is not the faintest suggestion of routine in the more familiar items. As a DG Double this is even more strongly recommendable.

Overtures and Preludes: *Alzira;* (Overture); *Attila* (Prelude); *La battaglia di Legnano* (Overture); *Il Corsaro; I due Foscari; Ernani* (Preludes); *Un giorno di regno (Il finto Stanislao); Giovanna d'Arco* (Overtures); *Macbeth* (Prelude with ballet music); *I Masnadieri* (Prelude); *Nabucco; Oberto* (Overtures).

*** Chandos Dig. CHAN 9510 [id.]. BBC Philh. O, Edward Downes.

Edward Downes's programme opens with the little-known *Oberto* and follows with the spirited *Un giorno di regno*; but its highlight is *Nabucco* with its dignified brass sonority. Throughout, these extremely lively performances combine panache and virtuosity with string playing which uses a very wide dynamic range. The crescendo at the opening of *Giovanna d'Arco* is most dramatic, and *La battaglia di Legnano* which ends the 76-minute programme has plenty of full-blooded brass at the opening and close. The recording shows Chandos engineering at its most spectacular, but where are *La forza del destino*, *I vespri siciliani* and *Luisa Miller*? All these are included in Karajan's comprehensive, mid-priced, two-disc DG set which, if not recorded as opulently as this Chandos CD, are marvellously authoritative (453 058-2).

String quartet in E min.

*** Collins Dig. 1267-2 [id.]. Britten Qt – CHERUBINI: *Quartet No. 1;* TURINA: *La Oración del Torero*. ***

*** CRD CRD 3366; *CRDC 4066* [id.]. Alberni Qt – DONIZETTI: *Quartet No. 13;* PUCCINI: *Crisantemi*. ***

(N) (B) **(*) Hyperion Helios Dig. CDH 55012 [id.]. Delmé Qt – R. STRAUSS: *Quartet*.

An outstanding performance of Verdi's only *String quartet* from the Britten group. They match polished energy in the outer movements with much warmth and elegance in the inner ones, particularly the charming Neapolitan serenade theme at the centre of the miniature scherzo. With full, immediate, yet transparent sound this is very impressive indeed.

The Alberni Quartet's performance is also strong and compelling, and it is most imaginatively and attractively coupled with the Puccini and Donizetti pieces.

The Delmé are not a 'high-powered', jet-setting ensemble and they give a very natural performance of the Verdi which will give much pleasure: there is the sense of music-making in the home among intimate friends, refreshingly unforced, even if the sound is on the dry side.

Requiem Mass.

*** Chandos Dig. CHAN 9490 [id.]. Michele Crider, Markella Hatziano, Gabriel Sade, Robert Lloyd, L. Symphony Ch., LSO, Hickox.

(B) *** EMI forte CZS5 68613-2 (2) [CDFB 68613]. Scotto, Baltsa, Luchetti, Nesterenko, Amb. Ch., Philh. O, Muti – CHERUBINI: *Requiem in C min.* ***

✿ (B) (***) DG Double mono 439 684-2 (2) [id.]. Stader, Dominguez, Carelli, Sardi, St Hedwig's Cathedral Ch., Berlin RIAS SO, Fricsay – ROSSINI: *Stabat Mater.* (***)

(M) (***) DG mono 447 442-2 [id.]. Stader, Radev, Krebs, Borg, St Hedwig's Cathedral Ch., Berlin RIAS O, Fricsay.

(M) (***) Dutton Lab. mono CDLX 7010 [id.]. Caniglia, Gigli, Stignani, Pinza, Rome Opera Ch. & O, Serafin.

**(*) Decca 411 944-2 (2) [id.]. Sutherland, Horne, Pavarotti, Talvela, V. State Op. Ch., VPO, Solti.

(i) *Requiem Mass;* (ii) *4 Sacred pieces.*

*** Ph. Dig. 442 142-2 (2). (i) Orgonasova, Von Otter, Canonici, Miles; (ii) Donna Brown; Monteverdi Ch., ORR, Gardiner.

*** DG Dig. 435 884-2 (2) [id.]. Studer, Lipovšek, Carreras, Raimondi, V. State Op. Ch., VPO, Abbado.

**(*) EMI CDS5 56250-2 (2) [Ang. CDCB 56250]. (i) Schwarzkopf, Ludwig, Gedda, Ghiaurov; (ii) J. Baker; Philh. Ch. & O, Giulini.

(BB) **(*) Naxos Dig. 8.550944/5 (2) [id.]. Filipova, Scalchi, Hernández, Colombara, Hungarian State Op. Ch. & O, Pier Giorgio Morandi.

(i) *Requiem Mass.* Choruses from: *Aida; Don Carlo; Macbeth; Nabucco; Otello.*

*** Telarc Dig. CD 80152 (2) [id.]. (i) Dunn, Curry, Hadley, Plishka; Atlanta Ch. & SO, Shaw.

It says much for Richard Hickox's recording for Chandos with the LSO and London Symphony Chorus that in important ways – not just practically as the only modern single-disc version – it marks the first of what could be a new generation of readings of Verdi's choral masterpiece. His pacing flows more freely than has become the rule in latterday performances, yet there is never a feeling of haste, simply of heightened intensity when his control of rubato and phrase is so warmly idiomatic. These are very much the speeds which made the vintage Serafin recording of 1939 so compelling (still available on a fine Dutton transfer), but with singing from the London Symphony Chorus infinitely finer than that of Serafin's Italian chorus. In their fire they rival Giulini's classic Philharmonia set, even outshining that in luminosity, thanks in part to the spacious and full recording which, in a reverberant church acoustic, yet reveals ample detail. The warm-toned soprano, Michele Crider, has a glorious chest register, and the mezzo, Markella Hatziano, is equally warm and characterful, while the tenor, Gabriel Sade, sings with clear, heady beauty, not least in a radiant *Ingemisco*, and Robert Lloyd gives one of his noblest, most commanding performances. A winning set in every way.

Gardiner, using period forces, is searingly dramatic and superbly recorded, with fine detail, combing transparent textures, weight and atmospheric bloom. It can still be recommended as a fine alternative among modern digital recordings even to collectors not drawn to period performance. The soloists make a characterful quartet, with the vibrant Orgonasova set against the rock-steady von Otter, and with Canonici bringing welcome Italianate colourings to the tenor role. The *Four Sacred pieces* are equally revealing. The longest and most complex, the final *Te Deum*, is the most successful of all, marked by thrillingly dramatic contrasts, as in the fortissimo cries of '*Sanctus*'.

With spectacular analogue sound – not always perfectly balanced, but vividly wide in its tonal spectrum – Muti's 1979 Kingsway Hall performance makes a tremendous impact and is in almost all respects preferable to his later version, recorded live eight years later at La Scala. Characteristically he prefers fast speeds, and in the *Dies irae* he rushes the singers dangerously, making the music breathless in its excitement. Unashamedly, from first to last this is an operatic performance, with a passionately committed quartet of soloists, underpinned by Nesterenko in glorious voice, giving priestly authority to the *Confutatis*. Scotto is not always sweet on top, but Baltsa is superb, and Luchetti sings freshly. Now offered very inexpensively, and aptly coupled with a splendid (digital) account of Cherubini's *C minor Requiem*, so admired by Berlioz, this makes an outstanding bargain.

Fricsay's second recording, which DG have now reissued on a bargain Double coupled with Rossini, is of a live performance given in 1960, the very last he conducted before his untimely death. In biting drama it has never been surpassed, and even though speeds are often measured when compared with his fine studio recording (which DG have also currently reissued on a single disc as an 'Original'), such is the voltage of this later performance that it doesn't sound slower. Moreover it is underpinned by a commanding gravity that plainly reflects the conductor's own emotions during his last illness. Like him, the two male soloists are Hungarian, and both are first rate, with the tenor, Gabor Carelli, pleasingly Italianate of tone (his *Ingemisco* is ravishing). Maria Stader, the soprano soloist as before, sings with clear, pure tone, and Oralia Dominguez is the rich mezzo. The chorus is superbly disciplined, yet ardent: the *Dies irae* is electrifying, the *Sanctus* is wonderfully light and joyful and the closing *Lux aeterna* raptly beautiful. The CD transfer enhances the bite of the choral projection without losing the atmospheric warmth of a recording which, even today, can startle by its immediacy of sound.

Fricsay's superb mono studio recording of Verdi's *Requiem* caused a sensation when it first appeared on LP in 1954. Its tingling drama anticipated the later version, and though tempi are generally faster than in that live account there is marginal extra precision and polish. This makes a worthy reissue in DG's 'Legendary Recordings' series, with the full, spacious mono recording already showing that the DG engineers, using mono techniques, could achieve a combination of clarity and atmosphere. The solo team is first class with the contribution of Kim Borg standing out, as in the live performance.

Claudio Abbado's DG live recording was taken from performances at the Vienna Musikverein with the Vienna Philharmonic and Vienna choirs, as well as Cheryl Studer, Marjana Lipovšek, José Carreras and Ruggero Raimondi, all in superb voice and finely matched, even if Carreras has to husband his resources. In detail Abbado's reading is little different from his earlier, La Scala version, but the sense of presence, of the tension of a live occasion, makes the later account far more magnetic from the hushed murmurings of the opening onwards. The Vienna forces are not only more expressive but more polished too. The *Four Sacred Pieces* are also superbly done in another live recording.

Robert Shaw, in the finest of his Atlanta recordings, may not have quite the same searing electricity as Toscanini's classic NBC recording (for which he trained the chorus), but it regularly echoes it in power and the well-calculated pacing. In the *Dies irae*, for example, like Toscanini he gains in thrust and power from a speed marginally slower than usual. With sound of spectacular quality, beautifully balanced and clear, the many felicities of the performance, not least the electricity of the choral singing and the consistency of the solo singing, add up to an exceptionally satisfying reading. The fill-up of five Verdi opera choruses is colourful, and again brings superb choral singing.

What Giulini proves is that refinement added to power can provide an even more intense experience than the traditional Italian approach. In this concept a fine English chorus and orchestra prove exactly right. The array of soloists could hardly be bettered. Schwarzkopf caresses each phrase, and the exactness of her voice matches the firm mezzo of Christa Ludwig in their difficult octave passages. Gedda is at his most reliable, and Ghiaurov with his really dark bass actually manages to sing the almost impossible *Mors stupebit* in tune without a suspicion of wobble. Giulini's set also finds space to include the *Four Sacred pieces* in polished and dramatic performances which bring out the element of greatness in often uneven works. The full-toned CD transfer of the 1963/4 recording reveals the occasional roughness in heavy climaxes of the *Requiem*.

Well recorded, with first-rate Hungarian chorus and orchestra, the Naxos version offers an enjoyable account of Verdi's *Requiem* which may lack something in dramatic intensity but which consistently brings out the work's lyrical warmth. Though the tenor, César Hernández, is at times coarse, the other three soloists are very good, notably the Bulgarian soprano, Elena Filipova, with her opulent tone. This is a performance which gains in intensity as it progresses and, if anything, the *Four Sacred pieces*, an apt fill-up, bring performances even more dedicated, with refined choral singing, with the chorus set slightly behind the orchestra. A good bargain version, though it is worth remembering that Richard Hickox's outstanding Chandos version of the *Requiem*, coming on a single full-priced disc, is also a bargain, with much more sharply detailed recording of the chorus.

The Dutton Sound transfer of Serafin's historic recording of 1939 relates the work to the Verdian operatic tradition more closely than most latter-day versions. The beefy, Italianate sound of the chorus is what Verdi himself no doubt had in mind, and the team of soloists is characterfully representative of the finest Italian singing at that period. The recording was built round Beniamino Gigli, singing with his most golden tone. Though his tendency to aspirate the vocal line and to bring his half-tone down to a gentle croon may upset the purists, few performances are as winning as his, and both Ebe Stignani and Ezio Pinza are at their supreme best, rarely matched since. The soprano, Maria Caniglia, is more variable but, always dramatic, she rises splendidly to the challenge of the final *Libera me*. Whether because of co-ordination problems between such distinguished soloists, a brief *a cappella* passage of 11 bars for mezzo, tenor and bass soloists is omitted towards the end of the *Lux aeterna*.

There is little or nothing reflective about Solti's Decca account, and those who criticize the work for being too operatic will find plenty of ammunition here. The team of soloists is a very strong one, though the matching of voices is not always ideal. It is a pity that the chorus is not nearly as incisive as the Philharmonia on the Giulini set. But if you want an extrovert performance, the firmness of focus and precise placing of forces in the Decca engineering of 1967 make for exceptionally vivid results on CD.

(i; ii) *Requiem Mass;* (iii; iv) *Inno delle nazione;* (ii) *Te Deum;* (iii) *Luisa Miller: Quando le sere al placido.* (iv) *Nabucco: Va pensiero.*
(M) (***) RCA mono GD 60299 (2) [60299-RG-2]. (i) Nelli, Barbieri, Di Stefano, Siepi; (ii) Robert Shaw Ch.; (iii) Jan Peerce; (iv) Westminster Ch.; NBC SO, Toscanini.

Toscanini's account of the *Requiem* brings a supreme performance, searingly intense. The opening of the *Dies irae* has never sounded more hair-raising, with the bass-drum thrillingly caught, despite the limitation of dry mono recording. And rarely has the chorus shone so brightly in this work on record, while the soloists are near-ideal, a vintage team. The other works make fascinating listening, too. The *Te Deum* was one of Toscanini's very last recordings, a performance more intense than usual with this work, and it is good to have the extra-ordinary wartime recording of the potboiling *Hymn of the Nations*. The *Internationale* is added to Verdi's original catalogue of national anthems, to represent the then ally, the USSR.

OPERA

Aida (complete).
(M) *** EMI CMS7 69300-2 (3) [CDMC 65423]. Freni, Carreras, Baltsa, Cappuccilli, Raimondi, Van Dam, V. State Op. Ch., VPO, Karajan.
(N) (B) *** Decca Double 460 765-2 (2) [id.]. Leontyne Price, Gorr, Vickers, Merrill, Tozzi, Rome Op. Ch. & O, Solti.
(M) *** Decca Legends 460 978-2 (3) [id.]. Tebaldi, Simionato, Bergonzi, MacNeil, Van Mill, Corena, V. Singverein, VPO, Karajan.
(M) (***) RCA mono GD 86652 (3) [6652-2-RG]. Milanov, Bjoerling, Barbieri, Warren, Christoff, Rome Op. Ch. & O, Perlea.
(**) EMI mono CDS5 56316-2 (3). Callas, Tucker, Barbieri, Gobbi, La Scala, Milan, Ch. & O, Serafin.
(M) (**) RCA mono GD 60300 (3) [60300-RG-2]. Nelli, Gustavson, Tucker, Valdengo, Robert Shaw Ch., NBC SO, Toscanini.

On EMI, Karajan's is a performance of *Aida* full of splendour and pageantry, which is yet fundamentally lyrical. On disc there is no feeling of Freni lacking power even in a role normally given to a larger voice, and there is ample gain in the tender beauty of her singing. Carreras makes a fresh, sensitive Radames, Raimondi a darkly intense Ramphis and Van Dam a cleanly focused King, his relative lightness no drawback. Cappuccilli gives a finely detailed performance as Amonasro, while Baltsa as Amneris crowns the whole performance with her fine, incisive singing. Despite some over-brightness on cymbals and trumpet, the Berlin sound for Karajan, as transferred to CD, is richly atmospheric, both in the intimate scenes and, most strikingly, in the scenes of pageant, reflecting the Salzburg Festival production which was linked to the recording. The set has been attractively re-packaged and remains a first choice, irrespective of price.

Leontyne Price is an outstandingly assured Aida on Decca, rich, accurate and imaginative, while Solti's direction is superbly dramatic, notably in the Nile Scene. Merrill is a richly secure Amonasro, Rita Gorr a characterful Amneris, and Jon Vickers is splendidly heroic as Radames. Though the digital transfer betrays the age of the recording (1962), making the result fierce at times to match the reading, Solti's version otherwise brings full, spacious sound, finer, more open and with greater sense of presence than most versions since. As a Double Decca reissue this is a formidable bargain and the new-style cued synopsis with 'listening guide' is a fair sustitute for a full libretto.

On Decca, as on EMI, Karajan was helped by having a Viennese orchestra and chorus; but most important of all is the musical teamwork of his soloists. Bergonzi in particular emerges here as a model among tenors, with a rare feeling for the shaping of phrases and attention to detail. Cornell MacNeil too is splendid. Tebaldi's creamy tone-colour rides beautifully over the phrases and she too acquires a new depth of imagination. Among the other soloists Arnold van Mill and Fernando Corena are both superb, and Simionato provides one of the finest portrayals of Amneris. The recording has long been famous for its technical bravura and flair. It has now been impressively remastered for Deca's current Legend series, and remains a remarkable technical achievement.

All four principals on the historic RCA set under Perlea are at their very finest, notably Milanov, whose poise and control in *O patria mia* are a marvel. Barbieri as Amneris is even finer here than in the Callas set, and it is good to hear the young Christoff resonant as Ramphis. A flamboyant performance.

The Nile Scene has never been performed more powerfully and characterfully on record than in this vintage La Scala set. Though Callas is not a sweet-toned Aida, her detailed imagination is irresistible, and she is matched by Tito Gobbi at the very height of his powers. Tucker gives one of his very finest performances on record, and Barbieri is a commanding Amneris. The mono sound is greatly improved in the latest transfer, but this remains at full price.

Toscanini's 1949 performance of *Aida* is the least satisfying of his New York opera recordings. Richard Tucker sings well but makes a relatively colourless Radames, and Herva Nelli lacks weight as Aida, neatly though she sings and with some touching moments. Eva Gustavson's Amneris lacks all menace, and Valdengo as Amonasro is the only fully satisfying principal. Yet Toscanini is so electrifying from first to last that his admirers will accept the limited, painfully dry recording.

Aida: highlights.
(M) *** Decca 458 206-2 [id.] (from above complete recording, with Leontyne Price, Jon Vickers, Rita Gorr, Robert Merrill, Giorgio Tozzi, Rome Op. Ch. & O, cond. Solti).

The selection from Solti's full-price recording is generous (71 minutes) and makes an obvious first choice, for not only is it handsomely packaged in a slipcase in Decca's Opera Gala series but it comes with full translation.

Aroldo (complete).
** Sony CD 79328 [M2K 39506] (2). Caballé, Cecchele, Lebherz, Pons, NY Oratorio Soc., Westminster Ch. Soc., NY Op. O, Queler.

Aroldo is Verdi's radical revision of his earlier unsuccessful opera, *Stiffelio*: he translated the story of a Protestant pastor with an unfaithful wife into this tale of a crusader returning from the Holy Land. Less compact than the original, it contains some splendid new material such as the superb aria for the heroine, beautifully sung by Caballé. The final scene too is quite new, for the denouement is totally different. The storm chorus (with echoes of *Rigoletto*) is most memorable – but so are the rum-ti-tum choruses common to both versions. This recording of a concert performance in New York is lively, though the tenor is depressingly coarse.

Attila (complete).
(M) *** Ph. 426 115-2 (2). Raimondi, Deutekom, Bergonzi, Milnes, Amb. S., Finchley Children's Music Group, RPO, Gardelli.

With its dramatic anticipations of *Macbeth* and musical ones of *Rigoletto*, the compression which (on record if not on the stage) becomes a positive merit. In a fine performance under Gardelli, this Philips set of *Attila* is intensely enjoyable set. Deutekom, not a sweet-toned soprano, has never sung better on record, and the rest of the cast is outstandingly good. The 1973 recording is well balanced and atmospheric.

Un ballo in maschera (complete).
*** Decca Dig. 410 210-2 (2) [id.]. Margaret Price, Pavarotti, Bruson, Ludwig, Battle, L. Op. Ch., Royal College of Music Junior Dept Ch., Nat. PO, Solti.
(M) *** DG Dig. 449 588-2 (2). Domingo, Barstow, Nucci, Quivar, Sumi Jo, V. State Op. Konzertvereinigung, VPO, Karajan.
(B) *** DG Double 453 148-2 (2) [id.]. Ricciarelli, Domingo, Bruson, Obraztsova, Gruberová, Raimondi, La Scala, Milan, Ch. & O, Abbado.
(M) *** RCA GD 86645 (2) [6645-2-RG]. L. Price, Bergonzi, Merrill, Grist, Verrett, Flagello, RCA Italiana Op. Ch. & O, Leinsdorf.
(***) EMI mono CDS5 56320-2 (2). Callas, Di Stefano, Gobbi, Ratti, Barbieri, La Scala, Milan, Ch. & O, Votto.
(N) (B) **(*) Decca Double 460 762-2 (2) [id.]. Tebaldi, Pavarotti, Milnes, Resnik, Donath, Santa Cecilia Academy, Rome Ch. & O, Bartoletti.

Shining out from the cast of Solti's set of *Ballo* is the gloriously sung Amelia of Margaret Price in one of her richest and most commanding performances on record, ravishingly beautiful, flawlessly controlled and full of unforced emotion. The role of Riccardo, pushy and truculent, is well suited to the extrovert Pavarotti, who swaggers through the part, characteristically clear of diction, challenged periodically by Price to produce some of his subtlest tone-colours. Bruson makes a noble Renato, Christa Ludwig an unexpected but intense and perceptive Ulrica, while Kathleen Battle is an Oscar whose coloratura is not just brilliant but sweet too. Solti is far more relaxed than he often is on record, presenting a warm and understanding view of the score. The recording is very vivid within a reverberant acoustic.

Recorded in Vienna early in 1989, *Un ballo in maschera* was Karajan's last opera recording. It makes a fitting memorial, characteristically rich and spacious, with a cast – if not ideal – which still makes a fine team, responding to the conductor's single-minded vision. Standing out vocally is the Gustavo of Plácido Domingo, strong and imaginative, dominating the whole cast. He may not have the sparkle of Pavarotti in this role, but the singing is richer, more refined and more thoughtful. This Amelia is Josephine Barstow's finest achievement on record, dramatically most compelling. Leo Nucci, though not as rough in tone as in some of his other recordings, is over-emphatic, with poor legato in his great solo, *Eri tu*. Sumi Jo, a Karajan discovery, gives a delicious performance as Oscar the page, coping splendidly with Karajan's slow speed for her Act I solo. Florence Quivar produces satisfyingly rich tone as Ulrica. Though the sound is not as cleanly focused as in the Decca recording for Solti, it is warm and full.

Abbado's powerful reading, admirably paced and with a splendid feeling for the sparkle of the comedy, remains highly recommendable as a DG Double. The cast is very strong, with Ricciarelli at her very finest and Domingo sweeter of tone and more deft of characterization than on the Muti set of five years earlier. Bruson as the wronged husband Renato (a role he also takes for Solti) sings magnificently, and only Obraztsova as Ulrica and Gruberová as Oscar are less consistently convincing. The analogue recording clearly separates the voices and instruments in different acoustics, distracting at first, brings the drama closer.

Leinsdorf's RCA set is one of his finest opera recordings. Leontyne Price is a natural for the part of Amelia, spontaneous-sounding and full of dramatic temperament. Only in the two big arias does Price for a moment grow self-conscious. Robert Merrill here seems to have acquired all sorts of dramatic, Gobbi-like overtones to add to the flow of firm, satisfying tone. Bergonzi is a model of sensitivity, while Reri Grist makes a light, bright Oscar, and the Ulrica of Shirley Verrett has a range of power, at once rich, firm and delicate. Excellent recording, hardly showing its age, with the voices rather forward.

Votto's 1956 mono recording, with voices set close but with a fair amount of space round them, is among the best of the sets with Callas from La Scala, and CD focuses its qualities the more sharply. Cast from strength with all the principals – notably Gobbi and Giuseppe di Stefano – on top form, this is indispensable for Callas's admirers.

The main interest in the earlier Decca set rests in the pairing of Tebaldi and Pavarotti. The latter was in young, vibrant voice, but Tebaldi made her recording in the full maturity of her career. She gives a commanding performance, but there is no mistaking that her voice here is not as even as it once was. The supporting cast is strong, not only Milnes as Renato and Donath as Oscar, but Resnik a dark-voiced Ulrica. Bartoletti directs the proceedings dramatically, and the (1970) Decca recording remains strikingly vivid and atmospheric. Now reissued as a Double Decca with new-style cued synopsis, this makes a good bargain recommendation.

La Battaglia di Legnano (complete).
(M) *** Ph. 422 435-2 (2) [id.]. Ricciarelli, Carreras, Manuguerra, Ghiuselev, Austrian R. Ch. & O, Gardelli.

La Battaglia di Legnano is a compact, sharply conceived piece, made the more intense by the subject's obvious relationship with the situation in Verdi's own time. One weakness is that the villainy is not effectively personalized, but the juxtaposition of the individual drama of supposed infidelity against a patriotic theme brings most effective musical contrasts. Gardelli directs a fine performance, helped by a strong cast of principals, with Carreras, Ricciarelli and Manuguerra all at their finest. Excellent recording, with the depth of perspective enhanced on CD.

Il Corsaro (complete).
(M) *** Ph. 426 118-2 (2). Norman, Caballé, Carreras, Grant, Mastromei, Noble, Amb. S., New Philh. O, Gardelli.

In *Il Corsaro*, though the characterization is rudimentary, the contrast between the two heroines is effective, with Gulnara, the Pasha's slave, carrying conviction in the *coup de foudre* which has her promptly worshipping the Corsair, an early example of the Rudolph Valentino figure. The rival heroines are taken splendidly here, with Jessye Norman as the faithful wife, Medora, actually upstaging Montserrat Caballé as Gulnara. Gardelli directs a vivid performance, with fine singing from the hero, portrayed by José Carreras. Gian-Piero Mastromei, not rich in tone, still rises to the challenge of the Pasha's music. Excellent, firmly focused and well-balanced Philips sound.

Don Carlos (complete).
(N) *** Ph. Dig. 454 463-2 (3) [id.]. Gorchakova, Borodina, Hvorostovsky, Margison, Scandiuzzi, Ch. & ROHCG O, Bernard Haitink.
*** EMI Dig. CDS5 56152-2 (3) [CDCC 56152]. Alagna, van Dam, Hampson, Mattila, Meier, Ch. de Théâtre du Châtelet, O de Paris, Antonio Pappano.
(M) *** EMI CMS7 69304-2 (3). Carreras, Freni, Ghiaurov, Baltsa, Cappuccilli, Raimondi, German Op. Ch., Berlin, BPO, Karajan.
*** EMI CDS7 47701-8 (3). Domingo, Caballé, Raimondi, Verrett, Milnes, Amb. Op. Ch., ROHCG O, Giulini.
(M) (**(*)) EMI mono CMS7 64642-2 (3). Christoff, Stella, Nicolai, Mario Filippeschi, Gobbi, Neri, Rome Op. Ch. & O, Santini.

The very opening of the Haitink set, based on the Covent Garden production, indicates a clear advantage over previous versions – the vividness of the sound, with off-stage choruses sharply focused left and right. If Haitink often takes a measured view, that matches the dramatic weight of this epic opera, with the pacing consistently reflecting experience in the opera-house. The three Slavonic singers heading the cast are all superb, with Galina Gorchakova a powerful Elisabetta, Olga Borodina a vibrant Eboli and Dmitri Hvorostovsky a moving and intense Posa. Though Richard Margison is too consistently loud in the title-role, he has a good heroic timbre; Roberto Scandiuzzi as Philip II, rather light for the role, and Robert Lloyd as the Grand Inquisitor, not quite as steady as he once was, are well contrasted and dramatically intense.

Recorded live at the Châtelet Théâtre in Paris, the EMI set of the full five-Act version makes a clear first choice for anyone wanting this epic opera in the original French. In the five-Act version Pappano may not include as much of the extra and optional material as Abbado has on his four-disc DG Scala set (the only rival in French), but his judgement on the text is good, with one or two variants included. The whole performance sounds more idiomatic, helped by a cast more fluent in

French than Abbado's. Regularly Pappano conveys the dramatic thrust more intensely. Naturally impetuous as well as expressive, he inspires his players as well as his singers, an exceptionally strong team. Roberto Alagna is both youthfully lyrical and heroic. Thomas Hampson as Posa and José van Dam as King Philip are both centrally strong and expressive, projecting firmly. Waltraud Meier is not caught at her best as Eboli, but relishes the drama of *O don fatale*. As the Grand Inquisitor, Eric Halfvarson is not quite steady enough, even if (thanks to Pappano) the confrontation with the King is thrilling. Crowning the whole performance is the Elisabeth of Karita Mattila, giving her most commanding performance to date, culminating in a magnificent account of her big Act V aria, sure and true as well as deeply moving. The live recording brings some odd balances, with the sound transferred at a lowish level, but the opera-house atmosphere, vividly caught, amply compensates for any shortcoming.

Karajan opts for the four-Act version of the opera, merely opening out the cuts he adopted on stage. The *Auto da fé* scene is here superb, while Karajan's characteristic choice of singers for refinement of voice rather than sheer size consistently pays off. Both Carreras and Freni are most moving. Baltsa is a superlative Eboli and Cappuccilli an affecting Rodrigo. Raimondi and Ghiaurov as the Grand Inquisitor and Philip II provide the most powerful confrontation. The sound is both rich and atmospheric and is made to seem even firmer and more vivid in its current remastering, giving great power to Karajan's uniquely taut account, full of panache.

There is extra joy in the *Auto da fé* scene as it is pointed by Giulini, who uses the full, five-Act text. Generally the cast is strong; the only vocal disappointment among the principals lies in Caballé's account of the big aria *Tu che le vanità* in the final Act. The CD transfer of the 1971 analogue recording brings astonishing vividness and realism, a tribute to the original engineering of Christopher Parker. Even in the big ensembles the focus is very precise, yet atmospheric too, not just analytic.

The vintage EMI mono recording offers a seriously cut version of the four-Act score. Indifferently conducted by Gabriele Santini, it is still an indispensable set, with performances from Tito Gobbi as Rodrigo and Boris Christoff as Philip that remain unsurpassed. Gobbi's singing in the Death scene is arguably the finest recorded performance that even this glorious artist ever made, with a wonderful range of tone and feeling for words. The bitingly dark tone of Christoff as the King also goes with intense feeling for the dramatic situation, making his big monologue one of the peaks of the performance. Antonietta Stella, never a distinctive artist, gives one of her finest recorded performances as Elisabetta. As Eboli, Elena Nicolai controls her fruity mezzo well, even if the vibrato becomes obtrusive; and the most serious blot is the singing of the tenor, Mario Filippeschi, too often strained.

Don Carlos: highlights.

(M) *** EMI (SIS) CDM7 63089-2 (from above recording, with Domingo, Caballé; cond. Giulini).

(M) **(*) Sony Dig. SMK 53507 [id.]. (from above recording, with Furlanetto, Millo, Zajick, Sylvester, Chernov; cond. Levine).

Giulini's disc of highlights can be highly recommended. In selecting from such a long opera, serious omissions are inevitable, but the *Auto da fé* scene is included. Vivid sound; the only reservation concerns Caballé's *Tu che le vanità*, which ends the selection disappointingly.

Although, like Levine's *Aida*, his Met. *Don Carlos* highlights was recorded in the Manhattan Center, the sound is full and vivid. Michael Sylvester (as Don Carlos) and Aprile Millo (as Elisabetta) are both well cast and, if the rest of the team are more uneven and Ferruccio Furlanetto is a less than ideal King Philip, this 74-minute selection makes an excellent mid-priced sampler.

I due Foscari (complete).

(M) *** Ph. 422 426-2 (2). Ricciarelli, Carreras, Cappuccilli, Ramey, Austrian R. Ch. & SO, Gardelli.

I due Foscari brings Verdian high spirits in plenty, erupting in swinging cabalettas and much writing that anticipates operas as late as *Simon Boccanegra* and *La forza del destino*. The cast here is first rate, with Ricciarelli giving one of her finest performances in the recording studio to date and with Carreras singing tastefully as well as powerfully. Crisp discipline from the Austrian, though this is less atmospheric than the earlier, London-made recordings in the series.

Ernani (complete).

(N) *** Decca Dig. 421 412-2 (2) [id.]. Luciano Pavarotti, Joan Sutherland, Leo Nucci, Paata Burchuladze, Welsh Nat. Op., Ch. & O, Richard Bonynge.

(M) *** RCA GD 86503 (2) [6503-2-RG]. Leontyne Price, Bergonzi, Sereni, Flagello, RCA Italiana Op. Ch. & O, Schippers.

**(*) EMI (SIS) Dig. CDS7 47083-2 (3) [Ang. CDC 47082]. Domingo, Freni, Bruson, Ghiaurov, La Scala, Milan, Ch. & O, Muti.

This is the Joan Sutherland opera recording that got away. Made in May 1987, it was the final collaboration between Sutherland and Luciano Pavarotti, yet for over ten years it remained on the shelf. Listening to the result – brilliantly recorded, vividly conducted and above all sung with winning character and flamboyance – it is hard to understand why. *Ernani*, the fifth of Verdi's operas, based on Victor Hugo's play, was the first to win him international success. The hero is a nobleman who becomes a bandit after the death of his father, offering Verdi what William Weaver in his note describes as 'a kind of rough draft for Manrico in *Il Trovatore*'. Yet it is the heroine, Elvira, with her challenging aria, *Ernani involami*, who captures first attention. Here Sutherland gives a commanding account of the role, and though the beat in the voice betrays her age, that showpiece aria brings not just power but all the old flexibility. Helped by the sympathetic conducting of her husband, Richard Bonynge, she endearingly throws caution to the wind, in a way that neither Mirella Freni on Muti's EMI set nor even Leontyne Price in Schippers' RCA version does.

Pavarotti too, balanced rather close, gives a vividly characterful portrayal of Ernani himself, always ready to shade down his tone, characteristically bringing out word-meaning. Leo Nucci as Don Carlo, the King, his rival in love, is also firmer and more characterful than others on disc, and Paata Burchuladze as the vengeful de Silva was caught here at the brief peak of his career with his dark, sinister bass well controlled. On sound the new set easily outshines its rivals, including Muti's on EMI, recorded live at La Scala in 1982 with curious stage balances. Richard Bonynge draws from his Welsh National Opera forces warmly; dramatic playing and singing, urgent and idiomatic.

At mid-price, Schippers' set, recorded in Rome in 1967, is an outstanding bargain. Leontyne Price may take the most celebrated aria, *Ernani involami*, rather cautiously, but the voice is gloriously firm and rich, and Bergonzi is comparably strong and vivid, though Mario Sereni, vocally reliable, is dull, and Ezio Flagello gritty-toned. With Schippers drawing the team powerfully together, it remains a highly enjoyable set, with the digital transfer making voices and orchestra sound full and vivid.

The great merit of Muti's set, recorded live at a series of performances at La Scala, is that the ensembles have an electricity rarely achieved in the studio, even if the results may not always be so precise and stage noises are often obtrusive. The singing, generally strong and characterful, is yet flawed. The strain of the role of Elvira for Mirella Freni is plain from the big opening aria, *Ernani involami*, onwards. Even in that aria there are cautious moments. Bruson is a superb Carlo and Ghiaurov a characterful Silva, but his voice now betrays signs of wear. As Ernani himself, Plácido Domingo gives a commanding performance, but under pressure there are hints of tight tone. The CD version gives greater immediacy and presence, but also brings out the inevitable flaws of live recording the more clearly.

Falstaff (complete).

*** DG Dig. 410 503-2 (2) [id.]. Bruson, Ricciarelli, Nucci, Hendricks, Egerton, Valentini Terrani, Boozer, LA Master Ch., LAPO, Giulini.

(N) (M) (***) EMI CMS5 67083-2 (2) [Ang. CDCB 67162]. Gobbi, Schwarzkopf, Zaccaria, Moffo, Panerai, Philh. Ch. & O, Karajan.

(M) **(*) Decca 417 168-2 (2) [id.]. Sir Geraint Evans, Ligabue, Freni, Kraus, Elias, Simionato, RCA Italiana Op. Ch. & O, Solti.

(M) (***) RCA mono GD 60251 (2) [60251-RG-2]. Valdengo, Nelli, Merriman, Elmo, Guarrera, Stich-Randall, Robert Shaw Ch., NBC SO, Toscanini.

Giulini's *Falstaff* brings a care for musical values which at times undermines the knockabout comic element, yet the clarity and beauty of the playing are caught superbly on CD. Bruson, hardly a comic actor, is impressive on record for his fine incisive singing, giving tragic implications to the monologue at the start of Act III after Falstaff's dunking. The Ford of Leo Nucci, impressive in the theatre, is thinly caught, where the heavyweight quality of Ricciarelli as Alice comes over well, if at times her singing lacks purity. Barbara Hendricks is a charmer as Nannetta, but she hardly sounds fairy-like in her Act III aria. The conviction of the performance puts it high amongst modern digital versions.

The earlier (1956) Karajan recording (now reissued as one of EMI's 'Great Recordings of the Century') presents not only the most pointed account orchestrally of Verdi's comic masterpiece (the Philharmonia Orchestra at its very peak) but the most sharply characterful cast ever gathered for a recording. If you relish the idea of Tito Gobbi as Falstaff (his many-coloured voice, not quite fat-sounding in humour, presents a sharper character than usual), then this is clearly the best choice. The rest of the cast too is a delight, with Schwarzkopf a tinglingly masterful Mistress Ford, Anna Moffo sweet as Nannetta and Rolando Panerai a formidable Ford. On CD the digital transfer is sharply focused.

Sir Geraint Evans's assumption of the role of Verdi's Falstaff, in partnership with Sir Georg Solti, was originally issued by RCA, and here it comes up as sparkling as ever on a pair of mid-priced CDs. There is an energy, a sense of fun, a sparkle that outshines rival versions, outstanding as they may be. Evans never sounded better on record, and the rest of the cast live up to his example admirably. Solti drives hard, but it is an exciting and well-pointed performance, and the rest of the cast well contrasted.

Toscanini's fizzing account of Verdi's last masterpiece has never been matched as a performance, the most high-spirited ever, beautifully paced for comedy. Even without stereo, and recorded with typical dryness, the clarity and sense of presence in this live concert performance set the story in relief. The cast is excellent, led by the ripe, firm baritone, Giuseppe Valdengo. Such singers as Nan Merriman as Mistress Page, Cloe Elmo as a wonderfully fruity Mistress Quickly and Frank Guarrera as Ford match or outshine more recent interpreters. Toscanini's favourite soprano in his last years, Herva Nelli, is less characterful as Mistress Ford, over-parted but still fresh and reliable.

La forza del destino (complete).

(M) *** RCA 74321 39502-2 (3). Leontyne Price, Domingo, Milnes, Cossotto, Giaiotti, Bacquier, Alldis Ch., LSO, Levine.

*** DG Dig. 419 203-2 (3) [id.]. Plowright, Carreras, Bruson, Burchuladze, Baltsa, Amb. Op. Ch., Philh. O, Sinopoli.

(M) *** RCA GD 87971 (3). Leontyne Price, Tucker, Merrill, Tozzi, Verrett, Flagello, Foiani, RCA Italiana Op. Ch. & O, Schippers.

(N) (M) **(*) EMI CMS5 67124-2 (3) [CDMB 67124]. Arroyo, Bergonzi, Cappuccilli, Raimondi, Casoni, Evans, Amb. Op. Ch., RPO, Gardelli.

James Levine directs a superb performance. The results are electrifying. Leontyne Price recorded the role of Leonora in an earlier RCA version made in Rome in 1956, but the years hardly touched her voice. The roles of Don Alvaro and Don Carlo are ideally suited to the team of Plácido Domingo and Sherrill Milnes so that their confrontations are the cornerstones of the dramatic structure. Fiorenza Cossotto makes a formidable rather than a jolly Preziosilla, while on the male side the line-up of Bonaldo Giaiotti, Gabriel Bacquier, Kurt Moll and Michel Sénéchal is far stronger than on rival sets. In a vivid transfer of the mid-1970s sound, this is a strong, well-paced version with an exceptionally good and consistent cast. Now reissued at mid-price in RCA's UK Opera Treasury series, it makes an unmissable bargain.

Sinopoli draws out phrases lovingly, sustaining pauses to the limit, putting extra strain on the singers. Happily, the whole cast thrives on the challenge, and the spaciousness of the recording acoustic not only makes the dramatic interchanges the more realistic, it brings out the bloom on all the voices, above all the creamy soprano of Rosalind Plowright. Though José Carreras is sometimes too conventionally histrionic, even strained, it is a strong, involved performance. Renato Bruson is a thoughtful Carlo, while some of the finest singing of all comes from Agnes Baltsa as Preziosilla and Paata Burchuladze as the Padre Guardiano, uniquely resonant.

On RCA, Leontyne Price's voice (in 1964) was fresher and more open; on balance this is a more tender and delicate performance than the weightier one she recorded with Levine. Richard Tucker as Alvaro is here far less lachrymose and more stylish than he was earlier in the Callas set, producing ample, heroic tone, if not with the finesse of a Domingo. Robert Merrill as Carlo also sings with heroic strength, consistently firm and dark of tone; while Shirley Verrett, Giorgio Tozzi and Ezio Flagello stand up well against any rivalry. The sound is remarkably full and vivid.

Gardelli, normally a reliable recording conductor in Italian opera, here gives a disappointing account of a vividly dramatic score. The cast is vocally strong and each member of it lives up to expectations. Moreover the recording – made in 1969 in Watford Town Hall – is first rate, vivid, full and atmospheric. But it is vital in so long and episodic a work that overall dramatic control should be firm. Admirers of the individual artists will find much to enjoy when the sound is so flattering to the voices. The layout places Acts I and II on the first disc, while Acts III and IV are each allotted a CD apiece.

La forza del destino (slightly abridged).

(***) EMI mono CDS5 56323-2 (3). Callas, Tucker, Tagliabue, Nicolai, Rossi-Lemeni, Capecchi, La Scala, Milan, Ch. & O, Serafin.

Though there are classic examples of Callas's raw tone on top notes, they are insignificant next to the wealth of phrasing which sets a totally new and individual stamp on even the most familiar passages. Apart from his tendency to disturb his phrasing with sobs, Richard Tucker sings superbly; but not even he – and certainly none of the others (including the baritone Carlo Tagliabue, well past his prime) – begin to rival the dominance of Callas. Serafin's direction is crisp, dramatic and well paced, again drawing the threads together. The 1955 mono sound is less aggressive than many La Scala recordings of this vintage and has been freshened on CD.

Un giorno di regno (complete).

(M) *** Ph. 422 429-2 (2). Cossotto, Norman, Carreras, Wixell, Sardinero, Ganzarolli, Amb. S., RPO, Gardelli.

Un giorno di regno may not be the greatest comic opera of the period, but this scintillating performance under Gardelli clearly reveals the young Verdi as more than an imitator of Rossini and Donizetti, and there are striking passages which clearly give a foretaste of such numbers as the duet *Si vendetta* from *Rigoletto*. Despite the absurd plot, this is as light and frothy an entertainment as anyone could want. Excellent singing from a fine team, with Jessye Norman and José Carreras outstanding. The recorded sound is vivid.

Giovanna d'Arco (complete).

(M) **(*) EMI CMS7 63226-2 (2) [CDMB 632262]. Caballé, Domingo, Milnes, Amb. Ch., LSO, Levine.

The seventh of Verdi's operas, based very loosely indeed on Schiller's drama, is typical of the works which the master was writing during his 'years in the galleys', exuberantly melodic. James Levine, a youthful whirlwind in his very first opera recording, presses on too hard in fast music, with the rum-ti-tum hammered home, but is warmly sympathetic in melodic writing, particularly when Caballé is singing. What had become a standard trio of principals for the 1970s here gives far more than a routine performance. With fine recording there is much to enjoy, even when the plot – involving merely Joan, her father (who betrays her) and the King – is so naïve.

I Lombardi (complete).
(N) *** Decca Dig. 455 287-2 (2) [id.]. Pavarotti, Anderson, Leech, Ramey, Met Opera Ch. and O, Levine.
(M) *** Ph. 422 420-2 (2). Deutekom, Domingo, Raimondi, Amb. S., RPO, Gardelli.

Levine proves a forceful, incisive interpreter of Verdi's fourth opera, set at the time of the Crusades, often reflecting the influence of Toscanini. With the help of brilliant Decca recording, Levine consistently brings out this early work's adventurousness, its striking anticipations of *La forza del destino*. Based on the staging of the opera at the Met. in New York, the chief glory of the set is the casting of Pavarotti as the hero, Oronte. As Oronte does not appear until Act II and dies at the end of Act III (signal for the *Great Trio*, much the finest number in the opera), it is not a role one would have expected Pavarotti to take on at this stage of his career. He does it masterfully, on the whole, with even more imagination than the young Domingo on the rival Philips set under Gardelli. Unfortunately, the visionary appearance of the dead hero in Act IV (*Benedetto del cielo*) has the singer placed far too close, a very corporeal ghost. Samuel Ramey sings strongly in the baritone role of the evil brother, Pagano (who appears later as a Hermit), but vocally cannot quite match Ruggero Raimondi on Philips. On the other hand June Anderson as the heroine, Giselda, is both sweeter and more sympathetic than Cristina Deutekom on Philips.

I Lombardi reaches its apotheosis in the famous *Trio*, well known from the days of 78-r.p.m. recordings. By those standards, Cristina Deutekom is not an ideal Verdi singer: her tone is sometimes hard and her voice is not always perfectly under control. Domingo as Oronte is in superb voice, and the villain Pagano is well characterized by Raimondi. Impressive singing too from Stafford Dean and Clifford Grant. Gardelli conducts dramatically, heightening the impact of the plot.

Luisa Miller (complete).
*** Sony Dig. S2K 48073 (2) [id.]. Domingo, Millo, Chernov, Rootering, Quivar, Plishka, Met. Op. O and Ch., Levine.
*** Decca 417 420-2 (2). Caballé, Pavarotti, Milnes, Reynolds, L. Op. Ch., Nat. PO, Maag.
*** DG (IMS) 423 144-2 (2). Ricciarelli, Obraztsova, Domingo, Bruson, ROHCG Ch. & O, Maazel.
(M) *** RCA GD 86646 (2) [6646-2-RG]. Moffo, Bergonzi, Verrett, MacNeil, Tozzi, Flagello, RCA Italiana Op. Ch. & O, Cleva.

Levine conducts his forces from the Met. in a red-blooded, exceptionally high-powered reading of this elusive opera. In the role of Miller, the heroine's father, Chernov is even more characterful and musically more individual than any of his main rivals on other sets, with the power of his singing brought home by the close balance of the voice. Though the sound tends to make Levine's direction seem less subtle than it is, the impact of the score is brought home formidably. It is significant how Plácido Domingo, who takes the role of the hero Rodolfo for both Maazel and Levine, sings with much greater animation in the New York recording. Among the others Jan-Henrik Rootering, Florence Quivar and Paul Plishka all sing powerfully, even if all three suffer from occasional unsteadiness. The snag is the variable quality of Aprile Millo's singing in the title-role. She is more girlish-sounding than her rivals, but in Act I the coloratura taxes her severely, even if by the final Act she produces some beautifully floated high *pianissimos*.

On Decca, Caballé, not flawless vocally, yet gives a splendidly dramatic portrait of the heroine and Pavarotti's performance is full of creative, detailed imagination. As Federica, Anna Reynolds underlines the light and shade, consistently bringing out atmospheric qualities. Vividly transferred to CD.

Though taut in his control, Maazel uses his stage experience of working with these soloists to draw them out to their finest, most sympathetic form. Ricciarelli gives one of her tenderest and most beautiful performances on record, Domingo is in glorious voice and Bruson as Luisa's father sings with velvet tone. Gwynne Howell is impressive as the Conte di Walter and Wladimiro Ganzarolli's vocal roughness is apt for the character of Wurm. The snag is the abrasive Countess Federica of Elena Obraztsova.

In many ways the Cleva RCA set provides a performance to compete with the full-price versions and is just as stylish, with Moffo at her very peak, singing superbly, Carlo Bergonzi unfailingly intelligent and stylish, and Verrett nothing less than magnificent in her role as a quasi-Amneris. MacNeil and Tozzi are also satisfyingly resonant, and Fausto Cleva tellingly reveals his experience directing the opera at the Met. Good recording.

Macbeth (complete).
*** Ph. Dig. 412 133-2 (3) [id.]. Bruson, Zampieri, Shicoff, Lloyd, German Op. Ch. & O, Berlin, Sinopoli.
(M) *** DG 449 732-2 (2). Cappuccilli, Verrett, Ghiaurov, Domingo, La Scala, Milan, Ch. & O, Abbado.
(M) *** EMI CMS5 67128-2 (2) [CDMB 67128].

Milnes, Cossotto, Raimondi, Carreras, Amb. Op. Ch., New Philh. O, Muti.
(M) **(*) RCA GD 84516 (2) [4516-2-RG]. Warren, Rysanek, Bergonzi, Hines, Met. Op. Ch. & O, Leinsdorf.
(M) (*(**)) EMI mono CMS5 66447-2 (2) [CDMB 66447]. Callas, Mascherini, Tajo, Penno, Della Pergola, La Scala, Milan, Ch. & O, Victor de Sabata.

Sinopoli presents *Macbeth* as a searing Shakespearean inspiration, scarcely more uneven than much of the work of the Bard himself. In the Banqueting scene, for example, Sinopoli creates extra dramatic intensity by his concern for detail and his preference for extreme dynamics, and Renato Bruson and Mara Zampieri respond vividly. Zampieri's voice may be biting rather than beautiful, but, with musical precision an asset, she matches exactly Verdi's request for the voice of a she-devil. Neil Shicoff as Macduff and Robert Lloyd as Banquo make up the excellent quartet of principals, while the high voltage of the whole performance clearly reflects Sinopoli's experience with the same chorus and orchestra at the Deutsche Oper in Berlin. CD adds vividly to the realism of a recording that is well balanced and focused but atmospheric.

At times Abbado's tempi are unconventional, but with slow speeds he springs the rhythm so infectiously that the results are most compelling. Together making a fine team, each of the principals is meticulous about observing Verdi's detailed markings, above all those for *pianissimo* and *sotto voce*. Verrett, powerful above the stave, yet makes a virtue out of necessity in floating glorious half-tones, and with so firm and characterful a voice she makes a highly individual Lady Macbeth. Cappuccilli has never sung with a finer range of tone or more imagination on record than here, and Plácido Domingo makes a real, sensitive character out of the small role of Macduff. Excellent recording, splendidly remastered as one of the first operas to be included in DG's 'Legendary Recordings' series, and now at mid-price on two discs.

Muti's 1976 version of *Macbeth*, made at Abbey Road, appeared within weeks of Abbado's, confirming that, in this opera, new standards were being set on record. Though Muti and his team do not quite match the supreme distinction of Abbado and, later, Sinopoli, they provide a strong alternative. Both Milnes and Cossotto sing warmly and are richly convincing in their relatively conventional views of their roles, while the comfortable reverberation and warmth of the EMI recording conceal any slight shortcomings of ensemble. The reissue therefore provides another mid-priced recommendation for this opera, neatly fitted on two CDs, but without the supplementary items originally included as an appendix.

Leinsdorf's vintage version brings a large-scale performance featuring three favourite principals from the Met. Leonie Rysanek here gives one of her finest performances on record, producing her firmest, creamiest sound for the Sleepwalking scene, even though the coloratura taxes her severely. Leonard Warren, much admired in this part before his untimely death (on stage, singing Don Carlo in *La forza del destino*), gives a strong, thoughtful reading, marred by the way the microphone exaggerates his vibrato. Carlo Bergonzi is a stylish, clear-toned Macduff. Good sound for its period.

The role of Lady Macbeth could hardly have been more perfectly suited to Maria Callas, and though there are serious flaws in this live recording of 1952 – evidently taken off a radio relay – the commanding presence, the magnetic musical imagination and the abrasive tones make this a unique experience. In 1952 the vocal flaws that beset Callas were largely in the future, with thrilling sound in every register. Also Victor de Sabata, despite some odd misjudgements like his brisk tempo for the Sleepwalking scene, is comparably incisive. Sadly, nothing else in the performance matches such mastery, with Enzo Mascherini a dull, uncharacterful Macbeth and only the resonant Italo Tajo as Banquo otherwise commanding attention. Scrubby, limited sound which most ears will still accommodate for the sake of such a performance.

I Masnadieri (complete).
(M) *** Ph. 422 423-2 (2). Caballé, Bergonzi, Raimondi, Cappuccilli, Amb. S., New Philh. O, Gardelli.

Few will seriously identify with the hero-turned-brigand of *I Masnadieri* who stabs his beloved rather than lead her into a life of shame; but, on record, flaws of motivation are of far less moment than on stage. The melodies may only fitfully be of Verdi's more memorable quality, but the musical structure and argument often look forward to a much later period with hints of *Forza*, *Don Carlo* and even *Otello*. With Gardelli as ever an urgently sympathetic Verdian, and a team of four excellent principals, splendidly recorded, the set can be warmly welcomed.

Nabucco (complete).
*** DG Dig. 410 512-2 (2) [id.]. Cappuccilli, Dimitrova, Nesterenko, Domingo, Ch. & O of German Op., Berlin, Sinopoli.
*** Decca 417 407-2 (2) [id.]. Gobbi, Suliotis, Cava, Previdi, V. State Op. Ch. & O, Gardelli.

With Sinopoli one keeps hearing details normally obscured. Even the thrill of the great chorus *Va, pensiero* is the greater when the melody first emerges at a hushed *pianissimo*, as marked. Dimitrova is superb in Abigaille's big Act II aria, noble in her evil, as is Cappuccilli as Nabucco, less intense than Gobbi was on Gardelli's classic set for Decca, but stylistically pure. The rest of the cast is strong too, including Domingo in the unusually small tenor role and Nesterenko superb as the High Priest, Zaccaria. Bright and forward digital sound, less atmospheric than the 1965 Decca set with Gobbi and Suliotis, conducted by Gardelli.

On Decca, the Viennese chorus lacks bite in *Va, pensiero*; but in every other way this is a masterly performance, with dramatically intense and deeply imaginative contributions from Tito Gobbi as Nabucco and Elena Suliotis as the evil Abigaille. Suliotis made this the one totally satisfying performance of an all-too-brief recording career, wild in places but no more than is dramatically necessary. Though Carlo Cava as Zaccaria is not ideally rich of tone, it is a strong performance, and Gardelli, as in his later Verdi recordings for both Decca and Philips, showed what a Verdian master he is, whether in pointing individual phrases or whole scenes, simply and naturally. Vivid and atmospheric 1965 Decca recording.

Nabucco: highlights.

(N) (M) *** Decca 458 246-2 [id.]. (from above recording with Suliotis; Gobbi; cond. Gardelli).

Suliotis's impressive contribution is well represented on the Decca highlights disc, and there are fine contributions too from Gobbi. Needless to say the chorus *Va, pensiero* is given its place of honour and the reissued selection now runs for 69 minutes. As in other Opera Gala reissues, a full translation is now included.

Otello (complete).

*** DG Dig. 439 805-2 (2) [id.]. Domingo, Studer, Leiferkus, Ch. & O of Bastille Opera, Myung-Whun Chung.

(M) *** RCA 74321 39501-2 (2) [RCD2-2951 full price]. Domingo, Scotto, Milnes, Amb. Op. Ch., Nat. PO, Levine.

*** Decca Dig. 433 669-2 (2) [id.]. Pavarotti, Te Kanawa, Nucci, Rolfe Johnson, Chicago SO & Ch., Solti.

(M) *** RCA GD 09026 63180-2 (2) [id.]. Vickers, Rysanek, Gobbi, Rome Op. Ch. & O, Serafin.

(N) (B) **(*) Music & Arts CD 1043 (2) [971150]. Plácido Domingo, Mirella Freni, Cappuccilli, Giuliano Ciannella, Dano Raffanti, La Scala Milan Ch. & O, Carlos Kleiber.

(M) (***) EMI mono CHS5 65751-2 (2). Vinay, Martinis, Schoefler, Dermota, V. State Op. Ch., VPO, Furtwängler.

(N) (B) **(*) Decca Double 460 756-2 (2) [id.]. Cossutta, Margaret Price, Bacquier, V. Boys' Ch., V. State Op. Ch., VPO, Solti.

(M) (**(*)) RCA mono GD 60302 (2) [60302-2-RG]. Vinay, Valdengo, Nelli, Merriman, Assandri, NBC Ch. & SO, Toscanini.

Plácido Domingo's third recording of *Otello* proves to be his finest yet, more freely expressive, even more involved than his previous ones. In the earliest, with James Levine conducting (RCA), the voice may be more ringingly heroic, but the baritonal quality of his tenor has here developed to bring extra darkness, with the final solo, *Niun mi tema*, poignantly tender. Cheryl Studer gives one of her finest performances as Desdemona, the tone both full and pure, while Sergei Leiferkus makes a chillingly evil Iago, the more so when his voice is the opposite of Italianate, verging on the gritty, which not everyone will like. With plenty of light and shade, Myung-Whun Chung is an urgent Verdian, adopting free-flowing speeds yet allowing Domingo full expansiveness in the death scene. The Chorus and Orchestra of the Bastille Opera excel themselves, setting new standards for an opera recording from Paris, and the sound is first rate, though transferred at a slightly low level.

On RCA, Domingo as Otello combines glorious heroic tone with lyrical tenderness. Scotto is not always sweet-toned in the upper register, and the big ensemble at the end of Act III brings obvious strain; nevertheless, it is a deeply felt performance which culminates in a most affecting account of the all-important Act IV solos, the *Willow song* and *Ave Maria*. Milnes makes a powerful Iago, a handsome, virile creature beset by the biggest of chips on the shoulder. In the transfer of the 1977 analogue original the voices are caught vividly and immediately, and the orchestral sound too is fuller and cleaner than in many more recent versions. Now reissued in RCA's Opera Treasury series, it is a clear first choice among mid-priced versions. In the USA it remains at full price for the moment.

In the Decca Chicago set the key element is the singing of Pavarotti, new to his role of Otello, as was Nucci as Iago. In obedience to Solti, Pavarotti often adopts faster speeds than usual. Whatever the detailed reservations, this is a memorable reading, heightened by Pavarotti's keen feeling for the words and consistently golden tone. With a close microphone-balance, like the others he is prevented from achieving genuine pianissimos; but above all he offers a vital, animated Otello, always individual. Dame Kiri Te Kanawa produces consistently sumptuous tone; the *Willow song* is glorious. The impact of the whole is greatly enhanced by the splendid singing of the Chicago Symphony Chorus, helped by digital sound that is fuller and more vivid than on any rival set.

No conductor is more understanding of Verdian pacing than Serafin and, with sound that hardly shows its age (1960), this alternative RCA set presents two of the finest solo performances on any *Otello* recording of whatever period: the Iago of Tito Gobbi has never been surpassed for vividness of characterization and tonal subtlety; while the young Jon Vickers, with a voice naturally suited to this role, was in his prime as the Moor. Leonie Rysanek is a warm and sympathetic Desdemona, not always ideally pure-toned but tender and touching in one of her very finest recorded performances. The sense of presence in the open, well-balanced recording is the more vivid on CD, thanks to a first-rate transfer.

Music and Arts offers a live recording of the legendary performance in December 1976, when Carlos Kleiber conducted at the opening night of a new production at La Scala, Milan. If Kleiber can often sound cold or even uninvolved in his studio recordings, this demonstrates the high voltage electricity he can produce on a big occasion, here matching the seering intensity of Toscanini in this work. Plácido Domingo, having just completed a series of performances in Hamburg and Paris, is in superb form, with the voice at its finest, and his personal magnetism as an actor heightened by the conductor's challenge. Mirella Freni as Desdemona is at her freshest, sweet and vulnerable, while Cappuccilli sings with keen incisiveness as Iago, not always sinister-sounding but musically superb. Stage noises are endlessly intrusive, but the atmosphere of a great occasion is vividly caught.

Furtwängler, dedicated to the German repertory, at the 1951 Salzburg Festival broke with tradition by presenting Verdi's masterpiece, no doubt intending to rival the pre-war Toscanini. The result is incandescent, a performance of extremes. Set against rapt concentration and tender expressiveness in such passages as the Act I love duet and Desdemona's final scene, the fierily dramatic attack of the main drama is heightened all the more. So the oath duet of Otello and Iago in Act II is thrilling, and the clarity of both Ramon Vinay in the title-role and of Paul Schoeffler as a clean-cut, Germanic Iago adds to the bite. Vinay, who recorded the role with Toscanini four years earlier, has a focus and power ideally suited to the role, even if the voice is rarely beautiful. Sadly, the Austrian Radio recording of the stage production often balances him distantly. Dragica Martinis, whose career was sadly short, is here revealed as a tender and charming Desdemona, a match for her more celebrated colleagues. The orchestral sound is limited and dim, with intrusive stage-noises, but the result is atmospheric and electrifying.

The warmth and tenderness of Solti's Vienna reading of *Otello* as well as its incisive sense of drama take one freshly by surprise. The recording is bright and atmospheric to match. As Desdemona Margaret Price gives a ravishing performance, with the most beautiful and varied tonal quality allied to deep imagination. Carlo Cossutta as Otello is not so characterful a singer but he sings sensitively with clear, incisive tone. Gabriel Bacquier gives a thoughtful, highly intelligent performance as Iago, but he is disappointingly weak in the upper register. The Decca recording is full and vivid, and in its new Double Decca format this can be counted excellent value. The libretto is replaced by Decca's new-style synopsis with 'listening guide'.

Toscanini's historic 1947 reading suffers more than usual from dry, limited sound but in magnetic intensity it is irresistible, bringing home the biting power of Verdi's score as few other recorded performances ever have. Ramon Vinay makes a commanding Otello, baritonal in vocal colouring but firm and clear, with a fine feeling for words. Giuseppe Valdengo had few rivals among baritones of the time in this role, strong, animated and clean in attack, though the vocal differentiation between hero and villain is less marked than usual. Herva Nelli is sweet and pure if a little colourless as Desdemona. The recording prevents her from achieving a really gentle pianissimo, and Toscanini, for all his flowing lines, fails to allow the full repose needed.

Rigoletto (complete).

(B) *** Ph. Dig. Duo 462 158-2 (2) [id.]. Bruson, Gruberová, Shicoff, Fassbaender, Lloyd, St Cecilia Ac., Rome, Ch. & O, Sinopoli.

*** Decca 414 269-2 (2) [id.]. Milnes, Sutherland, Pavarotti, Talvela, Tourangeau, Amb. Op. Ch., LSO, Bonynge.

(N) *** DG Dig. 447 064-2 (2) [id.]. Vladimir Chernov, Luciano Pavarotti, Cheryl Studer, Roberto Scandiuzzi, Denyce Graves, Met. Op. Ch. & O, Levine.

(***) EMI mono CDS5 56327-2 (2) [id.]. Gobbi, Callas, Di Stefano, La Scala, Milan, Ch. & O, Serafin.

(M) **(*) RCA GD 86506 (2) [6506-2-RG]. Merrill, Moffo, Kraus, Elias, Flagello, RCA Italiana Op. Ch. & O, Solti.

Edita Gruberová might have been considered an unexpected choice for Gilda, remarkable for her brilliant coloratura rather than for deeper expression, yet here she makes the heroine a tender, feeling creature, emotionally vulnerable yet vocally immaculate. Similarly, Renato Bruson as Rigoletto does far more than produce a stream of velvety tone, detailed and intense, responding to the conductor and combining beauty with dramatic bite. Even more remarkable is the brilliant success of Neil Shicoff as the Duke, more than a match for his most distinguished rivals. Here the *Quartet* becomes a genuine climax. Brigitte Fassbaender as Maddalena is sharply unconventional but vocally most satisfying. Sinopoli's speeds, too, are unconventional at times, but the fresh look he provides is most exciting, helped by full and vivid recording, consistently well balanced.

Just over ten years after her first recording of this opera, Sutherland appeared in it again, this time with Pavarotti who is an intensely characterful Duke: an unmistakable rogue but an unmistakable charmer, too. Thanks to him and to Bonynge above all, the *Quartet*, as on the Sinopoli set, becomes a genuine musical climax. Sutherland's voice has acquired a hint of a beat, but there is little of the mooning manner which disfigured her earlier assumption, and the result is glowingly beautiful as well as supremely assured technically. Milnes makes a strong Rigoletto, vocally masterful rather than strongly characterful. The digital transfer is exceptionally vivid and atmospheric.

With an excellent cast James Levine conducts a thrustful, exceptionally high-powered reading of *Rigoletto*, vividly dramatic. The sound is full and immediate, with the solo voices in sharp focus, enhancing the power. Vladimir Chernov is a firm, clear, virile Rigoletto, not as searchingly characterful as some, but maybe because he sings with no hint of strain, with the beauty and accuracy of the singing consistently satisfying. Cheryl Studer is a tenderly affecting Gilda, singing with a bright, girlish tone, at once youthful and mature, defying age. Pavarotti was fresher in his earlier recording with Bonynge, but heard in close-up his is a thrillingly involving performance still, and the rest of the cast are first rate too. Not a first choice perhaps, but a strong and sound one.

There has never been a more compelling performance of the title-role in *Rigoletto* than that of Gobbi on his classic La Scala set of the 1950s. At every point, in almost every single phrase, Gobbi finds extra meaning in Verdi's vocal lines, with the widest range of tone-colour employed for expressive effect. Callas, though not naturally suited to the role of the wilting Gilda, is compellingly imaginative throughout, and Di Stefano gives one of his finest performances. The transfer of the original mono recording is astonishingly vivid in capturing the voices. This remains at full price.

Anna Moffo makes a charming Gilda in the Solti set of 1963. Solti at times presses too hard, but this is a strong and dramatic reading, with Robert Merrill producing a glorious flow of dark, firm tone in the name-part. Alfredo Kraus is as stylish as ever as the Duke, and this rare example of his voice at its freshest should not be missed. A good bargain, though there are statutory cuts in the text.

Rigoletto: highlights.
(N) (M) (***) EMI mono CDM5 66667-2 [id.]. (from above recording with Callas, Gobbi, di Stefano, cond. Serafin).

The 58-minute selection from the Gobbi/Callas *Rigoletto* is well chosen to represent an extremely compelling performance, and the synopsis is properly cued.

Simon Boccanegra (complete).
✽ (M) *** DG Originals 449 752-2 (2) [id.]. Freni, Cappuccilli, Ghiaurov, Van Dam, Carreras, La Scala, Milan, Ch. and O, Abbado.
(M) (***) EMI mono CMS7 63513-2 (2). Gobbi, Christoff, de los Angeles, Campora, Monachesi, Dari, Rome Op. Chor & O, Santini.
(BB) **(*) Discover Dig. DICD 920225/6 [id.]. Tumagian, Gauci, Aragall, Mikulas, Sardinero, BRTN Philharmonic Ch. and O, Alexander Rahbari.

Abbado's 1977 recording of *Simon Boccanegra* is one of the most beautiful Verdi sets ever made. The playing of the orchestra is brilliantly incisive as well as refined, so that the drama is underlined by extra sharpness of focus. The cursing of Paolo after the great Council Chamber scene makes the scalp prickle, with the chorus muttering in horror and the bass clarinet adding a sinister comment, here beautifully moulded. Cappuccilli, always intelligent, gives a far more intense and illuminating performance than the one he recorded for RCA earlier in his career. He may not match Gobbi in range of colour and detail, but he too gives focus to the performance; and Ghiaurov as Fiesco sings beautifully too. Freni as Maria Boccanegra sings with freshness and clarity, while Van Dam is an impressive Paolo. With electrically intense choral singing as well, this is a set to outshine even Abbado's superb *Macbeth*, and it is superbly transferred to CD. The set is now all the more desirable at mid-price.

Tito Gobbi's portrait of the tragic Doge of Genoa is one of his greatest on record, and it emerges all the more impressively when it is set against equally memorable performances by Boris Christoff as Fiesco and Victoria de los Angeles as Amelia. The Recognition scene between father and daughter has never been done more movingly on record; nor has the great ensemble, which crowns the Council Chamber scene, been so powerfully and movingly presented, and that without the help of stereo recording. The transfer is full and immediate, giving a vivid sense of presence to the voices, though tape-hiss is on the high side.

On the Discover bargain label Rahbari's well-paced reading is newly recorded in good digital sound with strong casting. Excellent East European principals are joined by the long-established Spanish tenor, Giacomo Aragall, and the baritone, Vincente Sardinero. Miriam Gauci is a vibrant, sympathetic Amelia, and though Eduard Tumagian is not the most characterful Boccanegra and Peter Mikulas could be darker-toned in the bass role of Fiesco, their voices are clear and well-focused, despite backward balance. Libretto in Italian only. Good value.

Stiffelio (complete).
(M) *** Ph. 422 432-2 (2). Carreras, Sass, Manuguerra, Ganzarolli, Austrian R. Ch. & SO, Gardelli.

Coming just before the great trio of masterpieces,

Rigoletto, *Il Trovatore* and *La Traviata*, *Stiffelio* is still a sharply telling work, largely because of the originality of the relationships and the superb final scene in which Stiffelio reads from the pulpit the parable of the woman taken in adultery. Gardelli directs a fresh performance, at times less lively than Queler's of *Aroldo* but with more consistent singing, notably from Carreras and Manuguerra. First-rate recording from Philips, typical of this fine series.

La Traviata (complete).
❁ *** Decca Dig. 448 119-2 (2) [id.]. Gheorghiu, Lopardo, Nucci, ROHCG Ch. & O, Solti.
*** Decca Dig. 430 491-2 (2) [id.]. Sutherland, Pavarotti, Manuguerra, L. Op. Ch., Nat. PO, Bonynge.
(M) **(*) EMI Dig. CDS7 47538-8 (2). Scotto, Kraus, Bruson, Amb. Op. Ch., Philh. O, Muti.
*** Teldec/Warner Dig. 9031 76348-2 (2) [id.]. Gruberová, Shicoff, Zancanaro, Amb. S., LSO, Rizzi.
(N) (B) **(*) Decca Double 460 759-2 (2) [id.]. Sutherland, Bergonzi, Merrill, Ch. & O of Maggio Musicale Fiorentino, Pritchard.
(B) **(*) DG Double 453 115-2 (2) [id.]. Scotto, Raimondi, Bastianini, La Scala, Milan, Ch. & O, Votto.
(M) (*(**)) EMI mono CMS5 66450-2 (2) [CDMB 66450-2]. Callas, Di Stefano, Bastianini, La Scala Ch. & O, Giulini.
(M) (**) RCA mono GD 60303 (2) [60303-2-RG]. Albanese, Peerce, Merrill, NBC Ch. & SO, Toscanini.

Defying the problems of recording opera live at Covent Garden, the Decca engineers here offer one of the most vivid and involving versions ever of *La Traviata*, full and immediate in sound. In a magnetic reading Solti treats the piece, not with his old fierceness, but with refinement and tenderness as well as emotional weight from the ravishingly hushed opening of the Prelude onwards. The intensity of a live occasion comes over consistently, with little or no intrusion from stage or audience noises. As on stage, Gheorghiu brings heartfelt revelations, using her rich and vibrant, finely shaded soprano with consistent subtlety. Youthfully vivacious in the first Act, dazzling in her coloratura, she already reveals the depths of feeling which compel her later self-sacrifice. In Act II she finds ample power for the great outburst of '*Amami, Alfredo*', and in Act III almost uniquely uses the second stanza of *Addio del passato* (often omitted) to heighten the intensity of the heroine's emotions. Frank Lopardo emerges as a fresh, lyrical Alfredo with a distinctive timbre, passionate and youthful-sounding too. Leo Nucci, a favourite baritone with Solti, provides a sharp contrast as a stolid but convincing Germont. A video version – taken from a single performance, not (like the CDs) an edited compendium of a series – is also offered (VHS 071 431-3; Laserdisc 071 428-1), letting one appreciate how Gheorghiu's physical beauty matches her voice, and how elegant and atmospheric Richard Eyre's Covent Garden production is, with sets by Bob Crowley.

Sutherland's second recording of the role of Violetta has a breadth and exuberance beyond her achievement in the earlier version of 1963, conducted by John Pritchard, and the richness and command of the singing put this among the very finest of her later recordings. Pavarotti too, though he overemphasizes *Di miei bollenti spiriti*, sings with splendid panache as Alfredo. Manuguerra as Germont lacks something in authority, but the firmness and clarity are splendid. Bonynge's conducting is finely sprung, the style direct, the speeds often spacious in lyrical music, generally undistracting. The digital recording is outstandingly vivid and beautifully balanced but the CD booklet is not ideal.

Muti has no concern for tradition; at the start of the Act I party music, he is even faster than Toscanini, but the result is dazzling; and when he needs to give sympathetic support to his soloists, above all in the great Act II duet between Violetta and Germont, there is no lack of tenderness. Overall, it is an intensely compelling account, using the complete text (like Bonynge), and it gains from having three Italy-based principals. Scotto and Kraus have long been among the most sensitive and perceptive interpreters of these roles, and so they are here; with bright digital recording, however, it is obvious that these voices are no longer young, with Scotto's soprano spreading above the stave and Kraus's tenor often sounding thin. Bruson makes a fine, forthright Germont, though it does not add to dramatic conviction that his is the youngest voice. Small parts are well taken, and the stage picture is projected clearly on CD in a pleasantly reverberant acoustic.

Carlo Rizzi draws subtle, refined playing from the LSO, which in turn brings refined singing from a well-matched cast. Giorgio Zancanaro is a characterful Germont, giving depth of feeling to the first scene of Act II up to *Di Provenza il mar*. Though Edita Gruberová's bright soprano acquires an unevenness under pressure, she is freshly expressive and increasingly through the opera, up to the great challenge of the death scene, produces the most delicate pianissimos, with phrasing and tone exquisitely shaded. She may not match the finest Violettas of the past, and the tenor, Neil Shicoff, sings with less finesse than the other principals, but this stands high in the list of modern, digital versions.

In Sutherland's 1963 recording of *La Traviata*, it is true that her diction is poor, but it is also true that she has rarely sung on record with such deep feeling as in the final scene. The *Addio del passato* (both stanzas included and sung with an unexpected lilt) merely provides a beginning, for the duet with

Bergonzi is most winning, and the final death scene, *Se una pudica vergine*, is overwhelmingly beautiful. This is not a sparkling Violetta, but it is vocally close to perfection. Bergonzi is an attractive Alfredo and Merrill a clean-cut Germont.

This is excellent value as a Decca Double, although now the libretto has been replaced with Decca's cued synopsis and 'listening guide'.

It is worth having the 1962 DG La Scala set for the moving and deeply considered singing of Renata Scotto as Violetta, fresher in voice than in her later, HMV set. In a role which has usually eluded the efforts of prima donnas on record, she gives one of the most complete portraits, with thrilling coloratura in Act I and with the closing scene unforgettably moving. It is sad that the rest of the cast is largely undistinguished. Gianni Raimondi as Alfredo is stirring if not refined, and Bastianini is a coarse Germont *père*. The conductor, Antonino Votto, gives routine direction but keeps the music alive. The usual stage cuts are observed. The recording is vividly atmospheric, a fair bargain on a DG Double. There are good notes and a well-cued synopsis.

Callas's version with Giulini was recorded in 1955, three years before the Ghione Lisbon set, when the voice was fresher. There is no more vividly dramatic a performance on record than this, unmatchable in conveying Violetta's agony; sadly, the sound, always limited, grows crumbly towards the end. It is sad too that Bastianini sings so lumpishly as Germont *père*, even in the great duet of Act II, while di Stefano also fails to match his partner in the supreme test of the final scene. The transfer is fair.

Toscanini's live recording, made in December 1946, was one of the first he made of complete operas in his final years in New York, following after *La Bohème* in the previous February. Here, even more than in the Puccini and certainly more than in his later Verdi recordings, his speeds are not just fast but relentless. Even so, the high tension of the drama is hair-raising, and both Licia Albanese and Jan Peerce respond impressively, not letting the strict discipline mar their vocal production. The sound, as always with Toscanini recordings of this period, is painfully dry but very clear and forward.

La Traviata (complete in English).
(N) (M) *** Chandos CHAN 3023 (2) [id.]. Valerie Masterson, John Brecknock, Christian Du Plessis, E. Nat. Op. Ch. & O, Mackerras.

Mackerras directs a vigorous, colourful reading which brings out the drama, and Valerie Masterson is given the chance on record she has so long deserved. The voice is caught beautifully, if not always very characterfully, and John Brecknock makes a fine Alfredo, most effective in the final scene. Christian Du Plessis's baritone is less suitable for recording. The conviction of the whole enterprise is infectious – but be warned, Verdi in English has a way of sounding rather like Gilbert and Sullivan on record.

La Traviata: highlights.
(M) *** Decca 458 211-2 [id.] (from above complete set, with Sutherland, Bergonzi, Merrill; cond. Pritchard).

Decca's highlights from Sutherland's first (1963) recording make a clear first choice. They come handsomely packaged in Decca's Opera Gala series, with a generous selection (73 minutes) and including a full translation. Sutherland is in ravishing voice, and Bergonzi is also in excellent form. The set is discussed more fully above.

Il Trovatore (complete).
❁ (M) *** RCA 74321 39504-2. Leontyne Price, Domingo, Milnes, Cossotto, Amb. Op. Ch., New Philh. O, Mehta.
*** DG Dig. 423 858-2 (2). Plowright, Domingo, Fassbaender, Zancanaro, Nesterenko, Ch. & O of St Cecilia Academy, Rome, Giulini.
*** Sony Dig. S2K 48070 (2) [id.]. Millo, Domingo, Chernov, Zajick, Morris, Kelly, Met. Op. Ch. & O, Levine.
(***) EMI mono CDS5 56333-2 (2) [id.]. Callas, Barbieri, Di Stefano, Panerai, La Scala, Milan, Ch. & O, Karajan.
(M) (***) RCA mono GD 86643 (2) [6643-2-RG]. Milanov, Bjoerling, Warren, Barbieri, Robert Shaw Ch., RCA Victor O, Cellini.
(B) *** DG Double 453 118-2 (2) [id.]. Stella, Bergonzi, Cossotto, Bastianini, La Scala, Milan, Ch. & O, Serafin.
(N) (M) **(*) RCA 71321 61951-2 (2) [id.]. Raina Kabaiwanska, Plácido Domingo, Fiorenza, Cossotto, Piero Cappuccilli, José van Dam, V. State Op. Ch. & O, Karajan (with Karajan interview).

The soaring curve of Leontyne Price's rich vocal line is immediately thrilling in her famous Act I aria, and it sets the style of the RCA performance, full-bodied and with dramatic tension consistently high. The choral contribution is superb; the famous *Soldiers'* and *Anvil choruses* are marvellously fresh and dramatic. When *Di quella pira* comes, the orchestra opens with great gusto and Domingo sings with a ringing, heroic quality worthy of Caruso himself. There are many dramatic felicities, and Sherrill Milnes is in fine voice throughout; but perhaps the highlight of the set is the opening section of Act III, when Azucena finds her way to Conte di Luna's camp. The ensuing scene with Fiorenza Cossotto is vocally and dramatically electrifying.

Giulini flouts convention at every point. The opera's white-hot inspiration comes out in the intensity of the playing and singing, but the often slow tempi and refined textures present the whole work in new and deeper detail. Rosalind Plowright, sensuous yet ethereal in *Tacea la notte*, confidently brings together not just sweetness and purity but brilliant coloratura, flexibility and dramatic bite. Plácido Domingo sings Manrico as powerfully as he did in the richly satisfying Mehta set on RCA, but the voice is even more heroic in an Otello-like way, only very occasionally showing strain. Giorgio Zancanaro proves a firm and rounded Count di Luna and Evgeny Nesterenko a dark, powerful Ferrando, while Brigitte Fassbaender, singing her first Azucena, sings with detailed intensity, matching Giulini's freshness. The recording is warm and atmospheric with a pleasant bloom on the voices, naturally balanced and not spotlit.

James Levine conducts his Met. cast in a performance that with full, forward sound brings out the blood-and-thunder of the piece, not least in ensembles. Plácido Domingo as Manrico shows few if any signs of wear in the voice, even in relation to his singing on his two fine earlier sets – with both Mehta on RCA and Giulini on DG. Aprile Millo as Leonora has never been more impressive on record, disciplining a voice that can often sound unruly. Vladimir Chernov is a magnificent Count di Luna, with James Morris formidably cast as Ferrando. Dolora Zajick is aptly fruity-toned as Azucena, but heavy vibrato in the voice disturbs her legato singing. Strong as the performance is, it yields before both the vintage Mehta and the inspired Giulini.

The combination of Karajan and Callas is formidably impressive. There is toughness and dramatic determination in Callas's singing, whether in the coloratura or in the dramatic passages, and this gives the heroine an unsuspected depth of character which culminates in Callas's fine singing of an aria which used often to be cut entirely – *Tu vedrai che amore in terra*, here with its first stanza alone included. Barbieri is a magnificent Azucena, Panerai a strong, incisive Count, and di Stefano at his finest as Manrico. On CD the 1956 mono sound, now greatly improved, is one of the more vivid from La Scala at that period.

Though dating from 1952, using a cut text as in the Met. production, the Cellini version brings a vivid reminder of that great opera house at a key period. Milanov, though at times a little raw in Leonora's coloratura, gives a glorious, commanding performance, with the voice at its fullest. Bjoerling and Warren too are in ringing voice, and Barbieri is a superb Azucena, with Cellini – rarely heard on record – proving an outstanding Verdian.

There is room for a recommendable bargain set of *Il Trovatore*, and Serafin's splendidly red-blooded La Scala version on a DG Double fits the bill well. For the present DG Double reissue, the documentation has been improved with the synopsis well cued, but with no libretto. The performance is most enjoyable, with the contributions of Cossotto as Azucena and Carlo Bergonzi, splendid as Manrico, matching almost any rival. Stella and Bastianini give flawed performances, but they have many impressive moments; as Leonora's opening aria readily demonstrates, Stella is in full voice and identifies strongly with the heroine. The conducting of Serafin is crisp and stylish, and the 1963 recording is vividly transferred to CD with plenty of atmosphere.

The RCA live recording, made by Austrian Radio, celebrates Karajan's much-acclaimed return to the Vienna State Opera in 1978, following his success in this opera the previous year. After a reticent start, the thrust of the drama is unerringly brought home. Domingo is caught here just as he was developing into the greatest *Otello* tenor of our time, delivering a ringingly heroic account of the role of Manrico. The wonder is that he took over only at the last minute from Franco Bonisolli, who had then recently recorded the role with Karajan for EMI. Fiorenza Cossotto makes a tangy and tough Azucena, not always subtle, and Piero Cappuccilli characteristically brings out a streak of nobility in di Luna, no conventional villain. José van Dam sings incisively as Ferrando, the key figure in the first scene. Raina Kabaiwanska is in many ways well-suited to the role of Leonora, but with the pronounced flutter in her voice exaggerated by the microphone, she is not pure or poised enough in the great lyrical passages, phrasing so broadly she almost brings her Act IV aria to a halt. Her cabaletta, *Tu vedrei che amor in terra*, is unfortunately omitted. As a bonus the second disc contains an interview with Karajan on his love for this opera, translated in the booklet, which otherwise contains no libretto or translation of the opera itself, although there is a cued synopsis.

Il Trovatore: highlights.

(N) (M) *** DG 457 908-2 [id.]. (from above recording with Plowright, Domingo, Fassbaender, Zancanaro; cond. Giulini).

(N) (M) (***) EMI mono CDM5 66669-2 [id.]. (from above recording with Callas, di Stefano, Panerei, Barbieri, cond. Karajan).

(N) (M) ** Decca 458 227-2 [id.]. (from complete recording with Sutherland, Pavarotti, Horne, Wixell; cond. Bonynge).

Many collectors who have opted for the Mehta RCA set will want a reminder of Giulini's masterly, individual and highly compelling alternative interpretation. This Galleria disc is a straight reissue taken from a 1984 LP, and the content (just over an hour) seems less generous than it did then. The synopsis is cued.

The Callas/Karajan set is also represented by an hour of music, and this highly dramatic partnership comes over as strongly in excerpts as it does in the complete recording.

The selection from Bonynge's 1976 Decca set offers a useful reminder of Sutherland's Leonora.

The size of the voice and its flexibility are splendidly caught, though a latter-day beat afflicts the more sustained passages and Bonynge does not conduct with his usual urgency. Pavarotti may be stretched by the role of Manrico, but he is nearly always magnificent. Horne is represented by her powerful *Stride la vampa*, Wixell by a warm but dramatically undernourished *Il Balen*. A full translation is included.

I vespri siciliani (complete).
**(*) RCA RD 80370 (3). Arroyo, Domingo, Milnes, Raimondi, Ewing, Alldis Ch., New Philh. O, Levine.
**(*) EMI CDS7 54043-2 (3). Merritt, Studer, Zancanaro, Furlanetto, Ch. & O of La Scala, Milan, Muti.

This opera has been sadly neglected on record; Levine's 1974 RCA set, made in London, remains a first choice, dominated by the partnership of Plácido Domingo and Sherrill Milnes. Their Act II duet, using a melody well known from the *Overture*, is magnificent, with both singers at their very peak. Though Martina Arroyo is less responsive than Studer on Muti's EMI alternative version, Domingo, Milnes and the young Ruggero Raimondi are all preferable to the La Scala singers, and the sharpness of focus in both performance and recording exposes the relative fuzziness of Muti's live account. The rest of the singing in the RCA cast is good if rarely inspired, although James Levine's direction is colourful and urgent. Good recording, vividly remastered.

The EMI set is among the most successful of the live recordings made by Muti at La Scala, Milan, plagued by a difficult acoustic. The atmosphere is well caught and, though Muti can be too tautly urgent a Verdian, his pacing here is well geared to bring out the high drama. Outstanding in the cast is Cheryl Studer as the heroine, Elena, singing radiantly; while the tenor Chris Merritt as Arrigo sounds less coarse and strained than he has in the past. Giorgio Zancanaro also responds to the role of Monforte – the governor of Sicily, discovered to be Arrigo's father – with new sensitivity, and though Ferruccio Furlanetto as Procida lacks the full weight to bring out the beauty of line in the great aria, *O tu Palermo*, his is a warm performance too.

COLLECTIONS

Arias: *Aida: Ritorna vincitor!; Qui Radamès verrà! O patria mia. Il Trovatore: Che più t'arresti; Tacea la notte;* (i) *Di tale amor. Timor di me?; D'amor sull'ali rosee.*
(M) *** RCA 09026 68883-2 [id.]. Leontyne Price, Rome Opera O, Oliviero de Fabritiis or Artur Basile; (i) with Laura Londi – PUCCINI: *Arias.* **(*)

This recital, known as the 'blue album' (the colour of the original LP is reproduced on the CD), has justly become a collector's item, for the glorious flow of tone makes one understand why, even if tension is lower than in Price's performances of the complete operas. CD brings added bloom to the excellent recording.

Arias from: *Aida; Un ballo in maschera; I due Foscari; Luisa Miller; Macbeth; Rigoletto; La Traviata; Il Trovatore.*
(N) (M) *** Decca Analogue/Dig. 458 244-2 [id.]. Luciano Pavarotti with various orchestras and conductors.

Taken partly from a recital which Pavarotti put on disc early in his career, conducted by Edward Downes in 1968 (*I due Foscari, Luisa Miller* and *Macbeth*), and from others in 1969 and 1971 (*Il Trovatore*) and 1974 (*Aida*), this Verdi Opera Gala collection can be warmly recommended to anyone wanting a survey of the tenor's recording career, confirming that his vocal timbre was very consistent over the years. The *Rigoletto* excerpts come from the complete set directed by Bonynge in 1971 and the *Un ballo* scenes from the Solti set, and were the last to be recorded (in 1982/3). Vivid transfers and full translations.

Arias: *Don Carlo: Son io, mio Carlo . . . Per me giunto . . . O Carlo, ascolta. Luisa Miller: Sacra la scelta. Macbeth: Perfidi! All'anglo contra me v'unite . . . Pietà, rispetto, amore. La Traviata: Di Provenza il mar. Il Trovatore: Tutto è deserto . . . Il balen.*
*** Ph. (IMS) Dig. 426 740-2 [id.]. Dmitri Hvorostovsky, Rotterdam PO, Gergiev – TCHAIKOVSKY: *Arias.* ***

With a glorious voice, dark and characterful, and with natural musical imagination, Dmitri Hvorostovsky on this disc made his recording début in the West not just in Tchaikovsky arias, but here in Verdi, stylishly sung. With a voice of such youthful virility, he hardly sounds like the father-figure of the *Traviata* and *Luisa Miller* items, but the legato in Macbeth's Act IV aria is most beautiful. He also brings the keenest intensity to Posa's death-scene aria from *Don Carlo*.

Arias: *Don Carlos: Tu che le vanità. La Traviata: Ah fors'è lui. Il Trovatore: Timor di me.*
*** Sony Dig. CD 37298 [id.]. Kiri Te Kanawa, LPO, Pritchard – PUCCINI: *Arias.* ***

The Verdi part of Kiri Te Kanawa's Verdi–Puccini recital brings three substantial items, less obviously apt for the singer, but in each the singing is felt as well as beautiful. The coloratura of the *Traviata* and *Trovatore* items is admirably clean, and it is a special joy to hear Elisabetta's big aria from *Don Carlos* sung with such truth and precision. Good recording, enhanced on CD.

Choruses from: *Aida; La Battaglia di Legnano; Don Carlo; Ernani; La forza del destino;*

Macbeth; Nabucco; Otello; La Traviata; Il Trovatore.
(BB) *** Naxos Dig. 8.550241; *4.550241* [id.]. Slovak Philharmonic Ch. & RSO, Oliver Dohnányi.

Under Oliver Dohnányi's lively direction the chorus sings with fervour. The collection ends resplendently with the Triumphal scene from *Aida*, omitting the ballet but with the fanfare trumpets blazing out on either side most tellingly. With a playing time of 56 minutes this is an excellent bargain, with naturally balanced recording from the Bratislava Radio Concert Hall.

'*Gala*': *Aida*: (i) *Ritorna vincitor*; (ii) *Celeste Aida*. (iii) *Un ballo in maschera: Sapper vorreste. Don Carlo*: (iv) *Ella giammai m'amò!*; (v) *O don fatale*. (vi) *La forza del distino: Pace, pace mio Dio!*. (vii) *Luisa Miller: Quando le sere al placido*. (viii) *Otello: Willow song and Ave Maria. Rigoletto*: (ix) *La donna è mobile*; (x) *Caro nome. Il Trovatore: Di quella pira*. (xi) *I vespri siciliani: Mercé dilette amiche*.
(N) (M) *** Decca 458 226-2 [id.]. (i) Leontyne Price; (ii) Jon Vickers; (iii) Kathleen Battle; (iv) Ghiaurov; (v) Grace Bumbry; (vi) Tebaldi; (vii) Bergonzi; (viii) Kiri Te Kanawa; (ix) Pavarotti; (x) June Anderson; (xi) Maria Chiara.

The Verdi 'Gala', is a companion to a similar Puccini programme and is also full of memorable performances. The programme opens and closes with Pavarotti, crisply stylish in *La donna è mobile*, uninhibited in *Di quella pira*. Among the highlights are excerpts from Solti's *Aida* (with Leontyne Price and Jon Vickers), Kiri Te Kanawa's very beautiful *Willow song and Ave Maria* from *Otello*, Grace Bumbry's commanding *O don fatale* from *Don Carlo*, and, in a wholly different style, Kathleen Battle's engaging portrayal of Oscar in *Un ballo in maschera*. Maria Chiara offers a sparkling *Bolero* from *I vespri siciliani*; and another unexpected choice is June Anderson's *Caro nome* taken from the 1988 Chailly *Rigoletto*. Full translations are included.

Scenes and duets from: *Aida; Don Carlos; I Lombardi; I masnadieri; Otello; Rigoletto; Simon Boccanegra; La Traviata; Il Trovatore; I vespri siciliani; etc*
(N) *** EMI Dig. CDC5 56656-2 [id.]. Angela Gheorghiu, Roberto Alagna, L. Voices, BPO, Abbado.

Whatever the hype surrounding this starry operatic couple, this is an imaginatively planned collection of relative rarities as well as favourites, which inspires some ravishing singing. It helps that the presentation is lavish, with the chorus contributing far more than is common on such a disc, setting each duet in context. Dramatically and musically, Gheorghiu is very much the dominant partner, using the widest range of dynamic and tone-colour, not just exploiting her voice in every register, but turning each phrase with memorable individuality. Though Alagna is not quite so inspired, and such a role as Otello is not quite his yet, there are few tenors today who could match him. The disc is crowned by the ripe and responsive playing of the Berlin Philharmonic under Abbado, opulently recorded. An operatic feast!

Victoria, Tomás Luis de
(*c*. 1548–1611)

Ascendens Christus (motet); *Missa Ascendis Christus in altum; O Magnum mysterium* (motet); *Missa O Magnum mysterium*.
*** Hyperion Dig. CDA 66190 [id.]. Westminster Cathedral Ch., David Hill.

Missa Ave maris stella; O quam gloriosum est regnum (motet); *Missa O quam gloriosum*.
❁ *** Hyperion Dig. CDA 66114 [id.]. Westminster Cathedral Ch., David Hill.

The Latin fervour of the singing here is very involving; some listeners may initially be surprised at the volatile way David Hill moves the music on, with the trebles eloquently soaring aloft on the line of the music. The spontaneous ebb and flow of the pacing is at the heart of David Hill's understanding of this superb music. The recording balance is perfectly judged, with the Westminster acoustic adding resonance (in both senses of the word) to singing of the highest calibre, combining a sense of timelessness and mystery with real expressive power.

Ave Maria; Ave Maris stella (hymn). *Missa Vidi speciosam. Ne timeas, Maria; Sancta Maria, succurre miseris; Vidi speciosam* (motets).
*** Hyperion Dig. CDA 66129 [id.]. Westminster Cathedral Ch., David Hill.

An outstanding collection of some of Victoria's most beautiful music celebrating the Virgin Mary. The four-part *Ave Maria* may not be authentic, but the composer would surely not be reluctant to own it. The Westminster Choir again show their flexibly volatile response to this music with that special amalgam of fervour and serenity that Victoria's writing demands. The acoustics of Westminster Cathedral add the right degree of resonance to the sound without clouding.

Mass and Motet: *O magnum mysterium*. Mass and Motet: *O quam gloriosum. Ardens est cor meum; Ave Maria*.
(BB) *** Naxos Dig. 8.550575 [id.]. Oxford Camerata, Jeremy Summerly (with Alonso LOBO: *Versa est in luctum* ***).

These Masses are already familiar from recordings by David Hill's Westminster Cathedral Choir. But this Naxos coupling is by no means second best. Like David Hill, Jeremy Summerly moves the music of each Mass on fairly briskly until the *Sanctus* and *Agnus Dei*, when the spacious *espressivo* of the singing makes a poignant contrast. The two motets on which the Masses are based are sung as postludes and very beautiful they are, especially the idyllic *O magnum mysterium*. Finally the short *Versa est in luctum* (a setting of a section of the Requiem Mass) by Alonso Lobo, a Spanish contemporary, ends the concert serenely. The recording is excellent and this is a fine bargain.

Mass and Motet: *O quam gloriosum*.
(BB) *** Belart 461 018-2. Mary Thomas, Jean Allister, Edgar Fleet, Christopher Keyte, Carmelite Priory Ch., London, John McCarthy – PALESTRINA: Masses: *Ecce ego Joannes; Sine nomine*. ***

Like the Palestrina couplings, this paired Mass and motet are exceptionally distinguished performances, and they are made the more attractive (in all three cases) by this ideal recorded presentation which couples the motet which is musically connected with each Mass, something which we expect these days as a matter of course but which happened less frequently in the early 1960s, when these recordings first appeared. The sound is remarkably fine, with the part-writing clearly defined.

Officium defunctorum.
*** Gimell/Ph. Dig. 454 912-2 [id.]. Tallis Scholars, Phillips (with LOBO: Motet: *Versa est in luctum* ***).
*** Hyperion Dig. CDA 66250 [id.]. Westminster Cathedral Ch., David Hill.

The *Officium defunctorum* was Victoria's swan-song – he died only six years later. It is a work of great serenity and beauty. Honours are fairly evenly divided between the Westminster Cathedral Choir on Hyperion and the Tallis Scholars under Peter Phillips. The Westminster Choir has the advantage of boys' voices and larger forces; they are recorded in a warmer, more spacious acoustic. By comparison with the Gimell recording, the sound seems a little less well focused, but on its own terms it is thoroughly convincing. They permit themselves greater expressiveness, too. Moreover the *Requiem* is set in the wider liturgical context by the use of some chants.

The Tallis Scholars achieve great clarity of texture; they are 12 in number and, as a result, the polyphony is clearer, and so too are their words. They offer also a short and deeply felt motet by Alonso Lobo (*c*. 1555–1617). The recording has a warm, glowing sound which almost persuades you that you are in the imperial chapel.

Responsories for Tenebrae.
*** Hyperion Dig. CDA 66304 [id.]. Westminster Cathedral Ch., David Hill.
** Gimell/Ph. Dig. 454 922-2 [id.]. Tallis Scholars, Peter Phillips.

The *Tenebrae responsories* are so called because of the tradition of performing them in the evening in increasing darkness as the candles were extinguished one by one. The Tallis Scholars are flawless in both blend and intonation but are curiously uninvolving. They are beautifully recorded and technically immaculate but lack intensity of feeling. The Westminster Cathedral Choir under David Hill on Hyperion find far more atmosphere in this music and bring a sense of spontaneous feeling to their performance. Of recent versions, this can be welcomed without reservation.

Vierne, Louis (1870–1937)

Suite No. 3, Op. 54: Carillon de Westminster.
*** DG Dig. 413 438-2 [id.]. Simon Preston (organ of Westminster Abbey) – WIDOR: *Symphony No. 5*. ***

The Vierne *Carillon de Westminster* is splendidly played by Simon Preston and sounds appropriately atmospheric in this spacious acoustic and well-judged recording. It makes an attractive makeweight to the Widor *Fifth Symphony*.

Symphonies Nos. 1 in D min., Op. 14; 2 in E min., Op. 20.
*** Mer. CDE 84192 [id.]. David Sanger (organ of La Chiesa Italiana di San Pietro, London).

Symphonies Nos. 3 in F sharp min., Op. 28; 4 in G min., Op. 32.
*** Mer. CDE 84176 [id.]. David Sanger (organ of La Chiesa Italiana di San Pietro, London).

Symphonies Nos. 5 in A min., Op. 47; 6 in B min., Op. 59.
*** Mer. CDE 84171 [id.]. David Sanger (organ of La Chiesa Italiana di San Pietro, London).

David Sanger's recordings of the Vierne *Organ symphonies* are highly rewarding and can be strongly recommended, especially as Marie-Claire Alain's set on Erato has been withdrawn, and some listeners are likely to prefer the very appealing sound of the San Pietro organ. The sound quality maintains the high standards Meridian have set themselves: the resonance of the pedals is very telling without muddying the overall sound-picture.

Vieuxtemps, Henri (1820–81)

Violin concertos Nos. 2 in F sharp min., Op. 19; 3 in A, Op. 25.
(BB) *** Naxos Dig. 8.554114 [id.]. Misha Keylin, Janáček PO, Dennis Burkh.

Vieuxtemps wrote seven violin concertos and, on the evidence of this fine Naxos coupling, Nos. 2 and 3 are by no means inferior to the better-known Nos. 4 and 5. They are full of good tunes, both slow movements are warmly touching and finales have lyrical as well as histrionic appeal. Misha Keylin (Russian by birth but now an American émigré) gives highly persuasive performances that are technically dazzling and constantly tickle the ear in their subtlety of bowing and colour, easy rubato and imaginative dynamic shading. Dennis Burkh provides the strongest backing: his spirited introductions for both works (and especially the *Third*, with its throbbing drama) are arresting, and the orchestral playing, somewhat leonine in timbre, is excellent. So too is the recording, made in the Janáček Concert Hall, Ostrava, with the soloist not too close for comfort in his Paganinian flights into the stratosphere. An excellent bargain.

Violin concertos Nos. 4 in D min., Op. 31; 5 in A min. (Grétry), Op. 37.

(M) *** EMI (SIS) CDM5 66058-2. Itzhak Perlman, O de Paris, Barenboim – RAVEL: *Tzigane;* SAINT-SAENS: *Havanaise.* ***

Violin concerto No. 4 in D min., Op. 31.

(M) (***) EMI (SIS) mono CDH7 64251-2 [id.]. Heifetz, LPO, Barbirolli – SAINT-SAENS: *Havanaise* etc.; SARASATE: *Zigeunerweisen;* WIENIAWSKI: *Concerto No. 2.* (***)

Violin concerto No. 5 in A min., Op. 37.

(M) (***) EMI mono CDH5 65191-2 [id.]. Heifetz, LSO, Sargent – MENDELSSOHN: *Concerto* (**(*)); MOZART: *Concerto No. 5.* (***)

This coupling of the two best-known Vieuxtemps violin concertos is not only apt; it presents superbly stylish readings, with Perlman both aristocratically pure of tone and intonation and passionate of expression. In his accompaniments Barenboim draws warmly romantic playing from the Paris orchestra. The 1976–7 recording, as usual with Perlman, balancing the soloist well forward, now sounds a little dated, with a touch of shrillness on the upper range of the violin. However, this remains a three-star record, the more so for its inclusion of two of Perlman's very finest recordings as couplings.

The Vieuxtemps concertos are not great music, but, when played like this by Heifetz, one is almost convinced that they are. His account of *No. 4 in D minor* with Barbirolli, made in 1935, is coupled with other dazzling performances. Heifetz and Barbirolli had a good rapport when they first collaborated the previous year – which was just as well, as Barbirolli only learnt at 11 o'clock on the morning of the recording that he was due to record the Vieuxtemps *Fourth Concerto* (which he had not directed before) that very afternoon. The results are amazing.

Heifetz's recording of the *Fifth Concerto in A minor* was made in London just after the war with Sir Malcolm Sargent. This comes together with Heifetz's celebrated account of the Mendelssohn (made with Beecham and the RPO in 1949) and the 1934 recording with Barbirolli and the LPO of Mozart's *Turkish Concerto*. There are some cuts, but Heifetz's playing is glorious and the sound excellent for its period.

Violin concerto No. 5 in A min., Op. 37.

*** EMI Dig. CDC5 55292-2 [id.]. Sarah Chang, Philh. O, Dutoit – LALO: *Symphonie espagnole.* ***

(M) *** Sony Dig. SMK 64250. Cho-Liang Lin, Minnesota O, Marriner – BRUCH; MENDELSSOHN: *Concertos.* ***

(M) *** DG Dig. 457 896-2. Mintz, Israel PO, Mehta – LALO: *Symphonie espagnole;* SAINT-SAENS: *Introduction & Rondo capriccioso.* ***

(M) *** RCA 09026 61745-2 [id.]. Heifetz, New SO of L, Sargent – BRUCH: *Violin concerto No. 1* etc. ***

(M) *** Decca Dig. 460 007-2. Kyung Wha Chung, LSO, Foster – LALO: *Symphonie espagnole;* RAVEL: *Tzigane.* ***

(B) **(*) Sony SBK 48274 [id.]. Zukerman, LSO, Mackerras – BRUCH: *Concerto No. 1;* LALO: *Symphonie espagnole.* **(*)

Sarah Chang's recording, coupling a scintillating account of the Lalo *Symphonie espagnole*, goes readily to the top of the list. It is beautifully recorded, with a perfect balance, in an agreeably warm acoustic. Chang's vitality is matched by Dutoit and her playing has a magically gentle tenderness in presenting the engaging lyrical themes of the first movement and the *Adagio*. The brief finale has splendid élan.

Cho-Liang Lin plays with flair and zest and is well supported by Sir Neville Marriner and the Minnesota Orchestra. The recording is first class, and the couplings of the more famous concertos of Bruch and Mendelssohn could not be more appropriate.

Mintz's performance has enormous dash and also real lyrical magic. Mehta, obviously caught up in the inspiration of the solo playing, provides an excellent accompaniment. This is another example of a memorable live performance 'recorded on the wing' and, if the acoustic is not very flattering, the sound is truthful and well balanced.

The quicksilver of Heifetz is well suited to the modest but attractive *Fifth Concerto* of Vieuxtemps, and Sir Malcolm again provides a musical and well-recorded accompaniment. The balance of the soloist is rather close but the digital remastering is successful, and the couplings are both attractive and generous.

Even more than the Lalo *Symphonie espagnole* which forms the major coupling, the Vieuxtemps

No. 5 needs persuasive advocacy, and that is certainly what Kyung Wha Chung provides, not just in her passionate commitment in the bravura sections but also in the tender expressiveness of the slow movement, so much more compelling than the usual, more extrovert manner. The 1974 Kingsway Hall recording has perhaps lost a little of its original allure in the matter of the solo violin timbre but is otherwise very satisfactory.

Zukerman provides here an enjoyable bonus to his dazzling accounts of the Bruch and Lalo works. There is comparable dash for Vieuxtemps, yet he coaxes the *Adagio* tenderly. Again a very forward balance, but the ear adjusts.

Viola sonata in B flat, Op. 36; Elégie, Op. 30; Morceaux, Op. 61.

(N) *** Chandos Dig. CHAN 8873 [id.]. Nobuko Imai, Roger Vignoles – FRANCK: *Viola sonata in A.* ***

(N) *** Simax Dig. PSC 1126 [id.]. Lars Anders Tomter, Håvard Gimse – FRANCK: *Viola sonata in A.* ***

The Vieuxtemps *Sonata* is expertly crafted and well laid out for the instruments but it is no masterpiece. Nobuko Imai and Roger Vignoles give an exemplary account of it and are given expert recording from the Chandos engineers.

The Norwegian, Lars Anders Tomter is hardly less accomplished and every bit as eloquent a player as his celebrated rival, and his countryman, Håvard Gimse is a first-rate pianist. There is absolutely nothing to choose between them, and both couple the Vieuxtemps with the Franck sonata arranged for viola.

Villa-Lobos, Heitor (1887–1959)

Alvorada na floresta tropical (Dawn in a tropical rainforest); Bachianas brasileiras No. 2 (for orchestra) includes: *The little train of the Caipira. Dança frenética;* (i) *Mômoprecóce (fantasy for piano and orchestra).*

(BB) *** Arte Nova Dig. 73421 54465-2 [id.]. (i) Marco Antonio de Almeida; Jena PO, David Montgomery.

The enterprising Arte Nova label almost upstages the competition with a super-budget collection that is in every way recommendable. Like Cristina Ortiz (below), Marco Antonio de Almeida is Brazilian born, and he and Montgomery give an invigorating account of the *Mômoprecóce* ('Carnival King'). If the Jena Philharmonic strings lack a little in body of tone, the often glittering detail is very effectively projected by the modern digital recording, and the notes with the disc give useful programmatic detail. The exotic sounds of the tropical rainforest are also vividly caught, and the energetic toccata rhythms have plenty of energy. The sultry, jazzy atmosphere of *The song of the vagabond*, the first movement of the *Bachianas brasileiras No. 2*, is seductive, and the catchy trombone tune of the fourth (*Song of the desert*) is equally engaging, famous mainly for its charming portrayal of *The little train of the Caipira*.

Amazonas; Dawn in a tropical forest; Erosão; Gênesis.

*** Marco Polo Dig. 8.223357 [id.]. Czecho-Slovak RSO (Bratislava), Roberto Duarte.

These are imaginative scores with tropical colouring and exotic textures, all sounding rather similar in their luxuriance – but who cares! *Amazonas* is the earliest and most astonishing score, dating from the First World War, and in its vivid sonorities affirms Villa-Lobos's contention that his first harmony book was the map of Brazil. The Bratislava strings could be more opulent, but the performances under a Brazilian conductor are very good indeed as is the recording.

Bachianas brasileiras Nos. 1 for cellos; 2 for orchestra; (i) *5 for soprano and 8 cellos; 9 for string orchestra.*

(N) (M) (**(*)) EMI mono CDM5 66912-2 [CDMS 66964]. Fr. R & TV O, composer; (i) with Victoria de los Angeles.

Understandably, this EMI 'Great recordings of the century' reissue opens with No. 5, with its floating line melodic so delicately and ravishingly sustained by Victoria de los Angeles. Elsewhere the dry, lustreless orchestral recording will limit the appeal of this disc for the general, rather than the historically minded collector, for the composer's direction of the orchestra is of documentary rather than inpirational interest.

Bachianas brasileiras Nos. (iii) *1;* (i; iii) *5;* (i; ii) *Suite for voice and violin.* (iii) arr. of BACH: *The Well-tempered clavier: Prelude in D min., BWV 583; Fugue in B flat, BWV 846; Prelude in G min., BWV 867; Fugue in D, BWV 874.*

*** Hyperion Dig. CDA 66257 [id.]. (i) Jill Gomez, (ii) Peter Manning, (iii) Pleeth Cello Octet.

Jill Gomez is outstanding in the popular *Fifth Bachianas brasileiras* and with the violinist, Peter Manning, in the *Suite* (1923). Villa-Lobos' favourite 'orchestra of cellos' produce sumptuous sounds in both the *Bachianas brasileiras*, and an added point of interest is the effective transcriptions for cellos of unrelated Bach preludes and fugues. A most attractive introduction to this most colourful of composers.

Bachianas brasileiras No. 2: The little train of the Caipira.

(*) Everest EVC 9007 [id.]. LSO, Sir Eugene Goossens – ANTILL: *Corroboree* **(*); GINASTERA: *Estancia; Panambi.* *

It is good to have a recommendable mid-priced version of Villa-Lobos's engaging tone-picture of a little country train in São Paulo, Brazil, with Brazilian percussion instruments suggesting train noises. The performance is excellent and the recording vivid, if slightly over-resonant, with a slight edge to the violins.

(i–ii) *Bachianas brasileiras No. 3;* (iii) *Guitar concerto;* (iv) *Fantasia for soprano saxophone and chamber orchestra;* (i) Piano music: *A próle do bébé No. 1* (suite); *A lenda de caboclo; Alma brasiliera (Chorus No. 5); Cicio brasileiro: Festa no sertão; Impressões seresteiras.*
(B) *** EMI forte CZS5 72670-2 (2). (i) Cristina Ortiz; (ii) New Philh. O, Ashkenazy; (iii) Angel Romero, LPO, Jésus López-Cobos; (iv) John Harle, ASMF, Marriner.

In many ways this is the finest Villa-Lobos collection in the catalogue, certainly the most varied. His rather melancholy piano piece, *A lenda de caboclo* ('Legend of a half-caste') gives a clue to the unique identity of this music, for the composer's mother was Hispanic, his father of Indian descent. No. 3 of the *Bachianas brasileiras*, which dates from 1938, is the only one of the series to involve the piano. The *Mômoprecóce* began life in 1920 (while the composer was living in Paris) as the set of piano pieces called *Carnaval das Crianças*, and it was reworked in its concertante form later. Like so much of Villa-Lobos's music, the score is rowdy and colourful. Cristina Ortiz, herself Brazilian, is a natural choice for this repertoire. She plays with appropriate vigour, reflective feeling and colour, and Ashkenazy gives splendid support. The late-1970s recording is excellent, with the CD transfer adding a little edge to high violins. Ortiz is equally impressive in the solo piano pieces (again very well recorded), which she plays with flair and at times with touching tenderness, as in Villa-Lobos's portaits of the *Clay* and *Rag dolls*, the third and and sixth members of *A próle do bébé* ('Baby's family'). Angel Romero makes the very most of the comparatively slight *Guitar concerto*, bringing out its Latin feeling. The *Fantasia for soprano saxophone* is a more substantial piece with three well-defined movements, contrasted in invention. John Harle is a perceptive soloist with a most appealing timbre; one of the highlights of the set. The recordings in both these concertante works (made in 1984 and 1990 respectively) are well up to the best Abbey Road analogue standards.

Guitar concerto.
(M) *** Sony SMK 60022 [id.]. John Williams, ECO, Barenboim – CASTELNUOVO-TEDESCO: *Guitar concerto;* RODRIGO: *Concierto de Aranjuez.* ***
(BB) *** Naxos Dig. 8.550729 [id.]. Norbert Kraft, Northern CO, Nicholas Ward – CASTELNUOVO-TEDESCO: *Concerto* ***; RODRIGO: *Concierto de Aranjuez.* ***

John Williams's compulsive performance makes the very most of the finer points of Villa-Lobos's comparatively slight concerto, and especially the rhapsodic quality of the *Andantino*. The recording is bright and fresh, the soloist characteristically close, but the effect is vividly present.

An excellent account from Norbert Kraft, spontaneous and catching well the music's colour and atmosphere. If it is not quite as individual as Bream's version, it has the advantage of vivid, well-balanced, modern, digital recording and excellent couplings. Another genuine Naxos bargain.

(i) *Guitar concerto. 12 Etudes; 5 Preludes.*
(M) *** RCA 09026 61604-2. Julian Bream, (i) LSO, André Previn.

A highly distinguished account of the *Guitar concerto* from Bream, magnetic and full of atmosphere in the slow movement and finale. Previn accompanies sympathetically and with spirit. The rest of the programme also shows Bream in inspirational form. He engages the listener's attention from the opening of the first study and holds it to the last. The recording has a nice intimacy in the concerto and the solo items have fine presence against an attractive ambience.

Piano concertos Nos. 1–5.
(B) *** Decca Double Dig. 452 617-2 (2) [id.]. Cristina Ortiz, RPO, Miguel Gómez-Martínez.

What emerges from the series of concertos, as played by Cristina Ortiz here, is that the first two are the most immediately identifiable as Brazilian in their warm colouring and sense of atmosphere, even though the eclectic borrowings are often more unashamed than later, with many passages suggesting Rachmaninov with a Brazilian accent. No. 3, the work Villa-Lobos found it hard to complete, tends to sound bitty in its changes of direction. No. 4, more crisply conceived, has one or two splendid tunes, but it is in No. 5 that Villa-Lobos becomes most warmly convincing again, returning unashamedly to more echoes of Rachmaninov. With Ortiz articulating crisply, there is much to enjoy from such colourful, undemanding music, brilliantly recorded and sympathetically performed.

Discovery of Brazil: suites Nos. 1–3; (i) *4.*
**(*) Marco Polo Dig. 8.223551 [id.]. Slovak RSO (Bratislava), Roberto Duarte; (i) with Adam Blazo, Slovak Philharmonic Ch.

The *Discovery of Brazil* derives from an ambitious film project and Villa-Lobos fashioned three orchestral suites from it, plus a fourth which employs a soloist and choir. Though there are good things in this music and some exotic orchestral effects, the colours are not quite as vivid and dazzling as one would have expected from this prolific Brazilian master. Enjoyable performances

CHAMBER MUSIC

5 Preludes for guitar.
(B) *** Sony SBK 62425 [id.]. John Williams (guitar) – GIULIANI: *Variations on a theme by Handel;* PAGANINI: *Caprice No. 24; Grand sonata;* D. SCARLATTI: *Sonatas.* ***

Although John Williams is balanced a shade too closely, he is very well recorded; his playing, improvisationally spontaneous and full of magical evocation, is of the highest level of mastery. A lower-level setting compensates for the balance and enables this artist's playing to register effectively. These are as perfect and as finely turned as any performances in the catalogue.

String quartets Nos. 4 (1917); 6 (Quarteto brasileiro) (1938); 14 (1953).
*** Marco Polo Dig. 8.223391 [id.]. Danubius Qt.

The three quartets recorded here are all well crafted and their ideas are of quality. The *Fourth* is perhaps the most Gallic; the *Sixth* (*Quarteto brasileiro*) is one of the most individual and rewarding. It makes intelligent use of Brazilian folk-material. The *Fourteenth*, like so much of Villa-Lobos, is not entirely free from note-spinning. The Danubius Quartet are an accomplished ensemble and play with evident commitment. The recording places them rather forward in the aural picture.

String quartet No. 6 (Quarteto brasileiro).
(***) Testament mono SBT 1053 [id.]. Hollywood Qt – CRESTON: *Quartet;* DEBUSSY: *Danses sacrées;* RAVEL: *Intro and allegro;* TURINA: *La Oración.* (***)

The *Sixth Quartet* is a slight but amiable score, ultimately facile but pleasing and well crafted. It would be hard to imagine a finer performance than this.

Suite populaire brésilienne; Etudes Nos. 5 in C; 7 in E.
(M) *** RCA 09026 61596-2. Julian Bream – Recital: *'Twentieth-century guitar II'.* ***

The *Suite populaire brésilienne* is deservedly among Villa-Lobos's most popular music. The composer disclaims the idea that these four chôros (pieces in the style of Brazilian street-bands) were intended as a suite, but they fit together remarkably well. Bream plays them with his usual flair and brings out all their vivid colouring. The two contrasted *Etudes* are also fine pieces. Excellent late-1970s recording.

PIANO MUSIC

Alma brasileira, Bachiana brasileira No. 4; Ciclo brasileiro; Chôros No. 5; Valsa da dor (Waltz of sorrows).
*** ASV Dig. CDDCA 607 [id.]. Alma Petchersky.

Alma Petchersky's style is romantic, and some might find her thoughtful deliberation in the *Preludio* of the *Bachianas brasileira No. 4* overdone. Her very free rubato is immediately apparent in the *Valsa da dor* which opens the recital. Yet she clearly feels all this music deeply, and the playing is strong in personality and her timbre is often richly coloured. She is at her finest in the *Brazilian cycle*. The recording is first class.

Cirandas; Rudepoêma.
*** ASV Dig. CDDCA 957 [id.]. Alma Petchersky.

Not only is the playing here first class, but the music itself is of much interest. *Rudepoêma* (1921–6) is a musical portrait of Artur Rubinstein and is full of temperament and virtuosity. Alma Petchersky rises to its innumerable challenges with great spirit and panache. The *Cirandas* (1926), which make formidable technical demands on the pianist, are despatched with great brilliance and poetic feeling. Alma Petchersky is very well recorded and, if the standards of this series are maintained, future issues will be self-recommending.

VOCAL MUSIC

Bachianas brasileiras No. 5 for soprano and cellos.
(B) *** Decca Double Dig. 444 995-2 (2) [id.]; *444 995-4.* Kiri Te Kanawa, Lynn Harrell and instrumental ens. – CANTELOUBE: *Songs of the Auvergne.* ***
(M) *** RCA 09026 62600-2 [id.]. Anna Moffo, American SO, Stokowski – CANTELOUBE: *Chants d'Auvergne;* RACHMANINOV: *Vocalise.* ***

The Villa-Lobos piece makes an apt fill-up for the Canteloube songs, completing Kiri Te Kanawa's recording of all five books. It is, if anything, even more sensuously done, well sustained at a speed far slower than one would normally expect. Rich recording to match.

Anna Moffo gives a seductive performance of the most famous of the *Bachianas brasileiras*, adopting a highly romantic style (matching the conductor) and warm tone-colour.

Viotti, Giovanni Battista
(1755–1824)

Violin concerto No. 13 in A.
*** Hyperion Dig. CDA 66210 [id.]. Oprean, European Community CO, Faerber – FIORILLO: *Violin concerto No. 1.* ***

Viotti wrote a great many violin concertos in much the same mould, but this is one of his best. Adelina

Oprean's quicksilver style and light lyrical touch give much pleasure – she has the exact measure of this repertoire and she is splendidly accompanied and well recorded. The measure, though, is short.

Vivaldi, Antonio (1675–1741)

Philips Vivaldi Edition, Volume 1: Concertos: (i) *L'Estro armonico, Op. 3;* (ii) *La Stravaganza, Op. 4;* (iii) *6 Violin concertos, Op. 6.* Chamber music: (iv) *12 Sonatas for 2 violins, Op. 1;* (v) *12 Violin sonatas, Op. 2;* (vi) *6 Sonatas for 1 or 2 violins, Op. 5.*

(B) *** Ph. 456 185-2 (10) [id.]. (i) Michelucci; (ii) Ayo; (iii) Carmirelli; (i–iii) I Musici; (iv–vi) Accardo, Canino, De Saram; (iv) Gulli; (vi) Gazeau.

Philips Vivaldi Edition, Volume 2: Concertos: (i–ii) *12 Concertos for oboe or violin, Op. 7;* (iii) *Il Cimento dell'armonia e dell'inventione* (*The Trial between harmony and invention,* including *The Four Seasons*), *Op. 8; La Cetra, Op. 9;* (iv) *6 Flute concertos, Op. 10;* (i) *6 Violin concertos, Op. 11; 6 Violin concertos, Op. 12.*

(B) *** Ph. 456 186-2 (9) [id.]. I Musici, with (i) Accardo; (ii) Holliger; (iii) Ayo; (iv) Gazzelloni.

Philips's Vivaldi Edition is very competitively priced, and any reservations tend to be swept aside when the coverage is so uniquely comprehensive and the music-making so warmly enjoyable. These are refreshing and lively performances, and the current transfers offer gleaming tuttis, while the soloists are realisically placed and cleanly focused.

The reissue of the chamber music is particularly welcome, as these sonatas are not otherwise readily obtainable. In any case it is unlikely that Accardo's performances, so ably supported by Franco Gulli (in Op. 1), Rohan de Saram (cello) and Bruno Canino (harpsichord) could be surpassed in terms of fluency, musicianship and sheer beauty of tone.

The Opp. 11 and 12 *Violin concertos* were recorded in 1974–5. The best of them are very rewarding indeed and, played superlatively by Salvatore Accardo, they are likely to beguile the most reluctant listener.

L'Estro armonico (12 Concertos), Op. 3.

*** DG Dig. (IMS) 423 094-2 (2) [id.]. Standage & soloists, E. Concert, Trevor Pinnock.

(N) *** Virgin/Veritas/EMI VMD5 45315-2 (2) [id.]. Biondi, Longo, Casazza, Negri, Naddeo, Europa Galante.

L'Estro armonico, Op. 3; (i) *Bassoon concerto in A min., RV 498;* (ii) *Flute concerto in C min., RV 441;* (iii) *Oboe concerto in F, RV 456;* (i; iii; iv) *Concerto in F for 2 oboes, bassoon, 2 horns and violin, RV 574.*

(B) *** Decca Double 443 476-2 (2) [id.]. ASMF, Marriner; with (i) Martin Gatt; (ii) William Bennett; (iii) Neil Black; (iv) Celia Nicklin, Timothy Brown, Robin Davis, Iona Brown.

Vivaldi's *L'Estro armonico* includes some of his finest music. The chamber version from Pinnock (with one instrument to a part) brings together the best features from past versions: there is as much sparkle and liveliness as with Hogwood, for rhythms are consistently resilient, ensemble crisp and vigorous. Yet in slow movements there is that expressive radiance and sense of enjoyment of beauty without unstylish indulgence that one expects from the ASMF. The recording was made in EMI's Abbey Road studio, atmospheric and perfectly balanced.

Faio Biondi and Europe Galante start with No. 2, whose arresting opening *Adagio e spiccato* is very dramatic indeed. Indeed these performances are tremendously alert, crisply rhythmic and marvellously played, with the lyrical writing always winningly expressive. Almost all of these works are for two or more soloists, and here the concertino work splendidly together. But when Biondi plays alone his contribution is very stylish indeed and the *Largo* of the solo concerto, RV 356 (No. 6) is exquisite. Equally Biondi and Isabella Longo make a captivating partnership in the *Double violin concerto*, RV 519 (No. 7). Period instrument playing of Vivaldi has clearly matured and with first-class modern recording this offers a strong challenge to both Pinnock and Hogwood.

Those who have not been won over to the more abrasive sound of period instruments will find Marriner's set no less stylish. As so often, he directs the Academy in radiant and imaginative performances of baroque music and yet observes scholarly good manners. The delightful use of continuo – lute and organ as well as harpsichord – the sharing of solo honours and the consistently resilient string playing of the ensemble make for compelling listening. The 1972 recording, made in St John's, Smith Square, is immaculately transferred, and as a bonus come four of Vivaldi's most inventive concertos, each with its own special effects. The *A minor Bassoon concerto* has a delightful sense of humour and in RV 441 the flute chortles like a bird. The work for oboes and horns is agreeably robust, with a charming slow movement. The recording is a model of clarity and definition, warm and atmospheric.

(i) *L'Estro armonico (12 Concertos), Op. 3*; (ii) *6 Flute concertos, Op. 10.*

(N) (B) *** Decca Double 458 078-2 (2) [id.]. (i) Holloway, Huggett, Mackintosh, Wilcock; (ii) Simon Preston; AAM, Hogwood.

There is no question about the sparkle of Christopher Hogwood's performance with the Academy of Ancient Music. The captivating lightness of the solo playing and the crispness of articulation of the accompanying group bring music-making that combines joyful vitality with the authority of scholarship. Hogwood's continuo is first class, varying between harpsichord and organ, the latter used to add colour as well as substance. The balance is excellent, and the whole effect is exhilarating. In Op. 10 Stephen Preston plays a period instrument, a Schuchart, and the Academy of Ancient Music likewise play old instruments. Their playing is eminently stylish, but also spirited and expressive, and they are admirably recorded, with the analogue sound enhanced further in the CD format. A first choice among period instrument performances, this makes a more than generous coupling for Op. 3.

L'Estro armonico, Op. 3/1, 2, 4, 7, 8 & 10–11.
(BB) *** Naxos Dig. 8.550160 [id.]. Capella Istropolitana, Jozef Kopelman.

Jozef Kopelman and the Capella Istropolitana are robustly competitive with their bargain disc. The performances are lively, and the recording has warmth and presence. Good value for money.

La Stravaganza (12 concertos), *Op. 4* (complete).
✿ (B) *** Decca Double 444 821-2 (2). Soloists, ASMF, Marriner.

Marriner's performances make the music irresistible. The solo playing of Carmel Kaine and Alan Loveday is superb and, when the Academy's rhythms have such splendid buoyancy and lift, it is easy enough to accept Marriner's preference for a relatively sweet style in the often heavenly slow movements. The contribution of an imaginatively varied continuo (which includes cello and bassoon, in addition to harpsichord, theorbo and organ) adds much to the colour of Vivaldi's score. The recording, made in St John's, Smith Square, in 1973/4, is of the highest quality, with CD transfers in the demonstration class.

The Trial between harmony and invention (12 Concertos), Op. 8.
(B) **(*) Ph. Duo 438 344-2 (2). Felix Ayo, I Musici.

Felix Ayo recorded the first four concertos (*The Four Seasons*) in 1959 and his was one of the finest of the early versions, although the recording was rather resonant. The remaining concertos in the set – full of typically Vivaldian touches which stamp these works as among the best of their time – date from 1961/2 and the recording, though still full-bodied, is less reverberant. The solo playing is attractively fresh, although Maria Teresa Garatti's continuo fails to come through adequately. Good value.

The Four Seasons, Op. 8/1–4.
(M) *** Decca Penguin Classics 460 613-2 [id.]. Alan Loveday, ASMF, Marriner.
*** DG Dig. 439 933-2 [id.]. Gil Shaham, Orpheus CO – KREISLER: *Violin concerto in the style of Vivaldi.* ***

The Four Seasons, Op. 8/1–4; Violin concerto in D, RV 171; Concerto for strings in B flat (Concha), RV 163.
(N) *** Opus 111 Dig. OPS 912 [id.]. Fabio Biondi, Europe Galante.

The Four Seasons, Op. 8/1–4; Violin concertos: in E flat (La tempesta di mare), RV 253; in C (Il piacere), RV 108, Op. 8/5–6.
*** Teldec/Warner Dig. 4509 91683-2. Marieke Blankestijn, COE.
*** Ph. Dig. 446 699-2 [id.]. Mariana Sirbu, I Musici.

The Four Seasons, Op. 8/1–4; Violin concertos: in E flat (La tempesta di mare), RV 253; in C (Il Piacare), RV 108; in B flat (La Caccia), RV 362; in D, RV 210, Op. 8/5–6, 10–11.
(M) *** Virgin Veritas/EMI Dig. VER5 61172-2 [id.]. Monica Huggett, Raglan Bar. Players, Nicholas Kraemer.

(i; ii) *The Four Seasons, Op. 8/1–4;* (i; iii) *Violin concerto in E flat (La tempesta di mare), Op. 8/5, RV 253;* (iv) *Triple concerto in F for flute, oboe and bassoon, RV 570; Double concerto in G min. for flute and bassoon (La Notte), RV 104.*
(BB) *** ASV Quicksilva Dig. CDQS 6148 [id.]. (i) José-Luis Garcia; (ii) ECO; (iii) Fort Worth CO, Giordano; (iv) William Bennett, Neil Black, Robin O'Neill, ECO, Malcolm.

(i) *The Four Seasons, Op. 8/1–4;* (ii) *Violin concertos: L'Estro armonico: in A min., Op. 3/6. La Stravaganza: in A, Op. 4/5. Concerto in C min. (Il sospetto), RV 199.*
(M) *** EMI CDM7 64333-2. Perlman, (i) LPO; (ii) Israel PO.

The Four Seasons; (i) *L'Estro armonico: Quadruple violin concerto in B min., RV 580, Op. 3/10. Sinfonia in B min. (Al Santo Sepolcro), RV 169.*
✿ *** Sony Dig. SK 48251 [id.]. Jeanne Lamon, Tafelmusik.

(i) *The Four Seasons, Op. 8/1–4; Quadruple violin concerto in B flat, RV 553. Concerto for strings in G (alla rustica), RV 151; Sinfonia in G, RV 146.*
(M) *** Virgin/EMI VC5 45117-2. (i) Chiara Banchini, Alison Bury, John Holloway, Elizabeth Wallfisch; Taverner Players, Andrew Parrott.

(i) *The Four Seasons, Op. 8/1–4;* (ii) *Mandolin concerto in C, RV 425*; (iii) *Double mandolin concerto in G, RV 532;* (iv) *Double trumpet concerto in C, RV 537.*
(M) *** Ph. Dig/Analogue 442 393-2. (i) Salvatore Accardo, I Solisti delle Settimane Internazionali di Napoli; (ii) Parisi; (iii) Del

Vescovo, Ruta; (iv) Adelbrecht, Mathez; (ii-iv) I Musici.

There are innumerable recordings of Vivaldi's *Four Seasons* and nowadays those versions offered without fill-ups in a crowded marketplace seem uncompetitive. Yet Marriner's 1970 Academy of St Martin-in-the-Fields version with Alan Loveday is an exception and still remains at the top of the list. The performance is as satisfying as any and will surely delight all but those who are ruled by the creed of authenticity. It has an element of fantasy that makes the music sound utterly new; it is full of imaginative touches, with Simon Preston subtly varying the continuo between harpsichord and organ. The opulence of string tone may have a romantic connotation, but there is no self-indulgence in the interpretation, no sentimentality, for the contrasts are made sharper and fresher, not smoothed over. This has now appeared as one of the Penguin Classics at mid-price. The author's note is a fascinating reminiscence by Seamus Deane. However as we go to print, Decca have given advance notice of a further reissue of this Marriner performance on the Legends label (466 232-2) including as a bonus concertos for bassoon, piccolo and two oboes.

Tafelmusik offer a superbly imaginative version of Vivaldi's *Four Seasons* on period instruments, which is for the 1990s what Marriner's famous ASMF version was for the '70s. The playing is at once full of fantasy and yet has a robust gusto that is irresistible. The opening of *Spring*, with its chirruping bird calls, sets the scene and the second movement brings a lovely cantilena from Jeanne Lamon, while the barking dog is as musical as he is gruff. The performances throughout are full of dramatic contrasts. After *Winter*'s boisterous finale comes the hauntingly austere texture of the opening of the highly original *Sinfonia al Sepulcro*; and the famous *Concerto for four violins* makes a fitting finale. The Sony recording is first class, absolutely clean in focus, with plenty of body and the most refined detail.

Fabio Biondi and his similarly excellent period-instrument group, Europe Galante have already given us an outstanding set of *L'Estro armonico,* and their account of *The Four Seasons* is equally fresh. There is not a hint of routine anywhere, the solo playing is often exquisite; and even if the soloist nearly gets blown away by the gusto of the summer winds, the central reverie *Autumn* is hauntingly gentle and serene. *Winter* opens very dramatically indeed and the solo roulades have great bravura; the central movement makes a charmingly relaxed contrast. The bonuses are imaginative and include another of Vivaldi's most individual violin concertos and the *concerto for strings* given the nickname *Concha* because it is supposed to simulate a primitive instrument made from a seashell, notably in the central *Andante* with its echoing fifth (B flat and F). Again the performances are strongly characterized and very well recorded.

For those still preferring the fuller texture of modern instruments, the Teldec version with COE provides the perfect alternative. The chimerical solo playing of Marieke Blankestijn is a delight and her clean style shows that she has learned from authentic manners. There is more imaginative delicacy here, particularly in the improvisatory central movement of *Summer* and the gentle haze of *Autumn*, where the gutsy finale has splendid bite and energy. The opening of *Winter* mirrors the impressionism of the Tafelmusik version, but the cheerful COE approach to the *Largo* central movement is even more attractive than with Tafelmusik. With two extra concertos from Op. 8 also included, this is now also a very strong recommendation. The Teldec recording is superb.

Monica Huggett's Virgin Veritas CD makes a fine mid-priced alternative to the premium version by Tafelmusik, even if she does not quite match it in exuberant pictorialism. The shepherd's dog on Virgin is in a mellower mood, but the light texture and dancing tempo of the finale of *Spring* is matched by the sense of fantasy in the central movement of *Summer*, while the rumbustious energy of the latter's last movement is invigorating. Four other concertos from Op. 8 are also included, all played in fine style, with Monica Huggett's easy, supple bravura well matched by Raglan's zestful accompaniments.

Salvatore Accardo's version is of special interest in that he uses a different Stradivarius for each of the four concertos. Thanks to this aristocrat of violinists, the sounds are of exceptional beauty. The performances are much enhanced, too, by the imaginative continuo playing of Bruno Canino, who is not given a credit in the booklet. The notes also neglect to say that these were live performances, recorded digitally at the Cremona Festival in 1987. They have all the virtues of live music-making but none of the drawbacks. The other concertos are excellently played, and the analogue recording is first class.

The Taverner Players offer yet another authentic version which stimulates the ear without acerbity. They are not the first group to use a different soloist for each of Vivaldi's *Four Seasons*, and this works well, with plenty of tingling vitality overall and a good deal of imaginative freedom from each in turn, with Chiara Banchini setting the style in her duets with the leader in her volatile account of *Spring*. In the *Adagio* of *Summer*, Alison Bury's timbre is pure with a minimum of vibrato, yet the playing is appealingly expressive. The four players join together for the *Concerto for four violins in B flat*, offered as the principal bonus; it is an interesting work, if not quite as memorable as its more familiar companion in B minor, but it demands and receives virtuosity from its soloists. The *Sinfonia* and *Con-*

certo alla rustica are played with energy and tonal bite, and the recording is suitably vivid throughout.

The ASV version of *The Four Seasons*, with José-Luis Garcia as soloist and musical director, is very pleasing, with the violins of the accompanying group sweetly fresh and the soloist nicely balanced. The overall pacing is beautifully judged, and each movement takes its place naturally and spontaneously in relation to its companions. The one drawback is that there is only one track for each of the *Four Seasons*. The new couplings add two versions of *La tempesta del mare*, both the one with solo violin (from Op. 8) and the even more engaging triple concerto arrangement for flute, oboe and bassoon. The equally attractive flute/bassoon version of *La Notte* completes the collection. The wind soloists are all celebrated, and George Malcolm's accompaniments are a model of baroque style.

Mariana Sirbu has a beautiful tone and an admirable line, and she can be expressive and vigorous by turn, without putting the timbre under strain. I Musici are thoroughly at home and sound fresh in a work which they must have played countless times. All the points of programmatic detail are nicely observed, from the bold shepherd's dog onwards. This is a first-class modern-instrument performance if not as characterful as some, with the lute and harpsichord continuo adding to the effect of slow movements. The two bonus concertos are equally well played, and the recording is natural, with fine projection.

Gil Shaham and the excellent, conductorless Orpheus Chamber Orchestra combine to present a strongly characterized, eminently musical set of *Seasons* which seeks in some ways to emulate period-instrument performances with bright, bracingly athletic string-textures – sample the opening movement of *Autumn* – and gutsy virility when called for, as in the summer storms (tracks 5–6). Gil Shaham plays beautifully and with freshness. First-rate sound with plenty of presence.

Perlman's imagination holds the sequence together superbly, and there are many passages of pure magic, as in the central *Adagio* of *Summer*. The digital remastering of the 1976 recording is managed admirably, the sound firm, clear and well balanced, with plenty of detail. Now this record has been made much more competitive by the addition of three extra violin concertos, all fine works. Although the acoustic is somewhat dryish, this does not prevent these extra works from sounding very good.

The Four Seasons, Op. 8/1–4 (arr. for flute and strings).
(M) *** RCA GD 60748 [60748-2-RG]. James Galway, Zagreb Soloists.

James Galway's sensitive transcription is so convincing that at times one is tempted to believe that the work was conceived in this form. The playing is marvellous, full of detail and imagination, and the recording is excellent, even if the flute is given a forward balance, the more striking on CD.

La Cetra (12 Violin concertos), Op. 9.
(N) (BB) *** Virgin Veritas Dig. Double VBD5 61594-2 (2). Huggett, Raglan Bar. Players, Kraemer.
*** O-L (IMS) Dig. 421 366-2 (2). Standage, AAM, Hogwood.

(i) *La Cetra;* (ii) *Double oboe concerto in D min., RV 535;* (iii) *Piccolo concerto in C, RV 443.*
❁ (B) *** Decca Double 448 110-2 (2) [id.]. (i) Iona Brown, ASMF; (ii) Neil Black; (iii) Celia Nicklin; both with ASMF, Marriner.

La Cetra (The Lyre) was the last set of violin concertos Vivaldi published. Iona Brown, for some years the leader of St Martin's Academy, here acts as director in the place of Sir Neville Marriner. So resilient and imaginative are the results that one hardly detects any difference from the immaculate and stylish Vivaldi playing in earlier Academy Vivaldi sets. There is some wonderful music here; the later concertos are every bit the equal of anything in *The Trial between harmony and invention*, and they are played gloriously. The recording too is outstandingly rich and vivid, even by earlier Argo standards with this group, and the Decca transfer to CD retains the demonstration excellence of the original analogue LPs, with a yet greater sense of body and presence. For the Double Decca reissue, two of Vivaldi's most engaging wind concertos have been added, winningly played by two fine Academy soloists and made the more attractive in slow movements by the imaginative continuo from Kenneth Heath (cello), Christopher Hogwood (harpsichord) and Colin Tilney (organ). The sound is just as fine as in the concertos for violin.

Monica Huggett and the Raglan Baroque Players offer performances so accomplished and in such good style that they are unlikely to be surpassed in authentic-instrument versions of *La Cetra*. She is in excellent form and her virtuosity always appears effortless. The Raglan Baroque Players are of the same size as the Academy of Ancient Music and some players are common to both groups. First-class recording.

On Oiseau-Lyre, Simon Standage gives an attractive and fluent account of the set, and the recording is excellent, slightly dry but very clean.

6 Flute concertos, Op. 10.
(N) (B) *** Ph. Virtuoso 422 620-2. Gazzelloni, I Musici.
*** DG (IMS) Dig. 437 839-2 [id.]. Patrick Gallois, Orpheus CO.
*** DG (IMS) Dig. 423 702-2. Liza Beznosiuk, E. Concert, Pinnock.
(M) *** Carlton Dig. 30367 0021-2 [id.]. Judith Hall, Divertimenti of L., Paul Barritt.

Severino Gazzelloni's version of the six *Concertos*, Op. 10 is a safer recommendation for the general collector than the authentic rivals, good though the best of these is. With fresh, remastered sound this is an excellent bargain-price recommendation.

The Gallois/Orpheus version on DG is the lightest and most spirited of any, be they on period instruments or not. Collectors who recall Gallois's dazzling account of the Nielsen *Concerto* will know what to expect: effortless virtuosity, refined musicianship, intelligence and taste. He has an excellent rapport with the splendid Orpheus Chamber Orchestra and is very well served too by the engineers. A most distinguished issue.

There is some expressive as well as brilliant playing on the DG Archiv CD, which should delight listeners. Try track 8 (the *Largo* movement of *Concerto No. 2 in G minor, La Notte*) for an example of the beautifully refined and cool pianissimo tone that Liza Beznosiuk can produce – and almost any of the fast movements for an example of her virtuosity. Trevor Pinnock and the English Concert provide unfailingly vital and, above all, imaginative support. The DG recording is exemplary in its clarity. Recommended with enthusiasm.

Judith Hall's record of the Op. 10 *Flute concertos* is fresh and brightly recorded, and she plays with great virtuosity and fine taste. The Divertimenti of London is a modern-instrument group and the players are both sensitive and alert. At mid-price this is very competitive.

6 Flute concertos, Op. 10; Flute concertos: in A min., RV 108; in D, RV 429; in G, RV 438; in A min., RV 440; in C min., RV 441; (i) *Double flute concerto in C, RV 533. Piccolo concerto in A min., RV 445.*

(B) *** Ph. Duo 454 256-2 (2) [id.]. Severino Gazzelloni, I Musici; (i) with Marja Steinberg.

This Duo set purports to contain Vivaldi's 'complete flute concertos', but it is an unlikely claim: the works for sopranino recorder, RV 443 and 444, are not here, nor is the arrangement of *La Notte* (RV 104) which includes also a bassoon. However, the solo flute version is (Op. 10/2) and, with its movements representing ghosts (*Fantasmi*) and sleep (*Il sonno*), is a masterpiece by any standards. A Duo collection entirely made up of concertante works for flute might be thought a rather daunting prospect, but Gazzelloni is an artist of such quality and poetry that such doubts are banished. And it must be added that these concertos all show Vivaldi in the best light, not only in the best-known, *La tempesta di mare* and *Il gardellino*, from Op. 10, but in many of the miscellaneous concertos, too: witness the delicate slow movement of the *A minor*, RV 440, the touching *Largo* of the *C minor*, RV 441, or the lively opening movements of the *D major*, RV 429, and *A minor*, RV 108. In these modern-instrument performances Gazzelloni's tone is admirably fresh and clean, with I Musici giving him splendid support. The analogue recordings (from the 1960s and 1970s) are first-rate.

(i; ii) *Flute concertos, Op. 10: Nos. 1 in F (La tempesta di mare), RV 433: 2 in G min. (La notte), RV 439; 3 in D (Il gardellino), RV 428*; (i; iii) *5 in F, RV 434. Flute concerto in A min., RV 108; Sopranino recorder (Piccolo) concertos: in C, RV. 443 & RV 444; in A min., RV 445.* (iv) *Double flute concerto in C, RV 533.*

(BB) *** Naxos Dig. 8.554053 [id.]. Soloists; (i) Capella Istropolitana, (ii) Jaroslav Krechek; (i; iii) Oliver Dohnányi; (iv) City of L. Sinfonia, Kraemer.

An attractive and generous regrouping of Naxos recordings (78 minutes) brings a particularly generous clutch of modern-instrument performances which will especially suit those who want only the most famous named concertos from Op. 10. They are most persuasively played and the recording is excellent throughout.

Complete bassoon concertos

Bassoon concertos: in C, RV 466; in C, RV 467; in C, RV 469; in C, RV 470; in C, RV 471; in C, RV 472; in C, RV 473; in C, RV 474; in C, RV 475; in C, RV 476; in C, RV 477; in C, RV 478; in C, RV 479; in C min., RV 480; in D min., RV 481; in E flat, RV 483; in E min., RV 484; in F, RV 485; in F, RV 486; in F, RV 487; in F, RV 488; in F, RV 489; in F, RV 490; in F, RV 491; in G, RV 492; in G, RV 493; in G, RV 494; in G min., RV 495; in G min., RV 496; in A min., RV 497; in A min., RV 498; in A min., RV 499; in A min., RV 500; in B flat (La notte), RV 501; in B flat, RV 502; in B flat, RV 503; in B flat, RV 504.

(M) *** ASV Dig. CDDCX 625 (6). Daniel Smith, ECO, Ledger; Zagreb Soloists, Ninic.

The bassoon brought out a generous fund of inspiration in Vivaldi, for few of his 37 concertos for that instrument are in any way routine. Daniel Smith plays with constant freshness and enthusiasm. His woody tone is very attractive and he is very well caught by the engineers. This set can be welcomed almost without reservation and, dipped into, the various recordings will always give pleasure. Even if some of the more complicated roulades are not executed with exact precision, Smith's playing has undoubted flair.

For the last three CDs of the series the Zagreb Soloists take over the accompaniments and offer alert, vivacious playing that adds to the pleasure of these warm, affectionate performances. Daniel Smith, too, responds with vigour and polish.

Bassoon concertos: in C, RV 472; in D min., RV 482; in E min., RV 484; in F, RV 491; in G, RV 494; in G min., RV 495; in A min., RV 499.

*** Ph. Dig. (IMS) 446 066-2. Klaus Thunemann, I Musici.

In the late 1980s Klaus Thunemann gave us an excellent first instalment of Vivaldi's *Bassoon concertos* (Ph. 416 355-2). This second bunch is no less outstanding. He makes every work seem a masterpiece. His virtuosity is remarkable, and it is always at the composer's service. Moreover the polish of the playing is matched by its character and warmth. I Musici are on their finest form, and all the slow movements here are touchingly expressive, with Thunemann's ease of execution adds to enjoyment. The Philips recording, ideally balanced, is in the demonstration bracket.

Bassoon concerto in F, RV 485; (i) *Double concerto in G min., for recorder and bassoon (La Notte), RV 104.*
*** BIS Dig. CD 271 [id.]. McGraw, (i) Pehrsson, Drottningholm Bar. Ens. – TELEMANN: *Concertos*. ***

The concerto subtitled *La Notte* exists in three versions: one for flute (the most familiar), RV 439; another for bassoon, RV 501; and the present version, RV 104. Clas Pehrsson, Michael McGraw and the Drottningholm Baroque Ensemble give a thoroughly splendid account of it, and the *Bassoon concerto in F major* also fares well. Excellent recording.

Complete cello concertos

Volume 1: *Cello concertos: in C, RV 398; in C, RV 399; in D, RV 404; in D min., RV 406; in F, RV 410; in F, RV 412; in A min., RV 419.*
(BB) *** Naxos Dig. 8.550907 [id.]. Raphael Wallfisch, City of L. Sinfonia, Nicholas Kraemer.

Volume 2: *Cello concertos: in C, RV 400; in C min., RV 401; in E flat, RV 408; in G, RV 413; in A min., RV 422;* (i) *Double cello concerto in G min., RV 531.*
(BB) *** Naxos Dig. 8.550908 [id.]. Raphael Wallfisch, (i) with Keith Harvey; City of L. Sinfonia, Nicholas Kraemer.

Volume 3: *Cello concertos: in C min., RV 402; in D, RV 403; in D min., RV 407;* (i) *in E min., RV 409; in A min., RV 418; in B flat, RV 423; in B min., RV 424.*
❁ (BB) *** Naxos Dig. 8.550909 [id.]. Raphael Wallfisch, (i) with Johanna Graham; City of L. Sinfonia, Nicholas Kraemer.

Volume 4: *Cello concertos: in D min., RV 405; in F, RV 411; in G, RV 414; in G min., RV 416 & RV 417; in A min., RV 420 & RV 421.*
(BB) *** Naxos Dig. 8. 550910 [id.]. Raphael Wallfisch, City of L. Sinfonia, Nicholas Kraemer.

Vivaldi liked to write for instruments playing in the middle to lower register, and he left 27 solo concertos for the cello, all of which are here. This Naxos series is part of an overall survey, with plans eventually to record every one of the Vivaldi concertos. The company has begun admirably and the choice of Raphael Wallfisch as soloist could hardly have been bettered. He forms an admirable partnership with the City of London Sinfonia, directed from the harpsichord or chamber organ by Nicholas Kraemer. The first concerto of Volume 1, the fine *F major*, RV 412, sets off with great energy and produces a characteristically atmospheric central *Larghetto*. Wallfisch plays with restrained use of vibrato and a nicely judged expressive feeling. In the *A minor* work which follows (RV 419), Kraemer effectively uses an organ continuo to enliven the opening tutti and underpin the singing cello line in the *Andante*. The alert, resilient orchestral string-playing in the allegros is a pleasure in itself.

Besides several very striking solo works, Volume 2 of the Naxos series includes Vivaldi's only *Double cello concerto*, with much bustling interchange in the outer movements and the soloists answering each other eloquently in the *Largo*. In the *G major* solo *Concerto*, RV 413, there is a brilliantly articulated *moto perpetuo* semiquaver theme which alternates between soloist and orchestra; then follows a thoughtful slow movement, improvisatory in feeling, in which Wallfisch is in his element, over Kraemer's gentle organ continuo. Bravura passage-work returns in the finale. Throughout one admires the soloist's subtle use of light and shade and his understanding partnership with his accompanists.

Volume 3 is a particularly fine collection and as good a place to start as any. The soloist's bravura staccato playing at the opening on the *B flat major*, RV 423, commands the listener's attention at the very beginning of the disc, and this work has a matching good-humoured finale. The *Concerto in D minor*, RV 407, is one of Vivaldi's very best, and its central *Largo e sempre piano* again brings a touching solo response. Vivaldi is never predictable, and perhaps the most striking work of all here is the *E minor Concerto*, RV 409, where the cello is joined by a subservient and somewhat doleful solo bassoon. In the *Adagio–Allegro molto* opening movement, the two soloists wind their way through a melancholy recitativo, regularly interrupted by bursts of energy from the string tutti, reminding one of *The Four Seasons*; then in the much briefer *Allegro–Adagio* slow movement the procedure is reversed.

Volume 4 brings a further batch of concertos notable for their vitality and the vigorous bravura demanded from the soloist. Throughout these four discs there is never a hint of routine. Wallfisch's playing has extraordinary precision, and both he and the accompanying group continually communicate their enthusiasm for this endlessly inventive music.

The recording is vividly realistic and the balance seems very well judged indeed within the warm but never clouding ambience of All Saints' Church or Conway Hall, London. A remarkable achievement, standing very high indeed in the Vivaldi discography. We award a Rosette to Volume 3, but the final volume is hardly less attractive.

Cello concertos: in C, RV 398; in G, RV 413.
(B) *** DG Double 437 952-2 (2) [id.]. Rostropovich, Zurich Coll. Mus., Sacher – BERNSTEIN: *3 Meditations;* BOCCHERINI: *Cello concerto No. 2;* GLAZUNOV: *Chant du Ménestrel;* SHOSTAKOVICH: *Cello concerto No. 2;* TARTINI: *Cello concerto;* TCHAIKOVSKY: *Andante cantabile* etc. ***

Performances of great vigour and projection from Rostropovich; every bar comes fully to life. Spendidly lively accompaniments and excellent CD transfers, bright and clean with no lack of depth. Rostropovich's performances come as part of a very generous Double DG compilation, with the two discs offered for the price of one.

Cello concertos: in C, RV 399; in C min., RV 401; in D min., RV 405; in B flat, RV 423; in F, RV 538; Largo. (i) *Concerto in E min. for cello and bassoon, RV 409.*
*** RCA Dig. RD 87774 [7774-2-RC]. Harnoy, (i) or McKay, Toronto CO, Robinson.

Cello concertos: in C min., RV 402; in D, RV 403; in D min., RV 406; in F, RV 412; in G, RV 414; in A min., RV 422; in B min., RV 424.
*** RCA Dig. RD 60155 [60155-2-RC]. Ofra Harnoy, Toronto CO, Paul Robinson.

Cello concertos: in D, RV 404; D min., RV 407; F, RV 411; G min., RV 417; A min., RV 420; (i) *Double concerto for violin, cello and strings in F (Il Proteo o sia il mondo), RV 544.*
*** RCA Dig. 09026 61578-2 [id.]. Ofra Harnoy, (i) with Igor Oistrakh; Toronto CO, Paul Robinson.

Ofra Harnoy's are traditional performances with modern instruments; she plays with style, impeccable technique and eloquence. Her strength lies not so much in her tone, which is not big, but in her selfless approach to this repertoire. She does not regard this music as a vehicle for her own personality but plays it with an agreeable dedication and a delight in its felicities. The *Double concerto* brings an excellent partnership with Igor Oistrakh, and here the *Adagio* is particularly touching. She is given good support from the Toronto Chamber Orchestra under Paul Robinson, and is very well recorded.

Cello concerto in D min., RV 406.
(N) *** Teldec/Warner Dig. 9031 77311-2. Rostropovich, Saint Paul CO, Hugh Wolff – C. P. E. BACH; TARTINI: *Concertos.* ***

Who says that modern chamber orchestras cannot achieve the same transparency as period ensembles? Admittedly the Saint Paul Chamber Orchestra have had the advantage of Christopher Hogwood's presence, but the sound they produce blends transparency of texture with warmth and subtlety of colouring. Rostropovich is as masterly and eloquent as one could imagine, and he is accorded excellently balanced sound.

Cello concertos: in G, RV 413; in G min., RV 417.
(M) **(*) EMI CDM7 64326-2 [id.]. Lynn Harrell, ECO, Zukerman – HAYDN: *Concertos.* **(*)

Though Lynn Harrell is hardly a classical stylist among cellists (as he shows in the Haydn coupling), he gives imaginative performances of two fine Vivaldi concertos (the *G major* particularly attractive) and is well accompanied by Zukerman. The sound is lively and full, if not as smooth as on the Haydn concertos, which are interspersed with Vivaldi on the generous (74-minute) CD.

Flute concertos, Volume 1: *Chamber concertos: in C, for flute, oboe, violin, bassoon & continuo, RV 88; in D, for flute & 2 violins, RV 89; in D, for flute, violin, bassoon & continuo (Il gardellino), RV 90; in D, RV 91; in D min., RV 96 (both for flute, violin, bassoon & continuo); in F, RV 99; in G min., RV 107 (both for flute, oboe, violin, bassoon & continuo).*
(BB) *** Naxos Dig. 8.553365 [id.]. Béla Drahos and soloists, Nicolaus Esterházy Sinf.

The first of a series, this Naxos disc collects multiple concertos, but with a continuo instead of an orchestra. Although not to be played at a single sitting, these works offer a great deal of pleasure stemming from their rich textural interplay with plenty of imitation among the soloists. The quality of invention is astonishingly high. *Il gardellino* (which opens the programme) is justly famous, but the *G minor* work, RV 107, is also remarkable, with a touching *Siciliano* slow movement; it ends with a chaconne which maintains the minor key. RV 88 has a strikingly cheerful opening movement, then gives prominence to the flute both in its central *Largo cantabile* and in another chirping finale. RV 89 effectively brings a change of colour in the use of a pair of violins in juxtaposition to the flute. The performances here are admirable and the recording is most effectively balanced.

Flute concertos: in A min., RV 108; in F, RV 434; Double flute concerto in C, RV 533; Sopranino recorder concertos: in C, RV 443 & RV 444; in A min., RV 445.
(BB) *** Naxos Dig. 8.550385; *4550385* [id.]. Jálek, Novotny, Stivin, Capella Istropolitana, Oliver Dohnányi.

The Capella Istropolitana, who are drawn from the

excellent Slovak Philharmonic, play with vitality and sensitivity for Oliver Dohnányi and the soloists show appropriate virtuosity and flair. As always, there are rewards and surprises in this music. The sound is very good indeed, and so is the balance.

Flute concertos in D, RV 427; in D (Il gardellino), RV 428; in D, RV 429; in G, RV 436; in G, RV 438; in A min., RV 440; (i) *in C, for 2 flutes, RV 533.*
*** HM Dig. HMC 905193 [id.]. Janet See, (i) S. Schultz; Philh. Bar. O, McGegan.

Janet See is not only a first-class player but also an artist whose phrasing is alive and imaginative. Moreover the Philharmonia Baroque Orchestra, a West Coast American group, give her excellent support. The diversity and range of these pieces is astonishing. Highly enjoyable.

Guitar concertos in C, RV 82; in D, RV 93.
(M) *** DG (IMS) 439 984-2. Siegfried Behrend, I Musici – CARULLI: *Concerto in A;* GIULIANI: *Concerto in A, Op. 30.* ***

Both these concertos are transcriptions of chamber works intended for the lute. They work well on guitar and are most elegantly played here. Although – as the opening of the *D major* shows – there is no lack of life in these smooth, elegant performances, though a more robust and sinewy approach can be more telling in this repertoire.

Guitar concertos in D, RV 93; in B flat, RV 524; in G min., RV 531; in G, RV 532. Trios: in C, RV 82; in G min., RV 85.
*** DG Dig. (IMS) 415 487-2. Söllscher, Bern Camerata, Füri.

Göran Söllscher further enhances his reputation both as a master-guitarist and as an artist on this excellently recorded issue, in which he has first-class support from the Camerata Bern under Thomas Füri. In RV 532, Söllscher resorts to technology and plays both parts. The DG balance is admirably judged.

Guitar concertos: in D, RV 93; in A min., RV 108; (i) *with bassoon: in E, RV 265; in G, RV 435;* (ii) *Double guitar concerto in G, RV 532;* (iii) *Double concerto in D min. for viola d'amore and guitar, RV 540;* (iv) *Trio for violin, guitar and continuo in C, RV 82.*
*** RCA Dig. 09026 68291-2 [id.]. Angel Romero, ASMF; with (i) Graham Sheen; (ii) Lito Romero; (iii) Norbert Blume; (iv) Kenneth Sillito, John Constable.

Most of the Vivaldi concertos which are played on the guitar are arrangements. RV 93 and RV 532 were originally written for mandolins, and RV 540 was conceived for viola d'amore and lute. The other works were written for various instruments, usually flute or violin. However, they all work well on the guitar – and especially as presented here by Angel Romero and members of the ASMF, who seek to convey a transparency normally associated with period instruments. Romero produces a light, mandolin-like sound on his guitar, and the Academy players scale down their timbres to match. The result is delightful. Both *Double concertos* come off particularly well, with Norbert Blume playing gently and sweetly on the viola d'amore. The recording is first class.

Guitar concertos: in D, RV 93 (arr. Malipiero); *in A* (arr. Pujol from *Trio sonata in C, RV 82*); (i) *Double concerto for guitar and viola d'amore in D min., RV 540* (arr. Malipiero).
(B) **(*) Decca Eclipse 448 709-2. Eduardo Fernández, ECO, Malcolm, (i) with Norbert Blume – GIULIANI: *Concerto;* PAGANINI: *Sonata.* **(*)

Eduardo Fernández is a musician's guitarist whose playing is consistently refined and sensitive, always responsive to the composer's needs, if at times perhaps a little too self-effacing. The performance of the *Double concerto for guitar and viola d'amore* is winningly intimate, particularly in the very gentle central *Largo,* in which Fernández is perfectly balanced with Norbert Blume. The solo concertos are similarly refined, with bravura unexaggerated and Malcolm always providing the most understanding and polished accompaniments. The recording is first class and beautifully balanced.

Concertos for lute and mandolin: *Lute concerto in D, RV 93; Mandolin concerto in C, RV 425; Double mandolin concerto in G, RV 532; Double concerto in D min. for viola d'amore, lute and strings, RV 540; Concerto in C for 2 recorders, 2 violins 'in tromba marina', 2 mandolins, 2 theorbos, 2 salmoé, cello and strings, RV 558. Trios: in C, RV 82; in G min., RV 85, for violin, lute and continuo.*
**(*) Teldec/Warner Dig. 4509 91182-2. Il Giardino Armonico, Giovanni Antonini.

In these period performances from the pioneering Italian group in this field the opening of the multiple-instrument concerto, with two long, single-string violins '*in tromba marina*', is strikingly gutsy. The playing throughout has plenty of energy, and textures are fresh and transparent, with slow movements appealingly fragile. The *Largo* duet between lute and viola d'amore in RV 540 is delightful, as are the pair of *Trios* which bring similar delicacy of texture. The one snag is the curious flowing dynamic surge in the allegros which some listeners will find disconcerting. Otherwise, with the excellent recording we take for granted with Das Alte Werk, this can be recommended.

Mandolin concerto in C, RV 425; Double mandolin concerto in G, RV 532; (Soprano) Lute concerto in D, RV 93; Double concerto in D min.

for viola d'amore and lute, RV 540. Trios: in C, RV 82; in G min., RV 85.

*** Hyperion CDA 66160 [id.]. Jeffrey, O'Dette, Parley of Instruments, Goodman and Holman.

These are chamber performances, with one instrument to each part, providing an ideal balance for the *Mandolin concertos*. An organ continuo replaces the usual harpsichord, and very effective it is; in the *Trios* and the *Lute concerto* (but not in the *Double concerto*, RV 540) Paul O'Dette uses a gut-strung soprano lute. The delightful sounds here, with all players using period instruments, are very convincing. The recording is realistically balanced within an attractively spacious acoustic.

Oboe concertos: in C, RV 447 & RV 451; in F, RV 455 & RV 457; in A min., RV 461 & RV 463.

(BB) *** Naxos Dig. 8.550860 [id.]. Stefan Schilli, Budapest Failoni CO, Béla Nagy.

Oboe concertos: in C, RV 450 & RV 452; in D, RV 453; in D min., RV 454; (i) *Double oboe concertos: in C, RV 534; D min., RV 535; A min., RV 536.*

(BB) *** Naxos Dig. 8.550859 [id.]. Stefan Schilli; (i) with Diethelm Jonas; Budapest Failoni CO, Béla Nagy.

Excellent playing from these Budapest musicians in their survey of Vivaldi's concertante works for oboe. The second of these two discs offers the three *Double concertos*, and the two CDs between them include half the solo works. They are often surprisingly florid, requiring considerable bravura from the soloist. A good example is the Minuet finale of RV 447, which is a cross between a Rondo and a theme and variations. Vivaldi is never entirely predictable, except that his invention never seems to flag, and many of the simple *Grave*, *Larghetto* and *Largo* slow movements are very pleasing indeed.

(i) *Oboe concertos: in C, RV 540; in D min., RV 454; in F, RV 457;* (i–ii) *Double oboe concerto in D min., RV 535;* (i; iii) *Double concerto for oboe, bassoon and orchestra in G, RV 545;* (i–iii) *Concerto for 2 oboes, 2 violins, bassoon and orchestra, RV 557;* (i) *Recorder concerto in F, RV 442.*

(B) *** HM Dig. HMA 1903018 [id.]. (i) Marie Wolf (oboe or recorder); (ii) Márton Brandisz; (iii) Paul Tognon; Capella Savaria, Pál Németh.

While two of the solo oboe concertos here were conceived for bassoon, Marie Wolf with her warm phrasing and clean tonguing makes them all sound custom-made for her principal instrument. The tone of her baroque oboe is robust yet creamy, especially in the *Largo* of RV 454, while the chromatic 'slides' in the work's first movement are most seductively managed. In the double concertos the other wind soloists produce equally characterful timbres: the two oboes blend well together, yet have individuality, while the combination of oboe and the woody bassoon is specially felicitous. Then Marie Wolf turns to her recorder and charms us yet again. There are few more appealing bargain collections of Vivaldi wind concertos played on period instruments than this. The recording is beautifully balanced and truthful.

Concertos for strings: in C, RV 113 & RV 114; in D min., RV 127; in F, RV 138; in G (Alla Rustica), RV 151; in G min., RV 153, RV 156 & RV 157; in A min., RV 161; in B flat, RV 167.

(BB) **(*) Naxos Dig. 8.553742 [id.]. Accademia I Filarmonici, Alberto Martini.

The Accademia I Filarmonica is Italy's equivalent of the North American Orpheus group, a conductorless chamber orchestra, to some extent led from the bow by Alberto Martini. They do not use period instruments, but their style, brisk and athletic, with comparatively lean textures, is well removed from that of I Musici. They make the most of this group of Vivaldi's string concertos – which might equally well have been called sinfonias. The only famous one is *Alla Rustica*, which is vigorously done. Slow movements are delicate in texture with the harpsichord continuo coming through naturally. Not all this music is equally appealing, but the best movements are memorable, for instance the jogging opening allegro of RV 113 and its minor-key *Grave* slow movement. Excellent recording.

Viola d'amore concertos: in D, RV 392; in D min., RV 393, RV 394 & RV 395; in A, RV 396; in D min., RV 397.

**(*) Hyperion Dig. CDA 66795 [id.]. Catherine Mackintosh, OAE.

The viola d'amore was greatly admired in Vivaldi's time for its tone, apparently sweeter than that of the contemporary violin. Yet to today's ears its character is more plangent, and that especially applies to performance style on a baroque instrument. As can be seen, Vivaldi favoured the key of D minor above others for his concertos for that instrument, which are generally less striking than most of his violin concertos. Catherine Mackintosh gives expert performances with the Orchestra of the Age of Enlightenment, using rather astringent tone.

Violin concertos

'*Dresden Violin concertos*', Volume 1: *Violin concertos: in C, RV 170; in G, RV 314a; in G min., RV 319; in A, RV 341; in B flat (Il Carbonelli), RV 366; in B flat, RV 383.*

(N) (BB) *** Naxos Dig. 8.553792 [id.]. Alberto Martini, with Accademia I Filarmonici.

This latest Naxos Vivaldi series concentrates on concertos which survive in manuscript in the Dresden Saxony Landesbibliothek, and which were used by the Court Orchestra. They do not derive from the composer's residence in the city, and the sleeve note suggests that their existence may be connected with Vivaldi's association with an influential group of Dresden musicians, and most notably the violinist, Johanne Pisendel, who visited and studied under the composer during the latter part of 1716, and to whom Vivaldi dedicated a number of his concertos. The quality of these works is often remarkably high, reflecting the calibre of the orchestra and indeed Pisendel's virtuosity and musicianship. They sound extremely well in these excellent modern-instrument performances.

Volume 1 gets off to very good start indeed. Alberto Martini directs bright, resilient performances, aptly paced, and he also proves a splendid soloist. There is nothing routine about any of these six works as is demonstrated by the opening movements of RV 319 and RV 314a, with the following *Adagio* – a simple aria – quite lovely. And the haunting *Largo* of the *A major*, RV 341, where the soloist plays over a gentle quasi-tremolando, is exquisite. Both are ravishingly played, yet never romanticized. The recording acoustic and balance is ideal. Detail is clear yet there is plenty of warmth.

'*Dresden violin concertos', Volume 2: Violin concertos: in C, RV 184; in D min., RV 241; in E, RV 267; in F, RV 292; in G min., RV 329; in B flat (Posthorn), RV 363.*

(N) (BB) *** Naxos Dig. 8.553793 [id.]. Roberto Baraldi, Accademia I Filarmonici, Alberto Martini.

The concertos on the second disc are full of surprises, and Roberto Baraldi gives them the strongest profile. He is a very positive soloist, with a bolder sound image than Martini, which is not to say he is in the least insensitive. He likes to echo phrases, followed by the orchestra. His strength of purpose is especially telling in the *Posthorn concerto*, which features octave rhythmic figures on B flat, and also just right for the *D minor concerto*, RV 241, which brings a slow movement where the soloist steps out gravely. But perhaps the most striking work here is the *F major*, RV 292, where the six-minute first movement interpolates a slow central section and is virtually a miniature concerto in itself. The *E major concerto* goes one further with four tempo changes, *Allegro–Adagio–Largo–Allegro* while the *C major*, not to be outdone, has its opening and closing ritornello interrupted by a two-bar *Adagio* from the soloist; it also has a very lively and highly inventive finale. Again excellent sound.

'*Dresden concertos', Volume 3: Violin concertos: in D, RV 228; in D min., RV 245; in E flat, RV 262; in F, RV 285; in G min., RV 323; in B min., RV 384.*

(N) (BB) *** Naxos Dig. 8. 553860 [id.]. Marco Fornaciari, Accademia, I Filarmonici, Alberto Martini.

One is struck by the vigour of the *allegros* in *Volume 3*, emphasized by Marco Fornaciari's extrovert style and very open timbre. Yet in slow movements he fines down his tone most beautifully. The *Largo* of the *B minor Concerto*, accompanied solely by the basso continuo, is particularly moving while RV 262 brings a memorable central siciliana. The first movement of the *F major*, RV 285 introduces a second solo violin to echo the first, and the central melody of slow movement is framed by a remarkable chromatic series of repeated descending chords.

'*Dresden concertos',* Volume 4: *Violin concertos: in D, RV 213; in D, RV 219; in D, RV 224; in D min., RV 240; D in E flat, RV 260; in A, RV 344; in B min., RV 388.*

(N) (BB) *** Naxos Dig. 8. 554310 [id.]. Cristiano Rossi, Accademia I Filarmonici, Alberto Martini.

The use of a different soloist for each of these Naxos Dresden collections adds to their variety and interest. Cristiano Rossi's style is more intimate than that of Marco Fornaciari, yet his playing is by no means without personality and rhythmic flair. *Allegros* bustle with life in the orchestra, and Vivaldi's slow movements never fail to bring textural interest, apart from their melodic appeal. The last three of the seven concertos on this disc are all in D major, yet there is no sense of monotony, and RV 213 brings a stimulating close.

Violin concertos 'for Anna Maria': in D, RV 229; in D min., RV 248; in E, RV 267a; in E flat, RV 260; in B flat (Posthorn), RV 363; in A, RV 349.

(N) *** Ph. Dig. 454 459-2 [id.]. Mariana Sirbu, I Musici.

Anna Maria, a foundling, was one of the star pupils of Vivaldi's Pietá and as a teenager was to become a famous soloist (and she played other instruments besides the violin, including the lute and theorbo). Whatever Vivaldi's personal relationship with her was, he wrote at least two dozen concertos specifically for her to play. She did not have a monopoly on them, for two of those included here are also found in the Dresden collection above. The *E major Concerto*, RV 267a, however is fascinatingly different from the Dresden manuscript, RV 267. Not only does it have an alternative, more ambitious slow movement but the first movement has its tempo changes further extended. Mariana Sirbu takes on the mantle of her celebrated predecessor very persuasively. Her tone is enticingly beautiful, her bravura unostentatiously sparkling, and she brings memorable delicacy to slow movements, while in the *Largo* of the *Posthorn* she bounces the rhythmic main theme with engaging buoyancy. I Musici give her splendid support and the recording balance is particularly pleasing. So is the overall sound, with sunshine in the place of period-instrument acidity. Highly recommended.

Violin concertos, Op. 8, Nos. 5 in E flat (La Tempesta di mare), RV 253; 6 in C (Il Piacere), RV 180; 10 in B flat (La Caccia), RV 362; 11 in D, RV 210; in C min. (Il Sospetto), RV 199.
(B) *** CfP Dig. CD-CFP 4522. Lord Menuhin, Polish CO, Jerzy Maksymiuk.

Menuhin's collection of five concertos – four of them with nicknames and particularly delightful – brings some of his freshest, most intense playing. Particularly in slow movements – notably that of *Il Piacere* ('Pleasure') – he shows afresh his unique insight in shaping a phrase. Fresh, alert accompaniment and full digital recording.

6 Violin concertos, Op. 12.
(N) ** O-L Dig. 443 556-2 [id.]. Pavlo Beznosiuk, AAM, Hogwood.

It is good to have, at last, a period-instrument performance of Op. 12, but in the event it proves disappointing. Although there are no complaints about the quality of the recording, Beznosiuk's timbre is meagre and if not edgy, quite unseductive, especially when compared with Accardo's ravishing modern-instrument performances in Philips's Vivaldi Edition. Not surprisingly Hogwood's pacing is consistently much swifter than the tempi chosen by I Musici, and while this means that *allegros* are vividly alert, slow-movement lengths are reduced by about a third, and in the case of *No. 4 in C major* by half. So if by the side of his 'authentic' colleague Accardo does seem to languish a little, there is no question that he brings out the music's *espressivo* far more affectingly.

Miscellaneous concerto collections

(i) *The Trial between harmony and invention: Violin concertos Nos. 5 in E flat (La tempesta di mare); 6 in C (Il piacere), Op. 8/5–6;* (ii) *Bassoon concertos: in C, RV 472; in C min., RV 480; in A min., RV 498; in B flat, RV 504.*
(M) *** Chandos CHAN 6529 [id.]. (i) Ronald Thomas, Bournemouth Sinf.; (ii) Robert Thompson, L. Mozart Players, Ledger.

The two concertos included here from *The Trial between harmony and invention* were among the best of the complete set recorded by Ronald Thomas in 1980. The use of modern instruments does not preclude a keen sense of style, and the balance is convincing. The bassoonist Robert Thompson turns a genial eye on his four concertos. He is rather forwardly projected but the performances are, like the sound, agreeably fresh, among the most attractive accounts of Vivaldi's bassoon concertos available on CD.

Bassoon concerto in A min., RV 498; Flute concerto in C min., RV 108; Double horn concerto in F, RV 539; Oboe concerto in F, RV 456; Double oboe concerto in D min., RV 535; 2 Concertos for 2 oboes, bassoon, 2 horns & violin in F, RV 569 & RV 574; Piccolo concerto in C, RV 208.
(B) *** Decca Double 452 943-2 (2) [id.]. Soloists, ASMF, Marriner – BELLINI: *Oboe concerto in E flat;* HANDEL: *Oboe concertos* etc. ***

Marriner's modern-instrument performances of favourite Vivaldi wind concertos, made between 1965 and 1977, have long been praised. The soloists are all distinguished and the playing here is splendidly alive and alert, with crisp, clean articulation and well-pointed phrasing, full of imagination, yet free from over-emphasis. The *A minor Bassoon concerto* has a delightful sense of humour. Although the musical substance may not be very weighty, Vivaldi was never more engaging than when writing for wind instruments, particularly if he had more than one in his team of soloists, as in the two attractive composite works included in the programme. The vintage recordings remain in the demonstration bracket.

Concerti 'con molti instromenti': Bassoon concerto in E min., RV 484; Flute concerto in G min. (La notte), Op. 10/2, RV 439; Double mandolin concerto in G, RV 532; Concerto con multi instromenti in C, RV 558; Double concerto for oboe and violin in B flat, RV 548; Concerto for strings (alla rustica), RV 151; Concerto for 2 violins and two cellos in G, RV 575; L'Estro armonico: Concerto for 4 violins in D, Op. 3/1, RV 549.
(M) *** DG Dig. 447 301-2. Soloists, E. Concert, Pinnock.

This extremely generous 72-minute collection of varied works is very enticing at mid-price, showing Pinnock and the English Concert at their liveliest and most refreshing, although not always so strong on charm. The *Concerto for four violins* is very lithe, and throughout the concert the solo playing is most expert. The orchestral concerto, RV 558, involves an astonishing array of instruments.

(i) *Bassoon concertos: in C, RV 474; in F, RV 489; in A min., RV 498; Concerto for violin, 2 horns, cello, bassoon & strings in F, RV 571; Concerto for violin, 2 oboes, 2 recorders, bassoon & strings, RV 577; Concerto for violin, 3 oboes, 2 recorders, bassoon & strings, RV 576.*
*** O-L Dig. (IMS) 436 867-2. (i) Danny Bond; soloists, AAM, Hogwood.

Vivaldi's music was never more attractive than in his composite concertos for multiple instruments, when his ear obviously revelled in the contrasting timbres of recorder, bassoon, sometimes horns, and stringed instruments. The opening movement of the *G minor Concerto*, RV 576 (which is presented first on the disc), is particularly ear-catching. Here the wind also play in the slow movement, and the organ continuo adds further colour, whereas in RV 571 Simon Standage takes a solo violin role. In the outer movements of this concerto the horns make an attractively robust contribution. To provide extra variety here, three fine *Bassoon concertos* are interspersed among the multiple works, with Danny Bond providing a woodily authentic timbre. A collection which in its piquant variety of colouring will appeal to all Vivaldians who enjoy period instruments.

Cello concertos: in A min., RV 419; in D, RV 403; in B min., RV 424; Concerto for cello, bassooon and strings, RV 409; Concertos for strings: in D min., RV 127; in G min. (Alla Rustica), RV 151, 152 & RV 157; Concerto for 2 oboes, RV 535; Concerto for 2 oboes, 2 violins, bassoon and strings in C, RV 557; Concerto for 2 violins, 2 cellos and strings in D, RV 564.
(N) **(*) Sony SK 62719 [id.]. Anner Bylsma, Tafelmusik, Jeanne Lanon.

A well-planned concert dominated by Bylsma's bravura performances of three cello concertos and one for cello and bassoon. They are interspersed by concertos for strings, including the well-known *Alla Rustica* and a colourful display of baroque woodwind, with the work for oboes, violins and bassoon bringing more remarkable virtuosity. If you like the dry vintage of Anner Bylsma's period cello timbre, and authentic string playing with plenty of life and edge, this generous and well-recorded collection can be strongly recommended, but we found it just a little wanting in charm.

Double cello concerto in G min., RV 531; Flute concerto in C min., RV 441; Concerto in G min., for flute and bassoon (La notte), RV 104; Concerto in F for flute, oboe and bassoon (La tempesta di mare), RV 570; Guitar concerto in D, RV 93; Concerto in F for 2 horns, RV 539; Concerto in B flat for violin and cello, RV 547.
*** ASV Dig. CDDCA 645 [id.]. Soloists, ECO, Malcolm.

With George Malcolm in charge it is not surprising that this 65-minute collection of seven diverse concertos is as entertaining as any in the catalogue. Perhaps most striking of all is the *Double cello concerto*, vigorously energetic in outer movements, but with a short, serene central *Largo*, with overlapping phrases at the beginning, to remind one of the slow movement of Bach's *Double violin concerto*. The concert ends with the duet version of *La Notte*, which has much to charm the ear. Accompaniments are sympathetic and stylish, and the whole programme brims with vitality. The digital sound is vivid and realistic.

Double cello concerto in G min., RV 531; Lute concerto in G, RV 93; Double mandolin concerto in G, RV 532; Recorder concertos: in C min., RV 441; in C, RV 443. Trio for violin, lute & continuo in G min., RV 85.
(M) *** DG Dig. 445 602-2 [id.]. Demenga, Häusler, Söllscher, Copley, Camerata Bern, Füri.

An excellent mid-priced digital collection, assembled from various records made by the Camerata Bern, which will especially suit those who like their Vivaldi on original instruments. Söllscher's account of the *Duet concerto* for mandolins (in which he takes both solo roles) is quite outstanding, and there is some breathtaking virtuosity from Michael Copley in the *Recorder concertos*. Further variety is provided by the *Trio*, which is also an attractive work. The well-balanced recording has splendid presence and realism.

Double cello concerto in G min., RV 531; Lute (Guitar) concerto in D, RV 93; Oboe concerto in F, F.VII, No. 2 (R.455); Double concerto for oboe and violin; Trumpet concerto in D (trans. Jean Thilde); *Violin concerto in G min., Op. 12/1; RV 317.*
(BB) *** Naxos Dig. 8.550384; *4550384* [id.]. Capella Istropolitana, Jaroslav Krechek.

This is a recommendable disc from which to set out to explore the Vivaldi concertos, especially if you are beginning a collection. Gabriela Krcková makes a sensitive contribution to the delightful *Oboe concerto in F major*, F.VII, No. 2 (R.455), and the other soloists are pretty good too.

Double concertos: for 2 cellos in G min., RV 531; for violin, cello and strings in F (Il Proteo ò sia il mondo rovescio), RV 544; in A for 2 violins (per eco in lontano), RV 552; Triple concertos: for 3 violins in F, RV 551; for violin and 2 cellos in C, RV 561. Quadruple concerto for 2 violins & 2 cellos in D, RV 564.
*** Teldec/Warner Dig. 4509 94552-2 [id.]. Christophe Coin and soloists, Il Giardina Armonico, Antonini.

An exceptionally rewarding collection of concertos for multiple, stringed instruments, made the more striking by the inclusion of RV 544 with its curious subtitle evoking Proteus and an upside-down world. All the concertos here show Vivaldi's invention at its most diverse, with textures ever intriguing the ear (not least the work which features a favourite baroque device by designating one violin '*per eco in lontano*'). Christophe Coin leads an excellent team of soloists and the imaginative continuo (organ, harpsichord and arch-lute) adds to the colour of performances which are full of life, yet which also reveal the music's more subtle touches and are remarkably free from the exaggerated stylistic devices too often associated with period instruments. The recording is excellent.

Double concertos: for 2 cellos in G min., RV 531; for 2 oboes in D min., RV 523; for 2 violins in C, RV 505; in D, RV 511; Triple concerto for oboe & 2 violins, RV 554.
*** Chandos Dig. CHAN 0528 [id.]. Coe, Warkin, Robson, Latham, Standage, Comberti, Coll. Mus. 90, Standage.

Period-instrument performances are increasingly identified with the style of their performing groups, and that of Simon Standage's Collegium Musicum 90 is most invigorating, stylish with no lack of expressive feeling. The rhythmic crispness and buoyancy and the plangent string-sound make for characterful performances. The ripe sound of the baroque oboes and the crunchy cello timbre are particularly attractive, although the tingling astringency characteristic of the accompanying group is even more strongly focused in the solo playing for the concertos for two violins, and especially in the busy finale of RV 511. Outstanding Chandos sound.

Double concertos: for 2 flutes in C, RV 533; for 2 horns in F, RV 538 & RV 539; for 2 trumpets in C, RV 537; for oboe and bassoon in G, RV 545; Concerto (Sinfonia in D) for strings, RV 122; Quadruple concerto for 2 oboes and 2 clarinets, RV 560.
(BB) *** Naxos Dig. 8.553204 [id.]. Soloists, City of L. Sinfonia, Nicholas Kraemer.

A lively clutch of concertos, very well recorded in All Saints' Church, East Finchley. The opening double concertos for two horns, RV 539, two flutes, RV 533, and two trumpets, RV 537, all go well enough and offer expert solo contributions, but then at the arrival of the *Quadruple concerto for two oboes and two clarinets* the playing suddenly sparks into extra exuberance, and one senses the musicians' enjoyment of one of Vivaldi's most imaginatively scored multiple works. The *Concerto for two horns* which follows (RV 538) has a similar ebullience, and the concert is rounded off by a captivating account of RV 545, where both the oboe and bassoon clearly relish every bar of their engaging dialogue. Kraemer's accompaniments are polished and spirited.

Flute concerto in G min. (La notte), Op. 10/2, RV 439; Concertos for strings: in D min. (Madrigalesco), RV 129; in G (Alla rustica), RV 151. Violin concertos: in D (L'Inquietudine), RV 234; in E (L'Amoroso), RV 271. Double violin concerto in A, RV 523; Sinfonia in B min. (Al Santo Sepolcro), RV 169.
(B) **(*) DG Classikon 449 851-2 [(M) id. import]. Soloists, BPO, Karajan.

This collection dates from 1971 (except for the *Flute concerto*, which was recorded a decade later) and shows Karajan indulging himself in repertoire which he clearly loves but for which he does not have the stylistic credentials. Yet the charismatic playing and the glorious body of tone is irresistible. The orchestra dominates even the solo concertos and the soloists seem to float, concertante style, within the glowing acoustic.

Double flute concerto in C, RV 533; Double horn concerto in F, RV 539; Double mandolin concerto in G, RV 536; Double oboe concerto in A min., RV 536; Concerto for oboe and bassoon in G, RV 545; Double trumpet concerto in D, RV 563.
*** Ph. (IMS) Dig. 412 892-2 [id.]. Soloists, ASMF, Marriner.

Apart from the work for two horns, where the focus of the soloists lacks a degree of sharpness, the recording often reaches demonstration standard. On CD, the concerto featuring a pair of mandolins is particularly vivid, with the balance near perfect, the solo instruments in proper scale yet registering admirable detail. The concertos for flutes and oboes are played with engaging finesse, conveying a sense of joy in the felicity of the writing. As ever, Marriner makes a very good case for the use of modern wind instruments in this repertoire.

Fourteen concertos: Disc 1: (i–ii) *Lute concerto in D, RV 93; Double concerto for 2 mandolins in G, RV 532;* (i; iii) *Recorder concertos: in A min., RV. 108; in G min. (La notte);* (iv) *Violin concerto in D (Grosso Mogull), RV 208.* Disc 2: Double concertos: (v) *Double concertos: for 2 cellos in G min., RV 531; 2 flutes in C, RV 533; 2 trumpets in C, RV 537. Concerto for Flautino (sopranino recorder) in C, RV 443; Concertos for strings: in D min. (Madrigalesco), RV 129; in G (Alla rustica), RV 151; in G min., RV 153; Quadruple concerto for 2 violins & 2 cellos in D, RV 564; L'Estro armonico: Quadruple violin concerto in B min., Op. 3/10, RV 580.*
(B) *** O-L Double Dig./Analogue 455 703-2 [id.]. (i) New London Cons., Pickett, with (ii) Tom Finucane; (iii) Philip Pickett; (iv) Stanley Ritchie, Bach Ens., Rifkin; (v) Soloists, AAM, Hogwood.

The 14 concertos on this Oiseau-Lyre Double readily demonstrate the extraordinary diversity of Vivaldi's musical ideas and in many cases his originality too. None more so than the remarkable *Violin concerto*, RV 208 (written about 1710), nicknamed – probably not by the composer – '*Grosso Mogull*'. The outer movements with their *moto perpetuo* arpeggios demand great virtuosity from the soloist, and the slow movement is a long Recitativo, more like an improvisation. The remarkable seven-minute finale, perhaps the longest in any Vivaldi concerto, has a central cadenza which demands and is given a performance of dazzling virtuosity by the soloist here, Stanley Ritchie. An unforgettable performance, very well recorded. The concertos for lute, mandolin and recorder are also expertly and pleasingly played by Philip Pickett and his group, whose brand of authenticity is rather less abrasive than Hogwood's. The digital sound is first class. The *Concerto for two flutes* has great charm and is dispatched with vigour and aplomb. Performances and recording alike are first rate. For the reissue, three extra works have been added, most notably the famous *Quadruple violin concerto* from *L'Estro armonico*, taken from the Academy's splendid complete set, with John Holloway, Monica Huggett, Catherine Mackintosh and Elizabeth Wilcock the excellent soloists.

Double mandolin concerto in G, RV 532; Oboe concertos: in A min., RV 461; in B flat, RV 548; Concertos for strings: in G (Alla rustica), RV 151; in C (con molti stromenti), RV 558; Double violin concerto in G, RV 516.
(N) (M) *** DG Dig. 457 897-2 [id.]. E. Concert, Pinnock.

Taking its title, '*Alla rustica*', from the charming little *G major Concerto*, RV 151, with its drone in the finale, this collection is a straight reissue of a 1986 CD, offering only six concertos and a playing time of barely 53 minutes. Nevertheless, it makes up in quality for what it lacks in quantity, finding Pinnock and English Concert at their liveliest and most refreshing. Outstanding in a nicely balanced programme is the *C minor Concerto*, RV 558, involving a remarkable array of concertino instruments including two violins (in 'tromba marina') and pairs of recorders, mandolins and theorbos, plus one cello. Excellent recording, giving a most realistic perspective.

Concerto per l'Orchestra di Dresda in G min. (for 2 recorders, 2 oboes & bassoon), RV 577; Concerto per la Solennità di S. Lorenzo in C, RV 556; Chamber concerto for recorder, oboe, violin, bassoon & continuo in D (La pastorella), RV 95; Flute concerto in G min. (La Notte), Op. 10/2, RV 439; Concerto for strings (Sinfonia) in C, RV 114; Quadruple concerto for 2 violins and 2 cellos in G, RV 575.
(M) *** Virgin Veritas/EMI Dig. VER5 61275-2. Soloists, Taverner Players, Andrew Parrott.

This is a particularly winning collection – an hour of Vivaldi at his most creative. The opening Dresden concerto with its interplay between the wind groups, but including also solo violin obbligati, is particularly original; then comes the delightful pastoral chamber concerto, with its rustic woodwind charm. The two-movement 'Sinfonia', RV 114, is also notable for its inventive finale – in the form of a ciaconna. *La Notte* is (by common consent) among Vivaldi's most imaginative works for flute; its descriptive evocations are atmospherically caught by the Taverner Players, notably '*Ghosts*' and '*Sleep*' which is so reminiscent of the *Four Seasons*, The following concerto for a pair each of violins and echoing cellos at times sounds more like a concerto grosso. The grand opening of the *Concerto for S. Lorenzo* is Handelian, but Vivaldi's own personality reasserts itself firmly in the following allegro. The work is richly scored and, apart from the main protagonists – a pair of solo violins – features recorders, oboes and (a great novelty at that time) clarinets, with ear-catching results. This is its first recording in its original form; Vivaldi, for practical reasons, later dispensed with the clarinets. It makes a splendid conclusion to an outstanding concert, excellently recorded.

Concertos for strings: in D min. (Concerto madrigalesco), RV 129; in G (Alla rustica), RV 151; in G min., RV 157. (i) Motet: *In turbato mare irato, RV 627;* Cantata: *Lungi dal vago volto, RV 680. Magnificat, RV 610.*
*** Hyperion Dig. CDA 66247 [id.]. (i) Kirkby, Leblanc, Forget, Cunningham, Ingram, Tafelmusik Ch. & Bar. O, Lamon.

Mingling vocal and instrumental items, and works both well-known and unfamiliar, Jean Lamon provides a delightful collection, with Emma Kirkby a sparkling, pure-toned soloist in two items never recorded before: the motet, *In turbato mare irato*, and the chamber cantata, *Lungi dal vago volto*. The performance is lively, with fresh choral sound. The Tafelmusik performers come from Canada, and though the use of period instruments has some roughness, their vigour and alertness amply make up for that. Good, clear recorded sound.

CHAMBER MUSIC

Chamber concertos: in C for recorder, oboe, 2 violins, cello, harpsichord and lute, RV 87; in D for flute, violin, and cello, RV 92; in G min. for flute, oboe, bassooon, cello, organ and lute, RV 107; in D min. for solo organ and flute, 2 violins, viola, cello, violone and lute, RV 541; in F for organ and violin solo, 2 violins, viola, cello, violone and lute, RV 542. Trio sonata in D min. (La Folia), RV 65.
(N) *** Channel Classics Dig. CCS 8495 [id.]. Florilegium.

These are among the finest and most imaginatively scored of all Vivaldi's concertos and they could hardly be played more persuasively (one instrument to each part), than by Florilegium, an outstanding period-instrument ensemble. The concertos which include a solo organ are enchanting in their piquant colouring, and are full of splendid ideas. The finale of RV 107 for instance is a kaleidoscopic chaconne, in effect a chimerical set of variations. But every work here is inspired and aurally stimulating, and they could hardly be better played. The programme ends with Vivaldi's extensive variations on *La Folia* in the form of a *Trio sonata*, which is presented with bravura, a wide range of dynamic and a sense of fantasy. The group, led by Ashley Solomon (flute/recorder), are all masters of their instruments and play infectiously together as a team. The recording is ideally balanced, within an acoustic with just the right feeling of ambient space.

Cello sonatas Nos. 1–9, RV 39/47.
(M) *** CRD Dig. CRD 3440; *CRDC 4140* [id.]. (*Nos. 1–4*); CRD 3441; *CRDC 4141* [id.]. (*Nos. 5–9*); L'Ecole d'Orphée.

All nine *Sonatas* are given highly musical performances on CRD; they do not set out to impress by grand gestures but succeed in doing so by their dedication and sensitivity. Susan Sheppard is a thoughtful player and is well supported by her continuo team, Lucy Carolan and Jane Coe. The CRD recording is well focused with fine presence.

Cello sonatas Nos. 1 in B flat, RV 47; 3 in A min., RV 43; 4 in B flat, RV 45; 5 in E min., RV 40; 6 in B flat, RV 46.
*** RCA Dig. 09026 60430-2 [id.]. Ofra Harnoy, Colin Tilney, Miham Tetel.

Vivaldi's nine *Cello sonatas* are among his most inspired chamber works. Ofra Harnoy plays five of them with a deftly paced vigour and brings to the slow movements beautiful tone and a restrained simplicity of line which catches their expressive feeling to perfection. Here Colin Tilney's discreet continuo support is played on the organ, very effectively balanced; it also blends admirably with the cello. In allegros the harpsichord comes through less tellingly. In all other respects the recording is excellent.

2 Chamber sonatas for 2 violins and continuo in D min., Op. 1/8 & 12 (La Folia), RV 63 & RV 64; 4 Chamber sonatas for 2 violins: in F, RV 68 & RV 70; in G, RV 71; in E flat, RV 77.
(B) *** HM Dig. HMX 290853.55 (3) [(M) id.]. Ens. 315 (Chiara Banchieri, Véronique Méjean, Käthi Gohl, Jesper Christensen) – CORELLI: *Trio sonatas, Op. 5/1–6*. TARTINI: *Concerti grossi* etc. ***

This is the most winning of the three CDs of baroque music gathered together in a slip-case in Harmonia Mundi's bargain-price Trio format. Vivaldi's variations on *La Folia* extend to 11 minutes and are highly inventive, while Op. 1/12 also includes an extended set of variations, all in the key of D minor, with the two violins sometimes in dialogue with each other. The remaining four *Chamber sonatas* were not published until after the composer's death. They are genuine duet sonatas, written in the three-movement format which Vivaldi favoured in his concertos, with the interplay between the two violins often demanding considerable bravura. Vivaldi indicated the bass line as optional, and it is omitted here. It is not missed, and these works might be compared (if not quite in the same breath) with Bach's sonatas for a single, unaccompanied violin. These expert musicians certainly convey their enjoyment of this rewarding music. The recording has striking presence and realism.

'Manchester' violin sonatas (for violin and continuo) *Nos. 1–12* (complete).
**(*) Arcana Dig. A 4/5 [id.]. Fabio Biondi, Alessandri, Naddeo, Pandolfo, Lislevand.
** HM Dig. HMU 907089/90 [id.]. Romanesca.

The so-called 'Manchester' *Sonatas* were discovered as recently as 1973 in Manchester's Henry Watson Music Library. All the works are in four movements, with an opening Prelude, a following Corrente or Allemanda, then a slow movement, and a closing dance movement, often a Corrente or a Giga; but in three instances the Allemanda forms the finale. Within these simple structures Vivaldi wrote fine music offering much refreshment. Neither disc is ideal. Romanesca are recorded fairly dryly, though they are very well balanced. Nigel North's archlute, theorbo or guitar makes a very pleasing contribution and John Toll's harpsichord is nicely in the picture, but the sound of Andrew Manze's baroque violin is rather raw. On the other hand, the Romanesca phrasing has marginally less of that curious accented lunging often favoured by period groups, which is at times more noticeable on the Arcana set. However, one adjusts to this when Fabio Biondi's tone is so much sweeter and her colleagues are afforded an altogether warmer sound by the more expansive Arcana recording. Tempi are generally faster with Romanesca, appreciably so in the Correntes, but overall the Arcana set is the more persuasive.

VOCAL MUSIC

Sacred music, Volume 1: *Credo in unum Deum, RV 591; Dixit Dominus, RV 594; Kyrie eleison, RV 587; Lauda Jerusalem, RV 608; Magnificat, RV 610.*
*** Hyperion Dig. CDA 66769 [id.]. Susan Gritton, Lisa Milne, Caroline Denley, Lynton Atkinson, David Wilson-Johnson, Choristers and Ch., King's Consort, Robert King.

Hyperion's series aims to cover all the key sacred choral works of Vivaldi, and this first volume could not be more promising. Negri's fine analogue series for Philips revealed how inspired so much of this repertoire is, and the present disc readily bears this out. All the music here is for double choir except the simple *Credo*, which is without soloists but has great intensity of feeling expressed in the *Et incarnatus est* and *Crucifixus*. Apart from the splendidly grand and masterly *Dixit Dominus,* RV 594 (gloriously sung here), there are two fine, shorter works which also include double string orchestra:

the *Kyrie eleison* and the *Lauda Jerusalem*. But most striking of all is Vivaldi's first setting of the *Magnificat* – in G minor, dating from around 1715 although revised in the 1720s – made memorable by its highly individual chromatic writing, but also adding to the poignancy of the *Et misericordia*. Robert King has gathered an excellent team of soloists for this collection (witness the following soprano duet, *Esurientes*, which is delightful), but it is the stirringly eloquent choral singing one remembers most, vividly directed by King and splendidly balanced and recorded.

Sacred music, Volume 2: Motets: (i) *Canta in prato, ride in monte, RV 623;* (ii) *Clarae stellae, scintillate, RV 625;* (ii) *Filiae maestae Jerusalem, RV 638;* (i) *In furore iustissimae irae, RV 626;* (iii) *Longe mala, unbrae, terrores, RV 629;* (i) *Nulla in mundo pax sincera, RV 630.*

*** Hyperion Dig. CDA 66779 [id.]. (i) Deborah York; (ii) James Bowman; (iii) Catherine Denley; King's Consort, Robert King.

The quality of Vivaldi's motets emerged on an excellent Erato recital disc which offers a quartet of them, sung with agile charm by Cecilia Gasdia (see below). That is exactly what they require, for they are in essence concertos for voice, generally with a recitative between the first movement and slow movement. All the appealing works here are very well sung indeed, with those for the soprano, the very agile Deborah York, the most memorable. The opening of *In furore iustissimae irae* ('In wrath and most just anger') is delivered with dramatic venom, but then the Largo, *Tune meus fletus* ('Then shall my weeping'), follows exquisitely. The closing staccato *Alleluia* might have been conceived for a solo violin, and Vivaldi uses the same device for the opening of *Canto in prato*, which has no slow movement; here the *Alleluia* is engagingly melismatic. The other highlight of the collection is James Bowman's *Filiae maestae Jerusalem* which brings a touching Larghetto, *Silenti Zephyri* ('Let the winds be hushed'). The closing soprano cantata opens with a gentle siciliana with a typically evocative string accompaniment. The nimble following aria depicts a hidden snake waiting for the unwary, and the closing, fast-flowing *Alleluia* requires virtuosity from the singer, sparklingly delivered here. A first-class collection, excellently recorded.

Sacred music, Volume 3: *Beatus vir* (two versions), *RV 597 & RV 598; Crediti propter quod, RV 605; Dixit Dominus, RV 595; Domine ad adjuvandum, RV 593.*

*** Hyperion Dig. CDA 66789 [id.]. Susan Gritton, Catrin Wyn-Davies, Catherine Denley, Charles Daniels, Neal Davies, Michael George, King's Consort and Ch., Robert King.

Vivaldi's two settings of the *Beatus vir* are quite different. RV 597 is for double choir and is on an ambitious scale, with a refrain that reappears in various sections of the work. RV 598 is in a single movement and is written for soloists and a single choir, rather in the manner of a concerto grosso. The present setting of *Dixit Dominus* for single chorus (but with sopranos sometimes divided) was rediscovered only in the late 1960s – in Prague's National Library. *Domine ad adjuvandum* is a superbly concentrated short work for double choir, based on Psalm 69. It is in three brief sections and, after the soprano's *Gloria patri*, there is a spectacular contrapuntal bustling closing section. The performances here are well up to the standard of this excellent series, and the soloists sing with bravura, especially in duets. The Hyperion recording is of high quality, although ideally one would have welcomed more choral bite.

Sacred music, Volume 4: *Juditha Triumphans* (complete).

(N) *** Hyperion Dig. CDA 67281/2 [id.]. Ann Murray, Susan Bickley, Maria Cristina Kiehr, Sarah Connolly, Jean Rigby, Ch. & King's Consort, Robert King.

Juditha Triumphans, Vivaldi's only surviving oratorio, works well on disc, with its elaborate instrumental textures. Written for the Ospedale di Pietà in Venice, a home for foundlings, it involves only women's voices in the solo roles and here is exceptionally well cast. Ann Murray, in one of her most beautiful performances on disc, is seductive as Judith rather than sharply dramatic, and it is left to Susan Bickley as the tyrannical general, Holofernes, to steal first honours, strong and incisive. The others are excellent too, with the chorus (involving male voices as well as female) heightening the drama from the opening martial chorus onwards. Robert King relishes the rich instrumentation with its brilliant and original obbligato solos, beautifully caught in vivid, atmospheric recording.

Sacred music, Volume 5: *Confitebor tibi, Domine; Deus tuorum Militum; In turbato mare, RV 627; Non in pratis aut in hortis, RV 641; O qui coeli terraeque serenitas, RV 631; Stabat Mater, RV.621.*

(N) *** Hyperion Dig. CDA 66799 [id.]. Susan Gritton, Jean Rigby, Robin Blaze, Charkes Daniels, Neal Davis, King's Consort, Robert King.

Volume 5 of this excellent Hyperion series offers two solo motets, a simple Vesper hymn (*Deus tuorum militum*) sung as a contralto/tenor duet, and ends with a very fine three-voice setting of Psalm 110, *Confitebor tibi Domine*, which in its final movement draws on a sparkling terzet from Vivaldi's opera *La fida Ninfa*. It makes a satisfying close to a progamme which has as its centre-piece the glorious *Stabat Mater* (1712), very beautifully sung here by the male alto, Robin Blaze. As an ideal prelude to this masterpiece Jean Rigby sings most movingly the 'Introduzione to the Miserere', *Non in pratis aut in hortis*, which has a beautiful lament as its solo aria. To open the concert Susan Gritton despatches *In turbato mare irato* with biting bravura, but is later able to show her lovely lyrical style in *O qui colei terraeque serenitas*.

Beatus vir, RV 597; Credo, RV 592; Magnificat, RV 610.

(M) *** Ph. (IMS) 420 651-2. Soloists, Alldis Ch., ECO, Negri.

Beatus vir, RV 598; Dixit Dominus in D, RV 594; Introduzione al Dixit: Canta in prato in G, RV 636 (ed. Geigling); *Magnificat in G min., RV 611* (ed. Negri).

(M) *** Ph. (IMS) 420 649-2. Lott, Burgess, Murray, Daniels, Finnie, Collins, Rolfe Johnson, Holl, Alldis Ch., ECO, Negri.

Crediti propter quod, RV 105; Credo, RV 591; Introduction to Gloria, RV 639; Gloria, RV 588; Kyrie, RV 587; Laetatus sum, RV 607.

(M) *** Ph. (IMS) 420 650-2. M. Marshall, Lott, Finnie, Rolfe Johnson, Alldis Ch., ECO, Negri.

Dixit dominus, RV 595; In exitu Israel, RV 604; Sacrum, RV 586.

(M) *** Ph. (IMS) 420 652-2. Alldis Ch., ECO, Negri.

Introduction to Gloria, RV 642; Gloria in D, RV 589; Lauda Jerusalem in E min., RV 609; Laudate Dominum in D min., RV 606; Laudati pueri Dominum in A, RV 602.

(M) *** Ph. (IMS) 420 648-2. Marshall, Lott, Collins, Finnilä, Alldis Ch., ECO, Negri.

These Philips recordings come from the late 1970s. Vittorio Negri does not make use of period instruments, but he penetrates as deeply into the spirit of this music as many who do, and they come up splendidly in their new format, digitally refurbished. Any lover of Vivaldi is likely to be astonished that not only the well-known works but the rarities show him writing with the keenest originality and intensity. There is nothing routine about any of this music, nor any of the performances either.

Beatus vir, RV 597; Gloria in D, RV 589.

(BB) **(*) Naxos 8.550767 [id.]. Anna Crookes, Jayne Quitaker, Carys-Anne Lane, Caroline Trevor, Oxford Schola Cantorum, N. CO, Ward.

This Naxos coupling of what are probably the two favourite Vivaldi choral works is beautifully recorded and well worth its modest cost. Although some listeners will want greater attack in the famous opening and closing sections of the *Gloria* and in the *Potens in terra* in the companion work, these spacious performances, directed by Nicholas Ward, are still warmly enjoyable, partly because of the freshness of the solo contributions, but also because the choral singing has considerable intensity, especially in the continual return of the haunting *Beatus vir* chorale in RV 597. The *Paratum cor eius*, too, brings a surge of choral feeling, and the chorus rises to the occasion for the splendid closing *Gloria Patri*. Full translations are included.

Cantatas: (i) *All'ombra di sospetto, RV 678;* (ii–iii) *Amor hai vinto, RV 651;* (i) *Lungi dal vago volto, RV 680; Vengo a voi, luci adorate, RV 682.* (iv) *Gloria in D, RV 589;* (v; iii) *Nisi Dominus (Psalm 127), RV 608;* (ii–iii) *Nulla in mundo pax sincera, RV 630.* (vi) *Trio sonata (La Folia), RV 63.*

(B) *** O-L Double Analogue/Dig. 455 727-2 (2) [id.]. (i) Catherine Bott, New London Cons., Pickett; (ii) Emma Kirkby; (iii) AAM, Hogwood (iv) Judith Nelson, Kirkby, Carolyn Watkinson, Christ Church Cathedral Ch., AAM, Preston; (v) James Bowman; (vi) Simon Standage, Catherine Mackintosh, Christopher Hogwood.

Vivaldi's secular cantatas are lightweight but have much charm. The present group were written in Mantua between 1718 and 1720. Combining recitative and a pair of arias, they usually express the dolours of unrequited love in an Arcadian setting. The exception here is *Lungi dal vago volta*, in which the lovers are apart; but they are reunited before the end. In each case the words are written from the male point of view, yet here they are treated as soprano solos – delightfully so, for, after Emma Kirkby has opened the programme with a characteristically fresh-voiced *Amor, hai vento*, Catherine Bott takes over with her softer focus and more plaintive style. As a central instrumental interlude we are offered a lively and stylish account of the *Trio sonata* which Vivaldi based on *La Folia*, in essence a set of variations, almost a chaconne, following closely after Corelli's similar exercise which ends his Op. 5. The first CD opens with the familiar *Gloria*, also available separately, coupled with Handel. The choristers of Christ Church Cathedral excel themselves and the recording is remarkably fine. The solo motet, *Nulla in mundo pax sincera*, brings back Emma Kirkby, who copes splendidly with the bravura writing for soprano. James Bowman is also a persuasive soloist in the more extended, operatic-styled setting of Psalm 127. But since Vivaldi probably wrote *Nisi Dominus* for the Pietà, a Venetian orphanage for girls, there is a case here for preferring a woman soloist.

Motets: *Canto in prato, RV 623; In furore giustissimae irae, RV 626; Longa mala umbrae tertores, RV 640; Vos aurae per montes (per la solennita di S. Antonio), RV 634.*

(M) *** Erato/Warner Dig. 4509 96966-2. Cecilia Gasdia, Sol. Ven., Scimone.

Though the booklet for this collection of Vivaldi rarities fails to provide texts for these four solo motets, they make a delightful collection, also displaying the formidable talent of a rising star among Italian sopranos, Cecilia Gasdia. Vivaldi's solo motets might be described structurally as concertos for voice, but generally with a recitative between first movement and slow movement. *Canto in prato* is the exception, with three jolly, rustic allegros in succession. Lively performances and well-balanced recording.

(i) *Dixit Dominus in D, RV 594;* (ii) *Stabat Mater, RV 621.*

(B) **(*) Sony SBK 48282 [id.]. (i) Hill Smith, Bernardin, Partridge, Caddy; (i–ii) Watts; E. Bach Festival ((i) Ch.) O, Malgoire – D. SCARLATTI: *Stabat Mater.* **(*)

Malgoire's overemphatic style of baroque playing, with first beats of bars heavily underlined, is inclined to be wearing, but these fine works make an excellent coupling, and the singing is first rate, from both the chorus and the soloists in the better-known setting of *Dixit Dominus*, and particularly from Helen Watts in the moving sequence of solo items that makes up the *Stabat Mater*. Reverberant, church-like acoustic.

(i) *Gloria in D, RV 588; Gloria in D, RV 589;* (ii) *Concerto for guitar and viola d'amore, RV 540.*

(B) *** Decca Eclipse Dig. 448 223-2. (i) Russell, Kwella, Wilkens, St John's College, Cambridge, Ch., Wren O, Guest; (ii) Fernández, Blume, ECO, Malcolm.

(i) *Gloria in D, RV 588; Gloria in D, RV 589;* (ii; iii) *Beatus vir in C, RV 597; Dixit dominus in D, RV 594;* (iv; iii) *Magnificat in G min., RV 610.*

(B) *** Decca Double Dig./Analogue 443 455-2 (2) [id.]. (i) Russell, Kwella, Wilkens, Bowen, St John's College, Cambridge, Ch., Wren O, Guest; (ii) Jennifer Smith, Buchanan, Watts, Partridge, Shirley-Quirk, ECO, Cleobury; (iii) King's College, Cambridge, Ch.; (iv) Castle, Cockerham, King, ASMF, Ledger.

The two settings of the *Gloria* make an apt and illuminating pairing. Both in D major, they have many points in common, presenting fascinating comparisons, when RV 588 is as inspired as its better-known companion. Guest directs strong and well-paced readings, with RV 588 the more lively. Good, warm recording to match the performances. *Dixit dominus* cannot fail to attract those who have enjoyed the better-known *Gloria*. Both works are powerfully inspired and are here given vigorous and sparkling performances with King's College Choir in excellent form under Philip Ledger. The soloists are a fine team, fresh, stylish and nimble, nicely projected on CD. What caps this outstanding Vivaldi compilation is the earlier King's account of the inspired *Magnificat in G minor*. Ledger uses the small-scale setting and opts for boys' voices in the solos such as the beautiful duet (*Esurientes*) which is most winning. The performance overall is very compelling and moving, and the singing has all the accustomed beauty of King's. The transfer of an outstanding (1976) analogue recording to CD is admirable, even richer than its digital companions.

As can be seen, those seeking an inexpensive disc of the two *Glorias* will find the Eclipse CD a satisfactory alternative, and the *Concerto for guitar and viola d'amore* makes an attractively lightweight interlude between the two.

Gloria in D, RV 589.

*** EMI (SIS) Dig. CDC7 54283-2 [id.]. Hendricks, Murray, Rigby, Heilmann, Hynninen, ASMF Ch. & O, Marriner – BACH: *Magnificat.* ***

(M) *** Decca 421 146-2. Vaughan, J. Baker, King's College, Cambridge, Ch., ASMF, Willcocks – HAYDN: *Nelson Mass.* ***

*** DG Dig. (IMS) 423 386-2 [id.]. Argenta, Attrot, Denley, Ch. & E. Concert, Pinnock – A. SCARLATTI: *Dixit Dominus.* ***

(BB) *** Naxos Dig. 8.554056 [id.]. Oxford Schola Cantorum, N. CO, Nicholas Ward – BACH: *Magnificat.* ***

Gloria, RV 589; Ostro picta, armata spina, RV 642.

*** Chandos Dig. CHAN 0518 [id.]. Kirkby, Bonner, Chance, Coll. Mus. 90, Hickox – BACH: *Magnificat.* ***

Both Richard Hickox and Neville Marriner couple the more popular of the two *D major Glorias* with the Bach *Magnificat* and offer a clear choice between period and modern instruments. Honours are evenly divided between them: Hickox's purposeful account has the benefit of a fine team of soloists and good Chandos recording; Marriner's performance with the Academy on modern instruments is well paced, as is the Bach *Magnificat*. His soloists are also very fine, and the recording has warmth and immediacy. Both can be strongly recommended.

The CD remastering of the stylish 1962 Willcocks recording of Vivaldi's *Gloria* is strikingly vivid and, with excellent choral and solo singing, this makes a fine and generous bonus for the Haydn *Nelson Mass*.

Trevor Pinnock directs a bright, refreshing account of the grander and better known of Vivaldi's *Gloria* settings, with excellent playing and singing from the members of the English Concert. Unusually but attractively coupled with the rare Scarlatti setting of *Dixit Dominus*, and very well recorded, it makes a first-rate alternative recommendation.

On Naxos it is most refreshing to have a performance of Vivaldi's most popular choral work that with modern instruments and a relatively small choir clarifies textures, revealing inner detail usually obscured. With Jeremy Summerly directing the choir and Nicholas Ward conducting the orchestra, the rhythmic point of the writing is reinforced, helped by superb sound, fresh, clear and immediate.

Gloria in D, RV 589; Magnificat, RV 611.
(N) (M) ** EMI CDM5 66987-2 [CDM5 76002]. Berganza, Terrani, New Philh. Ch. & O, Muti.

Muti offers the more expansive version of the *Magnificat*, including extended solo arias. His approach, both in that work and the *Gloria*, is altogether blander than the more authentic style adopted by Preston and Guest, let alone Pinnock. Muti's expansiveness undoubtedly suits the larger-scaled *Magnificat* better than the *Gloria*, which lacks incisiveness. The 1977 analogue recording has been effectively remastered, but this is a curious choice for EMI's 'Great recordings of the century' series.

Laudate pueri dominum, RV 601; Nisi Dominus, RV 608.
*** Mer. Dig. CDE 84129 [id.]. Lynne Dawson, Christopher Robson, King's Consort, Robert King.

The present setting of Psalm 113, RV 601, is a strong, consistently inspired work; Lynne Dawson sings with an excellent sense of style and is given splendid support. The coupling, the *Nisi Dominus*, a setting of Psalm 127, is much better known but makes an attractive makeweight. It is also given an excellent performance by Christopher Robson. Good recording.

(i) *Nisi dominus (Psalm 127), RV 608*; (ii) *Nulla in mundo pax sincera, RV 630.*
(M) *** O-L 443 199-2 [id.]. (i) James Bowman; (ii) Emma Kirkby; AAM, Preston – BACH: *Magnificat*; KUHNAU: *Der Gerechte kommt um*. ***

The solo motet, *Nulla in mundo pax sincera*, has Emma Kirkby as soloist coping splendidly with the bravura writing for soprano. James Bowman is also a persuasive soloist in the more extended, operatic-styled setting of Psalm 127. But since Vivaldi probably wrote *Nisi Dominus* for the Pietà, a Venetian orphanage for girls, readers might prefer a soprano voice.

Nisi Dominus in G min., RV 608; Salve regina in C min., RV 616; Stabat Mater in F min., RV 621; Concerto for strings in D min. RV 128; Sinfonia al Santo Sepulcro for strings, RV 169.
(N) *** DG Dig. 453 428-2 [id.]. (i) Michael Chance; E. Concert, Trevor Pinnock.

Michael Chance's superb performance of the *G minor Nisi Dominus* is not only probably the finest on record but shows this distinguished counter-tenor at his most eloquent, the voice at its most beautiful, especially in the ravishing *Cum dederit dilectis suis somnum* ('For he giveth his beloved sleep'). His account of the *Stabat Mater* comes up against stiff competition from Andreas Scholl – see below – but is movingly beautiful in its own terms, especially in the *Cuius animam*, sung on a thread of tone, the lovely *Quis est homo* and the following gentle *Quis non posset*. And how delicately Pinnock manages the very Vivaldian rhythmic figure which accompanies the *Eja Mater*. The orchestral colour (with flute and recorders) also illuminates the *Salve regina*, a work offering greater variety of tempi, again splendidly sung. The *Sinfonia* and *Concerto* act as effective interludes and are most stylishly done. The recording is first class, but collectors interested in the three vocal works will find them included in an inexpensive DG Double set called '*The art of counter tenor*' which also surveys Michael Chance's other DG Archiv recordings (DG 463 042-2).

Stabat mater, RV 621.
(M) **(*) Ph. Dig. 462 054-2. Kowalski, Concg. CO, Negri – PERGOLESI: *Stabat Mater*. **(*)

The coupling here may be apt, but it was a curious decision to pair Maazel's highly romantic performance of Pergolesi with a much more authentic approach to Vivaldi's setting from a counter-tenor. Negri's accompaniment also uses modern instruments, and what appears to be a chamber-organ continuo; but it is altogether more restrained and stylish, while matching the warmth of the soloist. Jochen Kowakski is a highly expressive singer with a rich timbre. There is a tiny lapse of pitching in the brief *Fac ut ardeat*, but otherwise this performance cannot be faulted. The recording is excellent, but as this reissue comes as part of the Philips Choral Collection, there are no texts.

(i) *Stabat Mater in F min., RV 621; Cessate omai cessate, RV 684; Filiae mestae in C min., RV 638; Concerto for strings in C, RV 114; Sonata al Santo Sepolcro in E flat, RV 130.*
*** HM Dig. HMC 901571 [id.]. (i) Andreas Scholl; Ens. 415, Banchini.

Chiara Banchini and Ensemble 415 have given us some fine period-instrument performances, but none is finer than this, earning it – thanks to the superb contribution of counter-tenor Andreas Scholl - the *Gramophone*'s Baroque Vocal Award Winner in 1996. His tenderly expressive account of the *Stabat Mater* is infinitely touching, while the pastoral cantata, *Cessate omai cessate*, is, dramatically and lyrically, no less involving. Here Vivaldi's imaginative accompaniments are relished by the instrumental ensemble, and they are equally on their toes in the similarly contrasted string works. Strongly communicative music-making, very well recorded, though the programme lasts less than an hour.

OPERA

Opera Overtures and Sinfonias: Bajazet: Sinfonia in F. La Dorilla: Sinfonia in C. Il Farnace: Sinfonia in C. Il Giustino: Sinfonia in C. L'Olimpiade: Sinfonia in C. Ottone in Villa: Sinfonia in C. La vertia' in cimento: Sinfonia in G. Chamber concerto in D min., RV 128; Concerto in F for violin, 2 oboes, 2 horns & bassoon, RV 571; Violin concerto in C min.(Amato bene). Sinfonia in G, RV 149.

(N) **(*) DHM/BMG 05472 77501-2 [id.]. L'Arte Dell'Arco, Christopher Hogwood.

Although little of this music is top-drawer Vivaldi, all of it is of interest. Except for *L'Olimpiade* (which includes a *tempesta di mare* and is in four sections), and *Ottone in Villa* (which is a concertante piece for violins and oboes and is in two), these are all typical three-movement Italian overtures. *Bajazet* (because of the plot) features hunting horns in the outer sections, but they are used even more spectacularly in the *Concerto in F*, RV 571 (which is associated with a Venetian performance of the opera *Arsilda, Regina di Ponto*), while its finale is based on the Storm aria from *Ottone in Villa*. The finale of the *Sinfonia* for *La Dorilla* brings a surprise appearance of the introduction of *Spring* from *The Four Seasons*. The period performances here are highly energetic and certainly stylish, but a bit gruff. One might have thought Harnoncourt, rather than Hogwood, was in charge. Excellent documentation.

L'Incoronazione di Dario (complete).

(B) **(*) HM Dig. HMC 1901235/7 [id.]. Elwes, Visse, Lesne, Ledroit, Verschaeve, Poulenard, Mellon, Nice Bar. Ens., Bezzina.

Set in the fifth century B.C. at the Persian court, this Vivaldi opera involves the conflict which followed the death of King Cyrus and the succession of Darius. Written in 1717, it is one of Vivaldi's earlier operas, in places reflecting the great oratorio he had written the year before, *Juditha triumphans*, reworking three numbers. The opera here receives a lively performance, generally well sung. John Elwes as Darius himself, though stylish, does not sound as involved as some of the others, notably the male alto, Dominique Visse, who is superb both vocally and dramatically as the female confidante, Flora. Reliable singing from the whole cast, and first-rate recording. The full libretto is provided only in Italian, with translated summaries of the plot in English, French and German. A very welcome reissue on Harmonia Mundi's bargain Musique d'abord label.

Orlando Furioso (complete).

*** Erato/Warner 2292 45147-2 (3) [id.]. Horne, de los Angeles, Valentini Terrani, Gonzales, Kozma, Bruscantini, Zaccaria, Sol. Ven., Scimone.

Outstanding in a surprisingly star-studded cast is Marilyn Horne in the title-role, rich and firm of tone, articulating superbly in divisions, notably in the hero's two fiery arias. In the role of Angelica, Victoria de los Angeles has many sweetly lyrical moments, and though Lucia Valentini Terrani is less strong as Alcina, she gives an aptly clean, precise performance. The remastering has freshened a recording which was not outstanding in its analogue LP form.

Orlando Furioso: highlights.

(N) (M) *** Erato/Warner 0630 13819-9. (from above complete recording with Horne, de los Angeles, Valentini Terrani; cond. Scimone).

This 73-minute selection makes a fine sampler for Vivaldi's opera for those not wanting to stretch to the three discs of the complete set. A full narrative is conveyed in between the translated texts of the arias.

Ottone in Villa (complete).

(N) *** Chandos Dig. CHAN 0614 (2) [id.]. Monica Groop, Susan Gritton, Nancy Argenta, Mark Padmore, Sophie Daneman, Collegium Musicum 90, Richard Hickox.

Ottone in Villa was Vivaldi's very first opera, produced in 1713. It follows the conventions of the day in a sequence of da capo arias linked by recitatives, with no ensemble up until the final number for the characters in unison. With only five singers required, the scale of the piece is modest in treating the subject of the Emperor Ottone and the way he is fooled by the flirtatious Cleonilla. Vivaldi is here at his most tuneful and inventive, and Richard Hickox with an excellent cast of soloists and his fine period-instrument group, Collegium Musicum 90, presents the opera with a freshness and vigour that makes one forget the work's formal limitations. Susan Gritton sings charmingly as the provocative Cleonilla, and Nancy Argenta brings flawless control to the castrato role of Caio Sillo, with the mezzo, Monica Groop strong and firm in the title-role of the Emperor. Fine production and sound add to the compulsion of the performance.

Voříšek, Jan Václav (1791–1825)

Symphony in D, Op. 24.

*** Hyperion Dig. CDA 66800 [id.]. SCO, Sir Charles Mackerras – ARRIAGA: *Symphony in D min.* etc. ***

Voříšek is as close as the Czechs got to producing a Beethoven, and this remarkably powerful work has many fingerprints of the German master everywhere while displaying some individuality. The slow movement is impressive and, after an attractive Scherzo, the finale has something in common with that of Beethoven's *Fourth*. Mackerras offers the finest account this work has received on record so far. The Hyperion recording is warmly reverberant, but this serves to increase the feeling of Beethovenian weightiness, and the Scherzo is particularly imposing. The Arriaga coupling is indispensable.

Fantasia in C, Op. 12; Impromptus Nos. 1–6, Op. 7; Piano sonata in B flat min., Op. 19; Variations in B flat, Op. 19.
*** Unicorn Dig. DKPCD 9145 [id.]. Radoslav Kvapil.
*** Collins Dig. 1458-2 [id.]. Artur Pizarro.

Jan Václav Voříšek is among the most interesting of Beethoven's Bohemian contemporaries and, had he lived longer, might have developed into a major creative figure. His *Sonata in B flat minor* (1820), like his *D major Symphony*, is one of his most representative and well-argued works and is the centrepiece of this beautifully played recital on Unicorn. Radoslav Kvapil is a sensitive and imaginative artist, deeply committed to this repertoire. The slightly later *B flat variations* will be a welcome discovery for those who do not know them, and Kvapil's accounts of the *Impromptus* are as good as, if not better than, any predecessor's. The recording, though not outstanding, serves him well.

Artur Pizarro offers exactly the same programme as Raduslav Kvapil on Unicorn, and the two make interesting and in some ways complementary alternatives. Broadly, Pizarro lays greater stress on the poetic and inward-looking side of Voříšek's personality, while Kvapil gives greater weight to classical symmetry and restraint. The recording is exemplary.

12 Rhapsodies, Op. 1; Le Désir, Op. 3; Le Plaisir, Op. 4.
*** Collins Dig. 1477-2 [id.]. Artur Pizarro.

In 1813 Voříšek left Prague to study law in Vienna, but he lost no time in furthering his musical studies with Hummel. In 1814 he met Beethoven, who found his 12 *Rhapsodies*, Op. 1, 'well worked out' (*brav gearbeitet*) for so young a man. Some of the pieces are Beethovenian and others, like Nos. 8 and 9, even look forward to Schumann. *Le Désir* and *Le Plaisir* were published in 1820 and their poetic fantasy is well conveyed by Pizarro in this excellently recorded and highly recommendable disc.

Wagner, Richard (1813–83)

(i) *A Faust overture; Overtures: Der fliegende Holländer; Rienzi; Lohengrin: Prelude to Act I;* (ii) *Prelude to Act III. Tannhäuser: Overture and Grand march.*
(B) *** Sony SBK 62403 [id.]. (i) Cleveland O, Szell; (ii) Phd. O, Ormandy.

Szell's Wagner collection, recorded in Severance Hall in 1965, remains one of his most impressive records and is worthy to rank alongside his electrifying programme of excerpts from the *Ring* (SBK 48175 – see below). The inclusion of the still rarely heard *Faust overture* is most welcome. Hearing this searingly dramatic and intense work, one again wonders why it has not become a repertory piece. To describe the playing of the Cleveland Orchestra as brilliant is inadequate, for the precision and beauty of tone clothe deeper understanding. The concert opens with Ormandy's physically thrilling account of the *Tannhäuser overture*, followed by the *Grand march* (sumptuous Philadelphia strings), and he also contributes an ebullient *Lohengrin* Act III *Prelude*. The Philadelphia recordings are less refined but the concert overall makes for a rich experience.

Siegfried idyll.
(M) *** DG 449 725-2 [id.]. BPO, Karajan – R. STRAUSS: *Ein Heldenleben.* ***
❁ (M) *** Decca Legends 460 311-2 [id.]. VPO, Solti – SCHUBERT: Symphony No. 9. *** ❁
(N) (M) *** EMI CMS5 67036-2 (2). Philh. O, Klemperer – MAHLER: *Symphony No. 9;* R. STRAUSS: *Metamorphosen.* ***
(B) *** Carlton IMP Classics Dig. 30367 0029-2. SCO, Jaime Laredo – DVORAK: *String serenade* etc. ***

Karajan's account of Wagner's wonderful birthday present to Cosima is unsurpassed; it has never sounded better than in this transfer for DG's series of 'Originals', aptly coupled with Strauss's *Ein Heldenleben*, Karajan's very first stereo recording for DG.

So rich is the sound that Decca provided for Solti (in 1965) that one can hardly believe that this is a chamber performance. The playing is similarly warm and committed and this coupling with Schubert's *Great C major Symphony*, reissued in Decca's Legends series, is one of Solti's finest records.

Klemperer also favours the original chamber-orchestra scoring and the Philharmonia players are very persuasive, especially in the score's gentler moments. The balance is forward and, although the sound is warm, some ears may crave a greater breadth of string tone at the climax. However this triptych from the 'Klemperer Legacy' shows the conductor at his most compelling.

A beautiful performance from Jaime Laredo and the Scottish Chamber Orchestra, warm and poised, ending serenely, yet moving to a strong central climax. The recording, made in Glasgow City Hall, is pleasingly expansive, yet textures are clear.

Siegfried idyll. Die fliegende Holländer: Overture. Lohengrin: Prelude to Act III. Rienzi: Overture. Tannhäuser: Overture.
(BB) *** Tring Dig. TRP 008 [id.]. RPO, Vernon Handley.

The *Siegfried idyll* is beautifully played and radiantly recorded, but the highlight is Handley's rumbustious account of the *Rienzi overture* with thrilling brass and an exuberant contribution from the side-drum – a demonstration item. The heavy brass also makes a splendidly weighty contribution to the *Lohengrin* Act III *Prelude* and is no less effective at the climax of the *Ride of the Valkyries*. Handley uses the concert ending in both these pieces, and his spacious treatment of the reprise of the Pilgrim's chorale at the close of the *Tannhäuser overture* makes a satisfying close to a programme which is played as well as it is recorded, in the resonant acoustic of St Augustine's Church, Kilburn.

Siegfried idyll (with rehearsal); *Der fliegende Holländer: Overture; Die Meistersinger: Prelude to Act I; Lohengrin: Prelude to Act I; Parsifal: Prelude to Act I and Good Friday music; Tannhäuser:* (i) *Overture and Venusberg music*.
(M) *** Sony SMK 64456 (2) [id.]. (i) Occidental College Ch.; Columbia SO, Bruno Walter.

Walter's is above all a gentle performance of the *Siegfried idyll*. The 1963 recording seems fuller and more atmospheric than before, especially at the ardent climax, while the rapt closing ritenuto is magical. Before the performance, comes an extended rehearsal sequence lasting three-quarters of an hour, which most listeners will find fascinating. The rest of the programme was recorded in 1959. Highlights include the glowing *Parsifal Prelude* and *Good Friday music*, matching Jochum in its simple intensity, and the superb account of the *Tannhäuser Overture* and *Venusberg music* with its thrillingly sensuous climax, and the closing pages – the Occidental College Choir distantly balanced – bringing a radiant hush. Both here and in the *Flying Dutchman* and *Meistersinger overtures* the orchestra has more body and weight, while the *Lohengrin Prelude*, relaxed but beautifully controlled, sounds radiant.

Siegfried idyll. Götterdämmerung: Siegfried's Rhine journey; Siegfried's funeral music; Immolation scene. Siegfried: Forest murmurs. Die Walküre: Ride of the Valkyries; Wotan's farewell and magic fire music.
(N) *** Teldec/Warner Dig. 0630 17109-2 [id.]. Dresden State O, Donald Runnicles.

The present excerpts are taken from an orchestral concert in the Dresden State Opera House, which with richly expansive acoustics seems an ideal recording venue. At the opening of the programme the Valkyries ride in with great vigour and power. *Wotan's farewell* conveys at first the warmest human tenderness, and then great excitement at the climax of the *Fire music*, with glorious string playing throughout. *Forest murmurs* becomes here an atmospheric central interlude, yet ending exultantly. The mood darkens as Siegfried prepares for his Rhine journey after his reluctant parting from Brünnhilde. Runnicles builds a hugely passionate climax, with a thrilling accelerando before Siegfried sounds his famous horn call and the Dresden Orchestra create grippingly powerful sonorities in strings and brass in the following death/funeral sequence. The *Immolation scene* finalizes the narrative, with a gripping apotheosis. Wagner's beautiful *Siegfried idyll* then acts as a touching and ravishing epilogue. Again the orchestra plays very beautifully indeed. Overall this is one of the finest and most satisfying single-disc orchestral summations of what Wagner's Ring is all about.

Siegfried idyll. Lohengrin: Preludes to Acts I & III. Die Meistersinger: Prelude to Act I. Parsifal: Prelude to Act I. Tristan und Isolde: Prelude and Liebestod.
(B) *** Ph. 420 886-2. Concg. O, Haitink.

The addition of Haitink's simple, unaffected reading of the *Siegfried idyll* to his 1975 collection of *Preludes* enhances the appeal of a particularly attractive concert. The rich acoustics of the Concertgebouw are ideal for *Die Meistersinger*, given a spacious performance, and Haitink's restraint adds to the noble dignity of *Parsifal*. The *Lohengrin* excerpts are splendidly played. The digital remastering is first-rate.

Siegfried idyll. Lohengrin: Prelude to Acts I & III. Die Meistersinger: Overture. Die Walküre: Ride of the Valkyries; (i) *Wotan's farewell and Magic fire music*.
*** ASV Dig. CDDCA 666 [id.]. Philh. O, Francesco d'Avalos, (i) with John Tomlinson.

The opening *Siegfried idyll* has all the requisite serenity and atmosphere; here, as elsewhere, the Philharmonia play most beautifully. The sumptuous recording gives a thrilling resonance and amplitude to the brass, especially trombones and tuba, and in the expansive *Meistersinger overture*, and again in *Wotan's farewell* the brass entries bring a physical frisson. John Tomlinson's noble assumption of the role of Wotan, as he bids a loving farewell to his errant daughter, is very moving here, and the response of the Philharmonia strings matches his depth of feeling.

Siegfried idyll. Tannhäuser: overture. (i) *Tristan: Prelude and Liebestod*.
*** DG Dig. 423 613-2 [id.]. (i) Jessye Norman; VPO, Karajan.

This superb Wagner record was taken live from a unique concert conducted by Karajan at the Salzburg Festival in August 1987. The *Tannhäuser overture* has never sounded so noble, and the *Siegfried idyll* has rarely seemed so intense and dedicated behind its sweet lyricism; while the *Prelude and Liebestod*, with Jessye Norman as soloist, bring the richest culmination, sensuous and passionate, remarkable as much for the hushed, inward moments as for the massive building of climaxes.

OTHER ORCHESTRAL EXCERPTS FROM THE OPERAS

Der fliegende Holländer: Overture. Lohengrin: Preludes to Acts I & III. Die Meistersinger: Overture; Dance of the apprentices; Entry of the masters. Rienzi: Overture; Tannhauser: Overture.
(M) *** EMI CDM5 66805-2 [id.]. Philh. O, Klemperer.

Götterdämmerung: Siegfried's funeral music and Rhine journey. Parsifal: Prelude. Das Rheingold: Entry of the Gods into Valhalla. Siegfried: Forest murmurs. Tannhäuser: Prelude to Act III. Tristan und Isolde: Prelude and Liebestod. Die Walküre: Ride of the Valkyries.
(M) *** EMI CDM5 66806-2 [id.]. Philh. O, Klemperer.

It is good to have Klemperer's view of Wagner. Most of the performances reissued here as part of EMI's 'Klemperer legacy' have the kind of incandescent glow one associated with really great conductors, and the Philharmonia play immaculately. The *Tristan Prelude* and *Liebestod* do not have the sense of wonder that Toscanini and Furtwängler brought, but the noble passion at the climax communicates strongly. The characteristically spacious and superbly shaped *Parsifal* and *Lohengrin Preludes* are a highlight for similar reasons. Elsewhere, if the level of tension is more variable, Klemperer's readings are always solidly concentrated, even if this means that the plodding *Meistersingers* seem a bit too full of German pudding. Yet there is no lack of zest in the *Lohengrin Prelude to Act III*. The remastering for CD has brought a gloriously full sound-picture, clearer than on the original LPs.

Overtures and Preludes: *Der fliegende Holländer: Overture. Lohengrin: Preludes to Acts I & III; Parsifal: Prelude. Rienzi: Overture. Tannhäuser: Overture* (original version).
(M) *** DG (IMS) 453 989-2. VPO, Karl Boehm.

Under Boehm, the Vienna Philharmonic Orchestra plays beautifully in a choice of overtures and preludes spanning Wagner's full career, from *Rienzi* to *Parsifal* – in which the performance of the *Prelude* is superbly eloquent. Above all, Boehm's approach is spacious with speeds broad rather than urgent, yet there is no lack of concentration, and the account of *Rienzi* has striking life and vigour. All the performances – and especially the *Lohengrin Prelude to Act I* and the *Tannhäuser overture* – show a compulsive inevitability in their forward flow. The recording is full and vivid, even if some balances do not seem quite natural. The recordings, made in the Musikverein between 1975 and 1980, include two items from the very end of Boehm's recording career.

Der fliegende Holländer: Overture. Parsifal: Preludes to Acts I & III.
(M) *** EMI CDM5 66108-2 [id.]. BPO, Karajan – R. STRAUSS: *Ein Heldenleben.* ***

These recordings come from 1974 and are magnificently played and sumptuously recorded. There is urgency and edge in *The Flying Dutchman*, which is very exciting, and the string playing in the *Parsifal Preludes* is nobly shaped; if here perhaps the very last degree of tension is missing, the Berlin strings create a glorious sound.

Götterdämmerung: Siegfried's funeral music. Lohengrin, Act I: Prelude. Die Meistersinger, Act III: Prelude. Parsifal: Good Friday music. Siegfried: Forest murmurs. Tristan und Isolde: Prelude and Liebestod. Die Walküre: Ride of the Valkyries.
(N) *** DG Dig. 447 764-2 [id.]. NY Met. O, James Levine.

Levine's performances are admirably paced, tingling with life, with climaxes finely graduated; and he secures sumptuously passionate playing from the Met. strings. The richly full-bodied and atmospheric recording is just about the best yet to have come from the New York Manhattan Center. The cymbals at the climax of the *Lohengrin Prelude* could ideally be more present, but otherwise the balance is realistically managed, and when the Valkyries ride in with splendid vigour, the sound avoids any sense of brashness. Jochum achieved a spiritual dimension in the *Good Friday music* from *Parsifal* which is missing here, but taken as a whole this 75-minute programme is a great success.

Götterdämmerung: Dawn and Siegfried's Rhine journey. Lohengrin: Preludes to Acts I & III. Die Meistersinger: Prelude to Act I. Das Rheingold: Entry of the Gods into Valhalla. Rienzi: Overture. Siegfried: Forest murmurs. Tannhäuser: Overture. Die Walküre: Ride of the Valkyries; Wotan's farewell and Magic fire music.
(B) *** EMI forte (SIS) Dig. CZS5 68616-2 (2) [CDFB 68616]. BPO, Tennstedt.

This EMI forte double combines two highly successful collections from the early days of the digital era. The recordings were made in the Philharmonie between 1981 and 1983; they could ideally be more opulent in the middle and bass, but there is brilliance, weight and fine detail, especially in the atmospheric *Forest murmurs*. The orchestral playing is superb, with Tennstedt amalgamating something from the combined Furtwängler and Klemperer traditions in his broad, spacious readings, which are also electrifying. The opening and closing sections of the *Tannhäuser overture* are given a restrained nobility of feeling without any loss of power or impact. Similarly the gorgeous string melody at the opening of *Rienzi* is elegiacally moulded, and later when the brass enter in the allegro there is no suggestion of the bandstand.

Götterdämmerung: Siegfried's Rhine journey and Funeral music; Die Meistersinger: Preludes to Acts I & III; Dance of the apprentices; Procession of the Masters.
(N) (M) **(*) RCA 09026 63301-2 [id.]. Chicago SO, Fritz Reiner – R. STRAUSS: *Don Juan.* ***

In previous incarnations, on both LP and CD, Reiner's Wagner sessions of 1959 have always tended to sound a bit inflated, but the current remastering (by Hsi-Ling Chang) has greatly improved the balance. The bass remains weighty, but without the effect of too much amplitude and too little brightness. The *Götterdämmerung* excerpts are particularly impressive, the *Rhine journey* buoyant and joyous, the *Funeral music* powerful and sombre. Reiner choses spacious tempi in the *Meistersinger* excerpts with a further broadening at the (similar) climax of both the *Overture* and the *Procession of the Masters*: the result is very German in character. There is very fine playing from the horns in the *Prelude to Act III* from the same opera.

Götterdämmerung: Dawn and Siegfried's Rhine journey; Siegfried's death and funeral march. Lohengrin: Prelude to Act I. Tannhäuser: Overture and Venusberg music. Tristan und Isolde: Liebestod. Die Walküre: Ride of the Valkyries.
(M) (***) RCA mono GD 60306 [09026 60306-2]. NBC SO, Toscanini.

Götterdämmerung: Dawn; (i; ii) *Zu neuen Taten; Willst du mir Minne schenken; O heilige Götter; Siegfried's Rhine journey; Brünnhilde's immolation:* (i) *Starke Scheite schichtet mir dort; Wie Sonne lauter strahlt mir sein Licht; Mein Erbe nun nehm'ich zu eigen; Fliegt heim ihr Raben!; Grane, Mein Ross, sei mir gegrüsst. Siegfried: Forest murmurs.*
(M) (***) RCA mono GD 60304 [09026 60304-2]. (i) Helen Traubel; (ii) Lauritz Melchior; NBC SO, Toscanini.

Toscanini's special brand of electricity comes over vividly in these characteristic Wagner performances. The *Lohengrin Prelude* and the soaring *Tristan Liebestod* have keen intensity and, although the dynamic range is compressed, the sound is surprisingly good, as it is in the tenderly sensuous *Venusberg* sequence in *Tannhäuser*. One is offered a choice here of the *Götterdämmerung Dawn* sequence with or without the vocal contribution in which both Helen Traubel and Melchior are strong enough musical personalities to stand up against Toscanini. The recordings date from the 1940s and 1950s and, as transferred, are surprisingly full, with something of a concert-hall effect in the Carnegie Hall *Immolation* sequence of 1941. Traubel rides masterfully over the orchestra.

Götterdämmerung: Dawn and Siegfried's Rhine journey; Siegfried's death and funeral march; (i) *Brünnhilde's immolation. Siegfried: Forest murmurs. Die Walküre: Ride of the Valkyries.*
*** Erato/Warner Dig. 2292 45786-2 [id.]. (i) Deborah Polaski; Chicago SO, Barenboim.

Here Barenboim dons his Furtwänglerian mantle in spacious performances. Even with tempi measured, he secures playing of great concentration and excitement from the Chicago orchestra, and the recording is one of the finest made in Chicago's Orchestra Hall. Deborah Polaski makes a bold, passionate Brünnhilde, and if her voice is not flattered by the microphones, and under pressure her vibrato widens, this is still histrionically thrilling, and Barenboim and the orchestra provide an overwhelming final apotheosis to the *Immolation scene.*

Götterdämmerung: Dawn and Siegfried's Rhine journey; Siegfried's death and funeral music. Die Meistersinger: Prelude. Das Rheingold: Entry of the Gods into Valhalla. Siegfried: Forest murmurs. Tristan und Isolde: Prelude & Liebestod. Die Walküre: Wotan's farewell and Magic fire music.
❀ (M) *** SBK 48175 [id.]. Cleveland O, Szell.

The orchestral playing here is breathtaking in its virtuosity. Szell generates the greatest tension, particularly in the two scenes from *Götterdämmerung*, while the *Liebestod* from *Tristan* has never been played on record with more passion and fire. The *Tristan* and *Meistersinger* excerpts (from 1962) have been added to the contents of the original LP, which contained the *Ring* sequences made later (in 1968), much improved on CD. This is well worthy of Szell's extraordinary achievement in Cleveland in the 1960s, even if the forward balance of the recording places a limit on the dynamic range.

Götterdämmerung: Siegfried's Rhine journey & Funeral music. Parsifal: Prelude to Act I. Siegfried: Forest murmurs. Tristan und Isolde: Prelude & Liebestod. Die Walküre: Ride of the Valkyries.
*** Collins Dig. 1207-2 [id.]. Philh. O, Yuri Simonov.

If you want a spectacular, modern, digital recording of Wagnerian orchestral excerpts, this one is hard to beat. The magnificent account of *Siegfried's Rhine journey* (with a splendid horn solo) is followed by a performance of the *Funeral music* which has blazing drama and enormously expansive sound, with the brass biting venomously at Siegfried's betrayal. The *Prelude and Liebestod* from *Tristan* brings playing of great ardour from the Philharmonia strings, while – at a very spacious tempo – they find great intensity in the *Parsifal Prelude*.

Lohengrin: Preludes to Acts I & III. Parsifal: Preludes to Acts I & III.
(BB) *** EMI Seraphim CES5 69092 (2). BPO, Karajan (with BRUCKNER: *Symphony No. 8*. ***).

Karajan's Act I *Lohengrin Prelude* is graduated superbly; the *Parsifal* excerpts, too, are nobly shaped, yet here the tension is held at a marginally lower level. The *Parsifal* excerpts bring rapt serenity. This is magnificent playing, and the 1975 recording has an attractively wide amplitude.

Lohengrin: Preludes to Acts I & III. Tristan und Isolde: Prelude & Liebestod.
(M) *** EMI (SIS) CDM5 66107-2 [id.]. BPO, Karajan – R. STRAUSS: *Sinfonia domestica*. ***

These Karajan performances (again from 1974) are in a class of their own. The body of tone produced by the Berlin Philharmonic gives a breathtaking richness to the climaxes, and in the *Tristan Liebestod* the orgasmic culmination is quite overwhelming, as is the thrilling brass playing in the famous *Lohengrin* Act III *Prelude*.

Die Meistersinger: Overture. (i) *Tannhäuser: Overture and Venusberg music.*
(M) *** EMI (SIS) CDM5 66106-2 [id.]. BPO, Karajan, (i) with German Op. Ch. – R. STRAUSS: *Don Quixote*. ***

Further excerpts from Karajan's outstanding (1974) sessions: a superb sense of timing and spaciousness is applied to the *Tannhäuser* excerpts, and the *Die Meistersinger Prelude* has a similar imposing breadth. The sound is excellent.

Die Meistersinger: Prelude to Act III. Tannhäuser: Overture and Venusberg music. Tristan und Isolde: Prelude and Liebestod.
**(*) DG (IMS) Dig. Gold 439 022-2 [id.]. BPO, Karajan.

In Karajan's digital concert the orchestral playing is superlative. But, in spite of the reprocessing, the upper strings lack space, and climaxes should be freer. The overall effect is rather clinical in its detail, instead of offering a resonant panoply of sound, but the playing is eloquent and powerful. The measure is not very generous for a reissued premium-price CD.

Die Meistersinger: suite from Act III (arr. Barbirolli) (*Prelude; Dance of the apprentices; Entry of the Masters*).
(B) (***) Dutton Lab. mono CDEA 5504 [(M) id.]. Hallé O, Barbirolli – BERLIOZ: *Symphonie fantastique*. (***)

Barbirolli's own suite from *Meistersinger*, Act III, was a favourite work with him, and this recording, made in 1944, just over a year after he took over the Hallé, brings out the warmth and resonance of the playing under his guidance. The sound is astonishingly full and rich for the period, as transferred by Dutton, a cherishable coupling for Barbirolli's fine 1947 version of the *Symphonie fantastique*.

Parsifal, Act III: symphonic synthesis. Tristan und Isolde: Symphonic synthesis. Die Walkure: Wotan's farewell and magic fire music (all arr. Stokowski).
(N) *** Chandos Dig. CHAN 9686 [id.]. BBC PO, Matthias Bamert.

Stokowski's recordings of Wagner excerpts always treated the voices as a kind of adjunct to the orchestra, and he loved best to play the orchestral music without them. So he made a series of symphonic syntheses, joining scenes together in a continuous sensuous and dramatic melodic flow, leaving the orchestra to convey the full narrative. *Parsifal* includes tolling bells and rich mysticism, and in *Tristan* Stokowski frames the *Liebesnacht* (including the distant hunting horns heralding the return of Tristan) with the passionate *Prelude* and *Liebestod*. Best of all he creates a symphonic poem out of Wotan's sad, loving farewell to his beloved Brünnhilde, making a great climax out of the *Fire music*. Bamert is passionate and tender by turns and the BBC Philharmonic readily respond to the luscious orchestration. Perhaps the last degree of Stokowskian intensity is missing here, but with superbly spacious Chandos sound this is easy to enjoy.

VOCAL MUSIC

Lieder: *Les deux Grenadiers; Lied des Mephistopheles (Es war einmal ein König; Was machst du mir); Mignonne; Der Tannenbaum; Tout n'est qu'images fugitives.*
✿ *** EMI (SIS) Dig. CDC5 55047-2 [id.]. Thomas Hampson, Geoffrey Parsons – BERLIOZ: *Irlande;* LISZT: *Lieder*. *** ✿

Starting with a charming French salon piece, *Mignonne*, to words by Ronsard, the Hampson collection presents an almost unknown side of the composer. As well as another French love-song, there is a setting in French of the Goethe poem about the two grenadiers, not as subtle as Schumann's version but building to a tremendous climax with a reference to the *Marseillaise*. Two of Mephistopheles' songs from *Faust* (in German) date from earlier, including a jaunty setting of the *Song of the flea*. With Hampson in magnificent voice, powerfully accompanied by Geoffrey Parsons, this makes up a winning disc, very well recorded.

Wesendonk Lieder.
(N) (M) ** EMI CDM5 67037-2. Christa Ludwig,

Philh. O, Klemperer – BRUCKNER: *Symphony No. 6.* ***

Christa Ludwig is less successful here in her partnership with Klemperer than in the Brahms *Alto rhapsody* also dating from 1962. In Wagner she seems to be thinking in operatic terms. She has a rich and beautiful vocal quality, but seems unable or unwilling to always reduce the tone sufficiently for the more intimate effect required in Lieder. The orchestral accompaniment is very well done.

Wesendonk Lieder: Der Engel; Stehe still; Im Treibhaus; Schmerzen; Träume. Götterdämmerung: Starke Scheite schichet mir dort. Siegfried: Ewig war ich. Tristan: Doch nun von Tristan?; Mild und leise.

(***) EMI (SIS) mono CDH7 63030-2 [id.]. Kirsten Flagstad, Philh. O, Furtwängler, Dobrowen.

Recorded in the late 1940s and early '50s, a year or so before Flagstad did *Tristan* complete with Furtwängler, these performances show her at her very peak, with the voice magnificent in power as well as beautiful and distinctive in every register. The *Liebestod* (with rather heavy surface noise) may be less rapt and intense in this version with Dobrowen than with Furtwängler but is just as expansive. For the *Wesendonk Lieder* she shades the voice down very beautifully, but this is still monumental and noble rather than intimate Lieder-singing.

OPERA

Der fliegende Holländer (complete).

(N) *** DG Dig. 437 778-2 (2) [id.]. Bernd Weikl, Cheryl Studer, Hans Sotin, Plácido Domingo, Peter Seiffert, Ch. & O of German Op., Berlin, Sinopoli.

(M) *** Ph. Dig. 434 599-2 (2) [id.]. Estes, Balslev, Salminen, Schunk, Bayreuth Festival (1985) Ch. & O, Nelsson.

*** Sony Dig. S2K 66342 (2) [id.]. Morris, Voigt, Heppner, Rootering, Svendén, Groves, Met. Op. Ch. & O, James Levine.

(B) *** Naxos Dig. 8.660025/6 [id.]. Muff, Haubold, Knodt, Seiffert, Budapest R. Ch., Vienna ORF SO, Steinberg.

The very opening of the overture alerts you at once to the high drama of Sinopoli's reading, violent in its portrayal of a storm at sea. This is an intensely involving performance, volatile in the choice of often extreme speeds, slow as well as fast, but with fine playing from the orchestra of the Deutsche Oper, Berlin, it never sounds forced, with rhythms crisply sprung, making others seem dull or even pedestrian. The choral singing too is electrifying, and the line-up of principals is arguably finer than any. Cheryl Studer is a deeply moving Senta, not just immaculate vocally but conveying the intense vulnerability of the character in finely detailed singing. Bernd Weikl is a dark-toned, firmly focused Dutchman, strong and incisive. Hans Sotin is similarly firm and dark, nicely contrasted as Daland, and the luxury casting may be judged from the choice of Plácido Domingo as an impressive, forthright Erik and Peter Seiffert (the fine *Lohengrin* in Barenboim's Teldec set) as a ringing Steersman. Full, vivid sound. A clear first choice.

Woldemar Nelsson, with the team he had worked with intensively through the Bayreuth season, conducts a performance even more glowing and responsively paced than those of his starrier rivals. The cast is more consistent than any, with Lisbeth Balslev as Senta firmer, sweeter and more secure than any current rival, raw only occasionally, and Simon Estes a strong, ringing Dutchman, clear and noble of tone. Matti Salminen is a dark and equally secure Daland and Robert Schunk an ardent, idiomatic Erik. The veteran, Anny Schlemm, as Mary, though vocally overstressed, adds pointful character, and the chorus is superb, wonderfully drilled and passionate with it. Though inevitably stage noises are obtrusive at times, the recording is exceptionally vivid and atmospheric. On two mid-priced discs only, it makes an admirable alternative choice.

James Levine directs his Metropolitan Opera forces in a weighty, exceptionally spacious reading, warmly and atmospherically recorded, with a first-rate cast of soloists. Levine's speeds are even slower than Karajan's in his EMI recording, and markedly slower than those of Woldemar Nelsson in his live Bayreuth recording, which is otherwise a preferable choice. Levine sustains concentration strongly, even when – as in the Spinning Chorus – the speed is eccentrically slow. His springing of rhythms too helps to disguise slow speeds. His view is clearly that this early opera should be treated as being in the same bracket as the mature Wagner, and his principals respond to the challenge in performances that bring out the brooding intensity of both the Dutchman and Senta. So James Morris in the title-role makes the Dutchman into a Wotan-like figure, weighty if slightly gritty of tone. Deborah Voigt finds a stillness and repose in Senta's meditations in her Ballad, producing radiant sounds. Ben Heppner is a superb Erik, with heroic tone clear and fresh, while Jan-Hendrik Rootering is a warm, benevolent Daland. Excellent choral singing and fine playing. The Nelsson version remains a safer recommendation, more bitingly dramatic (unless you find stage noises too distracting), but this Levine set makes a powerful alternative.

Pinchas Steinberg, who has been outstandingly successful as music director of the ORF Orchestra and who was responsible for RCA's brilliant recording of Massenet's *Cherubin*, here proves a warmly sympathetic Wagnerian. More than most rivals, he brings out the light and shade of this earliest of the regular Wagner canon, helped by the refined, well-balanced recording, and by brilliant, sharply dramatic playing from the orchestra. His speeds are more urgent than most, with rhythms well sprung and melodic lines sympathetically moulded. The chorus too sings with a bite and precision to match any rival. The cast of soloists may not be in that league, but they sing clearly and on the whole freshly, avoiding most of the cardinal faults of Wagner singers today. Alfred Muff as the Dutchman attacks the notes cleanly, with vibrato only occasionally intrusive. The vibrato of Ingrid Haubold is more of a problem but, except under pressure, it is well controlled, and she begins *Senta's Ballad* with a meditative pianissimo. Both tenors are excellent, Peter Seiffert as Erik and Joerg Hering as the Steersman, and though Erich Knodt, rather gritty in tone, is an uncharacterful Daland, his Act II aria is light and refreshing, thanks to Steinberg's fine rhythmic pointing. The recording is both atmospheric and clear, and the set comes with libretto, translation, notes and detailed synopsis, an outstanding bargain.

Götterdämmerung (complete).

*** Decca 455 569-2 (4). Nilsson, Windgassen, Fischer-Dieskau, Frick, Neidlinger, Watson, Ludwig, V. State Op. Ch., VPO, Solti.

(N) (M) *** DG 457 795-2 (4) [id.]. Dernesch, Janowitz, Brilioth, Stewart, Kelemen, Ludwig, Ridderbusch, German Op. Ch., BPO, Karajan.

*** Ph. (IMS) 412 488-2 (4). Nilsson, Windgassen, Greindl, Mödl, Stewart, Neidlinger, Dvořáková, Bayreuth Festival (1967) Ch. & O, Boehm.

*** Teldec/Warner Dig. 4509 94194-2 (4) [id.]. Jerusalem, Anne Evans, Kang, Von Kannen, Bundschuh, Meier, Turner, Bayreuth (1991) Festival Ch. & O, Barenboim.

*** EMI (SIS) Dig. CD7 54485-2 (4) [Ang. CDCD 54485]. Marton, Jerusalem, Tomlinson, Adam, Hampson, Bundschuh, Lipovšek, Bav. R. Ch., RSO, Haitink.

(B) *** RCA Dig. 74321 45421-2 (4). Kollo, Altmeyer, Salminen, Wenkel, Nocker, Nimsgern, Sharp, Popp, Leipzig R. Ch., Berlin R. Ch., Dresden State Op. Ch., Dresden State O, Janowski.

(N) (B) (*(*)) Naxos mono 8.11041/3 (3) [id.]. Lauritz Melchior, Marjorie Lawrence, Ludwig Hoffman, Edward Habich, Friedrich Schorr, Met. Op. Ch. & O, Artur Bodanzky.

Solti's *Götterdämmerung* represented the peak of his achievement in recording the *Ring* cycle. His reading had matured before the recording was made. He presses on still, but there is no feeling of over-driving, and even the *Funeral march* is made into a natural, not a forced, climax. There is not a single weak link in the cast. Nilsson surpasses herself in the magnificence of her singing: even Flagstad in her prime would not have been more masterful as Brünnhilde. As in *Siegfried*, Windgassen is in superb voice; Frick is a vivid Hagen, and Fischer-Dieskau achieves the near impossible in making Gunther an interesting and even sympathetic character. As for the recording quality, it surpasses even Decca's earlier achievement, and the current remastering has further improved the sound. The layout, too, is ideal, and the box is illustrated with the original LP artwork.

Karajan's singing cast is marginally even finer than Solti's, and his performance conveys the steady flow of recording sessions prepared in relation to live performances. Ultimately he falls short of Solti's achievement in the thrusting, orgasmic quality of the music. Karajan is a degree less committed, beautifully as the players respond, and warm as his overall approach is. Dernesch's Brünnhilde is warmer than Nilsson's, with a glorious range of tone. Brilioth as Siegfried is fresh and young-sounding, while the Gutrune of Gundula Janowitz is far preferable to that of Claire Watson on Decca. The matching is otherwise very even. The new transfer has both freshened and filled out the sound. Now reissued as one of DG's Originals, the set finally reverts to upper mid-price.

Boehm's urgently involving reading of *Götterdämmerung*, very well cast, is crowned by an incandescent performance of the final *Immolation scene* from Birgit Nilsson as Brünnhilde. It is an astonishing achievement that she could sing with such biting power and accuracy in a live performance, coming to it at the very end of a long evening. The excitement of that is matched by much else in the performance, so that incidental stage noises and the occasional inaccuracy, almost inevitable in live music-making, matter hardly at all. Josef Greindl is rather unpleasantly nasal in tone as Hagen, and Martha Mödl as Waltraute is unsteady; but both are dramatically involving. Thomas Stewart is a gruff but convincing Gunther and Dvořáková, as Gutrune, strong if not ideally pure-toned. Neidlinger as ever is a superb Alberich.

Recorded at the 1991 Bayreuth Festival, a year earlier than *Siegfried*, Barenboim's live recording is not quite the culmination one had hoped for in his cycle for Teldec. There is also the problem in this opera, more than the rest of the *Ring*, of stage noises, particularly at the end of the Immolation scene, rather undermining its rapt intensity, when the fulfilment motif enters at last. Anne Evans sweetly and purely rises to the challenge of that radiant close of the tetralogy, compensating for any lack of power in the clarity of focus and expressive intensity of her singing, making Brünnhilde a very human figure to excite the deepest sympathy. The recording is satisfyingly weighty and has more presence than its direct digital rivals, recorded in the studio under Haitink (EMI) and Levine (DG). On balance, it stands as the most recommendable of latterday versions of this final opera, thanks not only to the beauty as well as the imagination of Evans's singing, more satisfying than that of her squally rivals, but also to the superb singing of Siegfried Jerusalem who outshines his already outstanding achievement in the same role in the Haitink version, even if the stresses of a long evening begin to show by the end. Eva-Maria Bundschuh makes a fresh, bright Gutrune and Waltraud Meier a powerful Waltraute, giving an animated account of her Act I narration. Bodo Brinkmann is an old-sounding, rather uneven Gunther, Philip Kang a powerful but gritty Hagen and Gunter von Kannen an unsinister Alberich. Any disappointment there is small compared to the keen tension and excitement of this live recording under Barenboim, consistently gripping. As a performance it may not outshine either Solti's pioneering version or Karl Boehm's live account from Bayreuth – both of which still sound splendid – but it satisfyingly completes the finest of modern *Ring* cycles on disc.

Haitink's reading is magnificent. In its strength, nobility and thrustfulness it crowns all his previous Wagner, culminating in a forceful and warmly expressive account of the final Immolation scene. Siegfried Jerusalem clearly establishes himself as the finest latterday Siegfried, both heroic and sweet of tone. Thomas Hampson is a sensitive and virile Gunther, John Tomlinson a sinister but human Hagen, Marjana Lipovšek a warmly intense Waltraute and Eva-Maria Bundschuh a rich, rather fruity Gutrune. The obvious reservation to make is with the singing of Eva Marton as Brünnhilde, when the unevenness of the vocal production is exaggerated by the microphone in a way that at times comes close to pitchless yelping. That drawback is clearly outweighed by the set's positive qualities, and the scale of her singing is in no doubt, an archetypal Brünnhilde voice in timbre if not in firmness.

With sharply focused yet warmly ambient sound, Janowski's *Götterdämmerung* hits refreshingly hard, at least as much so as in the earlier operas in the cycle. Speeds rarely linger but, with some excellent casting – consistent with the earlier operas – the result is rarely lightweight. Jeannine Altmeyer as Brünnhilde rises to the challenge, not so much in strength as in feeling, and here, as throughout the series, she consistently avoids the kind of squally and ill-focused – if powerful – tone-production that puts some listeners off Wagner altogether. She is ecstatic in Act I, bitter in Act II, dedicated in the Immolation scene. Kollo is a fine Siegfried, only occasionally raw-toned, and Salminen a magnificent Hagen, with Nimsgern an incisive Alberich on his brief appearances. Despite an indifferent Gunther and Gutrune and a wobbly if characterful Waltraute, the impression is of clean, strong vocalization matched by finely disciplined and dedicated playing, all recorded in faithful stereo, with very good detail. A remarkable achievement and a fine bargain.

On Naxos, the 1936 radio transmission, roughly recorded, may often bring excruciating sound, with high surfaces and heavy interference, and Bodansky's conducting may often be perfunctory, but the thrill of a great Wagnerian occasion featuring some of the finest Wagner singers of the day certainly comes over. Bodansky, who sanctions substantial cuts, even gallops through Brünnhilde's final Immolation scene, but the glory of Marjorie Lawrence's singing at the beginning of her all-too-brief career has never been so vividly captured. Equally, to hear Melchior as Siegfried – even fuzzily – is not to be missed by any Wagnerian. The others make a strong team, with voices rather clearer than the muddy orchestra.

The Twilight of the Gods (Götterdämmerung): Act III: excerpts (in English).

(M) *** Chandos CHAN 6593 [id.]. Rita Hunter, Alberto Remedios, Norman Bailey, Clifford Grant, Margaret Curphey, Sadler's Wells Opera Ch. & O, Goodall.

Originally recorded by Unicorn in the early 1970s, even before the Sadler's Wells company had changed its name to the English National Opera, this single Chandos CD brings an invaluable reminder of Reginald Goodall's performance of the *Ring* cycle when it was in its first flush of success. The two-LP set is here transferred on to a single CD, lasting 66 minutes and covering the closing two scenes. In many ways it possesses an advantage over even the complete live recording of the opera, made at the Coliseum five years later, when Rita Hunter and Alberto Remedios are here obviously fresher and less stressed than at the end of a full evening's performance. It is good too to have this sample, however brief, of Clifford Grant's Hagen and Norman Bailey's Gunther, fine performances both. Fresh, clear recording, not as full as it might be. At mid-price this CD is well worth investigating.

Lohengrin (complete).

*** DG Dig. 437 808-2 (3) [id.]. Jerusalem, Studer, Meier, Welker, Moll, Schmidt, V. State Op. Ch., VPO, Claudio Abbado.

*** Decca Dig. 421 053-2 (4) [id.]. Domingo, Norman, Nimsgern, Randová, Sotin, Fischer-Dieskau, V. State Op. Concert Ch., VPO, Solti.

(N) *** Teldec/Warner Dig. 3984 21484-2 (3). Peter Seiffert, Emily Magee, Falk Struckmann, Deborah Polaski, René Pape, Ch. & O of German Op.,Berlin, Barenboim.

*** EMI CDS7 49017-2 (3) [Ang. CDCC 49017]. Jess Thomas, Grümmer, Fischer-Dieskau, Ludwig, Frick, Wiener, V. State Op. Ch., VPO, Kempe.

Claudio Abbado adds another magnificent reading

to set alongside such classic performances as Kempe's and Solti's. But where Solti takes a very measured view, Abbado keeps Wagner's square rhythms flowing more freely, allowing himself a greater measure of rubato. That in turn reflects his experience with these same performers at the Vienna State Opera, and throughout the set one registers that, though this has all the benefits of a studio performance in precision, it consistently reflects stage experience, never more so than in the final denouement and Lohengrin's departure. That Abbado's speeds are generally faster than Solti's (with the Act III *Prelude* a notable exception) means that the complete opera is squeezed on to three instead of four discs, giving it the clearest advantage. As Elsa, matching her earlier, Bayreuth performance on Philips, Cheryl Studer is at her sweetest and purest, bringing out the heroine's naïvety more touchingly than Jessye Norman, whose weighty, mezzo-ish tone is thrillingly rich but is more suited to portraying other Wagner heroines than this. Though there are signs that Siegfried Jerusalem's voice is not as fresh as it once was, he sings commandingly, conveying both beauty and a true Heldentenor quality. Where Plácido Domingo for Solti, producing even more beautiful tone, tends to use a full voice for such intimate solos as *In fernem Land* and *Mein lieber Schwann*, Jerusalem sings there with tender restraint and gentler tone. Among the others, Waltraud Meier as Ortrud and Kurt Moll as King Heinrich are both superb, as fine as any predecessor, and though in the role of Telramund Hartmut Welker's baritone is not ideally steady, that tends to underline the weakness of the character next to the positive Ortrud.

It is Plácido Domingo's achievement singing Lohengrin that the lyrical element blossoms so consistently, with no hint of Heldentenor barking; at whatever dynamic level, Domingo's voice is firm and unstrained. Jessye Norman, not naturally suited to the role of Elsa, yet gives a warm, commanding performance, always intense, full of detailed insights into words and character. Eva Randová's grainy mezzo does not take so readily to recording, but as Ortrud she provides a pointful contrast, even if she never matches the firm, biting malevolence of Christa Ludwig on the Kempe set. Siegmund Nimsgern, Telramund for Solti, equally falls short of Fischer-Dieskau, his rival on the Kempe set; but it is still a strong, cleanly focused performance. Fischer-Dieskau here sings the small but vital role of the Herald, while Hans Sotin makes a comparably distinctive King Henry. Radiant playing from the Vienna Philharmonic, and committed chorus work too. This is one of the crowning glories of Solti's long recording career.

The first glory of Barenboim's set is the sound, full and upfront, with the voices clearly focused and with plenty of bloom, set against a rich, incandescent orchestra. Having voices relatively close adds immediacy to the drama, and Barenboim's pacing adds warmth and often urgency, even if Elsa's dream sounds a little sluggish. Emily Magee's full, rich tone makes the heroine sound rather too mature, and the voice is not well contrasted with the Ortrud of Deborah Polaski, a soprano rather lacking the sinister chest-tones apt for this evil character, hardly conveying her full villainy. Peter Seiffert makes an outstanding Lohengrin, not as honey-toned as Wolfgang Wingassen, the Heldentenor with whom he is sometimes compared, but lyrical as well as heroic, with no hint of strain. He is at his finest in strong, incisive outbursts, not as happy in the half-tones needed for such passages as the opening of *In fernem Land*. One merit of the set is that the text is absolutely complete, including the extended solo after that Act III aria. The Telramund of Falk Strickmann is rather gritty, lacking weight, and Roman Trekel is a strained Herald, but René Pape is magnificent as the King, a fine successor to Kurt Moll.

Kempe directs a rapt account of *Lohengrin*, a fine monument to a great Wagnerian. The singers seem uplifted, Jess Thomas singing more clearly and richly than usual, Elisabeth Grümmer unrivalled as Elsa in her delicacy and sweetness, Gottlob Frick gloriously resonant as the king. But it is the partnership of Christa Ludwig and Fischer-Dieskau as Ortrud and Telramund that sets the seal on this superb performance, giving the darkest intensity to their machinations in Act II, their evil heightening the beauty and serenity of so much in this opera. Though the digital transfer on CD reveals roughness (even occasional distortion) in the original recording, the glow and intensity of Kempe's reading come out all the more involvingly in the new format. The set is also very economically contained on three CDs instead of the four for most rivals, though inevitably breaks between discs come in the middle of Acts.

Die Meistersinger von Nürnberg (complete).

*** Decca Dig. 452 606-2 (4) [id.]. Van Dam, Heppner, Mattila, Opie, Lippert, Vermillion, Pape, Chicago SO Ch. & O, Solti.

*** DG 415 278-2 (4) [id.]. Fischer-Dieskau, Ligendza, Lagger, Hermann, Domingo, Laubenthal, Ludwig, German Op. Ch. & O, Berlin, Jochum.

*** Calig CAL 50971-74 (4) [id.]. Stewart, Crass, Hemsley, Konya, Unger, Janowitz, Fassbaender, Bav. R. Ch. & O, Kubelik.

*** EMI (SIS) CDS5 55142-2 (4) [id.]. Weikl, Heppner, Studer, Moll, Lorenz, Van der Walt, Kallisch, Bav. State Op. Ch., Bav. State O, Sawallisch.

(M) (***) EMI mono CHS7 63500-2 (4) [CDHD 63500]. Schwarzkopf, Edelmann, Kunz, Hopf, Unger, Bayreuth Festival Ch. & O, Karajan.

(N) (M) **(*) EMI CMS5 67086-2 [CDMB

67148] (4) [id.]. Theo Adam, René Kollo, Helen Donath, Karl Ridderbusch, Sir Geraint Evans, Peter Schreier, Ruth Hesse, Leipzig R. Ch., Dresden State Op. Ch. & O, Karajan.

This is the only Wagner opera that Sir Georg Solti has recorded a second time, a work which 'I think I love more than anything else which Wagner wrote'. That love comes over from first to last in this glowing performance. By comparison, his earlier, Vienna recording is stiff and metrical, often fierce, with bright, upfront recording, where this new live recording, made in Orchestra Hall, Chicago, is mellower, with plenty of air round the sound, enhancing the extra warmth, relaxation and subtlety of the performance. Though speeds are often a shade faster than before, the degree of urgency also reflects the new warmth and flexibility. Central to the success of the later performance is the singing of Ben Heppner as Walther, not just heroic but clear and unstrained, ardently following Solti's urgency in the *Prize song*, a performance more beautiful than any of recent years except his own for Sawallisch. Karita Mattila sings with comparable beauty as Eva. Though she is still young, her firm, clear voice is more mature, almost mezzo-ish at times, than one expects of an Eva, and she too naturally surges forward in the great solo of the *Quintet*. For some the controversial element will be the Sachs of José van Dam, clean and sharply focused rather than weighty, not quite the wise, old, genial Sachs in his duet with Eva in Act II. This is again unconventional casting which yet brings new beauty and new revelation, as in the hushed pianissimo at the end of the *Fliedermonolog* when he tells of the bird singing. With René Pape a powerful Pogner, Alan Opie a clean-cut, unexaggerated Beckmesser with plenty of projection, and Herbert Lippert and Iris Vermillion excellent as David and Magdalene, it is a cast to rival any on disc, making this a clear recommendation if you want a digital recording.

Jochum's is a performance which, more than any, captures the light and shade of Wagner's most warmly approachable score, its humour and tenderness as well as its strength. Above all, Jochum is unerring in building long Wagnerian climaxes and resolving them – more so than his recorded rivals. The cast is the most consistent yet assembled on record. Though Caterina Ligendza's big soprano is a little ungainly for Eva, it is an appealing performance, and the choice of Domingo for Walther is inspired. The key to the set is the searching and highly individual Sachs of Fischer-Dieskau, and Horst Laubenthal's finely tuned David matches this Sachs in applying Lieder style. The recording balance favours the voices, but on CD they are made to sound slightly ahead of the orchestra. There is a lovely bloom on the whole sound and, with a recording which is basically wide-ranging and refined, the ambience brings an attractively natural projection of the singers.

The Calig issue, belatedly issued on commercial disc, offers one of the very finest performances of *Meistersinger* ever recorded, with a cast unmatched on record for its characterful consistency. It is a radio recording, made in Munich in October 1967, and the vividness of the sound is astonishing, with more realism and presence than in almost any digital recording. There is plenty of body in the orchestral and choral sound; but what above all makes the results so involving is the immediacy of the voices, placed in front of the orchestra but with plenty of bloom, so that one registers their expressions, as though face to face. Even the mêlée at the end of Act II emerges vividly. This is also one of Kubelik's most inspired recordings, incandescent in the way it builds up to the big emotional climaxes, just as in a live performance. When it comes to the casting, every single voice has been chosen not only for its firmness and clarity, with no wobbling or straining, but also for the central aptness of voice to character. It would be hard to think of a more radiant and girlish Eva than Gundula Janowitz, and the Hungarian tenor, Sandor Konya, too little heard on record, is a glowing Walther, beautiful in every register if not quite as subtle as the leading Walther today, Ben Heppner. Thomas Stewart as Hans Sachs is similarly unstrained, using his firm, dark baritone with warm expressiveness, while Thomas Hemsley has rarely been so impressive on disc, a sharp-focused Beckmesser who conveys the ironic humour but who never guys the role. Franz Crass is a fine, dark Pogner, and it would be hard to find a match for Gerhard Unger as David or Brigitte Fassbaender as Magdalene, with the upfront sound heightening their subplot. A Wagner production as consistent as this is rare, the more surprising to find in a radio recording.

Sawallisch's fine set was the first studio recording of *Meistersinger* to be made in digital sound, with ensembles of glorious warmth and fullness. Sawallisch also paces the work in reflection of his long experience of performing it in the opera house with the same musicians. Add to that the most radiant and free-toned Walther on disc, the Canadian, Ben Heppner, and you have a superb set. In tonal beauty Heppner matches Plácido Domingo on Jochum's DG set, as he does in variety of expression and feeling. Cheryl Studer's contribution is hardly less remarkable than Heppner's, at once powerful and girlishly tender, with the voice kept pure. If she is less affecting than she might be in the poignant duet with Sachs in Act II and in the great *Quintet* of Act III, that has something to do with a limitation in Sawallisch's reading, fine as it is. It rarely brings a gulp to the throat, rarely finds the poetic magic that this of all Wagner's operas can convey, and Act II, with the opening prelude too soft-grained for this buoyant music, rather lacks freshness. Bernd Weikl makes a splendid Sachs, firm and true of voice, but something of the nobility of the master-shoemaker is missing. Deon van der Walt is a strong David, clear-cut and fresh, with Cornelia Kallisch making a traditionally fruity yet firm Magdalene. Siegfried Lorenz is a well-focused Beckmesser who refuses to caricature the much-mocked Town Clerk, and Kurt Moll is a magnificent Pogner. The chorus (balanced a little backwardly) and orchestra play with the warmth and radiance associated with recordings made in the Herkulessaal in Munich.

Recorded live at the 1951 Bayreuth Festival, Karajan's EMI version has never quite been matched since for its involving intensity. The mono sound may be thin and the stage noises often distracting, but, with clean CD transfers, the sense of being present at a great event is irresistible, with the big emotional moments – both between Eva and Walther and, even more strikingly, between Eva and Sachs – bringing a gulp in the throat. The young Elisabeth Schwarzkopf makes the most radiant Eva, singing her Act III solo *O Sachs, mein Freund!* with touching ardour before beginning the Quintet with flawless legato. Hans Hopf is here less gritty than in his other recordings, an attractive hero; while Otto Edelmann makes a superb Sachs, firm and virile, the more moving for not sounding old. There are inconsistencies among the others but, in a performance of such electricity generated by the conductor in his early prime, they are of minimal importance. The four mid-priced CDs are generously indexed and come with a libretto but no translation. EMI should have indicated the index points not just in the libretto, but in the English synopsis as well.

In setting up their later star-studded stereo version, EMI fell down badly in the choice of Sachs. Theo Adam, promising in many ways, has quite the wrong voice for the part, in one way too young-sounding, in another too grating, not focused enough. However, after that keen disappointment there is much to enjoy, for in a modestly reverberant acoustic (a smallish church was used) Karajan draws from the Dresden players and chorus a rich performance which retains a degree of bourgeois intimacy. Donath is a touching, sweet-toned Eva, Kollo here is as true and ringing a Walther as one could find today, Sir Geraint Evans is an incomparably vivid Beckmesser, and Ridderbusch a glorious-toned Pogner. The current CD transfer gives a new realism and presence to a recording not especially impressive on LP. Anyone wanting a widely expansive sound will be disappointed, but Karajan's thoughtful approach and the presence of perhaps the finest Eva on any current set makes this a good choice for those who are not upset by Adam's ungenial Sachs. However whether this is one of the 'Great Recordings of the Century' is much less sure. This description might much more readily have been applied to Karajan's earlier mono version.

Parsifal (complete).

❀ *** DG Dig. 413 347-2 (4) [id.]. Hofmann, Vejzovic, Moll, Van Dam, Nimsgern, Von Halem, German Op. Ch., BPO, Karajan.

*** Teldec Dig. 9031 74448-2 (4). Jerusalem, Van Dam, Hölle, Meier, Von Kannen, Tomlinson, Berlin State Op. Ch., BPO, Barenboim.

*** Decca 417 143-2 (4) [id.]. Kollo, Ludwig, Fischer-Dieskau, Hotter, Kelemen, Frick, V. Boys' Ch., V. State Op. Ch., VPO, Solti.

Communion, musical and spiritual, is what this intensely beautiful Karajan set provides. The playing of the Berlin orchestra is consistently beautiful, enhanced by the clarity and refinement of the recording. Kurt Moll as Gurnemanz is the singer who, more than any other, anchors the work vocally, projecting his voice with firmness and subtlety. José van Dam as Amfortas is also splendid. The Klingsor of Siegmund Nimsgern could be more sinister, but the singing is admirable. Dunja Vejzovic makes a vibrant, sensuous Kundry who rises superbly to the moment in Act II when she bemoans her laughter in the face of Christ. Only Peter Hofmann as Parsifal brings any disappointment; at times he develops a gritty edge on the voice, but his natural tone is admirably suited to the part and he is never less than dramatically effective. He is not helped by the relative closeness of the solo voices, but otherwise the recording is near the atmospheric ideal, a superb achievement.

With Siegfried Jerusalem a superb Parsifal, one of the finest ever, both characterful and mellifluous, Daniel Barenboim's is a dedicated version with an excellent cast. Like Karajan, Barenboim draws glorious sounds from the Berlin Philharmonic, even if he cannot quite match his predecessor in concentrated intensity, well sustained as his control of long paragraphs is. Waltraud Meier as in rival versions is an outstanding, darkly intense Kundry, and José van Dam is superb as Amfortas, clean of attack, as he was for Karajan. John Tomlinson is a resonant, if young-sounding Titurel, and Gunther von Kannen a clear and direct, if unvillainous, even noble Klingsor. The relatively weak link is the Gurnemanz of Matthias Hölle, warm-toned but slightly unsteady, not quite in character. The four-disc format is more convenient than most, with Acts II and III each complete on a single disc.

Solti's singing cast could hardly be stronger, every one of them pointing words with fine, illuminating care for detail; and the complex balances of sound, not least in the *Good Friday music*, are beautifully caught; throughout, Solti shows his sustained intensity in Wagner. What is rather missing is a rapt, spiritual quality. The remastering for CD, as with Solti's other Wagner recordings, opens up the sound, and the choral climaxes are superb.

Das Rheingold (complete).
*** Decca 455 556-2 (2) [id.]. London, Flagstad, Svanholm, Neidlinger, VPO, Solti.
*** Teldec/Warner Dig. 4509 91185-2 (2) [id.]. Tomlinson, Brinkmann, Schreibmayer, Clark, Finnie, Johansson, Svendén, Von Kannen, Pampuch, Hölle, Kang, Liedland, Küttenbaum, Turner, (1991) Bayreuth Festival O, Barenboim.
(M) **(*) DG 457 781-2 (2). Fischer-Dieskau, Veasey, Stolze, kelemen, BPO, Karajan.
(B) **(*) RCA Dig. 74321 45418-2 (2). Adam, Nimsgern, Stryczek, Schreier, Bracht, Salminen, Vogel, Büchner, Minton, Popp, Priew, Schwarz, Dresden State O & Ch., Janowski.
(N) (BB) *(*) Arte Nova Dig. 74321 63650-2 (2). Albert Dohmen, Nadja Michael, Andrea Martin, Witold Zaladkiewicz, Arnold Bezuyen, San Carlo O, Naples, Gustav Kuhn.

The first of Solti's cycle, recorded in 1958, *Rheingold* remains a spectactular recording achievement, the more so on CD, a fine memorial to the brilliant recording producer, John Culshaw. The immediacy and precise placing are thrilling, while the sound-effects of the final scenes, including Donner's hammer-blow and the Rainbow bridge, have never been matched since. Solti gives a magnificent reading of the score, crisp, dramatic and direct. Vocally, the set is held together by the unforgettable singing of Neidlinger as Alberich. He vocalizes with wonderful precision and makes the character of the dwarf develop from the comic creature of the opening scene to the demented monster of the last. Flagstad learned the part of Fricka specially for this recording, and her singing makes one regret that she never took the role on the stage. George London is sometimes a little rough, but this is a dramatic portrayal of the young Wotan. Svanholm could be more characterful as Loge, but again it is a relief to hear the part really sung. An outstanding achievement. Newly remastered and with the original artwork restored, the set has now been fitted on to a pair of CDs (instead of three).

Barenboim's recording of the *Ring* cycle for Teldec, made during the 1991 Bayreuth Festival, may not outshine the finest of previous versions but is most welcome as easily the most involving of modern versions. When Barenboim as Wagnerian has at times seemed lethargic, what is particularly surprising is the dramatic tension of the performance. Even with slow speeds, the sense of flow carries the ear on, where neither of the two most recent rival recordings, Haitink's for EMI and Levine's for DG, ever quite lets you forget the atmosphere of the studio. Even with often-thunderous stage noises, the Barenboim performances magnetize you much more consistently, with the atmosphere of the Festspielhaus well caught by the engineers. It is very satisfying too to have on disc John Tomlinson's magnificent performance as Wotan, Graham Clark as an electrifying, dominant Loge and Linda Finnie a thoughtful, intense Fricka.

Now reissued (at upper mid-price) on two instead of three CDs, Karajan's set is a good deal more competitive than it was. Yet the conductor's reflectiveness of approach has its less welcome side, for the tension rarely varies. One finds such incidents as Alberich's stealing of the gold or Donner's hammer-blow passing by without one's pulse quickening as it should. On the credit side however, the singing cast has hardly any flaw at all, and Fischer-Dieskau's Wotan is a brilliant and memorable creation, virile and expressive. Among the others, Veasey is excellent, though obviously she cannot efface memories of Flagstad; Gerhard Stolze with his flickering almost *Sprechstimme* as Loge gives an immensely vivid, if (for some) controversial interpretation. The 1968 sound has been clarified and further opened up in the new transfer.

Janowski's distinguished *Rheingold* is now the least expensive recommendable set on CD. The studio sound, nicely ambient, has the voices close and vivid, with the orchestra in the background. If the result lacks the atmospheric qualities which make the Solti *Rheingold* still the most compelling in sound, the effect still grips the listener, though Donner's hammer-blow brings only a very ordinary anvil stroke. Theo Adam, in spite of some grittiness of tone, makes a fine Wotan and the set is consistently well cast, including Peter Schreier, Matti Salminen, Yvonne Minton and Lucia Popp, as well as East German singers of high calibre. The current transfer is very impressive and the set is very well documented.

A recommendable super-bargain version of *Rheingold* would be very welcome, but this live recording made at the Tirol festival, is very flawed. The playing of the Naples Orchestra is limp at times, failing to create dramatic tension, and though the recording is full and immediate, it is too dry to convey much atmosphere or to put bloom on the voices. Albert Dohmen is a strong, virile Wotan, but his firm baritone grows gritty under pressure; Nadja Michael is a fruity-toned Fricka, Andrea Martin is a clear, incisive Alberich, and Arnold Bezuyen a characterful, snarling Loge. Otherwise a middling cast, reliable but with few beautiful voices. Libretto in German with synopsis in English. Janowski's bargain set on RCA is well worth the extra money.

Rienzi (complete).
(M) ** EMI CMS7 67131-2 (3) [CDMB 67131]. Kollo, Wennberg, Martin, Adam, Hillebrand, Vogel, Schreier, Leipzig R. Ch., Dresden State Op. Ch., Dresden State O, Hollreiser.

It is sad that the flaws in this ambitious opera prevent the unwieldy piece from having its full dramatic impact. This recording is not quite complete, but the cuts are unimportant and most of the set numbers make plain the youthful exuberance of the ambitious composer. Except in the recitative, Heinrich Hollreiser's direction is strong and purposeful, but much of the singing is disappointing. René Kollo sounds heroic, but the two women principals are poor. Janis Martin in the breeches role of Adriano produces tone that does not record very sweetly, while Siv Wennberg as the heroine, Rienzi's sister, slides unpleasantly between notes in the florid passages. Despite good recording, this is only a stop-gap.

Der Ring des Nibelungen: an introduction to *The Ring* by Deryck Cooke, with 193 music examples.
(M) *** Decca 443 581-2 (2) [id.]. VPO, Solti.

The reissue in Decca's Classic Sound series of Deryck Cooke's fascinating and scholarly lecture is most welcome. Even though the CD reissue omits the printed text, the principal musical motives are all printed out in the accompanying booklet and they demonstrate just how the many leading ideas in *The Ring* develop from one another, springing from an original germ.

Der Ring des Nibelungen (complete).
✿ (M) *** Decca 455 555-2 (14) [id.]. Nilsson, Windgassen, Flagstad, Fischer-Dieskau, Hotter, London, Ludwig, Neidlinger, Frick, Svanholm, Stolze, Böhme, Hoffgen, Sutherland, Crespin, King, Watson, Ch. & VPO, Solti.
(B) *** Ph. 446 057-2 (14) [(M) 420 325-2]. Nilsson, Windgassen, Neidlinger, Adam, Rysanek, King, Nienstedt, Esser, Talvela, Böhme, Silja, Dernesch, Stewart, Hoeffgen, (1967) Bayreuth Festival Ch. & O, Boehm.
(B) *** EMI CZS 72731-2 (14) [id.]. Behrens, Varady, Lipovšek, Schwarz, Hale, Kollo, Wlaschiha, Schunk, Tear, Rootering, Bav. State Opera Ch. & O, Sawallisch.
(B) *** RCA Dig. 74321 45417-2 (14). Jeannine Altmeyer, René Kollo, Theo Adam, Peter Schreier, Siegmund Nimsgern, Siegfried Vogel, Yvonne Minton, Ortrun Wenkel, Matti Salminen, Lucia Popp, Siegfried Jerusalem, Jessye Norman, Kurt Moll, Cheryl Studer, Leipzig R. Ch., Dresden State Op. Ch. & O, Janowski.
(N) (M) *** DG 457 780-2 (14). Veasey, Fischer-Dieskau, Stolze, Kelemen, Dernesch, Dominguez, Jess Thomas, Stewart, Crespin, Janowitz, Vickers, Talvela, Brilioth, Ludwig, Ridderbusch, BPO, Karajan.
(M) **(*) EMI Dig. CMS7 64775-2 (14). Eva Marton, James Morris, Marjana Lipovšek, Heinz Sednik, Theo Adam, Peter Haage, Siegfried Jerusalem, Kiri Te Kanawa, Kurt Rydl, Jadwiga Rappé, Cheryl Studer, Reiner Goldberg, Waldtraud Meier, Matti Salminen, Thomas Hampson, John Tomlinson, Eva-Maria Bundschuh, Bav. R. Ch. & SO, Haitink.
(M) (***) EMI (SIS) mono CZS7 67123-2 (13). Suthaus, Mödl, Frantz, Patzak, Neidlinger, Windgassen, Konetzni, Streich, Jurinac, Frick, RAI Ch. & Rome SO, Furtwängler.

Solti's was the first recorded *Ring* cycle to be issued. Whether in performance or in vividness of sound, it remains the most electrifying account of the tetralogy on disc, sharply focused if not always as warmly expressive as some. Solti himself developed in the process of making the recording, and *Götterdämmerung* represents a peak of achievement for him, commanding and magnificent. Though CD occasionally reveals bumps and bangs inaudible on the original LPs, this is a historic set that remains as central today as when it first appeared. The latest remastering is very impressive and the layout is improved, with the set now on 14 discs. The original artwork is used throughout on the boxes.

Anyone who prefers the idea of a live recording of the *Ring* cycle can be warmly recommended to Boehm's fine set, more immediately involving than any. Recorded at the 1967 Bayreuth Festival, it captures the unique atmosphere and acoustic of the Festspielhaus very vividly. Birgit Nilsson as Brünnhilde and Wolfgang Windgassen as Siegfried are both a degree more volatile and passionate than they were in the Solti cycle. Gustav Neidlinger as Alberich is also superb, as he was too in the Solti set; and the only major reservation concerns the Wotan of Theo Adam, in a performance searchingly intense and finely detailed but often unsteady of tone even at that period. The sound, only occasionally constricted, has been vividly transferred. In the UK Philips are offering this version of the *Ring* in a 14-disc limited edition (in effect for a limited time) at bargain price. Waverers should snap this up while it is still around and before it returns to mid-price under its earlier catalogue number (420 325-2).

On 14 discs at bargain price, the Sawallisch version of the *Ring* makes an excellent recommendation. This is the sound-track of the Bavarian State Opera production by Nikolaus Lehnhoff, as recorded in 1989 for television. The cast is as fine as any in rival versions of the digital age, the performances gain in dramatic momentum and expressive spontaneity from being recorded live, and – rather surprisingly – the sound is outstandingly rich, warm and spaciously atmospheric, in many ways outshining rival digital recordings.

Hildegard Behrens may not be a weighty Brünnhilde, with some unevenness of production, but, as in Levine's DG *Ring* cycle from the Met., she rises superbly to the big challenges at the end of both

Siegfried and *Götterdammerung*. No libretto is provided, but the synopses are linked to plentiful cue-points. An excellent, keenly enjoyable set.

Dedication and consistency are the hallmarks of the RCA *Ring*, a series of studio recordings made between 1980 and 1983 with German thoroughness by the then East German record company, Eurodisc. Voices tend to be balanced well forward of the orchestra, but the digital sound is admirably full as well as clear. The clarity has one concentrating on the words, helped by Janowski's vividly direct approach to the score. Overall this is more rewarding than many of the individual sets that have been issued at full price over the years since it first appeared. The documentation is first class. The set is not available in the USA.

Karajan's version of *The Ring* is now reissued as part of DG's catalogue of Originals, with the complete set at lower mid-price and the operas all available separately, but somewhat more expensively. The DG recording originally followed close on the heels of Solti's for Decca, providing a good alternative studio version which equally stands the test of time, even if *Siegfried* has its disappointments. The manner is smoother, the speeds generally broader, yet the tension and concentration of the performances are maintained more consistently than in most modern studio recordings. Casting is not quite consistent between the operas, with Régine Crespin as Brünnhilde in *Walküre*, but Helga Dernesch at her very peak in the last two operas. The casting of Siegfried is changed between *Siegfried* and *Götterdämmerung*, from Jess Thomas to Helge Brilioth, just as strong but sweeter of tone.

Haitink recorded the *Ring* cycle in the years when he was emerging as an inspired Wagner conductor. Strong and purposeful, he takes a thoughtful view which in each music-drama nevertheless builds up unerringly in tension and power, with the beauty of Wagner's orchestration consistently brought out. The recordings are warm and full, if not as sharply defined as they might be, and the principal snags lie in some of the casting, notably with Eva Marton as Brünnhilde, too often gusty and ill-focused. Theo Adam too is a disappointing Alberich, dramatically intense but unable any longer to sustain a steady line. James Morris as Wotan is here more sympathetic than in the Levine set, dating from the same period, but he yields to other singers in the role. For the rest, a strong and compelling issue, still (arguably) technically the best studio recording of the *Ring* in digital sound, the more welcome in this 14-disc package at mid-price.

When in 1972 EMI first transferred the Italian Radio tapes of Furtwängler's studio performances of 1953, the sound was disagreeably harsh, making sustained listening unpleasant. In this digital transfer, the boxiness of the studio sound and the closeness of the voices still take away some of the unique Furtwängler glow in Wagner, but the sound is acceptable and benefits in some ways from extra clarity.

Siegfried (complete).

*** Decca 455 564-2 (4). Windgassen, Nilsson, Hotter, Stolze, Neidlinger, Böhme, Hoffgen, Sutherland, VPO, Solti.

*** Teldec/Warner Dig. 4509 94193-2 (4) [id.]. Jerusalem, Anne Evans, Tomlinson, Clark, Von Kannen, Philip King, Svendén, Leidland, (1992) Bayreuth Festival Ch. & O, Barenboim.

*** Ph. (IMS) 412 483-2 (4) [id.]. Windgassen, Nilsson, Adam, Neidlinger, Soukupová, Köth, Böhme, (1967) Bayreuth Festival Ch. & O, Boehm.

(B) *** RCA Dig. 74321 45420-2 (4). Kollo, Altmeyer, Adam Schreier, Nimsgern, Wenkel, Salminen, Sharp, Dresden State O, Janowski.

(N) (M) ** DG 457 790-2 (4). Dernesch, Dominguez, Jess Thomas, Stolze, Stewart, Kelemen, BPO, Karajan.

Siegfried has too long been thought of as the grimmest of the *Ring* cycle, but a performance as buoyant as Solti's reveals that, more than in most Wagner, the message is one of optimism. Each of the three Acts ends with a scene of triumphant joy. Solti's array of singers could hardly be bettered. Windgassen is at the very peak of his form, lyrical as well as heroic. Hotter has never been more impressive on record, his Wotan at last captured adequately. Stolze, Neidlinger and Böhme are all exemplary, and predictably Joan Sutherland makes the most seductive of woodbirds. With singing finer than any opera house could normally provide, with masterly playing from the Vienna Philharmonic and with Decca's most vivid recording, this is still unsurpassed. As with the rest of the series, the present newly remastered and enhanced CDs have cleaned up background noises.

Barenboim's live recording of *Siegfried*, made at the Bayreuth Festival in 1992, is the finest of latterday digitally recorded versions. There is no finer interpreter of the role of Mime today than Graham Clark. On disc the characterization may sometimes sound extreme, but here is a powerful, clean-cut tenor voice that makes the dwarf into an intensely compelling character. In the title-role Siegfried Jerusalem completely outshines his already fine performance on Haitink's studio recording for EMI. His voice has grown fuller and more powerful without losing any beauty, and the recording helps to give it more weight. Few Siegfrieds since Wolfgang Windgassen begin to match him, and John Tomlinson is the firmest, most darkly projected Wanderer among current rivals. You may argue that the older Wotan should not sound so virile, but Tomlinson's superb singing goes with keen musical imagination and concern for word-meaning. As for Anne Evans as Brünnhilde, she too brings out the beauty of Wagner's lines, focusing cleanly and purely, with some thrilling top notes and not a suspicion of a wobble. The fifth principal is the splendid Erda of Brigitta Svendén, with other roles cast well, if not outstandingly. But what confirms this, recorded last in the series, as the high point in Barenboim's Bayreuth cycle is the incandescence of his conducting, given extra impact by the vivid sound and consistently reflecting his experience of working with these musicians.

The natural-sounding quality of Boehm's live recording from Bayreuth, coupled with his determination not to let the music lag, makes his account of *Siegfried* as satisfying as the rest of his cycle, vividly capturing the atmosphere of the Festspielhaus, with voices well ahead of the orchestra. Windgassen is at his peak here, if anything more poetic in Acts II and III than he is in Solti's studio recording, and vocally just as fine. Nilsson, as in *Götterdämmerung*, gains over her studio recording from the extra flow of adrenalin in a live performance; and Gustav Neidlinger is unmatchable as Alberich. Erika Köth is disappointing as the woodbird, not sweet enough, and Soukupová is a positive, characterful Erda. Theo Adam is at his finest as the Wanderer, less wobbly than usual, clean and incisive.

Janowski's *Siegfried* is in almost every way impressive. The singing is generally first rate with Kollo fine in the name role, hardly ever strained, and Peter Schreier a superb Mime, using Lieder-like qualities in detailed characterization. Siegmund Nimsgern is a less characterful Alberich, but the voice is excellent, and Theo Adam concludes his portrayal of Wotan/Wanderer with his finest performance of the series. There are a few less effective moments (Act II rather scurries to a close with Siegfried in pursuit of a rather shrill woodbird in Norma Sharp), but this is a small blot on a performance that brings cumulative tension in the splendid final scene. The relative lightness of Jeannine Altmeyer's Brünnhilde comes out in this love duet, but this matters far less on record than it would in the theatre. The tenderness and femininity are most affecting, as at the entry of the idyll motif, where Janowski in his dedicated simplicity is also at his most compelling, so that the opera moves to a thrilling close, with both singers at their finest. Clear, beautifully balanced, digital sound with voices and orchestra firmly placed. At bargain price this is splendid value.

When Siegfried is outsung by Mime, it is time to complain, and though Karajan's DG set has many fine qualities – not least the Brünnhilde of Helga Dernesch – it hardly rivals the Solti or Boehm versions. Windgassen on Decca gave a classic performance, and any comparison highlights the serious shortcomings of Jess Thomas. Even when voices are balanced forward, the digital transfer helps little to make Thomas's singing as Siegfried any more acceptable. Otherwise, the vocal cast is strong, and Karajan provides the seamless playing which characterizes his performances. Recommended only to those irrevocably committed to the Karajan cycle, even though the current remastering is very successful.

Tannhäuser (Paris version; complete).

*** DG. Dig. 427 625-2 (3) [id.]. Domingo, Studer, Baltsa, Salminen, Schmidt, Ch. & Philh. O, Sinopoli.

*** Decca 414 581-2 (3) [id.]. Kollo, Dernesch, Ludwig, Sotin, Braun, Hollweg, V. State Op. Ch., VPO, Solti.

Plácido Domingo as Tannhäuser for Sinopoli brings balm to ears wounded by the general run of German heroic tenors, producing sounds of much power as well as beauty. Sinopoli here makes one of his most passionately committed opera recordings, warmer and more flexible than Solti's Decca version, always individual, with fine detail brought out, always persuasively, and never wilful. Agnes Baltsa is not ideally opulent of tone as Venus, but she is the complete seductress. Cheryl Studer – who sang the role of Elisabeth for Sinopoli at Bayreuth – gives a most sensitive performance, not always ideally even of tone but creating a movingly intense portrait of the heroine, vulnerable and very feminine. Matti Salminen in one of his last recordings makes a superb Landgrave and Andreas Schmidt a noble Wolfram, even though the legato could be smoother in *O star of Eve*.

Solti gives one of his very finest Wagner performances to date, helped by superb playing from the Vienna Philharmonic and an outstanding cast, superlatively recorded. Dernesch as Elisabeth and Ludwig as Venus outshine all rivals; and Kollo, though not ideal, makes as fine a Heldentenor as we are currently likely to hear. The compact disc transfer reinforces the brilliance and richness of the performance. The sound is outstanding for its period (1971), and Ray Minshull's production adds to the atmospheric intensity.

Tristan und Isolde (complete).

(M) *** EMI CMS7 69319-2 (4) [Ang. CDMD 69319]. Vickers, Dernesch, Ludwig, Berry, Ridderbusch, German Op. Ch., Berlin, BPO, Karajan.

*** Teldec/Warner Dig. 4509 94568-2 (4). Meier, Jerusalem, Lipovšek, Salminen, Struckmann, Berlin State Op. Ch., BPO, Barenboim.

(M) *** DG 449 772-2 (3) [id.]. Windgassen, Nilsson, Ludwig, Talvela, Waechter, Bayreuth Festival (1966) Ch. & O, Boehm.

(M) *** Decca (IMS) 430 234-2 (4) [id.]. Uhl, Nilsson, Resnik, Van Mill, Krause, VPO, Solti.

(***) EMI mono CDS5 56254-2 (4) [Ang. CDC56254]. Suthaus, Flagstad, Thebom,

Greindl, Fischer-Dieskau, ROHCG Ch., Philh. O, Furtwängler.

Karajan's is a sensual performance of Wagner's masterpiece, caressingly beautiful and with superbly refined playing from the Berlin Philharmonic. Dernesch as Isolde is seductively feminine, not as noble as Flagstad, not as tough and unflinching as Nilsson; but the human quality makes this account if anything more moving still, helped by glorious tone-colour through every range. Jon Vickers matches her in what is arguably his finest performance on record, allowing himself true pianissimo shading. The rest of the cast is excellent too. The recording has been remastered again for the present reissue and the 1972 sound has plenty of body, making this an excellent first choice, with inspired conducting and the most satisfactory cast of all. The set has also been attractively repackaged.

Daniel Barenboim follows up his live recording of the *Ring* cycle, made at Bayreuth, with this glowing account of *Tristan*, recorded in opulent sound under studio conditions in the Philharmonie. As a Furtwängler devotee, Barenboim has learnt much from that master's classic recording, and Act I is comparably spacious. After that the urgency of the drama prompts speeds that move forward more readily than Furtwängler's. The cast is an exceptionally strong one, with Waltraud Meier as Isolde graduating from mezzo soprano to full soprano, breasting the top Cs easily, showing no sign of strain, and bringing a weight and intensity to the role that reflect her earlier experience. The vibrato sometimes grows obtrusive, and even in the final *Liebestod* there is a touch of rawness under pressure; but the feeling for line is masterly, always with words vividly expressed. Siegfried Jerusalem, with a more beautiful voice than most latterday Heldentenoren, makes a predictably fine Tristan, not quite as smooth of tone as he once was and conveying the poignancy of the hero's plight in Act III rather than his suffering. Marjana Lipovšek is among the most characterful of Brangänes, strong and vehement, while Matti Salminen is a resonant, moving King Mark. Only the gritty tones of Falk Struckmann as Kurwenal fall short. With weighty, full-ranging and well-balanced sound, this is a first-rate recommendation for a modern digital set.

Boehm's Bayreuth performance offers one great benefit in presenting this without any breaks at all, with each Act uninterrupted. Boehm is on the urgent side in this opera and the orchestral ensemble is not always immaculate; but the performance glows with intensity from beginning to end, carried through in the longest spans. Birgit Nilsson sings the *Liebestod* at the end of the long evening as though she was starting out afresh, radiant and with not a hint of tiredness, rising to an orgasmic climax and bringing a heavenly pianissimo on the final rising octave to F sharp. Opposite Nilsson is Wolfgang Windgassen, the most mellifluous of Heldentenoren; though the microphone balance sometimes puts him at a disadvantage to his Isolde, the realism and sense of presence of the whole set bathes you in the authentic atmosphere of Bayreuth. Making up an almost unmatchable cast are Christa Ludwig as Brangaene, Eberhard Waechter as Kurwenal, and Martti Talvela as King Mark, with the young Peter Schreier as the Young Sailor. The remastering for DG's 'Originals' series has further refined the CD transfer.

Solti's performance is less flexible and sensuous than Karajan's, but he shows himself ready to relax in Wagner's more expansive periods. On the other hand the end of Act I and the opening of the Love duet have a knife-edged dramatic tension. Nilsson is masterly in her conviction and she never attacks below the note, so that at the end of the Love duet the impossibly difficult top Cs come out and hit the listener crisply and cleanly, dead on the note; and the *Liebestod* is all the more moving for clean attack at the climax. Fritz Uhl is a sensitive Heldentenor, rather lightweight, but his long solo passages in Act III are superb. The Kurwenal of Tom Krause and the King Mark of Arnold van Mill are both excellent and it is only Regina Resnik as Brangäne who gives any disappointment. The production has the usual Decca/Culshaw imaginative touch, and the recording matches brilliance and clarity with satisfying co-ordination and richness.

Wilhelm Furtwängler's concept is spacious from the opening *Prelude* onwards, but equally the bite and colour of the drama are vividly conveyed, matching the nobility of Flagstad's portrait of Isolde. The richly commanding power of her singing and her always distinctive timbre make it a uniquely compelling performance. Suthaus is not of the same calibre as Heldentenor, but he avoids ugliness and strain. Among the others, the only remarkable performance comes from the young Fischer-Dieskau as Kurwenal, not ideally cast but keenly imaginative. One endearing oddity is that – on Flagstad's insistence – the top Cs at the opening of the Love duet were sung by Elisabeth Schwarzkopf. The Kingsway Hall recording was admirably balanced, catching the beauty of the Philharmonia Orchestra at its peak. The CDs have opened up the original mono sound and it is remarkable how little constriction there is in the biggest climaxes, mostly shown in the *fortissimo* violins above the stave.

Die Walküre (complete).

*** Ph. (IMS) 412 478-2 (4). King, Rysanek, Nienstedt, Nilsson, Adam, Burmeister, (1967) Bayreuth Festival Ch. & O, Boehm.

*** Decca 455 559-2 (4) [id.]. Nilsson, Crespin, Ludwig, King, Hotter, Frick, VPO, Solti.

*** Teldec/Warner Dig. 4509 91186-2 (4). Elming, Hölle, Tomlinson, Secunde, A. Evans, Finnie, Johansson, Floeren, Close, (1992) Bayreuth Festival O, Barenboim.

(M) (***) EMI (SIS) mono CHS7 63045-2 (3). Mödl, Rysanek, Frantz, Suthaus, Klose, Frick, VPO, Furtwängler.

(B) *** RCA Dig. 74321 45419-2 (4). Altmeyer, Norman, Minton, Jerusalem, Adam, Moll, Dresden State O, Janowski.

(N) (M) **(*) DG 457 785-2 (4). Crespin, Janowitz, Veasey, Vickers, Stewart, Talvela, BPO, Karajan.

(N) ** Decca Dig. 440 371-2 (4) [id.]. Poul Elming, Alessandra Marc, Gabriele Schnaut, Robert Hale, Alfred Muff, Anja Silja, Karin Goltz, Cleveland O, Christoph von Dohnányi.

Rarely if ever does Boehm's preference for fast speeds undermine the music; on the contrary, it adds to the involvement of the performance, which never loses its concentration. Theo Adam is in firmer voice here as Wotan than he is in *Rheingold*, hardly sweet of tone but always singing with keen intelligence. As ever, Nilsson is in superb voice as Brünnhilde. Though the inevitable noises of a live performance occasionally intrude, this presents a more involving experience than any rival complete recording. The CD transfer transforms what on LP seemed a rough recording, even if passages of heavy orchestration still bring some constriction of sound.

Solti sees Act II as the kernel of the work, with the conflict of wills between Wotan and Fricka making for one of Wagner's most deeply searching scenes. That is the more apparent when the greatest of latterday Wotans, Hans Hotter, takes the role, and Christa Ludwig sings with searing dramatic sense as his wife. Before that, Act I seems a little underplayed. This is partly because of Solti's deliberate lyricism – apt enough when love and spring greetings are in the air – but also (on the debit side) because James King fails both to project the character of Siegmund and to delve into the word-meanings as all the other members of the cast consistently do. As Sieglinde Crespin has never sung more beautifully on record. As for Nilsson's Brünnhilde, it has grown mellower, the emotions are clearer. Newly remastered, the sound is more vivid than ever and the layout is admirable. The original artwork is used on the box.

Barenboim's reading of *Die Walküre* is the most involving of modern versions, with orchestra and soloists after four years of the same production totally in sympathy. Barenboim's control of dramatic tension is masterly. Even with characteristically slow speeds, the results are magnetic. Consistently there is a natural sense of flow so that, despite intrusive stage noises, Barenboim compels attention from first to last. It could not be more welcome to have on disc John Tomlinson's magnificent performance as Wotan, even more demanding in *Walküre* than in *Rheingold*. The other British singer who stands out in this opera is Anne Evans, showing her paces on disc as a radiant Brünnhilde. Maybe she is not as powerful as such loud ladies as Eva Marton and Hildegard Behrens, but she is far truer and clearer in focusing notes, singing with more expressive variety. With Barenboim conveying the full emotional thrust, the final duet between Brünnhilde and Wotan has rarely been so moving on disc. Also outstanding is the Danish tenor, Poul Elming, as Siegmund. Again the Bayreuth atmosphere is very well caught.

Furtwängler, an excellent cast and the Vienna Philharmonic in radiant form match any of their successors. Ludwig Suthaus proves a satisfyingly clear-toned Heldentenor, never strained, with the lyricism of *Wintersturme* superbly sustained. Neither Léonie Rysanek as Sieglinde nor Martha Mödl as Brünnhilde is ideally steady, but the intensity and involvement of each is irresistible, classic performances both. Similarly, the mezzo of Margarete Klose may not be very beautiful, but the projection of words and the fire-eating character match the conductor's intensity. Gottlob Frick is as near an ideal Hunding as one will find, sinister but with the right streak of arrogant sexuality; while the Wotan of Ferdinand Frantz may not be as deeply perceptive as some, but to hear the sweep of Wagner's melodic lines so gloriously sung is a rare joy. The 1954 sound is amazingly full and vivid, with voices cleanly balanced against the inspired orchestra. The only snag of the set is that, to fit the whole piece on to only three CDs, breaks between discs come in mid-Act.

As in the rest of the tetralogy, in *Die Walküre* Janowski's direct approach matches the clarity of the recording, with voices well forward of the orchestra but not aggressively so. The balance allows full glory for the singing from a satisfyingly consistent cast. Jessye Norman might not seem an obvious choice for Sieglinde, but the sound is glorious, the expression intense and detailed, making her a fine match for the good if less imaginative Siegmund of Siegfried Jerusalem. The one snag from so commanding a Sieglinde is that she dramatically overtops the Brünnhilde of Jeannine Altmeyer, who yet conveys a touching measure of feminine vulnerability in the leading Valkyrie, even in her godhead days. The beauty and the frequent sensuousness of her singing are the more telling against the strong, gritty Wotan of Theo Adam, and the illumination of the narrative is consistent and intense, well supported by Janowski with surges of orchestral tone, especially in the great closing duet with the fire music which ends the opera, in which Adam sings so tenderly that one almost forgets his slow vibrato. Kurt Moll is a gloriously firm Hunding, and Yvonne Minton a searingly effective Fricka. Very satisfyingly transferred to CD, this makes a splendid bargain.

The great merits of Karajan's version are the refinement of the orchestral playing and the heroic strength of Jon Vickers as Siegmund. With that underlined, one cannot help but note that the vocal shortcomings here are generally more marked, and the total result does not add up to quite so compelling a dramatic experience: one is less involved. Thomas Stewart may have a younger, firmer voice than Hotter, but the character of Wotan emerges only partially; it is not just that he misses some of the word-meaning, but that on occasion – as in the kissing away of Brünnhilde's godhead – he underlines too crudely. Josephine Veasey as Fricka conveys the biting intensity of the part. Gundula Janowitz's Sieglinde has its beautiful moments, but it is not a dynamic performance. Crespin's Brünnhilde is impressive, but nothing like as satisfying as her study of Sieglinde on the Decca set. The DG recording is very good, but not quite in the same class as the Decca, though with the current remastering the sound is warmer and fuller, and the lightness of bass is less noticeable.

Die Walküre: Act III (complete).
(M) *** Decca 448 575-2 [id.]. Flagstad, Edelmann, Schech, VPO, Solti.

The Solti recording was made in 1957. Flagstad came out of retirement to make it, and Decca put us in their debt for urging her to do so. She sings radiantly. The meticulousness needed in the recording studio brought out all her finest qualities, and there is no more than a touch of hardness on some of the top notes to show that the voice was no longer as young as it had been. Edelmann is not the ideal Wotan, but he has a firm, well-focused voice, singing straight, without sliding up or sitting under the note. But it is Solti's conducting that prevents any slight blemishes from mattering. The recording too is remarkably vivid, anticipating the excellence of the great *Ring* project which was to follow, and so makes a good choice for reissue in Decca's 'Classic Sound' series.

VOCAL COLLECTIONS

(i) *Der fliegende Holländer: Overture.* (ii) *Götterdämmerung*; *Siegfried's funeral music*; (ii; iii; iv) *Immolation scene.* (ii; v) *Lohengrin: Prelude to Act III; Bridal chorus.* (i) *Die Meistersinger: Prelude to Act III.* (ii; vi) *Siegfried: Forest murmurs.* (ii; vii) *Tannhäuser: Pilgrim's chorus.* (ii; iii) *Tristan und Isolde: Liebestod.* (ii) *Die Walküre: Ride of the Valkyries.*
(N) (M) *** Penguin Classics Decca 460 610-2 [id.]. (i) Chicago SO; (ii) VPO; (iii) Nilsson; (iv) Frick); (v) V. State. Op. Konzertvereinigung; (vi) Windgassen; (vii) V, State Op. Ch., Solti.

This well-organized, often very gripping, and (it hardly needs saying) very well-recorded collection, is essentially a sampler of Solti's Wagner – often showing him at his very best. The vocal excerpts come from his superb complete recordings, and this means they usually have to be judiciously faded at the end, although Birgit Nilsson's superb *Liebestod* from *Tristan* has a closing cadence, and of course the *Immolation scene* from *Götterdämmerung* is the masterful climax of *The Ring*. But never mind if these are 'bleeding chunks': the *Ride of the Valkyries* is so much more effective when heard with the voices of Wotan's formidable brood, and even *Forest murmurs* from *Siegfried* (often played as an orchestral piece) here has a warmly lyrical contribution from Wolfgang Windgassen. The only snag, and it is a considerable one, is the inadequate documentation. The author's note (from Paul Johnson) concentrates on the sensuality and impact of Wagner's sound world and perhaps that is enough: this music certainly makes a huge impact on the listener, even with limited knowledge of what these artists are being so passionate about!

'Wagner singing on record': Excerpts from: (i) *Der fliegende Holländer;* (ii) *Götterdämmerung;* (iii) *Lohengrin;* (iv) *Die Meistersinger von Nürnberg;* (v) *Parsifal;* (vi) *Das Rheingold;* (vii) *Siegfried;* (viii) *Tannhäuser;* (ix) *Tristan und Isolde;* (x) *Die Walküre.*
(M) (***) EMI mono/stereo CMS7 640082 (4) [id.]. (i) Hermann, Nissen, Endrèze, Fuchs, Beckmann, Rethberg, Nilsson, Hotter; (ii) Austral, Widdop, List, Weber, Janssen, Lawrence; (iii) Rethberg, Pertil, Singher, Lawrence, Spani, Lehmann, Lemnitz, Klose, Wittrisch, Rosavaenge; (iv) Schorr, Thill, Martinelli, Bockelmann, Parr, Williams, Ralf, Lemnitz; (v) Leider, Kipnitz, Wolff; (vi) Schorr; (vii) Nissen, Olszewska, Schipper, Leider, Laubenthal, Lubin; (viii) Müller, Lorenz, Janssen, Hüsch, Flagstad; (ix) Leider, Marherr, Larsen-Todsen, Helm, Melchior, Seinemeyer, Lorenz; (x) Lawrence, Journet, Bockelmann.

This collection, compiled in Paris as '*Les Introuvables du Chant Wagnerien*', contains an amazing array of recordings made in the later years of 78-r.p.m. recording, mostly between 1927 and 1940. In 49 items, many of them substantial, the collection consistently demonstrates the reliability of the Wagner singing at that period, the ability of singers in every register to produce firm, well-focused tone of a kind too rare today. Some of the most interesting items are those in translation from French sources, with Germaine Lubin as Isolde and Brünnhilde and with Marcel Journet as Wotan, both lyrical and clean-cut. The ill-starred Marjorie Lawrence, a great favourite in France, is also represented by recordings in French, including Brünnhilde's Immolation scene from *Götterdämmerung*. Not only are such celebrated Wagnerians as Lauritz Melchior, Friedrich Schorr, Frida Leider, Lotte Lehmann and Max Lorenz very well represented, but also singers one might not expect, including the Lieder specialist,

Gerhard Husch, as Wolfram in *Tannhäuser* and Aureliano Pertile singing in Italian as *Lohengrin*. Meta Seinemeyer, an enchanting soprano who died tragically young, here gives lyric sweetness to the dramatic roles of Brünnhilde and Isolde; and among the baritones and basses there is none of the roughness or ill-focus that marks so much latter-day Wagner singing. It is a pity that British-based singers are poorly represented, but the Prologue duet from *Götterdämmerung* brings one of the most impressive items, sung by Florence Austral and Walter Widdop. First-rate transfers and good documentation.

Waldteufel, Emile (1837–1915)

Polkas: *Les Bohémiens; Retour des champs; Tout ou rien*. Waltzes: *Ange d'amour; Dans des nuages; España; Fontaine lumineuse; Je t'aime; Tout-Paris*.
** Marco Polo Dig. 8.223438 [id.]. Slovak State PO (Košler), Alfred Walter.

Polkas: *Camarade; Dans les bois; Jeu d'esprit*. Waltzes: *Bien aimés; Chantilly; Dans tes yeux; Estudiantina; Hommage aux dames; Les Patineurs*.
** Marco Polo Dig. 8.223433 [id.]. Slovak State PO (Košice), Walter.

Polkas: *L'esprit français; Par-ci, par-là; Zig-zag*. Waltzes: *Hébé; Les Fleurs; Fleurs et baisers; Solitude; Toujours ou jamais; Toujours fidèle*.
**(*) Marco Polo Dig. 8.223450 [id.]. Slovak State PO (Košice), Walter.

Invitation à la gavotte; Polkas: *Joyeux Paris; Ma Voisine*. Waltzes: *Pluie de diamants; Les Sirènes; Les Sourires; Soirée d'été; Très jolie; Tout en rose*.
** Marco Polo Dig. 8.223441 [id.]. Slovak State PO (Košice), Alfred Walter.

Béobile pizzicato. Polka-mazurka: *Bella*. Polka: *Château en Espagne*. Waltzes: *Acclamations; La barcarolle; Brune ou blonde; Flots de joie; Gaîté; Tout à vous*.
**(*) Marco Polo Dig. 8.223684 [id.]. Slovak State PO (Košice), Alfred Walter.

Grand vitesse galop. Mazurka: *Souveraine*. Polka: *Les folies*. Waltzes: *Amour et printemps; Dolorès; Mello; Mon rêve; Pomone; Sous la voûte étoilée*.
** Marco Polo Dig. 8.223451 [id.]. Slovak State PO (Košice), Alfred Walter.

Galop: *Prestissimo*. Polkas: *Bella bocca; Nuée d'oiseaux*. Waltzes: *Au revoir; Coquetterie; Jeunesse dorée; Un premier bouquet; Rêverie; Trésor d'amour*.
**(*) Marco Polo Dig. 8. 223685 [id.]. Slovak State PO (Košice), Alfred Walter.

Grand Galop du chemin de fer; Polkas: *Désirée; Jou-jou* (all arr. Christian Pollack). Waltzes: *Le Berceuse; Entre nous; Illusion; Joie envolée; Mariana; Sur le plage*.
(N) *** Marco Polo Dig. 8.223686 [id.]. Slovak State PO (Košice), Alfred Walter.

Waldteufel's music, if not matching that of the Strauss family in range and expressive depth, has grace and charm and is prettily scored in the way of French ballet music. Moreover its lilt is undeniably infectious. The most famous waltz, *Les Patineurs*, is mirrored in style here by many of the others (*Dans les nuages*, for instance), and there are plenty of good tunes. *Plus de diamants*, with lots of vitality, is among the more familiar items, as is the sparkling *Très jolie*, but many of the unknown pieces are equally engaging. Like Strauss, Waldteufel usually introduces his waltzes with a section not in waltz-time, and he is ever resourceful in his ideas and in his orchestration. The polkas are robust, but the scoring has plenty of character.

Waltzes: *Acclamations; España; Estudiantina; Les Patineurs*.
(M) *** EMI CDM7 63136-2. Monte Carlo Nat. Op. O, Boskovsky – OFFENBACH: *Gaîté parisienne*. **

Boskovsky's collection has the advantage of including, besides the three favourites, *Acclamations*, which he opens very invitingly. His manner is *echt*-Viennese, but *The Skaters* responds well to his warmth and there is no lack of sparkle here. The remastering of the mid-1970s recording is admirably fresh.

Wallace, William (1860–1940)

Symphonic poems Nos. 1, The Passing of Beatrice; 3, Sister Helen; 5, Sir William Wallace; 6, Villon.
*** Hyperion Dig. CDA 66848 [id.]. BBC Scottish SO, Martyn Brabbins.

This highly enjoyable Hyperion collection is something of a surprise. Like Hamish McCunn, William Wallace was born in Greenock, near Glasgow. The fifth of his symphonic poems was premièred at Sir Henry Wood's Queen's Hall Promenade Concerts in 1905, only a month after the 600th anniversary of the death of his eponymous Scottish hero, whose name has recently been made famous again by the film, *Braveheart*. The composition's full title is *Sir William Wallace, Scottish hero, freedom-fighter, beheaded and dismembered by the English*. The music is not as melodramatic as it sounds. Its Scottish character is immediately obvious at the brooding opening; the main theme, 'Scots wha' hae', emerges only slowly but is celebrated more openly towards the end of a piece which does not close with triumphant celebration, as there was nothing triumphant about the hero's fate. *Villon*, an irreverent medieval poet, was a hero of a different kind, and Wallace's programme draws on the thoughts of his philosophical ballads (which are named in the synopsis) in music which is both reflective and vividly colourful. The very romantic *Passing of Beatrice* is a sensuous vision of Paradise, lusciously Wagnerian with an unashamedly Tristanesque close, reflecting the heroine's final transformation. The final piece here is based on Rossetti and its full title is *Sister Helen, Villainess, murdering by sorcery; insane with jealous and frustrated love*. What is so remarkable is not only the quality of the musical material throughout these works, but also the composer's skill and confidence in handling it: they are musically every bit as well crafted as the symphonic poems of Liszt. Clearly the BBC Scottish Symphony Orchestra enjoy playing them, and Martyn Brabbins shapes the musical episodes skilfully to balance the warm lyricism and drama without becoming too histrionically melodramatic. The result is remarkably satisfying.

Wallace, William Vincent (1812–65)

Maritana (opera; complete).

**(*) Marco Polo Dig. 8.223406-7 [id.]. Cullagh, Lee, Clarke, Caddy, RTE Philharmonic Choir and Concert O, O Duinn.

Along with Balfe's *Bohemian Girl* and Benedict's *Lily of Killarney*, Wallace's *Maritana* marked a breakthrough in opera in Britain, and it held the stage for over 50 years. This lively recording, with Irish artists celebrating this nineteenth-century Irish composer, helps to explain the work's attractions, regularly reminding the modern listener of Gilbert and Sullivan. The big difference is that where G & S present a parody of grand opera, with tongue firmly in cheek, Wallace is intensely serious, with the big melodramatic moments quickly becoming unintentionally comic. To compound the similarity with G & S, the story, like that of the *Yeomen of the Guard*, depends on the heroine, by contract, marrying a man condemned to death who then escapes his punishment. What matters is that there are many more good tunes than that of the still-remembered aria for the heroine, *Scenes that are brightest*, and the ensembles in this winning performance are always fresh and lively. The soloists too all have voices which focus cleanly, even if they are not specially distinctive. The recording is bright and forwardly balanced, with words crystal clear. Worth investigating as a period piece.

Walton, William (1902–83)

(i) *Anniversary fanfare; Coronation marches: Crown imperial; Orb and sceptre;* (ii; v) *Cello concerto;* (v) *Symphony No. 1 in B flat min.;* (iii–v) *Belshazzar's feast;* (iv; v) *Coronation Te Deum*.

(N) (B) ** Chandos 2-for-1 Analogue/Dig. 241-10 (2) [id.]. (i) Philh. O, Willcocks; (ii) Kirshbaum; (iii) Milnes; (iv) RSNO Ch.; (v) RSNO, Gibson.

Sir David Willcocks conducts performances of the two *Coronation marches* full of panache, with the brass superbly articulated and inner detail well caught. The *Anniversary fanfare* is designed to lead directly into *Orb and sceptre*, which is what it does here. However the Kirshbaum/Gibson reading of the *Cello concerto* is disappointing, lacking the warmth, weight and expressiveness that so ripe an example of late romanticism demands. And while Gibson's is a well-paced, convincingly idiomatic view of the *First Symphony*, ensemble is not always bitingly precise enough for this darkly intense music (malice prescribed for the Scherzo, melancholy for the slow movement). Recording first rate, but with less body than usual from Chandos and with timpani resonantly obtrusive. Gibson's view of Walton's brilliant oratorio *Belshazzar's feast* tends towards brisk speeds, but is no less dramatic for that. It remains individually competitive, particularly with so magnificent a baritone as Sherrill Milnes as soloist, but overall this is not one of the more enticing issues in Chandos's 2-for-1 series.

Anniversary fanfare; Crown imperial; March for the history of the English-speaking peoples; Orb and sceptre; A Queen's fanfare; (i) *Antiphon; 4 Christmas carols: All this time; King Herod and his cock; Make we now this feast; What cheer?. In honour of the City of London; Jubilate Deo; Where does the uttered music go?.*

*** Chandos Dig. CHAN 8998 [id.]. (i) Bach Ch.; Philh. O, Willcocks.

Sir David Willcocks conducts performances of the two *Coronation marches* full of panache, with the brass superbly articulated and inner detail well caught. Also the *March for the history of the English-speaking peoples*. The *a cappella* choral items are very well done too, if less intimately than on the Conifer disc of Walton choral music from Trinity College Choir. With the original organ parts orchestrated, the *Jubilate* and *Antiphon* gain greatly from having full instrumental accompaniment. The brief fanfares, never previously recorded, are a welcome makeweight, with the *Anniversary fanfare*, designed to lead directly into *Orb and sceptre*, which is what it does here.

Capriccio burlesco; The First shoot (orch. Palmer); *Granada* (Prelude for orchestra); *Johannesburg festival overture; Music for children. Galop finale* (orch. Palmer); *Portsmouth Point: overture; Prologo e fantasia; Scapino.*

*** Chandos Dig. CHAN 8968 [id.]. LPO, Bryden Thomson.

The *Capriccio burlesco* is ravishingly orchestrated, with some apt echoes of Gershwin, and the *Prologo e fantasia* completes an American group. The *Granada* Prelude, written for the television company, taps Walton's patriotic march vein in a jaunty way. *The First shoot* comes in Christopher Palmer's brilliant orchestration of the brass band suite. The opening *Giocoso* is a re-run of *Old Sir Faulk*, and the other movements bring more echoes of *Façade*. As for the other novelty, the ten brief movements of *Music for children* are here supplemented by a *Galop finale*. Palmer has here orchestrated the piano score. Though the opulent Chandos recording tends to take some of the bite away from Walton's jazzily accented writing, the richness of the orchestral sound is consistently satisfying.

Cello concerto.

(N) *** Ph. Dig. 454 442-2 [id.]. Julian Lloyd Webber, ASMF, Marriner – BRITTEN: *Symphony for cello and orchestra, Op. 68.* ***

(M) *** Sony Dig. SMK 53333 [SK 39451]. Yo-Yo Ma, LSO, Previn – ELGAR: *Cello concerto.* ***

(BB) *** RCA Navigator 74321 29248-2. Piatigorsky, Boston SO, Munch – VAUGHAN WILLIAMS: *Sinfonia Antartica.* ***

(M) *** RCA 09026 61498-2. Piatigorsky, Boston SO, Munch – DVORAK: *Concerto.* **(*)

(N) **(*) RCA Dig. 09026 61695-2 [id.]. Janos Starker, Philharmonia Orch, Slatkin – DELIUS: *Caprice & Elegy* ***; ELGAR: *Cello concerto.* **(*)

Though Walton's *Cello concerto*, written for Piatigorsky, and Britten's tough and gritty *Cello Symphony*, written for Rostropovich, are strongly contrasted in mood and style, Julian Lloyd Webber in a unique coupling, passionately performed, draws fascinating parallels. Helped by sumptuous recording, his reading of the Walton firmly establishes this as a worthy counterpart to Walton's two pre-war *concerto* masterpieces for viola and violin, bringing out the beauty as well as the romantic warmth, helped by fine playing from Marriner and the Academy.

Yo-Yo Ma and Previn give a sensuously beautiful performance. With speeds markedly slower than usual in the outer movements, the meditation is intensified to bring a mood of ecstasy, quite distinct from other Walton, with the central allegro becoming the symphonic kernel of the work, far more than just a scherzo. In the excellent CBS recording, the soloist is less forwardly and more faithfully balanced than is common.

The *Cello concerto* was written for Piatigorsky and he plays it with a gripping combination of full-blooded eloquence and subtlety of feeling, readily capturing the bitter-sweet melancholy of its flowing lyrical lines. The closing pages of the final variations are particularly haunting. Munch provides a totally understanding accompaniment, with the strings of the Boston Symphony finding the lyrical ecstasy which is such a distinctive part of this concerto. The 1957 recording is close, but the improvement of the CD over the old LP is enormous, and the ambience of Symphony Hall is much more apparent than before. This performance is also available coupled to Previn's fine account of Vaughan Williams's *Sinfonia Antartica* on RCA's bargain Navigator label.

Janos Starker, not usually associated with British music, here takes a relatively tough, objective view of the romantic Walton work, superficially cooler but with emotion clearly implied. Playing with his characteristically firm, slightly wiry tone, he provides a clear alternative for those who resist a freely expressive approach. The Delius miniature makes a welcome bonus to the apt Walton/Elgar coupling.

(i; ii) *Cello concerto;* (ii) *Improvisations on an impromptu of Benjamin Britten; Partita for orchestra;* (i) *Passacaglia for solo cello.*

*** Chandos Dig. CHAN 8959 [id.]. (i) Raphael Wallfisch; (ii) LPO, Bryden Thomson.

With his rich, even tone, Wallfisch is just as warm and purposeful in the solo *Passacaglia* as in the *Concerto*, while Thomson relishes the vivid orchestral colours in both the *Improvisations*, here wider-ranging in expression than usual, and the brilliant *Partita*. Excellent Chandos sound.

Viola concerto.

(N) *** RCA Dig. 09026 63292-2 [id.]. Yuri Bashmet, LSO, Previn – BRUCH: *Concerto for violin and viola; Kol Nidrei; Romance.* ***

Yuri Bashmet with his opulent viola tone warmly relishes the ripe romanticism of the Walton concerto as well as the high-voltage electricity of its jazz-based writing. Like other latterday interpreters he opts for a daringly spacious speed for the haunting opening melody, but avoids any hint of sluggishness, relishing the bravura of the contrasting sections. The central scherzo brings a dazzling display, with the fun of the scherzando passages winningly brought out, as it is too in the finale. Bashmet ends with another daringly slow speed for the wistful epilogue, again superbly sustained, thanks also to the ideal accompaniment of Previn and the LSO. First-rate sound. The coupling may seem odd, but all three Bruch works will delight anyone who enjoys romantic viola music.

Viola concerto; Violin concerto.

*** EMI Dig. CDC7 49628-2 [id.]. Kennedy, RPO, Previn.

Kennedy's achievement in giving equally rich and expressive performances of both works makes for an ideal coupling, helped by the unique insight of André Previn as Waltonian. Kennedy on the viola produces tone as rich and firm as on his usual violin. The scherzo has never been recorded with more panache than here, and the finale brings a magic moment in the return of the main theme from the opening, hushed and intense. In the *Violin concerto* too, Kennedy gives a warmly relaxed reading, in which he dashes off the bravura passages with great flair. He may miss some of the more searchingly introspective manner of Chung in her 1971 version, but there are few Walton records as richly rewarding as this, helped by warm, atmospheric sound.

(i) *Viola concerto. Johannesburg festival overture; Symphony No. 2.*
(BB) *** Naxos Dig. 8.553402 [id.]. (i) Tomter; E. N. Philh. O, Paul Daniel.

With Paul Daniel drawing brilliantly pointed, keenly idiomatic playing from the English Northern Philharmonia, this first of the Naxos Walton series could not be more promising, helped by warm, clear and well-balanced recording. Pride of place goes to the thoughtful, deeply felt reading of the *Viola concerto* with the Norwegian viola-player, Lars Anders Tomter. Though Tomter's tight vibrato is at times prominent, he brings out the tender poetry of this most elusive of Walton's string concertos, with its mixture of melancholy and wit. More than others, Tomter observes pianissimo markings, and rightly he adopts a flowing speed for the first movement while refusing to be rushed in the Scherzo and finale, which with delectable pointing acquire extra scherzando sparkle. The overture is given the most exuberant performance, rivalling the composer's own, with the orchestra's soloists playing brilliantly. In the *Symphony No. 2* Daniel gives extra transparency to the often heavy orchestration, making the work less weighty than usual but just as warmly expressive. A superb bargain.

(i) *Viola concerto; Sonata for string orchestra; Variations on a theme of Hindemith.*
*** Chandos Dig. CHAN 9106 [id.]. (i) Nobuko Imai; LPO, Jan Latham-Koenig.

Imai is satisfyingly firm and true in all her playing, keenly confident in the virtuoso passages, with the central Scherzo not at all breathless-sounding. Imai uses a very broad *Andante* to bring out the full lyrical warmth, but it means that the following bravura section enters with a jolt rather than developing naturally. The movement is not helped either by the forward balance of the soloist. Jan Latham-Koenig secures crisply rhythmic playing from the orchestra in all three movements. The main theme of the finale is even jauntier than usual, again at a speed fractionally slower than normal.

The warmth of the LPO string-tone comes over impressively in the *Sonata for strings*. Though the extra weight and tonal warmth are often very satisfying, as in the opening of the slow movement, the contrast between the passages for solo string quartet (echoing the original quartet version) and the full string ensemble is too extreme. Latham-Koenig is also warmly expressive in the *Hindemith variations*, which is not as lightly pointed or cleanly detailed as it might be, partly a question of the recording. The three works on the disc not only make an exceptionally generous triptych, but one which reflects Walton's mastery throughout his long career.

(i) *Viola concerto;* (ii) *Symphony No. 1;* (iii) *3 Songs from Façade.*
❀ (M) (***) Dutton Laboratories mono CDAX 8003 [id.]. (i) Riddle, LSO, composer; (ii) LSO, Harty; (iii) Dora Stevens, Foss.

This first ever recording of the *Viola concerto*, made for Decca in December 1937 with Walton conducting the LSO and with Frederick Riddle as soloist, puts a totally different complexion on the piece from usual. Riddle's performance has never been surpassed by even the starriest viola-players since for, unlike almost every rival today, he takes the first movement, *Andante comodo*, at a flowing speed that avoids over-romanticizing the yearning melody at the start. Yet Riddle finds a poignant tenderness in the concerto. In the central Scherzo he is more relaxed, with wittily sprung rhythms, while after a fast, spiky account of the finale the epilogue is wistful rather than tragic. Amazingly, this historic recording was never transferred to LP, making the superb transfer from Dutton Laboratories doubly welcome. It is coupled ideally with the very first recording of Walton's *First Symphony*, made in 1935 by the LSO under Sir Hamilton Harty. Though the playing is not always as polished as in modern versions, the emotional thrust under Harty has never been surpassed. Again the sound is beefy and full, amazingly so when you think that Decca's improvised studio was in a warehouse building near Cannon Street station. The songs, with Dora Stevens accompanied by her husband, Hubert Foss, Walton's publisher from OUP, are a charming makeweight.

Violin concerto.
(N) *** Decca Dig. 452 051-2 [id.]. Joshua Bell; Baltimore SO, Davis Zinman – BARBER: *Violin concerto*; BLOCH: *Baal Shem.* ***
(M) *** Decca 460 014-2 [id.]. Kyung Wha Chung, LSO, André Previn – BEETHOVEN: *Violin concerto.* **
(M) *** EMI CDM7 64202-2. Ida Haendel, Bournemouth SO, Berglund – BRITTEN: *Violin concerto.* ***
(***) Biddulph mono WHL 016. Heifetz, Cincinnati SO, Goossens – VAUGHAN WILLIAMS: *A London Symphony (No. 2)* (***) (with Concert (***)).
(N) **(*) Classico Dig. CLASSCD 233. Sergeij Azizjan, Copenhagen PO, Giordano Bellincamp – BRITTEN: *Violin concerto.* ***

From an American perspective, Walton's *Violin concerto* can well be seen as a British counterpart of the Barber, similarly romantic, written at exactly the same period. This prizewinning Decca disc has Bell giving a commanding account of the solo part, even matching Heifetz himself in the ease of his virtuosity. Playing with rapt intensity, Bell treats the central cadenza of the first movement expansively, making it more deeply reflective than usual. Rich and brilliant sound, with the violin balanced forward, but not aggressively so.

In the brooding intensity of the opening, Kyung Wha Chung presents the first melody with a depth of expression, tender and hushed, that has never been matched on record. With Previn as guide and with the composer himself a sympathetic observer at the recording sessions, Chung then builds up a performance which remains a classic, showing the *Concerto* as one of the greatest of the century. Outstandingly fine recording, sounding the more vivid in its CD format. This now comes generously coupled with the Beethoven *Concerto*, not an ideal choice, when it is not among Chung's most successful recordings.

A sunny, glowing, Mediterranean-like view of the concerto from Ida Haendel, with brilliant playing from the soloist and eloquent orchestral support from the Bournemouth orchestra under Paavo Berglund. The CD transfer of the fine (1977) recording, made in the Guildhall, Southampton, brings a brilliant orchestral tapestry to provide the necessary contrast and, given the quality of the playing (as well as the interest of the equally successful Britten coupling), this is an eminently desirable reissue.

Jascha Heifetz made the very first recording in 1941 with Eugene Goossens and the Cincinnati orchestra, and it has never quite been matched since for its passionate urgency as well as its brilliance. Speeds are much faster than has latterly become the norm, but the romantic warmth of the work has never been more richly conveyed. Here in an excellent CD transfer it is coupled with the only existing recording of the original score of Vaughan Williams's *London Symphony*, plus other British music.

Sergej Azizjan, the Leningrad-trained concertmaster of the Copenhagen Philharmonic, has a superb technique, marked by flawless intonation and a wide tonal range. His reading of the Walton is passionate in an aptly extrovert way, an excellent choice for anyone wanting this coupling, though the orchestra is a degree recessed, and such passages as the rhythmic opening of the Walton finale lack something in bite. It is an astonishing coincidence (unless Britten was somehow looking over Walton's shoulder) that both composers in 1939 not only completed violin concertos for performance in America, but adopted a remarkably similar structure – so Britten's *concerto* makes a particularly apt pairing.

Violin concerto; 2 Pieces for violin and orchestra; Sonata for violin and orchestra (both orch. Palmer).
*** Chandos Dig. CHAN 9073 [id.].
Mordkovitch, LPO, Jan Latham-Koenig.

Lydia Mordkovitch gives the most expansive account of the Walton *Violin concerto* on disc, sustaining spacious speeds warmly and persuasively. Latham-Koenig may not have quite the spark that Previn brings to the orchestral writing in both the Chung and Kennedy versions but he is keenly idiomatic, both in his feeling for sharply syncopated rhythms and in flexible rubato for Walton's romantic melodies. The characteristically warm Chandos recording is also a help, allowing plenty of detail to be heard, but helping to give extra cohesion to such a passage as the final march coda. Christopher Palmer's scoring of the *Sonata* offers a sensuousness of sound comparable with that in the opera *Troilus and Cressida*. Though his use of the harp or pizzicato strings for arpeggio accompaniments is not always comfortable, Palmer is right in seeing much of the piano part as already implying orchestration. With Mordkovitch just as powerful and rich-toned as in the regular concerto, the work makes a far bigger impact than in its original chamber form, a valuable addition to the Walton repertory. The two shorter pieces make an agreeable supplement, with Palmer's lush orchestration removing them even further from their medieval source-material.

Façade (absolutely complete).
(B) *** Discover Dig. DICD 920125 [id.].
Hunter, Melologos Ens., Van den Broeck.

Enterprisingly the Discover International label at bargain price offers the most complete version of Walton's Entertainment yet, using a group of Belgian instrumentalists, the Melologos Ensemble, under Silveer van den Broeck. When the reciter, Pamela Hunter, has made a speciality of reciting these Edith Sitwell poems, not exactly imitating Dame Edith herself but observing the strictly stylized, rhythmically crisp manner originally laid down, it makes a welcome and delightful disc. Five items appear here for the first time, adding to those resurrected by Walton himself in *Façade 2*. What one registers here, even more than with *Façade 2* alone, is that the early settings are more experimental and less sharply parodistic than the later, well-known ones, though in the accompaniment to one of them, *Aubade* ('Jane, Jane, tall as a crane'), there is a clear tongue-in-cheek reference to Stravinsky's *Rite of spring*. The recording is cleanly focused, balanced with the voice in front of the players yet obviously in the same acoustic, not superimposed; and the clarity and point of the solo playing, notably from the flute and clarinet, are splendid. Pamela Hunter is excellent too, happily characterizing with a minimum of 'funny voices'. At the price, a disc to recommend to all.

Façade 1 & 2 and other Edith Sitwell poems.
(N) *** Arabesque Dig. Z 6699 [id.]. Lynn Redgrave, Chamber Music Society of Lincoln Center, David Shifrin.

With Lynn Redgrave an excellent reciter, characterful and sharply rhythmic, the ensemble from Lincoln Center under Joseph Silverstein give a virtuoso performance of the quirky score, both crisply disciplined and idiomatic. Far more than usual, the recording gets the balance right between voice and instruments, with words splendidly clear yet with no unnatural highlighting of the reciter. She also recites 11 *Façade* poems without music, a random choice, not those which Walton set, but for which the music is lost. Some may feel that Redgrave overdoes the characterizations, but she gets a very acceptable balance between expressive word-pointing and formality, characterizing precisely in different, stylized accents, as in the Noel Coward accent she adopts for the *Tango* and *Popular song*.

Façade: suites Nos. 1–3; Overture Portsmouth Point (arr. LAMBERT); *Siesta;* (i) *Sinfonia concertante.* WALTON/ARNOLD: *Popular birthday.*
*** Chandos Dig. CHAN 9148 [id.]. (i) Eric Parkin; LPO, Latham-Koenig or Thomson.

Adapted from a ballet score written for Diaghilev (but then rejected), the *Sinfonia concertante*, with its sharply memorable ideas in each movement and characteristically high voltage, has never had the attention it deserves. Like the Conifer issue with Kathryn Stott as soloist, the Chandos recording restores the original version. Eric Parkin as soloist is perfectly attuned to the idiom, warmly melodic as well as jazzily syncopated, making this a most sympathetic account, even if the *Maestoso* introduction is hardly grand enough. The recording sets the piano a little more backwardly, no doubt to reflect the idea that this is not a full concerto. Jan Latham-Koenig gives the witty *Façade* movements just the degree of jazzy freedom they need. The third suite, devised and arranged by Christopher Palmer, draws on three apt movements from the *Façade* entertainment, ending riotously with the rag-music of *Something lies beyond the scene*. That is a first recording, and so is Constant Lambert's arrangement for small orchestra of the *Overture Portsmouth Point*, clearer than the original. *Siesta* is given an aptly cool performance under Bryden Thomson, and the *Popular birthday* is Malcolm Arnold's fragmentary linking of 'Happy birthday to you' with the *Popular song* from *Façade*, originally written for Walton's 20th birthday.

Façade: suites 1 & 2.
*** Hyperion Dig. CDA 66436 [id.]. E. N. Philh. O, Lloyd-Jones (with BLISS: *Checkmate* ***) – LAMBERT: *Horoscope.* *** ❁

Brilliantly witty and humorous performances of the two orchestral suites which Walton himself fashioned from his 'Entertainment'. This is music which, with its outrageous quotations, can make one chuckle out loud. Moreover it offers, to quote Constant Lambert, 'one good tune after another', all scored with wonderful felicity. The playing here could hardly be bettered, and the recording is in the demonstration bracket with its natural presence and bloom.

Film scores

As you like it: suite. The Battle of Britain: suite. Henry V: suite. History of the English speaking peoples: March. Troilus and Cressida (opera): *Interlude.*
(M) *** EMI Dig. CDM5 65585-2. LPO Ch. & O, Carl Davis.

The Battle of Britain suite presents the music that (for trumpery reasons) was rejected for the original film, including a Wagnerian send-up and a splendid final march. Another vintage Walton march here was written for a television series based on Churchill's history, but again was never used. It is a pity that the *Henry V suite* does not include the Agincourt charge, but it is good to have the choral contributions to the opening and closing sequences. Most welcome is the long-buried music for the 1926 Paul Czinner film of *As You Like It*. Warm, opulent recording.

Film music: As you like it (Poem for orchestra); Hamlet (Shakespeare scenario in 9 movements) (both arr. Christopher Palmer).
(N) (BB) **(*) Naxos Dig. 8.553344 [id.]. Michael Sheen, Dublin RTE Concert O, Andrew Penny.

In adaptations of film music for concert performance by the late Christopher Palmer, both Penny and the RTE Concert Orchestra give warm, sympathetic performances. Michael Sheen recites the Hamlet soliloquies with the ardour of youth, and the unnamed soprano soloist in the *As you like it* song, *Under the greenwood tree*, sings with fresh, girlish tone. With recording a little recessed, and with thinnish strings, this cannot match the Chandos issue of the same coupling at full-price, but it makes a good bargain.

The Battle of Britain (suite); Escape me never (suite); The First of the Few: Spitfire prelude and fugue; Three Sisters; A Wartime sketchbook.
*** Chandos Dig. CHAN 8870 [id.]. ASMF, Marriner.

The Spitfire prelude and fugue, from *The First of the Few*, was immediately turned into a highly successful concert-piece, but we owe it to Christopher Palmer that there is the 'Wartime Sketchbook', drawing material from three of the wartime films, plus scraps that Colin Matthews did not use in the suite from the much later *Battle of Britain* film music and not least in the stirring theme from the credits of the film, *Went the day well*. The brief suite from the music for Olivier's film of Chekhov's *The Three Sisters*, from much later, brings more than one setting of the *Tsar's Hymn* and a charming imitation of *Swan Lake*. Earliest on the disc is *Escape me never*, the first of Walton's film-scores, written in 1935 in a more popular idiom; but the war-inspired music is what this delightful disc is really about. Marriner and the Academy give richly idiomatic performances, full of panache. Aptly opulent recording.

Henry V: A Shakespeare scenario (arr. Christopher Palmer).
*** Chandos Dig. CHAN 8892 [id.]. Christopher Plummer (nar.), Westminster Cathedral Ch., ASMF, Marriner.

Few film-scores can match Walton's for the Olivier film of *Henry V* in its range and imagination, the whole of the 'Scenario' devised by Christopher Palmer lasting just over an hour. The most controversial change is to 'borrow' the first section of the march which Walton wrote much later for a projected television series on Churchill's *History of the English-speaking peoples*; otherwise, the chorus's call to arms, *Now all the youth of England is on fire*, would have had no music to introduce it. As an appendix, three short pieces are included which Walton quoted in his score. Sir Neville Marriner caps even his previous recordings in this series, with the Academy and Westminster Choir producing heartfelt playing and singing in sumptuous sound. As narrator, Christopher Plummer makes an excellent substitute for Olivier, unselfconsciously adopting a comparably grand style.

Henry V: Passacaglia; The Death of Falstaff; Touch her soft lips and part.
(M) *** DG 439 529-2. ECO, Barenboim – DELIUS: *Aquarelles* etc.; VAUGHAN WILLIAMS: *Oboe concerto* etc. ***

These two fine Walton string pieces make an admirable complement to a sensuously beautiful collection of English music, with Barenboim at his most affectionately inspirational and the ECO very responsive, and with the 1975 recording retaining its warmth and bloom.

The Quest (ballet): complete; *The Wise Virgins* (ballet): suite.
*** Chandos Dig. CHAN 8871 [id.]. LPO, Bryden Thomson.

Walton's two wartime ballet-scores make an attractive coupling. Walton, even in a hurry, could not help creating memorable ideas and, with the help of Constant Lambert – not to mention Christopher Palmer, who has expanded the instrumentation in line with the suite – the orchestral writing is often dazzling. Quite apart from the dramatic power of the performance, the recording is superb, among the fullest and clearest from Chandos. The sound for *The Wise Virgins* is more reverberant and the performance has less electricity, though Walton's distinctive arrangements of Bach cantata movements – including *Sheep may safely graze* – remain as fresh as ever.

Sinfonia concertante for piano & orchestra (original version).
*** Conifer Dig. 74321 15007-2 [id.]. Kathryn Stott, RPO, Handley – BRIDGE: *Phantasm;* IRELAND: *Piano concerto.* ***

Kathryn Stott, warmly and strongly accompanied by Vernon Handley and the RPO, gives an outstanding reading of the work's original version, and the result seems to strengthen what is a consistently memorable work, built from vintage Walton material. First-rate recorded sound, and a coupling both generous and apt.

(i) *Sinfonia concertante. Spitfire Prelude & Fugue; Variations on a theme of Hindemith; March: The History of the English-speaking peoples.*
(N) (BB) *** Naxos Dig. 8.553869 [id.]. (i) Peter Donohoe, E. Northern Philh., Paul Daniel.

Following up his outstanding Naxos versions of the Walton symphonies, Paul Daniel conducts the English Northern Philharmonia in electrifying performances of this varied group of orchestral works. As before he is splendid at interpreting Walton's jazzy syncopations with the right degree of freedom. Following the composer's own suggestion, the original version of the *Sinfonia concertante* is preferred to the revision, fuller and more brilliant. The performance is excellent, despite the placing of the soloist, Peter Donohoe, too far forward. Daniel draws playing both warm and scintillating from the orchestra in the *Hindemith variations* – no finer version exists – while the *March* and the *Spitfire* music hit home all the harder through Daniel's refusal to dawdle.

Symphony No. 1 in B flat min.; (i) *Belshazzar's Feast.*
(N) ✿ *** EMI Dig. CDC5 56592-2 [id.]. CBSO, Rattle (i) with Thomas Hampson, CBSO Ch., Cleveland O Ch.

Symphony No. 1; Overture Scapino; Siesta.
(BB) *** BMG Arte Nova Dig. 74321 39124-2 [id.]. Gran Canaria PO, Adrian Leaper.

Symphony No. 1; Partita for orchestra.
(BB) *** Naxos Dig. 8.553180 [id.]. E. N. PO, Paul Daniel.

Symphony No. 1; Varii Capricci.
*** Chandos Dig. CHAN 8862 [id.]. LPO, Bryden Thomson.

It is Rattle's gift as a Walton interpreter that he can combine pin-point precision of ensemble with expressive freedom, making Walton's jazzy syncopations sound idiomatic. This ideal coupling brings together two bitingly intense masterpieces of the 1930s. *Belshazzar's Feast*, dating from 1931, has never been given quite so spectacular a recording as here, spacious and full yet meticulously detailed with the widest dynamic range thrillingly caught. With the Birmingham Symphony Chorus joined by the visiting Cleveland Orchestra Chorus, the recording clearly defines the many dramatic antiphonal effects. Interpretatively, where readings of this brilliant oratorio have tended to grow broader and slower than the composer's own, Rattle tautly echoes Walton's example, and the extra bite and urgency are thrilling – not that Rattle rushes at all in such beautiful choruses as *By the waters of Babylon*. Thomas Hampson is the resonant baritone soloist, not as chilling as some in his account of the writing on the wall, but firm and dramatic. Rattle's version of the *First Symphony*, also taut and intense, originally appeared in 1992, but the recoupling with *Belshazzar* is both more generous and more apt.

If anything even more clearly than on his first Naxos disc of Walton, Paul Daniel demonstrates his natural affinity with this composer's music. In the *First Symphony* he knows unerringly how to build up tension to breaking point before resolving it and then building again. He is also freer than many in his use of rubato, as well as in the degree of elbow-room he allows for jazzy syncopations, always idiomatic. The *Scherzo* is sparkily witty, not just full of malice. In the slow movement, after the poised opening, Daniel tends to press ahead slightly for the sections which follow, agonizingly intense. The finale with its brassy, more extrovert manner has plenty of panache, and though textures could be more transparent – largely a question of the reverberant Leeds Town Hall acoustic – the weight and bite of the sound are excellent. This is a version that vies with even the finest at whatever price, and it outshines most. Daniel's reading of the *Partita* brings out above all the work's joyfulness, with the outer movements relaxed in their brilliance and the central slow movement warmly expressive.

Leaper's disc of Walton's *First* may be on a super-budget label and the orchestra may not be familiar, but it competes very well with almost any version in the catalogue. With finely disciplined playing, the reading is fresh and alert, idiomatic in its rhythmic pointing and with intense poetry in such key moments as the distant trumpet-call in the final coda. Starting almost inaudibly at the very start, Leaper seems intent on making the music emerge from mists, then he quickly builds up tension and momentum, even if in the first movement his reading is not as weighty as many. The clarity of the recording compensates and there is no lack of weight in the heavy brass, which has impressive bite. The slow movement brings inspired wind solos, and the Scherzo and finale are crisp and resilient, with busy ensembles made unusually clear, even transparent, a point that also marks Leaper's witty and sparkling account of the *Scapino overture*, in which the cello solo is most beautifully done. *Siesta* is aptly dreamy, not literal or chilly, making this a disc to recommend to Waltonians and newcomers alike.

Thomson's is a warmly committed, understandingly idiomatic account of the work, weighty and rhythmically persuasive, if not as biting as some. In the slow movement his tender expressiveness goes with a flowing speed, well judged to avoid exaggeration. If the Scherzo is a degree less demonic than it might be, at a speed fractionally slower than usual, it is infectiously sprung. The Chandos coupling is not as generous as some but is very welcome when it brings the first recording of *Varii capricci*, the orchestral suite in five compact movements which Walton developed from his set of guitar *Bagatelles*, written for Julian Bream. With a brilliant performance and sumptuous sound, it makes a fine supplement.

Symphony No. 2; Partita for orchestra; Variations on a theme by Hindemith.
✿ (B) *** Sony SBK 62753. Cleveland O, Szell.

In a letter to the conductor, Walton expressed himself greatly pleased with Szell's performance of the *Second Symphony*: 'It is a quite fantastic and stupendous performance from every point of view. Firstly it is absolutely right musically speaking, and the virtuosity is quite staggering, especially the Fugato; but everything is phrased and balanced in an unbelievable way.' Listening to the splendidly remastered CD of this 1961 recording, one cannot but join the composer in responding to the wonderfully luminous detail in the orchestra. Szell's performance of the *Hindemith variations* is no less remarkable. Finally comes the *Partita*, which was commissioned by the Cleveland Orchestra and given its première a year before the recording was made. The recordings are bright, in the CBS manner, but the ambience of Severance Hall brings a backing warmth and depth, and these are technically among the finest of Szell's recordings in this venue.

The Wise virgins (ballet suite arr. from Bach).
(M) *** EMI CDM5 65911-2. Concert Arts O, Robert Irving – GLAZUNOV: *The Seasons;* SCARLATTI/TOMMASINI: *Good humoured ladies*. ***

Walton's orchestral arrangements of Bach created a score for the Sadler's Wells ballet in 1940. All the music except the second piece, a chorale-prelude, is extracted from cantatas, and the delightful '*Sheep may safely graze*' (richly presented here) is a highlight, alongside the tranquil '*See what His love can do*' from Cantata No. 85. However, some of the flamboyant brass writing and Walton's unashamedly anachronistic treatment brought the score into critical disfavour in the 1960s; and only more recently has public opinion (after acknowledging the pleasures of Stokowski's Bach transcriptions) taken Walton's ballet excursion back into favour. It could not be better presented than it is here, and the resonant recording emphasizes the ebullience of the uninhibited moments, especially the robust finale.

CHAMBER MUSIC

(i) *5 Bagatelles for solo guitar;* (ii; iii) *Duets for children;* (iv; ii) *2 Pieces for violin and piano; Toccata for violin and piano;* (ii) (Piano) *Façade: Valse;* (v; i) *Anon in love* (for tenor & guitar); (v; ii) *2 Songs for tenor: The Winds, The Tritons*.
*** Chandos Dig. CHAN 9292 [id.]. (i) Carlos Bonell; (ii) Hamish Milne; (iii) Gretel Dowdeswell; (iv) Kenneth Sillito; (v) John Mark Ainsley.

The *Toccata for violin and piano* is a curious mixture of cadenza and rhapsody of 15 minutes in a disconcertingly un-Waltonian style. Two songs for tenor are fascinating too, with a rushing accompaniment for *The Winds*, while *The Tritons* is chaconne-like, with a melody quite untypical of Walton. Milne and Dowdeswell bring out what charming, sharply focused ideas are contained in the ten *Duets for children*. The piano arrangement of the *Valse* from *Façade* is so thorny that even Hamish Milne has to go cautiously. The two violin pieces – using French troubadour songs – are spin-offs from the *Henry V* incidental music and, in the second, *Scherzetto*, reflect what their composer had learnt, writing for Heifetz. The two works with guitar are well known in Julian Bream's performances and recordings. Bonell is lighter and more delicate than Bream (see under Concerts, below), both in the *Bagatelles* and in *Anon in Love*, but is no less persuasive. Similarly, John Mark Ainsley lacks some of the punch of Peter Pears, for whom the cycle was written, but in a gentler way taps the wit and point of these Elizabethan conceits. A delightful collection, full of revealing insights into the composer's complex character.

Passacaglia for solo cello.
*** Chandos Dig. CHAN 8499 [id.]. Raphael Wallfisch – BAX: *Rhapsodic ballad;* BRIDGE: *Cello sonata;* DELIUS: *Cello sonata*. ***

William Walton's *Passacaglia* for solo cello was composed in the last year of his life. It has restraint and eloquence, and Raphael Wallfisch gives a thoroughly sympathetic account of it. Excellent recording.

Piano quartet; Violin sonata.
*** Chandos Dig. CHAN 8999 [id.]. Sillito, Smissen, Orton, Milne.

This performance of the *Piano quartet* with Hamish Milne as pianist makes one marvel that such music could have been the inspiration of a 16-year-old. Admittedly Walton revised the piece, but here is music which instantly grabs the ear, with striking ideas attractively and dramatically presented in each movement. This is a more sharply focused reading than the rival Meridian one, both in the performance and in the recorded sound, with speeds generally flowing more freely and strongly and the string sound more satisfyingly resonant. The two principal performers from the quartet make a warmly sympathetic rather than high-powered duo for the *Violin sonata* of 1949. Yet the combination of Sillito's ripely persuasive style and Milne's incisive power, clarifying textures and giving magic to the phrasing, keeps tensions sharp. The satisfyingly full sound helps too.

String quartet No. 1 (ed. Christopher Palmer); *String quartet in A min.*
*** Chandos Dig. CHAN 8944 [id.]. Gabrieli Qt.

Coupled ideally with the mature *String quartet in A minor*, completed in 1946, is the atonal *First quartet*, long thought to be lost, which Walton wrote when an undergraduate at Oxford. The result is hardly recognizable as Walton at all but is full of fire and imagination. The first movement is 'pastoral-atonal', lyrical in its counterpoint, but the Scherzo, built on vigorously rhythmic motifs and jagged ostinatos, has much more of Bartók in it than of Schoenberg, while the fugue of the finale seeks to emulate Beethoven's *Grosse Fuge* in its complexity and massive scale, alone lasting almost 16 minutes. The Gabrieli performance brings out all the latent power and lyrical warmth, often implying an underlying anger. It provides a fascinating contrast with the highly civilized *A minor* work of 25 years later. That comes in a red-blooded Gabrieli recording of 1986, earlier available in coupling with the Elgar *Quartet*. Both recordings were made in the warm, rich acoustic of The Maltings, Snape, with little discrepancy between them.

String quartet in A min.
*** Hyperion Dig. CDA 66718 [id.]. Coull Qt – BRIDGE: *3 Idylls;* *** ELGAR: *Quartet*. **(*)
*** Collins Dig. 1280-2 [id.]. Britten Qt – ELGAR: *Quartet*. ***
❁ *** Testament mono SBT 1052 [id.]. Hollywood Qt – HINDEMITH: *Quartet No. 3;* PROKOFIEV: *Quartet No. 2*. (***) ❁

The Elgar and Walton *Quartets* make an apt and attractive coupling, and here the Coulls, unlike their direct rivals, offer as bonus a fine example of Frank Bridge's quartet-writing. In the Walton, the reading captures movingly the spirit of Waltonian melancholy, bringing out the elegiac intensity of the extended *Lento* slow movement, taken at a very measured pace. The Coulls are splendid too in capturing the element of fun in Walton's scherzando ideas. The Brittens on Collins, also offering the Elgar, find less fantasy.

The Britten Quartet, bitingly powerful, bring out the emotional intensity, playing with refinement and sharp focus, finding a repose and poise in the slow movement that bring it close to late Beethoven. The contrasts of wistful lyricism and scherzando bite in the first movement make most other versions seem clumsy by comparison, and the incisiveness of Walton's jaggedly rhythmic writing is a delight.

In many ways the pioneering account by the Hollywood Quartet, made in 1950, has still not been surpassed. It first appeared on a Capitol LP in harness with the Villa-Lobos *Sixth Quartet*. The sound comes up very well, though it is not, of course, state of the art. Moreover it comes with equally strong couplings and cannot be too strongly recommended.

Sonata for strings.
(N) (M) **(*) EMI Dig. CDM5 66761-2 [id.]. City of L. Sinfonia, Hickox – ELGAR: *Introduction and allegro for strings*; VAUGHAN WILLIAMS: *Fantasia on a theme by Thomas Tallis*. **(*)

Walton's *Sonata for strings* (an arrangement of the 1947 *String quartet*) is made to sound highly effective in this outstanding performance under Hickox. The passionate account of the third movement *Lento* is a highlight of a reading which is full of intensity, and Hickox's athletic style and the bright, clearly focused digital sound suit this work better than the Elgar or Vaughan Williams couplings.

Violin sonata.
(BB) *** ASV Quicksilva CDQS 6191 [id.]. McAslan, Blakely – ELGAR: *Violin sonata*. ***
(M) (**) EMI mono CDM5 66122-2. Yehudi Menuhin, Louis Kentner – ELGAR; WALTON: *Sonatas*. **(*)

Lorraine McAslan gives a warmly committed performance of Walton's often wayward *Sonata*, coping well with the sharp and difficult changes of mood in both of the two long movements. The romantic melancholy of the piece suits her well and, though the recording does not make her tone as rounded as it should be, she produces some exquisite pianissimo playing, making this a very impressive début recording. John Blakely is a most sympathetic partner, particularly impressive in crisply articulated scherzando passages. At its modest cost this is very highly recommendable.

The Menuhins commissioned this sonata to be premièred by the present performers, and it was dedicated jointly to their wives. It was completed in 1940 but the composer withdrew it, and the present two-movement version was recorded in 1950. First recordings are always special, and this one is no exception; but it is a pity that the very forward recording tends to treble emphasis, which is unflattering to Menuhin's upper register in its CD transfer.

CHORAL MUSIC

Anon in love (song-cycle).
(M) *** RCA 09026 61601-2. Peter Pears, Julian Bream (guitar) – BRITTEN: *Songs from the Chinese* etc; SEIBER: *Four French folk songs*. ***

Walton wrote his cycle, *Anon in love*, for these same artists, and the melisma of the opening song, *Fain would I change that note*, soars aloft in a way that Pears made his own. The other songs progress from nostalgia and romantic feeling to jolly revelry (*I gave her cakes and ale*) and consummation (*To couple is a custom*), with the closing number in the form of a brilliantly earthy scherzando. With attractive couplings this (Volume 18) is one of the most attractive and valuable reissues in the Julian Bream Edition, providing an entire programme played and sung by the artists who inspired the music.

Belshazzar's Feast.
(B) *** Sony SBK 63039. Walter Cassel, Rutgers University Ch., Phd. O, Ormandy – MAHLER: *Kindertotenlieder; 3 Rückert Lieder*. ***

(i) *Belshazzar's Feast. Coronation march: Crown Imperial; Henry V* (film incidental music): *suite*.
*** Decca Dig. 448 134-2. (i) Bryn Terfel, Bournemouth Symphony Ch., Waynflete Singers, L'Inviti; Bournemouth SO, Litton.

(i) *Belshazzar's Feast. Henry V* (film score): *suite*.
(M) *** Carlton Dig. 30367 01862 [id.]. (i) Luxon, Brighton Festival Ch., L. Coll. Mus., RPO, Previn.

(i) *Belshazzar's Feast. Improvisations on an impromptu of Benjamin Britten; Overtures: Portsmouth Point; Scapino.*
(M) *** EMI CDM7 64723-2. LSO, Previn, (i) with John Shirley-Quirk, L. Symphony Ch.

(i) *Belshazzar's Feast. In honour of the City of London.*
(M) *** EMI Dig. CD-EMX 2225 [id.]. (i) David Wilson-Johnson; L. Symphony Ch., LSO, Hickox.

Belshazzar's Feast; Coronation Te Deum; Gloria.
**(*) Chandos Dig. CHAN 8760 [id.]. Howell,

Gunson, Mackie, Roberts, Bach Ch., Philh. O, Willcocks.

Richard Hickox not only conducts one of the most sharply dramatic accounts of *Belshazzar's Feast* currently available, even crisper and keener (if less jazzy) than Previn's superb (1971) EMI version; but he couples it with his long-neglected cantata, *In honour of the City of London*. With forces almost as lavish as those in the oratorio, its vitality and atmospheric colour come over on this record to a degree generally impossible in live performance. As for *Belshazzar* under Hickox, its voltage has never seemed higher on record, thanks not just to the LSO and Chorus – in far sharper form than for Previn, 17 years earlier – but also to the full and brilliant digital recording. The dramatic soloist is David Wilson-Johnson, colouring his voice with chilling menace in the writing-on-the-wall sequence. Now reissued on EMI's Eminence label, this makes a very strong recommendation.

Where the first two of Litton's Walton discs were recorded in the helpful acoustic of the Southampton Guildhall, *Belshazzar's Feast* was put into the grander setting of Winchester Cathedral. The reverberation time is formidably long, yet, thanks to brilliant balancing, there is ample detail and fine focus in exceptionally incisive choral and orchestral sound. The great benefit is that this emerges as a performance on a bigger scale than its rivals, with the contrasts between full chorus and semi-chorus the more sharply established. The vividly dramatic soloist is Bryn Terfel, pointing the words as no one else ever has. He was magnetic enough in his 1994 Last Night of the Proms performance with Andrew Davis (issued on Teldec), but his expressive colourings are even more individual here, both in the 'shopping-list' – 'Babylon was a great city' – and in his spine-chilling narration describing the writing on the wall. The other items, the *Henry V suite* and *Crown Imperial*, were recorded, like *Belshazzar*, in Winchester Cathedral, but sadly the opportunity was not taken for using a chorus in *Henry V*. The fanfares have never been more evocative, and the build-up of the Agincourt charge is thrilling. Despite the reverberation, *Crown Imperial* is also given a stirring performance.

Previn's EMI version of *Belshazzar's Feast* remains among the most spectacular yet recorded. The digital remastering has not lost the body and atmosphere of the sound but has increased its impact. This fine performance was recorded with Walton present on his seventieth birthday and, though Previn's tempi are slower than those set by Walton himself in his two recordings, the authenticity is clear, with consistently sharp attack and with dynamic markings meticulously observed down to the tiniest hairpin markings. Chorus and orchestra are challenged to their finest standards, and John Shirley-Quirk proves a searching and imaginative soloist. The *Improvisations*, given a first recording, make a generous fill-up alongside the two overtures in which Previn, the shrewdest and most perceptive of Waltonians, finds more light and shade than usual. Again the remastered sound is excellent.

André Previn's digital version of Walton's oratorio on Carlton brings a performance in some ways even sharper and more urgent than his fine earlier version for EMI with the LSO. The chorus, singing with biting intensity, is set cleanly and realistically behind the orchestra, though that gives the impression of a smaller, less weighty group than is ideal. Benjamin Luxon – who earlier sang in Solti's Decca version – is a characterful soloist, but his heavy vibrato is exaggerated by too close a balance. The five-movement suite from Walton's film-music for *Henry V* makes an attractive coupling. Previn was the first conductor on record since Walton himself to capture the full dramatic bite and colour of this music, with the cavalry charge at Agincourt particularly vivid.

Willcocks scores over some rivals in his pacing which, far more than is common, follows the example set by the composer himself in his two recordings. Speeds tend to be a degree faster, as in *By the waters of Babylon* which flows evenly yet without haste. The soloist, Gwynne Howell, firm and dark of tone, is among the finest of all exponents but, with the Bach Choir placed rather more distantly than in most versions, this is not as incisive as its finest rivals. The *Coronation Te Deum* receives a richly idiomatic performance, and Willcocks also gives weight and thrust to the *Gloria*, with the tenor, Neil Mackie, outstanding among the soloists. The microphone unfortunately catches an unevenness in Ameral Gunson's mezzo. The recording is warmly reverberant, not ideally clear on choral detail but easy to listen to.

The 1961 Ormandy account is fervent and atmospheric. The choral singing may not be absolutely refined but it has great enthusiasm, the words are clear and the effect is most invigorating, often thrilling. Walter Cassel makes an attractively robust contribution, and he also projects his words well. The balance has the orchestra well forward – although not at the expense of the choral bite – and the orchestral and percussive detail is fully and tinglingly conveyed. The spaciousness of the recording is also impressive. The coupling is hardly apt, but it offers some memorable singing from Jennie Tourel on her finest form.

(i) *Christopher Columbus (suite of incidental music);* (ii) *Anon in love;* (iii) *4 Songs after Edith Sitwell: Daphne; Through gilded trellises; Long steel grass; Old Sir Faulk. A Song for the Lord Mayor's table; The Twelve (an anthem for the Feast of any Apostle).*

*** Chandos Dig. CHAN 8824 [id.]. (i) Linda Finnie, Arthur Davies; (ii) Martyn Hill; (iii)

Jill Gomez; Westminster Singers, City of L. Sinfonia, Hickox.

The composer's own orchestral versions of his song-cycles *Anon in love* (for tenor) and *A Song for the Lord Mayor's table* (for soprano) are so beautifully judged that they transcend the originals, and the strength and beauty of these strongly characterized songs is enormously enhanced, particularly in performances as positive as these by Martyn Hill and Jill Gomez. The anthem, *The Twelve*, also emerges far more powerfully with orchestral instead of organ accompaniment. The four Sitwell songs were orchestrated by Christopher Palmer, who also devised the suite from Walton's incidental music to Louis MacNeice's wartime radio play, *Christopher Columbus*, buried for half a century. It is a rich score which brings more happy anticipations of the *Henry V* film-music in the choral writing, and even of the opera *Troilus and Cressida*, as well as overtones of *Belshazzar's Feast*. Warmly committed performances, opulently recorded.

OPERA

The Bear (complete).
*** Chandos Dig. CHAN 9245 [id.]. Della Jones, Opie, Shirley-Quirk, Northern Sinfonia, Hickox.

The one-Acter *The Bear*, based on Chekhov, matches in its point and flair Britten's own chamber operas also written for Aldeburgh, with Walton producing textures that are sumptuous rather than spare. It is a masterly score, with the farcical element reflected in dozens of parodies and tongue-in-cheek musical references, starting cheekily with echoes of Britten's own *Midsummer Night's Dream*. Richard Hickox with members of the Northern Sinfonia paces the music superbly, flexibly heightening the moments of mock-melodrama that punctuate this tale of a mourning widow who faces the demands of one of her dead husband's creditors. The casting of the three characters is ideal, with Della Jones commanding as the affronted widow, all her words crystal clear, Alan Opie clean-cut and incisive as the creditor or 'Bear' of the title, and with John Shirley-Quirk as the old retainer. In many ways this is a piece – with its climactic duel scene leading to an amorous *coup-de-foudre* – which comes off even better on disc than on stage.

Troilus and Cressida (complete).
✿ *** Chandos Dig. CHAN 9370/1 (2) [id.]. Arthur Davies, Howarth, Howard, Robson, Opie, Bayley, Thornton, Owen-Lewis, Opera North Ch., English N. Philh. O, Richard Hickox.

Few operas since Puccini have such a rich store of memorable tunes as *Troilus and Cressida*. As Chandos's magnificent recording shows, based on Opera North's 1995 production – using Walton's tautened score of 1976 but with the original soprano register restored for Cressida – this red-bloodedly romantic opera on a big classical subject deserves to enter the regular repertory. Judith Howarth portrays the heroine as girlishly vulnerable, rising superbly to the big challenges of the love duets and final death scene. Arthur Davies is an aptly Italianate Troilus, an ardent lover, and there is not a weak link in the rest of the characterful cast, with Nigel Robson a finely pointed Pandarus, comic but not camp, avoiding any echoes of Peter Pears, the originator. As Evadne, Cressida's maid, Yvonne Howard produces firm, rich mezzo tone, and the role of Calkas, Cressida's father, is magnificently sung by Clive Bayley. The role of Diomede, Cressida's Greek suitor, can seem one-dimensional but Alan Opie, in one of his finest performances on record, sharpens the focus, making him a genuine threat, a noble enemy. Richard Hickox draws magnetic performances from chorus and orchestra alike, bringing out the many parallels with the early Walton of *Belshazzar's Feast* and the *Symphony No. 1*. As for the recorded sound, the bloom of the Leeds Town Hall acoustic allows the fullest detail from the orchestra, enhancing the Mediterranean warmth of the score, helped by the wide dynamic range. The many atmospheric effects, often offstage, are clearly and precisely focused, and the placing of voices on the stereo stage is also unusually precise.

Ward, John (1571–1638)

Madrigals: *Come sable night; Cruel unkind; Die not, fond man; Hope of my heart; If heaven's just wrath; If the deep sighs; I have retreated; My breast I'll set; Oft have I tender'd; Out from the vale; Retire, my troubled soul; Sweet Philomel.*
*** Hyperion Dig. CDA 66256 [id.]. Consort of Musicke, Anthony Rooley.

Ward speaks with a distinctive voice. He chooses poetry of high quality, his music is always finely proportioned, and such is the quality of this music and the accomplishment with which it is presented, these settings represent the madrigal tradition at its finest.

Warlock, Peter (1894–1930)

(i) *Capriol suite; 6 English tunes; 6 Italian dance tunes; Serenade for strings;* (ii) *The Curlew* (song-cycle).
(BB) *** Arte Nova Dig. 74321 37868-2 [id.]. (i) L. Festival O, Ross Pople; (ii) Martyn Hill, Edward Beckett, Alison Alty, Robert Gibbs, Amanda Smith, Peter Stevens, Ferenc Szucs.

Warlock's two most important works, the colourful *Capriol suite* and searchingly intense setting of Yeats's *The Curlew*, are here very well coupled with the *Six English tunes* and the *Six Italian dance tunes*, both miniature suites on the lines of *Capriol*, but with movements barely a minute long unpretentiously making colourful points and moving on. The *Serenade* – lusciously echoes Delius in its string writing. Ross Pople directs clean-cut, consciously small-scale readings that rightly bring out the emotion of the writing. The tenor, Martyn Hill, placed well forward in *The Curlew*, similarly brings out the emotional thrust of the words with commendably clear diction. Warm recording to match.

Capriol suite (orchestral version); *Serenade for strings (for the sixtieth birthday of Delius).*
*** Chandos Dig. CHAN 8808 [id.]. Ulster O, Vernon Handley – MOERAN: *Serenade* etc. ***

The effect of the present full orchestral score of the *Capriol suite* is to rob the music of some of its astringency. A dryish wine is replaced with one with the fullest bouquet, for the wind instruments make the textures more rococo in feeling as well as increasing the colour. Handley's fine performance, is made to sound opulent by the acoustics of Ulster Hall, Belfast. The lovely *Serenade*, for strings alone, is also played and recorded very beautifully.

'Centenary collection': (i) *Capriol suite;* (ii) *Serenade to Frederick Delius on his 60th birthday.* Songs: (iii) *Adam lay ybounden;* (iv) *Autumn twilight;* (v) *Balulalow;* (vi) *Bethlehem Down;* (vii) *Captain Stratton's fancy;* (viii) *The Curlew* (song-cycle); (ix) *I saw a fair maiden;* (x) *The Lady's birthday* (arrangement); (v) *Pretty ring time;* (x) *The shrouding of the Duchess of Malfi;* (xi) *Where riches is everlasting;* (xii) *Yarmouth Fair.*
(M) *** EMI CDM5 65101-2 [id.]. (i) E. Sinf., Neville Dilkes; (ii) Bournemouth Sinf., Norman Del Mar; (iii) Robert Hammersley, Gavin Williams; (iv) Frederick Harvey, Gerald Moore; (v) Janet Baker, Philip Ledger; (vi) Guildford Cathedral Ch., Barry Rose; (vii) Robert Lloyd, Nina Walker; (viii) Ian Partridge, Music Group of London; (ix) Westminster Abbey Ch., Douglas Guest; (x) Baccholian Singers, Jennifer Partridge; (xi) King's College, Cambridge, Ch., Willcocks; (xii) Owen Brannigan, Ernest Lush.

Opening with one of our favourite versions of the *Capriol suite* from the English Sinfonia under Neville Dilkes, followed by Warlock's touchingly tender tribute to Delius, this selection ranges over a well-chosen selection of favourite songs, solo and choral. The other key item is *The Curlew*, Warlock's setting of a sequence of poems by Yeats which reflect the darker side of his complex personality. Ian Partridge, with the most sensitive response to word-meanings, gives an intensely poetic performance, beautifully recorded. Among other performances those of Dame Janet Baker stand out, but many of the songs here are persuasively beautiful. The transfers are consistently well managed.

(i) *Capriol suite;* (ii) *The Curlew* (song-cycle); *5 Nursery jingles. The Birds; Chopcherry; Fairest May; Mourn no moe; My gostly fader; Sleep; The water lilly.*
(BB) **(*) ASV Quicksilva CDQS 6143 [id.]. (i) RPO, Barlow; (ii) James Griffett, Haffner Qt; Mary Murdoch, Mary Ryan.

Though Griffett's performance of *The Curlew* is not so beautiful or so imaginative as Ian Partridge's, each one of these songs is a miniature of fine sensitivity, and James Griffett sings them with keen insight, pointing the words admirably. The instrumental playing is most sensitive, and the recording is warmly atmospheric yet clear. The performance of the *Capriol suite* is also a very good one, and the digital recording is first rate. This CD is well worth its modest cost.

Adam lay ybounden; As dew in Aprylle; Benedicamus Domino; Bethlehem Down; The Birds; Born is the babe; Balulalow; Carillon, Carilla; A Cornish Christmas carol; A Cornish carol; Corpus Christi; The First mercy; The Five lesser joys of Mary; The Frostbound wood; I saw a fair maiden; My little sweet darling; Out of the Orient crystal skies; The Rich cavalcade; Song for Christmas Day; Sweet was the song the Virgin sang; The Sycamore tree; Tyrley Tyrlow; What cheer? Good cheer!; Where riches is everlastingly.
(N) *** Somm Dig. SOMMCD 011 [id.]. Allegri Singers, Halsey; with Margaret Cable, Julian Empett; Rosamunde Qt; Matthew Barnes, Rosemary Barnes.

Most of these Christmas settings are little known, many are quite simple, but all are quite lovely. Among the more extended pieces the *Cornish Christmas carol* is strophic but the harmonic setting is constantly varied, while the ravishing *Corpus Christi* carol and simpler *Born is the babe* are set for solo voices and string quartet. *Out of the Orient crystal skies* and the gentle *Bethlehem down* are particularly haunting and the concert ends with the brief *Sycamore Tree*, as joyful as an English carol can be. Fine, lively, dedicated performances throughout, with excellent accompaniments from all concerned.

Songs: *As ever I saw; Autumn twilight; The bachelor; The bayly berith the bell away; Captain Stratton's fancy; First mercy; The fox; Hey, trolly, loly lo; Ha'nacker Mill; I held love's head; The jolly shepherd; Late summer; Lullaby; Milkmaids; Mourne no more; Mr Belloc's fancy; My gostly fader; My own country; The night; Passing by; Piggesnie; Play-acting; Rest, sweet*

nymphs; Sleep; Sweet content; Take, o take those lips away; There is a lady sweet and fair; Thou gav'st me leave to kiss; Walking the woods; When as the rye; The wind from the west; Yarmouth Fair.
*** Chandos Dig. CHAN 8643 [id.]. Benjamin Luxon, David Willison.

Songs like *Autumn twilight*, the powerfully expressive *Late summer* and *Captain Stratton's fancy* are appealing in utterly different ways, and there is not a single number in this programme that does not show the composer either in full imaginative flow or simply enjoying himself, as in *Yarmouth Fair*. Luxon's performances are first class and David Willison provides sensitive and sparkling accompaniments. The recording is first class.

Wassenaer, Unico Wilhelm
(1692–1766)

Concerti armonici Nos. 1–6.
*** Hyperion Dig. CDA 66670 [id.]. Brandenburg Cons., Goodman.

Long attributed to Pergolesi, these splendid concertos were in truth written by Unico Wilhelm, Graf von Wassenaer, a Dutch part-time composer of remarkable accomplishment. Their invention, vigorous and expressive, is sustained by a remarkably harmonic individuality: in short they are first-class works, almost on a par with the *concerti grossi* of Handel. These fine new performances are most presentable, and Hyperion's recording is very good indeed, to eclipse previous issues of this rewarding repertoire.

Waxman, Franz (1906–67)

The Song of Terezin (Das Lied von Terezin).
(N) *** Decca Dig. 460 211-2 [id.]. Della Jones, Berlin R. Ch., Children's Ch., & SO, Lawrence Foster – ZEISL: *Requiem Ebraico.*

Dating from 1964, only three years before he died, Franz Waxman's *The Song of Terezin* is a moving setting of poems and other material left by children imprisoned in the notorious concentration camp of Terezin. Waxman's style, with its Schoenbergian echoes, is far more uncompromising than in his film music but still approachable, helped by superb performances and opulent sound. In such a context the settings of lighter poems are all the more poignant.

Weber, Carl Maria von (1786–1826)

Andante and Hungarian rondo in E flat, Op. 35; Bassoon concerto in F, Op. 75.
(N) *** Chandos Dig. CHAN 9656 [id.]. Valeri Popov, Russian State SO, Polyansky – HUMMEL; MOZART: *Bassoon concertos.* ***

Valeri Popov is in his element here. There is some astonishing spiccato bravura in the finale of the *Hungarian Rondo*, and both he and his accompanying orchestra under Polyansky capture the grand manner of the first movement of the concerto and are quite touching in the romantic cantabile of the *Andantino*. The finale then brings both a genial wit and more solo fireworks. The recording is full-bodied and resonant, but clearly detailed in the Chandos manner.

Clarinet concertino in E flat, Op. 26.
*** ASV Dig. CDDCA 559 [id.]. Emma Johnson, ECO, Groves – CRUSELL: *Concerto No. 2* *** ✪; BAERMANN: *Adagio* ***; ROSSINI: *Introduction, theme and variations.* ***

Emma Johnson is in her element here. Her phrasing is wonderfully beguiling and her use of light and shade agreeably subtle, while she finds a superb lilt in the final section, pacing the music to bring out its charm rather than achieve breathless bravura. Sir Charles Groves provides an admirable accompaniment, and the recording is eminently realistic and naturally balanced.

Clarinet concerto No. 1 in F min., Op. 73.
*** EMI Dig. CDC 55155-2 [id.]. Sabine Meyer, Dresden State O, Blomstedt – MOZART; STAMITZ: *Concertos* ***.

Sabine Meyer gives a lusciously seductive account of the *F minor concerto*, accompanying herself with aplomb. She is beautifully recorded.

Clarinet concertos Nos. 1 in F min., Op. 73; 2 in E flat, Op. 74; Clarinet concertino in E flat, Op. 26.
(M) *** Classic fM Dig. 75605 57019-2. Colin Lawson, Hanover Band, Goodman – SPOHR: *Clarinet concerto No. 1.* ***
(N) (BB) *** Virgin Veritas Dig. Double VBD5 61585-2 (2) [id.]. Antony Pay, OAE – CRUSELL: *Clarinet concertos Nos. 1–3.* ***
(BB) *** Naxos Dig. 8.550378 [id.]. Ernst Ottensamer, Slovak State PO (Košice), Johannes Wildner.

Stylish and imaginative period performances of all three works from Colin Lawson with the Hanover Band, vividly recorded, generously supplemented by the Spohr *First Concerto*. With his attractively reedy tone Lawson is a most persuasive soloist, moulding Weber's melodies seductively and pointing rhythms jauntily, with brilliant feats of tonguing in the light-hearted finales of each work.

Antony Pay uses a copy of a seven-keyed clarinet by Simiot of Lyons from 1800. The sonority is cleaner and less bland than can be the case in modern performances, and the solo playing is both expert and sensitive. A further gesture to authenticity is the absence of a conductor; however, the ensemble might have been even better and the texture more finely judged and balanced had there been one. The recordings are vivid and truthful and those attracted to the coupling with Crusell, should be well satisfied.

Ernst Ottensamer is a highly sensitive clarinettist, who is a member of the Vienna Wind Ensemble. His account of the two *Clarinet concertos* can hold its own against nearly all the competition, the Košice orchestra also responds well to Johannes Wildner's direction, and the recorded sound is very natural and well balanced. A real bargain.

Clarinet concertos Nos. (i) *1 in F min., Op. 73;* (ii) *2 in E flat, Op. 74;* (iii) *Clarinet concertino, Op. 26.* (iv) *Grand duo concertante for clarinet and piano, Op. 48.*

✿ *** ASV CDDCA 747 [id.]. Emma Johnson, (i–iii) ECO, cond. (i) Yan Pascal Tortelier; (ii) Gerard Schwarz; (iii) Sir Charles Groves; (iv) with Gordon Black.

Emma Johnson's scintillating accounts of these three Weberian showpieces were made at different times and with different conductors, all of whom prove to be highly sympathetic to their young soloist. Her subtlety of expression is remarkable, with pianissimos more daringly extreme and with distinctly persuasive phrasing in slow movements treated warmly and spaciously. In the sparkling finales she is wittier than almost any, plainly enjoying herself to the full. The *Concertino*, in some ways the most delightful work of the three, especially its delicious finale, is hardly less beguiling; and as a bonus we are offered a brilliant and individually expressive account of the *Grand duo concertante* for clarinet and piano. Here she finds an admirable partner in Gordon Black, who accompanies with equal flair.

(i) *Clarinet concertos Nos. 1–2;* (ii) *Grand duo concertant for clarinet and piano, Op. 48.*

(N) **(*) Teldec/Warner Dig. 0630 15428-2 [id.]. Sharon Kam, (i) Leizig Gewandhaus O, Masur.

Having heard this young clarinettist in Israel, Kurt Masur invited her to Leipzig as a soloist, an imaginative and individual artist with a very sure technique. As the opening movement of the *First concerto* demonstrates, she has the gift of 'magicking' a phrase, regularly holding tension over an exaggerated pause or tenuto. Most remarkable of all is the dark intensity of Kam's account of the slow, minor-key *Romanza* of the *Second concerto*, taken at a measured tempo. She is similarly impressive in the *Grand duo concertant*, though there the piano tone of Itamar Golan is on the shallow side. The orchestral sound is warm, if rather opaque in tuttis. Emma Johnson's rival disc on ASV, with the *Clarinet concertino* as an extra, remains marginally preferable.

Piano concertos Nos. 1 in C, Op. 18; 2 in E flat, Op. 32; Konzertstück, Op. 79.

(B) **(*) Discovery Dig. DICD 920222 [id.]. Dana Protopopescu, Belgian R. & TV O, Rahbari.

Piano concertos Nos. 1–2; Konzertstück, Op. 79; Polacca brillante (L'hilarité), Op. 72 (orch. Liszt).

(BB) *** Naxos Dig. 8.550959 [id.]. Benjamin Frith, Dublin R. & TV Sinf., Prionnsias O'Duinn.

The young Hungarian pianist, Dana Protopopescu, plays all three works with striking freshness and an almost Chopinesque feeling in the lyrical music. Her sparkling passage-work and the chimerical changes of tempo and character of the *Konzertstück* are deftly managed. She is persuasively partnered by Alexander Rahbari, who enters fully into the spirit of her romantic style, convincing the listener that these works gain much from the added colour of a modern piano. Excellent recording.

However, Benjamin Frith's accounts are even finer and he receives splendid support from O'Duinn and the excellent Dublin Sinfonietta. In consequence, these performances all have more depth (the *Konzertstück* is particularly fine). Frith's playing has plenty of dash, yet its impetuosity is never inclined to run away with itself (as from time to time it almost does with Dana Protopopescu). The Naxos CD is not only better recorded and less expensive, it also includes the appropriately named *L'hilarité Polacca brillante*, which Frith plays with attractive panache.

Konzertstück in F min., Op. 79.

*** Ph. 412 251-2 [id.]. Brendel, LSO, Abbado – SCHUMANN: *Piano concerto.* ***

This Philips version of Weber's programmatic *Konzertstück* is very brilliant indeed, and finds the distinguished soloist in his very best form: Brendel is wonderfully light and invariably imaginative. In every respect, including the recording quality, this is unlikely to be surpassed for a long time.

(i) *Konzertstück for piano and orchestra; Invitation to the Dance; Overtures: Der Freischütz; Euryanthe; Oberon; The Ruler of the spirits; Die drei Pintos: Entr'acte.*

(N) *** DG Dig. 453 486-2 [id.]. (i) Mikhail Pletnev; Russian National Orchestra.

These are splendid performances, free from expressive exaggeration but excellently characterized in every way. Pletnev's account of the *Konzertstück*, which he directs from the keyboard, is quite simply dazzling – and arguably the best ever! Very good recorded sound too.

Overtures: *Abu Hassan; Der Beherrscher der Geister; Euryanthe; Der Freischütz; Oberon;*

Peter Schmoll; Invitation to the dance (orch. Berlioz), *Op. 65.*
❁ *** Nimbus Dig. NI 5154 [id.]. Hanover Band, Roy Goodman.

Goodman and the Hanover Band give persuasively delectable performances of the six Weber overtures (plus *Invitation to the dance* in Berlioz's arrangement) which are likely to convert even those who resist new-style authenticity. The rasp of trombones at the start of *Euryanthe* has a thrilling tang, and the warm acoustic ensures that the authentic string-players sound neither scrawny nor abrasive, yet present rapid passage-work with crystal clarity. Of feathery lightness, the scurrying of violins in the *Abu Hassan overture* is a delight, and each item – including a rarity in *Der Beherrscher der Geister* – brings its moments of magic, with Goodman, both fresh and sympathetic, securing consistently lively and alert playing from his team.

Overtures: *Der Freischütz; Oberon.*
*** DG Dig. 449 216-2 [id.]. Dresden State O, Sinopoli – R. STRAUSS: *Feuersnot* etc. ***

It is good too, to have fine, modern, digital recordings of these two masterly overtures. With finely moulded slow introductions leading to exhilarating allegros, the results are equally warm and refined.

Symphonies Nos. 1 in C; 2 in C.
**(*) ASV Dig. CDDCA 515 [id.]. ASMF, Marriner.

Symphonies Nos. 1 in C; 2 in C, J.50/51. Die Drei Pintos: Entr'acte. Silvana: Dance of the young nobles; Torch dance. Turandot: Overture; Act II: *March;* Act V: *Funeral march.*
❁ (BB) *** Naxos Dig. 8.550928 [id.]. Queensland PO, John Georgiadis.

Weber wrote his two symphonies in the same year (1807) and, though both are in C major, each has its own individuality. The witty orchestration and operatic character of the writing are splendidly caught in these sparkling Queensland performances, while in the slow movements the orchestral soloists relish their solos, for all the world like vocal cantilenas. Weber's scoring finds plentiful opportunities for the horns to shine, especially in the playful main theme of the *Presto* finale of No. 1. The Naxos recording is in the demonstration class, and the disc is made the more attractive for the inclusion of orchestral excerpts from two little-known operas and incidental music from *Turandot*. The *Entr'acte* from the incomplete *Die Drei Pintos* was put together by Mahler from Weber's sketches.

Sir Neville Marriner also has the full measure of Weber's two symphonies; these performances combine vigour and high spirits with the right degree of gravitas (not too much) in the slow movements. The recording is clear and full in the bass, but the bright upper range brings a touch of digital edge to the upper strings.

CHAMBER AND INSTRUMENTAL MUSIC

Cello sonata in A; Adagio & Rondo.
(N) (***) Testament mono SBT 2158 [id.]. Piatigorsky, Ivor Newton – BEETHOVEN: *Cello sonatas* (***); BRAHMS *Sonata No. 1.* (***)

These records were made in 1934–5 and are arrangements by Piatigorsky of the *Fifth* of Weber's *violin sonatas* Op. 10. The playing has an impressive eloquence.

Clarinet quintet in B flat, Op. 34.
(N) *** RCA Dig. 09026 68033-2 [id.]. Richard Stolzman, Tokyo Qt. – BRAHMS: *Clarinet quintet.* ***
(M) *** O-L (IMS) 444 167-2 [id.]. Alan Hacker, The Music Party – HUMMEL: *Clarinet quartet.* ***
(M) **(*) EMI CDM5 65995-2. Gervase de Peyer, Melos Ens. – BERWALD: *Septet* ***; SPOHR: *Double quartet.* **

(i) *Clarinet quintet; Introduction, theme and variations for clarinet and string quartet, Op. posth.;* (ii) *Grand duo concertante in E flat, Op. 48; 7 Variations on a theme from Silvana in B flat, Op. 33* (both for clarinet and piano).
(BB) *** Naxos Dig. 8.553122 [id.]. Kálmán Berkes, with (i) Auer Qt; (ii) Jenö Jandó.

Clarinet quintet; Flute trio in G min., Op. 63 (for flute, cello and piano).
(M) *** CRD CRD 3398; *CRDC 4098* [id.]. Nash Ens.

(i) *Clarinet quintet;* (ii) *Grand duo concertante, Op. 48; 7 Variations on a theme from Silvana, Op. 33.*
**(*) Chandos Dig. CHAN 8366 [id.]. Hilton, (i) Lindsay Qt; (ii) Keith Swallow.

This highly imaginative new RCA version of Weber's *Clarinet quintet* is in a class of its own. Richard Stolzman's lovely tone and his vocal sense of line (so important in Weber) constantly ravishes the ear, while he gets superbly sensitive support from the Tokyo Quartet. As in the coupled Brahms, their refined textures combine warmth with transparency. The slow movement opens quite ethereally, the fragility of the string playing, matched by exquisitely delicate solo playing, the clarinet timbre at times reduced to a whisper. Then comes the deliciously jocular Minuet followed by the rollicking finale with its good-humoured virtuosity and refinement of detail. The recording is in the demonstration bracket and beautifully balanced.

If you want to hear how Weber's *Clarinet quintet* must have sounded during his lifetime, Alan Hacker and the Music Party will probably be your first choice. The Gerock clarinet Hacker uses is from 1804, 11 years before the first complete performance of the *Quintet*. Hacker plays with his customary artistry and sensitivity, and with lots of bite and sparkle in the bravura passages. The recording is clear and vivid. Hacker has a price advantage and an ideal coupling.

On the CRD version, Antony Pay (playing a modern instrument) makes the very most of the work's bravura, catching the exuberance of the *Capriccio* third movement and the breezy gaiety of the finale. The Nash players provide an admirable partnership and then adapt themselves readily to the different mood of the *Trio*, another highly engaging work with a picturesque slow movement, described as a *Shepherd's lament*. The recording is first class, vivid yet well balanced.

However Naxos conveniently gather together expert and winning performances of all Weber's major chamber works featuring the clarinet, even if the amiable *Introduction, theme and variations* is now considered spurious. The *Quintet* is particularly successful with a lusciously appealing account af the *Adagio* and the finale chortles with great zest in its sparkling virtuosity. With Jandó an admirable partner, the *Grand duo concertante* is hardly less successful, and the two sets of variations are presented with both elegance and panache. The recording is realistic if too resonant, but the charisma and spontaneity of this Hungarian music-making carry the day in spite of this.

The Melos performance, with its extrovert dotted rhythms in the first movement and almost bucolic Scherzo, is very assured, and Gervase de Peyer's bravura playing in the finale is memorable. However, there is a slight lack of warmth here, caused partly by the recording acoustic, which is vivid but slightly dry.

Janet Hilton plays with considerable authority and spirit though she is not always as mellifluous as her rivals. However, her account of the *Grand duo concertante* is a model of fine ensemble, as are the *Variations on a theme from Silvana* of 1811, in both of which Keith Swallow is an equally expert partner.

7 Variations on a theme from Silvana in B flat, Op. 33.

*** Chandos Dig. CHAN 8506 [id.]. Gervase de Peyer, Gwenneth Pryor – SCHUBERT: *Arpeggione sonata;* SCHUMANN: *Fantasiestücke* etc. ***

These engaging Weber *Variations* act as a kind of encore to Schubert's *Arpeggione sonata* and with their innocent charm they follow on naturally. They are most winningly played by Gervase de Peyer; Gwenneth Pryor accompanies admirably. The recording is first class.

PIANO MUSIC

Piano sonatas Nos. 1–2; Rondo brillante in E flat (La Gaîté), Op. 52; Invitation to the dance, Op. 65.

(M) *** CRD Dig. CRD 3485; *CRDC 4185* [id.]. Hamish Milne.

Piano sonata Nos. 3 in D min., Op. 49; 4 in E min., Op. 70; Polacca brillante in E (L'Hilarité) (with LISZT: *Introduzione (Adagio)).*

(M) *** CRD Dig. CRD 3486; *CRDC 4186* [id.]. Hamish Milne.

These two Weber *Sonatas* are not easy to bring off, with their classical heritage and operatic freedom of line. Hamish Milne's performances have a lightness of touch that is most appealing, without ever being superficial, and his playing in the slow movements has attractive lyrical feeling. Moreover he also provides a sparkling account of the *Rondo brillante* and, as a final encore, a totally captivating account of the charming *Invitation to the dance*. He makes a sterner approach to the opening *Allegro feroce* of *No. 3 in D minor*, cast in an almost Beethovenian mould, while the last sonata is more introspective in its colouring and feeling, and concludes with a ruthless Tarantella, driven on by its own restless energy. The *Polacca brillante* returns to the world of dazzling articulation and sparkling display. Hamish Milne's playing is thoroughly inside Weber's world and technically equal to the composer's prodigious demands. He is very well recorded.

OPERA

Abu Hassan (opera; complete).

(M) *** CPO/EMI CPO 999 551-2 [id.]. Forster, Gedda, Edda Moser, Moll, Bav. State Op. Ch. & O, Sawallisch.

(M) *** RCA 74321 40577-2. Schreier, Hallstein, Adam, Dresden State Op. Ch., Dresden State O, Heinz Rogner.

Written in 1810, this frothy little farce reflects the then-current fashion for 'Turkish' themes. The overture is fizzingly brilliant, leading to a sequence of ten numbers, only three of them arias, including two for Abu Hassan's wife, Fatime. The plot involves the machinations of Abu Hassan to get himself out of debt, with the Caliph (one of three speaking roles) finally awarding him a thousand gold pieces. Sawallisch conducts a brilliant performance, with Nicolai Gedda in the title-role pointing his music lightly, with Edda Moser vibrantly expressive as his wife, and with Kurt Moll superb as the grasping money-lender, Omar. First-rate sound, engineered in 1975 by an EMI–Electrola team.

The alternative Eurodisc version, reissued on BMG/RCA, is not as starrily cast as its CPO/EMI competitor, but the singing of soloists and chorus is consistently pleasing. As with the reissued EMI set, the narrative and dialogue are often cued separately and can be omitted at will. The RCA libretto with translation omits this dialogue, assuming that the non-German listener will dispense with it. The

1971 recording is transferred smoothly and pleasingly.

Die drei Pintos (complete; adapted Mahler).
(M) *** RCA 74321 32246-2 (2) [id.]. Popp, Hollweg, Prey, Scovotti, Moll, Munich PO, Bertini.

Die drei Pintos was left unfinished by Weber; Mahler completed it in the 1880s, by adding re-arrangements of other Weber. The performance here is recorded complete with the spoken dialogue separately cued so that one can bypass it if necessary. The soloists are excellent with Werner Hollweg a fresh-voiced Gaston, and the whole production is lively and dramatic, while the orchestral support under Gary Bertini is first rate. The sound is excellent, warmly atmospheric yet clear, but the libretto only includes a German text.

Der Freischütz (complete).
*** Teldec/Warner Dig. 4509 97758-2 (2). Orgonasova, Schäfer, Wottrich, Salminen, Berlin R. Ch., BPO, Harnoncourt.
(M) *** EMI (SIS) CMS7 69342-2 (2). Grümmer, Otto, Schock, Prey, Wiemann, Kohn, Frick, German Op. Ch., Berlin, BPO, Keilberth.
(N) (M) *** DG 457 736-2 (2) [id.]. Janowitz, Mathis, Schreier, Adam, Vogel, Crass, Leipzig R Ch., Dresden State O, Carlos Kleiber.

Harnoncourt's electrifying and refreshing version of this operatic warhorse was recorded live at concert performances in the Philharmonie in Berlin in 1995 and the engineers have done wonders in conveying the atmosphere of a stage performance rather than a concert one, not least in the Wolf's glen scene, helped by recording of a very wide dynamic range. Harnoncourt clarifies textures and paces the drama well, making it sound fresh and new. The cast is first rate, with Orgonasova singing radiantly as Agathe, not just pure but sensuous of tone, floating high pianissimos ravishingly. Christine Schäfer, sweet and expressive, makes Aennchen into far more than just a soubrette character, and Erich Wottrich as Max is aptly heroic and unstrained, if hardly beautiful. The line-up of baritones and basses is impressive too, all firm and clear, contrasting sharply with one another, a team unlikely to be bettered today. A clear first choice among modern, digital recordings.

Keilberth's is a warm, exciting account of Weber's masterpiece which makes all the dated conventions of the work seem fresh and new. In particular the Wolf's glen scene on CD acquires something of the genuine terror that must have struck the earliest audiences. The casting of the magic bullets with each one numbered in turn, at first in eerie quiet and then in crescendo amid the howling of demons, is superbly conveyed. Elisabeth Grümmer sings more sweetly and sensitively than one ever remembers before, with Agathe's prayer exquisitely done. Lisa Otto is really in character, with genuine coquettishness. Schock is not an ideal tenor, but he sings ably enough. The Kaspar of Karl Kohn is generally well focused, and the playing of the Berlin Philharmonic has plenty of polish. The overall effect is immensely atmospheric and enjoyable.

The DG set, dating from 1973, marked Carlos Kleiber's first major recording venture, and now it is reissued as one of DG's Originals to stand beside the same conductor's equally powerful version of Brahms's *Fourth Symphony*. Kleiber's fine, incisive account of Weber's atmospheric and adventurous score fulfilled all expectations. With the help of an outstanding cast, excellent work by the recording producer, Eberhard Geller, and transparently clear recording, this is a most compelling version of an opera which transfers well to the gramophone. Only occasionally does Kleiber betray a fractional lack of warmth, but the full drama of the work is splendidly projected in the enhancement of the newly remastered sound.

Der Freischütz: highlights.
(B) *** DG Classikon 439 440-2 [id.] (from above recording, with Janowitz, Mathis; cond. Carlos Kleiber).

Anyone looking for a set of highlights from *Der Freischütz* cannot better this bargain Classikon disc. The 73-minute selection includes the full Wolf's Glen scene at the end of Act II, and the 1973 recording still sounds very well indeed.

Oberon (complete).
(M) *** DG 419 038-2 (2) [id.]. Grobe, Nilsson, Domingo, Prey, Hamari, Schiml, Bav. R. Ch. & SO, Kubelik.

Weber's delicately conceived score is a sequence of illogical arias, scenas and ensembles strung together by an absurd pantomime plot.The original issue included dialogue and a narrative spoken by one of Oberon's fairy characters. In the reissue this is omitted, cutting the number of discs from three to two, yet leaving the music untouched. With Birgit Nilsson commanding in *Ocean, thou mighty monster*, and excellent singing from the other principals, this performance is both stylish and refined, helped by Kubelik's ethereally light handling of the orchestra. The set can be recommended without reservation, for the recording remains of excellent quality.

Webern, Anton (1883–1945)

(i) *Concerto for nine instruments, Op. 24; 5 Movements for string quartet* (orchestral version), *Op. 5; Passacaglia, Op. 1; 6 Pieces for large orchestra, Op. 6; 5 Pieces for orchestra, Op. 10; Symphony, Op. 21; Variations for orchestra, Op.*

30. Arrangements of: BACH: *Musical offering: Fugue* (1935). (ii) SCHUBERT: *German dances* (for small orchestra), *Op. posth*. Chamber music: (iii) *6 Bagatelles for string quartet, Op. 9; 5 Movements for string quartet, Op. 5;* (iv; v) *4 Pieces for violin and piano, Op. 7;* (v; vi) *3 Small pieces for cello and piano, Op. 11;* (v; vii) *Quartet, Op. 22* (for piano, violin, clarinet & saxophone); (iii) *String quartet, Op. 28; String trio, Op. 20;* (v) *Variations for piano, Op. 27*. (Vocal) (viii; i) *Das Augenlicht, Op. 26;* (ix; x) *5 Canons on Latin texts, Op. 16;* (viii; ix; i) *Cantata No. 1, Op. 29;* (viii; ix; xi; i) *Cantata No. 2, Op. 31;* (viii) *Entflieht auf leichten Kähnen, Op. 2;* (ix; x) *5 Sacred songs, Op. 15;* (xii; v) *5 Songs, Op. 3; 5 Songs, Op. 4;* (xii; x) *2 Songs, Op. 8;* (xii; v) *4 Songs, Op. 12;* (xii; x) *4 Songs, Op. 13; 6 Songs, Op. 14;* (ix; x; xiii) *3 Songs, Op. 18;* (viii; i) *2 Songs, Op. 19;* (xii; v) *3 Songs, Op. 23;* (ix; v) *3 Songs, Op. 25;* (ix; x) *3 Traditional rhymes, Op. 17*.

(M) *** Sony SM3K 45845 (3) [id.]. (i) LSO (or members), Pierre Boulez; (ii) Frankfurt R. O, composer (recorded December 1932); (iii) Juilliard Qt (or members); (iv) Stern; (v) Rosen; (vi) Piatigorsky; (vii) Majeske, Marcellus, Weinstein; (viii) John Alldis Ch.; (ix) Lukomska; (x) with Ens., Boulez; (xi) McDaniel; (xii) Harper; (xiii) with John Williams. Overall musical direction: Boulez.

What Pierre Boulez above all demonstrates in the orchestral works (including those with chorus) is that, for all his seeming asceticism, Webern was working on human emotions. The Juilliard Quartet and the John Alldis Choir convey comparable commitment; though neither Heather Harper nor Halina Lukomska is ideally cast in the solo vocal music, Boulez brings out the best in both of them in the works with orchestra. Rarely can a major composer's whole *oeuvre* be appreciated in so compact a span. A rare recording of Webern himself conducting his arrangement of Schubert dances is also included. There are excellent notes, every item is cued, and perhaps it is carping to regret that the *Passacaglia* and *Variations for orchestra* were not indexed.

Concerto for 9 instruments, Op. 24.

(M) *** Chandos CHAN 6534 [id.]. Nash Ens., Simon Rattle – SCHOENBERG: *Pierrot Lunaire*. ***

This late Webern piece, tough, spare and uncompromising, makes a valuable fill-up for Jane Manning's outstanding version of Schoenberg's *Pierrot Lunaire*, a 1977 recording originally made for the Open University. First-rate sound and a beautifully clean CD transfer.

Langsamer satz (arr. Schwarz).

*** Delos Dig. DE 3121 [id.]. Seattle SO, Gerard Schwarz – HONEGGER: *Symphony No. 2;* R. STRAUSS: *Metamorphosen*. ***

The slow movement Webern composed in 1905 for string quartet sounds even more Mahlerian in Gerard Schwarz's transcription for full strings, which is eloquently played and sumptuously recorded.

5 Movements, Op. 5; Passacaglia, Op. 1; 6 Pieces for orchestra, Op. 6; Symphony, Op. 21.

(M) *** DG 427 424-2 (3). BPO, Karajan – BERG: *Lyric suite; 3 Pieces;* SCHOENBERG: *Pelleas und Melisande; Variations; Verklaerte Nacht*. ***

(M) *** DG (IMS) 423 254-2. BPO, Karajan.

Available either separately or within Karajan's three-CD compilation, this collection, devoted to four compact and chiselled Webern works, is in many ways the most remarkable of all. Karajan secures a highly sensitive response from the Berlin Philharmonic, who produce sonorities as seductive as Debussy. A strong recommendation, with excellent sound.

Passacaglia for orchestra, Op. 1.

(BB) *** RCA Navigator 74321 29243-2. Cologne RSO, Wakasugi – BERG: *Violin concerto;* SCHOENBERG: *Verklärte Nacht*. ***

(N) *(*) Koch Dig. 3-7316-2 [id.]. Houston SO, Eschenbach – SCHOENBERG: *Pelleas und Melisande*. *(*)

The Cologne Radio Symphony Orchestra understand what this music is about and under Hiroshi Wakasugi give a powerfully committed and very well-played account of Webern's most spectacular orchestral work. The 1977 recording is full and atmospheric, but documentation is inadequate.

Recorded at a live concert, this Koch version should be a more involving experience than it is. Karajan, Boulez or Abbado are more persuasive in this piece.

CHAMBER MUSIC

6 Bagatelles, Op. 9; 5 Movements, Op. 5 for string quartet.

(B) *** DG Classikon 439 470-2. LaSalle Qt – SCHOENBERG: *Verklaerte Nacht* etc. **(*)

Webern's six *Bagatelles*, written between 1911 and 1913, are characteristic of his brevity and density of expression; the earlier (1909) *Five Movements*, although succinct, are slightly more expansive. They are superbly played here and, while this is not easy music, it is certainly atmospheric and as arresting in impact as on the day it was written.

6 Bagatelles, Op. 9; 5 Movements, Op. 5; Quartet, Op. 28.

(M) *** Teldec/Warner 3984 21967-2. Alban Berg Qt – BERG: *Lyric suite* etc.; URBANNER: *String quartet No. 3*. ***

Really outstanding playing of the Webern pieces by the Berg Quartet makes this a first choice in this repertoire as the recording is impeccable and the LaSalle CD above omits the Op. 28 *Quartet*. The Berg couplings are hardly less fine, although the somewhat Schoenbergian quartet by the Austrian composer, Erich Urbanner, is less memorable.

Slow movement for string quartet (1905).
*** DG Dig. (IMS) 437 836-2 [id.]. Hagen Qt – DEBUSSY; RAVEL: *Quartets.* ***

The single-movement Webern *Quartet* was composed in Carinthia in the summer of 1905 and was first heard in the 1960s. It has an intense and chromatic study, and is played with great refinement by the Hagen Quartet and beautifully recorded. An excellent *bonne bouche*, if that term is appropriate, for a superb Debussy and Ravel coupling.

Weill, Kurt (1900–1950)

(i) *Violin concerto* (for violin, wind instruments and percussion), *Op. 12. Kleine Dreigroschenmusik (suite for wind from The Threepenny Opera)*. (Vocal): (ii–iv) *Berlin Requiem*; (iii–vii) *Happy End* (concert version); (ii–vii) *Mahagonny-Singspiel*; (iii–vi) *Der Protagonist* (opera): *Pantomime I*; (iv) *Von Tod in Wald (Death in the Forest), Op. 23.*
✽ (M) *** DG 459 442-2 (2) [id.]. L. Sinfonietta, David Atherton; with (i) Nona Liddell; (ii) Philip Langridge; (iii) Benjamin Luxon; (iv) Michael Rippon; (v) Mary Thomas; (vi) Ian Partridge; (vii) Meriel Dickinson.

This superb collection has been locked away in DG's vaults for over two decades! Now it re-emerges as a superb mid-priced Double, with full documentation, texts and translations, and in vividly real sound approaching demonstration quality. The music readily demonstrates that Kurl Weill had an imaginative range far wider than is generally realized. David Atherton and the London Sinfonietta recorded it all (on three LPs) immediately after returning from the Berlin Festival of 1975, and it will be a revelation for many to hear performances of such stylish incisiveness which put weight on purely musical as well as dramatic values. That remark covers all the clear-toned British soloists, who sound completely at home, while singing the notes with unusual precision. The real rarities here include the *Berlin Requiem*, rising intensely in tension, *Death in the Forest*, equally stark in the use of voices and wind, as well as the *Pantomime* from *Der Protagonist*. The early *Violin concerto*, with Nona Liddell as a sensitive soloist, already underlines the compactness of Weill's writing, while the relatively well-known works all emerge with new freshness. *Happy End*, for example, is performed at original pitch, with the voices the composer intended, though sadly the hit number, the *Bilbao song*, is left out. Excellent notes by David Drew who prepared the texts. Highly recommended.

Concerto for violin and winds, Op. 12.
*** Virgin/EMI Dig. VC5 45056-2. Christian Tetzlaff, Deutsche Kammerphilharmonie Wind – HINDEMITH: *Septet;* TOCH: *5 Pieces for wind and percussion.* ***
** Decca 452 481-2 [id.]. Chantal Juillet, Berlin RSO, Mauceri – KORNGOLD: *Violin concerto;* KRENEK: *Violin concerto.* ***

Weill's *Concerto for violin and winds* has a seriousness of purpose and an originality that are persuasive, no doubt much helped by the highly sensitive and imaginative performance given by Christian Tetzlaff and the winds of the Deutsche Kammerphilharmonie; it is coupled with most interesting repertoire. It will surely convert any doubters about the quality of this work as it has us.

This concerto asks for rather tougher, less soft-grained treatment than it receives from the expressive, poetic Juillet, whose style is better attuned to the more openly romantic works with which it is coupled. Nevertheless a valuable companion-piece for the other two concertos, also written by Central Europeans who found refuge in America.

STAGE WORKS

The Ballad of Magna Carta; Der Lindberghflug.
*** Capriccio Dig. 60012-1 [id.]. Henschel, Tyl, Calaminus, Clemens, Cologne Pro Musica Ch. & RSO, Latham-König; Wirl, Schmidt, Feckler, Minth, Scheeben, Berlin R. Ch. & O, Scherchen.

Der Lindberghflug ('The Lindbergh Flight') is a curiosity, a radio entertainment on the subject which was then (in 1927) hitting the headlines. Brecht wrote the text, but only later did Weill set the complete work, and that is how it is given in this excellent Cologne recording. A historic 1930 performance of the original Weill–Hindemith version, conducted by Hermann Scherchen, is given as an appendix, recorded with a heavy background roar but with astonishingly vivid voices. The fine, very German tenor who sang Lindbergh in 1930 was Erik Wirl and the tenor in the new recording is not nearly so sweet-toned, and the German narrator delivers his commentary in a casual, matter-of-fact way. Otherwise the performance under Jan Latham-König fully maintains the high standards of Capriccio's Weill series; and the other, shorter item, *The Ballad of Magna Carta* is most enjoyable too, a piece never recorded before. Clear, if rather dry, recording with voices vivid and immediate.

Die Dreigroschenoper (The Threepenny Opera): complete.

*** Decca Dig. 430 075-2 [id.]. Kollo, Lemper, Milva, Adorf, Dernesch, Berlin RIAS Chamber Ch. & Sinf., Mauceri.
*** Sony MK 42637 [id.]. Lenya, Neuss, Trenk-Trebisch, Hesterberg, Schellow, Koczian, Grunert, Ch. & Dance O of Radio Free Berlin, Brückner-Rüggeberg.

On Decca there are obvious discrepancies between the opera-singers, René Kollo and Helga Dernesch, and those in the cabaret tradition, notably the vibrant and provocative Ute Lemper (Polly Peachum) and the gloriously dark-voiced and characterful Milva (Jenny). That entails downward modulation in various numbers, as it did with Lotte Lenya, but the changes from the original are far less extreme. Kollo is good, but Dernesch is even more compelling. The co-ordination of music and presentation makes for a vividly enjoyable experience, even if committed Weill enthusiasts will inevitably disagree with some of the controversial textual and interpretative decisions.

The CBS alternative offers a vividly authentic abridged recording, darkly incisive and atmospheric, with Lotte Lenya giving an incomparable performance as Jenny. All the wrong associations, built up round the music from indifferent performances, melt away in the face of a reading as sharp and intense as this. Bright, immediate, real stereo recording, made the more vivid on CD.

Happy End (play by Brecht with songs); *Die sieben Todsünden (The Seven deadly sins)*.
(M) *** Sony mono/stereo MPK 45886 [id.]. Lotte Lenya, male quartet & O, Ch. & O, Brückner-Rüggeberg.

In the Sony/CBS performance of *The Seven deadly sins*, with the composer's widow as principal singer, the rhythmic verve is irresistible and, though Lenya had to have the music transposed down, her understanding of the idiom is unique. The recording is forward and slightly harsh, though Lenya's voice is not hardened, and the effect is undoubtedly vivid. *Happy end* was made in Hamburg-Harburg in 1960. Lenya turned the songs into a kind of cycle (following a hint from her husband), again transposing where necessary, and her renderings in her individual brand of vocalizing are so compelling they make the scalp tingle.

The Rise and fall of Mahagonny (complete).
**(*) Sony MK 77341 (2) [M2K 37874]. Lenya, Litz, Gunter, Mund, Gollnitz, Markworth, Saverbaum, Roth, Murch (speaker), NW German R. Ch. and O, Brückner-Rüggeberg.

Though Lotte Lenya, with her metallic rasping voice, was more a characterful *diseuse* than a singer, and again this bitterly inspired score had to be adapted to suit her limited range, it remains a most memorable performance. The recording lacks atmosphere, with voices (Lenya's in particular) close balanced. Yet even now one can understand how this cynical piece caused public outrage when it was first performed in Leipzig in 1930.

Der Silbersee (complete).
*** Capriccio Dig. 60011-2 (2) [id.]. Heichele, Tamassy, Holdorf, Schmidt, Mayer, Korte, Thomas, Cologne Pro Musica Ch., Cologne RSO, Latham-König.

This restoration of the original score of *Der Silbersee* aims to cope with the basic problem presented by having Weill's music as adjunct to a full-length play by Georg Kaiser. Between Weill's numbers a smattering of the original dialogue is here included to provide a dramatic thread and the speed of delivery adds to the effectiveness. Led by Hildegard Heichele, bright and full-toned as the central character, Fennimore, the cast is an outstanding one, with each voice satisfyingly clean-focused, while the 1989 recording is rather better-balanced and kinder to the instrumental accompaniment than some from this source, with the voices exceptionally vivid.

(i) *Die sieben Todsünden (The seven deadly sins); Kleine Dreigroschenmusik.*
(M) *** Sony Dig. SMK 44529 [id.]. (i) Migenes, Tear, Kale, Opie, Kennedy; LSO, Tilson Thomas.

(i) *Die sieben Todsünden (The seven deadly sins);* (ii) *Mahagonny Singspiel.*
*** Decca Dig. 430 168-2 [id.]. Lemper, Wildhaber, Haage, Mohr, Jungwirth, Berlin RIAS Chamber Ens., Mauceri, (ii) with J. Cohen.

Using the lower-pitch version of *The Seven deadly sins* originally designed for Lotte Lenya, but with Weill's original instrumentation, the Decca issue presents Ute Lemper in one of her finest performances on record. Her sensuous, tough voice exactly suits the role of the first Anna, who does all the singing. Mauceri's speeds, consistently slower than those of Rattle or Tilson Thomas, also enhance the sensuous element while bringing out the strange poignancy of the Prologue and Epilogue. The chattering ensemble of four male singers is well cast, and John Mauceri equally brings out the tang of the instrumental writing. He is rather less successful in the Singspiel, perhaps reflecting the fact that Lemper's role – mainly in duet with a singer of similar timbre – is less distinctive. Yet with similar forces required, it makes the ideal coupling. Full, bright sound to bring out the bite of the music.

In Tilson Thomas's performance with the LSO, Julia Migenes also uses the lower version of the score, colouring the voice even more boldly than Ute Lemper, echoing, even imitating, Lenya closely. With voices and instruments forwardly focused in the same consistent acoustic, the bite of the writing and its tangy beauty are put over powerfully, with

Tilson Thomas's relatively brisk speeds adding to the power rather than to the poignancy. This makes a formidable mid-priced alternative to the Mauceri version, in some ways more forceful but with a coupling, apt as it is, rather less generous.

Street scene (opera): complete.
*** TER Dig. CDTER2 1185 (2) [id.]. Kristine Ciesinski, Janis Kelly, Bottone, van Allan, ENO Ch. and O, Carl Davis.

Street scene was Kurt Weill's attempt, late in his Broadway career, to write an American opera as distinct from a musical. The TER set was made with the cast of the ENO production at the Coliseum, and the idiomatic feeling and sense of flow consistently reflect that. Some of the solo singing in the large cast is flawed, but never seriously, and the principals are all very well cast – Kristine Ciesinski as the much-put-upon Anna Maurrant, Richard van Allan as her sorehead husband, Janis Kelly sweet and tender as the vulnerable daughter, and Bonaventura Bottone as the diffident young Jewish neighbour who loves her. Those are only a few of the sharply drawn characters, and the performance on the discs, with dialogue briskly paced, reflects the speed of the original ENO production. Warm, slightly distanced sound.

Der Zar lässt sich Photographieren (complete).
**(*) Capriccio Dig. 60 007-1 [id.]. McDaniel, Pohl, Napier, Cologne R. O, Latham-König.

This curious one-Act *opera buffa* is a wry little parable about assassins planning to kill the Tsar when he has his photograph taken. Angèle, the photographer, is replaced by the False Angèle, but the Tsar proves to be a young man who simply wants friendship, and the would-be assassin, instead of killing him, plays a tango on the gramophone, before the Tsar's official duties summon him again. Jan Latham-König in this 1984 recording directs a strong performance, though the dryly recorded orchestra is consigned to the background. The voices fare better, though Barry McDaniel is not ideally steady as the Tsar.

'Kurt Weill on Broadway': excerpts from: *The Firebrand of Florence; Johnny Johnson (Johnny's song); Knickerbocker Holiday; Love Life; One Touch of Venus (Westwind).*
*** EMI Dig. CDC5 55563-2 [id.]. Thomas Hampson, Elizabeth Futral, Jerry Hadley, Jeanne Lehman, L. Sinf. Ch., L. Sinf., John McGlinn.

Thomas Hampson's magical collection of Weill numbers reveals what richness there is even in the least-known of Weill's Broadway scores. So a full 40 minutes are devoted to Weill's biggest flop, *The Firebrand of Florence*, an offbeat biography of Benvenuto Cellini, and the selection here is a delight. The very start of the disc on *One touch of Venus* establishes instantly that poetry is the keynote of the American Weill. One of the numbers in the 20-minute selection from *Love Life* (lyrics by Alan Jay Lerner) is a duet, *I remember it well.* Only later did Lerner adapt it for Gingold and Chevalier in *Gigi*, for here it is a dreamy slow waltz. The only well-known number is *It never was you* from *Knickerbocker Holiday*, and even that comes as a duet, not a solo. Hampson sings superbly, and McGlinn draws deeply sympathetic performances from the London Sinfonietta and the other soloists. Scholarly and informative notes add greatly to enjoyment, as well as the texts.

Weinberger, Jaromír (1896–1967)

Schwanda the Bagpiper: Polka and fugue.
(M) *** RCA 09026 62587-2 [id.]. Chicago SO, Fritz Reiner – DVORAK: *Symphony No. 9* etc.; SMETANA: *Bartered Bride: overture.* ***

This infectious orchestral display-piece was better known in the days of 78s. Reiner and his fine orchestra give a bravura performance, building to a huge climax. The Chicago recording is excellent and this CD overall is most attractive.

Weiner, Leó (1885–1960)

Hungarian folkdance suite, Op. 18.
*** Chandos Dig. CHAN 9029 [id.]. Philh. O, Järvi – BARTOK: *Miraculous Mandarin.* **(*)

Weiner here remained orientated towards the German and French schools, and this charming suite represents a Hungarian folk style far milder than Bartók's; but, with purposeful direction from Järvi, fine dramatic playing from the orchestra and ripely resonant recording, the full range of colour is brought out in these four movements lasting almost half an hour.

Serenade for small orchestra, Op. 3.
(N) *** Decca Dig. 458 929-2 [id.]. Budapest Festival O, Sir Georg Solti – BARTOK: *Cantata profana*; KODALY: *Psalmus hungaricus, Op. 13.* ***

Solti's very last recording sessions in Budapest in June, 1997, resulted in inspired performances, designed as a tribute to his three teachers at the Liszt Academy, not just Bartók and Kodály but his favourite teacher, the far less well known Leó Weiner. Weiner's *Serenade* proves a charmer, not so clearly Hungarian as Bartók or Kodály, but in its amiable way cleanly built on crisply conceived ideas.

Weir, Judith (born 1954)

OPERA

Blond Eckbert (complete).
*** Collins Dig. 1461-2 [id.]. Nerys Jones, Owens, Ventris, Folwell, ENO Ch. & O, Sian Edwards.

Not everyone will respond to the bald style of the libretto, here, yet the bright clarity and fresh invention of Weir's writing follows on the style she has adopted with such success in previous operas and mini-operas and this disc lets one appreciate the musical qualities without distraction. The singing is clean-cut and generally fresh, with Christopher Ventris excellent in multiple tenor roles, but with Nicholas Folwell gruff-sounding in the title-role. Excellent sound.

(i) *The Consolations of scholarship;* (ii) *Missa del Cid;* (iii) *King Harald's Saga.*
*** United Dig. 88040 CD [id.]. (i) Linda Hirst, Lontano, Odaline de la Martinez; (ii) Herrett, Combattimento, Mason; (iii) Jane Manning.

King Harald's Saga is a 13-minute sequence in three Acts, based on the Norwegian invasion of Britain under Harald Hardradi in 1066. With Jane Manning the magnetic soloist, it has the singer unaccompanied in a virtuoso performance. In the other two operas on this disc, Weir again uses spoken dialogue freely, with the solitary singer in each freely ringing the changes, but the chamber accompaniments expand the range of expression. *The Consolations of scholarship* has a libretto reflecting the style of the oldest form of Chinese play, about a boy thwarting a wicked general's plot against the Emperor. The *Missa del Cid* of 1988 is simpler in outline, with the exploits of El Cid told by an Evangelist in a sequence built on the six sections of the Latin Mass. Performances and recording are excellent, with Linda Hirst joined by Odaline de la Martinez in *Consolations* and Nick Herrett with Combattimento under David Mason in the *Missa*.

Wellesz, Egon (1885–1974)

Prospero's spell (Prosperos Beschwörungen), Op. 53; (i) *Violin concerto, Op. 84.*
(N) *** Orfeo Dig. C478 981A [id.]. Vienna Radio SO, Gerd Albrecht; (i) with Andrea Duka Löwenstein.

Egon Wellesz pursued a dual career as a scholar and composer. He was professor of musicology at Vienna and the leading authority on Byzantine hymnology in his day and on early opera, as well as the first biographer of Schoenberg, with whom he studied. It was in 1938 while he was in Amsterdam for the première of *Prosperos Beschwörungen* under Bruno Walter that he heard news of the *Anschluss* and took refuge in England. He remained in Oxford for the rest of his life. His output includes several stage works, the most impressive being the operas, *Alkestis* and *Die Bacchantinen* and his ballet, *Die Opferungen die Gefangenen*. Although his *Octet* written for the Vienna Octet in 1949 was recorded, none of his nine symphonies or other major works have yet been. *Prosperos Beschwörungen* (1935) is a highly imaginative score; Wellesz had toyed with the idea of writing an opera on *The Tempest* but these five orchestral pieces were the result. They are quite individual though they are closer to Hindemith than to the second Viennese school. The *Violin concerto* (1961) is a made of sterner stuff and it provides a formidable challenge to the soloist to which Andrea Duka Löwenstein rises triumphantly. Good playing from the ORF (Oesterreiches Rundfunk) or Vienna Radio Orchestra under Gerd Albrecht. Good sound though perhaps a little studio bound.

Wert, Giaches de (1535–96)

Il settimo libro de madrigali.
(M) *** Virgin Veritas/EMI Dig. VER5 61177-2 [id.]. Consort of Musicke, Anthony Rooley.

Giaches de Wert was Monteverdi's predecessor in Mantua at the court of Count Alfonso Gonzaga: this is the seventh of twelve books of madrigals, published in 1581. The opening madrigal is celebratory: *Sorgi e rischiara* ('Arise, light up the sky with thy approach, Holy Mother of love, lead in the day'), but many of the other varied settings are concerned with the trials and disappointments of love. De Wert certainly emerges here as a composer of expressive depth and personality and with a fine feeling for words. He is not another Monteverdi but his art is well worth knowing, and the singing here is persuasive, expressively responsive and beautifully blended, even if it does not always make the music project irresistibly. The recording is well up to the high standard of this stimulating Veritas series.

Westlake, Nigel (born 1958)

Antarctica (suite for guitar and orchestra).
*** Sony Dig. SK 53361 [id.]. John Williams, LSO, Paul Daniel – SCULTHORPE: *Nourlangie* etc. ***

Antarctica is a film-score written to accompany an Imax large-screen documentary about the frozen continent. Westlake's music is highly imaginative and inventive and stands up memorably on its own. The guitar is used both with the orchestra and to play haunting, improvisatory-styled interludes. John Williams clearly relishes the considerable demands of the solo part, and Paul Daniel shapes the music spontaneously and skilfully. The recording is in the demonstration bracket, though the solo guitar is very forwardly balanced.

White, Robert (*c.* 1538–74)

Motets: *Christe qui lux es; Domine quis habitavit; Portio mea Domine; Regina coeli.*
✿ (M) *** Cal. CAL 6623 [id.]. Clerkes of Oxenford, David Wulstan – TALLIS: *Mass Puer natus est* etc. *** ✿

Robert White's style of writing has a basic restraint and often shows a gentle, Dowland-like melancholy, so striking at the opening of *Domine quis habitavit*. But this is often offset by the soaring trebles, especially in the ravishing *Portio mea Domine*, while *Christe qui lux es*, the last motet on this record, is very touching indeed. Glorious performances by Wulstan and the Clerkes of Oxenford, who have the full measure of this repertoire. The analogue recording could hardly be bettered. Not to be missed.

Widor, Charles-Marie (1844–1937)

Symphony No. 3 in E minor, Op. 13/2: excerpts *(Prélude; Adagio; Finale); Symphony No. 4 in F min., Op. 13/4; Symphony No. 9 in C min.(Gothique), Op. 70.*
(N) (M) *** Erato/Warner 4509 98534-2 [id.]. Marie-Claire Alain (Cavaillé-Coll organ of L'Eglise St-Germain, St-Germain-en-Laye).

In the hands of Marie-Claire Alain the St-Germain organ sounds very orchestral, and her colouring of the gentle *Adagio* (a perpetual canon) of the *Third Symphony* and the *Andante cantabile* of No. 4 is quite haunting. The spectacular Wagnerian finale of this *E minor Symphony* – played in the revised 1901 version – with its cascading sextuplets, is not musically as well focused as the more famous *Toccata* which closes its successor, but it sounds very exciting here, and as it ends gently, the opening *Toccata* of No. 4 makes a bold contrast. The *Gothic Symphony* has a notable third movement where a Christmas chant (*Puer natus est nobis*) is embroidered fugally. The finale section is a set of variations, and the Gregorian chant is reintroduced in the pedals. These are classic performances, given spacious analogue sound, with just a touch of harshness to add a little edge to *fortisssimos*.

Organ symphony No. 5 in F min., Op. 42/1.
*** DG Dig. 413 438-2 [id.]. Simon Preston (organ of Westminster Abbey) – VIERNE: *Carillon de Westminster*. ***
*** Chandos Dig. CHAN 9271 [id.]. Ian Tracey (organ of Liverpool Cathedral), BBC PO, Yan Pascal Tortelier – GUILMANT: *Symphony No. 1 for organ and orchestra* ***; POULENC: *Concerto*. **(*)

Simon Preston gives a masterly account of the Widor *Fifth Symphony*, with a fine sense of pace and command of colour; there is a marvellous sense of space in this DG recording.

The long reverberation-period of Liverpool Cathedral gives a special character to Widor's *Fifth Symphony*, especially the mellow central movements. Ian Tracey makes the most of the colouristic possibilities of his fine instrument and also uses the widest possible range of dynamics, with the tone at times shaded down to a distant whisper. Yet the famous *Toccata* expands gloriously if without the plangent bite of a French instrument.

Symphonies Nos. 5 in F min. Op. 42/1; 7 in A min., Op. 42/3.
(N) *** ASV Dig. CDDCA 958 [id.]. Jane Parker-Smith (Van Den Heuvel organ), St Eustache, Paris.

It is good to have a demonstration-worthy modern digital recording of what must be counted two of Widor's very best symphonies. Jane Parker-Smith is a complete master of this repertoire and she shows that it does not always have to be played on a traditional Cavaillé-Coll instrument. The organ at St Eustache, Paris is new (1967), and is Netherlands-built. It is magnificent. Not only are the big tuttis, as in the finale of the *Seventh Symphony*, superbly expansive, but the organ has a ravishingly rich palette and a warm sonority to deal with Widor's gentler ideas, like the *Andante cantabile* and *Adagio* of the *Fifth* and the inner movements of No. 7, and particularly the *Allegro ma non troppo*, where the gently murmuring semiquavers flow along sensuously like a warm summer breeze. Because of this natural clarity of internal focus Jane Parker-Smith is able to use a very wide dynamic range and in the supreme test, the masterly *Toccata* which closes the *Fifth*, the calm at the centre of the storm does not lose contact with the listener, and the great reprise of the main theme, with thundering pedals, is unforgettable.

Symphony No. 10 in D (Romane), Op. 73; Suite Latine, Op. 86.
(N) *** MDG Dig. Ben van Oosten (Cavaillé-Coll organ, at Sermin, Toulouse).

Ben van Oosten is in the process of recording all Widor's organ music and we hope to cover his complete survey in a future edition. Meanwhile this coupling augurs well for the project. His gleaming registration at the opening of the *Symphony Romane* is quite dazzling, yet the central *Choral* and *Cantilène* (both based on plainchant from the Easter liturgy) are wonderfully serene. The cascading finale achieves a spectacular climax (still featuring the plainsong) then makes an extended diminuendo, culminating when the opening theme is reintroduced. The *Suite Latine*, one of Widor's last works and written when he was 83, again uses plainsong, but more introspectively. In van Oosten's hands the central *Beatus vir, Lamento* and *Adagio* are gently withdrawn in colour and feeling, so that the exuberant finale is the more telling. These are undoubtedly distinguished performances, very well recorded on an impressively sonorous Cavaillé-Coll organ.

Wieniawski, Henryk (1835–80)

(i) *Violin concertos Nos. 1–2;* (ii) *Caprice in A min.* (arr. Kreisler); *Obertass-Mazurka, Op. 19/1; Polonaise de concert No. 1 in D, Op. 4; Polonaise brillante No. 2, Op. 21; Scherzo–tarantelle, Op. 16.*
(M) *** EMI CDM5 66059-2 [id.]. Itzhak Perlman; (i) LPO, Ozawa; (ii) Samuel Sanders.

Violin concertos Nos. 1 in F sharp min., Op. 14; 2 in D min., Op. 22; Légende, Op. 17.
*** DG Dig. 431 815-2 [id.]. Gil Shaham, LSO, Lawrence Foster – SARASATE: *Zigeunerweisen.* ***

The Paganinian pyrotechnics in the first movement of Wieniawski's *First Violin concerto* , as Shaham readily demonstrates can be made to dazzle. Both soloist and orchestra are equally dashing, and lyrically persuasive in the better known *D minor Concerto*, while making an engaging encore out of the delightful *Légende*. With first-class DG recording this record is very recommendable.

Perlman gives scintillating performances, full of flair, and is excellently accompanied. The recording, from 1973, is warm, vivid and well balanced. It is preferable to Perlman's digital remake of the *Second Concerto*. The mid-priced reissue includes a mini-recital of shorter pieces, often dazzling, but losing some of their appeal from Perlman's insistence on a microphone spotlight. Samuel Sanders comes more into the picture in the introductions for the two *Polonaises*, although the violin still remains far too near the microphone.

Violin concerto No. 2 in D min., Op. 22.
*** Decca Dig. 421 716-2 [id.]. Joshua Bell, Cleveland O, Ashkenazy – TCHAIKOVSKY: *Violin concerto.* ***
(M) (***) EMI mono CDH7 64251-2 [id.]. Heifetz, LPO, Barbirolli – SAINT-SAENS: *Havanaise* etc.; SARASATE: *Zigeunerweisen;* VIEUXTEMPS: *Concerto No. 4.* (***)
(M) **(*) Sony Stern Edition I SMK 66830 [id.]. Stern, Phd. O, Ormandy – BRUCH: *Violin concerto No. 1* **(*); TCHAIKOVSKY: *Méditation; Sérénade mélancolique.* ***

Joshua Bell gives a masterly performance, full of flair, even if he does not find quite the same individual poetry in the big second-subject melody or in the central *Romance* as Shaham. Excellent recording, brilliant and full.

Everything that Heifetz touched turned to gold. He is as much in a class of his own here as he is elsewhere on this CD. The concerto was recorded in 1935 with the young John Barbirolli, with whom Heifetz formed a strong rapport. It is doubtful that this performance has ever been bettered on record. The sound is perhaps less vivid than the best recordings of the day, but the transfers are very good.

Stern's recording comes from 1957, and the very close balance is not flattering to his upper range (although of course this playing can stand any kind of scrutiny). The songful slow movement is played simply and beautifully, and the finale is very *energico* indeed. Ormandy, as usual, provides fine support and the orchestra, though also balanced artificially, plays against a warm ambience.

Wikmanson, Johan (1753–1800)

String quartet No. 2 in E min., Op. 1/2.
(M) *** CRD CRD 3361; *CRDC 4061* [id.]. Chilingirian Qt – BERWALD: *Quartet.* ***
(M) *** CRD CRD 33123 (2) [id.]. Chilingirian Qt – ARRIAGA: *String quartets Nos. 1–3.* ***

Wikmanson was a cultured musician, but little of his music survives and two of his five *Quartets* are lost. The overriding influence here is that of Haydn and the finale of the present quartet even makes a direct allusion to Haydn's *E flat Quartet*, Op. 33, No. 2. The Chilingirian make out a persuasive case for this piece and are very well recorded. As can be seen, this work is available coupled with either Arriaga or Berwald.

Wilbye, John (1574–1638)

Madrigals (First Set, 1598): excerpts: *Adieu sweet Amaryllis; Alas what a wretched life; Cruel behold my ending; Die hapless man; Lady when I behold the roses* (2 versions); *Lady, your words do spite me; My throat is sore; Of joys and pleasing pains; Thus saith my Cloris bright; Thou art but young; Weep O mine eyes; When shall my wretched life; Why dost thou shoot.* (Second Set, 1609): excerpts: *Ah cannot sighs, nor tears; Draw on sweet night; O wretched man; Softly, of softly, drop my eyes; Stay, Corydon; Sweet honey-sucking bee; Yes sweet, take heed; Ye that do live in pleasures.*
(N) (B) *** Decca Double 458 093-2 (2) Consort of Musicke, Anthony Rooley – GIBBONS; WILBYE: *Madrigals.* ***

John Wilbye was one of the major figures in the English music of the period and this selection made from both his major sets of madrigals must be counted the best current available introduction to his art. The most famous madrigals such as *Draw on sweet night* and *Stay, Corydon stay* are matched by other sad settings like *O wretched man* and *Softly softly drop, mine eyes*, and while a lighter note is caught with *Adieu sweet Amaryllis* and *Sweet honey-sucking bee*, it is the melancholic nature of his finest works that give them their special character. The performances here are appealingly fresh rather than profound in their depth, but they are beautifully recorded and this anthology overall is a most important addition to the catalogue.

Willaert, Adrian (*c*.1490–1562)

Ave Maria; Magnificat sexti toni; Missa Christus resurgens.

(N) (B) *** Naxos Dig. 8.553211 [id.]. Oxford Camerata, Summerly (with RICHAFORT: *Motet: Christus resurgens.* ***)

Over the first half of the sixteenth century this Flemish composer was one of the key figures in Western music, instrumental in the development both of the madrigal and of church music for double chorus. From 1527 until his death he was Maestro di capella at St Mark's in Venice, but this music, dates mainly from his earlier years, when he achieved nine settings of the Mass. This splendid offering from Summerly and his Oxford Camerata is the only one available, a magnificent 'parody mass', using as its base a motet by Jean Richafort, a piece included here as a prelude. Willaert's setting rises to a sublime conclusion in the extended *Agnus Dei*, in flowing polyphony. The *Magnificat* and *Ave Maria* offer inspired music too, performed with equal freshness and dedication. Vividly atmospheric sound. At Naxos price, not to be missed.

Williams, Grace (1906–1977)

(i) *Carillons for oboe and orchestra;* (ii) *Trumpet concerto. Fantasia on Welsh nursery rhymes;* (iii) *Penillion;* (iv) *Sea sketches* (for string orchestra).

*** Lyrita SRCS 323 [id.]. (i) Anthony Camden: (ii) Howard Blake; both with LSO; (iii) RPO; all cond. Groves; (iv) ECO, David Atherton.

It is good to have this attractive programme of works by a woman composer who (rarely among twentieth-century feminist musicians) glowingly shows that she believes in pleasing the listener's ear. No lack of imaginative resource either, particularly in the memorably individual *Sea sketches*, a masterly suite of five contrasted movements which catch the sea's unpredictability as well as its formidable energy, while the two slow sections, the seductive *Channel sirens* and the *Calm sea in summer*, are balmily, impressionistic and poetic. The other works here range attractively from the simple *Nursery-rhyme Fantasia* to *Penillion,* a set of four colourful, resourceful pieces, easy on the ear but full of individual touches retaining the idea of a central melodic line. The trumpet and oboe concertante pieces are superbly played by soloists from the LSO of the early 1970s – both show the affection and understanding of individual instrumental timbre which mark the composer's work. Excellent performances throughout, and very good analogue sound.

(i) *Symphony No. 2; Ballads for orchestra;* (ii) *Fairest of stars* (for soprano and orchestra).

*** Lyrita SRCS 327 [id.]. (i) BBC Welsh SO, Handley; (ii) Janet Price, LSO, Groves.

In her *Second Symphony*, Grace Williams's most ambitious orchestral work, the writing is sharp and purposeful, relaxing more towards lyricism in the slow movement (which produces an endearing pastoral oboe theme) and the finale with its darkly Mahlerian overtones. The *Ballades* of 1968, characteristically based on Welsh ballad and 'penillion' forms, also reveal the darker side of Grace Williams's writing. The performances, originally recorded for radio, are expressive and convincing. *Fairest of stars*, too, is a relatively tough setting of Milton, and is strongly sung by Janet Price. The recordings are all of good quality.

Williamson, Malcolm (born 1931)

Lento for strings. (i) *The World at the Manger* (cantata); *Agnus Dei; Easter Carol; Epiphany carol; Procession of Palms; Harvest thanksgiving; Jesu, lover of my soul; Love's redeeming work is done.*

(N) (M) *** Carlton Dig. 30366 01172. E. N. Philh. O (members), with (i) Mastersingers, Battiwalla, Alan Simmons.

The music of Malcolm Williamson, Master of the Queen's Music, has been shockingly neglected in the age of CD. During the LP era his symphonies, concertos and operas were available, but they have never been transferred to the new medium. This charming collection of short choral and instrumental works, including the Christmas cantata, *The World at the Manger*, shows how tuneful and approachable he can be, using conventional harmony and tonality in new and distinctive ways. Fresh singing from the Mastersingers under Alan Simmons, with Darius Battiwalla on the organ, as well as a group of players from the English Northern Philharmonia.

Wirén, Dag (1905–86)

Serenade for strings in G, Op. 11.

(BB) *** Naxos Dig. 8.553106 [id.]. Bournemouth Sinf., Richard Studt – Concert: *Scandinavian string music.* ***

The engaging *String serenade* is Dag Wirén's one claim to international fame, and it is good to welcome an outstanding super-bargain version. The finale certainly earns its hit status, full of spontaneous, lilting energy. First-rate recording within an entirely recommendable concert of Scandinavian string music, not all of it familiar.

(i–ii) *Miniature suite* (for cello & piano), *Op. 8b;* (ii) (Piano) *Improvisations; Little suite; Sonatina, Op. 25; Theme and variations, Op. 5;* (iii) *3 Sea poems;* (iv; ii) *2 Songs from Hösthorn, Op. 13.*
*** BIS Dig. CD 797 [id.]. (i) Torleif Thedéen; (ii) Stefan Bojsten; (iii) Jubilate Ch., Riska; (iv) Christina Högman.

Dag Wirén was a miniaturist *par excellence* and few of the individual movements recorded here detain the listener for more than two or three minutes. The early (and inventive) *Theme and variations*, Op. 5, is the longest work. Although it is slight, the *Sonatina for piano* often touches a deeper vein of feeling than one might expect to encounter. Good performances from all concerned, and the usual truthful BIS recording.

Wolf, Hugo (1860–1903)

Italian serenade in G.
(***) Biddulph mono LAB 098 [id.]. Budapest Qt – GRIEG; SIBELIUS: *Quartets.* ***

A welcome transfer – the first on CD – of the 1933 pioneering *Italian serenade.* It has a spring in its step and a lightness of touch that are almost unique, and it is well transferred here by Ward Marston. The couplings also show how special this ensemble was in the 1930s.

String quartet in D min.; Intermezzo in E flat; Italian serenade in G.
(N) *** CPO Dig. CPO 999 529-2 [id.]. Auryn Qt.

Hugo Wolf's massive *String quartet* may be a student work, but in its concentration and complexity it harks back to late Beethoven, as well as to Wagner. The formidable first movement leads to a slow movement of heavenly length, here interpreted with hushed intensity by the young Auryn Quartet. Both in the *Quartet* and in the other two works, including the winningly exuberant *Italian serenade*, the playing amply makes up in its warmth and spontaneity for any slight lack of polish. Warm, full sound.

Lieder: *Frage nicht; Frühling übers Jahr; Gesang Weylas; Kennst du das Land? (Mignon); Heiss mich nicht reden (Mignon I); Nur wer die Sehnsucht kennt (Mignon II); So lasst mich scheinen (Mignon III); Der Schäfer; Die Spröde.*
*** DG Dig. (IMS) 423 666-2. Anne Sofie von Otter, Rolf Gothoni – MAHLER: *Das Knaben Wunderhorn* etc. ***

Anne Sofie von Otter presents Wolf's *Mignon* songs with firm, persuasive lines. The gravity of *Kennst du das Land?* is then delightfully contrasted against the delicacy of *Frühling übers Jahr* or *Die Spröde.* The sensitivity and imagination of Rolf Gothoni's accompaniment add enormously to the performances in a genuine two-way partnership. Well-balanced recording.

Eichendorf Lieder: *Nachtzauber; Die Zigeunerin.* Mörike Lieder: *Elfenlied; Der Genesene an die Hoffnung; Lebewohl; Storchenbotschaft.* Lieder from *Italienisches Liederbuch: Du sagst mir; Ich esse nun mein Brot; Ich hab' in Penna; Nein, junger Herr; Nur lass uns Frieden schliessen; O wär' dein Haus durchsichtig; Schweig' einmal still; Verschling' der Abgrund; Wer rief dich denn?* Lieder from *Spanisches Liederbuch: Bedeckt mich mit Blumen; Geh', Geliebter, geh' jetzt; Herr, was trägt der Boden hier; In dem Schatten meiner Locken; Klinge klinge mein Pandero; Mögen alle bösen Zungen; Sie blasen zum Abmrarsch.* Encores: *Trau' nicht der Liebe.* Mörike Lieder: *Der Knabe und das Immelein; Nimmersatte Liebe; Selbstgeständnis.*
(M) (***) EMI mono CDH5 65749-2. Elisabeth Schwarzkopf, Gerald Moore.

In many ways the extra degree of freedom in Schwarzkopf's performances here, recorded live at Salfurg recitals in 1957 and 1963, adds to the intensity of the experience, both in weighty songs and in lighter ones such as *Wer rief dich denn?* (uniquely vehement) and *Ich hab' in Penna.* The recordings, originally made by Austrian Radio, capture the voice beautifully, with words crystal clear. Texts are given but no translation.

Goethe Lieder: *Anakreons Grab; Blumengruss; Erschaffen und Beleben; Gleich und gleich; Harfenspieler I, II & III; Ob der Koran von Ewigkeit sei?; Phänomen; Der Rattenfänger; Sie haben wegen der Trunkenheit; So lang man nüchtern ist; Spottlied; Trunken müssen wir alle sein!; Was in der Schenke waren heute.* Mörike Lieder: *Abschied; An die Geliebte; An eine Aolsharfe; Auf ein altes Bild; Bei einer Trauung; Elfenlied; Er ist's; Fussreise; Der Gärtner; Gebet; Gesang Weylas; Heimweh; Jägerlied; Nimmersatte Liebe; Der Tambour; Verborgenheit.*
(BB) *** Virgin Classics Dig. Double VBD5 61418-2 (2) [CVBD 61418]. Thomas Allen, Geoffrey Parsons – BRAHMS: *Lieder.* ***

This is an exceptionally generous (74-minute) collection of Wolf's Goethe and Mörike settings, which are much rarer, both on disc and in the recital room. Allen enters fully into the spirit of each song, and Geoffrey Parsons accompanies with characteristic imagination. Whether the words convey ardour (as in one of the best known, *An die Geliebte*), are hauntingly evocative (as in the remarkable *Harfenspieler* settings) or are exuberantly extrovert (*Der Rattenfänger*), these artists unerringly project their mood. Alas, this inexpensive reissue includes neither translations nor song summaries, but the vocal treasure offered here and the excellence both of performances and of Andrew Keener's recording balance at Abbey Road carries the day.

Italienisches Liederbuch (complete).
(M) *** EMI CDM7 63732-2 [id.]. Elisabeth Schwarzkopf, Dietrich Fischer-Dieskau, Gerald Moore.
*** Hyperion Dig. CDA 66760 [id.]. Felicity Lott, Peter Schreier, Graham Johnson.
(M) *** Ph. (IMS) 442 744-2 (2). Elly Ameling, Gérard Souzay, Dalton Baldwin – R. STRAUSS: *Lieder*. ***
**(*) Teldec/Warner Dig. 9031 72301. Barbara Bonney, Håkan Hagegård, Geoffrey Parsons.

On EMI all 46 songs of Wolf's *Italienisches Liederbuch* are sung by Schwarzkopf and Fischer-Dieskau on a CD playing for two seconds over 79 minutes, generous measure at mid-price! Few artists today can match the searching perception of these two great singers in this music, with Fischer-Dieskau using his sweetest tones and Schwarzkopf ranging through all the many emotions inspired by love. Gerald Moore is at his finest, and Walter Legge's translations will help bring the magic of these unique songs even to the newcomer. The well-balanced 1969 recording has been admirably transferred, giving the artists a fine presence.

Elly Ameling, delicately sweet and precise, contrasts well with Souzay, with his fine-drawn sense of line. The charm and point of these brief but intensely imaginative songs are well presented, with perceptive accompaniment from Dalton Baldwin. The coupled Richard Strauss recital also shows Souzay at his most perceptive. However, the unforgettable 1969 version with Schwarzkopf and Fischer-Dieskau has the advantage of being offered uncoupled, on a single, mid-priced CD.

Barbara Bonney uses her bright, clear soprano with keen imagination, often with echoes of Schwarzkopf, but with many individual insights. Håkan Hagegård is less individual but still gives a strong, firm reading, even if his baritone has often sounded more beautiful on disc. Geoffrey Parsons is the keenly responsive accompanist, sharply reflecting his singers' approach to each poem. First-rate sound.

Graham Johnson conjures up music-making full of magic, compelling from first to last. Yet, so far from being intrusive in his playing, he consistently heightens the experience, drawing out from Felicity Lott one of her most intense and detailed performances on record, totally individual. Peter Schreier, one of the supreme masters of Lieder today, also responds to this characterful accompanist; and having a tenor instead of the usual baritone brings many benefits in this sharply pointed sequence. The triumph of this issue is crowned by the substantial booklet provided in the package, containing Johnson's uniquely perceptive commentary on each song – alone worth the price of the disc. Excellent sound.

Mörike Lieder: Michelangelo Lieder: Alles endet, was entstehet; Fühlt meine Seele; Wohl denk' ich oft. Mörike Lieder: Abschied; An de Schlaf; An die Geliebte; Auf eine altes Bild; Auf eine Christblume I & II; Auf einer Wanderung; Auftrag; Begegnung; Bei einer Trauung; Denk' es, o Seele!; Der Feuerreiter; Füssreise; Der Gärtner; Gebet; Die Geister am Mummelsee; Der Genesene an die Hoffnung; Gesang Weyla's; Heimwek; Im Frühling; In der Fru'he; Der Jäger; Jägerlieg; Karwoche; Der König bei der Krönung; Lebe wohl; Lied eines Verliebten; Neue Liebe; Nimmersatte Liebe; Peregrina I & II; Schlafendes Jesuskind; Selbstgeständnis; Seufzer; Storchenbotschaft; Der Tambour; Um Mitternacht; Wo find' ich Trost; Verborgenheit; Zitronnenfalter im April; Zur Warnung.
(M) (***) EMI mono/stereo CMS7 63563-2 (2). Dietrich Fischer-Dieskau, Gerald Moore.

This collection of Wolf's settings of Mörike, 44 songs, was recorded in 1957, with four songs completing the collection, added two years later. Those four are in stereo but, so compelling is Fischer-Dieskau's singing, one hardly worries that the others are all in mono only. The experience is the more vivid thanks to the close placing of the singer, as though face to face. Texts and translations are given.

Spanisches Liederbuch (complete).
(M) *** DG 457 726-2 (2) [id.]. Schwarzkopf, Fischer-Dieskau, Moore.
*** EMI CDS5 55325-2 (2) [id.]. Anne Sofie von Otter, Olaf Bär, Geoffrey Parsons.

In this superb DG reissue, the sacred songs provide a dark, intense prelude, with Fischer-Dieskau at his very finest, sustaining slow tempi impeccably. Schwarzkopf's dedication comes out in the three songs suitable for a woman's voice; but it is in the secular songs, particularly those which contain laughter in the music, where she is at her most memorable. Gerald Moore is balanced rather too backwardly – something the transfer cannot correct – but gives superb support.

Completed barely six months before Geoffrey Parsons's untimely death, the EMI set of the *Spanish Songbook* makes a superb memorial to that great accompanist, here working with two of the most searching and stylish Lieder singers of the present generation. They opt for an order of the songs quite different from the original published order, seeking to find 'a dramatic shape that worked in the atmosphere of a concert'. Quite apart from Parsons's superb contribution, the performances of both soloists vie with those on the classic DG set with Schwarzkopf and Fischer-Dieskau. For the lighter songs von Otter uses a much brighter tonal range than elsewhere, though in such a song as *In dem Schatten meiner Locken* she remains more intimate than Schwarzkopf, pointing the words and phrases with comparable character.

Wolf-Ferrari, Ermanno (1876–1948)

L'amore medico: Overture. Il Campiello: Intermezzo; Ritornello. La Dama Bomba: Overture. I gioielli della Madonna (suite). I quattro rusteghi: Prelude & Intermezzo. Il segreto di Susanna: Overture.
*** ASV Dig. CDDCA 861 [id.]. RPO, José Serebrier.

Although this situation is currently changing, Wolf-Ferrari has long held a permanent place in the catalogue only with recordings of his operatic *intermezzi* – not surprising, perhaps, when they are so readily tuneful and charmingly scored. Serebrier conjures at times exquisite playing from the RPO (especially the strings) and, even though he takes Susanna's sparkling overture slightly slower than usual, it is hardly less successful. What is specially memorable is his delicate treatment of the gossamer string-pieces from *I quattro rusteghi* and the *Ritornello* from *Il Campiello* which almost have a Beecham touch. The ASV recording, made in the Henry Wood Hall, is slightly more open and indeed marginally more transparent and fresh.

Il Campiello: Prelude; Ritornello; Intermezzo. The Inquisitive Woman: Overture. Jewels of the Madonna: Neapolitan dance; The School for Fathers: Intermezzo. Susanna's Secret: Overture. Serenade for strings.
(N) (M) *** Berlin Classics Dig. 0091772BC [id.]. Berlin RSO, Heinz Rögner.

Rögner's collection comes from the late 1970s and has the advantage of natural, warmly resonant analogue sound which gives these attractive pieces a pleasing hall ambience. He offers an aptly paced, sparkling account of *Susanna's Secret*, while the sprightly *Inquisitive Woman overture*, with its songful theme for the oboe, is hardly less winning, and a real find. The Berlin Orchestra play it with the lightest rhythmic touch, and are hardly less persuasive in the *Neapolitan dance*, a brilliant show-piece of which they take full advantage. The charming *Intermezzo* from *The School for fathers* is given with fragile delicacy and the music from *Il Campiello* is just as delectable; both the *Prelude* and *Ritornello* have a haunting atmosphere. The programme ends with a captivating account of the *String Serenade*, which charms and touches the listener by turns.

(i) *Cello concerto in C (Invocazione), Op. 31. Symphonia Brevis in E flat, Op. 28.*
(N) *** CPO Dig.CPO 999 278-2 [id.]. (i) Gustav Rivinius; Frankfurt RSO, Alun Francis.

We are beginning to discover that Wolf-Ferrari, with his ready fund of appealing melody, is a great deal more than a composer of dainty operatic intermezzi. His *Cello concerto*, like the *Violin concerto*, is a considerable work and its title *Invocazione* is well chosen. The opening movements are both marked *Tranquillo*, and even the use of a theme very like 'Three blind mice' does not rob the first of its serenity. The gentle slow movement then has an exquisitely sustained gentility, within which the soloist ruminates ethereally, often playing on a thread of tone. The gay, dancing finale maintains the work's lightness of texture and feeling. The first movement of the *Sinfonia brevis* tries to sustain this tranquil mood, and finally does so at the close, after frequent interruptions, often quite boisterous. The jaunty *Capriccio* which follows acts as a colourful scherzo and might well be another of those intermezzi. The *Adagio* is both a barcarolle and a threnody, and again features a solo cello, pensive and darker-voiced than in the concerto. The finale dances away in a jiggy tarantella rhythm and ends in cheerful buoyancy. The performances here are full of life and feeling, and are given a vividly spacious recording.

(i) *Violin concerto in D, Op. 26; Serenade for strings in E flat.*
(N) ❁ *** CPO Dig. CPO 999 271-2 [id.]. (i) Ulf Hoelscher, Frankfurt RSO, Alaun Francis.

With its ardently sinuous lyricism, Wolf-Ferrari's warmly romantic *Violin concerto* (which might be compared to the Max Bruch concerto in its glowing romanticism) was up till now an undiscovered masterpiece. It captures the listener's ear from the very opening, and Ulf Hoelscher is a superbly responsive soloist. The *Romanza* opens with ethereal delicacy, but passion soon comes to the surface and is always ready to burst into the *Improviso* third movement. The jolly, sparkling Rondo finale is in the best traditional mode of classical concerto finales, with Hungarian influences, but there is also a playful element and expressive lyrical interludes special to the composer. Again Hoelscher is on his mettle: he never made a better record than this, and his exquisite playing of the long cadenza–soliloquy towards the movement's close is especially fine. The *String Serenade* is an extraordinarily accomplished and individual four-movement student work, genuinely inspired, and it is most persuasively played here, with a more passionate less innocent performance than Heinz Rögner gives in his collection below. First-class recording.

Piano trios Nos. 1 in D, Op. 5; 2 in F sharp, Op. 7.
*** ASV Dig. CDDCA 935 [id.]. Raphael Trio.

Ermanno Wolf-Ferrari, half-German, half-Italian, wrote these two ambitious *Piano trios* at the very beginning of his career. They may not be masterpieces, but the large-scale first movements show him as a fine craftsman, and more importantly, his themes already show the gift of easy memorability which marks his other major works. So the slow movement of No. 1 is like a Mascagni lament, and the chattering finale might be a sketch for an operatic interlude. No. 2 is even odder in its layout, with the first movement twice as long as the other two put together, but with well-disciplined performances from the Raphael Trio – an American group – the colour and charm of the writing is persuasively brought out.

Wood, Hugh (born 1932)

Piano concerto, Op. 31.
*** Collins Single Dig. 2007-2 [id.]. Joanna MacGregor, BBC SO, Sir Andrew Davis.

Hugh Wood's *Piano concerto*, written for Joanna MacGregor, who studied with him at Cambridge, is a three-movement piece whose central movement is a haunting set of variations on *Sweet Lorraine*, the song popularized in the 1950s by Nat King Cole. Expert playing from both the soloist and the BBC Symphony Orchestra under Andrew Davis, and first-class recorded sound.

Wordsworth, William (1908–88)

Symphonies Nos. 2 in D, Op. 34; 3 in C, Op. 48.
*** Lyrita Dig. SRCD 207 [id.]. LPO, Nicholas Braithwaite.

William Wordsworth (a direct descendant of the poet's brother, Christopher) was a real symphonist. The *Second*, dedicated to Tovey is distinctly Nordic in atmosphere and there is an unhurried sense of growth. It is serious, thoughtful music, both well crafted and well laid out for the orchestra, and the writing is both powerful and imaginative. The *Third* is less concentrated and less personal in utterance, but all the same this is music of integrity, and readers who enjoy, say, the symphonies of Edmund Rubbra should sample the *Second Symphony*. Nicholas Braithwaite gives a carefully prepared and dedicated account of it, and the recording is up to the usual high standard one expects from this label.

Ysaÿe, Eugène (1858–1931)

6 Sonatas for solo violin, Op. 27.
*** Chandos Dig. CHAN 8599 [id.]. Lydia Mordkovitch.
*** Nimbus Dig. NI 7715 [id.]. Oscar Shumsky.

Lydia Mordkovitch plays with great character and variety of colour and she characterizes No. 4 (the one dedicated to Kreisler, with its references to Bach and the *Dies Irae*) superbly. These *Sonatas* can seem like mere exercises, but in her hands they sound really interesting. Natural, warm recorded sound. Recommended.

Oscar Shumsky is a player of the old school. His artistry is everywhere in evidence in this 1982 recording, in the authority and naturalness of his phrasing, the sweetness of his tone and the security of his technique. True, there are one or two moments of imperfect intonation, but there are very few performances (as opposed to recordings) where every note in these impossibly demanding pieces is in perfect place. It is all wonderfully musical and splendidly free as if Shumsky is improvising these pieces.

Zandonai, Riccardo (1883–1944)

Francesca da Rimini: excerpts from Acts II, III & IV.
(M) **(*) Decca 433 033-2 (2) [id.]. Olivero, Del Monaco, Monte Carlo Op. O, Rescigno – GIORDANO: *Fedora.* **(*)

Magda Olivero is a fine artist who has not been represented nearly enough on record, and this rare Zandonai selection, like the coupled set of Giordano's *Fedora*, does her some belated justice. Decca opted to have three substantial scenes recorded rather than snippets and, though Mario del Monaco as Paolo is predictably coarse in style, his tone is rich and strong and he does not detract from the achievement, unfailingly perceptive and musicianly, of Olivero as Francesca herself. Excellent, vintage 1969, Decca sound.

Zeisl, Eric (1905–59)

Requiem Ebraico (92nd Psalm).
(N) *** Decca Dig. 460 211-2 [id.]. Della Jones, Berlin R. Ch., Children's Ch., & SO, Lawrence Foster – WAXMAN: *The Song of Terezin.* ***

Eric Zeisl, like Franz Waxman, had a successful career as a Hollywood composer, and in this *Hebrew requiem* he translates his film style into a warm and lyrical work, written in memory of his father killed in a concentration camp, and using a Hebrew text from Psalm 92. It may not be as original as the

Waxman work with which it is coupled, but with a similarly warm and committed performance, richly recorded, it is a welcome novelty.

Zelenka, Jan (1679–1745)

Concerto a 8 concertanti in G, ZWV 186; Hipocondrie a 7 concertanti in A, ZWV 187; Ouverture a 7 concertanti in F, ZWV 188; Simphonia a 8 concertanti in A min.

(N) (M) *** Vanguard Dig. 99724 [id.]. Il Fondamento, Paul Dombrecht.

A very strong recommendation for this Vanguard disc as a splendid representative collection of Zelenka's lively orchestral music. Paul Dombrecht's period-instrument group play with a pleasing rhythmic buoyancy, the strings ever-zestful. There is just as much bounce as with Harnoncourt and even more lift, without over-forceful accents. The oboe sounds are delightful, and the solo bassoon is engagingly lugubrious in the *Largo cantabile* of the *Concerto a 8*. This is a three-movement work in the form of a French overture, as in the *Hipocondrie*, and for that matter the attractive opening movement of the *Ouverture a 7*. Perhaps finest of all is the *Simphonia*, with its opening *Allegro* full of vitality and a crisply pointed central *Gavotte*. The eloquent following *Aria da Capriccio* opens as a concertante cello soliloquy, and after alternating slow and fast sections, ends with a spirited tutti. The work then closes with a pair of Minuets. Excellent recording.

Hipocondrie à 7 in A, ZWV 187; Overture à 7 concertanti in F, ZWV 188; Sonata No. 2 in G min. for 2 oboes, bassoon and continuo, ZWV 181.

(M) **(*) Teldec/Warner 0630 17386-2. VCM, Harnoncourt.

No one could accuse Harnoncourt of a lack of vitality in his performances of this lively, inventive and often unpredictable music by one of Bach's most remarkable contemporaries. There is some fine oboe-playing too, and the strings are brightly alert throughout. As usual with this conductor, accents are strong and rhythms bounce firmly, yet there is also some fine, expressive playing. The five-movement *Overture* (or suite), which shows well the diversity of Zelenka's invention, is particularly characterful. Recording (dating from 1980) is characteristically bright and forward, yet the range of dynamic is wide.

Trios sonatas Nos. 1–6.

(N) *** ECM Dig. 462 454-2 (2) [id.]. Holliger, Bourgue, Zehetmair, Thuneman, Stoll, Rubin, Jaccotte.

With such a starry team it is not surprising that these performances of Zelenka's *Trio sonatas* are so spirited and accomplished. They are scored for various colourful combinations of (almost always) two oboes and bassoon, with continuo, the violin taking the upper voice in No. 3. Zelenka's fast movements proceed with breathless polyphony of mounting intensity, granting neither players nor listeners any respite. So these works are better approached one at a time, stimulating as they are. Excellent if forward recording.

Missa dei Filii; Litaniae Laurentanae.

*** HM/BMG Dig. RD 77922 [7922-2-RC]. Argenta, Chance, Prégardien, Gordon Jones, Stuttgart Chamber Ch., Tafelmusik, Bernius.

The *Missa dei Filii* (Mass for the Son of God), is a 'short' Mass, consisting of *Kyrie* and *Gloria* only. It seems that Zelenka never heard that Mass, but his *Litany*, another refreshing piece, was specifically written when the Electress of Saxony was ill. Zelenka, like Bach, happily mixes fugal writing with newer-fangled concertato movements. Bernius provides well-sprung support with his period-instrument group, Tafelmusik, and his excellent soloists and choir.

Zemlinsky, Alexander von
(1871–1942)

Die Seejungfrau (The Mermaid); (i) *Psalms 13, 23.*

*** Decca 444 969-2 [id.]. (i) Ernst Senff Chamber Ch.; Berlin RSO, Chailly.

Zemlinsky's three-movement symphonic fantasy, based on the Hans Andersen story of the mermaid, is an exotic piece full of sumptuous orchestral writing. It is beautifully performed here, with ample recording to match. *Psalm 23* is warm in expression, airy and beautiful. But do not expect a religious atmosphere: this is sensuous music, beautifully played and sung. *Psalm 13*, presented first on the disc, still reveals the urgency of Zemlinsky's inspiration – never a revolutionary in the way Schoenberg was, but always inventive and imaginative. The choral sound is not as full as that of the orchestra, but this remains an excellent introduction to the composer.

Lyrische Symphonie, Op. 18.

(BB) *** Arte Nova Dig. 74321 27768-2 [id.]. Vlatka Orsanic, James Johnson, SWFSO, Gielen – BERG: *Lyric suite: 3 Pieces* etc. ***

**(*) DG Dig. 449 179-2 [id.]. Voigt, Terfel, VPO, Sinopoli.

(i) *Lyrische Symphonie, Op. 18;* (ii) *Sinfonische Gesänge, Op. 20.*

*** Decca (IMS) Dig. 443 569-2 [id.]. Concg. O, Chailly, with (i) Alessandra Marc, Håkan Hagegård; (ii) Willard White.

With the help of opulent and finely detailed recording of vivid immediacy, Chailly conducts a performance which on balance is the most powerful yet, moving and passionate on the one hand, rapt and poetic on the other, with the Concertgebouw producing ravishing sounds in playing marked by pin-point ensemble. Håkan Hagegård is an outstanding baritone soloist, illuminating in his pointing of words; Alessandra Marc may not have quite such clear diction, but she combines warmth and power with an ability to produce the most beautiful pianissimos. Zemlinsky's setting of the words from the anthology of black poets in German translation, *Afrika singt* brings a much more astringent style which yet conveys powerful emotions, helped by the fine, intense singing of Willard White.

At speeds markedly faster than usual, Michael Gielen conducts an exceptionally powerful and purposeful account of Zemlinsky's *Lyric symphony*. Here the work emerges as very fresh and distinctive in its own right. The playing of the orchestra is outstanding and the two soloists are ideal, singing with clean attack and fresh tone. First-rate recording too. An outstanding bargain, well coupled with the Berg works. The only snag is that the booklet is totally inadequate, with poor notes and no texts or translations, and not even any identification of the seven Tagore poems used by Zemlinsky in the symphony.

Sinopoli's is a sensuous, expansive reading, bringing out its links with Mahler's *Lied von der Erde*. Bryn Terfel is excellent, even if the darkness of the voice is not always an advantage in bringing out the meaning of the text. The dramatic soprano, Deborah Voigt, rides easily over the richest textures, but she misses the beauty of the gentler moments, with the top of the voice spreading. No coupling is provided.

String quartets Nos. 1 in A, Op. 4; 2, Op. 15.
(N) *** Nimbus Dig. NI5563 [id.]. Artis Qt.

String quartets Nos. 3, Op. 19; 4, Op. 25.
(N) *** Nimbus Dig. NI5604 [id.]. Artis Qt.

String quartets Nos. 1 in A, Op. 4; 4, Op. 25. 2 Movements.
(N) ** Praga Dig. PRD 250107 [id.]. Pražák Qt.

The Zemlinsky quartets were long represented in the catalogue by the LaSalle Quartet on DG but this has now been deleted. Of the two new sets (the Artis now offer fine performances of all four works) the Nimbus is the one to have. The *First Quartet* is very much in the received Brahmsian tradition and the Artis bring much warmth to it. The Pražák seem less authoritative and their tone is both less rich and not as well blended. They make a good showing in the demanding *Fourth*, and include two movements from a quartet of 1927 which Zemlinsky put to one side and never completed.

VOCAL MUSIC

Complete choral works: *Aurikelchen; Frühlingsbegräbnis; Frühlingsglaube; Geheimnis; Hochzeitsgesang; Minnelied; Psalms 13, 23 & 83.*
(N) *** EMI Dig. CDC5 56783-2 [id.]. Deborah Voigt, Donnie Ray Albert, Dusseldorf State Musikverein Ch., Mülheimer Kantorei, Gürzenich O & Cologne PO, James Conlon.

The major works here are Zemlinsky's passionate and intense settings of the three *Psalms*. If in a manner recognizable from his operas, the first two bring sensuous writing more apt for the Song of Solomon than the Psalms, the third, *Psalm 83*, brings dramatic martial music. Those three items as well as the cantata, *The burial of Spring*, in seven compact movements, were recorded live in Cologne, and bring warm, committed performances under Conlon as a dedicated Zemlinsky interpreter. The other lighter items were recorded later in the studio. Opulent sound to match.

Gesänge Op. 5, Books 1–2; Gesänge (Waltz songs on Tuscan folk-lyrics), Op. 6; Gesänge, Opp. 7–8, 10 & 13; Lieder, Op. 2, Books 1–2; Op. 22 & Op. 27.
*** DG Dig. (IMS) 427 348-2 (2). Barbara Bonney, Anne Sofie von Otter, Hans Peter Blochwitz, Andreas Schmidt, Cord Garben.

This two-disc DG collection of songs can be warmly recommended for the fresh tunefulness of dozens of miniatures. With Cord Garben accompanying four excellent soloists, the charm of these chips from the workbench comes over consistently. Best of all is von Otter, more sharply imaginative than the others, making the one consistent cycle that Zemlinsky ever wrote, the six Maeterlinck Songs, Op. 13, the high-point of the set.

6 Maeterlinck Lieder, Op. 13.
(B) *** Decca Double 444 871-2 (2) [id.]. Jard van Nes, Concg. O, Chailly – MAHLER: *Symphony No. 6.* ***

Beautifully sung by Jard van Nes in her finest recording to date, these ripely romantic settings of Maeterlinck make an unusual but valuable fill-up for Chailly's rugged and purposeful reading of the Mahler *Symphony*. The rich, vivid recording captures van Nes's full-throated singing with new firmness.

Psalm 83.
(N) *** Decca Dig. 460 213-2 [id.]. Slovak Philharmonic Ch., VPO, Chailly – JANACEK: *Glagolitic mass.* KORNGOLD: *Passover psalm.* ***

Zemlinsky's aptly dramatic setting of *Psalm 83*, beautifully performed and richly recorded, makes an unusual and attractive coupling for the Janáček.

Eine florentinische Tragödie (opera; first version).
*** Schwann Dig. CD 11625 [id.]. Soffel, Riegel, Sarabia, Berlin RSO, Albrecht.

A Florentine Tragedy presents a simple love triangle: a Florentine merchant returns home to find his sluttish wife with the local prince; but the musical syrup which flows over all the characters makes them repulsive, with motives only dimly defined. The score itself is most accomplished; it is compellingly performed here, more effective on disc than it is in the opera house. First-rate sound.

Der Zwerg (Der Geburtstag der Infantin).
(M) *** EMI CDM5 66247-2 (2) [id.]. Isokoski, Martinez, Kuebler, Collis, Cologne PO, Conlon.

Der Zwerg, 'The Dwarf', is the preferred title for the definitive edition of this most striking yet most disturbing of Zemlinsky's operas. The text here was prepared for Conlon from the autograph score, revised in detail by the composer. The version recorded previously was seriously cut, which means that this one-Acter, at 85 minutes, is too long for a single CD. Hence the two-disc format at mid-price. Deeply moving as Kenneth Riegel's performance is on the earlier recording, David Kuebler here has the advantage of a more beautiful, younger-sounding voice, making the portrait more tenderly moving, bringing out the character's vulnerability. Nor is passion lacking, and Soile Isokoski makes an excellent Princess, with Iride Martinez also singing beautifully as her favourite maid. Live recording on the dry side, but still vivid and full.

Zwilich, Ellen (born 1939)

Symphony No. 2.
** First Edition LCD 002 [id.]. Louisville O, Leighton Smith – HINDEMITH: *Piano concerto* *** (with LAWHEAD: *Aleost.* *(*))

Ellen Taaffe Zwilich was a pupil of Dohnányi. She is an accomplished musician. Her *First Symphony* (1982) won a Pulitzer Prize and prompted the San Francisco Orchestra to commission the *Second Symphony* in 1985. The work is called a 'cello symphony', since the cellos play a dominant role in the musical argument. The invention is solid and well argued, rather than inspired; it is music that commands respect though it is not easy to discern a voice of strong individuality. Good playing and decent recording.

'Great Pianists of the Twentieth Century'

Tom Deacon's celebration of the hundred greatest pianists of the twentieth century is a laudable enterprise – to some extent inhibited by the availability of recordings. Of course, not everyone will agree with all his choices of artists for inclusion (or omission!), but certainly most of the CDs in this series are of great interest and many of the performances are of very high quality. No one could quarrel with the attractive presentation, which moves away from the ubiquitous jewel-case. Documentation is satisfactory, and the generous presentation in each volume of 'two discs for the price of one' reminds us that it was Philips who conceived the idea of a Duo format for reissued material. The only snag is that while for newcomers to CDs this could prove a treasure trove, piano buffs who already have extensive collections will find that the duplication of recordings which are already available may consistently present a problem.

Argerich, Martha

Volume 2: (with (i) LSO; (ii) BPO, Abbado; (iii) Berlin RSO Berlin, Chailly). LISZT: (i) *Piano concerto No. 1 in E flat*. RAVEL: (ii) *Piano concerto in G. Gaspard de la nuit. Sonatine.* RACHMANINOV: (iii) *Piano concerto No. 3 in D min., Op. 30*. BACH: *Partita No. 2 in C min., BWV 826*. PROKOFIEV: (ii) *Piano concerto No. 3 in C, Op. 26*.

(N) (B) *** Ph. 456 700-2 (2) [id.].

No one could possibly quarrel with the choice here, which shows Argerich forming a splendid artistic partnership with Abbado in Liszt, Prokofiev and Ravel, while with Chailly she is electrifying in Rachmaninov. But all these recordings are already in the catalogue, and few experienced collectors will have ignored all of them. Splendid value, just the same.

Arrau, Claudio

Volume 4: BALAKIREV: *Islamey*. LISZT: *Rhapsodie espagnole; Années de pèlerinages: Les jeux d'eaux à la Villa d'Este. Bénédiction de Dieu; Danse le solitude:* BACH: *Chromatic Fantasia and fugue, BWV 903*. ALBENIZ: *Iberia* (Book 1): *Evocación; El puerto; Féte-Dieu á Seville*. BRAHMS: (i) *Piano concerto No. 1 in D min., Op. 15* (with Concg. O, Haitink). *Variations on a theme by Paganini, Op. 35.*

(N) (B) **(*) Ph. mono/stereo 456 706-2 (2) [id.].

Starting with a breathtaking performance of Balakirev's *Islamey* – recorded in the 1920s – the first of these two discs is a revelation, presenting Arrau in his earlier years as a dazzling virtuoso, evidently uninhibited in the recording studio. That is so, whether in the Bach *Chromatic fantasia* (aptly improvisatory in tone, with textures crystal clear), in Liszt (the *Spanish rhapsody* given astonishing lightness and clarity in this 1936 performance), or Albéniz (with the mystery and keen originality of the piano-writing heightened). Rounding off the first disc, the three Liszt performances, recorded between 1969 and 1976, are among the finest Arrau did for Philips. The second disc of Brahms is more questionable. The 1969 account of the *First concerto* sounds sluggish in the first two movements, though in the *Paganini variations,* speeds on the slow side go with sprung rhythms and persuasive phrasing.

Volume 5: BEETHOVEN: *Piano concerto No. 5 in E flat, (Emperor), Op. 73* (with Dresden State O, Sir Colin Davis). *Piano sonata No. 21 in C, (Waldstein), Op. 53. Andante favori in F, WoO 57*. CHOPIN: *Fantaisie in F min., Op. 49*. LISZT: *Piano sonata in B min., S.178*. SCHUMANN: *Fantasie in C, Op. 17*.

(N) (B) *** Ph. Dig./Analogue 456 709 (2) [id.].

Arrau's superb digital Dresden account of the *Emperor*, made in 1984 when he was 81, surpassed his earlier versions and is a truly great performance. It still holds its place in the catalogue at premium price, so the present set, at a similar cost, is an ideal way of getting it. The *Waldstein Sonata* (recorded in 1963) is at a lower voltage, but is scrupulous in matters of dynamic and attention to detail. The Chopin *Fantasy* (1977) has much perception and full colouring; the Schumann *Fantasie* however, recorded a decade earlier, is disappointing, lacking the spaciousness and breadth so striking in the Chopin performance. In the Liszt *Sonata*, Arrau returns to form: it has genuine eloquence and power, even if the style is somewhat deliberate, even pontifical. The resonant, full-bodied 1970 recording suits it admirably, and this set certainly gives a rounded picture of Arrau's achievements in the recording studio over two decades.

Ashkenazy, Vladimir

Volume 7: CHOPIN: *Barcarolle in F sharp, Op. 60; 3 Nouvelles études, Op. posth.; Mazurka in A flat, Op. 59/2; Nocturne in B, Op. 62/1; Scherzo No. 4 in E, Op. 54.* LISZT: *Mephisto waltz; Transcendant studies Nos. 1, Preludio; 2, Fusées; 3, Paysage; 5, Feux follets; 8, Wilde Jagd; 10, Appassionata; 11, Harmonies du soir.* RAVEL: *Gaspard de la nuit.* SCHUMANN: *Humoresque, Op. 20.* RACHMANINOV: *Variations on a theme of Corelli, Op. 42.* PROKOFIEV: *Romeo and Juliet* (before parting). BORODIN: *Scherzo in A flat.*
(N) (B) *** Ph. Analogue./Dig. 456 715-2 (2) [id.].

These performances derive from Decca recordings made from 1964 to 1983. Ashkenazy's Chopin hardly needs further advocacy. The *Scherzo* is played with impeccable technique and taste, and the *B major Nocturne* is given with aristocratic distinction; the *Barcarolle* and *Nouvelles études* are hardly less beautiful. The Liszt (1970) brings pianism of outstanding brilliance and eloquence, with an underlying vein of poetry throughout. *Harmonies du soir* is a marvellously penetrating account, and even the much recorded *Mephisto waltz* is strikingly fresh. The recording is almost excessively bright and immediate, but about the playing there are no reservations whatsoever. Perhaps the most memorable performance here is of Ravel's *Gaspard de la nuit*, recorded in 1965, which remains among the very finest in the catalogue, and is not even surpassed by Gieseking's 78-rpm set. The Rachmaninov *Corelli variations* too, are superb and are given the benefit of Kingsway Hall ambience. The Schumann *Humoreske* (1972) is highly eloquent, but let down by reverberant, rather clangorous sound. But this recital has been well chosen to show the range of Ashkenazy's keyboard prowess.

Backhaus, Wilhelm

Volume 8: BEETHOVEN: *Piano sonatas Nos. 8 in C min. (Pathétique), Op. 13; 17 in D min. (Tempest), Op. 31/2; 25 in G, Op. 79; 26 in E flat (Les adieux), Op. 81a; 32 in C min., Op. 111.* SCHUBERT: *Impromptu in E flat, D. 899/2.* SCHUMANN: *Warum, Op. 12/3.* LISZT: *Soirées de Vienne (after Schubert): Valse-Caprice No. 6, S.427.* CHOPIN: *Etude in F min., Op. 25/2.* BRAHMS: *Intermezzo in C, Op. 119/3*; (i) *Piano concerto in B flat, Op. 83* (with VPO, Carl Schuricht).
(N) (M) **(*) Ph. mono 456 718-2 (2) [id.].

Backhaus's plainspun style and literal dedication to each composer he surveyed had an emotional directness, even brusqueness, that gained him a reputation for powerful authority. Particularly so in the Viennese classics, and with Beethoven and Brahms in particular, where his unadorned manner appealed to his public for its self-confident, purposeful interpretations without frills. Some listeners find this approach marmoreal, but there is an undeniable strength of purpose here, even if the element of charm is almost entirely absent, notably so in Schubert. His interpretation of the Brahms *B flat Concerto* has a deserved reputation for rugged potency: this is the earlier mono Decca version, which is some ways is fresher than his later stereo account. Indeed all the recordings here are Decca-sourced and, coming from the last years of his life, do not really present a complete picture of what he was like in his youthful prime.

Brendel, Alfred

Volume 12: HAYDN: *Piano sonatas Nos. 53 in E min., Hob XV1/34; 45 in E flat, Hob XV1/52; 54 in G, Hob XV1/40; 56 in D, Hob 42.* MOZART: *Fantasia in C min., K.475.* SCHUBERT: *Impromptus Nos. 1–4, D.899; Impromptus Nos. 1–4, D.935.* SCHUMANN: *Fantasiestücke Op. 12 Nos: 1, Des Abends; 2, Warum; 3, In der nacht; 8, Ende vom lied.*
(N) (B) *** Ph. Dig. 456 727-2 (2) [id.].

Brendel's Haydn offers playing of real distinction, aristocratic without being aloof, concentrated without being too intense. Everything is cleanly articulated and finely characterized, and he is generous with repeats. Schumann's *Fantasiestücke* brings magically spontaneous playing, full of imaginative touches of colour, but for the Schubert *Impromptus* Brendel himself chose the later 1988 digital set. This offers many characteristic insights, and has the benefit of immaculate recorded sound. However, in some respects his earlier analogue recordings (see under Schubert in the Composer Index) were more affecting; not that the later versions are lacking in warmth, but there is just a hint of didacticism.

Volume 13: BEETHOVEN: 6 *Bagatelles, Op. 126; Piano sonatas Nos. 29 in B flat (Hammerklavier), Op. 106; 32 in C min., Op. 111; 33 Variations on a waltz by Diabelli, Op. 120; 10 Variations on Salieri's Air 'La stessa la stessima'.*
(N) (M) *** Ph. Dig./Analogue 456 730-2 (2) [id.].

Brendel has here chosen his earlier 1976 recording of the *Diabelli variations*. Recorded live, it has a striking urgency and concentration; the playing is understandably not flawless, but the tensions are superbly conveyed. The *Salieri variations* look back to 1963, and offer a sampler of Brendel's earliest recording sessions for Vox Turnabout. They are refreshingly spontaneous; the late Sonatas are among his most recent and most penetrating Beethoven recordings.

Bruk, Lyubov and Mark Taimanov

Volume 15: ARENSKY: *Suites Nos. 1 & 2.* BUSONI: *Duettino concertante.* CHOPIN: *Rondo in C.* MILHAUD: *Scaramouche.* MOZART: *Double concerto in E flat, K.365* (with Leningrad CO, Lazar Gozman). POULENC: *Double concerto in D min.* (with Leningrad PO, Arnold Katz); *Sonata for 2 pianos.* RACHMANINOV: *Suites Nos. 1 & 2.*

(N) (B) (***) Ph. mono 456 736-2 (2) [id.].

Lyubov Bruk and Mark Taimanov, the principal duo partnership included in the series, are little known outside Russia. Both born in Kharkov, they were trained in St Petersburg and their partnership flourished until the 1970s. (Mark Taimanov pursued a parallel career as a chess grandmaster.) They produce a beautifully balanced and cultured sound, and possess a flawless sense of ensemble and sophistication of tone. The Arensky *Second suite* and the Rachmaninov *First* were recorded in 1959 and the remainder of the programme at various times during the 1960s. The sound is variable but pleasure at this level of music-making far outweighs sonic limitations.

Cortot, Alfred

Volume 20: CHOPIN: *12 Etudes, Op. 10; 12 Etudes, Op. 25.* LISZT: *Hungarian rhapsodies Nos. 2, 11; Concert paraphrase on Verdi's Rigoletto.* RAVEL: *Jeux d'eau.* SCHUMANN: *Carnaval, Op. 9; Etudes symphoniques, Op. 13; Kreisleriana, Op. 16.*

(N) (B) (***) Ph. mono 456 751-2 (2) [id.].

Cortot made a name for himself as a Wagner conductor at the turn of the century and introduced *Götterdämmerung* to French audiences. He resumed his pianistic career in 1905 and established himself as a Chopin interpreter of note. (Cortot had studied with Emile Decombes, a pupil of the composer.) The *Etudes* were recorded in the early 1930s and demand to be heard. Everyone knows about the odd wrong notes that distinguished his music-making, but his playing has a certain air of authenticity and a powerful sense of harmonic direction that carries all before it. His *Jeux d'eau* is quite special.

Curzon, Clifford

Volume 22: SCHUBERT: *Fantasia in C (Wanderer), D. 960; Impromptus Op. 90.* MOZART: *Piano concertos Nos. 26 in D (Coronation), K.537; 27 in B flat, K.595* (with LSO, István Kertész).

(N) (B) *** Ph. mono/stereo 456 757-2 (2) [id.].

Clifford Curzon was a natural recording pianist, sharing with Kempff that supreme gift of being able to create the spontaneity of live performance in the recording studio. It is no better conveyed than in the freshness of his early mono recordings of the Schubert *Impromptus* and the superb account of the *Wanderer fantasia*, truthfully recorded in the 1940s. Curzon found a natural Mozartian partnership with István Kertesz and the pair of Mozart concertos – of which the *Coronation* was previously unpublished – were recorded in the Kingsway Hall in 1967 stereo, and combine warmth with a refreshing simplicity of manner.

Cziffra, György

Volume 23: CHOPIN: *Etudes, Opp. 10 & 25; Polonaise No. 6 in A flat, Op. 53.* LISZT: *Etudes de concert Nos. 2 (La leggierezza) & 3 (Un sospiro); Etude d'exécution transcendante No. 12 (Chasse-neige); Fantasy and fugue on the name B-A-C-H; Légende No. 2 (St François de Paule marchant sur les flots); Mephisto Waltz No. 1; Polonaise No. 2 in E; Années de pélerinage Sonetto 123 del Petrarca;* Supplement: *Tarantella di bravura.*

(N) (B) *** Ph. 456 760-2 (2) [id.].

A pupil of Dohnányi when he was nine, Cziffra's studies were broken off by military service during the Second World War and resumed in 1947–50, when he was arrested for political reasons. He won the Hungarian Liszt Prize two years before the 1956 uprising but his chequered career only took off after his escape from Hungary that year. These recordings made in 1958–63 show Cziffra at his most dazzling and virtuosic. Not only are they exciting and brilliant in the true Hungarian style but distinguished by great finesse and good taste. This set should do much to redress the disgraceful campaign of denigration to which this artist was subjected in the 1970s and '80s. Marvellous, exhilarating playing and very acceptable sound too.

Fischer, Edwin

Volume 25: BACH: *Well-Tempered Clavier, Books I & II*: excerpts; *Clavier concertos Nos. 1 in D min., BWV 1052; 4 in A, BWV 1055; 5 in F min., BWV 1056* (with Edwin Fischer Chamber Orchestra); *Chromatic fantasia and fugue, BWV 903; Fantasia in A min., BWV 992; Fantasia and fugue in A min., BWV 904.* BACH/BUSONI: *Chorale: Ich ruf zu dir Herr Jesu Christ.*

(N) (B) (***) Ph. mono 456 666-2 (2) [id.].

The first CD of this very distinguished set offers

eight *Preludes and Fugues* from Book I and five from Book II of Edwin Fischer's pioneering complete set of the '*48*', made in the 1930s. The second disc carries the three concertos and the remaining keyboard pieces. A useful sampler for those who do not already have, or cannot find these famous recordings elsewhere.

Fleisher, Leon

Volume 27: COPLAND: *Sonata.* LISZT: *Sonata in B minor.* MOZART: *Sonata No. 10 in C, K.330.* RACHMANINOV: (i) *Rhapsody on a theme of Paganini* (with Cleveland O, George Szell). RAVEL: *Alborada del gracioso; Piano concerto for the left hand* (with Baltimore SO, Sergiu Commissiona); *Sonatine.* ROREM: *3 Barcarolles.* WEBER: *Sonata No. 4 in E min., Op. 70.*
(N) (B) *** Ph. 456 775-2 (2) [id.].

One of the most valuable of the '*Great Pianists*' series, as it restores recordings which are not otherwise available. His admirers will recall Leon Fleisher's wonderful set of the Beethoven concertos with Szell and the Cleveland Orchestra, or his magisterial Brahms concertos with the same forces, before a nervous disorder affected his right hand and forced him to concentrate on repertoire for the left hand only. All these performances come from the period 1957–62 with the exception of the Baltimore account of the Ravel, which comes from 1982 and emanates from the Vanguard label. Of particular interest is the authoritative and powerful account of the Copland *Sonata*, which has scarcely been surpassed on disc.

Friedman, Ignaz

Volume 30: BEETHOVEN: *Piano sonata No. 14 (Moonlight), Op. 27/2.* CHOPIN: *Ballade No. 3 in A flat, Op. 47; Berceuse, Op. 57; Piano sonata No. 2: Marche funèbre and finale* (only); *Etudes; Préludes; Mazurkas and Waltzes* (selections); *Polonaises No. 6 and 9.* HUMMEL: *Rondo favori.* LISZT: *Paganini study: La Campanella; Hungarian rhapsody No. 12; Concert paraphrase of Schubert's Ständchen.* MENDELSSOHN: *Songs without words* (selection). RUBINSTEIN: *Valse caprice.* WEBER: *Invitation to the dance.*
(N) (B) (***) Ph. mono 456 784-2 [id.].

Ignaz Friedman was born in Podgórze near Cracow, which was also the birthplace of Josef Hofmann. He was a Leschetizky pupil and spent the pre-First-World-War years in Berlin and settled in the United States after a tour there in 1920. Although he gave some 3,000 recitals he made relatively few gramophone records though it is evident from the Chopin *Mazurkas* that his talent was quite special, as indeed was his delicacy of touch. Many of these recordings come from the 1920s, the earliest from 1923 and the last from 1936 so that the actual sound is variable and in the earlier discs frail. Nothing frail or variable about the playing though!

Gieseking, Walter

Volume 32: BEETHOVEN: *Piano concertos Nos. 4 in G; 5 in E flat (Emperor).* FRANCK: *Variations symphoniques.* MOZART: *Piano concertos Nos. 23 in A, K488; 24 in C min., K491* (all with Philharmonia O, Herbert von Karajan). CHOPIN: *Berceuse.* SCHUMANN *Schlummerlied.* SCRIABIN: *Poéme in F sharp, Op. 32/1; Prelude in E, Op. 15/4.*
(N) (B) (***) Ph. mono 456 811-2 (2) [id.].

Gieseking first recorded the two Beethoven concertos with Alceo Galliera and the Philharmonia, but these performances and the Mozart *A major*, K.488, come from 1951 and the *C minor*, K.491 two years later. The Beethoven were included in EMI's Karajan edition, as indeed was the Franck, also from 1951, about which we expressed enthusiasm in an earlier volume. It was presumably withheld from publication at the time, since once or twice the last note of a phrase does not 'speak' as Gieseking might have wished it to, and more disturbingly the piano has one or two notes that are not in perfect condition and which might be thought to prove irksome on repetition. Wonderful orchestral support from the Philharmonia and Karajan throughout. Playing of distinction and poetic feeling even if neither of the Beethoven concertos, beautiful though they are, is quite as special as Gieseking's Debussy. The Scriabin was among his last recordings.

Gilels, Emil

Volume 34: BACH: *French suite No. 5 in G, BWV 816; Prelude and Fugue in D, BWV 532.* MOZART: (i) *Piano concerto in B flat, KV. 595* (with VPO, Karl Boehm). BEETHOVEN: (ii) *Piano concerto No. 4 in G, Op. 58* (with Philharmonia O, Leopold Ludwig). WEBER: *Piano sonata No. 2 in A flat, Op. 39.* DEBUSSY: *Images: Book 1.* RAVEL: *Jeux d'eau; Le tombeau de Couperin: Toccata; Miroirs: Alborada del gracioso.*
(N) ✿ (B) *** Ph. 456 793-2 (2) [id.].

Now here is a *great* pianist if ever there was one. The 1957 Beethoven *G major concerto* with Leopold Ludwig and the Philharmonia, and the 1973 Mozart *B flat concerto,* K.595 with the Vienna Philharmonic under Karl Boehm, are classics of the gramophone and remain yardsticks by which others are judged. The Beethoven has been hailed in some quarters as 'perhaps the most perfect' recording of the *Fourth* ever made, from which one might be tempted to delete 'perhaps'. Even if you have acquired Testament's transfer, which comes with his magisterial *Emperor*, this is worth duplicating for the sake of the Bach and his incomparable Debussy.

Volume 35: STRAVINSKY: *3 movements from Petrushka*. MEDTNER: *Sonata-reminiscenza in A min., Op. 38/1*. PROKOFIEV: *March from The love for three oranges; Sonatas Nos. 3 in A min.; 8 in B flat, Op. 84; 8 Visions fugitives, Opp. 2/ 1, 3, 5, 7, 8, 10, 11 &17*. LISZT/BUSONI: *Fantasia on two motives from Mozart's Le nozze di Figaro*. LISZT: *Hungarian rhapsody No. 9 (Carnaval at Pest); Spanish rhapsody; Valse oubliée No. 1*. TCHAIKOVSKY: *Piano concerto No. 2 in G, Op. 44* (with New Philharmonia O, Maazel). BACH/SILOTI: *Prelude in B min*.
(N) (B) **(*) Ph. 456 796-2 (2) [id.].

The *Petrushka*, given in Prague in 1973 is stunning, and the Medtner *Sonata reminiscenza* (1968) enshrines the essential Gilels – a complete identification with the composer, and an ability to discern his depths without a trace of the self-conscious. The Prokofiev *Eighth*, of which he was every bit as masterly an interpreter as Richter, and the *Visions fugitives* also derive from 1974 Czech broadcasts. There is an example, too, of the youthful Gilels, the Liszt–Busoni *Fantasia* comes from 1935 when he was nineteen. The only surprise is the Tchaikovsky *Second Concerto* in the Siloti edition with the New Philharmonia under Lorin Maazel, a very curious inclusion. Gilels himself was far from enthusiastic about this recording.

Godowsky, Leopold

Volume 38: BEETHOVEN: (i) *Piano sonata No. 26 in E flat (Les adieux), Op. 81a*. CHOPIN: *Etudes: in G flat, Op. 10/5; G flat, Op. 25/9; Nocturnes Nos. 1 in B flat min. & 2 in E flat, Op. 9/1–2; 4 in F, 5 in F sharp, Op. 15/1–2; 7 in C sharp min., 8 in D flat, Op. 15/1–2; 9 in B, Op. 32/1; 11 in G min.; 12 in G, Op. 37/1–2; 14 in F sharp min., Op. 48/2; 15 in F min. Op. 55/1; 19 in E min., Op. 72/1; Scherzo No. 4 in E, Op. 54; Sonata No. 2 in B flat min., Op. 35*. GRIEG: *Ballade in G min., Op. 24*. LISZT: *Concert paraphrase on Rigoletto*. SCHUBERT arr. GODOWSKY: *Morgengrüss; Gute nacht*. SCHUMANN *Carnaval, Op. 9*.
(N) (B) (***) Ph. mono 456 805–2 (2) [id.].

Born near Vilnius in Lithuania, Godowsky's gifts soon attracted wide attention and by the time he was twenty, he had established an international reputation, made his début in the USA and assumed American citizenship. In 1909 he succeeded Busoni as head of piano master-classes in Vienna but settled permanently in the USA in 1914. Although the excellent notes speak of Godowsky's position in the pantheon of great pianists as 'unassailable', they quote Josef Hofmann as saying, 'it is tragic that the public has never heard [Godowsky] as only he can play'. His legendary pianistic finish and mastery of texture are represented, albeit fitfully, on records. This anthology of recordings made between 1925 and 1930 brings sterling testament to his keyboard prowess and musical insight: the Chopin *Scherzo* and the *Sonata* are ample vindication of his admirers' claims, and the 1929 Grieg *Ballade* has never been surpassed artistically.

Gould, Glenn

Volume 39: BYRD: *First Pavane and Galliard, Hughe Ashton's Ground, 6h. Pavane and Galliard, A Voluntary, Sellinger's Round*. GIBBONS: *Fantasy in C, Allemande on an Italian Ground, 'Lord of Salisbury' Pavane and Ground*. Domenico SCARLATTI: *Sonatas in D, L.413; D, L.463; G, L. 486*. MOZART: *Fantasy and fugue in C, K.394*. HAYDN: *Sonata in E flat*. BIZET: *Variations chromatiques*. R. STRAUSS: *5 piano pieces, Op. 3*. SCRIABIN: *2 preludes, Op. 57*. BERG: *Sonata, Op. 1*. PROKOFIEV: *Sonata No. 7 in B flat, Op. 83*.
(N) (B) (***) Ph. 456 808-2 (2) [id.].

Even those who do not normally respond to Glenn Gould's eccentric pianism may find a lot to interest them here. The 1967 recording of the Prokofiev is pretty amazing and his advocacy of the English virginal repertory has much delicacy and individuality to commend it. Likewise his championship of the Bizet *Variations chromatiques* has great style. An interesting set.

Gulda, Friedrich

Volume 40: DEBUSSY: *L'isle joyeuse; Pour le piano; Préludes, Books I & II; Reflets dans l'eau; Suite bergamasque*. RAVEL: *Gaspard de la nuit; Sonatine; Valses nobles et sentimentales*.
(N) (B) (**) Ph. mono 456 817-2 (2) [id.].

The Viennese-born Friedrich Gulda came into prominence after he won the Geneva piano competition in 1946, but he has never enjoyed the exposure to which perhaps his gifts entitle him. True, since after the late 1960s he has pursued a dual career as a jazz pianist, particularly in partnership with Chick Corea, and has made fewer records. However, those who recall these rather elegant but not exceptional performances from the 1950s will perhaps be surprised to find them keeping such company. Good but not great playing. The sound is inclined to be dryish and monochrome.

Volume 41: BEETHOVEN: *Piano concerto No. 1 in C, Op. 15* (with VPO, Karl Böehm). WEBER: *Konzertstück in F min., Op. 79* (with VPO,

Volkmar Andrea). STRAUSS: *Burlesque* (with LSO, Collins). CHOPIN: *Piano concerto No. 1 in E min.* (arr. BALAKIREV; with LPO, Boult). *4 Ballades*. SHEARING/FORSTER: *Lullaby of birdland.*
(N) (B) **(*) Ph. mono/stereo 456 820-2 (2) [id.].

The second Gulda Volume presents this pianist to rather greater effect .The present recordings all come from 1951–6 and show his youthful pianism at its best. One point of interest is that the Balakirev elaboration of Chopin's orchestration of the *E minor Piano concerto* is used. *The Record Guide* much admired the delicacy of Gulda's playing, though not in preference to Mewton Wood's poetic account; but compared with performances from later and greater pianists, there seems less cause for rapture. The Beethoven concerto is a very fluent and straightforward account, though the *Guide* was very critical of the somewhat shrill recording. The Strauss *Burlesque* is one of the more striking performances; obviously the partnership with Collins proved fruitful. But admirable though he is and of fine musical intelligence, one must question whether these performances can rank alongside the likes of Arrau, Gilels and Solomon.

Haebler, Ingrid

Volume 42: BACH: *French suite No. 6 in E, BWV 817*. HAYDN: *Piano concerto in D, Hob XVIII:11; Variations in F min., Hob. XVII: 6*. MOZART: *Piano concerto No. 18 in B flat, K.456* (with LSO, Sir Colin Davis). *9 Variations on a minuet by Duport, K.573*. SCHUBERT: *Sonata No. 14 in A min., D.784*. SCHUMANN: *Kinderszenen, Op. 15*. CHOPIN: *Waltz in E flat, Op. 18*.
(N) (B) **(*) Ph. 456 823-2 (2) [id.].

There is some musical playing here, but whether it can be described as great is a moot point! Ingrid Haebler has elegance and nimble fingers but many (including her admirers) would hesitate before placing her alongside such exalted company as Perahia, Richter and Horowitz. Having said that, this pair of CDs will undoubtedly give pleasure – particularly the *B flat concerto*, K.456 – but that is another matter.

Haskil, Clara

Volume 43: MOZART: *Piano concertos Nos. 13 in C, K.415* (with Lucerne Festival Strings, Rudolph Baumgartner); *20 in D min., K.491; 24 in C min., K.491* (with Lamoureux Orchestra of Paris, Markevitch); *23 in A, K.488* (with Vienna SO, Paul Sacher); *27 in B flat, K. 595* (with Bavarian State O, Fricsay). *Rondo in A, K.386* (with VSO, Bernhard Paumgartner).
(N) (B) **(*) Ph. mono/stereo 456 826-2 (2) [id.].

Clara Haskil is a much venerated pianist and some of these recordings have already appeared in the Philips *'Clara Haskil Legacy'*. Her refinement and grace are heard at their best in these Mozart concertos and the accompaniments are, on the whole, worthy of her. The performances are strong and classical, almost totally devoid of romanticism, but with the dramatic contrasts of light and shade made positive by the orchestra, especially under Markevitch and Fricsay. The recordings date from between 1954 and 1960: the coupling of K.466 and K.491 was made in the month before her death. Her somewhat cool approach rather suits the *Larghetto* of the *C minor* and, if some may find her a trifle unyielding in the slow movement of the *D minor*, K.488, suits her especially well. She is always stylish and musical, and there is usually ample spontaneity. Very good recording balances.

Volume 44: MOZART: *Sonatas Nos. 2 in F, K.280; 10 in C, K.330; 12 variations in C, K.265*. BEETHOVEN: *Sonatas Nos. 17 in D min. (Tempest), Op. 31/2; 18 in E flat, Op. 31/3*. SCHUMANN: *Abegg variations, Op. 1; Kinderszenen, Op. 15*. SCHUBERT: *Sonata No. 21 in B flat, D.960*.
(N) (B) **(*) Ph. mono/stereo 456 829-2 (2) [id.].

This second Haskil collection again draws on material included in the Philips '*Clara Haskil Legacy*'. The Schubert sonata and Schumann *Abegg variations* come from 1951, the Mozart and Beethoven sonatas from 1960, the year of her death. Her playing has a special kind of intimacy, more private than public; hers is a reflective, inward-looking sensibility with nothing of the virtuoso or showman, not even in Beethoven's *D minor Sonata*. Her musical dedication is total. Her Schumann is particularly searching and penetrating, And there is an innocence about her Schubert and her Mozart which makes both very fresh and immediate.

Horowitz, Vladimir

Volume 48: LISZT: *Hungarian rhapsodies Nos. 2* (arr. HOROWITZ); *6; Années de Pélerinages: Au bord d'une source; Petrarch Sonnet No. 104. Paganini étude No. 2 in E flat; Valse oubliée No. 1*. LISZT/SCHUBERT: *Soiree de Vienne No. 6 (Valse caprice)*. RACHMANINOV: *Sonata No. 2, Op. 36*. PROKOFIEV: *Sonata No. 7 in B flat, Op. 83*. SCRIABIN: *Sonata No. 5, Op. 53*. CHOPIN: *Fantaisie in F min., Op. 49; Polonaise-fantaisie, Op. 61*.
(N) (B) *** Ph. mono/stereo; analogue/Dig. 456 844-2 (2) [id.].

Some famous and formidable performances from the Horowitz discography are served up here, including the legendary Prokofiev *Seventh* from 1951. Let us hope that the pioneering disc of the

Barber will be included in a later anthology though it is of course available in RCA's Horowitz Edition.

Janis, Byron

Volume 50: BACH: *Prelude and fugue in A min., BWV 543.* BEETHOVEN: *Piano sonata No. 17 in D min. (Tempest), Op. 31/2.* SCHUBERT: *Impromptu in E flat, D.899/2.* BRAHMS: *Waltzes Op. 39 Nos. 1 in B, 2 in E, 6 in C sharp, 15 in A flat.* Johann STRAUSS/SCHULZ-EVLER: *Arabesques on An der schönen, blauen Donau.* LISZT: *Consolation No. 5 in E, (Andantino); Hungarian rhapsody No. 6 in D flat; Liebestraum No. 3 in A flat; Rigoletto concert paraphrase; Années de pélerinage: Sonetto 104 Petrarca.* CHOPIN: *Ballade No. 1 in G min., Op. 23; Etudes in E (Tristesse), Op. 10/3; G flat, (Black keys), Op. 10/5; F, Op. 10/8; F, Op. 25/3; Impromptu No. 1 in A flat, Op. 29; Mazurka in A min., Op. 67/4; Scherzo No. 3 in C sharp min., Op. 39; Sonata No. 2 in B fla min., (Funeral march), Op. 35; Waltzes in E min., Op. post.; A min., Op. 34/2.*
(N) (B) (***) Ph. mono/stereo 456 847 (2) [id.].

Byron Janis was a protégé of Horowitz and possessed an altogether outstanding virtuosity. This issue justifies its inclusion in this series in a way that many others don't. It presents us with material that has not been in circulation for many years and some recordings appear for the first time. A pupil of Josef and Rosina Lhévinne, Janis attracted Horowitz's attention in 1944 when he was sixteen and was hailed by Olin Downes in ecstatic terms. His career was cut short in the 1973 by psoriatic arthritis. The present survey includes recordings from the late 1940s and early '50s of Chopin, Liszt and Beethoven which are both remarkable and new to CD.

Katchen, Julius

Volume 53: BRAHMS: *Hungarian dances, Vol. 1; Piano sonata in F min., Op. 5; Variations on an original theme, Op. 21/1.* ROREM: *Piano sonata No. 2.* MENDELSSOHN: *Prelude and fugue in E min., Op. 35/1; Rondo capriccioso in E, Op. 14.* LISZT: *Hungarian rhapsody No. 12.* BALAKIREV: *Islamey.* FRANCK: *Prélude, choral et fugue.* CHOPIN: *Ballade No. 3 in A flat, Op. 47; Fantasy in F min., Op. 49.*
(N) (B) (***) Ph. mono/stereo 456 856-2 (2) [id.].

Born in New Jersey in 1926, Julius Katchen had a brief but meteoric recording career with Decca in the early LP era. His stereo Brahms survey has appeared in a six-CD bargain box, and this set is valuable in offering the early 1949 mono version of the *F minor Sonata*; it is also particularly valuable in exploring other areas of his discography such as Ned Rorem's *Second sonata* recorded in 1952 that briefly appeared on a mono Decca LP. Katchen's 1959 account of Balakirev's *Islamey* enjoyed classic status in its day. A most worthwhile collection.

Volume 54: GERSHWIN: *Rhapsody in Blue.* RAVEL: *Piano concerto for the left hand; Piano concerto in G.* PROKOFIEV: *Piano concerto No. 3 in C, Op. 26* (all with LSO, Kertész). LISZT: (iii) *Piano concerto No. 2 in A* (with LSO, Argenta). BEETHOVEN: *Rondo in B flat, WoO6* (with LSO, Piero Gamba). RACHMANINOV: *Rhapsody on a theme of Paganini.* DOHNANYI: *Variations on a nursery tune, Op. 25* (both with LPO, Sir Adrian Boult).
(N) (B) *** Ph. 456 859-2 (2) [id.].

Katchen's career was sadly cut short by his premature early death in 1969. Listening to his charismatic recordings of Gershwin and Prokofiev, both so vivid and exciting, and which date from 1968, no one would suspect that his health was anything but robust. The Ravel *Left hand concerto* was his last recording: it is a brilliant account and is most expertly accompanied by Kertész, and equally well served by the Decca enginerrs. The Liszt *A major concerto* (with Argenta) is hardly less impressive, but perhaps his most successful coupling was of Rachmaninov and Dohnànyi, with Boult and the LPO. The Rachmaninov is notable, not just for its virtuosity and romantic flair, but also for the diversity and wit displayed in the early variations. He made the Dohnànyi *Nursery rhyme variations* his very own, recording the work twice with Boult, once in mono and once in stereo, and it is difficult to decide which is the more enjoyable.

Kempff, Wilhelm

Volume 55: BRAHMS: *4 Ballades, Op. 10; 7 Fantasias, Op. 116; 3 Intermezzi, Op. 117; 8 Pieces, Op. 76; 6 Pieces, Op. 118; 4 Pieces, Op. 119.* SCHUMANN: *Arabeske in C, Op. 18; Kreisleriana, Op. 16.*
(N) (B) *** Ph. mono 456 862-2 (2) [id.].

We owe it to Alfred Brendel that this first of three Kempff collections planned for the Philips 'Great Pianists' series is devoted to Brahms and Schumann. All the recordings here – except for the final item, Schumann's *Kreisleriana* – were recorded not for Kempff's regular recording company, DG, but for Decca, filling in on repertory he had not previously tackled. Brendel counts that Decca period as 'in many ways the high point of Kempff's work in the recording studio', at once authoritative yet spontaneous-sounding, consistently bringing out his gift of producing a singing legato, while using the pedal lightly. The Philips transfers of mono recordings are superb, full and firm, bringing out the resonance and warmth of Kempff's piano sound, often giving the illusion of full stereo.

Volume 56: SCHUBERT: *Sonata No. 16 in A min., D.845.* BEETHOVEN: *Sonata No. 27 in E min., Op. 90.* MOZART: *Piano concerto No. 23 in A, K.488* (with BPO, Ferdinand Leitner). LISZT: *Legends Nos. 1, St. Francis of Assisi preaching to the birds; 2 St. Francis of Paola walking on the waves. Années de Pélerinage*, 1st Year: *Eglogue; Au lac de Wallenstadt; Au bord d'une source;* 2nd Year: *Il penseroso; Canzonetta del Salvator Rosa; Sonetti del Petrarca Nos. 47; 104; 123; Supplement: Gondoliera.* BACH, arr. KEMPFF: Chorales: *Jesu, Joy of man's desiring; Nun komm' der heiden Heiland; Watchet auf, ruft uns die stimme.*
(N) (B) *** Ph. 456 865-2 (2) [id.].

This second of the Kempff offerings in the Philips 'Great Pianists' series, like the first, includes Decca recordings he made in the 1950s, less well-known than those for DG. Guided by Alfred Brendel, the choice is weighted towards Kempff's poetry, notably in the Liszt and best of all in the two Legends based on the two St Francises. Kempff's evocation of *St Francis of Assisi preaching to the birds* has never been matched on disc, a miraculous performance. Kempff's 1953 Decca recording of the Schubert *A minor Sonata*, D.845, provides a contrast with the one he recorded later for DG in his Schubert sonata cycle. Here in 1953, with speeds marginally broader, he is lighter and more transparent, bringing out the poetry more intensely. Among much else, the DG Mozart concerto recording is also uniquely individual. Excellent transfers. An even more revealing choice than the first Kempff volume in this series.

Kissin, Evgeny

Volume 58: LISZT: *Etudes d'exécution transcendante Nos. 10 in F min.; 11, Harmonies du soir; 12, Chasse-neige; Hungarian rhapsody No. 12; Liebestraume No. 3 in A flat; Spanish rhapsody.* SCHUBERT/LISZT: *Concert paraphrases: Auf dem Wasser zu singen; Die forelle; Gretchen am spinnrade.* LISZT (after SCHUBERT): *Valse-caprice No. 6, S.427.* SCHUBERT/TAUSIG: *Marche militaire.* PROKOFIEV: (i) *Piano concerto No. 3 in C, Op. 26* (with BPO, Claudio Abbado); *Etude in C min., Op. 2/3; Overture on Hebrew themes, Op. 34; Piano sonata No. 6 in A, Op. 82; Visions fugitives, Op. 22 Nos. 10 (Ridicolosamente); 11 (Con vivacitá); 16 (Dolente); 17 (Poetico).*
(N) (B) *** Ph. Dig. 456 871 (2) [id.].

This remarkable pianist is not yet thirty and most of the performances collected here were made when he was not out of his teens; the Prokofiev *Visions fugitives* when he was in his fourteenth year. Of the two versions he has recorded of the Prokofiev *Sixth Sonata*, the producer has rightly chosen the RCA Carnegie Hall account made when he was nineteen in preference to the even wilder (but less accurate) version he put on disc four years earlier in Tokyo for Sony. The Liszt is pretty breathtaking, but in the Prokofiev concerto with Abbado a little more abandon would have been appropriate in the outer movements. No doubts here about the wisdom of Tom Deacon's choice.

Kocsis, Zoltán

Volume 59: GRIEG: *Lyric pieces, Op. 43, Nos. 1, Butterfly; 2, Solitary traveller; 3, In my native country; 4, Little bird; 5, Erotikon; 6, To the spring.* BARTOK: *Romanian folk dances, Sz.56.* LISZT: *Années de Pélerinages: Les jeux d'eaux á la Villa d'este.* DEBUSSY: *2 Arabesques; Estampes: Pagodes; Soirée dans Grenade; Jardins sous la pluie; Suite bergamasque. Fantaisie for piano and orchestra.* DOHNANYI: *Variations on a nursery song* (both with Budapest Festival O, Iván Fischer). RACHMANINOV: *Piano concerto No. 4 in G min., Op. 40* (with San Francisco SO, Edo de Waart); *Prelude in C sharp min., Op. 3/2; Vocalise, Op. 34/14* (arr. KOCSIS).
(N) (B) *** Ph. Dig. Duo 456 874 (2) [id.].

On the whole a well-chosen anthology, though it is a pity that one of the leading Bartók interpreters of the day is not represented by something more substantial than the *Romanian folk dances*. A Bartók concerto would have made a better choice than his Debussy *Fantaisie*. All the same, the Debussy items are excellent and so is his Grieg and Dohnànyi. The Rachmaninov *Fourth Concerto* is a particularly successful account which has been rather underrated. All the recordings are of a very high standard.

Kovacevich, Stephen

Volume 60: BEETHOVEN: *Piano sonatas Nos. 8 in C min. (Pathétique), Op. 13; 17 in D min. (Tempest), Op. 31/2; 18 in E flat, Op. 31/3; 28 in A, Op. 101; 30 in E, Op. 109; 31 in A flat, Op. 110; 32 in C min., Op. 111.*
(N) (BB) *** Ph. 456 877-2 (2) [id.].

Now that Kovacevich is re-recording the Beethoven sonatas for EMI, the reappearance of his earlier analogue Philips versions is the more valuable. The *Pathétique* is characteristically unmannered and refreshing and in his coupling of two of the Op. 31 sonatas he plays with all his habitual concentraton, pursuing the argument forcefully, never giving a Mendelssohnian tinge to the romanticism of the *D minor*, yet with the second and fourth movements of the *E flat major* superbly sprung. He goes on to give deeply satisfying accounts of the later sonatas, particularly the last two. Characteristically he uses a dramatically wide dynamic range down to the most hushed *pianissimo*, and the degree of expressive restraint – as in the other-worldly playing of the lovely opening theme of Op. 110 – actually adds to the intensity of the performances. In Op. 111 the crispness and clarity of the first movement make even more telling the contrast with the great set of variations, here set out as the noblest of musical spans. Clear, clean recording.

Volume 61: BEETHOVEN: *Piano Sonata No. 5 in C min., Op. 10/1.* Richard Rodney BENNETT: *Piano concerto* (with LSO, Sir Alexander Gibson). STRAVINSKY: *Concerto for piano and wind.* BARTOK: *Piano concerto No. 2 in G* (both with BBC SO, Sir Colin Davis). *Out of doors; Sonatina.* BRAHMS: *Pieces, Op. 119.* CHOPIN: *Nocturnes Nos. 17–18, Op. 62; Impromptu No. 3 in G flat.*
(N) (B) *** Philips 456 880-2 (2) [id.].

A useful addition to this series, in that it restores to circulation the recording of Richard Rodney Bennett's *Piano concerto* which Stephen Kovacevich dispatches with great flair, and some of his exemplary Bartók (above all *Out of doors*, which is of an artistry comparable with Perahia's) made in the late 1960s. Kovacevich's account of the *Second Piano concerto* with the BBC Symphony Orchestra and Sir Colin Davis is also among the finest accounts of this piece, though the piano is perhaps just a little too prominent. This gives a good cross-section of this artist's work in the studios in 1969–72 (save only for the Brahms which comes from 1983).

Larrocha, Alicia de

Volume 62: M.ALBENIZ: *Piano sonata in D.* SOLER: *Piano sonatas in C sharp min.; F; D.* GRANADOS: *Goyescas: El fandango de Candil; Quejas – la maja y el ruiseñor; El pelele (Escena goyesca); Spanish dance (Andaluza), Op. 37/5.* ALBENIZ: *Iberia: Book I: Evocación; El puerto; Féte-Dieu à Seville. Book II: Rondeña; Almeria; Triana. Book III: El Albaicin; El Polo; Lavapies. Book IV: Màlaga; Jérez; Eritaña. Navarra.* HALFFTER: *Sonatina (ballet): Danza de la Pastora.* MOMPOU: *Cançons i dansas (excerpts) Nos. 1–6; 14.*
(N) (BB) *** Ph. Analogue/Dig. 456 883-2 (2) [id.].

Most of this programme is already available reissued in Decca's '*Moesica española*' series and is discussed above within the Composer Index. Born in Barcelona, Alicia de Larrocha is uniquely equipped to play everything here, and she does so with distinction, and the fullest Mediterranean atmosphere. She is given first-class recording too, but it seems a pity to duplicate so much repertoire rather than give a broader picture of her talents.

Lhévinne, Rosina and Josef

Volume 64: (i) Rosina Lhévinne, Juillard O, Jean Morel; (ii) Josef and Rosina Lhévinne; (iii) Josef Lhévinne; (iv) Rosina Lhévinne, Alumini of the Nat. Orchestral Association, John Barnett: MOZART: (i) *Piano concerto No. 21 in C, KV.467;* (ii) *Sonata for two pianos in D, KV.448.* SCHUMANN: (iii) *Toccata in C, Op. 7.* SCHUMANN/LISZT: (iii) *Frühlingsnacht.* CHOPIN: (iv) *Piano concerto No. 1 in E min., Op. 11;* (iii) *Etudes in E flat, Op. 10/11; G sharp min., Op. 25/6; B min., Op. 25/10; A min., Op. 26/11; Polonaise in A flat, Op. 53; Preludes in B flat min., Op. 28/16; A flat, Op. 28/17.* J. STRAUSS/SCHULTZ-EVLER: (iii) *Arabesques on An der schönen, blauen Donau.* DEBUSSY, orch. RAVEL: (ii) *Fêtes.* BEETHOVEN/BUSONI: (iii) *Ecossaises.* SCHUMANN/TAUSIG: (iii) *Der Kontrabandiste.* TCHAIKOVSKY: (iii) *Trepak.* RACHMANINOV: (iii) *Prelude in G min., Op. 23/5.*
(N) (B) *** Ph. 456 889-2 (2) [id.].

Josef Lhévinne was a fellow student of Scriabin and Rachmaninov in Moscow, and after an international career, settled in New York, teaching at the Juilliard School until his death in 1944. Rosina, whom he married in 1898, survived him and lived into her late 90s. This set includes all their commercial recordings, few of which are otherwise available. Josef's pianism is refined and the virtuosity effortless and unostentatious. The husband and wife collaboration is heard in a fine account of the Mozart K.448 and an exhilarating performance of Ravel's transcription of Debussy's *Fêtes*. The earliest recording here is the Schumann, dating from 1920, though the majority come from the 1930s. Rosa made her remarkably cultured and elegant account of the Mozart concerto in 1961, when she was 81. The recordings, though a bit frail in tone, come over well.

Lipatti, Dinu

Volume 65: BACH: *Partita in B flat, BVW 825.* MOZART: *Piano sonata in A min., KV.310.* BRAHMS: *Waltzes Op. 39 Nos. 1–2, 5–6, 10, 14–15* (with Nadia Boulanger). CHOPIN: *Barcarolle in F sharp, Op. 60; Nocturne in D flat, Op. 27/2; Piano sonata in B min., Op. 58. RAVEL: Miroirs: Alborada del gracioso.* SCHUMANN: *Piano Concerto in A min., Op.54 (with Philharmonia O, Karajan).* GRIEG: *Piano concerto in A min., Op. 16* (with Philharmonia O, Galliera). SCHUBERT: *Impromptus in E flat, D.899/2; G flat, D.899/3.*

BACH, arr. Myra HESS: *Jesu, joy of man's desiring.*
(N) (B) (***) Ph. mono 456 892-2 (2) [id.].

Here is another instance where the repertoire (from the EMI archives) is duplicated in other collections. However this programme is certainly both representative and generous, and there is no doubt about Lipatti's claims to greatness.

Lupu, Radu

Volume 66: BEETHOVEN: *Sonata No. 14 (Moonlight), Op. 27/2; 32 Variations on an original theme.* BRAHMS: *3 Intermezzi, Op. 117; Theme and variations, Op. 18.* SCHUMANN: *Kinderszenen, Op. 15.* SCHUBERT: *6 Moments musicaux; Sonata in A min., D.784.* GRIEG: *Piano concerto in A min., Op. 16* (with LSO, Previn).
(N) (B) **(*) Ph. 456 895-2 (2) [id.].

The selection here is less perceptive than usual. The opening *Moonlight sonata* does not show this pianist at his very best and the Grieg concerto, though bright and fresh, is not really distinctive either. But his Schubert and Brahms do not disappoint.

Michelangeli, Arturo Benedetti

Volume 68: DEBUSSY: *Images, Books I–II; Preludes, Book 1: Danseuses de Delphes; Les sons e les parfums tournent dansl'air du soir; Des pas sur la neige; La fille aux cheveux de lin; La cathédrale engloutie; Minstrels. Book II: La Puerta del Vino; 6 Général Lavine; La terrasse des audiences du clair de lune; Ondine; Hommage á Samuel Pickwick, Esq. P.P.M.P.C.; Feux d'artifice.* GALUPPI: *Sonata No. 5 in C.* D.SCARLATTI: *Sonatas in C min., K.11; C, K.159; A, K.322.* RAVEL: *Gaspard de la nuit.* (i) *Piano concerto in G* (with Philharmonia O, Ettore Gracis).
(N) (B) *** Ph. 456 901-2 (2) [id.].

Michelangeli's Debussy is very distinguished indeed, if a little cool. His Galuppi and Scarlatti sonatas have the lightest touch and superb poise – they derive (surprisingly) from a vintage Decca stereo recital. But the highlight here is the Ravel *Piano concerto*, which in some ways has never been surpassed, especially the exquisite slow movement.

Moiseiwitsch, Benno

Volume 70: CHOPIN: *Ballades Nos. 3 in A flat, Op. 47; 4 in F min., Op. 52; Barcarolle in F sharp min., Op. 60; Fantaisie Impromptu in C sharp min., Op. 66; Nocturnes Nos. 12 in G, Op. 37/2; 18 in E, Op. 62/2; Scherzi Nos. 2 in B flat min., Op. 31; 4 in E, Op. 54.* MENDELSSOHN (arr. RACHMANINOV) *Scherzo from A Midsummer Night's Dream.* LISZT: *Etude de concert No. 2 in F min., La leggierezza.* KABALEVSKY: *Sonata No. 3, Op. 46.* MEDTNER: *Sonata in G min., Op. 22.* RACHMANINOV: *Moment musical in E min., Op. 16/4; Piano concerto No. 2 in C min., Op. 18* (with Philharmonia O, Hugo Rignold); *Prelude in G, Op. 32/5.*
(N) (B) *** Ph. mono/stereo 456 907-2 (2) [id.].

Given the towering position he assumed on the musical scene during the immediate pre-war years and through to the 1950s, it is surprising that Moiseiwitsch's recording legacy has suffered periodic neglect since his death in 1963. Things have improved in recent years, though his 1955 account of the Rachmaninov *Second Concerto* had to wait until 1991 before it was issued in stereo. This anthology is particularly welcome: it restores the authoritative set of Medtner's *G minor Sonata*, which has not been in circulation for many years, as well as his post-war account of the Kabalevsky *Third*. All these performances are distinguished by Moiseiwitsch's outsize personality and keyboard elegance.

Moravec, Ivan

Volume 71: CHOPIN: *Ballade No. 4 in F min., Op. 52; Barcarolle in F sharp, Op. 60; Mazurkas in E min., Op. 41/2; in C sharp min., Op. 50/3; in C, Op. 56/2; in F min., Op. 63/2; in C sharp min., Op. 63/3; in A min., Op. 68/2; in F min., Op. 68/4; Nocturnes Op. 62, Nos. 1 in B; 2 in E; Polonaise-fantaisie in A flat, Op. 61; Scherzo No. 2 in B flat min., Op. 31.* FRANCK: *Prélude, choral et fugue.* DEBUSSY: *Images Books 1–2; Pour le piano.* RAVEL: *Sonatine.*
(N) (B) *** Ph. analogue/Dig. 456 910 (2) [id.].

An artist of great distinction who has consistently eschewed publicity and dedicated himself to purely artistic goals. He produces a cultured sound of great purity and tonal refinement. Born in Prague, where he now teaches, Ivan Moravec is a relatively rare visitor to Britain and none of these recordings emanates from the major labels. Much of the Chopin comes from the 1960s, the rest from 1983; it is cultivated, restrained playing completely shorn of egocentricity, and the same must be said of the Franck and Debussy. Variable sound quality but the collection gives a highly positive portrait of a pianist of consummate artistry and dedication.

Ogdon, John

Volume 72: RACHMANINOV: *Piano sonata No. 2 in B flat min., Op. 36* (1931 revised version). SCRIABIN: *Piano sonata No. 4 in F sharp, Op. 30.* ALKAN: *Concerto pour piano seul.*

BUSONI: *Piano concerto, Op. 39* (with John Alldis Ch., RPO, Daniell Revenaugh); *Variations and fugue on prelude in C minor by Chopin.*
(N) (B) **(*) Ph. 456 913 (2) [id.]

In some ways, partly because of ill health, John Ogdon never quite fulfilled the promise of sharing the first prize in the 1962 Moscow Tchaikovky Competition with Askenazy. But he made some striking recordings, including in 1967 the Busoni *Piano concerto*, which has not since been surpassed. It is very welcome back in the catalogue, as are the Alkan *Concerto* and Rachmaninov *Second sonata.*

Paderewski, Ignacy

Volume 74: CHOPIN: *Berceuse, Op. 57; Etudes in E; in G flat (Black keys); C min. (Revolutionary), Op. 10/3, 5, & 10; in A flat, F min., G sharp min.; G flat (Butterfly); A min. (Winter wind), Op. 25/1, 2, 7, 9 & 11; Mazurkas in A min., Op. 17/4; in F sharp, Op. 59/3; in C sharp min., Op. 63/3; Nocturnes in E flat, Op. 9/2; in F; in F sharp, Op. 15/1–2; Polonaise in A, Op. 40; Waltzes in E flat, Op. 18; & A flat, Op. 42.* CHOPIN/LISZT: *The maiden's wish; My joys.* LISZT: *Etude de concert No. 2 in F min.* (ending altered cf. Moiseiwitsch); *Paganini étude (La campanella); Hungarian rhapsodies Nos. 2 & 10.* WAGNER/LISZT: *Concert paraphrase: Spinning chorus from The Flying Dutchman.* SCHUBERT: *Impromptus in A flat; in B flat; D.935/2 & 3.* PADEREWSKI: *Minuet in G, Op. 14/1.*
(N) (B) (**(*)) Ph. mono 456 919-2 (2) [id.].

It is open to question whether his records conveyed the real stature of Paderewski the pianist, but they certainly convey something of his delicacy and spirit. The recordings range from 1911 to 1930 and are pretty variable in quality though they are lovingly transferred. Paderewski was a phenomenon but the sense of presence he had in recital does not always come across on shellac and thus not on CD either.

Perahia, Murray

Volume 75: D.SCARLATTI: *Sonatas in B min., K.27; A, K.212.* MENDELSSOHN: *Variations sérieuses, Op. 54.* SCHUBERT: *Impromptu in B flat, D. 935/3.* CHOPIN: *Ballade No. 1 in G min., Op. 23.* BRAHMS: *Rhapsody in B min., Op. 79/1.* LISZT: *Consolation No. 3 in D flat.* BARTOK: *Improvisations on Hungarian peasant songs, Op. 20/1–8.* MOZART: (i) *Piano concerto No. 25 in C, KV. 503* (with ECO). BEETHOVEN: *Variations in C min., WoO 80.* GRIEG: *Piano concerto in A min., Op. 16* (with Bavarian RSO, Sir Colin Davis).
(N) (B) *** Ph. Dig./Analogue 456 922-2(2) [id.].

Murray Perahia's spontaneous imagination lights up everything he plays. He is surely among the greatest and most perceptive artists of our time. The snag about this recital is that it is too much like a sampler, and cuts across many CDs which collectors will already have purchased, or plan to do so.

Pletnev, Mikhail

Volume 77: TCHAIKOVSKY: *Capriccio in G flat, Op. 8; Piano concerto No. 2 in G, Op. 44* (with Philharmonia Orchestra, Fedoseyev); *Nutcracker* (concert suite) arr. Pletnev; *Romance in F min., Op. 5; The seasons, Op. 37b; Sleeping Beauty* (excerpts) arr. Pletnev; *Valse-scherzo in A, Op. 7.*
(N) (B) *** Ph. Dig. 456 931-2 (2) [id.].

Pletnev's playing here is not only masterly but demonstrates an exceptional affinity with Tchaikovsky. His performance of *The Seasons* is wonderfully poetic and illuminating, while the ballet transcriptions glitter and glow under his fingers. The one snag is that in the otherwise highly recommendable version of the *Second Piano concerto,* there is a small cut in the slow movement.

Pollini, Maurizio

Volume 78: SCHUMANN: *Arabeske in C, D.946; Piano sonata No. 1 in F sharp min., Op. 11.* LISZT: *Piano sonata in B min.* CHOPIN: *Scherzo No. 1 in B min., Op. 20.* SCHUBERT: *3 Klavierstücke, D.946 Nos. 1 in E flat min.; 2 in E flat, 3 in C.* WEBERN: *Piano variaions, Op. 27.* DEBUSSY: *Etudes for piano pour les: egrés chromatiques; agréments; notes répétées; opposées sonorités; arpéges composés; accords.* STRAVINSKY: *Petrushka (3 movements): Russian dance; Petrushka's room; The Shrovetide fair.*
(N) (B) *** Ph. Analogue/Dig. 456 937-2 (2) [id.].

An outstanding collection, restoring to the catalogue some of Pollini's finest performances, and reminding us of others. If his Chopin *Scherzo* is brilliantly hard-edged, his account of the *F sharp Minor Sonat*a is among the most distinguished Schumann interpretations on disc. The playing throughout has both command and authority, and deep poetic feeling. The *Arabeske* is comparably fine, and the glorious *Drei Klavierstücke* of Schubert are hardly less masterly. Some might feel that in the *B minor Sonata* of Liszt the consistent rush of adrenalin sweeps the music forward too unrelentingly. But Pollini has a firm grasp on the structure and the final denouement is most compelling. *Petrushka* is simply dazzling, and the Webern *Variations* have never been presented with greater perception or given a stronger advocacy. Excellent sound throughout.

Previn, André

Volume 80: GERSHWIN: *Boy! What Love has done to me!; Embraceable You; I got rhythm; I've got a crush on you; Piano concerto in F; Rhapsody in Blue* (with Pittsburgh SO); *Someone to watch over me; The Man I love.* MOZART: *Piano concerto No. 17 in G, K453* (with Vienna PO). POULENC: *Mélancolie; Presto in B flat; Trois piéces; Suite française.* SHOSTAKOVICH: *Piano concerto No. 1* (with NYPO, Leonard Bernstein).
(N) (B) *** Ph. 456 934-2 (2) [id.].

A superb all-round musician and fine pianist, Previn's accounts of these pieces have all been much admired – and rightly so. They remain hugely enjoyable. Whether he warrants inclusion with the greats of the century is a different matter, although he has something special to contribute to Gershwin and, in partnership with Bernstein, the Shostakovich concerto. Indeed, those wanting these performances need not hesitate.

Rachmaninov, Sergei

Volume 81: BEETHOVEN: *Variations in C min., WoO* 80 (excerpts). CHOPIN: *Ballade No. 3 in A flat, Op. 47; Scherzo No. 3 in C sharp min., Op. 64/2; Piano sonata in B flat min. (Funeral march), Op. 35; Waltzes Nos. 7 in C sharp min., Op. 64/2; 8 in A flat, Op. 64/3.* SCHUMANN: *Carnaval, Op. 9.* LISZT/CHOPIN: *Chants polonais Nos. 1, 6.* BACH: *Preludio, Gavotte and Gigue* (from *Violin Partita No. 3 in E, BWV 1006*) (arr. RACHMANINOV). RIMSKY-KORSAKOV: *Flight of the bumble-bee* (arr. RACHMANINOV). MENDELSSOHN: *A Midsummer Night's Dream: scherzo* (arr. RACHMANINOV). Johann STRAUSS: *Valse caprice, Op. 167/2* (arr. TAUSIG). TCHAIKOVSKY: *Lullaby, Op. 16/1* (arr. RACHMANINOV); *The Seasons, Op. 37b*, (arr. RACHMANINOV); *November.* RACHMANINOV: *Daisies, Op. 38/3; Etude-tableaux in C, Op. 33/2; E flat, Op. 33/7; Oriental sketch; Polka de W.R.; Preludes in C sharp min., Op. 3/2; G flat, Op. 23/10; E, Op. 32/3; F min., Op. 32/6; F, Op. 32/7; Melody in E, Op. 3/3; Humoresque in G, Op. 10/5; Moment musical in E flat min., Op. 16/2.* KREISLER: *Liebesleid, Liebesfreud* (arr. RACHMANINOV).
(N) (B) (***) Ph. mono 456 943-2 (2) [id.].

Along with Hoffman, arguably the greatest and most distinctive pianist of the century, Rachmaninov is heard here in a wide range of solo repertoire. If you don't have access to the complete RCA ten-CD box, these classics of the gramophone will be a mandatory acquisition.

Richter, Sviatoslav

Volume 82: MUSSORGSKY: *Pictures at an exhibition.* SCHUBERT: *Impromptus in E flat, D.899/2; A flat, D.899/4; Moment musical in C, D.780/1.* CHOPIN: *Etude in E, Op. 10/3.* LISZT: *Etudes d'exécuion transcendante Nos. 5, Feux follets; 11, Harmonies du soir. Valses oubliées Nos. 1 in F sharp; 2 in A flat.* RACHMANINOV: *Prelude in G sharp min., Op. 32/12.* PROKOFIEV: *Piano sonatas Nos. 6 in A, Op. 82; 7 in B flat, Op. 83; 8 in B flat, Op. 84.*
(N) (B) (***) Ph. 456 956-2 (2) [id.].

Pictures at an exhibition is very special to Richter; even Horowitz does not quite match his interpretative detail and power. The present writer has heard him play it live – an unforgettable experience. The performance here is also live, and totally compelling, wonderfully imaginative in detail. The closing *Great Gate of Kiev* is electrifying, triumphing over the indifferent, resonant, and slightly blurred piano focus, and the asthmatic problems of the the Sofia audience. The Schubert, Chopin, Liszt and Rachmaninov items also come from this same 1958 recital, and bring more dazzling playing: here the sound is for the most part, firmer. The uniquely authoritative performances of the three Prokofiev Sonatas have an arresting dynamism and electricity, to say nothing of poetic feeling (No. 7 is the BMG/Melodiya recording). Here the sound is clear and well focused, quite satisfactory. This is a set that no serious collector can ignore.

Volume 83: BEETHOVEN: *Piano sonatas Nos. 12 in A flat, Op. 26; 17 in D min.(Tempest), Op. 31/2; 23 in F min. (Appassionata), Op. 57; 30 in E, Op. 109; 31 in A flat, Op. 110; 32 in C min., Op. 111. Rondo in B for piano and orchestra, WoO 6* (with VSO, Sanderling).
(N) (B) *** Ph. 456 949 (2) [id.].

Richter's Beethoven had concentration and eloquence. His account of the *D minor, Op. 31, No. 2* was a legend in its day though the late sonatas, recorded in 1991 in Ludwigshafen, enjoyed less exposure and are at times somewhat remote, as he could be in his last years. Not everyone will feel this of course and his admirers should not overlook these performances – particularly the *Appassionata.*

Rubinstein, Artur

Volume 85: CHOPIN: *Andante spianato and grande polonaise brillante, Op. 22; Ballades Nos. 3 in A flat, Op. 47; 4 in F min., Op. 52; Berceuse in D flat, Op. 57; Fantaisie-impromptu in C sharp min., Op. 66; Impromptus Nos. 1 in A flat, Op. 29; 2 in F sharp. Op. 36; 3 in G flat, Op. 51; Mazurkas, Op. 68/1–4; Nocturnes in C sharp min., D flat, Op. 27/1–2; C min., F sharp min.,*

Op. 48/1–2; Polonaises in A, (Military), Op. 40/1; A flat, (Heroic), Op. 53; Scherzo No. 3 in C sharp min., Op. 39; Piano sonata No. 2 in B flat min. (Funeral march), Op. 35; Trois nouvelles études, Op. post.; Waltz in A flat, Op. 34/1; A flat, Op. 42; D flat, (Minute), Op. 64/1.
(N) (B) *** Ph. 456 955-2 (2) [id.].

Born in Lodz in 1887, Artur Rubinstein emigrated to the USA in 1937 and became an American citizen in 1946. He gave his last recital at London's Wigmore hall in June 1979, at the age of 89. His musical range was wide. Between October and December 1961 he played 90 works by 70 composers. But above all his art was celebrated for his magical Chopin performances, many of which RCA captured in stereo, often of very good quality. Even for those who especially admire his earlier, more youthful mono records, the present selection demonstrates that in the late 1950s and early 1960s, when these recordings were made, his technique remained absolutely assured while the poetic imagination and romantic fire were distilled as headily as ever. The programme opens with a delightful account of the *Andante spianato*, surveys all Chopin's major dance forms, and includes the almost improvisational *Berceuse* and the unsurpassed *Funeral march Sonata* and ends heroically with the *A flat major Polonaise*.

Schnabel, Artur

Volume 89: BEETHOVEN: *Piano concerto No. 4 in G, Op. 58* (with LPO, Sir Malcolm Sargent). *Piano sonatas Nos. 21 in C, (Waldstein), Op. 53; 30 in E, Op. 109; 32 in C min., Op. 111; 33 Variations on a waltz by Diabelli, Op. 120.*
(N) (B) (***) Ph. mono 456 961 (2) [id.].

It is arguable whether Schnabel's account of the *Diabelli variations* has ever been equalled in depth and insight, let alone surpassed, and both Opp. 109 and 111 are in a class of their own. He finds a depth and subtlety of tone in the slow movement of Op. 111 that is awesome. The *G major concerto* comes from his pre-war set made in 1934 with Sargent rather than either of the later ones with Frederick Stock or Issay Dobrowen.

Serkin, Rudolf

Volume 90: BEETHOVEN: *Sonata No. 23 in F min. (Appassionata), Op. 57.* MOZART: *Piano concerto No. 14 in E flat, K.449* (with Adolf Busch Chamber Players). *Piano concertos Nos. 12 in A, K.424; 16 in D, K.451; 17 in G, K.453; 19 in F, K. 459* (with LSO, Abbado).
(N) (B) (**) Ph. mono analogue/Dig. stereo 456 964-2 (2) [id.].

Few artists are displayed to less advantage than Rudolf Serkin by the juxtaposition here of his superb *Appassionata* and elegantly perceptive Mozart *E flat major Concerto*, K.449, (recorded by EMI in 1936 and 1938, respectively), and his performances of the other three Mozart concertos, recorded five decades later, with Abbado for DG. His intellectual command remains, but the actual playing is less supple and wanting in the grace he so obviously commanded earlier, and his passage-work is often uneven. Refined accompaniments from Abbado, and excellent stereo do little to compensate.

Sofronitzky, Vladimir

Volume 91: CHOPIN: *Barcarolle in F sharp, Op. 60; Impromptu in G flat, Op. 51; Mazurkas in B min., D flat & C sharp min., Op. 30/2–4; in C & B min., Op. 33/3–4; C sharp min & E min., Op. 41/1–2; F min., C sharp min, Op. 50/3; Op. 63/2; Nocturnes in C sharp min., D flat, Op. 27/1–2; Polonaise in C sharp min., Op. 26/1; Waltzes in A flat, Op. 69/1; F min., Op. 70/2; D flat, Op. 70/3.* SCRIABIN: *Deux Danses, Op. 73; Etude in F sharp min. Op. 42/3; Deux Poémes, Op. 32; Preludes in B flat min., Op. 11/16; B flat, Op. 35/2; B flat, Op. 37/1. Sonatas Nos. 2 in G sharp min. Op. 19: Andante; 3 in F sharp min. Op. 23; 4 in F sharp, Op. 30. 9, Op. 68 (Black Mass).*
(N) ❁ (B) **(*) Ph. 456 970-2 (2) [id.].

Sofronitzky is best remembered as a Scriabin interpreter (he married the composer's daughter and was hailed by Tatiana Schloezer, Scriabin's widow, as the finest interpreter of her husband's music). These performances have been available from time to time on Chant du Monde and other specialist labels but they are a valuable addition to this series. Only the *Fourth Sonata* of Scriabin is duplicated from the two-CD compilation in BMG's Russian Piano School. Sofronitzky was never cultivated by the Soviet regime and rarely appeared in the West. All these performances come from his last years (1959–61) and are an indispensable part of the Scriabin discography. He plays as if he is possessed and combines a mystic fervour with great pianistic refinement. The recordings call for a little tolerance but that is well worth extending.

Tureck, Rosalyn

Volume 93: BACH: *Partitas Nos. 1–6, BWV 825–30.*
(N) ❁ (B) *** Ph. mono 456 976-2 (2) [id.].

Too many issues in this 'Great Pianists' anthology offer recordings that are already available elsewhere. The present issue is valuable in that it restores to circulation these classic 1956–8 recordings which EMI have not already reissued on CD. Tureck's is playing of extraordinary style and refined musicianship, and her elegant phrasing, mastery of part-writing and keyboard colour are a joy in themselves. In order to accommodate all six *Partitas* on two CDs the repeats of the Sarabande of No. 4 in D have been excised. Totally compelling playing and good, clear mono sound.

Uchida, Mitsuko

Volume 95: MOZART: *Adagio in B min., K.540; Rondo in A min., K.511; Sonata in D, K.311; 10 Variations in G 'Unser dummer Pabel meint', K.455;* (i) *Piano concerto No. 9 in E flat (Jeunehomme), K.271* (with ECO, Jeffrey Tate). DEBUSSY: *12 Etudes*. SCHOENBERG: *3 Klavierstücke, Op. 12.*

(N) (B) *** Ph. Dig. 456 982-2 (2) [id.].

Mitsuko Uchida, first prizewinner in the 1975 Leeds competition, came to public notice as a Mozartian when in 1985–6 she played all the Mozart concertos with the ECO. But on record it was a complete set of the sonatas which established her reputation as an impeccable Mozartian stylist, with slow movements bringing a sensibility of the highest order. She was equally impressive in the shorter pieces, and the present lightweight set of *Variations* is expertly managed, with absolutely no suggestion of triviality. The '*Jeunehomme*' *Concerto* suits her especially well. Jeffrey Tate draws first-class playing from the orchestra and Uchida's response is spirited and elegant, while the *Andantino* brings lovely, refined playing, yet never sounds over-civilized. But it is her account of the Debussy *Etudes* which represents the very peak of her recording career so far, and is unsurpassed on CD. The Schoenberg *Klavierstücke*, recorded especially for this edition, are hardly less impressive, and throughout she is given the most natural piano recording, vividly coloured and beautifully focused.

Watts, André

Volume 96: LISZT: *Piano concerto No. 1 in E flat* (with NYPO, Bernstein), *Hungarian rhapsody No. 13; Paganini étude (La campanella). Totentanz* (with LSO, Leinsdorf). *Transcendental étude No. 10, in F min.* SCHUBERT: *Fantasy in C (Wanderer), D.760.* GERSHWIN: *13 songs* (arr. Gershwin): BEETHOVEN: *32 variations in C min.* CHOPIN: *Etudes in C, in C sharp min., C min., Op. 10/1; Op. 25/7 & 12.* DEBUSSY: *Children's corner suite.* RACHMANINOV: *Variations on a theme of Corelli, Op. 42.*

(N) (B) *** Ph. 456 985-2 (2) [id.].

André Watts was a teenage prodigy, and his Liszt *E flat concerto* with Bernstein was recorded in 1963 when he was seventeen. He made all the other recordings included here between 1968–1974 while he was still in his twenties, the sole exception being Debussy's *Children's Corner* which comes from 1980. He has made quite a number of records subsequently, some Liszt, Beethoven, Chopin and Rachmaninov but his more recent work is unrepresented. He is a fine player and his Liszt certainly has great brilliance.

Wild, Earl

Volume 98: '*The Art of the transcription*': GLUCK/SGAMBATI: *Melodie d'Orphée.* RAMEAU/GODOWSKY: *3 pieces: Rigaudon, Elegie, Tambourin.* BACH/TAUSIG: *Toccata and fugue in D min.* WAGNER/MOSZKOWSKI: *Liebestod from Tristan und Isolde.* RIMSKY-KORSAKOV/RACHMANINOV: *Scherzo from A Midsummer Night's Dream.* ROSSINI/THALBERG: *Grande fantasie sur l'opera Semiramide.* CHOPIN/LISZT: *3 Polish songs.* TCHAIKOVSKY/WILD: *Pas de quatre from Swan Lake.* STRAUSS/SCHUTZ-EVLER: *Concert arabesques on themes of The beautiful blue Danube.* GLINKA/BALAKIREV: *A Life for the Tsar.* HERZ: *Variations on 'Non piu mesta' from Rossini's La Cenerentola.* THALBERG: *Fantasy on Donizetti's Don Pasquale, Op. 67.* STRAUSS/GODOWSKI: *Symphonic metamorphosis on An Artist's life waltz.* GERSHWIN/WILD: *7 Etudes on popular songs.*

(N) (B) *** Ph. 456 991-2 (2) [id.].

Earl Wild possesses a virtuosity that is second to none and a refined musicianship. This set concentrates on the transcriptions with which he dazzles his public. Unfortunately he has never enjoyed the advocacy of a major record company. The recordings on offer here emanate from the period 1964–76 and also include part of a live Carnegie Hall recital from 1981. His playing radiates a delight and pleasure in every bar.

Yudina, Maria

Volume 99: BACH: *Goldberg variations, BWV 988.* BEETHOVEN: *Variations and fugue on a theme from Prometheus (Eroica variations), Op. 35; Variations on a waltz by Diabelli, Op. 120.*

(N) (B) ** Ph. 456 994-2 (2) [id.].

Maria Yudina studied with the legendary Essipova in St Petersburg and was particularly open to new music thanks to her contact with Klemperer and Hindemith. Her repertoire included Krenek, Bartók and Stravinsky; she had an extensive correspondence with the latter and played at his 80th birthday celebrations in 1962. (When Stalin heard a broadcast of her Mozart K.488, he asked Moscow Radio for a recording; not daring to confess that they did not have one, Yudina was summoned back to record it through the night!) The present recordings made in

1961 (Beethoven) and 1968 (Bach) show her in perhaps a less flattering light than the Hindemith, Krenek, Bartók and Stravinsky included in the BMG 'Great Russian Pianists'. The *Goldberg variations* are very plain and unadorned (there is none of Tureck's elegance and mastery of part writing) and the piano in both sets of the Beethoven cries out for the ministrations of a technician.

Zimerman, Krystian

Volume 100: BRAHMS: *Piano concerto No. 2 in B flat, Op. 83* (with Vienna PO, Bernstein); *Scherzo in E flat min., Op. 4*. CHOPIN: *Ballade No. 4 in F min., Op. 52; Fantaisie in F min., Op. 49*. LISZT: *Harmonies poéiques et religieuses: Funérailles*; (ii) *Totentanz* (with Boston SO, Ozawa). DEBUSSY: *Préludes, Book 1: Danseuses de Delphes; Les collines d'Anacapri; La cathédrale engloutie; La danse de Puck; Minstrels; Book 2: Hommage á Samuel Pickwick Esq., P.P.M.P.C.; Feux d'artifice.*

(N) (B) **(*) Ph. Dig. 456 997-2 (2) [id.].

Krystian Zimerman's Chopin is undoubtedly touched with distinction as is his Liszt: the *Totentanz* is very exciting yet fully controlled. The Debussy *Préludes*, though also very highly charged, are compellingly evocative and full of detailed insights. Only the Brahms concerto, in partnership with Bernstein, brings a measure of disappointment. Here the constant fluctuations of tempo in the first movement are disturbing, although there is charisma to spare from both artists, and no one could complain that this is dull, or indeed that there is a lack of poetic lyrical feeling. The recordings are all of high quality.

Other piano recitals

Katchen, Julius

The Art of Julius Katchen

Volume 1: BEETHOVEN: *Piano concertos Nos. 1–3; 5 (Emperor), Rondo in B flat for piano and orchestra* (with LSO, Piero Gamba).
(N) (B) *** Australian Decca Double 460 822–2 (2).

Volume 2: BEETHOVEN: *Piano concerto No. 4, Op. 58* (with LSO, Gamba); *Choral fantasia, Op. 80* (also with LSO Ch.). MOZART: *Piano concertos No. 13 in C, K.415* (with New SO of London, Peter Maag); *20 in D min., K. 466; 25 in C, K. 503* (with Stuttgart Chamber Orchestra. Karl Münchinger).
(N) (B) *** Australian Decca Double 460 825–2 (2).

Volume 3: BRAHMS: *Piano concertos Nos. 1* (with LSO, Monteux); *2* (with LSO, János Ferencsik). SCHUMANN: *Piano concerto in A min.* (with Israel PO, Kertesz); *Fantasia in C, Op. 17.*
(N) (B) *** Australian Decca Double 460 828–2 (2).

Volume 4: LISZT: *Piano concerto Nos. 1–2* (with LPO, Argenta). *Mephisto waltz No. 1 Harmonies poétiques et religieuses: Funérailles. Hungarian rhapsody No. 12.* GRIEG: *Piano concerto in A min., Op. 16* (with Israel PO, István Kertész). BALAKIREV: *Islamey.* MUSSORGSKY: *Pictures at an exhibition*
(N) (B) *** Australian Decca Double stereo/mono 460 831–2 (2).

Volume 5: TCHAIKOVSKY: *Piano concerto No. 1 in B flat min., Op. 23.* LISZT: *Hungarian fantasia* (both with LSO, Gamba). PROKOFIEV: *Piano concerto No. 3 in C, Op. 26* (with LSO, Kertéz). RACHMANINOV: *Piano concerto No. 2 in C min., Op. 18* (with LSO, Solti). *Rhapsody on a theme of Paganini, Op. 43.* DOHNANYI: *Variations on a nursery theme* (both with LPO, Sir Adrian Boult).
(N) (B) *** Australian Decca Double mono/stereo 460 834–2 (2).

Volume 6: GERSHWIN: *Piano concerto in F* (with Mantovani and his Orchestra). BARTOK: *Piano concerto No. 3.* RAVEL: *Piano concerto in G; Piano concerto for the left hand* (all with LSO, Kertész). BRITTEN:*Diversions for piano (left hand) and orchestra, Op. 21* (with SO, composer).
(N) (B) *** Australian Decca Double 460 837–2 (2).

Katchen's very distinguished 15-year recording career spanned the end of the mono LP era and the first decade of stereo. He was for most of that time Decca's star pianist, and we must be grateful to the Australian Repertoire Manager of Universal Music, Cyrus Meher-Homji, for providing what is to become a complete survey of his Decca recordings on a series of well-filled Doubles with the brightly lit transfers adding to the vividness, and the piano timbre of consistent high quality. As can be seen above, and from the four CDs (2 Volumes) included in Philips's '*Great Pianists*' series below, Katchen's range of repertoire was as wide as his technique was brilliant, and he never delivered an unstimulating or unspontaneous performance. For his concerto recordings Decca provided him with a fine roster of conductors. The unexpected choice of Mantovani for the early LP of Gershwin's *Concerto in F* worked quite well, for he had fine soloists in his orchestra, and many may prefer the compilations offered here on Volumes 5 and 6 to the content of Volume 54 of the Philips series, particularly as the wonderfully imaginative performance of Britten's *Diversions* (with the composer conducting) is an indispensable highlight.

In the Beethoven concertos Katchen's partnership with Gamba worked particularly well, and the performances are fresh and commanding. Tempi are often on the fast side, but Katchen keeps a classical firmness and provides the necessary contrast in relaxed, poetic accounts of slow movements and sparkling readings of finales. In No. 1 he uses the longest and most impressive of Beethoven's own cadenzas for the first movement. The opening atmosphere of No. 4 is beautifully caught, while the *Emperor* is characteristically full of animal energy. The first and last movements are taken at a spanking pace, but not so that Katchen sounds at all rushed. Plainly he enjoyed himself all through, and in the very relaxed slow movement he seems to be coaxing the orchestra into matching his own delicacy, with the tension admirably sustained. The *Rondo* and the *Choral fantasia* too, are both very successful.

In the Brahms *First Concerto* the solo playing is superb, especially in the first movement, and Katchen is well partnered by Monteux (with the LSO), as he is by Ferencsik in No. 2, where he again gives an impassioned and exciting account of the solo piano part, here combining tremendous drive with the kind of ruminating delicacy Brahms so often calls for. These recordings are less successfully balanced than the Beethoven. However in the Grieg and Schumann concertos the sound is clear and brilliant, with both performances strong, any wilfulness tempered by a natural flexibility and the feeling for the music's poetry. Kertesz provides plenty of life in the accompaniments. In Schumann Katchen's virtuosity does not eschew romantic charm, the first movement more rhapsodical than usual, and throughout there is a pervading freshness. The Mozart performances, with Münchinger not always an ideally resilient conductor, yet have character (as does the solo sonata), and in the *D minor* there is strength as well as plenty of life and spirit.

In Liszt Katchen is in his element. He is superb in the *E flat concerto* and by any standards these are commanding performances.The Bartók, Prokofiev and Ravel concertos are among his finest records, with Kertesz especially compelling in his native Hungarian music, the playing combining intensity with brilliance and sparkle, and the Rachmaninov and Dohnányi performances are hardly less celebrated. The Tchaikovsky *Piano concerto* offers equally prodigious pianism, but is alas mono, and although the recording is basically rich and full, and the piano timbre is real and well balanced, the high violin timbre is thin and glassy, though not disasterously so, except perhaps at the very opening. Some might feel that in the finale Gamba broadens the reprise of the grand tune rather more than necessary. An exciting account just the same. Of the other solo performances Katchen's almost unbelievable technique is well demonstrated in Balakirev's *Islamey*. Even in an age of technicians few pianists could play the piece like this. The *Mephisto waltz* and Mussorgsky *Pictures* are also pretty remarkable, but in the latter the rather dry mono sound does not help Katchen to colour the music as he might. *Goldenberg and Schmuyle* and the *Chicks*, are highlights, but the finale could ideally be more expansive.

The final Volumes (7 and 8), due for release towards the end of 1999, contain more major piano works by Beethoven, including the *Diabelli variations*, and Mozart, plus the last two Chopin *Sonatas*, Schubert's *Wanderer Fantasia*, Schumann's *Carnaval*, Mendelssohn (showing Katchen at his most chimerical), plus other encores. All these recordings can be obtained to special order from the UK source given in the Introduction.